THE HOME BOOK OF QUOTATIONS

THE HOME BOOK OF QUOTATIONS

Classical & Modern

SELECTED AND ARRANGED BY

BURTON STEVENSON

I can tell thee where that saying was born
SHAKESPEARE, *Twelfth Night*
Act i, sc. 5, l. 9

TENTH EDITION

GREENWICH HOUSE
Distributed by Crown Publishers, Inc.
New York

To

FRANK C. DODD

Who suggested this book, and whose
faith in it made it possible

This 1984 edition is published by Greenwich House, a division of Arlington House, Inc., distributed by Crown Publishers, Inc., by arrangement with Dodd, Mead & Company.

Manufactured in the United States of America

LIBRARY OF CONGRESS CATALOGING IN PUBLICATION DATA

The Home book of quotations, classical and modern.

Reprint. Originally published: New York : Dodd, Mead, 1967.
Includes indexes.
1. Quotations. I. Stevenson, Burton Egbert, 1872-1962.
II. Title.
[PN6081.H635 1984] 808.88'2 83-20509

ISBN: 0-517-431300

h g f e d c b a

PREFATORY NOTE TO THE SECOND EDITION

The welcome which The Home Book of Quotations has received is especially pleasing to its compiler because of the public's quick appreciation of what may be called its human quality. It was this quality which he worked hardest to achieve, for what he was striving to produce was not merely another dictionary of quotations—a work of reference to be consulted on occasion—but a book with personality and interest, to be read, lingered over and enjoyed.

Another pleasant feature of the book's reception has been the general recognition of the fact that it is by no means dead and done with, but is a living thing, with endless possibilities of growth and improvement. It should grow better and wiser as it grows older and larger—each edition nobler than the last, like Dr. Holmes's nautilus. At least, its compiler intends to try to make it so.

Already in the brief time which has elapsed since the final reading of the proofs for the first edition, a surprisingly large amount of new material has become available. There is "Ike" Hoover's *Forty-Two Years in the White House,* with its apparently well-based contention that Calvin Coolidge did not in the least mean his "I do not choose" to be taken as final. There is Stanley Walker's *City Editor,* with its assertion that the famous "man bites dog" definition of news was not an invention of Charles A. Dana, as generally supposed, nor of his city editor, John B. Bogart, as Frank O'Brien, the present editor of the *Sun,* believes, but of Amos Cummings, another of Dana's editors. There is David Muzzey's life of Blaine, with many citations, one of which sent the compiler digging back into the pages of the *Congressional Globe* for April 30, 1866, to read for himself the official account of one of the most amusing orgies of recrimination which ever took place on the floor of the House. There is the assertion by H. G. Wells in *Liberty* for December 29, 1934, "I launched the phrase 'The War to End War.'" These are only examples of a mass of material, in almost every item of which a nugget or two may be turned up by careful digging.

Most valuable of all have been the suggestions from readers and reviewers. Almost everyone has his favorite quotations, and when any of them have been found missing from this collection, its compiler has been promptly informed—exactly as he had hoped he would be. A number of these suggestions have been included in the present edition, such errors corrected as have been discovered, certain ambiguities made clear, many new entries added to the Concordance, and definite dates given for forty or fifty additional names in the Index of Authors. These are but the first steps in a sort of continuing life-process of renewal and regeneration, which will carry on indefinitely.

It should be noted that the word "familiar" has been carefully excluded from the title of this book. Apart from the fact that the phrase "familiar quotations" is all but meaningless, it is surely the duty of a compiler to rescue from obscurity sayings which deserve to be preserved either because of their own merit or because they indicate the origin and development of those more widely known. The present compiler has spent a great deal of time in searching for such waifs, and also in retrieving hundreds of others which have hitherto been considered too banal or too vulgar to merit attention, for he has felt that "baloney" and "bonehead" and "stuffed shirt" deserve a place here no less than "magic casements."

Chillicothe, Ohio
January 15, 1935

PREFATORY NOTE TO THE THIRD EDITION

With this edition, THE HOME BOOK OF QUOTATIONS reaches what is, in all essentials, its definitive form. It has been checked through for errors from end to end, nearly a thousand new quotations have been added, explanatory notes have been rewritten and where necessary expanded in the APPENDIX, the INDEX OF AUTHORS has been revised and the limit for the citation of quotations under each writer raised from forty to one hundred and fifty, and, finally, the CONCORDANCE has been nearly doubled in size by the addition of approximately fifty thousand entries. Four pages of familiar political phrases and ten of popular song refrains have been added to those quoted in the earlier editions, and innumerable minor changes in text and arrangement have been made.

In a word, the editor has done everything he could to improve the book. Of course he expects to keep polishing away at it, but future changes will be very largely confined to the correction of such errors as may hereafter be discovered, and to the addition in the APPENDIX of such new material as may demand inclusion.

There has been some inquiry from English users of the book as to why English spelling was not used throughout, since it is used in more than half of the quotations, but in this the editor followed what seemed to him the only logical method, and used the spelling which the writer himself used. This means, of course, English spelling for English writers and American spelling for American ones. Since the editor is himself an American, he has naturally used American spelling for his own notes and for translations from foreign languages. With a few of the older writers, such as Chaucer, the spelling has been sufficiently modernized to make it intelligible to the average reader, and obsolete spellings have been dropped except in cases where there was some special point in retaining them.

During the two years which have elapsed since the first edition was published, the editor has had the benefit of criticisms and suggestions from hundreds of readers both in this country and in England, with the result that many omissions have been repaired, uncertainties concerning the origin of a considerable number of quotations have been cleared up, and three or four hoaxes have been uncovered. For all this assistance he is most grateful.

Chillicothe, Ohio
June 15, 1937

PREFATORY NOTE TO THE FIFTH EDITION

Advantage has been taken of a new printing of THE HOME BOOK OF QUOTATIONS to make a number of corrections in the text, and to add certain quotations and phrases which have become familiar during the past few years, especially those which have arisen from World War II. These have been grouped at the end of the Appendix, and a separate index for them will be found at the end of the regular index. The biographical data have been brought up to date, and some needed entries inserted in the index—all of which it is hoped, will increase the usefulness of the book.

Chillicothe, Ohio
January 10, 1946

PREFATORY NOTE TO THE NINTH EDITION

When the first edition of this book was published in 1934, its compiler little thought he would still be working at it a quarter of a century later. He realizes now that he will probably be doing just that for the rest of his life, and that it will never really be finished, for new phrases are constantly being coined which demand inclusion—such phrases as "privileged sanctuary," "massive retaliation," "brink of war," "modern Republicanism" and so on; biographies, autobiographies, diaries, collections of letters, and what not are constantly being published which shed new light on older sayings as well as more recent ones; and finally the compiler, in his readings and re-readings, quite often digs up a nugget which he had previously overlooked.

And then he has had help, generous help. For example, General Courtney Whitney was good enough to furnish the exact text of General MacArthur's communiqué in which "privileged sanctuary" first appeared; an attaché of the State Department supplied the text of the "massive retaliation," "agonizing reappraisal" and "brink of war" statements; Mr. Herbert Bayard Swope, in a personal letter, described the genesis of "cold war"; Mr. Elliott M. Sanger, Jr., of the *New York Times,* detailed the circumstances which led to the adoption of the slogan, "All the news that's fit to print"; Mr. Arthur H. (Pop) Momand explained how he hit upon the phrase "Keeping up with the Joneses"; Mr. George W. Cecil told how he happened to write "The Plains of Hesitation" thirty-five years ago, which somehow stuck in Mr. Adlai Stevenson's memory until just the other day; Mr. H. G. Wells's coining of the phrase "The war to end war" has been verified—it was Mr. Wells, by the way, who also coined "iron curtain" forty years before Mr. Churchill used it at Fulton, Missouri; the origin of the phrase "The Constitution follows the flag," which Mr. Dooley later on made famous, has been tracked down, thanks to a hint from Mr. Henry F. Woods, editor of *American Sayings,* and so on in many other instances. Small triumphs, perhaps, but the source of considerable satisfaction to the compiler.

The reference departments of many public libraries have been especially helpful. Mr. Henry J. Dubester and his staff in the General Reference Division of the Library of Congress, have been unstinting of their assistance, not only for this edition but for all the preceding ones; Mrs. Ruth L. Douthit, reference librarian of the Ohio State Library, has also been indefatigable; Miss Mary N. Barton, head of the General Reference Department of the Enoch Pratt Free Library of Baltimore, Mr. A. P. DeWeese, chief of the Information Division of the New York Public Library, Miss Evelyn Kirkland, of the Brooklyn Business Reference Library, Mr. Hobart F. Berolzheimer, head of the Literature Department of the Free Library of Philadelphia, and Miss Lois M. Jones, of the Los Angeles Public Library, submitted much-valued lists of quotations which they had run down after long search and would like to see included, and there were scattered suggestions from many others, including the lynx-eyed users of this book.

In consequence this revision is exceptionally thorough, embodying, as it does, over five hundred new entries, the clarification of scores of others, the bringing of the Index of Authors up to date, and the preparation of an entirely new index of the changes and additions, which will be found following the main index. What the compiler would really like is to do the whole book over, from A to Izzard, and do it better. But, alas! Time's wingèd chariot.

Chillicothe, Ohio
May 6, 1958

PREFATORY NOTE TO THE TENTH EDITION

Burton Stevenson thought of his HOME BOOK OF QUOTATIONS, as he wrote in the prefatory note to the second edition, as "a living thing, with endless possibilities of growth and improvement. It should grow better and wiser as it grows older." That early expectation has now crystallized into a tradition in this tenth edition of the famous work. In it Bruce Bohle, newspaper and magazine man, dictionary and encyclopedia editor, has added several hundred new quotations, in accordance with Stevenson's intention of making the book a reflection of the times. Prominent world figures now appearing in its pages for the first time include Lyndon B. Johnson, John F. Kennedy, Dwight D. Eisenhower, and Nikita S. Khrushchev, along with many other famous people from all walks of life. Thus brought up to date in this tenth edition, the book again moves forward "in a sort of continuing life process of renewal which will carry on indefinitely" as its original compiler planned.

THE HOME BOOK OF QUOTATIONS

SUGGESTIONS FOR USING
THE HOME BOOK OF QUOTATIONS

THE quotations in this book are arranged alphabetically by subject, and, under each subject, alphabetically by author; except that quotations which are merely variations of the same phrase are arranged chronologically, with dates to indicate priority of authorship.

The more important subjects are divided into sections in which cognate quotations are grouped together. This division follows a uniform plan, the first section comprising definitions of the subject; the second, apothegms about it; the third, praise; the fourth, criticism. "Painting" is an example of this arrangement. Sometimes, instead of Praise and Criticism, the division is Virtue and Folly (as in "Ambition"), or Blessing and Curse (as in "Adversity"), or Compensations and Penalties (as in "Age"). The purpose has been to set the quotations for and against any subject in a sort of deadly parallel, which will be found both interesting and amusing.

The major subjects are still further divided in considerable detail. "Age," for example, has seventeen sub-divisions; "Man" has nineteen; "Life" has thirty; and "Love" has thirty-seven; the purpose being not only to make any quotation more easy to find, but also to present to the reader all related quotations in a single group. An elaborate system of cross-references works to the same end.

In looking for a particular quotation, the reader should turn directly to the subject, if the subject is a short one, such as "Abstinence" or "Advantage." But if it is a long one, the CONCORDANCE on page 2419 should be consulted. Here the quotations are grouped by leading words and phrases, with a reference not only to the page, but to the number of the quotation on the page, so that it may be turned to instantly. The CONCORDANCE is really a word-index to the quotations, and identifying words, with a few words of context, are generously given, in order that a quotation which is not exactly remembered may be traced through a number of channels. Detailed suggestions for the use of the CONCORDANCE will be found on the page preceding it, and these should be carefully read, as it is impossible to get the full benefit of this book unless one understands thoroughly how to use it.

Key-words are sometimes incorrectly remembered, in which case, of course, the CONCORDANCE will be of no assistance; but there is another resource, provided the author of the desired quotation is known. Preceding the CONCORDANCE is an INDEX OF AUTHORS, which gives the pages on which the quotations from the works of every author may be found—except in the case of a few authors, such as Shakespeare and Pope, where the quotations are so numerous that to list them in this way would be an absurdity. Full directions for the use of this index will be found on page 2300r, and should also be carefully read. If no clue to the desired quotation can be found either in the CONCORDANCE or the INDEX OF AUTHORS, the final resource is, of course, to turn to the subject where it would naturally be found, and to run through the entries there.

A

ABILITY

1
Natural abilities are like natural plants, that need pruning by study.
FRANCIS BACON, *Essays: Of Studies.*

2
There never was a bad man that had ability for good service.
EDMUND BURKE, *Impeachment of Warren Hastings.* Third day.

3
You are a devil at everything, and there is nothing in the whole world but what you can turn your hand to.
CERVANTES, *Don Quixote.* Pt. i, ch. 25.

"Lippen all to him," he [Corp] said with grand confidence, "he'll find a wy."
J. M. BARRIE, *Sentimental Tommy.* Ch. 21.

He was capable of imagining all, of arranging all, and of doing everything. (Il était capable de tout imaginer, de tout arranger, et de tout faire.)
VOLTAIRE, *Précis de Siècle de Louis XV.* Referring to the Chevalier de Belle-Isle.

4
As we advance in life, we learn the limits of our abilities.
J. A. FROUDE, *Short Studies: Education.*

5
Every person is responsible for all the good within the range of his abilities, and for no more, and none can tell whose sphere is the largest.
GAIL HAMILTON, *Country Living and Country Thinking: Men and Women.*

6
Beyond one's powers. (Supra vires.)
HORACE, *Epistles.* Bk. i, epis. 18, l. 22.

7
The heart to conceive, the understanding to direct, or the hand to execute.
JUNIUS, *Letters.* Letter 37, 19 March, 1770.

He [Hampden] had a head to contrive, a tongue to persuade, and a hand to execute any mischief.
EDWARD HYDE, EARL OF CLARENDON, *History of the Rebellion,* iii, vii, 84. (1702)

In every deed of mischief he [Commenus] had a heart to resolve, a head to contrive, and a hand to execute.
EDWARD GIBBON, *Decline and Fall of the Roman Empire.* Ch. 48. (1776)

8
A Traveller at Sparta, standing long upon one leg, said to a Lacedæmonian, "I do not believe you can do as much." "True," said he, "but every goose can."
PLUTARCH, *Laconic Apothegms.* Sec. 233B.

9
No one knows what he can do till he tries. (Quid quisque posset, nisi temptando nesciit.)
PUBLILIUS SYRUS, *Sententiæ.* No. 786. (c. 50 B. C.)

10
A man's ability cannot possibly be of one sort and his soul of another. If his soul be well-ordered, serious, and restrained, his ability also is sound and sober. Conversely, when the one degenerates, the other is contaminated. (Non potest alius esse ingenio, alius animo color. . . . Illo vitiato hoc quoque adflatur.)
SENECA, *Epistulæ ad Lucilium.* Epis. cxiv, 3.

11
I am as able and as fit as thou.
SHAKESPEARE, *Titus Andronicus.* Act ii, sc. 1, l. 33.

12
Let every man be *occupied,* and occupied in the highest employment of which his nature is capable, and die with the consciousness that he has done his best.
SYDNEY SMITH, *Of Occupation.* (LADY HOLLAND, *Memoir.* Vol. i, p. 121.)

13
Men of great abilities are generally of a large and vigorous animal nature.
SIR HENRY TAYLOR, *The Statesman,* p. 229.

14
They can because they think they can. (Possunt, quia posse videntur.)
VERGIL, *Æneid.* Bk. v, l. 231.

What a man *kens* he *cans.*
CARLYLE, *French Revolution.* Pt. iii, bk. 3, ch. 4.

15
We cannot all do all things. (Non omnia possumus omnes.)
VERGIL, *Eclogues.* No. viii, l. 63.

Everyone excels in something in which another fails. (In aliis rebus alius est præstantior.)
PUBLILIUS SYRUS, *Sententiæ.* No. 17.

I never learned how to tune a harp, or play upon a lute; but I know how to raise a small and obscure city to glory and greatness.
THEMISTOCLES, on being taunted with his lack of social accomplishments. (PLUTARCH, *Lives: Cimon.* Ch. 9, sec. 2.)

16
Man's capacities have never been measured; nor are we to judge of what he can do by any precedents, so little has been tried.
H. D. THOREAU, *Walden.* Ch. 1.

17
And all may do, what has by man been done.
YOUNG, *Night Thoughts.* Night vi, l. 607.

ABSENCE

See also Parting, Separation

I—Absence: Apothegms

1
Brutus and Cassius shone by their absence.
CHÉNIER, *Tiberius.* Act i, sc. 1. A paraphrase of Tacitus (*Annals.* Bk. iii, sec. 76), who, speaking of the funeral procession of Junia, sister of Brutus and wife of Cassius, says, "Brutus and Cassius shone with preëminent lustre for the very reason that their images were not displayed."

Among the defects of the bill, which were numerous, one provision was conspicuous by its presence, and one by its absence.
LORD JOHN RUSSELL, *Address to the Electors of the City of London,* 6 April, 1859, referring to Lord Derby's Reform Bill.

2
Friends, though absent, are still present. (Et absentes adsunt.)
CICERO, *De Amicitia.* Ch. vii, sec. 23.

Absent in body, but present in spirit.
New Testament: I Corinthians, v, 3.

3
To him that absent is All things succeed amiss.
CERVANTES, *Don Quixote.* Pt. i, ch. 25.

4
The Lord watch between me and thee, when we are absent one from another.
Old Testament: Genesis, xxxi, 49.

5
The absent party is still faulty.
GEORGE HERBERT, *Jacula Prudentum.*

Never was the absent in the right. (Nunca los ausentes se hallaron justos.)
UNKNOWN. A Spanish proverb.

The absent shall not be made heir. (Absens hæres non erit.)
UNKNOWN. A Latin proverb.

6
Achilles absent was Achilles still.
HOMER, *Iliad.* Bk. xxii, l. 418. (Pope, tr.)

This is not the son of Achilles, but Achilles himself.
PLUTARCH, *Lives: Alcibiades.* A Greek proverb.

7
"Presents," I often say, "endear absents."
CHARLES LAMB, *Essays of Elia: A Dissertation upon Roast Pig.*

8
Let no one be willing to speak ill of the absent. (Absenti nemo non nocuisse velit.)
PROPERTIUS, *Elegies.* Bk. ii, eleg. 19, l. 32.

Everyone agrees that the absent are warned by a ringing in the ears when they are being talked about. (Absentes tinnitu aurium præsentire sermones de se receptum est.)
PLINY, *Naturalis Historia.* Bk. xxviii, sec. 2.

9
There is not one among them but I dote on his very absence.
SHAKESPEARE, *The Merchant of Venice.* Act i, sc. 2, l. 121.

10
Greater things are believed of those who are absent. (Majora credi de absentibus.)
TACITUS, *History.* Bk. ii, sec. 83.

11
Far from our eyes th' Enchanting Objects set,
Advantage by the friendly distance get.
UNKNOWN, *A Poem Against Fruition,* from *Poems by Several Hands* (1685). *See also under* DISTANCE.

12
He rages against the absent. (Sævit in absentis.)
VERGIL, *Æneid.* Bk. ix, l. 63.

II—Absence and Love

13
Until she come again
The May is not the May,
And what she calls a week
Is forever and a day!
THOMAS BAILEY ALDRICH, *Forever and a Day.*

14
Absence makes the heart grow fonder.
T. H. BAYLY, *Isle of Beauty.* The line is not original with Bayly, for it was the first line of an anonymous poem published in Davison's *Poetical Rhapsody,* 1602.

Distance only lends enchantment,
Though the ocean waves divide;
Absence makes the heart grow fonder,
Longing to be near your side.
ARTHUR GILLESPIE, *Absence Makes the Heart Grow Fonder.* (1900)

Absence makes the heart grow fonder—
Of the other fellow!
UNKNOWN, *Absence.*

15
But ay the tear comes in my ee,
To think on him that's far awa.
BURNS, *The Bonie Lad That's Far Awa.*

And my heart falls back to Erin's Isle,
To the girl I left behind me.
UNKNOWN, *The Girl I Left Behind Me.*

16
Absence! is not the soul torn by it
From more than light, or life, or breath?
'Tis Lethe's gloom, but not its quiet,—
The pain without the peace of death!
THOMAS CAMPBELL, *Absence.*

17
Absence from whom we love is worse than death,
And frustrate hope severer than despair.
COWPER, *Despair at His Separation,* l. 35.

18
Our hours in love have wings; in absence crutches.
COLLEY CIBBER, *Xerxes.* Act iv, sc. 3.

Love reckons hours for months, and days for years;
And every little absence is an age.
DRYDEN, *Amphitryon.* Act iii, sc. 1.

1
Though absent, present to desires they be;
Our soul much further than our eyes can see.
MICHAEL DRAYTON, *The Barons' Wars*. Bk. iii, l. 20. (1603)

2
Absence sharpens love, presence strengthens it.
THOMAS FULLER, *Gnomologia*. No. 755.

I find that absence still increases love.
CHARLES HOPKINS, *To C. C.*

Absences are a good influence in love and keep it bright and delicate.
R. L. STEVENSON, *Virginibus Puerisque*. Pt. i.

3
Think not, O thou guide of my youth, that absence can impair my respect, or interposing trackless deserts blot your reverend figure from my memory. . . . By every remove, I only drag a greater length of chain.
GOLDSMITH, *The Citizen of the World*. Letter 3.

Where'er I roam, whatever realms to see,
My heart untravell'd fondly turns to thee;
Still to my brother turns with ceaseless pain,
And drags at each remove a lengthening chain.
GOLDSMITH, *The Traveller*, l. 7.

4
The farther off, the more desired; thus lovers
tie their knot.
HENRY HOWARD, EARL OF SURREY, *The Faithfull Lover Declareth His Paines*. (c. 1540)

5
Distance sometimes endears friendship, and absence sweeteneth it.
JAMES HOWELL, *Familiar Letters*. Bk. i, sec. 1, let. 6. (1655)

Absent or dead, still let a friend be dear
(A sigh the absent claims, the dead a tear).
POPE, *Epistle to Robert Earl of Oxford*, l. 13.

6
My mother bids me bind my hair
With bands of rosy hue,
Tie up my sleeves with ribbands rare,
And lace my bodice blue;

For why, she cries, sit still and weep,
While others dance and play?
Alas, I scarce can go or creep,
While Lubin is away.
ANNE HUNTER, *My Mother Bids Me Bind My Hair*.

7
Ever absent, ever near;
Still I see thee, still I hear;
Yet I cannot reach thee, dear!
FRANCIS KAZINCZY, *Separation*.

8
What shall I do with all the days and hours
That must be counted ere I see thy face?
FRANCES ANNE KEMBLE, *Absence*.

9
What's this dull town to me?
Robin's not near—
He whom I wished to see,
Wished for to hear;
Where's all the joy and mirth
Made life a heaven on earth?
O! they're all fled with thee,
Robin Adair.
CAROLINE KEPPEL, *Robin Adair*.

10
Absence diminishes little passions and increases great ones, just as the wind blows out a candle and fans a fire. (L'absence diminue les médiocres passions, et augmente les grandes, comme le vent éteint les bougies et allume le feu.)
LA ROCHEFOUCAULD, *Maximes*. No. 276.

Absence is to love what wind is to a fire; it puts out the little, it kindles the great.
ROGER DE BUSSY-RABUTIN, *Epigram*.

11
Absence quickens our love and elevates our affections. Absence is the invisible and incorporeal mother of ideal beauty.
W. S. LANDOR, *Imaginary Conversations: Kosciusko and Poniatowski*.

12
Tho' lost to sight, to mem'ry dear
Thou ever wilt remain.
GEORGE LINLEY, *Tho' Lost to Sight*. Written by Linley, probably about 1830, for Augustus Braham, and sung by him with great success. The first line is much older and of unknown origin. It was quoted as an axiom in the *Monthly Magazine*, Jan., 1827.

Perchance all des'late and forlorn
These eyes shall miss thee many a year;
But unforgotten every charm—
Tho' lost to sight, to mem'ry dear.
RUTHVEN JENKINS, *Sweetheart, Good-Bye*. This poem was published in London in 1880 by Horace F. Cutler, who claimed to have discovered it in the *Greenwich Magazine for Marines* for 1803, but it was eventually proved that no such magazine existed, and that Cutler's claim was a hoax. (See *Notes and Queries*, 27 March, 1909, p. 249; 21 Oct., 1916, p. 336.)

Tho' lost to sight, within this filial breast
Hendrick still lives in all his might confest.
WILLIAM RIDER, *Tho' Lost to Sight*. (*London Magazine*, 1755, p. 589.)

13
Thou art gone from my gaze like a beautiful
dream,
And I seek thee in vain by the meadow and
stream.
GEORGE LINLEY, *Thou Art Gone*.

Ever of thee I'm fondly dreaming,
Thy gentle voice my spirit can cheer.
GEORGE LINLEY, *Ever of Thee*.

See also under MEMORY.

14
Absence not long enough to root out quite
All love, increases love at second sight.
THOMAS MAY, *Henry II*.

15
For there's nae luck about the house,
There's nae luck ava',

There's little pleasure in the house
When our gudeman's awa'.
WILLIAM JULIUS MICKLE, *The Sailor's Wife*. Sometimes attributed with slight foundation to Jean Adam.

1
But O the heavy change, now thou art gone,
Now thou art gone, and never must return!
JOHN MILTON, *Lycidas*, l. 37.

2
With what a deep devotedness of woe
I wept thy absence—o'er and o'er again
Thinking of thee, still thee, till thought grew pain,
And mem'ry, like a drop that, night and day,
Falls cold and ceaseless, wore my heart away!
THOMAS MOORE, *Lalla Rookh: The Veiled Prophet of Khorassan*, l. 510.

3
A boat at midnight sent alone
To drift upon the moonless sea,
A lute, whose leading chord is gone,
A wounded bird, that hath but one
Imperfect wing to soar upon,
Are like what I am, without thee.
THOMAS MOORE, *Loves of the Angels: The Second Angel's Story*, l. 1533.

4
But love will long for the absent things,
Ever the old earth over.
J. U. NICOLSON, *String Stars for Pearls*.

5
Ye flowers that droop, forsaken by the spring,
Ye birds that, left by Summer, cease to sing,
Ye trees, that fade when Autumn-heats remove,
Say, is not absence death to those who love?
POPE, *Pastorals: Autumn*, l. 27.

Condemn'd whole years in absence to deplore,
And image charms he must behold no more.
POPE, *Eloisa to Abelard*, l. 361.

6
When those who love are severed, love's tide stronger flows. (Semper in absentes felicior æstus amantes.)
PROPERTIUS, *Elegies*. Bk. ii, eleg. 33, l. 43.

7
What, keep a week away? seven days and nights?
Eight score eight hours? and lovers' absent hours,
More tedious than the dial eight score times?
O weary reckoning!
SHAKESPEARE, *Othello*. Act iii, sc. 4, l. 173.

All days are nights to see till I see thee,
And nights bright days when dreams do show thee me.
SHAKESPEARE, *Sonnets*. No. xliii.

How like a winter hath my absence been
From thee, the pleasure of the fleeting year!
SHAKESPEARE, *Sonnets*. No. xcvii.

8
She only said, "My life is dreary,
He cometh not," she said;
She said, "I am aweary, aweary,
I would that I were dead!"
TENNYSON, *Mariana*.

Jest a-wearyin' fer you—
All the time a-feelin' blue.
FRANK L. STANTON, *Wearyin' fer You*.

9
'Tis said that absence conquers love,
But oh! believe it not;
I've tried, alas! its power to prove,
But thou art not forgot.
FREDERICK WILLIAM THOMAS, *Song*.

10
Since you have waned from us,
Fairest of women!
I am a darkened cage
Songs cannot hymn in.
My songs have followed you,
Like birds the summer;
Ah! bring them back to me,
Swiftly, dear comer!
FRANCIS THOMPSON, *A Carrier Song*.

III—Absence: Out of Sight Out of Mind

11
Times daily change and we likewise in them;
Things out of sight do straight forgotten die.
WILLIAM ALEXANDER, *Aurora*. Sonnet lxiii.

12
To men a man is but a mind. Who cares
What face he carries or what form he wears?
But woman's body is the woman. O
Stay thou, my sweetheart, and do never go,
But heed the warning words the sage hath said:
A woman absent is a woman dead.
AMBROSE BIERCE, *The Devil's Dictionary*, p. 15.

13
Distance makes the heart less fond. (Spatio debilitatur amor.)
CLAUDIAN, *Epistula ad Olybrium*, l. 12. (c. 400 A. D.)

Absence is the enemy of love. (Assenza nemica di amore.)
UNKNOWN. An Italian proverb.

14
The rarer seen, the less in mind,
The less in mind, the lesser pain.
BARNABE GOOGE, *Out of Sight, Out of Mind*.

15
Out of sight, out of mind. (ἄιστος ἄπυστος.)
HOMER, *Odyssey*. Bk. i, l. 242.

As soon as the breath is out of their bodies, it is "Out of sight, out of mind." (ἄιστοι, ἄπυστοι.)
MARCUS AURELIUS, *Meditations*. Bk. iv, sec. 33.

16
Tis sweet to think, that, where'er we rove,
We are sure to find something blissful and dear;
And that, when we're far from the lips we love,

We've but to make love to the lips we are near.
THOMAS MOORE, *'Tis Sweet to Think.*

Wives in their husbands' absences grow subtler,
And daughters sometimes run off with the butler.
BYRON, *Don Juan.* Canto iii, st. 22.

'Tis ever common
That men are merriest when they are from home.
SHAKESPEARE, *Henry V.* Act i, sc. 2, l. 271.

1
A short absence is safest: affection wanes with lapse of time: an absent love vanishes, and a new one takes its place. (Sed mora tuta brevis: lentescunt tempore curæ, Vanescitque absens et novus intrat amor.)
OVID, *Ars Amatoria.* Bk. ii, l. 357.

2
Far as I journey from thy sight, so far
Shall love too journey from my mind.
(Quantum oculis, animo tam procul ibit amor.)
PROPERTIUS, *Elegies.* Bk. iii, eleg. 21, l. 10.

3
Indeed, sir, you'll find they will not be missed.
SHERIDAN, *The Critic.* Act ii, sc. 2.

He's got 'em on the list—he's got 'em on the list;
And they'll none of 'em be missed.
W. S. GILBERT, *The Mikado.* Act i.

4
And when man is out of sight, quickly also is he out of mind.
THOMAS À KEMPIS, *De Imitatione Christi.* Pt. i, ch. 23. (1460)

Out of sight, out of mind.
JOHN HEYWOOD, *Proverbs.* Pt. i, ch. 3. (1546)

Out of mind as soon as out of sight.
SIR FULKE GREVILLE, *Sonnets.* No. lvi. (c. 1600)

Out of sight out of mind seems to be a proverb which applies to enemies as well as friends.
SYDNEY SMITH, *Peter Plymley Letters.* No. 2.

That out of sight is out of mind
Is true of most we leave behind.
ARTHUR HUGH CLOUGH, *Songs in Absence.* No. 9.

I do perceive that the old proverb be not always true, for I do find that the absence of my Nath. doth breed in me the more continual remembrance of him.
ANNE, LADY BACON, *Letter,* to Jane, Lady Cornwallis. (1613) Bacon himself had quoted the proverb. (*Private Correspondence of Lady Cornwallis,* p. 19.)

5
He that is absent is soon forgotten.
UNKNOWN, *Proverbs of Alfred.* No. 134. (c. 1270)

Far from eyes, far from heart, quoth Hendyng.
UNKNOWN, *Proverbs of Hendyng.* (c. 1320)

6
Heart soon forgets what the eye sees not.
UNKNOWN, *Cursor Mundi,* l. 4508. (c. 1250)

See also under EYES: APOTHEGMS.

IV—Absence: Absence of Mind

7
My friend, Will Honeycomb, is one of those sort of men who are very often absent in conversation, and what the French call a *reveur* and a *distrait.*
ADDISON, *The Spectator,* 29 May, 1711.

8
What is commonly called an absent man, is commonly either a very weak or a very affected man; but be he which he will, he is, I am sure, a very disagreeable man in company.
LORD CHESTERFIELD, *Letters,* 9 Oct., 1746.

I would rather be in company with a dead man than with an absent one; for if the dead man gives me no pleasure, at least he shows me no contempt; whereas, the absent man, silently indeed, but very plainly, tells me that he does not think me worth his attention.
LORD CHESTERFIELD, *Letters,* 22 Sept., 1749.

9
But my thoughts ran a wool-gathering; and I did like the countryman, who looked for his ass while he was mounted on his back.
CERVANTES, *Don Quixote.* Pt. ii, ch. lvii.

Have you summoned your wits from wool-gathering?
MIDDLETON, *The Family of Love.* Act v, sc. 3.

10
For with G. D., to be absent from the body is sometimes (not to speak it profanely) to be present with the Lord.
CHARLES LAMB, *Essays of Elia: Oxford in the Vacation.*

Your absence of mind we have borne, till your presence of body came to be called in question by it.
CHARLES LAMB, *Last Essays of Elia: Amicus Redivivus.*

ABSTINENCE

See also Temperance, Prohibition

11
Abstinence sows sand all over
The ruddy limbs and flaming hair,
But Desire gratified
Plants fruits of life and beauty there.
WILLIAM BLAKE, *Gnomic Verses.* No. 10.

12
Touch not; taste not; handle not.
New Testament: Colossians, ii, 21.

Thou shalt abstain, Renounce, refrain.
(Entbehren sollst du! sollst entbehren.)
GOETHE, *Faust.* Pt. i, sc. 4.

13
Call'd to the temple of impure delight,
He that abstains, and he alone, does right.
If a wish wander that way, call it home;
He cannot long be safe whose wishes roam.
COWPER, *The Progress of Error,* l. 584.

14
Refin'd himself to Soul, to curb the Sense;
And made almost a Sin of Abstinence.
DRYDEN, *The Character of a Good Parson,* l. 10.

1
Abstinence is whereby a man refraineth from anything which he may lawfully take.
Sir Thomas Elyot, *The Governour*. Pt. iii, ch. 16. (1531)

2
Against diseases here the strongest fence
Is the defensive virtue, abstinence.
Robert Herrick, *Abstinence*.

3
Abstinence is as easy to me as temperance would be difficult.
Samuel Johnson. (More, *Johnsoniana*, 467.)

4
All is, I never drink no sperit,
Nor I haint never signed no pledge.
J. R. Lowell, *The Biglow Papers*. Ser. i, No. 7, st. 9.

5
The lean and sallow abstinence.
Milton, *Comus*, l. 709.

6
To abstain that we may enjoy is the epicurianism of reason. (L'abstenir pour jouir, c'est l'épicurisme de la raison.)
J.-J. Rousseau.

7
Refrain to-night,
And that shall lend a kind of easiness
To the next abstinence: the next more easy;
For use almost can change the stamp of nature.
Shakespeare, *Hamlet*. Act iii, sc. 4, l. 165.

8
And must I wholly banish hence
These red and golden juices,
And pay my vows to Abstinence,
That pallidest of Muses?
William Watson, *To a Fair Maiden Who Bade Me Shun Wine*.

ACCIDENT

See also Chance

9
Chapter of accidents.
Edmund Burke, *Notes for Speeches*. Vol. ii, p. 426.

The chapter of accidents is the longest chapter in the book.
John Wilkes. (Southey, *The Doctor*. Ch. 118.)

10
For things said false and never meant,
Do oft prove true by accident.
Samuel Butler, *Satire Upon the Weakness and Misery of Man*, l. 157.

11
I think it a very happy accident.
Cervantes, *Don Quixote*. Pt. ii, ch. 58.

By many a happy accident.
Thomas Middleton, *No Wit Like a Woman's*. Act ii, sc. 2.

12
By some fortuitous concourse of atoms. (Fortuito quodam concursu atomorum.)
Cicero, *De Natura Deorum*. Bk. i, ch. 24, sec. 66. Adapted. The words in Cicero are, "Nulla cogente natura, sed concursu quodam fortuito."

How comes it to pass, if they be only moved by chance and accident, that such regular mutations and generations should be begotten by a fortuitous concourse of atoms?
John Smith, of Cambridge, *Select Discourses*. Vol. iii, p. 48. (1669)

A blind, fortuitous concourse of atoms, not guided by an understanding agent.
John Locke, *An Essay Concerning Human Understanding*. Bk. iv, ch. 20, sec. 15. (1690)

Epicureans, that ascribed the origin and frame of the world not to the power of God, but to the fortuitous concourse of atoms.
Richard Bentley, *Sermons*. Vol. iii, p. 147. Preached in 1692.

To what a fortuitous concurrence do we not owe every pleasure and convenience of our lives.
Oliver Goldsmith, *Vicar of Wakefield*. Ch. 31.

See also under Circumstance.

13
Accidents, accidents will happen.
George Colman the Elder, *The Deuce is in Him*. Act i.

Accidents will happen—best regulated families.
Dickens, *Pickwick Papers*. Ch. 2.

Accidents will occur in the best regulated families.
Dickens, *David Copperfield*. Ch. 28. Scott, *Peveril of the Peak*. Last ch.

14
Our wanton accidents take root, and grow
To vaunt themselves God's laws.
Charles Kingsley, *The Saint's Tragedy*. Act ii, sc. 4.

15
Nothing under the sun is accidental.
Lessing, *Emilia Galotti*. Act iv, sc. 3.

At first laying down, as a fact fundamental,
That nothing with God can be accidental.
Longfellow, *The Golden Legend*. Pt. vi.

16
There's many a slip 'twixt the cup and the lip. (Πολλὰ μεταξὺ πέλει κύλικος, καὶ χείλεος ἄκρου.)
Palladas. (*Greek Anthology*. Bk. x, epig. 32.) A very ancient proverb, sometimes attributed to Homer, and frequently quoted. See Aulus Gellius, *Noctes Atticæ*. Bk. xiii, ch. 18, sec. 3.

Between the mouth and the morsel many things may happen. (Inter os atque offam multa intervenire posse.)
Cato the Censor, *On the Improper Election of Ædiles*. (Aulus Gellius, *Noctes Atticæ*. Bk. xiii, ch. 18, sec. 1.)

Many things fall between the cup and mouth.
Richard Taverner, *Proverbs*. Fo. 15. (1539)

Oft times many things fall out between the cup and the lip.
Robert Greene, *Perimedes the Blacksmith*. (1588)

Many things happen between the cup and the lip.
Robert Burton, *Anatomy of Melancholy*. Pt. ii, sec. ii, mem. 3. (1621)

1
What the reason of the ant laboriously drags into a heap, the wind of accident will collect in one breath.

SCHILLER, *Fiesco*. Act ii, sc. 4.

2
Wherein I spake of most disastrous chances,
Of moving accidents by flood and field.

SHAKESPEARE, *Othello*. Act i, sc. 3, l. 134.

3
The accident of an accident.

LORD EDWARD THURLOW, *Speech*, in reply to the Duke of Grafton. Grafton had taunted Thurlow, then Lord Chancellor, on his humble origin. Thurlow, advancing on Grafton, expressed his amazement at the speech and added: "The noble lord cannot look before him, behind him, or on either side of him without seeing some noble peer who owes his seat in this House to his successful exertions in the profession to which I belong. Does he not feel that it is as honourable to owe it to these as to being the accident of an accident?"

ACT, ACTION

See also Deed

4
Action is but coarsened thought—thought become concrete, obscure, and unconscious.

AMIEL, *Journal*, 30 Dec., 1850.

See also THOUGHT AND ACT.

5
The best way to keep good acts in memory is to refresh them with new.

CATO. (BACON, *Apothegms*. No. 247. Quoting Plutarch.)

Actions of the last age are like almanacs of the last year.

SIR JOHN DENHAM, *The Sophy*.

Good actions still must be maintained with good,
As bodies nourished with resembling food.

DRYDEN, *Coronation of Charles II*, l. 77.

6
He is at no end of his actions blest
Whose ends will make him greatest and not best.

GEORGE CHAPMAN, *Tragedy of Charles, Duke of Byron*. Act v, sc. 1.

See also END: MEANS AND END.

7
The only things in life in which we can be said to have any property, are *our actions*.

C. C. COLTON, *Lacon: Reflections*. No. 52.

8
Action! Action! Action!

DEMOSTHENES, when asked what were the three essentials of oratory. (PLUTARCH, *Lives of the Ten Orators*.) The saying has often been imitated. When Louis XI asked what was needed to make war, Marshal Trivulce replied, "Three things: money, more money, always money." (De l'argent, encore de l'argent, et toujours de l'argent.) Danton, in a speech before the National Assembly, August, 1792, said three things were needed to save France, "Boldness, more boldness, and always boldness." (De l'audace, encore de l'audace, et toujours de l'audace.) Gambetta (*Speech*, 24 June, 1872) prescribed, "Work, more work, and always work," to achieve success. Daniel O'Connell, when asked how to free Ireland, replied, "Agitate, agitate, agitate!" and was himself known as "the great agitator." Parnell changed the prescription to "Organize, organize, organize!"

For as action follows speeches and votes in the order of time, so does it precede and rank before them in force.

DEMOSTHENES, *Olynthiaca*. No. iii, sec. 6.

See also WORD AND DEED.

9
Prodigious actions may as well be done
By weaver's issue, as by prince's son.

DRYDEN, *Absalom and Achitophel*. Pt. i, l. 638.

10
Why should we be cowed by the name of Action? . . . The rich mind lies in the sun and sleeps, and is Nature. To think is to act.

EMERSON, *Essays, First Series: Spiritual Laws*.

11
I see how many firm acts have been done; how many valiant *noes* have this day been spoken, when others would have uttered ruinous *yeas*.

EMERSON, *Essays, Second Series: Character*.

12
We are taught by great actions that the universe is the property of every individual in it.

EMERSON, *Nature, Addresses, and Lectures: Beauty*.

13
Act, if you like,—but you do it at your peril. Men's actions are too strong for them. Show me a man who has acted and who has not been the victim and slave of his action.

EMERSON, *Representative Men: Goethe*.

14
Great actions speak great minds.

JOHN FLETCHER, *The Prophetess*. Act ii, sc. 3.

Great acts grow out of great occasions and great occasions spring from great principles, working changes in society, and tearing it up by the roots.

WILLIAM HAZLITT, *Table Talk*. Pt. i, ser. ii.

15
Our acts our angels are, or good or ill,
Our fatal shadows that walk by us still.

JOHN FLETCHER, *Upon an Honest Man's Fortune*.

16
Action is the proper fruit of knowledge.

THOMAS FULLER, *Gnomologia*. No. 760.

The great end of life is not knowledge, but action.

T. H. HUXLEY, *Technical Education*.

17
It is not book learning young men need, nor instruction about this and that, but a stiffening of the vertebræ which will cause them to be loyal to a trust, to act promptly, concen-

trate their energies, do a thing—"carry a message to Garcia."

ELBERT HUBBARD, *A Message to Garcia,* first printed in *The Philistine,* March, 1900. The man who carried the message to Garcia was Lieut. Andrew S. Rowan, of the Bureau of Military Intelligence. It was delivered 1 May, 1898.

1
A man's acts are usually right, but his reasons seldom are.

ELBERT HUBBARD, *The Philistine.* Vol. xix, p. 143.

2
Although men flatter themselves with their great actions, they are usually the result of chance and not of design. (Quoique les hommes se flattent de leurs grandes actions, elles ne sont pas souvent les effets d'un grand dessein, mais des effets du hasard.)

LA ROCHEFOUCAULD, *Maximes.* No. 57.

We would often be ashamed of our finest actions if the world understood all the motives which produced them. (Nous aurions souvent honte de nos plus belles actions, si le monde voyait tous les motifs qui les produisent.)

LA ROCHEFOUCAULD, *Maximes.* No. 409.

3
No action, whether foul or fair,
Is ever done, but it leaves somewhere
A record, written by fingers ghostly,
As a blessing or a curse, and mostly
In the greater weakness or greater strength
Of the acts which follow it.

LONGFELLOW, *The Golden Legend.* Pt. ii.

4
Trust no Future, howe'er pleasant!
Let the dead Past bury its dead!
Act,—act in the living Present!
Heart within, and God o'erhead!

LONGFELLOW, *A Psalm of Life.*

5
Every man feels instinctively that all the beautiful sentiments in the world weigh less than a single lovely action.

J. R. LOWELL, *Among My Books: Rousseau and the Sentimentalists.*

Actions speak louder than words.

A sentiment which appears in the proverbial literature of all languages. *See* WORD AND DEED.

6
Execute every act of thy life as though it were thy last. (*Ὡς ἐσχάτην τοῦ βίου ἑκάστην πρᾶξιν ἐνεργῆς.*)

MARCUS AURELIUS, *Meditations.* Bk. ii, sec. 5. His prescription for a life of tranquillity and godliness.

Let thine every act and word and thought be those of a man who can depart from life this moment. (*Ὡς ἤδη δυνατοῦ ὄντος ἐξιέναι τοῦ βίου, οὕτως ἕκαστα ποιεῖν καὶ λέγειν καὶ διανοεῖσθαι.*)

MARCUS AURELIUS, *Meditations.* Bk. ii, sec. 11.

7
A due sense of value and proportion should regulate the care bestowed on every action.

MARCUS AURELIUS, *Meditations.* Bk. iv, sec. 32.

8
So much one man can do
That doth both act and know.

ANDREW MARVELL, *Horatian Ode Upon Cromwell's Return from Ireland.*

9
Life is Act, and not to Do is Death.

LEWIS MORRIS, *The Epic of Hades: Sisyphus.*

10
Not always actions show the man: we find
Who does a kindness is not therefore kind.

POPE, *Moral Essays.* Epis. i, l. 109.

11
Before you begin, get good counsel; then, having decided, act promptiy. (Prius quam incipias consulto, et ubi consulueris mature facto opus est.)

SALLUST, *Catilina.* Sec. i.

12
Our actions are honorable, but not the actual things which we do. (Actiones nostræ honestæ sunt, non ipsa quæ agentur.)

SENECA, *Epistulœ ad Lucilium.* Epis. xcii, sec. 13.

13
Action is eloquence.

SHAKESPEARE, *Coriolanus.* Act iii, sc. 2, l. 76.

14
It is no act of common passage, but
A strain of rareness.

SHAKESPEARE, *Cymbeline.* Act iii, sc. 4, l. 94.

All your acts are queens.

SHAKESPEARE, *The Winter's Tale.* Act iv, sc. 4, l. 146.

15
What act
That roars so loud and thunders in the index?

SHAKESPEARE, *Hamlet.* Act iii, sc. 4, l. 51.

16
Heaven ne'er helps the men who will not act.

SOPHOCLES, *Fragments,* No. 288.

17
I myself must mix with action, lest I wither by despair.

TENNYSON, *Locksley Hall,* l. 98.

18
If we would really know our heart, let us impartially view our actions.

BISHOP THOMAS WILSON, *Maxims of Piety,* 151.

19
Action is transitory, a step, a blow,
The motion of a muscle—this way or that.

WORDSWORTH, *The Borderers.* Act iii.

ACTING

See also Stage; Life: A Play; World: A Stage

20
An actor is a sculptor who carves in snow.

LAWRENCE BARRETT. (Ascribed to him by Wilton Lackaye in conversation with George C. Tyler.)

1
Farce follow'd Comedy, and reach'd her prime,
In ever-laughing Foote's fantastic time: . . .
"Alas, poor Yorick!" now forever mute!
Whoever loves a laugh must sigh for Foote.
We smile, perforce, when histrionic scenes
Ape the swoln dialogue of kings and queens,
When "Chrononhotonthologos must die,"
And Arthur struts in mimic majesty.

BYRON, *Hints from Horace*, l. 329.

To see Kean act was like reading Shakespeare by flashes of lightning.

S. T. COLERIDGE, *Table Talk*.

He doesn't act on the stage; he behaves.

OSCAR WILDE, of George Alexander. (HARRIS, *Oscar Wilde*, p. 342.)

2
Never meddle with actors, for they are a favored class. . . . Remember that, as they are merry folk who give pleasure, everyone favors and protects them.

CERVANTES, *Don Quixote*. Pt. ii, ch. 11.

3
Then there are no more actors.

RUFUS CHOATE, when told of the death of Junius Brutus Booth, 30 Nov., 1852.

It's a great loss—there's damned few of us left.

JOHN L. SULLIVAN, when told of the death of Edwin Booth.

4
On this great stage, the world, no monarch e'er
Was half so haughty as a monarch player.

CHARLES CHURCHILL, *The Apology*, l. 254.

See also under KING.

5
And what the actor could effect,
The scholar could presage.

THOMAS CAMPBELL, *Stanzas to J. P. Kemble*.

6
The Poet, to the end of time,
Breathes in his works and lives in rhyme;
But, when the Actor sinks to rest,
And the turf lies upon his breast,
A poor traditionary fame
Is all that's left to grace his name.

WILLIAM COMBE, *Dr. Syntax in Search of the Picturesque*. Canto xxiv.

7
Massive and concrete.

DICKENS, *Great Expectations*. Ch. 31. Herbert Pocket's whispered prompting of Pip, to compliment Wopsle's acting of Hamlet.

8
No! I am not Prince Hamlet, nor was meant to be;
Am an attendant lord, one that will do
To swell a progress, start a scene or two.

T. S. ELIOT, *The Love Song of J. Alfred Prufrock*.

Tom Goodwin was an actor-man,
Old Drury's pride and boast,
In all the light and sprite-ly parts,
Especially the Ghost.

J. G. SAXE, *The Ghost-Player*. St. 1.

9
"He the best player!" cries Partridge, with a contemptuous sneer. "Why, I could act as well as he myself. I am sure, if I had seen a ghost, I should have looked in the very same manner, and done just as he did. . . . The king for my money! He speaks all his words distinctly, half as loud again as the other. Anybody may see he is an actor."

HENRY FIELDING, *Tom Jones*. Bk. xvi, ch. 5.

10
Everybody has his own theatre, in which he is manager, actor, prompter, playwright, sceneshifter, boxkeeper, doorkeeper, all in one, and audience into the bargain.

J. C. and A. W. HARE, *Guesses at Truth*. Ser. ii.

11
It worries me to beat the band
To hear folks say our life is grand;
Wish they'd try some one-night stand—
Ain't it awful, Mabel?

JOHN EDWARD HAZZARD, *Ain't It Awful, Mabel?* Referring to the actor's life.

12
It's very hard! Oh, Dick, my boy,
It's very hard one can't enjoy
A little private spouting;
But sure as Lear or Hamlet lives,
Up comes our master, Bounce, and gives
The tragic muse a routing.

THOMAS HOOD, *The Stage-Struck Hero*.

13
Beggars, actors, buffoons, and all that breed.
(Mendici, mimæ, balatrones, hoc genus omne.)

HORACE, *Satires*. Bk. i, sat. 2, l. 2.

The strolling tribe; a despicable race.

CHARLES CHURCHILL, *Apology*, l. 206. (1761)

Peel'd, patch'd, and piebald, linsey-woolsey brothers,
Grave Mummers! sleeveless some and shirtless others.

POPE, *The Dunciad*. Bk. iii, l. 115. (1712)

14
And on the last day when we leave those we love
And move in a mournful procession,
I hope we'll both play star engagements above,
For I'm sure they "admit the profession."

JOSEPH JEFFERSON, *Letter*, to Laurence Hutton.

15
Does over-act prodigiously.

BEN JONSON, *The Staple of News: Induction*.

Emotional stilts.

THOMAS WALLACE KEENE, his description of his style of acting. (*Dictionary Amer. Biog.*, x, 285.)

I will do it in King Cambyses' vein.

SHAKESPEARE, *I Henry IV*. Act ii, sc. 4, l. 426. Cambyses was a pompous, ranting character in Thomas Preston's "lamentable tragedy" of that name.

1
Acting is therefore the lowest of the arts, if it is an art at all.
GEORGE MOORE, *Mummer-worship.*

2
To wake the soul by tender strokes of art,
To raise the genius, and to mend the heart;
To make mankind, in conscious virtue bold,
Live o'er each scene, and be what they behold:
For this the Tragic Muse first trod the stage.
POPE, *Prologue to Addison's Cato,* l. 1.

3
Like a dull actor now,
I have forgot my part, and I am out,
Even to a full disgrace.
SHAKESPEARE, *Coriolanus.* Act v, sc. 3, l. 40.

As an unperfect actor on the stage
Who with his fear is put besides his part.
SHAKESPEARE, *Sonnets.* No. xxiii.

One that never trod the stage before.
RICHARD STEELE, *Spectator.* No. 22.

4
Good my lord, will you see the players well bestowed? Do you hear, let them be well used; for they are the abstract and brief chronicles of the time: after your death you were better have a bad epitaph than their ill report while you live.
SHAKESPEARE, *Hamlet.* Act ii, sc. 2, l. 545.

5
Is it not monstrous that this player here,
But in a fiction, in a dream of passion,
Could force his soul so to his own conceit
That from her working all his visage wann'd,
Tears in his eyes, distraction in 's aspect,
A broken voice, and his whole function suiting
With forms to his conceit? and all for nothing!
For Hecuba!
What's Hecuba to him, or he to Hecuba,
That he should weep for her? What would he do,
Had he the motive and the cue for passion
That I have? He would drown the stage with tears.
SHAKESPEARE, *Hamlet.* Act ii, sc. 2, l. 577.

To make the weeper laugh, the laugher weep,
He had the dialect and different skill,
Catching all passions in his craft of will.
SHAKESPEARE, *A Lover's Complaint,* l. 124.

6
Speak the speech, I pray you, as I pronounced it to you, trippingly on the tongue: but if you mouth it, as many of your players do, I had as lief the town-crier spoke my lines. Nor do not saw the air too much with your hand, thus, but use all gently; for in the very torrent, tempest, and, as I may say, the whirlwind of passion, you must acquire and beget a temperance that may give it smoothness. O, it offends me to the soul to hear a robustious periwig-pated fellow tear a passion to tatters, to very rags, to split the ears of the groundlings. . . . Be not too tame, neither, but let your own discretion be your tutor: suit the action to the word, the word to the action; with this special observance, that you o'erstep not the modesty of nature: for any thing so overdone is from the purpose of playing, whose end, both at the first and now, was and is, to hold, as 'twere, the mirror up to nature; to show virtue her own feature, scorn her own image, and the very age and body of the time his form and pressure. Now this overdone, or come tardy off, though it make the unskilful laugh, cannot but make the judicious grieve; the censure of the which one must in your allowance o'erweigh a whole theatre of others. O, there be players that I have seen play, and heard others praise, and that highly, not to speak it profanely, that, neither having the accent of Christians nor the gait of Christian, pagan, nor man, have so strutted and bellowed that I have thought some of nature's journeymen had made men and not made them well, they imitated humanity so abominably. . . . And let those that play your clowns speak no more than is set down for them; for there be of them that will themselves laugh, to set on some quantity of barren spectators to laugh too; though, in the mean time, some necessary question of the play be then to be considered: that's villanous, and shows a most pitiful ambition in the fool that uses it.
SHAKESPEARE, *Hamlet.* Act iii, sc. 2, l. 1.

Who teach the mind its proper face to scan,
And hold the faithful mirror up to man.
ROBERT LLOYD, *The Actor,* l. 265.

7
Play out the play.
SHAKESPEARE, *I Henry IV.* Act ii, sc. 4, l. 531.

8
As in a theatre, the eyes of men,
After a well-graced actor leaves the stage,
Are idly bent on him that enters next,
Thinking his prattle to be tedious.
SHAKESPEARE, *Richard II.* Act v, sc. 2, l. 23.

9
A part to tear a cat in, to make all split.
SHAKESPEARE, *A Midsummer Night's Dream.* Act i, sc. 2, l. 32.

I can counterfeit the deep tragedian;
Speak and look back, and pry on every side,
Tremble and start at wagging of a straw,
Intending deep suspicion.
SHAKESPEARE, *Richard III.* Act iii, sc. 5, l. 5.

Like a strutting player, whose conceit
Lies in his hamstring, and doth think it rich
To hear the wooden dialogue and sound
'Twixt his stretch'd footing and the scaffoldage.
SHAKESPEARE, *Troilus and Cressida.* Act i, sc. 3, l. 153.

"Ham," a poor and generally fatuous performer, was originally "ham fatter," a neophyte in the minstrel ranks, forced to sing "Ham Fat," an old ditty of the George Christy days.
EDWARD B. MARKS, *They All Sang*, p. 66.

1
If one tolerable page appears
In folly's volume, 'tis the actor's leaf,
Who dries his own by drawing others' tears,
And, raising present mirth, makes glad his future years.
HORACE SMITH, *Rejected Addresses: Cui Bono?*

2
The purple robe and silver's shine
More fit an actor's needs than mine.
SOCRATES. (DIOGENES LAERTIUS, *Socrates*. Sec. 8.)

3
The play is done; the curtain drops,
Slow falling to the prompter's bell:
A moment yet the actor stops,
And looks around, to say farewell.
It is an irksome word and task:
And, when he's laughed and said his say,
He shows, as he removes the mask,
A face that's anything but gay.
THACKERAY, *The End of the Play*.

ADAM AND EVE

See also Ancestry: Children of Adam

4
Adam was. ('Αδὰμ ἦν ζο.)
UNKNOWN, *On the Transfiguration*. (*Greek Anthology*. Bk. i, epig. 48.)

5
Grant that the old Adam in these persons may be so buried, that the new man may be raised up in them.
Book of Common Prayer: Baptism of Those of Riper Years.

Consideration, like an angel, came
And whipp'd the offending Adam out of him.
SHAKESPEARE, *Henry V*. Act i, sc. 1, l. 29.

6
'Tis old to you
As the story of Adam and Eve, and possibly quite as true.
ROBERT BROWNING, *Ivàn Ivànovitch*, l. 16.

7
That Adam, called "the happiest of men."
BYRON, *Don Juan*. Canto xiv, st. 55.

8
The High God, when he hadde Adam maked,
And saw him all alone, belly-naked,
God of his greate goodness sedye then,
"Let us now make a help unto this man
Like to himself;" and then he made him Eve.
CHAUCER, *The Marchantes Tale*, l. 81.

Our grandsire Adam, ere of Eve possess'd,
Alone, and ev'n in Paradise unbless'd,
With mournful looks the blissful scene survey'd,
And wander'd in the solitary shade.
The Maker saw, took pity, and bestow'd
Woman, the last, the best reserv'd of God.
POPE, *January and May*, l. 59. (CHAUCER, *The Marchantes Tale.*)

9
The fall of the first Adam was the end of the beginning; the rise of the second Adam was the beginning of the end.
S. W. DUFFIELD, *Fragments*.

10
'Tis Lilith. . . . Adam's first wife is she.
Beware the lure within her lovely tresses.
GOETHE, *Faust*: Sc. 21, *Walpurgisnacht*. (Bayard Taylor, tr.)

Of Adam's first wife, Lilith, it is told
(The witch he loved before the gift of Eve)
That, ere the snake's, her sweet tongue could deceive
And her enchanted hair was the first gold.
And still she sits, young while the earth is old,
And, subtly of herself contemplative,
Draws men to watch the bright web she can weave,
Till heart and body and life are in its hold.
DANTE GABRIEL ROSSETTI, *Body's Beauty*.

11
That the woman was made of a rib out of the side of Adam . . . to be equal with him, under his arm to be protected, and near his heart to be loved.
MATTHEW HENRY, *Commentaries: Genesis*, ii, 21. *See also* WOMAN: HER CREATION.

12
Eve, with her basket, was
Deep in the bells and grass
Wading in bells and grass
Up to her knees,
Picking a dish of sweet
Berries and plums to eat,
Down in the bells and grass
Under the trees.
RALPH HODGSON, *Eve*.

Picture that orchard sprite,
Eve, with her body white,
Supple and smooth to her
Slim finger tips.
RALPH HODGSON, *Eve*.

13
Was the apple applesauce
Eve ate in the garden?
Aren't you all a total loss?
No? I beg your pardon!
SAMUEL HOFFENSTEIN, *Poems in Praise of Practically Nothing*. No. 4.

14
All the world was Adam once, with Eve by his side.
JEAN INGELOW, *Like a Laverock in the Lift*.

15
Adam, whiles he spake not, had paradise at will.
WILLIAM LANGLAND, *Piers Plowman*. Passus xiv, l. 226.

16
Adam the goodliest man of men since born
His sons, the fairest of her daughters Eve.
MILTON, *Paradise Lost*. Bk. iv, l. 323.

For contemplation he and valour form'd,
For softness she and sweet attractive grace.
MILTON, *Paradise Lost*. Bk. iv, l. 297.

1 Her rash hand in evil hour
Forth reaching to the fruit, she pluck'd, she eat:
Earth felt the wound, and Nature from her seat
Sighing through all her works gave signs of woe,
That all was lost.
MILTON, *Paradise Lost*. Bk. ix, l. 780.

2
When Eve upon the first of Men
The apple press'd with specious cant,
Oh, what a thousand pities then
That Adam was not Adam-ant!
THOMAS HOOD, *A Reflection*.

Adam was but human—this explains it all. He did not want the apple for the apple's sake, he wanted it only because it was forbidden.
MARK TWAIN, *Pudd'nhead Wilson's Calendar*.

What you have told us is all very good. It is indeed bad to eat apples. It is better to make them all into cider.
BENJAMIN FRANKLIN, *Remarks Concerning the Savages of North America*. Reply of an Indian orator, after hearing a missionary's story of the fall of man.

3
There is no ancient gentlemen but gardeners, ditchers, and grave-makers; they hold up Adam's profession.
SHAKESPEARE, *Hamlet*. Act v, sc. 1, l. 35.

And Adam was a gardener.
SHAKESPEARE, *II Henry VI*. Act iv, sc. 2, l. 142.

The gardener Adam and his wife.
TENNYSON, *Lady Clara Vere de Vere*. St. 7.

The first men in the world were a Gardener, a Ploughman and a Grazier.
THOMAS FULLER, *Gnomologia*.

WHEN ADAM DELVED, *see under* ANCESTRY.

4
Whoever has lived long enough to find out what life is, knows how deep a debt of gratitude we owe to Adam, the first great benefactor of our race. He brought death into the world.
MARK TWAIN, *Pudd'nhead Wilson's Calendar*.

Of man's first disobedience, and the fruit
Of that forbidden tree, whose mortal taste.
Brought death into the world, and all our woe.
MILTON, *Paradise Lost*. Bk. i, l. 1.

5
Think how poor Mother Eve was brought
To being as God's afterthought.
ANNA WICKHAM, *To Men*.

6
Whilst Adam slept, Eve from his side arose:
Strange his first sleep should be his last repose.
UNKNOWN, *The Consequence*.

What? Rise again with *all* one's bones?
Quoth Giles, I hope you fib.
I trusted when I went to Heaven
To go without my rib.
S. T. COLERIDGE, *Epigram*.

He knew the seat of Paradise, . . .
What Adam dreamt of when his bride
Came from her closet in his side: . . .
If either of them had a navel.
BUTLER, *Hudibras*, Pt. i, canto i, l. 173.

7
In Adam's fall We sinnèd all.
UNKNOWN, *The New England Primer*.

8
Not without wisdom was Adam so called, for the four letters represent the four quarters of the earth. The Alpha is from Anatolé, the East; the Delta from Dysis, the West; the second Alpha from Arctus, the North; and the Mu from Mesembria, the South.
UNKNOWN, *On Adam*. (*Greek Anthology*. Bk. i, epig. 108.)

9
Adam
Had 'em.
STRICKLAND GILLILAN, *Lines on the Antiquity of Microbes*. Said to be the shortest poem in the language.

ADAPTABILITY

10
Nothing is more politic than to make the wheels of the mind concentric and voluble with the wheels of fortune.
FRANCIS BACON, *Advancement of Learning: Of the Understanding*.

11
You shall see a bold fellow many times do Mahomet's miracle. Mahomet made the people believe that he would call an hill to him, and from the top of it offer up his prayers, for the observers of his law. The people assembled; Mahomet called the hill to come to him, again and again; and when the hill stood still, he was never a whit abashed, but said: If the hill will not come to Mahomet, Mahomet will go to the hill.
FRANCIS BACON, *Essays: Of Boldness*.

12
I am of a constitution so general, that it consorts and sympathiseth with all things. I have no antipathy, or rather idiosyncrasy, in diet, humour, air, any thing.
SIR THOMAS BROWNE, *Religio Medici*. Pt. ii, sec. 1.

13
I am made all things to all men.
New Testament: I Corinthians, ix, 22.

If they, directed by Paul's holy pen,
Become discreetly all things to all men,
That all men may become all things to them,
Envy may hate, but Justice can't condemn.
CHURCHILL, *The Prophecy of Famine*, l. 211.

Mrs. Akemit was not only like St. Paul, "all things to all men," but she had gone a step beyond that excellent theologue. She could be all things to one man.
HARRY LEON WILSON, *The Spenders*, p. 241.

I have been all things and it has availed nothing. (Omnia fui et nihil expedit.)
SEPTIMIUS SEVERUS. (*Historia Augusti*, x, 18.)

1
He was capable of adapting himself to place, time and person, and of playing his part appropriately under whatever circumstances.
DIOGENES LAERTIUS, *Aristippus*. Bk. ii, sec. 66.

2
The wise man does no wrong in changing his habits with the times. (Temporibus mores sapiens sine crimine mutat.)
DIONYSIUS CATO, *Disticha de Moribus*. Bk. i, No. 7.

3
Were I a nightingale, I would act the part of a nightingale; were I a swan, the part of a swan. (Εἰ γοῦν ἀηδὼν ἤμην, ἐποίουν τὰ τῆς ἀηδόνος, εἰ κύκνος, τὰ τοῦ κύκνου.)
EPICTETUS, *Discourses*. Bk. i, ch. 16, sec. 20.

4
Every tree and shrub is a distaff for holding, and every twig a spindle for spinning, the material with which God invests it.
J. G. HOLLAND, *Gold-Foil: Exordial Essay*.

5
Don't vie with me, he says, and he says true;
My wealth will bear the silly things I do;
Yours is a slender pittance at the best:
A wise man cuts his coat—you know the rest. (Meæ contendere noli
Stultitiam patiuntur opes; tibi parvola res est.
Arta decet sanum comitem toga.)
HORACE, *Epistles*. Bk. i, epis. 18, l. 28. (Conington, tr.)

Cut my coat after my cloth.
UNKNOWN, *Godly Queene Hester: Interlude*. (1530) The phrase is said to be a relic of the sumptuary laws.

I shall cut my coat after my cloth.
JOHN HEYWOOD, *Proverbs*. Pt. i, ch. 8. (1546)

They must shape their coats, good men, according to their cloth.
THOMAS NASHE, *Unfortunate Traveller*. (1594)

Conform thyself to thy present fortune, and cut thy coat according to thy cloth.
ROBERT BURTON, *Anatomy of Melancholy*. Pt. i, sec. 2, mem. 3. (1621)

Cut your cloth, sir, according to your calling.
BEAUMONT AND FLETCHER, *The Beggar's Bush*. Act iv, sc. 1. (1622)

According to her cloth she cut her coat.
DRYDEN, *The Cock and the Fox*, l. 20. (1700)

We must cut our coat according to our cloth, and adapt ourselves to changing circumstances.
DEAN W. R. INGE, *Lay Thoughts*, p. 187.

6
Adapt thyself to the estate which is thy portion. (Οἷς συγκεκλήρωσαι πραγμασι, τούτοις συνάρμοζε σεαυτόν.)
MARCUS AURELIUS, *Meditations*. Bk. vi, sec. 39.

Every man must fashion his gait according
To his calling.
BEAUMONT AND FLETCHER, *Love's Cure*. Act i, sc. 2.

7
Treat a thousand dispositions in a thousand ways. (Mille animos excipe mille modis.)
OVID, *Ars Amatoria*. Bk. i, l. 756.

Who to mankind will not adapt himself,
For his disdain must pay the penalty.
(Humanitati qui se non accommodat,
Plerumque poenas oppetit superbiæ.)
PHÆDRUS, *Fables*. Bk. iii, fab. 16, l. 7.

8
A man of all hours: i. e., ready for anything. (Omnium horarum homo.)
QUINTILIAN, *De Institutione Oratoria*. Bk. vi, ch. 3. See also APPENDIX, p. 2296.

9
My nature is subdued
To what it works in, like the dyer's hand.
SHAKESPEARE, *Sonnets*. No. cxi.

10
It is safest to be moderately base—to be flexible in shame, and to be always ready for what is generous, good, and just, when anything is to be gained by virtue.
SYDNEY SMITH, *Essays: The Catholic Question*.

ADDISON, JOSEPH

11
Whoever wishes to attain an English style, familiar but not coarse, and elegant but not ostentatious, must give his days and nights to the volumes of Addison.
SAMUEL JOHNSON, *Lives of the Poets: Addison*.

12
No whiter page than Addison remains.
He from the taste obscene reclaims our youth,
And sets the passions on the side of Truth,
Forms the soft bosom with the gentlest Art,
And pours each human virtue in the heart.
POPE, *Imitations of Horace: Epistles*. Bk. ii, epis. 1, l. 216.

Were there one whose fires
True Genius kindles, and fair Fame inspires,
Bless'd with each talent and each art to please,
And born to write, converse, and live with ease;
Should such a man, too fond to rule alone,
Bear, like the Turk, no brother near the throne;
View him with scornful, yet with jealous eyes,
And hate for arts that caus'd himself to rise;
Damn with faint praise, assent with civil leer,
And without sneering teach the rest to sneer;
Willing to wound, and yet afraid to strike,
Just hint a fault, and hesitate dislike;
Alike reserv'd to blame or to commend,
A tim'rous foe, and a suspicious friend;
Dreading ev'n fools, by flatterers besieged,
And so obliging that he ne'er obliged,
Like Cato, give his little Senate laws,
And sit attentive to his own applause:
While Wits and Templars ev'ry sentence raise,
And wonder with a foolish face of praise—
Who but must laugh if such a man there be?
Who would not weep, if Atticus were he?
POPE, *Epistle to Dr. Arbuthnot*, l. 193. (Atticus: i. e., Addison.)

1
When panting Virtue her last efforts made,
You brought your Clio to the virgin's aid.
WILLIAM SOMERVILLE, *Poetical Address to Mr. Addison*. A reference to the fact that Addison signed his papers in *The Spectator* with one or other of the letters making up the name of Clio, the Muse of history. Dr. Johnson said of this couplet: "The couplet which mentions Clio is written with the most exquisite delicacy of praise; it exhibits one of those happy strokes which are seldom attained."

2
If business calls, or crowded courts invite,
Th' unblemish'd statesman seems to strike my sight;
If in the stage I seek to soothe my care,
I meet his soul which breathes in Cato there;
If pensive to the rural shades I rove,
His shape o'ertakes me in the lonely grove;
'Twas there of just and good he reason'd strong,
Clear'd some great truth, or rais'd some serious song:
There patient show'd us the wise course to steer,
A candid censor and a friend severe.
THOMAS TICKELL, *To the Earl of Warwick, on the Death of Mr. Addison.*

Nor e'er was to the bowers of bliss convey'd
A fairer spirit or more welcome shade.
THOMAS TICKELL, *To the Earl of Warwick, on the Death of Mr. Addison.*

ADMIRATION

3
A fool always finds a greater fool to admire him. (Un sot trouve toujours un plus sot qui l'admire.)
BOILEAU, *L'Art Poétique*. Pt. i, l. 232.

4
Then take what gold could never buy—
An honest bard's esteem.
BURNS, *To John McMurdo.*

5
No nobler feeling than this of admiration for one higher than himself dwells in the breast of man.
CARLYLE, *Heroes and Hero-Worship: The Hero as Divinity.*

6
There is an admiration which is the daughter of knowledge. (Il est une admiration qui est fille du savoir.)
JOUBERT, *Pensées*. No. 77.

7
That I may admire you, and not your belongings. (Ut miremur te, non tua.)
JUVENAL, *Satires*. Sat. viii, l. 68.

9
Lues Boswelliana, or disease of admiration.
MACAULAY, *Essays: William Pitt*. Par. 2.

10
Yet let not each gay turn thy rapture move;
For fools admire, but men of sense approve.
POPE, *Essay on Criticism*. Pt. ii, l. 190.

11
For all who understood, admired,
And some who did not understand them.
WINTHROP MACKWORTH PRAED, *The Vicar.*

12
We are interested in others when they are interested in us.
PUBLILIUS SYRUS, *Sententiæ*. No. 16.

We always love those who admire us, but we do not always love those whom we admire. (Nous aimons toujours ceux qui nous admirent, et nous n'aimons pas toujours ceux que nous admirons.)
LA ROCHEFOUCAULD, *Maximes*. No. 294.

13
To admire (or wonder at) nothing. (Μηδὲν θαυμάζειν.)
PYTHAGORAS, *Maxim*. A caution against undue enthusiasm. See PLUTARCH, *Moralia: On Listening to Lectures*. Sec. 44B. CICERO, *Tusculanarum Disputationum*, bk. iii, ch. 14, sec. 30, gives the Latin, "Nihil admirari." Dr. Arnold called it "the devil's favourite text."

Nil admirari: a very necessary lesson.
LORD CHESTERFIELD, *Letters*, 27 Sept., 1748.

14
To admire nothing, (as most are wont to do;)
Is the only method that I know
To make men happy, and to keep them so.
(Nil admirari prope res et una, Numici,
Solaque quæ possit facere et servare beatum.)
HORACE, *Epistles*. Bk. i, epis. 6, l. 1. (Creech, tr.)

Not to admire, is all the art I know
To make men happy and to keep them so.
POPE, *Imitations of Horace*. Adapted from Creech's translation.

"Not to admire is all the art I know
(Plain truth, dear Murray, needs few flowers of speech)
To make men happy, or to keep them so"
(So take it in the very words of Creech)—
Thus Horace wrote, we all know, long ago;
And thus Pope quotes the precept, to re-teach
From his translation; but had *none admired,*
Would Pope have sung, or Horace been inspired?
BYRON, *Don Juan*. Canto v, st. 101.

And I must say, I ne'er could see the very
Great happiness of the "Nil Admirari."
BYRON, *Don Juan*. Canto v, st. 100.

15
Season your admiration for a while.
SHAKESPEARE, *Hamlet*. Act i, sc. 2, l. 192.

Admiration did not hoop at them.
SHAKESPEARE, *Henry V*. Act ii, sc. 2, l. 108.

16
We hear it not seldom said that ignorance is the mother of admiration. No falser word was ever spoken, and hardly a more mischievous one.
R. C. TRENCH, *The Study of Words: Introductory Lecture.*

1
We live by Admiration, Hope, and Love.
WORDSWORTH, *The Excursion*. Bk. iv, l. 763.

The freshness, the everlasting youth,
Of admiration sprung from truth;
From beauty infinitely growing
Upon a mind with love o'erflowing.
WORDSWORTH, *On the Banks of the Bran.*

ADULTERY, see Love and Lust

ADVANTAGE

2
Advantage is a better soldier than rashness.
H. G. BOHN, *Hand-Book of Proverbs*, p. 305.

3
Let nothing pass that will advantage you. (Rem tibi quam nosces aptam dimittere noli.)
DIONYSIUS CATO (?), *Disticha Moralia*. Bk. ii, No. 26.

Let not advantage slip.
SHAKESPEARE, *Venus and Adonis*, l. 129.

See also under OPPORTUNITY.

4
It's them as take advantage that get advantage i' this world.
GEORGE ELIOT, *Adam Bede*. Ch. 32.

5
Regula regularum, to seek and enforce all possible advantage.
GABRIEL HARVEY, annotation in Foorth's *Synopsis Politica.*

6
Every advantage has its disadvantage. (Omnis commoditas sua fert incommoda secum.)
UNKNOWN. A Latin proverb.

See also under COMPENSATION.

ADVENTURE

7
Adventure is the vitaminizing element in histories both individual and social.
WILLIAM BOLITHO, *Twelve Against the Gods: Introduction.*

8
The adventurer is an outlaw. Adventure must start with running away from home.
WILLIAM BOLITHO, *Twelve Against the Gods: Introduction.*

The life of an adventurer is the practice of the art of the impossible.
WILLIAM BOLITHO, *Twelve Against the Gods: Charles XII of Sweden.*

It is always the adventurers who accomplish great things. (Ce sont toujours les aventuriers qui font de grandes choses.)
MONTESQUIEU.

9
In the Law of Adventure, male adventure, love is no more than gold or fame—all three, glitterings on the horizon, beckoning constellations. But with the woman-adventurer all is love or hate. Her adventure is man; her type is not the prospector, but the courtesan. That is, her adventure is an escape, developing inevitably into a running fight with the institution of marriage.
WILLIAM BOLITHO, *Twelve Against the Gods: Lola Montez.*

10
Are there not, dear Michal,
Two points in the adventure of the diver,
One—when, a beggar, he prepares to plunge,
One—when, a prince, he rises with his pearl?
ROBERT BROWNING, *Paracelsus*. Pt. i, end.

Once more on my adventure brave and new.
ROBERT BROWNING, *Rabbi Ben Ezra*. St. 14.

11
Good aventure, O bele nece, have ye
Full lightly founden, and ye conne it take.
CHAUCER, *Troilus and Criseyde*. Bk. ii, l. 288. (c. 1380) The first use, perhaps, of "You can take it."

12
The fruit of my tree of knowledge is plucked, and it is this, "Adventures are to the adventurous."
BENJAMIN DISRAELI, *Ixion in Heaven*, ii, 2; also in *Coningsby*, iii, 1.

13
The thirst for adventure is the vent which Destiny offers; a war, a crusade, a gold mine, a new country, speak to the imagination and offer swing and play to the confined powers.
EMERSON, *Natural History of Intellect: Boston.*

14
Some bold adventurers disdain
The limits of their little reign,
And unknown regions dare descry.
THOMAS GRAY, *Ode on a Distant Prospect of Eton College*, l. 35.

15
Who seeks adventures finds blows.
GEORGE HERBERT, *Jacula Prudentum*. The French form is, "En aventure gisent beau coups."

16
The day shall not be up so soon as I,
To try the fair adventure of to-morrow.
SHAKESPEARE, *King John*. Act v, sc. 5, l. 21.

17
Her father loved me; oft invited me;
Still question'd me the story of my life, . . .
Wherein I spake of most disastrous chances,
Of moving accidents by flood and field.
SHAKESPEARE, *Othello*. Act i, sc. 3, l. 128.

ADVERSITY

See also Misfortune; Prosperity and Adversity

I—Adversity: A Blessing

18
Calamity is man's true touchstone.
BEAUMONT AND FLETCHER, *The Triumph of Honour*. Sc. 1.

19
Now let us thank th' eternal power, convinced
That Heaven but tries our virtue by affliction:

That oft the cloud that wraps the present hour
Serves but to brighten all our future days!
JOHN BROWN, *Barbarossa*. Act v, sc. 3.

Then welcome each rebuff
That turns earth's smoothness rough,
Each sting that bids nor sit nor stand but go!
Be our joys three-parts pain!
Strive, and hold cheap the strain;
Learn, nor account the pang; dare, never grudge the throe!
ROBERT BROWNING, *Rabbi Ben Ezra*. St. 6.

1
Adversity is the first path to truth.
BYRON, *Don Juan*. Canto xii, st. 50.

2
The adversities to which we are accustomed do not disturb us. (Damna minus consueta movent.)
CLAUDIAN, *In Eutropium*. Bk. ii, l. 149.

A man used to vicissitudes is not easily dejected.
SAMUEL JOHNSON, *Rasselas*. Ch. xii.

3
If aught can teach us aught, Affliction's looks,
(Making us pry into ourselves so near),
Teach us to know ourselves, beyond all books,
Or all the learnèd schools that ever were.
SIR JOHN DAVIES, *Nosce Teipsum: Introduction*. Sec. i, st. 38.

4
Bad times have a scientific value. These are occasions a good learner would not miss.
EMERSON, *Conduct of Life: Considerations by the Way*.

5
Adversity makes a man wise, though not rich.
THOMAS FULLER, *Gnomologia*. No. 764.

6
I have chosen thee in the furnace of affliction.
Old Testament: Isaiah, xlviii, 10.

He was afflicted, yet he opened not his mouth: he is brought as a lamb to the slaughter, and as a sheep before her shearers is dumb, so he openeth not his mouth.
Old Testament: Isaiah, liii, 7.

7
Feed him with bread of affliction, and with water of affliction.
Old Testament: I Kings, xxii, 27; *II Chronicles*, xviii, 26.

8
Adversity reminds men of religion.
LIVY, *History*. Bk. v, ch. 51.

9
For thine own purpose, thou hast sent
The strife and the discouragement!
LONGFELLOW, *The Golden Legend*. Pt. ii.

Let us be patient! These severe afflictions
Not from the ground arise,
But oftentimes celestial benedictions
Assume this dark disguise.
LONGFELLOW, *Resignation*.

Are afflictions aught But blessings in disguise?
DAVID MALLET, *Amyntor and Theodora*.

10
Who would have known of Hector, if Troy had been happy? The road to valor is builded by adversity. (Hectora quis nosset, si felix Troia fuisset? Publica virtutis per mala facta via est.)
OVID, *Tristia*. Bk. iv, eleg. 3, l. 75.

11
An undisturbed mind is the best sauce for adversity. (Animus æquos optimum est ærumnæ condimentum.)
PLAUTUS, *Rudens*, l. 402. (Act ii, sc. 3.)

Adversity's sweet milk, philosophy.
SHAKESPEARE, *Romeo and Juliet*. Act iii, sc. 3, l. 55.

12
If thou faint in the day of adversity, thy strength is small.
Old Testament: Proverbs, xxiv, 10.

13
The Good are better made by Ill,
As odours crushed are sweeter still.
SAMUEL ROGERS, *Jacqueline*. Pt. iii, l. 18.

As aromatic plants bestow
No spicy fragrance while they grow;
But crush'd, or trodden to the ground,
Diffuse their balmy sweets around.
OLIVER GOLDSMITH, *The Captivity*. Act i.

It loves to be trodden and bruised under foot, and the more it is destroyed the better it thrives. (Gaudet calcari et atteri, pereundoque melius provenit.)
PLINY, *Historia Naturalis*. Bk. xxi, sec. 6. The reference is to the crocus.

The camomile, the more it is trodden and pressed down, the more it spreadeth.
JOHN LYLY, *Euphues*, p. 46.

The camomile, the more it is trodden on the faster it grows.
SHAKESPEARE, *I Henry IV*. Act ii, sc. 4, l. 439.

14
Animals whose hoofs are hardened on rough ground can travel any road. (Quamlibet viam jumenta patiuntur, quorum durata in aspero ungula est.)
SENECA, *Epistulæ ad Lucilium*. Epis. li, sec. 10.

15
Gold is tried by fire, brave men by adversity. (Ignis aurum probat, miseria fortes viros.)
SENECA, *De Providentia*. Ch. v, sec. 9.

Some souls we see
Grow hard, and stiffen with adversity.
JOHN DRYDEN, *Hind and Panther*. Pt. i, l. 444.

16
Sweet are the uses of adversity,
Which, like the toad, ugly and venomous,
Wears yet a precious jewel in his head.
SHAKESPEARE, *As You Like It*. Act ii, sc. 1, l. 12. (1599)

The foul Toad hath a fair stone in his head.
JOHN LYLY, *Euphues*, p. 53. (1579)

Of the uses of adversity which are sweet, none

are sweeter than those which grow out of disappointed love.
Sir Henry Taylor, *Notes from Life*, p. 78.

1 His overthrow heap'd happiness upon him;
For then, and not till then, he felt himself,
And found the blessedness of being little.
Shakespeare, *Henry VIII*. Act iv, sc. 2, l. 64.

2 O benefit of ill! now I find true
That better is by evil still made better.
Shakespeare, *Sonnets*. No. cxix.

3 Affliction is not sent in vain, young man,
From that good God who chastens whom he
loves.
Southey, *Madoc in Wales*. Pt. iii, l. 165.

4 The Lord gets his best soldiers out of the highlands of affliction.
C. H. Spurgeon, *Sorrow's Discipline*.

5 For a man to rejoice in adversity is not grievous to him who loves; for so to joy is to joy in the cross of Christ.
Thomas à Kempis, *De Imitatione Christi*. Pt. ii, ch. 6.

6 Till from the straw the flail the corn doth
beat,
Until the chaff be purgèd from the wheat,
Yea, till the mill the grains in pieces tear,
The richness of the flour will scarce appear.
George Wither, *Fragmenta Poetica*.

II—Adversity: A Curse

7 Afflictions induce callosities.
Sir Thomas Browne, *Hydriotaphia*. Ch. v, 10.

8 Daughter of Jove, relentless power,
Thou tamer of the human breast,
Whose iron scourge and tort'ring hour
The bad affright, afflict the best.
Thomas Gray, *Hymn to Adversity*.

9 Unrighteous fortune seldom spares the noblest virtue; no one with safety can expose himself to frequent danger. Adversity finds at last the man whom she has often passed by. (Iniqua raro maximis virtutibus Fortuna parcit; nemo se tuto diu Periculis offerre tam crebris potest. Quem sæpe transit casus, aliquando invenit.)
Seneca, *Hercules Furens*, l. 325.

10 A wretched soul, bruis'd with adversity,
We bid be quiet when we hear it cry;
But were we burden'd with like weight of
pain,
As much, or more, we should ourselves complain.
Shakespeare, *The Comedy of Errors*. Act ii, sc. 1, l. 34. *See also* Friends and Adversity; Misfortunes of Others.

11 Let me embrace thee, sour adversity,
For wise men say it is the wisest course.
Shakespeare, *III Henry VI*. Act iii, sc. 1, l. 24.

Henceforth I'll bear
Affliction till it do cry out itself
"Enough, enough," and die.
Shakespeare, *King Lear*. Act iv, sc. 6, l. 76.

12 Thou art a soul in bliss; but I am bound
Upon a wheel of fire, that mine own tears
Do scald like molten lead.
Shakespeare, *King Lear*. Act iv, sc. 7, l. 46.

Affliction is enamour'd of thy parts,
And thou art wedded to calamity.
Shakespeare, *Romeo and Juliet*. Act iii, sc. 3, l. 2.

One writ with me in sour misfortune's book!
Shakespeare, *Romeo and Juliet*. Act v, sc. 3, l. 82.

A man I am cross'd with adversity.
Shakespeare, *The Two Gentlemen of Verona*. Act iv, sc. 1, l. 12.

Whom unmerciful disaster
Followed fast and followed faster.
Edgar Allan Poe, *The Raven*.

They seemed Like old companions in adversity.
Bryant, *A Winter Piece*.

13 What time to tardy consummation brings
Calamity, like to a frosty night
That ripeneth the grain, completes at once.
Sir Henry Taylor, *Philip von Artevelde*. Pt. i, act iv, sc. 2.

14 What region of earth is not full of our calamities? (Quæ regio in terris nostri non plena laboris?)
Vergil, *Æneid*. Bk. i, l. 460.

III—Adversity and Man

15 We cannot be more faithful to ourselves,
In anything that's manly, than to make
Ill fortune as contemptible to us
As it makes us to others.
Beaumont and Fletcher, *Honest Man's Fortune*. Act i, sc. 1.

16 Strong men greet war, tempest, hard times. They wish, as Pindar said, "to tread the floors of hell, with necessities as hard as iron."
Emerson, *Letters and Social Aims: Progress of Culture*.

17 In adversity a man is saved by hope. ("Ανθρωπος ἀτυχῶν σώζεθ' ὑπὸ τῆς ἐλπίδος.)
Menander, *Fragments*. No. 813.

18 Do they not seek occasion of new quarrels
On my refusal to distress me more,
Or make a game of my calamities?
Milton, *Samson Agonistes*, l. 1329.

1
Great men rejoice in adversity just as brave soldiers triumph in war.
SENECA, *De Providentia.* Sec. 4.
2
Behold a worthy sight, to which the God . . . may direct his gaze. Behold a thing worthy of a God, a brave man matched in conflict with adversity. (Ecce spectaculum dignum, ad quod respeciat . . . Deus. Ecce par Deo dignum, vir fortis cum mala fortuna compositus.)
SENECA, *De Providentia.* Sec. 4.

The bravest sight in all this world is a man fighting against odds.
FRANKLIN K. LANE, *The Unconquerable Soul.*
3
Seneca thinks the gods are well pleased when they see great men contending with adversity.
ROBERT BURTON, *Anatomy of Melancholy.* Pt. ii, sec. iii, mem. 1, subs. 1.

A wise man struggling with adversity is said by some heathen writer to be a spectacle on which the gods might look down with pleasure.
SYDNEY SMITH, *Sermon on the Duties of the Queen.*
4
A brave man struggling in the storms of fate,
And greatly falling with a falling state.
POPE, *Prologue to Mr. Addison's Cato,* l. 21.
5
The greatest object in the universe, says a certain philosopher, is a good man struggling with adversity; yet there is a still greater, which is the good man that comes to relieve it.
GOLDSMITH, *The Vicar of Wakefield.* Ch. 30.

ADVERTISEMENT, see Publicity

ADVICE

See also Woman: Her Advice

6
Bad counsel confounds the adviser. (Malum consilium consultori pessimum est.)
AULUS GELLIUS, *Noctes Atticæ.* Bk. iv, ch. 5, sec. 5. Quoted as a proverb. The rendering is Emerson's (*Essays, First Series: Compensation*). Attributed to Verrius Flaccus.

Those who give base counsel to cautious men lose their labor. (Consilia qui dant prava cautis hominibus, Et perdunt operam.)
PHÆDRUS, *Fables.* Bk. i, fab. 25.
7
Ask counsel of both times: of the ancient time what is best; and of the latter time what is fittest.
FRANCIS BACON, *Essays: Of Great Place.*

Consult the dead upon the things that were,
But the living only on things that are.
LONGFELLOW, *The Golden Legend.* Pt. i.
8
When all is done, the help of good counsel is that which setteth business straight.
FRANCIS BACON, *Essays: Of Friendship.*
9
The worst men often give the best advice.
P. J. BAILEY, *Festus: A Village Feast,* l. 917.

A fool sometimes gives a weighty suggestion. (Un fat quelquefois ouvre un avis important.)
BOILEAU, *L'Art Poétique.* Pt. iv, l. 50.

Good counsel failing men may give, for why?
He that's aground knows where the shoal doth lie. . . .
Thus, like the whetstone, many men are wont
To sharpen others while themselves are blunt.
BENJAMIN FRANKLIN, *Poor Richard,* 1734.
10
Advice: the smallest current coin.
AMBROSE BIERCE, *The Devil's Dictionary,* p. 20.
11
In ploughman phrase, "God send you speed,"
Still daily to grow wiser;
And may ye better reck the rede
Than ever did th' adviser!
BURNS, *Epistle to a Young Friend.*
12
He loves who advises. Farewell and beware. (Qui monet amat. Ave et cave.)
ROBERT BURTON, *The Anatomy of Melancholy.* Pt. i, sec. ii, mem. 2, subs. 4. Quoted.

Take the advice of a faithful friend, and submit thy inventions to his censure.
THOMAS FULLER, *Holy State: Of Fancy.*
13
Who cannot give good counsel? 'Tis cheap, it costs them nothing.
ROBERT BURTON, *Anatomy of Melancholy.* Pt. ii, sec. ii, mem. 3.

She had a good opinion of advice,
Like all who give and eke receive it gratis,
For which small thanks are still the market price.
BYRON, *Don Juan.* Canto xv, st. 29.
14
My counsel is a kind one; for 'tis even
Given chiefly at my own expense: 'tis true,
'Twill not be followed, so there's little lost.
BYRON, *Cain.* Act ii, sc. 2.
15
Good but rarely came from good advice.
BYRON, *Don Juan.* Canto xiv, st. 66.
16
But counselling is no commandement.
CHAUCER, *Wife of Bath's Prologue,* l. 67.

Counsel breaks not the head.
GEORGE HERBERT, *Jacula Prudentum.*
17
Advice is seldom welcome; and those who want it the most always like it the least.
LORD CHESTERFIELD, *Letters,* 29 Jan., 1748.
18
Dare to give true advice with all frankness. (Consilium verum dare audeamus libere.)
CICERO, *De Amicitia.* Ch. 13, sec. 44.
19
Nobody can give you wiser advice than yourself.
CICERO, *Epistolæ ad Atticum.* Bk. ii, epis. 7.

Let the counsel of thine own heart stand: for there is no man more faithful unto thee than it. For a man's mind is sometime wont to tell him

more than seven watchmen, that sit above in an high tower.
Apocrypha: Ecclesiasticus, xxxvii, 13, 14.

1
To ask advice is in nine cases out of ten to tout for flattery.
CHURTON COLLINS, *Maxims*. No. 59.

We ask advice, but we mean approbation.
C. C. COLTON, *Lacon: Reflections*. Vol. i, No. 190.

2
'Twas good advice, and meant, "My son, be good."
GEORGE CRABBE, *The Learned Boy*, l. 188.

3
They first condemn that first advis'd the ill.
DRYDEN, *Absalom and Achitophel*. Pt. ii, l. 183.

4
No gift is more precious than good advice. (Bono consilio nullum est munus pretiosius.)
ERASMUS, *Colloquia: Convivium Religiosum*.

There ne'er came ill after gude advisement.
JOHN RAY, *Proverbs: Scottish*.

Good advice Is beyond price.
W. G. BENHAM, *Quotations*, p. 768.

5
Beware lest clamour be taken for counsel. (Cavendum ne fiat pro consilio convicium.)
ERASMUS, *Colloquia: Senatulus*.

6
Easier to advise than suffer and be strong. (Ῥᾷον παραινεῖν ἢ παθόντα καρτερεῖν.)
EURIPIDES, *Alcestis*, l. 1078.

7
He that will not be counselled cannot be helped.
THOMAS FULLER, *Gnomologia*. No. 2350.

He that won't be counselled can't be helped.
BENJAMIN FRANKLIN, *Poor Richard*, 1747.

If the counsel be good, no matter who gave it.
THOMAS FULLER, *Gnomologia*. No. 2704.

8
If a man love to give advice, it is a sure sign that he himself wanteth it.
LORD HALIFAX, *Works*, p. 244.

9
Extremely foolish advice is likely to be uttered by those who are looking at the labouring vessel from the land.
ARTHUR HELPS, *Friends in Council*. Bk. ii, 2.

The toad beneath the harrow knows
Exactly where each tooth-point goes,
The butterfly upon the road
Preaches contentment to that toad.
RUDYARD KIPLING, *Pagett, M. P.*

Many masters, quoth the toad to the harrow, when every tine turn'd her over.
THOMAS FULLER, *Gnomologia*. No. 3354.

One can advise comfortably from a safe port. (Vom sichern Port lässt sich's gemächlich rathen.)
SCHILLER, *Wilhelm Tell*. Act i, sc. 1, l. 146.

When we are well it is easy to give good advice to the sick. (Facile omnes quom valemus recta consilia ægrotis damus.)
TERENCE, *Andria*, l. 309. (Act ii, sc. 1.)
See also under MISFORTUNE.

10
Know when to speak—for many times it
brings
Danger, to give the best advice to kings.
ROBERT HERRICK, *Caution in Counsel*.

11
Whatever advice you give, be brief. (Quidquid præcipies, esto brevis.)
HORACE, *Ars Poetica*, l. 335.

12
Advice is offensive, . . . because it shows us that we are known to others as well as to ourselves.
SAMUEL JOHNSON, *The Rambler*. No. 155.

13
There is often as much good sense required in knowing how to profit from good advice as there is to give it. (Il n'y a pas quelquefois moins d'habilité à savoir profiter d'un bon conseil, qu'à se bien conseiller soi-même.)
LA ROCHEFOUCAULD, *Maximes*. No. 283.

To profit from good advice requires more wisdom than to give it.
CHURTON COLLINS, *Aphorisms*.

14
One gives nothing so liberally as advice. (On ne donne rien si libéralement que ses conseils.)
LA ROCHEFOUCAULD, *Maximes*. No. 110.

We give advice, but we cannot give conduct. (On donne des conseils, mais on n'inspire point de conduite.)
LA ROCHEFOUCAULD, *Maximes*. No. 378.

15
In great straits and when hope is small, the boldest counsels are the safest. (In rebus asperis et tenui spe fortissima quæque consilia tutissima sunt.)
LIVY, *History*. Bk. xxv, ch. 38.

For when last need to desperation driveth,
Who dareth most he wisest counsel giveth.
TASSO, *Jerusalem Delivered*. Bk. vi, st. 6.

16
I tell ye wut, my jedgment is you're pooty
sure to fail,
Ez long 'z the head keeps turnin' back for
counsel to the tail.
J. R. LOWELL, *Biglow Papers*. Ser. ii, No. 3.

17
Slow-footed counsel is much the best, for swift counsel ever drags repentance behind it. (Ἡ βραδύπους βουλὴ μέγ' ἀμείνων· ἡ δὲ ταχεῖα αἰὲν ἐφελκομένη τὴν μετάνοιαν ἔχει.)
LUCIAN. (*Greek Anthology*. Bk. x, epig. 37.)

18
Hazard not your wealth on a poor man's advice. (No adventures mucho tu riqueza Por consejo de hombre que ha pobreza.)
MANUEL, *Conde Lucanor*.

19
It is the part of a fool to give advice to others and not himself to be on his guard. (Sibi non cavere, et aliis consilium dare, Stultum esse.)
PHÆDRUS, *Fables*. Bk. i, fab. 9.

1
He who counsels, aids. (Qui monet quasi adjuvat.)
PLAUTUS, *Curculio*, l. 460. (Act iii, sc. 1.) Quoted as a proverb.

2
Advice has greater strength coming from divine sources. (Consilia formiora sunt de divinis locis.)
PLAUTUS, *Mostellaria*, l. 1104. (Act v, sc. 1.)

3
A detestable counsel. (Fœdum consilium.)
PLINY, *History*. Bk. xxvi, sec. 38.

4
Be niggards of advice on no pretence,
For the worst avarice is that of sense.
POPE, *Essay on Criticism*. Pt. iii, l. 19.

5
In the multitude of counsellors there is safety.
Old Testament: Proverbs, xi, 14; xxiv, 6.

6
However harsh an adviser is, he injures no one. (Quamvis acerbus qui monet, nulli nocet.)
PUBLILIUS SYRUS, *Sententiæ*. No. 620. Loeb.

7
It is too late to seek advice after you have run into danger. (Sero in periclis est concilium quærere.)
PUBLILIUS SYRUS, *Sententiæ*. No. 673.

Advice comes too late when a thing is done.
SAMUEL RICHARDSON, *Clarissa Harlowe*. Bk. iv, 119. Quoting an old saying which appeared in Ray's *English Proverbs*.
See also WISDOM: AFTER THE EVENT.

8
It is bad advice that cannot be altered. (Malum est consilium quod mutari non potest.)
PUBLILIUS SYRUS, *Sententiæ*. No. 403. Loeb.

It is an ill counsel that hath no escape.
GEORGE HERBERT, *Jacula Prudentum*.

9
Advice when most needed is least heeded.
W. G. BENHAM, *Quotations*, p. 731.

10
Counsel over cups is crazy.
JOHN RAY, *English Proverbs*.

Wine-counsels seldom prosper.
GEORGE HERBERT, *Jacula Prudentum*.

11
To one who knows, it is superfluous to give advice; to one who does not know, it is insufficient. (Præcepta dare scienti supervacuum est, nescienti parum.)
SENECA, *Epistulæ ad Lucilium*. Epis. xciv, 11.

12
Share the advice betwixt you: if both gain, all
The gift doth stretch itself as 'tis receiv'd,
And is enough for both.
SHAKESPEARE, *All's Well that Ends Well*. Act ii, sc. 1, l. 3.

13
Friendly counsel cuts off many foes.
SHAKESPEARE, *I Henry VI*. Act iii, sc. 1, l. 185.

14
Bosom up my counsel,
You'll find it wholesome.
SHAKESPEARE, *Henry VIII*. Act i, sc. 1, l. 112.

When a wise man gives thee better counsel, give me mine again.
SHAKESPEARE, *King Lear*. Act ii, sc. 4, l. 76.

15
Counsel may stop awhile what will not stay;
For when we rage, advice is often seen
By blunting us to make our wits more keen.
SHAKESPEARE, *A Lover's Complaint*, l. 159.

16
Here comes a man of comfort, whose advice
Hath often still'd my brawling discontent.
SHAKESPEARE, *Measure for Measure*. Act iv, sc. i, l. 8.

17
I pray thee, cease thy counsel,
Which falls into mine ears as profitless
As water in a sieve.
SHAKESPEARE, *Much Ado About Nothing*. Act v, sc. 1, l. 3.

Direct not him whose way himself will choose:
'Tis breath thou lack'st, and that breath wilt thou lose.
SHAKESPEARE, *Richard II*. Act ii, sc. 1, l. 29.

18
Good advice is one of those injuries which a good man ought, if possible, to forgive, but at all events to forget at once.
HORACE SMITH, *The Tin Trumpet: Advice*.

19
In giving advice, seek to help, not to please, your friend.
SOLON. (DIOGENES LAERTIUS, *Solon*. Sec. 16.)

20
How is it possible to expect that mankind will take advice, when they will not so much as take warning?
SWIFT, *Thoughts on Various Subjects*.

21
Advice was forthcoming from all; few accepted the danger. (Consilium ab omnibus datum est, periculum pauci sumsere.)
TACITUS, *History*. Bk. iii, sec. 69.

22
He minded not his friends' advice
But followed his own wishes.
JANE TAYLOR, *The Little Fisherman*.

23
He had only one vanity, he thought he could give advice better than any other person.
MARK TWAIN, *The Man that Corrupted Hadleyburg*. Ch. 1.

24
It is always a silly thing to give advice, but to give good advice is absolutely fatal.
OSCAR WILDE, *Portrait of Mr. W. H.*

25
He is the best of all men who follows good advice. (Κεῖνος μὲν πανάριστος ὃς εὖ εἰπόντι πίθηται.)
ZENO, amending a line of Hesiod. (DIOGENES LAERTIUS, *Zeno*. Bk. vii, sec. 26.)

I shall know if I have rightly advised you, if you rightly beware. (Recte monuisse, si tu recte caveris.)
PLAUTUS, *Menæchmi*, l. 347. (Act ii, sc. 2.)

Many receive advice, only the wise profit by it. (Consilium inveniunt multi sed docti explicant.)
PUBLILIUS SYRUS, *Sententiæ*. No. 124.

AERONAUTICS, see Flying

AFFECTATION, see Pretence

AFFECTION

See also Love

1
There are wonders in true affection: it is a body of enigmas, mysteries, and riddles; wherein two so become one, as they both become two.
SIR THOMAS BROWNE, *Religio Medici*. Pt. ii, sec. 6.

2
Alas! our young affections run to waste,
Or water but the desert.
BYRON, *Childe Harold*. Canto iv, st. 120.

Talk not of wasted affection, affection never was wasted;
If it enrich not the heart of another, its waters, returning
Back to their springs, like the rain, shall fill them full of refreshment.
LONGFELLOW, *Evangeline*. Pt. ii, st. 1.

3
Set your affection on things above, not on things on the earth.
New Testament: Colossians, iii, 2.

4
Affection bends the judgment to her ply.
DANTE, *Inferno*. Canto xiii, l. 115. (Cary, tr.)

5
With affection beaming in one eye and calculation shining out of the other.
DICKENS, *Martin Chuzzlewit*. Ch. 8.

6
If you could see my legs when I take my boots off, you'd form some idea of what unrequited affection is.
DICKENS, *Dombey and Son*. Ch. 48.

7
The effect of the indulgence of this human affection is a certain cordial exhilaration.
EMERSON, *Essays, First Series: Friendship*.

What is so pleasant as these jets of affection which make a young world for me again? . . . The moment we indulge our affections, the earth is metamorphosed; there is no winter and no night; all tragedies, all ennuis, vanish,—all duties even.
EMERSON, *Essays, First Series; Friendship*.

Heraclitus looked upon the affections as dense and colored mists. In the fog of good and evil affections it is hard for man to walk forward in a straight line.
EMERSON, *Essays, First Series: Intellect*.

8
Affection, like melancholy, magnifies trifles.
LEIGH HUNT, *Table-Talk: Magnifying Trifles*.

9
As the rolling stone gathers no moss, so the roving heart gathers no affections.
ANNA JAMESON, *Studies: Sternberg's Novels*.

10
Tenderness is the repose of passion. (La tendresse est le repos de la passion.)
JOUBERT, *Pensées*. No. 68.

11
I never heard
Of any true affection but 'twas nipped.
THOMAS MIDDLETON, *Blurt, Master-Constable*. Act iii, sc. 2.

12
When affection only speaks,
Truth is not always there.
MIDDLETON, *The Old Law*. Act iv, sc. 2.

13
Happy is he the palace of whose affection is founded upon virtue, walled with riches, glazed with beauty, and roofed with honour.
FRANCIS QUARLES, *Enchiridion*. Cent. ii, No. 94.

14
My affection hath an unknown bottom, like the bay of Portugal.
SHAKESPEARE, *As You Like It*. Act iv, sc. 1, l. 212.

15
And keep you in the rear of your affection.
SHAKESPEARE, *Hamlet*. Act i, sc. 3, l. 34.

For affection,
Mistress of passion, sways it to the mood
Of what it likes or loathes.
SHAKESPEARE, *The Merchant of Venice*. Act. iv, sc. 1, l. 50.

16
But can you affection the 'oman?
SHAKESPEARE, *The Merry Wives of Windsor*. Act i, sc. 1, l. 234.

A mountain of affection.
SHAKESPEARE, *Much Ado About Nothing*. Act ii, sc. 1, l. 382.

Fair encounter Of two most rare affections!
SHAKESPEARE, *The Tempest*. Act iii, sc. 1, l. 75.

17
Affection is a coal that must be cool'd;
Else, suffer'd, it will set the heart on fire.
SHAKESPEARE, *Venus and Adonis*, l. 387.

18
Of such affection and unbroken faith
As temper life's worst bitterness.
SHELLEY, *The Cenci*. Act iii, sc. 1, l. 312.

19
One in whose heart Affection had no root.
SOUTHEY, *Joan of Arc*. Bk. i, l. 204.

20
Entire affection hateth nicer hands.
SPENSER, *The Faerie Queene*. Bk. i, canto viii, st. 40.

21
'Tis sweet to feel by what fine-spun threads our affections are drawn together.
LAURENCE STERNE, *A Sentimental Journey: The Fille de Chambre, Paris*.

For the affection of young ladies is of as rapid growth as Jack's beanstalk, and reaches up to the sky in a night.
THACKERAY, *Vanity Fair*. Ch. iv.

1
Yet would I not be of such wintry bareness
But that some leaf of your regard should hang
Upon my naked branches.
WORDSWORTH, *The Excursion*. Bk. iii, l. 491.

AFFLICTION, see Adversity

AGE

I—AGE: Age and Youth

2
Young men soon give, and soon forget, affronts;
Old age is slow in both.
ADDISON, *Cato*. Act ii, sc. 5.

3
Age is more just than youth. (Γῆρας γὰρ ἥβης ἐστὶν ἐνδικώ τερον.)
ÆSCHYLUS, *Fragments*. Frag. 228.

4
He carries an old mind with a youthful body. (Γέροντα τὸν νοῦν, σάρκα δ' ἡβῶσαν φύει.)
ÆSCHYLUS, *Seven Against Thebes*, l. 622.

A man that is young in years may be old in hours, if he have lost no time.
FRANCIS BACON, *Essays: Of Youth and Age*.

Nature is full of freaks, and now puts an old head on young shoulders, and then a young heart beating under fourscore winters.
EMERSON, *Society and Solitude: Old Age*.

Young in limbs, in judgement old.
SHAKESPEARE, *The Merchant of Venice*. Act ii, sc. 7, l. 71.

I never knew so young a body with so old a head.
SHAKESPEARE, *The Merchant of Venice*. Act iv, sc. 1, l. 163.

5
Old age is more suspicious than the free
And valiant heart of youth, or manhood's firm,
Unclouded reason.
MATTHEW ARNOLD, *Merope*, l. 156.

6
The child's toys and the old man's reasons
Are the fruits of the two seasons.
WILLIAM BLAKE, *Auguries of Innocence*.

7
Young, all lay in dispute; I shall know, being old.
ROBERT BROWNING, *Rabbi Ben Ezra*. St. 15

8
Let age approve of youth, and death complete the same!
ROBERT BROWNING, *Rabbi Ben Ezra*. Last line.

9
It was an old, old, old, old lady,
And a boy who was half-past three.
H. C. BUNNER, *One, Two, Three*.

10
The arrogance of age must submit to be taught by youth.
EDMUND BURKE, *Letter to Fanny Burney*.

The rev'rend grey-beards rav'd and storm'd,
That beardless laddies
Should think they better were inform'd
Than their auld daddies.
ROBERT BURNS, *Epistle to Simpson: Postscript*.

Young folks are smart, but all ain't good thet's new,
I guess the gran'thers they knowed sunthin', tu.
J. R. LOWELL, *The Biglow Papers*: Ser. ii, *Mason and Slidell*.

11
Yes, Life in Youth-tide standeth still; in Manhood streameth soft and slow;
See, as it nears th' abysmal goal how fleet the waters flash and flow!
SIR RICHARD BURTON, *The Kasîdah*. Pt. iii, st. 28.

The more we live, more brief appear
Our life's succeeding stages;
A day to childhood seems a year,
And years like passing ages. . . .

Heaven gives our years of fading strength
Indemnifying fleetness;
And those of Youth, a seeming length,
Proportioned to their sweetness.
THOMAS CAMPBELL, *A Thought Suggested by the New Year*.

12
'Tis the defect of age to rail at the pleasures of youth.
SUSANNAH CENTLIVRE, *The Basset Table*. Act i.

13
Young men think old men are fools; but old men *know* young men are fools.
GEORGE CHAPMAN, *All Fools*. Act v, sc. 1, l. 292. (1605) WILLIAM CAMDEN (*Remains*, 1605) quotes this, in slightly different form, as a saying of Dr. Metcalf.

14
Old age may be sweet, if it is made like youth; but youth is burdensome if it be like old age. (Grata senectus homini, quæ parilis juventæ; Illa juventa est gravior, quæ similis senectæ.)
CHILON. (AUSONIUS [?], *Septem Sapientum Sententiæ*, l. 41.)

15
Rashness is a quality of the budding-time of youth, prudence of the harvest-time of old age. (Temeritas est florentis ætatis, prudentia senescentis.)
CICERO, *De Senectute*. Ch. vi, sec. 20.

From thoughtless youth to ruminating age.
COWPER, *The Progress of Error*, l. 24.

No life is perfect that has not been lived youth in feeling, manhood in battle, old age in meditation.
WILFRID SCAWEN BLUNT, *The Perfect Life*.

Old the proverb, old, but true;—
Age should think, and Youth should do.
D'ARCY THOMPSON, *Sales Attici*.

1
For just as I approve of a young man in whom there is a touch of age, so I approve of the old man in whom there is some of the flavor of youth. He who strives thus to mingle youthfulness and age may grow old in body, but old in spirit he will never be. (Ut enim adulescentem in quo est senile aliquid, sic senem in quo est aliquid adulescentis probo, quod qui sequitur, corpore senex esse poterit, animo numquam erit.)
CICERO, *De Senectute*. Ch. xi, sec. 38.

The true way to render age vigorous is to prolong the youth of the mind.
MORTIMER COLLINS, *The Village Comedy*, i. 56.

If within the old man there is not a young man, —within the sophisticated, one unsophisticated, —then he is but one of the devil's angels.
H. D. THOREAU, *Journal*, 26 Oct., 1853.

2
Age, out of heart, impatient, sighed:—
"I ask what will the *Future* be?"
Youth laughed contentedly, and cried:—
"The future leave to me!"
FLORENCE EARLE COATES, *Youth and Age*.

3
Youth beholds happiness gleaming in the prospect. Age looks back on the happiness of youth, and, instead of hopes, seeks its enjoyment in the recollections of hope.
S. T. COLERIDGE, *Table Talk: Youth and Age*.

Youth with swift feet walks onward in the way;
The land of joy lies all before his eyes;
Age, stumbling, lingers slowly day by day,
Still looking back, for it behind him lies.
Fail not for sorrow, falter not for sin,
But onward, upward, till the goal ye win!
FRANCES ANNE KEMBLE, *Lines to the Young Gentlemen Leaving Lenox Academy*.

4
'Tis well to give honour and glory to Age,
With its lessons of wisdom and truth;
Yet who would not go back to the fanciful page,
And the fairy tale read but in youth?
ELIZA COOK, *Stanzas*, l. 1.

5
Read, ye that run, the awful truth,
With which I charge my page;
A worm is in the bud of youth,
And at the root of age.
COWPER, *Stanzas Subjoined to the Yearly Bill of Mortality of the Parish of All Saints, Northampton, A. D. 1787*.

6
When youth is fallen, there's hope the young may rise,
But fallen age for ever hopeless lies.
GEORGE CRABBE, *The Borough*. Letter 21.

7
The spring, like youth, fresh blossoms doth produce,
But autumn makes them ripe and fit for use:
So Age a mature mellowness doth set
On the green promises of youthful heat.
SIR JOHN DENHAM, *Cato Major*. Pt. iv, l. 47.

8
Youth is a blunder; Manhood a struggle; Old Age a regret.
BENJAMIN DISRAELI, *Coningsby*. Bk. iii, ch. 1.

The blunders of youth are preferable to the triumphs of manhood, or the success of old age.
BENJAMIN DISRAELI, *Lothair*. Ch. 31.

The disappointment of Manhood succeeds to the delusion of Youth; let us hope that the heritage of Old Age is not despair.
BENJAMIN DISRAELI, *Vivian Grey*. Bk. viii, ch. 4.

9
O Youth must bleed and measure
The days that span the sea—
But Age will keep for pleasure
What Youth thought misery.
GLENN WARD DRESBACH, *Youth and Age*.

10
For all their courteous words they are not one,
This Youth and Age, but civil strangers still;
Age with the best of all his seasons done,
Youth with his face towards the upland hill.
JOHN DRINKWATER, *Olton Pools: Dedication*.

11
When youth is spent, a penny at a fair,
The old men tell of the bargains there.
There was this and that for a price and a wage,
But when they came away they had all bought age.
LOUISE DRISCOLL, *Bargain*.

12
In youth, we clothe ourselves with rainbows, and go as brave as the zodiac. In age, we put out another sort of perspiration,—gout, fever, rheumatism, caprice, doubt, fretting, avarice.
EMERSON, *Conduct of Life: Fate*.

Youth is everywhere in place. Age, like woman, requires fit surroundings.
EMERSON, *Society and Solitude: Old Age*.

13
An angelic boyhood becomes a satanic old age. (Angelicus juvenis senibus satanizat in annis.)
ERASMUS, *Adagia*. Quoted as a proverb invented by Satan.

It is a common proverb, young saint old devil.
UNKNOWN, *Dives et Pauper*. Fo. 34. (1493)

Fie upon such as say, young saints, old devils: it is no doubt a devilish and damnable saying.
ROBERT GREENE, *Works*. Vol. x, p. 239. (1592)

Of a young hermit, an old devil. (De jeune hermite, vieil diable.)
RABELAIS, *Works*. Vol. ii. Quoted as a proverb.

14
If youth but knew; if old age could! (Si jeunesse savoit, si vieillesse pouvoit.)
HENRI ÉTIENNE, *Les Prémices*.

If I were a man and a young man,
And knew what I know today.
ELLA WHEELER WILCOX.

1
If youth knew what age would crave,
It would both get and save.
THOMAS FULLER, *Gnomologia*. No. 6085.

While strength and years permit, endure labor; soon bent old age will come with silent foot. (Dum vires annique sinunt, tolerate labores. Jam veniet tacito curva senecta pede.)
OVID, *Ars Amatoria*. Bk. ii, l. 669.

When we are young we lay up for old age; when we are old we save for death.
LA BRUYÈRE, *Les Caractères: Des Biens de Fortune.*

2
Old men have in some degree their reprisals upon younger, by making nicer observations upon them.
LORD HALIFAX, *Works*, p. 256.

3
Struggle and turmoil, revel and brawl—
Youth is the sign of them, one and all.
A smoldering hearth and a silent stage—
These are a type of the world of Age.
W. E. HENLEY, *Ballad of Youth and Age: Envoy.*

4
Boys must not have th' ambitious care of men,
Nor men the weak anxieties of age.
HORACE, *Ars Poetica*. l. 176. (Dillon, tr.)

5
'Tis time for thee to be gone, lest, when you have drunk too freely, youth mock and jostle you off the stage, playing the wanton with better grace. (Tempus abire tibi est, ne potum largius æquo Rideat et pulset lasciva decentius ætas.)
HORACE, *Epistles*. Bk. ii, epis. 2, l. 215.

"Let me not live," quoth he,
"After my flame lacks oil, to be the snuff
Of younger spirits."
SHAKESPEARE, *All's Well that Ends Well*. Act. i, sc. 2, l. 58.

The luck will turn. . . . Presently the younger generation will come knocking at my door.
IBSEN, *The Master Builder*. Act i.

As newer comers crowd the fore,
We drop behind—
We who have laboured long and sore
Times out of mind,
And keen are yet, must not regret
To drop behind.
THOMAS HARDY, *The Superseded.*

6
All the world's a mass of folly,
Youth is gay, age melancholy:
Youth is spending, age is thrifty,
Mad at twenty, cold at fifty;
Man is nought but folly's slave,
From the cradle to the grave.
W. H. IRELAND, *Of the Folly of all the World.*

7
Your old men shall dream dreams, your young men shall see visions.
Old Testament: Joel, ii, 28.

Youth lives on hope, old age on remembrance. (La jeunesse vit d'esperance, la vieillesse de souvenir.)
UNKNOWN. A French proverb.

8
The conversation of the old and the young ends generally with contempt or pity on either side.
SAMUEL JOHNSON, *The Rambler*. No. 69.

9
Power pleases the violent and proud; wealth delights the placid and the timorous. Youth therefore flies at power, and age grovels after riches.
SAMUEL JOHNSON, *Works*. Vol. x, p. 431.

10
Young men differ in various ways, but old men all look alike. (Plurima sunt juvenum discrimina, . . . una senum facies.)
JUVENAL, *Satires*. Sat. x, l. 196.

11
Around the child bend all the three
Sweet Graces—Faith, Hope, Charity.
Around the man bend other faces—
Pride, Envy, Malice are his Graces.
WALTER SAVAGE LANDOR, *Around the Child.*

12
He who hath braved Youth's dizzy heat
Dreads not the frost of Age.
WALTER SAVAGE LANDOR, *To Age.*

13
And boasting youth, and narrative old age,
Their pleas were diff'rent, their request the same;
For good and bad alike are fond of fame.
POPE, *The Temple of Fame*, l. 291.

14
Where the older age sins, the younger is led astray. (Quod ætas vitium posuit, ætas auferet.)
PUBLILIUS SYRUS, *Sententiæ*. No. 557.

Where old age is evil, youth can learn no good.
JOHN RAY, *English Proverbs.*

15
To love is natural in a young man, a crime in an old one. (Amare juveni fructus est, crimen seni.)
PUBLILIUS SYRUS, *Sententiæ*. No. 29.

Who early loves, though young, is wise—
Who old, though grey, a fool.
COWPER, *Upon a Venerable Rival.*

Youth is the proper time for love,
And age is virtue's season.
GEORGE GRANVILLE, *Corinna.*

16
They who would be young when they are old, must be old when they are young.
JOHN RAY, *English Proverbs.*

17
Of young men die many; of old escape not any.
JOHN RAY, *English Proverbs.*

1
O, roses for the flush of youth,
And laurel for the perfect prime;
But pluck an ivy branch for me,
Grown old before my time.
CHRISTINA ROSSETTI, *Song.*

2
The young man who has not wept is a savage, and the old man who will not laugh is a fool.
GEORGE SANTAYANA, *Dialogues in Limbo.*

3
A very riband in the cap of youth,
Yet needful too; for youth no less becomes
The light and careless livery that it wears
Than settled age his sables and his weeds,
Importing health and graveness.
SHAKESPEARE, *Hamlet.* Act iv, sc. 7, l. 78.

4
Thou art thy mother's glass, and she in thee
Calls back the lovely April of her prime:
So thou through windows of thine age shall see,
Despite of wrinkles this thy golden time.
SHAKESPEARE, *Sonnets.* No. iii.

5
Crabbed age and youth cannot live together:
Youth is full of pleasance, age is full of care;
Youth like summer morn, age like winter weather;
Youth like summer brave, age like winter bare.
Youth is full of sport, age's breath is short;
Youth is nimble, age is lame;
Youth is hot and bold, age is weak and cold;
Youth is wild, and age is tame.
Age, I do abhor thee; youth, I do adore thee.
SHAKESPEARE [?], *The Passionate Pilgrim,* l. 157.

6
Youth is the time for the adventures of the body, but age for the triumphs of the mind.
LOGAN PEARSALL SMITH, *On Reading Shakespeare,* p. 36.

7
In the days of my youth I remembered my God,
And He hath not forgotten my age.
SOUTHEY, *The Old Man's Comforts.*

8
All sorts of allowances are made for the illusions of youth; and none, or almost none, for the disenchantments of age.
R. L. STEVENSON, *Virginibus Puerisque: Crabbed Age and Youth.*

When an old gentleman waggles his head and says: "Ah, so I thought when I was your age," it is not thought an answer at all if the young man retorts: "My venerable sir, so shall I most probably think when I am yours." And yet the one is as good as the other.
R. L. STEVENSON, *Virginibus Puerisque: Crabbed Age and Youth.*

Age may have one side, but assuredly Youth has the other. There is nothing more certain than that both are right, except perhaps that both are wrong.
R. L. STEVENSON, *Virginibus Puerisque: Crabbed Age and Youth.*

9
A full, busy youth is your only prelude to a self-contained and independent age; and the muff inevitably develops into the bore.
R. L. STEVENSON, *Virginibus Puerisque. Crabbed Age and Youth.*

10
A young man will be wiser by and by;
An old man's wit may wander ere he die.
TENNYSON, *The Coming of Arthur,* l. 403.

11
The tears of the young who go their way,
Last a day;
But the grief is long of the old who stay.
J. T. TROWBRIDGE, *A Home Idyll* Pt. xv.

12
Youth is confident, manhood wary, and old age confident again.
MARTIN FARQUHAR TUPPER, *Proverbial Philosophy: Of Experience.*

13
Youth, large, lusty, loving—youth full of grace, force, fascination,
Do you know that Old Age may come after you with equal grace, force, fascination?
WALT WHITMAN, *Youth, Day, Old Age and Night.*

14
A happy youth, and their old age
Is beautiful and free.
WORDSWORTH, *The Fountain,* l. 43.

II—Age: Middle Age

See also Birth: Birthday

15
Of all the barbarous middle ages, that
Which is most barbarous is the middle age
Of man; it is—I really scarce know what;
But when we hover between fool and sage.
BYRON, *Don Juan.* Canto xii, st. 1.

16
Since more than half my hopes came true
And more than half my fears
Are but the pleasant laughing-stock
Of these my middle years:— . . .
Shall I not bless the middle years?
Not I for youth repine
While warmly round me cluster lives
More dear to me than mine.
SARAH N. CLEGHORN, *Contented at Forty.*

17
In the middle of the journey of our life. (Nel mezzo del cammin di nostra vita.)
DANTE, *Inferno.* Canto i, l. 1.

Thyself no more deceive, thy youth hath fled.
PETRARCH, *To Laura in Death.* Sonnet 82.

18
So take the hint, the hands of Time
Are pointing, not unkindly,
Back to the hills we used to climb

While prospects beckoned blindly.
LAURENCE HOUSMAN, *Farewell to Town.*

The pools of art and memory keep
Reflections of our fallen towers,
And every princess there asleep,
Whom once we kissed, is always ours.
E. B. C. JONES, *Middle-Age.*

1
Sweet is the infant's waking smile,
And sweet the old man's rest—
But middle age by no fond wile,
No soothing calm is blest.
JOHN KEBLE, *The Christian Year: St. Philip and St. James.* St. 3.

I may not be Meethosalem, but I am not a child in arms.
DICKENS, *Dombey and Son.* Bk. i, ch. 44.

2
Of middle age the best that can be said is that a middle-aged person has likely learned how to have a little fun in spite of his troubles.
DON MARQUIS, *The Almost Perfect State.*

3
Let us, then, love the perfect day,
The twelve o'clock of life, and stop
The two hands pointing to the top,
And hold them tightly while we may.
JOAQUIN MILLER, *The Sea of Fire.* Canto xxiii.

4
Thou'lt find thy Manhood all too fast—
Soon come, soon gone! and age at last
A sorry *breaking-up!*
THOMAS MOORE, *Ode: Clapham Academy.*

5
To be interested in the changing seasons is, in this middling zone, a happier state of mind than to be hopelessly in love with spring.
GEORGE SANTAYANA, *Little Essays,* p. 277.

6
On his bold visage middle age
Had slightly press'd its signet sage,
Yet had not quench'd the open truth
And fiery vehemence of youth;
Forward and frolic glee was there,
The will to do, the soul to dare.
SCOTT, *Lady of The Lake.* Canto i, st. 21. (1810)

Age has now
Stamped with its signet that ingenuous brow.
SAMUEL ROGERS, *Human Life.* (1819)

7
Your lordship, though not clean past your youth, hath yet some smack of age in you, some relish of the saltness of time.
SHAKESPEARE, *II Henry IV.* Act i, sc. 2, l. 108.

8
Pass, thou wild heart,
Wild heart of youth that still
Hast half a will
To stay.
I grow too old a comrade, let us part:
Pass thou away.
WILLIAM WATSON, *Leavetaking.*

Once he sang of summer,
Nothing but the summer;
Now he sings of winter,
Of winter bleak and drear;
Just because there's fallen
A snowflake on his forehead
He must go and fancy
'Tis winter all the year!
THOMAS BAILEY ALDRICH, *A Snowflake.*

9
Among the peaceful harvest days,
An Indian Summer comes at last!
ADELINE D. T. WHITNEY, *Equinoctial.*

10
Ho, pretty page with the dimpled chin
That never has known the barber's shear,
All your wish is woman to win,
This is the way that boys begin,—
Wait till you come to Forty Year.

Forty times over let Michaelmas pass;
Grizzling hair the brain doth clear,—
Then you know a boy is an ass,
Then you know the worth of a lass,
Once you have come to Forty Year.
THACKERAY, *The Age of Wisdom.*

Forty years on, growing older and older,
Shorter in wind and in memory long,
Feeble of foot and rheumatic of shoulder,
What will it help you that once you were young?
UNKNOWN, *Harrow School Song.*

11
Be wise with speed;
A fool at forty is a fool indeed.
YOUNG, *Love of Fame.* Satire ii, l. 281.

He who at fifty is a fool
Is far too stubborn grown for school.
NATHANIEL COTTON, *Slander.*

12
A boy may still detest age,
But as for me I know
A man has reached his best age
At forty-two or so.
R. C. LEHMANN, *Middle Age.*

III—Age: Old Age

13
To know how to grow old is the master-work of wisdom, and one of the most difficult chapters in the great art of living.
AMIEL, *Journal,* 21 Sept., 1874.

Few people know how to be old. (Peu de gens savent être vieux.)
LA ROCHEFOUCAULD, *Maximes.* No. 423.

14
Age has crept upon thee unperceived, nor canst thou call back the days that are gone. (Obrepsit non intellecta senectus Nec revocare potes, qui periere, dies.)
AUSONIUS, *Epigrams.* No. xxxiv, l. 3.

Whilst we drink, and call for garlands, for perfumes, and for maidens,
Old age is creeping on us unperceived.

(Dum bibimus, dum serta unguenta puellas
Poscimus, obrepit non intellecta senectus.)

JUVENAL, *Satires*. Sat. ix, l. 128.

But on us both did haggish age steal on.

SHAKESPEARE, *All's Well that Ends Well*. Act i, sc. 2, l. 29.

For Age, with stealing steps,
Hath clawed me with his clutch.

THOMAS VAUX, *The Aged Lover Renounceth Love* (c. 1550). Quoted by Shakespeare, *Hamlet*. Act v, sc. 1, l. 79.

Old age comes on apace to ravage all the clime.

JAMES BEATTIE, *The Minstrel*. Bk. i, st. 25.

1
I am too old, and the seas are too long, for me to double the Cape of Good Hope.

FRANCIS BACON, *Memorial of Access*.

Age will not be defied.

BACON, *Essays: Of Regimen of Health*.

2
What's a man's age? He must hurry more,
that's all;
Cram in a day what his youth took a year to
hold.

ROBERT BROWNING, *The Flight of the Duchess*.

I am long on ideas, but short on time. I expect to live to be only about a hundred.

THOMAS A. EDISON. (*Golden Book*, April, 1931.)

3
This I know without being told,
'Tis time to live as I grow old.
'Tis time short pleasures now to take,
Of little Life the best to make,
And manage wisely the last stake.

ABRAHAM COWLEY, *Age*.

4
Age is like love, it cannot be hid.

THOMAS DEKKER, *Fortunatus*. Act ii, sc. 1.

5
Few envy the consideration enjoyed by the oldest inhabitant.

EMERSON, *Society and Solitude: Old Age*.

We do not count a man's years, until he has nothing else to count.

EMERSON, *Society and Solitude: Old Age*.

6
It is time to be old, To take in sail.

EMERSON, *Terminus*.

7
Sir, you shall taste my *anno domini*.

FARQUHAR, *The Beaux' Stratagem*. Act i, sc. 1.

8
Old and well stricken in age.

Old Testament: Genesis, xviii, 11.

9
And if I should live to be
The last leaf upon the tree
In the spring,
Let them smile, as I do now,
At the old forsaken bough
Where I cling.

OLIVER WENDELL HOLMES, *The Last Leaf*.

10
Age is rarely despised but when it is contemptible.

SAMUEL JOHNSON, *The Rambler*. No. 50.

11
Is age a sorrow, then, too great to share?
Or to be old, perhaps, is not to care.

EDWARD D. KENNEDY, *Strange, Is It Not?*

12
We dread old age, yet how few attain it! . . . We hope to grow old and we dread old age; that is to say, we love life and flee from death. (L'on espère de vieillir, et l'on craint la vieillesse.)

LA BRUYÈRE, *Les Caractères*. Pt. xi.

Every man desires to live long; but no man would be old.

SWIFT, *Thoughts on Various Subjects*.

All would live long, but none would be old.

BENJAMIN FRANKLIN, *Poor Richard*, 1749.

13
Age loves to give good precepts to console itself for being no longer able to give bad examples. (Les vieillards aiment à donner de bons préceptes, pour se consoler de n'être plus en état de donner de mauvais exemples.)

LA ROCHEFOUCAULD, *Maximes*. No. 93.

14
In growing old, one grows more foolish and more wise. (En vieillissant, on devient plus fou et plus sage.)

LA ROCHEFOUCAULD, *Maximes*. No. 210. The shorter proverbial form is, "Old age makes us wiser and more foolish."

15
For we are old, and on our quick'st decrees
The inaudible and noiseless foot of Time
Steals ere we can effect them.

SHAKESPEARE, *All's Well that Ends Well*. Act v, sc. 3, l. 40.

16
I confess that I am old; Age is unnecessary.

SHAKESPEARE, *King Lear*. Act ii, sc. 4, l. 156.

I am declined Into the vale of years.

SHAKESPEARE, *Othello*. Act iii, sc. 3, l. 265.

17
Give me a staff of honour for mine age,
But not a sceptre to control the world.

SHAKESPEARE, *Titus Andronicus*. Act i, sc. 1, l. 198.

18
Old men and comets have been reverenced for the same reason: their long beards, and pretences to foretell events.

JONATHAN SWIFT, *Works*. Vol. iii, p. 409.

The older I grow the more I distrust the familiar doctrine that age brings wisdom.

H. L. MENCKEN, *Prejudices*. Ser. iii, p. 311.

IV—Age: Senility

19
Everyone knows that old men are twice boys. (Ἐγὼ δέ γ' ἀντείποιμ' ἂν ὡς δὶς παῖδες οἱ γέροντες.)

ARISTOPHANES, *The Clouds*, l. 1417.

Old men are children for the second time. (Δὶς παῖδες οἱ γέροντες.)
MENANDER, *Xera: Fragment.*

Once a man reaches the witless stage, without senses or mentality, they say that he has grown a child again. (Senex quom extemplo est, jam nec sentit nec sapit, Aiunt solere eum rusum repuerascere.)
PLAUTUS, *Mercator*, l. 295. (Act ii, sc. 2.)

Old men are twice children.
THOMAS RANDOLPH, *Jealous Lovers*, iii, 6.

An old man is twice a child.
SHAKESPEARE, *Hamlet*. Act ii, sc. 2, l. 404. TAYLOR, *The Old, Old, Very Old Man.*

1
Old Age, a second child, by Nature curst,
With more and greater evils than the first:
Weak, sickly, full of pains, in every breath
Railing at life and yet afraid of death.
CHARLES CHURCHILL, *Gotham*. Bk. i, l. 215.

2
Senile debility, usually called "dotage," is a characteristic, not of all old men, but only of those who are weak in mind and will. (Ista senilis stultitia, quæ deliratio appelari solet, senum levium est, non omnium.)
CICERO, *De Senectute*. Ch. xi, sec. 36.

3
The ruins of himself! now worn away
With age, yet still majestic in decay.
HOMER, *Odyssey*. Bk. xxiv, l. 271. (Pope, tr.)

And a crook is in his back,
And a melancholy crack
In his laugh.
OLIVER WENDELL HOLMES, *The Last Leaf.*

A poor, weak, palsy-stricken, churchyard thing.
KEATS, *The Eve of St. Agnes*. St. 18.

4
On his last legs.
THOMAS MIDDLETON, *The Old Law*. Act v, sc. 1.

Went on three feet, and sometimes crept on four,
His withered fist still knocking at death's door.
THOMAS RANDOLPH, *Mirror for Magistrates: Old Age.*

5
Last scene of all,
That ends this strange, eventful history,
Is second childishness and mere oblivion,
Sans teeth, sans eyes, sans taste, sans everything.
SHAKESPEARE, *As You Like It*. Act ii, sc. 7, l. 163.

6
Nature in you stands on the very verge
Of her confine.
SHAKESPEARE, *King Lear*. Act ii, sc. 4, l. 149.

A poor, infirm, weak, and despised old man.
SHAKESPEARE, *King Lear*. Act iii, sc. 2, l. 20.

Palsied eld.
SHAKESPEARE, *Measure for Measure*. Act iii, sc. 1, l. 36.

The lean and slippered pantaloon.
SHAKESPEARE, *As You Like It*. Act ii, sc. 7, l. 158

The oldest man he seemed that ever wore grey hairs.
WORDSWORTH, *Resolution and Independence.*

V—Age: Facing the Sunset

7
Beyond the ever and the never,
I shall be soon.
Love, rest, and home!
Sweet hope!
Lord, tarry not, but come.
HORATIUS BONAR, *Beyond the Smiling and the Weeping.*

Abide with me, fast falls the eventide;
The darkness deepens; Lord, with me abide.
HENRY FRANCIS LYTE, *Eventide.*

8
I stand upon the summit of my years;
Behind, the toil, the camp, the march, the strife,
The wandering and the desert; vast, afar,
Beyond this weary way, behold! the Sea!
JOSEPH BROWNLEE BROWN, *Thalatta! Thalatta!*

9
And he died in a good old age, full of days, riches, and honour.
Old Testament: I Chronicles, xxix, 28.

10
Drawing near her death, she sent most pious thoughts as harbingers to heaven; and her soul saw a glimpse of happiness through the chinks of her sickness-broken body.
THOMAS FULLER, *Life of Monica*. Bk. i, ch. 2.

To vanish in the chinks that Time has made.
SAMUEL ROGERS, *Italy: Pæstum*, l. 59. (c. 1820)

No, no; he cannot long hold out these pangs;
The incessant care and labour of his mind
Hath wrought the mure, that should confine it in,
So thin that life looks through and will break out.
SHAKESPEARE, *II Henry IV*. Act iv, sc. 4, l. 117. (1597)

The soul's dark cottage, batter'd and decay'd,
Lets in new light through chinks that Time hath made;
Stronger by weakness, wiser men become,
As they draw near to their eternal home.
Leaving the old, both worlds at once they view,
That stand upon the threshold of the new.
EDMUND WALLER, *Of the Last Verses in the Book.* (1645)

The robe of flesh wears thin, and with the years
God shines through all things.
JOHN BUCHAN, *The Wise Years.*

11
So peaceful shalt thou end thy blissful days,
And steal thyself from life by slow decays.
HOMER, *Odyssey*. Bk. xi, l. 164. (Pope, tr.)

An age that melts with unperceiv'd decay,
And glides in modest innocence away.
SAMUEL JOHNSON, *Vanity of Human Wishes*, l. 293.

Bends to the grave with unperceiv'd decay,
While Resignation gently slopes the way;

And, all his prospects bright'ning to the last,
His Heaven commences ere the world be pass'd.
GOLDSMITH, *The Deserted Village*, l. 109.

1
When he's forsaken, Wither'd and shaken,
What can an old man do but die?
THOMAS HOOD, *Ballad: Spring It Is Cheery*.

2
Superfluous lags the vet'ran on the stage,
Till pitying Nature signs the last release,
And bids afflicted worth retire to peace.
SAMUEL JOHNSON, *Vanity of Human Wishes*, l. 308.

3
I strove with none, for none was worth my strife.
Nature I loved, and, next to Nature, Art;
I warmed both hands before the fire of Life;
It sinks, and I am ready to depart.
W. S. LANDOR, *The Last Fruit of an Old Tree: Dedication*.

4
For you the To-come,
But for me the Gone-by;
You are panting to live,
I am waiting to die.
RICHARD LE GALLIENNE, *An Old Man's Song*.

5
The course of my long life hath reached at last,
In fragile bark o'er a tempestuous sea,
The common harbor, where must rendered be,
Account of all the actions of the past.
LONGFELLOW, *Old Age*.

6
Youth having passed, there is nothing to lose but memory. Cherishing the past without regrets and viewing the future without misgivings, we wait, then, for the nightfall when one may rest and call it a life.
GEORGE E. MACDONALD, *Fifty Years of Freethought*. Vol. ii, p. 635.

7
So mays't thou live till, like ripe fruit, thou drop
Into thy mother's lap, or be with ease
Gather'd, not harshly pluck'd, for death mature:
This is old age.
MILTON, *Paradise Lost*. Bk. xi, l. 532.

8
Would that by no disease, no cares opprest,
I in my sixtieth year were laid to rest.
MIMNERMUS. (DIOGENES LAERTIUS, *Solon*. Sec. 17.)

Surely a wiser wish were thus expressed,
At eighty years let me be laid to rest.
SOLON, *Fragments*. Frag. 20.

9
I'm wearin' awa', John,
Like snaw-wreaths in thaw, John,
I'm wearin' awa'
To the land o' the leal.
CAROLINA NAIRNE, *The Land o' the Leal*.

11
Old age hath yet his honour and his toil;
Death closes all.
ALFRED TENNYSON, *Ulysses*, l. 50.

12
For my eightieth year warns me to pack up my baggage before I leave life. (Annus enim octogesimus admonet me, ut sarcinas colligam, antequam proficiscare vita.)
VARRO, *De Re Rustica*, i, 1.

At seventy-seven it is time to be earnest.
SAMUEL JOHNSON. (BOSWELL, *Life*, v, 288.)

13
A little more tired at close of day,
A little less anxious to have our way;
A little less ready to scold and blame;
A little more care of a brother's name;
And so we are nearing the journey's end,
Where time and eternity meet and blend.
ROLLIN J. WELLS, *Growing Old*.

14
Then Old Age and Experience, hand in hand,
Lead him to Death, and make him understand,
After a search so painful and so long,
That all his life he has been in the wrong.
JOHN WILMOT, EARL OF ROCHESTER, *A Satire Against Mankind*, l. 25.

VI—Age: Its Love of Life

15
No one is so old as to think he cannot live one more year. (Nemo est tam senex qui se annum non putet posse vivere.)
CICERO, *De Senectute*. Ch. vii, sec. 24.

For never any man was yet so old
But hoped his life one winter more might hold.
SIR JOHN DENHAM, *Of Old Age*. Pt. i, l. 135.

16
With lying lips prays eld for death's release,
Plaining of age and weary-wearing time.
Let death draw near—who hails his coming? None:
No more is age a burden.
EURIPIDES, *Alcestis*, l. 669.

17
Yet we hope and hope, and fancy that he who has lived to-day may live to-morrow.
SAMUEL JOHNSON. (BOSWELL, *Life*. Vol. iv, p. 270.)

18
There is no man so decrepit, whilst he has Methuselah before him, who does not think he has still twenty years of life in his body. (N'est homme si decrepite, tant qu'il veoid Mathusalem devant, qui ne pense avoir encores vingt ans dans le corps.)
MONTAIGNE, *Essays*. Bk. i, ch. 19.

19
The tree of deepest root is found
Least willing still to quit the ground;
'Twas therefore said by ancient sages
That love of life increased with years,
So much that in our later stages,

When pains grow sharp, and sickness rages,
The greatest love of life appears.

HESTER LYNCH PIOZZI, *The Three Warnings.*

1
No man is so old that it is improper for him to hope for another day of existence. And one day, mind you, is a stage on life's journey. (Deinde nemo tam senex est, ut inprobe unum diem speret. Unus autem dies gradus vitæ est.)

SENECA, *Epistulæ ad Lucilium.* Epis. xii, sec. 6.

2
They that went on crutches ere he was born,
desire yet their life to see him a man.

SHAKESPEARE, *Winter's Tale.* Act i, sc. 1, l. 44.

3
Since, my last moments to assuage,
Your Majesty's humane decree
Has deign'd to leave the choice to me,
I'll die, so please you, of old age.

HORACE SMITH, *Jester Condemned to Death.*

4
Nobody loves life like an old man.

SOPHOCLES, *Acrisius.* Frag. 63.

5
O! why do wretched men so much desire
To draw their days unto the utmost date?

SPENSER, *Faerie Queene.* Bk. iv, canto iii, st. 1.

VII—Age: Its Compensations

6
In seventy or eighty years, a man may have a deep gust of the world; know what it is, what it can afford, and what 'tis to have been a man.

SIR THOMAS BROWNE, *Christian Morals.* Pt. iii, sec. 22.

7
Grow old along with me!
The best is yet to be,
The last of life, for which the first was made:
Our times are in his hand
Who saith, "A whole I planned,
Youth shows but half; trust God: see all, nor be afraid!"

ROBERT BROWNING, *Rabbi Ben Ezra.* St. 1.

8
For out of old fields, as men saith,
Cometh all this new corn fro year to year.

CHAUCER, *The Parlement of Foules,* l. 22.

Though summer goes, remember
The harvest fields;
The color-work of autumn
And what it yields.

FREDERICK HERBERT ADLER, *To One Who Fears Old Age.*

9
Old age lacks the heavy banquet, the loaded table, and the oft-filled cup; therefore it also lacks drunkenness, indigestion, and loss of sleep.

CICERO, *De Senectute.* Ch. xiii, sec. 44.

I am profoundly grateful to old age, which has increased my eagerness for conversation and taken away that for food and drink. (Habeoque senectuti magnam gratiam, quæ mihi sermonis aviditatem auxit, potionis et cibi sustulit.)

CICERO, *De Senectute.* Ch. xiv, sec. 46.

10
Old age, especially when crowned with honor, enjoys an authority which is of more value than all the sensual pleasures of youth. (Habet senectus, honorata præsertim, tantem auctoritatem, ut ea pluris sit quam omnes adulescentiæ voluptates.)

CICERO, *De Senectute.* Ch. xvii, sec. 61.

It is in old men that reason and judgment are found, and had it not been for old men no state would have existed at all. (Mens enim et ratio et consilium in senibus est, qui si nulli fuissent, nullæ omnino civitates fuissent.

CICERO, *De Senectute.* Ch. xix, sec. 67.

The fruit of old age is the memory of abundant blessings previously acquired. (Fructus autem senectutis est, ante partorum bonorum memoria et copia.)

CICERO, *De Senectute.* Ch. xix, sec. 71.

11
We come now to the third ground for abusing old age, and that is, that it is devoid of sensual pleasures. O glorious boon of age, if it does indeed free us from youth's most vicious fault!

CICERO, *De Senectute.* Ch. xii, sec. 39.

If age had no other pleasure than this, . . . it were a great one to have left all my painful and troublesome lusts behind me.

SENECA, *Epistulæ ad Lucilium.* Epis. xii, sec. 5.

Heaven forbid! I have fled from them as from a harsh and cruel master! (Di meliora! ego vero istinc sicut a domino agresti ac furioso profugi.)

SOPHOCLES, when asked if he indulged in the delights of love in his old age. (CICERO, *De Senectute.* Ch. xiv, sec. 47.)

The seas are quiet when the winds give o'er:
So, calm are we when passions are no more!

EDMUND WALLER, *Of the Last Verses in the Book.*

12
Come, Captain Age,
With your great sea-chest full of treasure!
Under the yellow and wrinkled tarpaulin
Disclose the carved ivory
And the sandalwood inlaid with pearl:
Riches of wisdom and years.

SARAH N. CLEGHORN, *Come, Captain Age.*

Then welcome age, and fear not sorrow;
Today's no better than tomorrow. . . .
I know we grow more lovely
Growing wise.

ALICE CORBIN, *Two Voices.*

13
And not by eastern windows only,
When daylight comes, comes in the light;
In front, the sun climbs slow, how slowly,
But westward, look, the land is bright.

ARTHUR HUGH CLOUGH, *Say Not the Struggle Nought Availeth.*

Suffer, O silent one, that I remind thee
Of the great hills that stormed the sky behind thee,
Of the wild winds of power that have resigned thee.

ALICE MEYNELL, *Letter from a Girl to Her Old Age.*

1
The year grows rich as it groweth old,
And life's latest sands are its sands of gold!

JULIA C. R. DORR, *To the "Bouquet Club."*

2
[Age] has weathered the perilous capes and shoals in the sea whereon we sail, and the chief evil of life is taken away in removing the grounds of fear. . . . At every stage we lose a foe. At fifty years, 'tis said, afflicted citizens lose their sick-headaches.

EMERSON, *Society and Solitude: Old Age.*

Old age brings along with its ugliness the comfort that you will soon be out of it. . . . To be out of the war, out of debt, out of the drouth, out of the blues, out of the dentist's hands, out of the second thoughts, mortifications, and remorses that inflict such twinges and shooting pains,—out of the next winter, and the high prices!

EMERSON, *Journals.* Vol. x, p. 51.

3
O blest retirement, friend to life's decline,
Retreats from care, that never must be mine,
How blest is he who crowns in shades like these,
A youth of labour with an age of ease;
Who quits a world where strong temptations try,
And, since 'tis hard to combat, learns tc fly!

GOLDSMITH, *The Deserted Village,* l. 97.

4
God on our Youth bestows but little ease,
But on our Age most sweet indulgences.

ROBERT HERRICK, *Youth and Age.*

5
Many blessings do the advancing years bring with them; many, as they retire, they take away. (Multa ferunt anni venientes commoda secum, Multa recedentes adimunt.)

HORACE, *Ars Poetica,* l. 175.

6
Light heart, light foot, light food, and slumber light,
These lights shall light us to old age's gate,
While monarchs, whom rebellious dreams affright,
Heavy with fear, death's fearful summons wait.

EDWARD HOVELL-THURLOW, *When In the Woods I Wander All Alone.*

7
With the ancient is wisdom; and in length of days understanding.

Old Testament: Job, xii, 12.

The essence of age is intellect.

EMERSON, *Society and Solitude: Old Age.*

Old age takes from the man of intellect no qualities save those which are useless to wisdom. (La vieillesse n'ôte à l'homme d'esprit que des qualités inutiles à la sagesse.)

JOUBERT, *Pensées.* No. 87.

As you are old and reverend, you should be wise.

SHAKESPEARE, *King Lear.* Act i, sc. 4, l. 262.

8
In the decline of life, shame and grief are of short duration.

SAMUEL JOHNSON, *Rasselas.* Ch. 4.

We grow with years more fragile in body, but morally stouter, and we can throw off the chill of a bad conscience almost at once.

LOGAN PEARSALL SMITH, *Afterthoughts.*

9
It is too late! Ah, nothing is too late
Till the tired heart shall cease to palpitate.
Cato learned Greek at eighty; Sophocles
Wrote his grand Œdipus, and Simonides
Bore off the prize of verse from his compeers,
When each had numbered more than four-score years, . . .
Chaucer, at Woodstock with the nightingales,
At sixty wrote the Canterbury Tales;
Goethe at Weimar, toiling to the last,
Completed Faust when eighty years were past.
These are indeed exceptions; but they show
How far the gulf-stream of our youth may flow
Into the arctic regions of our lives. . . .
For age is opportunity no less
Than youth itself, though in another dress,
And as the evening twilight fades away
The sky is filled with stars, invisible by day.

LONGFELLOW, *Morituri Salutamus,* l. 238.

10
Age is not all decay; it is the ripening, the swelling, of the fresh life within, that withers and bursts the husk.

GEORGE MACDONALD, *The Marquis of Lossie.* Ch. 40.

11
Not till the fire is dying in the grate,
Look we for any kinship with the stars.

GEORGE MEREDITH, *Modern Love.* St. 4.

12
We age inevitably:
The old joys fade and are gone:
And at last comes equanimity and the flame burning clear.

JAMES OPPENHEIM, *New Year's Eve.*

13
Certainly old age has a great sense of calm and freedom; when the passions relax their hold, then, as Sophocles says, you have escaped from the control not of one master, but of many.

PLATO, *The Republic.* Bk. i, sec. 329.

14
Why will you break the Sabbath of my days,
Now sick alike of Envy and of Praise?

POPE, *Imitations of Horace: Epistles.* Bk. i, epis. 1. l. 3.

In life's cool ev'ning, satiate of applause.
POPE, *Imitations of Horace: Epistles*. Bk. i, epis. 1, l. 9.

1
Life is most delightful when it is on the downward slope. (Jucundissima est ætas devexa jam.)
SENECA, *Epistulæ ad Lucilium*. Epis. xii, sec. 5.

2
Let us cherish and love old age; for it is full of pleasure, if one knows how to use it. . . . The best morsel is reserved to the last. (Conplectamur illam at amemus; plena est voluptatis, si illa scias uti. . . . Quod in se jucundissimum omnis voluptas habet, in finem sui differt.)
SENECA, *Epistulæ ad Lucilium*. Epis. xii, sec. 4.

Of earthly blessing age is not the least,
Serene its twilight sky, the journey past;
Like that rare draught at Cana's marriage feast,
Life's best wine is the last.
FRANCES E. POPE, *The End of the Road*.

The daintiest last, to make the end most sweet.
SHAKESPEARE, *Richard II*. Act i, sc. 3, l. 68.

3
More are men's ends mark'd than their lives before:
The setting sun, and music at the close,
As the last taste of sweets, is sweetest last,
Writ in remembrance more than things long past.
SHAKESPEARE, *Richard II*. Act ii, sc. 1, l. 11.

4
The day becomes more solemn and serene
When noon is past: there is a harmony
In Autumn, and a lustre in its sky
Which through the Summer is not heard or seen,
As if it could not be, as if it had not been!
SHELLEY, *Hymn to Intellectual Beauty*. St. 7.

5
Old age and the wear of time teach many things. (Γῆρας διδάσκει πολλὰ καὶ χρόνου τριβή.)
SOPHOCLES, *Tyro*. Frag. 586.

6
No wise man ever wished to be younger.
SWIFT, *Thoughts on Various Subjects*.

7
Old men view best at a distance, with the eyes of understanding, as well as with those of nature.
SWIFT, *Thoughts on Various Subjects*.

Observation is an old man's memory.
SWIFT, *Thoughts on Various Subjects*.

8
I shall grow old, but never lose life's zest,
Because the road's last turn will be the best.
HENRY VAN DYKE, *The Zest of Life*.

9
Old age is no such uncomfortable thing, if one gives oneself up to it with a good grace, and don't drag it about "To midnight dances and the public show."
HORACE WALPOLE, *Letter to the Countess of Ailesbury*, 7 Nov., 1774.

10
I see in you the estuary that enlarges and spreads itself grandly as it pours in the great sea.
WALT WHITMAN, *To Old Age*.

The lights indeed from them—old age's lambent peaks.
WALT WHITMAN, *Old Age's Lambent Peaks*.

11
Honorable age is not that which standeth in length of time, nor that is measured by number of years. But wisdom is the gray hair unto men, and an unspotted life is old age.
Apocrypha: Wisdom of Solomon, iv, 8, 9.

VIII—Age: Its Penalties

12
What is it to grow old? . . .
Ah, 'tis not what in youth we dreamed 'twould be!
'Tis not to have our life
Mellowed and softened as with sunset glow,
A golden day's decline. . . .
It is to spend long days
And not once feel that we were ever young; . . .
It is—last stage of all!— . . .
To hear the world applaud the hollow ghost
Which blamed the living man.
MATTHEW ARNOLD, *Growing Old*.

The foot less prompt to meet the morning dew,
The heart less bounding at emotion new,
And hope, once crushed, less quick to spring again.
MATTHEW ARNOLD, *Thyrsis*. St. 14.

The slow dull sinking into withered age.
SIR EDWIN ARNOLD, *The Light of Asia*. Bk. iv.

13
Men of age object too much, consult too long, adventure too little, repent too soon.
FRANCIS BACON, *Essays: Of Youth and Age*.

14
Remember age, and thou canst not be proud,
For age pulls down the pride of every man.
RICHARD BARNFIELD, *The Affectionate Shepherd*. St. 31.

15
Old age doth in sharp pains abound;
We are belabored by the gout,
Our blindness is a dark profound,
Our deafness each one laughs about.
Then reason's light with falling ray
Doth but a trembling flicker cast.
Honor to age, ye children pay!
Alas! my fifty years are past!
BÉRANGER, *Cinquante Ans*. (C. L. Betts, tr.)

16
Old age is the harbor of all ills. (Τὸ γῆρας ἔλεγεν ὅρμον εἶναι τῶν κακῶν.)
BION. (DIOGENES LAERTIUS, *Bion*. Bk. iv, sec. 48.)

17
When ance life's day draws near the gloamin',

Then fareweel vacant, careless roamin';
An' fareweel cheerfu' tankards foamin';
An' social noise;
An' fareweel dear, deluding Woman,
The joy of joys!
BURNS, *Epistle to James Smith*. St. 14.

1
I've seen sae monie changefu' years,
On earth I am a stranger grown;
I wander in the ways of men,
Alike unknowing and unknown.
BURNS, *Lament for James, Earl of Glencairn.*

What is the worst of woes that wait on age?
What stamps the wrinkle deeper on the brow?
To view each loved one blotted from life's page,
And be alone on earth, as I am now.
BYRON, *Childe Harold*. Canto ii, st. 98.

How strange it seems, with so much gone
Of life and love, to still live on!
WHITTIER, *Snow-Bound*, l. 181.

2
He, who grown aged in this world of woe,
In deeds, not years, piercing the depths of life.
BYRON, *Childe Harold*. Canto iii, st. 5.

3
Years steal
Fire from the mind as vigour from the limb,
And life's enchanted cup but sparkles near the brim.
BYRON, *Childe Harold*. Canto iii, st. 8.

4
Just as old age is creeping on apace,
And clouds come o'er the sunset of our day,
They kindly leave us, though not quite alone,
But in good company—the gout or stone.
BYRON, *Don Juan*. Canto iii, st. 59.

My days are in the yellow leaf;
The flowers and fruits of love are gone;
The worm, the canker, and the grief
Are mine alone!
BYRON, *On This Day I Complete My Thirty-sixth Year.*

Though the night was made for loving,
And the day returns too soon,
Yet we'll go no more a roving
By the light of the moon.
BYRON, *So We'll Go No More A Roving.*

5
Old age has disgraces of its own; do not add to them the shame of vice. (Πολλὰ ἔχοντι τῷ γήρᾳ τὰ αἰσχρὰ μὴ προστίθει τὴν ἀπὸ τῆς κακίας αἰσχύνην.)
MARCUS CATO. (PLUTARCH, *Lives: Marcus Cato*. Ch. ix, sec. 6.)

'Tis unseemly for the old man to love. (Turpe senilis amor.)
OVID, *Amores*. Bk. i, eleg. 9, l. 4.

6
Old boys have their playthings as well as young ones; the difference is only in the price.
BENJAMIN FRANKLIN, *Poor Richard*, 1752.

There are few things that we so unwillingly give up, even in advanced age, as the supposition that we have still the power of ingratiating ourselves with the fair sex.
SAMUEL JOHNSON, *Miscellanies*. Vol. ii, p. 326.

A head that's white
To maids brings no delight.
UNKNOWN. (*Berkeley MSS.*, iii, 30.)

7
Ah, that I might strip off again this old age!
(Ἃ πάντως ἵνα γῆρας αὖθι τόδ' ἐκδύοιμι.)
CALLIMACHUS, *Fragmenta Incertæ*. No. 106.

8
Statesmen and beauties are very rarely sensible of the gradations of their decay; and, too sanguinely hoping to shine on in their meridian, often set with contempt and ridicule.
LORD CHESTERFIELD, *Letters*, 26 Feb., 1754.

9
The heart never grows better by age; I fear rather worse; always harder. A young liar will be an old one; and a young knave will only be a greater knave as he grows older.
LORD CHESTERFIELD, *Letters*, 17 May, 1750.

Many foxes grow gray, but few grow good.
BENJAMIN FRANKLIN, *Poor Richard*, 1749.

Men become old but they never become good.
OSCAR WILDE, *Lady Windermere's Fan*. Act i.

10
Old age makes me sour. (Amariorem enim me senectus facit.)
CICERO, *Epistulæ ad Atticum*. Bk. xiv, epis. 21.

11
Age and wedlock bring a man to his night-cap.
JOHN CLARKE, *Parœmiologia A.-L.*, 279.

Age and wedlock tame man and beast.
WILLIAM CAMDEN, *Remains*, 317.

Age and wedlock we all desire and repent of.
THOMAS FULLER, *Gnomologia*. No. 780.

12
When I was young?—Ah, woeful When!
Ah! for the change 'twixt Now and Then!
This breathing house not built with hands,
This body that does me grievous wrong,
O'er aery cliffs and glittering sands,
How lightly then it flashed along:—
Like those trim skiffs, unknown of yore,
On winding lakes and rivers wide,
That ask no aid of sail or oar,
That fear no spite of wind or tide!
S. T. COLERIDGE, *Youth and Age*, l. 6.

Flowers are lovely; Love is flower-like;
Friendship is a sheltering tree;
O! the joys that came down shower-like,
Of Friendship, Love, and Liberty,
Ere I was old!
S. T. COLERIDGE, *Youth and Age*, l. 18.

Like some poor nigh-related guest,
That may not rudely be dismissed,
Yet hath outstay'd his welcome while,
And tells the jest without the smile.
S. T. COLERIDGE, *Youth and Age*, l. 46.

Oh! better, then, to die and give
The grave its kindred dust,

Than live to see Time's bitter change
In those we love and trust.
ELIZA COOK, *Time's Changes.*

1
But age is froward, uneasy, scrutinous,
Hard to be pleased, and parsimonious.
SIR JOHN DENHAM, *Of Old Age.* Pt. iii, l. 235.

Old men are testy, and will have their way.
SHELLEY, *The Cenci.* Act i, sc. 2.

2
Nature abhors the old.
EMERSON, *Essays, First Series: Circles.*

3
What else is an old man but voice and shadow?
EURIPIDES, *Melanippe.* Frag. 18.

An old man is a bed full of bones.
JOHN RAY, *English Proverbs.*

4
Slow-consuming Age.
THOMAS GRAY, *On a Distant Prospect of Eton College.* St. 9.

5
That age is best which is the first,
When youth and blood are warmer;
But being spent, the worse, and worst
Times still succeed the former.
ROBERT HERRICK, *To the Virgins, to Make Much of Time.* St. 3.

6
Youth longs and manhood strives, but age remembers,
Sits by the raked-up ashes of the past,
Spreads its thin hands above the whitening embers
That warm its creeping life-blood till the last.
OLIVER WENDELL HOLMES, *The Iron Gate.*

7
Nay, and thou too, old man, in former days wast as we hear, happy. (*Καὶ σέ γέρον, τὸπρὶν μὲν ἀκσύομεν ὄλβιον ἔιναι.*)
HOMER, *Iliad.* Bk. xxiv, 1, 543.

How rare to find old age and happiness in one! (Rarum est felix idemque senex.)
SENECA, *Hercules Œtæus,* l. 643.

8
And bended Age, whose rusted sickle lies
In the scant harvest of remembered days.
R. U. JOHNSON, *Youth and the Sea.*

9
Hides from himself his state, and shuns to know
That life protracted is protracted woe.
Time hovers o'er, impatient to destroy,
And shuts up all the passages of joy.
SAMUEL JOHNSON, *Vanity of Human Wishes,* l. 257.

10
There is a wicked inclination in most people to suppose an old man decayed in his intellects. If a young or middle-aged man, when leaving a company, does not recollect where he laid his hat, it is nothing; but if the same inattention is discovered in an old man, people will shrug up their shoulders, and say "His memory is going."
SAMUEL JOHNSON. (BOSWELL, *Life,* iv, 181.)

11
Young men have more virtue than old men; they have more generous sentiments in every respect.
SAMUEL JOHNSON. (BOSWELL, *Life,* i, 445.)

I hope our young men will not grow into such dodgers as these old men are.
BENJAMIN JOWETT, *Letters.* No. 250.

Every man over forty is a scoundrel.
BERNARD SHAW, *Maxims for Revolutionists.*

12
How great and unceasing are the miseries of age! (Quam continuis et quantis longa senectus Plena malis!)
JUVENAL, *Satires.* Sat. x, l. 190.

Such are the penalties of the old man: he sees calamity after calamity befall his house, he lives in a world of sorrow, he grows old amid continual lamentation and in the garb of woe. (Hæc data poena diu viventibus, ut renovata Semper clade domus multis in luctibus inque Perpetuo mærore et nigra veste senescant.)
JUVENAL, *Satires.* Sat. x, l. 243.

13
Old age, more to be feared than death. (Morte magis metuenda senectus.)
JUVENAL, *Satires.* Sat. xi, l. 45.

O what a thing is age! Death without death's quiet.
LANDOR, *Imaginary Conversations: Epicurus, Leontion, and Ternissa.*

14
When all the world is old, lad,
And all the trees are brown;
And all the sport is stale, lad,
And all the wheels run down:
Creep home, and take your place there,
The spent and maimed among:
God grant you find one face there
You loved when all was young.
CHARLES KINGSLEY, *Young and Old.* (*The Water-Babies.* Ch. 2.)

15
Old age is a tyrant who forbids, upon pain of death, all the pleasures of youth. (La vieillesse est un tyran qui défend, sur peine de la vie, tous les plaisirs de la jeunesse.)
LA ROCHEFOUCAULD, *Maximes.* No. 461.

16
Whatever poet, orator, or sage
May say of it, old age is still old age.
It is the waning, not the crescent moon;
The dusk of evening, not the blaze of noon;
It is not strength, but weakness; not desire,
But its surcease; not the fierce heat of fire,
The burning and consuming element,
But that of ashes and of embers spent.
LONGFELLOW, *Morituri Salutamus,* l. 262.

The sunshine fails, the shadows grow more dreary.
LONGFELLOW, *Canzone.*

1
As life runs on, the road grows strange
With faces new, and near the end
The milestones into headstones change,
'Neath every one a friend.
J. R. LOWELL, *Sixty-eighth Birthday.*

The days grow shorter, the nights grow longer,
The headstones thicken along the way;
And life grows sadder, but love grows stronger
For those who walk with us day by day.
ELLA WHEELER WILCOX, *Interlude.*

Men drop so fast, ere life's mid stage we tread,
Few know so many friends alive, as dead.
YOUNG, *Love of Fame.* Sat. v, l. 97.

After a certain distance, every step we take in life we find the ice growing thinner below our feet, and all around us and behind us we see our contemporaries going through.
STEVENSON, *Virginibus Puerisque: Æs Triplex.*

2
When the body is assailed by the force of time,
And the limbs weaken from exhausted strength,
The mind breaks down, and thought and speech fail.
(Ubi jam validis quassatum est viribus ævi
Corpus et obtusis ceciderunt viribus artus,
Claudicat ingenium delirat lingua, labat mens.)
LUCRETIUS, *De Rerum Natura.* Bk. iii, l. 451.

3
Old age, thou enemy of mortal frames, 'tis thou dost plunder all that's fair from shapes of loveliness.
MENANDER, *Fragments.* No. 552.

O burdensome old age, thou dost bring never a blessing, but, while life lasts, many an annoyance and sorrow!
MENANDER, *Fragments.* No. 555.

4
Set is the sun of my years,
And over a few poor ashes,
I sit in darkness and tears.
GERALD MASSEY, *A Wail.*

5
Old age plants more wrinkles in the mind than in the face. (La vieillesse nous attache plus des rides en l'esprit qu'en visage.)
MONTAIGNE, *Essays.* Bk. i, ch. 57.

6
The uselessness of men above sixty years of age and the incalculable benefit it would be in commercial, in political, and in professional life, if as a matter of course, men stopped work at this age.
WILLIAM OSLER, *Address,* Johns Hopkins University, 22 Feb., 1905. It was this statement, together with a jesting quotation from Anthony Trollope's *The Fixed Period,* that "it might be a good thing if all were peacefully chloroformed at sixty," which caused Dr. Osler to be headlined throughout the country as the advocate of chloroform after sixty and the enemy of old age. (See *Medical Record,* 4 March, 1905; CUSHING, *Life of Osler,* vol. i, ch. 29; REID, *The Great Physician,* p. 173.)

7
And oh! I shall find how, day by day,
All thoughts and things look older;
How the laugh of pleasure grows less gay,
And the heart of friendship colder.
W. M. PRAED, *Twenty-eight and Twenty-nine*

8
Now Time has fled—the world is strange,
Something there is of pain and change;
My books lie closed upon the shelf;
I miss the old heart in myself.
ADELAIDE ANN PROCTER, *A Student.*

9
What makes old age so sad is, not that our joys but that our hopes cease. (Das Alter ist nicht trübe weil darin unsere Freuden, sondern weil unsere Hoffnungen aufhören.)
JEAN PAUL RICHTER, *Titan.* Zykel 34.

10
I'm growing fonder of my staff;
I'm growing dimmer in the eyes;
I'm growing fainter in my laugh;
I'm growing deeper in my sighs;
I'm growing careless of my dress;
I'm growing frugal of my gold;
I'm growing wise, I'm growing—yes,
I'm growing old.
JOHN G. SAXE, *I'm Growing Old.*

11
Thus pleasures fade away;
Youth, talents, beauty, thus decay,
And leave us dark, forlorn, and grey.
SCOTT, *Marmion:* Canto ii, *Introduction.* St. 7.

12
Thus aged men, full loth and slow,
The vanities of life forego,
And count their youthful follies o'er,
Till Memory lends her light no more.
SCOTT, *Rokeby.* Canto v, st. 1.

13
Old age is an incurable disease. (Senectus insanabilis morbus est.)
SENECA, *Epistulæ ad Lucilium.* Epis. cviii, 28.

Old age in itself is a disease. (Senectus ipsast morbus.)
TERENCE, *Phormio,* l. 575. (Act iv, sc. 1.)

Old age itself is a disease.
BEN JONSON, *Explorata: Sed Seculi Morbus.*

Old age is sickness enough of itself.
WALKER, *Parœmiologia,* 33.

14
And so, from hour to hour, we ripe and ripe,
And then, from hour to hour, we rot and rot.
SHAKESPEARE, *As You Like It.* Act ii, sc. 7, l. 26.

15
There is an old poor man, . . .
Oppress'd with two weak evils, age and hunger.
SHAKESPEARE, *As You Like It.* Act ii, sc. 7, l. 129.

These tedious old fools!
SHAKESPEARE, *Hamlet.* Act ii, sc. 2, l. 223.

NO FOOL LIKE AN OLD FOOL, *see under* FOOL.

16
The satirical rogue says here, that old men have grey beards; that their faces are wrinkled; their eyes purging thick amber and

plum-tree gum; and that they have a plentiful lack of wit, together with most weak hams: all which, sir, though I most powerfully and potently believe, yet I hold it not honesty to have it thus set down; for you yourself, sir, should be old as I am, if, like a crab, you could go backward.

SHAKESPEARE, *Hamlet*. Act ii, sc. 2, l. 198.

At your age,
The hey-day in the blood is tame, it's humble,
And waits upon the judgement.

SHAKESPEARE, *Hamlet*. Act iii, sc. 4, l. 68.

And 'tis not hard, I think,
For men so old as we to keep the peace.

SHAKESPEARE, *Romeo and Juliet*. Act i, sc. 2, l. 3.

1

Falstaff: You that are old consider not the capacities of us that are young; you do measure the heat of our livers with the bitterness of your galls; and we that are in the vaward of our youth, I must confess, are wags too.

Chief Justice: Do you set down your name in the scroll of youth, that are written down old with all the characters of age? Have you not a moist eye? a dry hand? a yellow cheek? a white beard? a decreasing leg? an increasing belly? is not your voice broken? your wind short? your chin double? your wit single? and every part about you blasted with antiquity? and will you yet call yourself young? Fie, fie!

SHAKESPEARE, *II Henry IV*. Act i, sc. 2, l. 197.

2

Pray, do not mock me:
I am a very foolish fond old man,
Fourscore and upward; not an hour more nor less,
And, to deal plainly,
I fear I am not in my perfect mind.

SHAKESPEARE, *King Lear*. Act iv, sc. 7, l. 59.

3

I have lived long enough; my way of life
Is fall'n into the sear, the yellow leaf;
And that which should accompany old age,
As honour, love, obedience, troops of friends,
I must not look to have; but in their stead,
Curses, not loud but deep; mouth-honour, breath,
Which the poor heart would fain deny, and dare not.

SHAKESPEARE, *Macbeth*. Act v, sc. 3, l. 24.

That time of year thou mayst in me behold
When yellow leaves, or none, or few, do hang
Upon those boughs which shake against the cold,—
Bare ruin'd choirs, where late the sweet birds sang.

SHAKESPEARE, *Sonnets*. No. lxxiii.

4

When thou art old and rich,
Thou hast neither heat, affection, limb, nor beauty,
To make thy riches pleasant.

SHAKESPEARE, *Measure for Measure*. Act iii, 1, 36.

5

When the age is in, the wit is out.

SHAKESPEARE, *Much Ado About Nothing*. Act iii, sc. 5, l. 37. A play upon the proverb, "When the wine is in, the wit is out."

6

The eternal dawn, beyond a doubt,
Shall break on hill and plain,
And put all stars and candles out
Ere we be young again.

R. L. STEVENSON, *To Minnie*.

7

When men grow virtuous in their old age they are merely making a sacrifice to God of the devil's leavings.

SWIFT, *Thoughts on Various Occasions*.

8

Fires that shook me once, but now to silent ashes fall'n away.
Cold upon the dead volcano sleeps the gleam of dying day.

TENNYSON, *Locksley Hall Sixty Years After*. St. 21.

9

Old age brings this one vice to mankind, that we all think too much of money. (Solum unum hoc vitium adfert senectus hominibus: adtentiores sumus ad rem omnes, quam sat est.)

TERENCE, *Adelphi*, l. 833. (Act v, sc. 3.)

A man can no more separate age and covetousness than a' can part young limbs and lechery.

SHAKESPEARE, *II Henry IV*. Act i, sc. 2, l. 256.

That disease
Of which all old men sicken,—avarice.

MIDDLETON, *The Roaring Girl*. Act i, sc. 1.

So for a good old-gentlemanly vice,
I think I must take up with avarice.

BYRON, *Don Juan*. Canto i, st. 216.

Avarice is the vice of declining years.

GEORGE BANCROFT, *History of U. S.* Ch. 17.

Generally money lies nearest them that are nearest their graves.

WILLIAM PENN, *Fruits of Solitude*, p. 151.

The avaricious man will show his avarice as he gets into years, because avarice is a passion compatible with old age,—and will become more avaricious as his other passions fall off from him.

ANTHONY TROLLOPE, *Ralph the Heir*. Ch. 1.

10

How earthy old people become,—mouldy as the grave! Their wisdom smacks of the earth. There is no foretaste of immortality in it. They remind me of earthworms and mole crickets.

H. D. THOREAU, *Journal*, 16 Aug., 1853.

11

Age steals away all things, even the mind. (Omnia fert ætas, animum quoque.)

VERGIL, *Eclogues*. No. ix, l. 51.

12

The choicest days of hapless human life
Fly first; disease and bitter eld succeed,

And toil, till harsh death rudely snatches all.
(Optima quæque dies miseris mortalibus ævi
Prima fugit; subeunt morbi tristisque senectus
Et labor, et duræ rapit inclementia mortis.)
VERGIL, *Georgics*. Bk. iii, l. 66.

There dwelleth pale disease and bitter eld.
(Pallentesque habitant morbi tristisque senectus.)
VERGIL, *Æneid*. Bk. vi, l. 275.

1
The loss of youth is melancholy enough, but to enter into old age through the gate of infirmity most disheartening.
WALPOLE, *Letters: To George Montagu*, 28 July, 1765.

2
Nothing is so ridiculous as an antique face in a juvenile drawing-room.
WALPOLE, *Letter to Sir Horace Mann*, 31 Dec., 1780.

3
Thus fares it still in our decay,
And yet the wiser mind
Mourns less for what age takes away
Than what it leaves behind.
WORDSWORTH, *The Fountain*. St. 9.

4
Waters on a starry night
Are beautiful and fair;
The sunshine is a glorious birth:
But yet I know, where'er I go,
That there hath passed away a glory from the earth.
WORDSWORTH, *Intimations of Immortality*, l. 14.

5
O Man, that from thy fair and shining youth
Age might but take the things Youth needed not!
WORDSWORTH, *The Small Celandine*.

6
I heard the old, old men say,
"All that's beautiful drifts away
Like the waters."
W. B. YEATS, *The Old Men Admiring Themselves in the Water*.

IX—Age: Green and Lusty

7
His head,
Not yet by time completely silver'd o'er,
Bespoke him past the bounds of freakish youth,
But strong for service still, and unimpair'd.
COWPER, *The Task*. Bk. ii, l. 702.

8
His eye was not dim, nor his natural force abated.
Old Testament: Deuteronomy, xxxiv, 7.

9
Father Time is not always a hard parent, and, though he tarries for none of his children, often lays his hand lightly on those who have used him well.
DICKENS, *Barnaby Rudge*. Ch. 2.

10
Spring still makes spring in the mind
When sixty years are told;
Love makes anew this throbbing heart,
And we are never old.
Over the winter glaciers
I see the summer glow,
And through the wild-piled snowdrift,
The warm rosebuds below.
EMERSON, *The World-Soul*. St. 14.

11
In a good old age.
Old Testament: Genesis, xv, 15.

12
Alike all ages. Dames of ancient days
Have led their children through the mirthful maze;
And the gay grandsire, skill'd in gestic lore,
Has frisk'd beneath the burthen of threescore.
GOLDSMITH, *The Traveller*, l. 251.

When age is jocund it makes sport for death.
GEORGE HERBERT, *Jacula Prudentum*.

13
To be seventy years young is sometimes far more cheerful and hopeful than to be forty years old.
O. W. HOLMES, *Letter to Julia Ward Howe*, on her 70th birthday, 27 May, 1889.

14
Call him not old whose visionary brain
Holds o'er the past its undivided reign.
For him in vain the envious seasons roll
Who bears eternal summer in his soul.
O. W. HOLMES, *The Old Player*.

15
A green old age, unconscious of decays,
That proves the hero born in better days.
HOMER, *Iliad*. Bk. xxiii, l. 929. (Pope, tr.)

His hair just grizzled As in a green old age.
DRYDEN, *Œdipus*. Act iii, sc. 1.

That in my age as cheerful I might be
As the green winter of the Holly Tree.
ROBERT SOUTHEY, *The Holly Tree*.

His old age was still fresh and green. (Cruda deo viridisque senectus.)
VERGIL, *Æneid*. Bk. vi, l. 304. Vergil is speaking of Charon, the ferryman of the nether regions. In describing the Britons preparing to give battle to the Roman legions at the foot of the Grampians, Cæsar uses the same phrase: "Quibus cruda ac viridis senectus."

16
Our hearts are young 'neath wrinkled rind:
Life's more amusing than we thought.
ANDREW LANG, *Ballade of Middle Age*.

17
His leaf also shall not wither.
Old Testament: Psalms, i, 3.

18
Though I look old, yet I am strong and lusty;
For in my youth I never did apply
Hot and rebellious liquors in my blood,
Nor did not with unbashful forehead woo

The means of weakness and debility;
Therefore my age is as a lusty winter,
Frosty, but kindly.

SHAKESPEARE, *As You Like It.* Act ii, sc. 3, l. 47.

1
You are old, Father William, the young man cried,
The few locks which are left you are grey;
You are hale, Father William, a hearty old man,
Now tell me the reason, I pray.

In the days of my youth, Father William replied,
I remember'd that youth would fly fast,
And abused not my health and my vigour at first,
That I never might need them at last.

ROBERT SOUTHEY, *The Old Man's Comforts.*

"You are old, Father William," the young man said,
"And your hair has become very white;
And yet you incessantly stand on your head—
Do you think, at your age, it is right?"

"In my youth," Father William replied to his son,
"I feared it might injure the brain;
But, now that I'm perfectly sure I have none,
Why, I do it again and again."

LEWIS CARROLL, *Alice's Adventures in Wonderland.* Ch. 5.

2
Grave was the man in years, in looks, in word,
His locks were gray, yet was his courage green.
(Ei di virilità grave e maturo,
Mostra in fresco vigor chiome canute.)

TASSO, *Jerusalem Delivered.* Bk. i, st. 53.

I'll out a while, an' see the young anes play.
My heart's still light, albeit my locks be grey.

ALLAN RAMSAY, *The Gentle Shepherd.* Act iii, sc. 2.

3
You have seen the old age of an eagle, as the saying is. (Visa verost, quod dici solet, Aquilæ senectus.)

TERENCE, *Heauton Timorumenos,* l. 520. (Act iii, sc. 2.)

The old age of an eagle is better than the youth of a sparrow. (Ἀετοῦ γῆρας, κορύδου νεότης.)

UNKNOWN. A Greek proverbial saying.

4
Venerable men! you have come down to us from a former generation. Heaven has bounteously lengthened out your lives, that you might behold this joyous day.

DANIEL WEBSTER, *Address, at Laying the Corner-stone of the Bunker Hill Monument,* 17 June, 1825.

5
But an old age serene and bright,
And lovely as a Lapland night,
Shall lead thee to thy grave.

WORDSWORTH, *To a Young Lady.*

6
The monumental pomp of age
Was with this goodly Personage;
A stature undepressed in size,
Unbent, which rather seemed to rise,
In open victory o'er the weight
Of seventy years, to loftier height.

WORDSWORTH, *The White Doe of Rylstone.* Canto iii, l. 737.

7
Age . . . is a matter of feeling, not of years.

GEORGE WILLIAM CURTIS, *Prue and I.* Ch. vi.

O wherefore our age be revealing?
Leave that to the registry books!
A man is as old as he's feeling,
A woman as old as she looks.

MORTIMER COLLINS, *How Old Are You?*

One is as old as one's heart. (On a l'age de son cœur.)

ALFRED D'HOUDETOT, *Age.*

A man is as old as his arteries.

DR. PIERRE J. G. CABANIS, *Epigram.* (a. 1800) Frequently quoted.

X—Age: Its Crown of Glory

See also Hair: Gray

8
The hoary head is a crown of glory, if it be found in the way of righteousness.

Old Testament: Proverbs, xvi, 31.

The beauty of old men is the gray head.

Old Testament: Proverbs, xx, 29.

Thy white locks, the blossom of old age.

SOPHOCLES, *Electra,* l. 42.

9
But now your brow is beld, John,
Your locks are like the snow;
But blessings on your frosty pow,
John Anderson my jo.

ROBERT BURNS, *John Anderson My Jo.*

Nor can the snow, which now cold Age does shed
Upon thy reverend head,
Quench or allay the noble fires within.

ABRAHAM COWLEY, *To Mr. Hobs.* St. 6.

10
A little more toward the light;—
Me miserable! Here's one that's white;
And one that's turning;
Adieu to song and "salad days";
My Muse, let's go at once to Jay's,
And order mourning.

AUSTIN DOBSON, *Growing Gray.*

Come let me pluck that silver hair
Which 'mid thy clustering curls I see;
The withering type of time or care
Has nothing, sure, to do with thee.

ALARIC ALEX WATTS, *The Grey Hair.*

11
We grizzle every day. I see no need of it.

EMERSON, *Essays, First Series: Circles.*

He is more than halfway
On the road from Grizzle to Grey.

ROBERT SOUTHEY, *Robert the Rhymer's Account of Himself.*

1
"Gray temples at twenty?"—Yes! *white* if
we please!
Where the snow-flakes fall thickest there's
nothing can freeze!

OLIVER WENDELL HOLMES, *The Boys.*

2
Though Time has touched it in his flight,
And changed the auburn hair to white.

LONGFELLOW, *The Golden Legend.* Pt. iv, l. 388.

3
Remote from cities liv'd a Swain,
Unvex'd with all the cares of gain;
His head was silver'd o'er with age,
And long experience made him sage.

JOHN GAY, *Fables:* Pt. i, *Introduction.*

4
My whitening hair softens a spirit prone to strife and wanton brawling; I had not brooked such insult when hot with youth, in the consulship of Plancus. (Lenit albescens animos capillus Litium et rixæ cupidos protervæ; Non ego hoc ferrem calidus juventa Consule Planco.)

HORACE, *Odes.* Bk. ii, ode 14, l. 25.

5
The snows of the head. (Capitis nives.)

HORACE, *Odes.* Bk. iv, ode 13, l. 12.

6
Consider my gray hairs. (Meum caput contemples.)

PLAUTUS, *Asinaria,* l. 539. (Act iii, sc. 1.)

7
Darling, I am growing old,
Silver threads among the gold
Shine upon my brow today;
Life is fading fast away.

EBEN E. REXFORD, *Silver Threads Among the Gold.* (1873)

8
The silver livery of advised age.

SHAKESPEARE, *II Henry VI.* Act v, sc. 2, l. 47.

How ill white hairs become a fool and jester!

SHAKESPEARE, *II Henry IV.* Act v, sc. 5, l. 52.

9
When white hairs thatch the furrowed
brow
Crowns come too late!

RICHARD HENRY STODDARD, *Threescore and Ten.*

XI—Age and Learning

10
It is always in season for the old to learn. (Καλὸν δὲ καὶ γέροντα μανθάνειν σοφά.)

ÆSCHYLUS, *Fragments.* Frag. 224.

11
Nor does age prevent our persisting in the study of other matters, and especially agriculture, even to the latest period of old age. (Nec ætas impedit quo minus et ceterarum rerum, et in primis agri colendi studia teneamus, usque ad ultimum tempus senectutis.)

CICERO, *De Senectute.* Ch. 17, sec. 60.

12
If I were running in the stadium, ought I to slacken my pace when approaching the goal? ought I not rather to put on speed?

DIOGENES, when told that he should take a rest, since he was an old man. (DIOGENES LAERTIUS, *Diogenes.* Sec. 34.)

The riders in a race do not stop short when they reach the goal. There is a little finishing canter before coming to a standstill. There is time to hear the kind voice of friends and to say to one's self: "The work is done."

JUSTICE OLIVER WENDELL HOLMES, *Radio Address* on his 90th birthday, 8 March, 1931.

13
Nothing is more dishonorable than an old man, heavy with years, who has no other evidence of having lived long except his age.

SENECA, *De Tranquillitate.* Ch. iii, sec. 7.

An old man learning his A B C is a disgraceful and absurd object; the young man must store up, the old man must use. (Turpis et ridicula res est elementarius senex; juveni parandum, seni utendum est.)

SENECA, *Epistulæ ad Lucilium.* Epis. xxxvi, 4.

What a stupid thing is an old man learning an alphabet! (La sotte chose qu'un vieillard abecedaire!)

MONTAIGNE, *Essays.* Bk. ii, ch. 28.

14
The head grey, and no brains yet.

THOMAS FULLER, *Gnomologia.* No. 4587.

15
But I grow old ever learning many things. (Γηράσκω δ' αἰεὶ πολλὰ διδασκόμενος.)

SOLON. (PLUTARCH, *Lives: Solon.* Sec. 31.)

I am still learning. (Ancora imparo.)

MICHELANGELO. His motto.

16
The latter part of a wise man's life is taken up in curing the follies, prejudices, and false opinions he had contracted in the former.

SWIFT, *Thoughts on Various Subjects.*

XII—Age: Its Garrulity

17
When a man fell into his anecdotage it was a sign for him to retire from the world.

BENJAMIN DISRAELI, *Lothair.* Ch. 28. "The world in its anecdotage" is referred to in the preface to Isaac D'Israeli's *Curiosities of Literature.*

But oh! the biggest muff afloat
Is he who takes to anecdote.

HENRY SAMBROOKE LEIGH, *Men I Dislike.*

18
Miss not the discourse of the elders.

Apocrypha: Ecclesiasticus, viii, 9.

19
Talking age.

GOLDSMITH, *The Deserted Village,* l. 14.

Narrative old age.

POPE, *The Temple of Fame,* l. 291.

20
Chiefs who no more in bloody fights engage,
But, wise thro' time, and narrative with age,

In summer-days like grasshoppers rejoice,
A bloodless race, that send a feeble voice.
HOMER, *Iliad*. Bk. iii, l. 199. (Pope, tr.)

As ancient Priam at the Scæan gate
Sat on the walls of Troy in regal state
With the old men, too old and weak to fight,
Chirping like grasshoppers in their delight
To see the embattled hosts, with spear and shield,
Of Trojans and Achaians in the field.
LONGFELLOW, *Morituri Salutamus*, l. 78.

1
It was near a miracle to see an old man silent, since talking is the disease of age.
BEN JONSON, *Explorata: Homeri Ulysses*.

A fond old man is often as full of words as a woman.
SIR THOMAS MORE, *English Works*, p. 1169.

A good old man, sir: he will be talking.
SHAKESPEARE, *Much Ado About Nothing*, iii, 5, 36.

2
What should we speak of
When we are old as you? When we shall hear
The rain and wind beat dark December.
SHAKESPEARE, *Cymbeline*. Act iii, sc. 3, l. 36.

3
Age too shines out: and, garrulous, recounts
The feats of youth.
THOMSON, *The Seasons: Autumn*, l. 1231.

XIII—Age: In Women: Its Beauty

4
The autumn of the beautiful is beautiful. (Pulchrorum autumnus pulcher.)
FRANCIS BACON, *Essays: Of Beauty*. Quoted.

5
And there is healing in old trees,
Old streets a glamour hold;
Why may not I, as well as these,
Grow lovely, growing old?
KARLE WILSON BAKER, *Let Me Grow Lovely*.

6
Laura was blooming still, had made the best
Of time, and time return'd the compliment.
BYRON, *Beppo*. St. 23.

7
As a white candle in a holy place,
So is the beauty of an aged face.
JOSEPH CAMPBELL, *The Old Woman*.

As the clear light is upon the holy candlestick; so is the beauty of the face in ripe age.
Apocrypha: Ecclesiasticus, xxvi, 17.

8
No Spring nor Summer Beauty hath such grace
As I have seen in one Autumnal face.
JOHN DONNE, *Elegies*: No. 9, *Autumnal*.

9
It may be, old age is gentle and fair . . .
Still I shall tremble at a gray hair.
DOROTHY DOW, *Unbeliever*.

10
The dear old ladies whose cheeks are pink
In spite of the years of Winter's chill,
Are like the Autumn leaves, I think,
A little crumpled, but lovely still.
JANIE SCREVEN HEYWARD, *Autumn Leaves*.

11
You are beautiful and faded,
Like an old opera tune
Played upon a harpsichord.
AMY LOWELL, *A Lady*.

12
To me, fair friend, you never can be old,
For as you were when first your eye I eyed,
Such seems your beauty still.
SHAKESPEARE, *Sonnets*. No. civ.

But spite of Heaven's fell rage,
Some beauty peep'd through lattice of sear'd age.
SHAKESPEARE, *A Lover's Complaint*, l. 13.

13
Women sit or move to and fro, some old, some young,
The young are beautiful—but the old are more beautiful than the young.
WALT WHITMAN, *Beautiful Women*.

XIV—Age: In Women: Its Ugliness

14
By candle-light nobody would have taken you for above five-and-twenty.
ISAAC BICKERSTAFFE, *Maid of the Mill*. Act i, sc. 2. (c. 1760)

And a very nice girl you'll find her!
She may pass very well for forty-three
In the dusk, with a light behind her.
W. S. GILBERT, *Trial by Jury*.

15
A lady of a "certain age," which means
Certainly agèd.
BYRON, *Don Juan*. Canto vi, st. 69.

She was not old, nor young, nor at the years
Which certain people call a *"certain age,"*
Which yet the most uncertain age appears.
BYRON, *Beppo*. St. 22.

16
There are three classes into which all elderly women that I ever knew were to be divided: first, that dear old soul; second, that old woman; third, that old witch.
S. T. COLERIDGE, *Table-Talk*.

17
She might be young, some forty years ago.
COWPER, *Truth*, l. 132.

18
Old women sit, stiffly, mosaics of pain, . . .
Their memories: a heap of tumbling stones,
Once builded stronger than a city wall.
BABETTE DEUTSCH, *Old Women*.

Once they were flowers, and flame, and living bread;
Now they are old and brown and all but dead!
MARYA ZATURENSKA, *Spinners at Willowsleigh*.

19
Phyllis! 'tis true thy glass does run,
But since mine too keeps equal pace,
My silver hair may trouble thee,
As much as me thy ruined face.
THOMAS FLATMAN, *The Resolve*.

20
To everybody's prejudice I know a thing or two;

I can tell a woman's age in half a minute—
and I do.

W. S. Gilbert, *Princess Ida*. Act i.

One should never trust a woman who tells one her real age. A woman who would tell one that would tell one anything.

Oscar Wilde, *A Woman of No Importance*. Act i.

1
What though she be toothless and bald as a coote?

John Heywood, *Proverbs*. Bk. i, ch. v.

2
Ladies, stock and tend your hive,
Trifle not at thirty-five;
For howe'er we boast and strive,
Life declines from thirty-five.

Samuel Johnson, *To Mrs. Thrale, When Thirty-five*, l. 11.

3
The hell of women is old age. (L'enfer des femmes, c'est la vieillesse.)

La Rochefoucauld, *Maximes Posthumes*. No. 562. Said to have been addressed by La Rochefoucauld to his former mistress, Ninon de l'Enclos, who died in 1705 at the age of 90.

4
When you try to conceal your wrinkles, Polla, by the use of bean-meal, you deceive yourself, not me. Let a blemish, which perhaps is small, be undisguised. A fault which is hidden is deemed greater than it is. (Lomento rugas uteri quod condere temptas, Polla, tibi ventrem, non mihi labra linis. Simpliciter pateat vitium fortasse pusillum: Quod tegitur, majus creditur esse malum.)

Martial, *Epigrams*. Bk. iii, ep. 42.

Double we see those faults which art would mend.

Martial, *Epigrams*, iii, 42. (Sedley, tr.)

Sovereigns may sway materials, but not matter,
And wrinkles, the d——d democrats, won't flatter.

Byron, *Don Juan*. Canto x, st. 24.

My aunt! my poor deluded aunt!
Her hair is almost gray;
Why will she train that winter curl
In such a spring-like way?

O. W. Holmes, *My Aunt*.

5
The time will come when it will vex you to look at a mirror, and grief will prove a second cause of wrinkles. (Tempus erit, quo vos speculum videsse pigebit, Et veniet rugis altera causa dolor.)

Ovid, *De Medicamine Faciei*, l. 47.

Here, Cyprian, is my jeweled looking-glass,
My final gift to bind my final vow:
I cannot see myself as I once was;
I would not see myself as I am now.

Aline Kilmer, *To Aphrodite: With a Mirror*.

6
She's six-and-forty, and I wish nothing worse to happen to any woman.

Pinero, *The Second Mrs. Tanqueray*. Act ii.

7
Fat, fair and forty.

Scott, *St. Ronan's Well*. Ch. 7. The Prince Regent's description of what a wife should be.

A fat, fair and fifty card-playing resident of the Crescent.

Melesina Trench, *Letter*, 18 Feb., 1816.

I am resolved to grow fat and look young till forty, and then slip out of the world with the first wrinkle and the reputation of five-and-twenty.

Dryden, *The Maiden Queen*. Act iii, sc. 1.

8
Even in the afternoon of her best days.

Shakespeare, *Richard III*. Act iii, sc. 7, l. 186.

By the sharp tooth of cankering eld defaced.

William Shenstone, *The Schoolmistress*. St. 16.

9
I swear she's no chicken; she's on the wrong side of thirty, if she be a day.

Swift, *Polite Conversation*. Dial. 1.

10
So grieve not, Ladies, if at night
You wake to feel the cold December;
Rather recall the early light,
And in your loved one's arms, remember.

Anna Hempstead Branch, *Grieve Not Ladies*.

XV—Age: Old Things Are Best

11
Alonso of Aragon was wont to say in commendation of age, that age appears to be best in four things,—old wood best to burn, old wine to drink, old friends to trust, and old authors to read.

Francis Bacon, *Apothegms*. No. 97.

Old wood to burn! Old wine to drink! Old friends to trust! Old authors to read!—Alonso of Aragon was wont to say in commendation of age, that age appeared to be best in these four things.

Melchior, *Floresta Española de Apothegmas o Sentencias*, ii, 1, 20.

One who professes the maxim of King Alphonso of Castille—old wood to burn—old books to read—old wine to drink—and old friends . . . to converse with.

Scott, *The Antiquary*. Ch. 6.

12
Our nature here is not unlike our wine;
Some sorts when old continue brisk and fine.

Sir John Denham, *Of Old Age*. Pt. iii, l. 245.

As for age, what that's worth depends on the quality of the liquor.

George Eliot, *Adam Bede*. Bk. ii, ch. 21.

13
I love everything that's old: old friends, old times, old manners, old books, old wine.

Goldsmith, *She Stoops to Conquer*. Act i, sc. 1.

Old loves, old aspirations, and old dreams,
More beautiful for being old and gone.

J. R. Lowell, *The Parting of the Ways*.

Old thanks, old thoughts, old aspirations,
Outlive men's lives and lives of nations.
A. C. SWINBURNE, *Age and Song.*

1
No man also having drunk old wine straightway desireth new; for he saith, The old is better.
New Testament: Luke, v, 39. (Vetus melius est.—*Vulgate.*)

2
What find you better or more honourable than age? . . . Take the preëminence of it in everything: in an old friend, in old wine, in an old pedigree.
SHACKERLEY MARMION, *The Antiquary.* Act ii, sc. 1. (1635)

3
Old wine to drink! . . .
Old wood to burn! . . .
Old books to read! . . .
Old friends to talk! . . .
R. H. MESSINGER, *Give Me the Old.*

4
So Life's year begins and closes;
Days, though short'ning, still can shine;
What though youth gave love and roses,
Age still leaves us friends and wine.
THOMAS MOORE, *Spring and Autumn.*

A man not old, but mellow, like good wine.
STEPHEN PHILLIPS, *Ulysses.* Act iii, sc. 2.

5
With years a richer life begins,
The spirit mellows:
Ripe age gives tone to violins,
Wine, and good fellows.
JOHN TOWNSEND TROWBRIDGE, *Three Worlds.*

6
Is not old wine wholesomest, old pippins toothsomest, old wood burn brightest, old linen wash whitest? Old soldiers, sweetheart, are surest, and old lovers are soundest.
JOHN WEBSTER, *Westward Hoe!* Act ii, sc. 2. (1603)

XVI—Age: The Age

7
The age of great men is going; the epoch of the ant-hill, of life in multiplicity, is beginning.
AMIEL, *Journal,* 6 Sept., 1851.

8
Years hence, perhaps, may dawn an age
More fortunate, alas! than we,
Which without hardness will be sage,
And gay without frivolity.
MATTHEW ARNOLD, *Grande Chartreuse.* St. 27.

9
Why slander we the times?
What crimes
Have days and years, that we
Thus charge them with iniquity?
If we would rightly scan,
It's not the times are bad, but man.
DR. JOSEPH BEAUMONT, *The Times.*

10
Every age has its pleasures, its style of wit, and its own ways.
NICHOLAS BOILEAU-DESPREAUX, *The Art of Poetry.* Canto iii, l. 374.

11
Every age,
Heroic in proportions, double-faced,
Looks backward and before, expects a morn
And claims an epos. Ay, but every age
Appears to souls who live in 't (ask Carlyle)
Most unheroic. Ours, for instance, ours:
The thinkers scout it, and the poets abound
Who scorn to touch it with a finger-tip:
A pewter age,—mixed metal, silver-washed;
An age of scum, spooned off the richer past.
E. B. BROWNING, *Aurora Leigh.* Bk. v, l. 152.

12
Every age
Through being beheld too close, is ill-discerned.
E. B. BROWNING, *Aurora Leigh.* Bk. v, l. 167.

13
To complain of the age we live in, to murmur at the present possessors of power, to lament the past, to conceive extravagant hopes of the future, are the common dispositions of the greatest part of mankind.
EDMUND BURKE, *Thoughts on the Cause of the Present Discontents.*

The world always had the same bankrupt look, to foregoing ages as to us,—as of a failed world just re-collecting its old withered forces to begin again and try to do a little business.
EMERSON, *Papers from the Dial: Past and Present.*

What age was not dull? When was not the majority wicked? or what progress was ever made by society?
EMERSON, *Journals.* Vol. iv, p. 85.

The illusion that times that were are better than those that are, has probably pervaded all ages.
HORACE GREELEY, *The American Conflict.* Ch. 1, p. 21. *See also under* ANTIQUITY.

14
This Age will serve to make a very pretty farce for the next.
SAMUEL BUTLER, *Remains.* Vol. ii, p. 475.

While sacred temples burn you dance and sing.
MARY SINTON LEITCH, *To the Modern Spirit.*

They are like rats crawling about the club of Hercules.
SCHILLER, *Die Räuber.* Act i, sc. 2. Referring to the present generation.

15
Oh, this age! how tasteless and ill-bred it is!
(O sæclum insapiens et infacetum!)
CATULLUS, *Odes.* Ode xliii, l. 8.

16
One does not blame an epoch; one congratulates oneself on not having belonged to it.
JEAN COCTEAU, *Le Rappel à l'Ordre.*

17
The press, the pulpit, and the stage,

Conspire to censure and expose the age.
WENTWORTH DILLON, *Essay on Translated Verse,* l. 7.

1
The frigid theories of a generalising age.
BENJAMIN DISRAELI, *Coningsby*. Bk. ix, ch. 7.

Of Paris Balzac once said, "It is a city where great ideas perish, done to death by a witticism." This is an age when great spirits perish, done to death by a formula.
FRANK K. NOTCH, *King Mob*, p. 151.

2
The riddle of the age has for each a private solution.
EMERSON, *Conduct of Life: Fate.*

Every Age, like every human body, has its own distemper.
EMERSON, *Nature, Addresses and Lectures: Lecture on the Times.*

3
Ye unborn ages, crowd not on my soul.
THOMAS GRAY, *The Bard,* l. 108.

4
In this Age, when it is said of a man, He knows *how to live,* it may be implied he is not very honest.
LORD HALIFAX, *Works*, p. 232.

What an age is this and what a world is this! that a man cannot live without playing the knave and dissimulation.
SAMUEL PEPYS, *Diary,* 1 Sept., 1661.

5
What has this unfeeling age of ours left untried? What wickedness has it shunned? (Quid nos dura refugimus ætas? Quid intactum nefasti liquimus?)
HORACE, *Odes*. Bk. i, ode 35, l. 34.

6
We live in an age in which superfluous ideas abound and essential ideas are lacking. (Nous vivons dans un siècle où les idées superflues surabondent, et qui n'a pas les idées nécessaires.)
JOUBERT, *Pensées*. No. 243.

7
Twenty centuries sunk in eternal night,
Forever without movement, noise, or light.
(Vingt siècles descendus dans l'éternelle nuit,
Y sont sans mouvement, sans lumière, et sans bruit.)
LÉMOINE, *Saint Louis.*

8
End of the Century. (Fin de Siècle.)
F. DE JOUVENOT and H. MICARD. Title of comedy. (1888)

It may indeed be something more than a coincidence that placed this decade at the close of a century, and *fin de siècle* may have been at once a swan song and a death-bed repentance.
HOLBROOK JACKSON, *The Eighteen-Nineties.*

9
The ages roll
Forward; and forward with them, draw my soul
Into time's infinite sea.
OWEN MEREDITH, *The Wanderer*, iv, 9.

10
For each age is a dream that is dying,
Or one that is coming to birth.
ARTHUR O'SHAUGHNESSY, *The Music-Makers.*

11
I have known this age, and what its customs are.
(Novi ego hoc sæculum, moribus quibus siet.)
PLAUTUS, *Trinummus*. Act ii, sc. 2, l. 6.

12
One is always of his age, and especially he who least appears so.
SAINTE-BEUVE. (EMERSON, *Journals,* 1867.)

13
The age is grown so picked that the toe of the peasant comes so near the heel of the courtier, he galls his kibe.
SHAKESPEARE, *Hamlet*. Act v, sc. 1, l. 150.

O miserable age!
SHAKESPEARE, *II Henry VI*. Act iv, sc. 2, l. 11.

15
It is grown a word of course for writers to say, This critical age, as divines say, This sinful age.
SWIFT, *Thoughts on Various Subjects.*

16
I, the heir of all the ages, in the foremost files of time.
ALFRED TENNYSON, *Locksley Hall,* l. 178.

Neither you nor I know what is to befall us in two, three, or four years. *Centuries are not for us.* (Ne savons ce qui arrivera dans deux, trois, ou quatre ans. *Les siècles ne sont pas à nous.*)
NAPOLEON BONAPARTE, *Letter,* to his brother Joseph, King of Naples, 2 Sept., 1806, urging him to build an impregnable fortress at Castellamare, near Naples, as an asylum where he could "defy the rigors of Fortune, and await the return of her favor." (THIERS, *Consulate and Empire,* bk. xxv.)

17
Who stemm'd the torrent of a downward age.
THOMSON, *The Seasons: Summer,* l. 1516.

18
The great course of the ages begins anew.
(Magnus ab integro sæclorum nascitur ordo.)
VERGIL, *Eclogues*. No. iv, l. 5.

19
He who has not the spirit of his age,
Of his age has all the misery.
(Qui n'a pas l'esprit de son âge,
De son âge a tout le malheur.)
VOLTAIRE, *Letter to Cideville.*

20
And, cast in some diviner mould,
Let the new cycle shame the old!
WHITTIER, *Centennial Hymn.*

21
Born in an age more curious than devout.
YOUNG, *Night Thoughts*. Night ix, l. 1852.

XVII—Age: The Golden Age

22
Now sloth triumphs over energy, indolence over exertion, vice over virtue, arrogance over courage, and theory over practice in arms.

which flourished and shone only in the golden ages.

CERVANTES, *Don Quixote*. Pt. ii, ch. 1.

1
The golden age only comes to men when they have, if only for a moment, forgotten gold.

G. K. CHESTERTON. (*N. Y. Times Magazine*, 3 May, 1931.)

2
The golden age never was the present age.

BENJAMIN FRANKLIN, *Poor Richard*, 1750.

3
The age of gold was the age when gold did not rule. (L'âge d'or était l'âge où l'or ne règnait pas.)

ADRIEN DE LÉZAY-MARNÉSIA, *Pensées*.

4
Those who compare the age in which their lot has fallen with a golden age which exists only in imagination, may talk of degeneracy and decay; but no man who is correctly informed as to the past, will be disposed to take a morose or desponding view of the present.

MACAULAY, *History of England*. Vol. i, ch. 1.

5
Time will run back and fetch the age of gold.

MILTON, *Hymn on the Morning of Christ's Nativity*, l. 53.

6
We must not look for a golden life in an iron age.

JOHN RAY, *English Proverbs*.

7
The golden age is before, not behind us.

SAINT SIMON. (EMERSON, *Uncollected Lectures: Resources*.)

8
The lament for a golden age is only a lament for golden men.

H. D. THOREAU, *Journal*, 5 April, 1841.

AGRICULTURE, see Farming

AIM, see Purpose

ALE AND BEER

See also Drinking, Wine

9
And brought of mighty ale a large quart.

CHAUCER, *The Milleres Tale*, l. 311.

A quart of ale is a dish for a king.

SHAKESPEARE, *Winter's Tale*. Act iv, sc. 3, l. 8.

10
Good ale, the true and proper drink of Englishmen. He is not deserving of the name of Englishman who speaketh against ale, that is good ale.

GEORGE BORROW, *Lavengro*. Ch. 48.

I have fed purely upon ale; I have eat my ale, drank my ale, and I always sleep upon ale.

FARQUHAR, *The Beaux' Stratagem*. Act i, sc. 1.

Good ale is meat, drink, and cloth.

JOHN RAY, *English Proverbs*.

11
Give me a bumper, fill it up:
See how it sparkles in the cup;
O how shall I regale!
Can any taste this drink divine,
And then compare rum, brandy, wine,
Or aught with happy Ale?

JOHN GAY, *A Ballad on Ale*.

Ev'n while these stanzas I indite,
The bar-bell's grateful sounds invite
Where joy can never fail.
Adieu, my Muse! adieu, I haste
To gratify my longing taste
With copious draughts of Ale.

JOHN GAY, *A Ballad on Ale*.

12
Hundreds of men were turned into beasts,
Like the guests of Circe's horrible feasts,
By the magic of ale and cider.

THOMAS HOOD, *Miss Kilmansegg: Her Birth*.

13
Say, for what were hopyards meant,
Or why was Burton built on Trent?
Oh many a peer of England brews
Livelier liquor than the Muse,
And malt does more than Milton can
To justify God's ways to man.
Ale, man, ale's the stuff to drink
For fellows whom it hurts to think:
Look into the pewter pot
To see the world as the world's not.

A. E. HOUSMAN, *A Shropshire Lad*. No. 62.

14
As he brews, so shall he drink.

BEN JONSON, *Every Man in His Humour*. Act ii, sc. 1.

She brews good ale—and thereof comes the proverb,
"Blessing of your heart, you brew good ale."

SHAKESPEARE, *The Two Gentlemen of Verona*. Act iii, sc. 1, l. 304.

15
Then to the spicy nut-brown ale.

JOHN MILTON, *L'Allegro*, l. 100.

16
He that buys land buys many stones,
He that buys flesh buys many bones,
He that buys eggs buys many shells,
But he that buys good ale buys nothing else.

JOHN RAY, *English Proverbs*.

Bring us in no beef, for there is many bones,
But bring us in good ale, for that go'th down at once.

UNKNOWN, *Bring Us in Good Ale*. c. 1390. (WRIGHT, *Songs and Carols*.)

17
I would give all my fame for a pot of ale and safety.

SHAKESPEARE, *Henry V*. Act iii, sc. 2, l. 13.

18
Do you look for ale and cakes here, you rude rascals?

SHAKESPEARE, *Henry VIII*. Act v, sc. 4, l. 11.

Sir Toby: Dost thou think, because thou art virtuous, there shall be no more cakes and ale?

Clown: Yes, by Saint Anne, and ginger shall be hot i' the mouth too.
SHAKESPEARE, *Twelfth Night*. Act ii, sc. 3, l. 123.

1
Back and side go bare, go bare;
Both foot and hand go cold;
But, belly, God send thee good ale enough,
Whether it be new or old.
JOHN STILL [attr.], *Song: Gammer Gurton's Needle*. Act ii.

2
The hop for his profit I thus do exalt,
It strengtheneth drink, and it flavoureth malt:
And being well brewed, long kept it will last,
And drawing abide—if you draw not too fast.
THOMAS TUSSER, *Five Hundred Points of Good Husbandrie*. Ch. 43.

3
When treading London's well-known ground
If e'er I feel my spirits tire,
I haul my sail, look up around,
In search of Whitbread's best entire.
UNKNOWN, *A Pot of Porter, Ho!*

4
How easy can the barley-bree
Cement the quarrel!
It's aye the cheapest lawyer's fee
To taste the barrel.
ROBERT BURNS, *Scotch Drink*. St. 13.

The cock may craw, the day may daw,
And aye we'll taste the barley-bree.
BURNS, *Willie Brew'd a Peck o' Maut*.

We three and the barley-bree.
RICHARD HOVEY, *The Kavanagh*.

5
Here with my beer I sit,
While golden moments flit:
Alas! they pass unheeded by:
And as they fly,
I, being dry, sit, idly sipping here
My beer.
GEORGE ARNOLD, *Beer*.

And when I think upon a pot of beer.
BYRON, *Don Juan*. Canto x, st. 77.

Yes, my soul sentimentally craves British beer.
THOMAS CAMPBELL, *Epistle from Algiers*.

6
A double glass o' the inwariable.
DICKENS, *Pickwick Papers*. Ch. 33.

7
God made yeast, as well as dough, and loves fermentation just as dearly as he loves vegetation.
EMERSON, *Essays, Second Series: New England Reformers*.

8
They who drink beer will think beer.
WASHINGTON IRVING, *Sketch Book: Stratford*. Quoted.

9
The man who called it "near beer" was a bad judge of distance.
PHILANDER JOHNSON, *Shooting Stars*. Attributed also to Luke McLuke, columnist for the Cincinnati *Enquirer*.

10
That questionable superfluity—small beer.
DOUGLAS JERROLD, *The Tragedy of the Till*.

11
Doth it not show vilely in me to desire small beer?
SHAKESPEARE, *II Henry IV*. Act ii, sc. 2, l. 7.

By my troth, I do now remember the poor creature, small beer.
SHAKESPEARE, *II Henry IV*. Act ii, sc. 2, l. 12.

She was a wight, if ever such wight were . . .
To suckle fools and chronicle small beer.
SHAKESPEARE, *Othello*. Act ii, sc. 1, l. 159.

12
What two ideas are more inseparable than beer and Britannia? What event more awfully important to an English colony than the erection of its first brewhouse?
SYDNEY SMITH. (LADY HOLLAND, *Memoir*.)

13
For drink, there was beer which was very strong when not mingled with water, but was agreeable to those who were used to it. They drank this with a reed, out of the vessel that held the beer, upon which they saw the barley swim.
XENOPHON, *Anabasis*. Bk. iv, ch. 5.

14
While beer brings gladness, don't forget
That water only makes you wet.
HARRY LEON WILSON, *The Spenders*, p. 237. Quoted.

15
Here sleeps in peace a Hampshire grenadier,
Who caught his death by drinking cold small beer;
Soldiers, take heed from his untimely fall,
And when you're hot, drink strong, or not at all.
UNKNOWN, *Epitaph*, in churchyard at Winchester, England. (1764)

ALEXANDER THE GREAT

16
Verily, if I were not Alexander, I would be Diogenes. (Ἀλλὰ μὴν ἐγώ, εἰ μὴ Ἀλέξανδρος ἤμην, Διογένης ἂν ἤμην.)
ALEXANDER THE GREAT. (PLUTARCH, *Lives: Alexander*. Ch. 14, sec. 3.) It was at this interview that Diogenes, when Alexander asked if there was anything he could do for him, replied, "Yes; stand a little out of my sun." (Μικρὸν ἀπὸ τοῦ ἡλίου μετάστηθι.)

Were I not Napoleon, I would be Alexander.
NAPOLEON BONAPARTE, in 1814, speaking of Alexander of Russia.

17
So would I, by heaven, if I were Parmenio. (Κἀγώ, νὴ Δία, εἰ Παρμενίων.)
ALEXANDER THE GREAT, to his friend Parmenio, who said that, if he were Alexander, he would accept the offer made by Darius to share his empire. Alexander declined the offer, saying, "Heaven cannot support two

suns, nor earth two masters." (PLUTARCH, *Lives: Alexander*, 29, 4.)

So would I, were I Cleander.

LYSANDER, when advised to accept a bribe. Eteocles afterward said of him, "Greece cannot bear two Lysanders." (PLUTARCH, *Life*.)

1

O Athenians, what toil do I undergo to please you!

ALEXANDER THE GREAT. (PLUTARCH, *Lives: Alexander*. Ch. 60, sec. 3.)

2

The whole world was not half so wide
To Alexander, when he cried
Because he had but one to subdue,
As was a paltry narrow tub to
Diogenes.

BUTLER, *Hudibras*. Pt. i, canto iii, l. 1021.

3

Graceless son of graceless sire to graceless wight by graceless squire. (Ἄθλιος παρ' ἀθλίου δι' ἀθλίου πρὸς ἄθλιον.)

DIOGENES, of Alexander the Great, when the latter sent a letter to Antipater at Athens by a certain Athlios. (DIOGENES LAERTIUS, *Diogenes*. Sec. 44.)

4

One globe is all too little for the youth of Pella; he chafes uneasily within the narrow limits of the world. (Unus Pellæo juveni non sufficit orbis; Æstuat infelix angusto limite mundi.)

JUVENAL, *Satires*. Sat. x, l. 168. Alexander was born at Pella, 356 B.C.; died at Babylon, 323 B.C.

Alexander wept when he heard from Anaxarchus that there was an infinite number of worlds, and his friends asking him if any accident had befallen him, he returned this answer: Do you not think it is a matter worthy of lamentation that, where there is such a vast multitude of worlds, we have not yet conquered one?

PLUTARCH, *On the Tranquillity of the Mind*.

5

Philip fought men, but Alexander women.

NATHANIEL LEE, *Rival Queens*. Act. iv, sc. 2.

6

He dared well to despise vain things. (Bene ausus vana contemnere.)

LIVY, *History*. Bk. ix, sec. 17. Of Alexander.

7

Alexander, the conqueror of so many kings and nations, was laid low by anger and grief. (Alexander . . . victor tot regnum atque populorum, iræ tristiæque succumbens.)

SENECA, *Epistulæ ad Lucilium*. Epis. cxiii, 29.

8

When in the world I lived, I was the world's commander;
By east, west, north, and south, I spread my conquering might:
My scutcheon plain declares that I am Alisander.

SHAKESPEARE, *Love's Labour's Lost*. Act v, sc. 2, l. 565.

The crown will find an heir: great Alexander
Left his to the worthiest; so his successor
Was like to be the best.

SHAKESPEARE, *Winter's Tale*. Act v, sc. 1, l. 47.

9

How big was Alexander, Pa,
That people call him great?

UNKNOWN, *The Child's Inquiry*. (MCGUFFEY, *Third Reader*, p. 69.)

10

If Alexander wishes to be a god, let him set up as a god. (Εἰ Ἀλέξανδρος βουλέται εἶναι θεὸς, θεὸς ἐστῶ.)

UNKNOWN, *Lacedæmonian Edict on Alexander's Claim to Divinity*.

11

A tomb now suffices him for whom the whole world was not sufficient. (Sufficit huic tumulus, cui non suffecerit orbis.)

UNKNOWN, *Epitaph on Alexander the Great*.

ALMS, see Charity

AMBER

12

We see spiders, flies, or ants entombed and preserved forever in amber, a more than royal tomb.

FRANCIS BACON, *Historia Vitæ et Mortis*. Same idea BACON'S *Sylvia Sylvarum*. Century i, 100.

I saw a fly within a bead
Of amber cleanly buried.

ROBERT HERRICK, *The Amber Bead*.

13

Embalmed in amber every pirate lies.

VACHEL LINDSAY, *The Chinese Nightingale*.

14

The bee is enclosed, and shines preserved, in a tear of the sisters of Phaëton, so that it seems enshrined in its own nectar. It has obtained a worthy reward for its labors; methinks the bee itself would have desired such a death.

MARTIAL, *Epigrams*. Bk. iv, ep. 32.

The bee enclosed and through the amber shown,
Seems buried in the juice which was his own.

MARTIAL, *Epigrams*, iv, 32. (Hay, tr.)

While an ant was wandering under the shade of a tree of Phaëton, a drop of amber enveloped the tiny insect; thus she, who in life was disregarded, became precious by death.

MARTIAL, *Epigrams*. Bk. vi, ep. 15.

15

Let opening roses knotted oaks adorn,
And liquid amber drop from ev'ry thorn!

POPE, *Pastorals: Autumn*, l. 37.

16

Pretty! in amber to observe the forms
Of hairs, or straws, or dirt, or grubs, or worms!
The things, we know, are neither rich nor rare,
But wonder how the devil they got there.

POPE, *Epistle to Dr. Arbuthnot*, l. 169.

He is a fly in amber, nobody cares about the fly;

the only question is, How the Devil did it get there?
SYDNEY SMITH, *Peter Plymley Letters*. No. 7. Referring to Canning.

And wonders how the devil they durst come there.
JOHN DRYDEN, *The Husband His Own Cuckold: Prologue.*

AMBITION

See also Aspiration, Fame

I—Ambition: Definitions

1
Ambition is the growth of every clime.
WILLIAM BLAKE, *King Edward the Third*. Sc. iv, l. 2.

2
Ambition, a proud covetousness, or a dry thirst of honour, a great torture of the mind, composed of envy, pride, and covetousness, a gallant madness, one defines it a pleasant poison.
ROBERT BURTON, *Anatomy of Melancholy*. Pt. i, sec. ii, mem. 3, subs. 11.

Ambition is but avarice on stilts and masked.
WALTER SAVAGE LANDOR, *Imaginary Conversations: Brooke and Sidney.*

3
The passion of ambition is the same in a courtier, a soldier, or an ecclesiastic; but, from their different educations and habits, they will take very different methods to gratify it.
LORD CHESTERFIELD, *Letters*, 2 Oct., 1747.

4
Ambition aspires to descend. (Il aspire à descendre.)
CORNEILLE, *Cinna*. Act i, sc. 2.

5
Ambition is the mind's immodesty.
SIR WILLIAM D'AVENANT, *Gondibert.*

6
Ambition, like a torrent, ne'er looks back;
And is a swelling, and the last affection
A high mind can put off.
BEN JONSON, *Catiline*. Act iii, sc. 2.

Ambition dares not stoop.
BEN JONSON, *Cynthia's Revels*. Act iv, sc. 1.

7
The wise man is cured of ambition by ambition.
LA BRUYÈRE, *Les Caractères: Du Mérite Personnel.*

8
Ambition first sprung from your blest abodes,
The glorious fault of Angels and of Gods;
Thence to their images on earth it flows,
And in the breasts of Kings and Heroes glows.
Most souls, 'tis true, but peep out once an age,
Dull sullen pris'ners in the body's cage.
POPE, *Elegy to the Memory of an Unfortunate Lady.*

9
The very substance of the ambition is merely the shadow of a dream. . . . I hold ambition of so airy and light a quality that it is but a shadow's shadow.
SHAKESPEARE, *Hamlet*. Act ii, sc. 2, l. 264.

10
Ambition is our idol, on whose wings
Great minds are carry'd only to extreme;
To be sublimely great, or to be nothing.
SOUTHERNE, *The Loyal Brother*. Act i, sc. 1.

11
Ambition
Is like the sea wave, which the more you drink
The more you thirst—yea—drink too much, as men
Have done on rafts of wreck—it drives you mad.
TENNYSON, *The Cup*. Act i, sc. 3.

12
The true ambition there alone resides,
Where justice vindicates, and wisdom guides; . . .
Where public blessings public praise attend;
Where glory is our motive, not our end.
YOUNG, *Love of Fame*. Satire vii, l. 175.

Ambition! powerful source of good and ill!
YOUNG, *Night Thoughts*. Night vi, l. 399.

II—Ambition: Small Town, Great Renown

13
I would rather be the first man here than the second at Rome. (Ἐγὼ μὲν ἐβουλόμην παρὰ τούτοις εἶναι μᾶλλον πρῶτος ἢ παρὰ Ῥωμαίοις δεύτερος.)
JULIUS CÆSAR, referring to a little village, while crossing the Alps on his way to Spain, 61 B.C. (PLUTARCH, *Lives: Cæsar*. Ch. 11, 2.)

Cæsar, when he went first into Gaul, made no scruple to profess that he would rather be first in a village than second at Rome.
BACON, *Advancement of Learning*. Bk. ii, 23.

14
It is the true cry of nature; wherever we are we wish to be first.
LACORDAIRE, *Conférences.*

15
Just contrary to the other, I should like much better to be second or third at Périgueux than first at Paris. (Tout à l'opposite de l'autre, m'aimerois à l'avanture mieux deuxième ou troisième à Périgueux que premier à Paris.)
MONTAIGNE, *Essays*. Bk. iii, ch. 7.

16
Small town, great renown. (Petite ville, grand renom.)
RABELAIS, *Works*. Bk. v, ch. 35. Of Chinon, Rabelais' native town. Or, in the American vulgar phrase, "The big toad in the little puddle."

III—Ambition: Its Virtue

17
My father was an eminent button maker . . . but I had a soul above buttons. . . . I panted for a liberal profession.
GEORGE COLMAN THE YOUNGER, *Sylvester Daggerwood*. Act i, sc. 10.

1
All ambitions are lawful except those which climb upward on the miseries or credulities of mankind.

JOSEPH CONRAD, *A Personal Record: Preface.*

2
What shall I do to be for ever known,
And make the age to come my own?

ABRAHAM COWLEY, *The Motto.*

It is not necessary to live,
But to carve our names beyond that point,
This is necessary. (Non è necessario
Vivere, si scolpire olte quel termine
Nostro nome: quæsto è necessario.)

GABRIELE D'ANNUNZIO, *Canzone di Umberto Cagni.*

3
When a man is no longer anxious to do better than well, he is done for.

B. R. HAYDON, *Table-Talk.*

4
Oft have I levell'd, and at last have learn'd
That peril is the chiefest way to happiness,
And resolution honour's fairest aim.
What glory is there in a common good,
That hangs for every peasant to achieve?
That like I best that flies beyond my reach.

MARLOWE, *The Massacre at Paris*, l. 94.

5
Such joy ambition finds.

MILTON, *Paradise Lost.* Bk. iv, l. 92.

6
How can I mend my title then? Where can
Ambition find a higher style than man?

FRANCIS QUARLES, *Emblems.* Bk. iii, emb. 5.

7
Though ambition is itself a vice, it is often the parent of virtues. (Licet ipsa vitium sit ambitio, frequenter tamen causa virtutum est.)

QUINTILIAN, *De Institutione Oratoria.* Bk. i, ch. 2, sec. 22.

Though ambition itself be a vice, it is often the cause of great virtue. Give me that wit whom praise excites, glory puts on, or disgrace grieves; he is to be nourished with ambition, pricked forward with honour, checked with reprehension, and never to be suspected of sloth.

BEN JONSON, *Explorata: Imò Serviles.*

Ambition, in a private man a vice,
Is, in a prince, a virtue.

MASSINGER, *The Bashful Lover.* Act i, sc. 2.

The same ambition can destroy or save,
And makes a patriot as it makes a knave.

POPE, *Essay on Man.* Epis. ii, l. 201.

Our glories float between the earth and heaven
Like clouds which seem pavilions of the sun,
And are the playthings of the casual winds;
Still, like the cloud which drops on unseen crags
The dews the wild-flower feeds on, our ambition
May from its airy height drop gladness down
On unsuspected virtue;—and the flower
May bless the cloud when it hath passed away.

BULWER-LYTTON, *Richelieu.* Act v, sc. 3, Conclusion.

8
Hardly anything will bring a man's mind into full activity if ambition be wanting.

SIR HENRY TAYLOR, *The Statesman*, p. 132.

IV—Ambition: Its Folly

See also Greatness: Its Penalties

9
He that plots to be the only figure among ciphers, is the decay of a whole age.

FRANCIS BACON, *Essays: Of Ambition.*

See also under CÆSAR.

10
Ambition has no rest!

BULWER-LYTTON, *Richelieu.* Act iii, sc. 1.

11
Well is it known that ambition can creep as well as soar.

BURKE, *Letters on a Regicide Peace.* No. 3.

But what will not ambition and revenge
Descend to? who aspires must down as low
As high he soar'd.

MILTON, *Paradise Lost.* Bk. ix, l. 168.

Ambition often puts men upon doing the meanest offices: so climbing is performed in the same posture with creeping.

SWIFT, *Thoughts on Various Subjects.*

The same sun which gilds all nature, and exhilarates the whole creation, does not shine upon disappointed ambition.

EDMUND BURKE, *Observations on a Publication "The Present State of the Nation."*

This Siren song of Ambition.

EDMUND BURKE, *Speech*, at Bristol, 1780.

12
Or mad Ambition's gory hand,
  Sending, like bloodhounds from the slip,
Woe, want, and murder o'er a land.

BURNS, *A Winter Night.* St. 7.

13
There shall they rot, Ambition's honour'd fools!

BYRON, *Childe Harold.* Canto i, st. 42.

Low ambition's honours lost.

BYRON, *Childe Harold.* Canto i, st. 84.

Ambition's less than littleness.

BYRON, *Ode to Bonaparte.* St. 2.

14
Mad Ambition ever doth caress
Its own sure fate, in its own restlessness.

COLERIDGE, *Zapolya.* Pt. ii, act iv.

15
On what strange stuff Ambition feeds!

ELIZA COOK, *Thomas Hood.*

16
But let eternal infamy pursue
The wretched to nought but his ambition true
Who, for the sake of filling with one blast
The post-horns of all Europe, lays her waste

COWPER, *Table Talk*, l. 29.

Low ambition and the thirst of praise.

COWPER, *Table Talk*, l. 591.

  Leave all meaner things
To low ambition, and the pride of Kings.

POPE, *Essay on Man.* Epis. i, l. 2.

17
Nor think ambition wise because 'tis brave.

SIR WILLIAM D'AVENANT, *Gondibert.* Bk. i canto 5, st. 75.

18
But wild Ambition loves to slide, not stand,

And Fortune's Ice prefers to Virtue's land.
DRYDEN, *Absalom and Achitophel*. Pt. i, l. 198.

It has never, we believe, been remarked that two of the most striking lines in the description of Achitophel are borrowed, and from an obscure quarter. In Knolles' *History of the Turks*, printed more than sixty years before the appearance of *Absalom and Achitophel*, are the following verses, under a portrait of Sultan Mustapha I:

Greatness on goodness loves to slide, not stand,
And leaves for Fortune's ice Virtue's firm land.

The circumstance is the more remarkable, because Dryden has really no couplet more intensely Drydenian, both in thought and expression, than this, of which the whole thought, and almost the whole expression, are stolen.
T. B. MACAULAY, *Essays: Sir William Temple*.

1
Look not too high, Lest a chip fall in your eye.
THOMAS DYKES, *Moral Reflections*. (1708)

Nor strive to wind ourselves too high
For sinful man beneath the sky.
JOHN KEBLE, *Christian Year: Morning*.

2
Ambition has its disappointments to sour us, but never the good fortune to satisfy us.
BENJAMIN FRANKLIN, *On True Happiness*.

3 What madness is ambition!
What is there in that little breath of men
Which they call Fame, that should induce the brave
To forfeit ease and that domestic bliss
Which is the lot of happy ignorance?
PHILIP FRENEAU, *Columbus in Chains*.

4
Ambition sufficiently plagues her proselytes, by keeping them always in show and in public, like a statue in a street.
FULLER, *Introductio ad Prudentiam*, ii, 130.

5
For mortal daring nothing is too high.
In our blind folly we storm heaven itself.
(Nil mortalibus ardui est;
Cælum ipsum petimus stultitia.)
HORACE, *Odes*. Bk. i, ode 3, l. 37.

Still to new heights his restless wishes tower,
Claim leads to claim, and power advances power.
SAMUEL JOHNSON, *Vanity of Human Wishes*.

6
Such is the life of men set free from the burden of unhappy ambition. (Hæc est Vita solutorum misera ambitione gravique.)
HORACE, *Satires*. Bk. i, sat. 6, l. 128.

7
Go, madman, and race over the wildest Alps, that you may delight schoolboys, and become a subject for a declamation! (I demens et sævas curre per Alpes, Ut pueris placeas et declamatio fias!)
JUVENAL, *Satires*. Sat. x, l. 166.

Here runs the mountainous and craggy ridge
That tempts ambition. On the summit see
The seals of office glitter in his eyes;
He climbs, he pants, he grasps them! At his heels,
Close at his heels, a demagogue ascends,
And with a dext'rous jerk soon twists him down.
WILLIAM COWPER, *The Task*. Bk. iv, l. 57.

8
A purchased slave has but one master; an ambitious man must be a slave to all who may conduce to his aggrandizement.
LA BRUYÈRE, *Les Caractères: De la Cour*.

The shackled slave who 'tends his master's call
Has but one master at whose feet to fall,
But who has made ambition for his god
Fears many more than one tyrannic rod.
EDWARD OLDHAM, *Ambition*.

9
Most people would succeed in small things if they were not troubled with great ambitions.
LONGFELLOW, *Drift-Wood: Table-Talk*.

Let proud Ambition pause
And sicken at the vanity that prompts
His little deeds.
DAVID MALLET, *The Excursion*. Canto ii, l. 221.

10
How vainly men themselves amaze
To win the palm, the oak, or bays.
ANDREW MARVELL, *The Garden*.

11
Ambition sigh'd: she found it vain to trust
The faithless column and the crumbling bust.
POPE, *Epistle to Mr. Addison*, l. 19.

12
Men would be Angels, Angels would be Gods.
POPE, *Essay on Man*. Epis. i, l. 125. See 1609:17.

Oh, sons of earth! attempt ye still to rise
By mountains pil'd on mountains to the skies?
Heav'n still with laughter the vain toil surveys,
And buries madmen in the heaps they raise.
POPE, *Essay on Man*. Epis. iv, l. 73.

13
Who knows but He, whose hand the lightning forms,
Who heaves old ocean, and who wings the storms,
Pours fierce ambition in a Cæsar's mind,
Or turns young Ammon loose to scourge mankind?
POPE, *Essay on Man*. Epis. 1, l. 157.

When Catiline by rapine swell'd his store,
When Cæsar made a noble dame a whore,
In this the Lust, in that the Avarice
Were means, not ends, Ambition was the vice.
POPE, *Moral Essays*. Epis. i, l. 212.

But see how oft ambition's aims are cross'd,
And chiefs contend till all the prize is lost!
POPE, *Rape of the Lock*. Canto v, l. 107.

14
The trap to the high-born is ambition.
JOHN RAY, *English Proverbs*.

15
My Lord Ambition passed, and smiled in scorn;
I plucked a rose, and, lo! it had no thorn.
GEORGE JOHN ROMANES, *Simple Nature*.

16
Ambition so frenzied that you regard your-

self last in the race if there is anyone in front of you. (Tantus erit ambitionis furor, ut nemo tibi post te videatur, si aliquis ante te fuerit.)

SENECA, *Epistulæ ad Lucilium*. Epis. civ, sec. 10.

1
Ill-weaved ambition, how much thou art shrunk!
When that this body did contain a spirit,
A kingdom for it was too small a bound;
But now two paces of the vilest earth
Is room enough.

SHAKESPEARE, *I Henry IV*. Act v, sc. 4, l. 88.

Ambition's debt is paid.

SHAKESPEARE, *Julius Cæsar*. Act iii, sc. 1, l. 83.

O fading honours of the dead!
O high ambition, lowly laid!

SCOTT, *Lay of the Last Minstrel*. Canto ii, 10.

2
Banish the canker of ambitious thoughts.

SHAKESPEARE, *II Henry VI*. Act i, sc. 2, l. 18.

Virtue is chok'd with foul ambition.

SHAKESPEARE, *II Henry VI*. Act iii, sc. 1, l. 143.

3
Cromwell, I charge thee, fling away ambition:
By that sin fell the angels; how can man, then,
The image of his Maker, hope to win by it?

SHAKESPEARE, *Henry VIII*. Act iii, sc. 2, l. 440.

I had Ambition, by which sin
The angels fell;
I climbed and, step by step, O Lord,
Ascended into Hell.

Returning now to peace and quiet,
And made more wise,
Let my descent and fall, O Lord,
Be into Paradise.

WILLIAM H. DAVIES, *Ambition*.

4
Lowliness is young ambition's ladder,
Whereto the climber-upward turns his face;
But when he once attains the upmost round,
He then unto the ladder turns his back,
Looks in the clouds, scorning the base degrees
By which he did ascend.

SHAKESPEARE, *Julius Cæsar*. Act ii, sc. 1, l. 22.

Such a nature,
Tickled with good success, disdains the shadow
Which he treads on at noon.

SHAKESPEARE, *Coriolanus*. Act i, sc. 1, l. 263.

Th' aspirer, once attain'd unto the top,
Cuts off those means by which himself got up.

SAMUEL DANIEL, *Civil War*. Bk. ii.

Men do not heed the rungs by which they climb.

JOHN MASEFIELD, *Biography*.

5 The noble Brutus
Hath told you Cæsar was ambitious:
If it were so, it was a grievous fault,
And grievously hath Cæsar answer'd it. . . .
When that the poor have cried, Cæsar hath wept:
Ambition should be made of sterner stuff:
Yet Brutus says he was ambitious;
And Brutus is an honourable man.

SHAKESPEARE, *Julius Cæsar*. Act iii, sc. 2, l. 82.

6
How far your eyes may pierce I cannot tell:
Striving to better, oft we mar what's well.

SHAKESPEARE, *King Lear*. Act i, sc. 4, l. 368.

And he that strives to touch the stars
Oft stumbles at a straw.

SPENSER, *Shepherd's Calendar*. July, l. 99.

7
Vaulting ambition, which o'erleaps itself,
And falls on the other.

SHAKESPEARE, *Macbeth*. Act i, sc. 7, l. 27.

Thriftless ambition, that wilt ravin up
Thine own life's means.

SHAKESPEARE, *Macbeth*. Act ii, sc. 4, l. 28.

8
Few live exempt
From disappointment and disgrace, who run
Ambition's rapid course.

SMOLLETT, *The Regicide*. Act iv, sc. 2.

9
In Heaven Ambition cannot dwell,
Nor Avarice in the vaults of Hell;
Earthly these passions of the Earth,
They perish where they have their birth.

SOUTHEY, *The Curse of Kehama*. Pt. x, st. 10.

10
O sacred hunger of ambitious minds,
And impotent desire of men to reign.

SPENSER, *Faerie Queene*. Bk. v, canto xii, st. 1.

Vain the ambition of kings
Who seek by trophies and dead things
To leave a living name behind,
And weave but nets to catch the wind.

JOHN WEBSTER, *Song*.

11
Ambition destroys its possessor.

The Talmud. Yoma 86.

12
How like a mounting devil in the heart
Rules the unrein'd ambition!

N. P. WILLIS, *Parrhasius*.

And mad ambition trumpeteth to all.

N. P. WILLIS, *Poem Delivered at the Departure of the Senior Class of Yale College*, 1827.

13
Ambition has but one reward for all:
A little power, a little transient fame,
A grave to rest in, and a fading name!

WILLIAM WINTER, *The Queen's Domain*, l. 90.

14
And this is the moral,—Stick to your sphere;
Or, if you insist, as you have the right,
On spreading your wings for a loftier flight,
The moral is,—Take care how you light.

J. T. TROWBRIDGE, *Darius Green*. Last lines.

V—Ambition and Love

15
Love is not to be reason'd down, or lost
In high ambition or a thirst of greatness.

ADDISON, *Cato*. Act i, sc. 1.

Affection chain'd her to that heart;
Ambition tore the links apart.
BYRON, *The Bride of Abydos*. Canto i, st. 6.

1
Ambition is the only power that combats love.
COLLEY CIBBER, *Cæsar in Egypt*. Act i.

Ambition is no cure for love.
SCOTT, *Lay of the Last Minstrel*. Canto i, st. 27.

2
Love's but the frailty of the mind
When 'tis not with ambition join'd.
CONGREVE, *The Way of the World*. Act iii, sc. 12.

3
One often passes from love to ambition, but one rarely returns from ambition to love. (On passe souvent de l'amour à l'ambition; mais on ne revient guère de l'ambition à l'amour.)
LA ROCHEFOUCAULD, *Maximes*. No. 490.

4
Love is wiser than ambition.
BRYAN WALLER PROCTER, *A Vision*.

AMERICA

I—America: Songs of Praise

5
O, Columbia, the gem of the ocean,
The home of the brave and the free,
The shrine of each patriot's devotion,
A world offers homage to thee.
THOMAS À BECKET, *Columbia, the Gem of the Ocean*. Probably written in 1843 by Becket, a young English actor playing at the Chestnut Street Theatre, Philadelphia, for another English actor named David Taylor Shaw, to be sung at the latter's benefit. Shaw published it first as "written, composed and sung by David T. Shaw, and arranged by T. à Becket, Esq.," and then Becket published it as "written and composed by T. à Becket, and sung by D. T. Shaw." The song is said to have been taken to London by E. L. Davenport, and sung there under the title, *Britannia, the Pride of the Ocean*. Some authorities assert that the song was sung first by Shaw in England, and afterwards adapted by him to American use, but the second line, "the home of the brave and the free," is identical in both versions, and is so similar to a line in *The Star-Spangled Banner* that it would seem to indicate that the American version was the first, though it is difficult to understand why anyone should refer to a country the size of America as a "gem of the ocean," a phrase which would apply much more reasonably to an island like England. (See BANKS, *Immortal Songs of Camp and Field*, p. 77; *Notes and Queries*, 26 Aug., 1899.)

Columbia, Columbia, to glory arise,
The queen of the world and the child of the skies!
Thy genius commands thee; with rapture behold,
While ages on ages thy splendors unfold.
TIMOTHY DWIGHT, *Columbia*.

6
Hail, Columbia! happy land!
Hail, ye heroes! heaven-born band!
Who fought and bled in Freedom's cause,
Who fought and bled in Freedom's cause,
And when the storm of war was gone,
Enjoyed the peace your valor won.
Let independence be our boast,
Ever mindful what it cost;
Ever grateful for the prize,
Let its altar reach the skies!
JOSEPH HOPKINSON, *Hail, Columbia*. (May, 1798.)

The land of the free and the home of the brave.
FRANCIS SCOTT KEY, *The Star-Spangled Banner*. *See also* FLAG: AMERICAN.

7
O Land, the measure of our prayers,
Hope of the world in grief and wrong!
Be thine the blessing of the years,
The gift of faith, the crown of song.
JULIA WARD HOWE, *Our Country*.

8
I do not know beneath what sky
Nor on what seas shall be thy fate;
I only know it shall be high,
I only know it shall be great.
RICHARD HOVEY, *Unmanifest Destiny*.

9
Long as thine Art shall love true love,
Long as thy Science truth shall know,
Long as thine Eagle harms no Dove,
Long as thy law by law shall grow,
Long as thy God is God above,
Thy brother every man below,
So long, dear Land of all my love,
Thy name shall shine, thy fame shall grow!
SIDNEY LANIER, *The Centennial Meditation of Columbia*.

10
O Beautiful! my Country! ours once more!
Smoothing thy gold of war-dishevelled hair
O'er such sweet brows as never others wore,
And letting thy set lips,
Freed from wrath's pale eclipse,
The rosy edges of thy smile lay bare,
What words divine of lover or of poet
Could tell our love and make thee know it,
Among the nations bright beyond compare?
J. R. LOWELL, *Commemoration Ode*. Sec. 12.

America! America!
God shed His grace on thee
And crown thy good with brotherhood
From sea to shining sea!
KATHARINE LEE BATES, *America the Beautiful*.

11
The eagle's song:
To be stanch, and valiant, and free, and strong
RICHARD MANSFIELD, *The Eagle's Song*.

12
My country, 'tis of thee,
Sweet land of liberty,
Of thee I sing;
Land where my fathers died,

Land of the pilgrims' pride,
From every mountain side
  Let freedom ring.

SAMUEL FRANCIS SMITH, *America*. First printed on a broadside in connection with an Independence Day celebration by the Boston Sabbath School Union, 4 July, 1831.

O beautiful and grand,
My own, my Native Land!
  Of thee I boast:
Great Empire of the West,
The dearest and the best,
Made up of all the rest,
  I love thee most.

ABRAHAM COLES, *My Native Land.*

1

How sure the bolt that Justice wings;
How weak the arm a traitor brings;
How mighty they, who steadfast stand
For Freedom's Flag and Freedom's Land!

BAYARD TAYLOR, *To the American People.*

2

So it's home again, and home again, America for me!
My heart is turning home again, and there I long to be
In the land of youth and freedom beyond the ocean bars,
Where the air is full of sunlight, and the flag is full of stars.

HENRY VAN DYKE, *America for Me.*

But the glory of the Present is to make the Future free,—
We love our land for what she is and what she is to be.

HENRY VAN DYKE, *America for Me.*

Home from the lonely cities, time's wreck, and the naked woe,
Home through the clean great waters where freemen's pennants blow,
Home to the land men dream of, where all the nations go.

G. E. WOODBERRY, *Homeward Bound.*

3

And thou, America,
Thy offspring towering e'er so high, yet higher Thee above all towering,
With Victory on thy left, and at thy right hand Law;
Thou Union holding all, fusing, absorbing, tolerating all,
Thee, ever thee, I sing.

WALT WHITMAN, *Song of the Exposition*. Sec. 8.

A grand, sane, towering, seated Mother,
Chair'd in the adamant of Time.

WALT WHITMAN, *America.*

4

Thou, too, sail on, O Ship of State!
Sail on, O Union, strong and great!
Humanity with all its fears,
With all the hopes of future years,
Is hanging breathless on thy fate! . . .
Sail on, nor fear to breast the sea!
Our hearts our hopes, are all with thee,
Our hearts, our hopes, our prayers, our tears,
Our faith triumphant o'er our fears,
Are all with thee,—are all with thee!

LONGFELLOW, *The Building of the Ship.*

Sail, sail thy best, ship of Democracy,
Of value is thy freight, 'tis not the Present only,
The Past is also stored in thee.
Thou holdest not the venture of thyself alone, not of the Western continent alone.
Earth's *résumé* entire floats on thy keel O ship, is steadied by thy spars, . . .
With all their ancient struggles, martyrs, heroes, epics, wars, thou bear'st the other continents.

WALT WHITMAN, *Thou Mother with Thy Equal Brood*. Sec. 4.

II—America: Ideals

5

Driven from every other corner of the earth, freedom of thought and the right of private judgment in matters of conscience direct their course to this happy country as their last asylum.

SAMUEL ADAMS, *Speech*, Phila., Pa., 1 Aug., 1776.

6

Westward the course of empire takes its way;
  The first four acts already past,
A fifth shall close the drama with the day;
  Time's noblest offspring is the last.

BISHOP GEORGE BERKELEY, *On the Prospect of Planting Arts and Learning in America.* Bishop Berkeley wrote these verses under the inspiration of a project formed in his youth—the establishment of a college in Bermuda to train young Indians as missionaries to their fellow-tribesmen. The project was finally abandoned for lack of money. The first line is frequently misquoted, "Westward the star of empire takes its way," due probably to the fact that it was so given in the epigraph stamped on the back cover of the early editions of Bancroft's *History of the United States.*

Young man, there is America, which at this day serves for little more than to amuse you with stories of savage men and uncouth manners, yet shall, before you taste of death, show itself equal to the whole of that commerce which now attracts the envy of the world.

EDMUND BURKE, *Conciliation with America.*

The next Augustine Age will dawn on the other side of the Atlantic. There will perhaps be a Thucydides at Boston, a Xenophon at New York.

HORACE WALPOLE, *Letter to Sir Horace Mann*, 24 Nov., 1774.

7

Here the free spirit of mankind, at length,
  Throws its last fetters off; and who shall place
A limit to the giant's unchained strength,
  Or curb his swiftness in the forward race?

BRYANT, *The Ages*. St. 33.

8

England may as well dam up the waters of the Nile with bulrushes as to fetter the step of Freedom, more proud and firm in this youthful land than where she treads the sequestered glens of Scotland, or couches herself among the magnificent mountains of Switzerland.

LYDIA MARIA CHILD, *The Rebels*. Ch. 4. Mrs. Child puts this flamboyant speech into the mouth of James Otis, one of the historical characters in her romance.

Sad was the year, by proud oppression driven,
When Transatlantic Liberty arose.

THOMAS CAMPBELL, *Gertrude of Wyoming*. Pt. iii, st. 6.

1
We set out to Oppose Tyranny in all its Strides, and I hope we shall persevere.

ABRAHAM CLARK, *Letter to John Hart*, 8 Feb., 1777.

2
I feel that you are justified in looking into the future with true assurance, because you have a mode of living in which we find the joy of life and the joy of work harmoniously combined. Added to this is the spirit of ambition which pervades your very being, and seems to make the day's work like a happy child at play.

ALBERT EINSTEIN, *New Year's Greeting*, 1931.

Looking forward beyond my stay on earth, I can see our country becoming richer and more powerful. But to make her prosperity more than superficial, her moral and intellectual development should keep pace with her material wealth.

GEORGE PEABODY. Inscribed on tablet beneath his bust, Hall of Fame, New York.

3
America means opportunity, freedom, power.

EMERSON, *Uncollected Lectures: Public and Private Education.*

While European genius is symbolized by some majestic Corinne crowned in the capitol at Rome, American genius finds its true type in the poor negro soldier lying in the trenches by the Potomac with his spelling book in one hand and his musket in the other.

EMERSON, *Uncollected Lectures: Books.*

4
American life storms about us daily, and is slow to find a tongue.

EMERSON, *Letters and Social Aims: Poetry and Imagination.*

The reason American cities are prosperous is that there is no place to sit down.

ALFRED J. TALLEY, *Interview, on returning from Europe.*

5
America is a country of young men.

EMERSON, *Society and Solitude: Old Age.*

A people who are still, as it were, but in the gristle, and not yet hardened into the bone of manhood.

EDMUND BURKE, *Conciliation with America.*

The youth of America is their oldest tradition. It has been going on now for three hundred years.

OSCAR WILDE, *A Woman of No Importance.* Act i.

6
Our country has liberty without license and authority without despotism.

JAMES, CARDINAL GIBBONS, *Address*, at Rome, 25 March, 1887.

7
America is the only place where man is full-grown!

O. W. HOLMES, *The Professor at the Breakfast-Table.* Ch. 4.

8
Equal and exact justice to all men, . . . freedom of religion, freedom of the press, freedom of person under the protection of the habeas corpus; and trial by juries impartially selected,—these principles form the bright constellation which has gone before us.

THOMAS JEFFERSON, *First Inaugural Address*, 4 March, 1801. It was perhaps from this that a sentence attributed to Jefferson was derived, "Equal rights for all, special privileges for none."

9
They [the Americans] equally detest the pageantry of a king, and the supercilious hypocrisy of a bishop.

JUNIUS, *Letters*. No. 35, 19 Dec., 1769.

We grant no dukedoms to the few,
We hold like rights and shall;
Equal on Sunday in the pew,
On Monday in the mall.
For what avail the plough or sail,
Or land, or life, if freedom fail?

EMERSON, *Boston*. St. 5.

Titles are abolished; and the American Republic swarms with men claiming and bearing them.

THACKERAY, *Round Head Papers: On Ribbons.*

10
Intellectually I know that America is no better than any other country; emotionally I know she is better than every other country.

SINCLAIR LEWIS, *Interview in Berlin*, 29 Dec., 1930.

America is the last abode of romance and other medieval phenomena.

ERIC LINKLATER, *Juan in America.*

11
Earth's biggest country's gut her soul
An' risen up Earth's Greatest Nation.

J. R. LOWELL, *Biglow Papers*. Ser. ii, No. 7.

The soil out of which such men as he are made is good to be born on, good to live on, good to die for and to be buried in.

J. R. LOWELL, *Among My Books: Second Series: Garfield.*

12
I believe in the United States of America as a government of the people, by the people, for the people; whose just powers are derived from the consent of the governed; a democracy in a republic; a sovereign nation of many sovereign states; a perfect union, one and inseparable; established upon those principles of freedom, equality, justice and humanity for which American patriots sacrificed

their lives and fortunes. I therefore believe it is my duty to my country to love it, to support its constitution, to obey its laws, to respect its flag, and to defend it against all enemies.

WILLIAM TYLER PAGE, *The American's Creed.* Accepted by House of Representatives, on behalf of the American people, 3 April, 1918.

1
Let us raise a standard to which the wise and honest can repair; the event is in the hands of God.

GEORGE WASHINGTON, *Remark,* during discussion, Constitutional Convention. (1787)

2
The preservation of the sacred fire of liberty, and the destiny of the republican model of government, are justly considered as deeply, perhaps as finally staked, on the experiment entrusted to the hands of the American people.

GEORGE WASHINGTON, *First Inaugural,* 1789.

What constitutes the bulwark of our own liberty and independence? It is not our frowning battlements, our bristling sea coasts. . . . Our reliance is in the love of liberty which God has planted in us. Our defense is in the spirit which prized liberty as the heritage of all men, in all lands everywhere.

ABRAHAM LINCOLN, *Speech,* Edwardsville, Ill., 13 Sept., 1858.

Liberty has still a continent to live in.

HORACE WALPOLE, *Letter,* 17 Feb., 1779.

This great spectacle of human happiness.

SYDNEY SMITH, *Essays: Waterton's Wanderings.*

3
Let our object be, our country, our whole country, and nothing but our country. And, by the blessing of God, may that country itself become a vast and splendid monument, not of oppression and terror, but of wisdom, of peace, and of liberty, upon which the world may gaze with admiration forever.

DANIEL WEBSTER, *Speech,* Charlestown, Mass., 17 June, 1825, at laying of cornerstone of the Bunker Hill Monument.

When honored and decrepit age shall lean against the base of this monument, and troops of ingenuous youth shall be gathered round it, and when the one shall speak to the other of its objects, the purposes of its construction, and the great and glorious events with which it is connected, there shall rise from every youthful breast the ejaculation, "Thank God, I—I also—am an American!"

DANIEL WEBSTER, *Address,* Charlestown, Mass., 17 June, 1843, at completion of the Bunker Hill Monument.

I shall know but one country. The ends I aim at shall be my country's, my God's, and Truth's. I was born an American; I live an American; I shall die an American.

DANIEL WEBSTER, *Speech,* 17 July, 1850.

4
The only thing that has ever distinguished America among the nations is that she has shown that all men are entitled to the benefits of the law.

WOODROW WILSON, *Address,* New York, 14 Dec., 1906.

America lives in the heart of every man everywhere who wishes to find a region where he will be free to work out his destiny as he chooses.

WOODROW WILSON, *Speech,* Chicago, 6 April, 1912.

The interesting and inspiring thought about America is that she asks nothing for herself except what she has a right to ask for humanity itself.

WOODROW WILSON, *Speech,* New York, 17 May, 1915.

5
Just what is it that America stands for? If she stands for one thing more than another, it is for the sovereignty of self-governing people.

WOODROW WILSON, *Speech,* Pittsburgh, 29 Jan., 1916.

America is not anything if it consists of each of us. It is something only if it consists of all of us; and it can consist of all of us only as our spirits are banded together in a common enterprise. That common enterprise is the enterprise of liberty and justice and right.

WOODROW WILSON, *Speech,* Pittsburgh, 29 Jan., 1916.

America is a tune. It must be sung together.

GERALD STANLEY LEE, *Crowds.* Bk. v, iii, 12.

6
Americanism consists in utterly believing in the principles of America.

WOODROW WILSON, *Address,* West Point, 13 June, 1916.

7
The right is more precious than peace.

WOODROW WILSON, *Address to Congress,* 2 Apr., 1917.

8
I tell you, fellow citizens, that the war was won by the American spirit. . . . You know what one of our American wits said, that it took only half as long to train an American army as any other, because you had only to train them to go one way.

WOODROW WILSON, *Speech,* Kansas City, Mo., 6 Sept., 1919.

9
Sometimes people call me an idealist. Well, that is the way I know I am an American. America is the only idealistic nation in the world.

WOODROW WILSON, *Speech,* Sioux Falls, N. D., 8 Sept., 1919.

10
O America because you build for mankind I
build for you.

WALT WHITMAN, *By Blue Ontario's Shore.*

1
There is nothing the matter with Americans except their ideals. The real American is all right; it is the ideal American who is all wrong.

G. K. CHESTERTON. (*New York Times*, 1 Feb., 1931.)

2
Oh, America, the sun sets in you.
Are you the grave of our day?

D. H. LAWRENCE, *The Evening Land.*

III—America: The Melting-Pot

3
Here [in America] individuals of all nations are melted into a new race of men.

MICHEL GUILLAUME JEAN DE CREVECŒUR, *Letters from an American Farmer.* Let. iii. (1782)

America is God's Crucible, the great Melting-Pot where all the races of Europe are melting and re-forming! . . . God is making the American.

ISRAEL ZANGWILL, *The Melting-Pot.* Act i. Produced in New York City, Oct., 1908.

There is here a great melting pot in which we must compound a precious metal. That metal is the metal of nationality.

WOODROW WILSON, *Address,* Washington, 19 April, 1915.

We Americans are children of the crucible.

THEODORE ROOSEVELT, *Speech,* 9 Sept., 1917.

4
America! half brother of the world!
With something good and bad of every land.

P. J. BAILEY, *Festus: The Surface,* l. 340.

5
There's freedom at thy gates and rest
For Earth's down-trodden and oppressed,
A shelter for the hunted head,
For the starved laborer toil and bread.

BRYANT, *Oh Mother of a Mighty Race.*

Asylum of the oppressed of every nation.

UNKNOWN, *Democratic Platform,* 1856.

6
She of the open soul and open door,
With room about her hearth for all mankind!

J. R. LOWELL, *Commemoration Ode.*

8
I do not think that you can do better than to fix here for a while, till you can become again Americanized.

THOMAS JEFFERSON, *Letter to Barlow,* 20 April, 1802.

We go to Europe to be Americanized.

EMERSON, *Conduct of Life: Culture.*

9
We have room in this country for but one flag, the Stars and Stripes. . . . We have room for but one loyalty, loyalty to the United States. . . . We have room for but one language, the English language.

THEODORE ROOSEVELT, *The Great Adventure.* Also last message to the American Defense Society, 3 Jan., 1919, two days before his death.

America is not to be made a polyglot boarding-house for money hunters of twenty different nationalities who have changed their former country for this country only as farmyard beasts change one feeding-trough for another.

THEODORE ROOSEVELT, *Speech,* Bridgeport, Conn.

There can be no fifty-fifty Americanism in this country. There is room here for only 100 per cent Americanism, only for those who are Americans and nothing else.

THEODORE ROOSEVELT, *Speech,* Republican Convention, Saratoga. Also in *Foes of Our Own Household.*

10
I will put in my poems that with you is heroism upon land and sea,
And I will report all heroism from an American point of view.

WALT WHITMAN, *Starting from Paumanok.*

11
Some Americans need hyphens in their names because only part of them has come over.

WOODROW WILSON, *Address,* Washington, 16 May, 1914.

There are a great many hyphens left in America. For my part, I think the most un-American thing in the world is a hyphen.

WOODROW WILSON, *Speech,* St. Paul, Minn., 9 Sept., 1919.

Hyphenated Americans.

THEODORE ROOSEVELT, *Metropolitan Magazine,* Oct., 1915.

When two flags are hoisted on the same pole, one is always hoisted undermost. The hyphenated American always hoists the American flag undermost.

THEODORE ROOSEVELT, *Fear God and Take Your Own Part.* Ch. v.

12
O Liberty, white Goddess! is it well
To leave the gates unguarded? On thy breast
Fold Sorrow's children, soothe the hurts of Fate,
Lift the down-trodden, but with hand of steel
Stay those who to thy sacred portals come
To waste the gifts of Freedom.

T. B. ALDRICH, *Unguarded Gates.*

IV—America: The American

13
Most Americans are born drunk. . . . They have a sort of permanent intoxication from within, a sort of invisible champagne. . . . Americans do not need to drink to inspire them to do anything.

G. K. CHESTERTON. (*N. Y. Times Magazine,* 28 June, 1931.)

14
Lords of an empire wide as Shakespeare's soul,
Sublime as Milton's immemorial theme,
And rich as Chaucer's speech, and fair as Spenser's dream.

SYDNEY DOBELL, *America.*

1
In America, the geography is sublime, but the men are not; the inventions are excellent, but the inventors one is sometimes ashamed of.
EMERSON, *Conduct of Life: Considerations by the Way.*

The Americans have many virtues, but they have not Faith and Hope.
EMERSON, *Nature, Addresses and Lectures: Man the Reformer.*

I hate this shallow Americanism which hopes to get rich by credit, to get knowledge by raps on midnight tables, to learn the economy of the mind by phrenology, or skill without study, or mastery without apprenticeship.
EMERSON, *Society and Solitude: Success.*

I often think, when we are reproached with brag by the peoples of a small home-territory, like the English, that ours is only the gait and bearing of a tall boy by the side of small boys.
EMERSON, *Uncollected Lectures: Public and Private Education.*

2
I esteem it a chief felicity of this country that it excels in women.
EMERSON, *Essays, Second Series: Manners.*

She behaves as if she were beautiful. Most American women do. It is the secret of their charm.
OSCAR WILDE, *Picture of Dorian Gray.* Ch. 3.

3
Bring me men to match my mountains;
Bring me men to match my plains,—
Men with empires in their purpose,
And new eras in their brains.
SAM WALTER FOSS, *The Coming American.*

4
Emerson says that the Englishman of all men stands most firmly on his feet. But it is not the whole of man's mission to be found standing, even at the most important post. Let him take one step forward,—and in that advancing figure you have the American.
T. W. HIGGINSON, *Americanism in Literature.*

5
This will never be a civilized country until we expend more money for books than we do for chewing-gum.
ELBERT HUBBARD, *The Philistine.* Vol. xxv, p. 1.

All Wrigley had was an idea. He was the first man to discover that American jaws must wag. So why not give them something to wag against?
WILL ROGERS, *The Illiterate Digest,* p. 89.

6
Enslaved, illogical, elate,
He greets the embarrassed Gods, nor fears
To shake the iron hand of Fate
Or match with Destiny for beers.
RUDYARD KIPLING, *An American.*

7
First, the sweetheart of the nation, then her aunt, woman governs America because America is a land of boys who refuse to grow up.
SALVADOR DE MADARIAGA, *Americans Are Boys.*

In America . . . where law and custom alike are based upon the dreams of spinsters.
BERTRAND RUSSELL, *Marriage and Morals,* p. 75.

8
We have exchanged the Washingtonian dignity for the Jeffersonian simplicity, which was in truth only another name for the Jacksonian vulgarity.
BISHOP HENRY C. POTTER, *Address,* Washington Centennial Service, New York, 30 April, 1889.

9
The first requisite of a good citizen in this republic of ours is that he shall be able and willing to pull his weight.
THEODORE ROOSEVELT, *Address,* New York, 11 Nov., 1902.

Our average fellow-citizen is a sane and healthy man, who believes in decency and has a wholesome mind.
THEODORE ROOSEVELT, *Address,* Syracuse, Labor Day, 1903.

10
The American people never carry an umbrella. They prepare to walk in eternal sunshine.
ALFRED E. SMITH, in syndicate article, 1931.

11
Be proud of those strong sons of thine
Who wrenched their rights from thee!
TENNYSON, *England and America in 1782.*

V—America: The Union

12
E Pluribus Unum. (Cne from many.)
Motto, used on the title page of the *Gentleman's Journal,* Jan., 1692. Motto for seal of the United States proposed originally on 10 Aug., 1776, by a committee composed of Benjamin Franklin, John Adams and Thomas Jefferson. Adopted 20 June, 1782. The motto was added to certain coins in 1796. The actual selection of the motto has been claimed for Pierre Eugène du Simitière, a Swiss artist, who was employed by the committee, shortly after the Declaration of Independence, to submit a design for the seal—a design which was not accepted.

The many colors blend into one. (Color est e pluribus unus.)
VERGIL (attr.), *Moretum,* l. 104.

From many to make one. (Ex pluribus unum facere.)
ST. AUGUSTINE, *Confessions.* Bk. iv, sec. 8.

13
Then join hand in hand, brave Americans all,—
By uniting we stand, by dividing we fall!
JOHN DICKINSON, *Liberty Song.* First published in the Boston *Gazette,* 18 July, 1768.

A song for our banner! The watchword recall
Which gave the Republic her station:
"United we stand, divided we fall!"
It made and preserves us a nation!
The union of lakes, the union of lands,
The union of States none can sever,

The union of hearts, the union of hands,
And the flag of our union forever!

GEORGE P. MORRIS, *The Flag of Our Union.*

1
I never use the word "Nation" in speaking of the United States; I always use the word "Union," or "Confederacy." We are not a Nation, but a Union, a confederacy of equal and sovereign States.

JOHN C. CALHOUN, *Letter to Oliver Dyer,* 1 Jan., 1849.

2
The Constitution, in all its provisions, looks to an indissoluble Union composed of indestructible States.

SALMON P. CHASE, *Decision,* in Texas v. White, 7 Wallace, 725.

3
We join ourselves to no party that does not carry the flag and keep step to the music of the Union.

RUFUS CHOATE, *Letter to Whig Convention,* Worcester, Mass., 1 Oct., 1855.

4
I have heard something said about allegiance to the South. I know no South, no North, no East, no West, to which I owe any allegiance.

HENRY CLAY, *Speech,* in U. S. Senate, 1848.

The gentleman speaks of Virginia being my country. The Union, sir, is my country.

HENRY CLAY, on the same occasion.

I am not a Virginian, but an American.

PATRICK HENRY, *Speech,* Continental Congress, 5 Sept., 1774.

I have neither been false to the North nor to the South, to the East nor to the West.

ROBERT C. WINTHROP, *Speech,* in Congress, 21 Feb., 1850.

5
The North! the South! the West! the East!
No one the most and none the least,
But each with its own heart and mind,
Each of its own distinctive kind,
Yet each a part and none the whole,
But all together form one soul;
That soul Our Country at its best,
No North, no South, no East, no West,
No yours, no mine, but always Ours,
Merged in one Power our lesser powers,
For no one's favor, great or small,
But all for Each and each for All.

EDMUND VANCE COOKE, *Each for All.*

6
This glorious Union shall not perish! Precious legacy of our fathers, it shall go down honored and cherished to our children. Generations unborn shall enjoy its privileges as we have done; and if we leave them poor in all besides, we will transmit to them the boundless wealth of its blessings!

EDWARD EVERETT, *Speech,* at Union Meeting in Faneuil Hall.

7
Our Union is river, lake, ocean and sky:
Man breaks not the medal when God cuts the die!

O. W. HOLMES, *Brother Jonathan's Lament for Sister Caroline.*

One flag, one land, one heart, one hand,
One nation, evermore!

O. W. HOLMES, *Voyage of the Good Ship Union.*

One heart, one hope, one destiny, one flag from sea to sea.

KATE BROWNLEE SHERWOOD, *Albert Sidney Johnston.*

8
Our federal Union, it must be preserved.

ANDREW JACKSON, *Toast,* at a banquet at Washington on Jefferson's birthday, 13 April, 1830. The preceding toasts had savored of nullification, and Jackson's, which came last, electrified the country. (BASSETT, *Life,* p. 555.)

9
The cement of this Union is the heart blood of every American.

THOMAS JEFFERSON, *Writings.* Vol. xiv, p. 252.

When any one State in the American Union refuses obedience to the Confederation by which they have bound themselves, the rest have a natural right to compel obedience.

THOMAS JEFFERSON, *Writings.* Vol. xvii, p. 121.

10
This government, with its institutions, belongs to the people who inhabit it. Whenever they shall grow weary of the existing government, they can exercise their constitutional right of amending it, or their revolutionary right to dismember or overthrow it.

ABRAHAM LINCOLN, *Speech,* at first Republican State Convention in Illinois, 1856. Quoted by Theodore Roosevelt in address before Ohio Constitutional Convention, Columbus, Feb., 1912.

It [secession] is an issue which can only be tried by war and decided by victory.

ABRAHAM LINCOLN, *Message to Congress,* 1864.

11
The mystic chords of memory, stretching from every battlefield and patriot grave to every living heart and hearthstone all over this broad land, will yet swell the chorus of the Union, when again touched, as surely they will be by the better angels of our nature.

ABRAHAM LINCOLN, *Inaugural Address.* 4 Mar., 1861.

12
The advice nearest to my heart and deepest in my convictions is, that the Union of the states be cherished and perpetuated. Let the open enemy of it be regarded as a Pandora with her box opened, and the disguised one as the serpent creeping with his deadly wiles into paradise.

JAMES MADISON, *Advice to My Country: Conclusion.* Found among his papers after his death. (*Dictionary of American Biography.* Vol. xii, p. 193.)

1
If this bill [for the admission of Orleans Territory as a State] passes, it is my deliberate opinion that it is virtually a dissolution of the Union; that it will free the States from their moral obligation; and, as it will be the right of all, so it will be the duty of some, definitely to prepare for a separation,—amicably if they can, violently if they must.

JOSIAH QUINCY, *Speech,* House of Representatives, 14 Jan., 1811.

The gentleman [Josiah Quincy] cannot have forgotten his own sentiment, uttered even on the floor of this House, "Peaceably if we can, forcibly if we must."

HENRY CLAY, *Speech,* in Congress, on the New Army Bill, 8 Jan., 1813.

2
Liberty and Union, now and forever, one and inseparable!

DANIEL WEBSTER, *Speech,* on Foote's Resolution, 26 Jan., 1830.

When my eyes shall be turned to behold, for the last time, the sun in heaven, may I not see him shining on the broken and dishonored fragments of a once glorious Union; on States dissevered, discordant, belligerent; on a land rent with civil feuds, or drenched, it may be, in fraternal blood!

DANIEL WEBSTER, *Second Speech on Foote's Resolution,* 26 Jan., 1830.

Let us then stand by the constitution as it is, and by our country as it is, one, united, and entire; let it be a truth engraven on our hearts; let it be borne on the flag under which we rally in every exigency, that we have one country, one constitution, one destiny.

DANIEL WEBSTER, *Speech,* New York, 15 March, 1837.

3
Till North and South together brought
Shall own the same electric thought,
In peace a common flag salute,
And, side by side in labor's free
And unresentful rivalry,
Harvest the fields wherein they fought.

WHITTIER, *Snow-Bound,* l. 504.

I accept your nomination in the confident trust that the masses of our countrymen, North and South, are eager to clasp hands across the bloody chasm which has so long divided them.

HORACE GREELEY, accepting the Liberal nomination for President, 1872.

4
It [the Civil War] created in this country what had never existed before—a national consciousness. It was not the salvation of the Union; it was the rebirth of the Union.

WOODROW WILSON, *Memorial Day Address,* 1915.

5
Let us keep our eyes and our hearts steadily fixed upon the old flag of our fathers. . . . It has a star for every State. Let us resolve that there shall be a State for every star!

ROBERT C. WINTHROP, *Speech,* at mass meeting on Boston Common, 22 Aug., 1862.

VI—America and Europe

6
America, in the assembly of nations, since her admission among them, has invariably, though often fruitlessly, held forth to them the hand of honest friendship, of equal freedom, of generous reciprocity. She has uniformly spoken among them, though often to heedless and often to disdainful ears, the language of equal liberty, equal justice, and equal rights.

JOHN QUINCY ADAMS, *Address,* 4 July, 1821.

Oh mother of a mighty race,
Yet lovely in thy youthful grace!
The elder dames, thy haughty peers,
Admire and hate thy blooming years.
With words of shame
And taunts of scorn they join thy name.

BRYANT, *Oh Mother of a Mighty Race.*

7
I called the New World into existence to redress the balance of the Old.

GEORGE CANNING, *King's Message,* 12 Dec., 1826.

8
There is no calamity which a great nation can invite which equals that which follows a supine submission to wrong and injustice and the consequent loss of national self-respect and honor, beneath which are shielded and defended a people's safety and greatness.

GROVER CLEVELAND, *Message to Congress,* 17 Dec., 1895, referring to Great Britain's refusal to arbitrate the Venezuelan boundary dispute.

Three thousand miles of ocean make any permanent political union between an European and an American state unnatural and inexpedient.

RICHARD OLNEY, *Draft of Venezuelan Message.*

9
That is the point which decides the welfare of a people; *which way does it look?* If to any other people, it is not well with them. If occupied with their own affairs and thoughts and men . . . they are sublime.

EMERSON, *Letters and Social Aims: Social Aims.*

The less America looks abroad, the grander its promise.

EMERSON, *Uncollected Lectures: Character.*

One day we will cast out the passion for Europe, by the passion for America.

EMERSON, *Conduct of Life: Considerations by the Way.*

There is much in the calamities we have suffered which is disinfecting. We have learned to forget foreign nations.

EMERSON, *Uncollected Lectures: Books.*

Amidst the calamities which war has brought on our country this one benefit has accrued—that our eyes are withdrawn from England, withdrawn from France, and look homeward. We have come to feel that "by ourselves our safety may be bought."

EMERSON, *Letters and Social Aims: Social Aims.*

1
Peace, commerce, and honest friendship with all nations,—entangling alliances with none.

THOMAS JEFFERSON, *First Inaugural,* 4 Mar., 1801.

We owe gratitude to France, justice to England, good will to all, and subservience to none.

THOMAS JEFFERSON, *Writings.* Vol. ix, p. 420.

2
The less we have to do with the enmities of Europe the better. Not in our day, but at no distant one, we may shake a rod over the heads of all, which may make the stoutest tremble. But I hope our wisdom will grow with our power, and teach us that the less we use our power the greater it will be.

THOMAS JEFFERSON, *Writings.* Vol. xiv, p. 308.

I have ever deemed it fundamental for the United States never to take active part in the quarrels of Europe. Their political interests are entirely distinct from ours. . . . They are nations of eternal war. All their energies are expended in the destruction of the labor, property and lives of their people.

THOMAS JEFFERSON, *Writings.* Vol. xv, p. 436.

The day is not distant when we may formally require a meridian of partition through the ocean which separates the two hemispheres, on the hither side of which no European gun shall ever be heard, nor an American on the other.

THOMAS JEFFERSON, *Writings.* Vol. xv, p. 263.

3
We must meet our duty and convince the world that we are just friends and brave enemies.

THOMAS JEFFERSON, *Writings.* Vol. xix, p. 156.

Peace and friendship with all mankind is our wisest policy, and I wish we may be permitted to pursue it.

JEFFERSON, *Letter to C. W. F. Dumas,* 1786.

4
Our difficulties are indeed great . . . but when viewed in comparison to those of Europe, they are the joys of paradise. . . . Happily for us the Mammoth [Napoleon] cannot swim, nor the Leviathan [England] move on dry land; and if we will keep out of their way, they cannot get at us.

THOMAS JEFFERSON, *Writings.* Vol. xii, p. 372.

An American coming to Europe for his education, loses in his knowledge, in his morals, in his health, in his habits, and in his happiness. I had entertained only doubts on this head before I came to Europe; what I see and hear, since I came here, proves more than I had even suspected.

THOMAS JEFFERSON, *Writings.* Vol v, p. 185.

5
At what point then is the approach of danger to be expected? I answer if it ever reach us it must spring up amongst us; it cannot come from abroad. If destruction be our lot, we must ourselves be its author and finisher. As a nation of free men, we must live through all time or die by suicide.

ABRAHAM LINCOLN, *Perpetuation of Our Political Institutions.*

6
John Bull, looking o'er the Atlantic, in choler
At your aptness for trade, says you worship
 the dollar;
But to scorn such eye-dollar-try's what very
 few do,
And John goes to that church as often as
 you do.

J. R. LOWELL, *A Fable for Critics,* l. 1075.

It don't seem hardly right, John,
 When both my hands was full,
To stump me to a fight, John,—
 Your cousin, tu, John Bull!
 Ole Uncle S. sez he, "I guess
 We know it now," sez he,
 "The lion's paw is all the law,
 According to J. B.,
 Thet's fit for you an' me!"

J. R. LOWELL, *Jonathan to John.* St. 1.

7
In the wars of the European powers in matters relating to themselves we have never taken any part, nor does it comport with our policy so to do. It is only when our rights are invaded or seriously menaced that we resent injuries or make preparation for our defence.

JAMES MONROE, *Message to Congress,* 2 Dec., 1823.

We owe it, therefore, to candor, and to the amicable relations existing between the United States and those [European] powers, to declare that we should consider any attempt on their part to extend their system to any portion of this hemisphere, as dangerous to our peace and safety.

JAMES MONROE, *Message to Congress,* 2 Dec., 1823, in which he enunciated what has come to be known as the "Monroe Doctrine."

8
Why is it, whenever a group of internationalists get together, they always decide that Uncle Sam must be the goat?

BERTRAND H. SNELL, *Interview,* 7 May, 1931.

If disease spread among the livestock, the goats would get it first and die. That gave rise to the expression, "I'll be the goat."

ALFRED E. SMITH, *Interview,* New York *Herald Tribune,* 5 March, 1935, p. 38.

9
Why forego the advantages of so peculiar a situation? Why quit our own to stand upon foreign ground? Why, by interweaving our destiny with that of any part of Europe, entangle our peace and prosperity in the toils of European ambition, rivalship, interest, humor or caprice?

GEORGE WASHINGTON, *Farewell Address,* 17 Sept., 1796.

Against the insidious wiles of foreign influence, . . . the jealousy of a free people ought to be constantly awake, since history and experience prove that foreign influence is one of the most baneful foes of republican government.

WASHINGTON, *Farewell Address*, 17 Sept., 1796.

'Tis our true policy to steer clear of permanent alliances, with any portion of the foreign world.

WASHINGTON, *Farewell Address*, 17 Sept., 1796.

1
America can not be an ostrich with its head in the sand.

WOODROW WILSON, *Address*, Des Moines, 1 Feb., 1916.

Every time Europe looks across the Atlantic to see the American eagle, it observes only the rear end of an ostrich.

H. G. WELLS, *America*.

2
The best way to help mankind is to begin at home and put our own house in order. . . . Internationalism, as it is practised, is another name for money juggling and the operations of bankers. . . . I am ready and eager for Uncle Sam to turn over the job of being catspaw for the world to someone else.

W. E. WOODWARD, *Money for Tomorrow*, p. 218.

VII—America: Foreign Opinion

3
The capital defect of life in America: namely, that compared with life in England it is so uninteresting, so without savour and without depth.

MATTHEW ARNOLD, *Letter*, written in 1886, during his second visit to America.

4
A dirty chimney on fire.

THOMAS CARLYLE, *Letter*, referring to the American Civil War.

He was probably fond of them, but he was always able to conceal it.

MARK TWAIN, *My First Lie*. Referring to Thomas Carlyle and Americans.

5
The American never imitates the Englishman in simply taking for granted both his own patriotism and his own superiority.

G. K. CHESTERTON, *Generally Speaking*, p. 234.

6
I cannot conclude without mentioning how sensibly I feel the dismemberment of America from this empire, and that I should be miserable indeed if I did not feel that no blame on that account can be laid at my door, and did I not also know that knavery seems to be so much the striking feature of its inhabitants that it may not in the end be an evil that they will become aliens to this kingdom.

GEORGE III OF ENGLAND, *Letter to Shelburne*, 10 November, 1782.

7
Thou, O my country, hast thy foolish ways,
Too apt to purr at every stranger's praise!

O. W. HOLMES, *An After-Dinner Poem*.

8
The fact is that the Americans are not a thoughtful people: they are too busy to stop and question their values.

DEAN W. R. INGE. (MARCHANT, *Wit and Wisdom of Dean Inge*. No. 217.)

9
I am willing to love all mankind, except an American.

SAMUEL JOHNSON. (BOSWELL, *Life*, iii, 290.)

10
For some reason or other, the European has rarely been able to see America except in caricature. . . . We do not ask to be sprinkled with rosewater, but may perhaps fairly protest against being drenched with the rinsings of an unclean imagination.

J. R. LOWELL, *On a Certain Condescension in Foreigners*.

11
If I were an American as I am an Englishman while a foreign troop was landed in my country I never would lay down my arms,—never! never! never!

WILLIAM PITT, EARL OF CHATHAM, *Speech*, 18 Nov., 1777.

12
The desire for riches is their ruling passion.

DUC DE LA ROCHEFOUCAULT-LIANCOURT, *Travels Throughout the United States of North America*, 1798.

All the men in America make money their pursuit.

RICHARD PARKINSON, *A Tour of America*, 1805.

The most materialistic people in the world.

G. W. STEEVENS, *The Land of the Dollar*.

Huge American rattle of gold.

HENRY JAMES, *The American Scene*.

In hardness and materialism, exaggeration and boastfulness; in a false smartness, a false audacity, a want of soul and delicacy.

MATTHEW ARNOLD, *Discourses on America*, 1884. For "Kipling's curse" see APPENDIX.

13
To rouse their [the Americans'] eager interest, their distinguished consideration and their undying devotion, all that is necessary is to hold them up to the ridicule of the rest of the universe. Dickens won them to him forever by merciless projections of typical Americans as windbags, swindlers and assassins.

BERNARD SHAW. Commenting on award of Nobel prize to Sinclair Lewis, 1931.

You are right in your impression that a number of persons are urging me to come to the United States. But why on earth do you call them my friends?

BERNARD SHAW, *Letter to Oswald Garrison Villard*, 4 August, 1921.

14
In the four quarters of the globe, who reads an American book? or goes to an American play? or looks at an American picture or statue? What does the world yet owe to American physicians or surgeons? What new substances have their chemists discovered?

or what old ones have they analyzed? What new constellations have been discovered by the telescopes of Americans? What have they done in mathematics? Who drinks out of American glasses? or eats from American plates? or wears American coats or gowns? or sleeps in American blankets? Finally, under which of the old tyrannical governments of Europe is every sixth man a slave, whom his fellow-creatures may buy, and sell, and torture?

SYDNEY SMITH, *Review of Seybert's Annals of the U. S. Edinburgh Review*, Jan., 1820.

1
Gigantic daughter of the West
We drink to thee across the flood. . . .
For art not thou of English blood?

ALFRED TENNYSON, *Hands All Round*. First published in the London *Examiner*, 1862.

Yet, still, from either beach,
The voice of blood shall reach,
More audible than speech,
"We are one!"

WASHINGTON ALLSTON, *America to Great Britain.*

2
How frantically have the French acted, and how rationally the Americans! But Franklin and Washington were great men. None have appeared yet in France.

HORACE WALPOLE, *Letter to H. S. Conway*, 1 July, 1790.

3
Thou sit'st between thy oceans; but when Fate
Was at thy making, and endowed thy soul
With many gifts and costly, she forgot
To mix with these a genius for repose.

WILLIAM WATSON, *To the Invincible Republic.*

3a
America is one long expectoration.

OSCAR WILDE, *Newspaper Interview*, during his visit to America in 1882.

4
I do not know the method of drawing up an indictment against a whole people.

EDMUND BURKE, *Conciliation with America.*

VIII—America: Some Famous Phrases in American History

See also Politics: Familiar Phrases

5
No ill luck stirring but what lights upon Uncle Sam's shoulders.

UNKNOWN, *Editorial*, Troy, N. Y., *Post*, 7 Sept., 1813. The earliest known use of "Uncle Sam." There is a legend that the original Uncle Sam was Samuel Wilson, of Troy, N. Y., an army contractor, b. 1766, d. 1854.

Uncle Sam and John Bull.

UNKNOWN, *Editorial, Columbia Centinel*, Dec., 1814.

U. S or Uncle Sam—a cant term in the army for the United States.

UNKNOWN, *Niles' Register*, 1815.

6
We must consult Brother Jonathan.

GEORGE WASHINGTON. Said to be a frequent remark of his, during the Revolution, referring to his secretary and aide-de-camp, Col. Jonathan Trumbull, of Connecticut. It is alleged to be the origin of "Brother Jonathan," as typifying America.

The Diverting History of John Bull and Brother Jonathan.

JAMES KIRKE PAULDING. Title of book, 1812.

John Bull christened this son of his by the name of Jonathan; but by and by when he became a man grown, his friends and neighbors gave him the nickname of Uncle Sam, a sure sign they liked him, for I never knew a respectable nickname given to a scurvy fellow in my life.

JAMES KIRKE PAULDING, *John Bull in America.*

7
Yankee Doodle, keep it up,
Yankee Doodle, dandy;
Mind the music and the step,
And with the girls be handy.

EDWARD BANGS, *The Yankee's Return to Camp.* This is the chorus of the first version of *Yankee Doodle*, attributed to Bangs on the authority of Dr. Edward Everett Hale. Other authorities attribute it to Dr. Richard Shuckburg, an officer in the British army under Lord Amherst, stationed at Albany in 1758, during the French and Indian War. Said to have been inspired by the ungainliness of the American recruits. The tune is an old one, perhaps of Dutch origin, well known in the time of Charles II, under the name of *Lydia Fisher's Jig*, with the following chorus:

Lucy Locket lost her pocket,
Kitty Fisher found it;
Nothing in it, nothing on it,
But the binding round it.

8
In the name of the Great Jehovah and the Continental Congress.

ETHAN ALLEN, reputed answer to Captain de la Place, when the latter asked in whose name Allen demanded the surrender of Fort Ticonderoga, 10 May, 1775. Many authorities suspect the answer was far more profane.

9 Men, you are all marksmen—don't one of you fire until you see the white of their eyes.

ISRAEL PUTNAM, at the Battle of Bunker Hill, 17 June, 1775. (FROTHINGHAM, *History of the Siege of Boston*, p. 140, footnote. "Philip Johnson states of Putnam, "I distinctly heard him say, 'Men' " etc., as quoted above.) Also ascribed to Colonel William Prescott.

Boys, aim at their waistbands.

JOHN STARK, at Bunker Hill, 17 June, 1775.

10
I only regret that I have but one life to lose for my country.

NATHAN HALE, *Speech*, upon the gallows just before being hanged as a spy by the British, New York, 22 Sept., 1776.

Every kind of service, necessary to the public good, becomes honorable by being necessary.

NATHAN HALE, 10 Sept., 1776, when his friend,

Captain William Hull, protested against his entering the British lines as a spy.

What pity is it
That we can die but once to serve our country!
ADDISON, *Cato*. Act iv, sc. 4.

Witness to the world that I die like a man.
MAJOR JOHN ANDRÉ, just before he was hanged as a spy, 2 Oct., 1780.

1
Don't give up the ship! You will beat them off!
CAPTAIN JAMES MUGFORD, of the schooner *Franklin,* 19 May, 1776, his dying words during a British attack in Boston Harbor.

Crying, with death-white lip,
"Boys, don't give up the ship!"
His soul struck out for heaven's peaceful shore.
J. W. CHADWICK, *Mugford's Victory*.

Keep the guns going! Fight her till she strikes or sinks! Don't give up the ship!
Attributed to CAPTAIN JAMES LAWRENCE, commander of the American frigate, *Chesapeake,* during her fight with the British ship, *Shannon,* 1 June, 1813. Fatally wounded early in the action, he is said to have kept crying these words from the cockpit until the last. They seem to rest on the testimony of Dr. John Dix, at the trial of Lieut. Cox, 14 April, 1814, that "Captain Lawrence ordered me to go on deck, and tell the men to fire faster and not give up the ship." A daughter of Benjamin Russell, editor of the Boston *Centinel* at the time, is authority for the statement that her father coined the phrase in his account of Lawrence's death. (BOMBAUGH, *Facts and Fancies for the Curious,* p. 388.)

Don't give up the ship!
Signal floated at the masthead of Commodore Oliver Hazard Perry's flagship, the *Lawrence,* during the battle of Lake Erie, 10 Sept., 1813.

2
There, I guess King George will be able to read that.
JOHN HANCOCK, *Remark,* on signing the Declaration of Independence, July 4, 1776. His was the first signature, and in so bold a hand that "John Hancock" became the synonym for a signature.

3
Don't tread on me.
Motto of the first flag of the Revolution, raised on Paul Jones's ship, the *Alfred,* in 1776. The flag showed a pine tree with a rattlesnake coiled at its foot.

4
These are the times that try men's souls. The summer soldier and the sunshine patriot will, in this crisis, shrink from the service of their country; but he that stands it *now,* deserves the love and thanks of man and woman. Tyranny, like hell, is not easily conquered; yet we have this consolation with us, that the harder the conflict, the more glorious the triumph.
THOMAS PAINE, *The Crisis: Intro.,* Dec., 1776.

It is the object only of war that makes it honorable. And if there was ever a just war since the world began, it is this in which America is now engaged. . . . We fight not to enslave, but to set a country free, and to make room upon the earth for honest men to live in.
THOMAS PAINE, *The Crisis.* (1776)

5
Put none but Americans on guard to-night.
GEORGE WASHINGTON. Based upon his circular letter to regimental commanders, dated 30 April, 1777, regarding recruits for his bodyguard, "You will therefore send me none but natives." A short time before, a deserter from the British army, named Thomas Hickey, had tried to poison Washington, and had been convicted and hanged.

6
There, my boys, are your enemies, red-coats and Tories. You must beat them—or Molly Stark is a widow to-night.
Attributed to COL. JOHN STARK, at the battle of Bennington, 16 Aug., 1777.

See there the enemy, my boys!
Now strong in valor's might,
Beat them, or Molly Stark will sleep
In widowhood to-night.
THOMAS P. RODMAN, *The Battle of Bennington.*

7
I have not yet begun to fight.
JOHN PAUL JONES, when summoned to surrender as his ship, the *Bonhomme Richard,* was sinking under him in his fight with the British forty-four, *Serapis,* 23 Sept., 1779.

8
Put Watts into 'em, boys! Give 'em Watts!
Attributed to REV. JAMES CALDWELL, when giving the American troops a pile of hymnbooks to serve as wadding, 23 June, 1780. Caldwell's wife had been killed by a British soldier.

He ran to the church,
Broke the door, stripped the pews, and dashed out in the road
With his arms full of hymn-books, and threw down his load
At their feet! Then above all the shouting and shots,
Rang his voice,—"Put Watts into 'em! Boys, give 'em Watts!"
BRET HARTE, *Caldwell of Springfield.*

9
He defeated the Americans with great slaughter.
UNKNOWN, *Inscription,* on the tomb of Lord Cornwallis, in Westminster Abbey. The surrender of Cornwallis at Yorktown, 17 Oct., 1781, virtually ended the Revolution.

10
A National debt, if it is not excessive, will be to us a national blessing.
ALEXANDER HAMILTON, *Letter to Robert Morris,* 30 April, 1781.

At the time we were funding our national debt, we heard much about "a public debt being a public blessing"; that the stock representing it was a creation of active capital for the aliment of commerce, manufactures, and agriculture.

THOMAS JEFFERSON, *Letter to John W. Epps*, 6 Nov., 1813.

The gentleman has not seen how to reply to this, otherwise than by supposing me to have advanced the doctrine that a national debt is a national blessing.

DANIEL WEBSTER, *Second Speech on Foote's Resolution*, 26 Jan., 1830. (*Works*, iii, 303.)

1

The Government of the United States of America is not, in any sense, founded on the Christian religion.

UNKNOWN, *Treaty with Tripoli*, 1796.

2

Millions for defense but not a cent for tribute.

ROBERT GOODLOE HARPER, *Toast*, at the dinner given by Congress at Philadelphia, 18 June, 1798, in honor of John Marshall upon his return from France. It was the thirteenth toast in a list of sixteen, as published in the *American Daily Advertiser*, 20 June, 1798. (See BEVERIDGE, *Life of John Marshall*, ii, 349.) Robert Goodloe Harper was a member of Congress from South Carolina, and the ascription to him is confirmed by Mr. A. S. Salley, Secretary of the Historical Commission of South Carolina. Many of the other toasts at the dinner were also defiances of France, the eleventh being, "The American eagle; may it regard with disdain the crowing of the Gallic cock."

No, no; not a penny!

CHARLES COTESWORTH PINCKNEY, American ambassador to France, in answer to a demand for a bribe of $250,000, made on behalf of Talleyrand, French foreign minister, by a secret agent named Hottenguer, 26 October, 1797. Pinckney, together with John Marshall and Elbridge Gerry, as envoys from the United States, were endeavoring to secure a cessation of French attacks on American shipping, and Hottenguer had informed them that the French Directory would not receive them until the bribe was paid. Pinckney has been credited with having said, "Millions for defense, but not a cent for tribute," but he denied it, saying, "No, my answer was not a flourish like that, but simply, 'Not a penny; not a penny.'" The more dramatic saying undoubtedly originated at the dinner to Marshall, and Harper afterwards explained that what he had in mind was not the demanded bribe, but that, instead of permitting France to plunder American merchant vessels of millions in tribute, he would spend them in defense.

3

We give up the fort when there's not a man left to defend it.

CAPTAIN GEORGE CROGHAN, to the British General Proctor, at Fort Stephenson, Lower Sandusky, 1 August, 1813. Proctor was preparing to attack the fort at the head of a large force, and was beaten off after two days' desperate fighting.

4

We have met the enemy and they are ours—two ships, two brigs, one schooner and one sloop.

OLIVER HAZARD PERRY, *Dispatch*, to Gen. William Henry Harrison, announcing his victory at the battle of Lake Erie, 10 Sept., 1813.

5

General Washington set the example of voluntary retirement after eight years. I shall follow it. And a few more precedents will oppose the obstacle of habit to any one who after a while shall endeavor to extend his term.

THOMAS JEFFERSON, *Writings*. Vol. xi, p. 58.

6

Our country! in her intercourse with foreign nations may she always be in the right; but our country, right or wrong!

STEPHEN DECATUR, *Toast*, at a dinner in his honor at Norfolk, Va., April, 1816. (MACKENZIE, *Life of Decatur*. Ch. 14.)

I hope to find my country in the right: however, I will stand by her, right or wrong.

JOHN J. CRITTENDEN, of Kentucky, *Speech*, in Congress, May, 1846, when President Polk sent a message relating to War with Mexico.

Our country, right or wrong! When right, to be kept right; when wrong, to be put right!

CARL SCHURZ, *Speech*, U. S. Senate, 1872.

"My country, right or wrong," is a thing that no patriot would think of saying except in a desperate case. It is like saying, "My mother, drunk or sober."

G. K. CHESTERTON, *The Defendant*.

7

The Era of Good Feelings.

BENJAMIN RUSSELL. Title of an article on Monroe's administration in the Boston *Columbian Centinel*, of which Russell was editor, 12 July, 1817. (*Dict. Amer. Biog*. xvi, 239.)

8

This bill is an attempt to reduce the country south of Mason and Dixon's line to a state of worse than colonial bondage.

JOHN RANDOLPH of Roanoke, *Speech*, in Congress, 15 April, 1824, referring to the Missouri Compromise. Mason and Dixon's line was the boundary line between Pennsylvania and Maryland, as surveyed by Charles Mason and Jeremiah Dixon, two English surveyors, in 1763–7, to settle the disputes between the Penn family and Lord Baltimore. It lies in 39° 43′ 26″ north latitude, and as it separated the free state of Pennsylvania from the then slave states of Maryland and Virginia, it came to be regarded as the line north of which, as extended across the continent, slavery should not be permitted.

9

He who dallies is a dastard; he who doubts is damned.

Attributed to GEORGE MCDUFFIE, of South Carolina. It was quoted by James Hamilton, while governor of South Carolina, in 1831, during the excitement of the nullification period. Quoted in Congress by J. C. S. Blackburn, of Kentucky, Feb., 1877, during the

Hayes-Tilden controversy, and used in the Louisville *Courier-Journal* by Col. Henry Watterson, who had proposed that a hundred thousand Kentuckians march on Washington and seat Mr. Tilden.

1
Our manifest destiny to overspread the continent allotted by Providence for the free development of our yearly multiplying millions.

JOHN L. O'SULLIVAN, *United States Magazine and Democratic Review*, vol. xvii, p. 5–10, July–August, 1845. O'Sullivan was editor of the *Review*, and the above phrase appeared in an editorial article denouncing opposition to annexation of Texas. The first known published use of "manifest destiny." (J. W. PRATT, *American Historical Review*, xxxii, 795.)

There is one element of our title [to Oregon] . . . to which I may not have done entire justice. I mean that new revelation of right which has been designated as the right of our manifest destiny to spread over this whole continent.

ROBERT C. WINTHROP, *Speech*, House of Representatives, 3 Jan., 1846.

In the autumn of 1844 the question of annexation [of Texas] was one of the chief issues of the presidential campaign. The Democrats made "Manifest Destiny" the cornerstone of their political philosophy for the moment.

W. E. WOODWARD, *Meet General Grant*, p. 73.

It is our manifest destiny to lead and rule all other nations.

JAMES GORDON BENNETT, *Editorial* in *The New York Herald*, 3 April, 1865.

That word, "manifest destiny," which is profanely used, signifies the sense all men have of the prodigious energy and opportunity lying idle here.

EMERSON, *Journals*, 1865.

Manifest destiny.

WILLIAM MCKINLEY, *Remark*, to his secretary, George Cortelyou, referring to the annexation of the Hawaiian Islands. (STODDARD, *As I Knew Them*, p. 251.)

Unmanifest Destiny.

RICHARD HOVEY. Title of poem.

2
Our country: whether bounded by the St. John's and the Sabine, or however otherwise bounded or described, and be the measurements more or less;—still our country, to be cherished in all our hearts, to be defended by all our hands!

ROBERT C. WINTHROP, *Toast*, at dinner in Faneuil Hall, Boston, 4 July, 1846, referring to the annexation of Texas. Frequently quoted as: "Our country, however bounded."

3
A little more grape, Captain Bragg.

Attributed to GENERAL ZACHARY TAYLOR, at the battle of Buena Vista, 22 Feb., 1847. It has been denied that Taylor ever said it, but that when Captain Braxton Bragg reported that he would have to fall back with his battery or lose it, Taylor replied, "Captain Bragg, it is better to lose a battery than a battle." Which is quite as good!

Bliss tells me that the stories of the General in connection with Bragg are all false. He never said, "A little more grape, Captain Bragg," nor did he say, "Major Bliss and I will support you."

ETHAN ALLEN HITCHCOCK, *Diary*, 29 Dec., 1848. General Hitchcock was Inspector-General of Scott's army in Mexico and a friend of Taylor. William Wallace Smith Bliss was Taylor's Adjutant-General and son-in-law.

4
General Taylor never surrenders.

THOMAS L. CRITTENDEN, reply, on behalf of General Zachary Taylor, at the battle of Buena Vista, 22 Feb., 1847, when summoned to surrender by General Santa Ana, the Mexican commander. The phrase became the slogan of the presidential campaign of 1848, when Taylor was elected. See 2127:4.

5
I shall defer my visit to Faneuil Hall, the cradle of American liberty, until its doors shall fly open upon golden hinges to lovers of Union as well as lovers of liberty.

DANIEL WEBSTER, *Letter*, April, 1851, in reply to an invitation to speak in Boston extended by his friends, who reported, however, that they had been refused the use of Faneuil Hall by the mayor and aldermen. This was just after Massachusetts had been exasperated by Webster's 7th of March speech.

6
Cotton is King; or Slavery in the Light of Political Economy.

DAVID CHRISTY. Title of book, 1855.

You dare not make war on cotton. Cotton is king.

JAMES H. HAMMOND, *Speech*, U. S. Senate, March, 1858.

Cotton is King.

GOVERNOR MANNING, of South Carolina, *Speech*, at Columbia, S. C., 1858.

7
An irrepressible conflict between opposing and enduring forces.

WILLIAM H. SEWARD, *Speech*, 25 Oct., 1858. Referring to the antagonism between freedom and slavery.

8
Den I wish I was in Dixie! Hooray! Hooray!
In Dixie's land we'll took our stand,
To lib an' die in Dixie!

DANIEL DECATUR EMMETT, *Dixie*. (1859) There are many stories to explain the derivation of "Dixie" as a synonym for the South, none of them convincing. The compiler's guess is that it derives from Mason and Dixon's line.

To arms! To arms! To arms, in Dixie! . . .
For Dixie's land we take our stand,
And live or die for Dixie!

ALBERT PIKE, *Dixie*. (1861)

9
If any one attempts to haul down the American flag, shoot him on the spot.

GENERAL JOHN A. DIX, while Secretary of the Treasury, 29 Jan., 1861, in a telegram from

Washington, to William Hemphill Jones, who had been sent to New Orleans as a treasury clerk, ordering the arrest of Captain Breshwood, commander of the revenue cutter *McClennand,* which it was feared he would turn over to the Confederates. The telegram sounds well, but considering that Jones was alone and unarmed, and perhaps never in his life had handled a gun, was merely a gesture, intended, perhaps, to bolster up Union sentiment in the North.

1
Say to the seceded States: "Wayward sisters, depart in peace!"

WINFIELD SCOTT, *Letter to W. H. Seward,* 3 March, 1861.

2
On to Richmond!

FITZ-HENRY WARREN. Headline, New York *Tribune,* June, 1861. Adopted by Mr. Dana as a standing head before the McDowell campaign.

3
All we ask is to be let alone.

JEFFERSON DAVIS, *Inaugural Address,* as President of the Confederate States of America, 18 Feb., 1861, stating that the attitude of the Southern States was purely one of self-defence.

"In a veek or so I expects to come
And turn you out of your 'ouse and 'ome;—
I'm a quiet old cove," says he, with a groan:
"All I axes is—Let me alone!"

HENRY HOWARD BROWNELL, *The Old Cove.*

4
A rich man's war and a poor man's fight.

UNKNOWN. Slogan of protest in Confederacy in 1861 against various laws favoring large slave-owners.

5
All quiet along the Potomac to-night.

ETHEL LYNN BEERS, *All Quiet along the Potomac.* A phrase supposed to have been originated by Gen. George B. McClellan, in command of the Army of the Potomac, and repeated so often that it exasperated the country, which was demanding action.

6
It would be superfluous in me to point out to your Lordship that this is war.

CHARLES FRANCIS ADAMS, U. S. Minister to England, *Despatch,* to Earl Russell, 5 Sept., 1863, protesting against permitting the Confederate ironclads, then building in England, to depart from Liverpool.

7
No terms except an unconditional and immediate surrender can be accepted. I propose to move immediately upon your works.

U. S. GRANT, reply to General Simon B. Buckner, at Fort Donelson, Ky., 16 Feb., 1862. (BADEAU, *Military History of U. S. Grant,* p. 48.)

8
I propose to fight it out on this line if it takes all summer.

U. S. GRANT, to General Henry W. Halleck, 11 May, 1864.

9
Damn the torpedoes!

DAVID GLASGOW FARRAGUT, at the battle of Mobile Bay, 5 Aug., 1864.

10
Hold the fort, for I am coming!

What GENERAL WILLIAM TECUMSEH SHERMAN really signalled to General Corse from the top of Kenesaw Mountain, when Corse was attacked at Allatoona, 5 Oct., 1864, was "Hold out; relief is coming." But "Hold the fort, for I am coming" is the accepted version, and was made the refrain of a popular gospel-song by Philip Paul Bliss.

11
Fellow-citizens: Clouds and darkness are around Him; His pavilion is dark waters and thick clouds; justice and judgment are the establishment of His throne; mercy and truth shall go before His face! God reigns and the Government at Washington lives.

JAMES A. GARFIELD, *Address,* April, 1865, from the balcony of the New York Custom House to a crowd, excited by the news of President Lincoln's assassination.

One of the noblest sentences ever uttered was uttered by Mr. Garfield before he became President. He was a Member of Congress, as I remember it, at the time of Mr. Lincoln's assassination. He was at the old Fifth Avenue Hotel and they begged him to go out and say something to the people. He went out and after he had attracted their attention, he said this beautiful thing: "My fellow citizens, the President is dead, but the Government lives and God Omnipotent reigns." America is the place where you cannot kill your government by killing the men who conduct it.

WOODROW WILSON, *Address,* Helena, Mont., 11 Sept., 1919.

God lives and reigns! He built and lent
The heights for Freedom's battlement,
Where floats her flag in triumph still!

WILL HENRY THOMPSON, *The High Tide at Gettysburg.*

12
Waving the bloody shirt.

The phrase as applied to American politics is attributed to OLIVER P. MORTON, U. S. Senator from 1867–1879, and one of the presidential candidates at the Cincinnati convention of 1876. (See FARMER, *Americanisms,* p. 9.) For twenty years after the Civil War, Republican campaigns were based upon the record of the party in saving the Union, denunciation of the Democrats for bringing on the war. It was these tactics which were described as "waving the bloody shirt."

With a crutch by way of a pole,
With artistic flutter and flirt,
A Senator in the Senate sat
Waving a bloody shirt.

GEORGE THOMAS LANIGAN, *The Bloody Shirt.* The reference is to Senator Oliver P. Morton, whose legs were crippled and who had a stationary bracket at the side of his desk upon which he could lean while speaking.

It is a relief to remember that this phrase [waving the bloody shirt] is no invention of our politics. It dates back to Scotland three centuries ago. After a massacre in Glenfruin, not so savage as has stained our annals, two hundred and twenty widows rode on white palfreys to Stirling Tower, bearing each on a spear her husband's bloody shirt.

ROSCOE CONKLING, *Speech,* New York, 17 Sept., 1880.

Having no banners but bloody shirts hanged upon long staves.

SIR PHILIP SIDNEY, *Arcadia.* Bk. i.

The bloody shirt of the martyr was exposed in the mosch of Damascus.

GIBBON, *Decline and Fall.* Vol. vi, p. 277.

It is by spreading out the miseries of the workmen, the bloody shirt of some victim, that the people are excited to take arms.

LEON FOUCHER, *Review* of Guizot's translation of SPARKS's *Life of Washington.*

1

The way to resumption is to resume.

SALMON P. CHASE, *Letter to Horace Greeley,* 17 May, 1866.

I am thankful I have lived to see the day when the greenback can raise its right hand and declare "I know that my Redeemer liveth."

R. G. INGERSOLL, *Speech,* from sub-Treasury steps in Wall Street, 1 Jan., 1879, upon resumption of specie payments.

2

Well, isn't this a billion dollar country?

Attributed to CHARLES FOSTER, Secretary of the Treasury under Harrison, retorting to the Democratic gibe about a "billion dollar Congress."

The 51st was promptly dubbed "The Billion Dollar Congress." "This is a Billion Dollar Country" was the retort almost universally attributed to Reed [Thomas B. Reed] himself, although in an article in the *North American Review* for March, 1892, he lays no claim to its authorship and praises it as containing "both wit and wisdom" and "the best in kind ever evoked."

W. A. ROBINSON, *Thomas B. Reed.*

3

I have considered the pension list of the republic a roll of honor.

GROVER CLEVELAND, *Veto of Mary Ann Dougherty's Pension,* 5 July, 1888.

4

We want no war of conquest. . . . War should never be entered upon until every agency of peace has failed.

WILLIAM MCKINLEY, *Inaugural Address,* 4 Mar., 1897.

5

Remember the Maine!

The slogan of the Spanish-American War. On 15 Feb., 1898, the American battleship Maine was destroyed by a mine in the harbor of Havana, Cuba.

In a Broadway bar an unknown man raised his glass and solemnly said: "Gentlemen, remember the Maine!" and furnished a slogan that was to ring around the world.

JOHN K. WINKLER, *W. R. Hearst,* p. 154.

6

Please remain. You furnish the pictures and I'll furnish the war.

WILLIAM RANDOLPH HEARST, *Telegram,* to Frederic Remington, when the latter wished to come home from Cuba, March, 1898. (WINKLER, *Hearst,* p. 144.)

Ye who made war that your ships
Should lay to at the beck of no nation,
Make war now on Murder, that slips
The leash of her hounds of damnation;
Ye who remembered the Alamo,
Remember the Maine!

RICHARD HOVEY, *The Word of the Lord from Havana.*

7

You may fire when you are ready, Gridley.

ADMIRAL GEORGE DEWEY, to the Captain of his flagship, at the battle of Manila, 1 May, 1898. (*Autobiography,* p. 214.)

8

Don't cheer, boys; the poor devils are dying.

CAPTAIN JOHN WOODWARD PHILIP, of the battleship *Texas,* as his ship swept past the burning Spanish ship *Vizcaya,* battle of Santiago, 4 July, 1898. (LODGE, *War with Spain.*)

9

The open door.

JOHN HAY. On 2 Jan., 1900, Hay, then Secretary of State, announced to the cabinet that he had completed negotiations for the "open door" in China; i. e., that no country would be discriminated against by tariff laws or other conditions.

10

We want Perdicaris alive or Raisuli dead.

JOHN HAY, *Cablegram,* to American consul to Morocco, 22 June, 1904. Ion H. Perdicaris, an American citizen, had been kidnapped by a Moroccan bandit named Raisuli and held for ransom. "It was Roosevelt [who acted], though Hay coined the telegraphic phrase." —*Dict. American Biog.*, viii, 435. Perdicaris was released two days later. According to *AP, The Story of the News,* p. 188, the phrase was suggested to Hay by Edwin M. Hood, an Associated Press reporter in Washington, in place of the long dispatch Hay had prepared.

It is curious how a concise impropriety hits the public.

12 JOHN HAY, *Diary,* 23 June, 1904.

Remember, my son, that any man who is a bear on the future of this country will go broke.

J. PIERPONT MORGAN. Quoted by his son in talk at the Chicago Club, 10 Dec., 1908. J. P. Morgan was paraphrasing his father, Junius Spencer Morgan, who is credited with the injunction, "Never sell a bear on the United States." (*Dict. Amer. Biog.*, xiii, 182.)

13

We shall not, I believe, be obliged to alter our policy of watchful waiting.

WOODROW WILSON, *Message to Congress,* 2 Dec., 1913, referring to Mexico.

We must be impartial in thought as well as in action. The United States must be neutral in fact as well as in name.
WOODROW WILSON, *Proclamation*, 19 Aug., 1914.

Hold the Imperial German Government to strict accountability.
WOODROW WILSON, *Note to German Government*, 10 Feb., 1915.

1
Our whole duty, for the present, at any rate, is summed up in the motto: America first.
WOODROW WILSON, *Speech*, New York, 20 April, 1915.

There is such a thing as a man being too proud to fight.
WOODROW WILSON, *Speech*, at Philadelphia, 10 May, 1915. "I suppl'ed the President through Tumulty with a phrase which brought down upon him a storm of abuse and denunciation. The words 'too proud to fight' were mine."—O. G. VILLARD, *Fighting Years*, p. 256.

A little group of wilful men.
WOODROW WILSON, *Statement*, 3 March, 1916, referring to a group of eleven senators who, by filibustering tactics, had prevented the passage of a bill authorizing Wilson to arm American merchantmen.

2
Wake up America.
AUGUSTUS P. GARDNER, *Speech*, 16 Oct., 1916.

3
We have five hundred thousand and one lamp-posts in America, and that is where the German reservists will find themselves if they try any uprising.
AMBASSADOR JAMES W. GERARD, when told by Zimmermann, the German Foreign Minister, that there were 500,000 German reservists in America who would rise in arms if the American government entered the war. (GERARD, *My Four Years in Germany*, p. 237.)

4
Lafayette, we are here.
COLONEL C. E. STANTON, *Address*, delivered at the grave of Lafayette in the Picpus Cemetery, Paris, 4 July, 1917. Often wrongly attributed to General John J. Pershing, who has himself disclaimed it, stating that Colonel Stanton was its author. (PERSHING, *My Experiences in the World War*. Vol. i, p. 93.)

5
Come on, you sons of bitches! Do you want to live forever?
GUNNERY SERGEANT DANIEL DALY, U. S. Marine Corps, at Lucy-le-Bocage, on the fringe of Belleau Wood, 4 June, 1918.

Gunnery Sergeant Daly, however, writes me that the exclamation he made was, "For Christ's sake, men, come on! Do you want to live forever?" Obviously he is very loath to admit, as most of us would be, in writing, that he used the sobriquet of sons of bitches.
MAJOR E. N. MCCLELLAN, U. S. Marine Corps, *Letter to the Compiler*, 26 Jan., 1932.

I could ask people to throw ashes on their heads
In the name of that sergeant at Belleau Woods,
Walking into the drumfires, calling his men,
"Come on, you ——! Do you want to live forever?"
CARL SANDBURG, *Losers*.

Dogs, would you live forever? (Hunde, wollt ihr ewig leben?)
FREDERICK THE GREAT, to his wavering troops, at Kolin, 18 June, 1757. (MARTIN, *Hist. of France*, xv, 98.) Carlyle in his *Frederick the Great* (Bk. xviii, ch. 4) says this "is to be counted pure myth," but in his *French Revolution* (Pt. ii, bk. i, ch. 4) he writes, "There were certain runaways whom Fritz the Great bullied back into the battle with a: 'R——, wollt ihr ewig leben, Unprintable Offscouring of Scoundrels, would ye live forever!'" (The "R——" perhaps for Rindviehe.) The phrase has been common to all wars.

6
The legend, "Heaven, Hell, or Hoboken by Christmas," on a tent near General Headquarters of our Expeditionary Force in France reflected the spirit of the whole American Army.
GREGORY MASON, *How America Finished*, Paris, 7 Dec., 1918.

It's Heaven, Hell or Hoboken before next Christmas Day.
ALBERT JAY COOK, *Heaven, Hell, or Hoboken*.

7
America's present need is not heroics but healing; not nostrums but normalcy; not revolution but restoration; . . . not surgery but serenity.
WARREN G. HARDING, *Speech*, Boston, May, 1920.

AMUSEMENT

See also Game, Sport

8
Certain bounds must be observed in our amusements, and we must be careful not to carry things too far and, swept away by our passions, lapse into shameful excess. (Ludendi etiam est quidam modus retinendus, ut ne nimis omnia profundamus elatique voluptate in aliquam turpitudinem delabamur.)
CICERO, *De Officiis*. Bk. i, ch. 29, sec. 104.

9
Whoe'er was edified, themselves were not.
COWPER, *The Task*. Bk. ii, l. 444.

We are not amused.
QUEEN VICTORIA, after watching an imitation of her royal self by Alec Yorke, a young equerry, at Buckingham Palace, in 1889. There are other explanations of the phrase, for example that it was a warning the Queen gave whenever, in her opinion, the conversation in her presence grew a little too broad.

10
"There are amusing people who do not interest," said the Monsignore, "and interesting people who do not amuse."
BENJAMIN DISRAELI, *Lothair*. Ch. 41.

11
If you would rule the world quietly, you must keep it amused.
EMERSON, *Essays, Second Series: New Eng-*

land Reformers. Quoted as the maxim of a tyrant.

1
A man cannot spend all this life in frolic.
SAMUEL JOHNSON, *The Rambler*. No. 31.

If I had no duties, and no reference to futurity, I would spend my life in driving briskly in a post-chaise with a pretty woman.
SAMUEL JOHNSON. (BOSWELL, *Life*.)

2
I am a great friend to public amusements, for they keep people from vice.
SAMUEL JOHNSON. (BOSWELL, *Life*, 1772.)

Give 'em but a May-pole . . . 'tis meat, drink, washing, and lodging to 'em.
STERNE, *Tristram Shandy*. Vol. vii, ch. 38.

3
The only ground, therefore, on which restrictions on Sunday amusements can be defended must be that they are religiously wrong; a motive of legislation which can never be too earnestly protested against.
JOHN STUART MILL, *On Liberty*. Ch. 4.

4
Men spend their time following a ball or a hare; it is the pleasure even of kings.
PASCAL, *Pensées*. Sec. ii, No. 141.

5
Amusement is the happiness of those who cannot think.
POPE, *Thoughts on Various Subjects*.

Behold the child, by Nature's kindly law,
Pleas'd with a rattle, tickled with a straw:
Some livelier plaything gives his youth delight,
A little louder, but as empty quite:
Scarfs, garters, gold, amuse his riper stage,
And beads and prayer-books are the toys of age:
Pleas'd with this bauble still, as that before,
Till tired he sleeps, and life's poor play is o'er.
POPE, *Essay on Man*. Epis. ii, l. 275.

6
What revels are in hand? Is there no play
To ease the anguish of a torturing hour?
SHAKESPEARE, *A Midsummer-Night's Dream*. Act v, sc. i, l. 35.

Sir Andrew: I delight in masques and revels sometimes altogether.
Sir Toby: Art thou good at these kickshawses, knight?
SHAKESPEARE, *Twelfth Night*. Act i, sc. 3, l. 120.

7
We cry for mercy to the next amusement;
The next amusement mortgages our fields.
YOUNG, *Night Thoughts*. Night ii, l. 131.

O ye Lorenzos of our age! who deem
One moment unamus'd, a misery.
YOUNG, *Night Thoughts*. Night ii, l. 245.

ANCESTRY

See also Posterity; Titles; Virtue and Nobility

I—Ancestry: Apothegms

8
There was a young man in Rome, that was very like Augustus Cæsar; Augustus took knowledge of it, and sent for the man, and asked him, "Was your mother never at Rome?" He answered, "No, sir; but my father was."
FRANCIS BACON, *Apothegms*, No. 87.

9
Gentility is nothing else but ancient riches.
LORD BURGHLEY. (Peck, *Desiderata Curiosa*, 48.) Lord Burghley was quoting a proverb which was included by George Herbert in his *Jacula Prudentum*, published in 1640.

Honour was but ancient riches.
NICHOLAS BRETON, *Courtier and Countryman*.

10
A branch of one of your antediluvian families, fellows that the flood could not wash away.
CONGREVE, *Love for Love*. Act v, sc. 1.

I am, in point of fact, a particularly haughty and exclusive person, of pre-Adamite ancestral descent. You will understand this when I tell you that I can trace my ancestry back to a protoplasmal primordial atomic globule.
W. S. GILBERT, *The Mikado*. Act i.

Look in the chronicles; we came in with Richard Conqueror.
SHAKESPEARE, *Taming of the Shrew: Induction*. Sc. 1, l. 4.

Such is the stock from which I spring. (Eo sum genere gnatus.)
PLAUTUS, *Pseudolus*, l. 590. (Act ii, sc. 1.)

11
Earls that dated from early years.
HOOD, *Miss Kilmansegg: Her Fancy Ball*.

Nobles by the right of an earlier creation, and priests by the imposition of a mightier hand.
MACAULAY, *Essays: Milton*.

A penniless lass wi' a lang pedigree.
CAROLINA NAIRNE, *The Laird of Cockpen*.

12
Hereditary nobility is due to the presumption that we shall do well because our fathers have done well. (La noblesse est une dignité due à la présomption que nous ferons bien, parce que nos pères ont bien fait.)
JOUBERT, *Pensées*. No. 218.

13
Who is well-born? He who is by nature well fitted for virtue. (Quis est generosus? Ad virtutem bene a natura compositus.)
SENECA, *Epistulæ ad Lucilium*. Epis. xliv, sec. 5.

For all that fair is, is by nature good;
That is a sign to know the gentle blood.
SPENSER, *An Hymne in Honour of Beautie*, l. 139.

14
He who boasts of his descent, praises the deeds of another. (Qui genus jactat suum, Aliena laudat.)
SENECA, *Hercules Furens*, l. 340.

He stands for fame on his forefathers' feet,
By heraldry prov'd valiant or discreet.
YOUNG, *Love of Fame*. Sat. i, l. 131.

1
Our ancestors are very good kind of folks; but they are the last people I should choose to have a visiting acquaintance with.

SHERIDAN, *The Rivals*. Act iv, sc. 1.

2
Who breaks his birth's invidious bar.

TENNYSON, *In Memoriam*. Sec. lxiv.

3
You should study the Peerage, Gerald. . . . It is the best thing in fiction the English have ever done.

OSCAR WILDE, *A Woman of No Importance*. Act iii.

II—Ancestry: Heredity

4
That they breed in and in, as might be shown,
Marrying their cousins—nay, their aunts and nieces,
Which always spoils the breed, if it increases.

BYRON, *Don Juan*. Canto i, st. 57.

This heathenish cross restored the breed again,
Ruined its blood, but much improved its flesh.

BYRON, *Don Juan*. Canto i, st. 58.

5
How shall a man escape from his ancestors. or draw off from his veins the black drop which he drew from his father's or his mother's life? It often appears in a family, as if all the qualities of the progenitors were potted in several jars—some ruling quality in each son or daughter of the house,—and sometimes the unmixed temperament, the rank unmitigated elixir, the family vice, is drawn off in a separate individual, and the others are proportionally relieved.

EMERSON, *Conduct of Life: Fate*.

What can I do against the influence of Race, in my history? What can I do against heredity and constitutional habits; against scrofula, lymph. impotence?

EMERSON, *Representative Men: Montaigne*.

6
Men resemble their contemporaries even more than their progenitors.

EMERSON, *Representative Men: Uses of Great Men*.

7
It will not out of the flesh that is bred in the bone.

JOHN HEYWOOD, *Proverbs*. Pt. ii, ch. 8.

What is bred in the bone will never come out of the flesh.

PILPAY, *Two Fishermen*. Fable xiv.

It will never come out of the flesh that's bred in the bone.

BEN JONSON, *Every Man in His Humour*. Act ii, sc. 1.

8
This body in which we journey across the isthmus between the two oceans is not a private carriage, but an omnibus.

OLIVER WENDELL HOLMES, *The Guardian Angel*. Ch. 3. Quoted as "from a work which will be repeatedly referred to in this narrative." Sometimes condensed to: "We are omnibuses in which our ancestors ride."

See also LIFE: AN ISTHMUS.

9
What we have inherited from our fathers and mothers is not all that "walks" in us. There are all sorts of dead ideas and lifeless old beliefs. They have no tangibility but they haunt us all the same and we cannot get rid of them. Whenever I take up a newspaper I seem to see Ghosts gliding between the lines. Ghosts must be all over the country, as thick as the sands of the sea.

HENRIK IBSEN, *Ghosts*. Act ii.

Year by year, in pious patience, vengeful Mrs. Boffkin sits
Waiting for the Sleary babies to develop Sleary's fits.

RUDYARD KIPLING, *The Post That Fitted*.

10
They often repeat the form [i. e., peculiarities] of their progenitors. (Referant proavorum sæpe figuras.)

LUCRETIUS, *De Rerum Natura*. Bk. iv, l. 213.

11
One always retains the traces of one's origin. (On garde toujours la marque de ses origines.)

ERNEST RENAN, *La Vie de Jésus*.

12
He's a chip o' the old block.

WILLIAM ROWLEY, *A Match at Midnight*, Act i. (1633)

How well dost thou now appear to be a chip of the old block?

MILTON, *Apology for Smectymnuus*. Sec. 7. (1642)

Not merely a chip of the old block, but the old block itself.

EDMUND BURKE, referring to Pitt on the occasion of his first speech, 26 Feb., 1781. (WRAXALL, *Memoirs*. Vol. ii, pt. ii, p. 78.)

I look upon you as a gem of the old rock.

SIR THOMAS BROWNE, *Hydriotaphia*.

She's a chick of the old cock.

APHRA BEHN, *Sir Patient Fancy*. Act iv, sc. 4.

13
Bull Jove, sir, had an amiable low;
And some such strange bull leap'd your father's cow,
And got a calf in that same noble feat
Much like to you, for you have just his bleat.

SHAKESPEARE, *Much Ado About Nothing*. Act v, sc. 4, l. 48.

But where the bull and cow are both milk-white,
They never do beget a coal-black calf.

SHAKESPEARE, *Titus Andronicus*. Act v, sc. 1, l. 31.

Nor do fierce eagles produce the peaceful dove. (Neque imbellem feroces Progenerant aquilæ columbam.)

HORACE, *Odes*. Bk. iv, ode 4, l. 31.

1
Alas, our frailty is the cause, not we!
For such as we are made of, such we be.
SHAKESPEARE, *Twelfth Night*. Act ii, sc. 2, l. 32.

III—Ancestry: Its Worth

2
Nobility is a graceful ornament to the civil order. It is the Corinthian capital of polished society.
EDMUND BURKE, *Reflections on the Revolution in France*.

3
His father's name was José—*Don*, of course,
A true Hidalgo, free from every stain
Of Moor or Hebrew blood, he traced his source
Through the most Gothic gentlemen of Spain.
BYRON, *Don Juan*. Canto i, st. 9.

4
A great distinction, and amongst mankind
The most conspicuous, is to spring from sires
Renowned for virtue.
(*Δεινὸς χαρακτὴρ καπίσημος ἐν βροτοῖς
ἐσθλῶν γενέσθαι, κἀπὶ μεῖζον ἔρχεται
τῆς εὐγενείας ὄνομα τοῖσιν ἀξίοις.*)
EURIPIDES, *Hecuba*, l. 379. (Woodhull, tr.)

5
Spurn not the nobly born with love affected!
Nor treat with virtuous scorn the well-connected!
W. S. GILBERT, *Iolanthe*. Act ii.

I think you ought to recollect
You cannot show too much respect
Towards the highly-titled few;
But nobody does, and why should you?
W. S. GILBERT, *The Mikado*. Act i.

6
The fairest flower
That ever blossomed on ancestral timber.
W. S. GILBERT, *H. M. S. Pinafore*. Act. i.

He combines the manners of a Marquis with the morals of a Methodist.
W. S. GILBERT, *Ruddigore*. Act i.

7
No, my friends, I go (always other things being equal) for the man who inherits family traditions and the cumulative humanities of at least four or five generations.
O. W. HOLMES, *The Autocrat of the Breakfast-Table*. Ch. 1.

8
O Damsel Dorothy! Dorothy Q.!
Strange is the gift that I owe to you; . . .
What if, a hundred years ago,
Those close-shut lips had answered No,
When forth the tremulous question came
That cost the maiden her Norman name,
And under the folds that look so still
The bodice swelled with the bosom's thrill?
Should I be I, or would it be
One-tenth another, to nine-tenths me?
O. W. HOLMES, *Dorothy Q*. St. 5.

9
The brave are born from the brave and good.
(Fortes creantur fortibus et bonis.)
HORACE, *Odes*. Bk. iv, ode 4, l. 29.

Nothing like blood, sir, in hosses, dawgs, and men.
THACKERAY, *Vanity Fair*. Ch. 35.

10
Let wealth and commerce, laws and learning die,
But leave us still our old nobility.
LORD JOHN MANNERS, *England's Trust*. Bk. iii, l. 227.

Be aristocracy the only joy:
Let commerce perish—let the world expire.
UNKNOWN, *Modern Gulliver*, p. 192.

11
'Tis a high virtue to tread in the steps of our ancestors, when they have gone before us in the right path. (Invenio autem apud sapientes honestissimum esse majorum vestigia sequi, si modo recto itinere præcesserint.)
PLINY THE YOUNGER, *Epistles*. Bk. v, epis. 8.

It is indeed a desirable thing to be well descended, but the glory belongs to our ancestors.
PLUTARCH, *On the Training of Children*.

Birth and ancestry, and that which we have not ourselves achieved, we can scarcely call our own. (Nam genus et proavos et quæ non fecimus ipsi, Vix ea nostra voco.)
OVID, *Metamorphoses*. Bk. xiii, l. 140.

12
Ancestral glory is, as it were, a lamp to posterity. (Majorum gloria posteris quasi lumen est.)
SALLUST, *Jugurtha*. Ch. 85, sec. 23.

13
Brave peers of England, pillars of the state.
SHAKESPEARE, *II Henry VI*. Act i, sc. 1, l. 75.

14
Never unworthy my great ancestors. (Magnorum haud umquam indignus avorum.)
VERGIL, *Æneid*. Bk. xii, l. 649.

Do as your great progenitors have done,
And, by their virtues, prove yourself their son.
DRYDEN, *The Wife of Bath, Her Tale*, l. 398.

15
Bishop Warburton is reported to have said that high birth was a thing which he never knew any one to disparage except those who had it not, and he never knew any one make a boast of it who had anything else to be proud of.
RICHARD WHATELY, *Annotation on Bacon's Essay, Of Humility*.

IV—Ancestry: Its Emptiness

16
Nobility of birth commonly abateth industry; and he that is not industrious envieth him that is. Besides, noble persons cannot go much higher; and he that standeth at a stay when others rise can hardly avoid motions of envy.
FRANCIS BACON, *Essays: Of Nobility*.

Idleness is an appendix to nobility.
ROBERT BURTON, *Anatomy of Melancholy*. Pt. i, sec. ii, mem. 2, subs. 6.

It becomes noblemen to do nothing well.
GEORGE CHAPMAN, *The Gentleman Usher*. Act i, sc. 1.

The nobility think scorn to go in leather aprons.
SHAKESPEARE, *II Henry VI*. Act iv, sc. 2, l. 12.

1 Most lords are feeble and forlorn.
WALTER BAGEHOT, *English Constitution*, p. 122.

Peers are not always gen'rous as well-bred.
COWPER, *Retirement*, l. 597.

All baronets are bad.
W. S. GILBERT, *Ruddigore*. Act i.

When I'm a bad Bart, I will tell taradiddles.
W. S. GILBERT, *Ruddigore*. Act i.

Good families are generally worse than any others.
ANTHONY HOPE, *The Prisoner of Zenda*. Ch. 1.

Earls as goes mad in their castles,
And females what settles their hash.
GEORGE ROBERT SIMS, *Dagonet Ballads: Polly*.

Mongrel beef-witted lord.
SHAKESPEARE, *Troilus and Cressida*. Act ii, sc. 1, l. 14.

This lord . . . who wears his wit in his belly and his guts in his head.
SHAKESPEARE, *Troilus and Cressida*. Act ii, sc. 1, l. 79.

Your lord is a leaden shilling, which you bend every way, and debases the stamp he bears.
WYCHERLEY, *Plain-Dealer*. Act i, sc. 1.

See also under TITLES.

2 Sorry pre-eminence of high descent,
Above the vulgar born, to rot in state!
ROBERT BLAIR, *The Grave*, l. 154.

3 Almost in every kingdom the most ancient families have been at first princes' bastards; their worthiest captains, best wits, greatest scholars, bravest spirits in all our annals, have been base [born].
ROBERT BURTON, *Anatomy of Melancholy*. Pt. ii, sec. ii, mem. 1, subs. 1.

Great families of yesterday we show,
And lords whose parents were the Lord knows who.
DANIEL DEFOE, *The True-Born Englishman*. Pt. i, l. 374.

Who, fond of pedigree, derive
From the most noted whore alive.
MATTHEW GREEN, *The Spleen*, l. 324.

4 So that the branch a goodly verdure flings,
I reck not if an acorn gave it birth.
BYRON, *Don Juan*. Canto xiv, st. 59.

5 The pedigree of honey
Does not concern the bee;
A clover, any time, to him
Is aristocracy.
EMILY DICKINSON, *Poems*. Pt. ii, No. 56.

6 Then what can birth, or mortal men, bestow,
Since floods no higher than their fountains flow?
DRYDEN, *The Wife of Bath, Her Tale*, l. 388.

They talk about their Pilgrim blood,
Their birthright high and holy!
A mountain-stream that ends in mud
Methinks is melancholy.
J. R. LOWELL, *An Interview with Miles Standish*. St. 11.

7 Nor stand so much on your gentility,
Which is an airy, and mere borrowed thing,
From dead men's dust, and bones, and none of yours,
Except you make, or hold it.
BEN JONSON, *Every Man in His Humour*. Act i, sc. 1.

8 What do pedigrees avail? What boots it, Ponticus, to possess ancient blood, and show the painted features of ancestors? (Stemmata quid faciunt? Quid prodest, Pontice, longo Sanguine censeri, pictos ostendere vultus Majorum?)
JUVENAL, *Satires*. Sat. viii, l. 1.

"Your ancient house!" No more—I cannot see
The wondrous merits of a pedigree:
No, Ponticus; nor of a proud display
Of smoky ancestors in wax or clay.
JUVENAL, *Satires*, viii, 1. (Gifford, tr.)

Be not deluded by ancient masks about the hall. Take thy grandfathers and go. (Nec te decipiant veteres circum atria ceræ. Tolle tuos tecum avos!)
OVID, *Amores*. Bk. i, eleg. 8, l. 65.

A hall full of smoke-begrimed busts do not make a nobleman. (Non facit nobilem atrium plenum fumosis imaginibus.)
SENECA, *Epistulæ ad Lucilium*. Epis. xliv, sec. 5.

9 I don't know who my grandfather was; I am much more concerned to know what his grandson will be.
ABRAHAM LINCOLN. (GROSS, *Lincoln's Own Stories*, p. 12.)

10 Somehow I've always had a sort of sneakin'
Idee that peddygrees is purty much
Like monkeys' tails—so long they're apt to weaken
The yap that drags 'em round.
ROBERTUS LOVE, *The Boy from Hodgensville*.

11 Fine B—— observes no other rules
Than those the coterie prize;
She thinks, whilst lords continue fools,
'Tis vulgar to be wise.
EDWARD LOVIBOND, *On a Very Fine Lady*.

12 Sence I've ben here, I've hired a chap to look about for me

To git me a transplantable an' thrifty fem'ly-tree.

J. R. LOWELL, *Biglow Papers*. Ser. ii, No. 3.

1

The man who has not anything to boast of but his illustrious ancestors is like a potato,—the only good belonging to him is under ground.

SIR THOMAS OVERBURY, *Characters*. (1614)

A degenerate nobleman, or one that is proud of his birth, is like a turnip. There is nothing good of him but that which is underground.

SAMUEL BUTLER, *"Characters": A Degenerate Nobleman*. (c. 1660)

2

Aristocracy is always cruel.

WENDELL PHILLIPS, *Speeches: Toussaint L'Ouverture*.

3

A noble fool was never in a fault.

POPE, *January and May*, l. 165.

What woful stuff this madrigal would be
In some starv'd hackney sonnetteer or me!
But let a Lord once own the happy lines,
How the wit brightens! how the style refines!

POPE, *Essay on Criticism*. Pt. ii, l. 218.

'Tis from high life high characters are drawn;
A saint in crape is twice a saint in lawn; . . .
Wise if a minister; but if a king,
More wise, more learn'd, more just, more ev'ry-thing.

POPE, *Moral Essays*. Epis. i, l. 135.

4

But by your fathers' worth if yours you rate,
Count me those only who were good and great.
Go! if your ancient but ignoble blood
Has crept thro' scoundrels ever since the flood,
Go! and pretend your family is young,
Nor own your fathers have been fools so long.
What can ennoble sots, or slaves, or cowards?
Alas! not all the blood of all the *Howards*.

POPE, *Essay on Man*. Epis. iv, l. 209.

No tenth transmitter of a foolish face.

RICHARD SAVAGE, *The Bastard*, l. 7

And ever since the Conquest have been fools.

JOHN WILMOT, EARL OF ROCHESTER, *Artemisia in the Town to Chloe in the Country*.

Of a very old stock a most eminent scion,— . . .
Whose pedigree, traced to earth's earliest years,
Is longer than anything else but their ears.

J. R. LOWELL, *A Fable for Critics*, l. 110.

5

Here and there a cotter's babe is royal-born by right divine;
Here and there my lord is lower than his oxen or his swine.

TENNYSON, *Locksley Hall Sixty Years After*. St. 63.

The castle-bred brat is a senator born,
Or a saint, if religion's in vogue.

CHARLES KINGSLEY, *Saint's Tragedy*. Act ii, sc. 2.

6

Those transparent swindles—transmissible nobility and kingship.

MARK TWAIN, *A Connecticut Yankee at King Arthur's Court*. Ch. 28.

7

Men should press forward in fame's glorious chase;
Nobles look backward, and so lose the race. . . .
They that on glorious ancestors enlarge,
Produce their debt, instead of their discharge.

YOUNG, *Love of Fame*. Satire i, l. 137.

To Virtue's humblest son let none prefer
Vice, though descended from the Conqueror.

YOUNG, *Love of Fame*. Sat. i, l. 141.

V—Ancestry: Noblesse Oblige

8

Relationship compels. (Τὸ . . . συγγενὲς . . . ἐσαναγκάζει.)

ÆSCHYLUS, *Prometheus Bound*, l. 291.

9

If there be any good in nobility, I trow it to be only this, that it imposeth a necessity upon those which are noble, that they should not suffer their nobility to degenerate from the virtues of their ancestors. (Quod si quid est in nobilitate bonum, id esse arbitror solum, ut inposita nobilibus necessitudo videatur ne a majorum virtute degeneret.)

BOËTHIUS, *De Consolatione Philosophæ*. Bk. iii, ch. 6, sec. 25.

10

The nobly born must nobly meet their fate.

EURIPIDES, *Alcmene*. Frag. 100.

11

Superior worth your rank requires;
For that mankind reveres your sires:
If you degenerate from your race,
Their merits heighten your disgrace.

JOHN GAY, *Fables*. Pt. ii, No. 11, l. 43.

12

Noblesse oblige. (Birth compels it. Nobility constrains us. Noble birth imposes the obligation of noble actions.)

DUC DE LEVIS, *Maxims*. No. 73. (1808) Said by the Comte de Laborde to be the first occurrence of the phrase in this form. (*Notice to French Historical Society*, 1865.)

Noblesse oblige; or, superior advantages bind you to larger generosity.

EMERSON, *Letters and Social Aims: Progress of Culture*.

VI—Ancestry: Children of Adam

13

When Adam dalfe and Eve spane
So spire if thou may spede,
Whare was then the pride of man,
That now merres his mede?

RICHARD ROLLE DE HAMPOLE. (*Early English Text Society Reprints*, No. 26, p. 79. c. 1330.) The first line of this quatrain had been long in use as a proverb, but this is its first appearance in English literature.

1
When Adam dolve and Eve span,
Who was then the gentleman?

JOHN BALL, *Text*, used by him for his speech at Blackheath to the rebels in Wat Tyler's insurrection, 12 June, 1381. Ball was afterwards hanged. (WALSINGHAM, *Historia Anglicana;* HUME, *History of England*. Vol. i, ch. 17, note.)

When Adam delved and Eve span,
Where was then the gentleman?
Upstart a churl, and gathered good,
And thence did spring our gentle blood.

JOHN RAY, *English Proverbs*. (1678)

2
Say, when the ground our father Adam tilled,
And mother Eve the humble distaff held,
Who then his pedigree presumed to trace,
Or challenged the prerogative of place?
(Primus Adamus duro cum verterat arva ligone,
Pensaque de vili deceret Eva colo:
Ecquis in hoc poterat vir nobilis orbe videri?
Et modo quisquam alios ante locandus erir?)

FRIEDRICH DEDEKIND, *Grobianus*. Bk. i, sec. 4.

3
That all from Adam first begun,
None but ungodly Woolston doubts,
And that his son, and his son's sons
Were all but ploughmen, clowns and louts.
Each when his rustic pains began,
To merit pleaded equal right,
'Twas only who left off at noon,
Or who went on to work till night.
(D'Adam nous sommes tous enfants,
La preuve en est connue,
Et que tous, nos première parents
Ont mené la charrue.
Mais, las de cultiver enfin
La terre labourée,
L'une a dételé le matin,
L'autre l'après-dinée.)

PHILIPPE DE COULANGES, *L'Origine de la Noblesse*. (Matthew Prior, tr.)

4
As he said in Machiavel, *omnes eodem patre nati,* Adam's sons, conceived all and born in sin, etc. "We are by nature all as one, all alike, if you see us naked; let us wear theirs and they our clothes, and what is the difference?"

ROBERT BURTON, *Anatomy of Melancholy*. Pt. ii, sec. ii, mem. 2.

5
All blood is alike ancient.

THOMAS FULLER, *Gnomologia*. No. 505.

6
Nobles and heralds, by your leave,
Here lies what once was Matthew Prior;
The son of Adam and of Eve:
Can Bourbon or Nassau claim higher?

MATTHEW PRIOR, *Epitaph: Extempore*.

John Carnegie lies here,
Descended from Adam and Eve.
If any can boast of a pedigree higher,
He will willingly give them leave.

UNKNOWN. An ancient Scottish epitaph.

7
Every king springs from a race of slaves, and every slave has had kings among his ancestors.

PLATO, *Thæstetus*. Sec. 174.

8
We have all had the same number of forefathers. (Omnibus nobis totidem ante nos sunt.)

SENECA, *Epistulæ ad Lucilium*. Epis. xliv, sec. 4.

9
Each has his own tree of ancestors, but at the top of all sits Probably Arboreal.

R. L. STEVENSON, *Memories and Portraits: Pastoral*.

10
From yon blue heavens above us bent,
The gardener Adam and his wife
Smile at the claims of long descent.
Howe'er it be, it seems to me
'Tis only noble to be good.
Kind hearts are more than coronets,
And simple faith than Norman blood.

TENNYSON, *Lady Clara Vere de Vere*. St. 7.

VII—Ancestry: Its Beginning

11
My nobility begins in me, but yours ends in you.

IPHICRATES, a shoemaker's son, when reviled by Harmodius for his mean birth. (PLUTARCH, *Apothegms*.)

Very likely; my ancestry begins where yours ends.

Attributed to ALEXANDRE DUMAS, when asked if he were not descended from an ape, a covert sneer at his negro grandmother.

12
I am my own ancestor. (Moi je suis mon ancêtre.)

MARSHAL ANDOCHE JUNOT, when created by Napoleon Duke of Abrantès, and sneeringly asked by one of the old régime what was his ancestry. The whole reply was, "Ah, ma foi, je n'en sais rien; moi je suis mon ancêtre," Faith, I know nothing about it, I am my own ancestor.

Sire, I am my own Rudolph of Hapsburg.

NAPOLEON BONAPARTE, to his prospective father-in-law, the Emperor of Austria, when the latter wished to trace his ancestry to a prince. Rudolph was the founder of the Hapsburg family.

Friend, my patent of nobility comes from Montenotte.

NAPOLEON BONAPARTE, to a genealogist, referring to his first victory.

13
i have often noticed that
ancestors never boast
of the descendants who boast
of ancestors i would
rather start a family than

finish one blood will tell but often
it tells too much
DON MARQUIS, *a roach of the taverns.*

1
The Smiths never had any arms, and have invariably sealed their letters with their thumbs.
SYDNEY SMITH. (*Lady Holland, Memoir.* Vol. i, p. 244.)

2
Curtius Rufus seems to me to be descended from himself.
TIBERIUS. (TACITUS, *Annals.* Bk. xi, ch. 21.)

3
The first king was a successful soldier;
He who serves his country well has no need of ancestors.
(Le premier qui fut roi, fut un soldat heureux;
Qui sert bien son pays, n'a pas besoin d'aïeux.)
VOLTAIRE, *Mérope.* Act i, sc. 3.

Yet what can they see in the longest kingly line in Europe, save that it runs back to a successful soldier?
SCOTT, *Woodstock.* Ch. 37.

4
The stream is brightest at its spring,
And blood is not like wine;
Nor honored less than he who heirs
Is he who founds a line.
J. G. WHITTIER, *Amy Wentworth.* Pt. ii.

VIII—Ancestry: Its End

5
Rarely into the branches of the tree
Doth human worth mount up.
DANTE, *Purgatorio.* Canto vii, l. 122.

The sap which at the root is bred
In trees, through all the boughs is spread;
But virtues which in parents shine
Make not like progress through the line.
EDMUND WALLER, *To Zelinda.*

6
And seldom three descents continue good.
DRYDEN, *The Wife of Bath, Her Tale,* l. 403.

What's ill-got scarce to a third heir descends,
Nor wrongful booty meets with prosperous ends.
(De male quæsitis vix gaudet non tertius hæres,
Nec habet eventus sordida præda bonos.)
THOMAS WALSINGHAM, *Historia Anglicana,* p. 260. Quoted.

Three generations from shirtsleeves to shirtsleeves.
Attributed to ANDREW CARNEGIE, but the nearest approach in his published writings is in a letter in which he says, "Even in Yorkshire the proverb is, 'Three generations from clogs to clogs.'" (HENDRICK, *Life.* Vol. ii, p. 175.)

There's nobbut three generations atween clog and clog.
A Lancashire proverb. (*Notes and Queries,* iv, vii, 472.)

Hence the Lancashire proverb, "Twice clogs, once boots."
SAMUEL SMILES, *Thrift,* p. 292.

7
Little like Tydeus is his father's son. (Ἦ ὀλίγον οἱ παῖδα ἐοικότα γείνατο Τυδεύς.)
HOMER, *Iliad.* Bk. v, l. 800.

He follows his father with unequal steps.
(Sequiturque patrem non passibus æquis.)
VERGIL, *Æneid.* Bk. ii, l. 724.

It is disgraceful when the passers-by exclaim, "O ancient house! alas, how unlike is thy present master to thy former one."
CICERO, *De Officiis.* Bk. i, ch. 39, sec. 139.

8
Who can be called noble who is unworthy of his race, and distinguished in nothing but his name? (Quis enim generosum dixerit hunc qui Indignus genere et præclaro nomine tantum Insignis?)
JUVENAL, *Satires.* Sat. viii, l. 30.

And were thy fathers gentle? that's their praise;
No thanks to thee by whom their name decays.
JUVENAL, *Satires,* viii, 30. (Hall, tr.)

ANGEL

I—Angel: The Guardian Angel

9
Every man hath a good and a bad angel attending on him in particular, all his life long.
ROBERT BURTON, *Anatomy of Melancholy.* Pt. i, sec. ii, mem. 1, subs. 2.

I guess one angel in another's hell:
The truth I shall not know, but live in doubt,
Till my bad angel fire my good one out.
SHAKESPEARE, *The Passionate Pilgrim,* l. 26.

10
Was there no star that could be sent,
No watcher in the firmament,
No angel from the countless host
That loiters round the crystal coast,
Could stoop to heal that only child?
EMERSON, *Threnody.* St. 6.

11
How did he git thar? Angels.
He could never have walked in that storm.
They jest scooped down and toted him
To whar it was safe and warm.
And I think that saving a little child,
And fotching him to his own,
Is a derned sight better business
Than loafing around the Throne.
JOHN HAY, *Little Breeches.*

12
I am thy evil genius, Brutus, and thou shalt see me at Philippi. (Ὁ σός, ὦ Βροῦτε, δαίμων κακός· ὄψει δέ με περὶ Φιλίππους.)
PLUTARCH, *Lives: Cæsar.* Ch. 69, sec. 7. The threat of the spectre which appeared to Brutus in his tent at Abydos, 42 B C., an omen that Caesar's murder was not pleasing to the gods. Brutus answered boldly, "I shall see thee there," and when the spectre reappeared at Philippi, Brutus, having been defeated, "put his naked sword to his breast and so died."

1
A guardian angel o'er his life presiding,
Doubling his pleasures, and his cares dividing.
SAMUEL ROGERS, *Human Life*, l. 353.

Dear and great Angel, wouldst thou only leave
That child, when thou hast done with him, for me!
ROBERT BROWNING, *The Guardian-Angel.*

2
This sight would make him do a desperate turn,
Yea, curse his better angel from his side,
And fall to reprobation.
SHAKESPEARE, *Othello*. Act v, sc. 2, l. 207.

3
How oft do they their silver bowers leave
To come to succour us, that succour want!
SPENSER, *Faerie Queene*. Bk. ii, canto viii, st. 2.

4
Sweet souls around us watch us still,
Press nearer to our side;
Into our thoughts, into our prayers,
With gentle helpings glide.
HARRIET BEECHER STOWE, *The Other World.*

5
Some angel guide my pencil, while I draw,
What nothing less than angel can exceed.
YOUNG, *Night Thoughts*. Night viii, l. 1079.

II—Angel: The Recording Angel

6
A demon holds a book, in which are written the sins of a particular man; an Angel drops on it from a phial, a tear which the sinner had shed in doing a good action, and his sins are washed out.
ALBERIC, MONK OF MONTE-CASSINO. (*Edinburgh Review*, vol. i, p. 67.)

7
But, sad as angels for the good man's sin,
Weep to record, and blush to give it in.
CAMPBELL, *Pleasures of Hope*. Pt. ii, l. 357.

8
When a man dies they who survive him ask what property he has left behind. The angel who bends over the dying man asks what good deeds he has sent before him.
The Koran.

9
There are two angels, that attend unseen
Each one of us, and in great books record
Our good and evil deeds. He who writes down
The good ones, after every action closes
His volume, and ascends with it to God.
The other keeps his dreadful day-book open
Till sunset, that we may repent; which doing,
The record of the action fades away,
And leaves a line of white across the page.
LONGFELLOW, *Christus*. Pt. ii, *The School of Salerno.*

10
There written, all,
Black as the damning drops that fall
From the denouncing Angel's pen
Ere Mercy weeps them out again.
THOMAS MOORE, *Lalla Rookh: Paradise and the Peri*, l. 426.

11
"He shall not die, by G—," cried my uncle Toby. The Accusing Spirit, which flew up to heaven's chancery with the oath, blushed as he gave it in; and the Recording Angel, as he wrote it down, dropped a tear upon the word and blotted it out for ever.
STERNE, *Tristram Shandy*. Bk. vi, ch. 8.

The accusing Byers* "flew up to Heaven's Chancery,"
Blushing like scarlet with shame and concern;
The Archangel took down his tale, and in answer he
Wept—(See the works of the late Mr. Sterne).
Indeed, it is said, a less taking both were in
When, after a lapse of a great many years,
They book'd Uncle Toby five shillings for swearing,
And blotted the fine out again with their tears.
R. H. BARHAM, *Ingoldsby Legends: A Lay of St. Nicholas*. St. 27, 28. (* The Prince of Peripatetic Informers, and the terror of Stage Coachmen, when such things were. Alack! alack! the Railroads have ruined his "vested interest."—Barham's note.)

III—Angels: Their Visits

12
Once at the Angelus (Ere I was dead),
Angels all glorious came to my Bed;
Angels in blue and white crowned on the Head.
AUSTIN DOBSON, *Good-night, Babette!*

13
And he [the angel] said, Let me go, for the day breaketh. And he [Jacob] said, I will not let thee go, except thou bless me.
Old Testament: Genesis, xxxii, 26.

Hold the fleet angel fast until he bless thee.
NATHANIEL COTTON, *To-morrow*, l. 36.

Like the patriarch's angel hold it fast
Till it gives its blessing.
WHITTIER, *My Soul and I.*

14
Be not forgetful to entertain strangers: for thereby some have entertained angels unawares.
New Testament: Hebrews, xiii, 2.

Unbless'd thy hand, if, in this low disguise,
Wander, perhaps, some inmate of the skies.
HOMER, *Odyssey*. Bk. xvii, l. 576. (Pope, tr.)

In this dim world of clouding cares,
We rarely know, till 'wildered eyes
See white wings lessening up the skies,
The angels with us unawares.
GERALD MASSEY, *Ballad of Babe Christabel.*

15
But all God's angels come to us disguised:
Sorrow and sickness, poverty and death,
One after other lift their frowning masks,
And we behold the Seraph's face beneath,

All radiant with the glory and the calm
Of having looked upon the front of God.
J. R. LOWELL, *On the Death of a Friend's Child.*

With silence only as their benediction,
God's angels come
Where, in the shadow of a great affliction,
The soul sits dumb!
WHITTIER, *To My Friend on the Death of His Sister.*

1
An angel stood and met my gaze,
Through the low doorway of my tent;
The tent is struck, the vision stays;—
I only know she came and went.
J. R. LOWELL, *She Came and Went.*

I have no angels left
Now, Sweet, to pray to:
Where you have made your shrine
They are away to.
They have struck Heaven's tent,
And gone to cover you:
Whereso you keep your state
Heaven is pitched over you!
FRANCIS THOMPSON, *A Carrier Song.*

2
For God will deign
To visit oft the dwellings of just men
Delighted, and with frequent intercourse
Thither will send his winged messengers
On errands of supernal grace.
MILTON, *Paradise Lost.* Bk. vii, l. 569.

3
Like angels' visits, short and bright.
JOHN NORRIS, *The Parting.* (c. 1700)

Angels, as 'tis but seldom they appear,
So neither do they make long stay;
They do but visit and away.
JOHN NORRIS, *To the Memory of His Niece.*

Visits
Like those of angels, short and far between.
ROBERT BLAIR, *The Grave.* Pt. ii, l. 586. (1743)

What though my winged hours of bliss have been
Like angel-visits, few and far between?
THOMAS CAMPBELL, *Pleasures of Hope.* Pt. ii, l. 377. (1799)

Mr. Campbell in altering the expression has spoilt it. "Few" and "far between" are the same thing.
WILLIAM HAZLITT, *Lectures on the English Poets.* Hazlitt points out Campbell's indebtedness to Blair, and notes elsewhere that Campbell never forgave him for this bit of literary detective work.

4
And flights of angels sing thee to thy rest!
SHAKESPEARE, *Hamlet.* Act v, sc. 2, l. 371.

5
Around our pillows golden ladders rise,
And up and down the skies,
With winged sandals shod,
The angels come, and go, the Messengers of God!
R. H. STODDARD, *Hymn to the Beautiful.*

IV—Angels: In Heaven

6
I know that they are happy
With their angel-plumage on.
PARK BENJAMIN, *The Departed.*

See also DEATH: "THEY ARE ALL GONE."

7
'Tis only when they spring to Heaven that angels
Reveal themselves to you.
ROBERT BROWNING, *Paracelsus.* Pt. v.

8
This world has angels all too few,
And heaven is overflowing.
S. T. COLERIDGE, *To a Young Lady.*

In heaven an angel is nobody in particular.
BERNARD SHAW, *Maxims for Revolutionists.*

9
We trust, in plumed procession,
For such the angels go,
Rank after rank, with even feet
And uniforms of snow.
EMILY DICKINSON, *Poems.* Pt. i, No. 16.

10
In merest prudence men should teach . . .
That science ranks as monstrous things
Two pairs of upper limbs; so wings—
E'en angels' wings!—are fictions.
AUSTIN DOBSON, *A Fairy Tale.*

11
Writ in the climate of heaven, in the language spoken by angels.
LONGFELLOW, *The Children of the Lord's Supper,* l. 262.

12
How sweetly did they float upon the wings
Of silence through the empty-vaulted night,
At every fall smoothing the raven down
Of darkness till it smiled!
MILTON, *Comus,* l. 249.

The helmed Cherubim,
The sworded Seraphim,
Are seen in glittering ranks with wings display'd.
MILTON, *Hymn on the Nativity,* l. 112.

Hear all ye Angels, progeny of light,
Thrones, Dominations, Princedoms, Virtues, Powers.
MILTON, *Paradise Lost.* Bk. v, l. 600.

13
Look homeward, Angel, now, and melt with ruth.
MILTON, *Lycidas,* l. 163.

As far as angels' ken.
MILTON, *Paradise Lost.* Bk. i, l. 59.

14
Speak ye who best can tell, ye sons of light,
Angels, for ye behold him, and with songs
And choral symphonies, day without night,
Circle his throne rejoicing.
MILTON, *Paradise Lost.* Bk. v, l. 160.

The angels all were singing out of tune,
And hoarse with having little else to do,
Excepting to wind up the sun and moon,
Or curb a runaway young star or two.
BYRON, *The Vision of Judgment.* St. 2.

1
And with the morn those angel faces smile
Which I have loved long since, and lost awhile.

JOHN HENRY NEWMAN, *The Pillar of the Cloud.*

2
All angel now—yet little less than all,
While still a pilgrim in this world below!

SCOTT, *Lord of the Isles: Conclusion,* l. 10. Referring to Harriet, Duchess of Buccleugh.

Sleep on in peace, await thy Maker's will,
Then rise unchanged, and be an Angell still.

UNKNOWN, *Epitaph,* on the tomb of Mary Angell, in St. Mary's church, Nottingham, England.

3
Angels are bright still, though the brightest fell.

SHAKESPEARE, *Macbeth.* Act iv, sc. 3, l. 22.

If angels fight,
Weak men must fall, for heaven still guards the right.

SHAKESPEARE, *Richard II.* Act iii, sc. 2, l. 62.

4
Angels from friendship gather half their joy.

YOUNG, *Night Thoughts.* Night ii, l. 575.

Angels are men of a superior kind;
Angels are men in lighter habit clad.

YOUNG, *Night Thoughts.* Night iv, l. 533.

V—Angels: On Earth

5
When one that holds communion with the skies
Has fill'd his urn where these pure waters rise,
And once more mingles with us meaner things,
'Tis ev'n as if an angel shook his wings.

COWPER, *Charity,* l. 435.

6
We are ne'er like angels till our passion dies.

THOMAS DEKKER, *The Honest Whore.* Pt. ii, act i, sc. 2.

7
Let old Timotheus yield the prize
Or both divide the crown:
He rais'd a mortal to the skies;
She drew an angel down.

DRYDEN, *Alexander's Feast,* l. 167.

8
An angel! or, if not, An earthly paragon!

SHAKESPEARE, *Cymbeline.* Act iii, sc. 6, l. 43.

A ministering angel shall my sister be.

SHAKESPEARE, *Hamlet.* Act v, sc. 1, l. 264.

9
An angel is like you, Kate, and you are like an angel.

SHAKESPEARE, *Henry V.* Act v, sc. 1, l. 110.

Thou hast the sweetest face I ever look'd on.
Sir, as I have a soul, she is an angel.

SHAKESPEARE, *Henry VIII.* Act iv, sc. 1, l. 43.

O, the more angel she,
And you the blacker devil!

SHAKESPEARE, *Othello.* Act v, sc. 2, l. 130.

10
Like outcast spirits, who wait,
And see, through heaven's gate,
Angels within it.

THACKERAY, *The Church Porch.* (*Pendennis.* Ch. 31.)

11
When I see angels in pettycoats I'm always sorry they hain't got wings so they kin quietly fly off whare thay will be appreshiated.

ARTEMUS WARD, *Piccolomini.*

12
Not Angles, but Angels! (Non Angli, sed Angeli!)

Attributed to GREGORY THE GREAT, on seeing some handsome British captives offered for sale at Rome.

To equip a dull, respectable person with wings would be but to make a parody of an angel.

R. L. STEVENSON, *Virginibus Puerisque: Crabbed Age and Youth.*

ANGER

See also Hatred, Passion

I—Anger: Apothegms

13
And being exceedingly mad against them, I persecuted them even unto strange cities.

New Testament: Acts, xxvi, 11.

14
Anger makes dull men witty, but it keeps them poor.

FRANCIS BACON, *Apothegms.* No. 4. Quoted as by Queen Elizabeth.

Few men can afford to be angry.

AUGUSTINE BIRRELL, *Obiter Dicta: Edmund Burke.*

Anger is an expensive luxury in which only men of a certain income can indulge.

GEORGE WILLIAM CURTIS, *Prue and I.* Ch. 6.

Anger costs a man nothing.

BEN JONSON, *Every Man in His Humour.* Act iv. sc. 6.

15
Nine-tenths of mankind are more afraid of violence than of anything else.

WALTER BAGEHOT, *Biographical Studies,* p. 193.

16
Nursing her wrath to keep it warm.

BURNS, *Tam o' Shanter,* l. 12.

17
Your ladyship's absolutely in alt.

GEORGE COLMAN THE ELDER, *The Musical Lady.* Act i.

Come, please be a little less in alt.

MADAME D'ARBLAY, *Camilla.* Bk. ii, ch. 5.

"Hoity toity!" cries Honour, "Madam is in her airs, I protest."

FIELDING, *Tom Jones.* Bk. vii, ch. 8.

Like women's anger, impotent and loud.

DRYDEN, *To Sir Godfrey Kneller,* l. 84.

18
Beware the fury of a patient man.

DRYDEN, *Absalom and Achitophel.* Pt. i, l. 1005

Beware of him that is slow to anger; anger, when it is long in coming, is the stronger when it comes, and the longer kept.
FRANCIS QUARLES, *Enchiridion*. Cent. ii, No. 67.

1
Let not the sun go down upon your wrath.
New Testament: Ephesians, iv, 26.

Anger may repast with thee for an hour, but not repose for a night; the continuance of anger is hatred, the continuance of hatred turns malice. That anger is not warrantable which hath seen two suns.
FRANCIS QUARLES, *Enchiridion*. Cent. ii, No. 60.

2
Anger raiseth invention, but it overheateth the oven.
LORD HALIFAX, *Works*, p. 237.

Anger is never without an argument, but seldom with a good one.
LORD HALIFAX, *Works*, p. 237.

3
Let anger's fire be slow to burn.
GEORGE HERBERT, *Jacula Prudentum*.

4
He has hay on his horns. (Fœnum habet in cornu.)
HORACE, *Satires*. Bk. i, sat. 4, l. 34.

5
The one that fust gits mad's most ollers wrong.
J. R. LOWELL, *Biglow Papers*. Ser. ii, *Mason and Slidell*.

6
We have nettled him. Had we stung him to death it were but justice.
MASSINGER, *Parliament of Love*. Act iii, sc. 1.

7
So frown'd the mighty combatants, that hell
Grew darker at their frown.
MILTON, *Paradise Lost*. Bk. ii, l. 719.

He may look as black as midnight at Martinmas.
SCOTT, *Waverley*. Ch. 48.

8
Inextinguishable rage.
MILTON, *Paradise Lost*. Bk. vi, l. 217.

9
As one disarm'd, his anger all he lost.
MILTON, *Paradise Lost*. Bk. x, l. 945.

No anger find in thee, but pity and ruth.
MILTON, *Sonnets: To a Virtuous Lady*.

10
Like fragile ice, anger in time passes away. (Ut fragilis glacies, interit ira mora.)
OVID, *Ars Amatoria*. Bk. i, l. 374.

11
Biting his thumb to the quick. (Pollice usque ad periculum roso.)
PETRONIUS, *Fragments*. No. 3. Of a man in anger.

So angry it affected my sight. (Ita iracundia obstitit oculis.)
PLAUTUS, *Asinaria*, l. 451. (Act ii, sc. 4.)

12
A soft answer turneth away wrath: but grievous words stir up anger.
Old Testament: Proverbs, xv, 1.

As fire kindled by bellows, so is anger by words.
THOMAS FULLER, *Gnomologia*. No. 677.

13
It is hidden wrath that harms. (Ira quæ tegitur nocet.)
SENECA, *Medea*, l. 153.

I was angry with my friend:
I told my wrath, my wrath did end.
I was angry with my foe:
I told it not, my wrath did grow.
WILLIAM BLAKE, *A Poison Tree*. St. 1.

14
O, that I were
Upon the hill of Basan, to outroar
The horned herd! for I have savage cause.
SHAKESPEARE, *Antony and Cleopatra*. Act iii, sc. 13, l. 126.

Prithee, go hence;
Or I shall show the cinders of my spirits
Through the ashes of my chance.
SHAKESPEARE, *Antony and Cleopatra*. Act v, sc. 2, l. 172.

15
I love to cope him in these sullen fits,
For then he's full of matter.
SHAKESPEARE, *As You Like It*. Act ii, sc. 1, l. 67.

Being once chaf'd, he cannot
Be rein'd again to temperance; then he speaks
What's in his heart.
SHAKESPEARE, *Coriolanus*. Act iii, sc. 3, l. 27.

Never forget what a man says to you when he is angry.
HENRY WARD BEECHER, *Life Thoughts*.

16
It would make a man mad as a buck to be so bought and sold.
SHAKESPEARE, *Comedy of Errors*. Act iii, sc. 1, l. 72.

Anger's my meat; I sup upon myself.
SHAKESPEARE, *Coriolanus*. Act iv, sc. 2, l. 50.

The flash and outbreak of a fiery mind,
A savageness in unreclaimed blood.
SHAKESPEARE, *Hamlet*. Act ii, sc. 1, l. 33.

17
What, drunk with choler?
SHAKESPEARE, *I Henry IV*. Act i, sc. 3, l. 129.

Aggravate your choler.
SHAKESPEARE, *II Henry IV*. Act ii, sc. 4, l. 176.

Let's purge this choler without letting blood.
SHAKESPEARE, *Richard II*. Act i, sc. 1, l. 153.

Be not so hot.
SHAKESPEARE, *Measure for Measure*. Act v, sc. 1, l. 315.

18
Rancour will out.
SHAKESPEARE, *II Henry VI*. Act i, sc. 1, l. 142.

19
O Cassius, you are yoked with a lamb
That carries anger as the flint bears fire;
Who, much enforced, shows a hasty spark,
And straight is cold again.
SHAKESPEARE, *Julius Cæsar*. Act iv, sc. 3, l. 110.

20
Come not between the dragon and his wrath.
SHAKESPEARE, *King Lear*. Act i, sc. 1, l. 124.

Come not within the measure of my wrath.
SHAKESPEARE, *The Two Gentlemen of Verona*. Act v, sc. 4, l. 127.

1
The brain may devise laws for the blood, but a hot temper leaps o'er a cold decree.
SHAKESPEARE, *The Merchant of Venice*. Act i, sc. 2, l. 19.

High stomach'd are they both, and full of ire,
In rage deaf as the sea, hasty as fire.
SHAKESPEARE, *Richard II*. Act i, sc. 1, l. 18.

2
Put not another sin upon my head
By urging me to fury.
SHAKESPEARE, *Romeo and Juliet*. Act v, sc. 3, l. 62.

3
He chew'd
The thrice-turn'd cud of wrath, and cook'd his spleen.
TENNYSON, *The Princess*. Pt. i, st. 5.

4
What vexed and riled him (to use his own expression), was the infernal indifference . . . of Clavering.
THACKERAY, *Pendennis*. Ch. 64.

Thar ain't no sense in gittin' riled.
BRET HARTE, *Jim*.

II—Anger: Its Virtue

5
The tigers of wrath are wiser than the horses of instruction.
WILLIAM BLAKE, *Proverbs of Hell*.

6
Anger edgeth valour.
JOHN CLARKE, *Parœmiologia*, 178.

Valour's whetstone, anger,
Which sets an edge upon the sword, and makes it
Cut with a spirit.
THOMAS RANDOLPH, *The Muses' Looking-Glass*. Act iii, sc. 2.

7
Severity is allowable where mildness is in vain. (La violence est juste où la douceur est vaine.)
CORNEILLE, *Héraclius*. Act i, sc. 2.

8
Anger is one of the sinews of the soul; he that wants it hath a maimed mind.
THOMAS FULLER, *The Holy State: Of Anger*.

9
His nose should pant and his lip should curl,
His cheeks should flame and his brow should furl,
His bosom should heave and his heart should glow,
And his fist be ever ready for a knock-down blow.
W. S. GILBERT, *H. M. S. Pinafore*. Act i.

His energetic fist
Should be ready to resist
A dictatorial word.
W. S. GILBERT, *H. M. S. Pinafore*. Act i.

10
Anger, far sweeter than trickling honey, rises like smoke in the breasts of men.
HOMER, *Iliad*. Bk. xviii, l. 108.

11
Anger in its time and place
May assume a kind of grace.
It must have some reason in it,
And not last beyond a minute.
CHARLES AND MARY LAMB, *Anger*.

12
The flame of anger, bright and brief,
Sharpens the barb of love.
W. S. LANDOR, *Miscellaneous Poems*. No. 66.

13
Every normal man must be tempted, at times, to spit on his hands, hoist the black flag, and begin slitting throats.
H. L. MENCKEN, *Prejudices*. Ser. i, p. 90.

14
However weak the hand, anger gives it strength. (Quamlibet infirmas adjuvat ira manus.)
OVID, *Amores*. Bk. i, eleg. 7, l. 66.

Anger brings back his strength. (Ac vim suscitat ira.)
VERGIL, *Æneid*. Bk. v, l. 454.

Their rage supplies them with weapons. (Furor arma ministrat.)
VERGIL, *Æneid*. Bk. i, l. 150.

15
Touch me with noble anger!
SHAKESPEARE, *King Lear*. Act ii, sc. 4, l. 279.

'Tis the noblest mood
That takes least hold on anger; those faint hearts
That hold least fire are fain to show it first.
SWINBURNE, *Bothwell*. Act ii, sc. 4.

Anger is a noble infirmity.
MARTIN F. TUPPER, *Of Hatred and Anger*.

III—Anger: Its Folly

16
The angry man always thinks he can do more than he can. (Iratus semper plus putat posse facere quam possit.)
ALBERTANO OF BRESCIA, *Liber Consolationis*.

He that asketh counsel of himself, certes he must be without ire, for many causes. The first is this: he that hath great ire and wrath in himself, he weeneth alway that he may do things that he may not do. And secondly, he that is irate and wroth, he may not well deem, and he that may not well deem, may not well counsel.
CHAUCER, *The Tale of Melibeus*. Sec. 18.

17
The thing I pity most
In men is—action prompted by surprise
Of anger.
ROBERT BROWNING, *A Forgiveness*.

18
He that strives not to stem his anger's tide,
Does a wild horse without a bridle ride.
COLLEY CIBBER, *Love's Last Shift*. Act iii, sc. 7.

A man in a passion rides a mad horse.
BENJAMIN FRANKLIN, *Poor Richard*, 1749.

When a man grows angry, his reason rides out.
THOMAS FULLER, *Gnomologia*. No. 5533.

When anger rushes, unrestrained, to action,
Like a hot steed, it stumbles on its way.
RICHARD SAVAGE, *Sir Thomas Overbury*.

Anger is like
A full-hot horse, who being allow'd his way,
Self-mettle tires him.
SHAKESPEARE, *Henry VIII*. Act i, sc. 1, l. 132.

1
Rage supplies all with arms. When an angry man thirsts for blood, anything will serve him as a spear. (Omnibus armatur rabies. Pro cuspide ferri Cuncta volant, dum dextra ferox in vulnera sævit.)
CLAUDIAN, *Rimanti Telum Ira Facit*, l. 2.

Anger seeks its prey,—
Something to tear with sharp-edged tooth and claw.
GEORGE ELIOT, *Spanish Gypsy*. Bk. i.

2
Anger and folly walk cheek by jole; repentance treads on both their heels.
BENJAMIN FRANKLIN, *Poor Richard*, 1741.

3
Act nothing in furious passion; it's putting to sea in a storm.
THOMAS FULLER, *Introductio ad Prudentiam*.

Anger is a sworn enemy.
THOMAS FULLER, *Gnomologia*. No. 793.

4
He who curbs not his anger will wish undone that which vexation and wrath prompted. (Qui non moderabitur iræ, Infectum volet esse, dolor quod suaserit et mens.)
HORACE, *Epistles*. Bk. i, epis. 2, l. 59.

5
Anger is momentary madness. (Ira furor brevis est.)
HORACE, *Epistles*. Bk. i, epis. ii, l. 62.

Anger sets the house on fire; . . . it is a short madness, and an eternal enemy to discourse and sober counsels and fair conversation.
JEREMY TAYLOR, *Sermons*.

6
Says he, "I reckon I'm a ding-dang fool
For gettin' het up when I might stay cool:
If you are a hoss—then I'm a mule,"
Under the Joshua tree.
HENRY H. KNIBBS, *Under the Joshua Tree*.

7
Every stroke our fury strikes is sure to hit ourselves at last.
WILLIAM PENN, *Some Fruits of Solitude*, 57.

Anger punishes itself.
THOMAS FULLER, *Gnomologia*. No. 799.

To be angry is to revenge the faults of others upon ourselves.
POPE, *Thoughts on Various Subjects*.

8
"All this is madness," cries a sober sage:
But who, my friend, has reason in his rage?
POPE, *Moral Essays*. Epis. iii, l. 151.

9
Anger and haste hinder good counsel.
H. G. BOHN, *Handbook of Proverbs*, p. 313.

Angry men seldom want woe.
JOHN RAY, *English Proverbs*.

10
Anger is like those ruins which break themselves upon what they fall. (Ira ruinis simillima, quæ super id quod oppressere, franguntur.)
SENECA, *De Ira*. Bk. i, sec. 1.

11
Never anger Made good guard for itself.
SHAKESPEARE, *Antony and Cleopatra*. Act iv, sc. 1, l. 9.

12
Give not reins to your inflamed passions; take time and a little delay; impetuosity manages all things badly.
STATIUS, *Thebais*. Bk. x, l. 703.

13
Fury and anger carry the mind away. (Furor iraque mentem præcipitant.)
VERGIL, *Æneid*. Bk. ii, l. 316.

14
The elephant is never won with anger,
Nor must that man who would reclaim a lion
Take him by the teeth.
JOHN WILMOT, *Valentinian*. Act i, l. 1.

IV—Anger: Its Control

15
Anybody can become angry—that is easy; but to be angry with the right person, and to the right degree, and at the right time, and for the right purpose, and in the right way—that is not within everybody's power and is not easy.
ARISTOTLE, *Nicomachean Ethics*. Bk. ii, ch. 9.

16
Remember, when you are angry, to say or do nothing until you have repeated the four-and-twenty letters to yourself.
ATHENODORUS, to Cæsar Augustus. (PLUTARCH, *Lives: Cæsar Augustus*.)

Take a little time—count five-and-twenty, Tattycoram.
CHARLES DICKENS, *Little Dorrit*. Pt. i, ch. 14.

When angry, count ten before you speak; if very angry, an hundred.
THOMAS JEFFERSON, *Writings*. Vol. xvi, p. 111.

While one with moderate haste might tell a hundred.
SHAKESPEARE, *Hamlet*. Act i, sc. 2, l. 238.

When angry, count four; when very angry, swear.
MARK TWAIN, *Pudd'nhead Wilson's Calendar*.

See also under SELF-CONTROL.

17
Truly to moderate your mind and speech when you are angry, or else to hold your peace, betokens no ordinary nature. (Moderari vero et animo tacere, . . . est non mediocris ingenii.)
CICERO, *Epistolæ ad Quintum Fratrem*. Bk. i, ch. 1, sec. 13.

1
A man should study ever to keep cool. He makes his inferiors his superiors by heat.
EMERSON, *Uncollected Lectures: Social Aims.*

2
Whenever you are angry, be assured, that it is not only a present evil, but that you have increased a habit, and added fuel to a fire. . . . If you would not be of an angry temper, then, do not feed the habit. Give it nothing to help its increase. Be quiet at first, and reckon the days in which you have not been angry. "I used to be angry every day; now every other day; then every third and fourth day." And if you miss it so long as thirty days, offer a sacrifice of thanksgiving to God.
EPICTETUS, *Discourses.* Bk. ii, ch. 18.

3
Place a curb and drag on your wrath. (Pone iræ frena modumque.)
JUVENAL, *Satires.* Sat. viii, l. 88.

4
When thou art above measure angry, bethink thee how momentary is man's life.
MARCUS AURELIUS, *Meditations.* Bk. xi, ch. 18, sec. 6.

Bethink thee how much more grievous are the consequences of our anger than the acts which arouse it.
MARCUS AURELIUS, *Meditations.* Bk. xi, ch. 18, sec. 8.

Let this truth be present to thee in the excitement of anger, that to be moved by passion is not manly, but that mildness and gentleness, as they are more human, so also are they more manly.
MARCUS AURELIUS, *Meditations.* Bk. xi, ch. 18, sec. 10.

5
Never to master one's anger is a mark of intemperance and lack of training; but always to do so is difficult, and for some impossible.
PLUTARCH, *Lives: Solon.* Sec. 21.

6
The greatest remedy for anger is delay. (Maximum remedium est iræ mora.)
SENECA, *De Ira.* Bk. ii, sec. 28.

ANGLING, see Fishing

ANIMAL

7
God made all the creatures and gave them our love and our fear,
To give sign, we and they are his children, one family here.
ROBERT BROWNING, *Saul.* St. vi.

8
Animals are such agreeable friends—they ask no questions, they pass no criticisms.
GEORGE ELIOT, *Scenes of Clerical Life: Mr. Gilfil's Love Story.*

9
No flocks, that range the valley free,
To slaughter I condemn;
Taught by that Power that pities me,
I learn to pity them.
GOLDSMITH, *A Ballad.* (*Vicar of Wakefield.* Ch. 8.)

10
Beasts of each kind their fellows spare,
Bear lives in amity with bear.
SAMUEL JOHNSON, *The Rambler,* No. 160. (After Juvenal.) See 1955:11.

Beasts, urged by us, their fellow beasts pursue,
And learn of man each other to undo.
POPE, *Windsor Forest,* l. 123.

Who ever knew an honest brute
At law his neighbour prosecute? . . .
Brutes never meet in bloody fray,
Nor cut each others' throats, for pay.
GOLDSMITH, *The Logicians Refuted.*

11
Scripture foretells for them [animals] a "glorious liberty," and we are assured that the compassion of heaven will not be wanting to them.
JOHN KEBLE, *Lectures on Poetry.* No. 19. (1841)

All animals are equal, but some animals are more equal than others.
GEORGE ORWELL, *Animal Farm.* Ch. 10. (1945)

12
The cattle upon a thousand hills.
Old Testament: Psalms, l, 10.

The cattle are grazing,
Their heads never raising:
There are forty feeding like one!
WORDSWORTH, *Written in March.*

13
The beasts, which nature has fashioned grovelling and slaves to the belly. (Quæ natura prona atque ventri obœdientia finxit.)
SALLUST, *Catiline,* sec. 1.

14
Nature teaches beasts to know their friends.
SHAKESPEARE, *Coriolanus.* Act ii, sc. 1, l. 6.

15
A beast, that wants discourse of reason.
SHAKESPEARE, *Hamlet.* Act i, sc. 2, l. 150.

He is only an animal, only sensible in the duller parts.
SHAKESPEARE, *Love's Labour's Lost.* Act iv, sc. 2, l. 27.

Like brute-beasts that have no understanding.
Book of Common Prayer: Solemnization of Matrimony.

16
Since men prove beasts, let beasts bear gentle minds.
SHAKESPEARE, *The Rape of Lucrece,* l. 1148.

17
The behaviour of men to the lower animals, and their behaviour to each other, bear a constant relationship.
HERBERT SPENCER, *Social Statics.* Pt. iv, ch. 30, sec. 2.

18
Even savage animals, if kept shut up, forget their courage. (Etiam fera animalia, si clausa teneas, virtutis obliviscuntur.)
TACITUS, *History.* Bk. iv, sec. 64.

1
I envy not the beast that takes
His license in the field of time,
Unfetter'd by the sense of crime,
To whom a conscience never wakes.
TENNYSON, *In Memoriam*. Pt. xxvii.

2
Hurt not animals.
TRIPTOLEMUS, *Precepts*. (PLUTARCH.)

A righteous man regardeth the life of his beast.
Old Testament: Proverbs, xii, 10.

Physiological experiment on animals is justifiable for real investigation, but not for mere damnable and detestable curiosity.
DARWIN, *Letter to E. Ray Lankester*.

3
I think I could turn and live with animals, they are so placid and self-contain'd,
I stand and look at them long and long.
They do not sweat and whine about their condition,
They do not lie awake in the dark and weep for their sins,
They do not make me sick discussing their duty to God,
Not one is dissatisfied, not one is demented with the mania of owning things,
Not one kneels to another, nor to his kind that lived thousands of years ago,
Not one is respectable or unhappy over the whole earth.
WALT WHITMAN, *Song of Myself*. Sec. 32.

4
Behold a beast of nature black;
When one attacks it, it fights back!
(Cet animal est très méchant:
Quand on l'attaque il se defend.)
UNKNOWN, *La Ménagerie*. A burlesque upon a passage in Walckenaer's *Histoire Générale des Voyages:* "Ces animaux sont si furieux, qu'ils se défendent contre ceux qui les attaquent."

ANTICIPATION, see Expectation

ANTIPATHY, see Dislike

ANTIQUITY

See also Past

I—Antiquity: Definitions

5
Antiquities are history defaced, or some remnants of history which have casually escaped the shipwrecks of time.
BACON, *Advancement of Learning*. Bk. ii.

6
And to speak truly, "Antiquitas sæculi juventus mundi," These times are the ancient times, when the world is ancient, and not those which we account ancient ordine retrogrado, by a computation backward from ourselves.
BACON, *Advancement of Learning*. Bk. i.

As in the little, so in the great world, reason will tell you that old age or antiquity is to be accounted by the farther distance from the beginning and the nearer approach to the end, —the times wherein we now live being in propriety of speech the most ancient since the world's creation.
GEORGE HAKEWILL, *An Apologie or Declaration of the Power and Providence of God in the Government of the World.* (1627)

For as old age is that period of life most remote from infancy, who does not see that old age in this universal man ought not to be sought in the times nearest his birth, but in those most remote from it?
PASCAL, *Treatise on Vacuum: Preface*.

All this cant about our ancestors is merely an abuse of words. . . . We are the only white-bearded, silver-headed ancients, who have treasured up, and are prepared to profit by, all the experience human life can supply.
SYDNEY SMITH, *Peter Plymley Letters*. No. 5.

It is worthy of remark that a thought which is often quoted from Francis Bacon occurs in [Giordano] Bruno's *Cena di Cenere*, published in 1564: I mean the notion that the later times are more aged than the earlier.
WILLIAM WHEWELL, *Philosophy of the Inductive Sciences*. Vol. ii, p. 198.

We are Ancients of the earth,
And in the morning of the times.
TENNYSON, *The Day Dream: Envoi*.

7
In the morning of the world
When earth was nigher heaven than now.
ROBERT BROWNING, *Pippa Passes*. Pt. iii.

8
Age shakes Athena's tower, but spares grey Marathon.
BYRON, *Childe Harold*. Canto ii, st. 88.

9
An acute and experienced critic of antiques.
(Subtilis veterum judex et callidus.)
HORACE, *Satires*. Bk. ii, sat. 7, l. 101.

Critics in rust.
ADDISON, *Essays: Ancient Medals*.

Because thou prizest things that are
Curious and unfamiliar.
ROBERT HERRICK, *Oberon's Feast*.

With sharpen'd sight pale antiquaries pore,
Th' inscription value, but the rust adore.
This the blue varnish, that the green endears,
The sacred rust of twice ten hundred years!
POPE, *Epistle to Mr. Addison*, l. 35.

My copper-lamps, at any rate,
For being true antique, I bought;
Yet wisely melted down my plate,
On modern models to be wrought;
And trifles I alike pursue,
Because they're old, because they're new.
MATTHEW PRIOR, *Alma*. Canto iii.

10
The ancient and honourable.
Old Testament: Isaiah, ix, 15.

1
It was a mighty while ago.
BEN JONSON, *Every Man in His Humour*. Act i, sc. 3.

2
It seems to me much harder to be a modern than an ancient. (Il me semble beaucoup plus difficile d'être un moderne que d'être un ancien.)
JOUBERT, *Pensées*. No. 233.

3
Asleep in lap of legends old.
KEATS, *The Eve of St. Agnes*. St. 15.

This—all this—was in the olden
Time long ago.
EDGAR ALLAN POE, *The Haunted Palace*.

The spirit of antiquity.
WORDSWORTH, *Bruges*.

4
Antiquity! thou wondrous charm, what art thou? that, being nothing, art everything! When thou *wert*, thou wert not antiquity—then thou wert nothing, but hadst a remoter *antiquity*, as thou calledst it, to look back to with blind veneration; thou thyself being to thyself flat, jejune, *modern!*
LAMB, *Essays of Elia: Oxford in the Vacation*.

5
In ancient times all things were cheap.
MARTIN PARKER, *Roxburghe Ballads: An Excellent New Medley*.

6
Remove not the ancient landmark.
Old Testament: Proverbs, xxii, 28; xxiii, 10.

7
Antiquity is not always a mark of verity.
JOHN RAY, *English Proverbs*.

8
Miniver loved the Medici,
Albeit he had never seen one;
He would have sinned incessantly
Could he have been one.
E. A. ROBINSON, *Miniver Cheevy*.

9
In the dark backward and abysm of time.
SHAKESPEARE, *The Tempest*. Act i, sc. 2, l. 50.

10
Thou wert dead, and buried and embalmed,
Ere Romulus and Remus had been suckled:
Antiquity appears to have begun
Long after that primeval race was run.
HORACE SMITH, *Address to a Mummy*.

11
For now I see the true old times are dead,
When every morning brought a noble chance,
And every chance brought out a noble knight.
TENNYSON, *The Passing of Arthur*, l. 397.

A goodly place, a goodly time,
For it was in the golden prime
Of good Haroun Alraschid.
TENNYSON, *Recollections of the Arabian Nights*.

12
Nor rough, nor barren, are the winding ways
Of hoar antiquity, but strewn with flowers.
THOMAS WARREN, *Written on a Blank Leaf of Dugdale's Monasticon*.

II—Antiquity: Praise and Criticism

See also Age: The Age

13
They that reverence too much old times are but a scorn to the new.
FRANCIS BACON, *Essays: Of Innovations*.

14
Veneration of antiquity is congenial to the human mind.
EDMUND BURKE, *Tracts on the Popery Laws*. Ch. iii, pt. 2.

Our admiration of the antique is not admiration of the old, but of the natural.
EMERSON, *Essays, First Series: History*.

15
Speak of the moderns without contempt, and of the ancients without idolatry; judge them all by their merits, and not by their age.
LORD CHESTERFIELD, *Letters*, 22 Feb., 1748.

16
O, to bring back the great Homeric time,
The simple manners and the deeds sublime:
When the wise Wanderer, often foiled by Fate,
Through the long furrow drave the ploughshare straight.
MORTIMER COLLINS, *Letter to Benjamin Disraeli*, 1869.

17
Be eloquent in praise of the very dull old days which have long since passed away,
And convince 'em, if you can, that the reign of good Queen Anne was Culture's palmiest day.
W. S. GILBERT, *Patience*. Act i.

The idiot who praises, with enthusiastic tone,
All centuries but this and every country but his own.
W. S. GILBERT, *The Mikado*. Act i.

He disdaineth all things above his reach, and preferreth all countries before his own.
SIR THOMAS OVERBURY, *Characters: An Affectate Traveler*.

18
The fleets of Nineveh and Tyre
Are down with Davy Jones, Esquire,
And all the oligarchies, kings,
And potentates that ruled these things
Are gone! But cheer up; don't be sad;
Think what a lovely time they had!
ARTHUR GUITERMAN, *Elegy*.

19
You praise the fortune and manners of the men of old, and yet, if on a sudden some god were for taking you back to those days, you would refuse every time.
HORACE, *Satires*. Bk. ii, sat. 7, l. 23.

To look back to antiquity is one thing; to go back to it is another.
C. C. COLTON, *Lacon: Reflections*. No. 148.

20
With weeping and with laughter
Still is the story told,

How well Horatius kept the bridge
In the brave days of old.
MACAULAY, *Horatius*. St. 70.

1
Whoever saw old age which did not praise the past time, and blame the present? (Qui veid jamais vieillesse qui ne louast le temps passé, et ne blamast le present?)
MONTAIGNE, *Essays*. Bk. ii, ch. 13.

2
Let ancient times delight other folk; I rejoice that I was not born till now; this age suits my nature. (Prisca juvent alios: ego me nunc denique natum Gratulor: hæc ætas moribus apta meis.)
OVID, *Ars Amatoria*. Bk. iii, l. 121.

The good of ancient times let others state;
I think it lucky I was born so late.
OVID, *Ars Amatoria*, iii, 121. (Sydney Smith, tr.)

We praise the past, but use our present years. (Laudamus veteres, sed nostris utimur annis.)
OVID, *Fasti*. Bk. i, l. 225.

Praise they that will times past, I joy to see
My self now live: this age best pleaseth me.
ROBERT HERRICK, *The Present Time Best Pleaseth*.

3
We extol ancient things, regardless of our own age. (Vetera extollimus, recentium incuriosi.)
TACITUS, *Annals*. Bk. ii, sec. 88.

The fault lies in the carping spirit of mankind, that we are always praising what is old and scorning what is new. (Vitio autem malignitatis humanæ vetera semper in laude, præsentia in fastidio esse.)
TACITUS, *Dialogus de Oratoribus*. Sec. 18.

Antiquity surrenders, defeated by new things. (Cedit rerum novitate extrusa vetustas.)
LUCRETIUS, *De Rerum Natura*. Bk. iii, l. 964.

ANVIL

4
Men's hammers break, God's anvil stands.
SAMUEL V. COLE, *The Unthwarted Plan*.

5
The noise of the hammer and the anvil is ever in his ears.
Apocrypha: Ecclesiasticus, xxxviii, 28.

6
When you are an anvil, hold you still;
When you are a hammer, strike your fill.
JOHN FLORIO, *Second Frutes*, 101. (1591)

7
The anvil fears no blows.
THOMAS FULLER, *Gnomologia*. No. 4398.

The anvil is not afraid of the hammer.
C. H. SPURGEON, *John Ploughman*. Ch. 21.

8
Thou must (in commanding and winning, or serving and losing, suffering or triumphing) be either anvil or hammer.
GOETHE, *Der Gross-Cophta*. Act ii.

In this world a man must either be anvil or hammer.
LONGFELLOW, *Hyperion*. Bk. iv, ch. 7.

In the struggle between nationalities, one nation is the hammer and the other the anvil: one is the victor and the other the vanquished.
BERNHARD VON BÜLOW, *Imperial Germany*.

9
Every man who strikes blows for power, for influence, for institutions, for the right, must be just as good an anvil as he is a hammer.
HOLLAND, *Gold-Foil: Anvils and Hammers*.

10
For all your days prepare,
And meet them all alike:
When you are the anvil, bear—
When you are the hammer, strike.
EDWIN MARKHAM, *Preparedness*.

11
Lay me on an anvil, O God.
Beat me and hammer me into a crowbar.
Let me pry loose old walls;
Let me lift and loosen old foundations.
CARL SANDBURG, *Prayers of Steel*.

12
For a hard anvil, a hammer of feathers.
WODROEPHE, *Spared Houres*, 508. (1623)

ANXIETY, see Fear, Worry

APE

13
He doth like the ape, that the higher he climbs the more he shows his ars.
FRANCIS BACON, *Promus*. No. 924.

The higher the ape goes, the more he shows his tail.
GEORGE HERBERT, *Jacula Prudentum*. This is a proverb in all languages: Italian, "Tu fai come la simia, chi più va in alto più mostra il culo"; French, "Plus le singe s'elève, plus il montre son cul pelé"; German, "Je höher der Affe steigt, je mehr er den Hintern zeigt."

'Tis not till the ape has mounted the tree that she shows her tail so plain.
READE, *The Cloister and the Hearth*. Ch. 52.

As free as an ape is of his tail.
JOHN RAY, *English Proverbs*, 205.

14
An old ape has an old eye.
RICHARD BROME, *Damoiselle*. Act iii, sc. 2.

15
The ape, vilest of beasts, how like to us! (Simia, quam similis turpissuma bestia, nobis!)
ENNIUS. (CICERO, *De Natura Deorum*. Bk. i, ch. 35.)

16
It is a trite proverb that an ape will be an ape, though clad in purple.
ERASMUS, *Praise of Folly*, 23.

An ape's an ape, a varlet's a varlet,
Tho' they be clad in silk or scarlet.
THOMAS FULLER, *Gnomologia*. No. 6391.

Howsoever clothed like an ape in purple.
SIR JOHN HARINGTON, *Ulysses Upon Ajax*, 18.

Apes are apes, though clothed in scarlet.
BEN JONSON, *The Poetaster*. Act v, sc. 3.

An ape's an ape though he wears a gold ring.
JOHN RAY, *English Proverbs*.

1
Apes are never more beasts than when they wear men's clothes.
THOMAS FULLER, *Gnomologia*. No. 807.

An ape is ne'er so like an ape,
As when he wears a doctor's cap.
THOMAS FULLER, *Gnomologia*. No. 6382.

Though he endeavour all he can,
An ape will never be a man.
GEORGE WITHER, *First Lottery*. Emblem 14.

2
More new-fangled than an ape; more giddy in my desires than a monkey.
SHAKESPEARE, *As You Like It*. Act iv, sc. 1, l. 153.

3
I must dance barefoot on her wedding day,
And for your love to her, lead apes in hell.
SHAKESPEARE, *The Taming of the Shrew*. Act ii, sc. 1, l. 33. (1596)

'Tis an old proverb, and you know it well,
That women dying maids lead apes in hell.
UNKNOWN, *The London Prodigal*. Act i, sc. 2. (1605)

I'd rather die Maid, and lead apes in Hell,
Than wed an inmate of Silenus' cell.
RICHARD BRATHWAITE, *English Gentelman and Gentelwoman*. (1640)

Miss, you may say what you please; but faith you'll never lead apes in hell.
SWIFT, *Polite Conversation*. Dial. 1.

I'm sadly afraid that she died an old maid, . . .
So they say she is now leading apes.
R. H. BARHAM, *Bloudie Jacke*.

APOLOGY, see Excuse

APPAREL, see Dress

APPARITION, see Ghost

APPEARANCE

I—Appearance: Its Value

4
Personal beauty is a greater recommendation than any letter of introduction. (Τὸ κάλλος παντὸς ἐπιστολίου συστατικώτερον.)
ARISTOTLE. (DIOGENES LAERTIUS, *Aristotle*. Bk. v, sec. 18.)

It was the saying of an ancient philosopher, which I find some of our writers have ascribed to Queen Elizabeth, that a good face is a letter of recommendation.
ADDISON, *The Spectator*, 13 Nov., 1711.

5
A beautiful face is a silent commendation. (Formosa facies muta commendatio est.)
BACON, *Ornamenta Rationalia*. No. 12.

Whosoever hath a good presence and a good fashion, carries continual letters of recommendation.
ISABELLA OF SPAIN. (BACON, *Apothegms*. No. 99.)

Good looks are a great recommendation in the business of mankind. (La beauté est une pièce de grande recommendation au commerce des hommes.)
MONTAIGNE, *Essays*. Bk. ii, ch. 17.

A pleasing countenance is no slight advantage. (Auxilium non leve vultus habet.)
OVID, *Epistulæ ex Ponto*. Bk. ii, epis. 8, l. 54.

A comely face is a silent recommendation. (Formosa facies muta commendatio est.)
PUBLILIUS SYRUS, *Sententiæ*. No. 207.

Though you cannot know wine by the barrel, a good appearance is a letter of recommendation.
C. H. SPURGEON, *John Ploughman*. Ch. 3.

An honest good look covereth many faults.
THOMAS FULLER, *Gnomologia*. No. 609.

6
To be plain with you, friend, you don't carry in your countenance a letter of recommendation.
DICKENS, *Barnaby Rudge*. Ch. 2.

That there is falsehood in his looks,
I must and will deny;
They say their master is a knave—
And sure they do not lie.
BURNS, *The Parson's Looks*.

7
If a good face is a letter of recommendation, a good heart is a letter of credit.
BULWER-LYTTON, *What Will He Do With It?* Bk. ii, ch. 11, title.

8
His was the lofty port, the distant mien,
That seems to shun the sight, and awes if seen.
BYRON, *The Corsair*. Canto i, st. 16.

9
There is a great deal in the first impressions.
CONGREVE, *Way of the World*. Act iv, sc. 1.

10
For what is form, or what is face,
But the soul's index, or its case?
NATHANIEL COTTON, *Pleasure*.

The outward forms the inward man reveal,—
We guess the pulp before we cut the peel.
O. W. HOLMES, *A Rhymed Lesson*, l. 418.

11
Appearance, Sir, bears away the bell, almost in everything.
JOHN GAY, *Wife of Bath*. Act iv, sc. 1.

12
Beauty itself doth of itself persuade
The eyes of men without an orator.
SHAKESPEARE, *The Rape of Lucrece*, l. 29.

13
Even virtue is fairer in a fair body. (Gratior et pulchro veniens in corpore virtus.)
VERGIL, *Æneid*. Bk. v, l. 344.

14
All is not false that seems at first a lie.
ROBERT SOUTHEY, *St. Gualberto*. St. 28.

15
It is only shallow people who do not judge by appearances.
OSCAR WILDE, *Picture of Dorian Gray*. Ch. 2.

After all, you can't expect men not to judge by appearances.
ELLEN GLASGOW. *The Sheltered Life*, p. 15.

Hit look lak sparrer-grass, hit feel like sparrer-grass, hit tas'e lak sparrer-grass, en I bless ef 'taint sparrer-grass.
JOEL CHANDLER HARRIS, *Nights with Uncle Remus*. Ch. 27.

II—Appearance: Its Deceitfulness

1
We should look to the mind, and not to the outward appearance. (Ἀφορᾶν οὖν, δεῖ εἰς τὸν νοῦν, καὶ μὴ εἰς τὴν ὄψιν.)
ÆSOP, *Fables*.

2
Men are valued not for what they are, but for what they seem to be.
BULWER-LYTTON, *Money*. Act i, sc. 1.

Think not I am what I appear.
BYRON, *The Bride of Abydos*. Canto i, st. 12.

3
Habit maketh no monk, ne wearing of gilt spurs maketh no knight.
THOS. USK, *Testament of Love*. Bk. ii. (c. 1387)

A holy habit cleanseth not a foul soul.
GEORGE HERBERT, *Jacula Prudentum*.
See also under MONK.

4
Good and bad men are each less so than they seem.
S. T. COLERIDGE, *Table Talk*, 19 Apr., 1830.

5
They take chalk for cheese, as the saying is.
NICHOLAS GRIMAUD, *Three Books of Duties to Marcus His Son: Preface*.

6
We are deceived by the appearance of right. (Decipimur specie recti.)
HORACE, *Ars Poetica*, l. 25.

7
Under this rough exterior lies hid a mighty genius. (Ingenium ingens Inculto latet hoc sub corpore.)
HORACE, *Satires*. Bk. i, sat. 3, l. 33.

It follows not, because
The hair is rough, the dog's a savage one.
SHERIDAN KNOWLES, *The Daughter*. Act i, sc. 1.

Mellow nuts have hardest rind.
SCOTT, *Lord of the Isles*. Canto iii, st. 21.

8
Judge not according to the appearance.
New Testament: John, vii, 24.

Beware, as long as you live, of judging people by appearances. (Garde-toi, tant que tu vivras, De juger des gens sur la mine.)
LA FONTAINE, *Fables*. Bk. vi, fab. 5.

There is no trusting to appearances.
SHERIDAN, *The School for Scandal*. Act v, sc. 2.

Appearances are very deceitful.
LE SAGE, *Gil Blas*. Bk. iii, ch. 7. (Smollett, tr.)

Don't rely too much on labels,
For too often they are fables.
C. H. SPURGEON, *Salt-Cellars*.

9
He seem'd
For dignity compos'd and high exploit:
But all was false and hollow.
MILTON, *Paradise Lost*. Bk. ii, l. 110.

He had the air of his own statue erected by national subscription.
TURGENEV. (HOLMES, *The Poet at the Breakfast-Table*. Ch. 4.)

10
O that such an imposing appearance should have no brain! (O quanta species cerebrum non habet!)
PHÆDRUS, *Fables*. Bk. i, fab. 7, l. 2.

You look wise. Pray correct that error.
CHARLES LAMB, *Essays of Elia: All Fools' Day*.

Boobies have looked as wise and bright
As Plato or the Stagyrite;
And many a sage and learned skull
Has peeped through windows dark and dull!
THOMAS MOORE, *Nature's Labels*.

11
I have often found persons of handsome appearance to be the worst, and those of evil appearance the best. (Formosos sæpe inveni pessimos, Et turpi facie multos cognovi optimos.)
PHÆDRUS, *Fables*. Bk. iii, fab. 46.

12
Things are not always what they seem. (Non semper ea sunt quæ videntur.)
PHÆDRUS, *Fables*. Bk. iv, fab. 2, l. 5.

Things are seldom what they seem.
Skim milk masquerades as cream.
W. S. GILBERT, *H. M. S. Pinafore*. Act ii.

And things are not what they seem.
LONGFELLOW, *A Psalm of Life*.

13
We should strip the mask not only from men, but from things, and restore to each object its own aspect (Non hominibus tantum, sed rebus persona demenda est et reddenda facies sua.)
SENECA, *Epistulæ ad Lucilium*. Epis. xxiv, 13.

Black Tragedy lets slip her grim disguise
And shows you laughing lips and roguish eyes;
But when, unmasked, gay Comedy appears,
How wan her cheeks are, and what heavy tears!
THOMAS BAILEY ALDRICH, *Masks*.

Hast ever thought that beneath a gay and frivolous exterior there may lurk a cankerworm which is slowly but surely eating its way into one's very heart?
W. S. GILBERT, *H. M. S. Pinafore*. Act i.

14
We'll have a swashing and a martial outside,
As many other mannish cowards have
That do outface it with their semblances.
SHAKESPEARE, *As You Like It*. Act i, sc. 3, l. 122.

15
Mine eyes
Were not in fault, for she was beautiful;
Mine ears, that heard her flattery; nor my heart,
That thought her like her seeming.
SHAKESPEARE, *Cymbeline*. Act v, sc. 5, l. 63.

16
Seems, madam! nay, it is; I know not "seems."
SHAKESPEARE, *Hamlet*. Act i, sc. 2, l. 76.

1
Look how we can, or sad or merrily,
Interpretation will misquote our looks.
SHAKESPEARE, *I Henry IV*. Act v, sc. 2, l. 12.

2
O what a goodly outside falsehood hath!
SHAKESPEARE, *The Merchant of Venice*. Act i, sc. 3, l. 103.

Oh, that deceit should steal such gentle shapes,
And with a virtuous vizard hide foul guile!
SHAKESPEARE, *Richard III*. Act ii, sc. 2, l. 27.

O serpent heart, hid with a flowering face!
Did ever a dragon keep so fair a cave?
SHAKESPEARE, *Romeo and Juliet*. Act iii, sc. 2, l. 73.

Was ever book containing such vile matter
So fairly bound? O, that deceit should dwell
In such a gorgeous palace!
SHAKESPEARE, *Romeo and Juliet*. Act iii, sc. 2, l. 83.

3
So may the outward shows be least themselves:
The world is still deceived with ornament. . . .
Thus ornament is but the guiled shore
To a most dangerous sea; the beauteous scarf
Veiling an Indian beauty; in a word,
The seeming truth which cunning time puts on
To entrap the wisest.
SHAKESPEARE, *The Merchant of Venice*. Act iii, sc. 2, l. 73.

Nor more can you distinguish of a man
Than of his outward show; which, God he knows,
Seldom or never jumpeth with the heart.
SHAKESPEARE, *Richard III*. Act iii, sc. 1, l. 9.

When devils will the blackest sins put on,
They do suggest at first with heavenly shows.
SHAKESPEARE, *Othello*. Act ii, sc. 3, l. 357.

4
She began to ask herself whether she had not over-rated white beards and old age and nightshirts as divine credentials.
BERNARD SHAW, *The Adventures of the Black Girl in Her Search for God*.

5
We must see if he is worth rearing, or is only a wind-bag and a sham.
SOPHOCLES. (PLATO, *Theætetus*. Sec. 160.)

6
Ain't he the damnedest simulacrum!
WALT WHITMAN, commenting on Swinburne, when the latter had turned viciously against him.

7
All things are less dreadful than they seem.
WORDSWORTH, *Ecclesiastical Sonnets*. Pt. i, No. 7.

It is only by a wide comparison of facts that the wisest full-grown man can distinguish well-rolled barrels from more supernal thunder.
GEORGE ELIOT.

III—Appearance: All is not Gold that Glisters

8
Do not hold everything as gold which shines like gold. (Non teneas aurum totum quod splendet ut aurum.)
ALANUS DE INSULIS, *Parabolea*. (*Winchester College Hall-book*, 1401.)

9
It is not all gold that glareth.
CHAUCER, *House of Fame*. Bk. i, l. 272. (1383)

But all thing which that shineth as the gold
Is not gold, as that I have heard it told.
CHAUCER, *The Chanouns Yemannes Tale*, l. 962. (c. 1390)

10
Everything is not gold that one sees shining. (Que tout n'est pas or qu'on voit luire.)
UNKNOWN, *Li Diz de Freire Denise, Cordelier*. (c. 1300)

All is not gold that outward sheweth bright.
JOHN LYDGATE, *On the Mutability of Human Affairs*. (1440)

All is not gold that sheweth goldish hue.
JOHN LYDGATE, *Chorle and Byrde*.

11
All that glitters is not gold. (No es Oro todo que reluce.)
CERVANTES, *Don Quixote*. Pt. ii, ch. 33.

All, as they say, that glitters is not gold.
DRYDEN, *The Hind and the Panther*. Pt. ii, l. 215. (1687)

12
Black sheep dwell in every fold,
All that glitters is not gold;
Storks turn out to be but logs;
Bulls are but inflated frogs.
W. S. GILBERT, *H. M. S. Pinafore*. Act ii.

13
Dirt glitters as long as the sun shines.
GOETHE, *Sprüche in Prosa*.

14
Not all that tempts your wandering eyes
And heedless hearts is lawful prize,
Nor all that glisters gold.
THOMAS GRAY, *On a Favourite Cat*.

15
All is not gold that glisters.
JOHN HEYWOOD, *Proverbs*. Bk. i, ch. 10 (1546); BEN JONSON, *Tale of a Tub*. Act ii, sc. 1; THOMAS MIDDLETON, *Fair Quarrel*. Act v, sc. 1.

All that glisters is not gold;
Often have you heard that told.
SHAKESPEARE, *The Merchant of Venice*. Act ii, sc. 7, l. 65.

16
Yet gold all is not, that doth golden seem.
SPENSER, *The Faerie Queene*. Bk. ii, canto viii, st. 14. (1589)

17
Not everything that gives
A gleam and glittering show
Is to be counted gold, indeed,

This proverb well you know.
GEORGE TURBERVILLE, *The Answer of a Woman to Her Lover.*

IV—Appearance: Appearances

1
Keep up appearances; there lies the test;
The world will give thee credit for the rest.
Outward be fair, however foul within;
Sin, if thou wilt, but then in secret sin.
CHARLES CHURCHILL, *Night,* l. 311.

Appearances to save, his only care;
So things seem right, no matter what they are.
CHARLES CHURCHILL, *The Rosciad,* l. 299.
See also SIN: THE ELEVENTH COMMANDMENT.

2
The final good and the supreme duty of the wise man is to resist appearances. (Extremum bonorum et summus munus esse sapientis obsistere visis.)
CICERO, *De Finibus.* Bk. iii, ch. 9, sec. 31.

3
Always scorn appearances and you always may.
EMERSON, *Essays, First Series: Self-Reliance.*

4
Appearances to the mind are of four kinds: Things either are what they appear to be; or they neither are, nor appear to be; or they are, and do not appear to be; or they are not, and yet appear to be. Rightly to aim in all these cases is the wise man's task.
EPICTETUS, *Discourses.* Bk. i, ch. 27, sec. 1.

5
We see the sun, the moon and the stars revolving, as it seems to us, round us. That is false. We feel that the earth is motionless. That is false, too. We see the sun rise above the horizon. It is beneath us. We touch what we think is a solid body. There is no such thing.
CAMILLE FLAMMARION, *The Unknown.* Ch. 1.

6
Those awful goddesses, Appearances, are to us what the Fates were to the Greeks.
ARTHUR HELPS, *Friends in Council.* Bk. i, ch. 5.

7
Unduly concerned for outward appearances. (In cute curanda plus æquo operata.)
HORACE, *Epistles.* Bk. i, epis. 2, l. 29.

8
If Nature be a phantasm, as thou say'st,
A splendid figment and prodigious dream,
To reach the real and true I'll make no haste,
More than content with worlds that only seem.
WILLIAM WATSON, *Epigrams.*

9
Of the terrible doubt of appearances,
Of the uncertainty after all, that we may be deluded,
That may-be reliance and hope are but speculations after all,
That may-be identity beyond the grave is a beautiful fable only,
May-be the things I perceive, the animals, plants, men, hills, shining and flowing waters,
The skies of day and night, colors, densities, forms, may-be these are (as doubtless they are) only apparitions, and the real something has yet to be known.
WALT WHITMAN, *Of the Terrible Doubt of Appearances.*

APPETITE

See also Eating

I—Appetite for Food

10
That sought for no other sauce thereto except appetite.
JOHN BARBOUR, *Bruce.* Pt. iii, l. 540. (c. 1375)
See also under HUNGER.

11
And so leave with an appetite.
RICHARD BULLEIN, *Government of Health.* Fo. 37. (1558)

The surest way in feeding is to leave with an appetite.
THOMAS COGAN, *Haven of Health,* p. 167. (1588)

Go to your banquet, then, but use delight,
So as to rise still with an appetite.
ROBERT HERRICK, *Hesperides.* Pt. i, No. 236. (1648)

If thou rise with an appetite, thou art sure never to sit down without one.
WILLIAM PENN, *Fruits of Solitude.* (1693)

Who riseth from a feast
With that keen appetite that he sits down?
SHAKESPEARE, *The Merchant of Venice.* Act ii, sc. 6, l. 8.

12
Their hearts and sentiments were free, their appetites were hearty.
ROBERT BUCHANAN, *City of the Saints.*

13
And gazed around them to the left and right
With the prophetic eye of appetite.
BYRON, *Don Juan.* Canto v, st. 50.

14
There's no stomach a hand's breadth bigger than another.
CERVANTES, *Don Quixote.* Pt. ii, ch. 33.

15
Short are his meals, and homely is his fare;
His thirst he slakes at some pure neighbouring brook,
Nor asks for sauce where appetite stands cook.
CHARLES CHURCHILL, *Gotham.* Bk. iii, l. 132.

16
Poor men want meat for their stomachs, rich men stomachs for their meat.
ANTHONY COPLEY, *Wits, Fits, etc.,* p. 105.

Some people have food, but no appetite; others have an appetite, but no food. I have both. The Lord be praised.
OLIVER CROMWELL, *Grace.* (Attr.)

Some hae meat and canna eat,
And some wad eat that want it;
But we hae meat and we can eat,
And sae the Lord be thankit.
ROBERT BURNS, *The Selkirk Grace.*

Some have meat but cannot eat;
Some could eat but have no meat;
We have meat and can all eat;
Blest, therefore, be God for our meat.
UNKNOWN, *The Selkirk Grace.* (From MS. of about 1650.)

1
That heavenly food, which gives new appetite.
DANTE, *Purgatorio.* Canto xxxi, l. 128.

New dishes beget new appetites.
THOMAS FULLER, *Gnomologia.* No. 3534.

2
I find no abhorring in mine appetite.
JOHN DONNE, *Devotions.* Sec. 10.

3
What one relishes, nourishes.
BENJAMIN FRANKLIN, *Poor Richard,* 1734.

4
Nothing more shameless is than Appetite,
Who still, whatever anguish load our breast,
Makes us remember in our own despite
Both food and drink.
HOMER, *Odyssey.* Bk. vii, l. 216. (Worsley, tr.)

5
The best things beyond their measure cloy.
HOMER, *Iliad.* Bk. xiii, l. 795. (Pope, tr.)

Or cloy the hungry edge of appetite.
SHAKESPEARE, *Richard II.* Act i, sc. 3, l. 296.

6
Seek an appetite by hard toil. (Tu pulmentaria quære sudando.)
HORACE, *Satires.* Bk. ii, sat. ii, l. 20.

7
A stomach that is seldom empty despises common food. (Jejunus raro stomachus vulgaria temnit.)
HORACE, *Satires.* Bk. ii, sat. 2, l. 38.

8
There never lived a mortal man who bent
His appetite beyond his natural sphere,
But starved and died.
JOHN KEATS, *Endymion.* Bk. iv, l. 646.

9
I have no wish to waste my appetite. (Perdere nolo famem.)
MARTIAL, *Epigrams.* Bk. xiii, epig. 53.

10
That which is not good is not delicious
To a well-governed and wise appetite.
MILTON, *Comus,* l. 704.

11
The Receipts of Cookery are swelled to a Volume, but a good Stomach excels them all.
WILLIAM PENN, *Fruits of Solitude.*

12
The full stomach turns from the honey of Hybla. (Hyblæum refugit satur liquorem.)
PETRONIUS, *Fragments.* No. 120.

What is nourishment to a hungry man becomes a burden to a full stomach. (Quæ desiderantibus alimenta erant, onera sunt plenis.)
SENECA, *Epistulæ ad Lucilium.* Epis. xcv, sec. 16.

The sweetest honey
Is loathsome in its own deliciousness,
And in the taste confounds the appetite.
SHAKESPEARE, *Romeo and Juliet.* Act ii, sc. 6, l. 11.

13
Appetite comes with eating, says Angeston, but thirst departs with drinking. (L'appétit vient en mangeant, disoit Angeston, mais la soif, s'en va en beuvant.)
RABELAIS, *Works.* Bk. i, ch. 5. By "Angeston" Rabelais referred to Jerome de Hangeste, a scholar who died in 1538.

I have made this paction and covenant with my appetite, that it always lieth down and goes to bed with myself, then the next morning it also riseth with me, and gets up when I am awake.
RABELAIS, *Works.* Bk. i, ch. 41.

14
It is the sign of an over-nice appetite to toy with many dishes. (Fastidientis stomachi est multa degustare.)
SENECA, *Epistulæ ad Lucilium.* Epis. ii, sec. 4.

15
Poor wretches, do you not know that your appetites are bigger than your bellies? (Infelices, ecquid intellegitis majorem vos famem habere quam ventrem?)
SENECA, *Epistulæ ad Lucilium.* Epis. lxxxix, sec. 22.

16
A sick man's appetite, who desires most that
Which would increase his evil.
SHAKESPEARE, *Coriolanus.* Act i, sc. 1, l. 183.

Why, she would hang on him
As if increase of appetite had grown
By what it fed on.
SHAKESPEARE, *Hamlet.* Act i, sc. 2, l. 143.

17
A good digestion to you all.
SHAKESPEARE, *Henry VIII.* Act i, sc. 4, l. 62.

Now good digestion wait on appetite,
And health on both!
SHAKESPEARE, *Macbeth.* Act iii, sc. 4, l. 38.

Keen appetite and quick digestion wait on you and yours.
DRYDEN, *Cleomenes.* Act iv, sc. 1.

18
Doth not the appetite alter? a man loves the meat in his youth that he cannot endure in his age.
SHAKESPEARE, *Much Ado About Nothing.* Act ii, sc. 3, l. 247.

19
To make our appetites more keen,
With eager compounds we our palates urge.
SHAKESPEARE, *Sonnets.* No. cxviii.

1
And through the Hall there walked to and fro
A jolly Yeoman, marshall of the same,
Whose name was Appetite.
SPENSER, *Faerie Queene*. Bk. ii, canto ix, st. 28.

2
'Tis not the meat, but 'tis the appetite
Makes eating a delight.
SIR JOHN SUCKLING, *Of Thee, Kind Boy*.

3
Long graces do
But keep good stomachs off, that would fall to.
SIR JOHN SUCKLING, *To His Much Honoured the Lord Lepington*.

He made it a part of his religion, never to say grace to his meat.
SWIFT, *Tale of a Tub*. Sec. 11.

4
God sendeth and giveth both mouth and meat.
THOMAS TUSSER, *Hundred Points of Good Husbandrie*.

II—Appetite for Pleasure

5
Lo, here hath lust his domination,
And appetite flemeth discretion.
CHAUCER, *The Maunciples Tale*, l. 181.

6
Let the appetites be subject to reason. (Appetitus rationi obediant.)
CICERO, *De Officiis*. Bk. i, ch. 29, sec. 102.

Subdue your appetites, my dears, and you've conquered human natur'.
DICKENS, *Nicholas Nickleby*. Ch. 5.

7
Govern well thy appetite, lest Sin
Surprise thee, and her black attendant, Death.
MILTON, *Paradise Lost*. Bk. vii, l. 546.

8
Put a knife to thy throat, if thou be a man given to appetite.
Old Testament: Proverbs, xxiii, 2.

9
Satiety is a neighbor to continued pleasures. (Continuis voluptatibus vicina satietas.)
QUINTILIAN, *Declamationes*. Bk. xxx, sec. 6.

10
New meat begets new appetite.
JOHN RAY, *English Proverbs*.

11
O appetite, from judgement stand aloof!
The one a palate hath that needs will taste,
Though Reason weep, and cry, "It is thy last."
SHAKESPEARE, *A Lover's Complaint*, l. 166.

12
A mortified appetite is never a wise companion.
R. L. STEVENSON, *Ethical Studies*, p. 69.

APPLAUSE

See also Praise

13
Applause: the echo of a platitude.
AMBROSE BIERCE, *The Devil's Dictionary*, p. 25.

14
Do what thy manhood bids thee do, from none but self expect applause;
He noblest lives and noblest dies who makes and keeps his self-made laws.
SIR RICHARD BURTON, *The Kasîdah*, viii, 37.

15
Applause is the spur of noble minds, the end and aim of weak ones.
C. C. COLTON, *Lacon*. No. 205.

16
The silence that accepts merit as the most natural thing in the world, is the highest applause.
EMERSON, *Nature, Addresses and Lectures: Address*, 15 July, 1838.

17
Unruly murmurs, or ill-timed applause
Wrong the best speaker, and the justest cause.
HOMER, *Iliad*. Bk. xix, l. 85. (Pope, tr.)

At the conclusion of one of Mr. Burke's eloquent harangues, Mr. Cruger, finding nothing to add, or perhaps as he thought to add with effect, exclaimed earnestly, in the language of the counting-house, "I say ditto to Mr. Burke! I say ditto to Mr. Burke!"
MATTHEW PRIOR, *Life of Burke*, p. 152.

18
The applause of a single human being is of great consequence.
SAMUEL JOHNSON. (BOSWELL, *Life*, 1780.)

19
Fate cannot rob you of deserved applause,
Whether you win or lose in such a cause.
MASSINGER, *The Bashful Lover*. Act i, sc. 2.

20
In those days the applause was without art. (Plausus tunc arte carebant.)
OVID, *Ars Amatoria*. Bk. i, l. 113.

21
From the very applause and glad approval of the people any talent can catch the flame. (Plausibus ex ipsis populi lætoque favore Ingenium quodvis incaluisse potest.)
OVID, *Epistulæ ex Ponto*. Bk. iii, epis. 4, l. 29.

The glorious meed of popular applause.
BYRON, *Don Juan*. Canto iii, st. 82.

O Popular Applause! what heart of man
Is proof against thy sweet, seducing charms?
COWPER, *The Task*. Bk. ii, l. 481.

I have been nourished by the sickly food
Of popular applause.
WORDSWORTH, *The Borderers*. Act iv, l. 1821.

See also under PEOPLE.

22
Dare you say that any man will disown the wish to earn the applause of men? (An erit qui velle recuset os populi meruisse?)
PERSIUS, *Satires*. Sat. i, l. 41.

23
Ah me! ah me! this applause has ruined him! (Ei mihi, ei mihi, istæc illum perdidit assentatio.)
PLAUTUS, *Bacchides*, l. 411. (Act iii, sc. 3.)

1
Like Cato, give his little Senate laws,
And sit attentive to his own applause.
POPE, *Epistle to Dr. Arbuthnot*, l. 209.

The applause of listening senates to command.
THOMAS GRAY, *Elegy Written in a Country Church-yard*.

2
They threw their caps
As they would hang them on the horns o' the moon,
Shouting their emulation.
SHAKESPEARE, *Coriolanus*. Act i, sc. 1, l. 216.

Such a noise arose
As the shrouds make at sea in a stiff tempest,
As loud, and to as many tunes: hats, cloaks,—
Doublets, I think,—flew up; and had their faces
Been loose, this day they had been lost.
SHAKESPEARE, *Henry VIII*. Act iv, sc. 1, l. 71.

3
I would applaud thee to the very echo,
That should applaud again.
SHAKESPEARE, *Macbeth*. Act v, sc. 3, l. 53.

4
I love the people
But do not like to stage me to their eyes;
Though it do well, I do not relish well
Their loud applause, and Aves vehement.
SHAKESPEARE, *Measure for Measure*. Act i, sc. 1, l. 68.

And give to dust that is a little gilt
More laud than gilt o'er-dusted.
SHAKESPEARE, *Troilus and Cressida*. Act iii, sc. 3, l. 178.

5
The applause of the crowd makes the head giddy, but the attestation of a reasonable man makes the heart glad.
RICHARD STEELE, *The Spectator*. No. 188.

6
Farewell, and give us your applause. (Vos valete et plaudite.)
TERENCE, *Eunuchus*, l. 1094. Concluding words of several comedies.

7
Nay, who dare shine, if not in virtue's cause?
That sole proprietor of just applause.
YOUNG, *Epistles to Mr. Pope*. No. ii, l. 19.

8
When most the world applauds you, most beware;
'Tis often less a blessing, than a snare.
YOUNG, *Love of Fame*. Sat. vi, l. 231.

The melancholy ghosts of dead renown,
Whisp'ring faint echoes of the world's applause.
YOUNG, *Night Thoughts*. Night ix, l. 119.

APPLE

9
How we apples swim!
JOHN CLARKE, *Parœmiologia*, 32. (1639) SWIFT, *Brother Protestants*. (1710)

While tumbling down the turbid stream,
Lord love us, how we apples swim!
DAVID MALLET, *Tyburn*.

10
Apples are thought to quench the flame of Venus, according to that old English saying, He that will not a wife wed, Must eat a cold apple when he goeth to bed, though some turn it to a contrary purpose.
THOMAS COGAN, *Haven of Health*, p. 88. (1588)

Ait a happle avore gwain to bed,
An' you'll make the doctor beg his bread.
or, as the more popular version runs: An apple a day keeps the doctor away.
E. M. WRIGHT, *Rustic Speech*, p. 238. The couplet is from Devonshire.

Eat an apple on going to bed,
And you'll keep the doctor from earning his bread.
UNKNOWN. (*Notes and Queries*. Ser. iii, ix, 153.)

11
An apple may happen to be better given than eaten.
THOMAS FULLER, *Gnomologia*. No. 581.

An apple, an egg, and a nut
You may eat after a slut.
THOMAS FULLER, *Gnomologia*. No. 6250.

An apple, an egg, an orange, and a nut,
These four things you may take from a slut.
UNKNOWN, *Four Clean Things*.

12
Oh! happy are the apples when the south winds blow.
WILLIAM WALLACE HARNEY, *Adonais*.

13
What is more melancholy than the old apple-trees that linger about the spot where once stood a homestead, but where there is now only a ruined chimney rising out of a grassy and weed-grown cellar? They offer their fruit to every wayfarer—apples that are bitter-sweet with the moral of time's vicissitude.
HAWTHORNE, *Mosses from an Old Manse: The Old Manse*.

14
He pares his apple that will cleanly feed.
GEORGE HERBERT, *The Church-Porch*. St. 11.

15
The apples on the other side of the wall are the sweetest.
W. G. BENHAM, *Proverbs*, p. 837. *See also under* PROHIBITION.

16
She is lost with an apple, and won with a nut.
JOHN HEYWOOD, *Proverbs*. Pt. 1, ch. 10.

He that is won with a nut may be lost with an apple.
THOMAS FULLER, *Gnomologia*. No. 2201.

17
The apple blossoms' shower of pearl,
Though blent with rosier hue,
As beautiful as woman's blush,—
As evanescent too.
LETITIA ELIZABETH LANDON, *Apple Blossoms*.

1
I have upset my apple-cart; I am done for. ("Ολην τὴν α ἅμαξαν ἐπεσπάσω.)
LUCIAN, *Pseudolus*, l. 32.

I've upset the apple-cart! (Plaustrum perculi.)
PLAUTUS, *Epidicus*, l. 592. (Act iv, sc. 2.)

The Apple-Cart.
BERNARD SHAW. Title of play.

2
To satisfy the sharp desire I had
Of tasting those fair apples, I resolv'd
Not to defer; hunger and thirst at once,
Powerful persuaders, quicken'd at the scent
Of that alluring fruit, urg'd me so keen.
MILTON, *Paradise Lost*. Bk. ix, l. 584.

The apples that grew on the fruit-tree of knowledge
By woman were pluck'd, and she still wears the prize
To tempt us in theatre, senate, or college—
I mean the love-apples that bloom in the eyes.
HORACE AND JAMES SMITH, *Living Lustres*.

All the evil in the world was brought in by means of an apple. (Mala mali malo mala contulit omnia mundo.)
UNKNOWN. A medieval proverb.

3
It is more pleasant to pluck an apple from the branch than to take one from a graven dish.
OVID, *Epistulæ ex Ponto*. Bk. iii, epis. 5, l. 19.

The apples she had gathered smelt most sweet.
MATTHEW PRIOR, *Solomon*. Bk. ii, l. 495.

4
Like the sweet apple which reddens upon the topmost bough
A-top on the topmost twig—which the pluckers forgot, somehow—
Forgot it not, nay, but got it not, for none could get it till now.
D. G. ROSSETTI, *Beauty: A Combination from Sappho*.

Art thou the topmost apple
The gatherers could reach,
Reddening on the bough?
Shall I not take thee?
SAPPHO, *Odes*. No. 53. (Bliss Carman, tr.)

5
I often wished that all my causes were apple-pie causes.
JOHN SCOTT, LORD ELDON, referring to a complaint made to him when he was resident fellow of University College. Some of the undergraduates complained that the cooks had sent to table an apple-pie which could not be eaten. Lord Eldon ordered the cook to bring the pie before him, but the cook informed him that the pie was eaten, whereupon Lord Eldon gave judgment for the defendant, saying to complainants: "You complain that the pie could not be eaten, but the pie *has* been eaten, and therefore *could* be eaten."

But I, when I undress me
Each night, upon my knees
Will ask the Lord to bless me
With apple pie and cheese!
EUGENE FIELD, *Apple Pie and Cheese*.

6
A goodly apple rotten at the heart.
SHAKESPEARE, *The Merchant of Venice*. Act i, sc. 3, l. 102.

7
There's plenty of boys that will come hankering and gruvvelling around when you've got an apple, and beg the core off you; but when *they've* got one, and you beg for the core, and remind them how you give them a core one time, they make a mouth at you, and say thank you 'most to death, but there ain't a-going to *be* no core.
MARK TWAIN, *Tom Sawyer Abroad*. Ch. 1.

8
The apples lie scattered here and there, each under its own tree. (Strata jacent passim sua quæque sub arbore poma.)
VERGIL, *Eclogues*. No. vii, l. 54.

Old Fortune, like sly Farmer Dapple,
Where there's an orchard, flings an apple.
JOHN CLARE, *Rural Life*, l. 114.

9
With a heart that is true,
I'll be waiting for you,
In the shade of the old apple tree.
HARRY WILLIAMS, *In the Shade of the Old Apple Tree*. (1905)

10
"Very astonishing indeed! strange thing!"
(Turning the Dumpling round, rejoined the King), . . .
"But, Goody, tell me where, where, where's the Seam?"
"Sire, there's no Seam," quoth she; "I never knew
That folks did Apple-Dumplings sew."
"No!" cried the staring Monarch with a grin;
"How, how the devil got the Apple in?"
JOHN WOLCOT, *The Apple Dumplings and the King*.

APRIL

See also Spring

11
Blossom of the almond trees,
April's gift to April's bees.
EDWIN ARNOLD, *Almond Blossoms*.

12
And blossoming boughs of April in laughter shake:
Awake, O heart, to be loved, awake, awake!
ROBERT BRIDGES, *Awake, My Heart*.

13
Oh, to be in England
Now that April's there.
ROBERT BROWNING, *Home Thoughts from Abroad*.

14
Make me over, Mother April,
When the sap begins to stir!
Make me man or make me woman,

Make me oaf or ape or human,
Cup of flower or cone of fir;
Make me anything but neuter
When the sap begins to stir!
  BLISS CARMAN, *Spring Song.*

Once more in misted April
  The world is growing green,
Along the winding river
  The plumey willows lean.
  BLISS CARMAN, *An April Morning.*

1
One of love's April fools.
  CONGREVE, *The Old Batchelor.* Act i, sc. 1.

On the first of Aprile
Hunt the gowke another mile.
  JOHN DENHAM, *Proverbs.* No. 41.

The first of April, some do say,
Is set apart for All Fool's day;
But why the people call it so,
Nor I, nor they themselves, do know.
  UNKNOWN, *Poor Robin's Almanac,* 1760.

When beans are in flower, fools are in power.
(Quand les fèvres sont en fleur,
Les fous sont en vigeur.)
  UNKNOWN, *Poisson d'Avril.*

2
April comes in with his hack and his bill
And sets a flower on every hill.
  SIR JOHN DENHAM, *Proverbs.* No. 41.

3
April's amazing meaning doubtless lies
  In tall, hoarse boys and slips
Of slender girls with suddenly wider eyes
  And parted lips.
  GEORGE DILLON, *April's Amazing Meaning.*

The April winds are magical,
  And thrill our tuneful frames;
The garden-walks are passional
  To bachelors and dames.
  EMERSON, *April.*

4
April is the cruelest month, breeding
Lilacs out of the dead land, mixing
Memory and desire, stirring
Dull roots with spring rain.
  T. S. ELIOT, *The Waste Land.*

5
Sweet April! many a thought
Is wedded unto thee, as hearts are wed.
  LONGFELLOW, *An April Day.*

6
I have seen the lady April bringing the daffodils,
Bringing the springing grass and the soft warm April rain.
  JOHN MASEFIELD, *Beauty.*

7
When April rain had laughed the land
  Out of its wintry way,
And coaxed all growing things to greet
  With gracious garb the May.
  SHAEMAS O'SHEEL, *While April Rain Went By.*

8
Oh, hush, my heart, and take thine ease,
  For here is April weather!
The daffodils beneath the trees
  Are all a-row together.
  LIZETTE WOODWORTH REESE, *April Weather.*

9
Winter's done, and April's in the skies,
Earth, look up with laughter in your eyes.
  CHARLES G. D. ROBERTS, *An April Adoration.*

10
The lyric sound of laughter
  Fills all the April hills,
The joy-song of the crocus,
  The mirth of daffodils.
  CLINTON SCOLLARD, *April Music.*

11
The April's in her eyes: it is love's spring,
And these the showers to bring it on.
  SHAKESPEARE, *Antony and Cleopatra.* Act iii, sc. 2, l. 43.

12
When well-apparel'd April on the heel
Of limping winter treads.
  SHAKESPEARE, *Romeo and Juliet.* Act i, sc. 2, l. 27.

Proud-pied April dress'd in all his trim
Hath put a spirit of youth in every thing.
  SHAKESPEARE, *Sonnets.* No. xcviii.

Thy banks with pioned and twilled brims,
Which spongy April at thy hest betrims.
  SHAKESPEARE, *The Tempest.* Act iv, sc. 1, l. 64.

13
The uncertain glory of an April day!
  SHAKESPEARE, *The Two Gentlemen of Verona.* Act i, sc. 3, l. 85.

Oh, the lovely fickleness of an April day!
  W. H. GIBSON, *Pastoral Days: Spring.*

April's rare capricious loveliness.
  JULIA C. R. DORR, *November.*

14
Sweet April's tears,
Dead on the hem of May.
  ALEXANDER SMITH, *A Life Drama.* Sc. viii, l. 308.

15
A gush of bird-song, a patter of dew,
  A cloud, and a rainbow's warning,
Suddenly sunshine and perfect blue—
  An April day in the morning.
  HARRIET PRESCOTT SPOFFORD, *April.*

16
O sweet wild April came over the hills,
He skipped with the winds and he tripped with the rills;
His raiment was all of daffodils.
  Sing hi, sing hey, sing ho!
  WILLIAM FORCE STEAD, *Sweet Wild April.*

17
April warms the world anew.
  SWINBURNE, *The Year of Love.*

18
April, April,
Laugh thy girlish laughter;
Then, the moment after,
Weep thy girlish tears!
  WILLIAM WATSON, *Song.*

1
When April's silver showers so sweet
Can make May flowers to spring.

UNKNOWN, *Philip and Mary.* (c. 1560)

Sweet April showers Do bring May flowers.

THOMAS TUSSER, *Five Hundred Points of Good Husbandry,* 103. (1580)

I'll show you how April showers bring May flowers.

LODOWICK BARRY, *Ram-Alley.* Act v. (1611)

As Jupiter
On Juno smiles, when he impregns the clouds
That shed May flow'rs.

MILTON, *Paradise Lost.* Bk. iv, l. 499.

ARCADIA

2
Arcadia.

SIR PHILIP SIDNEY. Title of a medley of prose romance and pastoral eclogues written for the amusement of his sister, the Countess of Pembroke, first published in 1590. Vergil had sung Arcadia, a district of the Peloponnesus, as the home of pastoral simplicity and happiness, and the word was soon generally adopted into English.

Those golden times,
And those Arcadian scenes that Maro sings,
And Sidney, warbler of poetic prose.

COWPER, *The Task.* Bk. iv, l. 515.

Feign'd Arcadian scenes.

COWPER, *Hope,* l. 9.

3
The Arcadians were chestnut-eaters.

ALCÆUS, *Fragment.* No. 86.

4
What, know you not, old man (quoth he)—
Your hair is white, your face is wise—
That Love must kiss that mortal's eyes
Who hopes to see fair Arcady?

H. C. BUNNER, *The Way to Arcady.*

5
I too was born in Arcadia.

BARTOLOMEO SCHIDONI (c. 1600), on a painting in the Colonna Collection, Rome; NICHOLAS POUSSIN, on a painting in the Louvre, Paris; SIR JOSHUA REYNOLDS, on his portrait of Mrs. Crewe.

Auch ich war in Arkadien geboren.

GOETHE, *Travels in Italy: Motto.*

Auch ich war in Arkadien.

E. T. A. HOFFMANN, *Lebensansichten des Kater Murr,* i, 2: *Motto.*

Moi aussi, je fus pasteur dans l'Arcadie.

DE LILLE, *Les Jardins.*

I, too, shepherd, in Arcadia dwelt.

FELICIA DOROTHEA HEMANS, *Song.*

I dwell no more in Arcady,
But when the sky is blue with May,
And birds are blithe and winds are free,
I know what message is for me,
For I have been in Arcady.

LOUISE CHANDLER MOULTON, *Arcady.*

6
I envied not the happiest swain
That ever trod th' Arcadian plain.

SMOLLETT, *Ode to Leven Water.*

7
Both in the flower of youth, Arcadians both, equal in song and ready in response. (Ambo florentes ætatibus, Arcades ambo, Et cantare pares et respondere parati.)

VERGIL, *Eclogues.* No. vii, l. 4. That is, both poets or musicians, with voices matched to sing together or alternately.

Each pull'd different ways with many an oath,
"Arcades ambo," *id est*—blackguards both.

BYRON, *Don Juan.* Canto iv, st. 93.

Arcades ambo. Scotchies both.

J. M. BARRIE, *What Every Woman Knows.* Act iv.

8
Ye, O Arcadians, will sing my woes upon your hills; only Arcadians know how to sing! How softly shall my bones repose if, in future days, your pipes should tell my loves. (Tamen cantabitis, Arcades, Montibus hæc vestris, soli cantare periti Arcades. O mihi tum quam molliter ossa quiescant, Vestra meos olim si fistula dicat amores.)

VERGIL, *Eclogues.* No. x, l. 31.

ARCHITECTURE

I—Architecture: Definitions

9
Houses are built to live in, and not to look on: therefore let use be preferred before uniformity.

FRANCIS BACON, *Essays: Of Building.*

He that builds a fair house upon an ill seat, committeth himself to prison.

FRANCIS BACON, *Essays: Of Building.*

10
Architecture is preëminently the art of significant forms in space—that is, forms significant of their functions.

CLAUDE BRAGDON, *Wake Up and Dream.* (*Outlook,* 27 May, 1931.)

11
The Gothic cathedral is a blossoming in stone subdued by the insatiable demand of harmony in man. The mountain of granite blooms into an eternal flower.

EMERSON, *Essays, First Series: History.*

Giotto's tower,
The lily of Florence blossoming in stone.

LONGFELLOW, *Giotto's Tower.*

A style of Architecture [the Gothic] which, to me at least, is, in comparison with all others, the most beautiful of all, and by far the most in harmony with the mysteries of religion.

JOHN KEBLE, *Lectures on Poetry.* No. 3.

12
An arch never sleeps.

JAMES FERGUSSON, *History of Indian and Eastern Architecture,* p. 210, repeating a Hindu aphorism.

13
Too many stairs and back-doors makes thieves and whores.

BALTHAZAR GERBIER, *Discourse of Building.* Ch. 14. (1662)

A postern door makes thief and whore.
WILLIAM CAMDEN, *Remains*, p. 334.

1
Architecture is frozen music. (Die Baukunst ist eine ertarrte Musik.)
GOETHE, *Conversations with Eckermann*, 23 March, 1829.

Architecture is music in space, as it were a frozen music.
SCHELLING, *Philosophie der Kunst*, p. 576.

The sight of such a monument is like a continuous and stationary music.
MADAME DE STAËL, *Corinne*. Bk. iv, ch. 3.

2
For which of you, intending to build a tower, sitteth not down first and counteth the cost, whether he have sufficient to finish it?
New Testament: Luke, xiv, 28.

When we mean to build,
We first survey the plot, then draw the model;
And when we see the figure of the house,
Then must we rate the cost of the erection.
SHAKESPEARE, *II Henry IV*. Act i, sc. 3, l. 41.

The man who builds, and wants wherewith to pay,
Provides a home from which to run away.
YOUNG, *Love of Fame*, Sat. i, l. 171.

3
The building which is fitted accurately to its end will turn out to be beautiful, though beauty is not intended.
GEORG MOLLER, *Essay on Architecture*. (EMERSON, *Conduct of Life: Fate*.)

Better the rudest work that tells a story or records a fact, than the richest without meaning.
RUSKIN, *Seven Lamps of Architecture: The Lamp of Memory*.

4
To talk of architecture is a joke
Till you can build a chimney that won't smoke.
JAMES ROBINSON PLANCHÉ, paraphrasing Aristophanes, *The Birds*, l. 1034.

5
As if the story of a house
Were told, or ever could be.
E. A. ROBINSON, *Eros Turannos*.

6
When we build, let us think that we build for ever.
RUSKIN, *Seven Lamps of Architecture: The Lamp of Memory*.

7
We require from buildings, as from men, two kinds of goodness: first, the doing their practical duty well: then that they be graceful and pleasing in doing it; which last is itself another form of duty.
RUSKIN, *Stones of Venice*. Vol. i, ch. 2.

No architecture is so haughty as that which is simple.
RUSKIN, *Stones of Venice*. Vol. ii, ch. 6, sec. 73.

Ornamentation is the principal part of architecture, considered as a subject of fine art.
RUSKIN, *True and Beautiful: Sculpture*.

8
Architecture is the work of nations.
RUSKIN, *True and Beautiful: Sculpture*.

9
Architecture aims at Eternity; and therefore is the only thing incapable of modes and fashions in its principles.
CHRISTOPHER WREN, *Parentalia*.

10
Builds himself a name; and, to be great,
Sinks in a quarry an immense estate.
YOUNG, *Love of Fame*. Sat. i, l. 163.

11
To build many houses is the readiest road to poverty. (Δώματα πόλλ' ἀνεγείρειν ἀτραπὸς εἰς πενίην ἐστὶν ἑτοιμοτάτη.)
UNKNOWN. (*Greek Anthology*. Bk. x, epig. 119.)

Old houses mended,
Cost little less than new, before they're ended.
COLLEY CIBBER, *Double Gallant: Prol.*, l. 15.

Men who love building are their own undoers, and need no other enemies.
MARCUS CRASSUS. (PLUTARCH, *Lives: Marcus Crassus*. Ch. 2, sec. 5.)

To build is to be robbed.
SAMUEL JOHNSON, *The Idler*. No. 62.

12
That was a happy day, before the days of architects, before the days of builders! (Felis illud sæculum ante architectos fuit, ante tectores.)
SENECA, *Epistulæ ad Lucilium*. Epis. xc, sec. 9.

EVERY ONE THE ARCHITECT OF HIS OWN FORTUNE, *see under* FORTUNE.

II—Architecture: Description

13
It is a reverend thing to see an ancient castle or building, not in decay
FRANCIS BACON, *Essays: Of Nobility*.

How reverend is the face of this tall pile, . . .
Looking tranquillity!
CONGREVE, *The Mourning Bride*. Act ii, sc. 1.

14
Earth proudly wears the Parthenon,
As the best gem upon her zone,
And Morning opes with haste her lids
To gaze upon the Pyramids;
O'er England's abbeys bends the sky,
As on its friends, with kindred eye;
For out of Thought's interior sphere
These wonders rose to upper air;
And Nature gladly gave them place,
Adopted them into her race,
And granted them an equal date
With Andes and with Ararat.
EMERSON, *The Problem*.

The hand that rounded Peter's dome,
And groined the aisles of Christian Rome,
Wrought in a sad sincerity;
Himself from God he could not free;
He builded better than he knew;—
The conscious stone to beauty grew.
EMERSON, *The Problem*.

1
Gloom lends solemnity. (Σεμνότητ' ἔχει σκότος.)
EURIPIDES, *Bacchides*, l. 486.

In dim cathedrals, dark with vaulted gloom,
What holy awe invests the saintly tomb!
O. W. HOLMES, *A Rhymed Lesson*, l. 207.

Thus when we view some well-proportion'd dome . . .
No single parts unequally surprise,
All comes united to th' admiring eyes.
POPE, *Essay on Criticism*. Pt. ii, l. 47.

2
When I lately stood with a friend before [the cathedral of] Amiens, . . . he asked me how it happens that we can no longer build such piles? I replied: "Dear Alphonse, men in those days had convictions (Ueberzeugungen), we moderns have opinions (Meinungen) and it requires something more than an opinion to build a Gothic cathedral."
HEINRICH HEINE, *Confidential Letters to August Lewald on the French Stage*. No. 9.

3
And the house, when it was in building, was built of stone made ready before it was brought thither: so that there was neither hammer nor axe nor any tool of iron heard in the house, while it was in building.
Old Testament: I Kings, vi, 7.

No hammers fell, no ponderous axes rung,
Like some tall palm the mystic fabric sprung.
REGINALD HEBER, *Palestine*, l. 163. Bishop Heber is describing the building of Solomon's temple, as above.

Silently as a dream the fabric rose;
No sound of hammer or of saw was there.
COWPER, *The Task*. Bk. 5, l. 144. Cowper is describing the ice palace reared for Catherine of Russia.

No man saw the building of the New Jerusalem, the workmen crowded together, the unfinished walls and unpaved streets; no man heard the clink of trowel and pickaxe; it descended *out of heaven from God*.
JOHN ROBERT SEELEY, *Ecce Homo*. Ch. xxiv.

Anon out of the earth a fabric huge
Rose like an exhalation, with the sound
Of dulcet symphonies and voices sweet.
MILTON, *Paradise Lost*. Bk. i, l. 710.

4
Ah, to build, to build!
That is the noblest art of all the arts.
Painting and sculpture are but images,
Are merely shadows cast by outward things
On stone or canvas, having in themselves
No separate existence. Architecture,
Existing in itself, and not in seeming
A something it is not, surpasses them
As substance shadow.
LONGFELLOW, *Michael Angelo*. Pt. i, sec. 2, l. 54.

5
The architect
Built his great heart into these sculptured stones,
And with him toiled his children, and their lives
Were builded, with his own, into the walls,
As offerings unto God.
LONGFELLOW, *The Golden Legend*: Pt. iii, *In the Cathedral*.

In the elder days of Art,
Builders wrought with greatest care
Each minute and unseen part;
For the Gods see everywhere.
LONGFELLOW, *The Builders*.

A man who could build a church, as one may say, by squinting at a sheet of paper.
DICKENS, *Martin Chuzzlewit*. Pt. ii, ch. 6 .

6
But let my due feet never fail
To walk the studious cloisters pale,
And love the high embowed roof,
With antique pillars massy proof,
And storied windows richly dight,
Casting a dim religious light.
MILTON, *Il Penseroso*, l. 155.

Rich windows that exclude the light,
And passages that lead to nothing.
THOMAS GRAY, *A Long Story*.

7
Nor did there want
Cornice or frieze with bossy sculpture graven.
MILTON, *Paradise Lost*. Bk. i, l. 715.

The hasty multitude
Admiring enter'd, and the work some praise,
And some the architect.
MILTON, *Paradise Lost*. Bk. i, l. 730.

8
In the greenest of our valleys
By good angels tenanted,
Once a fair and stately palace
(Radiant palace) reared its head.
In the monarch Thought's dominion
It stood there!
Never seraph spread a pinion
Over fabric half so fair.
POE, *The Haunted Palace*. From *The Fall of the House of Usher*.

9
The stone which the builders refused is become the head stone of the corner.
Old Testament: Psalms, cxviii, 22.

10
In Saxon strength that abbey frowned,
With massive arches broad and round.
Built ere the art was known
By pointed aisles, and shafted stalk,
The arcades of an alleyed walk
To emulate in stone.
SCOTT, *Marmion*. Canto ii, st. 10.

11
Yon towers, whose wanton tops do buss the clouds.
SHAKESPEARE, *Troilus and Cressida*. Act iv, sc. 5, l. 220.

12
Mankind was never so happily inspired as when it made a cathedral: a thing as single and specious as a statue to the first glance, and

yet on examination, as lively and interesting as a forest in detail.

R. L. STEVENSON, *An Inland Voyage: Noyon Cathedral.*

1
Simple was its noble architecture. Each ornament arrested, as it were, in its position, seemed to have been placed there of necessity.

VOLTAIRE, *Le Temple du Goût.*

2
Behold, ye builders, demigods who made England's Walhalla.

THEODORE WATTS-DUNTON, *The Minster Spirits.* Referring to Westminster Abbey.

They dreamt not of a perishable home
Who thus could build.

WORDSWORTH, *King's College Chapel.* Sonnet iii.

3
There was King Bradmond's palace,
Was never none richer, the story says:
For all the windows and the walls
Were painted with gold, both towers and halls;
Pillars and doors all were of brass;
Windows of latten were set with glass;
It was so rich, in many wise,
That it was like a paradise.

UNKNOWN, *Sir Bevis of Hampton.* (c. 1325)

ARGUMENT

See also Reason

I—Argument: Apothegms

4
Testimony is like the shot of a long-bow, which owes its efficacy to the force of the shooter; argument is like the shot of the cross-bow, equally forcible whether discharged by a giant or a dwarf.

FRANCIS BACON. (As quoted by Samuel Johnson, *Dictionary: Cross-bow,* taken from Robert Boyle, and credited to Bacon. See TWISTLETON, *Handwriting of Junius: Preface,* xiv.)

5
Where we desire to be informed, 'tis good to contest with men above ourselves; but to confirm and establish our opinions, 'tis best to argue with judgements below our own, that the frequent spoils and victories over their reasons may settle in ourselves an esteem and confirmed opinion of our own.

SIR THOMAS BROWNE, *Religio Medici.* Pt. i, sec. 6.

6
So soon as the man overtook me, he was but a word and a blow.

BUNYAN, *Pilgrim's Progress.* Pt. i.

A knock-down argument; 'tis but a word and a blow.

DRYDEN, *Amphitryon.* Act i, sc. 1. (1690)

This is manhood to make thee bold,
Let there be but a word and a blow.

WILLIAM WAGER, *The Longer Thou Livest.* (c. 1568)

And but one word with one of us? couple it with something; make it a word and a blow.

SHAKESPEARE, *Romeo and Juliet.* Act iii, sc. 1, l. 43. (1595)

7
I've heard old sunning stagers
Say, fools for arguments use wagers.

BUTLER, *Hudibras.* Pt. ii, canto i, l. 297.

8
To "get out of my house" and "what do you want with my wife?" there's no answer.

CERVANTES, *Don Quixote.* Pt. ii, ch. 43.

9
Never maintain an argument with heat and clamour, though you think or know yourself to be in the right.

LORD CHESTERFIELD, *Letters,* 16 Oct., 1747.

Be calm in arguing: for fierceness makes
Error a fault and truth discourtesy. . . .
Calmness is great advantage: he that lets
Another chafe, may warm him at his fire.

GEORGE HERBERT, *The Church-Porch.* St. 52.

A modesty in delivering our sentiments leaves us a liberty of changing them without blushing.

THOMAS WILSON, *Maxims of Piety,* p. 127.

10
A noisy man is always in the right.

COWPER, *Conversation,* l. 114.

Asseveration blust'ring in your face
Makes contradiction such a hopeless case.

COWPER, *Conversation,* l. 59.

A contentious man will never lack words.

JOHN JEWEL, *A Defence of the Apology for the Church of England.*

11
Debate destroys despatch.

SIR JOHN DENHAM, *Of Prudence,* l. 63.

12
Burning is no answer. (Brûler n'est pas répondre.)

CAMILLE DESMOULINS, to Robespierre, when the latter proposed to burn the numbers of the moderate journal, *Le Vieux Cordelier.* The retort became proverbial.

13
Argeyment is a gift of Natur.

DICKENS, *Barnaby Rudge.* Ch. 1.

Rather a tough customer in an argeyment, Joe, if anybody was to try and tackle him.

DICKENS, *Barnaby Rudge.* Ch. 1.

14
The noble Lord is the Prince Rupert of parliamentary discussion.

BENJAMIN DISRAELI, *Speech,* House of Commons, April, 1844, referring to Edward Geoffrey, Earl of Derby, then Lord Stanley. Prince Rupert, the nephew of Charles I, was distinguished for his rash pursuit of a part of Cromwell's army at Naseby, which gave the victory to the Parliamentarians. So Disraeli added, "His charge is resistless; but when he returns from the pursuit, he always finds his camp in possession of the enemy."

Here Stanley meets,—how Stanley scorns, the glance!

The brilliant chief, irregularly great,
Frank, haughty, rash,—the Rupert of Debate.
BULWER-LYTTON, *The New Timon*. Pt. i, st. 6, l. 144. (1846)

1
In arguing, answer your opponent's earnest with jest and his jest with earnest. (Σπουδῆν διαφθείρειν τῶν ἐναντίων γέλωτι τὸν δὲ γέλωτα σπουδῇ.)
LEONTINUS GORGIAS. (ARISTOTLE, *Rhetoric*. Bk. iii, ch. 18, sec. 7.)

2
He argued high, he argued low,
He also argued round about him.
W. S. GILBERT, *Sir Macklin.*

3
His conduct still right, with his argument wrong.
GOLDSMITH, *Retaliation*, l. 46.

4
Slow to argue, but quick to act.
BRET HARTE, *John Burns of Gettysburg.*

5
When a thing ceases to be a subject of controversy, it ceases to be a subject of interest.
WILLIAM HAZLITT, *Works*. Vol. xii, p. 384.

6
Though we cannot out-vote them, we will out-argue them.
SAMUEL JOHNSON. (BOSWELL, *Life*, 1778.)

7
Treating your adversary with respect is giving him an advantage to which he is not entitled.
SAMUEL JOHNSON. (BOSWELL, *Life*, 1779.)

8
I have found you an argument; but I am not obliged to find you an understanding.
SAMUEL JOHNSON. (BOSWELL, *Life*, 1784.)

I am bound to furnish my antagonists with arguments, but not with comprehension.
BENJAMIN DISRAELI, *Speech*, House of Commons.

"Very well," cried the Squire, speaking very quick, "the premises being thus settled, I proceed to observe that the concatenation of self-existences, proceeding in a reciprocal duplicate ratio, naturally produces a problematical dialogism, which in some measure proves that the essence of spirituality may be referred to the second predicable. . . . Answer me directly to what I propose: Whether do you judge the analytical investigation of the first part of my enthymem deficient secundum quoad, or quoad minus; and give me your reasons." "I protest," cried Moses, "I don't rightly comprehend the force of your reasoning." . . . "Oh, Sir," cried the Squire, "I find you want me to furnish you with argument and intellects too. No, Sir; there I protest you are too hard for me."
GOLDSMITH, *The Vicar of Wakefield*. Ch. 7.

9
Men may be convinced, but they cannot be pleased, against their will.
JOHNSON, *Lives of the Poets: Congreve.*

We may convince others by our arguments; but we can only persuade them by their own. (On peut convaincre les autres par ses propres raisons; mais on ne les persuade que par les leurs.)
JOUBERT, *Pensées*. No. 106.

You have not converted a man because you have silenced him.
JOHN MORLEY, *On Compromise*, p. 246.

See also BUTLER *under* ARGUMENT: APOTHEGMS.

10
If he take you in hand, sir, with an argument,
He'll bray you in a mortar.
BEN JONSON, *The Alchemist*. Act ii, sc. 1.

Brief and bitter the debate.
ROBERT BROWNING, *Hervé Riel*. St. 4.

11
It is better to debate a question without settling it, than to settle it without debate. (Il vaut mieux remuer une question sans le décider que la décider sans le remuer.)
JOUBERT, *Pensées*. No. 115.

12
There is no good in arguing with the inevitable. The only argument available with an east wind is to put on your overcoat.
J. R. LOWELL, *Democracy and Other Addresses: Democracy.*

13
There are fagots and fagots. (Il y a fagots et fagots.)
MOLIÈRE, *Le Médicin Malgré Lui*. Act i, sc. 5.

14
What quoth the protector thou servest me I ween with iffs and with ands.
SIR THOMAS MORE, *Works*, p. 54. (1513)

Well, well, with *ifs* and *ands*
Mad men leave rocks and leap in the sands.
ROBERT DAVENPORT, *King John and Matilda*. Act i, sc. 2. (c. 1624)

If ifs and ands were pots and pans
There'd be no work for the tinkers.
PEACOCK, *Manley, etc., Glossary*, 286.

"In your propositions," said Pantagruel, "there are so many ifs and buts that I know not how to make anything of them."
RABELAIS, *Works*. Bk. iii, ch. 10.

Much virtue in If.
SHAKESPEARE, *As You Like It*. Act v, sc. 4, l. 107.

But me no buts.
HENRY FIELDING, *Rape upon Rape*. Act ii, sc. 2.
AARON HILL, *Snake in the Grass*. Sc. 1.

15
We should not investigate facts by the light of arguments, but arguments by the light of facts.
MYSON. (DIOGENES LAERTIUS, *Myson*. Sec. 3.)

16
Who over-refines his argument brings himself to grief. (Chi troppo s'assottiglia, si scavezza.)
PETRARCH, *To Laura in Life*. Canzone xi, l. 48.

17
To make the weaker argument the stronger. (Τὸν ἥττω λόγον κρείττω ποιῶν.)
PLATO, *Apology of Socrates*. Sec. 18.

To make the worse appear the better reason. (Λογον κρείττω ποιοῦντα.)

DIOGENES LAERTIUS, *Socrates*. Sec. 3.

Though his tongue
Dropt manna, and could make the worse appear
The better reason, to perplex and dash
Maturest counsels.

MILTON, *Paradise Lost*. Bk. ii, l. 112.

1

It is a tiresome way of speaking, when you should dispatch the business, to beat about the bush. (Odiosast oratio, cum rem agas longinquum loqui.)

PLAUTUS, *Mercator*, l. 608. (Act iii, sc. 4.)

And while I at length debate and beat the bush,
There shall step in other men and catch the birds.

JOHN HEYWOOD, *Proverbs*. Pt. i, ch. 3. (1546)

2

In argument
Similes are like songs in love:
They must describe; they nothing prove.

MATTHEW PRIOR, *Alma*. Canto iii, l. 211.

One single positive weighs more,
You know, than negatives a score.

MATTHEW PRIOR, *Epistle to Fleetwood Shepherd*, l. 131.

3

There are two sides to every question. (Δύο λόγους εἶναι περὶ παντὸς πράγματος.)

PROTAGORAS. (DIOGENES LAERTIUS, *Protagoras*. Bk. ix, sec. 51.) The first to maintain this.

Sir Roger told them, with the air of a man who would not give his judgement rashly, that much might be said on both sides.

ADDISON, *The Spectator*. No. 122.

Much may be said on both sides.

FIELDING, *Covent Garden Tragedy*. Act i, sc. 8

If he [Phil Gentle] is obliged to speak, he then observes that the question is difficult; that he never received so much pleasure from a debate before; that neither of the controvertists could have found his match in any other company; that Mr. Wormwood's assertion is very well supported, and yet there is great force in what Mr. Scruple has advanced against it.

SAMUEL JOHNSON, *The Idler*. No. 83.

The man who sees both sides of a question is a man who sees absolutely nothing at all.

OSCAR WILDE, *The Critic as Artist*. Pt. ii.

4

Whenever you argue with another wiser than yourself, in order that others may admire your wisdom, they will discover your ignorance.

SADI, *Gulistan*. Ch. 8. Maxim 37.

5

To strive with an equal is a doubtful thing to do; with a superior, a mad thing; with an inferior, a vulgar thing. (Cum pare contendere, anceps est; cum superiore, furiosum; cum inferiore, sordidum.)

SENECA, *De Ira*. 2, 34, 1. (Quoted by CHAUCER, *Melibeus*. Sec. 46.)

6

He draweth out the thread of his verbosity finer than the staple of his argument.

SHAKESPEARE, *Love's Labour's Lost*. Act v, sc. i, l. 18.

In some places he draws the thread of his verbosity finer than the staple of his argument.

RICHARD PORSON, *Letter to George Travis*, 1789. Referring to Gibbon's *Decline and Fall of the Roman Empire*.

7

And sheath'd their swords for lack of argument.

SHAKESPEARE, *Henry V*. Act iii, sc. 1, l. 21.

8

Let thy tongue tang with arguments of state.

SHAKESPEARE, *Twelfth Night*. Act iii, sc. 4, l. 78; act ii, sc. 5, l. 164.

9

You are fond of argument, and now you fancy that I am a bag full of arguments.

SOCRATES. (PLATO, *Theætetus*. Sec. 161.)

10

Ye may say, I am hot; I say I am not,
Only warm, as the subject on which I am got.

SWIFT, *The Famous Speechmaker*.

11

And friendly free discussion, calling forth
From the fair jewel, Truth, its latent ray.

JAMES THOMSON, *Liberty*. Pt. ii, l. 220.

12

I am not arguing with you—I am telling you.

J. MCNEILL WHISTLER, *The Gentle Art of Making Enemies*, p. 51. Quoted.

13

Ah, don't say that you agree with me. When people agree with me I always feel that I must be wrong.

OSCAR WILDE, *The Critic as Artist*. Pt. ii. *Lady Windermere's Fan*. Act ii.

II—Argument: Its Futility

14

Our disputants put me in mind of the scuttle-fish, that when he is unable to extricate himself, blackens the water about him till he becomes invisible.

ADDISON, *The Spectator*. No. 476.

15

Let the long contention cease!
Geese are swans and swans are geese!

MATTHEW ARNOLD, *The Last Word*.

16

In all disputes, so much as there is of passion, so much there is of nothing to the purpose.

SIR THOMAS BROWNE, *Religio Medici*. Pt. ii, sec. 4.

Iteration, like friction, is likely to generate heat instead of progress.

GEORGE ELIOT, *The Mill on the Floss*. Bk. ii, ch. 2.

17

Altogether they puzzle me quite,
They all seem wrong and they all seem right.

ROBERT BUCHANAN, *Fine Weather on the Digentia*. St. 6.

1
And there began a lang digression
About the lords o' the creation.
ROBERT BURNS, *The Twa Dogs*, l. 45.

Great contest follows, and much learned dust
Involves the combatants; each claiming truth,
And truth disclaiming both.
COWPER, *The Task*. Bk. iii, l. 161.

2
He'd undertake to prove, by force
Of argument, a man's no horse;
He'd prove a buzzard is no fowl,
And that a Lord may be an owl,
A calf an Alderman, a goose a Justice,
And rooks, Committee-men or Trustees.
BUTLER, *Hudibras*. Pt. i, canto i, l. 71.

3
This is no time nor fitting place to mar
The mirthful meeting with a wordy war.
BYRON, *Lara*. Canto i, st. 23.

4
We arg'ed the thing at breakfast, we arg'ed the thing at tea,
And the more we arg'ed the question, the more we didn't agree.
WILL CARLETON, *Betsy and I Are Out*. St. 5.

5
Her reasoning is full of tricks
And butterfly suggestions,
I know no point to which she sticks;
She begs the simplest questions,
And, when her premises are strong
She always draws her inference wrong.
ALFRED COCHRANE, *Upon Lesbia Arguing*.
See also under QUESTION.

6
But yet beware of councils when too full;
Number makes long disputes.
SIR JOHN DENHAM, *Of Prudence*, l. 59.

The tree of knowledge blasted by dispute,
Produces sapless leaves instead of fruit.
SIR JOHN DENHAM, *Progress of Learning*, l. 43.

7
Reproachful speech from either side
The want of argument supplied;
They rail, reviled: as often ends
The contests of disputing friends.
JOHN GAY, *Fables*: Pt. ii, *The Ravens, the Sexton, and the Earth-Worm*, l. 117.

8
In arguing, too, the parson own'd his skill,
For e'en though vanquish'd, he could argue still;
While words of learned length, and thund'ring sound,
Amazed the gazing rustics rang'd around;
And still they gaz'd, and still the wonder grew,
That one small head could carry all he knew.
GOLDSMITH, *The Deserted Village*, l. 211.

9
A dispute begun in jest . . . is continued by the desire of conquest, till vanity kindles into rage, and opposition rankles into enmity.
SAMUEL JOHNSON, *The Idler*. No. 23.

So high at last the contest rose,
From words they almost came to blows.
JAMES MERRICK, *The Chameleon*.

10
Anything that argues me into his idea of perfect social and political equality with the Negro is but a specious and fantastic arrangement of words, by which a man can prove a horse-chestnut to be a chestnut horse.
ABRAHAM LINCOLN, *Speech*, at Ottawa, Ill., 21 Aug., 1858.

11
Others apart sat on a hill retir'd,
In thoughts more elevate, and reason'd high
Of providence, foreknowledge, will and fate,
Fix'd fate, free will, foreknowledge absolute;
And found no end, in wand'ring mazes lost.
MILTON, *Paradise Lost*. Bk. ii, l. 557.

Myself when young did eagerly frequent
Doctor and Saint, and heard great argument
About it and about; but evermore
Came out by the same door wherein I went.
OMAR KHAYYÁM, *Rubáiyát*. St. 27. (Fitzgerald, tr.)

12
Con was a thorn to brother Pro—
On Pro we often sicked him:
Whatever Pro would claim to know
Old Con would contradict him!
CHRISTOPHER MORLEY, *The Twins*.

13
It were endless to dispute upon everything that is disputable.
WILLIAM PENN, *Fruits of Solitude*.

14
So spins the silkworm small its slender store,
And labours till it clouds itself all o'er.
POPE, *The Dunciad*. Bk. iv, l. 253.

Like doctors thus, when much dispute has past,
We find our tenets just the same at last.
POPE, *Moral Essays*. Epis. iii, l. 15.

15
Soon their crude notions with each other fought;
The adverse sect denied what this had taught;
And he at length the amplest triumph gain'd,
Who contradicted what the last maintain'd.
MATTHEW PRIOR, *Solomon*. Bk. i, l. 717.

16
In a heated argument we are apt to lose sight of the truth. (Nimium altercando veritas amittitur.)
PUBLILIUS SYRUS, *Sententiæ*. No. 326.

Heat is in proportion to the want of true knowledge.
STERNE, *Tristram Shandy*. Bk. iv, ch. 1.

17
It would be argument for a week, laughter for a month, and a good jest for ever.
SHAKESPEARE, *I Henry IV*. Act ii, sc. 2, l. 100.

And such a deal of skimble-skamble stuff
As puts me from my faith.
SHAKESPEARE, *I Henry IV*. Act iii, sc. 1, l. 155.

For they are yet but ear-kissing arguments.
SHAKESPEARE, *King Lear*. Act ii, sc. 1, l. 9.

1
Could we forbear dispute, and practise love,
We should agree as angels do above.
EDMUND WALLER, *Of Divine Love.* Canto iii.

2
An argument in a circle. (Circulus in probando.)
UNKNOWN. A Latin proverb.

ARISTOCRACY, see Ancestry

ART AND ARTISTS

See also Painting, Sculpture, Skill

I—Art: Definitions

3
The art which is grand and yet simple is that which presupposes the greatest elevation both in artist and in public.
AMIEL, *Journal,* 9 Dec., 1877.

Art strives for form, and hopes for beauty.
GEORGE BELLOWS. (STANLEY WALKER, *City Editor,* p. 152.)

4
Art, unless quickened from above and from within, has in it nothing beyond itself which is visible beauty.
JOHN BROWN, *Horæ Subsecivæ: Notes on Art.*

The beautiful is the most useful in art; but the sublime is the most helpful to morals, for it elevates the mind. (Le beau est plus utile à l'art; mais le sublime est plus utile aux mœurs, parce qu'il élève les esprits.)
JOUBERT, *Pensées.* No. 326.

It is the treating of the commonplace with the feeling of the sublime that gives to art its true power.
J. F. MILLET, *MS. Note,* accompanying unpublished sketches.

5
What is art
But life upon the larger scale, the higher,
When, graduating up in a spiral line
Of still expanding and ascending gyres,
It pushes toward the intense significance
Of all things, hungry for the Infinite?
Art's life,—and where we live, we suffer and toil.
E. B. BROWNING, *Aurora Leigh.* Bk. iv, l. 1151.

The secret of life is in art.
OSCAR WILDE, *The English Renaissance.*

6
It is the glory and good of Art,
That Art remains the one way possible
Of speaking truth, to mouths like mine at least.
ROBERT BROWNING, *The Ring and the Book.* Pt. xii, l. 837.

7
All the arts relating to human life are linked together by a subtle bond of mutual relationship. (Omnes artes, quæ ad humanitatem pertinent, habent quoddam commune vinculum et quasi cognatione quadam inter se continentur.)
CICERO, *Pro Archia Poeta.* Ch. i, sec. 2.

8
Art is science in the flesh.
JEAN COCTEAU, *Le Rappel à l'Ordre,* p. 7.

9
Art is an absolute mistress; she will not be coquetted with or slighted; she requires the most entire self-devotion, and she repays with grand triumphs.
CHARLOTTE CUSHMAN. (*American Actors.* Ch. 10.)

Art is a jealous mistress, and if a man have a genius for painting, poetry, music, architecture, or philosophy, he makes a bad husband and an ill provider.
EMERSON, *Conduct of Life: Wealth.*

10
'Tis the privilege of Art
Thus to play its cheerful part,
Man on earth to acclimate
And bend the exile to his fate.
EMERSON, *Essays, First Series: Art.*

11
Art is the path of the creator to his work.
EMERSON, *Essays, Second Series: The Poet.*

Classic art was the art of necessity: modern romantic art bears the stamp of caprice and chance.
EMERSON, *Journals,* 1856.

Perpetual modernness is the measure of merit in every work of art.
EMERSON, *Representative Men: Plato.*

The conscious utterance of thought, by speech or action, to any end, is Art. . . . From its first to its last works, Art is the spirit's voluntary use and combination of things to serve its end.
EMERSON, *Society and Solitude: Art.*

12
The highest problem of every art is, by means of appearances, to produce the illusion of a loftier reality.
GOETHE, *Truth and Poetry.* Bk. xi.

13
The temple of art is built of words. Painting and sculpture and music are but the blazon of its windows, borrowing all their significance from the light, and suggestive only of the temple's uses.
J. G. HOLLAND, *Plain Talks on Familiar Subjects: Art and Life.*

14
Great art is an instant arrested in eternity.
JAMES HUNEKER, *Pathos of Distance,* p. 120.

15
Art is not a thing: it is a way.
ELBERT HUBBARD, *Epigrams.*

16
An art is a handicraft in flower.
GEORGE ILES, *Jottings.*

17
Art is nothing more than the shadow of humanity.
HENRY JAMES, *Lectures: University in Arts.*

18
Art is power.
LONGFELLOW, *Hyperion.* Bk. iii, ch. v.

Art is the gift of God, and must be used
Unto His glory.

LONGFELLOW, *Michael Angelo*. Pt. i, sec. 2.

1
Art is the desire of a man to express himself, to record the reactions of his personality to the world he lives in.

AMY LOWELL, *Tendencies in Modern American Poetry*, p. 7.

2
Art is the conveyance of spirit by means of matter.

SALVADOR DE MADARIAGA, *Americans Are Boys*.

3
And now too late, we see these things are one:
That art is sacrifice and self-control,
And who loves beauty must be stern of soul.

ALICE DUER MILLER, *An American to France*.

4
Art is a reaching out into the ugliness of the world for vagrant beauty and the imprisoning of it in a tangible dream.

GEORGE JEAN NATHAN, *Critic and the Drama*.

Great art is as irrational as great music. It is mad with its own loveliness.

GEORGE JEAN NATHAN, *House of Satan*, p. 18.

5
Art is a form of catharsis.

DOROTHY PARKER, *Art*.

6
Art does not represent things falsely, but truly as they appear to mankind.

RUSKIN, *Stones of Venice: The Fall*. Ch. 2.

Fine art is that in which the hand, the head and the heart go together.

RUSKIN, *The Two Paths*. Lecture ii.

7
That which takes effect by chance is not an art. (Non est ars, quæ ad effectum casu venit.)

SENECA, *Epistulæ ad Lucilium*. Epis. xxix, sec. 3.

8
Art has been maligned. . . . She is a goddess of dainty thought—reticent of habit, abjuring all obtrusiveness, purposing in no way to better others.

J. MCNEILL WHISTLER, *"Ten O'Clock."*

Art happens—no hovel is safe from it, no Prince may depend upon it, the vastest intelligence cannot bring it about.

J. MCNEILL WHISTLER, *"Ten O'Clock."*

9
The moral life of a man forms part of the subject-matter of the artist, but the morality of art consists in the perfect use of an imperfect medium.

OSCAR WILDE, *The Picture of Dorian Gray: Preface*.

II—Art: Apothegms

10
Art is far feebler than necessity. (Τέχνη δ' ἀνάγκης ἀσθενεστέρα μακρῷ.)

ÆSCHYLUS, *Prometheus Bound*, l. 514.

11
Art can never give the rules that make an art.

EDMUND BURKE, *On the Sublime and Beautiful*. Pt. i, sec. 9.

12
The history of art is the history of revivals.

SAMUEL BUTLER THE YOUNGER, *Note-Books*, p. 130.

13
The fine arts once divorcing themselves from *truth*, are quite certain to fall mad, if they do not die.

CARLYLE, *Latter-Day Pamphlets*. No. 8.

May the Devil fly away with the fine arts!

CARLYLE, *Latter-Day Pamphlets*. No. 8. Quoted as the exclamation of "one of our most distinguished public men."

14
Art for art's sake. (L'art pour l'art.)

VICTOR COUSSIN, *Lecture xxii*, Sorbonne, 1818.

Venerate art as art.

WILLIAM HAZLITT, *On Patronage*.

All loved Art in a seemly way
With an earnest soul and a capital A.

JAMES JEFFREY ROCHE, *The V-a-s-e*.

15
Art thrives most
Where commerce has enrich'd the busy coast.

COWPER, *Charity*, l. 113.

16
Blest be the art that can immortalise.

COWPER, *On the Receipt of My Mother's Picture*, l. 8.

17
New arts destroy the old.

EMERSON, *Essays, First Series: Circles*.

The arts and inventions of each period are only its costume, and do not invigorate men.

EMERSON, *Essays, First Series: Self-Reliance*.

Life too near paralyses art.

EMERSON, *Journals*. Vol. v, p. 292.

18
Painting was called "silent poetry," and poetry "speaking painting." The laws of each art are convertible into the laws of any other.

EMERSON, *Society and Solitude: Art*.

19
Art is either a plagiarist or a revolutionist.

PAUL GAUGUIN. (HUNEKER, *Pathos of Distance*, p. 128.)

20
All passes. Art alone
Enduring stays to us:
The Bust outlasts the throne,—
The Coin, Tiberius.
(Tout passe,—L'art robuste
Seul a l'éternité,
Le buste
Survit à la cité.)

THÉOPHILE GAUTIER, *L'Art*. (Austin Dobson, tr.)

21
When they talk'd of their Raphaels, Correggios, and stuff,

He shifted his trumpet, and only took snuff.
GOLDSMITH, *Retaliation*, l. 145.

I do not want Michael Angelo for breakfast—for luncheon—for dinner—for tea—for supper—for between meals.
MARK TWAIN, *Innocents Abroad*. Ch. 3.

To my mind the old masters are not art; their value is in their scarcity.
THOMAS A. EDISON. (*Golden Book*, April, 1931.)

1
His art is of the lambent and not of the forked kind.
ARTHUR HELPS, *Friends in Council*. Bk. ii, ch. 2.

2
A fine judgment in discerning art. (Judicium subtile videndis artibus.)
HORACE, *Epistles*. Bk. ii, epis. 1, l. 242.

3
Build your art horse-high, pig-tight and bull-strong.
ELBERT HUBBARD, *Epigrams*. "Horse-high, pig-tight and bull-strong," the definition of a legal boundary fence.

4
Art has its fanatics and even its monomaniacs.
VICTOR HUGO, *Ninety-three*. Pt. ii, bk. iii, ch. 6.

5
Piety in art—poetry in art—Puseyism in art—let us be careful how we confound them.
ANNA JAMESON, *Memoirs and Essays: The House of Titian*.

6
Art hath an enemy called ignorance.
BEN JONSON, *Every Man Out of His Humour: Induction*, l. 216.

Art hath no enemy but ignorance.
JOHN TAYLOR, *To John Booker*. Quoting the Latin proverb, *Ars non habet inimicum nisi ignorantem*.

7
We have learned to whittle the Eden Tree to the shape of a surplice-peg,
We have learned to bottle our parents twain in the yelk of an addled egg,
We know that the tail must wag the dog, for the horse is drawn by the cart;
But the Devil whoops, as he whooped of old: "It's clever, but is it Art?"
RUDYARD KIPLING, *The Conundrum of the Workshops*.

8
As the sun colours flowers so does art colour life.
SIR JOHN LUBBOCK, *Pleasures of Life*. Ch. 5.

9
Art must be parochial in the beginning to be cosmopolitan in the end.
GEORGE MOORE, *Ave*, p. 5.

Blessed are the innocent, for theirs is the kingdom of Art!
GEORGE MOORE, *Ave*, p. 165.

10
If the art is concealed, it succeeds. (Si latet ars, prodest.)
OVID, *Ars Amatoria*. Bk. ii, l. 313. The source, perhaps, of the epigram, "Art consists in concealing art." (Ars est celare artem.) The art referred to here, of course, is that of deceit or cunning.

It is a chief point of art to dissemble art.
BRIAN MELBANCKE, *Philotinus*. Sig. G 1. (1583)

It is art to conceal art.
NICHOLAS BRETON, *Works*. Vol. ii, p. 11. (1637)

For art in the sense of artifice, *see* CUNNING.

11
Nothing is so poor and melancholy as art that is interested in itself and not in its subject.
SANTAYANA, *Life of Reason*. Vol. iv, p. 152.

12
Seraphs share with thee Knowledge;
But Art, O Man, is thine alone!
SCHILLER, *The Artists*. St. 2.

13
And Art made tongue-tied by Authority.
SHAKESPEARE, *Sonnets*. No. lxvi.

14
Fashion is a potency in art, making it hard to judge between the temporary and the lasting.
E. C. STEDMAN, *Poets of America*. Ch. 2.

15
This thing which you would almost bet
Portrays a Spanish omelette,
Depicts instead, with wondrous skill,
A horse and cart upon a hill.

Now, Mr. Dove has too much art
To show the horse or show the cart;
Instead, he paints the *creak* and *strain*.
Get it? No pike is half as plain.
BERT LESTON TAYLOR, *Post-Impressionism*.

16
Statues and pictures and verse may be grand,
But they are not the life for which they stand.
JAMES THOMSON (B. V.), *Sunday Up the River*.

17
All the arts are brothers; each one is a light to the others.
VOLTAIRE, *Note to Ode on the Death of the Princess de Bareith*.

All arts are one,—all branches on one tree;
All fingers, as it were, upon one hand.
W. W. STORY, *A Contemporary Criticism*.

18
Listen! There never was an artistic period.
There never was an Art-loving nation.
J. MCNEILL WHISTLER, *"Ten O'Clock."*

Art is upon the Town!—to be chucked under the chin by the passing gallant.
J. MCNEILL WHISTLER, *"Ten O'Clock."*

19
Art never expresses anything but itself.
OSCAR WILDE, *The Decay of Lying*.

20
Art! would that thou wert able to paint character and spirit; then there would be on earth no fairer picture. (Ars utinam mores

animumque effingere posses; Pulchrior in terris nulla tabella foret.)

UNKNOWN. *Inscription,* on portrait of Giovanna Tornabouni, by Ghirlandaio, dated 1488. Formerly in Morgan Library, N. Y.

III—Art is Long

1
Life is short, the art long, opportunity fleeting, experience treacherous, judgment difficult. (Ὁ βίος βραχύς, ἡ δὲ τέχνη μακρή, ὁ δὲ καιρὸς ὀξύς, ἡ δὲ πεῖρα σφαλερή, ἡ δέ κρίσις χαλεπή.)

HIPPOCRATES, *Aphorisms.* Sec. i, No. 1. Hippocrates is writing of the art of healing.

This is the utterance of the greatest of physicians, that life is short and art long. (Illa maximi medicorum exclamatio est, Vitam brevem est, longam artem.)

SENECA, *De Brevitate Vitæ.* Sec. 1.

Art is long, life short, experience deceiving.

RICHARD BRATHWAITE, *English Gentleman,* 74. (1630)

Art is long, life short; judgment difficult, opportunity transient.

GOETHE, *Wilhelm Meister.* Bk. vii, ch. ix.

Art is long, and Time is fleeting.

LONGFELLOW, *A Psalm of Life.*

2
The life so short, the craft so long to learn,
Th' assay so hard, so sharp the conquering.

CHAUCER, *The Parlement of Foules: Proem,* l. 1. (1380)

3
Art is difficult, transient is her reward. (Schwer ist die Kunst, vergänglich ist ihr Preis.)

SCHILLER, *Wallenstein: Prolog,* l. 40.

4
Skill comes so slow, and life so fast doth fly,
We learn so little and forget so much.

SIR JOHN DAVIES, *Nosce Teipsum.* Sec. i, st. 19.

5
One science only will one genius fit:
So vast is art, so narrow human wit.

POPE, *Essay on Criticism.* Pt. i, l. 60.

6
The day is short, the work is much.

BEN SYRA, *Sayings.*

7
So many worlds, so much to do,
So little done, such things to be.

TENNYSON, *In Memoriam.* Sec. lxxiii.

So much to do; so little done.

CECIL RHODES, *Last words.*

IV—Art and Nature

8
It is the fashion to talk as if art were a sort of addition to nature, with power to perfect what nature has begun or correct her when going aside. . . . In truth man has no power over nature except that of motion,—the power of putting natural bodies together or separating them; nature performs all the rest within herself.

FRANCIS BACON, *Description of the Intellectual Globe.* Ch. 2.

9
That hunger of the heart
Which comes when Nature man deserts for
Art.

BULWER-LYTTON, *The New Timon.* Pt. i, sec. iv, l. 69.

Nature I loved, and, next to Nature, Art.

W. S. LANDOR, *The Last Fruit of an Old Tree: Dedication.*

10
No work of art can be great but as it deceives; to be otherwise, is the prerogative of nature only.

EDMUND BURKE, *On the Sublime and Beautiful.* Pt. ii, sec. 11.

11
Not without art, but yet to Nature true.

CHARLES CHURCHILL, *The Rosciad,* l. 699.

12
Things perfected by nature are better than those finished by art. (Meliora sunt ea quæ natura quam illa quæ arte perfecta sunt.)

CICERO, *De Natura Deorum.* Bk. ii, ch. 34, sec. 87.

13
By viewing nature, nature's handmaid, art,
Makes mighty things from small beginnings
grow;
Thus fishes first to shipping did impart,
Their tail the rudder, and their head the
prow.

DRYDEN, *Annus Mirabilis.* St. 155.

14
Art may err, but nature cannot miss.

DRYDEN, *The Cock and the Fox,* l. 452.

Nothing but Nature can give a sincere pleasure; where that is not imitated, 'tis grotesque painting; the fine woman ends in a fish's tail.

DRYDEN, *Essays.* Vol. ii, p. 161.

Men at first produce effect by studying nature, and afterwards look at nature only to produce effect.

HAZLITT, *Lectures on Dramatic Literature,* 139.

15
Nature paints the best part of the picture, carves the best part of the statue, builds the best part of the house, speaks the best part of the oration.

EMERSON, *Essays, First Series: Art.*

And in their vaunted works of Art,
The master-stroke is still her part.

EMERSON, *Nature.* Pt. ii.

These temples grew as grows the grass;
Art might obey, but not surpass.

EMERSON, *The Problem.*

16
To me nature is everything that man is born to, and art is the difference he makes in it.

JOHN ERSKINE, *Gentle Reader,* Dec., 1931.

17
As all Nature's thousand changes
But one changeless God proclaim;

So in Art's wide kingdom ranges
One sole meaning still the same:
This is Truth, eternal Reason,
Which from Beauty takes its dress,
And serene through time and season
Stands for aye in loveliness.
GOETHE, *Wilhelm Meister's Travels*. Ch. 14.

1
Art may make a suit of clothes: but Nature must produce a man.
DAVID HUME, *Essays:* No. xv, *The Epicurean*.

2
Nature is a revelation of God;
Art a revelation of man.
LONGFELLOW, *Hyperion*. Bk. iii, ch. 5.

Art is the child of Nature; yes,
Her darling child, in whom we trace
The features of the mother's face,
Her aspect and her attitude;
All her majestic loveliness
Chastened and softened and subdued
Into a more attractive grace,
And with a human sense imbued.
He is the greatest artist, then,
Whether of pencil or of pen,
Who follows Nature. Never man,
As artist or as artisan,
Pursuing his own fantasies,
Can touch the human heart, or please,
Or satisfy our nobler needs,
As he who sets his willing feet
In Nature's footprints, light and fleet,
And follows fearless where she leads.
LONGFELLOW, *Kéramos*, l. 382.

3
Art is consummate when it seems to be nature. (Ἡ τέχνη τέλειος, ἡνίκ' ἂν φύσις εἶναι δοκῇ.)
LONGINUS, *De Sublimitate*. Ch. xxii, sec. 2.

4
Nature in no case cometh short of art, for the arts are copiers of natural forms. (Οὐκ ἔστι χείρων οὐδεμία φύσις τέχνης.)
MARCUS AURELIUS, *Meditations*. Bk. xi, sec. 10. The first phrase is quoted, apparently, from some unknown poet.

All art is but imitation of nature. (Omnis ars naturæ imitatio est.)
SENECA, *Epistulæ ad Lucilium*. Epis. lxv, sec. 3.

Whoe'er from Nature takes a view,
Must copy and improve it too.
WILLIAM COMBE, *Dr. Syntax in Search of the Picturesque*. Canto ii.

Art, as far as it can, follows nature, as a pupil imitates his master; thus your art must be, as it were, God's grandchild.
(L'arte vostra quella, quanto puote,
Segue, come il maestro fa il discente,
Sì che vostr' arte a Dio quasi è nipote.)
DANTE, *Inferno*. Canto xi, l. 103.

Art imitates nature.
RICHARD FRANCK, *Northern Memoirs*, p. 52.

Wherein the Graver had a strife
With Nature, to out-do the life.
BEN JONSON, *Shakespeare's Portrait*.

5
Art is Nature made by Man
To Man the interpreter of God.
OWEN MEREDITH, *The Artist*. St. 26.

6
Nature is God's, Art is man's instrument.
SIR THOMAS OVERBURY, *A Wife*. St. 8. (1614)

Nature is not at variance with Art, nor Art with Nature. . . . Art is the perfection of Nature. . . . Nature hath made one world and Art another. In brief, all things are artificial; for Nature is the Art of God.
SIR THOMAS BROWNE, *Religio Medici*. Pt. i, sec. 16. (1642) Thomas Hobbes quotes the last sentence without acknowledgment at the beginning of his introduction to *Leviathan*.

Art is man's nature; nature is God's art.
P. J. BAILEY, *Festus: Proem*.

Nature is the art of God. (Deus æternus, arte sua, quæ natura est.)
DANTE, *De Monarchia*. Pt. i, l. 3.

7
All nature is but art.
POPE, *Essay on Man*. Epis. i, l. 289.

8
Art is the right hand of nature. The latter only gave us being, but 'twas the former made us men.
SCHILLER, *Fiesco*. Act ii, sc. 17.

When nature conquers, Art must then give way. (Und siegt Natur, so muss die Kunst entweichen.)
SCHILLER, to Goethe when he staged Voltaire's *Mahomet*.

9
New Art would better Nature's best,
But Nature knows a thing or two.
OWEN SEAMAN, *Ars Postera*.

10
Nature's above art in that respect.
SHAKESPEARE, *King Lear*. Act iv, sc. 6, l. 86.

In scorn of nature, art gave lifeless life.
SHAKESPEARE, *The Rape of Lucrece*. St. 197.

Look, when a painter would surpass the life,
In limning out a well-proportion'd steed,
His art with nature's workmanship at strife,
As if the dead the living should exceed.
SHAKESPEARE, *Venus and Adonis*, l. 289.

Over that art
Which, you say, adds to nature, is an art
That nature makes. . . . The art itself is nature.
SHAKESPEARE, *Winter's Tale*. Act iv, sc. 4, l. 90.

11
When Love owes to Nature his charms,
How vain are the lessons of Art!
HORACE SMITH, *Horace in London*. Bk. i, 19.

12
But who can paint
Like Nature? Can Imagination boast,
Amid its gay creation, hues like hers?
Or can it mix them with that matchless skill?
THOMSON, *The Seasons: Spring*, l. 468.

13
Nature is usually wrong.
J. MCNEILL WHISTLER, *"Ten O'Clock."*

1
Nature contains the elements, in colour and form, of all pictures, as the keyboard contains the notes of all music. But the artist is born to pick, and choose, and group with science, these elements, that the result may be beautiful.

J. McNEILL WHISTLER. Inscribed beneath his bust in the Hall of Fame.

V—Art: The Artist

2
What is the Artist's duty? . . .
To praise and celebrate,
Because his love is great,
The lively miracle
Of Universal Beauty.

WILLIAM ALLINGHAM, *The Artist's Duty.*

3
The great artist is the simplifier.

AMIEL, *Journal*, 25 Nov., 1861.

4
Who of the gods first taught the artist's craft
Laid on the human race their greatest curse.
("Οστις τέχνην κατέδειξε πρῶτος τῶν θεῶν, οὗτος μέγιστον εὗρεν ἀνθρώποις κακόν.)

ANTIPHANES, *Knapheus*, Frag., l. 1.

5
Let each man exercise the art he knows.
("Ερδοι τις ἣν ἕκαστος εἰδείν τέχνην.)

ARISTOPHANES, *The Wasps*, l. 1431. CICERO (*Tusculanarum Disputationum.* Bk. i, ch. 18, sec. 41) puts this into Latin: "Quam quisque norit artem, in hac se exerceat."

6
To be an artist is a great thing, but to be an artist and not know it is the most glorious plight in the world.

J. M. BARRIE, *Sentimental Tommy*, p. 436.

An artist without sentiment is a painter without colours.

J. M. BARRIE, *Tommy and Grizel*, p. 24.

7
The study of the beautiful is a duel in which the artist cries out with terror before he is vanquished.

CHARLES BAUDELAIRE, *An Artist's Confession.*

8
Every artist dips his brush in his own soul, and paints his own nature into his pictures.

HENRY WARD BEECHER, *Proverbs from Plymouth Pulpit.*

Every artist writes his own autobiography.

HAVELOCK ELLIS, *The New Spirit*, p. 178.

9
The man who never in his mind and thought travelled to heaven, is no artist. . . . Mere enthusiasm is the all in all. . . . Passion and expression are beauty itself.

WILLIAM BLAKE. (GILCHRIST, *Life*, i, 310.)

10
None but blockheads copy each other.

WILLIAM BLAKE. (GILCHRIST, *Life*, ii, 174.)

To admire on principle is the only way to imitate without loss of originality.

S. T. COLERIDGE, *Biographia Literaria.* Ch. iv.

11
And you, great sculptor—so, you gave
A score of years to Art, her slave,
And that's your Venus, whence we turn
To yonder girl that fords the burn!

ROBERT BROWNING, *The Last Ride Together.*

Artists! Margaret's smile receive,
And on canvas show it;
But for perfect worship leave
Dora to her poet.

THOMAS CAMPBELL, *Margaret and Dora.*

12
Does he paint? he fain would write a poem—
Does he write? he fain would paint a picture,
Put to proof art alien to the artist's,
Once, and only once, and for one only,
So to be the man and leave the artist,
Gain the man's joy, miss the artist's sorrow.

ROBERT BROWNING, *One Word More.* St. 8.

13
An artist has liberty, if he is free to create any image in any material that he chooses.

G. K. CHESTERTON, *Generally Speaking*, p. 125.

14
Work thou for pleasure! Sing or paint or carve
The thing thou lovest, though the body starve.
Who works for glory misses oft the goal;
Who works for money coins his very soul.
Work for the work's sake, then, and it may be
That these things shall be added unto thee.

KENYON COX, *The Gospel of Art.* (*Century Magazine*, Feb., 1895.)

There is no way to success in art but to take off your coat, grind paint, and work like a digger on the railroad, all day and every day.

EMERSON, *Conduct of Life; Power.* Quoted as having been said by "a brave painter."

He that seeks popularity in art closes the door on his own genius: as he must needs paint for other minds, and not for his own.

ANNA JAMESON, *Memoirs and Essays: Washington Allston.*

Art should never try to be popular.

OSCAR WILDE, *The Soul of Man under Socialism.*

15
The torpid artist seeks inspiration at any cost, by virtue or by vice, by friend or by fiend, by prayer or by wine.

EMERSON, *Conduct of Life: Power.*

You cannot hide any secret. If the artist succor his flagging spirits by opium or wine, his work will characterize itself as the effect of opium or wine.

EMERSON, *Conduct of Life: Worship.*

16
Artists must be sacrificed to their art. Like bees, they must put their lives into the sting they give.

EMERSON, *Letters and Social Aims: Inspiration.*

Every artist was first an amateur.

EMERSON, *Letters and Social Aims: Progress of Culture.*

1
The true artist has the planet for his pedestal; the adventurer, after years of strife, has nothing broader than his shoes.

EMERSON, *Representative Men: Uses of Great Men.*

2
A man may be an artist though he have not his tools about him.

THOMAS FULLER, *Gnomologia.* No. 288.

3
And I thought, like Dr. Faustus, of the emptiness of art,
How we take a fragment for the whole, and call the whole a part.

O. W. HOLMES, *Nux Postcœnatica.* St. 2.

4
The artist needs no religion beyond his work.

ELBERT HUBBARD, *The Philistine.* Vol. xi, p. 136.

5
Scratch an artist and you surprise a child.

JAMES HUNEKER, *Chopin,* p. 25.

6
To draw a moral, to preach a doctrine, is like shouting at the north star. Life is a vast and awful business. The great artist sets down his vision of it and is silent.

LUDWIG LEWISOHN, *Modern Drama,* p. 109.

7
Emigravit is the inscription on the tombstone where he lies;
Dead he is not, but departed,—for the artist never dies.

LONGFELLOW, *Nuremberg.* St. 13.

And it came to pass that after a time the artist was forgotten, but the work lived.

OLIVE SCHREINER, *The Artist's Secret.*

But he is dust; we may not know
His happy or unhappy story:
Nameless, and dead these centuries,
His work outlives him,—there's his glory!

THOMAS BAILEY ALDRICH, *On an Intaglio Head of Minerva.*

8
Nothing can come out of an artist that is not in the man.

H. L. MENCKEN, *Prejudices.* Ser. v, p. 90.

9
The learned understand the theory of art, the unlearned its pleasure. (Docti rationem artis, intelligunt, indocti voluptatem.)

QUINTILIAN, *De Institutione Oratoria.* Bk. ii, ch. 17, sec. 42.

10
Back of the canvas that throbs the painter is hinted and hidden;
Into the statue that breathes the soul of the sculptor is bidden.

RICHARD REALF, *Indirection.*

Behind the poem is the poet's soul;
Behind the canvas throbs the artist's heart.

CHARLES HANSON TOWNE, *Manhattan.*

11
People always confuse the man and the artist because chance has united them in the same body. (On confond toujours l'homme et l'artist sous pretexte que le hasard les a réunis dans le même corps.)

JULES RENARD, *Journal.* Referring to Verlaine.

The artist and censor differ in this wise: that the first is a decent mind in an indecent body and that the second is an indecent mind in a decent body.

G. J. NATHAN, *The Autobiography of an Attitude.*

12
It is futile to assign the place an artist is likely to take in the future. There are fashions in immortality as there are trivial fashions. . . . Books and pictures read differently to different generations.

WILLIAM ROTHENSTEIN, *Men and Memories.* Vol. i, p. 66.

13
He is the greatest artist who has embodied in the sum of his works, the greatest number of the greatest ideas.

RUSKIN, *Modern Painters.* Vol. i, pt. i, ch. 2, 9.

If it is the love of that which your work represents—if, being a landscape painter, it is love of hills and trees that moves you—if, being a figure painter, it is love of human beauty, and human soul that moves you—if, being a flower or animal painter, it is love, and wonder, and delight in petal and in limb that move you, then the Spirit is upon you, and the earth is yours, and the fullness thereof.

RUSKIN, *The Two Paths.* Lect. i.

14
An artist is a dreamer consenting to dream of the actual world.

GEORGE SANTAYANA, *The Life of Reason,* p. 39.

Choice is what separates the artist from the common herd.

MORDAUNT SHAIRP, *The Green Bay Tree.* Act i.

15
Good material often stands idle for want of an artist. (Sæpe bona materia cessat sine artifice.)

SENECA, *Epistulæ ad Lucilium.* Epis. xlvii, 16.

16
In framing an artist, art hath thus decreed,
To make some good, but others to exceed.

SHAKESPEARE, *Pericles.* Act ii, sc. 3, l. 15.

17
The true artist will let his wife starve, his children go barefoot, his mother drudge for his living at seventy, sooner than work at anything but his art.

BERNARD SHAW, *Man and Superman.* Act i.

18
In fields of air he writes his name,
And treads the chambers of the sky;
He reads the stars, and grasps the flame
That quivers round the throne on high.

CHARLES SPRAGUE, *Art.*

19
There is no such thing as a dumb poet or a handless painter. The essence of an artist is that he should be articulate.

SWINBURNE, *Essays and Studies: Matthew Arnold's New Poems.*

1
The Grecian artist gleaned from many faces,
And in a perfect whole the parts combined.
H. T. TUCKERMAN, *Mary.*

2
A great artist can paint a great picture on a small canvas.
C. D. WARNER, *Washington Irving.* Ch. 6.

3
A life passed among pictures makes not a painter—else the policeman in the National Gallery might assert himself. As well allege that he who lives in a library must needs die a poet.
JAMES MCNEILL WHISTLER, *The Gentle Art of Making Enemies,* p. 26.

4
Around the mighty master came
The marvels which his pencil wrought,
Those miracles of power whose fame
Is wide as human thought.
WHITTIER, *Raphael.*

5
Artists, like the Greek gods, are only revealed to one another.
OSCAR WILDE, *The English Renaissance.*

6
High is our calling, Friend!—Creative Art
(Whether the instrument of words she use,
Or pencil pregnant with ethereal hues,)
Demands the service of a mind and heart.
Though sensitive, yet, in their weakest part
Heroically fashioned.
WORDSWORTH, *Miscellaneous Sonnets.* Pt. ii, No. 3.

VI—Art: Bohemia

7
I'd rather live in Bohemia than in any other land.
JOHN BOYLE O'REILLY, *Bohemia.*

8
We all draw a little and compose a little, and none of us have any idea of time or money.
DICKENS, *Bleak House.* Ch. 43.

9
One of those queer artistic dives,
Where funny people had their fling.
Artists, and writers, and their wives—
Poets, all that sort of thing.
OLIVER HERFORD, *The Women of the Better Class.*

10
Bohème is not down on the map because it is not a money-order office.
ELBERT HUBBARD, *The Philistine.* Vol. xi, p. 189.

11
Authors and actors and artists and such
Never know nothing and never know much . . .
Playwrights and poets and such horses' necks
Start off from anywhere, end up at sex.
Diarists, critics, and similar roe
Never say nothing, and never say no.
People Who Do Things exceed my endurance:
God, for a man that solicits insurance!
DOROTHY PARKER, *Bohemia.*

ASPIRATION

See also Ambition, Purpose

12
By aspiring to a similitude of God in goodness, or love, neither man nor angel ever transgressed, or shall transgress.
BACON, *Advancement of Learning.* Bk. ii.

As the hart panteth after the waterbrooks, so panteth my soul after Thee, O God.
Old Testament: Psalms, xlii, 1.

13
Let each man think himself an act of God,
His mind a thought, his life a breath of God;
And let each try, by great thoughts and good deeds,
To show the most of Heaven he hath in him.
P. J. BAILEY, *Festus: Proem.*

14
Alas, that the longest hill
Must end in a vale; but still,
Who climbs with toil, wheresoe'er,
Shall find wings waiting there.
H. C. BEECHING, *Going Down Hill on a Bicycle.*

God, give me hills to climb,
And strength for climbing!
ARTHUR GUITERMAN, *Hills.*

He that stays in the valley shall never get over the hill.
JOHN RAY, *English Proverbs.* No. 152.

Man can climb to the highest summits, but he cannot dwell there long.
BERNARD SHAW, *Candida.* Act iii.

And the most difficult of tasks to *keep*
Heights which the soul is competent to gain.
WORDSWORTH, *The Excursion.* Bk. iv, l. 138.

15
No bird soars too high if he soars with his own wings.
WILLIAM BLAKE, *Proverbs of Hell.*

16
Oh that men would seek immortal moments!
WILLIAM BLAKE. (GILCHRIST, *Life.* Vol. i, p. 65.)

17
The high that proved too high, the heroic for earth too hard,
The passion that left the ground to lose itself in the sky,
Are music sent up to God by the lover and the bard;
Enough that he heard it once: we shall hear it by and by.
ROBERT BROWNING, *Abt Vogler.*

Burrow awhile and build, broad on the roots of things.
ROBERT BROWNING, *Abt Vogler.* St. 2.

Ah, but a man's reach should exceed his grasp,
Or what's a heaven for?
ROBERT BROWNING, *Andrea del Sarto.*

Like plants in mines, which never saw the sun,
But dream of him, and guess where he may be,
And do their best to climb, and get to him.
ROBERT BROWNING, *Paracelsus*. Pt. v, l. 870.

1
What I aspired to be,
And was not, comforts me:
A brute I might have been, but would not sink
i' the scale.
ROBERT BROWNING, *Rabbi Ben Ezra*. St. 7.

'Tis not what man Does which exalts him, but what man Would do.
ROBERT BROWNING, *Saul*. St. 18.

2
When human power and failure
Are equalized forever,
And the great Light that haloes all is the passionate bright endeavour.
ROBERT BUCHANAN, *To David in Heaven*. St. 22.

3
Strong souls
Live like fire-hearted suns; to spend their strength
In furthest striving action.
GEORGE ELIOT, *The Spanish Gypsy*. Bk. iv.

4
Everything good in man leans on what is higher. All our strength and success in the work of our hands depend on our borrowing the aid of the elements. You have seen a carpenter on a ladder with a broad-axe chopping upward chips from a beam. How awkward! But see him on the ground, dressing his timber under him. Now, not his feeble muscles but the force of gravity brings down the axe; that is to say, the planet itself splits his stick. . . . I admire the skill which, on the sea-shore, makes the tides drive wheels and grind corn, and which thus engages the assistance of the moon, like a hired hand. Now that is the wisdom of a man, in every instance of his labor, to hitch his wagon to a star, and see his chore done by the gods themselves.
EMERSON, *Society and Solitude: Civilization*.

Hitch your wagon to a star. Let us not fag in paltry works which serve our pot and bag alone. Let us not lie and steal. No god will help. We shall find all their teams going the other way: every god will leave us. Work rather for those interests which the divinities honor and promote, —justice, love, freedom, knowledge, utility.
EMERSON, *Society and Solitude: Civilization*.

Raise thy head; Take stars for money.
GEORGE HERBERT, *The Church-Porch*. St. 29.

I should delight to have my curls half drowned
In Tyrian dews, and head with roses crowned;
And once more yet, ere I am laid out dead,
Knock at a star with my exalted head.
ROBERT HERRICK, *The Bad Season Makes the Poet Sad*.

Too low they build, who build beneath the stars.
YOUNG, *Night Thoughts*. Night viii, l. 215.

5
No one regards what is before his feet; we all gaze at the stars. (Quod est ante pedes, nemo spectat, cæli scrutantur plagas.)
ENNIUS, *Iphigenia*. (CICERO, *De Divinatione*. Bk. ii, ch. 13, sec. 30.)

Stretching his hand out to catch the stars, he forgets the flowers at his feet.
JEREMY BENTHAM, *Deontology*. Ch. 1, p. 52.

Why thus longing, thus forever sighing
For the far-off, unattain'd, and dim,
While the beautiful all round thee lying
Offers up its low, perpetual hymn?
HARRIET W. SEWALL, *Why Thus Longing?*

6
I drink the wine of aspiration and the drug of illusion. Thus I am never dull.
JOHN GALSWORTHY, *The Wine Horn Mountain*.

7
A good man, through obscurest aspirations,
Has still an instinct of the one true way.
GOETHE, *Faust: Prologue in Heaven*, l. 88.

The restless throbbings and burnings
That hope unsatisfied brings;
The weary longings and yearnings
For the mystical better things.
A. L. GORDON, *Wormwood and Nightshade*.

8
Heaven is not reached at a single bound;
But we build the ladder by which we rise
From the lowly earth to the vaulted skies,
And we mount to its summit round by round.
JOSIAH GILBERT HOLLAND, *Gradatim*. *See also under* VICE.

9
You know the proverb, "Corinth town is fair,
But 'tis not every man that can get there."
(Non cuivis homini contingit adire Corinthum.)
HORACE, *Epistles*. Bk. i, epis. 17, l. 36. (Conington, tr.)

I know full well that here below
Bliss unalloyed there is for none;
My prayer would else fulfilment know—
Never have I seen Carcassonne!
GUSTAVE NADAUD, *Carcassonne*. (Thompson, tr.)

10
Think not of rest; though dreams be sweet,
Start up, and ply your heavenward feet.
JOHN KEBLE, *The Christian Year: Second Sunday in Advent*.

11
Nemesis hangs over men who are overbold in aspiration, whether, like Prometheus, they devise methods and expedients for alleviation of common ills, or, as Io, indulge in building castles in the air.
JOHN KEBLE, *Lectures on Poetry*. No. 23.

12
Lightly I sped when hope was high
And youth beguiled the chase,—
I follow, follow still: but I
Shall never see her face.
F. LOCKER-LAMPSON, *The Unrealized Ideal*.

1
The shades of night were falling fast,
As through an Alpine village passed
A youth, who bore, 'mid snow and ice,
A banner with the strange device,
Excelsior!
LONGFELLOW, *Excelsior.*

Press on!—"for in the grave there is no work
And no device"—Press on! while yet ye may!
N. P. WILLIS, *Press On!* Poem delivered at the departure of the Senior Class of Yale College, in 1827.

2
I see, but cannot reach, the height
That lies forever in the light,
And yet forever and forever,
When seeming just within my grasp,
I feel my feeble hands unclasp,
And sink discouraged into night!
LONGFELLOW, *The Golden Legend: A Village Church.*

My . . . aspirations are my only friends.
LONGFELLOW, *Masque of Pandora.* Pt. iii, l. 74.

3
The thing we long for, that we are
For one transcendent moment.
J. R. LOWELL, *Longing.*

4
A fierce unrest seethes at the core
Of all existing things:
It was the eager wish to soar
That gave the gods their wings. . . .
There throbs through all the worlds that are
This heart-beat hot and strong,
And shaken systems, star by star,
Awake and glow in song.
DON MARQUIS, *Unrest.*

5
Better a brutal starving nation,
Than men with thoughts above their station.
JOHN MASEFIELD, *The Everlasting Mercy,* l. 965.

But all men praise some beauty, tell some tale,
Vent a high mood which makes the rest seem pale.
JOHN MASEFIELD, *Ships.*

6
Yet some there be that by due steps aspire
To lay their just hands on that golden key
That opes the palace of Eternity.
MILTON, *Comus,* l. 12.

Enflamed with the study of learning, and the admiration of virtue; stirred up with high hopes of living to be brave men, and worthy patriots, dear to God, and famous to all ages.
MILTON, *Tractate on Education.*

7
You cannot demonstrate an emotion or prove an aspiration.
JOHN MORLEY, *Rousseau,* p. 402.

8
The road to the heavens remains, and thither will we attempt to go. (Restat iter cæli: cælo temptabimus ire.)
OVID, *Ars Amatoria.* Bk. ii, l. 37.

Let fowk bode weel, an' strive to do their best;
Nae mair's required—let Heav'n mak out the rest.
ALLAN RAMSAY, *The Gentle Shepherd.* Act i, sc. 2.

Who does the best his circumstance allows
Does well, acts nobly; angels could no more.
YOUNG, *Night Thoughts.* Night ii, l. 91.

9
I have Immortal longings in me.
SHAKESPEARE, *Antony and Cleopatra.* Act v, sc. 2, l. 282.

10
'Twere all one,
That I should love a bright particular star,
And think to wed it
SHAKESPEARE, *All's Well that Ends Well.* Act i, sc. 1, l. 96.

The desire of the moth for the star,
Of the night for the morrow,
The devotion to something afar
From the sphere of our sorrow.
SHELLEY, *One Word Is too Often Profaned.*

11
He rises on the toe: that spirit of his
In aspiration lifts him from the earth.
SHAKESPEARE, *Troilus and Cressida.* Act iv, sc. 5, l. 15.

12
Who digs hills because they do aspire,
Throws down one mountain to cast up a higher.
SHAKESPEARE, *Pericles.* Act i, sc. 4, l. 5.

13
And thou my mind aspire to higher things;
Grow rich in that which never taketh rust.
SIR PHILIP SIDNEY, *Sonnet: Leave Me, O Love.*

14
Who shoots at the midday sun, though he be sure he shall never hit the mark, yet as sure he is he shall shoot higher than who aims but at a bush.
SIR PHILIP SIDNEY, *Arcadia.* Bk. ii. (1590)

Sink not in spirit; who aimeth at the sky
Shoots higher much than he that means a tree.
GEORGE HERBERT, *The Church-Porch.* St. 56. (1633)

He shoots higher, that threatens the moon, than he that aims at a tree.
GEORGE HERBERT, *A Priest to the Temple: Preface.*

It is best for great men to shoot over, and for lesser men to shoot short.
LORD HALIFAX, *Works,* p. 245.

15
Sky, be my depth;
Wind, be my width and my height;
World, my heart's span:
Loneliness, wings for my flight!
LEONORA SPEYER, *Measure Me, Sky.*

16
It was my duty to have loved the highest;
It surely was my profit had I known;
It would have been my pleasure had I seen.
We needs must love the highest when we see it.
TENNYSON, *Guinevere,* l. 652.

And ah for a man to arise in me,
That the man I am may cease to be!
TENNYSON, *Maud*. Pt. i, sec. 10, st. 6.

Man is complete and upstanding only when he would be more than man.
MIGUEL DE UNAMUNO, *Life of Don Quixote*.

1
A lover of Jesus and of truth . . . can lift himself above himself in spirit. (Amator Jesu et veritatis . . . potest se elevare supra seipsum in spiritu.)
THOMAS À KEMPIS, *De Imitatione Christi*. Bk. ii, sec. 1.

2
Ah! whither now are fled
Those dreams of greatness? those unsolid hopes
Of happiness? those longings after fame?
Those restless cares? those busy bustling days?
Those gay-spent festive nights?
THOMSON, *The Seasons: Winter*, l. 1033.

3
Ye skies, drop gently round my breast
And be my corselet blue;
Ye earth, receive my lance in rest,
My faithful charger you.
H. D. THOREAU, *The Great Adventure*.

4
All great ideas, the races' aspirations,
All heroisms, deeds of rapt enthusiasts,
Be ye my Gods.
WALT WHITMAN, *Gods*.

5
Better with naked nerve to bear
The needles of this goading air,
Than, in the lap of sensual ease, forego
The godlike power to do, the godlike aim to know.
J. G. WHITTIER, *Last Walk in Autumn*. St. 20.

Let the thick curtain fall;
I better know than all
How little I have gained,
How vast the unattained.
WHITTIER, *My Triumph*. St. 7.

6
Yet was there surely then no vulgar power
Working within us,—nothing less, in truth,
Than that most noble attribute of man, . . .
That wish for something loftier, more adorned,
Than is the common aspect, daily garb,
Of human life.
WORDSWORTH, *The Prelude*. Bk. v, l. 571.

ASS

7
When the prophet beats the ass,
The angel intercedes.
E. B. BROWNING, *Aurora Leigh*. Bk. viii, l. 795.

8
Other folks' burdens kill the ass.
CERVANTES, *Don Quixote*. Pt. ii, ch. 13.

The ass endures the load, but not the overload. (El Asno sufre la carga, mas no la sobrecarga.)
CERVANTES, *Don Quixote*. Pt. ii, ch. 71.

9
Fools! For I also had my hour;
One far fierce hour and sweet:
There was a shout about my ears,
And palms before my feet.
G. K. CHESTERTON, *The Donkey*.

To me the wonderful charge was given,
I, even a little ass, did go
Bearing the very weight of heaven;
So I crept cat-foot, sure and slow.
KATHARINE TYNAN HINKSON, *The Ass Speaks*.

10
The ass thinks one thing, and he that rides him another.
THOMAS D'URFEY, *Quixote*. Pt. iii, act iii, sc. 2.

Better strive with an ill ass than carry the wood one's self.
THOMAS FULLER, *Gnomologia*. No. 930.

11
An ass may bray a good while before he shakes the stars down.
GEORGE ELIOT, *Romola*. Bk. iii, ch. 50.

12
About a donkey's taste why need we fret us?
To lips like his a thistle is a lettuce.
WILLIAM EWART. A free translation of the witticism, "Similem habent labra lactucam," which made Crassus laugh the only time in his life, on seeing an ass eating thistles. (See CICERO, *De Finibus*, v, 30, 92.) Ewart's couplet is quoted by Moore in his diary.

Honey is not for the ass's mouth. (No es la Miel para la boca del asno.)
CERVANTES, *Don Quixote*. Pt. i, ch. 52.

Give an ass oats and he runs after thistles.
GEORGE HERBERT, *Jacula Prudentum*.

13
Who washes an ass's head loseth both labour and soap.
JOHN FLORIO, *First Fruites*. Fo. 34.

14
A dull ass near home needs no spur.
THOMAS FULLER, *Gnomologia*. No. 83.

15
An ass is but an ass, though laden with gold.
THOMAS FULLER, *Gnomologia*. No. 585.

By outward show let's not be cheated;
An ass should like an ass be treated.
JOHN GAY, *Fables: The Packhorse and Carrier*.
See also APE; APPEARANCE.

16
Every ass loves to hear himself bray.
THOMAS FULLER, *Gnomologia*. No. 1404.

17
He that makes himself an ass, must not take it ill if men ride him.
THOMAS FULLER, *Gnomologia*. No. 2232.

We may make ourselves asses, and then everybody will ride us.
C. H. SPURGEON, *John Ploughman*. Ch. 4.

18
Until the Donkey tried to clear
The Fence, he thought himself a Deer.
ARTHUR GUITERMAN, *A Poet's Proverbs*, p. 48.

1
If a donkey bray at you, don't bray at him.
GEORGE HERBERT, *Jacula Prudentum.* (1640)

Because a Donkey takes a whim
To Bray at You, why Bray at Him?
ARTHUR GUITERMAN, *A Poet's Proverbs*, p. 37.

When all tell thee thou art an ass, 'tis time for thee to bray.
JOHN HEYWOOD, *Proverbs.*

2
I had rather ride on an ass that carries me than a horse that throws me.
GEORGE HERBERT, *Jacula Prudentum.*

Better an ass that carries us than a horse that throws us.
J. G. HOLLAND, *Gold-Foil: The Infallible.*

3
God did forbid the Israelites to bring
An Ass unto Him for an offering,
Only, by this dull creature, to express
His detestation to all slothfulness.
ROBERT HERRICK, *The Ass.*

4
The ass often carries gold on his back, yet feeds on thistles.
JAMES HOWELL, *Parly of Beasts*, 17. (1660)

The ass that carrieth wine drinketh water.
THOMAS FULLER, *Gnomologia.*

5
He shall be buried with the burial of an ass.
Old Testament: Jeremiah, xxii, 19.

Asses die and wolves bury them.
THOMAS FULLER, *Gnomologia.* No. 821.

6
Hood an ass with rev'rend purple,
So you can hide his two ambitious ears,
And he shall pass for a cathedral doctor.
BEN JONSON, *Volpone.* Act i, sc. 1.

7
Clad in a lion's shaggy hide
An ass spread terror far and wide.
(De la peau de lion l'âne s'étant vêtu
Étoit craint partout à la ronde.)
LA FONTAINE, *Fables: The Ass in the Lion's Skin.*

What good can it do an ass to be called a lion?
THOMAS FULLER, *Gnomologia.* No. 5490.

8
What has the ass to do with a lyre?
LUCIAN. (THOMAS FRANCKLIN, *Lucian's Works*, ii, 109.)

9
An ass among apes. (Ὄνος ἐν πιθήκοις.)
MENANDER, *Plocium.* Frag. 402.

10
When a jackass brays, no one pays any attention to him, not even other jackasses. But when a lion brays like a jackass, even the lions in the neighborhood may be pardoned for exhibiting a little surprise.
G. J. NATHAN, *Testament of a Critic*, p. 24.

11
Who is there that has not the ears of an ass? (Auriculas asini quis non habet?)
PERSIUS, *Satires.* Sat. i, l. 121.

I am an ass, indeed; you may prove it by my long ears.
SHAKESPEARE, *The Comedy of Errors.* Act iv, sc. 4, l. 29.

The ass is known by his ears. (Ex auribus cognoscitur asinus.)
UNKNOWN. A Latin proverb.

12
A man who cannot beat his ass, beats the saddle. (Sed qui asinum non potest, stratum cædit.)
PETRONIUS, *Satyricon.* Sec. 45.

The fault of the ass must not be laid upon the pack-saddle.
CERVANTES, *Don Quixote.* Pt. ii, ch. 66.

13
An ass laden with gold can enter the gates of any city.
PHILIP OF MACEDON. (PLUTARCH, *Apothegms.*)

An ass loaded with gold goes lightly up a mountain.
CERVANTES, *Don Quixote.* Pt. ii, ch. 35.

There's no fence or fortress against an ass laden with gold.
JAMES HOWELL, *Familiar Letters.* Bk. i, sec. 2, ch. 9.

There is not any place so high whereunto an ass laden with gold will not get up.
JAMES MABBE, *Celestina*, 72. (1631)

See also GOLD: ITS POWER.

14
An ass is beautiful to an ass, and a pig to a pig.
JOHN RAY, *English Proverbs.*

15
Your dull ass will not mend his pace with beating.
SHAKESPEARE, *Hamlet.* Act v, sc. 1, l. 64.

A sharp goad for a stubborn ass. (À dur âne, dur aiguillon.)
UNKNOWN. A French proverb.

16
Methinks I have a great desire to a bottle of hay; good hay, sweet hay, hath no fellow.
SHAKESPEARE, *A Midsummer-Night's Dream.* Act iv, sc. 1, l. 36.

17
O that he were here to write me down an ass!
But, masters, remember that I am an ass;
though it be not written down, yet forget not that I am an ass.
SHAKESPEARE, *Much Ado About Nothing*, Act iv, sc. 2, l. 78.

Egregiously an ass.
SHAKESPEARE, *Othello.* Act ii, sc. 1, l. 318.

My foes tell me plainly that I am an ass; so that by my foes, sir, I profit in the knowledge of myself.
SHAKESPEARE, *Twelfth Night.* Act v, sc. i, l. 21.

18
To the great he is great; to the fool he's a fool:
In the world's dreary desert a crystalline pool,
Where a lion looks in and a lion appears;
But an ass will see only his own ass's ears.
J. T. TROWBRIDGE, *On Amos Bronson Alcott.*

1
One ass names another "Long-ears." (Ein Esel schimpft den andern Lang-ohr.)
UNKNOWN. A German proverb. *See also under* POT.

2
The asses' bridge. (Pons Asinorum.)
Applied to the fifth proposition of the first book of Euclid.

3
The mule is haf hoss and haf jackass, and then kums a full stop, natur discovering her mistake.
JOSH BILLINGS, *On Mules*.

ATHEISM

See also Doubt

4
Atheism is rather in the lip than in the heart of man.
FRANCIS BACON, *Essays: Of Atheism*.

They that deny a God destroy man's nobility; for certainly man is of kin to the beasts by his body; and if he be not of kin to God by his spirit, he is a base and ignoble creature.
FRANCIS BACON, *Essays: Of Atheism*.

5
God never wrought miracle to convince atheism, because his ordinary works convince it.
FRANCIS BACON, *Essays: Of Atheism*.

There was never miracle wrought by God to convert an atheist, because the light of nature might have led him to confess a God.
BACON, *Advancement of Learning*. Bk. ii.

6
Atheism leaves a man to sense, to philosophy, to natural piety, to laws, to reputation; all which may be guides to an outward moral virtue.
FRANCIS BACON, *Essays: Of Superstition*.

Great hypocrites are the real atheists. (Magni hypocritæ sunt veri atheistæ.)
FRANCIS BACON, *De Augmentis Scientiarum*. Pt. i, sec. 13.

7
Mock on, mock on, Voltaire, Rousseau;
Mock on, mock on; 'tis all in vain!
You throw the sand against the wind,
And the wind blows it back again.
WILLIAM BLAKE, *Mock On*.

8
All we have gained then by our unbelief
Is a life of doubt diversified by faith,
For one of faith diversified by doubt:
We called the chess-board white,—we call it black.
ROBERT BROWNING, *Bishop Blougram's Apology*.

Just when we're safest, there's a sunset-touch,
A fancy from a flower-bell, some one's death,
A chorus-ending from Euripides,—
And that's enough for fifty hopes and fears. . . .
The grand Perhaps!
ROBERT BROWNING, *Bishop Blougram's Apology*.

9
An atheist-laugh's a poor exchange
For Deity offended!
BURNS, *Epistle to a Young Friend*.

A Scoffer, always on the grin.
THOMAS HOOD, *Ode to Rae Wilson*, l. 152.

A man whom they had, you see,
Marked as a Sadducee.
R. H. BARHAM, *The Black Mousquetaire*.

10
He who does not believe that God is above all is either a fool or has no experience of life.
CÆCILIUS STATIUS, *Fragments*. No. 15.

11
Who seeks perfection in the art
Of driving well an ass and cart,
Or painting mountains in a mist,
Seeks God although an Atheist.
FRANCIS CARLIN, *Perfection*.

12
There is no unbelief;
Whoever plants a seed beneath the sod
And waits to see it push away the clod,
He trusts in God.
LIZZIE YORK CASE, *There Is No Unbelief*. Sometimes erroneously attributed to Bulwer-Lytton. (*See* STEVENSON, *Famous Single Poems*.)

The fearful Unbelief is unbelief in yourself.
CARLYLE, *Sartor Resartus: The Everlasting No*. Bk. ii, ch. 7.

13
Now who that runs can read it,
The riddle that I write
Of why this poor old sinner
Should sin without delight?
But I, I cannot read it
(Although I run and run)
Of them that do not have the faith
And will not have the fun.
G. K. CHESTERTON, *The Song of the Strange Ascetic*.

14
Forth from his dark and lonely hiding-place,
(Portentous sight!) the owlet Atheism,
Sailing on obscene wings athwart the noon,
Drops his blue-fringèd lids, and holds them close,
And hooting at the glorious sun in Heaven,
Cries out, "Where is it?"
S. T. COLERIDGE, *Fears in Solitude*, l. 81.

15
Blind unbelief is sure to err,
And scan his work in vain;
God is his own interpreter,
And he will make it plain.
COWPER, *Light Shining Out of Darkness*.

The wildest scorner of his Maker's laws
Finds in a sober moment time to pause.
COWPER, *Tirocinium*, l. 55.

16
Atheism is the last word of theism.
HEINRICH HEINE, *MS. Papers*.

1
The devil divides the world between atheism and superstition.
GEORGE HERBERT, *Jacula Prudentum.*

2
The infidels of one age have been the aureoled saints of the next. The destroyers of the old are the creators of the new.
R. G. INGERSOLL, *The Great Infidels.*

3
I do not know, sir, that the fellow is an infidel; but if he be an infidel, he is an infidel as a dog is an infidel; that is to say, he has never thought upon the subject.
SAMUEL JOHNSON. (BOSWELL, *Life,* 1769.)

4
Some believe that all things are subject to the chances of fortune, and that the world has no governor to move it. (Sunt in fortunæ qui casibus omnia ponant Et nullo credant mundum rectore moveri.)
JUVENAL, *Satires.* Sat. xiii, l. 86.

5
Fools! who fancy Christ mistaken;
Man a tool to buy and sell;
Earth a failure, God-forsaken,
Ante-room of Hell.
CHARLES KINGSLEY, *The World's Age.*

6
Sire, I had no need for that hypothesis. (Sire, je n'avais besoin de cet hypothèse.)
LA PLACE, to Napoleon, when the latter asked why God was not mentioned in the *Traité de la Mécanique Céleste.*

7
God is not dumb, that He should speak no more;
If thou hast wanderings in the wilderness
And find'st not Sinai, 'tis thy soul is poor.
J. R. LOWELL, *Bibliolatres.*

8
There is no strength in unbelief. Even the unbelief of what is false is no source of might. It is the truth shining from behind that gives the strength to disbelieve.
GEORGE MACDONALD, *The Marquis of Lossie.* Ch. 42.

Unbelief is blind.
JOHN MILTON, *Comus,* l. 519.

9
There are two things which I abhor: the learned in his infidelities, and the fool in his devotions.
MAHOMET. (EMERSON, *Conduct of Life: Worship.*)

10
A man cannot become an atheist merely by wishing it. (N'est pas athée qui veut.)
NAPOLEON BONAPARTE, *Sayings of Napoleon.*

11
Infidelity does not consist in believing or in disbelieving: it consists in professing to believe what one does not believe.
THOMAS PAINE, *Age of Reason.* Pt. i.

12
It is ridiculous to suppose that the great head of things, whatever it be, pays any regard to human affairs.
PLINY THE ELDER, *Historia Naturalis.* Bk. ii, sec. 1.

13
The fool hath said in his heart, There is no God.
Old Testament: Psalms, xiv, 1; liii, 1.

"There is no God," the foolish saith,
But none, "There is no sorrow":
And nature oft the cry of faith
In bitter need will borrow.
Eyes, which the preacher could not school,
By wayside graves are raisèd;
And lips say, "God be pitiful,"
Who ne'er said, "God be praisèd."
E. B. BROWNING, *The Cry of the Human.*

"There is no God," the wicked saith,
"And truly it's a blessing,
For what He might have done with us
It's better only guessing." . . .
And almost every one, when age,
Disease, or sorrows strike him,
Inclines to think there is a God,
Or something very like Him.
ARTHUR HUGH CLOUGH, *Dipsychus.* Pt. i, sc. 5.

14
Pests of society; because their endeavours are directed to loosen the bands of it, and to take at least one curb out of the mouth of that wild beast man.
HENRY ST. JOHN, *Letter,* 12 Sept., 1724. Referring to free-thinkers.

15
We are not to be guilty of that practical atheism, which, seeing no guidance for human affairs but its own limited foresight, endeavours itself to play the god, and decide what will be good for mankind and what bad.
HERBERT SPENCER, *Social Statics.* Pt. iv, ch. 32, sec. 8.

16
There are some spirits so atheistical that they . . . search their houses with a sunbeam, that they may be instructed in all the corners of nastiness.
JEREMY TAYLOR, *Holy Living.* Ch. ii, sec. 3.

17
I did it ignorantly in unbelief.
New Testament: I Timothy, i, 13.

18
He hath denied the faith, and is worse than an infidel.
New Testament: I Timothy, v, 8.

19
What behaved well in the past or behaves well to-day is not such a wonder,
The wonder is always and always how there can be a mean man or an infidel.
WALT WHITMAN, *Song of Myself.* Pt. xxii, l. 28.

20
By night an atheist half-believes a God.
YOUNG, *Night Thoughts.* Night v, l. 176.

1
A daring infidel (and such there are,
From pride, example, lucre, rage, revenge,
Or pure heroical defect of thought),
Of all earth's madmen, most deserves a chain.
YOUNG, *Night Thoughts*. Night vii, l. 201.

2
Selfishness is the only real atheism; aspiration, unselfishness, the only real religion.
ISRAEL ZANGWILL, *Children of the Ghetto*. Ch. 16.

ATHENS, see Greece

AUDACITY, see Boldness

AURORA, see Dawn

AUTHORITY

3
Who holds a power but newly gained is ever stern of mood. (Ἅπας δὲ τραχὺς, ὅστις ἂν νέον κρατῇ.)
ÆSCHYLUS, *Prometheus Bound*, l. 35.

None is more severe than he of humble birth when raised to high estate. (Aspersius nihil est humili, cum surgit in altum.)
CLAUDIAN, *In Eutropium*. Bk. i, l. 181.

4
Authority intoxicates,
And makes mere sots of magistrates;
The fumes of it invade the brain,
And make men giddy, proud, and vain.
SAMUEL BUTLER, *Miscellaneous Thoughts*, l. 282.

5
He who is firmly seated in authority soon learns to think security, and not progress, the highest lesson of statecraft.
J. R. LOWELL, *Among My Books: New England Two Centuries Ago.*

6
For he taught them as one having authority, and not as the scribes.
New Testament: Matthew vii, 29.

I am a man under authority, having soldiers under me: and I say to this man, Go, and he goeth; and to another, Come, and he cometh.
New Testament: Matthew, viii, 9.

7
To exercise authority with cruel claws. (Exercere imperium sævis unguibus.)
PHÆDRUS, *Fables*. Bk. i, fab. 31, l. 12.

8
Authority melts from me.
SHAKESPEARE, *Antony and Cleopatra*. Act iii, sc. 13, l. 90.

Authority forgets a dying king.
TENNYSON, *The Passing of Arthur*, l. 289.

9
Shall remain!
Hear you this Triton of the minnows? mark you
His absolute "shall"?
SHAKESPEARE, *Coriolanus*. Act iii, sc. 1, l. 88.

Must? Why, colonel, must's for the King.
SWIFT, *Polite Conversation*. Dial. i.

10
Thou hast seen a farmer's dog bark at a beggar? . . . And the creature run from the cur? There thou might'st behold the great image of authority: a dog's obeyed in office.
SHAKESPEARE, *King Lear*. Act iv, sc. 6, l. 159.

Thus can the demigod Authority
Make us pay down for our offence by weight
The words of heaven.
SHAKESPEARE, *Measure for Measure*. Act i, sc. 2, l. 124.

11
Drest in a little brief authority.
SHAKESPEARE, *Measure for Measure*. Act ii, sc. 2, l. 118.

12
Though authority be a stubborn bear, yet he is oft led by the nose with gold.
SHAKESPEARE, *The Winter's Tale*. Act iv, sc. 4, l. 831.

AUTHORS, AUTHORSHIP, see Writing

AUTUMN

See also Seasons.

I—Autumn: Its Beauty

13
O Autumn, laden with fruit, and stainèd
With the blood of the grape, pass not, but sit
Beneath my shady roof; there thou may'st rest
And tune thy jolly voice to my fresh pipe,
And all the daughters of the year shall dance!
Sing now the lusty song of fruits and flowers.
WILLIAM BLAKE, *To Autumn.*

14
Earth's crammed with heaven,
And every common bush afire with God.
E. B. BROWNING, *Aurora Leigh*. Bk. vii, l. 821.

We lack but open eye and ear
To find the Orient's marvels here;
The still small voice in autumn's hush,
Yon maple wood the burning bush.
WHITTIER, *The Chapel of the Hermits*. St. 16.

15
Autumn wins you best by this, its mute
Appeal to sympathy for its decay.
ROBERT BROWNING, *Paracelsus*. Pt. i, l. 25.

16
All-cheering Plenty, with her flowing horn,
Led yellow Autumn, wreath'd with nodding corn.
BURNS, *The Brigs of Ayr*, l. 221.

17
There is something in the autumn that is native to my blood—
Touch of manner, hint of mood;
And my heart is like a rhyme,
With the yellow and the purple and the crimson keeping time.
BLISS CARMAN, *A Vagabond Song.*

The scarlet of the maples can shake me like a cry

Of bugles going by.
And my lonely spirit thrills
To see the frosty asters like a smoke upon the hills.
BLISS CARMAN, *A Vagabond Song.*

1
A haze on the far horizon,
The infinite, tender sky,
The ripe, rich tint of the cornfields,
And the wild geese sailing high,—
And all over upland and lowland
The charm of the goldenrod,—
Some of us call it Autumn,
And others call it God.
WILLIAM HERBERT CARRUTH, *Each in His Own Tongue.*

The red upon the hill
Taketh away my will;
If anybody sneer,
Take care, for God is here,
That's all.
EMILY DICKINSON, *Mysteries.*

O be less beautiful, or be less brief!
WILLIAM WATSON, *Autumn.*

2
These are the days when skies put on
The old, old sophistries of June,—
A blue and gold mistake.
EMILY DICKINSON, *Indian Summer.*

The morns are meeker than they were.
EMILY DICKINSON, *Autumn.*

3
How bravely Autumn paints upon the sky
The gorgeous fame of Summer which is fled!
THOMAS HOOD, *Written in a Volume of Shakespeare.*

4
Fruit-bearing autumn. (Pomifer autumnus.)
HORACE, *Odes.* Bk. iv, ode 7, l. 11.

Autumn into earth's lap does throw
Brown apples gay in a game of play,
As the equinoctials blow.
DINAH MARIA MULOCK CRAIK, *October.*

5
Season of mists and mellow fruitfulness,
Close bosom-friend of the maturing sun;
Conspiring with him how to load and bless
With fruit the vines that round the thatch-eaves run;
To bend with apples the moss'd cottage-trees,
And fill all fruit with ripeness to the core.
JOHN KEATS, *To Autumn.* St. 1.

Who hath not seen thee oft amid thy store?
Sometimes whoever seeks abroad may find
Thee sitting careless on a granary floor,
Thy hair soft-lifted by the winnowing wind.
JOHN KEATS, *To Autumn.* St. 2.

6
The world puts on its robes of glory now;
The very flowers are tinged with deeper dyes;
The waves are bluer, and the angels pitch
Their shining tents along the sunset skies.
ALBERT LAIGHTON, *Autumn.*

7
Third act of the eternal play!
In poster-like emblazonries
"Autumn once more begins today"—
'Tis written all across the trees
In yellow letters like Chinese
RICHARD LE GALLIENNE, *The Eternal Play.*

8
Behold congenial Autumn comes,
The Sabbath of the year!
JOHN LOGAN, *Ode Written on a Visit to the Country in Autumn.*

9
It was Autumn, and incessant
Piped the quails from shocks and sheaves,
And, like living coals, the apples
Burned among the withering leaves.
LONGFELLOW, *Pegasus in Pound.*

10
What visionary tints the year puts on,
When falling leaves falter through motionless air
Or numbly cling and shiver to be gone!
How shimmer the low flats and pastures bare,
As with her nectar Hebe Autumn fills
The bowl between me and those distant hills,
And smiles and shakes abroad her misty, tremulous hair!
J. R. LOWELL, *An Indian Summer Reverie.*

11
Autumn, the fairest season of the year. (Autumnum, cum formossisimus annus.)
OVID, *Ars Amatoria.* Bk. ii, l. 315.

12
O, it sets my heart a clickin' like the tickin' of a clock,
When the frost is on the punkin and the fodder's in the shock.
JAMES WHITCOMB RILEY, *When the Frost is on the Punkin.*

13
The teeming autumn, big with rich increase.
SHAKESPEARE, *Sonnets.* No. xcvii.

14
There is a harmony
In Autumn, and a lustre in its sky,
Which thro' the Summer is not heard or seen,—
As if it could not be, as if it had not been!
SHELLEY, *Hymn to Intellectual Beauty.* St. 7.

15
Autumnal frosts enchant the pool,
And make the cart-ruts beautiful.
R. L. STEVENSON, *The House Beautiful.*

16
How are the veins of thee, Autumn, laden?
Umbered juices, And pulpèd oozes
Pappy out of the cherry-bruises,
Froth the veins of thee, wild, wild maiden!
With hair that musters
In globèd clusters,
In tumbling clusters, like swarthy grapes.
FRANCIS THOMPSON, *A Corymbus for Autumn.*

1
While Autumn, nodding o'er the yellow plain,
Comes jovial on.
THOMSON, *The Seasons: Autumn*, l. 2.

2
The tints of autumn—a mighty flower garden blossoming under the spell of the enchanter, Frost.
WHITTIER, *Patucket Falls*.

II—Autumn: Its Sadness

3
Now Autumn's fire burns slowly along the woods,
And day by day the dead leaves fall and melt,
And night by night the monitory blast
Wails in the key-hole, telling how it pass'd
O'er empty fields, or upland solitudes,
Or grim wide wave; and now the power is felt
Of melancholy, tenderer in its moods
Than any joy indulgent Summer dealt.
WILLIAM ALLINGHAM, *Autumnal Sonnet*.

4
The melancholy days are come, the saddest of the year,
Of wailing winds, and naked woods, and meadows brown and sear.
BRYANT, *The Death of the Flowers*.

5
When chill November's surly blast
Made fields and forests bare.
BURNS, *Man Was Made to Mourn*.

No Park—no Ring—no afternoon gentility—
No company—no nobility—
No warmth, no cheerfulness, no healthful ease,
No comfortable feel in any member—
No shade, no shine, no butterflies, no bees,
No fruits, no flowers, no leaves, no birds—
November!
THOMAS HOOD, *No!*

November's sky is chill and drear,
November's leaf is red and sear.
SCOTT, *Marmion:* Canto i, *Introduction*.

6
A breath, whence no man knows,
Swaying the grating weeds, it blows;
It comes, it grieves, it goes.
Once it rocked the summer rose.
JOHN VANCE CHENEY, *Passing of Autumn*.

7
My sorrow when she's here with me,
Thinks these dark days of autumn rain
Are beautiful as days can be;
She loves the bare, the withered tree;
She walks the sodden pasture lane.
ROBERT FROST, *My November Guest*.

8
I saw old Autumn in the misty morn
Stand shadowless like Silence, listening
To silence, for no lonely bird would sing
Into his hollow ear from woods forlorn.
THOMAS HOOD, *Ode to Autumn*, l. 1.

Boughs are daily rifled by the gusty thieves,
And the Book of Nature getteth short of leaves.
THOMAS HOOD, *The Seasons*.

9
Dread autumn, harvest-season of the Goddess of Death. (Autumnusque gravis, Libitinæ quæstus acerbæ.)
HORACE, *Satires*. Bk. ii, sat. 6, l. 19.

10
Sorrow and the scarlet leaf,
Sad thoughts and sunny weather;
Ah me! this glory and this grief
Agree not well together!
T. W. PARSONS, *A Song for September*.

11
End of autumn.
The hop of a wild rabbit
Scuttling through dead leaves.
FLORENCE B. SPILGER, *November*.

12
Cold autumn, wan with wrath of wind and rain.
A. C. SWINBURNE, *Autumn and Winter*. St. 1

AVARICE

See also Gold: The Lust for Gold; Money.

13
Vile avarice and pride. from Heaven accurst,
In all are ill, but in a church-man worst.
WILLIAM ALEXANDER, *Doomsday: The Sixth Hour*. St. 86.

14
Covetousness breaks the sack.
FRANCIS BACON, *Promus*. No. 616. (1594)

Covetousness bursts the bag.
CERVANTES, *Don Quixote*. Pt. i, ch. 20.

15
He has not acquired a fortune; the fortune has acquired him.
BION, of a miser. (DIOGENES LAERTIUS, *Bion*. Bk. iv, sec. 50.)

Covetousness cracks the sinews of faith; numbs the apprehension of anything above sense, and only affected with the certainty of things present, makes a peradventure of things to come.
SIR THOMAS BROWNE, *Christian Morals*. Pt. i, sec. 8.

16
Covetous desires, and inordinate love of riches.
Book of Common Prayer: St. Matthew's Day.

17
And were it not that they are loath to lay out money on a rope, they would be hanged forthwith, and sometimes die to save charges.
ROBERT BURTON, *Anatomy of Melancholy*. Pt. i, sec. ii, mem. 3, subs. 12.

Spare all I have, and take my life!
FARQUHAR, *The Beaux' Stratagem*. Act v, sc. 2.

18
The very suspicion of avarice is to be avoided. (Vitanda tamen est suspicio avaritiæ.)
CICERO, *De Officiis*. Bk. ii, ch. 17, sec. 58.

19
If you would abolish avarice, you must abolish its mother, luxury. (Avaritium si tollere vultia, mater ejus est tollenda, luxuries.)
CICERO, *De Oratore*. Bk. ii, sec. 40.

1
He who covets is always poor. (Semper inops quicumque cupit.)
CLAUDIAN, *In Rufinum*. Bk. i, l. 200.

Avarice of all is ever nothing's father.
GEORGE CHAPMAN, *The Revenge of Bussy D'Ambois*. Act v, sc. 1.

Covetousness, as well as prodigality, brings a man to a morsel of bread.
THOMAS FULLER, *Gnomologia*. No. 1173.

2
Avarice, mother of crimes, greedy for more the more she possesses, ever searching open-mouthed for gold. (Schelerum matrem, quæ semper habendo Plus sitiens patulis rimatur faucibus aurum, Trudis Avaritium.)
CLAUDIAN, *De Consulatu Stilichonis*. Bk. ii, l. 111.

3
Avarice and happiness never saw each other, how then should they become acquainted?
BENJAMIN FRANKLIN, *Poor Richard*, 1734.

If I knew a miser, who gave up every kind of comfortable living, all the pleasure of doing good to others, all the esteem of his fellow-citizens, and the joys of benevolent friendship, for the sake of accumulating wealth, Poor man, said I, you pay too much for your whistle.
BENJAMIN FRANKLIN, *The Whistle*.

4
A covetous man does nothing well till he dies.
THOMAS FULLER, *Gnomologia*. No. 51.

For Age and Avarice, *see* AGE: ITS PENALTIES.

5
The devil lies brooding in the miser's chest.
THOMAS FULLER, *Gnomologia*. No. 4484.

6
Avarice, sphincter of the heart.
MATTHEW GREEN, *The Spleen*, l. 697.

7
Punishment of a miser,—to pay the drafts of his heir in his tomb.
HAWTHORNE, *American Note-Books*, 10 July, 1838.

8
He'd drive a louse a mile for the skin and tallow of 'en.
W. C. HAZLITT, *English Proverbs*, 198.

He would have flayed a louse to save the skin of it.
JOHN FLORIO, *Second Frutes*, 117. (1591)

He would have flayed a louse for her skin, he was so covetous.
WODROEPHE, *Spared Houres*, 285. (1623)

Thrifty! Man, she'd skin a flea for his hide.
DUFFY, *The Coiner*. Sc. 7.

9
You cannot flay a stone.
GEORGE HERBERT, *Jacula Prudentum*.

To skin a stone for a penny, and break a knife of twelve-pence.
JAMES HOWELL, *Proverbs*, 11.

He would skin a flint.
BERTHELSON, *Eng.-Danish Dict.*, s.v. "skin."

10
Never was scraper brave man. Get to live;
Then live, and use it. . . . Surely use alone
Makes money not a contemptible stone. . . .
Gold thou mayst safely touch; but if it stick
Unto thy hands, it woundeth to the quick.
GEORGE HERBERT, *The Church-Porch*. St. 26.

11
The miser acquires, yet fears to use his gains. (Quærit, et inventis miser abstinet, ac timet uti.)
HORACE, *Ars Poetica*, l. 170.

12
Though your threshing-floor grind out a hundred thousand bushels of grain, not on that account will your stomach hold more than mine. (Milia frumenti tua triverit area centum, Non tuus hoc capiet venter plus ac meus.)
HORACE, *Satires*. Bk. i, sat. 1, l. 45.

13
The people hiss me, but at home I clap my hands for myself, once I gaze on the moneys in my chest. (Populus me sibilat, at mihi plaudo Ipse domi, simul ac nummos contemplor in arca.)
HORACE, *Satires*. Bk. i, sat. 1, l. 66.

Poor worms, they hiss at me, whilst I at home
Can be contented to applaud myself, . . . with joy
To see how plump my bags are and my barns.
BEN JONSON, *Every Man Out of His Humour*. Act i, sc. 1.

The unsunn'd heaps Of miser's treasures.
MILTON, *Comus*, l. 398.

14
Avarice, the spur of industry.
DAVID HUME, *Of Civil Liberty*.

15
Woe unto them that join house to house, that lay field to field, till there be no place!
Old Testament: Isaiah, v. 8.

16
Some men make fortunes, but not to enjoy them;
Blinded by avarice, they live to make fortunes.
(Non propter vitam faciunt patrimonia quidam,
Sed vitio cæci propter patrimonia vivunt.)
JUVENAL, *Satires*. Sat. xii, l. 50.

17
It is plain madness to live in want that you may die rich. (Manifesta phrenesis, Ut locuples moriaris, egentis vivere facto.)
JUVENAL, *Satires*. Sat. xiv, l. 136.

To famish in plenty, and live poorly to die rich, were a multiplying improvement in madness, and use upon use in folly.
SIR THOMAS BROWNE, *Christian Morals*. Pt. i, sec. 7.

A mere madness, to live like a wretch, and die rich.
ROBERT BURTON, *Anatomy of Melancholy*. Pt. i, sec. ii, mem. 3, subs. 12.

Some men choose to be miserable that they may

be rich, rather than be happy with the expense of money and doing noble things.
JEREMY TAYLOR, *Holy Living*. Ch. iv, sec. 8.

1
The love of pelf increases with the pelf. (Crescit amor nummi quantum ipsa pecunia crescit.)
JUVENAL, *Satires*. Sat. xiv, l. 139.

The more a man hath, the more he desireth.
JOHN FLORIO, *First Fruites*. Fo. 32.

Much would have more, but often meets with less.
THOMAS FULLER, *Gnomologia*. No. 3487.

Hoards after hoards his rising raptures fill;
Yet still he sighs, for hoards are wanting still.
GOLDSMITH, *The Traveller*, l. 53.

Poorly rich, so wanteth in his store,
That, cloy'd with much, he pineth still for more.
SHAKESPEARE, *The Rape of Lucrece*, l. 97.

2
Avarice is more opposed to economy than liberality is. (L'avarice est plus opposée à l'économie que la libéralité.)
LA ROCHEFOUCAULD, *Maximes*. No. 167.

3
Excess of wealth is cause of covetousness.
MARLOWE, *The Jew of Malta*. Act i, sc. 2.

4
The beautiful eyes of my money-box!
He speaks of it as a lover of his mistress.
(Les beaux yeux de ma cassette!
Il parle d'elle comme un amant d'une maîtresse.)
MOLIÈRE, *L'Avare*. Act v, sc. 3.

5
The mischief of grudging and the marring of grasping.
WILLIAM MORRIS, *Story of Child Christopher*.

6
He was always ready to pick a halfpenny out of the dirt with his teeth. (Paratus fuit quadrantem de stercore mordicus tollere.)
PETRONIUS, *Satyricon*. Sec. 43.

7
True it is that avarice is rich, modesty starves. (Verum est aviditas dives, et pauper pudor.)
PHÆDRUS, *Fables*. Bk. ii, fab. 1, l. 12.

8
Since you will go where all have gone before, why torment your disgraceful life with such mean ambitions? Tell me, O miser. (Abiturus illuc priores abierunt, Quid mente cæca torques spiritum? Tibi dico, avare.)
PHÆDRUS, *Fables*. Bk. iv, fab. 19, l. 16.

9
You might as well seek water from a pumice stone, that's thirsty itself. (Nam tu aquam a pumice nunc postulas, qui ipsius sitiat.)
PLAUTUS, *Persa*, l. 41. (Act i, sc. 1.)

For who'll wrest water from a flinty stone?
JOHN WEEVER, *Epigrammes*, 17.

There's no getting blood out of a turnip.
FREDERICK MARRYAT, *Japhet*. Ch. 4.

10
Which is the happier or the wiser,
A man of merit, or a miser?
POPE, *Imitations of Horace: Satires*. Bk. ii, sat. 6, l. 147.

11
The miser is as much in want of what he has as of what he has not. (Tam deest avaro quod habet, quam quod non habet.)
PUBLILIUS SYRUS, *Sententiæ*. No. 440.

Poverty wants much, but avarice everything. (Desunt inopiæ multa, avaritiæ omnia.)
PUBLILIUS SYRUS, *Sententiæ*. No. 441.

The avaricious man is good to no one, but he is worst of all to himself. (In nullam avarus bonus est, in se pessimus.)
PUBLILIUS SYRUS, *Sententiæ*. No. 442.

12
His money comes from him like drops of blood.
JOHN RAY, *English Proverbs*, 90. (1678)

13
Covetous of the property of others and prodigal of his own. (Alieni appetens, sui profusus.)
SALLUST, *Catilina*. Ch. 5, sec. 4.

14
To greed, all nature is insufficient. (Avidis natura parum est.)
SENECA, *Hercules Œtæus*, l. 631.

15
How quickly nature falls into revolt
When gold becomes her object!
For this the foolish over-careful fathers
Have broke their sleep with thoughts, their brains with care,
Their bones with industry.
SHAKESPEARE, *II Henry IV*. Act iv, sc. 5, l. 66.

Doth, like a miser, spoil his coat with scanting
A little cloth.
SHAKESPEARE, *Henry V*. Act ii, sc. 4, l. 47.

16
Happy always was it for that son
Whose father for his hoarding went to hell.
SHAKESPEARE, *III Henry VI*. Act ii, sc. 2, l. 45.

17
When Marcus Brutus grows so covetous,
To lock such rascal counters from his friends,
Be ready, gods, with all your thunderbolts:
Dash him to pieces!
SHAKESPEARE, *Julius Cæsar*. Act iv, sc. 3, l. 79.

This avarice
Sticks deeper, grows with more pernicious root.
SHAKESPEARE, *Macbeth*. Act iv, sc. 3, l. 84.

18
An old miser kept a tame jackdaw, that used to steal pieces of money, and hide them in a hole, which a cat observing, asked, "Why he would hoard up those round shining things that he could make no use of?" "Why," said the jackdaw, "my master has a whole chest-full, and makes no more use of them than I do."
SWIFT, *Thoughts on Various Subjects*.

1
Covetousness has such a blinding power that all the arguments in the world will not convince a man that he is covetous.
THOMAS WILSON, *Maxims of Piety*, 29.

2
Covetousness is the root of all evil, the ground of all vice.
LEONARD WRIGHT, *Display of Dutie*, 10. (1589)
See also MONEY: THE ROOT OF EVIL.

B

BABY AND BABYHOOD

See also Birth; Death and the Child

3
Have you not heard the poets tell
How came the dainty Baby Bell
Into this world of ours?
The gates of heaven were left ajar: . . .
Oh, earth was full of singing-birds
And opening springtide flowers,
When the dainty Baby Bell
Came to this world of ours.
THOMAS BAILEY ALDRICH, *Baby Bell.*

4
He smiles and clasps his tiny hand,
With sunbeams o'er him gleaming,—
A world of baby fairyland
He visits while he's dreaming.
JOSEPH ASHBY-STERRY, *King of the Cradle.*

5
Only a baby small dropped from the skies,
Only a laughing face, two sunny eyes;
Only two cherry lips, one chubby nose;
Only two little hands, ten little toes. . . .
Only a baby small, never at rest;
Small, but how dear to us, God knoweth best.
MATTHIAS BARR, *Only a Baby Small.* Sometimes attributed to Addie Layton.

6
Babies are bits of star-dust blown from the hand of God. Lucky the woman who knows the pangs of birth for she has held a star.
LARRY BARRETTO, *The Indiscreet Years*, p. 99.

The god in babe's disguise.
ROBERT BROWNING, *James Lee's Wife.* Pt. vi.

His flesh is angels' flesh, all alive.
EMERSON, *Society and Solitude: Domestic Life.*

7
Of all earth's songs God took the half
To make the ripple of her laugh.
HERBERT BASHFORD, *Alice.*

Oh, mother! laugh your merry note,
Be gay and glad, but don't forget
From baby's eyes look out a soul
That claims a home in Eden yet.
ETHEL LYNN BEERS, *Weighing the Baby.*

8
Loveliness beyond completeness,
Sweetness distancing all sweetness,
Beauty all that beauty may be—
That's May Bennett, that's my baby.
WILLIAM COX BENNETT, *Baby May.*

9
Sweet babe, in thy face
Soft desires I can trace,
Secret joys and secret smiles,
Little pretty infant wiles.
WILLIAM BLAKE, *A Cradle Song.*

10
"I have no name;
I am but two days old."
What shall I call thee?
"I happy am,
Joy is my name."
Sweet joy befall thee!
WILLIAM BLAKE, *Infant Joy.*

11
How lovely he appears! his little cheeks
In their pure incarnation, vying with
The rose leaves strewn beneath them.
BYRON, *Cain.* Act iii, sc. 1, l. 10.

12
There came to port last Sunday night
The queerest little craft,
Without an inch of rigging on;
I looked and looked—and laughed.
It seemed so curious that she
Should cross the unknown water,
And moor herself within my room—
My daughter! O my daughter!
GEORGE W. CABLE, *The New Arrival.*

Now from the coasts of morning pale
Comes safe to port thy tiny sail.
Now have we seen by early sun
Thy miracle of life begun.
GRACE HAZARD CONKLING, *To a New-Born Baby Girl.*

13
He is so little to be so large!
Why, a train of cars, or a whale-back barge
Couldn't carry the freight of the monstrous weight
Of all his qualities, good and great.
EDMUND VANCE COOKE, *The Intruder.*

14
Which is the way to Baby-land?
Any one can tell;
Up one flight,
To your right;
Please to ring the bell.
GEORGE COOPER, *Babyland.*

15
Every baby born into the world is a finer one than the last.
DICKENS, *Nicholas Nickleby.* Ch. 36.

16
When you fold your hands, Baby Louise, . . .
Are you trying to think of some angel-taught prayer
You learned above, Baby Louise?
MARGARET EYTINGE, *Baby Louise.*

1
Some admiring what motives to mirth infants meet with in their silent and solitary smiles, have resolved (how truly I know not) that then they converse with angels.
THOMAS FULLER, *A Pisgah Sight of Palestine.*

He smiles, and sleeps!—sleep on
And smile, thou little, young inheritor
Of a world scarce less young: sleep on and smile!
BYRON, *Cain.* Act iii, sc. 1, l. 18.

Her beads while she numbered,
The baby still slumbered,
And smiled in her face, as she bended her knee;
Oh! bless'd be that warning,
My child's sleep adorning,
For I know that the angels are whispering with thee.
SAMUEL LOVER, *The Angel's Whisper.*

The smile that flickers on baby's lips when he sleeps—does anybody know where it was born? Yes, there is a rumor that a young pale beam of a crescent moon touched the edge of a vanishing autumn cloud, and there the smile was first born in the dream of a dew-washed morning.
RABINDRANATH TAGORE, *Gitanjali.* No. 61.

See also SLEEP: LULLABYS.

2
A little child born yesterday,
A thing on mother's milk and kisses fed.
(Ὧδε νεογνὸς ἐὼν καὶ νήπιος.)
HOMER, *Hymn to Hermes,* l. 406. (Shelley, tr., *Hymn to Mercury.* St. 69.)

A babe is fed with milk and praise.
CHARLES AND MARY LAMB, *The First Tooth.*

3
What is the little one thinking about?
Very wonderful things, no doubt! . . .
Who can tell what a baby thinks?
Who can follow the gossamer links
By which the mannikin feels his way
Out from the shore of the great unknown,
Blind, and wailing, and alone,
Into the light of day?
J. G. HOLLAND, *Bitter-Sweet.* Pt. i.

4
God one morning, glad of heaven,
Laughed—and that was you!
BRIAN HOOKER, *A Little Person.*

5
About the only thing we have left that actually discriminates in favor o' the plain people is the stork.
KIN HUBBARD, *Sayings.*

6
Babies do not want to hear about babies; they like to be told of giants and castles, and of somewhat which can stretch and stimulate their little minds.
SAMUEL JOHNSON, *Miscellanies.* Vol. i, p. 156.

7
Fragoletta is so small,
We wonder that she lives at all—
Tiny alabaster girl,
Hardly bigger than a pearl.
RICHARD LE GALLIENNE, *Songs for Fragoletta.*

8
A tight little bundle of wailing and flannel,
Perplex'd with the newly-found fardel of life.
F. LOCKER-LAMPSON, *The Old Cradle.*

The hair she means to have is gold,
Her eyes are blue, she's twelve weeks old,
Plump are her fists and pinky.
She fluttered down in lucky hour
From some blue deep in yon sky bower—
I call her "Little Dinky."
F. LOCKER-LAMPSON, *Little Dinky.*

9
O child! O new-born denizen
Of life's great city! on thy head
The glory of the morn is shed,
Like a celestial benison!
LONGFELLOW, *To a Child.*

10
Where did you come from, baby dear?
Out of the Everywhere into the here. . . .
How did they all just come to be you?
God thought about me and so I grew.
GEORGE MACDONALD, *At the Back of the North Wind.* Ch. 33.

11
Who can foretell for what high cause
This darling of the gods was born?
ANDREW MARVELL, *The Picture of Little T. C.*

12
Whenever a little child is born
All night a soft wind rocks the corn;
One more buttercup wakes to the morn,
Somewhere, Somewhere.
AGNES CARTER MASON, *Somewhere.*

13
A sweet, new blossom of Humanity,
Fresh fallen from God's own home to flower on earth.
GERALD MASSEY, *Wooed and Won.*

Small traveler from an unseen shore,
By mortal eye ne'er seen before,
To you, good-morrow.
COSMO MONKHOUSE, *To a New-Born Child.*

14
The greatest poem ever known
Is one all poets have outgrown:
The poetry, innate, untold,
Of being only four years old.
CHRISTOPHER MORLEY, *To a Child.*

15
Borne to us hitherward,
Ah! from what shore?
Voyaging whitherward,
Child, evermore?
F. W. H. MYERS, *Harold at Two Years Old.*

16
For what she does not know, she eats,
A worm, a twig, a block, a fly,
And every novel thing she meets
Is bitten into bye and bye.
ROBERT NATHAN, *The Daughter at Evening.*

17
As living jewels dropped unstained from heaven.
POLLOCK, *The Course of Time.* Bk. v, l. 158.

1
Out of the mouth of babes and sucklings hast thou ordained strength.
Old Testament: Psalms, viii, 2.

He that of greatest works is finisher
Oft does them by the weakest minister:
So holy writ in babes hath judgement shown,
When judges have been babes.
SHAKESPEARE, *All's Well that Ends Well,* ii, 1, 139.

2
We still maun luve the Giver mair,
An' see Him in the given;
An' sae she'll lead us up to Him,
Our babie straight frae Heaven.
JEREMIAH EAMES RANKIN, *The Babie.*

3
At first the infant,
Mewling and puking in the nurse's arms.
SHAKESPEARE, *As You Like It.* Act ii, sc. 8, l. 143.

A grievous burthen was thy birth to me;
Tetchy and wayward was thy infancy.
SHAKESPEARE, *Richard III.* Act iv, sc. 4, l. 167.

Thou wast the prettiest babe that e'er I nursed:
SHAKESPEARE, *Romeo and Juliet.* Act i, sc. 3, 60.

4
Something to live for came to the place,
Something to die for maybe,
Something to give even sorrow a grace,
And yet it was only a baby!
HARRIET PRESCOTT SPOFFORD, *Only.*

5
Sweetest li'l' feller, everybody knows;
Dunno what to call him, but he's mighty lak' a rose.
FRANK L. STANTON, *Mighty Lak' a Rose.*

But ven he vash asleep in ped,
So quiet as a mouse,
I prays der Lord, "Dake anyding,
But leaf dot Yawcob Strauss."
CHARLES FOLLEN ADAMS, *Yawcob Strauss.*

6
The world has no such flower in any land,
And no such pearl in any gulf the sea,
As any babe on any mother's knee.
SWINBURNE, *Pelagius.* St. 2.

The sweetest flowers in all the world—
A baby's hands.
SWINBURNE, *Étude Réaliste.*

Man, a dunce uncouth,
Errs in age and youth:
Babies know the truth.
SWINBURNE, *Cradle Songs.* No. 4.

7
A babe in a house is a well-spring of pleasure.
MARTIN F. TUPPER, *Of Education.*

No merry frolics after tea,
No baby in the house.
CLARA DOLLIVER, *No Baby in the House.*

BACHELOR, see Marriage and Celibacy

BACON, SIR FRANCIS

8
In Bacon see the culminating prime
Of British intellect and British crime.
He died, and Nature, settling his affairs,
Parted his powers among us, his heirs:
To each a pinch of common-sense for seed,
And, to develop it, a pinch of greed.
Each frugal heir, to make the gift suffice,
Buries the talent to manure the vice.
AMBROSE BIERCE, *Sir Francis Bacon. The Lantern,* 15 July, 1874.

9
Let Bacon speak and wise men would rather listen, though the revolution of kingdoms was on foot.
EMERSON, *Society and Solitude: Eloquence.*

The reputations that were great and inaccessible change and tarnish. How great were once Lord Bacon's dimensions! he is now reduced almost to the middle height; and many another star has turned out to be a planet or an asteroid.
EMERSON, *Lecture on the Times.*

10
England's high Chancellor, the destined heir,
In his soft cradle, to his father's chair,
Whose even thread the Fates spin round and full
Out of their choicest and their whitest wool.
BEN JONSON, *On Lord Bacon's Sixtieth Birthday,* 22 Jan., 1621.

His hearers could not cough or look aside from him without loss. . . . The fear of every man that heard him was lest he should make an end.
BEN JONSON, *On the Lord St. Albans.*

In his adversity I ever prayed that God would give him strength; for greatness he could not want.
BEN JONSON, *On the Lord St. Albans.*

Bacon's sentence bends beneath the weight of his thought, like a branch beneath the weight of its fruit.
ALEXANDER SMITH, *Dreamthorp: On the Writing of Essays.*

11
If parts allure thee, think how Bacon shined,
The wisest, brightest, meanest of mankind.
POPE, *Essay on Man.* Epis. iv, l. 281.

12
The great secretary of Nature,—Sir Francis Bacon.
IZAAK WALTON, *Life of Herbert.*

Plato . . . Aristotle . . . Socrates . . . These great secretaries of Nature.
JAMES HOWELL, *Familiar Letters.* Bk. ii, let. 11.

BALDNESS, see Hair

BALLAD

See also Song

13
The farmer's daughter hath soft brown hair;
(Butter and eggs and a pound of cheese)
And I met a ballad, I can't say where,
Which wholly consisted of lines like these.
C. S. CALVERLEY, *Ballad.*

14
In this spacious isle I think there is not one
But he hath heard some talk of Hood and Little John,
Of Tuck, the merry friar, which many a sermon made

In praise of Robin Hood, his outlaws, and their trade.
MICHAEL DRAYTON, *Poly-Olbion.*

A famous man is Robin Hood,
The English ballad-singer's joy.
WORDSWORTH, *Rob Roy's Grave*, l. 1.

1
Thespis, the first professor of our art,
At country wakes sung ballads from a cart.
DRYDEN, *Sophonisba: Prologue.*

2
I knew a very wise man who believed that . . . if a man were permitted to make all the ballads, he need not care who should make the laws of a nation. And we find that most of the ancient legislators thought they could not well reform the manners of any city without the help of a lyric, and sometimes of a dramatic poet.
ANDREW FLETCHER, of Saltoun, *Letter to the Marquis of Montrose.* (*An Account of a Conversation Concerning a Right Regulation of Governments for the Common Good of Mankind.* 1704.) *Works*, p. 266. The reference is supposed to be to the Earl of Cromarty, though some authorities had guessed that John Selden was the "very wise man."

Confucius may indeed be said to have anticipated the apothegm.
HERBERT A. GILES, *History of Chinese Literature.* But, though often attributed to Confucius, the quotation in this form is not found in his works.

3
Some people resemble ballads which are only sung for a certain time. (Il y a des gens qui ressemblent aux vaudevilles, qu'on ne chante qu'un certain temps.)
LA ROCHEFOUCAULD, *Maximes.* No. 211.

4
I have a passion for ballads. . . . They are the gypsy-children of song, born under green hedgerows, in the leafy lanes and bypaths of literature.
H. W. LONGFELLOW, *Hyperion.* Bk. ii, ch. 2.

5
For a ballad's a thing you expect to find lies in.
SAMUEL LOVER, *Paddy Blake's Echo.*

6
Though some make slight of libels, yet you may see by them how the wind sits: as, take a straw and throw it up into the air, you shall see by that which way the wind is, which you shall not do by casting up a stone. Solid things do not show the complexion of the times so well as ballads and libels.
JOHN SELDEN, *Table-Talk: Libels.* By libels, Selden means lampoons.

7
An I have not ballads made on you all and sung to filthy tunes, let a cup of sack be my poison.
SHAKESPEARE, *I Henry IV.* Act ii, sc. 2, l. 48.

I had rather be a kitten and cry mew,
Than one of these same metre ballad-mongers:
I had rather hear a brazen canstick turn'd,
Or a dry wheel grate on the axle-tree;
And that would set my teeth nothing on edge,
Nothing so much as mincing poetry.
SHAKESPEARE, *I Henry IV.* Act iii, sc. 1, l. 128.

8
Armado: Is there not a ballad, boy, of the King and the Beggar?
Moth: The world was very guilty of such a ballad some three ages since: but I think now 'tis not to be found.
SHAKESPEARE, *Love's Labour's Lost.* Act i, sc. 2, l. 114.

I read that once in Africa
A princely wight did reign,
Who had to name Cophetua,
As poets they did feign. . . .
But, mark, what happened on a day,
As he out of his window lay,
He saw a beggar all in gray,
The which did cause his pain.
UNKNOWN, *King Cophetua and the Beggar-Maid.* (PERCY, *Reliques.* Bk. ii, No. 6.)

9
My mother had a maid call'd Barbara;
She was in love; and he she lov'd prov'd mad,
And did forsake her: she had a song of 'willow';
An old thing 'twas, but it express'd her fortune,
And she died singing it.
SHAKESPEARE, *Othello.* Act iv, sc. 3, l. 26.

He sighed in his singing and after each groan,
Come willow, willow, willow!
I'm dead to all pleasure, my true love is gone;
Oh willow, willow, willow!
UNKNOWN, *Willow, Willow, Willow.*

On a tree by a river a little tom-tit
Sang, "Willow, titwillow, titwillow!"
W. S. GILBERT, *The Mikado.* Act ii.

10
Now, good Cesario, but that piece of song,
That old and antique song we heard last night:
Methought it did relieve my passion much,
More than light airs and recollected terms
Of these most brisk and giddy-paced times. . . .
Mark it, Cesario, it is old and plain;
The spinsters and the knitters in the sun
And the free maids that weave their thread with bones
Do use to chant it: it is silly sooth,
And dallies with the innocence of love,
Like the old age.
SHAKESPEARE, *Twelfth Night.* Act ii, sc. 4, l. 2.

It hath been sung at festivals,
On ember eves and holy ales;
And lords and ladies of their lives
Have read it for restoratives.
SHAKESPEARE [?], *Pericles.* Act i, prol., l. 5.

11
He sings several times faster than you'll tell money; he utters them as he had eaten ballads and all men's ears grew to his tunes.
SHAKESPEARE, *Winter's Tale.* Act iv, sc. 4, l. 184.

In chords that tenderest be,
He played an ancient ditty, long since mute,
In Provence called, "La belle dame sans merci."
KEATS, *The Eve of St. Agnes*. St. 33.

1
I love a ballad but even too well, if it be doleful matter, merrily set down, or a very pleasant thing indeed, and sung lamentably.
SHAKESPEARE, *Winter's Tale*. Act iv, sc. 4, l. 187.

I love a ballad in print o' life, for then we are sure they are true.
SHAKESPEARE, *Winter's Tale*. Act iv, sc. 4, l. 263.

2
I never heard the old song of Percy and Douglass, that I found not my heart moved more than with a trumpet.
SIR PHILIP SIDNEY, *Defence of Poesy*.

The grand old ballad of Sir Patrick Spence.
S. T. COLERIDGE, *Dejection*. St. 1.

They'll cry "What expression is in it!"
Don't sing English ballads to me!
T. H. BAYLY, *Don't Sing English Ballads to Me!*

3
Build, build, but never monument of stone shall last as long
As one old soldier's ballad borne on breath of battle-song.
MAURICE THOMPSON, *The Ballad of Chickamauga.*

4
Yesterday I was walking under the fence; and I heard the peasant boys here, instead of some old ballad, bawling a street-song. That's what progress is.
TURGENEV, *Fathers and Children*. Ch. 27.

BANISHMENT, see Exile

BANK and BANKER, see Finance

BANNER, see Flag

BARBER

5
And thou, son of man, take thee a sharp knife, take thee a barber's razor, and cause it to pass upon thine head, and upon thy beard.
Old Testament: Ezekiel, v, 1.

6
Since I have dealt in suds, I could never discover more than two reasons for shaving; the one is to get a beard, the other is to get rid of one.
HENRY FIELDING, *Tom Jones*. Bk. viii, ch. 4.

7
And the barber kept on shaving.
JAMES T. FIELDS, *The Owl-Critic.*

8
One barber shaves not so close but another finds work.
THOMAS FULLER, *Gnomologia*. No. 3737.

Of a thousand shavers, two do not shave so much alike as not to be distinguished.
SAMUEL JOHNSON. (BOSWELL, *Life*, 1777.)

9
Well lathered is half shaven.
THOMAS FULLER, *Gnomologia*. No. 5472.

"A good lather is half the shave," is a very old remark among the trade [barbers].
HONE, *Every-Day Book*, i, 1269.

10
Every barber knows that. (Omnibus notum tonsoribus.)
HORACE, *Satires*. Bk. i, sat. 7, l. 3.

11
But he shaved with a shell when he chose,
'Twas the manner of primitive man.
ANDREW LANG, *Double Ballad of Primitive Man.*

12
How wonderful it is to have a perfectly safe place to throw worn-out safety razor blades.
ROSS W. LYNN, *Letter to F. P. A.*, from Hotel El Tovar, Grand Canyon of the Colorado, 5 Oct., 1916.

13
With odorous oil thy head and hair are sleek;
And then thou kemb'st the tuzzes on thy cheek:
Of these, my barbers take a costly care.
PERSIUS, *Satires*, iv, 89. (Dryden, tr.)

14
The first [barbers] that entered Italy came out of Sicily and it was in the 454 year after the foundation of Rome. . . . The first that was shaven every day was Scipio Africanus, and after him cometh Augustus the Emperor, who evermore used the rasor.
PLINY THE ELDER, *Historia Naturalis*. Bk. vii, sec. 59.

15
Like a barber's chair, that fits all buttocks.
SHAKESPEARE, *All's Well that Ends Well*. Act ii, sc. 2, l. 17. *See also under* VENUS.

16
Our courteous Antony . . .
Being barber'd ten times o'er, goes to the feast.
SHAKESPEARE, *Antony and Cleopatra*. Act ii, sc. 2, l. 227.

Fresh as a bridegroom; and his chin new reap'd
Show'd like a stubble-land at harvest-home.
SHAKESPEARE, *I Henry IV*. Act i, sc. 3, l. 34.

17
My master preaches patience to him and the while
His man with scissors nicks him like a fool.
SHAKESPEARE, *The Comedy of Errors*. Act v, sc. 1, l. 174.

Accept a proverb out of Wisdom's schools—
"Barbers first learn to shave by shaving fools."
JOHN WOLCOT, *Works*. Vol. ii, p. 446. The proverb appears in Cotgrave's *French-English Dictionary*, 1611.

18
I must to the barber's, monsieur; for methinks I am marvellous hairy about the face.
SHAKESPEARE, *A Midsummer-Night's Dream*. Act iv, sc. 1, l. 25.

19
A Fellow in a market town,
Most musical, cried Razors up and down.
JOHN WOLCOT, *Farewell Odes*. Ode iii.

1
The fellow will get a dry shave.
JOHN WOLCOT, *Great Cry and Little Wool.*

I'll shave her, like a punished soldier, dry.
JOHN WOLCOT, *The Louisad.* Canto ii.

2
When your razor is dull
And you need to shave
Think of the man
That lays in this grave,
For there was a time
It might have been whet,
You was afeard of a dime
And now its too late.
UNKNOWN, *Epitaph,* on tombstone of August Hefner, in cemetery at Waverly, Ohio. Hefner died 17 Sept., 1856, and the tombstone states, "The deceased being asked on his arrival in Waverly, O., where he was going, answered, Here and no farther."

BARGAIN

3
He who buys and lies feels it in his purse.
CERVANTES, *Don Quixote.* Pt. i, ch. 25.

4
Here's the rule for bargains: "Do other men, for they would do you." That's the true business precept.
DICKENS, *Martin Chuzzlewit.* Ch. 11.

5
A man loseth his time that comes early to a bad bargain.
THOMAS FULLER, *Gnomologia.* No. 286.

It is a silly bargain where nobody gains.
THOMAS FULLER, *Gnomologia.* No. 2878.

6
On a good bargain think twice.
GEORGE HERBERT, *Jacula Prudentum.*

A good bargain is a pick-purse.
GEORGE HERBERT, *Jacula Prudentum.*

7
For Diomed's brass arms, of mean device,
For which nine oxen paid (a vulgar price),
He gave his own, of gold divinely wrought;
An hundred beeves the shining purchase bought.
HOMER, *Iliad.* Bk. vi, l. 292. (Pope, tr.) Hence, "Diomedian swap," an exchange in which all the benefit is on one side.

Fair Diomed, you do as chapmen do,
Dispraise the thing that you desire to buy;
But we in silence hold this virtue well,
We'll not commend what we intend to sell.
SHAKESPEARE, *Troilus and Cressida.* Act iv, sc. 1, l. 75.

8
I . . . therefore am resolved to make the best of a bad market.
PEPYS, *Diary,* 14 Aug., 1663.

Her aunt seemed determined to make the best of a bad bargain.
SCOTT, *Quentin Durward.* Ch. 36.

9
The bargain is not a bargain, or what was not a bargain is a bargain, just as you please. (Pactum non pactum est, non pactum pactum est, quod vobis lubet.)
PLAUTUS, *Aulularia,* l. 260. (Act ii, sc. 1.)

'Tis ill luck to go back upon a bargain.
READE, *The Cloister and the Hearth.* Ch. 36.

A bargain is a bargain, and must stand without all exception.
THOMAS WILSON, *Arte of Rhetorique,* 34. (1560)

10
A dear bargain is always disagreeable, because it is a reflection upon the judgment of the buyer. (Nam mala emptio semper ingrata est eo maxime, quod exprobrare stultitiam domino videtur.)
PLINY THE YOUNGER, *Epistles.* Bk. i, epis. 24.

11
Make every bargain clear and plain,
That none may afterwards complain.
JOHN RAY, *English Proverbs.*

12
Lest the bargain should catch cold and starve.
SHAKESPEARE, *Cymbeline.* Act i, sc. 4, l. 179.

13
But in the way of bargain, mark ye me,
I'll cavil on the ninth part of a hair.
SHAKESPEARE, *I Henry IV.* Act iii, sc. 1, l. 139.

To sell a bargain well is as cunning as fast and loose.
SHAKESPEARE, *Love's Labour's Lost.* Act iii, sc. 1, l. 104.

14
And seal the bargain with a holy kiss.
SHAKESPEARE, *The Two Gentlemen of Verona.* Act ii, sc. 2, l. 6.

15
There never was a better bargain driven.
SIR PHILIP SIDNEY, *My True Love Hath My Heart.*

16
There's two words to that bargain.
SWIFT, *Polite Conversation.* Dial. iii.

17
The timely buyer Hath cheaper his fire.
THOMAS TUSSER, *Five Hundred Points of Good Husbandry: January's Abstract.*

18
A blind bargain.
UNKNOWN, *Merrie Tales of the Mad Men of Gottam.* No. 13. (1630)

BASHFULNESS, see Timidity

BATHING

19
Do you think that I, then, am taking pleasure in my bath?
GAUTEMOZIN, successor of Montezuma, to his companion, the cacique of Tacuba, while being tortured by Cortez. (PRESCOTT, *Conquest of Mexico,* bk. vii, ch. 1.) Usually quoted, "Am I, then, lying on a bed of roses?"

Hercules! How cold is this bath of yours!
JUGURTHA, when thrown into a subterranean

dungeon half full of water, 104 B.C. (SALLUST, *Jugurtha.*)

1
They who bathe in May will soon be laid in clay;
They who bathe in June will sing a merry tune;
They who bathe in July will dance like a fly.
WILLIAM HONE, *Table-Book,* p. 315.

2
Many recite their writings in the bath. How pleasantly the vaulted space echoes the voice!
HORACE, *Satires.* Bk. i, sat. 4, l. 75.

I fly to the hot baths, there you din my ears; I seek the cold bath, there I cannot swim for your noise.
MARTIAL, *Epigrams.* Bk. iii, ep. 44.

The man who always likes to hear his own voice in the bathroom. (Illum cui vox sua in balieno placet.)
SENECA, *Epistulæ ad Lucilium.* Epis. lvi, sec. 2.

3
If you wish, Faustinus, that a bath, so hot that even Julianus could scarcely get into it, should be cooled, ask the rhetorician Sabineius to bathe in it. He makes icy the warm baths of Nero.
MARTIAL, *Epigrams.* Bk. iii, epig. 25.

4
In the height of this bath, where I was more than half stewed in grease, like a Dutch dish.
SHAKESPEARE, *The Merry Wives of Windsor.* Act iii, sc. 5, l. 120.

Perspiration should flow only after toil. (Omnis sudor per laborem exeat.)
SENECA, *Epistulæ ad Lucilium.* Epis. li, sec. 6.

5
A seething bath, which yet men prove
Against strange maladies a sovereign cure . . .
And healthful remedy For men diseased.
SHAKESPEARE, *Sonnets.* No. cliii, cliv.

BATTLE, see War

BATTLE, see War

BEAR

6
One thing thinketh the bear, but another thinketh his leader.
CHAUCER, *Troilus and Criseyde.* Bk. iv, l. 1453.

7
I am as loath to go to it, as a bear is to go to the stake.
JOHN FLORIO, *Second Frutes,* 89.

If he goes, yet it is as a bear to the stake.
DANIEL ROGERS, *Naaman.* Sig. D5.

8
He must have iron nails that scratcheth with a bear.
THOMAS FULLER, *Gnomologia.* No. 1991.

Tho' the bear be gentle, don't bite him by the nose.
THOMAS D'URFEY, *Quixote.* Pt. iii, act i, sc. 1.

9
The bear wants a tail and cannot be a lion.
THOMAS FULLER, *Worthies of England.* Vol. iii, p. 271.

10
He is not worthy to carry guts to a bear.
JAMES HOWELL, *Proverbs.* No. 17.

George thinks us scarcely fit ('tis very clear)
To carry guts, my brethren, to a bear.
JOHN WOLCOT, *Works.* Vol. i, p. 198.

11
We roar all like bears.
Old Testament: Isaiah, lix, 11.

12
Make ye no truce with Adam-zad—the Bear that walks like a Man!
RUDYARD KIPLING, *The Truce of the Bear.* Referring to Russia.

The rugged Russian bear.
SHAKESPEARE, *Macbeth.* Act iii, sc. 4, l. 100.

13
I trusted so much that I sold the skin before the bear was taken.
JOHN LYLY, *Euphues,* p. 273.

He bade me have a care for the future, to make sure of the bear before I sell his skin.
L'ESTRANGE, *Æsop,* p. 270.

Indeed the devil may be said to sell the bear-skin, whatever he buys.
DANIEL DEFOE, *History of the Devil.* Pt. ii, ch. 8.

14
Are you there with your bears?
JOHN LYLY, *Mother Bombie.* Act ii, sc. 3. (1592)

15
As savage as a bear with a sore head.
FREDERICK MARRYAT, *The King's Own.* Ch. 26.

16
Bears when first born are little shapeless masses of white flesh a little larger than mice, their claws alone being prominent. Their mother then gradually licks them into proper shape.
PLINY THE ELDER, *Historia Naturalis.* Bk. viii, sec. 36.

Bears leisurely lick their cubs into form.
MONTAIGNE, *Essays.* Bk. ii, ch. 12.

Like to the bear which bringeth forth
In the end of thirty days a shapeless birth;
But after licking, it in shape she draws,
And by degrees she fashions out the paws,
The head, and neck, and finally doth bring
To a perfect beast that first deformèd thing.
DU BARTAS, *Devine Weeks and Works.* Week i, day 1.

Like to a chaos, or an unlick'd bear-whelp,
That carries no impression like the dam.
SHAKESPEARE, *III Henry VI.* Act iii, sc. 2, l. 161.

So watchful Bruin forms, with plastic care,
Each growing lump and brings it to a bear.
POPE, *The Dunciad.* Bk. i, l. 101.

See also WRITING: CAREFUL WRITING.

1 He hath as many tricks as a dancing bear.
JOHN RAY, *English Proverbs*, p. 163.

You have more tricks than a dancing bear.
SWIFT, *Polite Conversation*. Dial. i.

2 If it had been a bear it would have bit you!
SWIFT, *Polite Conversation*. Dial. i.

BEARD

3 Like the goat, you'll mourn for your beard. (Τράγος γένειον ἄρα πενθήσεις σύ γε.)
ÆSCHYLUS, *Prometheus the Fire-Kindler*. Frag. 117.

4 A beard creates lice, not brains. (Ὁ πώγων φθειρῶν ποιητής, οὐχὶ φρενῶν γέγονεν.)
AMMIANUS. (*Greek Anthology*. Bk. xi, epig. 156.)

'Tis not the beard that makes the philosopher.
THOMAS FULLER, *Gnomologia*. No. 5102.

If you think that to grow a beard is to acquire wisdom, a goat is at once a complete Plato.
LUCIAN. (*Greek Anthology*. Bk. xi, epig. 430.)

If the beard were all, a goat might preach.
UNKNOWN. A Danish proverb.

Wise as far as the beard. (Barbæ tenus sapientes.)
UNKNOWN. A Latin proverb.

5 Men for their sins
Have shaving, too, entailed upon their chins,—
A daily plague.
BYRON, *Don Juan*. Canto xiv, st. 23.

6 The soft down of manhood was just springing on his cheek. (Ἁρμοῖ που κἀκείνῳ ἐπέτρεχεν ἁβρὸς ἴουλος.)
CALLIMACHUS, *Hecale*. Frag. 4.

Ere on thy chin the springing beard began
To spread a doubtful down, and promise man.
MATTHEW PRIOR, *An Ode to the Memory of the Honourable Colonel George Villiers*, l. 5.

Small show of man was yet upon his chin;
His phœnix down began but to appear.
SHAKESPEARE, *A Lover's Complaint*, l. 92.

7 To cultivate a wise man's beard. (Sapientem pascere barbam.)
HORACE, *Satires*. Bk. ii, sat. 3, l. 35.

8 There was an old man with a beard,
Who said: "It is just as I feared—
Two Owls and a Hen,
Four Larks and a Wren
Have all built their nests in my beard."
EDWARD LEAR, *Book of Nonsense*.

9 He has singed the beard of the king of Spain.
LONGFELLOW, *A Dutch Picture*.

Sir Francis Drake entered the harbour of Cadiz, April 19, 1587, and destroyed shipping to the amount of ten thousand tons lading. To use his own expressive phrase, he had "singed the Spanish king's beard."
KNIGHT, *Pictorial History of England*. Vol. iii, p. 215.

10 Does he offer you his foolish beard to pluck at? (Stolidam præbet tibi vellere barbam?)
PERSIUS, *Satires*. Sat. ii, l. 28.

Pulling his beard because he had no heir.
THOMAS HOOD, *The Stag-Eyed Lady*.

11 Tarry at Jericho until your beards be grown.
Old Testament: II Samuel, x, 5. This was King David's advice to his servants, who had been mistaken for spies by Hanun and sent back from the land of Ammon with one half of their beards shaved off.

12 Beard of formal cut.
SHAKESPEARE, *As You Like It*. Act ii, sc. 7, l. 155.

Hoary whiskers and a forky beard.
POPE, *Rape of the Lock*. Canto iii, l. 38.

And slight Sir Robert with his watery smile
And educated whisker.
TENNYSON, *Edwin Morris*, l. 128.

13 *Hamlet*. His beard was grizzled,—no?
Horatio. It was, as I have seen it in his life,
A sable silver'd.
SHAKESPEARE, *Hamlet*. Act i, sc. 2, l. 240.

His beard was as white as snow,
All flaxen was his poll.
SHAKESPEARE, *Hamlet*. Act iv, sc. 5, l. 195.

Whose beard the silver hand of peace hath touch'd.
SHAKESPEARE, *II Henry IV*. Act iv, sc. 1, l. 43.

Thy father's beard is turned white with the news.
SHAKESPEARE, *I Henry IV*. Act ii, sc. 4, l. 393.

A black beard will turn white.
SHAKESPEARE, *Henry V*. Act v, sc. 1, l. 168.

14 Thy face is valanced since I saw thee last; comest thou to beard me?
SHAKESPEARE, *Hamlet*. Act ii, sc. 2, l. 442.

15 You must not think
That we are made of stuff so flat and dull
That we can let our beard be shook with danger
And think it pastime.
SHAKESPEARE, *Hamlet*. Act iv, sc. 7, l. 30.

16 You should be women,
And yet your beards forbid me to interpret
That you are so.
SHAKESPEARE, *Macbeth*. Act i, sc. 3, l. 45.

What a beard hast thou got! thou hast got more hair on thy chin than Dobbin my fill-horse has on his tail.
SHAKESPEARE, *The Merchant of Venice*. Act ii. sc. 2, l. 99.

17 How many cowards, whose hearts are all as false

As stairs of sand, wear yet upon their chins
The beards of Hercules and frowning Mars,
Who, inward search'd, have livers white as
milk?

SHAKESPEARE, *The Merchant of Venice*. Act iii. sc. 2, l. 83.

1
A little yellow beard, a Cain-coloured beard.

SHAKESPEARE, *The Merry Wives of Windsor*. Act i, sc. 4, l. 23.

Bottom: What beard were I best to play it in?
Quince: Why, what you will.
Bottom: I will discharge it in either your straw-colour beard, your orange-tawny beard, your purple-in-grain beard, or your French-crown-colour beard, your perfect yellow.

SHAKESPEARE, *A Midsummer-Night's Dream*. Act i, sc. 2, l. 92.

2
Lord, I could not endure a husband with a beard on his face: I had rather lie in the woollen.

SHAKESPEARE, *Much Ado About Nothing*. Act ii, sc. 1, l. 32.

He that hath a beard is more than a youth, and he that hath no beard is less than a man.

SHAKESPEARE, *Much Ado About Nothing*. Act ii, sc. 1, l. 38.

Claudio. The old ornament of his cheek hath already stuffed tennis-balls.
Leonato. Indeed, he looks younger than he did by the loss of a beard.

SHAKESPEARE, *Much Ado About Nothing*. Act iii, sc. 2, l. 46.

3
His beard, all silver white, Wagg'd up and down.

SHAKESPEARE, *The Rape of Lucrece*, l. 1405.

'Tis merry in hall Where beards wag all.

THOMAS TUSSER, *Hundred Points of Good Husbandry: August's Abstract*.

Merry swithe it is in halle
When the beards waveth alle.

UNKNOWN, *Alisaunder*. (c. 1308) Formerly attributed to Adam Davy.

4
He has not past three or four hairs on his chin.

SHAKESPEARE, *Troilus and Cressida*. Act i, sc. 2, l. 122.

Alas, poor chin! many a wart is richer.

SHAKESPEARE, *Troilus and Cressida*. Act i, sc. 2, l. 154.

Now Jove, in his next commodity of hair, send thee a beard!

SHAKESPEARE, *Twelfth Night*. Act iii, sc. 1, l. 50.

BEAUTY

See also Death and Beauty; Dress: Beauty Unadorned; World: Its Beauty

I—Beauty: Definitions

5
Beauty is the gift of God. (*Θεοῦ δῶρον*)

ARISTOTLE. (DIOGENES LAERTIUS, *Aristotle*. Bk. v, sec. 19.)

Beauty is heaven's gift, and how few can boast of beauty! (Forma dei munus: forma quota quæque superbit!)

OVID, *Ars Amatoria*. Bk. iii, l 103.

6
There is no excellent beauty that hath not some strangeness in the proportion.

FRANCIS BACON, *Essays: Of Beauty*.

The best part of beauty is that which a picture cannot express.

FRANCIS BACON, *Apothegms*. No. 64.

7
The beautiful is as useful as the useful. More so, perhaps. (Le beau est aussi utile que l'utile. Plus peut-être.)

HUGO, *Les Misérables: Fantine*. Bk. i, ch. 6.

Here below, the beautiful is the necessary. (Ici-bas, le joli c'est le nécessaire.)

MATILDA BETHAM-EDWARDS, *Heart of the Vosges: Montauban*. Paraphrasing Hugo.

Beauty rests on necessities. The line of beauty is the line of perfect economy.

EMERSON, *Conduct of Life: Beauty*.

The beautiful rests on the foundations of the necessary.

EMERSON, *Essays, Second Series: The Poet*.

8
Beauty is another's good. (*Τὸ κάλλος ἀλλότριον ἀγαθόν*.)

BION. (DIOGENES LAERTIUS, *Bion*. Bk. iv., sec. 48.)

9
Exuberance is Beauty.

WILLIAM BLAKE, *Proverbs of Hell*.

10
For beauty being the best of all we know
Sums up the unsearchable and secret aims
Of nature.

ROBERT BRIDGES, *The Growth of Love*.

11
Too much beauty, I reckon, is nothing but
too much sun.

E. B. BROWNING, *Lord Walter's Wife*.

12
Beauty is like the surf that never ceases,
Beauty is like the night that never dies,
Beauty is like a forest pool where peace is
And a recurrent waning planet lies.

STRUTHERS BURT, *I Know a Lovely Lady Who is Dead*.

13
Beauty has no relation to price, rarity, or age.

JOHN COTTON DANA, *Libraries*.

14
Beauty is not caused, It is.

EMILY DICKINSON, *Further Poems*. No. xlix.

15
Beauty, what is that? There are phalanxes of beauty in every comic show. Beauty neither buys food nor keeps up a home.

MAXINE ELLIOTT, *Newspaper Interview*, 1908.

16
The absence of flaw in beauty is itself a flaw.

HAVELOCK ELLIS, *Impressions and Comments*. Ser. i, p. 217. *See also under* FAULT.

1
Beauty—what is it? A perfume without
name:
A sudden hush where clamor was before:
Across the darkness a faint ghost of flame:
A far sail, seen from a deserted shore.

ARTHUR D. FICKE, *Epitaph for the Poet V.*

2
Wisdom is the abstract of the past, but beauty is the promise of the future.

O. W. HOLMES, *The Professor at the Breakfast-Table*. Ch. 2.

Beauty is the index of a larger fact than wisdom.

O. W. HOLMES, *The Professor at the Breakfast-Table*. Ch. 2.

3
A ship under sail, a man in complete armour, and a woman with a big belly, are the three handsomest sights in the world.

JAMES HOWELL, *Proverbs*, 2.

A ship under sail and a big-bellied woman
Are the handsomest two things that can be seen
common.

BENJAMIN FRANKLIN, *Poor Richard*, 1735.

Man nor king can see unmoved the coming of a wind-filled sail, the coming of a lovely lady, the coming of a horse in speed.

JAMES STEPHENS, *In the Land of Youth.*

4
Beauty, the smile of God, Music, His voice.

R. U. JOHNSON, *Goethals of Panama.*

5
Beauty from order springs.

WILLIAM KING, *Art of Cookery*, l. 55.

6
Beauty is something wonderful and strange that the artist fashions out of the chaos of the world in the torment of his soul.

W. S. MAUGHAM, *The Moon and Sixpence.*

It is in rare and scattered instants that beauty smiles even on her adorers, who are reduced for habitual comfort to remembering her past favours.

GEORGE SANTAYANA, *Little Essays*, p. 117.

7
Beauty is the purgation of superfluities.

MICHELANGELO. (EMERSON, *Conduct of Life: Beauty.*)

We ascribe beauty to that which is simple; which has no superfluous parts; which exactly answers its end.

EMERSON, *Conduct of Life: Beauty.*

8
Beauty stands
In the admiration only of weak minds
Led captive; cease to admire, and all her
plumes
Fall flat and shrink into a trivial toy,
At every sudden slighting quite abash'd.

MILTON, *Paradise Regained*. Bk. ii, l. 220.

9
Three of these points are white: the skin, the teeth, the hands. Three black: the eyes, the eyelashes, the eyebrows. Three red: lips, cheeks, nails. Three long: body, hair, hands. Three short: ears, teeth, chin. Three wide: the breast, the forehead, the space between the eyes. Three narrow: the waist, the hands, the feet. Three thin: the fingers, the ankles, the nostrils. Three plump: the lips, the arms, the hips.

MORESCO, *Twenty-seven Canons of Beauty.*

10
Beauty is ever to the lonely mind
A shadow fleeting; she is never plain.
She is a visitor who leaves behind
The gift of grief, the souvenir of pain.

ROBERT NATHAN, *Beauty is Ever.*

11
Beauty is a natural superiority. (Προτέρημα φύσεως.)

PLATO. (DIOGENES LAERTIUS, *Aristotle*. Bk. v, sec. 19.)

The beautiful consists in utility and the power to produce some good.

PLATO, *Hippias Major*. Sec. 295C.

12
In wit, as nature, what affects our hearts
Is not th' exactness of peculiar parts;
'Tis not a lip or eye we beauty call,
But the joint force and full result of all.

POPE, *Essay on Criticism*, Pt. ii, l. 43.

13
Beauty comes, we scarce know how, as an emanation from sources deeper than itself.

SHAIRP, *Studies in Poetry and Philosophy: Moral Motive Power.*

14
Beauty is bought by judgement of the eye,
Not utter'd by base sale of chapmen's
tongues.

SHAKESPEARE, *Love's Labour's Lost*. Act ii, sc. 1, l. 15.

Beauty is altogether in the eye of the beholder.

LEW WALLACE, *The Prince of India*. Bk. iii, ch. 6, p. 178.

15
Beauty is a mute deception. (Σιωπῶσαν ἀπατην.)

THEOPHRASTUS. (DIOGENES LAERTIUS, *Aristotle*. Bk. v, sec. 19.)

Yet is beauty the pleasing trickery that cheateth
half the world.

MARTIN FARQUHAR TUPPER, *Proverbial Philosophy: Of Immortality.*

16
Beauty is an evil in an ivory setting. (Ἐλεφαντίνην ζημίαν.)

THEOCRITUS. (DIOGENES LAERTIUS, *Aristotle*. Bk. v, sec. 19.)

17
The only beautiful things are the things that do not concern us.

OSCAR WILDE, *The Decay of Lying.*

18
Beauty is a form of Genius—is higher, indeed, than Genius, as it needs no explanation.

OSCAR WILDE, *The Picture of Dorian Gray*, Ch. 2.

1
Beauty is the flower of chastity. (Τὸ κάλλος εἶπε τῆς σωφροσύνης ἄνθος εἶναι.)
ZENO. (DIOGENES LAERTIUS, *Zeno*. Bk. vii, sec. 23.)

2
Ask of thyself what beauty is.
P. J. BAILEY, *Festus: A Party*.

Who hath not proved how feebly words essay
To fix one spark of Beauty's heavenly ray?
BYRON, *The Bride of Abydos*. Canto i, st. 6.

To draw true beauty shows a master's hand.
DRYDEN, *Epistles: To Mr. Lee*, l. 54.

II—Beauty: Its Praise

3
Too late I loved Thee, O Beauty of ancient days, yet ever new! too late I loved thee! And lo! Thou wert within, and I abroad searching for Thee. Thou wert with me, but I was not with Thee.
ST. AUGUSTINE, *Confessions*. Bk. x, sec. 38.

The Beauty which old Greece or Rome
Sung, painted, wrought, lies close at home.
WHITTIER, *To ——*.

4
If you get simple beauty and naught else,
You get about the best thing God invents.
ROBERT BROWNING, *Fra Lippo Lippi*.

5
And behold there was a very stately palace before him, the name of which was Beautiful.
BUNYAN, *Pilgrim's Progress*. Pt. i.

The Beautiful! it is beauty seen with the eye of the soul. (Le Beau! c'est la beauté vue avec les yeux de l'âme.)
JOUBERT, *Pensées*. No. 273.

6
Everything has its beauty but not everyone sees it.
CONFUCIUS, *Analects*.

He hath made every thing beautiful in his time.
Old Testament: Ecclesiastes, iii, 11.

I have then with pleasure concluded with Solomon,
"Everything is beautiful in his season."
IZAAK WALTON, *Compleat Angler: The Angler's Wish*.

7
Beauty crowds me till I die,
Beauty, mercy have on me!
Yet if I expire to-day
Let it be in sight of thee!
EMILY DICKINSON, *Poems*. Pt. v, No. 43.

8
Rhodora! if the sages ask thee why
This charm is wasted on the earth and sky,
Tell them, dear, that if eyes were made for seeing,
Then Beauty is its own excuse for being.
EMERSON, *The Rhodora*.

Art's perfect forms no moral need,
And beauty is its own excuse.
WHITTIER, *Songs of Labor: Dedication*. (For the idea of this line, I am indebted to Emerson.—*Whittier's note*.)

9
My faith in beauty shall not fail
Because I fail to understand.
EDMUND GOSSE, *Epilogue*.

10
Who walks with beauty holds inviolate
The guarded secrets of the years to come,
Sees unborn Aprils crowding at the gate
Of living gardens white with petaled plum.
DANIEL WHITEHEAD HICKY, *Who Walks With Beauty*.

Who walks with Beauty has no need of fear;
The sun and moon and stars keep pace with him,
Invisible hands restore the ruined year,
And time, itself, grows beautifully dim.
DAVID MORTON, *Who Walks With Beauty*.

11
In beauty's cause illustriously he fails.
HOMER, *Odyssey*. Bk. xi, l. 358. (Pope, tr.)

He thought it happier to be dead,
To die for Beauty, than live for bread.
EMERSON, *Beauty*, l. 25.

12
Does not beauty confer a benefit upon us, even by the simple fact of being beautiful?
VICTOR HUGO, *Toilers of the Sea*. Pt. i, bk. iii, ch. 1.

13
Beauty, you lifted up my sleeping eyes
And filled my heart with longing with a look.
JOHN MASEFIELD, *Sonnets*. No. i.

If I could come again to that dear place
Where once I came, where Beauty lived and moved,
Where, by the sea, I saw her face to face,
That soul alive by which the world has loved; . . .
Joy with its searing-iron would burn me wise,
I should know all; all powers, all mysteries.
JOHN MASEFIELD, *Sonnets*. No. iv.

14
Euclid alone
Has looked on Beauty bare. Fortunate they
Who, though once only and then but far away,
Have heard her massive sandal set on stone.
EDNA ST. VINCENT MILLAY, *Sonnets*.

Such sights as youthful poets dream
On summer eves by haunted stream.
MILTON, *L'Allegro*, l. 129.

15
Praised be the gods that made my spirit mad;
Kept me aflame and raw to beauty's touch.
ANGELA MORGAN, *June Rapture*.

16
Take from our hearts the love of the beautiful, and you take away all the charm of life. (Ôtez de nos cœurs cet amour du beau, vous ôtez tout le charme de la vie.)
ROUSSEAU, *Émile*. Bk. iv.

1
Our hearts were drunk with a beauty
Our eyes could never see.
GEORGE WILLIAM RUSSELL (A. E.), *The Unknown God.*

2
All things of beauty are not theirs alone
Who hold the fee; but unto him no less
Who can enjoy, than unto them who own,
Are sweetest uses given to possess.
J. G. SAXE, *The Beautiful.*

3
Spirit of Beauty, whose sweet impulses,
Flung like the rose of dawn across the sea,
Alone can flush the exalted consciousness
With shafts of sensible divinity—
Light of the world, essential loveliness.
ALAN SEEGER, *Ode to Natural Beauty.*

4
And beauty, making beautiful old rhyme.
SHAKESPEARE, *Sonnets.* No. cvi.

5
Grave is all beauty, Solemn is joy.
WILLIAM WATSON, *England My Mother.* Pt. iv.

6
O Beauty, old yet ever new!
Eternal Voice and Inward Word.
WHITTIER, *The Shadow and the Light.*

Elysian beauty, melancholy grace,
Brought from a pensive though a happy place.
WORDSWORTH, *Laodamia,* l. 95.

7
Doth perfect beauty stand in need of praise? Nay; no more than law, no more than truth, no more than loving kindness, nor than modesty.
MARCUS AURELIUS, *Meditations.* Bk. iv., sec. 20.

III—Beauty and Goodness: A Reality

8
Beautiful faces are those that wear
Whole-souled honesty printed there.
ELLEN P. ALLERTON, *Beautiful Things.*

9
In beauty, that of favour is more than that of colour, and that of decent and gracious motion more than that of favour.
FRANCIS BACON, *Essays: Of Beauty.*

10
The beautiful seems right
By force of beauty, and the feeble wrong
Because of weakness.
E. B. BROWNING, *Aurora Leigh.* Bk. i., l. 753.

11
Beauty, alone, may please, not captivate;
If lacking grace, 'tis but a hookless bait.
CAPITO, *Epigrams.* Bk. v, l. 67. (Lilla Cabot Perry, tr., *Garden of Hellas,* p. 105.)

Beauty without grace is the hook without the bait. Beauty, without expression, tires.
EMERSON, *Conduct of Life: Beauty.*

12
Beauty is part of the finished language by which goodness speaks.
GEORGE ELIOT, *Romola.* Ch. 19.

13
Any extraordinary degree of beauty in man or woman involves a moral charm.
EMERSON, *Conduct of Life: Worship.*

14
Beauty is the virtue of the body, as virtue is the beauty of the soul.
EMERSON, *Natural History of Intellect: Michael Angelo.*

Beauty is the mark God sets upon virtue.
EMERSON, *Nature, Addresses, and Lectures: Beauty.*

Chant the beauty of the good.
EMERSON, *Society and Solitude: Success.*

15
Nothing in human life, least of all in religion, is ever right until it is beautiful.
HARRY EMERSON FOSDICK, *As I See Religion.*

16
Beauty without virtue is a flower without perfume. (La beauté sans vertu est une fleur sans parfum.)
UNKNOWN. A French proverb.

17
How near to good is what is fair!
BEN JONSON, *Love Freed from Ignorance.*

18
Beauté sans bonté, blessed were it never.
WILLIAM LANGLAND, *Piers Plowman,* xviii, 162. (1362.)

Kindness is worth more than beauty. (Bonté vaut mieux que beauté.)
JEAN D'ARRAS, *Melusine.* (c. 1393.)

Beautiful enough if good enough. (Sat pulchra si sat bona.)
UNKNOWN. A Latin proverb.

19
But a celestial brightness—a more ethereal beauty—
Shone on her face and encircled her form when, after confession,
Homeward serenely she walked with God's benediction upon her.
When she had passed, it seemed like the ceasing of exquisite music.
LONGFELLOW, *Evangeline.* Pt. i.

The beauty of a lovely woman is like music; what can one say more?
GEORGE ELIOT, *Adam Bede.*

When Nature's happiest touch could add no more,
Heaven lent an angel's beauty to her face.
W. S. MICKLE, *Mary, Queen of Scots.*

A form so fair, that, like the air,
'Tis less of earth than heaven.
EDWARD COATE PINKNEY, *A Health.*

20
I want to help you to grow as beautiful as God meant you to be when he thought of you first.
GEORGE MACDONALD, *The Marquis of Lossie.* Ch. 22.

21
An' fair was her sweet bodie,
Yet fairer was her mind.
ROBERT NICOLL, *Menie.*

1
Beauty is certainly a soft, smooth, slippery thing, and, therefore, of a nature which easily slips in and permeates our souls. And I further add that the good is the beautiful.

PLATO, *Lysis*, sec. 216. (Jowett, tr.)

2
When a beautiful soul harmonizes with a beautiful form, and the two are cast in one mould, that will be the fairest of sights to him who has the eye to contemplate the vision.

PLATO, *The Republic*. Bk. iii, sec. 402.

For, when with beauty we can virtue join,
We paint the semblance of a form divine.

MATTHEW PRIOR, *To the Countess of Oxford.*

3
Beauty is the flower of virtue.

JOHN RAY, *English Proverbs.*

The ancients called beauty the flowering of virtue.

EMERSON, *Essays, First Series: Love.*

4
She was good as she was fair,
None, none on earth above her!
As pure in thought as angels are:
To know her was to love her.

SAMUEL ROGERS, *Jacqueline*. St. 1.

5
I have always believed that good is only beauty put into practice. (J'ai toujours cru que le bon n'etait que le beau mis en action)

ROUSSEAU, *Julie*. Pt. i, letter 12.

6
What is beautiful is good, and who is good will soon also be beautiful.

SAPPHO, *Fragments*. No. 101.

7
Physical beauty is the sign of an interior beauty, a spiritual and moral beauty which is the basis, the principle, and the unity of the beautiful.

SCHILLER, *Essays, Esthetical and Philosophical: Introduction.*

8
The hand that hath made you fair hath made you good.

SHAKESPEARE, *Measure for Measure*. Act iii, sc. 1, l. 184.

9
He hath a daily beauty in his life.

SHAKESPEARE, *Othello*. Act v, sc. 1, l. 19.

10
There's nothing ill can dwell in such a temple:
If the ill spirit have so fair a house,
Good things will strive to dwell with 't.

SHAKESPEARE, *The Tempest*. Act i, sc. 2, l. 457.

It becomes possible to admit that plainness may coexist with nobility of nature, and fine features with baseness; and yet to hold that mental and physical perfection are fundamentally connected, and will, when the present causes of incongruity have worked themselves out, be ever found united.

HERBERT SPENCER, *Essays: Personal Beauty.*

11
Beauty is not, as fond men misdeem,
An outward show of things that only seem.

SPENSER, *Hymne in Honour of Beautie*, l. 90.

12
Virtue lives when Beauty dies.

H. K. WHITE, *Additional Stanza to Waller's "Go, Lovely Rose."*

13
What's female beauty, but an air divine,
Thro' which the mind's all gentle graces shine?
They, like the sun, irradiate all between;
The body charms because the soul is seen.

YOUNG, *Love of Fame*. Satire vi, l. 150.

14
Not that which is great is beautiful, but that which is beautiful is great. (Non id quod magnum est, pulchrum est, sed id quod pulchrum, magnum.)

UNKNOWN. A Latin proverb.

IV—Beauty and Goodness: An Illusion

15
Too dear I prized a fair enchanting face:
Beauty unchaste is beauty in disgrace.

HOMER, *Odyssey*. Bk. viii, l. 359. (Pope, tr.)

16
Christian endeavor is notoriously hard on female puchritude.

H. L. MENCKEN, *The Aesthetic Recoil*. (*American Mercury*, July, 1931.)

17
Would you were either less beautiful or less base;
Beauty so fair mates not with evil ways.
(Aut formosa fores minus, aut minus improba, vellem;
Non facit ad mores tam bona forma malos.)

OVID, *Amores*. Bk. iii, eleg. 11, l. 41.

As a jewel of gold in a swine's snout, so is a fair woman which is without discretion.

Old Testament: Proverbs, xi, 22.

18
O Hero, what a Hero hadst thou been
If half thy outward graces had been placed
About thy thoughts and counsels of thy heart!
But fare thee well, most foul, most fair! farewell,
Thou pure impiety and impious purity!

SHAKESPEARE, *Much Ado About Nothing*. Act iv, sc. i, l. 101.

The ornament of beauty is suspect,
A crow that flies in heaven's sweetest air.

SHAKESPEARE, *Sonnets*. No. lxx.

19
What a strange illusion it is to suppose that beauty is goodness.

LEO TOLSTOY, *The Kreutzer Sonata*. Ch. 5.

1
It is better to be beautiful than to be good, but it is better to be good than to be ugly.

OSCAR WILDE, *The Picture of Dorian Gray.*

2
Say not of Beauty she is good,
Or aught but beautiful.

ELINOR WYLIE, *Beauty.*

V—Beauty and Truth

3
I must not say that thou wert true,
Yet let me say that thou wert fair;
And they that lovely face who view,
They will not ask if truth be there.

MATTHEW ARNOLD, *Indifference.* St. 1.

4
Beauty and Truth, tho' never found, are worthy to be sought.

ROBERT BUCHANAN, *To David in Heaven.*

5
If I were called upon to choose between beauty and truth, I should not hesitate; I should hold to beauty, being confident that it bears within it a truth both higher and deeper than truth itself. I will go so far as to say there is nothing true in the world save beauty.

ANATOLE FRANCE. (COURNOS, *Modern Plutarch,* p. 25.)

6
"Beauty is truth, truth beauty,"—that is all
Ye know on earth, and all ye need to know.

JOHN KEATS, *Ode on a Grecian Urn.*

7
Goodness is a special kind of truth and beauty. It is truth and beauty in human behavior.

H. A. OVERSTREET, *The Enduring Quest,* p. 163.

8
Truth exists for the wise, beauty for the feeling heart.
(Die Wahrheit ist vorhanden für den Weisen.
Die Schönheit für ein fühlend Herz.)

SCHILLER, *Don Carlos.* Act iv, sc. 21, l. 186.

9
O, how much more doth beauty beauteous seem
By that sweet ornament which truth doth give!

SHAKESPEARE, *Sonnets.* No. liv.

10
If thou art beautiful, and youth
And thought endue thee with all truth—
Be strong;—be worthy of the grace
Of God.

WORDSWORTH, *The White Doe of Rylstone.* Canto ii, l. 581.

11
The identification of the true and good is but a pious wish.

MIGUEL DE UNAMUNO, *Tragic Sense of Life,* p. 93.

VI—Beauty and Love

12
The essence of all beauty, I call love.
The attribute, the evidence, and end,
The consummation to the inward sense
Of beauty apprehended from without,
I still call love.

E. B. BROWNING, *A Drama of Exile,* l. 777.

13
All kinds of beauty do not inspire love; there is a kind which only pleases the sight, but does not captivate the affections.

CERVANTES, *Don Quixote.* Pt. ii, ch. 6.

14
Beauty is the lover's gift.

CONGREVE, *The Way of the World.* Act ii, sc. 2.

15
Love built on beauty, soon as beauty, dies.

JOHN DONNE, *Elegies:* No. 2, *The Anagram,* l. 27.

16
When beauty fires the blood, how love exalts the mind!

DRYDEN, *Cymon and Iphigenia,* l. 41.

17
Beauty is the child of love.

HAVELOCK ELLIS, *The New Spirit,* p. 280.

18
Beauty brings its own fancy price, for all that a man hath will he give for his love.

EMERSON, *Uncollected Lectures: Social Aims.*

19
Fair is my love for April's in her face,
Her lovely breasts September claims his part,
And lordly July in her eyes takes place,
But cold December dwelleth in her heart;

ROBERT GREENE, *Perimedes.*

Tender—but her hands can
Tear a soul apart!
He who follows Beauty
Breaks his foolish heart.

B. Y. WILLIAMS, *Song Against Beauty.*

20
Where beauty is, there will be love.
Nature, that wisely nothing made in vain,
Did make you lovely to be loved again.

ROBERT HEATH, *To Clarastella.*

21
Yet beauty, tho' injurious, hath strange power,
After offence returning, to regain
Love once possess'd.

MILTON, *Samson Agonistes,* l. 1003.

22
Were beauty under twenty locks kept fast,
Yet love breaks through and picks them all at last.

SHAKESPEARE, *Venus and Adonis,* l. 575.

23
Love is a flame, and therefore we say beauty is attractive; because physicians observe that fire is a great drawer.

SWIFT, *Thoughts on Various Subjects.*

1
O beauty, are you not enough?
Why am I crying after love?
SARA TEASDALE, *Spring Night.*

2
Be she fairer than the day,
Or the flowery meads in May,
If she be not so to me,
What care I how fair she be?
GEORGE WITHER, *The Lover's Resolution.*

3
True beauty dwells in deep retreats,
Whose veil is unremoved
Till heart with heart in concord beats,
And the lover is beloved.
WORDSWORTH, *To ——.*

4
And beauty, for confiding youth,
Those shocks of passion can prepare
That kill the bloom before its time,
And blanch, without the owner's crime,
The most resplendent hair.
WORDSWORTH, *Lament of Mary Queen of Scots.*

5
Oh gracious, why wasn't I born old and ugly?
DICKENS, *Barnaby Rudge.* Ch. 70.

VII—Beauty and Riches

6
A beautiful girl, though poor indeed, is yet abundantly dowered. (Virgo formosa etsi sit oppido pauper, tamen abunde dotata est.)
APULEIUS, *De Magia.* Sec. 92.

She that is fair hath half her portion.
THOMAS DRAXE, *Bibliotheca Schol. Instr.*, 15.

7
Beauty carries its dower in its face.
UNKNOWN.

A good face needs no band and a pretty wench no land.
JOHN RAY, *English Proverbs.*

"What is your fortune, my pretty maid?"
"My face is my fortune, sir," she said.
UNKNOWN. Old nursery rhyme.

8
A poor beauty finds more lovers than husbands.
GEORGE HERBERT, *Jacula Prudentum.*

Beauty without bounty avails not.
JOHN LYLY, *Euphues*, 295.

Beauty is potent, but money is omnipotent.
JOHN RAY, *English Proverbs.* No. 122.

The mate for beauty
Should be a man, and not a money-chest!
BULWER-LYTTON, *Richelieu.* Act i, sc. 2.

9
All heiresses are beautiful.
DRYDEN, *King Arthur.* Act i, sc. 1.

No woman can be a beauty without a fortune.
FARQUHAR, *The Beaux' Stratagem.* Act ii, sc. 2.

VIII—Beauty: Its Power

10
There's nothing that allays an angry mind
So soon as a sweet beauty.
BEAUMONT AND FLETCHER, *Elder Brother*, iii, 5.

11
Such man, being but mere man ('twas all she knew),
Must be made sure by beauty's silken bond,
The weakness that subdues the strong, and bows
Wisdom alike and folly.
ROBERT BROWNING, *The Ring and the Book.* Pt. ix, l. 440.

12
Beauty in distress is much the most affecting beauty.
EDMUND BURKE, *On the Sublime and Beautiful.* Pt. iii, sec. 9.

Nor be, what man should ever be,
The friend of Beauty in distress?
BYRON, *To Florence.*

13
Who doth not feel, until his failing sight
Faints into dimness with its own delight,
His changing cheek, his sinking heart confess,
The might, the majesty of Loveliness?
BYRON, *The Bride of Abydos.* Canto i, st. 6.

Who hath not paused while Beauty's pensive eye
Asked from his heart the homage of a sigh?
CAMPBELL, *The Pleasures of Hope.* Pt. ii, l. 3.

14
I pour into the world the eternal streams
Wan prophets tent beside, and dream their dreams.
JOHN VANCE CHENEY, *Beauty.*

15
Beauties are tyrants, and if they can reign
They have no feeling for their subjects' pain;
Their victim's anguish gives their charms applause,
And their chief glory is the woe they cause.
GEORGE CRABBE, *Tales: The Patron*, l. 199.

16
Ah, Beauty! Syren, fair enchanting Good,
Sweet silent Rhetoric of persuading eyes;
Dumb Eloquence, whose power doth move the Blood,
More than the Words or Wisdom of the Wise;
Still Harmony, whose Diapason lies
Within a Brow; the Key which Passions move
To ravish Sense, and play a World in love.
SAMUEL DANIEL, *The Complaint of Rosamund.* St. 19.

17
Beauty hath created been
T' undo or be undone.
SAMUEL DANIEL, *Ulysses and the Syren*, l. 71.

18
Things that are lovely
Can tear my heart in two—
Moonlight on still pools,
You.
DOROTHY DOW, *Things.*

1
Old as I am, for ladies' love unfit,
The power of beauty I remember yet,
Which once inflam'd my soul, and still inspires my wit.
DRYDEN, *Cymon and Iphigenia*, l. 1.

2
Who gave thee, O Beauty,
The keys of this breast,—
Too credulous lover
Of blest and unblest?
Say, when in lapsed ages
Thee knew I of old?
Or what was the service
For which I was sold?
EMERSON, *Ode to Beauty.*

3
'Tis true, gold can do much,
But beauty more.
MASSINGER, *The Unnatural Combat.* Act i, sc. 1.

Beauty provoketh thieves sooner than gold.
SHAKESPEARE, *As You Like It.* Act i, sc. 3, l. 111.

4
Beauty makes idiots sad and wise men merry.
GEORGE JEAN NATHAN, *House of Satan*, p. 82.

5 Beauty draws more than oxen.
GEORGE HERBERT, *Jacula Prudentum.* No. 687. (1640)

Beauty can pierce like a pain.
THOMAS MANN, *Buddenbrooks.* Pt. xi, ch. 2. (1903)

6
Beauty doth varnish age, as if new-born,
And gives the crutch the cradle's infancy.
SHAKESPEARE, *Love's Labour's Lost.* Act iv, sc. 3, l. 244.

Beauty is a witch,
Against whose charms faith melteth into blood.
SHAKESPEARE, *Much Ado About Nothing.* Act ii, sc. 1, l. 186.

Beauty itself doth of itself persuade
The eyes of men without an orator.
SHAKESPEARE, *The Rape of Lucrece*, l. 29.

All orators are dumb when beauty pleadeth.
SHAKESPEARE, *The Rape of Lucrece*, l. 268.

7
Men have no sense now but for the worthless flower of beauty.
SHERIDAN, *The Rivals.* Act iii, sc. 3.

8
O how can beauty master the most strong!
SPENSER, *Faerie Queene.* Bk. i, canto iii, st. 6.

9
Sacharissa's beauty's wine,
Which to madness doth incline:
Such a liquor as no brain
That is mortal can sustain.
EDMUND WALLER, *Amoret*, l. 43.

10
Beauty with a bloodless conquest finds
A welcome sovereignty in rudest minds.
EDMUND WALLER, *Upon Her Majesty's Repairing of St. Paul's*, l. 41.

IX—Beauty Draws With a Single Hair

11
And from that luckless hour my tyrant fair
Has led and turned me by a single hair.
ROBERT BLAND, *Anthology*, p. 20. (1813)

12
No cord nor cable can so forcibly draw, or hold so fast, as love can do with a twined thread.
ROBERT BURTON, *Anatomy of Melancholy.* Pt. iii, sec. ii, mem. 1, subs. 2.

13
Ten teams of oxen draw much less
Than doth one hair of Helen's tress.
JOHN FLORIO, *Second Frutes*, l. 183. (1603)

14
'Tis a powerful sex; they were too strong for the first, the strongest and wisest man that was; they must needs be strong, when one hair of a woman can draw more than a hundred pair of oxen.
JAMES HOWELL, *Familiar Letters.* Bk. ii, letter 4.

Not ten yoke of oxen
Have the power to draw us
Like a woman's hair!
LONGFELLOW, *The Saga of King Olaf.* Pt. xvi, st. 23.

15
She knows her man, and when you rant and swear,
Can draw you to her with a single hair.
(Ne trepidare velis atque artos rodere casses.)
PERSIUS, *Satires.* Sat. v, l. 170. (Dryden, tr., l. 246.)

16
Fair tresses man's imperial race ensnare,
And beauty draws us with a single hair.
POPE, *Rape of the Lock.* Canto ii, l. 27. (1712)

X—Beauty: Its Permanence

17
What is lovely never dies,
But passes into other loveliness,
Star-dust, or sea-foam, flower or wingèd air.
T. B. ALDRICH, *A Shadow of the Night.*

And Beauty immortal awakes from the tomb.
JAMES BEATTIE, *The Hermit.* St. 6.

18
All that is beautiful shall abide,
All that is base shall die.
ROBERT BUCHANAN, *Balder the Beautiful.*

19
When death hath poured oblivion through my veins,
And brought me home, as all are brought, to lie
In that vast house, common to serfs and thanes,—
I shall not die, I shall not utterly die,
For beauty born of beauty—*that* remains.
MADISON CAWEIN, *Beauty.*

20
A thing of beauty is a joy for ever:
Its loveliness increases; it will never

Pass into nothingness; but still will keep
A bower quiet for us, and a sleep
Full of sweet dreams, and health, and quiet breathing.
JOHN KEATS, *Endymion*. Bk. i, l. 1.

1
Wherever beauty has been quick in clay
Some effluence of it lives, a spirit dwells,
Beauty that death can never take away,
Mixed with the air that shakes the flower bells.
JOHN MASEFIELD, *Sonnets*. No. xxxv.

2
Beauty is momentary in the mind—
The fitful tracing of a portal;
But in the flesh it is immortal.
WALLACE STEVENS, *Peter Quince at the Clavier*.

3
Beauty remains, but we are transitory.
Ten thousand years from now will fall the dew,
And high in heaven still hang that arch of blue;
The rose will still repeat its perfect story.
CHARLES HANSON TOWNE, *Enigma*.

4
Beauty seen is never lost.
WHITTIER, *Sunset on the Bearcamp*.

Beauty is the only thing that time cannot harm.
OSCAR WILDE, *The English Renaissance*.

5
Beauty abides, nor suffers mortal change,
Eternal refuge of the orphaned mind.
G. E. WOODBERRY, *The North Shore Watch*.

6
Who dreamed that beauty passes like a dream?
W. B. YEATS, *The Rose of the World*.

XI—Beauty: Its Impermanence

7
Beauty soon grows familiar to the lover,
Fades in his eye, and palls upon the sense.
ADDISON, *Cato*. Act i, sc. 4.

Beauty is all very well at first sight; but who ever looks at it when it has been in the house three days?
BERNARD SHAW, *Man and Superman*. Act iv.

8
Beauty is as summer-fruits, which are easy to corrupt, and cannot last.
FRANCIS BACON, *Essays: Of Beauty*.

Too bright, too beautiful to last.
BRYANT, *The Rivulet*.

9
Beauty,—thou pretty plaything, death, deceit!
That steals so softly o'er the stripling's heart,
And gives it a new pulse, unknown before,
The grave discredits thee.
ROBERT BLAIR, *The Grave*, l. 337.

10
Beauty's of a fading nature—
Has a season, and is gone!
BURNS, *Will Ye Go and Marry Katie?*

11
Decay's effacing fingers
Have swept the lines where beauty lingers.
BYRON, *The Giaour*, l. 72.

12
Beauty's witching sway
Is now to me a star that's fallen—a dream that's passed away.
THOMAS CAMPBELL, *Farewell to Love*.

13
Beauty, sweet Love, is like the morning dew,
Whose short refresh upon the tender green
Cheers for a time, but till the sun doth show:
And straight 'tis gone, as it had never been.
SAMUEL DANIEL, *To Delia*.

14
Art quickens nature; care will make a face;
Neglected beauty perisheth apace.
ROBERT HERRICK, *Neglect*.

15
Ah, lovely boy, trust not too much to your bloom!
The white privets fall, the dark hyacinths are culled.
(O formose puer, numium ne crede colori:
Alba ligustra cadunt, vaccina nigra leguntur.)
VERGIL, *Eclogues*, No. ii, l. 17.

Trust not too much to that enchanting face:
Beauty's a charm; but soon the charm will pass.
VERGIL, *Eclogues*, ii, 17. (Dryden, tr.)

16
Brittle beauty, that nature made so frail,
Whereof the gift is small, and short the season;
Flowering to-day, to-morrow apt to fail;
Fickle treasure, abhorred of reason.
THOMAS HOWARD, EARL OF SURREY, *The Frailty and Hurtfulness of Beauty*.

17
Beauty is a fading flower. (Flori decidenti.)
Old Testament: Isaiah, xxviii, 1.

Beauty is but a flower,
Which wrinkles will devour.
THOMAS NASHE, *Summer's Last Will and Testament*, l. 600.

Beauty's a flower.
SHAKESPEARE, *Twelfth Night*. Act i, sc. 5, l. 57.

18
She that a clinquant outside doth adore,
Dotes on a gilded statue and no more.
SIR RICHARD LOVELACE, *Song*.

19
What's beauty but a corse?
What but fair sand-dust are earth's purest forms?
Queens' bodies are but trunks to put in worms.
MIDDLETON AND DEKKER, *The Honest Whore*, Pt. i, act i, sc. 1.

20
Beauty has wings, and too hastily flies.
EDWARD MOORE, *Song*.

1
A frail gift is beauty, which grows less as time draws on, and is devoured by its own years. (Forma bonum fragile est, quantumque accedit ad annos, Fit minor, et spatio carpitur ipsa suo.)
OVID, *Ars Amatoria*. Bk. i, l. 113.

Trust little to treacherous beauty. (Fallaci timide confide figuræ.)
OVID, *Ars Amatoria*. Bk. ii, l. 143.

That comely face will be marred by the long years; and the wrinkles of old age will be upon your brow.
(Ista decens facies longis vitiabitur annis;
Rugaque in antiqua fronte senilis erit.)
OVID, *Tristia*. Bk. iii, eleg. 7, l. 33.

The flowers anew returning seasons bring
But beauty faded has no second spring.
AMBROSE PHILIPS, *Pastoral*.

2
To bring your beauty back to you
Would be to lift so soft a thing
As only on a day of blue
Only a thrush could sing.
EDWIN QUARLES, *Prelude*.

3
Beauty is but a vain and doubtful good;
A shining gloss that vadeth suddenly;
A flower that dies when first it 'gins to bud;
A brittle glass that's broken presently:
A doubtful good, a gloss, a glass, a flower,
Lost, vaded, broken, dead within an hour.
SHAKESPEARE [?], *Passionate Pilgrim*, l. 169.

Since brass, nor stone, nor earth, nor boundless sea,
But sad mortality o'ersways their power,
How with this rage shall beauty hold a plea,
Whose action is no stronger than a flower?
SHAKESPEARE, *Sonnets*. No. lxv.

For he being dead, with him is beauty slain;
And beauty dead, black chaos comes again.
SHAKESPEARE, *Venus and Adonis*, l. 1019.

4
Beauty is a short-lived reign. (Ὀλιγοχρόνιον Τυραννίδα.)
SOCRATES. (DIOGENES LAERTIUS, *Aristotle*. Bk. v, sec. 19.)

5
Beauty vanishes like a vapor,
Preach the men of musty morals.
HARRIET PRESCOTT SPOFFORD, *Evanescence*.

6
Beauty is not immortal. In a day
Blossom and June and rapture pass away.
ARTHUR STRINGER, *A Fragile Thing is Beauty*.

7
Though one were fair as roses
His beauty clouds and closes.
SWINBURNE, *The Garden of Proserpine*.

8
In the body itself what is beauty save a little skin, well colored? (In corpore ipso quid forma est, nempe cuticula bene colorata?)
LUDOVICUS VIVES, *Works: Introduction*. Vol. ii, p. 61. (1555)

Beauty's but skin deep.
JOHN DAVIES, *A Select Second Husband for Sir Thomas Overburie's Wife*, vi. (1606)

And all the carnal beauty of my wife
Is but skin deep.
SIR THOMAS OVERBURY, *A Wife*. St. 16. (1614)

All the beauty in the world 'tis but skin-deep, a sunblast defaceth it.
RALPH VENNING, *Orthodoxe Paradoxes*, p. 41. (1650)

Beauty of face is a frail ornament,
A passing flower, a brightness momentary—
A thing belonging only to the skin.
(La beauté du visage est un frêle ornement,
Une fleur passagère, un éclat d'un moment,
Et qui n'est attaché qu'à la simple épiderme.)
MOLIÈRE, *Les Femmes Savantes*. Act iii, sc. 4, l. 19. (1672)

Beauty's only skin deep, but ugly goes to the bone.
A. B. EVANS, *Leicestershire Words*, p. 101.

The saying that beauty is but skin deep is but a skin-deep saying.
HERBERT SPENCER. (*Home Life with Herbert Spencer*. Ch. 4.)

XII—Beauty: Its Penalties

9
Women's beauty, like men's wit, is generally fatal to the owners.
LORD CHESTERFIELD, *Misc. Works*. Vol. ii, p. 101.

Thou who hast The fatal gift of beauty.
BYRON, *Childe Harold*. Canto iv, st. 42.

10
Beauty will buy no beef.
THOMAS FULLER, *Gnomologia*. No. 956.

Beauty is no inheritance.
JOHN RAY, *English Proverbs*, 2.

11
In beauty, faults conspicuous grow;
The smallest speck is seen on snow.
JOHN GAY, *The Peacock, Turkey and Goose*.

Would it were I had been false, not you!
I that am nothing, not you that are all;
I, never the worse for a touch or two
On my speckled hide; not you, the pride
Of the day, my swan, that a first fleck's fall
On her wonder of white might unswan, undo!
ROBERT BROWNING, *The Worst of It*.

12
What ills from beauty spring.
SAMUEL JOHNSON, *The Vanity of Human Wishes*, l. 319.

13
Rare is the union of beauty and modesty. (Rara est adeo concordia formæ Atque pudicitiæ.)
JUVENAL, *Satires*. Sat. x, l. 297.

Great is the strife between beauty and modesty. (Lis est cum forma magna pudicitiæ.)
OVID, *Heroides*. No. xvi, l. 290.

Rarely do great beauty and great virtue dwell together. (Raro admodum forma, insignis, honestasque uno sub lare habitant.)
PETRARCH, *De Remediis*. Bk. ii.

1
It is worth nothing to be young without being beautiful, nor to be beautiful without being young. (Il ne sert de rien d'être jeune sans être belle, ni d'être belle sans être jeune.)
LA ROCHEFOUCAULD, *Maximes*. No. 497.

2
Beauty and sadness always go together.
Nature thought Beauty too rich to go forth
Upon the earth without a meet alloy.
GEORGE MACDONALD, *Within and Without*. Pt. iv, sc. 3.

Beauty and anguish walking hand in hand
The downward slope to death.
TENNYSON, *A Dream of Fair Women*. St 4.

3
Beauty, like the fair Hesperian tree
Laden with blooming gold had need the guard
Of dragon-watch with unenchanted eye,
To save her blossoms and defend her fruit.
MILTON, *Comus*, l. 393.

4
Trust not to the treacherous lamp; darkness and drink impair your judgment of beauty. (Hic tu fallaci nimium ne crede lucernæ: Judicio formæ noxque merumque nocent.)
OVID, *Ars Amatoria*. Bk. i, l. 245.

When the candles are out all women are fair.
PLUTARCH, *Conjugal Precepts*.

5
Beauty, if you do not open your doors, takes age from lack of use. (Forma, nisi admittas, nullo exercente senescit.)
OVID, *Amores*. Bk. i, eleg. 8, l. 53.

What is hidden is unknown; what is unknown none desires; naught is gained when a lovely face has none to see it. (Quod latet, ignotum est; ignoti nulla cupido: Fructus abest, facies cum bona teste caret.)
OVID, *Ars Amatoria*. Bk. iii, l. 397.

Where none admire, 'tis useless to excel;
Where none are beaux, 'tis vain to be a belle.
Beauty, like wit, to judges should be shown;
Both most are valued where they best are known.
GEORGE LYTTELTON, *Soliloquy of a Beauty in the Country*, l. 11.

Beauty is Nature's coin, must not be hoarded,
But must be current, and the good thereof
Consists in mutual and partaken bliss. . . .
Beauty is Nature's brag, and must be shown
In courts, at feasts, and high solemnities,
Where most may wonder at the workmanship;
It is for homely features to keep home,
They had their name hence.
JOHN MILTON, *Comus*, l. 739.

Small is the worth
Of beauty from the light retired;
Bid her come forth,
Suffer herself to be desired,
And not blush so to be admired.
EDMUND WALLER, *Go, Lovely Rose*.

6
Beauty's elixir vitæ, praise.
COVENTRY PATMORE, *The Angel in the House*: Bk. ii, *Prologue*.

7
Beauty and wisdom are rarely conjoined. (Raram fecit mixturam cum sapientia forma.)
PETRONIUS, *Satyricon*. Sec. 94, l. 2.

O that such beauty should be so brainless! (O quanta species cerebrum non habet!)
PHÆDRUS, *Fables*. Bk. i, fab. 7, l. 2.

Beauty and folly are old companions.
BENJAMIN FRANKLIN, *Poor Richard*, 1734.

8
Favour is deceitful, and beauty is vain.
Old Testament: Proverbs, xxxi, 30.

9
She never yet was foolish that was fair,
For even her folly helped her to an heir.
SHAKESPEARE, *Othello*. Act ii, sc. l, l. 137.

10
No hollow wiles, nor honeyed smiles,
Of ladies fair I follow;
For beauty sweet still hides deceit,
'Tis hollow, hollow, hollow.
UNKNOWN, *Deceitful Beauty*. (MCGUFFEY, *Third Reader*, p. 84.)

11
Let it be given to the more beautiful. (Detur pulchriori.)
Inscription on the Apple of Discord.

XIII—Beauty in Women

12
Not more the rose, the queen of flowers,
Outblushes all the bloom of bowers,
Than she unrivall'd grace discloses,
The sweetest rose, where all are roses.
ANACREON, *Odes*. No. 66. (Moore, tr.)

A lovely being, scarcely formed or moulded,
A rose with all its sweetest leaves yet folded.
BYRON, *Don Juan*. Canto xv, st. 43.

And she was fair as is the rose in May.
CHAUCER, *The Legend of Good Women: Cleopatra*, l. 34.

Proserpine gathering flowers
Herself a fairer flower.
MILTON, *Paradise Lost*. Bk. iv, l. 269.

Of Nature's gifts thou may'st with lilies boast
And with the half-blown rose.
SHAKESPEARE, *King John*. Act iii, sc. 1, l. 53.

She wears a rose in her hair,
At the twilight's dreamy close:
Her face is fair,—how fair
Under the rose!
R. H. STODDARD, *Under the Rose*.

13
No gems, no gold she needs to wear;
She shines intrinsically fair.
THOMAS BEDINGFIELD, *The Lover's Choice*.

1
So fair,
She takes the breath of men away
Who gaze upon her unaware.
E. B. BROWNING, *Bianca Among the Nightingales*. St. 12.

Beauty's chiefest maid of honour,
You may break Lent with looking on her.
JOHN CLEVELAND, *To the State of Love.*

Beauty enough to make a world to dote.
JAMES I OF SCOTLAND, *The King's Quair*. St. 28.

We cannot choose; our faces madden men!
STEPHEN PHILLIPS, *Paolo and Francesca*. Act ii, sc. 1.

2
Fair, as the first that fell of womankind.
BYRON, *The Bride of Abydos*. Canto i, st. 6.

Her glossy hair was cluster'd o'er a brow
Bright with intelligence, and fair and smooth;
Her eyebrow's shape was like the aërial bow,
Her cheek all purple with the beam of youth,
Mounting, at times, to a transparent glow,
As if her veins ran lightning.
BYRON, *Don Juan*. Canto i, st. 61.

And beauteous, even where beauties most abound.
BYRON, *Don Juan*. Canto xiii, st. 2.

She was a form of life and light
That, seen, became a part of sight;
And rose, where'er I turned mine eye,
The Morning-star of Memory!
BYRON, *The Giaour*, l. 1127.

3
She walks in beauty, like the night
Of cloudless climes and starry skies;
And all that's best of dark and bright
Meet in her aspect and her eyes:
Thus mellow'd to that tender light
Which heaven to gaudy day denies.
BYRON, *She Walks in Beauty.*

4
Exceeding fair she was not; and yet fair
In that she never studied to be fairer
Than Nature made her; beauty cost her nothing,
Her virtues were so rare.
GEORGE CHAPMAN, *All Fools*. Act i, sc. 1.

She is not fair to outward view
As many maidens be;
Her loveliness I never knew
Until she smiled on me:
Oh! then I saw her eye was bright,
A well of love, a spring of light. . . .
Her very frowns are fairer far
Than smiles of other maidens are.
HARTLEY COLERIDGE, *Song.*

She was not fair,
Nor beautiful;—those words express her not.
But, oh, her looks had something excellent,
That wants a name!
LONGFELLOW, *Hyperion*. Bk. iii, ch. iv.

5
A beautiful woman is a practical poet, taming her savage mate, planting tenderness, hope, and eloquence in all whom she approaches.
EMERSON, *Conduct of Life: Beauty.*

6
Beauty to no complexion is confined,
Is of all colours, and by none defined.
GEORGE GRANVILLE, *Progress of Beauty*, l. 77.

7
Beauty should be kind, as well as charm.
GEORGE GRANVILLE, *To Myra.*

Beauty and beauteous words should go together.
GEORGE HERBERT, *The Forerunners.*

8
Beauty's the thing that counts
In women; red lips
And black eyes are better than brains.
MARY J. ELMENDORF, *Beauty's the Thing.*

9
And matchless Ganymede, divinely fair.
(Ἀντίθεος Γανυμήδης, ὃς δὴ κάλλιστος γένετο θνητῶν ἀνθρώπων.)
HOMER, *Iliad*. Bk. xx, l. 232. (Pope, tr., l. 278.)

She fair, divinely fair, fit love for gods.
MILTON, *Paradise Lost*. Bk. ix, l. 489.

At length I saw a lady within call,
Stiller than chisell'd marble, standing there;
A daughter of the gods, divinely tall
And most divinely fair.
TENNYSON, *A Dream of Fair Women*. St. 22.

10
Beautiful in form and feature,
Lovely as the day,
Can there be so fair a creature
Formed of common clay?
LONGFELLOW, *The Masque of Pandora*. Pt. i.

11
What is your sex's earliest, latest care,
Your heart's supreme ambition? To be fair.
GEORGE LYTTELTON, *Advice to a Lady.*

Every woman would rather be beautiful than good. (Jedes Weib will lieber schön als fromm sein.)
UNKNOWN. A German proverb.

12
The most beautiful object in the world, it will be allowed, is a beautiful woman.
MACAULAY, *Criticisms on Italian Writers: Dante.*

13
O thou art fairer than the evening air,
Clad in the beauty of a thousand stars.
CHRISTOPHER MARLOWE, *Faustus*. Act v, sc. 2.

14
But the loveliest things of beauty God ever has showed to me
Are her voice, and her hair, and eyes, and the dear red curve of her lips.
JOHN MASEFIELD, *Beauty.*

15
She's all my fancy painted her;
She's lovely, she's divine.
WILLIAM MEE, *Alice Gray.*

Whate'er is lovely or divine.
ROBERT BURTON, *Anatomy of Melancholy: The Author's Abstract.*

1
Hung over her enamour'd, and beheld
Beauty, which, whether waking or asleep,
Shot forth peculiar graces.
MILTON, *Paradise Lost*. Bk. v, l. 13.

Grace was in all her steps, heav'n in her eye,
In every gesture dignity and love.
MILTON, *Paradise Lost*. Bk. viii, l. 488.

2
To weave a garland for the rose,
And think thus crown'd 'twould lovelier be,
Were far less vain than to suppose
That silks and gems add grace to thee.
THOMAS MOORE, *Songs from the Greek Anthology: To Weave a Garland.*

3
Even honest maids love to hear their charms extolled; even to the chaste their beauty is a care and a delight. (Delectant etiam castas præconia formæ; Virginibus curæ grataque forma sua est.)
OVID, *Ars Amatoria*. Bk. i, l. 623.

Dear to the heart of girls is their own beauty. (Virginibus cordi grataque forma sua est.)
OVID, *De Medicamine Faciei*, l. 32.

4
Here is all the beauty of the world. (Hæc habet quicquid in orbe fuit.)
OVID, *Ars Amatoria*. Bk. i, l. 56.

All the eminent and canonised beauties,
By truth recorded, or by poets feigned.
MASSINGER, *The Bashful Lover*. Act iv, sc. 1.

5
Outward beauty is not enough. . . . Words, wit, play, sweet talk and laughter, surpass the work of too simple nature. For all device of art seasons beauty.
PETRONIUS, *Fragments*. No. 89.

The beauty that addresses itself to the eyes is only the spell of the moment; the eye of the body is not always that of the soul.
GEORGE SAND, *Handsome Lawrence*. Ch. 1.

Beauty, madam, pleases the eyes only; sweetness of disposition charms the soul. (La beauté, madame, Ne plaît qu'aux yeux; la douceur charme l'âme.)
VOLTAIRE, *Nanine*. Act i, sc. 1.

6
Helen, thy beauty is to me
Like those Nicæan barks of yore,
That gently, o'er a perfumed sea,
The weary, wayworn wanderer bore
To his own native shore.
EDGAR ALLAN POE, *To Helen.*

On desperate seas long wont to roam,
Thy hyacinth hair, thy classic face,
Thy naiad airs have brought me home
To the glory that was Greece
And the grandeur that was Rome.
EDGAR ALLAN POE, *To Helen.*

7
God made my lady lovely to behold.
D. G. ROSSETTI, *How My Songs of Her Began.*

8
Is she not more than painting can express,
Or youthful poets fancy when they love?
NICHOLAS ROWE, *Fair Penitent*. Act iii, sc. 1.

9
And ne'er did Grecian chisel trace
A Nymph, a Naiad, or a Grace
Of finer form or lovelier face. . . .
A foot more light, a step more true,
Ne'er from the heath-flower dash'd the dew.
SCOTT, *Lady of the Lake*. Canto i, st. 18.

There was a soft and pensive grace,
A cast of thought upon her face,
That suited well the forehead high,
The eyelash dark, and downcast eye.
SCOTT, *Rokeby*. Canto iv, st. 5.

10
For her own person,
It beggar'd all description.
SHAKESPEARE, *Antony and Cleopatra*. Act ii, sc. 2, l. 202.

Is she not passing fair?
SHAKESPEARE, *The Two Gentlemen of Verona*. Act iv, sc. 4, l. 153.

The most peerless piece of earth, I think,
That e'er the sun shone bright on.
SHAKESPEARE, *Winter's Tale*. Act v, sc. 1, l. 94.

11
O, she is rich in beauty, only poor,
That when she dies with beauty dies her store.
SHAKESPEARE, *Romeo and Juliet*. Act i, sc. 1, l. 221.

O, she doth teach the torches to burn bright!
It seems she hangs upon the cheek of night
Like a rich jewel in an Ethiope's ear:
Beauty too rich for use, for earth too dear!
SHAKESPEARE, *Romeo and Juliet*. Act i, sc. 5, l. 46.

Her beauty makes
This vault a feasting presence full of light.
SHAKESPEARE, *Romeo and Juliet*. Act v, sc. 3, l. 85.

12
If I could write the beauty of your eyes,
And in fresh numbers number all your graces,
The age to come would say, "This poet lies;
Such heavenly touches ne'er touch'd earthly faces."
SHAKESPEARE, *Sonnets*. No. xvii.

13
It is one of the mysterious ways of Allah to make women troublesome when he makes them beautiful.
BERNARD SHAW, *The Adventures of the Black Girl in Her Search for God.*

14
A lovely Lady garmented in light
From her own beauty.
SHELLEY, *The Witch of Atlas*. St. 5.

For she was beautiful: her beauty made
The bright world dim, and everything beside
Seemed like the fleeting image of a shade.
SHELLEY, *The Witch of Atlas*. St. 12.

1
As the lily among thorns, so is my love among the daughters.
Old Testament: Song of Solomon, ii, 2.

2
Her face so fair as flesh it seemed not,
But heavenly portrait of bright angels' hue,
Clear as the sky, withouten blame or blot,
Through goodly mixture of complexion's dew;
And in her cheeks the vermeil red did shew
Like roses in a bed of lilies shed,
The which ambrosial odours from them threw,
And gazers' sense with double pleasure fed,
Able to heal the sick, and to revive the dead.
SPENSER, *Faerie Queene*. Bk. ii, canto iii, st. 22.

3
But there has never been a woman born
Who was so beautiful, not one so beautiful
Of all the women born.
JAMES STEPHENS, *Deirdre*.

4
Thy cradled brows and loveliest loving lips,
The floral hair, the little lightening eyes,
And all thy goodly glory.
SWINBURNE, *Atalanta in Calydon: Althæa*.

5
A surpassing beauty and in the bloom of youth. (Egregia forma atque ætate integra.)
TERENCE, *Andria*, l. 74. (Act i, sc.1.)

6
Thoughtless of beauty, she was Beauty's self.
THOMSON, *The Seasons: Autumn*, l. 207.

7
Her eyes as stars of Twilight fair;
Like Twilight's, too, her dusky hair;
But all things else about her drawn
From May-time and the cheerful Dawn.
WORDSWORTH, *She Was a Phantom of Delight*.

8
Sweet harmonist! and beautiful as sweet!
And young as beautiful! and soft as young!
And gay as soft! and innocent as gay!
YOUNG, *Night Thoughts*. Night iii, l. 81.

9
The pale unripen'd beauties of the North.
ADDISON, *Cato*. Act i, sc. 4.

10
Women have, in general, but one object, which is their beauty; upon which, scarce any flattery is too gross for them to swallow.
LORD CHESTERFIELD, *Letters*, 16 Oct., 1747.

BED

See also Rising, Sleep

11
Matthew, Mark, Luke, and John,
The bed be blest that I lie on.
THOMAS ADY, *A Candle in the Dark*, p. 58. (1655)

Matthew, Mark, Luke, and John,
Bless the bed that I lie on;
Four corners to my bed,
Four angels round my head,
One to watch, and one to pray,
And two to bear my soul away.
UNKNOWN, *Old Nursery Rhyme*.

12
Warm beds, beds to charm away fatigue. (Θερμὰ λουτρὰ καὶ πόνων θελκτηρία στρωμνή.)
ÆSCHYLUS, *Choephoroi*, l. 670.

13
In bed we laugh, in bed we cry;
And born in bed, in bed we die;
The near approach a bed may show
Of human bliss to human woe.
(Théâtre des ris et des pleurs,
Lit! où je nais, et où je meurs,
Tu nous fais voir comment voisins
Sont nos plaisirs et nos chagrins.)
ISAAC DE BENSERADE, *À Son Lit*. (Samuel Johnson, tr.)

The bed comprehends our whole life, for we were born in it, we live in it, and we shall die in it.
GUY DE MAUPASSANT, *The Bed*.

14
Would you have a settled head,
You must early go to bed;
I tell you, and I tell 't again,
You must be in bed at ten.
NICHOLAS CULPEPER. (SWIFT, *Letters: To Stella*, 19 Jan., 1710.)

Ten, struck the church clock, straight to bed went he.
ROBERT BROWNING, *How it Strikes a Contemporary*.

15
My bed itself is like the grave,
My sheets the winding-sheet,
My clothes the mould which I must have,
To cover me most meet.
The hungry fleas, which frisk so fresh,
To worms I can compare,
Which greedily shall gnaw my flesh
And leave the bones full bare.
GEORGE GASCOIGNE, *Good-night*.

16
He that makes his bed ill, lies there.
GEORGE HERBERT, *Jacula Prudentum*. *See also under* RETRIBUTION.

17
Oh, bed, oh, bed! delicious bed!
That heaven upon earth to the weary head.
THOMAS HOOD, *Miss Kilmansegg: Her Dream*.

Stretch the tired limbs and lay the head
Down on our own delightful bed.
JAMES MONTGOMERY, *Night*.

18
If a bed would tell all it knows, it would put many to the blush.
JAMES HOWELL, *Proverbs*, 4.

19
And so to bed.
SAMUEL PEPYS, *Diary*, 2 Jan., 1659.

And so to bed. Pray wish us all good rest.
ROBERT HERRICK, *Epitaph on Sir Edward Giles*.

1
She knows the heat of luxurious bed.
SHAKESPEARE, *Much Ado About Nothing*. Act iv, sc. 1, l. 42.

You rise to play and go to bed to work.
SHAKESPEARE, *Othello*. Act ii, sc. 1, l. 116.

There's millions now alive
That nightly lie in those unproper beds
Which they dare swear peculiar.
SHAKESPEARE, *Othello*. Act iv, sc. 1, l. 68.

2
I was in love with my bed.
SHAKESPEARE, *The Two Gentlemen of Verona*. Act ii, sc. 1, l. 87.

3
Or go to bed now, being two hours to day.
SHAKESPEARE, *The Merchant of Venice*. Act v, sc. 1, l. 303.

Goes, with the fashionable owls, to bed.
YOUNG, *Love of Fame*. Sat. v, l. 210.

4
To go to bed after midnight is to go to bed betimes.
SHAKESPEARE, *Twelfth Night*. Act ii, sc. 3, l. 8.

Whoever thinks of going to bed before twelve o'clock is a scoundrel.
SAMUEL JOHNSON, *Miscellanies*. Vol. ii, p. 19.

No civilized person ever goes to bed the same day he gets up.
RICHARD HARDING DAVIS, *Gallegher*.

5
Take thou of me, sweet pillows, sweetest bed;
A chamber deaf to noise, and blind to light,
A rosy garland and a weary head.
SIR PHILIP SIDNEY, *Astrophel and Stella*. Sonnet xxxix.

6
In winter I get up at night
And dress by yellow candle-light.
In summer, quite the other way,
I have to go to bed by day.
R. L. STEVENSON, *Bed in Summer*.

The pleasant Land of Counterpane.
R. L. STEVENSON, *The Land of Counterpane*.

7
'Tis very warm weather when one's in bed.
SWIFT, *Letters: To Stella*, 8 Nov., 1710.

8
Before he retired to his virtoous couch.
ARTEMUS WARD, *Edwin Forrest as Othello*.

9
Bed is a medicine. (El leto xe' una medicina.)
UNKNOWN. A Venetian proverb.

BEE

See also Amber

10
The poison of the honey-bee
Is the artist's jealousy.
WILLIAM BLAKE, *Ideas of Good and Evil*.

11
The honey-bee that wanders all day long . . .
Seeks not alone the rose's glowing breast,
The lily's dainty cup, the violet's lips,
But from all rank and noxious weeds he sips
The single drop of sweetness closely pressed
Within the poison chalice.
ANNE BOTTA, *The Lesson of the Bee*.

Even bees, the little almsmen of spring bowers,
Know there is richest juice in poison-flowers.
JOHN KEATS, *Isabella*. St. 13.

In the nice bee, what sense, so subtly true,
From pois'nous herbs extracts the healing dew?
POPE, *Essay on Man*. Epis. i, l. 219.

Thus may we gather honey from the weed,
And make a moral of the devil himself.
SHAKESPEARE, *Henry V*. Act iv, sc. 1, l. 11.

12
For aye as busy as bees Been they.
CHAUCER, *The Marchantes Tale: Epilogue*, l. 4. (1388)

A comely old man as busy as a bee.
JOHN LYLY, *Euphues and His England*, p. 252. (1580)

13
Nature's confectioner, the bee.
JOHN CLEVELAND, *Fuscara*. (1653)

14
The murmur of a bee
A witchcraft yieldeth me.
If any ask me why,
'Twere easier to die
Than tell.
EMILY DICKINSON, *Poems*. Pt. ii, No. 54.

Oh, for a bee's experience
Of clovers and of noon!
EMILY DICKINSON, *Poems*. Pt. ii, No. 65.

How many cups the bee partakes,—
The debauchee of dews!
EMILY DICKINSON, *Poems*. Pt. ii, No. 39.

15
For where's the state beneath the firmament
That doth excel the bees for government?
DU BARTAS, *Devine Weeks and Works*. Week i, day 5.

So work the honey-bees,
Creatures that by a rule in nature teach
The act of order to a peopled kingdom.
They have a king and officers of sorts,
Where some, like magistrates, correct at home,
Others, like merchants, venture trade abroad,
Others, like soldiers, armed in their stings,
Make boot upon the summer's velvet buds,
Which pillage they with merry march bring home.
SHAKESPEARE, *Henry V*. Act i, sc. 2, l. 187.

Neither Egypt nor mighty Lydia show such homage to their king [as do the bees.] . . . He is the guardian of their toils; to him they do reverence; all stand round him in clamorous crowd, and attend him in throngs. Often they lift him on their shoulders, for him expose their bodies to battle, and seek amid wounds a glorious death.
VERGIL, *Georgics*. No. iv, l. 210.

A king in a hive of bees.
FRANCIS BACON, *Apothegms*.

For among Bees and Ants are social systems
found
so complex and well-order'd as to invite offhand
a pleasant fable enough: that once upon a time,
or ever a man was born to rob their honeypots,
bees were fully endow'd with Reason and only
lost it
by ordering so their life as to dispense with it;
whereby it pined away and perish'd of disuse.

ROBERT BRIDGES, *The Testament of Beauty*. Bk. ii, l. 188.

1

Burly, dozing humble-bee,
Where thou art is clime for me.
Let them sail for Porto Rique,
Far-off heats through seas to seek;
I will follow thee alone,
Thou animated torrid-zone!

EMERSON, *The Humble-Bee*.

Wiser far than human seer,
Yellow-breeched philosopher!
Seeing only what is fair,
Sipping only what is sweet,
Thou dost mock at fate and care,
Leave the chaff, and take the wheat.

EMERSON, *The Humble-Bee*.

2

The careful insect 'midst his works I view,
Now from the flowers exhaust the fragrant dew,
With golden treasures load his little thighs,
And steer his distant journey through the skies.

JOHN GAY, *Rural Sports*. Canto i, l. 83.

3

While Honey lies in Every Flower, no doubt,
It takes a Bee to get the Honey out.

ARTHUR GUITERMAN, *A Poet's Proverbs*, p. 13.

4

From Beavers, Bees should learn to mend their ways;
A Bee just Works; a Beaver Works and Plays.

ARTHUR GUITERMAN, *A Poet's Proverbs*, p. 31.

5

Bees work for man, and yet they never bruise
Their Master's flower, but leave it, having done,
As fair as ever and as fit to use;
So both the flower doth stay, and honey run.

GEORGE HERBERT, *Providence*. St. 17.

6

Every bee's honey is sweet.

GEORGE HERBERT, *Jacula Prudentum*.

7

Ah! woe is me; woe, woe is me,
Alack and well-a-day!
For pity, Sir, find out that bee
Which bore my love away.
I'll seek him in your bonnet brave,
I'll seek him in your eyes;
Nay, now I think th'ave made his grave
I' th' bed of strawberries.

ROBERT HERRICK, *The Mad Maid's Song*. (1646)

He has a bee in his bonnet.

JOHN RAY, *English Proverbs*. (1670)

8

Their hearts full heavy, their heads be full of bees, *i.e.*, cares or fancies.

JOHN HEYWOOD, *Proverbs*. Pt. i, ch. 12. (1546)

9

But when was ever honey made
With one bee in a hive?

THOMAS HOOD, *The Last Man*.

10

No good sensible working bee listens to the advice of a bedbug on the subject of business.

ELBERT HUBBARD, *Epigrams*.

11

God's little epigrams, the Bees,
Are pointed and impartial.
Could Martial rival one of these?
No, not even Martial.

RICHARD R. KIRKE, *The Bees*.

12

The bee that hath honey in her mouth, hath a sting in her tail.

JOHN LYLY, *Euphues*, 79. (1579)

Honey is sweet, but the bee stings.

GEORGE HERBERT, *Jacula Prudentum*. (1640)
FRANKLIN, *Poor Richard*, 1758.

The honey of a crowded hive,
Defended by a thousand stings.

COWPER, *Olney Hymns*, No. 7.

Some say the bee stings: but I say, 'tis the bee's wax.

SHAKESPEARE, *II Henry VI*. Act iv, sc. 2, l. 88.

I think the honey guarded with a sting.

SHAKESPEARE, *The Rape of Lucrece*, l. 493.

Full merrily the humble-bee doth sing,
Till he hath lost his honey and his sting;
And being once subdued in armed tail,
Sweet honey and sweet notes together fail.

SHAKESPEARE, *Troilus and Cressida*. Act v, sc. 10, l. 42.

He is not worthy of the honey-comb
Who shuns the hives because the bees have stings.

UNKNOWN, *Locrine*. Act iii, sc. 2. One of the spurious plays attributed to Shakespeare.

13

That which is not good for the swarm, neither is it good for the bee. (Τὸ τῷ σμήνει μὴ συμφέρον οὐδὲ τῇ μελίσσῃ συμφέρει.)

MARCUS AURELIUS, *Meditations*. Bk. vi, sec. 54.

No matter how you seem to fatten on a crime, that can never be good for the bee which is bad for the hive.

EMERSON, *Lectures and Biographical Studies: The Sovereignty of Ethics*.

14

The bee and the serpent often sip from the selfsame flower. (L'ape e la serpe spesso Suggon l'istesso umore.)

METASTASIO, *Morte d'Abele*. Pt. i.

15

As bees
In spring-time, when the sun with Taurus rides,

Pour forth their populous youth about the hive.
MILTON, *Paradise Lost*. Bk. i, l. 768.

1
The arts of building from the bee receive.
POPE, *Essay on Man*. Epis. iii, l. 175.

3
Where the bee sucks, there suck I;
In a cowslip's bell I lie.
SHAKESPEARE, *The Tempest*. Act v, sc. 1, l. 88.

4
My banks they are furnished with bees,
Whose murmur invites one to sleep.
WILLIAM SHENSTONE, *A Pastoral Ballad*. Pt. ii.

And murmuring of innumerable bees.
ALFRED TENNYSON, *The Princess*. Pt. vii, l. 207.

Here ever hum the golden bees
Underneath full-blossomed trees.
J. R. LOWELL, *The Sirens*, l. 94.

5
The little bee returns with evening's gloom,
To join her comrades in the braided hive,
Where, housed beside their mighty honey-comb,
They dream their polity shall long survive.
C. T. TURNER, *Summer Night in the Bee Hive*.

6
How doth the little busy bee
Improve each shining hour,
And gather honey all the day
From every opening flower!
ISAAC WATTS, *Against Idleness*.

The busy bee has no time for sorrow.
WILLIAM BLAKE, *Proverbs of Hell*.

7
The wild bee reels from bough to bough
With his furry coat and his gauzy wing,
Now in a lily-cup, and now
Setting the jacinth bell a-swing.
OSCAR WILDE, *Her Voice*.

8
A swarm of bees in May is worth a cow and a bottle of hay, whereas a swarm in July is not worth a fly.
UNKNOWN, *Reformed Commonwealth of Bees*, 26. (1655)

A swarm of bees in May
Is worth a load of hay;
A swarm of bees in June
Is worth a silver spoon;
A swarm of bees in July
Is not worth a fly.
UNKNOWN, *Old Rhyme*. (Quoted *London Times*, 7 Oct., 1921.)

BEECHER, HENRY WARD

9
Mankind fell in Adam, and has been falling ever since, but never touched bottom till it got to Henry Ward Beecher.
TOM APPLETON, *More Uncensored Recollections*, p. 137.

10
All those who came here this morning to worship Henry Ward Beecher may now withdraw from the church; all who came to worship God may remain.
THOMAS BEECHER, in Plymouth Church, Brooklyn, when some of the congregation, who had expected to hear his brother, Henry Ward, preach, started to walk out.

11
The Reverend Henry Ward Beecher
Called a hen a most elegant creature.
The hen, pleased with that,
Laid two eggs in his hat,
And thus did the hen reward Beecher.
O. W. HOLMES, *An Eggstravagance*. Usually ascribed to Holmes, but Edward P. Mitchell asserts (*Memoirs of an Editor*, p. 89) that the author was Alphonso Ross, managing editor of the Boston *Daily Advertiser* in 1872.

12
Henry Ward Beecher was born in a Puritan penitentiary, of which his father was one of the wardens. Under its walls were the rayless, hopeless and measureless dungeons of the damned, and on its roof fell the shadow of God's eternal frown.
R. G. INGERSOLL, *Henry Ward Beecher*.

13
A dunghill covered with flowers.
HENRY WATTERSON. Referring to Henry Ward Beecher. (*Beecher-Tilton Scandal*, p. 143.)

BEER, see Ale and Beer

BEGGAR AND BEGGING

14
A beggar's life is for a king.
FRANCIS DAVISON, *Song*. (c. 1613)

The real beggar is indeed the true and only king.
(Der wahre Bettler ist Doch einzig und allein der wahre König.)
LESSING, *Nathan der Weise*. Act ii, sc. 9.

I'd just as soon be a beggar as king,
And the reason I'll tell you for why:
A king cannot swagger, nor drink like a beggar,
Nor be half so happy as I.
UNKNOWN. (SHARPE, *Folk Songs from Somerset*.)

None but beggars live at ease.
A. W., *Song*. (DAVISON, *Rhapsody*.)

I fear no plots against me, I live in open cell;
Then who would be a king, when beggars live so well?
And a-begging we will go, will go,
And a-begging we will go!
UNKNOWN, *The Jovial Beggar*.

15
Beggars, beggars, are the happy folk;
They love one another. Long live beggars!
(Les gueux, les gueux, Sont les gens heureux;
Ils s'aiment entre eux. Vivent les gueux!)
BÉRANGER, *Les Gueux*.

16
Better it is to die than to beg.
Apocrypha: Ecclesiasticus, xl, 28.

For not to ask, is not to be denied.
DRYDEN, *Hind and the Panther*. Pt. iii, l. 242

A shameless beggar must have a short denial.
THOMAS FULLER, *Gnomologia*. No. 392.

1
Better to die a beggar than live a beggar.
THOMAS FULLER, *Gnomologia*. No. 888. *See also under* AVARICE.

2
Sue a beggar and get a louse.
EDMUND GAYTON, *Festivous Notes on Don Quixote*, 83. (1654)

A beggar pays a benefit with a louse.
THOMAS FULLER, *Gnomologia*. No. 10.

Gie a beggar a bed and he'll repay you with a louse.
JOHN RAY, *Proverbs: Scottish.*

What think ye as the proverb goes that beggars have no lice?
ROBERT WILSON THE ELDER, *Cobblers Prophecy*, l. 836. (1594)

3
The long-remembered beggar was his guest,
Whose beard descending swept his aged breast.
GOLDSMITH, *The Deserted Village*, l. 151.

4
Jacob God's Beggar was, and so we wait
(Though ne'er so rich) all beggars at His Gate.
ROBERT HERRICK, *Beggars.*

5
Beggar is jealous of beggar, and minstrel of minstrel.
(Πτωχὸς πτωχῷ φθονέει καὶ ἀοιδὸς ἀοιδῷ.)
HESIOD, *Works and Days*, l. 26.

One beggar bideth woe that another by the door should go.
ERASMUS, *Adagia*. (Taverner, tr.)

6
The petition of an empty hand is dangerous. (Vacuæ manus temeraria petitio est.)
JOHN OF SALISBURY, *Policraticus*, v, 10. (1476)

7
Beggars should be no choosers.
JOHN HEYWOOD, *Proverbs*. Pt. i, ch. 10. (1546) In frequent use thereafter.

8
Better a living beggar than a dead emperor. (Mieux vaut goujat debout qu'empereur enterré.)
LA FONTAINE, *La Matrone d'Ephèse.*

9
The highest price we can pay for anything, is to ask it.
W. S. LANDOR, *Imaginary Conversations: Eschines and Phocion.*

What is got by begging costs dear. (Caro costa quel che con preghi si comprà.)
UNKNOWN. An Italian proverb. Common to all languages.

10
The Book blameth all beggary, it banneth it thus: I have been young and now am old, yet have I not seen the righteous forsaken or his seed begging their bread.
WILLIAM LANGLAND, *Piers Plowman: God's Bill of Pardon.*

11
A beggar through the world am I,
From place to place I wander by.
Fill up my pilgrim's scrip for me,
For Christ's sweet sake and charity!
J. R. LOWELL, *The Beggar.*

12
This is neither begging, borrowing, nor robbery;
Yet it hath a twang of all of them.
PHILIP MASSINGER, *The Guardian*. Act v, sc. 4.

13
Pity the sorrows of a poor old man,
Whose trembling limbs have borne him to your door,
Whose days are dwindled to the shortest span;
Oh give relief, and Heaven will bless your store.
THOMAS MOSS, *The Beggar.*

14
I am ashamed always to be begging for the same thing. (Pudet et metuo semperque eademque precari.)
OVID, *Epistulæ ex Ponto*. Bk. iv, epis. 15, l. 29.

15
The peer and the beggar are often of the same family.
THOMAS PAINE, *Rights of Man*. Pt. ii, ch. v. *See also under* ANCESTRY.

16
That beggar of mine pleases me, as her king pleases a queen. (Placet ille meus mihi mendicus, suus rex reginæ placet.)
PLAUTUS, *Stichus*. Act i, sc. 2.

17
Characteristic of Solon also was his regulation of the practice of eating at the public table at the town-hall, for which his word was parasite. (παρασιτεῖν.)
PLUTARCH, *Lives: Solon*. Sec. 24.

18
The horseleech hath two daughters, crying, Give, give.
Old Testament: Proverbs, xxx, 15.

All genuine descendants of the daughter of the horseleech, whose cry is "Give, give."
SCOTT, *Peveril of the Peak*. Ch. 27.

19
Beggars breed and rich men feed.
JOHN RAY, *English Proverbs*, 60.

20
Beggary is valiant.
SHAKESPEARE, *II Henry VI*. Act iv, sc. 2, l. 59.

21
Beggars mounted run their horse to death.
SHAKESPEARE, *III Henry VI*. Act i, sc. 4, l. 127. (1591)

Set a beggar on horseback and they say he will never light.
ROBERT GREENE, *Orpharion*. (1599)

Such beggars
Once set o' horseback, you have heard, will ride.
BEAUMONT AND FLETCHER, *The Scornful Lady*. Act iv, sc. 2. (1616)

Set a beggar on horseback, and he will ride a gallop.

ROBERT BURTON, *Anatomy of Melancholy*. Pt. ii, sec. iii, mem. 2. (1621)

Such is the sad effect of wealth—rank pride—
Mount but a beggar, how the rogue will ride!

JOHN WOLCOT, *Epistle to Lord Lonsdale*.

1
A beggar's book Outworths a noble's blood.

SHAKESPEARE, *Henry VIII*. Act i, sc. 1, l. 122.

When beggars die, there are no comets seen;
The heavens themselves blaze forth the death of princes.

SHAKESPEARE, *Julius Cæsar*. Act ii, sc. 2, l. 30.

2
Well, whiles I am a beggar I will rail
And say there is no sin but to be rich;
And being rich, my virtue then shall be
To say there is no vice but beggary.

SHAKESPEARE, *King John*. Act ii, sc. 1, l. 593.

3
You taught me first to beg, and now, methinks,
You teach me how a beggar should be answer'd.

SHAKESPEARE, *The Merchant of Venice*. Act iv, sc. 1, l. 439.

Speak with me, pity me, open the door:
A beggar begs that never begg'd before.

SHAKESPEARE, *Richard II*. Act v, sc. 3, l. 77.

4
Begging is a trade unknown in this empire.

SWIFT, *Gulliver's Travels: Voyage to Lilliput*.

5
A beggar's scrip is never filled.

RICHARD TAVERNER, *Proverbs*. Fo. 39. (1539)

BEGINNING

6
The beginning, as the proverb says, is half the whole. (Ἡ δ' ἀρχὴ λέγεται ἥμισυ εἶναι παντός.)

ARISTOTLE, *Politics*. Bk. v, ch. 3, sec. 30.

7
Begin: to have commenced is half the deed. Half yet remains: begin again on this and thou wilt finish all. (Incipe: dimidium facti est coepisse. Superfit dimidium rursum hoc incipe et efficies.)

AUSONIUS, *Epigrams*. No. xv. From the Greek of Lucian.

Well begun is half done. (Dimidium facti qui cœpit habet.)

HORACE, *Epistles*. Bk. i, epis. 2, l. 40.

As the proverb says, "a good beginning is half the business," and "to have begun well" is praised by all.

PLATO, *Laws*. Bk. vi, sec. 2.

Laertius ascribeth to him [Socrates] this saying also: To have well begun is a thing half done. . . . The saying is half of a verse of the Greek poet, Hesodius, Beginning is half of the whole.

NICHOLAS UDALL, *Erasmus' Apothegms*. No. 17.

8
My way is to begin with the beginning.

BYRON, *Don Juan*. Canto i, st. 7.

"Where shall I begin, please your Majesty?" he asked. "Begin at the beginning," the King said, very gravely, "and go on till you come to the end: then stop."

LEWIS CARROLL, *Alice's Adventures in Wonderland*. Ch. 12.

9
The beginnings of all things are small. (Omnium enim rerum principia parva sunt.)

CICERO, *De Finibus*. Bk. v, ch. 21, sec. 58. *See also under* TRIFLES.

10
Before beginning, prepare carefully. (Prius quam aggrediare, adhibenda est præparatio diligens.)

CICERO, *De Officiis*. Bk. i, ch. 21, sec. 73.

11
The first step is as good as half over.

JOHN CLARKE, *Par. Anglo-Latina*, 171. (1639)

The hardest step is that over the threshold.

JAMES HOWELL, *Proverbs*. No. 7. (1659)

It is only the first step that costs. (Il n'y a que le premier pas que coûte.)

MADAME DU DEFFAND, *Letter to Horace Walpole*, 6 June, 1767; also *Letter to d'Alembert*, 7 July, 1763. Voltaire tells the story in a note to the first canto of *La Pucelle:* The Cardinal de Polignac was relating the history of St. Denis, who, it will be remembered, after being decapitated on Montmartre, is said to have picked up his head and carried it two leagues to the spot north of Paris where the cathedral dedicated to him now stands, and added that it was only at first that Denis found the journey difficult, to which Madame du Deffand replied, "Je le crois bien, il n'y a dans de telles affaires que le premier pas que coûte."

It is only the first obstacle which counts to conquer modesty. (Il n'y a que le premier obstacle qui coûte à vaincre la pudeur.)

BOSSUET, *Pensées Chrétiennes et Morales*, ix.

12
Run a moist pen slick through everything and start afresh.

DICKENS, *Martin Chuzzlewit*. Ch. 17.

13
Only engage, and then the mind grows heated:
Begin it, and the work will be completed!

GOETHE, *Faust: Prelude at the Theatre*, l. 306. John Anster, tr. *See* p. 2298g:3.

14
To win a race, the swiftness of a dart
Availeth not without a timely start.
(Rien ne sert de courir: Il faut partir à point.)

LA FONTAINE, *Fables*. Bk. vi, fab. 10.

15
Resist beginnings. (Principiis obsta.)

OVID, *Remediorum Amoris*, l. 91.

We shut our eyes to the beginnings of evil because they are small, and in this weakness lies the germ of our defeat. *Principiis obsta:* this maxim closely followed would preserve us from almost all our misfortunes.

AMIEL, *Journal*, 23 Feb. 1870.

We must be watchful, especially in the beginning of temptation, because then the enemy is more easily overcome, if he is not suffered to come in at all at the door of the soul, but is kept out and resisted at his first knock. Whence a certain man said, *"Withstand the beginning:* after remedies come too late."

THOMAS À KEMPIS, *De Imitatione Christi*. Bk. i, ch. 13.

1
Things are always at their best in their beginning. (Les choses valent toujours mieux dans leur source.)

PASCAL, *Lettres Provinciales*. No. 2.

2
Take care not to begin anything of which you may repent. (Cave quicquam incipias, quod pœniteat postea.)

PUBLILIUS SYRUS, *Sententiæ*. No. 122.

3
Whilst we deliberate how to begin a thing, it grows too late to begin it. (Dum deliberamus quando incipiendum sit, incipiere jam serum est.)

QUINTILIAN, *De Institutione Oratoria*. Bk. xii, ch. 6, sec. 3.

4
Things bad begun make strong themselves by ill.

SHAKESPEARE, *Macbeth*. Act iii, sc. 2, l. 55.

5
Each goodly thing is hardest to begin.

SPENSER, *Faerie Queene*. Bk. i, canto x, st. 6.

6
The first step, my son, which one makes in the world, is the one on which depends the rest of our days.

VOLTAIRE, *L'Indiscret*. Act i, sc. 1.

7
All glory comes from daring to begin.

EUGENE F. WARE, *John Brown*.

II—Beginning and Ending

8
Evil beginning hours may end in good.

BEAUMONT AND FLETCHER, *The Knight of Malta*. Act ii, sc. 5.

9
Still ending, and beginning still.

COWPER, *The Task*. Bk. iii, l. 627.

10
Better is the end of a thing than the beginning thereof.

Old Testament: Ecclesiastes, vii, 8.

11
A bad beginning makes a bad ending. (Κακῆς ἀπ' ἀρχῆς γίγνεται κακὸν τέλος.)

EURIPIDES, *Æolus*. Frag. 32.

If you miss the first button-hole, you will not succeed in buttoning up your coat.

GOETHE, *Sprüche in Prosa*.

12
Better never begin than never make an end.

GEORGE HERBERT, *Jacula Prudentum*.

13
It's a long road from the inception of a thing to its realization. (Le chemin est long du projet à la chose.)

MOLIÈRE, *Le Tartuffe*. Act iii, sc. 1, l. 8.

14
You began better than you end. (Cœpisti melius quam desinis.)

OVID, *Heroides*. Epis. ix, l. 23.

15
It's much easier to begin a thing than to finish it. (Incipere multost quam impetrare facilius.)

PLAUTUS, *Pœnulus*, l. 974. (Act v, sc. 2.)

Anybody can start something.

JOHN A. SHEDD, *Salt from My Attic*, p. 21.

16
From the end spring new beginnings. (Alia initia e fine.)

PLINY THE ELDER, *Historia Naturalis*. Bk. ix, sec. 65.

17
Everything ends that has a beginning. (Deficit omne quod nascitur.)

QUINTILIAN, *De Institutione Oratoria*. Bk. v, ch. 10, sec. 71.

Whatever begins, also ends. (Quidquid cœpit, et desinit.)

SENECA, *Ad Polybium de Consolatione*. Sec. 1.

18
The end may be inferred from the beginning; as in the common saying, I cannot expect a toga prætexta when I see the commencement of the web black; or the beginning may be argued from the end.

QUINTILIAN, *De Institutione Oratoria*. Bk. v, ch. 10, sec. 71.

What begins with tow won't end with silk.

JOHN RAY, *English Proverbs*.

19
I am Alpha and Omega, the beginning and the ending, saith the Lord.

New Testament: Revelation, i, 8.

You, my origin and ender.

SHAKESPEARE, *A Lover's Complaint*, l. 222.

20
That is the true beginning of our end.

SHAKESPEARE, *A Midsummer-Night's Dream*. Act v, sc. 1, l. 111.

It seems to me, sire, to be the beginning of the end.

TALLEYRAND, to Napoleon, after the battle of Leipsig. (LOCKHART, *Life of Napoleon*, ii, 205.) Fournier asserts, on the authority of Talleyrand's brother, that Talleyrand was an assiduous reader of a collection of anecdotes in twenty-one volumes called *L'Improvisateur Français*, and that he quickly adopted any bon mot which he found wandering about in search of a parent. "C'est le commencement de la fin" seems to have been one of these.

21
Keen in commencing, negligent in concluding. (Acribus initiis, incurioso fine.)

TACITUS, *Annals*. Bk. vi, sec. 17.

1
Good beginning maketh good ending.
UNKNOWN, *Proverbs of Hendyng*. Bk. ii (c. 1300); *Reliq. Antiquæ*, i, 109. (c. 1320)

Who that well his work beginneth
The rather a good end he winneth.
JOHN GOWER, *Confessio Amantis*.

Of a good beginning cometh a good end.
JOHN HEYWOOD, *Proverbs*. Pt. i, ch. 10.

A hard beginning maketh a good ending.
JOHN HEYWOOD, *Proverbs*. Pt. i, ch. 10.

Good onset bodes good end.
J. W. WARTER, *Last of the Old Squires*, 48.

2
A fool beholdeth only the beginning of his works, but a wise man taketh heed to the end.
UNKNOWN, *Dialogues of Creatures*, ccvii. (1535)

BEHAVIOR

See also Manners

I—Behavior: Definitions

3
Conduct is three-fourths of our life and its largest concern.
MATTHEW ARNOLD, *Literature and Dogma*. Ch. 1.

4
The sum of behaviour is to retain a man's own dignity, without intruding upon the liberty of others.
FRANCIS BACON, *Advancement of Learning: Civil Knowledge*. Sec. 3.

5
Behaviour seemeth to me as a garment of the mind, and to have the conditions of a garment. For it ought to be made in fashion; it ought not to be too curious; it ought to be shaped so as to set forth any good making of the mind, and hide any deformity; and above all, it ought not to be too strait, or restrained for exercise or motion.
FRANCIS BACON, *Advancement of Learning: Civil Knowledge*. Sec. 3.

Men's behaviour should be like their apparel, not too strait, or point device, but free for exercise or motion.
BACON, *Essays: Of Ceremonies and Respects*.

6
For behaviour, men learn it, as they take diseases, one of another.
BACON, *Advancement of Learning*. Bk. ii.

7
Put himself upon his good behaviour.
BYRON, *Don Juan*. Canto v, st. 47.

8
As the occasion, so the behavior. (Cual el Tiempo, tal el tiento.)
CERVANTES, *Don Quixote*. Pt. ii, ch. 50.

9
"And how did little Tim behave?" asked Mrs. Cratchit. . . ."As good as gold," said Bob.
DICKENS, *A Christmas Carol*. Stave 3.

10
Gentle Jane was as good as gold,
She always did as she was told.
She never spoke when her mouth was full,
Or caught blue-bottles their legs to pull.
W. S. GILBERT, *Patience*. Act ii.

11
The laws of behavior yield to the energy of the individual.
EMERSON, *Essays, Second Series: Manners*.

A beautiful form is better than a beautiful face; a beautiful behavior is better than a beautiful form: . . . it is the finest of the fine arts.
EMERSON, *Essays, Second Series: Manners*.

12
What is natural is never disgraceful. (Οὐκ αἰσχρὸν οὐδὲν τῶν ἀναγκαίων βροτοῖς.)
EURIPIDES, *Fragments*. Frag. 863.

Nothing so much prevents one's being natural as the desire to appear so. (Rien n'empêche tant d'être naturel que l'envie de le paraître.)
LA ROCHEFOUCAULD, *Maximes*. No. 431.

13
Behavior is a mirror in which every one shows his image. (Das Betragen ist ein Spiegel in welchem jeder sein Bild zeigt.)
GOETHE, *Die Wahlverwandtschaften* (*Elective Affinities*). Bk. ii, ch. 5.

14
I am never to act otherwise than so that I could also will that my maxim should become a universal law. (Ich soll niemals anders verfahren, als so, dass ich auch wollen könne, meine Maxime solle ein allgemeines Gesetz werden.
KANT, *Grundlegung zur Metaphysic der Sitten*. Abschnitt 1. This is Kant's "Categorical Imperative," as translated by T. K. Abbott (*Kant's Theory of Ethics*, p. 18). It has been more freely rendered, "Make the maxim of thy conduct such that it might become a universal law."

15
Acting without design, occupying oneself without making a business of it, finding the great in what is small and the many in the few, repaying injury with kindness, effecting difficult things while they are easy, and managing great things in their beginnings: this is the method of Tao.
LAO-TSZE, *The Simple Way*. (Old, tr.) The religion called Taoism claims Lao-tsze as its founder.

16
What a man does, not what he feels, thinks, or believes, is the universal yardstick of behavior.
BENJAMIN C. LEEMING, *Imagination*.

17
Nothing is more adroit than irreproachable conduct.
MADAME DE MAINTENON, *Maxims*. The maxim which governed her life.

1
I see the right, and I approve it, too;
Condemn the wrong, and yet the wrong pursue.
(Video meliora proboque, Deteriora sequor.)
OVID, *Metamorphoses*. Bk. vii, l. 20. (Tate, tr.)

I know and love the good, yet, ah! the worst pursue.
PETRARCH, *To Laura in Life*. Sonnet ccxxv.

For the good that I would, I do not: but the evil which I would not, that I do.
New Testament: Romans, vii, 19.

Every one of us, whatever our speculative opinions, knows better than he practices, and recognizes a better law than he obeys.
FROUDE, *Short Studies on Great Subjects: On Progress*. Pt. ii.

See also WORDS: WORD AND DEED.

2
Bad conduct soils the finest ornament more than filth. (Pulchrum ornatum turpes mores pejus cœno collinunt.)
PLAUTUS, *Epidicus*. Act v, sc. 2, l. 53.

3
Behaviour, what wert thou
Till this madman show'd thee?
SHAKESPEARE, *Love's Labour's Lost*. Act v, sc. 2, l. 337.

Unweighed behaviour.
SHAKESPEARE, *The Merry Wives of Windsor*. Act ii, sc. 1, l. 23.

4
There is a fair behaviour in thee.
SHAKESPEARE, *Twelfth Night*. Act i, sc. 2, l. 47.

Is there no respect of place, persons, nor time in you?
SHAKESPEARE, *Twelfth Night*. Act ii, sc. 3, l. 98.

5
Would to God we had behaved ourselves well in this world, even for one day.
THOMAS À KEMPIS, *De Imitatione Christi*. Pt. i, ch. 23, sec. 6.

6
As a rule, there is no surer way to the dislike of men than to behave well where they have behaved badly.
LEW WALLACE, *Ben Hur*. Bk. iv, ch. 9.

7
During good behaviour. (Quando se bene gesserit.)
UNKNOWN, *Statutes 12 and 13, William III*, ii, 3.

II—Behavior: Admonitions

8
Dread God, do law, love truth and worthiness.
CHAUCER, *Lack of Steadfastness*, l. 27.

9
Make yourself necessary to somebody. Do not make life hard to any.
EMERSON, *Conduct of Life: Considerations by the Way*.

10
Hast thou named all the birds without a gun?
Loved the wood-rose and left it on its stalk?
At rich men's tables eaten bread and pulse?
Unarmed, faced danger with a heart of trust?
And loved so well a high behavior,
In man or maid, that thou from speech refrained,
Nobility more nobly to repay?
O, be my friend, and teach me to be thine!
RALPH WALDO EMERSON, *Forbearance*.

11
Be civil to all; sociable to many; familiar with few; friend to one; enemy to none.
BENJAMIN FRANKLIN, *Poor Richard*, 1756.

Call no man foe, but never love a stranger.
Build up no plan, nor any star pursue.
Go forth with crowds, in loneliness is danger.
Thus nothing Fate can send,
And nothing Fate can do
Shall pierce your peace, my friend.
STELLA BENSON, *This is the End*.

12
Four precepts: to break off customs; to shake off spirits ill-disposed; to meditate on youth; to do nothing against one's genius.
HAWTHORNE, *American Note-Books*, 25 Oct., 1836.

Walk groundly, talk profoundly, drink roundly, sleep soundly.
W. C. HAZLITT, *English Proverbs*. No. 446.

Fear less, hope more; eat less, chew more; whine less, breathe more; talk less, say more; hate less, love more; and all good things are yours.
LORD FISHER. (Quoted in *Records*, 25 Nov., 1919.)

13
Let every man be swift to hear, slow to speak, slow to wrath.
New Testament: James, i, 19.

14
Let what will be said or done, preserve your sang-froid immovable, and to every obstacle oppose patience, perseverance and soothing language.
THOMAS JEFFERSON, *Writings*. Vol. viii, p. 316.

15
If not seemly, do it not; if not true, say it not. (Εἰ μὴ καθήκει, μὴ πράξῃς· εἰ μὴ ἀληθές ἐστι, μὴ εἴπῃς.)
MARCUS AURELIUS, *Meditations*. Bk. xii, sec. 17.

If thou wouldst not be known to do anything, never do it.
EMERSON, *Essays, First Series: Spiritual Laws*.

Never suffer a thought to be harbored in your mind which you would not avow openly. When tempted to do anything in secret, ask yourself if you would do it in public. If you would not, be sure it is wrong.
THOMAS JEFFERSON, *Writings*. Vol. xix, p. 241.

16
Be not careless in deeds, nor confused in words, nor rambling in thought.
MARCUS AURELIUS, *Meditations*. Bk. viii, sec. 51.

Blot out vain pomp; check impulse; quench appetite; keep reason under its own control.
MARCUS AURELIUS, *Meditations*. Bk. ix, sec. 7.

1
My code of life and conduct is simply this: work hard; play to the allowable limit; disregard equally the good and bad opinion of others; never do a friend a dirty trick; . . . never grow indignant over anything; . . . live the moment to the utmost of its possibilities, . . . and be satisfied with life always, but never with oneself.

George Jean Nathan, *Testament of a Critic*, p. 14.

2
Do what you like. (Fais ce que voudras.)

Rabelais, *Works*. Bk. i, ch. 57. The rule of life of the Thelemites.

3
Neither crow nor croak.

W. G. Benham, *Proverbs*, p. 814.

4
Behave yoursel' before folk;
Whate'er ye do, when out o' view,
Be cautious aye before folk.

Alexander Rodger, *Behave Yoursel' Before Folk*.

5
Love all, trust a few,
Do wrong to none: be able for thine enemy
Rather in power than use.

Shakespeare, *All's Well that Ends Well*. Act i, sc. 1, l. 73.

Love thyself last: cherish those hearts that hate thee:
Corruption wins not more than honesty.
Still in thy right hand carry gentle peace,
To silence envious tongues. Be just, and fear not:
Let all the ends thou aim'st at be thy country's,
Thy God's, and truth's.

Shakespeare, *Henry VIII*. Act iii, sc. 2, l. 443.

Keep thy foot out of brothels, thy hand out of plackets, thy pen from lenders' books, and defy the foul fiend.

Shakespeare, *King Lear*. Act iii, sc. 4, l. 99.

6
Live pure, speak true, right wrong, follow the King—
Else, wherefore born?

Tennyson, *Gareth and Lynette*, l. 117.

7
Four things a man must learn to do
If he would make his record true:
To think without confusion clearly;
To love his fellow-men sincerely;
To act from honest motives purely;
To trust in God and Heaven securely.

Henry van Dyke, *Four Things*.

8
Then bless thy secret growth, nor catch
At noise, but thrive unseen and dumb;
Keep clean, bear fruit, earn life, and watch
Till the white-wing'd Reapers come!

Henry Vaughan, *The Seed Growing Secretly*.

Heed how thou livest. Do no act by day
Which from the night shall drive thy peace away.

Whittier, *Conduct*.

9
Do all the good you can,
In all the ways you can,
In all the places you can,
At all the times you can,
To all the people you can,
As long as ever you can.

John Wesley, *Rules of Conduct*. Perhaps an expansion of a proverbial stanza sometimes used on tombstones. Adopted by the Rev Dwight L. Moody as his motto.

BELGIUM

10
After years of bondage, the Belgian, rising from the tomb, has reconquered by his courage, his name, his rights and his flag; and your hand, kingly and proud, people hereafter unconquerable, writes upon your flag, King, Law, and Liberty.
(Après des siècles d'esclavage,
Le Belge sortant du tombeau,
A reconquis par son courage,
Son nom, ses droits et son drapeau;
Et ta main, souveraine et fière,
Peuple désormais indompté,
Grava sur ta vieille bannière
Le Roi, la loi, la liberté.

Louis Dechez, *La Brabançonne*. The Belgian national anthem, written during the revolution of 1830.

11
And now I have gained the cockpit of the Western world, and academy of arms for many years.

James Howell, *Vocall Forest*. (c. 1640) Belgium has been called the cockpit of Europe because it has been the scene of so many wars.

12
The little white ewe lamb of Europe.

Father Vincent McNabb, *Open Letter to the Kaiser*, August, 1914.

13
I dislike Belgium and think the Belgians, on the whole, the most contemptible people in Europe.

Matthew Arnold, *Letter to Miss Arnold*, 1859.

BELIEF

See also Creeds, Faith, Trust

14
I believe without bother
In This, That, and T'other;
Whatever is current, no matter.
I believe in Success,
And in Comfort no less;
I believe all the rest is but patter.

William Allingham, *Blackberries*.

15
A belief is not true because it is useful.

Amiel, *Journal*, 15 Nov., 1876.

1
Strong beliefs win strong men, and then make them stronger.
WALTER BAGEHOT, *Physics and Politics*, p. 76.

2
Why first, you don't believe, you don't and can't,
(Not statedly, that is, and fixedly
And absolutely and exclusively)
In any revelation called divine.
No dogmas nail your faith.
ROBERT BROWNING, *Bishop Blougram's Apology*.

And set you square with Genesis again.
ROBERT BROWNING, *Bishop Blougram's Apology*.

3
Men freely believe that which they desire. (Libenter homines id quod volunt credunt.)
CÆSAR, *De Bello Gallico*. Bk. iii, sec. 18.

Man prefers to believe what he prefers to be true.
FRANCIS BACON, *Aphorisms*. No. 49.

With how much ease believe we what we wish!
DRYDEN, *All for Love*. Act iv, sc. 1.

What the wretched wish for intensely, that they easily believe. (Quod nimis miseri volunt, Hoc facile credunt.)
SENECA, *Hercules Furens*, l. 313.

What ardently we wish, we soon believe.
YOUNG, *Night Thoughts*. Night vii, l. 1233.

4
No iron chain, or outward force of any kind, could ever compel the soul of man to believe or to disbelieve.
THOMAS CARLYLE, *Heroes and Hero-Worship: The Hero as Priest*.

5
Each man's belief is right in his own eyes.
COWPER, *Hope*, l. 283.

Can this be true?—an arch observer cries;
Yes (rather mov'd), I saw it with these eyes.
Sir! I believe it on that ground alone;
I could not, had I seen it with my own.
COWPER, *Conversation*, l. 231.

6
"I make it a rule only to believe what I understand," replied Proserpine.
BENJAMIN DISRAELI, *The Infernal Marriage*. Pt. i, ch. 4.

7
We are born believing. A man bears beliefs, as a tree bears apples.
EMERSON, *Conduct of Life: Worship*.

Belief consists in accepting the affirmations of the soul; unbelief, in denying them.
EMERSON, *Representative Men: Montaigne*.

We believe that mustard bites the tongue, that pepper is hot, friction-matches incendiary, revolvers are to be avoided, and suspenders hold up pantaloons.
EMERSON, *Representative Men: Montaigne*.

8
He does not believe that does not live according to his belief.
THOMAS FULLER, *Gnomologia*.

9
And as with guns we kill the crow,
For spoiling our relief,
The devil so must we o'erthrow,
With gunshot of belief.
GEORGE GASCOIGNE, *Good-morrow*.

10
Though dead to the faith that assured me of God,
I mourn to the end the delights of belief.
(Quoique mort à la foi qui m'assurait de Dieu
Je regrette toujours la volupté de croire.)
CHARLES M. GUERIN, *Quoique Mort*.

11
He that believes all, misseth; he that believes nothing, hits not.
GEORGE HERBERT, *Jacula Prudentum*.

12
Fields are won by those who believe in the winning.
T. W. HIGGINSON, *Americanism in Literature*.

13
Ignorance is preferable to error; and he is less remote from truth who believes nothing, than he who believes what is wrong.
THOMAS JEFFERSON, *Writings*. Vol. ii, p. 43.

14
Jesus saith unto him, Thomas, because thou hast seen me, thou hast believed: blessed are they that have not seen, and yet have believed.
New Testament: John, xx, 29.

Birds sing on a bare bough;
O believer, canst not thou?
C. H. SPURGEON, *Salt-Cellars*.

Believing where we cannot prove.
TENNYSON, *In Memoriam: Introduction*. St. 1.

15
They believed—faith, I'm puzzled—I think I may call
Their belief a believing in nothing at all,
Or something of that sort; I know they all went
For a general union of total dissent.
J. R. LOWELL, *A Fable for Critics*, l. 734.

16
O thou, whose days are yet all spring,
Faith, blighted once, is past retrieving;
Experience is a dumb, dead thing;
The victory's in believing.
J. R. LOWELL, *To ——*.

17
Lord, I believe; help thou mine unbelief.
New Testament: Mark, ix, 24.

Believing hath a core of unbelieving.
ROBERT BUCHANAN, *Songs of Seeking*.

Nor can belief touch, kindle, smite, reprieve
His heart who has not heart to disbelieve.
SWINBURNE, *In the Bay*. St. 31.

18
I wiil not believe it until I have read it. (Non credam nisi legero.)
MARTIAL, *Epigrams*. Bk. xii, epig. 73.

1
It is easier to believe than to doubt.
E. D. MARTIN, *The Meaning of a Liberal Education*. Ch. 5.

2
Nothing is so firmly believed as that which we least know.
MONTAIGNE, *Essays*. Bk. i, ch. 31.

Men are most apt to believe what they least understand.
MONTAIGNE, *Essays*. Bk. iii, ch. 11.

O belief! how much you block our way. (O cuider! combien tu nous empesches.)
MONTAIGNE, *Essays*. Bk. ii, ch. 12.

3
Believe! No storm harms a man who believes. (Credite! Credenti nulla procella nocet.)
OVID, *Amores*. Bk. ii, eleg. 11, l. 22.

Do not believe hastily. (Nec cito credere.)
OVID, *Ars Amatoria*. Bk. iii, l. 685.

Quick believers need broad shoulders.
GEORGE HERBERT, *Jacula Prudentum*.

4
Where belief is painful, we are slow to believe. (Tarde, quæ credita lædunt, Credimus.)
OVID, *Heroides*. Epis. ii, l. 9.

Somewhat costive of belief.
BEN JONSON, *The Alchemist*. Act ii, sc. 1.

5
Whoever has even once become notorious by base fraud, even if he speaks the truth, gains no belief.
PHÆDRUS, *Fables*. Bk. i, fab. 10.

6
And when religious sects ran mad,
He held, in spite of all his learning,
That if a man's belief is bad,
It will not be improved by burning.
W. M. PRAED, *The Vicar*. St. 9.

7
For, dear me, why abandon a belief
Merely because it ceases to be true?
Cling to it long enough, and not a doubt
It will turn true again, for so it goes.
Most of the change we think we see in life
Is due to truths being in and out of favour.
ROBERT FROST, *The Black Cottage*, l. 105.

8
Every man, wherever he goes, is encompassed by a cloud of comforting convictions, which move with him like flies on a summer day.
BERTRAND RUSSELL, *Sceptical Essays*, p. 28.

9
The brute necessity of believing something so long as life lasts does not justify any belief in particular.
GEORGE SANTAYANA, *Scepticism*, p. 9.

10
All which, sir, though I most powerfully and potently believe, yet I hold it not honesty to have it thus set down.
SHAKESPEARE, *Hamlet*. Act ii, sc. 2, l. 204.

Stands not within the prospect of belief.
SHAKESPEARE, *Macbeth*. Act i, sc. 3, l. 74.

11
A thing that nobody believes cannot be proved too often.
BERNARD SHAW, *The Devil's Disciple*. Act iii.

12
He in his heart
Felt that misgiving which precedes belief
In what was disbelieved.
SOUTHEY, *Joan of Arc*. Bk. i, l. 75.

13
The want of belief is a defect that ought to to concealed when it cannot be overcome.
SWIFT, *Thoughts on Religion*. *See also under* HERESY.

14
I believe because it is impossible. (Credo quia impossibile.)
TERTULLIAN, *De Carne Christi*. Pt. ii, ch. 5. Tertullian's "rule of faith," sometimes given, "Certum est quia impossibile est," It is certain because it is impossible.

It is believable because unbelievable. (Ideo credendum quod incredibile.)
ROBERT BURTON, *Anatomy of Melancholy*, paraphrasing Tertullian.

15
I know whom I have believed.
New Testament: II Timothy, i, 12. (Scio cui credidi.—*Vulgate*.)

16
Conviction is the Conscience of the Mind.
MRS. HUMPHRY WARD, *Robert Elsmere*. Bk. iv, ch. 26.

17
I have believed the best of every man,
And find that to believe it is enough
To make a bad man show him at his best,
Or even a good man swing his lantern higher.
WILLIAM BUTLER YEATS, *Deirdre*.

18
Who knows much believes the less. (Chi più sa, meno crede.)
UNKNOWN. An Italian proverb.

BELL

19
They tune like bells, and want but hanging.
THOMAS ADAMS, *Works*, p. 192. (1630)

They agree like bells, they want nothing but hanging.
GEORGE MERITON, *Yorkshire Ale*, 83. (1683)

20
And all went merry as a marriage bell.
BYRON, *Childe Harold*. Canto iii, st. 21.

Hear the mellow wedding bells, Golden bells!
What a world of happiness their harmony foretells.
EDGAR ALLAN POE, *The Bells*.

21
And let see which of you shall bear the bell
To speak of love a-right!
CHAUCER, *Troilus and Criseyde*. Bk. iii, l. 198 (1379)

So vices brag, but virtue bears the bell.
GEORGE GASCOIGNE, *Glasse of Government.* Act iii, sc. 6. (1575)

1
He was a rationalist, but he had to confess that he liked the ringing of church bells.
ANTON CHEKHOV, *Notebook.*

The cheerful Sabbath bells, wherever heard,
Strike pleasant on the sense, most like the voice
Of one, who from the far-off hills proclaims
Tidings of good to Zion.
CHARLES LAMB, *The Sabbath Bells.*

And the Sabbath bell,
That over wood and wild and mountain dell
Wanders so far, chasing all thoughts unholy
With sounds most musical, most melancholy.
SAMUEL ROGERS, *Human Life*, l. 517.

2
Each matin bell, the Baron saith,
Knells us back to a world of death.
S. T. COLERIDGE, *Christabel.* Pt. ii, st. 1.

The bell invites me.
Hear it not, Duncan; for it is a knell
That summons thee to heaven or to hell.
SHAKESPEARE, *Macbeth.* Act ii, sc. 1, l. 62.

Hark, how chimes the passing bell!
There's no music to a knell.
JAMES SHIRLEY, *The Passing Bell.*

They went and told the sexton, and
The sexton toll'd the bell.
THOMAS HOOD, *Faithless Sally Brown.*

3
How soft the music of those village bells,
Falling at intervals upon the ear
In cadence sweet, now dying all away,
Now pealing loud again, and louder still,
Clear and sonorous, as the gale comes on!
With easy force it opens all the cells
Where Mem'ry slept.
COWPER, *The Task.* Bk. vi, l. 6.

Dear bells! how sweet the sounds of village bells
When on the undulating air they swim!
Now loud as welcomes! faint, now, as farewells!
And trembling all about the breezy dells
As flutter'd by the wings of Cherubim.
THOMAS HOOD, *Ode to Rae Wilson*, l. 159.

4
But the sound of the church-going bell
These valleys and rocks never heard;
Ne'er sigh'd at the sound of a knell,
Or smil'd when a Sabbath appear'd.
COWPER, *Alexander Selkirk.*

Bell! thou soundest merrily,
When the bridal party
To the church doth hie!
Bell! thou soundest solemnly,
When, on Sabbath morning,
Fields deserted lie!
LONGFELLOW, *Hyperion.* Bk. iii, ch. 3. Quoted as by a Swiss poet.

The vesper bell from far,
That seems to mourn for the expiring day.
DANTE, *Purgatorio.* Canto viii, l. 6. (Cary, tr.)

The curfew tolls the knell of parting day.
THOMAS GRAY, *Elegy Written in a Country Church-yard.* Probably Upton Church, near Slough, not Stoke Pogis.

Your voices break and falter in the darkness,—
Break, falter, and are still.
BRET HARTE, *The Angelus.*

And she breathed the husky whisper:—
"Curfew must not ring to-night."
ROSE HARTWICK THORPE, *Curfew Must Not Ring To-night.* Mrs. Thorpe later changed "must" to "shall" in signed quotations from the poem.

6
If you love not the noise of bells, why do you pull the ropes?
THOMAS FULLER, *Gnomologia.* No. 2767.

A crackt bell can never sound well.
THOMAS FULLER, *Gnomologia.* No. 6358.

7
Bells call others, but themselves enter not into the Church.
GEORGE HERBERT, *Jacula Prudentum.*

The Bell calls others to Church, but itself never minds the Sermon.
BENJAMIN FRANKLIN, *Poor Richard*, 1754.

8
While the steeples are loud in their joy
To the tune of the bell's ring-a-ding,
Let us chime in a peal, one and all,
For we all should be able to sing
Hullahbaloo!
THOMAS HOOD, *A Song for the Million.*

9
Play uppe, play uppe, O Boston bells!
Ply all your changes, all your swells,
Play uppe "The Brides of Enderby."
JEAN INGELOW, *The High Tide on the Coast of Lincolnshire.* St. 1.

10
Bells, the music bordering nearest heaven.
LAMB, *Essays of Elia: New Year's Eve.*

For bells are Music's laughter.
HOOD, *Miss Kilmansegg: Her Marriage.*

11
For bells are the voice of th church;
They have tones that touch and search
The hearts of young and old.
LONGFELLOW, *The Bells of San Blas.* St. 3.

These bells have been anointed.
LONGFELLOW, *The Golden Legend: Prologue.*

He heard the convent bell
Suddenly in the silence ringing.
LONGFELLOW, *The Golden Legend.* Pt. iii.

12
The bells themselves are the best of preachers,
Their brazen lips are learned teachers,
From their pulpits of stone, in the upper air,
Sounding aloft, without crack or flaw,
Shriller than trumpets under the Law.
Now a sermon and now a prayer.
LONGFELLOW, *The Golden Legend.* Pt. iii.

13
The bells of Shandon, That sound so grand on

The pleasant waters of the river Lee.
FRANCIS SYLVESTER MAHONY, *The Bells of Shandon.*

1
Those evening bells! those evening bells!
How many a tale their music tells!
Of youth, and home, and that sweet time
When last I heard their soothing chime.
THOMAS MOORE, *Those Evening Bells.*

2
The bell never rings of itself; unless some one swings it, it is dumb. (Nunquam ædepol temere tinnit tintinnabulum; Nisi quis illud tractat aut movet, mutum est.)
PLAUTUS, *Trinummus.* Act iv, sc. 2, l. 162.

3
Keeping time, time, time
In a sort of Runic rhyme
To the tintinnabulation that so musically wells
From the bells, bells, bells.
EDGAR ALLAN POE, *The Bells.*

4
And now the chapel's silver bell you hear,
That summons you to all the pride of prayer.
Light quirks of music, broken and uneven,
Make the soul dance upon a jig to Heav'n.
POPE, *Moral Essays.* Epis. iv, l. 141.

5
And this be the vocation fit,
For which the founder fashioned it:
High, high above earth's life, earth's labor,
E'en to heaven's blue vault to soar,
To hover as the thunder's neighbor,
The very firmament explore;
To be a voice as from above,
Like yonder stars so bright and clear,
And praise their Maker as they move,
And usher in the circling year.
SCHILLER, *Song of the Bell.* (Bowring, tr.)

I call the living; I mourn the dead; I break the lightning. (Vivos voco; mortuos plango; fulgura frango.)
UNKNOWN, *Inscription,* on the great bell of Schaffhausen minster. Used by Schiller as the motto of his poem, *The Bell.*

Funera plango, fulgura frango, sabbato pango;
Excito lentos, dissipo ventos, paco cruentos.
Another form of the above, meaning, "I toll for funerals, I break the lightning, I announce the Sabbath; I wake the lazy, I dissipate the winds, I pacify the quarrelsome."

6
Like sweet bells jangled, out of tune and harsh.
SHAKESPEARE, *Hamlet.* Act iii, sc. 1, l. 166.

7
Bid the merry bells ring to thine ear.
SHAKESPEARE, *II Henry IV.* Act iv, sc. 5, l. 112.

8
Silence that dreadful bell: it frights the isle
From her propriety.
SHAKESPEARE, *Othello.* Act ii, sc. 3, l. 175.

9
They may ring their bells now; before long they will be wringing their hands.
SIR ROBERT WALPOLE, when the bells were rung in London on the declaration of war against Spain, in 1739. (COXE, *Life of Walpole,* i, 579.)

10
The bells of Rylston seemed to say,
While she sate listening in the shade,
With vocal music, "God us ayde;"
And all the hills were glad to bear
Their part in this effectual prayer.
WORDSWORTH, *The White Doe of Rylstone.* Canto vii, l. 1772.

BELLY

11
Every investigation which is guided by the principles of nature fixes its ultimate aim upon gratifying the stomach.
ATHENÆUS, *Deipnosophists.* Bk. vii, ch. 2.

"Little Mary."
J. M. BARRIE. Title of play. A euphemism for the stomach.

12
It is a difficult matter, my fellow citizens, to argue with the belly, since it has no ears. (*Χαλεπὸν μέν ἐστιν, ὦ πολῖται, πρὸς γαστέρα λέγειν ὦτα οὐκ ἔχουσαν.*)
MARCUS CATO. (PLUTARCH, *Lives: Marcus Cato.* Ch. viii, sec. 1.)

The hungry belly has no ears. (La ventre affamé n'a point d'oreilles.)
RABELAIS, *Works.* Bk. iii, ch. 15.

The belly will not listen to advice. (Venter præcepta non audit.)
SENECA, *Epistulæ ad Lucilium.* Epis. xxi, 11.

13
Let Martha die, but let her die with a full belly.
CERVANTES, *Don Quixote.* Pt. ii, ch. 59.

14
Never did he kiss a strange hand for his belly's sake. (*Οὔποτε δ' ὀθνείην ἔκυσεν χέρα γαστρὸς ἕκητι.*)
ISIDORUS OF ÆGÆ, *Epigram.* (*Greek Anthology.* Bk. vii, No. 156.)

15
A gross belly does not produce a refined mind. (*Παχεῖα γαστὴρ λεπτὸν οὐ τίκτει νόον.*)
ST. JEROME, quoting an old Greek proverb.

The vilest of beasts is the belly. (*Ὡς κάκιστον θηρίον ἐστὶν ἡ γαστήρ.*)
UNKNOWN. A Greek proverb.

16
He who does not mind his belly will hardly mind anything else.
SAMUEL JOHNSON. (BOSWELL, *Life,* 1763.)

17
What comedy, what actor is better than a disappointed belly? (Quæ comœdia, mimus Quis melior plorante gula?)
JUVENAL, *Satires.* Sat. v, l. 157.

1
It once happened that all the other members of a man mutinied against the stomach, which they accused as the only idle, uncontributing part of the whole body, while the rest were put to hardships and expense of much labor to supply and minister to its appetites.
MENENNIUS AGRIPPA, recounting an old fable. (PLUTARCH, *Lives: Coriolanus.*)

2
What avails it us to have our bellies full of meat if it be not digested?
MONTAIGNE, *Essays.* Bk. i, ch. 24.

3
That master of arts, that dispenser of genius, the Belly. (Magister artis ingenique largitor Venter.)
PERSIUS, *Satires: Prologue,* l. 10.

The master of art and giver of wit, Their belly.
BEN JONSON, *The Poetaster: To the Reader.*

4
Do not mourn the dead with the belly. (Οὐ γὰρ ἔοικεν γαστέρι πενθῆσαι νεκρόν.)
PALLADAS, quoting Homer. (*Greek Anthology.* Bk. x, epig. 47.)

5
It's the tripes that carry the feet, not the feet the tripes. (Tripas llevan piés, que no piés á tripas.)
CERVANTES, *Don Quixote.* Pt. ii, ch. 34.

The belly carries the legs, and not the legs the belly.
CERVANTES, *Don Quixote.* Pt. ii, ch. 34.

Let the guts be full, for it's they that carry the legs.

6
I can reason down or deny everything except this perpetual belly: feed he must and will, and I cannot make him respectable.
EMERSON, *Representative Men: Montaigne.*

7
A full belly makes a dull brain.
BENJAMIN FRANKLIN, *Poor Richard,* 1758.

A belly full of gluttony will never study willingly.
THOMAS FULLER, *Gnomologia.* No. 6115.

A full belly neither fights nor flies well.
GEORGE HERBERT, *Jacula Prudentum.*

8
Your belly will never let your back be warm.
THOMAS FULLER, *Gnomologia.* No. 6043.

The belly robs the back.
JAMES HOWELL, *Proverbs,* 33. (1659)

If it were not for the belly, the back might wear gold.
THOMAS FULLER, *Gnomologia.* No. 2690

9
The eye is bigger than the belly.
GEORGE HERBERT, *Jacula Prudentum.*

10
May God look with hatred on the belly and its food; it is through them that chastity breaks down.
PALLADAS. (*Greek Anthology.* Bk. x, epig. 57.)

When the belly is full the mind is amongst the maids.
UNKNOWN. *MS. Proverbs,* c. 1645.

A full Belly is the Mother of all Evil.
BENJAMIN FRANKLIN, *Poor Richard,* 1744.

11
Whose God is their belly.
New Testament: Philippians, iii, 19.

Such as for their bellies' sake
Creep and intrude, and climb into the fold.
MILTON, *Lycidas,* l. 114.

Men given up to the belly. (Mortales dediti ventri.)
SALLUST, *Catilina.* Ch. ii, sec. 8.

12
I say, whatever you maintain
Of Alma in the heart or brain,
The plainest man alive may tell ye
Her seat of empire is the belly.
From hence she sends out those supplies
Which make us either stout or wise;
The strength of every other member
Is founded on your belly-timber.
MATTHEW PRIOR, *Alma.* Canto iii, l. 196.

13
The belly is not filled with fair words.
RABELAIS, *Works.* Bk. iv, ch. 62.

Promises don't fill the belly.
C. H. SPURGEON, *Ploughman's Pictures,* p. 18.

14
No clock is more regular than the Belly.
RABELAIS, *Works.* Bk. iv, ch. 64.

Your belly chimes, it's time to go to dinner.
JOHN RAY, *English Proverbs,* 66.

See also under APPETITE.

15
What is got over the Devil's back is spent under the Devil's belly.
RABELAIS, *Works.* Bk. v, ch. 11.

Isocrates was in the right to insinuate, in his elegant Greek expression, that what is got over the Devil's back is spent under his belly.
LE SAGE, *Gil Blas.* Bk. viii, ch. 9.

16
A bellyfull is a bellyfull.
RABELAIS, *Works.* Bk. v, ch. 23.

A wamefou is a wamefou.
SCOTT, *St. Ronan's Well.* Ch. x.

17
When belly with bad pains doth swell,
It matters nought what else goes well.
SADI, *The Gulistan.* Pt. iii, No. 9. (Arnold, tr.)

18
How many men are kept busy to humor a single belly! (Quantum hominem unus venter exercet!)
SENECA, *Epistulæ ad Lucilium.* Epis. xcv, 24.

19
In fair round belly with good capon lined.
SHAKESPEARE, *As You Like It.* Act ii, sc. 7, l. 154.

He had a broad face and a little round belly,
That shook, when he laughed, like a bowlful of jelly.
CLEMENT CLARKE MOORE, *A Visit from St. Nicholas.*

1
My belly's as cold as if I had swallowed snowballs for pills.

SHAKESPEARE, *The Merry Wives of Windsor*. Act iii, sc. 5, l. 23.

2
Who wears his wit in his belly and his guts in his head.

SHAKESPEARE, *Troilus and Cressida*. Act ii, sc. 1, l. 80.

No barricado for a belly; know't;
It will let in and out the enemy
With bag and baggage.

SHAKESPEARE, *Winter's Tale*. Act i, sc. 2, l. 204.

3
When the belly is full, the bones would be at rest.

SWIFT, *Polite Conversation*. Dial. ii.

4
Better belly burst than good liquor be lost.

SWIFT, *Polite Conversation*. Dial. ii.

5
Evil beasts, slow bellies. (Γαστέρες ἀργαί.)

New Testament: Titus, i, 12. Paul is quoting a Cretan poet.

6
O importunate belly, through whom parasite fawners sell for a sop the law of liberty. (Ὦ γαστὴρ κυκόμυια, δι' ἣν κόλακες παράσιτοι ζωμοῦ πωλοῦσιν θεσμὸν ἐλευθερίης.)

UNKNOWN, *Epigram*. (*Greek Anthology*. Bk. xvi, No. 9.)

BENEDICTION, see Blessing

BENEFITS

See also Favor, Gifts, Injuries and Benefits, Kindness

7
He who confers a benefit on any one loves him better than he is beloved.

ARISTOTLE, *Nicomachean Ethics*. Bk. ix, sec. 7. Quoted by MONTAIGNE, *Essays*, ii, 8.

8
If you confer a benefit, never remember it; if you receive one, never forget it. (Tu bene si quid facias, nec meminisse fas est; Quæ bene facta accipias, perpetuo memento.)

CHILON. (AUSONIUS [?], *Septem Sapientum Sententiæ*, l. 39.)

Let him who has conferred the benefit conceal it; let him who has accepted it disclose it. (Qui dedit beneficium taceat; narret, qui accepit.)

SENECA, *De Beneficiis*. Bk. ii, sec. 11.

When befriended, remember it; when you befriend, forget it.

BENJAMIN FRANKLIN, *Poor Richard*, 1740.

9
He that has once done you a kindness will be more ready to do you another, than he whom you yourself have obliged.

BENJAMIN FRANKLIN, *Autobiography*. Ch. 1. Quoted as a maxim.

10
Write injuries in dust, benefits in marble.

BENJAMIN FRANKLIN, *Poor Richard*, 1747. *See also under* INJURIES.

11
Benefits please like flowers while they are fresh.

GEORGE HERBERT, *Jacula Prudentum*.

12
A chief source for evils among men are benefits, excessive benefits. (Ἀρχὴ μεγίστη τῶν ἐν ἀνθρώποις κακῶν ἀγαθά, τὰ λίαν ἀγαθά.)

MENANDER, *Fragments*. No. 724.

13
That man is worthless who knows how to receive a benefit, but not how to return one. (Nam improbus est homo qui beneficium scit accipere et reddere nescit.)

PLAUTUS, *Persa*, l. 762. (Act v, sc. 1.)

14
To accept a benefit is to sell one's freedom. (Beneficium accipere, libertatem est vendere.)

PUBLILIUS SYRUS, *Sententiæ*. No. 58.

There is a hook in every benefit, that sticks in his jaws that takes that benefit, and draws him whither the benefactor will.

JOHN DONNE, *Sermons*, p. 550.

15
When you confer a benefit on a worthy man you oblige all men. (Beneficium dignis ubi des, omnes obliges.)

PUBLILIUS SYRUS, *Sententiæ*. No. 88.

16
A benefit is a good office, done with intention and judgment; . . . it is a voluntary and benevolent action that delights the giver, in the comfort it brings to the receiver.

SENECA, *De Beneficiis*. Bk. i, sec. 1.

A benefit is estimated according to the mind of the doer. . . . It consists not in what is done, but in what is intended. (Eodem animo beneficium debetur, quo datur . . . Beneficium non in eo quod fit aut datur consistit, sed in ipso dantis aut facientis animo.)

SENECA, *De Beneficiis*. Bk. i, sec. 4.

17
Benefits are only so far acceptable as they seem capable of being requited; beyond that point, they excite hatred instead of gratitude. (Beneficia eo usque læta sunt, dum videntur exsolvi posse: ubi multum antevenere, pro gratia odium redditur.)

TACITUS, *Annals*. Bk. iv, sec. 18.

Benefits, says Tacitus through the mouth of Montaigne, are only agreeable as long as one can repay them.

ANDRÉ GIDE, *The Counterfeiters*. Pt. ii, ch. 3.

Benefits too great
To be repaid, sit heavy on the soul,
As unrequited wrongs.

THOMAS GRAY, *Agrippina*. Act i, sc. 1. (1742)

Every one takes pleasure in returning small obligations; many go so far as to acknowledge moderate ones; but there is hardly any one who does not repay great ones with ingratitude.

LA ROCHEFOUCAULD, *Maximes*. No. 299.

BENEVOLENCE, see Philanthropy

BIBLE, THE

I—Bible: Praise

1
After the sacred volumes of God and the Scriptures, study, in the second place, that great volume of the works and creatures of God, strenuously, and before all books, which ought to be only regarded as commentaries.

FRANCIS BACON, *Letters: To Trinity College, Cambridge.*

2
Sir John Rainsford besought the queen [Elizabeth] aloud "That four prisoners, among the rest, might likewise have their liberty." The queen asked who they were. And he said, "Matthew, Mark, Luke, and John, who had long been imprisoned in the Latin tongue; and now he desired that they might go abroad among the people in English."

FRANCIS BACON, *Apothegms.*

The sacred book no longer suffers wrong,
Bound in the fetters of an unknown tongue,
But speaks with plainness art could never mend,
What simplest minds can soonest comprehend.

COWPER, *Hope,* l. 449.

What sages would have died to learn,
Now taught by cottage dames.

JOHN KEBLE, *The Christian Year: Catechism.*

It was a crime in a child to read by the bedside of a sick parent one of those beautiful collects which had soothed the griefs of forty generations of Christians.

MACAULAY, *History of England.* Ch. 2.

He who guides the plough, or wields the crook,
With understanding spirit now may look
Upon her records, listen to her song.

WORDSWORTH, *Translation of the Bible.*

3
The sire turns o'er, wi' patriarchal grace,
The big ha' Bible, ance his father's pride.

BURNS, *The Cotter's Saturday Night.* St. 12.

4
Holy Bible, book divine,
Precious treasure, thou art mine;
Mine to teach me whence I came,
Mine to teach me what I am.

JOHN BURTON, *Holy Bible, Book Divine.*

5
In the poorest cottage are Books: is one Book, wherein for several thousands of years the spirit of man has found light, and nourishment, and an interpreting response to whatever is Deepest in him.

CARLYLE, *Essays: Corn-Law Rhymes.*

6
What built St. Paul's Cathedral? Look at the heart of the matter, it was that divine Hebrew Book,—the word partly of the man Moses, an outlaw tending his Midianitish herds, four thousand years ago, in the wildernesses of Sinai! It is the strangest of things, yet nothing is truer.

CARLYLE, *Heroes and Hero-Worship: The Hero as Man of Letters.*

7
A glory gilds the sacred page,
Majestic like the sun,
It gives a light to ev'ry age,
It gives, but borrows none.

COWPER, *Olney Hymns.* No. 30.

8
Just knows, and knows no more, her Bible true, . . .
And in that charter reads, with sparkling eyes,
Her title to a treasure in the skies.

COWPER, *Truth,* l. 327.

9
Lo, here a little volume, but great book!
(Fear it not, sweet, It is no hypocrite),
Much larger in itself than in its look.

RICHARD CRASHAW, *Prayer Prefixed to a Little Prayer-Book,* l. 1.

It is an armoury of light;
Let constant use but keep it bright,
You'll find it yields
To holy hands and humble hearts,
More swords and shields
Than sin hath snares, or hell hath darts.

RICHARD CRASHAW, *Prayer Prefixed to a Little Prayer-Book,* l. 24.

10
The Scriptures, though not everywhere
Free from corruption, or entire, or clear,
Are uncorrupt, sufficient, clear, entire
In all things which our needful faith require.

DRYDEN, *Religio Laici,* l. 297.

11
The Bible is like an old Cremona; it has been played upon by the devotion of thousands of years until every word and particle is public and tunable.

EMERSON, *Letters and Social Aims: Quotation and Originality.*

12
Out from the heart of nature rolled
The burdens of the Bible old.

EMERSON, *The Problem.*

The word unto the prophet spoken
Was writ on tables yet unbroken:
The word by seers or sibyls told,
In groves of oak, or fanes of gold,
Still floats upon the morning wind,
Still whispers to the willing mind.

EMERSON, *The Problem.*

13
The music of the Gospel leads us home.

F. W. FABER, *Hymn: Hark, Hark, My Soul!*

14
It is a plain old book, modest as nature itself, and as simple, too, a book of an unpretending work-day appearance, like the sun that warms or the bread that nourishes us. . . . And the name of this book is simply—the Bible.

HEINE, *Scintillations: Religion.*

1
It was a common saying among the Puritans, "Brown bread and the Gospel is good fare."
MATTHEW HENRY, *Commentaries: Isaiah xxx.*

2
Shallows where a lamb could wade and depths where an elephant would drown.
MATTHEW HENRY, *Commentaries: Of Solomon's Song.*

3
The book of books, the storehouse and magazine of life and comfort, the Holy Scriptures.
GEORGE HERBERT, *A Priest to the Temple.* Ch. 4.

Stars are poor books, and oftentimes do miss:
This book of stars lights to eternal bliss.
GEORGE HERBERT, *The Holy Scriptures.* Sonnet ii.

Bibles laid open, millions of surprises.
GEORGE HERBERT, *Sin.*

4
There is a book, who runs may read,
Which heavenly truth imparts,
And all the lore its scholars need,
Pure eyes and Christian hearts.
JOHN KEBLE, *The Christian Year: Septuagesima.*

5
The English Bible,—a book which if everything else in our language should perish, would alone suffice to show the whole extent of its beauty and power.
MACAULAY, *Essays: John Dryden.*

6
What is home without a Bible?
'Tis a home where daily bread
For the *body* is provided,
But the *soul* is never fed.
C. D. MEIGS, *Home Without a Bible.*

7
The history of every individual man should be a Bible.
NOVALIS, *Christianity or Europe.* (Carlyle, tr.)

8
But the word of the Lord endureth for ever.
New Testament: I Peter, i, 25.

Most wondrous book! bright candle of the Lord!
Star of Eternity! The only star
By which the bark of man could navigate
The sea of life, and gain the coast of bliss
Securely.
POLLOK, *The Course of Time.* Bk. ii, l. 270.

9
Thy word is a lamp unto my feet, and a light unto my path.
Old Testament: Psalms, cxix, 105.

10
Within that awful volume lies
The mystery of mysteries!
Happiest they of human race,
To whom God has granted grace
To read, to fear, to hope, to pray,
To lift the latch and force the way;
And better had they ne'er been born,
Who read to doubt, or read to scorn.
SCOTT, *The Monastery.* Bk. i, ch. 12.

11
The stars, that in their courses roll,
Have much instruction given;
But thy good Word informs my soul
How I may climb to heaven.
ISAAC WATTS, *The Excellency of the Bible.*

How glad the heathens would have been,
That worship idols, wood and stone,
If they the book of God had seen,
Or Jesus and his gospel known!
ISAAC WATTS, *Praise for the Gospel.*

Dear Lord, this Book of thine
Informs me where to go,
For grace to pardon all my sin,
And make me holy too.
ISAAC WATTS, *Praise to God for Learning to Read.*

12
The Bible is a book of faith, and a book of doctrine, and a book of morals, and a book of religion, of special revelation from God; but it is also a book which teaches man his own individual responsibility, his own dignity, and his equality with his fellow-man.
DANIEL WEBSTER, *Speech,* at Bunker Hill Monument, 17 June, 1843.

13
We search the world for truth; we cull
The good, the pure, the beautiful,
From graven stone and written scroll,
From all old flower-fields of the soul;
And, weary seekers of the best,
We come back laden from our quest,
To find that all the sages said
Is in the Book our mothers read.
WHITTIER, *Miriam.*

My mother's hands this Bible clasped;
She, dying, gave it me.
GEORGE POPE MORRIS, *My Mother's Bible.*

II—Bible: Criticism

14
His study was but little on the bible.
CHAUCER, *Canterbury Tales: Prologue,* l. 440.

15
Is there to be no such thing as advance beyond any portion of the Bible? . . . Were the ideas of inspired persons upon all subjects absolutely right?
ARTHUR HELPS, *Friends in Council.* Bk. iii, ch. 2.

16
The Old Testament is tribal in its provinciality; its god is a local god, and its village police and sanitary regulations are erected into eternal laws.
JOHN MACY, *The Spirit of American Literature.* Ch. 1.

17
As long as woman regards the Bible as the charter of her rights, she will be the slave of man. The Bible was not written by a woman.

Within its lids there is nothing but humiliation and shame for her.

R. G. INGERSOLL, *The Liberty of Man, Woman and Child.*

1
O Bible! say I, "What follies and monstrous barbarities are defended in *thy* name."

WALT WHITMAN, paraphrasing Madame Roland. *See under* LIBERTY. (*Uncollected Prose.* Vol. i, p. 103.)

III—Bible: Its Perversion

2
And of all arts sagacious dupes invent,
To cheat themselves and gain the world's assent,
The worst is—Scripture warp'd from its intent.

COWPER, *The Progress of Error,* l. 435.

The Scripture was his jest-book.

COWPER, *Truth,* l. 307. Referring to Voltaire.

3
You rule the Scripture, not the Scripture you.

DRYDEN, *Hind and the Panther.* Pt. ii, l. 187.

4
The New Testament was less a Christiad than a Pauliad to his intelligence.

THOMAS HARDY, *Tess of the D'Urbervilles.* Phase iv, ch. 1.

There's a great text in Galatians,
Once you trip on it, entails
Twenty-nine distinct damnations,
One sure, if another fails.

ROBERT BROWNING, *Soliloquy in a Spanish Cloister.*

5
All is not Gospel that thou doest speak.

JOHN HEYWOOD, *Proverbs.* Pt. ii, ch. 2.

6
On Bible stilts I don't affect to stalk,
Nor lard with Scripture my familiar talk.

THOMAS HOOD, *Ode to Rae Wilson.*

7
Not versions, but perversions. (Non versiones, sed eversiones.)

ST. JEROME, of the versions of the Bible current in his day.

8
So *we* 're all right, an' I, fer one,
Don't think our cause 'll lose in vally
By rammin' Scriptur' in our gun,
An' gittin' Natur' fer an ally.

J. R. LOWELL, *The Biglow Papers.* Ser. ii, No. vii, l. 129.

9
One day at least in every week,
The sects of every kind
Their doctrines here are sure to seek,
And just as sure to find.

AUGUSTUS DE MORGAN. (C. D., From *Matter to Spirit: Preface.*)

10
Scrutamini Scripturas. These two words have undone the world.

JOHN SELDEN, *Table-Talk: Bible, Scripture.*

11
The Scripture, in time of disputes, is like an open town in time of war, which serves indifferently the occasions of both parties.

SWIFT, *Thoughts on Various Subjects.*

BIOGRAPHY

See also Death: De Mortuis

12
One of the new terrors of death.

JOHN ARBUTHNOT, referring to Edmund Curll's practice of issuing catch-penny lives of eminent persons immediately upon their decease. (ROBERT CARRUTHERS, *Life of Pope,* p. 149.)

Death was now armed with a new terror.

LORD BROUGHAM. (CAMPBELL, *Lives of the Chancellors,* vii, 163.)

13
There is no life of a man, faithfully recorded, but is a heroic poem of its sort, rhymed or unrhymed.

CARLYLE, *Essays: Memoirs on the Life of Scott.*

A well-written life is almost as rare as a well-spent one.

CARLYLE, *Essays: State of German Literature.*

Biography is the only true history.

CARLYLE, *Journal,* 13 Jan., 1832.

See also HISTORY: DEFINITIONS.

14
The real source of all biography is the confession of the man himself to somebody.

EMERSON, *Uncollected Lectures: Table-Talk.*

15
Here is biography—a field, a spade,
Digging of roots, and gathering of flowers:
Desire of shade—*and then the fear of shade,*
As night sweeps up the hours.

GERALD GOULD, *Biography.*

16
The poor dear dead have been laid out in vain;
Turn'd into cash, they are laid out again!

THOMAS HOOD, *On Reading a Diary Lately Published.*

17
If thou didst ever hold me in thy heart,
Absent thee from felicity awhile,
And in this harsh world draw thy breath in pain
To tell my story.

SHAKESPEARE, *Hamlet.* Act v, sc. 2, l. 357.

After my death I wish no other herald,
No other speaker of my living actions,
To keep mine honour from corruption,
But such an honest chronicler as Griffith.

SHAKESPEARE, *Henry VIII.* Act iv, sc. 2, l. 69.

18
The great and good do not die even in this world. Embalmed in books, their spirits walk abroad. The book is a living voice. It is an intellect to which one still listens.

SAMUEL SMILES, *Character.* Ch. 10. *See also* POETS AND FAME.

1
Make bare the poor dead secrets of his heart,
Strip the stark-naked soul, that all may peer,
Spy, smirk, sniff, snap, snort, snivel, snarl,
and sneer.
SWINBURNE, *In Sepulcretis*. St. 2.

Shame, such as never yet dealt heavier stroke
On heads more shameful, fall on theirs through whom
Dead men may keep inviolate not their tomb,
But all its depths these ravenous grave-worms choke.
SWINBURNE, *In Sepulcretis*. St. 4.

2
For since he would sit on a prophet's seat,
As a lord of the human soul,
We needs must scan him from head to feet,
Were it but for a wart or a mole?
TENNYSON, *The Dead Prophet*. St. 14.

For now the Poet cannot die,
Nor leave his music as of old,
But round him ere he scarce be cold
Begins the scandal and the cry.
TENNYSON, *To ——, after Reading a Life and Letters*. St. 4.

3
Why should the stranger peer and pry
One's vacant house of life about,
And drag for curious ear and eye
His faults and follies out?

Why stuff, for fools to gaze upon,
With chaff of words, the garb he wore,
As corn-husks when the ear is gone
Are rustled all the more?
WHITTIER, *My Namesake*. Sts. 6, 7.

BIRDS

Quotations relating to the more important birds will be found under their several names, Blackbird, Lark, Nightingale, etc.

I—Birds: Apothegms

4
I am no bird to be taken with chaff.
WILLIAM CAMDEN, *Reynard the Fox*, 110. (1481)

You must not think, sir, to catch old birds with chaff.
CERVANTES, *Don Quixote*. Bk. iv, ch. 5.

5
The early bird catches the worm.
WILLIAM CAMDEN, *Remains*, 333. (1605) In frequent use thereafter.

The first bird gets the first grain. (Den först: Fugl fanger det förste Korn.)
UNKNOWN. A Danish proverb.

6
The little birds of the field have God for their caterer.
CERVANTES, *Don Quixote*. Pt. ii, ch. 33.

God gives every bird its food, but does not throw it into the nest.
J. G. HOLLAND, *Gold Foil: Providence*.

Learn from the birds what food the thickets yield.
POPE, *Essay on Man*. Epis. iii, l. 173.

My sisters, the birds, ye are greatly beholden to God for the element of the air.
Attributed to ST. FRANCIS OF ASSISI.

7
There are no birds this year in last year's nests. (En los Nidos de antaño no hay pajaros hogaño.)
CERVANTES, *Don Quixote*. Pt. ii, ch. 74.

Enjoy the Spring of Love and Youth,
To some good angel leave the rest;
For Time will teach thee soon the truth,
There are no birds in last year's nest!
LONGFELLOW, *It Is Not Always May*.

8
For one reward to pursue two things. (Una mercede duas res adsequi.)
CICERO, *Pro Roscio Amerino*. Ch. 29, sec. 80.

Now for a neat job of catching two wild boars in one brake. (Jam ego uno in saltu lepide apros capiam duos.)
PLAUTUS, *Casina*, l. 476. (Act ii, sc. 7.)

I should kill two birds with one stone, as that excellent thrifty proverb says.
THOMAS SHADWELL, *The Miser*. Act ii. (1671)

9
I shall not ask Jean-Jacques Rousseau
If birds confabulate or no.
COWPER, *Pairing Time Anticipated*, l. 1.

10
A bird of the air shall carry the voice, and that which hath wings shall tell the matter.
Old Testament: Ecclesiastes, x, 20.

I did lately hear . . . by one bird that in my ear was late chaunting.
JOHN HEYWOOD, *Proverbs*. Pt. ii, ch. 5. (1546)

I had a little bird, that brought me news of it.
BRIAN MELBANCKE, *Philotinus*. Sig. F3. (1583)

I heard a bird so sing.
SHAKESPEARE, *II Henry IV*. Act v, sc. 5, l. 113.

I heard the little bird say so.
SWIFT, *Letter to Stella*. 23 May, 1711.

11
The birds are down.
JOHN HEYWOOD, *Three Hundred Epigrams*. No. 280. (1562)

12
It is a foul bird that defileth his own nest.
JOHN HEYWOOD, *Proverbs*. Pt. ii, ch. 5.

That bird is not honest
That fyleth his own nest.
JOHN SKELTON, *Poems Against Garnesche*. No. 3.

Jay-bird don't rob his own nes'.
JOEL CHANDLER HARRIS, *Plantation Proverbs*.

13
Each bird loves to hear himself sing.
JAMES HOWELL, *Proverbs*, 11. (1659).

14
A rare bird upon the earth. (Rara avis in terris.)
JUVENAL, *Satires*. Sat. vi, l. 165.

Rare bird as it would be. (Quando hæc rara avis est.)
PERSIUS, *Satires*. Sat. i, l. 46.

1
Even when the bird walks one feels that it has wings. (Même quand l'oiseau marche on sent qu'il a des ailes.)

LEMIÈRRE, *Fastes*. Chant. i.

2
The bird avoids the nets that show too plainly. (Quæ nimis apparent retia, vitat avis.)

OVID, *Remediorum Amoris*, l. 516.

Surely in vain the net is spread in the sight of any bird.

Old Testament: Proverbs, i, 17.

Vainly the fowler's eye
Might mark thy distant flight to do thee wrong,
As, darkly painted on the crimson sky,
Thy figure floats along.

BRYANT, *To a Waterfowl*.

A bird may be caught with a snare that will not be shot.

THOMAS FULLER, *Gnomologia*. No. 13.

3
He is a fool who leaves things close at hand to follow what is out of reach. (Νήπιος, ὃς τὰ ἕτοιμα λιπὼν ἀνέτοιμα διώκει.)

PLUTARCH, *Moralia: Of Garrulity*. Sec. 505D. Plutarch is quoting an unknown poet. *See also* 330:18.

That proverb, "A bird in the hand is worth two in the bush," is of more authority with them [the men of this world] than are all the divine testimonies of the good of the world to come.

JOHN BUNYAN, *The Pilgrim's Progress*. Pt. i.

A bird in hand is better than three in the wood

RICHARD HILLS, *Common-place Book*, p. 128. (c. 1530)

Better one bird in hand than ten in the wood.

JOHN HEYWOOD, *Witty and Witles*, 213. (1530)

Better sparrow in hand than vulture on wing.

CERVANTES, *Don Quixote*. Pt. i, ch. 31.

One thing that you have, they say, is worth more than two things that you may have. The one is sure, the other is not. (Un Tiens vaut, ce dit-on, mieux que deux Tu l'auras.)

LA FONTAINE, *Fables*. Bk. v, fab. 3. Paraphrasing CORROZET, fable 70, "Mieux vaut un Tiens que deux fois Tu l'auras."

4
He would beat the bushes without catching the birds. (Il battoit les buissons sans prendre les ozillons.)

RABELAIS, *Works*. Bk. i, ch. 11.

5
To fright a bird is not the way to catch her.

JOHN RAY, *English Proverbs*.

He that will take the bird must not scare it.

GEORGE HERBERT, *Jacula Prudentum*.

6
The bird that can sing and won't sing must be made to sing.

JOHN RAY, *English Proverbs*.

Such bird, such song. (Qualis avis, talis cantus.)

UNKNOWN. A Latin proverb.

7
The birds nor sow nor reap, yet sup and dine,
The flowers without clothes live,
Yet Solomon was never dressed so fine.

HENRY VAUGHAN, *Man*. *See also under* DRESS.

8
Birds in their little nests agree.

ISAAC WATTS, *Love Between Brothers and Sisters*.

With Nature never do *they* wage
A foolish strife; they see
A happy youth, and their old age
Is beautiful and free

WORDSWORTH, *The Fountain*. St. 11.

9
Then said the wren, I am called the hen
Of our Lady most comely.

UNKNOWN, *Harmony of Birds*, 10. (c. 1555)

The robin and the wren
Are God Almighty's cock and hen;
The martin and the swallow
Are God Almighty's bow and arrow.

WILLIAM HONE, *Every-Day Book*. Vol. i, p. 647.

BIRDS OF A FEATHER, etc.: *See under* COMPANY.

II—Birds: Description

10
Near all the birds
Will sing at dawn—and yet we do not take
The chaffering swallow for the holy lark.

E. B. BROWNING, *Aurora Leigh*. Bk. i, l. 951.

Oh, the little birds sang east, and the little birds sang west.

E. B. BROWNING, *Toll Slowly*.

11
Take any bird, and put him in a cage,
And do all thine intent, and thy coráge,
To foster it tenderly with meat and drink,
And eke with all the dainties thou canst think,
And keep it all so kindly as thou may;
Although his cage of gold be never so gay,
Yet hath this bird, by twenty thousand fold,
Far rather in a forest, wild and cold,
Go eten worms and suche wretchedness.

CHAUCER, *The Mauncipes Tale*, l. 161.

Just as a bird that flies about
And beats itself against the cage,
Finding at last no passage out,
It sits and sings, and so o'ercomes its rage.

ABRAHAM COWLEY, *Friendship in Absence*.

12
Dame nature's minstrels.

GAVIN DOUGLAS, *Morning in May*.

13
And as a bird each fond endearment tries
To tempt its new-fledg'd offspring to the skies.

GOLDSMITH, *The Deserted Village*, l. 167.

The shell must break before the bird can fly.

TENNYSON, *The Ancient Sage*, l. 154.

14
Many strange birds are on the air abroad,
Nor are all of one flight or of one force,

But each after his kind dissimilar.
GUINICELLI, *Of Moderation and Tolerance.*

1
When the little birds sweetly did sing
Lauds to their Maker early i' the morning.
STEPHEN HAWES, *Passetyme of Pleasure.* (1506)

The little birds that tune their morning's joy.
SHAKESPEARE, *The Rape of Lucrece.* St. 159.

2
The dear Lord God, of His glories weary—
Christ our Lord had the heart of a boy—
Made Him birds in a moment merry,
Bade them soar and sing for his joy.
KATHERINE TYNAN HINKSON, *The Making of Birds.*

3
And all the little birds had laid their heads
Under their wings—sleeping in feather beds.
THOMAS HOOD, *Bianca's Dream,* l. 111.

4
Be like the bird which on frail branches balanced
A moment sits and sings;
He feels them tremble, but he sings unshaken,
Knowing that he has wings.
VICTOR HUGO, *Wings.* (Edwin Arnold, tr.)

5
A bird appears a thoughtless thing, . . .
No doubt he has his little cares,
And very hard he often fares,
The which so patiently he bears.
CHARLES LAMB, *Crumbs to the Birds.*

6
Do you ne'er think what wondrous beings these?
Do you ne'er think who made them, and who taught
The dialect they speak, where melodies
Alone are the interpreters of thought?
Whose household words are songs in many keys,
Sweeter than instrument of man e'er caught!
LONGFELLOW, *The Birds of Killingworth.* St. 15.

A bird knows nothing of gladness,
Is only a song machine.
GEORGE MACDONALD, *Book of Dreams.* Pt. ii.

7
By shallow rivers, to whose falls
Melodious birds sing madrigals.
CHRISTOPHER MARLOWE, *The Passionate Shepherd to His Love.* SHAKESPEARE, *Merry Wives of Windsor.* Act iii, sc. 1.

8
Yet this was but a simple bird,
Alone, among dead trees.
W. A. PERCY, *Overtones.*

9
Gone to the world where birds are blest!
Where never cat glides o'er the green.
SAMUEL ROGERS, *Epitaph on a Robin.*

10
Gay, guiltless pair,
What seek ye from the fields of Heaven?
Ye have no need of prayer,
Ye have no sins to be forgiven.
CHARLES SPRAGUE, *The Winged Worshippers.*

11
O delicate chain over all the ages stretched,
O dumb tradition from what far darkness fetched:
Each little architect with its one design
Perpetual, fixed, and right in stuff and line,
Each little ministrant who knows one thing,
One learnèd rite to celebrate the spring.
Whatever alters else on sea or shore,
These are unchanging: man must still explore.
J. C. SQUIRE, *The Birds.*

12
Hark, by the bird's song ye may learn the nest.
TENNYSON, *The Marriage of Geraint,* l 359.

What does little birdie say
In her nest at peep of day?
TENNYSON, *Sea Dreams,* l. 281.

13
The birds know when the friend they love is nigh,
For I am known to them, both great and small.
JONES VERY, *Nature.*

14
You alone can lose yourself
Within a sky, and rob it of its blue!
MAXWELL BODENHEIM, *Advice to a Blue-Bird.*

The bluebird carries the sky on his back.
THOREAU, *Journal.* (EMERSON, *Thoreau.*)

15
And all it lends to the eye is this—
A sunbeam giving the air a kiss.
HARRY KEMP, *The Hummingbird.*

16
The linnet's lay of love.
JAMES BEATTIE, *The Minstrel.* Bk. i, l. 38.

17
Then from the neighboring thicket the mocking-bird, wildest of singers,
Swinging aloft on a willow spray that hung o'er the water,
Shook from his little throat such floods of delirious music,
That the whole air and the woods and the waves seemed silent to listen.
LONGFELLOW, *Evangeline.* Pt. ii, sec. 2.

Winged mimic of the woods! thou motley fool!
Who shall thy gay buffoonery describe?
Thine ever-ready notes of ridicule
Pursue thy fellows still with jest and jibe:
Wit, sophist, songster, Yorick of thy tribe;
Thou sportive satirist of Nature's school;
To thee the palm of scoffing we ascribe,
Arch-mocker and mad abbot of misrule!
ROBERT WYLDE, *To the Mocking-Bird.*

18
The bird forlorn
That singeth with her breast against a thorn.
THOMAS HOOD, *Plea of the Midsummer Fairies.*

1
Across the narrow beach we flit,
One little sand-piper and I;
And fast I gather, bit by bit,
The scattered drift-wood, bleached and dry,
The wild waves reach their hands for it,
The wild wind raves, the tide runs high,
As up and down the beach we flit,
One little sand-piper and I.
CELIA THAXTER, *The Sand-Piper.*

2
Seagulls . . . slim yachts of the element.
ROBINSON JEFFERS, *Pelicans.*

3
How joyously the young sea-mew
Lay dreaming on the waters blue
Whereon our little bark had thrown
A little shade, the only one,
But shadows ever man pursue.
E. B. BROWNING, *The Sea-Mew.*

BIRTH AND BIRTHDAY

See also Baby; Birth and Death. For Birth in the sense of rank or nobility, see Ancestry.

I—Birth

4
The infant, as soon as Nature with great pangs of travail hath sent it forth from the womb of its mother into the regions of light, lies, like a sailor cast out from the waves, naked upon the earth, in utter want and helplessness, and fills every place around with mournful wailings and piteous lamentations, as is natural for one who has so many ills of life in store for him, so many evils which he must pass through and suffer.
FRANCIS BACON, *De Rerum Natura.* Pt. v, sec. 223.

He is born naked, and falls a whining at the first.
ROBERT BURTON, *Anatomy of Melancholy.* Pt. i, sec. ii, mem. 3, subs. 10.

Man alone at the very moment of his birth, cast naked upon the naked earth, does she abandon to cries and lamentations.
PLINY THE ELDER, *Historia Naturalis.* Bk. vii, sec. 2.

5
You have given yourself the trouble to be born. (Vous vous êtes donné la peine de naître.)
BEAUMARCHAIS, *Mariage de Figaro.* Act v, sc. 3.

6
Every night and every morn
Some to misery are born;
Every morn and every night
Some are born to sweet delight.
WILLIAM BLAKE, *Auguries of Innocence.*

7
I came upstairs into the world, for I was born in a cellar.
CONGREVE, *Love for Love.* Act ii, sc. 7.

Born in a cellar and living in a garret.
SAMUEL FOOTE, *The Author.* Act ii.

Born in the garret, in the kitchen bred.
BYRON, *A Sketch,* l. 1.

8
When each comes forth from his mother's womb, the gate of gifts closes behind him.
EMERSON, *Conduct of Life: Fate.*

9
For we should mourn in sorrowing throngs the house
Where a man child is born to light of day.
(Nam nos decebat cœtus celebrantes domum
Lugere, ubi esset aliquis in lucem editus.)
EURIPIDES, *Cresphontes.* As translated by CICERO, *Tusculanarum Disputationum.* Bk. i, ch. 48, sec. 115.

10
Zoë, the fourth wife of Leo VI, gave birth to the future Emperor Constantine Porphyrogenitus in the purple chamber of the imperial palace.
GEORGE FINLAY, *Byzantine and Greek Empires,* i. Porphyrogenitus, or born in the purple, has nothing to do with purple robes of royalty, but refers to the porphyry-lined chamber in which Constantine was born.

11
A man is not completely born until he be dead.
BENJAMIN FRANKLIN, *Letters: To Miss Hubbard. See also* DEATH AND BIRTH.

12
Into the world we come like ships,
Launch'd from the docks, and stocks, and slips,
For fortune fair or fatal!
THOMAS HOOD, *Miss Kilmansegg: Her Birth.*

13
Let the day perish wherein I was born, and the night in which it was said, There is a man-child conceived.
Old Testament: Job, iii, 3.

14
You were born of a white hen. (Gallinæ filius albæ.)
JUVENAL, *Satires.* Sat. xiii, l. 141.

He was born with a penny in 's mouth.
JOHN CLARKE, *Par. Anglo-Latina,* 39.

One man, says the auld proverb, is born wi' a silver spoon in his mouth, and another wi' a wudden ladle.
JOHN WILSON, *Noctes Ambrosianæ.* Nov., 1831.

Plutus, as sponsor, stood at her font,
And Midas rocked the cradle.
THOMAS HOOD, *Miss Kilmansegg: Her Birth.*

15
Naked I alighted on the earth and naked shall I go beneath it. (Γῆς ἐπεβην γυμνός, γυμνός θ' ὑπὸ γαῖαν ἄπειμι.)
PALLADAS. (*Greek Anthology.* Bk. x, No. 58.)

Naked came I out of my mother's womb, and naked shall I return thither: the Lord gave and the Lord hath taken away; blessed be the name of the Lord.

Old Testament: Job, i, 21.

For we brought nothing into this world, and it is certain we can carry nothing out.

New Testament: I Timothy, vi, 7.

Naked was I born, naked I am; I neither lose nor gain. (Desnudo nací, desnudo me hallo; ni pierdo ni gano.)

CERVANTES, *Don Quixote*. Pt. i, ch. 25; Pt. ii, chs. 8, 53, 55, 57.

1

Blest indeed are those who were never born to see the sun! (*Φεῦ μακαριστοί, ὅσσοι ἀπ' ὠδίνων οὐκ ἴδον ἠέλιον.*)

PHILIPPUS OF THESSALONICA, *Epigram*. (*Greek Anthology*. Bk. vii, No. 383.)

Who breathes, must suffer; and who thinks, must mourn;
And he alone is bless'd, who ne'er was born.

MATTHEW PRIOR, *Solomon on the Vanity of the World*. Bk. iii, l. 240.

2

From the womb of the morning: thou hast the dew of thy youth.

Old Testament: Psalms, cx, 3.

Her birth was of the womb of morning dew
And her conception of the joyous prime.

SPENSER, *Faerie Queene*. Bk. iii, canto vi, st. 3.

3

Infinitely more important than any other question in this country—that is the question of race suicide, complete or partial.

THEODORE ROOSEVELT, *Letter to Bessie Van Vorst*, 18 Oct., 1902. Reprinted as a preface to her *The Woman Who Toils*.

We want far better reasons for having children than not knowing how to prevent them.

DORA RUSSELL, *Hypatia*, p. 46.

4

I was born about three of the clock in the afternoon, with a white head and something a round belly.

SHAKESPEARE, *II Henry IV*. Act i, sc. 2, l. 210.

There was he born, under a hedge.

SHAKESPEARE, *II Henry VI*. Act iv, sc. 2, l. 54.

5

Thou must be patient; we came crying hither:
Thou know'st the first time that we smell the air,
We wawl and cry. . . .
When we are born, we cry that we are come
To this great stage of fools.

SHAKESPEARE, *King Lear*. Act iv, sc. 6, l. 182.

6

I 'spect I growed. Don't think nobody never made me.

HARRIET BEECHER STOWE, *Uncle Tom's Cabin*. Ch. 21.

7

When I was born, I did lament and cry,
And now each day doth show the reason why.

RICHARD WATKYNS, *Flamma Sine Fumo*. (1662)

8

And when I was born, I drew in the common air, and fell upon the earth, which is of like nature, and the first voice which I uttered was crying, as all others do. . . . For there is no king had any other beginning of birth. For all men have one entrance into life, and the like going out.

Apocrypha: Wisdom of Solomon, vii, 3–6.

9

My father got me strong and straight and slim
And I give thanks to him.
My mother bore me glad and sound and sweet,
I kiss her feet!

MARGUERITE WILKINSON, *The End*.

10

Our birth is but a sleep and a forgetting;
The Soul that rises with us, our life's Star,
Hath had elsewhere its setting,
And cometh from afar:
Not in entire forgetfulness,
And not in utter nakedness,
But trailing clouds of glory do we come
From God, who is our home.

WORDSWORTH, *Intimations of Immortality*, l. 58.

11

Born of a Monday, fair in the face,
Born of a Tuesday, full of God's grace,
Born of a Wednesday, merry and glad,
Born of a Thursday, sour and sad,
Born of a Friday, Godly given,
Born of a Saturday, work for your living,
Born of a Sunday, ne'er shall you want,
So ends the week, and there's an end on't.

UNKNOWN. (BRAND, *Popular Antiquities. Notes and Queries*, ser. v, vii, 424.)

Monday's child is fair of face,
Tuesday's child is full of grace,
Wednesday's child is full of woe,
Thursday's child has far to go,
Friday's child is loving and giving,
Saturday's child works hard for its living,
And a child that's born on the Sabbath day
Is fair and wise and good and gay.

UNKNOWN. (BRAY, *Traditions of Devon*, ii, 288.)

II—Birth: Birthday

See also Age: Middle Age

12

What different dooms our birthdays bring!
For instance, one little mannikin thing
Survives to wear many a wrinkle;
While Death forbids another to wake,
And a son that it took nine moons to make,
Expires without even a twinkle!

THOMAS HOOD, *Miss Kilmansegg: Her Birth*

13

Do you count your birthdays thankfully? (Natalis grate numeras?)

HORACE, *Epistles*. Bk. ii, epis. 2, l. 210.

1
The return of my birthday, if I remember it, fills me with thoughts which it seems to be the general care of humanity to escape.
SAMUEL JOHNSON. (BOSWELL, *Life*, v, 222.)

My birthday!—what a different sound
That word had in my youthful ears;
And how each time the day comes round,
Less and less white its mark appears.
THOMAS MOORE, *My Birthday*.

2
Believing hear, what you deserve to hear:
Your birthday as my own to me is dear. . . .
But yours gives most; for mine did only lend
Me to the world; yours gave to me a friend.
MARTIAL, *Epigrams*. Bk. ix, epig. 52.

3
Is that a birthday? 'tis, alas! too clear;
'Tis but the funeral of the former year.
POPE, *To Mrs. M. B. on Her Birthday*.

4
This day I breathed first: time is come round,
And where I did begin, there shall I end;
My life is run his compass.
SHAKESPEARE, *Julius Cæsar*. Act v, sc. 3, l. 23.

5
How soon hath Time, the subtle thief of youth,
Stol'n on his wing my three-and-twentieth year!
MILTON, *Sonnet: On His Being Arrived to the Age of Twenty-three*.

6
Through life's road, so dim and dirty,
I have dragged to three-and-thirty;
What have these years left to me?
Nothing, except thirty-three.
BYRON, *Diary*. 22 Jan., 1821. (MOORE, *Life of Byron*. Vol. ii, p. 414.)

I am thirty-three—the age of the good *sans-culotte* Jesus; an age fatal to revolutionists.
CAMILLE DESMOULINS, when asked his age by the French Revolutionary Tribunal, 3 April, 1794. He was guillotined two days later. *Sans-culotte*, without breeches, was the popular name for the Revolutionaries, presumably because they had discarded knee-breeches—*culottes*—for pantaloons. (*Aperçus sur Camille Desmoulins*. Carlyle, *French Revolution*. Vol. iii, bk. vi, ch. 2.)

7
Make me content
With fading light;
Give me a glorious sunset
And a peaceful night.
NORMAN B. HALL, *A Thought on My Forty-fifth Birthday*.

8
Fifty years spent, and what do they bring me?
Now I can buy the meadow and hill:
Where is the heart of the boy to sing thee?
Where is the life for thy living to fill?
STRUTHERS BURT, *Fifty Years Spent*.

Old Age, on tiptoe, lays her jewelled hand
Lightly in mine.
GEORGE SANTAYANA, *A Minuet on Reaching the Age of Fifty*.

I keep some portion of my early dream;
Brokenly light, like moonbeams on a river,
It lights my life, a far elusive gleam,
Moves as I move, and leads me on forever.
J. T. TROWBRIDGE, *Twoscore and Ten*. St. 29.

9
Past my next milestone waits my seventieth year.
I mount no longer when the trumpets call;
My battle-harness idles on the wall,
The spider's castle, camping-ground of dust,
Not without dints, and all in front, I trust.
J. R. LOWELL, *Epistle to George William Curtis: Postscript, 1887*.

III—Birth: Birthright

10
And he sold his birthright unto Jacob.
Old Testament: Genesis, xxv, 33.

Better a mess of pottage than nothing, pardie.
UNKNOWN, *The Historie of Jacob and Esau*. (1557) The expression, "a mess of pottage," does not occur in the authorized version of the Bible, but seems to have been derived from the heading of the 25th chapter of Genesis in the Genevan version, printed in 1537: "Esau selleth his birthright for a mess of pottage."

11
His birthright sold, some pottage so to gain.
WILLIAM ALEXANDER, *Doomsday: The Sixth Hour*. St. 39.

Lest, selling that noble inheritance for a poor mess of pottage, you never enter into his eternal rest.
WILLIAM PENN, *No Cross, No Crown*. Pt. ii, ch. 20.

Shall we sell our birthrite for a mess of potash?
ARTEMUS WARD, *Lecture*.

12
Where'er a single slave doth pine,
Where'er one man may help another,—
Thank God for such a birthright, brother,—
That spot of earth is thine and mine!
There is the true man's birthplace grand,
His is a world-wide fatherland!
J. R. LOWELL, *The Fatherland*.

13
Bearing their birthrights proudly on their backs.
SHAKESPEARE, *King John*. Act ii, sc. 1, l. 70.

IV—Birth: Birth-stones

14
January

By her who in this month is born,
No gems save *Garnets* should be worn;
They will insure her constancy,
True friendship and fidelity.

February
The February born will find
Sincerity and peace of mind;
Freedom from passion and from care,
If they the *Pearl* will always wear.
March
Who in this world of ours their eyes
In March first open shall be wise;
In days of peril firm and brave,
And wear a *Bloodstone* to their grave.
April
She who from April dates her years,
Diamonds should wear, lest bitter tears
For vain repentance flow; this stone,
Emblem of innocence is known.
May
Who first beholds the light of day
In Spring's sweet flowery month of May
And wears an *Emerald* all her life,
Shall be a loved and happy wife.
June
Who comes with Summer to this earth
And owes to June her day of birth,
With ring of *Agate* on her hand,
Can health, wealth, and long life command.
July
The glowing *Ruby* should adorn
Those who in warm July are born,
Then will they be exempt and free
From love's doubt and anxiety.
August
Wear a *Sardonyx* or for thee
No conjugal felicity.
The August-born without this stone
'Tis said must live unloved and lone.
September
A maiden born when Autumn leaves
Are rustling in September's breeze,
A *Sapphire* on her brow should bind,
'Twill cure diseases of the mind.
October
October's child is born for woe,
And life's vicissitudes must know;
But lay an *Opal* on her breast,
And hope will lull those woes to rest.
November
Who first comes to this world below
With drear November's fog and snow
Should prize the *Topaz'* amber hue—
Emblem of friends and lovers true.
December
If cold December gave you birth,
The month of snow and ice and mirth,
Place on your hand a *Turquoise* blue,
Success will bless whate'er you do.

UNKNOWN, (*Notes and Queries,* 11 May, 1889, p. 371.)

BLACK

1
Black is a pearl in a woman's eye.

GEORGE CHAPMAN, *An Humorous Day's Mirth.*

2
Above black there is no colour, and above salt no savour.

JOHN FLORIO, *First Fruites.* Fo. 33. (1578)

3
Black will take no other hue. (Lanæ nigræ nullum colorem bibunt.)

PLINY THE ELDER, *Naturalis Historia.* Bk. viii. JOHN HEYWOOD, *Proverbs.* Pt. ii, ch. 9. (1546)

4
Having no colours but only white and black,
To the tragedies which that I shall write.

JOHN LYDGATE, *Fall of Princes.* Bk. i, l. 465. (c. 1440)

I have it here in black and white.

BEN JONSON, *Every Man in His Humour.* Act iv, sc. 2. (1598)

Which, indeed, is not under white and black.

SHAKESPEARE, *Much Ado About Nothing.* Act v, sc. 1, l. 314. (1599)

We have gotten it under black and white.

BISHOP JOSEPH HALL, *Works,* p. 166. (c. 1656)

5
A black plum is as sweet as a white.

JOHN RAY, *English Proverbs,* 63.

6
They'll . . . pinch us black and blue.

SHAKESPEARE, *The Comedy of Errors.* Act ii, sc. 2, l. 194.

7
Black as hell.

SHAKESPEARE, *Hamlet.* Act iii, sc. 3, l. 94.

Thou'rt damn'd as black—nay, nothing is so black.

SHAKESPEARE, *King John.* Act iv, sc. 3, l. 121.

Black is the badge of hell,
The hue of dungeons and the suit of night.

SHAKESPEARE, *Love's Labour's Lost.* Act iv, sc. 3, l. 254.

8
By heaven, thy love is black as ebony.

SHAKESPEARE, *Love's Labour's Lost.* Act iv, sc. 3, l. 247.

To look like her are chimney-sweepers black.

SHAKESPEARE, *Love's Labour's Lost.* Act iv, sc. 3, l. 266.

9
Is black so base a hue?

SHAKESPEARE, *Titus Andronicus.* Act iv, sc. 2, l. 71.

Coal-black is better than another hue,
In that it scorns to bear another hue.

SHAKESPEARE, *Titus Andronicus.* Act iv, sc. 2, l. 99.

10
No one can say black is her eye.

STEELE, *The Spectator.* No. 1711.

I defy anybody to say black's my nail.

JOHN REED, *Registry Office.* Act i.

11
Every white will have its black
And every sweet its sour.

UNKNOWN, *Sir Cauline.* (15th century ballad.)

Sweet meat must have sour sauce.

BEN JONSON, *Poetaster.* Act iii, sc. 1.

See also under SWEET AND BITTER.

1
As black as any coal.
UNKNOWN, *King Horn,* l. 590. (c. 1260)

As black as any crow.
UNKNOWN, *Horn Childe,* l. 1049. (c. 1320)

As black he lay as any coal or crow.
CHAUCER, *The Knightes Tale,* l. 1834. (1386)

Black as a sloe.
CHAUCER, *The Milleres Tale,* l. 60. (c. 1386)

2
At every tempest they be as black as ink.
ALEXANDER BARCLAY, *Egloges,* 30. (c. 1510)

Deformed monsters, foul and black as ink.
SPENSER, *Faerie Queene.* Bk. i, canto i, st. 22.

How black?—Why, as black as ink.
SHAKESPEARE, *The Two Gentlemen of Verona.* Act iii, sc. 1, l. 288.

3
It cometh out of Ethiope and Ind,
Black as is jet.
JOHN LYDGATE, *Troy Book.* Bk. ii, l. 987. (1412)

Two proper palfreys, black as jet.
SHAKESPEARE, *Titus Andronicus.* Act v, sc. 2, l. 50.

Their nails and teeth as black as jet.
JOHN EVELYN, *Diary,* 19 June, 1682.

4
His steed was black as raven.
ROBERT MANNYNG (ROBERT DE BRUNNE), tr. Langtoft's *Chronicles,* 295. (c. 1300)

He looks as black as thunder.
J. R. PLANCHÉ, *Extravaganza,* ii, 56.

His face was as black as a devil in a play
SIR HENRY SPELMAN, *Dialogue,* 42. (c. 1580)

BLACKBIRD

5
I value my garden more for being full of blackbirds than of cherries, and very frankly give them fruit for their songs.
ADDISON, *The Spectator.* No. 477.

6
Strange, beautiful, unquiet thing,
Lone flute of God.
JOSEPH AUSLANDER, *A Blackbird Suddenly.*

7
Ov all the birds upon the wing
Between the zunny showers o' spring, . . .
The blackbird, whisslèn in among
The boughs, do zing the gayest song.
WILLIAM BARNES, *The Blackbird.*

8
O blackbird, who hath taught thee
The heartbreak in thy song?
F. W. BOURDILLON, *The Blackbird.*

9
The nightingale has a lyre of gold,
The lark's is a clarion call,
And the blackbird plays but a boxwood flute,
But I love him best of all.
W. E. HENLEY, *Echoes.* No. 18.

10
The blackbird in the coppice
Looked out to see me stride,
And hearkened as I whistled
The trampling team beside,
And fluted and replied.
A. E. HOUSMAN, *A Shropshire Lad.* No. 7.

11
Wet your feet, wet your feet,
This is what he seems to say,
Calling from the dewy thicket
At the breaking of the day.
JAMES MCALPINE, *To an Irish Blackbird.*

12
Quaintest, richest carol of all the singing throats.
GEORGE MEREDITH, *Love in the Valley.* St. 17.

13
The birds have ceased their songs,
All save the blackbird, that from yon tall ash, . . .
In adoration of the setting sun,
Chants forth his evening hymn.
DAVID MOIR, *An Evening Sketch.*

14
Let thy loud and welcome lay
Pour alway
Few notes but strong.
JAMES MONTGOMERY, *The Blackbird.*

15
O Blackbird! sing me something well:
While all the neighbours shoot thee round,
I keep smooth plats of fruitful ground,
Where thou may'st warble, eat and dwell.
ALFRED TENNYSON, *The Blackbird.*

16
The Blackbird sings along the sunny breeze
His ancient song of leaves, and summer boon.
FREDERICK TENNYSON, *The Blackbird.*

His bill's so yellow,
his coat's so black,
that he makes a fellow
whistle back.
HUMBERT WOLFE, *The Blackbird.*

BLACKSMITH, see Smith

BLAKE, WILLIAM

17
Blake saw a treeful of angels at Peckham Rye,
And his hands could lay hold on the tiger's terrible heart.
Blake knew how deep is Hell, and Heaven how high,
And could build the universe from one tiny part.
WILLIAM ROSE BENÉT, *Mad Blake.*

18
Be a god, your spirit cried;
Tread with feet that burn the dew;
Dress with clouds your locks of pride;
Be a child, God said to you.
OLIVE DARGAN, *To William Blake.*

19
This seer's ambition soared too far;
He sank, on pinions backward blown;

But, tho' he touched nor sun nor star,
He made a world his own.
EDMUND GOSSE, *William Blake*.

1
How shall a wise man, babbling like a child,
Tame jungle tigers and make lambkins wild?
JOHN MACY, *Couplets in Criticism: Blake*.

2
He came to the desert of London town,
Gray miles long;
He wandered up and he wandered down,
Singing a quiet song.
He came to the desert of London town,
Mirk miles broad;
He wandered up and he wandered down,
Ever alone with God.
JAMES THOMSON THE YOUNGER, *William Blake*.

BLESSING

3
Bless me in this life with but peace of my conscience, command of my affections, the love of Thyself and my dearest friends, and I shall be happy enough to pity Cæsar.
SIR THOMAS BROWNE, *Religio Medici*. Pt. ii, conclusion.

4
Come what may, I *have been* blessed.
BYRON, *The Giaour*, l. 1115.

5
Blessed are the valiant that have lived in the Lord.
CARLYLE, *Cromwell's Letters and Speeches*. Vol. v, pt. 10.

For blessings ever wait on virtuous deeds.
CONGREVE, *The Mourning Bride*. Act v, sc. 12.

6
A spring of love gush'd from my heart,
And I bless'd them unaware.
S. T. COLERIDGE, *Ancient Mariner*. Pt. iv, st. 14.

7
Blessed shall be thy basket and thy store.
Old Testament: Deuteronomy, xxviii, 5.

8
"God bless us every one!" said Tiny Tim, the last of all.
DICKENS, *A Christmas Carol*. Stave 3.

God bless us every one, prayed Tiny Tim,
Crippled and dwarfed of body, yet so tall
Of soul, we tiptoe earth to look on him,
High towering over all.
J. W. RILEY, *God Bless Us Every One*.

9
Blessings are not valued till they are gone.
THOMAS FULLER, *Gnomologia*. No. 989.

Like birds, whose beauties languish half conceal'd,
Till, mounted on the wing, their glossy plumes
Expanded, shine with azure, green and gold;
How blessings brighten as they take their flight!
YOUNG, *Night Thoughts*. Night ii, l. 597.

10
May fortune bless you! may the middle distance
Of your young life be pleasant as the foreground.
W. S. GILBERT, *The Sorcerer*. Act i.

11
Bless the four corners of this little house,
And be the lintel blest;
And bless the hearth. and bless the board,
And bless each place of rest.
ARTHUR GUITERMAN, *House Blessing*.

12
To heal divisions, to relieve th' oppress'd,
In virtue rich; in blessing others. bless'd.
HOMER, *Odyssey*. Bk. vii, l. 95. (Pope, tr.)

In proportion as it blesses, blest.
POPE, *Essay on Man*. Epis. iii, l. 300.

He who blesses most is blest:
And God and man shall own his worth
Who toils to leave as his bequest
An added beauty to the earth.
WHITTIER, *Lines for the Agricultural Exhibition at Amesbury*.

13
Nothing is blessed in every respect. (Nihil est ab omni Parte beatum.)
HORACE, *Odes*. Bk. ii, ode 16, l. 27.

'Tis not for mortals always to be blest.
JOHN ARMSTRONG, *Art of Preserving Health*. Bk. iv, l. 260.

14
Out of the same mouth proceedeth blessing and cursing.
New Testament: James, iii, 10.

He whom thou blesseth is blessed, and he whom thou cursest is cursed. . . . Blessed is he that blesseth thee, and cursed is he that curseth thee.
Old Testament: Numbers, xxii, 6; xxiv, 9.

15
Blessed is he that cometh in the name of the Lord.
New Testament: Matthew, xxiii, 39; *Mark*, xi, 10; *Luke*, xiii, 35.

16
My blessings have banished fear. (Excessere metum mea jam bona.)
OVID, *Metamorphoses*. Bk. vi, l. 197.

17
No human blessing lasts forever. (Nullum homini est perpetuom bonum.)
PLAUTUS, *Curculio*, l. 189. (Act i, sc. 3.)

18
The blest to-day is as completely so,
As who began a thousand years ago.
POPE, *Essay on Man*. Epis. i, l. 75.

19
Blest be those,
How mean soe'er, that have their honest wills.
SHAKESPEARE, *Cymbeline*. Act i, sc. 6, l. 7.

The benediction of these covering heavens
Fall on their heads like dew!
SHAKESPEARE, *Cymbeline*. Act v, sc. 5, l. 350.

The dews of heaven fall thick in blessings on her!
SHAKESPEARE, *Henry VIII*. Act iv, sc. 2, l. 133.

20
A double blessing is a double grace.
SHAKESPEARE, *Hamlet*. Act i, sc. 3, l. 53.

And when you are desirous to be bless'd,
I'll blessing beg of you.
SHAKESPEARE, *Hamlet*. Act iii, sc. 4, l. 171.

I had most need of blessing, and "Amen"
Stuck in my throat.
SHAKESPEARE, *Macbeth*. Act ii, sc. 2, l. 32.

1
Bless thee, Bottom! bless thee! thou art translated.
SHAKESPEARE, *A Midsummer-Night's Dream*. Act iii, sc. 1, l. 119.

A pack of blessings lights upon thy back.
SHAKESPEARE, *Romeo and Juliet*. Act iii, sc. 3, l. 141.

2
Got pless my heart, liver, and lungs.
SMOLLETT, *Roderick Random*. Ch. 26.

3
The three blessings for which I am most grateful to Fortune are: first, that I was born a human being and not one of the brutes; second, that I was born a man and not a woman; third, that I was born a Greek and not a barbarian.
THALES. (DIOGENES LAERTIUS, *Thales*. Sec. 33.)

Amid my list of blessings infinite,
Stand this the foremost, "That my heart has bled."
YOUNG, *Night Thoughts*. Night ix, l. 496.

BLINDNESS

I—Blindness: Apothegms

4
How blind is he that sees not light through the bottom of a sieve!
CERVANTES, *Don Quixote*. Pt. ii, ch. 1.

5
We'll follow the blind side of him.
GEORGE CHAPMAN, *Gentleman Usher*. Act i, sc. 1. (1606)

The rascals have a blind side, as all conceited coxcombs have.
APHRA BEHN, *The Rover*. Pt. ii, act i, sc. 1.

6
But as a blind man start an hare.
CHAUCER, *The Hous of Fame*. Bk. ii, l. 173.

By wondrous accident perchance one may
Grope out a needle in a load of hay;
And though a white crow is exceeding rare,
A blind man may, by fortune, catch a hare.
JOHN TAYLOR, *A Kicksey Winsey*. Pt. vii.

7
A blind man cannot judgen well in hues.
CHAUCER, *Troilus and Criseyde*. Bk. ii, l. 21. (1374)

The blind man of colours all wrong deemeth.
THOMAS HOCCLEVE, *De Regimine Principum*, 36. (1411)

8
As blind as a bat at noon.
JOHN CLARKE, *Parœmiologia*, 52. (1639)

In this wisdom he is as blind as a beetle.
HUGH LATIMER, *Seven Sermons*, p. 90. (1549)

In the water as blind as a mole.
UNKNOWN, *Euterpe*, p. 68. (1584)

Blinder Than a trebly-bandaged mole.
C. S. CALVERLEY, *Lines on Hearing an Organ*.

9
A pebble and a diamond are alike to a blind man.
THOMAS FULLER, *Gnomologia*. No. 340.

10
Better be blind than to see ill.
GEORGE HERBERT, *Jacula Prudentum*.

Better one-eyed than stone blind.
JOHN RAY, *English Proverbs*.

11
Folk oft times are most blind in their own cause.
JOHN HEYWOOD, *Proverbs*. Pt. ii, ch. 5.

Every man's blind in his ain cause.
JOHN RAY, *Proverbs: Scottish*.

12
Who is so deaf or blind as is he
That wilfully will neither hear nor see?
JOHN HEYWOOD, *Proverbs*. Pt. ii, ch. 9. (1546)

Who is blinder than he that will not see?
ANDREW BOORDE, *Breviary of Helthe*. Bk. ii, fo. 6. (1547)

There is none so blind as they that won't see.
SWIFT, *Polite Conversation*. Dial. iii.

Being too blind to have desire to see.
TENNYSON, *The Holy Grail*, l. 868.

13
I was eyes to the blind, and feet was I to the lame.
Old Testament: Job, xxix, 15.

14
I read each a blind buzzard.
WILLIAM LANGLAND, *Piers Plowman*. Passus x, l. 267. (1377)

Wept till blind as a buzzard.
THOMAS OTWAY, *Soldier's Fortune*. Act iv, sc. 3.

15
The blind eat many a fly.
JOHN LYDGATE, *Ballade*. (c. 1430)

16
They be blind leaders of the blind. And if the blind lead the blind, both shall fall into the ditch.
New Testament: Matthew, xv, 14.

Can the blind lead the blind? shall they not both fall into the ditch?
New Testament: Luke, vi, 39.

When the blind leads the blind, no wonder they both fall into—matrimony.
FARQUHAR, *Love and a Bottle*. Act v, sc. 1.

17
In the country of the blind, the one-eyed man is king. (Cæcorum in patria luscus rex imperat omnis.)
MICHAEL APOSTOLIUS, *Proverbs*. An old proverb, taken from the Greek, its earliest English use probably in the translation by John Palsgrave, in 1540, of the *Comedye of Acolastus*, by Fullenius. In frequent use thereafter, with minor variations.

Among the blind, the one-eyed man is king. (Scitum est inter cæcos luscum regnare posse.)
ERASMUS, *Adagia: Excellentia et Inequalitas*. (c. 1500)

Blessed are the one-eyed in the country of the blind. (Beati monoculi in regione cæcorum.)
FREDERICK THE GREAT, quoting a proverb. (CARLYLE, *Frederick the Great*. Bk. iv, ch. 11.)

Among the blind the one-eyed blinkard reigns.
ANDREW MARVELL, *Character of Holland.*

But have ye not heard this,
How an one-eyed man is
Well sighted when
He is among blind men?
JOHN SKELTON, *Why Come Ye Not to Courte?*

1
The eyes are blind when the mind is elsewhere. (Cæci sunt oculi cum animus alias res agit.)
PUBLILIUS SYRUS, *Sententiæ*. No. 126.

2
Blind-man's holiday, when it is too dark to see to work.
UNKNOWN, *Dictionary Canting Crew*. Sig. B6. (1690)

II—Blindness: Its Misery

3
For Blindness is the first born of Excess.
BYRON, *Heaven and Earth*. Pt. i, sc. 3, l. 807.

4
Oh, say! what is that thing call'd light,
Which I must ne'er enjoy?
What are the blessings of the sight?
Oh, tell your poor blind boy.
COLLEY CIBBER, *The Blind Boy.*

5
As blind as are these three to me,
So, blind to Some-one I must be.
WALTER DE LA MARE. *All But Blind.*

6
Dispel this cloud, the light of Heav'n restore;
Give me to see, and Ajax asks no more.
HOMER, *Iliad*. Bk. xvii, l. 729. (Pope, tr.)

7
Mild light, and by degrees, should be the plan
To cure the dark and erring mind;
But who would rush at a benighted man,
And give him two black eyes for being blind?
THOMAS HOOD, *Ode to Rae Wilson*, l. 273.

8
Thus with the year
Seasons return, but not to me returns
Day, or the sweet approach of ev'n or morn,
Or sight of vernal bloom, or summer's rose,
Or flocks, or herds, or human face divine;
But cloud instead, and ever-during dark, . . .
And wisdom at one entrance quite shut out.
MILTON, *Paradise Lost*. Bk. iii, l. 40.

O, loss of sight, of thee I most complain!
Blind among enemies, O worse than chains,
Dungeons, or beggary, or decrepit age!
MILTON, *Samson Agonistes*, l. 67.

O dark, dark, dark, amid the blaze of noon,
Irrecoverably dark, total eclipse
Without all hope of day!
MILTON, *Samson Agonistes*, l. 80.

9
When I consider how my light is spent,
E'er half my days, in this dark world and wide, . . .
Doth God exact day-labour, light denied,
I fondly ask.
MILTON, *Sonnets*. No. xvi.

These eyes, though clear
To outward view, of blemish or of spot,
Bereft of light, their seeing have forgot,
Nor to their idle orbs doth sight appear
Of sun, or moon, or star, throughout the year,
Or man, or woman. Yet I argue not
Against Heaven's hand or will, nor bate a jot
Of heart or hope; but still bear up and steer
Right onward.
MILTON, *To Mr. Cyriack Skinner.*

10
He from thick films shall purge the visual ray,
And on the sightless eyeball pour the day.
POPE, *Messiah*, l. 39.

11
He that is strucken blind can not forget
The precious treasure of his eyesight lost.
SHAKESPEARE, *Romeo and Juliet*. Act i, sc. 1, l. 238.

12
A blind man is a poor man, and blind a poor man is;
For the former seeth no man, and the latter no man sees.
FRIEDRICH VON LOGAU, *Sinngedichte*. (Longfellow, tr.)

BLISS

See also Delight, Joy

13
To bliss unknown my lofty soul aspires,
My lot unequal to my vast desires.
JOHN ARBUTHNOT, *Gnothi Seaton*, l. 3.

14
The bliss e'en of a moment still is bliss.
JOANNA BAILLIE, *The Beacon*. Act i, sc. 2.

One moment may with bliss repay
Unnumbered hours of pain.
THOMAS CAMPBELL, *The Ritter Bann*, l. 173.

15
It was a dream of perfect bliss,
Too beautiful to last.
T. H. BAYLY, *It Was a Dream.*

Thus ever fade my fairy dreams of bliss.
BYRON, *The Corsair*. Canto i, st. 14.

16
All indistinctly apprehend a bliss,
On which the soul may rest; the hearts of all
Yearn after it.
DANTE, *Purgatorio*. Canto xvii, l. 124. (Cary, tr.)

17
Is bliss, then, such abyss
I must not put my foot amiss
For fear I spoil my shoe?
EMILY DICKINSON, *Poems*. Pt. i, No. 135.

1
The hues of bliss more brightly glow,
Chastis'd by sabler tints of woe.
THOMAS GRAY, *Ode on the Pleasure Arising from Vicissitude*, l. 41.

2
And my heart rocked its babe of bliss,
And soothed its child of air,
With something 'twixt a song and kiss,
To keep it nestling there.
GERALD MASSEY, *On a Wedding Day*. St. 3.

3
But such a sacred and home-felt delight,
Such sober certainty of waking bliss,
I never heard till now.
MILTON, *Comus*, l. 262.

The sum of earthly bliss.
MILTON, *Paradise Lost*. Bk. viii, l. 522.

4
Some place the bliss in action, some in ease,
Those call it pleasure, and contentment these.
POPE, *Essay on Man*. Epis. iv, l. 21.

Condition, circumstance, is not the thing;
Bliss is the same in subject or in king.
POPE, *Essay on Man*. Epis. iv, l. 57.

5
Man looks at his own bliss, considers it,
Weighs it with curious fingers; and 'tis gone.
WILLIAM WATSON, *Epigrams*.

6
The spider's most attenuated thread
Is cord, is cable, to man's tender tie
On earthly bliss; it breaks at every breeze.
YOUNG, *Night Thoughts*. Night i, l. 178.

BLOCKHEAD, see Fool

BLOOD

7
The blood is the life.
Old Testament: Deuteronomy, xii, 23.

Blood is a juice of rarest quality. (Blut ist ein ganz besondrer Saft.)
GOETHE, *Faust*. Pt. i, sc. 4, l. 214.

8
Something will come of this. I hope it mayn't be human gore.
DICKENS, *Barnaby Rudge*. Ch. 4.

9
What coast knows not our blood? (Quæ caret ora cruore nostro?)
HORACE, *Odes*. Bk. ii, ode. 1, l. 36.

10
Human blood is all of a color.
THOMAS FULLER, *Gnomologia*. No. 2560.

11
And in the midst, 'mong thousand heraldries,
And twilight saints, and dim emblazonings,
A shielded scutcheon blush'd with blood of queens and kings.
KEATS, *The Eve of St. Agnes*. St. 24.

12
His blood be on us and on our children.
New Testament: Matthew, xxvii, 25.

Blood will have blood.
SOUTHEY, *Madoc in Wales*. Sec. vii, l. 45.

See also under RETRIBUTION.

13
First Moloch, horrid King, besmear'd with blood.
MILTON, *Paradise Lost*. Bk. i, l. 392.

14
I am in blood
Stepp'd in so far that, should I wade no more,
Returning were as tedious as go o'er.
SHAKESPEARE, *Macbeth*. Act iii, sc. 4, l. 136.

Yet who would have thought the old man to have had so much blood in him?
SHAKESPEARE, *Macbeth*. Act v, sc. 1, l. 44.

15
A compact sealed in blood. (In sanguine fœdus.)
UNKNOWN. A Latin proverb.

For blood in the sense of birth, *see* ANCESTRY.

II—Blood Is Thicker Than Water

16
For naturally blood will aye of kind
Draw unto blood, where he may it find.
JOHN LYDGATE, *Troy Book*. Bk. iii, l. 2071. (1412)

17
No distance breaks the tie of blood;
Brothers are brothers evermore.
JOHN KEBLE, *The Christian Year: Second Sunday After Trinity*.

Yet, still, from either beach,
The voice of blood shall reach.
ALLSTON, *America to Great Britain*.

18
Blood is thicker than water.
JOHN RAY, *English Proverbs*. (1670)

Blood is thicker than water.
COMMODORE JOSIAH TATTNALL, *Despatch*, to U. S. Secretary of the Navy, justifying assistance to the British fleet in the Pei-ho, June, 1859.

Bluid is thicker than water.
SCOTT, *Guy Mannering*. Ch. 38.

19
Hands across the sea,
Feet on English ground,
The old blood is bold blood, the wide world round.
BYRON WEBBER, *Hands Across the Sea*.

BLUNDER, see Error; Mistake

BLUSHING

20
Now the red wins upon her cheek;
Now white with crimson closes
In desperate struggle—so to speak,
A War of Roses.
THOMAS BAILEY ALDRICH, *On Her Blushing*.

21
The very sight of his scarlet coat made me blush as red as a turkey-cock.
BEAUMONT AND FLETCHER, *Faithful Friends*. Act iii, sc. 2.

22
Girls blush, sometimes, because they are alive,

Half wishing they were dead to save the shame.
The sudden blush devours them, neck and brow;
They have drawn too near the fire of life, like gnats,
And flare up bodily, wings and all.
E. B. BROWNING, *Aurora Leigh*. Bk. ii, l. 732.

1
So sweet the blush of bashfulness,
E'en pity scarce can wish it less!
BYRON, *The Bride of Abydos*. Canto i, st. 8.

2
I would rather see a young man blush than turn pale. (*Τῶν δὲ νέων χαίρειν τοῖς ἐρυθριῶσι μᾶλλον ὃ τοῖς ὠχριῶσι.*)
MARCUS CATO. (PLUTARCH, *Lives: Marcus Cato*. Ch. ix, sec. 4.)

Better a blush on the cheek than a spot in the heart.
CERVANTES, *Don Quixote*. Pt. ii, ch. 44.

3
And of his own thought he wex all reed.
CHAUCER, *The Shipmannes Tale*, l. 111.

"Nay, nay," quod she, and waxed as red as rose.
CHAUCER, *Troilus and Criseyde*. Bk. ii, l. 1256. (c. 1374)

His blood began to change, and he woxe red as a rose.
WILLIAM CAXTON, *Jason*, 156. (c. 1477)

Red as a rose is she.
S. T. COLERIDGE, *Ancient Mariner*. Pt. i, st. 9.

The rising blushes, which her cheek o'er-spread,
Are opening roses in the lily's bed.
JOHN GAY, *Dione*. Act ii, sc. 3.

While, mantling on the maiden's cheek,
Young roses kindled into thought.
THOMAS MOORE, *Evenings in Greece*. Evening ii, Song 2.

And ever and anon, with rosy red
The bashful blood her snowy cheeks did dye.
SPENSER, *Faerie Queene*. Bk. ii, canto ix, st. 41.

4
I always take blushing either for a sign of guilt or ill-breeding.
CONGREVE, *The Way of the World*. Act i, sc. 9.

5
We griev'd, we sigh'd, we wept; we never blush'd before.
ABRAHAM COWLEY, *A Discourse by Way of Vision Concerning the Government of Oliver Cromwell*. Poem ii, st. 7. The line was quoted in the House of Commons by Sir Robert Peel, replying to an attack by William Cobbett.

6
I pity bashful men, who feel the pain
Of fancied scorn and undeserv'd disdain,
And bear the marks, upon a blushing face,
Of needless shame, and self-impos'd disgrace.
COWPER, *Conversation*, l. 347.

Forgot the blush that virgin fears impart
To modest cheeks, and borrow'd one from art.
COWPER, *Expostulation*, l. 47.

7
The question about everything [with Mr. Podsnap] was, would it bring a blush to the cheek of a young person?
DICKENS, *Our Mutual Friend*. Bk. i, ch. 11.

Mr. Phunky, blushing into the very whites of his eyes, tried to look as if he didn't know that everybody was gazing at him: a thing which no man ever succeeded in doing yet, or, in all reasonable probability, ever will.
DICKENS, *Pickwick Papers*. Ch. 34.

8
Courage! that is the hue of virtue. (*Θάρρει, τοιοῦτόν ἐστι τῆς ἀρετῆς τὸ χρῶμα.*)
DIOGENES, to a young man who blushed. (DIOGENES LAERTIUS, *Diogenes*. Sec. 54.)

Blushing is the colour of virtue.
MATHEW HENRY, *Commentaries; Jeremiah*, iii.

The man that blushes is not quite a brute.
YOUNG, *Night Thoughts*. Night vii, l. 496.

When guilty men begin to blush, it is a sign of grace.
UNKNOWN, *School of Slovenrie*, 96. (1605)

9
A blush is no language: only a dubious flag-signal which may mean either of two contradictories.
GEORGE ELIOT, *Daniel Deronda*. Bk. v, ch. 35.

10
The blush is beautiful, but it is sometimes inconvenient. (Bello è il rossore, ma è incommodo qualche volta.)
GOLDONI, *Pamela*. Act i, sc. 3.

11
To read my book, the virgin shy
May blush while Brutus standeth by;
But when he's gone, read through what's writ,
And never stain a cheek for it.
ROBERT HERRICK, *On His Book*.

The modest fan was lifted up no more,
And virgins smil'd at what they blush'd before.
POPE, *Essay on Criticism*. Pt. ii, l. 342.

A virtue but at second-hand;
They blush because they understand.
SWIFT, *Cadenus and Vanessa*.

12
Men blush less for their crimes than for their weaknesses and vanity. (Les hommes rougissent moins de leur crimes que de leurs faiblesses et de leur vanité.)
LA BRUYÈRE, *Les Caractères*. Pt. ii.

13
Innocence is not accustomed to blush. (L'innocence à rougir n'est point accoutumée.)
MOLIÈRE, *Don Garcie de Navarre*. Act ii, sc. 5.

Whoso blushes is guilty already; true innocence is ashamed of nothing. (Quiconque rougit est déjà coupable; la vraie innocence n'a honte de rien.)
ROUSSEAU, *Émile*. Bk. iv.

14
Rather bring the blood into a man's cheek

than let it out of his body. (Suffundere malis hominis sanguinèm, quam effundere.)
TERTULLIAN, *Apologetics*. Quoted by MONTAIGNE, *Essays*, bk. i, ch. 15.

1
Blushes become a pale face, but the blush one feigns is the one that profits. (Decet alba quidem pudor ora, si simules, prodest.)
OVID, *Amores*. Bk. i, eleg. viii, l. 35.

2
From every blush that kindles in thy cheeks,
Ten thousand little loves and graces spring
To revel in the roses.
NICHOLAS ROWE, *Tamerlane*. Act i, sc. 1.

3
I will go wash;
And when my face is fair, you shall perceive
Whether I blush or no.
SHAKESPEARE, *Coriolanus*. Act i, sc. 9, l. 68.

4
Now, if you can blush and cry, "guilty," cardinal,
You'll show a little honesty.
SHAKESPEARE, *Henry VIII*. Act iii, sc. 2, l. 305.

Lay by all nicety and prolixious blushes,
That banish what they sue for.
SHAKESPEARE, *Measure for Measure*. Act ii, sc. 4, l. 162.

5
Her blush is guiltiness, not modesty.
SHAKESPEARE, *Much Ado About Nothing*. Act iv, sc. 1, l. 43.

By noting of the lady, I have mark'd
A thousand blushing apparitions
To start into her face, a thousand innocent shames
In angel whiteness beat away those blushes.
SHAKESPEARE, *Much Ado About Nothing*. Act iv, sc. i, l. 160.

Her pure, and eloquent blood
Spoke in her cheeks, and so distinctly wrought,
That one might almost say, her body thought.
JOHN DONNE, *Of the Progress of the Soul*. Pt. ii, l. 244. (*Written by Occasion of the Religious Death of Mistress Elizabeth Drury*.)

6
Yet will she blush, here be it said,
To hear her secrets so bewray'd.
SHAKESPEARE [?], *Passionate Pilgrim*, l. 351.

Thou know'st the mask of night is on my face;
Else would a maiden blush bepaint my cheek.
SHAKESPEARE, *Romeo and Juliet*. Act ii, sc. 2, l. 85.

7
What, canst thou say all this and never blush?
SHAKESPEARE, *Titus Andronicus*. Act v, sc. 1, l. 121.

And bid the cheek be ready with a blush
Modest as morning when she coldly eyes
The youthful Phœbus.
SHAKESPEARE, *Troilus and Cressida*. Act i, sc. 3, l. 228.

Come, quench your blushes and present yourself
That which you are, mistress o' the feast.
SHAKESPEARE, *Winter's Tale*. Act iv, sc. 4, l. 67.

8
He blushes: all is well. (Erubuit: salva res est.)
TERENCE, *Adelphi*, l. 643. (Act iv, sc. 5.)

9
Blushes are badges of imperfection.
WYCHERLEY, *Love in a Wood*. Act i, sc. 1.

BOASTING

See also Praise: Self-Praise

10
Youth, thy words need an army.
AGESILAÜS II, to a youth talking boastfully. (PLUTARCH, *Life*.) Also told of Lysander.

Friend, thy words need an army and a treasure.
AGIS II, of an ambitious plan to free Greece. (PLUTARCH, *Laconic Apothegms*.)

The phrase would be more german to the matter, if we could carry cannon by our sides.
SHAKESPEARE, *Hamlet*. Act v, sc. 2, l. 166.

11
You were best take heed the next time you run away, how you look back.
JULIUS CÆSAR, to a soldier, boasting of a wound in the face. (FRANCIS BACON, *Apothegms*, No. 41.)

A vaunter and a liar, all is one.
CHAUCER, *Troilus and Criseyde*. Bk. iii, l. 309.

12
Great boast and small roost.
ROBERT COPLAND, *Spyttel House*, l. 978. (c. 1532)

There was great boast and little roast.
SIR JOHN HARINGTON, *Orlando Furioso*. Bk. xxv, st. 66.

13
To compare Demosthenes to me is like comparing a sow to Minerva. ('Εμὲ Δημοσθένης, ἡ ὖς τὴν 'Αθηνᾶν.)
DEMADES. (PLUTARCH, *Lives: Demosthenes*. Sec. 11.)

14
Sooth'd with the sound, the king grew vain;
Fought all his battles o'er again;
And thrice he routed all his foes, and thrice he slew the slain.
DRYDEN, *Alexander's Feast*, l. 66.

16
Cunning egotism. If I cannot brag of knowing something, then I brag of not knowing it. At any rate, brag.
EMERSON, *Journals*, 1866.

17
Yet if thou sin in wine or wantonness,
Boast not thereof; nor make thy shame thy glory.
GEORGE HERBERT, *The Church-Porch*. St. 9.

18
Ye deedless boasters!
HOMER, *Odyssey*. Bk. i, l. 470. (Pope, tr.)

What will this boaster produce worthy of such inflated language? (Quid dignum tanto feret hic promissor hiatu?)
HORACE, *Ars Poetica*, l. 138.

See also WORD AND DEED.

1
Every other enjoyment malice may destroy; every other panegyric envy may withhold; but no human power can deprive the boaster of his own encomiums.

Samuel Johnson, *The Rambler*. No. 193.

2
If you stop to consider the work you have done
And to boast what your labour is worth, dear,
Angels may come for you, Willie, my son,
But you'll never be wanted on Earth, dear!

Rudyard Kipling, *Mary's Son*.

3
The empty vessel giveth a greater sound than the full barrel.

John Lyly, *Euphues*, p. 15. (1579)

Empty barrels make the most noise.

E. M. Wright, *Rustic Speech*, 171

4
If you would keep your ears from jeers,
These things keep meekly hid:
Myself and me, or my and mine,
And how I do or did.

W. E. Norris, *Thirlby Hall*. Vol. i, p. 315.

5
A man destitute of courage, but boasting of his glorious achievements, imposes on strangers, but is the derision of those who know him.

Phædrus, *Fables*. Bk. i, fab. 11, l. 1.

6
He changes a fly into an elephant.

John Ray, *English Proverbs*, 75.

7
He who blushes at riding in a rattle-trap, will boast when he rides in style. (Qui sordido vehiculo erubescit, pretioso gloriabitur.)

Seneca, *Epistulæ ad Lucilium*. Epis. 87, sec. 4.

8
Who knows himself a braggart,
Let him fear this, for it will come to pass
That every braggart shall be found an ass.

Shakespeare, *All's Well that Ends Well*. Act iv, sc. 3, l. 369. *See also under* Ass.

To such as boasting show their scars
A mock is due.

Shakespeare, *Troilus and Cressida*, iv, 5, 290.

Show them the unaching scars which I should hide.

Shakespeare, *Coriolanus*, ii, 2, 152.

9
It out-herods Herod.

Shakespeare, *Hamlet*. Act iii, sc. 2, l. 16.
Shakespeare alludes, not to any villainy, but to the vain rantings of Herod in the old mystery plays.

I am the greatest above degree
That is, or was, or ever shall be;
The sun it dare not shine on me
And I bid him go down.

Unknown, *The Offering of the Three Kings*.
It is Herod speaking.

10
I am not yet of Percy's mind, the Hotspur of the north; he that kills me some six or seven dozen of Scots at a breakfast, washes his hands, and says to his wife "Fie upon this quiet life! I want work." "O my sweet Harry," says she, "how many hast thou killed to-day?" "Give my roan horse a drench," says he; and answers "Some fourteen," an hour after; "a trifle, a trifle."

Shakespeare, *I Henry IV*. Act ii, sc. 4, l. 114.

Here's a large mouth, indeed,
That spits forth death, and mountains, rocks, and seas;
Talks as familiarly of roaring lions,
As maids of thirteen do of puppy-dogs!

Shakespeare, *King John*. Act ii, sc. 2, l. 457.

O, I could play the woman with mine eyes
And braggart with my tongue.

Shakespeare, *Macbeth*. Act iv, sc. 3, l. 231.

11
Faith, that's as well said as if I had said it myself.

Swift, *Polite Conversation*. Dial. ii.

12
A good name is seldom got by giving it one's self; and women, no more than honour, are compassed by bragging.

Wycherley, *The Country Wife*. Act i.

13
Where boasting ends, there dignity begins.

Young, *Night Thoughts*. Night viii, l. 509.

BOAT AND BOATING, see Ship

BOBOLINK

14
When Nature had made all her birds,
With no more cares to think on,
She gave a rippling laugh and out
There flew a Bobolinkon.

C. P. Cranch, *The Bobolinks*.

15
The crack-brained bobolink courts his crazy mate,
Poised on a bulrush tipsy with his weight.

O. W. Holmes, *Spring*.

16
Merrily swinging on brier and weed,
Near to the nest of his little dame,
Over the mountain-side or mead,
Robert of Lincoln is telling his name:
Bob-o'-link, bob-o'-link,
Spink, spank, spink;
Snug and safe is this nest of ours,
Hidden among the summer flowers.
Chee, chee, chee.

Bryant, *Robert of Lincoln*.

17
There were Bobolincon, Wadolincon, Winterseeble, Conquedle,—
A livelier set was never led by tabor, pipe, or fiddle,—
Crying, "Phew, shew, Wadolincon, see, see, Bobolincon, . . .
Bobbing in the clover there—see, see, see!"

Wilson Flagg, *The O'Lincoln Family*.

1
Bobolink! still may thy gladness
Take from me all taint of sadness.
THOMAS HILL, *The Bobolink.*

Why art thou but a nest of gloom
While the bobolinks are singing?
W. D. HOWELLS, *The Bobolinks Are Singing.*

2
June's bridesman, poet o' the year,
Gladness on wings, the bobolink, is here;
Half-hid in tip-top apple-blooms he swings,
Or climbs against the breeze with quiverin' wings,
Or, givin' way to 't in a mock despair,
Runs down, a brook o' laughter, thru the air.
J. R. LOWELL, *Biglow Papers.* Ser. ii, No. 6.

BODY

See also Mind and Body; Soul and Body

3
I built a house of sticks and mud,
And God built one of flesh and blood.
How queer that was, how strange that is,
That my poor house should shelter His. . . .
And yet my house of sticks and clay
Is standing sturdy still today;
While God's house in a narrow pit
Is rotting where men buried it.
N. D. ANDERSON, *The Two Houses.*

4
Can anyone foretell in what condition his body will be, I do not say a year hence, but this evening? (An id exploratum cuiquam potest esse, quomodo se hoc habiturum sit corpus non dico ad annum, sed ad vesperum?)
CICERO, *De Finibus.* Bk. ii, ch. 28, sec. 92.

Every body is subject to change, so comes it to pass that every body is mortal. (Omne corpus mutabile est; . . . ita efficitur ut omne corpus mortale est.)
CICERO, *De Natura Deorum.* Bk. iii, sec. 12.

Who can put trust in strength of body? (Qui poterit corporis firmitate confidere?)
CICERO, *Tusculanarum Disputationum.* Bk. v, ch. 14.

5
But I keep under my body, and bring it into subjection.
New Testament: I Corinthians, ix, 27.

6
Never a slave but in body, now has she won freedom for her body, too. (Ἡ πρὶν ἐοῦσα μόνῳ τῷ σώματι δούλη, καὶ τῷ σώματι νῦν εὗρεν ἐλευθερίην.)
DAMASCIUS, *Epitaph.* (*Greek Anthology.* Bk. vii, epig. 553.)

7
Our bodies do not fit us, but caricature and satirize us. Man is physically as well as metaphysically a thing of shreds and patches, borrowed unequally from good and bad ancestors, and a misfit from the start.
EMERSON, *Conduct of Life: Beauty.*

What a plastic little creature he is! so shifty, so adaptive! his body a chest of tools.
EMERSON, *Letters and Social Aims: Resources.*

The body of man is the type after which a dwelling house is built.
EMERSON, *Representative Men: Montaigne.*

The human body is the magazine of inventions, the patent office, where are the models from which every hint is taken. All the tools and engines on earth are only extensions of its limbs and senses.
EMERSON, *Society and Solitude: Works and Days.*

The body borrows the elements of its blood from the whole world, and the mind its belief.
EMERSON, *Journals,* 1864.

8
Since the body is the pipe through which we tap all the succors and virtues of the material world, it is certain that a sound body must be at the root of any excellence in manners and actions.
EMERSON, *Lectures and Biographical Studies: Aristocracy. See also under* HEALTH.

9
No more was seen the human form divine.
HOMER, *Odyssey.* Bk. x, l. 278. (Pope, tr.)

Human face divine.
MILTON, *Paradise Lost.* Bk. iii, l. 44.

10
I believe in the flesh and the body, which is worthy of worship—to see a perfect human body unveiled causes a sense of worship. . . . Increase of physical beauty is attended by increase of soul beauty. The soul is the higher even by gazing on beauty. Let me be fleshly perfect.
RICHARD JEFFERIES, *The Story of My Heart.*

The body is the temple of the Holy Spirit, and is the means whereby alone the soul can establish relations with the universe.
HARRY ROBERTS, *Letter.* (*New Statesman,* 29 Aug., 1931.)

11
My poor gentlemanlike carcass.
BEN JONSON, *Every Man in His Humour.* Act iv, sc. 5.

12
Death alone discloses how insignificant are the puny bodies of men. (Mors sola fatetur quantula sint hominum corpuscula.)
JUVENAL, *Satires.* Sat. x, l. 172.

13
Whether our bodies are burnt on the pyre or decompose with time matters not at all: nature finds room for them all in her gentle arms. (Tabesne cadavera solvat An rogus, haud refert: placido natura receptat.)
LUCAN, *De Bello Civili.* Bk. vii, l. 809.

To what vulture shall this carcass be given? (Cujus vulturis hoc erit cadaver?)
MARTIAL, *Epigrams.* Bk. vi, epig. 62.

14
For the body at best
Is a bundle of aches,

Longing for rest;
It cries when it wakes.
EDNA ST. VINCENT MILLAY, *Moriturus.*

1
The body is an affliction of the soul; it is Hell, Fate, a burden, a necessity, a strong chain, and a tormenting punishment. (Σῶμα, πάθος ψυχῆς, ἅδης, μοῖρ', ἄχθος, ἀνάγκη, καὶ δεσμὸς κρατερός, καὶ κόλασις βασάνων.)
PALLADAS. (*Greek Anthology*. Bk. x, epig. 88.)

2
She whose body's young and cool
Has no need of dancing-school.
DOROTHY PARKER, *Salome's Dancing Lesson.*

3
Our vile body.
New Testament: Philippians, iii, 21.

4
Pocahontas' body, lovely as a poplar, sweet as a red haw in November or a pawpaw in May, did she wonder? does she remember? . . . in the dust, in the cool tombs?
CARL SANDBURG, *Cool Tombs.*

5
Would you be free from the restraint of your body? Live in it as if you were about to leave it. (Vis adversus hoc corpus liber esse? Tanquam migraturus habita.)
SENECA, *Epistulæ ad Lucilium*. Epis. lxx, sec. 17.

6
Our bodies are our gardens, to which our wills are gardeners.
SHAKESPEARE, *Othello*. Act i, sc. 3, l. 323.

7
Ah beautiful passionate body
That never has ached with a heart!
SWINBURNE, *Dolores*. St. 11.

8
The beautiful body on the oblong bed
Beautiful as a sword, that has for hilt
Arms whitely crossed behind a silver head.
WINIFRED WELLES, *Design for a Blade.*

9
If anything is sacred the human body is sacred.
WALT WHITMAN, *I Sing the Body Electric*. Sec. 6.

The man's body is sacred and the woman's body is sacred.
WHITMAN, *I Sing the Body Electric*. Sec. 6.

Have you ever loved the body of a woman?
Have you ever loved the body of a man?
Do you not see that these are exactly the same to all in all nations and times all over the earth?
WHITMAN, *I Sing the Body Electric*. Sec. 6.

Sacred is the dust
Of this heaven-labour'd form, erect, divine!
This heaven-assum'd majestic robe of earth.
YOUNG, *Night Thoughts*, Night iii, l. 191.

BOLDNESS

I—Boldness: Its Virtues

10
Push on, pursue, in no wise faint of foot!
(Ἕλα, δίωκε, μή τι μαλκίων ποδί.)
ÆSCHYLUS, *Fragments*. Frag. 185.

Not for laggards doth a contest wait. (Ἀγὼν γὰρ ἄνδρας οὐ μένει λελειμένους.)
ÆSCHYLUS, *Glaucus of Potniæ*. Frag. 21.

11
What action is to the orator, that is boldness to the public man; first, second, third.
FRANCIS BACON, *De Augmentis Scientiarum: Audacia.*

Boldness in business is the first, second, and third thing.
THOMAS FULLER, *Gnomologia*. No. 1006.

12
Dare, will, keep silence. (Oser, vouloir, se taire.)
WILLIAM BOLITHO, *Twelve Against the Gods*, p. 190. "The inscription over the little side door where Cagliostro dangled the key."

13
He most prevails who nobly dares.
WILLIAM BROOME, *Courage in Love.*

14
He ruled them—man may rule the worst,
By ever daring to be first.
BYRON, *The Siege of Corinth*. St. 12.

15
There are periods when the principles of experience need to be modified, . . . when in truth to *dare* is the highest wisdom.
WILLIAM ELLERY CHANNING, *Works*, p. 641.

16
'Tis boldness, boldness, does the deed in the Court.
GEORGE CHAPMAN, *Monsieur d'Olive*. Act iii, sc. 1.

17
He which that nothing undertaketh,
Nothing ne achieveth, be he looth or dere.
CHAUCER, *Troilus and Criseyde*. Bk. ii, l. 807. (c. 1374)

For he who naught dare undertake,
By right he shall no profit take.
JOHN GOWER, *Confessio Amantis*. Bk. iv, l. 319.

Naught venture naught have.
JOHN HEYWOOD, *Proverbs*. Pt. i, ch. 11. (1546)

He that nothing ventures, hath neither horse nor mule, (says Solomon): He who adventureth too much (said Echephron) loseth both horse and mule, answered Malchon.
RABELAIS, *Works*. Bk. i, ch. 33.

18
The gods look with favor on superior daring.
CIVILIS, to his legions. (TACITUS, *History*. Bk. iv, sec. 17.)

Even God lends a hand to honest boldness. (Τόλμῃ δικαίᾳ καὶ θεὸς συλλαμβάνει.)
MENANDER, *Fragments*. No. 572.

God himself favors the bold. (Audentes deus ipse juvat.)
OVID, *Metamorphoses*. Bk. x, l. 586.

Fortune favors the bold, *see under* FORTUNE.

19
To dare, and again dare, and forever dare! (De l'audace, et encore de l'audace, et toujours de l'audace!)
GEORGE JACQUES DANTON, *Speech*, to the Legislative Committee of General Defence,

2 Sept., 1792, when the tocsin gave the signal for the slaughter of the royalists who crowded the prisons of Paris. The entire sentence is: "Legislators! it is not the alarm-cannon that you hear: it is the *pas-de-charge* against our enemies. To conquer them, to hurl them back, what do we require? To dare, and again dare, and forever dare!" (*Le Moniteur: Hist. Parl.*, xvii, 347. CARLYLE, *French Revolution*. Vol. iii, bk. i, ch. 4.)

1
Finite to fail, but infinite to venture.
EMILY DICKINSON, *Poems*, p. 52.

2
And though he stumbles in a full career,
Yet rashness is a better fault than fear.
DRYDEN, *Tyrannic Love: Prologue*, l. 20.

Boldness has genius, power, and magic in it.
GOETHE, *Faust: Prelude at the Theatre*, l. 305. John Anster, tr. *See* p. 2298g:3.

4
He either fears his fate too much,
Or his deserts are small,
That dares not put it to the touch,
To gain or lose it all.
JAMES GRAHAM, MARQUIS OF MONTROSE, *I'll Never Love Thee More*.

5
On the neck of the young man sparkles no gem so gracious as enterprise.
HAFIZ. (EMERSON, *Conduct of Life: Power.*)

6
Towards great persons use respective boldness.
GEORGE HERBERT, *The Church-Porch*. St. 43.

Be not too bold with your betters.
JAMES HOWELL, *Proverbs*, 3. (1659)

7
Tender-handed stroke a nettle,
And it stings you for your pains;
Grasp it like a man of mettle,
And it soft as silk remains.
'Tis the same with common natures;
Use 'em kindly, they rebel;
But be rough as nutmeg-graters,
And the rogues obey you well.
AARON HILL, *Verses Written on a Window in Scotland*.

8
A decent boldness ever meets with friends.
HOMER, *Odyssey*. Bk. vii, l. 67. (Pope, tr.)

9
Begin, be bold, and venture to be wise. (Sapere aude; Incipe!)
HORACE, *Epistles*. Bk. i, epis. 2, l. 40.

10
By boldness great fears are concealed. (Audendo magnus tegitur timor.)
LUCAN, *De Bello Civili*. Bk. iv, l. 702.

He died . . . as bold as brass.
GEORGE PARKER, *Life's Painter*, 162.

11
Daring leads a man to heaven and to hell. (Τόλμα καὶ εἰς ἀΐδαν καὶ ἐς οὐρανὸν ἄνδρα κομίζει.)
NICANDER OF COLOPHON, *Epitaph*. (*Greek Antholoigy*. Bk. vii, epig, 529.)

12
The bold persist even against misfortune; the timorous and abject yield to despair through fear alone.
PLOTIUS FIRMUS, to Emperor Otho. (TACITUS, *History*. Bk. ii, sec. 46.)

13
What though strength fails? Boldness is certain to win praise. In mighty enterprises, it is enough even to have willed success. (Quod si deficiant vires, audacia certe Laus erit: in magnis et voluisse sat est.)
PROPERTIUS, *Elegies*. Bk. ii, eleg. 10, l. 5.

14
No one reaches a high position without boldness. (Nemo timendo ad summum pervenit locum.)
PUBLILIUS SYRUS, *Sententiæ*. No. 463.

15
Vogue la galère! (On with the galley! Row on, whatever happens! Come what may!)
RABELAIS, *Works*. Bk. i, ch. 40. MOLIÈRE, *Le Tartuffe*. Act i, sc. 1. MONTAIGNE, *Essays*.

My fearful trust "en vogant la galère."
SIR THOMAS WYATT, *The Lover Prayeth Venus*.

16
Boldness is a bulwark. (Audacia pro muro habetur.)
SALLUST, *Bellum Catilinæ*. Ch. lviii, sec. 17.

17
"Dash! and through with it!"—That's the better watchword.
SCHILLER, *Die Piccolomini*. Act i, sc. 2. (Coleridge, tr.)

18
Fortune fears the brave, the cowardly overwhelms. (Fortuna fortes metuit, ignavos premit.)
SENECA, *Medea*, l. 159.

19
Boldness be my friend!
Arm me, audacity, from head to foot!
SHAKESPEARE, *Cymbeline*. Act i, sc. 6, l. 18.

Some enterprise That hath a stomach in 't.
SHAKESPEARE, *Hamlet*. Act i, sc. 1, l. 99.

20
Fearless minds climb soonest unto crowns.
SHAKESPEARE, *III Henry VI*. Act iv, sc. 7, l. 62.

Be stirring as the time; be fire with fire;
Threaten the threat'ner and outface the brow
Of bragging horror: so shall inferior eyes,
That borrow their behaviours from the great,
Grow great by your example and put on
The dauntless spirit of resolution.
SHAKESPEARE, *King John*. Act v, sc. 1, l. 48.

Show boldness and aspiring confidence.
SHAKESPEARE, *King John*. Act v, sc. 1, l. 56.

21
I dare do all that may become a man;
Who dares do more is none.
SHAKESPEARE, *Macbeth*. Act i, sc. 7, l. 46.

What man dare, I dare.
SHAKESPEARE, *Macbeth*. Act iii, sc. 4, l. 99.

1
A jewel in a ten-times-barr'd-up chest
Is a bold spirit in a loyal breast.
SHAKESPEARE, *Richard II*. Act i, sc. 1, l. 180.

2
Who is so faint, that dares not be so bold
To touch the fire, the weather being cold?
SHAKESPEARE, *Venus and Adonis*, l. 401.

Boldness comes to me now and brings me heart.
SHAKESPEARE, *Troilus and Cressida*, iii, 2, 121.

3
And as she lookt about, she did behold
How over that same door was likewise writ,
Be bold, be bold, and everywhere *Be bold,*
That much she mus'd, yet could not construe it
By any riddling skill or common wit.
At last she spied at that room's upper end
Another iron door, on which was writ,
Be not too bold; whereto though she did bend
Her earnest mind, yet wist not what it might intend.
SPENSER, *Faerie Queene*. Bk. iii, canto xi, st. 54.

One would say he had read the inscription on the gates of Busyrane,—"Be bold;" and on the second gate,—"Be bold, be bold, and evermore be bold;" and then again had paused well at the third gate,—"Be not too bold."
EMERSON, *Representative Men: Plato*.

Write on your doors the saying wise and old,
"Be bold! be bold!" and everywhere, "Be bold;
Be not too bold!" Yet better the excess
Than the defect; better the more than less;
Better like Hector in the field to die,
Than like a perfumed Paris turn and fly.
LONGFELLOW, *Morituri Salutamus*, l. 100.

4
If we must fall, we should boldly meet our fate. (Si cadere necesse est, occurendum discrimini.)
TACITUS, *History*. Bk. i, sec. 33.

In rashness there is hope. (Ex temeritate spes.)
TACITUS, *History*. Bk. iii, sec. 26.

The only hope of safety was in boldness. (Unam in audacia spem salutis.)
TACITUS, *History*. Bk. iv, sec. 49.

5
I drink, I huff, I strut, look big and stare,
And all this I can do, because I dare.
GEORGE VILLIERS, *The Rehearsal*.

I cowhearted? I'm as bold as a lion.
UNKNOWN, *Terence Made English*, 84. (1694)

6
Yet a rich guerdon waits on minds that dare,
If aught be in them of immortal seed.
WORDSWORTH, *Miscellaneous Sonnets*. Pt. ii, No. 4.

II—Boldness: Its Faults

7
What first? *Boldness;* What second and third? *Boldness.* And yet boldness is a child of ignorance and baseness, far inferior to other parts.
FRANCIS BACON, *Essays: Of Boldness*.

Boldness is an ill keeper of promise.
FRANCIS BACON, *Essays: Of Boldness*.

Great boldness is seldom without some absurdity.
FRANCIS BACON, *Essays: Of Boldness*.

Boldness is ever blind, for it seeth not dangers and inconveniences. Therefore, it is ill in counsel, good in execution.
FRANCIS BACON, *Essays: Of Boldness*.

8
He has no hearing on the prudent side.
COWPER, *The Progress of Error*, l. 549.

9
Bold knaves thrive, without one grain of sense,
But good men starve for want of impudence.
DRYDEN, *Constantine the Great: Epilogue*.

10
In conversation boldness now bears sway;
But know, that nothing can so foolish be
As empty boldness.
GEORGE HERBERT, *The Church-Porch*. St. 35.

11
Rashness is not always fortunate. (Non semper temeritas est felix.)
LIVY, *History*. Bk. xxx, ch. 42.

Rashness brings success to few, misfortune to many. (Paucis temeritas est bono, multis malo.)
PHÆDRUS, *Fables*. Bk. v, fab. iv, l. 1.

12
And dar'st thou then
To beard the lion in his den,
The Douglas in his hall?
SCOTT, *Marmion*, canto vi, st. 14.

13
You call honourable boldness impudent sauciness.
SHAKESPEARE, *II Henry IV*. Act ii, sc. 1, l. 134.

14
A bold, bad man!
SPENSER, *The Faerie Queene*. Bk. i, canto 1, st. 37. (1590)

This bold bad man.
SHAKESPEARE, *Henry VIII*. Act ii, sc. 2, l. 44; MASSINGER, *A New Way to Pay Old Debts*. Act iv, sc. 2; CHURCHILL, *Duellist*. Bk. ii, 278.

Please do not think I'm bad or bold,
But where it's deep it's awful cold!
UNKNOWN, *Couplet*, celebrating Paul Chabas' *Matinée de Septembre*, brought into public notice in May, 1913, by Anthony Comstock's denunciation, "There's too little morning and too much maid!"

BONAPARTE, see NAPOLEON

BONE

See also Flesh and Bone

15
Which may be a bone for you to pick on.
JAMES CALFHILL, *Answer to Martiall*, 277. (1565)

But here's a bone for ye to pick.
SIR ROGER L'ESTRANGE, *The Observator*. Vol. i, No. 64. (1681)

There is a bone for the gastronomers to pick.
SIR WALTER SCOTT. (LOCKHART, *Life*, vii, 215.)

1
I have a bone in my throat and cannot speak.
DEMOSTHENES, having been bribed not to speak. (ERASMUS, *Adagia*, 375.)
See also under BRIBERY.

2
It is the soundness of the bones that ultimates itself in the peach-bloom complexion.
EMERSON, *Conduct of Life: Beauty*.

BRED IN THE BONE, *see* ANCESTRY: HEREDITY.

3
Bone of my bones.
Old Testament: Genesis, ii, 23. *See also* FLESH AND BONE.

4
He that gives thee a bone would not have thee die.
GEORGE HERBERT, *Jacula Prudentum*.

5
I may tell all my bones: they look and stare upon me.
Old Testament: Psalms, xxii, 17.

6
They have made no bones at it.
RICHARD SHACKLOCK, *Hatcher of Heresies*. (1565)

Making no bones of it.
ROBERT ARMIN, *Nest of Ninnies*, 27. (1608)

7
Fair fall the bones that took the pains for me!
SHAKESPEARE, *King John*. Act i, sc. 1, l. 78.

8
Thy bones are marrowless.
SHAKESPEARE, *Macbeth*. Act iii, sc. 4, l. 94.

Thy bones are hollow.
SHAKESPEARE, *Measure for Measure*. Act i, sc. 2, l. 56.

9
Bones bring meat to town: meaning difficult and hard things are not altogether to be rejected.
UNKNOWN. (*Berkeley MSS.*, iii, 31. 1639)

We have an English proverb that bones bring meat to town.
THOMAS FULLER, *Profane State: "Andronicus."*

10
Bones for those who come late. (Sero venientibus ossa.)
UNKNOWN. A Latin proverb.

BOOKS

See also Library, Reading, Writing
For Novels, see Fiction

I—Books: Definitions

11
Books are the legacies that a great genius leaves to mankind, which are delivered down from generation to generation, as presents to the posterity of those who are yet unborn.
ADDISON, *The Spectator*. No. 166.

12
That is a good book which is opened with expectation and closed with profit.
AMOS BRONSON ALCOTT, *Table Talk:* Bk. i, *Learning-Books*.

The test of a first-rate work, and a test of your sincerity in calling it a first-rate work, is that you finish it.
ARNOLD BENNETT, *Things That Have Interested Me*, p. 90.

There is no quite good book without a good morality; but the world is wide, and so are morals.
R. L. STEVENSON, *A Gossip on a Novel of Dumas's*.

The good book is always a book of travel; it is about a life's journey.
H. M. TOMLINSON, *Out of Soundings*, p. 192.

13
Books are the shrine where the saint is, or is believed to be.
FRANCIS BACON, *Letter to Sir Thomas Bodley*, 1605.

The images of men's wits and knowledges remain in books, exempted from the wrong of time, and capable of perpetual renovation.
BACON, *Advancement of Learning*. Bk. i.

Books are ships which pass through the vast seas of time.
BACON, *Advancement of Learning*. Bk. i.

14
Books are the compasses and telescopes and sextants and charts which other men have prepared to help us navigate the dangerous seas of human life.
JESSE LEE BENNETT, *Books as Guides*.

15
Books are men of higher stature,
And the only men that speak aloud for future times to hear.
E. B. BROWNING, *Lady Geraldine's Courtship*. St. 49.

16
You, O Books, are the golden vessels of the temple, . . . burning lamps to be held ever in the hand.
RICHARD DE BURY, BISHOP OF DURHAM, (born Richard Aungerville), *Philobiblon*. Ch. 15. (1345)

Ye are the tree of life and the fourfold river of Paradise, by which the human mind is nourished, and the thirsty intellect is watered and refreshed; . . . fig-trees that are never barren.
RICHARD DE BURY, *Philobiblon*. Ch. 12.

Wells of living waters, delightful ears of corn, combs of honey, golden pots in which manna is stored, udders of milk.
RICHARD DE BURY, *Philobiblon*. Ch. 12.

All the glory of the world would be buried in oblivion, unless God had provided mortals with the remedy of books.
RICHARD DE BURY, *Philobiblon*. Ch. 9.

17
O blessed letters! that combine in one
All ages past, and make one live with all.
SAMUEL DANIEL, *Musophilus*.

18
In Books lies the *soul* of the whole Past Time; the articulate audible voice of the Past, when the body and material substance

of it has altogether vanished like a dream. . . . All that Mankind has done, thought, gained or been: it is lying as in magic preservation in the pages of Books. They are the chosen possession of men.

CARLYLE, *On Heroes and Hero-Worship: The Hero as Man of Letters.*

The assembled souls of all men held wise, imprisoned until some one takes them down from a shelf and reads them.

SAMUEL BUTLER THE YOUNGER, *Note-Books,* p. 95.

The monument of vanish'd minds.

SIR WILLIAM D'AVENANT, *Gondibert.* Bk. ii, canto 5.

1
Of the things which man can do or make here below, by far the most momentous, wonderful, and worthy are the things we call Books!

CARLYLE, *On Heroes and Hero-Worship: The Hero as Man of Letters.*

2
Books are the blessed chloroform of the mind.

ROBERT CHAMBERS, *What English Literature Gives Us. See also* Diodorus Siculus under LIBRARY: DEFINITIONS.

3
Of all the inanimate objects, of all men's creations, books are the nearest to us, for they contain our very thoughts, our ambitions, our indignations, our illusions, our fidelity to truth, and our persistent leaning toward error. But most of all they resemble us in their precarious hold on life.

JOSEPH CONRAD, *Notes on Life and Letters,* p. 5.

4
Wise books
For half the truths they hold are honoured tombs.

GEORGE ELIOT, *Spanish Gypsy.* Bk. ii, l. 14.

Books are sepulchres of thought;
The dead laurels of the dead.

LONGFELLOW, *Wind Over the Chimney.* St. 8.

5
In the highest civilization, the book is still the highest delight. He who has once known its satisfactions is provided with a resource against calamity.

EMERSON, *Letters and Social Aims: Quotation and Originality.*

6
The virtue of books is to be readable.

EMERSON, *Society and Solitude: Eloquence.*

Of all the needs a book has, the chief need is, that it be readable.

ANTHONY TROLLOPE, *Autobiography.* Ch. 19.

7
Books, those miraculous memories of high thoughts and golden moods; those magical shells, tremulous with the secrets of the ocean of life; . . . those honeycombs of dreams; those orchards of knowledge; those still-beating hearts of the noble dead; . . . prisms of beauty; urns stored with all the sweets of all the summers of time; immortal nightingales that sing for ever to the rose of life.

RICHARD LE GALLIENNE, *Prose Fancies,* p. 114.

8
For books are more than books, they are the life
The very heart and core of ages past,
The reason why men lived and worked and died,
The essence and quintessence of their lives.

AMY LOWELL, *The Boston Athenæum.*

9
Books are not absolutely dead things, but do contain a progeny of life in them to be as active as that soul was whose progeny they are; nay, they do preserve as in a vial the purest efficacy and extraction of that living intellect that bred them.

MILTON, *Areopagitica.* Sec. 6.

As good almost kill a man as kill a good book: who kills a man kills a reasonable creature, God's image; but he who destroys a good book, kills reason itself, kills the image of God, as it were, in the eye.

MILTON, *Areopagitica.* Sec. 6.

10
A good book is the precious life-blood of a master spirit, imbalmed and treasured up on purpose to a Life beyond Life.

MILTON, *Areopagitica.* Sec. 6.

That seasoned life of man preserved and stored up in books.

MILTON, *Areopagitica.* Sec. 6.

For books are as meats and viands are; some of good, some of evil substance.

MILTON, *Areopagitica.* Sec. 20.

11
Books are a part of man's prerogative;
In formal ink they thoughts and voices hold,
That we to them our solitude may give,
And make time present travel that of old;
Our life fame pieceth longer at the end,
And books it farther backward do extend.

SIR THOMAS OVERBURY, *The Wife.*

12
A book may be a flower that blows;
A road to a far town;
A roof, a well, a tower;
A book
May be a staff, a crook.

LIZETTE WOODWORTH REESE, *Books.*

13
Books are a finer world within the world. . . . When I go to my long sleep, on a book will my head be pillowed.

ALEXANDER SMITH, *Dreamthorp: Men of Letters.*

14
Books, the children of the brain.

SWIFT, *The Tale of a Tub.* Sec. 1.

15
Books are the treasured wealth of the world, the fit inheritance of generations and nations.

THOREAU, *Walden: Reading.*

1
Bright books: the perspectives to our weak sights,
The clear projections of discerning lights,
Burning and shining thought, man's posthume day,
The track of fled souls in their Milky Way,
The dead alive and busy, the still voice
Of enlarged spirits, kind Heaven's white decoys.

HENRY VAUGHAN, *To His Books.*

They are not dead, but full of blood again,
I mean the sense, and every line a vein.

HENRY VAUGHAN, *On Sir Thomas Bodley's Library.*

2
Books are life's best business: vocation to these hath more emolument coming in, than all the other busy terms of life. They are . . . of easy access and kind expedition, never sending away empty any client or petitioner, nor by delay making their δῶρα ἄδωρα, Courtesies injurious.

RICHARD WHITLOCK, *Zoötomia,* p. 246. (Ζωοτόμια, London, 1654.)

Books are for company, the best friends; in doubts counsellors, in damps comforters; Time's perspective, the home traveller's ship, or horse; the busy man's best recreation, the opiate of idle weariness, the mind's best ordinary, nature's garden and seed-plot of immortality.

RICHARD WHITLOCK, *Zoötomia,* p. 248.

3
There is no such thing as a moral or an immoral book. Books are well written, or badly written. That is all.

OSCAR WILDE, *The Picture of Dorian Gray: Preface.*

We call some books immoral! *Do they live?*
If so, believe me, TIME hath made them pure.
In Books, the veriest wicked rest in peace.

BULWER-LYTTON, *The Souls of Books.* St. 3.

4
What holy cities are to nomadic tribes—a symbol of race and a bond of union—great books are to the wandering souls of men: they are the Meccas of the mind.

G. E. WOODBERRY, *Torch,* p. 176.

5
Dreams, books, are each a world; and books, we know,
Are a substantial world, both pure and good:
Round these, with tendrils strong as flesh and blood,
Our pastime and our happiness will grow.

WORDSWORTH, *Personal Talk.* St. 3.

II—Books: Apothegms

6
I am a man of one book. (Homo unius libri.)

ST. THOMAS AQUINAS, referring to the fact that he read only the Bible.

Aquinas was once asked, with what compendium a man might become learned. He answered, "By reading of one book."

JEREMY TAYLOR, *Life of Christ.* Pt. ii, sec. 12.

Beware the man of one book. (Cave ab homine unius Libri.)

ISAAC D'ISRAELI, *Curiosities of Literature.*

The *homo unius libri* is indeed proverbially formidable to all conversational figurantes.

SOUTHEY, *The Doctor,* p. 164.

Woe be to him that reads but one book.

GEORGE HERBERT, *Jacula Prudentum.*

It is our duty to live among books; especially to live by one book, and a very old one.

JOHN HENRY NEWMAN, *Tracts for the Times.*

7
Books must follow sciences, and not sciences books.

FRANCIS BACON, *A Proposal for Amending the Laws of England.*

8
There is no Past, so long as Books shall live!

BULWER-LYTTON, *The Souls of Books.* St. 4.

9
Laws die, Books never.

BULWER-LYTTON, *Richelieu.* Act i, sc. 2.

The one invincible thing is a good book; neither malice nor stupidity can crush it.

GEORGE MOORE, *Impressions and Opinions: A Great Poet.*

10
Blessings upon Cadmus, the Phœnicians, or whoever it was that invented books.

THOMAS CARLYLE, *Early Letters: To R. Mitchell.*

11
Due attention to the inside of books, and due contempt for the outside, is the proper relation between a man of sense and his books.

LORD CHESTERFIELD, *Letters,* 10 Jan., 1749.

Buy good books and read them; the best books are the commonest, and the last editions are always the best, if the editors are not blockheads, for they may profit of the former.

LORD CHESTERFIELD, *Letters,* 19 March, 1750.

12
A room without books is as a body without a soul.

CICERO. (LUBBOCK, *Pleasures of Life.* Ch. 3.)

Far more seemly to have thy study full of books, than thy purse full of money.

JOHN LYLY, *Euphues.*

A house full of books, and a garden of flowers.

ANDREW LANG, *Ballade of True Wisdom.*

No furniture so charming as books.

SYDNEY SMITH. (LADY HOLLAND, *Memoir.* Vol. i.)

13
"Gracious heavens!" he cries out, leaping up and catching hold of his hair, "what's this? Print!"

DICKENS, *Somebody's Luggage.* Ch. 3.

1
Of making many books there is no end.
Old Testament: Ecclesiastes, xii, 12.

2
A book may be as great a thing as a battle.
BENJAMIN DISRAELI, *Memoir of Isaac D'Israeli: Introduction.*

3
Some books leave us free and some books make us free.
EMERSON, *Journals*, 22 Dec., 1839.

The colleges, whilst they provide us with libraries, furnish no professor of books; and I think no chair is so much wanted.
EMERSON, *Society and Solitude: Books.*

4
Now go, write it before them in a table, and note it in a book.
Old Testament: Isaiah, xxx, 8.

5
Oh that my words were now written! oh that they were printed in a book!
Old Testament: Job, xix, 23.

6
Even the world itself could not contain the books that should be written.
New Testament: John, xxi, 25.

7
A book that is shut is but a block.
THOMAS FULLER, *Gnomologia.* No. 23.

8
Learning hath gained most by those books by which the printers have lost.
THOMAS FULLER, *The Holy State: Of Books.*

9
A book may be amusing with numerous errors, or it may be very dull without a single absurdity.
GOLDSMITH, *The Vicar of Wakefield: Preface.*

10
A book is never a masterpiece; it becomes one.
EDMOND AND JULES DE GONCOURT, *Journal.*

11
There be some men are born only to suck out the poison of books.
BEN JONSON, *Explorata: De Malign. Studentium.*

12
Every age hath its book.
Koran. Ch. xiii.

13
Why have we no grace for books, those spiritual repasts—a grace before Milton—a grace before Shakespeare—a devotional exercise proper to be said before reading the "Faerie Queene"?
CHARLES LAMB, *Essays of Elia: Grace Before Meat.*

14
I can read anything which I call *a book.* There are things in that shape which I cannot allow for such. In this catalogue of *books which are no books—biblia a-biblia*—I reckon Court Calendars, Directories, . . . Almanacs. Statutes at Large, the works of Hume, Gibbon, Robertson, Beattie, Soame Jenyns, and, generally, all those volumes which "no gentleman's library should be without."
CHARLES LAMB, *Last Essays of Elia: Detached Thoughts on Books and Reading.*

15
If books did good, the world would have been converted long ago.
GEORGE MOORE, *Impressions and Opinions.*

16
If a book is worth reading, it is worth buying.
RUSKIN, *Sesame and Lilies*, p. 55.

If I were asked what book is better than a cheap book, I should answer that there is one book better than a cheap book, and that is a book honestly come by.
J. R. LOWELL, before U. S. Senate Committee on Patents, 29 Jan., 1886.

17
I see, lady, the gentleman is not in your books.
SHAKESPEARE, *Much Ado About Nothing.* Act i, sc. 1, l. 79.

He comes not in my books.
BEAUMONT AND FLETCHER, *The Widow.* Act i, sc. 1.

18
The reader's fancy makes the fate of books. (Pro captu lectoris habent sua fata libelli.)
TERENTIANUS MAURUS, *De Litteris, de Syllabis, de Metris*, l. 1286. (*De Syllabis*, l. 1008.)

19
Few, but full of understanding, are the books of the library of God.
MARTIN FARQUHAR TUPPER, *Proverbial Philosophy: Of Recreation.*

20
It is with books as with men: a very small number play a great part, the rest are lost in the multitude.
VOLTAIRE, *Philosophical Dictionary: Books.*

III—Books: Their Influence

21
Books will speak plain, when counsellors blanch.
FRANCIS BACON, *Essays: Of Counsel.*

22
There is no mood to which a man may not administer the appropriate medicine at the cost of reaching down a volume from his bookshelf.
ARTHUR BALFOUR, *Essays and Addresses*, p. 36.

To divert at any time a troublesome fancy, run to thy books; they always receive thee with the same kindness.
THOMAS FULLER, *The Holy State: Of Books.*

23
Books that purify the thought,
Spirits of the learned dead,
Teachers of the little taught,
Comforters when friends are fled.
WILLIAM BARNES, *My Books.*

1
Without books God is silent, justice dormant, natural science at a stand, philosophy lame, letters dumb, and all things involved in Cimmerian darkness.

THOMAS BARTHOLIN, *De Libris Legendis.*

2
Hark! the world so loud,
And they, the movers of the world, so still!

BULWER-LYTTON, *The Souls of Books.* St. 3.

3
No good Book, or good thing of any sort, shows its best face at first.

CARLYLE, *Essays: Novalis.*

4
If a book come from the heart, it will contrive to reach other hearts; all art and authorcraft are of small amount to that.

CARLYLE, *Heroes and Hero-Worship: The Hero as Man of Letters.*

5
It is chiefly through books that we enjoy intercourse with superior minds. . . . In the best books, great men talk to us, give us their most precious thoughts, and pour their souls into ours.

WILLIAM ELLERY CHANNING, *On Self-Culture.*

Books are the true levellers. They give to all, who will faithfully use them, the society, the spiritual presence, of the best and greatest of our race.

WILLIAM ELLERY CHANNING, *On Self-Culture.*

6
It is saying less than the truth to affirm that an excellent book (and the remark holds almost equally good of a Raphael as of a Milton) is like a well-chosen and well-tended fruit tree. Its fruits are not of one season only. With the due and natural intervals, we may recur to it year after year, and it will supply the same nourishment and the same gratification, if only we ourselves return to it with the same healthful appetite.

S. T. COLERIDGE, *Prospectus of Lectures.*

7
Books are a guide in youth and an entertainment for age.

JEREMY COLLIER, *Of the Entertainment of Books.*

8
Books should, not Business, entertain the Light;
And Sleep, as undisturb'd as Death, the Night.

ABRAHAM COWLEY, *Of Myself.*

9
Books are not seldom talismans and spells.

COWPER, *The Task.* Bk. vi, l. 98.

'Twere well with most if books that could engage
Their childhood, pleas'd them at a riper age.

COWPER, *Tirocinium,* l. 147.

10
But what strange art, what magic can dispose
The troubled mind to change its native woes? . . .
This, books can do;—nor this alone; they give
New views to life, and teach us how to live;
They soothe the griev'd, the stubborn they chastise,
Fools they admonish, and confirm the wise.

GEORGE CRABBE, *The Library,* l. 37.

Books should to one of these four ends conduce,
For wisdom, piety, delight, or use.

SIR JOHN DENHAM, *Of Prudence,* l. 83.

11
He ate and drank the precious words,
His spirit grew robust;
He knew no more that he was poor,
Nor that his frame was dust.
He danced along the dingy days,
And this bequest of wings
Was but a book. What liberty
A loosened spirit brings!

EMILY DICKINSON, *Poems.* Pt. i, No. 21.

There is no frigate like a book
To take us lands away,
Nor any coursers like a page
Of prancing poetry.

EMILY DICKINSON, *Poems.* Pt. i, No. 99.

12
Who, without books, essays to learn,
Draws water in a leaky urn.

AUSTIN DOBSON, *A Bookman's Budget,* 188.

13
They support us in solitude. . . . They help us to forget the coarseness of men and things, compose our cares and our passions, and lay our disappointments to sleep.

COMTESSE DE GENLIS, *Mémoires.*

14
I have ever gained the most profit, and the most pleasure also, from the books which have made me think the most.

J. C. AND A. W. HARE, *Guesses at Truth,* p. 458.

The books which help you most are those which make you think the most.

THEODORE PARKER, *World of Matter and World of Men.*

15
Books give not wisdom where was none before,
But where some is, there reading makes it more.

SIR JOHN HARINGTON, *Epigrams.* Bk. i, epig. 2.

16
Dear little child, this little book
Is less a primer than a key
To sunder gates where wonder waits
Your "Open Sesame!"

RUPERT HUGHES, *With a First Reader.*

17
The globe we inhabit is divisible into two worlds: the common geographical world, and the world of books; . . . if habit and perception between real and unreal, we may say that we more frequently wake out of

common life to them, than out of them to common life.

LEIGH HUNT, *Monthly Repository: Farewell Address*, 1828.

1

Dear, human books,
With kindly voices, winning looks!
Enchant me with your spells of art,
And draw me homeward to your heart.

LIONEL JOHNSON, *Oxford Nights.*

2

Books have always a secret influence on the understanding; we cannot at pleasure obliterate ideas: he that reads books of science, though without any desire fixed of improvement, will grow more knowing; he that entertains himself with moral or religious treatises, will imperceptibly advance in goodness; the ideas which are often offered to the mind, will at last find a lucky moment when it is disposed to receive them.

SAMUEL JOHNSON, *The Adventurer*. No. 137.

3

Many readers judge of the power of a book by the shock it gives their feelings.

LONGFELLOW, *Kavanagh*. Ch. 13.

4

All books are either dreams or swords,
You can cut, or you can drug, with words.

AMY LOWELL, *Sword Blades and Poppy Seed*, l. 292.

5

We profit little by books we do not enjoy.

SIR JOHN LUBBOCK, *Pleasures of Life*. Ch. 3.

6

He fed his spirit with the bread of books,
And slaked his thirst at all the wells of thought.

EDWIN MARKHAM, *Young Lincoln.*

7

The book is doubly gifted: it moves to laughter, and by its counsel teaches a wise man how to live. (Duplex libelli dos est: quod risum movet, Et quod prudenti vitam consilio monet.)

PHÆDRUS, *Fables:* Bk. i, *Prologue.*

8

No book is so bad but some profit may be gleaned from it. (Nullum esse librum tam malum, ut non aliqua parte prodesset.)

PLINY THE ELDER. (PLINY THE YOUNGER, *Epistles*. Bk. iii, epis. 5.)

There's no book so bad but has some good in it.

CERVANTES, *Don Quixote*. Pt. ii, ch. 3.

Take up any book, even down to a jest-book, it is still better than nothing.

LORD CHESTERFIELD, *Letters*, 30 Oct., 1747.

The foolishest book is a kind of leaky boat on a sea of wisdom; some of the wisdom will get in anyhow.

HOLMES, *Poet at the Breakfast-Table*. Ch. 11.

A wise man, like a good refiner, can gather gold out of the drossiest volume.

MILTON, *Areopagitica*. Sec. 28.

9

There exists one book, which, to my taste, furnishes the happiest treatise of natural education. What then is this marvellous book? Is it Aristotle? Is it Pliny, is it Buffon? No,—it is *Robinson Crusoe.* (Il en existe un [livre] qui fournit, à mon gré, le plus heureux traité d'éducation naturelle . . . Quel est donc ce merveilleux livre? Est-ce Aristote? est-ce Pline, est-ce Buffon? Non; c'est *Robinson Crusoe.*)

ROUSSEAU, *Émile*. Bk. iii.

That wonderful book, while it obtains admiration from the most fastidious critics, is loved by those who are too simple to admire it.

MACAULAY, *Essays: Bunyan's Pilgrim's Progress.*

10

Let your bookcases and your shelves be your gardens and your pleasure-grounds. Pluck the fruit that grows therein, gather the roses, the spices, and the myrrh.

JUDAH IBN TIBBON. (ABRAHAMS, *Jewish Life in the Middle Ages*, p. 354.)

11

By sucking you, the wise, like bees, do grow
Healing and rich, though this they do most slow,
Because most choicely; for as great a store
Have we of books as bees of herbs, or more:
And the great task to try, then know, the good,
To discern weeds and judge of wholesome food,
Is a rare scant performance. For man dies
Oft ere 'tis done, while the bee feeds and flies.

HENRY VAUGHAN, *To His Books.*

IV—Books as Friends and Companions

12

Books are the most mannerly of companions, accessible at all times, in all moods, frankly declaring the author's mind, without offence.

AMOS BRONSON ALCOTT, *Concord Days.*

Books
Are not companions—they are solitudes;
We lose ourselves in them, and all our cares.

P. J. BAILEY, *Festus: A Village Feast: Evening.*

13

Alonso of Arragon was wont to say of himself "That he was a great necromancer, for that he used to ask counsel of the dead," meaning books.

FRANCIS BACON, *Apothegms*. No. 105.

My days among the Dead are passed,
Around me I behold,
Where'er these casual eyes are cast,
The mighty minds of old:
My never-failing friends are they,
With whom I converse day by day.

ROBERT SOUTHEY, *My Days Among the Dead Are Passed.*

Studious let me sit,
And hold high converse with the mighty Dead.
THOMSON, *The Seasons: Winter*, l. 431.

Dead counsellors are likewise most instructive, because they are heard with patience and with reverence.
SAMUEL JOHNSON, *The Rambler*. No. 87.

1 That place that does contain
My books, the best companions, is to me
A glorious court, where hourly I converse
With the old sages and philosophers.
BEAUMONT AND FLETCHER, *The Elder Brother*. Act i, sc. 2, l. 177.

2
The best companions are the best books.
LORD CHESTERFIELD, *Letters to Lord Huntingdon*. No. 3.

We should choose our books as we would our companions, for their sterling and intrinsic merit.
C. C. COLTON, *Lacon: Reflections*. No. 181.

Books and friends should be few and good. (Libros y amijos pocos y buenos.)
UNKNOWN. A Spanish proverb.

3
I can study my books at any time, for they are always disengaged.
CICERO, *De Re Publica*. Bk. i, sec. 9.

Books are the quietest and most constant of friends; they are the most accessible and wisest of counsellors, and the most patient of teachers.
CHARLES W. ELIOT, *The Happy Life*.

4
Come, my best friends, my books, and lead me on.
ABRAHAM COWLEY, *The Motto*.

5
A man's library is a sort of harem, and tender readers have a great pudency in showing their books to a stranger.
EMERSON, *Society and Solitude: Books*.

Women are by nature fickle, and sc are men. . . . Not so with books, for books cannot change. A thousand years hence they are what you find them today, speaking the same words, holding forth the same comfort.
EUGENE FIELD, *Love Affairs of a Bibliomaniac*, p. 11.

6
I . . . showed her that books were sweet unreproaching companions to the miserable, and that, if they could not bring us to enjoy life, they would at least teach us to endure it.
GOLDSMITH, *The Vicar of Wakefield*. Ch. 22.

7
My masters and companions, my books.
JOSEPH HALL, *Epistle to Lord Denny*.

8
A blessed companion is a book,—a book that, fitly chosen, is a lifelong friend, . . . a book that, at a touch, pours its heart into our own.
DOUGLAS JERROLD, *Specimens of Jerrold's Wit: Books*.

9
When I would know thee . . . my thought looks
Upon thy well-made choice of friends and books;
Then do I love thee, and behold thy ends
In making thy friends books, and thy books friends.
BEN JONSON, *Epigrams*. No. 86.

10
We enter our studies, and enjoy a society which we alone can bring together. We raise no jealousy by conversing with one in preference to another; we give no offence to the most illustrious by questioning him as long as we will, and leaving him as abruptly. Diversity of opinion raises no tumult in our presence; each interlocutor stands before us, speaks or is silent, and we adjourn or decide the business at our leisure.
LANDOR, *Imaginary Conversations: Milton and Andrew Marvell*.

The debt which he owes to them is incalculable; they have guided him to truth; they have filled his mind with noble and graceful images; they have stood by him in all vicissitudes, comforters in sorrow, nurses in sickness, companions in solitude. These friendships are exposed to no danger from the occurrences by which other attachments are weakened or dissolved. Time glides on; fortune is inconstant; tempers are soured; bonds which seemed indissoluble are daily sundered by interest, by emulation, or by caprice. But no such cause can affect the silent converse which we hold with the highest of human intellects.
MACAULAY, *Essays: Lord Bacon*.

11
A book is a friend whose face is constantly changing. If you read it when you are recovering from an illness, and return to it years after, it is changed surely, with the change in yourself.
ANDREW LANG, *The Library*. Ch. 1.

Three kinds of companions, men, women, and books,
Were enough, said the elderly Sage, for his ends.
And the women we deem that he chose for their looks,
The men for their cellars: the books were his friends:
"Man delights me not," often, "nor women," but books
Are the best of good comrades in loneliest nooks.
ANDREW LANG, *To the Gentle Reader*.

12
A wise man will select his books, for he would not wish to class them all under the sacred name of friends. Some can be accepted only as acquaintances. The best books of all kinds are taken to the heart, and cherished as his most precious possessions. Others to be chatted with for a time, to spend a few

pleasant hours with, and laid aside, but not forgotten.

John Alfred Langford, *The Praise of Books: Preliminary Essay.*

1
What are my books? My friends, my loves,
My church, my tavern, and my only wealth;
My garden, yea, my flowers, my bees, my doves,
My only doctor, and my only health.

Richard Le Gallienne, *My Books.*

I feel your great hearts throbbing deep in quire,
And hear your breathing round me in the gloom.

Richard Le Gallienne, *Confessio Amantis.*

All round the room my silent servants wait,
My friends in every season.

Bryan Waller Procter, *Autobiographical Fragment.*

2
The pleasant books, that silently among
Our household treasures take familiar places,
And are to us as if a living tongue
Spake from the printed leaves or pictured faces!

Longfellow, *The Seaside and the Fireside: Dedication.*

3
While you converse with lords and dukes,
I have their betters here—my books.

Thomas Sheridan, *My Books.*

4
A good book is the best of friends, the same to-day and forever.

Martin F. Tupper, *Proverbial Philosophy: Of Reading.*

V—Books: Their Shortcomings

5
Most books, indeed, are records less
Of fulness than of emptiness.

William Allingham, *Writing.*

Some books are lies frae end to end.

Burns, *Death and Dr. Hornbook,* l. 1.

6
Epitomes are the moths and corruptions of learning.

Francis Bacon, *Of the Colours of Good and Evil.*

Every summary of a good book is a stupid summary. (Tout abbregé sur un bon livre est un sot abbregé.)

Montaigne, *Essays.* Bk. iii, ch. 8.

Abstracts, abridgements, please the fickle times.

George Crabbe, *The Library.*

There's more ado to interpret interpretations, than to interpret things: and more books upon books, than upon any other subject.

Montaigne, *Essays.* Bk. iii, ch. 13.

A dedication is a wooden leg.

Edward Young, *Love of Fame.* Sat. iv, l. 192.

7
"What is the use of a book," thought Alice, "without pictures or conversations?"

Lewis Carroll, *Alice's Adventures in Wonderland,* p. 1.

8
Books cannot always please, however good;
Minds are not ever craving for their food.

George Crabbe, *The Borough,* l. 24.

9
Books are fatal: they are the curse of the human race. . . . The greatest misfortune that ever befell man was the invention of printing.

Benjamin Disraeli, *Lothair.* Ch. 24.

The multitude of books is making us ignorant.

Voltaire.

10
Books are for the scholar's idle times. When he can read God directly, the hour is too precious to be wasted in other men's transcripts of their reading.

Emerson, *Nature, Addresses and Lectures: The American Scholar.*

When the mind wakes, books are set aside as impertinent.

Emerson, *Uncollected Lectures: Books.*

One master could so easily be conceived as writing all the books of the world. They are all alike.

Emerson, *Journals.* Vol. vii, p. 297.

11
Books are the best things, well used: abused, among the worst.

Emerson, *Nature, Addresses and Lectures: The American Scholar.*

Good books are the most precious of blessings to a people; bad books are among the worst of curses.

E. P. Whipple, *Essays: Romance of Rascality.*

No worse thief than a bad book.

Unknown. An Italian proverb.

12
He that takes up conclusions on the trust of authors, . . . loses his labour, and does not know anything, but only believeth.

Thomas Hobbes, *Leviathan.* Pt. i, ch. 5.

13
No book is of much importance, the vital thing is, What do you yourself think?

Elbert Hubbard, *Philistine.* Vol. xviii, p. 19.

14
The best book ever written by a man on the wrong side of a question of which the writer was profoundly ignorant.

Macaulay, *Essays: Atterbury's Defense of the Letters of Phalaris.*

15
Away with thy books! Be no longer drawn aside by them: it is not allowed. (*Ἄφες τὰ βιβλία· μηκέτι σπῶ· οὐ δέδοται.*)

Marcus Aurelius, *Meditations.* Bk. ii, sec. 2.

16
Books have led some to learning and others

to madness, when they swallow more than they can digest.

PETRARCH, *On Fortune.*

1
What need of books these truths to tell,
Which folks perceive who cannot spell?

MATTHEW PRIOR, *Alma.* Canto iii, l. 590.

2
Some books are drenchèd sands,
On which a great soul's wealth lies all in heaps,
Like a wrecked argosy.

ALEXANDER SMITH, *A Life Drama.* Sc. 2.

3
To mind the inside of a book is to entertain one's self with the forced product of another man's brain.

SIR JOHN VANBRUGH, *The Relapse.*

VI—Books and Men

4
Many are perfect in men's humours, that are not greatly capable of the real part of business; which is the constitution of one, that hath studied men, more than books.

FRANCIS BACON, *Essays: Of Cunning.*

5
I have rather studied books than men.

FRANCIS BACON, *Advice to Sir George Villiers.*

The proper study of mankind is books.

ALDOUS HUXLEY, *Chrome Yellow.*

See also MAN: THE STUDY OF MAN.

6
Learning is acquired by reading books; but the much more necessary learning, the knowledge of the world, is only to be acquired by reading men, and studying all the various editions of them.

LORD CHESTERFIELD, *Letters,* 16 March, 1752.

7
Sleep over books, and leave mankind unknown.

CHARLES CHURCHILL, *The Author,* l. 20.

We can not learn men from books.

BENJAMIN DISRAELI, *Vivian Grey.* Bk. v, ch. 1.

8
Books are a triviality. Life alone is great.

THOMAS CARLYLE, *Journal,* 29 May, 1839.

Books are good enough in their way, but they are a mighty bloodless substitute for life. . . . There are not many works extant, if you look the alternative all over, which are worth the price of a pound of tobacco to a man of limited means.

R. L. STEVENSON, *Virginibus Puerisque: An Apology for Idlers.*

We are vessels of a very limited content. Not all men can read all books; it is only in a chosen few that any man will find his appointed food.

R. L. STEVENSON, *Books Which Have Influenced Me.*

9
Books teach us very little of the world.

OLIVER GOLDSMITH, *Letter to Henry Goldsmith,* Feb., 1759.

His knowledge of books had in some degree diminished his knowledge of the world.

WILLIAM SHENSTONE, *A Character.*

10
The years know more than books.

GEORGE HERBERT, *Jacula Prudentum.*

11
Books without the knowledge of life are useless.

SAMUEL JOHNSON. (MRS. PIOZZI, *Johnsoniana.*)

12
The earth has had to forget its books that it might recover its men.

F. D. MAURICE, *The Friendship of Books,* p. 62.

VII—Books Old and New

13
Of all odd crazes, the craze to be forever reading new books is one of the oddest.

AUGUSTINE BIRRELL, *Essays: Books Old and New.*

14
All books grow homilies by time; they are Temples, at once, and Landmarks.

BULWER-LYTTON, *The Souls of Books.* St. 4.

15
Old Books are best! With what delight
Does "Faithorne fecit" greet our sight.

BEVERLY CHEW, *Old Books Are Best. See also under* AGE.

16
Some will read old books, as if there were no valuable truths to be discovered in modern publications.

ISAAC D'ISRAELI, *Literary Miscellanies,* p. 183.

17
Old age is a good advertisement.

EMERSON, *Journals.* Vol. x, p. 312.

18
Books, like metals, require to be stamped with some valuable effigies before they become popular and current.

FARQUHAR, *The Twin Rivals: Preface.*

19
The volumes of antiquity, like medals, may very well serve to amuse the curious; but the works of the moderns, like the current coin of a kingdom, are much better for immediate use.

GOLDSMITH, *Citizen of the World.* Letter 75.

Books, like proverbs, receive their chief value from the stamp and esteem of ages through which they have passed.

SIR WILLIAM TEMPLE, *Ancient and Modern Learning.*

20
In proportion as society refines, new books must ever become more necessary. . . . Books are necessary to correct the vices of the polite; but those vices are ever changing, and the antidote should be changed accordingly—should still be new.

GOLDSMITH, *Citizen of the World.* Letter 75.

21
One would imagine that books were, like

women, the worse for being old; that they have a pleasure in being read for the first time; that they open their leaves more cordially; that the spirit of enjoyment wears out with the spirit of novelty; and that, after a certain age, it is high time to put them on the shelf.

WILLIAM HAZLITT, *Essays: On Reading New Books.*

New-fangled books are also like made-dishes in this respect, that they are generally little else than hashes and *rifaccimenti* of what has been served up entire and in a more natural state at other times.

HAZLITT, *The Plain Speaker: On Reading Old Books.*

1
The praise of ancient authors proceeds not from the reverence of the dead, but from the competition and mutual envy of the living.

THOMAS HOBBES, *Leviathan: Conclusion.*

2
Old books, as you well know, are books of the world's youth, and new books are fruits of its age.

O. W. HOLMES, *The Professor at the Breakfast-Table.* Ch. 9.

3
The great drawback in new books is that they prevent our reading the old ones. (Le grand inconvénient des livres nouveaux, c'est qu'ils nous empêchent de lire les anciens.)

JOUBERT, *Pensées.* No. 250.

4
What a sense of security in an old book which Time has criticised for us!

J. R. LOWELL, *My Study Windows: Library of Old Authors.*

And the loved books that younger grow with years.

J. R. LOWELL, *Epistle to George William Curtis: Postscript, 1887.*

5
Nothing so old as a new book.

MARK PATTISON, *Books and Critics.*

6
For some in ancient books delight;
Others prefer what moderns write:
Now I should be extremely loth
Not to be thought expert in both.

MATTHEW PRIOR, *Alma.* Canto i, l. 517.

7
All books are divisible into two classes, the books of the hour, and the books of all time.

RUSKIN, *Sesame and Lilies.* Pt. i.

VIII—Books: The Book-Lover

8
I love my books as drinkers love their wine;
The more I drink, the more they seem divine.

FRANCIS BENNOCH, *My Books.*

9
Books we must have though we lack bread.

ALICE WILLIAMS BROTHERTON, *Ballade of Poor Bookworms.*

10
With faded yellow blossoms 'twixt page and page,
To mark great places with due gratitude.

ROBERT BROWNING, *Pippa Passes.* Pt. ii.

The peace of great books be for you,
Stains of pressed clover leaves on pages,
Bleach of the light of years held in leather.

CARL SANDBURG, *For You.*

11
And as for me, though that my wit be light,
On bookës for to read I me delight,
And to them give I faith and full credence,
And in my heart have them in reverence
So heartily, that there is gamë none
That from by bookës maketh me to goon.

CHAUCER, *The Legend of Good Women: Prologue,* l. 29.

12
His delight
Was all in books; to read them or to write;
Women and men he strove alike to shun,
And hurried homeward when his tasks were done.

GEORGE CRABBE, *The Parish Register.* Pt. iii.

And so his blameless years rolled by,
To-day the double of to-morrow;
No wish to smile, no need to sigh,
No heart for mirth, no time for sorrow.

ROBERT CREWE-MILNES, *The Bookworm.*

13
Golden volumes! richest treasures!
Objects of delicious pleasures!
You my eyes rejoicing please,
You my hands in rapture seize!
Brilliant wits and musing sages,
Lights who beamed through many ages,
Left to your conscious leaves their story,
And dared to trust you with their glory;
And now their hope of fame achieved,
Dear volumes, you have not deceived!

ISAAC D'ISRAELI, *Curiosities of Literature: Libraries.*

14
We prize books, and they prize them most who are themselves wise.

EMERSON, *Letters and Social Aims: Quotation and Originality.*

There are books . . . which take rank in our life with parents and lovers and passionate experiences.

EMERSON, *Society and Solitude: Books.*

15
The Love of Books, the Golden Key
That opens the Enchanted Door.

ANDREW LANG, *Ballade of the Bookworm.*

17
But whether it be worth or looks
We gently love or strongly,
Such virtue doth reside in books
We scarce can love them wrongly.

COSMO MONKHOUSE, *De Libris.*

1
Knowing I loved my books, he furnish'd me
From mine own library with volumes that
I prize above my dukedom.
SHAKESPEARE, *The Tempest*. Act i, sc. 2, l. 166.

I never knew
More sweet and happy hours than I employ'd
Upon my books.
JAMES SHIRLEY, *Lady of Pleasure*. Act ii, sc. 1.

2
Take thou a book in thine hands as Simon the Just took the Child Jesus into his arms to carry him and kiss him.
THOMAS À KEMPIS, *Doctrinale Juvenum*.

3
Everywhere have I sought rest and found it not, except sitting apart in a nook with a little book. (In omnibus requiem quæsivi et non inveni, nisi seorsum sedans in angulo cum libello.)
THOMAS À KEMPIS, *Inscription*, on his picture at Zwoll, Holland, where he is buried. Supposed to have been written by him in a copy of his *De Imitatione Christi*. Credited to him by Rosweyd in his *Preface* to the 1617 edition of the book.

With spots of sunny openings, and with nooks
To lie and read in, sloping into brooks.
LEIGH HUNT, *The Story of Rimini*.

The love of learning, the sequestered nooks,
And all the sweet serenity of books.
LONGFELLOW, *Morituri Salutamus*, l. 232.

4
O for a Booke and a shadie nooke,
Eyther in-a-doore or out;
With the grene leaves whispering overhede,
Or the streete cryes all about;
Where I maie Reade all at my ease,
Both of the Newe and Olde,
For a jollie goode Booke whereon to looke
Is better to me than golde.
JOHN WILSON. On the authority of Austin Dobson, to whom Wilson, an old London bookseller, stated that he had written this stanza as a motto for one of his second-hand book catalogues. First published in Alexander Ireland's *Book Lover's Enchiridon*, 1883, as an "old English song," and was so called by Sir John Lubbock, who used it as the heading for Ch. iii, *The Pleasures of Life*, 1887. (See *Notes and Queries*, Nov., 1919, p. 297.)

5
Often have I sighed to measure
By myself a lonely pleasure,
Sighed to think I read a book
Only read, perhaps, by me.
WORDSWORTH, *To the Small Celandine*.

6
My Book and Heart Shall never part.
UNKNOWN, *The New England Primer*.

IX—Books: Bibliomania

7
As it hath been wisely noted, the most corrected copies are commonly the least correct.
BACON, *Advancement of Learning*. Bk. ii.

8
A big book is a great evil. (Μέγα βιβλίον μέγα κακόν.)
CALLIMACHUS, *Fragmenta Incertæ*. No. 359.

A fig for big books! We like only the little format which slips into the pocket. (Fi des gros livres! Nous ne voulons plus que de petit format qui marche avec nous.)
JULES JANIN, *Le Livre*, 109.

Books that you may carry to the fire, and hold readily in your hand, are the most useful after all.
SAMUEL JOHNSON. (HAWKINS, *Johnsoniana*. No. 197.)

9
Great collections of books are subject to certain accidents besides the damp, the worms, and the rats; one not less common is that of the *borrowers*, not to say a word of the *purloiners*.
ISAAC D'ISRAELI, *Curiosities of Literature: The Bibliomania*.

I mean your borrowers of books—those mutilators of collections, spoilers of the symmetry of shelves, and creators of odd volumes.
CHARLES LAMB, *Essays of Elia: The Two Races of Men*.

Such is the sad fate of each lent book—often it is lost, always it is spoilt. (Tel est le triste sort de tout livre prêté, Souvent il est perdu, toujours il est gâté.)
NODIER, *Lines Written for Pixerecourt*.

10
Not as ours the books of old—
Things that steam can stamp and fold;
Not as ours the books of yore—
Rows of type, and nothing more.
AUSTIN DOBSON, *To a Missal of the Thirteenth Century*.

11
What wild desires, what restless torments seize
The hapless man, who feels the book-disease!
JOHN FERRIAR, *The Bibliomania*, l. 1.

How pure the joy when first my hands unfold
The small, rare volume, black with tarnished gold.
JOHN FERRIAR, *The Bibliomania*.

The princeps copy, clad in blue and gold.
JOHN FERRIAR, *The Bibliomania*.

In red morocco drest he loves to boast
The bloody murder; or the yelling ghost;
Or dismal ballads, sung to crowds of old,
Now cheaply bought for thrice their weight in gold.
JOHN FERRIAR, *The Bibliomania*.

12
Yon second-hand bookseller is second to none in the worth of the treasures which he dispenses.
LEIGH HUNT, *On the Beneficence of Bookstalls*.

13
Blest be the hour wherein I bought this book;
His studies happy that composed the book,

And the man fortunate that sold the book.
BEN JONSON, *Every Man Out of His Humour*. Act i, sc. 1.

1
Wear the old coat and buy the new book.
AUSTIN PHELPS, *The Theory of Preaching*.

2
A book? O rare one!
Be not, as is our fangled world, a garment
Nobler than that it covers.
SHAKESPEARE, *Cymbeline*. Act v, sc. 4, l. 133.

3
You two are book-men.
SHAKESPEARE, *Love's Labour's Lost*. Act iv, sc. 2, l. 35.

We turn'd o'er many books together.
SHAKESPEARE, *The Merchant of Venice*. Act iv, sc. 1, l. 156.

The bookish theoric.
SHAKESPEARE, *Othello*. Act i, sc. 1, l. 24.

That book in many's eyes doth share the glory,
That in gold clasps locks in the golden story.
SHAKESPEARE, *Romeo and Juliet*. Act i, sc. 3, l. 91.

4
You shall see them on a beautiful quarto page, where a neat rivulet of text shall meander through a meadow of margin.
SHERIDAN, *The School for Scandal*. Act i, sc. 1.

But every page having an ample marge,
And every marge enclosing in the midst
A square of text that looks a little blot.
TENNYSON, *Merlin and Vivien*, l. 667.

Or where the pictures for the page atone,
And Quarles is sav'd by beauties not his own.
POPE, *The Dunciad*. Bk. i, l. 139.

5
Thee will I sing, in comely wainscot bound,
And golden verge enclosing thee around;
The faithful horn before, from age to age
Preserving thy invaluable page;
Behind, thy patron saint in armour shines,
With sword and lance, to guard thy sacred lines; . . .
Th' instructive handle 's at the bottom fix'd
Lest wrangling critics should pervert the text.
THOMAS TICKELL, *The Hornbook*, l. 7.

Their books of stature small they take in hand,
Which with pellucid horn securèd are;
To save from fingers wet the letters fair.
WILLIAM SHENSTONE, *The Schoolmistress*. St. 18.

6
This boke is one thing, the halter another;
He that stealeth the one may be sure of the other.
UNKNOWN, *Inscription*, dating from 1578.

Steal not this book, my honest friend,
For fear the gallows be thine end.
UNKNOWN, *Book Inscription*.

Steal not this book, for fear of shame,
For it is in the owner's name;
And when you're dead, the Lord will say,
"Where is that book you stole away?"
UNKNOWN, *Book Inscription*.

X—Books: The Author and His Book

7
When I am dead, I hope it may be said:
"His sins were scarlet, but his books were read."
HILAIRE BELLOC, *On His Books*.

8
Some said, John, print it; others said, Not so;
Some said, It might do good; others said, No.
BUNYAN, *The Pilgrim's Progress. The Author's Apology for His Book*.

9
Go now, my little Book, to every place
Where my first Pilgrim has but shown his face.
Call at their door. If any say, "Who's there?"
Then answer thou "Christiana is here."
BUNYAN, *The Pilgrim's Progress: The Author's Way of Sending Forth His Second Part*.

Now may this little Book a blessing be
To those that love this little Book and me:
And may its buyer have no cause to say,
His money is but lost or thrown away.
BUNYAN, *The Pilgrim's Progress: The Author's Way of Sending Forth His Second Part*.

10
'Tis pleasant, sure, to see one's name in print;
A book's a book, although there's nothing in't.
BYRON, *English Bards and Scotch Reviewers*, l. 51.

11
O little book, thou art so unconning,
How dar'st thou put thyself in press for dread?
CHAUCER [?], *The Flower and the Leaf*, l. 591.

Go, little book, go little mine tragedy,
Ther God thy maker yet, ere that he die.
CHAUCER, *Troilus and Criseyde*. Bk. v, l. 256.

12
Wouldst thou find my ashes? Look
In the pages of my book;
And, as these thy hands doth turn,
Know here is my funeral urn.
ADELAIDE CRAPSEY, *The Immortal Residue*.

13
Better 'twere my book were dead
Than to live not perfected.
ROBERT HERRICK, *His Request to Julia*.

Thou art a plant sprung up to wither never,
But, like a laurel, to grow green forever.
ROBERT HERRICK, *To His Booke*.

14
The best part of every author is in general to be found in his book.
SAMUEL JOHNSON. (HILL, *Johnsonian Miscellanies*, ii, 310.)

15
Pray thee, take care, that tak'st my book in hand,
To read it well; that is, to understand.
BEN JONSON, *Epigrams*. No. 1.

16
All the doings of mankind, their vows, their fears, their angers and their pleasures their

joys and their goings to and fro, shall form the motley subject of my book. (Quidquid agunt homines, votum tomor ira voluptas Gaudia discursus, nostri farrago libelli est.)

JUVENAL, *Satires.* Sat. i, l. 85.

1
I like you and your book, ingenious Hone!
In whose capacious all-embracing leaves
The very marrow of tradition's shown;
And all that history, much that fiction, weaves.

CHARLES LAMB, *To the Editor of the Every-Day Book.*

2
The readers and the hearers like my books,
And yet some writers cannot them digest;
But what care I? for when I make a feast,
I would my guests should praise it, not the cooks.
(Lector et auditor nostros probat, Aule, libellos,
Sed quidam exactos esse poeta negat.
Non nimium curo: nam cenæ fercula nostræ
Malim convivis quam placuisse cocis.)

MARTIAL, *Epigrams.* Bk. ix, epig. 81. (Sir John Harington, tr.)

3
I have not made my book more than my book has made me. (Je n'ay pas plus faict mon livre, que mon livre m'a faict.)

MONTAIGNE, *Essays.* Bk. ii, ch. 18.

All the world may know me by my book, and my book by me.

MONTAIGNE, *Essays.* Bk. iii, ch. 5.

4
Go, little Book! from this my solitude;
I cast thee on the waters,—go thy ways:
And if, as I believe, thy vein be good,
The World will find thee after many days.
Be it with thee according to thy worth:
Go, little Book! in faith I send thee forth.

SOUTHEY, *Lay of the Laureate: L'Envoi.*

"Go, little book, from this my solitude!
I cast thee on the waters,—go thy ways!
And if, as I believe, thy vein be good,
The world will find thee after many days."
When Southey's read, and Wordsworth understood,
I can't help putting in my claim to praise—
The first four rhymes are Southey's, every line:
For God's sake, reader! take them not for mine.

BYRON, *Don Juan.* Canto i, st. 222.

5
O, let my books be then the eloquence
And dumb presagers of my speaking breast; . . .
O, learn to read what silent love hath writ:
To hear with eyes belongs to love's fine wit.

SHAKESPEARE, *Sonnets.* No. xxiii.

6
Go, little book, and wish to all
Flowers in the garden, meat in the hall,
A bit of wine, a spice of wit,
A house with lawns enclosing it,
A living river by the door,
A nightingale in the sycamore!

R. L. STEVENSON, *Envoy.*

7
Go, songs, for ended is our brief, sweet play;
Go, children of swift joy and tardy sorrow:
And some are sung, and that was yesterday,
And some unsung, and that may be tomorrow.

FRANCIS THOMPSON, *Envoy.*

8
Then falter not, O book, fulfil your destiny,
You not a reminiscence of the land alone,
You too as a lone bark cleaving the ether, purpos'd
I know not whither, yet ever full of faith.

WALT WHITMAN, *In Cabin'd Ships at Sea.*

Camerado, this is no book,
Who touches this touches a man, . . .
It is I you hold and who holds you,
I spring from the pages into your arms.

WALT WHITMAN, *So Long.*

9
Go forth, my little book! pursue thy way;
Go forth, and please the gentle and the good.

WORDSWORTH, *Memorials of a Tour on the Continent.* No. 37.

Reader, farewell! My last words let them be—
If in this book Fancy and Truth agree;
If simple Nature trained by careful Art
Through It have won a passage to thy heart;
Grant me thy love, I crave no other fee!

WORDSWORTH, *Miscellaneous Sonnets.* Pt. iii, No. 39.

BOOTH, EDWIN

10
That face which no man ever saw
And from his memory banished quite,
With eyes in which are Hamlet's awe
And Cardinal Richelieu's subtle light.

THOMAS BAILEY ALDRICH, *Sargent's Portrait of Edwin Booth at "The Players."*

In narrow space, with Booth, lie housed in death
Iago, Hamlet, Shylock, Lear, Macbeth.
If still they seem to walk the painted scene,
'Tis but the ghosts of those that once have been.

T. B. ALDRICH, *The Grave of Edwin Booth.*

11
Take with thee, too, our bond of gratitude
That in a cynic and a tattling age
Thou didst consent to write, in missal script,
Thy name on the poor players' slandered page,
And teach the lords of empty birth a king may walk the stage.

ALICE BROWN, *Edwin Booth.*

12
The Artist is a rare, rare breed. There were but two, forsooth,
In all me time (the stage's prime!) and The Other One was Booth.

EDMUND VANCE COOKE, *The Other One Was Booth.*

BORES

1
Bore: a person who talks when you wish him to listen.

AMBROSE BIERCE, *The Devil's Dictionary*.

A bore is a man who, when you ask him how he is, tells you.

BERT LESTON TAYLOR, *The So-Called Human Race*, p. 163.

2
For ennui is a growth of English root,
Though nameless in our language: we retort
The fact for words, and let the French translate
That awful yawn which sleep can not abate.

BYRON, *Don Juan*. Canto xiii, l. 101.

3
Description is always a bore, both to the describer and to the describee.

BENJAMIN DISRAELI, *Home Letters*. Letter vii.

4
The bore is usually considered a harmless creature, or of that class of irrational bipeds who hurt only themselves.

MARIA EDGEWORTH, *Thoughts on Bores*.

5
To inflict anyone with a compulsory interview of more than ten minutes indicates a crude state of civilization.

EMERSON, *Uncollected Lectures: Social Aims*.

6
And she became a bore intense
Unto her love-sick boy.

W. S. GILBERT, *Trial by Jury*.

7
All men are bores, except when we want them.

O. W. HOLMES, *The Autocrat of the Breakfast-Table*. Ch. 1.

8
A tedious person is one a man would leap a steeple from, gallop down any steep hill to avoid.

BEN JONSON, *Explorata: Impertinens*.

9
We often pardon those who bore us, but never those whom we bore. (Nous pardonnons souvent à ceux qui nous ennuient, mais nous ne pouvons pardonner à ceux que nous ennuyons.)

LA ROCHEFOUCAULD, *Maximes*. No. 304.

One is bored almost always by those persons with whom one is not permitted to be bored. (On s'ennuie presque toujours avec les gens avec qui il n'est pas permis de s'ennuyer.)

LA ROCHEFOUCAULD, *Maximes*. No. 352.

We are nearly always most bored by those whom we bore. (On s'ennuie presque toujours avec ceux que l'on ennuie.)

LA ROCHEFOUCAULD, *Maximes Posthumes*. No. 555.

Extreme boredom serves to cure boredom. (L'extrême ennui sert à nous désennuyer.)

LA ROCHEFOUCAULD, *Maximes Posthumes*. No. 532.

10
And so dull that the men who retailed them out-doors
Got the ill name of augurs, because they were bores.

J. R. LOWELL, *A Fable for Critics*, l. 54.

There was one feudal custom worth keeping, at least,
Roasted bores made a part of each well-ordered feast.

J. R. LOWELL, *A Fable for Critics*, l. 1226.

11
Meanwhile I inly curse the bore
Of hunting still the same old coon.

J. R. LOWELL, *Without and Within*.

12
The well bred man should never consent to become a bore. (Dedecet ingenuos tædia ferre sui.)

OVID, *Ars Amatoria*. Bk. ii, l. 530.

13
So sweetly mawkish, and so smoothly dull.

POPE, *The Dunciad*. Bk. iii, l. 171.

14
That old hereditary bore, the steward.

SAMUEL ROGERS, *A Character*.

15
Again I hear that creaking step!—
He's rapping at the door!
Too well I know the boding sound
That ushers in a bore.

J. G. SAXE, *My Familiar*.

I do not tremble when I meet
The stoutest of my foes,
But Heaven defend me from the friend
Who comes—but never goes!

J. G. SAXE, *My Familiar*.

He says a thousand pleasant things,—
But never says "Adieu."

J. G. SAXE, *My Familiar*.

In vain I speak of urgent tasks;
In vain I scowl and pout;
A frown is no extinguisher—
It does not put him out!

J. G. SAXE, *My Familiar*.

16
O, he is as tedious
As a tired horse, a railing wife;
Worse than a smoky house: I had rather live
With cheese and garlic in a windmill, far,
Than feed on cates and have him talk to me
In any summer-house in Christendom.

SHAKESPEARE, *I Henry IV*. Act iii, sc. 1, l. 159.

Faith! he must make his stories shorter
Or change his comrades once a quarter.

SWIFT, *On the Death of Dr. Swift*, l. 95.

17
The secret of being a bore is to tell everything. (Le secret d'ennuyer est celui de tout dire.)

VOLTAIRE, *L'Enfant Prodigue: Preface*.

Every species of mankind is good except the bore species. (Tous les genres sont bons hors le genre ennuyeux.)

VOLTAIRE, *L'Enfant Prodigue: Preface*.

One must always aim at being interesting rather than exact; for the spectator forgives everything except dreariness. (Il faut toujours songer à être intérressant plutôt qu'exact; car le spectateur pardonne tout, hors la langueur.)
VOLTAIRE, *Œdipe*. Lettre iv.

1
Repose is a good thing, but boredom is its brother. (Le repos est un bon chose, mais l'ennui est son frère.)
VOLTAIRE.

BORROWING AND LENDING

See also Debt. For literary borrowing see Plagiarism

I—Borrowing

2
Borrow from yourself. (A te mutuum sumes.)
CATO, *Fragments*. No. 79. (SENECA, *Epistulæ ad Lucilium*. Epis. cxix, sec. 2.)

3
Be not made a beggar by banqueting upon borrowing.
Apocrypha: Ecclesiasticus, xviii, 33.

The borrower runs in his own debt.
EMERSON, *Essays, First Series: Compensation.*

4
Borrowing thrives but once. (Borgen thut nur einmal wohl.)
UNKNOWN. A German proverb.

5
Two things thou shalt not long for, if thou love a mind serene:—
A woman to thy wife, though she were a crownèd queen;
And the second, borrowed money,—though the smiling lender say
That he will not demand the debt until the Judgment Day.
IBN JEMIN, *Epigram*. (Emerson, tr.)

6
Borrowing is not much better than begging. (Borgen ist nicht viel besser als betteln.)
LESSING, *Nathan der Weise*. Act ii, sc. 9.

7
Money borrowed is soon sorrowed.
JOHN RAY, *English Proverbs*.

Who goeth a-borrowing, goeth a-sorrowing.
THOMAS TUSSER, *Five Hundred Points of Good Husbandrie: June's Abstract*. (1580)

He that goes a-borrowing, goes a-sorrowing.
BENJAMIN FRANKLIN, *Poor Richard*, 1758.

8
Who quick be to borrow, and slow be to pay,
Their credit is naught, go they never so gay.
THOMAS TUSSER, *Five Hundred Points of Good Husbandrie*, 83.

9
Let us all be happy, and live within our means, even if we have to borrow the money to do it.
ARTEMUS WARD, *Natural History*.

II—Borrowing: Lending

10
Give, and you may keep your friend if you lose your money; lend, and the chances are that you lose your friend if ever you get back your money.
BULWER-LYTTON, *Caxtoniana*. Essay xxi.

Lend money to an enemy, and thou'lt gain him; to a friend, and thou'lt lose him.
BENJAMIN FRANKLIN, *Poor Richard*, 1740.

11
A small sum makes a debtor, a larger sum an enemy. (Æs debitorem leve, gravius inimicum facit.)
LABERIUS. *See also under* BENEFIT.

12
He who prefers to give Linus the half of what he wishes to borrow, rather than lend him the whole, prefers to lose only the half. (Dimidium donare Lino quam credere totum Qui mavolt, mavolt perdere dimidium.)
MARTIAL, *Epigrams*. Bk. i, epig. 75.

What you lend is lost.
PLAUTUS, *Trinummus*. Act iv, sc. 3, l. 43.

Lend only what you can afford to lose.
GEORGE HERBERT, *Jacula Prudentum*.

Who lends loseth double.
TORRIANO, *Piazza Universale*, 217.

Very often he that his money lends
Loses both his gold and his friends.
C. H. SPURGEON, *John Ploughman*. Ch. 4.

What we spent we had; what we gave we have; what we lent is lost.
UNKNOWN, *New Help to Discourse*, 250. (1669)
See also under GIFT.

13
A good man sheweth favour, and lendeth.
Old Testament: Psalms, cxii, 5.

14
In low simplicity
He lends out money gratis and brings down
The rate of usance here with us in Venice.
SHAKESPEARE, *The Merchant of Venice*. Act i, sc. 3, l. 44.

15
If thou wilt lend this money, lend it not
As to thy friends; for when did friendship take
A breed for barren metal of his friend?
But lend it rather to thine enemy;
Who, if he break, thou mayst with better face
Exact the penalty.
SHAKESPEARE, *The Merchant of Venice*. Act i, sc. 3, l. 133.

Out of my lean and low ability
I'll lend you something.
SHAKESPEARE, *Twelfth Night*. Act iii, sc. 4, l. 378.

16
That may be claim'd again which was but lent,
And should be yielded with no discontent,
Nor surely can we find herein a wrong,
That it was left us to enjoy it long.
RICHARD CHENEVIX TRENCH, *The Lent Jewels*.

1
The holy passion of Friendship is of so sweet and steady and loyal and enduring a nature that it will last through a whole lifetime, if not asked to lend money.
MARK TWAIN, *Pudd'nhead Wilson's Calendar.*

2
Seldom comes a loan laughing home.
UNKNOWN, *Reliq. Antiquæ.* i, 113. (c. 1320.)

3
God bless pawnbrokers!
They are quiet men.
MARGUERITE WILKINSON, *Pawnbrokers.*

Brothers, Wardens of City Halls,
And Uncles, rich as three Golden Balls
From taking pledges of nations.
THOMAS HOOD, *Miss Kilmansegg,* l. 275

III—Borrowing and Lending

4
I hae naething to lend—
I'll borrow frae naebody.
BURNS, *I Hae a Wife.*

5
I come to borrow what I'll never lend
And buy what I'll never pay for.
SIR WILLIAM D'AVENANT, *The Wits.* Act i, sc. 1.

6
Generally speaking, among sensible persons, it would seem that a rich man deems that friend a sincere one who does not want to borrow his money; while, among the less favored with fortune's gifts, the sincere friend is generally esteemed to be the individual who is ready to lend it.
BENJAMIN DISRAELI, *Tancred.* Bk. v, ch. 1.

7
Creditors have better memories than debtors.
BENJAMIN FRANKLIN, *Poor Richard,* 1758.

8
The best way to keep your friends is to never owe them anything and never lend them anything. (Le meilleur moyen de conserver vos amis est de rien leur devoir et de ne jamais leur prêter.)
PAUL DE KOCK, *L'Homme aux Trois Culottes.* Ch. 3.

9
The human species, according to the best theory I can form of it, is composed of two distinct races, the men who borrow, and the men who lend.
LAMB, *Essays of Elia: The Two Races of Men.*

10
The borrower is the servant to the lender.
Old Testament: Proverbs, xxii, 7.

11
Believe me, 'tis a godlike thing to lend; to owe is a heroic virtue. (Croyez que chose divine est prester; debvoir est vertu heroïque.)
RABELAIS, *Works.* Bk. iii, ch. 4.

Nature hath created man to no other end but to lend and to borrow. (Nature n'a crée l'homme que pour prester et emprunter.)
RABELAIS, *Works.* Bk. iii, ch. 4.

No man is so rich that he may not sometimes owe, and none so poor but that one may sometimes borrow of him. (Il n'est si riche qui quelquefois ne doibve; il n'est si pauvre de qui quelquefois on ne puisse emprunter.)
RABELAIS, *Works.* Bk. iii, ch. 5.

12
Neither a borrower nor a lender be:
For loan oft loses both itself and friend,
And borrowing dulls the edge of husbandry.
SHAKESPEARE, *Hamlet.* Act i, sc. 3, l. 75.

Lend less than thou owest.
SHAKESPEARE, *King Lear.* Act i, sc. 4, l. 133.

13
'Tis a very good world that we live in,
To lend, or to spend, or to give in;
But to beg or to borrow, or get a man's own,
'Tis the very worst world that ever was known.
JOHN WILMOT, EARL OF ROCHESTER, *Epigram.*

BOSTON

14
A Boston man is the east wind made flesh.
THOMAS APPLETON. (Attr.)

15
And this is good old Boston,
The home of the bean and the cod,
Where the Lowells talk to the Cabots,
And the Cabots talk only to God.
J. C. BOSSIDY, *On the Aristocracy of Harvard.*

Then here's to the City of Boston,
The town of the cries and the groans,
Where the Cabots can't see the Kabotschniks,
And the Lowells won't speak to the Cohns.
FRANKLIN P. ADAMS, *Revised.*

Here's to the town of New Haven,
The home of the Truth and the Light,
Where God talks to Jones in the very same tones
That He uses with Hadley and Dwight.
F. S. JONES, *On the Democracy of Yale.*

I've never seen a Lowell walk,
Nor heard a Cabot speak with God,
But I enjoy good Boston talk
And Boston beans and Boston cod.
R. H. BRUCE LOCKHART, *In Praise of Boston.*

16
Boston's a hole, the herring-pond is wide,
V-notes are something, liberty still more.
ROBERT BROWNING, *Mr. Sludge "The Medium."*

17
The rocky nook with hill-tops three
Looked eastward from the farms,
And twice each day the flowing sea
Took Boston in its arms.
EMERSON, *Boston.* St. 1.

The sea returning day by day
Restores the world-wide mart;
So let each dweller on the Bay
Fold Boston in his heart,
Till these echoes be choked with snows,
Or over the town blue ocean flows.
EMERSON, *Boston.* St. 20.

18
We say the cows laid out Boston. Well, there are worse surveyors.
EMERSON, *Conduct of Life: Wealth.*

One day, through the primeval wood,
A calf walked home, as good calves should;
But made a trail all bent askew,
A crooked trail, as all calves do. . . .
This forest trail became a lane,
That bent, and turned, and turned again, . . .
And this, before men were aware,
A city's crowded thoroughfare; . . .
And men two centuries and a half
Trod in the footsteps of that calf.

SAM WALTER FOSS, *The Calf-Path.*

1
Boston State-house is the hub of the solar system. You couldn't pry that out of a Boston man if you had the tire of all creation straightened out for a crow-bar.

O. W. HOLMES, *The Autocrat of the Breakfast-Table.* Ch. 6.

The axis of the earth sticks out visibly through the center of each and every town and city.

O. W. HOLMES, *The Autocrat of the Breakfast-Table.* Ch. 6.

2
Full of crooked little streets; but I tell you Boston has opened, and kept open, more turnpikes that lead straight to free thought and free speech and free deeds than any other city of live men or dead men.

O. W. HOLMES, *The Professor at the Breakfast-Table.* Ch. 1.

That's all I claim for Boston,—that it is the thinking center of the continent, and therefore of the planet.

O. W. HOLMES, *The Professor at the Breakfast-Table.* Ch. 4.

I never thought he would come to good, when I heard him attempting to sneer at an unoffending city so respectable as Boston.

O. W. HOLMES, *The Professor at the Breakfast-Table.* Ch. 11.

The heart of the world beats under the three hills of Boston.

O. W. HOLMES, *The Professor at the Breakfast-Table,* Ch. 12.

3
Solid men of Boston, banish long potations!
Solid men of Boston, make no long orations!

CHARLES MORRIS, *Pitt and Dundas's Return to London from Wimbledon.* (*Lyra Urbanica,* 1840.) Referring to Boston, Lincolnshire, England, after which Boston, Mass., was named.

Solid men of Boston, make no long orations;
Solid men of Boston, drink no long potations;
Solid men of Boston, go to bed at sundown;
Never lose your way like the loggerheads of London.

UNKNOWN, *Billy Pitt and the Farmer.* (DEBRETT, *Asylum for Fugitive Pieces,* 1786.) Daniel Webster, in a letter to Rev. C. B. Haddock (9 March, 1849), quoted the first two lines and added with seeming seriousness, "I take them to myself."

A solid man of Boston;
A comfortable man with dividends,
And the first salmon and the first green peas.

LONGFELLOW, *John Endicott.* Act iv.

4
Boston is a state of mind.

MARK TWAIN [?]. Also attributed to Emerson and Thomas G. Appleton.

5
Massachusetts has been the wheel within New England, and Boston the wheel within Massachusetts. Boston therefore is often called the "hub of the world," since it has been the source and fountain of the ideas that have reared and made America.

REV. F. B. ZINCKLE, *Last Winter in the United States.* (1868)

BOY AND BOYHOOD

See also Children, Youth

6
My object will be, if possible, to form Christian men, for Christian boys I can scarcely hope to make.

THOMAS ARNOLD, *Letter,* written in 1828 when appointed headmaster of Rugby.

7
And six little singing boys—dear little souls!
In nice clean faces, and nice white stoles.

R. H. BARHAM, *The Jackdaw of Rheims.*

8
Ah! happy years! once more who would not be a boy!

BYRON, *Childe Harold.* Canto ii, st. 23.

One of the best things in the world to be is a boy; it requires no experience, but needs some practice to be a good one.

CHARLES DUDLEY WARNER, *Being a Boy.* Ch. 1.

9
Few boys are born with talents that excel,
But all are capable of living well.

COWPER, *Tirocinium.* l. 509.

10
I only know two sorts of boys. Mealy boys and beef-faced boys.

DICKENS, *Oliver Twist.* Ch. 14.

11
That boy is blest,
Whose infant lips have drain'd a mother's breast;
But happier far are those, (if such be known),
Whom both a father and a mother own.

JOHN GAY, *Trivia.* Bk. ii, l. 177.

12
God bless all little boys who look like Puck,
With wide eyes, wider mouths and stick-out ears,
Rash little boys who stay alive by luck
And Heaven's favor in this world of tears.

ARTHUR GUITERMAN, *Blessing on Little Boys.*

13
The boy stood on the burning deck
Whence all but him had fled;
The flame that lit the battle's wreck,
Shone round him o'er the dead.

FELICIA DOROTHEA HEMANS, *Casabianca.* The original version. In later ones Mrs. Hemans sometimes preferred the ungrammatical, "Whence all but he had fled."

1
Has there any old fellow got mixed with the boys?
If there has, take him out, without making a noise.
O. W. HOLMES, *The Boys.*

Shall we always be youthful, and laughing, and gay,
Till the last dear companion drops smiling away?
Then here's to our boyhood, its gold and its gray!
The stars of its winter, the dews of its May!
O. W. HOLMES, *The Boys.*

2
O for one hour of youthful joy!
Give back my twentieth spring!
I'd rather laugh, a bright-haired boy,
Than reign, a gray-beard king.
O. W. HOLMES, *The Old Man Dreams.*

Oh, would I were a boy again,
When life seemed formed of sunny years,
And all the heart then knew of pain
Was wept away in transient tears!
MARK LEMON, *Oh, Would I Were a Boy Again.*

3
I remember, I remember
The fir trees dark and high;
I used to think their slender tops
Were close against the sky;
It was a childish ignorance,
But now 'tis little joy
To know I'm farther off from heav'n
Than when I was a boy.
THOMAS HOOD, *I Remember, I Remember.*

Oh, when I was a tiny boy
My days and nights were full of joy,
My mates were blithe and kind!
No wonder that I sometimes sigh
And dash a tear-drop from my eye
To cast a look behind!
THOMAS HOOD, *A Retrospective Review.*

My eyes are dim with childish tears,
My heart is idly stirred,
For the same sound is in my ears
Which in those days I heard.
WORDSWORTH, *The Fountain,* l. 29.

5
Let no foul word or sight cross the threshold wherein there is a boy. . . . Great reverence is due to boyhood. (Nil dictu fœdum visuque hæc limina tangat, intra quæ puer est. . . . Maxima debetur puero reverentia.)
JUVENAL, *Satires.* Sat. xiv, l. 44.

6
I do be thinking God must laugh
The time He makes a boy;
All element the creatures are,
And divilment and joy.
WINIFRED M. LETTS, *Boys.*

7
I remember the gleams and glooms that dart
Across the school-boy's brain;
The song and the silence in the heart,
That in part are prophecies, and in part
Are longings wild and vain.
And the voice of that fitful song
Sings on, and is never still:
"A boy's will is the wind's will,
And the thoughts of youth are long, long thoughts."
LONGFELLOW, *My Lost Youth.* St. 7.

Perhaps there lives some dreamy boy, untaught
In schools, some graduate of the field or street,
Who shall become a master of the art,
An admiral sailing the high seas of thought.
LONGFELLOW, *Possibilities.*

8
When I was a beggarly boy
And lived in a cellar damp,
I had not a friend nor a toy,
But I had Aladdin's lamp.
J. R. LOWELL, *Aladdin.*

I knew the streets of Rome and Troy,
I supp'd with Fates and Furies;
Twelve years ago I was a boy,
A happy boy, at Drury's.
W. M. PRAED, *School and Schoolfellows.*

9
The smiles and tears of boyhood's years,
The words of love then spoken.
THOMAS MOORE, *Oft in the Stilly Night.*

10
O, 'tis a parlous boy;
Bold, quick, ingenious, forward, capable;
He's all the mother's, from the top to toe.
SHAKESPEARE, *Richard III.* Act iii, sc. 1, l. 154.

Tush, tush! fear boys with bugs.
SHAKESPEARE, *The Taming of the Shrew.* Act i, sc. 2, l. 211.

11
When that I was and a little tiny boy,
With hey, ho, the wind and the rain,
A foolish thing was but a toy,
For the rain it raineth every day.
SHAKESPEARE, *Twelfth Night.* Act v, sc. 1, l. 398.

Two lads that thought there was no more behind,
But such a day to-morrow as to-day,
And to be boy eternal.
SHAKESPEARE, *Winter's Tale.* Act i, sc. 2, l. 63.

12
What are little boys made of, made of?
What are little boys made of?
Snips and snails and puppy-dog tails,
And such are little boys made of.
ROBERT SOUTHEY, *What All the World Is Made Of.* (c. 1820)

What are young women made of? . . .
Sugar and spice and all things nice,
And such are young women made of.
SOUTHEY, *What All the World Is Made Of.*

How rude are the boys that throw pebbles and mire.
ISAAC WATTS, *Innocent Play.*

13
Blessings on thee, little man,
Barefoot boy, with cheek of tan!
With thy turned-up pantaloons,
And thy merry whistled tunes.
WHITTIER, *The Barefoot Boy.*

Oh, for boyhood's time of June,
Crowding years in one brief moon.
WHITTIER, *The Barefoot Boy.*

1
The sweetest roamer is a boy's young heart.
GEORGE E. WOODBERRY, *Agathon.*

2
O dearest, dearest boy! my heart
For better lore would seldom yearn,
Could I but teach the hundredth part
Of what from thee I learn.
WORDSWORTH, *Anecdote for Fathers,* l. 57.

3
Boys are boys, and employ themselves with boyish matters. (Sunt pueri pueri, pueri puerilia tractant.)
UNKNOWN. A Latin proverb.

Boys will be boys.
BULWER-LYTTON, *The Caxtons.* Pt. xv, ch. 1.

Boys will be men one day.
THOMAS FULLER, *Gnomologia.* No. 1014.

"Boys will be boys." "And even that," I interposed, "wouldn't matter if we could only prevent girls from being girls."
ANTHONY HOPE, *The Dolly Dialogues.* No. 16.

BRAIN, see Mind

BRAVERY, see Courage

BREAD

4
Acorns were good until bread was found.
FRANCIS BACON, *Colours of Good and Evil.* Sec. 6.

5
All goes well here; bread is not to be had. (Tout va bien ici; le pain manque.)
PIERRE BAILLE, *Letter,* from Paris, 1792. (CARLYLE, *French Revolution.* Vol. ii, bk. v, ch. 8.)

6
Better half a loaf than no bread.
WILLIAM CAMDEN, *Remains,* p. 293. (1605)

Half a loaf is better than no bread.
JOHN HEYWOOD, *Proverbs.* Pt. i, ch. 11.

Something is better than nothing. (Mas vale Algo que nada.)
CERVANTES, *Don Quixote.* Pt. i, ch. 21.

"Better," they say, "a bad 'scuse than none."
NICHOLAS UDALL, *Ralph Roister Doister.* Act v, sc. 2. (c. 1540)

A bad shift is better than none at all.
HENRY PORTER, *The Two Angry Women of Abington.* (1599)

7
A loaf of bread, the Walrus said,
Is what we chiefly need:
Pepper and vinegar besides
Are very good indeed.
LEWIS CARROLL, *The Walrus and the Carpenter.* (*Through the Looking-Glass.* Ch. 4.)

8
To look for better bread than ever came of wheat. (Buscar Pan de trastrigo.)
CERVANTES, *Don Quixote.* Pt. i, ch. 7.

9
The bread eaten and the company dispersed. (El Pan comido y la compania deshecha.)
CERVANTES, *Don Quixote.* Pt. ii, ch. 7.

Eaten bread is forgotten.
JOHN RAY, *English Proverbs.*
See also under DEVIL.

11
With his bread let him eat it. (Con su Pan se lo come.) *i.e.,* That's his look-out.
CERVANTES, *Don Quixote.* Pt. ii, ch. 25.

12
Man doth not live by bread only.
Old Testament: Deuteronomy, viii, 3.

Man shall not live by bread alone.
New Testament: Matthew, iv, 4.

Man does not live by bread alone, but by faith, by admiration, by sympathy.
EMERSON, *Lectures, and Biographical Studies: The Sovereignty of Ethics.*

Man is a creature who lives not upon bread alone, but principally by catch-words.
R. L. STEVENSON, *Virginibus Puerisque.* Pt. ii.
See also under HYACINTH.

13
Secure of bread as of returning light.
DRYDEN, *Eleonora,* l. 16.

14
Cast thy bread upon the waters: for thou shalt find it after many days.
Old Testament: Ecclesiastes, xi, 1.

He who casts his bread upon the water will surely find it again; for though it falleth to the bottom, it sinks but like the ax of the prophet, to arise again unto him.
SIR THOMAS BROWNE, *Christian Morals.* Pt. i, sec. 6.

What bread men break is broke to them again.
JOHN TAYLOR THE WATER-POET, *Works,* p. 186. (1630)

15
Will it bake bread?
EMERSON, *Essays, First Series: Prudence.* "A prudence which asks but one question of any project,—Will it bake bread?"

16
They that have no other meat,
Bread and butter are glad to eat.
THOMAS FULLER, *Gnomologia.* No. 6128.

I won't quarrel with my bread and butter.
SWIFT, *Polite Conversation.* Dial. 1.

He who turns up his nose at his work quarrels with his bread and butter.
C. H. SPURGEON, *John Ploughman.* Ch. 19.

17
Of all smells, bread; of all tastes, salt.
GEORGE HERBERT, *Jacula Prudentum.*

18
I know which side my bread is buttered.
JOHN HEYWOOD, *Proverbs.* Pt. ii, ch. 8. (1546)

His bread is buttered on both sides.
THOMAS FULLER, *Gnomologia.* No. 6044.

19
Two things only the people anxiously desire—

bread and circus games. (Duas tantum res anxius optat, Panem et circenses.)
JUVENAL, *Satires*. Sat. x, l. 80. Hence the phrase, "Bread and circuses."

1
I have broken the staff of your bread.
Old Testament: Leviticus, xxvi, 26.

He brake the whole staff of bread.
Old Testament: Psalms, cv, 16.

Behold, I will break the staff of bread in Jerusalem: and they shall eat bread by weight, and with care; and they shall drink water by measure, and with astonishment.
Old Testament: Ezekiel, iv, 16. *See also Ezekiel*, v, 16; xiv, 13.

The stay and the staff, the whole stay of bread, and the whole stay of water.
Old Testament: Isaiah, iii, 1.

Corn, which is the staff of life.
EDWARD WINSLOW, *Good Newes from New England*, p. 47. (1624)

Here is bread, which strengthens man's heart, and therefore called the staff of life.
MATTHEW HENRY, *Commentaries: Psalm civ.*

"Bread," says he, "dear brothers, is the staff of life."
SWIFT, *Tale of a Tub*. Sec. iv.

2
When you came, you were like red wine and honey,
And the taste of you burnt my mouth with its sweetness.
Now you are like morning bread,
Smooth and pleasant.
I hardly taste you at all, for I know your savor;
But I am completely nourished.
AMY LOWELL, *A Decade*.

3
Give us this day our daily bread.
New Testament: Matthew, vi, 11.

Back of the loaf is the snowy flour,
And back of the flour the mill,
And back of the mill is the wheat and the shower
And the sun and the Father's will.
MALTBIE D. BABCOCK, *Give Us This Day Our Daily Bread*.

4
Bread and cheese be two targets against death.
THOMAS MOFFETT, *Health's Improvement*, p. 236. (1655)

I love not the humour of bread and cheese.
SHAKESPEARE, *The Merry Wives of Windsor* Act ii, sc. 1, l. 140.

Be fair conditioned and eat bread with your pudding.
JOHN RAY, *English Proverbs*, 79.

5
In one hand he carries a stone, and with the other offers bread. (Altera manu fert lapidem, panem ostentat altera.)
PLAUTUS, *Aulularia*, l. 195. (Act ii, sc. 2.)

A favor roughly bestowed by a hard man is bread made of stone.
FABIUS VERRUCOSUS. (SENECA, *De Beneficiis*, ii, 7.)

What man is there of you, whom if his son ask bread, will he give him a stone?
New Testament: Matthew, vii, 9.

The poet's fate is here in emblem shown,
He asked for bread, and he received a stone.
SAMUEL WESLEY, *Epigrams: On Butler's Monument in Westminster Abbey*.

Robbie asked for bread when he was alive; now that he is dead, they give him a stone.
Comment attributed to Burns's mother when informed that a monument was to be erected to him by his countrymen.

BREEDING, see Manners

BREVITY

6
Here comes my pruning-knife. (Ἡ *τῶν ἐμῶν λόγων κοπὶς πάρεστιν*.)
DEMOSTHENES, referring to Phocion, who was celebrated for his conciseness. (PLUTARCH, *Lives: Phocion*. Ch. 5, sec. 4.)

Bilin' down his repoort, wuz Finnigin!
An' he writed this here: "Musther Flannigan:
Off agin, on agin,
Gone agin.—Finnigin."
STRICKLAND GILLILAN, *Finnigin to Flannigan*.

7
Let thy speech be short, comprehending much in few words.
Apocrypha: Ecclesiasticus, xxxii, 8.

8
A good discourse is that from which nothing can be retrenched without cutting into the quick.
ST. FRANCIS DE SALES, *On Eloquence*.

9
Few were his words, but wonderfully clear. (Π*αῦρα μέν, ἀλλὰ μάλα λιγέως*.)
HOMER, *Iliad*. Bk. iii, l. 214.

10
Every word that is superfluous flows away from the full mind. (Omne supervacuum pleno de pectore manat.)
HORACE, *Ars Poetica*, l. 337.

There is need of brevity, that the thought may run on. (Est brevitate opus, ut currat sententia.)
HORACE, *Satires*. Bk. i, sat. 10, l. 9.

You reply, as your custom is, in few words. (Respondes, ut tuus est mos, Pauca.)
HORACE, *Satires*. Bk. i, sat. 6, l. 60.

11
In laboring to be brief, I become obscure. (Brevis esse laboro, obscurus fio.)
HORACE, *Ars Poetica*, l. 25.

For brevity is very good,
Where we are, or are not understood.
BUTLER, *Hudibras*. Pt. i, canto 1, l. 669.

12
Let your yea be yea; and your nay, nay.
New Testament: James, v, 12.

Let your communication be, Yea, yea; Nay, nay.
New Testament: Matthew, v, 37.

Use not vain repetitions.
New Testament: Matthew, vi, 7.

1
It is a foolish thing to make a long prologue, and to be short in the story itself.
Apocrypha: II Maccabees, ii, 32.

2
He who writes couplets wishes, I suppose, to please by brevity. But what is the use of brevity, tell me, when there is a whole book of it? (Disticha qui scribit, puto, vult brevitate placere. Quid prodest brevitas, dic mihi, si liber est?)
MARTIAL, *Epigrams*. Bk. viii, epig. 29.

3
In the eloquence of the bar, nothing pleases so much as brevity. (Nihil æque in causis agendis, ut brevitas, placet.)
PLINY THE YOUNGER, *Epistles*. Bk. i, epis. 20.

4
As man is now constituted, to be brief is almost a condition of being inspired.
GEORGE SANTAYANA, *Little Essays*, p. 141.

5
Since brevity is the soul of wit,
And tediousness the limbs and outward flourishes,
I will be brief.
SHAKESPEARE, *Hamlet*. Act ii, sc. 2, l. 90.

Brevity is the soul of drinking, as of wit.
CHARLES LAMB, *John Woodvil*. Ch. iii.

6
It is better to be brief than tedious.
SHAKESPEARE, *Richard III*. Act i, sc. 4, l. 88.

7
Not that the story need be long, but it will take a long while to make it short.
H. D. THOREAU, *Letter to a friend*.

BRIBERY

See also Gold: Its Power; Price

8
The man was clever, but of his hand had no control. (Σοφὸς γὰρ ἀνήρ, τῆς δὲ χειρὸς οὐ κρατῶν.)
ARISTIDES, of Themistocles. (PLUTARCH, *Lives: Aristides*. Ch. 4, sec. 2.)

9
He lied with such a fervour of intention—
There was no doubt he earn'd his laureate pension.
BYRON, *Don Juan*. Canto iii, st. 80.

A moderate pension shakes full many a sage
BYRON, *Don Juan*. Canto viii, st. 14.

Pension: An allowance made to anyone without an equivalent. In England it is generally understood to mean pay given to a state hireling for treason to his country.
SAMUEL JOHNSON, *Dictionary*.

Where Young must torture his invention
To flatter knaves, or lose his pension.
SWIFT, *Poetry, a Rhapsody*, l. 279.

Poor pensioner on the bounties of an hour.
YOUNG, *Night Thoughts*. Night i, l. 67.

10
For a crust of bread he can be hired either to keep silence or to speak. (Frusto panis conduci potest, vel uti taceat vel uti loquatur.)
CATO, referring to Marcus Cælius. (AULUS GELLIUS, *Noctes Atticæ*. Bk. i, ch. 15, sec. 10.)

A hoarseness caused by swallowing gold and silver.
The silver quinsy. (ἀργυράγχης.)
PLUTARCH, of Demosthenes, when the latter, who had been bribed not to speak against Harpalus, pretended to have lost his voice. (*Lives: Demosthenes*. Ch. 25, sec. 5.)

Moved by the rhetoric of a silver fee.
JOHN GAY, *Trivia*. Bk. iii, l. 318.

11
And they will best succeed, who best can pay:
Those who would gain the votes of British tribes,
Must add to force of merit, force of bribes.
CHARLES CHURCHILL, *The Rosciad*, l. 16.

Our supple tribes repress their patriot throats,
And ask no questions but the price of votes.
SAMUEL JOHNSON, *Vanity of Human Wishes*, l. 95.

12
To refuse with the right and take with the left.
JOHN CLARKE, *Parœmiologia*. (1639)

He refuseth the bribe, but putteth forth his hand.
THOMAS FULLER, *Gnomologia*. No. 2009.

13
It is patent to the mob,
That my being made a nob,
Was effected by a job.
W. S. GILBERT, *Trial by Jury*.

14
Too poor for a bribe, and too proud to importune,
He had not the method of making a fortune.
THOMAS GRAY, *Sketch of His Own Character*.

15
Turn from the glitt'ring bribe thy scornful eye,
Nor sell for gold what gold could never buy.
SAMUEL JOHNSON, *London*, l. 87.

Won by bribes, by flatteries implor'd,
The groom retails the favours of his lord.
SAMUEL JOHNSON, *London*, l. 180.

16
Bribes, believe me, buy both gods and men. (Munera, crede mihi, capiunt hominesque deosque.)
OVID, *Ars Amatoria*. Bk. iii, l. 653.

All those men have their price.
SIR ROBERT WALPOLE. *See under* PRICE.

17
Alas! the small discredit of a bribe
Scarce hurts the lawyer, but undoes the scribe.
POPE, *Epilogue to Satires*. Dial. ii, l. 46.

Then give humility a coach and six,
Justice a conqueror's sword, or truth a gown,
Or public spirit its great cure, a crown.
POPE, *Essay on Man*. Epis. iv, l. 170.

1
Honesty stands at the gate and knocks, and bribery enters in.
BARNABE RICH, *Irish Hubbub*. Ch. 9.

2
Let me tell you, Cassius, you yourself
Are much condemn'd to have an itching palm;
To sell and mart your offices for gold
To undeservers.
SHAKESPEARE, *Julius Cæsar*. Act iv, sc. 3, l. 9.

3
For a con-si-de-ra-tion.
SCOTT, *Fortunes of Nigel*. Ch. 22.

4
There is gold for you;
Sell me your good report.
SHAKESPEARE, *Cymbeline*. Act ii, sc. 3, l. 87.

Shall we now
Contaminate our fingers with base bribes?
SHAKESPEARE, *Julius Cæsar*. Act iv, sc. 3, l. 24.

But they wavered not long, for conscience was strong,
And they thought they might get more;
And they refused the gold, but not
So rudely as before.
ROBERT SOUTHEY, *The Surgeon's Warning*. St. 29.

5
Few men have virtue to withstand the highest bidder.
GEORGE WASHINGTON, *Moral Maxims: Virtue and Vice*.

6
Yet one of them, more hard of heart,
Did vow to do his charge,
Because the wretch, that hired him,
Had paid him very large.
UNKNOWN, *The Children in the Wood*. St. 12.

BRIDE and BRIDEGROOM, see Marriage: The Wedding Day

BRITANNIA, see England

BROOK

7
A noise like of a hidden brook
In the leafy month of June,
That to the sleeping woods all night
Singeth a quiet tune.
S. T. COLERIDGE, *Ancient Mariner*. Pt. v, st. 18.

Over the stones to lull and leap
Herding the bubbles like white sheep;
The claims of worry to deny,
And whisper sorrow into sleep.
GRACE HAZARD CONKLING, *The Whole Duty of Berkshire Brooks*.

8
Shallow brooks that flow'd so clear
The bottom did the top appear.
DRYDEN, *To the Pious Memory of Mrs. Anne Killigrew*, l. 110.

9
The streams, rejoic'd that winter's work is done,
Talk of to-morrow's cowslips as they run.
EBENEZER ELLIOTT, *Village Patriarch: Spring*.

And in the hush we joined to make
We heard, we knew we heard the brook.
ROBERT FROST, *Going for Water*.

10
From Helicon's harmonious springs
A thousand rills their mazy progress take.
THOMAS GRAY, *The Progress of Poesy*, l. 3.

Myriads of rivulets hurrying thro' the lawn.
TENNYSON, *The Princess*. Pt. vii, l. 205.

11
Sweet are the little brooks that run
O'er pebbles glancing in the sun,
Singing in soothing tones.
THOMAS HOOD, *Town and Country*. St. 9.

I heard a little water, and oh, the sky was blue,
A little water singing as little waters do.
R. C. LEHMANN, *Singing Water*.

The music of the brook silenced all conversation.
LONGFELLOW, *Kavanagh*. Ch. 21.

First of earthly singers, the sun-loved rill.
GEORGE MEREDITH, *Phœbus with Admetus*. St. 3.

12
Better to hearken to a brook
Than watch a diamond shine.
GEORGE MACDONALD, *Better Things*. St. 1.

And pore upon the brook that babbles by.
THOMAS GRAY, *Elegy Written in a Country Church-yard*, l. 104.

13
I wandered by the brookside,
I wandered by the mill;
I could not hear the brook flow,
The noisy wheel was still.
RICHARD MONCKTON MILNES, *The Brookside*.

14
And liquid lapse of murmuring streams.
MILTON, *Paradise Lost*. Bk. viii, l. 263.

15
He makes sweet music with th' enamell'd stones,
Giving a gentle kiss to every sedge
He overtaketh in his pilgrimage,
And so by many winding nooks he strays
With willing sport to the wild ocean.
SHAKESPEARE, *The Two Gentlemen of Verona*. Act ii, sc. 7, l. 28. (1594)

Gently running, made sweet music with the enamel'd stones and seemed to give a gentle kiss to every sedge he overtook in his watery pilgrimage.
RICHARD JOHNSON, *Seven Champions of Christendom*. (1597)

16
I chatter, chatter, as I flow
To join the brimming river,
For men may come and men may go,
But I go on for ever.
TENNYSON, *The Brook*, l. 47.

1
Brook! whose society the poet seeks,
Intent his wasted spirits to renew;
And whom the curious painter doth pursue
Through rocky passes, among flowery creeks,
And tracks thee dancing down thy water-breaks.

WORDSWORTH, *Miscellaneous Sonnets*. Pt. ii, No. 31.

2
Few men, drinking at a rivulet, stop to consider its source.

M. F. TUPPER, *Proverbial Philosophy: Of Gifts*.

Before we drink much at a brook, it is well to know its source.

JOHN A. SHEDD, *Salt from My Attic*, p. 19.

BROTHER AND BROTHERHOOD

See also Companionship, Philanthropy

3
O men, this man in brotherhood your weary paths beguiling,
Groaned inly while he taught you peace, and died while ye were smiling!

E. B. BROWNING, *Cowper's Grave*. St. 2.

4
I think, am sure, a brother's love exceeds
All the world's loves in its unworldliness.

ROBERT BROWNING, *A Blot in the 'Scutcheon*. Act ii, sc. 1.

5
Affliction's sons are brothers in distress;
A brother to relieve, how exquisite the bliss!

ROBERT BURNS, *A Winter Night*. St. 8.

And when with grief you see your brother stray,
Or in a night of error lose his way,
Direct his wandering and restore the day. . . .
Leave to avenging Heaven his stubborn will,
For, O, remember, he's your brother still.

SWIFT, *The Swan Tripe Club in Dublin*.

6
Of a truth, men are mystically united: a mysterious bond of brotherhood makes all men one.

CARLYLE, *Essays: Goethe's Works*.

7
Here's the sweet brotherhood of the proverb! (Hoc est, quod dicitur, illud Fraternum vere dulce sodalitium.)

CATULLUS, *Odes*. Ode c, l. 3.

8
Yes, you'd know him for a heathen
If you judged him by the hide,
But bless you, he's my brother,
For he's just like me inside.

ROBERT FREEMAN, *The Heathen*.

9
"Men work together," I told him from the heart,
"Whether they work together or apart."

ROBERT FROST, *The Tuft of Flowers*.

10
The right hands of fellowship.

New Testament: Galatians, ii, 9.

Out upon this half-fac'd fellowship!

SHAKESPEARE, *I Henry IV*. Act i, sc. 3, l. 208.

11
Am I my brother's keeper?

Old Testament: Genesis, iv, 9.

12
I do not hunger for a well-stored mind,
I only wish to live my life, and find
My heart in unison with all mankind.

EDMUND GOSSE, *Lying in the Grass*.

13
Let brotherly love continue.

New Testament: Hebrews, xiii, 1.

14
To-day, old friend, remember still
That I am Joe and you are Bill.

O. W. HOLMES, *Bill and Joe*.

15
There with a communal zeal we both had strove
In acts of dear benevolence and love;
Brothers in peace, not rivals in command.

HOMER, *Odyssey*. Bk. iv, l. 241. (Pope, tr.)

Between them was mutual love, and side by side they were wont to rush into battle. (His amor unus erat pariterque in bella ruebant.)

VERGIL, *Æneid*. Bk. ix, l. 182.

16
Forget the brother and resume the man.

HOMER, *Odyssey*. Bk. iv, l. 732. (Pope, tr.)

17
A noble pair of brothers. (Par nobile fratrum.)

HORACE, *Satires*. Bk. ii, sat. 3, l. 243.

18
Down in their hearts, wise men know this truth: the only way to help yourself is to help others.

ELBERT HUBBARD, *The Philistine*. Vol. 18, p. 12.

19
It is through fraternity that liberty is saved.

VICTOR HUGO, *Speech*, Paris, 1870.

The amiable age when man said to man,
Let us be brothers—or I'll knock you on the head.
(L'amiable siècle où l'homme dit à l'homme,
Soyons frères,—ou je t'assomme.)

E. LEBRUN, *Sur la Fraternité ou la Morte*.

20
We should be low and love-like, and leal, each man to other,
And patient as pilgrims, for pilgrims are we all.

WILLIAM LANGLAND, *Piers Plowman*. Passus xiii, l. 129.

21
A brother is a friend given by nature. (Un frère est un ami donné par la nature.)

LEGOUVÉ (père), *Maximes*.

22
Wherefore to colliers, carters, and cokes,
To Jack and Tom my rhyme shall be directed.

SIR DAVID LINDSAY, *Dialog Betwixt Experience and a Courteour*. Sig. A 8. (1552)

Of the maimed, of the halt and the blind in the rain and the cold—
Of these shall my songs be fashioned, my tales be told.

JOHN MASEFIELD, *A Consecration*.

1
Then none was for a party;
Then all were for the state;
Then the great man helped the poor,
And the poor man loved the great:
Then lands were fairly portioned;
Then spoils were fairly sold:
The Romans were like brothers
In the brave days of old.
MACAULAY, *Horatius*. St. 32.

2
The crest and crowning of all good,
Life's final star, is Brotherhood.
EDWIN MARKHAM, *Brotherhood*.

There is a destiny which makes us brothers;
None goes his way alone.
EDWIN MARKHAM, *A Creed*.

3
We two have talked our hearts out to the embers,
And now go hand in hand down to the dead.
JOHN MASEFIELD, *The Faithful*.

4
The time shall come
When man to man shall be a friend and brother.
GERALD MASSEY, *Hope On, Hope Ever*.

Throw out the life-line across the dark wave,
There is a brother whom someone must save.
EDWARD SMITH UFFORD, *Throw Out the Life-Line*. (1884) A favorite Moody and Sankey hymn.

5
Fellowship is heaven, and lack of fellowship is hell; fellowship is life, and lack of fellowship is death; and the deeds that ye do upon the earth, it is for fellowship's sake that ye do them.
WILLIAM MORRIS, *A Dream of John Ball*. Ch. 4.

6
To count the life of battle good,
And dear the land that gave you birth;
And dearer yet the brotherhood
That binds the brave of all the earth.
HENRY NEWBOLT, *Clifton Chapel*.

7
So great is the strife between brothers. (Tanta est discordia fratrum.)
OVID, *Metamorphoses*. Bk. i, l. 60.

8
We two form a multitude. (Nos duo turba sumus.)
OVID, *Metamorphoses*. Bk. i, l. 355. Referring to Deucalion and Pyrrha after the deluge.

One man with a dream, at pleasure,
Shall go forth and conquer a crown;
And three with a new song's measure
Can trample an empire down.
ARTHUR O'SHAUGHNESSY, *The Music-Makers*.

Three men, together riding,
Can win new worlds at their will;
Resolute, ne'er dividing,
Lead, and be victors still.
Three can laugh and doom a king,
Three can make the planets sing.
MARY CAROLYN DAVIES, *Three*.

9
Heav'n forming each on other to depend,
A master, or a servant, or a friend,
Bids each on other for assistance call,
Till one man's weakness grows the strength of all.
POPE, *Essay on Man*. Epis. ii, l. 249.

10
The younger brother hath the more wit.
JOHN RAY, *English Proverbs*.

11
We few, we happy few, we band of brothers.
SHAKESPEARE, *Henry V*. Act iv, sc. 3, l. 60.

Finds brotherhood in thee no sharper spur?
SHAKESPEARE, *Richard II*. Act i, sc. 2, l. 9.

12
Every man shift for all the rest, and let no man take care for himself.
SHAKESPEARE, *The Tempest*. Act v, sc. 1, l. 256.

13
No one can be perfectly free till all are free; no one can be perfectly moral till all are moral; no one can be perfectly happy till all are happy.
SPENCER, *Social Statics*. Pt. iv, ch. 30, sec. 16.

While there is a lower class I am in it. While there is a criminal class I am of it. While there is a soul in prison I am not free.
EUGENE V. DEBS, *Labor and Freedom*.

Whoever degrades another degrades me,
And whatever is done or said returns at last to me.
WALT WHITMAN, *Song of Myself*. Sec. 24.

14
Go, poor devil; get thee gone! why should I hurt thee? This world surely is wide enough to hold both thee and me!
STERNE, *Tristram Shandy*. Vol. ii, ch. 12.

15
There is a fellowship more quiet even than solitude, and which, rightly understood, is solitude made perfect.
R. L. STEVENSON, *Travels with a Donkey: A Night Among the Pines*.

16
No blast of air or fire of sun
Puts out the light whereby we run
With girdled loins our lamplit race,
And each from each takes heart of grace
And spirit till his turn be done.
SWINBURNE, *Songs Before Sunrise: Prelude*.

17
The little brown brother.
WILLIAM HOWARD TAFT, in 1900, referring to the Filipinos.

He may be a brother of Big Bill Taft,
But he ain't no brother of mine.
ROBERT F. MORRISON, in *Manila Sunday Sun*.

18
Not till the sun excludes you do I exclude you,
Not till the waters refuse to glisten for you and the leaves to rustle for you, do my words refuse to glisten and rustle for you.
WALT WHITMAN, *To a Common Prostitute*.

19
O love that passes the love of woman!
Who that hath felt it shall ever forget,

When the breath of life with a throb turns
human,
And a lad's heart is to a lad's heart set?
G. E. WOODBERRY, *Comrades.*

BROWN, JOHN

1
I am fully persuaded that I am worth inconceivably more to hang than for any other purpose.
JOHN BROWN, *Speech,* at his trial, 2 Nov., 1859.

2
John Brown's body lies a-mouldering in the
grave,
His soul is marching on!
CHARLES SPRAGUE HALL, *John Brown's Body.* Sometimes attributed to Frank E. Jerome.

John Brown died on the scaffold for the slave;
Dark was the hour when we dug his hallowed
grave;
Now God avenges the life he gladly gave,
Freedom reigns to-day!
EDNA DEAN PROCTOR, *John Brown.*

3
The death of Brown is more than Cain killing Abel: it is Washington slaying Spartacus.
VICTOR HUGO, *A Word Concerning John Brown to Virginia,* 2 Dec., 1859.

4
But, Virginians, don't do it! for I tell you that
the flagon,
Filled with blood of Old Brown's offspring,
was first poured by Southern hands;
And each drop from Old Brown's life-veins,
like the red gore of the dragon,
May spring up a vengeful Fury, hissing
through your slave-worn lands:
And Old Brown, Osawatomie Brown,
May trouble you more than ever, when you've
nailed his coffin down!
E. C. STEDMAN, *How Old Brown Took Harper's Ferry.* Written Nov., 1859, during Brown's trial.

But high let our standard flout it!
"Sic semper"—the drop comes down—
And (woe to the rogues that doubt it!)
There's an end of old John Brown!
HENRY HOWARD BROWNELL, *The Battle of Charlestown.*

5
John Brown of Ossawatomie, they led him out
to die;
And lo! a poor slave-mother with her little
child pressed nigh.
Then the bold, blue eye grew tender, and the
old harsh face grew mild,
As he stooped between the jeering ranks and
kissed the negro's child!
The shadows of his stormy life that moment
fell apart;
And they who blamed the bloody hand forgave the loving heart.
That kiss from all its guilty means redeemed
the good intent,
And round the grisly fighter's hair the martyr's
aureole bent!
WHITTIER, *Brown of Ossawatomie.*

Compassionate eyes had our brave John Brown,
And a craggy stern forehead, a militant frown;
He, the storm-bow of peace, give him volley on
volley,
The fool who redeemed us once of our folly,
And the smiter that healed us, our right John
Brown!
LOUISE IMOGEN GUINEY, *John Brown: A Paradox.*

6
I, John Brown, am now quite certain that the crimes of this guilty land will never be purged away but with Blood.
JOHN BROWN, *Last Statement,* made in writing the day of his execution, 2 Dec., 1859.

BROWNING, ROBERT

7
Or from Browning some "Pomegranate,"
which, if cut deep down the middle,
Shows a heart within blood-tinctured, of a
veined humanity.
E. B. BROWNING, *Lady Geraldine's Courtship.* St. 41.

You, Fitzgerald, whom by ear and eye
She never knew, "thanked God my wife was dead."
ROBERT BROWNING, *To Edward Fitzgerald.* Fitzgerald had written, "No more Aurora Leighs, thank God!" For Browning's verses see APPENDIX.

8
And, Robert Browning, you writer of plays,
Here's a subject made to your hand!
ROBERT BROWNING, *A Light Woman.*

9
Great-hearted son of the Titan mother, Earth,
Fed at her breast,
He builded upward from the solid ground,
While listening ever for the heavenly sound
Of higher voices, to his soul addressed.
FLORENCE EARLE COATES, *Robert Browning.*

10
Still fares he forth from dawn-lit paths dew-
pearled,
A singing pilgrim through a sighing world.
JAMES B. KENYON, *Robert Browning.*

11
Browning! Since Chaucer was alive and hale,
No man hath walk'd along our roads with
step
So active, so inquiring eye, or tongue
So varied in discourse.
W. S. LANDOR, *To Robert Browning.*

12
Yet few poets were so mated before and no poet was so mated afterward, until Browning stooped and picked up a fair-coined soul that lay rusting in a pool of tears.
FRANCIS THOMPSON, *Shelley,* p. 38.

13
He used poetry as a medium for writing in prose.
OSCAR WILDE, *The Critic as Artist.* Pt. i. Referring to Browning.

BRYAN, WILLIAM JENNINGS

1
The boy orator of the Platte.

W. J. CONNELL. Derisive description given to Bryan during Congressional campaign of 1890.

The Platte—six inches deep and six miles wide at the mouth.

SENATOR JOSEPH B. FORAKER, *Speech*, during campaign against Bryan, 1896.

1a
His civic laurels will not yield in splendor to the brightest chaplet that ever bloomed upon a warrior's brow.

HENRY T. LEWIS, *Speech*, nominating Bryan, 11 July, 1896. Lewis was quoting Prentiss, who said the same thing of Henry Clay.

2
Bryan's hold on the West lay in the fact that he was in himself the average man of a large part of that country; he did not merely resemble that average man, he was that average man.

CHARLES WILLIS THOMPSON, *Presidents I've Known*, p. 41.

George Harvey, with sarcastic intent, once alleged mendaciously that Bryan became a white ribboner because he heard a little girl recite, "The Lips That Touch Liquor Shall Never Touch Mine."

THOMPSON, *Presidents I've Known*, p. 42.

He [Bryan] was a progressive who never progressed—mentally. I never saw the least indication that he ever learned anything, either in Europe or at home, at any time in his mature life.

THOMPSON, *Presidents I've Known*, p. 91.

3
Would that we could do something at once dignified and effective to knock Mr. Bryan once for all into a cocked hat.

WOODROW WILSON, *Letter to Adrian H. Joline*, 29 April, 1907. Given to public by Joline in January, 1912. (See *Literary Digest*, 20 Jan., 1912.)

BURDEN

See also Care

4
Oh, there are moments for us here, when seeing
Life's inequalities, and woe, and care,
The burdens laid upon our mortal being
Seem heavier than the human heart can bear.

WILLIS G. CLARK, *A Song of May*.

5
But wilt thou measure all thy road,
See thou lift the lightest load.

EMERSON, *Conduct of Life: Considerations by the Way*.

6
Every horse thinks his own pack heaviest.

THOMAS FULLER, *Gnomologia*.

Each one thinks his lot the worst; but he is mistaken. If he thought himself the worst of the lot he might be right.

C. H. SPURGEON, *Salt-Cellars*.

7
And when the porter bends beneath his load,
And pants for breath, clear thou the crowded road.

JOHN GAY, *Trivia*. Bk. ii, l. 49.

Respect the burden, Madam.

NAPOLEON, to Mrs. Balcombe, at St. Helena, when some servants carrying heavy boxes, passed in their way. (O'MEARA, *Napoleon at St. Helena*.)

8
Bear ye one another's burdens.

New Testament: Galatians, vi, 2.

Every man shall bear his own burden.

New Testament: Galatians, vi, 5.

9
None knows the weight of another's burden.

GEORGE HERBERT, *Jacula Prudentum*.

Light burdens, long borne, grow heavy.

GEORGE HERBERT, *Jacula Prudentum*.

10
I would rather have a big burden and a strong back, than a weak back and a caddy to carry life's luggage.

ELBERT HUBBARD, *The Philistine*. Vol. xx, p. 26.

11
Money and time are the heaviest burdens of life, and the unhappiest of all mortals are those who have more of either than they know how to use.

SAMUEL JOHNSON, *The Idler*. No. 30.

12
How many weak shoulders have craved heavy burdens! (Combien d'épaules sans force ont demandé de lourds fardeaux!)

JOUBERT, *Pensées*. No. 201.

God giveth the shoulder according to the burden. (Gott giebt die Schultern nach der Bürde.)

UNKNOWN. A German proverb.

The back is made for the burden.

CARLYLE. Quoted as "a pious adage."

13
Take up the White Man's burden—
Send forth the best ye breed—
Go bind your sons to exile
To serve your captives' need;
To wait, in heavy harness,
On fluttered folk and wild—
Your new-caught, sullen peoples,
Half-devil and half-child.

RUDYARD KIPLING, *The White Man's Burden*.

Half angel and half bird.

ROBERT BROWNING, *The Ring and the Book*. Pt. i, l. 1391. See 1193:1.

15
Light grows the burden which is well borne. (Leve fit, quod bene fertur, onus.)

OVID, *Amores*. Bk. i, eleg. 2, l. 10.

The burden one likes is cheerfully borne.

JOHN RAY, *English Proverbs*.

16
To support the burden, you must strive with head erect; if your sinews yield, you will fall. (Sustineas ut onus, nitendum vertice pleno est, Aut, flecti nervos si patiere, cades.)

OVID, *Epistulæ ex Ponto*. Bk. ii, epis. 7, l. 77.

1
It is base to flinch under a burden. (Turpe est cedere oneri.)
SENECA, *Epistulæ ad Lucilium*. Epis. xxii, sec. 7.

2
A load would sink a navy, too much honour;
O, 'tis a burden, Cromwell, 'tis a burden
Too heavy for a man that hopes for heaven!
SHAKESPEARE, *Henry VIII*. Act iii, sc. 2, l. 383.

3
The burden is equal to the horse's strength.
Talmud. Sota 13.

An ass endures his burden, but not more than his burden.
GEORGE HERBERT, *Jacula Prudentum*.

4
The strength will with the burden grow.
TOM TAYLOR, *Abraham Lincoln*.

5
Place the burden on the slow-paced ass. (Onus segni impone asello.)
UNKNOWN. A Latin proverb. *See also* Ass.

BURKE, EDMUND

6
Here lies our good Edmund, whose genius was such,
We scarcely can praise it, or blame it too much;
Who, born for the Universe, narrow'd his mind,
And to party gave up what was meant for mankind:
Though fraught with all learning, yet straining his throat
To persuade Tommy Townshend to lend him a vote; . . .
Though equal to all things, for all things unfit;
Too nice for a statesman, too proud for a wit;
For a patriot, too cool; for a drudge, disobedient;
And too fond of the right to pursue the expedient.
In short, 'twas his fate, unemploy'd or in place, Sir,
To eat mutton cold, and cut blocks with a razor.
OLIVER GOLDSMITH, *Retaliation*, l. 29.

7
Burke, sir, is such a man that if you met him for the first time in the street, when you were stopped by a drove of oxen, and you and he stepped aside to take shelter but for five minutes, he'd talk to you in such a manner that when you parted you would say, "This is an extraordinary man."
SAMUEL JOHNSON. (BOSWELL, *Life*.)

8
We could only wish that the years had brought to him . . . a disposition to happiness, a composed spirit to which time has made things clear, an unambitious temper, and hopes undimmed for mankind.
JOHN MORLEY, *Burke*, p. 299.

9
And the final event to himself has been that, as he rose like a rocket, he fell like a stick.
THOMAS PAINE, *Letter to the Addressers*. Referring to Edmund Burke. The phrase was afterwards appropriated by Lockhart. *See under* DICKENS.

BURNS, ROBERT

10
Oh, but the mountain breeze must have been pleasant
Upon the sunburnt brow
Of that poetic and triumphant peasant
Driving his laureled plow!
WILLIAM ALEXANDER, *Robert Burns*.

11
The poor inhabitant below
Was quick to learn and wise to know,
And keenly felt the friendly glow,
And softer flame;
But thoughtless follies laid him low,
And stain'd his name.
ROBERT BURNS, *A Bard's Epitaph*.

12
Misled by a Fancy's meteor ray,
By Passion driven;
But yet the light that led astray,
Was light from Heaven.
ROBERT BURNS, *The Vision*. Duan ii, st. 18.

But ne'er to a seductive lay
Let faith be given,
Nor deem that "light which leads astray
Is light from heaven."
WORDSWORTH, *To the Sons of Burns*.

13
And rustic life and poverty
Grew beautiful beneath his touch. . . .
Whose lines are mottoes of the heart,
Whose truths electrify the sage.
CAMPBELL, *Ode to the Memory of Burns*.

14
A Burns is infinitely better educated than a Byron.
THOMAS CARLYLE, *Note Book*, 2 Nov., 1831.

Burns of all poets is the most a Man.
DANTE GABRIEL ROSSETTI, *On Burns*.

15
Such graves as his are pilgrim shrines,
Shrines to no code or creed confined,—
The Delphian vales, the Palestines,
The Meccas of the mind.
FITZ-GREENE HALLECK, *Burns*. St. 32.

16
The century shrivels like a scroll,—
The past becomes the present,—
And face to face, and soul to soul,
We greet the monarch-peasant. . . .

We praise him, not for gifts divine,—
His Muse was born of woman,—

His manhood breathes in every line,—
Was ever heart more human?

O. W. Holmes, *For the Burns Centennial Celebration.*

1
'Tis but a cot roofed in with straw, a hovel built of clay;
One door shuts out the snow and storm, one window greets the day.
And yet I stand within this room and hold all thrones in scorn,
For here, beneath this lowly thatch, love's sweetest bard was born.

R. G. Ingersoll, *The Burns Cottage in Ayr.*

2
Each little lyrical
Grave or satirical
Musical miracle!

F. L. Knowles, *On a Fly-Leaf of Burns's Songs.*

3
A dreamer of the common dreams,
A fisher in familiar streams,
He chased the transitory gleams
That all pursue;
But on his lips the eternal themes
Again were new.

William Watson, *The Tomb of Burns.*

He came when poets had forgot
How rich and strange the human lot;
How warm the tints of Life; how hot
Are Love and Hate:
And what makes Truth divine, and what
Makes Manhood great.

William Watson, *The Tomb of Burns.*

His greatness, not his littleness,
Concerns mankind.

William Watson, *The Tomb of Burns.*

4
Give lettered pomp to teeth of Time,
So "Bonnie Doon" but tarry:
Blot out the epic's stately rhyme,
But spare his Highland Mary!

Whittier, *Burns.* St. 29.

5
I mourned with thousands, but as one
More deeply grieved, for he was gone
Whose light I hailed when first it shone,
And showed my youth
How verse may build a princely throne
On humble truth.

Wordsworth, *At the Grave of Burns.* St. 6.

BUSINESS

See also Commerce, Corporations, Finance

I—Business: Apothegms

6
Business tomorrow. (Οὐκοῦν εἰς αὔριον τὰ σπουδαῖα.)

Archias, to a messenger who arrived during a banquet with a letter which he said should be read at once, since it was on serious business. It contained warning of a plot to assassinate Archias, but he slipped it unread under the pillow of his couch, and a few minutes later the assassins broke in and killed him. "Wherefore," says Plutarch, "these words of his are a current proverb to this day among the Greeks." (Plutarch, *Lives: Pelopidas.* Ch. 10, sec. 4.)

7
The playthings of our elders are called business. (Majorum nugæ negotia vocantur.)

St. Augustine, *Confessions.* Bk. i, sec. 15.

8
Come home to men's business and bosoms.

Francis Bacon, *Essays: Dedication to the Duke of Buckingham.*

9
Mr. Morgan buys his partners; I grow my own.

Andrew Carnegie. (Hendrick, *Life.*)

10
Steel is Prince or Pauper.

Andrew Carnegie. (Hendrick, *Life.*)

Homestead, Braddock, Birmingham, they make their steel with men.
Smoke and blood is the mix of steel.

Carl Sandburg, *Smoke and Steel.*

11
Keep thy shop, and thy shop will keep thee.

George Chapman, *Eastward Hoe.* Act i, sc. 1. (1610) Attributed to Sir William Temple by Steele. (*Spectator*, No. 509.)

Mind your till and till your mind.

C. H. Spurgeon, *Salt-Cellars.*

12
You foolish man, you don't even know your own foolish business.

Lord Chesterfield, to John Amstis, the Garter King of Arms. (Jesse, *Memories of the Courts of the Stuarts: Nassau and Hanover.*)

You silly old fool, you don't even know the alphabet of your own silly business.

Attributed to Judge William Henry Maule, speaking to a witness in his court.

A silly old man who does not understand even his silly old trade.

Attributed to Richard Bethell, first Baron Westbury, while Lord Chancellor, speaking of a witness from the Herald's College.

13
This business will never hold water.

Colley Cibber, *She Wou'd and She Wou'd Not.* Act iv.

14
Like inscriptions over the graves of dead businesses.

Dickens, *Our Mutual Friend.* Bk. i, ch. 14.

15
Whose talk is of bullocks.

Apocrypha: Ecclesiasticus, xxxviii, 25.

16
Sir, it was my partner made that bargain, not myself; and I don't hold myself bound by it, for he is the sleeping partner only, and not empowered to act in the way of business.

Maria Edgeworth, *The Absentee.* Ch. 1.

1
Drive thy business or it will drive thee.
BENJAMIN FRANKLIN, *Poor Richard*, 1758.

2
The citizen is at his business before he rises.
GEORGE HERBERT, *Jacula Prudentum*.

3
Ask the grave tradesman to direct thee right;
He ne'er deceives but when he profits by 't.
JOHN GAY, *Trivia*. Bk. ii, l. 71.

4
And, if you want it, he
Makes a reduction on taking a quantity.
W. S. GILBERT, *The Sorcerer*. Act i.

5
Business is other people's money. (Les affaires, c'est l'argent des autres.)
MADAME DE GIRARDIN, *Marguerite*. Vol. ii, p. 104. (1852)

Business? That's very simple—it's other people's money. (Les affaires? C'est bien simple, c'est l'argent des autres.)
ALEXANDRE DUMAS, fils, *La Question d'Argent*. Act ii, sc. 7. (1857)

6
Lord Stafford mines for coal and salt,
The Duke of Norfolk deals in malt,
The Douglas in red herrings.
FITZ-GREENE HALLECK, *Alnwick Castle*.

7
I attend to the business of other people, having lost my own. (Aliena negotia curo, Excussus propriis.)
HORACE, *Satires*. Bk. ii, sat. 3, l. 19.

Have you so much time to spare from your own business that you can attend to another man's with which you have no concern? (Tantumne ad re tuast oti tibi Aliena ut cures ea quæ nil ad te attinent?)
TERENCE, *Heauton Timorumenos*, l. 75. (Act i, sc. 1.)

Let every man mind his own business.
CERVANTES, *Don Quixote*. Pt. i, ch. 8.

Each one to his trade; then would the cows be well cared for.
FLORIAN, *Le Vacher et le Garde-chasse*.

"If everybody minded their own business," the Duchess said, in a hoarse growl, "the world would go round a great deal faster than it does."
LEWIS CARROLL, *Alice's Adventures in Wonderland*, p. 84.

8
Never fear the want of business. A man who qualifies himself well for his calling, never fails of employment.
THOMAS JEFFERSON, *Writings*. Vol. viii, p. 385.

9
The ugliest of trades have their moments of pleasure. Now, if I were a grave-digger, or even a hangman, there are some people I could work for with a great deal of enjoyment.
DOUGLAS JERROLD, *Jerrold's Wit: Ugly Trades*.

10
The sign brings customers.
LA FONTAINE, *Fables*. Bk. vii, fab. 15.

11
Business today consists in persuading crowds.
GERALD STANLEY LEE, *Crowds*. Bk. ii, ch. 5.

A man's success in business today turns upon his power of getting people to believe he has something that they want.
GERALD STANLEY LEE, *Crowds*. Bk. ii, ch. 9.

12
When I see a merchant over-polite to his customers, begging them to taste a little brandy and throwing half his goods on the counter—thinks I, that man has an axe to grind.
CHARLES MINER, *Essays from the Desk of Poor Robert the Scribe: Who'll Turn Grindstones?* (1815) in Luzerne *Federalist*, 7 Sept., 1810.

13
Business is business. (Les affaires sont les affaires.)
OCTAVE MIRBEAU. Title of play, produced at Comédie Française, Paris, 20 April, 1903.

"Business is business," the Little Man said,
"A battle where 'everything goes,'
Where the only gospel is 'get ahead,'
And never spare friends or foes."
BERTON BRALEY, *Business is Business*.

14
Strife never; business seldom; a quiet mind. (Lis numquam, toga rara, mens quieta.)
MARTIAL, *Epigrams*. Bk. x, epig. 47, l. 5. A prescription for a happy life.

15
Good merchandise finds a ready buyer. (Proba mers facile emptorem reperit.)
PLAUTUS, *Pœnulus*, l. 342. (Act i, sc. 2.)

Ill ware is never cheap. Pleasing ware is half sold.
GEORGE HERBERT, *Jacula Prudentum*.

16
Not slothful in business; fervent in spirit.
New Testament: Romans, xii, 11.

17
We demand that big business give people a square deal.
THEODORE ROOSEVELT, *Letter*, when suit was brought to dissolve the Steel Trust.

18
It is easy to escape from business, if you will only despise the rewards of business. (Facile est autem occupationes evadere, si occupationum pretia contempseris.)
SENECA, *Epistulæ ad Lucilium*. Epis. xxii, sec. 9.

19
Every man has business and desire,
Such as it is.
SHAKESPEARE, *Hamlet*. Act i, sc. 5, l. 130.

Has this fellow no feeling of his business?
SHAKESPEARE, *Hamlet*. Act v, sc. 1, l. 73.

This weighty business will not brook delay.
SHAKESPEARE, *II Henry VI*. Act i, sc. 1, l. 170.

20
I am ill at reckoning; it fitteth the spirit of a tapster.
SHAKESPEARE, *Love's Labour's Lost*. Act i, sc. 2, l. 42.

1
To things of sale a seller's praise belongs.
SHAKESPEARE, *Love's Labour's Lost*. Act iv, sc. 3, l. 240.

2
A man who has no office to go to—I don't care who he is—is a trial of which you can have no conception.
BERNARD SHAW, *The Irrational Knot*. Ch. 18.

3
Except during the nine months before he draws his first breath, no man manages his affairs as well as a tree does.
BERNARD SHAW, *Maxims for Revolutionists*.

4
Everyone lives by selling something.
R. L. STEVENSON, *Beggars*.

5
Neither above nor below his business. (Par negotiis neque supra.)
TACITUS, *Annals*. Bk. vi, sec. 39.

He who thinks his business below him, will always be above his business.
THOMAS FULLER, *Gnomologia*. No. 2333.

Those that are above business.
MATTHEW HENRY, *Commentaries: Matthew xx*.

6
We are all proud or humble, according as our business prospers or fails. (Omnibus nobis ut res dant sese, ita magni atque humiles sumus.)
TERENCE, *Hecyra*, l. 380. (Act iii, sc. 2.)

7
And that ye study to be quiet, and to do your own business.
New Testament: I Thessalonians, iv, 11.

8
I have postponed my serious business for their sport. (Posthabui tamen illorum mea seria ludo.)
VERGIL, *Eclogues*. No. vii, l. 17.

9
I remember that a wise friend of mine did usually say, "That which is everybody's business is nobody's business."
IZAAK WALTON, *The Compleat Angler*. Pt. i, ch. 2. (Third edition.)

Everybody's business is nobody's business.
MACAULAY, *Essays: Hallam's Constitutional History*. (1828) Quoted as an "old maxim."

10
I cannot sit still, James, and hear you abuse the shopocracy.
JOHN WILSON, *Noctes Ambrosianæ*. No. 39.

11
Go to your business, pleasure, whilst I go to my pleasure, business.
WYCHERLEY, *The Country Wife*. Act ii.

Business was his aversion; pleasure was his business.
MARIA EDGEWORTH, *The Contrast*. Ch. 1.
See also under PLEASURE.

II—Business: Its Virtues

12
Business is really more agreeable than pleasure; it interests the whole mind . . . more deeply. But it does not *look* as if it did.
WALTER BAGEHOT, *English Constitution*, p. 117.

13
I have always recognized that the object of business is to make money in an honorable manner. I have endeavored to remember that the object of life is to do good.
PETER COOPER, *Speech*, at a reception given in his honor in 1874. (*Dict. of American Biog.*, iv, 410.)

14
A business with an income at its heels
Furnishes always oil for its own wheels.
COWPER, *Retirement*, l. 615.

15
Business is the salt of life.
THOMAS FULLER, *Gnomologia*. No. 1026.

16
Without business, debauchery.
GEORGE HERBERT, *Jacula Prudentum*. *See also under* DEVIL.

17
The aim of all legitimate business is service, for profit, at a risk.
BENJAMIN C. LEEMING, *Imagination*.

18
There is no better ballast for keeping the mind steady on its keel, and saving it from all risk of *crankiness*, than business.
J. R. LOWELL, *Among My Books: New England Two Centuries Ago*.

19
Cherish the little trade which thou hast learned and be content therewith. (Τὸ τεχνίον, ὃ ἔμαθες, φίλει, τούτῳ προσαναπαύου.)
MARCUS AURELIUS, *Meditations*. Bk. iv, sec. 31

20
Seest thou a man diligent in his business? he shall stand before kings; he shall not stand before mean men.
Old Testament: Proverbs, xxii, 29.

21
To business that we love we rise betime,
And go to 't with delight.
SHAKESPEARE, *Antony and Cleopatra*. Act iv, sc. 4, l. 20.

III—Business: Its Faults

22
The market is a place set apart where men may deceive each other.
ANACHARSIS. (DIOGENES LAERTIUS, *Anacharsis* Sec. 5.)

23
Look round, look up, and feel, a moment's space,
That carpet-dusting, though a pretty trade,
Is not the imperative labour after all.
E. B. BROWNING, *Aurora Leigh*. Bk. i, l. 878.

The buying and the selling, and the strife
Of little natures.
ROBERT BUCHANAN, *De Berney*.

1
I care not a fig for the cares of business;
Politics fill me with doubt and dizziness.
ROBERT BUCHANAN, *Fine Weather on the Digentia*. St. 4.

2
Thou shalt not covet: but tradition
Approves all forms of competition.
ARTHUR HUGH CLOUGH, *The Latest Decalogue*.

3
Hackney'd in business, wearied at that oar
Which thousands, once fast chain'd to, quit
no more.
COWPER, *Retirement*, l. 1.

Stamps God's own name upon a lie just made,
To turn a penny in the way of trade.
COWPER, *Table Talk*, l. 420.

4
We must hold a man amenable to reason for the choice of his daily craft or profession. It is not an excuse any longer for his deeds that they are the custom of his trade. What business has he with an evil trade? Has he not a *calling* in his character?
EMERSON, *Essays, First Series: Spiritual Laws*.

The ways of trade are grown selfish to the borders of theft, and supple to the borders (if not beyond the borders) of fraud.
EMERSON, *Nature Addresses and Essays: Man the Reformer*.

5
Why so serious, why so grave?
Man of business, why so muddy?
Thyself from chance thou canst not save
With all thy care and study.
Look merrily then, and take thy repose;
For 'tis to no purpose to look so forlorn,
Since the world was as bad before thou wert
born,
And when it will mend who knows?
THOMAS FLATMAN, *The Whim*.

6
When a man's business does not fit him, 'tis as ofttimes with a shoe—if too big for the foot it will trip him, if too small, will chafe. (Cui non conveniet sua res, ut calceus olim, Si pede major erit, subvertet, si minor, uret.)
HORACE, *Epistles*. Bk. i, epis. 10, l. 42.

7
The rust of business is sometimes polished off in a camp, but never in a court. (L'air bourgeois se perd quelquefois à l'armée, mais il ne se perd jamais à la cour.)
LA ROCHEFOUCAULD, *Maximes*. No. 393.

8
Curse on the man who business first designed,
And by 't enthralled a free-born lover's mind!
JOHN OLDHAM, *Complaining of Absence*.

The lover too shuns business.
COWPER, *Retirement*, l. 219.

9
Swear, fool, or starve; for the dilemma's
even;
A tradesman thou! and hope to go to Heav'n?
PERSIUS, *Satires*. Sat. v, l. 168. (Dryden, tr., l. 204.)

He looked upon the whole generation of woollen-drapers to be such despicable wretches that no gentleman ought to pay them.
SAMUEL JOHNSON, *The Rambler*. No. 9.

10
How happy the life unembarrassed by the cares of business! (Quam est felix vita, quæ sine odiis transiit.)
PUBLILIUS SYRUS, *Sententiæ*. No. 725.

11
Bad is the trade that must play fool to
sorrow.
SHAKESPEARE, *King Lear*. Act iv, sc. 1, l. 40.

Half way down
Hangs one that gathers samphire, dreadful trade!
SHAKESPEARE, *King Lear*. Act iv, sc. 6, l. 14.

12
Of all the damnable waste of human life that ever was invented, clerking is the very worst.
BERNARD SHAW, *Misalliance*, p. 70.

This counter-caster.
SHAKESPEARE, *Othello*. Act i, sc. 1, l. 31.

IV—Business: Its Dispatch

13
Talk of nothing but business and dispatch that business quickly.
ALDUS, placard on the door of his printing office. (T. F. DIBDIN, *Introduction to the Knowledge of Rare and Valuable Editions of the Greek and Latin Classics*, p. 436.)

14
There is nothing more requisite in business than despatch.
ADDISON, *The Drummer*. Act v, sc. 1.

15
Of all virtues for rising to honour, quickness of despatch is the best; for superiors many times love not to have those they employ too deep or too sufficient, but ready and diligent.
FRANCIS BACON, *Advancement of Learning: Civil Knowledge*. Sec. 9.

16
Business dispatched is business well done, but business hurried is business ill done.
BULWER-LYTTON, *Caxtoniana: Readers and Writers*.

17
Despatch is the soul of business.
LORD CHESTERFIELD, *Letters*, 5 Feb., 1750.

18
Cecil's despatch of business was extraordinary, his maxim being, "The shortest way to do many things is to do only one thing at once."
SAMUEL SMILES, *Self-Help*. Ch. 9.

V—Business and Busyness

19
Nowhere so busy a man as he there was,
And yet he seemed busier than he was.
CHAUCER, *Canterbury Tales: Prologue*, l. 321.

1
Who more busy than he that hath least to do?
THOMAS DRAXE, *Biblio. Scho. Inst.*, 20. (1633)

2
To be too busy gets contempt.
GEORGE HERBERT, *Jacula Prudentum.*

3
Without any sort of business, is forever busy. (Sans aucune affaire, est toujours affairé.)
MOLIÈRE, *Le Misanthrope.* Act ii, sc. 4, l. 30.

4
Nor will he be in business for the mere sake of being busy. (Nec in negotiis erit negotii causa.)
SENECA, *Epistulæ ad Lucilium.* Epis. xxii, 8.

5
No one is so busy as the man who has nothing to do. (Il n'y a pas de gens plus affairés que ceux qui n'ont rien à faire.)
UNKNOWN. A French proverb. *See also* LEISURE.

BUTCHER

6
He would have made a good butcher, but for the by-blow.
JOHN CLARKE, *Parœmiologia,* 77. (1639)

7
Butchers! whose hands are dy'd with blood's foul stain,
And always foremost in the hangman's train.
JOHN GAY, *Trivia.* Bk. ii, l. 43.

8
Whoe'er has gone thro' London Street,
Has seen a Butcher gazing at his meat,
And how he keeps
Gloating upon a sheep's
Or bullock's personals, as if his own;
How he admires his halves
And quarters—and his calves,
As if in truth upon his own legs grown;—
His fat! *his* suet!
His kidneys peeping elegantly thro' it!
THOMAS HOOD, *A Butcher.*

Of brutal juices the whole man is full.—
In fact, fulfilling the metempsychosis,
The Butcher is already half a Bull.
THOMAS HOOD, *A Butcher.*

9
A sturdy man he look'd to fell an ox,
Bull-fronted, ruddy, with a formal streak
Of well-greas'd hair down either cheek.
THOMAS HOOD, *Ode to Rae Wilson,* l. 428.

10
Where is that devil's butcher?
SHAKESPEARE, *III Henry VI.* Act v, sc. 5, l. 77.

Like to a mortal butcher bent to kill.
SHAKESPEARE, *Venus and Adonis,* l. 618.

11
The butcher looked for his knife and it was in his mouth.
SWIFT, *Polite Conversation.* Dial. 1.

He'd with his candle look for his knife,
Which he had in his mouth.
UNKNOWN, *Roxburghe Ballads,* iii, 321.

12
Beef on the butcher's stall, the slaughter-house of the butcher, the butcher in his killing-clothes.
WALT WHITMAN, *A Song For Occupations.* Sec. v, l. 26.

13
Begot by butchers, but by bishops bred,
How high his honour holds his haughty head.
UNKNOWN, *Epigram on Wolsey.*

BUTTERCUP

14
The royal kingcup bold
Dares not don his coat of gold.
EDWIN ARNOLD, *Almond Blossoms.*

15
He likes the poor things of the world the best;
I would not, therefore, if I could, be rich.
It pleasures him to stoop for buttercups.
E. B. BROWNING, *Aurora Leigh.* Bk. iv, l. 210.

16
All will be gay when noontide wakes anew
The buttercups, the little children's dower.
ROBERT BROWNING, *Home Thoughts from Abroad.*

17
When daisies and buttercups gladdened my sight,
Like treasures of silver and gold.
THOMAS CAMPBELL, *Field Flowers.*

18
The buttercups across the field
Made sunshine rifts of splendor.
DINAH MARIA MULOCK CRAIK, *A Silly Song.*

19
The buttercups, bright-eyed and bold,
Held up their chalices of gold
To catch the sunshine and the dew.
JULIA C. R. DORR, *Centennial Poem,* l. 165.

20
I'm called little Buttercup,
Dear little Buttercup,
Though I could never tell why.
W. S. GILBERT, *H.M.S. Pinafore.* Act i.

21
Buttercups and daisies,
Oh, the pretty flowers;
Coming ere the spring time,
To tell of sunny hours. . . .
He who gave them hardships
And a life of care,
Gave them likewise hardy strength
And patient hearts to bear.
MARY HOWITT, *Buttercups and Daisies.*

22
And O the buttercups! that field
O' the cloth of gold, where pennons swam— . . .
What was it to their matchless sheen,
Their million million drops of gold
Among the green!
JEAN INGELOW, *The Letter L: Present.* St. 3.

23
And still a tiny fan turns
Above a forge of gold.

To keep, with fairy lanterns,
The world from growing old.
WILFRED THORLEY, *Buttercups.*

BUTTERFLY

1
I'd be a butterfly, born in a bower,
Where roses and lilies and violets meet.
THOMAS HAYNES BAYLY, *I'd Be a Butterfly.*

2
And all about her wheeled and shone
Butterflies all gold.
JOHN DAVIDSON, *Butterflies.*

3
I'll make my joy like this
Small Butterfly;
Whose happy heart has power
To make a stone a flower.
WILLIAM H. DAVIES, *The Example.*

4
Thou spark of life that wavest wings of gold,
Thou songless wanderer mid the songful birds,
With Nature's secrets in thy tints unrolled. . . .
Thou wingèd blossom, liberated thing, . . .
But thou art Nature's freeman.
T. W. HIGGINSON, *Ode to a Butterfly.*

5
We saw a snow-white butterfly
Dancing before the fitful gale,
Far out at sea.
RICHARD HENGIST HORNE, *Genius.*

6
There was never a Queen like Balkis,
From here to the wide world's end;
And Balkis talked to a butterfly
As you would talk to a friend.
RUDYARD KIPLING, *Just-So Stories: The Butterfly that Stamped.*

7
There will be butterflies,
There will be summer skies
And flowers upthrust,
When all that Cæsar bids,
And all the pyramids
Are dust.
HANIEL LONG, *Butterflies.*

8
The butterfly, an idle thing,
Nor honey makes, nor yet can sing. . . .
And though from flower to flower I rove,
My stock of wisdom I'll improve,
Nor be a butterfly.
ADELAIDE O'KEEFE, *The Butterfly.*

9
Who breaks a butterfly upon a wheel?
POPE, *Epistle to Dr. Arbuthnot,* l. 308.

10
Exquisite child of the air.
ALICE FREEMAN PALMER, *The Butterfly.*

11
This was your butterfly, you see—
His fine wings made him vain:
The caterpillars crawl, but he
Passed them in rich disdain.—
My pretty boy says, "Let him be
Only a worm again!"
SARAH M. B. PIATT, *After Wings.*

12
What more felicity can fall to creature
Than to enjoy delight with liberty,
And to be lord of all the works of Nature?
EDMUND SPENSER, *Muiopotmos, Or the Fate of the Butterflie,* l. 209.

13
Fly away, butterfly, back to Japan,
Tempt not a pinch at the hand of a man,
And strive not to sting ere you die away.
So pert and so painted, so proud and so pretty,
To brush the bright down from your wings were a pity—
Fly away, butterfly, fly away!
SWINBURNE, *To James McNeill Whistler.*

14
Much converse do I find in thee,
Historian of my infancy!
Float near me; do not yet depart!
Dead times revive in thee:
Thou bring'st, gay creature as thou art!
A solemn image to my heart.
WORDSWORTH, *To a Butterfly.*

What joy awaits you, when the breeze
Hath found you out among the trees,
And calls you forth again!
WORDSWORTH, *To a Butterfly.*

BYRON, GEORGE GORDON

15
And poor, proud Byron, sad as grave
And salt as life; forlornly brave,
And quivering with the dart he gave.
E. B. BROWNING, *A Vision of Poets,* l. 412.

16
And be the Spartan's epitaph on me—
"Sparta hath many a worthier son than he."
BYRON, *Childe Harold.* Canto iv, st. 10.

Even I,—albeit I'm sure I did not know it,
Nor sought of foolscap subjects to be king,—
Was reckon'd, a considerable time,
The grand Napoleon of the realms of rhyme.
BYRON, *Don Juan.* Canto xi, st. 55.

17
'Twas his to mourn Misfortune's rudest shock,
Scourged by the winds, and cradled on the rock.
CAMPBELL, *The Pleasures of Hope.* Pt. i, l. 105.

18
He might have soared, a miracle of mind,
Above the doubts that dim our mental sphere,
And poured from thence, as music on the wind,
Those prophet tones, which men had turned to hear,
As if an angel's harp had sung of bliss
In some bright world beyond the tears of this
WALTER COLTON, *Byron.*

1
Oh, Night doth love her! Oh, the clouds
They do her form environ!
The lightning weeps—it hears her sob,
"Speak to me, Lord Byron!"
EBENEZER ELLIOTT, *Speak to Me, Lord Byron.* Referring to the story that Byron refused to speak to his sister for many years before she died.

2
He had a head which statuaries loved to copy, and a foot the deformity of which the beggars in the street mimicked.
MACAULAY, *Essays: Moore's Life of Byron.*

3
From the poetry of Lord Byron they drew a system of ethics, compounded of misanthropy and voluptuousness,—a system in which the two great commandments were, to hate your neighbour, and to love your neighbour's wife.
MACAULAY, *Essays: Moore's Life of Lord Byron.*

4
Yes, Byron, thou art gone,
Gone like a star that through the firmament
Shot and was lost, in its eccentric course
Dazzling, perplexing. Yet thy heart, methinks,
Was generous, noble—noble in its scorn
Of all things low or little; nothing there
Sordid or servile.
SAMUEL ROGERS, *Italy: Bologna.*

5
O mighty mind, in whose deep streams this age
Shakes like a reed in the unheeding storm,
Why dost thou curb not thine own sacred rage?
SHELLEY, *Fragment: Addressed to Byron.*

6
Too avid of earth's bliss, he was of those
Whom Delight flies because they give her chase.
Only the odour of her wild hair blows
Back in their faces hungering for her face.
WILLIAM WATSON, *Byron the Voluptuary.*

7
My friend the apothecary o'er the way
Doth in his window Byron's bust display.
Once, at Childe Harold's voice, did Europe bow:
He wears a patent lung-protector now.
WILLIAM WATSON, *The Fall of Heroes.*

C

CAB

8
Does nobody know where these gondolas of Paris came from? (Ne sait on pas où viennent ces gondoles Parisiennes?)
BALZAC, *Physiologie du Mariage.* (1827) See *Notes and Queries.* Ser. v, vol. iv, p. 499; vol. v, p. 195.

There beauty half her glory veils
In cabs, those gondolas on wheels.
UNKNOWN, *May Fair.* (1827)

Those gondolas on wheels, called hansoms.
H. SCHÜLTZ WILSON, *The Three Paths.* (1859)

The gondola of London.
BENJAMIN DISRAELI, *Lothair.* Ch. 27.

9
Go, call a coach, and let a coach be called;
And let the man who calleth be the caller;
And in the calling, let him nothing call,
But coach! coach! coach! O for a coach, ye gods!
HENRY CAREY, *Chrononhotonthologos.* Act ii, sc. 4.

CÆSAR

I—Cæsar: Apothegms

10
I appeal unto Cæsar.
New Testament: Acts, xxv, 11.

11
What millions died—that Cæsar might be great!
CAMPBELL, *The Pleasures of Hope.* Pt. ii, l. 174.

12
Cæsarism is democracy without liberty. (Le Césarisme, c'est la démocratie sans la liberté.)
TAXILE DELORD, *History of the Second Empire.*

13
Born, Cæsar-like, to write and act great deeds.
DRYDEN, *Annus Mirabilis.* St. 175.

14
Where's Cæsar gone now, in command high and able?
JACOPONE, *De Contemptu Mundi.* (Coles, tr.)

Imperious Cæsar, dead and turn'd to clay,
Might stop a hole to keep the wind away:
O, that that earth, which kept the world in awe,
Should patch a wall to expel the winter's flaw!
SHAKESPEARE, *Hamlet.* Act v, sc. 1, l. 236.

15
Render therefore unto Cæsar the things which are Cæsar's, and unto God the things that are God's.
New Testament: Matthew, xxii, 21.

16
No bending knee will call thee Cæsar now.
SHAKESPEARE, *III Henry VI.* Act iii, sc. 1, l. 18.

Thou'rt an emperor, Cæsar, Keisar, and Pheezar.
SHAKESPEARE, *Merry Wives of Windsor.* Act i, sc. 3, l. 9.

17
One Cæsar lives; a thousand are forgot.
YOUNG, *Night Thoughts.* Night viii, l. 202.

18
Hail Cæsar, those who are about to die salute

thee! (Ave, Cæsar, morituri te salutant!)

The salutation used by the Roman gladiators, as they filed past the imperial box before fighting in the circus. Sometimes given, "Ave, Imperator, morituri te salutamus." (SUETONIUS, *Lives of the Cæsars: Claudius.* Ch. xxi, sec. 6.)

Like a parrot, I will learn from you the names of others; but I have learned of myself to say, "Hail, Cæsar." (Psittacus a vobis aliorum nomina discam: Hoc didici per me dicere "Cæsar have.")

MARTIAL, *Epigrams.* Bk. xiv, epig. 73.

For other names your lessons may avail:
I taught myself to carol, "Cæsar! hail!"

MARTIAL. xiv, 73. (Elphinston, tr.)

"O Cæsar, we who are about to die
Salute you!" was the gladiators' cry
In the arena, standing face to face
With death and with the Roman populace.

LONGFELLOW, *Morituri Salutamus,* l. 1.

1
Either Cæsar or nothing. (Aut Cæsar aut nihil.)

The device of Cæsar Borgia.

Cæsar or nothing? We are nothing loath
Thus to acclaim him; Cæsar Borgia's both.
(Aut nihil aut Cæsar vult dici Borgia. Quidni?
Cum simul et Cæsar possit et esse nihil.)

JACOPO SANNAZZARO, *De Cæsar Borgia.* (*Carmina Poetarum Italorum.* Vol. viii, p. 444.)

Either Pontifex Maximus or an exile. (Nisi pontificem non reversurum.)

JULIUS CÆSAR, to his mother, on the morning of the election. (SUETONIUS, *Lives of the Cæsars: Julius.* Sec. 13.)

II—Cæsar, Julius

2
Cæsar's wife must be above suspicion. (Tum Cæsar . . . respondit: quia suam uxorem etiam suspicione vacare vellet.)

PLUTARCH, *Lives: Julius Cæsar.* Sec. 10.

Cæsar, however, when summoned as a witness, gave no testimony against Clodius, and denied that he had condemned his wife for adultery, but said that he had put her away because Cæsar's wife must be free not only from shameful conduct, but even from shameful report.

PLUTARCH, *Lives: Cicero.* Ch. 29, sec. 7.

He took to wife Pompeia, daughter of Quintus Pompeius and granddaughter of Lucius Sulla. But he afterward divorced her, suspecting her of adultery with Publius Clodius. . . . When summoned as a witness against Clodius, Cæsar declared that he had no evidence, although both his mother Aurelia and his sister Julia had given the jurors a faithful account of the whole affair; and on being asked why it was then that he had put away his wife, he replied, "Because I maintain that the members of my family should be free from suspicion, as well as from guilt." (Quoniam meos tam suspicione quam crimine judico carere oportere.)

SUETONIUS, *Lives of the Cæsars: Julius.* Secs. 6 and 74.

3
I hold thee fast, Africa. (Teneo te, Africa.)

JULIUS CÆSAR, when he fell on landing in Africa. (SUETONIUS, *Lives of the Cæsars: Julius.* Sec. 59.)

By the splendor of God, I have taken seizin of my kingdom: the earth of England is in my two hands.

WILLIAM THE CONQUEROR, as he slipped and fell when landing at Pevensey, England, 28 Sept., 1066. (FREEMAN, *Norman Conquest.* Vol. iii, ch. 15.)

4
No honor shall make thee worthy of Cæsar's wrath. (Dignum te Cæsaris ira Nullus honor faciet.)

JULIUS CÆSAR, to Metellus. (LUCAN, *De Bello Civili.* Bk. iii, l. 136.)

5
Cæsar, in modesty mixed with greatness, did for his pleasure apply the name of a Commentary to the best history of the world.

FRANCIS BACON, *Advancement of Learning.* Bk. ii.

The commentaries Cæsar writ.

SHAKESPEARE, *II Henry VI.* Act iv, sc. 7, l. 65.

6
Every woman's man and every man's woman. (Omnium mulierum virum et omnium virorum mulierum.)

CURIO, of Julius Cæsar. (SUETONIUS, *Lives of the Cæsars: Julius.* Sec. 52.)

They are men to women, and women to men. (Ἀνέρες εἰσὶ γυναιξί, καὶ ἀνδράσιν εἰσὶ γυναῖκες.)

UNKNOWN, *On Cinædi.* (*Greek Anthology.* Bk. xi, epig. 272.)

7
Give, you gods,
Give to your boy, your Cæsar,
This rattle of a globe to play withal,
This gewgaw world, and put him cheaply off.

DRYDEN, *All for Love.* Act ii, sc. 1.

8
No chief has Rome so loved, nor thee so much, Cæsar, as now; thee too, albeit she would, she cannot now love more. (Nullum Roma ducem, nec te sic, Cæsar, amavit: Te quoque jam non plus, ut velit ipsa, potest.)

MARTIAL, *Epigrams.* Bk. viii, epig. 11.

Not that I loved Cæsar less, but that I loved Rome more.

SHAKESPEARE, *Julius Cæsar.* Act iii, sc. 2, l. 23.

9
Ask why from Britain Cæsar would retreat?
Cæsar himself might whisper he was beat.
Why risk the world's great empire for a punk?
Cæsar perhaps might answer, he was drunk.

POPE, *Moral Essays.* Epis. i, l. 129.

10
Cæsar was held great because of his benefactions and lavish generosity. Cæsar gained glory by giving, helping, and forgiving. Finally, Cæsar had schooled himself to work hard and sleep little, to devote himself to the welfare of his friends and neglect his own, to refuse nothing that was worth the giving.

He longed for great power, an army, a new war to give scope to his merit.
SALLUST, *Catilina*. Ch. 54, sec. 2.

1
Julius Cæsar, whose remembrance yet
Lives in men's eyes and will to ears and tongues
Be theme and hearing ever.
SHAKESPEARE, *Cymbeline*. Act iii, sc. 1, l. 2.

There be many Cæsars, Ere such another Julius.
SHAKESPEARE, *Cymbeline*. Act iii, sc. 1, l. 11.

There is no moe such Cæsars: others of them may have crook'd noses, but to owe such straight arms, none.
SHAKESPEARE, *Cymbeline*. Act iii, sc. 1, l. 36.

The scarce-bearded Cæsar.
SHAKESPEARE, *Antony and Cleopatra*, i, 1, 21.

2
Cæsar's ambition,
Which swell'd so much that it did almost stretch
The sides o' the world.
SHAKESPEARE, *Cymbeline*. Act iii, sc. 1, l. 49.

See AMBITION: SMALL TOWN GREAT RENOWN.

3
Now in the names of all the gods at once,
Upon what meat doth this our Cæsar feed,
That he is grown so great?
SHAKESPEARE, *Julius Cæsar*. Act i, sc. 2, l. 148.

Cæsar was mighty, bold, royal, and loving.
SHAKESPEARE, *Julius Cæsar*. Act iii, sc. 1, l. 127.

I come to bury Cæsar, not to praise him.
SHAKESPEARE, *Julius Cæsar*. Act iii, sc. 2, l. 79.

4
That Julius Cæsar was a famous man;
With what his valour did enrich his wit,
His wit set down to make his valour live.
SHAKESPEARE, *Richard III*. Act iii, sc. 1, l. 84.

Alas! thou know'st not Cæsar's active soul,
With what a dreadful course he rushes on
From war to war. In vain has nature form'd
Mountains and oceans to oppose his passage;
He bounds o'er all; victorious in his march,
The Alps and Pyreneans sink before him;
Through winds and waves, and storms he works his way,
Impatient for the battle.
ADDISON, *Cato*. Act i, sc. 2.

5
Great Julius, on the mountains bred,
A flock, perhaps, or herd had led;
He that the world subdued had been
But the best wrestler on the green.
EDMUND WALLER, *To Zelinda*, l. 19.

For RUBICON *see under* DECISION.

CALAMITY, see Adversity

CALMNESS, see Serenity

CALUMNY

See also Rumor, Scandal, Slander

6
Hurl your calumnies boldly; something is sure to stick. (Audacter calumniare, semper aliquid hæret.)
BACON, *De Augmentis Scientiarum*. Pt. viii, sec. 2. Quoted as a Latin proverb.

Calumniate, calumniate; some of it will always stick. (Calomniez, calomniez; il en reste toujours quelque chose.)
BEAUMARCHAIS, *Barbier de Séville*. Act iii.

Lie lustily, some filth will stick.
THOMAS HALL, *Funebria Floræ*, 38. (1660)

The scandal of others is mere dirt—throw a great deal, and some of it will stick.
GEORGE COLMAN THE ELDER, *Man and Wife: Prelude*.

Only throw dirt enough and some of it is sure to stick.
THOMAS HUGHES, *Tom Brown*. Pt. i, ch. 9.

7
Nothing is so swift as calumny; nothing is more easily uttered; nothing more readily received; nothing more widely dispersed. (Nihil est autem tam volucre, quam maledictum; nihil facilius emittitur; nihil citius excipitur, nihil latius dissipatur.)
CICERO, *Pro Cnæo Plancio*. Sec. 23.

8
As long as there are readers to be delighted with calumny, there will be found reviewers to calumniate.
S. T. COLERIDGE, *Biographia Literaria*. Ch. 3.

9
Calumny always makes the calumniator worse, but the calumniated—never.
C. C. COLTON, *Lacon: Reflections*. No. 172.

10
Blush, Calumny! and write upon his tomb,
If honest eulogy can spare thee room,
Thy deep repentance of thy thousand lies.
COWPER, *Hope*, l. 588.

11
A nickname a man may chance to wear out; but a system of calumny, pursued by a faction, may descend even to posterity.
ISAAC D'ISRAELI, *Amenities of Literature: The First Jesuits in England*.

12
Whom does lying calumny alarm except the liar? (Mendax infamia terret Quem nisi mendosum?)
HORACE, *Epistles*. Bk. i, epis. 16, l. 39.

13
Calumny differs from most other injuries in this dreadful circumstance: he who commits it can never repair it.
SAMUEL JOHNSON, *Wit and Wisdom*, p. 36.

14
I am beholden to calumny, that she hath so endeavoured and taken pains to belie me. It shall make me set a surer guard on myself, and keep a better watch upon my actions.
BEN JONSON, *Explorata: Calumniæ Fructus*.

15
Calumnies are answered best with silence.
BEN JONSON, *Volpone*. Act ii, sc. 1.

To persevere in one's duty and be silent is the best answer to calumny.
GEORGE WASHINGTON, *Moral Maxims*.

1
If nobody took calumny in and gave it lodging, it would starve and die of itself.
ARCHBISHOP ROBERT LEIGHTON, *Works*, iv, 162.

2
Nothing is more distressing than calumny. (Οὐδέν διαβολῆς ἐστιν ἐπιπονώτερον.)
MENANDER, *Fragments*. No. 576.

There are calumnies against which even innocence loses courage.
NAPOLEON BONAPARTE, *Sayings of Napoleon*.

3
It is right to give a tardy hearing to calumnies. (Difficilem habere oportet aurem ad crimina.)
PUBLILIUS SYRUS, *Sententiæ*. No. 153.

4
Be thou as chaste as ice, as pure as snow, thou shalt not escape calumny.
SHAKESPEARE, *Hamlet*. Act iii, sc. 1, l. 140.

Calumny will sear
Virtue itself: these shrugs, these hums and ha's.
SHAKESPEARE, *Winter's Tale*. Act ii, sc. 1, l. 73.

If a cherub in the shape of woman
Should walk this world, yet defamation would,
Like a vile cur, bark at the angel's train.
JOHN HOME, *Douglas*. Act iii.

Like all rogues, he was a great calumniator of the fair sex.
WALTER SCOTT, *Heart of Midlothian*. Ch. 18.

5
My unsoil'd name, the austereness of my life,
My vouch against you, and my place i' the state,
Will so your accusation overweigh,
That you shall stifle in your own report,
And smell of calumny.
SHAKESPEARE, *Measure for Measure*. Act ii, sc. 4, l. 155.

6
No might nor greatness in mortality
Can censure 'scape; back-wounding calumny
The whitest virtue strikes.
SHAKESPEARE, *Measure for Measure*. Act iii, sc. 2, l. 196.

CAMEL

7
The black camel.
ABD-EL-KADER, referring to death. Title of novel by Earl Derr Biggers.

8
With strength and patience all his grievous loads are borne,
And from the world's rose-bed he only asks a thorn.
W. R. ALGER, *Mussud's Praise of the Camel*.

9
Yon dumb patient camel,
Keeping a reserve of scanty water,
Meant to save his own life in the desert;
Ready in the desert to deliver
(Kneeling down to let his breast be opened)
Hoard and life together for his mistress.
ROBERT BROWNING, *One Word More*. Sec. 11.

10
There's never a question About *my* digestion,
Anything does for me!
C. E. CARRYL, *The Plaint of the Camel*.

A Camel's all lumpy And bumpy and humpy—
Any shape does for me!
C. E. CARRYL, *The Plaint of the Camel*.

11
The camel, desiring horns, was shorn of even his ears. (Camelus desiderans cornua etiam aures perdidit.)
ERASMUS, *Adagia*. Cent. v, sec. 8. A translation of a Greek proverb, Apostolius, ix, 8, 43.

The camel set out to get him horns and was shorn of his ears.
Babylonian Talmud: Sanhedrin, p. 106a.

12
'Tis the last feather that breaks the horse's back.
THOMAS FULLER, *Gnomologia*. No. 5120.

As the last straw breaks the laden camel's back.
DICKENS, *Dombey and Son*. Ch. 2.

13
Old camels carry young camels' skins to market.
GEORGE HERBERT, *Jacula Prudentum*.

14
The camel at the close of day
Kneels down upon the sandy plain
To have his burden lifted off,
And rest again.
ANNA TEMPLE, *The Kneeling Camel*.

15
Patient of thirst and toil, Son of the desert.
THOMSON, *The Seasons: Summer*, l. 965.

16
The camel, even when mangy, bears the burden of many asses. (Κάμηλος καὶ ψωριῶσα πολλῶν ὄνων ἀνατίθεται φορτία.)
ERASMUS, *Adagia*. Chil. i, cent. ix, No. 58.

17
The camel is dancing. (Camelus saltat.)
UNKNOWN. A Latin proverb, applied to a person disporting himself in some ridiculous way.

CANDLE

18
A candle lights others and consumes itself.
H. G. BOHN, *Hand-Book of Proverbs*, 283.

19
I light my candle from their torches.
ROBERT BURTON, *Anatomy of Melancholy*. Pt. iii, sec. ii, mem. 5, subs. 1.

Light another's candle, but don't put out your own.
UNKNOWN.

20
To enlarge or illustrate this . . . is to set a candle in the sun.
ROBERT BURTON, *Anatomy of Melancholy*. Pt. iii, sec. ii, mem. 1, subs. 2.

Like his that lights a candle to the sun.
ANDREW FLETCHER, *Letter to Sir Walter Aston*.

But it is not necessary to light a candle to the sun.
ALGERNON SIDNEY, *Discourses on Government* Ch. ii, sec. 23.

1
And hold up to the sun my little taper.
BYRON, *Don Juan*. Canto xii, st. 21.

Oh! rather give me commentators plain,
Who with no deep researches vex the brain;
Who from the dark and doubtful love to run,
And hold their glimmering tapers to the sun.
GEORGE CRABBE, *The Parish Register: Introduction*. Pt. i.

Some future strain in which the muse shall tell
How science dwindles and how volumes swell.
How commentaries each dark passage shun,
And hold their farthing candle to the sun.
YOUNG, *Love of Fame*. Sat. vii, l. 95.

2
How inferior for *seeing* with, is your brightest train of fireworks to the humblest farthing candle!
CARLYLE, *Essays: Diderot*.

3
Then he never snuffed a candle with his fingers.
CHARLES I, of Spain, reading upon the tombstone of a Spanish grandee, "Here lies one who never knew fear." (BOSWELL, *Johnson*, 1769.)

4
His candle burns within the socket.
JOHN CLARKE, *Parœm. Anglo-Latina*, 279.

5
The smallest candle fills a mile with its rays, and the papillæ of a man run out to every star.
EMERSON, *Conduct of Life: Fate*.

6
Tace, madam, is Latin for candle.
FIELDING, *Amelia*. Bk. i, ch. 10.

Brandy is Latin for a goose and Tace is Latin for a candle.
SWIFT, *Polite Conversation*. Dial. i. (According tc *Notes and Queries*, 6 Dec., 1851, this expression is much older and occurs in Dampier's *Voyages*, 1686.)

7
He consuming just like a candle on both ends, between wine and women.
RICHARD FLECKNOE, *Enigmatic Characters*, p. 64. (1658)

The butler and steward were in a confederacy and burnt the candle at both ends.
LE SAGE, *Gil Blas*, iii, 116. (Smollet, tr.)

My candle burns at both ends;
It will not last the night;
But ah, my foes, and oh, my friends—
It gives a lovely light!
EDNA ST. VINCENT MILLAY, *A Few Figs from Thistles: First Fig*.

8
Sith Nature thus gave her the praise,
To be the chiefest work she wrought,
In faith, methink, some better ways
On your behalf might well be sought,
Than to compare, as ye have done,
To match the candle with the sun.
HENRY HOWARD, *Sonnet to the Fair Geraldine*.

9
Be of good comfort, Master Ridley, and play the man. We shall this day light such a candle, by God's grace, in England, as I trust shall never be put out.
HUGH LATIMER, at the stake, to Nicholas Ridley, who was burned with him, 16 Oct., 1555. (*The Martyrdom*, p. 523.) Hume (*History of England*. Ch. 37) gives a slightly different version.

10
Neither do men light a candle, and put it under a bushel, but on a candlestick, and it giveth light unto all that are in the house.
New Testament: Matthew, v, 15.

Is a candle brought to be put under a bushel, or under a bed? and not to be set on a candlestick?
New Testament: Mark, iv, 21.

And useless as a candle in a skull.
WILLIAM COWPER, *Conversation*, l. 785.

11
He that is worst may still hold the candle.
JOHN RAY, *English Proverbs*.

Must I hold a candle to my shames?
SHAKESPEARE, *The Merchant of Venice*. Act ii, sc. 6, l. 41.

I'll be a candle-holder, and look on.
SHAKESPEARE, *Romeo and Juliet*. Act i, sc. 4, l. 38.

12
Thus hath the candle singed the moth.
SHAKESPEARE, *The Merchant of Venice*. Act ii, sc. 9, l. 79.

13
And then, exulting in their taper, cry,
"Behold the sun;" and, Indian-like, adore!
YOUNG, *Night Thoughts*. Night iv, l. 779.

CANDOR

See also Heart: The Speaking Heart; Sincerity

I—Candor: Definitions

14
'Tis not my talent to conceal my thoughts,
Or carry smiles and sunshine in my face,
When discontent sits heavy at my heart.
ADDISON, *Cato*. Act i, sc. 4.

You know I say
Just what I think, and nothing more nor less, . . .
I cannot say one thing and mean another.
LONGFELLOW, *Giles Corey*. Act ii, sc. 3.

15
Gracious to all, to none subservient,
Without offence he spake the word he meant.
T. B. ALDRICH, *The Sisters' Tragedy*.

16
To talk like a Scythian.
ANACHARSIS, who was a Scythian, and so frank, that this phrase became a synonym for frankness. (DIOGENES LAERTIUS, *Anacharsis*, 1.)

17
Without, or with, offence to friends or foes,

I sketch your world exactly as it goes.
BYRON, *Don Juan*. Canto viii, st. 89.

But now I'm going to be immoral; now
I mean to show things really as they are,
Not as they ought to be.
BYRON, *Don Juan*. Canto xii, st. 40.

1
I was so free with him as not to mince the matter.
CERVANTES, *Don Quixote: Author's Preface*.

2
We use great plainness of speech.
New Testament: II Corinthians, iii, 12.

3
"Not to put too fine a point upon it"—a favourite apology for plain-speaking with Mr. Snagsby.
DICKENS, *Bleak House*. Ch. 11.

4
Speak boldly, and speak truly, shame the devil.
JOHN FLETCHER, *Wit Without Money*. Act iv, sc. 4. See also 2057:15.

5
Do all things like a man, not sneakingly:
Think the king sees thee still; for his King does.
GEORGE HERBERT, *The Church-Porch*. St. 21.

Frankness is a natural quality. (La franchise est une qualité naturelle.)
JOUBERT, *Pensées*. No. 108.

6
Speak out, hide not thy thoughts. (Ἐξαύδα, μὴ κεῦθε νόῳ.)
HOMER, *Iliad*. Bk. i, l. 363.

He spake, and into every heart his words
Carried new strength and courage.
HOMER, *Iliad*. Bk. v, l. 586. (Bryant, tr.)

7
Be not ashamed to say what you are not ashamed to think. (Non pudeat dicere, quod non pudet sentire.)
MONTAIGNE, *Essays*. Bk. iii, ch. 5. Quoted.

8
His heart's his mouth:
What his breast forges, that his tongue must vent.
SHAKESPEARE, *Coriolanus*. Act iii, sc. 1, l. 257.

He hath a heart as sound as a bell, and his tongue is the clapper, for what his heart thinks his tongue speaks.
SHAKESPEARE, *Much Ado About Nothing*. Act iii, sc. 2, l. 13.

He speaks home, madam; you may relish him more in the soldier than in the scholar.
SHAKESPEARE, *Othello*. Act ii. sc. 1, l. 166.

9
I want that glib and oily art,
To speak and purpose not.
SHAKESPEARE, *King Lear*. Act 1, sc. 1, l. 227.

Henceforth my wooing mind shall be expressed
In russet yeas and honest kersey noes.
SHAKESPEARE, *Love's Labour's Lost*. Act v, sc. 2, l. 412.

10
He was wont to speak plain, and to the purpose, like an honest man and a soldier; and now is he turned orthographer; his words are a very fantastical banquet, just so many strange dishes.
SHAKESPEARE, *Much Ado About Nothing*. Act ii, sc. 3, l. 19.

11
I will begin at thy heel, and tell what thou art by inches, thou thing of no bowels, thou!
SHAKESPEARE, *Troilus and Cressida*. Act ii, sc. 1, l. 53.

Speak frankly as the wind.
SHAKESPEARE, *Troilus and Cressida*. Act i, sc. 3, l. 253.

II—Candor: Its Virtues

12
Always be ready to speak your mind, and a base man will avoid you.
WILLIAM BLAKE, *Proverbs of Hell*.

13
Candour, who, with the charity of Paul,
Still thinks the best, whene'er she thinks at all,
With the sweet milk of human kindness bless'd,
The furious ardour of my zeal repress'd.
CHARLES CHURCHILL, *Epistle to Hogarth*, l. 55.

14
Blunt tools are sometimes found of use where sharper instruments would fail.
DICKENS, *Barnaby Rudge*. Ch. 24.

15
There is no wisdom like frankness.
BENJAMIN DISRAELI, *Sybil*. Bk. iv, ch. 9.

Frankness invites frankness.
EMERSON, *Essays, First Series: Prudence*.

16
Feign'd Zeal, you saw, set out with speedier pace,
But, the last heat, Plain Dealing won the race.
DRYDEN, *Albion and Albanus: Epilogue*.

Nothing astonishes men so much as common sense and plain dealing.
EMERSON, *Essays, First Series: Art*.

17
There's a brave fellow! There's a man of pluck!
A man who's not afraid to say his say,
Though a whole town's against him.
LONGFELLOW, *John Endicott*. Act ii, sc. 2.

18
I blurt ungrateful truths, if so they be,
That none may need to say them after me.
J. R. LOWELL, *Epistle to George William Curtis*.

19
We drank the pure daylight of honest speech.
GEORGE MEREDITH, *Modern Love*. St. 48.

20
Open rebuke is better than secret love.
Old Testament: Proverbs, xxvii, 5.

21
For when I dinna clearly see,
I always own I dinna ken,
An' that's the way o' wisest men.
ALLAN RAMSAY, *The Clock and Dial*

1
I had rather seal my lips, than, to my peril,
Speak that which is not.
SHAKESPEARE, *Antony and Cleopatra*. Act v, sc. 2, l. 145.

2
Innocence in genius and candor in power are both noble qualities.
MADAME DE STAËL, *Germany*. Pt. ii, ch. 8.

3
On an occasion of this kind it becomes more than a moral duty to speak one's mind. It becomes a pleasure.
OSCAR WILDE, *The Importance of Being Earnest*. Act ii.

4
Come, give us your plain-dealing fellows,
Who never from honesty shrink,
Not thinking of all they should tell us,
But telling us all that they think.
UNKNOWN, *The Broderer's Song*.

III—Candor: Its Dangers

5
Candor, my tepid Friend,
Come not to play with me!
The Myrrhs and Mochas of the Mind
Are its Iniquity.
EMILY DICKINSON, *Poems*. Pt. v, No. 109.

6
A man that should call everything by its right name, would hardly pass the streets without being knocked down as a common enemy.
LORD HALIFAX, *Works*, p. 246.

7
Nothing is more useful to man than to speak truly, yet candor is apt to be twisted to its own destruction. (Utilius homini nihil est, quam recte loqui; Sed ad perniciem solet agi sinceritas.)
PHÆDRUS, *Fables*. Bk. iv, fab. 12, l. 1.

8
Plain-dealing is a jewel, and he that useth it shall die a beggar.
HENRY PORTER, *Two Angry Women of Abington*. (1599)

Plain-dealing is a jewel.
WYCHERLEY, *Country Wife*. Act iv, sc. 3.

Plain dealing is the best when all is done.
WILLIAM PRYNNE, *Histriomastix*, iii, 1.

9
Candor and generosity, unless tempered by due moderation, lead to ruin. (Simplicitas ac liberalitas, ni adsit modus, in exitium vertuntur.)
TACITUS, *History*. Bk. iii, sec. 86.

10
Complaisance gets us friends, plain-speaking hate. (Obsequium amicos, veritas odium parit.)
TERENCE, *Andria*. Act i, sc. 1, l. 41.

If he persists in saying to me what he likes, he shall hear what he does not like. (Si mihi perget quæ volt dicere, ea quæ non volt audiet.)
TERENCE, *Andria*, l. 920. (Act v, sc. 4.) Said to be an Eastern proverb.

He that speaketh what he will shall hear what he would not.
RICHARD TAVERNER, *Proverbs*, 2. (1539)

11
To be intelligible is to be found out.
OSCAR WILDE, *Lady Windermere's Fan*. Act i.

IV—Candor: Spades are Spades

12
To call a fig a fig, and a skiff a skiff. (Τὰ σῦκα σῦκα, τὴν σκάφην δὲ σκάφην ὀνομάσων.)
ARISTOPHANES. (LUCIAN, *De Conscribend. Hist.*, 41.) Erasmus (*Colloquies: Philetymus et Pseudocheus*) puts the phrase into Latin: "Ficum vocamus ficum, et scapham scapham."

Confutation is my name, the friend of truth and frankness. . . . I call a fig a fig; a skiff a skiff. (Τὰ σῦκα σῦκα, τὴν σκάφην σκάφην λέγων.)
MENANDER, *Fragments*. No. 545.

The world's too squeamish now to bear plain words;
Concerning deeds it acts with gust enough:
But, thanks to wine-lees and democracy,
We've still our stage where truth calls spade a spade!
ROBERT BROWNING, *Aristophanes' Apology*.

13
A fig's a fig, he calls a spade a spade. (Ficus ficus, ligonem ligonem vocat.)
ERASMUS, *Adagiorum Chiliades: Veritas*.

14
Which can call . . . a spade a spade.
RICHARD TAVERNER, *Garden of Wysdome*. Sig. C 4. (1539)

A loose, plain, rude writer, I call a spade a spade.
ROBERT BURTON, *Anatomy of Melancholy: Democritus to the Reader*.

I cannot say the crow is white,
But needs must call a spade a spade.
HUMPHREY GIFFORD, *A Woman's Face is Full of Wiles*.

15
Faith we do call a spade a spade in Cornwall.
BEN JONSON, *The Magnetic Lady*. Act i.

Ramp up my genius, be not retrograde,
But boldly nominate a spade a spade.
BEN JONSON, *The Poetaster*. Act v, sc. 3.

I have learned to call wickedness by its own terms: a fig a fig; and a spade a spade.
JOHN KNOX.

16
The Macedonians are a rude and clownish people that call a spade a spade.
PHILIP OF MACEDON. (PLUTARCH, *Apothegms of Kings and Great Commanders: Philip*.)

Brought up like a rude Macedon, and taught to call a spade a spade.
STEPHEN GOSSON, *Ephemerides of Phialo*. (1579)

1
I think it good plain English, without fraud,
To call a spade a spade, a bawd a bawd.
JOHN TAYLOR THE WATER-POET, *A Kicksey Winsey.*

2
I'll give you leave to call me anything, if you don't call me spade.
SWIFT, *Polite Conversation.* Dial. ii.

3
"Ye can call it influenza if ye like," said Mrs. Machin. "There was no influenza in my young days. We called a cold a cold."
ARNOLD BENNETT, *The Card.* Ch. 8.

4
I call a cat a cat and Rolet a rascal. (J'appelle un chat un chat, et Rolet un fripon.)
BOILEAU, *Satires.* Sat. i, l. 52.

5
I don't complain of Betsy or any of her acts
Exceptin' when we've quarreled and told each other facts.
WILL CARLETON, *Betsy and I Are Out.*

V—Candor: The Candid Friend

6
There is no man so friendless but what he can find a friend sincere enough to tell him disagreeable truths.
BULWER-LYTTON, *What Will He Do with It?* Bk. ii, ch. 14.

7
Give me the avowed, the erect, the manly foe,
Bold I can meet,—perhaps may turn his blow;
But of all plagues, good Heaven, thy wrath can send,
Save, save, oh, save me from the Candid Friend.
GEORGE CANNING, *The New Morality.*

Many a friend will tell us our faults without reserve, who will not so much as hint at our follies.
LORD CHESTERFIELD, *Letters,* July 1, 1748.

8
I hate him that my vices telleth me.
CHAUCER, *Wife of Bath's Prologue,* l. 662.

To a poor man, men should his vices tell,
But not to a lord, though he should go to hell.
CHAUCER, *The Somnours Tale,* l. 369.

9
Truly, sir, when a man is ruined, 'tis but the duty of a Christian to tell him of it.
FARQUHAR, *The Twin-Rivals.* Act i, sc. 1.

10
If a friend telleth thee a fault, imagine always that he telleth thee not the whole.
FULLER, *Introductio ad Prudentiam,* i, 47.

CANT, see Hypocrisy

CARDS AND CARD-PLAYING

See also Gambling

11
There be that can pack the cards, and yet cannot play well.
FRANCIS BACON, *Essays: Of Cunning.*

As much is lost by a card too many as a card too few. (Tanto se pierde por Carta de mas como por Carta de menos.)
CERVANTES, *Don Quixote.* Pt. ii, ch. 17.

12
Patience and shuffle the cards. (Paciencia y barajar.)
CERVANTES, *Don Quixote.* Pt. ii, ch. 23.

13
With spots quadrangular of diamond form,
Ensanguined hearts, clubs typical of strife,
And spades, the emblem of untimely graves.
COWPER, *The Task.* Bk. iv, l. 217.

14
Cards were at first for benefits designed,
Sent to amuse, not to enslave the mind.
DAVID GARRICK, *Epilogue to Ed. Moore's Gamester.*

15
When in doubt, win the trick.
EDMOND HOYLE, *Twenty-Four Rules for Learners.*

16
"A clear fire, a clean hearth, and the rigour of the game." This was the celebrated wish of old Sarah Battle (now with God), who, next to her devotions, loved a good game of whist. She was none of your lukewarm gamesters, your half-and-half players. . . They do not play at cards, but only play at playing at them. . . . All people have their blind side—their superstitions; and I have heard her declare, under the rose, that Hearts was her favourite suit.
CHARLES LAMB, *Essays of Elia: Mrs. Battle's Opinions on Whist.*

17
If dirt was trumps, what hands you would hold!
CHARLES LAMB, *Lamb's Suppers.* Vol. ii, last ch.

Soiled by rude hands, who cut and come again.
GEORGE CRABBE, *Tales of the Hall: The Widow's Tale,* l. 26.

18
It is an old courtesy at the cards, perdy, to let the loser have his word.
SIR THOMAS MORE, *Works,* p. 1018. (1533)

19
See how the world its veterans rewards!
A youth of frolics, an old age of cards.
POPE, *Moral Essays.* Epis. ii, l. 243.

You do not play then at whist, sir? Alas, what a sad old age you are preparing for yourself! (Vous ne jouez donc pas le whist, monsieur? Hélas! quelle triste vieillesse vous vous préparez!)
TALLEYRAND, *Retort,* when reproached for his addiction to cards.

20
Ere he took me, I put him to his trumps.
THOMAS SACKVILLE, *Mirrour for Magistrates: Jack Cade.* (1559)

It has put him to his trumps.
BEAUMONT AND FLETCHER, *Cupid's Revenge.* Act iv, sc. 1.

I will not play my ace of trumps yet.
THOMAS FULLER, *Gnomologia,* 2647. (1732)

1
Have I not here the best cards for the game,
To win this easy match play'd for a crown?
SHAKESPEARE, *King John*. Act v, sc. 2, l. 105.

As sure a card as ever won the set.
SHAKESPEARE, *Titus Andronicus*, v, 1, 100.

He's a sure card.
DRYDEN, *The Spanish Friar*. Act ii, sc. 2.

2
I must complain the cards are ill shuffled till I have a good hand.
SWIFT, *Thoughts on Various Subjects*.

3
Damn your cards, said he, they are the devil's books.
SWIFT, *Polite Conversation*. Dial. iii.

Cards are the devil's books.
BULWER-LYTTON, *Money*. Act iv, sc. 2.

Or lee-lang nights, wi' crabbit leuks,
Pore owre the devil's pictured beuks.
ROBERT BURNS, *The Twa Dogs*.

CARE

See also Burden, Trouble, Worry.

5
But what is past my help is past my care.
BEAUMONT AND FLETCHER, *The Double Marriage*. Act i.

Things past redress are now with me past care.
SHAKESPEARE, *Richard II*. Act ii, sc. 3, l. 171.

6
Ye banks and braes o' bonie Doon,
How can ye bloom sae fresh and fair?
How can ye chant, ye little birds,
And I sae weary fu' o' care?
BURNS, *The Banks o' Doon*.

Carking cares.
BURNS, *The Cotter's Saturday Night*.

7
Great waves of care. (Magnis curarum undis.)
CATULLUS, *Odes*. No. lxiv, l. 62.

8
An essential of a happy life is freedom from care. (Caput enim esse ad beate vivendum securitatem.)
CICERO, *De Amicitia*. Ch. 13, sec. 45.

9
Care lives with all; no rules, no precepts save
The wise from woe, no fortitude the brave.
GEORGE CRABBE, *The Library*.

10
Euripides did well and wisely say
Man's life and care are twins, and born one day.
ALEXANDER CRAIG, *The Misery of Man*.

11
Care draws on care, woe comforts woe again;
Sorrow breeds sorrow, one grief brings forth twain.
MICHAEL DRAYTON, *Henry Howard to the Lady Geraldine*, l. 87.

12
Cast away care; he that loves sorrow
Lengthens not day, nor can buy tomorrow.
FORD AND DEKKER, *The Sun's Darling*.

13
Restless Anxiety, forlorn Despair,
And all the faded family of Care.
SAMUEL GARTH, *Dispensary*. Canto vi, l. 137.

14
Behind the horseman sits black care. (Post equitem sedet atra Cura.)
HORACE, *Odes*. Bk. iii, ode 1, l. 40.

Care, looking grim and black, doth sit
Behind his back that rides from it.
FLORIO, tr., *Montaigne*, i, 38. After Horace.

Care jumps up behind and gallops with him. (Le chagrin monte en croupe et galope avec lui.)
BOILEAU, *Epistle*. No. 5, l. 44.

Black Care rarely sits behind a rider whose pace is fast enough.
THEODORE ROOSEVELT, *Ranch Life*, p. 59.

15
Vile care boards even the brass-bound galley, nor fails to overtake the troop of horse, swifter than stags, swifter than the wind which drives the clouds. (Scandit æratas vitiosa naves Cura nec turmas equitum relinquit, Ocior cervis et agente nimbos Ocior Euro.)
HORACE, *Odes*. Bk. ii, ode 16, l. 21.

16
Care that is entered once into the breast
Will have the whole possession ere it rest.
BEN JONSON, *Tale of a Tub*. Act i, sc. 4.

17
Telling lies and scraping siller, heaping cares on cares.
CHARLES KINGSLEY, *The Outlaw*.

Old Care has a mortgage on every estate,
And that's what you pay for the wealth that you get.
J. G. SAXE, *Gifts of the Gods*.

18
And the night shall be filled with music
And the cares, that infest the day,
Shall fold their tents, like the Arabs,
And as silently steal away.
LONGFELLOW, *The Day is Done*.

19
Ye pallid cares, far hence away! (Pallentes procul hinc abite curæ.)
MARTIAL, *Epigrams*. Bk. xi, epig. 6, l. 6.

Begone, old Care, and I prithee begone from me;
For i' faith, old Care, thee and I shall never agree.
JOHN PLAYFORD, *Musical Companion*. Song 13.

20
If every man's internal care
Were written on his brow,
How many would our pity share,
Who have our envy now!
(Se a ciascun l'interno affano
Si leggesse in fronte scritto,
Quanti mai, che invidia fanno,
Ci farebbero pietà!)
PIETRO METASTATIO, *Giuseppe Riconosciuto*. Pt. i. (*Opere*, vii, 266.) For other renderings see APPENDIX, p. 2273.

21
Care Sat on his faded cheek.
MILTON, *Paradise Lost*. Bk. i, l. 601.

Care is beauty's thief.
SHACKERLEY MARMION, *Cupid and Psyche.*

1
For other things mild Heav'n a time ordains,
And disapproves that care, though wise in show,
That with superfluous burden loads the day.
MILTON, *Sonnet xviii: To Cyriac Skinner.*

2
O human cares! What emptiness in the affairs of men! (O curas hominum, O quantum est in rebus inane!)
PERSIUS, *Satires.* Sat. i, l. 1.

3
Banish care from your mind. (Ejicite ex animo curam.)
PLAUTUS, *Casina: Prologue,* l. 23.

Eat not thy heart, which forbids to afflict our souls, and waste them with vexatious cares.
PLUTARCH, *Morals: Of the Training of Children.*

Eat not thy heart, that is to say, consume not thyself with cares.
RICHARD TAVERNER, *Proverbs.* Fo. 54.

4
Fretting cares make grey hairs.
W. G. BENHAM, *English Proverbs,* p. 763.

Care makes white hairs. (Cura facit canos.)
UNKNOWN. A Latin proverb.

5
So shaken as we are, so wan with care.
SHAKESPEARE, *I Henry IV.* Act i, sc. 1, l. 1.

6
O polish'd perturbation! golden care!
That keep'st the ports of slumber open wide
To many a watchful night!
SHAKESPEARE, *II Henry IV.* Act iv, sc. 5, l. 22.

Care keeps his watch in every old man's eye,
And where care lodges, sleep will never lie.
SHAKESPEARE, *Romeo and Juliet.* Act ii, sc. 3, l. 35.

7
His cares are now all ended.
SHAKESPEARE, *II Henry IV.* Act v, sc. 2, l. 3.

8
Care is no cure, but rather corrosive,
For things that are not to be remedied.
SHAKESPEARE, *I Henry VI.* Act iii, sc. 3, l. 3.

9
Deep-drenched in a sea of care.
SHAKESPEARE, *The Rape of Lucrece,* l. 1100.

10
Comfort's in heaven; and we are on the earth,
Where nothing lives but crosses, cares, and grief.
SHAKESPEARE, *Richard II.* Act ii, sc. 2, l. 78.

And is there care in Heaven?
SPENSER, *Faerie Queene.* Bk. ii, canto viii, st. 1.

11
Care's an enemy to life.
SHAKESPEARE, *Twelfth Night.* Act i, sc. 3, l. 3.

12
I could lie down like a tired child
And weep away the life of care
Which I have borne and yet must bear.
SHELLEY, *Stanzas Written in Dejection Near Naples.*

13
Those little cares and visionary joys
That so perplex the fond impassion'd heart
Of ever-cheated, ever-trusting man.
JAMES THOMSON, *To the Memory of Sir Isaac Newton,* l. 154.

14
And care, whom not the gayest can outbrave,
Pursues its feeble victim to the grave.
HENRY KIRKE WHITE, *Childhood.* Pt. ii, l. 17.

15
Care to our coffin adds a nail, no doubt;
But every grin so merry draws one out.
JOHN WOLCOT, *Expostulatory Odes.* Ode 15.

16
Let care kill a cat, We'll laugh and grow fat.
UNKNOWN, *Shirburn Ballads,* 91. (1585)

What though care killed a cat, thou hast mettle enough in thee to kill care.
SHAKESPEARE, *Much Ado About Nothing.* Act v, sc. 1, l. 135.

Hang sorrow, care'll kill a cat.
BEN JONSON, *Every Man in His Humour.* Act i, sc. 3.

Hang sorrow! care will kill a cat,
And therefore let's be merry.
GEORGE WITHER, *Christmas.*

CARLYLE, THOMAS

17
A spectre moving in a world of spectres.
THOMAS CARLYLE, *Description of himself.*

18
He is like a lover or an outlaw who wraps up his message in a serenade, which is nonsense to the sentinel, but salvation to the ear for which it is meant.
EMERSON, *Papers from the Dial: Past and Present.*

Carlyle, in his strange, half-mad way, has entered the Field of the Cloth of Gold . . . the indubitable champion of England.
EMERSON, *Papers from the Dial: Past and Present.*

19
A trip-hammer, with an Æolian attachment.
EMERSON, after meeting Carlyle in 1848.

20
These deathless names by this dead snake defiled
Bid memory spit upon him for their sake.
SWINBURNE, *After Looking into Carlyle's Reminiscences.*

CASTLE

I—Castles on Earth

21
Castles are forests of stone.
GEORGE HERBERT, *Jacula Prudentum.*

22
A castle, after all, is but a house—
The dullest one when wanting company.
J. S. KNOWLES, *The Hunchback.* Act iv, sc. 1.

1
This castle hath a pleasant seat; the air
Nimbly and sweetly recommends itself
Unto our gentle senses.
SHAKESPEARE, *Macbeth*. Act i, sc. 6, l. 1.

The rude ribs of that ancient castle.
SHAKESPEARE, *Richard II*. Act iii, sc. 3, l. 32.

2
A castle girt about and bound
With sorrow, like a spell.
SWINBURNE, *The Tale of Balen*. Pt. vi, st. 25.

II—Castles in the Air

3
The bonnie, bonnie bairn who sits poking in the ase,
Glowering in the fire wi' his wee round face,
Laughing at the fuffin' lowe—what sees he there?
Ha! the young dreamer's bigging castles in the air.
JAMES BALLANTINE, *Castles in the Air*.

For a' sae sage he looks, what can the laddie ken?
He's thinkin' upon naething, like mony mighty men;
A wee thing maks us think, a sma' thing maks us stare;
There are mair folks than him biggin' castles in the air.
JAMES BALLANTINE, *Castles in the Air*.

4
Castles in the air cost a vast deal to keep up.
BULWER-LYTTON, *Lady of Lyons*. Act i, sc. 3.

5
When I build castles in the air,
Void of sorrow, void of fear.
ROBERT BURTON, *Anatomy of Melancholy: The Author's Abstract*. (1621)

6
Building castles in the air, and making yourself a laughing-stock.
CERVANTES, *Don Quixote*. Pt. ii, ch. 31.

7
I find the gayest castles in the air that were ever piled, far better for comfort and for use, than the dungeons in the air that are daily dug and caverned out by grumbling, discontented people.
EMERSON, *Conduct of Life: Considerations by the Way*.

8
And castles built above in lofty skies,
Which never yet had good foundation.
GEORGE GASCOIGNE, *Steel Glass*, p. 55. (1576)

9
There is more pleasure in building castles in the air than on the ground.
EDWARD GIBBON, *Miscellaneous Works*, i, 278.

10
Castles in the air—they are so easy to take refuge in. And so easy to build, too.
HENRIK IBSEN, *The Master Builder*. Act iii.

11
Alerand was a building of castles in the air.
WILLIAM PAINTER, *The Palace of Pleasure*, i, 266. (1566) This is the earliest known instance of the use in English of this proverbial phrase, of which many examples could be quoted.

As we are wont to say by them that build castles in the air.
SIR PHILIP SIDNEY, *Apology for Poetry*. Par. 12. (1595)

'Tis best to build no castles in the air.
MADAME D'ARBLAY, *Diary*. Vol. ii, p. 424.

12
If one advances confidently in the direction of his dreams, and endeavors to live the life which he has imagined, he will meet with a success unexpected in common hours. . . . If you have built castles in the air, your work need not be lost; that is where they should be. Now put the foundations under them.
HENRY DAVID THOREAU, *Walden*. Ch. 18.

III—Castles in Spain

13
Thou shalt make castles then in Spain,
And dream of joy, all but in vain.
CHAUCER, *Romaunt of the Rose*, l. 2573. (c. 1400)
This is the earliest use in English of this proverbial phrase, whose origin is obscure. Storer (*Peter the Cruel*, p. 280) ascribes it to the lavish favors bestowed by Don Enrique of Spain. It has been traced back in French literature to the thirteenth century, and Littré thinks the idea is simply that of an imaginary castle in any foreign country. It may have originated from the boastings of Spanish adventurers in France of their lordly residences, which existed only in the imagination.

He began to make castles in Spain, as lovers do.
WILLIAM CAXTON, *Jason*, 25. (c. 1477)

14
I fell asleep in the very act of building castles in Spain.
LE SAGE, *Gil Blas*. Bk. iii, ch. 76.

15
When I could not sleep for cold,
I had fire enough in my brain,
And builded, with roofs of gold,
My beautiful castles in Spain.
J. R. LOWELL, *Aladdin*. St. 1.

16
Let me think of building castles in Spain. (Faire des châteaux en Espagne.)
MONTAIGNE, *Essays*. Bk. iii, ch. 4.

CAT

17
An old cat laps as much milk as a young.
WILLIAM CAMDEN, *Remains*, p. 318.

18
What a monstrous tail our cat hath got!
HENRY CAREY, *Dragon of Wantley*. Act ii, sc. 1.

19
Who shall hang the bell about the cat's neck?
CERVANTES, *Don Quixote*. Pt. ii, ch. 43

It is weel said, but wha will bell the cat?
JOHN RAY. *Scottish Proverbs*.

But when the bell was brought and on a collar hung, was no rat in the rout, for all the realm of France, that durst have bound the bell about the cat's neck.

WILLIAM LANGLAND, *Piers Plowman: The Vision of the Field Full of Folk*, l. 180. Langland tells the whole fable of the mice who decided to hang a bell to the cat's neck in order to be warned of her approach.

1
Let take a cat, and foster him well with milk
And tender flesh, and make his couch of silk,
And let him see a mouse go by the wall,
Anon he waveth milk, and flesh, and all,
And every dainty which is in that house,
Such appetite hath he to eat a mouse.

CHAUCER, *Maunciples Tale*, l. 71.

The cat, if you but singe her tabby skin,
The chimney keeps, and sits content within:
But once grown sleek, will from her corner run,
Sport with her tail and wanton in the sun:
She licks her fair round face, and frisks abroad
To show her fur, and to be catterwaw'd.

POPE, *The Wife of Bath. Prologue*, l. 142.

2
Ere a cat could lick his ear.

CHARLES COTTON, *Vergil Travestied*. Bk. iv. (1664)

3
Mrs. Crupp had indignantly assured him that there wasn't room to swing a cat there; but as Mr. Dick justly observed to me, sitting down on the foot of the bed, nursing his leg, "You know, Trotwood, I don't want to swing a cat. I never do swing a cat. Therefore what does that signify to *me!*"

DICKENS, *David Copperfield*. Vol. ii, ch. 6.

4
Confound the cats! All cats—alway—
Cats of all colours, black, white, grey;
By night a nuisance and by day—
Confound the cats!

ORLANDO DOBBIN, *A Dithyramb on Cats.*

5
Turn cat in the pan very prettily.

RICHARD EDWARDS, *Damon and Pithias.*

6
A cat gloved catcheth no mice.

JOHN FLORIO, *First Fruites*. Fo. 30. (1578)

The Cat in Gloves catches no Mice.

BENJAMIN FRANKLIN, *Poor Richard*, 1754.

The Cat that always wears Silk Mittens
Will catch no Mice to feed her Kittens.

ARTHUR GUITERMAN, *A Poet's Proverbs*, p. 94.

A muzzled cat never was a good mouser.

WILLIAM CAMDEN, *Remains*, p. 317. (1605)

7
When the cat is abroad the mice play.

JOHN FLORIO, *First Fruites*. Fo. 33. (1578)

When the cat's away The mice will play.

JOHN RAY, *English Proverbs*. (1670)

When the cat's gone, the mice grow saucy.

THOMAS FULLER, *Gnomologia*. No. 5572. (1732)

Well wots the mouse The cat's out of house.

JOHN RAY, *Proverbs: Scottish*. (1670)

So it is, and such is life. The cat's away, and the mice they play.

DICKENS, *Bleak House*. Ch. 54.

Playing the mouse in absence of the cat.

SHAKESPEARE, *Henry V*. Act i, sc. 2, l. 172.

8
Is the cat to blame,
If maids be fools with shame?

JOHN FLORIO, *Second Fruites*. Fo. 41. (1591)

9
Cats hide their claws.

THOMAS FULLER, *Gnomologia*. No. 1072.

The cat invites the mouse to a feast.

THOMAS FULLER, *Gnomologia*. No. 4441.

When the cat winketh,
Little wots the mouse what the cat thinketh.

THOMAS FULLER, *Gnomologia*. No. 6453.

Let the cat wink and let the mouse run.

UNKNOWN, *World and the Child*. (1522)

10
Far in the stillness a cat Languishes loudly.

W. E. HENLEY, *In Hospital: Vigil*.

the great open spaces
where cats are cats

DON MARQUIS, ***mekitabel has an adventure.***

11
An old cat sports not with her prey.

GEORGE HERBERT, *Jacula Prudentum*.

The devil playeth oft . . . as doth the cat with the mouse.

UNKNOWN, *Ayenbite*, 179. (1340)

12
The cat would eat fish, and would not wet her feet.

JOHN HEYWOOD, *Proverbs*. Pt. i, ch. 11. (1546)
A medieval proverb: "Catus amat pisces, sed non vult tangere plantas."

Fain would the cat fish eat,
But she's loath to wet her feet.

THOMAS FULLER, *Gnomologia*. No. 6130.

Letting "I dare not" wait upon "I would,"
Like the poor cat i' the adage.

SHAKESPEARE, *Macbeth*. Act i, sc. 7, l. 44.

What cat's averse to fish?

THOMAS GRAY, *On Death of a Favourite Cat*.

13
When all candles be out all cats be grey.

JOHN HEYWOOD, *Proverbs*. Pt. i, ch. 5. (1546)

All cats are grey in the dark.

THOMAS LODGE, *A Marguerite of America*, l. 56.

By night all cats are gray. (De noche todos los Gatos son pardos.)

CERVANTES, *Don Quixote*. Pt. ii, ch. 33.

14
A cat may look on a king.

JOHN HEYWOOD, *Proverbs*. Pt. ii, ch. 5. (1546)

A halfpenny cat may look at a king.

JOHN RAY, *Proverbs: Scottish*. (1670)

15
There are more ways of killing a cat than choking her with cream.

CHARLES KINGSLEY, *Westward Ho*. Ch. 20.

16
To pull the chestnuts from the fire with the

cat's paw. (Tirer les marrons de la patte du chat.)

MOLIÈRE, *L'Étourdi*. Act iii, sc. 5. The story of the ape using the whelp's foot to get chestnuts out of the fire was told in 1586 by GEOFFREY WHITNEY, *Choice of Emblems*, p. 58. It was from this book that Shakespeare gained his knowledge of the foreign emblematists of the sixteenth century.

Some few that . . . make use of us, as the monkey did of the cat's paw, to scrape the nuts out of the fire.

JOHN WILSON, *The Cheats*. Act v, sc. 4. (1664)

To take the nuts from the fire with the dog's foot.

GEORGE HERBERT, *Jacula Prudentum*. (1640)

1 When I play with my cat, who knows whether I do not make her more sport than she makes me?

MONTAIGNE, *Essays*. Bk. ii, ch. 12. (1580)

When my Cat and I entertain each other with mutual apish tricks (as playing with a garter), who knows but that I make her more sport than she makes me?

IZAAK WALTON, *Compleat Angler*. Ch. 1. (1653)

2 A baited cat may grow as fierce as a lion.

SAMUEL PALMER, *Moral Essays*, p. 305.

3 It has been the providence of Nature to give this creature nine lives instead of one.

PILPAY, *The Greedy Cat*. Fable iii.

Good king of cats, nothing but one of your nine lives.

SHAKESPEARE, *Romeo and Juliet*. Act iii, sc. 1, l. 80.

As many lives as a cat.

BUNYAN, *The Pilgrim's Progress*. Pt. ii.

With new reversions of nine lives,
Starts up, and like a cat revives.

BUTLER, *Hudibras*. Pt. iii, canto 2, l. 1629.

4 It would make a cat laugh.

J. R. PLANCHÉ, *Extravaganza*, iv, 148.

5 But thousands die without or this or that,
Die, and endow a college or a cat.

POPE, *Moral Essays*. Epis. iii, l. 95. The Duchess of Richmond left annuities for the maintenance of her cats.

6 Never wake a sleeping cat. (N'eveille point le chat qui dort.)

RABELAIS, *Works*. Bk. i. *See also under* DOG.

7 The more you rub a cat on the rump, the higher she sets her tail.

JOHN RAY, *English Proverbs*, 109.

8 He's like a cat; fling him which way you will, he'll light on his legs.

JOHN RAY, *English Proverbs*, 282. (1678)

9 I would like to be there, were it but to see how the cat jumps.

WALTER SCOTT, *Journal*, 7 Oct., 1826.

10 I am as vigilant as a cat to steal cream.

SHAKESPEARE, *I Henry IV*. Act iv, sc. 2, l. 64.

11 A harmless necessary cat.

SHAKESPEARE, *Merchant of Venice*. Act iv, sc. 1, l. 55.

The cat, with eyne of burning coal.

SHAKESPEARE, *Pericles:* Act iii, *Prelude*.

12 She watches him as a cat would watch a mouse.

SWIFT, *Polite Conversation*. Dial. iii.

13 Stately, kindly, lordly friend, Condescend
Here to sit by me.

SWINBURNE, *To a Cat*.

14 I like little Pussy, her coat is so warm,
And if I don't hurt her, she'll do me no harm.

JANE TAYLOR, *I Like Little Pussy*.

15 For oft museth the cat after her mother.

UNKNOWN, *Proverbs of Alfred*, 296. (c. 1275)

The cat will after kind.

SHAKESPEARE, *As You Like It*. Act iii, sc. 2, l. 109.

16 A good cat deserves a good rat. (À bon chat bon rat.)

UNKNOWN. A French proverb. There is also its opposite: "À mauvais chat mauvais rat."

CAUSE

I—Cause: Apothegms

17 Home of lost causes, and forsaken beliefs, and unpopular names, and impossible loyalties!

MATTHEW ARNOLD, *Essays in Criticism: Preface*. Referring to Oxford University.

Oxford! of whom the poet said
That one of your unwritten laws is
To back the weaker side, and wed
Your gallant heart to wobbling causes.

OWEN SEAMAN, *The Scholar Farmer*.

18 Greatly unfortunate, he fights the cause
Of honour, virtue, liberty and Rome.

JOSEPH ADDISON, *Cato*. Act i, sc. 1.

19 A cause may be inconvenient, but it's magnificent. It's like champagne or high shoes, and one must be prepared to suffer for it.

ARNOLD BENNETT, *The Title*.

20 Presume to lay their hand upon the ark
Of her magnificent and awful cause.

COWPER, *The Task*. Bk. ii, l. 231.

21 Great causes are never tried on their merits.

EMERSON, *Essays, Second Series: Nature*.

22 Seeing the root of the matter is found in me.

Old Testament: Job, xix, 28.

23 This cause is to be fought, not pleaded.

PHILIP MASSINGER, *Bashful Lover*. Act i, sc. 2.

And, confident we have the better cause,
Why should we fear the trial?

PHILIP MASSINGER, *Bashful Lover*. Act i, sc. 2.

1
Cause me no causes.

PHILIP MASSINGER, *A New Way to Pay Old Debts*. Act i, sc. 3.

2
To set the Cause above renown,
To love the game beyond the prize,
To honour, while you strike him down,
The foe that comes with fearless eyes.

HENRY NEWBOLT, *Clifton Chapel*.

3
A man is a lion in his own cause.

H. G. BOHN, *Hand-Book of Proverbs*, p. 294.

4
Your cause doth strike my heart.

SHAKESPEARE, *Cymbeline*. Act i, sc. 6, l. 101.

5
Hear me for my cause, and be silent, that you may hear.

SHAKESPEARE, *Julius Cæsar*. Act iii, sc. 2, l. 13.

Mine's not an idle cause.

SHAKESPEARE, *Othello*. Act i, sc. 2, l. 95.

II—Cause: The Good Cause

6
A good cause needs not to be patron'd by passion, but can sustain itself upon a temperate dispute.

SIR THOMAS BROWNE, *Religio Medici*. Pt. i, sec. 5.

7
They never fail who die in a great cause.

BYRON, *Marino Faliero*. Act ii, sc. 2.

In such a cause they could not dare to fear.

COWPER, *Expostulation*, l. 621.

8
Our cause is just, our union is perfect.

JOHN DICKINSON, *Declaration on Taking up Arms*, 1775. Formerly attributed to Jefferson, but occurs in original manuscript draft in Dickinson's handwriting.

9
A good cause makes a stout heart and a strong arm.

THOMAS FULLER, *Gnomologia*. No. 140.

That cause is strong which has not a multitude, but one strong man behind it.

J. R. LOWELL, *Democracy: Books and Libraries*.

A just cause is strong.

THOMAS MIDDLETON, *A Trick to Catch the Old One*. Act iii, l. 3.

10
Pledged to the glory of a mighty cause.

ANGELA MORGAN, *Conquerors*.

11
The cause is gude and the word's "Fa' on."

JOHN RAY, *Proverbs: Scottish*.

12
God befriend us, as our cause is just!

SHAKESPEARE, *I Henry IV*. Act v, sc. 1, l. 120.

13
A noble cause doth ease much a grievous case.

SIR PHILIP SIDNEY, *Arcadia*. Bk. i.

14
For my sake, do get it into your minds that my cause is a just one. (Mea causa causam hanc justum esse animum inducite.)

TERENCE, *Heauton Timorumenos: Prologue*, l. 41.

15
The homely beauty of the good old cause.

WORDSWORTH, *Sonnet: O Friend! I Know Not*.

III—Cause: The Bad Cause

16
Defend not my deed; a bad cause should be silent. (Nec factum defende meum: mala causa silenda est.)

OVID, *Epistulæ ex Ponto*. Bk. iii, epis. 1, l. 147.

17
A bad cause will ever be supported by bad means and bad men.

THOMAS PAINE, *The Crisis*. No. ii.

18
It is a bad cause that asks for mercy. (Mala causa est quæ requirit misericordiam.)

PUBLILIUS SYRUS, *Sententiæ*. No. 346.

19
It's a bad cause that none dare speak in.

JOHN RAY, *English Proverbs*.

IV—Cause and Effect

20
To know truly is to know by causes. (Vere scire, esse per causas scire.)

FRANCIS BACON, *De Augmentis Scientiarum*. Pt. ii, bk. ii, aphor. 1. Quoted.

21
The causes of events are ever more interesting than the events themselves. (Semper causæ eventorum magis movent quam ipsa eventa.)

CICERO, *Epistolæ ad Atticum*. Bk. ix, sec. 5.

22
Behind the coarse effect is a fine cause. . . . Cause and effect are two sides of one fact.

EMERSON, *Essays, First Series: Circles*.

Cause and effect, means and ends, seed and fruit, cannot be severed; for the effect already blooms in the cause, the end preëxists in the means, the fruit in the seed.

EMERSON, *Essays, First Series: Compensation*.

23
Do not clutch at sensual sweetness until it is ripe on the slow tree of cause and effect.

EMERSON, *Essays, First Series: Prudence*.

Cause and effect, the chancellors of God.

EMERSON, *Essays, First Series: Self-Reliance*.

Everything is the cause of itself.

EMERSON, *Journals*, 1856.

24
To all facts there are laws,
The effect has its cause, and I mount to the cause.

OWEN MEREDITH, *Lucile*. Pt. ii, canto iii, st. 8.

25
That which follows ever conforms to that which went before. (Τὰ ἑξῆς ἀεὶ τοῖς προηγησαμένοις οἰκείως ἐπιγίνεται.)

MARCUS AURELIUS, *Meditations*. Bk. iv, sec. 45.

1
Their cause is hidden, but our woes are clear. (Causa latet, mala nostra patent.)
OVID, *Heroides*. Eleg. xxi, l. 53.

The cause is hidden, but the result is known. (Causa latet, vis est notissima.)
OVID, *Metamorphoses*. Bk. iv, l. 287.

2
And now remains
That we find out the cause of this effect;
Or, rather say, the cause of this defect,
For this effect defective comes by cause.
SHAKESPEARE, *Hamlet*. Act ii, sc. 2, l. 100.

3
There is occasions and causes why and wherefore in all things.
SHAKESPEARE, *Henry V*. Act v, sc. 1, l. 3.

It is the cause, it is the cause, my soul,—
Let me not name it to you, you chaste stars!—
It is the cause.
SHAKESPEARE, *Othello*. Act v, sc. 2, l. 1.

Thou art the cause, and most accursed effect.
SHAKESPEARE, *Richard III*. Act i, sc. 2, l. 120.

4
Happy the man who has been able to understand the causes of things. (Felix, qui potuit rerum cognoscere causas.)
VERGIL, *Georgics*. Bk. ii, l. 490.

5
After this, therefore on account of this. (Post hoc, ergo propter hoc.) False argument from cause to effect from mere precedence of circumstance.
RICHARD WHATELY, *Logic*, p. 135.

V—Cause: First Cause

6
The parent of the universe . . . fixed for eternity the causes whereby he keeps all things in order. (Parens rerum . . . Fixit in æternum causas, qui cuncta coercet.)
LUCAN, *De Bello Civili*. Bk. ii, l. 7.

Even from the first beginnings of the world descends a chain of causes. (A prima descendit origine mundi Causarum series.)
LUCAN, *De Bello Civili*. Bk. vi, l. 608.

7
The Universal Cause
Acts to one end, but acts by various laws.
POPE, *Essay on Man*. Epis. iii, l. 1.

The Universal Cause
Acts not by partial but by gen'ral laws.
POPE, *Essay on Man*. Epis. iv, l. 35.

8
Thou Great First Cause, least understood.
POPE, *Universal Prayer*.

CAUTION, see Prudence

CELIBACY, see Marriage and Celibacy

CENSURE, see Criticism

CENTURY, see Age: The Age

CERTAINTY

9
To be positive: to be mistaken at the top of one's voice.
AMBROSE BIERCE, *The Devil's Dictionary*.

10
As certain as a gun.
BUTLER, *Hudibras*. Pt. i, canto iii, l. 11.

As sure as a gun.
CONGREVE, *Double Dealer*. Act v; DRYDEN, *Spanish Friar*. Act iii. sc. 2; RICHARD STEELE, *Tender Husband*. Act iii, sc. 2. "As sure as shooting" is the modern form.

As sure as death.
BEN JONSON, *Every Man in His Humour*, ii, 1.

Sure as God made little apples.
NORTHALL, *Folk Phrases*, p. 11.

Sure as the coat on your back.
JOHN RAY, *English Proverbs*, 208.

11
Never take anything for granted.
BENJAMIN DISRAELI, *Speech*, 5 Oct., 1864.

12
No great deed is done
By falterers who ask for certainty.
GEORGE ELIOT, *Spanish Gypsy*. Bk. i, last sc.

13
In this world, nothing is certain but death and taxes.
BENJAMIN FRANKLIN, *Letter to M. Leroy*, 1789.

There's nothing certain in man's life but this:
That he must lose it.
OWEN MEREDITH, *Clytemnestra*. Pt. xx.

One thing at least is certain—*this* life flies:
One thing is certain, and the rest is lies.
OMAR KHAYYÁM, *Rubáiyát*. St. 63. (Fitzgerald, tr.)

14
How shall I hedge myself with certainties?
HELEN FRAZEE-BOWER, *Certainties*.

But I have certainty enough
For I am sure of you.
AMELIA JOSEPHINE BURR, *Certainty Enough*.

15
Such sober certainty of waking bliss.
MILTON, *Comus*, l. 263.

16
I will maintain it before the whole world. (Je le soutiendrai devant tout le monde.)
MOLIÈRE, *Le Bourgeois Gentilhomme*. Act iv, sc. 3.

17
All cares of mortal men did they forget,
Except the vague desire not to die,
The hopeless wish to flee from certainty,
That sights and sounds we love will bring on us
In this sweet fleeting world and piteous.
WILLIAM MORRIS, *Life and Death of Jason*. Bk. v, l. 385.

18
I'll make assurance double sure,
And take a bond of fate.
SHAKESPEARE, *Macbeth*. Act iv, sc. 1, l. 83.

1
Wisely and slow: they stumble that run fast.
SHAKESPEARE, *Romeo and Juliet*. Act ii, sc. 3, l. 94. (1591)

Slowness is sure.
THOMAS DRAXE, *Bibliotheca Scholastica Instructissima*, 111. (1633)

These, though slow, were sure.
FULLER, *Holy War*. Bk. iii, ch. 5. (1639)

As he is slow he is sure.
STEELE, *The Spectator*. No. 140. (1711)

I may be slow, but I am precious sure.
DICKENS, *Our Mutual Friend*. Bk. ii, ch. 5.

2
It is certain because it is impossible. (Certum est quia impossible est.)
TERTULLIAN, *De Carne Christi*. Pt. ii, ch. 5. *See under* BELIEF.

II—Certainty and Uncertainty

3
If a man will begin with certainties, he will end with doubts; but if he will be content to begin with doubts, he shall end in certainties.
BACON, *Advancement of Learning*. Bk. i. *See also under* DOUBT.

4
What is more unwise than to mistake uncertainty for certainty, falsehood for truth? (Quid enim stultius quam incerta pro certis habere, falso pro veris?)
CICERO, *De Senectute*. Ch. xix, sec. 68.

5
Certainty is the mother of Quietness and Repose; and Incertainty the cause of variance and contentions.
COKE, *The Institutes*. No. iii, p. 302.

6
He is a fool who leaves certainties for uncertainties. (Νήπιος ὃς τὰ ἕτοιμα λιπὼν τ' ἀνέτοιμα διώκει.)
HESIOD. (Attribution by PLUTARCH, ii, 505.)

He that leaves certainty and sticks to chance,
When fools pipe he may dance.
THOMAS FULLER, *Gnomologia*. No. 6439.

He is no wise man that will quit a certainty for an uncertainty.
SAMUEL JOHNSON, *The Idler*. No. 57.

7
We lose certainties whilst we seek uncertainties. (Certa mittimus, dum incerta petimus.)
PLAUTUS, *Pseudolus*, l. 685. (Act ii, sc. 3.)

8
The only certainty is that nothing is certain. (Solum certum nihil esse certi.)
PLINY THE ELDER, *Historia Naturalis*. Bk. ii, 7.

Nothing is more certain than incertainties.
BARNFIELD, *The Shepherd's Content*. St. 11.

Nothing is certain but uncertainty. (Rien n'est sûr que la chose incertaine.)
UNKNOWN. A French proverb.

9
I am not so nice,
To change true rules for old inventions.
SHAKESPEARE, *Taming of the Shrew*. Act iii, sc. 1, l. 80.

CERVANTES SAAVEDRA, MIGUEL DE

10
Cervantes smiled Spain's chivalry away;
A single laugh demolished the right arm
Of his own country.
BYRON, *Don Juan*. Canto xiii, st. 11.

11
Cervantes on his galley sets the sword back in the sheath
(*Don John of Austria rides homeward with a wreath.*)
And sees across a weary land a straggling road in Spain,
Up which a lean and foolish knight forever rides in vain.
G. K. CHESTERTON, *Lepanto*.

12
Alas! poor Knight! Alas! poor soul possessed!
Yet would to-day, when Courtesy grows chill,
And life's fine loyalties are turned to jest,
Some fire of thine might burn within us still!
Ah! would but one might lay his lance in rest,
And charge in earnest—were it but a mill.
AUSTIN DOBSON, *Don Quixote*.

Thou wert a figure strange enough, good lack!
To make Wiseacredom, both high and low,
Rub purblind eyes, and (having watched thee go),
Dispatch its Dogberrys upon thy track.
AUSTIN DOBSON, *Don Quixote*.

13
Dearest of all the heroes! Peerless knight
Whose follies sprang from such a generous blood!
Young, young must be the heart that in thy fight
Beholds no trace of its own servitude.
ARTHUR DAVISON FICKE, *Don Quixote*.

14
The peerless knight of La Mancha, whom, by the bye, with all his follies, I love more, and would actually have gone farther to have paid a visit to, than the greatest hero of antiquity.
STERNE, *Tristram Shandy*. Bk. i, ch. 10.

15
I only desire to have follies that are amusing, and am sorry Cervantes laughed chivalry out of fashion.
WALPOLE, *Letter to Sir Horace Mann*, 10 July, 1774.

CHANCE

See also Accident, Fortune, Gambling, Luck

I—Chance: Definitions

16
Chance is a nickname of Providence. (Le hasard est un sobriquet de la Providence.)
SEBASTIAN-ROCH-NICHOLAS DE CHAMFORT.

1
The ancients . . . exalted Chance into a divinity.
EMERSON, *Essays, Second Series: Experience.*

2
Chance is perhaps the pseudonym of God when He did not want to sign. (Le hasard c'est peut-être le pseudonyme de Dieu, quand il ne veut pas signer.)
ANATOLE FRANCE, *Le Jardin d'Epicure*, p. 132.

3
That Power Which erring men call Chance.
MILTON, *Comus*, l. 587.

4
All chance, direction, which thou canst not see.
POPE, *Essay on Man*. Epis. i, l. 290.

5
What is chance but the rude stone which receives its life from the sculptor's hand? Providence gives us chance—and man must mould it to his own designs.
SCHILLER, *Don Carlos*. Act iii, sc. 9, l. 13.

6
Chance and valor are blended in one. (Fors et virtus miscentur in unum.)
VERGIL, *Æneid*. Bk. xii, l. 714.

7
To a sensible man, there is no such thing as chance. (Für den Vernünftigen Menschen giebt gar keinen Zufall.)
LUDWIG TIECK, *Fortunat.*

Chance is a word void of sense; nothing can exist without a cause.
VOLTAIRE, *A Philosophical Dictionary.*

Things do not happen in this world—they are brought about.
WILL H. HAYS, *Speech*, during campaign of 1918. Featured in *New York American*, 10 Dec., 1922.

II—Chance: Apothegms

8
"I care not," said Richard, "hap as it hap will."
WILLIAM CAXTON, *Sonnes of Aymon*, 332. (1489)

Therefore hap good, or hap ill, I will walk on still.
NICHOLAS BRETON, *Works*, ii, 7. (1599)

9
One hopeless, dark idolater of Chance.
CAMPBELL, *The Pleasures of Hope*. Pt. ii, l. 296.

10
Probabilities direct the conduct of the wise man. (Probabilia . . . sapientis vita regeretur.)
CICERO, *De Natura Deorum*. Bk. i, ch. 5, sec. 12.

Almost all human life depends on probabilities.
VOLTAIRE, *Essays: Probabilities.*

11
Work and acquire, and thou hast chained the wheel of Chance.
EMERSON, *Essays, First Series: Self-Reliance.*

12
Chance fights ever on the side of the prudent. (Πᾶσιν γὰρ εὖ φρονοῦσι συμμαχεῖ τύχη.)
EURIPIDES, *Pirithous*. (Adapted.)

Chance usually favors the prudent. (Le hasard est ordinairement heureux pour l'homme prudent.)
JOUBERT, *Pensées*. No. 147.

13
Chance cannot touch me! Time cannot hush me!
MARGARET WITTER FULLER, *Dryad Song.*

14
His own chance no man knoweth
But as Fortune it on him throweth.
JOHN GOWER, *Confessio Amantis*, vi. (Hence: You never know your luck.)

15
He that leaveth nothing to Chance will do few things ill, but he will do very few things.
LORD HALIFAX, *Works*, p. 247.

16
There is no chance which does not return. (Il n'est pas chance qui ne retourne.)
UNKNOWN. A French proverb.

17
A certain man drew a bow at a venture, and smote the King of Israel.
Old Testament: I Kings, xxii, 34.

Let my disclaiming from a purposed evil
Free me so far in your most generous thoughts,
That I have shot mine arrow o'er the house,
And hurt my brother.
SHAKESPEARE, *Hamlet*. Act v, sc. 2, l. 252.

I shot an arrow into the air
It fell to earth, I knew not where;
For, so swiftly it flew, the sight
Could not follow it in its flight.
LONGFELLOW, *The Arrow and the Song.*

I shot a rocket in the air,
It fell to earth, I knew not where
Until next day, with rage profound,
The man it fell on came around.
TOM MASSON, *Enough.*

18
What Chance has made yours is not really yours. (Non est tuum, fortuna quod fecit tuum.)
LUCILIUS. (SENECA, *Epistulæ ad Lucilium*. Epis. viii, sec. 10.)

19
Chance contrives better than we ourselves. (Τὸ αὐτόματον ἡμῶν καλλίω βουλεύεται.)
MENANDER, *Fragments.*

20
Everything may happen (Omnia fieri possent.)
SENECA, *Epistulæ ad Lucilium*. Epis. lxx, 9.

21
Whom chance often passes by, it finds at last (Quem sæpe transit casus, aliquando invenit.)
SENECA, *Hercules Furens*, l. 328.

22
I shall show the cinders of my spirits

Through the ashes of my chance.
SHAKESPEARE, *Antony and Cleopatra*. Act v, sc. 2, l. 173.

1
If chance will have me king, why, chance may crown me.
SHAKESPEARE, *Macbeth*. Act i, sc. 3, l. 143.

Even in the force and road of casualty.
SHAKESPEARE, *The Merchant of Venice*. Act ii, sc. 9, l. 30.

2
The dice of Zeus have ever lucky throws. (Ἀεὶ γὰρ εὖ πίπτουσιν οἱ Διὸς κύβοι.)
SOPHOCLES, *Fragments*. No. 763.

The dice of God are always loaded. (Οἱ κύβοι Διὸς ἀεὶ εὐπίπτουσι.)
Proverbial form of the above.

3
A chance may win that by mischance was lost.
ROBERT SOUTHWELL, *Times Go by Turns*.

4
Whatever chance shall bring, we will bear it philosophically. (Quod fors feret feremus æquo animo.)
TERENCE, *Phormio*, l. 138. (Act i, sc. 2.)

5
Through divers mishaps, through so many perilous chances. (Per varios casus, per tot discrimina rerum.)
VERGIL, *Æneid*. Bk. i, l. 204.

6
Use thou thy chance. (Utere sorte tua.)
VERGIL, *Æneid*. Bk. xii, l. 932.

Grasps the skirts of happy chance.
TENNYSON, *In Memoriam*. Pt. lxiv.

III—Chance: Its Power

7
We do not what we ought,
What we ought not, we do,
And lean upon the thought
That Chance will bring us through.
MATTHEW ARNOLD, *Empedocles on Etna*, l. 237.

Yet they, believe me, who await
No gifts from Chance, have conquer'd Fate.
MATTHEW ARNOLD, *Resignation*, l. 245.

8
How slight a chance may raise or sink a soul!
P. J. BAILEY, *Festus: A Country Town*.

And we cry, though it seems to our dearest of foes,
"God, give us another chance."
RICHARD BURTON, *Song of the Unsuccessful*.

9
Revolving in his altered soul
The various turns of chance below.
DRYDEN, *Alexander's Feast*. St. 4.

10
There is a master who, without an effort, surpasses us all, and that master is chance.
ÉMILE GABORIAU, *File 113*. Ch. 11.

11
Chances rule men and not men chances.
HERODOTUS, *History*. Bk. vii, ch. 49.

12
Blind chance sweeps the world along (Cum caeco rapiantur saecula casu.)
LUCAN, *De Bello Civili*. Bk. vii, l. 446.

Chance and whim govern the world. (La fortune et l'humeur gouvernent le monde.)
LA ROCHEFOUCAULD, *Maximes*. No. 435.

Chance governs all.
MILTON, *Paradise Lost*. Bk. ii, l. 910.

Everlasting Fate shall yield to fickle Chance.
MILTON, *Paradise Lost*. Bk. ii, l. 232.

Chance everywhere has power. (Casus ubique valet.)
OVID, *Ars Amatoria*. Bk. iii, l. 425.

Chance is another master. (Magister alius casus.)
PLINY THE ELDER, *Historia Naturalis*.

13
Chance dispenses life with unequal justice. (Fortuna arbitriis tempus dispensat iniquis.)
OVID, *Consolatio ad Livium*, l. 371.

All the affairs of men hang by a slender thread; and sudden chance brings to ruin what once was strong. (Omnis sunt hominum tenui pendentia filo, Et subito casu, quæ valere, ruunt.)
OVID, *Epistulæ ex Ponto*. Bk. iv, epis. 3, l. 35.

Chance is blind and is the sole author of creation.
J. X. B. SAINTINE, *Picciola*. Ch. 3.

14
How Chance whirls round the affairs of men! (Quanti casus humana rotant!)
SENECA, *Hippolytus*, l. 1123.

15
But as the unthought-on accident is guilty
To what we wildly do, so we profess
Ourselves to be the slaves of chance, and flies
Of every wind that blows.
SHAKESPEARE, *The Winter's Tale*. Act iv, sc. 4, l. 548.

16
How often things occur by the merest chance, which we dared not even hope for! (Quam sæpe forte temere Eveniunt quæ non audeas optare!)
TERENCE, *Phormio*, l. 757. (Act v, sc. 1.)

A lucky chance, that oft decides the fate
Of mighty monarchs.
THOMSON, *The Seasons: Summer*, l. 1285.

17
Chance will not do the work—Chance sends the breeze;
But if the pilot slumber at the helm,
The very wind that wafts us towards the port
May dash us on the shelves.
SCOTT, *The Fortunes of Nigel*. Ch. 22. Quoted as from an old play.

18
What disturbance can result from the instability of Chance, if you are sure in the face of what is unsure?
SENECA, *Epistulæ ad Lucilium*. Epis. ci, sec. 9.

IV—Chance: The Main Chance

1
Let me stand to the main chance.
JOHN LYLY, *Euphues*, p. 104. (1580)

2
Always have an eye to the main, whatsoever thou art chanced at the buy.
JOHN LYLY, *Euphues*, p. 430. (1580)

I know what's what, and have always taken care of the main chance.
CERVANTES, *Don Quixote*. Pt. i, ch. 9.

3
Be careful still of the main chance, my son.
PERSIUS, *Satires*. Sat. vi. (Dryden, tr., l. 158.)

Have a care o' the main chance.
BUTLER, *Hudibras*. Pt. ii, canto ii, l. 499.

4
Main chance, father, you meant!
SHAKESPEARE, *II Henry VI*. Act i, sc. 1, l. 212.

CHANGE

See also Consistency, Constancy

5
Change doth unknit the tranquil strength of
men.
MATTHEW ARNOLD, *A Question*.

6
It is sufficiently clear that all things are changed, and nothing really perishes, and that the sum of matter remains absolutely the same.
FRANCIS BACON, *De Natura Rerum*.

The more it changes, the more it's the same thing. (Plus ça change, plus c'est la même chose.)
ALPHONSE KARR, *Les Guêpes; Les Femmes*, Jan., 1849. (Edition Levy, vol. vi, p. 304.) See APPENDIX.

7
The changes and chances of this mortal life.
Book of Common Prayer: Collect.

The sundry manifold changes of the world.
Book of Common Prayer: Fourth Sunday After Easter.

8
This world has been harsh and strange;
Something is wrong; there needeth a change.
ROBERT BROWNING, *Holy-Cross Day*.

9
Rejoice that man is hurled
From change to change unceasingly,
His soul's wings never furled.
ROBERT BROWNING, *James Lee's Wife*. Pt. vi.

Weep not that the world changes—did it keep
A stable, changeless state, 'twere cause indeed
to weep.
BRYANT, *Mutation*.

Fallow and change we need, nor constant toil,
Not always the same crop on the same soil.
W. W. STORY, *A Contemporary Criticism*.

10
Look abroad thro' Nature's range,
Nature's mighty law is change.
BURNS, *Let Not Women E'er Complain*.

11
He was a man who had seen many changes,
And always changed as true as any needle.
BYRON, *Don Juan*. Canto iii, st. 80. See also POLITICS: EXPEDIENCY.

12
To-day is not yesterday: we ourselves change; how can our Works and Thoughts, if they are always to be the fittest, continue always the same? Change, indeed, is painful; yet ever needful; and if Memory have its force and worth, so also has Hope.
CARLYLE, *Essays: Characteristics*.

13
They must often change who would be constant in happiness or wisdom.
CONFUCIUS. (GOLDSMITH, *Citizen of the World*. No. 123.)

14
If he's a change, give me a constancy.
DICKENS, *Dombey and Son*. Bk. i, ch. 18.

15
Change is inevitable in a progressive country,
Change is constant.
BENJAMIN DISRAELI, *Speech*, 20 Oct., 1867.

16
All things do willingly in change delight,
The fruitful mother of our appetite.
JOHN DONNE, *Elegies*: No. 17, *Variety*, l. 9.

17
The least change in our point of view gives the whole world a pictorial air.
EMERSON, *Nature, Addresses: Idealism*.

18
Change in all things is sweet. (Μεταβολὴ πάντων γλυκύ.)
ARISTOTLE, *Rhetoric*. Bk. i, ch. 11, sec. 20.

19
There is danger in reckless change; but greater danger in blind conservatism.
HENRY GEORGE, *Social Problems*.

20
Thus times do shift; each thing his turn does
hold;
New things succeed, as former things grow
old.
HERRICK, *Ceremonies for Candlemas Eve*.

21
Change is not made without inconvenience, even from worse to better.
RICHARD HOOKER. (SAMUEL JOHNSON, *Preface to Dictionary*.)

22
Times change, and we change with them. (Tempora mutantur, nos et mutantur in illis.)
RAPHAEL HOLINSHED, *Chronicles of England*. Fo. 99b. (1577); JOHN OWEN, *Epigrammata*, i, 58. (1624); CELLARIUS, *Harmonica Macrocosmica: Preface*. (1661) Quoted as "common and very true words of wisdom."

Times change and men deteriorate. (Tempora mutantur et homines detiorantur.)
UNKNOWN, *Gesta Romanorum*. (c. 1300) *Harl. MS*. 7833.

All things are changed, and with them we, too,
change;
Now this way and now that turns fortune's
wheel.

(Omnia mutantur nos et mutamur in illis;
Illa vices quasdam res habet, illa vices.)

LOTHARIUS I, of Germany. (MATTHIAS BORBONIUS, *Deliciæ Poetarum Germanorum*. Vol. i, p. 585.)

Things do not change; we change.

H. D. THOREAU, *Walden: Conclusion*.

1
He changes squares into circles. (Mutat quadrata rotundis.)

HORACE, *Epistles*. Bk. i, epis. i, l. 100.

2
Change generally pleases the rich. (Plerumque gratæ divitibus vices.)

HORACE, *Odes*. Bk. iii, ode 29, l. 13.

3
I am not what I once was under the sway of kindly Cynara. (Non sum qualis eram bonæ Sub regno Cinaræ.)

HORACE, *Odes*. Bk. iv, ode 1, l. 3. Title of poem by Ernest Dowson.

I am not now That which I have been.

BYRON, *Childe Harold*. Canto iv, st. 185.

I am not what I have been; what I should be.

JOHN HOME, *Douglas*. Act ii, sc. 1.

Do not think that years leave us and find us the same!

OWEN MEREDITH, *Lucile*. Pt. ii, canto ii, st. 3.

Nor the exterior nor the inward man
Resembles that it was.

SHAKESPEARE, *Hamlet*. Act ii, sc. 2, l. 6.

Presume not that I am the thing I was.

SHAKESPEARE, *II Henry IV*. Act v, sc. 5, l. 60.

4
There is a certain relief in change, even though it be from bad to worse; as I have found in travelling in a stage-coach, that it is often a comfort to shift one's position and be bruised in a new place.

WASHINGTON IRVING, *Tales of a Traveller: Preface*.

So when a raging fever burns,
We shift from side to side by turns;
And 'tis a poor relief we gain
To change the place, but keep the pain.

ISAAC WATTS, *Hymns and Spiritual Songs*, 146.

5
The world goes up and the world goes down,
And the sunshine follows the rain;
And yesterday's sneer and yesterday's frown
Can never come over again.

CHARLES KINGSLEY, *Dolcino to Margaret*.

6
All things must change
To something new, to something strange.

LONGFELLOW, *Kéramos*, l. 32.

O visionary world, condition strange,
Where naught abiding is but only change.

J. R. LOWELL, *Commemoration Ode*.

7
Unceasingly contemplate the generation of all things through change, and accustom thyself to the thought that the Nature of the Universe delights above all in changing the things that exist and making new ones of the same pattern. For everything that exists is the seed of that which shall come out of it.

MARCUS AURELIUS, *Meditations*. Bk. iv, sec. 36.

Everything changes. Thou thyself art undergoing a continuous change, and, in some sort, decay: aye, and the whole Universe as well.

MARCUS AURELIUS, *Meditations*. Bk. ix, sec. 19.

All things change them to the contrary.

SHAKESPEARE, *Romeo and Juliet*, iv, 5, 90.

Mark this, that there is change in all things. (Omnium rerum, heus, vicissitudo est!)

TERENCE, *Eunuchus*, l. 276. (Act ii, sc. 2.)

In a higher world it is otherwise; but here below to live is to change, and to be perfect is to have changed often.

JOHN HENRY NEWMAN, *Development of Christian Doctrine*, p. 40.

8
Change, the strongest son of life.

GEORGE MEREDITH, *The Woods of Westermain*.

9
Tomorrow to fresh woods, and pastures new.

MILTON, *Lycidas*, l. 193. Often misquoted, "to fresh fields."

10
In dim eclipse, disastrous twilight sheds
On half the nations, and with fear of change
Perplexes monarchs.

MILTON, *Paradise Lost*. Bk. i, l. 597.

With delight he snuffed the smell
Of mortal change on earth.

MILTON, *Paradise Lost*. Bk. x, l. 272.

11
We have changed all that. (Nous avons changé tout cela.)

MOLIÈRE, *Le Médicin Malgré Lui*. Act ii, sc. 4. Sganarelle, the pretended physician, declares that the liver is on the left side and the heart on the right, and is asked to account for such an inversion of the usual arrangement. He answers, "Oui, cela étoit autrefois ainsi; mais nous avons changé tout cela." Yes, it used to be that way, but we have changed all that.

12
O Death in life, O sure pursuer, Change,
Be kind, be kind, and touch me not.

WILLIAM MORRIS, *The Earthly Paradise: Bellerophon in Lycia*, l. 3485.

13
We shall all be changed, In a moment, in the twinkling of an eye.

New Testament: I Corinthians, xv, 51, 52.

14
All things change, nothing perishes. (Omnia mutantur, nihil interit.)

OVID, *Metamorphoses*. Bk. xv, l. 165.

There 's nothing constant in the universe,
All ebb and flow, and every shape that 's born
Bears in its womb the seeds of change.
(Nihil est toto, quod perstet, in orbe.
Cuncta fluunt, omnisque vagans formatur imago;
Ipsa quoque adsiduo labuntur tempora motu.)

OVID, *Metamorphoses*. Bk. xv, l. 177.

1
The strength of nature lies not in holding on one even way, but she loves to change the fashion of her laws. (Non uno contenta valet natura tenore, Sed permutatas gaudet habere vices.)
PETRONIUS, *Fragments*. No. 90.

2
It is a maxim here [at Venice], handed down from generation to generation, that change breeds more mischief from its novelty than advantage from its utility.
HESTER LYNCH PIOZZI, *Observations on a Journey through Italy.*

3
Manners with fortunes, humours turn with climes,
Tenets with books, and principles with times.
POPE, *Moral Essays*. Epis. i, l. 172.

4
It is a bad plan that admits of no modification. (Malum est consilium, quod mutari non potest.)
PUBLILIUS SYRUS, *Sententiæ*. No. 469.

5
To some will come a time when change
Itself is beauty, if not heaven.
E. A. ROBINSON, *Llewellyn and the Tree.*

6
They are the weakest-minded and the hardest-hearted men, that most love variety and change.
RUSKIN, *Modern Painters*. Pt. ii, ch. 6, sec. 7.

O people keen
For change, to whom the new looks always green!
WORDSWORTH, *Ecclesiastical Sonnets*. Pt. ii, No. 33.

7
Every change of scene becomes a delight. (Omnis mutatio loci jucunda fiet.)
SENECA, *Epistulæ ad Lucilium*. Epis. xxviii, 4.

8
Nothing of him that doth fade
But doth suffer a sea-change
Into something rich and strange.
SHAKESPEARE, *The Tempest*. Act i, sc. 2, l. 400.

9
There is nothing permanent except change.
HERACLITUS. The central idea of his philosophy. (ROGERS, *Students' History of Philosophy*, p. 15.)

Nought may endure but Mutability.
SHELLEY, *Mutability*. St. 4.

10
Times go by turns, and chances change by course,
From foul to fair, from better hap to worse. . . .
No joy so great but runneth to an end,
No hap so hard but may in fine amend.
ROBERT SOUTHWELL, *Times Go by Turns.*

In the course of time, we grow to love things we once hated and hate things we loved.
R. L. STEVENSON, *Crabbed Age and Youth.*

11
Change lays not her hand upon truth.
A. C. SWINBURNE, *Poems: Dedication.*

12
Not in vain the distance beacons. Forward, forward let us range,
Let the great world spin for ever down the ringing grooves of change.
TENNYSON, *Locksley Hall*. St. 91. Dr. Alfred Gatty (*Notes and Queries*, ser. viii, vol. 2, p. 387) states that the phrase "ringing grooves of change" was due to a misconception on the part of Tennyson, who had been present at the opening of the Manchester-Liverpool railway, and, being short-sighted, thought the wheels ran in grooved rails.

13
The world was never made;
It will change, but it will not fade. . . .
Nothing was born, Nothing will die;
All things will change.
TENNYSON, *Nothing Will Die.*

14
The old order changeth, yielding place to new,
And God fulfils himself in many ways,
Lest one good custom should corrupt the world.
TENNYSON, *Morte d'Arthur*, l. 291. (1842) Also *The Passing of Arthur*, l. 408; *The Coming of Arthur*, l. 508. (1869)

15
All things change, creeds and philosophies and outward system—but God remains!
MRS. HUMPHRY WARD, *Robert Elsmere*. Bk. iv, ch. 27.

16
It is not now as it hath been of yore;—
Turn wheresoe'er I may,
By night or day,
The things which I have seen I now can see no more.
WORDSWORTH, *Intimations of Immortality.*

CHANTICLEER

17
I heard nae mair, for Chanticleer
Shook off the pouthery snaw,
And hailed the morning with a cheer,
A cottage-rousing craw.
ROBERT BURNS, *A Winter Night*. St. 9.

18
A yard she had, enclosed all about
With sticks, and a dry ditch without,
In which she had a cock, hight Chauntecleer
In all the land of crowing n'as his peer.
His voice was merrier than the merry organ
On mass-days that in the churche gon.
CHAUCER, *The Nonne Preestes Tale*, l. 27.

19
Hail chanticleer! (Χαῖρε ἀλέκτορ.)
DIOGENES, to a musician whose audience always deserted him, explaining that it was because the musician's song "made everybody get up." (DIOGENES LAERTIUS, *Diogenes*. 48.)

20
And hark! how clear bold chanticleer,
Warmed with the new wine of the year,

Tells all in his lusty crowing!
J. R. LOWELL, *The Vision of Sir Launfal: Prelude.*

1
While the cock with lively din
Scatters the rear of darkness thin,
And to the stack, or the barn door,
Stoutly struts his dames before.
MILTON, *L'Allegro,* l. 49.

2
Bold chanticleer proclaims the dawn
And spangles deck the thorn.
JOHN O'KEEFFE, *Tzar Peter.* Act. i, sc. 4.

3
Ah, God! Stab upward with your noise;
Tear at the sky.
With the day gone molten down his throat
And his spine a tilted flame,
What singer could not make one song
As fine as fire?
GEORGE O'NEIL, *The White Rooster.*

4
I recoil dazzled at beholding myself all rosy red, at having, I myself, caused the sun to rise. (Je recule Ébloui de me voir moi même tout vermeil Et d'avoir, moi, le coq, fait élever le soleil.)
EDMOND ROSTAND, *Chanticler.* Act ii, sc. 3.

And sounding in advance its victory,
My song jets forth so clear, so proud, so peremptory,
That the horizon, seized with a rosy trembling,
Obeys me.
EDMOND ROSTAND, *Chanticler.* Act ii, sc. 3.

He's welly like a cock as thinks the sun's rose o' purpose to hear him crow.
GEORGE ELIOT, *Adam Bede.* Ch. 33.

5
Every cock is at his best on his own dunghill. (Gallum in suo sterquilinio plurimum posse.)
SENECA, *Apocolocyntosis,* vii, 3.

Every cock will fight upon his own dunghill.
CONGREVE, *The Old Batchelor.* Act ii, sc. 2.

Every cock is proud on his own dunghill.
JOHN HEYWOOD, *Proverbs.* Pt. i, ch. 11.

6
The cock, that is the trumpet to the morn,
Doth with his lofty and shrill-sounding throat
Awake the god of day.
SHAKESPEARE, *Hamlet.* Act i, sc. 1, l. 150.

The early village cock
Hath twice done salutation to the morn.
SHAKESPEARE, *Richard III.* Act v, sc. 3, l. 209.

7
Some say that ever 'gainst that season comes
Wherein our Saviour's birth is celebrated,
The bird of dawning singeth all night long.
SHAKESPEARE, *Hamlet.* Act i, sc. 1, l. 158.

8
Hark, hark! I hear
The strain of strutting chanticleer
Cry, Cock-a-diddle-dow.
SHAKESPEARE, *The Tempest.* Act i, sc. 2, l. 384.

9
He is the sun's brave herald
That, ringing his blithe horn,
Calls round a world dew-pearled
The heavenly airs of morn.
KATHERINE TYNAN HINKSON, *Chanticleer.*

CHAOS

10
The wrecks of matter, and the crush of worlds.
ADDISON, *Cato.* Act v, sc. 1.

Temple and tower went down, nor left a site:—
Chaos of ruins!
BYRON, *Childe Harold.* Canto iv, st. 80.

The world was void,
The populous and the powerful was a lump,
Seasonless, herbless, treeless, manless, lifeless—
A lump of death—a chaos of hard clay.
BYRON, *Darkness,* l. 69.

11
The chaos of events.
BYRON, *Prophecy of Dante.* Canto ii, l. 6.

12
Star after star from heaven's high arch shall rush,
Suns sink on suns, and systems systems crush,
Headlong, extinct, in one dark centre fall,
And death, and night, and chaos, mingle all!
ERASMUS DARWIN, *Economy of Vegetation.* Canto iv.

13
And the earth was without form, and void; and darkness was upon the face of the deep.
Old Testament: Genesis, i, 2.

14
No arts, no letters, no society, and which is worst of all, continual fear and danger of violent death, and the life of man solitary, poor, nasty, brutish and short.
THOMAS HOBBES, *Leviathan.* Ch. 18.

15
Even so, when the framework of the world is dissolved, and the final hour, closing so many ages, reverts to pristine chaos (antiquum chaos), then the fiery stars will drop into the sea, and earth will shake off the ocean, . . . and the whole distracted fabric of the shattered firmament will overthrow its laws.
LUCAN, *De Bello Civili.* Bk. i, l. 72.

16
Abomination of desolation.
New Testament: Matthew, xxiv, 15; *Mark,* xiii, 14.

17
Chaos, that reigns here
In double night of darkness and of shades.
MILTON, *Comus,* l. 334.

Fate shall yield
To fickle Chance, and Chaos judge the strife.
MILTON, *Paradise Lost.* Bk. ii, l. 232.

18
Chaos umpire sits,
And by decision more embroils the fray
By which he reigns.
MILTON, *Paradise Lost.* Bk. ii, l. 907.

1
Then rose the seed of Chaos, and of Night,
To blot out order and extinguish light.
POPE, *The Dunciad*. Bk. iv, l. 13.

Lo! thy dread empire, Chaos! is restor'd;
Light dies before thy uncreating word:
Thy hand, great Anarch! lets the curtain fall,
And universal darkness buries all.
POPE, *The Dunciad*. Bk. iv, l. 653.

2
Nay, had I the power, I should
Pour the sweet milk of concord into hell,
Uproar the universal peace, confound
All unity on earth.
SHAKESPEARE, *Macbeth*. Act iv, sc. 3, l. 97.

3
Chaos is come again.
SHAKESPEARE, *Othello*. Act iii, sc. 3, l. 92.

CHARACTER

I—Character: Definitions

4
Our characters are the result of our conduct.
ARISTOTLE, *Nicomachean Ethics*. Bk. iii, ch. 5, sec. 12.

5
A character is like an acrostic—read it forward, backward, or across, it still spells the same thing.
EMERSON, *Essays, First Series: Self-Reliance*.

6
Character,—a reserved force which acts directly by presence and without means.
EMERSON, *Essays, Second Series: Character*.

Character is centrality, the impossibility of being displaced or overset.
EMERSON, *Essays, Second Series: Character*.

Character is higher than intellect. . . . A great soul will be strong to live, as well as to think.
EMERSON, *Nature, Addresses, and Lectures: The American Scholar*.

Character, that sublime health which values one moment as another, and makes us great in all conditions.
EMERSON, *Society and Solitude: Works and Days*.

Character is that which can do without success.
EMERSON, *Uncollected Lectures: Character*.

7
In my opinion the best character is generally that which is the least talked about.
SIR WILLIAM EARLE, *Decision*, Queen v. Rowton. (34 L.J.M.C. 63.)

8
A great character . . . is a dispensation of Providence, designed to have not merely an immediate, but a continuous, progressive, and never-ending agency. It survives the man who possessed it; survives his age,—perhaps his country, his language.
EDWARD EVERETT, *Speech*, 4 July, 1835.

9
Talent is nurtured aye in solitude,
But Character 'mid the tempests of the world.
(Es bildet ein Talent sich in der Stille,
Sich ein Charakter in dem Strom der Welt.)
GOETHE, *Torquato Tasso*. Act i, sc. 2, l. 66.

No talent, but yet a character. (Kein Talent, doch ein Charakter.)
HEINRICH HEINE, *Atta Troll*. Ch. 24.

10
Character is Destiny.
HERACLITUS. (MULLACH, *Fragments of Greek Philosophy*.)

Habits form character, and character is destiny.
JOSEPH KAINES, *Address: Our Daily Faults and Failings*.

Character is simply habit long continued. (Τὸ ἦθος ἔθος ἐστὶ πολυχρόνιον.)
PLUTARCH, *Morals: On Moral Virtue*. Sec. 4. *See also under* HABIT.

11
We must have a weak spot or two in a character before we can love it much. People that do not laugh or cry, or take more of anything than is good for them, or use anything but dictionary-words, are admirable subjects for biographies. But we don't always care most for those flat pattern-flowers that press best in the herbarium.
O. W. HOLMES, *The Professor at the Breakfast-Table*. Ch. 3.

12
Character is like a tree and reputation like its shadow. The shadow is what we think of it; the tree is the real thing.
ABRAHAM LINCOLN. (GROSS, *Lincoln's Own Stories*, p. 109.) *See also under* REPUTATION.

13
Character is what you are in the dark.
DWIGHT L. MOODY, *Sermons: Character*.

14
To my mind, the best and most faultless character is his who is as ready to pardon the rest of mankind, as though he daily transgressed himself; and at the same time as cautious to avoid a fault as if he never forgave one.
PLINY THE YOUNGER, *Epistles*. Bk. viii, epis. 22.

15
Character is the governing element of life, and is above genius.
FREDERICK SAUNDERS, *Stray Leaves: Life's Little Day*.

16
It is energy—the central element of which is will—that produces the miracles of enthusiasm in all ages. Everywhere it is the main-spring of what is called force of character, and the sustaining power of all great action.
SAMUEL SMILES, *Self-Help*. Ch. 5.

The things that really move liking in human beings are the gnarled nodosities of character, vagrant humours, freaks of generosity, some little

unextinguishable spark of the aboriginal savage, some little sweet savour of the old Adam.
ALEXANDER SMITH, *Dreamthorp: On Vagabonds.*

1
Fame is what you have taken,
Character's what you give;
When to this truth you waken,
Then you begin to live.
BAYARD TAYLOR, *Improvisations.* Sec. 11.

2
Character is a by-product; it is produced in the great manufacture of daily duty.
WOODROW WILSON, *Address,* Arlington, 31 May, 1915.

II—Character: Apothegms

3
No better than you should be.
BEAUMONT AND FLETCHER, *The Coxcomb.* Act iv, sc. 3.

On ev'ry hand it will allow'd be
He's just—nae better than he should be.
BURNS, *A Dedication to Gavin Hamilton.*

The shepherd thought her no better than she should be, a little loose in the hilts, and free of her hips.
CERVANTES, *Don Quixote.* Pt. i, ch. 3. (Motteux, tr.)

She's loose i' the hilts.
JOHN WEBSTER, *Duchess of Malfi.* Act ii, sc. 5.

She is no better than she should be.
FIELDING, *The Temple Beau.* Act iv, sc. 3.

Some might suspect the nymph not over good—
Nor would they be mistaken, if they should.
YOUNG, *Love of Fame.* Sat. vi, l. 75.

4
Happiness is not the end of life: character is.
HENRY WARD BEECHER, *Life Thoughts.*

5
Some men are like pyramids, which are very broad where they touch the ground, but grow narrow as they reach the sky.
HENRY WARD BEECHER, *Life Thoughts.*

Many men build as cathedrals were built—the part nearest the ground finished, but that part which soars toward heaven, the turrets and the spires, forever incomplete.
HENRY WARD BEECHER, *Life Thoughts.*

6
Character must be kept bright, as well as clean.
LORD CHESTERFIELD, *Letters,* 8 Jan., 1750.

7
Or if, once in a thousand years,
A perfect character appears.
CHARLES CHURCHILL, *The Ghost.* Bk. iii, l. 207.

8
"Hard," replied the Dodger. "As nails," added Charley Bates.
DICKENS, *Oliver Twist.* Ch. 9.

My landlord is as rich as a Jew and as hard as nails.
BERNARD SHAW, *You Never Can Tell.* Act i

9
There is a great deal of unmapped country within us.
GEORGE ELIOT, *Daniel Deronda.* Bk. iii, ch. 24.

What does Africa,—what does the West stand for? Is not our own interior white on the chart? black though it may prove, like the coast, when discovered.
H. D. THOREAU, *Walden: Conclusion.*

10
Character gives splendor to youth and awe to wrinkled skin and gray hairs.
EMERSON, *Conduct of Life: Beauty.*

11
Use what language you will, you can never say anything but what you are.
EMERSON, *Conduct of Life: Worship.*

We pass for what we are. Character teaches above our wills.
EMERSON, *Essays, First Series: Self-Reliance.*

Human character evermore publishes itself. The most fugitive deed and word, the intimated purpose, expresses character.
EMERSON, *Essays, First Series: Spiritual Laws.*

Don't *say* things. What you *are* stands over you the while, and thunders so that I cannot hear what you say to the contrary.
EMERSON, *Letters and Social Aims: Social Aims.*

12
The force of character is cumulative.
EMERSON, *Essays, First Series: Self-Reliance.*

No change of circumstances can repair a defect of character.
EMERSON, *Essays, Second Series: Character.*

13
The Porcupine, whom one must Handle, gloved,
May be respected, but is never Loved.
ARTHUR GUITERMAN, *A Poet's Proverbs.*

14
Such a man, in truth, am I. (Nimirum hic ego sum.)
HORACE, *Epistles.* Bk. i, epis. 15, l. 42.

15
A very unclubbable man.
SAMUEL JOHNSON. (BOSWELL, *Life,* 1764.)
Johnson was referring to Sir John Hawkins, and must have been proud of the remark for he repeated it to Fanny Burney, who recorded it in her diary (3 Aug., 1778) as "Sir John was a most unclubbable man."

16
To be capable of respect is almost as rare as to be worthy of it. (Être capable de respect est aujourd'hui presque aussi rare qu'en être digne.)
JOUBERT, *Pensées.* No. 247.

17
No man can climb out beyond the limitations of his own character.
JOHN MORLEY, *Miscellanies: Robespierre.*

18
Character is much easier kept than recovered.
THOMAS PAINE, *The Crisis.* No. xv

1
He is pepper, not a man. (Piper, non homo.)
PETRONIUS, *Satyricon*. Hence, "full of pep."

2
I would rather be adorned by beauty of character than by jewels. Jewels are the gift of fortune, while character comes from within. (Bono me esse ingenio ornatum quam auro multo movolo: Aurum id fortuna invenitur, natura ingenium bonum.)
PLAUTUS, *Pœnulus*, l. 301. (Act i, sc. 2.)

3
A man's own character is the arbiter of his fortune. (Cuique hominum mores fingunt fortunam sui.)
PUBLILIUS SYRUS, *Sententiæ*. No. 141.

4
It matters not what you are thought to be, but what you are.
PUBLILIUS SYRUS, *Sententiæ*. No. 785.

It's not what you were, it's what you are to-day.
DAVID MARION. Title of song. (1898)

5
See thou character.
SHAKESPEARE, *Hamlet*. Act i, sc. 3, l. 59.

Come, give us a taste of your quality.
SHAKESPEARE, *Hamlet*. Act ii, sc. 2, l. 452.

Put thyself into the trick of singularity.
SHAKESPEARE, *Twelfth Night*. Act ii, sc. 5, l. 164; act iii, sc. 4, l. 79.

6
I'm called away by particular business. But I leave my character behind me.
SHERIDAN, *School for Scandal*. Act. ii, sc. 2. *See also under* REPUTATION.

7
Put more trust in nobility of character than in an oath.
SOLON. (DIOGENES LAERTIUS, *Solon*. Sec. 16.)

8
"High characters," cries one, and he would see
Things that ne'er were, nor are, nor e'er will be.
SIR JOHN SUCKLING, *The Goblins: Epilogue*.

9
A man should endeavor to be as pliant as a reed, yet as hard as cedar-wood.
Talmud: Taanith, xx.

10
How can we expect a harvest of thought who have not had a seed-time of character?
H. D. THOREAU, *Journal*. (EMERSON, *Thoreau*.)

11
What thou art, that thou art; that God knoweth thee to be and thou canst be said to be no greater.
THOMAS À KEMPIS, *De Imitatione Christi*. Pt. ii, ch. 6.

12
Happy for us if the grace of God enables us to live so that we retain innocency and freshness of character down to old age.
MARY ANN WENDELL, *Private letter*.

13
So build we up the being that we are.
WORDSWORTH, *The Excursion*. Bk. iv, l. 1264.

14
When wealth is lost, nothing is lost;
When health is lost, something is lost;
When character is lost, all is lost!
UNKNOWN. Motto on the wall of a school in Germany.

III—Character: Judgment of Character

15
To judge human character rightly, a man may sometimes have very small experience, provided he has a very large heart.
BULWER-LYTTON, *What Will He Do With It?* Bk. v, ch. 4.

16
We are firm believers in the maxim that, for all right judgment of any man or thing, it is useful, nay, essential, to see his good qualities before pronouncing on his bad.
CARLYLE, *Essays: Goethe*.

17
Those who deserve a good character, ought to have the satisfaction of knowing that they have it, both as a reward and as an encouragement.
LORD CHESTERFIELD, *Letters*, 6 March, 1747.

Colonel Chartres . . . was once heard to say that although he would not give one farthing for virtue, he would give ten thousand pounds for a character; because he should get a hundred thousand pounds by it.
LORD CHESTERFIELD, *Letters*, 8 Jan., 1750.

18
By nothing do men show their character more than by the things they laugh at.
GOETHE, *Sprüche in Prosa*.

A man never shows his own character so plainly as by the way he portrays another's.
RICHTER, *Titan*. Zykel 110.

19
Men are more lovable for the bad qualities they don't possess than for the good ones they do.
E. P. OPPENHEIM, *Simple Peter Cradd*, p. 60.

20
O think not of his errors now; remember
His greatness, his munificence, think on all
The lovely features of his character,
On all the noble exploits of his life,
And let them, like an angel's arm, unseen,
Arrest the lifted sword.
SCHILLER, *The Death of Wallenstein*. Act iii, sc. 8. (Coleridge, tr.)

21
There is a kind of character in thy life,
That to the observer doth thy history
Fully unfold.
SHAKESPEARE, *Measure for Measure*. Act i, sc. 1, l. 28.

IV—Character: Good and Bad

See also Goodness: Good and Evil

22
In him, inexplicably mixed, appeared

Much to be loved and hated, sought and feared.
BYRON, *Lara*. Canto i, st. 17.

1
A man so various, that he seem'd to be
Not one, but all mankind's epitome;
Stiff in opinions, always in the wrong,
Was everything by starts, and nothing long;
But, in the course of one revolving moon,
Was chymist, fiddler, statesman, and buffoon.
DRYDEN, *Absalom and Achitophel*. Pt. i, l. 545.

So over violent, or over civil,
That every man, with him, was God or Devil.
DRYDEN, *Absalom and Achitophel*. Pt. i, l. 557.

2
This scholar, rake, Christian, dupe, gamester and poet.
DAVID GARRICK, *Jupiter and Mercury*.

3
A man not perfect, but of heart
So high, of such heroic rage,
That even his hopes became a part
Of earth's eternal heritage.
RICHARD WATSON GILDER, *At the President's Grave*. Referring to James Abram Garfield.

4
Captious, yet gracious, sweet and bitter too,
I cannot with thee live, nor yet without thee.
(Difficilis facilis, jucundus acerbus es idem:
Nec tecum possum vivere, nec sine te.)
MARTIAL, *Epigrams*. Bk. xii, ep. 47, l. 1.

Thus neither with thee, nor without thee, can I live. (Sic ego non sine te, nec tecum vivere possum.)
OVID, *Amores*. Bk. iii, elegy 11, l. 39.

In all thy humours, whether grave or mellow,
Thou'rt such a touchy, testy, pleasant fellow,
Hast so much wit, and mirth, and spleen about thee,
There is no living with thee, nor without thee.
ADDISON, *The Spectator*. No. 68. A free translation of Martial.

5
Some squire, perhaps, you take delight to rack,
Whose game is whist, whose treat a toast in sack;
Who visits with a gun, presents you birds,
Then gives a smacking buss, and cries, No words!
Or with his hounds comes hollowing from the stable,
Makes love with nods, and knees beneath a table.
POPE, *Epistle to Mrs. Teresa Blount on Her Leaving Town*, l. 23.

6
Many men have been capable of doing a wise thing, more a cunning thing, but very few a generous thing.
POPE, *Thoughts on Various Subjects*.

7
His legs bestrid the ocean; his rear'd arm
Crested the world: his voice was propertied
As all the tuned spheres, and that to friends;
But when he meant to quail and shake the orb,
He was as rattling thunder.
SHAKESPEARE, *Antony and Cleopatra*. Act v, sc. 2, l. 82.

8
Alas! 'tis true I have gone here and there,
And made myself a motley to the view,
Gored mine own thoughts, sold cheap what is most dear,
Made old offences of affections new;
Most true it is that I have looked on truth
Askance and strangely.
SHAKESPEARE, *Sonnets*. No. cx.

9
O, tell her, Swallow, thou that knowest each,
That bright and fierce and fickle is the South,
And dark and true and tender is the North.
TENNYSON, *The Princess*. Pt. iv, l. 78.

10
I am as bad as the worst, but thank God I am as good as the best.
WALT WHITMAN.

Here's to you, as good as you are,
And here's to me, as bad as I am;
But as good as you are, and as bad as I am,
I am as good as you are, as bad as I am.
UNKNOWN. Old Scotch Toast.

11
Fair and foolish, little and loud,
Long and lazy, black and proud;
Fat and merry, lean and sad,
Pale and pettish, red and bad.
THOMAS WRIGHT, *Passions of the Mind*. (1604)

If long, she is lazy, if little, she is loud;
If fair, she is sluttish, if foul, she is proud.
JOHN FLORIO, *Second Frutes*, 189.

With a red man rede thy rede;
With a brown man break thy bread;
At a pale man draw thy knife;
From a black man keep thy wife.
THOMAS WRIGHT, *Passions of the Mind*.

V—Character: Good

See also Goodness

12
An easy-minded soul, and always was. (Ὁ δ' εὔκολος μὲν ἐνθάδ', εὔκολος δ' ἐκεῖ.)
ARISTOPHANES, *The Frogs*, l. 82. (Frere, tr.)

And certainly, he was a good felawe.
CHAUCER, *Canterbury Tales: Prologue*, l. 395.

In other respects the best fellow in the world.
(Au demeurant, le meilleur fils du monde.)
CLEMENT MAROT, *Letter to Francis I*.

A glass is good, and a lass is good,
And a pipe to smoke in cold weather;
The world is good, and the people are good,
And we're all good fellows together.
JOHN O'KEEFFE, *Sprigs of Laurel*. Act ii, sc. 1.

Hail fellow, *see under* PROVERBS.

1
Zealous, yet modest; innocent, though free;
Patient of toil; serene amidst alarms;
Inflexible in faith; invincible in arms.
JAMES BEATTIE, *The Minstrel*. Bk. i, st. 11.

2
With more capacity for love than earth
Bestows on most of mortal mould and birth,
His early dreams of good out-stripp'd the truth,
And troubled manhood follow'd baffled youth.
BYRON, *Lara*. Canto i, st. 18.

3
The ideal of courtesy, wit, grace, and charm. (Specimen fuisse humanitatis, salis, suavitatis, leporis.)
CICERO, *Tusculanarum Disputationum*. Bk. v, ch. 19, sec. 55

4
A man of letters, manners, morals, parts.
COWPER, *Tirocinium*, l. 673

5
Even children follow'd with endearing wile,
And pluck'd his gown, to share the good man's smile.
GOLDSMITH, *The Deserted Village*, l. 183.

6
A nice unparticular man.
THOMAS HARDY, *Far From the Madding Crowd*.

7
Time could not chill him, fortune sway,
Nor toil with all its burdens tire.
O. W. HOLMES, *F. W. C.*

8
He is so good that no one can be a better man. (Est bonus, ut melior vir Non alius quisquam.)
HORACE, *Satires*. Bk. i, sat. 3, l. 32.

9
A Soul of power, a well of lofty Thought
A chastened Hope that ever points to Heaven.
JOHN HUNTER, *A Replication of Rhymes*.

10
One that feared God and eschewed evil.
Old Testament: Job, i, 1.

He was a good man, and a just.
New Testament: Luke, xxiii, 50.

Mark the perfect man, and behold the upright.
Old Testament: Psalms, xxxvii, 37.

Rich in good works.
New Testament: I Timothy, vi, 18.

He was his Maker's image undefaced.
S. T. COLERIDGE, *Remorse*. Act ii, sc. 1.

11
A frame of adamant, a soul of fire,
No dangers fright him, and no labours tire.
SAMUEL JOHNSON, *The Vanity of Human Wishes*, l. 191.

12
Stiff-necked Glasgow beggar! I've heard he's prayed for my soul,
But he couldn't lie if you paid him, and he'd starve before he stole.
RUDYARD KIPLING, *The "Mary Gloster."*

13
Free from self-seeking, envy, low design,
I have not found a whiter soul than thine.
CHARLES LAMB, *To Martin Charles Burney*.

14
Other hope had she none, nor wish in life, but to follow
Meekly, with reverent steps, the sacred feet of her Saviour.
LONGFELLOW, *Evangeline*. Pt. ii, sec. 5, l. 35.

15
His magic was not far to seek,—
He was so human! Whether strong or weak,
Far from his kind he neither sank nor soared,
But sate an equal guest at every board:
No beggar ever felt him condescend,
No prince presume; for still himself he bare
At manhood's simple level, and where'er
He met a stranger, there he left a friend.
J. R. LOWELL, *Agassiz*. Pt. ii, sec. 2.

16
The wisest man could ask no more of Fate
Than to be simple, modest, manly, true,
Safe from the Many, honored by the Few;
To count as naught in World, or Church, or State,
But inwardly in secret to be great.
J. R. LOWELL, *Sonnet: Jeffries Wyman*.

17
Who knows nothing base, Fears nothing known.
OWEN MEREDITH, *A Great Man*. St. 8.

18
To those who know thee not, no words can paint;
And those who know thee know all words are faint.
HANNAH MORE, *Sensibility*.

19
He was straight; you could trust him. (Sed rectus, sed certus.)
PETRONIUS, *Satyricon*. Sec. 44.

20
Unlearn'd, he knew no schoolman's subtle art,
No language, but the language of the heart.
By nature honest, by experience wise,
Healthy by temperance, and by exercise.
POPE, *Epistle to Dr. Arbuthnot*, l. 398.

But where's the man who counsel can bestow,
Still pleas'd to teach, and yet not proud to know? . . .
Tho' learn'd, well bred; and tho' well bred, sincere;
Modestly bold, and humanly severe;
Who to a friend his faults can freely show,
And gladly praise the merit of a foe?
POPE, *Essay on Criticism*. Pt. iii, l. 72.

21
Of manners gentle, of affections mild;
In wit a man; simplicity a child:
With native humour temp'ring virtuous rage,
Form'd to delight at once and lash the age:
Above temptation, in a low estate,

And uncorrupted ev'n among the great:
A safe companion, and an easy friend,
Unblamed thro' life, lamented in thy end.
POPE, *Epitaph on John Gay.*

1
Devout yet cheerful, active yet resigned,
Grant me, like thee whose heart knew no disguise,
Whose blameless wishes never aimed to rise,
To meet the changes Time and Chance present,
With modest dignity and calm content.
SAMUEL ROGERS, *Pleasures of Memory.* Pt. ii.

Devout, yet cheerful; pious, not austere;
To others lenient, to himself severe.
JOHN MILTON HARNEY, *On a Friend.*

2
He preferred to be, rather than to seem, good; hence the less he sought fame, the more it pursued him.
SALLUST, *Catilina.* Ch. 54, sec. 6. Of Cato.

3
Heaven never meant him for that passive thing
That can be struck and hammered out to suit
Another's taste and fancy. He'll not dance
To every tune of every minister.
It goes against his nature—he can't do it.
SCHILLER, *Die Piccolomini.* Act i, sc. 4. (Coleridge, tr.)

4
Look here, upon this picture, and on this,
The counterfeit presentment of two brothers.
See, what a grace was seated on this brow:
Hyperion's curls; the front of Jove himself;
An eye like Mars, to threaten and command;
A station like the herald Mercury
New-lighted on a heaven-kissing hill;
A combination and a form indeed,
Where every god did seem to set his seal,
To give the world assurance of a man.
SHAKESPEARE, *Hamlet.* Act iii, sc. 4, l. 53.

A man of sovereign parts he is esteem'd;
Well fitted in arts, glorious in arms:
Nothing becomes him ill that he would well.
SHAKESPEARE, *Love's Labour's Lost.* Act ii, sc. 1, l. 44.

Manhood, learning, gentleness, virtue, youth, liberality, and such like, the spice and salt that season a man.
SHAKESPEARE, *Troilus and Cressida.* Act i, sc. 2, l. 276.

5
Horatio, thou art e'en as just a man
As e'er my conversation coped withal.
SHAKESPEARE, *Hamlet.* Act iii, sc. 2, l. 59.

6
One of those happy souls
Which are the salt of the earth, and without whom
This world would smell like what it is—a tomb.
SHELLEY, *Letter to Maria Gisborne,* l. 209.

7
Not a kindlier life or sweeter
Time, that lights and quenches men,
Now may quench or light again.
A. C. SWINBURNE, *Epicede for J. L. Graham.*

8
She has more goodness in her little finger than he has in his whole body.
SWIFT, *Polite Conversation.* Dial. ii.

9
So his life has flowed
From its mysterious urn a sacred stream,
In whose calm depth the beautiful and pure
Alone are mirrored.
THOMAS NOON TALFOURD, *Ion.* Act i, sc. 1.

10
I would be true, for there are those who trust me;
I would be pure, for there are those that care.
I would be strong, for there is much to suffer,
I would be brave, for there is much to dare.
I would be friend to all—the foe, the friendless;
I would be giving, and forget the gift.
I would be humble, for I know my weakness;
I would look up—and laugh—and love—and lift.
HOWARD ARNOLD WALTER, *My Creed.*

11
But God, who is able to prevail, wrestled with him, as the angel did with Jacob, and marked him; marked him for his own.
IZAAK WALTON, *Life of John Donne.*

12
His daily prayer, far better understood
In acts than words, was simply doing good.
WHITTIER, *Daniel Neall.*

A silent, shy, peace-loving man,
He seemed no fiery partisan.
WHITTIER, *The Tent on the Beach.* St. 11.

13
And therefore does not stoop, nor lie in wait
For wealth, or honours, or for worldly state.
WORDSWORTH, *Character of the Happy Warrior,* l. 41.

And, through the heat of conflict, keeps the law
In calmness made, and sees what he foresaw.
WORDSWORTH, *Character of the Happy Warrior,* l. 53.

Whom neither shape of danger can dismay,
Nor thought of tender happiness betray.
WORDSWORTH, *Character of the Happy Warrior,* l. 72.

But who, if he be called upon to face
Some awful moment to which Heaven has joined
Great issues, good or bad for human kind,
Is happy as a lover.
WORDSWORTH, *Character of the Happy Warrior,* l. 48.

1
Thy nature is not therefore less divine:
Thou liest in Abraham's bosom all the year,
And worship'st at the Temple's inner shrine,
God being with thee when we know it not.
WORDSWORTH, *It Is a Beauteous Evening.*

2
Horses he loved, and laughter, and the sun,
A song, wide spaces and the open air;
The trust of all dumb living things he won,
And never knew the luck too good to share:
Now, though he will not ride with us again,
His merry spirit seems our comrade yet,
Freed from the power of weariness and pain,
Forbidding us to mourn or to forget.
W. KERSLEY HOLMES, *Jimmy—Killed in Action.* (1917)

VI—Character: Bad

3
A demd damp, moist, unpleasant body.
DICKENS, *Nicholas Nickleby.* Ch. 34.

4
Of these the false Achitophel was first,
A name to all succeeding ages curst.
For close designs and crooked counsels fit,
Sagacious, bold, and turbulent of wit,
Restless, unfixt in principles and place,
In pow'r unpleased, impatient of disgrace;
A fiery soul, which working out its way,
Fretted the pigmy body to decay.
DRYDEN, *Absalom and Achitophel.* Pt. i, l. 150. Referring to Shaftesbury.

Crouching at home, and cruel when abroad.
DRYDEN, *Annus Mirabilis.* St. 1.

5
Three sorts of men my soul hateth: . . . a poor man that is proud, a rich man that is a liar, and an old adulterer that doateth.
Apocrypha: Ecclesiasticus, xxv, 2.

The Twelve Evils of the Age: 1, A wise man without good works; 2, An old man without religion; 3, A young man without obedience; 4, A rich man without charity; 5, A woman without modesty; 6, A lord without virtue; 7, A quarrelsome Christian; 8, A poor man who is proud; 9, An unjust King; 10, A negligent Bishop; 11, A populace without discipline; 12, A people without law.
UNKNOWN, *De Octo Viciis.* c.1200. (*E. E. T. S.,* xxxiv, 107.)

6
Green indiscretion, flattery of greatness,
Rawness of judgment, wilfulness in folly,
Thoughts vagrant as the wind, and as uncertain.
JOHN FORD, *The Broken Heart.* Act ii, sc. 2.

7
He was not a sweet-tempered man, nor one of gentle mood. (Οὐ γάρ τι γλυκύθυμος ἀνὴρ ἦν οὐδ' ἀγανόφρων.)
HOMER, *Iliad.* Bk. xx, l. 467. Referring to Achilles.

8
He was a scoundrel and a coward: a scoundrel for charging a blunderbuss against religion and morality; a coward, because he had not resolution to fire it off himself, but left half a crown to a beggarly Scotchman to draw the trigger at his death.
SAMUEL JOHNSON. (BOSWELL, *Life,* 1754.) Johnson is referring to Henry Saint-John, first Viscount Bolingbroke, whose works were edited by David Mallet after his death.

9
He is awkward and out of place in the society of his equals . . . He cannot meet you on the square.
CHARLES LAMB, *Essays of Elia: The Old and the New Schoolmaster.*

10
In prosperity he is brave, in adversity a runaway. (Re secunda fortis est, dubia fugax.)
PHÆDRUS, *Fables.* Bk. v, fab. 2, l. 13.

11
I know him a notorious liar,
Think him a great way fool, solely a coward;
Yet these fix'd evils sit so fit in him,
That they take place, when virtue's steely bones
Look bleak i' the cold wind.
SHAKESPEARE, *All's Well that Ends Well.* Act i, sc. 1, l. 111.

He is deformed, crooked, old and sere,
Ill-faced, worse-bodied, shapeless everywhere;
Vicious, ungentle, foolish, blunt, unkind,
Stigmatical in making, worse in mind.
SHAKESPEARE, *The Comedy of Errors.* Act iv, sc. 2, l. 19.

A fellow of no mark nor likelihood.
SHAKESPEARE, *I Henry IV.* Act iii, sc. 2, l. 45.

I grant him bloody,
Luxurious, avaricious, false, deceitful,
Sudden, malicious, smacking of every sin
That has a name.
SHAKESPEARE, *Macbeth.* Act iv, sc. 3, l. 57.

A man whose blood
Is very snow-broth; one who never feels
The wanton stings and motions of the sense.
SHAKESPEARE, *Measure for Measure.* Act i, sc. 4, l. 57.

A very superficial, ignorant, unweighing fellow.
SHAKESPEARE, *Measure for Measure.* Act iii, sc. 2, l. 147.

12
When he is best, he is a little worse than a man, and when he is worst, he is little better than a beast.
SHAKESPEARE, *The Merchant of Venice.* Act i, sc. 2, l. 94.

A stony adversary, an inhuman wretch
Uncapable of pity, void and empty
From any dram of mercy.
SHAKESPEARE, *The Merchant of Venice.* Act iv, sc. 1, l. 4.

13
I am very proud, revengeful, ambitious; with more offences at my beck, than I have

thoughts to put them in, imagination to give them shape, or time to act them in.

SHAKESPEARE, *Hamlet*. Act iii, sc. 1, l. 127.

1
High-stomach'd are they both and full of ire,
In rage deaf as the sea, hasty as fire.

SHAKESPEARE, *Richard II*. Act i, sc. 1, l. 18.

2
He was a man
Hard, selfish, loving only gold,
Yet full of guile: his pale eyes ran
With tears, which each some falsehood told.

SHELLEY, *Rosalind and Helen*, l. 248.

3
Lax in their gaiters, laxer in their gait.

HORACE AND JAMES SMITH, *Rejected Addresses: The Theatre.*

4
A man of plots,
Craft, poisonous counsels, wayside ambushings.

TENNYSON, *Gareth and Lynette*, l. 423.

CHARITY

See also Gifts and Giving; Philanthropy

For Charity of Judgment, see Tolerance

I—Charity: Definitions

5
Charity is a virtue of the heart, and not of the hands.

ADDISON, *The Guardian*. No. 166.

6
The desire of power in excess caused the angels to fall; the desire of knowledge in excess caused man to fall; but in charity there is no excess, neither can angel or man come in danger by it.

FRANCIS BACON, *Essays: Of Goodness*. *See also* AMBITION: ITS FOLLY.

7
For this I think charity, to love God for himself, and our neighbour for God.

SIR THOMAS BROWNE, *Religio Medici*. Pt. ii, sec. 14.

True charity is sagacious, and will find out hints for beneficence.

SIR THOMAS BROWNE, *Christian Morals*. Pt. i, sec. 6.

8
Charity is, indeed, a great thing, and a gift of God, and when it is rightly ordered, likens us to God himself, as far as that is possible; for it is charity which makes the man.

ST. JOHN CHRYSOSTOM, *True Almsgiving*.

9
Though I speak with the tongues of men and of angels, and have not charity, I am become as sounding brass or a tinkling cymbal.
And though I have the gift of prophecy, and understand all mysteries, and all knowledge; and though I have all faith, so that I could remove mountains, and have not charity, I am nothing.
And though I bestow all my goods to feed the poor, and though I give my body to be burned, and have not charity, it profiteth me nothing.
Charity suffereth long, and is kind; charity envieth not; charity vaunteth not itself, is not puffed up. . . .
And now abideth faith, hope, charity, these three; but the greatest of these is charity.

New Testament: I Corinthians, xiii, 1–4, 13.

Meek and lowly, pure and holy,
Chief among the "blessed three."

CHARLES JEFFERYS, *Charity.*

In Faith and Hope the world will disagree,
But all mankind's concern is Charity.

POPE, *Essay on Man*. Epis. iii, l. 307.

Hell bade all its millions rise; Paradise sends three:
Pity, and Self-sacrifice, and Charity.

THEODOSIA GARRISON, *These Shall Prevail.*

10
True Charity, a plant divinely nurs'd.

COWPER, *Charity*, l. 573.

11
Charity is indeed a noble and beautiful virtue, grateful to man, and approved by God. But charity must be built on justice. It cannot supersede justice.

HENRY GEORGE, *The Condition of Labor*, p. 92.

12
The best form of charity is extravagance. . . . The prodigality of the rich is the providence of the poor.

R. G. INGERSOLL, *Hard Times and the Way Out.*

13
Charity, decent, modest, easy, kind,
Softens the high, and rears the abject mind;
Knows with just reins, and gentle hand to guide,
Betwixt vile shame and arbitrary pride.

MATTHEW PRIOR, *Charity.*

Soft peace she brings, wherever she arrives:
She builds our quiet, as she forms our lives:
Lays the rough paths of peevish Nature even,
And opens in each heart a little Heaven.

MATTHEW PRIOR, *Charity.*

14
Charity itself fulfills the law,
And who can sever love from charity?

SHAKESPEARE, *Love's Labour's Lost*, iv, 3, 364.

Charity,
Which renders good for bad, blessings for curses.

SHAKESPEARE, *Richard III*. Act i, sc. 2, l. 68.

15
True charity is the desire to be useful to others without thought of recompense.

SWEDENBORG, *Arcana Cœlesta*. Sec. 3419.

The charities that soothe and heal and bless
Are scattered at the feet of Man—like flowers.

WORDSWORTH, *The Excursion*. Bk. ix, l. 239.

16
What is faith? What you do not see.
What is hope? A great thing.

What is charity? A great rarity.
(Quid est fides? Quod non vides.
Quid est spes? Magna res.
Quid est caritas? Magna raritas.)

UNKNOWN, *Facetiæ Cantabrigiensis.*

Alas! for the rarity, Of Christian charity
Under the sun!

THOMAS HOOD, *The Bridge of Sighs.*

II—Charity: Apothegms

1
Now there was at Joppa a certain disciple named Tabitha, which by interpretation is called Dorcas: this woman was full of good works and almsdeeds which she did.

New Testament: Acts, ix, 36.

2
It was the man and not his character that I pitied.

ARISTOTLE, when reproached for having given alms to a bad man. (DIOGENES LAERTIUS, *Aristotle*. Sec. 17.)

3
The living need charity more than the dead.

GEORGE ARNOLD, *The Jolly Old Pedagogue.*

4
He that defers his charity until he is dead is, if a man weighs it rightly, rather liberal of another man's than of his own.

FRANCIS BACON, *Collection of Sentences.* No. 55.

5
Be charitable before wealth make thee covetous, and lose not the glory of the mite.

SIR THOMAS BROWNE, *Christian Morals.* Pt. i, sec. 5.

6
He who bestows his goods upon the poor,
Shall have as much again, and ten times more.

JOHN BUNYAN, *The Pilgrim's Progress.* Pt. ii.
See also GIFTS: GIVING AND RECEIVING.

7
No sound ought to be heard in the church but the healing voice of Christian charity.

EDMUND BURKE, *Reflections on the Revolution in France.*

8
Did universal charity prevail, earth would be a heaven, and hell a fable.

C. C. COLTON, *Lacon.* Vol. i, No. 160.

9
Why, 'tis a point of faith. Whate'er it be,
I'm sure it is no point of charity.

RICHARD CRASHAW, *On a Treatise of Charity.*

10
Soft-handed Charity,
Tempering her gifts, that seem so free,
By time and place,
Till not a woe the bleak world see,
But finds her grace.

JOHN KEBLE, *The Christian Year: The Sunday After Ascension Day.*

11
He told me of Charity, the beautiful story of Charity.

WILLIAM LANGLAND, *Piers Plowman: Do-Better*, l. 19

12
With malice toward none; with charity for all.

ABRAHAM LINCOLN, *Second Inaugural Address*, 4 March, 1865.

In charity to all mankind, bearing no malice or ill-will to any human being.

JOHN QUINCY ADAMS, *Letter to A. Bronson*, 30 July, 1838.

13
Verily I say unto you, Inasmuch as ye have done it unto one of the least of these my brethren, ye have done it unto me.

New Testament: Matthew, xxv, 40.

14
In necessary things, unity; in doubtful things, liberty; in all things, charity. (In necessariis, unitas; in dubias, libertas; in omnibus, caritas.)

Attributed to Melanchthon by W. L. Bowles, who had it inscribed over the door of his house in Salisbury Close; also to Rupertus Meldenius by Canon Farrar, Croyden Church Conference, 1877.

15
I do not give alms; I am not poor enough for that.

FRIEDRICH NIETZSCHE, *Thus Spake Zarathustra: Introductory.* Sec. 2.

Give no bounties: make equal laws: secure life and prosperity and you need not give alms.

EMERSON, *Conduct of Life: Wealth.*

16
In this cold world where Charity lies bleating
Under a thorn, and none to give him greeting.

EDNA ST. VINCENT MILLAY, *Love Sonnet.*

17
Charity shall cover the multitude of sins.

New Testament: I Peter, iv, 8.

Charity creates a multitude of sins.

OSCAR WILDE, *The Soul of Man under Socialism.*

18
He hath a tear for pity, and a hand
Open as day for melting charity.

SHAKESPEARE, *II Henry IV.* Act iv, sc. 4, l. 31

19
To do him any wrong was to beget
A kindness from him, for his heart was rich,
Of such fine mould that if you sowed therein
The seed of Hate, it blossomed Charity.

TENNYSON, *Queen Mary.* Act iv, sc. 1.

20
He is truly great who hath a great charity.

THOMAS À KEMPIS, *De Imitatione Christi.* Pt. i, ch. 3.

21
All hearts confess the saints elect,
Who, twain in faith, in love agree,
And melt not in an acid sect
The Christian pearl of charity!

WHITTIER, *Snow-Bound*, l. 670.

1
Whate'er we look on, at our side
Be Charity,—to bid us think
And feel, if we would know.

WORDSWORTH, *Composed in One of the Catholic Cantons.*

III—Charity Begins at Home

2
Help thy kin, Christ biddeth, for there beginneth Charity.

WILLIAM LANGLAND, *Piers Plowman.* Passus xviii, l. 61. (1362)

Charity beginneth first at itself.

THOMAS WILSON, *Discourse Upon Usury,* l. 235.

Charity should begin at himself.

JOHN WYCLIFFE, *Works,* p. 76. (c. 1380)

3
Charity begins at home. (Proximus sum egomet mihi.)

TERENCE, *Andria,* l. 635. (Act iv, sc. 1.); BEAUMONT AND FLETCHER, *Wit Without Money;* ROBERT BROME, *Jovial Crew,* ii.

Charity well directed should begin at home. (Charité bien ordonné commence par soi même.)

MONTLUC, *La Comédie de Proverbes.* Act iii, 7.

Charity begins at home, and justice begins next door.

DICKENS, *Martin Chuzzlewit.* Ch. 27.

4
Let them learn first to show piety at home.

New Testament: I Timothy, v, 4.

5
Rowley: I believe there is no sentiment he has such faith in as that "charity begins at home."
Sir Oliver: And his, I presume, is of that domestic sort which never stirs abroad at all.

SHERIDAN, *School for Scandal.* Act v, sc. 1.

6
Our charity begins at home,
And mostly ends where it begins.

HORACE SMITH, *Horace in London.* Bk. ii, ode 15.

IV—Charity: Organized Charity

7
And fevered him with dreams of doing good
For good-for-nothing people.

E. B. BROWNING, *Aurora Leigh.* Bk. ii, l. 645.

The worst of charity is, that the lives you are asked to preserve are not worth preserving.

EMERSON, *Conduct of Life: Considerations by the Way.*

8
No rich man's largesse may suffice his soul,
Nor are the plundered succored by a dole.

EDMUND VANCE COOKE, *From the Book of Extenuations.*

9
This seems to me to be ambition, not charity. (Hæc mihi videtur ambitio, non eleemosyna.)

ERASMUS, *Convivium Religiosum.* He is speaking of charitable bequests.

Charity and Pride have different aims, yet both feed the poor.

THOMAS FULLER, *Gnomologia.* No. 1084.

It is better that ten drones be fed than one bee be famished.

THOMAS FULLER, *Worthies of England,* 33.

10
I have no great confidence in organized charities. Money is left and buildings are erected and sinecures provided for a good many worthless people. Those in immediate control are almost, or when they were appointed were almost, in want themselves, and they naturally hate other beggars.

R. G. INGERSOLL, *Organized Charities.*

11
I deem it the duty of every man to devote a certain portion of his income for charitable purposes; and that it is his further duty to see it so applied as to do the most good of which it is capable. This I believe to be best insured by keeping within the circle of his own inquiry and information the subjects of distress to whose relief his contributions should be applied.

THOMAS JEFFERSON, *Writings.* Vol. xi, p. 92.

12
I had much rather not to live at all, than to live by alms. (J'aime bien mieulx ne vivre point que de vivre d'aulmosne.)

MONTAIGNE, *Essays.* Bk. iii, ch. 5.

13
The organized charity, scrimped and iced,
In the name of a cautious, statistical Christ.

JOHN BOYLE O'REILLY, *In Bohemia.*

14 With one hand he put
A penny in the urn of poverty,
And with the other took a shilling out.

ROBERT POLLOK, *The Course of Time.* Bk. viii, l. 634.

15
God's servants making a snug living
By guiding Mammon in smug giving.

KEITH PRESTON, *Professional Welfare Workers.*

16
Cold is thy hopeless heart, even as charity.

SOUTHEY, *The Soldier's Wife.*

17
To be supported by the charity of friends or a government pension is to go into the almshouse.

H. D. THOREAU, *Journal,* 13 March, 1853.

CHARLES I and II

18
Mr. Dick had been for upwards of ten years endeavouring to keep King Charles the First out of the Memorial; but he had been constantly getting into it, and was there now.

DICKENS, *David Copperfield.* Ch. 15.

19
Great, good, and just, could I but rate
My grief with thy too rigid fate,
I'd weep the world in such a strain

As it should deluge once again;
But since thy loud-tongued blood demands supplies
More from Briareus' hands than Argus' eyes,
I'll sing thy obsequies with trumpet sounds
And write thy epitaph in blood and wounds.

JAMES GRAHAM, MARQUIS OF MONTROSE, *To Charles I.*

1
Vanquished in life, his death
By beauty made amends:
The passing of his breath
Won his defeated ends.

LIONEL JOHNSON, *By the Statue of King Charles at Charing Cross.*

King, tried in fires of woe!
Men hunger for thy grace:
And through the night I go,
Loving thy mournful face.

LIONEL JOHNSON, *By the Statue of King Charles at Charing Cross.*

2
He nothing common did or mean
Upon that memorable scene;
But with his keener eye
The axe's edge did try.

ANDREW MARVELL, *Execution of Charles I.*

3
Old times were changed, old manners gone;
A stranger filled the Stuarts' throne;
The bigots of the iron time
Had called his harmless art a crime.

SCOTT, *Lay of the Last Minstrel: Introduction.*

4
The royal refugee our breed restores
With foreign courtiers and with foreign whores,
And carefully repeopled us again,
Throughout his lazy, long, lascivious reign.

DANIEL DEFOE, *The True-Born Englishman*, l. 234. Referring to Charles II.

5
He was utterly without ambition. He detested business, and would sooner have abdicated his crown than have undergone the trouble of really directing the administration.

MACAULAY, *History of England*. Vol. i, ch. 2. Referring to Charles II.

6
A merry monarch, scandalous and poor.

JOHN WILMOT, EARL OF ROCHESTER, *On the King.*

7
Here lies our Sovereign Lord, the King,
Whose word no man relies on:
He never says a foolish thing,
Nor ever does a wise one.

JOHN WILMOT, EARL OF ROCHESTER, *Epitaph on Charles II.* These lines are said to have been written by Rochester on the door of the king's bedchamber. The first line is sometimes quoted: "Here lies our mutton-eating king."

That is very true: for my sayings are my own, my actions are my ministers'.

CHARLES II, In reply to the above. (HUME, *History of England*. Vol. viii, p. 312.)

CHARM

I—Charm: Attraction

8
It's a sort of bloom on a woman. If you have it, you don't need to have anything else; if you don't have it, it doesn't much matter what else you have.

J. M. BARRIE, *What Every Woman Knows.* Act i. Referring to Charm.

It's that damned charm.

BARRIE, *What Every Woman Knows.* Act iii.

9
He touches nothing but he adds a charm.

FÉNELON, *Eulogy of Cicero.*

10
To me more dear, congenial to my heart,
One native charm, than all the gloss of art.

GOLDSMITH, *The Deserted Village*, l. 253.

11
There are charms made only for distant admiration.

SAMUEL JOHNSON, *Works*. Vol. ii, p. 228.

12
Charms strike the sight, but merit wins the soul.

POPE, *The Rape of the Lock*. Canto v, l. 34.

13
All the charm of all the Muses.

TENNYSON, *To Virgil.*

Or loftier Mantuan, more divinely sweet,
Lord of the incommunicable charm.

WILLIAM WATSON, *Ode*. Referring to Vergil.

14
All charming people, I fancy, are spoiled. It is the secret of their attraction.

OSCAR WILDE, *The Portrait of Mr. W. H.*

When men give up saying what is charming, they give up thinking what is charming.

OSCAR WILDE, *Lady Windermere's Fan.* Act ii.

II—Charm: Spell

15
They charmed it with smiles and soap.

LEWIS CARROLL, *Hunting of the Snark.*

16
Enter'd the very lime-twigs of his spells,
And yet came off.

MILTON, *Comus*, l. 646.

17
They are like the deaf adder that stoppeth her ear; which will not harken to the voice of charmers, charming never so wisely.

Old Testament: Psalms, lviii, 4, 5.

18
I know of a charm by way of a prayer that will preserve a man from the violence of guns and all manner of fire-weapons and engines, but it will do me no good because I do not believe it.

RABELAIS, *Works*. Bk. i, ch. 42. A monk is speaking.

1
Fair is foul, and foul is fair.
SHAKESPEARE, *Macbeth*. Act i, sc. 1, l. 11.

Eye of newt and toe of frog,
Wool of bat and tongue of dog.
SHAKESPEARE, *Macbeth*. Act iv, sc. 1, l. 14.

2
Charm ache with air and agony with words.
SHAKESPEARE, *Much Ado About Nothing*. Act v, sc. 1, l. 26.

3
The charm dissolves apace.
SHAKESPEARE, *The Tempest*. Act v, sc. 1, l. 64.

CHASE, THE, see Hunting

CHASTITY

See also Purity; Woman: Her Virtue

4
Who is the chaste woman? She about whom scandal fears to lie. (Quæ casta est? De qua mentiri fama veretur.)
BIAS. (AUSONIUS [?], *Septem Sapientum Sententiæ*, l. 5.)

Chaste women are often proud and froward, as presuming upon the merit of their chastity.
BACON, *Essays: Of Marriage and Single Life*.

5
That chastity of honour which felt a stain like a wound.
EDMUND BURKE, *Reflections on the Revolution in France*.

6
"Keep your good name, though Eve herself once fell."
"Nay," quoth the maid, "the Sultan's self shan't carry me,
Unless his highness promises to marry me."
BYRON, *Don Juan*. Canto v, st. 84.

But, whatsoe'er she wished, she acted right;
And whether coldness, pride, or virtue, dignify
A woman, so she's good, what does it signify?
BYRON, *Don Juan*. Canto xiv, st. 57.

Be warm, but pure; be amorous, but be chaste.
BYRON, *English Bards and Scotch Reviewers*.

7
So a maiden, while she remains untouched, remains dear to her own; but when she has lost her chaste flower with sullied body, she remains neither lovely to boys nor dear to girls. (Sic virgo dum intacta manet, dum cara suis est; Cum castum amisit polluto corpore florem, Nec pueris jucunda manet nec cara puellis.)
CATULLUS, *Odes*. Ode lxii, l. 45.

8
There is no jewel in the world so valuable as a chaste and virtuous woman.
CERVANTES, *Don Quixote*. Pt. i, ch. 33.

9
There said once a clerk in two verses: "what is better than gold? Jasper. What is better than jasper? Wisdom. And what is better than wisdom? Woman. And what is better than a good woman? No-thing."
CHAUCER, *The Tale of Melibeus*, l. 2297.

A good woman is a hidden treasure; who discovers her will do well not to boast about it. (Une honnête femme est un trésor caché; celui qui l'a trouvé fait fort bien de ne s'en pas vanter.)
LA ROCHEFOUCAULD, *Maximes Posthumes*. No. 552.

God's rarest blessing is, after all, a good woman.
GEORGE MEREDITH, *Richard Feverel*. Ch. 34.

Who can find a virtuous woman? for her price is far above rubies.
Old Testament: Proverbs, xxxi, 10.

A good woman is worth, if she were sold,
The fairest crown that's made of purest gold.
WODROEPHE, *Spared Houres*, 484. (1623)

10
You see me with child, and you want me a virgin.
CERVANTES, *Don Quixote*. Pt. ii, ch. 41.

11
In vain to honour they pretend
Who guard themselves with ramparts and with walls.
Them only fame the truly valiant calls
Who can an open breach defend.
ABRAHAM COWLEY, *Maidenhead*.

12
Chastity and Beauty, which were deadly foes,
Live reconcilèd friends within her brow;
SAMUEL DANIEL, *To Delia*.

13
A foolish female nice and shy,
That never yet trod shoe awry.
THOMAS D'URFEY, *Richmond Heiress*. Act ii, sc. 2.

No woman . . . but such one as hath trod her shoe amiss. [*i. e.*, lapsed from virtue.]
THOMAS HOCCLEVE, *Minor Poems*, xxiv, 66. (c. 1422)

14
For me it will be enough that a marble stone should declare that a queen having reigned such a time, lived and died a virgin.
QUEEN ELIZABETH, in answer to a petition from the House of Commons, in 1559, that she should consider marriage. (HUME, *History of England*. Ch. 38.)

15
Chastity, they admit, is very well—but then think of Mirabeau's passion and temperament!
EMERSON, *Letters and Social Aims: Poetry and Imagination*.

16
Not lightly be thy citadel subdued;
Not ignobly, not untimely,
Take praise in solemn mood;
Take love sublimely.
RICHARD WATSON GILDER, *Ah, Be Not False*.

17
A woman's chastity consists, like an onion, of a series of coats.
HAWTHORNE, *Journals*, 16 March, 1854.

18
Beware of lust: it doth pollute and foul. . . .
Wholly abstain, or wed. Thy bounteous Lord

Allows thee choice of paths: take no by-
ways. . . .
Continence hath his joy: weigh both; and so
If rottenness have more, let Heaven go.

GEORGE HERBERT, *The Church-Porch*. Sts. 2, 3.

1
She who keeps chastely to her husband's side
Is not for one but every night his bride:
And stealing still with love and fear to bed,
Brings him not one, but many a maidenhead.

ROBERT HERRICK, *Julia's Churching*.

2
Men are virtuous because women are; women are virtuous from necessity.

E. W. HOWE, *A Letter from Mr. Biggs*.

3
Chastity enables the soul to breathe a pure air in the foulest places. (Par la chasteté, l'âme respire un air pur dans les lieux les plus corrompus.)

JOUBERT, *Pensées*. No. 78.

4
Whole towns worship the dog, but no one worships Diana (*i.e.*, Chastity). (Oppida tota canem venerantur, nemo Dianam.)

JUVENAL, *Satires*. Sat. xv, l. 8.

5
Chastity without charity lies chained in hell,
It is but an unlighted lamp.
Many chaplains are chaste, but where is their
charity?
There are no harder, hungrier men than men
of Holy Church.

WILLIAM LANGLAND, *Piers Plowman*. Pt. ii.

6
Virtue in women is often merely love of their reputation and of their repose. (L'honnêteté des femmes est souvent l'amour de leur réputation et de leur repos.)

LA ROCHEFOUCAULD, *Maximes*. No. 205.

There are few good women who are not weary of their trade. (Il y a peu d'honnêtes femmes qui ne soient lasses de leur métier.)

LA ROCHEFOUCAULD, *Maximes*. No. 367.

7
And virtue flies when love once blows the
sail.

SHACKERLEY MARMION, *Cupid and Psyche*.

8
Chaste in morals and spotless in modesty. (Casta moribus et integra pudore.)

MARTIAL, *Epigrams*.

9
Thy beauty shall no more be found,
Nor, in thy marble vault, shall sound
My echoing song: then worms shall try
That long preserved virginity,
And your quaint honour turn to dust,
And into ashes all my lust:
The grave's a fine and private place,
But none, I think, do there embrace.

ANDREW MARVELL, *To His Coy Mistress*.

10
And fifteen arms went round her waist.
(And then men ask, Are Barmaids chaste?)

JOHN MASEFIELD, *The Everlasting Mercy*.

11
Virgin me no virgins.

PHILIP MASSINGER, *New Way to Pay Old Debts*. Act iii, sc. 2.

12
'Tis chastity, my brother, chastity:
She that has that is clad in complete steel,
And, like a quiver'd nymph with arrows keen,
May trace huge forests, and unharbour'd
heaths,
Infamous hills, and sandy perilous wilds;
Where, through the sacred rays of chastity,
No savage fierce, bandite, or mountaineer,
Will dare to soil her virgin purity.

MILTON, *Comus*, l. 420.

Some say no evil thing that walks by night,
In fog or fire, by lake or moorish fen,
Blue meagre hag, or stubborn unlaid ghost
That breaks his magic chains at curfew time,
No goblin, or swart fairy of the mine,
Hath hurtful power o'er true virginity.

MILTON, *Comus*, l. 432.

So dear to heav'n is saintly chastity,
That when a soul is found sincerely so,
A thousand liveried angels lackey her,
Driving far off each thing of sin and guilt,
And in clear dream and solemn vision,
Tell her of things that no gross ear can hear,
Till oft converse with heav'nly habitants
Begin to cast a beam on th' outward shape.

MILTON, *Comus*, l. 453.

13
Belike we must be incontinent that we may be continent; burning is quenched by fire.

MONTAIGNE, *Essays*. Bk. iii, ch. 5.

14
Do I counsel you to chastity? Chastity is a virtue in some, but in many almost a vice. These, it is true, are abstinent; but from all that they do the bitch of sensuality looks out with envious eyes.

NIETZSCHE, *Thus Spake Zarathustra*.

15
Chaste is she whom no one has asked. (Casta est, quam nemo rogavit.)

OVID, *Amores*. Bk. i, eleg. 8, l. 43.

She is chaste who was never asked the question.

CONGREVE, *Love for Love*. Act iii, sc. 3.

An unattempted woman cannot boast of her chastity.

MONTAIGNE, *Essays*. Bk. iii, ch. 5.

16
If she is chaste when there is no fear of detection, she is truly chaste; she who sins not because she dares not, does the sin. (Siqua metu dempto casta est, ea denique casta est; Quæ, quia non liceat, non facit, illa facit!)

OVID, *Amores*. Bk. iii, eleg. 4, l. 3.

17
Women always live chastely enough, so that they live charily enough.

GEORGE PETTIE, *Petite Pallace*, i, 32. (1576)

I learned this old saying in Latin, *Caute, si non caste*. Live charily, if not chastely.
UNKNOWN, *Tinker of Turvey,* 36. (1630)

If not chastely, at all events cautiously. (Nisi casta, saltem caute.)
UNKNOWN. A Latin proverb.

1
What guards the purity of melting maids,
In courtly balls, and midnight masquerades,
Safe from the treacherous friend, the daring spark,
The glance by day, the whisper in the dark;
When kind occasion prompts their warm desires,
When music softens, and when dancing fires?
'Tis but their Sylph, the wise Celestials know,
Tho' Honour is the word with men below.
POPE, *The Rape of the Lock*. Canto i, l. 71.

2
I envy not their bliss, if he or she
Think fit to live in perfect chastity:
Pure let them be, and free from taint or vice;
I for a few slight spots am not so nice.
POPE, *Wife of Bath's Prologue,* l. 36.

Full many a saint, since first the world began,
Lived an unspotted maid in spite of man:
Let such (a God's name) with fine wheat be fed,
And let us honest wives eat barley bread.
POPE, *Wife of Bath's Prologue,* l. 46.

3
Not that I mistrust her virtue, but—she is a woman. There lies the suspicion.
RABELAIS.

4
If she seem not chaste to me,
What care I how chaste she be?
SIR WALTER RALEIGH, *Shall I, Like a Hermit, Dwell?*

5
They are thorns which produce roses.
SCHOPENHAUER, of virgins. (EMERSON, *Journals,* 1864.)

6
Helena: Man is enemy to virginity; how may we barricado it against him?
Parolles: Keep him out.
SHAKESPEARE, *All's Well that Ends Well.* Act i, sc. 1, l. 123.

7
There was never virgin got till virginity was first lost . . . Virginity breeds mites, much like a cheese consumes itself to the very paring, and so dies with feeding its own stomach. Besides, virginity is peevish, proud, idle, made of self-love, which is the most inhibited sin in the canon.
SHAKESPEARE, *All's Well that Ends Well.* Act i, sc. 1, l. 140.

8
My chastity's the jewel of our house,
Bequeathed down from many ancestors.
SHAKESPEARE, *All's Well that Ends Well.* Act iv, sc. 2, l. 46.

9
A very honest woman, but something given to lie.
SHAKESPEARE, *Antony and Cleopatra.* Act v, sc. 2, l. 252.

Well, I am not fair, and therefore I pray the gods make me honest.
SHAKESPEARE, *As You Like It.* Act iii, sc. 3, l. 34.

10
Run, run, Orlando: carve on every tree
The fair, the chaste, and unexpressive she.
SHAKESPEARE, *As You Like It.* Act iii, sc. 2, l. 9.

11
The very ice of chastity is in them.
SHAKESPEARE, *As You Like It.* Act iii, sc. 4, l. 18.

Chaste as the icicle
That's curdied by the frost from purest snow.
SHAKESPEARE, *Coriolanus.* Act v, sc. 3, l. 66.

As chaste as unsunn'd snow.
SHAKESPEARE, *Cymbeline.* Act ii, sc. 5, l. 14.

As chaste as a picture cut in alabaster.
HENRY WOODFALL, *Darby and Joan.*

Chaste as morning dew.
YOUNG, *Night Thoughts.* Night v, l. 600.

12
There my white stole of chastity I daff'd,
Shook off my sober guards and civil fears.
SHAKESPEARE, *A Lover's Complaint,* l. 297.

13
I will find you twenty lascivious turtles ere one chaste man.
SHAKESPEARE, *The Merry Wives of Windsor.* Act ii, sc. 1, l. 82.

14
You seem to me as Dian in her orb,
As chaste as is the bud ere it be blown.
SHAKESPEARE, *Much Ado About Nothing.* Act iv, sc. 1, l. 58.

15
Her honour is an essence that's not seen;
They have it very oft that have it not.
SHAKESPEARE, *Othello.* Act iv, sc. 1, l. 14.

16
Young budding virgin, fair and fresh and sweet,
Whither away, or where is thy abode?
Happy the parents of so fair a child;
Happier the man, whom favourable stars
Allot thee for his lovely bed-fellow!
SHAKESPEARE, *The Taming of the Shrew.* Act iv, sc. 5, l. 37.

Lady, you are the cruell'st she alive,
If you will lead these graces to the grave
And leave the world no copy.
SHAKESPEARE, *Twelfth Night.* Act i, sc. 5, l. 259.

Fruitless chastity,
Love-lacking vestals and self-loving nuns,
That on the earth would breed a scarcity
And barren dearth of daughters and of sons.
SHAKESPEARE, *Venus and Adonis,* l. 751.

17
Women may, as Napoleon said, be the occupation of the idle man, just as men are the preoccupation of the idle woman; but the

mass of mankind is too busy and too poor for the long and expensive sieges which the professed libertine lays to virtue.

BERNARD SHAW, *Overruled: Preface.*

1
Could women but our secret counsel scan—
Could they but reach the deep reserve of man—
To keep our love they'd rate their virtue high:
They live together, and together die.

SHERIDAN, *A Trip to Scarborough.* Act v, sc. 1.

2
O Chastity, the chief of heavenly lights,
Which mak'st us most immortal shape to wear,
Hold thou my heart, establish thou my sprites;
To only thee my constant course I bear.

SIR PHILIP SIDNEY, *Arcadia.* Bk. ii.

Who doth desire that chaste his wife should be,
First be he true, for truth doth truth deserve.

SIR PHILIP SIDNEY, *Arcadia.* Bk. ii.

3
A woman who has sacrificed her chastity will hesitate at no other iniquity. (Neque femina, amissa pudicitia, alia abnuerit.)

TACITUS, *Annals.* Bk. iv, sec. 3.

4
Virginity is a life of angels, the enamel of the soul.

JEREMY TAYLOR, *Holy Living.* Ch. ii, sec. 3.

Chastity is either abstinence or continence. Abstinence is that of virgins or widows; continence, of married persons.

JEREMY TAYLOR, *Holy Living.* Ch. ii, sec. 3.

5
Then she rode forth, clothed on with chastity.

TENNYSON, *Godiva,* l. 53.

6
To lead sweet lives in purest chastity.

TENNYSON, *Guinevere,* l. 471.

I know the Table Round, my friends of old;
All brave, and many generous, and some chaste.

TENNYSON, *Merlin and Vivien,* l. 814.

7
Even from the body's purity, the mind
Receives a secret sympathetic aid.

THOMSON, *The Seasons: Summer,* l. 1267.

8
I would wring your neck with my own hands rather than permit an attempt on your honor; for, look you, I love you well enough for that. (Je te tordrai le cou de mes propres mains plutôt que de souffrir qu'on attente à ton honneur; car, vois-tu, je t'aime assez pour cela.)

VOLTAIRE, *La Échange.* Act ii, sc. 7. Le Baron de la Canardière to his daughter.

9
I have been so misused by chaste men with one wife
That I would live with satyrs all my life.

ANNA WICKHAM, *Ship Near Shoals.*

10
Acquainted with the world, and quite well-bred,
Drusa receives her visitants in bed;
But, chaste as ice, this Vesta, to defy
The very blackest tongues of calumny,
When from the sheets her lovely form she lifts,
She begs you just would turn you, while she shifts.

YOUNG, *Love of Fame.* Satire vi, l. 36.

11
Beneath this stone I lie, the famous woman who loosed her zone to one man only. ("Ἀδ' ἐγὼ ἁ περίβωτος ὑπὸ πλακὶ τῇδε τέθαμμαι, μούνῳ ἐνὶ ζώναν ἀνέρι λυσαμένα.)

UNKNOWN, *Epigram.* (*Greek Anthology.* Bk. vii, No. 324.)

CHAUCER, GEOFFREY

12
And Chaucer, with his infantine
Familiar clasp of things divine;
That mark upon his lip is wine.

E. B. BROWNING, *A Vision of Poets,* l. 388.

13
Chaucer is glad and erect.

EMERSON, *Representative Men: Shakespeare.*

14
He is the poet of the dawn, who wrote
The Canterbury Tales, and his old age
Made beautiful with song; and as I read
I hear the crowing cock, I hear the note
Of lark and linnet, and from every page
Rise odors of ploughed field or flowery mead.

LONGFELLOW, *Chaucer.*

15
Sith of our language he was the lodestar. . . .
Sith he in Englishmaking was the best,
Pray unto God to give his soul good rest.

JOHN LYDGATE, *The Falls of Princes.*

16
Old Chaucer, . . . that broad famous English poet.

THOMAS MIDDLETON, *More Dissemblers Besides Women.* Act i, sc. 4.

17
Or call up him that left half told
The story of Cambuscan bold.

MILTON, *Il Penseroso,* l. 109. Referring to the unfinished *Squire's Tale.*

18
Dan Chaucer, well of English undefiled,
On Fame's eternal beadroll worthy to be filed.

SPENSER, *The Faerie Queene.* Bk. iv, canto ii, st. 32. (Dan, *i.e.,* Master.)

And in our tongue was well of eloquence.

UNKNOWN, *The Book of Courtesye.* St. 50. (c. 1470) The reference is also to Chaucer.

From purest wells of English undefiled
None deeper drank than he, the New World's child.

J. G. WHITTIER, *James Russell Lowell.*

1
Dan Chaucer, the first warbler, whose sweet
breath
Preluded those melodious bursts that fill
The spacious times of great Elizabeth
With sounds that echo still.

TENNYSON, *A Dream of Fair Women*. St. 2.

2
Some kind person has sent me Chawcer's poems. Mr. C. had talent, but he couldn't spel. No man has a right to be a lit'rary man onless he knows how to spel. It is a pity that Chawcer, who had geneyus, was so unedicated. He's the wus speller I know of.

ARTEMUS WARD, *Chaucer's Poems*.

Chaucer, I confess, is a rough diamond; and must first be polish'd e'er he shines.

DRYDEN, *Fables: Preface*.

CHEATING

3
Like strawberry wives, that laid two or three great strawberries at the mouth of their pot, and all the rest were little ones.

FRANCIS BACON, *Apothegms*. No. 54.

4
The first and worst of all frauds is to cheat one's self.

P. J. BAILEY, *Festus: Anywhere*.

He is most cheated who cheats himself. (Den sviges vaerst, som sviger sig selv.)

UNKNOWN. A Danish proverb.

5
This is a pretty flimflam.

BEAUMONT AND FLETCHER, *The Little French Lawyer*. Act iii, sc. 3.

'Twas a most notorious flam.

BUTLER, *Hudibras*. Pt. ii, canto iii, l. 887.

6
Don't steal; thou'lt never thus compete
Successfully in business. Cheat.

AMBROSE BIERCE, *The Devil's Dictionary: The Decalogue Revised*.

Thou shalt not steal: an empty feat,
When it's so lucrative to cheat.

ARTHUR HUGH CLOUGH, *The Latest Decalogue*.

7
To suppose one cheat
Can gull all these, were more miraculous far
Than aught we should confess a miracle.

ROBERT BROWNING, *Mr. Sludge "The Medium."*

8
Doubtless the pleasure is as great
Of being cheated, as to cheat;
As lookers on feel most delight
That least perceive a juggler's sleight,
And still, the less they understand,
The more they admire his sleight of hand.

BUTLER, *Hudibras*. Pt. ii, canto 3, l. 1.

First wish to be imposed on, and then are.

COWPER, *The Progress of Error*, l. 290.

9
He is not cheated who knows he is being cheated. (Non decipitur qui scit se decipi.)

SIR EDWARD COKE, *Institutes*.

10
There are a thousand methods of cheating your creditors. (Ut ludas creditores, mille sunt artes.)

ERASMUS, *Hippeus Anippos*.

Bankruptcy, full of ease and health,
And wallowing in well-saved wealth.

CHARLES CHURCHILL, *The Ghost*. Bk. iv, l. 1661.

11
Three things are men most likely to be cheated in, a horse, a wig, and a wife.

BENJAMIN FRANKLIN, *Poor Richard*, 1736.

12
Cheat me in the price but not in the goods.

THOMAS FULLER, *Gnomologia*. No. 1090.

He that cheateth in small things is a fool; but in great ones is a rogue.

THOMAS FULLER, *Gnomologia*. No. 2066.

He that will cheat at play
Will cheat you any way.

THOMAS FULLER, *Gnomologia*. No. 6302.

In the kingdom of a cheater, the wallet is carried before.

GEORGE HERBERT, *Jacula Prudentum*.

13
I hope I shall never be deterred from detecting what I think a cheat, by the menaces of a ruffian.

SAMUEL JOHNSON, *Letter to James Macpherson*.

14
The stupid makes a disturbance; the fool laments; the honest man, when he is cheated, retires and says not a word (Le bruit est pour le fat, la plainte est pour le sot; l'hônnete homme trompé s'éloigne et ne dit mot.)

LA NOUÉ, *La Coquette Corrigée*. Act i, sc. 3.

If thou art cheated by a great man, lose thy money, and say nothing.

FULLER, *Introductio ad Prudentiam*, i, 19.

Many men *swallow* the being cheated, but no man can ever endure to chew it.

LORD HALIFAX, *Works*, p. 247.

15
We know that there are chiselers. At the bottom of every case of criticism and obstruction we have found some selfish interest, some private axe to grind.

FRANKLIN D. ROOSEVELT, *Radio Address*, 22 Oct., 1933. The first official use of a word used to indicate employers who were not keeping their pledges under the National Recovery Administration. The revival of a slang term used in the Western United States as early as 1848, probably originating in Louisiana, and derived from the French verb "ciseler," meaning to cut, to trim.

16
They cheat . . . worse than Cross I win, Pile you lose; but there are some left that can lose upon the square.

THOMAS SHADWELL, *Epsom Wells*. Act ii, sc. 1. (1672)

A game which a sharper once play'd with a dupe, intitled, "Heads I win, tails you lose."
UNKNOWN, *Croker Papers,* iii, 59.

It's heads Law wins, tails they lose.
WILLIAM DE MORGAN, *It Never Can Happen Again.* Ch. 38.

1
My revenue is the silly cheat.
SHAKESPEARE, *Winter's Tale.* Act iv, sc. 3, l. 28.

2
She cheats horse and foot.
WALPOLE, *Letters: To Richard West,* 2 Oct., 1740.

3
To a cheat, a cheat and a half. (À trompeur, trompeur et demi.)
UNKNOWN. A French proverb.

CHEERFULNESS

See also Merriment, Mirth, Optimism

4
A cheerful temper joined with innocence will make beauty attractive, knowledge delightful, and wit good-natured.
ADDISON, *The Tatler.* No. 192.

5
Health and cheerfulness mutually beget each other.
ADDISON, *The Spectator.* No. 387.

Health is the condition of wisdom, and the sign is cheerfulness,—an open and noble temper.
EMERSON, *Society and Solitude: Success.*

Cheerfulness, sir, is the principal ingredient in the composition of health.
ARTHUR MURPHY, *The Apprentice.* Act ii, sc. 4.

6
Cheered up himself with ends of verse
And sayings of philosophers.
BUTLER, *Hudibras.* Pt. i, canto iii, l. 1011.

"And yet," demanded Councillor Barlow, . . . "what great cause is he identified with?"—"He is identified," said the speaker, "with the great cause of cheering us all up."
ARNOLD BENNETT, *Denry the Audacious. (The Card.)* Ch. 12.

7
Cheerful without mirth.
BYRON, *Don Juan.* Canto vi, st. 53.

8
So of cheerfulness, or a good temper, the more it is spent, the more of it remains.
EMERSON, *Conduct of Life: Considerations by the Way.*

9
That which befits us is cheerfulness and courage.
EMERSON, *Essays, Second Series: New England Reformers.*

Cheerfulness, without which no man can be a poet—for beauty is his aim.
EMERSON, *Representative Men: Shakespeare.*

How often it seems the chief good to be born with a cheerful temper . . . Like Alfred, "good fortune accompanies him like a gift of God."
EMERSON, *Society and Solitude: Success.*

10
Cheerful at morn he wakes from short repose,
Breasts the keen air, and carols as he goes.
GOLDSMITH, *The Traveller,* l. 185.

11
We ought to feel a deep cheerfulness, as I may say, that a happy Providence kept it from being any worse.
THOMAS HARDY, *Far From the Madding Crowd.* Ch. 8.

12
A cheerful look makes a dish a feast.
GEORGE HERBERT, *Jacula Prudentum.*

13
Cheer up! the worst is yet to come!
PHILANDER JOHNSON, *Shooting Stars.* (See *Everybody's Magazine,* May, 1920.)

The worst is yet to come.
TENNYSON, *Sea Dreams,* l. 301.

14
Be of good cheer.
New Testament: Matthew, xiv, 27.

15
The most manifest sign of wisdom is a continual cheerfulness.
MONTAIGNE, *Essays.* Bk. i, ch. 25.

16
Good humour only teaches charms to last,
Still makes new conquests and maintains the past.
POPE, *Epistle to Mrs. Blount with the Works of Voiture,* l. 61.

Thus wisely careless, innocently gay,
Cheerful he play'd the trifle, Life, away.
POPE, *Epistle to Mrs. Blount with the Works of Voiture,* l. 11. Of Voiture.

O! bless'd with temper, whose unclouded ray
Can make to-morrow cheerful as to-day.
POPE, *Moral Essays.* Epis. ii, l. 257.

17
What then remains, but well our power to use,
And keep good humour still whate'er we lose?
And trust me, dear, good humour can prevail,
When airs, and flights, and screams, and scolding fail.
POPE, *The Rape of the Lock.* Canto v, l. 29.

18
Lay aside life-harming heaviness
And entertain a cheerful disposition.
SHAKESPEARE, *Richard II.* Act ii, sc. 2, l. 3.

Look cheerfully upon me.
SHAKESPEARE, *The Taming of the Shrew.* Act iv, sc. 3, l. 38.

19
Good humour may be said to be one of the very best articles of dress one can wear in society.
THACKERAY, *On Tailoring and Toilets.*

20
Cheerfulness in most cheerful people, is the

rich and satisfying result of strenuous discipline.
E. P. WHIPPLE, *Success and Its Conditions: Cheerfulness.*

1
A cheerful life is what the Muses love,
A soaring spirit is their prime delight.
WORDSWORTH, *From the Dark Chambers.*

CHICAGO, ILL.

2
Queen of the West! by some enchanter taught
To lift the glory of Aladdin's court.
BRET HARTE, *Chicago.*

3
Sputter, city! Bead with fire
Every ragged roof and spire; . . .
Burst to bloom, you proud, white flower,
But—remember that hot hour
When the shadow of your brand
Laps the last cool grain of sand—
You will still be just a scar
On a little, lonesome star.
MILDRED PLEW MERRYMAN, *To Chicago at Night.*

4
O great city of visions, waging the war of the free,
Beautiful, strong and alert, a goddess in purpose and mien.
WALLACE RICE, *Chicago.*

5
Hog-Butcher for the World,
Tool-maker, Stacker of Wheat,
Player with Railroads and the Nation's Freight-handler;
Stormy, husky, brawling,
City of the Big Shoulders.
CARL SANDBURG, *Chicago.*

6
Then lift once more thy towers on high,
And fret with spires the western sky,
To tell that God is yet with us,
And love is still miraculous.
WHITTIER, *Chicago.* The reference is to the great fire of 1871.

CHILDHOOD

See also Boyhood, Youth

7
When I was a child, I spake as a child, I understood as a child, I thought as a child; but when I became a man, I put away childish things.
New Testament: I Corinthians, xiii, 11.

The sports of children satisfy the child.
GOLDSMITH, *The Traveller,* l. 154.

8
Childhood and youth are vanity.
Old Testament: Ecclesiastes, xi, 10.

9
Childhood has no forebodings.
GEORGE ELIOT, *Mill on the Floss.* Bk. i, ch. 9.

10
The growth of flesh is but a blister;
Childhood is health.
GEORGE HERBERT, *Holy Baptism.*

11
Childhood, whose very happiness is love.
LETITIA ELIZABETH LANDON, *Erinna.*

12
He who gives a child a treat
Makes joy-bells ring in Heaven's street,
And he who gives a child a home
Builds palaces in Kingdom come,
And she who gives a baby birth
Brings Saviour Christ again to Earth,
For life is joy, and mind is fruit,
And body's precious earth and root.
JOHN MASEFIELD, *The Everlasting Mercy.*

Lord, give to men who are old and rougher
The things that little children suffer,
And let keep bright and undefiled
The young years of the little child.
JOHN MASEFIELD, *The Everlasting Mercy.*

13
The childhood shows the man,
As morning shows the day.
MILTON, *Paradise Regained.* Bk. iv, l. 220.

The child is father of the man.
WORDSWORTH, *My Heart Leaps Up.*

Our days, our deeds, all we achieve or are,
Lay folded in our infancy; the things
Of good or ill we choose while yet unborn.
J. T. TROWBRIDGE, *Sonnet: Nativity.*

14
The greatest poem ever known
Is one all poets have outgrown:
The poetry, innate, untold,
Of being only four years old.
CHRISTOPHER MORLEY, *To a Child.*

15
I remember, I remember
How my childhood fleeted by,—
The mirth of its December,
And the warmth of its July.
W. M. PRAED, *I Remember, I Remember.*

16
Childhood is the sleep of reason.
ROUSSEAU, *Émile.* Bk. ii.

17
'Tis the eye of childhood
That fears a painted devil.
SHAKESPEARE, *Macbeth.* Act ii, sc. 2, l. 54.

"My children," said an old man to his boys, scared by a figure in the dark entry, "my children, you will never see anything worse than yourselves."
EMERSON, *Essays, First Series: Spiritual Laws.*

18
Childhood is a stage in the process of that continual remanufacture of the Life Stuff by which the human race is perpetuated.
BERNARD SHAW, *Parents and Children.*

19
The days of childhood are but days of woe.
SOUTHEY, *The Retrospect.* St. 9.

1
The hills are dearest which our childish feet
Have climbed the earliest; and the streams most sweet
Are ever those at which our young lips drank.

WHITTIER, *The Bridal of Pennacook:* Pt. vi, *At Pennacook,* l. 1.

How dear to this heart are the scenes of my childhood,
When fond recollection recalls them to view;
The orchard, the meadow, the deep-tangled wild-wood,
And every loved spot which my infancy knew.

SAMUEL WOODWORTH, *The Old Oaken Bucket.* First published in *The Post-Chaise Annual,* Baltimore, 1819.

2
Sweet childish days, that were as long
As twenty days are now.

WORDSWORTH, *To a Butterfly.*

3
There was a time when meadow, grove, and stream,
The earth, and every common sight,
To me did seem
Apparelled in celestial light.

WORDSWORTH, *Intimations of Immortality.* St. 1.

CHILDREN

See also Youth

I—Children: Apothegms

4
The noblest works and foundations have proceeded from childless men.

BACON, *Essays: Of Parents and Children.*

Certainly, the best works, and of greatest merit for the public, have proceeded from the unmarried or childless men.

BACON, *Essays: Of Marriage and Single Life.*

5
Be kind to those dear little folks,
When our toes are turned up to the daisies!

R. H. BARHAM, *The Babes in the Wood.*

6
Children mothered by the street. . . .
Blossoms of humanity!
Poor soiled blossoms in the dust!

MATHILDE BLIND, *The Street-Children's Dance.*

7
Cornelia kept her in talk till her children came from school, "and these," said she. "are my jewels."

ROBERT BURTON, *Anatomy of Melancholy.* Pt. iii, sec. ii, mem. 2, subs. 3. Burton is quoting Seneca, who tells the story of how Cornelia, daughter of Scipio Africanus, and wife of Sempronius Gracchus, presented her sons to a lady who had been displaying her jewels, and asking Cornelia about hers.

Pointing to such, well might Cornelia say,
When the rich casket shone in bright array,
"These are my jewels!"

SAMUEL ROGERS, *Human Life,* l. 210.

My jewels are my husband and his triumphs. ('Εμοὶ δέ κόσμος ἐστὶ Φωκίων.)

The wife of Phocian. (PLUTARCH, *Lives: Phocian.* Ch. 19, sec. 3.)

8
Woe to thee, O land, when thy king is a child.

Old Testament: Ecclesiastes, x, 16.

Woe to that land that's governed by a child!

SHAKESPEARE, *Richard III.* Act ii, sc. 3, l. 11.

9
A cheel that can tell afore he can go
Is sure to have naught but sorrow and woe.

ELWORTHY, *West Somerset Word-Book,* 290. Cited as a common proverb.

10
Children and chicken must be always pickin'.

THOMAS FULLER, *Gnomologia.* No. 6078.

11
Bachelors' wives and maids' children be well taught.

JOHN HEYWOOD, *Proverbs.* Pt. ii, ch. 6. (1546)

The maid's child is ever best taught.

HUGH LATIMER, *Seven Sermons,* p. 138. (1549)

A bachelor's children are always young.

GEORGE ELIOT, *Felix Holt.* Ch. 22.

12
Nothing seems to have been more universally dreaded by the ancients than orbity, or want of children.

SAMUEL JOHNSON, *The Rambler.* No. 69.

13
Is it well with the child?

Old Testament: II Kings, iv, 26.

14
Children divine those who love them; it is a gift of nature which we lose as we grow up. (Les enfants devinent ceux qui les aiment; c'est un don de la nature que l'on perd en grandissant.)

PAUL DE KOCK, *L'Homme aux Trois Culottes.* Ch. 12.

And children know,
Instinctive taught, the friend and foe.

SCOTT, *The Lady of the Lake.* Canto ii, st. 14.

15
It were better for him that a millstone were hanged about his neck, and he cast into the sea, than that he should offend one of these little ones.

New Testament: Luke, xvii, 2.

Better to be driven out from among men than to be disliked of children.

R. H. DANA, *The Idle Man: Domestic Life.*

16
Of all people children are the most imaginative.

MACAULAY, *Essays: Milford's Greece.*

17
Suffer the little children to come unto me, and forbid them not; for of such is the kingdom of God.

New Testament: Mark, x, 14; *Luke,* xviii, 16.

Suffer little children, and forbid them not, to

come unto me; for of such is the kingdom of heaven.
New Testament: Matthew, xix, 14.

Whosoever therefore shall humble himself as this little child, the same is greatest in the kingdom of heaven.
New Testament: Matthew, xviii, 4.

For such a child I bless God, in whose bosom he is! May I and mine become as this little child.
JOHN EVELYN, *Diary,* 27 Jan., 1658.

Gentle Jesus, meek and mild,
Look upon a little child,
Pity my simplicity,
Suffer me to come to Thee.
CHARLES WESLEY, *Gentle Jesus.*

1
Ah, there are no children nowadays. (Ah, il n'y a plus d'enfants.)
MOLIÈRE, *Le Malade Imaginaire.* Act ii, sc. 8, l. 118.

2
Who knows the thoughts of a child?
NORA PERRY, *Who Knows?*

3
For a little child a little mourning.
JOHN RAY, *English Proverbs.* The French form is: "De petit enfant petit deuil." *See also* DEATH AND THE CHILD.

THE BURNT CHILD DREADS THE FIRE. *See under* EXPERIENCE.

II—Children: Blessings

4
Infantine Art divinely artless.
ROBERT BROWNING, *Red Cotton Night-cap Country.* Bk. ii.

5
A little curly-headed, good-for-nothing,
And mischief-making monkey from his birth.
BYRON, *Don Juan.* Canto i, st. 25.

6
In praise of little children I will say
God first made man, then found a better way
For woman, but his third way was the best.
Of all created things, the loveliest
And most divine are children.
WILLIAM CANTON, *Laus Infantium.*

7
Of all nature's gifts to the human race, what is sweeter to a man than his children? (Quid dulcius hominum generi ab natura datum est quam sui cuique liberi?)
CICERO, *Post Reditum ad Quirites.* Ch. i, sec. 2.

They are idols of hearts and of households;
They are angels of God in disguise;
The sunlight still sleeps in their tresses,
His glory still gleams in their eyes;
These truants from home and from Heaven,
They have made me more manly and mild;
And I know now how Jesus could liken
The kingdom of God to a child.
CHARLES M. DICKINSON, *The Children.*

8
Little children are still the symbol of the eternal marriage between love and duty.
GEORGE ELIOT, *Romola: Proem.*

9
Children are poor men's riches.
THOMAS FULLER, *Gnomologia.* No. 1094.

10
One laugh of a child will make the holiest day more sacred still.
R. G. INGERSOLL, *The Liberty of Man, Woman and Child.*

11
Ah! what would the world be to us
If the children were no more?
We should dread the desert behind us
Worse than the dark before.
LONGFELLOW, *Children.* St. 4.

Ye are better than all the ballads
That ever were sung or said;
For ye are living poems,
And all the rest are dead.
LONGFELLOW, *Children.* St. 9.

Between the dark and the daylight,
When the night is beginning to lower,
Comes a pause in the day's occupations,
That is known as the Children's Hour.
LONGFELLOW, *The Children's Hour.*

12
Lo, children are a heritage of the Lord: and the fruit of the womb is his reward. As arrows are in the hand of a mighty man; so are children of the youth. Happy is the man that hath his quiver full of them.
Old Testament: Psalms, cxxvii, 3–5.

Thy children like olive plants round about thy table.
Old Testament: Psalms, cxxviii, 3.

13
Children are the keys of Paradise.
R. H. STODDARD, *The Children's Prayer.*

If there is anything that will endure
The eye of God, because it still is pure,
It is the spirit of a little child,
Fresh from his hand, and therefore undefiled.
R. H. STODDARD, *The Children's Prayer.*

14
Where children are not, heaven is not.
SWINBURNE, *A Song of Welcome,* l. 37.

15
We need love's tender lessons taught
As only weakness can;
God hath His small interpreters;
The child must teach the man.
WHITTIER, *Child-Songs.*

16
O blessed vision! happy child!
Thou art so exquisitely wild,
I think of thee with many fears
For what may be thy lot in future years.
WORDSWORTH, *To Hartley Coleridge Six Years Old.*

III—Children: Curses

17
Children sweeten labours, but they make misfortunes more bitter: they increase the cares

of life, but they mitigate the remembrance of death.
BACON, *Essays: Of Parents and Children.*

1
Children reflect constant cares, but uncertain comforts.
RICHARD BRATHWAITE, *English Gentleman*, p. 27. (1641)

Besides, they always smell of bread and butter.
BYRON, *Beppo*. St. 39.

2
Children bring with them innumerable cares. (Innumeras curas secum adferunt liberi.)
ERASMUS, *Procus et Puella.*

3
He that hath children, all his morsels are not his own.
GEORGE HERBERT, *Jacula Prudentum.*

4
Children, ay, forsooth,
They bring their own love with them when they come,
But if they come not, there is peace and rest.
JEAN INGELOW, *Supper at the Mill.*

5
A rascal of a child—that age is without pity. (Un fripon d'enfant—cet age est sans pitié.)
LA FONTAINE, *Fables*. Bk. ix, fab. 2.

6
Alas! thrice wretched he who weds, though poor, And children gets.
(Ὦ τρισκακοδαίμων, ὅστις ὢν πένης γαμεῖ καὶ παιδοποιεῖθ'.)
MENANDER, *Plokion. Frag.* 404.

Unfortunate in truth the man, who poor
Yet children gets to share his poverty.
(Is demum infortunatas est homo,
Pauper qui educit in egestatem liberos.)
CÆCILIUS STATIUS, *Plocium*, l. 169.

7
Children blessings seem, but torments are;
When young, our folly, and when old, our fear.
THOMAS OTWAY, *Don Carlos.*

8
Little children, little sorrows; big children, big sorrows.
JOHN RAY, *English Proverbs.*

Children suck the mother when they are young, and the father when they are old.
JOHN RAY, *English Proverbs.*

Children when they are little make parents fools, when great, mad.
RICHARDSON, *Clarissa Harlowe*. Bk. iv, 120.

9
How many troubles are with children born!
Yet he that wants them counts himself forlorn.
SIR JOHN SCOT, *Verses*. (Drummond, tr.)

10
Briefly die their joys
That place them on the truth of girls and boys.
SHAKESPEARE, *Cymbeline*. Act v, sc. 5, l. 106.

11
How sharper than a serpent's tooth it is
To have a thankless child!
SHAKESPEARE, *King Lear*. Act i, sc. 4, l. 310.

Grieved I, I had but one?
Chid I for that at frugal nature's frame?
O, one too much by thee! Why had I one?
SHAKESPEARE, *Much Ado About Nothing*. Act iv, sc. 1, l. 129.

Wife, we scarce thought us blest
That God had lent us but this only child;
But now I see this one is one too much.
SHAKESPEARE, *Romeo and Juliet*. Act iii, sc. 5, l. 165.

12
Unruly children make their sire Stoop.
SHAKESPEARE, *Richard II*. Act iii, sc. 4, l. 30.

Your children were vexation to your youth,
But mine shall be a comfort to your age.
SHAKESPEARE, *Richard III*. Act iv, sc. 4, l. 305.

13
Children are a torment and nothing more.
LEO TOLSTOY, *The Kreutzer Sonata*. Ch. 14.

IV—Children: Their Behavior

14
Eat no green apples or you'll droop,
Be careful not to get the croup,
Avoid the chicken-pox and such,
And don't fall out of windows much.
EDWARD ANTHONY, *Advice to Small Children.*

15
In silence I must take my seat, . . .
I must not speak a useless word,
For children must be seen, not heard.
B. W. BELLAMY, *Open Sesame*. Vol. i, p. 167. Quoted as from *Table Rules for Little Folks.*

16
Children use the fist
Until they are of age to use the brain.
E. B. BROWNING, *Casa Guidi Windows*. Pt. i, l. 685.

17
When children stand still,
They have done some ill.
A. B. CHEALES, *Proverbial Folk-Lore*, 47.

When children are doing nothing, they are doing mischief.
FIELDING, *Tom Jones*. Bk. xv, ch. 2.

18
The dutifulness of children is the foundation of all virtues. (Pietas fundamentum est omnium virtutum.)
CICERO, *Pro Cnœo Plancio*. Ch. xii, sec. 29.

19
Speak when you are spoken to, come when you are called.
THOMAS FULLER, *Gnomologia*. No. 4244.

Come when you're called,
And do as you're bid;
Shut the door after you,
And you'll never be chid.
MARIA EDGEWORTH, *The Contrast*. Ch. 1.

20
Alas! regardless of their doom,
The little victims play;

No sense have they of ills to come,
  Nor care beyond to-day.
  GRAY, *On a Distant Prospect of Eton College.*

Children think not of what is past, nor what is to come, but enjoy the present time, which few of us do.
  LA BRUYÈRE, *Les Caractères: De L'Homme.*

1
Then wicked children wake and weep,
  And wish the long black gloom av ay;
But good ones love the dark, and find
  The night as pleasant as the day.
  THOMAS HOOD, *Queen Mab.*

2
Even a child is known by his doings.
  Old Testament: Proverbs, xx, 11.

3
How pleasant is Saturday night,
  When I've tried all the week to be good,
Not spoken a word that is bad,
  And obliged every one that I could.
  NANCY DENNIS SPROAT, *How Pleasant is Saturday Night.*

4
Cruel children, crying babies,
All grow up as geese and gabies,
Hated, as their age increases,
By their nephews and their nieces.
  R. L. STEVENSON, *Good and Bad Children.*

5
When I am grown to man's estate
I shall be very proud and great,
And tell the other girls and boys
Not to meddle with my toys.
  R. L. STEVENSON, *Looking Forward.*

6
The child that is not clean and neat,
With lots of toys and things to eat,
He is a naughty child, I'm sure—
Or else his dear papa is poor.
  R. L. STEVENSON, *System.*

7
It is very nice to think
The world is full of meat and drink,
With little children saying grace
In every Christian kind of place.
  R. L. STEVENSON, *A Thought.*

8
A child should always say what's true
And speak when he is spoken to,
And behave mannerly at table;
At least as far as he is able.
  R. L. STEVENSON, *Whole Duty of Children.*

9
Let dogs delight to bark and bite,
  For God hath made them so;
Let bears and lions growl and fight,
  For 'tis their nature, too.

But, children, you should never let
  Such angry passions rise;
Your little hands were never made
  To tear each other's eyes.
  ISAAC WATTS, *Against Quarrelling and Fighting.* The last word of the fourth line is persistently misquoted "to."

  'Tis a shameful sight,
When children of one family
  Fall out, and chide, and fight.
  ISAAC WATTS, *Love Between Brothers and Sisters.*

10
While others early learn to swear,
  And curse, and lie, and steal;
Lord, I am taught Thy name to fear,
  And do Thy holy will.
  ISAAC WATTS, *Praise for Mercies Spiritual and Temporal.*

V—Children: Their Training

See also Education of Children

11
You can do anything with children if you only play with them.
  BISMARCK, *Sayings of Bismarck.*

12
  Women know
The way to rear up children (to be just);
They know a simple, merry, tender knack
Of tying sashes, fitting baby-shoes,
And stringing pretty words that make no sense,
And kissing full sense into empty words;
Which things are corals to cut life upon,
Although such trifles.
  E. B. BROWNING, *Aurora Leigh.* Bk. i, l. 48.

He that cockers his child provides for his enemy.
  GEORGE HERBERT, *Jacula Prudentum.*

A spoilt child never loves its mother.
  SIR HENRY TAYLOR, *Notes from Life,* p. 123.

13
  Go practise if you please
With men and women: leave a child alone
For Christ's particular love's sake!
  ROBERT BROWNING, *The Ring and the Book.* Pt. iii, l. 88.

14
Speak roughly to your little boy,
  And beat him when he sneezes:
He only does it to annoy,
  Because he knows it teases.
  LEWIS CARROLL, *Alice's Adventures in Wonderland.* Ch. 6.

15
Respect the child. Be not too much his parent. Trespass not on his solitude.
  EMERSON, *Lectures and Biographical Sketches: Education.*

16
Let thy child's first lesson be obedience, and the second will be what thou wilt.
  BENJAMIN FRANKLIN, *Poor Richard.*

17
Children learn to creep ere they can learn to go.
  JOHN HEYWOOD, *Proverbs.* Pt. i, ch. 11.

The wee birdie fa's when it tries ower soon to flee,
Folks are sure to tumble, when they climb ower hie;

They wha cannot walk right are sure to come to wrang,
Creep awa', my bairnie, creep afore ye gang.
JAMES BALLANTINE, *Creep Afore Ye Gang.*

1
Children have more need of models than of critics. (Les enfants ont plus besoin de modèles que de critiques.)
JOUBERT, *Pensées.* No. 261.

2
Whilst that the child is young, let him be instructed in virtue and literature.
JOHN LYLY, *Euphues: Of the Education of Youth.*

Just as the twig is bent the tree's inclined.
POPE, *Moral Essays.* Epis. i, l. 150.
See also under TREE.

3
Give thy child what he will crave,
And thy whelp what he will have,
Then mayst thou make you a stounde,
A foul child and a fair hounde.
ROBERT MANNYNG (ROBERT DE BRUNNE), *Handlyng Synne,* l. 7240. (1303)

Give a child his will and a whelp his fill,
Both will surely turn out ill.
C. H. SPURGEON, *Ploughman's Pictures,* p. 70.

4
Children are to be won to follow liberal studies by exhortations and rational motives and on no account to be forced thereto by whipping.
PLUTARCH, *Of the Training of Children.*

Those that do teach young babes
Do it with gentle means and easy tasks.
SHAKESPEARE, *Othello.* Act iv, sc. 2, l. 111.

5
Train up a child in the way he should go; and when he is old, he will not depart from it.
Old Testament: Proverbs, xxii, 6.

6
Why does the nurse tell the child of Rawhead and Bloody-bones? To keep it in awe.
JOHN SELDEN, *Table-Talk: Priests of Rome.*

7
Better a little chiding than a great deal of heart-break.
SHAKESPEARE, *The Merry Wives of Windsor.* Act v, sc. 3, l. 11.

8
It is better to bind your children to you by respect and gentleness, than by fear. (Pudore et liberalitate liberos Retinere satius esse credo quam metu.)
TERENCE, *Adelphi,* l. 57. (Act i, sc. 1.)

9
As each one wishes his children to be, so they are. (Ut quisque suom volt esse, itast.)
TERENCE, *Adelphi,* l. 399. (Act iii, sc. 3.)

VI—Children: Spare the Rod and Spoil the Child

10
Diogenes struck the father when the son swore.
ROBERT BURTON, *Anatomy of Melancholy.* Pt. iii, sec. ii, mem. 2, subs. 5.

11
O ye! who teach the ingenuous youth of nations,
Holland, France, England, Germany, or Spain,
I pray ye flog them upon all occasions,
It mends their morals, never mind the pain.
BYRON, *Don Juan.* Canto ii, st. 1.

12
He that will not use the rod on his child, his child shall be used as a rod on him.
THOMAS FULLER, *The Holy State: The Good Parent.*

Better the child should cry than the father. (Es ist besser das Kind weine, denn der Vater.)
UNKNOWN. A German proverb.

13
He never spoils the child and spares the rod,
But spoils the rod, and never spares the child.
THOMAS HOOD, *The Irish Schoolmaster.* St. 12.

That sour tree of knowledge—now a birch.
THOMAS HOOD, *The Irish Schoolmaster.* St. 6.

There is now less flogging in our great schools than formerly,—but then less is learned there; so that what the boys get at one end they lose at the other.
SAMUEL JOHNSON. (BOSWELL, *Life,* 1775.)

14
Whoso spareth the spring spoileth his children.
WILLIAM LANGLAND, *Piers Plowman.* Passus v, l. 41. (1377)

They spare the rod and spoil the child.
RALPH VENNING, *Mysteries and Revelations,* p. 5. (1649)

Spare the rod and spoil the child.
BUTLER, *Hudibras.* Pt. ii, canto i, l. 844. (1664)

15
The man that's ne'er been flogged has ne'er been taught. (Ὁ μὴ δαρεὶς ἄνθρωπος οὐ παιδεύεται.)
MENANDER, *Rapizomene.* Frag. 422. (*The Girl Who Gets Flogged.*)

16
He that spareth his rod hateth his son.
Old Testament: Proverbs, xiii, 24.

As he spared his rod, he hated his child.
ÆLFRIC, *Homilies.* Bk. ii, l. 324. (c. 1000)

Who spareth the yard hateth the child. (Qui parsit virge odit filium.)
UNKNOWN, *Governance of Princes,* 161. (1422) Quoted as a precept of Solomon.

17
If you strike a child, take care that you strike it in anger, even at the risk of maiming it for life. A blow in cold blood neither can nor should be forgiven.
BERNARD SHAW, *Maxims for Revolutionists.*

18
There is nothing that more displeaseth God,
Than from their children to spare the rod.
JOHN SKELTON, *Magnyfycence,* l. 1954.

VII—Children: Little Pitchers

1
Teach your child to hold his tongue; he'll learn fast enough to speak.
BENJAMIN FRANKLIN, *Poor Richard*, 1734.

2
Children have wide ears and long tongues.
THOMAS FULLER, *Gnomologia*. No. 1097.

3
The child says nothing but what it heard by the fire.
GEORGE HERBERT, *Jacula Prudentum*.

4
Avoid your children: small pitchers have wide ears.
JOHN HEYWOOD, *Proverbs*. Pt. ii, ch. 5. (1546)

Pitchers have ears, and I have many servants.
JOHN LACY, *Sauny the Scot*. Pt. iv.

Pitchers have ears.
SHAKESPEARE, *The Taming of the Shrew*. Act iv, sc. 4, l. 52. *Richard III*. Act ii, sc. 4, l. 37.

5
Children pick up words as pigeons peas,
And utter them again as God shall please.
JOHN RAY, *English Proverbs*, 213. (1670)

VIII—Children and Parents

See also Father, Mother, Parents

6
"Late children," says the Spanish proverb, "are early orphans."
BENJAMIN FRANKLIN, *Letter to John Alleyn*, on early marriages.

7
Happy is he that is happy in his children.
THOMAS FULLER, *Gnomologia*. No. 1787.

8
He that wipes the child's nose kisseth the mother's cheek.
GEORGE HERBERT, *Jacula Prudentum*.

9
Lost in the children of the present spouse,
They slight the pledges of their former vows.
HOMER, *Odyssey*. Bk. xv, l. 25. (Pope, tr.)

Put another man's child in your bosom and he'll creep out at your elbow.
JOHN RAY, *English Proverbs*.

10
This child is not mine as the first was,
I cannot sing it to rest,
I cannot lift it up fatherly
And bliss it upon my breast:
Yet it lies in my little one's cradle
And sits in my little one's chair,
And the light of the heaven she's gone to
Transfigures its golden hair.
J. R. LOWELL, *The Changeling*.

11
Never a head is dimmed with gray but another is sunned with curls;
She was a girl and he was a boy, but yet there are boys and girls.
COSMO MONKHOUSE, *A Dead March*.

12
A mother's pride, a father's joy.
WALTER SCOTT, *Rokeby*. Canto iii, st. 15.

13
A child and weak,
Mine, a delight to no man, sweet to me.
SWINBURNE, *Atalanta in Calydon*.

14
Oh, how very thankful I always should be,
That I have kind parents to watch over me,
Who teach me from wickedness ever to flee!
ANN AND JANE TAYLOR, *Poor Children*.

15
Children begin by loving their parents. After a time they judge them. Rarely, if ever, do they forgive them.
OSCAR WILDE, *A Woman of No Importance*. Act ii.

16
And when with envy time transported,
Shall think to rob us of ou. joys,
You'll in your girls again be courted,
And I'll go wooing in my boys.
UNKNOWN, *Winifreda*. Claimed for Gilbert Cooper by JOHN AIKIN (*Collection of English Songs*) and WALTER THORNBURY (*Two Centuries of Song*). First appeared in *Miscellaneous Poems by Several Hands*, 1726. Included in PERCY'S *Reliques*, bk. iii, No. 13.

IX—Children: The Lad That Is Gone

17
When I was as you are now, towering in the confidence of twenty-one, little did I suspect that I should be at forty-nine, what I now am.
SAMUEL JOHNSON, *Letter to Bennet Langton*. (BOSWELL, *Life*, 1758.)

18
Across the fields of yesterday
He sometimes comes to me,
A little lad just back from play—
The lad I used to be.

And yet he smiles so wistfully
Once he has crept within,
I wonder if he hopes to see
The man I might have been.
THOMAS S. JONES, JR., *Sometimes*.

19
Each one has been a little child,
A little child with laughing look,
A lovely white unwritten book;
A book that God will take, my friend,
As each goes out at journey's end.
JOHN MASEFIELD, *The Everlasting Mercy*. St. 27.

20
Where is the promise of my years,
Once written on my brow?
Ere errors, agonies, and fears
Brought with them all that speaks in tears,
Ere I had sunk beneath my peers;
Where sleeps that promise now?
ADAH ISAACS MENKEN, *Infelix*.

21
How different is the man you are from the

child you were. (Dissimiles hic vir et ille puer.)
OVID, *Heroides*. Epis. ix, l. 24.

1
Looking on the lines
Of my boy's face, methoughts I did recoil
Twenty-three years, and saw myself unbreech'd,
In my green velvet coat, my dagger muzzled,
Lest it should bite its master, and so prove,
As ornaments oft do, too dangerous.
SHAKESPEARE, *Winter's Tale*. Act i, sc. 2, l. 153.

2
Sing me a song of a lad that is gone;
Say, could that lad be I?
Merry of soul he sailed on a day
Over the sea to Skye.
R. L. STEVENSON, *A Lad That is Gone*.

3 I called the boy to my knee one day,
And I said: "You're just past four;
Will you laugh in the same lighthearted way
When you've turned, say, thirty more?"
Then I thought of a past I'd fain erase—
More clouded skies than blue—
And I anxiously peered in his upturned face
For it seemed to say: "Did you?"
CARL WERNER, *The Questioner*.

4
But still I dream that somewhere there must be
The spirit of a child that waits for me.
BAYARD TAYLOR, *The Poet's Journal: Third Evening*.

CHIVALRY

5
The world's male chivalry has perished out,
But women are knight-errants to the last.
E. B. BROWNING, *Aurora Leigh*. Bk. vii, l. 224.

6
The age of chivalry is gone; that of sophisters, economists, and calculators has succeeded.
EDMUND BURKE, *Reflections on the Revolution in France*.

The unbought grace of life, the cheap defence of nations, the nurse of manly sentiment and heroic enterprise, is gone!
BURKE, *Reflections on the Revolution in France*.

"The age of chivalry is past," said Miss Dacre. "Bores have succeeded to dragons."
BENJAMIN DISRAELI, *Young Duke*. Bk. ii, ch. 5.

Some say that the age of chivalry is past, that the spirit of romance is dead. The age of chivalry is never past so long as there is a wrong left unredressed on earth.
CHARLES KINGSLEY, *Life*. Vol. ii, ch. 28.

For now I see the true old times are dead,
When every morning brought a noble chance,
And every chance brought out a noble knight.
TENNYSON, *The Passing of Arthur*, l. 397.

7
The Knight of the Rueful Countenance. (El Caballero de la Triste Figura)
CERVANTES, *Don Quixote*. Pt. i, ch. 19. *See also* CERVANTES.

8
A Knight there was, and that a worthy man,
That from the time that he first began
To riden out, he loved chivalry,
Truth and honour, freedom and courtesy. . . .
And though that he was worthy, he was wise,
And of his port as meek as is a maid.
He never yet no villany had said
In all his life, unto no manner wight.
He was a very parfit gentle knight.
CHAUCER, *Canterbury Tales: Prologue*, l. 43.

The Knight's bones are dust,
And his good sword rust;—
His soul is with the saints, I trust.
S. T. COLERIDGE, *The Knight's Tomb*.

9
The whole of heraldry and of chivalry is in courtesy.
EMERSON, *Essays, First Series: History*.

10
And hearts were soft, though blows were hard;
But when the fight was over,
A brimming goblet cheered the board,
His Lady's smile the lover.
EDWARD FITZGERALD, *Chivalry at a Discount*.

11
Chivalry is an ingredient
Sadly lacking in our land.
Sir, I am your most obedient,
Most obedient to command!
W. S. GILBERT, *The Sorcerer*. Act i.

12
He loved the twilight that surrounds
The border-land of old romance;
Where glitter hauberk, helm, and lance,
And banner waves, and trumpet sounds,
And ladies ride with hawk on wrist,
And mighty warriors sweep along,
Magnified by the purple mist,
The dusk of centuries and of song.
LONGFELLOW, *Tales of a Wayside Inn*: Pt. i, *Prelude*, l. 130.

13
Forward, each gentleman and knight!
Let gentle blood show generous might,
And chivalry redeem the fight!
SCOTT, *The Lord of the Isles*. Canto vi, st. 24.

For lady's suit, and minstrel's strain,
By knight should ne'er be heard in vain.
SCOTT, *Marmion*. Canto i, st. 13.

14
His square-turned joints, and strength of limb,
Showed him no carpet knight so trim,
But, in close fight, a champion grim,
In camps, a leader sage.
SCOTT, *Marmion*. Canto i, st. 5.

For CARPET KNIGHT, *see under* FOP.

1
So faithful in love, and so dauntless in war,
There never was knight like the young Lochinvar.
SCOTT, *Marmion*. Canto v, st. 12.

2
Dread thou to speak presumptuous doom
On noble Marmion's lowly tomb;
But say, "He died a gallant knight,
With sword in hand, for England's right."
SCOTT, *Marmion*. Canto vi, st. 37.

3
I may speak it to my shame,
I have a truant been to chivalry.
SHAKESPEARE, *I Henry IV*. Act v, sc. 1, l. 94.

4
And there at Venice gave
His body to that pleasant country's earth,
And his pure soul unto his captain Christ,
Under whose colours he had fought so long.
SHAKESPEARE, *Richard II*. Act iv, sc. 1, l. 97.

And on his breast a bloody cross he bore,
The dear remembrance of his dying Lord,
For whose sweet sake that glorious badge he wore.
SPENSER, *Faerie Queene*. Bk. i, canto i, st. 2.

For I was of Christ's choosing, I God's knight,
No blinkard heathen stumbling for scant light.
SWINBURNE, *Laus Veneris*. St. 53.

5
A true knight,
Not yet mature, yet matchless, firm of word,
Speaking in deeds and deedless in his tongue;
Not soon provoked nor being provoked soon calm'd;
His heart and hand both open and both free.
SHAKESPEARE, *Troilus and Cressida*. Act iv, sc. 5, l. 96.

6
Thy necessity is yet greater than mine.
SIR PHILIP SIDNEY, handing to a wounded soldier a bottle of water which had been brought him to allay his burning thirst, as he was being carried, mortally wounded, from the battlefield of Zutphen, 22 Sept., 1586. (GREVILLE, *Life of Sidney;* HUME, *History of England*. Ch. 18.)

As he was putting the bottle to his mouth, he saw a poor Soldier carried along, who had eaten his last at the same Feast, ghastly casting up his eyes at the bottle. Which Sir Philip perceiving, took it from his head before he drank, and delivered it to the poor man with these words, Thy necessity is yet greater than mine. And when he had pledged this poor soldier, he was presently carried to Arnheim.
SIR FULKE GREVILLE, *Life of Sidney*.

Battles nor songs can from oblivion save,
But Fame upon a white deed loves to build:
From out that cup of water Sidney gave,
Not one drop has been spilled.
LIZETTE WOODWORTH REESE, *Immortality*.

Ay, not yet may the land forget that bore and loved thee and praised and wept,
Sidney, lord of the stainless sword, the name of names that her heart's love kept.
SWINBURNE, *Astrophel*. Pt. ii, l. 4. After reading Sidney's *Arcadia*.

7
A gentle knight was pricking on the plain.
SPENSER, *Faerie Queene*. Bk. i, canto i, st. 1.

Yet was he but a squire of low degree.
SPENSER, *Faerie Queene*. Bk. iv, canto vii, st. 15.

8
A kingly flower of knights, a sunflower,
That shone against the sunlight like the sun.
SWINBURNE, *The Complaint of Lisa*.

9
And indeed he seems to me
Scarce other than my own ideal knight,
"Who reverenced his conscience as his king;
Whose glory was, redressing human wrong;
Who spake no slander, no, nor listened to it."
TENNYSON, *Idylls of the King: Dedication*, l. 6.

10
Oh for a knight like Bayard,
Without reproach or fear;
My light glove on his casque of steel,
My love-knot on his spear!
J. G. WHITTIER, *The Hero*.

11
Who passes by this road so late?
Compagnon de la Majolaine!
Who passes by this road so late?
Always gay!
Of all the king's knights 'tis the flower,
Compagnon de la Majolaine,
Of all the king's knights 'tis the flower,
Always gay!
UNKNOWN, *Compagnon de la Majolaine*. An old French song quoted by DICKENS, *Little Dorrit*. Ch. 1.

12
Knight without fear and without reproach.
(Chevalier sans peur et sans reproche.)
Applied to PIERRE DU TERRAIL, CHEVALIER DE BAYARD.

Mourn, Columbia! for one of thy brightest stars has set, a son without fear and without reproach.
UNKNOWN, *National Intelligencer*, 24 Mar., 1820, on the death of Stephen Decatur, as the result of a duel with Capt. Barron.

CHOICE

13
My death and life,
My bane and antidote, are both before me.
ADDISON, *Cato*. Act v, sc. 1.

14
White shall not neutralize the black, nor good
Compensate bad in man, absolve him so:
Life's business being just the terrible choice.
BROWNING, *The Ring and the Book: The Pope*, l. 1236.

15
The strongest principle of growth lies in human choice.
GEORGE ELIOT, *Daniel Deronda*. Bk. vi, ch. 42.

16
God offers to every mind its choice between truth and repose.
EMERSON, *Essays, First Series: Intellect*.

And but two ways are offered to our will,
Toil with rare triumph, ease with safe disgrace,
The problem still for us and all of human race.
LOWELL, *Under the Old Elm*. Pt. vii, st. 3.

1
I say, do not choose.
EMERSON, *Essays, First Series: Spiritual Laws*.

2
Everything has two handles, by one of which it ought to be carried and by the other not. (Πᾶν πρᾶγμα δύο ἔχει λαβάς, τὴν μὲν φορητήν, τὴν δὲ ἀφόρητον.)
EPICTETUS, *Encheiridion*. Sec. 43. Quoted by BURTON, *Anatomy of Melancholy*, ii, 2, 3.

3
The king of Babylon stood at the parting of the way.
Old Testament: Ezekiel, xxi, 21.

4
Any color, so long as it's red,
Is the color that suits me best,
Though I will allow there is much to be said
For yellow and green and the rest.
EUGENE FIELD, *Red*.

5
But it is said and ever shall,
Between two stools lieth the fall.
JOHN GOWER, *Confessio Amantis: Prologue*, l. 336. (1390)

While between two stools, my tail go to the ground.
JOHN HEYWOOD, *Proverbs*. Pt. i, ch. 3. (1546)

One falls to the ground in trying to sit between two stools. (S'asseoir entre deux selles le cul à terre.)
RABELAIS, *Works*. Bk. i, ch. 2.

6
Or fight or fly,
This choice is left you to resist or die.
HOMER, *Odyssey*. Bk. xxii, l. 79. (Pope, tr.)

7
God had sifted three kingdoms to find the wheat for this planting.
LONGFELLOW, *The Courtship of Miles Standish*. Pt. iv, st. 8.

God sifted a whole nation that he might send choice grain over into this wilderness.
WILLIAM STOUGHTON, *Election Sermon*. Boston, 29 April, 1669.

8
But one thing is needful; and Mary hath chosen that good part, which shall not be taken away from her.
New Testament: Luke, x, 42.

The Sons of Mary seldom bother, for they have inherited that good part;
But the Sons of Martha favour their Mother of the careful soul and the troubled heart.
KIPLING, *The Sons of Martha*. See 2232:7.

9
Where there is no choice, we do well to make no difficulty.
GEORGE MACDONALD, *Sir Gibbie*. Ch. xi.

10
I never knows the children. It's just six of one and half-a-dozen of the other.
FREDERICK MARRYAT, *The Pirate*. Ch. iv.

11
Many are called but few are chosen.
New Testament: Matthew, xxii, 14.

12
Rather than be less
Car'd not to be at all.
MILTON, *Paradise Lost*. Bk. ii, l. 47.

13
The difficulty in life is the choice.
GEORGE MOORE, *Bending of the Bough*. Act iv.

14
There's small choice in rotten apples.
SHAKESPEARE, *Taming of the Shrew*. Act i, sc. 1, l. 138.

15
There is such a choice of difficulties that I am myself at a loss how to determine.
JAMES WOLFE, *Despatch*, to Pitt, 2 Sept., 1759.

16
Hobson's choice.
Tobias Hobson (d. 1630) was the first man in England that let out hackney horses. When a man came for a horse, he was led into the stable, where there was a great choice, but he obliged him to take the horse that stood next to the stable-door; . . . from whence it became a proverb when what ought to be your election was forced upon you, to say, "Hobson's choice."—RICHARD STEELE, *The Spectator*, No. 509. Hobson's first name was really Thomas, he was born in 1544, and died at Cambridge in 1631.

Where to elect there is but one,
'Tis Hobson's choice,—take that or none.
THOMAS WARD, *England's Reformation*. Ch. 4. (1630)

II—Choice: Of Evils

17
Of evils we must choose the least. (Τὰ ἐλάχιστα ληπτέον τῶν κακῶν.)
ARISTOTLE, *Nicomachean Ethics*. Bk. ii, ch. 9, sec. 4. Quoted as a saying.

Of harmes two the less is for to choose.
CHAUCER, *Troilus and Criseyde*. Bk. ii, l. 470.

Of two evils, the lesser should be chosen. (E duobus malis minimum eligendum.)
ERASMUS, *Adagia*.

Of two evils we take the less.
RICHARD HOOKER, *Laws of Ecclesiastical Polity*. Bk. v, ch. 81.

Of two evils, the less is always to be chosen. (De duobus malis, minus est semper eligendum.)
THOMAS À KEMPIS, *De Imitatione Christi*. Bk. iii, ch. 13, sec. 3.

18
I have learned from philosophers that among evils one ought not only to choose the least. but also to extract even from these any element of good that they may contain. (Quia sic ab hominibus doctis accepimus, non solum ex malis eligere minima oportere, sed etiam excerpere ex his ipsis, si quid inesset boni.)
CICERO, *De Officiis*. Bk. iii, ch. 1, sec. 3.

1
Life too often presents us with a choice of evils, rather than of goods.
C. C. COLTON, *Lacon*. Vol. ii, No. 102.

When better choices are not to be had,
We needs must take the seeming best of bad.
SAMUEL DANIEL, *The History of the Civil War*. Bk. ii, st. 24.

2
When compelled to choose one of two evils, no one will choose the greater when he may choose the lesser. ("Οταν τε ἀναγκασθῇ δυοῖν κακοῖν, τὸ ἕτερον αἱρεῖσθαι, οὐδεὶς τὸ μεῖζον αἱρήσεται εξὸν τὸ ἔλαττον.)
SOCRATES. (PLATO, *Protagoras*. Sec. 358 D.)

3
Of two evils, choose neither.
C. H. SPURGEON, *John Ploughman*.

CHRIST

I—Christ: His Birth

4
Trumpets! Lightnings! The earth trembles! But into the Virgin's womb thou didst descend with noiseless tread.
AGATHIAS SCHOLASTICUS, *On the Birth of Christ*. (*Greek Anthology*. Bk. i, epig. 37.)

The manger is Heaven, yes, greater than Heaven.
Heaven is the handiwork of this child.
AGATHIAS SCHOLASTICUS, *On the Birth of Christ*. (*Greek Anthology*. Bk. i, epig. 38.)

5
Of the offspring of the gentleman Jafeth come Abraham, Moses, Aaron, and the prophets, also the King of the right line of Mary, of whom that gentleman Jesus was borne.
JULIANA BERNERS, *Blasyng of Armys*. (c. 1375)

Welcome, all wonders in one sight!
Eternity shut in a span!
Summer in Winter, Day in Night!
Heaven in earth, and God in man!
Great little One! whose all-embracing birth
Lifts Earth to Heaven, stoops Heaven to Earth.
RICHARD CRASHAW, *In the Holy Nativity of Our Lord God*.

6
To work a wonder, God would have her shown,
At once, a Bud, and yet a Rose full-blown.
ROBERT HERRICK, *The Virgin Mary*.

7
Behold, a virgin shall conceive and bear a son, and shall call his name Immanuel.
Old Testament: Isaiah, vii, 14.

Now all this was done, that it might be fulfilled which was spoken of the Lord by the prophet, saying, Behold, a virgin shall be with child, and shall bring forth a son, and they shall call his name Emmanuel, which being interpreted is, God with us.
New Testament: Matthew, i, 23.

8
He is despised and rejected of men: a man of sorrows, and acquainted with grief.
Old Testament: Isaiah, liii, 3.

9
"Isn't this Joseph's son?"—ay, it is He;
Joseph the carpenter—same trade as me.
CATHERINE C. LIDDELL, *Jesus the Carpenter*.

10
A virgin shall conceive, a virgin bear a son!
From Jesse's root behold a branch arise,
Whose sacred flower with fragrance fills the skies.
POPE, *Messiah*, l. 8.

Hark! a glad voice the lonely desert cheers:
Prepare the way! a God, a God appears!
A God, a God! the vocal hills reply;
The rocks proclaim th' approaching Deity.
Lo, earth receives him from the bending skies!
Sink down, ye mountains, and, ye valleys, rise;
With heads declin'd, ye cedars, homage pay;
Be smooth, ye rocks; ye rapid floods, give way!
The Saviour comes, by ancient bards foretold!
Hear him, ye deaf, and all ye blind, behold!
POPE, *Messiah*, l. 29.

Now the Virgin returns, and the reign of Saturn;
Now descends from heaven a new generation. . . .
His shall be the gift of life divine.
(Jam redit et Virgo, redeunt Saturnia regna;
Jam nova progenies cælo demittitur alto. . . .
Ille deum vitam accipiet.)
VERGIL, *Eclogues*. No. iv, l. 6. Referring to Astrea, or Justice, last of the immortals to leave the earth.

11
Little Jesus, was Thou shy
Once, and just so small as I?
And what did it feel like to be
Out of Heaven, and just like me?
FRANCIS THOMPSON, *Ex Ore Infantium*.

The Christ-child stood at Mary's knee,
His hair was like a crown,
And all the flowers looked up at Him,
And all the stars looked down.
G. K. CHESTERTON, *A Christmas Carol*.

12
Mother and maiden Was never none but she!
Well might such a lady God's mother be.
UNKNOWN, *A Carol*.

II—Christ: His Life

13
The best of men
That e'er wore earth about him was a sufferer;
A soft, meek, patient, humble, tranquil spirit,
The first true gentleman that ever breathed.
THOMAS DEKKER, *The Honest Whore*. Pt. i, act 1, sc. 12. (In some editions Pt. i, act v, sc. 2.)

14
Then came Jesus forth, wearing the crown of thorns and the purple robe. And Pilate saith unto them, Behold the man! (Ecce homo.)
New Testament: John, xix, 5.

15
Into the woods my Master went,
Clean forspent, forspent.
Into the woods my Master came,
Forspent with love and shame.
SIDNEY LANIER, *Ballad of Trees and the Master*.

16
It is I; be not afraid.
New Testament: Matthew, xiv, 27.

1
Two thousand years ago there was One here on this earth who lived the grandest life that ever has been lived yet,—a life that every thinking man, with deeper or shallower meaning, has agreed to call divine.

F. W. ROBERTSON, *Lectures and Addresses: Skeptical Publications.*

2
He went about, he was so kind,
To cure poor people who were blind;
And many who were sick and lame,
He pitied them and did the same.

ANN AND JANE TAYLOR, *About Jesus Christ.*

III—Christ: His Death

3
There is a green hill far away,
Without a city wall,
Where the dear Lord was crucified,
Who died to save us all.

CECIL FRANCES ALEXANDER, *There Is a Green Hill.*

4
Now he is dead. Far hence he lies
In the lorn Syrian town;
And on his grave, with shining eyes,
The Syrian stars look down.

MATTHEW ARNOLD, *Obermann Once More,* l. 173.

Where Life was slain and Truth was slandered
On that one holier hill than Rome.

G. K. CHESTERTON, *To F. C. in Memoriam Palestine.*

Lovely was the death
Of Him whose Life was Love!

S. T. COLERIDGE, *Religious Musings,* l. 29.

5
When Jesus came to Golgotha,
They hanged him on a tree,
They drove great nails through hands and feet,
And made a Calvary;
They crowned him with a crown of thorns,
Red were his wounds and deep,
For those were crude and cruel days,
And human flesh was cheap.

G. A. STUDDERT-KENNEDY, *Indifference.*

6
By the Cross, on which suspended,
With his bleeding hands extended,
Hung that Son she so adored,
Stood the mournful Mother weeping,
She whose heart, its silence keeping,
Grief had cleft as with a sword.

(Stabat mater dolorosa
Iuxta crucem lacrimosa,
Dum pendebat filius,
Cuius animam gementem,
Contristantem et dolentem
Pertransivit gladius.)

JACOPONE DA TODI, *Stabat Mater.* (D. F. Maccarthy, tr.)

7
The man, the Christ, the soldier.
Who from his cross of pain
Cried to the dying comrade,
"Lad, we shall meet again!"

WILLARD WATTLES, *Comrades of the Cross.*

8
Had Christ the death of death to death
Not given death by dying,
The gates of life had never been
To mortals open lying.

UNKNOWN, *Epitaph.* On tombstone in Castle-Camps churchyard, Cambridgeshire, England.

Death when to death a death by death hath given
Then shall be oped the long-shut gates of Heaven.
(Mors, mortis morti mortem nisi morte dedisset.)

THOMAS HEYWOOD, *Of the Sybells.*

9
God bought men here with His heart's blood expense;
And man sold God here for base thirty pence.

ROBERT HERRICK, *God's Price and Man's Price.*

Betrayer of the Master,
He sways against the sky
A black and broken body,
Iscariot—or I?

CAROLINE GILTINAN, *Identity.*

IV—Christ: His Influence

10
Speak low to me, my Saviour, low and sweet
From out the hallelujahs, sweet and low,
Lest I should fear and fall, and miss Thee so
Who art not missed by any that entreat.

E. B. BROWNING, *Comfort.*

11
In every pang that rends the heart
The Man of Sorrows has a part.

MICHAEL BRUCE, *Christ Ascended.*

12
The difference between Socrates and Jesus Christ? The great Conscious; the immeasurably great Unconscious.

THOMAS CARLYLE, *Journal,* 28 Oct., 1833.

13
He was the Word, that spake it;
He took the bread and brake it;
And what that Word did make it,
I do believe and take it.

JOHN DONNE, *On the Sacrament.* (1633)

Christ was the word that spake it;
He took the bread and brake it;
And what that word did make it,
That I believe and take it.

Attributed to QUEEN ELIZABETH, of England, when, before her coronation in 1558, twenty-five years before Donne was born, she parried the question of a Catholic priest as to whether she believed in the real Presence in the communion bread.

14
The vine-wreathed god
Rising, a stifled question from the silence,
Fronts the pierced Image with the crown of thorns.

GEORGE ELIOT, *Spanish Gypsy.* Bk. i, l. 103.

1
Christ preached the greatness of man: We preach the greatness of Christ. The first is affirmative; the last negative.
EMERSON, *Journals,* 1867.

2
Jesus, whose name is not so much written as ploughed into the history of this world.
EMERSON, *Nature, Addresses, and Lectures: Address.*

3
Jesus was Jesus because he refused to listen to another and listened at home.
EMERSON, *Uncollected Lectures: Natural Religion;* also *The Sovereignty of Ethics.*

An era in human history is the life of Jesus, and its immense influence for good leaves all the perversion and superstition that has accrued almost harmless.
EMERSON, *Uncollected Lectures: Natural Religion.*

4
He is a path, if any be misled;
He is a robe, if any naked be;
If any chance to hunger, he is bread;
If any be a bondman, he is free;
If any be but weak, how strong is he!
To dead men life is he, to sick men health;
To blind men sight, and to the needy wealth;
A pleasure without loss, a treasure without stealth.
GILES FLETCHER, *Excellency of Christ.*

5
I have prayed in her fields of poppies,
I have laughed with the men who died—
But in all my ways and through all my days
Like a friend He walked beside.
I have seen a sight under Heaven
That only God understands,
In the battle's glare I have seen Christ there
With the Sword of God in His hand.
GORDON JOHNSTONE, *On Fields of Flanders.*

Now we remember over here in Flanders,
(It isn't strange to think of You in Flanders!)
This hideous warfare seems to make things clear.
We never thought about You much in England,
But now that we are far away from England
We have no doubts, we know that You are here.
MRS. C. T. WHITMELL, *Christ in Flanders.*

6
In darkness there is no choice. It is light that enables us to see the differences between things; and it is Christ that gives us light.
J. C. AND A. W. HARE, *Guesses at Truth.*

7
Shepherd of mortals, here behold
A little flock, a wayside fold
That wait thy presence to be blest—
O Man of Nazareth, be our guest.
DANIEL HENDERSON, *Hymn for a Household.*

8
Mine eyes have seen the glory of the coming of the Lord;
He is trampling out the vintage where the grapes of wrath are stored;
He hath loosed the fateful lightning of His terrible swift sword;
His truth is marching on.
JULIA WARD HOWE, *Battle-Hymn of the Republic.*

9
Whose shoe's latchet I am not worthy to unloose.
New Testament: John, i, 27.

10
He that lends
To Him, need never fear to lose his venture.
CHARLES KINGSLEY, *The Saint's Tragedy.* Act ii, sc. 8.

11
But Thee, but Thee, O sovereign Seer of time,
But Thee, O poets' Poet, Wisdom's Tongue,
But Thee, O man's best Man, O love's best Love,
O perfect life in perfect labor writ,
O all men's Comrade, Servant, King, or Priest,— . . .
Oh, what amiss may I forgive in Thee,
Jesus, good Paragon, thou Crystal Christ?
SIDNEY LANIER, *The Crystal.* Last lines.

12
When Pilate heard of Galilee, he asked whether the man were a Galilean.
New Testament: Luke, xxiii, 6.

Thou hast conquered, O Galilean! (Vicisti, Galilæe!)
EMPEROR JULIAN, "The Apostate," his dying words, addressed to the Christ he had denied. (THEODORET, *Historia Eccles.,* iii, 20.) The story is probably without authenticity. Gibbon (Ch. 23) affirms that Julian remained a Platonist to the last. Montaigne (Bk. ii, ch. 19) states that the words are also given, "Content thyself, O Nazaræan."

Thou hast conquered, O pale Galilean; the world has grown grey from thy breath;
We have drunken of things Lethean, and fed on the fullness of death.
Laurel is green for a season, and love is sweet for a day;
But love grows bitter with treason, and laurel outlives not May.
SWINBURNE, *Hymn to Proserpine,* l. 35.

13
Lo, I am with you alway, even unto the end of the world.
New Testament: Matthew, xxviii, 20.

14
With this ambiguous earth
His dealings have been told us. There abide:
The signal to a maid, the human birth,
The lesson, and the young Man crucified.
ALICE MEYNELL, *Christ in the Universe.*

15
The hands of Christ seem very frail,
For they were broken by a nail.
But only they reach Heaven at last
Whom these frail, broken hands hold fast.
JOHN RICHARD MORELAND, *His Hands.*

Love cannot die, nor truth betray;
Christ rose upon an April day.
JOHN RICHARD MORELAND, *Resurgam.*

1
Ah! what if some unshamed iconoclast
Crumbling old fetish raiments of the past,
Rises from dead cerements the Christ at last?
What if men take to following where He leads,
Weary of mumbling Athanasian creeds?
RODEN NOËL, *The Red Flag.*

2
Only a Christ could have conceived a Christ.
JOSEPH PARKER, *Ecce Deus.* Ch. 11.

3
To live is Christ, and to die is gain.
New Testament: Philippians, i, 21.

4
I see His blood upon the rose
And in the stars the glory of His eyes,
His body gleams amid eternal snows,
His tears fall from the skies.
JOSEPH M. PLUNKETT, *I See His Blood.*

5
Therefore, friends,
As far as to the sepulchre of Christ,
Whose soldier now, under whose blessed cross
We are impressed and engaged to fight . . .
To chase these pagans in those holy fields
Over whose acres walk'd those blessed feet,
Which fourteen hundred years ago were nail'd
For our advantage on the bitter cross.
SHAKESPEARE, *I Henry IV.* Act i, sc. 1, l. 18.

6
Our fair father Christ.
TENNYSON, *Guinevere,* l. 559.

7
And so the Word had breath, and wrought
With human hands the creed of creeds
In loveliness of perfect deeds,
More strong than all poetic thought.
TENNYSON, *In Memoriam.* Sec. xxxvi.

8
All His glory and beauty come from within, and there He delights to dwell, His visits there are frequent, His conversation sweet, His comforts refreshing; and His peace passing all understanding.
THOMAS À KEMPIS, *De Imitatione Christi.* Pt. ii, ch. 1.

His love, at once, and dread, instruct our thought;
As man He suffer'd, and as God He taught.
EDMUND WALLER, *Of Divine Love.* Canto iii, l. 41.

9
This ae nighte, this ae nighte,
Every nighte and all;
Fire and sleete, and candle lighte,
And Christe receive thy saule.
UNKNOWN, *Lyke-Wake Dirge.* (SCOTT, *Minstrelsy of the Scottish Border.* Vol. iii, p. 163.)

V—Christ: Hymns of Praise

10
Hail, O bleeding Head and wounded,
With a crown of thorns surrounded.
ST. BERNARD OF CLAIRVAUX, *Passion Hymn* (Coles, tr.)

11
Just as I am, without one plea
But that Thy blood was shed for me,
And that Thou bid'st me come to Thee,
O Lamb of God, I come!
CHARLOTTE ELLIOTT, *Just As I Am.*

12
Blest be the tie that binds
Our hearts in Jesus' love;
JOHN FAWCETT, *Blest Be the Tie That Binds.*

13
The Son of God goes forth to war,
A kingly crown to gain;
His blood-red banner streams afar!
Who follows in His train?
REGINALD HEBER, *The Son of God.*

14
One Name above all glorious names
With its ten thousand tongues
The everlasting sea proclaims,
Echoing angelic songs.
JOHN KEBLE, *The Christian Year: Septuagesima Sunday.* St. 9.

Sun of my soul! Thou Saviour dear,
It is not night if Thou be near.
JOHN KEBLE, *The Christian Year: Evening.*

15
The head that once was crowned with thorns
Is crowned with glory now.
THOMAS KELLEY, *Hymn.*

16
Near, so very near to God,
Nearer I cannot be;
For in the person of his Son
I am as near as he.
CATESBY PAGET, *Hymn.*

17
All hail the power of Jesus' name!
Let angels prostrate fall;
Bring forth the royal diadem,
To crown Him Lord of all!
EDWARD PERRONET, *Coronation.*

18
Jesus, lover of my soul,
Let me to Thy bosom fly,
While the nearer waters roll,
While the tempest still is high!
CHARLES WESLEY, *In Temptation.*

For additional hymns see APPENDIX.

CHRISTIANITY

See also Religion

I—Christianity: Apothegms

19
If a man cannot be a Christian in the place where he is, he cannot be a Christian anywhere.
HENRY WARD BEECHER, *Life Thoughts.*

1
A Christian is one who rejoices in the superiority of a rival.
EDWIN BOOTH. (W. L. PHELPS, *Jealousy*.)

2
I dare without usurpation assume the honourable style of a Christian.
SIR THOMAS BROWNE, *Religio Medici*. Pt. i, 1.

3
And the disciples were called Christians first in Antioch.
New Testament: Acts, xi, 26.

4
Then Agrippa said unto Paul, Almost thou persuadest me to be a Christian.
New Testament, Acts, xxvi, 28.

5
His Christianity was muscular.
BENJAMIN DISRAELI, *Endymion*. Ch. 14.

6
The whole religious complexion of the modern world is due to the absence from Jerusalem of a lunatic asylum.
HAVELOCK ELLIS, *Impressions and Comments*. Ser. iii, p. 130.

7
A local thing called Christianity.
THOMAS HARDY, *The Dynasts: Spirit of the Years*. Sc. 6.

8
That Christian principle, conciliation.
THOMAS HOOD, *Ode to Rae Wilson*, l. 417.

What was invented two thousand years ago was the spirit of Christianity.
GERALD STANLEY LEE, *Crowds*. Bk. ii, ch. 18.

9
You are Christians of the best edition, all picked and culled.
RABELAIS, *Works*. Bk. iv, ch. 50.

10
Bend thy neck, meek Sicambrian: adore what thou hast burned, burn what thou hast adored.
ST. REMI, at the baptism of Clovis I, 496. (GREGORY OF TOURS, *Ecclesiastical History of the Franks*, ii, ch. 31.) By a curious change of meaning, "meek" has become "proud," in the French proverb, "Fléchis le cou, fier Sicambre!"

11
Neither having the accent of Christians, nor the gait of Christian, pagan or man.
SHAKESPEARE, *Hamlet. Act* iii, sc. 2, l. 34.

Some Christians have a comfortable creed.
BYRON, *Don Juan*. Canto ii, st. 86.

12
The Hebrew will turn Christian: he grows kind.
SHAKESPEARE, *The Merchant of Venice*. Act i, sc. 3, l. 179.

13
This making of Christians will raise the price of hogs: if we grow all to be pork-eaters, we shall not shortly have a rasher on the coals for money.
SHAKESPEARE, *The Merchant of Venice*. Act iii, sc. 5, l. 24.

In converting Jews to Christians, you raise the price of pork.
SHAKESPEARE, *The Merchant of Venice*. Act iii, sc. 5, l. 38.

14
It is spoke as a Christians ought to speak.
SHAKESPEARE, *The Merry Wives of Windsor*. Act i, sc. 1, l. 103.

Christ bless thee, brother, for that Christian speech!
SOUTHEY, *Roderick*. Sec. 5, l. 45.

15
As to the Christian creed, if true
Or false, I never questioned it;
I took it as the vulgar do.
SHELLEY, *Rosalind and Helen*, l. 512.

16
A Christian is the highest style of man.
YOUNG, *Night Thoughts*. Night iv, l. 788.

A Christian is God Almighty's gentleman.
A. W. AND J. C. HARE, *Guesses at Truth*.

His tribe were God Almighty's gentlemen.
DRYDEN, *Absalom and Achitophel*. Pt. i, l. 645.

17
Scratch the Christian and you find the pagan —spoiled.
ISRAEL ZANGWILL, *Children of the Ghetto*. Bk. ii, ch. 6.

A pagan heart, a Christian soul had he.
He followed Christ, yet for dead Pan he sighed.
As if Theocritus in Sicily
Had come upon the Figure crucified.
MAURICE FRANCIS EGAN, *Maurice de Guërin*.

II—Christianity: Its Virtues

18
There was never law, or sect, or opinion did so much magnify goodness, as the Christian religion doth.
FRANCIS BACON, *Essays: Of Goodness*.

Philosophy makes us wiser, but Christianity makes us better men.
FIELDING, *Tom Jones*. Bk. viii, ch. 13.

19
That though you hunt the Christian man
Like a hare in the hill-side,
The hare has still more heart to run
Than you have heart to ride.
G. K. CHESTERTON, *Ballad of the White Horse*.

20
Two inestimable advantages Christianity has given us; first the Sabbath, the jubilee of the whole world; . . . and secondly, the institution of preaching.
EMERSON, *Nature, Addresses, and Lectures: Address*.

21
He who shall introduce into public affairs the principles of primitive Christianity will change the face of the world.
FRANKLIN, *Letter*, to the French ministry, March, 1778.

22
To the corruptions of Christianity I am, indeed, opposed; but not to the genuine

precepts of Jesus himself. I am a Christian in the only sense in which he wished any one to be; sincerely attached to his doctrines in preference to all others; ascribing to himself every human excellence; and believing he never claimed any other.

THOMAS JEFFERSON, *Writings*. Vol. x, p. 379.

Of all the systems of morality, ancient or modern, which have come under my observation, none appear to me so pure as that of Jesus.

THOMAS JEFFERSON, *Writings*. Vol. xiii, p. 377.

In extracting the pure principles which [Jesus] taught, we should have to strip off the artificial vestments in which they have been muffled by priests, who have travestied them into various forms, as instruments of riches and power to themselves . . . there will be found remaining the most sublime and benevolent code of morals which has ever been offered to man.

THOMAS JEFFERSON, *Writings*. Vol. xiii, p. 389.

The doctrines which flowed from the lips of Jesus himself are within the comprehension of a child; but thousands of volumes have not yet explained the Platonisms engrafted on them.

THOMAS JEFFERSON, *Writings*. Vol. xiv, p. 149.

1
Christianity is the highest perfection of humanity.

SAMUEL JOHNSON. (BOSWELL, *Life*. Vol. ii, p. 27.)

2
A wise man will always be a Christian, because the perfection of wisdom is to know where lies tranquillity of mind, and how to attain it, which Christianity teaches.

W. S. LANDOR, *Imaginary Conversations: Marvel and Parker*.

3
Silence the voice of Christianity, and the world is well-nigh dumb, for gone is that sweet music which kept in order the rulers of the people, which cheers the poor widow in her lonely toil, and comes like light through the windows of morning, to men who sit stooping and feeble, with failing eyes and a hungering heart.

THEODORE PARKER, *Critical and Miscellaneous Writings: A Discourse of the Transient and Permanent in Christianity*.

4
In the ethic of Christianity, it is the relation of the soul to God that is important, not the relation of man to his fellow man.

BERTRAND RUSSELL, *Marriage and Morals*, p. 175.

5
Whatever makes men good Christians, makes them good citizens.

DANIEL WEBSTER, *Speech*, Plymouth, 22 Dec., 1820.

III—Christianity: Its Faults

See also Church: Its Faults; Religion: Its Dissensions

6
I hold that the Christian religion is the best yet promulgated, but do not thence infer that it is not susceptible of improvement; nor do I wish to confound its doctrines with its founder, and to worship one of my fellow-beings.

AMOS BRONSON ALCOTT, *Diary*.

7
Christians and camels receive their burdens kneeling.

AMBROSE BIERCE, *The Devil's Dictionary*.

8
The religion of Jesus is a threat, that of Mohammed is a promise.

NAPOLEON BONAPARTE. (O'MEARA, *Napoleon in Exile*.)

Mohammed's truth lay in a holy Book,
Christ's in a sacred Life.

RICHARD MONCKTON MILNES, *Mohammedanism*.

9
We all have known . . .
Good popes who brought all good to jeopardy,
Good Christians who sat still in easy chairs
And damned the general world for standing up.

E. B. BROWNING, *Aurora Leigh*. Bk. iv, l. 498.

Christians have burnt each other, quite persuaded
That all the Apostles would have done as they did.

BYRON, *Don Juan*. Canto i, st. 83.

Millions of innocent men, women and children, since the introduction of Christianity, have been burned, tortured, fined and imprisoned, yet we have not advanced one inch toward uniformity. What has been the effect of coercion? To make one-half of the world fools and the other half hypocrites.

THOMAS JEFFERSON, *Notes on Virginia*.

10
He who begins by loving Christianity better than Truth will proceed by loving his own sect or church better than Christianity, and end in loving himself better than all.

S. T. COLERIDGE, *Aids to Reflection: Aphorisms*.

11
Every Stoic was a Stoic; but in Christendom, where is the Christian?

EMERSON, *Essays, First Series: Self-Reliance*.

12
Yes,—rather plunge me back in Pagan night,
And take my chance with Socrates for bliss,
Than be the Christian of a faith like this,
Which builds on heavenly cant its earthly sway,
And in a convert mourns to lose a prey.

THOMAS MOORE, *Intolerance*, l. 68.

13
Christianity has ever been the enemy of human love. . . . Christianity has made of death a terror which was unknown to the gay calmness of the Pagan.

OUIDA, *The Failure of Christianity*.

1
Christianity is the world's monumental fraud if there be no future life.

MARTIN J. SCOTT, *Religion and Commonsense*, p. 120.

2
O father Abram, what these Christians are,
Whose own hard dealings teaches them suspect
The thoughts of others!

SHAKESPEARE, *The Merchant of Venice*, i, 3, 161.

3
Many Christians are like chestnuts—very pleasant nuts, but enclosed in very prickly burrs, which need various dealings of Nature and her grip of frost before the kernel is disclosed.

HORACE SMITH, *The Tin Trumpet: Christians.*

4
Christian, what of the night?—
I cannot tell; I am blind.
I halt and hearken behind
If haply the hours will go back
And return to the dear dead light,
To the watchfires and stars that of old
Shone where the sky now is black,
Glowed where the earth now is cold.

SWINBURNE, *Watch in the Night*. St. 10.

5
"See," they say, "how these Christians love one another," for themselves hate one another; "and how they are ready to die for each other," for themselves will be readier to kill each other. (Vide, inquiunt, ut invicem se diligant; ipsi enim invicem oderunt; et ut pro alterutro mori sint parati; ipsi enim ad accidendum alterutrum paratiores erunt.)

TERTULLIAN, *Apologeticus*. Ch. 39, sec. 7.

6
You say that you believe the Gospel: you live as if you were sure not one word of it is true.

THOMAS WILSON, *Maxims of Piety*, p. 44.

7
Great God! I'd rather be
A Pagan, suckled in a creed outworn;
So might I, standing on the pleasant lea,
Have glimpses that would make me less forlorn;
Have sight of Proteus rising from the sea,
Or hear old Triton blow his wreathèd horn.

WORDSWORTH, *Miscellaneous Sonnets*. Pt. i, No. 33.

Triton, blowing loud his wreathed horne.

SPENSER, *Colin Clout*, l. 245. (1595)

From thy dead lips a clearer note is born
Than ever Triton blew from wreathèd horn.

O. W. HOLMES, *The Chambered Nautilus*.

IV—Christianity: The Cross

8
Onward, Christian soldiers!
Marching as to war,
With the Cross of Jesus
Going on before.

SABINE BARING-GOULD, *Onward, Christian Soldiers.*

9
Through this sign thou shalt conquer. (In hoc signo vinces.)

CONSTANTINE THE GREAT. Motto which he is said to have seen in the sky in his march toward Rome, and which he placed upon the Laburum, or Roman standard over the monogram of Christ, after his victory over Maxentius, at Saxa Rubra, near Rome, 27 Oct., 312.

10
The Cross!
There, and there only (though the deist rave,
And atheist, if Earth bear so base a slave);
There, and there only, is the power to save.

COWPER, *The Progress of Error*, l. 613.

11
The cross is the ladder of heaven.

THOMAS DRAXE, *Biblioth. Scholas. Instr.*, 36.

Crosses are the ladders that lead to heaven.

SAMUEL SMILES, *Self-Help*, p. 341.

12
But God forbid that I should glory, save in the cross of our Lord Jesus Christ.

New Testament: Galatians, vi, 14.

Nothing except in the cross. (Nil nisi cruce.)

Motto founded on the text from Galatians.

In the cross there is safety. (In cruce salus.)

THOMAS À KEMPIS, *De Imitatione Christi*. Pt. ii, ch. 12.

13
Take up the Cross if thou the Crown would'st gain (Tolle crucem, qui vis auferre coronam.)

Attributed to ST. PAULINUS, BISHOP OF NOLA.

14
No pain, no palm; no thorns, no throne; no gall, no glory; no cross, no crown.

WILLIAM PENN, *No Cross, No Crown*. (1668)

The way to bliss lies not on beds of down,
And he that has no cross deserves no crown.

FRANCIS QUARLES, *Esther*.

There are no crown-wearers in heaven who were not cross-bearers here below.

C. H. SPURGEON, *Gleanings Among the Sheaves: Cross-Bearers.*

See also under COMPENSATION.

15
The moon of Mahomet Arose, and it shall set:
While blazoned as on Heaven's immortal noon,
The cross leads generations on.

SHELLEY, *Hellas*, l. 221.

16
Christianity without the Cross is nothing. The Cross was the fitting close of a life of rejection, scorn, and defeat. But in no true sense have these things ceased or changed. Jesus is still He whom man despiseth, and the rejected of men.

JAMES THOMSON, *The Great Argument*.

CHRISTMAS

I—Christmas: Bethlehem.

17
Oh, the Shepherds in Judea!—
Do you think the Shepherds know

How the whole round world is brightened
In the ruddy Christmas glow?
MARY AUSTIN, *The Shepherds in Judea.*

1
O little town of Bethlehem,
How still we see thee lie!
Above thy deep and dreamless sleep
The silent stars go by.
PHILLIPS BROOKS, *O Little Town of Bethlehem.*

2
No trumpet-blast profaned
The hour in which the Prince of Peace was born;
No bloody streamlet stained
Earth's silver rivers on that sacred morn.
BRYANT, *Christmas in 1875.*

3
The King of Kings, He is so sweet and small.
GERALD BULLETT, *Carol.*

4
Christians awake, salute the happy morn
Whereon the Saviour of the world was born.
JOHN BYROM, *Hymn for Christmas Day.*

5
When 'twas bitter winter,
Houseless and forlorn
In a star-lit stable
Christ the Babe was born.
WILLIAM CANTON, *Carol.*

Welcome, heavenly lambkin;
Welcome, golden rose;
Alleluia, Baby,
In the swaddling clothes!
WILLIAM CANTON, *Carol.*

6
Glory to God, this wondrous morn,
On earth the Saviour Christ is born.
BLISS CARMAN, *Bethlehem.*

7
There fared a mother driven forth
Out of an inn to roam;
In the place where she was homeless
All men are at home.
The crazy stable close at hand,
With shaking timber and shifting sand,
Grew a stronger thing to abide and stand
Than the square stones of Rome.
G. K. CHESTERTON, *The House of Christmas.*

8
The night that erst no name had worn,
To it a happy name is given;
For in that stable lay new-born
The peaceful Prince of Earth and Heaven,
In the solemn midnight Centuries ago.
ALFRED DOMETT, *A Christmas Hymn.*

9
Run, shepherds, run where Bethlem blest appears,
We bring the best of news; be not dismay'd:
A Saviour there is born, more old than years,
Amidst heaven's rolling heights this earth who stay'd.
WILLIAM DRUMMOND, *Flowers of Sion.* No. 9.

10
What babe new born is this that in a manger cries?
Near on her lowly bed his happy mother lies.
Oh, see the air is shaken with white and heavenly wings—
This is the Lord of all the earth, this is the King of Kings.
R. W. GILDER, *A Christmas Hymn.*

Fra Lippo, we have learned from thee
A lesson of humanity:
To every mother's heart forlorn,
In every house the Christ is born.
R. W. GILDER, *A Madonna of Fra Lippo Lippi.*

11
There's a song in the air!
There's a star in the sky!
There's a mother's deep prayer
And a Baby's low cry!
And the star rains its fire where the Beautiful sing,
For the manger of Bethlehem cradles a King.
J. G. HOLLAND, *A Christmas Carol.*

12
When mother-love makes all things bright,
When joy comes with the morning light,
When children gather round their tree,
Thou Christmas Babe, we sing of thee!
TUDOR JENKS, *A Christmas Song*

13
I sing the birth was born to-night,
The author both of life and light.
BEN JONSON, *A Hymn of the Nativity.*

14
Hail to the King of Bethlehem,
Who weareth in his diadem
The yellow crocus for the gem
Of his authority!
LONGFELLOW, *The Golden Legend: The Nativity.* Pt. ix.

15
"What means this glory round our feet,"
The Magi mused, "more bright than morn?"
And voices chanted clear and sweet,
"To-day the Prince of Peace is born!"
J. R. LOWELL, *A Christmas Carol.*

16
Unto you is born this day in the city of David a Saviour, which is Christ the Lord.
New Testament, Luke, ii, 11.

17
Away in a manger, no crib for a bed,
The little Lord Jesus laid down His sweet head.
MARTIN LUTHER, *Cradle Hymn.*

18
They all were looking for a king
To slay their foes and lift them high;
Thou cam'st, a little baby thing,
That made a woman cry.
GEORGE MACDONALD, *That Holy Thing.* From *Paul Faber.*

1
New every year,
New born and newly dear,
He comes with tidings and a song,
The ages long, the ages long.
ALICE MEYNELL, *Unto Us a Son is Given.*

2
This is the month, and this the happy morn
Wherein the Son of Heaven's Eternal King,
Of wedded maid and virgin mother born,
Our great redemption from above did bring.
MILTON, *On the Morning of Christ's Nativity.*

3
God rest ye, little children; let nothing you affright,
For Jesus Christ, your Saviour, was born this happy night;
Along the hills of Galilee the white flocks sleeping lay,
When Christ, the Child of Nazareth, was born on Christmas day.
DINAH MARIA MULOCK CRAIK, *Christmas Carol.*

4
Peace to the byre, peace to the fold,
For that they housed Him from the cold!
LIZETTE WOODWORTH REESE, *A Christmas Folk-Song.*

5
Born in a stable,
Cradled in a manger,
In the world His hands had made,
Born a stranger.
CHRISTINA ROSSETTI, *Before the Paling of the Stars.*

6
It came upon the midnight clear,
That glorious song of old.
EDMUND HAMILTON SEARS, *Christmas Carols.*

Calm on the listening ear of night
Came Heaven's melodious strains,
Where wild Judea stretches far
Her silver-mantled plains.
EDMUND HAMILTON SEARS, *Christmas Song.*

7
All glory be to God on high,
And to the earth be peace;
Good-will henceforth, from Heaven to men,
Begin and never cease.
NAHUM TATE, *While Shepherds Watched.*

8
To-day He makes his entrance here,
But not as monarchs do.
No gold, nor purple swaddling-bands,
Nor royal shining things;
A manger for His cradle stands,
And holds the King of Kings.
ISAAC WATTS, *Shepherds, Rejoice.*

9
Hark the herald angels sing,
Glory to the new-born King;
Peace on earth, and mercy mild,
God and sinners reconciled!
CHARLES WESLEY, *Christmas Hymn.*

Hark how all the welkin rings,
Glory to the King of kings!
CHARLES WESLEY, *Christmas Hymn.* (The original version of the first two lines.)

10
God rest you merry, gentlemen,
Let nothing you dismay,
For Jesus Christ, our Saviour,
Was born upon this day,
UNKNOWN, *Old Carol.*

11
He came all so still
Where His mother was,
As dew in April
That falleth on the grass.
UNKNOWN, *Old Carol.*

12
As Joseph was a-waukin',
He heard an angel sing,
"This night shall be the birthnight
Of Christ our heavenly King."
UNKNOWN, *Christmas Carol.*

II—Christmas: Its Celebration

13
I have often thought, says Sir Roger, it happens very well that Christmas should fall out in the middle of winter.
ADDISON, *The Spectator.* No. 269.

14
The mistletoe hung in the castle hall,
The holly branch shone on the old oak wall.
THOMAS HAYNES BAYLY, *The Mistletoe Bough.*

15
Not believe in Santa Claus! You might as well not believe in fairies. . . . Nobody sees Santa Claus, but that is no sign there is no Santa Claus. The most real things in the world are those which neither children nor men can see. No Santa Claus! Thank God! he lives and he lives forever.
FRANK CHURCH, *Is There a Santa Claus?* (*N. Y. Sun,* 21 Sept., 1897.)

16
Many merry Christmases, friendships, great accumulation of cheerful recollections, affection on earth, and Heaven at last for all of us.
CHARLES DICKENS, *Christmas Message,* to John Forster, 1846. (FORSTER, *Life of Dickens;* also in Dickens's *Dr. Marigold's Prescription.*)

17
'Most all the time, the whole year round, there ain't no flies on me,
But jest 'fore Christmas I'm as good as I kin be!
EUGENE FIELD, *Jest 'fore Christmas.*

18
How bless'd, how envied, were our life,
Could we but scape the poulterer's knife!
But man, curs'd man, on Turkeys preys,
And Christmas shortens all our days:
Sometimes with oysters we combine,
Sometimes assist the savoury chine;

From the low peasant to the lord,
The Turkey smokes on every board.
JOHN GAY, *Fables: The Turkey and the Ant.*

1
They talk of Christmas so long that it comes.
GEORGE HERBERT, *Jacula Prudentum.*

Coming! ay, so is Christmas.
SWIFT, *Polite Conversation.* Dial i.

2
Come, bring with a noise,
My merry, merry boys,
The Christmas log to the firing;
While my good dame, she
Bids ye all be free;
And drink to your hearts' desiring.
ROBERT HERRICK, *Ceremonies for Christmas.*

3
Glorious time of great Too-Much, . . .
Right thy most unthrifty glee,
And pious thy mince-piety.
LEIGH HUNT, *Christmas.*

4
On Christmas day in the morning.
WASHINGTON IRVING, *Sketch Book: The Sunny Bank.* Quoting an old Worcestershire song.

5
While rich men sigh and poor men fret,
Dear me! we can't spare Christmas yet!
EDWARD S. MARTIN, *Christmas, 1898.*

6
I heard the bells on Christmas Day
Their old, familiar carols play,
And wild and sweet
The words repeat
Of peace on earth, good-will to men!
LONGFELLOW, *Christmas Bells.*

7
'Twas the night before Christmas, when all through the house
Not a creature was stirring, not even a mouse.
CLEMENT CLARKE MOORE, *A Visit from St. Nicholas.* Erroneously claimed for Henry Livingston by his descendants. (See STEVENSON, *Famous Single Poems.*)

8
Have you seen God's Christmas tree in the sky,
With its trillions of tapers blazing high?
ANGELA MORGAN, *Christmas Tree of Angels.*

9
After a Christmas comes a Lent.
JOHN RAY, *English Proverbs.*

10
Heap on more wood!—the wind is chill;
But let it whistle as it will,
We'll keep our Christmas merry still.
SCOTT, *Marmion:* Canto vi, *Introduction,* l. 1.

England was merry England, when
Old Christmas brought his sports again.
'Twas Christmas broached the mightiest ale,
'Twas Christmas told the merriest tale;
A Christmas gambol oft could cheer
The poor man's heart through half the year.
SCOTT, *Marmion:* Canto vi, *Introduction,* l. 80.

11
And after him came next the chill December:
Yet he, through merry feasting which he made
And great bonfires, did not the cold remember;
His Saviour's birth his mind so much did glad.
SPENSER, *Faerie Queene.* Bk. vii, canto vii, st. 41.

12
A hot Christmas makes a fat churchyard.
SWAN, *Speculum Mundi,* 161. (1635)

A green Christmas is neither handsome nor healthful.
THOMAS FULLER, *Holy State: Of Time-Serving.* (1642)

13
Christmas is here:
Winds whistle shrill,
Icy and chill,
Little care we:
Little we fear
Weather without,
Sheltered about
The Mahogany-Tree.
THACKERAY, *The Mahogany-Tree.*

As fits the holy Christmas birth,
Be this, good friends, our carol still—
Be peace on earth, be peace on earth,
To men of gentle will.
THACKERAY, *The End of the Play.*

14
At Christmas play and make good cheer,
For Christmas comes but once a year.
THOMAS TUSSER, *Hundreth Good Pointes of Husbandrie.* Ch. 12. (1557)

You merry folk, be of good cheer,
For Christmas comes but once a year.
From open door you'll take no harm
By winter if your hearts are warm.
GEOFFREY SMITH, *At the Sign of the Jolly Jack.*

For Christmas comes but once a year,
And then they shall be merry.
GEORGE WITHER, *Christmas Carol.*

15
They keep Christmas all the year.
EDWARD WALKER, *Parœmiologia,* 25. (1672)

16
Life still hath one romance that naught can bury—
Not Time himself, who coffins Life's romances—
For still will Christmas gild the year's mischances,
If Childhood comes, as here, to make him merry.
THEODORE WATTS-DUNTON, *The Christmas Tree.*

17
Blow, bugles of battle, the marches of peace;
East, west, north, and south let the long quarrel cease;
Sing the song of great joy that the angels began,

Sing the glory of God and of good-will to man!
WHITTIER, *A Christmas Carmen.*

1
So now is come our joyfull'st feast;
Let every man be jolly;
Each room with ivy leaves is drest,
And every post with holly.
GEORGE WITHER, *Christmas Carol.*

2
Christmas is coming, the geese are getting fat,
Please to put a penny in the old man's hat;
If you haven't got a penny, a ha'penny will do,
If you haven't got a ha'penny, God bless you!
UNKNOWN, *Beggar's Rhyme.*

CHURCH

I—Church: Apothegms

3
They build not castles in the air who would build churches on earth: and though they leave no such structures here, may lay good foundations in Heaven.
SIR THOMAS BROWNE, *To a Friend.* Sec. 23.

Who builds a church to God, and not to Fame,
Will never mark the marble with his name.
POPE, *Moral Essays.* Epis. iii, l. 285.

4
We are ready to proclaim in Italy this principle. A free church in a free state. (Libera chiesa in libero stato.)
CAMILLE CAVOUR, *Speech,* in the Italian Parliament, 27 March, 1861. Montalambert used the same phrase in an address at Malines, 20 Aug., 1863, and is sometimes erroneously credited with originating it.

5
Bred to the church, and for the gown decreed,
Ere it was known that I should learn to read.
CHARLES CHURCHILL, *The Author,* l. 342.

6
What is a church?—Our honest sexton tells,
" 'Tis a tall building, with a tower and bells."
CRABBE, *The Borough.* Letter ii, l. 11.

7
Let the church have leave to stand in the churchyard.
THOMAS FULLER, *Gnomologia.* No. 3192.

8
When once thy foot enters the church, be bare;
God is more there than thou.
GEORGE HERBERT, *The Church-Porch.* St. 68.

Kneeling ne'er spoiled silk stocking: quit thy state.
All equal are within the church's gate.
GEORGE HERBERT, *The Church-Porch.* St. 68.

9
Nothing lasts but the Church.
GEORGE HERBERT, *Jacula Prudentum.*

11
And I say also unto thee, That thou art Peter, and upon this rock I will build my church; and the gates of hell shall not prevail against it.
New Testament: Matthew, xvi, 18.

It was founded upon a rock.
New Testament: Matthew, vii, 25; *Luke,* vi, 48.

Christ's famous pun, "Upon this rock I will build my church."
BERNARD SHAW, *John Bull's Other Island: Preface.*

See the Gospel Church secure,
And founded on a Rock!
All her promises are sure;
Her bulwarks who can shock?
CHARLES WESLEY, *The Church.* St. 9.

12
Some to church repair
Not for the doctrine, but the music there.
POPE, *Essay on Criticism.* Pt. ii, l. 142.

Constant at Church and 'Change.
POPE, *Moral Essays.* Epis. iii, l. 347.

13
An I have not forgotten what the inside of a church is made of, I am a pepper-corn.
SHAKESPEARE, *I Henry IV.* Act iii, sc. 3, l. 9.

14
The itch of disputation will prove the scab of the Church.
SIR HENRY WOTTON, *Panegyric to King Charles.*

He directed the stone over his grave to be thus inscribed:
Hic jacet hujus Sententiæ primus Author:
Disputandi pruritus ecclesiarum scabies.
Nomen alias quære.
Here lies the first author of this sentence:
"The itch of disputation will prove the scab of the Church." Inquire his name elsewhere.
IZAAK WALTON, *Life of Wotton.*

The itch of disputation will break out
Into a scab of error.
ROWLAND WATKYNS, *Flamma Sine Fumo: The New Illiterate Late Teachers.*

II—Church: Its Virtues

See also Christianity: Its Virtues

15
A church is God between four walls.
VICTOR HUGO, *Ninety-Three.* Pt. ii, bk. iii, ch. 2.

Why where's the need of Temple, when the walls
O' the world are that?
ROBERT BROWNING, *Dramatis Personæ: Epilogue.*

16
Bless all the churches, and blessed be God, who, in this our great trial, giveth us the churches.
ABRAHAM LINCOLN, attributed to him in replying to a Methodist delegation, 14 May, 1864.

17
No silver saints, by dying misers giv'n,
Here brib'd the rage of ill-requited Heav'n;
But such plain roofs as Piety could raise,

And only vocal with the Maker's praise.
POPE, *Eloisa to Abelard*, l. 137.

III—Church: Its Faults

See also Christianity: Its Faults; Religion: Its Dissensions

1
The multitude of false churches accredits the true religion.
EMERSON, *Essays, Second Series: Nature.*

If I should go out of church whenever I hear a false sentiment I could never stay there five minutes. But why come out? The street is as false as the church.
EMERSON, *Essays, Second Series: New England Reformers.*

2
The church alone beyond all question
Has for ill-gotten goods the right digestion.
(Die Kirch' allein, meine lieben Frauen,
Kann ungerechtes Gut verdauen.)
GOETHE, *Faust*. Pt. i, sc. 9, l. 35.

3
The nearer the church, the farther from God.
JOHN HEYWOOD, *Proverbs*. Pt. i, ch. 9. Quoted by Bishop Andrews in sermon before James I, 1622; by FULLER, *Worthies*, ii, 5; and by many others.

It is common for those that are farthest from God, to boast themselves most of their being near to the Church.
MATHEW HENRY, *Commentaries: Jeremiah vii.*

To kerke the narre, from God more farre,
Has bene an old-sayd sawe.
SPENSER, *The Shepheardes Calender: Julye*, l. 97.

4
Go tell the Church it shows
What's good, and doth no good.
SIR WALTER RALEIGH, *The Lie.*

5
You have made
The cement of your churches out of tears
And ashes, and the fabric will not stand.
EDWIN ARLINGTON ROBINSON, *Captain Craig.*

6
The Churches must learn humility as well as teach it.
BERNARD SHAW, *Saint Joan: Preface.*

7
The church and clergy here, no doubt,
Are very much akin;
Both weather-beaten are without,
Both empty are within.
SWIFT, *Extempore Verses.*

8
Christian love among the Churches look'd the twin of heathen hate.
TENNYSON, *Locksley Hall Sixty Years After*, l. 86.

But the churchmen fain would kill their church,
As the churches have killed their Christ.
TENNYSON, *Maud*, l. 266.

IV—Church: The Spire

9
An instinctive taste teaches men to build their churches in flat countries with spire-steeples, which, as they cannot be referred to any other object, point as with silent finger to the sky and stars.
S. T. COLERIDGE, *The Friend*. Sec. i, No. 14.

And O, ye swelling hills and spacious plains!
Besprent from shore to shore with steeple-towers,
And spires whose "silent finger points to heaven."
WORDSWORTH, *The Excursion*. Bk. vi, l. 17.

Accepts the village church as part of the sky.
EMERSON, *Journals*, 1867.

10
A beggarly people, A church and no steeple.
EDMUND MALONE. (PRIOR, *Life of Swift*, p. 381.) The reference is to St. Ann's church, Dublin.

11
Who taught that heaven-directed spire to rise?
POPE, *Moral Essays*. Epis. iii, l. 261.

12
How the tall temples, as to meet their gods,
Ascend the skies!
YOUNG, *Night Thoughts*. Night vi, l. 781.

V—Church and Chapel

13
For commonly, wheresoever God buildeth a church, the devil will build a chapel just by.
THOMAS BECON, *Catechism*, 361. (1560)

Where Christ erecteth his church, the devil in the same churchyard will have his chapel.
RICHARD BANCROFT, *Sermon Against Puritans*, 9 Feb., 1588.

14
Where God hath a temple, the Devil will have a chapel.
ROBERT BURTON, *Anatomy of Melancholy*. Pt. iii, sec. iv, mem. 1, subs. 7.

15
Wherever God erects a house of prayer,
The Devil always builds a chapel there;
And 'twill be found, upon examination,
The latter has the largest congregation.
DANIEL DEFOE, *The True-Born Englishman*. Pt. i, l. 1.

16
God never had a church but there, men say,
The Devil a chapel hath rais'd by some wiles.
I doubted of this saw, till on a day
I westward spied great Edinburgh's Saint Giles.
WILLIAM DRUMMOND, *A Proverb.*

17
No sooner is a temple built to God, but the Devil builds a chapel hard by.
GEORGE HERBERT, *Jacula Prudentum*. (1640)

18
For where God built a church there the Devil would also build a chapel. . . . Thus is the Devil ever God's ape.
MARTIN LUTHER, *Table-Talk: Of God's Works*. No. 67.

1
As, like a church and an ale-house, God and the Devil they many times dwell near to either.

THOMAS NASHE, *Have with You to Saffron-Walden.*

2
There can be no church in which the demon will not have his chapel.

CARDINAL PALEOTTI. (DIGBY, *Compitum.* Vol. ii, p. 297.)

CIRCLES

3
Do not disturb my circles. (Noli disturbare circulos meos.)

ARCHIMEDES, to the Roman soldier who, during the siege of Syracuse, 212 B.C., burst into his study to find him figuring some circles, and, being unable to obtain a satisfactory reply to his questions, put him to death. (VALERIUS MAXIMUS, viii, 7.)

4
The nature of God is a circle whose centre is everywhere and its circumference nowhere.

ST. AUGUSTINE. (EMERSON, *Essays: Circles.*)

5
Circles and right lines limit and close all bodies, and the mortal right-lined circle * must conclude and shut up all.

SIR THOMAS BROWNE, *Hydriotaphia.* Ch. v. (*The character of death.)

6
We all of us live too much in a circle.

BENJAMIN DISRAELI, *Sybil.* Bk. iii, ch. 7.

7
A circle may be small, yet it may be as mathematically beautiful and perfect as a large one.

ISAAC D'ISRAELI, *Miscellanies.*

8
Circles are prais'd, not that abound
In largeness, but th' exactly round:
So life we praise, that does excel
Not in much time, but acting well.

EDMUND WALLER, *Long and Short Life.*

Circles though small are yet complete.

UNKNOWN, *Inscription,* on a monument to two children, Northleigh Church, Oxon.

Round as the O of Giotto.

Pope Benedict XI once asked Giotto for a proof of his skill. Giotto sent him in reply an O drawn with a free sweep of the brush.

9
The eye is the first circle; the horizon which it forms is the second; and throughout nature this primary figure is repeated without end. It is the highest emblem in the cipher of the world.

EMERSON, *Essays, First Series: Circles.*

Nature centers into balls,
And her proud ephemerals,
Fast to surface and outside,
Scan the profile of the sphere.

EMERSON, *Essays, First Series: Circles.*

10
Every man is the center of a circle, whose fatal circumference he can not pass.

JOHN JAMES INGALLS, *Eulogy on Benjamin Hill,* U. S. Senate, 23 Jan., 1882.

11
He drew a circle that shut me out—
Heretic, rebel, a thing to flout.
But Love and I had the wit to win:
We drew a circle that took him in!

EDWIN MARKHAM, *Outwitted.*

12
As the small pebble stirs the peaceful lake;
The centre mov'd, a circle straight succeeds,
Another still, and still another spreads.

POPE, *Essay on Man.* Epis. iv, l. 364.

As on the smooth expanse of crystal lakes,
The sinking stone at first a circle makes;
The trembling surface by the motion stirr'd,
Spread in a second circle, then a third;
Wide, and more wide, the floating rings advance,
Fill all the wat'ry plain, and to the margin dance.

POPE, *Temple of Fame,* l. 436.

I watch'd the little circles die;
They passed into the level flood.

TENNYSON, *The Miller's Daughter.* St. 10.

13
I'm up and down and round about,
Yet all the world can't find me out;
Though hundreds have employed their leisure,
They never yet could find my measure.

SWIFT, *On a Circle.*

CIRCUMSTANCE

See also Chance, Destiny, Fate, Providence

14
He fixed thee 'mid this dance
Of plastic circumstance.

ROBERT BROWNING, *Rabbi Ben Ezra.* St. 28.

15
Circumstance, that unspiritual god
And miscreator, makes and helps along
Our coming evils.

BYRON, *Childe Harold.* Canto iv, st. 125.

16
Men are the sport of circumstances, when
The circumstances seem the sport of men.

BYRON, *Don Juan.* Canto v, st. 17.

I am the very slave of circumstance.

BYRON, *Sardanapalus.* Act iv, sc. 1.

Man is the creature of circumstance.

ROBERT OWEN, *The Philanthropist.*

Man, without religion, is the creature of circumstances.

J. C. AND A. W. HARE, *Guesses at Truth.*

Man is not the creature of circumstances, circumstances are the creatures of men. We are free agents, and man is more powerful than matter.

BENJAMIN DISRAELI, *Vivian Grey.* Bk. vi, ch. 7.

17
A "strange coincidence," to use a phrase
By which such things are settled nowadays.

BYRON, *Don Juan.* Canto vi, st. 78. Byron is

referring to the expression of Queen Caroline's advocate in the House of Lords, who spoke of circumstances in her association with Bergami as "odd instances of strange coincidence."

The long arm of coincidence has reached after me.
C. HADDON CHAMBERS, *Captain Swift*, Act ii.

1
A certain concurrence of circumstances.
LORD CHESTERFIELD, *Letters*, 9 Dec., 1746.

Fortuitous combination of circumstances.
DICKENS, *Our Mutual Friend*. Vol. ii, ch. 7.

The happy combination of fortuitous circumstances.
WALTER SCOTT, *Answer of the Author of Waverley to the Letter of Captain Clutterbuck: The Monastery*.

2
Circumstances alter cases.
DICKENS, *Edwin Drood*. Ch. 9.

3
Circumstances are beyond the control of man; but his conduct is in his own power.
BENJAMIN DISRAELI, *Contarini Fleming*. Pt. vii, ch. 2.

4
Tyrannical Circumstance!
EMERSON, *Conduct of Life: Fate*.

5
Under all this running sea of circumstance, whose waters ebb and flow with perfect balance, lies the aboriginal abyss of real Being.
EMERSON, *Essays, First Series: Compensation*.

You think me the child of my circumstances: I make my circumstance.
EMERSON, *Nature, Addresses, and Lectures: The Transcendentalist*.

6
The necessity of circumstances proves friends and detects enemies.
EPICTETUS, *Fragments*. No. 154.

7
I endeavor to subdue circumstances to myself, and not myself to circumstances. (Mihi res, non me rebus, subjungere conor.)
HORACE, *Epistles*. Bk. i, epis. 1, l. 19.

Men's plans should be regulated by the circumstances, not circumstances by the plans.
LIVY, *History*. Bk. xxii, ch. 39.

8
What the discordant harmony of circumstances would and could effect. (Quid velit et possit rerum concordia discors.)
HORACE, *Epistles*. Bk. i, epis. 12, l. 19.

9
Circumstances never made the man do right who didn't do right in spite of them.
COULSON KERNAHAN, *A Book of Strange Sins*.

10
Circumstances are things *round about;* we are *in* them, not *under* them.
W. S. LANDOR, *Imaginary Conversations: Samuel Johnson and John Horne*.

11
The circumstances of others seem good to us, while ours seem good to others. (Alienum nobis, nostrum plus aliis placet.)
PUBLILIUS SYRUS, *Sententiæ*. No. 28.

12
Leave frivolous circumstances.
SHAKESPEARE, *The Taming of the Shrew*. Act v, sc. 1, l. 27.

13
I don't believe in circumstances. The people who get on in this world are the people who get up and look for the circumstances they want.
BERNARD SHAW, *Mrs. Warren's Profession*. Act ii.

14
The changeful chance of circumstances. (Varia sors rerum.)
TACITUS, *History*. Bk. ii, sec. 70.

15
Breasts the blows of circumstance.
TENNYSON, *In Memoriam*. Pt. lxiv.

16
This fearful concatenation of circumstances.
DANIEL WEBSTER, *Argument*, on the murder of Captain White, 1830. (*Works*, vi, 88.)

17
F. M. the Duke of Wellington presents his compliments to Mr. ——, and declines to interfere in circumstances over which he has no control.
DUKE OF WELLINGTON, *Letter*, written in 1839, with reference to a business complication in which his son was involved. According to George Augustus Sala (*Echoes of the Week, London Illustrated News*, 23 Aug., 1884) this is the first recorded use of the phrase. (See FRASER, *Words on Wellington*, p. 10.)

Circumstances beyond my individual control.
DICKENS, *David Copperfield*. Ch. 20.

CITIES

I—Cities: Apothegms

18
Cities should be walled with the courage of their inhabitants.
AGESILAÜS II. (PLUTARCH, *Apothegms: Agesilaüs*.) When shown a walled city, he said: "It is for women, not men, to live in." To a stranger visiting Sparta, he showed the citizens in arms, saying: "These are the walls of Sparta."

Fighting men are the city's fortress.
ALCÆUS, *Fragment*. No. xxii.

A city will be well fortified which is surrounded by brave men and not by bricks. (Οὐκ ἂν εἴν ἀτείχιστος πόλις ἅτις ἄνδρεσσι, καὶ οὐ πλίνθοις ἐστεφάνωται.)
LYCURGUS, when asked to fortify the city. (PLUTARCH, *Lives: Lycurgus*. Ch. 19, sec. 4.)

If the inhabitants are of good morals I consider the place handsomely fortified. (Si incolæ bene sunt morati, pulchre munitum arbitror.)
PLAUTUS, *Persa*, l. 554. (Act iv, sc. 3.)

19
The Bible shows how the world progresses. It

begins with a garden, but ends with a holy city.

PHILLIPS BROOKS. (ALLEN, *Life and Letters.*)

1
If you would be known, and not know, *vegetate* in a village; if you would know, and not be known, *live* in a city.

C. C. COLTON, *Lacon.* Vol. i, No. 334.

2
The first requisite to a man's happiness is birth in a famous city. (Χρῆναι τῷ εὐδαίμονι πρῶτον ὑπάρξαι τὰν πόλιν εὐδόκιμον.)

EURIPIDES. (PLUTARCH, *Lives: Demosthenes.* Ch. 1, sec. 1.)

Surely in toil or fray, Under an alien sky,
Comfort it is to say, "Of no mean city am I!"

RUDYARD KIPLING, *Seven Seas: Dedication.*

I live in a small city, and I prefer to dwell there that it may not become smaller still.

PLUTARCH, *Lives: Demosthenes.* Ch. 2, sec. 2.

3
Where are the cities of old time?

EDMUND GOSSE, *The Ballade of Dead Cities.*

Even cities have their graves!

LONGFELLOW, *Amalfi.*

4
Cities are immortal.

GROTIUS, *De Jure Belli et Pacis.* Bk. ii, ch. 9.

For here we have no continuing city, but we seek one to come.

New Testament: Hebrews, xiii, 14.

5
Your weakness, city, Is that you have a soul.

LAURENCE HARTMUS, *City.*

6
The chicken is the country's, but the city eats it.

GEORGE HERBERT, *Jacula Prudentum.* No. 113.

The city is recruited from the country.

EMERSON, *Essays, Second Series: Manners.*

7
Far from gay cities and the ways of men.

HOMER, *Odyssey.* Bk. xiv, l. 410. (Pope, tr.)

8
Farmer Jake Bentley talks some o' movin' to the city so he kin keep a son.

KIN HUBBARD, *Abe Martin's Broadcast.*

9
The zenith city of the unsalted seas.

THOMAS FOSTER, *Speech,* referring to Duluth, Minn., 4 July, 1868. See *Duluth Minnesotean,* 1 May, 1869. Usually attributed to Proctor Knott, who quoted it in the House of Representatives, 27 January, 1871.

10
City of magnificent vistas.

PIERRE CHARLES L'ENFANT, the architect-engineer who planned the city of Washington and began its building. Afterwards corrupted to "City of magnificent distances."

11
A city that is set on a hill cannot be hid.

New Testament: Matthew, v, 14.

Beautiful for situation . . . is Mount Zion, . . . the city of the great King.

Old Testament: Psalms, xlviii, 2.

12
Where now the city stands, there was once naught but the city's site. (Hic, ubi nunc urbs est, tum locus urbis erat.)

OVID, *Fasti.* Bk. ii, l. 280.

13
The people are the city.

SHAKESPEARE, *Coriolanus.* Act iii, sc. 1, l. 200.

A great city is that which has the greatest men
and women,
If it be a few ragged huts it is still the greatest
city in the whole world.

WHITMAN, *Song of the Broad-Axe.* Sec. 4.

14
That city is the best to live in, in which those who are not wronged, no less than those who are wronged, exert themselves to punish the wrongdoers.

SOLON. (PLUTARCH, *Lives: Solon.* Sec. 18.)

15
Unless the Lord keepeth the city, the watchman waketh in vain. (Nisi Dominus fustra.)

Motto of the city of Edinburgh.

II—Cities: Their Virtues

16
And the need of a world of men for me.

ROBERT BROWNING, *Parting at Morning.*

17
Match me such marvel save in Eastern
clime—
A rose-red city, half as old as time.

JOHN WILLIAM BURGON, *Petra.*

18
I love capitals. Everything is best at capitals.

LORD CHESTERFIELD, *Letters,* 2 Oct., 1749.

The centre of a thousand trades.

COWPER, *Hope,* l. 246.

Golden towns where golden houses are.

JOYCE KILMER, *Roofs.*

19
Cities and Thrones and Powers
Stand in Time's eye
Almost as long as flowers,
Which daily die:
But, as new buds put forth
To glad new men,
Out of the spent and unconsidered Earth,
New Cities rise again.

RUDYARD KIPLING, *Cities and Thrones and Powers.* (*Puck of Pook's Hill: Prelude.*)

20
Let them sing who will of the gurgling rill,
Or the woodbird's note so wild;
My heart still sticks to the good red bricks—
For I was a city child.

WALTER LINDSAY, *O Patria Mia.*

21
I said, "Let me walk in the fields;"
He said, "Nay, walk in the town;"
I said, "There are no flowers there;"
He said, "No flowers, but a crown."

GEORGE MACDONALD, *What Christ Said.*

22
Towered cities please us then,

And the busy hum of men.
MILTON, *L'Allegro*, l. 117.

In the busy haunts of men.
FELICIA DOROTHEA HEMANS, *Tale of the Secret Tribunal*, l. 203.

'Midst the crowd, the hum, the shock of men.
BYRON, *Childe Harold*. Canto ii, st. 26.

1
For students of the troubled heart
Cities are perfect works of art.
CHRISTOPHER MORLEY, *John Mistletoe*, p. 27.

O praise me not the country—
The meadows green and cool,
The solemn glow of sunsets, the hidden silver pool!
The city for my craving,
Her lordship and her slaving,
The hot stones of her paving
For me, a city fool!
CHRISTOPHER MORLEY, *O Praise Me Not the Country*.

All cities are mad: but the madness is gallant. All cities are beautiful: but the beauty is grim.
CHRISTOPHER MORLEY, *Where the Blue Begins*, p. 55.

2
A house is much more to my taste than a tree,
And for groves, O! a good grove of chimneys for me.
CHARLES MORRIS, *The Contrast*.

3
Though the latitude's rather uncertain,
And the longitude also is vague,
The persons I pity who know not the City,
The beautiful City of Prague.
W. J. PROWSE, *The City of Prague*.

4
Fields and trees teach me nothing, but the people in a city do. (Τὰ μὲν οὖν χωρία καὶ τὰ δένδρα οὐδέν μ' ἐθέλει διδάσκειν, οἱ δ' ἐν τῷ ἄστει ἄνθρωποι.)
SOCRATES, explaining why he rarely left the city. PLATO, *Phædrus*. Sec. 230.

5
The city is built
To music, therefore never built at all,
And therefore built for ever.
TENNYSON, *Gareth and Lynette*, l. 272.

6
For the earth that breeds the trees
Breeds cities, too, and symphonies.
JOHN HALL WHEELOCK, *Earth*.

III—Cities: Their Faults

7
Cambridge people rarely smile,
Being urban, squat, and packed with guile.
RUPERT BROOKE, *The Old Vicarage, Grantchester*.

8
How fast the flitting figures come!
The mild, the fierce, the stony face;
Some bright with thoughtless smiles, and some
Where secret tears have left their trace.

These struggling tides of life that seem
In wayward, aimless course to tend,
Are eddies of the mighty stream
That rolls to its appointed end.
BRYANT, *The Crowded Street*.

9
High mountains are a feeling, but the hum
Of human cities torture.
BYRON, *Childe Harold*. Canto iii, st. 72.

10
To fly from the town to the country as though from chains. (Evolare rus ex urbe tanquam ex vinculis.)
CICERO, *De Oratore*. Bk. ii, sec. 6.

11
Well then; I now do plainly see
This busy world and I shall ne'er agree;
The very honey of all earthly joy
Does of all meats the soonest cloy;
And they, methinks, deserve my pity,
Who for it can endure the stings,
The crowd, the buzz, the murmurings
Of this great hive, the city.
ABRAHAM COWLEY, *The Wish*.

From cities humming with a restless crowd,
Sordid as active, ignorant as loud,
Whose highest praise is that they live in vain,
The dupes of pleasure or the slaves of gain;
Where works of man are clustered close around,
And works of God are hardly to be found.
COWPER, *Retirement*, l. 21.

12
In cities vice is hidden with most ease,
Or seen with least reproach.
COWPER, *The Task*. Bk. i, l. 689.

13
Cities give not the human senses room enough.
EMERSON, *Essays, Second Series: Nature*.

Cities force growth and make men talkative and entertaining, but they make them artificial.
EMERSON, *Society and Solitude: Farming*.

14
The modern town-dweller has no God and no Devil; he lives without awe, without admiration, without fear.
DEAN WILLIAM RALPH INGE, *Outspoken Essays:* Ser. i, *Our Present Discontents*.

15
The mobs of great cities add just so much to the support of pure government as sores do to the strength of the human body.
THOMAS JEFFERSON, *Writings*. Vol. ii, p. 229.

16
Who's ground the grist of trodden ways—
The gray dust and the brown—
May love red tiling two miles off,
But cannot love a town.
LESLIE NELSON JENNINGS, *Highways*.

17
The gloom and glare of towns.
ANDREW LANG, *Ballade of the Midnight Forest*

1
When ye go out of that city, shake off the very dust from your feet for a testimony against them.

New Testament: Luke, ix, 5.

2
Go down into the city. Mingle with the details; . . . your elation and your illusion vanish like ingenuous snowflakes that have kissed a hot dog sandwich on its fiery brow.

DON MARQUIS, *The Almost Perfect State.*

3
As one who long in populous city pent,
Where houses thick and sewers annoy the air.

MILTON, *Paradise Lost*. Bk. ix, l. 445.

4
To cities and to courts repair,
Flattery and falsehood flourish there;
There all thy wretched arts employ,
Where riches triumph over joy,
Where passion does with interest barter,
And Hymen holds by Mammon's charter;
Where truth by point of law is parried,
And knaves and prudes are six times married.

MATTHEW PRIOR, *Turtle and Sparrow*, l. 437.

5
I have, I said, found in Holy Scripture that Cain was the first builder of towns. (J'ay, dis je, trouvé en Escriture sacrée que Cayn fut le premier battisseur de villes.)

RABELAIS, *Works*. Bk. v, ch. 35.

God the first garden made, and the first city Cain.

ABRAHAM COWLEY, *The Garden.*

Divine Nature gave us fields; man's art built cities. (Divina natura dedit agros, ars humana ædificavit urbes.)

VARRO, *De Re Rustica*, iii. 1.

God made the country and man made the town.

COWPER, *The Task*. Bk. i, l. 749.

6
Cities are the sink of the human race. (Les villes sont le gouffre de l'espèce humaine.)

ROUSSEAU, *Émile*. Bk. i.

7
The City is of Night, but not of Sleep;
There sweet sleep is not for the weary brain;
The pitiless hours like years and ages creep,
A night seems termless hell.

JAMES THOMSON, *The City of Dreadful Night*. Pt. i, st. 11.

8
As for these communities, I think I had rather keep bachelor's hall in hell than go to board in heaven.

H. D. THOREAU, *Journal*, 3 March, 1841.

9
In great cities culture is diffused but vulgarized. . . . In great cities proud natures become vain. . . . If you want to submerge your own "I," better the streets of a great city than the solitudes of the wilderness.

MIGUEL DE UNAMUNO, *Essays and Soliloquies*, p. 127.

A great city, a great loneliness. (Magna civitas, magna solitudo.)

UNKNOWN. A Latin proverb taken from the Greek.

CIVILIZATION

I—Civilization: Definitions

10
The three great elements of modern civilisation, gunpowder, printing, and the Protestant religion.

CARLYLE, *Essays: German Literature.*

Increased means and increased leisure are the two civilizers of man.

BENJAMIN DISRAELI, *Speech*, 3 April, 1872.

11
There is nothing so fragile as civilization, and no high civilization has long withstood the manifold risks it is exposed to.

HAVELOCK ELLIS, *Impressions and Comments*. Ser. i, p. 105.

12
What is civilization? I answer, the power of good women.

EMERSON, *Miscellanies: Woman.*

13
The true test of civilization is, not the census, nor the size of cities, nor the crops,—no, but the kind of man the country turns out.

EMERSON, *Society and Solitude: Civilization.*

The test of civilization is the power of drawing the most benefit out of cities.

EMERSON, *Journals*, 1864.

A decent provision for the poor is the true test of civilization.

SAMUEL JOHNSON. (BOSWELL, *Life*, ii, 130.)

14
The highest civility has never loved the hot zones.
Wherever snow falls there is usually civil freedom.
Where the banana grows, man is sensual and cruel.

EMERSON, *Society and Solitude: Civilization.*

15
Civilization is paralysis.

PAUL GAUGUIN. (COURNOS, *Modern Plutarch*, p. 43.)

16
Civilization is simply a series of victories over nature.

WILLIAM HARVEY, *Where Are We and Whither Tending?* Lect. 1.

17
No one is so savage that he cannot become civilized, if he will lend a patient ear to culture. (Nemo adeo ferus est, ut non mitescere possit, Si modo culturæ patientem commodet aurem.)

HORACE, *Epistles*. Bk. i, epis. 1, l. 39.

18
Jesus wept; Voltaire smiled. Of that divine tear and of that human smile is composed the sweetness of the present civilization.

VICTOR HUGO, *Centenary Oration on Voltaire*, 30 May, 1878.

1
The true civilization is where every man gives to every other every right that he claims for himself.

R. G. INGERSOLL, *Interview*, Washington *Post*, 14 Nov., 1880.

The history of civilization is the history of the slow and painful enfranchisement of the human race.

INGERSOLL, *The Declaration of Independence.*

Civilization was thrust into the brain of Europe on the point of a Moorish lance.

INGERSOLL, *Address*, New York, 24 Jan., 1888.

2
Civilization is the making of civil persons.

JOHN RUSKIN, *The Crown of Wild Olive.*

3
Does the thoughtful man suppose that . . . the present experiment in civilization is the last the world will see?

GEORGE SANTAYANA, *Life of Reason.* Vol. ii, 127.

4
Our existing civilisations, described quite justifiably by Ruskin as heaps of agonizing human maggots, struggling with one another for scraps of food.

BERNARD SHAW, *Parents and Children.*

Those who admire modern civilization usually identify it with the steam engine and the electric telegraph.

BERNARD SHAW, *Maxims for Revolutionists.*

5
Civilization is a progress from an indefinite, incoherent homogeneity toward a definite, coherent heterogeneity.

SPENCER, *First Principles.* Ch. 16, par. 138.

II—Civilization: Its Faults

6
Civilization degrades the many to exalt the few.

AMOS BRONSON ALCOTT, *Table-Talk: Pursuits.*

7
Wealth may not produce civilization, but civilization produces money.

HENRY WARD BEECHER, *Proverbs from Plymouth Pulpit.*

8
It is a law of life and development in history that where two national civilizations meet they fight for ascendency.

BERNHARD VON BÜLOW, *Imperial Germany.*

9
They revenged themselves on tyranny by destroying civilisation.

BENJAMIN DISRAELI, *Contarini Fleming.* Pt. v, ch. 12.

10
Every prison is the exclamation point and every asylum is the question mark in the sentences of civilization.

S. W. DUFFIELD, *Essays: Righteousness.*

11
The civilized man has built a coach, but has lost the use of his feet.

EMERSON, *Essays, First Series: Self-Reliance.*

12
As long as our civilization is essentially one of property, of fences, of exclusiveness, it will be mocked by delusions.

EMERSON, *Representative Men: Napoleon.*

Is civilization only a higher form of idolatry, that man should bow down to a flesh-brush, to flannels, to baths, diet, exercise, and air?

MARY BAKER EDDY, *Science and Health*, p. 174.

13
Comfort, opportunity, number, and size are not synonymous with civilization.

ABRAHAM FLEXNER, *Universities*, p. 40.

14
Civilization is being poisoned by its own waste products.

DEAN W. R. INGE. (MARCHANT, *Wit and Wisdom of Dean Inge.* No. 195.)

15
Our civilization is a dingy ungentlemanly business: it drops so much out of a man.

R. L. STEVENSON, *Letters.*

CLEANLINESS

16
Cleanness of the body was ever deemed to proceed from a due reverence to God.

FRANCIS BACON, *Advancement of Learning* Bk. ii.

Slovenliness is no part of religion; neither this, nor any text of Scripture, condemns neatness of apparel. Certainly this is a duty, not a sin; "cleanliness is, indeed, next to godliness."

JOHN WESLEY, *Sermons:* No. xciii, *On Dress.* The text referred to is *I Peter*, iii, 3–4, "Whose adorning, let it not be that outward adorning," etc. Wesley puts the last phrase into quotation marks, indicating that it did not originate with him, but gives no indication as to its source.

17
He that toucheth pitch shall be defiled therewith.

Apocrypha: Ecclesiasticus, xiii, 7.

18
With unwashed feet. (Inlotis pedibus.)

AULUS GELLIUS, *Noctes Atticæ.* Bk. xvii, ch. 5, sec. 14. Referred to as a proverb, meaning irreverently.

19
Beauty will fade and perish, but personal cleanliness is practically undying, for it can be renewed whenever it discovers symptoms of decay.

W. S. GILBERT, *The Sorcerer.* Act ii.

20
Cleanliness is a fine life-preserver.

UNKNOWN.

One keep-clean is better than ten make-cleans

UNKNOWN.

21
Unless the vessel is clean, whatever you pour into it turns sour. (Sincerum est nisi vas, quodcumque infundis acescit.)

HORACE, *Epistles.* Bk. i, epis. 2, l. 54.

1
Above all things, keep clean. It is not necessary to be a pig in order to raise one.

R. G. INGERSOLL, *About Farming in Illinois.*

2
Be thou clean.

New Testament: Luke, v, 13. (Mundare.—*Vulgate.*) Christ to the leper.

God loveth the clean.

The Koran. Ch. 9.

3
Empty, swept, and garnished.

New Testament: Matthew, xii, 44; *Luke,* xi, 25.

4
Bid them wash their faces
And keep their teeth clean.

SHAKESPEARE, *Coriolanus.* Act ii, sc. 3, l. 68.

5
I'll purge and leave sack and live cleanly.

SHAKESPEARE, *I Henry IV.* Act v, sc. 4, l. 168.

6
The doctrines of religion are resolved into carefulness; carefulness into vigorousness; vigorousness into guiltlessness; guiltlessness into abstemiousness; abstemiousness into cleanliness; cleanliness into godliness.

Talmud: Mishna. (Dr. A. S. Bettelheim, tr.)

Religious zeal leads to cleanliness, cleanliness to purity, purity to godliness.

RABBI PHINEHAS-BEN-JAÏR, *Commentary on the Talmud.*

Poverty comes from God, but not dirt.

The Talmud.

7
Whoever eats bread without first washing his hands is as though he had sinned with a harlot.

Babylonian Talmud: Sotah, p. 4b.

To have not only clean hands, but clean minds. (Non solum manus, sed etiam mentes puras habere.)

THALES. (VALERIUS MAXIMUS. Bk. vii, ch. 2, sec. 8.)

8
Keep clean, bear fruit, earn life, and watch
Till the white-wing'd reapers come!

HENRY VAUGHAN, *The Seed Growing Secretly.*

CLERGYMEN, see Preachers

CLEVELAND, GROVER

9
Whatever you do, tell the truth.

GROVER CLEVELAND, to Charles W. Goodyear, when asked what should be done about the story of his liaison with Maria Halpin, sprung by the Republicans during the Presidential campaign of 1884. (NEVINS, *Grover Cleveland,* p. 163.) *See under* POLITICS: SLOGANS, and 452:12.

10
The other side can have a monopoly of all the dirt in this campaign.

GROVER CLEVELAND, during the campaign of 1884, when destroying a packet of "evidence" relating to the private life of James G. Blaine. (NEVINS, *Grover Cleveland,* p. 169.)

11
I feel like a locomotive hitched to a boy's express wagon.

GROVER CLEVELAND, in 1897, when asked how he felt with no Senate to fight and no official responsibility to bear. (MCELROY, *Grover Cleveland,* ii, 269.)

12
I have tried so hard to do right.

GROVER CLEVELAND, last words. (MCELROY, *Grover Cleveland,* ii, 385.)

13
They love him, gentlemen, and they respect him, not only for himself, but for his character, for his integrity and judgment and iron will; but they love him most for the enemies he has made.

GEN. EDWARD S. BRAGG, Governor of Wisconsin, *Speech,* seconding the nomination of Grover Cleveland for the Presidency, at the Democratic National Convention, Chicago, 9 July, 1884. (See *Wisconsin State Journal,* 10 July, 1884.) "They" referred to the young men of Wisconsin; "enemies" to Tammany Hall, which was bitterly fighting Cleveland's nomination. The phrase became one of the slogans of the campaign, and was usually quoted, "We love him for the enemies he has made." (MCELROY, *Grover Cleveland,* i, 81.)

14
For his was that best courage peace tries best,—
Sedate defiance of all clamors shrill;
Scorn of mere shows; stern putting to the test
Of men and causes, and unconquered will.

WM. GOLDSMITH BROWN, *Grover Cleveland.*

15
So long as the helm of state is entrusted to his hands we are sure that, should the storm come, he will say with Seneca's Pilot, "O Neptune! you may save me if you will; you may sink me if you will; but whatever happens I shall keep my rudder true."

JAMES RUSSELL LOWELL, *Address,* at celebration of 250th anniversary of Harvard College, 1886.

16
Let who has felt compute the strain
Of struggle with abuses strong,
The doubtful course, the helpless pain
Of seeing best intents go wrong;
We, who look on with critic eyes
Exempt from action's crucial test,
Human ourselves, at least are wise
In honoring one who did his best.

JAMES RUSSELL LOWELL, *Verses,* sent to Grover Cleveland, 10 December, 1889, with his regrets for non-attendance at a meeting in Boston which Cleveland had addressed.

17
He restored honesty and impartiality to government at a time when the service had become indispensable to the health of the re-

public. . . . To have bequeathed a nation such an example of iron fortitude is better than to have swayed parliaments or to have won battles or to have annexed provinces.

ALLAN NEVINS, *Grover Cleveland*, p. 766.

1

To nominate Grover Cleveland would be to march through a slaughter house into an open grave.

HENRY WATTERSON, *Editorial, Louisville Courier-Journal,* referring to nomination of 1892.

CLEVERNESS

See also Intelligence

2

Cleverness is serviceable for everything, sufficient for nothing.

AMIEL, *Journal.* 16 Feb., 1868.

3

And nobody calls you a dunce,
And people suppose me clever.

ROBERT BROWNING, *Youth and Art.*

Clever to a fault.

BROWNING, *Bishop Blougram's Apology.*

Too clever is dumb.

OGDEN NASH, *When the Moon Shines.*

4

Clever men are good, but they are not the best.

CARLYLE, *Essays: Goethe.*

I never heard tell of any clever man that came of entirely stupid people.

CARLYLE, *Inaugural Address,* Edinburgh, 1865.

5

"Brooks of Sheffield": "'Somebody's sharp.' 'Who is?'" asked the gentleman, laughing. I looked up quickly, being curious to know. "Only Brooks of Sheffield," said Mr. Murdstone. I was glad to find it was only Brooks of Sheffield; for at first I really thought that it was I.

DICKENS, *David Copperfield.* Ch. 2.

I know that man; he comes from Sheffield.

SYDNEY GRUNDY, *A Pair of Spectacles.*

6

Be good, sweet maid, and let who can be clever.

CHARLES KINGSLEY, *A Farewell.*

Here is a startling alternative which to the English, alone among great nations, has been not startling but a matter of course. Here is a casual assumption that a choice must be made between goodness and intelligence; that stupidity is first cousin to moral conduct, and cleverness the first step into mischief; that reason and God are not on good terms with each other.

JOHN ERSKINE, *The Moral Obligation to be Intelligent.*

7

It's clever, but is it art?

RUDYARD KIPLING, *The Conundrum of the Workshops.*

8

The wish to appear clever often prevents one from being so. (Le désir de paraître habile empêche souvent de le devenir.)

LA ROCHEFOUCAULD, *Maximes.* No. 199.

The supreme cleverness consists in knowing perfectly the price of things. (La souveraine habilité consiste à bien connaître le prix des choses.)

LA ROCHEFOUCAULD, *Maximes.* No. 244.

It is great cleverness to know how to conceal one's cleverness. (C'est une grande habilité que de savoir cacher son habilité.)

LA ROCHEFOUCAULD, *Maximes.* No. 245.

9

Cleverness is an attribute of the selecter missionary lieutenants of Satan.

GEORGE MEREDITH, *Diana of the Crossways.* Ch. 1.

10

The Athenians do not mind a man being clever, so long as he does not impart his cleverness to others.

PLATO, *Euthyphro.* Sec. 3.

11

Mr. Hannaford's utterances have no meaning; he's satisfied if they sound clever.

ALFRED SUTRO, *The Walls of Jericho.* Act i.

12

The wicked are always surprised to find ability in the good. (Les méchants sont toujours surpris de trouver de l'habileté dans les bons.)

VAUVENARGUES, *Réflexions.* No. 103.

13

If all good people were clever,
And all clever people were good,
The world would be nicer than ever
We thought that it possibly could.

But somehow, 'tis seldom or never
The two hit it off as they should;
The good are so harsh to the clever,
The clever so rude to the good.

ELIZABETH WORDSWORTH, *St. Christopher and Other Poems: The Clever and the Good.*

CLOUDS

14

I saw two clouds at morning
Tinged by the rising sun,
And in the dawn they floated on
And mingled into one.

JOHN G. C. BRAINARD, *I Saw Two Clouds at Morning.*

15

Were I a cloud I'd gather
My skirts up in the air,
And fly I well know whither,
And rest I well know where.

ROBERT BRIDGES, *Elegy: The Cliff Top.*

16

Our fathers were under the cloud.

New Testament: I Corinthians, x, 1.

17

The Lord went before them by day in a pillar of a cloud, to lead them the way; and by night in a pillar of fire.

Old Testament: Exodus, xiii, 21.

The Pillar of the Cloud.
JOHN HENRY NEWMAN. Title of hymn beginning, "Lead, kindly Light."

1
One cloud is enough to eclipse all the sun.
THOMAS FULLER, *Gnomologia*. No. 3743.

2
When clouds appear like rocks and towers,
The earth's refreshed by frequent showers.
WILLIAM HONE, *Year Book*, 1831, p. 300.

When mountains and cliffs in the clouds appear,
Some sudden and violent showers are near.
INWARDS, *Weather Lore*, p. 96.

A round-topped cloud with flattened face
Carries rainfall in its face.
INWARDS, *Weather Lore*, p. 96.

3
The clouds,—the only birds that never sleep.
VICTOR HUGO, *The Vanished City*.

4
"Only disperse the cloud," they cry,
"And if our fate be death, give light, and let us die."
JOHN KEBLE, *The Christian Year: Sixth Sunday after Epiphany*.

5
Behold, there ariseth a little cloud out of the sea, like a man's hand.
Old Testament: I Kings, xviii, 44.

6
The sun is set; and in his latest beams
Yon little cloud of ashen gray and gold,
Slowly upon the amber air unrolled,
The falling mantle of the Prophet seems.
LONGFELLOW, *A Summer Day by the Sea*.

7
The clouds in thousand liveries dight.
MILTON, *L'Allegro*, l. 62.

8
The low'ring element
Scowls o'er the darken'd landscape.
MILTON, *Paradise Lost*. Bk. ii, l. 490.

9
So clouds replenish'd from some bog below,
Mount in dark volumes, and descend in snow.
POPE, *The Dunciad*. Bk. ii, l. 363.

10
Who maketh the clouds his chariot.
Old Testament: Psalms, civ, 3.

Oh that a chariot of cloud were mine!
Of cloud which the wild tempest weaves in air.
SHELLEY, *Fragment: A Cloud-Chariot*.

In the clouds. (In nubibus.)
UNKNOWN. A Latin proverb.

11
If there were no clouds, we should not enjoy the sun.
JOHN RAY, *English Proverbs*.

12
We often praise the evening clouds,
And tints so gay and bold,
But seldom think upon our God,
Who tinged these clouds with gold.
SCOTT, *On the Setting Sun*.

13
A little gale will soon disperse that cloud . . .
For every cloud engenders not a storm.
SHAKESPEARE, *III Henry VI*. Act v, sc. 3, l. 10.

When clouds appear, wise men put on their cloaks.
SHAKESPEARE, *Richard III*. Act ii, sc. 3, l. 32.

14
The more fair and crystal is the sky,
The uglier seem the clouds that in it fly.
SHAKESPEARE, *Richard II*. Act i, sc. 1, l. 41.

15
I bring fresh showers for the thirsting flowers,
From the seas and the streams;
I bear light shade for the leaves when laid
In their noonday dreams.
From my wings are shaken the dews that waken
The sweet buds every one,
When rocked to rest on their mother's breast,
As she dances about the sun.
I wield the flail of the lashing hail,
And whiten the green plains under,
And then again I dissolve it in rain,
And laugh as I pass in thunder.
SHELLEY, *The Cloud*.

16
The clouds consign their treasures to the fields,
And, softly shaking on the dimpled pool
Prelusive drops, let all their moisture flow
In large effusion, o'er the freshen'd world.
THOMSON, *The Seasons: Spring*, l. 173.

17
A cloud lay cradled near the setting sun,
A gleam of crimson tinged its braided snow; . . .
Tranquil its spirit seemed and floated slow!
Ev'n in its very motion there was rest;
While every breath of eve that chanced to blow
Wafted the traveller to the beauteous west.
JOHN WILSON, *The Evening Cloud*.

The clouds that gather round the setting sun
Do take a sober colouring from an eye
That hath kept watch o'er man's mortality.
WORDSWORTH, *Intimations of Immortality*, l. 200.

18
I wandered lonely as a cloud
That floats on high o'er vales and hills.
WORDSWORTH, *Poems of the Imagination*, xii.

II—Clouds: Their Shape

19
The fair, frail palaces,
The fading Alps and archipelagoes,
The great cloud-continents of sunset-seas.
T. B. ALDRICH, *Sonnet: Miracles*.

20
Didst thou never espy a cloud in the sky
Which a centaur or leopard might be,
Or a wolf, or a cow?
ARISTOPHANES, *The Clouds*, l. 346.

Sometime we see a cloud that's dragonish;
A vapour sometime like a bear or lion,

A tower'd citadel, a pendant rock,
A forked mountain, or blue promontory.
SHAKESPEARE, *Antony and Cleopatra*. Act iv, sc. 14, l. 2.

Hamlet: Do you see yonder cloud that's almost in shape of a camel?
Polonius: By the mass, and 't is like a camel, indeed.
Hamlet: Methinks, it is like a weasel.
Polonius: It is backed like a weasel.
Hamlet: Or like a whale?
Polonius: Very like a whale. . . .
Hamlet: They fool me to the top of my bent.
SHAKESPEARE, *Hamlet*. Act iii, sc. 2, l. 393.

1
O, it is pleasant, with a heart at ease,
Just after sunset, or by moonlight skies,
To make the shifting clouds be what you please,
Or let the easily persuaded eyes
Own each quaint likeness issuing from the mould
Of a friend's fancy.
S. T. COLERIDGE, *Fancy in Nubibus*.

2
Thou must have marked the billowy clouds,
Edged with intolerable radiancy,
Towering like rocks of jet
Crowned with a diamond wreath. . . .
When those far clouds of feathery gold,
Shaded with deepest purple, gleam
Like islands on a dark-blue sea. . . .
Yet not the golden islands
Gleaming in yon flood of light,
Nor the feathery curtains
Stretching o'er the sun's bright couch,
Nor the burnished ocean-waves
Paving that gorgeous dome,
So fair, so wonderful a sight
As Mab's ethereal palace could afford.
SHELLEY, *Queen Mab*. Pt. ii, l. 9.

3
Becalmed along the azure sky,
The argosies of cloudland lie,
Whose shores, with many a shining rift,
Far off their pearl-white peaks uplift.
J. T. TROWBRIDGE, *Midsummer*.

III—Clouds: The Silver Lining

4
Was I deceiv'd, or did a sable cloud
Turn forth her silver lining on the night?
MILTON, *Comus*, l. 221.

I expand, I open, I turn my silver lining outward, like Milton's cloud.
DICKENS, *Bleak House*. Ch. 18.

Don't let's be down-hearted! There's a silver lining to every cloud.
W. S. GILBERT, *The Mikado*. Act ii.

5
Though outwardly a gloomy shroud,
The inner half of every cloud
Is bright and shining:
I therefore turn my clouds about
And always wear them inside out
To show the lining.
ELLEN THORNEYCROFT FOWLER, *The Wisdom of Folly*.

6
Nature is always kind enough to give even her clouds a humorous lining.
J. R. LOWELL, *My Study Windows: Thoreau*

7
every cloud
has its silver
lining but it is
sometimes a little
difficult to get it to
the mint
DON MARQUIS, *certain maxims of archy*.

8
There's a silver lining
Through the dark cloud shining,
Turn the dark cloud inside out,
Till the boys come home.
IVOR NOVELLO AND LENA GUILBERT FORD, *Keep the Home Fires Burning*. (1915)

9
After the greatest clouds the sun. (Post maxima nubila Phœbus.)
ALANUS DE INSULIS, *Liber Parabolarum*.

After clouds black, we shall have weather clear.
JOHN HEYWOOD, *Proverbs*. Pt. i, ch. 11.

After clouds comes clear weather.
SMOLLETT, *Sir Launcelot Greaves*. Ch. 10.

10
No cloud across the sun
But passes at the last, and gives us back
The face of God once more.
CHARLES KINGSLEY, *The Saint's Tragedy*. Act iii, sc. 2.

11
Be still, sad heart! and cease repining;
Behind the clouds is the sun still shining.
LONGFELLOW, *The Rainy Day*.

Never once, since the world began,
Has the sun ever stopped shining;
His face very often we could not see,
And we grumbled at his inconstancy,
But the clouds were really to blame, not he,
For behind them he was shining.
JOHN OXENHAM, *God's Sunshine*.

See also under COMPENSATION.

12
Behind the cloud the starlight lurks,
Through showers the sunbeams fall;
For God, who loveth all His works,
Has left His hope with all!
WHITTIER, *A Dream of Summer*.

13
Wait till the clouds roll by, Jenny,
Wait till the clouds roll by;
Jenny, my own true loved one,
Wait till the clouds roll by.
J. T. WOOD, *Wait Till the Clouds Roll By*. (1881)

CLOVER

14
Crimson clover I discover

By the garden gate,
And the bees around her hover,
But the robins wait.
Dora Reed Goodale, *Red Clover.*

1
Clouds of bees are giddy with clover.
Jean Ingelow, *Divided.*

2
The clover blossoms kiss her feet,
She is so sweet, she is so sweet.
While I, who may not kiss her hand,
Bless all the wild flowers in the land.
Oscar Laighton, *Clover Blossoms.*

3
He's in clover.
John Ray, *English Proverbs,* p. 57.

4
The clover is a homely little flower, but which flower has more honey?
John A. Shedd, *Salt from My Attic,* p. 36.

5
Flocks thick-nibbling through the clovered vale.
Thomson, *The Seasons: Summer,* l. 1234.

6
With airs outblown from ferny dells
The clover-bloom and sweetbrier smells.
Whittier, *The Last Walk in Autumn.*

COAL

7
Salt to Dysart, or coals to Newcastle.
Sir James Melville, *Autobiography,* i, 163. (1583)

To send you our news from England, were to carry coals to Newcastle.
Thoresby Correspondence, i, 16. (1682) Newcastle is a great British coal port.

So far from being needless pains, it may bring considerable profit to carry char-coals to Newcastle.
Thomas Fuller, *Pisgah Sight,* 128. (1650)

Labour in Vain, or Coals to Newcastle.
Unknown. Title of sermon announced in *Daily Courant,* London, 6 Oct., 1709.

To bring owls to Athens. (Γλαῦκ' εἰς 'Αθήνας.)
Aristophanes, *Aves,* l. 301. The Athenian coins were stamped with an owl.

To bear pots to Samos isle, . . . owls to Athens, crocodiles to Nile.
Sir John Harington, *Orlando Furioso,* xl, 1.

It is foolish to carry timber to a wood. (In silvam non ligna feras insanius.)
Horace, *Satires.* Bk. i, sat. 10, l. 34.

8
We may well call it black diamonds. Every basket is power and civilization. For coal is a portable climate. It carries the heat of the tropics to Labrador and the polar circle; and it is the means of transporting itself whithersoever it is wanted.
Emerson, *Conduct of Life: Wealth.*

9
The best sun we have is made of Newcastle coal, and I am determined never to reckon upon any other.
Walpole, *Letter to George Montagu,* 15 June, 1768.

COBBLERS, see Shoemakers

COCK, see Chanticleer

COLERIDGE, SAMUEL TAYLOR

10
Stop, Christian passer-by!—Stop, child of God,
And read with gentle breast. Beneath this sod
A poet lies, or that which once seem'd he.
O, lift one thought in prayer for S. T. C.;
That he who many a year with toil of breath
Found death in life, may here find life in death!
Mercy for praise—to be forgiven for fame
He ask'd, and hoped, through Christ. Do thou the same!
S. T. Coleridge, *Epitaph.* Six manuscript versions of this epitaph are extant, all showing minor variations.

11
He talked on for ever; and you wished him to talk on for ever.
William Hazlitt, *The Living Poets: Coleridge.*

12
He was a mighty poet and
A subtle-souled psychologist;
All things he seemed to understand,
Of old or new, on sea or land,
Save his own soul, which was a mist.
Charles Lamb, *Coleridge.*

13
It [*The Ancient Mariner*] is marvellous in its mastery over that delightfully fortuitous inconsequence that is the adamantine logic of dreamland.
J. R. Lowell, *Among My Books: Coleridge.*

14
You will see Coleridge—he who sits obscure
In the exceeding lustre and the pure
Intense irradiation of a mind
Which, with its own internal lightning blind,
Flags wearily through darkness and despair—
A cloud-encircled meteor of the air,
A hooded eagle among blinking owls.
Shelley, *Letter to Maria Gisborne,* l. 202.

Those songs half-sung that yet were all-divine—
That woke Romance, the queen, to reign afresh—
Had been but preludes from that lyre of thine,
Could thy rare spirit's wings have pierced the mesh
Spun by the wizard who compels the flesh,
But lets the poet see how heav'n can shine.
Theodore Watts-Dunton, *Coleridge.*

15
A noticeable man with large grey eyes,
And a pale face that seemed undoubtedly
As if a blooming face it ought to be,
Heavy his low-hung lip did oft appear,

Deprest by weight of musing Phantasy;
Profound his forehead was, though not severe.

WORDSWORTH, *Stanzas, Written in My Pocket Copy of Thomson's "Castle of Indolence."*

COLLEGE, see University

COLUMBIA, see America

COLUMBUS, CHRISTOPHER

1
O patient master, seer,
For whom the far is near,
The vision true, and the mere present pales.

LOUIS JAMES BLOCK, *The New World.*

2
Columbus! Other title needs he none.

FLORENCE EARLE COATES, *Columbus.*

3
Every ship that comes to America got its chart from Columbus.

EMERSON, *Representative Men: Uses of Great Men.*

4
Columbus discovered no isle or key so lonely as himself.

EMERSON, *Society and Solitude.*

5
He dreads no tempests on the untravell'd deep,
Reason shall steer, and skill disarm the gale.

PHILIP FRENEAU, *Columbus to Ferdinand.*

6
Well! but *I* saw It. Wait! the Pinta's gun!
Why look, 'tis dawn, the land is clear: 'tis done!
Two dawns do break at once from Time's full hand—
God's, East—mine, West: good friends, behold my Land!

SIDNEY LANIER, *Hymn of the West.*

7
Would that we had the fortunes of Columbus.
Sailing his caravels a trackless way,
He found a Universe—he sought Cathay.
God give such dawns as when, his venture o'er,
The Sailor looked upon San Salvador.
God lead us past the setting of the sun
To wizard islands, of august surprise;
God make our blunders wise.

VACHEL LINDSAY, *Litany of the Heroes.*

8
He gained a world; he gave that world
Its grandest lesson: "On! sail on!"

JOAQUIN MILLER, *Columbus.*

He gave the world another world, and ruin
Brought upon blameless, river-loving nations,
Cursed Spain with barren gold, and made the Andes
Fiefs of Saint Peter.

GEORGE SANTAYANA, *Odes.*

9
Into Thy hands, O Lord,
Into Thy hands I give my soul.

EDNA DEAN PROCTOR, *Columbus Dying.* "In manus tuas, Domine, commendo spiritum meum," were Columbus's last words.

10
Columbus found a world, and had no chart,
Save one that faith deciphered in the skies;
To trust the soul's invincible surmise
Was all his science and his only art.

GEORGE SANTAYANA, *O World.*

11
Then first Columbus, with the mighty hand
Of grasping genius, weigh'd the sea and land.

JAMES MONTGOMERY, *The West Indies.* Pt. i, l. 31.

Steer, bold mariner, on! albeit witlings deride thee,
And the steersman drop idly his hand at the helm.
Ever and ever to westward! there must the coast be discovered,
If it but lie distinct, luminous lie in thy mind.
Trust to the God that leads thee, and follow the sea that is silent;
Did it not yet exist, now would it rise from the flood.

SCHILLER, *Steer, Bold Mariner, On!*

12
Courage, World-finder! Thou hast need!
In Fate's unfolding scroll
Dark woes and ingrate wrongs I read
That rack the noble soul.

LYDIA HUNTLEY SIGOURNEY, *Columbus.*

13
From his adventurous prime
He dreamed the dream sublime:
Over his wandering youth
It hung, a beckoning star.
At last the vision fled,
And left him in its stead
The scarce sublimer truth,
The world he found afar.

WILLIAM WATSON, *Columbus.*

When shall the world forget
The glory and our debt;
Indomitable soul,
Immortal Genoese?

WILLIAM WATSON, *Columbus.*

14
What treasure found he? Chains and pains and sorrow—
Yea, all the wealth those noble seekers find
Whose footfalls mark the music of mankind!
'Twas his to lend a life: 'twas Man's to borrow:
'Twas his to make, but not to share, the morrow.

THEODORE WATTS-DUNTON, *Columbus.*

COMFORT

15
It's grand, and you canna expect to be baith grand and comfortable.

BARRIE, *The Little Minister.* Ch. 10.

1
We have all sinned and come short of the glory of making ourselves as comfortable as we easily might have done.

SAMUEL BUTLER THE YOUNGER, *The Way of All Flesh*, p. 82.

2
The villager, born humbly and bred hard,
Content his wealth, and Poverty his guard,
In action simply just, in conscience clear,
By guilt untainted, undisturb'd by fear,
His means but scanty, and his wants but few,
Labour his business, and his pleasure too,
Enjoys more comforts in a single hour
Than ages give the wretch condemn'd to power.

CHARLES CHURCHILL, *Gotham*. Bk. iii, l. 117.

They have most satisfaction in themselves, and consequently the sweetest relish of their creature comforts.

MATTHEW HENRY, *Commentaries*. Psalm 37.

See also GREAT AND SMALL.

3
Is there no balm in Gilead?

Old Testament: Jeremiah, viii, 22.

Is there no treacle in Gilead?

Old Testament: Jeremiah, viii, 22. Version in the "Treacle Bible," 1568.

Is there, is there balm in Gilead?

EDGAR ALLAN POE, *The Raven*. St. 15.

5
Thy rod and thy staff they comfort me.

Old Testament: Psalms, xxiii, 4.

6
Thou art all the comfort
The gods will diet me with.

SHAKESPEARE, *Cymbeline*. Act iii, sc. 4, l. 182.

O, my good lord, that comfort comes too late;
'Tis like a pardon after execution;
That gentle physic, given in time, had cur'd me;
But now I am past all comforts here but prayers.

SHAKESPEARE, *Henry VIII*. Act iv, sc. 2, l. 120.

I beg cold comfort; and you are so strait,
And so ingrateful, you deny me that.

SHAKESPEARE, *King John*. Act v, sc. 7, l. 42.

He receives comfort like cold porridge.

SHAKESPEARE, *The Tempest*. Act ii, sc. 1, l. 10.

7
Most of the luxuries and many of the so-called comforts of life are not only not indispensable, but positive hindrances to the elevation of mankind.

H. D. THOREAU, *Walden*: Ch. 1, *Economy*.

COMMAND, see Obedience

COMMERCE

See also Business

8
For Commerce, tho' the child of Agriculture,
Fosters his parent, who else must sweat and toil
And gain but scanty fare.

WILLIAM BLAKE, *King Edward the Third*. Sc. 2.

9
It is the interest of the commercial world that wealth should be found everywhere.

EDMUND BURKE, *Letter to Samuel Span, Esq.*

10
When we speak of the commerce with our colonies, fiction lags after truth, invention is unfruitful, and imagination cold and barren.

EDMUND BURKE, *Conciliation with America*.

11
In matters of commerce the fault of the Dutch
Is offering too little and asking too much.
The French are with equal advantage content,
So we clap on Dutch bottoms just twenty per cent.

GEORGE CANNING, *Dispatch*, in cipher, to Sir Charles Bagot, English Ambassador at The Hague, 31 Jan., 1826. Original attributed to Andrew Marvell. (See London *Morning Post*, 25 May, 1904; also *Notes and Queries*, ser. ix, vol. x, p. 270.) A paper on the subject was read before the Royal Historical Society by Sir Harry Poland, 16 Nov., 1905.

12
God is making commerce his missionary.

COOK, *Boston Monday Lectures: Conscience*.

13
It is well known what a middleman is: he is a man who bamboozles one party and plunders the other.

BENJAMIN DISRAELI, *Speech*, 11 April, 1845.

14
Trade which, like blood, should circularly flow.

DRYDEN, *Annus Mirabilis*. St. 2.

15
And where they went on trade intent
They did what freemen can,
Their dauntless ways did all men praise,
The merchant was a man.
The world was made for honest trade—
To plant and eat be none afraid.

EMERSON, *Boston*.

16
The craft of the merchant is this bringing a thing from where it abounds, to where it is costly.

EMERSON, *Conduct of Life: Wealth*.

There are geniuses in trade, as well as in war, or the State, or letters. . . . Nature seems to authorize trade, as soon as you see a natural merchant, who appears not so much a private agent as her factor and Minister of Commerce.

EMERSON, *Essays, Second Series: Character*.

17
Commerce is of trivial import; love, faith, truth of character, the aspiration of man, these are sacred.

EMERSON, *Essays, First Series: Circles*.

Trade, that pride and darling of our ocean, that educator of nations, that benefactor in spite of

itself, ends in shameful defaulting, bubble, and bankruptcy, all over the world.
EMERSON, *Society and Solitude: Works and Days.*

1
The most advanced nations are always those who navigate the most.
EMERSON, *Society and Solitude: Civilization.*

The greatest meliorator of the world is selfish, huckstering trade.
EMERSON, *Society and Solitude: Works and Days.*

Commerce is the great civilizer. We exchange ideas when we exchange fabrics.
R. G. INGERSOLL, *Reply to the Indianapolis Clergy.*

2
No nation was ever ruined by trade.
BENJAMIN FRANKLIN, *Thoughts on Commercial Subjects.*

Commerce proudly flourish'd through the state;
At her command the palace learn'd to rise,
Again the long-fall'n column sought the skies;
The canvas glow'd beyond e'en Nature warm,
The pregnant quarry teem'd with human form;
Till, more unsteady than the southern gale,
Commerce on other shores display'd her sail.
GOLDSMITH, *The Traveller,* l. 134.

3
And honour sinks where commerce long prevails.
GOLDSMITH, *The Traveller,* l. 92.

And trade's proud empire hastes to swift decay.
SAMUEL JOHNSON, line added to Goldsmith's *Deserted Village.*

In vain the state where merchants gild the top.
JOHN MARSTON, *What You Will.* Act i.

4
Perish commerce. Let the constitution live!
GEORGE HARDINGE, *Debate,* House of Commons, 22 March, 1793.

5
Who hath taken this counsel against Tyre, the crowning city, whose merchants are princes, whose traffickers are the honourable of the earth.
Old Testament: Isaiah, xxiii, 8.

Strike, louder strike, th' ennobling strings
To those whose Merchant Sons were Kings.
WILLIAM COLLINS, *Ode to Liberty,* l. 42.

A true-bred merchant is the best gentleman in the nation.
DANIEL DEFOE, *Robinson Crusoe: Farther Adventures.*

6
The merchant has no country.
THOMAS JEFFERSON, *Writings.* Vol. xiv, p. 119.

7
Is it not a common proverb amongst us when any man hath cozened or gone beyond us, to say, He hath played the merchant with us?
THOMAS NASHE, *Works,* iv, 240. (1593)

Merchant and pirate were for a long period one and the same person. Even today mercantile morality is really nothing but a refinement of piratical morality.
NIETZSCHE, *Thus Spake Zarathustra.*

8
What war could ravish, commerce could bestow,
And he returned a friend, who came a foe.
POPE, *Essay on Man.* Epis. iii, l. 205.

9
The merchant, to secure his treasure,
Conveys it in a borrow'd name.
MATTHEW PRIOR, *An Ode,* l. 1.

10
A merchant of great traffic through the world.
SHAKESPEARE, *The Taming of the Shrew.* Act i, sc. 1, l. 12.

Traffic's thy god; and thy god confound thee!
SHAKESPEARE, *Timon of Athens.* Act i, sc. 1, l. 246.

11
Hence Commerce springs, the venal interchange
Of all that human art or Nature yield; . . .
Commerce! beneath whose poison-breathing shade
No solitary virtue dares to spring,
But Poverty and Wealth with equal hand
Scatter their withering curses.
SHELLEY, *Queen Mab.* Canto v, l. 38.

12
The propensity to truck, barter, and exchange one thing for another . . . is common to all men, and to be found in no other race of animals.
ADAM SMITH, *Wealth of Nations.* Bk. i, ch. 2.

13
No man is a better merchant than he that lays out his time upon God and his money upon the poor.
JEREMY TAYLOR, *Holy Living and Dying.* Ch. 1.

14 Generous commerce binds
The round of nations in a golden chain.
THOMSON, *The Seasons: Summer,* l. 138.

Trade, the calm health of nations.
BULWER-LYTTON, *Richelieu.* Act iv, sc. 1.

COMPANIONS, COMPANIONSHIP

See also Brotherhood

I—Companions: Apothegms

15
A crowd is not company, and faces are but a gallery of pictures.
FRANCIS BACON, *Essays: Of Friendship.*

16
Endeavour, as much as you can, to keep company with people above you.
LORD CHESTERFIELD, *Letters,* 9 Oct., 1747.

Be the tail of lions rather than the head of foxes.
Babylonian Talmud: Pirke Aboth. Ch. 4, sec. 20.

I love good creditable acquaintance; I love to be the worst of the company.
SWIFT, *Letter to Stella,* 17 Apr., 1710.

17
Take the tone of the company you are in.
LORD CHESTERFIELD, *Letters,* 16 Oct., 1747.

18
Pleasures afford more delight when shared

with others; to enjoy them in solitude is a dreary thing.

DIO CHRYSOSTOM, *Third Discourse on Kingship*. Sec. 96.

There is no satisfaction in any good without a companion. (Nullius boni sine socio jucunda possessio est.)

SENECA, *Epistulæ ad Lucilium*. Epis. vi, sec. 4.

Who can enjoy alone,
Or all enjoying, what contentment find?

MILTON, *Paradise Lost*. Bk. viii, l. 365.

1
It brings comfort and encouragement to have companions in whatever happens.

DIO CHRYSOSTOM, *Third Discourse on Kingship*. Sec. 103.

MISERY LOVES COMPANY, *see under* MISERY.

2
We are in the same boat.

POPE CLEMENT I, *Epistle to the Church of Corinth*.

3
Ah, hideous company! but, in church with saints,
And with guzzlers in the taverns.
(Ahi fiera compagnia! ma nella chiesa
Coi santi ed in taverna coi ghiottoni.)

DANTE, *Inferno*. Canto xxii, l. 14.

4
Two are better than one. (Melius est ergo duos esse simul.)

Old Testament: Ecclesiastes, iv, 9.

One's too few, three too many.

JOHN RAY, *English Proverbs*, p. 173.

Two is company, but three is none.

W. C. HAZLITT, *Proverbs*, p. 442. A variant is, "Two is company but three is a crowd."

Two is company, three is trumpery, as the proverb says.

EDNA LYALL, *Wayfaring Men*. Ch. 24.

5
Men who know the same things are not long the best company for each other.

EMERSON, *Representative Men: Uses of Great Men*.

6
Better your room than your company.

SIMON FORMAN, *Marriage of Wit and Wisdom*. (c. 1570)

His room is better than his company.

ROBERT GREENE, *Works*. Vol. xi, p. 255.

7
The company makes the feast.

HACKWOOD, *Good Cheer*, p. 361. *See under* DINING.

8
Ez soshubble ez a baskit er kittens.

JOEL CHANDLER HARRIS, *Legends of the Old Plantation*. Ch. 3.

9
He cleaves to me like Alcides' shirt.

BEN JONSON, *The Poetaster*. Act iii, sc. 1.

10
To no man make yourself a boon companion:
Your joy will be less, but less will be your grief.
(Nulli te facias nimis sodalem:
Gaudibis minus et minus dolebis.)

MARTIAL, *Epigrams*. Bk. xii, epig. 34.

11
For we were nursed upon the self-same hill.

MILTON, *Lycidas*, l. 23.

12
Present company excepted.

JOHN O'KEEFFE, *The London Hermit*. (1793)

13
Companionship with a powerful person is never to be trusted. (Numquam est fidelis cum potente societas.)

PHÆDRUS, *Fables*. Bk. i, fab. 5, l. 1.

14
We still have slept together,
Rose at an instant, learn'd, play'd, eat together;
And whereso'er we went, like Juno's swans,
Still we went coupled and inseparable.

SHAKESPEARE, *As You Like It*. Act i, sc. 3, l. 75.

15
To make society
The sweeter welcome, we will keep ourself
Till supper-time alone.

SHAKESPEARE, *Macbeth*. Act iii, sc. 1, l. 42.

16
Nature hath fram'd strange fellows in her time.

SHAKESPEARE, *The Merchant of Venice*. Act i, sc. 1, l. 51.

Lion and stoat have isled together, knave,
In time of flood.

TENNYSON, *Gareth and Lynette*, l. 871.

17
I thought you and he were hand-in-glove.

SWIFT, *Polite Conversation*. Dial. ii.

18
No man can be provident of his time that is not prudent in the choice of his company.

JEREMY TAYLOR, *Holy Living and Dying*. Ch. i, sec. 1.

19
Good company and good discourse are the very sinews of virtue.

IZAAK WALTON, *The Compleat Angler*. Pt. i, ch. 2.

20
Company keeps our rind from growing too coarse and rough.

WALPOLE, *Letter to George Montagu*, 22 Sept., 1765.

21
When a university course convinces like a slumbering woman and child convince,
When the minted gold in the vault smiles like the night-watchman's daughter,
When warrantee deeds loafe in chairs opposite and are my friendly companions,
I intend to reach them my hand, and make as much of them as I do of men and women like you.

WALT WHITMAN, *A Song for Occupations*. Sec. 6.

II—Companions: A Man is Known By

1 Tell me what company thou keepest, and I'll tell thee what thou art. (Dime con quien Andas, decirte he quien eres.)

CERVANTES, *Don Quixote*. Pt. ii, ch. 10.

There is a Spanish proverb, which says very justly, Tell me who you live with and I will tell you who you are.

LORD CHESTERFIELD, *Letters*, 9 Oct., 1747.

2 Every man is like the company he is wont to keep.

EURIPIDES, *Phœnissæ*. Frag. 809.

He is known by his companions. (Noscitur a sociis.)

UNKNOWN. A Latin proverb.

3 If one wishes to be esteemed, one must live with estimable people. (Si l'on voulait être estimé, il faudrait vivre avec des personnes estimables.)

LA BRUYÈRE, *Les Caractères*. Pt. ii, No. 58.

4 A man's mind is known by the company it keeps.

J. R. LOWELL, *My Study Windows: Pope*.

5 A man is known by the paper he pays for.

JOHN A. SHEDD, *Salt from My Attic*, p. 19.

6 "A man is known by the company he keeps" —it is the motto of a prig. Little men with foot rules six inches long, applied their measuring sticks in this way to One who lived nineteen centuries ago. "He sit at meat with publicans and sinners," they tauntingly said, assuming that his character was smirched thereby.

ELBERT HUBBARD, *The Philistine*. Vol. xii, p. 62.

III—Companions: Evil Communications

7 Keep good men company, and thou wilt become one of them. (Júntate á los Buenos y serás uno dellos.)

CERVANTES, *Don Quixote*. Pt. ii, ch. 32.

8 Go with mean people and you think life is mean.

EMERSON, *Representative Men: Plutarch*.

9 Company makes cuckolds.

THOMAS FULLER, *Gnomologia*. No. 1132.

10 Keep not ill men company lest you increase the number.

GEORGE HERBERT, *Jacula Prudentum*.

11 Evil communications corrupt good character. (Φθείρουσιν ἤθη χρήσθ' ὁμιλίαι κακαί.)

MENANDER, *Thaïs: Fragment*.

Evil communications corrupt good manners.

New Testament: I Corinthians, xv, 33.

Evil communications corrupt good mutton.

GEORGE WILLIAM CURTIS, *Nile Notes of a Howadji*. Ch. 3.

See also under MANNERS.

12 This forbids a good man to consort for any purpose with an evildoer. (Interdecit ne cum maleficio Usum bonus consociet ullius rei.)

PHÆDRUS, *Fables*. Bk. iv, fab. 10, l. 20.

13 If you live with a lame person you will learn to limp. (Si claudo cohabites, subclaudicare disces.)

PLUTARCH, *The Education of Children*. Quoted.

14 The more closely you associate yourself with the good, the better. (Quam ad probos propinquitate proxime te adjunxeris, Tam optumum est.)

PLAUTUS, *Aulularia*, l. 236. (Act ii, sc. 2.)

15 Live with a hangman, and you will never be rid of your cruelty; if an adulterer be your club-mate, he will kindle the baser passions. If you would be stripped of your faults, leave far behind you the patterns of the faults. (Numquam sævitiam in tortoris contubernio pones. Incendent libidines tuas adulterorum sodalicia. Si velis vitiis exui, longe a vitiorum exemplis recedendum est.)

SENECA, *Epistulæ ad Lucilium*. Epis. civ., 21.

16 O, thou hast damnable iteration, and art indeed able to corrupt a saint. Thou hast done much harm upon me, Hal; God forgive thee for it! Before I knew thee, Hal, I knew nothing; and now am I, if a man should speak truly, little better than one of the wicked.

SHAKESPEARE, *I Henry IV*. Act i, sc. 2, l. 101.

I have forsworn his company hourly, any time this two-and-twenty years, and yet I am bewitch'd with the rogue's company. If the rascal have not given me medicines to make me love him, I'll be hanged.

SHAKESPEARE, *I Henry IV*. Act ii, sc. 2, l. 16.

Company, villanous company, hath been the spoil of me.

SHAKESPEARE, *I Henry IV*. Act iii, sc. 3, l. 11.

17 It is certain that either wise bearing or ignorant carriage is caught, as men take diseases, one of another: therefore let men take heed of their company.

SHAKESPEARE, *II Henry IV*. Act v, sc. 1, l. 83.

Therefore it is meet
That noble minds keep ever with their likes;
For who so firm that cannot be seduced?

SHAKESPEARE, *Julius Cæsar*. Act i, sc. 2, l. 315

18 Shun evil company. (Μὴ κακοῖς ὁμίλει.)

SOLON. (DIOGENES LAERTIUS, *Solon*. Bk. i, 60.)

19 Ill company is like a dog, who dirts those most whom he loves best.

SWIFT, *Thoughts on Various Subjects*.

IV—Companions: Like to Like

1
Like to like; jackdaw to jackdaw. (Τὸν ὅμοιόν ὡς τὸν ὅμοιον, καὶ κολοιὸν ποτὶ κολοιόν.)
ARISTOTLE, *Nicomachean Ethics*. Bk. vii, ch. 1, sec. 6.

Like to like. (Ὡς αἰεὶ τὸν ὁμοῖον.)
ARISTOTLE, *Rhetoric*. Bk. i, ch. 11, sec. 25. Quoted as a proverb.

As ever, the god is bringing like and like together. (Ὡς αἰεὶ τὸν ὁμοῖον ἄγει θεὸς ὡς τὸν ὁμοῖον.)
HOMER, *Odyssey*. Bk. xvii, l. 218.

How universally God joineth like to like!
MENANDER, *The Man from Sicyon: Fragment*.

Like with like most readily foregathers. (Pares cum paribus facillime congregantur.)
CATO, quoting an old proverb. (CICERO, *De Senectute*. Ch. iii, sec. 7.)

Like will to like.
JOHN HEYWOOD, *Proverbs*. Pt. i, ch. 4. (1546)

Like to like, the proverb saith.
SIR THOMAS WYATT, *The Lover Complaineth*.

2
Beast knows beast; birds of a feather flock together. (Ἔγνω δὲ θὴρ θῆρα, ἀεὶ κολοιὸς παρὰ κολοιόν.)
ARISTOTLE, *Rhetoric*. Bk. i, ch. 11, sec. 25. Quoted as proverbs.

Birds of a feather best fly together.
GEORGE WHETSTONE, *Promos and Cassandra*. (1578)

Birds of a feather will gather together.
ROBERT BURTON, *Anatomy of Melancholy*. Pt. iii, sec. i, mem. 2, subs. 1.

Then let's flock hither,
Like birds of a feather.
THOMAS RANDOLPH, *Aristippus*.

3
Things that have a common quality quickly seek their kind. (Ὅσα κοινοῦ τινος μετέχει, πρὸς τὸ ὁμογενὲς σπεύδει.)
MARCUS AURELIUS, *Meditations*. Bk. ix, sec. 9.

For as saith the proverb notable,
Each thing seeketh its semblable.
SIR THOMAS WYATT, *Re-cured Lover*. (1525)

V—Companions on a Journey

4
Good company is a good coach.
JOHN CLARKE, *Par. Anglo-Latina*, 291. (1639)

Good company upon the road, says the proverb, is the shortest cut.
OLIVER GOLDSMITH, *Vicar of Wakefield*. Ch. 18.

Good company in a journey makes the way to seem the shorter.
IZAAK WALTON, *Compleat Angler*. Pt. i, ch. 1. A proverb in all languages.

5
A man knows his companion in a long journey and a little inn.
THOMAS FULLER, *Gnomologia*. No. 284.

6
A merry companion is as good as a wagon.
JOHN LYLY, *Woman in the Moon*. Act iv. (1597)

A merry companion is music in a journey.
JOHN RAY, *English Proverbs*.

With merry company, the dreary way is endured. (Con alegre compania se sufre la triste via.)
UNKNOWN. A Spanish proverb.

7
A witty comrade at your side,
To walk's as easy as to ride.
(Comes facundus in via pro vehiculo est.)
PUBLILIUS SYRUS, *Sententiæ*. No. 104.

8
Most people sulk in stage-coaches; I always talk.
SYDNEY SMITH, *Sayings*. (LADY HOLLAND, *Memoir*. Vol. i.)

VI—Companions Lost

9
Whene'er with haggard eyes I view
This dungeon that I'm rotting in,
I think of those companions true
Who studied with me at the U-
Niversity of Göttingen.
GEORGE CANNING, *Song: Of One Eleven Years in Prison*.

10
Dear lost companions of my tuneful art,
Dear as the light that visits these sad eyes,
Dear as the ruddy drops that warm my heart.
THOMAS GRAY, *The Bard*, l. 39.

11
I have had playmates, I have had companions,
In my days of childhood, in my joyful school-days—
All, all are gone, the old familiar faces.
CHARLES LAMB, *The Old Familiar Faces*.

12
And the bright faces of my young companions
Are wrinkled like my own, or are no more.
LONGFELLOW, *The Spanish Student*. Act iii, sc. 3.

13
When, musing on companions gone,
We doubly feel ourselves alone.
SCOTT, *Marmion: Canto ii, Introduction*, l. 134.

COMPARISONS

14
To liken them to your auld-warld squad,
I must needs say comparisons are odd.
ROBERT BURNS, *The Brigs of Ayr*, l. 177.

15
Some say, compared to Bononcini,
That Mynheer Handel's but a ninny;
Others aver that he to Handel
Is scarcely fit to hold a candle.
Strange all this difference should be
'Twixt Tweedledum and Tweedledee.
JOHN BYROM. *On the Feud Between Handel and Bononcini*. The original version which appeared in the *London Journal*, 5 June, 1725, differs slightly from this. It was published with the heading: "The Contest. By the Author of the Celebrated Pastoral, My Time, O Ye Muses, Was Happily Spent." The last two lines were attributed to Swift and Pope in Scott's edition of the former

and Dyce's edition of the latter. (See *Notes and Queries*, Ser. x, 2, 7; 8, 47; and 11, 426.)

Est-ce Gluck, est-ce Piccinni,
Que doit couronner Polymnie?
Donc, entre Gluck et Piccinni
Tout le Parnasse est désuni;
L'un soutient ce que l'autre nie,
Et Clio veut battre Uranie.
Pour moi, qui crains toute manie,
Plus irrésolu que Babouc,
N'épousant Piccinni ni Gluck,
Je n'y connais rien; ergo, Gluck.

C. C. de la Ruthière, *Epigram*. This followed Byrom by fifty years, and was evoked by the quarrel between the followers of Gluck and Piccinni in Paris.

1

Is it possible your pragmatical worship should not know that the comparisons made between wit and wit, courage and courage, beauty and beauty, birth and birth, are always odious and ill taken?

Cervantes, *Don Quixote*. Pt. ii, ch. 1.

All comparisons are odious. (Toda Comparacion es odiosa.)

Cervantes, *Don Quixote*. Pt. ii, ch. 23.

She, and comparisons are odious.

Donne, *Elegies:* No. 8, *The Comparison*, l. 54.

Comparisons are odious.

John Fortescue, *De Laudibus Legum Angliæ*. Ch. 19. (1471); Burton, *Anat. of Melancholy*, iii, iii, 1, 2; Marlowe, *Lust's Dominion*, iii, 4; Carew, *Describing Mt. Edgcumbe;* Harvey, *Archaica*, ii, 23; Herbert, *Jacula Prudentum;* Heywood, *Woman Killed with Kindness*, i, 2; and many others.

2

Odious of old been comparisons.

John Lydgate, *Political Poems*. No. xxii. (c. 1440)

Comparisons are odorous.

Shakespeare, *Much Ado About Nothing*. Act iii, sc. 5, l. 18.

We own your verses are melodious,
But then comparisons are odious.

Swift, *Answer to Sheridan's Simile.*

3

Half-happy, by comparison of bliss,
Is miserable.

Keats, *Endymion*. Bk. ii, l. 371.

4

Comparisons do ofttime great grievence.

John Lydgate, *Bochas*. Bk. iii, ch. 8. (c. 1440)

5

Comparisons make enemies of our friends. (Ἐχθροὺς ποιοῦσι τοὺς φίλους αἱ συγκρίσεις.)

Philemon, *Fabulæ Incerta*. Frag. 17.

6

Another, yet the same.

Pope, *The Dunciad*. Bk. iii, l. 40.

In a deep pool, by happy chance we saw
A twofold Image; on a grassy bank
A snow-white Ram, and in the crystal flood
Another and the same!

Wordsworth, *The Excursion*. Bk. ix, l. 439.

7

Comparing what thou art,
With what thou mightst have been.

Walter Scott, *The Field of Waterloo*, l. 396.

8

Hyperion to a satyr.

Shakespeare, *Hamlet*. Act i, sc. 2, l. 140.

My father's brother, but no more like my father
Than I to Hercules.

Shakespeare, *Hamlet*. Act i, sc. 2, l. 152.

9

I have been studying how I may compare
This prison where I live unto the world:
And for because the world is populous
And here is not a creature but myself,
I cannot do it; yet I'll hammer it out.

Shakespeare, *Richard II*. Act v, sc. 5, l. 1.

No caparisons, miss, if you please. Caparisons don't become a young woman.

Sheridan, *The Rivals*. Act iv, sc. 2.

10

Knowing pups are like dogs and kids like goats,
So used I to compare great things with small.
(Sic canibus catulos similes, sic matribus hædos
Noram; sic parvis componere magna solebam.)

Vergil, *Eclogues*. No. i, l. 23.

If we may compare small things with great. (Si parva licet componere magnis.)

Vergil, *Georgics*. Bk. iv, l. 176.

To compare Great things with small.

Milton, *Paradise Lost*. Bk. ii, l. 921.

COMPASSION, see Pity

COMPENSATION

See also Gain and Loss; Good and Evil; Sweet and Sour

11

Night brings out stars as sorrow shows us truths.

P. J. Bailey, *Festus: Water and Wood.*

12

He who makes,
Can make good things from ill things, best from worst,
As men plant tulips upon dunghills when
They wish them finest.

E. B. Browning, *Aurora Leigh*. Bk. ii, l. 284.

Whosoe'er would reach the rose,
Treads the crocus under foot.

E. B. Browning, *Bertha in the Lane*. St. 26.

13

Each loss has its compensation;
There is healing for every pain;
But the bird with the broken pinion
Never soars so high again.

Hezekiah Butterworth, *The Broken Pinion.*

14

One moment may with bliss repay
Unnumber'd hours of pain.

Thomas Campbell, *The Ritter Bann*, l. 173.

A day in such serene enjoyment spent
Were worth an age of splendid discontent!

Montgomery, *Greenland*. Canto ii, l. 224.

1
O Lady! we receive but what we give,
And in our life alone doth Nature live;
Ours is her wedding-garment, ours her shroud!
S. T. COLERIDGE, *Dejection: An Ode*, l. 47.

2
How could a little tinker
Ever hope to sing
Without prison, or at least,
Grief and suffering.
POWER DALTON, *Flail.*

3
The wings of Time are black and white,
Pied with morning and with night.
Mountain tall and ocean deep
Trembling balance duly keep.
In changing moon, in tidal wave,
Glows the feud of Want and Have.
RALPH WALDO EMERSON, *Compensation.*

4
Evermore in the world is this marvellous balance of beauty and disgust, magnificence and rats.
EMERSON, *Conduct of Life: Considerations by the Way.*

5
Forever and ever it takes a pound to lift a pound.
EMERSON, *Lectures and Biographical Studies: Aristocracy.*

6
If severe, short; if long, light. (Si gravis brevis, si longus levis.)
EPICURUS, referring to pain. (CICERO, *De Finibus,* Bk. ii, sec. 7.)

Pain is generally light if long and short if strong, so that its intensity is compensated by its brief duration and its continuance by diminishing severity. (Dolor in longinquitate levis, in gravitate brevis soleat esse, ut ejus magnitudinem celeritas, diuturnitatem allevatio consoletur.)
CICERO, *De Finibus.* Bk. i, ch. 12, sec. 40.

The fiercest agonies have shortest reign.
BRYANT, *Mutation,* l. 4.

Long pains are light ones,
Cruel ones are brief!
J. G. SAXE, *Compensation.*

7
I know that any weed can tell
And any red leaf knows
That what is lost is found again
To blossom in a rose.
LOUIS GINSBERG, *I Know That Any Weed.*

8
As some tall cliff, that lifts its awful form,
Swells from the vale, and midway leaves the storm,
Though round its breast the rolling clouds are spread,
Eternal sunshine settles on its head.
GOLDSMITH, *The Deserted Village,* l. 189.

9
Oh, every heart hath its sorrow.
And every heart hath its pain—
But a day is always coming
When the birds go north again.
ELLA HIGGINSON, *When the Birds Go North Again.*

10
Good to the heels the well-worn slipper feels
When the tired player shuffles off the buskin;
A page of Hood may do a fellow good
After a scolding from Carlyle or Ruskin.
O. W. HOLMES, *How Not to Settle It.* St. 3.

11
Give unto them beauty for ashes, the oil of joy for mourning, the garment of praise for the spirit of heaviness.
Old Testament: Isaiah, lxi, 3.

12
It is a comfort that the medal has two sides. There is much vice and misery in the world, I know; but more virtue and happiness, I believe.
THOMAS JEFFERSON, *Writings.* Vol. xii, p. 379.

13
But the nearer the dawn the darker the night,
And by going wrong all things come right;
Things have been mended that were worse,
And the worse, the nearer they are to mend.
LONGFELLOW, *Tales of a Wayside Inn: The Baron of St. Castine,* l. 265.

14
Alas! by some degree of woe
We every bliss must gain;
The heart can ne'er a transport know
That never feels a pain.
GEORGE LYTTELTON, *Song.*

Our days and nights
Have sorrows woven with delights.
MALHERBE, *To Cardinal Richelieu.*

15
But many that are first shall be last; and the last shall be first.
New Testament: Matthew, xix, 30; *Mark,* x, 31; *Luke,* xiii, 30.

16
On the fall of an oak every man gathers wood. (Δρυὸς πεσούσης πᾶς ανὴρ ξυλεύεται.)
MENANDER, *Monostikoi.* No. 123.

17
Time still, as he flies, brings increase to her truth,
And gives to her mind what he steals from her youth.
EDWARD MOORE, *The Happy Marriage.*

18
Love, hope, and joy, fair pleasure's smiling train,
Hate, fear, and grief, the family of pain,
These mix'd with art, and to due bounds confin'd,
Make and maintain the balance of the mind;
The lights and shades, whose well-accorded strife
Gives all the strength and colour of our life.
POPE, *Essay on Man.* Epis. ii, l. 117.

1
There is no evil without its compensation. Avarice promises money; luxury, pleasure; ambition, a purple robe. (Nullum sine auctoramento malum est. Avaritia pecuniam promittit, luxuria voluptates, ambitio purpuram.)
SENECA, *Epistulæ ad Lucilium*. Epis. lxix, sec. 4.

2
As surfeit is the father of much fast,
So every scope by the immoderate use
Turns to restraint.
SHAKESPEARE, *Measure for Measure*, i, 2, 130.

3
Nought so vile that on the earth doth live
But to the earth some special good doth give,
Nor aught so good but strain'd from that fair use
Revolts from true birth, stumbling on abuse.
SHAKESPEARE, *Romeo and Juliet*. Act ii, sc. 3, 17.

4
Life may change, but it may fly not;
Hope may vanish, but can die not;
Truth be veiled, but still it burneth;
Love repulsed,—but it returneth!
SHELLEY, *Hellas*, l. 34.

4a
Every way we look we see even-handed nature administering her laws of compensation.
ALEXANDER SMITH, *Dreamthorp: On the Writing of Essays*.

5
Them ez wants, must choose.
Them ez hez, must lose.
Them ez knows, won't blab.
Them ez guesses, will gab.
Them ez borrows, sorrows.
Them ez lends, spends.
Them ez gives, lives.
Them ez keeps dark, is deep.
Them ez kin earn, kin keep.
Them ez aims, hits.
Them ez hez, gits.
Them ez waits, win.
Them ez *will*, *kin*.
EDWARD ROWLAND SILL, *A Baker's Duzzen Uv Wize Sawz*.

6
There is no felicity upon earth, which carries not its counterpoise of misfortunes; no happiness which mounts so high, which is not depressed by some calamity.
JEREMY TAYLOR, *Contemplation of the State of Man*. Bk. i, ch. 2.

7
Not a moth with vain desire
Is shrivel'd in a fruitless fire,
Or but subserves another's gain.
TENNYSON, *In Memoriam* Sec. liv.

8
We should have been undone, but for our undoing. (Ἀπωλόμεθα ἄν, εἰ μὴ ἀπωλόμεθα.)
THEMISTOCLES, to his children, when, after being exiled, he was entertained splendidly by Artaxerxes. (PLUTARCH, *Lives: Themistocles*. Ch. 19, sec. 7.)

9
If you rightly bear your cross, it will bear you. (Si libenter crucem portas, portabit te.)
THOMAS À KEMPIS, *De Imitatione Christi*. Bk. 2, ch. 5.

"The cross, if rightly borne, shall be
No burden, but support to thee;"
So, moved of old time for our sake,
The holy monk of Kempen spake.
J. G. WHITTIER, *The Cross*.

Though good things answer many good intents,
Crosses do still bring forth the best events.
ROBERT HERRICK, *Crosses*.

See also CHRISTIANITY: THE CROSS.

10
One plucked, another fills its room
And burgeons with like precious bloom.
(Primo avolso non deficit alter
Aureus, et simili frondescit virga metallo.)
VERGIL, *Æneid*. Bk. vi, l. 143.

11
Since I must be old and have the gout, I have long turned those disadvantages to my own account, and plead them to the utmost when they will save me from doing anything I dislike.
WALPOLE, *Letter to Sir Horace Mann*, 30 Oct., 1785.

12
And light is mingled with the gloom,
And joy with grief;
Divinest compensations come,
Through thorns of judgment mercies bloom
In sweet relief.
WHITTIER, *Anniversary Poem*. St. 15.

God's ways seem dark, but, soon or late,
They touch the shining hills of day.
WHITTIER, *For Righteousness' Sake*.

13
As high as we have mounted in delight,
In our dejection do we sink as low.
WORDSWORTH, *Resolution and Independence*, l. 24.

II—Compensation: Sun and Rain

14
There is a day of sunny rest
For every dark and troubled night:
And grief may bide an evening guest.
But joy shall come with early light.
BRYANT, *Blessed Are They That Mourn*.

15
Somewhere the sun is shining,
Somewhere a little rain.
CHARLES K. HARRIS, *Somewhere*. (1906)

Tho' the rain is on the river,
Yet the sun is on the hill.
F. WYVILLE HOME, *Sunshine and Rain*.

16
The world goes up, and the world goes down,
And the sunshine follows the rain;
And yesterday's sneer, and yesterday's frown

Can never come over again.
CHARLES KINGSLEY, *Dolcino to Margaret.*

1
Under the storm and the cloud to-day,
And to-day the hard peril and pain—
To-morrow the stone shall be rolled away,
For the sunshine shall follow the rain.
Merciful Father, I will not complain,
I know that the sunshine shall follow the rain.
JOAQUIN MILLER, *For Princess Maud.*

2
If you count the sunny and cloudy days throughout a year, you will find that the sunshine predominates. (Si numeres anno soles et nubilia toto, Invenies nitidum sæpius esse diem.)
OVID, *Tristia.* Bk. v, eleg. 8, l. 31.

O don't be sorrowful, darling!
And don't be sorrowful, pray;
Taking the year together, my dear,
There isn't more night than day.
REMBRANDT PEALE, *Don't Be Sorrowful, Darling.*

3
Day follows on the murkiest night, and, when the time comes, the latest fruits will ripen. (Tag wird es auf die dickste Nacht, und, kommt Die Zeit, so reifen auch die spät'sten Früchte.)
SCHILLER, *Jungfrau von Orleans.* Act iii, sc. 2.

COMPLIMENT

See also Flattery, Praise

4
You're exceedingly polite,
And I think it only right
To return the compliment.
W. S. GILBERT, *H. M. S. Pinafore.* Act i.

5
A compliment is usually accompanied with a bow, as if to beg pardon for paying it.
J. C. AND A. W. HARE, *Guesses at Truth.*

6
Compliments cost nothing, yet many pay dear for them.
THOMAS FULLER, *Gnomologia.* No. 1135.

7
What honour that,
But tedious waste of time, to sit and hear
So many hollow compliments and lies.
MILTON, *Paradise Regained.* Bk. iv, l. 122.

I have heard say that complimenting is lying.
SWIFT, *Polite Conversation.* Dial. i.

8
When quality meets compliments pass.
W. G. BENHAM, *Proverbs,* p. 870.

Compliments fly when gentlefolk meet.
R. L. STEVENSON, *St. Ives.* Ch. 28.

What compliments fly when beggars meet!
NORTHALL, *Folk Phrases,* 12.

9
Manhood is melted into courtesies, valour into compliment.
SHAKESPEARE, *Much Ado About Nothing.* Act iv, sc. 1, l. 321.

Fain would I dwell on form, fain, fain deny
What I have spoke: but farewell compliment!
SHAKESPEARE, *Romeo and Juliet.* Act ii, sc. 2, l. 88.

'Twas never merry world
Since lowly feigning was called compliment.
SHAKESPEARE, *Twelfth Night.* Act iii, sc. 1, l. 109.

10
Though compliments should arise naturally out of the occasion, they should not appear to be prompted by the spur of it; for then they seem hardly spontaneous. Applaud a man's speech at the moment when he sits down and he will take your compliment as exacted by the demands of common civility; but let some space intervene, and then show him that the merits of his speech have dwelt with you when you might have been expected to have forgotten them, and he will remember your compliment for a much longer time than you have remembered his speech.
SIR HENRY TAYLOR, *The Statesman,* p. 237.

11
This barren verbiage, current among men,
Light coin, the tinsel clink of compliment.
TENNYSON, *The Princess.* Pt. ii, l. 40.

12
I can live for two months on a good compliment.
MARK TWAIN. (PAINE, *Mark Twain.*)

COMPROMISE

13
The common problem, yours, mine, every one's,
Is—not to fancy what were fair in life
Provided it could be,—but, finding first
What may be, then find how to make it fair
Up to our means.
ROBERT BROWNING, *Bishop Blougram's Apology.*

And finds, with keen, discriminating sight,
Black's not so black,—nor white so *very* white.
GEORGE CANNING, *The New Morality.*

14
All government—indeed, every human benefit and enjoyment, every virtue and every prudent act—is founded on compromise and barter.
EDMUND BURKE, *Speech on Conciliation with America,* 22 March, 1775.

The concessions of the weak are the concessions of fear.
EDMUND BURKE, *Conciliation with America.*

15
Every compromise was surrender and invited new demands.
EMERSON, *Miscellanies: American Civilization.*

16
Everything yields. The very glaciers are viscous, or regelate into conformity, and the stiffest patriots falter and compromise.
EMERSON, *Miscellanies: The Fortune of the Republic.*

1
A lean compromise is better than a fat lawsuit.
GEORGE HERBERT, *Jacula Prudentum.*

2
Life cannot subsist in society but by reciprocal concessions.
SAMUEL JOHNSON, *Letter to Boswell,* 1766.

3
Man, a bear in most relations—worm and savage otherwise,—
Man propounds negotiations, Man accepts the compromise.
Very rarely will he squarely push the logic of a fact.
To its ultimate conclusion in unmitigated act.
RUDYARD KIPLING, *The Female of the Species.*

4
Heaven forbids, it is true, certain gratifications, but there are ways and means of compounding such matters. (Le Ciel défend, de vrai, certains contentements; Mais on trouve avec lui des accommodements.)
MOLIÈRE, *Le Tartuffe.* Act iv, sc. 5.

5
Basely yielded upon compromise
That which his noble ancestors achieved with blows.
SHAKESPEARE, *Richard II.* Act ii, sc. 1, l. 253.

6
All great alterations in human affairs are produced by compromise.
SYDNEY SMITH, *Essays: The Catholic Question.*

7
Is not Compromise of old a god among you?
SWINBURNE, *A Word from the Psalmist.* St. 4.

8
From compromise and things half done,
Keep me with stern and stubborn pride;
And when at last the fight is won,
God, keep me still unsatisfied.
LOUIS UNTERMEYER, *Prayer.*

Compromise is never anything but an ignoble truce between the duty of a man and the terror of a coward.
REGINALD WRIGHT KAUFFMAN, *The Way of Peace.*

COMRADE, see Brotherhood, Companionship

CONCEIT

See also Egotism, Self-Love, Vanity

9
Conceit is God's gift to little men.
BRUCE BARTON, *Conceit.*

10
Conceit is the most incurable disease that is known to the human soul.
HENRY WARD BEECHER, *Proverbs from Plymouth Pulpit.*

11
The world tolerates conceit from those who are successful, but not from anybody else.
JOHN BLAKE, *Uncommon Sense.*

Every man has a right to be conceited until he is successful.
BENJAMIN DISRAELI, *The Young Duke.*

12
Thus when we fondly flatter our desires
Our best conceits do prove the greatest liars.
DRAYTON, *The Barons' Wars.* Bk. vi, st. 94.

13
I laugh at the lore and the pride of man,
At the sophist schools, and the learned clan;
For what are they all, in their high conceit,
When man in the bush with God may meet?
RALPH WALDO EMERSON, *Good-Bye.*

Conceit, which destroys almost all the fine wits.
EMERSON, *Letters and Social Aims: Social Aims.*

14
We can bear to be deprived of everything but our self-conceit.
WILLIAM HAZLITT, *Characteristics.* No. 421.

15
Conceit is the finest armour a man can wear.
JEROME K. JEROME, *Idle Thoughts of an Idle Fellow: On Being Shy.*

16
Seest thou a man wise in his own conceit? there is more hope of a fool than of him.
Old Testament: Proverbs, xxvi, 12.

Wiser in his own conceit than seven men that can render a reason.
Old Testament: Proverbs, xxvi, 16.

Mind not high things, but condescend to men of low estate. Be not wise in your own conceits.
New Testament: Romans, xii, 16.

When Christian saw that the man was wise in his own conceit, he said to Hopeful whisperingly, There is more hopes of a fool than of him.
JOHN BUNYAN, *The Pilgrim's Progress.* Pt. i.

17
Conceit may puff a man up, but never prop him up.
RUSKIN, *True and Beautiful: Morals and Religion.*

18
Conceit in weakest bodies strongest works.
SHAKESPEARE, *Hamlet.* Act iii, sc. 4, l. 114.

There are a sort of men whose visages
Do cream and mantle like a standing pond,
And do a wilful stillness entertain,
With purpose to be dress'd in an opinion
Of wisdom, gravity, profound conceit.
SHAKESPEARE, *The Merchant of Venice,* i, 1, 88.

Conceit, more rich in matter than in words,
Brags of his substance, not of ornament.
SHAKESPEARE, *Romeo and Juliet,* ii, 6, 30.

19
Thy conceit is soaking.
SHAKESPEARE, *Winter's Tale.* Act i, sc. 2, l. 224

20
Still tempering, from the guilty forge
Of vain conceit, an iron scourge.
WORDSWORTH, *The Brownie's Cell,* l. 29.

CONDUCT, see Behavior, Manners

CONFESSION

1
Full sweetly heard he confession,
And pleasant was his absolution.
CHAUCER, *Canterbury Tales: Prologue*, l. 221.

2
May confession be a medicine to the erring. (Sit erranti medecina confessio.)
CICERO, *Ad Octavium*. Perhaps the original of the proverb, An open confession is good for the soul.

He oft finds med'cine who his grief imparts.
SPENSER, *The Faerie Queene*. Bk. i, canto ii, st. 34.

3
I destroy this man with his own confession. (Sua confessione hunc jugulo.)
CICERO, *In Verrem*. Oration ii, ch. 5, sec. 64.

4
Confess and be hanged.
ANTHONY COPLEY, *Wits, Fits and Fancies*, p. 148. (1594)

5
Come, now again thy woes impart,
Tell all thy sorrows, all thy sin;
We cannot heal the throbbing heart,
Till we discern the wounds within.
GEORGE CRABBE, *The Hall of Justice*. Pt. ii, l. 1.

6
Admissions are mostly made by those who do not know their importance.
CHARLES JOHN DARLING, *Scintillæ Juris*.

7
There are two confessionals, in one or the other of which we must be shriven.
EMERSON, *Essays, First Series: Self-Reliance*.

8
There are some things which men confess with ease, but others with difficulty. (Τῶν περὶ αὐτοὺς κακῶν τὰ μὲν ῥᾳδίως ὁμολογοῦσιν ἄνθρωποι, τὰ δ' οὐ ῥᾳδίως.)
EPICTETUS, *Discourses*. Bk. ii, ch. 21, sec. 1.

9
A generous confession disarms slander.
THOMAS FULLER, *Gnomologia*. No. 126.

10
Confession is the first step to repentance.
EDMUND GAYTON, *Festivous Notes on Don Quixote*, p. 66. (1654)

11
Of all unhappy sinners, I'm the most unhappy one!
The padre said, "Whatever have you been and gone and done?"
W. S. GILBERT, *Gentle Alice Brown*.

12
A fault confess'd was half amended.
SIR JOHN HARINGTON, *Epigrams*. Bk. iii, No. 25.

He's half absolv'd who has confessed.
MATTHEW PRIOR, *Alma*. Canto ii, l. 22.

13
Open confession is good for the soul.
H. G. BOHN. *Hand-Book of Proverbs*, p. 471.

14
Every one is wary in the confession; we should be as heedful in the action.
MONTAIGNE, *Essays*. Bk. iii, ch. 5.

15
They shall confess their sin which they have done.
Old Testament: Numbers, v, 7.

16
I will confess; if it advantages in aught to own one's faults. (Confiteor, si quid prodest delicta fateri.)
OVID, *Amores*. Bk. ii, eleg. 4, l. 3.

17
Confession of our faults is the next thing to innocency.
PUBLILIUS SYRUS, *Sententiæ*. No. 1060.

18
Confess yourself to heaven;
Repent what's past; avoid what is to come.
SHAKESPEARE, *Hamlet*. Act iii, sc. 4, l. 149.

Confess thee freely of thy sin.
SHAKESPEARE, *Othello*. Act v, sc. 2, l. 54.

19
I own the soft impeachment.
SHERIDAN, *The Rivals*. Act v, sc. 3.

CONFIDENCE

See also Self-Confidence, Trust

20
Sole friend to worth,
And patroness of all good spirits, Confidence.
CHAPMAN, *The Widow's Tears*. Act i, sc. 1.

21
Confidence is that feeling by which the mind embarks in great and honorable courses with a sure hope and trust in itself.
CICERO, *De Inventione Rhetorica*. Bk. i.

22
Confident because of our caution. (Δία τὴν εὐλάβειαν θαρραλέοι.)
EPICTETUS, *Discourses*. Bk. ii, ch. 1, sec. 7.

We should do everything both cautiously and confidently at the same time.
EPICTETUS, *Discourses*. Bk. ii, ch. 1, sec. 1.

23
Skill and confidence are an unconquered army.
GEORGE HERBERT, *Jacula Prudentum*.

24
By mutual confidence and mutual aid
Great deeds are done, and great discoveries made.
HOMER, *Iliad*. Bk. x, l. 265. (Pope, tr.)

25
Confidence does more to make conversation than wit. (La confiance fournit plus à la conversation que l'esprit.)
LA ROCHEFOUCAULD, *Maximes*. No. 421.

26
Confidence placed in another often compels confidence in return. (Habita fides ipsam plerumque obligat fidem.)
LIVY, *History*. Bk. xxii, ch. 22, sec. 20.

Confidence begets confidence. (Fides facit fidem.)
UNKNOWN. A Latin proverb.
See also under TRUST.

1
Confidence is wont to come slowly in matters of great moment. (Tarda solet magnis rebus inesse fides.)
OVID, *Heroides*. Epis. xvii, l. 130.

2
As to the present gentlemen, I cannot give them my confidence. Pardon me, gentlemen, confidence is a plant of slow growth in an aged bosom. Youth is the season of credulity.
WILLIAM PITT, EARL OF CHATHAM, *Speech*, House of Commons, 14 Jan., 1766.

I see before me the statue of a celebrated minister, who said that confidence was a plant of slow growth. But I believe, however gradual may be the growth of confidence, that of credit requires still more time to arrive at maturity.
BENJAMIN DISRAELI, *Speech*, House of Commons, 9 Nov., 1867.

3
My last confidence will be like my first. (Ultima talis erit quæ mea prima fides.)
PROPERTIUS, *Elegies*. Bk. ii, eleg. 20, l. 34.

4
Confidence, like the soul, never returns whence it has once departed. (Fides, sicut anima, unde abiit eo numquam redit.)
PUBLILIUS SYRUS, *Sententiæ*. No. 206.

5
Lack of confidence is not the result of difficulty; the difficulty comes from lack of confidence. (Non quia difficilia sunt, non audemus, sed quia non audemus, difficilia sunt.)
SENECA, *Epistulæ ad Lucilium*. Epis. civ, sec. 26.

6
Your wisdom is consum'd in confidence.
SHAKESPEARE, *Julius Cæsar*. Act ii, sc. 2, l. 49.

7
Confidence should arise from beneath, and power descend from above.
JOSEPH SIEYÈS. (THIERS, *Consulate and Empire*. Vol. i, p. 44.)

8
Confidence is conqueror of men; victorious
both over them and in them;
The iron will of one stout heart shall make a
thousand quail:
A feeble dwarf, dauntlessly resolved, will
turn the tide of battle,
And rally to a nobler strife the giants that
had fled.
MARTIN FARQUHAR TUPPER, *Proverbial Philosophy: Of Faith*, l. 11.

9
Alas! it is not wise to be confident when the gods are adverse. (Heu! nihil invitis fas quemquam fidere divis.)
VERGIL, *Æneid*. Bk. ii, l. 402.

Confidence is never secure. (Nunquam tuta fides.)
VERGIL, *Æneid*. Bk. iv, l. 373. Sometimes given: "Nusquam tuta fides," Nowhere is confidence secure.

10
Confidence is a thing not to be produced by compulsion. Men cannot be forced into trust.
DANIEL WEBSTER, *Speech*, U. S. Senate, 1833.

11
The most implicit confidence. (Uberrima fides.)
UNKNOWN. A Latin proverb.

CONQUERORS AND CONQUEST

For Self-Conquest see Self-Control

12
Quietly rested under the drums and tramplings of three conquests.
SIR THOMAS BROWNE, *Hydriotaphia*. Ch. 5.

13
What want these outlaws conquerors should
have
But History's purchased page to call them
great?
BYRON, *Childe Harold*. Canto iii, st. 48.

14
It is the right of war for conquerors to treat the conquered according to their pleasure. (Jus belli, ut qui vicissent, iis quos vicissent quæmadmodum vellent, imperarent.)
CÆSAR, *De Bello Gallico*. Bk. i, sec. 36.

15
The fame of a conqueror; a cruel fame, that arises from the destruction of the human species.
LORD CHESTERFIELD, *Letters*, 30 Sept., 1757.

16
Rats and conquerors must expect no mercy in misfortune.
C. C. COLTON, *Lacon*. Pt. i.

17
And though mine arm should conquer twenty
worlds,
There's a lean fellow beats all conquerors.
THOMAS DEKKER, *Old Fortunatus*. Act i, sc. 1.
See also DEATH THE INEVITABLE.

18
As conquerors will never want pretence,
When arm'd, to justify th' offence.
DRYDEN, *To the Pious Memory of Mrs. Anne Killigrew*, l. 96.

19
They can conquer who believe they can. It is he who has done the deed once who does not shrink from attempting it again.
EMERSON, *Society and Solitude: Courage*. *See also under* ABILITY.

20
I have lived enough, for I die unconquered. (Satis vixi, invictus enim morior.)
EPAMINONDAS. (CORNELIUS NEPOS, *Epaminondas*, 15.)

21
He that will conquer must fight.
THOMAS FULLER, *Gnomologia*. No. 2346.

22
Conquest pursues where courage leads the
way.
SAMUEL GARTH, *The Dispensary*. Canto iv, l. 99.

1
She Stoops to Conquer.
OLIVER GOLDSMITH. Title of comedy.

In this surrender, the National Government does not even stoop to conquer.
CHARLES SUMNER, *Speech*, U. S. Senate, 7 Jan., 1862.

2
Why read ye not the changeless truth,
The free can conquer but to save?
JOHN HAY, *Northward*. Quoted by President McKinley in a message on the Philippines.

3
The world is nowadays, God save the conqueror.
GEORGE HERBERT, *Jacula Prudentum*.

4
Like Douglas conquer, or like Douglas die.
JOHN HOME, *Douglas*. Act v, sc. 1, l. 100.

5
It is difficult to contend with a conqueror. (Contendere durum est cum victore.)
HORACE, *Satires*. Bk. i, sat. 9, l. 42.

6
A man may build himself a throne of bayonets, but he cannot sit on it.
DEAN W. R. INGE. (MARCHANT, *Wit and Wisdom of Dean Inge*. No. 108.)

7
To joy in conquest is to joy in the loss of human life.
LAO-TSZE, *The Simple Way*. No. 31.

8
The conquering cause was pleasing to the gods. (Victrix causa deis placuit.)
LUCAN, *De Bello Civili*. Bk. i, l. 128.

9
The conqueror would rather burst a city gate than find it open to admit him; he would rather ravage the land with fire and sword (ferri populetur et igni) than overrun it without protest from the husbandmen. He scorns to advance by an unguarded road or to act like a peaceful citizen.
LUCAN, *De Bello Civili*. Bk. ii, l. 443. Referring to Cæsar.

10
They'll wond'ring ask, how hands so vile
Could conquer hearts so brave.
THOMAS MOORE, *Weep On, Weep On*.

11
See the conquering hero comes!
Sound the trumpets, beat the drums!
DR. THOMAS MORELL, who wrote the text for Handel's oratorios, *Joshua* and *Judas Maccabeus*, in both of which this song was used. Also introduced into the later stage versions of Nathaniel Lee's *The Rival Queens*. Act ii, sc. 1.

Hail to the Chief who in triumph advances!
SCOTT, *The Lady of the Lake*. Canto ii, st. 19.

12
With the same hand with which he conquers he protects the conquered. (Qua vincit, victos protegit ille manu.)
OVID, *Amores*. Bk. i, eleg. 2, l. 52.

Humanity always becomes a conqueror.
SHERIDAN, *Pizarro*. Act i, sc. 1. (1799)

13
Yield if you are opposed: by yielding you conquer. (Cede repugnanti: cedendo victor abibis.)
OVID, *Ars Amatoria*. Bk. ii, l. 197.

The slender shrub which is seen to bend, conquers when it yields to the storm. (Sai che piegar si vede Il docile arboscello, Che vince allor che cede Dei turbini al furor.)
METASTASIO, *Il Trionfo di Clelia*, i, 8.

14
It is hard to conquer, but conquer you shall. (Male vincetis, sed vincite.)
OVID, *Metamorphoses*. Bk. viii, l. 509.

15
Conquered, we conquer. (Victi vicimus.)
PLAUTUS, *Casina*, l. 510. (Act i, sc. 1.)

He is hailed a conqueror of conquerors. (Victor victorum cluet.)
PLAUTUS, *Trinummus*. Act ii, sc. 2.

16
He went forth conquering and to conquer.
New Testament: Revelation, vi, 2.

17
The man is overcome without glory who is overcome without danger. (Sine gloria, qui sine periculo vincitur.)
SENECA, *De Providentia*. Sec. 3.

We triumph without glory when we conquer without danger. (A vaincre sans péril on triomphe sans gloire.)
CORNEILLE, *Le Cid*. Act ii, sc. 2.

The honor of the conquest is rated by the difficulty.
MONTAIGNE, *Essays*. Bk. iii, ch. 5.

18
We go to gain a little patch of ground,
That hath in it no profit but the name.
SHAKESPEARE, *Hamlet*. Act iv, sc. 4, l. 18.

It is a conquest for a prince to boast of.
SHAKESPEARE, *I Henry IV*. Act i, sc. 1, l. 77.

19
Conquest has explored more than ever curiosity has done; and the path of science has been commonly opened by the sword.
SYDNEY SMITH, *Table-Talk*.

20
For we by conquest, of our sovereign might,
And by eternal doom of Fate's decree,
Have won the Empire of the Heavens bright.
SPENSER, *Faerie Queene*. Bk. vii, canto vi, st. 33.

21
Arise, go forth, and conquer as of old.
TENNYSON, *The Passing of Arthur*, l. 64.

22
Which would you rather be,—a conqueror in the Olympic games, or the crier who proclaims him?
THEMISTOCLES, when asked whether he would rather be Achilles or Homer. (PLUTARCH, *Apothegms*.)

23
Drunk with the dream Of easy conquest.
JAMES THOMSON, *Britannia*, l. 70.

1
Not simple conquest, triumph is his aim.
YOUNG, *Night Thoughts*. Night v, l. 811.

2
Here lies one conquered that hath conquered kings,
Subdued large territories and done things
Which to the world impossible would seem
But the truth is held in more esteem.
UNKNOWN, *Inscription*, on tomb of Captain John Smith, Church of St. Sepulchre, London.

3
In this you shall conquer. (Ἐν τούτῳ νίκα.)
UNKNOWN. A Greek proverb. *See also under* CHRISTIANITY: THE CROSS.

II—Conquest: Veni, Vidi, Vici

4
I came, I saw, I conquered. (Veni, vidi, vici.)
JULIUS CÆSAR, *Letter to Amantius*, announcing his victory over Pharnaces at Zela in Pontus, 47 B. C.

In announcing the swiftness and fierceness of this battle to one of his friends at Rome, Amantius, Cæsar wrote three words: "Came, saw, conquered." (Ἦλθον, εἶδον, ἐνίκησα.)
PLUTARCH, *Lives: Cæsar*. Ch. 50, sec. 2.

In his Pontic triumph he displayed an inscription of but three words, "I came, I saw, I conquered" (Veni, Vidi, Vici), not indicating the events of the war, but the speed with which it was finished.
SUETONIUS, *Lives of the Cæsars: Julius*. Ch. 37, sec. 2. There is no authority for the frequent misstatement that the words were applied by Cæsar to his expedition to Britain (55 B. C.), which was only partly successful.

5
I came, I saw, God conquered.
JOHN SOBIESKI, to the Pope, with the Mussulman standards captured before Vienna.

The enemy came, was beaten, I am tired, good-night.
TURENNE, announcing his victory over the Spaniards at Dunkirk, June 14, 1658.

Hurrah! Prague! Suwarrow!
SUWARROW, announcing the capture of Prague, in 1794, to Catherine of Russia. Catherine's answer was, "Bravo! Field-marshal! Catherine!"

Peccavi!
SIR CHARLES NAPIER, announcing his victory at Hyderabad in 1843, meaning "I have Scinde."

6
Never shall the insolent barbarian say, "I came, I saw, I conquered." (Ne insolens barbarus dicat "Veni, vidi, vici.")
MARCUS ANNÆUS SENECA, *Suasoriæ*. Bk. ii, sec. 19. The earliest occurrence of the saying in literature, written by Seneca the Elder shortly before his death about A. D. 32.

7
Cæsar's thrasonical brag of 'I came, saw, and overcame.'
SHAKESPEARE, *As You Like It*. Act v, sc. 2, l. 34.

I may justly say, with the hook-nosed fellow of Rome, "I came, saw, and overcame."
SHAKESPEARE. *II Henry IV*. Act iv, sc. 3, l. 44.

He it was that might rightly say, Veni, vidi, vici; which to annothanize in the vulgar,—O base and obscure, vulgar!—videlicet, He came, saw, and overcame.
SHAKESPEARE, *Love's Labour's Lost*. Act iv, sc. 1, l. 67

CONSCIENCE

I—Conscience: Definitions

8
Conscience and reputation are two things. Conscience is due to yourself, reputation to your neighbor. (Duæ res sunt conscientia et fama. Conscientia tibi, fama proximo tuo.)
ST. AUGUSTINE, *Works*. Vol. xxi, p. 347.

There be two things that are necessary and needful, and that is good conscience and good report; that is to say, good conscience in thine own person inward, and good report for thy neighbour outward.
CHAUCER, *Melibeus*. Sec. 52. Quoting St. Augustine.

9
Conscience, which is a sparkle of the purity of his first estate.
BACON, *Advancement of Learning*. Bk. ii.

Labor to keep alive in your breast that little spark of celestial fire, called Conscience.
GEORGE WASHINGTON, *Moral Maxims: Conscience*.

10
The great beacon light God sets in all,
The conscience of each bosom.
ROBERT BROWNING, *Strafford*. Act iv, sc. 2.

11
Conscience was born when man had shed his fur, his tail, his pointed ears.
SIR RICHARD BURTON, *The Kasîdah*. Pt. v, st. 19.

12
Yet still there whispers the small voice within,
Heard through Gain's silence, and o'er Glory's din;
Whatever creed be taught or land be trod,
Man's conscience is the oracle of God.
BYRON, *The Island*. Canto i, st. 6.

Inexorable conscience holds his court,
With still, small voice the plot of guilt alarms.
ERASMUS DARWIN, *Mores Concluded*.

A still small voice spake unto me.
TENNYSON, *The Two Voices*, l. 1.

There is another man within me that's angry with me.
SIR THOMAS BROWNE, *Religio Medici*. Pt. ii.

13
Conscience, good my lord,
Is but the pulse of reason.
S. T. COLERIDGE, *Zapola*. Act i.

14
Conscience emphasizes the word ought.
JOSEPH COOK, *Boston Monday Lectures: Conscience*.

Our secret thoughts are rarely heard except in secret. No man knows what conscience is until he understands what solitude can teach him concerning it.

JOSEPH COOK, *Boston Monday Lectures: Conscience.*

1

In early days the Conscience has in most
A quickness which in later life is lost.

COWPER, *Tirocinium,* l. 109.

But at sixteen the conscience rarely gnaws
So much as when we call our old debts in
At sixty years, and draw the accounts of evil,
And find a deuced balance with the devil.

BYRON, *Don Juan.* Canto i, st. 167.

2

Oh! Conscience! Conscience! man's most faithful friend,
Him canst thou comfort, ease, relieve, defend;
But if he will thy friendly checks forego,
Thou art, oh! woe for me, his deadliest foe!

GEORGE CRABBE, *Tales:* No. xiv, *The Struggles of Conscience.* Last lines.

3

We must not harbor disconsolate consciences, borrowed too from the consciences of other nations. We must set up the strong present tense against all the rumors of wrath, past or to come.

EMERSON, *Essays, Second Series: Experience.*

The prosperous and beautiful
To me seem not to wear
The yoke of conscience masterful,
Which galls me everywhere.

EMERSON, *The Park.*

4

The man who acts never has any conscience; no one has any conscience but the man who thinks.

GOETHE, *Sprüche in Prosa.*

5

A man's conscience and his judgement is the same thing, and as the judgement, so also the conscience, may be erroneous.

THOMAS HOBBES, *Leviathan.* Pt. ii, ch. 29.

6

A man's vanity tells him what is honour; a man's conscience what is justice.

W. S. LANDOR, *Imaginary Conversations: Peter Leopold and President.*

7

Conscience is a God to all mortals. (Βροτοῖς ἅπασιν ἡ συνείδησις θεός.)

MENANDER, *Monostikoi.* No. 564.

8

The laws of conscience, which we pretend are born of nature, are born of custom. (Les loix de la conscience, que nous disons naistre de nature, naissent de la coustume.)

MONTAIGNE, *Essays.* Bk. i, ch. 22.

9

I ever understood an impartial liberty of conscience to be the natural rights of all men. . . . Liberty of conscience is the first step to having a religion.

WILLIAM PENN, *The People's Ancient and Just Liberties Asserted.* (1673)

10

Conscience is the voice of the soul, the passions are the voice of the body. (La conscience est la voix de l'âme, les passions sont la voix du corps.)

ROUSSEAU, *Émile.* Bk. iv.

11

I know thou art religious,
And hast a thing within thee called conscience,
With twenty popish tricks and ceremonies,
Which I have seen thee careful to observe.

SHAKESPEARE, *Titus Andronicus.* Act v, sc. 1, l. 74.

12

The conscience has morbid sensibilities; it must be employed but not indulged, like the imagination or the stomach.

R. L. STEVENSON, *Ethical Studies,* p. 84.

13

Conscience is God's presence in man.

SWEDENBORG, *Arcana Cœlesta.* Sec. 4299.

Conscience is, in most men, an anticipation of the opinion of others.

SIR HENRY TAYLOR, *The Statesman,* p. 63.

14

Conscience is instinct bred in the house,
Feeling and Thinking propagate the sin
By an unnatural breeding in and in.

H. D. THOREAU, *Conscience.* (*A Week on the Concord and Merrimack Rivers.*)

A conscience worth keeping,
Laughing not weeping;
A conscience wise and steady,
And forever ready;
Not changing with events,
Dealing in compliments;
A conscience exercised about
Large things that one *may* doubt.

H. D. THOREAU, *Conscience.* (*A Week on the Concord and Merrimack Rivers.*)

15

In matters of conscience that is the best sense which every wise man takes in before he hath sullied his understanding with the designs of sophisters and interested persons.

JEREMY TAYLOR, *Ductor Dubitantium.* Bk. i, ch. 1, rule 6. (1660)

16

The conscience is a thousand witnesses.

RICHARD TAVERNER, *Proverbs.* Fo. 29. (1539)

II—Conscience: Apothegms

17

He that loses his conscience has nothing left that is worth keeping.

CAUSSIN. (WALTON, *Compleat Angler.* Ch. 21.)

He who has no conscience has nothing. (Qui n'a conscience n'a rien.)

RABELAIS, *Works:* Bk. ii, *Prologue.*

18

Conscience, avaunt! Richard's himself again!

COLLEY CIBBER, *Richard III* (alt.). Act v, sc. 3.

1
Sell not your conscience; thus are fetters wrought.
What is a Slave but One who can be Bought?
ARTHUR GUITERMAN, *A Poet's Proverbs*, p. 80.

2
It is always term time in the court of conscience.
THOMAS FULLER, *Gnomologia*. No. 2914.

Why should not Conscience have vacation
As well as other Courts o' th' nation?
Have equal power to adjourn,
Appoint appearance and return?
BUTLER, *Hudibras*. Pt. ii, canto ii, l. 317.

3
Some make a conscience of spitting in the church, yet rob the altar.
GEORGE HERBERT, *Jacula Prudentum*. No. 646.

Once a year a man may say, "On his conscience."
GEORGE HERBERT, *Jacula Prudentum*. No. 964.

4
There is a spectacle more grand than the sea; it is heaven: there is a spectacle more grand than heaven; it is the conscience.
VICTOR HUGO, *Les Miserables: Fantine*. Bk. vii, ch. 3.

5
And crowneth Conscience king.
WILLIAM LANGLAND, *Piers Plowman*. Passus xxii, l. 256.

6
It is neither safe nor prudent to do aught against conscience.
MARTIN LUTHER, *Table-Talk*.

7
Help us to save free conscience from the paw
Of hireling wolves, whose gospel is their maw.
MILTON, *Sonnet: To Cromwell*.

8
Not as of the conscience of an angel or a horse, but of a man. (Non comme de la conscience d'un ange ou d'un cheval, mais comme de la conscience d'un homme.)
MONTAIGNE, *Essays*. Bk. iii, ch. 2.

9
According to the state of a man's conscience, so do hope and fear on account of his deeds arise in his mind. (Conscia mens ut cuique sua est, ita concipit intra Pectora pro facto spemque metumque suo.)
OVID, *Fasti*. Bk. i, l. 485.

10
What Conscience dictates to be done,
Or warns me not to do;
This teach me more than Hell to shun,
That more than Heav'n pursue.
POPE, *Universal Prayer*.

11
A scar on the conscience is the same as a wound. (Cicatrix conscientiæ pro vulnere est.)
PUBLILIUS SYRUS, *Sententiæ*.

12
Conscience places a bridle upon the tongue. (Frenos imponit linguæ conscientia.)
PUBLILIUS SYRUS, *Sententiæ*.

13
Passion is here a soilure of the wits,
We're told, and Love a cross for them to bear;
Joy shivers in the corner where she knits
And Conscience always has the rocking-chair,
Cheerful as when she tortured into fits
The first cat that was ever killed by Care.
E. A. ROBINSON, *New England*. *See also under* CARE.

14
Conscience has no more to do with gallantry than it has with politics.
SHERIDAN, *The Duenna*. Act ii, l. 4.

I will subdue my conscience to the plot.
SHERIDAN, *A Trip to Scarborough*. Act i.

15
Trust that man in nothing who has not a Conscience in everything.
STERNE, *Tristram Shandy*. Bk. ii, ch. 17.

16
As guardian of His Majesty's conscience.
LORD CHANCELLOR EDWARD THURLOW, *Speech*, House of Lords, 1780. (BUTLER, *Reminiscences*, p. 199.)

17
The conscience of the dying belies their life. (La conscience des mourants calomnie leur vie.)
VAUVENARGUES, *Réflexions*. No. 136.

18
Conscience makes egoists of us all.
OSCAR WILDE, *Portrait of Dorian Gray*. Ch. 8.

19
Their consciences are like cheverel skins, that will stretch every way.
UNKNOWN, *Discoverie of Knights of the Poste*. Sig. B4. (1597) A cheverel is a wild goat.

Which gifts,
Saving your mincing, the capacity
Of your soft cheveril conscience would receive,
If you might please to stretch it.
SHAKESPEARE, *Henry VIII*. Act ii, sc. 3, l. 30.

They have cheveril consciences that will stretch.
ROBERT BURTON, *Anatomy of Melancholy*. Pt. iii, sec. iv, mem. 2, subs. 3.

III—The Quiet Conscience

20
A conscience void of offence toward God, and toward men.
New Testament: Acts, xxiv, 16.

21
A quiet conscience makes one so serene!
BYRON, *Don Juan*. Canto i, st. 83.

22
A man that will enjoy a quiet conscience must lead a quiet life.
LORD CHESTERFIELD, *Letters*, 24 April, 1741.

23
O faithful conscience, delicately pure,
How doth a little failing wound thee sore!
(O dignitosa coscienza e netta,
Come t' è picciol fallo amaro morso.)
DANTE, *Purgatorio*. Canto iii, l. 8.

May heaven's grace so clear away the foam from the conscience, that the river of thy thoughts may roll limpid henceforth.
DANTE, *Purgatorio*. Canto xiii, l. 88.

1
Keep conscience clear, then never fear.
BENJAMIN FRANKLIN, *Poor Richard,* 1749.

2
A clear conscience can bear any trouble.
THOMAS FULLER, *Gnomologia*. No. 40.

A quiet conscience sleeps in thunder.
THOMAS FULLER, *Gnomologia*. No. 374.

A good conscience is a continual Christmas.
BENJAMIN FRANKLIN, *Poor Richard,* 1749.

3
A clear conscience is a sure card.
JOHN LYLY, *Euphues,* p. 207. (1580)

A clear conscience needeth no excuse.
JOHN LYLY, *Euphues,* p. 256.

See also under INNOCENCE.

4
A good conscience is a soft pillow.
JOHN RAY, *English Proverbs*.

What better bed than conscience good, to pass the night with sleep.
THOMAS TUSSER, *Posies for Thine Own Bed-Chamber*.

5
A peace above all earthly dignities,
A still and quiet conscience.
SHAKESPEARE, *Henry VIII*. Act iii, sc. 2, l. 379.

A very gentle beast, and of a good conscience.
SHAKESPEARE, *A Midsummer-Night's Dream*. Act v, sc. 1, l. 230.

6
The testimony of a good conscience is the glory of a good man; have a good conscience and thou shalt ever have gladness. A good conscience may bear right many things and rejoices among adversities.
THOMAS À KEMPIS, *De Imitatione Christi*. Pt. ii, ch. 6.

IV—The Guilty Conscience

See also Remorse

7
A burthen'd conscience
Will never need a hangman.
BEAUMONT AND FLETCHER, *Laws of Candy*. Act v, sc. 1.

8
Conscience wakened in a fever,
Just a day too late, as ever.
ROBERT BUCHANAN, *White Rose and Red*. Pt. ii, l. 5.

9
Those whom God forsakes, the devil by his permission lays hold on. Sometimes he persecutes them with that worm of conscience, as he did Judas, Saul, and others. The poets call it Nemesis.
ROBERT BURTON, *Anatomy of Melancholy*. Pt. iii, sec. iv, mem. 2, subs. 3.

The worm of conscience still begnaw thy soul!
SHAKESPEARE, *Richard III*. Act i, sc. 3, l. 222.

The worm of conscience consorts with the owl.
Sinners and evil spirits shun the light.
SCHILLER, *Kabale und Liebe*. Act v, sc. 1.

10
When Conscience wakens who can with her strive?
Terrors and troubles from a sick soul drive?
Naught so unpitying as the ire of sin,
The inappeas'ble Nemesis within.
ABRAHAM COLES, *The Light of the World*.

No hell like a bad conscience.
JOHN CROWNE, *The Ambitious Statesman*. Act v, sc. 3. (1679)

An evil conscience breaks many a man's neck.
THOMAS FULLER, *Gnomologia*. No. 602.

The disease of an evil conscience is beyond the practice of all the physicians of all the countries in the world.
W. E. GLADSTONE, *Speech,* Plumstead, 1878.

11
No guilty man is acquitted at the bar of his own conscience, though he win his cause by a juggling urn, and the corrupt favor of the judge. (Judice nemo nocens absolvitur, improba quamvis Gratia fallaci prætoris vicerit urna.)
JUVENAL, *Satires*. Sat. xiii, l. 3.

12
Now conscience wakes despair
That slumber'd, wakes the bitter memory
Of what he was, what is, and what must be
Worse; of worse deeds worse sufferings must ensue!
MILTON, *Paradise Lost*. Bk. iv, l. 23.

O conscience, into what abyss of fears
And horrors hast thou driven me!
MILTON, *Paradise Lost*. Bk. x, l. 842.

Let his tormentor conscience find him out.
MILTON, *Paradise Regained*. Bk. iv, l. 130.

13
Whom conscience, ne'er asleep,
Wounds with incessant strokes, not loud, but deep.
MONTAIGNE, *Essays:* Bk. ii, ch. 5.

14
Conscience, the bosom-hell of guilty man!
MONTGOMERY, *Pelican Island*. Canto v, l. 127.

15
Nothing is more wretched than the mind of a man conscious of guilt. (Nihil est miserius quam animus hominis conscius.)
PLAUTUS, *Mostellaria*. Act iii, sc. 1, l. 13.

A guilty conscience never feels secure.
PUBLILIUS SYRUS, *Sententiæ*. No. 617.

The guilt of conscience take thou for thy labour,
But neither my good word nor princely favour:
With Cain go wander thorough shades of night,
And never show thy head by day nor light.
SHAKESPEARE, *Richard II*. Act v, sc. 6, l. 41.

16
Some certain dregs of conscience are yet within me.
SHAKESPEARE, *Richard III*. Act i, sc. 4, l. 124

My conscience hath a thousand several tongues,
And every tongue brings in a several tale,
And every tale condemns me for a villain.
SHAKESPEARE, *Richard III*. Act v, sc. 3, l. 193.

And conscience, that undying serpent, calls
Her venomous brood to their nocturnal task.
SHELLEY, *Queen Mab*. Canto iii, l. 60.

1
I sat alone with my conscience
In a place where time had ceased,
And we talked of my former living
In the land where the years increased.
CHARLES WILLIAM STUBBS, *Alone with My Conscience*.

And I know of the future judgment
How dreadful so'er it be
That to sit alone with my conscience
Would be judgment enough for me.
CHARLES WILLIAM STUBBS, *Alone with My Conscience*.

2
The guilty conscience thinks what is said
Is always spoken himself to upbraid.
UNKNOWN, *Servingmans Comfort*. (1598)

V—The Coward Conscience

3
Conscience is a coward, and those faults it has not strength enough to prevent, it seldom has justice enough to accuse.
GOLDSMITH, *The Vicar of Wakefield*. Ch. 13.

4
Guilty consciences ever make people cowards.
PILPAY, *Fables: The Prince and the Minister*.

5
In every hedge and ditch both day and night
We fear our death, of every leaf affright;
A lamp appears a lion, and we fear
Each bush we see 's a bear.
FRANCIS QUARLES, *Emblems*. Bk. i, emb. 13.

Or in the night, imagining some fear,
How easy is a bush supposed a bear!
SHAKESPEARE, *A Midsummer-Night's Dream*. Act v, sc. 1, l. 21.

The guilty conscience fears, when there's no fear,
And thinks that every bush contains a bear.
ROWLAND WATKYNS, *Flamma Sine Fumo: The Righteous Is Confident as a Lion*.

6
The fond fantastic thing call'd conscience,
Which serves for nothing but to make men cowards.
THOMAS SHADWELL, *The Libertine*. Act i, sc. 1.

7
Thus conscience does make cowards of us all;
And thus the native hue of resolution
Is sicklied o'er with the pale cast of thought,
And enterprises of great pith and moment
With this regard their currents turn awry,
And lose the name of action.
SHAKESPEARE, *Hamlet*. Act iii, sc. 1, l. 83.

8
O coward conscience, how dost thou afflict me!
SHAKESPEARE, *Richard III*. Act v, sc. 3, l. 179.

I'll not meddle with it [conscience]: it is a dangerous thing: it makes a man a coward: a man cannot steal, but it accuseth him; he cannot swear, but it checks him; he cannot lie with his neighbour's wife, but it detects him: 'tis a blushing shamefast spirit that mutinies in a man's bosom; it fills one full of obstacles: . . . it beggars any man that keeps it.
SHAKESPEARE, *Richard III*. Act i, sc. 4, l. 137.

9
By the apostle Paul, shadows to-night
Have struck more terror to the soul of Richard
Than can the substance of ten thousand soldiers.
SHAKESPEARE, *Richard III*. Act v, sc. 3, l. 216.

10
Conscience is but a word that cowards use,
Devised at first to keep the strong in awe.
SHAKESPEARE, *Richard III*. Act v, sc. 3, l. 309.

11
O the cowardice of a guilty conscience.
SIR PHILIP SIDNEY, *Arcadia*. Bk. ii.

A guilty conscience never thinketh itself safe.
THOMAS FULLER, *Gnomologia*. No. 208.

Guilty consciences make men cowards.
VANBRUGH, *The Provok'd Wife*. Act v, sc. 6.

12
Conscience and cowardice are really the same things. Conscience is the trade-name of the firm. That is all.
OSCAR WILDE, *Picture of Dorian Gray*. Ch. 1.

13
Conscience, a terrifying little sprite,
That bat-like winks by day and wakes by night.
JOHN WOLCOT, *The Lousiad*. Canto ii.

CONSEQUENCES

14
Things and actions are what they are, and the consequences of them will be what they will be; why then should we desire to be deceived?
BISHOP JOSEPH BUTLER, *Sermons*. No. 7.

15
The pitcher that goes too often to the well leaves behind either the handle or the spout. (Cantarillo que muchas veces va á la fuente O deja el asa ó la frente.)
CERVANTES, *Don Quixote*. Pt. i, ch. 30.

Whether the pitcher hits the stone, or the stone hits the pitcher, it's a bad business for the pitcher.
CERVANTES, *Don Quixote*. Pt. i, ch. 20.

So long goeth the pot to the water, that it cometh broken home.
UNKNOWN, *Ayenbite*, 206. (1340)

The pot so long to the water goeth,
That home it cometh at the last y-broke.
THOMAS HOCCLEVE, *De Regimine Principum*, l. 4432. (1412)

The pitcher goes not so often to the well, but that it comes home cracked at last.
HEAD AND KIRKMAN, *English Rogue*, i, 69. (1665)

The old pitcher went to the well once too often, but I'm glad the championship remains in America.
JOHN L. SULLIVAN, when struggling to his feet after his defeat by James J. Corbett, 7 Sept., 1892.

1
The event is the print of your form. It fits you like your skin.
EMERSON, *Conduct of Life: Fate.*

What we call results are beginnings.
EMERSON, *Representative Men: Plato.*

2
Logical consequences are the scarecrows of fools and the beacons of wise men.
HUXLEY, *Science and Culture: Animal Automatism.*

3
There are in nature neither rewards nor punishments—there are consequences.
R. G. INGERSOLL, *Some Reasons Why.*

Attack is the reaction; I never think I have hit hard unless it rebounds.
SAMUEL JOHNSON. (BOSWELL, *Life*, 1775.)

4
Ye shall know them by their fruits. Do men gather grapes of thorns, or figs of thistles?
New Testament: Matthew, vii, 16.

By their fruits ye shall know them.
New Testament: Matthew, vii, 20.

5
The result proves the wisdom of the act. (Exitus acta probat.)
OVID, *Heroides*. Epis. ii, l. 85.

6
Can a man take fire in his bosom, and his clothes not be burned?
Old Testament: Proverbs, vi, 27. *See also under* RETRIBUTION.

7
O most lame and impotent conclusion!
SHAKESPEARE, *Othello*. Act ii, sc. 1, l. 162.

But this denoted a foregone conclusion.
SHAKESPEARE, *Othello*. Act iii, sc. 3, l. 428.

A Foregone Conclusion.
WILLIAM DEAN HOWELLS. Title of novel.

8
The blood will follow where the knife is driven,
The flesh will quiver where the pincers tear.
EDWARD YOUNG, *The Revenge*. Act v.

CONSERVATISM

9
I take my pleasures without change,
And as I lived I live.
WILFRID SCAWEN BLUNT, *The Old Squire.*

10
We are living in a phase of evolution which is known as the twentieth century and stands for a certain achieved growth of the human mind. But the enormous majority of the human race do not belong to that phase at all. . . . Victorians, Tudorians, ghosts surviving from the Middle Ages, and multitudes whose minds properly belong to palæolithic times, far outnumber the people who truly appertain to the twentieth century.
ROBERT BRIFFAULT, *Rational Evolution.*

11
"Old things need not be therefore true,"
O brother men, nor yet the new;
Ah! still awhile the old thought retain,
And yet consider it again.
ARTHUR HUGH CLOUGH, *Ah! Yet Consider It Again.*

12
We have a maxim in the House of Commons, and written on the walls of our house, that old ways are the safest and surest ways.
EDWARD COKE, *Speech*, 8 May, 1628.

13
We have always been conscientiously attached to what is called the Tory, and which might with more propriety be called the Conservative, party.
J. WILSON CROKER, *Article, Quarterly Review*, Jan., 1830, p. 276. Said to be the first use of the word in this connection.

14
It seems to me a barren thing, this Conservatism—an unhappy cross-breed, the mule of politics that engenders nothing.
BENJAMIN DISRAELI, *Coningsby*. Ch. 5.

A conservative government is an organized hypocrisy.
BENJAMIN DISRAELI, *Speech*, 17 March, 1845.

15
All conservatives are such from personal defects. They have been effeminated by position or nature, born halt and blind, through luxury of their parents, and can only, like invalids, act on the defensive.
EMERSON, *Conduct of Life: Fate.*

Men are conservative when they are least vigorous, or when they are most luxurious. They are conservatives after dinner.
EMERSON, *Essays, Second Series: New England Reformers.*

Conservatism tends to universal seeming and treachery, believes in a negative fate; . . . it distrusts nature.
EMERSON, *Nature, Addresses, and Lectures: The Conservative.*

16
I often think it's comical
How nature always does contrive
That every boy and every gal,
That's born into this world alive,
Is either a little Liberal,
Or else a little Conservative.
W. S. GILBERT, *Iolanthe*. Act ii.

17
Cried all, "Before such things can come,
You idiotic child,

You must alter Human Nature!"
And they all sat back and smiled.
Thought they, "An answer to that last
It will be hard to find!"
It was a clinching argument
To the Neolithic Mind!

CHARLOTTE PERKINS GILMAN, *Similar Cases.*

1
A conservative is a man who is too cowardly to fight and too fat to run.

ELBERT HUBBARD, *One Thousand and One Epigrams.*

2
What is conservatism? Is it not adherence to the old and tried, against the new and untried?

ABRAHAM LINCOLN, *Address,* Cooper Institute, N. Y., 27 Feb., 1860.

3
They have learned nothing and forgotten nothing. (Ils n'ont rien appris, ni rien oublié.)

CHEVALIER DE PANAT, *Letter to Mallet du Pan,* January, 1796, referring to the Bourbons. Attributed also to Talleyrand.

4
He learns how stocks will fall or rise;
Holds poverty the greatest vice;
Thinks wit the bane of conversation;
And says that learning spoils a nation.

MATTHEW PRIOR, *The Chameleon.*

5
The Atlantic Ocean beat Mrs. Partington.

SYDNEY SMITH, *Speech,* at Taunton, Oct., 1831. The story is that Mrs. Partington had a house on the beach at Sidmouth, Devon, England, and during a great storm in November, 1824, tried to mop up the waves which were driven into her house. Smith satirized the attempts in the House of Lords to stay the progress of reform by comparing them to Mrs. Partington. "In the midst of this sublime and terrible storm," said Smith, "Dame Partington was seen at the door of her house with mop and pattens, vigorously pushing away the Atlantic Ocean. The Atlantic was roused, Mrs. Partington's spirit was up; but I need not tell you that the contest was unequal. The Atlantic beat Mrs. Partington." Ever since, Mrs. Partington has been a synonym for a bigoted and incorrigible conservative.

The refinement of good breeding could go no further.

J. R. LOWELL, *On a Certain Condescension in Foreigners,* referring to the fact that when the Marquess of Hartington, later the Duke of Devonshire, visited America in 1862, he wore a secession badge in his buttonhole and President Lincoln persisted in calling him "Mr. Partington."

6
Conservatism defends those coercive arrangements which a still-lingering savageness makes requisite. Radicalism endeavours to realize a state more in harmony with the character of the ideal man.

HERBERT SPENCER, *Social Statics.* Pt. iv, ch. 32, sec. 5.

7
May Freedom's oak for ever live
With stronger life from day to day;
That man's the true Conservative
Who lops the moulder'd branch away.

TENNYSON, *Hands All Around.*

8
The staid, conservative,
Came-over-with-the-Conqueror type of mind.

WILLIAM WATSON, *A Study in Contrasts.* Pt. i, l. 42.

9
Generally young men are regarded as radicals. This is a popular misconception. The most conservative persons I ever met are college undergraduates.

WOODROW WILSON, *Address,* N. Y., 19 Nov., 1905.

CONSISTENCY AND INCONSISTENCY

10
Consistency, thou art a jewel.

The origin of this proverb is unknown. In 1867, a newspaper wag succeeded in hoaxing the unwary by announcing that he had discovered the line in an old ballad, *Jolly Robyn-Roughhead,* published in "Murtagh's *Collection of Ballads,* 1754," but no such book ever existed, and the ballad itself proved to be a fake. Its first four lines ran:

Tush! tush! my lassie, such thoughts resigne,
Comparisons are cruele:
Fine pictures suit in frames as fine,
Consistencie's a jewell.

11
No well-informed person ever imputed inconsistency to another for changing his mind. (Nemo doctus unquam mutationem consili inconstantiam dixit esse.)

CICERO, *Epistolæ ad Atticum.* Bk. xvi, epis. 7.

The absurd man is he who never changes. (L'homme absurde est celui qui ne change jamais.)

BARTHÉLEMY.

12
A foolish consistency is the hobgoblin of little minds, adored by little statesmen and philosophers and divines.

EMERSON, *Essays, First Series: Self-Reliance.*

With consistency a great soul has simply nothing to do. . . . Speak what you think to-day in words as hard as cannon balls, and to-morrow speak what to-morrow thinks in hard words again, though it contradict everything you said to-day.

EMERSON, *Essays, First Series: Self-Reliance.*

13
For sea and land don't understand
Nor skies without a frown
See rights for which the one hand fights
By the other cloven down.

EMERSON, *Ode.*

1
I think you will find that people who honestly mean to be true really contradict themselves much more rarely than those who try to be "consistent."
O. W. HOLMES, *The Professor at the Breakfast-Table*. Ch. 2.

2
In opinions look not always back,—
Your wake is nothing, mind the coming track;
Leave what you've done for what you have to do;
Don't be "consistent," but be simply true.
O. W. HOLMES, *A Rhymed Lesson*, l. 290.

3
With what knot shall I hold this Proteus, who so often changes his countenance? (Quo teneam voltus mutantem Protea nodo?)
HORACE, *Epistles*. Bk. i, epis. 1, l. 90.

4
He despises what he sought; and he seeks that which he lately threw away. (Quod petiit spernit, repetit quod nuper omisit.)
HORACE, *Epistles*. Bk. i, epis. 1, l. 98.

What our contempt doth often hurl from us,
We wish it ours again.
SHAKESPEARE, *Antony and Cleopatra*. Act i, sc. 2, l. 127.

5
Gineral C. is a dreffle smart man;
He's ben on all sides thet give places or pelf;
But consistency still wuz a part of his plan,—
He's been true to *one* party,—an' thet is himself.
J. R. LOWELL, *Biglow Papers*. Ser. i, No. 3: Referring to Caleb Cushing.

6
I mean not to run with the Hare and hold with the Hound.
JOHN LYLY, *Euphues: Euphues to Philautus*.

7
What boots it at one gate to make defence
And at another to let in the foe?
MILTON, *Samson Agonistes*, l. 560.

8
Unthought-of frailties cheat us in the wise:
The fool lies hid in inconsistencies.
See the same man in vigour, in the gout;
Alone, in company, in place, or out;
Early at business, and at hazard late,
Mad at a fox-chase, wise at a debate,
Drunk at a borough, civil at a ball,
Friendly at Hackney, faithless at Whitehall!
POPE, *Moral Essays*. Epis. i, l. 69.

Alas! in truth the man but changed his mind;
Perhaps was sick, in love, or had not dined.
POPE, *Moral Essays*. Epis. i, l. 127.

'Tis often constancy to change the mind.
METASTASIO, *Sieves*. (John Hoole, tr.)

9
I would always have one play but one thing.
SHAKESPEARE, *The Two Gentlemen of Verona*. Act iv, sc. 2, l. 71.

10
Inconsistency is the only thing in which men are consistent.
HORATIO SMITH, *Tin Trumpet*. Vol. i, p. 273.

11
Do I contradict myself?
Very well then I contradict myself.
(I am large, I contain multitudes.)
WALT WHITMAN, *Song of Myself*. Sec. 51.

CONSPIRACY

12
Conspiracies no sooner should be form'd
Than executed.
ADDISON, *Cato*. Act i, sc. 2.

13
Plot me no plots.
BEAUMONT AND FLETCHER, *Knight of the Burning Pestle*. Act ii, sc. 5.

14
Plots, true or false, are necessary things,
To raise up commonwealths, and ruin kings.
DRYDEN, *Absalom and Achitophel*. Pt. i, l. 83.

15
O the curst fate of all conspiracies!
They move on many springs; if one but fail
The restive machine stops.
DRYDEN, *Don Sebastian*. Act iv, sc. 1.

Machination ceases.
SHAKESPEARE, *King Lear*. Act v, sc. 1, l. 46.

16
O conspiracy,
Sham'st thou to show thy dangerous brow by night,
When evils are most free?
SHAKESPEARE, *Julius Cæsar*. Act ii, sc. 1, l. 76.

Take no care
Who chafes, who frets, or where conspirers are.
SHAKESPEARE, *Macbeth*. Act iv, sc. 1, l. 91.

17
Open-eye conspiracy His time doth take.
SHAKESPEARE, *The Tempest*. Act ii, sc. 1, l. 301.

CONSTANCY AND INCONSTANCY

See also Fidelity; Love: Constant and Inconstant; Woman: Her Inconstancy

18
Constancy is the foundation of virtues.
FRANCIS BACON, *De Augmentis Scientiarum*. Pt. i, bk. vi, sec. 23.

Constancy lives in realms above.
S. T. COLERIDGE, *Christabel*. Pt. ii, l. 410.

Still constant is a wondrous excellence.
SHAKESPEARE, *Sonnets*. No. cv.

19
I loathe inconstancy—I loathe, detest,
Abhor, condemn, abjure the mortal made
Of such quicksilver clay that in his breast
No permanent foundation can be laid.
BYRON, *Don Juan*. Canto ii, st. 209.

20
The world's a scene of changes, and to be
Constant, in Nature were inconstancy.
COWLEY, *Inconstancy*.

Constant in nothing but inconstancy.
POPE, *Moral Essays*. Epis. ii.

There is nothing in this world constant but inconstancy.
SWIFT, *On the Faculties of the Mind.*

Since 'tis Nature's law to change,
Constancy alone is strange.
JOHN WILMOT, *A Dialogue*, l. 31.

1
Constancy is never the virtue of a mortal;
To be constant one must be immortal.
(La constance n'èst point la vertu d'un mortel,
Et pour être constant it faut être immortel.)
COLLIN D'HARLEVILLE, *L'Inconstant*. Act i, sc. 10.

2
Changeless march the stars above,
Changeless morn succeeds to even;
And the everlasting hills,
Changeless watch the changeless heaven.
CHARLES KINGSLEY, *The Saint's Tragedy*. Act ii, sc. 2.

3
Wouldst thou approve thy constancy, approve
First thy obedience.
MILTON, *Paradise Lost*. Bk. ix, l. 367.

4
Expect not constancy from nightingales, who will every moment serenade a fresh rose.
SADI, *Gulistan*. Ch. vi, tale 2.

5
Now from head to foot
I am marble-constant: now the fleeting moon
No planet is of mine.
SHAKESPEARE, *Antony and Cleopatra*. Act v, sc. 2, l. 240.

O swear not by the moon, the inconstant moon,
That monthly changes in her circled orb,
Lest that thy love prove likewise variable.
SHAKESPEARE, *Romeo and Juliet*. Act ii, sc. 2, l. 109.

6
O constancy, be strong upon my side,
Set a huge mountain 'tween my heart and tongue!
SHAKESPEARE, *Julius Cæsar*. Act ii, sc. 4, l. 6.

7
O heaven! were man
But constant, he were perfect.
SHAKESPEARE, *The Two Gentlemen of Verona*. Act v, sc. 4, l. 109.

8
Ever the same. (Semper eadem.)
QUEEN ELIZABETH, *Motto*.

II—Constancy: The Needle and the Pole

9
True as the needle to the pole,
Or as the dial to the sun.
BARTON BOOTH, *Song*.

True as the dial to the sun,
Although it be not shin'd upon.
BUTLER, *Hudibras*. Part iii, canto ii, l. 175.

She was as true to her husband as the dial to the sun.
FIELDING, *Joseph Andrews*. Bk. i, ch. 18.

10
My heart is feminine, nor can forget—
To all, except one image, madly blind;
So shakes the needle, and so stands the pole,
As vibrates my fond heart to my fix'd soul.
BYRON, *Don Juan*. Canto i, st. 196.

Change, as ye list, ye winds! my heart shall be
The faithful compass that still points to thee.
JOHN GAY, *Sweet William's Farewell to Black-eyed Susan*.

11
Nor ease nor peace that heart can know,
That like the needle true,
Turns at the touch of joy or woe;
But turning, trembles too.
FRANCES GREVILLE, *Prayer for Indifference*.

As still to the star of its worship, though clouded,
The needle points faithfully o'er the dim sea,
So dark when I roam in this wintry world shrouded,
The hope of my spirit turns trembling to Thee.
THOMAS MOORE, *The Heart's Prayer*.

12
Spontaneously to God should tend the soul,
Like the magnetic needle to the Pole.
THOMAS HOOD, *Ode to Rae Wilson*, l. 115.

13
Even here Thy strong magnetic charms I feel,
And pant and tremble like the amorous steel.
To lower good, and beauties less divine,
Sometimes my erroneous needle does incline;
But yet (so strong the sympathy)
It turns, and points again to Thee.
JOHN NORRIS of Bemerton, *Aspiration*. Norris was fond of this metaphor, which he used in *The Prayer*, and in *Contemplation and Love*.

And the touch'd needle trembles to the pole.
POPE, *The Temple of Fame*, l. 431.

14
Even as the needle that directs the hour,
(Touched with the loadstone) by the secret power
Of hidden Nature, points upon the pole;
Even so the wavering powers of my soul,
Touch'd by the virtue of Thy spirit, flee
From what is earth, and point alone to Thee.
FRANCIS QUARLES, *Emblems*. Bk. i, emb. 13.

15
I am constant as the northern star,
Of whose true-fix'd and resting quality
There is no fellow in the firmament.
SHAKESPEARE, *Julius Cæsar*. Act iii, sc. 1, l. 60.

16
Our life's a flying shadow, God the pole,
The needle pointing to Him is our soul.
UNKNOWN, *Inscription*, in Bishop Joceline's crypt, Glasgow cathedral.

The earliest known use of the simile of the soul and the magnetic needle is in *Memorials of a Christian Life* by Raimond Lull of Majorca, written about 1300.

CONSTITUTION

1
'Tis constitution governs us all.
ISAAC BICKERSTAFFE, *The Hypocrite*. Act ii, sc. 1.

2
Well can ye mouth fair Freedom's classic line,
And talk of Constitutions o'er your wine.
THOMAS CAMPBELL, *On Poland.*

3
What's the Constitution between friends?
TIMOTHY J. CAMPBELL, about 1885, to President Cleveland who refused to sign a bill on the grounds that it was unconstitutional. Campbell was a Tammany member of the House of Representatives, and the attribution to him is on the authority of William Tyler Page.

4
As the British Constitution is the most subtile organism which has proceeded from the womb and the long gestation of progressive history, so the American Constitution is, so far as I can see, the most wonderful work ever struck off at a given time by the brain and purpose of man.
W. E. GLADSTONE, *Kin beyond Sea.* (*North American Review,* Sept., 1878.)

5
Some men look at Constitutions with sanctimonious reverence, and deem them like the ark of the covenant, too sacred to be touched. They ascribe to the men of the preceding age a wisdom more than human, and suppose what they did to be beyond amendment. . . . Laws and institutions must go hand in hand with the progress of the human mind. . . . We might as well require a man to wear the coat that fitted him as a boy, as civilized society to remain ever under the regime of their ancestors.
THOMAS JEFFERSON, *Writings.* Vol. xv, p. 40.

6
All that is valuable in the United States Constitution is one thousand years old.
WENDELL PHILLIPS, *Speech,* Boston, 17 Feb., 1861.

7
It's got so it is as easy to amend the Constitution of the United States as it used to be to draw a cork.
THOMAS RILEY MARSHALL. (*Literary Digest,* 20 June, 1925, p. 45.)

8
There is a higher law than the Constitution.
WILLIAM H. SEWARD, *Speech,* U. S. Senate, March, 1850, condemning Daniel Webster for support of the Fugitive Slave Law.

9
No philosopher's stone of a constitution can produce golden conduct from leaden instincts.
HERBERT SPENCER, *Social Statics.* Pt. iii, ch. 21, sec. 7.

CONTEMPLATION

10
The act of contemplation then creates the thing contemplated.
ISAAC D'ISRAELI, *Literary Character.* Ch. xii.

11
All civil mankind have agreed in leaving one day for contemplation against six for practice.
EMERSON, *Lectures and Biographical Studies: The Preacher.*

If I were to compare action of a much higher strain with a life of contemplation, I should not venture to pronounce with much confidence in favor of the former.
EMERSON, *Representative Men: Goethe.*

12
Give me, kind Heaven, a private station,
A mind serene for contemplation.
JOHN GAY, *Fables:* Pt. ii, *The Vulture, the Sparrow, and Other Birds.*

13
He that contemplates hath a day without night.
GEORGE HERBERT, *Jacula Prudentum.* (1640)

14
Wisdom's . . . best nurse, Contemplation.
MILTON, *Comus,* l. 377.

But first and chiefest, with thee bring
Him that yon soars on golden wing,
Guiding the fiery-wheeled throne,
The Cherub Contemplation.
MILTON, *Il Penseroso,* l. 51.

15
So sweet is zealous contemplation.
SHAKESPEARE, *Richard III.* Act iii, sc. 7, l. 94.

16
Contemplation makes a rare turkey-cock of him:
How he jets under his advanced plumes.
SHAKESPEARE, *Twelfth Night.* Act ii, sc. 5, l. 35.

CONTEMPT

See also Ridicule, Scorn, Sneer

17
He that all despiseth all displeaseth. (Qui omnes despicit, omnibus displicet.)
ALBERTANO OF BRESCIA, *Liber Consolationis.* (CHAUCER, *Melibeus.* Sec. 15.)

18
Familiarity breeds contempt, while rarity wins admiration. (Parit enim conversatio contemptum, raritas conciliat ipsis rebus admirationem.)
APULEIUS, *De Deo Socratis.*

Familiarity breeds contempt. (Nimia familiaritas parit Contemptum.)
ST. THOMAS AQUINAS, *Ad Joannem Fratrem Monitio;* PUBLILIUS SYRUS, *Sententiæ,* No. 640; LIVY, *History,* bk. xxxv, ch. 10.

I find my familiarity with thee has bred contempt.
CERVANTES, *Don Quixote.* Pt. i, ch. 6.

I hope upon familiarity will grow more contempt.
SHAKESPEARE, *The Merry Wives of Windsor*. Act i, sc. 1, l. 253.

1
The Sacristan, he says no word that indicates a doubt,
But he puts his thumb unto his nose and spreads his fingers out.
RICHARD HARRIS BARHAM, *Nell Cook*.

2
Ay, do despise me, I'm the prouder for it;
I likes to be despised.
ISAAC BICKERSTAFFE, *The Hypocrite*. Act v, sc. 1.

3
As the air to a bird or the sea to a fish, so is contempt to the contemptible.
WILLIAM BLAKE, *Proverbs of Hell*.

4
Contempt will sooner kill an injury than revenge.
H. G. BOHN, *Hand-Book of Proverbs*.

5
I knew you once: but in Paradise,
If we meet, I will pass nor turn my face.
ROBERT BROWNING, *The Worst of It*.

6
Over-great homeliness engendereth dispraising.
CHAUCER, *Melibeus*. Sec. 55. (1386)

7
Contempt is a kind of gangrene, which, if it seizes one part of a character, corrupts all the rest.
SAMUEL JOHNSON, *Works*. Vol. iii, p. 186.

8
O Poverty, thy thousand ills combined
Sink not so deep into the generous mind,
As the contempt and laughter of mankind.
(Nil habet infelix paupertas durius in se,
Quam quod ridiculos homines facit.)
JUVENAL, *Satires*. Sat. iii, l. 152.

9
See how the mountain goat hangs from the summit of the cliff; you would expect it to fall; it is merely showing its contempt for the dogs. (Despicit illa canes.)
MARTIAL, *Epigrams*. Bk. xiii, epig. 98.

10
Grown all to all, from no one vice exempt,
And most contemptible, to shun contempt.
POPE, *Moral Essays*. Epis. i, l. 194.

11
Contempt is Failure's share.
G. L. SCARBOROUGH, *To the Vanquished*.

12
Contempt his scornful perspective did lend me.
SHAKESPEARE, *All's Well that Ends Well*. Act v, sc. 3, l. 48.

The senseless winds shall grin in vain,
Who in contempt shall hiss at thee again.
SHAKESPEARE, *II Henry VI*. Act iv, sc. 1, l. 77.

Let the foul'st contempt Shut door upon me.
SHAKESPEARE, *Henry VIII*. Act ii, sc. 4, l. 42.

13
Every puny whipster.
SHAKESPEARE, *Othello*. Act v, sc. 2, l. 244.

14
O, what a deal of scorn looks beautiful
In the contempt and anger of his lip!
SHAKESPEARE, *Twelfth Night*. Act iii, sc. 1, l. 156.

Wafting his eyes to the contrary and falling
A lip of much contempt.
SHAKESPEARE, *Winter's Tale*. Act i, sc. 2, l. 372

CONTENT

See also Happiness, Moderation, Wants

I—Content: Definitions

15
The all-in-all of life—Content.
CAMPBELL, *To a Lady on Receiving a Seal*.

16
He that is absolute, can do what he likes; he that can do what he likes, can take his pleasure; he that can take his pleasure, can be content; he that can be content, has no more to desire; and when there is nothing left to desire, the matter's over.
CERVANTES, *Don Quixote*. Pt. i, bk. iv, ch. 23.

17
Fortify yourself with contentment, for this is an impregnable fortress.
EPICTETUS, *Fragments*. No. 138.

18
Content is the Philosopher's Stone, that turns all it touches into gold.
BENJAMIN FRANKLIN, *Poor Richard*, 1758.

Content's a kingdom.
HEYWOOD, *Woman Kill'd with Kindness*, iii, 1.

19
Content is happiness.
THOMAS FULLER, *Gnomologia*. No. 1152.

We are contented because we are happy, and not happy because we are contented.
W. S. LANDOR, *Imaginary Conversations: Brooke and Sidney*.

20
Contentment consisteth not in adding more fuel, but in taking away some fire; not in multiplying of wealth, but in subtracting men's desires.
THOMAS FULLER, *The Holy State*.

21
Content layeth pleasure, nay virtue, in a slumber. . . . It is to the mind, like moss to a tree, it bindeth it up so as to stop its growth.
LORD HALIFAX, *Works*, p. 248.

22
Every man is either well or ill, according as he finds himself. Not he whom another thinks content, but he is content indeed, that thinks he is so himself.
MONTAIGNE, *Essays*. Bk. i, ch. 40.

23
My crown is in my heart, not on my head;
Not deck'd with diamonds and Indian stones,

Nor to be seen: my crown is called content;
A crown it is that seldom kings enjoy.
SHAKESPEARE, *III Henry VI*. Act iii, sc. 1, l. 62.

Our content Is our best having.
SHAKESPEARE, *Henry VIII*. Act ii, sc. 3, l. 23.

Best state, contentless,
Hath a distracted and most wretched being,
Worse than the worst, content.
SHAKESPEARE, *Timon of Athens*. Act iv, sc. 3, l. 245.

1
There is a jewel which no Indian mines can buy,
No chymic art can counterfeit;
It makes men rich in greatest poverty,
Makes water wine; turns wooden cups to gold;
The homely whistle to sweet music's strain:
Seldom it comes; to few from Heaven sent,
That much in little, all in naught, *Content*.
JOHN WILBYE, *Madrigales: There Is a Jewel*.

II—Content: Apothegms

2
Oh, bring again my heart's content,
Thou Spirit of the Summer-time!
WILLIAM ALLINGHAM, *Song*.

Ah, sweet Content, where doth thine harbour hold?
BARNABE BARNES, *Parthenophil and Parthenophe*.

He that commends me to my own content
Commends me to the thing I cannot get.
SHAKESPEARE, *The Comedy of Errors*. Act i, sc. 2, l. 33.

3
When we have not what we like, we must like what we have. (Quand on n'a pas ce que l'on aime, Il faut aimer ce que l'on a.)
BUSSY-RABUTIN, *Letter to Madame de Sévigné;* MARMONTEL, *Contes Moraux*.

Take the good the gods provide thee.
DRYDEN, *Alexander's Feast*, l. 106.

If you are wise, be wise; keep what goods the gods provide you. (Si sapias, sapias; habeas quod di dant boni.)
PLAUTUS, *Rudens*, l. 1229. (Act iv, sc. 7.)

4
'Tis want of courage not to be content.
CHARLES CHURCHILL, *The Farewell*, l. 70.

5
God hath made none (that all might be) contented.
GEORGE CHAPMAN, *The Tears of Peace*, l. 370.

6
Content is all.
JOHN CLARKE, *Paræmiologia*. (1639)

7
A good man is contented.
EMERSON, *Essays, First Series: Spiritual Laws*.

He that's content hath enough.
BENJAMIN FRANKLIN, *Poor Richard*, 1758.

8
Content lodges oftener in cottages than palaces.
THOMAS FULLER, *Gnomologia*. No. 1155.

9
Where wealth and freedom reign, contentment fails.
OLIVER GOLDSMITH, *The Traveller*, l. 91.

10
Let us draw upon content for the deficiencies of fortune.
GOLDSMITH, *The Vicar of Wakefield*. Ch. 3.

11
How comes it, Mæcenas, that no man living is content with the lot which either his choice has given him, or chance has thrown in his way? (Qui fit, Mæcenas, ut nemo, quam sibi sortem Seu ratio dederit seu fors, objecerit, illa Contentus vivat?)
HORACE, *Satires*. Bk. i, sat. 1, l. 1.

12
If some god were to say, "Here I am! I grant your prayers forthwith. You, who were but now a soldier, shall be a trader; you, but now a lawyer, shall be a farmer. Change parts; away with you—and with you! Well! Why standing still?" They would refuse.
HORACE, *Satires*. Bk. i, sat. 1, l. 15.

If all our misfortunes were laid in one common heap, whence every one must take an equal portion, most people would be content to take their own and depart.
SOCRATES. (PLUTARCH, *Ad Appolonium de Consolatione*.)

If, as Socrates said, All men in the world should come and bring their grievances together, of body, mind, fortune, . . . and lay them on a heap to be equally divided, wouldst thou share alike and take thy portion? or be as thou art? Without question thou wouldst be as thou art.
ROBERT BURTON, *Anatomy of Melancholy*. Pt. ii, sec. 3, mem. 1, subs. 1.

13
A sweet content
Passing all wisdom or its fairest flower.
R. H. HORNE, *Orion*. Bk. iii, canto ii.

14
That cloud, now! Just below that strip of blue!
You like it? That's mine too!
RICHARD R. KIRK, *We Visit My Estate*.

I do not own an inch of land,
But all I see is mine.
LUCY LARCOM, *A Strip of Blue*.

15
Let not thy thoughts run on what thou lackest as much as on what thou already hast.
MARCUS AURELIUS, *Meditations*. Bk. vii, sec. 27.

16
It is good for us to be here.
New Testament: Matthew, xvii, 4.

My cup runneth over.
Old Testament: Psalms, xxiii, 5.

1
I have learned, in whatsoever state I am, therewith to be content.
New Testament: Philippians, iv, 11.

2
Naught's had, all's spent,
Where our desire is got without content.
SHAKESPEARE, *Macbeth.* Act iii, sc. 2, l. 4.

3
The all-enclosing freehold of Content.
J. T. TROWBRIDGE, *Guy Vernon.*

4
What better fare than well content?
THOMAS TUSSER, *Hundred Pointes of Good Husbandrie: Posies for Thine Own Bed Chamber.*

III—Content: The Mind Content

5
Content is wealth, the riches of the mind;
And happy he who can such riches find.
JOHN DRYDEN, *Wife of Bath's Tale,* l. 466.

But all the pleasure that I find
Is to maintain a quiet mind.
EDWARD DYER, *My Mind to Me a Kingdom Is.*

6
Happy the man, of mortals happiest he,
Whose quiet mind from vain desires is free;
Whom neither hopes deceive, nor fears torment,
But lives at peace, within himself content;
In thought, or act, accountable to none
But to himself, and to the gods alone.
GEORGE GRANVILLE, *Epistle to Mrs. Higgons,* l. 79.

7
A mind content both crown and kingdom is.
ROBERT GREENE, *Farewell to Folly.*

Sweet are the thoughts that savour of content;
The quiet mind is richer than a crown;
Sweet are the nights in careless slumber spent;
The poor estate scorns fortune's angry frown:
Such sweet content, such minds, such sleep, such bliss,
Beggars enjoy, when princes oft do miss.
ROBERT GREENE, *Farewell to Folly.*

8
That best of blessings, a contented mind. (Æquum animum.)
HORACE, *Epistles.* Bk. i, epis. 18, l. 112.

9
It is great riches to a man to live sparingly with a quiet mind. (Divitiæ grandes homini sunt, vivere parce æquo animo.)
LUCRETIUS, *De Rerum Natura.* Bk. v, l. 1117.

Yet truest riches, would mankind their breasts
Bend to the precept, in a little lie,
With mind well-poised; here want can never come.
LUCRETIUS, *De Rerum Natura.* Bk. v, l. 1140. (Watson, tr.)

10
If you have a contented mind, you have enough to enjoy life with. (Si est animus æquos tibi, sat habes qui bene vitam colas.)
PLAUTUS, *Aulularia,* l. 187. (Act ii, sc. 2.)

11
The noblest mind the best contentment has.
SPENSER, *Faerie Queene.* Bk. i, canto i, st. 35.

12
This, this is all my choice, my cheer,—
A mind content, a conscience clear.
JOSHUA SYLVESTER, *A Contented Mind.*

13
A flower more sacred than far-seen success
Perfumes my solitary path; I find
Sweet compensation in my humbleness,
And reap the harvest of a quiet mind.
J. T. TROWBRIDGE, *Twoscore and Ten.* St. 28.

14
When all is done and said,
In the end this shall you find:
He most of all doth bathe in bliss
That hath a quiet mind.
THOMAS VAUX, *Of a Contented Mind.*

IV—Content: Better than Riches

15
To others let the glittering baubles fall,
Content shall place us far above them all.
CHARLES CHURCHILL, *Night,* l. 193.

16
Flee grandeur; beneath a humble roof you may, by your life, excel kings and the friends of kings. (Fuge magna: licet sub paupere tecto Reges et regum vita præcurrere amicos.)
HORACE, *Epistles.* Bk. i, epis. 10, l. 32.

In a cottage I live, and the cot of content,
Where a few little rooms for ambition too low,
Are furnish'd as plain as a patriarch's tent,
With all for convenience, but nothing for show:
Like Robinson Crusoe's, both peaceful and pleasant,
By industry stor'd, like the hive of a bee;
And the peer who looks down with contempt on a peasant,
Can ne'er be look'd up to with envy by me.
JOHN COLLINS, *Scripscrapologia: How to Be Happy.*

17
I have mental joys and mental health,
Mental friends and mental wealth,
I've a wife that I love and that loves me;
I've all but riches bodily.
WILLIAM BLAKE, *Mammon.*

18
For who did ever yet, in honour, wealth,
Or pleasure of the sense, contentment find?
JOHN DAVIES, *Nosce Teipsum.* Sec. xxx, st. 50.

And his best riches, ignorance of wealth.
GOLDSMITH, *The Deserted Village,* l. 61.

The greatest wealth is contentment with little.
JAMES HOWELL, *Proverbs.* (1659)

19
He who is content can never be ruined.
LAO-TSZE, *The Simple Way.* No. 44.

20
Content surpasses wealth. (Contentement passe richesse.)
MOLIÈRE, *Médecin Malgré Lui.* Act ii, sc. 1 l. 65.

1
He who is contented with his lot has the greatest and surest riches. (Qui suis rebus contentus est, huic maximæ ac certissimæ divitiæ.)
PUBLILIUS SYRUS, *Sententiæ*. No. 617.

2
This is the charm, by sages often told,
Converting all it touches into gold:
Content can soothe, where'er by fortune placed,
Can rear a garden in the desert waste.
HENRY KIRKE WHITE, *Clifton Grove*, l. 130.

3
What though, from fortune's lavish bounty,
No mighty treasures we possess;
We'll find, within our pittance, plenty,
And be content without excess.
UNKNOWN, *Winifreda*. Claimed for Gilbert Cooper. (PERCY, *Reliques*. Bk. iii, No. 13.)

V—Content With Little

4
But if I'm content with a little,
Enough is as good as a feast.
ISAAC BICKERSTAFFE, *Love in a Village*. Act iii, sc. 1. *See also under* MODERATION.

Contented wi' little, and cantie wi' mair.
BURNS, *Contented wi' Little*.

5
What happiness the rural maid attends,
In cheerful labour while each day she spends!
She gratefully receives what Heav'n has sent,
And, rich in proverty, enjoys content.
JOHN GAY, *Rural Sports*. Canto ii, l. 148.

6
May the proud chariot never be my fate,
If purchas'd at so mean, so dear a rate:
Or rather give me sweet content on foot,
Wrapt in my virtue and a good surtout!
JOHN GAY, *Trivia*. Bk. ii, l. 589.

7
Nature with little is content.
HERRICK, *No Want Where There's Little*.

Who with a little cannot be content,
Endures an everlasting punishment.
HERRICK, *Poverty and Riches*.

8
Content with little, I can piddle here
On brocoli and mutton round the year.
HORACE, *Satires*. Bk. ii, sat. 2, l. 137. (Pope, tr.)

9
Contented if he might enjoy
The things which others understand.
WORDSWORTH, *A Poet's Epitaph*. St. 14.

VI—Content: Its Virtues

10
From labour health, from health contentment springs;
Contentment opes the source of every joy.
JAMES BEATTIE, *The Minstrel*. Bk. i, st. 13.

11
Hope not sunshine every hour,
Fear not clouds will always lour.
Happiness is but a name,
Make content and ease thy aim.
BURNS, *Lines Written in Friars Carse Hermitage*. *See also* COMPENSATION: SUN AND RAIN.

12
Let me be deft and debonair,
I am content, I do not care!
JOHN BYROM, *Careless Content*.

With more of thanks and less of thought,
I strive to make my matters meet;
To seek what ancient sages sought,
Physic and food in sour and sweet,
To take what passes in good part,
And keep the hiccups from the heart.
JOHN BYROM, *Careless Content*.

13
How calm and quiet a delight
Is it alone
To read, and meditate, and write
By none offended, and offending none;
To walk, ride, sit, or sleep at one's own ease,
And pleasing a man's self, none other to displease!
CHARLES COTTON, *The Retirement*.

14
Whatever comes, let's be content withall:
Among God's blessings there is no one small.
ROBERT HERRICK, *Welcome What Comes*.

15
Contented with your lot, you will live wisely. (Lætus sorte tua vives sapienter.)
HORACE, *Epistles*. Bk. i, epis. x, l. 44.

16
Sense of pleasure we may well
Spare out of life, perhaps, and not repine
But live content, which is the calmest life.
MILTON, *Paradise Lost*. Bk. vi, l. 459.

17
Contentment furnishes constant joy. Much covetousness, constant grief. To the contented even poverty is joy. To the discontented, even wealth is a vexation.
UNKNOWN, *Ming-hsin pao-chien*. (William Milne, tr., in the *Indo-Chinese Gleaner*, Aug., 1818.)

18
No eye to watch and no tongue to wound us,
All earth forgot, and all heaven around us.
THOMAS MOORE, *Come o'er the Sea*.

19
Every man should remain within his own sphere. (Intra fortunam debet quisque manere suam.)
OVID, *Tristia*. Bk. iii, eleg. iv, l. 25.

Be content with what you are, and wish no change; nor dread your last day, nor long for it. (Quod sis esse velis nihilque malis; Summum nec metuas diem nec optes.)
MARTIAL, *Epigrams*. Bk. x, epig. 47.

Enjoy the present hour, be thankful for the past,
And neither fear nor wish th' approaches of the last.
MARTIAL, *Epigrams*, x, 47. (Cowley, tr.)

1
I earn that I eat, get that I wear, owe no man hate, envy no man's happiness; glad of other men's good, content with my harm.

SHAKESPEARE, *As You Like It*. Act iii, sc. 2, l. 77.

2
For mine own part, I could be well content
To entertain the lag-end of my life
With quiet hours.

SHAKESPEARE, *I Henry IV*, Act v, sc. 1, l. 23.

'Tis better to be lowly born,
And range with humble livers in content,
Than to be perk'd up in a glistering grief,
And wear a golden sorrow.

SHAKESPEARE, *Henry VIII*. Act ii, sc. 3, l. 19.

3
My soul hath her content so absolute,
That not another comfort like to this
Succeeds in unknown fate.

SHAKESPEARE, *Othello*. Act ii, sc. 1, l. 193.

Shut up In measureless content.

SHAKESPEARE, *Macbeth*. Act ii, sc. 1, l. 17.

4
Then be content, poor heart!
God's plans, like lilies pure and white, unfold:
We must not tear the close-shut leaves apart—
Time will reveal the calyxes of gold.

MARY LOUISE RILEY SMITH, *Sometime*.

5
For not that which men covet most is best,
Nor that thing worst which men do most refuse:
But fittest is, that all contented rest
With that they hold: each hath his fortune in his breast.

SPENSER, *Faerie Queene*. Bk. vi, canto ix, st. 29.

6
No chance is evil to him that is content.

JEREMY TAYLOR, *Holy Living: Of Contentedness*.

7
For what men call content,
And also that something may be sent
To be contented with, I ask of fate.

EDWARD THOMAS, *For These*.

CONTENTION, see Discord, Quarreling

CONVENTIONALITY, see Society

CONVERSATION

See also Speech, Talk

I—Conversation: Definitions

8
Method is not less requisite in ordinary conversation than in writing, provided a man would talk to make himself understood.

ADDISON, *The Spectator*. No. 476.

9
Debate is masculine; conversation is feminine.

AMOS BRONSON ALCOTT, *Concord Days: May*.

Many can argue, not many converse.

AMOS BRONSON ALCOTT, *Concord Days: May*.

10
The wisdom of Conversation ought not to be over much affected, but much less despised; for it hath not only an honour in itself, but an influence also in business and government.

FRANCIS BACON, *Advancement of Learning: Civil Knowledge*. Sec. 3.

11
It is not easy to say how far an affable and courteous manner in conversation may go toward winning the affections. (Tamen difficile dictu est, quantopere conciliet animos comitas affabilitasque sermonis.)

CICERO, *De Officiis*. Bk. ii, ch. 14, sec. 48.

12
Conversation, in its better part,
May be esteem'd a gift and not an art,
Yet much depends, as in the tiller's toil,
On culture, and the sowing of the soil.
Words learn'd by rote a parrot may rehearse,
But talking is not always to converse;
Not more distinct from harmony divine
The constant creaking of a country sign.

COWPER, *Conversation*, l. 3.

And finds a changing clime an happy source
Of wise reflection and well-timed discourse.

COWPER, *Conversation*, l. 387.

13
Conversation is an art in which a man has all mankind for his competitors, for it is that which all are practising every day while they live.

EMERSON, *Conduct of Life: Considerations by the Way*.

Conversation is a game of circles.

EMERSON, *Essays, First Series: Circles*.

In good conversation parties don't speak to the words, but to the meanings of each other.

EMERSON, *Letters and Social Aims: Social Aims*.

The conversation of men is a mixture of regrets and apprehensions.

EMERSON, *Natural History of Intellect: The Tragic*.

14
Wise, cultivated, genial conversation is the last flower of civilization. . . . Conversation is our account of ourselves.

EMERSON, *Miscellanies: Woman*.

Conversation is the vent of character as well as of thought.

EMERSON, *Society and Solitude: Clubs*.

Conversation is the laboratory and workshop of the student.

EMERSON, *Society and Solitude: Clubs*.

15
Men of great conversational powers almost universally practise a sort of lively sophistry and exaggeration which deceives for the moment both themselves and their auditors.

MACAULAY, *Essays: On the Athenian Orators*.

1
Silence and modesty are very valuable qualities in the art of conversation. (Le silence et la modestie sont qualités très commodes à la conversation.)
MONTAIGNE, *Essays*. Bk. i, ch. 25.

II—Conversation: Apothegms

2
Madam, I have but ninepence in ready money, but I can draw for a thousand pounds.
JOSEPH ADDISON, when a lady complained that he took little part in conversation. (BOSWELL, *Johnson*, 1773.) See also 805:2.

3
Their discourses are as the stars, which give little light, because they are so high.
BACON, *Advancement of Learning*. Bk. ii.

4
A sort of chit-chat, or small talk, which is the general run of conversation . . . in most mixed companies.
LORD CHESTERFIELD, *Letters*, 20 June, 1791.

The poor threadbare topics of half wits.
LORD CHESTERFIELD, *Letters*, 8 Jan., 1750.

The hare-brained chatter of irresponsible frivolity.
BENJAMIN DISRAELI, *Speech*, at Guildhall, London, 9 Nov., 1878.

But they couldn't chat together—they had not been introduced.
W. S. GILBERT, *Etiquette*.

The meaning doesn't matter if it's only idle chatter of a transcendental kind.
W. S. GILBERT, *Patience*. Act i.

To stuff his conversation full of quibble and of quiddity.
W. S. GILBERT, *Patience*. Act ii.

5
While conversation, an exhausted stock,
Grows drowsy as the clicking of a clock.
COWPER, *Hope*, l. 103.

Silence propagates itself, and the longer talk has been suspended, the more difficult it is to find anything to say.
SAMUEL JOHNSON, *The Adventurer*. No. 84.

We were so exceedingly genteel, that our scope was limited.
DICKENS, *David Copperfield*. Ch. 25.

6
He that converses not, knows nothing.
THOMAS FULLER, *Gnomologia*. No. 2070.

Knowledge begins a gentleman, but 'tis conversation that completes him.
THOMAS FULLER, *Gnomologia*. No. 3136.

7
Inject a few raisins of conversation into the tasteless dough of existence.
O. HENRY, *Complete Life of John Hopkins*.

8
His conversation does not show the *minute* hand; but he strikes the hour very correctly.
SAMUEL JOHNSON. (KEARSLEY, *Johnsoniana*, p. 604.)

9
Conversation seems to always tire me.
GEORGE W. LEDERER, *I'm Tired*. (1901)

10
His discourse sounds big, but means nothing.
SIR THOMAS OVERBURY, *Characters: An Affectate Traveller*.

11
Now is the time for converse. (Conloquii jam tempus adest.)
OVID, *Ars Amatoria*, l. 607.

Fly not conversation, nor let your door be closed. (Nec fuge conloquium, nec sit tibi janua clausa.)
OVID, *Remediorum Amoris*, l. 587.

12
I converse only with myself and my books. (Mecum tantum et cum libellis loquor.)
PLINY THE YOUNGER, *Epistles*. Bk. i, epis. 9.

13
They converse as those would who know that God hears. (Ita fabulantur, ut qui sciant dominum audire.)
TERTULLIAN, *Apologeticus*. Ch. 39, sec. 18.

III—Conversation: Admonitions

14
Discourse may want an animated "No"
To brush the surface, and to make it flow;
But still remember, if you mean to please,
To press your point with modesty and ease.
COWPER, *Conversation*, l. 101.

But conversation, choose what theme we may,
And chiefly when religion leads the way,
Should flow, like waters after summer showers,
Not as if raised by mere mechanic powers.
COWPER, *Conversation*, l. 703.

15
You may talk of all subjects save one, namely, your maladies.
EMERSON, *Conduct of Life: Behavior*.

There is one topic peremptorily forbidden to all rational mortals, namely, their distempers. If you have not slept, or if you have slept, or if you have headache, or sciatica, or leprosy, or thunder-stroke, I beseech you, by all angels, to hold your peace, and not pollute the morning by corruption and groans.
EMERSON, *Conduct of Life: Behavior*.

Never name sickness; and, above all, beware of unmuzzling the valetudinarian.
EMERSON, *Uncollected Lectures: Table-Talk*.

16
If thou hast a mind to get esteem in company, have the art to edge about, till thou canst get into a subject thou hast studied and art master of.
THOMAS FULLER, *Introductio ad Prudentiam*, i, 59.

Make not thy own person, family, relations or affairs the frequent subject of thy tattle. Say not, My manner and custom is to do thus. I neither eat nor drink in a morning. I am apt to be troubled with corns. My child said such a witty thing last night.
FULLER, *Introductio ad Prudentiam*, i, 195.

1
I never, with important air,
In conversation overbear. . . .
My tongue within my lips I rein;
For who talks much must talk in vain.

JOHN GAY, *Fables:* Pt. i, *Introduction*, l. 53.

2
In thy discourse, if thou desire to please:
All such is courteous, useful, new, or witty:
Usefulness comes by labour, wit by ease;
Courtesy grows in court; news in the city.
Get a good stock of these, then draw the card;
That suits him best, of whom thy speech is heard.

GEORGE HERBERT, *The Church-Porch*. St. 49.

All discourses but my own afflict me; they seem harsh, impertinent, and irksome.

BEN JONSON, *Epicœne; Or, The Silent Woman*. Act ii, sc. 1, l. 5.

3
And when you stick on conversation's burrs,
Don't strew your pathway with those dreadful *urs*.

O. W. HOLMES, *A Rhymed Lesson*, l. 414.

4
Let all thy converse be sincere.

THOMAS KEN, *Morning Hymn*.

5
Be humble and gentle in your conversation; and of few words, I charge you; but always pertinent when you speak.

WILLIAM PENN, *Letters to His Wife and Children*.

6
Would you both please and be instructed too,
Watch well the rage of shining to subdue;
Hear every man upon his favourite theme,
And ever be more knowing than you seem.

BENJAMIN STILLINGFLEET, *Essay on Conversation*.

7
Equality is the life of conversation; and he is as much out who assumes to himself any part above another, as he who considers himself below the rest of the society.

RICHARD STEELE, *The Tatler*. No. 225.

Conversation is but carving;
Carve for all, yourself is starving;
Give no more to every guest,
Than he's able to digest;
Give him always of the prime;
And but little at a time.
Carve to all but just enough:
Let them neither starve nor stuff:
And, that you may have your due,
Let your neighbours carve for you.

SWIFT, *To a Lady*, l. 124.

8
A dearth of words a woman need not fear,
But 'tis a task indeed to learn—to hear:
In that the skill of conversation lies;
That shows, or makes, you both polite and wise.

YOUNG, *Love of Fame*. Sat. v, l. 57.

IV—Conversation: Its Pleasures

9
The delights of a pleasant and improving conversation. (Laxantes jucundis honestisque sermonum.)

AULUS GELLIUS, *Noctes Atticæ*. Bk. xviii, ch. 2.

10
"Let me not live," saith Aretine's Antonia, "if I had not rather hear thy discourse than see a play."

ROBERT BURTON, *Anatomy of Melancholy*. Pt. iii, sec. 1, mem. 1, subs. 1.

11
Nor wanted sweet discourse, the banquet of the mind.

DRYDEN, *Flower and the Leaf*, l. 432. (1700)

Discourse, the sweeter banquet of the mind.

HOMER, *Odyssey*. Bk. xv, l. 433. (Pope, tr., 1714.)

12
The best of life is conversation.

EMERSON, *Conduct of Life: Behavior*.

13
With thee conversing I forget the way.

JOHN GAY, *Trivia*. Bk. ii, l. 480.

With thee conversing I forget all time.

MILTON, *Paradise Lost*. Bk. iv, l. 639.

14
A single conversation across the table with a wise man is better than ten years' study of books.

LONGFELLOW, *Hyperion*. Ch. vii. Quoted from the Chinese.

15
We took sweet counsel together.

Old Testament: Psalms, lv. 14.

16
Your fair discourse hath been as sugar,
Making the hard way sweet and delectable.

SHAKESPEARE, *Richard II*. Act ii, sc. 3, l. 6.

A kind Of excellent dumb discourse.

SHAKESPEARE, *The Tempest*. Act iii, sc. 3, l. 38.

17
Bid me discourse, I will enchant thine ear.

SHAKESPEARE, *Venus and Adonis*, l. 145.

18
One of the greatest pleasures in life is conversation.

SYDNEY SMITH, *Essays: Female Education*.

19
He has occasional flashes of silence, that make his conversation perfectly delightful.

SYDNEY SMITH, speaking of Macaulay. (LADY HOLLAND, *Memoir*, i, 363.)

He speaketh not; and yet there lies
A conversation in his eyes.

LONGFELLOW, *The Hanging of the Crane*. Sec. 3.

That silence is one of the great arts of conversation is allowed by Cicero himself, who says that there is not only an art, but even an eloquence in it.

HANNAH MORE, *Thoughts on Conversation*.

20
The world is best enjoyed and most immedi-

ately while we converse blessedly and wisely with men.

THOMAS TRAHERNE, *Centuries of Meditations.*

CONVICTION, see Belief

COOKS AND COOKING

I—Cooks

1
"I have been sent to procure an angel to do cooking."

EMERSON, *Conduct of Life: Considerations by the Way.* Quoting "a man of wit," who was asked what was his errand in the city.

2
A cook is known by his knife.

THOMAS FULLER, *Gnomologia.* No. 50.

Cooks are not to be taught in their own kitchen.

THOMAS FULLER, *Gnomologia.* No. 1160.

3
Many excellent cooks are spoiled by going into the arts.

PAUL GAUGUIN. (COURNOS, *Modern Plutarch,* p. 48.)

4
Too many cooks spoil the broth.

SIR BALTHAZAR GERBIER, *Discourse of Building.* (1662)

The more cooks the worse broth.

FULLER, *Gnomologia.* No. 4657. (1732)

5
Every cook commends his own sauce.

SIR BALTHAZAR GERBIER, *Counsel.* (1664)

6
Pure Cinna gets his wife a maiden cook
With red cheeks, yellow locks, and cheerful look;
What might he mean thereby? I hold my life,
She dresseth flesh for him, not for his wife.

SIR JOHN HARINGTON, *Of Cinna.* (*Epigrams.* Bk. iv, epig. 285.)

7
'Tis by his cleanliness a cook must please.

WILLIAM KING, *Art of Cookery,* l. 603.

8
Digestion, much like Love and Wine, no trifling will brook:
His cook once spoiled the dinner of an Emperor of men;
The dinner spoiled the temper of his Majesty, and then
The Emperor made history—and no one blamed the cook.

F. J. MACBEATH, *Cause and Effect.*

9
I seem to you cruel and gluttonous, when I beat my cook for sending up a bad dinner. If that appears to you too trifling a cause, say for what cause you would have a cook flogged?

MARTIAL, *Epigrams.* Bk. viii, epig. 23.

10
A cook should double one sense have: for he
Should taster for himself and master be.
(Non satis est ars solo coco: servire palatum
Nolo: cocus domini debet habere gulam.)

MARTIAL, *Epigrams.* Bk. xiv, epig. 220.

11
Nobody ever escaped punishment for unrighteous treatment of a cook. That guild is sacrosanct.

MENANDER, *Dyskolos.* Frag. 130.

12
We may live without poetry, music, and art;
We may live without conscience and live without heart;
We may live without friends, we may live without books,
But civilized man cannot live without cooks.

OWEN MEREDITH, *Lucile.* Pt. i, canto 2, st. 19.

13
He is a sorry cook that may not lick his own finger.

JOHN RAY, *Proverbs: Scottish.*

He is an evil cook that cannot lick his own lips.

JOHN STANBRIDGE, *Vulgaria.* (c. 1520)

A bad cook licks his own fingers.

JOHN TAYLOR THE WATER-POET, *Penniless Pilgrimage.*

14
You need not wonder that diseases are beyond counting: count the cooks! (Innumerabiles esse morbos non miraberis: cocos numera.)

SENECA, *Epistulæ ad Lucilium.* Epis. xcv, 23.

Look at our kitchens and our cooks, who bustle about over so many fires; is it, think you, for a single belly that all this preparation of food takes place?

SENECA, *Epistulæ ad Lucilium.* Epis. cxiv, 26.

15
Epicurean cooks
Sharpen with cloyless sauce his appetite.

SHAKESPEARE, *Antony and Cleopatra.* Act ii, sc. 1, l. 24.

A crier of green sauce.

RABELAIS, *Works.* Bk. ii, ch. 31.

16
Would the cook were of my mind!

SHAKESPEARE, *Much Ado About Nothing.* Act i, sc. 3, l. 74.

She would have made Hercules have turned spit.

SHAKESPEARE, *Much Ado About Nothing.* Act ii, sc. 1, l. 260.

Let housewives make a skillet of my helm.

SHAKESPEARE, *Othello.* Act i, sc. 3, l. 273.

17
Where's the cook? is supper ready, the house trimmed, rushes strewed, cobwebs swept?

SHAKESPEARE, *The Taming of the Shrew.* Act iv, sc. 1, l. 47.

II—Cooks: The Devil Sends Cooks

18
God sends meat and the devil sends cooks.

THOMAS DELONEY, *Works,* p. 221 (1600); JOHN TAYLOR THE WATER-POET, *Works,* ii, 85. (1630)

Bad commentators spoil the best of books,
So God sends meat, (they say,) the devil cooks.
BENJAMIN FRANKLIN, *Poor Richard*, 1735.

Heaven sends us good meat, but the Devil sends cooks.
DAVID GARRICK, *Epigram on Goldsmith's Retaliation.*

1
The most disagreeable thing at sea is the cookery; for there is not, properly speaking, any professional cook on board. The worse sailor is generally chosen for that purpose. Hence comes the proverb used among the English sailors, that "God sends meat, and the Devil sends cooks."
BENJAMIN FRANKLIN, *Precautions to be Used by Those Who are About to Undertake a Sea Voyage.*

I must here observe that this double baked bread was originally the real biscuit prepared to keep at sea; for the word *biscuit*, in French, signifies twice baked.
BENJAMIN FRANKLIN, *Precautions to be Used by Those Who are About to Undertake a Sea Voyage.*

2
The waste of many good materials, the vexation that frequently attends such mismanagements, and the curses not unfrequently bestowed on cooks with the usual reflexion, that whereas God sends good meat, the devil sends cooks.
EDWARD SMITH, *The Compleat Housewife.* (1727)

3
Great pity were it if this beneficence of Providence should be marr'd in the ordering, so as to justly merit the reflection of the old proverb, that though God sends us meat, yet the Devil does cooks.
UNKNOWN, *Cooks' and Confectioners' Dictionary.* (1724)

III—Cooking

4
The discovery of a new dish does more for the happiness of man than the discovery of a star.
BRILLAT-SAVARIN, *Physiologie du Goût.*

5
Cookery has become an art, a noble science; cooks are gentlemen.
ROBERT BURTON, *Anatomy of Melancholy.* Pt. i, sec. ii, mem. 2, subs. 2.

6
In a house where there is plenty, supper is soon cooked.
CERVANTES, *Don Quixote.* Pt. ii, ch. 30.

Quicker than you can cook asparagus. (Celerius quam asparagi cocuntur.)
AUGUSTUS CÆSAR, to express the speed of a hasty action. (SUETONIUS, *Lives of the Cæsars: Augustus.* Ch. 87, sec. 1.)

7
A highly geological home-made cake.
DICKENS, *Martin Chuzzlewit.* Ch. 5.

8
A fat kitchen, a lean will.
BENJAMIN FRANKLIN, *Poor Richard*, 1733.

9
"Very well," cried I, "that's a good girl; I find you are perfectly qualified for making converts, and so go help your mother to make the gooseberry pye."
GOLDSMITH, *The Vicar of Wakefield.* Ch. vii.

10
I doubt whether English cookery, for the very reason that it is so gross, is not better for man's moral and spiritual nature than French. In the former case, you know that you are gratifying your animal needs and propensities, and are duly ashamed of it; but, in dealing with these French delicacies, you delude yourself into the idea that you are cultivating your taste while filling your belly.
HAWTHORNE, *Journals*, 6 Jan., 1858.

Thirty two religions and but one course (*plat*) at dinner.
TALLEYRAND, of the United States.

There are in England sixty different religions and only one gravy, melted butter.
MARQUIS CARACCIOLI, Neapolitan ambassador.

11
The greatest animal in creation, the animal who cooks.
DOUGLAS JERROLD, *Jerrold's Wit.*

12
But, first Or last, your fine Egyptian cookery
Shall have the fame. I have heard that Julius Cæsar
Grew fat with feasting there.
SHAKESPEARE, *Antony and Cleopatra.* Act ii, sc. 6, l. 63.

13
The capon burns, the pig falls from the spit,
The clock hath strucken twelve.
SHAKESPEARE, *The Comedy of Errors.* Act i, sc. 2, l. 44.

'Tis burnt; and so is all the meat.
What dogs are these! Where is the rascal cook?
SHAKESPEARE, *The Taming of the Shrew.* Act iv, sc. 1, l. 164.

14
Let onion atoms dwell within the bowl,
And, scarce suspected, animate the whole.
SYDNEY SMITH, *Recipe for Salad Dressing.* (LADY HOLLAND, *Memoir.* Vol. i, p. 426.)

15
To make a ragout, first catch your hare. (Pour faire un civet, prenez un lièvre.)
LA VARENNE, *Le Cusinier Français*, p. 40. Quoted by Metternich from Marchioness of Londonderry. (*Narrative of a Visit to the Courts of Vienna.*) In a cook book published in 1747, attributed to Dr. Hill. (See *Notes and Queries*, 10 Sept., 1859, p. 206.)

COOPER, JAMES FENIMORE

16
He has drawn you one character, though, that is new,

One wildflower he's plucked that is wet with the dew
Of this fresh Western world, and, the thing not to mince,
He has done naught but copy it ill ever since; . . .
All his other men-figures are clothes upon sticks,
The *dernière chemise* of a man in a fix, . . .
And the women he draws from one model don't vary,
All sappy as maples and flat as a prairie.
When a character's wanted, he goes to the task
As a cooper would do in composing a cask;
He picks out the staves, of their qualities needful,
Just hoops them together as tight as is needful,
And, if the best fortune should crown the attempt, he
Has made at the most something wooden and empty.

J. R. LOWELL, *A Fable for Critics*, l. 1031.

1
In it [*Precaution*], Cooper carved the first of his long line of wooden women.

W. P. TRENT, *American Literature*, p. 236.

COQUETRY

See also Women: Their Fickleness

2
Or light or dark, or short or tall,
She sets a springe to snare them all;
All's one to her—above her fan
She'd make sweet eyes at Caliban.

THOMAS BAILEY ALDRICH, *Coquette*.

At first I enchant a fair Sensitive Plant,
Then I flirt with the Pink of Perfection:
Then I seek a Sweet Pea, and I whisper, "For thee
I have long felt a fond predilection."
A Lily I kiss, and exult in my bliss,
But I very soon search for a new lip;
And I pause in my flight to exclaim with delight,
"Oh! how dearly I love you, my Tulip!"

T. H. BAYLY, *The Butterfly Beau*.

3
Her pleasure is in lovers coy;
When hers, she gives them not a thought;
But, like the angler, takes more joy
In fishing, than in fishes caught.

GEORGE BIRDSEYE, *Coquette*.

4
Like a lovely tree
So grew to womanhood, and between whiles
Rejected several suitors, just to learn
How to accept a better in his turn.

BYRON, *Don Juan*. Canto ii, st. 128.

Such is your cold coquette, who can't say "No,"
And won't say "Yes," and keeps you on and off-ing
On a lee-shore, till it begins to blow—
Then sees your heart wreck'd, with an inward scoffing.

BYRON, *Don Juan*. Canto xii, st. 63.

5
I assisted at the birth of that most significant word "flirtation," which dropped from the most beautiful mouth in the world, and which has since received the sanction of our most accurate Laureate in one of his comedies. . . . Flirtation is short of coquetry, and indicates only the first hints of approximation.

LORD CHESTERFIELD, *The World*. No. 101. The "most beautiful mouth in the world" was that of Lady Frances Shirley, and Colley Cibber was the accurate Poet-Laureate.

Flirtation, attention without intention.

MAX O'RELL, *John Bull and His Island*.

What we find the least of in flirtation is love.

LA ROCHEFOUCAULD, *Réflexions Diverses: Des Coquettes*.

And so she flirted, like a true
Good woman, till we bade adieu.

CAMPBELL, *Lines on My New Child Sweetheart*.

6
Careless she is with artful care,
Affecting to seem unaffected.

WILLIAM CONGREVE, *Amoret*.

7
In the School of Coquettes
Madam Rose is a scholar;—
Oh, they fish with all nets
In the School of Coquettes!
When her brooch she forgets
'Tis to show a new collar.

AUSTIN DOBSON, *Circe*.

8
How happy could I be with either
Were t'other dear charmer away;
But now you both tease me together,
To neither a word will I say.

JOHN GAY, *The Beggar's Opera*. Act ii, sc. 2.

But Alice was a pious girl, who knew it wasn't wise
To look at strange young sorters with expressive purple eyes.

W. S. GILBERT, *Gentle Alice Brown*.

9
She who trifles with all is less likely to fall
Than she who but trifles with one.

JOHN GAY, *The Coquette*.

By keeping men off, you keep them on.

JOHN GAY, *The Beggar's Opera*. Act i.

10
A coquette's April-weather face.

MATTHEW GREEN, *The Spleen*, l. 121.

11
Coquettes, leave off affected arts,
Gay fowlers at a flock of hearts;
Woodcocks to shun your snares have skill,
You show so plain you strive to kill.
In love the artless catch the game,
And they scarce miss who never aim.

MATTHEW GREEN, *The Spleen*, l. 252.

1
He who wins a thousand common hearts is therefore entitled to some renown; but he who keeps undisputed sway over the heart of a coquette, is indeed a hero.

WASHINGTON IRVING, *The Legend of Sleepy Hollow.*

2
It is a species of coquetry to make a parade of never practising it. (C'est une espèce de coquetterie de faire remarquer qu'on n'en fait jamais.)

LA ROCHEFOUCAULD, *Maximes.* No. 107.

All women are coquettes, though all do not practise coquetry; some are restrained by fear and some by reason. (Le coquetterie est le fond de l'humeur des femmes; mais toutes ne la mettent pas en pratique, parce que la coquetterie de quelques-unes est retenue par la crainte ou par la raison.)

LA ROCHEFOUCAULD, *Maximes.* No. 241.

Women know not the whole of their coquetry. (Les femmes ne connaissent pas toute leur coquetterie.)

LA ROCHEFOUCAULD, *Maximes.* No. 332.

Women are less able to control their coquetry than their passion. (Les femmes peuvent moins surmonter leur coquetterie que leur passion.)

LA ROCHEFOUCAULD, *Maximes.* No. 334.

3
The greatest miracle of love is that it cures coquetry. (Le plus grand miracle de l'amour, c'est de guérir de la coquetterie.)

LA ROCHEFOUCAULD, *Maximes.* No. 349.

Envy is cured by true friendship, and coquetry by true love. (L'envie est détruite par la véritable amitié, et la coquetterie par le véritable amour.)

LA ROCHEFOUCAULD, *Maximes.* No. 376.

4
She has two eyes, so soft and brown,
Take care!
She gives a side-glance and looks down,
Beware! Beware!
Trust her not, She is fooling thee!

LONGFELLOW, *Beware.*

5
Not that I'd have my pleasure incomplete,
Or lose the kiss for which my lips beset you;
But that in suffering me to take it, Sweet,
I'd have you say, "No! no! I will not let you.

CLÉMENT MAROT, *A Love-Lesson.* (Leigh Hunt, tr.)

6
Coquetry whets the appetite; flirtation depraves it. Coquetry is the thorn that guards the rose—easily trimmed off when once plucked. Flirtation is like the slime on water-plants, making them hard to handle, and when caught, only to be cherished in slimy waters.

DONALD G. MITCHELL, *Reveries of a Bachelor: Sea-Coal.*

7
Lesbia hath a beaming eye,
But no one knows for whom it beameth.

THOMAS MOORE, *Song: Lesbia Hath.*

8
From a grave thinking mouser, she had grown
The gayest flirt that coach'd it round the town.

WILLIAM PITT, *Fable: The Young Man and His Cat.*

9
Fair to no purpose, artful to no end,
Young without lovers, old without a friend;
A Fop their passion, but their prize a Sot.

POPE, *Moral Essays.* Epis. ii, l. 245.

10
Euphelia serves to grace my measure,
But Chloe is my real flame.

MATTHEW PRIOR, *An Ode.*

11
In vain did she conjure him
To depart her presence so;
Having a thousand tongues to allure him,
And but one to bid him go:
Where lips invite, And eyes delight,
And cheeks, as fresh as rose in June,
Persuade delay; What boots, she say,
Forgo me now, come to me soon?

SIR WALTER RALEIGH [?], *Dulcina.* (PERCY, *Reliques.* Bk. ii, No. 13. Anonymous.)

12
With one she gossips full of art;
Her glances with a second flirt;
She holds another in her heart:
Whom does she love enough to hurt?

ARTHUR W. RYDER, *Whom Does She Love?*

13
There's language in her eye, her cheek, her lip,
Nay, her foot speaks; her wanton spirits look out
At every joint and motive of her body.

SHAKESPEARE, *Troilus and Cressida.* Act iv, sc. 5, l. 56.

Every little movement has a meaning all its own.

HARBACH AND HOSCHNA. The song hit of *Madame Sherry,* 1909.

14
So innocent-arch, so cunning simple.

TENNYSON, *Lilian.*

15
I hold my love but lightly For I know
Things with wings held tightly Want to go.

JEWELL BOTHWELL TULL, *Coquette.*

16
Ye belles, and ye flirts, and ye pert little things,
Who trip in this frolicsome round,
Pray tell me from whence this impertinence springs,
The sexes at once to confound?

PAUL WHITEHEAD, *Song for Ranelagh.*

1
Womankind more joy discovers
Making fools than keeping lovers.
JOHN WILMOT, *A Dialogue*, l. 71.

CORPORATIONS

2
Corporations cannot commit treason, nor be outlawed, nor excommunicated, for they have no souls.
SIR EDWARD COKE, *Case of Sutton's Hospital*, 1612. (5 Rep. 303; 10 Rep. 32 b)

Lord Coke gravely informs us that corporations cannot be excommunicated, because they have no souls, and they appear to be as destitute of every feeling as if they had also no bowels. . . . There is in truth but one point through which they are vulnerable, and that is the keyhole of the cash box.
GROTIUS, *De Jure Belli et Pacis*. Bk. ii, ch. 9.

3
They feel neither shame, remorse, gratitude, nor goodwill.
WILLIAM HAZLITT, *Table-Talk*. Essay 27. Referring to corporations.

4
When it is said that a corporation is immortal, we are to understand nothing more than that it is capable of an indefinite duration.
STEWART KYD, *On Corporations*, p. 17.

5
I see in the near future a crisis approaching that unnerves me and causes me to tremble for the safety of my country. As a result of the war, corporations have been enthroned, and an era of corruption in high places will follow. . . . I feel at this moment more anxiety for the safety of my country than ever before, even in the midst of war.
Attributed to ABRAHAM LINCOLN, but not found in his works and probably apocryphal.

6
As touching corporations, that they were invisible, immortal, and that they had no soul, therefore no subpœna lieth against them, because they have no conscience or soul.
SIR ROGER MANWOOD, Chief Baron of the Exchequer, 1592. (*Dict. National Biography*.)

7
The biggest corporation, like the humblest private citizen, must be held to strict compliance with the will of the people.
THEODORE ROOSEVELT, *Speech*, Cincinnati, 1902.

8
Did you expect a corporation to have a conscience, when it has no soul to be damned and no body to be kicked?
EDWARD THURLOW. (SAMUEL WILBERFORCE, *Life of Thurlow*. Vol. ii, Appendix.)

Why, you never expected justice from a company, did you? they have neither a soul to lose nor a body to kick.
SYDNEY SMITH, quoting Thurlow. (LADY HOLLAND, *Memoir*. Vol. i, p. 331, ch. 11.)

9
A corporation cannot blush. It is a body, it is true; has certainly a head—a new one every year; arms it has and very long ones, for it can reach at anything; . . . a throat to swallow the rights of the community, and a stomach to digest them! But who ever yet discovered, in the anatomy of any corporation, either bowels or a heart?
HOWEL WALSH, *Speech*, at the Tralee assizes. (WILLIAM HONE, Table Book.)

CORRUPTION

10
Corruption is a tree, whose branches are
Of an unmeasurable length: they spread
Ev'rywhere.
BEAUMONT AND FLETCHER, *Honest Man's Fortune*. Act iii, sc. 3.

11
The Interpreter has them first into a room where was a man who could look no way but downwards, with a muck-rake in his hand. . . . The man did neither look up nor regard, but raked to himself the straws, the small sticks, and dust of the floor.
JOHN BUNYAN, *The Pilgrim's Progress*, ii. This was the theme of President Roosevelt's speech at the dinner of the Gridiron Club in Washington, 17 March, 1906. Hence "muck-raker."

The men with the muck-rake are often indispensable to the well-being of society, but only if they know when to stop raking the muck.
THEODORE ROOSEVELT, *Address*, at Gridiron Club dinner, Washington, 14 April, 1906.

12
Corrupt influence, which is in itself the perennial spring of all prodigality, and of all disorder.
EDMUND BURKE, *Speech*, House of Commons, 11 Feb., 1780.

13
Corruption, the most infallible symptom of constitutional liberty.
EDWARD GIBBON, *Decline and Fall*. Ch. 21.

14
At length corruption, like a general flood,
(So long by watchful ministers withstood,)
Shall deluge all; and avarice, creeping on,
Spread like a low-born mist, and blot the sun.
POPE, *Moral Essays*. Epis. iii, l. 135.

15
So true is that old saying, Corruptio optima pessima. (The best things corrupted become the worst.)
SAMUEL PURCHAS, *Pilgrims: To the Reader: Of Religion*. (1625) The "old saying may be found in ST. THOMAS AQUINAS, *Prim. Soc.*, i, 5.

The opposite of the best must be the worst. (Κάκιστον τὸ ἐναντίον τῷ βελτίστῳ.)
ARISTOTLE, *Nicomachean Ethics*. Bk. viii, ch. 10, sec. 3.

'Tis the most certain sign, the world's accurst
That the best things corrupted are the worst.
Sir John Denham, *Progress of Learning.*

I know, when they prove bad, they are a sort of the vilest creatures: yet still the same reason gives it: for, Optima, corrupta, pessima: the best things corrupted become the worst.
Owen Feltham, *Resolves: Of Woman,* p. 70. (1620)

1
Corruption wins not more than honesty.
Shakespeare, *Henry VIII.* Act iii, sc. 2, l. 444.

Rank corruption, mining all within,
Infects unseen.
Shakespeare, *Hamlet.* Act iii, sc. 4, l. 148.

I have seen corruption boil and bubble
Till it o'er-run the stew.
Shakespeare, *Measure for Measure,* v, 1, 320.

Stew'd in corruption.
Shakespeare, *Hamlet.* Act iii, sc. 4, l. 93.

2
The foul, corruption-gender'd swarm of state.
Southey, *Joan of Arc.* Bk. iv, l. 94.

COSMOPOLITANISM

3
Where most I prosper, there's my fatherland. (Πατρὶς γάρ ἐστι πᾶσ' ἵν' ἂν πράττῃ τις εὖ.)
Aristophanes, *Plutus,* l. 1151.

One's country is wherever one is well off. (Patria est, ubicumque est bene.)
Pacuvius, *Teucer.* (Cicero, *Tusculanarum Disputationum.* Bk. v, ch. 37, sec. 108.)

Our country is wherever we are well off.
Milton, *Letter to P. Heinbach.* 15 Aug., 1666.

Every soil,
Where he is well, is to a valiant man
His natural country.
Massinger, *The Picture.* Act ii, sc. 2.

I count any place my country where I may live well and wealthily.
George Pettie, *Petite Pallace,* i, 40. (1576)

And where a man lives well, there is his country.
Thomas Kyd, *Solyman and Perseda.* Act iv.

4
If a man be gracious and courteous to strangers, it shows he is a citizen of the world.
Francis Bacon, *Essays: Of Goodness.*

5
To a resolved mind, his home is everywhere.
Beaumont and Fletcher, *The Knight of the Burning Pestle.* Act v.

6
All countries are a wise man's home,
And so are governments to some.
Butler, *Hudibras.* Pt. iii, canto 2, l. 1293.

7
I am a citizen of the world. (Κοσμοπολίτης.)
Diogenes, on being asked what his country was, and so originated "cosmopolitan." (Diogenes Laertius, *Diogenes.* Bk. vi, 63.)

I am not an Athenian nor a Greek, but a citizen of the world. (Οὐκ Ἀθηναῖος οὐδ' Ἕλλην ἀλλὰ κόσμιος.)
Socrates. (Plutarch, *Of Banishment,* 600.)

Socrates, on being asked to what country he claimed to belong, said, "To the world." (Socrates quidem cum rogaretur cuiatem se esse diceret, "Mundanum" inquit.)
Cicero, *Tusculanarum Disputationum.* Bk. v, ch. 37, sec. 108.

8
He made all countries where he came his own.
Dryden, *Astrea Redux,* l. 76.

9
Go where he will, the wise man is at home,
His hearth the earth, his hall her azure dome.
Emerson, *Woodnotes.* Pt. i, sec. 3.

10
Our country is the world—our countrymen are all mankind.
William Lloyd Garrison, *Motto of The Liberator.* In his prospectus for the new journal, in 1830, Mr. Garrison had written: "My country is the world; my countrymen are mankind."

11
The truth is that Mr. James's cosmopolitanism is, after all, limited; to be really cosmopolitan, a man must be at home even in his own country.
T. W. Higginson, *Short Studies of American Authors: Henry James, Jr.*

I hate the man that keeps his praise
For foreign policy and ways,
And shows his wit—and lack of sense—
At his own countrymen's expense.
D'Arcy Wentworth Thompson, *Sales Attici.*

I don't set up for being a cosmopolite, which to my mind signifies being polite to every country except your own.
Thomas Hood, *Up the Rhine.*

12
He has no home whose home is everywhere. (Quisquis ubique habitat, nusquam habitat.)
Martial, *Epigrams.* Bk. vii, epig. 73.

13
The sea's vast depths lie open to the fish;
Where'er the breezes blow the bird may roam;
So to the brave man every land's a home.
(Omne solum forti patria est, ut piscibus æquor,
Ut volucri, vacuo quicquid in orbe patet.)
Ovid, *Fasti.* Bk. i, l. 493.

Home is anywhere for me
On this purple-tented sea.
John G. Neihardt, *Outward.*

14
My country is the world, and my religion is to do good.
Thomas Paine, *Rights of Man.* Pt. ii, ch. v.

15
A brave man's country is wherever he chooses his abode. (Patria est ubicumque vir fortis sedem elegerit.)
Quintus Curtius Rufus, *De Rebus Gestis Alexandri Magni.* Bk. vi, sec. 4.

16
That man's the best cosmopolite
Who loves his native country best.
Tennyson, *Hands All Around.*

1
The world is my country. (Πατρίδα τον κόσμον.)
THEODORUS. (DIOGENES LAERTIUS, *Aristippus*. Bk. ii, sec. 99.)

All the world is the fatherland of a noble soul.
DEMOCRITUS, *Ethica*. Frag. 168.

I am not born for any one corner of the universe; the whole world is my country. (Non sum uni angulo natus; patria mea totus hic mundus est.)
SENECA, *Epistulæ ad Lucilium*. Epis xxviii, 5.

The whole world is a man's birthplace.
STATIUS, *Thebais*. Bk. viii, l. 320.

2
Anchorite, who didst dwell
With all the world for cell!
FRANCIS THOMPSON, *To the Dead Cardinal of Westminster*. St. 5.

3
O gentle hands that soothed the soldier's brow
And knew no service save of Christ's the Lord!
Thy country now is all humanity.
G. E. WOODBERRY, *Edith Cavell*.

COUNTRY, THE

For "Our Country" see Patriotism; for individual countries, see their names.

I—Country: Its Attractions

4
The country for a wounded heart.
A. C. BENSON, *College Window*, p. 107. Quoted as an old proverb.

5
And country life I praise,
And lead, because I find
The philosophic mind
Can take no middle ways.
ROBERT BRIDGES, *Spring*. Ode i, st. 7.

6
No one knows the countryside,
Deep and green and sweetly wide,
Until he loves it as a woman,
Something warm and dear and human.
STRUTHERS BURT, *No One Knows the Countryside*.

7
Nor rural sights alone, but rural sounds
Exhilarate the spirit, and restore
The tone of languid nature.
COWPER, *The Task*. Bk. i, l. 181.

God made the country, and man made the town.
What wonder then that health and virtue, gifts
That can alone make sweet the bitter draught
That life holds out to all, should most abound
And least be threaten'd in the fields and groves?
COWPER, *The Task*. Bk. i, l. 749.

See also under CITIES.

8
How blessed is he who leads a country life,
Unvexed with anxious cares, and void of strife!
Who, studying peace, and shunning civil rage,
Enjoyed his youth, and now enjoys his age:
All who deserve his love he makes his own;
And, to be loved himself, needs only to be known.
DRYDEN, *To John Driden of Chesterton*, l. 1.

9
A land flowing with milk and honey.
Old Testament: Exodus, iii, 8; *Jeremiah*, xxxii, 22.

10
A country man may be as warm in kersey as a king in velvet.
THOMAS FULLER, *Gnomologia*. No. 55.

11
To one who has been long in city pent,
'Tis very sweet to look into the fair
And open face of heaven,—to breathe a prayer
Full in the smile of the blue firmament.
KEATS, *Sonnet*.

12
The country is lyric,—the town dramatic. When mingled, they make the most perfect musical drama.
LONGFELLOW, *Kavanagh*. Ch. 13.

13
Country in town. (Rus in urbe.)
MARTIAL, *Epigrams*. Bk. xii, epig. 57, l. 21.

14
Before green apples blush,
Before green nuts embrown,
Why, one day in the country
Is worth a month in town.
CHRISTINA ROSSETTI, *Summer*.

15
Happy is he who knows the country divinities!
(Fortunatus et ille, deos qui novit agrestis.)
VERGIL, *Georgics*. Bk. ii, l. 493.

II—Country: Its Faults

16
He likes the country, but in truth must own,
Most likes it when he studies it in town.
COWPER, *Retirement*, l. 573.

17
I hate the country's dirt and manners, yet
I love the silence; I embrace the wit.
WILLIAM HABINGTON, *To My Noblest Friend, I. C., Esquire*.

18
There is nothing good to be had in the country, or, if there be, they will not let you have it.
WILLIAM HAZLITT, *Lectures: Mr. Wordsworth's "Excursion."*

All country people hate each other. They have so little comfort that they envy their neighbours the smallest pleasure or advantage.
WILLIAM HAZLITT, *Round-Table*. Vol. ii, p. 116.

19
My living in Yorkshire was so far out of the way, that it was actually twelve miles from a lemon.
SYDNEY SMITH. (LADY HOLLAND, *Memoir*. Vol. i, p. 262.)

You, who live fourteen miles from a market town, are become a kind of holy vegetable.
SYDNEY SMITH, *Peter Plymley Letters*. No. 1.

1
I have no relish for the country; it is a kind of healthy grave.
SYDNEY SMITH, *Letter to Miss Harcourt*, 1838.

I do all I can to love the country, and endeavour to believe those poetical lies which I read in Rogers and others, on the subject; which said deviations from the truth were, by Rogers, all written in St. James's Place.
SYDNEY SMITH, *Letter to Lady Holland*, 3 Jan., 1841.

2
The rustic has, in general, good principles, though he cannot control his animal habits; and, however loud he may snore, his face is perpetually turned toward the fountain of orthodoxy.
SYDNEY SMITH, *Peter Plymley Letters*. No. 1.

3
Anybody can be good in the country. There are no temptations there.
OSCAR WILDE, *Picture of Dorian Gray*. Ch. 19.

COURAGE

See also Boldness, Valor

I—Courage: Definitions

4
I think the Romans call it Stoicism.
ADDISON, *Cato*. Act i, sc. 4.

5
The brave man is not he who feels no fear,
For that were stupid and irrational;
But he, whose noble soul its fear subdues,
And bravely dares the danger nature shrinks from.
JOANNA BAILLIE, *Basil*. Act iii, sc. 1, l. 151.

6
Where true fortitude dwells, loyalty, bounty, friendship, and fidelity may be found.
SIR THOMAS BROWNE, *Christian Morals*. Pt. i, sec. 36.

The brave Love mercy, and delight to save.
JOHN GAY, *Fables: The Lion, Tiger and Traveller*, l. 33.

7
Courage is that virtue which champions the cause of right. (Fortitudo, eam virtutem propugnantem pro æquitate.)
CICERO, *De Officiis*. Bk. i, ch. 19, sec. 62. Quoted as a Stoic definition.

No man can be brave who thinks pain the greatest evil; nor temperate, who considers pleasure the highest good. (Fortis vero dolorem summum malum judicans aut temperans voluptatem summum bonum statuens esse certe nullo modo potest.)
CICERO, *De Officiis*. Bk. i, ch. 2, sec. 5.

8
Courage is generosity of the highest order, for the brave are prodigal of the most precious things.
C. C. COLTON, *Lacon*. Vol. i, No. 299.

9
Courage consists in equality to the problem before us.
EMERSON, *Society and Solitude: Courage*.

A great part of courage is the courage of having done the thing before.
EMERSON, *Society and Solitude: Courage*.

The charm of the best courages is that they are inventions, inspirations, flashes of genius.
EMERSON, *Society and Solitude: Courage*.

10
Who, then, is the invincible man? He whom nothing that is outside the sphere of his moral purpose can dismay.
EPICTETUS, *Discourses*. Bk. i, ch. 18, sec. 21.

11
Courage, the highest gift, that scorns to bend
To mean devices for a sordid end.
Courage—an independent spark from Heaven's bright throne,
By which the soul stands raised, triumphant, high, alone. . . .
Courage, the mighty attribute of powers above,
By which those great in war, are great in love.
The spring of all brave acts is seated here,
As falsehoods draw their sordid birth from fear.
FARQUHAR, *Love and a Bottle: Dedication*.

12
The greatest test of courage on the earth is to bear defeat without losing heart.
R. G. INGERSOLL, *The Declaration of Independence*.

13
True courage is to do without witnesses everything that one is capable of doing before all the world. (La parfaite valeur est de faire sans témoins ce qu'on serait capable de faire devant tout le monde.)
LA ROCHEFOUCAULD, *Maximes*. No. 216.

To fight aloud is very brave,
But gallanter, I know,
Who charge within the bosom
The cavalry of woe.
EMILY DICKINSON, *Poems*. Pt. i, No. 16.

14
Courage is the most common and vulgar of the virtues.
HERMAN MELVILLE. (COURNOS, *Modern Plutarch*, p. 86.)

15
Courage conquers all things: it even gives strength to the body. (Animus tamen omnia vincit: Ille etiam vires corpus habere facit.)
OVID, *Epistulæ ex Ponto*. Bk. ii, epis. vii, l. 75.

16
Courage is the best gift of all; courage stands before everything. It is what preserves our liberty, safety, life, and our homes and parents, our country and children. Courage comprises all things: a man with courage has every blessing.
PLAUTUS, *Amphitruo*, l. 646. (Act i, sc. 2.)

1
That's courage—to take hard knocks like a man when occasion calls. (Em ista virtus est, quando usust qui malum fert fortiter.)
PLAUTUS, *Asinaria*, l. 323. (Act ii, sc. 2.)

He's truly valiant, that can wisely suffer
The worst that man can breathe.
SHAKESPEARE, *Timon of Athens*. Act iii, sc. 5, l. 31.

2
Courage leads starward, fear toward death. (Virtus in astra tendit, in mortem timor.)
SENECA, *Hercules Œtæus*, l. 1971.

Now has my valor borne me to the stars and to the gods themselves. (Jam virtus mihi In astra et ipsos fecit ad superos iter.)
SENECA, *Hercules Œtæus*, l. 1943.

3
Courage is a scorner of things which inspire fear. (Fortitudo contemptrix timendorum est.)
SENECA, *Epistulæ ad Lucilium*. Epis. 88, sec. 29.

You can behold such sights,
And keep the natural ruby of your cheeks,
When mine is blanch'd with fear.
SHAKESPEARE, *Macbeth*. Act iii, sc. 4, l. 114.

4
Courage, the footstool of the Virtues, upon which they stand.
R. L. STEVENSON, *The Great North Road*.

5
Courage in strife is common enough; even the dogs have it. But the courage which can face the ultimate defeat of a life of good will, . . . that is different, that is victory.
H. M. TOMLINSON. (NEWTON, *My Idea of God*, p. 78.)

II—Courage: Apothegms

6
It is only from cold.
JEAN BAILLY, while waiting to be guillotined. (CARLYLE, *French Revolution*.) "Bailly, thou tremblest," someone said. "Mon ami, c'est de froid," Bailly replied.

Dick: Why dost thou quiver, man?
Say: The palsy, and not fear, provoke me.
SHAKESPEARE, *II Henry VI*. Act iv, sc. 7, l. 97.

If I tremble with cold, my enemies will say it was from fear: I will not expose myself to such reproaches.
CHARLES I, of England, as he put on two shirts the morning of his execution. (LINGARD, *History of England*. Vol. x, ch. 5.)

7
Courage is the thing. All goes if courage goes.
J. M. BARRIE, *Rectorial Address*, St. Andrew's, 3 May, 1922.

8
If not unmoved, yet undismayed.
BYRON, *Heaven and Earth*. Pt. i, sc. 3, l. 892.

9
And though hard be the task,
"Keep a stiff upper lip."
PHŒBE CARY, *Keep a Stiff Upper Lip*.

10
I prefer to strive in bravery with the bravest, rather than in wealth with the richest, or in greed with the greediest.
MARCUS CARO. (PLUTARCH, *Lives: Marcus Cato*. Ch. x, sec. 4.)

11
Impair my vigour!
SUSANNAH CENTLIVRE, *The Beau's Duel*. Act i. Favorite exclamation of Sir William Mode.

12
A stout heart breaks bad luck.
CERVANTES, *Don Quixote*. Pt. ii, ch. 10.

13
We are not downhearted.
JOSEPH CHAMBERLAIN, *Speech*, Southwick, 15 Jan., 1906.

Are we downhearted? No!
An expression which came into great vogue with the British soldiers during the World War, based, probably, upon these words of Mr. Chamberlain.

14
The bad man's courage still prepares the way
For its own outwitting.
S. T. COLERIDGE, *Zapolya*. Act i, sc. 1.

15
Brave men are brave from the very first. (Les hommes valeureux le sont au premier coup.)
CORNEILLE, *Le Cid*. Act ii, sc. 3.

16
For who gets wealth, that puts not from the shore?
Danger hath honour; great designs, their fame;
Glory doth follow, courage goes before.
SAMUEL DANIEL, *To Delia*. Sonnet xxx.

17
None but the brave deserves the fair.
DRYDEN, *Alexander's Feast*. St. 1.

The brave deserve the lovely—every woman may be won.
CHARLES GODFREY LELAND, *The Masher*.
See also WOOING: FAINT HEART AND FAIR LADY.

18
Whistling to keep myself from being afraid.
DRYDEN, *Amphitryon*. Act iii, sc. 1.

The schoolboy, with his satchel in his hand,
Whistling aloud to bear his courage up.
ROBERT BLAIR, *The Grave*. Pt. i, l. 58.

I am devilishly afraid, that's certain; but . . .
I'll sing, that I may seem valiant.
DRYDEN, *Amphitryon*. Act ii, sc. 1.

19
Presence of mind and courage in distress,
Are more than armies to procure success.
DRYDEN, *Aureng-Zebe*. Act ii, last lines.

20
Courage scorns the death it cannot shun.
DRYDEN, *The Conquest of Granada*. Pt. ii, act iv, sc. 2.

21
What a new face courage puts on everything!
EMERSON, *Letters and Social Aims: Resources*.

Have the courage not to adopt another's courage.

EMERSON, *Society and Solitude: Courage.*

1
A man of courage never wants weapons.

THOMAS FULLER, *Gnomologia.* No. 302.

Courage should have eyes as well as arms.

THOMAS FULLER, *Gnomologia.* No. 1188.

2
The brave are born from the brave. (Fortes creantur fortibus.)

HORACE, *Odes.* Bk. iv, ode 4, l. 29. *See also* ANCESTRY: HEREDITY.

3
Perfect courage and complete cowardice are two extremes which happen rarely. (La parfaite valeur et la poltronnerie complète sont deux extrémités où l'on arrive rarement.)

LA ROCHEFOUCAULD, *Maximes.* No. 215.

4
One can't answer for one's courage when one has never been in danger. (On ne peut répondre de son courage quand on n'a jamais été dans le péril.)

LA ROCHEFOUCAULD, *Maximes Supprimées.* No. 616.

5
Courage in danger is half the battle. (Bonus animus in mala re, dimidium est mali.)

PLAUTUS, *Pseudolus,* l. 452. (Act i, sc. 5.)

Who combats bravely is not therefore brave:
He dreads a death-bed like the meanest slave.

POPE, *Moral Essays.* Epis. i, l. 115.

6
Courage, like cowardice, is undoubtedly contagious, but some persons are not liable to catch it.

ARCHIBALD PRENTICE, *Prenticeana.*

7
He that has no Heart, ought to have Heels.

THOMAS FULLER, *Gnomologia.* No. 2146. The Italians say, "Chi non ha cuore abbia gambe"; French, "Qui n'a cœur a jambes."

8
Courage mounteth with occasion.

SHAKESPEARE, *King John.* Act ii, sc. 1, l. 82.

It is in great dangers that we see great courage.

JEAN FRANÇOIS REGNARD, *Le Légataire.*

9
Why, now I see there's mettle in thee.

SHAKESPEARE, *Othello.* Act iv, sc. 2, l. 205.

10
Fortune favours the brave. (Fortis fortuna adjuvat.)

TERENCE, *Phormio.* Act i, sc. 4.

God helps the brave. (Dem Muthigen hilft Gott.)

SCHILLER, *Wilhelm Tell.* Act i, sc. 2.

See also under BOLDNESS.

11
Bravery never goes out of fashion.

THACKERAY, *The Four Georges: George II.*

12
It is easier to use a gun than to show courage.

H. M. TOMLINSON, *Out of Soundings,* p. 79.

13
Recall your courage, and lay aside sad fear. (Revocate animos, mæstumque timorem Mittite.)

VERGIL, *Æneid.* Bk. i, l. 202.

14
Of small number, but their courage quick for war. (Exugui numero, sed bello vivida virtus.)

VERGIL, *Æneid.* Bk. v, l. 754.

Courage from hearts, and not from numbers, grows.

DRYDEN, *Annus Mirabilis.* St. 76.

15
We place at the top of our esteem those people who take chivalrously the heavy blows of life, who are not brave merely, but gallant.

OWEN WISTER, *Reminiscence with Postscript.*

III—Courage: Personal Courage

16
Unbounded courage and compassion join'd,
Temp'ring each other in the victor's mind,
Alternately proclaim him good and great,
And make the hero and the man complete.

JOSEPH ADDISON, *The Campaign,* l. 219.

17
Languor is not in your heart,
Weakness is not in your word,
Weariness not on your brow.

MATTHEW ARNOLD, *Rugby Chapel,* l. 193.

18
And she, whom once the semblance of a scar
Appall'd, an owlet's 'larum chill'd with dread,
Now views the column-scattering bay'net jar,
The falchion flash, and o'er the yet warm dead
Stalks with Minerva's step where Mars might quake to tread.

BYRON, *Childe Harold.* Canto i, st. 54.

Earth shakes beneath them, and heaven roars above;
But nothing scares them from the course they love.

COWPER, *Table Talk,* l. 460.

19
You cannot choose your battlefield,
The gods do that for you,
But you can plant a standard
Where a standard never flew.

NATHALIA CRANE, *The Colors.*

20
I think even lying on my bed I can still do something.

DOROTHEA LYNDE DIX, *Remark,* a few days before her death, 17 July, 1887.

21
The brave man seeks not popular applause,
Nor, overpower'd with arms, deserts his cause;
Unsham'd, though foil'd, he does the best he can;
Force is of brutes, but honour is of man.

DRYDEN, *Palamon and Arcite.* Bk. iii, l. 739.

Without a sign, his sword the brave man draws,
And asks no omen but his country's cause.
HOMER, *Iliad*. Bk. xii, l. 283. (Pope, tr.)

1
In cold blood he leapt into burning Ætna. (Ardentem frigidus Ætnam Insiluit.)
HORACE, *Ars Poetica*, l. 465.

Were the vault of heaven to break and fall upon him, its ruins would smite him undismayed. (Si fractus inlabatur orbis, Impravidum ferient ruinæ.)
HORACE, *Odes*. Bk. iii, ode 3, l. 7.

Should the whole frame of nature round him break
In ruin and confusion hurled,
He, unconcerned, would hear the mighty crack,
And stand secure amidst a falling world.
HORACE, *Odes*, iii, 3. (Addison, tr.)

2
Once I ha' laughed at the power of Love and twice at the grip of the Grave,
And thrice I ha' patted my God on the head that men might call me brave.
RUDYARD KIPLING, *Tomlinson*, l. 65.

3
This is another day! Are its eyes blurred
With maudlin grief for any wasted past?
A thousand thousand failures shall not daunt!
Let dust clasp dust, death, death; I am alive!
DON MARQUIS, *This Is Another Day*.

4
Being a man, ne'er ask the gods for life set free from grief, but ask for courage that endureth long.
MENANDER, *Fragments*. No. 549.

5
Ran on embattled armies clad in iron,
And, weaponless himself,
Made arms ridiculous.
MILTON, *Samson Agonistes*, l. 129.

Rushed where the thickest fire announced most foes.
BYRON, *Don Juan*. Canto vii, st. 32.

A man should stop his ears against paralysing terror, and run the race that is set before him with a single mind.
R. L. STEVENSON, *Virginibus Puerisque: Æs Triplex*.

Where there is a brave man there is the thickest of the fight, there the post of honor.
H. D. THOREAU, *Journal*, 2 Dec., 1839.

6
A courage mightier than the sun—
You rose and fought and, fighting, won!
ANGELA MORGAN, *Know Thyself*.

7
Almost every man covered with his body, when life was gone, the position which he had taken at the beginning of the conflict.
SALLUST, *Bellum Catilinæ*. Sec. 61.

8
He hath borne himself beyond the promise of his age, doing, in the figure of a lamb, the feats of a lion.
SHAKESPEARE, *Much Ado About Nothing*. Act i, sc. 1, l. 13.

IV—Courage: Exhortations

9
We have hard work to do, and loads to lift;
Shun not the struggle—face it; 'tis God's gift.
MALTBIE BABCOCK, *Be Strong*.

10
Be steadfast as a tower that doth not bend
Its stately summit to the tempest's shock.
(Sta come torre ferma, che non crolla
Giammai la cima per soffiar de' venti.)
DANTE, *Purgatorio*. Canto v, l. 14.

O friends, be men, and let your hearts be strong,
And let no warrior in the heat of fight
Do what may bring him shame in others' eyes;
For more of those who shrink from shame are safe
Than fall in battle, while with those who flee
Is neither glory nor reprieve from death.
HOMER, *Iliad*. Bk. v, l. 663. (Bryant, tr.)

11
No steps backward. (Vestigia . . . nulla retrorsum.)
HORACE, *Epistles*. Bk. i, epis. 1, l. 74.

12
Live as brave men, and oppose brave hearts to adverse fate. (Vivite fortes, Fortiaque adversis opponite pectora rebus.)
HORACE, *Satires*. Bk. ii, sat. 2, l. 135.

13
Oh, fear not in a world like this,
And thou shalt know erelong,
Know how sublime a thing it is
To suffer and be strong.
LONGFELLOW, *The Light of Stars*. St. 9.

14
What though the field be lost?
All is not lost; th' unconquerable will,
And study of revenge, immortal hate,
And courage never to submit or yield.
MILTON, *Paradise Lost*. Bk. i, l. 105.

Awake, arise, or be for ever fall'n!
MILTON, *Paradise Lost*. Bk. i, l. 330.

15
Be not afraid of every stranger;
Start not aside for every danger;
Things that seem are not the same;
Blow not a blast at every flame.
GEORGE PEELE, *The Old Wives' Tale*. (1595)

16
Courage, Father Joseph, Brisach is ours. (Courage, Père Joseph, Brisach est à nous.)
CARDINAL RICHELIEU. *Remark*, to his dying colleague, Joseph du Tremblay, 1638.

17
Be strong, and quit yourselves like men.
Old Testament: I Samuel, iv, 9.

The man so bravely played the man,
He made the fiend to fly.
JOHN BUNYAN, *The Pilgrim's Progress*. Pt. ii.

18
What's brave, what's noble,
Let's do it after the high Roman fashion,
And make death proud to take us.
SHAKESPEARE, *Antony and Cleopatra*. Act iv, sc. 15, l. 86.

O, the blood more stirs
To rouse a lion than to start a hare!
SHAKESPEARE, *I Henry IV*. Act i, sc. 3, l. 197.

1
Gloucester, 'tis true that we are in great danger;
The greater therefore should our courage be.
SHAKESPEARE, *Henry V*. Act iv, sc. 1, l. 1.

Why, courage then! what cannot be avoided
'Twere childish weakness to lament or fear.
SHAKESPEARE, *III Henry VI*. Act v, sc. 4, l. 37.

2
Muster your wits: stand in your own defence;
Or hide your heads like cowards, and fly hence.
SHAKESPEARE, *Love's Labour's Lost*, v, 2, 85.

Screw your courage to the sticking-place,
And we'll not fail.
SHAKESPEARE, *Macbeth*. Act i, sc. 7, l. 60.
Often misquoted, "sticking point."

COURT AND COURTIER

I—The Court

3
For friend in court aye better is
Than penny in purse, certis.
CHAUCER, *Romaunt of the Rose*, l. 5541. (c. 1367)

A friend in court is better than a penny in purse.
ALEXANDER BARCLAY, *Ship of Folys*, i, 70. (1509)

I shouldn't wonder—friends at court, you know.
DICKENS, *Dombey and Son*. Ch. 38.

It is good to have friends at court.
LAMB, *Last Essays of Elia: Popular Fallacies*.

If one has friends at court, he can easily become an officer. ('Chao chung yu jên 'hao wei kuan.)
UNKNOWN. A Chinese proverb.

4
The man that has no friend at court,
Must make the laws confine his sport;
But he that has, by dint of flaws,
May make his sport confine the laws.
THOMAS CHATTERTON, *The Revenge*. Act ii, sc. 3.

5
Falsehood and dissimulation are certainly to be found at courts; but where are they not to be found? Cottages have them, as well as courts, only with worse manners.
LORD CHESTERFIELD, *Letters*, 10 May, 1748.

Great courts are the seats of true good-breeding.
LORD CHESTERFIELD, *Letters*, 10 May, 1751.

6
Far from Court, far from care. (Loin de la cour, loin de souci.)
JAMES CLARKE, *Parœmiologia*, 205. (1639)

7
St. Paul hath fought with beasts at Ephesus, and I at Windsor.
RICHARD CORBET, *Letter to Lord Mordant*, referring to "court-wits," and other antagonists at the court.

8
At court everyone for himself.
GEORGE HERBERT, *Jacula Prudentum*.

9
I have many fair promises and holy water of court.
WILLIAM HORMAN, *Vulgaria*. Fo. 231. (1519)

There were we won with court holy water, that is, fair and flattering words.
RICHARD SHACKLOCK, *De Heresibus*. (1565)

10
A virtuous court a world to virtue draws.
BEN JONSON, *Cynthia's Revels*. Act v, sc. 3.

11
The court does not make us happy; it prevents our being so anywhere else. (La Cour ne rend pas content; elle empêche qu'on ne le soit ailleurs.)
LA BRUYÈRE, *Les Caractères: De la Cour*.

The court is like a palace built of marble, made up of very hard but very polished people. (La Cour est comme un édifice bâti de marbre, je veux qu'elle est composée d'hommes fort durs, mais fort polis.)
LA BRUYÈRE, *Les Caractères: De la Cour*.

Who has seen the court has seen the world.
(Qui a vu la Cour, a vu du monde.)
LA BRUYÈRE, *Les Caractères: De la Cour*.

12
Who for preferments at a court would wait,
Where every gudgeon's nibbling at the bait?
What fish of sense would on the shallow lie,
Amongst the little starving wriggling fry,
That throng and crowd each other for a taste
Of the deceitful, painted, poison'd paste;
When the wide river he behind him sees,
Where he may launch to liberty and ease?
THOMAS OTWAY, *Epistle to Mr. Duke*.

13
I was not born for courts or great affairs;
I pay my debts, believe, and say my prayers.
POPE, *Epistle to Dr. Arbuthnot*, l. 267.

Court-virtues bear, like gems, the highest rate,
Born where Heaven's influence scarce can penetrate.
In life's low vale, the soil the virtues like,
They please as beauties, here as wonders strike.
Tho' the same sun, with all-diffusive rays,
Blush in the rose and in the diamond blaze,
We prize the stronger effort of his power,
And justly set the gem above the flower.
POPE, *Moral Essays*. Epis. i, l. 141.

14
Are not these woods
More free from peril than the envious court?
SHAKESPEARE, *As You Like It*. Act ii, sc. 1, l. 2.

Lord, who would live turmoiled in the court,
And may enjoy such quiet walks as these?
SHAKESPEARE, *II Henry VI*. Act iv, sc. 10, l. 18.

15
This is the English, not the Turkish court;
Not Amurath an Amurath succeeds,
But Harry Harry.
SHAKESPEARE, *II Henry IV*. Act v, sc. 2, l. 47.

1
O, happy they that never saw the court,
Nor ever knew great men but by report.
JOHN WEBSTER, *The White Devil*. Act v, sc. 6.

2
The court affords
Much food for satire;—it abounds in lords.
YOUNG, *Love of Fame*. Sat. i, l. 197.

II—The Courtier

3
Such easy greatness, such a graceful port,
So turned and finished for the camp or court!
JOSEPH ADDISON, *The Campaign*.

4
To laugh, to lie, to flatter to the face,
Four ways in court to win men's grace.
ROGER ASCHAM, *The Schoolmaster*.

To shake with laughter ere the jest they hear,
To pour at will the counterfeited tear;
And, as their patron hints the cold or heat,
To shake in dog-days, in December sweat.
SAMUEL JOHNSON, *London*, l. 140.

Grin when he laughs that beareth all the sway,
Frown when he frowns, and groan when he is pale.
SIR THOMAS WYATT, *Of the Courtier's Life*.

5
Young courtiers be beggars in their age.
ALEXANDER BARCLAY, *Egloges*, 20. (c. 1510)

Whoso liveth in the court shall die in the straw.
JOHN LYLY, *Euphues: Euphues to Philautus*, p. 185. (1579) Quoted as a proverb.

And then do prove the proverb often told,
"A careless courtier young, a beggar old."
UNKNOWN, *Uncasing of Machivils Instruction to His Son*. (1613)

6
Heads bow, knees bend, eyes watch around a throne,
And hands obey—our hearts are still our own.
BYRON, *Don Juan*. Canto v, st. 127.

7
Near Death he stands, that stands too near a crown.
SAMUEL DANIEL, *The Tragedy of Cleopatra*. Act iv, sc. 1.

The greatest favorites are in most danger of falling.
THOMAS FULLER, *Gnomologia*.

8
If you think we are worked by strings,
Like a Japanese marionette,
You don't understand these things:
It is simply Court etiquette.
W. S. GILBERT, *The Mikado*. Act i.

9
Men at court think so much of their cunning that they forget other men's.
LORD HALIFAX, *Works*, p. 228.

10
So many men in court, and so many strangers.
GEORGE HERBERT, *Jacula Prudentum*.

11
Whoever prefers the service of princes before his duty to his Creator, will be sure, early or late, to repent in vain.
PILPAY, *Fables: The Prince and His Ministers*.

Lost is his God, his country, everything,
And nothing left but homage to a King!
POPE, *The Dunciad*. Bk. iv, l. 523.

12
Sir, I have lived a courtier all my days,
And studied men, their manners, and their ways;
And have observed this useful maxim still,
To let my betters always have their will.
POPE, *January and May*, l. 156.

13
Lordlings and witlings not a few,
Incapable of doing aught,
Yet ill at ease with nought to do.
SCOTT, *Bridal of Triermain*. Canto ii, l. 618.

14
There is, betwixt that smile we would aspire to,
That sweet aspect of princes, and their ruin,
More pangs and fears than wars or women have.
SHAKESPEARE, *Henry VIII*. Act iii, sc. 2, l. 368.

To dance attendance on their lordships' pleasures.
SHAKESPEARE, *Henry VIII*. Act v, sc. 2, l. 31.

15
The caterpillars of the commonwealth,
Which I have sworn to weed and pluck away.
SHAKESPEARE, *Richard II*. Act ii, sc. 3, l. 166.

A mere court butterfly,
That flutters in the pageant of a monarch.
BYRON, *Sardanapalus*. Act v, sc. 1.

16
Whoso betakes him to a prince's court,
Becomes his slave, albeit of free birth.
SOPHOCLES, *Fragments*. No. 789.

17
The two maxims of any great man at court are, always to keep his countenance, and never to keep his word.
SWIFT, *Thoughts on Various Subjects*.

18
At the throng'd levee bends the venal tribe:
With fair but faithless smiles each varnish'd o'er,
Each smooth as those that mutually deceive,
And for their falsehood each despising each.
JAMES THOMSON, *Liberty*. Pt. v, l. 190.

19
By being a willow, and not an oak.
WILLIAM, MARQUESS OF WINCHESTER, when asked how he managed to continue in the favor of divers princes. (CAMDEN, *Remains*, p. 313.)

COURTESY

See also Manners

I—Courtesy: Definitions

20
Of Courtesy, it is much less

Than Courage of Heart or Holiness,
Yet in my Walks it seems to me
That the Grace of God is in Courtesy.
HILAIRE BELLOC, *Courtesy.*

1
Politeness is artificial good humor; it covers the natural want of it, and ends by rendering habitual a substitute nearly equivalent to the real virtue.
THOMAS JEFFERSON, *Writings*. Vol. xii, p. 198.

2
Politeness . . . is fictitious benevolence.
SAMUEL JOHNSON. (BOSWELL, *Life*, v, 82.)

3
Politeness is the flower of humanity. He who is not polite enough is not human enough. (La politesse est la fleur de l'humanité. Qui n'est pas assez poli n'est pas assez humain.)
JOUBERT, *Pensées*. No. 120.

4
Politeness is to do and say
The kindest thing in the kindest way.
LUDWIG LEWISOHN [?], *Politeness.*

5
Now as to politeness . . . I would venture to call it benevolence in trifles.
WILLIAM PITT, EARL OF CHATHAM, *Correspondence*. Vol. i, p. 79.

Politeness has been well defined as benevolence in small things.
MACAULAY, *Essays: Samuel Johnson.*

6
True politeness consists in being easy one's self, and in making every one about one as easy as one can.
POPE, *Table-Talk.*

7
Politeness is to human nature what warmth is to wax.
SCHOPENHAUER, *Aphorisms on the Wisdom of Life.*

8
Deference is the most complicate, the most indirect, and the most elegant of all compliments.
WILLIAM SHENSTONE, *Of Men and Manners*, 66.

9
Politeness is the art of choosing among one's real thoughts.
ABEL STEVENS, *Life of Mme. de Staël*. Ch. 4.

II—Courtesy: Apothegms

10
It is nothing won to admit men with an open door, and to receive them with a shut and reserved countenance.
FRANCIS BACON, *Advancement of Learning: Civil Knowledge*. Sec. 3.

11
Curtsey while you're thinking what to say. It saves time.
LEWIS CARROLL, *Through the Looking-Glass*. Ch. 2.

12
She is mirror of all courtesy.
CHAUCER, *Tale of the Man of Law*, l. 68.

The mirror of all courtesy.
SHAKESPEARE, *Henry VIII*. Act ii, sc. 1, l. 53.

13
To be rude to him was courtesy. (E cortesia fu in lui esser villano.)
DANTE, *Inferno*. Canto xxxiii, l. 150.

14
Life is short, but there is always time for courtesy.
EMERSON, *Uncollected Lectures: Social Aims.*

15
Courtesy costs nothing.
W. G. BENHAM, *Proverbs*, p. 749.

Politeness costs nothing, and gains everything.
LADY MARY WORTLEY MONTAGU, *Letters.*

Cap in hand never did anyone harm. (Biretta in mano non fece mai danno.)
UNKNOWN. An Italian proverb.

16
Politeness of spirit consists in thinking of things which are fastidious and in good taste. (La politesse de l'esprit consiste à penser des choses honnêtes et délicates.)
LA ROCHEFOUCAULD, *Maximes*. No. 99.

17
Intelligence and courtesy not always are combined;
Often in a wooden house a golden room we find.
LONGFELLOW, *Art and Tact.*

18
Punctuality is the politeness of kings. (L'exactitude est la politesse des rois.)
LOUIS XVIII of France. His best-known saying. (*Fleurs Historique.*)

"Punctuality," said Louis XIV, "is the politeness of kings." It is also the duty of gentlemen, and the necessity of men of business.
SAMUEL SMILES, *Self-Help*. Ch. 9. The ascription to Louis XIV is an error.

Punctuality is a politeness which a man owes to his stomach.
ÉMILE GABORIAU, *Other People's Money*. Pt. ii, ch. 3.

19
When the king was horsed thore,
Launcelot lookys he upon,
How courtesy was in him more
Than ever was in any mon.
SIR THOMAS MALORY, *Morte d'Arthur.*

20
Do not limp before the lame. (Ne clochez pas devant les boyteux.)
RABELAIS, *Works*. Bk. i.

21
I am the king of courtesy.
SHAKESPEARE, *I Henry IV*. Act ii, sc. 4, l. 11.

Princes of courtesy, merciful, proud and strong.
HENRY NEWBOLT, *Craven.*

22
I am the very pink of courtesy.
SHAKESPEARE, *Romeo and Juliet*. Act ii, 4, 61.

He is the very pine-apple of politeness!
SHERIDAN, *The Rivals*. Act iii, sc. 3.

1
The greater man the greater courtesy.
TENNYSON, *The Last Tournament*, l. 628.

2
To all men the same. (Omnibus idem.)
VERGIL, *Æneid*. Bk. x, l. 112.

III—Courtesy: Its Virtues

3
Politeness and good-breeding are absolutely necessary to adorn any, or all other good qualities or talents. . . . The scholar, without good-breeding, is a pedant; the philosopher, a cynic; the soldier, a brute; and every man disagreeable.
LORD CHESTERFIELD, *Letters*, 9 Oct., 1747.

4
Fair and softly goes far.
CERVANTES, *Don Quixote*. Pt. i, ch. 2.

Soft and fair goes far.
JOHN DRYDEN, *Sir Martin Mar-All*. Act ii, sc. 2.

5
Nothing is more becoming in a great man than courtesy and forbearance. (Nihil mango et præclaro viro dignius placabilitate atque clementia.)
CICERO, *De Officiis*. Bk. i, ch. 25, sec. 87.

6
Her air, her manners, all who saw admired;
Courteous though coy, and gentle, though retired.
GEORGE CRABBE, *The Parish Register*. Pt. ii.

7
What boots it, thy virtue,
What profit thy parts,
While one thing thou lackest—
The art of all arts,
The only credentials,
Passport to success,
Opens castle and parlor,
Address, man, address?
EMERSON, *Tact*.

8
How sweet and gracious, even in common speech,
Is that fine sense which men call Courtesy!
Wholesome as air and genial as the light,
Welcome in every clime as breath of flowers,
It transmutes aliens into trusting friends,
And gives its owner passport round the globe.
JAMES T. FIELDS, *Courtesy*.

9
All doors open to courtesy.
THOMAS FULLER, *Gnomologia*. No. 512.

Hearts, like doors, will ope with ease
To very, very little keys,
And don't forget that two of these
Are "I thank you" and "If you please."
UNKNOWN, *Old Nursery Rhyme*.

10
There is great force hidden in a sweet command.
GEORGE HERBERT, *Jacula Prudentum*.

11
Politeness smoothes wrinkles. (La politesse aplanit les rides.)
JOUBERT, *Pensées*. No. 90.

12
Courtesy,
Which oft is sooner found in lowly sheds
With smoky rafters, than in tap'stry halls,
And courts of princes.
MILTON, *Comus*, l. 322.

13
Hail ye small sweet courtesies of life, for smooth do ye make the road of it!
STERNE, *A Sentimental Journey. The Pulse*.

14
Nothing is more valuable to a man than courtesy. (Facilitate nil esse homini melius.)
TERENCE, *Adelphi*, l. 861. (Act v, sc. 4.)

IV—Courtesy: Its Faults

15
Their accents firm and loud in conversation,
Their eyes and gestures eager, sharp and quick
Showed them prepared on proper provocation
To give the lie, pull noses, stab and kick!
And for that very reason it is said
They were so very courteous and well-bred.
JOHN HOOKHAM FRERE, *Prospectus and Specimen of an Intended National Work*.

16
He was so generally civil, that nobody thanked him for it.
SAMUEL JOHNSON. (BOSWELL, *Life*, 1777.)

None of your dam punctilio.
GEORGE MEREDITH, *One of Our Conquerors*. Ch. 1.

17
Glozing courtesy.
MILTON, *Comus*, l. 161.

18
Much courtesy, much subtlety.
THOMAS NASHE, *Unfortunate Traveller*.

Full of courtesy and full of craft.
JOHN RAY, *English Proverbs*, 73.

19
So obliging that he ne'er oblig'd.
POPE, *Epistle to Dr. Arbuthnot*, l. 208.

That's too civil by half.
SHERIDAN, *The Rivals*. Act iii, sc. 4.

20
Dissembling courtesy! How fine this tyrant
Can tickle where she wounds!
SHAKESPEARE, *Cymbeline*. Act i, sc. 1, l. 84.

The show Of smooth civility.
SHAKESPEARE, *As You Like It*. Act ii, sc. 7, l. 95.

Why, what a candy deal of courtesy
This fawning greyhound then did proffer me!
SHAKESPEARE, *I Henry IV*. Act i, sc. 3, l. 251.

How courtesy would seem to cover sin!
SHAKESPEARE, *Pericles*. Act i, sc. 1, l. 121.

21
Duck with French nods and apish courtesy.
SHAKESPEARE, *Richard III*. Act i, sc. 3, l. 49.

And rubbed his hands, and smiled aloud
And bowed, and bowed, and bowed, and bowed,
Like a man who is sawing marble.
THOMAS HOOD, *Miss Kilmansegg: Her Fancy Ball.*

1
Politeness is excellent, but it does not pay the bill.
C. H. SPURGEON, *Salt-Cellars.*

Less of your courtesy and more of your purse.
JOHN RAY, *English Proverbs.*

COURTSHIP, see Wooing

COW

I—Cow: Apothegms

2
Kiss till the cow comes home.
BEAUMONT AND FLETCHER, *The Scornful Lady.* Act iii, sc. 1. (1616)

Drinking, eating, feasting, and revelling, till the cows come home, as the saying is.
UNKNOWN. (*Harl. Miscell.*, iv, 125. 1625)

I warrant you lay abed till the cows came home.
SWIFT, *Polite Conversation.* Dial ii. (1738)

You may rezoloot till the cows come home.
JOHN HAY, *Little Breeches.* (c. 1873)

3
Cows are my passion.
DICKENS, *Dombey and Son.* Bk. i, ch. 21.

4
The gossiping sort have a cow's tongue, a smooth side and a rough side.
WILLIAM ELLIS, *Housewife's Companion.* Ch. 7. (1750)

5
A cow does not gaze at the rainbow, or show or affect any interest in the landscape, or a peacock, or the song of thrushes.
EMERSON, *Letters and Social Aims: Poetry and Imagination.*

6
The cross cow holds up her milk.
EMERSON, *Society and Solitude: Clubs.*

7
All is not butter that comes from the cow.
THOMAS FULLER, *Gnomologia.* No. 527.

8
God, they say, sendeth commonly a curst cow short horns.
JOHN HARVEY, *Discoursive Problems.* (1588)

It is said, "God sends a curst cow short horns," but to a cow too curst he sends none.
SHAKESPEARE, *Much Ado About Nothing.* Act ii, sc. 1, l. 25.

9
The cow knows not what her tail is worth till she have lost it.
GEORGE HERBERT, *Jacula Prudentum.* No. 864.

10
Many a good cow hath an evil calf.
JOHN HEYWOOD, *Proverbs.* Pt. i, ch. 10. (1546)

Thou art not the first good cow that hast had an ill calf.
GEORGE CHAPMAN, *Eastward Hoe.* Act iv, sc. 1. (1605)

11
Who'd keep a cow, when he may have a quart of milk for a penny?
THOMAS FULLER, *Gnomologia.* No. 5697.

12
A cow is a very good animal in the field; but we turn her out of a garden.
SAMUEL JOHNSON. (BOSWELL, *Life,* 1772.)

13
How now! whose cow has calv'd?
BEN JONSON, *Every Man in His Humour.* Act iv, sc. 1.

14
As becometh a cow to hop in a cage.
WILLIAM LANGLAND, *Richard the Redeless,* iii, 262. (1399)

As comely as a cow in a cage.
JOHN HEYWOOD, *Proverbs.* Pt. ii, ch. 1. (1546)

15
This town goes downhill like the calf's tail. (Hæc colonia retroversus crescit tanquam coda vituli.)
PETRONIUS, *Satyricon.* Sec. 44.

Which never grow but like cows' tails downwards.
RABELAIS, *Works.* Bk. ii, ch. 27.

You're growing downwards now
Like tail of heifer or of cow.
EDWARD WARD, *Nuptial Dialogues.* Pt. ii, l. 76.

Brother, thy tail hangs down behind.
KIPLING, *Road-Song of the Bandar-Log.*

16
Be not you like the cow, that gives a good sope of milk, and casts it down with her heels.
HENRY PORTER, *The Pleasant History of the Two Angry Women of Abington.* Sc. 10. (1599)

A cow that gives good milk, but kicks it to the ground.
EDWARD WARD, *Female Policy,* 84. (1716)

17
An herd of bulls, whom kindly rage doth sting,
Do for the milky mothers want complain,
And fill the fields with troublous bellowing.
SPENSER, *The Faerie Queene.* Bk. i, canto viii, st. 11. (1579)

As when the long-ear'd milky mothers wait
At some sick miser's triple-bolted gate.
POPE, *The Dunciad.* Bk. ii, l. 247. Pope called this "a simile, with a long tail, in the manner of Homer."

I am she, O most bucolical juvenal, under whose charge are placed the milky mothers of the herd.
SCOTT, *The Monastery.* Ch. 28.

18
Milk the cow which is near. Why pursue the one which runs away? (Τὰν παρεοῖσαν ἄμελγε' τί τὸν φεύγοντα διώκεις;)
THEOCRITUS, *Idylls.* No. xi, l. 75.

Milk the standing cow. Why follow you the flying?
FRANCIS BACON, *Promus.* No. 553. (c. 1594)

1
It is not all for the calf the cow loweth,
As it is for the green grass that in the meadow groweth.

UNKNOWN, *Epigram*, c. 1332. (WRIGHT, *Political Songs*, 332.)

A lowing cow soon forgets her calf.

NORTHALL, *Folk Phrases*, 6.

2
Everyone to their liking,
As the old woman said when she kissed her cow.

UNKNOWN, *Everyone to Their Liking*. (1810)

3
Jack Whaley had a cow,
And he had naught to feed her;
He took a pipe and played a tune,
And bid the cow consider.

UNKNOWN, *Jack Whaley*. Quoted in a letter by Lady Granville, 1836.

There was an old man and he had an old cow,
But he had no fodder to give her,
So he took up his fiddle, and played her a tune,
Consider, good cow, consider;
This isn't the time for the grass to grow;
Consider, good cow, consider.

UNKNOWN, *Old Ballad*. (*Notes and Queries*. Sec. ii, vol. 2, p. 309.) "The tune the old cow died of."

This tune . . . "which the old cow died of," as the saying is, used to be their horror.

FREDERICK MARRYAT, *Japhet*. Ch. 68.

II—Cow: Some Jingles

4
I never saw a PURPLE COW,
I never HOPE to see one;
But I can tell you, anyhow,
I'd rather SEE than BE one.

GELETT BURGESS, *The Purple Cow*. Appeared in *The Lark*, San Francisco, May, 1895, Burgess's first published writing.

Ah, Yes! I Wrote the PURPLE COW—
I'm Sorry, now, I Wrote it!
But I can Tell you Anyhow,
I'll KILL you if you QUOTE it!

GELETT BURGESS.

5
The moo-cow-moc's got a tail like a rope
En it's revelled down where it grows,
En it's just like feeling a piece of soap
All over the moo-cow's nose.

EDMUND VANCE COOKE, *The Moo-Cow-Moo*.

6
And when the Jug is empty quite,
I shall not mew in vain,
The Friendly Cow, all red and white,
Will fill her up again.

OLIVER HERFORD, *The Milk Jug*.

7
God's jolly cafeteria
With four legs and a tail.

E. M. ROOT, *The Cow*.

8
The friendly cow all red and white,
I love with all my heart:
She gives me cream with all her might
To eat with apple-tart.

R. L. STEVENSON, *The Cow*.

9
Thank you, pretty cow, that made
Pleasant milk to soak my bread.

ANN TAYLOR, *The Cow*.

COWARDS AND COWARDICE

See also Timidity

10
The coward calls himself wary, and the miser says he is frugal. (Timidus vocat se cautum, parcum sordidus.)

BACON, *Ornamenta Rationalia*. No. 35. Quoting PUBLILIUS SYRUS. See 2015:3.

11
For anything I know, I am an arrant coward.

BEAUMONT AND FLETCHER, *Little French Lawyer*. Act ii, l. 2.

12
Thou art a cat, and rat, and a coward to boot.

CERVANTES, *Don Quixote*. Pt. i, ch. 8.

13
To see what is right and not to do it is want of courage.

CONFUCIUS, *Analects*. Bk. ii, ch. 24.

14
The coward never on himself relies,
But to an equal for assistance flies.

GEORGE CRABBE, *Tales in Verse*. No. iii, l. 84.

15
Cowards do not count in battle; they are there, but not in it.

EURIPIDES, *Meleager*. Frag. 523.

That neither have the hearts to stay,
Nor wit enough to run away.

BUTLER, *Hudibras*. Pt. iii, canto ii, l. 569.

16
A coward's fear can make a coward valiant.

OWEN FELLTHAM, *Resolves: Of Cowardice*.

So cowards fight when they can fly no further;
So doves do peck the falcon's piercing talons;
So desperate thieves, all hopeless of their lives,
Breathe out invectives 'gainst the officers.

SHAKESPEARE, *III Henry VI*. Act i, sc. 4, l. 40.

Make a coward fight and he will kill the devil.

UNKNOWN, *New Help to Discourse*, 151. (1669)

Put a coward to his mettle and he'll fight the devil.

THOMAS FULLER, *Gnomologia*. No. 3980.

17
God Almighty hates a quitter.

GENERAL SAMUEL FESSENDEN, of Connecticut, at Republican National Convention, St. Louis, June, 1896, referring to Joseph Manley. *See* ROBINSON, *Life of Reed*.)

The blues of mental and physical wear and tear are not as devastating as the yellows of the quitter.

JAMES J. WALKER, *Interview*, 20 Sept., 1931.

18
The coward only threatens when he is safe.

GOETHE, *Torquato Tasso*. Act ii, sc. 3, l. 207.

19
Cowards in scarlet pass for men of war.

GEORGE GRANVILLE, *She Gallants*. Act v, sc. 1.

1
These are the wages of my cowardice,—
Too weak to face the world, too weak to leave it.
CHARLES KINGSLEY, *The Saint's Tragedy*. Act i, sc. 3.

2
Till I 'eard a beggar squealin' out for quarter as 'e ran,
An' I thought I knew the voice an'—it was me!
RUDYARD KIPLING, *That Day*.

3
Then to side with Truth is noble when we share her wretched crust,
Ere her cause bring fame and profit, and 'tis prosperous to be just;
Then it is the brave man chooses, while the coward stands aside,
Doubting in his abject spirit, till his Lord is crucified.
J. R. LOWELL, *The Present Crisis*. St. 11.

4
Ever will a coward shew no mercy.
SIR THOMAS MALORY, *Morte d'Arthur*. Bk. xviii, ch. 24.

Cowards are cruel, but the brave
Love mercy and delight to save.
JOHN GAY, *Fables*. Pt. i, fable 1, l. 33.

5
The brave word that I failed to speak
Will brand me dastard on the cheek.
JOHN MASEFIELD, *A Creed*.

6
Only the cowards are sinners,
Fighting the fight is all.
JOHN G. NEIHARDT, *Battle Cry*.

7
The coward is foiled by his faint heart. (Piger ipse sibi opstat.)
SENECA, *Epistulæ ad Lucilium*. Epis. xciv, 28.

8
He who can be coerced knows not how to die. (Cogi qui potest nescit mori.)
SENECA, *Hercules Furens*, l. 426.

9
You souls of geese,
That bear the shapes of men, how have you run
From slaves that apes would beat!
SHAKESPEARE, *Coriolanus*. Act i, sc. 4, l. 34.

So bees with smoke and doves with noisome stench
Are from their hives and houses driven away.
They call'd us for our fierceness English dogs;
Now, like to whelps, we crying run away.
SHAKESPEARE, *I Henry VI*. Act i, sc. 5, l. 23.

I know them to be as true-bred cowards as ever turned back.
SHAKESPEARE, *I Henry IV*. Act i, sc. 2, l. 202.
See also under DISCRETION.

10
A plague of all cowards, I say, and a vengeance, too!
SHAKESPEARE, *I Henry IV*. Act ii, sc. 4, l. 127.

What a slave art thou, to hack thy sword as thou hast done, and then say it was in fight!
SHAKESPEARE, *I Henry IV*. Act ii, sc. 4, l. 286.

I was now a coward on instinct.
SHAKESPEARE, *I Henry IV*. Act ii, sc. 4, l. 301.

11
Cowards die many times before their deaths;
The valiant never taste of death but once.
SHAKESPEARE, *Julius Cæsar*. Act ii, sc. 2, l. 32.

12
Thou slave, thou wretch, thou coward!
Thou little valiant, great in villainy!
Thou ever strong upon the stronger side!
Thou Fortune's champion, that dost never fight
But when her humorous ladyship is by
To teach thee safety!
SHAKESPEARE, *King John*. Act iii, sc. 1, l. 116.

Out, dunghill! dar'st thou brave a nobleman?
SHAKESPEARE, *King John*. Act iv, sc. 3, l. 87.

A coward, a most devout coward, religious in it.
SHAKESPEARE, *Twelfth Night*. Act iii, sc. 4, l. 427.

13
Art thou afeard
To be the same in thine own act and valour
As thou art in desire? Wouldst thou have that
Which thou esteem'st the ornament of life,
And live a coward in thine own esteem?
SHAKESPEARE, *Macbeth*. Act i, sc. 7, l. 39.

He who fears to venture as far as his heart urges and his reason permits, is a coward; he who ventures further than he intended to go, is a slave.
HEINE, *Wit, Wisdom, and Pathos: Letters on the French Stage*.

14
He was a coward to the strong:
He was a tyrant to the weak.
SHELLEY, *Rosalind and Helen*, l. 254.

15
There grows
No herb of help to heal a coward heart.
SWINBURNE, *Bothwell*, Act ii, sc. 13.

16
It is the misfortune of worthy people that they are cowards. (Un des plus grands malheurs des honnêtes gens c'est qu'ils sont des lâches.)
VOLTAIRE. (EMERSON, *Conduct of Life: Fate*.)

17
For all men would be cowards if they durst.
JOHN WILMOT, EARL OF ROCHESTER, *A Satire Against Mankind*, l. 157. (c. 1670)

That all men would be cowards if they dare,
Some men we know have courage to declare.
GEORGE CRABBE, *Tales in Verse*. No. iii, l. 11. (1812)

Many would be cowards if they had courage enough.
THOMAS FULLER, *Gnomologia*. No. 3366.

18
What easy, tame, suffering, trampled things does that little god of talking cowards make of us!
WYCHERLEY, *The Plain Dealer*. Act iv, sc. 1.
See also under BOASTING.

1
I confess myself the greatest coward in the world, for I dare not do an ill thing.

XENOPHANES. (PLUTARCH, *Morals: Of Bashfulness.*)

COWSLIP

2
Smiled like yon knot of cowslips on a cliff.

ROBERT BLAIR, *The Grave,* l. 523.

3
Yet soon fair Spring shall give another scene,
And yellow cowslips gild the level green.

ANN ELIZA BLEECKER, *Return to Tomhanick.*

And wild-scatter'd cowslips bedeck the green dale.

BURNS, *The Chevalier's Lament.*

4
Ilk cowslip cup shall kep a tear.

BURNS, *Elegy on Capt. Matthew Henderson.*

5
The nesh young cowslip bendeth with the dew.

THOMAS CHATTERTON, *Ælla.* (Nesh: tender.)

6
Then came the cowslip,
Like a dancer in the fair,
She spread her little mat of green,
And on it danced she.
With a fillet bound about her brow,
A fillet round her happy brow,
A golden fillet round her brow,
And rubies in her hair.

SYDNEY DOBELL, *Balder: A Chanted Calendar.*

7
The cowslip is a country wench.

THOMAS HOOD, *Flowers.*

8
The first wan cowslip, wet
With tears of the first morn.

OWEN MEREDITH, *Ode to a Starling.*

9
Thus I set my printless feet
O'er the cowslip's velvet head,
That bends not as I tread.

MILTON, *Comus: Song,* l. 897.

Cowslips wan that hang the pensive head.

MILTON, *Lycidas,* l. 147.

10
The cowslips tall her pensioners be:
In their gold coats spots you see;
Those be rubies, fairy favours,
In those freckles live their savours.

SHAKESPEARE, *A Midsummer-Night's Dream.* Act ii, sc. 1, l. 10.

The freckled cowslip.

SHAKESPEARE, *Henry V.* Act v, sc. 2, l. 49.

CREATOR, see God

CREDIT

11
A poor man has no credit. (Nulla fides inopi.)

AUSONIUS, *Epigrams.* No. xxiii, l. 4.

Every man's credit is proportioned to the cash which he has in his chest. (Quantum quisque sua nummorum servat in arca, Tantum habet et fidei.)

JUVENAL, *Satires.* Sat. iii, l. 143.

12
To lose a man's credit is the greatest loss.

JOHN CLARKE, *Parœmiologia,* 87. (1639)

He that has lost his credit is dead to the world.

GEORGE HERBERT, *Jacula Prudentum.* (1640)

13
Public credit means the contracting of debts which a nation never can pay.

WILLIAM COBBETT, *Advice to Young Men.*

14
Every innocent man has in his countenance a promise to pay, and hence credit.

EMERSON, *Letters and Social Aims: Social Aims.*

If a good face is a letter of recommendation, a good heart is a letter of credit.

BULWER-LYTTON, *What Will He Do With It?* Bk. ii, Ch. 11. *See also under* APPEARANCE.

15
Creditors are a superstitious set, great observers of set days and times.

BENJAMIN FRANKLIN, *Poor Richard.*

16
The only road, the sure road, to unquestioned credit and a sound financial condition is the exact and punctual fulfilment of every pecuniary obligation, public and private, according to its letter and spirit.

RUTHERFORD B. HAYES, *Speech,* Brooklyn, 21 Dec., 1880.

17
Men pay severely who require credit.

DOUGLAS JERROLD, *Specimens of Jerrold's Wit.*

18
Private credit is wealth; public honour is security. The feather that adorns the royal bird supports his flight. Strip him of his plumage, and you fix him to the earth.

JUNIUS, *Letters.* No. 42, 30 Jan., 1771.

19
Ah, take the cash and let the credit go.

OMAR KHAYYÁM, *Rubáiyát.* St. 13. (Fitzgerald, tr.)

20
Blest paper-credit! last and best supply!
That lends corruption lighter wings to fly!

POPE, *Moral Essays.* Epis. iii, l. 39.

That canker at the heart of national prosperity, the imaginary riches of paper credit.

T. L. PEACOCK, *Melincourt.* Ch. 26.

21
He who loses credit can lose nothing further. (Fidem qui perdit, ultra perdere nil potest.)

PUBLILIUS SYRUS, *Sententiæ.* No. 204.

22
So far as my coin would stretch; and where it would not, I have used my credit.

SHAKESPEARE, *I Henry IV.* Act i, sc. 2, l. 61.

23
Once I guessed right,
And I got credit by't;

Thrice I guessed wrong,
And I kept my credit on.

SWIFT, *Letter*. 1710. Quoted.

1
He smote the rock of the national resources, and abundant streams of revenue gushed forth. He touched the dead corpse of public credit, and it sprang upon its feet.

DANIEL WEBSTER, *Eulogy on Alexander Hamilton*, 10 March, 1831.

CREDULITY

For Incredulity, see Doubt

2
A credulous man is a deceiver.

BACON, *Advancement of Learning*. Bk. i.

3
There are a set of heads that can credit the relations of Mariners.

SIR THOMAS BROWNE, *Religio Medici*. Pt. i, 21. *See also under* TRAVEL.

4
He would believe, since he would be believed;
Your noblest natures are most credulous.

GEORGE CHAPMAN, *Revenge of Bussy d'Ambois*. Act iv, sc. 1.

That only disadvantage of honest hearts, credulity.

SIR PHILIP SIDNEY, *Arcadia*. Bk. ii.

5
The characteristic of the present age is craving credulity.

BENJAMIN DISRAELI, *Speech*, Oxford, 25 Nov., 1864.

To swallow and follow, whether old doctrine or new propaganda, is a weakness still dominating the human mind.

CHARLOTTE PERKINS GILMAN, *Human Work*.

6
A rational reaction against irrational excesses . . . readily degenerates into the rival folly of credulity.

GLADSTONE, *Time and Place of Homer: Introduction*.

7
Let the Jew Apella believe it. (Credat Judæus Apella.)

HORACE, *Satires*. Bk. i, sat. 5, l. 100.

Tell it to the Marines, *see under* PROVERBS.

8
Ye who listen with credulity to the whispers of fancy, and pursue with eagerness the phantoms of hope; who expect that age will perform the promises of youth, and that the deficiencies of the present day will be supplied by the morrow,—attend to the history of Rasselas, Prince of Abyssinia.

SAMUEL JOHNSON, *Rasselas*. Ch. 1.

9
When credulity comes from the heart it does no harm to the intellect. (La crédulité qui vient du cœur ne fait aucun mal à l'esprit.)

JOUBERT, *Pensées*. No. 160.

10
The incredulous are the most credulous. They believe the miracles of Vespasian that they may not believe those of Moses. (Incrédules les plus crédules. Ils croient les miracles de Vespasien, pour ne pas croire ceux de Moïse.)

PASCAL, *Pensées*. No. 816.

11
A man who is always ready to believe what is told him will never do well. (Nunquam autem recte facit, qui cito credit.)

PETRONIUS, *Satyricon*. Sec. 43.

12
Wearied from doubt to doubt to flee,
We welcome fond credulity,
Guide confident, though blind.

SCOTT, *Marmion*. Canto iii, st. 30.

13
Those old credulities to nature dear,
Shall they no longer bloom upon the stock
Of history?

WORDSWORTH, *Memorials of a Tour to Italy*. No. iv.

CREEDS

See also Religion: Its Unity; Theology

14
The whole history of civilization is strewn with creeds and institutions which were invaluable at first, and deadly afterwards.

WALTER BAGEHOT, *Physics and Politics*, p. 74.

15
Where I may see saint, savage, sage,
Fuse their respective creeds in one,
Before the general Father's throne.

ROBERT BROWNING, *Christmas Eve*. Pt. xix.

He knew
Behind all creeds the Spirit that is One.

ANDREW LANG, *Herodotus in Egypt*.

16
Sapping a solemn creed with a solemn sneer.

BYRON, *Childe Harold*. Canto iii, st. 107.

17
My creed is, he is safe that does his best,
And death's a doom sufficient for the rest.

COWPER, *Hope*, l. 395.

My creed is this:
Happiness is the only good.
The place to be happy is here.
The time to be happy is now.
The way to be happy is to help make others so.

ROBERT G. INGERSOLL, *Motto*, on title page of Vol. xii, *Works*. (Farrell, Ed.)

I belong to the Great Church which holds the world within its starlit aisles; that claims the great and good of every race and clime; that finds with joy the grain of gold in every creed, and floods with light and love the germs of good in every soul.

ROBERT G. INGERSOLL, *Declaration*, in discussion with REV. HENRY M. FIELD on *Faith and Agnosticism*. (FARRELL, *Life*. Vol. vi.)

I believe in one God and no more, and I hope for happiness beyond this life. I believe in the equality of man; and I believe that religious duties consist in doing justice, loving mercy, and in

endeavoring to make our fellow-creatures happy.
THOMAS PAINE, *The Age of Reason*. Ch. 1.

1
The Athanasian Creed is the most splendid ecclesiastical lyric ever poured forth by the genius of man.
BENJAMIN DISRAELI, *Endymion*. Ch. 54.

2
The maimed form
Of calmly joyous beauty, marble-limbed, . . .
Looks mild reproach from out its opened grave
At creeds of terror.
GEORGE ELIOT, *The Spanish Gypsy*. Bk. i, l. 99.

3
As men's prayers are a disease of the will, so are their creeds a disease of the intellect.
EMERSON, *Essays, First Series: Self-Reliance.*

4
Uncursed by doubt our earliest creed we take;
We love the precepts for the teacher's sake.
O. W. HOLMES, *A Rhymed Lesson*, l. 191.

5
My heart ferments not with the bigot's leaven,
All creeds I view with toleration thorough,
And have a horror of regarding heaven
As anybody's rotten borough.
THOMAS HOOD, *Ode to Rae Wilson*, l. 52.

Ev'n the poor Pagan's homage to the Sun
I would not harshly scorn, lest even there
I spurn'd some elements of Christian pray'r.
THOMAS HOOD, *Ode to Rae Wilson*, l. 212.

6
My brother kneels, so saith Kabir,
To stone and brass in heathen-wise,
But in my brother's voice I hear
My own unanswered agonies.
His God is as his fates assign,
His prayer is all the world's—and mine.
RUDYARD KIPLING, *The Prayer*.

7
As the forehead of Man grows broader, so do his creeds;
And his gods they are shaped in his image, and mirror his needs;
And he clothes them with thunders and beauty, he clothes them with music and fire;
Seeing not, as he bows by their altars, that he worships his own desire. . . .
For all of the creeds are false, and all of the creeds are true;
And low at the shrines where my brothers bow, there will I bow, too.
For no form of a god, and no fashion
Man has made in his desperate passion,
But is worthy some worship of mine;—
Not too hot with a gross belief,
Nor yet too cold with pride,
I will bow me down where my brothers bow,
Humble, but open eyed.
DON MARQUIS, *The God-Maker, Man.*

As skulls grow broader, so do faiths; as old tongues die, old gods die, too,
And only ghosts of gods and wraiths may meet the backward-gazer's view.
DON MARQUIS, *At Last.*

8
Shall I ask the brave soldier, who fights by my side
In the cause of mankind, if our creeds agree?
Shall I give up the friend I have valued and tried,
If he kneel not before the same altar with me?
From the heretic girl of my soul should I fly,
To seek somewhere else a more orthodox kiss?
No! perish the hearts, and the laws that try
Truth, valour, or love, by a standard like this!
THOMAS MOORE, *Come Send Round the Wine.*

Are we to stand examining our generals and armies as a bishop examines a candidate for holy orders; and to suffer no one to bleed for England who does not agree with you about the second of Timothy?
SYDNEY SMITH, *Peter Plymley Letters*. No. 1.

9
Together kneeling, night and day,
Thou, for *my* sake, at Allah's shrine,
And I—at *any* God's for thine.
THOMAS MOORE, *Lalla Rookh: The Fire-Worshippers*. Sec. iv, l. 309.

At the muezzin's call for prayer,
The kneeling faithful thronged the square,
And on Pushkara's lofty height
The dark priest chanted Brahma's might.
Amid a monastery's weeds
An old Franciscan told his beads;
While to the synagogue there came
A Jew to praise Jehovah's name.
The one great God looked down and smiled
And counted each His loving child;
For Turk and Brahmin, monk and Jew
Had reached Him through the gods they knew.
HARRY ROMAINE, *Ad Cœlum*. (*Munsey's Magazine*, Jan., 1895.)

10
Creeds grow so thick along the way,
Their boughs hide God; I cannot pray.
LIZETTE WOODWORTH REESE, *Doubt*.

11
From the dust of creeds out-worn.
SHELLEY, *Prometheus Unbound*. Act i, l. 697.

12
Creeds for the credulous; but not for me,
I choose to keep a mind alert and free.
Not Faith but Truth I set me for a goal:
Toward that shining mark God speed thee, Soul!
FRANK DEMPSTER SHERMAN, *The Goal*.

13
All creeds and opinions are nothing but the mere result of chance and temperament.
J. H. SHORTHOUSE, *John Inglesant*. Vol. i, ch. 6.

1
The Shadow cloak'd from head to foot,
Who keeps the keys of all the creeds.
TENNYSON, *In Memoriam*. Sec. xxiii.

2
Men have dulled their eyes with sin,
And dimmed the light of heaven with doubt,
And built their temple-walls to shut thee in,
And framed their iron creeds to shut thee out.
HENRY VAN DYKE, *God of the Open Air*.

3
Orthodoxy is my doxy; heterodoxy is another man's doxy.
WILLIAM WARBURTON, Bishop of Gloucester, to Lord Sandwich, c. 1770. (PRIESTLEY, *Memoirs*, i, 572.)

Orthodoxy is a corpse that does not know it is dead.
ELBERT HUBBARD, *Epigrams*.

4
Truth has never been, can never be, contained in any one creed.
MRS. HUMPHRY WARD, *Robert Elsmere*. Bk. vi, ch. 38.

5
How pitiful are little folk—
They seem so very small;
They look at stars, and think they are
Denominational.
WILLARD WATTLES, *Creeds*.

6
From the death of the old the new proceeds,
And the life of truth from the rot of creeds.
WHITTIER, *The Preacher*. St. 5.

7
The world has a thousand creeds, and never a one have I;
Nor church of my own, though a million spires are pointing the way on high.
But I float on the bosom of faith, that bears me along like a river;
And the lamp of my soul is alight with love, for life, and the world, and the Giver.
ELLA WHEELER WILCOX, *Heresy*.

So many gods, so many creeds—
So many paths that wind and wind
While just the art of being kind
Is all the sad world needs.
ELLA WHEELER WILCOX, *The World's Need*.

8
Creed and test
Vanish before the unreserved embrace
Of catholic humanity.
WORDSWORTH, *Ecclesiastical Sonnets*. Pt. iii, No. 36.

CRIME

9
Heaven takes care that no man secures happiness by crime. (Oh! ben provvide il cielo, Ch' uom per delitti mai lieto non sia.)
ALFIERI, *Oreste*. Act i, sc. 2.

10
Evil deeds are done for the mere desire of occupation.
AMMIANUS MARCELLINUS, *Historia*. Bk. 30.

The reason of idleness and crime is the deferring of our hopes. Whilst we are waiting we beguile the time with jokes, with sleep, with eating, and with crimes.
EMERSON, *Essays, Second Series: Nominalist and Realist*

11
There's not a crime
But takes its proper change out still in crime
If once rung on the counter of this world.
E. B. BROWNING, *Aurora Leigh*. Bk. iii, l. 870.

12
Why here you have the awfulest of crimes
For nothing! Hell broke loose on a butterfly!
A dragon born of rose-dew and the moon!
ROBERT BROWNING, *Ring and the Book*. Pt. iv, l. 1601.

13
A man who has no excuse for crime, is indeed defenceless!
BULWER-LYTTON, *The Lady of Lyons*. Act iv, sc. 1.

14
Crimes not against forms, but against those eternal laws of justice, which are our rule and our birthright.
EDMUND BURKE, *Impeachment of Warren Hastings*, 15 Feb., 1788.

15
Nor all that heralds rake from coffin'd clay,
Nor florid prose, nor honied lies of rhyme,
Can blazon evil deeds, or consecrate a crime.
BYRON, *Childe Harold*. Canto i, st. 3.

16
No one lives [who is] without a crime. (Nemo sine crimine vivit.)
DIONYSIUS CATO, *Disticha de Moribus*. Bk. i, No. 5.

His own crime besets each man. (Suum quemque scelus agitat.)
CICERO, *Pro Roscio Amerino*. Ch. 24, sec. 67.

17
A man may thrive on crime, but not for long. (Felix criminibus non erit hoc diu.)
CLEOBULUS. (AUSONIUS [?], *Septem Sapientum Sententiæ*, l. 17.)

18
But many a crime, deem'd innocent on earth,
Is registered in Heaven; and these, no doubt,
Have each their record, with a curse annex'd.
COWPER, *The Task*. Bk. vi, l. 439. *See also* ANGEL: RECORDING.

19
I will be brief nor have I heart to dwell
On crimes they almost share who paint too well.
GEORGE CRABBE, *The Sisters*.

20
Successful crimes alone are justified.
DRYDEN, *The Medal*, l. 208.

1
Men never speak of crime as lightly as they think.

EMERSON, *Essays, Second Series: Experience.*

2
Wherever a man commits a crime, God finds a witness. . . . Every secret crime has its reporter.

EMERSON, *Uncollected Lectures: Natural Religion.*

3
It is worse than a crime; it is a blunder—words which I record, because they have been attributed to others. (C'est plus qu'un crime; c'est une faute.)

JOSEPH FOUCHÉ, *Memoirs.* Fouché claimed to have originated this *mot* when referring to the political murder of the Duc d'Enghien by Napoleon in 1804. Sometimes quoted as "C'est pis qu'un crime," or "C'estoit pire qu'un crime." (See *Notes and Queries,* 14 Aug., 1915, p. 123; 28 Aug., p. 166.) Some authorities say that the expression was originated by Boulay de la Meurthe. It has also been attributed to Talleyrand.

"It is worse than a crime, it is a blunder," said Napoleon, speaking the language of the intellect.

EMERSON, *Essays, Second Series: Experience.*

The wine is drawn, it must be drunk.

TALLEYRAND, to Napoleon, referring to the arrest of the Duc d'Enghien. (LANFREY, *Life of Napoleon,* ii, 9.)

4
Crime is not punished as an offense against God, but as prejudicial to society.

FROUDE, *Short Studies on Great Subjects: Reciprocal Duties of State and Subjects.*

5
Every crime destroys more Edens than our own.

HAWTHORNE, *The Marble Faun.* Vol. i, ch. 23.

6
Bold to endure all things, mankind rushes on through every crime. (Audax omnia perpeti Gens humana ruit per vetitum nefas.)

HORACE, *Odes.* Bk. i, ode 3, l. 25.

7
If you wish to *be* anybody nowadays, you must dare some crime that merits banishment or imprisonment. (Aude aliquid brevibus Gyaris et carcere dignum, Si vis esse aliquid.)

JUVENAL, *Satires.* Sat. i, l. 73. Gyara was a small island in the Ægean, on which criminals were confined.

8
With a differing fate, men commit the same crimes: one man gets a cross, another a crown, as a reward of villainy. (Committunt eadem diverso crimina fato: Ille crucem sceleris pretium tulit, hic diadema.)

JUVENAL, *Satires.* Sat. xiii, l. 104.

9
Whoever meditates a crime has all the guiltiness of the deed. (Scelus intra se tacitum qui cogitat ullum, Facti crimen habet.)

JUVENAL, *Satires.* Sat. xiii, l. 209.

The guilty is he who meditates a crime; the punishment is his who lays the plot. (Il reo D'un delitto è chi'l pensa: a chi l' ordisce La pena spetta.)

ALFIERI, *Antigone.* Act ii, sc. 2.

10
What man have you ever seen who was contented with one crime only? (Quisnam hominum est quem tu contentum videris uno Flagitio?)

JUVENAL, *Satires.* Sat. xiii, l. 243.

11
We easily forget crimes that are known only to ourselves. (Nous oublions aisément nos fautes lorsqu'elles ne sont sues que de nous.)

LA ROCHEFOUCAULD, *Maximes.* No. 196.

12
No crime is founded upon reason. (Nullum scelus rationem habet.)

LIVY, *History.* Bk. xxviii, sec. 28.

13
Crime levels those whom it pollutes. (Facinus, quos inquinat, æquat.)

LUCAN, *De Bello Civili.* Bk. v, l. 290.

14
The contagion of crime is like that of the plague.

NAPOLEON BONAPARTE, *Sayings of Napoleon.*

15
Where crime is taught from early years, it becomes a part of nature. (Ars fit ubi a teneris crimen condiscitur annis.)

OVID, *Heroides.* Epis. iv, l. 25.

16
If you share your friend's crime, you make it your own. (Amici vitia nisi feras, facis tua.)

PUBLILIUS SYRUS, *Sententiæ.* No. 10.

17
Through crime is always the safe way for crime. (Per scelera semper sceleribus tutum est iter.)

SENECA, *Agamemnon,* l. 115.

It is unlawful to overcome crime by crime. (Nunquam scelus scelere vincendum est.)

SENECA, *De Moribus.* Sec. 139.

Crime must be concealed by crime. (Scelere velandum est scelus.)

SENECA, *Hippolytus,* l. 721.

18
Every man enjoys his own crimes. (Omnibus crimen suum voluptati est.)

SENECA, *Epistulæ ad Lucilium.* Epis. xcvii, 11.

19
Crime which is prosperous and lucky is called virtue. (Prosperum ac felix scelus virtus vocatur.)

SENECA, *Hercules Furens,* l. 251.

Success makes some crimes honorable. (Honesta quædam scelera successus facit.)

SENECA, *Hippolytus,* l. 598.

No crime has been without a precedent. (Nullum caruit exemplo nefas.)
SENECA, *Hippolytus*, l. 554.

1
Who profits by a crime commits the crime. (Cui podest scelus Is fecit.)
SENECA, *Medea*, l. 500.

He who does not prevent a crime when he can, encourages it. (Qui non vetat peccare, cum possit, jubet.)
SENECA, *Troades*, l. 291.

2
If little faults, proceeding on distemper,
Shall not be wink'd at, how shall we stretch our eye
When capital crimes, chew'd, swallow'd, and digested,
Appear before us?
SHAKESPEARE, *Henry V*. Act ii, sc. 2, l. 54.

3
Beyond the infinite and boundless reach
Of mercy, if thou didst this deed of death,
Art thou damn'd, Hubert.
SHAKESPEARE, *King John*. Act iv, sc. 3, l. 117.

Tremble, thou wretch,
That hast within thee undivulged crimes,
Unwhipp'd of justice.
SHAKESPEARE, *King Lear*. Act iii, sc. 2, l. 51.

If you bethink yourself of any crime
Unreconcil'd as yet to heaven and grace,
Solicit for it straight.
SHAKESPEARE, *Othello*. Act v, sc. 2, l. 26.

For I must talk of murders, rapes, and massacres,
Acts of black night, abominable deeds.
SHAKESPEARE, *Titus Andronicus*. Act v, sc. 1, l. 63.

4
They, sweet soul, that most impute a crime
Are pronest to it, and impute themselves,
Wanting the mental range.
TENNYSON, *Merlin and Vivien*, l. 823.

5
Had I a hundred tongues, a hundred mouths, and a voice of iron, I could not sum up all the forms of crime. (Non mihi si linguæ centum sint oraque centum, Ferrea vox, omnis scelerum comprendere formas.)
VERGIL, *Æneid*. Bk. vi, l. 625.

6
Divided by interests and united by crime.
(Divisés d'interêts, et pour le crime unis.)
VOLTAIRE, *Mérope*. Act i, sc. 1, l. 8.

7
He spared his fellow-men—his blows
Fell only on their crimes.
WHITTIER, *My Namesake*.

CRITICISM

I—Criticism: Definitions

8
Criticism is a disinterested endeavour to learn and propagate the best that is known and thought in the world.
MATTHEW ARNOLD, *Essays in Criticism*. No. 1.

9
As the arts advance towards their perfection, the science of criticism advances with equal pace.
EDMUND BURKE, *On the Sublime and Beautiful*. Pt. i, *Introduction*.

10
The most noble criticism is that in which the critic is not the antagonist so much as the rival of the author.
ISAAC D'ISRAELI, *Curiosities of Literature: Literary Journals*.

Criticism should not be querulous and wasting, all knife and root-puller, but guiding, instructive, inspiring, a south wind, not an east wind.
EMERSON, *Journals*.

11
The good critic is he who relates the adventures of his soul among masterpieces.
ANATOLE FRANCE.

A critic is a man who expects miracles.
JAMES HUNEKER, *Iconoclasts*, p. 139.

A wise scepticism is the first attribute of a good critic.
LOWELL, *Among My Books: Shakespeare Once More*.

12
It is through criticism . . . that the race has managed to come out of the woods and lead a civilized life. The first man who objected to the general nakedness, and advised his fellows to put on clothes, was the first critic.
E. L. GODKIN, *Problems of Modern Democracy*.

13
Criticism is the art wherewith a critic tries to guess himself into a share of the artist's fame.
G. J. NATHAN, *The House of Satan*, p. 98.

There are two kinds of dramatic critics: destructive and constructive. I am a destructive. There are two kinds of guns: Krupp and pop.
G. J. NATHAN, *The World in Falseface*.

14
A critic is a man whose watch is five minutes ahead of other people's watches.
SAINTE-BEUVE. (GIESE, *Sainte-Beuve*.)

The critic is only the secretary of the public, but a secretary who does not wait to take dictation, and who divines, who decides, who expresses every morning what everybody is thinking.
SAINTE-BEUVE. (GIESE, *Sainte-Beuve*.)

15
Criticism . . . is a serious and public function: it shows the race assimilating the individual, dividing the immortal from the mortal part of a soul.
GEORGE SANTAYANA, *Life of Reason*, iv, 151.

16
The aim of criticism is to distinguish what is essential in the work of a writer. It is the delight of a critic to praise; but praise is scarcely a part of his duty. . . . What we

ask of him is that he should find out for us more than we can find out for ourselves.

ARTHUR SYMONS, *Introduction to Coleridge's Biographia Literaria.*

1
Censure's to be understood,
Th' authentic mark of the elect;
The public stamp Heav'n sets on all that's great and good,
Our shallow search and judgment to direct.

SWIFT, *Ode to the Athenian Society.*

II—Criticism: Apothegms

2
He who discommendeth others obliquely commendeth himself.

SIR THOMAS BROWNE, *Christian Morals.* Pt. i, sec. 34.

3
Let dull critics feed upon the carcasses of plays; give me the taste and the dressing.

LORD CHESTERFIELD, *Letters,* 6 Feb., 1752.

4
I read Glenarvon too by Caro Lamb—
God damn!

BYRON, his comment on the novel in which Lady Caroline Lamb exposed the details of her passion for the poet.

Which not even critics criticise.

COWPER, *The Task.* Bk. iv, l. 51.

5
Criticism is easy, and art is difficult. (La critique est aisée, et l'art est difficile.)

DESTOUCHES, *Le Glorieux.* Act ii, sc. 5.

6
It is much easier to be critical than to be correct.

BENJAMIN DISRAELI, *Speech,* House of Commons, 24 Jan., 1860.

7
He wreathed the rod of criticism with roses.

ISAAC D'ISRAELI, *Miscellanies of Literature.* Referring to Pierre Bayle.

Yea, though he sang not, he was unto song
A light, a benediction.

JOHN DRINKWATER, *The Dead Critic.*

8
Let none presume to measure the irregularities of Michael Angelo or Socrates by village scales.

EMERSON, *Representative Men: Plato: New Readings.*

9
Blame-all and praise-all are two blockheads.

BENJAMIN FRANKLIN, *Poor Richard,* 1734.

10
The Stones that Critics hurl with Harsh Intent
A Man may use to build his Monument.

ARTHUR GUITERMAN, *A Poet's Proverbs,* p. 41.

11
I'll play a whetstone's part, which makes iron sharp, though unable itself to cut. (Fungar vice cotis, acutum Reddere quæ ferrum valet, exsors ipsa secandi.)

HORACE, *Ars Poetica,* l. 304.

12
I find the pain of a little censure, even when it is unfounded, is more acute than the pleasure of much praise.

THOMAS JEFFERSON, *Writings.* Vol. vii, p. 299.

The sting of a reproach is the Truth of it.

BENJAMIN FRANKLIN, *Poor Richard,* 1746.

13
Unmov'd, tho' witlings sneer and rivals rail;
Studious to please, yet not asham'd to fail.

SAMUEL JOHNSON, *Irene: Prologue.*

14
Blown about with every wind of criticism.

SAMUEL JOHNSON. (BOSWELL, *Life,* 1784.)

15
How many people have a good ear for literature but sing out of tune! (Que de gens, en littérature, ont l'oreille juste et chantent faux!)

JOUBERT, *Pensées.* No. 367.

16
Our censor absolves the crow and passes judgment on the pigeon. (Dat veniam corvis, vexat censura columbas.)

JUVENAL, *Satires.* Sat. ii, l. 63.

17
Criticism of our contemporaries is not criticism; it is conversation.

LEMAÎTRE. (BRANDER MATTHEWS, N. Y. *Times,* 2 April, 1922.)

18
He does ill who is hypercritical of another man's book. (Improbe facit qui in alieno libro ingeniosus est.)

MARTIAL, *Epigrams:* Bk. i, *Preface.*

19
I much prefer a compliment, insincere or not, to sincere criticism. (Equidem pol vel falso tamen laudari multo malo.)

PLAUTUS, *Mostellaria,* l. 179.

20
Cavil you may, but never criticise.

POPE, *Essay on Criticism.* Pt. i, l. 123.

21
The cant of criticism.

SIR JOSHUA REYNOLDS, *The Idler,* 29 Sept., 1759.

Of all the cants that are canted in this canting world, though the cant of hypocrisy may be the worst, the cant of criticism is the most tormenting.

STERNE, *Tristram Shandy.* Bk. iii, ch. 12.

22
For I am nothing, if not critical.

SHAKESPEARE, *Othello.* Act ii, sc. 1, l. 120.

The carping censures of the world.

SHAKESPEARE, *Richard III.* Act iii, sc. 5, l. 68.

23
When things are as pretty as that, criticism is out of season.

R. L. STEVENSON, *Some Portraits by Raeburn.*

24
Men sift all secrets, in their critic sieve.

SWINBURNE, *In Sepulcretis.* St. 1.

1
Really to stop criticism they say one must die.

VOLTAIRE, *Les Trois Empereurs en Sorbonne.*

2
When critics disagree the artist is in accord with himself.

OSCAR WILDE, *The Picture of Dorian Gray: Preface.*

III—Criticism: Its Rules

3
When I read rules of criticism, I immediately inquire after the works of the author who has written them, and by that means discover what it is he likes in a composition.

ADDISON, *The Guardian.* No. 115.

4
The critic in *The Vicar of Wakefield* lays down that you should *always* say that the picture would have been better if the painter had taken more pains; but in the case of the practised literary man, you should often enough say that the writings would have been much better if the writer had taken less pains.

WALTER BAGEHOT, *Literary Studies: Shakespeare.*

You should not say it is not good. You should say you do not like it; and then, you know, you're perfectly safe.

J. MCNEILL WHISTLER. (DON SEITZ, *Whistler Stories.*)

5
He was in Logic, a great critic,
Profoundly skill'd in Analytic;
He could distinguish, and divide
A hair 'twixt south and south-west side.

BUTLER, *Hudibras.* Pt. i, canto i, l. 65.

6
Fear not to lie—'twill seem a sharper hit;
Shrink not from blasphemy—'twill pass for wit;
Care not for feeling—pass your proper jest,
And stand a critic, hated yet caress'd.

BYRON, *English Bards and Scotch Reviewers,* l. 71.

7
To disparage scenery as quite flat is of course like disparaging a swan as quite white, or an Italian sky as quite blue.

G. K. CHESTERTON, *Robert Browning.* Ch. 6.

8
Some to the fascination of a name
Surrender judgment hoodwink'd. Some the style
Infatuates, and through labyrinths and wilds
Of error leads them by a tune entranc'd.

COWPER, *The Task.* Bk. vi, l. 101.

9
Blame is safer than praise.

EMERSON, *Essays, First Series: Compensation.*

Blame where you must, be candid where you can,
And be each critic the Good-natured Man.

GOLDSMITH, *The Good-Natured Man: Epilogue.*

10
I lose my patience, and I own it too,
When works are censur'd, not as bad, but new:
While, if our elders break all reason's laws,
These fools demand not pardon, but applause.
(Indignor quicquam reprehendi, non quia crasse
Compositum illepideve putetur, sed quia nuper,
Nec veniam antiquis, sed honorem et præmia posci.)

HORACE, *Epistles.* Bk. ii, epis. 1, l. 76. (Pope, tr., l. 115.)

While an author is yet living, we estimate his powers by his worst performance; and when he is dead, we rate them by his best.

SAMUEL JOHNSON, *Works.* Vol. ix, p. 240.

He could gauge the old books by the old set of rules,
And his very old nothings pleased very old fools;
But give him a new book, fresh out of the heart,
And you put him at sea without compass or chart.

J. R. LOWELL, *A Fable for Critics,* l. 205.

11
He that fears his blotches may offend,
Speaks gently of the pimples of his friend;
For reciprocity exacts her dues,
And they that need excuse must needs excuse.
(Qui ne tuberibus propriis offendat amicum
Postulat, ignoscet verrucis illius: æquum est
Peccatis veniam poscentem reddere rursus.)

HORACE, *Satires.* Bk. i, sat. 3, l. 73. (Conington, tr.)

12
When I take up the end of a web and find it pack-thread, I do not expect, by looking further, to find embroidery.

SAMUEL JOHNSON. (BOSWELL, *Life,* ii, 88.)

13
'Tis not the wholesome sharp morality,
Or modest anger of a satiric spirit,
That hurts or wounds the body of the state;
But the sinister application
Of the malicious, ignorant, and base
Interpreter; who will distort and strain
The general scope and purpose of an author
To his particular and private spleen.

BEN JONSON, *The Poetaster.* Act v. sc. 1.

14
I hold it
In some degree blasphemous to dispraise
What's worthy admiration: yet, for once,
I will dispraise a little.

MASSINGER, *Great Duke of Florence.* Act iii, sc. 1.

Since we cannot equal it, let us avenge ourselves by abusing it. (Puisque nous ne le pouvons aveindre, vengeons nous à en mesdire.)

MONTAIGNE, *Essays.* Bk. iii, ch. 7.

15
Reviewers are forever telling authors they

can't understand them. The author might often reply: Is that my fault?

J. C. AND A. W. HARE, *Guesses at Truth.*

The lot of critics is to be remembered by what they failed to understand.

GEORGE MOORE, *Impressions and Opinions: Balzac.*

They damn what they do not understand. (Damnant quod non intelligunt.)

QUINTILIAN, *De Institutione Oratoria.* Bk. x, ch. 1, sec. 26.

1

A perfect judge will read each work of wit
With the same spirit that its author writ;
Survey the whole, nor seek slight faults to find
When nature moves, and rapture warms the mind.

POPE, *Essay on Criticism.* Pt. ii, l. 33.

In every work regard the writer's end,
Since none can compass more than they intend.

POPE, *Essay on Criticism.* Pt. ii, l. 55.

Some ne'er advance a judgment of their own,
But catch the spreading notion of the town; . . .
Some judge of authors' names, not works, and then
Nor praise nor blame the writings, but the men.

POPE, *Essay on Criticism.* Pt. ii, l. 208.

Willing to wound, and yet afraid to strike,
Just hint a fault, and hesitate dislike.

POPE, *Epistle to Dr. Arbuthnot,* l. 203.

For, poems read without a name,
We justly praise, or justly blame;
And critics have no partial views,
Except they know whom they abuse.
And since you ne'er provoke their spite,
Depend upon't their judgement's right.

SWIFT, *On Poetry,* l. 129.

You don't expect me to know what to say about a play when I don't know who the author is, do you? . . . If it's by a good author, it's a good play, naturally. That stands to reason.

BERNARD SHAW, *Fanny's First Play: Epilogue.*

2

We'll cry both arts and learning down,
And hey! then up go we!

FRANCIS QUARLES, *Song of Anarchus.*

He gives directions to the town
To cry it up or run it down.

SWIFT, *On Poetry.*

3

A critic must accept what is best in a poet, and thus become his best encourager.

STEDMAN, *Poets of America.* Ch. 6.

4

Mediocrity flattered at acknowledging mediocrity, and mistaking mystification for mastery, enters the fog of dilettantism, and, graduating connoisseur, ends its days in a bewilderment of bric-à-brac and Brummagem!

J. MCNEILL WHISTLER, *The Gentle Art of Making Enemies,* p. 31.

IV—Critics: Their Limitations

5

Critics!—appalled, I venture on the name,
Those cut-throat bandits in the paths of fame.

ROBERT BURNS, *Third Epistle to Robert Graham.*

6

A man must serve his time to ev'ry trade
Save censure—critics all are ready made.

BYRON, *English Bards and Scotch Reviewers,* l. 63.

7

A servile race,
Who, in mere want of fault all merit place;
Who blind obedience pay to ancient schools,
Bigots to Greece, and slaves to musty rules.

CHARLES CHURCHILL, *The Rosciad,* l. 183.

8

Reviewers are usually people who would have been poets, historians, biographers, if they could: they have tried their talents at one or the other, and have failed; therefore they turn critics.

S. T. COLERIDGE, *Lectures: Shakespeare and Milton,* p. 36.

9

There are some Critics so with Spleen diseased,
They scarcely come inclining to be pleased:
And sure he must have more than mortal Skill,
Who pleases any one against his Will.

CONGREVE, *The Way of the World: Epilogue.*

10

You know who critics are?—the men who have failed in literature and art.

BENJAMIN DISRAELI, *Lothair.* Ch. 35.

11

They who write ill, and they who ne'er durst write,
Turn critics out of mere revenge and spite.

DRYDEN, *Conquest of Granada: Prologue.*

All who (like him) have writ ill plays before,
For they, like thieves, condemned, are hangmen made,
To execute the members of their trade.

DRYDEN, *The Rival Ladies: Prologue.*

When Poets' plots in plays are damn'd for spite,
They critics turn and damn the rest that write.

JOHN HAYNES, *Prologue: Oxford and Cambridge Miscellany Poems.*

12

Just then, with a wink and a sly normal lurch,
The owl very gravely got down from his perch,
Walked round, and regarded his fault-finding critic
(Who thought he was stuffed) with a glance analytic;
And then fairly hooted, as if he would say,
"Your learning's at fault *this* time, anyway,
I'm an owl; you're another. Sir Critic, good day!"
And the barber kept on shaving.

JAMES T. FIELDS, *The Owl-Critic.*

13

We do not say that a man to be a critic must

necessarily be a poet; but to be a good critic, he ought not to be a bad poet.

WILLIAM HAZLITT, *Characters of Shakespeare's Plays*, p. 17.

In truth it may be laid down as an almost universal rule that good poets are bad critics.

MACAULAY, *Criticisms on the Principal Italian Writers: Dante.*

1
What a blessed thing it is that Nature, when she invented, manufactured, and patented her authors, contrived to make critics out of the chips that were left!

O. W. HOLMES, *The Professor at the Breakfast-Table.* Ch. 1.

2
There is a certain race of men that either imagine it their duty, or make it their amusement, to hinder the reception of every work of learning or genius, who stand as sentinels in the avenues of fame, and value themselves upon giving Ignorance and Envy the first notice of a prey.

SAMUEL JOHNSON, *The Rambler.* No. 3.

Critics are sentinels in the grand army of letters, stationed at the corners of newspapers and reviews, to challenge every new author.

LONGFELLOW, *Kavanagh.* Ch. 13.

It is the business of reviewers to watch poets, not of poets to watch reviewers.

WILLIAM HAZLITT, *Lectures on the English Poets*, p. 296.

3
Nature fits all her children with something to do,
He who would write and can't write, can surely review,
Can set up a small booth as critic, and sell us his
Petty conceit and his pettier jealousies.

J. R. LOWELL, *A Fable for Critics*, l. 1784.

4
Every critic in the town
Runs the minor poet down;
Every critic—don't you know it?—
Is himself a minor poet.

ROBERT F. MURRAY, *Critic and Poet.*

Like curs, our critics haunt the poet's feast,
And feed on scraps refused by every guest;
From the old Thracian dog they learned the way
To snarl in want, and grumble o'er their prey.

WILLIAM PITT, *To Mr. Spence.* Zoïlus, a carping critic of ancient Greece, was called the Thracian dog.

5
A critic is a legless man who teaches running.

CHANNING POLLOCK, *The Green Book.*

6
'Tis hard to say if greater want of skill
Appear in writing or in judging ill;
But of the two less dangerous is th' offence
To tire our patience than mislead our sense:
Some few in that, but numbers err in this;
Ten censure wrong for one who writes amiss;
A fool might once himself alone expose;
Now one in verse makes many more in prose . . .
In poets as true genius is but rare,
True taste as seldom is the critic's share; . . .
Let such teach others who themselves excel,
And censure freely who have written well;
Authors are partial to their wit, 'tis true,
But are not critics to their judgment too?

POPE, *Essay on Criticism.* Pt. i, l. 1.

Nor in the Critic let the man be lost.

POPE, *Essay on Criticism.* Pt. ii, l. 323.

7
As a bankrupt thief turns thief-taker, so an unsuccessful author turns critic.

SHELLEY, *Adonais: Preface.* Cancelled passage.

8
A poet that fails in writing becomes often a morose critic; the weak and insipid white wine makes at length excellent vinegar.

WILLIAM SHENSTONE, *Essays: On Writing and Books.*

Turns vinegar, and comes again in play.

CHARLES SACKVILLE, *To Mr. Edward Howard.* See 2171:14.

Ill writers are usually the sharpest censors; for they (as the best Poet and the best Patron said), When in the full perfection of decay, turn vinegar, and come again in play. Thus the corruption of a poet is the generation of a critic.

DRYDEN, *Examen Poeticum: Dedication.*

9
I heard a whisper from a ghost who shall be nameless, "that these commentators always kept in the most distant quarters from their principals in the lower world, through a consciousness of shame and guilt, because they had so horribly misrepresented the meaning of those authors to posterity."

SWIFT, *Gulliver's Travels: Voyage to Laputa.*

10
The trade of critic, in literature, music, and the drama, is the most degraded of all trades.

MARK TWAIN, *Autobiography.* Vol. ii, p. 69.

11
Critics are like brushers of noblemen's clothes.

SIR HENRY WOTTON. (BACON, *Apothegms.* No. 64.)

V—Critics: Their Power

12
His "bravo" was decisive, for that sound
Hush'd "Academie" sigh'd in silent awe;
The fiddlers trembled as he look'd around,
For fear of some false note's detected flaw.
The "prima donna's" tuneful heart would bound,
Dreading the deep damnation of his "bah!"
Soprano, basso, even the contra-alto,
Wish'd him five fathom under the Rialto.

BYRON, *Beppo.* St. 32.

13
Who shall dispute what the Reviewers say?
Their word's sufficient; and to ask a reason,

In such a state as theirs, is downright treason.
CHARLES CHURCHILL, *The Apology*, l. 94.

Dull, superstitious readers they deceive,
Who pin their easy faith on critic's sleeve,
And, knowing nothing, every thing believe.
CHARLES CHURCHILL, *The Apology*, l. 99.

Though by whim, envy, or resentment led,
They damn those authors whom they never read.
CHARLES CHURCHILL, *The Candidate*, l. 57.

1
The British critics—be it to their glory,
When they abuse us, do it *con amore*.
A. J. H. DUGANNE, *Parnassus in Pillory*.

2
The opinion of a great body of the reading public is very materially influenced even by the unsupported assertions of those who assume a right to criticise.
MACAULAY, *Essays: Montgomery's Poems*.

3
He cannot 'scape their censures who delight
To misapply whatever he shall write.
MASSINGER, *The Emperor of the East: Prologue*.

4
To check young Genius' proud career,
The slaves who now his throne invaded,
Made Criticism his prime Vizier,
And from that hour his glories faded.
THOMAS MOORE, *Genius and Criticism*. St. 4.

5
And you, my Critics! in the checquer'd shade,
Admire new light thro' holes yourselves have made.
POPE, *The Dunciad*. Bk. iv, l. 125.

The generous Critic fann'd the Poet's fire,
And taught the world with reason to admire.
POPE, *Essay on Criticism*. Pt. i, l. 100.

6
It may be well said that these wretched men know not what they do. They scatter their insults and their slanders without heed as to whether the poisoned shaft lights on a heart made callous by many blows, or one, like Keats's, composed of more penetrable stuff.
SHELLEY, *Adonais: Preface*.

7
Why should the unborn critic whet
For me his scalping-knife?
WHITTIER, *My Namesake*.

8
From such sad readers Heaven the muse protect,
Proud to find faults and raptured with defect!
JOHN WOLCOT, *Benevolent Epistle to Sylvanus Urban*.

VI—Critics: Their Futility

9
If in your censure you prove sweet to me,
I little care, believe 't, how sour you be.
RICHARD BRATHWAITE, *A Boulster Lecture: Dedication*.

10
There spoke up a brisk little somebody,
Critic and whippersnapper, in a rage
To set things right.
ROBERT BROWNING, *Balaustion's Adventure*. Pt. i, l. 308.

The exhausted air-bell of the Critic.
ROBERT BROWNING, *Christmas-Eve*, Pt. xvi, l. 3.

11
As soon
Seek roses in December, ice in June;
Hope constancy in wind, or corn in chaff;
Believe a woman or an epitaph,
Or any other thing that's false, before
You trust in critics.
BYRON, *English Bards and Scotch Reviewers*, l. 75.

12
And still in the honest working world,
With posture and hint and smirk,
These sons of the devil are standing by
While Man does all the work.

They balk endeavor and baffle reform,
In the sacred name of law;
And over the quavering voice of Hem,
Is the droning voice of Haw.
BLISS CARMAN, *Hem and Haw*.

13
POSTSCRIPTUM.—And you, whom we all so adore,
Dear Critics, whose verdicts are always so new!—
One word in your ear. There were Critics before. . . .
And the man who plants cabbages imitates, too!
AUSTIN DOBSON, *Ballade of Imitation*.

14
The absence of humility in critics is something wonderful.
ARTHUR HELPS, *Friends in Council*. Bk. ii, ch. 2.

15
No critic has ever settled anything.
JAMES HUNEKER, *Pathos of Distance*, p. 281.

16
It is rarely that an author is hurt by his critics.
SAMUEL JOHNSON. (BOSWELL, *Life*, iii, 423.)

If an author have any least fibre of worth in him,
Abuse would but tickle the organ of mirth in him;
All the critics on earth cannot crush with their ban
One word that's in tune with the nature of man.
J. R. LOWELL, *A Fable for Critics*, l. 452.

17
You do not publish your own verses, Lælius; you criticise mine. Pray cease to criticise mine, or else publish your own.
MARTIAL, *Epigrams*. Bk. i, ep. 91.

18
It is impossible to think of a man of any actual force and originality . . . who spent his whole life appraising and describing the work of other men.
H. L. MENCKEN, *Prejudices*. Ser. iii, p. 87.

1
Some are bewilder'd in the maze of schools,
And some made coxcombs nature meant but fools:
In search of wit these lose their common sense,
And then turn critics in their own defence:
Each burns alike, who can or cannot write,
Or with a rival's or an eunuch's spite.

Pope, *Essay on Criticism*. Pt. i, l. 26.

Some have at first for wits, then poets pass'd
Turn'd critics next, and prov'd plain fools at last.

Pope, *Essay on Criticism*. Pt. i, l. 36.

2
Court not the critic's smile, nor dread his frown.

Scott, *Harold the Dauntless: Introduction.*

3
When you hark to the voice of the Knocker,
As you list to his hammer fall,
Remember the fact that the knocking act
Requires no brains at all.

Unknown, *The Quarrelsome Trio.*

CROMWELL, OLIVER

4
Cromwell was a man in whom ambition had not wholly suppressed, but only suspended, the sentiments of religion.

Edmund Burke, *Letter,* 1791.

5
How shall I then begin, or where conclude,
To draw a fame so truly circular?

Dryden, *Heroick Stanzas, Consecrated to the Memory of His Highness, Oliver, Late Protector of This Commonwealth.* St. 5.

His grandeur he deriv'd from Heav'n alone,
For he was great, ere Fortune made him so;
And wars, like mists that rise against the sun,
Made him but greater seem, not greater grow.

Dryden, *Heroick Stanzas.* St. 6.

Peace was the prize of all his toil and care.

Dryden, *Heroick Stanzas.* St. 16.

His ashes in a peaceful urn shall rest;
His name a great example stands, to show
How strangely high endeavours may be blest,
Where piety and valour jointly go.

Dryden, *Heroick Stanzas.* St. 37.

6
Unknown to Cromwell as to me
Was Cromwell's measure or degree;
Unknown to him as to his horse,
If he than his groom be better or worse.
He works, plots, fights, in rude affairs,
With squires, lords, kings, his craft compares,
Till late he learned, through doubt and fear,
Broad England harbored not his peer.

Emerson, *Fate.*

7
Some Cromwell guiltless of his country's blood.

Thomas Gray, *Elegy Written in a Country Church-yard.*

8
So restless Cromwell could not cease
In the inglorious arts of peace,
But through adventurous war
Urged his active star.

Andrew Marvell, *An Horatian Ode Upon Cromwell's Return from Ireland,* l. 9.

He nothing common did, or mean,
Upon that memorable scene,
But with his keener eye
The axe's edge did try.

Andrew Marvell, *An Horatian Ode,* l. 57.

9
Or, ravish'd with the whistling of a name,
See Cromwell damn'd to everlasting fame!

Pope, *Essay on Man.* Epis. iv, l. 283.

CROSS, See Christianity: The Cross; Compensation

CROW

10
With rakish eye and plenished crop,
Oblivious of the farmer's gun,
Upon the naked ash-tree top
The Crow sits basking in the sun.

William Canton, *The Crow.*

11
The black crow thinketh her own birds white.

Gavin Douglas, *Æneis:* Bk. ix, *Prologue,* l. 78. (1513)

I . . . like the foolish crow,
Believe my black brood swans.

Massinger, *The Unnatural Combat.* Act iii, sc. 2.

The crow thinketh her own birds fairest in the wood.

John Heywood, *Proverbs.* Pt. ii, ch. 4.

12
Crows are never the whiter for washing themselves.

Thomas Fuller, *Gnomologia.* No. 1210.

A craw's nae whiter for being washed.

John Ray, *Scottish Proverbs.*

13
To shoot at crows is powder flung away.

John Gay, *Epistles.* No. iv, last line.

14
Report makes the crows blacker than they are.

George Herbert, *Jacula Prudentum.*

Even the blackest of them all, the crow,
Renders good service as your man-at-arms,
Crushing the beetle in his coat of mail,
And crying havoc on the slug and snail.

Longfellow, *Birds of Killingworth.* St. 19.

15
The little crow, stripped of his stolen colors, excites our ridicule. (Moveat cornicula risum Furtivis nudata coloribus.)

Horace, *Epistles.* Bk. i, epis. 3, l. 19.

16
If the crow could feed in quiet, he would have more meat. (Tacitus pasci si possit corvus, haberet Plus dapis.)

Horace, *Epistles.* Bk. i, epis. 17, l. 50.

17
An evil crow an evil egg.

Hugh Latimer, *Sermons,* 42. (1536)

As the Greek proverb saith, Like crow, like egg.
THOMAS MOFFETT, *Health's Improvement*, 135. (1655)

1
As he that would say the crow is white.
SIR THOMAS MORE, *Works*, p. 207. (1528) *See also under* CANDOR.

2
We'll pluck a crow together.
SHAKESPEARE, *The Comedy of Errors*. Act iii, sc. 1, l. 83.

If not, resolve, before we go,
That you and I must pull a crow.
BUTLER, *Hudibras*. Pt. ii, canto ii, l. 499.

Na, na, abide; we have a crow to pull.
UNKNOWN, *Towneley Plays*, 18. (c. 1410); HEYWOOD, *Proverbs*, ii, 5. (1546); JOHN LYLY, *Mother Bombie*, ii, 1. (1592)

I've a crow to pluck w' ye.
JOHN WILSON, *Projectors*. Act v. (1665); DICKENS, *Barnaby Rudge*. Ch. 13.

3
The crow doth sing as sweetly as the lark,
When neither is attended.
SHAKESPEARE, *The Merchant of Venice*. Act v, sc. 1, l. 102.

4
The crow may bathe his coal-black wings in mire,
And unperceiv'd fly with the filth away;
But if the like the snow-white swan desire,
The stain upon his silver down will stay.
SHAKESPEARE, *The Rape of Lucrece*, l. 1009.

5
The many winter'd crow that leads the clanging rookery home.
TENNYSON, *Locksley Hall*, l. 68.

6
One crow does not make a winter. (Eine Krähe macht keinen Winter.)
UNKNOWN. A German proverb. *See also under* SWALLOW.

CROWD, THE, see People, The

CROWN

See also King

7
There is a crown for us all somewhere.
J. M. BARRIE, *Tommy and Grizel*, p. 27.

8
Many a crown Covers bald foreheads.
E. B. BROWNING, *Aurora Leigh*. Bk. i, l. 754.

9
Every noble crown is, and on Earth will forever be, a crown of thorns.
THOMAS CARLYLE, *Past and Present*. Bk. iii, Ch. 8.

A crown
Golden in show, is but a wreath of thorns,
Brings dangers, troubles, cares, and sleepless nights.
MILTON, *Paradise Regained*. Bk. ii, l. 458.

A crown, if it hurt us, is hardly worth wearing.
P. J. BAILEY, *Festus: A Large Party*.

10
They do it to obtain a corruptible crown; but we an incorruptible.
New Testament: I Corinthians, ix, 25.

11
The royal crown cures not the headache.
GEORGE HERBERT, *Jacula Prudentum*.

12
A crown! what is it?
It is to bear the miseries of a people!
To hear their murmurs, feel their discontents,
And sink beneath a load of splendid care!
HANNAH MORE, *Daniel*. Pt. vi.

So hard is height, so cruel is a crown.
STEPHEN PHILLIPS, *Ulysses*. Act iii, sc. 2.

13
Uneasy lies the head that wears a crown.
SHAKESPEARE, *II Henry IV*. Act iii, sc. 1, l. 31.

Why doth the crown lie there upon his pillow,
Being so troublesome a bedfellow?
O polish'd perturbation! golden care!
That keep'st the ports of slumber open wide,
To many a watchful night! sleep with it now!
Yet not so sound and half so deeply sweet
As he whose brow with homely biggen bound
Snores out the watch of night. O Majesty!
When thou dost pinch thy bearer, thou dost sit
Like a rich armour worn in heat of day,
That scalds with safety.
SHAKESPEARE, *II Henry IV*. Act iv, sc. 5, l. 21.

14
How sweet a thing it is to wear a crown,
Within whose circuit is Elysium,
And all that poets feign of bliss and joy.
SHAKESPEARE, *III Henry VI*. Act i, sc. 2, l. 29.

15
Upon my head they placed a fruitless crown,
And put a barren sceptre in my gripe,
Thence to be wrench'd with an unlineal hand,
No son of mine succeeding.
SHAKESPEARE, *Macbeth*. Act iii, sc. 1, l. 61.

For within the hollow crown
That rounds the mortal temples of a king
Keeps Death his court and there the antic sits,
Scoffing his state and grinning at his pomp, . . .
Comes at the last and with a little pin
Bores through his castle wall, and farewell king!
SHAKESPEARE, *Richard II*. Act iii, sc. 2, l. 160.

16
A crown and justice? Night and day
Shall first be yoked together.
SWINBURNE, *Marino Faliero*. Act iii, sc. 1.

17
Hail to the crown by Freedom shaped—to gird
An English Sovereign's brow.
WORDSWORTH, *The Excursion*. Bk. vi, l. 1.

18
Woe to the Crown that doth the Cowl obey!
WORDSWORTH, *Ecclesiastical Sonnets*. Pt. i, No. 29.

CRUELTY

19
You must be most miserable To be so cruel.
E. B. BROWNING, *Aurora Leigh*. Bk. iii, l. 781.

1
A man of cruelty is God's enemy.
THOMAS FULLER, *Gnomologia*. No. 303.

2
Weak men are apt to be cruel because they stick at nothing that may repair the ill effect of their mistakes.
LORD HALIFAX, *Works*, p. 235.

3
Cruelty ever proceeds from a vile mind, and often from a cowardly heart.
SIR JOHN HARINGTON, *Orlando Furioso:* Bk. xxxvi, *Notes*.

A cruel heart ill suits a manly mind.
HOMER, *Iliad*. Bk. ix, l. 619. (Pope, tr.)

4
Of all cruelties those are the most intolerable that come under the name of condolence and consolation.
W. S. LANDOR, *Letter to Robert Southey*, after the death of his son, 1816.

5
How I should like to see the grimace he is making at this moment upon that scaffold! (Je voudrais bien voir le grimace qu'il fait à cette heure sur cet échafaud.)
LOUIS XIII, referring to the Marquis de Cinq-Mars. (*Histoire de Louis XIII*, iv, 416.)

6
Cowardice, the mother of cruelty. (Couardise, mère de la cruauté.)
MONTAIGNE, *Essays*. Bk. ii, ch. 27. Heading.

Fear is the parent of cruelty.
J. A. FROUDE, *Short Studies on Great Subjects: Party Politics*.

Cruelty is a tyrant that's always attended with fear.
THOMAS FULLER, *Gnomologia*. No. 1213.

7
Cruelty was the vice of the ancient, vanity is that of the modern, world.
GEORGE MOORE, *Mummer-Worship*.

8
Each snivelling hero seas of blood can spill,
When wrongs provoke and honour bids him kill;—
Give me your through-paced rogue, who scorns to be
Prompted by poor revenge, or injury,
But does it of true inbred cruelty.
JOHN OLDHAM, *On the Jesuits*.

9
Clemency is the remedy of cruelty. (Atrocitatis mansuetudo est remedium.)
PHÆDRUS, *Fables*.

10
Let me be cruel, not unnatural.
SHAKESPEARE, *Hamlet*. Act iii, sc. 2, l. 413.

I must be cruel, only to be kind.
SHAKESPEARE, *Hamlet*. Act iii, sc. 4, l. 178.

It is cruelty to be humane to rebels, and humanity to be cruel. (Contre les rebelles c'est cruauté que d'être humain, et humanité d'être cruel.)
BISHOP CORNEILLE MUIS, *Sermon*. (FOURNIER, *L'Esprit dans l'Histoire*.) This sentence was quoted by Catherine de Medicis, to quiet the scruples of her son, Charles IX, against the massacre of St. Bartholomew.

11
'T is a cruelty To load a falling man.
SHAKESPEARE, *Henry VIII*. Act v, sc. 3, l. 76.

Oh, 'tis cruelty to beat a cripple with his own crutches.
THOMAS FULLER, *Holy and Profane States: Of Jesting*.

12
Come, you spirits . . .
And fill me from the crown to the toe, top-full
Of direst cruelty! make thick my blood;
Stop up the access and passage to remorse,
That no compunctious visitings of nature
Shake my fell purpose, nor keep peace between
The effect and it! Come to my woman's breasts,
And take my milk for gall, you murdering ministers!
SHAKESPEARE, *Macbeth*. Act i, sc. 5, l. 41.

13
I would find grievous ways to have thee slain,
Intense device, and superflux of pain.
SWINBURNE, *Anactoria*, l. 27.

14
As ruthless as a baby with a worm,
As cruel as a school-boy.
TENNYSON, *Walking to the Mail*, l. 98.

15
Your cruelty is our glory. (Crudelitas vestra gloria est nostra.)
TERTULLIAN, *Ad Scapulam*. Sec. 4.

CRYING, see Tears

CUCKOO

16
The tell-tale cuckoo: spring's his confidant,
And he lets out her April purposes.
ROBERT BROWNING, *Pippa Passes*. Pt. i, l. 355.

17
The Attic warbler pours her throat
Responsive to the cuckoo's note.
THOMAS GRAY, *Ode on the Spring*, l. 5.

18
It came, and with a strange, sweet cry,
A friend, but from a far-off land;
We stood and listened, hand in hand,
And heart to heart, my Love and I.
F. LOCKER-LAMPSON, *The Cuckoo*.

19
Sweet bird! thy bower is ever green,
Thy sky is ever clear;
Thou hast no sorrow in thy song,
No Winter in thy year!

O could I fly, I'd fly with thee!
We'd make, with joyful wing,
Our annual visit o'er the globe,
Companions of the Spring.
JOHN LOGAN, *To the Cuckoo*. Attributed also to Michael Bruce. (See *Notes and Queries*, April, 1902, p. 309; June 14, 1902, p. 469.)

1
The bird of passage known to us as the cuckoo.

PLINY THE ELDER, *Historia Naturalis*. Bk. xviii, sec. 249.

2
The cuckoo builds not for himself.

SHAKESPEARE, *Antony and Cleopatra*. Act ii, sc. 6, l. 28.

3
And being fed by us you used us so
As that ungentle gull, the cuckoo's bird,
Useth the sparrow.

SHAKESPEARE, *I Henry IV*. Act v, sc. 1, l. 59.

The hedge-sparrow fed the cuckoo so long,
That it had it head bit off by it young.

SHAKESPEARE, *King Lear*. Act i, sc. 4, l. 235.

4
The cuckoo then, on every tree,
Mocks married men; for thus sings he,
Cuckoo!
Cuckoo! Cuckoo! O word of fear,
Unpleasing to a married ear.

SHAKESPEARE, *Love's Labour's Lost*. Act v, sc. 2, l. 908.

5
The merry cuckow, messenger of Spring,
His trumpet shrill hath thrice already sounded.

SPENSER, *Amoretti*. Sonnet xix.

While I deduce,
From the first note the hollow cuckoo sings,
The symphony of spring.

THOMSON, *The Seasons: Spring*, l. 576.

6
And sweet to hear the cuckoo mock the spring
While the last violet loiters by the well.

OSCAR WILDE, *The Burden of Itys*. St. 10.

7
O blithe new-comer! I have heard,
I hear thee and rejoice.
O Cuckoo! Shall I call thee bird,
Or but a wandering voice?

WORDSWORTH, *To the Cuckoo*.

8
Sumer is icumen in,
Lhude sing cuccu!
Groweth sed, and bloweth med,
And springth the wude nu.

UNKNOWN, *Cuckoo Song*. (c. 1250) It is perhaps from this song, the earliest in English literature, that the proverb originated, "To fence in the cuckoo," referring to the attempt of the Wise Men of Gotham to preserve the summer by imprisoning the bird.

Cuccu, cuccu, well singes thu, cuccu:
Ne swike thu never nu;
Sing cuccu, nu, sing cuccu,
Sing cuccu, sing cuccu, nu!

UNKNOWN, *Cuckoo Song*. (Swike: cease.)

CULTURE

9
Culture is then properly described not as having its origin in curiosity, but as having its origin in the love of perfection: *it is a study of perfection.*

MATTHEW ARNOLD, *Culture and Anarchy*. Ch. 1.

There is no better motto which it [culture] can have than these words of Bishop Wilson, "To make reason and the will of God prevail."

MATTHEW ARNOLD, *Culture and Anarchy*. Ch. 1.

The men of culture are the true apostles of equality.

MATTHEW ARNOLD, *Culture and Anarchy*. Ch. 1.

10
Culture has one great passion—the passion for sweetness and light. It has one even yet greater, the passion for making them *prevail.*

MATTHEW ARNOLD, *Culture and Anarchy*. Ch. 1.

Culture is the passion for sweetness and light, and (what is more) the passion for making them prevail.

MATTHEW ARNOLD, *Literature and Dogma: Preface*.

Instead of dirt and poison, we have rather chosen to fill our hives with honey and wax; thus furnishing mankind with the two noblest of things, which are sweetness and light.

SWIFT, *Battle of the Books*.

The Greek word *euphuia*, a finely tempered nature, gives exactly the notion of perfection as culture brings us to conceive it; a harmonious perfection, a perfection in which the characters of beauty and intelligence are both present, which unites "the two noblest of things,"—as Swift, who of one of the two, at any rate, had himself all too little, most happily calls them in his *Battle of the Books*,—"the two noblest of things, sweetness and light." The *euphues*, I say, is the man who tends towards sweetness and light, the *aphues*, on the other hand, is our Philistine.

MATTHEW ARNOLD, *Culture and Anarchy*.

This divine ordinance imparts both light and sweetness to the soul which has eyes to see.

PHILO-JUDÆUS. (WALSH, *Curiosities of Literature*, p. 1043.)

11
Culture is "to know the best that has been said and thought in the world."

MATTHEW ARNOLD, *Literature and Dogma: Preface*.

Culture is reading.

MATTHEW ARNOLD, *Literature and Dogma: Preface*.

12
The acquiring of culture is the developing of an avid hunger for knowledge and beauty.

JESSE LEE BENNETT, *On Culture*.

13
Jackdaw culture, . . . a collection of charming miscomprehensions, untargeted enthusiasms, and a general habit of skimming.

WILLIAM BOLITHO, *Twelve Against the Gods: Isadora Duncan*.

In the room the women come and go

Talking of Michelangelo.

T. S. ELIOT, *The Love Song of J. Alfred Prufrock.*

1
The great law of culture is: Let each become all that he was created capable of being.

CARLYLE, *Essays: J. P. F. Richter.*

2
With culture spoil what else would flourish wild,
And rock the cradle till they bruise the child.

GEORGE VALENTINE COX, *Black Gowns and Red Coats.*

3
Culture with us . . . ends in a headache. . . . Do not craze yourself with thinking, but go about your business anywhere. Life is not intellectual or critical; but sturdy.

EMERSON, *Essays, Second Series: Experience.*

Culture is one thing, and varnish another.

EMERSON, *Journals,* 1868.

4
Culture implies all that which gives the mind possession of its own powers; as languages to the critic, telescope to the astronomer.

EMERSON, *Letters and Social Aims: Progress of Culture.*

The foundation of culture, as of character, is at last the moral sentiment.

EMERSON, *Letters and Social Aims: Progress of Culture.*

The triumph of culture is to overpower nationality.

EMERSON, *Uncollected Lectures: Table-Talk.*

5
Hoist all sail, my dear boy, and steer clear of culture. (Παιδείαν δὲ πᾶσαν, μακάριε, φεῦγε τἀκάτιον ἀράμενος.)

EPICURUS, *Letter to Pythocles.* (DIOGENES LAERTIUS, *Epicurus.* Sec. 6.)

6
Culture which smooth the whole world licks,
Also unto the devil sticks.
(Auch die Kultur, die alle Welt beleckt,
Hat auf den Teufel sich erstreckt.)

GOETHE, *Faust.* Pt. i, sc. 6, l. 160.

7
Men are so inclined to content themselves with what is commonest; the spirit and the senses so easily grow dead to the impressions of the beautiful and perfect, that every one should study, by all methods, to nourish in his mind the faculty of feeling these things. . . . For this reason, one ought every day at least, to hear a little song, read a good poem, see a fine picture, and, if it were possible, to speak a few reasonable words.

GOETHE, *Wilhelm Meister's Apprenticeship.* Bk. v, ch. 1. (Carlyle, tr.)

The soul is plastic, and a person who every day looks upon a beautiful picture, reads a page from some good book, and hears a beautiful piece of music will soon become a transformed person —one born again.

JOHN RUSKIN.

To have read the greatest works of any great poet, to have beheld or heard the greatest works of any great painter or musician, is a possession added to the best things of life.

SWINBURNE, *Essays and Studies: Victor Hugo*

8
Rather than by your culture spoiled,
Desist, and give us nature wild.

MATTHEW GREEN, *The Spleen,* l. 248.

9
No one is so savage that he cannot be civilized if he will lend a patient ear to culture. (Nemo adeo ferus est, ut non mitescere possit, Si modo culturæ patientem commodet aurem.)

HORACE, *Epistles.* Bk. i, epis. 1, l. 39.

10
To have known the best, and to have known it for the best, is success in life.

J. W. MACKAIL, *Classical Studies,* p. 207.

11
The essence of a self-reliant and autonomous culture is an unshakable egoism.

H. L. MENCKEN, *Prejudices.* Ser. ii, p. 93.

12
No man, however learned, can be called a cultured man while there remains an unbridged gap between his reading and his life.

J. C. POWYS, *The Meaning of Culture,* p. 22.

The purpose of culture is to enhance and intensify one's vision of that synthesis of truth and beauty which is the highest and deepest reality.

J. C. POWYS, *The Meaning of Culture,* p. 164.

Culture would not be culture if it were not an acquired taste.

J. C. POWYS, *The Meaning of Culture,* p. 196.

Culture is the bed-rock, the final wall, against which one leans one's back in a god-forsaken chaos.

J. C. POWYS, *The Meaning of Culture,* p. 262.

13
Culture is on the horns of this dilemma: if profound and noble it must remain rare, if common it must become mean.

GEORGE SANTAYANA, *The Life of Reason,* ii, 111.

The longing to be primitive is a disease of culture.

GEORGE SANTAYANA, *Little Essays,* p. 163.

14
The primary indication, to my thinking, of a well-ordered mind is a man's ability to remain in one place and linger in his own company.

SENECA, *Epistulæ ad Lucilium.* Epis. ii, sec. 1.

15
Culture is the habit of being pleased with the best and knowing why.

HENRY VAN DYKE. ("This is certainly mine, but I don't remember when, or where, I said it."—Letter to compiler.)

16
Those who find beautiful meanings in beautiful things are the cultivated. For these there is hope.

OSCAR WILDE, *The Picture of Dorian Gray: Preface.*

CUNNING

See also Deceit; Hypocrisy

1
We take cunning for a sinister or crooked wisdom.
FRANCIS BACON, *Essays: Of Cunning.*

There is a cunning which we in England call "the turning of the cat in the pan"; which is, when that which a man says to another, he lays it as if another had said it to him.
FRANCIS BACON, *Essays: Of Cunning.*

It is a good point of cunning for a man to shape the answer he would have in his own words and propositions, for it makes the other party stick the less.
FRANCIS BACON, *Essays: Of Cunning.*

Nothing doth more hurt in a state, than that cunning men pass for wise.
FRANCIS BACON, *Essays: Of Cunning.*

2
How like a hateful ape,
Detected, grinning, 'midst his pilfer'd hoard,
A cunning man appears, whose secret frauds
Are open'd to the day!
JOANNA BAILLIE, *Basil.* Act iii, sc. 1.

3
The weak in courage is strong in cunning.
WILLIAM BLAKE, *Proverbs of Hell.*

4
Refined policy ever has been the parent of confusion; and ever will be so, as long as the world endures.
EDMUND BURKE, *Conciliation with America.*

All policy's allowed in war and love.
SUSANNAH CENTLIVRE, *Love at a Venture.* Act i. (1706)

Where force hath failed,
Policy often hath prevailed.
CHARLES CHURCHILL, *The Ghost.* Bk. iv, l. 1215.

Turn him to any cause of policy,
The Gordian knot of it he will unloose,
Familiar as his garter.
SHAKESPEARE, *Henry V.* Act i, sc. 1, l. 45.

Policy sits above conscience.
SHAKESPEARE, *Timon of Athens,* iii, 2, 94.

5
[He] never ran away, except when running
Was nothing but a valorous kind of cunning.
BYRON, *Don Juan.* Canto viii, st. 35.

6
Cunning is the dark sanctuary of incapacity.
LORD CHESTERFIELD, *Letters,* p. 656.

7
Dumb's a sly dog.
COLLEY CIBBER, *Love Makes the Man.* Act iv, 1.

8
A sly old fish. too cunning for the hook.
GEORGE CRABBE, *The Parish Register.* Pt. ii.

9
That's the common fate of your Machiavellians; they draw their designs so subtle that their very fineness breaks them.
DRYDEN, *Sir Martin Mar-All.* Act v, sc. 1.

10
Which I wish to remark,
And my language is plain,
That for ways that are dark
And for tricks that are vain,
The heathen Chinee is peculiar,
Which the same I would rise to explain.
BRET HARTE, *Plain Language from Truthful James.*

11
The greatest cunning is to have none. (La plus grande finesse est de n'en avoir point.)
UNKNOWN. A French proverb.

12
Every man wishes to be wise, and they who cannot be wise are almost always cunning.
SAMUEL JOHNSON, *The Idler.* No. 92.

13
Too many expedients may spoil an affair. (Le trop d'expédients peut gâter une affaire.)
LA FONTAINE, *Fables.* Fab. lx, l. 14.

14
Art counterfeits chance. (Ars casu similis.)
OVID, *Ars Amatoria.* Bk. iii, l. 155.

So art lies hid by its own artifice. (Ars adeo latet arte sua.)
OVID, *Metamorphoses.* Bk. x, l. 252.

More matter, with less art.
SHAKESPEARE, *Hamlet.* Act ii, sc. 2, l. 95.

Fortune, my friend, I've often thought,
Is weak, if Art assist her not:
So equally all Arts are vain,
If Fortune help them not again.
SHERIDAN, *Love Epistles of Aristænetus,* xiii.

15
Well skilled in cunning wiles, he could make white of black and black of white. (Furtum ingeniosus ad omne, Candida de nigris et de candentibus atra Qui facere Adsuerat.)
OVID, *Metamorphoses.* Bk. xi, l. 313.

There is a demand nowadays for men who can make wrong appear right. (His nunc præmiumst, qui recta prava faciunt.)
TERENCE, *Phormio,* l. 771. (Act viii, sc. 2.)

16
Contrivance is better than force.
JOHN RAY, *English Proverbs.*

Machination is worth more than force. (Engin mieux vaut que force.)
RABELAIS, *Works.* Bk. ii, ch. 26.

17
His was the subtle look and sly,
That, spying all, seems nought to spy.
SCOTT, *Rokeby.* Canto v, st. 16.

18
Time will unfold what plaited cunning hides;
Who cover faults, at last shame them derides.
SHAKESPEARE, *King Lear.* Act i, sc. 1, l. 283.

19
I hold it ever,
Virtue and cunning were endowments greater
Than nobleness and riches: careless heirs
May the two latter darken and expend;
But immortality attends the former,
Making a man a god.
SHAKESPEARE, *Pericles.* Act iii, sc. 2, l. 26.

To cunning men I will be very kind.
SHAKESPEARE, *The Taming of the Shrew,* i, 1, 96.

1
The devil knew not what he did when he made man politic; he crossed himself by 't.
SHAKESPEARE, *Timon of Athens*. Act iii, sc. 3, l. 28.

1a
In Craven-street, Strand, ten attorneys find place,
And ten dark coal-barges are moor'd at its base.
Fly, Honesty, fly! seek some safer retreat;
For there's craft in the river and craft in the street.
JAMES SMITH, *Craven-Street, Strand.*

CUPID

2
To Chloe's breast young Cupid slily stole,
But he crept in at Myra's pocket-hole.
WILLIAM BLAKE, *Couplets and Fragments.* No. 4.

3
There is music even in the beauty, and the silent note which Cupid strikes, far sweeter than the sound of an instrument.
SIR THOMAS BROWNE, *Religio Medici*. Pt. ii, 9.

4
Archers ever
Have two strings to a bow; and shall great Cupid
(Archer of archers both in men and women),
Be worse provided than a common archer?
GEORGE CHAPMAN, *Bussy d'Ambois*. Act ii, sc. 1. *See also under* PRUDENCE.

5
So cold herself, whilst she such warmth expressed,
'Twas Cupid bathing in Diana's stream.
DRYDEN, *To the Pious Memory of Mrs. Anne Killigrew.*

6
Venus, when her son was lost,
Cried him up and down the coast,
In hamlets, palaces, and parks,
And told the truant by his marks,—
Golden curls, and quiver, and bow.
EMERSON, *The Initial Love.*

Cupid is a casuist,
A mystic and a cabalist,— . . .
He is versed in occult science,
In magic and in clairvoyance. . . .
All things wait for and divine him,—
How shall I dare to malign him?
EMERSON, *The Initial Love.*

Who drinks of Cupid's nectar cup
Loveth downward, and not up.
EMERSON, *To Rhea.*

7
Cupid is a blind gunner.
FARQUHAR, *Love and a Bottle*. Act i, sc. 1.

8
Whoe'er thou art, thy Lord and master see!
Thou wast my Slave, thou art, or thou shalt be!
GEORGE GRANVILLE, *Inscription for a Figure Representing the God of Love.* Paraphrase of an epigram from the *Greek Anthology*.

Whoe'er thou art, thy master see;
He was—or is—or is to be.
(Qui que tu sois, voici ton maître;
Il l'est—le fut—ou le doit être.)
VOLTAIRE, *Inscription for a Statue of Cupid*

9
Cupid and my Campaspe play'd
At cards for kisses; Cupid paid;
He stakes his quiver, bow and arrows,
His mother's doves, and team of sparrows;
Loses them too; then down he throws
The coral of his lip—the rose
Growing on 's cheek (but none knows how)
With these, the crystal of his brow,
And then the dimple of his chin;
All these did my Campaspe win.
At last he set her both his eyes,
She won, and blind did Cupid rise.
O Love! hath she done this to thee?
What shall, alas! become of me?
JOHN LYLY, *Alexander and Campaspe*. Act iii, sc. 5.

10
Cupid . . . whose humour is to strive,
Then yield, then stay, and play the fugitive.
SHACKERLEY MARMION, *Cupid and Psyche.*

11
No wonder Cupid is a murderous boy;
A fiery archer making pain his joy.
His dam, while fond of Mars, is Vulcan's wife,
And thus 'twixt fire and sword divides her life.
MELEAGER. (*Greek Anthology*. Bk. v, ep. 180.)

12
The frivolous bolt of Cupid.
MILTON, *Comus*, l. 445.

13
What will not blind Cupid do in the night, which is his blindman's holiday?
THOMAS NASHE, *Lenten Stuffe.* (1599)

But Cupid is a downy cove,
Wot it takes a deal to hinder;
And if you shuts him out o' the door,
Vy he valks in at the winder.
J R. PLANCHÉ, *The Discreet Princess.*

14
It may be said of him that Cupid hath clapped him o' the shoulder.
SHAKESPEARE, *As You Like It*. Act iv, sc. 1, l. 48.

15
Cupid's butt-shaft is too hard for Hercules' club.
SHAKESPEARE, *Love's Labour's Lost*, i, 2, 181.

This wimpled, whining, purblind wayward boy;
This senior-junior, giant-dwarf, Dan Cupid;
Regent of love-rhymes, lord of folded arms,
The anointed sovereign of sighs and groans,
Liege of all loiterers and malcontents.
SHAKESPEARE, *Love's Labour's Lost*, iii, 1, 181.

16
I swear to thee by Cupid's strongest bow,
By his best arrow with the golden head
By that which knitteth souls and prospers loves.
SHAKESPEARE, *A Midsummer-Night's Dream*

Act i, sc. 1, l. 169. Cupid's golden arrow, virtuous love; Cupid's leaden arrow, sensual passion.

But I might see young Cupid's fiery shaft
Quench'd in the chaste beams of the watery moon.

SHAKESPEARE, *A Midsummer-Night's Dream*. Act ii, sc. 1, l. 161.

1
Cupid is a knavish lad,
Thus to make poor females mad.

SHAKESPEARE, *A Midsummer-Night's Dream*. Act iii, sc. 2, l. 440.

2
Of this matter
Is little Cupid's crafty arrow made,
That only wounds by hearsay.

SHAKESPEARE, *Much Ado About Nothing*. Act iii, sc. 1, l. 22.

Loving goes by haps:
Some Cupid kills with arrows, some with traps.

SHAKESPEARE, *Much Ado About Nothing*. Act iii, sc. 1, l. 105.

He hath twice or thrice cut Cupid's bow-string and the little hangman dare not shoot at him.

SHAKESPEARE, *Much Ado About Nothing*. Act iii, sc. 2, l. 11.

3
Young Adam Cupid, he that shot so trim,
When King Cophetua loved the beggar-maid.

SHAKESPEARE, *Romeo and Juliet*. Act ii, sc. 1, l. 13.

The blinded boy, that shoots so trim,
From heaven down did hie;
He drew a dart and shot at him,
In place where he did lie.

UNKNOWN, *King Cophetua and the Beggar-Maid*. (PERCY, *Reliques*. Ser. i, bk. 2, No. 6.)

4
Sweet, rouse yourself; and the weak wanton Cupid
Shall from your neck unloose his amorous fold,
And, like a dewdrop from the lion's mane,
Be shook to air.

SHAKESPEARE, *Troilus and Cressida*. Act iii, sc. 3, l. 222.

5
Cupid "the little greatest god."

SOUTHEY, *Commonplace Book*. Ser. iv, p. 462.

Cupid "the little greatest enemy."

O. W. HOLMES, *The Professor at the Breakfast-Table*.

6
What easy, tame, suffering, trampled things does that little god of talking cowards make of us!

WILLIAM WYCHERLEY, *The Plain Dealer*. Act iv, sc. 1.

7
Take ye heed, nymphs, because Cupid is fair;
Love naked is complete, Love unarmed is the same.

UNKNOWN, *Pervigilium Veneris*. St. 9.

CURIOSITY

8
This disease of curiosity. (Hoc morbo cupiditatis.)

ST. AUGUSTINE, *Confessions*. Bk. x, ch. 35.

9
He fashioned hell for the inquisitive. (Scrutantibus gehennas parabat.)

ST. AUGUSTINE, *Confessions*. Bk. xi, ch. 12. Quoting an unnamed author, who made this reply when asked what God was doing before he made heaven and earth.

One demanding how God employed Himself before the world was made, had answer: that he was making Hell for curious questioners.

JOHN MILTON, *Works*. Vol. i, p. 362.

St. Austin might have returned another answer to him that asked him, "What God employed himself about before the world was made?" "He was making hell."

SOUTHEY, *Commonplace Book*. Ser. iv, p. 591.

10
Too much curiosity lost Paradise.

APHRA BEHN, *The Lucky Chance*. Act. iii, sc. 3.

11
I loathe that low vice curiosity.

BYRON, *Don Juan*. Canto i, st. 23.

12
Curiosity
Does, no less than devotion, pilgrims make.

ABRAHAM COWLEY, *Ode on a Chair Made of Sir Francis Drake's Ship*. Pt. iv.

13
The prospect of finding anybody out in anything would have kept Miss Miggs awake under the influence of henbane.

DICKENS, *Barnaby Rudge*. Ch. 9.

14
Be not curious in unnecessary matters: for more things are shewed unto thee than men understand.

Apocrypha: Ecclesiasticus, iii, 23.

Inquire not too curiously.

The Koran. Ch. 49.

15
There are three things about which I have curiosity, though I know nothing of them,—music, poetry, and love.

FONTENELLE. (EMERSON, *Success*.)

16
Take heed of a gluttonous curiosity to feed on many things, lest the greediness of the appetite of thy memory spoil the digestion thereof.

FULLER, *Holy and Profane States*. Bk. iii.

17
Curiosity is little more than another name for hope.

J. C. AND A. W. HARE, *Guesses at Truth*.

18
Much curiousness is a perpetual wooing,
Nothing with labour; folly long a doing.

GEORGE HERBERT, *The Church-Porch*. St. 32.

19
Avoid a questioner. for he is also a tattler. (Percontatorem fugito: nam garrulus idem est.)

HORACE, *Epistles*. Bk. i, epis. 18, l. 69.

Talk to him of Jacob's ladder, and he would ask the number of the steps.

DOUGLAS JERROLD, *A Matter-of-Fact Man.*

1
Curiosity is one of the most permanent and certain characteristics of a vigorous intellect.

SAMUEL JOHNSON, *The Rambler.* No. 103.

Curiosity is, in great and generous minds, the first passion and the last.

SAMUEL JOHNSON, *The Rambler.* No. 150.

2
I do love To note and to observe.

BEN JONSON, *Volpone.* Act ii, sc. 1.

3
The poorest of the sex still have an itch
To know their fortunes, equal to the rich.
The dairy-maid inquires if she shall take
The trusty tailor, and the cook forsake.
(Consulit ante falas delphinorumque columnas
An saga vendenti nubat caupone relicto.)

JUVENAL, *Satires.* Sat. vi, l. 590. (Dryden, tr.)

4
Keep your mouth shut, and close up the doors of sight and sound, and as long as you live you will have no vexation. But open your mouth, or become inquisitive, and you will be in trouble all your life long.

LAO-TSZE, *The Simple Way.* No. 52.

5
Remember Lot's wife.

New Testament: Luke, xvii, 32.

6
No state sorrier than that of the man who keeps up a continual round, and pries into "the secrets of the nether world," as saith the poet, and is curious in conjecture of what is in his neighbor's heart.

MARCUS AURELIUS, *Meditations.* Bk. ii, sec. 13.

7
Curiosity is born of jealousy. (La curiosité naît de la jalousie.)

MOLIÈRE, *Dom Garcie de Navarre.* Act ii, sc. 5, l. 22.

8
Plato holds that there is some vice of impiety in enquiring too curiously about God and the world. (Platon estime qu'il y ait quelque vice d'impiété à trop curieusement s'enquerir de Dieu et du monde.)

MONTAIGNE, *Essays.* Bk. ii, ch. 12.

'Twere to consider too curiously to consider so.

SHAKESPEARE, *Hamlet.* Act v, sc. 1, l. 225.

9
Our inquisitiveness is excited by having its gratification deferred. (Incitantur enim homines ad agnoscenda quæ differuntur.)

PLINY THE YOUNGER, *Epistles.* Bk. ix, epis. 27.

10
A spirit of inquiry is the great characteristic of the age we live in.

JOHN POOLE, *Paul Pry.*

I only ask for information.

DICKENS, *David Copperfield* Ch. 20.

11
I hope I don't intrude.

JOHN POOLE, *Paul Pry.* An apology always on the lips of the inquisitive and intrusive Paul Pry. Produced at Theatre Royal, Haymarket, 13 Sept., 1825. The phrase is also used, but without iteration, in Burgoyne's comedy, *Maid of the Oaks,* act ii.

Unmannerly intruder as thou art!

SHAKESPEARE, *Titus Andronicus.* Act ii, 3, 69.

The eye of Paul Pry often finds more than he wished to find. (Der Blick des Forschers fand Nicht selten mehr, als er zu finden wünschte.)

LESSING, *Nathan der Weise.* Act ii, sc. 8.

12
He that pryeth into every cloud may be struck with a thunderbolt.

JOHN RAY, *English Proverbs,* 134.

Where the apple reddens,
Never pry—
Lest we lose our Edens,
Eve and I.

ROBERT BROWNING, *A Woman's Last Word.*

13
Do not be inquisitive. He who asks what has been said about him, who digs out malicious talk, even if it has been private, disturbs his own peace.

SENECA, *De Ira.* Bk. iii, sec 11

14
For look where Beatrice, like a lapwing, runs
Close by the ground, to hear our conference.

SHAKESPEARE, *Much Ado About Nothing.* Act iii, sc. 1, l. 25.

The false lapwing, full of treachery.

CHAUCER, *The Parlement of Foules,* l. 47.

15
Curiosity is the direct incontinency of the spirit.

JEREMY TAYLOR, *Holy Living,* p. 129.

16
Let curiosities alone.

THOMAS À KEMPIS, *De Imitatione Christi.* Pt. i, ch. 20.

17
You know what a woman's curiosity is. Almost as great as a man's!

OSCAR WILDE, *An Ideal Husband.* Act i.

CURSE

For Cursing in the Sense of Swearing, see Swearing

18
Blessings star forth for ever; but a curse
Is like a cloud—it passes.

P. J. BAILEY, *Festus: Hades.*

19
The bad man's charity [cursing].

BEAUMONT AND FLETCHER, *The Spanish Curate.* Act i, sc. 2.

20
And oftentimes such cursing wrongfully returneth again to him that curseth, as a bird that returneth again to his own nest.

CHAUCER, *The Personnes Tale.* Sec. 41.

Curse away!
And let me tell thee, Beauseant, a wise proverb
The Arabs have,—"Curses are like young chickens,
And still come home to roost!"

BULWER-LYTTON, *Lady of Lyons*. Act v, sc. 2.

Curses are like young chickens; they always come home to roost.

ROBERT SOUTHEY, *Curse of Kehama: Motto*.

I have heard a good man say, that a curse was like a stone flung up to the heavens, and maist like to return on the head that sent it.

SCOTT, *Old Mortality*. Ch. 42.

See also under RETRIBUTION.

1
Curse not the king, no not in thy thought; and curse not the rich in thy bedchamber.

Old Testament: Ecclesiastes, x, 20.

2
Curse and be cursed! it is the fruit of cursing.

JOHN FLETCHER, *Rollo*. Act iii, sc. 1.

3
As the bird by wandering, as the swallow by flying, so the curse causeless shall not come.

Old Testament: Proverbs, xxvi, 2.

4
As he loved cursing, so let it come unto him: as he delighted not in blessing, so let it be far from him. As he clothed himself with cursing like as with his garment, so let it come into his bowels like water, and like oil into his bones.

Old Testament: Psalms, cix, 17.

5
I'll be damned for never a king's son in Christendom.

SHAKESPEARE, *I Henry IV*. Act i, sc. 2, l. 109.

Abuses me to damn me.

SHAKESPEARE, *Hamlet*. Act ii, sc. 2, l. 632.

6
Let this pernicious hour
Stand aye accursed in the calendar.

SHAKESPEARE, *Macbeth*. Act iv, sc. 1, l. 133.

7
Curses, not loud but deep.

SHAKESPEARE, *Macbeth*. Act v, sc. 3, l. 27.

8
The Curse shall be on thee Forever and ever.

SOUTHEY, *The Curse of Kehama*. Pt. ii, st. 14.

9
I sent down to the rum mill on the corner and hired an artist by the week to sit up nights and curse that stranger.

MARK TWAIN, *A Mysterious Visit*.

10
"A jolly place," said he, "in times of old!
But something ails it now; the spot is curst."

WORDSWORTH, *Hart-Leap Well*. Pt. ii, l. 123.

II—Curse: Some Examples

11
By thy cold breast and serpent smile,
By thy unfathom'd gulfs of guile,
By that most seeming virtuous eye,
By thy shut soul's hypocrisy; . . .
By thy delight in others' pain,
And by thy brotherhood of Cain,
I call upon thee! and compel
Thyself to be thy proper Hell!

BYRON, *Manfred*, l. 242. This "Incantation," as Byron called it, referred to his wife.

12
May God palsy the hand that wrote that order, may God palsy the brain that conceived it, and may God palsy the tongue that dictated it.

LUCIUS FAIRCHILD, of Wisconsin, National Commander of the Grand Army of the Republic, *Speech*, at a meeting in Harlem, June, 1887, referring to the order issued by President Cleveland restoring the captured Confederate flags in the possession of the Government to the Southern States. He was afterwards known as "Fairchild of the three palsies."

13
I shall curse you with book and bell and candle.

SIR THOMAS MALORY, *Morte d'Arthur*. Bk. xxi, ch. 1. (1470) Frequently thereafter. Alluding to the ancient method of excommunication practised by the Roman Catholic Church.

The Cardinal rose with a dignified look,
He call'd for his candle, his bell, and his book!
In holy anger, and pious grief,
He solemnly cursed that rascally thief!
He cursed him at board, he cursed him in bed;
From the sole of his foot to the crown of his head;
He cursed him in sleeping, that every night
He should dream of the devil, and wake in a fright;
He cursed him in eating, he cursed him in drinking,
He cursed him in coughing, in sneezing, in winking;
He cursed him in sitting, in standing, in lying;
He cursed him in walking, in riding, in flying;
He cursed him in living, he cursed him dying!—
Never was heard such a terrible curse!
But what gave rise
To no little surprise,
Nobody seem'd one penny the worse!

R. H. BARHAM, *The Jackdaw of Rheims*. Paraphrasing the famous "Curse of Bishop Ernulf," preserved in the cathedral at Rochester, England.

Mark, where she stands!—around her form I draw
The awful circle of our solemn Church!
Set but a foot within that holy ground,
And on thy head—yea, though it wore a crown—
I launch the curse of Rome!

BULWER-LYTTON, *Richelieu*. Act iv, sc. 2, l. 121.

14
Boils and plagues
Plaster you o'er, that you may be abhorr'd
Further than seen.

SHAKESPEARE, *Coriolanus*. Act i, sc. 4, l. 31.

Now the red pestilence strike all trades in Rome,
And occupations perish!

SHAKESPEARE, *Coriolanus*. Act iv, sc. 1, l. 13.

15
Therefore be gone
Without our grace, our love, our benizon.

SHAKESPEARE, *King Lear*. Act i, sc. 1, l. 267.

You nimble lightnings, dart your blinding flames
Into her scornful eyes!—Infect her beauty,
You fen-suck'd fogs, drawn by the powerful sun,
To fall and blast her pride!

SHAKESPEARE, *King Lear*. Act ii, sc. 4, l. 167.

Weary se'nnights nine times nine
Shall he dwindle, peak and pine.

SHAKESPEARE, *Macbeth*. Act i, sc. 3, l. 22.

All the infections that the sun sucks up
From bogs, fens, flats, on Prosper fall, and make him
By inch-meal a disease!

SHAKESPEARE, *The Tempest*. Act ii, sc. 2, l. 1.

1

Out, damned spot! out, I say.

SHAKESPEARE, *Macbeth*. Act v, sc. 1, l. 39.

Out! out! . . . accursed spot!

SOUTHEY, *All for Love*. Pt. vi, st. 16.

2

O villains, vipers, damn'd without redemption;
Dogs, easily won to fawn on any man;
Snakes in my heart-blood warm'd, that sting my heart;
Three Judases, each one thrice worse than Judas!

SHAKESPEARE, *Richard II*. Act iii, sc. 2, l. 129.

A plague o' both your houses!

SHAKESPEARE, *Romeo and Juliet*. Act iii, sc. 1, l. 94.

3

May the strong curse of crushed affections light
Back on thy bosom with reflected blight!
And make thee in thy leprosy of mind
As loathsome to thyself as to mankind!
Till all thy self-thoughts curdle into hate,
Black—as thy will for others would create:
Till thy hard heart be calcined into dust,
And thy soul welter in its hideous crust.
Oh, may thy grave be sleepless as the bed—
The widowed couch of fire, that thou hast spread!

SHELLEY, *To the Lord Chancellor*. Referring to Lord Eldon, who, on 17 March, 1816, had pronounced a decree depriving Shelley of the custody of his children by his wife Harriet, because of his flight from England with Mary Godwin. The poem was written "in his first resentment against the Chancellor," and there are several extant versions.

I curse thee by a parent's outraged love,
By hopes long cherished and too lately lost,
By gentle feelings thou couldst never prove,
By griefs which thy stern nature never crost.

SHELLEY, *To the Lord Chancellor*.

4

Cursed be the social wants that sin against the strength of youth!
Cursed be the social lies that warp us from the living truth!
Cursed be the sickly forms that err from honest Nature's rule!
Cursed be the gold that gilds the straighten'd forehead of the fool.

TENNYSON, *Locksley Hall*. St. 31.

CUSTOM

See also Habit

I—Custom: Definitions

5

Custom suffers naught to be strange to the eye. (Consuetudo oculis nil sinit esse novum.)

AUSONIUS [?], *Epigram*.

6

Custom which is before all law, Nature which is above all art.

SAMUEL DANIEL, *An Apology for Rhyme*.

Customs may not be as wise as laws, but they are always more popular.

BENJAMIN DISRAELI, *Speech*, House of Commons, 11 Mar., 1870.

Custom is another law. (Consuetudo est altera lex.)

UNKNOWN. A Latin proverb.

Custom rules the law. (Mos regit legem.)

UNKNOWN. A Latin proverb.

7

Custom, that unwritten law,
By which the people keep even kings in awe.

SIR WILLIAM D'AVENANT, *Circe*. Act ii, sc. 3.

8

A good custom is surer than law. (Τρόπος γε χρηστὸς ἀσφαλέστερος νόμου.)

EURIPIDES, *Pirithoüs*.

9

Custom without reason is but ancient error.

THOMAS FULLER, *Gnomologia*. No. 1226.

A deep meaning often lies in old customs. (Ein tiefer Sinn wohnt in den alten Bräuchen.)

SCHILLER, *Marie Stuart*. Act i, sc. 7, l. 131.

10

Custom is another nature. (Consuetudo est altera natura.)

GALEN, *De Tuenda Valetudine*. Ch. 1.

Custom becomes a sort of second nature. (Consuetudine quasi alteram quandam naturam effici.)

CICERO, *De Finibus* Bk. v, ch. 25, sec. 74.

Custom is almost a second nature.

PLUTARCH, *Rules for the Preservation of Health*.

11

Custom has furnished the only basis which ethics have ever had.

JOSEPH W. KRUTCH, *The Modern Temper*, p. 13.

12

Men's customs differ; different people honor different practices; but all honor the maintenence of their own peculiar ways.

PLUTARCH, *Lives: Themistocles*. Sec. 27.

13

Custom, the world's great idol.

JOHN POMFRET, *Reason*, l. 99.

14

Custom is the plague of wise men and the idol of fools.

JOHN RAY, *English Proverbs*.

II—Custom: Apothegms

15

Talk not of custom,—'tis the coward's plea.

CHARLES CHURCHILL, *Independence*, l. 345.

1
Never can custom conquer nature. (Numquam naturam mos vinceret.)
CICERO, *Tusculanarum Disputationum*. Bk. v, sec. 27.

2
Men's customs change like leaves on the bough; some go and others come.
DANTE, *Paradiso*. Canto xxvi, l. 137.

3
As the custom is. (Ut mos est.)
JUVENAL, *Satires*. Sat. vi, l. 392.

As the custom is.
SHAKESPEARE, *Romeo and Juliet*. Act iv, sc. 5, l. 80.

4
Let not things, because they are common, enjoy for that the less share of our consideration.
PLINY THE ELDER, *Historia Naturalis*. Bk. xix, sec. 59.

5
So many countries, so many customs.
JOHN RAY, *English Proverbs*.

Strange customs do not thrive in foreign soil. (Nicht fremder Brauch gedeiht in einem Lande.)
SCHILLER, *Demetrius*. Act i, sc. 1.

The custom of the country.
MARK TWAIN, *Innocents at Home*. Ch. 10.

6
Such is the custom of Branksome Hall.
SCOTT, *Lay of the Last Minstrel*. Canto i, st. 7.

7
Outside in accordance with custom; inside as we please. (Foris ut mos est, intus ut libet.)
SENECA, *Epistulæ ad Lucilium*. Epis. v, sec. 2.

8
But to my mind, though I am native here,
And to the manner born, it is a custom
More honour'd in the breach than the observance.
SHAKESPEARE, *Hamlet*. Act i, sc. 4, l. 15.

9
Nice customs curtsey to great kings.
SHAKESPEARE, *Henry V*. Act v, sc. 2, l. 293.

Wherefore should I
Stand in the plague of custom?
SHAKESPEARE, *King Lear*. Act i, sc. 2, l. 2.

A thing of custom: 't is no other;
Only it spoils the pleasure of the time.
SHAKESPEARE, *Macbeth*. Act iii, sc. 4, l. 97.

10
'Tis nothing when you are used to it.
SWIFT, *Polite Conversation*. Dial. iii.

There's nothing like being used to a thing.
SHERIDAN, *The Rivals*. Act v, sc. 1.

11
Old customs, habits, superstitions, fears,
All that lies buried under fifty years.
J. G. WHITTIER, *The Countess*.

III—Custom: Its Power

12
We think according to nature; we speak according to rules; we act according to custom.
FRANCIS BACON, *De Augmentis Scientiarum: Natura*.

13
What custom hath endeared
We part with sadly, though we prize it not.
JOANNA BAILLIE, *Basil*. Act i, sc. 2.

14
The deadliest foe to love is custom.
BULWER-LYTTON, *Devereux*. Bk. iii, ch. 5.

15
Custom reconciles us to everything.
EDMUND BURKE, *On the Sublime and Beautiful*. Pt. iv, sec. 18.

16
Custom is the master of all things. (Rerum omnium magister usus.)
CÆSAR, *Civil Wars*. Bk. ii, sec. 8.

Custom is the best master. (Usus magister est optimus.)
CICERO, *Pro Rabirio*. Ch. iv, sec. 9.

Custom is a very powerful master of all things. (Usus efficacissimus rerum omnium magister.)
PLINY, *Historia Naturalis*. Bk. xxvi, sec. 2.

Custom, towering master. (Usus magister egregius.)
PLINY THE YOUNGER, *Letters*. Bk. i, epis. 20.

17
An ancient custom obtains the force of nature. (Vetus consuetudo naturæ vim obtinet.)
CICERO, *De Inventione*.

18
Man yields to custom, as he bows to fate,
In all things ruled—mind, body, and estate;
In pain, in sickness, we for cure apply
To them we know not, and we know not why.
GEORGE CRABBE, *Tales in Verse*. Tale iii, l. 86.

19
Only that he may conform to tyrant custom.
DU BARTAS, *Devine Weekes and Dayes*. Week ii, day 3. (Sylvester, tr.)

The tyrant custom, most grave senators,
Hath made the flinty and steel couch of war
My thrice-driven bed of down.
SHAKESPEARE, *Othello*. Act i, sc. 3, l. 230.

When tyrant Custom had not shackled men.
THOMSON, *The Seasons: Autumn*, l. 222.

Custom is a tyrant. (Usus est tyrannus.)
UNKNOWN. A Latin proverb.

20
Custom, then, is the great guide of human life.
DAVID HUME, *Human Understanding*. Sec. v, pt. i.

21
Custom meets us at the cradle and leaves us only at the tomb.
ROBERT G. INGERSOLL, *Individuality*.

22
Long customs are not easily broken; he that attempts to change the course of his own life very often labors in vain.
SAMUEL JOHNSON, *Rasselas*. Ch. 29.

23
Great things astonish us, and small dishearten us. Custom makes both familiar.
LA BRUYÈRE, *Les Caractères: Des Jugements*.

What humanity abhors, custom reconciles and recommends to us.
JOHN LOCKE, *On Education*. Sec. 116.

The roots of cruelty come to perfection by means of custom.
MONTAIGNE, *Essays*. Bk. i, ch. 22.

1
Custom and use have power to enure and fashion us, not only to what form they please . . . but also to change and variation.
MONTAIGNE, *Essays*. Bk. iii, ch. 10.

2
We are more sensible of what is done against custom than against Nature.
PLUTARCH, *Of Eating of Flesh*. Tract i.

3
Very weighty is the authority of custom. (Gravissimum est imperium consuetudinis.)
PUBLILIUS SYRUS, *Sententiæ*. No. 236.

4
Choose what is best; custom will make it agreeable and easy. (Optimum elige; suave et facile illud faciet consuetudo.)
PYTHAGORAS, *Ethical Sentences from Stobæus*. Latinized by Bacon.

That monster, custom, who all sense doth eat,
Of habits devil, is angel yet in this,
That to the use of actions fair and good
He likewise gives a frock or livery,
That aptly is put on. Refrain tonight,
And that shall lend a kind of easiness
To the next abstinence; the next more easy;
For use almost can change the stamp of nature.
SHAKESPEARE, *Hamlet*. Act iii, sc. 4, l. 161.

Custom hath made it in him a property of easiness.
SHAKESPEARE, *Hamlet*. Act v, sc. 1, l. 75.

Custom makes all things easy.
JEAN INGELOW, *The Dreams That Come True*. St. 7.

5
Custom calls me to 't:
What custom wills, in all things should we do 't.
SHAKESPEARE, *Coriolanus*. Act ii, sc. 3, l. 124.

New customs,
Though they be never so ridiculous,
Nay, let 'em be unmanly, yet are follow'd.
SHAKESPEARE, *Henry VIII*. Act i, sc. 3, l. 2.

6
How many unjust and crooked things custom makes one do. (Quam multa injusta ac prava fiunt moribus!)
TERENCE, *Heauton Timorumenos*, l. 839.

IV—Custom: Its Faults

7
Cast away the bondage and the fear
Of rotten custom.
HARTLEY COLERIDGE, *Sonnets*. No. 38.

8
Such dupes are men to custom, and so prone
To reverence what is ancient, and can plead
A course of long observance for its use.
COWPER, *The Task*. Bk. v, l. 299.

Custom's idiot sway.
COWPER, *Retirement*, l. 49.

9
The slaves of custom and established mode,
With pack-horse constancy we keep the road
Crooked or straight, through quags or thorny dells,
True to the jingling of our leader's bells.
COWPER, *Tirocinium*, l. 251. *See also under* PRECEDENT.

10
The interrogation of custom at all points is an inevitable stage in the growth of every superior mind.
EMERSON, *Representative Men: Montaigne*.

11
The despotism of custom is everywhere the standing hindrance to human advancement.
JOHN STUART MILL, *On Liberty*. Ch. 3.

12
Nature is seldom in the wrong, custom always.
LADY MARY WORTLEY MONTAGU, *Letter to Miss Anne Wortley*, 8 Aug., 1709.

13
Custom is a violent and deceiving schoolmistress.
MONTAIGNE, *Essays*. Bk. i, ch. 22.

A bad custom is like a good cake, better broken than kept.
JOHN RAY, *English Proverbs*.

CYNICISM

14
Why should we strive, with cynic frown,
To knock their fairy castles down?
ELIZA COOK, *Oh! Dear to Memory*.

15
The royal cynic. (Βασιλικὸν κύνα.)
DIOGENES, of Aristippus, because of his attendance upon Dionysius, a sneering phrase which may also be translated, "The king's poodle," for κύων means dog as well as cynic, and indicates how much the Cynics gloried in snarling and biting. (DIOGENES LAERTIUS, *Aristippus*. Bk. ii, sec. 66.)

16
A cynic can chill and dishearten with a single word.
EMERSON, *Society and Solitude: Success*.

17
If to look truth in the face and not resent it when it's unpalatable, and take human nature as you find it, . . . is to be cynical, then I suppose I'm a cynic.
SOMERSET MAUGHAM, *The Back of Beyond*.

18
Cynicism is intellectual dandyism.
GEORGE MEREDITH, *The Egoist*. Ch. 7.

19
I hate cynicism a great deal worse than I do the devil; unless, perhaps, the two were the same thing?
R. L. STEVENSON, *An Inland Voyage*. Ch. 5.

20
Cecil Graham: What is a cynic?

Lord Darlington: A man who knows the price of everything, and the value of nothing.
OSCAR WILDE, *Lady Windermere's Fan.* Act iii.

Nowadays people know the price of everything, and the value of nothing.
OSCAR WILDE, *Picture of Dorian Gray.* Ch. 4.

D

DAFFODIL

1
The daffodil is our doorside queen;
She pushes upward the sward already,
To spot with sunshine the early green.
BRYANT, *An Invitation to the Country.*

2
O Love-star of the unbeloved March,
When cold and shrill,
Forth flows beneath a low, dim-lighted arch
The wind that beats sharp crag and barren hill,
And keeps unfilmed the lately torpid rill!
AUBREY DE VERE, *Ode to the Daffodil.*

3
What ye have been ye still shall be
When we are dust the dust among,
O yellow flowers!
AUSTIN DOBSON, *To Daffodils.*

4
There flames the first gay daffodil
Where winter-long the snows have lain!
RUTH GUTHRIE HARDING, *Daffodils.*

5
Fair daffodils, we weep to see
You haste away so soon;
As yet the early-rising sun
Has not attained his noon. . . .
We have short time to stay as you,
We have as short a spring;
As quick a growth to meet decay
As you, or any thing.
ROBERT HERRICK, *To Daffodils.*

6
O fateful flower beside the rill—
The Daffodil, the Daffodil!
JEAN INGELOW, *Persephone.* St. 16.

7
Now blow the daffodils on slender stalks,
Small keen flames that leap up in the mold
And run along the dripping garden walks.
LIZETTE WOODWORTH REESE, *Sweet Weather.*

8
When daffodils begin to peer,
With, heigh! the doxy over the dale,
Why, then comes in the sweet o' the year;
For the red blood reigns in the winter's pale.
SHAKESPEARE, *Winter's Tale.* Act iv, sc. 3, l. 1.

Daffodils
That come before the swallow dares, and take
The winds of March with beauty.
SHAKESPEARE, *Winter's Tale.* Act iv, sc. 4, l. 118.

9
Daffy-down-dilly came up in the cold,
Through the brown mould
Although the March breeze blew keen on her face,
Although the white snow lay in many a place.
ANNA WARNER, *Daffy-Down-Dilly.*

10
There is a tiny yellow daffodil,
The butterfly can see it from afar,
Although one summer evening's dew could fill
Its little cup twice over, ere the star
Had called the lazy shepherd to his fold
And be no prodigal.
OSCAR WILDE, *The Burden of Itys.* St. 17.

11
I wandered lonely as a cloud
That floats on high o'er vales and hills,
When all at once I saw a crowd,
A host, of golden daffodils;
Beside the lake, beneath the trees,
Fluttering and dancing in the breeze.

Continuous as the stars that shine
And twinkle in the milky way,
They stretched in never-ending line
Along the margin of a bay:
Ten thousand saw I at a glance,
Tossing their heads in sprightly dance.
WORDSWORTH, *I Wandered Lonely as a Cloud: Poems of the Imagination.* No. xii.

DAISY

12
Wee, modest, crimson-tippèd flow'r,
Thou's met me in an evil hour;
For I maun crush amang the stoure
Thy slender stem:
To spare thee now is past my pow'r,
Thou bonie gem.
ROBERT BURNS, *To a Mountain Daisy.* St. 1.

Ev'n thou who mourn'st the daisy's fate,
That fate is thine—no distant date;
Stern Ruin's ploughshare drives, elate,
Full on thy bloom,
Till crush'd beneath the furrow's weight
Shall be thy doom!
BURNS, *To a Mountain Daisy.* St. 9.

Myriads of daisies have shone forth in flower
Near the lark's nest, and in their natural hour
Have passed away, less happy than the One
That, by the unwilling ploughshare, died to prove
The tender charm of Poetry and Love.
WORDSWORTH, *Poems Composed or Suggested During a Tour, in the Summer of 1833.* No. 37.

13
The daisy's for simplicity and unaffected air.
BURNS, *The Posie.* St. 4.

Yet, all beneath th' unrivalled rose,
The lowly daisy sweetly blows.
BURNS, *The Vision*. Duan ii, st. 21.

1
Over the shoulders and slopes of the dune
I saw the white daisies go down to the sea. . . .
And all of their saying was, "Earth, it is well!"
And all of their dancing was, "Life, thou art good!"
BLISS CARMAN, *Daisies*.

2
With daisied mantles is the mountain dight.
THOMAS CHATTERTON, *Ælla*.

3
Of all the flowers in the mead,
Then love I most those flowers white and red,
Which that men callen daisies in our town.
CHAUCER, *Legend of Good Women: Prologue*, l. 41.

That well by reason men it callë may
The "day's-eye" or else the "eye of day,"
The emperice and flower of flowers all.
CHAUCER, *Legend of Good Women: Prologue*, l. 183.

4
Daisies infinite
Uplift in praise their little glowing hands,
O'er every hill that under heaven expands.
EBENEZER ELLIOTT, *Spring*, l. 13.

5
Daisies smell-less, yet most quaint.
JOHN FLETCHER, *The Two Noble Kinsmen*. Act i, sc. 1.

6
The daisy's cheek is tipp'd with a blush,
She is of such low degree.
THOMAS HOOD, *Flowers*.

And daisy stars, whose firmament is green.
THOMAS HOOD, *The Plea of the Midsummer Fairies*, l. 317.

Stars are the daisies that begem
The blue fields of the sky.
D. M. MOIR, *Stars*. (*Dublin University Magazine*, Oct., 1852.)

7
All summer she scattered the daisy leaves;
They only mocked her as they fell.
She said: "The daisy but deceives;
'He loves me not,' 'he loves me well,'
One story no two daisies tell."
Ah, foolish heart, which waits and grieves
Under the daisy's mocking spell.
HELEN HUNT JACKSON, *The Sign of the Daisy*.

8
There is a flower, a little flower
With silver crest and golden eye,
That welcomes every changing hour,
And weathers every sky.
JAMES MONTGOMERY, *A Field Flower*.

The Rose has but a summer-reign,
The daisy never dies.
JAMES MONTGOMERY, *A Field Flower*.

9
Sweet bunch of daisies, Brought from the dell,
Kiss me once, darling, Daisies won't tell.
ANITA OWEN, *Sweet Bunch of Daisies*. (1894)

10
Daisies, those pearled Arcturi of the earth,
The constellated flower that never sets.
SHELLEY, *The Question*.

11
She asked him but to stand beside her grave—
She said she would be daisies—and she thought
'Twould give her joy to feel that he was near.
ALEXANDER SMITH, *A Life-Drama*.

12
So dear a life your arms enfold,
Whose crying is a cry for gold.
TENNYSON, *The Daisy*. St. 24.

13
Ah, drops of gold in whitening flame
Burning, we know your lovely name—
Daisies, that little children pull!
FRANCIS THOMPSON, *To Daisies*.

14
Bright Flower! whose home is everywhere,
Bold in maternal Nature's care,
And all the long year through the heir
Of joy and sorrow;
Methinks that there abides in thee
Some concord with humanity,
Given to no other flower I see
The forest thorough!
WORDSWORTH, *To the Daisy*. No. 2.

Thou art indeed by many a claim.
The Poet's darling.
WORDSWORTH, *To the Daisy*. No. 1.

We meet thee, like a pleasant thought,
When such are wanted.
WORDSWORTH, *To the Daisy*. No. 1.

Thou unassuming Common-place
Of Nature, with that homely face,
And yet with something of a grace,
Which Love makes for thee!
WORDSWORTH, *To the Same Flower*.

A nun demure of lowly port;
Or sprightly maiden, of Love's court,
In thy simplicity the sport
Of all temptations;
A queen in crown of rubies drest;
A starveling in a scanty vest;
Are all, as seems to suit thee best,
Thy appellations.
WORDSWORTH, *To the Same Flower*.

Sweet silent creature!
That breath'st with me in sun and air,
Do thou, as thou art wont, repair
My heart with gladness, and a share
Of thy meek nature!
WORDSWORTH, *To the Same Flower*.

15
So fair, so sweet, withal so sensitive,
Would that the little Flowers were born to live,
Conscious of half the pleasure which they give;

That to this mountain-daisy's self were known
The beauty of its star-shaped shadow, thrown
On the smooth surface of this naked stone!
WORDSWORTH, *Poems of Sentiment and Reflection.* No. 42.

DANCING

I—Dancing: Definitions

1
A dance is a measured pace, as a verse is a measured speech.
FRANCIS BACON, *Advancement of Learning.* Bk. ii, sec. 13.

2
Dancing, the child of Music and of Love.
SIR JOHN DAVIES, *Orchestra.* St. 96.

3
The poetry of the foot.
DRYDEN, *The Rival Ladies.* Act iii, sc. 1.

4
Dancing's a touchstone that true beauty tries,
Nor suffers charms that nature's hand denies.
SOAME JENYNS, *The Art of Dancing.* Canto i, l. 119.

5
The Indian dances to prepare himself for killing his enemy: but while the beaux and belles of our assemblies dance, they are in the very act of killing theirs—TIME!—a more inveterate and formidable foe than any the Indian has to contend with; for, however completely and ingeniously killed, he is sure to rise again, "with twenty mortal murders on his crown," leading his army of blue devils, with ennui in the van and vapours in the rear.
T. L. PEACOCK, *Headlong Hall.* Ch. xiii.

II—Dancing: Apothegms

6
He dances like an angel.
ADDISON, *The Spectator.* No. 475.

7
O give me new figures! I can't go on dancing
The same that were taught me ten seasons ago;
The schoolmaster over the land is advancing,
Then why is the master of dancing so slow?
It is such a bore to be always caught tripping
In dull uniformity year after year;
Invent something new, and you'll set me a skipping:
I want a new figure to dance with my Dear!
T. H. BAYLY, *Quadrille à la Mode.*

Waltzing is fine, Bill, but not for mine, Bill;
It isn't in it with the two-step a minute.
BENJAMIN HAPGOOD BURT, *I'd Rather Two-Step than Waltz, Bill.* (1907)

8
When you go to dance, take heed whom you take by the hand.
JOHN CLARKE, *Paræmiologia,* 24.

9
But, by the Lord, though I should beg
Wi' lyart pow,
I'll laugh, an' sing, an' shake my leg
As lang's I dow!
BURNS, *Second Epistle to J. Lapraik.*

10
Let Angiolini bare her breast of snow,
Wave the white arm and point the pliant toe.
BYRON, *English Bards and Scotch Reviewers.*

11
On with the dance! let joy be unconfin'd;
No sleep till morn, when Youth and Pleasure meet
To chase the glowing Hours with flying feet.
BYRON, *Childe Harold.* Canto iii, st. 22.

12
They are waiting on the shingle—will you come and join the dance?
Will you, won't you, will you, won't you, will you join the dance?
Will you, won't you, will you, won't you, won't you join the dance?
LEWIS CARROLL, *Alice in Wonderland: The Whiting and the Snail.*

13
Custom has made dancing sometimes necessary for a young man; therefore mind it while you learn it that you may learn to do it well, and not be ridiculous, though in a ridiculous act.
LORD CHESTERFIELD, *Letters,* 9 Oct., 1746.

14
They love dancing well that dance barefoot upon thorns.
THOMAS FULLER, *Gnomologia.* No. 4966.

15
To brisk notes in cadence beating,
Glance their many-twinkling feet.
THOMAS GRAY, *The Progress of Poesy,* l. 34.

Muse of the many-twinkling feet, whose charms
Are now extending up from legs to arms.
BYRON, *The Waltz,* l. 1.

16
And how I once went down the middle
With the man who shot Sandy McGee.
BRET HARTE, *Her Letter.*

17
When fools pipe, by authority he may dance.
JOHN HEYWOOD, *Proverbs.* Pt. ii, ch. 11.

I will not dance to every fool's pipe.
THOMAS FULLER, *Gnomologia.* No. 2644.

18
Light is the dance, and doubly sweet the lays,
When, for the dear delight, another pays.
HOMER, *Odyssey.* Bk. i, l. 159. (Pope, tr.)

Always those that dance must pay the music.
JOHN TAYLOR THE WATER-POET, *Taylor's Feast,* p. 98. (1638)

I warrant you, if he danced till doomsday, he thought I was to pay the piper.
CONGREVE, *Love for Love.* Act ii, sc. 5.

19
Our dancers ennoble what is coarse, but they degrade what is heroic. (Nos danseurs ennoblissent ce qui est grossier; mais ils dégradent ce qui est héroique.)
JOUBERT, *Pensées.* No. 283.

1
The Congress of Vienna does not march but it dances. (Le Congrès ne marche pas, mais il danse.)

The PRINCE DE LIGNE. The pun is untranslatable. In French, the verb *marcher* means not only to walk or march, but also to progress.

One of the Prince de Ligne's speeches that will last forever.

UNKNOWN, *Edinburgh Review*, July, 1890, p. 244.

2
All be not merry that men see dance.

JOHN LYDGATE, *Daunce of Machabree*, l. 392. (c. 1430)

Everyone is not happy who dances. (Chacun n'est pas aisé qui danse.)

UNKNOWN. A French proverb.

3
My men, like satyrs grazing on the lawn,
Shall with their goat feet dance the antic hay.

CHRISTOPHER MARLOWE, *Edward II*. Act i, 1.

4
We have piped unto you, and ye have not danced.

New Testament: Matthew, xi, 17; *Luke*, vii, 32.

5
Come, and trip it as ye go,
On the light fantastic toe.

MILTON, *L'Allegro*, l. 33.

Come, knit hands, and beat the ground
In a light fantastic round.

MILTON, *Comus*, l. 143.

6
Casey would waltz with a strawberry blonde,
And the band played on.

JOHN F. PALMER, *The Band Played On*. Popular song set to music by Charles B. Ward in 1894.

Waltz me around again, Willie, around and around and around,
The music is dreamy, it's peaches and creamy,
Oh! don't let my feet touch the ground!

WILL D. COBB, *Waltz Me Around Again, Willie*. (1906)

Waltz, you siren of melody, soft and sweet,
Waltz, I follow you ever with tireless feet;
Waltz, you lure me away to a dream of bliss,
Waltz, you're like the soft glory of love's first kiss.

A translation by Carolyn Wells of a waltz song from an opera by Franz Lehar. (1914)

7
Those move easiest who have learn'd to dance.

POPE, *Essay on Criticism*. Pt. ii, l. 163; *Imitations of Horace: Epistles*. Bk. ii, epis. 2, l. 178.

Not to go back, is somewhat to advance,
And men must walk, at least, before they dance.

POPE, *Imitations of Horace: Epistles*. Bk. i, epis. 1, l. 53.

8
He, perfect dancer, climbs the rope,
And balances your fear and hope.

MATTHEW PRIOR, *Alma*. Canto ii, l. 9.

9
He dances well to whom Fortune pipes.

JOHN RAY, *English Proverbs*.

10
They have measured many a mile,
To tread a measure with you on this grass.

SHAKESPEARE, *Love's Labour's Lost*. Act v, sc. 2, l. 186.

11
For you and I are past our dancing days.

SHAKESPEARE, *Romeo and Juliet*. Act i, sc. 5, l. 33. (1592)

My dancing days are done.

BEAUMONT AND FLETCHER, *Scornful Lady*. Act v, sc. 3.

My dancing days are past.

MASSINGER, *The Picture*. Act ii, sc. 2.

I doubt her dancing days are over.

SWIFT, *Polite Conversation*. Dial. i.

12
While his off-heel, insidiously aside,
Provokes the caper which he seems to chide.

R. B. SHERIDAN, *Pizarro: Prologue*.

Inconsolable to the minuet in Ariadne.

SHERIDAN, *The Critic*. Act ii, sc. 2.

13
We are dancing on a volcano. (Nous dansons sur un volcan.)

M. LE COMTE DE SALVANDY, at a fête given to the King of Naples before the revolution of 1830.

14
Dance light, for my heart it lies under your feet, love.

JOHN FRANCIS WALLER, *Kitty Neil*.

15
Waltzes, polkas, lancers, gallops, glides;
Portland fancy, quadrilles, reels and slides!
High-lows, di-dos, how we danced them all!
I'll never forget that time, you may bet,
At the party at Odd Fellows' Hall

JACOB WENDELL, JR., *The Party at Odd Fellows' Hall*. Interesting as an enumeration of the dances popular in 1890, when the song was written.

16
Jack shall pipe, and Jill shall dance.

GEORGE WITHER, *Poem on Christmas*.

17
This dance of death which sounds so musically
Was sure intended for the corpse de ballet.

UNKNOWN, *On the Danse Macabre of Saint-Saëns*.

III—Dancing: Its Beauty

18
And then he danced,—all foreigners excel
The serious Angles in the eloquence
Of pantomime;—he danced, I say, right well,
With emphasis, and also with good sense—
A thing in footing indispensable:
He danced without theatrical pretence,
Not like a ballet-master in the van
Of his drill'd nymphs, but like a gentleman.

BYRON, *Don Juan*. Canto xiv, st. 38.

1
Merrily, merrily whirled the wheels of the dizzying dances
Under the orchard-trees and down the path to the meadows.
LONGFELLOW, *Evangeline*. Pt. i, sec. 4.

Meanwhile there is dancing in yonder green bower.
OWEN MEREDITH, *Midges*.

2
Dear creature!—you'd swear
When her delicate feet in the dance twinkle round,
That her steps are of light, that her home is the air,
And she only *par complaisance* touches the ground.
THOMAS MOORE, *Fudge Family in Paris*. Letter v, l. 50.

I saw her at the county ball;
There, when the sounds of flute and fiddle
Gave signal sweet in that old hall
Of hands across and down the middle,
Hers was the subtlest spell by far
Of all that sets young hearts romancing:
She was our queen, our rose, our star;
And then she danced—Oh, Heaven! her dancing!
W. M. PRAED, *The Belle of the Ball*.

3
To many a youth and many a maid,
Dancing in the chequer'd shade.
MILTON, *L'Allegro*, l. 95.

Anon they move
In perfect phalanx, to the Dorian mood
Of flutes and soft recorders.
MILTON, *Paradise Lost*. Bk. i, l. 549.

4
Come unto these yellow sands,
And then take hands:
Courtsied when you have, and kiss'd
The wild waves whist.
Foot it featly here and there;
And, sweet sprites, the burthen bear.
SHAKESPEARE, *The Tempest*. Act i, sc. 2, l. 376.

5
When you do dance, I wish you
A wave o' the sea, that you might ever do
Nothing but that.
SHAKESPEARE, *The Winter's Tale*. Act iv, sc. 4, l. 140.

6
But O! she dances such a way,
No sun upon an Easter day
Is half so fine a sight.
SIR JOHN SUCKLING, *Ballad Upon a Wedding*. St. 8. It was formerly a common belief that the sun danced on Easter Day.

7
And beautiful maidens moved down in the dance,
With the magic of motion and sunshine of glance.
WHITTIER, *Cities of the Plain*. St. 4.

IV—Dancing: Its Faults

8
And Clara dies that Claribel may dance.
ALFRED AUSTIN, *The Golden Age*.

9
How ill the motion to the music suits!
So Orpheus fiddled, and so danced the brutes.
EUSTACE BUDGELL, *On Bad Dancing to Good Music*.

10
Dancing? Oh, dreadful! How it was ever adopted in a civilized country I cannot find out; 'tis certainly a Barbarian exercise, and of savage origin.
FANNY BURNEY, *Cecilia*. Bk. iii, ch. 1.

11
Terpsichore! too long misdeem'd a maid—
Reproachful term bestow'd but to upbraid—
Henceforth in all the bronze of brightness shine,
The least a vestal of the virgin Nine.
BYRON, *The Waltz*, l. 3.

Endearing Waltz!—to thy more melting tune
Bow Irish jig and ancient rigadoon;
Scotch reels, avaunt! and country-dance, forego
Your future claims to each fantastic toe!
Waltz—Waltz alone—both legs and arms demands,
Liberal of feet and lavish of her hands;
Hands which may freely range in public sight
Where ne'er before—but—pray "put out the light."
BYRON, *The Waltz*, l. 109.

12
The rout is Folly's circle, which she draws
With magic wand. So potent is the spell,
That none, decoy'd into that fatal ring,
Unless by Heaven's peculiar grace, escape.
There we grow early gray, but never wise.
COWPER, *The Task*. Bk. ii, l. 629.

When an old man dances,
His locks with age are gray,
But he's a child in mind.
ANACREON, *Odes*. No. xxxix, l. 3.

See also AGE: ITS COMPENSATIONS.

13
The better, the worse.
DIOGENES, of a young woman who danced daintily and was much commended. (BACON, *Apothegms*. No. 266.)

She could dance more skilfully than an honest woman need. (Saltare elegantius, quam necesse est probæ.)
SALLUST, *Catiline*. Ch. 25, sec. 2.

14
What! the girl I adore by another embraced?
What! the balm of her breath shall another man taste?
What! pressed in the dance by another man's knee?
What! panting recline on another than me?
Sir, she's yours; you have pressed from the grape its fine blue,
From the rosebud you've shaken the tremulous dew;

What you've touched you may take. Pretty waltzer—adieu!

SIR HENRY ENGLEFIELD, *The Waltz*.

1
At their speed behold advancing
Modern men and women dancing;
Step and dress alike express
Above, below from heel to toe,
Male and female awkwardness.

CATHERINE FANSHAWE, *The Abrogation of the Birth-Night Ball*.

2
'Twas surely the devil that taught women to dance.

THOMAS FULLER, *Gnomologia*. No. 5319.

3
In dance the hand hath liberty to touch,
The eye to gaze, the arm for to embrace.

GEORGE GASCOIGNE, *The Grief of Joy*. (1575)

Hot from the hands promiscuously applied,
Round the slight waist, or down the glowing side.

BYRON, *The Waltz*, l. 234.

4
The greater the fool the better the dancer.

THEODORE EDWARD HOOK, *Epigram*. (BARHAM, *Life and Reminiscences*, p. 91.)

5
He who esteems the Virginia reel
A bait to draw saints from their spiritual weal,
And regards the quadrille as a far greater knavery
Than crushing his African children with slavery,
Since all who take part in a waltz or cotillon
Are mounted for hell on the devil's own pillion,
Who, as every true orthodox Christian well knows,
Approaches the heart through the door of the toes.

J. R. LOWELL, *A Fable for Critics*, l. 495.

6
Fat wet bodies go waddling by,
Girdled with satin, though God knows why;
Gripped by satyrs in white and black,
With a fat wet hand on the fat wet back.

ALFRED NOYES, *A Victory Dance*.

7
Once on a time, the wight Stupidity
For his throne trembled,
When he discovered in the brains of men
Something like thoughts assembled. . . .
At last he hit upon a way
For putting to rout, And driving out
From our dull clay
These same intruders new—
This Sense, these Thoughts, these Speculative ills—
What could he do? He introduced quadrilles.

JOHN RUSKIN, *The Invention of Quadrilles*.

8
To sing well and dance well are accomplishments which advance one very little in the world. (Qui bien chante et bien danse fait un métier qui peu avance.)

ROUSSEAU, *Confessions*. Ch. 5.

9
He capers nimbly in a lady's chamber
To the lascivious pleasing of a lute.

SHAKESPEARE, *Richard III*. Act i, sc. 1, l. 12.

10
[The] play of limbs succeeds the play of wit.

HORACE AND JAMES SMITH, *Cui Bono*.

DANDELION

11
A dandelion in his verse,
Like the first gold in childhood's purse.

ANNIE RANKIN ANNAN, *Dandelion*.

12
Those golden kisses all over the cheeks of the meadow, queerly called dandelions.

HENRY WARD BEECHER, *Star Papers: A Discourse of Flowers*.

13
Upon a showery night and still,
Without a sound of warning,
A trooper band surprised the hill,
And held it in the morning.
We were not waked by bugle notes,
No cheer our dreams invaded,
And yet at dawn their yellow coats
On the green slopes paraded.

HELEN GRAY CONE, *The Dandelions*.

14
Young Dandelion on a hedge-side,
Said young Dandelion, who'll be my bride?
Said young Dandelion, with a sweet air,
I have my eye on Miss Daisy fair.

DINAH M. M. CRAIK, *Young Dandelion*.

15
Star-disked dandelions, just as we see them lying in the grass, like sparks that have leaped from the kindling sun of summer.

O. W. HOLMES, *The Professor at the Breakfast-Table*. Ch. 10.

16
Dear common flower, that grow'st beside the way,
Fringing the dusty road with harmless gold,
First pledge of blithesome May,
Which children pluck, and, full of pride, uphold,
High-hearted buccaneers, o'erjoyed that they
An Eldorado in the grass have found,
Which not the rich earth's ample round
May match in wealth, thou art more dear to me
Than all the prouder summer-blooms may be.

J. R. LOWELL, *To the Dandelion*.

How like a prodigal doth nature seem,
When thou, for all thy gold, so common art!
Thou teachest me to deem
More sacredly of every human heart,
Since each reflects in joy its scanty gleam
Of heaven, and could some wondrous secret show,

Did we but pay the love we owe,
And with a child's undoubting wisdom look
On all these living pages of God's book.
J. R. LOWELL, *To the Dandelion.*

1
The robe of Spring was incomplete at dawn;
The needles of the Sun had done their best.
Gold buttons now are sewn upon the lawn—
Final touch to a green vest.
KENNETH W. PORTER, *Dandelions.*

2
With locks of gold today;
Tomorrow silver gray;
Then blossom-bald. Behold,
O man, thy fortune told!
JOHN B. TABB, *The Dandelion.*

DANDY, see Fop

DANGER

3
If the danger seems slight, then truly it is not slight. (Non jam leve est periculum, si leve videatur.)
FRANCIS BACON, *De Augmentis Scientiarum: Principiis Obstare.*

4
Dangers bring fears, and fears more dangers bring.
RICHARD BAXTER, *Love Breathing Thanks.*

5
Where Mars might quake to tread.
BYRON, *Childe Harold.* Canto i, st. 54.

6
I have not quailed to danger's brow
When high and happy—need I now?
BYRON, *The Giaour,* l. 1027.

For danger levels man and brute,
And all are fellows in their need.
BYRON, *Mazeppa.* St. 3.

7
Danger, the spur of all great minds.
CHAPMAN, *Bussy d'Ambois.* Act v, sc. 1.

8
Without danger the game grows cold. (Sine periculo friget lusus.)
CHAPMAN, *All Fools.* Act iii. Quoted. *See* GAME.

9
Where one danger's near,
The more remote, tho' greater, disappear.
So, from the hawk, birds to man's succour flee,
So from fir'd ships, man leaps into the sea.
ABRAHAM COWLEY, *Davideis.* Bk. iii, l. 31.

9a
He that loveth danger shall perish therein. (Qui amat periculum, in illo peribit.)
Vulgate: Ecclesiastici, ii, 27; *Apocrypha: Ecclesiasticus,* iii, 26.

10
As soon as there is life there is danger.
EMERSON, *Uncollected Lectures: Public and Private Education.*

11
Great things through greatest hazards are attained
And then they shine.
JOHN FLETCHER, *Loyal Subject.* Act i, sc. 5.

12
Dangers foreseen are the sooner prevented.
RICHARD FRANCK, *Northern Memoirs,* p. 95. (1658)

He that fears danger in time seldom feels it.
THOMAS FULLER, *Gnomologia.* No. 2099.

Danger is next neighbour to security.
THOMAS FULLER, *Gnomologia.* No. 1233.

13
He that bringeth himself into needless dangers, dieth the devil's martyr.
THOMAS FULLER, *Holy War.* Bk. ii, ch. 29.

14
All on a razor's edge it stands, either woeful ruin or life. (Δὴ πάντεσσιν ἐπὶ ξυροῦ ἵσταται ἀκμῆς ἢ μάλα λυγρος ὄλεθρος ἠὲ βιῶναι.)
HOMER, *Iliad.* Bk. x, l. 173. THEOCRITUS, *Idylls.* No. xxii, l. 6.

Ye see our danger on the utmost edge
Of hazard, which admits no long debate.
MILTON, *Paradise Regained.* Bk. i, l. 94.

Young man, you are standing on the brink of an abscess.
ANDREW FREEDMAN, owner of the New York Giants, in 1898, to Charley Dryden, a sports writer, who had offended him. (STANLEY WALKER, *City Editor,* p. 118.)

15
Sweet is danger. (Dulce periculum est.)
HORACE, *Odes.* Bk. iii, ode 25, l. 18.

Danger and delight grow on one stalk.
JOHN LYLY, *Euphues,* p. 226. (1580)

Everything is sweetened by risk.
ALEXANDER SMITH, *Dreamthorp: On Death and the Fear of Dying.*

16
Danger well past remembered works delight.
HENRY HOWARD, *Bonum est Mihi Quod Humilliasti Me.*

So—now, the danger dared at last,
Look back, and smile at perils past!
SCOTT, *The Bridal of Triermain: Introduction.* St. 2.

See also under REMEMBRANCE.

17
The mere apprehension of a coming peril has put many into a situation of the utmost danger. (Multos in summa pericula misit Venturi timor ipse mali.)
LUCAN, *De Bello Civili.* Bk. vii, l. 104.

He who sees danger perishes in it.
CERVANTES, *Don Quixote.* Pt. i, ch. 20.

18
Danger will wink on opportunity.
MILTON, *Comus,* l. 401.

19
Danger comes the sooner when despised. (Citius venit periculum, cum contemnitur.)
PUBLILIUS SYRUS, *Sententiæ.* No. 104.

Dangers by being despised grow great.
EDMUND BURKE, *Speech,* House of Commons, 11 May, 1792.

20
He who dares dangers overcomes them before he incurs them. (Pericula qui audet, ante vincit quam accipit.)
PUBLILIUS SYRUS, *Sententiæ.* No. 538.

A danger is never overcome without danger. (Numquam periculum sine periculo vincitur.)
PUBLILIUS SYRUS, *Sententiæ*. No. 420.

Dangers are overcome by dangers.
THOMAS FULLER, *Gnomologia*. No. 1232.

Danger itself is the best remedy for danger.
GEORGE HERBERT, *Jacula Prudentum*. (1651)

Without danger we cannot get beyond danger.
GEORGE HERBERT, *Jacula Prudentum*.

1
Oft beneath the sweetest flow'rs
Is couch'd the deadliest danger.
THOMAS LOVE PEACOCK, *Maria's Return to Her Native Cottage*.

SNAKE IN THE GRASS, *see* SERPENT.

2
The danger past and God forgotten.
JOHN RAY, *English Proverbs*, 6.

THE DEVIL WAS SICK, *see* DEVIL: ILL AND WELL.

3
Constant exposure to dangers will breed contempt for them. (Contemptum periculorum assiduitas periclitandi dabit.)
SENECA, *De Providentia*. Sec. iv.

4
Blind panic is incapable of providing even for its own safety, for it does not avoid danger, but runs away. Yet we are more exposed to danger when we turn our backs.
SENECA, *Epistulæ ad Lucilium*. Epis. civ, sec. 10.
See also under DISCRETION.

5
No one can with safety expose himself often to dange.. The man who has often escaped is caught at last.
SENECA, *Hercules Furens*, l. 326.

The danger that is nearest we least dread. (Levius solet timere, qui propius timet.)
SENECA, *Troades*, l. 515.

6
There is no person who is not dangerous for someone. (Il n'y a personne qui ne soit dangereux pour quelqu'un.)
MADAME DE SÉVIGNÉ, *Letters*.

For, though I am not splenitive and rash,
Yet have I something in me dangerous.
SHAKESPEARE, *Hamlet*. Act v, sc. 1, l. 284.

7
Send danger from the east unto the west,
So honour cross it from the north to south.
SHAKESPEARE, *I Henry IV*. Act i, sc. 3, l. 195.

Danger deviseth shifts; wit waits on fear.
SHAKESPEARE, *Venus and Adonis*, l. 690.

8
It is no jesting with edge tools.
UNKNOWN, *True Tragedy of Richard III*. (1594)

There is no jesting with edge tools.
BEAUMONT AND FLETCHER, *The Little French Lawyer*. Act ii, sc. 4.

All tools are in one sense edge-tools, and are dangerous.
EMERSON, *Society and Solitude: Works and Days*.

II—Danger: Scylla and Charybdis

9
Scylla guards the right side; insatiate Charybdis the left. (Dextrum Scylla latus, lævum implacata Charybdis.)
VERGIL, *Æneid*. Bk. iii, l. 420.

10
Thou wilt fall upon Scylla in seeking to shun Charybdis. (Incidis in Scyllam cupiens vitare Charybdis.)
PHILIPPE GAULTIER, *Alexandreis*. Bk. v, l. 301. (c. 1300) Alluding to the Homeric fable of Scylla and Charybdis, the first a rock, the second a whirlpool, in the straits of Messina.

When I shun Scylla, your father, I fall in Charybdis, your mother.
SHAKESPEARE, *Merchant of Venice*, iii, 5, 18.

11
In front a precipice, behind wolves. (À fronte præcipitium, à tergo lupi.)
ERASMUS, *Adagia*. Chil. iii, cent. iv, No. 94.

Between the wolf and the dog. (Hac urget lupus, hac canis, aiunt.)
HORACE, *Satires*. Bk. ii, sat. ii, l. 64.

Between altar and axe. (Inter sacrum saxumque.)
PLAUTUS, *Captivi*, l. 617. (Act iii, sc. 4.)

12
Thou'ldst shun a bear;
But if thy flight lay toward the raging sea,
Thou'ldst meet the bear i' the mouth.
SHAKESPEARE, *King Lear*. Act iii, sc. 4, l. 9.

DANTE

13
And Dante stern
And sweet, whose spirit was an urn
For wine and milk poured out in turn.
E. B. BROWNING, *A Vision of Poets*, l. 352.

14
Oh their Dante of the dread Inferno!
ROBERT BROWNING, *One Word More*. St. 19.

15
Ungrateful Florence! Dante sleeps afar,
Like Scipio, buried by the upbraiding shore.
BYRON, *Childe Harold*. Canto iv, st. 57.

16
Dante dared to write his autobiography in colossal cipher, or into universality.
EMERSON, *Essays, Second Series: The Poet*.

Dante's imagination is the nearest to hands and feet that we have seen. He clasps the thought as if it were a tree or a stone, and describes as mathematically.
EMERSON, *Essays: Natural History of Intellect*.

17
Thy sacred song is like the trump of doom;
Yet in thy heart what human sympathies,
What soft compassion glows, as in the skies
The tender stars their clouded lamps relume!
LONGFELLOW, *Dante*.

This man descended to the doomed and dead
For our instruction; then to God ascended;
Heaven opened wide to him its portals splendid,
Who from his country's, closed against him, fled.
LONGFELLOW, *Dante*.

1
Yet there is something round thy lips
That prophesies the coming doom,
The soft, gray herald-shadow ere the eclipse
Notches the perfect disk with gloom.
J. R. LOWELL, *On a Portrait of Dante.*

2
He used Rome's harlot for his mirth;
Plucked bare hypocrisy and crime;
But valiant souls of knightly worth
Transmitted to the rolls of Time.
T. W. PARSONS, *On a Bust of Dante.*

No dream his life was—but a fight!
Could any Beatrice see
A lover in that anchorite?
T. W. PARSONS, *On a Bust of Dante.*

3
Nay, then, what flames are these that leap
and swell
As 'twere to show, where earth's foundations
crack,
The secrets of the sepulchres of hell
On Dante's track?
A. C. SWINBURNE, *In Guernsey.* Pt. iv, st. 3.

DARING, see Boldness

DARKNESS

See also Night

4
All colours will agree in the dark.
FRANCIS BACON, *Essays: Of Unity in Religion.*

In the dark all cats are gray.
CERVANTES, *Don Quixote.* Pt. ii, ch. 33.

In darkness there is no choice.
J. C. AND A. W. HARE, *Guesses at Truth.*

By night are blemishes hid, and every fault forgiven. (Nocte latent mendæ, vitioque ignoscitur omni.)
OVID, *Ars Amatoria.* Bk. i, l. 249.

5
Ask what is darkness of the night.
P. J. BAILEY, *Festus: A Party.*

Defining night by darkness.
P. J. BAILEY, *Festus: Water and Wood.*

6
Dark as pitch.
BUNYAN, *Pilgrim's Progress.* Pt. i; JOHN RAY, *English Proverbs;* JOHN GAY, *Shepherd's Week: Wednesday.*

Got home well by coach, though as dark as pitch.
PEPYS, *Diary,* 18 Jan., 1666.

7
Darkness is more productive of sublime ideas than light.
EDMUND BURKE, *On the Sublime and Beautiful.* Pt. ii, sec. 14.

8
Cabin'd, cribb'd, confined
And bred in darkness.
BYRON, *Childe Harold.* Canto iv, st. 127.

The winds were wither'd in the stagnant air,
And the clouds perish'd; Darkness had no need
Of aid from them—She was the Universe.
BYRON, *Darkness,* l. 80.

9
"Timon—for thou art no more—which is most hateful to thee, darkness or light?" "Darkness; there is more of it in Hades."
CALLIMACHUS, *Epigram.* (*Greek Anthology.* Bk. vii, No. 317.)

Men loved darkness rather than light, because their deeds were evil.
New Testament: John, iii, 19.

10
The sun's rim dips; the stars rush out:
At one stride comes the dark.
S. T. COLERIDGE, *The Ancient Mariner.* Pt. iii.

11
Darkness our guide, Despair our leader was.
SIR JOHN DENHAM, *Essay: Vergil's Æneid.*

12
Come, blessed Darkness, come and bring thy
balm
For eyes grown weary of the garish day!
Come with thy soft, slow steps, thy garments gray,
Thy veiling shadows, bearing in thy palm
The poppy-seeds of slumber, deep and calm.
JULIA C. R. DORR, *Darkness.*

13
O radiant Dark! O darkly fostered ray!
Thou hast a joy too deep for shallow Day.
GEORGE ELIOT, *The Spanish Gypsy.* Bk. i.

14
Darkness which may be felt.
Old Testament: Exodus, x, 21.

15
Auld Daddy Darkness creeps frae his hole,
Black as a blackamoor, blin' as a mole:
Stir the fire till it lowes, let the bairnie sit,
Auld Daddy Darkness is no wantit yit.
JAMES FERGUSON, *Auld Daddy Darkness.*

16
Darkness of slumber and death, forever sinking and sinking.
LONGFELLOW, *Evangeline.* Pt. ii, sec. 5, l. 108.

17
Lo! darkness bends down like a mother of
grief
On the limitless plain, and the fall of her hair
It has mantled a world.
JOAQUIN MILLER, *From Sea to Sea.* St. 4.

18
A dungeon horrible on all sides round
As one great furnace flamed, yet from these
flames
No light but rather darkness visible.
MILTON, *Paradise Lost.* Bk. i, l. 61.

He sees enough who doth his darkness see.
LORD HERBERT OF CHERBURY, *To His Mistress for Her True Picture.*

Of darkness visible so much be lent.
POPE, *The Dunciad.* Bk. iv, l. 3.

19
And all around was darkness like a wall.
WILLIAM MORRIS, *Life and Death of Jason.* Bk. vii, l. 157.

1
Day is ended, Darkness shrouds
The shoreless seas and lowering clouds.
T. L. PEACOCK, *Rhododaphne*. Canto v, l. 264.

Darkness there, and nothing more.
EDGAR ALLAN POE, *The Raven*. St. 4.

2
He that gropes in the dark finds that he would not.
JOHN RAY, *English Proverbs*.

He that runs in the dark may well stumble.
JOHN RAY, *English Proverbs*.

It is sure to be dark if you shut your eyes.
JOHN RAY, *English Proverbs*.

3
Dark as a wolf's mouth.
SCOTT, *St. Ronan's Well*. Ch. 36.

Dark as the devil's mouth.
SCOTT, *Woodstock*. Ch. 12.

4
It was so dark, Hal, that thou couldst not see thy hand.
SHAKESPEARE, *I Henry IV*. Act ii, sc. 4, l. 247.

With hue like that when some great painter dips
His pencil in the gloom of earthquake and eclipse.
SHELLEY, *The Revolt of Islam*. Canto v, st. 23.

5
And out of darkness came the hands
That reach thro' nature, moulding men.
TENNYSON, *In Memoriam*. Sec. cxxiv.

6
I'm afraid to go home in the dark.
WILLIAMS-VAN ALSTYNE. Title and refrain of popular song. (1907) Parodied by O. Henry as he was dying. *See* p. 415:11.

DAUGHTER

7
Thy daughters bright thy walks adorn,
Gay as the gilded summer sky,
Sweet as the dewy, milk-white thorn,
Dear as the raptured thrill of joy.
BURNS, *Address to Edinburgh*. St. 4.

A lady with her daughters or her nieces
Shines like a guinea and seven-shilling pieces.
BYRON, *Don Juan*. Canto iii, st. 60.

8
You appear to me so superior, so elevated above other men; I contemplate you with such strange mixture of humility, admiration, reverence, love and pride, that very little superstition would be necessary to make me worship you as a superior being . . . I had rather not live than not be the daughter of such a man.
THEODOSIA BURR, *Letter to her Father*. (PARTON, *Life and Times of Aaron Burr*, ii, 188.)

9
Is thy face like thy mother's, my fair child,
Ada, sole daughter of my house and heart?
BYRON, *Childe Harold*. Canto iii, st. 1.

10
A country squire, with . . . a wife and two daughters . . . Oh God! two such unlicked cubs.
CONGREVE, *The Old Batchelor*. Act iv, sc. 8.
See also under BEAR.

11
An undutiful Daughter will prove an unmanageable Wife.
BENJAMIN FRANKLIN, *Poor Richard*, 1752.

12
Daughters and dead fish are no keeping wares.
THOMAS FULLER, *Gnomologia*. No. 1235.

13
I make presents to the mother, but think of the daughter. (Der Mutter schenk' ich, Die Tochter denk' ich.)
GOETHE, *Sprüche in Reimen*. Pt. iii.

He that would the daughter win,
Must with the mother first begin.
JOHN RAY, *English Proverbs*, p. 49.

14
Home-made by the homely daughters.
THOMAS HOOD, *Miss Kilmansegg*, l. 2043.

15
O daughter, lovelier than thy lovely mother. (O matre pulchra filia pulchrior.)
HORACE, *Odes*. Bk. i, ode 16, l. 1.

16
Then farewell, my dear; my loved daughter, adieu;
The last pang of life is in parting from you.
THOMAS JEFFERSON, *A Deathbed Advice from T. J. to M. R.*

17
You teach your daughters the diameters of the planets, and wonder what you have done that they do not delight in your company.
SAMUEL JOHNSON, *Miscellanies*. Vol. i, p. 160.

O, I see thee old and formal, fitted to thy petty part,
With a little hoard of maxims preaching down a daughter's heart!
TENNYSON, *Locksley Hall*. St. 47.

18
If I had a daughter, I would bring her up as a clinging vine.
MARY LATHROP, first woman member of the American Bar Association.

19
Filled her with thee, a daughter fair,
So buxom, blithe, and debonair.
MILTON, *L'Allegro*, l. 23.

20
Now such an one for daughter Creon had
As maketh wise men fools and young men mad.
WILLIAM MORRIS, *Life and Death of Jason*. Bk. xvii, l. 199.

21
Many daughters have done virtuously, but thou excellest them all.
Old Testament: Proverbs, xxxi, 29.

22
Twa daughters and a back door are three stark thieves.
JOHN RAY, *Proverbs: Scottish*.

1
Still harping on my daughter.
SHAKESPEARE, *Hamlet*. Act ii, sc. 2, l. 188.

My daughter! O my ducats! O my daughter!
Fled with a Christian! O my Christian ducats!
SHAKESPEARE, *Merchant of Venice*. Act ii, sc. 8, l. 15.

2
It was a lordling's daughter, the fairest one of three,
That liked of her master as well as well might be.
SHAKESPEARE [?], *Passionate Pilgrim*, l. 211.

3
I am all the daughters of my father's house,
And all the brothers too.
SHAKESPEARE, *Twelfth Night*. Act ii, sc. 4, l. 123.

A daughter and a goodly babe,
Lusty and like to live: the queen receives
Much comfort in 't.
SHAKESPEARE, *Winter's Tale*. Act ii, sc. 2, l. 26.

4
If a daughter you have, she's the plague of your life,
No peace shall you know, though you've buried your wife!
At twenty she mocks at the duty you taught her—
Oh, what a plague is an obstinate daughter!
SHERIDAN, *The Duenna*. Act i, sc. 3.

5
The mother says to her daughter: Daughter, bid thy daughter, to tell her daughter, that her daughter's daughter is crying.
(Mater ait natæ, die natæ filia natum
Ut moneat natæ, plangere filiolam.)
UNKNOWN, *Distich on a Lady Who Saw Her Descendants to the Sixth Generation*. (GRESWELL, *Account of Runcorn*, p. 34.)

The mother said to her daughter, "Daughter, bid thy daughter tell her daughter that her daughter's daughter hath a daughter."
GEORGE HAKEWILL, *Apologie of the Power and Providence of God*. Bk. iii, ch. 5, sec. 9.

6
Have you not heard these many years ago,
Jeptha was judge of Israel?
He had one only daughter and no mo,
The which he loved passing well.
UNKNOWN, *Jeptha Judge of Israel*. (PERCY, *Reliques*. Ser. i, bk. ii, No. 3.)

Hamlet: O Jephthah, judge of Israel, what a treasure hadst thou!
Polonius: What a treasure had he, my lord?
Hamlet: Why,
"One fair daughter, and no more,
The which he loved passing well."
SHAKESPEARE, *Hamlet*. Act ii, sc. 2, l. 422.

DAVIS, JEFFERSON

7
If I could take one wing and Lee the other, I think we could between us wrest a victory from those people.
JEFFERSON DAVIS, *Memoirs*. Vol. ii, p. 392.

8
Calm martyr of a noble cause,
Upon thy form in vain
The Dungeon clanks its cankered jaws,
And clasps its cankered chain;
For thy free spirit walks abroad,
And every pulse is stirred
With the old deathless glory thrill,
Whene'er thy name is heard.
W. M. BELL, *Jefferson Davis*.

9
He has made an army, has made a navy, and, more than that, has made a nation.
GLADSTONE, *Speech*, at Newcastle, 1862, referring to Jefferson Davis.

10
We'll hang Jeff Davis to a sour apple tree,
As we go marching on.
CHARLES SPRAGUE HALL, *John Brown's Body*.

11
Et arma cedunt toga,
Said a Roman of renown:
When the din of war is over,
Arms yield unto the gown.

But this motto Jeff reverses:
For, arrayed in female charms,
When the din of war is over,
In his gown he yields to arms.
CHARLES G. HALPINE, *An Old Maxim Reversed*. Referring to the report that Davis had been captured in a woman's clothes.

12
And he . . . now slinks through dark Oblivion's gate,
With this his epitaph: When others quailed,
He staked his all upon one cast of fate
And lost—and lived to know that he had failed!
HARRY THURSTON PECK, *Jefferson Davis*.

DAWN

See also Day: Its Beginning; Morning; Sunrise

13
Now had Aurora displayed her mantle over the blushing skies, and dark night withdrawn her sable veil.
CERVANTES, *Don Quixote*. Pt. i, ch. 6.

Aurora had but newly chased the night,
And purpled o'er the sky with blushing light.
DRYDEN, *Palamon and Arcite*. Bk. i, l. 186.

Aurora [Dawn] a friend to the Muses. (Aurora Musis amica.)
ERASMUS, *De Ratione Studii; Letter to Christian Northoff*, 1497.

But when Aurora, daughter of the dawn,
With rosy lustre purpled o'er the lawn.
HOMER, *Odyssey*. Bk. iii, l. 621. (Pope, tr.)

You cannot shut the windows of the sky
Through which Aurora shows her brightening face.
THOMSON, *Castle of Indolence*. Canto ii, st. 3.

14
When God sends the dawn, he sends it for all.
CERVANTES, *Don Quixote*. Pt. ii, ch. 49.

1
Slow buds the pink dawn like a rose
  From out night's gray and cloudy sheath;
Softly and still it grows and grows,
  Petal by petal, leaf by leaf.
SUSAN COOLIDGE, *The Morning Comes Before the Sun.*

2
Kathleen mavourneen! the grey dawn is breaking,
The horn of the hunter is heard on the hill.
LOUISA MACARTNEY CRAWFORD, *Kathleen Mavourneen.*

3
It is always darkest just before the day dawneth.
THOMAS FULLER, *Pisgah Sight*. Bk. ii, ch. 11. (1650)

4
The dawn is lonely for the sun,
  And chill and drear;
The one lone star is pale and wan,
  As one in fear.
RICHARD HOVEY, *Chanson de Rosemonde.*

5
Oh, the road to Mandalay, where the flyin'-fishes play,
An' the dawn comes up like thunder outer China crost the Bay!
RUDYARD KIPLING, *Mandalay.*

East, oh, east of Himalay
  Dwell the nations underground,
Hiding from the shock of day,
  For the sun's uprising sound. . . .
So fearfully the sun doth sound,
  Clanging up beyond Cathay;
For the great earthquaking sunrise
  Rolling up beyond Cathay.
FRANCIS THOMPSON, *The Mistress of Vision.*

6
Oft when the white, still dawn
Lifted the skies and pushed the hills apart,
I've felt it like a glory in my heart.
EDWIN MARKHAM, *Joy of the Morning.*

7
The wind that sighs before the dawn
  Chases the gloom of night,
The curtains of the East are drawn,
  And suddenly—'t is light.
LEWIS MORRIS, *Le Vent de l'Esprit.*

8
God, with sweet strength, with terror and with trancing,
  Spake in the purple mystery of dawn.
F. W. H. MYERS, *St. Paul.*

9
Clothing the palpable and familiar
With golden exhalations of the dawn.
SCHILLER, *Wallenstein's Tod*. Act i, sc. 1. (Coleridge, tr.)

10
Out of the scabbard of the night,
  By God's hand drawn,
Flashes his shining sword of light,
  And lo,—the dawn!
FRANK DEMPSTER SHERMAN, *Dawn.*

11
What humbugs we are, who pretend to live for Beauty, and never see the Dawn!
LOGAN PEARSALL SMITH, *Afterthoughts.*

12
Hail, gentle Dawn! mild blushing goddess, hail!
Rejoic'd I see thy purple mantle spread
O'er half the skies, gems pave thy radiant way,
And orient pearls from ev'ry shrub depend.
WILLIAM SOMERVILLE, *The Chase*. Bk. ii, l. 79.

13
Of all the fonts from which man's heart has drawn
  Some essence of the majesty of earth, . . .
I reckon first the sunset and the dawn.
GEORGE STERLING, *The Guerdon of the Sun.*

14
Dawn sleeps on the shadowy hills,
The stars hold their breath counting the hours.
RABINDRANATH TAGORE, *The Gardener.*

15
Now the frosty stars are gone:
I have watched them one by one,
Fading on the shores of Dawn.
Round and full the glorious sun
Walks with level step the spray,
Through his vestibule of Day.
BAYARD TAYLOR, *Ariel in the Cloven Pine.*

16
Dawn, meanwhile, had restored her gentle light to weary men, recalling them to task and toil. (Aurora interea miseris mortalibus alman Extulerat lucem, referens opera atque labores.)
VERGIL, *Æneid*. Bk. xi, l. 182.

17
Day's sweetest moments are at dawn.
ELLA WHEELER WILCOX, *Dawn.*

18
When, in extravagant revel, the Dawn, a Bacchante upleaping,
Spills, on the tresses of Night, vintages golden and red.
WILLIAM WATSON, *Hymn to the Sea*. Pt. iii, l. 13.

19
And down the long and silent street,
The dawn with silver-sandalled feet,
Crept like a frightened girl.
OSCAR WILDE, *The Harlot's House*. St. 12.

DAY

See also Night and Day

I—Day: Its Beginning

See also Dawn, Morning, Sunrise

20
The dawn is over-cast, the morning low'rs,
And heavily in clouds brings on the day,
The great, th' important day, big with the fate
Of Cato and of Rome.
JOSEPH ADDISON. *Cato*. Act i, sc. 1, l. 1.

Big with the fate of Europe.
THOMAS TICKELL, *Ode on Earl Stanhope's Voyage to France*. St. 1.

1
Day is a snow-white Dove of heaven
That from the East glad message brings.
T. B. ALDRICH, *Day and Night*.

2
Yet, behind the night,
Waits for the great unborn, somewhere afar,
Some white tremendous daybreak.
RUPERT BROOKE, *Second Best*.

3
Day! Faster and more fast,
O'er night's brim, day boils at last.
ROBERT BROWNING, *Pippa Passes: Introduction*.

4
Day breaks not, it is my heart.
JOHN DONNE, *Daybreak*.

5
Oh, tenderly the haughty day
Fills his blue urn with fire.
EMERSON, *Ode*. Concord, 4 July, 1857.

6
Out of the shadows of night
The world rolls into light;
It is daybreak everywhere.
LONGFELLOW, *Bells of San Blas*.

7
This is another day! And flushed Hope walks
Adown the sunward slopes with golden shoon.
DON MARQUIS, *This is Another Day*.

8
Phosphor, bring back the day! why delay our delight?
Cæsar returns; O Phosphor, bring back the day!
(Phosphore, redde diem! quid gaudia nostra moraris?
Cæsar venturo; Phosphore, redde diem!)
MARTIAL, *Epigrams*. Bk. viii, ep. 21, l. 1. [Phosphor, the morning star.]

Sweet Phosphor, bring the day,
Whose conqu'ring ray
May chase these fogs; sweet Phosphor, bring the day! . . .

Sweet Phosphor, bring the day;
Light will repay
The wrongs of night: sweet Phosphor, bring the day!
FRANCIS QUARLES, *Emblems*. Bk. i, Emb. 14.

9
Hide me from day's garish eye.
MILTON, *Il Penseroso*, l. 141.

10
How troublesome is day!
It calls us from our sleep away;
It bids us from our pleasant dreams awake,
And sends us forth to keep or break
Our promises to pay.
How troublesome is day!
THOMAS LOVE PEACOCK, *Fly-by-Night*. St. 1.

11
The day begins to break, and night is fled,
Whose pitchy mantle over-veil'd the earth.
SHAKESPEARE, *I Henry VI*. Act ii, sc. 2, l. 1.

The sun is in the heaven, and the proud day,
Attended with the pleasures of the world,
Is all too wanton and too full of gauds
To give me audience.
SHAKESPEARE, *King John*. Act iii, sc. 3, l. 34.

12
The wolves have prey'd: and look, the gentle day,
Before the wheels of Phœbus, round about,
Dapples the drowsy east with spots of grey.
SHAKESPEARE, *Much Ado About Nothing*. Act v, sc. 3, l. 25.

Look, love, what envious streaks
Do lace the severing clouds in yonder east:
Night's candles are burnt out, and jocund day
Stands tip-toe on the misty mountain tops.
SHAKESPEARE, *Romeo and Juliet*. Act iii, sc. 5, l. 6.

The busy day,
Wak'd by the lark, hath rous'd the ribald crows,
And dreaming night will hide our joys no longer.
SHAKESPEARE, *Troilus and Cressida*. Act iv, sc. 2, l. 8.

13
Only that day dawns to which we are awake. There is more day to dawn. The sun is but a morning star.
H. D. THOREAU, *Walden*. Closing lines. Quoted as closing lines of H. M. Tomlinson's *All Our Yesterdays*.

II—Day: Its Employment

14
Think in the morning. Act in the noon. Eat in the evening. Sleep in the night.
WILLIAM BLAKE, *Proverbs of Hell*.

15
Oh Day, if I squander a wavelet of thee,
A mite of my twelve-hours' treasure,
The least of thy gazes or glances . . .
One of thy choices, or one of thy chances . . .
Then shame fall on Asolo, mischief on me!
ROBERT BROWNING, *Pippa Passes*, l. 13.

16
One day well spent is to be preferred to an eternity of error. (Unus dies bene . . . actus peccanti immortalitate anteponendus.)
CICERO, *Tusculanarum Disputationum*. Bk. v, ch. 2, sec. 5.

17
He is only rich who owns the day. There is no king, rich man, fairy, or demon who possesses such power as that. . . . The days are made on a loom whereof the warp and woof are past and future time.
EMERSON, *Society and Solitude: Works and Days*.

18
One day is equal to every day. (Unus dies par omni est.)
HERACLITUS, *Fragments*. No. 106. (SENECA, *Epistulæ ad Lucilium*. Epis. xii, sec. 7.)

1
One day, with life and heart,
Is more than time enough to find a world.
JAMES RUSSELL LOWELL, *Columbus*.

2
Each morning gives thee wings to flee from hell,
Each night a star to guide thy feet to heaven.
WALTER MALONE, *Opportunity*.

3
Make it short, for this is my busy day. (Hunc pudet, . . . quaque id promisit die.)
PLAUTUS, *Pseudolus*, l. 279. (Act i, sc. 3.)

This is my busy day.
EUGENE FIELD, *Notice*, above his desk in the Denver *Tribune* office, 1882.

4
No day without its line. (Nulla dies sine linea.)
PLINY THE ELDER, *Historia Naturalis*. Bk. xxxv, ch. 36, sec. 10. This is a condensation of Pliny's statement that "It was Apelles' constant habit never to allow a day to be so fully occupied that he had not time for the exercise of his art, if only to the extent of one stroke of the brush."

Add a line every hour, and between whiles add a line.
EMERSON, *Essays, Second Series: Experience*.

5
Each day is the scholar of yesterday. (Discipulus est prioris posterior dies.)
PUBLILIUS SYRUS, *Sententiæ*. No. 143.

But you with pleasure own your errors past,
And make each day a critique on the last.
POPE, *Essay on Criticism*. Pt. iii, l. 11.

6
Every day should be passed as if it were to be our last.
PUBLILIUS SYRUS, *Sententiæ*. No. 633.

Write it on your heart that every day is the best day in the year. No man has learned anything rightly until he knows that every day is Doomsday.
EMERSON, *Society and Solitude: Works and Days*.

Each present day thy last esteem.
THOMAS KEN, *Morning Hymn*.

7
Better the day, better the deed.
THOMAS MIDDLETON, *Michaelmas Terme*. Act iii, sc. 1. (1607)

The beter day, the better deed.
SAMUEL ROWLANDS, *Knave of Hearts*, l. 46. (1612); See also SWIFT, *Polite Conversation*, dial. i (1738); GARRICK, *May-Day*, sc. 2 (1775).

I think the better day the better deed.
CHIEF JUSTICE SIR JOHN HOLT, *Judgment*, in Sir W. Moore's case. (1703) 2 Raym. 1028.

The better day, the worse deed.
MATTHEW HENRY, *Commentaries: Genesis*, iii.

The better the day the better the deed.
DICKENS, *Edwin Drood*. Ch. 10. (1870)

8
Golden days, fruitful of golden deeds.
MILTON, *Paradise Lost*. Bk. iii, l. 337.

9
A day differs not a whit from eternity. (Nihil interesse inter diem et sæculum.)
SENECA, *Epistulæ ad Lucilium*. Epis. ci, sec. 9.

A day is a miniature eternity.
EMERSON, *Journals*. Vol. iv, p. 26.

10
And here have sat The livelong day.
SHAKESPEARE, *Julius Cæsar*. Act i, sc. 1, l. 46.

11
We should hold day with the Antipodes,
If you would walk in absence of the sun.
SHAKESPEARE, *Merchant of Venice*, v, 1, 127.

12
Friends, I have lost a day! (Amici, diem perdidi!)
EMPEROR TITUS VESPASIANUS, his customary self-reproach when a day passed without his benefiting some one. (SUETONIUS, *Lives of the Cæsars: Titus*. Ch. 8, sec. 1.)

Whatever is is right.—This world, 'tis true,
Was made for Cæsar—but for Titus too:
And which more blest? who chained his country, say,
Or he whose virtue sighed to lose a day?
POPE, *Essay on Man*. Epis. iv, l. 145.

"I've lost a day,"—the prince who nobly cried,
Had been an emperor without his crown.
YOUNG, *Night Thoughts*. Night ii, l. 99.

13
Think that day lost whose low descending sun
Views from thy hand no worthy action done.
UNKNOWN. The earliest known instance of the use of this couplet is in the autograph album of David Krieg, in the British Museum, where it appears in quotation marks, signed James Bobart, with the caption, "Virtus sui gloria," and dated 8 Dec., 1697.

Count that day lost whose low descending sun
Views from thy hand no worthy action done.
The more familiar version, as given in Staniford's *Art of Reading*, p. 27 (Boston, 1803).

14
The day is short and the work is long.
UNKNOWN, *Beryn*, l. 3631. (1400) *See under* ART.

III—Days: Happy

15
The day which she marks with a whiter stone. (Quem lapide illa, dies, candidiore notat.)
CATULLUS, *Odes*. Ode lxviii, l. 108. (148)

Let not a day so fair lack its white chalk-mark. (Cressa ne careat pulchra dies nota.)
HORACE, *Odes*. Bk. i, ode 36, l. 10.

O happy day, to be marked with the whitest stone! (O diem lætum notandumque mihi candidissimo calculo!)
PLINY THE YOUNGER, *Epistles*. Bk. vi, epis. 11.

Pericles separated his whole force into eight divisions, had them draw lots, and allowed the division which got the white bean to feast and take their ease, while the others did the fighting. And this is the reason, as they say, why those who have had a gay and festive time call it a "white day," from the white bean.
PLUTARCH, *Lives: Pericles*. Ch. 27, sec. 2.

O festival day . . . worthy to be marked with a stone as white as snow!
JOHN PALSGRAVE, *Acolastus,* K 1. (1540)

This happy day to be enrolled
In rubric letters and in gold.
APHRA BEHN, *The City Heiress.* Act v, sc. 3.

1
Into which list are they to go? Marked with chalk as sane, or with charcoal? (Quorsum abeant? Sani ut creta, an carbone notati?)
HORACE, *Satires.* Bk. ii, sat. 3, l. 246.

Are we to mark this day with a white or a black stone?
CERVANTES, *Don Quixote.* Pt. ii, ch. 10.

2
On a good day good words must be spoken. (Dicenda bona sunt bona verba die.)
OVID, *Fasti.* Bk. i, l. 72.

3
O, such a day,
So fought, so follow'd and so fairly won.
SHAKESPEARE, *II Henry IV.* Act i, sc. 1, l. 20.

'Tis a lucky day, boy, and we'll do good deeds on it.
SHAKESPEARE, *Winter's Tale.* Act iii, sc. 3, l. 142.

4
A day, long to be remembered! (O longum memoranda dies!)
STATIUS, *Sylvarum.* Bk. i, 13.

5
Happy days
Roll onward, leading up the golden year.
TENNYSON, *The Golden Year,* l. 40.

When I said to her,
"A day for gods to stoop," she answered, "Ay,
And men to soar."
TENNYSON, *The Lover's Tale,* l. 297.

6
The longed for day is at hand. (Exspectata dies aderat.)
VERGIL, *Æneid.* Bk. v, l. 104.

7
One of those heavenly days that cannot die.
WORDSWORTH, *Nutting,* l. 2.

The immortal spirit of one happy day.
WORDSWORTH, *Miscellaneous Sonnets.* No. iv.

IV—Days: Unhappy

8
The long days are no happier than the short ones.
P. J. BAILEY, *Festus: A Village Feast: Evening.*

9
The poorest day that passes over us is the conflux of two eternities; it is made up of currents that issue from the remotest Past, and flow onwards to the remotest Future.
CARLYLE, *Signs of the Times.*

Is not every meanest day the confluence of two eternities?
CARLYLE, *French Revolution.* Pt. i, bk. vi, ch. 1.

10
Days that need borrow
No part of their good morrow,
From a fore-spent night of sorrow.
RICHARD CRASHAW, *Wishes to His (Supposed) Mistress.* St. 26.

11
Dullest of dull-hued days.
THOMAS HARDY, *A Commonplace Day.*

12
Every man hath his ill day.
GEORGE HERBERT, *Jacula Prudentum.*

No day passeth without some grief.
JOHN RAY, *English Proverbs,* 6. (1670)

13
How short our happy days appear!
How long the sorrowful!
JEAN INGELOW, *The Mariner's Cave.* St. 38.

14
This has certainly been a perverse and adverse day! (Edepol ne hic dies pervorsus atque advorsus.)
PLAUTUS, *Menæchmi,* l. 899. (Act v, sc. 5.)

15
The next day is never so good as the day before.
PUBLILIUS SYRUS, *Sententiæ.* No. 815.

16
What hath this day deserv'd? what hath it done,
That it in golden letters should be set
Among the high tides in the calendar?
SHAKESPEARE, *King John.* Act iii, sc. 1, l. 84.

17
So foul and fair a day I have not seen.
SHAKESPEARE, *Macbeth.* Act i, sc. 3, l. 38.

Come what come may,
Time and the hour runs through the roughest day.
SHAKESPEARE, *Macbeth.* Act i, sc. 3, l. 146.

18
We have seen better days.
SHAKESPEARE, *Timon of Athens.* Act iv, sc. 2, l. 27.

19
I hate the day, because it lendeth light
To see all things, and not my love to see.
EDMUND SPENSER, *Daphnaïda,* l. 407.

20
But the tender grace of a day that is dead
Will never come back to me.
TENNYSON, *Break, Break, Break. See also under* PAST.

V—Days: Their Passage

See also under Time

21
My days are swifter than a weaver's shuttle.
Old Testament: Job, vii, 6.

My days are swifter than a post.
Old Testament: Job, ix, 25.

22
What one day gives, another takes.
GEORGE HERBERT, *Jacula Prudentum.*

23
Day is pushed out by day. (Truditur dies die.)
HORACE, *Odes.* Bk. ii, ode 18, l. 15.

24
Daughters of Time, the hypocritic Days,

Muffled and dumb like barefoot dervishes,
And marching single in an endless file,
Bring diadems and fagots in their hands.
To each they offer gifts after his will,
Bread, kingdom, stars, and sky that holds them all.
I, in my pleached garden, watched the pomp,
Forgot my morning wishes, hastily
Took a few herbs and apples, and the Day
Turned and departed silent. I, too late,
Under her solemn fillet saw the scorn.

EMERSON, *Days.*

They [the days] come and go like muffled and veiled figures sent from a distant friendly party; but they say nothing, and if we do not use the gifts they bring, they carry them as silently away.

EMERSON, *Society and Solitude: Works and Days.*

1
Nor mourn the unalterable Days
That Genius goes and Folly stays.

EMERSON, *In Memoriam: Edward Bliss Emerson.*

2
A day to come shows longer than a year that's gone.

THOMAS FULLER, *Gnomologia.* No. 68.

3
My days are gone a-wandering. (Mes jours s'en sont allez errant.)

FRANÇOIS VILLON, *Le Grand Testament.*

4
There's one sun more strung on my bead of days.

HENRY VAUGHAN, *Rules and Lessons.* St. 20.

VI—Day: Its End

See also Night and Day; Evening; Sunset; Twilight

5
Parting day
Dies like the dolphin, whom each pang imbues
With a new colour as it gasps away,
The last still loveliest.

BYRON, *Childe Harold.* Canto iv, st. 29.

6
Beware of desp'rate steps. The darkest day
(Live but to-morrow) will have pass'd away.

COWPER, *The Needless Alarm: Moral.*

7
And all the dying day might be
Immortal in its dying!

AUBREY DE VERE, *Evening Melody.*

8
Be how so that the day be long,
The dark night cometh at last.

JOHN GOWER, *Confessio Amantis.* Bk. vi, l. 578. (1390)

For though the day be never so long,
At last the bells ringeth to evensong.

STEPHEN HAWES, *Passetyme of Pleasure.* Ch. 42, p. 207. (1517) Quoted at the stake by George Tankerfield, 1555. (Fox, *Book of Martyrs,* ch. 7.)

9
The curfew tolls the knell of parting day,
The lowing herd wind slowly o'er the lea,
The ploughman homeward plods his weary way,
And leaves the world to darkness and to me.

THOMAS GRAY, *Elegy Written in a Country Church-yard.* (1751)

Or when the ploughman leaves the task of day,
And trudging homeward whistles on the way.

JOHN GAY, *Rural Sports.* (1713)

10
Sweet day, so cool, so calm, so bright,
The bridal of the earth and sky,
The dew shall weep thy fall to-night;
For thou must die.

GEORGE HERBERT, *The Church: Virtue.*

11
As vanquished day lit camp-fires in the west.

JAMES BARRON HOPE, *Approach to Jamestown.*

12
Well, this is the end of a perfect day,
Near the end of a journey, too;
But it leaves a thought that is big and strong,
With a wish that is kind and true.
For mem'ry has painted this perfect day
With colors that never fade,
And we find at the end of a perfect day,
The soul of a friend we've made.

CARRIE JACOBS BOND, *A Perfect Day.*

13
Now in his Palace of the West,
Sinking to slumber, the bright Day,
Like a tired monarch fann'd to rest,
'Mid the cool airs of Evening lay;
While round his couch's golden rim
The gaudy clouds, like courtiers, crept—
Struggling each other's light to dim,
And catch his last smile e'er he slept.

THOMAS MOORE, *The Summer Fête.* St. 22.

14
Long is it to the ending of the day,
And many a thing may hap ere eventide.

WILLIAM MORRIS, *The Earthly Paradise: Bellerophon in Lycia,* l. 2857.

15
The longest day soon comes to an end. (Longissimus dies cito conditur.)

PLINY THE YOUNGER, *Epistles.* Bk. ix, epis. 36.

16
Day's lustrous eyes grow heavy in sweet death.

SCHILLER, *The Assignation.* St. 4.

17
The gaudy, blabbing and remorseful day
Is crept into the bosom of the sea.

SHAKESPEARE, *II Henry VI.* Act iv, sc. 1, l. 1.

18
In the posteriors of this day, which the rude multitude call the afternoon.

SHAKESPEARE, *Love's Labour's Lost.* v, 1, 94.

The west yet glimmers with some streaks of day:
Now spurs the lated traveller apace
To gain the timely inn.

SHAKESPEARE, *Macbeth.* Act iii, sc. 3, l. 4.

20
The lights begin to twinkle from the rocks;

The long day wanes; the slow moon climbs; the deep
Moans round with many voices.
TENNYSON, *Ulysses*, l. 54.

1
The spirit walks of ev'ry day deceased.
YOUNG, *Night Thoughts*. Night ii, l. 180.

2
For there is no day however beautiful which has not its night. (Car il n'est si beau jour qui n'amène pas sa nuit.)
UNKNOWN. *Inscription*, on tombstone of Jean d'Orbesan, at Padua.

DEAFNESS

3
He is as deaf as a door.
NICHOLAS BRETON, *Works*, ii, 49. (1599)

Dumb and deaf as a post.
THOMAS CHURCHYARD, *Chippes*, p. 136. (1575)

The userer is as deaf as a door nail.
THOMAS WILSON, *Discourse Upon Usury*, 224. (1572)

4
I fear we are deaf on that side.
JOHN CHAMBERLAIN, *Letters*. No. 12. (1598)

As deaf as adders upon that side of the head.
SCOTT, *Waverley*. Ch. 36.

They never would hear,
But turn the deaf ear,
As a matter they had no concern in.
SWIFT, *Dingley and Brent*.

5
Who is so deaf or so blind as is he
That wilfully will neither hear nor see?
JOHN HEYWOOD, *Proverbs*. Pt. ii, ch. 9. (1546)

None so deaf as those that will not hear.
MATTHEW HENRY, *Commentaries: Psalms*, lviii.

6
A deaf man went to law with another deaf man, and the judge was much deafer than either. One of them asserted that the other owed him five months' rent, and the other said that his opponent had been grinding corn at night to avoid the tax. The judge looked at them and said, "Why are you quarreling? She is your mother; you must both support her."
NICARCHUS. (*Greek Anthology*. Bk. xi, epig. 251.)

7
They are like the deaf adder that stoppeth her ear.
Old Testament: Psalms, lviii, 4.

Ears more deaf than adders.
SHAKESPEARE, *Troilus and Cressida*. Act ii, sc. 2, l. 172.

I will be deaf as an adder.
CHAPMAN, *Eastward Hoe*. Act v, sc. 2.

8
Your tale, sir, would cure deafness.
SHAKESPEARE, *The Tempest*. Act i, sc. 2, l. 106

9
Deaf, giddy, helpless, left alone,
To all my friends a burden grown;
No more I hear my church's bell
Than if it rang out for my knell;
At thunder now no more I start
Than at the rumbling of a cart;
And what's incredible, alack!
No more I hear a woman's clack.
JONATHAN SWIFT, *On His Own Deafness*.

He thinks himself deaf, because he no longer hears himself talked of.
TALLEYRAND, of Chateaubriand in his old age.

10
He tells his story to a deaf ear. (Surdo narret fabulam.)
TERENCE, *Heauton Timorumenos*, l. 222.

DEATH

See also Fame and Death; Goodness and Death; Life and Death; Love and Death; Soldier: How Sleep the Brave

I—Death: Definitions

11
Death is a black camel, which kneels at the gates of all.
ABD-EL-KADER, *Rappel à l'Intelligent*.

The Black Camel.
EARL DERR BIGGERS. Title of novel.

12
Death is the universal salt of states.
P. J. BAILEY, *Festus: A Country Town*.

O great corrector of enormous times,
Shaker of o'er-rank states, thou grand decider
Of dusty and old titles, that healest with blood
The earth when it is sick, and curest the world
O' the pleurisy of people!
BEAUMONT AND FLETCHER, *The Two Noble Kinsmen*. Act v, sc. 1.

13
Death hath not only particular stars in heaven, but malevolent places on earth, which single out our infirmities and strike at our weaker parts.
SIR THOMAS BROWNE, *To a Friend*. Sec. 4.

14
Death, . . . pale priest of the mute people.
ROBERT BROWNING, *Balaustion's Adventure*, l. 303.

15
Love, fame, ambition, avarice—'tis the same,
Each idle, and all ill, and none the worst—
For all are meteors with a different name,
And Death the sable smoke where vanishes the flame.
BYRON, *Childe Harold*. Canto iv, st. 124.

Yet what is
Death, so it be glorious? 'Tis a sunset.
BYRON, *Sardanapalus*. Act ii, sc. 1.

16
What is death? A bugbear. (Θάνατος τί ἐστιν; μορμολύκειον.)
EPICTETUS, *Discourses*. Bk. ii, ch. 1, sec. 17. Epictetus adds that Socrates did well to call all such things "bugbears." (PLATO, *Phædo*, 77e.)

1
Death, kind Nature's signal of retreat.
SAMUEL JOHNSON, *The Vanity of Human Wishes*, l. 364.

2
Death, like birth, is a secret of Nature. (Ὁ θάνατος τοιοῦτος, οἷον γένεσις, φύσεως μυστήριον.)
MARCUS AURELIUS, *Meditations*. Bk. iv sec. 5.

3
Death, however, Is a spongy wall,
Is a sticky river, Is nothing at all.
EDNA ST. VINCENT MILLAY, *Moriturus*.

4
Death is but a name, a date,
A milestone by the stormy road,
Where you may lay aside your load
And bow your face and rest and wait,
Defying fear, defying fate.
JOAQUIN MILLER, *A Song of Creation*. Canto iv, st. 12.

What is this rest of death, sweet friend?
What is the rising up, and where?
I say, death is a lengthened prayer,
A longer night, a larger end.
JOAQUIN MILLER, *A Song of the South*. Sec. vii.

5
Death is the scion Of the house of hope.
DOROTHY PARKER, *Death*.

6
Death's but a path that must be trod,
If man would ever pass to God.
THOMAS PARNELL, *A Night-Piece on Death*. l. 67.

7
Death is but crossing the world, as friends do the seas; they live in one another still.
WILLIAM PENN, *Fruits of Solitude*.

8
Death is sometimes a punishment, often a gift; to many it has been a favor. (Interim pœna est mori, Sed sæpe donum; pluribus veniæ fuit.)
SENECA, *Hercules Œtæus*, l. 930.

Death is fortunate for the child, bitter to the youth, too late to the old. (Mors infanti felix, juveni acerba, nimis sera seni.)
PUBLILIUS SYRUS, *Sententiæ*. No. 394.

9
Death is the veil which those who live call life:
They sleep, and it is lifted.
SHELLEY, *Prometheus Unbound*. Act iii, sc. 3.

10
Death is the ugly fact which nature has to hide, and she hides it well.
ALEXANDER SMITH, *Dreamthorp: On Death and the Fear of Dying*.

11
The sleeping partner of life.
HORACE SMITH, *The Tin Trumpet: Death*.

12
Death is the mother of beauty; hence from her
Alone shall come fulfillment to our dreams.
WALLACE STEVENS, *Sunday Morning*.

13
Death's truer name
Is "Onward," no discordance in the roll
And march of that Eternal Harmony
Whereto the world beats time.
TENNYSON, *Unpublished Sonnet*. (*Life*, vol. i.)

14
I am the Dark Cavalier; I am the Last Lover:
My arms shall welcome you when other arms are tired.
MARGARET WIDDEMER, *The Dark Cavalier*.

15
Death is an angel with two faces:
To us he turns
A face of terror, blighting all things fair;
The other burns
With glory of the stars, and love is there.
T. C. WILLIAMS, *A Thanatopsis*.

16
Death is the crown of life:
Were death denied, poor man would live in vain;
Were death denied, to live would not be life;
Were death denied, ev'n fools would wish to die.
YOUNG, *Night Thoughts*. Night iii, l. 526.

17
Who can take
Death's portrait true? The tyrant never sat.
YOUNG, *Night Thoughts*. Night vi, l. 52.

II—Death: Apothegms

18
Though this may be play to you,
'Tis death to us.
ÆSOP, *Fables: The Boys and the Frog*.

19
To die quickly is a privilege; I shall die by inches.
AMIEL, *Journal*, 1 Sept., 1874.

20
Drive your cart and your plow over the bones of the dead.
WILLIAM BLAKE, *Proverbs of Hell*.

21
The angel of Death has been abroad throughout the land: you may almost hear the beating of his wings.
JOHN BRIGHT, *Speech against the Crimean War*, House of Commons, 23 Feb., 1855.

The wind of Death's imperishable wing.
DANTE GABRIEL ROSSETTI, *The House of Life: Lovesight*.

22
To be content with death may be better than to desire it.
SIR THOMAS BROWNE, *To a Friend*. Sec. 26.

I do not wish to die, but care not if I were dead. (Emori nolo: sed me esse mortuum nihil æstimo.)
CICERO, *Tusculanarum Disputationum*. Bk. i, 8.

23
Death stepped tacitly and took them where they never see the sun.
ROBERT BROWNING, *A Toccata of Galuppi's*.

1
The dead ride fast. (Die Todten reiten schnell.)
GOTTFRIED AUGUSTUS BÜRGER, *Leonore.*

Tramp! tramp! across the land they speed,
Splash! splash! across the sea;
Hurrah! the dead can ride apace!
Dost fear to ride with me?
BÜRGER, *Leonore.* (William Taylor, tr.)

2
The crash of the whole solar and stellar systems could only kill you once.
THOMAS CARLYLE, *Letter to John Carlyle.*

Men die but once, and the opportunity
Of a noble death is not an everyday fortune:
It is a gift which noble spirits pray for.
CHARLES LAMB, *John Woodvil.* Act ii, sc. 2.

It is the lot of man but once to die.
FRANCIS QUARLES, *Emblems.* Bk. v, emb. 7.

3
The cup of death already drained. (Jam exhausto illo poculo mortis.)
CICERO, *Pro Cluentio.* Ch. 11, sec. 31.

4
These have not the hope of death. (Questi non hanno speranza di morte.)
DANTE, *Inferno.* Canto iii, l. 46.

5
O that . . . they would consider their latter end.
Old Testament: Deuteronomy, xxxii, 29.

6
He'd make a lovely corpse.
DICKENS, *Martin Chuzzlewit.* Ch. 19.

"Never see . . . a dead post-boy, did you?" inquired Sam. . . . "No," rejoined Bob, "I never did." "No!" rejoined Sam triumphantly. "Nor never vill; and there's another thing that no man never see, and that's a dead donkey."
DICKENS, *Pickwick Papers.* Ch. li.

8
In the jaws of death.
DU BARTAS, *Devine Weekes and Workes.* Week ii, day 1. (Sylvester, tr.)

This youth that you see here
I snatch'd one half out of the jaws of death.
SHAKESPEARE, *Twelfth Night.* Act iii, sc. 4, l. 394.

Into the jaws of death.
TENNYSON, *Charge of the Light Brigade.* St. 3.

9
When death puts out the flame, the snuff will tell
If we are wax or tallow, by the smell.
BENJAMIN FRANKLIN, *Poor Richard,* 1739.

10
"The Grecian Daughter's" being dead as dishwater after the first act.
DAVID GARRICK, *Correspondence.* Vol. i, p. 465.

He'd be sharper than a serpent's tooth, if he wasn't as dull as ditch water.
DICKENS, *Our Mutual Friend.* Bk. iii, ch. 10.

11
Deaths foreseen come not.
GEORGE HERBERT, *Jacula Prudentum.*

12
First Odius falls, and bites the bloody sand.
HOMER, *Iliad.* Bk. v, l. 51. (Pope, tr.)

A bullet whistled o'er his head;
The foremost Tartar bites the ground!
BYRON, *The Giaour.* Sec. 20.

Another Redskin bit the dust!
From the Nick Carter library.

13
Death o'ertakes the man who flees. (Mors et fugacem persequitur virum.)
HORACE, *Odes.* Bk. iii, ode 2, l. 14.

The coward flees in vain; death follows close behind;
It is in defying it that the brave escapes.
(Le lâche fuit en vain; la mort vole à sa suite;
C'est en la défiant que le brave l'evite.)
VOLTAIRE, *Le Triumvirat.* Pt. iv, l. 7.

14
He shall return no more to his house, neither shall his place know him any more.
Old Testament: Job, vii, 10; xvi, 22.

15
He said, It is finished, and he bowed his head and gave up the ghost. (Consummatum est.)
New Testament: John, xix, 30.

16
Death's pale flag advanced in his cheeks.
RICHARD JOHNSON, *Seven Champions of Christendom.* Pt. iii, ch. 11.

17
And, behold, this day I am going the way of all the earth.
Old Testament: Joshua, xxiii, 14.

Now the days of David drew nigh that he should die; and he charged Solomon his son, saying, I go the way of all the earth.
Old Testament: I Kings, ii, 1–2.

If I go by land, and miscarry, then I go the way of all flesh.
THOMAS HEYWOOD, *Golden Age.* Act iii. (1611)

I saw him even now going the way of all flesh.
JOHN WEBSTER, *Westward Hoe.* Act ii, sc. 2.

The Way of All Flesh.
SAMUEL BUTLER THE YOUNGER. Title of posthumous novel published in 1903.

18
Dead as a door nail.
WILLIAM LANGLAND, *Piers Plowman.* Pt. ii, l. 183. (1362)

As dead as a doornail.
SHAKESPEARE, *II Henry VI.* Act iv, sc. 10, l. 43.

Falstaff. What, is the old King dead?
Pistol. As nail in door.
SHAKESPEARE, *II Henry IV.* Act v, sc. 3, l. 126.

Marley was dead: to begin with . . . Old Marley was as dead as a door-nail.
CHARLES DICKENS, *A Christmas Carol.* Stave 1.

I'll warrant him as dead as a herring.
SMOLLETT, *Roderick Random.* Ch. iv.

19
Death itself has often fled from a man. (Mors ipsa refugit Sæpe virum.)
LUCAN, *De Bello Civili.* Bk. ii, l. 74.

1
So he blessed them, and was gathered to his fathers.
Apocrypha: I Maccabees, ii, 69.

Then Abraham gave up the ghost . . . and was gathered to his people.
Old Testament: Genesis, xxv, 8.

2
The dead have few friends.
ROBERT MANNYNG (ROBERT DE BRUNNE), *Handlyng Synne,* l. 6302. (1303)

Justice has bid the world adieu,
And dead men have no friends.
SIR CHARLES SEDLEY, *Ballad.*

3
"God help the fools who count on death for gain."
FRANK T. MARZIALS, *Death as the Fool.*

4
Let the dead bury their dead.
New Testament: Matthew, viii, 22; *Luke,* ix, 60.

5
A slight touch of apoplexy may be called a retaining fee on the part of death.
MÉNAGE, *Epigram.*

6
Not death is dreadful, but a shameful death. (Οὐ κατθανεῖν γὰρ δεινόν, ἀλλ' αἰσχρῶς θανεῖν.)
MENANDER, *Monostikoi.* No. 504.

7
Today if death did not exist, it would be necessary to invent it. (Aujourd'hui si la mort n'existait pas, il faudrait l'inventer.)
JEAN BAPTISTE MILHAUD, when voting for the death of Louis XVI, 19 Jan., 1793. (*Le Moniteur,* 20 Jan., 1793.)

8
Food of Acheron. (Pabulum Acheruntis.)
PLAUTUS, *Casina,* l. 157. (Act ii, sc. 1.) Acheron, a Greek word meaning "The River of Sorrows," the river flowing through Hades.

9
Gaily I lived as ease and nature taught,
And spent my little life without a thought,
And am amazed that Death, that tyrant grim,
Should think of me, who never thought of him.
RENÉ FRANÇOIS REGNIER, *Epigram.*

10
And I looked, and behold a pale horse: and his name that sat on him was Death.
New Testament: Revelation, vi, 8.

Behind her Death
Close following pace for pace, not mounted yet
On his pale horse.
MILTON, *Paradise Lost.* Bk. x, l. 588.

At my door the Pale Horse stands
To carry me to unknown lands.
JOHN HAY, *The Stirrup Cup.*

11
Who shall deliver me from the body of this death?
New Testament: Romans, vii, 24.

12
In yonder room he lies,
With pennies on his eyes.
LEW SARETT, *Requiem for a Modern Crœsus.*

13
On him does death lie heavily who, but too well known to all, dies to himself unknown. (Illi mors gravis incubat Qui, notus nimis omnibus, Ignotus moritur sibi.)
SENECA, *Thyestes,* l. 401.

14
I am dying, Egypt, dying.
SHAKESPEARE, *Antony and Cleopatra.* Act iv, sc. 15, l. 18.

I am dying, Egypt, dying,
Ebbs the crimson life-tide fast,
And the dark Plutonian shadows
Gather on the evening blast.
W. H. LYTLE, *Antony and Cleopatra.*

15
Dead, for a ducat, dead!
SHAKESPEARE, *Hamlet.* Act iii, sc. 4, l. 23.

As cold as any stone.
SHAKESPEARE, *Henry V.* Act ii, sc. 3, l. 27.

16
Those clamorous harbingers of blood and death.
SHAKESPEARE, *Macbeth.* Act v, sc. 6, l. 10.

17
Now our sands are almost run.
SHAKESPEARE, *Pericles,* Act v, sc. 2, l. 1.

Death has shaken out the sands of my glass.
JOHN G. C. BRAINARD, *Lament for Long Tom.*

18
Yes, all men are dust, but some are gold-dust.
JOHN A. SHEDD, *Salt from My Attic,* p. 45.

19
Death without phrases. (La mort sans phrase.)
JOSEPH SIEYÈS, voting for the death of Louis XVI. (*Le Moniteur,* 20 Jan., 1793.) It is probable that Sieyès said simply "La mort," and the reporter added in parenthesis, "sans phrase," but it became historic in the above form. Some of the other "phrases," as given in the *Moniteur,* were: "The blood of a king is not the blood of a man," by Bernardin de Saint-Pierre; "I will not commit a murder that Rome may make a saint," by Chaillon; "Seclusion; to make a Charles I. is to make a Cromwell," by Gentil, a prophecy, for Napoleon turned out to be the Cromwell; "No people free without a tyrant dead," by Jean-Bon Saint-André; "Death: while the tyrant breathes, liberty stifles," by Lavicomterie.

20
To have to die is a distinction of which no man is proud.
ALEXANDER SMITH, *Dreamthorp: On the Writing of Essays.*

21
I shall be like that tree—I shall die at the top.
JONATHAN SWIFT. (SCOTT, *Life of Swift.*)

22
An honorable death is better than a dishonored life. (Honesta mors turpi vita potior.)
TACITUS, *Agricola.* Sec. 33.

23
Let us have a quiet hour,
Let us hob-and-nob with Death.
TENNYSON, *The Vision of Sin.* Pt. iv, st. 3.

1
A dead man does not bite. (νεκρὸς οὐ δάκνει.)
THEODOTUS, when urging the assassination of Pompey. (37 B.C.) See PLUTARCH, *Pompey*, sec. 77. The Latin is "Mortui non mordent."

Knock out her brains! And then she'll never bite.
BEAUMONT AND FLETCHER, *The Coxcomb*, ii, 2.

A dog that's dead,
The Spanish proverb says, will never bite.
BEAUMONT AND FLETCHER, *The Custom of the Country*. Act iv, sc. 1.

Death biteth not. (La mort ny mord.)
SPENSER, *The Shepheardes Calender: November: Colin's Emblem.*

2
It would be better to eschew sin than to flee from death. (Melius esset peccata cavere quam mortem fugere.)
THOMAS À KEMPIS, *De Imitatione Christi*. Pt. i, ch. 23.

3
My God, my Father, and my Friend,
Do not forsake me in the end.
(Cor contritum quasi cinis,
Gere curam mei finis!)
TOMMÁSO DI CELANO, *Dies Iræ*. (Dillon, tr.)

4
I will die in the last ditch.
WILLIAM OF ORANGE. (HUME, *History of England*. Ch. 43.)

5
'Twere best to knock them in the head. . . .
The dead do tell no tales.
JOHN WILSON, *Andronicus Commenius*. Act i, sc. 4. (1664)

Dead men tell no tales.
JOHN DRYDEN, *Spanish Friar*. Act iv, sc. 1.

Death is deaf. (La muerta es sorda.)
CERVANTES, *Don Quixote*.

6
God made no Death: neither hath he pleasure in the destruction of the living.
Apocrypha: Wisdom of Solomon, i, 13.

7
Has death his fopperies?
YOUNG, *Night Thoughts*. Night ii, l. 232.

III—Death: a Debt

8
Death is a debt we all must pay. (Ὡς πᾶσιν ἡμῖν κατθανεῖν ὀφείλεται.)
EURIPIDES, *Alcestis*, l. 419.

9
Finally he paid the debt of nature.
ROBERT FABYAN, *Chronicles*, ii, xli, 28. (1494)

Your son, my lord, has paid a soldier's debt.
SHAKESPEARE, *Macbeth*. Act v, sc. 8, l. 39.

To die, is the great debt and tribute due unto nature.
STERNE, *Tristram Shandy*. Bk. v, ch. 3.

10
We and our works are a debt due to death. (Debemur morti nos nostraque.)
HORACE, *Ars Poetica*, l. 63.

Death, who sets all free,
Hath paid his ransom now, and full discharge.
MILTON, *Samson Agonistes*, l. 1572.

11
Death pays all debts. (La mort nous acquitte de toutes nos obligations.)
MONTAIGNE, *Essays*. Bk. i, ch. 7.

The debt which cancels all others.
C. C. COLTON, *Lacon: Reflections*. Vol. ii, 49.

Death quits all scores.
JAMES SHIRLEY, *Cupid and Death*. (1653)

12
Death is a debt due by all men. (Πᾶσι θανεῖν μερόπεσσιν ὀφείλεται.)
PALLADAS. (*Greek Anthology*. Bk. xi, epig. 62.)

13
The slender debt to Nature's quickly paid,
Discharged, perchance, with greater ease than made.
FRANCIS QUARLES, *Emblems*. Bk. ii, emb. 13.

14
A man can die but once: we owe God a death.
SHAKESPEARE, *II Henry IV*. Act iii, sc. 2, l. 250.

Why, thou owest God a death.
SHAKESPEARE, *I Henry IV* Act v, sc. 1, l. 126.

He owed a death, and he hath paid that debt.
HEYWOOD AND ROWLEY, *Fortune by Land and Sea*. Act i, sc. 1.

15
He that dies this year is quit for the next.
SHAKESPEARE, *II Henry IV*. Act iii, sc. 2, l. 254.

He that dies pays all debts.
SHAKESPEARE, *The Tempest*. Act iii, sc. 2, l. 140.

16
First our pleasures die—and then
Our hopes, and then our fears—and when
These are dead, the debt is due,
Dust claims dust—and we die too.
SHELLEY, *Death*. (1820)

17
We are all owed to death. (Θανάτῳ πάντες ὀφειλόμεθα.)
SIMONIDES. (*Greek Anthology*, Bk. x, 105.)

IV—Death: A Gate

18
Death the gate of life. (Mors janua vitæ.)
ST. BERNARD, *In Transitu S. Malachi*. Sermon i, sec. 4, *ad fin*.

And to the faithful, death the gate of life.
MILTON, *Paradise Lost*. Bk. xii, l. 571.

Death is life's gate.
P. J. BAILEY, *Festus: Colonnade and Lawn.*

19
The gate of death. (Janua lethi.)
LUCRETIUS, *De Rerum Natura*. Bk. i, l. 1113.

20
Death is for many of us the gate of hell; but we are inside on the way out, not outside on the way in.
BERNARD SHAW, *Parents and Children*.

21
And so thro' those dark gates across the wild
That no man knows.
TENNYSON, *The Princess*. Pt. vii, l. 341.

1
Death is only an old door.
Set in a garden wall.
NANCY BYRD TURNER, *Death is a Door.*

2
As soon as man, expert from time, has found
The key of life, it opes the gates of death.
YOUNG, *Night Thoughts.* Night iv, l. 122.

V—Death: A Voyage

3
Without a hail at parting,
Or any colors shown,
My friend has gone aboard her
For the Isles of the Unknown.
BLISS CARMAN, *Passing Strange.*

4
Now the labourer's task is o'er;
Now the battle day is past;
Now upon the farther shore
Stands the voyager at last.
EDWARD ELLERTON, *Hymn.*

5
God, I am travelling out to death's sea,
I, who exulted in sunshine and laughter,
Dreamed not of dying—death is such a waste of me!
JOHN GALSWORTHY, *Valley of the Shadow.* Used by Mrs. Galsworthy on card acknowledging letters of condolence.

6
To die is landing on some silent shore,
Where billows never break, nor tempests roar:
Ere well we feel the friendly stroke, 'tis o'er.
GARTH, *The Dispensary.* Canto iii, l. 225.

7
And I hear from the outgoing ship in the bay
The song of the sailors in glee:
So I think of the luminous footprints that bore
The comfort o'er dark Galilee,
And wait for the signal to go to the shore,
To the ship that is waiting for me.
BRET HARTE, *The Two Ships.*

8
Oh, in some morning dateless yet
I shall steal out in the sweet dark
And find my ship with sails all set
By the dim quayside, and embark.
KATHERINE TYNAN HINKSON, *The Last Voyage.*

9
When I have folded up this tent
And laid the soiled thing by,
I shall go forth 'neath different stars,
Under an unknown sky.
FREDERICK LAWRENCE KNOWLES, *Last Word.*

10
Death was a harbor and a transient goal
Wherefrom you pass now, with your skysail set
For ports beyond the margin of the stars.
ELOISE ROBINSON, *To-Day I Saw Bright Ships.*

11
It's far I must be going
Some night or morning gray,
Beyond the ocean's flowing,
Beyond the rim of day;
But sure it's not the going,
But that I find the way.
PATRICK MCDONOUGH, *Via Longa.*

12
When I drift out on the Silver Sea,
O may it be a blue night
With a white moon
And a sprinkling of stars in the cedar tree.
LEW SARETT, *The Great Divide.*

13
Here is my journey's end, here is my butt,
And very sea-mark of my utmost sail.
SHAKESPEARE, *Othello.* Act v, sc. 2, l. 267.

14
Sunset and evening star,
And one clear call for me!
And may there be no moaning of the bar
When I put out to sea. . . .
For tho' from out our bourne of Time and Place
The flood may bear me far,
I hope to see my Pilot face to face
When I have crost the bar.
TENNYSON, *Crossing the Bar.*

There came so loud a calling of the sea
That all the houses in the haven rang.
TENNYSON, *Enoch Arden,* l. 904. The "calling of the sea" is an old English term for a ground-swell.

15
Joy, shipmate, joy!
(Pleas'd to my soul at death I cry,)
Our life is closed, our life begins,
The long, long anchorage we leave,
The ship is clear at last, she leaps!
She swiftly courses from the shore,
Joy, shipmate, joy!
WALT WHITMAN, *Joy, Shipmate, Joy!*

16
I think of death as some delightful journey
That I shall take when all my tasks are done.
ELLA WHEELER WILCOX, *The Journey.*

Never any weary traveller complained that he came too soon to his journey's end.
THOMAS FULLER, *Good Thoughts in Bad Times,* 24.

VI—Death: Its Immanence

17
In the midst of life we are in death. (Media vita in morte sumus.)
Book of Common Prayer: Burial of the Dead. Origin uncertain, but dating from the Middle Ages. Found in choirbook of the Monks of St. Gall.

18
When swift the Camel-rider spans the howling waste, by Kismet sped,
And of his Magic Wand a wave hurries the quick to join the dead.
SIR RICHARD BURTON, *Kasîdah.* Pt. iii, st. 35.

19
Short shall this half-extinguished spirit burn

And soon these limbs to kindred dust return.
CAMPBELL, *Pleasures of Hope*. Pt. ii, l. 423.

1
Methinks I hear some gentle spirit say,
Be not fearful, come away!
THOMAS FLATMAN, *A Thought of Death.*

I hear a voice you cannot hear,
Which says, I must not stay;
I see a hand you cannot see,
Which beckons me away.
THOMAS TICKELL, *Colin and Lucy.*

2
Death rides on every passing breeze,
He lurks in every flower:
Each season has its own disease,
Its peril every hour.
REGINALD HEBER, *At a Funeral.*

3
Leaves have their time to fall,
And flowers to wither at the north-wind's breath,
And stars to set,—but all,
Thou hast all seasons for thine own, O Death!
FELICIA HEMANS, *The Hour of Death.*

4
Death is still working like a mole,
And digs my grave at each remove.
GEORGE HERBERT, *Grace.*

5
Prepare for death if here at night you roam,
And sign your will before you sup from home.
SAMUEL JOHNSON, *London.*

6
There is no confessor like unto Death!
Thou canst not see him, but he is near:
Thou needst not whisper above thy breath,
And he will hear.
LONGFELLOW, *The Golden Legend*. Pt. v.

7
And over them triumphant Death his dart
Shook, but delay'd to strike, though oft invok'd.
MILTON, *Paradise Lost*. Bk. xi, l. 488.

8
Live mindful of death; the hour flies. (Vive memor leti, fugit hora.)
PERSIUS, *Satires* Sat. v, l. 153.

Remember you must die. (Memento mori.)
Motto, Order of the Death's Head.

Look behind you. Remember you are but a man. (Respice post te. Hominem memento te.)
The warning whispered by a slave stationed behind the Roman general in his triumphal chariot.

9
If thou expect death as a friend, prepare to entertain it; if thou expect death as an enemy, prepare to overcome it; death has no advantage, but when it comes a stranger.
FRANCIS QUARLES, *Enchiridion*. Cent. iv, No. 37.

10
Soon the shroud shall lap thee fast,
And the sleep be on thee cast
That shall ne'er know waking.
SCOTT, *Guy Mannering*. Ch. 27.

11
It is uncertain where death may await thee, therefore expect it everywhere. (Incertum est, quo loco te mors expectet; itaque tu illam omni loco expecta.)
SENECA, *Epistulæ ad Lucilium*. Epis. xxvi, 7.

12
Come, let us take a muster speedily:
Doomsday is near; die all, die merrily.
SHAKESPEARE, *I Henry IV*. Act iv, sc. 1, l. 133.

And we shall feed like oxen at a stall,
The better cherish'd, still the nearer death.
SHAKESPEARE, *I Henry IV*. Act v, sc. 2, l. 14.

13
'Tis now dead midnight, and by eight tomorrow
Thou must be made immortal.
SHAKESPEARE, *Measure for Measure*. Act iv, sc. 2, l. 67.

14
Death is here and death is there,
Death is busy everywhere,
All around, within, beneath,
Above is death—and we are death.
SHELLEY, *Death*. (1820)

15
All buildings are but monuments of death,
All clothes but winding-sheets for our last knell,
All dainty fattings for the worms beneath,
All curious music but our passing bell:
Thus death is nobly waited on, for why?
All that we have is but death's livery.
JAMES SHIRLEY, *Death.*

16
He that would die well must always look for death, every day knocking at the gates of the grave.
JEREMY TAYLOR, *Holy Dying*. Ch. ii, sec. 1.

17
In mid whirl of the dance of Time ye start,
Start at the cold touch of Eternity,
And cast your cloaks about you, and depart:
The minstrels pause not in their minstrelsy.
WILLIAM WATSON, *Epigrams.*

18
He is look'd for in hovel, and dreaded in hall—
The king in his closet keeps hatchment and pall—
The youth in his birthplace, the old man at home,
Make clean from the door-stone the path to the tomb.
N. P. WILLIS, *The Death of Harrison.*

19
The rising morn cannot assure
That we shall end the day,
For Death stands ready at the door
To take our lives away.
UNKNOWN. *From an old sampler.*

VII—Death: Its Thousand Doors

20
Death hath so many doors to let out life.
BEAUMONT AND FLETCHER, *The Custom of the Country*. Act ii, sc. 2.

There are a thousand doors to let out life.
MASSINGER, *Parliament of Love*. Act iv, sc. 2.

Death hath a thousand doors to let out life.
I shall find one.
MASSINGER, *A Very Woman*. Act v, sc. 4.

1
Death's thousand doors stand open.
ROBERT BLAIR, *The Grave*, l. 394.

The thousand doors that lead to death.
SIR THOMAS BROWNE, *Religio Medici*. Pt. i, sec. 51.

Death with his thousand doors.
JOHN FLETCHER, *Loyal Subject*. Act i, sc. 2.

2
The best thing which eternal law ever ordained was that it allowed us one entrance into life, but many exits. (Nil melius æterna lex fecit, quam quod unum introitum nobis ad vitam dedit. exitus multos.)
SENECA, *Epistulæ ad Lucilium*. Epis. lxx, 15.

Death is everywhere. . . . Of life anyone can rob a man, but of death no one; to this a thousand doors lie open. (Ubique mors est. . . . Eripere vitam nemo non homini potest, At nemo mortem: mille ad hanc aditus patent.)
SENECA, *Phœnissæ*, l. 151.

The doors of death are ever open.
JEREMY TAYLOR, *Contemplation on the State of Man*. Bk. i, ch. 7.

3
I know death hath ten thousand several doors
For men, to take their exits.
JOHN WEBSTER, *Duchess of Malfi*. Act iv, sc. 2.

VIII—Death, the Inevitable

See also Mortality

4
Alone of the gods, Death loves not gifts; no, not by sacrifice, nor by libation, canst thou aught avail with him; he hath no altar nor hath he hymn of praise; from him, alone of gods, Persuasion stands aloof.
ÆSCHYLUS, *Niobe*. Frag. 82.

5
The man who to untimely death is doom'd,
Vainly you hedge him from the assault of harm:
He bears the seed of ruin in himself.
MATTHEW ARNOLD, *Merope*, l. 860.

6
Death comes even to the monumental stones, and the names inscribed thereon. (Mors etiam saxis nominibusque venit.)
AUSONIUS, *Epitaphs*. No. 32, l. 10.

7
"Nay," said Time, "we must not bide,
The way is long and the world is wide,
And we must be ready to meet the tide."
MICHAEL BEVERLY, *The River of Time*.

8
'Mid youth and song, feasting and carnival,
Through laughter, through the roses, as of old
Comes Death, on shadowy and relentless feet.
RUPERT BROOKE, *Second Best*.

9
There is a remedy for everything but death, which will be sure to lay us out flat some time or other.
CERVANTES, *Don Quixote*. Pt. ii, ch. 10.

Against Death is worth no medicine.
JOHN LYDGATE, *Daunce of Machabree*, l. 432. (c. 1430)

Against the evil of death there is no remedy in the gardens. (Contra malum mortis non est medicamen in hortis.)
UNKNOWN. A medieval proverb.

10
Nay, in death's hand, the grape-stone proves
As strong as thunder is in Jove's.
ABRAHAM COWLEY, *Elegy upon Anacreon*, l. 106.

11
All has its date below; the fatal hour
Was register'd in Heav'n ere time began.
We turn to dust, and all our mightiest works
Die too.
COWPER, *The Task*. Bk. v, l. 529.

12
The best of men cannot suspend their fate;
The good die early, and the bad die late.
DANIEL DEFOE, *Character of the Late Dr. S. Annesley*.

Stern fate and time
Will have their victims; and the best die first,
Leaving the bad still strong, though past their prime,
To curse the hopeless world they ever curs'd,
Vaunting vile deeds, and vainest of the worst.
EBENEZER ELLIOTT, *The Village Patriarch*. Bk. iv, pt. iv.

13
All human things are subject to decay,
And when fate summons, monarchs must obey.
DRYDEN, *MacFlecknoe*, l. 1.

14
One event happeneth to them all.
Old Testament: Ecclesiastes, ii, 14.

There is no discharge in that war.
Old Testament: Ecclesiastes. viii, 8.

15
Death takes no denial. (Θάνατος ἀπροφάσιστος.)
EURIPIDES, *Bacchæ*, l. 1002.

16
To this complexion thou must come at last.
DAVID GARRICK, *Epitaph on Quinn* (MURPHY, *Life of Garrick*. Vol. ii, p. 38.)

17
For dust thou art, and unto dust shalt thou return.
Old Testament: Genesis, iii, 19.

18
Where the brass knocker, wrapt in flannel band,
Forbids the thunder of the footman's hand,
Th' upholder, rueful harbinger of death,
Waits with impatience for the dying breath.
JOHN GAY, *Trivia*. Bk. ii, l. 467.

1
"Passing away" is written on the world and all the world contains.

FELICIA DOROTHEA HEMANS, *Passing Away.*

2
"Oh, nobody knows when de Lord is goin ter call, *Roll dem bones.*
It may be in de Winter time, and maybe in de Fall, *Roll dem bones.*
But yer got ter leabe yer baby and yer home an all—*So roll dem bones.*

DUBOSE HEYWARD, *Gamesters All.*

3
All, soon or late, are doom'd that path to tread. (Ἄλλοι ἅπαξ θνήσκουσ' ἄνθρωποι.)

HOMER, *Odyssey.* Bk. xii, l. 22. (Pope, tr.)

One night awaits us all, and the downward path must be trodden once. (Omnes una manet nox, Et calcanda semel via leti.)

HORACE, *Odes.* Bk. i, ode 28, l. 15.

4
Man, born of woman, must of woman die.

THOMAS HOOD, *A Valentine.*

5
Inasmuch as all creatures that live on earth have mortal souls, for neither great nor small is there escape from death. (Terrestria quando Mortalis animas vivunt sortita, neque ulla est Aut magno aut parvo leti fuga.)

HORACE, *Satires.* Bk. ii, sat. 6, l. 93.

6
We have made a covenant with death.

Old Testament: Isaiah, xxviii, 15.

I have a rendezvous with Death
At some disputed barricade, . . .
At midnight in some flaming town,
When Spring trips north again this year,
And I to my pledged word am true,
I shall not fail that rendezvous.

ALAN SEEGER, *I Have a Rendezvous with Death.*

I have a rendezvous with Life
In days I hope will come
Ere youth has sped and strength of mind,
Ere voices sweet grow dumb. . . .
Though wet, nor blow, nor space, I fear,
Yet fear I deeply, too,
Lest Death should greet and claim me ere
I keep Life's rendezvous.

COUNTEE CULLEN, *I Have a Rendezvous with Life.*

7
We all do fade as a leaf.

Old Testament: Isaiah, lxiv, 6.

8
We are but tenants, and . . . shortly the great Landlord will give us notice that our lease has expired.

JOSEPH JEFFERSON, *Inscription,* on his monument at Sandwich, Cape Cod, Mass.

9
Man dieth, and wasteth away: yea, man giveth up the ghost, and where is he?

Old Testament: Job, xiv, 10.

10
The young may die, but the old must!

H. W. LONGFELLOW, *The Golden Legend:* Pt. iv, *The Cloisters.*

11
Death is free from Fortune: the earth takes back everything which it has brought forth. (Libera fortunæ mors est; capit omnia tellus, Quæ genuit.)

LUCAN, *De Bello Civili.* Bk. vii, l. 818.

12
To every man upon this earth
Death cometh soon or late.

MACAULAY, *Horatius.* St. 27.

13
When Life knocks at the door no one can wait,
When Death makes his arrest we have to go.

JOHN MASEFIELD, *The Widow in the Bye Street.* Pt. ii.

14
Rome can give no dispensation from death. (On n'a point pour la mort de dispense de Rome.)

MOLIÈRE, *L'Étourdi.* Act ii, sc. 3, l. 6. Also attributed to Thomas à Kempis.

15
Depart, saith she [Nature], out of the world, even as you came into it.

MONTAIGNE, *Essays.* Bk. i, ch. 19.

16
All victory ends in the defeat of death. That's sure. But does defeat end in the victory of death? That's what I wonder!

EUGENE O'NEILL, *Mourning Becomes Electra: Homecoming.* Act iii.

17
We hasten to a common goal. Black Death summons all things under the sway of its laws. (Metam properamus ad unam, Omnia sub leges Mors vocat atra suas.)

OVID, *Consolatio ad Liviam,* l. 359.

18
We are all kept and fed for death, like a herd of swine to be slain without reason. (Πάντες τῷ θανάτῳ τηρούμεθα, καὶ τρεφόμεσθα ὡς ἀγέλη χοίρων σφαζομένων ἀλόγως.)

PALLADAS. (*Greek Anthology.* Bk. x, epig. 85.)

19
Death comes to all His cold and sapless hand
Waves o'er the world and beckons us away.

THOMAS LOVE PEACOCK, *Time.*

20
To each unthinking being, Heaven, a friend,
Gives not the useless knowledge of its end:
To man imparts it, but with such a view
As, while he dreads it, makes him hope it too:
The hour conceal'd, and so remote the fear,
Death still draws nearer, never seeming near.
Great standing miracle! that Heaven assign'd
Its only thinking thing this turn of mind.

POPE, *Essay on Man.* Epis. iii, l. 71.

21
In vain we think the free-will'd man has power

To hasten or protract th' appointed hour.
Our term of life depends not on our deed:
Before our birth our funeral was decreed.
PRIOR, *Ode to the Memory of Colonel Villiers.*

Nor aw'd by foresight, nor misled by chance,
Imperious Death directs his ebon lance.
PRIOR, *Ode to the Memory of Colonel Villiers.*

When obedient nature knows his will,
A fly, a grapestone, or a hair can kill.
PRIOR, *Ode to the Memory of Colonel Villiers.*

1
I have said, Ye are gods, . . . But ye shall die like men.
Old Testament: Psalms, lxxxii, 6, 7.

Whate'er thou lovest, man, that, too, become thou must—
God, if thou lovest God; dust, if thou lovest dust.
JOHANN SCHEFFLER, *The Cherubic Pilgrim.*

2
Make thine account with Heaven, governor,
Thou must away, thy sand is run.
(Mach deine Rechnung mit dem Himmel, Vogt!
Fort musst du, deine Uhr ist abgelaufen.)
SCHILLER, *Wilhelm Tell.* Act iv, sc. 3.

3
There is no man who does not die his own death. . . . No one dies except upon his own day. (Nemo moritur nisi sua morte; . . . nemo nisi suo die moritur.)
SENECA, *Epistulæ ad Lucilium.* Epis. lxix, 1, 6.

4
Death visits each and all; the slayer soon follows the slain. (Mors per omnes it; qui occidit, consequitur occisum.)
SENECA, *Epistulæ ad Lucilium.* Epis. xciii, 12.

The last hour reaches, but every hour approaches, death. Death wears us away, but does not whirl us away. (Ad mortem dies extremus pervenit, accedit omnis. Carpit nos illa, non corripit.)
SENECA, *Epistulæ ad Lucilium.* Epis. cxx, 18.

The major portion of death has already passed. Whatever years lie behind us are in death's hands. (Quicquid ætatis retro est, mors tenet.)
SENECA, *Epistulæ ad Lucilium.* Epis. i, sec. 2.

5
Golden lads and girls all must,
As chimney-sweepers, come to dust.
SHAKESPEARE, *Cymbeline.* Act iv, sc. 2 l. 262.

By medicine life may be prolonged, yet death
Will seize the doctor too.
SHAKESPEARE, *Cymbeline.* Act v, sc. 5, l. 29.

6
All that lives must die,
Passing through nature to eternity.
SHAKESPEARE, *Hamlet.* Act i, sc. 2, l. 72.

Now get you to my lady's chamber, and tell her, let her paint an inch thick, to this favour she must come.
SHAKESPEARE, *Hamlet.* Act v, sc. 1, l. 213.

Certain, 'tis certain; very sure, very sure: death, as the Psalmist saith, is certain to all; all shall die.
SHAKESPEARE, *II Henry IV.* Act iii, sc. 2, l. 40.

Death will have his day.
SHAKESPEARE, *Richard II.* Act iii, sc. 2, l. 103.

7
Here burns my candle out; ay, here it dies,
Which, whiles it lasted, gave King Henry light.
SHAKESPEARE, *III Henry VI.* Act ii, sc. 6, l. 1.

Why, what is pomp, rule, reign, but earth and dust?
And, live we how we can, yet die we must.
SHAKESPEARE, *III Henry VI.* Act v, sc. 2, l. 27.

8
That we shall die we know; 'tis but the time
The drawing days out, that men stand upon.
SHAKESPEARE, *Julius Cæsar.* Act iii, sc. 1, l. 99.

Men must endure
Their going hence, even as their coming hither;
Ripeness is all.
SHAKESPEARE, *King Lear.* Act v, sc. 2, l. 9.

It is a knell
That summons thee to heaven or to hell.
SHAKESPEARE, *Macbeth.* Act ii, sc. 1, l. 63.

That fell arrest Without all bail.
SHAKESPEARE, *Sonnets.* No. lxxiv.

9
Death's like the best bower anchor, as the saying is, it will bring us all up.
SMOLLETT, *Roderick Random.* Ch. 24.

10
Death, if thou wilt, fain would I plead with thee:
Canst thou not spare, of all our hopes have built,
One shelter where our spirits fain would be,
Death, if thou wilt?
SWINBURNE, *A Dialogue.* St. 1.

11
She throws a kiss, and bids me run
In whispers sweet as roses' breath;
I know I can not win the race,
And at the end, I know, is death.
MAURICE THOMPSON, *Atalanta's Race.*

12
Comes the supreme day and the inevitable hour. (Venit summa dies et ineluctabile tempus.)
VERGIL, *Æneid.* Bk. ii, l. 324; LUCAN, *De Bello Civili.* Bk. vii, l. 197.

Awaits alike the inevitable hour.
THOMAS GRAY, *Elegy Written in a Country Church-yard.*

13
Each has his appointed day; life is brief and irrevocable. (Stat sua cuique dies, breve et inreparabile tempus.)
VERGIL, *Æneid.* Bk. x l. 467.

14
Die we must, every mother's son of us.
THOMAS WILSON, *Rhetorique,* 72. (1560)

IX—Death: The Silent Majority

15
'Tis long since Death had the majority.
ROBERT BLAIR, *The Grave,* l. 449.

1
All that tread
The globe are but a handful to the tribes
That slumber in its bosom.
BRYANT, *Thanatopsis.*

2
The long, mysterious Exodus of Death.
LONGFELLOW, *The Jewish Cemetery at Newport.*

3
He went over to the majority. (Tamen abiit ad plures.)
PETRONIUS, *Satyricon.* Sec. 42.

Times before you, when even living men were antiquities; when the living might exceed the dead, and when to leave this world could not be properly said to go unto the greater number. (Abiit ad plures.)
SIR THOMAS BROWNE, *Hydriotaphia: Dedication.* (1658)

This Mirabeau's work, then, is done. He sleeps with the primeval giants. He has gone over to the majority: "Abiit ad plures."
CARLYLE, *Essays: Mirabeau.*

4
To our graves we walk
In the thick footprints of departed men.
ALEXANDER SMITH, *Horton,* l. 570.

5
Life is the desert, life the solitude;
Death joins us to the great majority.
EDWARD YOUNG, *Revenge.* Act iv, sc 1. (1721)

X—Death: The Leveler

See also Grave: Its Democracy

6
That fatal sergeant, Death, spares no degree.
WILLIAM ALEXANDER, *Doomsday: The Ninth Hour.* St. 114.

This fell sergeant, death, Is strict in his arrest.
SHAKESPEARE, *Hamlet.* Act v, sc. 2, l. 347.

7
The winds of Luxor fiercely blow
Against my cheeks the dust of kings,
Egyptians of the long ago,
Pharaohs and serfs, the overflow
And undertow of centuries—
Dust, dust, dust.
ROBERT CARY, *The Winds of Luxor.*

8
Death levels all things. (Omnia mors æquat.)
CLAUDIAN, *De Raptu Proserpinæ.* Bk. ii, l. 302.

Death and dice level all distinctions.
SAMUEL FOOTE, *The Minor.* Act i, sc. 1.

Death makes equal the high and low.
JOHN HEYWOOD, *Be Merry, Friends.*

Life levels all men: death reveals the eminent.
BERNARD SHAW, *Maxims for Revolutionists.*

9
Death levels master and slave, the sceptre and the law, and makes unlike like. (Mors dominos servis et sceptra ligionibus æquat, dissimiles simili conditione trahens.)
WALTER COLMAN, *La Danse Macabre.* (c. 1633) The phrase, "Mors sceptra ligionibus æquat," is included in *Vers Sur la Mort* of the 12th century, and has been used as a motto and inscription. (See *Notes and Queries,* May, 1917, p. 134.)

10
This quiet Dust was Gentlemen and Ladies,
And Lads and Girls;
Was laughter and ability and sighing,
And frocks and curls.
EMILY DICKINSON, *This Quiet Dust.*

The dust we tread upon was once alive.
BYRON, *Sardanapalus.* Act iv, sc. 1, l. 66.

The whole earth is a sepulchre for famous men.
THUCYDIDES, *History.* Bk. ii, sec. 43.

Where is the dust that has not been alive?
The spade, the plough, disturb our ancestors;
From human mould we reap our daily bread.
YOUNG, *Night Thoughts.* Night ix, l. 92.

11
The prince, who kept the world in awe,
The judge, whose dictate fix'd the law,
The rich, the poor, the great, the small,
Are levell'd: death confounds 'em all.
JOHN GAY, *Fables.* Pt. ii, fab. 16, l. 143.

All alike are rich and richer,
King with crown, and cross-legged stitcher,
When the grave hides all.
R. W. GILDER, *Drinking Song.*

12
One destin'd period men in common have,
The great, the base, the coward, and the brave,
All food alike for worms, companions in the grave.
GEORGE GRANVILLE, *Meditation on Death.*

13
Pale Death, with impartial step, knocks at the poor man's cottage and at the palaces of kings. (Pallida Mors æquo pulsat pede pauperum tabernas Regumque turres.)
HORACE, *Odes.* Bk. i, ode 4, l. 13.

14
They die
An equal death—the idler and the man
Of mighty deeds.
HOMER, *Iliad.* Bk. ix, l. 396. (Bryant, tr.)

With equal pace, impartial Fate
Knocks at the palace, as the cottage gate.
HORACE, *Odes.* Bk. i, ode 4. (Francis, tr.)

The equal earth is opened alike to the poor man and the sons of kings. (Æqua tellus Pauperi recluditur, regumque pueris.)
HORACE, *Odes.* Bk. ii, ode 18, l. 32.

15
We are all driven by the same force; our lots are cast into the urn, sooner or later to be drawn forth, to send us to Charon's boat for our eternal exile.
(Omnes eodem cogimur, omnium
Versatur urna serius ocius
Sors exitura et nos in æternum
Exsilium impositura cumbæ.)
HORACE, *Odes.* Bk. ii, ode 3, l. 25.

Alike for high and low
Death votes. His mighty urn will throw
Each name or soon or late.
(Æqua lege Necessitas
Sortitur insignes et imos:
Omne capax movet urna nomen.)

HORACE, *Odes*. Bk. iii, ode i, l. 16. (Marshall, tr.)

1

When death comes, he respects neither age nor merit. He sweeps from this earthly existence the sick and the strong, the rich and the poor, and should teach us to live to be prepared for death.

ANDREW JACKSON, *Letter: My Dear E.*, 12 Dec., 1824.

2

Where's Cæsar gone now, in command high and able?
Or Xerxes the splendid, complete in his table?
Or Tully, with powers of eloquence ample?
Or Aristotle, of genius the highest example?

JACOPONE DA TODI, *De Contemptu Mundi*. (Coles, tr.)

3

In life's last scene what prodigies surprise,
Fears of the brave, and follies of the wise!
From Marlborough's eyes the streams of dotage flow,
And Swift expires a driveller and a show.

SAMUEL JOHNSON, *The Vanity of Human Wishes*, l. 313.

4

Produce the urn that Hannibal contains,
And weigh the mighty dust which yet remains:
And is that all?
(Expende Hannibalem; quot libras in duce summo Invenies?)

JUVENAL, *Satires*. Sat. x, l. 147. (Gifford, tr.)

Here lies Tibullus: of all that he was there remains scarcely enough to fill a small urn. (Jacet, ecce, Tibullus; Vix manet e toto, parva quod urna capit!)

OVID, *Amores*. Bk. iii, eleg. 9, l. 39.

So peaceful rests, without a stone, a name,
What once had beauty, titles, wealth, and fame,
How lov'd, how honour'd once, avails thee not,
To whom related, or by whom begot;
A heap of dust alone remains of thee;
'Tis all thou art, and all the proud shall be!

POPE, *Elegy to the Memory of an Unfortunate Lady*, l. 69.

5

There is a Reaper, whose name is Death,
And, with his sickle keen,
He reaps the bearded grain at a breath,
And the flowers that grow between.

LONGFELLOW, *The Reaper and the Flowers*.

Oh, not in cruelty, not in wrath,
The Reaper came that day;
'Twas an angel visited the green earth,
And took the flowers away.

LONGFELLOW, *The Reaper and the Flowers*.

"Who gathered this flower?" The gardener answered, "The Master." And his fellow-servant held his peace.

UNKNOWN, *Epitaph*, Budock Churchyard, and elsewhere.

6

The timid and the brave alike must die. (Pavido fortique cadendum est.)

LUCAN, *De Bello Civili*. Bk. ix, l. 583.

7

Nay, the greatest wits and poets, too, cease to live;
Homer, their prince, sleeps now in the same forgotten grave as do the others.

LUCRETIUS, *De Rerum Natura*. Bk. iii, l. 1049.

Death reduced to the same condition Alexander the Macedonian and his muleteer.

MARCUS AURELIUS, *Meditations*. Bk. vi, sec. 24.

8

Since each trade's ending needs must be the same:
And we men call it Death.

WILLIAM MORRIS, *The Earthly Paradise: Epilogue*, l. 7.

9

The little broken bones of men,
They ride on every wind that blows,
With dust of Memphis whirled again
And this year's dust of last year's rose.

J. U. NICHOLSON, *I Would Remember Constant Things*.

The sun will rise, the winds that ever move
Will blow our dust that once were men in love.

JOHN MASEFIELD, *Sonnets*.

10

I sometimes think that never blows so red
The Rose as where some buried Cæsar bled;
That every Hyacinth the Garden wears
Dropped in her Lap from some once lovely Head.

OMAR KHAYYÁM, *Rubáiyát*. St. 19. (Fitzgerald, tr.)

He whom the harvest hath remembered not
Sleeps with the rose.

MARJORIE L. C. PICKTHALL, *The Lamp of Poor Souls*.

Each spot where tulips prank their state
Has drunk the life-blood of the great;
The violets yon field which stain
Are moles of beauties Time hath slain.

R. W. EMERSON, *From Omar Khay Yam*.

Lay her i' the earth:
And from her fair and unpolluted flesh
May violets spring!

SHAKESPEARE, *Hamlet*. Act v, sc. 1, l. 261.

And from his ashes may be made
The violet of his native land.

TENNYSON, *In Memoriam*. Pt. xviii, st. 1.

11

Death lays his impious touch on all things rare:
His shadowy hands no sacred office spare.
(Scilicet omne sacrum mors inportuna profanat,
Omnibus obscuras inicit illa manus!

OVID, *Amores*. Bk. iii, eleg. 9, l. 19.

1
Alike must every state and every age
Sustain the universal tyrant's rage:
Nor neither William's power nor Mary's charms,
Could, or repel, or pacify his arms.
PRIOR, *Ode to the Memory of Colonel Villiers.*

2
As men, we are all equal in the presence of death.
PUBLILIUS SYRUS, *Sententiæ*. No. 1.

3
It's all a world where bugs and emperors
Go singularly back to the same dust.
E. A. ROBINSON, *Ben Jonson Entertains a Man from Stratford.*

4
A man may fish with the worm that hath eat of a king, and eat of the fish that hath fed of that worm.
SHAKESPEARE, *Hamlet*. Act iv, sc. 3, l. 28.

5
To what base uses we may return, Horatio! Why may not imagination trace the noble dust of Alexander, till we find it stopping a bung-hole?
SHAKESPEARE, *Hamlet*. Act v, sc. 1, l. 222.

Imperious Cæsar, dead and turn'd to clay,
Might stop a hole to keep the wind away:
O, that that earth, which kept the world in awe,
Should patch a wall to expel the winter's flaw!
SHAKESPEARE, *Hamlet*. Act. v, sc. 1, l. 234.

Dead Cæsar who "stops bungholes" in the cask.
E. B. BROWNING, *Aurora Leigh*. Bk. iii, l. 556.

6
O proud death,
What feast is toward in thine eternal cell,
That thou so many princes at a shot
So bloodily hast struck?
SHAKESPEARE, *Hamlet*. Act v, sc. 2, l. 375.

7
The glories of our blood and state
Are shadows, not substantial things;
There is no armour against Fate,
Death lays his icy hand on kings.
Scepter and Crown
Must tumble down,
And in the dust be equal made
With the poor crooked scythe and spade.
JAMES SHIRLEY, *Death's Final Conquest*. From *The Contention of Ajax and Ulysses*. (PERCY, *Reliques*. Ser. i, bk. 3, No. 2.)

Death calls ye to the crowd of common men.
JAMES SHIRLEY, *Cupid and Death.*

How little room
Do we take up in death, that living know
No bounds!
JAMES SHIRLEY, *The Wedding.*

8
Sooner or later, all things pass away,
And are no more: The beggar and the king,
With equal steps, tread forward to their end.
THOMAS SOUTHERNE, *The Fatal Marriage*. Act ii, sc. 2.

9
Death is an equal doom
To good and bad, the common Inn of rest.
SPENSER, *Faerie Queene*. Bk. ii, canto ii, st. 59.

Death, the only immortal who treats us all alike, whose pity and whose peace and whose refuge are for all—the soiled and the pure, the rich and the poor, the loved and the unloved.
MARK TWAIN, *Memorandum*, written on his deathbed. (*Unpublished Diaries of Mark Twain.*)

10
Death is not rare, alas! nor burials few,
And soon the grassy coverlet of God
Spreads equal green above their ashes pale.
BAYARD TAYLOR, *The Picture of St. John*. Bk. iii, st. 84.

11
The tall, the wise, the reverend head,
Must be as low as ours.
ISAAC WATTS, *Hymns*. Bk. ii, hymn 63.

12
Why all this toil for triumphs of an hour?
What though we wade in wealth, or soar in fame?
Earth's highest station ends in, "Here he lies:"
And "dust to dust" concludes her noblest song.
YOUNG, *Night Thoughts*. Night iv, l. 97.

13
Xerxes the great did die;
And so must you and I.
UNKNOWN, *The New England Primer.*

XI—Death: Its Terrors

14
My God, how lonely The dead are!
GUSTAVO BÉCQUER, *They Closed Her Eyes.* (Masefield, tr.)

15
How shocking must thy summons be, O Death!
To him that is at ease in his possessions:
Who, counting on long years of pleasure here,
Is quite unfurnish'd for that world to come!
ROBERT BLAIR, *The Grave*, l. 350.

16
Oh! death will find me, long before I tire
Of watching you; and swing me suddenly
Into the shade and loneliness and mire
Of the last land!
RUPERT BROOKE, *Sonnet.*

17
Oh God! it is a fearful thing
To see the human soul take wing
In any shape, in any mood.
BYRON, *The Prisoner of Chillon*. Pt. viii.

18
Down to the dust!—and, as thou rott'st away,
Ev'n worms shall perish on thy poisonous clay.
BYRON, *A Sketch.*

Out—out are the lights—out all!
And, over each quivering form,
The curtain, a funeral pall,
Comes down with the rush of a storm,
And the angels, all pallid and wan,
Uprising, unveiling, affirm

That the play is the tragedy, "Man,"
And its hero the Conqueror Worm.
E. A. POE, *The Conqueror Worm*. St. 5.

The knell, the shroud, the mattock, and the grave;
The deep damp vault, the darkness, and the worm;
These are the bugbears of a winter's eve,
The terrors of the living, not the dead.
YOUNG, *Night Thoughts*. Night iv, l. 10.

1
This is the hour of lead
Remembered if outlived
As freezing persons recollect
The snow—
First chill, then stupor, then
The letting go.
EMILY DICKINSON, *After Great Pain.*

The world feels dusty
When we stop to die;
We want the dew then,
Honors taste dry.
EMILY DICKINSON, *Poems*, p. 331.

2
Death is king of the world; 'tis his park
Where he breeds life to feed him. Cries of pain
Are music for his banquet.
GEORGE ELIOT, *Spanish Gypsy*. Bk. ii, l. 446.

3
For who, to dumb Forgetfulness a prey,
This pleasing anxious being e'er resign'd,
Left the warm precincts of the cheerful day,
Nor cast one longing ling'ring look behind?
THOMAS GRAY, *Elegy Written in a Country Church-yard*. St. 22.

Whatever crazy sorrow saith,
No life that breathes with human breath
Has ever truly long'd for death.
TENNYSON, *The Two Voices*, l. 394.

4
Come to the bridal-chamber, Death!
Come to the mother's, when she feels,
For the first time, her first-born's breath! . . .
Come when the heart beats high and warm
With banquet-song, and dance, and wine,
And thou art terrible.
FITZ-GREENE HALLECK, *Marco Bozzaris.*

5
'Tis horrible to die
And come down with our little all of dust,
That Dun of all the duns to satisfy.
THOMAS HOOD, *Bianca's Dream.*

6
The king of terrors.
Old Testament: Job, xviii, 14.

The grisly terror.
MILTON, *Paradise Lost*. Bk. ii, l. 704.

Death gives us more than was in Eden lost.
This king of terrors is the prince of peace.
YOUNG, *Night Thoughts*. Night iii, l. 534.

7
All our knowledge merely helps us to die a more painful death than the animals that know nothing.
MAURICE MAETERLINCK, *Joyzelle*. Act i.

8
The mode of death is sadder than death itself. (Tristius est leto, leti genus.)
MARTIAL, *Epigrams*. Bk. xi, epig. 91.

More cruel than death itself was the moment of death. (O morte ipsa mortis tempus indignius!)
PLINY THE YOUNGER, *Epistles*. Bk. v, epis. 16.

It hath often been said that it is not death, but dying, which is terrible.
HENRY FIELDING, *Amelia*. Bk. iii, ch. 4.

9
Grim death.
MASSINGER, *The Roman Actor*. Act iv. sc. 2.

10
That must be our cure,
To be no more; sad cure; for who would lose,
Though full of pain, this intellectual being,
Those thoughts that wander through eternity,
To perish rather, swallowed up and lost
In the wide womb of uncreated night,
Devoid of sense and motion?
MILTON, *Paradise Lost*. Bk. ii, l. 145.

11
I fled, and cry'd out, Death!
Hell trembled at the hideous name, and sigh'd
From all her caves, and back resounded, Death!
MILTON, *Paradise Lost*. Bk. ii, l. 787.

Before mine eyes in opposition sits
Grim Death, my son and foe.
MILTON, *Paradise Lost*. Bk. ii, l. 803.

Death Grinned horrible a ghastly smile, to hear
His famine should be filled, and blessed his maw
Destined to that good hour.
MILTON, *Paradise Lost*. Bk. ii, l. 845.

12
The sorrows of death compassed me.
Old Testament: Psalms, xviii, 4.

13
Cut off even in the blossoms of my sin,
Unhouseled, disappointed, unaneled;
No reckoning made, but sent to my account
With all my imperfections on my head;
O horrible! O horrible! most horrible!
If thou hast nature in thee, bear it not.
SHAKESPEARE, *Hamlet*. Act i, sc. 5, l. 76.

Ah, what a sign it is of evil life
Where death's approach is seen so terrible!
SHAKESPEARE, *II Henry VI*. Act iii, sc. 3, l. 5.

'Tis a vile thing to die, my gracious lord,
When men are unprepared and look not for it.
SHAKESPEARE, *Richard III*. Act iii, sc. 2, l. 64.

14
Ay, but to die, and go we know not where;
To lie in cold obstruction, and to rot;
This sensible warm motion to become
A kneaded clod; and the delighted spirit
To bathe in fiery floods, or to reside
In thrilling region of thick-ribbed ice; . . .
Imagine howling!—'tis too horrible!

The weariest and most loathed worldly life
That age, ache, penury, and imprisonment
Can lay on nature, is a paradise
To what we fear of death.
SHAKESPEARE, *Measure for Measure*. Act iii, sc. 1, l. 118.

Death in itself is nothing; but we fear
To be we know not what, we know not where.
DRYDEN, *Aureng-Zebe*. Act iv, sc. 1.

1 Woe, destruction, ruin, and decay;
The worst is death, and death will have his day.
SHAKESPEARE, *Richard II*. Act iii, sc. 2, l. 102.

2
Who pass'd, methought, the melancholy flood
With that grim ferryman which poets write of,
Unto the kingdom of perpetual night.
SHAKESPEARE, *Richard III*. Act i, sc. 4, l. 45.

The Pilot of the Galilean lake,
Two massy keys he bore of metals twain,
(The golden opes, the iron shuts amain).
MILTON, *Lycidas*, l. 109.

3
What may we take into the vast Forever?
That marble door
Admits no fruit of all our long endeavor,
No fame-wreathed crown we wore,
No garnered lore.
EDWARD ROWLAND SILL, *The Future*.

XII—Death: The Fear of Death

4
Better die once for all than to live in continual terror. (Βέλτιον θανεῖν ἅπαξ ἢ διὰ βίον τρέμειν.)
ÆSOP, *Fables*.

It is better to die once for all than to live in constant expectation of death.
JULIUS CÆSAR. (PLUTARCH, *Lives of the Cæsars: Julius*. Ch. 57, sec. 5.)

He that fears death lives not.
GEORGE HERBERT, *Jacula Prudentum*.

That life is better life, past fearing death,
Than that which lives to fear.
SHAKESPEARE, *Measure for Measure*, v, 1, 402.

5
Of all things that are feared, the least is death.
WILLIAM ALEXANDER, *Doomsday: The Second Hour*. St. 73.

6
Why be afraid of death
As though your life were breath? . . .
Why should you fear to meet
The Thresher of the wheat?
MALTBIE D. BABCOCK, *Emancipation*.

7
Men fear death, as children fear to go in the dark: and as that natural fear in children is increased with tales, so is the other.
FRANCIS BACON, *Essays: Of Death*.

There is no passion in the mind of man so weak, but it mates and masters the fear of death. . . . Revenge triumphs over death; love slights it; honour aspireth to it; grief flieth to it.
FRANCIS BACON, *Essays: Of Death*.

8
I am not so much afraid of death as ashamed thereof; 'tis the very disgrace and ignominy of our natures.
SIR THOMAS BROWNE, *Religio Medici*. Pt. i, sec. 47.

9
Fear death?—to feel the fog in my throat,
The mist in my face,
When the snows begin, and the blasts denote
I am nearing the place,
The power of the night, the press of the storm,
The post of the foe;
Where he stands, the Arch Fear in a visible form,
Yet the strong man must go.
ROBERT BROWNING, *Prospice*.

10
Must I consume my life—this little life—
In guarding against all may make it less?
It is not worth so much! It were to die
Before my hour, to live in dread of death.
BYRON, *Sardanapalus*. Act i, sc. 2, l. 438.

11
He who cares naught for death cares naught for threats. (Qui ne craint point la mort ne craint point les menaces.)
CORNEILLE, *Le Cid*. Act ii, sc. 1.

12
Far happier are the dead, methinks, than they
Who look for death, and fear it every day.
WILLIAM COWPER, *On Invalids*.

13
In every hedge and ditch both day and night
We fear our death, of every leaf affright.
DU BARTAS, *Devine Weekes and Dayes*. Day i, pt. 3.

14
'Tis not to die we fear, but to die poorly,
To fall forgotten, in a multitude.
JOHN FLETCHER, *The Humorous Lieutenant*. Act ii, sc. 2.

15
What man can look on Death unterrified?
R. W. GILDER, *Love and Death*. St. 2.

16
The ancients dreaded death: the Christian can only fear dying.
J. C. AND A. W. HARE, *Guesses at Truth*.

17
Nay, why should I fear Death,
Who gives us life, and in exchange takes breath?
FREDERICK LAWRENCE KNOWLES, *Laus Mortis*.

18
Death stands above me, whispering low
I know not what into my ear;
Of his strange language all I know
Is, there is not a word of fear.
WALTER SAVAGE LANDOR, *Death*.

1
Neither the sun nor death can be regarded without flinching (Le soleil ni la mort ne se peuvent regarder fixement.)
La Rochefoucauld, *Maximes*. No. 26.

2
What tragic tears bedim the eyes!
What deaths we suffer ere we die!
John Logan, *On the Death of a Young Lady.*

So many are the deaths we die
Before we can be dead indeed.
W. E. Henley, *Rhymes and Rhythms*. No. xv.
See also Wilde *under* Life and Death.

3
Neither dread your last day nor desire it. (Summum nec metuas diem nec optas.)
Martial, *Epigrams*. Bk. x, epig. 47.

4
What fear of death is like the fear beyond it?
Montgomery, *Pelican Island*. Canto viii.

5
Yet as with morn my lad finds fears were vain,
So death shall give to age its toys again.
John Richard Moreland, *Gifts*.

6
Yea, though I walk through the valley of the shadow of death, I will fear no evil; for thou art with me.
Old Testament: Psalms, xxiii, 4.

7
The fear of death is worse than death itself. (Timor mortis morte pejor.)
Publilius Syrus, *Sententiæ*. No. 54.

8
Cowards may fear to die; but courage stout,
Rather than live in snuff, will be put out.
Sir Walter Raleigh, *On the Snuff of a Candle,* the night before his death. (Bayley, *Life of Raleigh*, p. 157.)

9
And come he slow, or come he fast,
It is but Death who comes at last.
Scott, *Marmion*. Canto ii, st. 30.

10
To die without fear of death is a desirable death. (Optanda mors est, sine metu mortis mori.)
Seneca, *Troades*, l. 869.

11
Cowards die many times before their deaths;
The valiant never taste of death but once.
Shakespeare, *Julius Cæsar*. Act ii, sc. 2, l. 32.

Fear is my vassal: when I frown, he flies;
A hundred times in life a coward dies.
John Marston, *The Insatiate Countess*.

12
It seems to me most strange that men should fear;
Seeing that death, a necessary end,
Will come when it will come.
Shakespeare, *Julius Cæsar*. Act ii, sc. 2, l. 35.

13
The sense of death is most in apprehension;
And the poor beetle that we tread upon,
In corporal sufferance finds a pang as great
As when a giant dies.
Shakespeare, *Measure for Measure*. Act iii, sc. 1, l. 78.

14
He that on his pillow lies,
Fear-embalmed before he dies,
Carries, like a sheep, his life,
To meet the sacrificer's knife,
And for eternity is prest,
Sad bell-wether to the rest.
James Shirley, *The Passing Bell*.

15
For him who has faith, death, so far as it is his own death, ceases to possess any quality of terror. The experiment will be over, the rinsed beaker returned to its shelf, the crystals gone dissolving down the waste-pipe; the duster sweeps the bench.
H. G. Wells, *First and Last Things*.

16
It is not the fear of death
That damps my brow.
N. P. Willis, *André*.

17
Man makes a death, which nature never made:
Then on the point of his own fancy falls;
And feels a thousand deaths, in fearing one.
Young, *Night Thoughts*. Night iv, l. 15.

XIII—Death: Its Finality

18
No lamentation can loose
Prisoners of death from the grave.
Matthew Arnold, *Merope*, l. 527.

19
It is only the dead who do not return. (Il n'y a que les morts qui ne reviennent pas.)
Bertrand Barère, *Speech*, in the Convention, 1794. A pun on revenir, to return, or to haunt; and so, sarcastically, "Only dead men's ghosts do not haunt us." (Carlyle, *French Revolution*. Vol. iii, bk. 6, ch. 3.) Napoleon used the expression in regard to himself on 17 July and 12 Dec., 1816. (O'Meara, *Napoleon in Exile*.)

20
Sure! 'tis a serious thing to die! My soul!
What a strange moment must it be, when, near
Thy journey's end, thou hast the gulf in view!
That awful gulf, no mortal e'er repass'd
To tell what's doing on the other side!
Robert Blair, *The Grave*, l. 369.

21
Who e'er returned to teach the Truth, the things of Heaven and Hell to limn?
And all we hear is only fit for grandam-talk and nursery-hymn.
Sir Richard Burton, *The Kasîdah*. Pt. viii, st. 8.

22
"What is it like down there, Charides?" "Very dark." "And what of return?" "All lies."

"And Pluto?" "A myth." "I am done for!" ('Απωλόμεθα.)
CALLIMACHUS. (*Greek Anthology*. Bk. vii, epig. 524.)

Hath any loved you well, down there,
Summer or winter through?
Down there, have you found any fair,
Laid in the grave with you?
Is death's long kiss a richer kiss
Than mine was wont to be—
Or have you gone to some far bliss
And quite forgotten me?
ARTHUR O'SHAUGHNESSY, *Chaitivel: Sarrazine's Song*.

1
Now he travels that dark road, whence, they say, no one returns. (Qui nunc it per iter tenebricosum Illuc, unde negant redire quemquam.)
CATULLUS, *Odes*. Ode iii, l. 11.

Back from the tomb No step has come.
GEORGE CROLY, *The Genius of Death*.

Ah, of the dead, who hath returned from Hades? (Καὶ τίς θανόντων ἦλθεν ἐξ Ἅιδου πάλιν.)
EURIPIDES, *Hercules Furens*, l. 297.

2
Can storied urn or animated bust
Back to its mansion call the fleeting breath?
Can Honour's voice provoke the silent dust,
Or Flattery soothe the dull cold ear of death?
THOMAS GRAY, *Elegy Written in a Country Church-yard*, l. 41.

3
We . . . dry away,
Like to the summer's rain;
Or as the pearls of morning's dew,
Ne'er to be found again.
ROBERT HERRICK, *To Daffodils*.

4
And not a man appears to tell their fate.
HOMER, *Odyssey*. Bk. x, l. 308. (Pope, tr.)

The unreturning brave.
BYRON, *Childe Harold*. Canto iii, st. 27.

5
Before I go whence I shall not return, even to the land of darkness and the shadow of death.
Old Testament: Job, x, 21.

I shall go the way whence I shall not return.
Old Testament: Job, xvi, 22.

6
But O the heavy change, now thou art gone,
Now thou art gone and never must return!
MILTON, *Lycidas*, l. 37.

7
When You and I behind the Veil are past,
Oh, but the long, long while the World shall last,
Which of our Coming and Departure heeds
As the Sea's self should heed a pebble-cast.
OMAR KHAYYÁM, *Rubáiyát*. St. 47. (Fitzgerald, tr.)

When you and I have ceased Champagne to Sup,
Be sure there will be More to Keep it Up;
And while we pat Old Tabby by the fire,
Full many a Girl will lead her Brindle Pup.
JOSEPHINE DASKAM BACON, *Omar for Ladies*.

8
Strange—is it not?—that of the myriads who
Before us passed the door of Darkness through,
Not one returns to tell us of the road
Which to discover we must travel too.
OMAR KHAYYÁM, *Rubáiyát*. St. 68. (Fitzgerald, tr.)

9
The ancient sage, who did so long maintain
That bodies die, but souls return again,
With all the births and deaths he had in store,
Went out Pythagoras, and came no more.
PRIOR, *Ode to the Memory of Colonel Villiers*.

10
The greedy Acheron does not relinquish his prey. (L'avare Achéron ne lâche pas sa proie.)
RACINE, *Phèdre*. Act ii, sc. 5.

Never the grave gives back what it has won!
SCHILLER, *Funeral Fantasy*. Last line.

11
Death,
The undiscover'd country, from whose bourne
No traveller returns.
SHAKESPEARE, *Hamlet*. Act iii, sc. 1, l. 79.

The wave from which there is no return. (Inremeabilis undæ.)
VERGIL, *Æneid*. Bk. vi, l. 425. The Styx.

12
Absence and death, how differ they? and how
Shall I admit that nothing can restore
What one short sigh so easily removed?
Death, life, and sleep, reality and thought—
Assist me, God, their boundaries to know,
O teach me calm submission to thy Will!
WORDSWORTH, *Maternal Grief*, l. 8.

13
And, round us, Death's inexorable hand
Draws the dark curtain close; undrawn no more.
YOUNG, *Night Thoughts*. Night vii, l. 812.

When one is dead, it is for a long time. (Quand on est mort, c'est pour longtemps.)
UNKNOWN. A French proverb.

XIV—Death: The Comforter

14
Death were great joy. (Θανεῖν πολλὴ χάρις.)
ÆSCHYLUS, *Agamemnon*, l. 550.

Men hate death unjustly; it is the greatest defence against their many ills.
ÆSCHYLUS, *Fragments*. Frag. 191.

Death is rather to be chosen than a toilsome life, and not to be born is better than to be born to misery.
ÆSCHYLUS, *Fragments*. Frag. 229.

15
Thou alone, O Death, art the healer of deadly ills. (Μόνος σύ, θάνατε, τῶν ἀνηκέστων κακῶν ἰατρός.)
ÆSCHYLUS, *Philoctetes*. Frag. 229.

O Death the Healer, scorn thou not, I pray,
To come to me: of cureless ills thou art
The one physician. Pain lays not its touch
Upon a corpse.
ÆSCHYLUS, *Philoctetes*. Fr. 229. (Plumptre, tr.)

We all labour against our own cure, for death is the cure of all diseases.
SIR THOMAS BROWNE, *Religio Medici*. Pt. ii, sec. 10.

Death is the receipt for all evils. (La mort est la recepte à touts maux.)
MONTAIGNE, *Essays*. Bk. ii, ch. 3.

Death is the common medicine for woe—
The peaceful haven, which the shatter'd bark
In tempest never seeks.
FREDERIC REYNOLDS, *Werter*. Act iii, sc. 1.

He had rather
Groan so in perpetuity, than be cured
By the sure physician, death.
SHAKESPEARE, *Cymbeline*. Act v, sc. 4, l. 6.

1 Why fear death, the mother of rest, death that puts an end to sickness and the pains of poverty? It happens but once to mortals, and no man ever saw it come twice.
AGATHIAS. (*Greek Anthology*. Bk. x, epig. 69.)

2 Death is the port where all may refuge find,
The end of labour, entry into rest.
WILLIAM ALEXANDER, *Tragedy of Darius*.

They rest from their labours.
Book of Common Prayer: Burial of the Dead.

3 Death is a friend of ours; and he that is not ready to entertain him is not at home.
FRANCIS BACON, *Remains: An Essay on Death.*

O Death! the poor man's dearest friend—
The kindest and the best.
BURNS, *Man Was Made to Mourn.*

The friend of those that have no friend but me.
FLORENCE EARLE COATES, *Death.*

Life that dares send A challenge to his end,
And when it comes say, "Welcome, friend!"
RICHARD CRASHAW, *Wishes to His (Supposed) Mistress*. St. 29.

And Death is beautiful as feet of friend
Coming with welcome at our journey's end.
LOWELL, *Epistle to G.W.Curtis: Postscript*, l. 51.

My name is Death: the last best friend am I.
SOUTHEY, *Carmen Nuptiale*. St. 87.

Death! to the happy thou art terrible;
But how the wretched love to think of thee,
O thou true comforter! the friend of all
Who have no friend beside!
SOUTHEY, *Joan of Arc*. Bk. i, l. 315.

4 Beyond the shining and the shading,
Beyond the hoping and the dreading
I shall be soon.
Love, rest and home!
Sweet hope!
Lord! tarry not, but come.
BONAR, *Beyond the Smiling and the Weeping.*

5 How he lies in his rights of a man!
Death has done all death can.
And, absorbed in the new life he leads,
He recks not, he heeds
Nor his wrong nor my vengeance; both strike
On his senses alike,
And are lost in the solemn and strange
Surprise of the change.
ROBERT BROWNING, *After.*

6 Raise then, the hymn to Death. Deliverer!
God hath anointed thee to free the oppressed
And crush the oppressor.
W. C. BRYANT, *Hymn to Death*, l. 33.

7 Now death as welcome to me comes
As e'er the month of May.
THOMAS CHATTERTON, *The Bristowe Tragedy.*

8 Death is rest from labor and misery. (Aut laborem ac miseriarum quietam.)
CICERO, *In Catilinam*. No. iv, ch. 4, sec. 7.

9 Death—Life's servitor and friend—the guide
That safely ferries us from shore to shore!
FLORENCE EARLE COATES, *Sleep.*

10 Two hands upon the breast,
And labour's done;
Two pale feet crossed in rest,—
The race is won.
DINAH MARIA MULOCK CRAIK, *Now and Afterwards*. Published with sub-title, "Two hands upon the breast, and labour is past"—*Russian Proverb*.

11 How can death be evil, when in its presence we are not aware of it?
DIOGENES. (DIOGENES LAERTIUS, *Diogenes*, 68.)

12 We are too stupid about death. We will not learn
How it is wages paid to those who earn,
How it is the gift for which on earth we yearn,
To be set free from bondage to the flesh;
How it is turning seed-corn into grain,
How it is winning Heaven's eternal gain,
How it means freedom evermore from pain,
How it untangles every mortal mesh.
WILLIAM CROSWELL DOANE, *Death.*

13 Past is the Fear of future Doubt;
The Sun is from the Dial gone;
The Sands are sunk, the Glass is out,
The Folly of the Farce is done.
THOMAS D'URFEY, *Pills to Purge Melancholy.*

14 Death, the great reconciler.
GEORGE ELIOT, *Adam Bede*. Ch. 4.

15 Better thou mayest, but worse thou canst not be
Than in this vale of tears and misery.
THOMAS FLATMAN, *A Thought of Death.*

When on my sick-bed I languish,
Full of sorrow, full of anguish,
Fainting, gasping, trembling, crying,
Panting, groaning, speechless, dying, . . .
Methinks I hear some gentle spirit say,
Be not fearful, come away.

THOMAS FLATMAN, *A Thought of Death.* (1674) *See also* Pope's paraphrase of Adrian, *under* SOUL.

1
Their tears, their little triumphs o'er,
Their human passions now no more.

THOMAS GRAY, *Ode for Music,* l. 48.

2
Forgetfulness and silence are the privileges of the dead. (Λήθη καὶ σιγὴ νεκύων γέρας.)

SAINT GREGORY THE THEOLOGIAN, *Epigram.* (*Greek Anthology.* Bk. viii, No. 236.)

3
When life is woe, And hope is dumb,
The World says, "Go!" The Grave says, "Come!"

ARTHUR GUITERMAN, *Betel-Nuts.*

4
From the winter's grey despair,
From the summer's golden languor,
Death, the lover of Life,
Frees us for ever.

W. E. HENLEY, *In Hospital: Ave, Cæsar!*

The ways of Death are soothing and serene,
And all the words of Death are grave and sweet.

W. E. HENLEY, *The Ways of Death.* (*Bric-à-Brac.* No. 21.)

5
Out of the strain of the Doing,
Into the peace of the Done;
Out of the thirst of Pursuing,
Into the rapture of Won.

W. M. L. JAY, *Harvest Home.* (Published in *Sunday at Home,* May, 1910.)

6
There the wicked cease from troubling; and there the weary be at rest.

Old Testament: Job, iii, 17.

And the wicked cease from troubling, and the weary are at rest.

TENNYSON, *The May Queen.* Last line.

7
Which long for death, but it cometh not; and dig for it more than for hid treasures.

Old Testament: Job, iii, 21.

8
How happier far than life, the end
Of souls that infant-like beneath their burden bend.

JOHN KEBLE, *Holy Innocents.*

9
And, as she looked around, she saw how Death, the consoler,
Laying his hand upon many a heart, had healed it forever.

LONGFELLOW, *Evangeline.* Pt. ii, sec. v, l. 88.

So Nature deals with us, and takes away
Our playthings one by one, and by the hand
Leads us to rest so gently, that we go
Scarce knowing if we wish to go or stay,
Being too full of sleep to understand
How far the unknown transcends the what we know.

LONGFELLOW, *Nature,* l. 9.

10
None but those shadowed by death's approach are suffered to know that death is a blessing; the gods conceal this from those who have life before them, in order that they may go on living. (Agnoscere solis Permissum, quos jam tangit vicinia fati, Victurosque dei celant, ut vivere durent, Felix esse mori.)

LUCAN, *De Bello Civili.* Bk. iv, l. 518.

No one knows but that death is the greatest of all human blessings. (Οἶδε μὲν, γὰρ οὐδεὶς τὸν θάνατον οὐδ' εἰ τυγχάνει τῷ ἀνθρώπῳ.)

PLATO, *Apologia of Socrates.* Sec. 29.

I am that blessing which men fly from—Death.

GEORGE HENRY BOKER, *Countess Laura.*

11
Think not disdainfully of death, but look on it with favor, for Nature wills it like all else. . . . Look for the hour when the soul shall emerge from this its sheath, as now thou awaitest the moment when the child she carries shall come forth from thy wife's womb.

MARCUS AURELIUS, *Meditations.* Bk. ix, sec. 3.

12
Love lent me wings; my path was like a stair;
A lamp unto my feet, that sun was given;
And death was safety and great joy to find;
But dying now, I shall not climb to Heaven.

MICHELANGELO, *Sonnet LXIII: After Sunset.*

13
Death is delightful. Death is dawn,
The waking from a weary night
Of fevers unto truth and light.

JOAQUIN MILLER, *Even So.* St. 35.

14
Life's race well run,
Life's work well done,
Life's victory won,
Now cometh rest.

Claimed for JOHN MILLS, a banker of Manchester, in *Life of John Mills,* by his widow, as having been written by him in 1878, in memory of a favorite brother who died in 1877. (See *Notes and Queries,* vol. iv, p. 167.) Claimed for DR. EDWARD HAZEN PARKER, by his brother, as having been used in his *Funeral Ode on President Garfield,* 1881. (See *Notes and Queries,* vol vii, p. 406.) Brought to public notice by Alexandra, Princess of Wales, who used verse on tombstone of an old nurse in Brampton cemetery and on cards accompanying funeral wreaths.

15
Hence, with denial vain, and coy excuse,
So may some gentle Muse
With lucky words favour my destined urn,
And as he passes turn,
And bid fair peace be to my sable shroud.

MILTON, *Lycidas,* l. 18.

Eas'd the putting off
These troublesome disguises which we wear.
MILTON, *Paradise Lost*. Bk. iv, l. 739.

1
How sweet is death to those who weep,
To those who weep and long to die!
THOMAS MOORE, *Elegiac Stanzas*.

Deep, deep—where never care or pain,
Shall reach her innocent heart again!
THOMAS MOORE, *Lalla Rookh: Prologue ii*.

2
At end of Love, at end of Life,
At end of Hope, at end of Strife,
At end of all we cling to so—
The sun is setting—must we go?

At dawn of Love, at dawn of Life,
At dawn of Peace that follows Strife,
At dawn of all we long for so—
The sun is rising—let us go.
LOUISE CHANDLER MOULTON, *At End*.

3
Death is not grievous to me, for it rids me of my pains. (Nec mihi mors gravis est posituro morte dolores.)
OVID, *Metamorphoses*. Bk. iii, l. 471.

4
For death betimes is comfort, not dismay,
And who can rightly die needs no delay.
PETRARCH, *To Laura in Death*. Canz. v, st. 6.

5
Good is a man's death which destroys the evils of life. (Bona mors est homini, vitæ qui exstinguit mala.)
PUBLILIUS SYRUS, *Sententiæ*. No. 64.

6
O eloquent, just, and mighty Death! whom none could advise, thou hast persuaded; what none hath dared, thou hast done; . . . thou hast drawn together all the far-stretched greatness, all the pride, cruelty, and ambition of man, and covered it over with these two narrow words, *Hic jacet!*
SIR WALTER RALEIGH, *History of the World*. Bk. v, pt. i, ch. 6, Conclusion.

7
Ye old, old dead, and ye of yesternight,
Chieftains, and bards, and keepers of the sheep,
By every cup of sorrow that you had,
Loose me from tears, and make me see aright
How each hath back what once he stayed to weep:
Homer his sight, David his little lad!
LIZETTE WOODWORTH REESE, *Tears*.

8
Death is the privilege of human nature,
And life without it were not worth our taking:
Thither the poor, the pris'ner and the mourner
Fly for relief, and lay their burthens down.
NICHOLAS ROWE, *The Fair Penitent*. Act v, sc. 1, l. 138.

9
Out of the chill and the shadow,
Into the thrill and the shine;
Out of the dearth and the famine,
Into the fulness divine.
MARGARET E. SANGSTER, *Going Home*.

10
If thou and nature can so gently part,
The stroke of death is as a lover's pinch,
Which hurts, and is desir'd.
SHAKESPEARE, *Antony and Cleopatra*. Act v, sc. 2, l. 297.

11
Vex not his ghost: O, let him pass! he hates him much
That would upon the rack of this tough world
Stretch him out longer.
SHAKESPEARE, *King Lear*. Act v, sc. 3, l. 313.

12
I have a strong feeling that I shall be glad when I am dead and done for—scrapped at last to make room for somebody better, cleverer, more perfect than myself.
BERNARD SHAW. (HENDERSON, *G. B. S.*, p. 484.)

13
He has out-soared the shadow of our night;
Envy and calumny, and hate and pain,
And that unrest which men miscall delight,
Can touch him not and torture not again;
From the contagion of the world's slow stain,
He is secure, and now can never mourn
A heart grown cold, a head grown grey in vain.
SHELLEY, *Adonais*. St. 40.

14
Peace, rest, and sleep are all we know of death,
And all we dream of comfort.
SWINBURNE, *In Memory of John William Inchbold*.

Out of the world's way, out of the light,
Out of the ages of worldly weather,
Forgotten of all men altogether.
SWINBURNE, *The Triumph of Time*. St. 15.

At the door of life, by the gate of breath,
There are worse things waiting for men than death.
SWINBURNE, *The Triumph of Time*. St. 20.

15
A sudden death is but a sudden joy, if it takes a man in the state and exercises of virtue.
JEREMY TAYLOR, *Holy Dying*. Ch. 3, sec. 9.

16
"Consider well," the voice replied,
"His face, that two hours since hath died;
Wilt thou find passion, pain, or pride?"
TENNYSON, *The Two Voices*, l. 241.

17
Each person is born to one possession which outvalues all the others—his last breath.
MARK TWAIN, *Pudd'nhead Wilson's Calendar*.

18
Dear, beauteous death, the jewel of the just!
Shining nowhere but in the dark;
What mysteries do lie beyond thy dust,
Could man outlook that mark!
HENRY VAUGHAN, *They Are All Gone*.

1
No more for him life's stormy conflicts,
Nor victory, nor defeat—no more time's dark events,
Charging like ceaseless clouds across the sky.
WALT WHITMAN, *Hush'd Be the Camps Today.*

2
Come lovely and soothing death,
Undulate round the world, serenely arriving, arriving,
In the day, in the night, to all, to each,
Sooner or later, delicate death.
WALT WHITMAN, *Memories of President Lincoln.* Sec. 14.

Prais'd be the fathomless universe
For life and joy, and for objects and knowledge curious,
And for love, sweet love—but praise! praise! praise!
For the sure-enwinding arms of cool-enfolding death.
WALT WHITMAN, *Memories of President Lincoln.* Sec. 14.

3
And I will show that there is no imperfection in the present, and can be none in the future,
And I will show that whatever happens to anybody it may be turn'd to beautiful results,
And I will show that nothing can happen more beautiful than death.
WALT WHITMAN, *Starting from Paumanok.* Sec. 12.

4
O heart sore-tried! thou hast the best,
That Heaven itself could give thee,—rest,
Rest from all bitter thoughts and things!
How many a poor one's blessing went
With thee beneath the low green tent
Whose curtain never outward swings!
J. G. WHITTIER, *Snow-Bound,* l. 386.

5
Death, of all pain the period, not of joy.
YOUNG, *Night Thoughts.* Night iii, l. 519.

XV—Death: Gentle Death

6
Her suffering ended with the day;
Yet lived she at its close,
And breathed the long, long night away
In statue-like repose.

But when the sun, in all his state,
Illumed the eastern skies,
She passed through Glory's morning gate,
And walked in Paradise.
JAMES ALDRICH, *A Death-bed.*

Her washing ended with the day,
Yet lived she at its close,
And passed the long, long night away
In darning ragged hose.
But when the sun in all its state
Illumed the Eastern skies,
She passed about the kitchen grate
And went to making pies.
PHŒBE CARY, *The Wife.*

7
Strew on her roses, roses,
And never a spray of yew.
In quiet she reposes:
Ah! would that I did too.
MATTHEW ARNOLD, *Requiescat.*

Her cabin'd, ample Spirit,
It flutter'd and fail'd for breath.
To-night it doth inherit
The vasty Hall of Death.
MATTHEW ARNOLD, *Requiescat.*

8
So fades a summer cloud away;
So sinks the gale when storms are o'er;
So gently shuts the eye of day;
So dies a wave along the shore.
ANNA L. BARBAULD, *The Death of the Virtuous.*

9
Aye, Death is tender, Death is fair—
A tall, pale one with spun-gold hair.
ELLEN M. CARROLL, *An Appreciation.*

10
She passed away like morning dew
Before the sun was high;
So brief her time, she scarcely knew
The meaning of a sigh.
HARTLEY COLERIDGE, *Early Death.*

Love was her guardian Angel here,
But Love to Death resigned her;
Though Love was kind, why should we fear
But holy Death is kinder?
HARTLEY COLERIDGE, *Early Death.*

11
So softly death succeeded life in her,
She did but dream of heaven, and she wa there.
DRYDEN, *Eleonora,* l. 315.

12
We watch'd her breathing thro' the night,
Her breathing soft and low,
As in her breast the wave of life
Kept heaving to and fro. . . .

Our very hopes belied our fears,
Our fears our hopes belied;
We thought her dying when she slept,
And sleeping when she died.
THOMAS HOOD, *The Death-bed.*

13
Then with no fiery, throbbing pain,
No cold gradations of decay,
Death broke at once the vital chain,
And freed his soul the nearest way.
SAMUEL JOHNSON, *On the Death of Dr. Robert Levet.*

14
Then fell upon the house a sudden gloom,
A shadow on those features fair and thin;
And softly, from the hushed and darkened room,
Two angels issued, where but one went in.
LONGFELLOW, *The Two Angels.* St. 9.

1
Lord, now lettest thou thy servant depart in peace, according to thy word.
New Testament: Luke, ii, 29.

2
Softly woo away her breath,
Gentle death!
BRYAN WALLER PROCTER, *Softly Woo Away Her Breath.*

3
When faith and love which parted from thee never,
Had ripened thy just soul to dwell with God,
Meekly thou didst resign this earthly load
Of death, called life; which us from life doth sever.
Thy works, and alms, and all thy good endeavour,
Stayed not behind, nor in the grave were trod;
But, as Faith pointed with her golden rod,
Followed thee up to joy and bliss for ever.
MILTON, *Sonnets: On the Memory of Mrs. Thomson.*

4
The breast where roses could not live
Has done with rising and with falling.
E. A. ROBINSON, *For a Dead Lady.*

5
Death, death; oh, amiable, lovely death!
SHAKESPEARE, *King John.* Act iii, sc. 4, l. 34.

6
Now is done thy long day's work;
Fold thy palms across thy breast,
Fold thine arms, turn to thy rest.
Let them rave.
TENNYSON, *A Dirge.*

7
God laid His fingers on the ivories
Of her pure members as on smoothèd keys.
And there out-breathed her spirit's harmonies.
FRANCIS THOMPSON, *Her Portrait.* St. 7.

8
Into the Silent Land!
Ah! who shall lead us thither? . . .
Into the land of the great Departed,
Into the Silent Land!
(Ins stille Land!
Wer leitet uns hinüber? . . .
Ins Land der grossen Toten,
Ins stille Land.)
JOHANN GAUDENZ VON SALIS-SEEWIS, *Lied.* (Longfellow, tr.)

9
His Maker kissed his soul away,
And laid his flesh to rest.
ISAAC WATTS, *The Presence of God.*

Died of the kisses of the lips of God.
FREDERIC W. H. MYERS, *St. Paul.* Of Moses.

10
Yet there was round thee such a dawn
Of light, ne'er seen before,
As fancy never could have drawn,
And never can restore.
CHARLES WOLFE, *To Mary.*

11
Come gentle death, the ebb of care;
The ebb of care, the flood of life.
UNKNOWN, *Upon Consideration of the State of This Life.* (TOTTEL, *Miscellany,* 1557.)

12
Is it then so sad a thing to die? (Usque adeone mori miserum est?)
VERGIL, *Æneid.* Bk. xii, l. 646.

XVI—Death: The Last Sleep

See also Sleep: Brother to Death

13
They do neither plight nor wed
In the city of the dead,
In the city where they sleep away the hours.
RICHARD BURTON, *The City of the Dead.*

14
The silence of that dreamless sleep
I envy now too much to weep.
BYRON, *And Thou Art Dead.*

Death, so called, is a thing which makes men weep,
And yet a third of life is passed in sleep.
BYRON, *Don Juan.* Canto xiv, st. 3.

15
He but sleeps the holy sleep. (Ἱερὸν ὕπνον κοιμᾶται.)
CALLIMACHUS, *Epigrams.* No. 11.

16
Sleep on, beloved, sleep, and take thy rest;
Lay down thy head upon thy Saviour's breast;
We love thee well, but Jesus loves thee best—
Good-night! Good-night! Good-night!
SARAH DOUDNEY, *The Christian's Good-Night.*
Ira D. Sankey wrote the music for this hymn, which was sung at the funeral of Dr. Charles H. Spurgeon, 3 Feb., 1892.

17
Father in thy gracious keeping
Leave we now thy servant sleeping.
JOHN LODGE ELLERTON, *Now the Laborer's Task is O'er.*

18
Death is an eternal sleep. (La mort est un sommeil éternel.)
JOSEPH FOUCHÉ, who, as minister of police under the Directory, in 1794, ordered this inscription placed on the gates of French cemeteries.

Who sleeps the longest is the happiest;
Death is the longest sleep.
THOMAS SOUTHERNE, *The Fatal Marriage.* Act v, sc. 2.

19
And wish my friend as sound a sleep
As lads' I did not know,
That shepherded the moonlit sheep
A hundred years ago.
A. E. HOUSMAN, *A Shropshire Lad.* No. 9.

20
They sleep beneath the shadows of the clouds, careless alike of sunshine or storm, each in the windowless palace of rest. Earth may run red with other wars—they are at peace. In

the midst of battles, in the roar of conflict, they found the serenity of death.
R. G. INGERSOLL, *Memorial Day Vision.*

1
She is not dead, but sleepeth.
New Testament: Luke, viii, 52; *Matthew,* ix, 24.

The report of my death was an exaggeration.
MARK TWAIN, *Cablegram,* from London to inquiring New York newspaper, 2 June, 1897.

2
A death-like sleep,
A gentle wafting to immortal life.
MILTON, *Paradise Lost.* Bk. xii, l. 434.

3
There's nothing terrible in death;
'Tis but to cast our robes away,
And sleep at night, without a breath
To break repose till dawn of day.
ROBERT MONTGOMERY, *In Memory of E. G.*

4
Till tired, he sleeps, and life's poor play is o'er.
POPE, *Essay on Man.* Epis. ii, l. 282.

5
Yet a little sleep, a little slumber, a little folding of the hands to sleep.
Old Testament: Proverbs, vi, 10; xxiv, 33.

6
He giveth his beloved sleep.
Old Testament: Psalms, cxxvii, 2.

Of all the thoughts of God that are
Borne inward into souls afar,
Along the Psalmist's music deep,
Now tell me if that any is,
For gift or grace, surpassing this:
"He giveth his belovèd—sleep"?
E. B. BROWNING, *The Sleep.* St. 1.

And friends, dear friends, when it shall be
That this low breath is gone from me,
And round my bier ye come to weep,
Let One, most loving of you all,
Say, "Not a tear must o'er her fall!
He giveth his belovèd sleep."
E. B. BROWNING, *The Sleep.* St. 9.

And if there be no meeting past the grave,
If all is darkness, silence, yet 'tis rest.
Be not afraid, ye waiting hearts that weep,
For still He giveth His beloved sleep,
And if an endless sleep He wills, 'tis best.
MRS. THOMAS HENRY HUXLEY, *Lines,* on the grave of Thomas Henry Huxley.

7
She slept the sleep of the just. (Elle s'endormit du sommeil des justes.)
RACINE, *Abrégé de l'Histoire de Port Royal.* Vol. iv, l. 517.

8
Sleep that no pain shall wake,
Night that no morn shall break,
Till joy shall overtake
Her perfect peace.
CHRISTINA ROSSETTI, *Dream-Land.*

Sleep the sleep that knows not breaking,
Morn of toil, nor night of waking.
SCOTT, *The Lady of the Lake.* Canto i, st. 31.

9
For a man who has done his natural duty, death is as natural and welcome as sleep.
GEORGE SANTAYANA. (*Greatest Thoughts on Immortality,* p. 115.)

10
To die: to sleep;
No more; and by a sleep to say we end
The heart-ache and the thousand natural shocks
That flesh is heir to, 'tis a consummation
Devoutly to be wish'd. To die, to sleep;
To sleep: perchance to dream: ay, there's the rub;
For in that sleep of death what dreams may come
When we have shuffled off this mortal coil,
Must give us pause: there's the respect
That makes calamity of so long life.
SHAKESPEARE, *Hamlet.* Act iii, sc. 1, l. 60.

11
Then death rock me asleep, abridge my doleful days!
SHAKESPEARE, *II Henry IV.* Act ii, sc. 4, l. 211.

This sleep is sound indeed, this is a sleep
That from this golden rigol hath divorc'd
So many English kings.
SHAKESPEARE, *II Henry IV.* Act iv, sc. 5, l. 35.

12
He gave his honours to the world again,
His blessed part to heaven, and slept in peace.
SHAKESPEARE, *Henry VIII.* Act iv, sc. 2, l. 29.

After life's fitful fever, he sleeps well;
Treason has done his worst: nor steel, nor poison,
Malice domestic, foreign levy, nothing,
Can touch him further.
SHAKESPEARE, *Macbeth.* Act iii, sc. 2, l. 23.

And the fever called "Living"
Is conquered at last.
EDGAR ALLAN POE, *For Annie.*

13
The best of rest is sleep,
And that thou oft provok'st; yet grossly fear'st
Thy death, which is no more.
SHAKESPEARE, *Measure for Measure,* iii, 1, 17.

14
That sweet sleep which medicines all pain.
SHELLEY, *Julian and Maddalo,* l. 499.

15
Yes, 'twill only be a sleep:
When, with songs and dewy light,
Morning blossoms out of Night,
She will open her blue eyes
'Neath the palms of Paradise,
While we foolish ones shall weep.
EDWARD ROWLAND SILL, *Sleeping.*

16
Sleep; and if life was bitter to thee, pardon;
If sweet, give thanks; thou hast no more to live;
And to give thanks is good, and to forgive.
SWINBURNE, *Ave Atque Vale.* St. 17.

Who knows but on their sleep may rise
Such light as never heaven let through
To lighten earth from Paradise?
SWINBURNE, *A Baby's Death.* Sec. 4.

1
The end is come of pleasant places,
The end of tender words and faces,
The end of all, the poppied sleep.
SWINBURNE, *Ilicet.* St. 1.

2
God's finger touched him, and he slept.
TENNYSON, *In Memoriam.* Pt. lxxxv, st. 5.

3
Sleep till the end, true soul and sweet.
Nothing comes to thee new or strange.
Sleep full of rest from head to feet;
Lie still, dry dust, secure of change.
TENNYSON, *To J. S.* St. 19.

XVII—Death: The Good Death

4
Nobly to die were better than to save one's life. (Καλῶς τεθνάναι κάλλιον ἂν μᾶλλον ἢ σεσῶσθαι.)
ÆSCHYLUS [?], *Fragments.* Frag. 235.

How beautiful is death, when earn'd by virtue!
ADDISON, *Cato.* Act iv, sc. 6.

5
That was indeed to live—
At one bold swoop to wrest
From darkling death the best
That Death to Life can give!
T. B. ALDRICH, *Shaw Memorial Ode.* Pt. iii.

6
Happy he who dies before he calls for death to take him away. (Mori est felicis antequam mortem invocet.)
FRANCIS BACON, *Ornamenta Rationalia.* No. 27.

7
But whether on the scaffold high,
Or in the battle's van,
The fittest place where man can die
Is where he dies for man.
MICHAEL BARRY, *The Place to Die.* (Dublin *Nation,* 28 Sept., 1844.)

8
We must all die!
All leave ourselves, it matters not where, when,
Nor how, so we die well.
BEAUMONT AND FLETCHER, *Valentinian,* iv, 4.

9
For I say, this is death and the sole death,
When a man's loss comes to him from his gain,
Darkness from light, from knowledge ignorance,
And lack of love from love made manifest.
ROBERT BROWNING, *A Death in the Desert.*

10
The finest sight beneath the sky
Is to see how bravely a man can die.
ROBERT BUCHANAN, *O'Murtogh.*

One likes to die where his father before him
Died, with the same sky shinin' o'er him.
ROBERT BUCHANAN, *White Rose and Red.* Pt. iii, 2.

11
He died, as erring man should die,
Without display, without parade;
Meekly had he bowed and prayed,
As not disdaining priestly aid,
Nor desperate of all hope on high.
BYRON, *Parisina.* St. 17.

12
Then is it best, as for a worthy fame,
To dyen when that he is best of name.
CHAUCER, *The Knightes Tale,* l. 2197.

And could we choose the time, and choose aright,
'Tis best to die, our honour at the height.
DRYDEN, *Palamon and Arcite.* Bk. iii, l. 1088.

It is better to die, since death comes surely,
In the full noon-tide of an honored name,
Than to lie at the end of years obscurely,
A handful of dust in a shroud of shame.
J. J. ROCHE, *Sir Hugo's Choice.*

13
At length, fatigued with life, he bravely fell,
And health with Boerhaave bade the world farewell.
BENJAMIN CHURCH, *The Choice.* (1754)

14
And, having lived a trifler, die a man.
COWPER, *Retirement,* l. 14.

15
So he died for his faith. That is fine—
More than most of us do.
But say, can you add to that line
That he lived for it, too?
ERNEST CROSBY, *Life and Death.*

Death comes with a crawl, or comes with a pounce,
And whether he's slow or spry,
It isn't the fact that you're dead that counts,
But only, how did you die?
EDMUND VANCE COOKE, *How Did You Die?*

16
Some men die early and are spared much care,
Some suddenly, escaping worse than death;
But he is fortunate who happens where
He can exult and die in the same breath.
LOUISE DRISCOLL, *The Good Hour.*

17
Of no distemper, of no blast he died,
But fell like autumn fruit that mellow'd long,—
Even wonder'd at, because he dropp'd no sooner.
Fate seem'd to wind him up for fourscore years,
Yet freshly ran he on ten winters more;
Till like a clock worn out with eating time,
The wheels of weary life at last stood still.
DRYDEN, *Œdipus.* Act iv, sc. 1.

18
The game of death was never played more nobly.
JOHN FLETCHER, *A Wife for a Month.* Act v, 1.

Death never won a stake with greater toil.
DRYDEN, *Threnodia Augustalis.* St. 5.

1
Those who have endeavoured to teach us to die well, have taught few to die willingly.
SAMUEL JOHNSON. (BOSWELL, *Life,* June, 1861.)

2
Yea, say that I went down to death
Serene and unafraid,
Still loving Song, but loving more
Life, of which Song is made!
HARRY KEMP, *Farewell.*

3
And grant that when I face the grisly Thing,
My song may trumpet down the gray Perhaps;
Let me be as a tune-swept fiddlestring
That feels the Master Melody—and snaps.
JOHN G. NEIHARDT, *Let Me Live Out My Years.*

4
So that he seemed to depart not from life, but from one home to another. (Ut non ex vita, sed ex domo in domum videretur migrare.)
CORNELIUS NEPOS, *Lives: Atticus.*

5
Let me die the death of the righteous, and let my last end be like his!
Old Testament: Numbers, xxiii, 10.

"O let me die his death!" all nature cries.
"Then live his life."—All nature falters there.
YOUNG, *Night Thoughts.* Night v, l. 367.

6
He died full of years and honors, as illustrious for those he refused as for those he accepted. (Et ille quidem plenus annis abiit, plenus honoribus, illis etiam, quos recusavit.)
PLINY THE YOUNGER, *Epistles.* Bk. ii, epis. 1, sec. 2. Referring to Virginius Rufus.

Thou shalt come to thy grave in a full age, like as a shock of corn cometh in in his season.
Old Testament: Job, v, 26.

The sweet wise death of old men honourable.
SWINBURNE, *Atalanta in Calydon: Althæa.*

7
Thou, Abelard! the last sad office pay,
And smooth my passage to the realms of day:
See my lips tremble, and my eyeballs roll,
Suck my last breath, and catch my flying soul!
Ah, no!—in sacred vestments mayst thou stand,
The hallow'd taper trembling in thy hand,
Present the cross before my lifted eye,
Teach me at once, and learn of me, to die.
POPE, *Eloisa to Abelard,* l. 321.

8
Blessed are the dead which die in the Lord from henceforth: Yea, saith the Spirit, that they may rest from their labours; and their works do follow them.
New Testament: Revelation, xiv, 13.

9
So die as though your funeral
Ushered you through the doors that led
Into a stately banquet hall
Where heroes banqueted.
ALAN SEEGER, *Maktoob.*
See also BRYANT *under* LIFE AND DEATH.

10
It is not a question of dying earlier or later, but of dying well or ill. And dying well means escape from the danger of living ill. (Citius mori aut tardius ad rem non pertinet, bene mori aut male ad rem pertinet. Bene autem mori est effugere male vivendi periculum.)
SENECA, *Epistulæ ad Lucilium.* Epis. lxx, sec. 6.

11
They say he made a good end.
SHAKESPEARE, *Hamlet.* Act iv, sc. 5, l. 186.

A' made a finer end and went away an it had been any christom child.
SHAKESPEARE, *Henry V.* Act ii, sc. 3, l. 11.

Mr. Badman died . . . as they call it, like a chrisom-child, quietly and without fear.
JOHN BUNYAN, *Mr. Badman,* p. 566.

12
And so espoused to death, with blood he sealed
A testament of noble-ending love.
SHAKESPEARE, *Henry V.* Act iv, sc. 6, l. 26.

And, to add greater honours to his age
Than man could give him, he died fearing God.
SHAKESPEARE, *Henry VIII.* Act iv, sc. 2, l. 67.

Nothing in his life
Became him like the leaving it; he died
As one that had been studied in his death
To throw away the dearest thing he owed,
As 't were a careless trifle.
SHAKESPEARE, *Macbeth.* Act i, sc. 4, l. 7.

They say he parted well, and paid his score;
And so, God be with him!
SHAKESPEARE, *Macbeth.* Act v, sc. 8, l. 52.

13
How oft, when men are at the point of death,
Have they been merry! which their keepers call
A lightning before death.
SHAKESPEARE, *Romeo and Juliet.* Act v, sc. 3, l. 88.

14
To die well is the chief part of virtue. (Καλῶς θνήσκειν ἀρετῆς μέρος ἐστὶ μὲγιστον.)
SIMONIDES, *Epitaph.* (*Greek Anthology.* Bk. vii, No. 253.)

15
Now sure 's the moment when I ought to die,
Lest some hereafter bitterness in life
Impair this joy.
(Nunc est perfecto, interfici quom perpeti me possum,
Ne hoc gaudium contaminet vita ægritudine aliqua.)
TERENCE, *Eunuchus,* l. 551. (Act iii, sc. 5.)

16
As the last bell struck, a peculiar sweet smile shone over his face, and he lifted up his head a little, and quickly said, "Adsum!" and fell

back. It was the word we used at school, when names were called; and lo, he, whose heart was as that of a little child, had answered to his name, and stood in the presence of The Master.

THACKERAY, *The Newcomes*. Bk. i, ch. 42.

1
How beautiful it is for man to die
Upon the walls of Zion! to be called,
Like a watch-worn and weary sentinel,
To put his armor off and rest—in heaven!

N. P. WILLIS, *On the Death of a Missionary*.

2
But when the great and good depart,
What is it more than this—
That Man, who is from God sent forth,
Doth yet again to God return?—
Such ebb and flow must ever be,
Then wherefore should we mourn?

WORDSWORTH, *Lines on the Expected Dissolution of Mr. Fox*.

XVIII—Death: One Fight More

3
And of all the ancient songs
Passing to the swallow-blue halls
By the dark streams of Persephone,
This only remains:
That in the end we turn to thee, Death,
That we turn to thee, singing One last song.

RICHARD ALDINGTON, *Choricos*.

4
To die would be an awfully big adventure.

JAMES M. BARRIE, *Peter Pan*. Act iii.

Why fear death? It is the most beautiful adventure in life.

CHARLES FROHMAN, his last words before going down with the *Lusitania*, torpedoed by the Germans, 7 May, 1915. (As reported by Rita Jolivet.) Mr. Frohman had produced Barrie's *Peter Pan*, and so was familiar with the preceding quotation.

Death is only an incident in life.

Message from Voltaire's Ghost. (DE MORGAN, *Joseph Vance*. Ch. 11.)

5
We shall go down with unreluctant tread
Rose-crowned into the darkness.

RUPERT BROOKE, *The Hill*.

Proud, then, clear-eyed and laughing, go to greet
Death as a friend!

RUPERT BROOKE, *Second Best*.

6
I was ever a fighter, so—one fight more,
The best and the last!
I would hate that death bandaged my eyes, and forbore,
And bade me creep past.
No! let me taste the whole of it, fare like my peers,
The heroes of old,
Bear the brunt, in a minute pay glad life's arrears
Of pain, darkness and cold.

ROBERT BROWNING, *Prospice*.

7
Like a led victim, to my death I'll go,
And dying, bless the hand that gave the blow.

DRYDEN, *The Spanish Friar*. Act ii, sc. 1, l. 64.

We bear it calmly, though a ponderous woe,
And still adore the hand that gives the blow.

JOHN POMFRET, *Verses to His Friend under Affliction*.

Pleas'd to the last he crops the flowery food,
And licks the hand just rais'd to shed his blood.

POPE, *Essay on Man*. Epis. i, l. 83.

8
So be my passing!
My task accomplished and the long day done,
My wages taken, and in my heart
Some late lark singing,
Let me be gathered to the quiet west,
The sundown splendid and serene,
Death.

W. E. HENLEY, *Margaritæ Sorori*.

9
I would always be in the thick of life,
Threading its mazes, sharing its strife;
Yet—somehow, singing!
When at the road's end shadows longer grow—
Into the last long shadow let me go,
Still—somehow, singing.

ROSELLE MERCIER MONTGOMERY, *Somehow, Singing*.

10
Give me my scallop-shell of quiet,
My staff of faith to walk upon,
My scrip of joy, immortal diet,
My bottle of salvation,
My gown of glory, hope's true gage;
And thus I'll take my pilgrimage.

SIR WALTER RALEIGH, *His Pilgrimage*.

11
'Tis but to die,
'Tis but to venture on that common hazard,
Which many a time in battle I have run;
'Tis but to do, what, at that very moment,
In many nations of the peopled earth,
A thousand and a thousand shall do with me.

NICHOLAS ROWE, *Jane Shore*. Act iv, sc. 1.

12
Death in my boots may-be, but fighting, fighting!

ROBERT W. SERVICE, *Song of the Soldier-Born*.

13
If I must die
I will encounter darkness as a bride,
And hug it in mine arms.

SHAKESPEARE, *Measure for Measure*. Act iii, sc. 1, l. 83.

14
We count it death to falter, not to die. (Οὐ τὸ θανεῖν, ἀλλὰ φυγεῖν θάνατος.)

SIMONIDES [?], *Epigram*. (*Greek Anthology*. Bk. vii, epig. 431.)

15
Each day, I gird my feeble soul with prayer:
May then the blood of Bayard be my own:

May I ride hard and straight and smite him
square,
And in a clash of arms be overthrown;
And as I fall hear through the evening air
The distant horn of Roland, faintly blown.
FREDERIC F. VAN DE WATER, *The Last Tourney.*

And when I face the tyrant Death, may Bok be with me in the gloom, to decorate my final breath with tassels and an ostrich plume.
WALT MASON, *Helpful Mr. Bok.*

1
My foothold is tenon'd and mortis'd in
granite,
I laugh at what you call dissolution,
And I know the amplitude of time.
WALT WHITMAN, *Song of Myself*. Sec. 20.

2
Farewell, sweet dust; I was never a miser:
Once, for a minute, I made you mine:
Now you are gone, I am none the wiser,
But the leaves of the willow are bright as
wine.
ELINOR WYLIE, *Farewell, Sweet Dust.*

XIX—Death and Fame

3
Above all, believe it, the sweetest canticle is "Nunc dimittis," when a man hath obtained worthy ends and expectations. Death hath this also: that it openeth the gate to good fame, and extinguisheth envy.
FRANCIS BACON, *Essays: Of Death.* (1597)

Death's a pleasant road that leads to fame.
GEORGE GRANVILLE, *Verses*, l. 48. (1690)

Death opens the gate of Fame and shuts the gate of Envy after it.
STERNE, *Tristram Shandy.* Vol. v, ch. 3.

4
Peace to the mighty dead!
THOMAS CAMPBELL, *Lines to Commemorate the Day of Victory in Egypt.*

There studious let me sit,
And hold high converse with the mighty dead.
THOMSON, *The Seasons: Winter*, l. 431.

5
The rest were vulgar deaths unknown to
fame.
HOMER, *Iliad.* Bk. ii, l. 394. (Pope, tr.)

6
No more famous shade will dwell in the house of death. (Non erit in Stygia notior umbra domo.)
MARTIAL, *Epigrams.* Bk. xii, epig. 52.

7
Weep him dead and mourn as you may,
Me, I sing as I must:
Blessed be Death, that cuts in marble
What would have sunk to dust!
EDNA ST. VINCENT MILLAY, *Keen.*

8
Death makes no conquest of this conqueror:
For now he lives in fame, though not in life.
SHAKESPEARE, *Richard III.* Act iii, sc. 1, l. 87.

9
A Power is passing from the earth.
WORDSWORTH, *Lines on the Expected Dissolution of Mr. Fox*, l. 17.

XX—Death and Beauty

11
Thy day without a cloud hath passed,
And thou wert lovely to the last.
BYRON, *And Thou Art Dead*, l. 50.

So fair, so calm, so softly seal'd,
The first, last look by death reveal'd!
BYRON, *The Giaour*, l. 88.

12
Oh, who will find a lover for Death and for
her only?
Though all men kiss her lips, they kiss against
their will.
Oh, pity Death! Wistful she is, and exquisite
and lonely
And all who sleep with her lie curiously still.
RALPH CHEYNEY, *A Lover for Death.*

13
One more Unfortunate,
Weary of breath,
Rashly importunate,
Gone to her death!

Take her up tenderly,
Lift her with care;
Fashion'd so slenderly,
Young, and so fair!
THOMAS HOOD, *The Bridge of Sighs.*

Past all dishonour,
Death has left on her
Only the beautiful.
THOMAS HOOD, *The Bridge of Sighs.*

14
In dreams she grows not older,
The lands of Dream among,
Though all the world wax colder,
Though all the songs be sung,
In dreams doth he behold her
Still fair and kind and young.
ANDREW LANG, *Lost Love.*

Stand close around, ye Stygian set,
With Dirce in one boat conveyed,
Or Charon, seeing, may forget
That he is old, and she a shade.
WALTER SAVAGE LANDOR, *Dirce.*

15
Die when you will, you need not wear
At Heaven's Court a form more fair
Than Beauty here on earth has given;
Keep but the lovely looks we see—
The voice we hear—and you will be
An angel ready-made for Heaven!
THOMAS MOORE, *To* ——. A translation of "Moria pur quando vuol, non è bisogna mutar ni faccia ni voce per esser un Angelo," the words addressed by Lord Herbert of Cherbury to the beautiful nun at Murano.

And should you visit now the seats of bliss,
You need not wear another form but this.
JOHN OLDHAM, *To Madam L. E.*

1
Death aims with fouler spite at fairer marks.
FRANCIS QUARLES, *Divine Poems.*

Death loves a shining mark, a signal blow.
YOUNG, *Night Thoughts.* Night v, l. 1010.

2
A most unspotted lily shall she pass
To the ground, and all the world shall mourn her.
SHAKESPEARE, *Henry VIII.* Act v, sc. 5, l. 62.

Death lies on her like an untimely frost
Upon the sweetest flower of all the field.
SHAKESPEARE, *Romeo and Juliet.* Act iv, sc. 5, l. 28.

Death, that hath suck'd the honey of thy breath,
Hath had no power yet upon thy beauty;
Thou art not conquer'd; beauty's ensign yet
Is crimson in thy lips, and in thy cheeks,
And death's pale flag is not advanced there.
SHAKESPEARE, *Romeo and Juliet,* v, 3, 92.

3
She died in beauty, like a rose
Blown from its parent stem.
C. D. SILLERY, *She Died in Beauty.*

4
Death has made
His darkness beautiful with thee.
TENNYSON, *In Memoriam.* Pt. lxxiv, st. 3.

The passing of the sweetest soul
That ever look'd with human eyes.
TENNYSON, *In Memoriam.* Pt. lvii, st. 3.

5
And as pale sickness does invade
Your frailer part, the breaches made
In that fair lodging still more clear
Make the bright guest, your soul, appear.
EDMUND WALLER, *À la Malade.*

6
She made the stars of heaven more bright
By sleeping under them at night.
GEORGE EDWARD WOODBERRY, *Wild Eden.*

XXI—Death: "They Are All Gone"

See also Friends: Their Loss

7
The white sail of his soul has rounded
The promontory—death.
WILLIAM ALEXANDER, *The Icebound Ship.*

8
The dead abide with us. Though stark and cold,
Earth seems to grip them, they are with us still:
They have forged our chains of being for good or ill,
And their invisible hands these hands yet hold.
MATHILDE BLIND, *The Dead.*

9
Fled, like the sun eclipsed as noon appears,
And left us darkling in a world of tears.
BURNS, *Third Epistle to Robert Graham,* l. 80.

10
The cold, the changed, perchance the dead, anew,
The mourn'd, the loved, the lost,—too many, yet how few!
BYRON, *Childe Harold.* Canto iv, st. 24.

11
Soul of the just! companion of the dead!
Where is thy home, and whither art thou fled?
CAMPBELL, *The Pleasures of Hope.* Pt. ii, l. 277

12
Ha! Dead! Impossible! It cannot be!
I'd not believe it though himself should swear it.
HENRY CAREY, *Chrononhotonthologos.* Act ii, sc. 4.

Is he then dead?
What, dead at last! quite, quite, for ever dead!
CONGREVE, *The Mourning Bride.* Act v, sc. 1.

13
It singeth low in every heart,
We hear it each and all,—
A song of those who answer not,
However we may call;
They throng the silence of the breast,
We see them as of yore,—
The kind, the brave, the true, the sweet,
Who walk with us no more.
JOHN WHITE CHADWICK, *Auld Lang Syne.*

14
You may give over plow, boys,
You may take the gear to the stead,
All the sweat o' your brow, boys,
Will never get beer and bread.
The seed's waste, I know, boys,
There's not a blade will grow, boys,
'Tis cropped out, I trow, boys,
And Tommy's dead.
SYDNEY DOBELL, *Tommy's Dead.*

But Tom's no more—and so no more of Tom.
BYRON, *Don Juan.* Canto xi, st. 20.

15
Covetous Death bereaved us all,
To aggrandize one funeral.
The eager fate which carried thee
Took the largest part of me:
For this losing is true dying;
This is lordly man's down-lying,
This his slow but sure reclining,
Star by star his world resigning.
EMERSON, *Threnody.*

16
Old Grimes is dead—that good old man,
We ne'er shall see him more:
He us'd to wear a long black coat,
All button'd down before. . . .

He modest merit sought to find,
And pay it its desert:
He had no malice in his mind,
No ruffles on his shirt.
ALBERT GORTON GREENE, *Old Grimes.* First published in the Providence, R. I. *Gazette,* 16 Jan., 1822, referring to the eccentric Ephriam Grimes, of Hubbardston, Mass., who did not really die, however, until 1844.

Old Rose is dead, that good old man,
We ne'er shall see him more;
He used to wear an old blue coat
All button'd down before.
UNKNOWN, *Old Rose*. (c. 1650)

Now let's go to an honest alehouse and sing *Old Rose*.
IZAAK WALTON, *Compleat Angler*. Ch. 2. (1653)

John Lee is dead, that good old man,—
We ne'er shall see him more:
He used to wear an old drab coat
All buttoned down before.
UNKNOWN, *Epitaph*, on a tomb in Matherne churchyard, in memory of John Lee, died 21 May, 1823.

1
The mossy marbles rest
On the lips that he has prest
In their bloom;
And the names he loved to hear
Have been carved for many a year
On the tomb.
O. W. HOLMES, *The Last Leaf*.

2
Fast as the rolling seasons bring
The hour of fate to those we love,
Each pearl that leaves the broken string
Is set in Friendship's crown above.
As narrower grows the earthly chain,
The circle widens in the sky;
These are our treasures that remain,
But those are stars that beam on high.
O. W. HOLMES, *F. W. C.* [Frederick W. Crocker.]

3
To bear, to nurse, to rear,
To watch and then to lose,
To see my bright ones disappear,
Drawn up like morning dews.
JEAN INGELOW, *Songs of Seven: Seven Times Six*.

4
The Lord gave, and the Lord hath taken away; blessed be the name of the Lord.
Old Testament: Job, i, 21.

The Lord giveth and the landlord taketh away.
JOHN W. RAPER, *Giving and Taking*.

5
All, all are gone, the old familiar faces.
CHARLES LAMB, *The Old Familiar Faces*.

6
Ah, what avails the sceptred race,
Ah, what the form divine!
What every virtue, every grace!
Rose Aylmer, all were thine.
Rose Aylmer, whom these wakeful eyes
May weep, but never see,
A night of memories and of sighs
I consecrate to thee.
W. S. LANDOR, *Rose Aylmer*. One of Landor's early loves, who died suddenly in India.

7
Sleep softly . . . eagle forgotten . . . under the stone.
Time has its way with you there, and the clay has its own.
VACHEL LINDSAY, *The Eagle That Is Forgotten*. [John P. Altgeld.]

He loved his fellows, and their love was sweet—
Plant daisies at his head and at his feet.
RICHARD REALF. Concluding couplet of sonnet found by his bedside after he had committed suicide, in a hotel at Oakland, Cal., 28 Oct., 1878.

8
There is no flock, however watched and tended,
But one dead lamb is there!
There is no fireside, howsoe'er defended,
But has one vacant chair!
H. W. LONGFELLOW, *Resignation*.

Take them, O Grave! and let them lie
Folded upon thy narrow shelves,
As garments by the soul laid by,
And precious only to ourselves!
LONGFELLOW, *Suspiria*.

9
When true hearts lie wither'd
And fond ones are flown,
Oh, who would inhabit
This bleak world alone?
THOMAS MOORE, *The Last Rose of Summer*.

10
For some we loved, the loveliest and the best
That from his Vintage rolling Time hath prest,
Have drunk their Cup a Round or two before,
And one by one crept silently to rest.
OMAR KHAYYÁM, *Rubáiyát*. St. 22. (Fitzgerald, tr.)

11
There is no music more for him;
His lights are out, his feast is done,
His bowl that sparkled to the brim
Is drained, is broken, cannot hold.
CHRISTINA ROSSETTI, *A Peal of Bells*.

12
Remember me when I am gone away,
Gone far away into the silent land.
CHRISTINA ROSSETTI, *Sonnet: Remember*.

13
Railroad brakemen taking trains across Nebraska prairies, lumbermen jaunting in pine and tamarack of the Northwest, stock ranchers in the middle west, mayors of southern cities
Say to their pals and wives now: I see by the papers Anna Held is dead.
CARL SANDBURG, *An Electric Sign Goes Dark*.

14
Like the dew on the mountain,
Like the foam on the river,
Like the bubble on the fountain,
Thou art gone, and for ever!
SCOTT, *The Lady of the Lake*. Canto iii, st. 16.

15
Fear no more the heat o' the sun
Nor the furious winter's rages;
Thou thy worldly task hast done,
Home art gone and ta'en thy wages.
SHAKESPEARE, *Cymbeline*. Act iv, sc. 2, l. 258

He is dead and gone, lady,
He is dead and gone;
At his head a grass-green turf,
At his heels a stone.
SHAKESPEARE, *Hamlet*. Act iv, sc. 5, l. 29.

1
We should profane the service of the dead,
To sing a requiem and such rest to her
As to peace-parted souls.
SHAKESPEARE, *Hamlet*. Act v, sc. 1, l. 259.

2
He dies, and makes no sign.
SHAKESPEARE, *II Henry VI*. Act iii, sc. 3, l. 29.

The ripest fruit first falls, and so doth he;
His time is spent.
SHAKESPEARE, *Richard II*. Act ii, sc. 1, l. 153.

3
Time takes them home that we loved, fair names and famous,
To the soft long sleep, to the broad sweet bosom of death.
SWINBURNE, *In Memory of Barry Cornwall.*

4
And the stately ships go on,
To their haven under the hill;
But O for the touch of a vanished hand,
And the sound of a voice that is still!
TENNYSON, *Break, Break, Break.*

5
Our father's dust is left alone
And silent under other snows.
TENNYSON, *In Memoriam*. Pt. cv.

6
As those we love decay, we die in part;
String after string is severed from the heart.
THOMSON, *On the Death of Mr. Aikman.*

7
They are all gone into the world of light,
And I alone sit ling'ring here;
Their very memory is fair and bright,
And my sad thoughts doth clear.
HENRY VAUGHAN, *Friends Departed.*

They are not gone who pass
Beyond the clasp of hand,
Out from the strong embrace.
HUGH ROBERT ORR, *They Softly Walk.*

8
Over the river they beckon to me,
Loved ones who've cross'd to the farther side.
NANCY P. WAKEFIELD, *Over the River.*

9
I long for household voices gone.
J. G. WHITTIER, *The Eternal Goodness*. St. 15.

I have friends in Spirit Land,
Not shadows in a shadowy band,
Not others but themselves are they.
And still I think of them the same
As when the Master's summons came.
J. G. WHITTIER, *Lucy Hooper*, l. 53.

10
Tender as woman, manliness and meekness
In him were so allied
That they who judged him by his strength or weakness,
Saw but a single side.
And now he rests; his greatness and his sweetness
No more shall seem at strife,
And death has moulded into calm completeness
The statue of his life.
WHITTIER, *In Remembrance of Joseph Sturge.*

11
'Tis infamy to die and not be missed.
CARLOS WILCOX, *The Religion of Taste.*

12
The high song is over. Silent is the lute now.
They are crowned forever and discrowned now.
Whether they triumphed or suffered they are mute now,
Or at the most they are only a sound now.
HUMBERT WOLFE, *Coda: The High Song.*

13
If I had thought thou couldst have died
I might not weep for thee;
But I forgot, when by thy side,
That thou couldst mortal be;
It never through my mind had past
The time would e'er be o'er,
And I on thee should look my last,
And thou shouldst smile no more!
CHARLES WOLFE, *To Mary.*

14
She lived unknown, and few could know
When Lucy ceased to be;
But she is in her grave, and oh,
The difference to me!
WORDSWORTH, *Poems Founded on the Affections*. No. viii.

How fast has brother followed brother,
From sunshine to the sunless land!
WORDSWORTH, *Extempore Effusion upon the Death of James Hogg.*

15
He first deceased; she for a little tried
To live without him, liked it not, and died.
HENRY WOTTON, *Upon the Death of Sir Albertus Morton's Wife.*

'Twas sung how they were lovely in their lives,
And in their deaths had not divided been.
THOMAS CAMPBELL, *Gertrude of Wyoming*. Pt. iii, st. 33.

XXII—Death: Not Lost, but Gone Before

16
The buried are not lost, but gone before.
EBENEZER ELLIOTT, *The Excursion.*

Thou art but gone before,
Whither the world must follow.
BEN JONSON, *Epitaph on Sir John Roe*. (DODD, *Epigrammatists*, p. 190.)

Gone before
To that unknown and silent shore.
CHARLES LAMB, *Hester.*

17
Oh! there at last, life's trials past,
We'll meet our loved once more,

Whose feet have trod the path to God—
"Not lost, but gone before."
CAROLINE ELIZABETH SARAH NORTON, *Not Lost, But Gone Before.*

Those that he loved so long and sees no more,
Loved and still loves—not dead, but gone before.
SAMUEL ROGERS, *Human Life,* l. 746.

Dear is the spot where Christians sleep,
And sweet the strain which angels pour;
Oh, why should we in anguish weep?
They are not lost, but gone before.
UNKNOWN, *Not Lost But Gone Before.* (SMITH, *Edinboro' Harmony,* 1829.)

1
He whom you say is passed away has simply posted on ahead. (Quem putas perisse, præmissus est.)
SENECA, *Epistulæ ad Lucilium.* Epis. xcix, 7.

They are not amissi, but præmissi;
Not lost, but gone before.
PHILIP HENRY. (MATTHEW HENRY, *Life of Philip Henry.*)

Not dead, but gone before.
MATTHEW HENRY, *Commentaries: Matthew ii.*

2
And perhaps, if only the tale told by the wise men is true and there is a bourne to welcome us, then he whom we think we have lost has only been sent on ahead. (Et fortasse, si modo vera sapientium fama est recipitque nos locus aliquis, quem putamus perisse, præmissus est.)
SENECA, *Epistulæ ad Lucilium.* Epis. lxiii, 16.

3
Then steal away, give little warning,
Choose thine own time;
Say not good-night. but in some brighter clime
Bid me good-morning!
ANNA LETITIA BARBAULD, *Life.*

4
O thou soul of my soul! I shall clasp thee again,
And with God be the rest!
ROBERT BROWNING, *Prospice.*

I know thou art gone to the home of thy rest—
Then why should my soul be so sad?
I know thou art gone where the weary are blest,
And the mourner looks up, and is glad;
I know thou hast drank of the Lethe that flows
In the land where they do not forget,
That sheds over memory only repose,
And takes from it only regret.
THOMAS KIBBLE HERVEY, *I Know Thou Art Gone.*

5
Oh, write of me, not "Died in bitter pains,"
But "Emigrated to another star!"
HELEN HUNT JACKSON, *Emigravit.*

Nor sink those stars in empty night:
They hide themselves in heaven's own light.
JAMES MONTGOMERY, *Friends.*

6
'Tis sweet, as year by year we lose
Friends out of sight, in faith to muse
How grows in Paradise our store.
JOHN KEBLE, *Burial of the Dead.*

7
It is an old belief
That on some solemn shore,
Beyond the sphere of grief,
Dear friends shall meet once more
J. G. LOCKHART, *Lines Sent in a Letter to Carlyle,* 1 April, 1842.

8
They are not dead; life's flag is never furled:
They passed from world to world.
EDWIN MARKHAM, *Our Dead, Overseas.*

9
And may we find, when ended is the page,
Death but a tavern on our pilgrimage.
JOHN MASEFIELD, *The Word.*

10
If we could know
Which of us, darling, would be first to go,
Who would be first to breast the swelling tide
And step alone upon the other side—
If we could know!
JULIA HARRIS MAY, *If We Could Know.*

11
They eat, they drink, and in communion sweet
Quaff immortality and joy.
MILTON, *Paradise Lost.* Bk. v, l. 637. (1674 ed.)

12
And with the morn those angel faces smile
Which I have loved long since and lost awhile.
JOHN HENRY NEWMAN, *Pillar of the Cloud.*

13
They that love *beyond* the *world,* cannot be separated. Death cannot kill what *never* dies. Nor can Spirits ever be divided that love and and live in the *same* Divine Principle; the Root and Record of their *Friendship.* Death is but *crossing* the *world,* as Friends do the Seas; they live in one another still.
WILLIAM PENN, *Fruits of Solitude.* Pt. ii.

14
I am borne darkly, fearfully, afar;
Whilst, burning through the inmost veil of Heaven,
The soul of Adonais, like a star,
Beacons from the abode where the Eternal are.
SHELLEY, *Adonais.* St. 55.

15
He is not dead, this friend; not dead,
But, in the path we mortals tread,
Got some few, trifling steps ahead,
And nearer to the end;
So that you, too, once past the bend,
Shall meet again, as face to face this friend
You fancy dead.
R. L. STEVENSON, *Verses Written in 1872.*

16
His time was come; he ran his race;
We hope he's in a better place.
SWIFT, *On the Death of Dr. Swift,* l. 241.

17
But trust that those we call the dead

Are breathers of an ampler day
For ever nobler ends.
TENNYSON, *In Memoriam*. Pt. cxviii, st. 2.

It may be we shall touch the Happy Isles,
And see the great Achilles whom we knew.
TENNYSON, *Ulysses*, l. 63.

1
Henceforward, listen as we will,
The voices of that hearth are still;
Look where we may, the wide earth o'er
Those lighted faces smile no more. . . .
Yet Love will dream, and Faith will trust
(Since He who knows our need is just)
That somehow, somewhere, meet we must.
J. G. WHITTIER, *Snow-Bound*, l. 187.

2
It is but crossing with a bated breath,
A white, set face, a little strip of sea—
To find the loved one waiting on the shore,
More beautiful, more precious than before.
ELLA WHEELER WILCOX, *The Crossing*. Inscribed upon a wreath sent by Queen Alexandra, to be laid on the coffin of Mrs. William Ewart Gladstone, in June, 1900.

3
Passed on, beyond our mortal vision,
But now the thought is robbed of gloom,
Within the Father's many mansions
Still dwelling in another room.

The one whose going left us lonely
Is scaling heights undreamed of yore,
And guided on by Love's unfolding,
Has gone upstairs and shut the door.
UNKNOWN, *Upstairs*.

XXIII—Death: Weep Not the Dead

See also Mourning

4
No funeral gloom, my dears, when I am gone,
Corpse-gazings, tears, black raiment, graveyard grimness;
Think of me as withdrawn into the dimness,
Yours still, you mine; remember all the best
Of our past moments, and forget the rest;
And so, to where I wait, come gently on.
WILLIAM ALLINGHAM, *No Funeral Gloom*. Copied by Ellen Terry on the flyleaf of her *Imitation of Christ*, and under it, "I should wish my children, relatives and friends to observe this when I die." This wish was carried out.

Weep awhile, if ye are fain,—
Sunshine still must follow rain;
Only not at death,—for death,
Now I know, is that first breath
Which our souls draw when we enter
Life, which is of all life centre.
EDWIN ARNOLD, *After Death in Arabia*.

5
He who died at Azan sends
This to comfort all his friends:
Faithful friends! It lies, I know,
Pale and white and cold as snow;
And ye say, "Abdallah's dead!"
Weeping at the feet and head,
I can see your falling tears,
I can hear your sighs and prayers;
Yet I smile and whisper this:
"*I* am not the thing you kiss;
Cease your tears and let it lie;
It *was* mine—it is not I."
EDWIN ARNOLD, *After Death in Arabia*.

Behold—not him we knew!
This was the prison which his soul looked through.
O. W. HOLMES, *The Last Look*.

6
But never be a tear-drop shed
For them, the pure, enfranchised dead.
MARY E. BROOKS, *Weep Not for the Dead*.

7
On that grave drop not a tear!
Else, though fathom-deep the place,
Through the woolen shroud I wear
I shall feel it on my face.
E. B. BROWNING, *Bertha in the Lane*. St. 31.

8
Him who is dead and gone, honour with remembrance, not with tears. (Τὸν δὲ ἀποιχόμενον μνήμῃ τιμᾶτε, μὴ δάκρυσιν.)
ST. CHRYSOSTOM, *Commentaries*. *See also under* MEMORY.

9
When I am dead, forget me, dear,
For I shall never know,
Though o'er my cold and lifeless hands
Your burning tears shall flow;
I'll cancel with my living voice
The debt you owe the dead—
Give me the love you'd show me then,
But give it now instead.
LADY CELIA CONGREVE, *When I Am Dead*.

10
Make little weeping for the dead, for he is at rest.
Apocrypha: Ecclesiasticus, xxii, 11.

When the dead is at rest, let his remembrance rest; and be comforted for him, when his spirit is departed from him.
Apocrypha: Ecclesiasticus, xxxviii, 23.

Weep ye not for the dead, neither bemoan him.
Old Testament: Jeremiah, xxii, 10.

11
When I am dead, no pageant train
Shall waste their sorrows at my bier,
Nor worthless pomp of homage vain
Stain it with hypocritic tear.
EDWARD EVERETT, *Alaric the Visigoth*.

12
Thou art gone to the grave! but we will not deplore thee,
Though sorrows and darkness encompass the tomb.
REGINALD HEBER, *Hymns: At a Funeral*.

13
Let dirges be absent from what you falsely deem my death, and unseemly show of grief

and lamentation! Restrain all clamor and forego the idle tribute of a tomb!
(Absint inani funere neniæ
Luctusque turpes et querimoniæ;
Compesce clamorem ac sepulcri
Mitte supervacuos honores.)
HORACE, *Odes*. Bk. ii, ode 20, l. 21.

1
You come not, as aforetime, to the headstone every day,
And I, who died, I do not chide because, my friend, you play;
Only, in playing, think of him who once was kind and dear,
And, if you see a beauteous thing, just say, he is not here.
WILLIAM JOHNSON CORY, *Remember*.

2
No chorus of loud dirges, no hysteria. (Μὴ συνεπιθρηνεῖν, μὴ σφύζειν.)
MARCUS AURELIUS, *Meditations*. Bk. vii, sec. 43.

3
Weep not for him who departs from life, for there is no suffering beyond death. (Οὐδὲν γάρ θανάτου δεύτερόν ἐστι πάθος.)
PALLADAS. (*Greek Anthology*. Bk. x, epig. 59.)

4
We have no need of strains of sorrow and lamentation.
PLATO, *The Republic*. Bk. iii, sec. 398.

The silent organ loudest chants
The master's requiem.
EMERSON, *Dirge*.

5
And when committed to the dust I'd have
Few tears, but friendly, dropped into my grave.
JOHN POMFRET, *The Choice*, l. 164.

6
Weep not, O friend, we should not weep:
Our friend of friends lies full of rest;
No sorrow rankles in her breast,
Fallen fast asleep, She sleeps below,
She wakes and laughs above;
To-day, as she walked, let us walk in love;
To-morrow, follow so.
CHRISTINA ROSSETTI, *My Friend*.

7
When I am dead, my dearest,
Sing no sad songs for me;
Plant thou no roses at my head,
Nor shady cypress tree:
Be the green grass above me
With showers and dewdrops wet;
And if thou wilt, remember,
And if thou wilt, forget.
CHRISTINA ROSSETTI, *Song*.

8
Let not the eyes be dry when we have lost a friend, nor let them overflow. We may weep, but we must not wail. (Nec sicci sint oculi amisso amico nec fluant. Lacrimandum est, non plorandum.)
SENECA, *Epistulæ ad Lucilium*. Epis. lxiii, sec. 1.

9
Moderate lamentation is the right of the dead; excessive grief the enemy to the living.
SHAKESPEARE, *All's Well that Ends Well*. Act i, sc. 1, l. 64.

10
No longer mourn for me when I am dead
Than you shall hear the surly sullen bell
Give warning to the world that I am fled
From this vile world, with vilest worms to dwell:
Nay, if you read this line, remember not
The hand that writ it; for I love you so
That I in your sweet thoughts would be forgot
If thinking on me then should make you woe.
SHAKESPEARE, *Sonnets*. No. lxxi.

11
Come not, when I am dead,
To drop thy foolish tears upon my grave,
To trample round my fallen head,
And vex the unhappy dust thou wouldst not save.
There let the wind sweep and the plover cry;
But thou, go by.
TENNYSON, *Come Not When I Am Dead*.

12
Oh, stanch thy bootless tears, thy weeping is in vain;
I am not lost, for we in heaven shall one day meet again.
UNKNOWN, *The Bride's Burial*. (*Roxburghe Ballads*.)

XXIV—Death: De Mortuis

13
Speak not evil of the dead, but call them blessed. (Τὸν τεθνηκότα μὴ κακολόγει, ἀλλὰ μακάριζε.)
CHILO. (STOBÆUS, *Florilegium*, cxxv, 15; DIOGENES LAERTIUS, *Chilo*, i, 69.) The Latin form of the proverb is, "De mortuis nil nisi bonum."

Speak no ill of the dead. (Τὸν τεθνηκότα κακῶς ἀγορεύειν.)
SOLON, one of his laws. (PLUTARCH, *Lives: Solon*. Sec. 21.)

14
Wherefore I praised the dead which are already dead, more than the living which are yet alive.
Old Testament: Ecclesiastes, iv, 2.

15
Let not thy jests, like mummy, be made of dead men's flesh. Abuse not any that are departed; for, to wrong their memories, is to rob their ghosts of their winding-sheets.
THOMAS FULLER, *The Holy State*, p. 146.

How can I speak into a grave? How can I battle with a shroud? Silence is a duty and a doom.
ROSCOE CONKLING, after Garfield's assassina-

tion. (STODDARD, *As I Knew Them*, p. 114.)

1
I war not with the dead.
HOMER, *Iliad*. Bk. vii, l. 485. (Pope, tr.) Said by Charles V of Luther.

It is not right to exult over slain men.
HOMER, *Odyssey*. Bk. xii, l. 412. Quoted by John Bright in his speech on America, 29 June, 1867.

Brave men ne'er warred with the dead and vanquished. (Nullum cum victis certamen et æthere cassis.)
VERGIL, *Æneid*. Bk. xi, l. 104.

2
The record of a generous life runs like a vine around the memory of our dead, and every sweet, unselfish act is now a perfumed flower.
R. G. INGERSOLL, *Tribute to Eben C. Ingersoll.*

3
He doth sin that doth belie the dead.
SHAKESPEARE, *II Henry IV*. Act i, sc. 1, l. 98.

Beat not the bones of the buried.
SHAKESPEARE, *Love's Labour's Lost*. Act v, sc. 2, l. 666.

Speak me fair in death.
SHAKESPEARE, *The Merchant of Venice*. Act iv, sc. 1, l. 275.

4
War not with the fallen, nor wound the dead.
What valour is there in slaying the slain?
SOPHOCLES, *Antigone*, l. 1029.

5
All men are wont to praise him who is no more.
THUCYDIDES, *History*. Bk. ii, ch. 45, sec. 1.

6
Nor shall thy death be without honor among the nations. (Neque hoc sine nomine letum Per gentis erit.)
VERGIL, *Æneid*. Bk. xi, l. 846.

7
Death softens all resentments, and the consciousness of a common inheritance of frailty and weakness modifies the severity of judgment.
J. G. WHITTIER, *Ichabod: Note.*

XXV—Death: Rest Lightly, Earth

8
Lie lightly on my ashes, gentle earth.
BEAUMONT AND FLETCHER, *Bonduca*. Act iv, sc. 3.

Upon thy buried body lie lightly, gentle earth.
BEAUMONT AND FLETCHER, *Maid's Tragedy*. Act ii, sc. 1.

9
Light lay the earth on Billy's breast,
His chicken heart's so tender;
But build a castle on his head,—
His skull will prop it under.
ROBERT BURNS, *On a Noted Coxcomb*. [Captain William Roddick, of Corbiston.]

10
May his body rest free from evil. (Corpus requiescat malis.)
ENNIUS, *Thyestes*. (CICERO, *Tusculanarum Disputationum*. Bk. i, ch. 44, sec. 107.)

11
Earth of Tarentum, keep gently this body of a good man. Lie not heavy upon the stranger. (Γαῖα Ταραντίνων, ἔχε μείλιχος ἀνέρος ἐσθλοῦ τόνδε νέκυν. . . . κείνῳ μὴ βαρὺς ἔσσο τάφος.)
LOLLIUS BASSUS, *Epigram*. (*Greek Anthology*. Bk. vii, No. 372.)

12
May the earth lie light upon you. (Sit tibi terra levis.)
MARTIAL, *Epigrams*. Bk. ix, epig. 29. An inscription frequently used on Roman tombstones, often indicated by the initials, S.T.T.L. "Requiescat in pace" was also frequently used, represented by R.I.P.

13
O bones, rest gently in protecting urn, and may the earth weigh light upon your ashes. (Ossa quieta, precor, tuta requiescite in urna, Et sit humus cineri non onerosa tuo!)
OVID, *Amores*. Bk. iii, eleg. 9, l. 67.

May his bones rest gently. (Molliter ossa cubent.)
OVID, *Heroides*. Epis. vii, l. 162.

14
Yet shall thy grave with rising flowers be drest,
And the green turf lie lightly on thy breast.
POPE, *Elegy to the Memory of an Unfortunate Lady.*

15
Sleep well and peacefully, and above thy untroubled ashes may the earth be light! (Bene placideque quiescas, Terraque securæ sit super ossa levis.)
TIBULLUS, *Odes*. Bk. ii, ode 4, l. 49.

To whom life is heavy, the earth will be light.
HENRYK SIENKIEWICZ, *With Fire and Sword*, p. 561.

XXVI—Death the Deathless

16
Death be not proud, though some have called thee
Mighty and dreadful, for, thou art not so,
For, those, whom thou think'st, thou dost overthrow,
Die not, poor death, nor yet canst thou kill me. . . .
One short sleep past, we wake eternally,
And death shall be no more; death, thou shalt die.
JOHN DONNE, *Holy Sonnets*. No. x.

Then, soul, live thou upon thy servant's loss. . . .
So shalt thou feed on Death, that feeds on men,
And Death once dead, there's no more dying then.
SHAKESPEARE, *Sonnets*. No. cxlvi.

17
Death is the final Master and Lord. But Death must await my good pleasure. I command Death because I have no fear of Death, but only love.
HAVELOCK ELLIS, *Impressions and Comments*. Ser. iii, p. 55.

18
If the red slayer think he slays,
Or if the slain think he is slain,
They know not well the subtle ways

I keep. and pass, and turn again.
EMERSON, *Brahma.*

1
Death is the only deathless one.
JOHN PAYNE, *Kyrielle.*

2
In adamantine chains shall Death be bound,
And Hell's grim tyrant feel th' eternal wound.
POPE, *Messiah,* l. 47.

3
Be absolute for death; either death or life
Shall thereby be the sweeter.
SHAKESPEARE, *Measure for Measure.* Act iii, sc. 1, l. 4.

XXVII—Death and Birth

See also Birth; Life and Death

4
We weep when we are born, Not when we die!
THOMAS BAILEY ALDRICH, *Metempsychosis.*

5
The end of birth is death; the end of death is birth: this is ordained!
EDWIN ARNOLD, *The Song Celestial.* Ch. ii.

6
It is as natural to die as to be born; and to a little infant, perhaps, the one is as painful as the other.
FRANCIS BACON, *Essays: Of Death.*

7
For what remains but that we still should cry
For being born, or, being born, to die?
FRANCIS BACON, *The World.* (1624)

I, when I was born, was born to die.
WILLIAM DRUMMOND, *Poems.* Sonnet xxxii. (1656); HENRY KING, BISHOP OF CHICHESTER, *Poems,* p. 145. (1657)

8
With what strife and pains we come into the world we know not, but 'tis commonly no easy matter to get out of it.
SIR THOMAS BROWNE, *To a Friend.* Sec. 5.

9
Death borders upon our birth, and our cradle stands in the grave.
JOSEPH HALL, *Epistles.* Epis. 2.

10
He that once is born, once must die.
GEORGE HERBERT, *Jacula Prudentum.*

11
On parent knees, a naked new-born child,
Weeping thou sat'st while all around thee smiled:
So live, that, sinking to thy life's last sleep,
Calm thou may'st smile, while all around thee weep.
SIR WILLIAM JONES, *On Parent Knees.* (From *Enchanted Fruit: Six Hymns to Hindu Deities.* See his *Life,* p. 110.)

When summoned hence to thine eternal sleep,
Oh, may'st thou smile while all around thee weep.
CHARLES WESLEY, *On an Infant.*

12
We begin to die as soon as we are born, and the end is linked to the beginning. (Nascentes morimur, finisque ab origine pendet.)
MANILIUS, *Astronomica.* Bk. iv, sec. 16.

13
Every one avoids seeing a man born, but all run hastily to see him die. To destroy him we seek a spacious field and a full light: but to construct him we hide ourselves in some dark corner, and work as close as we may.
MONTAIGNE, *Essays.* Bk. iii, ch. 5.

14
Dying is something ghastly, as being born is something ridiculous.
GEORGE SANTAYANA, *Little Essays,* p. 91.

15
The babe is at peace within the womb,
The corpse is at rest within the tomb;
We begin in what we end.
SHELLEY, *Fragment: From Rest to Rest.*

16
Death is the peak of a life-wave, and so is birth. Death and birth are one.
ABBA HILLEL SILVER. (*Greatest Thoughts on Immortality,* p. 40.)

17
Every minute dies a man,
Every minute one is born.
TENNYSON, *The Vision of Sin.* Pt. iv, st. 9. "Moment" in later editions.

Every minute dies a man,
And one and one-sixteenth is born.
UNKNOWN, *Parody by a Statistician.*

18
All goes onward and outward, nothing collapses,
And to die is different from what any one supposed, and luckier.
Has any one supposed it lucky to be born?
I hasten to inform him or her it is just as lucky to die, and I know it.
WALT WHITMAN, *Song of Myself.* Sec. 6–7.

20
To die is all as common as to live;
The one in choice, the other holds in chase;
For from the instant we begin to live
We do pursue and hunt the time to die.
UNKNOWN, *The Reign of King Edward III.* Act iv, sc. 4. (1596)

From the day of your birth you begin to die as well as to live.
MONTAIGNE, *Essays.* Bk. i, ch. 20.

XXVIII—Death and the Child

21
At last he came, the messenger,
The messenger from unseen lands:
And what did dainty Baby Bell?
She only crossed her little hands,
She only looked more meek and fair!
We parted back her silken hair,
We wove the roses round her brow—
White buds, the summer's drifted snow—
Wrapped her from head to foot in flowers . . .
And thus went dainty Baby Bell
Out of this world of ours.
THOMAS BAILEY ALDRICH, *Baby Bell.*

1
The little toy dog is covered with dust,
But sturdy and stanch he stands;
And the little toy soldier is red with rust,
And his musket moulds in his hands.
Time was when the little toy dog was new,
And the soldier was passing fair;
And that was the time when our Little Boy Blue
Kissed them and put them there.
EUGENE FIELD, *Little Boy Blue.*

2
Loveliest of lovely things are they
On earth that soonest pass away.
The rose that lives its little hour
Is prized beyond the sculptured flower.
BRYANT, *A Scene on the Banks of the Hudson.*

3
Ere sin could blight or sorrow fade,
Death came with friendly care;
The opening bud to Heaven conveyed,
And bade it blossom there.
S. T. COLERIDGE, *Epitaph on an Infant.*

4
When the lessons of life are all ended,
And death says: "The school is dismissed!"
May the little ones gather around me
To bid me good night and be kissed.
CHARLES MONROE DICKINSON, *The Children.*

5
For such a child I bless God. in whose bosom he is! May I and mine become as this little child.
JOHN EVELYN, *Diary,* 27 Jan., 1658.

6
Oh, call my brother back to me!
I cannot play alone:
The summer comes with flower and bee,—
Where is my brother gone?
FELICIA HEMANS, *The Child's First Grief.*

7
Here she lies a pretty bud,
Lately made of flesh and blood;
Who, as soon fell fast asleep
As her little eyes did peep.
Give her strewings, but not stir
The earth that lightly covers her.
ROBERT HERRICK, *Upon a Child that Died.*

8
But still when the mists of Doubt prevail,
And we lie becalmed by the shores of Age,
We hear from the misty troubled shore
The voice of the children gone before,
Drawing the soul to its anchorage.
BRET HARTE, *A Greyport Legend.*

9
Rachel weeping for her children refused to be comforted: because they were not.
Old Testament: Jeremiah, xxxi, 15; *New Testament: Matthew,* ii, 18.

10
He seemed a cherub who had lost his way
And wandered hither, so his stay
With us was short, and 'twas most meet,
That he should be no delver in earth's clod,
Nor need to pause and cleanse his feet
To stand before his God.
J. R. LOWELL, *Threnodia.*

11
A boy of five years old serene and gay,
Unpitying Hades hurried me away.
Yet weep not for Callimachus: if few
The days I lived, few were my sorrows too.
LUCIAN. (*Greek Anthology.* Bk. vii, epig. 308.)

12
My little daughter lieth at the point of death.
New Testament: Mark, v, 23.

13
She thought our good-night kiss was given,
And like a lily her life did close;
Angels uncurtain'd that repose,
And the next waking dawn'd in heaven.
GERALD MASSEY, *Babe Christabel.*

And thou hast stolen a jewel, Death!
Shall light thy dark up like a Star.
A Beacon kindling from afar
Our light of love and fainting faith.
GERALD MASSEY, *Babe Christabel.*

14
You scarce would think so small a thing
Could leave a loss so large;
Her little light such shadow fling
From dawn to sunset's marge.
In other springs our life may be
In bannered bloom unfurled,
But never, never match our wee
White Rose of all the world.
GERALD MASSEY, *Our Wee White Rose.*

Those who living fill the smallest space,
In death have often left the greatest void.
W. S. LANDOR, *Geri.*

We miss thy small step on the stair;
We miss thee at thine evening prayer;
All day we miss thee, everywhere.
DAVID MACBETH MOIR, *Casa Wappy.*

No sound of tiny footfalls filled the house
With happy cheer.
ROBERT BUCHANAN, *The Scaith o' Bartle.*

15
O fairest flower no sooner blown than blasted,
Soft silken Primrose fading timelessly.
MILTON, *On the Death of a Fair Infant,* l. 1.

Think what a present thou to God hast sent,
And render him with patience what he lent.
MILTON, *On the Death of a Fair Infant,* l. 74

16
With more fortitude does a mother mourn one out of many, than she who weeping cries, "Thou wert my only one." (Fortius e multis mater desiderat unum, Quam quæ flens clamat. Tu mihi solus eras.)
OVID, *Remediorum Amoris,* l. 463.

17
And, father cardinal, I have heard you say
That we shall see and know our friends in heaven:
If that be true, I shall see my boy again;
For since the birth of Cain, the first male child,

To him that did but yesterday suspire,
There was not such a gracious creature born.
SHAKESPEARE, *King John*. Act iii, sc. 4, l. 76.

1 All my pretty ones?
Did you say all? Oh, hell-kite! All?
What! all my pretty chickens and their dam
At one fell swoop?
SHAKESPEARE, *Macbeth*. Act iv, sc. 3, l. 216.

Death never takes one alone, but two!
Whenever he enters in at a door,
Under roof of gold or roof of thatch,
He always leaves it upon the latch,
And comes again ere the year is o'er.
Never one of a household only!
H. W. LONGFELLOW, *The Golden Legend:* Pt. vi, *The Farm-House in the Odenwald.*

Insatiate archer! could not one suffice?
Thy shaft flew thrice; and thrice my peace was slain!
YOUNG, *Night Thoughts*. Night i, l. 212.

2
Oh! when a Mother meets on high
The Babe she lost in infancy,
Hath she not then, for pains and fears,
The day of woe, the watchful night,
For all her sorrow, all her tears,
An over-payment of delight?
SOUTHEY, *The Curse of Kehama*. Pt. x, st. 11.

3
God, God, be lenient her first night there.
The crib she slept in was so near my bed;
Her blue and white wool blanket was so soft;
The pillow hollowed so it fit her head.
VIOLET STOREY, *A Prayer for a Very New Angel.*

4
A little soul scarce fledged for earth
Takes wing with heaven again for goal,
Even while we hailed as fresh from birth
A little soul.
A. C. SWINBURNE, *A Baby's Death*. St. 1.

5
But Thee, deep buried in the silent tomb,
That spot which no vicissitude can find.
Love, faithful love, recalled thee to my mind.
WORDSWORTH, *Miscellaneous Sonnets*. Pt. i, No. xxvii. Referring to his second daughter, Catherine, who died in 1812, at the age of four.

Three years she grew in sun and shower,
Then Nature said, "A lovelier flower
On earth was never sown;
This child I to myself will take;
She shall be mine, and I will make
A lady of my own."
WORDSWORTH, *Three Years She Grew.*

6 ———A simple child,
That lightly draws its breath,
And feels its life in every limb,
What should it know of death?
WORDSWORTH, *We Are Seven.*

"But they are dead; those two are dead!
Their spirits are in Heaven!"
'Twas throwing words away; for still
The little Maid would have her will,
And said, "Nay, we are seven!"
WORDSWORTH, *We Are Seven.*

XXIX—Death and Youth

See also Goodness and Death

7
Whom the gods love dies young. (Ὃν οἱ θεοὶ φιλοῦσιν ἀποθνήσκει νέος.)
MENANDER, *Dis Exapaton*. Frag. 125.

He whom the gods love dies young (Νέος δ' ἀπόλλυθ', ὅντινα φιλεῖ θεός.)
HYPSAEUS. (STOBAEUS, *Florilegium*, cxx, 1 .

He whom the gods love dies young, while he has his strength and senses and wits. (Quem di diligunt Adulescens moritur, dum valet sentit sapit.)
PLAUTUS, *Bacchides*, l. 816. (Act iv, sc. 7.)

8
"Whom the gods love die young," was said of yore,
And many deaths do they escape by this:
The death of friends, and that which slays even more,
The death of friendship, love, youth, all that is,
Except mere breath.
BYRON, *Don Juan*. Canto iv, st. 12.

Perhaps the early grave
Which men weep over may be meant to save.
BYRON, *Don Juan*. Canto iv, st. 12.

Heaven gives its favourites—early death.
BYRON, *Childe Harold*, iv, 102.

9
Those that God loves, do not live long.
GEORGE HERBERT, *Jacula Prudentum*.

Whom God loveth best, those he taketh soonest.
THOMAS WILSON, *Rhetorique*, p. 73.

10
Whom the gods love die young no matter how long they live.
ELBERT HUBBARD, *Philistine*. Vol. xxiv, cover.

The good die young, so men have sadly sung
Who do not know the happier reason why
Is never that they die while they are young,
But that the good are young until they die.
ARTHUR GUITERMAN, *Thus Spake Theodore Roosevelt.*

It has never been satisfactorily determined whether the saying about the darlings of the gods dying young means young in years or young in heart.
E. V. LUCAS, *Advisory Ben*. Ch. 10.

11
One of the fathers saith . . . that old men go to death, and death comes to young men.
FRANCIS BACON, *Apothegms*. No. 119.

12
To kill the emotions and so live to old age, or to accept the martyrdom of our passions and die young is our doom.
BALZAC, *La Peau de Chagrin*, p. 67.

13
Blow out, you bugles, over the rich Dead!
There's none of these so lonely and poor of old,
But, dying, has made us rarer gifts than gold.
These laid the world away: poured out the red
Sweet wine of youth; gave up the years to be
Of work and joy, and that unhoped serene

That men call age, and those who would have been
Their sons, they gave their immortality.
RUPERT BROOKE, *The Dead.* (1914)

1
But, oh! fell death's untimely frost
That nipt my flower sae early.
ROBERT BURNS, *Highland Mary.*

2
You also, laughing one,
Tosser of balls in the sun,
Will pillow your bright head
By the incurious dead.
BABETTE DEUTSCH, *A Girl.*

3
As precious gums are not for lasting fire,
They but perfume the temple, and expire,
So was she soon exhal'd; and vanish'd hence;
A short sweet odour, of a vast expense.
She vanish'd, we can scarcely say she died;
For but a Now, did Heav'n and Earth divide:
She pass'd serenely with a single breath,
This moment perfect health, the next was death.
JOHN DRYDEN, *Eleonora,* l. 301.

He was exhal'd; his great Creator drew
His spirit, as the sun the morning dew.
DRYDEN, *On the Death of a Very Young Gentleman.*

Early, bright, transient, chaste, as morning dew,
She sparkled, was exhal'd, and went to heaven.
YOUNG, *Night Thoughts.* Night v, l. 600.

4
Heav'n gave him all at once; then snatch'd away,
Ere mortals all his beauties could survey;
Just like the flower that buds and withers in a day.
DRYDEN, *On the Death of Amyntas.*

5
Earth laughs in flowers to see her boastful boys
Earth-proud, proud of the earth which is not theirs;
Who steer the plough, but cannot steer their feet
Clear of the grave.
EMERSON, *Hamatreya.*

6
Young Never-Grow-Old, with your heart of gold
And the dear boy's face upon you,
It is hard to tell, though we know it well,
That the grass is growing upon you.
ALICE FLEMING, *Spion Kop.*

7
Grieve not that I die young. Is it not well
To pass away ere life hath lost its brightness?
FLORA ELIZABETH HASTINGS, *Swan Song.*

8
As full-blown poppies, overcharg'd with rain,
Decline the head, and drooping kiss the plain,—
So sinks the youth; his beauteous head, deprest
Beneath his helmet, drops upon his breast.
HOMER, *Iliad.* Bk. viii, l. 371. (Pope, tr.)

9
Who dies in youth and vigour, dies the best,
Struck thro' with wounds, all honest on the breast.
HOMER, *Iliad.* Bk. xxii, l. 100. (Pope, tr.)

10
Life's pleasure hath he lost—escaped life's pain,
Nor wedded joys nor wedded sorrows knew.
JULIANUS, *On a Youth.* (Goldwin Smith, tr.)

We that survive perchance may end our days
In some employment meriting no praise;
They have outlived this fear, and their brave ends
Will ever be an honour to their friends.
PHINEAS JAMES, *Epitaph to His Stricken Comrades.* (1633) James was a shipmaster.

We, growing old, grow stranger to the College,
Symbol of youth, where we were young together,
But you, beyond the reach of time and weather,
Of youth in death forever keep the knowledge.
UNKNOWN, *V. D. F.*

11
Tenderly bury the fair young dead,
Pausing to drop on his grave a tear;
Carve on the wooden slab at his head,
"Somebody's darling slumbers here!"
MARIE R. LA COSTE, *Somebody's Darling.*

12
Is it not better at an early hour
In its calm cell to rest the weary head,
While birds are singing and while blooms the bower,
Than sit the fire out and go starved to bed?
WALTER SAVAGE LANDOR, *On Living Too Long.*

13
Oh, what hadst thou to do with cruel Death,
Who wast so full of life, or Death with thee,
That thou shouldst die before thou hadst grown old!
LONGFELLOW, *Three Friends of Mine.* Pt. ii.

14
Weep not for those whom the veil of the tomb,
In life's happy morning, hath hid from our eyes,
Ere sin threw a blight o'er the spirit's young bloom,
Or earth had profan'd what was born for the skies.
THOMAS MOORE, *Weep Not for Those.*

Death chill'd the fair fountain ere sorrow had stain'd it;
'Twas frozen in all the pure light of its course,
And but sleeps till the sunshine of Heaven has unchain'd it,
To water that Eden where first was its source.
THOMAS MOORE, *Weep Not for Those.*

15
Ah me! all praise and blame, they heed it not;

Cold are the yearning hearts that once were hot.
WILLIAM MORRIS, *The Earthly Paradise: Epilogue*, l. 83.

1
Precocious youth is a sign of premature death. (Senilem juventam prænaturæ mortis esse signum.)
PLINY, *Historia Naturalis*. Bk. vii, sec. 51.

A little too wise they say do ne'er live long.
THOMAS MIDDLETON, *The Phœnix*. Act i, sc. 1.

So wise so young, they say, do never live long.
SHAKESPEARE, *Richard III*. Act iii, sc. 1, l. 79.

2
A dirge for her, the doubly-dead,
In that she died so young.
EDGAR ALLAN POE, *Lenore*.

3
Hushed in the alabaster arms of Death,
Our young Marcellus sleeps.
JAMES RYDER RANDALL, *John Pelham*.

4
Fate cropped him short—for be it understood
He would have lived much longer, if he could!
W. B. RHODES, *Bombastes Furioso*.

5
I thought thy bride-bed to have deck'd, sweet maid,
And not have strew'd thy grave.
SHAKESPEARE, *Hamlet*. Act v, sc. 1, l. 268.

Then, after his brief range of blameless days,
The toll of funeral in an angel ear
Sounds happier than the merriest marriage bell.
TENNYSON, *The Death of the Duke of Clarence*.

6
The young gentleman, according to Fates and Destinies and such odd sayings, the Sisters Three and such branches of learning, is indeed deceased; or, as you would say in plain terms, gone to heaven.
SHAKESPEARE, *The Merchant of Venice*. Act ii, sc. 2, l. 64.

XXX—Death: Count No Man Happy

7
Only when a man's life comes to its end in prosperity dare we pronounce him happy. (Ὀλβίσαι δὲ χρὴ βίον τελευτήσαντ' ἐν εὐεστοῖ φίλῃ.)
ÆSCHYLUS, *Agamemnon*, l. 928.

8
Let no one till his death
Be called unhappy. Measure not the work
Until the day's out and the labour done.
E. B. BROWNING, *Aurora Leigh*. Bk. v, l. 76.

9
Judge none blessed before his death.
Apocrypha: Ecclesiasticus, xi, 28. (Ante mortem ne laudes hominem quemquam.—*Vulgate*.)

10
Account ye no man happy till he die. (Μηδένα νομίζετ' εὐτυχεῖν πρὶν ἂν θάνῃ.)
EURIPIDES, *Daughters of Troy*, l. 510.

Call no mortal blest till thou hast seen his dying day, and how he passed therethrough and came on death.
EURIPIDES, *Andromache*, l. 100.

11
Praise day at night, and life at end.
GEORGE HERBERT, *Jacula Prudentum*.

12
Our love is like our life;
There's no man blest in either till his end.
SHACKERLEY MARMION, *A Fine Companion*. Act i, sc. 1.

13
None must be counted happy till his death, till his last funeral rites are paid. (Dicique beatus Ante obitum nemo supremaque funera debet.)
OVID, *Metamorphoses*. Bk. iii, l. 136.

14
When the Deity bestows prosperity on a man up to the end, that man we consider happy; to pronounce anyone happy, however, while he is still living and running the risks of life, is like proclaiming an athlete victorious and crowning him while he is still contending for the prize.
SOLON, to Crœsus. (PLUTARCH, *Lives: Solon*. Sec. 27.) Crœsus paid no attention to this warning till he was conquered by Cyrus, and lay bound upon the pyre, when he called, "O Solon!" thrice in a loud voice. Cyrus inquired the reason for the cry, and when he learned it, released Crœsus and permitted him to live. "Thus," adds Plutarch, "Solon had the reputation of saving one king and instructing another by a single saying."

I bid all men watch life's end. (Ὅρα τέλος μακροῦ βίου.)
SOLON, to Crœsus. Ausonius puts this into Latin: Spectare vitæ jubeo cunctos terminum. (*Ludus Septem Sapientum*, l. 87.)

I call a life happy only after its fated course is run.
(Tunc beatem dico vitam, cum peracta fata sunt.)
SOLON. (AUSONIUS [?], *Septem Sapientum Sententiæ*, l. 29.)

15
Therefore wait to see life's ending ere thou count one mortal blest;
Wait till, free from pain and sorrow, he has gained his final rest.
(Ἡμέραν ἐπισκοποῦντα μηδέν' ὀλβίζειν, πρὶν ἂν τέρμα τοῦ βίου περάσῃ μηδὲν ἀλγεινὸν παθών.)
SOPHOCLES, *Œdipus Tyrannus*, l. 1529.

There is an old-world saying current still,
"Of no man canst thou judge the destiny
To call it good or evil, till he die."
(Λόγος μέν ἐστ' ἀρχαῖος ἀνθρώπων φανεὶς, ὡς οὐκ ἂν αἰῶν' ἐκμάθοις βροτῶν, πρὶν ἂν θάνῃ τις, οὔτ' εἰ χρηστὸς οὔτ' εἴ τῳ κακός.)
SOPHOCLES, *Trachiniæ*, l. 1.

Praise no man much until thou see his death.
(Μήπω μέγ' εἴπῃς πρὶν τελευτήσαντ' ἴδῃς.)
SOPHOCLES, *Fragment*. No. 520. (Plumptre, tr.)

XXXI—Death and Immortality

See also Immortality

16
Death is another life. We bow our heads

At going out, we think, and enter straight
Another golden chamber of the king's,
Larger than this we leave. and lovelier.

P. J. BAILEY, *Festus: Home.*

1

To die
Is to begin to live. It is to end
An old, stale, weary work and to commence
A newer and a better. 'Tis to leave
Deceitful knaves for the society
Of gods and goddesses.

BEAUMONT AND FLETCHER, *Four Plays in One.* (c. 1608)

2

Death with the might of his sunbeam,
Touches the flesh, and the soul awakes.

ROBERT BROWNING, *The Flight of the Duchess.* Pt. xv.

3

To himself every one is an immortal; he may know that he is going to die, but he can never know that he is dead.

SAMUEL BUTLER THE YOUNGER, *Note-Books,* p. 257.

4

The life of the dead is placed in the memory of the living. (Vita enim mortuorum in memoria vivorum est posita.)

CICERO, *Philippicæ.* No. xi, sec. 5.

To live in hearts we leave behind,
Is not to die.

THOMAS CAMPBELL, *Hallowed Ground.* St. 6.

I saw a dead man's finer part
Shining within each faithful heart
Of those bereft. Then said I, "This must be
His immortality."

THOMAS HARDY, *His Immortality.*

5

'Tis immortality to die aspiring,
As if a man were taken quick to heaven.

GEORGE CHAPMAN, *Conspiracy of Charles, Duke of Byron.* Act i, sc. 1.

6

The last day does not bring extinction, but change of place. (Supremus ille dies non exstinctionem, sed commutationem adfert loci.)

CICERO, *Tusculanarum Disputationum.* Bk. i, ch. 49, sec. 117.

7

So when this corruptible shall have put on incorruption, and this mortal shall have put on immortality, then shall be brought to pass the saying that is written, Death is swallowed up in victory.
O death, where is thy sting? O grave, where is thy victory?

New Testament: I Corinthians, xv, 54, 55.

How when the light and glow of life wax dim in thickly gathering gloom,
Shall mortal scoff at sting of Death, shall scorn the victory of the Tomb?

SIR RICHARD BURTON, *The Kasîdah.* Pt. ix, st. 3.

My sword I give to him that shall succeed me in my pilgrimage, and my courage and skill to him that can get it. My marks and scars I carry with me, to be a witness for me that I have fought his battles who now will be my rewarder When the day that he must go hence was come, many accompanied him to the riverside, into which as he went he said: "Death, where is thy sting?" And as he went down deeper, he said: "Grave, where is thy victory?" So he passed over, and all the trumpets sounded for him on the other side.

BUNYAN, *The Pilgrim's Progress.* Pt. ii. Such was the passing of Valiant-for-Truth.

The world recedes; it disappears;
Heav'n opens on my eyes; my ears
With sounds seraphic ring:
Lend, lend your wings! I mount! I fly!
O Grave! where is thy victory?
O Death! where is thy sting?

POPE, *The Dying Christian to His Soul.*

It is through death and rebirth that this corruptible shall become incorruptible, and this mortal put on immortality. . . . There is only one belief that can rob death of its sting and the grave of its victory; and that is the belief that we can lay down the burden of our wretched little makeshift individualities forever at each lift towards the goal of evolution.

BERNARD SHAW, *Parents and Children.*

8

Immortality
Alone could teach this mortal how to die.

DINAH MARIA MULOCK CRAIK, *Looking Death in the Face,* l. 77.

9

The quiet nonchalance of death
No daybreak can bestir;
The slow archangel's syllables
Must awaken her.

EMILY DICKINSON, *Poems.* Pt. iv, No. 5.

10

But all lost things are in the angels' keeping,
Love;
No past is dead for us, but only sleeping,
Love;
The years of Heaven with all earth's little pain
Make good,
Together there we can begin again
In babyhood.

HELEN HUNT JACKSON, *At Last.* St. 6.

11

Passed from death unto life.

New Testament: John, v, 24.

12

There is no Death! What seems so is transition;
This life of mortal breath
Is but a suburb of the life elysian,
Whose portal we call Death.

LONGFELLOW, *Resignation.* (1848)

There is no death! the stars go down
To rise upon some other shore,
And bright in Heaven's jeweled crown,
They shine for ever more.

JOHN LUCKEY MCCREERY, *There Is No Death.* (First published in *Arthur's Home Magazine,* July, 1863. Wrongly ascribed to Bulwer-Lytton. (See STEVENSON, *Famous Single Poems.*)

There is no such thing as death.
In nature nothing dies.
From each sad remnant of decay
Some forms of life arise.
CHARLES MACKAY, *No Such Thing as Death.*

1
Safe from temptation, safe from sin's pollution,
She lives, whom we call dead.
LONGFELLOW, *Resignation.* St. 7.

2
Emerge thou mayst from the last whelming sea,
And prove that death but routs life into victory.
J. R. LOWELL, *Epilogue.*

3
I came from God, and I'm going back to God, and I won't have any gaps of death in the middle of my life.
GEORGE MACDONALD, *Mary Marston.* Ch. 57.

4
Time brings not death, it brings but changes;
I know he rides, but rides afar,
To-day some other planet ranges
And camps to-night upon a star
Where all his other comrades are.
DOUGLAS MALLOCH, *A Comrade Rides Ahead.*

5
From out the throng and stress of lies,
From out the painful noise of sighs,
One voice of comfort seems to rise:
"It is the meaner part that dies."
WILLIAM MORRIS, *Comfort.*

6
This much, and this is all, we know,
They are supremely blest,
Have done with sin, and care, and woe,
And with their Saviour rest.
JOHN NEWTON, *Olney Hymns.*

7
The ear, the eye doth make us deaf and blind;
Else should we be aware of all our dead
Who pass above us, through us, and beneath us.
STEPHEN PHILLIPS, *Herod.* Act iii.

8
The righteous hath hope in his death.
Old Testament: Proverbs, xiv, 32.

9
This day, which thou fearest as thy last, is the birthday of eternity. (Dies iste, quem tamquam extremum reformidas, æterni natalis est.)
SENECA, *Epistulæ ad Lucilium.* Epis. cii, sec. 26.

10
Even through the hollow eyes of death
I spy life peering.
SHAKESPEARE, *Richard II.* Act ii, sc. 1, l. 270.

Mount, mount, my soul! thy seat is up on high;
Whilst my gross flesh sinks downward, here to die.
SHAKESPEARE, *Richard II.* Act v, sc. 5, l. 112.

11
And her immortal part with angels lives.
SHAKESPEARE, *Romeo and Juliet.* Act v, sc. 1, l. 19.

12
What a world were this,
How unendurable its weight, if they
Whom Death hath sundered did not meet again!
SOUTHEY, *Inscription XVII: Epitaph.*

13
Ah, well! for us all some sweet hope lies
Deeply buried from human eyes;
And, in the hereafter, angels may
Roll the stone from its grave away!
WHITTIER, *Maud Muller.*

14
Nothing is dead, but that which wished to die;
Nothing is dead, but wretchedness and pain.
YOUNG, *Night Thoughts.* Night vi, l. 41.

XXXII—Death: Last Words

Note:—The reputed last words of famous men are always open to suspicion, but the ones that follow are among the best known and best authenticated. Quotations from the Bible and mere exclamations have been omitted.

15
O, but they say the tongues of dying men
Enforce attention like deep harmony:
Where words are scarce, they are seldom spent in vain,
For they breathe truth that breathe their words in pain.
SHAKESPEARE, *Richard II.* Act ii, sc. 1, l. 5.

A death-bed's a detector of the heart.
YOUNG, *Night Thoughts.* Night ii, l. 639.

16
This is the last of earth! I am content.
JOHN QUINCY ADAMS. (JOSIAH QUINCY, *Life of John Quincy Adams.*)

17
I have sent for you that you may see how a Christian can die.
JOSEPH ADDISON, shortly before his death, July 17, 1719, to his step-son, Lord Warwick, a young man of irregular life, who himself died soon afterwards.

There taught us how to live; and (oh! too high
The price for knowledge!) taught us how to die.
THOMAS TICKELL, *To the Earl of Warwick, On the Death of Mr. Addison,* l. 81.

Come and see how a marshal of France can die.
MARSHAL NEY, at the close of the battle of Waterloo. (Venez voir comment meurt un maréchal de France!)

18
I have such sweet thoughts.
ALBERT, *Consort of Queen Victoria.*

I have had wealth, rank, and power; but if these were all I had, how wretched I should be!
ALBERT, *Consort of Queen Victoria.*

1
How tired you must be. (Que vous devez être fatiguée.)
ALEXANDER I of Russia, to his wife.

2
Clasp my hand, dear friend, I am dying.
VITTORIO ALFIERI.

3
Give the boys a holiday.
ANAXAGORAS, the philosopher, who taught school, when asked if he wished for anything.

4
Wait till I have finished my problem.
ARCHIMEDES, to the Roman soldier who ordered him to follow.

5
Now comes the mystery.
HENRY WARD BEECHER.

6
It is a great consolation to a poet at the point of death that he has never written a line injurious to good morals.
NICHOLAS BOILEAU.

7
I shall hear in heaven.
BEETHOVEN, referring to his deafness.

8
The executioner is, I believe, very expert, and my neck is very slender.
ANNE BOLEYN.

9
Tell mother—tell mother—I died for my country.
JOHN WILKES BOOTH. (*Dic. Am. Biog.* ii, 451.)

10
I have been dying for twenty years, now I am going to live.
JAMES DRUMMOND BURNS.

11
Don't let the awkward squad fire over my grave.
ROBERT BURNS.

12
I must sleep now.
GEORGE GORDON BYRON.

13
You, too, Brutus! (Et tu, Brute!)
JULIUS CÆSAR, as Brutus stabbed him.

14
The South, the poor South.
JOHN C. CALHOUN. (*Dic. Am. Biog.* iii, 419.)

15
I go from a corruptible to an incorruptible crown, where no disturbance can have place.
CHARLES I of England, on the scaffold. (HUME, *Hist. of Engl.*, ch. 22.)

Remember!
CHARLES I, to Juxon, Archbishop of Canterbury, just before he laid his head on the block. Readers of Dumas will remember the use he made of this word in the *Vicomte de Bragelonne.*

16
I fear, gentlemen, I am an unconscionable time a-dying.
CHARLES II of England.

Let not poor Nelly starve.
CHARLES II, referring to his mistress, Nell Gwynne. His last words.

17
Give Dayrolles a chair.
LORD CHESTERFIELD, polite to the last.

18
Remember, we meet again to celebrate the victory.
JOSEPH H. CHOATE, to Arthur Balfour, 13 May, 1917, at the close of exercises at the Cathedral of St. John the Divine. Mr. Choate died next day. (MARTIN, *Life of Joseph Hodges Choate*, iii, 391.)

19
What great God is this, that pulls down the strength of the strongest kings?
CLOTAIRE I. (GREGORY OF TOURS, *History*, iv, 21.)

20
One man have I slain to save a hundred thousand.
CHARLOTTE CORDAY, referring to her murder of Marat.

21
That unworthy hand! That unworthy hand!
THOMAS CRANMER, at the stake, as he thrust into the flames the hand that had signed his apostacy.

22
My desire is to make what haste I can to be gone.
OLIVER CROMWELL.

23
Nurse, it was I who discovered that leeches have red blood.
GEORGES CUVIER, the naturalist, to the nurse who was applying leeches.

24
Be sure you show my head to the mob. It will be a long time ere they see its like.
JACQUES DANTON, to the executioner, at the guillotine.

25
You may go home; the show is over.
DEMONAX, the philosopher, quoting Lucian.

26
Yes, on the ground.
CHARLES DICKENS, to his sister-in-law, who had urged him to lie down.

27
The first step toward philosophy is incredulity.
DENIS DIDEROT.

28
All my possessions for a moment of time.
QUEEN ELIZABETH of England.

29
A strange sight, sir, an old man unwilling to die.
EBENEZER ELLIOTT, the "corn-law rhymer."

30
I have had my span of life. All I want now is heaven.
MARSHAL FERDINAND FOCH.

31
I do not suffer, my friends: but I feel a certain

difficulty of existing. (Je ne souffre pas, mes amis, mais je sens une certaine difficulté d'être.)

Bernard de Fontanelle.

1
I die happy.

Charles James Fox.

2
If Mr. Selwyn calls, let him in; if I am alive I shall be very glad to see him, and if I am dead he will be very glad to see me.

Henry Fox, Baron Holland, referring to George Augustus Selwyn.

3
A dying man can do nothing easy.

Benjamin Franklin, to his daughter who advised him to change his position in bed, that he might breathe more easily.

4
We are over the mountain, we shall go better now. (La montagne est passée, nous irons mieux.)

Frederick the Great.

5
We are all going to heaven, and Van Dyck is of the company.

Thomas Gainsborough.

6
Wally, what is this? It is death, my boy: they have deceived me.

George IV of England, to his page, Sir Walthen Waller, who was assisting him to a seat when the end came.

8
Come, my son, and see how a Christian can die.

Sir Henry Havelock, to his son.

10
All is lost. Monks, monks, monks!

Henry VIII of England.

11
Turn up the lights. (Then, smiling he added the words of a popular song of the day) I don't want to go home in the dark.

O. Henry (W. S. Porter). His last words, just before he died, 5 June, 1910. *See* Smith, *O. Henry*, p. 250. The song was, "I'm afraid to go home in the dark." See p. 366:6. There is some difference of opinion as to the exact words. A nurse who was with him at the time reported next day that he had said, "Put up the shades. I don't want to go home in the dark."

12
I am about to take my last voyage, a great leap in the dark.

Thomas Hobbes. (1679) (Watkins, *Anecdotes of Men of Learning.*)

The "leap in the dark" is the least to be dreaded.

Byron, *Diary,* 5 Dec., 1813.

A little before you made a leap in the dark.

Sir Thomas Browne, *Letters from the Dead.*

Now I am for Hobbes' Voyage—a great leap in the dark.

Sir John Vanbrugh, *The Provoked Wife.* Act v, sc. 6. Referring to matrimony.

The spiritual life is a grand experiment which ends in an experience; but it is not merely a leap in the dark.

Dean W. R. Inge. (Marchant, *Wit and Wisdom of Dean Inge.* No. 3.)

13
I strike my flag.

Isaac Hull.

14
I must arrange my pillows for another weary night.

Washington Irving.

15
Let us cross the river and rest in the shade.

General "Stonewall" Jackson.

16
I resign my spirit to God, my daughter to my country.

Thomas Jefferson.

17
God bless you, my dear.

Samuel Johnson, to Miss Morris, who had come to ask his blessing. (Boswell, *Life.*)

18
I feel the flowers growing over me.

John Keats.

19
My bed-fellows are cramp and cough—we three all in one bed.

Charles Lamb.

20
I die content, I die for the liberty of my country. (Je meurs content, je meurs pour la liberté de mon pays.)

Marshal Lannes. Also attributed to Le Pelletier.

21
No one can be more willing to send me out of life than I am desirous to go.

Archbishop William Laud, at his execution, 1645. (Hume, *History of England.* Ch. 22.)

22
This side enough is toasted, so turn me, tyrant, eat,
And see whether raw or roasted I make the better meat.

St. Laurence, who was broiled alive on a gridiron. (Fox, *Book of Martyrs: St. Laurence.*)

23
Let the tent be struck.

General Robert E. Lee.

24
Why do you weep? Did you think I should live forever? I thought it was more difficult to die.

Louis XIV of France, to Madame de Maintenon. (Martin, *History of France,* xiv, 91.)

25
May my blood cement your happiness! (Puisse mon sang cimenter votre bonheur!)

Louis XVI of France, on the scaffold, 21 Jan., 1793.

26
I shall retire early; I am very tired.

Thomas Babington Macaulay.

1
It is God's way. His will, not ours, be done.
WILLIAM MCKINLEY. (*Dictionary of American Biog.*, xii, 109.)

2
I always talk better lying down.
JAMES MADISON.

3
I want to meet my God awake.
MARIA-THERESA, refusing to take a drug when dying (CARLYLE).

4
Farewell, my children, forever; I am going to your father.
MARIE ANTOINETTE.

5
I see no reason why the existence of Harriet Martineau should be perpetuated.
HARRIET MARTINEAU.

6
After I am dead you will find "Calais" written upon my heart.
MARY Queen of England, referring to the capture of Calais by the French.

7
Poor Carlotta!
EMPEROR MAXIMILIAN of Mexico, referring to his wife.

8
Let me die to the sounds of delicious music.
VICTOR, MARQUIS DE MIRABEAU.

9
See me safe up: for my coming down, I can shift for myself.
SIR THOMAS MORE, on ascending the scaffold. (FROUDE, *History of England*. Ch. 9.)

This hath not offended the king.
SIR THOMAS MORE, drawing his beard aside as he placed his head upon the block. (BACON, *Apothegms*. No. 22.)

10
I have too often braved death to fear it.
MURAT, King of Naples, on the scaffold, 13 Oct., 1815.

11
What an artist the world is losing! (Qualis artifex pereo!)
EMPEROR NERO, as he drove a dagger into his throat, rather than be taken alive. (SUETONIUS, *Lives of the Twelve Cæsars: Nero*. Sec. 49.)

12
Die, my dear doctor! That's the last thing I shall do!
VISCOUNT PALMERSTON

13
Oh, my country! how I leave my country!
WILLIAM PITT, referring to the shattering of the English coalition by the battle of Austerlitz. (*Dictionary of National Biography*.) Usually erroneously given as "How I love my country!" The authenticity of the phrase has been questioned, and there is some reason to believe that his last articulate utterance was, "I think I could eat one of Bellamy's veal pies."

14
Stay a little longer, Monsieur le Curé, and we will depart together.
MADAME DE POMPADOUR.

15
I am going to seek a grand perhaps; draw the curtain, the farce is played. (Je m'en vais chercher un grand peut-être; tirez le rideau, la farce est jouée.)
RABELAIS. (MOTTEUX, *Life*.) Motteux, strangely enough, translates this: "I am about to leap into the dark." The story that these were his last words has been pronounced apocryphal by some critics.

His religion, at best, is an anxious wish; like that of Rabelais, "a great Perhaps."
CARLYLE, *Burns*.

The grand Perhaps!
ROBERT BROWNING, *Bishop Blougram's Apology*.

Even going my journey; they have greased my boots already.
FRANÇOIS RABELAIS, on his death-bed, after receiving extreme unction, to a friend who inquired how he was. (BACON, *Apothegms*, No. 46.) Also attributed to Sir Samuel Garth.

16
'Tis a sharp remedy, but a sure one for all ills.
SIR WALTER RALEIGH, feeling the edge of the axe. (HUME, *History of England*. Ch. 20.)

So the heart is right, it is no matter which way the head lies.
SIR WALTER RALEIGH, at his execution, when asked on which side he preferred to lay his head on the block.

17
We perish, we disappear, but the march of time goes on forever.
ERNEST RENAN.

18
I know that all things on earth must have an end, and now I am come to mine.
SIR JOSHUA REYNOLDS.

19
So much to do; so little done!
CECIL RHODES.

20
O Liberty! how many crimes are committed in thy name!
MADAME ROLAND, from the scaffold.

21
Put out the light.
THEODORE ROOSEVELT.

22
I think I shall die to-night.
DANTE GABRIEL ROSSETTI.

23
I am going to see the sun for the last time. (Je m'em vais voir le soleil pour la dernière fois.)
JEAN-JACQUES ROUSSEAU

24
Leave the grass. (Laissez la verdure.)
GEORGE SAND, meaning that she did not wish her grave covered with bricks or stone

1
Ah, my children, you cannot cry for me as much as I have made you laugh.
PAUL SCARRON.

2
We slept reasonably, but on the next morning . . .
SIR WALTER SCOTT. Last and unfinished entry in his journal.

God bless you all; I feel myself again.
SIR WALTER SCOTT, to his family.

3
I have been all things, and it avails me naught. (Omnia fui, et nihil expediti.)
EMPEROR SEPTIMIUS SEVERUS. (EUTROPIUS, *History*, viii, 19.)

4
I die for the good old cause.
ALGERNON SIDNEY, on the scaffold, to which he had been condemned for complicity in the Rye House plot.

5
Crito, we owe a cock to Æsculapius! Be sure that it is paid! (Ὦ Κρίτων, τῷ Ἀσκληπιῷ ὀφείλομεν ἀλεκτρυόνα.)
SOCRATES, to the friend with whom he had been conversing after drinking the hemlock. (PLATO, *Phædo*. Sec. 118.) A cock was the usual offering made to Æsculapius, the Greek god of medicine and of healing. The phrase, "To sacrifice a cock to Æsculapius," meant to return thanks—to pay the doctor's bill, as it were—after recovery from illness.

6
I leave this world without a regret.
HENRY DAVID THOREAU.

7
Even in the valley of the shadow of death, two and two do not make six.
LEO TOLSTOY, when, as he was dying, he was urged to return to the fold of the Russian Orthodox Church.

8
Death is but a little word, but 'tis a great work to die.
SIR HARRY VANE, on the scaffold, 1662.

9
An emperor should die standing. (Imperatorem stantem mori oportere.)
VESPASIAN, his last words, as he tried to rise. (SUETONIUS, *Life*.)

A bishop ought to die on his legs.
JOHN WOOLTON, Bishop of Exeter, his last words. (1594)

A bishop should die preaching.
JOHN JEWEL, Bishop of Salisbury. (1571)

It becomes not a valiant man to die lying like a beast.
SIWARD, EARL OF NORTHUMBERLAND, rising from his deathbed, 1055, and putting on his armor. "And so he died standing." (CAMDEN, *Remains*, p. 261.)

10
Woe's me! I suppose I am becoming a god! (Væ, puto deus fio!)
EMPEROR VESPASIAN. (SUETONIUS, *Twelve Cæsars: Vespasian*. Sec. 23.)

11
Oh, that peace may come!
QUEEN VICTORIA, referring to the South African war.

12
It is today, my dear, that I take the perilous leap. (C'est aujourd'hui, ma belle amie, que je fais le saut perilleux.)
VOLTAIRE, quoting the words of Henry IV of France to Gabrielle d'Estrées, when about to enter the Catholic Church.

Do let me die in peace.
VOLTAIRE.

13
It is well. I die hard, but am not afraid to go.
GEORGE WASHINGTON.

14
I have known thee all the time.
JOHN GREENLEAF WHITTIER, to his niece.

15
Alas, I am dying beyond my means.
OSCAR WILDE.

16
Shoot, Walter, in heaven's name!
WILLIAM II of England (WILLIAM RUFUS), to Walter Tirel, while hunting in New Forest, in 1100. Tirel did shoot, and his arrow killed the king.

17
Can this last long?
WILLIAM III of England, to his physician. He had been thrown from his horse while riding at Hampton Court.

18
Bury me where the birds will sing over my grave.
ALEXANDER WILSON, the ornithologist.

19
I fear not this fire.
GEORGE WISHART, at the stake.

20
What, do they run already? Then I die happy!
GENERAL JAMES WOLFE, as he saw the French retreating at the battle of Quebec.

DEBATE, see Argument

DEBT

See also Borrowing

21
I hold every man a debtor to his profession.
FRANCIS BACON, *Elements of the Law: Preface.*

22
Not a *sou* had he got—not a guinea or note,
And he looked most confoundedly flurried,
As he bolted away without paying his shot,
And the landlady after him hurried.
R. H. BARHAM, *Parody on the Death of Sir John Moore.*

23
He is rich enough who owes nothing. (Il est assez riche qui ne doit rien.)
UNKNOWN. A French proverb.

24
He'd run in debt by disputation,
And pay by ratiocination.
BUTLER, *Hudebras*. Pt. i, canto i, l. 77.

1
Dreading that climax of all human ills,
The inflammation of his weekly bills.
BYRON, *Don Juan*. Canto iii, st. 35.

2
There are but two ways of paying debt—increase of industry in raising income, increase of thrift in laying out.
CARLYLE, *Past and Present*. Ch. 10.

3
A debt and gratitude are different things. (Quamquam dissimilis est pecuniæ debitio et gratiæ.)
CICERO, *Pro Cnæo Planco*. Ch. 18, sec. 68.

4
I owe you one.
GEORGE COLMAN THE YOUNGER, *The Poor Gentleman*. Act i, sc. 2.

5
Anticipated rents, and bills unpaid,
Force many a shining youth into the shade,
Not to redeem his time, but his estate,
And play the fool, but at the cheaper rate.
COWPER, *Retirement*, l. 559.

6
At the end of every seven years thou shalt make a release. And this is the manner of the release: Every creditor that lendeth aught unto his neighbour shall release it; he shall not exact it of his neighbour, or of his brother; because it is called the Lord's release.
Old Testament: Deuteronomy, xv, 1, 2.

7
Thou whom avenging pow'rs obey,
Cancel my debt (too great to pay)
Before the sad accounting day.
WENTWORTH DILLON, *On the Last Judgment*. St. 11.

8
Debt is a prolific mother of folly and of crime.
BENJAMIN DISRAELI, *Henrietta Temple*. Bk. ii, ch. 1.

9
One man thinks justice consists in paying debts. . . . But that second man . . . asks himself, Which debt must I pay first, the debt to the rich, or the debt to the poor? the debt of money, or the debt of thought to mankind?
EMERSON, *Essays, First Series: Circles*.

10
Always pay; for first or last you must pay your entire debt.
EMERSON, *Essays, First Series: Compensation*.

Wilt thou seal up the avenue of ill?
Pay every debt as if God wrote the bill!
EMERSON, *Suum Cuique*.

11
A poor man's debt makes a great noise.
THOMAS FULLER, *Gnomologia*. No. 355.

Debt is the worst poverty.
THOMAS FULLER, *Gnomologia*. No. 1258.

12
Don Pedro's out of debt, be bold to say it,
For they are said to owe, that mean to pay it.
SIR JOHN HARINGTON, *Of Don Pedro's Debts*. (*Epigrams*. Bk. i, epig. 64.)

Speak not of my debts unless you mean to pay them.
GEORGE HERBERT, *Jacula Prudentum*. No. 997.

13
Sleep without supping, and wake without owing.
GEORGE HERBERT, *Jacula Prudentum*. No. 93.

Rather go to bed supperless than rise in debt.
BENJAMIN FRANKLIN, *Poor Richard*, 1758.

14
He that gets out of debt grows rich.
GEORGE HERBERT, *Jacula Prudentum*. No. 9.

Out of debt out of danger.
JOHN RAY, *English Proverbs*.

15
Debtors are liars.
GEORGE HERBERT, *Jacula Prudentum*. No. 165.

Lying rides on debt's back.
H. G. BOHN, *Hand-Book of Proverbs*, p. 447.

Debts and lies are generally mixed together. (Debtes et mensonges sont ordinairement ensemble ralliés.)
RABELAIS, *Works*. Bk. iii, ch. 5.

The second vice is lying; the first is running in debt.
FRANKLIN, *Way to Wealth*, i, 449.

16
A pound of care pays not a dram of debt.
THOMAS DEKKER, *Shoemaker's Holiday*. Act iii, sc. 5. (1599) JOHN RAY, *English Proverbs*. (1670)

A hundred load of thought will not pay one of debts.
GEORGE HERBERT, *Jacula Prudentum*. No. 410. (1640)

17
I am poor in my own money. (Meo sum pauper in ære.)
HORACE, *Epistles*. Bk. ii, epis. 2, l. 12. Meaning "I am not in debt."

18
A mortgage casts a shadow on the sunniest field.
R. G. INGERSOLL, *About Farming in Illinois*.

19
Never spend your money before you have it.
THOMAS JEFFERSON, *Writings*. Vol xvi, p. 111.

20
Small debts are like small shot; they are rattling on every side, and can scarcely be escaped without a wound; great debts are like cannon, of loud noise but little danger.
SAMUEL JOHNSON, *Letter to Joseph Simpson*.

21
And looks the whole world in the face,
For he owes not any man.
LONGFELLOW, *The Village Blacksmith*.

22
May his debts torment him. (Torqueat hunc æris mutua summa sui.)
OVID, *Remediorum Amoris*, l. 562.

23
There died my father, no man's debtor,
And there I'll die, or worse or better.
POPE, *Imitations of Horace, Epistles*. Bk. i, epis. 7, l. 79.

24
Debt is a grievous bondage to an honorable

man. (Alienum æs homini ingenuo acerba est servitus.)
PUBLILIUS SYRUS, *Sententiæ*. No. 11.

A man in debt is so far a slave.
EMERSON, *Conduct of Life: Wealth.*

A man in debt is caught in a net.
JOHN RAY, *English Proverbs.*

1
Outrun the constable. (To run into debt.)
JOHN RAY, *English Proverbs.*

"How far have you over-run the Constable?" I told him that the debt amounted to eleven pounds.
SMOLLETT, *Roderick Random*. Ch. 23.

Friend Ralph, thou hast
Outrun the constable at last.
BUTLER, *Hudibras*. Pt. i, canto iii, l. 1367.

Outran the constable; lived *fast*, you know.
PLANCHÉ, *Extravaganza*. Pt. ii, p. 197.

2
Loans and debts make worries and frets.
W. G. BENHAM, *Proverbs*, p. 804.

3
I pay debts of honour—not honourable debts.
FREDERIC REYNOLDS, *The Will*. Act iii, sc. 2.

4
Owe no man anything, but to love one another.
New Testament: Romans, xiii, 8.

You shall owe to none (saith the Holy Apostle) anything save Love, Friendship, and a mutual Benevolence.
RABELAIS, *Works*. Bk. iii, ch. 5.

5
A trifling debt makes a man your debtor, a large one makes him your enemy. (Leve aes alienum debitorem facit, grave inimicum.)
SENECA, *Epistulæ ad Lucilium*. Epis. xix, 12.

6
There is more owing her than is paid; and more shall be paid her than she'll demand.
SHAKESPEARE, *All's Well that Ends Well*. Act i, sc. 3, l. 107.

7
It is characteristic of our present manners . . . that if anyone repays a debt, it must be regarded as an immense favor. (Præsertim ut nunc sunt mores, . . . Si quis quid reddit, magna habendast gratia.)
TERENCE, *Phormio*, l. 55. (Act i, sc. 2.)

Base is the slave that pays.
SHAKESPEARE, *Henry V*. Act ii, sc. 1, l. 100.

8
Better old debts than old grudges.
Attributed to PRINCE ALFRID, son of Oswy, King of Northumbria; also to Fithal, lawgiver to King Cormac macAirt.

A New Way to Pay Old Debts.
PHILIP MASSINGER. Title of play.

DECAY

9
A gilded halo hovering round decay.
BYRON, *The Giaour*, l. 99.

10
Something there is that doesn't love a wall,
That wants it down.
ROBERT FROST, *Mending Wall.*

11
A general flavor of mild decay,
But nothing local, as one might say.
O. W. HOLMES, *The Deacon's Masterpiece.*

12
While in the progress of their long decay,
Thrones sink to dust, and nations pass away.
FREDERICK HOWARD, EARL OF CARLISLE, *On the Ruins of Pæstum.*

13
There seems to be a constant decay of all our ideas; . . . the print wears out, and at last there remains nothing to be seen.
JOHN LOCKE, *Human Understanding*. Bk. ii, ch. 10.

14
Everything rises but to fall and increases but to decay. (Omnia orta occidunt et aucta secuntur.)
SALLUST, *Jugurtha*. Ch. ii, sec. 3.

15
Sullen presage of your own decay.
SHAKESPEARE, *King John*. Act i, sc. 1, l. 28.

16
And all our chants but chaplet some decay.
FRANCIS THOMPSON, *Ode to the Setting Sun*, l. 196.

17
The Night is Mother of the Day,
The Winter of the Spring,
And ever upon old Decay
The greenest mosses cling.
WHITTIER, *A Dream of Summer.*

DECEIT

See also Cheating; Cunning; Hypocrisy; Speech: To Conceal Thought; Treachery

18
From righteous deception God standeth not aloof. (Ἀπάτης δικαίας οὐκ ἀποστατεῖ θεός.)
ÆSCHYLUS, *Fragments*. Frag. 162.

There are times when God honoreth the season for untruth. (Ψευδῶν δὲ καιρὸν ἔσθ' ὅπου τιμᾷ θεός.)
ÆSCHYLUS, *Fragments*. Frag. 163.

19
Surely the continual habit of dissimulation is but a weak and sluggish cunning, and not greatly politic.
BACON, *Advancement of Learning*. Bk. ii.

Dissimulation invites dissimulation.
BACON, *De Augmentis Scientiarum*. Pt. i, bk. 6.

Dissimulation is the coward's virtue.
VOLTAIRE, *Don Pèdre*. Act ii, sc. 5.

Who does not know how to dissimulate does not know how to live. (Qui nescit dissimulare nescit vivere.)
PALINGENIUS, *Zodiacus Vitæ*. Bk. iv, 684. Quoted by Burton, (*Anatomy of Melancholy*, Pt. i, sec. ii, mem. 3, subs. 15) as a saying of Frederick Barbarossa.

See also KINGS: APOTHEGMS.

1
The deceits of the world, the flesh, and the devil.
Book of Common Prayer: Litany.

2
My great-grandfather was but a waterman, looking one way and rowing another; and I got most of my estate by the same occupation.
JOHN BUNYAN, *The Pilgrim's Progress.* Pt. i.

Like the watermen that row one way and look another.
BURTON, *Anatomy of Melancholy: Democritus to the Reader.*

Like the watermen who advance forward while they look backward.
MONTAIGNE, *Essays.* Bk. ii, ch. 29.

Like watermen who look astern while they row the boat ahead.
PLUTARCH, *Apothegms.*

3
Subtlety may deceive you; integrity never will.
OLIVER CROMWELL, *Letter to Robert Barnard,* Jan., 1642.

4
Fraud, that in every conscience leaves a sting. (La froda, ond' ogni coscïenza è morsa.)
DANTE, *Inferno.* Canto xi, l. 52.

5
But Esau's hands suit ill with Jacob's voice.
DRYDEN, *Absalom and Achitophel.* Pt. i, l. 982.

Orlando's helmet in Augustine's cowl.
HORACE AND JAMES SMITH, *Cui Bono.*

6
Let no man deceive you with vain words.
New Testament: Ephesians, v, 6.

7
The world wishes to be deceived. (Mundus vult decipi.)
SEBASTIAN FRANCK, *Paradoxi Ducenta Octoginta.* No. 238.

The people wish to be deceived; let them be deceived. (Populus vult decipi; decipiatur.)
CARDINAL CARLO CARAFFA, Legate of Paul IV., referring to the Parisians. (DE THOU, i, 17.) The German proverb, "Die Welt will betrogen sein," long antedates Caraffa.

If the world will be gulled, let it be gulled.
ROBERT BURTON, *Anatomy of Melancholy.* Pt. iii, sec. iv, mem. 1, subs. 2.

A certain portion of the human race
Has certainly a taste for being diddled.
THOMAS HOOD, *A Black Job.*

We seek and offer ourselves to be gulled.
MONTAIGNE, *Essays.* Bk. iii, ch. 11.

8
Pretexts are not wanting when one wishes to use them. (Non mancano pretesti quando si vuole.)
GOLDONI, *La Villeggiatura.* Act i, sc. 12.

9
To be deceived in your true heart's desire
Was bitterer than a thousand years of fire!
JOHN HAY, *A Woman's Love.*

10
Who dares think one thing, and another tell,
My heart detests him as the gates of hell.
HOMER, *Iliad.* Bk. ix, l. 412. (Pope, tr.)

Hateful to me as are the gates of hell,
Is he who, hiding one thing in his heart,
Utters another.
HOMER, *Iliad.* Bk. ix, l. 386. (Bryant, tr.)

I hate the man who is double-minded, kind in words, but a foe in his conduct.
PALLADAS. (*Greek Anthology.* Bk. x, epig. 95.)

My tongue may swear, but I act as I please. (Meus arbitratust, lingua quod juret mea.)
PLAUTUS, *Rudens,* l. 1355. (Act v, sc. 2.)

Words of his tongue can no man trust,
For in his heart there is deceitful thought.
PITTACUS. (DIOGENES LAERTIUS, *Pittacus.* Bk. i, sec. 78.)

11
Love no man: trust no man: speak ill of no man to his face, nor well of any man behind his back. . . . Spread yourself upon his bosom publicly, whose heart you would eat in private.
BEN JONSON, *Every Man Out of His Humour.* Act iii, sc. 1.

12
One never deceives for a good purpose; knavery adds malice to falsehood. (On ne trompe point en bien; la fourberie ajoute la malice au mensonge.)
LA BRUYÈRE, *Les Caractères.* Pt. xi.

You believe him your dupe; but if he is pretending to be so, who is the greater dupe, he or you? (Vous le croyez votre dupe; s'il feint de l'être, qui est plus dupe, de lui ou de vous?)
LA BRUYÈRE, *Les Caractères.* Pt. v.

13
Distrust justifies deceit. (Notre défiance justifie la tromperie d'autrui.)
LA ROCHEFOUCAULD, *Maximes.* No. 86.

14
It is in vain to find fault with those arts of deceiving wherein men find pleasure to be deceived.
JOHN LOCKE, *Human Understanding.* Bk. iii, ch. 10, sec. 34.

He speaks the kindest words, and looks such things,
Vows with such passion, swears with so much grace,
That it is Heaven to be deluded by him.
NATHANIEL LEE, *The Rival Queens.* Act i, sc. 1.

15
On such folk, plainly, is no trust,
That fire and water holden in their fist.
JOHN LYDGATE, *Troy Book.* Bk. iv, l. 4988. (1412)

Water in the one hand, fire in the other.
GABRIEL HARVEY, *Works.* Vol. ii, p. 317.

16
To sell smoke. (Fumos vendere.)
MARTIAL, *Epigrams.* Bk. iv, epig. 5.

17
We are easily deceived by that which we love. (On est aisément dupé par ce qu'on aime.)
MOLIÈRE, *Le Tartuffe.* Act iv, sc. 3, l. 82.

1
Deceive the deceivers: they are mostly an unrighteous sort. (Fallite fallentes: ex magna parte profanum.)
Ovid, *Ars Amatoria*. Bk. i, l. 645.

Fraud may be repelled by fraud, and the laws allow arms to be taken against an armed foe. (Fraus est concessa repellere fraudem, Armaque in armatos sumere jura sinunt.)
Ovid, *Ars Amatoria*. Bk. iii, l. 491.

To deceive a deceiver is no deceit.
Ulpian Fulwell, *Ars Adulandi*. (1580)

Deceiving of a deceiver is no knavery.
Thomas Fuller, *Gnomologia*. No. 1261.

It is doubly pleasant to deceive the deceiver. (C'est double plaisir de tromper le trompeur.)
La Fontaine, *Fables*. Bk. ii, fab. 15.

2
Individuals may deceive and be deceived; but no one ever deceived everybody, nor has everybody ever deceived any one. (Singuli enim decipere et decipi possunt; nemo omnes, neminem omnes fefellunt.)
Pliny the Younger, *Panegyrics: Trajan*, 62.

One may outwit another, but not all the others. (On peut être plus fin qu'un autre, mais non pas plus fin que tous les autres.)
La Rochefoucauld, *Maximes*. No. 394.

You can fool some of the people all of the time, and all of the people some of the time, but you cannot fool all of the people all the time.
Abraham Lincoln, *Speech*, Bloomington, Ill., 29 May, 1856. (On the authority of William P. Kellogg.) Credited to P. T. Barnum by Spofford.

There is no lie that many men will not believe; there is no man who does not believe many lies; and there is no man who believes only lies.
John Sterling, *Essays and Tales: Thoughts*.

3
Who tries with craft another to deceive,
Deceives himself, if he says he's deceived
Whom he'd deceive. For if whom you'd deceive
Perceives that he's deceived, the deceiver 'tis
Who is deceived, the other's not deceived.
(Nam qui lepide portulat alterum frustrari,
Quem frustratur, frustra eum dicit frustra esse;
Nam si se frustrari quem frustras sentit,
Qui frustratur frustrast, si non ille frustra est.)
Quintus Ennius, *Saturæ*, l. 59.

4
O, what a tangled web we weave,
When first we practise to deceive!
Scott, *Marmion*. Canto vi, st. 17.

Assumed despondence bent his head,
While troubled joy was in his eye,
The well-feigned sorrow to belie.
Scott, *Rokeby*. Canto i, st. 14.

5
By indirections find directions out.
Shakespeare, *Hamlet*. Act ii, sc. 1, l. 66.

A quicksand of deceit.
Shakespeare, *III Henry VI*. Act v, sc. 4, l. 26.

6
Sweet, sweet, sweet poison for the age's tooth:
Which, though I will not practise to deceive,
Yet, to avoid deceit, I mean to learn.
Shakespeare, *King John*. Act i, sc. 1, l. 213.

The seeming truth which cunning time puts on
To entrap the wisest.
Shakespeare, *The Merchant of Venice*. Act iii, sc. 2, l. 100.

7
To beguile many and be beguil'd by one.
Shakespeare, *Othello*. Act iv, sc. 1, l. 98.

Who makes the fairest show means most deceit.
Shakespeare, *Pericles*. Act i, sc. 4, l. 75.

See also Appearance: Its Deceitfulness.

8
And thus I clothe my naked villainy
With old odd ends, stol'n out of holy writ;
And seem a saint, when most I play the devil.
Shakespeare, *Richard III*. Act i, sc. 3, l. 336.

9
One dupe is as impossible as one twin.
John Sterling, *Essays and Tales: Crystals from a Cavern*.

10
O purblind race of miserable men,
How many among us at this very hour
Do forge a lifelong trouble for ourselves
By taking true for false, or false for true!
Tennyson, *Geraint and Enid*, l. 1.

11
Deceit and treachery skulk with hatred, but an honest spirit flieth with anger.
M. F. Tupper, *Proverbial Philosophy: Of Hatred and Anger*.

12
We must distinguish between speaking to deceive and being silent to be impenetrable. (Il faut distinguer entre parler pour tromper et se taire pour être impénétrable.)
Voltaire, *Essai sur les Mœurs*. Sec. 163.

13
One way they look, another way they steer.
Young, *Love of Fame*. Sat. i, l. 73.

14
Thou hast a crooked tongue, holding with hound and running with hare.
Unknown, *Jacob's Well*, 263. (c. 1440)

To hold with the hare and run with the hounds.
Humphrey Robert, *Complaint for Reformation*. (1572)

And both could run with hound and hold with hare.
Christopher Brooke, *Richard the Third*, 86. (1614)

II—Deceit: Self-Deception

15
The easiest person to deceive is one's self.
Bulwer-Lytton, *The Disowned*. Ch. 42.

16
We never are but by ourselves betrayed.
Congreve, *The Old Batchelor*. Act iii, sc. 1.

1
Yet still we hug the dear deceit.
NATHANIEL COTTON, *Content*. Vision iv.

2
The easiest thing of all is to deceive one's self; for what a man wishes he generally believes to be true.
DEMOSTHENES, *Olynthiaca*. No. iii, sec. 19.

3
Who hath deceived thee so often as thyself?
BENJAMIN FRANKLIN, *Poor Richard*, 1738.

4
We are never deceived; we deceive ourselves. (Man wird nie betrogen, man betrügt sich selbst.)
GOETHE, *Sprüche in Prosa*, iii.

5
Deceive, deceive me once again!
WALTER SAVAGE LANDOR, *To Ianthe*.

6
The surest way to be deceived is to think one's self more clever than others. (Le vrai moyen d'être trompé, c'est de se croire plus fin que les autres.)
LA ROCHEFOUCAULD, *Maximes*. No. 127.

7
Hoping at least she may herself deceive;
Against experience willing to believe.
MATTHEW PRIOR, *Solomon*. Bk. iii, l. 223.

8
We deceive and flatter no one by such delicate artifices as we do our own selves. (Wir betrügen und schmeicheln niemanden durch so feine Kunstgriffe als uns selbst.)
SCHOPENHAUER, *Die Welt als Wille*. Bk. i, 350.

DECEMBER

See also Winter

9
In a drear-nighted December,
Too happy, happy brook,
Thy bubblings ne'er remember
Apollo's summer look;
But with a sweet forgetting,
They stay their crystal fretting,
Never, never petting
About the frozen time.
KEATS, *Stanzas*.

10
Ah, distinctly I remember it was in the bleak December.
EDGAR ALLAN POE, *The Raven*.

11
In cold December fragrant chaplets blow,
And heavy harvests nod beneath the snow.
POPE, *The Dunciad*. Bk. i, l. 77.

12
When we shall hear
The rain and wind beat dark December, how,
In this our pinching cave, shall we discourse
The freezing hours away?
SHAKESPEARE, *Cymbeline*. Act iii, sc. 3, l. 36.

13
The sun that brief December day
Rose cheerless over hills of gray,
And, darkly circled, gave at noon
A sadder light than waning moon.
WHITTIER, *Snow-Bound*.

DECENCY

See also Modesty

14
Immodest words admit of no defence,
For want of decency is want of sense.
WENTWORTH DILLON, LORD ROSCOMMON, *Essay on Translated Verse*, l. 113. (1684) Often attributed to Pope.

15
My cares and my inquiries are for decency and truth, and in this I am wholly occupied. (Quid verum atque decens curo et rogo, et omnis in hoc sum.)
HORACE, *Epistles*. Bk. i, epis. i, l. 11.

16
Those thousand decencies, that daily flow
From all her words and actions.
MILTON, *Paradise Lost*. Bk. viii, l. 601.

17
Respectable means rich, and decent means poor. I should die if I heard my family called decent.
T. L. PEACOCK, *Crotchet Castle*. Ch. 3.

18
Virtue she finds too painful an endeavour,
Content to dwell in decencies forever.
POPE, *Moral Essays*. Epis. ii, l. 163.

19
You'll oft find in books, rather ancient than recent,
A gap in the page marked with *"cetera desunt,"* . . .
And may borrow, perhaps, a significant hint
That *desunt* means simply not decent to print.
JOHN GODFREY SAXE, *Lucas a Non*.

20
Decency is Indecency's Conspiracy of Silence.
BERNARD SHAW, *Maxims for Revolutionists*.

DECISION

21
The die is cast. (Jacta alea est.)
JULIUS CÆSAR, on crossing the Rubicon, after coming from Gaul, and advancing into Italy against Pompey. (SUETONIUS, *Twelve Cæsars: Julius*. Sec. 32.) The Rubicon has been identified as a brook now called the Fluminico (little river), and Mussolini has recently caused a monument to be erected on its bank, near the village of Savignano, to mark the spot where Cæsar crossed it. The honor has also been claimed for the Luso, a small stream which empties into the Adriatic near Rimini.

But finally, with a sort of passion, as if abandoning calculation and casting himself upon the future, and uttering the phrase with which men usually prelude their plunge into desperate and daring fortunes, "Let the die be cast," (Ἀνερρίφθω κύβος) he hastened to cross the Rubicon.
PLUTARCH, *Lives: Cæsar*. Ch. 32, sec. 6.

I answered that the die was now cast; I had passed the Rubicon. Sink or swim, live or die, survive or perish with my country was my unalterable determination.

JOHN ADAMS, *Conversation,* with Jonathan Sewall, 1774. (ADAMS, *Works.* Vol. iv, p. 8.)

1
He only is a well-made man who has a good determination.

EMERSON, *Conduct of Life: Culture.*

I like the sayers of No better than the sayers of Yes.

EMERSON, *Journals.*

2
The door must either be shut or be open.

GOLDSMITH, *Citizen of the World.* No. 51.

Il Faut qu'une Porte Soit Ouverte ou Fermé.

ALFRED DE MUSSET. Title of play.

3
Multitudes, multitudes in the valley of decision: for the day of the Lord is near in the valley of decision.

Old Testament: Joel, iii, 14. *The Valley of Decision* is the title of a novel by Edith Wharton.

4
Once to every man and nation comes the moment to decide,
In the strife of Truth with Falsehood, for the good or evil side;
Some great cause, God's new Messiah, offering each the bloom or blight,
Parts the goats upon the left hand, and the sheep upon the right,
And the choice goes by forever 'twixt that darkness and that light.

J. R. LOWELL, *The Present Crisis.* St. 5.

5
Men must be decided on what they will NOT do, and then they are able to act with vigor *in what they ought to do.*

MENCIUS, *Works.* Bk. iv, pt. ii, ch. 8.

6
Deliberate as often as you please, but when you decide it is once for all. (Deliberandum est sæpe, statuendum est semel.)

PUBLILIUS SYRUS, *Sententiæ.* No. 132.

He who considers too much will perform little. (Wer gar zu viel bedenkt wird wenig leisten.)

SCHILLER, *Wilhelm Tell.* Act iii, sc. 1.

7
Swift decisions are not sure. (Φρονεῖν γὰρ οἱ ταχεῖς, οὐκ ἀσφαλεῖς.)

SOPHOCLES, *Œdipus Tyrannus,* l. 617.

Decide not rashly. The decision made
Can never be recalled.

LONGFELLOW, *Masque of Pandora: Tower of Prometheus on Mount Caucasus.*

8
'Tis fix'd; th' irrevocable doom of Jove;
No force can bend me, no persuasion move.

STATIUS, *Thebais.* Bk. i, l. 413. (Pope, tr.)

9
"Settled once, settled forever," as the saying is. ("Actum" aiunt "ne agas.")

TERENCE, *Phormio,* l. 419. (Act ii, sc. 3.)

DEEDS

See also Action; Word and Deed

I—Deeds: Apothegms

10
What we have to learn to do we learn by doing. (Μαθόντας ποιεῖν, ταῦτα ποιοῦντες μανθάνομεν.)

ARISTOTLE, *Nicomachean Ethics.* Bk. ii, ch. 1, sec. 4.

11
Deeds let escape are never to be done.

ROBERT BROWNING, *Sordello.* Bk. iii. *See also under* OPPORTUNITY.

12
Let us do or die!

BURNS, *Bruce to His Men at Bannockburn;* CAMPBELL, *Gertrude of Wyoming,* iii, 37; FLETCHER, *Island Princess,* ii, 4.

This expression is a kind of common property, being the motto, we believe, of a Scottish family.

SCOTT, *Miscellanies: Review of Gertrude of Wyoming.* Vol. i, p. 153.

13
Everywhere in life, the true question is not what we *gain,* but what we *do.*

CARLYLE, *Essays: Goethe's Helena.*

The All of things is an infinite conjugation of the verb *To do.*

CARLYLE, *The French Revolution.* Vol. ii, bk. iii, ch. 1.

14
Whatever is worth doing at all, is worth doing well.

LORD CHESTERFIELD, *Letters,* 9 Oct., 1746.

15
The soul ever yearns to be doing something. (Animus agere semper aliquid.)

CICERO, *De Finibus.* Bk. v, ch. 20, sec. 55.

16
Whatever you do, do with all your might. (Quicquid agas agere pro viribus.)

CICERO, *De Senectute.* Ch. 9, sec. 27.

Whatsoever thy hand findeth to do, do it with thy might.

Old Testament: Ecclesiastes, ix, 10.

17
Let us do nothing abjectly, nothing timidly, nothing sluggishly. (Ne quid abjecte, ne quid timide, ne quid ignave . . . faciamus.)

CICERO, *Tusculanarum Disputationum.* Bk. ii, ch. 23, sec. 55.

18
This is the Thing that I was born to do.

SAMUEL DANIEL, *Musophilus.* St. 100.

19
What is well done is done soon enough.

DU BARTAS, *Devine Weekes and Workes.* Week i, day 1. (Sylvester, tr.)

20
As we are, so we do; and as we do, so is it done to us.

EMERSON, *Conduct of Life: Worship.*

21
Do the thing and you have still the power;

but they who do not the thing have not the power.

EMERSON, *Essays, First Series: Compensation.*

Only deeds give strength to life. (Nur Thaten geben dem Leben Stärke.)

JEAN PAUL RICHTER, *Titan*. Zykel 145.

1
Counsel that I once heard given to a young person, "Always do what you are afraid to do."

EMERSON, *Essays, First Series: Heroism.*

2
While you do that which no other man can do, every man is a willing spectator.

EMERSON, *Uncollected Lectures: Public and Private Education.*

3
If you'd have it done, Go: if not, Send.

BENJAMIN FRANKLIN, *Poor Richard*, 1743.

4
The shortest answer is doing.

GEORGE HERBERT, *Jacula Prudentum.*

5
Living requires but little life; doing requires much! (On a besoin pour vivre de peu de vie; il en faut beaucoup pour agir.)

JOUBERT, *Pensées*. No. 93.

6
Cæsar, headlong in everything, thought nothing done while anything remained to do. (Cæsar, in omnia præceps, Nil actum credens, cum quid superesset agendum.)

LUCAN, *De Bello Civili*. Bk. ii, l. 656.

He hath nothing done that doth not all.

SAMUEL DANIEL, *The History of the Civil War*. Bk. iv, st. 14.

Think nothing done while aught remains to do.

SAMUEL ROGERS, *Human Life*, l. 49.

7
As he pronounces lastly on each deed,
Of so much fame in Heaven expect thy meed.

MILTON, *Lycidas*, l. 83.

8
Goodly is he that goodly doeth.

ANTHONY MUNDAY, *Sundry Examples*, 78. (1580)

He is proper that proper doeth.

DEKKER, *Shoemaker's Holiday*, ii, 1. (1600)

He is handsome that handsome does.

GAY, *Wife of Bath*, iii, 1. (1713)

Handsome is that handsome does.

FIELDING, *Tom Jones*. Bk. iv, ch. 12. (1749); GOLDSMITH, *Vicar of Wakefield*. Ch. 1. (1768)

9
With deeds my life was filled, not with inactive years. (His ævom fuit implendum, non segnibus annis.)

OVID, *Consolatio ad Liviam*, l. 449.

We live in deeds, not years, in thoughts, not breaths.

P. J. BAILEY, *Festus: A Country Town.*

A life spent worthily should be measured by a nobler line,—by deeds, not years.

R. B. SHERIDAN, *Pizarro*. Act iv, sc. 1.

10
Men do not value a good deed unless it brings a reward. (Ipse decor, recte facti si præmia desint, non movet.)

OVID, *Epistulæ ex Ponto*. Bk. ii, epis. iii, l. 13.

He covets less
Than misery itself would give; rewards
His deeds with doing them.

SHAKESPEARE, *Coriolanus*. Act ii, sc. 2, l. 130.

The reward for a good deed is to have done it.

ELBERT HUBBARD, *Philistine*. Vol. xx, p. 139.

See also under REWARD.

11
The deed is forgotten, but its result remains. (Factum abiit, monumenta manent.)

OVID, *Fasti*. Bk. iv, l. 709.

12
The deeds of men never deceive the gods. (Acta deos numquam mortalia fallunt.)

OVID, *Tristia*. Bk. i, eleg. 2, l. 97.

13
Better not do the deed, than weep it done.

MATTHEW PRIOR, *Henry and Emma*, l. 308.

14
To do two things at once is to do neither.

PUBLILIUS SYRUS, *Sententiæ*. No. 7.

15
Their works do follow them.

New Testament: Revelation, xiv, 13.

Every man is the son of his own works. (Cada uno es hijo de sus obras.)

CERVANTES, *Don Quixote*. Bk. i, ch. 4.

16
What should be done must be learned from one who does it. (Quid faciendum sit, a faciente discendum est.)

SENECA, *Epistulæ ad Lucilium*. Epis. xcviii, 17.

17
Better to leave undone, than by our deed
Acquire too high a fame, when him we serve 's away.

SHAKESPEARE, *Antony and Cleopatra*. Act iii, sc. 1, l. 14.

18
Alone I did it.

SHAKESPEARE, *Coriolanus*. Act v, sc. 6, l. 117.

19
If it were done when 'tis done, then 'twere well
It were done quickly.

SHAKESPEARE, *Macbeth*. Act i, sc. 7, l. 1.

20
O, what men dare do! what men may do! what men daily do, not knowing what they do.

SHAKESPEARE, *Much Ado About Nothing*. Act iv, sc. 1, l. 19.

21
Things won are done, joy's soul lies in the doing.

SHAKESPEARE, *Troilus and Cressida*. Act i, sc. 2, l. 313.

22
How my achievements mock me!

SHAKESPEARE, *Troilus and Cressida*. Act iv, sc. 2, l. 71.

1
There are deeds which have no form.
SHELLEY, *The Cenci*. Act iii, sc. 1.

2
We do as we can, since we can't do as we would, as the saying is. (Ut quimus, aiunt, quando ut volumus non licet.)
TERENCE, *Andria*, l. 805. (Act iv, sc. 5.)

II—Deeds: Deed and Thought

3
Our deeds are sometimes better than our thoughts.
P. J. BAILEY, *Festus: A Village Feast*, l. 918.

4
'Tis not what man Does which exalts him, but what man Would do.
ROBERT BROWNING, *Saul*. Sec. xviii.

We know better than we do.
EMERSON, *Essays, First Series: The Over-Soul*.

5
Knowledge we ask not—knowledge Thou hast lent,
But, Lord, the will—there lies our bitter need,
Give us to build above the deep intent
The deed, the deed.
JOHN DRINKWATER, *A Prayer*.

6
Do noble things, not dream them.
CHARLES KINGSLEY, *A Farewell*.

To stretch the octave 'twixt the dream and deed,
Ah, that's the thrill!
RICHARD LE GALLIENNE, *The Decadent to His Soul*.

7
Thinking the deed, and not the creed,
Would help us in our utmost need.
LONGFELLOW, *Tales of a Wayside Inn: Prelude*, l. 221.

8
And what they dare to dream of, dare to do.
J. R. LOWELL, *Commemoration Ode*.

The dreaming doer is the master poet—
And lo, the perfect lyric is a deed!
JOHN G. NEIHARDT, *The Lyric Deed*.

9
Space is as nothing to spirit, the deed is outdone by the doing.
RICHARD REALF, *Indirection*.

10
He knows a baseness in his blood
At such strange war with something good,
He may not do the thing he would.
TENNYSON, *The Two Voices*, l. 301.

11
Forget the poet, but his warning heed,
And shame his poor word with your nobler deed.
WHITTIER, *The Panorama*. Last lines.

WILL FOR THE DEED, *see under* WILL.

III—Deeds: Great Deeds

12
Our wreaths may fade, our flowers may wane,
But his well-ripened deeds remain.
ALFRED AUSTIN, *At His Grave*.

But these are deeds that should not pass away,
And names that must not wither.
BYRON, *Childe Harold*. Canto iii, st. 67.

Things of to-day?
Deeds which are harvest for Eternity!
EBENEZER ELLIOTT, *Hymn*, l. 22.

13
There may be danger in the deed,
But there is honour too.
W. E. AYTOUN, *The Island of the Scots*, l. 43.

14
Great things are done when men and mountains meet;
This is not done by jostling in the street.
WILLIAM BLAKE, *Gnomic Verses*. No. 1.

15
Great deeds are reserved for great men.
CERVANTES, *Don Quixote*. Pt. ii, ch. 23.

His deeds inimitable.
CHAPMAN, *Bussy D'Ambois*. Act i, sc. 1.

16
Remember thine own verse: "Should heaven turn hell
For deeds well done, I would do ever well."
CHAPMAN, *The Tears of Peace: Induction*.

17
Born, Cæsar-like, to write and act great deeds.
DRYDEN, *Annus Mirabilis*. St. 175.

18
No great deed is done
By falterers who ask for certainty.
GEORGE ELIOT, *The Spanish Gypsy*. Bk. i.

19
Desperate deeds of derring do.
W. S. GILBERT, *Ruddigore*. Act i.

20
I count this thing to be grandly true:
That a noble deed is a step toward God.
J. G. HOLLAND, *Gradatim*.

Nor doubt that golden chords
Of good works, mingling with the visions, raise
The soul to purer worlds.
WORDSWORTH, *Ecclesiastical Sonnets*. Pt. i, 18.

21
First in the fight, and ev'ry graceful deed.
HOMER, *Iliad*. Bk. iv, l. 295. (Pope, tr.)

22
Oh! 'tis easy
To beget great deeds; but in the rearing of them— . . .
There lies the self-denial.
CHARLES KINGSLEY, *The Saint's Tragedy*. Act iv, sc. 3.

23
But the good deed, through the ages
Living in historic pages,
Brighter grows and gleams immortal,
Unconsumed by moth or rust.
LONGFELLOW, *The Norman Baron*.

Whene'er a noble deed is wrought,
Whene'er is spoken a noble thought,
Our hearts, in glad surprise,
To higher levels rise.
LONGFELLOW, *Santa Filomena*.

1
The gods see the deeds of the righteous. (Di pia facta vident.)
OVID, *Fasti*. Bk. ii, l. 117.

2
Your deeds are known,
In words that kindle glory from the stone.
SCHILLER, *The Walk*.

3
Things done well,
And with a care, exempt themselves from fear;
Things done without example, in their issue
Are to be fear'd.
SHAKESPEARE, *Henry VIII*. Act i, sc. 2, l. 88.

4
How far that little candle throws his beams!
So shines a good deed in a naughty world.
SHAKESPEARE, *The Merchant of Venice*. Act v, sc. 1, l. 90.

O, would the deed were good!
For now the devil, that told me I did well,
Says that this deed is chronicled in hell.
SHAKESPEARE, *Richard II*. Act v, sc. 5, l. 115.

5
Not till earth be sunless, not till death strike blind the skies,
May the deathless love that waits on deathless deeds be dead.
SWINBURNE, *Grace Darling*, l. 103.

6
Great deeds cannot die;
They with the sun and moon renew their light
For ever, blessing those that look on them.
TENNYSON, *The Princess*. Pt. iii, l. 237.

7
And do we still hesitate to extend our renown by deeds? (Et dubitamus adhuc virtutem extendere factis?)
VERGIL, *Æneid*. Bk. vi, l. 806.

It is valor's task to extend our fame by deeds. (Sed famam extendere factis, Hoc virtutis opus.)
VERGIL, *Æneid*, Bk. x, l. 468. "Famam extendere factis"—To extend fame by deeds—was the motto of Linnæus.

8
A deed well done pleaseth the heart.
UNKNOWN, *How the Good Wife*, l. 110. (1460)

IV—Deeds: Evil Deeds

9
When about to commit a base deed, respect thyself, though there is no witness. (Turpe quid ausurus, te sine teste time.)
ANACHARSIS. (AUSONIUS [?], *Septem Sapientum Sententiæ*, l. 43.)

10
Inasmuch as ill deeds spring up as a spontaneous crop, they are easy to learn.
CERVANTES, *Coloquio de los Perros*.

11
Men loved darkness rather than light, because their deeds were evil.
New Testament: John, iii, 19.

12
Every guilty deed
Holds in itself the seed
Of retribution and undying pain.
LONGFELLOW, *The Masque of Pandora*. Pt. viii. *See also under* RETRIBUTION.

13
Many things, base in the doing, please when done. (Multaque, dum fiunt, turpia, facta placent.)
OVID, *Ars Amatoria*. Bk. iii, l. 218.

14
Foul deeds will rise,
Though all the earth o'erwhelm them, to men's eyes.
SHAKESPEARE, *Hamlet*. Act i, sc. 2. *See also under* MURDER.

15
There shall be done A deed of dreadful note.
SHAKESPEARE, *Macbeth*. Act iii, sc. 2, l. 43.

A deed without a name.
SHAKESPEARE, *Macbeth*. Act iv, sc. 1, l. 49.

Deeds to make heaven weep, all earth amazed.
SHAKESPEARE, *Othello*. Act iii, sc. 3, l. 370.

16
Unnatural deeds Do breed unnatural troubles.
SHAKESPEARE, *Macbeth*. Act v, sc. 1, l. 79.

17
You undergo too strict a paradox,
Striving to make an ugly deed look fair.
SHAKESPEARE, *Timon of Athens*. Act iii, 5, 24.

18
Let guilty men remember their black deeds
Do lean on crutches made of slender reeds.
JOHN WEBSTER, *The White Devil*. Act v, sc. 6.

V—Deeds Done and Undone

19
We have left undone those things which we ought to have done; and we have done those things which we ought not to have done.
Book of Common Prayer: General Confession.

20
For deeds undone
Rankle and snarl and hunger for their due,
Till there seems naught so despicable as you
In all the grin o' the sun.
W. E. HENLEY, *Rhymes and Rhythms*. No. vii, st. 2.

21
It is a most mortifying reflection for a man to consider what he has done, compared with what he might have done.
SAMUEL JOHNSON. (BOSWELL, *Life*, 1770.)

22
It is done and cannot be undone. (Factum est illud: fieri infectum non potest.)
PLAUTUS, *Aulularia*, l. 741. (Act iv, sc. 10.)

The thing that is done cannot be undone.
RICHARD TAVERNER, *Proverbs*. No. 35. (1539)

What's done, cannot be undone.
SHAKESPEARE, *Macbeth*. Act v, sc. 1, 74. (1606)

Things without all remedy
Should be without regard; what's done is done.
SHAKESPEARE, *Macbeth*. Act iii, sc. 2, l. 11.

What is done cannot be now amended.
SHAKESPEARE, *Richard III*. Act iv, sc. 4, l. 291.

What's done can't be undone. (Ce qui est faict ne se peult desfaire.)
MONTAIGNE, *Essays*. Bk. iii, ch. 2.
See also under PROVIDENCE.

1
It is, no doubt, an immense advantage to have done nothing, but one should not abuse it.
RIVAROL, *Petit Almanach de nos Grands Hommes: Preface*.

Did nothing in particular, And did it very well.
W. S. GILBERT, *Iolanthe*. Act ii.

2
And all that you are sorry for is what you haven't done.
MARGARET WIDDEMER, *De Senectute*.

VI—Deed and Doer

3
Who doth right deeds
Is twice-born, and who doeth ill deeds vile.
EDWIN ARNOLD, *The Light of Asia*. Bk. vi, l. 78.

4
We are much beholden to Machiavel and others, that write what men do, and not what they ought to do.
BACON, *Advancement of Learning*. Bk. ii.

5
I did some excellent things indifferently,
Some bad things excellently. Both were praised,
The latter loudest.
E. B. BROWNING, *Aurora Leigh*. Bk. iii, l. 205.

6
Do what thy manhood bids thee do, from none but self expect applause.
SIR RICHARD BURTON, *The Kasîdah*. Canto viii, st. 37.

7
Our grand business undoubtedly is, not to *see* what lies dimly at a distance, but to *do* what lies clearly at hand.
CARLYLE, *Essays: Signs of the Times*.

Our works are the mirror wherein the spirit first sees its natural lineaments.
CARLYLE, *Sartor Resartus*. Bk. ii, ch. 7.

8
Our deeds determine us, as much as we determine our deeds.
GEORGE ELIOT, *Adam Bede*. Ch. 29.

Our deeds still travel with us from afar,
And what we have been makes us what we are.
GEORGE ELIOT, *Middlemarch:* Ch. 70, *Heading*.

Our deeds are like children born to us: they live and act apart from our own will. Children may be strangled, but deeds never.
GEORGE ELIOT, *Romola*. Ch. 16.

9
The manly part is to do with might and main what you can do.
EMERSON, *Conduct of Life: Wealth*.

10
For as one star another far exceeds,
So souls in heaven are placèd by their deeds.
ROBERT GREENE, *A Maiden's Dream*.

11
If thou do ill, the joy fades, not the pains:
If well, the pain doth fade, the joy remains.
GEORGE HERBERT, *The Church-Porch*. St. 77.

Do well and right, and let the world sink.
GEORGE HERBERT, *Priest to the Temple*. Ch. 29.

12
The readiness of doing doth express
No other but the doer's willingness.
ROBERT HERRICK, *Readiness*.

13
No deed that sets an example of evil brings joy to the doer. (Exemplo quodcumque malo committitur, ipsi displicet auctori.)
JUVENAL, *Satires*. Sat. xiii, l. 1.

14
He who does something at the head of one regiment will eclipse him who does nothing at the head of a hundred.
ABRAHAM LINCOLN, *Letter to General Hunter*.

15
Something attempted, something done,
Has earned a night's repose.
LONGFELLOW, *The Village Blacksmith*.

16
A good man makes no noise over a good deed, but passes on to another as a vine to bear grapes again in season.
MARCUS AURELIUS, *Meditations*. Bk. v, sec. 6.

Nobody enters his good deeds in his day-book. (Nemo beneficia in calendario scribit.)
SENECA, *De Beneficiis*. Bk. i, sec. 2.

To be nameless in worthy deeds, exceeds an infamous history.
SIR THOMAS BROWNE, *Hydriotaphia*. Ch. v.

17
We are our own fates. Our own deeds
Are our doomsmen. Man's life was made not for men's creeds,
But men's actions.
OWEN MEREDITH, *Lucile*. Pt. ii, canto v, sec. 8.

18
I . . . Us'd no ambition to commend my deeds;
The deeds themselves, though mute, spoke loud the doer.
MILTON, *Samson Agonistes*, l. 247.

19
From lowest place when virtuous things proceed,
The place is dignified by the doer's deed.
SHAKESPEARE, *All's Well that Ends Well*. Act ii, sc. 3, l. 132.

I never saw . . .
Such precious deeds in one that promis'd nought
But beggary and poor looks.
SHAKESPEARE, *Cymbeline*. Act v, sc. 5, l. 7.

20
I am in this earthly world; where to do harm
Is often laudable, to do good sometime
Accounted dangerous folly.
SHAKESPEARE, *Macbeth*. Act iv, sc. 2, l. 75.

21
They look into the beauty of thy mind,

And that, in guess, they measure by thy deeds.
SHAKESPEARE, *Sonnets*. No. lxix.

1
If one good deed in all my life I did,
I do repent it from my very soul.
SHAKESPEARE, *Titus Andronicus*. Act v, sc. 3, l. 189.

2
Go in, and cheer the town; we'll forth and fight;
Do deeds worth praise and tell you them at night.
SHAKESPEARE, *Troilus and Cressida*. Act v, sc. 3, l. 92.

3
Man is of soul and body, formed for deeds
Of high resolve; on fancy's boldest wing.
SHELLEY, *Queen Mab*. Canto iv, l. 160.

4
"The one may and the other may not, do this without harm," the difference lying not in the deed, but in the doer. ("Hoc licet inpune facere huic, illi non licet," Non quo dissimilis res sit sed quo is qui facit.)
TERENCE, *Adelphi*, l. 824. (Act v, sc. 3.)

DEFEAT, see Failure

DEFIANCE

5
An attitude not only of defence, but defiance.
THOMAS GILLESPIE, *The Mountain Storm*.

Defence, not defiance.
Motto adopted by the British Volunteer Movement, 1859.

6
He manned himself with dauntless air,
Returned the Chief his haughty stare,
His back against a rock he bore,
And firmly placed his foot before:—
"Come one, come all! this rock shall fly
From its firm base as soon as I!"
SCOTT, *The Lady of the Lake*. Canto v, st. 10.

Like rock engirdled by the sea,
Like rock immovable is he.
(Ille, velut pelagi rupes immota, resistit.)
VERGIL, *Æneid*. Bk. vii, l. 586. (Conington, tr.)

7
Fear we broadsides? no, let the fiend give fire.
SHAKESPEARE, *II Henry IV*. Act ii, sc. 4, l. 196.

Rather let my head
Stoop to the block than these knees bow to any
Save to the God of heaven and to my king.
SHAKESPEARE, *II Henry VI*. Act iv, sc. 1, l. 124.

I had rather chop this hand off at a blow,
And with the other fling it at thy face,
Than bear so low a sail, to strike to thee.
SHAKESPEARE, *III Henry VI*. Act v, sc. 1, l. 49.

8
Thou mayest hold a serpent by the tongue,
A chafed lion by the mortal paw,
A fasting tiger safer by the tooth,
Than keep in peace that hand which thou dost hold.
SHAKESPEARE, *King John*. Act iii, sc. 1, l. 258.

9
Blow, wind! come, wrack!
At least we'll die with harness on our back.
SHAKESPEARE, *Macbeth*. Act v, sc. 5, l. 51.

Lay on, Macduff,
And damn'd be him that first cries "Hold, enough!"
SHAKESPEARE, *Macbeth*. Act v, sc. 8, l. 33.

10
I do defy him, and I spit at him;
Call him a slanderous coward and a villain:
Which to maintain, I would allow him odds,
And meet him, were I tied to run afoot,
Even to the frozen ridges of the Alps.
SHAKESPEARE, *Richard II*. Act i, sc. 1, l. 60.

Who sets me else? by heaven, I'll throw at all;
I have a thousand spirits in one breast
To answer twenty thousand such as you.
SHAKESPEARE, *Richard II*. Act iv, sc. 1, l. 57.

He breathed defiance to my ears.
SHAKESPEARE, *Romeo and Juliet*. Act i, sc. 1, l. 117.

DEFINITIONS

11
Defining night by darkness, death by dust.
P. J. BAILEY, *Festus: Water and Wood*.

12
I have no great opinion of a definition, the celebrated remedy for the cure of this disorder [uncertainty and confusion].
EDMUND BURKE, *On the Sublime and Beautiful:* Pt. i, *Introduction*.

13
I hate definitions.
BENJAMIN DISRAELI, *Vivian Grey*. Bk. ii, ch. 6.

14
He shall be as a god to me, who can rightly divide and define.
EMERSON, *Representative Men: Plato*. Quoted.

He that can define . . . is the best man.
EMERSON, *Society and Solitude: Clubs*.

15
Every definition is dangerous. (Omnis definitio periculosa est.)
ERASMUS, *Adagia*.

16
Define, define, well-educated infant.
SHAKESPEARE, *Love's Labour's Lost*. Act i, sc. 2, l. 99.

If you wish to converse with me, define your terms.
VOLTAIRE.

DELAY

See also Procrastination

17
By delay he restored the state. (Cunctando restituit rem.)
ENNIUS, speaking of Quintus Fabius Maximus, "Cunctator." Hence the "Fabian policy" of waiting. (CICERO, *De Senectute*. Ch. iv, 10.)

He wore out the boyish impetuosity of Hannibal by his patient endurance. (Hannibalem juveniliter exsultantem patientia sua molliebat.)
CICERO, *De Senectute*. Ch. iv, sec. 10.

1
Delay in vengeance gives a heavier blow.
JOHN FORD, *'Tis Pity She's a Whore*. Act iv, 3.

2
Tear thyself from delay. (Eripe te moræ.)
HORACE, *Odes*. Bk. iii, ode 29, l. 5.

Away with delay; the chance of great fortune is short-lived. (Pelle moras; brevis est magni fortuna favoris.)
SILIUS ITALICUS, *Punica*. Bk. iv, l. 734.

Delay doth oft times prevent the performance of good things, for the wings of man's life are plumed with the feathers of Death!
SIR HUMPHREY GILBERT, *Discourse: How Her Majesty May Annoy the King of Spain*. (1577)

Do not delay,
Do not delay: the golden moments fly!
LONGFELLOW, *Masque of Pandora*. Pt. vii.

See also LIFE AND LIVING.

3
Delay is preferable to error.
THOMAS JEFFERSON, *Writings*. Vol. viii, p. 338.

4
When a man's life is at stake, no delay is too long. (Nulla umquam de morte hominis cunctatio longa est.)
JUVENAL, *Satires*. Sat. vi, l. 221.

Why, one that rode to 's execution, man,
Could never go so slow.
SHAKESPEARE, *Cymbeline*. Act iii, sc. 2, l. 72.

5
There is danger in delay. (Periculum in mora.)
LIVY, *History*. Bk. xxxviii, ch. 25, sec. 13.

Delay hath often injury wrought.
UNKNOWN, *Havelok*, l. 1352. (c. 1300)

Peril is with dreeching in y-drawe.
CHAUCER, *Troilus and Criseyde*. Bk. iii, l. 853. (c. 1384)

Delays breed dangers.
JOHN LYLY, *Euphues*, p. 65. (1579)

All delays are dangerous.
DRYDEN, *Tyrannic Love*. Act i, sc. 1.

Delays have dangerous ends.
SHAKESPEARE, *I Henry VI*. Act iii, sc. 2, l. 33.

6
Away with delay; it is always fatal to those who are prepared. (Tolle moras; semper nocuit differre paratis.)
LUCAN, *De Bello Civili*. Bk. i, l. 281.

To men prepared delay is always hurtful. (Il fornito Sempre con danno l' attender sofferse.)
DANTE, *Inferno*. Canto xxviii, l. 98.

7
And sweet reluctant amorous delay.
MILTON, *Paradise Lost*. Bk. iv, l. 311. (1667)

With sweet, reluctant, amorous delay.
HOMER, *Odyssey*. Bk. i, l. 22. The first book of Pope's *Odyssey* was translated by Elijah Fenton, and revised by Pope in 1725. This line was undoubtedly borrowed from Milton, but whether by Fenton or Pope is uncertain.

8
Delay is a great procuress. (Maxima lena mora est.)
OVID, *Ars Amatoria*. Bk. iii, l. 752.

9
Every delay that postpones our joys is long. (Longa mora est nobis omnis, quæ gaudia differt.)
OVID, *Heroides*. Epis. xix, l. 3.

Every delay is long to one who is in haste. (Omnis nimium longa properanti mora est.)
SENECA, *Agamemnon*, l. 426.

10
Delay gives strength, delay matures the tender grapes and ripens grass into lusty crops. (Mora dat vires, teneras mora percoquit uvas, Et validas segetes quæ fuit herba, facit.)
OVID, *Remediorum Amoris*, l. 83.

11
'Tis wisdom's use
Still to delay what we dare not refuse.
SCOTT, *Harold the Dauntless*. Canto iv, st. 11.

12
Give yourself time and room; what reason could not avoid, delay has often cured. (Da tempus ac spatium tibi: Quod ratio non quit sæpe sanavit mora.)
SENECA, *Agamemnon*, l. 129.

13
Dull not device by coldness and delay.
SHAKESPEARE, *Othello*. Act ii, sc. 3, l. 394.

Delay leads impotent and snail-paced beggary.
SHAKESPEARE, *Richard III*. Act iv, sc. 3, l. 53.

15
Long ailments wear out pain, and long hopes joy.
STANISLAUS, KING OF POLAND, *Maxims*.

16
And Mecca saddens at the long delay.
THOMSON, *The Seasons: Summer*, l. 979.

17
Naught of delay is there, nor of repose. (Nec mora, nec requies.)
VERGIL, *Georgics*. Bk. iii, l. 110.

DELIGHT

See also Bliss, Joy

18
A sip is the most that mortals are permitted from any goblet of delight.
A. B. ALCOTT, *Table Talk: Habits*.

19
The soul of sweet delight can never be defil'd.
WILLIAM BLAKE, *Proverbs of Hell*.

20
In ev'ry sorrowing soul I pour'd delight.
HOMER, *Odyssey*. Bk. xvii, l. 505. (Pope, tr.)

Yes, life then seemed one pure delight.
GEORGE LINLEY, *Tho' Lost to Sight*.

21
Not by appointment do we meet delight
Or joy; they heed not our expectancy;

But round some corner of the streets of life
They of a sudden greet us with a smile.

GERALD MASSEY, *The Bridegroom of Beauty.*

1
Delights, which to achieve, danger is nothing,
And loyalty but a word.

MASSINGER, *Great Duke of Florence.* Act ii, 3.

2
'Tis never too late for delight, my dear.

THOMAS MOORE, *The Young May Moon.*

3
There is also some little delight in having pleased one's self. (Est etiam placuisse sibi quotacumque voluptas.)

OVID, *De Medicamina Faciei,* l. 31.

4
For where is he that, knowing the height
And depth of ascertain'd delight,
Inhumanly henceforward lies
Content with mediocrities!

COVENTRY PATMORE, *The Victories of Love:* Bk. ii, *The Wedding Sermon.* Pt. xi.

Life is not life at all without delight.

COVENTRY PATMORE, *Victory in Defeat.*

5
Why, all delights are vain; but that most vain,
Which with pain purchas'd, doth inherit pain.

SHAKESPEARE, *Love's Labour's Lost.* Act i, sc. 1, l. 72.

These violent delights have violent ends,
And in their triumph die; like fire and powder,
Which, as they kiss, consume.

SHAKESPEARE, *Romeo and Juliet.* Act ii, sc. 6, l. 9.

6
Delight, the rootless flower,
And love, the bloomless bower;
Delight that lives an hour,
And love that lives a day.

SWINBURNE, *Before Dawn.* St. 1.

The delight that consumes the desire,
The desire that outruns the delight.

SWINBURNE, *Dolores.* St. 14.

DEMOCRACY

See also Government, Voting

I—Democracy: Definitions

7
Democracy arose from men's thinking that if they are equal in any respect, they are equal absolutely. (Δῆμος μὲν γὰρ ἐγένετο ἐκ τοῦ ἴσους ὁτιοῦν ὄντας οἴεσθαι ἁπλῶς ἴσους εἶναι.)

ARISTOTLE, *Politics.* Bk. v, ch. 1, sec. 2.

8
Democracy means government by the uneducated, while aristocracy means government by the badly educated.

G. K. CHESTERTON. (*N. Y. Times,* 1 Feb., 1931.)

We have sometimes been tempted to define democracy as an institution in which the whole is equal to the scum of all the parts.

KEITH PRESTON, *Pot Shots from Pegasus,* p. 138.

9
Democracy is the healthful life-blood which circulates through the veins and arteries, which supports the system, but which ought never to appear externally, and as the mere blood itself.

S. T. COLERIDGE, *Table Talk,* 19 Sept., 1830.

10
A monarchy is like a man-of-war,—bad shots between wind and water hurt it exceedingly; there is danger of capsizing. But democracy is a raft. You cannot easily overturn it. It is a wet place, but it is a pretty safe one.

JOSEPH COOK, *Boston Monday Lectures: Labor.*

Fisher Ames expressed the popular security more wisely, when he compared a monarchy and a republic, saying that a monarchy is a merchantman, which sails well, but will sometimes strike on a rock and go to the bottom; whilst a republic is a raft, which would never sink, but then your feet are always in the water.

EMERSON, *Essays, Second Series: Politics.*

11
The governments of the past could fairly be characterized as devices for maintaining in perpetuity the place and position of certain privileged classes. . . . The Government of the United States is a device for maintaining in perpetuity the rights of the people, with the ultimate extinction of all privileged classes.

CALVIN COOLIDGE, *Speech,* Phila., 25 Sept., 1924.

12
The democrat is a young conservative; the conservative is an old democrat. The aristocrat is the democrat ripe and gone to seed.

EMERSON, *Representative Men: Napoleon.*

13
Democracy is based upon the conviction that there are extraordinary possibilities in ordinary people.

HARRY EMERSON FOSDICK, *Democracy.*

14
A republic may be called the climate of civilization.

VICTOR HUGO, *Speech,* French Assembly, 1851.

15
Men, by their constitutions, are naturally divided into two parties: 1. Those who fear and distrust the people, and wish to draw all powers from them into the hands of the higher classes. 2. Those who identify themselves with the people, have confidence in them, cherish and consider them as the most honest and safe, although not the most wise, depository of the public interests. . . . In every country these two parties exist. . . . The appellation of Aristocrats and Democrats is the true one, expressing the essence of all.

THOMAS JEFFERSON, *Writings.* Vol. xvi, p. 73.

16
Democ'acy gives every man
The right to be his own oppressor.

J. R. LOWELL, *Biglow Papers.* Ser. ii, No. 7.

II—Democracy: Apothegms

1
The manners of women are the surest criterion by which to determine whether a republican government is practicable in a nation or not.

JOHN ADAMS, *Diary*, 2 June, 1778. (C. F. ADAMS, *Life of Adams*. Vol. iii, p. 171.)

2
You can never have a revolution in order to establish a democracy. You must have a democracy in order to have a revolution.

G. K. CHESTERTON, *Tremendous Trifles: Wind and the Trees.*

3
The Ship of Democracy, which has weathered all storms, may sink through the mutiny of those on board.

GROVER CLEVELAND, *Letter to Wilson S. Bissell*, 15 Feb., 1894.

4
Democracy is on trial in the world, on a more colossal scale than ever before.

C. F. DOLE, *The Spirit of Democracy.*

5
Would shake hands with a king upon his
  throne,
And think it kindness to his majesty.

FITZ-GREENE HALLECK, *Connecticut.*

6
I am a Democrat still—very still.

DAVID B. HILL, after the nomination of William Jennings Bryan in 1896. (NEVINS, *Grover Cleveland*, p. 705.)

7
An acrimonious and surly republican.

SAMUEL JOHNSON, *Lives of the Poets: Milton.*

8
Go thou, and first establish democracy in thy household. (Σὺ γάρ πρῶτος ἐν τῇ οἰκίᾳ σου ποίησον δημοκρατίαν.)

LYCURGUS, to a man who demanded the establishment of democracy in Sparta. (PLUTARCH, *Lives: Lycurgus.* Ch. 19.)

9
Thus our democracy was from an early period the most aristocratic, and our aristocracy the most democratic.

MACAULAY, *History of England.* Vol. i, p. 20.

10
It is easier for a republican form of government to be applauded than realized. (Respublicæ forma laudari facilius quam evenire.)

TACITUS, *Annals.* Bk. iv, sec. 33.

11
The only remedy for democrats is soldiers. (Gegen Demokraten Helfen nur Soldaten.)

WILHELM VON MERCHEL, *Die Fünfte Zunft.*

12
The world must be made safe for democracy.

WOODROW WILSON, *War Address to Congress*, 2 April, 1917.

The world was never more unsafe for democracy than it is today.

STANLEY BALDWIN, *Speech*, House of Commons, 12 March, 1935.

III—Democracy: Of the People, By the People

13
The government is a government of the people and for the people.

THOMAS COOPER, *Some Information Respecting America.* (London, 1795.)

14
The declaration that our People are hostile to a government made by themselves, for themselves, and conducted by themselves, is an insult.

JOHN ADAMS, *Address*, to the citizens of Westmoreland Co., Virginia, 1798.

15
The government of the Union, then, is emphatically and truly a government of the people. In form and in substance it emanates from them. Its powers are granted by them, and are to be exercised directly on them and for their benefit.

JOHN MARSHALL, *Case of McCulloch vs. Maryland*, 1819. (WHEATON, iv, 316.)

16
The people's government made for the people, made by the people, and answerable to the people.

DANIEL WEBSTER, *Second Speech on Foote's Resolution*, 26 Jan., 1830.

A body . . . representing the people, springing from the people, and sympathising with the people.

LORD JOHN RUSSELL, *Speech*, introducing the Reform Bill, 1831; referring to the House of Commons.

17
There is what I call the American idea. . . . This idea demands . . . a democracy,—that is, a government of all the people, by all the people, for all the people.

THEODORE PARKER, *Speech*, at Anti-Slavery Convention, Boston, 29 May, 1850.

For there is the democratic idea: that all men are endowed by their creator with certain natural rights; . . . that they are equal as men; . . . and therefore government is to be of all the people, by all the people, and for all the people.

THEODORE PARKER, *Address*, to the Anti-Slavery Society, Boston, 13 May, 1854.

Democracy is direct self-government, over all the people, for all the people, by all the people.

THEODORE PARKER, *Sermon*, delivered at Music Hall, Boston, 4 July, 1858. It was published as a pamphlet, *On the Effect of Slavery on the American People*, the above sentence occurring on page 5. Herndon, in his *Life of Lincoln*, asserts that he gave a copy of this pamphlet to Lincoln, who marked the above passage. There has been a tradition that "of the people, by the people, for the people" occurred in the introduction to the translation of the Bible made by John Wycliffe about 1384, but a careful examination has failed to disclose it. The nearest approach to it is the following quotation from Saint Jerome (vol. i, p. 56): "Hooly writ is the scripture of puplis, for it is maad, that alle puples schulden knowe it." The examination of the difficult text was made by the Legislative Reference Service of the Library of Congress, at the request of the compiler, using the Oxford edition of 1850.

1
The world will little note nor long remember what we say here, but it can never forget what they did here. . . . It is rather for us to be here dedicated to the great task remaining before us—that from these honored dead we take increased devotion to that cause for which they gave the last full measure of devotion; that we here highly resolve that these dead shall not have died in vain; that this nation, under God, shall have a new birth of freedom; and that government of the people, by the people, for the people, shall not perish from the earth.

ABRAHAM LINCOLN, *Address*, Gettysburg National Cemetery, 19 Nov., 1863.

2
President Lincoln defined democracy to be "the government of the people, by the people, for the people." This is a sufficiently compact statement of it as a political arrangement. Theodore Parker said that "Democracy meant not 'I'm as good as you are,' but 'You're as good as I am.'" And this is the ethical conception of it, necessary as a complement of the other.

JAMES RUSSELL LOWELL, *Essays: Democracy*

3
As the happiness of the people is the sole end of government, so the consent of the people is the only foundation of it, in reason, morality, and the natural fitness of things.

JOHN ADAMS, *Proclamation*, adopted by Council of Massachusetts Bay, 1774.

4
You cannot possibly have a broader basis for any government than that which includes all the people, with all their rights in their hands, and with an equal power to maintain their rights.

WILLIAM LLOYD GARRISON, *Life*. Vol. iv, p. 224.

5
I know no safe depository of the ultimate powers of society but the people themselves; and if we think them not enlightened enough to exercise their control with a wholesome discretion, the remedy is not to take it from them, but to inform their discretion by education.

THOMAS JEFFERSON, *Letter to W. C. Jarvis*, 28 Sept., 1820.

Governments are republican only in proportion as they embody the will of the people, and execute it.

THOMAS JEFFERSON, *Writings*. Vol. xv, p. 33.

No government can continue good but under the control of the people.

THOMAS JEFFERSON, *Writings*. Vol. xv, p. 234.

The qualifications of self-government in society are not innate. They are the result of habit and long training, and for these they will require time and probably much suffering.

THOMAS JEFFERSON, *Writings*. Vol. xvi, p. 22.

It is an axiom in my mind that our liberty can never be safe but in the hands of the people themselves.

THOMAS JEFFERSON, *Writings*. Vol. xix, p. 24.

6
This end was the representative sovereignty of all the citizens concentrated in an election as extensive as the people themselves, and acting by the people, and for the people in an elective council, which should be all the government.

LAMARTINE, *History of the Girondists*. Vol. iii, p. 104. Referring to Robespierre's ideas.

7
The problem of democracy is not the problem of getting rid of kings. It is the problem of clothing the whole people with the elements of kingship. To make kings and queens out of a hundred million people: that is the Problem of American democracy.

F. C. MOREHOUSE, *The Problem of Democracy*.

8
The estate goes before the steward; the foundation before the house, people before their representatives, and the creation before the creator. The steward lives by preserving the estate; the house stands by reason of its foundation; the representative depends upon the people, as the creature subsists by the power of its creator.

WILLIAM PENN, *England's Present Interest Considered*, p. 392. (1674)

9
In a government like ours, founded by the people, managed by the people.

JOSEPH STORY, *On the Constitution*. Sec. 304.

10
Democracy means simply the bludgeoning of the people by the people for the people.

OSCAR WILDE, *Soul of Man Under Socialism*.

IV—Democracy: Its Virtues

11
Will anybody deny now that the Government at Washington, as regards its own people, is the strongest government in the world at this hour? And for this simple reason, that it is based on the will, and the good will, of an instructed people.

JOHN BRIGHT, *Speech*, Rochdale, 24 Nov., 1863.

12
A representative democracy, where the right of election is well secured and regulated, and the exercise of the legislative, executive, and judiciary authorities is vested in select persons, chosen really and not nominally by the people, will, in my opinion, be most likely to be happy, regular, and durable.

ALEXANDER HAMILTON, *Works*. Vol. ix, p. 72.

13
The republican is the only form of govern-

ment which is not eternally at open or secret war with the rights of mankind.

THOMAS JEFFERSON, *Reply to Address*, 1790.

1
The love of equality, in a democracy, limits ambition to the sole desire, to the sole happiness, of doing greater services to our country than the rest of our fellow-citizens.

MONTESQUIEU, *Spirit of the Laws*. Bk. v, ch. 3.

2
Democracy is better than tyranny. (Δημοκρατία κρεῖττον τυραννίδος.)

PERIANDER. (DIOGENES LAERTIUS, *Periander*. 4.)

3
Freedom in a democracy is the glory of the State, and, therefore, in a democracy only will the freeman of nature deign to dwell.

PLATO, *The Republic*. Bk. ii, sec. 391.

4
The Republican form of government is the highest form of government: but because of this it requires the highest type of human nature—a type nowhere at present existing.

HERBERT SPENCER, *The Americans*.

5
He who would save liberty must put his trust in democracy.

NORMAN THOMAS. (*Saturday Review of Literature*, 7 June, 1930.)

6
I speak the pass-word primeval, I give the sign of democracy,
By God! I will accept nothing which all cannot have their counterpart of on the same terms.

WALT WHITMAN, *Song of Myself*. Sec. 24.

Thunder on! Stride on! Democracy. Strike with vengeful stroke!

WALT WHITMAN, *Rise O Days*. Sec. 3.

7
The beauty of a Democracy is that you never can tell when a youngster is born what he is going to do with you, and that, no matter how humbly he is born . . . he has got a chance to master the minds and lead the imaginations of the whole country.

WOODROW WILSON, *Address*, Columbus, O., 10 Dec., 1915.

I believe in Democracy because it releases the energies of every human being.

WOODROW WILSON, *Address*, New York, 4 Sept., 1912.

V—Democracy: Its Faults

8
A perfect democracy is the most shameless thing in the world.

EDMUND BURKE, *Reflections on the Revolution in France*.

9
That fatal drollery called a representative government.

BENJAMIN DISRAELI, *Tancred*. Bk. ii, ch. 13.

10
Drawn to the dregs of a democracy.

DRYDEN, *Absalom and Achitophel*. Pt. i, l. 227.

11
Democracy becomes a government of bullies tempered by editors.

EMERSON, *Journals*. Vol. vii, p. 193.

12
Humanity is singing everywhere
All men are equal. Dupes of democracy!

DONALD EVANS, *Bonfire of Kings*.

13
The great danger, as it appears to me, of representative government, is lest it should slide down from representative government to delegate government.

HELPS, *Friends in Council*. Bk. i, ch. 6.

14
It is not good that few should be governed by many; let there be one ruler only. (Οὐκ ἀγαθὸν πολυκοιρανίη· εἷς κοίρανος ἔστω.)

HOMER, *Iliad*. Bk. ii, l. 204.

Who can direct, when all pretend to know?

GOLDSMITH, *The Traveller*, l. 64.

15
Democracy—the ballot-box—has few worshippers any longer except in America.

DEAN W. R. INGE. (MARCHANT, *Wit and Wisdom of Dean Inge*. No. 216.)

16
Democracy which began by liberating man politically has developed a dangerous tendency to enslave him through the tyranny of majorities and the deadly power of their opinion.

LUDWIG LEWISOHN, *The Modern Drama*, p. 17.

17
Envy, the vice of republics.

LONGFELLOW, *Evangeline*. Pt. i, l. 35.

Envy is the basis of democracy.

BERTRAND RUSSELL, *The Conquest of Happiness*, p. 83.

18
The most popular man under a democracy is not the most democratic man, but the most despotic man. The common folk delight in the exactions of such a man. They like him to boss them. Their natural gait is the goose-step.

H. L. MENCKEN, *Prejudices*. Ser. ii, p. 221.

19
The tyranny of a prince in an oligarchy is not so dangerous to the public welfare as the apathy of a citizen in a democracy.

MONTESQUIEU, *Spirit of the Laws*.

20
The government will take the fairest of names, but the worst of realities—mob rule.

POLYBIUS, *History*. Bk. vi, sec. 57.

21
I have long been convinced that institutions purely democratic must, sooner or later, destroy liberty or civilization, or both.

MACAULAY, *Letter to H. S. Randall*, 23 May, 1857. (TREVELYAN, *Life and Letters of Lord Macaulay*, Appendix to vol. ii, p. 452. Cited in Lippman's *Method of Freedom*, p. 77.)

1
Democracy, which is more cruel than wars or tyrants. (In libertate bellis ac tyrannis sæviore.)

SENECA, *Epistulæ ad Lucilium*. Epis. civ, 27.

2
Democracies are prone to war, and war consumes them.

W. H. SEWARD, *Eulogy on John Quincy Adams*.

3
Democracy substitutes election by the incompetent many for appointment by the corrupt few.

BERNARD SHAW, *Maxims for Revolutionists*.

DENIAL, see Refusal

DESERT, THE

4
Slowly they wind athwart the wild, and while young Day his anthem swells,
Sad falls upon my yearning ear the tinkling of the Camel-bells.

SIR RICHARD BURTON, *The Kasîdah*. Pt. i, st. 6.

In these drear wastes of sea-born land, these wilds where none may dwell but He,
What visionary Pasts revive, what process of the Years we see.

SIR RICHARD BURTON, *The Kasîdah*. Pt. ii, st. 1.

5
O that the desert were my dwelling-place!

BYRON, *Childe Harold*. Canto i, l. 359.

6
That undefined and mingled hum,
Voice of the desert never dumb!

JAMES HOGG, *To Lady Anne Scott*.

7
The desert shall rejoice, and blossom as the rose.

Old Testament: Isaiah, xxxv, 1.

O see where wide the golden sunlight flows—
The barren desert blossoms like the rose!

R. W. GILDER, *The Smile of Her I Love*.

8
The sea-like, pathless, limitless waste of the desert.

LONGFELLOW, *Evangeline*. Pt. ii, sec. 4, l. 140.

9
A white tomb in the desert,
An Arab at his prayers,
Beside the Nile's dark water,
Where the lone camel fares;
An ibis on the sunset,
A slow shadouf at rest,
And in the caravansary
Low music for the guest.

CALE YOUNG RICE, *From a Felucca*.

10
O wilderness of drifting sands, O lonely caravan!
The desert heart is set apart, unknown to any man.

DAVID ROSS AND ARCHIE COATES, *Kismet*.

11
Some dark deep desert, seated from the way,
That knows not parching heat nor freezing cold,

SHAKESPEARE, *The Rape of Lucrece*, l. 1144.

12
The desert-circle spreads,
Like the round ocean, girdled with the sky.

SOUTHEY, *Thalaba*. Bk. i, l. 8.

DESERVING

See also Merit; Worth

13
No power or virtue of man could ever have deserved that what has been fated should not have taken place. (Nulla vis humana vel virtus meruisse unquam potuit, ut, quod præscripsit fatalis ordo, non fiat.)

AMMIANUS MARCELLINUS, *History*. Sec. 23.

14
Desert, how known soe'er, is long delayed;
And then, too, fools and knaves are better paid.

DRYDEN, *Epistles: To Mr. Lee*, l. 21.

15
God ne'er afflicts us more than our desert,
Though He may seem to overact His part:
Sometimes He strikes us more than flesh can bear,
But yet still less than Grace can suffer here.

ROBERT HERRICK, *Affliction*.

It is better to deserve without receiving, than to receive without deserving.

R. G. INGERSOLL, *The Children of the Stage*.

There is nothing an honest man should fear more timorously than getting and spending more than he deserves.

R. L. STEVENSON, *Morality of the Profession of Letters*.

16
Desert may make a sergeant to a colonel,
And it may hinder him from rising higher.

MASSINGER, *The Maid of Honour*. Act iii, sc. 1.

17
You would have it so, George Dandin, you would have it so; this suits you very nicely, and you are served right; you have precisely what you deserve. (Vous l'avez voulu, George Dandin, vous l'avez voulu; cela vous sied fort bien, et vous voilà ajusté comme il faut; vous avez justement ce que vous méritez.)

MOLIÈRE, *George Dandin*. Act i, sc. 7.

18
What is deservedly suffered must be borne with calmness. (Leniter ex merito quidquid patiare ferendum est.)

OVID, *Heroides*. Epis. v, l. 7.

Use every man after his desert, and who should 'scape whipping?

SHAKESPEARE, *Hamlet*. Act ii, sc. 2, l. 554.

19
O, your desert speaks loud; and I should wrong it
To lock it in the wards of covert bosom,
When it deserves, with characters of brass,

A forted residence 'gainst the tooth of time,
And razure of oblivion.

SHAKESPEARE, *Measure for Measure*. Act v, sc. 1, l. 9.

Thy desert may merit praise.

SHAKESPEARE [?], *Passionate Pilgrim*, l. 325.

1
All may be well; but, if God sort it so,
'Tis more than we deserve, or I expect.

SHAKESPEARE, *Richard III*. Act ii, sc. 3, l. 36.

2
They have ensured remembrance by their deserts. (Quique sui memores aliquos fecere merendo.)

VERGIL, *Æneid*. Bk. vi, l. 664.

3
Against me—if I deserve it. (Si mereor in me.)

Motto on coin struck at coronation of James I, with representation of hand holding a sword.

This inscription seemed also to presage the sentence of divine justice upon his son.

MILTON, *Tenure of Kings*. Referring to Charles I.

DESIRE

See also Wants, Wishes

I—Desire: Mental

4
We should aim rather at levelling down our desires than levelling up our means.

ARISTOTLE, *Politics*. Bk. ii, ch. 7, sec. 8.

5
Sooner murder an infant in its cradle than nurse unacted desires.

WILLIAM BLAKE, *Proverbs of Hell*.

He who desires but acts not, breeds pestilence.

WILLIAM BLAKE, *Proverbs of Hell*.

6
Heaven favors good desires. (Siempre favorece el cielo los buenos deseos.)

CERVANTES, *Don Quixote*. Pt. ii, ch. 43.

7
Nothing troubles you for which you do not yearn. (Nihil autem est molestum quod non desideres.)

CICERO, *De Senectute*. Ch. 14, sec. 47.

8
Passing into higher forms of desire, that which slumbered in the plant, and fitfully stirred in the beast, awakes in the man.

HENRY GEORGE, *Progress and Poverty*. Bk. ii, ch. 3.

9
Humble hearts have humble desires.

GEORGE HERBERT, *Jacula Prudentum*.

10
Naked I seek the camp of those who desire nothing. (Nil cupientium Nudus castra peto.)

HORACE, *Odes*. Bk. iii, ode xvi, l. 22 .

11
The desire of love, Joy;
The desire of life, Peace:
The desire of the soul, Heaven:
The desire of God—a flame-white secret forever.

WILLIAM SHARP, *Desire*.

12
The things that I can't have I want,
And what I have seems second-rate,
The things I want to do I can't,
And what I have to do I hate.

DON MARQUIS, *Frustration*.

13
We live in our desires rather than in our achievements.

GEORGE MOORE, *Ave*, p. 239.

14
There is no desire for what is unknown. (Ignoti nulla cupido.)

OVID, *Ars Amatoria*. Bk. iii, l. 397.

The jewel that we find, we stoop and take 't,
Because we see it; but what we do not see
We tread upon, and never think of it.

SHAKESPEARE, *Measure for Measure*. Act ii, sc. 1, l. 24.

See also HEYWOOD *under* EYES: APOTHEGMS.

15
Each man has his own desires. (Velle suum cuique est.)

PERSIUS, *Satires*. Sat. v, l. 53.

16
Let us pay with our bodies for our soul's desire.

THEODORE ROOSEVELT, *Foes of Our Own Household*. Ch. 2.

17
We desire nothing so much as what we ought not to have.

PUBLILIUS SYRUS, *Sententiæ*. No. 559.

See also under PROHIBITION.

18
Is it not strange that desire should so many years outlive performance?

SHAKESPEARE, *II Henry IV*. Act ii, sc. 4, l. 286.

19
At Christmas I no more desire a rose
Than wish a snow in May's new-fangled mirth.

SHAKESPEARE, *Love's Labour's Lost*. Act i, sc. 1, l. 105.

20
There are two tragedies in life. One is not to get your heart's desire. The other is to get it.

BERNARD SHAW, *Man and Superman*. Act iv.

21
The desire of the moth for the star,
Of the night for the morrow.

PERCY BYSSHE SHELLEY, *To ——*.

22
Here I possess—what more should I require?
Books, children, leisure,—all my heart's desire.

SOUTHEY, *The Poet's Pilgrimage to Waterloo: Proem*. St. 4.

23
His own desire leads every man. (Trahit sua quemque voluptas.)

VERGIL, *Eclogues*. No. ii, l. 65.

1
The fewer desires, the more peace.
THOMAS WILSON, *Maxims of Piety*, 27.

II—Desire: Physical

See also Love and Lust

2
You must learn to desire what you would have. Much wanting makes many a maid a wanton.
MAXWELL ANDERSON, *Elizabeth the Queen*. Act i.

3
[Desire] is a perpetual rack, or horsemill, according to Austin, still going round as in a ring.
ROBERT BURTON, *Anatomy of Melancholy*. Pt. i, sec. ii, mem. 3, subs. 11.

Desire hath no rest.
ROBERT BURTON, *Anatomy of Melancholy*. Bk. i, sec. 2, mem. 3, subs. 11. Quoted.

Though her years were waning,
Her climacteric teased her like her teens.
BYRON, *Don Juan*. Canto x, st. 47.

4
Where Desire doth bear the sway,
The heart must rule, the head obey.
FRANCIS DAVISON, *Desire's Government*.

5
Could swell the soul to rage, or kindle soft desire.
DRYDEN, *Alexander's Feast*, l. 160.

The bloom of young desire, and purple light of love.
THOMAS GRAY, *The Progress of Poesy*, l. 41.

6
Desire suffereth no delay.
GABRIEL HARVEY, *Marginalia*, 201. (c. 1582)

Desires are nourished by delays.
JOHN RAY, *English Proverbs*, 7. (1670)

7
Desire attained is not desire,
But as the cinders of the fire.
SIR WALTER RALEIGH, *A Poesy to Prove Affection is Not Love*.

8
The trustless wings of false desire.
SHAKESPEARE, *The Rape of Lucrece*, l. 2.

The sea hath bounds, but deep desire hath none.
SHAKESPEARE, *Venus and Adonis*, l. 389.

9
Till ev'ry woman wished her place,
And ev'ry man wished his.
SIR JOHN SUCKLING, *Ballad Upon a Wedding*.

10
Desire, The odor of the human flowers.
R. H. STODDARD, *The Squire of Low Degree*. Pt. i, l. 13.

11
There in the windy flood of morning
Longing lifted its weight from me,
Lost as a sob in the midst of cheering,
Swept as a sea-bird out to sea.
SARA TEASDALE, *Morning*.

DESPAIR

See also Misery, Sorrow

12
I will indulge my sorrows, and give way
To all the pangs and fury of despair.
JOSEPH ADDISON, *Cato*. Act iv, sc. 3.

There is no despair so absolute as that which comes with the first moments of our first great sorrow, when we have not yet known what it is to have suffered and be healed, to have despaired and have recovered hope.
GEORGE ELIOT, *Adam Bede*. Ch. 31.

13
Let me not know that all is lost,
Though lost it be—leave me not tied
To this despair, this corpse-like bride.
ROBERT BROWNING, *Easter Day*. Pt. xxxi.

14
The name of the Slough was Despond.
JOHN BUNYAN, *The Pilgrim's Progress*. Pt. i.

Now there was a castle, called Doubting Castle, the owner whereof was Giant Despair.
JOHN BUNYAN, *The Pilgrim's Progress*. Pt. i.

That domestic Irish Giant, named of Despair.
CARLYLE, *Latter-Day Pamphlets*. No. 3.

15
The nympholepsy of some fond despair.
BYRON, *Childe Harold*. Canto iv, st. 115.

16
They say Despair has power to kill
With her bleak frown; but I say No;
If life did hang upon her will,
Then Hope had perish'd long ago;
Yet still the twain keep up their "barful strife,"
For Hope Love's leman is, Despair his wife.
HARTLEY COLERIDGE, *Epigram*.

17
With woful measures wan Despair
Low sullen sounds his grief beguil'd,
A solemn, strange, and mingled air,
'T was sad by fits, by starts 't was wild.
WILLIAM COLLINS, *The Passions*, l. 25.

18
Invention flags, his brain grows muddy,
And black despair succeeds brown study.
WILLIAM CONGREVE, *An Impossible Thing*.

19
What do the damned endure, but to despair?
CONGREVE, *The Mourning Bride*. Act iii, sc. 1.

20
Me, howling blasts drive devious, tempest-toss'd,
Sails ripp'd, seams op'ning wide, and compass lost.
COWPER, *On the Receipt of My Mother's Picture*, l. 102.

I am driven
Into a desperate strait; and cannot steer
A middle course.
MASSINGER, *Great Duke of Florence*. Act iii, 1.

21
Despair ruins some, Presumption many.
BENJAMIN FRANKLIN, *Poor Richard*. 1747.

1
Despair in vain sits brooding over the putrid eggs of hope.
JOHN H. FRERE, *The Rovers*. Act i, sc. 2.

As an egg, when broken, never
Can be mended, but must ever
Be the same crushed egg for ever—
So shall this dark heart of mine!
T. H. CHIVERS, *To Allegra Florence in Heaven.*

2
There is no vulture like despair.
GEORGE GRANVILLE, *Peleus and Thetis.*

3
Anywhere, anywhere Out of the world.
THOMAS HOOD, *The Bridge of Sighs.*

4
Never despair. (Nil desperandum.)
HORACE, *Odes*. Bk. i, ode 7, l. 27.

It is not a matter for despair. (Non desperandum.)
BACON, *Impetus Philosophii.*

Give not thy heart to despair.
MATTHEW ARNOLD, *Merope*, l. 526.

5
Despair . . . is a wilful business, common to corrupt blood, and to weak woeful minds; native to the sentimentalist of the better order.
GEORGE MEREDITH, *Sandra Belloni*. Ch. 38.

6
Vaunting aloud, but racked with deep despair.
MILTON, *Paradise Lost*. Bk. i, l. 126.

7
Out of the depths have I cried unto thee, O Lord.
Old Testament: Psalms, cxxx, 1. (De profundis. —*Vulgate*.)

A cry goes up of great despair,—
Miserere, Domine!
ADELAIDE ANN PROCTER, *The Storm.*

8
An evil counsellor is despair.
SCOTT, *Harold the Dauntless*. Canto i, st. 21.

9
My desolation does begin to make
A better life.
SHAKESPEARE, *Antony and Cleopatra*. Act v, sc. 2, l. 1.

10
Grim and comfortless despair.
SHAKESPEARE, *The Comedy of Errors*. Act v, sc. 1, l. 80.

Grim-visag'd comfortless Despair.
THOMAS GRAY, *Ode on a Distant Prospect of Eton College*, l. 69.

11
Our hap is loss, our hope but sad despair.
SHAKESPEARE, *III Henry VI*. Act ii, sc. 3, l. 9.

Our final hope Is flat despair.
MILTON, *Paradise Lost*. Bk. ii, l. 142.

12
The lowest and most dejected thing of fortune.
SHAKESPEARE, *King Lear*. Act iv, sc. 1, l. 3.

Who calls that wretched thing that was Alphonso?
CONGREVE, *The Mourning Bride*. Act ii, sc. 2.

13
Had I but died an hour before this chance,
I had liv'd a blessed time; for, from this instant,
There's nothing serious in mortality:
All is but toys; renown and grace is dead;
The wine of life is drawn, and the mere lees
Is left this vault to brag of.
SHAKESPEARE, *Macbeth*. Act ii, sc. 3, l. 96.

The golden wine is drunk, the dregs remain,
Bitter as wormwood and as salt as pain;
And health and hope have gone the way of love
Into the drear oblivion of lost things.
ERNEST DOWSON, *Dregs.*

14
I am one, my liege,
Whom the vile blows and buffets of the world
Have so incens'd that I am reckless what
I do to spite the world.
SHAKESPEARE, *Macbeth*. Act iii, sc. 1, l. 108.

So weary with disasters, tugg'd with fortune,
That I would set my life on any chance,
To mend it, or be rid on 't.
SHAKESPEARE, *Macbeth*. Act iii, sc. 1, l. 112.

Rash-embraced despair.
SHAKESPEARE, *The Merchant of Venice*. Act iii, sc. 2, l. 110.

15
Nothing canst thou to damnation add
Greater than that.
SHAKESPEARE, *Othello*. Act iii, sc. 3, l. 372.

This is worst of all worst worsts that hell could have devised!
BEN JONSON, *Epicœne*. Act v, sc. 1.

16
Discomfort guides my tongue
And bids me speak of nothing but despair.
SHAKESPEARE, *Richard II*. Act iii, sc. 2, l. 65.

O, break, my heart! poor bankrupt, break at once!
To prison, eyes, ne'er look on liberty!
Vile earth, to earth resign; end motion here.
SHAKESPEARE, *Romeo and Juliet*. Act iii, sc. 2, l. 57.

Betake thee To nothing but despair.
SHAKESPEARE, *Winter's Tale*. Act iii, sc. 2, l. 210.

17
So is Hope
Changed for Despair: one laid upon the shelf,
We take the other.
SHELLEY, *Epigrams: From the Greek.*

18
No change, no pause, no hope! Yet I endure.
SHELLEY, *Prometheus Unbound*. Act i, l. 24.

Then black despair,
The shadow of a starless night, was hrown
Over a world in which I moved alone.
SHELLEY, *Revolt of Islam: Dedication*. St. 6.

19
Despair the twin-born of devotion.
SWINBURNE, *Dolores*. St. 14.

20
The mass of men lead lives of quiet desperation. What is called resignation is confirmed

desperation. . . . A stereotyped but unconscious despair is concealed even under what are called the games and amusments of mankind.
H. D. THOREAU, *Walden*. Ch. 1.

1
Despair not only aggravates our misery, but our weakness. (Le désespoir comble non seulement notre misère, mais notre faiblesse.)
VAUVENARGUES, *Réflexions*. No. 252.

2
Night was our friend, our leader was Despair.
VERGIL, *Æneid*. Bk. ii, l. 487. (Dryden, tr.)

Darkness our guide, Despair our leader was.
SIR JOHN DENHAM, *Essay on Virgil's Æneid*.

3
The vilest deeds like poison-weeds
Bloom well in prison-air:
It is only what is good in Man
That wastes and withers there:
Pale Anguish keeps the heavy gate
And the Warder is Despair.
OSCAR WILDE, *The Ballad of Reading Gaol*.

4
He soonest loseth that despairs to win.
UNKNOWN, *The Play of Stuckley*, l. 711.

II—Despair: Its Courage

5
Despair and confidence both banish fear.
WILLIAM ALEXANDER, *Doomsday: The Ninth Hour*. St. 55.

6
Our last and best defence, despair:
Despair, by which the gallant'st feats
Have been achiev'd in greatest straits.
BUTLER, *Hudibras*. Pt. iii, canto 2, l. 586.

7
Despair defies even despotism.
BYRON, *The Two Foscari*. Act i, sc. 1.

Despair alone makes wicked men be bold.
S. T. COLERIDGE, *Zapolya*. Act i, sc. 1.

Despair gives courage to a coward.
THOMAS FULLER, *Gnomologia*. No. 1272.

Despair doubles our strength. (Le désespoir redouble les forces.)
UNKNOWN. A French proverb.

8
Like strength is felt from hope, and from despair.
HOMER, *Iliad*. Bk. xv, l. 852. (Pope, tr.)

Despair has often gained battles.
VOLTAIRE, *Henriade*. Chant 10.

DESPOTISM, see Tyranny

DESTINY

See also Circumstance, Fate, Fortune, Providence

9
Nor sitting by his hearth at home doth man escape his appointed doom. (Οὔτ' ἐν στέγῃ τις ἥμενος παρ' ἑστίᾳ φεύγει τι μᾶλλον τὸν πεπρωμένον μόρον.)
ÆSCHYLUS, *Fragments*. Frag. 193.

10
Destiny has two ways of crushing us—by refusing our wishes and by fulfilling them.
AMIEL, *Journal*, 10 April, 1881.

11
Rarely man escapes his destiny. (Che l'uomo il suo destin fugge di raro.)
ARIOSTO, *Orlando Furioso*. Pt. xviii, l. 58.

12
We, in some unknown Power's employ,
Move on a rigorous line;
Can neither, when we will, enjoy,
Nor, when we will, resign.
MATTHEW ARNOLD, *Stanzas in Memory of the Author of Obermann*, l. 133.

For this and that way swings
The flux of mortal things,
Though moving inly to one far-set goal.
MATTHEW ARNOLD, *Westminster Abbey*.

Allons! through struggle and wars!
The goal that was named cannot be countermanded.
WALT WHITMAN, *Song of the Open Road*. Sec. 14.

13
As, when a thing is shapen, it shall be.
CHAUCER, *The Knightes Tale*, l. 608.

That shall be, shall be.
JOHN HEYWOOD, *Proverbs*. Pt. ii, ch. 1.

14
The Destiny, minister general,
That executeth in the world over-all
The purveyance, that God hath seen before,
So strong it is, that, though the world had sworn
The contrary of a thing, by yea or nay,
Yet sometime it shall fallen on a day
That falleth not eft within a thousand year.
For certainly, our appetites here,
Be it of war, or peace, or hate, or love,
All is thus rulèd by the sight above.
CHAUCER, *The Knightes Tale*, l. 805.

15
The irrevocable Hand
That opes the year's fair gate, doth ope and shut
The portals of our earthly destinies;
We walk through blindfold, and the noiseless doors
Close after us, forever.
DINAH MARIA MULOCK CRAIK, *April*.

Walk darkling to their doom.
BYRON, *Heaven and Earth*. Sc. 3.

16
Where'er she lie,
Lock'd up from mortal eye,
In shady leaves of destiny.
RICHARD CRASHAW, *Wishes to His (Supposed) Mistress*. St. 2.

17
A consistent man believes in destiny, a capricious man in chance.
BENJAMIN DISRAELI, *Vivian Grey*. Bk. vi, ch. 7.

1
How easy 'tis, when destiny proves kind,
With full-spread sails to run before the wind.
DRYDEN, *Astræa Redux*, l. 63.

2
Alas! that one is born in blight,
Victim of perpetual slight, . . .
And another is born
To make the sun forgotten.
EMERSON, *Destiny*.

No man can change the common lot to rare.
THOMAS HARDY, *To an Unborn Pauper Child*.

3
The bitterest tragic element in life is the belief in a brute Fate or Destiny.
EMERSON, *Natural History of Intellect: The Tragic*.

4
Events will take their course, it is no good
Our being angry at them; he is happiest
Who wisely turns them to the best account.
EURIPIDES, *Bellerophon*. Frag. 298.

Art and power will go on as they have done,—will make day out of night, time out of space, and space out of time.
EMERSON, *Society and Solitude: Works and Days*.

5
I am the dance of youth, and life is fair!
Footfall, footfall;
I am a dream, divinely unaware!
Footfall, footfall;
I am the burden of an old despair!
Footfall. . . .
HAZEL HALL, *Footsteps*.

6
These purblind Doomsters had as readily strown
Blisses about my pilgrimage as pain.
THOMAS HARDY, *Wessex Poems: Hap*.

7
By time and counsel do the best we can,
Th' event is never in the power of man.
ROBERT HERRICK, *Hesperides*. No. 295.

8
No man of woman born,
Coward or brave, can shun his destiny. (Μοῖραν δ' οὔ τινά φημι πεφυγμένον ἔμμεναι ἀνδρῶν, οὐ κακόν, οὐδὲ μὲν εσθλόν.)
HOMER, *Iliad*. Bk. vi, l. 488. (Bryant, tr.)

Shunless destiny.
SHAKESPEARE, *Coriolanus*. Act ii, sc. 2, l. 116.

The one inexorable thing!
LOUISE IMOGEN GUINEY, *A Friend's Song for Simoisius*.

'Tis vain to quarrel with our destiny.
THOMAS MIDDLETON, *A Trick to Catch the Old One*. Act iv, sc. 4.

9
The destiny assigned to every man is suited to him, and suits him to himself. (Ἡ γὰρ ἑκάστῳ νεμομένη μοῖρα συνεμφέρεταί τε καὶ συνεμφέρει.)
MARCUS AURELIUS, *Meditations*. Bk. iii, sec. 4.

Whatever befalls thee was preordained for thee from eternity. (Ὅ τι ἄν σοι συμβαίνῃ, τοῦτό σοι ἐξ αἰῶνος προκατεσκευάζετο.)
MARCUS AURELIUS, *Meditations*. Bk. x, sec. 5.

Ere suns and moons could wax and wane,
Ere stars were thundergirt, or piled
The heavens, God thought on me His child:
Ordained a life for me, arrayed
Its circumstances every one
To the minutest.
ROBERT BROWNING, *Johannes Agricola*.

Ere systemed suns were globed and lit
The slaughters of the race were writ.
THOMAS HARDY, *The Dynasts*. Act ii, sc. 5.

For in the time we know not of
Did fate begin
Weaving the web of days that wove
Your doom.
SWINBURNE, *Faustine*. St. 24.

10
Earth loves to gibber o'er her dross,
Her golden souls, to waste;
The cup she fills for her god-men
Is a bitter cup to taste.
DON MARQUIS, *Wages*.

11
We are but as the instrument of Heaven.
Our work is not design, but destiny.
OWEN MEREDITH, *Clytemnestra*. Pt. xix.

We are what we must And not what we would be.
OWEN MEREDITH, *Lucile*. Pt. i, canto iii, sec. 19.

We but catch at the skirts of the thing we would be,
And fall back on the lap of a false destiny.
OWEN MEREDITH, *Lucile*. Pt. i, canto v, l. 5.

Unseen hands delay
The coming of what oft seems close in ken,
And, contrary, the moment when we say
" 'Twill never come!" comes on us even then.
OWEN MEREDITH, *Thomas Muntzer to Martin Luther*, l. 379.

12
Why hast Thou made me so,
My Maker? I would know
Wherefore Thou gav'st me such a mournful dower;—
Toil that is oft in vain,
Knowledge that deepens pain,
And longing to be pure, without the power.
J. J. MURPHY, *Eternity*.

13
If God in His wisdom have brought close
The day when I must die,
That day by water or fire or air
My feet shall fall in the destined snare
Wherever my road may lie.
D. G. ROSSETTI, *The King's Tragedy*. St. 50.

14
I feel that I am a man of destiny. (Ich fühl's das ich der Mann des Schicksals bin.)
SCHILLER, *Wallenstein's Tod*. Act iii, sc. 15, 171.

15
I am hurried I know not whither, but I am hurried on. (Rapior et quo nescio, Sed rapior.)
SENECA, *Thyestes*, l. 261.

1
Let determined things to destiny
Hold unbewail'd their way.

SHAKESPEARE, *Antony and Cleopatra*. Act iii, sc. 6, l. 84.

2
Think you I bear the shears of destiny?
Have I commandment on the pulse of life?

SHAKESPEARE, *King John*. Act iv, sc. 2, l. 91.

3
A man whom both the waters and the wind,
In that vast tennis-court, hath made the ball
For them to play upon.

SHAKESPEARE, *Pericles*. Act ii, sc. 1, l. 62.

I am as a weed,
Flung from the rock on Ocean's foam to sail,
Where'er the surge may sweep, the tempest's breath prevail.

BYRON, *Childe Harold*. Canto iii, st. 2.

4
If your lot is certainly decreed, what profit to guard against it? Or if all is uncertain, what is the use of fear? (Certa si decreta sors est, quid cavere proderit? Sive sunt incerta cuncta, quid timere convenit?)

SOLON. (AUSONIUS [?], *Septem Sapientum Sententiæ*, l. 34.)

5
No one can be more wise than destiny.

TENNYSON, *A Dream of Fair Women*. St. 24.

And though his efforts never slack,
And though he twist, and twirl, and tack,
Alas! still faithful to his back,
The pigtail hangs behind him.

W. M. THACKERAY, *A Tragic Story*.

6
Each of us suffers his own destiny. (Quisque suos patimur Manis.)

VERGIL, *Æneid*. Bk. vi, l. 743.

7
Your destiny is that of a man, your vows those of a god. (Tes destins sont d'un homme, et tes vœux sont d'un dieu.)

VOLTAIRE, *La Liberté*.

8
A millstone and the human heart are driven ever round,
If they have nothing else to grind, they must themselves be ground.

FRIEDRICH VON LOGAU, *Sinnegedichte*. (Longfellow, tr.)

THE MILLS OF THE GODS GRIND SLOWLY, *see under* RETRIBUTION.

9
This day we fashion Destiny, our web of Fate we spin.

WHITTIER, *The Crisis*. St. 10.

10
To be a Prodigal's favourite,—then worse truth,
A Miser's Pensioner,—behold our lot!

WORDSWORTH, *The Small Celandine*.

MANIFEST DESTINY, *see* AMERICAN HISTORY.

DEVIL, THE

I—Devil: Apothegms

11
For John the Baptist came neither eating bread nor drinking wine; and ye say, He hath a devil.

New Testament: Luke, vii, 33. Taken as a wedding text by Parson William Smith, when he married his daughter, Abigail, to John Adams, 25 Oct., 1764. (MINNIGERODE, *Some American Ladies*, p. 56.)

12
The devil take the hindmost!

BEAUMONT AND FLETCHER, *Philaster*. Act v. (1610), *Bonduca*. Act iv, sc. 2; DRYDEN, *An Evening's Love*. Act iv, sc. 3. (1671); etc.

Plague seize the hindmost. (Occupet extremum scabies.)

HORACE, *Ars Poetica*, l. 417.

Bid the Devil take the slowest.

MATTHEW PRIOR, *On the Taking of Namur*.

'Tis myself, quoth he, I must mind most;
So the Devil may take the hindmost.

SOUTHEY, *The March to Moscow*. St. 10.

13
Grant that he may have power and strength to have victory, and to triumph, against the devil, the world, and the flesh. Amen.

Book of Common Prayer: Baptism of Infants.

Renounce the devil and all his works.

Book of Common Prayer: Baptism of Infants.

14
The devil's most devilish when respectable.

E. B. BROWNING, *Aurora Leigh*. Bk. 7, l. 105.

15
Behind the cross there's the devil. (Tras la cruz está el Diablo.)

CERVANTES, *Don Quixote*. Pt. i, ch. 6.

16
One devil is like another. (Un diablo Parece à otro.)

CERVANTES, *Don Quixote*. Pt. i, ch. 31.

17
Therefore behooveth him a full long spoon
That shall eat with a fiend, thus heard I say.

CHAUCER, *The Squieres Tale*, l. 594. (c. 1386)

He must have a long spoon that shall eat with the devil.

HEYWOOD, *Proverbs*, ii, 5. (1546); SHAKESPEARE, *Comedy of Errors*, iv, 3, 64. (1592)

This is a devil, and no monster; I will leave him; I have no long spoon.

SHAKESPEARE, *The Tempest*. Act ii, sc. 2, l. 102.

18
It is become a proverb, *as great as the devil and Dr. Foster*.

DEFOE, *History of the Devil*. Pt. ii, ch. 6. (1726)

What the devil and Doctor Faustus, shan't I do what I will with my own daughter?

FIELDING, *Tom Jones*. Bk. xviii, ch. 8.

19
Every devil has not a cloven foot.

DEFOE, *History of the Devil*. Pt. ii, ch. 6.

20
Keep up your spirits! Never say die! Bow,

wow, wow! I'm a devil, I'm a devil, I'm a devil!
DICKENS, *Barnaby Rudge*. Ch. 6.

1
Demon—with the highest respect for you—behold your work!
DICKENS, *Our Mutual Friend*. Bk. iv, ch. 5.

2
Better sit still, than rise to meet the devil.
MICHAEL DRAYTON, *The Owl*.

3
A religion can no more afford to degrade its Devil than to degrade its God.
HAVELOCK ELLIS, *Impressions and Comments*. Ser. i, p. 33.

4
If I am the Devil's child, I will live then from the Devil.
EMERSON, *Essays, First Series: Self-Reliance*.

5
Talk of the devil and he'll appear.
ERASMUS, *Adagia*. No. 17.

Speak o' the devil and behold his horns!
THOMAS KNIGHT, *Turnpike Gate*. Act ii, sc. 1.

Since therefore 'tis to combat evil,
'Tis lawful to combat the Devil;
Forthwith the Devil did appear,
For name him, and he's always near.
MATTHEW PRIOR, *Hans Carvel*.

Talk of the devil and he's presently at your elbow.
TORRIANO, *Piazza Universale*, 134. (1666)

The wolf in the story. (Lupus in fabula.)
TERENCE, *Adelphi*, l. 537. The wolf appeared when spoken of. Also CICERO, *Epistulæ ad Atticum*. Bk. xiii, epis. 33, sec. 4. A proverb, applied to the appearance of a person just as he is being spoken of. The Latin equivalent of, "Speak of the devil and he will appear."

6
'Tis an easier matter to raise the devil than to lay him.
ERASMUS, *Adagia*, 202.

The devil's sooner raised than laid.
DAVID GARRICK, *School for Scandal: Prologue*.

7
What a silly fellow must he be who would do the devil's work for nothing.
FIELDING, *Joseph Andrews*. Bk. ii, ch. 16.

8
In heaven they scorn to serve, so now in hell
they reign.
JOHN FLETCHER, *The Purple Island*. Canto vii. *See also under* AMBITION.

9
Each man for himself and the Devil for all.
JOHN FLORIO, *First Fruites*. Fo. 33. (1578)

Every man for himself, his own ends, the Devil for all.
ROBERT BURTON, *Anatomy of Melancholy*. Pt. iii, sec. 1, mem. 3.

Every man for himself and God for us all.
JOHN HEYWOOD, *Proverbs*. Pt. ii, ch. 9. (1546)

10
Better keep the devil at the door than turn him out of the house.
THOMAS FULLER, *Gnomologia*. No. 907.

11
If the devil catch a man idle, he'll set him at work.
THOMAS FULLER, *Gnomologia*. No. 2705. *See also* IDLENESS: APOTHEGMS.

12
The devil is an egotist. (Der Teufel ist ein Egoist.)
GOETHE, *Faust*. Act i, sc. 4, l. 124.

13
We must not so much as taste of the devil's broth, lest at last he bring us to eat of his beef.
THOMAS HALL, *Funebria Floræ*, 12. (1660)

One had as good eat the devil as the broth he's boiled in.
THOMAS D'URFEY, *Quixote*. Pt. iii, ch. 1.

14
Resist the devil, and he will flee from you.
New Testament: James, iv, 7.

15
Let him go abroad to a distant country; let him go to some place where he is not known. Don't let him go to the devil where he is known.
SAMUEL JOHNSON. (BOSWELL, *Life*, 1773.)

16
The Devil is an ass, I do acknowledge it.
BEN JONSON, *The Devil Is an Ass*. Act iv, sc. 1.

17
Whin a bad egg is shut av the army he says the devil's mass . . . an' manes swearin' at ivrything from the commandher-in-chief down to the room-corp'ril.
RUDYARD KIPLING, *Soldiers Three*, p. 95.

18
Sabbathless Satan! he who his unglad
Task ever plies 'mid rotatory burnings,
That round and round incalculably reel—
For wrath divine hath made him like a wheel—
In that red realm from which are no returnings.
CHARLES LAMB, *Work*.

19
And the Devil said to Simon Legree:
"I like your style, so wicked and free."
VACHEL LINDSAY, *A Negro Sermon*.

20
For it is often said of him that yet lives,
He must needs go that the devil drives.
JOHN LYDGATE, *Assembly of Gods*, iii, 2. (c. 1420)

There is a proverb which true now proveth,
He must needs go that the devil driveth.
JOHN HEYWOOD, *Johan the Husband*. (1553)

He must needs go that the devil drives.
CHRISTOPHER MARLOWE, *Dr. Faustus*. (1584); SHAKESPEARE, *All's Well that Ends Well*. Act i, sc. 3, l. 31. (1623)

Needs must when the Devil drives.
RABELAIS, *Works*. Bk. iv, ch. 57.

Scampering as if the Devil drove them.
RABELAIS, *Works*. Bk. iv, ch. 62.

1
Out of whom he had cast seven devils.
New Testament: Mark, xvi, 9.

Casting out devils is mere juggling; they never cast out any but what they first cast in.
JOHN SELDEN, *Table-Talk: Devils*.

I charge thee, Satan, hous'd within this man,
To yield possession to my holy prayers,
And to thy state of darkness hie thee straight;
I conjure thee by all the saints in heaven!
SHAKESPEARE, *The Comedy of Errors*. Act iv, sc. 4, l. 57.

2
The devil turned precisian!
PHILIP MASSINGER, *A New Way to Pay Old Debts*. Act i, sc. 1.

3
Get thee hence, Satan.
New Testament: Matthew, iv, 10. (Vade, Satanas.—*Vulgate*.)

Get thee behind me, Satan.
New Testament: Matthew, xvi, 23. (Vade, retro, Satanas.—*Vulgate*.) Christ said this to Peter.

4
To whom the Arch-Enemy,
And thence in Heaven call'd Satan.
MILTON, *Paradise Lost*. Bk. i, l. 82. In the Old Testament, the name Satan is usually applied to a human adversary, and only in the three examples which follow is it used to denote an evil spirit.

And he shewed me Joshua the high priest standing before the angel of the Lord, and Satan standing at his right hand to resist him.
Old Testament: Zechariah, iii, 1.

And Satan stood up against Israel.
Old Testament: I Chronicles, xxi, 1.

And Satan came also among them to present himself before the Lord.
Old Testament: Job, ii, 1.

5
Never hold a candle to the devil.
JOHN RAY, *English Proverbs*.

6
The devil is seldom outshot in his own bow.
DANIEL ROGERS, *Matrimonial Honour*, 42. (1642)

7
Nay, then, let the devil wear black, for I'll have a suit of sables.
SHAKESPEARE, *Hamlet*. Act iii, sc. 2, l. 137.

8
He will give the devil his due.
SHAKESPEARE, *I Henry IV*. Act i, sc. 2, l. 132.

Let every man speak as he finds and give the devil his due.
DRYDEN, *The Wild Gallant*. Act ii, sc. 2.

Being of that honest few,
Who give the Fiend himself his due.
TENNYSON, *To the Rev. F. D. Maurice*.

9
The devil rides upon a fiddlestick.
SHAKESPEARE, *I Henry IV*. Act ii, sc. 4, l. 534.

10
What, can the devil speak true?
SHAKESPEARE, *Macbeth*. Act i, 3, 106. (1606)

The devil sometimes speaks the truth.
HENRY GLAPTHORNE, *Lady Mother*. Act i, sc. 3. (1635)

Truth may sometimes come out of the devil's mouth.
THOMAS FULLER, *Gnomologia*, 5508. (1732)

11
'T is the eye of childhood
That fears a painted devil.
SHAKESPEARE, *Macbeth*. Act ii, sc. 2, l. 54.

12
The devil can cite Scripture for his purpose.
SHAKESPEARE, *The Merchant of Venice*. Act i, sc. 3, l. 99. (1595)

As devils, to serve their purpose, Scripture quote.
CHARLES CHURCHILL, *The Apology*, l. 313.

13
What, man! defy the devil: consider, he's an enemy to mankind.
SHAKESPEARE, *Twelfth Night*. Act iii, sc. 4, 107.

Zounds, sir, you are one of those that will not serve God, if the devil bid you.
SHAKESPEARE, *Othello*. Act i, sc. 1, l. 107.

14
The devil corrects sin.
TORRIANO, *Piazza Univ.*, 60. (1666)

How the devil rebukes sin!
APHRA BEHN, *Roundheads*. Act v, sc. 2. (1682)

That incident is one of the most deplorable examples I have ever known of Satan reproving sin.
RAMSAY MACDONALD, *Speech*, House of Commons, 23 Nov., 1922.

15
The bane of all that dread the Devil!
WORDSWORTH, *The Idiot Boy*. St. 67.

16
The devil will take his own.
THOMAS WRIGHT, *Essays on the Middle Ages*. Vol. i, p. 146.

17
Dear Tillotson! be sure the best of men;
Nor thought he more, than thought great Origen,
Though once upon a time he misbehaved;
Poor Satan! doubtless he'll at length be saved.
YOUNG, *Love of Fame*. Sat. vi, l. 447. John Tillotson, Archbishop of Canterbury, endorsed Origen's doctrine of the Apocatastasis or Final Restitution, which expressly included the devil and his angels.

18
The devil is dead.
UNKNOWN, *Mankind*. (c. 1470) (MANLY, *Specimens of Pre-Shakespearean Drama*, i, 337.)

The devil, they say, is dead, The devil is dead!
JOHN SKELTON, *Colin Clout*, l. 36. (c. 1529)

Courage, brave wife, the devil is dead.
READE, *Cloister and the Hearth*. Ch. 52.

19
Better were be at home for aye,

Than her to serve the devil to pay.
UNKNOWN, (*Reliq. Antiquæ*, i, 257. 1400)

Here's the devil to pay.
RICHARDSON, *Clarissa Harlowe*. Bk. vi, 87.

Here's the devil-and-all to pay.
CERVANTES, *Don Quixote*. Pt. ii, ch. 10.

1
God made bees, and bees made honey,
God made man, and man made money,
Pride made the devil, and the devil made sin;
So God made a cole-pit to put the devil in.
UNKNOWN. An old rhyme found on the flyleaf of a Bible belonging to a miner living near Hutton-Henry. Transcribed by James Henry Dixon.

II—Devil: Ill and Well

2
When the wolf was sick he would be a monk, but when he recovered he was a wolf again.
(Lupus languebat monachus tunc esse volebat,
Sed cum convaluit lupus ut ante fuit.)
WALTER BOWER, *Scotichronicon*, ii, 292. (c. 1450) A proverb circulated in the early Middle Ages in all languages. (*Notes and Queries*. Ser. viii, vol. 12, p. 331.)

The devil was sick, the devil a monk would be;
The devil was well, the devil a monk was he.
(Ægrotat Dæmon, monachus tunc esse volebat;
Dæmon convaluit, Dæmon ante fuit.)
UNKNOWN. A variation of the medieval Latin proverb quoted above. (Urquhart, tr.)

When the devil was sick, the devil a saint would be;
When the devil was well, the devil a saint was he.
SAMUEL SMILES, *Thrift*, p. 314. (1875)

3
And almost every one when age,
Disease, or sorrows strike him,
Inclines to think there is a God,
Or something very like him.
ARTHUR HUGH CLOUGH, *Dipsychus*. Pt. i, sc. 5.

There are few so confirmed in Atheism, that a pressing danger or the neighborhood of death will not force to a recognition of the divine power.
MONTAIGNE, *Essays*. Bk. ii, ch. 12.

4
The devil was sick and crazy;
Good would the monk be that was lazy.
LEWIS EVANS, *Withals Dictionary Revised*. Sig. K8. (1586)

5
We are never so virtuous as when we are ill. . . . It is then a man recollects that there are gods, and that he himself is mortal; . . . and he resolves that if he has the luck to recover, his life shall be passed in harmless happiness.
PLINY, THE YOUNGER, *Epistles*. Bk. vii, epis. 26.

6
God and the Doctor we alike adore
But only when in danger, not before;
The danger o'er, both are alike requited,
God is forgotten, and the Doctor slighted.
JOHN OWEN, *Epigram*.

7
He is resolved to make good the Italian proverb,
When the danger's past the saint is cheated.
(Passato el pericolo è gabato el Santo.)
RABELAIS, *Works*. Bk. iv, ch. 24.

Cross a bridge, then throw away the staff. ('Chiao kuo tiu 'kuai.)
UNKNOWN. A Chinese proverb.

III—Devil: His Faults

8
A winnock-bunker in the east,
There sat auld Nick, in shape o' beast;
A towzie tyke, black, grim and large.
BURNS, *Tam o' Shanter*.

9
The Devil himself, which is the author of confusion and lies.
ROBERT BURTON, *Anatomy of Melancholy*. Pt. iii, sec. iv, mem. 1, subs. 3.

10
When to sin our biass'd nature leans,
The careful devil is still at hand with means.
DRYDEN, *Absalom and Achitophel*. Pt. i, l. 79.

11
'Gainst the logic of the devil
Human logic strives in vain.
A. L. GORDON, *The Wayside House*.

12
Who is the most diligent bishop and prelate in England? . . . I will tell you. It is the devil. . . . He is never out of his diocese. . . . The devil is diligent at his plough.
HUGH LATIMER, *Sermon on Ploughers*. (1549)

13
Be sober, be vigilant; because your adversary the devil, as a roaring lion, walketh about, seeking whom he may devour.
New Testament: I Peter, v, 8.

14
No man means evil but the devil, and we shall know him by his horns.
SHAKESPEARE, *Merry Wives of Windsor*, v, 2, 12.

15
If there be devils, would I were a devil,
To live and burn in everlasting fire,
So I might have your company in hell!
SHAKESPEARE, *Titus Andronicus*. Act v, sc. 1, 147.

IV—Devil: His Virtues

16
The devil's ever kind to his own.
ALEXANDER BROME, *New Montebank*. (1660)

The devil has a care of his footmen.
MIDDLETON, *A Trick to Catch the Old One*, i, 4.

17
The Devil that old stager . . . who leads
Downward, perhaps, but fiddles all the way!
ROBERT BROWNING, *Red Cotton Night-cap Country*. Pt. ii, l. 264.

18
All the devils respect virtue.
EMERSON, *Essays, First Series: Spiritual Laws*.

The dear old devil.
EMERSON, *Essays, Second Series: Experience*.

1
Part of that Power am I, least understood,
Which always wills the Bad and always works
the Good.
GOETHE, *Faust*. (Bayard Taylor, tr.)

2
I call'd the devil, and he came;
With wonder his form did I closely scan;
He is not ugly, and is not lame,
But really a handsome and charming man.
HEINE, *Pictures of Travel: The Return Home.*

3
Devils are not so black as they are painted.
THOMAS LODGE, *A Margarite of America*, p. 57. (1596)

As if the devil was not so black as he was painted.
DEFOE, *History of the Devil*. Pt. ii, ch. 6.

We paint the devil foul, yet he
Hath some good in him, all agree.
GEORGE HERBERT, *The Church: Sin.*

4
It is Lucifer,
The son of mystery;
And since God suffers him to be,
He, too, is God's minister,
And labors for some good
By us not understood.
LONGFELLOW, *The Golden Legend: Epilogue.*

5
The virtue of the devil is in the loins. (Diaboli virtus in lumbis est.)
ST. JEROME, *Contra Jovimen*, ii, l. 2.

6
The spirit that I have seen
May be the devil: and the devil hath power
To assume a pleasing shape.
SHAKESPEARE, *Hamlet*. Act ii, sc. 2, l. 627.

7
The devil shall have his bargain; for he was never yet a breaker of proverbs.
SHAKESPEARE, *I Henry IV*. Act i, sc. 2, l. 131.

Now I perceive the devil understands Welsh;
And 'tis no marvel he is so humorous.
SHAKESPEARE, *I Henry IV*. Act iii, sc. 1, l. 233

8
The prince of darkness is a gentleman.
SHAKESPEARE, *King Lear*. Act iii, sc. 4, l. 147.
SIR JOHN SUCKLING, *The Goblins*. Act iii, sc. 2.

9
The devil is good when he is pleased.
SWIFT, *Polite Conversation*. Dial. ii.

10
From his brimstone bed at break of day
A-walking the Devil is gone,
To look at his little snug farm of the world,
And see how his stock went on. . . .
His coat was red and his breeches were blue,
And there was a hole where his tail came
through.
ROBERT SOUTHEY, *The Devil's Walk*. Sts. 1, 3. This poem was originally published by S. T. Coleridge, 6 Sept., 1799, under the title *The Devil's Thoughts*. It consisted of fourteen stanzas of which Southey had written the first three. It was reprinted in Coleridge's *Sibylline Leaves* (1817), with a statement of Southey's share in its composition. It is reprinted in Southey's works with many additional stanzas. It was imitated by Byron and claimed by Professor R. C. Porson, who was exposed as an impostor.

V—The Devil According to Milton

11
Th' infernal serpent; he it was whose guile,
Stirr'd up with envy and revenge, deceiv'd
The mother of mankind.
MILTON, *Paradise Lost*. Bk. i, l. 34.

12
Hail horrors, hail
Infernal world, and thou profoundest hell
Receive thy new possessor.
MILTON, *Paradise Lost*. Bk. i, l. 250.

13
His spear, to equal which the tallest pine
Hewn on Norwegian hills, to be the mast
Of some great ammiral, were but a wand,
He walk'd with to support uneasy steps
Over the burning marle.
MILTON, *Paradise Lost*. Bk. i, l. 292.

14
His form had yet not lost
All her original brightness, nor appear'd
Less than arch-angel ruin'd, and th' excess
Of glory obscur'd.
MILTON, *Paradise Lost*. Bk. i, l. 591.

15
High on a throne of royal state, which far
Outshone the wealth of Ormus and of Ind,
Or where the gorgeous East with richest hand
Showers on her kings barbaric pearl and gold,
Satan exalted sat, by merit rais'd
To that bad eminence.
MILTON, *Paradise Lost*. Bk. ii, l. 1.

16
The strongest and the fiercest Spirit
That fought in Heav'n, now fiercer by despair:
His trust was with th' Eternal to be deem'd
Equal in strength; and rather than be less
Car'd not to be at all.
MILTON, *Paradise Lost*. Bk. ii, l. 44.

17
Black it stood as night,
Fierce as ten furies, terrible as hell,
And shook a dreadful dart; what seem'd his
head
The likeness of a kingly crown had on.
Satan was now at hand.
MILTON, *Paradise Lost*. Bk. ii, l. 670.

18
Incens'd with indignation Satan stood
Unterrified, and like a comet burn'd.
MILTON, *Paradise Lost*. Bk. ii, l. 707.

19
O'er bog or steep, through strait, rough, dense,
or rare,
With head, hands, wings, or feet, pursues his
way,

And swims or sinks, or wades, or creeps, or flies.
MILTON, *Paradise Lost*. Bk. ii, l. 948.

1
Abash'd the Devil stood,
And felt how awful goodness is, and saw
Virtue in her shape how lovely; saw, and pin'd
His loss.
MILTON, *Paradise Lost*. Bk. iv, l. 846.

2
Satan, so call him now, his former name
Is heard no more in heav'n.
MILTON, *Paradise Lost*. Bk. v, l. 655.

3
Swinges the scaly horror of his folded tail.
MILTON, *Hymn on the Morning of Christ's Nativity*, l. 172.

DEVOTION

4
Compar'd with this, how poor Religion's pride,
In all the pomp of method and of art,
When men display to congregations wide,
Devotion's ev'ry grace, except the heart!
ROBERT BURNS, *The Cotter's Saturday Night*.

5
Devotion, mother of obedience.
SAMUEL DANIEL, *The History of the Civil War*. Bk. vi, st. 33. *See also under* IGNORANCE.

6
The image of devotion. (Pietatis imago.)
VERGIL, *Æneid*. Bk. vi, l. 405.

7
Devotion has mastered the hard way. (Vicit iter durum pietas.)
VERGIL, *Æneid*. Bk. vi, l. 688.

8
Devotion! daughter of Astronomy!
YOUNG, *Night Thoughts*. Night ix, l. 769.

DEW

9
The dew,
'Tis of the tears which stars weep, sweet with joy.
P. J. BAILEY, *Festus: Another and a Better World*.

Dewdrops, Nature's tears, which she
Sheds in her own breast for the fair which die.
The sun insists on gladness; but at night,
When he is gone, poor Nature loves to weep.
P. J. BAILEY, *Festus: Water and Wood*.

10
In lang, lang days o' simmer,
When the clear and cloudless sky
Refuses ae wee drap o' rain
To Nature parched and dry,
The genial night, wi' balmy breath,
Gars verdure spring anew,
An' ilka blade o' grass
Keps its ain drap o' dew.
JAMES BALLANTINE, *Its Ain Drap o' Dew*.

11
He lived upon dew, after the manner of a grasshopper. (Rore vixit more cicadæ.)
SIR THOMAS BROWNE, *Religio Medici*. Pt. ii, sec. 11.

12
The dews of the evening most carefully shun;
Those tears of the sky for the loss of the sun.
LORD CHESTERFIELD, *Advice to a Lady in Autumn*.

13
Dew-drops are the gems of morning,
But the tears of mournful eve!
S. T. COLERIDGE, *Youth and Age*.

14
Sudden perfect as the dew-bead,
Gem of earth and sky begotten.
GEORGE ELIOT, *Spanish Gypsy: Song*. Pt. i.

15
The world globes itself in a drop of dew.
EMERSON, *Essays, First Series: Compensation*.

The drop of dew which hangs from the blade of grass reflects a sky as vast and as pure as the immense ocean in its azure plains.
(La goutte de rosée à l'herbe suspendue,
Y réfléchit un ciel aussi vaste, aussi pur,
Que l'immense océan dans ses plaines d'azur.)
LAMARTINE.

Every dew-drop and rain-drop had a whole heaven within it.
LONGFELLOW, *Hyperion*. Bk. iii, ch. 7.

And every dew-drop paints a bow.
TENNYSON, *In Memoriam*. Pt. cxxii, st. 5.

16
The lovely varnish of the dew, whereby the old, hard, peaked earth and its old self-same productions are made new every morning, and shining with the last touch of the artist's hand.
EMERSON, *Nature Addresses: Literary Ethics*.

17
The wizard silence of the hours of dew.
EDMUND GOSSE, *Dejection and Delay*.

18
Brushing with hasty steps the dews away,
To meet the sun upon the upland lawn.
THOMAS GRAY, *Elegy Written in a Country Church-yard*. St. 25.

19
I've seen the dew-drop clinging
To the rose just newly born.
CHARLES JEFFERYS, *Mary of Argyle*.

20
Stars of morning, dew-drops which the sun
Impearls on every leaf and every flower.
MILTON, *Paradise Lost* Bk. v, l. 743.

21
The dew-drop in the breeze of morn,
Trembling and sparkling on the thorn,
Falls to the ground, escapes the eye,
Yet mounts on sunbeams to the sky.
JAMES MONTGOMERY, *Recollection of Mary F.*

22
That diamond dew, so pure and clear,
It rivals all but Beauty's tear.
SCOTT, *Lady of the Lake*. Canto v, st. 2.

1
I must go seek some dewdrops here,
And hang a pearl in every cowslip's ear.
SHAKESPEARE, *A Midsummer-Night's Dream*. Act ii, sc. 1, l. 14.

And like a dew-drop from the lion's mane,
Be shook to air.
SHAKESPEARE, *Troilus and Cressida*. Act iii, sc. 3, l. 224.

2
O Dewey was the morning
Upon the first of May,
And Dewey was the Admiral
Down in Manila Bay;
And Dewey were the Regent's eyes,
"Them" orbs of royal blue!
And Dewey feel discouraged?
I Dew not think we Dew.
EUGENE WARE, *Dewey*. (*Topeka Capital*, May 3, 1898.)

DIAMOND

3
Better a diamond with a flaw than a pebble without.
CONFUCIUS, *Analects*.

4
A diamond is valuable tho' it lie on a dunghill.
THOMAS FULLER, *Gnomologia*. No. 74.

5
The lively diamond drinks thy purest rays,
Collected light compact; that, polished bright,
And all its native lustre let abroad,
Dares, as it sparkles on the fair one's breast,
With vain ambition emulate her eyes.
THOMSON, *The Seasons: Summer*, l. 142.

6
Diamond me no diamonds! . . . prize me no prizes!
TENNYSON, *Lancelot and Elaine*, l. 501.

7
None cuts a diamond but a diamond.
WEBSTER AND MARSTON, *The Malcontent*. Act iv, sc. 3. (1604)

Diamonds cut diamonds.
JOHN FORD, *The Lover's Melancholy*. Act i, sc. 3. (1629)

Wit must be foiled by wit; cut a diamond with a diamond.
CONGREVE, *The Double-Dealer*. Act i, sc. 5.

Among such fellows, it was diamond cut diamond.
THACKERAY, *Barry Lyndon*. Ch. 10.

8
The tears of fallen women turned to ice
By man's cold pity for repentant vice.
ELLA WHEELER WILCOX, *Diamonds*.

DICKENS, CHARLES

9
Has Dickens turned his hinge
A-pinch upon the fingers of the great?
E. B. BROWNING, *Aurora Leigh*. Bk. iv, l. 403.

10
The good, the gentle, the high-gifted, ever-friendly, noble Dickens—every inch of him an Honest Man.
THOMAS CARLYLE. (FORSTER, *Life*, iii, 475.)

11
And on that grave where English oak and holly
And laurel wreaths entwine,
Deem it not all a too presumptuous folly—
This spray of Western pine!
BRET HARTE, *Dickens in Camp*.

12
He has risen like a rocket and he will come down like a stick.
JOHN GIBSON LOCKHART, in review of the *Pickwick Papers* in the *Quarterly Review*. The phrase stolen from Thomas Paine, who used it with reference to Edmund Burke.

I will watch for that stick, Mr. Lockhart, and when it comes down, I will break it across your back.
CHARLES DICKENS, on meeting Lockhart for the first time after the publication of the review referred to above.

13
He violated every rule of art
Except the feeling mind and thinking heart.
JOHN MACY, *Couplets in Criticism: Dickens*.

14
If Columbus found a new world, Dickens created one—and peopled it with men and women.
ARTHUR QUILLER-COUCH, *Address*, Dickens Fellowship dinner, 7 Feb., 1931.

DIFFERENCES

15
There's but the twinkling of a star
Between a man of peace and war, . . .
A formal preacher and a player,
A learn'd physician and man-slayer.
BUTLER, *Hudibras*. Pt. ii, canto iii, l. 957.

16
Strange! all this difference should be
'Twixt Tweedledum and Tweedledee.
JOHN BYROM, *On the Feuds between Handel and Bononcini*. Wrongly attributed to Pope and Swift. *See under* COMPARISONS.

17
The whole character and fortune of the individual are affected by . . . the perception of differences.
EMERSON, *Nature, Addresses: Discipline*.

18
Distinction without a difference.
FIELDING, *Tom Jones*. Bk. vi, ch. 13.

19
There are fagots and fagots. (Il y a fagots et fagots.)
MOLIÈRE, *Le Médicin Malgré Lui*. Act i, sc. 5.

20
The king can drink the best of wine—
So can I;
And has enough when he would dine—
So have I;
And can not order rain or shine—

Nor can I.
Then where's the difference—let me see—
Betwixt my lord the king and me?
CHARLES MACKAY, *Differences.*

1
Differing but in degree, of kind the same.
MILTON, *Paradise Lost.* Bk. v, l. 490.

2
All Nature's diff'rence keeps all Nature's peace.
POPE, *Essay on Man.* Epis. iv, l. 56.

3
The difference is as great between
The optics seeing as the objects seen.
POPE, *Moral Essays.* Epis. i, l. 31.

4
The difference is wide that the sheets will not decide.
JOHN RAY, *English Proverbs,* p. 201.

5
O, the difference of man and man!
SHAKESPEARE, *King Lear.* Act iv, sc. 2, l. 26.

6
Because it makes no difference. ("Οτι οὐδὲν διαφέρει.)
THALES, when asked why he did not die, after he had declared that there was no difference between life and death. (DIOGENES LAERTIUS, *Thales.* Bk. i, sec. 36.)

7
No difference will I make 'twixt Tyrian and Trojan. (Tros Turiusque mihi nullo discrimine agetur.)
VERGIL, *Æneid.* Bk. i, l. 574.

There's some difference between Peter and Peter. (Algo va de Pedro à Pedro.)
CERVANTES, *Don Quixote.* Pt. i, ch. 47.

8
Like—but oh! how different!
WORDSWORTH, *The Mountain Echo.*

DIFFICULTY

9
There's difficulty, there's danger, there's the dear spirit of contradiction in it.
ISAAC BICKERSTAFFE, *The Hypocrite.* Act i, sc. 1.

10
Difficulty is a severe instructor.
EDMUND BURKE, *Reflections on the Revolution in France.*

11
What is difficult? To keep a secret, to employ leisure well, to be able to bear an injury.
CHILON. (DIOGENES LAERTIUS, *Chilon.* Sec. 2.)

12
The greater the difficulty, the greater the glory. (Quo difficilius, hoc præclarius.)
CICERO, *De Officiis.* Bk. i, ch. 19, sec. 64.

13
It is difficulties which show what men are. (Αἱ περιστάσεις εἰσὶν αἱ τοὺς ἄνδρας δεικνύουσαι.)
EPICTETUS, *Discourses.* Bk. i, ch. 24.

A difficulty raiseth the spirits of a great man.
LORD HALIFAX, *Works,* p. 248.

14
All things are difficult before they are easy.
THOMAS FULLER, *Gnomologia.* No. 560.

A stumbler stumbles least in rugged way.
GEORGE HERBERT, *The Church-Porch.* St. 36.

15
Every difficulty yields to the enterprising.
J. G. HOLMAN, *Votary of Wealth.* Act iv, sc. 1.

16
To solve one difficulty by raising another. (Litem quod lite resolvit.)
HORACE, *Satires.* Bk. ii, sat. 2, l. 103.

17
Difficulty is, for the most part, the daughter of idleness.
SAMUEL JOHNSON, *The Rambler.* No. 129.

18
Many things difficult to design prove easy to performance.
SAMUEL JOHNSON, *Rasselas.* Ch. 13.

Hard things are compassed oft by easy means.
PHILIP MASSINGER, *A New Way to Pay Old Debts.* Act v, sc. 1.

19
He who accounts all things easy will have many difficulties.
LAO-TSZE, *The Simple Way.* No. 63.

20
So he with difficulty and labour hard
Mov'd on, with difficulty and labour he.
MILTON, *Paradise Lost.* Bk. ii, l. 1021.

21
What is worth while must needs be difficult. (Nulla, nisi ardua, virtus.)
OVID, *Ars Amatoria.* Bk. ii, l. 537.

The best things are most difficult.
PLUTARCH, *Morals: On Education.*

22
O Time, thou must untangle this, not I;
It is too hard a knot for me t' untie.
SHAKESPEARE, *Twelfth Night.* Act ii, sc. 2, l. 42.

23
For easy things, that may be got at will,
Most sorts of men do set but little store.
EDMUND SPENSER, *Amoretti.* Sonnet xxvi.

Sith never ought was excellent assayed
Which was not hard t' achieve and bring to end.
EDMUND SPENSER, *Amoretti.* Sonnet li.

24
Have the courage to face a difficulty, lest it kick you harder than you bargain for.
KING STANISLAUS of Poland, *Maxims.*

25
Nothing is so easy but it becomes difficult when done with reluctance. (Nullast tam facilis res quin difficilis siet, Quam invitus facias.)
TERENCE, *Heauton Timoroumenos,* l. 805.

CHOICE OF DIFFICULTIES, *see* CHOICE.

DIGESTION

See also Appetite

26
'Tis not *her* coldness, father,
That chills my labouring breast;

It's that confounded cucumber
I've ate and can't digest.
R. H. Barham, *The Confession.*

1
A good digestion turneth all to health.
George Herbert, *The Church-Porch.* St. 60

To eat is human, to digest divine.
Charles T. Copeland.

1a
Rustics, who have stomachs like ostriches, that can digest hard iron.
Thomas Cogan, *Haven of Health,* 33. (1584)
See 999:17.

2
Things sweet to taste prove in digestion sour.
Shakespeare, *Richard II.* Act i, sc. 3, l. 236

Unquiet meals make ill digestion.
Shakespeare, *Comedy of Errors.* Act v, sc. 1, l. 74

3
I am convinced digestion is the great secret of life.
Sydney Smith, *Letter to Arthur Kinglake,* 30 Sept., 1837.

DIGNITY

5
There is a certain dignity of manners absolutely necessary, to make even the most valuable character either respected or respectable.
Lord Chesterfield, *Letters,* 10 Aug., 1749.

6
With grave
Aspect he rose, and in his rising seem'd
A pillar of state; deep on his front engraven
Deliberation sat, and public care;
And princely counsel in his face yet shone
Majestic, though in ruin.
Milton, *Paradise Lost.* Bk. ii, l. 300.

7
Our dignity is not in what we do, but what we understand.
George Santayana, *Little Essays,* p. 202.

Perhaps the only true dignity of man is his capacity to despise himself.
George Santayana, *Little Essays,* p. 230.

8
It is easier to grow in dignity than to make a start. (Facilius enim crescit dignitas quam incipit.)
Seneca, *Epistulæ ad Lucilium.* Epis. ci, sec. 2.

9
But clay and clay differs in dignity,
Whose dust is both alike.
Shakespeare, *Cymbeline.* Act iv, sc. 2, l. 6.

10
My cloud of dignity
Is held from falling with so weak a wind
That it will quickly drop.
Shakespeare, *II Henry IV.* Act iv, sc. 5, l. 99.

11
Pistol, I will double-charge thee with dignities.
Shakespeare, *II Henry IV.* Act v, sc. 3, l. 130.
See also under Honors.

12
Too coy to flatter, and too proud to serve,
Thine be the joyless dignity to starve.
Tobias Smollett, *Advice,* l. 236.

13
True dignity abides with him alone
Who, in the silent hour of inward thought,
Can still suspect, and still revere himself,
In lowliness of heart.
Wordsworth, *Lines Left upon a Seat in a Yew Tree,* l. 61.

14
Beneath one's dignity. (Infra dig.: Infra Dignitatem.)
A proverbial expression, origin unknown.

DILEMMA, see Choice

DILIGENCE, see Industry

DIMPLES

15
Then did she lift her hands unto his chin,
And praised the pretty dimpling of his skin.
Francis Beaumont, *Salmacis and Hermaphroditus,* l. 661.

16
And love to live in dimple sleek.
Milton, *L'Allegro,* l. 30.

17
There's a boil on his ear; and a corn on his chin,—
He calls it a dimple—but dimples stick in—
Yet it might be a dimple turned over, you know!
James Whitcomb Riley, *The Man in the Moon.*

18
Pandarus: She puts her white hand to his cloven chin.
Cressida: Juno have mercy! how came it cloven.
Pandarus: Why, you know, 'tis dimpled.
Shakespeare, *Troilus and Cressida.* Act i, sc. 2, l. 132.

19
In each cheek appears a pretty dimple;
Love made those hollows; if himself were slain.
He might be buried in a tomb so simple;
Foreknowing well, if there he came to lie,
Why, there Love lived and there he could not die.
Shakespeare, *Venus and Adonis,* l. 242.

20
The pretty dimples of his chin and cheek.
Shakespeare, *Winter's Tale.* Act ii, sc. 3, l. 97.

And then the dimple on his chin.
John Lyly, *Cupid and Campaspe.*

DINING

See also Eating, Feast

I—Dining: Its Importance

21
That all-softening, overpowering knell,
The tocsin of the soul—the dinner bell.
Byron, *Don Juan.* Canto v, st. 49.

22
All human history attests
That happiness for man—the hungry sinner—

Since Eve ate apples, much depends on dinner!

BYRON, *Don Juan*. Canto xiii, st. 99.

1
All people are made alike.
They are made of bones, flesh and dinners.
Only the dinners are different.

GERTRUDE LOUISE CHENEY, *People*. The author of this was aged nine in 1927 when it was written.

2
My dinners have never interfered with my business. They have been my recreation. . . . A public banquet, if eaten with thought and care, is no more of a strain than a dinner at home.

CHAUNCEY DEPEW, *Interview,* on his 80th birthday.

3
To seek his dinner in poules with Duke Humphrey.

GABRIEL HARVEY, *Works,* i, 206. (1592)

One Diggory Chuzzlewit was in the habit of perpetually dining with Duke Humphrey.

DICKENS, *Martin Chuzzlewit*. Ch. 1. Humphrey, Duke of Gloucester, son of Henry IV, was renowned for his hospitality, was buried in St. Paul's, and when the promenaders left for dinner, the poor stay-behinds who had no dinner to go to, used to say that they were dining with Duke Humphrey. The expression was at one time very common.

4
'Tis not the food, but the content,
That makes the table's merriment.

ROBERT HERRICK, *Content not Cates*.

5
Among the great whom Heaven has made to shine,
How few have learned the art of arts,—to dine!
Nature, indulgent to our daily need,
Kind-hearted mother! taught us all to feed;
But the chief art,—how rarely Nature flings
This choicest gift among her social kings!

O. W. HOLMES, *The Banker's Secret*, l. 31.

6
A simple dinner in a poor man's house, without tapestries and purple, has smoothed the wrinkles from the anxious brow. (Mundæque parvo sub lare pauperum Cenæ sine aulæis et ostro Sollicitam explicuere frontem.)

HORACE, *Odes*. Bk. iii, ode 29, l. 14.

7
A man seldom thinks with more earnestness of anything than he does of his dinner.

SAMUEL JOHNSON, *Miscellanies*. Vol. i, p. 249.

This was a good dinner enough, to be sure, but it was not a dinner to *ask* a man to.

SAMUEL JOHNSON. (BOSWELL, *Life*. Ch. 9.)

8
What, did you not know, then, that to-day Lucullus dines with Lucullus? (Παρὰ Λουκούλλῳ δειπνεῖ Λούκουλλος.)

LUCIUS LUCULLUS, to the servant who had provided only a small repast when his master happened to dine alone (PLUTARCH, *Lives: Lucullus*. Ch. 41, sec. 2.)

9
Dr. Middleton misdoubted the future as well as the past of the man who did not, in becoming gravity, exult to dine. That man he deemed unfit for this world and the next.

GEORGE MEREDITH, *The Egoist*. Ch. 20.

10
He may live without books,—what is knowledge but grieving?
He may live without hope,—what is hope but deceiving?
He may live without love,—what is passion but pining?
But where is the man that can live without dining?

OWEN MEREDITH, *Lucile*. Pt. i, canto ii, st. 19.

O hour of all hours, the most bless'd upon earth,
Blessèd hour of our dinners!

OWEN MEREDITH, *Lucile*. Pt. i, canto ii, st. 18.

11
The true Amphitryon is the Amphitryon with whom we dine. (Le véritable Amphitryon est l'Amphitryon où l'on dîne.)

MOLIÈRE, *Amphitryon*. Act iii, sc. 5, l. 89. That is, the person who provides the dinner, whether the master of the house or not, is the real host. The story is that Jupiter assumed the likeness of Amphitryon in order to visit the latter's wife, Alcmena, and gave a banquet at his house, but Amphitryon came home unexpectedly and claimed the honor of being the host. The guests and servants decided that "he who gave the feast was to them the host."

I am the true Amphitryon.

DRYDEN, *Amphitryon*. Act v, sc. 1.

12
A good dinner, and company.

SAMUEL PEPYS, *Diary,* 19 July, 1668. *See also under* COMPANY.

13
Is this a cause why one should not dine? (Cur quis non prandeat hoc est?)

PERSIUS, *Satires*. Sat. iii, l. 85.

14
Judicious drank, and greatly daring din'd.

POPE, *The Dunciad*. Bk. iv, l. 318.

15
Better is a dinner of herbs where love is, than a stalled ox and hatred therewith.

Old Testament: Proverbs, xv, 17.

Oh, better, no doubt, is a dinner of herbs,
When season'd by love, which no rancour disturbs,
And sweeten'd by all that is sweetest in life
Than turbot, bisque, ortolans, eaten in strife!

OWEN MEREDITH, *Lucile*. Pt. i, canto ii, st. 22.

16
A very man—not one of nature's clods—
With human failings, whether saint or sinner:
Endowed perhaps with genius from the gods
But apt to take his temper from his dinner.

J. G. SAXE, *About Husbands*.

1
Little we fear Weather without,
Sheltered about The Mahogany Tree.
THACKERAY, *The Mahogany Tree.*

II—Dining: The Menu

2
A rich soup; a small turbot; a saddle of venison; an apricot tart: this is a dinner fit for a king.
BRILLAT-SAVARIN, *La Physiologie du Goût.*

3
A warmed-up dinner was never worth much. (Un dîner réchauffé ne valut jamais rien.)
BOILEAU, *Le Lutrin.* Pt. i, l. 104.

Like warmed-up cabbage served at each repast,
The repetition kills the wretch at last.
(Occidit miseros crambe repetitia magistros.)
JUVENAL, *Satires.* Sat. vii, l. 154. (Gifford, tr.)

4
You must reflect carefully beforehand with whom you are to eat and drink, rather than what you are to eat and drink. For a dinner of meats without the company of a friend is like the life of a lion or a wolf.
EPICURUS, *Fragments.* Frag. 542. (Quoted SENECA, *Epistulæ ad Lucilium.* Epis. xix, 10.)

He showed me his bill of fare to tempt me to dine with him. "Foh," said I, "I value not your bill of fare, give me your bill of company."
SWIFT, *Letter to Stella,* 2 Sept., 1711.

It isn't so much what 's on the table that matters, as what 's on the chairs.
W. S. GILBERT. (PEARSON, *Gilbert and Sullivan.*)

5
Dinners cannot be long where dainties want.
JOHN HEYWOOD, *Proverbs.* Pt. ii, ch. 1.

6
From the egg to the apples. (Ab ovo usque ad mala.)
HORACE, *Satires.* Bk. i, sat. iii, l. 6. Referring to the first and last dish of a dinner, the equivalent of "From soup to nuts."

The most nourishing meat is first to be eaten, that ancient proverb ratifieth Ab ovo ad mala; from the egg to the apples.
THOMAS MOFFETT, *Health's Improvement,* 295. (1639)

7
Corydon and Thyrsis met,
Are at their savoury dinner set,
Of herbs, and other country messes,
Which the neat-handed Phillis dresses.
MILTON, *L'Allegro,* l. 83.

8
And we meet, with champagne and a chicken,
at last.
MARY WORTLEY MONTAGU, *The Lover.*

What say you to such a supper with such a woman?
BYRON, *Note to a Letter on Bowles's Strictures.*

9
I will make an end of my dinner; there's pippins and cheese to come.
SHAKESPEARE, *Merry Wives of Windsor,* i, 2, 12.

10
Across the walnuts and the wine.
TENNYSON, *The Miller's Daughter,* l. 32.

You'll have no scandal while you dine,
But honest talk and wholesome wine.
TENNYSON, *To the Rev. F. D. Maurice.*

Dinner was made for eatin', not for talkin'.
THACKERAY, *Fashnable Fax.*

11
A puzzle dinner—where you'd be puzzled which dish to try first. (Cena dubia . . . ubi tu dubites quid sumas potissumum.)
TERENCE, *Phormio,* l. 342. Horace repeats the expression, *Satires.* Bk. ii, sat. 2, l. 77.

12
They make their pride in making their dinner cost much; I make my pride in making my dinner cost little.
H. D. THOREAU. (EMERSON, *Thoreau.*)

III—Dining: The Number at Table

13
The number at table should be three or four, or at most five.
ARCHESTRATUS. (ATHENÆUS, *Deipnosophists.* Bk. i.)

Not fewer than three, nor more than nine. (Neque pauciores tribus, neque plures novem.)
ERASMUS, *Adagia.* Quoting an old proverb.

14
Crowd not your table: let your numbers be
Not more than seven, and never less than
three.
WILLIAM KING, *Art of Cookery,* l. 259.

Best company consists of five persons.
RICHARD STEELE, *The Tatler.* No. 132.

Seven make a banquet; nine make a clamor. (Septem convivium; novem convicium.)
UNKNOWN. A Latin proverb.

15
I have chosen five; for six are suitable for a feast with a king: if more, it is a clamor. (Quinque advocavi; sex enim convivium Cum rege justum: si super, convicium est.)
UNKNOWN. A Latin proverb.

16
The more the merrier; the fewer, the better fare.
JOHN PALSGRAVE, *L'Éclair. Langue Française,* 885. (1530)

17
At a round table there's no dispute of place.
JOHN RAY, *English Proverbs.*

18
Heavenly Father, bless us,
And keep us all alive,
There's ten of us to dinner
And not enough for five.
UNKNOWN, *Hodge's Grace.*

IV—Dining: The Diner-Out

19
Solomon of saloons, And philosophic diner-out.
ROBERT BROWNING, *Mr. Sludge "The Medium."*

No dinner goes off well without him.
BENJAMIN DISRAELI, *Ixion in Heaven*. Jupiter refers to Apollo.

Ye diners-out from whom we guard our spoons.
MACAULAY, *Political Georgics*.

See also JOHNSON, *under* VICE AND VIRTUE.

1
Philosopher, whom dost thou most affect,
Stoics austere, or Epicurus' sect?
Friend, 'tis my grave infrangible design
With those to study and with these to dine.
RICHARD GARNETT, *Epigram*.

Catius is ever moral, ever grave,
Thinks who endures a knave, is next a knave,
Save just at dinner—then prefers, no doubt,
A rogue with venison to a saint without.
POPE, *Moral Essays*. Epis. i, l. 77.

2
At dinner my man appears.
GEORGE HERBERT, *Jacula Prudentum*.

Then from the Mint walks forth the man of rhyme,
Happy to catch me just at dinner-time.
POPE, *Epistle to Dr. Arbuthnot*, l. 13.

3
When a man is invited to dinner, he is disappointed if he does not get something good.
SAMUEL JOHNSON. (BOSWELL, *Life*, iii, 186.)

4
To eat at another's table is your ambition's height. (Bona summa putes aliena vivere quadra.)
JUVENAL *Satires*. Sat. v, l. 2.

It is the hope of a good dinner that beguiles you. (Spes bene cenendi vos decipit.)
JUVENAL, *Satires*. Sat. v, l. 166.

5
Philo swears that he has never dined at home, and it is so: he never dines at all unless invited out.
MARTIAL, *Epigrams*. Bk. v, ep. 47.

6
Who depends upon another man's table often dines late.
JOHN RAY, *English Proverbs*, 164.

V—Dining: After Dinner

7
Truth that peeps
Over the glass's edge when dinner's done,
And body gets its sop, and holds its noise,
And leaves soul free a little.
ROBERT BROWNING, *Bishop Blougram's Apology*, l. 17.

8
That old English saying: After dinner sit a while, and after supper walk a mile.
THOMAS COGAN, *Haven of Health*, 186. (1588)
See also HEALTH: ITS PRESERVATION.

9
Men are . . . conservatives after dinner.
EMERSON, *Essays, Second Series: New England Reformers*.

10
Strange to see how a good dinner and feasting reconciles everybody.
SAMUEL PEPYS, *Diary*. 9 Nov., 1665.

11
A dinner lubricates business.
WILLIAM SCOTT, BARON STOWELL. (BOSWELL, *Life of Johnson*, viii, 67, note.)

We were to do more business after dinner; but after dinner is after dinner—an old saying and a true.
SWIFT, *Letter to Stella*, 26 Feb., 1711.

12
Serenely full, the epicure would say,
"Fate cannot harm me, I have dined to-day."
SYDNEY SMITH, *A Recipe for Salad*.

13
After a good dinner, one can forgive anybody, even one's own relations.
OSCAR WILDE, *Woman of No Importance*. Act ii.

14
He that hath a good dinner knows better the way to supper.
UNKNOWN, *Fair Maid of Bristow*. (1605)

DIPLOMACY

See also Statesmanship

15
International arbitration may be defined as the substitution of many burning questions for a smouldering one.
AMBROSE BIERCE, *The Devil's Dictionary*.

16
A dull-eyed diplomatic corps.
CAMPBELL, *Jemima, Rose and Eleanore*.

17
You must look into people, as well as at them.
LORD CHESTERFIELD, *Letters*, 4 Oct., 1746.

18
It is fortunate that diplomats generally have long noses, since usually they cannot see beyond them.
Attributed to PAUL CLAUDEL, while Ambassador of the French Republic at Washington, but denied by him in a letter to the compiler.

19
American diplomacy is easy on the brain but hell on the feet.
CHARLES G. DAWES, American Ambassador to Great Britain, in talk at Washington, 2 June, 1931.

It depends on which you use.
HENRY PRATHER FLETCHER, ex-Ambassador to Italy, commenting on Mr. Dawes's epigram.

20
"Frank and explicit"—that is the right line to take when you wish to conceal your own mind and to confuse the minds of others.
BENJAMIN DISRAELI, *Sybil*. Bk. vi, ch. 1.

If you wish to preserve your secret, wrap it up in frankness.
ALEXANDER SMITH, *Dreamthorp: On the Writing of Essays*.

This is some fellow, . . . doth affect
A saucy roughness, and constrains the garb
Quite from his nature: he cannot flatter, he,
An honest mind and plain, he must speak truth!
An they will take it, so; if not, he's plain.

These kind of knaves I know, which in this plainness
Harbour more craft and more corrupter ends
Than twenty silly ducking observants
That stretch their duties nicely.
SHAKESPEARE, *King Lear*. Act ii, sc. 2, l. 101.

1
Ambassadors are the eye and ear of states. (Gli ambasciadori sono l'occhio e l'orecchio degli stati.)
GUICCIARDINI, *Storia d'Italia.*

2
There are three species of creatures who
when they seem coming are going,
When they seem going they come: Diplomats,
women, and crabs.
JOHN HAY, *Distichs.*

3
European Councils, where artful and refined plausibility is forever called in to aid the most pernicious designs.
RICHARD HENRY LEE, *Speech,* House of Representatives.

4
Spheres of action.
GEORGE LEVESON-GOWER, EARL GRANVILLE, *Letter to Count Münster*, 29 April, 1885.

Spheres of influence.
HERTSLET, *Map of Africa by Treaty*, p. 596.

5
The public weal requires that a man should betray, and lie, and massacre. (Le bien public requiert qu'on trahisse, et qu'on mente, et qu'on massacre.)
MONTAIGNE, *Essays*. Bk. iii, ch. 1.

6
Keep a good table and look after the ladies. (Tenez bonne table et soignez les femmes.)
NAPOLEON I, instructions to Abbé Dominique de Pradt, when sending him as ambassador to Warsaw in 1812.

7
The rulers of the State are the only ones who should have the privilege of lying, either at home or abroad; they may be allowed to lie for the good of the State.
PLATO, *The Republic*. Bk. iii, sec. 389.

An ambassador is an honest man, sent to lie abroad for the good of his country. (Legatus est vir bonus peregre missus ad mentiendum Reipublicæ causa.)
SIR HENRY WOTTON, written in the album of his friend, Christopher Fleckamore, in 1604, as he passed through Augsburg on his way to Venice to assume the English Ambassadorship there. It was published eight years later by Jasper Scioppius (*Eccleciasticus*, ch. 8), a scurrilous controversalist, with malicious intent, and raised a storm of disapproval in Europe, losing Wotton for a time the favor of King James I. Wotton apologized, insisting that the epigram was only "a merriment," and called attention to the double meaning of "lie," but this, unfortunately, was not present in the Latin in which he had written the jest. (WALTON, *Life*; *Reliquiæ Wottonianæ*; *Dict. Natl. Biog.*)

This merry definition of an ambassador I had chanced to set down at my friend's, Mr. Christopher Fleckamore, in his Album.
SIR HENRY WOTTON, *Letter to Velserus*, 1612.

8
Men, like bullets, go farthest when they are smoothest. (Die Menschen gehen wie Schiesskugeln weiter, wenn sie abgeglättet sind.)
JEAN PAUL RICHTER, *Titan*. Zykel. 26.

9 Touch sourest points with sweetest terms.
SHAKESPEARE, *Antony and Cleopatra*, ii, 2, 24.

Diplomacy is to do and say
The nastiest thing in the nicest way.
ISAAC GOLDBERG, *The Reflex*. (1933)

Be soople, Davie, in things immaterial.
R. L. STEVENSON, *Kidnapped*. Ch. i. (1886)

10
Alas! how should you govern any kingdom,
That know not how to use ambassadors.
SHAKESPEARE, *III Henry VI*. Act iv, sc. 3, l. 35.

11
All ambassadors make love and are very nice and useful to people who travel.
BERNARD SHAW, *Misalliance*, p. 102.

12
Tell the truth.
SIR HENRY WOTTON, when asked by a young diplomatist how best to puzzle his adversaries. (*Reliquæ Wottonianæ*.) *See also* 279:9.

DISAPPOINTMENT

13
The best-laid schemes o' mice an' men
Gang aft agley,
An' lea'e us nought but grief an' pain,
For promis'd joy!
BURNS, *To a Mouse.*

But evil fortune has decreed,
(The foe of mice as well as men)
The royal mouse at last should bleed,
Should fall—ne'er to arise again.
MICHAEL BRUCE, *The Musiad.*

14
Like to the apples on the Dead Sea's shore,
All ashes to the taste.
BYRON, *Childe Harold*. Canto iii, st. 34.

Greedily they pluck'd
The fruitage, fair to sight, like that which grew
Near that bituminous lake where Sodom flam'd:
This more delusive, not the touch, but taste
Deceiv'd; they fondly thinking to allay
Their appetite with gust, instead of fruit
Chew'd bitter ashes, which th' offended taste
With spattering noise rejected.
MILTON, *Paradise Lost*. Bk. x, l. 560.

Like Dead-Sea fruits that tempt the eye
But turn to ashes on the lips.
MOORE, *Lalla Rookh: The Fire-Worshippers.* The reference is to the so-called apples of Sodom, a yellow fruit which grows on the shores of the Dead Sea, beautiful to the eye, but bitter to the taste and filled with minute black seeds not unlike ashes.

15
Oh! ever thus, from childhood's hour,
I've seen my fondest hopes decay;

I never lov'd a tree or flow'r,
But 'twas the first to fade away.
I never nurs'd a dear gazelle,
To glad me with its soft black eye,
But when it came to know me well,
And love me, it was sure to die!

THOMAS MOORE, *Lalla Rookh: The Fire-Worshippers*, l. 279.

I never nursed a dear Gazelle to glad me with its soft black eye, but when it came to know me well, and love me, it was sure to marry a market-gardener.

DICKENS, *Old Curiosity Shop*. Ch. 56.

I never had a piece of toast,
Particularly long and wide,
But fell upon the sanded floor,
And always on the buttered side.

JAMES PAYN [?], *After Tom Moore*. (HAMILTON, *Parodies*. Vol. iii, p. 268.)

1
And still they dream that they shall still succeed,
And still are disappointed.

COWPER, *The Task*. Bk. iii, l. 128.

2
Nothing is so good as it seems beforehand.

GEORGE ELIOT, *Silas Marner*. Ch. 18.

3
As for disappointing them, I should not so much mind; but I can't abide to disappoint myself.

GOLDSMITH, *She Stoops to Conquer*. Act i.

DISASTER, see Misfortune

DISCONTENT

I—Discontent: Definitions

4
And sigh that one thing only has been lent
To youth and age in common—discontent.

MATTHEW ARNOLD, *Youth's Agitations*.

On every stage from youth to age
Still discontent attends.

SOUTHEY, *Remembrance*, l. 3.

5
Who hath so entire happiness that he is not in some part offended with the condition of his estate? (Quis est enim tam compositae felicitatis ut non aliqua ex parte cum status sui qualitate rixetur?)

BOËTHIUS, *Philosophiæ Consolationis*. Bk. ii, sec. 4, l. 41.

6
Does he paint? he fain would write a poem,—
Does he write? he fain would paint a picture.

ROBERT BROWNING, *One Word More*.

7
Discontent is the want of self-reliance: it is infirmity of will.

EMERSON, *Essays, First Series: Self-Reliance*.

The more discontent the better we like it.

EMERSON, *Papers from the Dial: A Letter*.

8
There are two kinds of discontent in this world: the discontent that works, and the discontent that wrings its hands. The first gets what it wants, and the second loses what it had. There is no cure for the first but success, and there is no cure at all for the second.

GORDON GRAHAM. (ELBERT HUBBARD, *Scrap-book*, p. 78.)

9
One who likes another's lot, of course dislikes his own. (Cui placet alterius, sua nimirum est odio sors.)

HORACE, *Epistles*. Bk. i, epis. 14, l. 11.

Admiring others' lots, our own we hate.

HORACE, *Epistles*, i, 14. (Conington, tr.)

The fat ox desires the trappings of the horse; the horse desires to plough. (Optat ephippia bos piger, optat arare caballus.)

HORACE, *Epistles*. Bk. i, epis. 14, l. 43.

We love in others what we lack ourselves,
And would be everything but what we are.

R. H. STODDARD, *Arcadian Idyl*, l. 30.

10
Our discontent is from comparison:
Were better states unseen, each man would like his own.

JOHN NORRIS, *The Consolation*. St. 2.

11
Now is the winter of our discontent
Made glorious summer by this sun of York.

SHAKESPEARE, *Richard III*. Act i, sc. 1, l. 1.

You've been to "Richard." Ah, you've seen
A noble play: I'm glad you went;
But what on earth does Shakespeare mean
By "*winter of our discontent*"?

THOMAS CONSTABLE, *Old October*.

12
Content you in my discontent.

SHAKESPEARE, *The Taming of the Shrew*. Act i, sc. 1, l. 80.

In pale contented sort of discontent.

KEATS, *Lamia*. Pt. ii, l. 135.

13
Dissemble all your griefs and discontents.

SHAKESPEARE, *Titus Andronicus*. Act i, sc. 1, l. 443.

Let thy discontents be thy secrets.

BENJAMIN FRANKLIN, *Poor Richard*, 1758.

II—Discontent: Its Virtues

14
Man is not so far lost but that he suffers ever the great Discontent which is the elegy of his loss and the prediction of his recovery.

EMERSON, *Papers from the Dial: Thoughts on Modern Literature*.

15
To be discontented with the divine discontent, and to be ashamed with the noble shame, is the very germ of the first upgrowth of all virtue.

CHARLES KINGSLEY, *Health and Education*.

16
Can you make no use of your discontent?

SHAKESPEARE, *Much Ado About Nothing*. Act i, sc. 3, l. 40.

1
The thirst to know and understand,
A large and liberal discontent:
These are the goods in life's rich hand,
The things that are more excellent.

WILLIAM WATSON, *The Things That Are More Excellent*. St. 8.

2
The splendid discontent of God
With Chaos, made the world; . . .
And from the discontent of man
The world's best progress springs.

ELLA WHEELER WILCOX, *Discontent*.

3
Discontent is the first step in the progress of a man or a nation.

OSCAR WILDE, *A Woman of No Importance*. Act ii.

III—Discontent: Its Faults

4
A perverse and fretful disposition makes any state of life unhappy. (Importunitas autem et inhumanitas omni ætati molesta est.)

CICERO, *De Senectute*. Ch. 3, sec. 7.

5
A man's discontent is his worst evil.

GEORGE HERBERT, *Jacula Prudentum*.

Men are suspicious; prone to discontent.

ROBERT HERRICK, *Hesperides*. No. 922.

6
A discontented man knows not where to sit easy.

GEORGE HERBERT, *Jacula Prudentum*.

The discontented Man finds no easy Chair.

BENJAMIN FRANKLIN, *Poor Richard*, 1753.

7
Fickle as the wind, at Rome loving Tibur, at Tibur Rome. (Romæ Tibur amem ventosus, Tibure Romam.)

HORACE, *Epistles*. Bk. i, epis. 8, l. 12.

At Rome you long for the country; in the country you extol to the stars the distant town. (Romæ rus optas; absentem rusticus urbem Tollis ad astra levis.)

HORACE, *Satires*. Bk ii, sat. 7, l. 28.

At Rome you hanker for your country home;
Once in the country, there's no place like Rome.

HORACE, *Satires*, ii, 7, 28. (Conington, tr.)

8
The fastidious are unfortunate: nothing can satisfy them. (Les délicats sont malheureux, Rien ne saurait les satisfaire.)

LA FONTAINE, *Fables*. Bk. ii, fab. 1.

9
Save me alike from foolish pride
Or impious discontent.

POPE, *Universal Prayer*.

10
For what's more miserable than discontent?

SHAKESPEARE, *II Henry VI*. Act iii, sc. 2, l. 201.

The murmuring lips of discontent.

SHAKESPEARE, *King John*. Act iv, sc. 2, l. 53.

Happy thou art not;
For what thou hast not, still thou striv'st to get,
And what thou hast, forget'st.

SHAKESPEARE, *Measure for Measure*, iii, 1, 21.

Brawling discontent.

SHAKESPEARE, *Measure for Measure*, iv, 1, 9.

11
Thou art the Mars of malcontents.

SHAKESPEARE, *The Merry Wives of Windsor*. Act i, sc. 3, l. 113.

I see your brows are full of discontent,
Your hearts of sorrow and your eyes of tears.

SHAKESPEARE, *Richard II*. Act iv, sc. 1, l. 331.

Happiness courts thee in her best array;
But, like a misbehav'd and sullen wench,
Thou pout'st upon thy fortune and thy love:
Take heed, take heed, for such die miserable.

SHAKESPEARE, *Romeo and Juliet*. Act iii, sc. 3, l. 142.

12
I know a discontented gentleman,
Whose humble means match not his haughty mind.

SHAKESPEARE, *Richard III*. Act iv, sc. 2, l. 36.

13
To waste long nights in pensive discontent.

SPENSER, *Mother Hubberds Tale*, l. 498.

14
Poor in abundance, famish'd at a feast.

YOUNG, *Night Thoughts*. Night vii, l. 44.

DISCORD

For Discord as related to Music,
see Music and Discord

15
And Doubt and Discord step 'twixt thine and thee.

BYRON, *The Prophecy of Dante*. Canto ii, l. 140.

16
The daughter of debate,
That discord aye doth sow.

QUEEN ELIZABETH, *A Sonnet*. (PERCY, *Reliques*. Ser. ii, bk. ii, 15.) The reference is to Mary Queen of Scots.

17
Concord can never join Minds so divided.

JOHN FLETCHER, *Rollo*. Act i, sc. 1.

18
Their discords sting through Burns and Moore
Like hedgehogs dressed in lace.

O. W. HOLMES, *The Music-Grinders*.

19
A discordant concord. (Concordia discors.)

HORACE, *Epistles*. Bk. i, epis. 12, l. 19. A reference to the main principle of Empedocles' philosophy that the life of the world is due to the perpetual conflict of the two principles of Love and Strife.

Inharmonious harmony. (Discors concordia.)

OVID, *Metamorphoses*. Bk. i, l. 433.

Agreement consists in disagreement. (Mansit concordia discors.)

LUCAN, *De Bello Civili*. Bk. i, l. 98.

All concord's born of contraries.

BEN JONSON, *Cynthia's Revels*. Act v, sc. 2.

All discord, harmony not understood.

POPE, *Essay on Man*. Epis. i, l. 291.

1
When dreadful Discord bursts her brazen bars,
And shatters locks to thunder forth her wars.
(Postquam Discordia tetra
Belli ferratos postis portasque refregit.)
HORACE, *Satires*. Bk. i, sat. iv, l. 60.

2
Is it, O man, with such discordant noises,
With such accursed instruments as these,
Thou drownest Nature's sweet and kindly voices,
And jarrest the celestial harmonies?
LONGFELLOW, *The Arsenal at Springfield.*

3
All your danger is in discord.
LONGFELLOW, *Hiawatha*. Pt. i, l. 113.

4
If a house be divided against itself, that house cannot stand.
New Testament: Mark, iii, 25.

5
Discord, with a thousand various mouths.
MILTON, *Paradise Lost*. Bk. ii, l. 967.

6
You are poking up a hornet's nest. (Inritabis crabones.)
PLAUTUS, *Amphitruo*, l. 707. (Act ii, sc. 2.)

7
The whole concord of the world consists in discord. (Tota hujus mundi concordia ex discord.)
SENECA, *Naturales Questiones*. Bk. vii, sec. 27.

8
How, in one house,
Should many people, under two commands,
Hold amity?
SHAKESPEARE, *King Lear*. Act ii, sc. 4, l. 243.

9
The Demon of Discord, with her sooty wings, had breathed her influence upon our counsels.
SMOLLETT, *Roderick Random*. Ch. 33.

Discord seemed to clap her sooty wings in expectation of battle.
SMOLLETT, *Launcelot Greaves*. Ch. 3.

10
Adverse fortune brought forth discord. (Res adversæ discordium peperere.)
TACITUS, *History*. Bk. iv, sec. 37.

11
Discord wild,
Her viper-locks with bloody fillets bound.
VERGIL, *Æneid*. Bk. iv, l. 300.

12
Discord, a sleepless hag who never dies,
With Snipe-like nose, and Ferret-glowing eyes,
Lean sallow cheeks, long chin with beard supplied,
Poor crackling joints, and wither'd parchment hide,
As if old Drums, worn out with martial din,
Had clubb'd their yellow heads to form her skin.
JOHN WOLCOT, *The Louisad*. Canto iii, l. 121.

DISCRETION

See also Prudence

I—Discretion and Valor

13
You put too much wind to your sail; discretion and hardy valour are the twins of honour.
BEAUMONT AND FLETCHER, *Bonduca*. Act i, 1.

14
He had a natural aversion to danger, and thought it below a man of wit or common sense to be guilty of that brutal thing called Courage, or Fighting. His philosophy told him, "It was safe sleeping in a whole skin."
APHRA BEHN, *The Lucky Mistake.*

15
And this, too, is a manly quality, namely, discretion. (Καὶ τοῦτό τοι τἀνδρεῖον, ἡ προμηθία.)
EURIPIDES, *Suppliants*, l. 510.

16
Valour would fight, but discretion would run away.
THOMAS FULLER, *Gnomologia*. No. 5344.

17
He led his regiment from behind
(He found it less exciting).
W. S. GILBERT, *The Gondoliers*. Act i.

18
Discreet women have neither eyes nor ears.
GEORGE HERBERT, *Jacula Prudentum.*

She that could think, and ne'er disclose her mind,
See suitors following, and not look behind.
SHAKESPEARE, *Othello*. Act ii, sc. 1, l. 157.

19
While the discreet advise, the fool doth his business.
GEORGE HERBERT, *Jacula Prudentum.* (1640)

20
There are things in the breast of mankind which are best
In darkness and decency hid,
For you never can tell, when you've opened a hell,
How soon you can put back the lid.
RUDYARD KIPLING.

The reticent volcano keeps
His never slumbering plan;
Confided are his projects pink
To no precarious man.
EMILY DICKINSON, *Poems*. Pt. i, No. 107.

20a
When you have got an elephant by the hind leg, and he is trying to run away, it 's best to let him run.
ABRAHAM LINCOLN, *Remark*, to Charles A. Dana, 14 April, 1865, when urged to arrest Jacob Thompson, a Confederate commissioner who was trying to escape to Europe. Lincoln was shot a few hours later, and this was probably his last aphorism. (WILSON, *Life of Charles A. Dana*, p. 358; Mitchell, *Memoirs of an Editor*, p. 35.)

21
Know not what you know, and see not what you see. (Etiam illud quod scies nesciveris Ne videris quod videris.)
PLAUTUS, *Miles Gloriosus*. l. 572. (Act ii, sc. 6.)

You, in truth, if you are wise, will not know what you do know. (Tu pol, si sapis, quod scis nescis.)
TERENCE, *Eunuchus*, l. 721. (Act iv, sc. 4.)

1
Discretion shall preserve thee.
Old Testament: Proverbs, ii, 11. (Consilium custodiet te.—*Vulgate*.)

2
An ounce of discretion is worth a pound of wit.
JOHN RAY, *English Proverbs*.

3
Valour can do little without discretion.
JOHN RAY, *English Proverbs*.

4
Let fools the name of loyalty divide:
Wise men and gods are on the strongest side.
SIR CHARLES SEDLEY, *Death of Marc Antony*. Act iv, sc. 2.

5
Therefore use thy discretion.
SHAKESPEARE, *As You Like It*. Act i, sc. 1, l. 152.

Let your own discretion be your tutor.
SHAKESPEARE, *Hamlet*. Act iii, sc. 2, l. 19.

6
The better part of valour is discretion.
SHAKESPEARE, *I Henry IV*. Act v, sc. 4, l. 122.

It shew'd discretion, the best part of valour.
BEAUMONT AND FLETCHER, *A King and No King*. Act iv, sc. 3.

Even in a hero's heart
Discretion is the better part.
CHARLES CHURCHILL, *The Ghost*. Bk. i, l. 233.

7
Covering discretion with a coat of folly.
SHAKESPEARE, *Henry V*. Act ii, sc. 4, l. 38.

8
Thou pigeon-egg of discretion.
SHAKESPEARE, *Love's Labour's Lost*. Act v, sc. 1, l. 75.

9
I have seen the day of wrong through the little hole of discretion.
SHAKESPEARE, *Love's Labour's Lost*. Act v, sc. 2, l. 734.

10
Lysander: This lion is a very fox for his valour.
Theseus: True; and a goose for his discretion.
Demetrius: Not so, my lord; for his valour cannot carry his discretion; and the fox carries the goose.
Theseus: His discretion, I am sure, cannot carry his valour, for the goose carries not the fox. It is well: leave it to his discretion.
SHAKESPEARE, *A Midsummer-Night's Dream*. Act v, sc. 1, l. 233.

11
Dogberry: You are to bid any man stand, in the prince's name.
Watchman: How if a' will not stand?
Dogberry: Why, then, take no note of him, but let him go; and presently call the rest of the watch together and thank God you are rid of a knave.
SHAKESPEARE, *Much Ado About Nothing*. Act iii, sc. 3, l. 26.

12
Let's teach ourselves that honourable stop
Not to outsport discretion.
SHAKESPEARE, *Othello*. Act ii, sc. 3, l. 2.

13
Ever since I came to years of discretion.
RICHARD STEELE, *Tender Husband*. Act ii, sc. 1.

14
Shoot not beyond the mark, as the proverb says. (Ita fugias ne præter casam.)
TERENCE, *Phormio*, l. 768. (Act v, sc. 2.)

O discretion, thou art a jewel!
UNKNOWN, *The Skylark*. (1772)

II—Discretion: They That Fight and Run Away

15
And by a prudent flight and cunning save
A life, which valour could not, from the grave.
A better buckler I can soon regain;
But who can get another life again?
ARCHILOCHUS, *Fragments*. No. 6.

Cowardice?
I only know we don't live twice,
Therefore—shun death, is my advice.
ROBERT BROWNING, *Arcades Ambo*.

16
In all the trade of war no feat
Is nobler than a brave retreat:
For those that run away and fly
Take place at least o' the enemy.
BUTLER, *Hudibras*. Pt. i, canto iii, l. 607.

17
Then as wise and discreet he withdrew him saying that more is worth a good retreat than a foolish abiding.
WILLIAM CAXTON, *Jason*, 23. (c. 1477)

18
To retire is not to flee, and there is no wisdom in waiting when danger outweighs hope, and it is the part of wise men to preserve themselves today for tomorrow, and not risk all in one day.
CERVANTES, *Don Quixote*. Pt. i, ch. 23.

19
There are worser ills to face
Than foemen in the fray;
And many a man has fought because—
He feared to run away.
RICHARD HOVEY, *The Marriage of Guenevere*. Act iv, sc. 3.

20
There's some say that we wan, some say that they wan,
Some say that nane wan at a', man,
But one thing I'm sure that at Sheriff-Muir,
A battle there was which I saw, man.
And we ran and they ran, and they ran and we ran,

And we ran, and they ran awa', man.

MURDOCH MCLENNAN, *Sheriff-Muir*. The reference is to the indecisive battle known as "The Bob of Dunblane" fought near Stirling, 12 Nov., 1715.

1

The man who runs away may fight again. (Ἀνὴρ ὁ φεύγων καὶ πάλιν μαχήσεται.)

MENANDER, *Monostikoi*. No. 45.

Demosthenes sought safety in flight from the battlefield [of Chæronea, 338 B.C.], and when he was bitterly taunted with his flight he jestingly replied in the well-known verse, "The man who runs away will fight again."

AULUS GELLIUS, *Noctes Atticæ*. Bk. xvii, ch. 21, sec. 31.

He who flees will fight again. (Qui fugiebat, rursus prœliabitur.)

TERTULLIAN, *De Fuga in Persecutione*. Sec. 10. The proverb is quoted by many authors.

That same man that runneth away
May fight again an other day.

ERASMUS, *Adagia*. No. 372. Quoted as a saying of Demosthenes.

2

He that fights and runs away
May live to fight another day.

The above couplet appeared in *Musarum Deliciæ*, a collection made by Sir John Mennes and Dr. James Smith, and published in 1656. No author was given. The lines were ascribed to Sir John Suckling, but no confirmation of this ascription was ever given.

For those that fly may fight again,
Which he can never do that's slain.

BUTLER, *Hudibras*. Pt. iii, canto iii, l. 243. (1668)

For those that save themselves and fly
Go halves at least i' the victory.

BUTLER, *Hudibras*. Pt. iii, canto iii, l. 269.

3

He that fights and runs away
May turn and fight another day;
But he that is in battle slain
Will never rise to fight again.

JAMES RAY, *A Complete History of the Rebellion*, p. 48. (1749)

For he who fights and runs away
May live to fight another day;
But he who is in battle slain
Can never rise and fight again.

This quatrain appeared without ascription of authorship in a book published by Newbery, in 1762, entitled, *The Art of Poetry on a New Plan*, ii, 147. It had been revised by Goldsmith, and it is thought he wrote the lines.

4

He can return who flies:
Not so with him who dies.
(Qui fuit peut revenir aussi:
Qui meurt, il n'en est pas ainsi.)

PAUL SCARRON, *Epigram*.

5

It is not seemly for any man who has weapons in his hands to resort to the help of his unarmed feet. (Nec quemquem decere, qui manus armaverit, ab inermis pedibus auxilium petere.)

SULLA. (SALLUST, *Jugurtha*. Ch. cvii, sec. 1.)

6

Prone to flight, and therefore more likely to survive. (Fugacissimi ideoque tam diu superstites.)

TACITUS, *Agricola*. Sec. 34.

7

Poor John was a gallant captain,
In battles much delighting;
He fled full soon
On the first of June—
But he bade the rest keep fighting.

UNKNOWN, *Elegy on the Death of Jean Bon Saint-André*. (*Anti-Jacobin*, 14 May, 1790.) Saint-André was beheaded at Algiers by the Dey's orders for forming a revolutionary club there, and this bit of doggerel is said to be the joint production of Canning, Ellis and Frere.

8

It is an old saw, he fighteth well that flyeth fast.

UNKNOWN, *Gesta Romanorum: The Wolf and Hare*.

9

Oft he that doth abide
Is cause of his own pain;
But he that flieth in good tide
Perhaps may fight again.
(Celui qui fuit de bonne heure
Peut combattre derechef.)

UNKNOWN, *Satyre Menipée*. (1595)

DISDAIN, see Scorn

DISEASE

See also Doctors; Medicine

I—Disease: Apothegms

10

There is no curing a sick man who believes himself in health.

AMIEL, *Journal*, 6 Feb., 1877.

11

Across the wires the electric message came:
"He is no better, he is much the same."

ALFRED AUSTIN, referring to the illness of the Prince of Wales, afterward Edward VII.

12

Cure the disease, and kill the patient.

FRANCIS BACON, *Essays: Of Friendship*.

THE REMEDY WORSE THAN THE DISEASE: *see under* MEDICINE.

13

Pale disease
Shall linger by thy side, and thou shalt know
Eternal autumn to thy day of death.

MAURICE BARING, *The Black Prince and the Astrologer*.

14

Some will allow no diseases to be new, others think that many old ones have ceased; and

that such which are esteemed new, will have but their time.
SIR THOMAS BROWNE, *To a Friend*. Sec. 14.

1 I think it frets the saints in heaven to see
How many desolate creatures on the earth
Have learnt the simple dues of fellowship
And social comfort, in a hospital.
E. B. BROWNING, *Aurora Leigh*. Bk. iii, l. 1121.

2 Diseases of their own accord,
But cures come difficult and hard.
SAMUEL BUTLER, *The Weakness and Misery of Man*, l. 82.

Sickness comes on horseback, but goes away on foot.
W. C. HAZLITT, *English Proverbs*, 336.

3 Despair of all recovery spoils longevity,
And makes men's miseries of alarming brevity.
BYRON, *Don Juan*. Canto ii, st. 64.

4 The beginning of health is to know the disease.
CERVANTES, *Don Quixote*. Pt. ii, ch. 60.

It is a step toward health to know the disease. (Ad sanitatem gradus est novisse morbum.)
ERASMUS, *Adagia*. No. 9.

Physicians consider that when the cause of a disease is discovered, the cure is discovered. (Medici causa morbi inventa curationem esse inventam putant.)
CICERO, *Tusculanarum Disputationum*. Bk. iii, ch. 10, sec. 23.

5 Physical ills are the taxes laid upon this wretched life; some are taxed higher, and some lower, but all pay something.
LORD CHESTERFIELD, *Letters*, 22 Nov., 1757.

6 No slow disease,
To soften grief by just degrees.
DRYDEN, *Threnodia Augustalis*. St. 1.

7 It is dainty to be sick, if you have leisure and convenience for it.
EMERSON, *Journals*. Vol. v, p. 162.

Some maladies are rich and precious and only to be acquired by the right of inheritance or purchased with gold.
HAWTHORNE, *Mosses from an Old Manse: The Procession of Life*.

Polite diseases make some idiots vain,
Which, if unfortunately well, they feign.
YOUNG, *Love of Fame*. Sat. i, l. 95.

8 There is no mortal whom sorrow and disease do not touch. (Ἔφυ μὲν οὐδεὶς ὅστις οὐ πονεῖ βροτῶν.)
EURIPIDES, *Fragments*. No. 757. Quoted by CICERO, *Tusculanarum Disputationum*, bk. iii, ch. 25, sec. 59: "Mortalis nemo est, quem non attingat dolor morbusque."

9 He who was never sick dies the first fit.
THOMAS FULLER, *Gnomologia*. No. 2409.

10 Sickness is felt, but health not at all.
THOMAS FULLER, *Gnomologia*. No. 4160.

11 I've that within for which there are no plasters.
DAVID GARRICK, GOLDSMITH'S *She Stoops to Conquer: Prologue*.

A malady
Preys on my heart that med'cine cannot reach.
CHARLES R. MATURIN, *Bertram*. Act iv, sc. 2.

12 We er sorter po'ly, Sis Tempy, I'm blige ter you. You know w'at de jay-bird say ter der squinch-owls, "I'm sickly but sassy."
JOEL CHANDLER HARRIS, *Nights With Uncle Remus*. Ch. 50.

13 Sick as a dog.
GABRIEL HARVEY, *Works*, i, 161. (1592)

As sick as a horse.
GEORGE MERITON, *Yorkshire Ale*, 71. (1685)

I am sick as a horse.
STERNE, *Tristram Shandy*. Vol. vii, ch. 11.

As sick as a cat.
C. H. SPURGEON, *John Ploughman*. Ch. 20.

Poor miss, she's sick as a cushion.
SWIFT, *Polite Conversation*. Dial. i.

14 Each season has its own disease,
Its peril every hour.
REGINALD HEBER, *At a Funeral*.

15 The whole head is sick, and the whole heart faint.
Old Testament: Isaiah, i, 5.

16 Illness makes a man a scoundrel.
SAMUEL JOHNSON. (TWINING, *Letter to Fanny Burney*, Jan., 1788.)

It is so very difficult for a sick man not to be a scoundrel.
SAMUEL JOHNSON, *Miscellanies*. Vol. i, p. 267.

17 Disease generally begins that equality which death completes.
SAMUEL JOHNSON, *Rambler*, No. 48.

18 What can a sick man say, but that he is sick?
SAMUEL JOHNSON. (BOSWELL, *Life*, iv, 362.)

19 When men a dangerous disease did 'scape,
Of old, they gave a cock to Æsculape.
BEN JONSON, *Epigram*. *See also* SOCRATES *under* DEATH: LAST WORDS.

20 Disease will have its course.
THOMAS MOFFETT, *Health's Improvement*, 8. (1655)

21 An incurable body. (Immedicabile corpus.)
OVID, *Metamorphoses*. Bk. i, l. 190.

1
Meet the disease on its way. (Venienti occurrite morbo.)
PERSIUS, *Satires*. Sat. iii, l. 64. A recommendation of preventive medicine.

2
Death's servant, sickness.
FRANCIS ROUS, *Thule*.

3
O, he's a limb, that has but a disease;
Mortal, to cut it off; to cure it, easy.
SHAKESPEARE, *Coriolanus*. Act iii, sc. 1, l. 296.

4
This sickness doth infect
The very life-blood of our enterprise.
SHAKESPEARE, *I Henry IV*. Act iv, sc. 1, l. 28.

5
Before the curing of a strong disease,
Even in the instant of repair and health,
The fit is strongest.
SHAKESPEARE, *King John*. Act iii, sc. 4, l. 112.

6
Maybe he is not well:
Infirmity doth still neglect all office
Whereto our health is bound.
SHAKESPEARE, *King Lear*. Act ii, sc. 4, l. 106.

7
Sickness is catching.
SHAKESPEARE, *A Midsummer-Night's Dream*. Act i, sc. 1, l. 186.

8
Loathsome canker lives in sweetest bud.
SHAKESPEARE, *Sonnets*. No. xxxv.

In the sweetest bud The eating canker dwells.
SHAKESPEARE, *The Two Gentlemen of Verona*. Act 1, sc. 1, l. 42.

As is the bud bit with an envious worm,
Ere he can spread his sweet leaves to the air,
Or dedicate his beauty to the sun.
SHAKESPEARE, *Romeo and Juliet*, i, 1, 157.

The canker which the trunk conceals is revealed by the leaves, the fruit, or the flower.
(D'ogni pianta palesa l'aspetto
Il difetto, che il tronco nasconde
Per le fronde, dal frutto, o dal fior.)
METASTASIO, *Giuseppe Riconosciuto*. Bk. i.

As killing as the canker to the rose.
MILTON, *Lycidas*, l. 45.

9
I'll sweat and seek about for eases,
And at that time bequeath you my diseases.
SHAKESPEARE, *Troilus and Cressida*, v, 10, 56.

10
He seems a little under the weather, somehow; and yet he's not sick.
WILLIAM DUNLAP, *The Memoirs of a Water Drinker*, i, 80. (1836)

A little under the weather.
DONALD G. MITCHELL, *The Lorgnette*. (1851)

11
We are so fond of each other, because our ailments are the same.
SWIFT, *Letter to Stella*, 1 Feb., 1710.

We con ailments, which makes us very fond of each other.
SWIFT, *Letter to Stella*, 14 Feb., 1710.

12
Ring out old shapes of foul disease.
TENNYSON, *In Memoriam*. Sec. 106.

13
To hide disease is fatal. (Occultare morbum funestam.)
UNKNOWN. A Latin Proverb.

II—Disease: Cause and Effect

14
[Diseases] crucify the soul of man, attenuate our bodies, dry them, wither them, shrivel them up like old apples, make them so many anatomies.
ROBERT BURTON, *Anatomy of Melancholy*. Pt. i, sec. 2, mem. 3, subs. 10.

15
Self-contemplation is infallibly the symptom of disease.
CARLYLE, *Characteristics*.

If the man thinks about his physical or moral state he nearly always discovers that he is ill.
GOETHE, *Sprüche in Prosa*.

16
Diseases of the soul are more dangerous and more numerous than those of the body. (Morbi perniciosiores pluresque sunt animi quam corporis.)
CICERO, *Tusculanarum Disputationum*. Bk. iii, ch. 3, sec. 5.

Philosophers apply the term disease to all disorders of the soul, and they say that no foolish person is free from such diseases; sufferers from disease are not sound, and the souls of all unwise persons are diseased.
CICERO, *Tusculanarum Disputationum*. Bk. iii, ch. 4, sec. 9.

A bodily disease which we look upon as whole and entire within itself, may, after all, be but a symptom of some ailment in the spiritual part.
HAWTHORNE, *The Scarlet Letter*. Ch. 10.

17
Disease can carry its ill-effects no farther than mortal mind maps out the way. . . . Disease is an image of thought externalized. . . . We classify disease as error, which nothing but Truth or Mind can heal. . . . Disease is an experience of so-called mortal mind. It is fear made manifest on the body.
MARY BAKER EDDY, *Science and Health*. Pages 176, 411, 483, 493.

Sickness, sin, and death, being inharmonious, do not originate in God nor belong to His government. His law, rightly understood, destroys them.
MARY BAKER EDDY, *Science and Health*, p. 472. *See also under* MEDICINE.

18
Languor seizes the body from bad ventilation. (Aëre non certo corpora languor habet.)
OVID, *Ars Amatoria*. Bk. ii, l. 318.

19
As man, perhaps, the moment of his breath,
Receives the lurking principle of death,
The young disease, that must subdue at length,

Grows with his growth, and strengthens with
his strength.
POPE, *Essay on Man*. Epis. ii, l. 133.

1
Diseases are the tax on pleasures.
JOHN RAY, *English Proverbs*, 7. (1670)

Diseases are the price of ill pleasures.
THOMAS FULLER, *Gnomologia*. No. 1297.

But just disease to luxury succeeds,
And ev'ry death its own avenger breeds.
POPE, *Essay on Man*. Epis. iii, l. 165.

2
A disease is farther on the road to being cured when it breaks forth from concealment and manifests its power.
SENECA, *Epistulæ ad Lucilium*. Epis. lvi, sec. 10.

3
Disease is not of the body but of the place. (Non corpore esse, sed loci morbum.)
SENECA, *Epistulæ ad Lucilium*. Epis. civ, sec. 1.

4
Will he steal out of his wholesome bed,
To dare the vile contagion of the night?
SHAKESPEARE, *Julius Cæsar*. Act ii, sc. 1, l. 264.

5
An' I thowt 'twur the will o' the Lord, but
Miss Annie she said it wur draäins,
For she hedn't naw coomfut in 'er, an' arn'd
naw thanks fur 'er paäins.
TENNYSON, *The Village Wife*.

6
My long sickness
Of health and living now begins to mend,
And nothing brings me all things.
SHAKESPEARE, *Timon of Athens*. Act v, sc. 1, l. 189.

7
See the wretch, that long has tost
On the thorny bed of pain,
At length repair his vigour lost,
And breathe and walk again:
The meanest flow'ret of the vale,
The simplest note that swells the gale,
The common sun, the air, the skies,
To him are opening Paradise.
THOMAS GRAY, *On the Pleasure Arising from Vicissitude*, l. 49.

III—Disease: Specific Ailments

8
The common fallacy of consumptive persons, who feel not themselves dying, and therefore still hope to live.
SIR THOMAS BROWNE, *To a Friend*. Sec. 2.

The ancient inhabitants of this island were less troubled with coughs when they went naked, and slept in caves and woods, than men now in chambers and feather-beds.
SIR THOMAS BROWNE, *To a Friend*. Sec. 14.

9
That dire disease, whose ruthless power
Withers the beauty's transient flower.
GOLDSMITH, *The Double Transformation*, l. 75.
Referring to the small-pox.

10
The daughter of limb-relaxing Bacchus and limb-relaxing Aphrodite is limb-relaxing Gout. (Λυσιμελοῦς βάκχου καὶ λυσιμελοῦς Ἀφροδίτης γεννᾶται θυγάτηρ λυσιμελὴς ποδάγρα.)
HEDYLUS. (*Greek Anthology*. Bk. xi, ep. 414.)

From pangs arthritic that infest the toe
Of libertine excess.
COWPER, *The Task*. Bk. i, l. 105.

If gentlemen love the pleasant titillation of the gout, it is all one to the Town Pump
NATHANIEL HAWTHORNE, *The Town Pump*.

For that old enemy the gout
Had taken him in toe.
THOMAS HOOD, *Lieutenant Luff*.

11
Another weepeth over chilblains fell,
Always upon the heel, yet never to be well!
THOMAS HOOD, *The Irish Schoolmaster*.

12
By self-indulgence the dreadful dropsy grows apace. (Crescit indulgens sibi dirus hydrops.)
HORACE, *Odes*. Bk. ii, ode 2, l. 13.

So with those whose bellies swell with dropsy, the more they drink, the more they thirst. (Sic quibus intumuit suffusa venter ab unda, quo plus sunt potæ, plus sitiuntur aquæ.)
OVID, *Fasti*. Bk. i, l. 215.

13
He has a rupture, he has sprung a leak.
BEN JONSON, *The Staple of News*. Act i, sc. 1.

14
A lazar-house it seem'd, wherein were laid
Numbers of all diseas'd, all maladies
Of ghastly spasm or racking torture, qualms
Of heart-sick agony, all feverous kinds,
Convulsions, epilepsies, fierce catarrhs,
Intestine stone and ulcer, colic pangs,
Demoniac phrenzy, moping melancholy,
And moon-struck madness, pining atrophy,
Marasmus, and wide-wasting pestilence,
Dropsies, and asthmas, and joint-racking
rheums.
Dire was the tossing, deep the groans; Des-
pair
Tended the sick, busiest from couch to couch.
MILTON, *Paradise Lost*. Bk. xi, l. 479.

15
Fever, the eternal reproach to the physicians.
MILTON, *Reason of Church Government: Preface*.

If you feed a cold, as is often done, you frequently have to starve a fever.
BERNARR MACFADDEN, *When a Cold is Needed*. (*Physical Culture*, Feb., 1934.) Mr. Macfadden's interpretation of the old adage, "Feed a cold and starve a fever," is undoubtedly the correct one.

He had a fever when he was in Spain,
And when the fit was on him, I did mark
How he did shake; 'tis true, this god did shake:
His coward lips did from their colour fly,
And that same eye whose bend doth awe the
world
Did lose his lustre.
SHAKESPEARE, *Julius Cæsar*. Act i, sc. 2, l. 119.

I've known my lady (for she loves a tune)
For *fevers* take an opera in June:
And, though perhaps you'll think the practice bold,
A midnight park is sov'reign for a *cold*.
YOUNG, *Love of Fame*. Sat. v, l. 185.

A person's age is not dependent upon the number of years that have passed over his head, but upon the number of colds that have passed through it.
DR. SHIRLEY W. WYNNE, Quoting Dr. Woods Hutchinson.

1
Bilious attack—black bile. (Atra bili percita est.)
PLAUTUS, *Amphitruo*, l. 727. (Act ii, sc. 2)

Every disease, but not disease of the bowels.
Babylonian Talmud: Shabbath, p. 11a.

2
Nor for the pestilence that walketh in darkness; nor for the destruction that wasteth at noonday.
Old Testament: Psalms, xci, 6.

3
This apoplexy is, as I take it, a kind of lethargy, an't please your lordship; a kind of sleeping in the blood, a whoreson tingling.
SHAKESPEARE, *II Henry IV*. Act i, sc. 2, l. 125.

The rotten diseases of the south, the guts-griping, ruptures, catarrhs, loads o' gravel i' the back, lethargies, cold palsies, raw eyes, dirt-rotten livers, wheezing lungs, bladders full of imposthume, sciaticas, limekilns i' the palm, incurable bone-ache.
SHAKESPEARE, *Troilus and Cressida*. Act v, sc. 1, l. 18.

A whoreson tisick, a whoreson rascally tisick so troubles me, and I have a rheum in mine eyes too.
SHAKESPEARE, *Troilus and Cressida*, v, 3, 101.

4
Did you ever have the measles, and if so, how many?
ARTEMUS WARD, *The Census*.

DISGRACE

See also Shame

5
Come, Death, and snatch me from disgrace.
BULWER-LYTTON, *Richelieu*. Act iv, sc. 1.

6
Infamy was never incurred for nothing.
EDMUND BURKE, *Impeachment of Warren Hastings*, 25 April, 1789.

Could he with reason murmur at his case,
Himself sole author of his own disgrace?
COWPER, *Hope*, l. 316.

7
To stumble twice against the same stone, is a proverbial disgrace. (Culpa enim illa, bis ad eundem, vulgari reprehensa proverbio est.)
CICERO, *Epistolæ ad Familiares*. Bk. x, epis. 20.

8
A wise and good man can suffer no disgrace.
FABIUS MAXIMUS. (PLUTARCH, *Lives*.)

9
Disgraces are like cherries—one draws another.
GEORGE HERBERT, *Jacula Prudentum*.

10
Who fears disgrace as worse than death. (Pejusque leto flagitium timet.)
HORACE, *Odes*. Bk. iv, ode ix, l. 45.

11
That and that alone is a disgrace to a man, which he has deserved to suffer. (Id demum est homini turpe, quod meruit pati.)
PHÆDRUS, *Fables*. Bk. iii, fab. 11, l. 7.

12
Disgrace is deathless. (Immortalis est infamia.)
PLAUTUS, *Persa*, l. 355. (Act iii, sc. 1.)

The pleasure is over, but the disgrace remains. (Voluptas abit, turpitudino manet.)
UNKNOWN. A Latin proverb.

13
It is better not to live at all than to live disgraced.
SOPHOCLES, *Peleus*. Frag. 445.

Live to be the show and gaze o' the time.
SHAKESPEARE, *Macbeth*. Act v, sc. 8, l. 24.

14
I have lived in such dishonour that the gods
Detest my baseness.
SHAKESPEARE, *Antony and Cleopatra*. Act iv, sc. 14, l. 57.

15
Like a dull actor now,
I have forgot my part, and I am out,
Even to a full disgrace.
SHAKESPEARE, *Coriolanus*. Act v, sc. 3, l. 40.

DISILLUSION

16
There's not a joy the world can give like that it takes away,
When the glow of early thought declines in feeling's dull decay;
'Tis not on youth's smooth cheek the blush alone, which fades so fast,
But the tender bloom of heart is gone, ere youth itself be past.
BYRON, *Stanzas for Music*.

17
Let me keep my eyes on yours;
I dare not look away
Fearing again to see your feet
Cloven and of clay.
CAROLINE GILTINAN, *Disillusioned*.

18
With all our most holy illusions knocked higher than Gilderoy's kite.
We have had a jolly good lesson, and it servès us jolly well right!
RUDYARD KIPLING, *The Lesson*.

19
Ah, what a dusty answer gets the soul
When hot for certainties in this our life!
GEORGE MEREDITH, *Modern Love*. St. 50.

Dusty Answer.
ROSAMOND LEHMANN. Title of Novel.

1
Alas, from what high hope to what relapse
Unlook'd for are we fallen!
MILTON, *Paradise Regained*. Bk. ii, l. 30.

2
The great events with which old story rings
Seem vain and hollow; I find nothing great;
Nothing is left which I can venerate:
So that a doubt almost within me springs
Of Providence, such emptiness at length
Seems at the heart of all things.
WORDSWORTH, *Poems Dedicated to National Independence*. Pt. i, No. 22.

DISLIKE

See also Hatred

3
I do not love thee, Sabidius, nor can I say why;
I can only say this: I do not love thee.
(Non amo te, Sabidi, nec possum dicere quare;
Hoc tantum possum dicere, non amo te.)
MARTIAL, *Epigrams*. Bk. i, epig. 32.

I do not love thee, Dr. Fell:
The reason why I cannot tell;
But this I know, and know full well:
I do not love thee, Dr. Fell.
THOMAS BROWN (1663–1704), had been threatened with expulsion from Christ Church College, Oxford, by the Dean, Dr. John Fell, who promised to forgive him if he would translate impromptu Martial's 32nd epigram, which he did as given above. (BROWN, *Works*. Vol. iv, p. 100.)

Je ne vous aime pas, Hylas;
Je n'en saurais dire la cause,
Je sais seulement une chose:
C'est que ne vous aime pas.
ROGER DE BUSSY, COMTE DE RABUTIN, paraphrase of Martial's epigram.

4
I love thee not, Nell,
But why I can't tell.
THOMAS FORDE, *Virtus Rediviva*.

5
I love him not, but show no reason can
Wherefore, but this, I do not love the man.
ROWLAND WATKYNS, *Antipathy*. (1662)

6
Whom she likes, she likes; whom she dislikes, she dislikes. (Quem amat, amat; quem non amat, non amat.)
PETRONIUS, *Satyricon*. Sec. 37.

7
Ask you what provocation I have had?
The strong antipathy of good to bad.
POPE, *Epilogue to Satires*. Dial. ii, l. 197.

8
Commonly, we say a judgment falls upon a man for something in him we cannot abide.
JOHN SELDEN, *Table-Talk: Judgments*.

9
I do desire we may be better strangers.
SHAKESPEARE, *As You Like It*. Act iii, 2, 274.

10
Some men there are love not a gaping pig;
Some, that are mad if they behold a cat;
And others, when the bagpipe sings i' the nose,
Cannot contain their urine. . . .
As there is no firm reason to be render'd,
Why he cannot abide a gaping pig;
Why he, a harmless necessary cat;
Why he, a woollen bag-pipe; but of force
Must yield to such inevitable shame
As to offend, himself being offended;
So can I give no reason, nor I will not,
More than a lodged hate, and a certain loathing
I bear Antonio, that I follow thus
A losing suit against him.
SHAKESPEARE, *The Merchant of Venice*. Act iv, sc. 1, l. 47.

There is one species of terror which those who are unwilling to suffer the reproach of cowardice have wisely dignified with the name of *antipathy*.
SAMUEL JOHNSON, *Rambler*. No. 126.

11
I see, lady, the gentleman is not in your books.
SHAKESPEARE, *Much Ado About Nothing*. Act i, sc. 1, l. 59.

12
My aversion, my aversion, my aversion of all aversions.
WYCHERLEY, *The Plain-Dealer*. Act ii, sc. 1.

DISPUTE, see Argument

DISRAELI, BENJAMIN

13
What Landor said of Canning is truer of Disraeli, that "he is an understrapper made an overstrapper."
EMERSON, *Journals*, 1868.

14
Then he calls me a traitor. My answer to that is, he is a liar. He is a liar in action and in words. His life is a living lie. He is a disgrace to his species. . . . He possesses just the qualities of the impenitent thief who died upon the Cross, whose name, I verily believe, must have been Disraeli.
DANIEL O'CONNELL, *Speech*, Dublin, 1835.

DISSENSION, see Discord, Quarreling

DISTANCE

15
Kings themselves cannot force the exquisite politeness of distance to capitulate, hid behind its shield of bronze.
HONORÉ DE BALZAC.

16
What looks dark in the distance may brighten as I draw near.
MARY GARDINER BRAINARD, *Not Knowing*. *See also under* TROUBLE.

1
'Tis distance lends enchantment to the view,
And robes the mountain in its azure hue.
CAMPBELL, *Pleasures of Hope*. Pt. i, l. 7.

Mountains when far away appear misty and smooth, but when near at hand they are rugged.
DIOGENES LAERTIUS, *Pyrrho*. Bk. ix, sec. 85.

2
To the vulgar eye, few things are wonderful that are not distant.
THOMAS CARLYLE, *Essays: Burns*.

3
A delusion that distance creates, and that contiguity destroys.
C. C. COLTON, *Lacon*. Vol. ii, No. 109.

So various is the human mind;
Such are the frailties of mankind!
What at a distance charmed our eyes,
Upon attainment, droops, and dies.
JOHN CUNNINGHAM, *Hymen*.

4
So little distant dangers seem:
So we mistake the future's face,
Ey'd thro' Hope's deluding glass;
As yon summits soft and fair,
Clad in colours of the air,
Which, to those who journey near,
Barren, brown and rough appear.
JOHN DYER, *Grongar Hill*, l. 884.

5
As distant prospects please us, but when near
We find but desert rocks, and fleeting air.
SAMUEL GARTH, *The Dispensary*. Can. iii, l. 27.

Love is like a landscape which doth stand
Smooth at a distance, rough at hand.
ROBERT HEGGE, *On Love*.

6
From a distance it is something; and nearby it is nothing. (De loin, c'est quelque chose; et de prés, ce n'est rien.)
LA FONTAINE, *Fables*. Bk. iv, fable 10.

7
The hills of manhood wear a noble face
When seen from far;
The mist of light from which they take their grace
Hides what they are.
RICHARD MONCKTON MILNES, *Carpe Diem*.

A man's best things are nearest him,
Lie close about his feet;
It is the distant and the dim
That we are sick to greet.
R. M. MILNES, *The Men of Old*.

8
Far off his coming shone.
MILTON, *Paradise Lost*. Bk. vi, l. 768.

9
There's a magic in the distance, where the sea-line meets the sky.
ALFRED NOYES, *Forty Singing Seamen*.

10
Some figures monstrous and misshaped appear,
Consider'd singly, or beheld too near,
Which, but proportion'd to their light or place,
Due distance reconciles to form and grace.
POPE, *Essay on Criticism*. Pt. i, l. 171.

11
Far fowls hae fair feathers.
JOHN RAY, *Proverbs: Scottish*.

12
Respect is greater from a distance. (Major e longinquo reverentia.)
TACITUS, *Annals*. Bk. iv, sec. 23. Adapted from "Quæ ex longinquo in majus audiebantur."

Reverent distance.
MASSINGER, *The Maid of Honour*. Act iii, sc. 3.

13
My soul goes out in a longing to touch the skirt of the dim distance.
RABINDRANATH TAGORE, *The Gardener*. No. 5.

14
Remotest Thule. (Ultima Thule.)
VERGIL, *Georgics*. Bk. i, l. 30. Thule, the most remote land known to the Greeks and Romans, may have been Norway or Iceland. Camden says it was one of the Shetland Islands.

Nor shall Thule be the extremity of the world. (Nec sit terris ultima Thule.)
SENECA, *Medea*, l. 375.

I have reached these lands but newly
From an ultimate dim Thule—
From a wild weird clime, that lieth, sublime,
Out of Space, out of Time.
EDGAR ALLAN POE, *Dreamland*. (*Graham's Magazine*, June, 1844.)

15
Glories, like glow-worms, afar off shine bright,
But look'd too near, have neither heat nor light.
JOHN WEBSTER, *The White Devil*. Act v, sc. 1.

16
Yon foaming flood seems motionless as ice . . .
Frozen by distance.
WORDSWORTH, *Address to Kilchurn Castle*.

17
Sweetest melodies
Are those that are by distance made more sweet.
WORDSWORTH, *Personal Talk*, l. 25.

In notes by distance made more sweet.
COLLINS, *The Passions*, l. 60.

18
We're charm'd with distant views of happiness,
But near approaches make the prospect less.
THOMAS YALDEN, *Against Enjoyment*, l. 23.

DISTRUST

See also Suspicion; Trust, Its Folly

19
Distrust yourself, and sleep before you fight.
'Tis not too late to-morrow to be brave.
JOHN ARMSTRONG, *Art of Preserving Health* Bk. iv, l. 456.

The first step to self-knowledge is self-distrust.
J. C. and A. W. Hare, *Guesses at Truth*, p. 454.

A certain amount of distrust is wholesome, but not so much of others as of ourselves.
Madame Necker.

1
Here must thou all distrust behind thee leave.
(Qui se convien lasciare ogni sospetto.)
Dante, *Inferno*. Canto iii, l. 14.

2
They were called Sceptics or inquirers because they were always looking for a solution and never finding one.
Diogenes Laertius, *Pyrrho*. Bk. ix, sec. 70.

3
What loneliness is more lonely than distrust?
George Eliot, *Middlemarch*. Bk. v, ch. 44.

4
Be sober and remember to distrust: these are the very mainsprings of understanding.
Epicharmus. (Ahreus, *De Dialecto Dorico*, 119.)

5
Hear all men speak; but credit few or none.
Robert Herrick, *Distrust*.

6
Once to distrust is never to deserve.
Richard Savage, *Volunteer Laureate*. No. 4.

7
I hold it cowardice
To rest mistrustful where a noble heart
Hath pawn'd an open hand in sign of love.
Shakespeare, *III Henry VI*. Act iv, sc. 2, l. 7.

8
Distrust that man who tells you to distrust.
Ella Wheeler Wilcox, *Distrust*.

DIVIDENDS

See also Money: Its Use

9
Usury is the taking of any interest whatever upon an unproductive loan.
Hilaire Belloc, *Economics for Helen*.

10
With loves and doves, at all events
With money in the Three per Cents.
Robert Browning, *Dîs Aliter Visum*. St. 13.

11
Year after year they voted cent. per cent.,
Blood, sweat, and tear-wrung millions—why? for rent!
Byron, *The Age of Bronze*. Sec. 14.

12
They hired the money, didn't they?
Calvin Coolidge, referring to the money borrowed during the World War by France and the other allies. (1925)

13
The widow and the orphan
That pray for ten per cent,
They clapped their trailers on us
To spy the road we went.
Rudyard Kipling, *The Broken Men*.

14
We have heard it said that five per cent. is the natural interest of money.
Macaulay, *Essays: Southey's Colloquies*.

15
Unearned increment.
John Stuart Mill, *Political Economy*. Bk. v, ch. ii, sec. 5. Phrase used in the land agitation of 1870–71, and probably original with Mill.

16
Do you know the only thing that gives me pleasure? It's to see my dividends coming in.
John D. Rockefeller. (Winkler, *John D.*)

17
The elegant simplicity of the three per cents.
William Scott, Baron Stowell. (Campbell, *Lives of the Chancellors*, x, 212.)

The sweet simplicity of the three per cents.
Benjamin Disraeli, *Speech*, 19 Feb., 1850; *Endymion*. Ch. 96.

18
Through life's dark road his sordid way he wends,
An incarnation of fat dividends.
Charles Sprague, *Curiosity*, l. 393.

19
It is always better policy to earn an interest than to make a thousand pounds.
R. L. Stevenson, *Lay Morals*.

DOCTORS

See also Disease, Medicine

I—Doctors: Apothegms

20
Agelaus killed Acestorides by operating on him, saying, "If he had lived, the poor fellow would have been lame."
Callicter. (*Greek Anthology*. Bk. xi, epig. 121.)

21
Few physicians live well.
William Camden, *Remains*, 322. (1605)

22
Will kicked out the doctor; but when ill indeed,
E'en dismissing the doctor don't always succeed.
George Colman the Younger, *Lodgings for Single Gentlemen*.

23
The first physicians by debauch were made:
Excess began, and sloth sustains the trade.
Dryden, *To John Driden*. Epis. xiv, l. 73.

24
A good bedside manner.
George du Maurier, under a picture in *Punch*, 15 March, 1884. The complete text was: "What sort of a doctor is he?" "Well, I don't know much about his ability, but he has a very good bedside manner."

25
Every physician, almost, hath his favourite disease.
Fielding, *Tom Jones*. Bk. ii, ch. 9.

1
From the physician and lawyer keep not the truth hidden.
JOHN FLORIO, *First Fruites*. Fo. 27. (1578)

From your confessor, lawyer and physician,
Hide not your case on no condition.
SIR JOHN HARINGTON, *Metamorphosis of Ajax*, 98. (1596)

2
God heals, and the Doctor takes the Fee.
BENJAMIN FRANKLIN, *Poor Richard*, 1744.

God heals, and the physician hath the thanks.
GEORGE HERBERT, *Jacula Prudentum*.

Kill thy physician, and the fee bestow
Upon thy foul disease.
SHAKESPEARE, *King Lear*. Act i, sc. 1, l. 164.

3
Physicians, like beer, are best when they are old.
THOMAS FULLER, *The Holy State*, 50. (1642)

Beware of the young doctor and the old barber.
BENJAMIN FRANKLIN, *Poor Richard*, 1733.

Talk of your science! after all is said
There's nothing like a bare and shiny head;
Age lends the graces that are sure to please;
Folks want their doctors mouldy, like their cheese.
O. W. HOLMES, *Rip Van Winkle, M.D.* Pt. ii.

4
After death the doctor. (Après la mort le médicin.)
GEORGE HERBERT, *Jacula Prudentum*.

5
While the doctors consult, the patient dies.
JOHN HEYWOOD, *English Proverbs*.

Who shall decide when doctors disagree,
And soundest casuists doubt, like you and me?
POPE, *Moral Essays*. Epis. iii, l. 1. (1733)

Well, doctors differ.
WYCHERLEY, *Plain-Dealer*. Act i, sc. 1. (1677)

6
Doctor So-much-the-Worse and Doctor-all-the-Better. (Le médecin Tant-pis et le médecin Tant-mieux.)
LA FONTAINE, *Fables*. Bk. v, fab. 12.

Good is a good doctor, but Bad is sometimes a better.
EMERSON, *Conduct of Life: Considerations by the Way*.

7
Diophantus saw Hermogenes, the doctor, in his sleep, and never woke up again, although he was wearing an amulet.
LUCILIUS. (*Greek Anthology*. Bk. xi, ep. 257.)

8
Physician, heal thyself. (Ἰατρὲ, θεράπευσον σεαυτόν.)
New Testament: Luke, iv, 23. (*Vulgate:* Medice, cura tiepsum); JOHN COLET, *Sermon*. (DUNTON, *Phenix*, ii, 8. 1511); THOMAS BECON, *Early Works*, 385. (1543); JOHN LYLY, *Euphues*, 118. (1579) In frequent use thereafter.

Good leech is he that can himself recure.
JOHN LYDGATE, *Daunce of Machabree*, l. 424. (c. 1430)

He is a good physician who cures himself.
TORRIANO. *Piazza Univ.*, 148. (1666)

Not one amongst the doctors, as you'll see,
For his own friends desires to prescribe.
PHILEMON, *Fabulæ Incertæ*. Frag. 46.

Do not imitate those unskilful physicians who profess to possess the healing art in the diseases of others, but are unable to cure themselves.
SULPICIUS. (CICERO, *Ad Familiares*, iv, 5.)

9
Remember how many physicians are dead after puckering up their brows so often over their patients.
MARCUS AURELIUS, *Meditations*. Bk. iv, sec. 48.

10
They that be whole need not a physician, but they that are sick.
New Testament: Matthew, ix, 12.

The physician is superfluous amongst the healthy. (Supervacuus . . . inter sanos medicus.)
TACITUS, *Dialogus de Oratoribus*. Sec. 41.

11
The book of Nature is that which the physician must read; and to do so he must walk over the leaves.
PARACELSUS, (*Encyclopædia Britannica*. Vol. xviii, p. 234. Ninth ed.)

12
A physician is nothing but a consoler of the mind. (Medicus nihil aliud est quam animi consolatio.)
PETRONIUS, *Satyricon*. Sec. 42.

13
A physician can sometimes parry the scythe of death, but has no power over the sand in the hourglass.
HESTER LYNCH PIOZZI, *Letter to Fanny Burney*, 12 Nov., 1781.

14
Banish'd the doctor, and expell'd the friend.
POPE, *Moral Essays*. Epis. iii, l. 330.

15
A sick man does ill for himself who makes the doctor his heir. (Male secum agit æger, medicum qui hæredem facit.)
PUBLILIUS SYRUS, *Sententiæ*. No. 366; FRANCIS BACON, *Ornamenta Rationalia*. No. 31.

He's a fool that makes his doctor his heir.
BENJAMIN FRANKLIN, *Poor Richard*, 1733.

That patient is not like to recover who makes the doctor his heir.
THOMAS FULLER, *Gnomologia*. No. 4368.

16
A hundred devils leap into my body, if there be not more old drunkards than old doctors.
RABELAIS, *Works*. Bk. i, ch. 41; FRANKLIN, *Poor Richard*, 1736.

17
Happy the physician who is called in at the end of the illness.
RABELAIS, *Works*. Bk. iii, ch. 41. Quoted as a proverb.

1
The physician cannot prescribe by letter, he must feel the pulse. (Non potest medicus per epistulas eligere, vena tangenda est.)

SENECA, *Epistulæ ad Lucilium*. Epis. xxii, sec. 1.

The physician prescribes hesitatingly out of his few resources . . . If the patient mends, he is glad and surprised.

EMERSON, *Considerations by the Way*.

If you must listen to his doubtful chest,
Catch the essentials and ignore the rest. . . .
So of your questions: don't, in mercy, try
To pump your patient absolutely dry;
He's not a mollusk squirming in a dish,
You're not Agassiz, and he's not a fish.

O. W. HOLMES, *The Morning Visit*.

2 If thou couldst, doctor, cast
The water of my land, find her disease,
And purge it to a sound and pristine health,
I would applaud thee to the very echo,
That should applaud again.

SHAKESPEARE, *Macbeth*. Act v, sc. 3, l. 50.

3
There are worse occupations in this world than feeling a woman's pulse.

STERNE, *A Sentimental Journey: The Pulse*.

And medical friction is, past contradiction,
Much better performed by a She than a He.

R. H. BARHAM, *The Black Mousquetaire*.

4
Every man at thirty is either a fool or a physician.

EMPEROR TIBERIUS. (PLUTARCH, *De Sanitate*, ii; SUETONIUS, *Tiberius*. Sec. 68.)

He was wont to mock at the arts of physicians, and to ridicule those who, after the age of thirty, needed counsel as to what was good or bad for their bodies.

TACITUS, *Annals*. Bk. vi, sec. 46. Of Tiberius.

Every man is a fool or a physician at forty.

THOMAS FULLER, *Gnomologia*. No. 1428.

5
A physician is a person who pours drugs of which he knows little into a body of which he knows less.

VOLTAIRE. (Helps, *Friends in Council*, ii, 10.)

He's the best physician that knows the worthlessness of the most medicines.

BENJAMIN FRANKLIN, *Poor Richard*, 1733.

There is a great difference between a good physician and a bad one; yet very little between a good one and none at all.

ARTHUR YOUNG, *Travels in France*, 9 Sept., 1787.

6
Medicine men have always flourished. A good medicine man has the best of everything and, best of all, he doesn't have to work.

JOHN B. WATSON, *Behaviorism*, p. 4.

7
In a good surgeon, a hawk's eye: a lion's heart: and a lady's hand.

LEONARD WRIGHT, *Display of Dutie*, 37. (1589)

The knife was still, the surgeon bore
The shattered arm away;
Upon his bed in painless sleep
The noble hero lay.

GEORGE COOPER, *Good-Bye, Old Arm*.

"What! don't you know what a Sawbones is, Sir?" inquired Mr. Weller. "I thought everybody know'd as a Sawbones was a Surgeon."

DICKENS, *Pickwick Papers*. Ch. 30.

A surgeon and not a gentleman.

UNKNOWN. Phrase used in Dominus Rex vs. Seaward (1727) 2 Strange, 739. (See *Illinois Law Review*, xxvii, 329.)

II—Doctors: Their Merits

8
Learn'd he was in medic'nal lore,
For by his side a pouch he wore,
Replete with strange hermetic powder
That wounds nine miles point-blank would solder.

BUTLER, *Hudibras*. Pt. i, canto ii, l. 223.

A skilful leech is better far
Than half a hundred men of war.

BUTLER, *Hudibras*. Pt. i, canto ii, l. 245.

9
This is the way physicians mend or end us,
Secundum artem: but although we sneer
In health,—when ill, we call them to attend us,
Without the least propensity to jeer.

BYRON, *Don Juan*. Canto x, st. 42.

There will be nothing else spoken about . . . till this is either ended or mended.

SCOTT, *Heart of Midlothian*. Ch. 3.

10
Even as a Surgeon, minding off to cut
Some cureless limb, before in use he put
His violent Engines on the vicious member,
Bringeth his Patient in a senseless slumber,
And grief-less then (guided by use and art),
To save the whole, saws off th' infected part.

DU BARTAS, *Devine Weekes and Workes*. Week i, day 6, l. 1018. (Sylvester, tr.)

11
Honour a physician with the honour due unto him for the uses which ye may have of him: for the Lord hath created him. For of the most High cometh healing, and he shall receive honour of the king. The skill of the physician shall lift up his head: and in the sight of great men he shall be in admiration.

Apocrypha: Ecclesiasticus, xxxviii, 1–3.

12
In the hands of the discoverer, medicine becomes a heroic art. . . . Wherever life is dear he is a demigod.

EMERSON, *Uncollected Lectures: Resources*.

13
Physicians are the cobblers, rather the botchers, of men's bodies; as the one patches our tattered clothes, so the other solders our diseased flesh.

JOHN FORD, *The Lover's Melancholy*. Act i, 2.

14
In misery's darkest cavern known,
His useful care was ever nigh. . . .

His virtues walk'd their narrow round,
 Nor made a pause, nor left a void;
And sure th' Eternal Master found
 The single talent well employ'd.

SAMUEL JOHNSON, *On the Death of Dr. Robert Levet.*

1 You behold in me
Only a travelling Physician;
One of the few who have a mission
To cure incurable diseases,
Or those that are called so.

LONGFELLOW, *The Golden Legend.* Pt. i.

2
How the Doctor's brow should smile,
Crown'd with wreaths of camomile.

THOMAS MOORE, *Wreaths for Ministers.*

3
It is not the same thing to feel diseases and to cure them; all men can feel, but the evil is removed only by skill. (Non eadem ratio est sentire et demere morbos; Sensus inest cunctis, tollitur arte malum.)

OVID, *Epistulae ex Ponto.* Bk. iii, epis. 9, l. 15.

4
To the sick man, the physician when he enters seems to have three faces, those of a man, a devil, and a god. When the physician first comes and announces the safety of the patient, then the sick man says: "Behold a god or a guardian angel." (Intrantis medici facies tres esse videntur Ægrotanti; hominis, Daemonis, atque Dei. Cum primum accessit medicus dixitque salutem, "En Deus aut custos angelus," æger ait.)

JOHN OWEN, *The Physician.* (1647)

5
A country doctor needs more brains to do his work passably than the fifty greatest industrialists in the world require.

WALTER B. PITKIN, *The Twilight of the American Mind,* p. 118.

6
There are men and classes of men that stand above the common herd: the soldier, the sailor, and the shepherd not unfrequently; the artist rarely; rarelier still, the clergyman; the physician almost as a rule. He is the flower (such as it is) of our civilisation.

R. L. STEVENSON, *Underwoods: Dedication.*

7
Removed from kind Arbuthnot's aid,
Who knows his art but not his trade,
Preferring his regard for me
Before his credit or his fee.

SWIFT, *In Sickness.* Oct., 1714.

8
To preserve a man alive in the midst of so many chances and hostilities, is as great a miracle as to create him.

JEREMY TAYLOR, *Holy Dying.* Ch. i, sec. 1.

9
But nothing is more estimable than a physician who, having studied nature from his youth, knows the properties of the human body, the diseases which assail it, the remedies which will benefit it, exercises his art with caution, and pays equal attention to the rich and the poor.

VOLTAIRE, *A Philosophical Dictionary: Physicians.* For Hippocratic oath see APPENDIX.

III—Doctors: Their Faults

10
The crowd of physicians has killed me.

EMPEROR ADRIAN, when dying. (MONTAIGNE, *Essays.* Bk. ii, ch. 37.)

But, when the wit began to wheeze,
 And wine had warm'd the politician,
Cur'd yesterday of my disease,
 I died last night of my physician.

PRIOR, *The Remedy Worse than the Disease.*

Physicians kill more than they cure.

EDWARD WARD, *Writings.* Vol. ii, p. 328.

11
Nor bring, to see me cease to live,
Some doctor full of phrase and fame,
To shake his sapient head, and give
The ill he cannot cure a name.

MATTHEW ARNOLD, *A Wish.*

12
A single doctor like a sculler plies,
And all his art and all his physic tries;
But two physicians, like a pair of oars,
Conduct you soonest to the Stygian shores.

JOHN BOOTH, *Epigrams Ancient and Modern,* p. 144.

One doctor, singly like the sculler plies,
The patient struggles, and by inches dies;
But two physicians, like a pair of oars,
Waft him right swiftly to the Stygian shores.

SAMUEL GARTH, *The Dispensary.* Quoted.

13
Though patients die, the doctor's paid.
Licens'd to kill, he gains a place
For what another mounts the gallows.

WILLIAM BROOME, *Poverty and Poetry.*

14
So liv'd our sires, ere doctors learn'd to kill,
And multiplied with theirs the weekly bill.

DRYDEN, *To John Driden, Esq.,* l. 71.

15
Ignorance is not so damnable as humbug, but when it prescribes pills it may happen to do more harm.

GEORGE ELIOT, *Felix Holt.*

16
The body is well, but the purse is sick. (Corpus valet sed ægrotat crumena.)

ERASMUS, *Adagia.*

"Is there no hope?" the sick man said;
The silent doctor shook his head,
And took his leave with signs of sorrow,
Despairing of his fee to-morrow.

JOHN GAY, *The Sick Man and the Angel.*

The alienist is not a joke;
He finds you cracked and leaves you broke.

KEITH PRESTON, *The Alienist.*

17
He doctors others, all diseased himself.

EURIPIDES. (PLUTARCH, *Morals.* Sec. 32.)

1
The patient's ears remorseless he assails;
Murders with jargon where his medicine
fails.

SAMUEL GARTH, *The Dispensary*. Pt. ii, l. 96.

2
The doctor found, when she was dead,
Her last disorder mortal.

GOLDSMITH, *Elegy on Mrs. Mary Blaize.*

3
In fact he did not find M.D.'s
Worth one D — M.

THOMAS HOOD, *Jack Hall.*

4
When people's ill, they comes to I,
I physics, bleeds, and sweats 'em;
Sometimes they live, sometimes they die.
What's that to I? I lets 'em.

DR. J. C. LETTSOM, *On Himself.*

5
Diaulus, lately a doctor, is now an undertaker; what he does as an undertaker, he used also to do as a doctor.

MARTIAL, *Epigrams*. Bk. i, epig. 47.

6
The sun doth always behold your good success, and the earth covers all your ignorance.

SIR JOHN MELTON, *Astrologaster*, 17. (1620) For Greek original of this saying, which was used by many of the seventeenth century writers, see *Notes and Queries*, Ser. viii, vol. 6, p. 246.

If the doctor cures, the sun sees it; if he kills, the earth hides it.

JAMES KELLY, *Scottish Proverbs*, p. 184.

Physicians, of all men, are most happy; whatever good success soever they have the world proclaimeth, and what faults they commit the earth covereth.

QUARLES, *Hieroglyphics of the Life of Man.*

7
That happens because you were never my doctor.

PAUSANIAS, to a physician who remarked on his great age. (PLUTARCH, *Apothegms: Of Pausanias.*)

8
You tell your doctor, that y' are ill,
And what does he, but write a bill,
Of which you need not read one letter:
The worse the scrawl, the dose the better.
For if you knew but what you take,
Though you recover, he must break.

MATTHEW PRIOR, *Alma*. Canto iii, l. 97.

9
I do remember an apothecary,—
And hereabouts he dwells,—which late I
noted
In tatter'd weeds, with overwhelming brows,
Culling of simples; meagre were his looks,
Sharp misery had worn him to the bones:
And in his needy shop a tortoise hung,
An alligator stuff'd, and other skins
Of ill-shaped fishes; and about his shelves
A beggarly account of empty boxes,
Green earthen pots, bladders and musty
seeds,
Remnants of packthread and old cakes of
roses,
Were thinly scatter'd, to make up a show.

SHAKESPEARE, *Romeo and Juliet*. Act v, sc. 1, l. 37.

So modern 'pothecaries, taught the art
By doctors' bills to play the doctor's part,
Bold in the practice of mistaken rules,
Prescribe, apply, and call their masters fools.

POPE, *Essay on Criticism*. Pt. i, l. 108.

10
Trust not the physician;
His antidotes are poison, and he slays
More than you rob.

SHAKESPEARE, *Timon of Athens*. Act iv, sc. 3, l. 434.

11
Apollo was held the god of physic, and sender of diseases. Both were originally the same trade, and still continue.

SWIFT, *Thoughts on Various Subjects.*

12
In fleeing disease you fall into the hands of the doctors. (Si morbum fugiens incidis in medicos.)

UNKNOWN. (Line sometimes added to HORACE, *Odes*, bk. ii, ode 1.)

13
I was well; I would be better; I am here. (Stavo bene; per star meglio; sto qui.)

UNKNOWN, *Epitaph*, on the monument of an Italian Valetudinarian. (ADDISON, *The Spectator*. No. 25.)

This comes of altering fundamental laws and overpersuading by his landlord to take physic (of which he died) for the benefit of the doctor. Stavo bene (was written on his monument) ma per star meglio, sto qui.

DRYDEN, *Dedication of the Æneid.*

DOCTRINE

See also Theology

14
Doctrine is nothing but the skin of truth set up and stuffed.

HENRY WARD BEECHER, *Life Thoughts.*

15
False doctrine, heresy, and schism.

Book of Common Prayer: Litany.

16
No dogmas nail your faith.

ROBERT BROWNING, *Bishop Blougram's Apology.*

17
And prove their doctrine orthodox,
By apostolic blows and knocks.

BUTLER, *Hudibras*. Pt. i, canto i, l. 199.

What makes all doctrines plain and clear?—
About two hundred pounds a year.
And that which was prov'd true before
Prove false again? Two hundred more.

BUTLER, *Hudibras*. Pt. iii, canto i, l. 1277.

1
Carried about with every wind of doctrine.
New Testament: Ephesians, iv, 14.

Carried away with every blast of vain doctrine.
Book of Common Prayer: St. Mark's Day.

Blown about with every wind of criticism.
SAMUEL JOHNSON. (BOSWELL, *Life*. 1784.)

2
Adieu, and remember my doctrines. (Χαίρετε καὶ μέμνησθε τὰ δόγματα.)
EPICURUS. (*Greek Anthology*. Bk. vii, epig. 106.)

3
Doctrines, as infections, fear,
Which are not steeped in vinegar.
MATTHEW GREEN, *The Spleen*, l. 339.

4
Any doctrine that will not bear investigation is not a fit tenant for the mind of an honest man.
R. G. INGERSOLL, *Intellectual Development*.

5
Though all the winds of doctrine were let loose to play upon the earth, so Truth be in the field, we do ingloriously, by licensing and prohibiting, to misdoubt her strength.
MILTON, *Areopagitica*.

6
He who receives
Light from above, from the Fountain of Light,
No other doctrine needs, though granted true.
MILTON, *Paradise Regained*. Bk. iv, l. 288.

7
From the age of fifteen, dogma has been the fundamental principle of my religion. I know of no other religion; I cannot enter into the idea of any other sort of religion; religion, as a mere sentiment, is to me a dream and a mockery.
JOHN HENRY NEWMAN, *Apologia pro Vita Sua*. Ch. 2.

But, whatsoe'er they do or say, I'll build a Christian's hope
On incense and on altar-lights, on chasuble and cope.
BRET HARTE, *The Ritualist*.

8
Live to explain thy doctrine by thy life.
MATTHEW PRIOR, *To Dr. Sherlock*.

No doctrine, however high, however true, can make men happy until it is translated into life.
HENRY VAN DYKE, *Joy and Power*.

DOGS

I—Dogs: Apothegms

9
Who loves me will love my dog also. (Qui me amat, amet et canem meum.)
ST. BERNARD, *In Festo Sancti Michaelis: Sermo Primus*. (c. 1150)

Who loves me loves my dog. (Qui m'aime il aime mon chien.)
LE ROUX DE LINCY, *Trésor de Jehan de Meung*, l. 1567. 13th century MS.

Whosoever loveth me loveth my hound.
SIR THOMAS MORE, *Sermon on the Lord's Prayer*. (c. 1530)

Love me, love my dog.
JOHN HEYWOOD, *Proverbs*. Pt. ii, ch. 9. (1546)

Who loves Jack, loves his dog. (Qui aime Jean, aime son chien.)
UNKNOWN. A French proverb.

10
A dog starved at his master's gate
Predicts the ruin of the state.
WILLIAM BLAKE, *Auguries of Innocence*.

11
Foxes, rejoice! here buried lies your foe.
ROBERT BLOOMFIELD, *The Farmer's Boy: Autumn*, l. 332. Quoted as inscribed on a stone in the wall of Euston Park, in memory of a hound.

12
Dogs begin in jest and end in earnest.
H. G. BOHN, *Hand-Book of Proverbs*, 345.

13
It is hard to teach an old dog tricks.
WILLIAM CAMDEN, *Remains*, p. 326. (1605)

An old dog will learn no new tricks.
THOMAS D'URFEY, *Quixote*. Pt. i, ii, 1.

We are an ancient and dignified people, and you cannot teach an old dog new tricks.
IAN HAY, *The Shallow End*, p. 5.

14
Mother of dead dogs.
CARLYLE, *Reminiscences*. Vol. i, p. 257. Quoted. FROUDE, *Life in London*. Vol. i, p. 196.

15
A dog's nose is ever cold.
JOHN CLARKE, *Parœmiologia*, 72. (1639)

16
Give a dog an ill name and hang him.
GEORGE COLMAN THE ELDER, *Polly Honeycombe*. Sc. 4. (1760)

17
Diogenes, a true-born son of Zeus, a hound of heaven. (Διογένης Ζανὸς γόνος οὐράνιός τε κύων.)
CERCIDAS of Crete. (DIOGENES LAERTIUS, *Diogenes*. Sec. 77.)

The Hound of Heaven.
FRANCIS THOMPSON. Title of poem.

I am called a dog because I fawn on those who give me anything, I yelp at those who refuse, and I set my teeth in rascals.
DIOGENES. (DIOGENES LAERTIUS, *Diogenes*. Sec. 60.)

18
Try that bone on some other dog.
CERVANTES, *Don Quixote*. Pt. i, ch. 32.

19
'Twould make a dog laugh.
J. P. COLLIER, *Roxburghe Ballads*, 158. (c. 1603)

To hear how W. Symons do commend and look sadly . . . would make a dog laugh.
PEPYS, *Diary*, 8 Jan., 1664.

20
Unmissed but by his dogs and by his groom.
COWPER, *The Progress of Error*, l. 95.

1
"I beg its little pardon," said Mr. Mantalini. . . . "It's all up with its handsome friend. He has gone to the demnition bow-wows."
DICKENS, *Nicholas Nickleby*. Pt. ii, ch. 32.

2
A living dog is better than a dead lion.
Old Testament: Ecclesiastes, ix, 4.

At this rate a dead dog would indeed be better than a living lion.
SAMUEL JOHNSON. (BOSWELL, *Life*, ii, 257.)

3
So, when two dogs are fighting in the streets,
With a third dog one of the two dogs meets;
With angry teeth he bites him to the bone,
And this dog smarts for what that dog has done.
FIELDING, *Tom Thumb the Great*. Act i, sc. 5.

Thus when a barber and a collier fight,
The barber beats the luckless collier—white;
The dusty collier heaves his ponderous sack,
And big with vengeance beats the barber—black.
In comes the brick-dust man, with grime o'er spread,
And beats the collier and the barber—red:
Black, red and white in various clouds are tost,
And in the dust they raise the combatants are lost.
CHRISTOPHER SMART, *The Trip to Cambridge*.

4
Who sleepeth with dogs shall rise with fleas.
JOHN FLORIO, *First Fruites*. Fo. 29. (1578)

5
The watch-dog's voice that bayed the whispering wind.
GOLDSMITH, *The Deserted Village*, l. 121.

'Tis sweet to hear the honest watch-dog's bark
Bay deep-mouth'd welcome as we draw near home.
BYRON, *Don Juan*. Canto i, st. 123.

6
And in that town a dog was found,
As many dogs there be,
Both mongrel, puppy, whelp, and hound,
And curs of low degree.
GOLDSMITH, *Elegy on the Death of a Mad Dog*.

7
When a dog is drowning, every one offers him drink.
GEORGE HERBERT, *Jacula Prudentum*.

8
Dogs, ye have had your day. (Ὦ κύνες.)
HOMER, *Odyssey*. Bk. xxii, l. 35. (Pope, tr.)

A dog hath a day.
JOHN HEYWOOD, *Proverbs*. Pt. i, ch. 11. (1546)

Let's spend while we may,
Each dog hath his day.
J. P. COLLIER, *Roxburghe Ballads*. Pt. i, p. 184.

Let Hercules himself do what he may,
The cat will mew, the dog will have his day.
SHAKESPEARE, *Hamlet*. Act v, sc. 1, l. 315.

I've heard a good old proverb say
That ev'ry dog has got his day.
EDWARD WARD, *Hudibras Redivivus*. Pt. ii, canto iii, l. 18.

9
It is bad to awaken a sleeping dog. (Il fait mal éveiller le chien qui dort.)
LE ROUX DE LINCY, *Trésor de Jehan de Meung*. 13th century MS. Quoted as a proverb. Used frequently by medieval writers.

It is nought good a sleeping hound to wake.
CHAUCER, *Troilus and Criseyde*. Bk. iii, l. 764.

It is evil waking of a sleeping dog.
JOHN HEYWOOD, *Proverbs*. Bk. i, ch. 10.

Wake not a sleeping wolf.
SHAKESPEARE, *II Henry IV*. Act i, sc. 2, l. 174; *Henry VIII*. Act i, sc. 1, l. 122.

Do not disturb the sleeping dog. (Non stuzzicare il cane che dorme.)
ALESSANDRO ALLEGRI, *Rime e Prose*.

Let sleeping dogs lie—who wants to rouse 'em?
DICKENS, *David Copperfield*. Ch. 39.

10
Killing the dog does not cure the bite.
ABRAHAM LINCOLN.

11
The dogs eat of the crumbs which fall from their masters' table.
New Testament: Matthew, xv, 27.

12
The censure of a dog is something no man can stand.
CHRISTOPHER MORLEY, *The Haunted Bookshop*, p. 193.

13
The wild boar is often held by a small dog. (A cane non magno sæpe tenetur aper.)
OVID, *Remediorum Amoris*, l. 422.

14
The dog is turned to his own vomit again.
New Testament: II Peter, ii, 22.

15
I have eaten the dog's tongue; I must speak the truth. (De re tamen ego verum dicam, qui linguam caninam comedi.)
PETRONIUS, *Satyricon*. Sec. 43.

16
I am his Highness' dog at Kew;
Pray tell me, sir, whose dog are you?
ALEXANDER POPE, *Engraved on the Collar of a Dog Which He Gave to His Royal Highness*. The Royal Highness in question was Frederick, Prince of Wales.

17
Brag's a good dog, but Holdfast is a better.
JOHN RAY, *English Proverbs*.

And holdfast is the only dog, my duck.
SHAKESPEARE, *Henry V*. Act ii, sc. 3, l. 53.

18
The more I see of men, the more I admire dogs. (Plus je vois les hommes, plus j'admire les chiens.)
MADAME ROLAND. Attributed also to Ouida and to Madame de Sévigné. (See *Notes and Queries*, ser. x, vol. xii, p. 292.)

The more I see of the representatives of the people, the more I admire my dogs. (Plus je vois des représentants du peuple, plus j'admire mes chiens.)
LAMARTINE. (COUNT D'ORSAY, *Letter to John Forster*, 1850.)

The best thing about man is the dog. (Ce qu'il y a de mieux dans l'homme, c'est le chien.)
BELLOY, *Siège de Calais*. Quoted by Voltaire.

The more one comes to know men, the more one admires dogs. (Plus on apprend à connaître l'homme, plus on apprend à estimer le chien.)
JOUSSENEL. (FRANCHE, *La Legende Dorée des Bêtes*, p. 191.)

1
A staff is quickly found to beat a dog.
SHAKESPEARE, *II Henry VI*. Act iii, sc. 1, l. 171.

2
Mine enemy's dog,
Though he had bit me, should have stood that night Against my fire.
SHAKESPEARE, *King Lear*. Act iv, sc. 7, l. 36.

3
A gentle hound should never play the cur.
JOHN SKELTON, *Garland of Laurell*, l. 1436.

I like a bit of a mongrel myself, whether it's a man or a dog: they're the best for everyday.
BERNARD SHAW, *Misalliance*, p. 19.

4
Every dog is a lion at home.
TORRIANO, *Piazza Universale*, 36. (1666)

5
Hunger and ease is a dog's life.
TORRIANO, *Piazza Universale*, 276. (1666)

6
To dog in the manger some liken I could.
THOMAS TUSSER, *Hundreth Good Pointes of Husbandrie*, 69 (1580). Gower (*Confessio Amantis*, ii, 84, c. 1390), and Caxton (*Æsope*, 1484), both tell the fable of the dog who kept the ox away from the hay (Lucian, *Timon*), but, so far as known, Tusser was the first to use the phrase, "dog in the manger."

Like a dog in the manger, he doth only keep it because it shall do nobody else good, hurting himself and others.
ROBERT BURTON, *Anatomy of Melancholy*. Pt. i, sec. ii, mem. 3, subs. 12.

Nothing in the world so hateful as a dog in the manger.
PEPYS, *Diary*, 25 Nov., 1663.

7
If you pick up a starving dog and make him prosperous, he will not bite you. That is the principal difference between a dog and a man.
MARK TWAIN, *Pudd'nhead Wilson's Calendar*.

8
A dog so called from its not singing. (Canis a non canendo.)
VARRO, *De Linguâ Latina*.

9
A reasonable amount o' fleas is good fer a dog —keeps him from broodin' over *bein'* a dog.
EDWARD NOYES WESTCOTT, *David Harum*, p. 284.

10
The spaniels of the world.
WYCHERLEY, *The Plain-Dealer*. Act i, sc. 1.

11
The yellowest cur I ever knew
Was to the boy who loved him true.
UNKNOWN. *The Dog*.

II—Dogs: Their Bark and Bite

12
Dogs barking aloof bite not at hand.
WILLIAM CAMDEN, *Remains*, 321. (1605)

Dogs that bark at a distance never bite.
THOMAS FULLER, *Gnomologia*. No. 1317.

13
Dogs bark as they are bred, and fawn as they are fed.
A. B. CHEALES, *Proverbial Folk-Lore*, 140.

At thieves I bark'd, at lovers wagg'd my tail,
And thus I pleased both Lord and Lady Frail.
JOHN WILKES, *Epitaph on the Lap-dog of Lady Frail*.

14
An old dog barks not in vain.
JOHN FLORIO, *First Fruites*. Fo. 28. (1578)

Old dogs bark not for nothing.
THOMAS FULLER, *Gnomologia*. No. 3711.

15
Presumed to bark the more that he might bite the less.
FULLER, *Church History*. Bk. viii, sec. 2. (1655)

His bark is worse than his bite.
GEORGE HERBERT, *Jacula Prudentum*.

Her new bark is worse than ten times her old bite.
J. R. LOWELL, *A Fable for Critics*, l. 28.

16
If the old dog bark, he gives counsel.
GEORGE HERBERT, *Jacula Prudentum*.

17
A dog will bark ere he bite.
JOHN HEYWOOD, *Proverbs*. Pt. ii, ch. 7.

Dogs ought to bark before they bite.
THOMAS FULLER, *Gnomologia*. No. 1316.

18
Those dogs bite least that greatest barkings keep.
THOMAS HOWELL, *H. His Devises*, 30. (1581)

19
They are all dumb dogs, they cannot bark.
Old Testament: Isaiah, lvi, 10.

20
A waking dog doth afar off bark at a sleeping lion.
JOHN LYLY, *Endymion*. Act iii, sc. 1. (1591)

21
Like dogs that bark by custom.
JAMES MABBE, *Celestina: Dedication*. (1631)

It is a common proverb, "Dogs bark more for custom than fierceness."
SIR GEORGE WHARTON, *Merlini Anglici: Preface*. (1647)

22
What! keep a dog and bark myself!
JOHN RAY, *English Proverbs*. (1670)

I won't keep a dog and bark myself.
SWIFT, *Polite Conversation*. Dial. i. (1738)

23
A cowardly cur barks more fiercely than it bites. (Canis timidus vehementius latrat quam mordet.)
QUINTUS CURTIUS RUFUS, *De Rebus Gestis Alexandri Magni*, vii, 14.

1
Dogs bark at me as I halt by them.
SHAKESPEARE, *Richard III*. Act i, sc. 1, l. 23.

2
Let dogs delight to bark and bite,
For God hath made them so;
Let bears and lions growl and fight,
For 'tis their nature. too.
ISAAC WATTS, *Divine Songs*. No. 16.

3
The bitch biteth ill when she berke still.
UNKNOWN, *Proverbs of Alfred*, 137. (c. 1270)

A still dog bites sore.
UNKNOWN, *Tell-Trothes*, 15. (1593)

The slowest barker is the surest biter.
D. TUVILL, *Vade Mecum*, 130. (1638)

It is the mute hound that bites the hardest.
A. CONAN DOYLE, *Sir Nigel*. Ch. 14. (1906)

III—Dogs: Friends and Companions

4
People who lived here long ago
Did by this stone, it seems, intend
To name for future times to know
The dachs-hound, Geist, their little friend.
MATTHEW ARNOLD, *Geist's Grave*.

5
He was such a dear little cock-tailed pup.
R. H. BARHAM, *Mr. Peter's Story*.

6
Nay, brother of the sod,
What part hast thou in God?
What spirit art thou of?
It answers, "Love."
KATHARINE LEE BATES, *Laddie*.

7
But the poor dog, in life the firmest friend,
The first to welcome, foremost to defend.
BYRON, *Inscription on a Newfoundland Dog*.

8
On the green banks of Shannon, when Sheelah was nigh,
No blithe Irish lad was so happy as I;
No harp like my own could so cheerily play,
And wherever I went was my poor dog Tray.
THOMAS CAMPBELL, *The Harper*.

Old dog Tray's ever faithful,
Grief cannot drive him away;
He's gentle, he is kind; I'll never, never find
A better friend than old dog Tray.
STEPHEN COLLINS FOSTER, *Old Dog Tray*.

9
His faithful dog salutes the smiling guest.
CAMPBELL, *Pleasures of Hope*. Pt. i, l. 86.

10
And still I like to fancy that,
Somewhere beyond the Styx's bound,
Sir Guy's tall phantom stoops to pat
His little phantom hound!
PATRICK R. CHALMERS, *"Hold."*

11
He's dead. Oh! lay him gently in the ground!
And may his tomb be by this verse renowned:
Here Shock, the pride of all his kind, is laid,
Who fawned like man, but ne'er like man betrayed.
JOHN GAY, *An Elegy on a Lap-Dog*.

12
In dreams I see them spring to greet,
With rapture more than tail can tell,
Their master of the silent feet
Who whistles o'er the asphodel,
And through the dim Elysian bounds
Leads all his cry of little hounds.
JOHN HALSHAM, *My Last Terrier*.

13
There is sorrow enough in the natural way
From men and women to fill our day;
And when we are certain of sorrow in store
Why do we always arrange for more?
Brothers and Sisters, I bid you beware
Of giving your heart to a dog to tear.
RUDYARD KIPLING, *"The Power of the Dog."*

Into the Presence, flattening while I crawl—
From head to tail, I do confess it all.
Mine was the fault—deal me the stripes—but spare
The Pointed Finger which I cannot bear!
The Dreadful Tone in which my Name is named,
That sends me 'neath the sofa-frill ashamed!
(Yet to be near thee I would face the woe.)
If Thou reject me, whither shall I go?
RUDYARD KIPLING, *Supplication of the Black Aberdeen*.

14
The curate thinks you have no soul;
I know that he has none.
ST. JOHN LUCAS, *The Curate Thinks*.

But in some canine Paradise
Your wraith, I know, rebukes the moon.
ST. JOHN LUCAS, *To a Dog*.

15
Fierce in the woods, gentle in the home.
(Silvis aspera, blanda domi.)
MARTIAL, *Epigrams*. Bk. xi, epig. 69, l. 2.

16
The dog is man's best friend.
He has a tail on one end.
Up in front he has teeth.
And four legs underneath.
OGDEN NASH, *An Introduction to Dogs*.

17
Histories are more full of examples of the fidelity of dogs than of friends.
POPE, *Letters to and from H. Cromwell, Esq.* Letter 10, 9 Oct., 1709.

18
I have a dog of Blenheim birth,
With fine long ears and full of mirth;
And sometimes, running o'er the plain,
He tumbles on his nose:
But quickly jumping up again,
Like lightning on he goes!
JOHN RUSKIN, *My Dog Dash*.

19
Two dogs of black St. Hubert's breed,
Unmatched for courage, breath, and speed.
SCOTT, *Lady of the Lake*. Canto i, st. 7.

1
The little dogs and all,
Tray, Blanche, and Sweetheart, see, they bark at me.
SHAKESPEARE, *King Lear*. Act iii, sc. 6, l. 65.

Mastiff, greyhound, mongrel grim,
Hound or spaniel, brach or lym,
Or bobtail tyke or trundle-tail.
SHAKESPEARE, *King Lear*. Act iii, sc. 6, l. 71.

Ay, in the catalogue ye go for men;
As hounds, and greyhounds, mongrels, spaniels, curs,
Shoughs, water-rugs and demi-wolves, are clept
All by the name of dogs: the valued file
Distinguishes the swift, the slow, the subtle,
The housekeeper, the hunter, every one
According to the gift which bounteous nature
Hath in him closed.
SHAKESPEARE, *Macbeth*. Act iii, sc. 1, l. 92.

2
Mine is no narrow creed,
And He who gave thee being did not frame
The mystery of life to be the sport
Of merciless Man. There is another world
For all that live and move,—a better one!
Where the proud bipeds, who would fain confine
Infinite goodness to the little bounds
Of their own charity, may envy thee.
SOUTHEY, *On the Death of a Favourite Spaniel*.

3
And the young man's dog [went] with them.
Apocrypha: Tobit, v, 16.

4
We are two travellers, Roger and I.
Roger's my dog.—Come here, you scamp!
Jump for the gentlemen,—mind your eye!
Over the table,—look out for the lamp!—
The rogue is growing a little old;
Five years we've tramped through wind and weather,
And slept out-doors when nights were cold,
And ate and drank—and starved—together.
J. T. TROWBRIDGE, *The Vagabonds*.

5
The stone tells that it covers the white Maltese dog, Eumelus' faithful companion. They called him Bull while he still lived, but now the silent paths of night possess his voice.
TYMNES, *Epitaph on a Dog*. (*Greek Anthology*. Bk. vii, No. 211.)

6
Gentlemen of the Jury: The one absolutely unselfish friend that man can have in this selfish world, the one that never deserts him, the one that never proves ungrateful or treacherous, is his dog.
SENATOR GEORGE GRAHAM VEST, *Eulogy on the Dog*. (ELBERT HUBBARD, *Pig-Pen Pete*, p. 178.)

7
His friends he loved. His fellest earthly foes—
Cats—I believe he did but feign to hate.
My hand will miss the insinuated nose,
Mine eyes the tail that wagged contempt at Fate.
WILLIAM WATSON, *An Epitaph*.

8
My little old dog:
A heart-beat At my feet.
EDITH WHARTON, *A Lyrical Epigram*.

9
Once he passed by as a dog was being beaten, and pitying it, spoke as follows: "Stop and beat it not; for the soul is that of a friend."
XENOPHANES, *Of Diogenes*. (*Greek Anthology*. Bk. vii, epig. 120.)

DOLLAR, THE

10
The Americans have little faith. They rely on the power of the dollar.
EMERSON, *Nature, Addresses and Lectures: Man the Reformer*.

11
You know a dollar would go much farther in those days.
W. M. EVARTS, to Lord Coleridge, during a visit to Mount Vernon, when the latter remarked that he had heard that Washington was able to throw a dollar across the Potomac. (LUCY, *Diary of Two Parliaments*.) "But," said Mr. Evarts, "I met a journalist just afterwards who said, 'Oh, Mr. Evarts, you should have said that it was a small matter to throw a dollar across the Potomac for a man who had chucked a Sovereign across the Atlantic.'" (*Collections and Recollections*, p. 181.)

12
"The American nation in the Sixth Ward is a fine people," he says. "They love th' eagle," he says, "on the back iv a dollar."
F. P. DUNNE, *Mr. Dooley in Peace and War: Oratory on Politics*.

13
The almighty dollar, that great object of universal devotion throughout our land, seems to have no genuine devotees in these peculiar villages.
WASHINGTON IRVING, *Wolfert's Roost: The Creole Village*. First appeared in the *Knickerbocker Magazine*, Nov., 1836.

As we swept away from the shore I cast back a wistful eye upon the moss grown roofs and ancient elms of the village and prayed that the inhabitants might long retain their happy ignorance—their absence of all enterprise and improvements—their respect for the fiddle and their contempt for the Almighty Dollar.
WASHINGTON IRVING, *The Crayon Papers: The Creole Village*. (1837)

"The Almighty Dollar" is the only object of worship.
UNKNOWN, *Editorial, Philadelphia Public Ledger*, 2 Dec., 1836.

15
Till he disbursed at Saint Colme's inch

Ten thousand dollars to our general use.

SHAKESPEARE, *Macbeth*. Act i, sc. 2, l. 61. Dollar was the English name of the large German silver coin called *thaler*, and also of the large silver Spanish coin called the Spanish dollar, or piece of eight, as containing eight reals.

Gonzalo: Comes to the entertainer—
Sebastian: A dollar.

SHAKESPEARE, *The Tempest*. Act ii, sc. 1, l. 18.

1
Dollar Diplomacy.

AUTHOR UNKNOWN. A term applied in 1910 to the activities of Philander Knox, Secretary of State, in securing opportunities for the employment of American capital abroad. (*Harper's Weekly*, 23 Apr., 1910, p. 8.)

DONKEY, see Ass

DOUBT

See also Atheism

I—Doubt: Apothegms

2
When in doubt do nowt.

BRIDGE, *Cheshire Proverbs*, 155.

3
Who knows most, doubts not.

ROBERT BROWNING, *Two Poets of Croisic*, l. 158.

4
He could raise scruples dark and nice,
And after solve 'em in a trice:
As if Divinity had catch'd
The itch, on purpose to be scratch'd.

BUTLER, *Hudibras*. Pt. i, canto 1, l. 163.

5
My mind is in a state of philosophical doubt.

S. T. COLERIDGE, *Table Talk*. 30 Apr., 1830.

6
I don't believe there's no sich a person.

DICKENS, *Martin Chuzzlewit*. Ch. 49. Betsy Prig, referring to an imaginary Mrs. Harris.

7
I am the doubter and the doubt.

EMERSON, *Brahma*.

8
Scepticism is unbelief in cause and effect.

EMERSON, *Conduct of Life: Worship*.

Scepticism is slow suicide.

EMERSON, *Essays, First Series: Self-Reliance*.

A skeptic is not one who doubts, but one who examines.

SAINTE-BEUVE.

9
He that casteth all doubts shall never be resolved.

THOMAS FULLER, *Gnomologia*. No. 2063.

10
Of that there is no manner of doubt—
No probable, possible shadow of doubt—
No possible doubt whatever.

W. S. GILBERT, *The Gondoliers*. Act i.

11
I will listen to any one's convictions, but pray keep your doubts to yourself.

GOETHE, *Conversations with Eckermann*.

12
Man may doubt here and there, but mankind does not doubt. The universal conscience is larger than the individual conscience, and that constantly comes in to correct and check our own infidelity.

H. R. HAWEIS, *Speech in Season*. Bk. iii, 328.

13
How prone to doubt, how cautious are the wise!

HOMER, *Odyssey*. Bk. xiii, l. 375. (Pope, tr.)

14
Human minds so move about,
Only if fenced round with doubt;
Only if denied their grasp
Gain the everlasting clasp.
Only streams which fettered be
Fret their way at last to sea.

LAURENCE HOUSMAN, *Bonds*.

15
I took thought, and invented what I conceived to be the appropriate title of "agnostic." It came into my head as suggestively antithetic to the "Gnostic" of Church history who professed to know so much about the very things of which I was ignorant, and I took the earliest opportunity of parading it at our society, to show that I, too, had a tail like the other foxes. To my great satisfaction, the term took; and when the *Spectator* had stood godfather to it, any suspicion in the minds of respectable people that a knowledge of its parentage might have awakened was, of course, completely lulled.

THOMAS HENRY HUXLEY, *Agnosticism*. (*Nineteenth Century*, Feb., 1889.)

16
There is no doubt in this book.

The Koran. Ch. 1.

17
An honest man can never surrender an honest doubt.

WALTER MALONE, *The Agnostic's Creed*.

18
O thou of little faith, wherefore didst thou doubt?

New Testament: Matthew, xiv, 31. (Modicæ fidei, quare dubitasti?—*Vulgate*.)

Though thus, my friend, so long employed,
And so much midnight oil destroyed,
I must confess, my searches past,
I only learned to doubt at last.

THOMAS MOORE, *Morality*.

19
She who, wise as she was fair,
For subtle doubts had simple clues.

COVENTRY PATMORE, *The Angel in the House: Epilogue*. Pt. iii.

20
I do not like, "but yet," it does allay
The good precedence; fie upon "but yet!"
"But yet" is as a gaoler to bring forth
Some monstrous malefactor.

SHAKESPEARE, *Antony and Cleopatra*. Act ii, sc. 5, l. 50.

And yet another yet.
SHAKESPEARE, *The Two Gentlemen of Verona*. Act ii, sc. 1, l. 126.

1
No hinge, nor loop To hang a doubt on.
SHAKESPEARE, *Othello*. Act iii, sc. 3, l. 366.

2
Cleave ever to the sunnier side of doubt.
TENNYSON, *The Ancient Sage*, l. 68.

For all my mind is clouded with a doubt.
TENNYSON, *The Passing of Arthur*, l. 426.

3
When the mind is in doubt, slight influences impel it hither and thither. (Dum in dubiost animus, paulo momento huc vel illuc inpellitur.)
TERENCE, *Andria*, l. 268. (Act i, sc. 5.)

4
I follow my law and fulfil it all duly—
And look! when your doubt runneth high,
North points to the needle!
EDITH M. THOMAS, *The Compass*.

5
The slow-consenting Academic doubt.
JAMES THOMSON, *Liberty*. Pt. ii, l. 240.

6
Doubt makes the mountain which faith can move.
UNKNOWN. (*Toledo* (Ohio) *Blade*. Jan., 1931.)

II—Doubt: Its Virtues

7
I love the doubt, the dark, the fear,
That still surroundeth all things here.
ALFRED AUSTIN, *Hymn to Death*.

8
Who never doubted never half believed;
Where doubt, there truth is,—'tis her shadow.
P. J. BAILEY, *Festus: A Country Town*.

9
Rather I prize the doubt
Low kinds exist without,
Finished and finite clods, untroubled by a spark.
ROBERT BROWNING, *Rabbi Ben Ezra*. St. 3.

I love not mystery or doubt.
SCOTT, *Rokeby*. Canto iii, st. 11.

10
Doubt charms me no less than knowledge. (Non menche saver, dubbiar m' aggrata.)
DANTE, *Inferno*. Canto xi, l. 93.

11
The first step towards philosophy is incredulity.
DENIS DIDEROT, *Last Conversation*.

By doubting we come at the truth. (Dubitando ad veritatem pervenimus.)
CICERO.

12
Doubt is the beginning, not the end, of wisdom.
GEORGE ILES, *Jottings*.

13
Too much doubt is better than too much credulity.
ROBERT G. INGERSOLL, *How to Reform Mankind*.

14
The man that feareth, Lord, to doubt,
In that fear doubteth thee.
GEORGE MACDONALD, *Disciple*. Pt. xxxii, st. 15.

15
To doubt is safer than to be secure.
PHILIP MASSINGER, *A Very Woman*. Act i, sc. 1.

16
William James used to preach the "will to believe." For my part, I should wish to preach the "will to doubt." . . . What is wanted is not the will to believe, but the wish to find out, which is the exact opposite.
BERTRAND RUSSELL, *Sceptical Essays*, p. 155.

17
To be once in doubt Is once to be resolv'd.
SHAKESPEARE, *Othello*. Act iii, sc. 3, l. 179.

The road to resolution lies by doubt.
FRANCIS QUARLES, *Emblems*. Bk. iv, emb. 2.

18
Modest doubt is call'd The beacon of the wise.
SHAKESPEARE, *Troilus and Cressida*. Act ii, sc. 2, l. 15.

19
To believe with certainty we must begin with doubting.
STANISLAUS, KING OF POLAND, *Maxims*. No. 61.

20
There lives more faith in honest doubt,
Believe me, than in half the creeds.
TENNYSON, *In Memoriam*. Pt. xcvi, st. 3.

21
Ever insurgent let me be,
Make me more daring than devout;
From sleek contentment keep me free,
And fill me with a buoyant doubt.
LOUIS UNTERMEYER, *Prayer*.

III—Doubt: Its Penalties

22
I hope, I fear, resolved, and yet I doubt,
I'm cold as ice, and yet I burn as fire;
I wot not what, and yet I much desire,
And trembling too, am desperately stout.
WILLIAM ALEXANDER, EARL OF STIRLING, *Aurora*. Sonnet lxviii.

23
Doubt is the accomplice of tyranny.
AMIEL, *Journal*, 30 Dec., 1866.

24
Through doubt error acquires honour; truth suffers repulse.
FRANCIS BACON, *De Augmentis Scientiarum*. Pt i, Bk. 4, ch. 1.

25
There are minutes that fix the fate
Of battles and of nations,
(Christening the generations,)
When valor were all too late,
If a moment's doubt be harbored.
HENRY HOWARD BROWNELL, *The Bay Fight*.

26
Melt, and dispel, ye spectre-doubts, that roll
Cimmerian darkness on the parting soul!
CAMPBELL, *The Pleasures of Hope*. Pt. ii, l. 263.

1
O Incredulity! the wit of fools,
That slovenly will split on all things fair;
The coward's castle, and the sluggard's cradle.
GEORGE CHAPMAN, *De Guiana*, l. 86.

2
Uncertain ways unsafest are,
And doubt a greater mischief than despair.
SIR JOHN DENHAM, *Cooper's Hill*.

3
You prove only too clearly that seeking to know is often but learning to doubt. (Vous ne prouvez que trop que chercher à connaître n'est souvent qu'apprendre à douter.)
ANTOINETTE DE DESHOULIÈRES, *Epigram*. Elaborating the French proverb: "Chercher à connaître c'est chercher à douter."

4
Doubt indulged soon becomes doubt realized.
FRANCES RIDLEY HAVERGAL, *Royal Bounty*.

5
Knowledge of divine things is lost to us by incredulity.
HERACLITUS. (PLUTARCH, *Lives: Coriolanus*.)

6
Chase Anguish and doubt and fear and sorrow and pain
From mortal or immortal minds.
MILTON, *Paradise Lost*. Bk. i, l. 557.

7
But the gods are dead—
Ay, Zeus is dead, and all the gods but Doubt,
And doubt is brother devil to Despair!
JOHN BOYLE O'REILLY, *Prometheus: Christ*.

8
Now conscience chills her, and now passion burns,
And atheism and religion take their turns;
A very heathen in the carnal part,
Yet still a sad, good Christian at her heart.
POPE, *Moral Essays*. Epis. ii, l. 65. Referring to the Duchess of Hamilton.

9
He that doubteth is damned.
New Testament: Romans, xiv, 23.

He who doubts is damned: *See* AMERICA: FAMOUS PHRASES.

10
We talk of a credulous vulgar without always recollecting that there is a vulgar incredulity, which . . . finds it easier to doubt than to examine.
SCOTT, *Fair Maid of Perth: Introduction*.

11
I am cabin'd, cribb'd, confined, bound in
To saucy doubts and fears.
SHAKESPEARE, *Macbeth*. Act iii, sc. 4, l. 24.

Doubts, horrors, superstitious fears
Saddened and dimmed descending years.
SCOTT, *Rokeby*. Canto i, st. 17.

12
Our doubts are traitors
And make us lose the good we oft might win
By fearing to attempt.
SHAKESPEARE, *Measure for Measure*. Act i, sc. 4, l. 77.

13
You tell me, doubt is Devil-born.
TENNYSON, *In Memoriam*. Pt. xcvi, st. 1.

Leave thou thy sister, when she prays,
Her early heaven, her happy views;
Nor thou with shadowed hint confuse
A life that leads melodious days.
TENNYSON, *In Memoriam*. Pt. xxxiii, st. 2.

DOVE

See also Eagle

14
And there my little dove did sit
With feathers softly brown.
E. B. BROWNING, *My Doves*.

15
Of doves I have a dainty pair
Which, when you please to take the air,
About your head shall gently hover.
Your clear brow from the sun to cover,
And with their nimble wings shall fan you
That neither cold nor heat shall tan you,
And like umbrellas, with their feathers
Shield you in all sorts of weathers.
MICHAEL DRAYTON, *My Doves*.

16
As when the dove returning bore the mark
Of earth restor'd to the long lab'ring ark,
The relics of mankind, secure of rest,
Oped every window to receive the guest,
And the fair bearer of the message bless'd.
DRYDEN, *To Her Grace of Ormond*, l. 70.

17
But the dove found no rest for the sole of her foot.
Old Testament: Genesis, viii, 9.

18
Listen, sweet Dove, unto my song,
And spread thy golden wings in me;
Hatching my tender heart so long,
Till it get wing and fly away with Thee.
GEORGE HERBERT, *The Church: Whitsunday*.

19
But who does hawk at eagles with a dove?
GEORGE HERBERT, *The Sacrifice*.

20
See how that pair of billing doves
With open murmurs own their loves
And, heedless of censorious eyes,
Pursue their unpolluted joys:
No fears of future want molest
The downy quiet of their nest.
MARY WORTLEY MONTAGU, *Verses Written in a Garden*.

21
The Dove,
On silver pinions, wing'd her peaceful way.
MONTGOMERY, *The Pelican Island*. Canto i, l. 173.

1
As the hawk is wont to pursue the trembling dove. (Ut solet accipiter trepidas agitare columbas.)
OVID, *Metamorphoses*. Bk. v, l. 606.

2
Doves have made a nest in the soldier's helmet: see how Venus loveth Mars. (Militis in galea nidum fecere columbæ: Apparet Marti quam sit amica Venus.)
PETRONIUS, *Fragments*. No. 96.

3
Not half so swift the trembling doves can fly,
When the fierce eagle cleaves the liquid sky;
Not half so swiftly the fierce eagle moves,
When thro' the clouds he drives the trembling doves.
POPE, *Windsor Forest*, l. 185.

And mine to fly like doves whom th' eagle doth affray.
SPENSER, *Faerie Queene*. Bk. v, canto xii, st. 5.

4
Oh that I had wings like a dove! for then would I fly away and be at rest.
Old Testament: Psalms, lv, 6.

The Wings of the Dove.
HENRY JAMES. Title of novel.

5
As patient as the female dove.
SHAKESPEARE, *Hamlet*. Act v, sc. 1, l. 309.

Thou wilt be as valiant as the wrathful dove, or most magnanimous mouse.
SHAKESPEARE, *II Henry IV*. Act iii, sc. 2, l. 171.

The dove and very blessed spirit of peace.
SHAKESPEARE, *II Henry IV*. Act iv, sc. 1, l. 46.

6
I will roar you as gently as any sucking dove.
SHAKESPEARE, *A Midsummer-Night's Dream*. Act i, sc. 2, l. 84.

Modest as the dove.
SHAKESPEARE, *The Taming of the Shrew*. Act ii, sc. 1, l. 295.

7
Doves will peck in safeguard of their brood.
SHAKESPEARE, *III Henry VI*. Act ii, sc. 2, l. 18.

8
Who will not change a raven for a dove?
SHAKESPEARE, *A Midsummer-Night's Dream*. Act ii, sc. 2, l. 114.

So shows a snowy dove trooping with crows.
SHAKESPEARE, *Romeo and Juliet*. Act i, 5, 50.

9
In the spring a livelier iris changes on the burnish'd dove.
TENNYSON, *Locksley Hall*, l. 19.

10
And oft I heard the tender dove
In firry woodlands making moan.
TENNYSON, *The Miller's Daughter*, l. 41.

I heard a Stock-dove sing or say
His homely tale, this very day;
His voice was buried among trees,
Yet to be come at by the breeze:
He did not cease; but cooed—and cooed;
And somewhat pensively he wooed:
He sang of love, with quiet blending,
Slow to begin, and never ending;
Of serious faith, and inward glee;
That was the song,—the song for me!
WORDSWORTH, *O Nightingale! Thou Surely Art*.

DOWRY

See also Marriage and Money

11
Often in marriage the dowry, if overlarge, becomes a cause of offense. (Sæpe in conjugiis fit noxia, si nimia est dos.)
AUSONIUS, *Technopaegnion*. Sec. vii, l. 1.

12
Then hey for a lass wi' a tocher,
The nice yellow guineas for me!
BURNS, *Hey for a Lass wi' a Tocher*.

Oh, gie me the lass that has acres o' charms,
Oh, gie me the lass wi' the weel-stockit farms.
BURNS, *Hey for a Lass wi' a Tocher*.

13
He who gets a dowry with his wife, sells himself for it.
EURIPIDES, *Phæthon: Fragment*.

I sold myself for a dowry. (Dote imperium vendidi.)
PLAUTUS, *Asinaria*, l. 87. (Act i, sc. 1.)

14
Old women's gold is not ugly.
THOMAS FULLER, *Gnomologia*.

15
There is no character so contemptible as a man that is a fortune-hunter.
GOLDSMITH, *Vicar of Wakefield*. Ch. 5.

16
A great dowry is a bed full of brabbles.
GEORGE HERBERT, *Jacula Prudentum*. No. 754.

17
I would rather be poor a thousand times over than grow wealthy through my wife.
ST. JOHN CHRYSOSTOM, *Marriages as They Were and as They Are*, ii, 355.

18
Nor has he pined under the darts of Venus; he was never burnt by her torch. It was the dowry that lighted his fires, the dowry that shot those arrows. (Nec pharetris Veneris macer est aut lampade fervet; Inde faces ardent, veniunt a dote sagittæ.)
JUVENAL, *Satires*. Sat. vi, l. 138.

19
Alas that I took Crobyle to wife,
With sixteen talents and a foot of nose.
MENANDER, *Plocium*. Frag. 402.

20
I do not consider that my dowry is that which people call a dowry, but purity and modesty and quiet desire.
PLAUTUS, *Amphitryon*, l. 839. (Act ii, sc. 2.)

She is herself a dowry.
SHAKESPEARE, *King Lear*. Act i, sc. 1, l. 244.

1
Money is a beautiful dowry. (Pulchra edepol dos pecuniast.)
PLAUTUS, *Epidicus*, l. 180. (Act ii, sc. 1.)

2
I'll give thee this plague for thy dowry.
SHAKESPEARE, *Hamlet*. Act iii, sc. 1, l. 140.

3
A dowry for a queen.
SHAKESPEARE, *Love's Labour's Lost*. Act ii, sc. 1, l. 8.

Her dowry shall weigh equal with a queen.
SHAKESPEARE, *King John*. Act ii, sc. 1, l. 486.

4
I tell you, he that can lay hold of her
Shall have the chinks.
SHAKESPEARE, *Romeo and Juliet*. Act i, sc. 5, l. 118.

5
Only this thing is said;
That white and gold and red,
God's three chief words, man's bread
And oil and wine,
Were given her for dowers.
A. C. SWINBURNE, *Madonna Mia*. St. 8.

DRAMA, see Stage

DREAMS

I—Dreams: Apothegms

6
I dreamt that I dwelt in marble halls,
With vassals and serfs at my side.
ALFRED BUNN, *Bohemian Girl: Song*.

7
Life and love are all a dream.
ROBERT BURNS, *The Lament*, l. 8.

I had a dream, which was not all a dream.
BYRON, *Darkness*, l. 1.

A change came o'er the spirit of my dream.
BYRON, *The Dream*. St. 3.

8
Thy wise dreams and fables of the sky.
HOMER, *Odyssey*. Bk. ii, l. 208. (Pope, tr.)

The vain dreams of a sick man. (Ægri somnia vanæ.)
HORACE, *Ars Poetica*, l. 7.

9
In solitude we have our dreams to ourselves, and in company we agree to dream in concert.
SAMUEL JOHNSON, *The Idler*. No. 32.

10
The more a man dreams, the less he believes.
H. L. MENCKEN, *Prejudices*, 2nd ser., p. 101.

11
It is the fault of dreamers to fear fate.
STEPHEN PHILLIPS, *Herod*. Act i.

12
Dreams grow holy put in action.
ADELAIDE ANN PROCTER, *Philip and Mildred*.

13
As a dream when one awaketh.
Old Testament: Psalms, lxxiii, 20.

We are near awakening when we dream that we dream.
NOVALIS, *Fragment*. (Carlyle, tr.)

14
Foolish men have foolish dreams.
W. G. BENHAM, *Proverbs*, p. 762.

15
A dream itself is but a shadow.
SHAKESPEARE, *Hamlet*. Act ii, sc. 2, l. 266.

Half our daylight faith's a fable;
Sleep disports with shadows too.
THOMAS CAMPBELL, *A Dream*, l. 5.

A dream's but the ghost of a shadow.
JOSEPH DEVLIN, *The Girl That I Loved When a Boy*.

16
Dreams are true while they last, and do we not live in dreams?
TENNYSON, *The Higher Pantheism*.

17
So runs my dream.
TENNYSON, *In Memoriam*. Pt. liv, st. 5.

II—Dreams: Their Cause

18
If ever I ate a good supper at night,
I dreamed of the Devil, and waked in a fright.
CHRISTOPHER ANSTEY, *The New Bath Guide*.

Like the dreams,
Children of night, of indigestion bred.
CHARLES CHURCHILL, *The Candidate*, l. 784.

19
Dreams in their development have breath,
And tears, and tortures, and the touch of joy;
They leave a weight upon our waking thoughts;
They take a weight from off our waking toils;
They do divide our being; they become
A portion of ourselves as of our time,
And look like heralds of eternity.
BYRON, *The Dream*. St. 1.

20
All dreams, as in old Galen I have read,
Are from repletion and complexion bred,
From rising fumes of indigested food,
And noxious humours that infect the blood.
DRYDEN, *Fables: The Cock and the Fox*, l. 140.

Dreams are but interludes which fancy makes:
When Monarch-Reason sleeps, this mimic wakes;
Compounds a medley of disjointed things,
A mob of cobblers and a court of kings:
Light fumes are merry, grosser fumes are sad;
Both are the reasonable soul run mad:
And many monstrous forms in sleep we see,
That neither were, nor are, nor e'er can be.
DRYDEN, *The Cock and the Fox*, l. 325. The fourth line is probably a misprint for "A court of cobblers and a mob of kings."

21
Two diverse gates there are of bodiless dreams,
These of sawn ivory, and those of horn.

Such dreams as issue where the ivory gleams
Fly without fate, and turn our hopes to scorn.
But dreams which issue through the burnished horn,
What man soe'er beholds them on his bed,
These work with virtue and of truth are born.
HOMER, *Odyssey*. Bk. xix, l. 562. (Worsley, tr.)

Two gates of Sleep there are, whereof the one is said to be of horn, and thereby an easy outlet is given to true shades; the other gleaming with the sheen of polished ivory, but false are the dreams sent by the spirits to the world above. (Sunt geminæ Somni portæ; quarum altera fertur
Cornea, qua veris facilis datur exitus umbris,
Altera candenti perfecta nitens elephanto,
Sed falsa ad cælum mittunt insomnia Manes.)
VERGIL, *Æneid*. Bk. vi, l. 893.

Sleep gives his name to portals twain:
One all of horn they say,
Through which authentic spectres gain
Quick exit into day,
And one which bright with ivory gleams,
Whence Pluto sends delusive dreams.
VERGIL, *Æneid*, vi, 893. (Conington, tr.)

Two gates the silent house of Sleep adorn:
Of polished ivory this, that of transparent horn:
True visions through transparent horn arise;
Through polished ivory pass deluding lies.
VERGIL, *Æneid*, vi, 893. (Dryden, tr.)

1 Some dreams we have are nothing else but dreams,
Unnatural and full of contradictions;
Yet others of our most romantic schemes
Are something more than fictions.
THOMAS HOOD, *The Haunted House*. Pt. i, st. 1.

2 How light
Must dreams themselves be; seeing they're more slight
Than the mere nothing that engenders them!
KEATS, *Endymion*. Bk. i, l. 754.

3 For what one has dwelt on by day, these things are seen in visions of the night. ("A γὰρ μεθ' ἡμέραν τις ἐσπούδα ταῦτ' εἶδε νύκτωρ.)
MENANDER, *Fragments*. No. 734.

4 It is not the shrines of the gods, nor the powers of the air, that send the dreams which mock the mind with flitting shadows: each man makes his own dreams. (Somnia quæ mentes ludunt volitantibus umbris, Non delubra deum nec ab æthere numina mittunt: Sed sibi quisque facit.)
PETRONIUS, *Fragments*. No. 121.

Dreams, which, beneath the hov'ring shades of night,
Sport with the ever-restless minds of men,
Descend not from the gods. Each busy brain
Creates its own.
PETRONIUS, *Fragments*. 121. (Peacock, tr.)

Those dreams, that on the silent night intrude,
And with false flitting shades our minds delude,
Jove never sends us downward from the skies;
Nor can they from infernal mansions rise;
But all are mere productions of the brain,
And fools consult interpreters in vain.
SWIFT, *On Dreams*.

5 You eat, in dreams, the custard of the day.
POPE, *The Dunciad*. Bk. i, l. 92.

6 I talk of dreams,
Which are the children of an idle brain,
Begot of nothing but vain fantasy;
Which is as thin of substance as the air
And more inconstant than the wind.
SHAKESPEARE, *Romeo and Juliet*. Act i, sc. 4, 96.

7 Dreams sport at random in a deceiving night, filling affrighted souls with false alarm. (Somnia fallaci ludunt temeraria nocte
Et pavidas mentes falsa timere jubent.)
TIBULLUS, *Elegies*. Bk. iii, eleg. 4, l. 7.

8 From dreams, where thought in fancy's maze runs mad.
YOUNG, *Night Thoughts*. Night iii, l. 1.

8a Don't tell me what you dream'd last night, for
I've been reading Freud.
FRANKLIN P. ADAMS, *Don't Tell Me What You Dream'd Last Night*. Music by Brian Hooker.

III—Dreams: Their Interpretation

9 So the visions of the night do often chance contrary.
APULEIUS, *The Golden Ass*. Bk. iv.

For commonly of these dreams the contrary men shall find.
UNKNOWN, *Beryn: Prologue*, l. 108. (c. 1400)

O strange! to see how dreams fall by contraries.
ROWLEY, *Match at Midnight*. Act iv. (1633)

Dreams go by the contraries.
WILLIAM WYCHERLEY, *The Gentleman Dancing-Master*. Act iv, sc. 1. (1673)

Dreams, you know, go always by contraries.
GOLDSMITH, *Citizen of the World*. No. 46.

"Now, Rory, I'll cry if you don't let me go;
Sure I drame ev'ry night that I'm hating you so!"
"Oh," says Rory, "that same I'm delighted to hear,
For drames always go by conthraries, my dear."
SAMUEL LOVER, *Rory O'More*.

Ground not upon dreams; you know they are ever contrary.
MIDDLETON, *The Family of Love*. Act iv, sc. 3.

Oh! the perjury of men! I find that dreams do not always go by contraries.
HENRY FIELDING, *Grub-Street Opera*. Act i, sc. 11.

10 [Dreams and predictions] ought to serve but for winter talk by the fireside.
FRANCIS BACON, *Essays: Of Prophecies*.

Man is but an ass, if he go about to expound this dream.
SHAKESPEARE, *A Midsummer-Night's Dream*. Act iv, sc. 1, l. 210.

Till their own dreams at length deceive 'em,
And oft repeating, they believe 'em.
MATTHEW PRIOR, *Alma*. Canto iii, l. 13.

1
That children dream not the first half-year; that men dream not in some countries, with many more, are unto me sick men's dreams; dreams out of the ivory gate, and visions before midnight.
SIR THOMAS BROWNE, *On Dreams*.

Some dreams I confess may admit of easy and feminine exposition: he who dreamed that he could not see his right shoulder, might easily fear to lose the sight of his right eye. . . . But why to dream of lettuce should presage some ensuing disease, why to eat figs should signify foolish talk, why to eat eggs great trouble, . . . I shall leave unto your divination.
SIR THOMAS BROWNE, *To a Friend*. Sec. 19.

2
After a dream of weddings comes a corse.
JOHN CLARKE, *Parœmiologia*, 236. (1639)

3
A Friday night's dream on the Saturday told,
Is sure to come true be it never so old.
WILLIAM HONE, *Every-Day Book*, 252.

4
After midnight, when dreams are true. (Post mediam noctem visus, cum somnia vera.)
HORACE, *Satires*. Bk. i, sat. 10, l. 33.

Those dreams are true which we have in the morning as the lamp begins to flicker. (Namque sub aurora, jam dormitante lucerna, Somnia quo cerni tempore vera solent.)
OVID, *Heroides*. Epis. xix, l. 195.

Oft morning dreams presage approaching fate,
For morning dreams, as poets tell, are true.
MICHAEL BRUCE, *Elegy on Spring*.

At break of day when dreams, they say, are true.
DRYDEN, *Spanish Friar*. Act iii, sc. 2.

And all the morning dreams are true.
BEN JONSON, *Love Restored*, last line.

This morn, as sleeping in my bed I lay,
I dreamt (and morning dreams come true they say).
W. B. RHODES, *Bombastes Furioso*.

In the morning, there happen more pleasant and certain dreams.
REGINALD SCOT, *Witchcraft*. Bk. x, ch. 7.

5
Dreams are the true interpreters of our inclinations, but art is required to sort and understand them.
MONTAIGNE, *Essays*. Bk. iii, ch. 13.

6
There is some ill a-brewing towards my rest,
For I did dream of money-bags to-night.
SHAKESPEARE, *The Merchant of Venice*. Act ii, sc. 5, l. 17.

7
I have had a dream past the wit of man to say what dream it was.
SHAKESPEARE, *A Midsummer-Night's Dream*. Act iv, sc. 1, l. 211.

The eye of man hath not heard, the ear of man hath not seen, man's hand is not able to taste, his tongue to conceive, nor his heart to report, what my dream was.
SHAKESPEARE, *A Midsummer-Night's Dream*. Act iv, sc. 1, l. 216.

8
If I may trust the flattering truth of sleep,
My dreams presage some joyful news at hand.
SHAKESPEARE, *Romeo and Juliet*. Act v, sc. 1, 1.

IV—Dreams: The Land of Dreams

9
Let us go in and dance once more
On the dream's glimmering floor,
CONRAD AIKEN, *Nocturne of Remembered Spring*.

10
When to soft Sleep we give ourselves away,
And in a dream as in a fairy bark
Drift on and on through the enchanted dark
To purple daybreak—little thought we pay
To that sweet bitter world we know by day.
T. B. ALDRICH, *Sonnet: Sleep*.

11
Sweet sleep be with us, one and all!
And if upon its stillness fall
The visions of a busy brain,
We'll have our pleasure o'er again,
To warm the heart, to charm the sight.
Gay dreams to all! good night, good night.
JOANNA BAILLIE, *The Phantom: Song*.

12
If there were dreams to sell,
Merry and sad to tell,
And the crier rung his bell,
What would you buy?
THOMAS LOVELL BEDDOES, *Dream-Pedlary*.

13
But I jumped to feel how sharp had been
The pain when it did live,
How the faded dreams of Nineteen-ten
Were Hell in Nineteen-five.
RUPERT BROOKE, *The One Before the Last*.

14
Nosegays! leave them for the waking,
Throw them earthward where they grew;
Dim as such, beside the breaking
Amaranths he looks unto:
Folded eyes see brighter colours than the open ever do.
E. B. BROWNING, *A Child Asleep*. St. 2.

15
We shall start up, at last awake
From Life, that insane dream we take
For waking now, because it seems.
ROBERT BROWNING, *Easter-Day*. Canto xiv.

We wake in a dream, and we ache in a dream,
And we break in a dream, and die!
ROBERT BUCHANAN, *Balder the Beautiful: Proem*.

16
[Her] sweet lips murmur'd like a brook

A wordless music, and her face so fair
Stirr'd with her dream, as rose-leaves with
the air.
BYRON, *Don Juan*. Canto iv, st. 29.

1
The fisher droppeth his net in the stream,
And a hundred streams are the same as
one;
And the maiden dreameth her love-lit dream;
And what is it all, when all is done?
The net of the fisher the burden breaks,
And always the dreaming the dreamer wakes.
ALICE CARY, *The Lover's Diary*.

2
Ah, how the years exile us into dreams.
JAMES CASSIDY, *Fire Island*.

3
Into the land of dreams I long to go.
Bid me forget!
MARY E. COLERIDGE, *Mandragora*.

In the music-land of dreams.
FELICIA DOROTHEA HEMANS, *The Sleeper*.

Ah, give us back our dear dead Land of Dreams!
HENRY MARTYN HOYT, *The Land of Dreams*.

4
This tale's a fragment from the life of
dreams.
S. T. COLERIDGE, *Phantom or Fact?*

5
A crooked street goes past my door, entwin-
ing love of every land;
It wanders, singing, round the world, to
Ashkelon and Samarkand.
To roam it is an ecstasy, each mile the
easier it seems,
And yet the longest street on earth is this—
the Street of Dreams.
CHARLES DIVINE, *The Crooked Street of Dreams*.

6
There's a long, long trail a-winding
Into the land of my dreams,
Where the nightingales are singing,
And a white moon beams.
There's a long, long night of waiting
Until my dreams all come true,
Till the day when I'll be going down
That long, long trail with you.
STODDARD KING, *There's a Long, Long Trail*. (1915) Music by Zo (Alonzo) Elliott.

7
Whence comes Solace? Not from seeing
What is doing, suffering, being;
Not from noting Life's conditions,
Not from heeding Time's monitions;
But in cleaving to the Dream
And in gazing at the Gleam
Whereby grey things golden seem.
THOMAS HARDY, *On a Fine Morning*.

8
In thoughts from the visions of the night,
when deep sleep falleth on men.
Old Testament: Job, iv, 13.

In a dream, in a vision of the night, when deep
sleep falleth upon men.
Old Testament: Job, xxxiii, 15.

9
O Thou, the Father of us all,
Whose many mansions wait,
To whose dream welcome each must come
A child, at Heaven's gate:
In that fair house not made with hands
Whatever splendor beams,
Out of Thy bounty keep for me
A little room of dreams.
R. U. JOHNSON, *The Little Room of Dreams*.

10
A house of dreams untold,
It looks out over the treetops,
And faces the setting sun.
EDWARD MACDOWELL, *From a Log Cabin: Heading*. These lines are inscribed on a memorial tablet at MacDowell's grave.

11
The dream that fires man's heart to make,
To build, to do, to sing or say
A beauty Death can never take,
An Adam from the crumbled clay.
JOHN MASEFIELD, *Fragments*.

12
But that a dream can die will be a thrust
Between my ribs forever of hot pain.
EDNA ST. VINCENT MILLAY, *Here is a Wound*.

13
A thousand creeds and battle-cries,
A thousand warring social schemes,
A thousand new moralities,
And twenty thousand thousand dreams!
ALFRED NOYES, *Forward*.

Enough of dreams! No longer mock
The burdened hearts of men!
Not on the cloud, but on the rock.
ALFRED NOYES, *The Secret Inn*.

14
That holy dream—that holy dream,
While all the world were chiding,
Hath cheered me as a lovely beam
A lonely spirit guiding.
EDGAR ALLAN POE, *A Dream*.

15
All that we see or seem
Is but a dream within a dream.
EDGAR ALLAN POE, *A Dream Within a Dream*.

And did not dream it was a dream.
TENNYSON, *The Two Voices*, l. 213.

16
I shall be satisfied
If only the dreams abide.
CLINTON SCOLLARD, *If Only the Dreams Abide*.

Yet after brick and steel and stone are gone,
And flesh and blood are dust, the dream lives on.
ANDERSON M. SCRUGGS, *Only the Dream is Real*.

Dream abides. It is the only thing that abides;
vision abides.
MIGUEL DE UNAMUNO, *Essays and Soliloquies*, p. 237.

17
I'll dream no more—by manly mind

Not even in sleep is will resigned.
My midnight orisons said o'er,
I'll turn to rest, and dream no more.
SCOTT, *Lady of the Lake*. Canto i, st. 35.

1
To sleep: perchance to dream: ay, there's the rub;
For in that sleep of death what dreams may come,
When we have shuffled off this mortal coil,
Must give us pause.
SHAKESPEARE, *Hamlet*. Act iii, sc. 1, l. 65.

2
Ah, the strange, sweet, lonely delight
Of the Valleys of Dream.
WILLIAM SHARP, *Dream Fantasy*.

From the dim blue Hills of Dream
I have heard the west wind blow.
WILLIAM SHARP, *From the Hills of Dream*.

3
A dream
Of youth, which night and time have quenched forever,
Still, dark, and dry, and unremembered now.
SHELLEY, *Alastor*, l. 669.

4
Dreams and the light imaginings of men,
And all that faith creates, or love desires,
Terrible, strange, sublime and beauteous shapes.
SHELLEY, *Prometheus Unbound*. Act i, l. 200.

5
In an ocean of dreams without a sound.
SHELLEY, *The Sensitive Plant*. Pt. i, st. 26.

6
A place of dream, the Holy Land
Hangs midway between earth and heaven.
HARRIET PRESCOTT SPOFFORD, *The Holy Land*.

7
In the world of dreams I have chosen my part.
To sleep for a season and hear no word
Of true love's truth or of light love's art,
Only the song of a secret bird.
SWINBURNE, *A Ballad of Dreamland: Envoi*.

I have put my days and dreams out of mind,
Days that are over, dreams that are done.
SWINBURNE, *The Triumph of Time*. St. 7.

8
Moreover, something is or seems,
That touches me with mystic gleams,
Like glimpses of forgotten dreams.
TENNYSON, *The Two Voices*, l. 379.

9
The chambers in the house of dreams
Are fed with so divine an air,
That Time's hoar wings grow young therein,
And they who walk there are most fair.
FRANCIS THOMPSON, *Dream-Tryst*. St. 3.

10
A pleasing land of drowsyhed it was,
Of dreams that wave before the half-shut eye;
And of gay castles in the clouds that pass,
For ever flushing round a summer sky.
JAMES THOMSON, *The Castle of Indolence*. Canto i, st. 6.

11
In dreams the exile cometh home;
In dreams the lost is found;
In dreams the captive's feet may roam
The world around.
WILLIAM WATSON, *In Dreams*.

12
Don't you ever try to go there—
It's to dream of, not to find.
Lovely things like that is always
Mostly in your mind.
JOHN V. A. WEAVER, *Legend*.

13
You might as well
Hunt half a day for a forgotten dream.
WORDSWORTH, *Hart-Leap Well*. Pt. ii, st. 9.

Whither is fled the visionary gleam?
Where is it now, the glory and the dream?
WORDSWORTH, *Intimations of Immortality*, l. 56.

V—Dreams: Pleasant Dreams

14
It was a dream of perfect bliss
Too beautiful to last.
T. H. BAYLY, *It Was a Dream*.

15
One of those passing, rainbow dreams,
Half light, half shade, which Fancy's beams
Paint on the fleeting mists that roll
In trance or slumber round the soul!
THOMAS MOORE, *Lalla Rookh: The Fire-Worshippers*. Pt. iii, l. 273.

Oh! that a dream so sweet, so long enjoy'd,
Should be so sadly, cruelly destroy'd!
MOORE, *Lalla Rookh: Veiled Prophet of Khorassan*. Pt. ii, l. 404.

None thrives for long upon the happiest dream.
COVENTRY PATMORE, *Tired Memory*.

16
O dream, how sweet, too sweet, too bitter sweet,
Whose wakening should have been in Paradise.
CHRISTINA ROSSETTI, *Echo*.

17
This is the rarest dream that e'er dull sleep
Did mock sad fools withal.
SHAKESPEARE, *Pericles*. Act v, sc. 1, l. 164.

All this is but a dream,
Too flattering-sweet to be substantial.
SHAKESPEARE, *Romeo and Juliet*. Act ii, sc. 2, l. 140.

18
If it be thus to dream, still let me sleep!
SHAKESPEARE, *Twelfth Night*, Act iv, sc. 1, l. 67.

Is this a dream? Oh, if it be a dream,
Let me sleep on, and do not wake me yet!
LONGFELLOW, *Spanish Student*. Act iii, sc. 5.

19
The dream
Dream'd by a happy man, when the dark East.

Unseen, is brightening to his bridal morn.
TENNYSON, *The Gardener's Daughter*, l. 71.

VI—Dreams: Unpleasant Dreams

1
Hence, babbling dreams! you threaten here in vain!
COLLEY CIBBER, *Richard III* (Alt.). Act v, sc. 3.

2
Dreams that bring us little comfort, heavenly promises that lapse
Into some remote It-may-be, into some forlorn Perhaps.
S. R. LYSAGHT, *A Confession of Unfaith*.

3
Dreams affright me, that mimic real dangers, and my senses wake to my misfortunes. (Somnia me terrent veros imitantia casus, Et vigilant sensus in mea damna mei.)
OVID, *Epistulæ ex Ponto*. Bk. i, epis. 2, l. 43.

4
Deep into that darkness peering, long I stood there, wondering, fearing,
Doubting, dreaming dreams no mortal ever dared to dream before.
EDGAR ALLAN POE, *The Raven*.

5
'Tis still a dream, or else such stuff as madmen
Tongue, and brain not.
SHAKESPEARE, *Cymbeline*. Act v, sc. 4, l. 146.

6
O God! I could be bounded in a nut-shell and count myself a king of infinite space, were it not that I have bad dreams.
SHAKESPEARE, *Hamlet*. Act ii, sc. 2, l. 260.

But as the fierce vexation of a dream.
SHAKESPEARE, *A Midsummer-Night's Dream*. Act iv, sc. 1, l. 72.

In the affliction of these terrible dreams
That shake us nightly.
SHAKESPEARE, *Macbeth*. Act iii, sc. 2, l. 17.

O, I have pass'd a miserable night,
So full of ugly sights, of ghastly dreams,
That, as I am a Christian faithful man,
I would not spend another such a night,
Though 't were to buy a world of happy days.
SHAKESPEARE, *Richard III*. Act i, sc. 4, l. 2.

For never yet one hour in his bed
Have I enjoy'd the golden dew of sleep,
But have been waked by his timorous dreams.
SHAKESPEARE, *Richard III*. Act iv, sc. 1, l. 83.

Lord! Lord! methought, what pain it was to drown!
What dreadful noise of waters in mine ears!
What ugly sights of death within mine eyes!
SHAKESPEARE, *Richard III*. Act i, sc. 4, l. 21.

Sometime she driveth o'er a soldier's neck,
And then dreams he of cutting foreign throats.
Of breaches, ambuscadoes, Spanish blades,
Of healths five-fathom deep; and then anon
Drums in his ear, at which he starts and wakes,
And being thus frighted, swears a prayer or two
And sleeps again.
SHAKESPEARE, *Romeo and Juliet*. Act i, sc. 4, 82.

7
May the dream never prove true which an evil sleep brought me yesternight. (Nec sint mihi somnia vera, Quæ tulit hesterna pessima nocte quies.)
TIBULLUS, *Elegies*. Bk. ii, eleg. 4, l. 1.

VII—Dreams of Love

8
Come to me in my dreams, and then
By day I shall be well again.
For then the night will more than pay
The hopeless longing of the day.
MATTHEW ARNOLD, *Longing*. St. 1.

Come to me, darling; I'm lonely without thee;
Daytime and nighttime I'm dreaming about thee.
JOSEPH BRENAN, *The Exile to His Wife*.

9
The glory dropped from their youth and love,
And both perceived they had dreamed a dream.
ROBERT BROWNING, *The Statue and the Bust*.

10
That just as her young lip began to ope
Upon the golden fruit the vision bore,
A bee flew out and stung her to the heart.
BYRON, *Don Juan*. Canto iv, st. 77.

11
A damsel with a dulcimer
In a vision once I saw:
It was an Abyssinian maid,
And on her dulcimer she played,
Singing of Mount Abora.
S. T. COLERIDGE, *Kubla Khan*.

Adieu! adieu!
Love's dreams prove seldom true.
S. T. COLERIDGE, *Il Zapolya*. Act ii, sc. 1.

12
The house of dreams in which I live
Has beamed old ceilings high,
It sits far back amid the trees
And a brook runs laughing by;
It has a quaint old-fashioned hall,
Where soft light filters through,
Red roses on the newel-post
And on the staircase, You.
ELIZABETH GORDON, *House of Dreams*.

13
Thou lovest what thou dreamest her;
I am thy very dream!
THOMAS HARDY, *The Well-Beloved*. St. 13.

14
In blissful dream, in silent night,
There came to me, with magic might,
With magic might, my own sweet love,
Into my little room above.
HEINE, *Youthful Sorrows*. Pt. iv, st. 1.

15
In dreams she grows not older
The lands of Dream among,
Though all the world wax colder,
Though all the songs be sung,

In dreams doth he behold her
  Still fair and kind and young.
  ANDREW LANG, *Lost Love.*

1
Ever of thee I'm fondly dreaming,
Thy gentle voice my spirit can cheer.
  GEORGE LINLEY, *Ever of Thee.*

2
With the first dream that comes with the first sleep,
I run, I run, I am gathered to thy heart.
  ALICE MEYNELL, *Renouncement.*

We that are twain by day, at night are one.
A dream can bring me to your arms once more.
  LIZETTE WOODWORTH REESE, *Compensation.*

Thou comest as the memory of a dream,
Which now is sad because it hath been sweet.
  SHELLEY, *Prometheus Unbound.* Act ii, sc. 1.

3
And all my days are trances,
  And all my nightly dreams
Are where thy gray eye glances
  And where thy footstep gleams—
In what ethereal dances
  By what eternal streams.
  EDGAR ALLAN POE, *To One in Paradise.*

4
Still on that breast enamour'd let me lie,
Still drink delicious poison from thy eye,
Pant on thy lip, and to thy heart be press'd;
Give all thou canst—and let me dream the rest.
  POPE, *Eloisa to Abelard,* l. 121.

5
I arise from dreams of thee
In the first sweet sleep of night,
When the winds are breathing low,
And the stars are shining bright.
  SHELLEY, *Lines to an Indian Air.*

6
Meet me in Dreamland, sweet dreamy Dreamland,
There let my dreams come true.
  BETH SLATER WHITSON, *Meet Me To-night in Dreamland.* (1909)

7
But I, being poor, have only my dreams.
I have spread my dreams under your feet;
Tread softly, because you tread on my dreams.
  W. B. YEATS, *Wind Among the Reeds.*

VIII—Dreams: The Dreamer

8
Back of the Job—the Dreamer
  Who's making the dream come true.
  BERTON BRALEY, *The Thinker.*

9
The soul hath need of prophet and redeemer:
  Her outstretched wings against her prisoning bars,
She waits for truth; and truth is with the dreamer,—
  Persistent as the myriad light of stars!
  FLORENCE EARLE COATES, *Dream the Great Dream.*

10
Behold, this dreamer cometh.
  Old Testament: Genesis, xxxvii, 19.

11
All men of action are dreamers.
  JAMES HUNEKER, *Pathos of Distance,* p. 111.

12
Yet to have greatly dreamed precludes low ends.
  J. R. LOWELL, *Columbus.*

13
Dreamer of dreams, born out of my due time,
Why should I strive to set the crooked straight?
  WILLIAM MORRIS, *The Earthly Paradise: Apology.*

14
For a dreamer lives forever,
  And a toiler dies in a day.
  JOHN BOYLE O'REILLY, *The Cry of the Dreamer.*

15
He whom a dream hath possessed knoweth no more of doubting.
  SHAEMAS O'SHEEL, *He Whom a Dream Hath Possessed.*

16
Some must delve when the dawn is nigh;
  Some must toil when the noonday beams;
But when night comes, and the soft winds sigh,
  Every man is a King of Dreams.
  CLINTON SCOLLARD, *The King of Dreams.*

IX—Dreams: Day-Dreams

17
Thou shalt make castles then in Spain,
And dream of joy all but in vain.
  CHAUCER, *Romaunt of the Rose,* l. 2573.

CASTLES IN SPAIN, CASTLES IN THE AIR, *see under* CASTLE.

18
My eyes make pictures, when they are shut.
  S. T. COLERIDGE, *A Day-Dream.*

Divert her eyes with pictures in the fire.
  POPE, *Epistle to Mrs. Blount.*

19
I walked beside the evening sea
And dreamed a dream that could not be;
The waves that plunged along the shore
Said only: "Dreamer, dream no more!"
  GEORGE WILLIAM CURTIS, *Ebb and Flow.*

20
I strongly wish for what I firmly hope;
Like the day-dreams of melancholy men,
I think and think on things impossible,
Yet love to wander in that golden maze.
  DRYDEN, *The Rival Ladies.* Act iii, sc. 1.

21
He dreams awake. (Vigilans somniat.)
  PLAUTUS, *Amphitryon,* l. 697. (Act ii, sc. 2.)

DRESS

See also Fashion, Tailor

I—Dress: Apothegms

1
The fair feathers still make the fair fowls.
JOHN DAVIES, *The Scourge of Folly*, 46. (1611)

They be fine feathers, that make a fine bird.
BUNYAN, *The Pilgrim's Progress*. Pt. i.

Fine feathers, they say, make fine birds.
ISAAC BICKERSTAFFE, *The Padlock*. Act i, sc. 1.

As everybody knows, fine feathers make fine birds.
THOMAS HARDY, *Tess*. Ch. 34.

A stick dressed up does not look like a stick.
CERVANTES, *Don Quixote*. Pt. ii, ch. 51.

2
The mother, wi' her needle an' her shears,
Gars auld claes look amaist as weel's the new.
BURNS, *The Cotter's Saturday Night*. St. 5.

3
His hump was subdued into a Grecian bend.
BENJAMIN DISRAELI, *Vivian Grey*. Bk. viii, ch. 1.

4
The Frenchman invented the ruffle, the Englishman added the shirt.
EMERSON, *English Traits*, p. 89.

It's like sending them ruffles, when wanting a shirt.
GOLDSMITH, *The Haunch of Venison*, l. 34.

5
It is only when mind and character slumber that the dress can be seen.
EMERSON, *Letters and Social Aims: Social Aims*.

6
Though manners make, yet apparel shapes.
JOHN FLORIO, *Second Frutes*, 115. (1591)

The hood makes not the monk, nor the apparel the man.
ROBERT GREENE, *Works*. Vol. ix, p. 19.

7
We are all Adam's children, but silk makes the difference.
THOMAS FULLER, *Gnomologia*. No. 5425.

8
They stript Joseph out of his coat, his coat of many colours.
Old Testament: Genesis, xxxvii, 23.

How his eyes languish! how his thoughts adore
That painted coat, which Joseph never wore!
He shows, on holidays, a sacred pin,
That touch'd the ruff, that touched Queen Bess' chin.
YOUNG, *Love of Fame*. Sat. iv, l. 119.

9
Nowadays, if men are more serious than women, it's because their clothes are darker.
ANDRÉ GIDE, *The Counterfeiters*. Pt. i, ch. 7.

The world must be getting old, I think; it dresses so very soberly now.
JEROME K. JEROME, *Idle Thoughts of an Idle Fellow: On Dress and Deportment*.

10
The nakedness of the indigent world may be clothed from the trimmings of the vain.
GOLDSMITH, *The Vicar of Wakefield*, ch. 4, *She Stoops to Conquer*, i, 1.

11
Meretricious arts of dress.
MATTHEW GREEN, *The Spleen*, l. 614.

12
All thing is the worse for the wearing.
JOHN HEYWOOD, *Proverbs*. Pt. ii, ch. 1.

13
I know it is a sin
For me to sit and grin
At him here;
But the old three-cornered hat,
And the breeches and all that,
Are so queer!
O. W. HOLMES, *The Last Leaf*.

14
Art may make a suit of clothes; but nature must produce a man.
DAVID HUME, *Essays: The Epicurean*.

15
Glorious in his apparel.
Old Testament: Isaiah, lxiii, 1.

I saw among the spoils a goodly Babylonish garment.
Old Testament: Joshua, vii, 21.

16
These my sky-robes spun out of Iris' woof.
MILTON, *Comus*, l. 83.

17
Then up he rose, and donn'd his clothes.
SHAKESPEARE, *Hamlet*. Act iv, sc. 5, l. 52.

18
I have no more doublets than backs, no more stockings than legs, nor no more shoes than feet.
SHAKESPEARE, *The Taming of the Shrew: Induction*. Sc. 2, l. 9.

19
I say, beware of all enterprises that require new clothes, and not rather a new wearer of clothes.
HENRY DAVID THOREAU, *Walden*. Ch. 1.

20
Dress does not give knowledge. (La ropa no da ciencia.)
YRIARTE, *Fables*. No. 27.

II—Dress: Its Philosophy

21
We must present an appearance of neatness, not too punctilious or exquisite, but just enough to avoid slovenliness. (Adhibenda præterea munditia est non odiosa necque exquisita nimis, tantum quæ fugiat agrestem.)
CICERO, *De Officiis*. Bk. i, ch. 36, sec. 130.

22
Any man may be in good spirits and good temper when he's well dressed. There ain't much credit in that.
DICKENS, *Martin Chuzzlewit*. Ch. 5.

The sense of being perfectly well-dressed gives a feeling of inward tranquillity which religion is powerless to bestow.
EMERSON, *Letters and Social Aims: Social*

Aims. Quoted as by a lady of his acquaintance, said to have been Mrs. Helen Bell.

1
Plain without pomp, and rich without a
show.

DRYDEN, *The Flower and the Leaf*, l. 187.

2
The least mistake in sentiment takes all the beauty out of your clothes.

EMERSON, *Journal*, 1860.

3
Good clothes open all doors.

THOMAS FULLER, *Gnomologia*. No. 1705.

There is one other reason for dressing well, namely that dogs respect it, and will not attack you in good clothes.

EMERSON, *Journal*, 1870.

4
Eat to please thyself, but dress to please others.

BENJAMIN FRANKLIN, *Poor Richard*, 1738.

5
Fine clothes are good only as they supply the want of other means of procuring respect.

SAMUEL JOHNSON. (BOSWELL, *Life*. 1776)

6
For he that's out of clothes is out of fashion,
And out of fashion is out of countenance,
And out of countenance is out of wit.

BEN JONSON, *The Staple of News*. Act i, sc. 1.

7
A peasant's dress befits a peasant's fortune.

SCOTT, *The Doom of Devorgoil*. Act iii, sc. 4.

Honest mean habiliments.

SHAKESPEARE, *The Taming of the Shrew*. Act iv, sc. 3, l. 172.

8
Dress doth make a difference, David.
'Tis all in all, I think.

SHERIDAN, *The Rivals*. Act iii, sc. 4.

9
As for Clothing, . . . perhaps we are led oftener by the love of novelty and a regard for the opinions of men, in procuring it, than by a true utility.

H. D. THOREAU, *Walden*. Ch. 1.

10
Costume is not dress.

J. MCNEILL WHISTLER, *"Ten O'Clock."*

III—Dress: Its Vanity

11
Thy clothes are all the soul thou hast.

BEAUMONT AND FLETCHER, *Honest Man's Fortune*. Act v, sc. 3, l. 170.

The soul of this man is his clothes.

SHAKESPEARE, *All's Well That Ends Well*. Act ii, sc. 5, l. 45.

All his reverend wit
Lies in his wardrobe.

JOHN WEBSTER, *The White Devil*. Act ii, sc. 1.

12
Our bravery's but a vain disguise,
To hide us from the world's dull eyes,
The remedy of a defect,
With which our nakedness is deckt.

SAMUEL BUTLER, *Satire Upon the Weakness and Misery of Man*, l. 88.

13
Let him wear brand-new garments still,
Who has a threadbare soul, I say.

BLISS CARMAN, *The Mendicants*.

No man ever stood the lower in my estimation for having a patch in his clothes; yet I am sure that there is a greater anxiety, commonly, to have fashionable, or at least clean and unpatched clothes, than to have a sound conscience.

H. D. THOREAU, *Walden*. Ch. 1.

14
And just when evening turns the blue vault
grey,
To spend two hours in dressing for the
day.

COWPER, *Hope*, l. 81.

Let the world go dine and dress.

LAMAN BLANCHARD, *Dolce far Niente*.

15
We sacrifice to dress, till household joys
And comforts cease. Dress drains our cellar
dry,
And keeps our larder lean; puts out our fires,
And introduces hunger, frost, and woe,
Where peace and hospitality might reign.

COWPER, *The Task*. Bk. ii, l. 614.

Many a one, for the sake of finery on the back, has gone with a hungry belly, and half-starved their families. "Silks and satins, scarlets and velvets, put out the kitchen fire," as Poor Richard says.

BENJAMIN FRANKLIN, *The Way to Wealth*.

16
Fond pride of dress is sure a very curse;
Ere fancy you consult, consult your purse.

BENJAMIN FRANKLIN, *The Way to Wealth*.

17
He that is proud of the rustling of his silks, like a madman, laughs at the rattling of his fetters. For indeed, Clothes ought to be our remembrances of our lost innocency.

THOMAS FULLER, *The Holy and Profane States: Apparel*.

18
Those who make their dress a principal part of themselves, will, in general, become of no more value than their dress.

WILLIAM HAZLITT, *Political Essays: On the Clerical Character*.

Not caring, so that sumpter-horse, the back
Be hung with gaudy trappings, in what coarse,
Yea, rags most beggarly, they clothe the soul.

J. R. LOWELL, *Cambridge Thirty Years Ago*. Quoted. This essay was originally called *Fireside Travels*.

19
Here everyone dresses above his means. (Hic ultra vires habitus nitor.)

JUVENAL, *Satires*. Sat. iii, l. 180.

20
What madness to carry whole incomes on

one's body! (Quis furor est census corpore ferre suos!)

OVID, *Ars Amatoria*. Bk. iii, l. 172.

A silk suit which cost me much money, and I pray God to make me able to pay for it.

SAMUEL PEPYS, *Diary*, 1 July, 1660.

1

Our purses shall be proud, our garments poor;
For 'tis the mind that makes the body rich;
And as the sun breaks through the darkest clouds,
So honour peereth in the meanest habit.
What is the jay more precious than the lark,
Because his feathers are more beautiful?

SHAKESPEARE, *The Taming of the Shrew*. Act iv, sc. 3, l. 173.

2

The tulip and the butterfly
Appear in gayer coats than I:
Let me be dressed fine as I will,
Flies, worms, and flowers exceed me still.

ISAAC WATTS, *Against Pride in Clothes*.

IV—Dress: For Women

3

There is not so variable a thing in Nature as a lady's head-dress.

JOSEPH ADDISON, *The Spectator*. No. 98.

4

Miss Flora McFlimsey, of Madison Square,
Has made three separate journeys to Paris,
And, her father assures me, each time she was there,
That she and her friend, Mrs. Harris . . .
Spent six consecutive weeks without stopping
In one continuous round of shopping . . .
For all manner of things that a woman can put
On the crown of her head or the sole of her foot,
Or wrap round her shoulders, or fit round her waist,
Or that can be sewed on, or pinned on, or laced,
Or tied on with a string, or stitched on with a bow,
In front or behind, above or below;
For bonnets, mantillas, capes, collars, and shawls;
Dresses for breakfasts and dinners and balls;
Dresses to sit in and stand in and walk in;
Dresses to dance in and flirt in and talk in;
Dresses in which to do nothing at all;
Dresses for winter, spring, summer, and fall; . . .
And yet, though scarce three months have passed since the day
This merchandise went, on twelve carts, up Broadway,
This same Miss McFlimsey, of Madison Square,
The last time we met was in utter despair
Because she had nothing whatever to wear!

WILLIAM ALLEN BUTLER, *Nothing to Wear*. Authorship claimed without foundation by Hattie (?) Peck. (See STEVENSON, *Famous Single Poems*.)

5

I for one venerate a petticoat.

BYRON, *Don Juan*. Canto xiv, st. 26.

A petticoat is no great shakes after all, when it hangs fluttering on a clothes line.

LORENZO DOW, *Potent Sermons*, iii, 133.

Without a whole tatter to her tail, but as ragged as one of the Muses.

CONGREVE, *Love for Love*. Act i, sc. 1.

6

Th' adorning thee with so much art
  Is but a barbarous skill;
'Tis like the poisoning of a dart
  Too apt before to kill.

ABRAHAM COWLEY, *The Waiting-Maid*.

7

The woman shall not wear that which pertaineth unto a man.

Old Testament: Deuteronomy, xxii, 5.

8

Each ornament about her seemly lies,
By curious chance, or careless art composed.

EDWARD FAIRFAX, *Godfrey of Bullogne*. (From TASSO, *Jerusalem Delivered*.)

9

If you wear your cambric ruffles as I do, and take care not to mend the holes, they will come in time to be lace; and feathers, my dear girl, may be had in America from every cock's tail.

BENJAMIN FRANKLIN, *Letter to his Daughter*, 3 June, 1779.

10

They sewed fig-leaves together and made themselves aprons.

Old Testament: Genesis, iii, 7.

All the costumes since Adam's, right or wrong,
From Eve's fig-leaf down to the petticoat,
Almost as scanty, of days less remote.

BYRON, *The Vision of Judgment*. St. 66.

11

But when those charms are past,—for charms are frail,—
When time advances, and when lovers fail,
She then shines forth, solicitous to bless,
In all the glaring impotence of dress.

GOLDSMITH, *The Deserted Village*, l. 291.

12

A sweet disorder in the dress
Kindles in clothes a wantonness.

ROBERT HERRICK, *Delight in Disorder*.

A winning wave, (deserving note,)
In the tempestuous petticoat,
A careless shoe-string, in whose tie
I see a wild civility,—
Do more bewitch me than when art
Is too precise in every part.

ROBERT HERRICK, *Delight in Disorder*.

1
Whenas in silks my Julia goes,
Then, then, methinks, how sweetly flows
That liquefaction of her clothes!
ROBERT HERRICK, *Upon Julia's Clothes.*

And ye sall walk in silk attire,
And siller hae to spare,
Gin ye'll consent to be his bride,
Nor think o' Donald mair.
SUSANNA BLAMIRE, *The Siller Crown.*

To show the form it seemed to hide.
SCOTT, *The Lord of the Isles.* Canto i, st. 5.

Silk was invented so that women could go naked in clothes.
MAHOMET.

2
'Tis not the robe or garment I affect;
For who would marry with a suit of clothes?
THOMAS HEYWOOD, *Royal King and Loyal Subject.* Act ii, sc. 2.

3
For gowns, and gloves, and caps, and tippets,
Are beauty's sauces, spice, and sippets.
THOMAS HOOD, *A Recipe.*

4
Plain in neatness. (Simplex munditiis.)
HORACE, *Odes.* Bk. i, ode 5, l. 5.

We are charmed by neatness. (Munditiis capimur.)
OVID, *Ars Amatoria.* Bk. iii, l. 133.

Still to be neat, still to be drest,
As you were going to a feast;
Still to be powder'd, still perfumed:
Lady, it is to be presumed,
Though art's hid causes are not found,
All is not sweet, all is not sound.

Give me a look, give me a face,
That makes simplicity a grace;
Robes loosely flowing, hair as free:
Such sweet neglect more taketh me
Than all th' adulteries of art;
They strike mine eyes, but not my heart.
BEN JONSON, *Epicœne, or, The Silent Woman.* Act i, sc. 1. An imitation of a Latin poem commencing "Semper munditias," printed at the end of the variorum edition of Petronius. *See* p. 2298.

5
It's not the skirt that breaks papa, it's the chiffon ruffles.
F. M. KNOWLES, *A Cheerful Year Book.*

6
Dwellers in huts and in marble halls—
From Shepherdess up to Queen—
Cared little for bonnets, and less for shawls,
And nothing for crinoline.
But now simplicity's *not* the rage,
And it's funny to think how cold
The dress they wore in the Golden Age
Would seem in the Age of Gold.
H. S. LEIGH, *The Two Ages.* St. 4.

In tea-cup times of hood and hoop,
Or while the patch was worn.
TENNYSON, *The Talking Oak,* l. 63.

7
A bevy of fair women, richly gay
In gems and wanton dress.
MILTON, *Paradise Lost.* Bk. xi, l. 578.

A lady so richly clad as she—
Beautiful exceedingly.
S. T. COLERIDGE, *Christabel.* Pt. i, l. 67.

8
But who is this, what thing of sea or land?
Female of sex it seems,
That so bedeck'd, ornate, and gay,
Comes this way sailing
Like a stately ship
Of Tarsus, bound for th' isles
Of Javan or Gadier
With all her bravery on, and tackle trim,
Sails fill'd, and streamers waving,
Courted by all the winds that hold them play.
MILTON, *Samson Agonistes,* l. 710.

9
Let him be inflamed by the love of your dress. (Uratur vestis amore tuæ.)
OVID, *Ars Amatoria.* Bk. iii, l. 448.

We are captivated by dress; all is concealed by gems and gold; a woman is the least part of herself. (Auferimur cultu; gemmis auroque teguntur Omnia; pars minima est ipsa puella sui.)
OVID, *Remediorum Amoris,* l. 343.

10
Who wishes to give himself an abundance of business let him equip these two things, a ship and a woman. These two things are never sufficiently adorned, nor is any excess of adornment enough for them.
(Negoti sibi qui volet vim parare,
Navem et mulierem, hæc duo comparato. . .
Neqúe unquam satis hæ duæ res ornatur,
Neque eis ulla ornandi satis satietas est.)
PLAUTUS, *Pœnulus,* l. 210 (Act i, sc. 2.)

A ship is sooner rigged by far than a gentlewoman made ready.
UNKNOWN, *Lingua; or, The Five Senses.* Act iv, sc. 5. Often erroneously attributed to Anthony Brewer.

Clothes introduced sewing, a kind of work which you may call endless; a woman's dress, at least, is never done.
H. D. THOREAU, *Walden.* Ch. 1.

11
To fifty chosen sylphs, of special note,
We trust th' important charge, the petticoat;
Oft have we known that sev'n-fold fence to fail,
Tho stiff with hoops, and arm'd with ribs of whale.
POPE, *The Rape of the Lock.* Canto ii, l. 117.

12
At sermons, too, I shone in scarlet gay:
The wasting moth ne'er spoil'd my best array:
The cause was this, I wore it every day.
POPE, *Wife of Bath: Prologue,* l. 287.

1
No longer shall the bodice aptly laced
From thy full bosom to thy slender waist,
That air and harmony of shape express,
Fine by degrees, and beautifully less.

MATTHEW PRIOR, *Henry and Emma*, l. 429.

2
She bears a duke's revenues on her back,
And in her heart she scorns our poverty.

SHAKESPEARE, *II Henry VI*. Act i, sc. 3, l. 83.

See where she comes, apparell'd like the spring.

SHAKESPEARE, *Pericles*. Act i, sc. 1, l. 12.

3
Set not thy sweet heart on proud array.

SHAKESPEARE, *King Lear*. Act iii, sc. 4, l. 84.

4
So tedious is this day,
As is the night before some festival
To an impatient child, that hath new robes,
And may not wear them.

SHAKESPEARE, *Romeo and Juliet*. Act iii, sc. 2, l. 28

With silken coats, and caps, and golden rings,
With ruffs, and cuffs, and fardingales, and things;
With scarfs, and fans, and double change of bravery,
With amber bracelets, beads, and all this knavery.

SHAKESPEARE, *The Taming of the Shrew*. Act iv, sc. 3, l. 55.

5
Thy gown? Why, ay: come, tailor, let us see't.
O mercy, God! what masquing stuff is here?
What's this? a sleeve? 'tis like a demi-cannon:
What, up and down, carv'd like an apple-tart?
Here's snip and nip and cut and slish and slash,
Like to a censer in a barber's shop:
Why, what i' devil's name, tailor, call'st thou this!

SHAKESPEARE, *The Taming of the Shrew*. Act iv, sc. 3, l. 86.

6
Lawn as white as driven snow.

SHAKESPEARE, *Winter's Tale*. Act iv, sc. 4, 220.

Her cap, far whiter than the driven snow,
Emblem right meet of decency does yield.

WILLIAM SHENSTONE, *The Schoolmistress*. St. 6.

7
Never teach false morality. How exquisitely absurd to tell girls that beauty is of no value, dress of no use! Beauty is of value; her whole prospects and happiness in life may often depend upon a new gown or a becoming bonnet, and if she has five grains of common sense she will find this out.

SYDNEY SMITH. (LADY HOLLAND, *Memoir*. Vol. i, ch. 11, p. 297.)

8
She wears her clothes as if they were thrown on her with a pitchfork.

SWIFT, *Polite Conversation*. Dial. i.

Will she pass in a crowd? Will she make a figure in a country church?

SWIFT, *Letter to Stella*, 9 Feb., 1710.

Looked as if she had walked straight out of the Ark.

SYDNEY SMITH. (LADY HOLLAND, *Memoir*, i, 7.)

9
So for thy spirit did devise
Its Maker seemly garniture,
Of its own essence parcel pure, . . .
Which woven vesture should subserve.
For outward robes in their ostents
Should show the soul's habiliments.

FRANCIS THOMPSON, *Gilded Gold*.

10
By God, those are bastard-concealers!

BRIAND DE VALLÉE, referring to hoopskirts. (LAMANDÉ, *Montaigne*, p. 22.)

11
All such dresses are forbidden, which incite irregular desires.

THOMAS WILSON, *Maxims of Piety*, p. 6.

12
Bloomers.

Named from Mrs. Amelia Jenks Bloomer, an American dress reformer, who first wore them in 1851. The garment consisted of a skirt reaching to the knees, over trousers cut full and gathered at the ankle.

Rainy-day skirt.

A skirt ending at the ankle for street wear in bad weather. Hence "rainy-daisies." (1900)

V—Dress: Beauty Unadorned

13
Who seems most hideous when adorned the most. (Che quant' era più ornata, era più brutta.)

ARIOSTO, *Orlando Furioso*. Canto xx, st. 116.

14
A gaudy dress and gentle air,
May slightly touch the heart,
But it's innocence and modesty
That polishes the dart.

BURNS, *My Handsome Nell*.

She just wore
Enough for modesty—no more.

ROBERT BUCHANAN, *White Rose and Red*.

15
Lack of adornment is said to become some women. (Mulieres esse dicuntur nonnullæ inornatæ.)

CICERO, *De Oratore*. Ch. xxiii, sec. 78.

Ornate for the very reason that ornaments had been neglected. (Ornata hoc ipso, quod ornamenta neglexerunt.)

CICERO, *Epistolæ ad Atticum*. Bk. ii, epis. 1, sec. 1.

16
Beauty when most unclothed is clothed best.

PHINEAS FLETCHER, *Sicelides*. Act ii, sc. 4.

In naked beauty more adorn'd,
More lovely than Pandora.

MILTON, *Paradise Lost*. Bk. iv, l. 713.

17
If she is beautiful, she is overdressed. (Si pulchra est, nimis ornata est.)

PLAUTUS, *Mostellaria*. Act i, sc. 3, l. 134.

2
Attired to please herself: no gems of any kind
She wore, nor aught of borrowed gloss in Nature's stead.
(Sine auro; tum ornatum ita uti quæ ornantur sibi,
Nulla mala re interpoltam mulierbri.)
TERENCE, *Heauton Timorumenos*, l. 288.

3
O fair undress, best dress! it checks no vein,
But every flowing limb in pleasure drowns,
And heightens ease with grace.
THOMSON, *Castle of Indolence*. Canto i, st. 26.

4 Her polished limbs,
Veiled in a simple robe, their best attire,
Beyond the pomp of dress; for Loveliness
Needs not the foreign aid of ornament,
But is, when unadorned, adorned the most.
THOMSON, *The Seasons: Autumn*, l. 202.

5 She's adorned
Amply, that in her husband's eye looks lovely,—
The truest mirror that an honest wife
Can see her beauty in!
JOHN TOBIN, *The Honeymoon*. Act iii, sc. 4.

VI—Dress: For Men

6
A civil habit Oft covers a good man.
BEAUMONT AND FLETCHER, *Beggars' Bush*. Act ii, sc. 3.

7
Without black velvet breeches, what is man?
JAMES BRAMSTON, *Man of Taste*.

The things named "pants" in certain documents,
A word not made for gentlemen, but "gents."
O. W. HOLMES, *A Rhymed Lesson*, l. 422.

8
His very serviceable suit of black
Was courtly once, and conscientious still.
ROBERT BROWNING, *How It Strikes a Contemporary*.

Whose coat was as bare of nap as a frog's is of feathers.
J. G. LOCKHART, *Reginald Dalton*, vi, 345.

His two-year coat so smooth and bare,
Through every thread it lets in air.
SWIFT, *Progress of Poetry*.

Be faithful to me, O poor coat that I love! Together we are growing old. For ten years I myself have brushed thee—Socrates would have done no better. Should fate make fresh assaults upon your thin cloth, imitate me, resist like a philosopher: old friend of mine, let us never part.
(Sois-moi fidèle, O pauvre habit que j'aime!
Ensemble nous devenons vieux.
Depuis dix ans je te brosse moi-même,
Et Socrate n'eut pas fait mieux.
Quand le sort à mince étoffe
Liverait de nouveaux combats,
Imite-moi, résiste en philosophe;
Mon vieil ami, ne nous séparons pas.
PIERRE JEAN DE BÉRANGER, *Mon Habit*.

"Ah, now, Laigle of the funeral oration, your coat is old." "I should hope so," retorted Laigle. "That's why we agree so well, my coat and I. It has got all my wrinkles, it doesn't bind me anywhere, it has fitted itself to all my deformities, it is complaisant to all my movements; I am only conscious of it because it keeps me warm. Old coats are just like old friends."
VICTOR HUGO, *Les Miserables: Saint Denis*. Bk. xii, sec. 11.

9
Take great care always to be dressed like the reasonable people of your own age, in the place where you are; whose dress is never spoken of one way or another, as either too negligent or too much studied.
LORD CHESTERFIELD, *Letters*, 9 Oct., 1746.

Any affectation whatsoever in dress implies, in my mind, a flaw in the understanding.
LORD CHESTERFIELD, *Letters*, 30 Dec., 1748.

A man of sense carefully avoids any particular character in his dress.
LORD CHESTERFIELD, *Letters*, 30 Dec., 1748.

10 A wig that flowed behind,
A hat not much the worse for wear,
Each comely in its kind.
COWPER, *John Gilpin*. St. 46.

11
They [the English] think him the best dressed man, whose dress is so fit for his use that you cannot notice or remember to describe it.
EMERSON, *English Traits*, p. 89.

I hold that gentleman to be the best dressed whose dress no one observes.
ANTHONY TROLLOPE, *Thackeray*. Ch. 9.

12
That garment best the winter's rage defends,
Whose shapeless form in ample plaits depends;
By various names in various counties known,
Yet held in all the true Surtout alone;
Be thine of kersey firm, though small the cost,
Then brave unwet the rain, unchill'd the frost.
JOHN GAY, *Trivia*. Bk. i, l. 55.

Be thou, for every season, justly drest,
Nor brave the piercing frost with open breast;
And when the bursting clouds a deluge pour,
Let thy surtout defend the drenching shower.
JOHN GAY, *Trivia*. Bk. i, l. 128.

13
I'd a swallow-tail coat of a beautiful blue,
A brief which I bought of a booby,
A couple of shirts, and a collar or two,
And a ring that looked like a ruby.
W. S. GILBERT, *Trial by Jury*.

14
Wear seemly gloves; not black, nor yet too light,
And least of all the pair that once was white; . . .
Shave like a goat, if so your fancy bids,
But be a parent,—don't neglect your kids.
O. W. HOLMES, *A Rhymed Lesson*, l. 444.

15
A vest as admired Vortiger had on,

Which from this Island's foes his grandsire won,
Whose artful colours pass'd the Tyrian dye,
Obliged to triumph in this legacy.

EDWARD HOWARD, *The British Princes*, p. 96. (1669)

A painted vest Prince Vortiger had on,
Which from a naked Pict his grandsire won.

This burlesque of Howard's lines is said to have been attributed to Sir Richard Blackmore by his enemies, as from his epic, *The Creation*, suppressed by him because of the outcry it occasioned. Boswell and Johnson discussed it (29 Oct., 1769), Boswell defending "Blackmore's supposed lines," as "a poetical conceit. A Pict being painted, if he is slain in battle, and a vest made of his skin, it is a painted vest won from him, though he was naked." They were quoted by Maria Edgeworth as an example of an Irish bull by an English writer. For discussion of authorship see *The European Magazine*, April, 1792.

They were attempting to put on
Raiment from naked bodies worn.

MATTHEW GREEN, *The Spleen*. Referring to the parody attributed to Blackmore.

If the Kings of Mexico changed four times a day, it was but an upper vest which they used to honour some meritorious servant with.

JOHN EVELYN, *Tyrannus*.

1
Let thy attire be comely but not costly.

JOHN LYLY, *Euphues*, p. 39. (1579)

Costly thy habit as thy purse can buy,
But not express'd in fancy; rich, not gaudy;
For the apparel oft proclaims the man.

SHAKESPEARE, *Hamlet*. Act i, sc. 3, l. 70.

Neat, not gaudy.

CHARLES LAMB, *Letter to Wordsworth*, 11 June, 1806. A meaningless misquotation of a good phrase.

The admiration of the "neat but not gaudy," which is commonly reported to have influenced the devil when he painted his tail pea-green.

JOHN RUSKIN, *Architectural Magazine*, Nov., 1838.

2
A negligent dress is becoming to men. (Forma viros neglecta decet.)

OVID, *Ars Amatoria*. Bk. i, l. 509.

An old suit, a battered hat, a perfect tie, and a good collar—that's what makes a well-dressed man.

BARON DE MEYER, International style expert, *Newspaper Interview*, 1930.

The essential thing for a necktie is style. A well-tied tie is the first serious step in life.

WILDE, *A Woman of No Importance*. Act iii.

3
Let your person please by cleanliness and be made swarthy by the campus; let your toga fit and be spotless; do not let your shoe-strap be wrinkled; let your teeth be free of rust, and your foot not float about in a shoe too large for you; nor let your stubborn locks be spoiled by bad cutting; let hair and beard be dressed by a skilled hand. Do not let your nails project, and keep them free of dirt, nor let any hair be in the hollow of your nostrils. Let not your breath be sour, nor permit the lord and master of the herd to offend the nose.

OVID, *Ars Amatoria*. Bk. i, l. 513.

4
My galligaskins, that have long withstood
The winter's fury, and encroaching frosts,
By time subdued (what will not time subdue?)
An horrid chasm disclosed.

JOHN PHILIPS, *The Splendid Shilling*, l. 121.

5
Thou knowest that the fashion of a doublet, or a hat, or a cloak, is nothing to a man.

SHAKESPEARE, *Much Ado About Nothing*. Act iii, sc. 3, l. 127.

6
King Stephen was a worthy peer,
His breeches cost him but a crown;
He held them sixpence all too dear,
With that he call'd the tailor lown.
He was a wight of high renown,
And thou art but of low degree:
'Tis pride that pulls the country down;
Then take thine auld cloak about thee.

SHAKESPEARE, *Othello*. Act ii, sc. 3, l. 92. This is a variation of an old ballad, *Take Thy Auld Cloak About Thee*, given in Percy, *Reliques*. "Lown" is probably a misprint for "clown," as given in the Percy manuscript.

7
He will come to her in yellow stockings, and 'tis a colour she abhors; and cross-gartered, a fashion she detests.

SHAKESPEARE, *Twelfth Night*. Act ii, sc. 5, l. 216.

8
Where did you get that hat?
Where did you get that tile?
Isn't it a nobby one,
And just the proper style?

JOSEPH J. SULLIVAN, *Where Did You Get That Hat?* A popular song, written in 1888.

DRINKING

See also Ale and Beer; Eating and Drinking; Wine

I—Drinking: Apothegms

9
To wet the lungs. (Τέγγε πνεύμονας.)

ALCÆUS, *Fragment*.

Let us wet our whistles. (Tengomenas faciamus.)

PETRONIUS, *Satyricon*. Sec. 34. A derivative of the phrase of Alcæus.

So was her jolly whistle well y-wet.

CHAUCER, *The Reeves Tale*, l. 235. (c. 1386)

All with wine their whistles wet.

BARNABE GOOGE, *Popish Kingdom*, 50. (1570)

Well may I my whistle wet, for sure the subject's dry.
SAMUEL WESLEY, *Maggots*, 64. (1685)

For, whether we're right or whether we're wrong,
There's a rose for every thistle.
Here's luck!
And a drop to wet your whistle!
RICHARD HOVEY, *At the Crossroads.*

1 The vine bears three kinds of grapes: the first of pleasure, the second of intoxication, the third of disgust.
ANACHARSIS. (DIOGENES LAERTIUS, *Anacharsis*. Sec. 3.)

At the first cup man drinks wine; at the second cup wine drinks wine; at the third cup wine drinks man.
UNKNOWN. A Japanese proverb.

At the punch-bowl's brink,
Let the thirsty think
What they say in Japan:
"First the man takes a drink,
Then the drink takes a drink,
Then the drink takes the man!"
E. R. SILL, *An Adage from the Orient.*

2 If you cannot carry your liquor when you are young, you will be a water-carrier when you are old.
ANACHARSIS. (DIOGENES LAERTIUS, *Anacharsis*. Sec. 5.)

3 When the liquor's out, why clink the cannikin?
ROBERT BROWNING, *The Flight of the Duchess*. Pt. xvi.

4 The Deil's awa wi' th' Exciseman.
BURNS, *The Deil's Awa Wi' the Exciseman.*

5 I drink when I have occasion, and sometimes when I have no occasion.
CERVANTES, *Don Quixote*. Pt. ii, ch. 33.

Under a bad cloak there is often a good drinker.
CERVANTES, *Don Quixote*. Pt. ii, ch. 33.

6 It seems to me that that rule which holds in the feasts of the Greeks, is to be observed, too, in life: "Either let him drink," they say, "or depart." And with justice. For either let a man enjoy with others the pleasure of drinking; or let him first depart. (Aut bibat, aut abeat.)
CICERO, *Tusculanarum Disputationum*. Bk. 5, ch. 41, sec. 118. The Greek proverb to which Cicero refers is: Ἢ πῖθι ἢ ἄπιθι.

We'll teach you to drink deep ere you depart.
SHAKESPEARE, *Hamlet*. Act i, sc. 2, l. 175.

7 Some men are like musical glasses,—to produce their finest tones you must keep them wet.
S. T. COLERIDGE, *Table Talk.*

8 He seldom went up to town without coming down "three sheets in the wind."
R. H. DANA, *Two Years Before the Mast*. Ch. 20.

9 Did you ever hear of Captain Wattle?
He was all for love and a little for the bottle.
CHARLES DIBDIN, *Captain Wattle and Miss Rol.*

Said Aristotle unto Plato,
"Have another sweet potato?"
Said Plato unto Aristotle,
"Thank you, I prefer the bottle."
OWEN WISTER, *Philosophy 4*. Quoted.

And I wish his soul in heaven may dwell,
Who first invented this leathern bottel!
UNKNOWN, *The Leathern Bottel.*

10 That which belongs to another.
DIOGENES, when asked which wines he liked best to drink. (DIOGENES LAERTIUS, *Diogenes*. Sec. 6.)

The rapturous, wild, and ineffable pleasure
Of drinking at somebody else's expense.
HENRY SAMBROOKE LEIGH, *Stanzas to an Intoxicated Fly.*

11 Among the Indians of the extreme north . . . there is a liquor made which . . . is called hoochinoo. The ingredients . . . are simple and innocent, being only yeast, flour, and either sugar or molasses.
EDWARD R. EMERSON, *Beverages, Past and Present*. (Hence, hooch.)

12 Here, tapster, broach number 1706, as the saying is.
Sir, you shall taste my *Anno Domini.*
FARQUHAR, *The Beaux' Stratagem*. Act i, sc. 1.

13 He is drinking at the Harrow when he should be at the plough.
THOMAS FULLER, *Gnomologia*. No. 2456.

14 You can have some home-brew, if you want to, you know.
THOMAS HARDY, *Mayor of Casterbridge*. Bk. i, p. 119.

15 Some say three fingers, some say two;
I'll leave the choice to you.
JOHN HAY, *The Mystery of Gilgal*. St. 5. (1871) Said to have been coined by Hay in Jack's Bar, in Paris.

16 I pray thee let me and my fellow have
A hair of the dog that bit us last night.
JOHN HEYWOOD, *Proverbs*, i, 11. Inebriates were always advised to drink in the morning some of the same liquor they had drunk to excess the night before.

'Twas a hot night with some of us last night, John: shall we pluck a hair of the same wolf to-day, proctor John?
BEN JONSON, *Bartholomew Fair*. Act i.

If they, in the morning, did fall to drinking again, taking a hair of the old dog.
HEAD AND KIRKMAN, *English Rogue*. iii, 91.

A hair of the same dog next morning
Is best to quench our fev'rish burning.
EDWARD WARD, *Brit. Wonders,* 17.

He poured out a large bumper of brandy, exhorting me to swallow "a hair of the dog that bit me."
SCOTT, *Rob Roy*. Ch. 12.

If any so wise is, that sack he despises,
Let him drink his small beer and be sober;
And while we drink and sing, as if it were spring,
He shall droop like the trees in October.
But be sure overnight, if this dog do you bite,
You may take it henceforth for a warning;
Soon as out of your bed, to settle your head,
Take a hair of his tail in the morning.
UNKNOWN, *Song*. (1650)

1
The flowing bowl—whom has it not made eloquent? Whom has it not made free, even amid pinching poverty? (Fecundi calices quem non fecere disertum? Contracta quem non in paupertate solutum?)
HORACE, *Epistles*. Bk. i, epis. 5, l. 19.

Come landlord fill a flowing bowl until it does run over,
Tonight we will all merry be—tomorrow we'll get sober.
JOHN FLETCHER, *The Bloody Brother*. Act ii, 2.

Be in their flowing cups freshly remembered.
SHAKESPEARE, *Henry V*. Act iv, sc. 3, l. 55.

It is rarely seldum that I seek consolation in the Flowin Bole.
ARTEMUS WARD, *On "Forts."*

2
There are some sluggish men who are improved by drinking, as there are fruits that are not good till they are rotten.
SAMUEL JOHNSON. (BOSWELL, *Life*, iii, 42.)

3
And man that boozed of that,
Fourpence a gallon.
WILLIAM LANGLAND, *Piers Plowman: Vision of the Seven Sins: Avarice*. (1370)

Booze and the blowens cop the lot. (Tout aux tavernes et aux fiells.)
W. E. HENLEY, *Villon's Straight Tip to All Cross Coves*.

If a man has a bit of conscience, it always takes him when he's sober; and then it makes him low-spirited. A drop of booze just takes that off and makes him happy.
BERNARD SHAW, *Pygmalion*. Act iii.

4
Over their cups. (Inter pocula.)
PERSIUS, *Satires*. Sat. i, l. 30.

5
There St. John mingles with my friendly bowl
The feast of reason and the flow of soul.
POPE, *Imitations of Horace: Satires*. Bk. ii, sat. 1, l. 127.

6
Thirst departs with drinking. (Le soif s'en va en beuvant.)
RABELAIS, *Works*. Bk. i, ch. 5.

Thirst comes with drinking, when the wine is good.
ÉMILE AUGIER, *La Ciguë*.

7
Come, let us drink. (Venite apotemus.)
RABELAIS, *Works*. Bk. i, ch. 42. The monk's invocation.

8
I do not drink more than a sponge. (Je ne boy en plus qu'une esponge.)
RABELAIS, *Works*. Bk. i, ch. 5.

I'll do anything, Nerissa, ere I'll be married to a sponge.
SHAKESPEARE, *The Merchant of Venice*. Act i, sc. 2, l. 107.

9
The great
Should be as large in liquor as in love.
E. A. ROBINSON, *Ben Jonson Entertains a Man from Stratford*.

11
And that he calls for drink, I'll have prepared him
A chalice for the nonce.
SHAKESPEARE, *Hamlet*. Act iv, sc. 7, l. 160.

12
Potations pottle-deep.
SHAKESPEARE, *Othello*. Act ii, sc. 3, l. 56.

Most potent in potting.
SHAKESPEARE, *Othello*. Act ii, sc. 3, l. 78.

13
I can drink like a fish.
JAMES SHIRLEY, *Works*. Vol. vi, p. 321. (1646)

Where I may drink like a fish, and swear like a devil.
FARQUHAR, *Sir Harry Wildair*. Act ii. (1701)

I shall have nothing to do but go to Bath and drink like a fish.
HANNAH MORE. (*Garrick Correspondence*. Vol. ii, p. 320. 1778.)

We can drink till all look blue.
JOHN FORD, *Lady's Trial*. Act iv, sc. 2.

To drink like a funnel.
JOHN RAY, *English Proverbs*, p. 191. (1670)

14
Fifteen men on the Dead Man's Chest—
Yo-ho-ho and a bottle of rum!
Drink and the devil had done for the rest—
Yo-ho-ho and a bottle of rum!
R. L. STEVENSON, *Treasure Island*. Formerly believed to be the refrain of an old chanty, but stated by Lloyd Osbourne to be incontestably by R.L.S. Used by Young E. Allison as refrain for his poem *Derelict*. (See STEVENSON, *Famous Single Poems*.) The Dead Man's Chest is one of the Virgin Islands.

Fifteen men on the Dead Man's Chest—
Yo-ho-ho and a bottle of rum!
Young E. Allison done all the rest!
Yo-ho-ho and a bottle of rum.
JAMES WHITCOMB RILEY, *Letter*, to Allison.

1
A bottle of sherry, a bottle of sham, a bottle of port, and a shass caffy.

THACKERAY, *Pendennis*. Ch. 4. Mr. Foker's idea of the drinks which should go with a dinner. Cordially approved by George Saintsbury in his *Notes on a Cellar-Book*.

2
Let them drink, since they will not eat. (Quasi ut biberent quaodo esse nolent.)

TIBERIUS, of the sacred chickens, who would not eat when he took the auspices, and which he threw into the sea. (SUETONIUS, *Tiberius*. Ch. ii, sec. 2.)

3
The Dutch their wine, and all their brandy lose,
Disarmed of that from which their courage grows.

EDMUND WALLER, *Instructions to a Painter for a Picture of the Victory over the Dutch*, 3 June, 1665. (Hence, "Dutch courage.")

4
They drink with impunity, or anybody who invites them.

ARTEMUS WARD, *Moses the Sassy: Programme*.

5
The dew was falling fast, the stars began to blink;
I heard a voice; it said, "Drink, pretty creature, drink!"

WORDSWORTH, *The Pet Lamb*.

5a
Shun not the mead, but drink in measure;
Speak to the point or be still.

UNKNOWN, *The Elder Edda: Hovamol*. Sec. 19. (HENRY ADAMS BELLOWS, tr., *Poetic Edda*.)

6
It's a long time between drinks.

The expression, "It is too long between drinks," "It's a long time between drinks," is undoubtedly an invention. There is no record of its having occurred in any conference between governors of the Carolinas. My guess is that when a convivial party was having a good time one night and matters became a little slow, some booster of the party asked the question, "What did the governor of North Carolina say to the Governor of South Carolina?" And when they all gave it up, he furnished the answer, "It is too long between drinks."—A. S. Salley, Secretary Historical Commission of South Carolina, in a letter to the compiler, 28 May, 1932. The expression antedates the Civil War, and many stories have been invented to explain it, but none of them has any historical foundation. John Motley Morehead states that there is a legend in his family that his grandfather was the governor of North Carolina who made the historic remark. Another legend credits it to Zebulon B. Vance, governor of North Carolina at the time Wade Hampton was governor of South Carolina.

II—Drinking: Its Pleasures

7
Fill up the goblet and reach to me some!
Drinking makes wise, but dry fasting makes glum.

W. R. ALGER, *Oriental Poetry: Wine Song of Kaitmas*.

8
The thirsty Earth soaks up the Rain,
And drinks, and gapes for Drink again;
The Plants suck in the Earth, and are
With constant drinking fresh and fair. . . .
Nothing in Nature's sober found,
But an eternal Health goes round.
Fill up the Bowl then, fill it high,
Fill all the Glasses there; for why
Should every Creature drink but I?
Why, Men of Morals, tell me why?

ANACREON, *Odes*. No. 21. (Cowley, tr.)

9
Weak withering age no rigid law forbids,
With frugal nectar, smooth and slow with balm,
The sapless habit daily to bedew,
And give the hesitating wheels of life
Gliblier to play.

JOHN ARMSTRONG, *Art of Preserving Health*. Pt. ii, l. 484. (1744)

10
We also had drink of three kinds, all wholesome and good; wine of the grape; a drink of grain, such as is with us our ale but more clear; and a kind of cider made of a fruit of that country, a wonderful pleasing and refreshing drink.

FRANCIS BACON, *New Atlantis*. Sec. 3.

11
We'll tak' a right gude-willie waught
For Auld Lang Syne.

ROBERT BURNS, *Auld Lang Syne*. Frequently misquoted "gude willie-waught." "Gude-willie waught" means good-will draught. The other is nonsense.

Just a wee deoch-an-doris, just a wee yin, that's a'.
Just a wee deoch-an-doris before we gang a-wa',
There's a wee wifie waitin', in a wee but-an-ben;
If you can say "It's a braw bricht moon-licht nicht,"
Y're a 'richt ye ken.

HARRY LAUDER, *Just a Wee Deoch-an-Doris*.

12
Food fills the wame, an' keep us livin'; . . .
But, oiled by thee,
The wheels o' life gae down-hill scrievin',
Wi' rattlin' glee.

ROBERT BURNS, *Scotch Drink*. St. 5.

Leeze me on drink! it gies us mair
Than either school or college:
It kindles wit, it waukens lair,
It pangs us fou o' knowledge.

ROBERT BURNS, *The Holy Fair*. St. 19.

13
Fill the goblet again! for I never before
Felt the glow which now gladdens my heart to its core;
Let us drink!—who would not?—since, through life's varied round,

In goblet alone no deception is found.
BYRON, *Fill the Goblet Again.*

1
To drink is a Christian diversion,
Unknown to the Turk or the Persian.
CONGREVE, *The Way of the World.* Act iv, sc. 2.

2
Then trust me there's nothing like drinking
So pleasant on this side the grave;
It keeps the unhappy from thinking,
And makes e'en the valiant more brave.
CHARLES DIBDIN, *Nothing Like Grog.*

3
"Mrs. Harris," I says, "leave the bottle on the chimley-piece, and don't ask me to take none, but let me put my lips to it when I am so dispoged."
DICKENS, *Martin Chuzzlewit.* Ch. 19.

4
The peculiar charm of alcohol lies in the sense of careless well-being and bodily and mental comfort which it creates. It unburdens the individual of his cares and his fears. . . . Under such conditions it is easy to laugh or to weep, to love or to hate, not wisely but too well.
DR. HAVEN EMERSON, *Alcohol and Man.*

5
The jolly god in triumph comes;
Sound the trumpets; beat the drums:
Flush'd with a purple grace
He shows his honest face:
Now give the hautboys breath; he comes, he comes!
Bacchus ever fair and young,
Drinking joys did first ordain;
Bacchus' blessings are a treasure,
Drinking is the soldier's pleasure:
Rich the treasure, Sweet the pleasure,
Sweet is pleasure after pain.
DRYDEN, *Alexander's Feast,* l. 49.

6
The man that isn't jolly after drinking
Is just a drivelling idiot, to my thinking.
EURIPIDES, *Cyclops,* l. 169. Quoted by Rabelais, *Works.* Bk. iv, ch. 65.

7
Drink to-day, and drown all sorrow;
You shall perhaps not do it to-morrow:
Best, while you have it, use your breath;
There is no drinking after death.
JOHN FLETCHER, *The Bloody Brother.* Act ii, sc. 2.

8
Let's warm our brains with half-a-dozen healths,
And then, hang cold discourse; for we'll speak fireworks.
JOHN FLETCHER, *The Elder Brother.* Act i, sc. 2.

9
Let schoolmasters puzzle their brain,
With grammar, and nonsense, and learning;
Good liquor, I stoutly maintain,
Gives *genus* a better discerning.
GOLDSMITH, *She Stoops to Conquer.* Act i, sc. 2.

10
There are bonds of all sorts in this world of ours,
Fetters of friendship and ties of flowers, . . .
But there's never a bond, old friend, like this,
We have drunk from the same canteen.
CHARLES GRAHAM HALPINE, *The Canteen.*

For it's always fair weather
When good fellows get together,
With a stein on the table and a good song ringing clear.
RICHARD HOVEY, *Spring.*

11
The warm, champagny, old-particular, brandy-punchy feeling.
O. W. HOLMES, *Nux Postcœnatica.*

12
Who, after his wine, prates of war's hardships or of poverty? (Quis post vina gravem militiam aut pauperiem crepat?)
HORACE, *Odes.* Bk. i, ode 18, l. 5.

'Tis mighty easy, o'er a glass of wine,
On vain refinements vainly to refine,
To laugh at poverty in plenty's reign,
To boast of apathy when out of pain.
CHARLES CHURCHILL, *The Farewell,* l. 47.

13
Now is the time for drinking, and now with sportive foot to beat the earth. (Nunc est bibendum, nunc pede libero pulsanda tellus.)
HORACE, *Odes.* Bk. i, ode 37, l. 1.

Bacchus scatters devouring cares. (Dissipat Evius Curas edaces.)
HORACE, *Odes.* Bk. ii, ode ii, l. 18.

14
They that love mirth, let them heartily drink,
'Tis the only receipt to make sorrow sink.
BEN JONSON, *Entertainments: The Penates.*

Nor shall our cups make any guilty men;
But at our parting, we will be as when
We innocently met.
BEN JONSON, *Epigrams.* No. 101.

15
Often I sung thus, and I will cry it from the tomb: "Drink ere ye put on this dusty garment." (Πολλάκι μὲν τόδ' ἄεισα, καὶ ἐκ τύμβου δε βοησω· "Πίνετε, πρὶν ταύτην ἀμφιβάλησθε κόνιν.")
JULIANUS, PREFECT OF EGYPT, *On Anacreon.* (*Greek Anthology.* Bk. vii, No. 32.)

Drink! for you know not whence you came, nor why;
Drink! for you know not why you go, nor where.
OMAR KHAYYÁM, *Rubáiyát.* St. 74. (Fitzgerald, tr.)

And when like her, oh Sákí, you shall pass
Among the Guests Star-scattered on the Grass,
And in your joyous errand reach the spot

Where I made One—turn down an empty Glass!
OMAR KHAYYÁM, *Rubáiyát*. Last stanza. (Fitzgerald, tr.)

1
O for a beaker full of the warm South,
Full of the true, the blushful Hippocrene,
With beaded bubbles winking at the brim,
And purple-stained mouth.
KEATS, *Ode to a Nightingale*.

2
The Elixir of Perpetual Youth,
Called Alcohol.
LONGFELLOW, *The Golden Legend*. Pt. i.

3
I intend to die in a tavern; let the wine be placed near my dying mouth, so that when the choirs of angels come, they may say, "God be merciful to this drinker!"
(Meum est propositum in taberna mori;
Vinum sit appositum morientis ori,
Ut dicant cum venerint angelorum chori,
"Deus sit propitius huic potatori!")
WALTER MAPES, *Goliæ Confessio*. (c. 1205) The attribution to Mapes has been disputed.

4
Oh some that's good and godly ones they hold that it's a sin
To troll the jolly bowl around, and let the dollars spin;
But I'm for toleration and for drinking at an inn,
Says the old bold mate of Henry Morgan.
JOHN MASEFIELD, *Captain Stratton's Fancy*.

5
One sip of this
Will bathe the drooping spirits in delight,
Beyond the bliss of dreams.
MILTON, *Comus*, l. 811.

6
Friend of my soul, this goblet sip,
'Twill chase that pensive tear;
'Tis not so sweet as woman's lip,
But, oh! 'tis more sincere.
Like her delusive beam,
'Twill steal away thy mind:
But, truer than love's dream,
It leaves no sting behind
THOMAS MOORE, *Anacreontic*.

If with water you fill up your glasses,
You'll never write anything wise;
For wine is the horse of Parnassus,
Which hurries a bard to the skies.
THOMAS MOORE, *Anacreontic*.

Fill the bumper fair!
Every drop we sprinkle
O'er the brow of Care
Smooths away a wrinkle.
THOMAS MOORE, *Fill the Bumper Fair*.

Wreath the bowl
With flowers of soul,
The brightest Wit can find us;
We'll take a flight
Tow'rds heaven to-night,
And leave dull earth behind us.
THOMAS MOORE, *Wreath the Bowl*.

7
There are two reasons for drinking: one is, when you are thirsty, to cure it; the other, when you are not thirsty, to prevent it. . . . Prevention is better than cure.
T. L. PEACOCK, *Melincourt*. Ch. 16.

If all be true that I do think,
There are five reasons we should drink;
Good wine—a friend—or being dry—
Or lest we should be by and by—
Or any other reason why.
(Si bene commemini, causæ sunt quinque bibendi;
Hospitis adventus, præsens sitis, atque futura,
Aut vini bonitas, aut quælibet altera causa.)
A Latin epigram attributed to PÈRE SIRMOND, 16th century. (MÉNAGE, *Menagiana*, i, 172.) Trans. by Henry Aldrich. (PLAYFORD, *Banquet of Music*, 1689.)

There are, unless my memory fail,
Five causes why we should not sail:
The fog is thick; the wind is high;
It rains; or may do by-and-by;
Or—any other reason why.
JOHN WESLEY, *When Delayed at Holyhead*.

8
A hot drink is as good as an overcoat. (Tamen calda potio vestiarius est.)
PETRONIUS, *Satyricon*. Sec. 41.

9
There is no deceit in a brimmer.
JOHN RAY, *English Proverbs*.

10
There is no money, among that which I have spent since I began to earn my living, of the expenditure of which I am less ashamed, or which gave me better value in return, than the price of the liquids chronicled in this booklet.
GEORGE SAINTSBURY, *Notes on a Cellar-Book*, p. 14.

There is absolutely no scientific proof of a trustworthy kind, that moderate consumption of sound alcoholic liquor does a healthy body any harm at all; while on the other hand there is the unbroken testimony of all history that alcoholic liquors have been used by the strongest, wisest, handsomest, and in every way best races of all times.
GEORGE SAINTSBURY, *Notes on a Cellar-Book*, p. 17.

11
Drink down all unkindness.
SHAKESPEARE, *The Merry Wives of Windsor*. Act i, sc. 1, l. 203.

12
And let me the canakin clink:
A soldier's but a man;
A life's but a span;
Why, then, let a soldier drink.
SHAKESPEARE, *Othello*. Act ii, sc. 3, l. 72.

Fill the can and fill the cup:
All the windy ways of men

Are but dust that rises up,
And is lightly laid again.
TENNYSON, *The Vision of Sin*, l. 131.

1
A bumper of good liquor
Will end a contest quicker
Than justice, judge, or vicar;
So fill a cheerful glass.
R. B. SHERIDAN, *The Duenna*. Act ii, sc. 3.

Candy Is dandy
But liquor Is quicker.
OGDEN NASH, *Reflection on Ice-Breaking*.

This bottle's the sun of our table,
His beams are rosy wine;
We, planets, that are not able
Without his help to shine.
R. B. SHERIDAN, *The Duenna*. Act iii, sc. 5.

2
And he thought that all the world over
In vain for a man you might seek,
Who could drink more like a Trojan
Or talk more like a Greek.
ROBERT SOUTHEY, *The Devil's Walk*. St. 50. The reference is to Prof. R. C. Porson, who claimed the authorship of *The Devil's Walk*.

3
I cannot eat but little meat,
My stomach is not good;
But sure I think that I can drink
With him that wears a hood.
JOHN STILL, *Gammer Gurton's Needle*. Act ii, l. 1. Said to be from a song older than the play. It is also uncertain whether Bishop Still wrote the play, which has been attributed to Nicholas Udall and to John Bridges, Dean of Salisbury. The authorship of the song has been claimed for William Stevenson, of Durham.

4
One top of Parnassus was sacred to Bacchus, the other to Apollo.
SWIFT, *Thoughts on Various Subjects*.

It is sometimes forgotten that only one of the two peaks of Parnassus was sacred to Apollo, the other belonging to Dionysus.
SAINTSBURY, *Notes on a Cellar-Book*, p. 21.

5
We drank the Libyan sun to sleep, and lit
Lamps which out-burn'd Canopus.
TENNYSON, *A Dream of Fair Women*, l. 145.

6
I'll look in thy purse by and by,
And if thou have any money in it,
We'll drink the devil dry.
ROBERT WILSON, *Cobbler's Prophecy*, l. 106

7
He that drinks well, sleeps well.
THOMAS WILSON, *Rule of Reason*. (1551)

He that eateth well, drinketh well; he that drinketh well, sleepeth well; he that sleepeth well, sinneth not; he that sinneth not goeth straight through Purgatory to Paradise.
WILLIAM LITHGOW, *Rare Adventures*. (1609)

He that drinks well, does sleep well;
He that sleeps well, doth think well;
He that thinks well, doth do well;
He that does well, must drink well.
UNKNOWN, *Loyal Garland*. Song 65. (1686)

8
Drinking will make a man quaff,
Quaffing will make a man sing,
Singing will make a man laugh,
And laughing long life doth bring,
Saith old Simon the King
UNKNOWN, *Old Simon the King*. (D'URFEY, *Pills to Purge Melancholy*.) The reference is said to be to Simon Wadloe, keeper of the Devil Tavern, in Fleet Street, about 1621.

9
We're gaily yet, and we're gaily yet;
And we're no very fou but we're gaily yet;
Then sit ye a while, and tipple a bit,
For we're no very fou, but we're gaily yet.
UNKNOWN. Introduced into the third act of Vanbrugh's *The Provoked Wife*, apparently by Fowler, the printer of the play, and called a Scotch medley.

III—Drinking: Its Penalties

10
Beware the deadly fumes of that insane elation
Which rises from the cup of mad impiety,
And go, get drunk with that divine intoxication
Which is more sober far than all sobriety.
W. R. ALGER, *Oriental Poetry: The Sober Drunkenness*.

11
For when the wine is in, the wit is out.
THOMAS BECON, *Catechism*, 375. (1558)

Where the drink goes in, there the wit goes out.
GEORGE HERBERT, *Jacula Prudentum*.

When the wine's in, murder will out.
Babylonian Talmud: Erubin, fo. 65b.

12
There's Death in the cup—so beware!
Nay, more—there is danger in touching;
But who can avoid the fell snare?
The man and his wine's so bewitching!
BURNS, *On a Goblet*.

13
For though within this bright seductive place
My dollars go not far,
I never more shall see them face to face,
When they have crossed the bar!
BLISS CARMAN, *Crossing the Bar*.

14
Ha! see where the wild-blazing Grog-Shop appears,
As the red waves of wretchedness swell.
How it burns on the edge of tempestuous years
The horrible Light-House of Hell!
M'DONALD CLARKE, *The Rum Hole*.

15
Ten thousand casks,
Forever dribbling out their base contents,
Touch'd by the Midas finger of the state,

Bleed gold for ministers to sport away.
Drink, and be mad then; 'tis your country bids!

COWPER, *The Task*. Bk. iv, l. 504.

1
Drink not the third glass, which thou canst not tame,
When once it is within thee; but before
Mayst rule it, as thou list; and pour the shame,
Which it would pour on thee, upon the floor.
It is most just to throw that on the ground,
Which would throw me there, if I keep the round.

GEORGE HERBERT, *The Church-Porch*. St. 5.

2
But they also have erred through wine, and through strong drink.

Old Testament: Isaiah, xxviii, 7.

3
Their sinfulness is greater than their use.

The Koran. Ch. 2. Of wine and gambling.

4
Dread the delight of drink and thou shalt do the better.
Though thou long for more, Measure is Medicine.
What the belly asketh is not all good for the ghost,
What the soul loveth is not all food for the body.

WILLIAM LANGLAND, *Piers Plowman: The Vision of Holy Church*, l. 29.

5
Touch the goblet no more!
It will make thy heart sore
To its very core!
Its perfume is the breath
Of the Angel of Death,
And the light that within it lies
Is the flash of his evil eyes.
Beware! Oh, beware!
For sickness, sorrow, and care
All are there!

LONGFELLOW, *The Golden Legend*. Pt. i.

6
Long quaffing maketh a short lyfe.

JOHN LYLY, *Euphues*.

7
Soon as the potion works, their human count'nance,
Th' express resemblance of the gods, is chang'd
Into some bruitish form of wolf or bear,
Or ounce or tiger, hog, or bearded goat,
All other parts remaining as they were;
And they, so perfect is their misery,
Not once perceive their foul disfigurement.

MILTON, *Comus*, l. 68.

O madness, to think use of strongest wines
And strongest drinks our chief support of health,
When God with these forbidden made choice to rear
His mighty Champion, strong above compare,
Whose drink was only from the liquid brook.

MILTON, *Samson Agonistes*, l. 553.

8
Indeed the Idols I have loved so long
Have done my credit in the World much wrong:
Have drown'd my Glory in a shallow Cup,
And sold my Reputation for a Song.

OMAR KHAYYÁM, *Rubáiyát*. St. 93. (Fitzgerald, tr.)

9
It has passed into a proverb that wisdom is clouded by wine. (In proverbium cessit, sapientiam vino obumbrari.)

PLINY THE ELDER, *Naturalis Historia*, Bk. xxiii, ch. 1, sec. 23.

10
They never taste who always drink.

MATTHEW PRIOR, *On a Passage in the Scaligerana*.

11
In vain I trusted that the flowing bowl
Would banish sorrow, and enlarge the soul.
To the late revel, and protracted feast,
Wild dreams succeeded, and disorder'd rest.

MATTHEW PRIOR, *Solomon*. Bk. ii, l. 106.

And in the flowers that wreathe the sparkling bowl
Fell adders hiss and poisonous serpents roll.

MATTHEW PRIOR, *Solomon*. Bk. ii, l. 140.

Thou sparkling bowl! thou sparkling bowl!
Though lips of bards thy brim may press . . .
I will not touch thee; for there clings
A scorpion to thy side, that stings!

JOHN PIERPONT, *The Sparkling Bowl*.

12
Men fished for women, and women for men, in muddy water, and drink was the bait they used.

WILLIAM ROTHENSTEIN, *Men and Memories, 1872–1900*, p. 71.

WINE AND WOMEN, *see under* WINE.

13
Just as I do not care to live in a place of torture, neither do I care to live in a café. (Quemadmodum inter tortores habitare nolim, sic ne inter popinas quidem.)

SENECA, *Epistulæ ad Lucilium*. Epis. li, sec. 4.

14
I have very poor and unhappy brains for drinking: I could well wish courtesy would invent some other custom of entertainment.

SHAKESPEARE, *Othello*. Act ii, sc. 3, l. 35.

15
O God, that men should put an enemy in their mouths to steal away their brains! that we should, with joy, pleasance, revel and applause, transform ourselves into beasts!

SHAKESPEARE, *Othello*. Act ii, sc. 3, l. 291.

16
Much drinking, little thinking.

SWIFT, *Letter to Stella*, 26 Feb., 1711.

1
The vials of summer never made a man sick, but those which he stored in his cellar. Drink the wines, not of your bottling, but Nature's bottling; not kept in goat-skins or pig-skins, but the skins of a myriad fair berries.

H. D. THOREAU, *Journal,* 23 Aug., 1853.

2
Drink makes men hungry, or it makes them
lie.

GEORGE WILKINS, *The Miseries of Enforced Marriage.* Act ii.

IV—Drinking: Brandy, Punch, Rum, Whiskey

See also Ale and Beer, Wine

3
There's some are fou o' love divine,
There's some are fou o' brandy.

ROBERT BURNS, *The Holy Fair.* St. 27.

4
I always had on my journeys a pocket pistol loaded with brandy and lemon juice.

EDWARD BURT, *Letters from a Gentleman in the North of Scotland.*

5
Mynheer Vandunck, though he never was
drunk,
Sipped brandy and water gayly.

GEORGE COLMAN THE YOUNGER, *Mynheer Vandunck.*

6
Call things by their right names. . . . Glass of brandy and water! That is the current but not the appropriate name: ask for a glass of liquid fire and distilled damnation.

REV. ROBERT HALL, to a man who asked for a glass of brandy. (GREGORY, *Life of Hall.*)

Liquid Madness sold at tenpence the quartern.

THOMAS CARLYLE, *Chartism.* Ch. 4.

A drunkard clasp his teeth and not undo 'em,
To suffer wet damnation to run through 'em.

CYRIL TOURNEUR, *Revenger's Tragedy.* Act iii, 1.

7
If wine tells truth,—and so have said the
wise,—
It makes me laugh to think how brandy lies!

O. W. HOLMES, *The Banker's Secret,* l. 161.

8
As for the brandy, 'nothing extenuate;' and the water, put naught in in malice.

DOUGLAS JERROLD, *Shakespeare Grog.*

9
Claret is the liquor for boys; port for men; but he who aspires to be a hero must drink brandy.

SAMUEL JOHNSON, *Remark,* at dinner with Sir Joshua Reynolds. (BOSWELL, *Life,* 1779.)

Forswear thin potations.

SHAKESPEARE, *II Henry IV.* Act iv, sc. 3, l. 133.

10
Did ye iver try a brandy cocktail, Cornel?

THACKERAY, *The Newcomes.* Ch. 13. Napoleon I is said to have invented the cocktail. His favorite "pick-me-up" was called a "Rose."

11
What makes the cider blow its cork
With such a merry din?
What makes those little bubbles rise
And dance like harlequin?
It is the fatal apple, boys,
The fruit of human sin.

CHRISTOPHER MORLEY, *A Glee Upon Cider.*

12
While briskly to each patriot lip
Walks eager round the inspiring flip;
Delicious draught, whose pow'rs inherit
The quintessence of public spirit!

JOHN TRUMBULL, *McFingal.* Canto iii, l. 21.

13
Meanwhile, my friend, 'twould be no sin
To mix more water in your gin.
We're neither saints nor Philip Sidneys,
But mortal men with mortal kidneys.

JOHN MASEFIELD, *The Everlasting Mercy.*

The shortest way out of Manchester is notoriously a bottle of Gordon's gin.

WILLIAM BOLITHO, *Twelve Against the Gods: Cagliostro (and Seraphina).*

14
'Tis grog, only grog,
Is his rudder, his compass, his cable, his log;
The sailor's sheet anchor is grog.

CHARLES DIBDIN, *The Sailor's Sheet Anchor.*

15
He drinketh strong waters which do bemuse a man, and make him even as the wild beasts of the desert.

W. S. GILBERT, *Ruddigore.* Act i.

16
This cordial julep here,
That flames and dances in his crystal bounds.

MILTON, *Comus,* l. 672.

17
There's nought, no doubt, so much the spirit
calms
As rum and true religion; thus it was,
Some plunder'd, some drank spirits, some
sung psalms.

BYRON, *Don Juan.* Canto ii, st. 34.

18
Oh some are fond of red wines, and some are
fond of white,
And some are all for dancing by the pale
moonlight;
But rum alone's the tipple, and the heart's
delight
Of the old bold mate of Henry Morgan.

JOHN MASEFIELD, *Captain Stratton's Fancy.*

But I'm for right Jamaica till I roll beneath the
bench,
Says the old bold mate of Henry Morgan.

JOHN MASEFIELD, *Captain Stratton's Fancy.*

19
The great utility of rum has given it the medical name of an antifogmatic. The quantity taken every morning is in exact proportion to the thickness of the fog.

UNKNOWN, *Massachusetts Spy,* 12 Nov., 1789.

1
What harm in drinking can there be,
Since punch and life so well agree?
THOMAS BLACKLOCK, *Epigram on Punch*, l. 15.

2
I got up to the Peacock, where I found everybody drinking hot punch in self-preservation.
DICKENS, *The Holly-Tree Inn*.

3
Though I already half seas over am,
If the capacious goblet overflow
With arrack punch—'fore George! I'll see it out.
FIELDING, *Tom Thumb the Great*. Act ii, sc. 2.

4
Many estates are spent in the getting,
Since women for tea forsook spinning and knitting,
And men for punch forsook hewing and splitting.
FRANKLIN, *Way to Wealth*. Vol. i, p. 446.

5
Those bottled windy drinks that laugh in a man's face and then cut his throat.
THOMAS ADAMS, *Works*, iii, 267.

6
Let half-starv'd slaves in warmer skies
See future wines, rich-clust'ring, rise;
Their lot auld Scotia ne'er envies,
But, blythe and frisky,
She eyes her freeborn, martial boys
Tak aff their whisky.
BURNS, *The Author's Earnest Cry and Prayer to the Scotch Representatives in the House of Commons: Postscript*.

Freedom and whisky gang thegither!—
Tak aff your dram!
ROBERT BURNS, *The Author's Earnest Cry*.

O Whisky! soul o' plays an' pranks!
Accept a Bardie's gratefu' thanks!
ROBERT BURNS, *Scotch Drink*. St. 18.

7
John Barleycorn was a hero bold,
Of noble enterprise,
For if you do but taste his blood,
'Twill make your courage rise.
BURNS, *John Barleycorn*. St. 13.

Inspiring bold John Barleycorn,
What dangers thou canst make us scorn!
Wi' tippenny, we fear nae evil;
Wi' usquebae, we'll face the devil!
ROBERT BURNS, *Tam o' Shanter*, l. 105.

8
When he chanced to have taken an overdose of the creature.
WALTER SCOTT, *Guy Mannering*. Ch. 44.

9
Whiskey is a bad thing—especially bad whiskey.
C. H. SPURGEON. Quoted as a Highland saying.

10
Let the farmer praise his grounds,
Let the huntsman praise his hounds,
The shepherd his dew-scented lawn;
But I, more blest than they,
Spend each happy night and day
With my charming little cruiskeen lawn, lawn, lawn,
My charming little cruiskeen lawn.
UNKNOWN, *The Cruiskeen Lawn*.

V—Drinking Healths

11
Waes-hael! for Lord and Dame!
O! merry be their Dole;
Drink-hael! in Jesu's name,
And fill the tawny bowl.
King Arthur's Waes-Hael.

12
Here's a health to them that's awa,
Here's a health to them that's awa;
And wha winna wish guid luck to our cause,
May never guid luck be their fa'!
ROBERT BURNS, *Here's a Health*.

13
My boat is on the shore,
And my bark is on the sea;
But, before I go, Tom Moore,
Here's a double health to thee! . . .

Were 't the last drop in the well,
As I gasp'd upon the brink,
Ere my fainting spirit fell,
'Tis to thee that I would drink.
BYRON, *My Boat is On the Shore*.

14
Drink ye to her that each loves best,
And, if you nurse a flame
That's told but to her mutual breast,
We will not ask her name.
THOMAS CAMPBELL, *Drink Ye to Her*.

15
To drink healths is to drink sickness.
THOMAS DEKKER, *II The Honest Whore*. Act iv, sc. 3. (1635)

We drink one another's healths and spoil our own.
JEROME K. JEROME, *Idle Thoughts of an Idle Fellow: On Eating and Drinking*.

So the sailors in this ship [the *Carouse*] have taken a use to drink other men's healths, to the amplifying of their own diseases.
JOHN TAYLOR, *A Navy of Landships*. (c. 1650)

16
But the standing toast that pleased the most
Was, "The wind that blows, the ship that goes,
And the lass that loves a sailor!"
CHARLES DIBDIN, *The Standing Toast*. From the comic opera, *The Round Robin*, produced 21 June, 1811.

17
And he that will this health deny,
Down among the dead men let him lie.
JOHN DYER, *Song*. Empty bottles were colloquially known as "dead men."

18
We drank Sir Condy's good health and the

downfall of his enemies till we could stand no longer ourselves.
MARIA EDGEWORTH, *Castle Rackrent: Continuation of Memoirs.*

1
Here's a health to you, Father O'Flynn,
Sláinte, and *sláinte,* and *sláinte* agin;
Powerfulest preacher, and
Tinderest teacher, and
Kindliest creature in ould Donegal.
ALFRED PERCEVAL GRAVES, *Father O'Flynn.*

2
Here's to your health and your family's good health. May you all live long and prosper.
JOSEPH JEFFERSON, *Rip Van Winkle.* A play from Irving's story.

3
To the old, long life and treasure;
To the young, all health and pleasure.
BEN JONSON, *Metamorphosed Gipsies: Third Song.*

4
Give me the cups;
And let the kettle to the trumpet speak,
The trumpet to the cannoneer without,
The cannons to the heavens, the heavens to earth,
"Now the king drinks to Hamlet."
SHAKESPEARE, *Hamlet.* Act v, sc. 2, l. 285.

I drink to the general joy o' the whole table.
SHAKESPEARE, *Macbeth.* Act iii, sc. 4, l. 89.

Here, with a cup that's stored unto the brim
. . . We drink this health to you.
SHAKESPEARE, *Pericles.* Act ii, sc. 3, l. 50.

5
Here's to the maiden of bashful fifteen;
Here's to the widow of fifty;
Here's to the flaunting, extravagant quean;
And here's to the housewife that's thrifty.
Let the toast pass,—
Drink to the lass,
I'll warrant she'll prove an excuse for the glass.
SHERIDAN, *The School for Scandal.* Act iii, sc. 3.

6
A health to the nut-brown lass,
With the hazel eyes: let it pass. . . .
As much to the lively grey
'Tis as good i' th' night as day: . . .
She's a savour to the glass,
An excuse to make it pass.
SIR JOHN SUCKLING, *The Goblins.* Act iii.

7
Wine fills the veins, and healths are understood
To give our friends a title to our blood.
EDMUND WALLER, *The Drinking of Healths.*

8
Here's a health to all those that we love,
Here's a health to all those that love us,
Here's a health to all those that love them that love those
That love them that love those that love us.
UNKNOWN, *Here's a Health.*

9
Merry met, and merry part.
I drink to thee with all my heart.
UNKNOWN, *Old Cup Inscription.*

DRUNKENNESS

I—Drunkenness: Apothegms

10
If fortune that helps frantic men and drunk
Had not him safe convey'd.
ARIOSTO, *Orlando Furioso.* Bk. xxx, st. 13. (Sir John Harington, tr., 1591)

That is well said, John, an honest man, that is not quite sober, has nothing to fear.
ADDISON, *The Drummer.* Act i, sc. 1. (1715)

A drunken man never takes harm.
UNKNOWN, *Meeting of Gallants,* 26. (1604)

The power that guards the drunk, his sleep attends.
JOHN GAY, *Shepherd's Week,* l. 127.

11
She pledged him once, and she pledged him twice,
And she drank as Lady ought not to drink.
R. H. BARHAM, *A Lay of St. Nicholas.*

12
They make a complete sentence by saying of a friend, "He is one who on the market day," and leaving the rest to the listener's common sense.
J. M. BARRIE, *Farewell, Miss Julie Logan,* p. 13.

13
I will be drunken as a rat.
ANDREW BOORD, *Introduction,* 147. (1542)

As drunk as a tinker.
CIBBER, *Love Makes a Man.* Act i. (1701)

Drunk as a fish.
CONGREVE, *Way of the World.* Act iv, 9. (1704)

To make a German general as drunk as a wheelbarrow.
THOMAS DILKE, *City Lady.* Act i, sc. 1. (1697)

Here's my brother as drunk as an emperor.
THOMAS DILKE, *City Lady.* Act iii, 2. (1697)

Drunk as a piper all day long.
JOHN GAY, *Fables.* (1720)

Drunk as a beggar.
MASSINGER, *Virgin Martyr.* Act iii, sc. 3. (1622)

They must be still drunk as owls.
R. L. STEVENSON, *Treasure Island.* Ch. 24.

I'm as drunk as a Plymouth fiddler.
STEVENSON AND HENLEY, *Admiral Guinea.* Act ii, sc. 4.

Thou comest home as dronken as a mouse.
CHAUCER, *Wife of Bath's Prologue,* l. 246. (1386)

As drunk as a lord.
UNKNOWN, *Somers Tracts,* vii, 184. (1659)

14
A whiff of stale debauch.
COWPER, *The Task.* Bk. iv, l. 469.

All learned, and all drunk!
COWPER, *The Task.* Bk. iv, l. 478.

1
It is most absurdly said, in popular language, of any man, that he is *disguised* in liquor; for, on the contrary, most men are disguised by sobriety.

THOMAS DE QUINCEY, *Confessions of an English Opium-Eater.*

2
That hasten to be drunk, the business of
the day.

DRYDEN, *Cymon and Iphigenia*, l. 408.

3
People can't tell us apart, we stagger so much alike.

FINLEY PETER DUNNE, *Cross-Examinations.*

4
There is this to be said in favor of drinking, that it takes the drunkard first out of society, then out of the world.

EMERSON, *Journal*, 1866.

5
Since the creation of the world there has been no tyrant like Intemperance, and no slaves so cruelly treated as his.

WILLIAM LLOYD GARRISON, *Life.* Vol. i, p. 268.

6
Alcoholic psychosis is nothin' more or less'n ole D.T.'s in a dinner suit.

KIN HUBBARD, *Abe Martin's Broadcast*, p. 20.

7
It is a kindness to lead the sober; a duty to lead the drunk.

W. S. LANDOR, *Imaginary Conversations: Don Victor Naez and El Rey, Nelto.*

8
Never go out drunk on a winter night. (*Χειμερίας μεθύων μηδαμὰ νμκτὸς ἴῃς.*)

LEONIDAS OF TARENTUM, *Epitaph*, for a man who died as the result of this indiscretion. (*Greek Anthology*. Bk. vii, epig. 660.)

9
I, for my part, can do nothing when sober. (Possum nil ego sobrius.)

MARTIAL, *Epigrams*. Bk. xi, ep. 6, l. 12.

10
He has come home late with staggering foot. (Sero domum est reversus titubanti pede.)

PHÆDRUS, *Fables*. Bk. iv, fab. 14, l. 10.

11
The penalty is doubled if the offender is drunk. (Τοῖς *μεθύουσι διῆλâ τὰ επιτίμια.*)

PITTACUS, *Politics*, ii, fin. One of his laws. (ARISTOTLE, *Nicomachean Ethics*, iii, 5.)

He that killeth a man drunk, sober shall be hanged.

THOMAS STARKEY, *England in the Reign of Henry VIII.* Bk. i, ch. 2.

Let him who sins when drunk be punished when sober. (Qui peccat ebrius, luat sobrius.)

Quoted in Kendrick v. Hopkins, 1580. (CARY'S *Rep.*, 133.)

12
Don't you see I'm just soaking soaked? (Non vides me ut mandide madeam?)

PLAUTUS, *Pseudolus*, l. 1297. (Act v, sc. 2.)

13
Drunkards beget drunkards. (Ebrii gignunt ebrios.)

PLUTARCH. (BURTON, *Anatomy of Melancholy.*)

14
He who quarrels with a drunken man injures one who is absent. (Absentem lædit, cum ebrio qui litigat.)

PUBLILIUS SYRUS, *Sententiæ*. No. 3.

15
'Tis not the drinking that is to be blamed, but the excess.

JOHN SELDEN, *Table-Talk: Humility.*

16 Sweet fellowship in shame!
One drunkard loves another of the name.

SHAKESPEARE, *Love's Labour's Lost*. Act iv, sc. 3, l. 49.

17
Full of supper and distempering draughts.

SHAKESPEARE, *Othello*. Act i, sc. 1, l. 99.

Do not think, gentlemen, I am drunk: this is my ancient; this is my right hand, and this is my left: I am not drunk now; I can stand well enough, and speak well enough.

SHAKESPEARE, *Othello*. Act ii, sc. 3, l. 116.

No man shall be held as mellow
Who can distinguish blue from yellow.

P. J. BAILEY, *Festus*. Sc. 15.

Not drunk is he, who from the floor
Can rise alone, and still drink more;
But drunk is he, who prostrate lies,
Without the power to drink or rise.
(Nid meddw y dyn a allo
Cwnu ei hun a rhodio,
Ac yved rhagor ddiawd:
Nid yw hyny yn veddwdawd.)

THOMAS LOVE PEACOCK, *The Misfortunes of Elphin*. Ch. 3, heading. Sometimes mistakenly attributed to Eugene Field.

18
And pavement, faithless to the fuddled foot.

THOMSON, *The Seasons: Autumn*, l. 537.

19
Every man that had any respect for himself would have got drunk, as was the custom of the country on all occasions of public moment.

MARK TWAIN, *Innocents at Home*. Ch. 10.

20
I would appeal to Philip, but to Philip sober. (Provocarem ad Philippum, sed sobrium.)

VALERIUS MAXIMUS. Bk. vi, ch. 2. Valerius gives this as the appeal of an old woman, against whom Philip of Macedon, sitting in judgment after dinner, had pronounced an unjust sentence. "I appeal!" she cried. "To whom?" asked Philip. "To Philip when sober," the woman replied. Philip allowed the appeal and when he recovered his senses, reversed the judgment. The incident has passed into a proverb, "To appeal from Philip drunk to Philip sober."

21
Better to trip with the feet than with the tongue. (*Κρεῖττον εἶναι τοῖς ποσὶν ὀλισθεῖν ἢ τῇ γλώττῃ.*)

ZENO, excusing drunkenness. (DIOGENES LAERTIUS, *Zeno*. Bk. vii, sec. 26.)

II—Drunkenness: Its Delights

1
Boy, us for plain myrtle, while under this fertile
Old grapevine myself I seclude.
For you and bibacious young Quintus Horatius—
Stewed.

F. P. ADAMS, *Persicos Odi.*

Simplici myrto nihil adlabores
Sedulus, cura: neque te ministrum
Decedet myrtus neque me sub arta
Vite bibentem.

HORACE, *Odes.* Bk. i, ode 38.

1a
The clachan yill had made me canty;
I was na fou, but just had plenty.

BURNS, *Death and Dr. Hornbook.* St. 3.

We are na fou, we're nae that fou,
But just a drappie in our e'e.

BURNS, *Willie Brew'd a Peck o' Maut.*

2
For ilka man that's drunk's a lord.

BURNS, *Guidwife, Count the Lawin'.*

He that is drunk is as great as a king.

UNKNOWN, *Westminster Drollery.* Pt. ii, l. 77. (1672) Said to have been quoted by Charles II to Sir Robert Viner, Lord Mayor of London, in 1674, when the latter appeared at an official function in a drunken condition.

3
There let him bowse, and deep carouse,
Wi' bumpers flowing o'er,
Till he forgets his loves or debts,
An' minds his griefs no more.

BURNS, *Scotch Drink: Motto.* A paraphrase of *Proverbs*, xxxi, 6–7.

Kings may be blest, but Tam was glorious,
O'er a' the ills o' life victorious.

BURNS, *Tam o' Shanter*, l. 57.

4
His ancient, trusty, drouthy crony;
Tam lo'ed him like a vera brither;
They had been fou for weeks thegither!

BURNS, *Tam o' Shanter*, l. 42.

5
Gloriously drunk, obey th' important call.

COWPER, *The Task.* Bk. iv, l. 510.

6
The secret of drunkenness is that it insulates us in thought, whilst it unites us in feeling.

R. W. EMERSON, *Journal*, 1857, quoting from a letter from "a man signing himself George R——, of Madison, Wis."

7
Petition me no petitions, Sir, to-day;
Let other hours be set apart for business,
To-day it is our pleasure to be drunk;
And this our queen shall be as drunk as we.

FIELDING, *Tom Thumb the Great.* Act i, sc. 2.

8
And he that will to bed go sober
Falls with the leaf still in October.

JOHN FLETCHER, *Bloody Brother.* Act ii, sc. 2.

He who goes to bed, and goes to bed sober,
Falls as the leaves do, and dies in October;
But he who goes to bed, and goes to bed mellow,
Lives as he ought to do, and dies an honest fellow.

UNKNOWN, an amplification of Fletcher's song, which was for a time a popular glee.

9
I went to Frankfort, and got drunk
With that most learn'd professor, Brunck;
I went to Worms, and got more drunken
With that more learn'd professor, Ruhncken.

RICHARD PORSON, *Facetiæ Cantab.*

10
He bids the ruddy cup go round,
Till sense and sorrow both are drowned.

SCOTT, *Rokeby.* Canto iii, st. 15.

11
I told you, sir, they were red-hot with drinking;
So full of valour that they smote the air
For breathing in their faces; beat the ground
For kissing of their feet.

SHAKESPEARE, *The Tempest.* Act iv, sc. 1, l. 171.

III—Drunkenness: Its Penalties

12
Where drunkenness reigneth in any route,
There is no counsel hid, withouten doubt.

CHAUCER, *Tale of the Man of Lawe*, l. 776.

For drunkenness is very sepulture
Of manne's wit and his discretion.

CHAUCER, *The Pardoneres Tale*, l. 230.

And drunkenness is eke a foul record
Of any man, and namely in a lord.

CHAUCER, *The Sumnours Tale*, l. 341.

13
Prudence must not be expected from a man who is never sober. (Non est ab homine nunquam sobrio postulanda prudentia.)

CICERO, *Philippicæ.* No. ii, sec. 32.

14
Drunk'ness, the darling favourite of hell.

DEFOE, *The True-born Englishman*, l. 51.

15
Drunkards have a fool's tongue and a knave's heart.

THOMAS FULLER, *Gnomologia.* No. 1342.

16
Licker talks mighty loud w'en it git loose from de jug.

JOEL CHANDLER HARRIS, *Plantation Proverbs.*

17
In shallow waters heav'n doth show;
But who drinks on, to hell may go.

GEORGE HERBERT, *Charms and Knots.*

18
He that is drunken, may his mother kill
Big with his sister: he hath lost the reins,
Is outlaw'd by himself: all kind of ill
Did with his liquor slide into his veins.

GEORGE HERBERT, *The Church-Porch.* St. 6.

Shall I, to please another wine-sprung mind,
Lose all mine own?

GEORGE HERBERT, *The Church-Porch.* St. 7.

Be not a beast in courtesy, but stay,
Stay at the third cup, or forego the place.
Wine above all things doth God's stamp deface.
GEORGE HERBERT, *The Church-Porch*. St. 8.

1
What does drunkenness not accomplish? It unlocks secrets, confirms our hopes, urges the indolent into battle, lifts the burden from anxious minds, teaches new arts. (Quid non ebrietas designat? Operta recludit, Spes jubet esse ratas, in prœlia trudit inertem, Sollicitis animis onus eximit, addocet artes.)
HORACE, *Epistles*. Bk. i, epis. 5, l. 16.

2
Racked by wine and anger. (Vino tortus et ira.)
HORACE, *Epistles*. Bk. i, epis. 18, l. 38. Thus induced to reveal another's secrets.

3
Woe unto them that rise up early in the morning, that they may follow strong drink.
Old Testament: Isaiah, v, 11.

But they also have erred through wine and through strong drink.
Old Testament: Isaiah, xxviii, 7.

4
They lay and slept like drunken swine.
JOHN LYDGATE, *Fall of Princes*. Bk. iii, l. 2369. (c. 1440)

5
Whatsoever is in the heart of the sober man, is in the mouth of the drunkard.
JOHN LYLY, *Euphues*, p. 146.

6
Your drunken banquets tell your vileness. (Nequitiam vinosa tuam convivia narrant.)
OVID, *Amores*. Bk. iii, eleg. i, l. 17.

Till the half-drunk lean over the half-dressed.
ALFRED AUSTIN, *The Season*.

7
There, with the wine before you, you will tell of many things. (Illic adposito narrabis multa Lyæo.)
OVID, *Amores*. Bk. ii, eleg. xi, l. 49.

8
Drunkenness is an expression identical with ruin.
PYTHAGORAS. (DIOGENES LAERTIUS, *Pythagoras*.)

9
Drunkenness is nothing but voluntary madness. (Nihil aliud est ebrietatem quam voluntariam insaniam.)
SENECA, *Epistulæ ad Lucilium*. Epis. lxxxiii, 18.

10
Drunkenness does not create vice; it merely brings it into view. (Non facit ebrietas vitia, sed protrahit.)
SENECA, *Epistulæ ad Lucilium*. Epis. lxxxiii, 20.

There is more of turn than of truth in a saying of Seneca, 'That drunkenness does not produce but discover faults.' Common experience teaches the contrary. Wine throws a man out of himself, and infuses qualities into the mind which she is a stranger to in her sober moments.
JOSEPH ADDISON, *The Spectator*. No. 569.

11
His two chamberlains
Will I with wine and wassail so convince,
That memory, the warder of the brain,
Shall be a fume, and the receipt of reason
A limbeck only.
SHAKESPEARE, *Macbeth*. Act i, sc. 7, l. 63.

Boundless intemperance
In nature is a tyranny; it hath been
Th' untimely emptying of the happy throne
And fall of many kings.
SHAKESPEARE, *Macbeth*. Act iv, sc. 3, l. 66.

Drunk? and speak parrot? and squabble? swagger? swear? and discourse fustian with one's own shadow?
SHAKESPEARE, *Othello*. Act ii, sc. 3, l. 280.

To be now a sensible man, by and by a fool, and presently a beast!
SHAKESPEARE, *Othello*. Act ii, sc. 3, l. 309.

12
Olivia: What's a drunken man like, fool?
Clown: Like a drowned man, a fool and a mad man: one draught above heat makes him a fool; the second mads him; and a third drowns him.
Olivia: Go thou and seek the crowner, and let him sit o' my coz; for he's in the third degree of drink, he's drowned.
SHAKESPEARE, *Twelfth Night*. Act i, sc. 5, l. 136.

13
No fool is silent over his cups.
SOLON, when asked whether he was silent over his cups for want of words, or because he was a fool. (EPICTETUS, *Fragments*, lxxvi.)

14
Drunkenness is an immoderate affection and use of drink. That I call immoderation that is besides or beyond that order of good things for which God hath given us the use of drink.
JEREMY TAYLOR, *Holy Living: Of Drunkenness*. Pt. ii, ch. 2.

IV—Drunkenness: The Morning After

15
A dark brown taste, a burning thirst,
A head that's ready to split and burst.
GEORGE ADE, *Remorse*, from *The Sultan of Sulu*.

The water-wagon is the place for me!
Last night my feelings were immense;
Today I feel like thirty cents!
No time for mirth, no time for laughter—
The cold gray dawn of the morning after.
GEORGE ADE, *Remorse*, from *The Sultan of Sulu*.

16
Who drinks one bowl hath scant delight; to poorest passion he was born;
Who drains the score must e'er expect to rue the headache of the morn.
SIR RICHARD BURTON, *Kasîdah*. Pt. viii, st. 11.

17
Man, being reasonable, must get drunk;
The best of life is but intoxication:
Glory, the grape, love, gold, in these are sunk
The hopes of all men and of every nation;

Without their sap, how branchless were the trunk
 Of life's strange tree, so fruitful on occasion:
But to return,—Get very drunk; and when
You wake with headache, you shall see what then.
BYRON, *Don Juan*. Canto ii, st. 179.

1
A drunken night makes a cloudy morning.
SIR WILLIAM CORNWALLIS, *Essays*. Pt. ii. (1601)

2
How gracious those dews of solace that over my senses fall
At the clink of the ice in the pitcher the boy brings up the hall.
EUGENE FIELD, *The Clink of the Ice*.

I've a head like a concertina: I've a tongue like a button-stick.
RUDYARD KIPLING, *Cells*, l. 1.

3
 On his weary couch
Fat Luxury, sick of the night's debauch,
Lay groaning, fretful at the obtrusive beam
That through his lattice peeped derisively.
POLLOK, *The Course of Time*. Bk. vii, l. 69.

4
 Will the cold brook,
Candied with ice, caudle thy morning taste,
To cure thy o'er-night's surfeit?
SHAKESPEARE, *Timon of Athens*. Act iv, sc. 3, l. 225.

5
Drunken days have all their tomorrows.
SAMUEL SMILES, *Thrift*, p. 167.

DRYDEN, JOHN

6
Dryden's genius was of that sort which catches fire by its own motion: his chariot-wheels got hot by driving fast.
S. T. COLERIDGE, *Table Talk*.

7
Behold, where Dryden's less presumptuous car,
Wide o'er the fields of glory bear
Two coursers of ethereal race,
With necks in thunder cloth'd and long-resounding pace.
THOMAS GRAY, *The Progress of Poesy*, l. 103.

8
I told him [Johnson] that Voltaire, in a conversation with me, had distinguished Pope and Dryden thus: "Pope drives a handsome chariot, with a couple of neat trim nags; Dryden, a coach and six stately horses." Johnson.—"Why, sir, the truth is. they both drive coaches and six; but Dryden's horses are either galloping or stumbling: Pope's go at a steady even trot."
SAMUEL JOHNSON. (BOSWELL, *Life*, Feb., 1766.)

The father of English criticism.
SAMUEL JOHNSON, *Lives of the Poets: Dryden*.

9
We feel that he [Dryden] never heartily and sincerely praised any human being, or felt any real enthusiasm for any subject he took up.
JOHN KEBLE, *Lectures on Poetry*.

10
Waller was smooth, but Dryden taught to join
The varying verse, the full resounding line,
The long majestic march, and energy divine.
POPE, *Imitations of Horace*. Bk. ii, epis. 1, l. 267.

Ev'n copious Dryden wanted, or forgot,
The last and greatest art,—the art to blot.
POPE, *Imitations of Horace*. Bk. ii, epis. 1, l. 280.

DUELLING

11
It has a strange, quick jar upon the ear,
 That cocking of a pistol, when you know
A moment more will bring the sight to bear
 Upon your person, twelve yards off or so.
BYRON, *Don Juan*. Canto iv, st. 41.

12
Some fiery fop, with new commission vain,
Who sleeps on brambles till he kills his man;
Some frolic drunkard, reeling from a feast,
Provokes a broil, and stabs you for a jest.
SAMUEL JOHNSON, *London*, l. 226.

13
Who dares this pair of boots displace
Must meet Bombastes face to face.
W. B. RHODES, *Bombastes Furioso*. Act i, sc. 4.

14
 I never in my life
Did hear a challenge urg'd more modestly,
Unless a brother should a brother dare
To gentle exercise and proof of arms.
SHAKESPEARE, *I Henry IV*. Act v, sc. 2, l. 52.

15
The passado he respects not, the duello he regards not.
SHAKESPEARE, *Love's Labour's Lost*. Act i, sc. 2, l. 185.

He fights as you sing prick-song, keeps time, distance, and proportion; rests me his minim rest, one, two, and the third in your bosom: the very butcher of a silk button, a duellist, a duellist; a gentleman of the very first house, of the first and second cause: ah, the immortal passado! the punto reverso! the hai!
SHAKESPEARE, *Romeo and Juliet*. Act ii, iv, 20.

16
If I were young again, the sword should end it.
SHAKESPEARE, *Merry Wives of Windsor*. Act i, sc. 1, l. 41.

 There I throw my gage,
To prove it on thee to the extremest point
Of mortal breathing.
SHAKESPEARE, *Richard II*. Act iv, sc. 1, l. 46.

17
Plague on't; an I thought he had been valiant, and so cunning in fence, I'ld have seen

him damned ere I'ld have challenged him.
SHAKESPEARE, *Twelfth Night*. Act iii, sc. 4, l. 311.

1
When you meet your antagonist, do everything in a mild and agreeable manner. Let your courage be as keen, but at the same time as polished, as your sword.
SHERIDAN, *The Rivals*. Act iii, sc. 4.

DULLNESS, see Stupidity

DUTY

2
Thanks to the gods! my boy has done his duty.
JOSEPH ADDISON, *Cato*. Act iv, sc. 4.

I've done my duty, and I've done no more.
FIELDING, *Tom Thumb the Great*. Act i, sc. 3.

It is my duty, and I will.
W. S. GILBERT, *Captain Reece*.

Here lies Henry Lawrence, who tried to do his duty.
SIR HENRY LAWRENCE, *Epitaph*. Lawrence, one of the heroes of the defence of Lucknow, desired this sentence engraved on his tomb.

I am quite happy, thank God, and, like Lawrence, I have *tried* to do my duty.
GENERAL CHARLES GEORGE GORDON, *Postscript*, to his last letter from Khartoum, 29 Dec., 1884.

Thank God, I have done my duty.
HORATIO NELSON, his last words. (HUME, *History of England*.)

3
In doing what we ought we deserve no praise, because it is our duty.
ST. AUGUSTINE, *Confessions*. Bk. x.

4
He who is false to present duty breaks a thread in the loom, and will find the flaw when he may have forgotten its cause.
HENRY WARD BEECHER, *Life Thoughts*.

5
Thine heart should feel what thou mayst
hourly see,
That Duty's basis is humanity.
ROBERT BLOOMFIELD, *The Farmer's Boy: Winter*, l. 105.

6
To do my duty in that state of life unto which it shall please God to call me.
Book of Common Prayer: Catechism.

7
He trespasses against his duty who sleeps upon his watch, as well as he that goes over to the enemy.
EDMUND BURKE, *Thoughts on the Cause of the Present Discontents*.

8
No phase of life, whether public or private, can be free from duty. (Nulla vitæ pars neque publicis neque privatis . . . vacare officio potest.)
CICERO, *De Officiis*. Bk. i, ch. 2, sec. 4.

9
Ponder not what you might do, but what you should do, and let regard for duty control your mind. (Nec tibi quid liceat, sed quid fecisse decebit Occurat, mentemque domet respectus honesti.)
CLAUDIAN, *Panegyricus de Quarto Consulatu Honorii Augusti*, l. 267.

10
God has never failed to make known to me the path of duty.
GROVER CLEVELAND, *Letter*, 18 March, 1906.

11
And rank for her meant duty, various,
Yet equal in its worth, done worthily.
GEORGE ELIOT, *Agatha*.

12
When a duty ceases to be a pleasure, then it ceases to exist.
NORMAN DOUGLAS, *Good-bye to Western Culture*.

13
What I must do is all that concerns me, not what the people think.
EMERSON, *Essays, First Series: Self-Reliance*.

14
So nigh is grandeur to our dust,
So near is God to man,
When Duty whispers low, *Thou must*,
The youth replies, *I can*.
EMERSON, *Voluntaries*. St. iii, l. 13.

15
Slight not what's near through aiming at what's far. (Μὴ νυν τὰ πόρρω ταγγύθεν μεθεὶς σκόπει.)
EURIPIDES, *Rhesus*, l. 482.

Do well the duty that lies before you. (Τὸ παρὸν εὖ ποιεῖν.)
PITTACUS. (DIOGENES LAERTIUS, *Pittacus*. Bk. i, sec. 77.)

Do the duty that lies nearest thee; which thou knowest to be a duty! The second duty will already become clearer.
THOMAS CARLYLE, *Sartor Resartus*. Bk. ii, ch. ix.

The only way to regenerate the world is to do the thing which lies nearest us, and not hunt after grand, far-fetched ones for ourselves.
CHARLES KINGSLEY, *Letters and Memories*.

16
For duty, duty must be done;
The rule applies to everyone,
And painful though that dutv be,
To shirk the task were fiddle-de-dee!
W. S. GILBERT, *Ruddigore*. Act i.

When stern Duty calls, I must obey.
W. S. GILBERT, *The Pirates of Penzance*. Act ii.

17
What, then, is your duty? What the day demands. (Was aber ist deine Pflicht? Die Forderung des Tages.)
GOETHE, *Sprüche in Prosa*, iii, 151.

No one will consider the day as ended, until the duties it brings have been discharged.
GENERAL JOSEPH HOOKER, *Order*, assuming com-

mand of the Dept. of the Northwest, 1865.

1
He were n't no saint,—but at jedgment
I'd run my chance with Jim,
'Longside of some pious gentlemen
That wouldn't shook hands with him.
He seen his duty, a dead-sure thing,—
And went for it thar and then;
And Christ ain't a-going to be too hard
On a man that died for men.
JOHN HAY, *Jim Bludso.*

2
Then on! then on! where duty leads,
My course be onward still.
REGINALD HEBER, *Journal.*

3
The straightest path perhaps which may be sought,
Lies through the great highway men call "I ought."
ELLEN STURGIS HOOPER, *The Straight Road.*

4
I slept, and dreamed that life was Beauty;
I woke, and found that life was Duty.
Was thy dream then a shadowy lie?
Toil on, sad heart, courageously,
And thou shalt find thy dream to be
A noonday light and truth to thee.
ELLEN STURGIS HOOPER, *Beauty and Duty.* First published, untitled, in *The Dial,* July, 1840.

Hath the spirit of all beauty
Kissed you in the path of duty?
ANNA KATHERINE GREEN, *On the Threshold.*

Straight is the line of Duty;
Curved is the line of Beauty;
Follow the straight line, thou shalt see
The curved line ever follow thee.
WILLIAM MACCALL, *Duty.*

Beauty, strength, youth, are flowers but fading seen;
Duty, faith, love, are roots, and ever green.
GEORGE PEELE, *A Farewell to Arms.*

5
The trivial round, the common task,
Would furnish all we ought to ask;
Room to deny ourselves; a road
To bring us, daily, nearer God.
JOHN KEBLE, *The Christian Year: Morning.*

6
Duty then is the sublimest word in our language. Do your duty in all things. You cannot do more. You should never wish to do less.
ROBERT E. LEE. Inscribed beneath his bust in Hall of Fame.

7
Thet tells the story! Thet's wut we shall git
By tryin' squirtguns on the burnin' Pit;
For the day never comes when it'll du
To kick off Dooty like a worn-out shoe.
J. R. LOWELL, *Biglow Papers.* Ser. ii, No. 11.

8
You would not think any duty small
If you yourself were great.
GEORGE MACDONALD, *Willie's Question.* Pt. iv.

9
Duty determines destiny.
WILLIAM MCKINLEY, *Speech,* Chicago, 19 Oct., 1898.

10
Truth is a divine word. Duty is a divine law.
DOUGLAS C. MACINTOSH. (NEWTON, *My Idea of God,* p. 142.)

11
Every mission constitutes a pledge of duty. Every man is bound to consecrate his every faculty to its fulfilment. He will derive his rule of action from the profound conviction of that duty.
MAZZINI, *Life and Writings: Young Europe.*

12
If a sense of duty tortures a man, it also enables him to achieve prodigies.
H. L. MENCKEN, *Prejudices.* Ser. i, p. 64.

God helps us do our duty and not shrink,
And trust His mercy humbly for the rest.
OWEN MEREDITH, *Imperfection.*

13
When Duty comes a-knocking at your gate,
Welcome him in; for if you bid him wait,
He will depart only to come once more
And bring seven other duties to your door.
EDWIN MARKHAM, *Duty.*

14
Knowledge is a steep which few may climb,
While Duty is a path which all may tread.
WILLIAM MORRIS, *The Epic of Hades: Heré.*

15
To an honest man, it is an honor to have remembered his duty.
PLAUTUS, *Trinummus.* Act iii, sc. 2, l. 71.

16
Thy sum of duty let two words contain;
(O may they graven in thy heart remain!)
Be humble, and be just.
MATTHEW PRIOR, *Solomon on the Vanity of the World.* Bk. iii, l. 867.

17
And I read the moral—A brave endeavor
To do thy duty, whate'er its worth,
Is better than life with love forever,
And love is the sweetest thing on earth.
JAMES JEFFREY ROCHE, *Sir Hugo's Choice.*

18
God never imposes a duty without giving time to do it.
JOHN RUSKIN, *Lectures on Architecture.* No. 2.

19
A categorical imperative crying in the wilderness, a duty which nobody need listen to, or suffer for disregarding, seemed rather a forlorn authority.
GEORGE SANTAYANA, *Essays: Kant.*

20
Alas! when duty grows thy law, enjoyment fades away.
SCHILLER, *The Playing Infant.*

21
'Tis praiseworthy to do not what one may,

but what one ought. (Id facere laus est quod decet, non quod licet.)
SENECA, *Octavia*, l. 454.

1
I owe him little duty and less love.
SHAKESPEARE, *I Henry VI*. Act iv, sc. 4, l. 34.

2
My ever esteemed duty pricks me on.
SHAKESPEARE, *Love's Labour's Lost*. Act i, sc. 1, l. 268.

And in the modesty of fearful duty
I read as much, as from the rattling tongue
Of saucy and audacious eloquence.
SHAKESPEARE, *A Midsummer-Night's Dream*. Act v, sc. 1, l. 101.

3
It is a man's office, but not yours.
SHAKESPEARE, *Much Ado About Nothing*. Act iv, sc. 1, l. 268.

I do perceive here a divided duty.
SHAKESPEARE, *Othello*. Act i, sc. 3, l. 181.

4
Of all the ways of life but one—
The path of duty—leads to happiness.
SOUTHEY, *Carmen Nuptiale*. St. 65.

There's life alone in duty done,
And rest alone in striving.
WHITTIER, *The Drovers*.

5
That peace
Which follows painful duty well perform'd.
SOUTHEY, *Roderick*. Pt. vii, l. 185.

6
Yea, let all things good await
Him who cares not to be great,
But as he saves or serves the state.
Not once or twice in our rough island-story,
The path of duty was the way to glory.
TENNYSON, *Ode on the Death of the Duke of Wellington*. St. 8.

7
I will perform a useless duty. (Fungar inani Munere.)
VERGIL, *Æneid*. Bk. vi, l. 885.

8
A sense of duty pursues us ever. It is omnipresent, like the Deity. If we take to ourselves the wings of the morning, and dwell in the uttermost parts of the sea, duty performed or duty violated is still with us, for our happiness or our misery. If we say the darkness shall cover us, in the darkness as in the light our obligations are yet with us.
DANIEL WEBSTER, *Argument on the Murder of Captain White*.

Simple duty hath no place for fear.
WHITTIER, *Abraham Davenport*. Last line.

9
Duty is what one expects from others.
OSCAR WILDE, *A Woman of No Importance*. Act ii.

10
There is no question what the roll of honor in America is. The roll of honor consists of the names of men who have squared their conduct by ideals of duty.
WOODROW WILSON, *Speech*, Washington, 27 Feb., 1916.

11
A light of duty shines on every day
For all; and yet how few are warmed or cheered!
WORDSWORTH, *The Excursion*. Bk. v, l. 383.

The primal duties shine aloft like stars.
WORDSWORTH, *The Excursion*. Bk. ix, l. 236.

12
Stern Daughter of the Voice of God!
O Duty! if that name thou lov
Who art a light to guide, a rod
To check the erring, and reprove;
Thou, who art victory and law
When empty terrors overawe;
From vain temptations dost set free;
And calm'st the weary strife of frail humanity!
WORDSWORTH, *Ode to Duty*. St. 1.

Left that command Sole daughter of his voice.
MILTON, *Paradise Lost*. Bk. ix, l. 652.

13
There are who ask not if thine eye
Be on them; who, in love and truth,
Where no misgiving is, rely
Upon the genial sense of youth:
Glad Hearts! without reproach or blot;
Who do thy work, and know it not:
Oh! if through confidence misplaced
They fail, thy saving arms, dread Power! around them cast.
WORDSWORTH, *Ode to Duty*. St. 2.

Serene will be our days and bright,
And happy will our nature be,
When love is an unerring light,
And joy its own security.
And they a blissful course may hold
Even now, who, not unwisely bold,
Live in the spirit of this creed;
Yet seek thy firm support, according to their need.
WORDSWORTH, *Ode to Duty*. St. 3.

Stern Lawgiver! yet thou dost wear
The Godhead's most benignant grace;
Nor know we anything so fair
As is the smile upon thy face:
Flowers laugh before thee on their beds
And fragrance in thy footing treads;
Thou dost preserve the stars from wrong;
And the most ancient heavens, through Thee, are fresh and strong.
WORDSWORTH, *Ode to Duty*. St. 6.

The confidence of reason give;
And in the light of truth thy Bondman let me live!
WORDSWORTH, *Ode to Duty*. St. 7.

E

EAGLE

See also Dove

1
And 'tis an added grief that with my own feathers I am slain. (Καὶ τοῦτό μοι ἑτέρα λύπη, τὸ τοῖς ἰδίοις πτεροῖς ἐναποθνήσκειν.)

ÆSOP, *Fables: The Eagle and the Arrow*. The idea of the eagle slain by a feather from his own wing is repeated many times in classical literature.

So, in the Libyan fable it is told
That once an eagle, stricken with a dart,
Said, when he saw the fashion of the shaft,
"With our own feathers, not by others' hand
Are we now smitten."

ÆSCHYLUS, *Fragments*. Frag. 63.

2
So the struck eagle, stretch'd upon the plain,
No more through rolling clouds to soar again,
View'd his own feather on the fatal dart,
And wing'd the shaft that quiver'd in his heart:
Keen were his pangs, but keener far to feel
He nursed the pinion which impell'd the steel,
While the same plumage that had warm'd his nest
Drank the last life-drop of his bleeding breast.

BYRON, *English Bards and Scotch Reviewers*, l. 841.

Like a young eagle, who has lent his plume
To fledge the shaft by which he meets his doom,
See their own feathers pluck'd, to wing the dart
Which rank corruption destines for their heart!

THOMAS MOORE, *Corruption*, l. 95.

That eagle's fate and mine are one,
Which, on the shaft that made him die,
Espied a feather of his own,
Wherewith he wont to soar so high.

EDMUND WALLER, *To a Lady Singing a Song of His Composing*.

3
The eagle never lost so much time as when he submitted to learn of the crow.

WILLIAM BLAKE, *Proverbs of Hell*.

4
When thou seest an eagle, thou seest a portion of Genius; lift up thy head!

WILLIAM BLAKE, *Proverbs of Hell*.

5
Perched on the eagle's towering wing
The lowly linnet loves to sing.

COLLEY CIBBER, *Birthday Ode*.

Fool that I was! upon my eagle's wings
I bore this wren, till I was tired with soaring,
And now he mounts above me.

DRYDEN, *All for Love*. Act ii, sc. 1.

Thus the fable tells us, that the wren mounted as high as the eagle, by getting upon his back.

RICHARD STEELE, *The Tatler*. No. 224.

6
As if an eagle flew aloft, and then—
Stoop'd from his highest pitch to pounce a wren.

COWPER, *Table Talk*, l. 552.

The eagle am I, with my fame in the world,
The wren is he, with his maiden face.

ROBERT BROWNING, *A Light Woman*.

7
Tho' he inherit
Nor the pride, nor ample pinion,
That the Theban eagle bear,
Sailing with supreme dominion
Thro' the azure deep of air.

THOMAS GRAY, *The Progress of Poesy*, l. 113.

8
The eagle does not catch flies. (Aquila non capit muscas.)

GABRIEL HARVEY, *Letter-Book*, 50. (1573) A medieval Latin proverb.

That proverb in this point might make thee wise,
That princely eagles scorn the catching flies.

SAMUEL ROWLANDS, *Guy of Warwick*, 12. (1607)

Eagles stoop not to flies.

JAMES SHIRLEY, *Opportunity*. Act v, 2. (1640)

The eagle flies not but at noble game.

JOSEPH GLANVILL, *Scepsis Scientifica*, p. 211.

The eagle does not make war against frogs. (L'aquila non fa' guerra ai ranocchi.)

UNKNOWN. An Italian proverb.

9
You cannot fly like an eagle with the wings of a wren.

W. H. HUDSON, *Afoot in England*. Ch. 6. Quoted as a proverb.

Eagles fly alone; they are but sheep that always flock together.

UNKNOWN, *Politeuphuia*, 185. (1669)

10
They shall mount up with wings as eagles.

Old Testament: Isaiah, xl, 31.

11
Wheresoever the carcass is, there will the eagles be gathered together

New Testament: Matthew, xxiv, 28.

Like an empty eagle
Tire on the flesh of me and of my son!

SHAKESPEARE, *III Henry VI*. Act i, sc. 1, l. 268.

12
Bird of the broad and sweeping wing,
Thy home is high in heaven,
Where wide the storms their banners fling,
And the tempest clouds are driven.

JAMES GATES PERCIVAL, *To the Eagle*.

13
If you have writ your annals true, 'tis there
That, like an eagle in a dove-cote, I
Flutter'd your Volscians in Corioli.

SHAKESPEARE, *Coriolanus*. Act v, sc. 6, l. 114.

14
I saw Jove's bird, the Roman eagle.

SHAKESPEARE, *Cymbeline*. Act iv, sc. 2, l. 348.

The bird of Jove, stoop'd from his æry tour.
MILTON, *Paradise Lost*. Bk. xi, l. 185.

1
Mount, eagle, to thy palace crystalline.
SHAKESPEARE, *Cymbeline*. Act v, sc. 4, l. 113.

The eagle, feather'd king.
SHAKESPEARE, *Phœnix and the Turtle*, l. 11.

2
Gnats are unnoted wheresoe'er they fly,
But eagles gaz'd upon with every eye.
SHAKESPEARE, *The Rape of Lucrece*, l. 1014.

More pity that the eagle should be mew'd,
While kites and buzzards prey at liberty.
SHAKESPEARE, *Richard III*. Act i, sc. 1, l. 132.

3
But flies an eagle flight, bold and forth on,
Leaving no track behind.
SHAKESPEARE, *Timon of Athens*. Act i, sc. 4, 49.

4
The eagle suffers little birds to sing,
And is not careful what they mean thereby.
SHAKESPEARE, *Titus Andronicus*. Act iv, sc. 4, 83.

5
Around, around, in ceaseless circles wheeling
With clang of wings and scream, the Eagle sailed
Incessantly—sometimes on high concealing
Its lessening orbs, sometimes as if it failed,
Drooped thro' the air.
SHELLEY, *The Revolt of Islam*. Canto i, st. 10.

6
He clasps the crag with crooked hands;
Close to the sun in lonely lands,
Ring'd with the azure world, he stands.

The wrinkled sea beneath him crawls:
He watches from his mountain walls,
And like a thunderbolt he falls.
TENNYSON, *The Eagle*.

7
Shall eagles not be eagles? wrens be wrens?
If all the world were falcons, what of that?
The wonder of the eagle were the less,
But he not less the eagle.
TENNYSON, *The Golden Year*, l. 37.

8
The Eagle he was lord above,
And Rob was lord below.
WORDSWORTH, *Rob Roy's Grave*, l. 59.

9
You are teaching an eagle to fly. (Ἀετὸν ἵπτασθαι διδάσκεις.)
UNKNOWN. A Greek proverb. The Latin form is, "Aquilam volare doces."

EARS

See also Deafness; Eyes and Ears

10
Within a bony labyrinthean cave,
Reached by the pulse of the aërial wave,
This sibyl, sweet, and Mystic Sense is found,
Muse, that presides o'er all the Powers of Sound.
ABRAHAM COLES, *Man, the Microcosm*.

11
You had on your harvest ears, thick of hearing.
JOHN HEYWOOD, *Proverbs*. Pt. ii, ch. 9.

12
There is always someone dinning in my well-rinsed ear. (Est mihi purgatum crebro qui personet aurem.)
HORACE, *Epistles*. Bk. i, epis. 1, l. 7.

13
When the ear heard me, then it blessed me.
Old Testament: Job, xxix, 11.

The ear trieth words, as the mouth tasteth meat.
Old Testament: Job, xxxiv, 3.

14
Where did you get that pearly ear?
God spoke, and it came out to hear.
GEORGE MACDONALD, *At the Back of the North Wind*. Ch. 33.

15
He that hath ears to hear, let him hear.
New Testament: Mark, iv, 9.

He that hath ears to hear, let him stuff them with cotton.
THACKERAY, *The Virginians*. Ch. 32.

16
I was all ear,
And took in strains that might create a soul
Under the ribs of death.
MILTON, *Comus*, l. 560.

When Adam first of men,
To first of women Eve, thus moving speech,
Turn'd him all ear to hear new utterance flow.
MILTON, *Paradise Lost*. Bk. iv, l. 408.

17
Of Forests, and enchantments drear,
Where more is meant than meets the ear.
MILTON, *Il Penseroso*, l. 120.

18
Let the ear despise nothing, nor yet believe anything forthwith. (Nil spernat auris, nec tamen credat statim.)
PHÆDRUS, *Fables*. Bk. iii, fab. 10, l. 51.

19
If your ear burns, some one is talking about you.
PLINY, *Historia Naturalis*. Bk. xxviii, sec. 2.

And we shall speak of thee somewhat, I trow,
When thou art gone, to do thine ears glow!
CHAUCER, *Troilus and Criseyde*. Bk. ii, l. 1021.

One ear tingles; some there be
That are snarling now at me.
ROBERT HERRICK, *On Himself*.

What fire is in mine ears? Can this be true?
SHAKESPEARE, *Much Ado About Nothing*. Act iii, sc. 1, l. 107.

20
In at one ear and out at the other. (Nec quæ dicentur superfluent aures.)
QUINTILIAN, *De Institutione Oratoria*. Bk. ii, ch. 5, sec. 13.

One ear it heard, at the other out it went.
CHAUCER, *Troilus and Criseyde*. Bk. iv, l. 434.

Went in at the one ear and out at the other.
JOHN HEYWOOD, *Proverbs*. Pt. ii, ch. 9.

He comes in at one year,
To go out by the other!
THOMAS HOOD, *Ode to the Late Lord Mayor*, l. 116.

1
Give every man thy ear, but few thy voice.
SHAKESPEARE, *Hamlet*. Act i, sc. 3, l. 68.

2
Whose warlike ears could never brook retreat.
SHAKESPEARE, *III Henry VI*. Act i, sc. 1, l. 5.

3
Friends, Romans, countrymen, lend me your ears.
SHAKESPEARE, *Julius Cæsar*. Act iii, sc. 2, l. 78.

4
Such an exploit have I in hand, Ligarius,
Had you a healthful ear to hear of it.
SHAKESPEARE, *Julius Cæsar*. Act ii, sc. 1, l. 318.

You have a quick ear.
SHAKESPEARE, *The Two Gentlemen of Verona*. Act iv, sc. 2, l. 63.

5
Take heed what you say. Walls have ears.
JAMES SHIRLEY, *A Bird in a Cage*. Act i, sc. 1.
PITCHERS HAVE EARS, *see under* CHILDREN.

6
Ears are eyes to the blind. (Θωνῇ γὰρ ὁρῶ.)
SOPHOCLES, *Œdipus Coloneus*, l. 138.

7
They stand by with ears pricked up. (Arrectis auribus adstant.)
VERGIL, *Æneid*. Bk. i, l. 152.

Like unbacked colts, they prick'd their ears.
SHAKESPEARE, *The Tempest*. Act iv, sc. 1, l. 176.

8
The ear is the road to the heart. (L'oreille est le chemin du cœur.)
VOLTAIRE, *Réponse au Roi de Prusse*.

9
Upon the pivot of his skull
Turns round his long left ear.
WORDSWORTH, *Peter Bell*. Pt. i.

10
We have two ears and one mouth that we may listen the more and talk the less. (Διὰ τοῦτο, δύο ὦτα ἔχομεν, στόμα δὲ ἕν, ἵνα πλείονα μὲν ἀκούωμεν, ἧττονα δὲ λέγωμεν.)
ZENO. (DIOGENES LAERTIUS, *Zeno*. Bk. vii, 24.)

Nature has given to men one tongue, but two ears, that we may hear from others twice as much as we speak.
EPICTETUS, *Fragments*. No. 113.

One pair of ears draws dry a hundred tongues.
GEORGE HERBERT, *Jacula Prudentum*.

The hearing ear is always found close to the speaking tongue.
EMERSON, *English Traits*. Ch. 4.

EARTH

See also World

11
So simple is the earth we tread,
So quick with love and life her frame:
Ten thousand years have dawned and fled,
And still her magic is the same.
STOPFORD A. BROOKE, *The Earth and Man*.

12
Earth's crammed with heaven,
And every common bush afire with God;
And only he who sees takes off his shoes;
The rest sit round it and pluck blackberries.
E. B. BROWNING, *Aurora Leigh*. Bk. vii, l. 821.

O earth, so full of dreary noises!
E. B. BROWNING, *The Cry of the Children*.

13
He findeth God who finds the earth He made.
JOHN BUCHAN, *The Wise Years*.

14
No command of art,
No toil, can help you hear;
Earth's minstrelsy falls clear
But on the listening heart.
JOHN VANCE CHENEY, *The Listening Heart*.

15
Earth, with her thousand voices, praises God.
S. T. COLERIDGE, *Hymn Before Sun-rise, in the Vale of Chamouni*, l. 85.

Earth! thou mother of numberless children, the nurse and the mother,
Sister thou of the stars, and beloved by the Sun, the rejoicer!
Guardian and friend of the moon, O Earth, whom the comets forget not,
Yea, in the measureless distance wheel round and again they behold thee!
S. T. COLERIDGE, *Hymn to the Earth*, l. 15.

16
Of the earth, earthy.
New Testament: I Corinthians, xv, 47.

17
The earth was made so various, that the mind
Of desultory man, studious of change
And pleased with novelty, might be indulged.
COWPER, *The Task*. Bk. i, l. 506.

18
One generation passeth away, and another generation cometh; but the earth abideth for ever.
Old Testament: Ecclesiastes, i, 4.

19
Earth is but the frozen echo of the silent voice of God.
S. M. HAGEMAN, *Silence*.

20
Recall the good Creator to his creature,
Making all earth a fane, all heav'n its dome!
THOMAS HOOD, *Ode to Rae Wilson*, l. 375.

21
Earth's the best shelter.
JAMES HOWELL, *Proverbs*, 38. (1659)

22
The heaven is my throne, and the earth is my footstool.
Old Testament: Isaiah, lxvi, 1.

Swear not at all: neither by heaven; for it is God's throne: Nor by the earth; for it is his footstool.
New Testament: Matthew, v, 34, 35.

23
O earth, earth, earth, hear the word of the Lord.
Old Testament: Jeremiah, xxii, 29.

1
Speak to the earth, and it shall teach thee.
Old Testament: Job, xii, 8.

2
The poetry of earth is never dead; . . .
The poetry of earth is ceasing never.
KEATS, *On the Grasshopper and Cricket.*

3
Fools! who fancy Christ mistaken;
Man a tool to buy and sell;
Earth a failure, God-forsaken,
Anteroom of Hell.
CHARLES KINGSLEY, *The World's Age.*

4
I am in love with this green earth.
LAMB, *Essays of Elia: New Year's Eve.*

Back to earth, the dear green earth.
WORDSWORTH, *Peter Bell: Prologue.*

5
O maternal earth which rocks the fallen leaf
to sleep!
EDGAR LEE MASTERS, *The Spoon River Anthology: Washington McNeely.*

6
Hail earth, Mother of all! (Παμμῆτορ γῆ, χαῖρε.)
MELEAGER. (*Greek Anthology.* Bk. vii, ep. 461.)

7
He who has looked upon Earth
Deeper than flower and fruit,
Losing some hue of his mirth,
As the tree striking rock at the root.
GEORGE MEREDITH, *The Day of the Daughter of Hades.* Pt. i.

8
Above the smoke and stir of this dim spot
Which men call Earth.
MILTON, *Comus*, l. 5.

This opacous earth.
MILTON, *Paradise Lost.* Bk. viii, l. 23.

9
Fragrant the fertile earth After soft showers.
MILTON, *Paradise Lost.* Bk. iv, l. 645.

Earth now
Seemed like to Heav'n, a seat where gods might
dwell.
MILTON, *Paradise Lost.* Bk. vii, l. 328.

10
Earth, left silent by the wind of night,
Seems shrunken 'neath the grey unmeasured
height.
WILLIAM MORRIS, *The Earthly Paradise: December.*

11
Earth, air, and ocean, glorious three.
ROBERT MONTGOMERY, *On Woman.*

Earth, Ocean, Air, belovèd brotherhood.
SHELLEY, *Alastor*, l. 1.

12
Man makes a great fuss
About this planet
Which is only a ball-bearing
In the hub of the universe.
CHRISTOPHER MORLEY, *The Hubbub of the Universe.*

13
An old saw, earth must to earth.
GEORGE PEELE, *Edward I.* Sc. 24. (1593)

The earth produces all things, and receives all again.
THOMAS FULLER, *Gnomologia.* No. 4493.

Weary the cloud falleth out of the sky,
Dreary the leaf lieth low.
All things must come to the earth by and by,
Out of which all things grow.
OWEN MEREDITH, *Earth's Havings.*

See also under MORTALITY.

14
The earth is the Lord's, and the fulness thereof.
Old Testament: Psalms, xxiv, 1; *New Testament: I Corinthians*, x, 26, 28.

The earth and the fulness thereof are mine, saith Monseigneur.
DICKENS, *A Tale of Two Cities.* Bk. ii, ch. 7.

15
He that loves but half of Earth
Loves but half enough for me.
A. T. QUILLER-COUCH, *The Comrade.*

16
Surely the earth, that's wise being very old,
Needs not our help.
D. G. ROSSETTI, *The House of Life: The Choice.*

17
The little O, the earth.
SHAKESPEARE, *Antony and Cleopatra.* Act v, sc. 2, l. 81.

18
The earth's a thief,
That feeds and breeds by a composture stolen
From general excrement.
SHAKESPEARE, *Timon of Athens.* Act iv, sc. 3, l. 443.

19
The world's great age begins anew,
The golden years return,
The earth doth like a snake renew
Her winter weeds outworn.
SHELLEY, *Hellas*, l. 1060.

20
O happy earth,
Whereon thy innocent feet do ever tread!
SPENSER, *The Faerie Queene.* Bk. i, canto 10, st. 9.

21
Even the linked fantasies, in whose blossomy
twist
I swung the earth a trinket at my wrist.
FRANCIS THOMPSON, *Hound of Heaven*, l. 126.

22
Grasshopper, your fairy song
And my poem alike belong
To the dark and silent earth
From which all poetry has birth.
JOHN HALL WHEELOCK, *Earth.*

Christ's love and Homer's art
Are but the workings of her heart.
JOHN HALL WHEELOCK, *Earth.*

Even as the growing grass
Up from the soil religions pass,
And the field that bears the rye
Bears parables and prophecy.
Out of the earth the poem grows

Like the lily, or the rose.
JOHN HALL WHEELOCK, *Earth.*

Yea, the quiet and cool sod
Bears in her breast the dream of God.
JOHN HALL WHEELOCK, *Earth.*

1
The green earth sends her incense up
From many a mountain shrine;
From folded leaf and dewy cup
She pours her sacred wine.
WHITTIER, *The Worship of Nature.* St. 5.

2
The common growth of mother-earth
Suffices me—her tears, her mirth,
Her humblest mirth and tears.
WORDSWORTH, *Peter Bell: Prologue.* St. 27.

3
Lean not on Earth; 'twill pierce thee to the heart;
A broken reed, at best; but, oft, a spear;
On its sharp point peace bleeds, and hope expires.
YOUNG, *Night Thoughts.* Night iii, l. 145.

EARTHQUAKE

4
I remember when our whole island was shaken with an earthquake some years ago, there was an impudent mountebank who sold pills, which, as he told the country people, were very good against an earthquake.
ADDISON, *The Tatler.* No. 240.

5
The earthquake that had the honour to be noticed by the Royal Society.
MARIA EDGEWORTH, *Essay on Irish Bulls.* Ch. 2. Quoted as "the exquisitely polite expression" of a correspondent of the English Royal Society.

6
Diseased nature oftentimes breaks forth
In strange eruptions; oft the teeming earth
Is with a kind of colic pinch'd and vex'd
By the imprisoning of unruly wind
Within her womb; which, for enlargement striving,
Shakes the old beldam earth and topples down
Steeples and moss-grown towers.
SHAKESPEARE, *I Henry IV.* Act iii, sc. 1, l. 27.

7
With hue like that when some great painter dips
His pencil in the gloom of earthquake and eclipse.
SHELLEY, *Revolt of Islam.* Canto v, st. 23.

8
With a voice, that like a bell
Toll'd by an earthquake in a trembling tower,
Rang ruin.
TENNYSON, *The Princess.* Pt. vi, l. 311.

The earth-ox changes his burden to the other shoulder. (Ti niu chuan chien.)
UNKNOWN. A Chinese proverb.

EASE, see Leisure

EAST, THE

9
The East bow'd low before the blast,
In patient, deep disdain.
She let the legions thunder past,
And plunged in thought again.
MATTHEW ARNOLD, *Obermann Once More,* l. 109.

10
'Tis light translateth night; 'tis inspiration
Expounds experience; 'tis the west explains
The East; 'tis time unfolds Eternity.
P. J. BAILEY, *Festus: A Ruined Temple.*

11
Ye orient realms, where Ganges' waters run!
Prolific fields! dominions of the sun!
CAMPBELL, *The Pleasures of Hope.* Pt. i, l. 535.

12
The farther I journey towards the West, the more convinced I am that the wise men came from the East.
WILLIAM DAVY, KING'S SERJEANT, 1762. (WOOLRYCH, *Lives of Eminent Serjeants at Law.* Vol. ii, p. 621.)

When I hear of high Devonian pretensions, I confess I am reminded of the celebrated saying of Serjeant Davy, that "the oftener he went into the West, he better understood how the Wise Men came from the East."
LORD JOHN CAMPBELL, *Lives of the Chief Justices of England.* Vol. i, p. 155.

I think it was Jekyll who used to say that the further he went west, the more convinced he felt that the wise men came from the East.
SYDNEY SMITH. (LADY HOLLAND, *Memoir.* Vol. i.) The reference is to Joseph Jekyll, wit and politician, but the epigram undoubtedly belongs to Serjeant Davy.

13
Oh, East is East, and West is West, and never the twain shall meet,
Till Earth and Sky stand presently at God's great Judgment Seat;
But there is neither East nor West, Border, nor Breed, nor Birth,
When two strong men stand face to face, though they come from the ends of the earth!
RUDYARD KIPLING, *The Ballad of East and West.*

14
An' I'm learnin' 'ere in London what the ten-year soldier tells:
"If you've 'eard the East a-callin', you won't never 'eed naught else."
RUDYARD KIPLING, *Mandalay.*

Ship me somewheres east of Suez, where the best is like the worst,
Where there aren't no Ten Commandments, an' a man can raise a thirst.
RUDYARD KIPLING, *Mandalay.*

15
Now it is not good for the Christian's health to hustle the Aryan brown,

For the Christian riles, and the Aryan smiles
and he weareth the Christian down;
And the end of the fight is a tombstone white
with the name of the late deceased,
And the epitaph drear: "A Fool lies here
who tried to hustle the East."
RUDYARD KIPLING, *The Naulahka*. Ch. 5, heading.

1
Big perilous theorem, hard for king and priest:
Pursue the West but long enough, 'tis East.
SIDNEY LANIER, *Psalm of the West.*

2
Men look to the East for the dawning things,
for the light of a rising sun
But they look to the West, to the crimson
West, for the things that are done, are done.
DOUGLAS MALLOCH, *East and West.*

3
From the East comes light, from the West
law. (Ex oriente lux, ex occidente lex.)
UNKNOWN. A Latin proverb.

EASTER

4
The golden gates are lifted up,
The doors are opened wide;
The King of Glory is gone in
Unto His Father's side.
CECIL FRANCES ALEXANDER, *Lift Up Our Hearts.*

5
The Son of David bowed to die,
For man's transgression stricken;
The Father's arm of power was nigh,
The Son of God to quicken.
Praise Him that He died for men:
Praise Him that He rose again.
JOSEPH ANSTICE, *Victor Funeris.*

6
Awake, thou wintry earth—
Fling off thy sadness!
Fair vernal flowers, laugh forth
Your ancient gladness!
Christ is risen.
THOMAS BLACKBURN, *An Easter Hymn.*

7
Tomb, thou shalt not hold Him longer;
Death is strong, but Life is stronger;
Stronger than the dark, the light;
Stronger than the wrong, the right;
Faith and Hope triumphant say
Christ will rise on Easter Day.
PHILLIPS BROOKS, *An Easter Carol.*

8
Hail, Day of days! in peals of praise
Throughout all ages owned,
When Christ, our God, Hell's empire trod,
And high o'er heaven was throned.
BISHOP FORTUNATUS OF POITIERS, *Hail, Day of Days.*

"Welcome, happy morning!" age to age shall say:
Hell today is vanquished; heaven is won today.
BISHOP FORTUNATUS OF POITIERS, *Welcome, Happy Morning.* (Ellerton, tr.)

9
You keep Easter, when I keep Lent.
THOMAS FULLER, *Gnomologia.* No. 5927.

10
Rise, heart; thy Lord is risen. Sing His praise
Without delays,
Who takes thee by the hand, that thou likewise
With Him mayst rise:
That, as His death calcined thee to dust,
His life may make thee gold, and, much more, just.
GEORGE HERBERT, *The Church: Easter.*

11
Easter so longed for is gone in a day.
JAMES HOWELL, *Proverbs,* 20. (1659)

12
I'll warrant you for an egg at Easter.
JAMES HOWELL, *Proverbs,* 2. (1659)

I suppose her ladyship plays sometimes for an egg at Easter.
SWIFT, *Polite Conversation.* Dial. iii.

A kiss at Christmas and an egg at Easter.
UNKNOWN, *Denham Tracts,* ii, 92.

13
Neither might the gates of death, nor the
tomb's dark portal,
Nor the watchers nor the seal, hold Thee as
a mortal.
But today amidst the Twelve Thou didst
stand, bestowing
That Thy peace, which evermore passeth
human knowing.
JOHN OF DAMASCUS, *Come, Ye Faithful.* (Neale, tr.)

The day of resurrection! Earth tell it out abroad;
The Passover of gladness, the Passover of God.
From death to life eternal, from this world to
the sky,
Our Christ hath brought us over, with hymns
of victory.
JOHN OF DAMASCUS, *The Day of Resurrection.* (Neale, tr.)

14
Thou art the Sun of other days,
They shine by giving back thy rays.
JOHN KEBLE, *The Christian Year: Easter Day.*

15
Come, ye saints, look here and wonder,
See the place where Jesus lay;
He has burst His bands asunder;
He has borne our sins away;
Joyful tidings,
Yes, the Lord has risen to-day.
THOMAS KELLY, *Come, Ye Saints.*

16
At Easter let your clothes be new,
Or else be sure you will it rue.
LEAN, *Collectanea.* Pt. i, p. 378.

Didst thou not fall out with a tailor for wearing his new doublet before Easter?
SHAKESPEARE, *Romeo and Juliet.* Act iii, sc. 1, l. 30.

1
'Twas Easter Sunday. The full blossomed trees
Filled all the air with fragrance and with joy.
LONGFELLOW, *The Spanish Student*. Act i, sc. 3.

2
O chime of sweet Saint Charity,
Peal soon that Easter morn
When Christ for all shall risen be,
And in all hearts new-born!
J. R. LOWELL, *Godminster Chimes*. St. 7.

3
In the bonds of Death He lay
Who for our offence was slain;
But the Lord is risen to-day,
Christ hath brought us life again,
Wherefore let us all rejoice,
Singing loud, with cheerful voice,
Hallelujah!
MARTIN LUTHER, *In the Bonds of Death*.

4
In vain with stone the cave they barred;
In vain the watch kept ward and guard;
Majestic from the spoilèd tomb.
In pomp of triumph Christ is come.
JOHN MASON NEALE, *Lift Up Your Voices*.

5
The fasts are done; the Aves said;
The moon has filled her horn,
And in the solemn night I watch
Before the Easter morn.
EDNA DEAN PROCTOR, *Easter Morning*.

I think of the garden after the rain;
And hope to my heart comes singing,
"At morn the cherry blooms will be white,
And the Easter bells be ringing!"
EDNA DEAN PROCTOR, *Easter Bells*.

6
Spring bursts to-day,
For Christ is risen and all the earth's at play.
CHRISTINA ROSSETTI, *Easter Carol*.

7
Angels, roll the rock away;
Death, yield up thy mighty prey:
See, He rises from the tomb,
Glowing with immortal bloom.
Al-le-lu-ia! Al-le-lu-ia!
Christ the Lord is risen to-day!
THOMAS SCOTT, *Easter Angels*.

8
God expects from men . . . that their Easter devotions would in some measure come up to their Easter dress.
ROBERT SOUTH, *Sermons*. Vol. ii, No. 8.

9
Lift your glad voices in triumph on high,
For Jesus hath risen, and man cannot die.
HENRY WARE, JR., *Lift Your Glad Voices*.

10
Hail the day that sees Him rise
To His throne above the skies;
Christ, awhile to mortals given,
Reascends His native Heaven.
CHARLES WESLEY, *Ascension*.

"Christ the Lord is risen to-day,"
Sons of men and angels say:
Raise your joys and triumphs high;
Sing, ye heavens, and earth, reply.
CHARLES WESLEY, *Christ the Lord Is Risen*.

11
Christ is risen, Christ the first-fruits
Of the holy harvest-field,
Which will of its full abundance
At His second coming yield.
CHRISTOPHER WORDSWORTH, *Christ Is Risen*.

He who on the cross a victim
For the world's salvation bled,
Jesus Christ, the King of Glory,
Now is risen from the dead.
CHRISTOPHER WORDSWORTH, *The Resurrection*.

12
Jesus Christ is risen to-day,
Our triumphant holy day;
Who did once upon the cross
Suffer to redeem our loss.
Hallelujah!
UNKNOWN, *Jesus Christ Is Risen To-day*.
Translation of 15th Century Latin hymn.

EATING

See also Dining, Feasts

I—Eating: Apothegms

13
Tell me what you eat, and I will tell you what you are. (Dis moi ce que tu manges, je te dirai ce que tu es.)
BRILLAT-SAVARIN, *Physiologie du Goût*. Ch. 36.

14
Not with whom thou art bred, but with whom thou art fed. (No con quien Naces, Sino con quien paces.)
CERVANTES, *Don Quixote*. Pt. ii, ch. 68.

15
Whether therefore ye eat, or drink, or whatsoever ye do, do all to the glory of God.
New Testament: 1 Corinthians, x, 31.

16
If a rich man, when you will; if a poor man, when you can. (Εἰ μὲν πλούσιος, ὅταν θέλῃ· εἰ δὲ πένης, ὅταν ἔχῃ.)
DIOGENES, when asked the proper time to eat. (DIOGENES LAERTIUS, *Diogenes*. Bk. vi, sec. 40.) The aphorism is quoted by Rabelais (*Works*, iv, 64).

17
My heart is Catholic, but my stomach Lutheran.
ERASMUS, *Colloquies*. Referring to his dislike of fish.

18
The way to a man's heart is through his stomach.
FANNY FERN, *Willis Parton*.

19
The proof of the pudding is in the eating.
HENRY GLAPTHORNE, *The Hollander*. Act iii. (1635); ADDISON, *The Spectator*. No. 567.

1
Who will eat the kernel of the nut must break the shell.
JOHN GRANGE, *The Golden Aphroditis.* (1577)

2
Lazy fokes' stummucks don't git tired.
JOEL CHANDLER HARRIS, *Plantation Proverbs.*

3
I wish that every peasant may have a chicken in his pot on Sundays. (Je veux que le dimanche chaque paysan ait sa poule au pot.)
HENRY IV of France, when he was crowned king.

4
The table robs more than a thief.
GEORGE HERBERT, *Jacula Prudentum.*

5
In order to know whether a human being is young or old, offer it food of different kinds at short intervals. If young, it will eat anything at any hour of the day or night. If old, it observes stated periods.
O. W. HOLMES, *The Professor at the Breakfast-Table.* Ch. 3.

6
A handful of meal in a barrel, and a little oil in a cruse.
Old Testament: I Kings, xvii, 12.

And the barrel of meal wasted not, neither did the cruse of oil fail.
Old Testament: I Kings, xvii, 16.

The smallest grain of meal would suit my necessity better (than this pearl). (Le moindre grain de mil Seroit bien mieux mon affaire.)
LA FONTAINE, *Fables.* Bk. i, fab. 20.

7
He hath a fair sepulchre in the grateful stomach of the judicious epicure—and for such a tomb might be content to die.
CHARLES LAMB, *Essays of Elia: Dissertation upon Roast Pig.*

8
What is food to one man may be fierce poison to others.
LUCRETIUS, *De Rerum Natura.* Bk. iv, l. 637.

What's one man's poison, signor,
Is another's meat or drink.
BEAUMONT AND FLETCHER, *Love's Cure.* Act iii, sc. 2.

The food that to him now is as luscious as locusts, shall be to him shortly as bitter as coloquintida.
SHAKESPEARE, *Othello.* Act i, sc. 3, l. 352.

9
I am glad that my Adonis hath a sweet tooth in his head.
JOHN LYLY, *Euphues and His England,* p. 308.

10
Eat enough and it will make you wise.
JOHN LYLY, *Midas.* Act iv, sc. 3. (1592) Quoted as "an old proverb."

11
Highly fed and lowly taught.
SHAKESPEARE, *All's Well that Ends Well.* Act ii, sc. 2, l. 3.

12
Sit down and feed, and welcome to our table.
SHAKESPEARE, *As You Like It.* Act ii, sc. 7, l. 106.

13
Unquiet meals make ill digestions.
SHAKESPEARE, *The Comedy of Errors.* Act v, sc. 1, l. 73.

To feed were best at home;
From thence the sauce to meat is ceremony;
Meeting were bare without it.
SHAKESPEARE, *Macbeth.* Act iii, sc. 4, l. 35.

14
But mice, and rats, and such small deer,
Have been Tom's food for seven long year.
SHAKESPEARE, *King Lear.* Act iii, sc. 4, l. 143. A quotation of a song found in the medieval manuscript, *Sir Bevis of Hamtoun,* l. 1427.

Titania: Or say, sweet love, what thou desirest to eat.
Bottom: Truly a peck of provender: I could munch your good dry oats. Methinks I have a great desire to a bottle of hay: good hay, sweet hay, hath no fellow.
SHAKESPEARE, *A Midsummer-Night's Dream.* Act iv, sc. 1, l. 32.

15
The nearest.
H. D THOREAU, when asked at table which dish he preferred. (EMERSON, *Thoreau.*)

16
The eye, can it feast when the stomach is starving?
Pray less of your gilding and more of your carving.
EGERTON WARBURTON, *On a Mean Host.*

Your supper is like the hidalgo's dinner, very little meat, and a great deal of tablecloth.
LONGFELLOW, *The Spanish Student.* Act i, sc. 4.

17
I were eaten out of house and of harbour.
UNKNOWN. (*Towneley Plays,* xiii, 124. c. 1400.)

Till we have eat him out of house and home.
JOHN DAY, *Blind Beggar.* Act iv, sc. 1. (1600)

They would eat me out of house and home, as the saying is.
SHADWELL, *The Sullen Lovers.* Act v, sc. 3.

He hath eaten me out of house and home.
SHAKESPEARE, *II Henry IV.* Act ii, sc. 1, l. 80.

II—Eating to Live, Living to Eat

18
Other men live to eat, while I eat to live. (Ἄλλους ἀνθρώπους ζῆν ἵν' ἐσθίοιεν· αὐτὸς δὲ ἐσθίειν ἵνα ζῴη.)
SOCRATES. (DIOGENES LAERTIUS, *Socrates.* Bk. ii, sec. 34; STOBÆUS, *Florilegium,* xvii, 22.)

Bad men live that they may eat and drink, whereas good men eat and drink that they may live.
SOCRATES. (PLUTARCH, *How a Young Man Ought to Hear Poems.*)

19
Thou shouldst eat to live, not live to eat. (Edere oportet ut vivas, non vivere ut edas.)
CICERO, *Rhetoricorum.* Bk. iv, sec. 7.

Do not live to eat, but eat that you may live. (Non vivas ut edas, sed edas ut vivere posses.)
DIONYSIUS, *Fragments*. Frag. 13.

Eat to live, and not live to eat.
BENJAMIN FRANKLIN, *Poor Richard*, 1733.

1
Cloyed with ragouts you scorn my simple food,
And think good eating is man's only good;
I ask no more than temperance can give;
You live to eat, I only eat to live.
RICHARD GRAVES, *Diogenes to Aristippus*.

2
One should eat to live, and not live to eat. (Il faut manger pour vivre, et non pas vivre pour manger.)
MOLIÈRE, *L'Avare*. Act iii, sc. 1, l. 140.

We must eat to live and live to eat.
FIELDING, *The Miser*. Act iii, sc. 2. It will be noted that Fielding, either wilfully or inadvertently, omits the "not" in this translation of Molière's line.

3
In compelling man to eat that he may live, Nature gives an appetite to invite him, and pleasure to reward him.
BRILLAT-SAVARIN, *Physiologie du Goût*. Ch. 36.

4
Not for renewal, but for eating's sake,
They stuff their bellies with to-morrow's ache.
EDMUND VANCE COOKE, *From the Book of Extenuations: Lazarus*.

5
Let the stoics say what they please, we do not eat for the good of living, but because the meat is savory and the appetite is keen.
EMERSON, *Essays, Second Series: Nature*.

6
Their sole reason for living lies in their palate. (In solo vivendi causa palato est.)
JUVENAL, *Satires*. Sat. xi, l. 11.

III—Eating: Eat, Drink and Be Merry

See also Life and Living

7
Drink, sport, for life is mortal, short upon earth our days;
But death is deathless, once a man is dead.
AMPHIS, *Gynæcocratia: Fragment*.

8
Eat, drink, and love; the rest's not worth a fillip.
BYRON, *Sardanapalus*. Act i, sc. 1.

"Eat, drink, and love, what can the rest avail us?"
So said the royal sage, Sardanapalus.
BYRON, *Don Juan*. Canto ii, st. 207.

9
"Eat, drink, and sport; the rest of life's not worth a fillip," quoth the King;
Methinks the saying saith too much: the swine would say the selfsame thing.
SIR RICHARD BURTON, *Kasîdah*. Pt. ii, st. 15.

10
Eat, drink, and play, and think that this is bliss.
There is no heaven but this;
There is no hell
Save earth, which serves the purpose doubly well.
ARTHUR HUGH CLOUGH, *Easter Day*. St. 9.

11
Although they say, "Come let us eat and drink;
Our life is but a spark, which quickly dies,"
Though thus they say, they know not what to think;
But in their minds ten thousand doubts arise.
SIR JOHN DAVIES, *Nosce Teipsum*. Sec. 30, st. 4.

12
Then I commended mirth, because a man hath no better thing under the sun, than to eat, and to drink, and to be merry: for that shall abide with him of his labour the days of his life.
Old Testament: Ecclesiastes, viii, 15.

Take thine ease, eat, drink, and be merry.
New Testament: Luke, xii, 19.

13
Yet some must swim when others sink;
And some must sink when others swim;
Make merry, comrades, eat and drink—
The lights are growing dim.
A. L. GORDON, *Sunlight on the Sea*.

14
Let us eat and drink; for to-morrow we shall die.
Old Testament: Isaiah, xxii, 13.

Let us eat and drink, for to-morrow we die.
New Testament: I Corinthians, xv, 32.

Eat thou and drink; to-morrow thou shalt die.
D. G. ROSSETTI, *The House of Life: The Choice*.

15
Drink and dance and laugh and lie,
Love, the reeling midnight through,
For tomorrow we shall die!
(But, alas, we never do.)
DOROTHY PARKER, *The Flaw in Paganism*.

16
It is good to be merry at meat.
JOHN RAY, *English Proverbs*, p. 18.

IV—Eating: Its Pleasures

17
Irks care the crop full bird? Frets doubt the maw-crammed beast?
ROBERT BROWNING, *Rabbi Ben Ezra*. St. 4.

18
No prince fares like him; he breaks his fast with Aristotle, dines with Tully, drinks tea at Helicon, sups with Seneca.
COLLEY CIBBER, *Love Makes the Man*. Act i, 1.

He breaks his fast
With Aristotle, dines with Tully, takes
His watering with the Muses, sups with Livy.
JOHN FLETCHER, *The Elder Brother*. Act i, 2.

19
Taking food and drink is a great enjoyment for healthy people, and those who do not

enjoy eating seldom have much capacity for enjoyment or usefulness of any sort.
CHARLES W. ELIOT, *The Happy Life.*

1
Plain fare gives as much pleasure as a costly diet, while bread and water confer the highest possible pleasure when they are brought to hungry lips.
EPICURUS, *Letter to Menœceus.* (DIOGENES LAERTIUS, *Epicurus.* Bk. x, sec. 130.)

We have water and porridge; let us rival Jove himself in happiness. (Habemus aquam, habemus polentam, Jovi ipsi controversiam de felicitate faciamus.)
SENECA, *Epistulæ ad Lucilium.* Epis. cx, 18.

2
Not in the costly savour lies the greatest pleasure [in eating], but in yourself. So earn your sauce with sweat. (Non in caro nidore voluptas Summa, sed in te ipso est. Tu pulmentaria quære Sudando.)
HORACE, *Satires.* Bk. ii, sat. 2, l. 19.

3
The whole of nature, as has been said, is a conjugation of the verb to eat, in the active and passive.
WILLIAM RALPH INGE, *Outspoken Essays:* Ser. ii, *Confessio Fidei.*

4
They eat, they drink, and in communion sweet
Quaff immortality and joy.
MILTON, *Paradise Lost.* Bk. v, l. 637. (Ed. 1674)

5
Timid roach, why be so shy?
We are brothers, thou and I.
In the midnight, like thyself,
I explore the pantry shelf!
CHRISTOPHER MORLEY, *Nursery Rhymes for the Tender-Hearted.*

6
Fame is at best an unperforming cheat;
But 'tis substantial happiness to eat.
POPE, *Prologue for Mr. D'Urfey's Last Play.*

7
Who satisfieth thy mouth with good things; so that thy youth is renewed like the eagle's.
Old Testament: Psalms, ciii, 5.

8
Breakfast makes good memory. (Le déjeuner fait bonne mémoire.)
RABELAIS, *Works.* Bk. i, ch. 21.

A good, honest, wholesome, hungry breakfast.
WALTON, *The Compleat Angler.* Ch. 5.

A meagre, unsubstantial breakfast causes a sinking sensation of the stomach and bowels. Robert Browning truly remarks that
"A sinking at the lower abdomen
Begins the day with indifferent omen."
PYE HENRY CHAVASSE, *Advice to a Wife.*

9
And men sit down to that nourishment which is called supper.
SHAKESPEARE, *Love's Labour's Lost.* Act i, sc. 1, l. 239.

10
Their tables were stor'd full, to glad the sight,
And not so much to feed on as delight.
SHAKESPEARE, *Pericles.* Act i, sc. 4, l. 28.

11
There is no love sincerer than the love of food.
BERNARD SHAW, *Man and Superman.* Act i.

V—Eating: Abstemiousness

See also Health: Its Preservation

12
And famish'd people must be slowly nurst,
And fed by spoonfuls, else they always burst.
BYRON, *Don Juan.* Canto ii, st. 158.

13
I'm not voracious; only peckish.
CERVANTES, *Don Quixote.* Pt. ii, ch. 41.

14
Just enough food and drink should be taken to restore our strength, and not to overburden it. (Tantum cibi et potionis adhibendum, ut reficiantur vires, non opprimantur.)
CICERO, *De Senectute.* Ch. 11, sec. 36.

15
If, after exercise, we feed sparingly, the digestion will be easy and good, the body lightsome, the temper cheerful, and all the animal functions performed agreeably.
BENJAMIN FRANKLIN, *The Art of Procuring Pleasant Dreams.*

16
To lengthen thy life, lessen thy meals.
BENJAMIN FRANKLIN, *Poor Richard,* 1733.

A little in the morning, nothing at noon, and a light supper doth make to live long.
UNKNOWN, *Reliq. Antiquæ.* Vol. i, p. 208. (c. 1550)

17
We never repent of having eaten too little.
THOMAS JEFFERSON, *Writings.* Vol. xvi, p. 111.

If you wish to grow thinner, diminish your dinner,
And take to light claret instead of pale ale;
Look down with an utter contempt upon butter,
And never touch bread till it's toasted—or stale.
H. S. LEIGH, *A Day for Wishing.*

18
Many dishes make many diseases.
THOMAS MOFFETT, *Healths Improvement,* 272.

19
Stop short of your appetite; eat less than you are able. (Desine citra Quam capis; es paulo quam potes esse minus.)
OVID, *Ars Amatoria.* Bk. iii, l. 757.

20
Their best and most wholesome feeding is upon one dish and no more and the same plain and simple: for surely this huddling of many meats one upon another of divers tastes is pestiferous. But sundry sauces are more dangerous than that.
PLINY, *Historia Naturalis.* Bk. xi, ch. 53.

VI—Eating: Gluttony

1
He who eats too much know not how to eat.
BRILLAT-SAVARIN, *Physiologie du Goût*. Ch. 36.

2
To kindle and blow the fire of lechery,
That is annexed unto gluttony.
CHAUCER, *The Pardoneres Tale*, l. 153.

O gluttony, full of cursedness,
O cause first of our confusion,
O original of our damnation.
CHAUCER, *The Pardoneres Tale*, l. 170.

3
He needs no more than birds and beasts to think,
All his occasions are to eat and drink.
DRYDEN, *Absalom and Achitophel*. Pt. ii, l. 423.

4
Who dainties love, shall Beggars prove.
BENJAMIN FRANKLIN, *Poor Richard*, 1749.

5
He that banquets every day never makes a good meal.
THOMAS FULLER, *Gnomologia*, No. 2043.
See also under APPETITE.

6
He will never have enough till his mouth is full of mould.
THOMAS FULLER, *Gnomologia*.

7
Who hastens a glutton, chokes him.
GEORGE HERBERT, *Jacula Prudentum*.

With eager feeding, food doth choke the feeder.
SHAKESPEARE, *Richard II*. Act ii, sc. 1, l. 37.

8
The first in banquets, but the last in fight.
HOMER, *Iliad*. Bk. iv, l. 401. (Pope, tr.)

Born but to banquet and to drain the bowl.
HOMER, *Odyssey*. Bk. x, l. 622. (Pope, tr.)

9
Clogged with yesterday's excess, the body drags the mind down with it, and fastens to the ground this fragment of divine spirit.
HORACE, *Satires*. Bk. ii, sat. 2, l. 77.

10
Greediness closed Paradise; it beheaded John Baptist. (Gula paradisum clausit; decollavit Baptistam.)
POPE INNOCENT III, *De Contemptu Mundi*. Bk. ii, ch. 18.

Herodes, (whoso well the story sought,)
When he of wine was réplete at his feast,
Right at his own table he gave his hest
To slay the baptist John full guiltless.
CHAUCER, *The Pardoneres Tale*, l. 160.

11
I will eat exceedingly, and prophesy.
BEN JONSON, *Bartholomew Fair*. Act i, sc. 1.

I eat and eat, I swear.
SHAKESPEARE, *Henry V*. Act v, sc. 1, l. 50.

12
O what gluttony is his who has whole boars served up for himself, an animal born for banquets. (Quanta est gula quæ sibi totos Ponit apros, animal propter convivia natum!)
JUVENAL, *Satires*. Sat. i, l. 140.

13
Afterward he wisheth that he had neck of crane and belly of cow, that the morsels might remain longer in the throat and be digested more.
FRÈRE LORENS, *Le Somme des Vices et des Vertus*. (1279)

I do not know who it was, in ancient days, who wished for a gullet lengthened out like a goose's neck, so that he might taste for a longer space of time what he devoured. (Je ne sçais qui, anciennement, desiroit le gosier allongé comme le col d'une grue, pour savourer plus longtemps ce qu'il avalloit.)
MONTAIGNE, *Essays*. Bk. iii, ch. 5.

14
Although Annius has almost three hundred tables, he has servants instead of tables, dishes run hither and thither and plates fly about. Keep such banquets to yourselves, ye pompous! We are annoyed by a dinner that walks.
MARTIAL, *Epigrams*. Bk. vii, epig. 48.

Ingenious is gluttony! (Ingeniosa gula est.)
MARTIAL, *Epigrams*. Bk. xiii, epig. 62.

15
Swinish gluttony
Ne'er looks to heav'n amidst his gorgeous feast,
But with besotted base ingratitude
Crams, and blasphemes his feeder.
MILTON, *Comus*, l. 776.

16
Ever a glutton, at another's cost,
But in whose kitchen dwells perpetual frost.
PERSIUS, *Satires*. Sat. iv, l. 58. (Dryden, tr.)

17
Greediness is rich and shame poor. (Est aviditas dives, et pauper pudor.)
PHÆDRUS, *Fables*. Bk. ii, fab. 1, l. 12.

18
When the tired glutton labours thro' a treat,
He finds no relish in the sweetest meat;
He calls for something bitter, something sour,
And the rich feast concludes extremely poor.
POPE, *Imitations of Horace: Satires*. Bk. ii, sat. 2, l. 31.

19
A greedy man God hates.
JOHN RAY, *Proverbs: Scottish*.

20
Let him herd with the dumb brutes—an animal whose delight is in fodder. (Mutis adgregetur animal pabulo lætum.)
SENECA, *Epistulæ ad Lucilium*. Epis. xcii, 7.

What is a man
If his chief good and market of his time
Be but to sleep and feed? a beast, no more.
SHAKESPEARE, *Hamlet*. Act iv, sc. 4, l. 33.

21
They are as sick that surfeit with too much, as they that starve with nothing.
SHAKESPEARE, *The Merchant of Venice*. Act i, sc. 2, l. 6.

A surfeit of the sweetest things

The deepest loathing to the stomach brings.
SHAKESPEARE, *A Midsummer-Night's Dream.* Act ii, sc. 2, l. 137.

1
He is a very valiant trencherman; he hath an excellent stomach.
SHAKESPEARE, *Much Ado About Nothing.* Act i, sc. 1, l. 51.

He was a man Of an unbounded stomach.
SHAKESPEARE, *Henry VIII.* Act iv, sc. 2, l. 33.

You would eat chickens i' the shell.
SHAKESPEARE, *Troilus and Cressida.* Act i, sc. 2, l. 147.

2
All day long they ate with the resolute greed of brutes.
R. L. STEVENSON, *Song of Rahéro.* Pt. ii.

3
The fool that eats till he is sick must fast till he is well.
WALTER THORNBURY, *The Jester's Sermon.*

4
Young children and chickens would ever be eating.
THOMAS TUSSER, *Points of Housewifery: Supper Matters.*

VII—Eating: Digging One's Grave

5
They have digged their grave with their teeth.
THOMAS ADAMS, *Works,* p. 108. (1630)

Who by intemperance in his diet, in some sort, digged his grave with his own teeth.
THOMAS FULLER, *Church History.* Bk. iv, sec. 3. (1655)

How many people daily dig their own graves, either with their teeth, their tongues, or their tails.
DYKES, *English Proverbs.* No. 173. (1709)

We each day dig our graves with our teeth.
SAMUEL SMILES, *Duty,* p. 418. (1880)

6
I saw few die of hunger; of eating, a hundred thousand.
BENJAMIN FRANKLIN, *Poor Richard,* 1736.

7
Hence [from gluttony] come sudden deaths and intestate old age. (Hinc subitæ mortes atque intestata senectus.)
JUVENAL, *Satires.* Sat. i, l. 144.

8
There is death in the pot.
Old Testament: II Kings, iv, 40. It should be noted that in this well-known quotation the reference is to eating and not to drinking, the pottage having been poisoned.

9
I have heard it remarked by a statesman of high reputation, that most great men have died of over eating themselves.
HENRY TAYLOR, *Sermons,* p. 230.

10
Surfeit has killed many more men than famine. (Πολλῷ τοι πλέονας λιμοῦ κόρος ὤλεσεν ἄνδρας.)
THEOGNIS, *Sententiæ.*

Gluttony kills more than the sword. (Gula plures occidit quam gladius.)
Attributed to PATRICIUS, Bishop of Gæta. GEORGE HERBERT, *Jacula Prudentum.*

More perish by a surfeit than the sword.
JOHN LYLY, *Euphues,* p. 275.

The board consumes more than the sword.
ROBERT BURTON, *Anatomy of Melancholy.*

More are slain by suppers than the sword.
JOHN RAY, *English Proverbs.*

Surfeit slays more than the sword.
JOHN RAY, *Proverbs: Scottish.*

Many more people by gluttony are slain
Than in battle or in fight, or with other pain.
UNKNOWN, *Dialogues of Creatures,* p. 128. (c. 1535)

VIII—Eating and Drinking

11
Eat when you're hungry, and drink when you're dry.
BRIDGE, *Cheshire Proverbs,* p. 52.

12
Never spare the parson's wine, nor the baker's pudding.
BENJAMIN FRANKLIN, *Poor Richard,* 1733.

13
Eat-well is drink-well's brother.
THOMAS FULLER, *Gnomologia.* No. 1357.

He that eats well and drinks well should do his duty well.
THOMAS FULLER, *Gnomologia.* No. 2095.

14
Eat less and drink less,
And buy a knife at Michaelmas.
JAMES HOWELL, *Proverbs,* 6. (1659)

15
Take no thought for your life, what ye shall eat, or what ye shall drink.
New Testament: Matthew, vi, 25.

There is nothing from without a man, that entering into him can defile him: but the things that cometh out of him, those are they that defile a man.
New Testament: Mark, vii, 15.

16
Their beer was strong; their wine was port;
Their meal was large; their grace was short.
MATTHEW PRIOR, *An Epitaph.*

17
A truce with thirst, a truce with hunger; they're strong, but wine and meat are stronger.
RABELAIS, *Works.* Bk. iv, ch. 65.

18
Eat thy meat and drink thy drink,
And stand thy ground, old Harry.
JOHN RAY, *English Proverbs,* p. 63. (1678)

Eat at pleasure, drink by measure.
JOHN RAY, *English Proverbs,* p. 29.

Eat an' drink measurely, an' defy the medicinérs.
JOHN RAY, *Scottish Proverbs,* p. 234.

1
Eat without surfeit: Drink without drunkenness.

HUGH RHODES, *Boke of Nurture. See also under* MODERATION.

2
The halls of the professor and the philosopher are deserted, but what a crowd there is in the cafés! (In rhetorum ac philosophorum scholis solitudo est; at quam celebres culinæ sunt.)

SENECA, *Epistulæ ad Lucilium*. Epis. xcv, 23.

3
It is meat and drink to me.

SHAKESPEARE, *As You Like It*. Act v, sc. 1, 11.

4
I told him . . . that we ate when we were not hungry, and drank without the provocation of thirst.

SWIFT, *Gulliver's Travels: Voyage to the Houyhnhnms*.

This eating and drinking takes away a body's stomach.

SWIFT, *Polite Conversation*. Dial. ii.

IX—Eating: Table Manners

5
Leave off first for manners' sake; and be not unsatiable, lest thou offend.

Apocrypha: Ecclesiasticus, xxxi, 17.

6
The man who bites his bread, or eats peas with a knife, I look upon as a lost creature.

W. S. GILBERT, *Ruddigore*. Act i.

7
Now when someone asked him how it was possible to eat acceptably to the gods, he said, If it is done graciously and fairly and restrainedly and decently, is it not also done acceptably to the gods?

EPICTETUS, *Discourses*. Bk. i, ch. 13, sec. 1.

8
Gather up the fragments that remain, that nothing be lost.

New Testament: John, vi, 12.

He that keeps nor crust nor crum,
Weary of all, shall want some.

SHAKESPEARE, *King Lear*. Act i, sc. 4, l. 216.

9
Manners in eating count for something. (Est quiddam gestus edendi.)

OVID, *Ars Amatoria*. Bk. iii, l. 755.

10
At table it becomes no one to be bashful. (Verecundari neminem apud mensam decet.)

PLAUTUS, *Trinummus*. Act iii, sc. 4.

11
Eat slowly; only men in rags
  And gluttons old in sin
Mistake themselves for carpet-bags
  And tumble victuals in.

SIR WALTER RALEIGH, *Stans Puer ad Mensam*.

12
They say fingers were made before forks, and hands before knives.

SWIFT, *Polite Conversation*. Dial. ii.

13
The frightful manner of feeding with their knives, till the whole blade seemed to enter into the mouth; and the still more frightful manner of cleaning the teeth afterwards with a pocket-knife.

FRANCES TROLLOPE, *Domestic Manners of the Americans*. Ch. 3.

X—Eating: Food for the Gods

14
Food for the gods. (Βρῶμα θεων.)

EMPEROR NERO, referring to mushrooms, by means of which Agrippina killed Claudius. The Latin form is "Deorum cibus."

A dish fit for the gods.

SHAKESPEARE, *Julius Cæsar*. Act ii, sc. 1, l. 173.

  Oh, dainty and delicious!
Food for the gods! Ambrosia for Apicius!
Worthy to thrill the soul of sea-born Venus,
Or titillate the palate of Silenus!

W. A. CROFFUT, *Clam Soup*.

There's food for gods!
There's nectar! there's ambrosium!
There's food for Roman Emperors to eat!

THOMAS HOOD, *The Turtles*.

15
For he on honey-dew hath fed,
And drunk the milk of Paradise.

S. T. COLERIDGE, *Kubla Khan*.

To eat the lotus of the Nile
  And drink the poppies of Cathay.

WHITTIER, *The Tent on the Beach*.

16
The pet of the harem, Rose-in-Bloom,
Orders a feast in his favorite room—
Glittering squares of colored ice,
Sweetened with syrup, tinctured with spice,
Creams, and cordials, and sugared dates,
Syrian apples, Othmanee quinces,
Limes and citrons and apricots,
And wines that are are known to Eastern princes.

T. B. ALDRICH, *When the Sultan Goes to Ispahan*.

17
Yielding more wholesome food than all the messes
That now taste-curious wanton plenty dresses.

DU BARTAS, *Devine Weekes and Workes*. Week ii, day 1. (Sylvester, tr.)

18
When I demanded of my friend what viands he preferred,
He quoth: "A large cold bottle, and a small hot bird!"

EUGENE FIELD, *The Bottle and the Bird*.

19
What will not luxury taste? Earth, sea, and air,
Are daily ransack'd for the bill of fare.
Blood stuffed in skins is British Christian's food,

And France robs marshes of the croaking brood.

John Gay, *Trivia*. Bk. iii, l. 199.

1
Yet shall you have, to rectify your palate,
An olive, capers, or some better salad
Ushering the mutton; with a short-legged hen,
If we can get her, full of eggs, and then,
Limons, and wine for sauce: to these a coney
Is not to be despaired of for our money;
And though fowl now be scarce, yet there are clerks,
The sky not falling, think we may have larks.

Ben Jonson, *Epigrams*. No. 101.

2
And lucent syrops, tinct with cinnamon.

Keats, *The Eve of St. Agnes*. St. 30.

3
Cornwall squab-pie, and Devon white-pot brings;
And Leicester beans and bacon, food of kings.

William King, *Art of Cookery*.

4
If my opinion is of any worth, the fieldfare is the greatest delicacy among birds, the hare among quadrupeds. (Inter aves turdus, si quid me judice certum est, Inter quadripedes mattea prima lepus.)

Martial, *Epigrams*. Bk. xiii, epig. 92.

When I can have a fat turtle-dove, good-bye, lettuce; and keep the snails for yourself. I have no wish to spoil my appetite. (Cum pinguis mihi turtur erit, lactuca, valebis; Et cocleas tibi habe. Perdere nolo famem.)

Martial, *Epigrams*. Bk. xiii, epig. 53.

5
Some pigeons, Davy, a couple of short-legged hens, a joint of mutton, and any pretty little tiny kickshaws, tell William cook.

Shakespeare, *II Henry IV*. Act v, sc. i, l. 27.

6
Though we eat little flesh and drink no wine,
Yet let's be merry: we'll have tea and toast;
Custards for supper, and an endless host
Of syllabubs and jellies and mince-pies,
And other such lady-like luxuries.

Shelley, *Letter to Maria Gisborne*, l. 302.

Now to the banquet we press;
Now for the eggs, the ham,
Now for the mustard and cress,
Now for the strawberry jam!
Now for the tea of our host,
Now for the rollicking bun,
Now for the muffin and toast,
Now for the gay Sally Lunn!

W. S. Gilbert, *The Sorcerer*. Act i.

XI—Eating: Individual Foods

7
Asparagus

C—— holds that a man cannot have a pure mind who refuses apple-dumpling. . . . Only I stick to asparagus, which still seems to inspire gentle thoughts.

Charles Lamb, *Essays of Elia: Grace Before Meat*.

8
Beans

If pale beans bubble for you in a red earthenware pot, you can often decline the dinners of sumptuous hosts. (Si spumet rubra conchis tibi pallida testa, Lautorum cenis sæpe negare potes.)

Martial, *Epigrams*. Bk. xiii, epig. 7.

9
Beef

When mighty roast beef was the Englishman's food
It ennobled our hearts and enriched our blood—
Our soldiers were brave and our courtiers were good.
Oh! the roast beef of England,
And Old England's roast beef.

Henry Fielding, *Grub Street Opera*. Act iii, sc. 2.

10
What say you to a piece of beef and mustard?

Shakespeare, *The Taming of the Shrew*. Act iv, sc. 3, l. 23.

There's nothing picturesque in beef.

William Combe, *Dr. Syntax in Search of the Picturesque*. Canto xiv.

11
One fat Sir Loin possesses more sublime
Than all the airy castles built by rhyme.

John Wolcot, *Bozzy and Piozzi*. Pt. ii.

For its merit, I will knight it and make it sir-loin!

Charles II, on being told that a piece of beef which particularly pleased him was called the loin. Attributed also to James I. A humorous invention, for the word is derived from sur-loin, the upper part of the loin.

12
Bouillabaisse

This Bouillabaisse a noble dish is—
A sort of soup, or broth, or brew,
Or hotchpotch of all sorts of fishes,
That Greenwich never could outdo;
Green herbs, red peppers, mussels, saffron,
Soles, onions, garlic, roach, and dace;
All these you eat at Terré's tavern
In that one dish of Bouillabaisse.

Thackeray, *Ballad of Bouillabaisse*.

13
Butter

She brought forth butter in a lordly dish.

Old Testament: Judges, v, 25.

14
Cheese

Cheese, that the table's closing rites denies,
And bids me with the unwilling chaplain rise.

John Gay, *Trivia*. Bk. ii, l. 255.

As after cheese, nothing to be expected.

Thomas Fuller, *Church History*. Bk. vi, 5.

1
Digestive cheese.

BEN JONSON, *Epigrams*. No. 101.

My cheese, my digestion.

SHAKESPEARE, *Troilus and Cressida*. Act ii, sc. 3, l. 44.

2
Cress

Eat well of the cresses.

JOHN GRANGE, *The Golden Aphroditis*. Sig. F3. (1577) Cress was supposed to help the memory.

3
Duck

Let a duck certainly be served up whole; but it is tasty only in the breast and neck: the rest return to the cook. (Tota quidem ponatur anas, sed pectore tantum Et cervice sapit: cetera redde coco.)

MARTIAL, *Epigrams*. Bk. xiii, epig. 52.

4
Leeks

Well loved he garlic, onions, and eke leeks,
And for to drinken strong wine, red as blood.

CHAUCER, *Canterbury Tales: Prologue*, l. 634.

5
As often as you have eaten the strong-smelling shoots of Tarentine leeks give kisses with shut mouth. (Fila Tarentini graviter redolentia porri Edisti quotiens, oscula clusa dato.)

MARTIAL, *Epigrams*. Bk. xiii, epig. 18. Nero ate them in oil to improve his voice. (PLINY, *Historia Naturalis*, xix, 33.)

6
Lettuce

After wine, lettuce rises on the acid stomach. (Lactuca innatat acri Post vinum stomacho.)

HORACE, *Satires*. Bk. ii, sat. 4, l. 59.

7
Tell me, why is it that lettuce, which used to end our grandsires' dinners, ushers in our banquets? (Cludere quæ cenas lactuca solebat avorum, Dic mihi, cur nostras inchoat illa dapes?)

MARTIAL, *Epigrams*. Bk. xiii, epig. 14.

First, there will be given you lettuce, useful for relaxing the bowels. (Prima tibi dabitur ventri lactuca movendo Utilis.)

MARTIAL, *Epigrams*. Bk. xi, epig. 52.

If the bowels be costive, limpet and common shell-fish will dispel the trouble, or low-growing sorrel. (Si dura morabitur alvus, Mitulus et voles pellent obstantia conchæ Et lapathi brevis herba.)

HORACE, *Satires*. Bk. ii, sat. 4, l. 27.

8
Liver

See how the liver is swollen larger than a fat goose! In wonder you will say, "Where, I ask, did this grow?" (Aspice quam tumeat magno jecur ansere majus! Miratus dices "Hoc, rogo, crevit ubi?")

MARTIAL, *Epigrams*. Bk. xiii, epig. 58.

9
Meat

And nearer as they came, a genial savour
Of certain stews, and roast-meats, and pilaus,
Things which in hungry mortals' eyes find
favour.

BYRON, *Don Juan*. Canto v, st. 47.

Yet smelt roast meat, beheld a clear fire shine,
And cooks in motion with their clean arms bared.

BYRON, *Don Juan*. Canto v, st. 50.

10
A friendly swarry, consisting of a boiled leg of mutton with the usual trimmings.

DICKENS, *Pickwick Papers*. Ch. 37.

There are wholesale eaters who can devour a leg of mutton and trimmings at a sitting.

THOMAS HOOD, *Review of Arthur Coningsby*, 1838.

11
Strong meat belongeth to them that are of full age.

Old Testament: Hebrews, v, 14.

Such as have need of milk, and not of strong meat.

New Testament: Hebrews, v, 12.

12
Out-did the meat, out-did the frolick wine.

ROBERT HERRICK, *Ode for Ben Jonson*.

13
You require flesh if you want to be fat. (Carne opus est, si satur esse velis.)

MARTIAL, *Epigrams*. Bk. xiii, epig. 2.

14
This dish of meat is too good for any but anglers, or very honest men.

WALTON, *The Compleat Angler*. Pt. i, ch. 8.

15
Mulberries

A man will pass his summers in health, who will finish his luncheon with black mulberries. (Ille salubris Æstates peraget, qui nigris prandia moris Finiet.)

HORACE, *Satires*. Bk. ii, sat. 4, l. 21.

16
Mutton

Of all birds give me mutton.

THOMAS FULLER, *Gnomologia*. No. 3695.

17
Partridge

Whether woodcock or partridge, what does it matter, if the flavor be the same? A partridge is dearer, and thus has better flavor. (Rustica sim an perdix quid refert, si sapor idem est? Carior est perdix; sic sapit illa magis.)

MARTIAL, *Epigrams*. Bk. xiii, epig. 76.

18
An honest fellow enough, and one that loves quails.

SHAKESPEARE, *Troilus and Cressida*. Act v, sc. 1, l. 58.

19
Pheasant

Pheasant exceedeth all fowls in sweetness and

wholesomeness, and is equal to capon in nourishment.

Sir Thomas Elyot, *The Castle of Helth*. Ch. 8. (1530)

1
Pudding

I sing the sweets I know, the charms I feel,
My morning incense, and my evening meal,
The sweets of Hasty Pudding.

Joel Barlow, *The Hasty Pudding*. Canto i.

2
Hallo! A great deal of steam! the pudding was out of the copper. A smell like a washing-day! That was the cloth. A smell like an eating-house and a pastrycook's next door to each other, with a laundress's next door to that. That was the pudding.

Dickens, *A Christmas Carol: Stave Three.*

3
One solid dish his week-day meal affords,
An added pudding solemniz'd the Lord's.

Pope, *Moral Essays*. Epis. iii, l. 345.

"Live like yourself," was soon my lady's word,
And lo! two puddings smok'd upon the board.

Pope, *Moral Essays*. Epis. iii, l. 359.

4
Salad

According to the Spanish proverb, four persons are wanted to make a good salad: a spendthrift for oil, a miser for vinegar, a counsellor for salt, and a madman to stir all up.

Abraham Hayward, *The Art of Dining*.

5
Salad, and eggs, and lighter fare,
Tune the Italian spark's guitar;
And, if I take Dan Congreve right,
Pudding and beef make Britons fight.

Matthew Prior, *Alma*. Canto iii, l. 246.

6
Oh, herbaceous treat!
'Twould tempt the dying anchorite to eat;
Back to the world he'd turn his fleeting soul,
And plunge his fingers in the salad bowl.

Sydney Smith, *A Receipt for a Salad*.

7
Tripe

How say you to a fat tripe finely broil'd?

Shakespeare, *The Taming of the Shrew*. Act iv, sc. 3, l. 20.

8
Turbot

However wide the dish that bears the turbot, yet the turbot is wider than the dish. (Quamvis lata gerat patella rhombum, Rhombus latior est tamen patella.)

Martial, *Epigrams*. Bk. xiii, epig. 81.

9
Turtle

A plate of turtle green and glutinous.

Robert Browning, *The Pied Piper of Hamelin.*

10
"Of all the things I ever swallow,—
Good well-dress'd turtle beats them hollow,—
It almost makes me wish, I vow,
To have *two* stomachs, like a cow! . . .
I almost think that I could eat one raw."

Thomas Hood, *The Turtles*.

The turtle lives 'twixt plated decks
Which practically conceal its sex.
I think it clever of the turtle
In such a fix to be so fertile.

Ogden Nash, *The Turtle.*

11
Venison

Come, we have a hot venison pasty to dinner.

Shakespeare, *The Merry Wives of Windsor.* Act i, sc. 1, l. 202.

12
One cut from ven'son to the heart can speak
Stronger than ten quotations from the Greek.

John Wolcot, *Bozzy and Piozzi*. Pt. ii.

13
Vermicelli

Ceres presents a plate of vermicelli,—
For love must be sustained like flesh and blood,—
While Bacchus pours out wine, or hands a jelly:
Eggs, oysters, too, are amatory food.

Byron, *Don Juan*. Canto ii, st. 170.

14
Wood-pigeon

Wood-pigeons check and blunt the manly powers: let him not eat this bird who wishes to be amorous. (Inguina torquati tardent hebetantque palumbi: Non edat hanc volucrem qui cupit esse salax.)

Martial, *Epigrams*. Bk. xiii, epig. 67.

XII—Eating: Vegetarianism

15
I once ate a pea.

George (Beau) Brummell, when asked at dinner if he never ate vegetables.

16
If meat make my brother to offend, I will eat no flesh while the world standeth, lest I make my brother to offend.

New Testament: I Corinthians, viii, 13.

But from the mountain's grassy side
A guiltless feast I bring;
A scrip with herbs and fruits supplied,
And water from the spring.

Goldsmith, *A Ballad*. (*Vicar of Wakefield,* ch. 8.)

17
Oh, how criminal it is for flesh to be stored away in flesh, for one greedy body to grow fat with food gained from another, for one live creature to go on living through the destruction of another living thing! And so in the midst of the wealth of food which Earth, the best of mothers, has produced, it

is your pleasure to chew the piteous flesh of slaughtered animals!
OVID, *Metamorphoses*. Bk. xv, l. 88.

Kill creatures that work you harm, but even in the case of these let killing suffice. Make not their flesh your food, but seek a more harmless nourishment. (Perdite siqua nocent, verum hæc quoque perdite tantum: Ora vacent epulis alimentaque mitia carpant.)
OVID, *Metamorphoses*. Bk. xv, l. 477.

Take not away the life you cannot give:
For all things have an equal right to live.
Kill noxious creatures, where 'tis sin to save;
This only just prerogative we have:
But nourish life with vegetable food,
And shun the sacrilegious taste of blood.
OVID, *Metamorphoses*, xv, 477. (Dryden, tr.)

1
It engenders choler, planteth anger;
And better 'twere that both of us did fast,
Since, of ourselves, ourselves are choleric,
Than feed it with such over-roasted flesh.
SHAKESPEARE, *The Taming of the Shrew*. Act iv, sc. 1, l. 175.

2
But man is a carnivorous production,
And must have meals, at least one meal a day; . . .
Although his anatomical construction
Bears vegetables in a grumbling way,
Your labouring people think, beyond all question,
Beef, veal, and mutton, better for digestion.
BYRON, *Don Juan*. Canto ii, st. 67.

ECHO

3
Let echo, too, perform her part,
Prolonging every note with art;
And in a low expiring strain,
Play all th' concert o'er again.
ADDISON, *Ode for St. Cecilia's Day*.

4
In shade affrighted Silence melts away.
Not so her sister.—Hark! for onward still,
With far-heard step, she takes her listening way,
Bounding from rock to rock, and hill to hill:
Ah, mark the merry maid, in mockful play,
With thousand mimic tones the laughing forest fill!
SIR EGERTON BRYDGES, *Echo and Silence*.

5
Hark! to the hurried question of Despair:
"Where is my child?" An Echo answers—"Where?"
BYRON, *The Bride of Abydos*. Canto ii, st. 27.

I came to the place of my birth and cried: "The friends of my youth, where are they?"—And an echo answered, "Where are they?"
SAMUEL ROGERS, *Pleasures of Memory*. Pt. i, l. 17, note. Quoted from an Arabic manuscript.

6
Mysterious haunts of echoes old and far,
The voice divine of human loyalty.
GEORGE ELIOT, *Spanish Gypsy*. Bk. iv, l. 149.

7
Echo waits with art and care
And will the faults of song repair.
EMERSON, *May-day*, l. 439.

8
Echo the mimic, the lees of the voice, the tail of a word. (Ἠχὼ μιμολόγον, φωνῆς τρύγα, ῥήμετος οὐρήν.)
EVODUS, *On a Statue of Echo*. (*Greek Anthology*. Bk. xvi, epig. 155.)

9
Echo is the voice of a reflection in the mirror.
HAWTHORNE, *American Note-Books*.

10
And when the echoes had ceased, like a sense of pain was the silence.
LONGFELLOW, *Evangeline*. Pt. ii, l. 56.

11
Sweet Echo, sweetest Nymph, that liv'st unseen
Within thy airy shell,
By slow Meander's margent green,
And in the violet-embroidered vale.
MILTON, *Comus*, l. 230.

12
How sweet the answer Echo makes
To music at night,
When, roused by lute or horn, she wakes,
And far away, o'er lawns and lakes,
Goes answering light.
THOMAS MOORE, *Echo*.

13
And all with pearl and ruby glowing
Was the fair palace door:
Through which came flowing, flowing, flowing,
And sparkling evermore,
A troop of Echoes, whose sweet duty
Was but to sing,
In voices of surpassing beauty,
The wit and wisdom of their king.
EDGAR ALLAN POE, *The Haunted Palace*.

14
And more than echoes talk along the walls
POPE, *Eloisa to Abelard*, l. 306.

15
It seemed the harmonious echo
From our discordant life.
ADELAIDE ANN PROCTER, *A Lost Chord*.

16
Even Echo speaks not on these radiant moors.
BRYAN WALLER PROCTER, *Sea in Calm*. Pt. iii.

17
True as the echo to the sound.
SAMUEL ROGERS, *Jacqueline*. Pt. ii, l. 8.

18
But her voice is still living immortal,
The same you have frequently heard,
In your rambles in valleys and forests,
Repeating your ultimate word.
J. G. SAXE, *The Story of Echo*.

1
Thy hounds shall make the welkin answer them,
And fetch shrill echoes from the hollow earth.
SHAKESPEARE, *The Taming of the Shrew: Induction*. Sc. 2, l. 47.

The babbling echo mocks the hounds,
Replying shrilly to the well-tun'd horns,
As if a double hunt were heard at once.
SHAKESPEARE, *Titus Andronicus*. Act ii, sc. 3, 17.

2
Halloo your name to the reverberate hills,
And make the babbling gossip of the air
Cry out, "Olivia."
SHAKESPEARE, *Twelfth Night*. Act i, sc. 5, 291.

3
Lost Echo sits among the voiceless mountains,
And feeds her grief.
SHELLEY, *Adonais*. St. 15.

4
The shadow of a sound,—a voice without a mouth, and words without a tongue.
HORACE SMITH, *The Tin Trumpet: Echo*.

5
Never sleeping, still awake,
Pleasing most when most I speak;
The delight of old and young,
Though I speak without a tongue.
SWIFT, *An Echo*.

6
I heard . . . the great echo flap
And buffet round the hills from bluff to bluff.
TENNYSON, *The Golden Year*, l. 75.

And a million horrible bellowing echoes broke
From the red-ribb'd hollow behind the wood,
And thunder'd up into Heaven.
TENNYSON, *Maud*. Pt. ii, sec. 1, l. 24.

7
Our echoes roll from soul to soul,
And grow for ever and for ever.
Blow, bugle, blow, set the wild echoes flying,
And answer, echoes, answer, dying, dying, dying.
TENNYSON, *The Princess*. Pt. iv, l. 362.

8
What would it profit thee to be the first
Of echoes, tho' thy tongue should live forever,
A thing that answers, but hath not a thought
As lasting but as senseless as a stone.
FREDERICK TENNYSON, *Isles of Greece: Apollo*, l. 367.

9
Like,—but oh how different!
WORDSWORTH, *Yes, It Was the Mountain Echo*.

ECONOMY

See also Moderation: Living on Little; Thrift; Trifles

10
Men do not realise how great a revenue economy is. (Non intelligunt homines quam magnum vectigal sit parsimonia.)
CICERO, *Paradoxa*, vi, 3.

Frugality is a handsome income.
ERASMUS, *Familiar Colloquies*, 491. (Bailey, tr.)

Economy is a great revenue.
JOHN RAY, *English Proverbs*.

Economy, the poor man's mint.
M. F. TUPPER, *Proverbial Philosophy: Of Society*, l. 191.

11
A man may, if he knows not how to save as he gets, keep his nose to the grindstone.
LORD CHESTERFIELD, *Letters*; FRANKLIN, *Poor Richard*, 1757.

12
Frugality embraces all the other virtues. (Reliquas etiam virtutes frugalitas continet.)
CICERO, *Tusculanarum Disputationum*. Bk. iii, ch. 8, sec. 16.

13
Though on pleasure she was bent,
She had a frugal mind.
COWPER, *John Gilpin*. St. 8.

14
As much wisdom may be expended on a private economy as on an empire, and as much wisdom may be drawn from it.
EMERSON, *Essays, First Series: Prudence*.

15
Mend your clothes and you may hold out this year.
GEORGE HERBERT, *Jacula Prudentum*.

16
Without frugality none can be rich, and with it very few would be poor.
SAMUEL JOHNSON, *The Rambler*. No. 57.

17
In enterprises like theirs parsimony is the worst profusion.
MACAULAY, *Essays: Hallam's Constitutional History*.

18
Frugality is good, if liberality be joined with it. The first is leaving off superfluous expenses; the last bestowing them to the benefit of others that need. The first without the last begets covetousness; the last without the first begets prodigality.
WILLIAM PENN, *Fruits of Solitude*.

The man who saves the pennies is a dandy and a duck—if he always has a quarter for the guy that's out of luck.
WALT MASON, *The Penny Saved*.

19
Frugality is misery in disguise. (Frugalitas miseria est rumoris boni.)
PUBLILIUS SYRUS, *Sententiæ*. No. 193.

20
To balance Fortune by a just expense,
Join with Economy, Magnificence.
POPE, *Moral Essays*. Epis. iii, l. 223.

A creative economy is the fuel of magnificence.
EMERSON, *Lectures and Biographical Sketches: Aristocracy*.

1
Economy is the science of avoiding unnecessary expenditure, or the art of managing our property with moderation.

SENECA, *De Beneficiis*. Bk. ii, sec. 34.

2
Economy is too late at the bottom of the purse. (Sera parsimonia in fundo est.)

SENECA, *Epistulæ ad Lucilium*. Epis. i, sec. 5.

3
Economy is the art of making the most of life. The love of economy is the root of all virtue.

BERNARD SHAW, *Maxims for Revolutionists*.

EDEN, see Paradise

EDUCATION

See also Teaching

I—Education: Definitions

4
What sculpture is to a block of marble, education is to the soul.

ADDISON, *The Spectator*. No. 215.

Then take him to develop, if you can,
And hew the block off, and get out the man.

POPE, *The Dunciad*. Bk. iv, l. 269. Pope is referring to a notion of Aristotle's that every block of marble contained a statue, which would appear when the superfluous parts were chipped away.

5
Education makes a people easy to lead, but difficult to drive; easy to govern, but impossible to enslave.

LORD BROUGHAM, *Speech*, House of Commons, 29 Jan., 1828.

6
The secret of education lies in respecting the pupil.

EMERSON, *Lectures and Biographical Sketches: Education*.

7
Most Americans do value education as a business asset, but not as the entrance into the joy of intellectual experience or acquaintance with the best that has been said and done in the past. They value it not as an experience, but as a tool.

W. H. P. FAUNCE, *Letter*, 16 Jan., 1928, to Abraham Flexner. (FLEXNER, *Universities*.)

8
Without ideals, without effort, without scholarship, without philosophical continuity, there is no such thing as education.

ABRAHAM FLEXNER, *Universities*, p. 97.

9
Technical education is the exaltation of manual labour, the bringing of manual labour up to the highest excellence of which it is susceptible.

W. E. GLADSTONE, *Speech*, Chester, 12 Sept., 1890.

10
The true purpose of education is to cherish and unfold the seed of immortality already sown within us; to develop, to their fullest extent, the capacities of every kind with which the God who made us has endowed us.

ANNA JAMESON, *Education*.

11
Finally, education alone can conduct us to that enjoyment which is, at once, best in quality and infinite in quantity.

HORACE MANN, *Lectures and Reports on Education*. Lecture 1.

12
That's what education means—to be able to do what you've never done before.

GEORGE HERBERT PALMER, *Life of Alice Freeman Palmer*. The above sentence was the exclamation of the cook when Mrs. Palmer went to the kitchen, and baked a loaf of bread, without previous experience.

13
Education is the only interest worthy the deep, controlling anxiety of the thoughtful man.

WENDELL PHILLIPS, *Speeches: Idols*.

14
The essence of education is that it is a change effected in the organism to satisfy the desires of the operator.

BERTRAND RUSSELL, *Sceptical Essays*, p. 210.

15
True education makes for inequality; the inequality of individuality, the inequality of success; the glorious inequality of talent, of genius; for inequality, not mediocrity, individual superiority, not standardization, is the measure of the progress of the world.

FELIX E. SCHELLING, *Pedagogically Speaking*.

16
Education has for its object the formation of character.

HERBERT SPENCER, *Social Statics*: Pt. ii, ch. 17, sec. 4.

Education makes the man.

JAMES CAWTHORN, *Birth and Education of Genius*.

Impartially their talents scan:
Just education forms the man.

JOHN GAY, *Fables: The Owl, Swan, Cock, Spider, Ass, and Farmer*, l. 9.

17
Only the refined and delicate pleasures that come from research and education can build up barriers between different ranks.

MADAME DE STAËL, *Corinne*. Bk. ix, ch. 1.

II—Education: Apothegms

18
Observation more than books, experience rather than persons, are the prime educators.

A. B. ALCOTT, *Table Talk*. Pt. ii.

The best university that can be recommended to a man of ideas is the gauntlet of the mob.

EMERSON, *Essays: Society and Solitude*.

1
Where do you suppose he got that high brow? (Πόθεν ἡμῖν αὕτη ἡ οφρυς?)

Epictetus, *Encheiridion.* Sec. 22. A jeering question asked concerning a person who has turned philosopher.

A highbrow is the kind of person who looks at a sausage and thinks of Picasso.

A. P. Herbert, *The Highbrow.*

A highbrow is a person educated beyond his intelligence.

Brander Matthews, *Epigram.*

What is a highbrow? He is a man who has found something more interesting than women.

Edgar Wallace, *Interview,* at Hollywood, Calif., Dec., 1931.

2
There is no royal road to geometry.

Euclid, to Ptolemy I, when the latter asked if there was not some easier way to master the science. (Proclus, *Commentaria in Euclidem.* Bk. ii, ch. 4.)

The prevailing philosophy of education tends to discredit hard work.

Abraham Flexner, *Universities,* p. 47.

3
All uneducated people are hypocrites.

William Hazlitt, *Table-Talk: On the Knowledge of Character.*

4
Men of polite learning and a liberal education.

Matthew Henry, *Commentaries: Acts,* x.

Of good natural parts and of a liberal education.

Cervantes, *Don Quixote.* Pt. i, ch. 8.

'Tis grand! 'tis solemn! 'tis an education of itself to look upon!

J. Fenimore Cooper, *The Deerslayer.* Ch. 2.

To love her is a liberal education.

Richard Steele, *The Tatler.* No. 49.

5
Now we must educate our masters.

Dr. Robert Lowe, after the Conservative party took the leap in the dark of passing in the late sixties the Household Suffrage bill.

6
'Tis education forms the common mind;
Just as the twig is bent the tree's inclined.

Pope, *Moral Essays.* Epis. i, l. 149. *See also under* Tree.

7
It is only the ignorant who despise education.

Publilius Syrus, *Sententiæ.* No. 571.

III—Education: Its Virtues

8
The roots of education are bitter, but the fruit is sweet.

Aristotle. (Diogenes Laertius, *Aristotle.* Sec. 18.)

Education is an ornament in prosperity and a refuge in adversity.

Aristotle. (Diogenes Laertius, *Aristotle,* 19.)

Educated men are as much superior to uneducated men as the living are to the dead.

Aristotle. (Diogenes Laertius, *Aristotle,* 19.)

Education is the best provision for old age.

Aristotle. (Diogenes Laertius, *Aristotle,* 21.)

9
Education is a controlling grace to the young, consolation to the old, wealth to the poor, and ornament to the rich.

Diogenes. (Diogenes Laertius, *Diogenes,* 68.)

10
Only the educated are free. (Μόνους τοὺς παιδευθέντας ἐλευθέρους εἶναι.)

Epictetus, *Discourses.* Bk. ii, ch. 1, sec. 23.

11
Instruction increases inborn worth, and right discipline strengthens the heart. (Doctrina sed vim promovet insitam, Rectique cultus pectora roborant.)

Horace, *Odes.* Bk. iv, ode 4, l. 33.

12
The right path of a virtuous and noble education, laborious indeed at the first ascent, but else so smooth, so green, so full of goodly prospect, and melodious sounds on every side, that the harp of Orpheus was not more charming.

Milton, *On Education.*

13
Education is a treasure, and culture never dies. (Litteræ thesaurum est, et artificium nunquam moritur.)

Petronius, *Satyricon.* Sec. 47.

14
The very spring and root of honesty and virtue lie in the felicity of lighting on good education.

Plutarch, *On the Training of Children.*

15
Hence you see why "liberal studies" are so called: it is because they are studies worthy of a free-born gentleman. But there is only one really liberal study,—that which gives a man his liberty. (Quare liberalia studia dicta sint, vides: quia homine libero digna sunt. Ceterum unum studium vere liberale est: quod liberum facit.)

Seneca, *Epistulæ ad Lucilium.* Epis. 88, sec. 2.

IV—Education: Its Faults

16
The chief wonder of education is that it does not ruin everybody concerned in it, teachers and taught.

Henry Adams, *Education of,* p. 55.

17
There's a new tribunal now,
Higher than God's—the educated man's!

Robert Browning, *The Ring and the Book.* Bk. x, l. 1976.

18
A set o' dull, conceited hashes
Confuse their brains in college-classes!
They gang in stirks, and come out asses,
Plain truth to speak;
An' syne they think to climb Parnassus
By dint o' Greek!

Burns, *First Epistle to J. Lapraik.* St. 12.

Gie me ae spark o' Nature's fire!
That's a' the learning I desire.
BURNS, *First Epistle to J. Lapraik*. St. 13.

1
What's a' your jargon o' your schools,
Your Latin names for horns an' stools;
If honest Nature made you fools.
BURNS, *First Epistle to J. Lapraik*. St. 11.

To them the sounding jargon of the schools
Seems what it is—a cap and bells for fools.
COWPER, *Truth*, l. 368.

What's all the noisy jargon of the schools,
But idle nonsense of laborious fools,
Who fetter reason with perplexing rules?
JOHN POMFRET, *Reason*.

All jargon of the schools.
MATTHEW PRIOR, *An Ode on Exodus* iii, 14.

2
Natural gifts without education have more often attained to glory and virtue than education without natural gifts. (Sæpius ad laudem atque virtutem naturam sina doctrina quam sine natura valuisse doctrinam.)
CICERO, *Pro Archia Poeta*. Ch. vii, sec. 15.

Nature has always been stronger than education. (La Nature a toujours été en eux plus forte que l'education.)
VOLTAIRE, *Life of Molière;* BENJAMIN DISRAELI, *Contarini Fleming*. Pt. i, ch. 13.

3
By education most have been misled;
So they believe, because they so were bred.
The priest continues what the nurse began,
And thus the child imposes on the man.
DRYDEN, *Hind and the Panther*. Pt. iii, l. 389.

4
After the education has gone far, such is the expensiveness oi America, that the best use to put a fine person to is, to drown him to save his board.
EMERSON, *Conduct of Life: Worship*.

In alluding just now to our system of education, I spoke of the deadness of its details. . . . It is a system of despair.
EMERSON, *Essays, Second Series: New England Reformers*.

We are students of words: we are shut up in schools and colleges and recitation-rooms for ten or fifteen years, and come out at last with a bag of wind, a memory of words, and do not know a thing.
EMERSON, *Essays, Second Series: New England Reformers*.

"Whom are you?" said he, for he had been to night school.
GEORGE ADE, *Bang! Bang: The Steel Box*.

5
Can a girl's trained intelligence be trusted to learn how to wash, feed, or clothe a baby? Certainly not: there is apparently no fund of experience upon which an educated person may draw! The girl's education may therefore be interrupted, suspended, or confused, in order that under artificial conditions she may be taught such things, probably by spinsters. Can the trained intelligence of a young man be trusted to learn salesmanship, marketing or advertising? Certainly not: the educational process has once more to be interrupted, suspended or confused, in order that he may learn the "principles" of salesmanship from a Ph.D. who has never sold anything, or the "principles" of marketing from a Ph.D. who has never marketed anything.
ABRAHAM FLEXNER, *Universities*, p. 71.

6
They [academies] commit their pupils to the theatre of the world, with just taste enough of learning to be alienated from industrious pursuits, and not enough to do service in the ranks of science.
THOMAS JEFFERSON, *Writings*. Vol. xiv, p. 150.

7
My foolish parents taught me to read and write. (Me literulas stulti docuere parentes.)
MARTIAL, *Epigrams*. Bk. ix, epig. 74, l. 7.

Smith: He can write and read and cast accompt.
Cade: O monstrous!
Smith: We took him setting of boys' copies.
Cade: Here's a villain!
SHAKESPEARE, *II Henry VI*. Act iv, sc. 2, l. 92.

God hath blessed you with a good name: to be a well-favoured man is the gift of fortune, but to write and read comes by nature.
SHAKESPEARE, *Much Ado About Nothing*. Act iii, sc. 3, l. 13.

8
A little of everything, and nothing at all. (Un peu de chaque chose, et rien de tout.)
MONTAIGNE, *Essays*. Bk. i, ch. 25. *Of the Education of Children*.

A smattering of everything, and a knowledge of nothing.
DICKENS, *Sketches by Boz: Sentiment*.

9
Too much and too little education hinder the mind.
PASCAL, *Pensées*. Sec. ii, No. 72.

Tell schools they want profoundness,
And stand too much on seeming.
SIR WALTER RALEIGH, *The Lie*.

There is nothing so stupid as an educated man, if you get off the thing that he was educated in.
WILL ROGERS. (DURANT, *On the Meaning of Life*, p. 61.)

We are faced with the paradoxical fact that education has become one of the chief obstacles to intelligence and freedom of thought.
BERTRAND RUSSELL, *Sceptical Essays*, p. 163.

10
The sentiments of an adult are compounded of a kernel of instinct surrounded by a vast husk of education.
BERTRAND RUSSELL, *Sceptical Essays*, p. 206

11
I respect no study, and deem no study good. which results in money-making. (Nullum

suspicio, nullum in bonis numero, quod ad æs exit.)

SENECA, *Epistulæ ad Lucilium*. Epis. 88, sec. 1.

1
Wisdom is ever a blessing; education is sometimes a curse.

JOHN A. SHEDD, *Salt From My Attic*, p. 29.

2
The school which they have set up may properly be called the Satanic school.

SOUTHEY, *A Vision of Judgment:* Pt. iii, *Preface*.

3
What does education often do? It makes a straight-cut ditch of a free, meandering brook.

H. D. THOREAU, *Journal*, Oct., 1850.

4
Soap and education are not as sudden as a massacre, but they are more deadly in the long run.

MARK TWAIN, *The Facts Concerning My Recent Resignation*.

V—Education: Public Education: Its Virtues

5
Surely, of all "rights of man" this right of the ignorant man to be guided by the wiser, to be, gently or forcibly, held in the true course by him is the indisputablest.

CARLYLE, *Chartism*. Ch. 6.

6
Better build schoolrooms for "the boy,"
Than cells and gibbets for "the man."

ELIZA COOK, *A Song for the Ragged Schools*.

7
The foundation of every state is the education of its youth.

DIOGENES. (STOBÆUS, *Florilegium*.)

8
Nations have recently been led to borrow billions for war; no nation has ever borrowed largely for education. Probably no nation is rich enough to pay for both war and civilization. We must make our choice; we cannot have both.

ABRAHAM FLEXNER, *Universities*, p. 302.

9
Next in importance to freedom and justice is popular education, without which neither freedom nor justice can be permanently maintained.

JAMES A. GARFIELD, *Letter*, accepting nomination for Presidency, 12 July, 1880. For an account of the origin of the phrase, "My definition of a University is Mark Hopkins at one end of a log and a student at the other," attributed to Garfield, see 2069:4.

The most significant fact in this world today is, that in nearly every village under the American flag, the school-house is larger than the church.

R. G. INGERSOLL, *Speech*, at Thirteen Club Dinner, 13 Dec., 1886.

Still sits the school-house by the road,
A ragged beggar sleeping;
Around it still the sumachs grow
And blackberry-vines are creeping.

WHITTIER, *In School-Days*. St. 1.

10
By far the most important bill in our whole code, is that for the diffusion of knowledge among the people. No other sure foundation can be devised for the preservation of freedom and happiness. If anybody thinks that kings, nobles, priests are good conservators of the public happiness, send him here [to Europe].

THOMAS JEFFERSON, *Writings*. Vol. v, p. 394.

Enlighten the people generally and tyranny and oppressions of both mind and body will vanish like evil spirits at the dawn of day.

THOMAS JEFFERSON, *Letter to Du Pont de Nemours*, 1816. (*Works*, xiv, 491.)

11
I desire to see the time when education, and by its means, morality, sobriety, enterprise and industry, shall become much more general than at present.

ABRAHAM LINCOLN, *Communication*, Sangamon *Journal*, 1832.

12
But it was in making education not only common to all, but in some sense compulsory on all, that the destiny of the free republics of America was practically settled.

J. R. LOWELL, *Among My Books: New England Two Centuries Ago*.

13
In our country and in our times no man is worthy the honored name of statesman who does not include the highest practicable education of the people in all his plans of administration.

HORACE MANN, *Lectures on Education*. Lect. 3.

The Common School is the greatest discovery ever made by man.

HORACE MANN. Inscribed beneath his bust in Hall of Fame.

14
Public instruction should be the first object of government.

NAPOLEON BONAPARTE, *Sayings of Napoleon*.

15
Slavery is but half abolished, emancipation is but half completed, while millions of freemen with votes in their hands are left without education. Justice to them, the welfare of the States in which they live, the safety of the whole Republic, the dignity of the elective franchise,—all alike demand that the still remaining bonds of ignorance shall be unloosed and broken, and the minds as well as the bodies of the emancipated go free.

ROBERT C. WINTHROP, *Yorktown Oration*, 19 Oct., 1881.

VI—Education: Public Education: Its Faults

1
Public schools are becoming a nuisance, a pest, an abomination; and it is fit that the eyes and noses of mankind should, if possible, be open to perceive it.

COWPER, *Tirocinium: Preface.*

Would you your son should be a sot or dunce,
Lascivious, headstrong, or all these at once;
That, in good time, the stripling's finish'd taste
For loose expense and fashionable waste,
Should prove your ruin, and his own at last,
Train him in public with a mob of boys.

COWPER, *Tirocinium*, l. 201.

2
The microcosm of a public school.

BENJAMIN DISRAELI, *Vivian Grey*. Bk. i, ch. 2.

3
With universal cheap education, we have stringent theology, but religion is low.

EMERSON, *Lectures and Biographical Sketches: The Man of Letters.*

4
The cult of the public schools, and the curious sentiment now attached to them, are fruits of the complicated emotionalism of the mid-Victorian epoch.

HUGH KINGSMILL, *Anthology of Invective and Abuse*, p. 108.

5
The idea that going to college is one of the inherent rights of man seems to have obtained a baseless foothold in the minds of many of our people.

A. LAWRENCE LOWELL, *Address*, Haverford College, 17 April, 1931.

6
He was the product of an English public school and university. . . . He had little education and highly developed muscles—that is to say, he was no scholar, but essentially a gentleman.

H. S. MERRIMAN, *The Sowers*. Ch. 1.

7
Thou hast most traitorously corrupted the youth of the realm in erecting a grammar-school.

SHAKESPEARE, *II Henry VI*. Act iv, sc. 7, l. 37.

Public schools are the nurseries of all vice and immorality.

FIELDING, *Joseph Andrews*. Bk. iii, ch. 5.

8
There is nothing on earth intended for innocent people so horrible as a school. To begin with, it is a prison. But it is in some respects more cruel than a prison. In a prison, for instance, you are not forced to read books written by the warders and the governor. . . . In prison they may torture your body; but they do not torture your brains.

BERNARD SHAW, *Parents and Children.*

9
You call this education, do you not?
Why, 'tis the forced march of a herd of bullocks
Before a shouting drover. The glad van
Move on at ease, and pause awhile to snatch
A passing morsel from the dewy greensward,
While all the blows, the oaths, the indignation,
Fall on the croupe of the ill-fated laggard
That cripples in the rear.

UNKNOWN. (Quoted by Scott, *The Monastery*, as from an old play.)

VII—Education: Self-Education

10
The only really educated men are self-educated.

JESSE LEE BENNETT, *Culture and A Liberal Education.*

11
The Self-Educated are marked by stubborn peculiarities.

ISAAC D'ISRAELI, *Literary Character*. Ch. 6.

12
Self-education is largely book-education.

BENJAMIN C. LEEMING, *Imagination.*

13
The better part of every man's education is that which he gives himself.

J. R. LOWELL, *My Study Windows: Lincoln.*

14
Self-education is fine when the pupil is a born educator.

JOHN A. SHEDD, *Salt from My Attic*, p. 28.

VIII—Education of Children

See also Children: Their Training

15
Those things which they will use when men.

ARISTIPPUS, when asked what boys should be taught. (DIOGENES LAERTIUS, *Aristippus.*) Also attributed to Agesilaus the Great. (PLUTARCH, *Laconic Apothegms.*)

The Roman rule was to teach a boy nothing that he could not learn standing.

EMERSON, *Essays, Second Series: New England Reformers.*

16
All those instances to be found in history, whether real or fabulous, of a doubtful public spirit, at which morality is perplexed, reason is staggered, and from which affrighted Nature recoils, are their chosen and almost sole examples for the instruction of their youth.

EDMUND BURKE, *On a Regicide Peace.*

17
He learned the arts of riding, fencing, gunnery,
And how to scale a fortress—or a nunnery.

BYRON, *Don Juan*. Canto i, st. 38.

18
"I only took the regular course," said the Mock Turtle. "What was that?" inquired Alice. "Reeling and Writhing, of course, to begin with," the Mock Turtle replied; "and then the different branches of Arithmetic—

Ambition, Distraction, Uglification, and Derision."

LEWIS CARROLL, *Alice's Adventures in Wonderland*. Ch. 10.

"That's the reason they're called lessons," the Gryphon remarked; "because they lessen from day to day."

LEWIS CARROLL, *Alice in Wonderland*. Ch. 9.

1
One should give one's daughters to their husbands maidens in years but women in wisdom.

CLEOBULUS, meaning that girls should be educated as well as boys. (DIOGENES LAERTIUS, *Cleobulus*. Sec. 4.)

2
The whining schoolboy, with his satchel
And shining morning face, creeping like snail
Unwillingly to school.

SHAKESPEARE, *As You Like It*. Act ii, sc. 7, 147.

But to go to school in a summer morn,
O! it drives all joy away;
Under a cruel eye outworn,
The little ones spend the day
In sighing and dismay.

WILLIAM BLAKE, *The Schoolboy*.

BETTER UNBORN THAN UNTAUGHT, *see* IGNORANCE.

EGGS

3
The egg is smooth and very pale;
It has no nose, it has no tail;
It has no ears that one can see;
It has no wit, no repartee.

ROY BISHOP, *The Inefficacious Egg*.

4
Going as if he trod upon eggs.

ROBERT BURTON, *Anatomy of Melancholy*. Pt. iii, sec. ii, mem. 3, subs. 1.

5
It will be seen in the frying of the eggs.

CERVANTES, *Don Quixote*. Bk. i, ch. 37.

6
The hen will lay on one egg.

CERVANTES, *Don Quixote*. Bk. ii, ch. 7.

7
It is the part of a wise man . . . not to venture all his eggs in one basket.

CERVANTES, *Don Quixote*. Bk. iii, ch. 9.

Don't venture all your eggs in one basket.

SAMUEL PALMER, *Moral Essays on Proverbs*.

Put all your eggs in one basket, and—watch the basket.

MARK TWAIN, *Pudd'nhead Wilson's Calendar*.

8
All the goodness of a good egg cannot make up for the badness of a bad one.

CHARLES A. DANA, *The Making of a Newspaper Man*. Maxim 5.

9
There is always a best way of doing everything, if it be to boil an egg.

EMERSON, *Conduct of Life: Behavior*.

10
There be many that will have both the egg and the hen.

JOHN FLORIO, *First Fruites*. Fo. 33.

11
It is very hard to shave an egg.

GEORGE HERBERT, *Jacula Prudentum*.

12
The more the eggs, the worse the hatch.

THOMAS HOOD, *Miss Kilmansegg: Her Courtship*.

13
Alas! my child, where is the Pen
That can do justice to the Hen?
Like Royalty she goes her way,
Laying foundations every day,
Though not for Public Buildings, yet
For Custard, Cake and Omelette.
Or if too old for such a use
They have their fling at some abuse. . . .
No wonder, Child, we prize the Hen,
Whose Egg is mightier than the Pen.

OLIVER HERFORD, *The Hen*.

14
I have both eggs on the spit, and iron in the fire.

BEN JONSON, *Bartholomew Fair*. Act i. (1614)

Half-frighted out on's little wit,
He now has eggs (i' faith) o' the spit.

CHARLES COTTON, *Scarronides*. Bk. iv. (1670)

15
As sure as eggs be eggs.

THOMAS OTWAY, *Caius Marius*. Act iv, sc. 2.

16
And new-laid eggs, with Baucis' busy care,
Turn'd by a gentle fire and roasted rare.

OVID, *Metamorphoses*, viii, 97. (Dryden, tr.)

The vulgar boil, the learned roast an egg.

POPE, *Imitations of Horace: Epistles*. Bk. ii, epis. ii, l. 85.

There's reason in roasting of eggs.

JAMES HOWELL, *English Proverbs*.

17
A black hen lays a white egg.

JOHN RAY, *English Proverbs*.

18
They know in France 685 different ways of dressing eggs. (On connoit en France 685 manières différentes d'accommoder les oeufs.)

DE LA REYNIÈRE.

Who can help loving the land that has taught us
Six hundred and eighty-five * ways to dress eggs?

THOMAS MOORE, *The Fudge Family in Paris*. Letter viii, l. 64. (1818) * The exact number mentioned by M. de la Reynière.

19
You can't make an omelette without breaking eggs. (On ne fait pas d'omelette sans casser des oeufs.)

ROBESPIERRE, *Epigram*. (c. 1790) See A. B. CHEALES, *Proverbial Folk Lore*, p. 131. (1874) Attributed also to Napoleon. But both were merely repeating an old saying.

You can't unscramble eggs.

J. PIERPONT MORGAN, when rejecting a proposal to dissolve the trusts. (c. 1905)

20 Not worth an egg.

SHAKESPEARE, *Coriolanus*. Act iv, sc. 4, l. 21.

21
Think him as a serpent's egg

Which, hatch'd, would, as his kind, grow mischievous,
And kill him in the shell.

SHAKESPEARE, *Julius Cæsar*. Act ii, sc. 1, l. 32.

What, you egg! Young fry of treachery!

SHAKESPEARE, *Macbeth*. Act iv, sc. 2, l. 83.

1
If you love an addle egg as well as you love an idle head, you would eat chickens i' the shell.

SHAKESPEARE, *Troilus and Cressida*. Act i, sc. 2, l. 146.

2
Will you take eggs for money?

SHAKESPEARE, *Winter's Tale*. Act i, sc. 2, l. 161.

3
As full as an egg is of meat. (E pieno quanto un uovo.)

UNKNOWN. An Italian proverb. *See under* LIE; QUARRELING; WISDOM.

EGOTISM

See also Boasting, Conceit, Self-Love, Vanity

4
His opinion of himself, having once risen, remained at "set fair."

ARNOLD BENNETT, *Denry the Audacious*. Ch. 1.

5
Because, however sad the truth may seem,
Sludge is of all-importance to himself.

ROBERT BROWNING, *Mr. Sludge "The Medium."*

6
The pest of society is egotists.

EMERSON, *Conduct of Life: Culture*.

It is an amiable illusion, which the shape of our planet prompts, that every man is at the top of the world.

EMERSON, *Uncollected Lectures: Table-Talk*.

7
We talk little, if we do not talk about ourselves.

WILLIAM HAZLITT, *Characteristics*. No. 172.

They talked together like two egotists,
In conversation made all up of *eyes*.

THOMAS HOOD, *Legend of Navarre*.

It makes dear self on well-bred tongues prevail,
And I the little hero of each tale.

YOUNG, *Love of Fame*. Sat. i, l. 115.

E is the Egotist dread
Who, as some one has wittily said,
Will talk till he's blue
About Himself when you
Want to talk about Yourself instead.

OLIVER HERFORD, *The Egotist*.

8
When a man tries himself, the verdict is usually in his favor.

E. W. HOWE. (*New American Literature*, 490.)

9
The world knows only two, that's Rome and I.

BEN JONSON, *Sejanus*. Act v, sc. 1.

10
Every man is of importance to himself.

SAMUEL JOHNSON, *Works*. Vol. iv, p. 53.

11
Of all speculations the market holds forth,
The best that I know, for the lover of pelf,
Is to buy Marcus up at the price he is worth,
And then sell him at that which he sets on himself.

THOMAS MOORE, *A Speculation*.

12
In men this blunder still you find,
All think their little set mankind.

HANNAH MORE, *Florio*. Pt. i.

13
We think that his too great opinion of his ability and valor was the chief cause of his disaster. (Huic maxime putamus malo fuisse nimiam opinionem ingenii atque virtutes.)

CORNELIUS NEPOS, *Lives: Themistocles*.

14
Losing, he wins, because his name will be
Ennobled by defeat, who durst contend with me.

OVID, *Metamorphoses*. Bk. xiii. (Dryden, tr.)

15
Egoism is hateful. (Le moi est haïssable.)

PASCAL, *Pensées*. Pt. i, art. ix, sec. 23.

16
I easily regain favor with myself. (Mecum facile redeo in gratiam.)

PHÆDRUS, *Fables*. Bk. v, fab. 3, l. 6.

17
Know Nature's children all divide her care;
The fur that warms a monarch warm'd a bear.
While Man exclaims, "See all things for my use!"
"See man for mine!" replies a pamper'd goose.
And just as short of reason he must fall,
Who thinks all made for one, not one for all.

POPE, *Essay on Man*. Epis. iii, l. 43.

When the loose mountain trembles from on high,
Shall gravitation cease if you go by?

POPE, *Essay on Man*. Epis. iv, l. 127.

18
To observations which ourselves we make,
We grow more partial for the observer's sake.

POPE, *Moral Essays*. Epis. i, l. 11.

19
Without doubt I can teach crowing, for I gobble. (Sans doute Je peux apprendre à coqueriquer: je glougloute.)

EDMOND ROSTAND, *Chanticler*. Act i, sc. 2.

And sounding in advance its victory,
My song jets forth so clear, so proud, so peremptory,
That the horizon, seized with a rosy trembling,
Obeys me.
(Et sonnant d'avance sa victoire,
Mon chant jaillit si net, si fier, si peremptoire,
Que l'horizon, saisi d'un rose tremblement,
M'obéit.)

EDMOND ROSTAND, *Chanticler*. Act ii, sc. 3.

See also under CHANTICLEER.

20
The egoist does not tolerate egoism.

JOSEPH ROUX, *Meditations of a Parish Priest*. Pt. ix, No. 11.

1
If I were a medical man, I would prescribe a holiday to any patient who considered his work important.

BERTRAND RUSSELL, *The Conquest of Happiness*, p. 74.

2
Intolerance itself is a form of egoism, and to condemn egoism intolerantly is to share it.

GEORGE SANTAYANA, *Words of Doctrine*, p. 151.

3
He that is giddy thinks the world turns round.

SHAKESPEARE, *The Taming of the Shrew*. Act v, sc. 2, l. 20.

4
There is nothing so monstrous but we can believe it of ourselves.

R. L. STEVENSON, *Virginibus Puerisque*. Ch. ii.

5
Like Joe Miller's friend, the Senior Wrangler, who bowed to the audience from his box at the play, because he and the king happened to enter the theatre at the same time.

THACKERAY, *Pendennis*. Bk. i, ch. 20.

6
When I'm playful, I use the meridians of longitude and parallels of latitude for a seine, and drag the Atlantic ocean for whales. I scratch my head with the lightning and purr myself to sleep with the thunder.

MARK TWAIN, *Life on the Mississippi*.

7
It is difficult to esteem a man as highly as he would wish. (Il est difficile d'estimer quelqu'un comme il veut l'être.)

VAUVENARGUES, *Réflexions*. No. 67.

8
Other people are quite dreadful. The only possible society is oneself.

OSCAR WILDE, *An Ideal Husband*. Act iii.

9
I and my king. (Ego et rex meus.)

CARDINAL WOLSEY, referring to Henry VIII. An example of bad taste but good Latin.

The most violent egotism I have met with in the course of my reading.

RICHARD STEELE, *The Spectator*. No. 562.

10
The man whose eye
Is ever on himself doth look or one,
The least of Nature's works.

WORDSWORTH, *Lines Left Upon a Seat in a Yew-tree*, l. 55.

12
Who venerate themselves, the world despise.

YOUNG, *Night Thoughts*. Night ii, l. 355.

13
Charms and a man I sing, to wit—a most superior person,
Myself, who bear the fitting name of George Nathaniel Curzon.

UNKNOWN, *Charma Virumque Cano*. (*Poetry of the Crabbet Club*, p. 36. 1892.)

EGYPT AND THE EGYPTIANS

See also Nile

14
Truly at weaving wiles the Egyptians are clever. (Δεινοὶ πλέκειν τοι μηχανὰς Αἰγύπτιοι.)

ÆSCHYLUS, *Fragments*. Frag. 206.

15
The tap'ring pyramid, the Egyptian's pride,
And wonder of the world! whose spiky top
Has wounded the thick cloud.

ROBERT BLAIR, *The Grave*, l. 190.

16
Since what unnumbered year
Hast thou kept watch and ward
And o'er the buried Land of Fear
So grimly held thy guard?

HENRY HOWARD BROWNELL, *The Sphynx*.

17
She has seen the mystery hid
Under Egypt's pyramid:
By those eyelids pale and close
Now she knows what Rhamses knows.

E. B. BROWNING, *Little Mattie*. St. 2.

Who shall doubt "the secret hid
Under Cheops' pyramid"
Was that the contractor did
Cheops out of several millions?
Or that Joseph's sudden rise
To Comptroller of Supplies
Was a fraud of monstrous size
On King Pharaoh's swart Civilians?

RUDYARD KIPLING, *A General Summary*.

18
Egypt! from whose all dateless tombs arose
Forgotten Pharaohs from their long repose,
And shook within their pyramids to hear
A new Cambyses thundering in their ear;
While the dark shades of forty ages stood
Like startled giants by Nile's famous flood.

BYRON, *The Age of Bronze*. Pt. v.

19
Egypt had maimed us,
offered dream for life,
an opiate for a kiss,
and death for both.

HILDA DOOLITTLE, *Egypt*.

20
And they spoiled the Egyptians.

Old Testament: Exodus, xii, 36.

21
The land of Egypt, when we sat by the flesh-pots, and when we did eat bread to the full.

Old Testament: Exodus, xvi, 3.

22
The Pyramids themselves, doting with age, have forgotten the names of their founders.

THOMAS FULLER, *The Holy and Profane States: Of Tombs*.

23
The mighty pyramids of stone
That wedge-like cleave the desert airs,
When nearer seen, and better known,
Are but gigantic flights of stairs.

LONGFELLOW, *The Ladder of St. Augustine*.

1
Sound the loud timbrel o'er Egypt's dark sea!
Jehovah has triumph'd—his people are free.
THOMAS MOORE, *Sound the Loud Timbrel.*

2
Soldiers, from these pyramids forty centuries look down upon you. (Soldats, du haut ces Pyramides quarante siècles vous contemplent.)
NAPOLEON, *Proclamation to His Army,* before the Battle of the Pyramids, 21 July, 1797.

3
Beside the eternal Nile
The Pyramids have risen.
Nile shall pursue his changeless way;
Those Pyramids shall fall;
Yea! not a stone shall stand to tell
The spot whereon they stood.
SHELLEY, *Queen Mab.* Pt. ii, l. 126.

4
Pigmies are pigmies still, tho' perch'd on alps;
And pyramids are pyramids in vales.
YOUNG, *Night Thoughts.* Night vi, l. 309.

ELECTRICITY

5
Stretches, for leagues and leagues, the Wire,
A hidden path for a Child of Fire—
Over its silent spaces sent,
Swifter than Ariel ever went,
From continent to continent.
W. H. BURLEIGH, *The Rhyme of the Cable.*

6
And fire a mine in China here
With sympathetic gunpowder.
BUTLER, *Hudibras.* Pt. ii, canto iii, l. 295.

7
Indebtedness to oxygen
The chemist may repay,
But not the obligation
To electricity.
EMILY DICKINSON, *Poems.* Pt. i, No. 109.

8
Electricity—carrier of light and power, devourer of time and space, bearer of human speech over land and sea, greatest servant of man, itself unknown.
CHARLES W. ELIOT, *Inscription,* Union Station, Washington, D. C.

A machine that is like the tools of the Titans put in your hands.
CHARLES FERGUSON, *Address.* (*Stevens' Indicator.* Vol. xxxiv, No. 1.)

What hath God wrought!
Old Testament: Numbers, xxiii, 23. Quoted by S. F. B. Morse in first message sent by him over the electric telegraph from the capitol at Washington, 24 May, 1844, to his partner, Alfred Vail, in Baltimore, Md.

9
Is it a fact—or have I dreamt it—that, by means of electricity, the world of matter has become a great nerve, vibrating thousands of miles in a breathless point of time? Rather, the round globe is a vast head, a brain, instinct with intelligence! Or, shall we say, it is itself a thought, nothing but thought, and no longer the substance that we dreamed it?
HAWTHORNE, *House of Seven Gables:* Ch. 17.

10
A million hearts here wait our call,
All naked to our distant speech—
I wish that I could ring them all
And have some welcome news for each.
CHRISTOPHER MORLEY, *Of a Telephone Directory.*

11
This is a marvel of the universe:
To fling a thought across a stretch of sky—
Some weighty message, or a yearning cry,
It matters not; the elements rehearse
Man's urgent utterance, and his words traverse
The spacious heav'ns like homing birds.
JOSEPHINE PRESTON PEABODY, *Wireless.*

An ideal's love-fraught, imperious call
That bids the spheres become articulate.
JOSEPHINE PRESTON PEABODY, *Wireless.*

ELEPHANT

12
When people call this beast to mind,
They marvel more and more
At such a LITTLE tail behind,
So LARGE a trunk before.
HILAIRE BELLOC, *The Elephant.*

13
The docile and ingenuous elephant
T' his own and only female is gallant;
And she as true and constant to his bed,
That first enjoy'd her single maidenhead.
BUTLER, *Miscellaneous Thoughts,* l. 379.

14
Th' unwieldy elephant,
To make them mirth, us'd all his might, and wreath'd
His lithe proboscis.
MILTON, *Paradise Lost.* Bk. iv, l. 345.

15
It was six men of Indostan
To learning much inclined,
Who went to see the Elephant
(Though all of them were blind);
That each by observation
Might satisfy his mind.
J. G. SAXE, *The Blind Men and the Elephant.*

16
Slow as the elephant.
SHAKESPEARE, *Troilus and Cressida.* Act i, sc. 2, l. 22.

The elephant hath joints, but none for courtesy: his legs are legs for necessity, not for flexure.
SHAKESPEARE, *Troilus and Cressida.* Act ii, sc. 3, l. 97.

17
The elephant is never won with Anger.
JOHN WILMOT, *Valentinian.* Act i, sc. 1.

18
And he swore like mad because he had

An elephant on his hands.

J. CHEEVER GOODWIN, *Wang: Elephant Song.* This comic opera opened in New York 4 May, 1891, and the song was made famous by De Wolf Hopper.

ELOQUENCE

See also Oratory, Speech, Tongue

I—Eloquence: Definitions

1
He is an eloquent man who can treat humble subjects with delicacy, lofty things impressively, and moderate things temperately. (Is enim est eloquens qui et humilia subtiliter, et magna graviter, et mediocria temperate potest dicere.)

CICERO, *Orator.* Sec. 29.

2
Eloquence is the child of Knowledge.

BENJAMIN DISRAELI, *Young Duke.* Bk. v, ch. 6.

3
Eloquence is the power to translate a truth into language perfectly intelligible to the person to whom you speak.

EMERSON, *Letters and Social Aims: Eloquence.*

4
Eloquence is a great and diverse thing: nor did she yet ever favour any man so much as to become wholly his.

BEN JONSON, *Explorata: Eloquentia.*

Talking and eloquence are not the same: to speak and to speak well, are two things. A fool may talk, but a wise man speaks.

BEN JONSON, *Explorata: Præcept. Element.*

5
Eloquence is to the sublime what the whole is to its part. (L'Éloquence est au sublime ce que le tout est à sa partie.)

LA BRUYÈRE, *Les Caractères.* Ch. 1.

6
There is no less eloquence in the tone of the voice, in the eyes and in the air of the speaker, than in his choice of words. (Il n'y a pas moins d'éloquence dans le ton de la voix, dans les yeux, et dans l'air de la personne, que dans le choix des paroles.)

LA ROCHEFOUCAULD, *Maximes.* No. 249.

Often there is eloquence in a silent look. (Sæpe tacens vocem verbaque vultus habet.)

OVID, *Ars Amatoria.* Bk. i, l. 574.

7
True eloquence consists in saying all that is necessary, and nothing but what is necessary. (La véritable éloquence consiste à dire tout ce qu'il faut, et à ne dire que ce qu'il faut.)

LA ROCHEFOUCAULD, *Maximes.* No. 250.

8
The finest eloquence is that which gets things done; the worst is that which delays them.

DAVID LLOYD GEORGE, *Speech,* at the Peace Conference, Paris, Jan., 1919.

9
Copiousness of words, however ranged, is always false eloquence, though it will ever impose on some sort of understandings.

MARY WORTLEY MONTAGU, *Letter to Lady Bute,* 20 July, 1754.

10
True eloquence scorns eloquence.

PASCAL, *Pensées.* No. 4.

Eloquence, which persuades by sweetness, not by authority.

PASCAL, *Pensées.* No. 15.

11
Eloquence is the art of saying things in such a way that those to whom we speak may listen to them with pleasure.

PASCAL, *Pensées.* No. 16.

Eloquence is a painting of thought; and thus those who, after having painted it, add something more, make a picture instead of a portrait.

PASCAL, *Pensées.* No. 26.

12
Eloquence, smooth and cutting, is like a razor whetted with oil.

SWIFT, *Thoughts on Various Subjects.*

13
Mistress of all the arts. (Omnium artium domina.)

TACITUS, *De Oratoribus.* Sec. 32. Referring to eloquence.

14
Great eloquence, like a flame, must have fuel to feed it, motion to excite it, and brightens by burning. (Magna eloquentia, sicut flamma, materia alitur, et moribus excitatur, et urendo clarescit.)

TACITUS, *De Oratoribus.* Sec. 36.

It is with eloquence as with a flame; it requires fuel to feed it, motion to excite it, and brightens as it burns.

WILLIAM PITT THE YOUNGER, *Paraphrase of Tacitus.*

15
Eloquence, the foster-child of license, which fools call liberty. (Eloquentia, alumna licentiæ, quam stulti libertatem vocabant.)

TACITUS, *De Oratoribus.* Sec. 46.

His eloquence is that of a drunken man, twisting, turning, and full of licence. (Eloquentiam ebrii hominis involutam et errantem et licentiæ plenam.)

SENECA, *Epistulæ ad Lucilium.* Epis. cxiv, 4.

II—Eloquence: Apothegms

16
He adorned whatever subject he either wrote or spoke upon, by the most splendid eloquence.

LORD CHESTERFIELD, *Character of Bolingbroke.*

He adorns all that he touches. (Il embellit tout ce qu'il touche.)

FÉNÉLON, *Lettre sur les Occupations de l'Académie Française.* Sec. 4.

He touched nothing that he did not adorn. (Nullum quod tetigit non ornavit.)

SAMUEL JOHNSON, *Epitaph on Goldsmith.*

1
I grew intoxicated with my own eloquence.
BENJAMIN DISRAELI, *Contarini Fleming*. Pt. i, ch. 7.

2
One of our statesmen said "The curse of this country is eloquent men."
EMERSON, *Society and Solitude: Eloquence.*

3
Their own eloquence is fatal to many. (Sua mortifera est facundia.)
JUVENAL, *Satires*. Sat. x, l. 9.

4
Profane eloquence is transferred from the Bar, where it has become obsolete, to the Pulpit, where it is out of place. (L'Eloquence profane est tranposée, pour ainsi dire, du Barreau, . . . à la Chaire où elle ne doit pas être.)
LA BRUYÈRE, *Les Caractères: De la Chaire.*

The deep soul-moving sense
Of religious eloquence.
WORDSWORTH, *Odes*. No. 45.

5
Till the sad breaking of that Parliament
Broke him, as that dishonest victory
At Chæronea, fatal to liberty,
Kill'd with report that old man eloquent.
MILTON, *Sonnet: To the Lady Margaret Ley.* Milton's reference is to Isocrates, the Athenian orator, who died four days after hearing of the defeat of the Athenians at Chæronea. The term was afterwards applied to John Quincy Adams and to W. E. Gladstone.

6
Everyone was eloquent in behalf of his own cause. (Proque sua causa quisque disertus erat.)
OVID, *Fasti*. Bk. iv, l. 112.

In an easy cause any man may be eloquent. (In causa facili cuivis licet esse diserto.)
OVID, *Tristia*. Bk. iii, eleg. 11, l. 21.

7
He is eloquent enough for whom truth speaks. (Satis est disertus, e quo loquitur veritas.)
PUBLILIUS SYRUS, *Sententiæ*. No. 681.

He who has the truth at his heart need never fear the want of persuasion on his tongue.
JOHN RUSKIN, *Stones of Venice*. Vol. ii, ch. vi, sec. 99.

Can there be a more horrible object in existence than an eloquent man not speaking the truth?
CARLYLE, *Address*, University of Edinburgh, 1866.

8
There would be no eloquence in the world if we were to speak only with one person at a time.
QUINTILIAN, *De Institutione Oratoria*. Bk. i, 2.

9
It is the heart which makes men eloquent. (Pectus est quod disertos facit.)
QUINTILIAN, *De Institutione Oratoria*. Bk. x, sec. 7. Quoted by MONTAIGNE, *Essays*. Bk. iii, ch. 5.

10
So much the more eloquent as I was less sincere. (D'autant plus éloquent que j'étais moins sincere.)
EDMOND ROSTAND, *Cyrano de Bergerac*. Act iii, sc. 1.

11
Plenty of eloquence, but little wisdom. (Satis eloquentiæ sapientiæ parum.)
SALLUST, *Catilina*. Sec. 5.

Eloquence may exist without a proportionable degree of wisdom.
EDMUND BURKE, *Reflections on the Revolution in France.*

III—Eloquence: Its Power

12
Tully was not so eloquent as thou,
Thou nameless column with the buried base.
BYRON, *Childe Harold*. Canto iv, st. 110.

13
Such was his force of eloquence, to make
The hearers more concerned than he that spake;
Each seemed to act the part he came to see,
And none was more a looker-on than he.
SIR JOHN DENHAM, *On the Earl of Strafford's Trial and Death*, l. 11.

14
Him of the Western dome, whose weighty sense
Flows in fit words and heavenly eloquence.
DRYDEN, *Absalom and Achitophel*. Pt. i, l. 868.

15
Eloquence a hundred times has turned the scale of war and peace at will.
EMERSON, *Letters and Social Aims: Progress of Culture.*

16
A man whose eloquence has power
To clear the fullest house in half an hour.
SOAME JENYNS, *Imitations of Horace*. Bk. ii, epis. 1.

17
A woman, no less than a populace, a grave judge, or a chosen senate, will surrender, defeated, to eloquence. (Quam populus judexque gravis lectusque senatus, Tam dabit eloquio victa puella manus.)
OVID, *Ars Amatoria*. Bk. i, l. 461.

Ulysses was not beautiful, but he was eloquent. (Non formosus erat, sed erat facundus Ulixes.)
OVID, *Ars Amatoria*. Bk. ii, l. 123.

18
Pour the full tide of eloquence along,
Serenely pure, and yet divinely strong.
POPE, *Imitations of Horace: Epistles*. Bk. ii, epis. ii, l. 171.

19
I have neither wit, nor words, nor worth,
Action, nor utterance, nor the power of speech,
To stir men's blood: I only speak right on.
SHAKESPEARE, *Julius Cæsar*. Act iii, sc. 2, l. 225.

Which his fair tongue, conceit's expositor,
Delivers in such apt and gracious words,

That aged ears play truant at his tales,
And younger hearings are quite ravished.
SHAKESPEARE, *Love's Labour's Lost*. Act ii, sc. 1, l. 72.

Every tongue that speaks
But Romeo's name speaks heavenly eloquence.
SHAKESPEARE, *Romeo and Juliet*. Act iii, sc. 2, l. 32.

1
A full-cell'd honeycomb of eloquence
Stored from all flowers. Poet-like he spoke.
TENNYSON, *Edwin Morris*, l. 26.

2
How the heart listened while he pleading spoke!
While on the enlightened mind, with winning art,
His gentle reason so persuasive stole,
That the charmed hearer thought it was his own.
THOMSON, *To Memory of Lord Talbot*, l. 103.

3
While listening senates hang upon thy tongue,
Devolving through the maze of eloquence
A roll of periods, sweeter than her song.
THOMSON, *The Seasons: Autumn*, l. 15.

4
But to a higher mark than song can reach,
Rose this pure eloquence.
WORDSWORTH, *The Excursion*. Bk. vii, l. 24.

EMERSON, RALPH WALDO

5
O monstrous, dead, unprofitable world,
That thou canst hear, and hearing, hold thy way!
A voice oracular hath peal'd to-day,
To-day a hero's banner is unfurl'd.
MATTHEW ARNOLD, *Written in a Volume of Emerson's Essays.*

6
Voice of the deeps thou art! . . . Light of the deeps thou art!
CRAVEN LANGSTROTH BETTS, *Emerson.*

7
His thought rounded the spheres, his dreams topped the Cosmos. He walks in ether and is part of the barred and crimson sunset.
BENJAMIN DE CASSERES, *Emerson*. (*The Philistine*. Vol. xx, No. 10.)

8
Dry lighted soul, the ray that shines in thee,
Shot without reflex from primeval sun.
ELLEN HOOPER, *To R. W. E.*

9
There comes Emerson first, whose rich words, every one,
Are like gold nails in temples to hang trophies on.
J. R. LOWELL, *A Fable for Critics*, l. 527.

For though he builds glorious temples, 'tis odd
He leaves never a doorway to get in a god.
'Tis refreshing to old-fashioned people like me
To meet such a primitive Pagan as he,
In whose mind all creation is duly respected
As parts of himself—just a little projected;
And who's willing to worship the stars and the sun,
A convert to—nothing but Emerson.
J. R. LOWELL, *A Fable for Critics*, l. 557.

10
A great interpreter of life ought not himself to need interpretation.
JOHN MORLEY, *Miscellanies: Emerson.*

11
A foul mouth is so ill-matched with a white beard that I would gladly believe the newspaper-scribes alone responsible for the bestial utterances which they declare to have dropped from a teacher whom such disciples as these exhibit to our disgust and compassion as performing on their obscene platform the last tricks of tongue now possible to a gap-toothed and hoary ape, carried at first into notice on the shoulder of Carlyle, and who now in his dotage spits and chatters from a dirtier perch of his own finding and fouling: coryphæus or choragus of his Bulgarian tribe of auto-coprophagous baboons, who make the filth they feed on.
A. C. SWINBURNE, *Letter to Ralph Waldo Emerson*, 30 Jan., 1874.

EMOTION, see Feeling

EMPEROR, see King

END

See also Beginning and End; Purpose. For End in the sense of Death, see Death

I—End: Apothegms

12
All is good that hath good end.
JOHN AWDELAY, *Poems*, p. 54. (c. 1426)

If the end be well, all will be well. (Si finis bonus est, totum bonum erit.)
UNKNOWN, *Gesta Romanorum*. Tale lxvii. (c. 1473)

All is well that ends well.
HEYWOOD, *Proverbs*. Pt. i, ch. 10. (1546)

All's well that ends well; still the fine's the crown;
Whate'er the course, the end is the renown.
SHAKESPEARE, *All's Well that Ends Well*, Act iv, sc. 4, l. 35. (1602)

13
Who keeps one end in view makes all things serve.
ROBERT BROWNING, *In a Balcony.*

14
With mortal crisis doth portend,
My days to appropinque an end.
BUTLER, *Hudibras*. Pt. i, canto iii, l. 589.

15
Some time an end there is of every deed.
CHAUCER, *The Knightes Tale*, l. 1778.

Everything hath end.
CHAUCER, *Troilus and Criseyde*. Bk. iii, l. 615.

Everything hath an end, and a pudding hath two.
THOMAS NASHE, *Strange Newes.*

A pudding merits double praise,
A pudding hath two ends.
THOMAS BASTARD, *Chrestoloros.* Bk. iii, ep. 12. (1598)

All things have end,
And that we call a pudding hath his two.
BEAUMONT AND FLETCHER, *The Knight of the Burning Pestle.* Act i, sc. 2.

1
Around the man who seeks a noble end,
Not angels but divinities attend.
R. W. EMERSON, *Life.*

2
He who has put a good finish to his undertaking is said to have placed a golden crown to the whole.
EUSTATHIUS, *Commentary on the Iliad.*

3
A morning Sun, and a Wine-bred child, and a Latin-bred woman seldom end well.
GEORGE HERBERT, *Jacula Prudentum.*

4
The end of things is at hand. (Finis adest rerum.)
LUCAN, *De Bello Civili.* Bk. iii, l. 328.

The end is not yet.
New Testament: Matthew, xxiv, 6.

5
Her end is bitter as wormwood.
Old Testament: Proverbs, v, 4.

We rode with two anchors ahead, and the cables veered out to the better end.
DEFOE, *Robinson Crusoe.* Ch. 1. The "better end" of a cable is the end which is secured within the vessel and little used. It is alleged by some authorities that "bitter end" is a corruption of this.

A bitter is but the turn of a cable about the bitts, and the bitter end is that part of the cable which doth stay within board.
CAPTAIN JOHN SMITH, *Seaman's Grammar.* (1627) This is another explanation of "bitter end."

6
All things move on to their end. (Toutes choses se meuvent à leur fin.)
RABELAIS, *Works.* Bk. ii, ch. 3.

And so on to the end of the chapter.
RABELAIS, *Works.* Bk. v, ch. 10.

7
Let the end try the man.
SHAKESPEARE, *II Henry IV.* Act ii, sc. 2, l. 50.

Let all the ends thou aim'st at be thy country's,
Thy God's, and Truth's.
SHAKESPEARE, *Henry VIII.* Act iii, sc. 2, l. 447.

8
O, that a man might know
The end of this day's business ere it come!
But it sufficeth that the day will end,
And then the end is known.
SHAKESPEARE, *Julius Cæsar.* Act v, sc. 1, l. 123.

9
Matters be ended as they are be-friended.
THOMAS STARKEY, *England in the Reign of Henry VIII.* Bk. i, ch. 3.

10
Big-endians and Little-endians.
SWIFT, *Gulliver's Travels: Voyage to Lilliput.* Pt. i, ch. 4. In the empire of Lilliput, the Big-endians belonged to the party which made it a matter of conscience to break their eggs at the big end, and were regarded as heretics by the orthodox party, who broke their eggs at the little end.

11
Thy works and mine are ripples on the sea.
Take heart, I say: we know not yet their end.
A. C. SWINBURNE, *Locrine.* Act iii, sc. 1.

12
Things will work to ends the slaves o' the world
Do never dream of.
WORDSWORTH, *The Borderers.* Act ii, l. 936.

II—End: The End Crowns All

13
It is the end that crowns us, not the fight.
ROBERT HERRICK, *Hesperides.* No. 309.

14
The end crowns the work. (Finis coronat opus.)
LEHMANN, *Florilegium Politicum.* (1630)

15
The last act crowns the play.
FRANCIS QUARLES, *Respice Finem.* (1640)

'Tis the last act which crowns the play.
NATHANIEL COTTON, *Death.* (1780)

16
The end crowns every action, stay till that;
Just judges will not be prejudicate.
THOMAS RANDOLPH, *The Muses' Looking-Glass.* Act iii, sc. 1.

17
The end crowns all.
SHAKESPEARE, *Troilus and Cressida.* Act iv, sc. 5, l. 224.

La fin couronne les œuvres.
SHAKESPEARE, *II Henry VI.* Act v, sc. 2, l. 28.

18
Integrity of Life is fame's best friend,
Which nobly, beyond death, shall crown the end.
JOHN WEBSTER, *Duchess of Malfi.* Act v, sc. 5.

III—End: Means and End

19
When the end is lawful, the means are also lawful. (Cum finis est licitus, etiam media sunt licita.)
H. BUSENBAUM, *Medulla Theologiæ.* (1650) Busenbaum was a Jesuit. Hence the doctrine that the end justifies the means.

20
He who does evil that good may come, pays a toll to the devil to let him into heaven.
J. C. AND A. W. HARE, *Guesses at Truth,* ii, 213.

21
Be virtuous ends pursued by virtuous means,

Nor think th' intention sanctifies the deed.
SAMUEL JOHNSON, *Irene.*

1
Ill comes from ill,
And as a thing begins, so ends it still.
WILLIAM MORRIS, *The Earthly Paradise: The Stealing of the Coif*, l. 140.

2
Whether with Reason or with Instinct blest,
Know all enjoy that power which suits them best;
To bliss alike by that direction tend,
And find the means proportion'd to their end.
POPE, *Essay on Man*. Epis. iii, l. 79.

3
The end must justify the means:
He only sins who ill intends:
Since therefore 'tis to combat evil,
'Tis lawful to employ the devil.
MATTHEW PRIOR, *Hans Carvel.*

4
As some affirm that we say, Let us do evil, that good may come.
New Testament: Romans, iii, 8. (Faciamus mala ut veniant bona.—*Vulgate.*)

5
No man is justified in doing evil on the ground of expediency.
THEODORE ROOSEVELT, *The Strenuous Life.*

6
The doing evil to avoid an evil
Cannot be good.
SCHILLER, *Wallenstein*. Act iv, 6. (Coleridge, tr.)

Perish with him the folly that seeks through evil good.
WHITTIER, *Brown of Ossawatomie.*

7
Nothing can seem foul to those that win.
SHAKESPEARE, *I Henry IV*. Act v, sc. 1, l. 8.

8
A little harm done to a great good end
For lawful policy remains enacted.
SHAKESPEARE, *The Rape of Lucrece*, l. 528.

9
The result justifies the deed. (Exitus acta probat.)
GEORGE WASHINGTON, *Motto*. (From OVID, *Heroides*. Eleg. ii, l. 85.)

10
The end directs and sanctifies the means.
SIR JOHN WILMOT, Collins v. Blantern, 1762. (*2 Wils. Rep.* 351.)

11
Him only pleasure leads, and peace attends,
Him, only him, the shield of Jove defends,
Whose means are fair and spotless as his ends.
WORDSWORTH, *Dion*. St. 6.

IV—End: Remember the End

12
Look to the end. (Τέλος σκοπεῖν.)
CHILON, the Spartan philosopher, and one of the seven wise men of Greece, who died 597 B.C. The phrase is said to have been inscribed on the wall of the temple at Delphi. Quoted by Solon to Crœsus. (PLUTARCH, *Lives: Solon*. Sec. 28. *See under* DEATH: COUNT NO MAN HAPPY.)

13
Whatsoever thou takest in hand, remember the end, and thou shalt never do amiss.
Apocrypha: Ecclesiasticus, vii, 36. (In omnibus operibus tuis memorare novissima tua, et in æternum non peccabis.—*Vulgate: Ecclesiastici*, vii, 40.)

14
In every thing you do, consider the matters which come first and those which follow after, and only then approach the thing itself.
EPICTETUS, *Discourses*. Bk. iii, ch. 15, sec. 1.

15
When any great design thou dost intend,
Think on the means, the manner, and the end.
SIR JOHN DENHAM, *Of Prudence*, l. 186.

16
In every thing one must consider the end. (En toute chose il faut considérer la fin.)
LA FONTAINE, *Fables*. Bk. iii, fab. 5.

17
In every enterprise consider where you would come out. (Quicquid conaris, quo pervenias cogites.)
PUBLILIUS SYRUS, *Sententiæ*. No. 777.

ENDURANCE

18
An anvil to receive the hammer's blows and to forge the red-hot ore, he, without a groan, endured in silence.
ÆSCHYLUS, *Fragments*. Frag. 167.

19
Behold, we live through all things,—famine, thirst,
Bereavement, pain; all grief and misery,
All woe and sorrow; life inflicts its worst
On soul and body,—but we can not die,
Though we be sick and tired and faint and worn,—
Lo, all things can be borne!
ELIZABETH AKERS ALLEN, *Endurance.*

20
'Tis the world the same
For my praise or blame,
And endurance is easy then.
ROBERT BROWNING, *Lovers' Quarrel*. St. 17.

21
The victory of endurance born.
BRYANT, *The Battle-Field*. St. 8.

22
'Tis not now who's stout and bold,
But who bears hunger best, and cold;
And he's approv'd the most deserving,
Who longest can hold out at starving.
BUTLER, *Hudibras*. Pt. iii, canto iii, l. 353.

23
Sorrow and silence are strong, and patient endurance is godlike.
LONGFELLOW, *Evangeline*. Pt. ii, sec. 1, l. 60.

24
Endurance is the crowning quality,

And patience all the passion of great hearts.
J. R. LOWELL, *Columbus.*

1
Nothing befalls any man which he is not fitted to endure. (Οὐδὲν οὐδενὶ συμβαίνει, ὃ οὐχὶ πέφυκε φέρειν.)
MARCUS AURELIUS, *Meditations.* Bk. v, sec. 18.

2
He that shall endure unto the end, the same shall be saved.
New Testament: Matthew, xxiv, 13.

He that endures is not overcome.
GEORGE HERBERT, *Jacula Prudentum.* No. 848.

3
Much and long have I endured. (Multa diuque tuli.)
OVID, *Amores.* Bk. iii, eleg. 11, l. 1.

Endure and persist; this pain will turn to your good by and by. (Perfer et obdura; dolor hic tibi proderit olim.)
OVID, *Amores.* Bk. iii, eleg. 11, l. 7.

4
O vile, Intolerable, not to be endured!
SHAKESPEARE, *The Taming of the Shrew.* Act v, sc. 2, l. 94.

5
Such was his life, gently to bear with and endure all men. (Sic vita erat; facile omnes perferre ac pati.)
TERENCE, *Andria,* l. 62. (Act i, sc. 1.)

6
Endure, and keep yourselves for days of happiness. (Durate, et vosmet rebus servate secundis.)
VERGIL, *Æneid.* Bk. i, l. 207.

7
Whatsoe'er it be, every fortune is to be overcome by bearing it. (Quidquid erit, superanda omnis fortuna ferendo est.)
VERGIL, *Æneid.* Bk. v, l. 710.

Every lot is to be overcome by endurance. (Omnis sors ferendo superanda est.)
W. G. BENHAM, *Proverbs,* p. 613.

8
More able to endure,
As more exposed to suffering and distress.
WORDSWORTH, *Character of the Happy Warrior.*

II—Endurance: What Can't Be Cured

9
What cannot be repaired is not to be regretted.
SAMUEL JOHNSON, *Rasselas.*

10
What can't be cured were best endured. (Optimum est pati, quod emendare non possis.)
SENECA, *Epistulæ ad Lucilium.* Epis. cvii, sec. 9.

11
What cannot be cured must be endured.
RABELAIS, *Works.* Bk. v, ch. 15; BURTON, *Anatomy of Melancholy.* Pt. ii, sec. ii, mem. 3.

12
What cannot be eschew'd, must be embraced.
SHAKESPEARE, *The Merry Wives of Windsor.* Act v, sc. 5, l. 251.

13
Better it were a little to feign,
And cleanly cover that cannot be cured:
Such ill as is forced must needs be endured.
SPENSER, *The Shepheardes Calender: September,* l. 137.

What's past help is beyond prevention.
MASSINGER, *Unnatural Combat:* Act ii, sc. 1.

14
I'll not willingly offend,
Nor be easily offended:
What's amiss I'll strive to mend,
And endure what can't be mended.
ISAAC WATTS, *Good Resolutions.*

ENEMY

See also Friend and Enemy

I—Enemy: Apothegms

15
Even from a foe a man may wisdom learn. (Μάθοι γὰρ ἄν τις κἀπὸ τῶν ἐχθρῶν σοφόν.)
ARISTOPHANES, *The Birds,* l. 382.

An enemy may chance to give good counsel.
THOMAS FULLER, *Gnomologia.* No. 600.

It is well to learn even from an enemy. (Fas est et ab hoste doceri.)
OVID, *Metamorphoses.* Bk. iv, l. 428. (A. D. 7)

16
Who shows mercy to an enemy, denies it to himself. (Qui misericordiam inimico impertit, sibi denegat.)
FRANCIS BACON, *De Augmentis Scientiarum: Crudelitas.*

17
I wish my deadly foe no worse
Than want of friends, and empty purse.
NICHOLAS BRETON, *A Farewell to Town.*

18
He has got beyond the gunshot of his enemies.
JOHN BUNYAN, *The Pilgrim's Progress.* Pt. i.

19
Quoth he, That man is sure to lose
That fouls his hands with dirty foes;
For where no honour's to be gained
'Tis thrown away in being maintained.
BUTLER, *Hudibras.* Pt. ii, canto ii, l. 849.

20
What mark is so fair as the breast of a foe?
BYRON, *Childe Harold.* Canto ii, st. 72.

21
Of enemies the fewer the better. (De los Enemigos los menos.)
CERVANTES, *Don Quixote.* Pt. ii, ch. 14.

22
Every wise man dreadeth his enemy.
CHAUCER, *Melibeus.* Sec. 31, l. 2505.

23
A weak invention of the enemy.
COLLEY CIBBER, *Richard III* (alt.). Act v, sc. 3.

Invented by the calumniating enemy. (Inventé par le caloumnateur ennemi.)
RABELAIS, *Works.* Bk. iii, ch. 11.

A thing devised by the enemy.
SHAKESPEARE, *Richard III.* Act v, sc. 3, l. 306.

1
There is more to be feared from unspoken and concealed, than from open and declared, hostility.
CICERO, *In Verrem*. No. ii, sec. 5.

Give me the avowed, the erect, the manly foe.
GEORGE CANNING, *New Morality*.

Secret path marks secret foe.
SCOTT, *Lady of the Lake*. Canto v, st. 8.

2
Enmity is anger watching the opportunity for revenge. (Inimicitia ira ulciscendi tempus observans.)
CICERO, *Tusculanarum Disputationum*. Bk. iv, ch. 9, sec. 21.

3
A man hath many enemies when his back is to the wall.
JOHN CLARKE, *Parœmiologia*, p. 166.

The base insulting foe.
COWPER, *Translation Psalm 137*.

As one that neither seeks, nor shuns his foe.
DRYDEN, *Annus Mirabilis*. St. 41.

4
He wants worth who dares not praise a foe.
DRYDEN, *The Conquest of Granada*. Pt. ii, act iv, sc. 3.

5
Rejoice not over thy greatest enemy being dead.
Apocrypha: Ecclesiasticus, viii, 7.

6
The assailant makes the strength of the defense. Therefore, we ought to pray, give us a good enemy.
EMERSON, *Journal*, 1865.

Love your Enemies, for they tell you your Faults.
BENJAMIN FRANKLIN, *Poor Richard*, 1756.

I love my best friend . . . my bravest enemy.
That is the man who keeps me up to the mark.
BERNARD SHAW, *Major Barbara*. Act iii.

7
Our enemies will tell the rest with pleasure.
WILLIAM FLEETWOOD, *The Spectator*. No. 384.
This phrase occurred in a preface to four sermons delivered while Fleetwood was Bishop of St. Asaph, and published in 1712. It was burned by order of the House of Commons, and afterwards published as No. 384 of *The Spectator*.

8
No man is without enemies.
UNKNOWN. An Arabian proverb.

Though thou art not to let the sun set on thy anger, yet thou art not to trust a deceiving treacherous enemy next morning.
THOMAS FULLER, *Gnomologia*.

9
We ne'er see our foes but we wish them to stay,
They never see us but they wish us away;
If they run, why, we follow, or run them ashore,
For if they won't fight us, we cannot do more.
DAVID GARRICK, *Hearts of Oak*.

10
One enemy is too much.
GEORGE HERBERT, *Jacula Prudentum*.

11
Our enemies come nearer the truth in the judgments they form of us, than we do in our judgment of ourselves. (Nos ennemis approchent plus de la vérité dans les jugements qu'ils font de nous, que nous n'en approchons nous-mêmes.)
LA ROCHEFOUCAULD, *Maximes*. No. 458.

12
A man's foes shall be they of his own household.
New Testament: Matthew, x, 36.

For in this world is no worse pestilence
Than homely foe all day in thy presence.
CHAUCER, *The Marchantes Tale*, l. 549.

13
An enemy hath done this.
New Testament: Matthew, xiii, 28.

14
Ye have heard that it hath been said, Thou shalt love thy neighbour, and hate thine enemy.
New Testament: Matthew, v, 43.

15
My nearest and dearest enemy.
THOMAS MIDDLETON, *Anything for a Quiet Life*. Act v, sc. 1.

'Twas one of my most intimate enemies.
D. G. ROSSETTI, *Fragment*.

16
You must not fight too often with one enemy, or you will teach him all your art of war.
NAPOLEON BONAPARTE. (EMERSON, *Representative Men: Uses of Great Men: Napoleon.*)

17
It is evil to trust the enemy. (Male creditur hosti.)
OVID, *Fasti*. Bk. ii, l. 226.

18
I fear no foe in shining armour.
EDWARD OXENFORD, *Song*.

19
A man's greatness can be measured by his enemy.
DONN PIATT, *Memories of Men Who Saved the Union: Appendix*.

20
"We are fallen among our enemies," said a soldier to Pelopidas. "How are we fallen among them more than they among us?" said he.
PLUTARCH, *Apothegms: Pelopidas*.

21
And deal damnation round the land,
On each I judge thy foe.
POPE, *Universal Prayer*.

22
His enemies shall lick the dust.
Old Testament: Psalms, lxxii, 9.

1
His must be a very wretched fortune who has no enemy. (Miserrima est fortuna quæ inimico caret.)
PUBLILIUS SYRUS, *Sententiæ*. No. 499.

The truly civilized man has no enemies.
C. F. DOLE, *The Smoke and the Flame*.

He has no enemy, you say;
My friend your boast is poor,
He who hath mingled in the fray
Of duty that the brave endure
Must have made foes. If he has none
Small is the work that he has done.
He has hit no traitor on the hip;
Has cast no cup from perjured lip;
Has never turned the wrong to right;
Has been a coward in the fight.
ANASTASIUS GRÜN, *No Enemies*.

The man who has no enemies has no following.
DONN PIATT, *Memories of the Men Who Saved the Union: Preface*.

2
A wise man fears his enemy, however insignificant. (Inimicum quamvis humilem docti est metuere.)
PUBLILIUS SYRUS, *Sententiæ*.

Scorn no man's love, though of a mean degree; . . .
Much less make any one thine enemy.
As guns destroy, so may a little sling.
The cunning workman never doth refuse
The meanest tool, that he may chance to use.
GEORGE HERBERT, *The Church-Porch*. St. 59.

Little enemies and little wounds are not to be despised. (Kleine Feinde und kleine Wunden sind nicht zu verachten.)
UNKNOWN. A German proverb.

There is no little enemy. (Il n'y a pas de petit ennemi.)
UNKNOWN. A French proverb.

3
Do not speak ill of an enemy, but think it. (De inimico non loquaris male, sed cogites.)
PUBLILIUS SYRUS, *Sententiæ*. No. 147.

4
No tears are shed when an enemy dies. (Inimico exstincto non habent lacrimæ exitum.)
PUBLILIUS SYRUS, *Sententiæ*. No. 376.

A dead body revenges not injuries.
WILLIAM BLAKE, *Proverbs of Hell*.

5
Take heed of enemies reconciled, and of meat twice boiled.
JOHN RAY, *Spanish Proverbs*.

6
How goes the enemy?
FREDERIC REYNOLDS, *The Will*. Act i, sc. 1. Said by Mr. Ennui, the "time-killer."

7
One may employ everything against one's enemies. (On peut tout employer contre ses ennemis.)
RICHELIEU, *Les Tuileries*.

8
If thine enemy hunger, feed him; if he thirst, give him drink: for in so doing thou shalt heap coals of fire on his head.
New Testament: Romans, xii, 20.

If thou must needs have thy revenge of thine enemy, with a soft tongue break his bones, heap coals of fire on his head, forgive him, and enjoy it.
SIR THOMAS BROWNE, *Christian Morals*. Pt. iii, sec. 12.

He doeth well who doeth good
To those of his own brotherhood;
He doeth better who doth bless
The stranger in his wretchedness;
Yet best, oh! best of all doth he
Who helps a fallen enemy.
UNKNOWN, *Best of All*.

9
I love to hear of worthy foes.
SCOTT, *Lady of the Lake*. Canto iv, st. 8.

The stern joy which warriors feel
In foemen worthy of their steel.
SCOTT, *Lady of the Lake*. Canto v, st. 10.

Yet, rest thee God! for well I know
I ne'er shall find a nobler foe.
SCOTT, *Lay of the Last Minstrel*. Canto v, st. 29.

Thus, then, my noble foe I greet:
Health and high fortune till we meet,
And then—what pleases Heaven.
SCOTT, *Lord of the Isles*. Canto iii, st. 6.

10
Would I had met my dearest foe in heaven
Or ever I had seen that day, Horatio.
SHAKESPEARE, *Hamlet*. Act i, sc. 2, l. 182.

11
In cases of defence 'tis best to weigh
The enemy more mighty than he seems.
SHAKESPEARE, *Henry V*. Act ii, sc. 4, l. 43.

Do not undervalue an enemy by whom you have been worsted.
JOHN SELDEN, *Table-Talk: War*.

12
He shall have the skins of our enemies to make dog's-leather of.
SHAKESPEARE, *II Henry VI*. Act iv, sc. 2, l. 25.

13
Heat not a furnace for your foe so hot
That it do singe yourself.
SHAKESPEARE, *Henry VIII*. Act i, sc. 1, l. 140.

14
You have many enemies, that know not
Why they are so, but, like to village-curs,
Bark when their fellows do.
SHAKESPEARE, *Henry VIII*. Act ii, sc. 4, l. 158.

Finding their enemy to be so curst,
They all strain curt'sy who shall cope him first.
SHAKESPEARE, *Venus and Adonis*. St. 148.

15
To exult
Even o'er an enemy oppressed, . . . is the mark
And the mean triumph of a dastard soul.
SMOLLETT, *The Regicide*. Act i, sc. 7.

16
Earth could not hold us both, nor can one Heaven

Contain my deadliest enemy and me!
SOUTHEY, *Roderick*. Sec. 21.

1
He was within a few hours of giving his enemies the slip for ever.
STERNE, *Tristram Shandy*. Vol. i, ch. 12

2
The body of a dead enemy always smells sweet. (Optime olere occisum hostem.)
AULUS VITELLIUS, when riding over the field of Beriacum, a few days after the battle, 14 April, 69. (SUETONIUS, *Lives of the Cæsars: Vitellius*. Sec. 10.) The saying has also been attributed to Vespasian and Charles IX of France.

Too many there be to whom a dead enemy smells well.
SIR THOMAS BROWNE, *Christian Morals*. Pt. iii, sec. 12.

And, as the soldiers bore dead bodies by,
He call'd them untaught knaves, unmannerly,
To bring a slovenly unhandsome corse
Betwixt the wind and his nobility.
SHAKESPEARE, *I Henry IV*. Act i, sc. 3, l. 42.

3
Fortune can give no greater advantage than discord among the enemy. (Nihil jam præstare fortuna majus potest, quam hostium discordiam.)
TACITUS, *Germania*. Sec. 33.

4
Who troubles himself either about valor or fraud in an enemy? (Dolus, an virtus, quis in hoste requirat?)
VERGIL, *Æneid*. Bk. ii, l. 390.

5
The enemy is at hand. (Hostis adest.)
VERGIL, *Æneid*. Bk. ix, l. 38.

While throng'd the citizens with terror dumb,
Or whispering with white lips—"The foe! they come! they come!"
BYRON, *Childe Harold*. Canto iii, st. 25.

The Spartans are not wont to ask how many the enemy are, but where they are.
KING AGIS II. (PLUTARCH, *Life*.)

6
I go to fight your majesty's enemies, and I leave you in the midst of my own. (Je vais combattre les ennemis de votre majesté, et je vous laisse au milieu des miens.)
MARECHAL DE VILLARS, to Louis XIV, as he started to join the Army of the Rhine. Attributed to Voltaire by Duvemet (*Vie de Voltaire*).

7
I'm lonesome. They are all dying. I have hardly a warm personal enemy left.
J. A. MCNEILL WHISTLER. (SEITZ, *Whistler Stories*.)

8
I choose my friends for their good looks, my acquaintances for their good characters, and my enemies for their good intellects. A man cannot be too careful in the choice of his enemies.
OSCAR WILDE, *Picture of Dorian Gray*. Ch. 1.

II—Enemy: Man His Own Enemy

9
What is man's chief enemy? Each man is his own. (Τί ἐστι πολέμιον ἀνθρώποις; αὐτοὶ ἑαυτοῖς.)
ANACHARSIS. (STOBÆUS, *Florilegium*. Pt. ii, l. 43.)

His father was no man's friend but his own, and he, saith the proverb, is no man's foe else.
THOMAS ADAMS, *Diseases of the Soul*, p. 53.

10
Yet is every man his own greatest enemy, and as it were his own executioner.
SIR THOMAS BROWNE, *Religio Medici*. Pt. ii, 4.

11
He is his own worst enemy. (Sibi est adversarius unus acerrimus.)
CICERO, *Epistolæ ad Atticum*. Bk. x, epis. 8. Referring to Julius Caesar.

12
It smarts not half so ill as the phrase, Every body's friend but his own.
CHARLES CORNWALLIS, *Essays*. No. 7. (1600)

Tom, though an idle, thoughtless, rattling rascal, was nobody's enemy but his own.
FIELDING, *Tom Jones*. Bk. iv, ch. 5.

13
Let me hack at my own vines. (Ut vineta egomet cædam mea.)
HORACE, *Epistles*. Bk. ii, epis. 1, l. 220.

He is not harmless who harms himself. (On n'est point innocent quand on nuit à soi-même.)
JOUBERT, *Pensées*. No. 134.

14
None but yourself, who are your greatest foe.
LONGFELLOW, *Michael Angelo*. Pt. ii, sec. 3.

15
None but myself ever did me any harm.
NAPOLEON BONAPARTE, at St. Helena, 6 April, 1817. (O'MEARA, *Napoleon in Exile*.)

16
Formidable is that enemy that lies hid in a man's own breast. (Gravis est inimicus is, qui latet in pectore.)
PUBLILIUS SYRUS, *Sententiæ*. No. 235.

III—Enemy: The Bridge of Silver

17
Instead of destroying that bridge, we should build another, that he may retire the more quickly from Europe.
ARISTIDES, referring to the proposal to destroy Xerxes' bridge of boats across the Hellespont. (PLUTARCH, *Lives: Themistocles*. Ch. 16, sec. 3.)

18
I tell thee, be not rash; a golden bridge
Is for a flying enemy.
BYRON, *The Deformed Transformed*. Act ii, 2.

To a flying enemy, a bridge of silver.
CERVANTES, *Don Quixote*. Pt. ii, ch. 58.

Build a bridge of gold for a flying enemy.
LOUIS II of France, to Brantôme. (BRANTÔME, *Memoirs*. Vol. i, p. 83.)

For a flying foe
Discreet and provident conquerors build up
A bridge of gold.
PHILIP MASSINGER, *The Guardian*. Act i, sc. 1.

1
Open unto your enemies all your gates and ways, and make for them a bridge of silver. rather than fail to get quit of them. (Ouvrez toujours à vos ennemis toutes les portes et chemins, et plutôt leurs faites un pont d'argent, afin de les renvoyer.)

RABELAIS, *Works*. Bk. i, ch. 43.

2
Give the enemy not only a road for flight, but also the means of defending it. (Hosti non solum dandam esse viam fugiendi verum etiam muniendam.)

SCIPIO AFRICANUS. (FRONTINUS, *Strategy*. Bk. iv, ch. 7, sec. 16.)

ENGLAND AND THE ENGLISH

I—England: Familiar Phrases

3
There are no countries in the world less known by the British than these self-same British Islands.

GEORGE BORROW, *Lavengro: Preface.*

What should they know of England who only England know?

RUDYARD KIPLING, *The English Flag.*

4
Ah! perfidious England! (Ah! la perfide Angleterre!)

JACQUES BOSSUET, *Sermon on the Circumcision.* His first sermon, preached at Metz, in 1652. The phrase was quoted by Napoleon on leaving England for St. Helena.

5
England is the mother of parliaments.

JOHN BRIGHT, *Speech,* at Birmingham, 18 Jan., 1865. (THOROLD ROGERS, *Speeches of John Bright*. Vol. ii, p. 112.)

The king, and his faithful subjects, the Lords and Commons of this realm—the triple cord, which no man can break.

EDMUND BURKE, *A Letter to a Noble Lord.*

England is not governed by logic, but by Acts of Parliament.

UNKNOWN, *Saying,* quoted in King's Bench, London, 13 April, 1923.

6
Still amorous, and fond, and billing,
Like Philip and Mary on a shilling.

SAMUEL BUTLER, *Hudibras*. Pt. iii, canto 1, l. 687. The reference is to coins struck in 1555, in which Mary and her consort were placed face to face and not cheek by jowl, as was customary.

Like Will. and Mary on the coin.

MATTHEW GREEN, *The Spleen,* l. 197.

7
Be England what she will,
With all her faults, she is my country still.

CHARLES CHURCHILL, *The Farewell,* l. 27. (1760)

England, with all thy faults, I love thee still.

COWPER, *The Task*. Bk. ii, l. 206. (1783)

8
The cat, the rat, and Lovell our dog,
Ruleth all England under a hog.

The which was meant that Catesby, Ratcliffe and the Lord Lovell ruleth the land under the king [Richard III].

ROBERT FABYAN, *The Concordance of Histories.* Fo. 468. (1542)

9
In these troublous days, when the great Mother Empire stands splendidly isolated in Europe.

HON. GEORGE EULAS FOSTER, *Speech,* Canadian House of Commons, 16 Jan., 1896.

Whether splendidly isolated or dangerously isolated, I will not now debate; but for my part, I think splendidly isolated, because this isolation of England comes from her superiority.

SIR WILFRID LAURIER, *Speech,* Canadian House of Commons, 5 Feb., 1896.

We have stood alone in that which is called isolation—our splendid isolation, as one of our Colonial friends was good enough to call it.

SIR WILLIAM EDWARD GOSCHEN, *Speech,* at Lewes, 26 Feb., 1896.

He was careful not to tear England from the splendid isolation in which she had wrapped herself.

RAYMOND POINCARÉ, *Speech,* at Cannes, 13 April, 1912. Referring to King Edward VII.

10
He whom I favor wins. (Cui adhæreo præest.)

HENRY VIII of England, *Motto,* on his tent in the Field of the Cloth of Gold, June, 1520.

11
God of our fathers, known of old,
Lord of our far-flung battle-line,
Beneath whose awful Hand we hold
Dominion over palm and pine—
Lord God of Hosts, be with us yet,
Lest we forget—lest we forget!

RUDYARD KIPLING, *Recessional.* Written in celebration of Queen Victoria's Diamond Jubilee, and first published in the London *Times,* 17 July, 1897.

12
England expects every man to do his duty.

LORD NELSON, *Signal,* to the fleet at the battle of Trafalgar, 21 Oct., 1805. (SOUTHEY, *Life of Nelson*. Ch. 9.) There are several versions of this famous sentence. In the London *Times,* 26 Dec., 1805, it was given: "England expects every officer and man to do his duty this day." William Pryce Cunby, First Lieutenant of the *Bellerophon,* reported it: "England expects that every man will do his duty." Captain Pasco, Nelson's flag-lieutenant, stated that Nelson's order was: "Say to the fleet, England confides that every man will do his duty," and that he suggested the substitution of "expects" for "confides." (See *Notes and Queries*. Ser. vi, vol. ix, pp. 261, 283.)

13
It cannot be made, it shall not be made, it will not be made; but if it were made there would be a war between France and England for the possession of Egypt.

LORD PALMERSTON, *Speech,* 1851, during the

debate in Parliament concerning the Suez Canal. An outstanding example of indiscreet prophecy.

1
From old Bellerium to the northern main.

POPE, *Windsor Forest*, l. 316. (Bellerium: Land's End.)

2
God and my right. (Dieu et mon droit.)

RICHARD I of England, at the battle of Gisors, in 1198, chose this phrase as his parole, or battle-word, meaning that he was not a vassal of France, but owed his royalty to God alone. He won a great victory, in memory of which the phrase was made the motto of the royal arms of England.

3
It is beginning to be hinted that we are a nation of amateurs.

LORD ROSEBERY, *Rectorial Address*, Glasgow, 16 Nov., 1900.

4
Child Rowland to the dark tower came,
His word was still,—Fie, foh and fum,
I smell the blood of a British man.

SHAKESPEARE, *King Lear*. Act iii, sc. 4, l. 187.

With fi, fi, fo, and fum,
I smell the blood of a Christian man.

UNKNOWN, *Old Scottish Ballad*. (JAMIESON, *Illustrations of Northern Antiquities*.)

5
The spacious times of great Elizabeth.

TENNYSON, *A Dream of Fair Women*, l. 7.

6
In this country they put an admiral to death from time to time to encourage the others. (Dans ce pays-ci il est bon de tuer de temps en temps un amiral pour encourager les autres.)

VOLTAIRE, *Henriade: Preface. Candide*. Ch. 23. Referring to the execution of the English admiral, John Byng, for failing to relieve Minorca, besieged by the French, in 1756.

7
My good associates, by whose light and leading I have walked.

SIR HENRY WOTTON, *Letter to James I*, 1651. (*Reliquiæ Wottonianæ*.)

The men of England, the men, I mean, of light and leading in England.

EDMUND BURKE, *Reflections on the Revolution in France*. Disraeli used the expression, "men of light and leading," a number of times: *Speech*, House of Commons, 28 Feb., 1859; *Letter to Duke of Marlborough*, 10 March, 1880; *Sybil*. Bk. v, ch. i.

8
St. George he was for England: St. Dennis was for France.
Sing, Honi soit qui mal y pense.

UNKNOWN, *St. George He Was for England*. (Black-Letter Ballad, London, 1512.)

Thou *Saint George* shalt callèd be,
Saint George of Merry England, the sign of victory.

SPENSER, *The Faerie Queene*. Bk. i, canto x, st. 61. (1594)

Romulus and Remus were those that Rome did build,
But St. George, St. George, the dragon he hath killed.

THOMAS D'URFEY, *Pills to Purge Melancholy*. (1661)

II—England: John Bull

9
John Bull.

DR. JOHN ARBUTHNOT, *The History of John Bull*. (1712) A political allegory designed to ridicule the Duke of Marlborough and to render the Continental War, then raging, unpopular. Each European nation was given a nickname by Arbuthnot: "Lewis Baboon" for the French; "Nicholas Frog" for the Dutch, and so on; but "John Bull" for the British was the only one which stuck. It caught the British imagination and has been in use ever since.

Law is a bottomless pit. Exemplified in the case of Lord Strutt, John Bull, Nicholas Frog, and Lewis Baboon, who spent all they had in a lawsuit.

DR. JOHN ARBUTHNOT, *The History of John Bull*. Ch. 24.

10
The world is a bundle of hay,
Mankind are the asses who pull;
Each tugs it a different way,—
And the greatest of all is John Bull!

BYRON, *Epigram*.

11
Not a Bull of them all but is persuaded he bears Europa upon his back.

J. R. LOWELL, *On a Certain Condescension in Foreigners*.

12
John Bull was in his very worst of moods,
Raving of sterile farms and unsold goods.

SCOTT, *The Search After Happiness*, l. 230.

III—England: God Save the King

13
God save our gracious king,
Long live our noble king,
God save the king.

HENRY CAREY [?], *God Save the King*. Said to have been first sung by Carey, as his own composition, in 1740. (*Gentleman's Magazine*, ii, 1075.) Also credited, both words and music, to Dr. John Bull (1563?–1628), composer and singer. Claimed also by James Oswald, chamber composer to George III, 1742. The earliest known version was printed in *Harmonia Anglicana* (1742), and the three verses usually sung appeared in the *Gentleman's Magazine*, Oct., 1745. They began, "God save great George our King."

14
Now let us sing long live the King.

COWPER, *History of John Gilpin*. St. 63.

15
That Bogie, the National Anthem!

W. S. GILBERT, *His Excellency*. Act i.

16
The national anthem belongs to the eight-

eenth century. In it you find us ordering God about to do our political dirty work.

BERNARD SHAW, *The Adventures of the Black Girl in Her Search for God.*

IV—England: On Which the Sun Never Sets

1
Till now the name of names, England, the name of might,
Flames from the austral fires to the bounds of the boreal night,
And the call of her morning drum goes in a girdle of sound,
Like the voice of the sun in song, the great globe round and round.

W. E. HENLEY, *Rhymes and Rhythms.* No. 2.

2
Old England is our home and Englishmen are we,
Our tongue is known in every clime, our flag on every sea.

MARY HOWITT, *Old England is Our Home. See also* FLAG: BRITISH.

3
The martial airs of England
Encircle still the earth.

AMELIA B. RICHARDS, *The Martial Airs of England.*

Take 'old o' the Wings o' the Mornin',
An' flop round the earth till you're dead;
But you won't get away from the tune that they play
To the bloomin' old rag over'ead.

RUDYARD KIPLING, *The Widow at Windsor.*

A power which has dotted over the surface of the whole globe with her possessions and military posts, whose morning drum-beat, following the sun, and keeping company with the hours, circles the earth with one continuous and unbroken strain of the martial airs of England.

DANIEL WEBSTER, *Speech,* 7 May, 1834. *Works.* Vol. iv, p. 110.

4
Never was isle so little, never was sea so lone,
But over the scud and the palm-trees an English flag was flown.

RUDYARD KIPLING, *The English Flag.*

5
That island queen who sways the floods and lands
From Ind to Ind.

TENNYSON, *Buonaparte.*

6
His Majesty's dominions, on which the sun never sets.

JOHN WILSON, *Noctes Ambrosianæ.* No. 42, April, 1829.

"The sun never sets on his empire" was applied originally to the King of Spain. See HOWELL, *Familiar Letters,* (1623), and THOMAS FULLER, *Holy State,* p. 107. (1642) *See also under* SPAIN. Claudian (*see under* ROME) applied the idea to Rome.

V—England: Britannia Rules the Waves

7
Britain's best bulwarks are her wooden walls.

THOMAS AUGUSTINE ARNE, *Britain's Best Bulwarks.* (c. 1760)

The royal navy of England has ever been its greatest defence and ornament; it is its ancient and natural strength; the floating bulwark of the island.

SIR WILLIAM BLACKSTONE, *Commentaries.* Vol. i, bk. 1, ch. 13. (1765)

The dominion of the sea, as it is an ancient and undoubted right of the crown of England, so is it the best security of the land. The wooden walls are the best walls of this kingdom.

THOMAS COVENTRY, Lord Keeper of the Great Seal, *Speech,* 17 June, 1635. (GARDINER, *History of England,* iii, 79.)

You truly have fortified Britain with wooden walls. (Tu certe Ligneis Muris Britanniam munivisti.)

UNKNOWN, *Latin Address,* sent to Samuel Pepys by the Univ. of Oxford, Oct., 1702.

See also under SHIP: APOTHEGMS.

8
Britannia needs no bulwarks,
No towers along the steep;
Her march is o'er the mountain waves,
Her home is on the deep.

THOMAS CAMPBELL, *Ye Mariners of England.*

9
And trident-bearing queen of the wide seas.

COWPER, *Expostulation,* l. 275.

10
The British cannon formidably roars,
While starting from his oozy bed,
Th' asserted Ocean rears his reverend head,
To view and recognise his ancient lord again;
And, with a willing hand, restores
The fasces of the main.

DRYDEN, *Threnodia Augustalis,* l. 512.

11
When Britain first, at Heaven's command,
Arose from out the azure main,
This was the charter of the land,
And guardian angels sung this strain—
"Rule, Britannia, rule the waves;
Britons never will be slaves."

JAMES THOMSON, *Rule, Britannia!* This ode appeared originally in the last scene (Act ii, sc. 5) of *Alfred, A Masque,* a dramatic piece in which David Mallet collaborated and which was published in 1740. The ode has sometimes been attributed to Mallet, but the evidence is in favor of Thomson's authorship.

With Freedom's lion-banner
Britannia rules the waves.

THOMAS CAMPBELL, *Ode to the Germans.* (1832)

Englishmen never will be slaves; they are free to do whatever the Government and public opinion allow them to do.

BERNARD SHAW, *Man and Superman.* Act i.

1
Providence has given to the French the empire of the land; to the English that of the sea; to the Germans that of—the air!

JEAN PAUL FRIEDRICH RICHTER, as reported by Madame de Staël. (CARLYLE, *Essays: Richter.*) A better prophecy than Richter supposed.

The English, a nation over-proud, claim the empire of the sea; the French, a flighty nation, assume that of the air.
(Les Anglais, nation trop fière,
S'arrogent l'empire des mers;
Les Français, nation légère,
S'emparent de celui des airs.)

LOUIS XVIII of France, when Comte de Provence in 1783, *Impromptu Sur Nos Découvertes Aérostatiques.* Referring to the balloon flights of Montgolfier and other Frenchmen. The attribution has been questioned.

2
Others may use the ocean as their road,
Only the English make it their abode, . . .
Our oaks secure, as if they there took root,
We tread on billows with a steady foot.

EDMUND WALLER, *Of a War with Spain,* l. 25.

They that the whole world's monarchy designed,
Are to their ports by our bold fleet confined.

EDMUND WALLER, *Of a War with Spain,* l. 21.

Guarded with ships, and all our sea our own.

EDMUND WALLER, *Epistle to My Lord of Falkland.*

3
Oh, Britannia, the pride of the ocean,
The home of the brave and the free,
The shrine of the sailor's devotion,
No land can compare unto thee.

The authorship and even the inception of this song is in dispute. It is generally held to be an adaptation of *Columbia, the Gem of the Ocean,* a song written in 1843 by Thomas à Becket, a young English actor playing at the Chestnut Street Theatre, Philadelphia, and sung there by another English actor named David Taylor Shaw, who afterwards claimed its authorship. It is said to have been taken to London by E. L. Davenport and sung there under the title, *Britannia, the Pride of the Ocean.* Some authorities assert that the British version was the first, and was sung by Shaw in England before he came to America. (*See* BANKS, *Immortal Songs of Camp and Field,* p. 77; *Notes and Queries,* 26 Aug., 1899.) For *Columbia, the Gem of the Ocean, see* AMERICA: SONGS OF PRAISE.

VI—England: A Nation of Shopkeepers

4
A shopkeeper will never get the more custom by beating his customers, and what is true of a shopkeeper is true of a shopkeeping nation.

JOSIAH TUCKER, *Four Tracts on Political and Commercial Subjects.* (1766)

5
To found a great empire for the sole purpose of raising up a people of customers, may at first sight appear a project fit only for a nation of shopkeepers. It is, however, a project altogether unfit for a nation of shopkeepers, but extremely fit for a nation whose government is influenced by shopkeepers.

ADAM SMITH, *Wealth of Nations.* Vol. ii, bk. iv, ch. 7. (1775)

6
A nation of shopkeepers.

SAMUEL ADAMS, *Oration,* delivered in the State House at Philadelphia, 1 Aug., 1776. Referring to England. There is some doubt as to whether this oration was really delivered. It exists only in a professed English reprint (Philadelphia, printed; London, reprinted for E. Johnson, No. 4 Ludgate Hill, 1776), of which a number of copies are known. W. V. Wells, in his life of Adams, states that "No such American edition has ever been seen."

7
Let Pitt then boast of his victory to his shopkeeping nation. (Nation boutiquière.)

BERTRAND BARRÈRE, *Speech,* before the French National Convention, 11 June, 1794.

England is a nation of shopkeepers. (L'Angleterre est une nation de boutiquiers.)

NAPOLEON BONAPARTE, *Remark,* at St. Helena. *See* O'MEARA, *Napoleon at St. Helena,* ii. Napoleon perhaps spoke in Italian, using a phrase of Paoli, "Sono mercanti." *See* GOURGAUD, i, 69. SCOTT, *Life of Napoleon,* also attributes the phrase to him.

We are indeed a nation of shopkeepers.

BENJAMIN DISRAELI, *Young Duke.* Bk. i, ch. 11.

The Continent will not suffer England to be the workshop of the world.

DISRAELI, *Speech,* 15 Mar., 1838.

9
Governments of nations of shopkeepers must keep shop also.

EMERSON, *Journal,* 1862.

10
The first of all English games is making money.

RUSKIN, *Crown of Wild Olive: Work.*

It may be doubted whether nature intended the Englishman to be a money-making animal.

DEAN W. R. INGE. (MARCHANT, *Wit and Wisdom of Dean Inge.* No. 194.)

11
We are not cotton-spinners all,
But some love England and her honour yet.

TENNYSON, *The Third of February.*

12
Tartuffe has emigrated to England and opened a shop.

OSCAR WILDE, *Picture of Dorian Gray.* Ch. 17.

13
Down the river did glide, with wind and with tide,
A pig with vast celerity;

And the Devil look'd wise as he saw how the while
It cut its own throat. "There!" quoth he, with a smile,
"Goes 'England's commercial prosperity.'"
S. T. COLERIDGE, *The Devil's Thoughts*. St. 8.

VII—England: The Paradise of Women

1
England is the paradise of women, the purgatory of men, and the hell of horses,
JOHN FLORIO, *Second Frutes*, p. 205. (1591)

England, they say, is the only hell for horses, and only paradise for women.
THOMAS DEKKER, *II The Honest Whore*. Act iv, sc. 1. (1604)

England is termed by foreigners the paradise of women, as it is by some accounted the hell of horses, and purgatory of servants.
UNKNOWN, *New Help to Discourse*, 51. (1619)

2
England is a paradise for women, and hell for horses: Italy is a paradise for horses, hell for women.
ROBERT BURTON, *Anatomy of Melancholy*. Pt. iii, sec. iii, mem. 1, subs. 2. (1621)

3
England is a prison for men, a paradise for women, a purgatory for servants, a hell for horses.
THOMAS FULLER, *Holy State*. (1642) Quoted as a proverb.

4
The wife of every Englishman is counted blessed.
THOMAS DELONEY, *Works*, p. 377. (c. 1593)

5
How often have I told you that English women are not to be treated like Circassian slaves. We have the protection of the world; we are to be won by gentle means only, and not to be hectored, and bullied, and beat into compliance.
FIELDING, *Tom Jones*. Bk. x, ch. 8.

VIII—England: Fast-Anchor'd Isle

6
And now last, this most happy and glorious event, that this island of Britain, divided from all the world, should be united in itself.
BACON, *Advancement of Learning*. Bk. ii.

7
Through many a storm
His isles had floated on the abyss of time;
For the rough virtues chose them for their clime.
BYRON, *The Vision of Judgment*. St. 42. "His" refers to George III.

8
Fast-anchor'd isle.
COWPER, *The Task*. Bk. ii, l. 151. (1783)

The silver-coasted isle.
TENNYSON, *Ode on the Death of the Duke of Wellington*, l. 136.

9
O, it's a snug little island!
A right little, tight little island!
Search the globe round, none can be found
So happy as this little island.
THOMAS DIBDIN, *The Snug Little Island.*

10
Our Isle, indeed, too fruitful was before;
But all uncultivated lay
Out of the solar walk and heaven's highway.
DRYDEN, *Threnodia Augustalis*, l. 351.

11
This, in England, (commonly called the "ringing-island") was done with tolling a bell.
THOMAS FULLER, *Church History*. Bk. vi, 2.

12
Streak of silver sea.
W. E. GLADSTONE, writing of the English Channel, *Edinburgh Review*, 18 Oct., 1870.

The Channel is that silver strip of sea which severs merry England from the tardy realms of Europe.
UNKNOWN. (*Church and State Review*, 1 April, 1863.)

13
Tut! the best thing I know between France and England is the sea.
DOUGLAS JERROLD, *Jerrold's Wit: The Anglo-French Alliance.*

A tunnel underneath the sea, from Calais straight to Dover, Sir,
That qualmish folks may cross by land from shore to shore,
With sluices made to drown the French, if e'er they would come over, Sir,
Has long been talk'd of, till at length 'tis thought a *monstrous bore.*
THEODORE HOOK, *Bubbles of 1825.*

14
O thou dear and happy Isle
The garden of the world erewhile,
Thou Paradise of the four seas,
Which Heaven planted us to please,
But, to exclude the world, did guard
With watery if not flaming sword.
ANDREW MARVELL, *A Garden.*

15
Rejoice, O Albion! severed from the world,
By Nature's wise indulgence.
JOHN PHILIPS, *Cider*. Bk. ii.

16
Your isle, which stands
As Neptune's park, ribbed and paled in
With rocks unscalable and roaring waters.
SHAKESPEARE, *Cymbeline*. Act iii, sc. 1, l. 18.

You shall find us in our salt-water girdle.
SHAKESPEARE, *Cymbeline*. Act iii, sc. 1, l. 81.

17
That pale, that white-faced shore,
Whose foot spurns back the ocean's roaring tides
And coops from other lands her islanders. . . ,

That England, hedged in with the main,
That water-walled bulwark, still secure
And confident from foreign purposes, . . .
The utmost corner of the west.
SHAKESPEARE, *King John*. Act ii, sc. 1, l. 23.

1
This royal throne of kings, this scepter'd isle,
This earth of majesty, this seat of Mars,
This other Eden, demi-paradise,
This fortress built by Nature for herself
Against infection and the hand of war,
This happy breed of men, this little world,
This precious stone set in the silver sea,
Which serves it in the office of a wall
Or as a moat defensive to a house,
Against the envy of less happier lands,
This blessed plot, this earth, this realm, this England.
SHAKESPEARE, *Richard II*. Act ii, sc. 1, l. 40.

England, bound in with the triumphant sea,
Whose rocky shore beats back the envious siege
Of watery Neptune.
SHAKESPEARE, *Richard II*. Act ii, sc. 1, l. 61.

2
Hail, happy Britain! highly favoured isle,
And Heaven's peculiar care!
WILLIAM SOMERVILLE, *The Chase*. Bk. i.

3
Hope knows not if fear speak truth, nor fear whether hope be not blind as she:
But the sun is in heaven that beholds her immortal, and girdled with life by the sea.
SWINBURNE, *England: An Ode*. Sec. 3, ch. 7.

4
Thank Him who isled us here, and roughly set
His Briton in blown seas and storming showers.
TENNYSON, *Ode on the Death of the Duke of Wellington*, l. 154. "Briton" is so printed, but is evidently a mistake for Britain.

God bless the narrow sea which keeps her off,
And keeps our Britain, whole within herself,
A nation yet, the rulers and the ruled.
TENNYSON, *The Princess: Conclusion*, l. 51. The reference is to France.

Compass'd by the inviolate sea.
TENNYSON, *To the Queen*. St. 9.

5
Island of bliss! amid the subject seas,
That thunder round thy rocky coasts, set up,
At once the wonder, terror, and delight
Of distant nations, whose remotest shore
Can soon be shaken by thy naval arm;
Not to be shook thyself, but all assaults
Baffling, like thy hoar cliffs the loud sea-wave.
THOMSON, *The Seasons: Summer*, l. 1595.

It is now three centuries since an English pig has fallen in a fair battle upon English ground, or a clergyman's wife been submitted to any other proposals of love than the connubial endearments of her sleek and orthodox mate.
SYDNEY SMITH, *Peter Plymley Letters*. No. 5.

6
The Britons, wholly sundered from all the world. (Penitus toto divisos orbe Britannos.)
VERGIL, *Eclogues*. Ecl. i, l. 66.

The sea which, according to Virgil's famous line, divided the poor Britons utterly from the world, proved to be the ring of marriage with all nations.
EMERSON, *English Traits*, p. 47.

7
Whether this portion of the world were rent,
By the rude ocean, from the continent,
Or thus created, it was sure designed
To be the sacred refuge of mankind.
EDMUND WALLER, *Panegyric to My Lord Protector*, l. 25.

Rome, though her eagle through the world had flown,
Could never make this island all her own.
EDMUND WALLER, *Panegyric to My Lord Protector*, l. 67.

8
Look, where clothed in brightest green
Is a sweet Isle, of isles the Queen;
Ye fairies, from all evil keep her!
WORDSWORTH, *Peter Bell: Prologue*, l. 63.

9
His home!—the Western giant smiles,
And twirls the spotty globe to find it;—
This little speck the British Isles?
'Tis but a freckle,—never mind it!
O. W. HOLMES, *A Good Time Going*.

IX—England: Her Virtues

10
England! my country, great and free!
Heart of the world, I leap to thee!
P. J. BAILEY, *Festus: The Surface*, l. 376.

11
Man is the nobler growth our realms supply,
And souls are ripened in our northern sky.
ANNA LETITIA BARBAULD, *The Invitation*.

12
In spite of their hats being terribly ugly,
God-damn! I love the English!
(Quoique leurs chapeaux soient bien laids,
Goddam! moi j'aime les Anglais.)
BÉRANGER, *Les Boxeurs*. (1814)

How I love English boldness! how I love the people who say what they think.
VOLTAIRE.

13
Oh, to be in England
Now that April's there,
And whoever wakes in England
Sees, some morning, unaware,
That the lowest boughs and the brush-wood sheaf,
Round the elm-tree bole are in tiny leaf,
While the chaffinch sings on the orchard bough

In England—now!
ROBERT BROWNING, *Home Thoughts from Abroad.*

"Here and here did England help me: how can I help England?"—say,
Whoso turns as I, this evening, turn to God to praise and pray,
While Jove's planet rises yonder, silent over Africa.
ROBERT BROWNING, *Home Thoughts from the Sea.*

1
Her women fair; her men robust for toil;
Her vigorous souls, high-cultured as her soil;
Her towns, where civic independence flings
The gauntlet down to senates, courts, and kings.
THOMAS CAMPBELL, *Theodric*, l. 160.

2
Liberty is the idol of the English, under whose banner all the nation lists.
SUSANNAH CENTLIVRE, *Wonder.* Act i, sc. 1.

3
A song of hate is a song of Hell;
Some there be who sing it well.
Let them sing it loud and long,
We lift our hearts in a loftier song:
We lift our hearts to Heaven above,
Singing the glory of her we love,
England!
HELEN GRAY CONE, *A Chant of Love for England.*

Bind her, grind her, burn her with fire,
Cast her ashes into the sea,—
She shall escape, she shall aspire,
She shall arise to make men free;
She shall arise in a sacred scorn,
Lighting the lives that are yet unborn,
Spirit supernal, splendour eternal,
England!
HELEN GRAY CONE, *A Chant of Love for England.*

See also LISSAUER *under* GERMANY.

4
Kent, sir—everybody knows Kent—apples, cherries, hops, and women.
DICKENS, *Pickwick Papers.* Ch. 2.

That shire which we the heart of England well may call.
MICHAEL DRAYTON, *Poly-olbion.* Song 13. Referring to Warwickshire.

I love thee, Cornwall, and will ever,
And hope to see thee once again!
For why?—thine equal knew I never
For honest minds and active men.
THOMAS FREEMAN, *Encomion Cornubiæ.* (1614)

An acre in Middlesex is better than a principality in Utopia.
MACAULAY, *Essays: Lord Bacon.*

And Devon was heaven to him.
WALLACE RICE, *The First American Sailors.*

5
But who did ever, in French authors, see
The comprehensive English energy?
WENTWORTH DILLON, *Essay on Translated Verse*, l. 51.

6
England is a domestic country; there the home is revered, the hearth sacred.
BENJAMIN DISRAELI, *Speech*, 3 April, 1872.

The stately Homes of England!
How beautiful they stand,
Amidst their tall ancestral trees,
O'er all the pleasant land!
FELICIA HEMANS, *The Homes of England.*

7
What of the bow?
The bow was made in England:
Of true wood, of yew-wood,
The wood of English bows;
So men who are free
Love the old yew-tree
And the land where the yew-tree grows.
A. CONAN DOYLE, *The Song of the Bow.* (*The White Company.*)

England were but a fling,
Save for the crooked stick and the grey-goose wing.
THOMAS FULLER, *Worthies of England.* Vol. i, p. 116.

8
Freedom! which in no other land will thrive,
Freedom! an English subject's sole prerogative.
DRYDEN, *Threnodia Augustalis*, l. 300.

9
The land of scholars and the nurse of arms.
GOLDSMITH, *The Traveller*, l. 356.

10
What have I done for you,
England, my England?
What is there I would not do,
England, my own?
With your glorious eyes austere,
As the Lord were walking near,
Whispering terrible things and dear,
As the Song on your bugles blown,
England—
Round the world on your bugles blown!
W. E. HENLEY, *England, My England.*

Ever the faith endures,
England, my England:—
"Take and break us: we are yours,
England, my own!
Life is good, and joy runs high
Between English earth and sky:
Death is death; but we shall die
To the Song on your bugles blown,
England—
To the stars on your bugles blown!"
W. E. HENLEY, *England, My England.*

11
Take of English earth as much
As either hand may rightly clutch. . . .
Lay that earth upon thy heart,
And thy sickness shall depart!
RUDYARD KIPLING, *A Charm.*

Land of our Birth, our faith, our pride,
For whose dear sake our fathers died;
O Motherland, we pledge to thee
Head, heart, and hand through the years to be!
RUDYARD KIPLING, *The Children's Song.*

There is but one task for all—
One life for each to give.
Who stands if Freedom fall?
Who dies if England live?
RUDYARD KIPLING, *For All We Have and Are.*

1
The strength of England lies not in armaments and invasions; it lies in the omnipotence of her industry, and in the vivifying energies of her high civilisation.
W. S. LANDOR, *Imaginary Conversations: Lascy and Merino.*

2
The history of England is emphatically the history of progress.
MACAULAY, *Essays: Mackintosh's History of the Revolution.*

Attend, all ye who list to hear our noble England's praise;
I tell of the thrice famous deeds she wrought in ancient days.
MACAULAY, *The Armada.*

3
There she sits in her Island-home,
Peerless among her Peers!
And Liberty oft to her arms doth come,
To ease its poor heart of tears.
Old England still throbs with the muffled fire
Of a Past she can never forget:
And again shall she banner the World up higher;
For there's life in the Old Land yet.
GERALD MASSEY, *Old England.*

4
An old and haughty Nation proud in arms.
MILTON, *Comus*, l. 33.

Methinks I see in my mind a noble and puissant nation rousing herself like a strong man after sleep, and shaking her invincible locks. Methinks I see her as an eagle mewing her mighty youth, and kindling her undazzled eyes at the full midday beam.
MILTON, *Areopagitica.*

5
Britain scorns to yield.
THOMAS OLIPHANT, *March of the Men of Harlech.* St. 1.

6
Bid harbours open, public ways extend,
Bid temples, worthier of the God, ascend;
Bid the broad arch the dangerous flood contain,
The mole projected break the roaring main,
Back to his bounds their subject sea command,
And roll obedient rivers thro' the land.
These honours Peace to happy Britain brings;
These are imperial works, and worthy Kings
POPE, *Moral Essays.* Epis. iv, l. 197.

7
Britain is
A world by itself; and we will nothing pay
For wearing our own noses.
SHAKESPEARE, *Cymbeline.* Act iii, sc. 1, l. 12.

8
O England! model to thy inward greatness,
Like little body with a mighty heart.
SHAKESPEARE, *Henry V.* Act ii, prologue, l. 16.

Upon this land a thousand thousand blessings.
SHAKESPEARE, *Henry VIII.* Act v, sc. 5, l. 20.

9
This England never did, nor never shall,
Lie at the proud foot of a conqueror,
But when it first did help to wound itself. . . .
Come the three corners of the world in arms,
And we shall shock them. Nought shall make us rue,
If England to itself do rest but true.
SHAKESPEARE, *King John.* Act v, sc. 7, l. 112.

All our past acclaims our future: Shakespeare's voice and Nelson's hand,
Milton's faith and Wordsworth's trust in this our chosen and chainless land,
Bear us witness: come the world against her, England yet shall stand.
SWINBURNE, *England: An Ode.* Pt. ii, st. 5.

10
First pledge our Queen this solemn night,
Then drink to England, every guest; . . .
Hands all round!
God the traitor's hope confound!
To this great cause of Freedom drink, my friends,
And the great name of England, round and round.
TENNYSON, *Hands All Round.* (*Memoirs of Tennyson*, by his son. Vol. i, p. 345.) First printed in the London *Examiner*, 7 Feb., 1852.

O Statesmen, guard us, guard the eye, the soul
Of Europe, keep our noble England whole.
TENNYSON, *Ode on the Death of the Duke of Wellington.* Pt. vii.

11
It is the land that freemen till,
That sober-suited Freedom chose;
The land, where, girt with friends or foes,
A man may speak the thing he will;

A land of settled government,
A land of just and old renown,
Where Freedom slowly broadens down
From precedent to precedent.
TENNYSON, *You Ask Me Why.*

12
I thank the goodness and the grace
Which on my birth have smiled,
And made me, in these Christian days,
A happy English child.
ANN AND JANE TAYLOR, *A Child's Hymn of Praise.*

O, how good should we be found

Who live on England's happy ground!
JANE TAYLOR, *The English Girl.*

1
'Tis to thy sov'reign grace I owe
That I was born on British ground!
ISAAC WATTS, *Praise for Birth in a Christian Land.*

Lord, I ascribe it to thy grace,
And not to chance, as others do,
That I was born of Christian race,
And not a Heathen or a Jew.
ISAAC WATTS, *Praise for the Gospel.*

But I count the grey barbarian lower than the Christian child.
TENNYSON, *Locksley Hall,* l. 174.

2
O Englishmen!—in hope and creed,
In blood and tongue our brothers!
We too are heirs of Runnymede;
And Shakespeare's fame and Cromwell's deed
Are not alone our mother's.
WHITTIER, *To Englishmen.*

The New World's Sons, from England's breasts we drew
Such milk as bids remember whence we came;
Proud of her Past, wherefrom our Present grew,
This window we inscribe with Raleigh's name.
J. R. LOWELL, *Inscription,* On the Raleigh window in St. Margaret's, Westminster.

3
Hail to the crown by Freedom shaped—to gird
An English Sovereign's brow! and to the throne
Whereon he sits! whose deep foundations lie
In veneration and the people's love.
WORDSWORTH, *The Excursion.* Bk. vi, l. 1.

I travelled among unknown men
In lands beyond the sea;
Nor, England! did I know till then
What love I bore to thee.
WORDSWORTH, *I Travelled Among Unknown Men.* (*Poems Founded on the Affections.* No. 9.)

4
Thou art free,
My Country! and 'tis joy enough and pride
For one hour's perfect bliss, to tread the grass
Of England once again.
WORDSWORTH, *Poems Dedicated to National Independence.* Pt. i, No. 10.

We must be free or die, who speak the tongue
That Shakespeare spake; the faith and morals hold
Which Milton held.—In every thing we are sprung
Of Earth's first blood, have titles manifold.
WORDSWORTH, *Poems Dedicated to National Independence.* Pt. i, No. 16.

X—England: Her Faults

5
A race that binds
Its body in chains and calls them Liberty,
And calls each fresh link Progress.
ROBERT BUCHANAN, *Titan and Avatar.*

6
For 'tis a low, newspaper, humdrum, lawsuit Country.
BYRON, *Don Juan.* Canto xii, st. 65.

I am sure my bones would not rest in an English grave, or my clay mix with the earth of that country. . . . I would not even feed her worms if I could help it.
BYRON, *Letters.*

7
The world's busybody.
CARLYLE, *Latter-Day Pamphlets: Downing Street.*

8
England, a happy land we know,
Where follies naturally grow,
Where without culture they arise,
And tower above the common size;
England, a fortune-telling host
As numerous as the stars, could boast;
Matrons, who toss the cup, and see
The grounds of fate in grounds of tea;
Who, versed in every modest lore,
Can a lost maidenhead restore,
Or, if their pupils rather choose it,
Can show the readiest way to lose it.
CHARLES CHURCHILL, *The Ghost.* Bk. i, l. 111.

9
We justly boast
At least superior jockeyship, and claim
The honours of the turf as all our own!
COWPER, *The Task.* Bk. ii, l. 275.

England is unrivalled for two things—sporting and politics.
BENJAMIN DISRAELI, *Coningsby.* Bk. ii, ch. 1.

10
Alas the Church of England! What with Popery on one hand, and schismatics on the other, how has she been crucified between two thieves!
DEFOE, *The Shortest Way with the Dissenters.*

"The Church of England," I said, seeing that Mr. Inglesant paused, "is no doubt a compromise."
SHORTHOUSE, *John Inglesant.* Bk. ii, ch. 19.

11
Wealth, howsoever got, in England makes
Lords of mechanics, gentlemen of rakes:
Antiquity and birth are needless here;
'Tis impudence and money makes a peer.
DANIEL DEFOE, *The True-Born Englishman.* Pt. i, l. 360.

It was not the custom in England to confer titles on men distinguished by peaceful services, however good and great; unless occasionally, when they consisted of the accumulation of some very large amount of money.
DICKENS, *Bleak House.* Ch. 35.

12
But English gratitude is always such,
To hate the hand which doth oblige too much.
DANIEL DEFOE, *The True-Born Englishman* Pt. ii, l. 409.

1
England has no higher worship than Fate. She lives in the low plane of the winds and waves, watches like a wolf a chance for plunder; . . . never a lofty sentiment, never a duty to civilization, never a generosity, a moral self-restraint.

EMERSON, *Journal*, 1862.

2
Long beards heartless, painted hoods witless,
Gay coats graceless, make England thriftless.

THOMAS FULLER, *Worthies of England*. Vol. i, p. 119. (1662)

3
It is one of the happiest characteristics of this glorious country that official utterances are invariably regarded as unanswerable.

W. S. GILBERT, *H. M. S. Pinafore*. Act ii.

4
O England! full of sin, but most of sloth;
Spit out thy phlegm, and fill thy breast with glory:
Thy gentry bleats, as if thy native cloth
Transfus'd a sheepishness into thy story:
Not that they all are so; but that the most
Are gone to grass, and in the pasture lost.

GEORGE HERBERT, *The Church-Porch*. St. 16.

5
By no stretch of charity, and by no violence to grammar can you call the British Nation a Christian people. The British leaders have an itch for dictation, and their chief vice is a thirst for power.

ELBERT HUBBARD, *The Philistine*. Vol. xi, p. 32.

6
This is the true character of the English Government, and it presents the singular phenomenon of a nation, the individuals of which are as faithful to their private engagements and duties, as honorable, as worthy as those of any Nation on earth, and yet whose government is the most unprincipled at this day known.

THOMAS JEFFERSON, *Writings*. Vol. xii, p. 376.

It may be asked, what, in the nature of her government, unfits England for the observation of moral duties? . . . The real power and property of the government is in the great aristocratical families of the nation. The nest of office being too small for all of them to cuddle into it at once, the contest is eternal which shall crowd the other out. For this purpose they are divided into two parties, the INS and the OUTS.

THOMAS JEFFERSON, *Writings*. Vol. xii, p. 376.

We are going on here in the same spirit still. The Anglophobia has seized violently on three members of our council.

THOMAS JEFFERSON, *Writings*, 1793.

7
Of all the sarse thet I can call to mind,
England *doos* make the most onpleasant kind:
It 's you 're the sinner ollers, she 's the saint;
Wut 's good 's all English, all thet is n't ain't;
Wut profits her is ollers right an' just,
An' ef you don't read Scriptur so, you must;
She 's praised herself cntil she fairly thinks
There ain't no light in Natur when she winks; . . .
She 's all thet 's honest, honnable, an' fair,
An' when the vartoos died they made her heir.

J. R. LOWELL, *The Biglow Papers: Mason and Slidell*.

8
Better a brutal starving nation,
Than men with thoughts above their station.

JOHN MASEFIELD, *Everlasting Mercy*, l. 965.

9
And shall not Britain now reward his toils,
Britain, that pays her patriots with her spoils?

POPE, *Moral Essays*. Epis. iii, l. 215.

10
Its people curbed and broken to the ring,
Packed with a caste and saddled with a King.

JAMES JEFFREY ROCHE, *Washington*.

11
It was always yet the trick of our English nation, if they have a good thing, to make it too common.

SHAKESPEARE, *II Henry IV*. Act i, sc. 2, l. 240.

12
Half of it has been incurred in putting down the Bourbons, and the other half in setting them up.

R. B. SHERIDAN, referring to England's public debt. (MOORE, *Life of Sheridan*. Vol. ii, p. 218.)

13
England is the land of sects. An Englishman, like a free man, goes to heaven by the way which pleases him. . . . If there was only one religion in England its despotism would be a matter for fear; if two, they would cut each other's throats; but there are thirty, and they live in peace, and happy.

VOLTAIRE, *Letters on the English*. Nos. 5 and 6.

In England there are sixty different religions, and only one sauce. (Il y a en Angleterre soizante sectes religieuses différentes, et une seule sauce.)

Attributed to Prince Francesco Caraccioli.

14
Minds like ours, my dear James, must always be above national prejudices, and in all companies it gives me true pleasure to declare that, as a people, the English are very little indeed inferior to the Scotch.

JOHN WILSON, *Noctes Ambrosianæ*. No. 9.

15
O Britain! infamous for suicide!
An island in thy manners! far disjoin'd
From the whole world of rationals beside!

YOUNG, *Night Thoughts*. Night v, l. 442.

16
I will not cease from mental fight,
Nor shall my sword sleep in my hand,

Till we have built Jerusalem
  In England's green and pleasant land.
  WILLIAM BLAKE, *Milton*, l. 13.

XI—England: Her Mission

1
The most eloquent voice of our century uttered, shortly before leaving the world, a warning cry against the "Anglo-Saxon contagion."
  MATTHEW ARNOLD, *Essays on Criticism: Milton*. The probability seems to be that Arnold referred to Emerson, but the reference has also been claimed for Coleridge and Victor Hugo.

2
Yes, we arraign her! but she,
The weary Titan! with deaf
Ears, and labour-dimm'd eyes,
Regarding neither to right
Nor left, goes passively by,
Staggering on to her goal;
Bearing on shoulders immense,
Atlanteän, the load,
Well-nigh not to be borne,
Of the too vast orb of her fate.
  MATTHEW ARNOLD, *Heine's Grave*, l. 87.

3
O praise the Lord with one consent,
And in this great design
Let Britain and the Colonies
Unanimously jine.
  WILLIAM BILLINGS, *The New-England Psalm-Singer*, 1770.

England's done the right thing,
she's never done a wrong—
and this is merely one more way
to start the same old song.
  ALFRED KREYMBORG, *Rule Britannia.*

4
Did Peace descend, to triumph and to save,
When freeborn Britons crossed the Indian wave?
Ah, no!—to more than Rome's ambition true,
The Nurse of Freedom gave it not to you!
She the bold route of Europe's guilt began,
And, in the march of nations, led the van!
  CAMPBELL, *The Pleasures of Hope*. Pt. i, l. 555.

5
The earth is a place on which England is found,
And you find it however you twirl the globe round;
For the spots are all red and the rest is all grey,
And that is the meaning of Empire Day.
  G. K. CHESTERTON, *Songs of Education.*

6
            Doing good,
Disinterested good, is not our trade.
  COWPER, *The Task*. Bk. i, l. 673.

The real policy of England—apart from questions which involve her own particular interests, political or commercial—is to be the champion of justice and right.
  LORD PALMERSTON, *Speech*, on Polish question, 1848.

A small boy with diamonds is no match for a large burglar with experience.
  UNKNOWN. A reference to the British victory over the Boers, which appeared in *Life*, 15 Nov., 1900.

7
Without one friend, above all foes,
Britannia gives the world repose.
  COWPER, *To Sir Joshua Reynolds*, l. 41.

8
If England's head and heart were one,
Where is that good beneath the sun
Her noble hands should leave undone!
  SYDNEY DOBELL, *A Shower in War Time.*

9
Rous'd by the lash of his own stubborn tail,
Our lion now will foreign foes assail.
  DRYDEN, *Astræa Redux*, l. 117.

The British lion always rouses itself to fresh efforts by lashing itself with its tail.
  DEAN W. R. INGE. (MARCHANT, *Wit and Wisdom of Dean Inge*. No. 159.)

10
The stability of England is the security of the modern world.
  EMERSON, *English Traits*, p. 143.

Far fall the day when England's realm shall see
The sunset of dominion!
  G. E. WOODBERRY, *Sonnets Written in the Fall of 1914.*

11
A Nation spoke to a Nation,
  A Throne sent word to a Throne:
"Daughter am I in my mother's house,
  But mistress in my own."
  RUDYARD KIPLING, *Our Lady of the Snows*. St. 6. Referring to Canada. (1897)

12
England, so strong to slay, be strong to spare;
England, have courage even to forgive;
Give back the little nation leave to live.
  RICHARD LE GALLIENNE, *Christmas in War-Time*. (1899)

13
Now, victory to our England!
  And where'er she lifts her hand
In Freedom's fight, to rescue Right,
  God bless the dear Old Land!
  GERALD MASSEY, *England Goes to Battle.*

Where might is, the right is:
  Long purses make strong swords.
Let weakness learn meekness:
  God save the House of Lords!
  SWINBURNE, *A Word for the Country*. St. 1.

14
Let not England forget her precedence of teaching nations how to live.
  MILTON, *Doctrine and Discipline of Divorce.*

15
England! on thy knees to-night,

Pray that God defend the Right.
HENRY NEWBOLT, *The Vigil.*

1
England has saved herself by her exertions, and will, I trust, save Europe by her example.
WILLIAM PITT, *Speech,* at Lord Mayor's banquet at Guildhall, London, 9 Nov., 1805. This was Pitt's last speech, and the above sentence has been variously reported. The above version is from Stanhope's *Life of Pitt* (vol. iv, p. 346), as told him by the Duke of Wellington. Macaulay (*Miscellaneous Writings*. Vol. ii, p. 368) gives the following: "Let us hope that England, having saved herself by her energy, may save Europe by her example." Still different versions were given in the newspapers commenting on the speech.

Herself by fortitude, Europe by example. (Seipsum constantia Europam exemplo.)
Inscription, on medal struck in 1814 to commemorate the Treaty of Paris.

2
Certainly England for the English goes without saying: it is the simple law of nature. But this woman denies to England her legitimate conquests, given her by God because of her peculiar fitness to rule over less civilized races for their own good.
BERNARD SHAW, *Saint Joan*. Act iv.

3
No little German state are we,
But the one voice in Europe; we *must* speak.
TENNYSON, *The Third of February, 1852*. Protesting against the *coup d'état* of Louis Napoleon.

4
Remote compatriots, whereso'er ye dwell,
By your prompt voices, ringing clear and true,
We know that with our England all is well.
WILLIAM WATSON, *Ver Tenebrosum: Last Word: To the Colonies.*

Sons of the Empire, Britain's sons,
Here, as the darkness falls,
Over your grey Sea-Mother's guns
The warning clarion calls;
O, and I bid you now "God speed,
Quit you like men, be true";
Stand by us in the hour of need
And we shall stand by you.
J. C. SQUIRE, *The Hands-Across-the-Sea Poem*

5
I believe England will be conquered some day or other in New England or Bengal.
WALPOLE, *Letter to Sir Horace Mann,* 2 Feb., 1774.

6
Where now is Britain? . . .
Even as the savage sits upon the stone
That marks where stood her capitols, and hears
The bittern booming in the weeds, he shrinks
From the dismaying solitude.
HENRY KIRKE WHITE, *Time.*

7
Set in this stormy Northern sea,
Queen of these restless fields of tide,
England! what shall men say of thee,
Before whose feet the worlds divide?
OSCAR WILDE, *Ave Imperatrix.*

XII—England: Her Soldiers

8
In joys of conquest he resigns his breath,
And, fill'd with England's glory, smiles in death.
ADDISON, *The Campaign,* l. 313. Of Philip Dormer.

9
With proud thanksgiving, a mother for her children,
England mourns for her dead across the sea.
Flesh of her flesh they were, spirit of her spirit,
Fallen in the cause of the free.
LAURENCE BINYON, *For the Fallen.*

10
If I should die, think only this of me:
That there's some corner of a foreign field
That is for ever England. There shall be
In that rich earth a richer dust concealed;
A dust whom England bore, shaped, made aware,
Gave, once, her flowers to love, her ways to roam,
A body of England's, breathing English air,
Washed by the rivers, blest by suns of home.
RUPERT BROOKE, *1914: The Soldier.*

11
Be Britain still to Britain true,
Amang oursels united;
For never but by British hands
Maun British wrangs be righted!
ROBERT BURNS, *The Dumfries Volunteers.*

12
Bitterly, England, must thou grieve—
Though none of these poor men who died
But did within his soul believe
That death for thee was glorified.
WALTER DE LA MARE, *"How Sleep the Brave."*

13
Go, stranger! track the deep,
Free, free, the white sail spread!
Wave may not foam, nor wild wind sweep,
Where rest not England's dead.
FELICIA DOROTHEA HEMANS, *England's Dead.*

14
Never the lotos closes, never the wild-fowl wake,
But a soul goes out on the East Wind that died for England's sake—
Man or woman or suckling, mother or bride or maid—
Because on the bones of the English the English Flag is stayed.
RUDYARD KIPLING, *The English Flag*. St. 12.

15
You are ordered abroad as a soldier of the King to help our French comrades against the invasion of a common enemy. You have to

perform a task which will need your courage, your energy, and your patience. Remember that the honour of the British Army depends on your individual conduct. . . . Do your duty bravely. Fear God and honour the King.

LORD KITCHENER, *Address to the British Expeditionary Force*, 1914.

1
Napoleon's troops fought in bright fields where every helmet caught some beams of glory; but the British soldier conquered under the cold shade of aristocracy.

SIR W. F. P. NAPIER, *History of the Peninsular War*. Bk. ii, p. 401.

2
And, if I take Dan Congreve right,
Pudding and beef make Britons fight.

MATTHEW PRIOR, *Alma*. Canto iii, l. 248.

3
Warriors!—and where are warriors found,
If not on martial Britain's ground?
And who, when waked with note of fire,
Love more than they the British lyre?

SCOTT, *Lord of the Isles*. Canto iv, st. 20.

But say, "He died a gallant knight,
With sword in hand, for England's right."

SCOTT, *Marmion*. Canto vi, st. 37.

4
I thought upon one pair of English legs
Did march three Frenchmen.

SHAKESPEARE, *Henry V*. Act iii, sc. 6, l. 158.

That silly, sanguine notion, which is firmly entertained here, that one Englishman can beat three Frenchmen, encourages, and has sometimes enabled, one Englishman, in reality, to beat two.

LORD CHESTERFIELD, *Letters*, 7 Feb., 1749.

5
England we love; and for that England's sake
With burden of our armour here we sweat.

SHAKESPEARE, *King John*. Act ii, sc. 1, l. 91.

6
The British soldier can stand up to anything—except the British War Office.

BERNARD SHAW, *The Devil's Disciple*. Act iii.

The British blockade won the war; but the wonder is that the British blockhead did not lose it.

BERNARD SHAW, *O'Flaherty, V. C.: Preface*.

7
It was not British blood which had been spilt, but it was British honour that bled at every vein.

R. B. SHERIDAN, *Speech*, House of Commons, 29 Oct., 1795, referring to conduct of Commodore Warren at Quiberon two days previously.

England's far, and Honour a name.

HENRY NEWBOLT, *Vitaï Lampada*.

8
The last great Englishman is low.

TENNYSON, *Ode on the Death of the Duke of Wellington*, l. 18.

9
Thus did England fight:
And shall not England smite
With Drake's strong sword in battles yet to be?

THEODORE WATTS-DUNTON, *Christmas at the Mermaid: Chorus*.

Yea, he sent out his arrows, and scattered them.

Old Testament: Psalms, xviii, 14. This text was used on the medal struck to commemorate the defeat of the Spanish Armada, August, 1588.

10
Whate'er the bans the winds may waft her,
England's true men are we, and Pope's men after.

THEODORE WATTS-DUNTON, *When England Calls*.

11
Not in the Abbey proudly laid
Find they a place or part;
The gallant boys of the Old Brigade
They sleep in Old England's heart.

F. E. WEATHERLY, *They All Love Jack*.

12
Soldiers, we must never be beat—what will they say in England?

DUKE OF WELLINGTON, *Remark*, attributed to him at Waterloo.

13
He [the British officer] muffs his real job without a blush, and yet he would rather be shot than do his bootlaces up criss-cross.

H. G. WELLS, *Mr. Britling Sees It Through*. Bk. ii, ch. 4, sec. 3.

14
It is my royal and imperial command . . . that you address all your skill, and all the valor of my soldiers, to exterminate the treacherous English, and to walk over General French's contemptible little army.

KAISER WILHELM II [?], *Army Order*, Aix, 19 Aug., 1914. Hence the title "Old Contemptibles" given to the first British expeditionary force. The Kaiser actually said "negligible," not "contemptible." "Contemptible" was either an error in translation or the invention of a British propagandist. Years before, in answer to a question, "What would you do if England landed an army on the coast of Germany?" Bismarck had replied, "I would call out the police to arrest them."

O little Force that in your agony
Stood fast while England girt her armour on,
Held high our honour in your wounded hands,
Carried our honour safe with bleeding feet—
We have no glory great enough for you,
The very soul of Britain keeps your day.

UNKNOWN, *O Little Force*. (1917)

The English Infantry is the most formidable in Europe, but fortunately there is not much of it. (L'infanterie anglaise est la plus redoubtable de l'Europe; heureusement, il n'y en a pas beaucoup.)

MARSHAL BUGEAUD, *Œuvres Militaires*.

15
Some talk of Alexander, and some of Hercules;

Of Hector and Lysander, and such great names as these;
But of all the world's brave heroes, there's none that can compare
With a tow, row, row, row, row, row, for the British Grenadier.

UNKNOWN, *The British Grenadier.*

XIII—England: Her Climate

1
I like the weather, when it's not too rainy,
That is, I like two months of every year.

BYRON, *Beppo.* St. 48.

Our cloudy climate and our chilly women.

BYRON, *Beppo.* St. 49.

The English winter—ending in July,
To recommence in August.

BYRON, *Don Juan.* Canto xiii, st. 42.

2
Though thy clime
Be fickle, and thy ear, most part deform'd
With dripping rains, or wither'd by a frost,
I would not yet exchange thy sullen skies,
And fields without a flower, for warmer France,
With all her vines.

COWPER, *The Task.* Bk. ii, l. 209.

3
The expression "as right as rain" must have been invented by an Englishman.

WILLIAM LYON PHELPS, *The Country or the City.*

4
Hath Britain all the sun that shines?

SHAKESPEARE, *Cymbeline.* Act iii, sc. 4, l. 139.

5
We are all well, and keep large fires, as it behoveth those who pass their summers in England.

SYDNEY SMITH, *Letter to Mrs. Meynell,* 1820.

6
Say, Britain, could you ever boast,
Three poets in an age at most?
Our chilling climate hardly bears
A sprig of bays in fifty years.

SWIFT, *On Poetry.*

7
My suit had wither'd, nipt to death by him
That was a god, and is a lawyer's clerk,
The rent-roll Cupid of our rainy isles.

TENNYSON, *Edwin Morris,* l. 101.

8
In a fine day, looking up a chimney; in a foul day, looking down one.

UNKNOWN, *Epigram,* on the English climate, quoted Emerson, *English Traits,* p. 45.

XIV—England: The English: Their Virtues

9
My general impression is that Englishmen act better than Frenchmen, and Frenchwomen better than Englishwomen.

ARNOLD BENNETT, *The Crisis in the Theatre.* (Preface to *Cupid and Commonsense.*)

10
There is a peculiarity in the countenance, as everybody knows, which, though it cannot be described, is sure to betray the Englishman.

GEORGE BORROW, *The Bible in Spain.* Ch. 2.

11
Bright Thoughts, clear Deeds, Constancy, Fidelity, Bounty, and generous Honesty are the Gems of noble Minds: wherein (to derogate from none) the true Heroic English Gentleman hath no Peer.

SIR THOMAS BROWNE, *Christian Morals.* Pt. i, sec. 36.

The greatest benefit of the Eton school, says the report in an English blue book, is the serenity and repose of character which it gives to its graduates, and which, as the document says, without intent of irony, is a well-known trait of the character of the English gentleman.

EMERSON, *Uncollected Lectures: Public and Private Education.* The document in question is by S. Hawtrey, Provost of Eton.

Ye gentlemen of England
That live at home at ease.

MARTIN PARKER, *Ye Gentlemen of England.*

12
Cool, and quite English, imperturbable.

BYRON, *Don Juan.* Canto xiii, st. 14.

13
Men of England! who inherit
Rights that cost your sires their blood.

THOMAS CAMPBELL, *Men of England.*

14
Of all the nations in the world, at present, the English are the stupidest in speech, the wisest in action.

THOMAS CARLYLE, *Past and Present.* Bk. iii, ch. 5.

15
A glorious charter, deny it who can,
Is breathed in the words, "I'm an Englishman."

ELIZA COOK, *The Englishman.*

Some people . . . may be Rooshans, and others may be Prooshans; they are born so, and will please themselves. Them which is of other naturs thinks different.

DICKENS, *Martin Chuzzlewit.* Ch. 19.

He is an Englishman!
For he himself has said it,
And it's greatly to his credit,
That he is an Englishman!
For he might have been a Roosian,
A French or Turk or Proosian,
Or perhaps Itali-an.
But in spite of all temptations
To belong to other nations,
He remains an Englishman.

W. S. GILBERT, *H. M. S. Pinafore.* Act ii.

Never, even when the storm-clouds appear blackest, have I been tempted to wish that I was other than an Englishman.

DEAN W. R. INGE. (MARCHANT, *Wit and Wisdom of Dean Inge.* No. 166.)

A stern, *true-born Englishman.*

SAMUEL JOHNSON. (BOSWELL, *Life.* 1783.)

No little lily-handed baronet he,
A great broad-shoulder'd genial Englishman.
TENNYSON, *The Princess: Conclusion*, l. 84.

1
The ancient . . . spirit of Englishmen was once expressed by our proverb, "Better be the head of a dog than the tail of a lion"; i.e. the first of the yeomanry rather than the last of the gentry.
ISAAC D'ISRAELI, *Curiosities of Literature*. Ser. ii, p. 447.

2
I find the Englishman to be him of all men who stands firmest in his shoes.
EMERSON, *English Traits*, p. 106.

An Englishman has firm manners. He rests secure on the reputation of his country, on his family, and his expectations at home. There is in his manners a suspicion of insolence. If his belief in the Thirty-nine Articles does not bind him much, his belief in the fortieth does:—namely, that he shall not find his superiors elsewhere.
EMERSON, *Journal*, 1868.

3
The most honest people in the world are the French who think and the British who talk. (Les plus honnêtes gens du monde, ce sont les Français qui pensent et les Anglais qui parlent.)
SAINT-ÉVREMOND. (INGE, *Wit and Wisdom: Preface*.)

4
Not Angles, but Angels! (Non Angli, sed Angeli!)
POPE GREGORY I., remarking upon the beauty of some English captives exposed for sale in the market-place at Rome. (FREEMAN, *Old English History*, 44.)

5
He [the Englishman] is like a stout ship, which will weather the roughest storm uninjured, but roll its masts overboard in the succeeding calm.
WASHINGTON IRVING, *Sketch Book: John Bull*.

His very faults smack of the raciness of his good qualities.
WASHINGTON IRVING, *Sketch Book: John Bull*.

6
A Frenchman must be always talking, whether he knows anything of the matter or not; an Englishman is content to say nothing when he has nothing to say.
SAMUEL JOHNSON. (BOSWELL, *Life*, 1779.)

I hope we English will long maintain our *grand talent pour le silence*.
CARLYLE, *Heroes and Hero-Worship*. Lect. 6.

The English are a dumb people.
CARLYLE, *Past and Present*. Bk. iii, ch. 5.

Silence—a conversation with an Englishman.
HEINRICH HEINE.

7
The whole nation, beyond all other mortal men, is most given to banqueting and feasts.
PAULUS JOVIUS, *History*. Bk. ii. (Burton, tr.)

If an earthquake were to engulf England tomorrow, the English would manage to meet and dine somewhere among the rubbish, just to celebrate the event.
DOUGLAS JERROLD, *Remark*, made in the Museum Club. (BLANCHARD JERROLD, *Life*.)

8
An Englishman hath three qualities, he can suffer no partner in his love, no stranger to be his equal, nor to be dared by any.
JOHN LYLY, *Euphues and His England*.

9
The Rev. Doctor was a fine old picture; a specimen of art peculiarly English; combining in himself piety and epicurism, learning and gentlemanliness, with good room for each and a seat at one another's table.
GEORGE MEREDITH, *The Egoist*. Ch. xx.

10
The people of England are never so happy as when you tell them they are ruined.
ARTHUR MURPHY, *The Upholsterer*. Act ii, 1.

How hard it is to make an Englishman acknowledge that he is happy!
THACKERAY, *Pendennis*. Bk. ii, ch. 31.

11
Not only England, but every Englishman is an island. (Non seulement l'Angleterre, mais chaque anglais est une île.)
NOVALIS, *Fragments*. (1799)

Every one of these islanders is an island himself, safe, tranquil, incommunicable.
EMERSON, *English Traits*, p. 109.

The Englishman's strong point is a vigorous insularity which he carries with him, portable and sometimes insupportable.
T. W. HIGGINSON, *Americanism in Literature*.

12
But we, brave Britons, foreign laws despised,
And kept unconquered and uncivilized.
POPE, *Essay on Criticism*. Pt. iii, l. 156.

13
The English people fancy they are free; it is only during the election of Members of Parliament that they are so. As soon as these are elected the people are slaves, they are nothing. In the brief moments of their liberty the use made of it fully deserves that it should be lost. (Le peuple anglais pense être libre, il se trompe fort; il ne l'est que durant l'élection des membres du parlement. Sitôt qu'ils sont élus, il est esclave, il n'est rien. Dans les courts moments de sa liberté, l'usage qu'il en fait mérite bien qu'il en perde.)
ROUSSEAU, *Contrat Social*. Bk. iii, ch. 15.

Great eaters of meat are in general more cruel and ferocious than other men. The cruelty of the English is known. (Les grands mangeurs de viande sont en général cruels et féroces plus que les autres hommes. . . . La barbarie anglaise est connue.)
ROUSSEAU, *Émile*. Bk. ii.

14
We Englishmen, trim, correct,

All minted in the self-same mould,
Warm hearted but of semblance cold,
All-courteous out of self-respect.
CHRISTINA ROSSETTI, *Enrica.*

1
It is to the middle class we must look for the safety of England.
THACKERAY, *The Four Georges: George III.*

They are like their own beer: froth on top, dregs at the bottom, the middle excellent.
VOLTAIRE, referring to the British.

2
The English people are people who defend themselves. (Les gens Anglais sont gens qui se défendent.)
VOLTAIRE, *La Pucelle.* Canto x.

XV—England: The English: Their Faults

3
An English tourist's preconceived idea of us is a thing he brings over with him on the steamer and carries home again intact.
T. B. ALDRICH, *Ponkapog Papers,* p. 70.

4
No good man is a Briton. (Nemo bonus Brito est.)
AUSONIUS, *Epigrams.* No. 110.

5
Frenchmen sin in lechery,
Englishmen in ennui.
ROBERT DE BRUNNE, *Handlyng Synne,* l. 4156.

6
An Englishman,
Being flatter'd, is a lamb; threaten'd, a lion.
GEORGE CHAPMAN, *Alphonsus.* Act i, sc. 2.

7
Wise men affirm it is the English way
Never to grumble till they come to pay.
DEFOE, *Britannia,* l. 84.

That vain, ill-natured thing, an Englishman.
DEFOE, *The True-Born Englishman.* Pt. i, l. 133.

No panegyric needs their praise record;
An Englishman ne'er wants his own good word.
DEFOE, *The True-Born Englishman.* Pt. ii, l. 152.

For Englishmen are ne'er contented long.
DEFOE, *The True-Born Englishman.* Pt. ii, l. 244.

Thus from a mixture of all kinds began
That heterogeneous thing, an Englishman:
In eager rapes and furious lust begot
Between a painted Briton and a Scot;
Whose gendering offspring quickly learnt to bow
And yoke their heifers to the Roman plough;
From whence a mongrel half-bred race there came,
With neither name nor nation, speech nor fame;
In whose hot veins new mixtures quickly ran,
Infus'd between a Saxon and a Dane.
DEFOE, *The True-Born Englishman.* Pt. i, l. 279.

8
The English are not an inventive people; they don't eat enough pie.
THOMAS A. EDISON. (*Golden Book,* April, 1931.)

9
There is a prose in certain Englishmen which exceeds in wooden deadness all rivalry with other countrymen.
EMERSON, *English Traits.* Ch. 6.

The common Englishman is prone to forget a cardinal article in the bill of social rights, that every man has a right to his own ears.
EMERSON, *English Traits.* Ch. 8.

Englishmen are not made of polishable substance.
HAWTHORNE, *Journals,* 13 Feb., 1854.

10
The English (it must be owned) are rather a foul-mouthed nation.
WILLIAM HAZLITT, *Table-Talk: On Criticism.*

11
The English race is the best at weeping and the worst at laughing. (Anglica gens est optima flens et pessima ridens.)
THOMAS HEARNE, *Reliquiæ Hearnianæ.* Vol. i, p. 136. A medieval Latin proverb quoted in Kornmannus, *De Linea Amoris.* Ch. ii, p. 47.

12
If ever a people required to be amused, it is we sad-hearted Anglo-Saxons—heavy eaters, hard thinkers, often given up to a peculiar melancholy of our own, with a climate that for months together would frown away mirth if it could; many of us with very gloomy thoughts about our hereafter.
ARTHUR HELPS, *Friends in Council.* Bk. i, ch. 4.

The English amuse themselves sadly according to the custom of their country. (Les Anglais s'amusent tristement selon l'usage de leur pays.)
DUC DE SULLY, *Memoirs.* (c. 1630)

They amused themselves sadly after the custom of their country. (Ils s'amusaient tristement selon la coutume de leur pays.)
FROISSART, referring to the English. (EMERSON, *English Traits,* ch. 8; HAZLITT, *Sketches and Essays: Merry England.*) In spite of the fact that both Emerson and Hazlitt quote this as coming from Froissart, it is not to be found in his writings, but was probably derived from Sully, as given above. Hazlitt gives "se rejouissoient" instead of "s'amusaient."

13
The King blew his nose twice, and wiped the royal perspiration repeatedly from a face which is probably the largest uncivilized spot in England.
O. W. HOLMES, *Life and Letters,* l. 135. Referring to William IV.

14
You are a right Englishman, you cannot tell when you are well.
JAMES HOWELL, *Proverbs,* 10. (1659)

15
When two Englishmen meet, their first talk is of the weather.
SAMUEL JOHNSON, *The Idler.* No. 11.

1
As thorough an Englishman as ever coveted his neighbour's goods.

CHARLES KINGSLEY, *The Water Babies*. Ch. 1.

2
For Allah created the English mad—the maddest of all mankind!

RUDYARD KIPLING, *Kitchener's School.*

3
We know no spectacle so ridiculous as the British public in one of its periodical fits of morality.

MACAULAY, *Essays: Moore's Life of Lord Byron.* For full quotation, see APPENDIX.

The unctuous rectitude of my countrymen.

CECIL RHODES, *Speech,* at Port Elizabeth, 24 Dec., 1896.

An Englishman thinks he is moral when he is only uncomfortable.

BERNARD SHAW, *Man and Superman.* Act iii.

It is the habit of the Englishman to sniff for doctrine everywhere.

HENRY ARTHUR JONES, *The Triumph of the Philistines: Preface.*

4
The fickleness which is attributed to us as we are islanders.

JOHN MILTON, *Ready and Easy Way.*

5
But Lord! to see the absurd nature of Englishmen, that cannot forbear laughing and jeering at everything that looks strange.

SAMUEL PEPYS, *Diary,* 28 Nov., 1662.

6
Drunk as an Englishman. (Sot comme un Anglois.)

RABELAIS, *Works.* Bk. i, ch. 15.

7
The only letter which Englishmen write in capitals is I. This I think is the most pointed comment on their national character.

Attributed to RUBINSTEIN.

8
England, where, indeed, they are most potent in potting: your Dane, your German, and your swag-bellied Hollander, are nothing to your English.

SHAKESPEARE, *Othello.* Act ii, sc. 3, l. 78.

9
No Englishman has any common sense, or ever had, or ever will have.

BERNARD SHAW, *John Bull's Other Island,* i.

There is nothing so bad or so good that you will not find Englishmen doing it; but you will never find an Englishman in the wrong. He does everything on principle. He fights you on patriotic principles; he robs you on business principles; he enslaves you on imperial principles.

BERNARD SHAW, *The Man of Destiny,* p. 213.

How can what an Englishman believes be heresy? It is a contradiction in terms.

BERNARD SHAW, *Saint Joan.* Act iv.

No Englishman is ever fairly beaten.

BERNARD SHAW, *Saint Joan.* Act iv.

10
I cannot but conclude the bulk of your natives to be the most pernicious race of little odious vermin that nature ever suffered to crawl upon the surface of the earth.

SWIFT, *Gulliver's Travels: Voyage to Brobdingnag.*

If a traveller were informed that such a man was leader of the House of Commons, he may begin to comprehend how the Egyptians worshipped an insect.

BENJAMIN DISRAELI, *On Lord John Russell.*

11
The self-complaisant British sneer.

TOM TAYLOR, *Abraham Lincoln.*

And curving a contumelious lip,
Gorgonized me from head to foot
With a stony British stare.

TENNYSON, *Maud.* Sec. xiii, st. 2.

12
Whenever he met a great man he grovelled before him, and my-lorded him as only a free-born Briton can do.

THACKERAY, *Vanity Fair.* Ch. 13.

13
The English are mentioned in the Bible: Blessed are the meek, for they shall inherit the earth.

MARK TWAIN, *Pudd'nhead Wilson's New Calendar.*

14
The gloomy Englishman, even in his loves, always wants to reason. We are more reasonable in France.

(Le sombre Anglais, même dans ses amours,
Veut raisonner toujours.
On est plus raisonable en France.)

VOLTAIRE, *Les Originaux: Entrée des Diverses Nations.* Last lines.

15
A perfect Englishman, travelling without motive, buying modern antiques at great cost, looking at everything in a superior manner, and despising the saints and their relics.

(Parfait Anglais, voyageant sans dessin,
Achetant cher de modernes antiques,
Regardant tout avec un air hautain,
Et méprisant les saints et leurs reliques.)

VOLTAIRE, *La Pucelle.* Canto viii.

An Englishman does not travel to see Englishmen.

LAURENCE STERNE, *A Sentimental Journey: Preface: In the Désobligeant.*

The English are generally the most extraordinary persons that we meet with, even out of England.

HORACE WALPOLE, *Letters.*

16
I should like my country well enough, if it were not for my countrymen.

HORACE WALPOLE, *Letters.*

17
They feared the "low" and they hated and despised the "stuck up" and so they "kept

themselves to themselves," according to the English ideal.
H. G. WELLS, *Kipps*. Bk. i, ch. 1.

1
He was inordinately proud of England and he abused her incessantly.
H. G. WELLS, *Mr. Britling Sees It Through*. Bk. i, ch. 2, sec. 2.

That favourite topic of all intelligent Englishmen, the adverse criticism of things British.
H. G. WELLS, *Mr. Britling Sees It Through*. Bk. i, ch. 1, sec. 6.

2
Those things which the English public never forgives—youth, power, and enthusiasm.
OSCAR WILDE, *The English Renaissance*.

3
The Englishman greets, the Irishman sleeps, but the Scotchman gangs till he gets it.
UNKNOWN, *Denham Tracts*. Vol. i, p. 302.

XVI—England: The English: Hearts of Oak

4
Hem once or twice like hearts of oak.
RABELAIS, *Works:* Bk. v, *Prologue*. (1562)

Here is a dozen of yonkers that have hearts of oak at fourscore years.
UNKNOWN, *Old Meg of Herefordshire*. (1609)

He was heart of oak; he wore like iron.
WALKER, *Paræmiologia*, 24. (1672)

5
Where are the rough brave Britons to be found
With Hearts of Oak, so much of old renowned?
SUSANNAH CENTLIVRE, *The Cruel Gift*. (1717)

6
Heart of oak are our ships,
Heart of oak are our men,
We always are ready:
Steady, boys, steady!
We'll fight and we'll conquer again and again.
DAVID GARRICK, *Heart of Oak*. (c. 1770)

Britannia triumphant, her ships sweep the sea;
Her standard is Justice—her watchwo.d, "Be free."
DAVID GARRICK, *Heart of Oak*.

7
Those pigmy tribes of Panton street,
Those hardy blades, those hearts of oak,
Obedient to a tyrant's yoke.
UNKNOWN, *A Monstrous Good Lounge*, p. 5. (1777)

8
Our ships were British oak,
And hearts of oak our men.
SAMUEL J. ARNOLD, *The Death of Nelson*.

So small a nation of hearts of oak.
DICKENS, *Edwin Drood*. Ch. 12.

9
Vain, mightiest fleets of iron framed;
Vain, those all-shattering guns;
Unless proud England keep, untamed,
The strong heart of her sons.
FRANCIS HASTINGS DOYLE, *The Private of the Buffs*. St. 5.

10
Their hearts were made of English oak, their swords of Sheffield steel.
SCOTT, *The Bold Dragoon*.

11
And broad-based under all
Is planted England's oaken-hearted mood,
As rich in fortitude
As e'er went worldward from the island-wall.
BAYARD TAYLOR, *America*.

12
There is no land like England,
Where'er the light of day be;
There are no hearts like English hearts,
Such hearts of oak as they be.
TENNYSON, *The Foresters: Song*.

XVII—England: The English: Mostly Fools

13
Consider, in fact, a body of six hundred and fifty-eight miscellaneous persons set to consult about "business" with twenty-seven millions, mostly fools, assiduously listening to them, and checking and criticising them:—was there ever since the world began, will there ever be till the world end, any "business" accomplished in these circumstances?
CARLYLE, *Latter-Day Pamphlets:* No. 6.

14
England has been divided into three classes: Knaves, Fools, and Revolutionists.
G. K. CHESTERTON, *Victorian Age in English Literature*, p. 233.

15
Let but thy wicked men from out thee go,
And all the fools that crowd thee so,
Even thou who dost thy millions boast,
A village less than Islington will grow,
A solitude almost.
ABRAHAM COWLEY, *Of Solitude*.

16
At least eighty out of a hundred adults . . . returned in the last census are neither extraordinarily silly, nor extraordinarily wicked, nor extraordinarily wise.
GEORGE ELIOT, *Scenes of Clerical Life: The Sad Fortunes of the Reverend Amos Barton*. Ch. 5.

17
He gave the little Wealth he had
To build a House for Fools and Mad;
And shew'd, by one satiric Touch,
No Nation wanted it so much.
SWIFT, *On the Death of Dr. Swift*, l. 479.

18
O fruitful Britain! doubtless thou wast meant
A nurse of fools, to stock the continent.
YOUNG, *Love of Fame*. Sat. iii, l. 113.

19
You will always be fools; we shall never be gentlemen.
Quoted by Lord Fisher as "a classic," in the

Times, 16 June, 1919, as the remark of a German naval officer to an English one. "On the whole," Lord Fisher commented, "I think I prefer to be the fool."

ENJOYMENT, see Pleasure

ENTHUSIASM

1
It is unfortunate, considering that enthusiasm moves the world, that so few enthusiasts can be trusted to speak the truth.

A. J. BALFOUR, *Letter to Mrs. Gladstone,* 1891.

2
The sallow, virgin-minded, studious
Martyr to mild enthusiasm.

ROBERT BROWNING, *Christmas Eve.* Sec. 14.

3
Enthusiasm is the genius of sincerity, and truth accomplishes no victories without it.

BULWER-LYTTON, *The Last Days of Pompeii.* Bk. i, ch. 8.

The prudent man may direct a state; but it is the enthusiast who regenerates it, or ruins.

BULWER-LYTTON, *Rienzi.* Bk. i, ch. 2.

4
Rash enthusiasm in good society
Were nothing but a moral inebriety.

BYRON, *Don Juan.* Canto xiii, st. 35.

5
No wild enthusiast ever yet could rest,
Till half mankind were like himself possess'd.

COWPER, *The Progress of Error,* l. 470.

6
Every production of genius must be the production of enthusiasm.

ISAAC D'ISRAELI, *Curiosities of Literature: Solitude.*

Enthusiasm is that secret and harmonious spirit which hovers over the production of genius, throwing the reader of a book, or the spectator of a statue, into the very ideal presence whence these works have really originated. A great work always leaves us in a state of musing.

ISAAC D'ISRAELI, *Literary Character.* Ch. xii.

7
Nothing great was ever achieved without enthusiasm.

EMERSON, *Essays, First Series: Circles.*

Enthusiasm is the leaping lightning, not to be measured by the horse-power of the understanding.

EMERSON, *Letters and Social Aims: Progress of Culture.*

Every great and commanding moment in the annals of the world is the triumph of some enthusiasm.

EMERSON, *Nature, Addresses, and Lectures: Man the Reformer.*

8
Two dry Sticks will burn a green One.

BENJAMIN FRANKLIN, *Poor Richard,* 1755.

9
Enthusiasm without imagination tends to make a man a crank.

BENJAMIN C. LEEMING, *Imagination.*

10
A little ginger 'neath the tail
Will oft for lack of brains avail.

T. F. MACMANUS, *Cave Sedem.*

11
An ounce of enterprise is worth a pound of privilege.

FREDERIC R. MARVIN, *The Companionship of Books,* p. 318.

12
I love enthusiasts; exalted people frighten me.

JOSEPH ROUX, *Meditations of a Parish Priest.* Pt. ix, No. 19.

13
Enthusiast most strange! (Sonderbarer Schwärmer!)

SCHILLER, *Don Carlos.* Act iii, sc. 10, l. 277.

14
There is a melancholy which accompanies all enthusiasm.

LORD SHAFTESBURY, *Characteristics.* Vol. i, p. 13.

15
I see you stand like greyhounds in the slips,
Straining upon the start.

SHAKESPEARE, *Henry V.* Act iii, sc. 1, l. 31.

16
His rash fierce blaze of riot cannot last,
For violent fires soon burn out themselves;
Small showers last long, but sudden storms are short;
He tires betimes that spurs too fast betimes.

SHAKESPEARE, *Richard II.* Act ii, sc. 1, l. 33.

17
Put down enthusiasm.

ARCHBISHOP MANNERS-SUTTON, *Valedictory Sermon,* on Bishop Heber's consecration to the see of Calcutta.

"Put down enthusiasm"—the Church of England in a nutshell.

MRS. HUMPHRY WARD, *Robert Elsmere.* Bk. ii, ch. 16.

18
Enthusiasm is that temper of the mind in which the imagination has got the better of the judgment.

BISHOP WILLIAM WARBURTON, *Divine Legation.* Bk. v.

ENVY

See also Jealousy

19
Envy has no holidays.

FRANCIS BACON, *De Augmentis Scientiarum.* Pt. i, bk. vi, sec. 16.

There be none of the affections which have been noted to fascinate, or bewitch, but Love and Envy.

FRANCIS BACON, *Essays: Of Envy.*

20
Neither can he, that mindeth but his own business, find much matter for Envy. For Envy is a gadding passion, and walketh the streets, and doth not keep at home.

FRANCIS BACON, *Essays: Of Envy.*

Envy, which is proud weakness, and deserveth to be despised.
FRANCIS BACON, *Filum Labyrinthi.*

1
It is not given to the children of men to be philosophers without envy. Lookers-on can hardly bear the spectacle of the great world.
WALTER BAGEHOT, *Literary Studies.* Vol. ii, p. 286.

2
Envy's a coal comes hissing hot from hell.
P. J. BAILEY, *Festus: A Country Town.*

Envy! eldest-born of hell!
CHARLES JENNENS, *Saul: Chorus.* Jennens, who was a friend of Handel, wrote the words for his famous oratorio.

3
Envy is the most corroding of the vices, and also the greatest power in any land.
J. M. BARRIE, *Address,* Edinburgh University.

4
From envy, hatred, and malice, and all uncharitableness.
Book of Common Prayer: The Litany.

5
Envy never dies.
JOHN BOURCHIER, *Froissart.* Sec. 428. (1523)

The envious will die, but envy never. (Les envieux mourront, mais non jamais l'envie.)
MOLIÈRE, *Le Tartuffe.* Act v, sc. 3, l. 25.

6
Let age not envy draw wrinkles on thy cheeks; be content to be envied, but envy not.
SIR THOMAS BROWNE, *Christian Morals.* Pt. i, sec. 13.

7
The envious man shall never want woe.
WILLIAM CAMDEN, *Remains,* p. 333. (1605)

8
With that malignant envy which turns pale,
And sickens, even if a friend prevail,
Which merit and success pursues with hate,
And damns the worth it cannot imitate.
CHARLES CHURCHILL, *The Rosciad,* l. 127.

9
Nothing can allay the rage of biting envy. (Rabiem livoris acerbi Nulla potest placare quies.)
CLAUDIAN, *De Raptu Proserpinæ.* Bk. iii, l. 290.

10
Envy and fear are the only passions to which no pleasure is attached.
CHURTON COLLINS, *Aphorisms.*

11
Expect not praise without envy until you are dead.
C. C. COLTON, *Lacon.* No. 245.

12
A man shall never be enriched by envy.
DRAXE, *Biblio. Schol. Instr.,* 52. (1633)

13
Envy and wrath shorten the life.
Apocrypha: Ecclesiasticus, xxx, 24.

14
There is a time in every man's education when he arrives at the conviction that envy is ignorance.
EMERSON, *Essays, First Series: Self-Reliance.*

15
Some folks rail against other folks because other folks have what some folks would be glad of.
FIELDING, *Joseph Andrews.* Bk. iv, ch. 6.

16
An envious man is a squint-eyed fool.
THOMAS FULLER, *Gnomologia.* No. 601.

Nothing sharpens sight like envy.
THOMAS FULLER, *Gnomologia.* No. 3674.

17
Fools may our scorn, not envy, raise.
For envy is a kind of praise
JOHN GAY, *The Hound and the Huntsman.*

Envy is the sincerest form of flattery.
CHURTON COLLINS, *Aphorisms.*

18
What mighty magic can assuage
A woman's envy and a bigot's rage?
GEORGE GRANVILLE, *Progress of Beauty,* l. 161.

19
Envy is but the smoke of low estate,
Ascending still against the fortunate.
SIR FULKE GREVILLE, *Alaham.* *See also* GREATNESS: ITS PENALTIES.

20
Envy, among other ingredients, has a mixture of the love of justice in it. We are more angry at undeserved than at deserved good fortune.
WILLIAM HAZLITT, *Characteristics.* No. 19.

21
Envy not greatness: for thou mak'st thereby
Thyself the worse, and so the distance greater.
GEORGE HERBERT, *The Church-Porch.* St. 44.

22
It is better to be envied than pitied.
HERODOTUS, *Thalia.* Bk. iii, sec. 52.

Envy is better than pity. Those who are envied lead a splendid life, while our pity is for the unfortunate.
PALLADAS, quoting Pindar. (*Greek Anthology.* Bk. x, epig. 51.)

23
Beneficent this bitter envy burns—
Thus emulous his wheel the potter turns,
The smith his anvil beats, the beggar throng
Industrious ply, the bards contend in song. . . .
The artist envies what the artist gains,
The bard the rival bard's successful strains.
HESIOD, *Works and Days,* l. 33.

In ev'ry age and clime we see
Two of a trade can ne'er agree.
JOHN GAY, *The Rat-Catcher and the Cats.*

24
Lo! ill-rejoicing Envy, winged with lies,
Scattering calumnious rumours as she flies.
HESIOD, *Works and Days,* l. 172.

1
Than envy Sicilian tyrants have invented no worse torture. (Invidia Siculi non invenere tyranni Majus tormentum.)
HORACE, *Epistles*. Bk. i, epis. 2, l. 58.

2
The envious man grows thin at another's prosperity. (Invidus alterius macrescit rebus opimis.)
HORACE, *Epistles*. Bk. i, epis. 2, l. 57.

An envious man waxes lean with the fatness of his neighbor.
H. G. BOHN, *Hand-Book of Proverbs*, 311.

He sicken'd at all triumphs but his own.
CHARLES CHURCHILL, *The Rosciad*, l. 64.

Such men as he be never at heart's ease
Whiles they behold a greater than themselves.
SHAKESPEARE, *Julius Cæsar*. Act i, sc. 2, l 208.

Base Envy withers at another's joy,
And hates that excellence it cannot reach.
THOMSON, *The Seasons: Spring*, l. 284.

3
Here is the very ink of the cuttlefish; here is envy unadulterate. (Hic nigræ sucus lolliginis, hæc est Ærugo mera.)
HORACE, *Satires*. Bk. i, sat. 4, l. 100.

4
Are you attempting to appease envy by abandoning virtue? (Invidiam placere paras virtute relicta?)
HORACE, *Satires*. Bk. ii, sat. 3, l. 13.

5
Things we haven't got we disparage.
ELBERT HUBBARD, *The Philistine*. Vol. 27, p. 42.

6
Envy is almost the only vice which is practicable at all times, and in every place; the only passion which can never lie quiet from want of irritation.
SAMUEL JOHNSON, *The Rambler*. No. 183.

7
And the crop of our neighbor seems greater and better than our own. (Majorque videtur Et melior vicina seges.)
JUVENAL, *Satires*. Sat. xiv, l. 142.

The crops are ever more abundant in other people's fields. (Fertilior seges est alienis semper in agris.)
OVID, *Ars Amatoria*. Bk. i, l. 349.

8
Envy is more irreconcilable than hate. (L'envie est plus irréconciliable que la haine.)
LA ROCHEFOUCAULD, *Maximes*. No. 328.

The truest sign of being born with great qualities is to be born without envy. (La plus véritable marque d'être né avec de grandes qualités, c'est d'être né sans envie.)
LA ROCHEFOUCAULD, *Maximes*. No. 433.

9
Envy, like fire, soars upward. (Invidiam, tamquam ignem, summa petere.)
LIVY, *History*. Bk. viii, sec. 31.

10
Envy the living, not the dead, doth bite,
For after death all men receive their right.
RICHARD LOVELACE, *On Sanazar's Being Honoured with 600 Ducats*.

For something in the envy of the small
Still loves the vast Democracy of Death!
BULWER-LYTTON, *The Bones of Raphael*.

Envy feeds on the living; it ceases when they are dead. (Pascitur in vivis Livor; post fata quiescit.)
OVID, *Amores*. Bk. i, eleg. 15, l. 39.

When one told Pleistarchus that a notorious railer spoke well of him, "I'll lay my life," said he, "somebody hath told him I am dead, for he can speak well of no man living."
PLUTARCH, *Sayings of Spartans: Pleistarchus*.

11
I envy no man, no, not I,
And no man envies me!
CHARLES MACKAY, *The Miller of the Dee*.

12
Men always hate most what they envy most.
H. L. MENCKEN, *Prejudices*. Ser. iv, p. 130.

13
That most odious and anti-social of all passions—envy.
JOHN STUART MILL, *On Liberty*. Ch. 4.

14
I . . . do this under the nose of the envious.
MILTON, *Apology for Smectymnuus*.

15
We are all clever enough at envying a famous man while he is yet alive, and at praising him when he is dead.
MIMNERMUS, *Fragments*. No. 1.

16
The vulture who explores our inmost liver, and drags out our heart and nerves, is not the bird of whom our poets talk, but those diseases of the soul, envy and wantonness.
PETRONIUS, *Fragments*. No. 25.

17
I would rather that my enemies envy me than that I should envy my enemies. (Mavelim mihi inimicos invidere, quam me inimicis meis.)
PLAUTUS, *Truculentus*. Act iv, sc. 2, l. 30.

18
Envy will Merit, as its shade, pursue;
But, like a shadow, proves the substance true.
POPE, *Essay on Criticism*. Pt. ii, l. 266.

Envy, to which th' ignoble mind's a slave,
Is emulation in the learn'd or brave.
POPE, *Essay on Man*. Epis. ii, l. 191.

19
A brave man or a fortunate one is able to bear envy. (Invidiam ferre aut fortis aut felix potest.)
PUBLILIUS SYRUS, *Sententiæ*. No. 277.

20
The green sickness.
SHAKESPEARE, *Antony and Cleopatra*. Act iii. sc. 2, l. 6.

21
Men that make

Envy and crooked malice nourishment,
Dare bite the best.

SHAKESPEARE, *Henry VIII*. Act v, sc. 3, l. 43.

No metal can,
No, not the hangman's axe, bear half the keenness
Of thy sharp envy.

SHAKESPEARE, *The Merchant of Venice*. Act iv, sc. 1, l. 124.

1

The general's disdain'd
By him one step below; he by the next,
That next by him beneath; so every step,
Exampled by the first pace that is sick
Of his superior, grows to an envious fever
Of pale and bloodless emulation.

SHAKESPEARE, *Troilus and Cressida*. Act i, sc. 3, l. 129.

2

There is nothing more universally commended than a fine day; the reason is, that people can commend it without envy.

WILLIAM SHENSTONE, *Essays: On Men and Manners*.

3

Vile is the vengeance on the ashes cold;
And envy base to bark at sleeping fame.

SPENSER, *Faerie Queene*. Bk. ii, canto 8, st. 13.

4

Envy slays itself by its own arrows. (Ὁ φθόνος αὐτὸς ἑαυτὸν ἑοῖς βελέεσσι δαμάζει.)

UNKNOWN. (*Greek Anthology*. Bk. x, ep. 111.)

Envy shooteth at others, but hitteth and woundeth herself.

GABRIEL HARVEY, *Marginalia*, p. 103. (1590)

An envious heart procures mickle smart.

UNKNOWN, *Plasidas*, p. 167. (1597)

EPIGRAM, THE

Definitions only. Epigrams themselves will be found under appropriate headings, or under Proverbs

5

The diamond's virtues well might grace
The epigram, and both excel
In brilliancy in smallest space,
And power to cut, as well.

GEORGE BIRDSEYE, *The Epigram*.

6

What is an epigram? A dwarfish whole,
Its body brevity, and wit its soul.

Attributed to S. T. COLERIDGE, but not found in his works. (See MATTHEWS, *American Epigrams, Harper's Monthly*, Nov., 1903.)

7

Paradoxes are useful to attract attention to ideas.

MANDELL CREIGHTON. (CREIGHTON, *Life*.)

8

The epigram has been compared to a scorpion, because as the sting of the scorpion lieth in the tail, the force of the epigram is in the conclusion.

LILIUS GYRALDUS, *De Poetica Historia*. Dial 10. (1545); EDWARD TOPSELL, *The Historie of Serpents*, p. 756. (1653)

9

A thought must tell at once, or not at all.

WILLIAM HAZLITT, *Characteristics*.

10

In general I don't see how an epigram, being a pure bolt from the blue, with no introduction or cue, gets itself writ.

WILLIAM JAMES, *Letters*. Vol. ii, p. 142.

11

The sharp, the rapier-pointed epigram.

KEATS, *Letters: Epistle to C. C. Clarke*.

12

You complain Velox, that I write long epigrams. You yourself write nothing, so yours are shorter. (Scribere me quereris, Velox, epigrammata longa. Ipse nihil scribis; tu breviora facis.)

MARTIAL, *Epigrams*. Bk. i, epig. 110.

Although you ask for lively epigrams, you propose lifeless subjects. (Vivida cum poscas epigrammata, mortua ponis Lemmata.)

MARTIAL, *Epigrams*. Bk. xi, epig. 42.

13

But, with the imprecisive arrow
The intended acorn fairly struck—
Such is epigram, requiring
Wit, occasion, and good luck!

CHRISTOPHER MORLEY, *The Epigram*.

14

Sure if they cannot cut, it may be said
His saws are toothless, and his hatchet's lead.

POPE, *Epilogue to Satires*. Dial. ii, l. 148.

15

No epigram contains the whole truth.

C. W. THOMPSON, *Presidents I've Known*, p. 271.

16

Somewhere in the world there is an epigram for every dilemma.

H. W. VAN LOON, *Tolerance*, p. 197.

17

The qualities rare in a bee that we meet,
In an epigram never should fail;
The body should always be little and sweet,
And a sting should be felt in its tail.

TOMAS DE YRIARTE, *The Epigram*. (See MATTHEWS, *American Epigrams, Harper's Monthly*, Nov., 1903.)

18

Beware of cultivating this delicate art.

JOHN MORLEY, *Studies in Literature*, p. 88.

EPITAPHS

Epitaphs of persons who have subject-headings will be found under their respective names

I—Epitaphs: Apothegms

19

Julius Scaliger, who in a sleepless fit of the gout could make two hundred verses in a night, would have but five plain words upon his tomb. [Julii Cæsaries Scaligeri quod fuit.]

SIR THOMAS BROWNE, *To a Friend*. Sec. 21.

20

Gravestones tell truth scarce forty years.

SIR THOMAS BROWNE, *Hydriotaphia*. Ch. 5.

Old gravestones were taken up and other bodies laid under them.

1
Kind Reader! take your choice to cry or laugh;
Here Harold lies—but where's his Epitaph?
If such you seek, try Westminster, and view
Ten thousand just as fit for him as you.
BYRON, *Substitute for an Epitaph.*

2
Having read the inscriptions
Upon the tombstones
Of the Great and the Little Cemeteries,
Wang Peng advised the Emperor
To kill all the living
And resurrect the dead.
PAUL ELDRIDGE, *Wang Pen, Famous Sociologist, Suggests to the Emperor the Only Possible Means of Improving the People of the Empire.*

3
Let there be no inscription upon my tomb. Let no man write my epitaph. No man can write my epitaph. I am here ready to die. I am not allowed to vindicate my character; and when I am prevented from vindicating myself, let no man dare to calumniate me. Let my character and motives repose in obscurity and peace, till other times and other men can do them justice.
ROBERT EMMET, *Speech,* on his conviction for treason, Sept., 1803.

Let no man write my epitaph; let my grave
Be uninscribed, and let my memory rest
Till other times are come, and other men,
Who then may do me justice.
SOUTHEY, *Written after Reading the Speech of Robert Emmet.*

4
When fades at length our lingering day,
Who cares what pompous tombstones say?
Read on the hearts that love us still,
Hic jacet Joe. *Hic jacet* Bill.
O. W. HOLMES, *Bill and Joe.*

5
In lapidary inscriptions a man is not upon oath.
SAMUEL JOHNSON. (BOSWELL, *Life,* 1775.)

Friend, in your epitaphs I'm grieved
So very much is said:
One-half will never be believed,
The other never read.
UNKNOWN, *On Too-Wordy Epitaphs.* Sometimes ascribed to Pope, but not found in his works.

6
The hobby-horse, whose epitaph is, "For, O, for, O, the hobby-horse is forgot."
SHAKESPEARE, *Hamlet.* Act iii, sc. 2, l. 144.

7
Adieu, and take thy praise with thee to heaven!
Thy ignominy sleep with thee in the grave,
But not remember'd in thy epitaph.
SHAKESPEARE, *I. Henry IV.* Act v, sc. 4, l. 99.

Either our history shall with full mouth
Speak freely of our acts, or else our grave,
Like Turkish mute, shall have a tongueless mouth,
Not worshipp'd with a waxen epitaph.
SHAKESPEARE, *Henry V.* Act i, sc. 2, l. 230.

8
You cannot better be employ'd, Bassanio,
Than to live still and write mine epitaph.
SHAKESPEARE, *The Merchant of Venice.* Act iv, sc. 1, l. 117.

And if your love
Can labour aught in sad invention,
Hang her an epitaph upon her tomb.
SHAKESPEARE, *Much Ado About Nothing.* Act v. sc. 1, l. 292.

9
Let's talk of graves, of worms, and epitaphs.
SHAKESPEARE, *Richard II.* Act iii, sc. 2, l. 145.

10
Build me no comic tombstone, lying half,
And half glozed over with unmeaning words,
But a brave fountain. Let my epitaph
Be sung by birds.
HUGH WESTERN, *My Testament.*

II—Epitaphs: Some Famous Examples

11
Here Huntington's ashes long have lain
Whose loss is our own eternal gain,
For while he exercised all his powers,
Whatever he gained, the loss was ours.
AMBROSE BIERCE, *Epitaph on Collis P. Huntington.* (*The Devil's Dictionary,* p. 202.)

12
Underneath this sable hearse
Lies the subject of all verse:
Sidney's sister, Pembroke's mother:
Death, ere thou hast slain another,
Fair, and learn'd, and good as she,
Time shall throw a dart at thee.
WILLIAM BROWNE, *On the Countess Dowager of Pembroke.* The stanza as engraved on the tomb varies slightly from the above, which is the version given in the edition of Browne's poems edited by Gordon Goodwin. There is a second stanza, sometimes attributed to William, Earl of Pembroke, the son of the Countess. The first publication of the famous epitaph was in Osborne's *Traditional Memoirs of the Reign of King James,* 1658, but with no ascription of authorship. It was claimed for Ben Jonson by Peter Whalley, who published a collected edition of his works in 1756, but with no authority except popular tradition.

And since my weak and saddest verse
Was worthy thought thy grandam's hearse,
Accept of this! Just tears my sight
Have shut for thee—dear Lord—good night.
WILLIAM BROWNE, *On the Right Honourable Charles, Lord Herbert of Cardiff and Shurland.* Lord Herbert was the grandson of the Countess of Pembroke, and this explicit claim of Browne to the authorship of her famous epitaph should settle the question.

Browne was a protégé of William, Earl of Pembroke, the Countess's son.

1

This is the tomb of Callimachus that thou art passing.
He could sing well, and laugh well at the right time over the wine.

CALLIMACHUS, *His Own Epitaph*. (*Greek Anthology*. Bk. vii, epig. 415.)

2

Lo, here the precious dust is laid,
Whose purely-temper'd clay was made
So fine, that it the guest betray'd.
Else, the soul grew so fast within,
It broke the outward shell of sin,
And so was hatch'd a Cherubin.

THOMAS CAREW, *Epitaph on Lady Maria Wentworth*.

3

And when I lie in the green kirkyard,
With the mould upon my breast,
Say not that she did well or ill,
Only, "She did her best."

DINAH MARIA MULOCK CRAIK, *Epitaph*.

4

His form was of the manliest beauty,
His heart was kind and soft,
Faithful, below, he did his duty;
But now he's gone aloft. . . .
For though his body's under hatches,
His soul has gone aloft.

CHARLES DIBDIN, *Tom Bowling*. Written on the occasion of the death of his brother, for many years master of a merchant vessel. The first stanza is inscribed on Charles Dibdin's gravestone in the cemetery of St. James, Camden Town, London.

5

Never be vexed at not getting something, but rejoice in all the gifts of God. Wise Periander died of disappointment at not attaining the thing he wished.

DIOGENES LAERTIUS, *Epitaph for Periander*. (*Greek Anthology*. Bk. vii, epig. 620.)

6

If e'er she knew an evil thought
She spoke no evil word:
Peace to the gentle! She has sought
The bosom of her Lord.

EBENEZER ELLIOTT, *Epitaph on Hannah Ratcliff*.

7

Under this stone, reader, survey
Dead Sir John Vanbrugh's house of clay.
Lie heavy on him, earth! for he
Laid many heavy loads on thee.

ABEL EVANS, *On Sir John Vanbrugh*. Vanbrugh was the architect of Blenheim Palace.

Lie light upon him, earth, tho' he
Laid many a heavy load on thee.

The foregoing epitaph as quoted by SNUFFLING, *Epitaphia: Architects*.

8

Alas, poor Tom! how oft, with merry heart,
Have we beheld thee play the Sexton's part;
Each comic heart must now be grieved to see
The Sexton's dreary part performed on thee.

ROBERT FERGUSSON, *Epigram on the Death of Mr. Thomas Lancashire, Comedian*.

9

When I shall be there, I shall be without care.
(Quand je serai la, je serai sans souci.)

FREDERICK THE GREAT, *Inscription*, written at the foot of the statue of Flora at Sans Souci.

10

"Fuller's earth."

THOMAS FULLER, *Epitaph Written by Himself*.

11

Here lies James Quinn. Deign, Reader, to be taught,
Whate'er thy strength of body, force of thought,
In Nature's happiest mould however cast,
To this complexion thou must come at last.

DAVID GARRICK, *Epitaph on James Quinn*. In the abbey church at Bath, England. (MURPHY, *Life of Garrick*. Vol. ii, p. 38.) The last line is often attributed to Shakespeare, perhaps in confused remembrance of *Hamlet*, act v, sc. 1, l. 186: "Now get you to my lady's chamber, and tell her, let her paint an inch thick, to this favour she must come."

12

Here Reynolds is laid, and, to tell you my mind,
He has not left a wiser or better behind:
His pencil was striking, resistless, and grand;
His manners were gentle, complying, and bland.

OLIVER GOLDSMITH, *On Sir Joshua Reynolds*.

13

His foe was folly and his weapon wit.

ANTHONY HOPE HAWKINS, *Epitaph on William Schwenck Gilbert*. Inscribed on the tablet placed in memory of Gilbert on the Victoria Embankment, London, 31 Aug., 1915.

14

But here's the sunset of a tedious day.
These two asleep are; I'll but be undrest,
And so to bed. Pray wish us all good rest.

ROBERT HERRICK, *Epitaph on Sir Edward Giles*.

15

Her face was fair, her person pleasing, her temper amiable, her heart kind. . . . To the poor she was a benefactor, to the rich an example, to the wretched a comforter, to the prosperous an ornament.

ANDREW JACKSON, *Epitaph for his Wife, Rachel*, inscribed on her tomb at their home, The Hermitage, near Nashville, Tenn.

16

The hand of him here torpid lies,
That drew th' essential form of grace;
Here closed in death th' attentive eyes
That saw the manners in the face.

SAMUEL JOHNSON,. *Epitaph for William Hogarth*.

1
Phillips! whose touch harmonious could remove
The pangs of guilty power and hapless love,
Rest here, distress'd by poverty no more;
Find here that calm thou gav'st so oft before;
Sleep undisturb'd within this peaceful shrine,
Till angels wake thee with a note like thine!
SAMUEL JOHNSON, *Epitaph on Claudius Phillips, the Musician.*

2
Underneath this stone doth lie
As much beauty as could die;
Which in life did harbour give
To more virtue than doth live.
If at all she had a fault,
Leave it buried in this vault.
One name was ELIZABETH,
The other let it sleep in death.
BEN JONSON, *Epitaph on Elizabeth, L. H.*

3
Gentle Lady, may thy grave
Peace and quiet ever have.
MILTON, *Epitaph on Lady Winchester,* l. 47.

4
I have found the haven; Hope and Fortune, farewell!
You have mocked me long enough; mock others now!
(Inveni portum; Spes et Fortuna valete!
Sat me lusistis; ludite nunc alios.)
JANUS PANNONIUS, *Onofrio.* A Latin version of a Greek epitaph. (LAURENTIUS SCHRADERN, *Monumenta Italiæ: Folio Helmæstadii,* p. 164.) Quoted in this form by Le Sage, *Gil Blas,* bk. ix, ch. 10, last lines.

Fortune and Hope farewell! I've found the port;
You've done with me: go, now, with others sport.
(Jam portum inveni, Spes et Fortuna valete.
Nil mihi vobiscum est, ludite nunc alios.)
SIR THOMAS MORE, *Progymnasmata.* Latin version of Greek epitaph prefixed to More's *Epigrams,* 1520. English version by John Herman Merivale.

Mine haven's found; Fortune and Hope, adieu.
Mock others now, for I have done with you.
(Inveni portum Spes et Fortuna valete
Nil mihi vobiscum ludite nunc alios.)
Latin version of Greek epitaph as inscribed on the tomb of Francesco Pucci, church of St. Onofrio, Rome. English version by ROBERT BURTON (*Anatomy of Melancholy.* Pt. ii, sec. iii, mem. 6), who credits the authorship to Prudentius.

Avete multum, Spesque, Forsque; sum in vado.
Qui pone sint illudite; haud mea interest.
Latin version of Greek epitaph, given by Dr. HENRY WELLESLEY, *Anthologia Polyglotta,* p. 464.

5
Excuse my dust.
DOROTHY PARKER, *Her Own Epitaph.*

6
He kept at true good humour's mark
The social flow of pleasure's tide:
He never made a brow look dark,
Nor caused a tear, but when he died.
THOMAS LOVE PEACOCK, *Headlong Hall: Song.*

7
Here Rufus lies, who raised in victory's hour
His country, not himself, to sovran power.
(Hic situs est Rufus, pulso qui Vindice quondam
Imperium adseruit non sibi, sed patriæ.)
PLINY THE YOUNGER, *Epistles.* Bk. ix, epis. 19.

8
Here rests a Woman, good without pretence,
Bless'd with plain Reason and with sober Sense:
No Conquests she but o'er herself desired,
No Arts essay'd but not to be admired.
Passion and Pride were to her soul unknown,
Convinc'd that Virtue only is her own.
So unaffected, so composed, a mind,
So firm, yet soft, so strong, yet so refin'd,
Heaven, as its purest gold, by Tortures tried:
The Saint sustain'd it, but the Woman died.
POPE, *Epitaph on Mrs. Corbet, Who Died of a Cancer in Her Breast.*

9
Here lies Lord Coningsby—be civil!
The rest God knows—perhaps the Devil.
POPE, *Epitaph on Lord Coningsby.*

10
Statesman, yet friend to truth; of soul sincere,
In action faithful, and in honour clear;
Who broke no promise, serv'd no private end,
Who gain'd no title, and who lost no friend;
Ennobled by himself, by all approv'd,
And prais'd, unenvied by the Muse he lov'd.
POPE, *Epistle to Mr. Addison,* l. 67. Referring to James Craggs. The line on his tomb in Westminster Abbey reads: "Prais'd, wept, and honour'd, by the Muse he lov'd."

11
This modest stone, what few vain marbles can,
May truly say, Here lies an Honest Man;
A Poet bless'd beyond the Poet's fate,
Whom Heav'n kept sacred from the proud and great;
Foe to loud Praise, and friend to learned Ease,
Content with Science in the vale of peace.
Calmly he look'd on either life, and here
Saw nothing to regret, or there to fear;
From Nature's temp'rate feast rose satisfied,
Thank'd Heav'n that he had liv'd, and that he died.
POPE, *Epitaph on Mr. Elijah Fenton.*

12
To this sad shrine, whoe'er thou art, draw near;
Here lies the Friend most lov'd, the Son most dear;
Who ne'er knew Joy but Friendship might divide,
Or gave his father grief but when he died.
POPE, *Epitaph on the Hon. Simon Harcourt.*

1
Kneller, by Heav'n, and not a master, taught,
Whose Art was Nature, and whose pictures thought. . . .
Living, great Nature fear'd he might outvie
Her works; and, dying, fears herself may die.

POPE, *Epitaph on Sir Godfrey Kneller*. Inscribed on his monument in Westminster. An imitation of an epitaph on Raphael, Pantheon, Rome.

2
She was—but room forbids to tell thee what—
Sum all perfection up, and she was—that.

FRANCIS QUARLES, *Epitaph on Lady Luchyn*.

3
Warm summer sun, shine friendly here;
Warm western wind, blow kindly here;
Green sod above, rest light, rest light—
Good-night, Annette! Sweetheart, good-night.

ROBERT RICHARDSON, *Requiem*. (*Willow and Wattle*, p. 35.)

Warm summer sun Shine kindly here;
Warm southern wind Blow softly here;
Green sod above Lie light, lie light—
Good night, dear heart, Good night, good night.

MARK TWAIN, *Epitaph for His Daughter, Susy*. Inscribed on her tombstone. A variation of the lines by Robert Richardson.

4
Hotten
Rotten
Forgotten

G. A. SALA, *Epitaph for John Camden Hotten*.

5
Traveller, let your step be light,
So that sleep these eyes may close,
For poor Scarron, till to-night,
Ne'er was able e'en to doze.

PAUL SCARRON, *Epitaph Written by Himself*.

6
These are two friends whose lives were undivided;
So let their memory be, now they have glided
Under the grave; let not their bones be parted,
For their two hearts in life were single-hearted.

SHELLEY, *Epitaph*.

7
Stranger, bear this message to the Spartans, that we lie here obedient to their laws. ('Ω ξεῖν', ἄγγειλον Λακεδαιμονίοις ὅτι τῇδε κείμεθα, τοῖς κείνων ῥήμασι πειθόμενοι.)

SIMONIDES, *Epitaph*, on the monument of the Spartans who fell at Thermopylæ. (*Greek Anthology*. Bk. vii, No. 249.) The noblest group of words ever uttered by man.—RUSKIN.

Stranger, to Lacedæmon go, and tell
That here, obedient to her words, we fell.

SIMONIDES OF CHIOS, *Fragment*. (Burges, tr.)

Go tell the Spartans, thou that passest by,
That here, obedient to their laws, we lie.

SIMONIDES OF CHIOS, *Fragment*.

Tell Britain, ye who mark this monument,
Faithful to her we fell, and rest content.

UNKNOWN, *Inscription*, World War Memorial, Southport, England.

Tell England, ye who pass this monument,
That we who rest here, die content.

UNKNOWN, *Inscription*, at entrance to Waggon Hill Cemetery, Ladysmith, South Africa, commemorating British soldiers who fell in the Boer War.

8
Here lies one who meant well, tried a little, failed much.

R. L. STEVENSON, *Christmas Sermon*.

I, whom Apollo sometimes visited,
Or feigned to visit, now, my day being done,
Do slumber wholly, nor shall know at all
The weariness of changes; nor perceive
Immeasurable sands of centuries
Drink up the blanching ink, or the loud sound
Of generations beat the music down.

R. L. STEVENSON, *Epitaph for Himself*.

9
Under the wide and starry sky,
Dig the grave and let me lie.
Glad did I live and gladly die,
And I laid me down with a will.

This be the verse you grave for me:
Here he lies where he longed to be;
Home is the sailor, home from sea,
And the hunter home from the hill.

ROBERT LOUIS STEVENSON, *Requiem*. Written for himself and engraved on his tombstone.

10
Ubi sæva indignatio ulterius cor lacerare nequit.
(Where fierce indignation can no longer tear my heart.)

JONATHAN SWIFT, *Epitaph for Himself*. Inscribed on his tomb in St. Patrick's Cathedral, Dublin.

11
Thou third great Canning, stand among our best
And noblest, now thy long day's work hath ceased,
Here silent in our Minster of the West
Who wert the voice of England in the East.

TENNYSON, *Epitaph on Stratford Canning, First Viscount Stratford de Redcliffe*.

12
Here in this place sleeps one whom love
Caused, through great cruelty, to fall;
A little scholar, poor enough,
Whom François Villon men did call.
No scrap of land or garden small
He owned; he gave his goods away,
Table and trestles, baskets—all;
For God's sake say for him this lay.

FRANÇOIS VILLON, *His Own Epitaph*.

13
Under this stone there lieth at rest
A friendly man, a worthy knight;
Whose heart and mind was ever prest
To favour truth, to further right.

THOMAS WYATT, *Epitaph on Sir Thomas Gravener*.

14
In this grave are the bones of the venerable

Bede. (Hac sunt in fossa Bedæ venerabilis ossa.)

UNKNOWN, *Epitaph of Bede*, Durham Cathedral.

1

O man! whosoever thou art, and whencesoever thou comest, for come I know thou wilt, I am Cyrus, founder of the Persian empire. Envy me not the little earth that covers my body. (*Ὦ ἄνθρωπε, ὅστις εἶ καὶ ὅθεν ἥκεις, ὅτι μεν γὰρ ἥξεις, οἶδα, ἐγὼ Κῦρος εἰμὶ ὁ Πέρσαις κτησάμενος τὴν ἀρχην. μὴ οὖν τῆς ὀλίγης μοι ταύτης γῆς φθονήσῃς ἣ τοὐμὸν σῶμα περικαλύπτει.*)

UNKNOWN, *Epitaph of Cyrus*. (PLUTARCH, *Lives: Alexander*. Sec. 69.)

2

Say, dog, I pray, what guard you in that tomb?
"A dog." His name? "Diogenes." From far?
"Sinopê." He who made a tub his home?
"The same. Now, dead, among the stars a star."

UNKNOWN, *Inscription*, on pillar, surmounted by a dog, raised at Athens to the memory of Diogenes. (*Greek Anthology*.)

3

Her name was Margaret Lucas, youngest sister to the Lord Lucas of Colchester, a Noble Familie: for all the brothers were valiant and all the sisters virtuous.

UNKNOWN, *Epitaph on Margaret, Duchess of Newcastle*, Westminster Abbey.

4

Farewell, vain world, I've had enough of thee,
And Values't not what thou Can'st say of me;
Thy Smiles I count not, nor thy frowns I fear,
My days are past, my head lies quiet here.
What faults you saw in me take Care to shun,
Look but at home, enough is to be done.

UNKNOWN, *Epitaph* on tombstone of William Harvey, Greasley churchyard, England. (STAPLETON, *The Churchyard Scribe*, p. 95.)

5

Here lies Tom Hyde;
It's a pity he died;
We had rather
It had been his father;
If it had been his sister
We had not missed her;
If the whole generation,
It had been better for the nation.

UNKNOWN, *Epitaph on Thomas Hyde*, son of Edward Hyde, Lord Chancellor of England. (ROBERT BOWERS, *Letter to Robert Southwell*, 9 July, 1667.) This epitaph and the one which follows are probably versions of a French epigram, "Colas est morte de maladie." (JEAN OGIER GOMBAULD, *Epigrammes*. 1658)

Here lies Fred,
Who was alive and is dead;
Had it been his father,
I had much rather;
Had it been his brother,
Still better than another;
Had it been his sister,
No one would have missed her;
Had it been the whole generation,
Still better for the nation:
But since 'tis only Fred
Who was alive and is dead,
There's no more to be said.

UNKNOWN, *Epitaph on Frederick, Prince of Wales*, father of George III. (THACKERAY, *Four Georges: George III*. Also preserved in Walpole. See *Notes and Queries*, 3 May, 1902.)

6

In sex a woman, in abilities a man. (Sexu femina, ingenio vir.)

UNKNOWN, *Epitaph of Maria Theresa of Austria*.

7

Here lies one who was nothing. (Ci-gît qui ne fut rien.)

UNKNOWN, *Piron's Epitaph*. Cited by Voltaire, in *La Vanité*, as happy and worthy of Piron's tomb.

8

Born in America, in Europe bred,
In Africa travelled, in Asia wed,
Where long he lived and thrived, in London dead;
Much good, some ill he did, so hope all's even,
And that his soul through mercy's gone to heaven.

UNKNOWN, *Epitaph*, on tomb of Elihu Yale, founder of Yale University, in the churchyard of Wrexham, North Wales.

III—Epitaphs: "Revised by the Author"

9

The *World's* a *Printing-House*, our *words*, our *thoughts*,
Our *deeds*, are *characters* of several sizes.
Each *Soul* is a *Compos'tor*, of whose faults
The *Levites* are *Correctors; Heaven Revises*.
Death is the *common Press*, from whence being driven,
We're *gather'd*, Sheet by Sheet, and bound for *Heaven*.

FRANCIS QUARLES, *Divine Fancies*. (1635)

The world's a *book*, writ by th' *eternal Art*
Of the great Maker; printed in man's heart;
'Tis falsely *printed* though divinely penn'd,
And all the *Errata* will appear at th' *end*.

FRANCIS QUARLES, *Divine Fancies*. (1635)

See also under FRANKLIN.

10

A living, breathing Bible; tables where
Both Covenants at large engraven were.
Gospel and law, in 's heart, had each its column;
His head an index to the sacred volume;
His very name a title-page; and, next,
His life a commentary on the text.
O what a monument of glorious worth,
When, in a new edition, he comes forth!

Without errata may we think he'll be,
In leaves and covers of eternity!

BENJAMIN WOODBRIDGE, *Epitaph on Himself*. Though born in England, Woodbridge was a member of the first graduating class of Harvard College, 1642. He afterwards returned to England and in 1660 was chaplain to Charles II. His epitaph was quoted in Cotton Mather's *Magnalia Christi*, and so gained wide circulation.

1
Yet at the resurrection we shall see
A fair edition, and of matchless worth,
Free from erratas, new in heaven set forth.

JOSEPH CAPEN, *Lines upon Mr. John Foster*.

2
Like a worn out type, he is returned to the Founder in the hope of being recast in a better and more perfect mould.

UNKNOWN, *Epitaph on Peter Gedge*. Parish church, Bury St. Edmund's.

He died pied.
Reset and stet,
HE NAPS IN CAPS.

DAVID MCCORD, *Remainders*.

3
He will be weighed again
At the Great Day,
His rigging refitted,
And his timbers repaired,
And with one broadside
Make his adversary
Strike in his turn.

TOBIAS SMOLLETT, *Peregrine Pickle: Epitaph on Commodore Trunnion*. Bk. iii, ch. 7.

4
Then haste, kind Death, in pity to my age,
And clap the Finis to my life's last page.
May Heaven's great *Author my foul proof revise*,
Cancel the *page* in which my *error* lies,
And *raise my form* above the ethereal skies. . . .
The stubborn *pressman's* form I now may scoff;
Revised, corrected, finally *worked off!*

UNKNOWN. (TIMBERLEY, *Songs of the Press*.)

5
Here lies the remains of James Pady, Brickmaker, in hope that his clay will be remoulded in a workmanlike manner, far superior to his former perishable materials.

UNKNOWN, *Epitaph of James Pady*. Addiscombe churchyard, Devonshire, England.

IV—Epitaphs: Curiosa

6
To say an angel here interred doth lie
May be thought strange, for angels never die,
Indeed some fell from heaven to hell;
Are lost to rise no more.
This only fell from death to earth,
Not lost, but gone before.

Epitaph on tomb of Mary Angell, Stepney, d. 1693.

Rest, gentle Shade, await thy Master's will;
Then rise unchanged and be an angel still.

Epitaph of Richard Jebb, Chirk Church, North Wales.

7
As I walked by myself I talked to myself,
And thus myself said to me,
Look to thyself and take care of thyself
For nobody cares for thee.
So I turned to myself, and I answered myself
In the self-same reverie
Look to myself or look not to myself
The self-same thing will it be.

Epitaph of Robert Crytoft, Hornersfield, Suffolk, England. (WILLIAM H. BEABLE, *Epitaphs*, p. 139.)

8
Here lies Thomas Dudley, that trusty old stud—
A bargain's a bargain, and must be made good.

Epitaph on Governor Dudley, attributed to Governor Belcher.

9
Here lies DuVall; reader, if male thou art,
Look to thy purse; if female, to thy heart.

Epitaph of the famous highwayman, Claude DuVall, in Covent Garden church.

10
Here lie I, Martin Elginbrodde.
Have mercy o' my soul, Lord God,
As I would do were I Lord God,
And ye were Martin Elginbrodde.

One of many variants of an epitaph frequently found in British and American graveyards. GEORGE MACDONALD cites it in this form in his novel, *David Elginbrod*.

If I were Thou and Thou wert I,
I would resign the Deity;
Thou shouldst be God, I would be man—
Is't possible that Love more can?

JAMES HOWELL, *Familiar Letters*. Bk. ii, sec. 7, No. 53. A versification of a passage in St. Augustine.

Were I thou, Agni, and wert thou I, this aspiration should be fulfilled.

Rig Veda. viii, 19, 25.

11
Here rests one fortune never favored,
He grew no wiser from the past;
But e'er with perseverance labored
And still contended to the last.

JOSEPH EVE, *His Epitaph*.

12
Beneath this stone lies Catherine Gray,
Changed to a lifeless lump of clay.
By earth and clay she got her pelf,
And now she's turned to earth herself.
Ye weeping friends let me advise,
Abate your tears and dry your eyes;
For what avails a flood of tears?
Who knows but in a course of years,
In some tall pitcher or brown pan,
She in her shop may be again?

Epitaph, in a Church at Chester, England.

1
Beneath these green trees rising to the skies,
The planter of them, Isaac Greentree, lies;
The time shall come when these green trees
shall fall,
And Isaac Greentree rise above them all.
Epitaph of Isaac Greentree, Harrow.

2
Here lies Sir Jenkin Grout, who loved his friend and persuaded his enemy: what his mouth ate, his hand paid for: what his servants robbed, he restored: if a woman gave him pleasure, he supported her in pain: he never forgot his children; and whoso touched his finger, drew after it his whole body.
EMERSON, *Essays, Second Series: Manners*. Quoted.

3
Pray for the soul of Gabriel John,
Who died in the year eighteen-hundred and
one
You may if you please, or let it alone,
For it's all one To Gabriel John,
Who died in the year eighteen-hundred and
one.
UNKNOWN, *Old Rhyme*.

4
Here lie the bones of Robert Lowe:
Where he's gone to I don't know.
If to the realms of peace and love,
Farewell to happiness above.
If he's gone to a lower level,
I can't congratulate the devil.
E. KNATCHBULL-HUGESSEN, *Epitaph on Robert Lowe*.

5
Here lies Anne Mann; she lived an
Old maid and died an old Mann.
Epitaph of Anne Mann, Bath Abbey.

6
Beneath this stone old Abraham lies;
Nobody laughs and nobody cries.
Where he is gone, and how he fares,
Nobody knows, and nobody cares.
ABRAHAM NEWLAND, *His Own Epitaph*. Newland, who died in 1807, was chief cashier of the Bank of England.

7
Under this sod
And under these trees
Lieth the bod-
y of Solomon Pease.
He's not in this hole,
But only his pod;
He shelled out his soul
And went up to his God.
On a tombstone in Ohio. (J. R. KIPPAX, *Churchyard Literature*, p. 163.)

8
Stranger, pause and shed a tear
For one who leaves no mourners.
D. F. Sapp reposes here:
He would cut corners.
Here lies G. Whilliken's friends, all five.
He took them along when he learned to drive.
LEONARD H. ROBBINS, *Epitaphs for the Speed Age*.

9
In heart a Lydia, and in tongue a Hannah,
In zeal a Ruth, in wedlock a Susanna,
Prudently simple, providently wary,
To the world a Martha, and to heaven a
Mary.
Epitaph on Dame Dorothy Selby (d. 1641), Ightham Church, near Sevenoaks, England.

10
Here lies who, born a man, a grocer died. (Né homme—mort épicier.)
ALFRED AUSTIN, *Golden Age*.

11
Man's life is like unto a summer's day
Some break their fast and so away;
Others stay dinner, then depart full fed;
The longest age but sups and goes to bed:
O reader then behold and see:
As we are now, so must you be.
Attributed to JOSEPH HENSHAW, BISHOP OF PETERBOROUGH. Found with variations in many churches.

12
Here lies a poor woman, who always was
tired;
She lived in a house where help was not
hired.
Her last words on earth were: "Dear friends,
I am going
Where washing ain't done, nor sweeping, nor
sewing;
But everything there is exact to my wishes;
For where they don't eat there's no washing
of dishes.
I'll be where loud anthems will always be
ringing,
But, having no voice, I'll be clear of the
singing.
Don't mourn for me now; don't mourn for
me never—
I'm going to do nothing for ever and ever."
UNKNOWN, *The Tired Woman's Epitaph*.

13
She took the cup of life to sip,
Too bitter 'twas to drain;
She meekly put it from her lip,
And went to sleep again.
UNKNOWN, *Epitaph*, Meole Churchyard. (*Sabrinæ Corolla*, p. 246.)

14
Here lies the mother of children seven,
Four on earth and three in heaven;
The three in heaven preferring rather
To die with mother than live with father.
UNKNOWN, *Epitaph*, in a graveyard at Birmingham, Eng.

15
Bland, Passionate, and Deeply Religious; also she painted in Water Colours, and sent several Pictures to the Exhibition. She was the first

cousin to Lady Jones; and of such is the Kingdom of Heaven.

UNKNOWN, *Epitaph of Lady O'Looney*, Pewsey church-yard. (*Spectator*, London, 21 Dec., 1934, p. 971.)

EQUALITY

2
Your abundance may be a supply for their want, that their abundance also may be a supply for your want; that there may be equality.

New Testament: II Corinthians, viii, 14.

3
As a man is equal to the Church and equal to the State, so he is equal to every other man.

EMERSON, *Essays, Second Series: New England Reformers.*

The Spartan principle of "calling that which is just, equal; not that which is equal, just."

EMERSON, *Essays, Second Series: Politics.*

4
There is a little formula, couched in pure Saxon, which you may hear in the corners of streets and in the yard of the dame's school, from very little republicans: "I'm as good as you be," which contains the essence of the Massachusetts Bill of Rights and of the American Declaration of Independence.

EMERSON, *Natural History of Intellect: Boston.*

5
Men are made by nature unequal. It is vain, therefore, to treat them as if they were equal.

J. A. FROUDE, *Short Studies on Great Subjects: Party Politics.*

That all men are equal is a proposition to which, at ordinary times, no sane individual has ever given his assent.

ALDOUS HUXLEY, *Proper Studies*, p. 23.

I am an aristocrat. I love liberty; I hate equality.

JOHN RANDOLPH OF ROANOKE. (BRUCE, *Randolph of Roanoke*. Vol. ii, p. 203.)

Inequality is as dear to the American heart as liberty itself.

W. D. HOWELLS, *Impressions and Experiences: New York Streets*, p. 202.

6
One place there is—beneath the burial sod,
Where all mankind are equalized by death;
Another place there is—the Fane of God,
Where all are equal who draw living breath.

THOMAS HOOD, *Ode to Rae Wilson*, l. 133.

7
We are all born equal, and are distinguished alone by virtue. (Omnes pari sorte nascimur, sola virtute distinguimur.)

UNKNOWN. A Latin proverb.

8
When people have to obey other people's orders, equality's out of the question.

W. S. GILBERT, *H. M. S. Pinafore*. Act i.

9
We hold these truths to be self-evident, that all men are created equal.

THOMAS JEFFERSON, *Declaration of Independence*. See 975:4.

I leave you, hoping that the lamp of liberty will burn in your bosoms, until there shall no longer be a doubt that all men are created free and equal.

LINCOLN, *Speech*, Chicago, Ill., 10 July, 1858.

Fourscore and seven years ago, our fathers brought forth on this continent a new nation, conceived in liberty, and dedicated to the proposition that all men are created equal.

LINCOLN, *Gettysburg Address*, 19 Nov., 1863.

All men are equal before the natural law. (Quod ad jus naturale attinet, omnes homines æquales sunt.)

UNKNOWN, *Legal Maxim.*

All men are equal on the turf and under it.

LORD GEORGE BENTINCK.

10
Your levellers wish to level *down* as far as themselves; but they cannot bear levelling *up* to themselves.

SAMUEL JOHNSON. (BOSWELL, *Life*, 1763.)

It is better that some should be unhappy, than that none should be happy, which would be the case in a general state of equality.

SAMUEL JOHNSON. (BOSWELL, *Life*, 1776.)

No two men can be half an hour together but one shall acquire an evident superiority over the other.

SAMUEL JOHNSON, combating the theory that all men are equal. (BOSWELL, *Life*, 1776.)

11
Equality in society beats inequality, whether the latter be of the British-aristocratic sort or of the domestic-slavery sort.

LINCOLN, *Speech*, Peoria, Ill., 16 Oct., 1854.

12
The odds for high and low's alike.

SHAKESPEARE, *Winter's Tale*. Act v, sc. 1, l. 207.

The trickling rain doth fall
Upon us one and all;
The south-wind kisses
The saucy milkmaid's cheek,
The nun's, demure and meek,
Nor any misses.

E. C. STEDMAN, *A Madrigal.*

13
Equality breeds no war. ("Ισον πόλεμον οὐ ποιεῖ.)

SOLON. (PLUTARCH, *Lives: Solon*. Sec. 14.)

Equality of two domestic powers
Breeds scrupulous faction.

SHAKESPEARE, *Antony and Cleopatra*, i, 3, 47.

14
One man is as good as another—and a great dale betther, as the Irish philosopher said.

THACKERAY, *Roundabout Papers: On Ribbons.*

15
I celebrate myself, and sing myself,
And what I assume you shall assume,
For every atom belonging to me as good as belongs to you.

WALT WHITMAN, *Song of Myself*, l. 1.

ERIN, see Ireland

ERROR

See also Mistake

I—Error: Apothegms

1
He who errs quickly, is quick in correcting the error.
FRANCIS BACON, *De Augmentis Scientiarum: Promptitudo.*

2
No man prospers so suddenly as by others' errors.
FRANCIS BACON, *Essays: On Fortune.*

Sometimes we may learn more from a man's errors than from his virtues.
LONGFELLOW, *Hyperion.* Bk. iv, ch. 3.

3
Error is worse than ignorance.
P. J. BAILEY, *Festus: A Mountain Sunrise.*

4
Error has no end.
ROBERT BROWNING, *Paracelsus.* Pt. iii.

5
There is no anguish like an error of which we feel ashamed.
BULWER-LYTTON, *Ernest Maltravers.* Bk. ii, ch. 3.

6
They defend their errors as if they were defending their inheritance.
EDMUND BURKE, *Speech,* House of Commons, 11 Feb., 1780.

7
Who errs and mends, to God himself commends.
CERVANTES, *Don Quixote.* Pt. ii, ch. 28.

8
Error is the discipline through which we advance.
WILLIAM ELLERY CHANNING, *The Present Age.*

9
Honest error is to be pitied, not ridiculed.
LORD CHESTERFIELD, *Letters,* 16 Feb., 1748.

10
I would rather err with Plato than perceive the truth with others. (Errare malo cum Platone, quam cum istis vera sentire.)
CICERO, *Tusculanarum Disputationum.* Bk. i, ch. 17, sec. 39.

Better to err with Pope than shine with Pye.
BYRON, *English Bards and Scotch Reviewers,* l. 102.

If I have erred, I err in company with Abraham Lincoln.
THEODORE ROOSEVELT, *Speech,* campaign of 1912.

If frequently I fret and fume,
And absolutely will not smile,
I err in company with Hume,
Old Socrates and T. Carlyle.
FRANKLIN P. ADAMS, *Erring in Company.*

11
Ignorance is a blank sheet on which we may write; but error is a scribbled one from which we must first erase.
C. C. COLTON, *Lacon.* No. 1.

12
Error lives ere reason can be born.
CONGREVE, *The Mourning Bride.* Act iii, sc. 1.

13
Yesterday's errors let yesterday cover.
SUSAN COOLIDGE, *New Every Morning.*

14
Man, on the dubious waves of error toss'd.
COWPER, *Truth,* l. 1.

15
Errors, like straws, upon the surface flow;
He who would search for pearls, must dive below.
DRYDEN, *All for Love: Prologue.*

16
No one who lives in error is free. (Οὐδεὶς τοίνυν ἁμαρτάνων ἐλεύθερος ἐστιν.)
EPICTETUS, *Discourses.* Bk. ii, ch. 1, sec. 24.

17
Error is prolific. (Fecundus est error.)
ERASMUS, *Epicureus.*

18
No vehement error can exist in this world with impunity.
J. A. FROUDE, *Spinoza.*

19
A most pleasing error of the mind. (Mentis gratissimus error.)
HORACE, *Epistles.* Bk. ii, epis. 2, l. 140.

Happy in their error. (Felices errore suo.)
LUCAN, *De Bello Civili.*

For his was the error of head, not of heart.
THOMAS MOORE, *The Irish Slave,* l. 45.

20
One goes to the right, the other to the left; both err, but in different ways. (Ille sinistrorsum, hic dextrorsum abit, unus utrique Error, sed variis illudit partibus.)
HORACE, *Satires.* Bk. ii, sat. 3, l. 50.

Brother, brother; we are both in the wrong.
JOHN GAY, *The Beggar's Opera.* Act ii, sc. 2

21
I shall try to correct errors when shown to be errors, and I shall adopt new views so fast as they shall appear to be new views.
ABRAHAM LINCOLN, *Letter to Horace Greeley,* 22 Aug., 1862.

22
So the last error shall be worse than the first.
New Testament: Matthew, xxvii, 64.

A double error sometimes sets us right.
P. J. BAILEY, *Festus: Il Heaven.*

23
The fatal tendency of mankind to leave off thinking about a thing, when it is no longer doubtful, is the cause of half their errors.
J. S. MILL, *On Liberty.* Ch. 2.

24
Error by his own arms is best evinc'd.
MILTON, *Paradise Regained.* Bk. iv, l. 235.

25
The shortest errors are always the best. (Les

plus courtes erreurs sont toujours les meilleures.)

MOLIÈRE, *L'Étourdi*. Act iv, sc. 3, l. 24; CHARRON, *La Sagesse*. Bk. i, ch. 38.

1
Remote from liberty and truth,
By fortune's crime, my early youth
Drank error's poisoned springs.

ROBERT NUGENT, *Ode to William Pulteney*. Referring to the poet's renunciation of Catholicism.

2
If it was an error, its causes were honorable. (Si fuit errandum, causas habet error honestas.)

OVID, *Heroides*. Epis. vii, l. 109.

3
Those oft are stratagems which errors seem.

POPE, *Essay on Criticism*. Pt. i, l. 179.

4
When people once are in the wrong,
Each line they add is much too long;
Who fastest walks, but walks astray,
Is only furthest from his way.

PRIOR, *Alma*. Canto iii, l. 194.

5
Who can discern his errors?

Old Testament: Psalms, xix, 12.

6
Giant Error, darkly grand,
Grasped the globe with iron hand.

SAMUEL ROGERS, *Ode to Superstition*, ii, 1.

7
The dust on antique time would lie unswept,
And mountainous error be too highly heapt
For truth to o'er-peer.

SHAKESPEARE, *Coriolanus*. Act ii, sc. 3, l. 125.

8
O hateful error, melancholy's child!
Why dost thou shew to the apt thoughts of men
The things that are not? O error, soon conceiv'd,
Thou never com'st unto a happy birth,
But kill'st the mother that engender'd thee.

SHAKESPEARE, *Julius Cæsar*. Act v, sc. 3, l. 67.

The error of our eye directs our mind:
What error leads must err.

SHAKESPEARE, *Troilus and Cressida*. Act v, sc. 2, l. 110.

9
If this be error, and upon me proved,
I never writ, nor no man ever loved.

SHAKESPEARE, *Sonnets*. No. cxvi.

10
O my princess! true she errs,
But in her own grand way.

TENNYSON, *The Princess*. Pt. iii, l. 91.

11
Error is a hardy plant; it flourisheth in every soil.

MARTIN F. TUPPER, *Proverbial Philosophy: Of Truth in Things False*.

12
Believe me, error also has its merit. (Croyez moi, l'erreur aussi a son merite.)

VOLTAIRE. (EMERSON, *Natural History of Intellect*.)

13
The progress of rivers to the ocean is not so rapid as that of man to error.

VOLTAIRE, *A Philosophical Dictionary: Rivers*.

14
When the learned man errs, he errs with a learned error. (Cum errat eruditus, errat errore erudito.)

UNKNOWN. An Arabic proverb published in translation in 1623.

II—Error: To Err Is Human

15
The wisest of the wise may err. (Ἁμαρτάνει τοι καὶ σοφοῦ σοφώτερος.)

ÆSCHYLUS, *Fragments*. Frag. 219.

The best may err.

ADDISON, *Cato*. Act v, sc. 4.

The best may slip, and the most cautious fall;
He's more than mortal that ne'er err'd at all.

JOHN POMFRET, *Love Triumphant over Reason*, l. 145.

16
It is human to err; it is devilish to remain wilfully in error. (Humanum fuit errare, diabolicum est per animositatem in errore manere.)

ST. AUGUSTINE, *Sermons*. No. 164, sec. 14.

Man-like it is to fall into sin,
Fiend-like it is to dwell therein;
Christ-like it is for sin to grieve,
God-like it is all sin to leave.

FRIEDRICH VON LOGAU, *Sinnegedichte*.

To step aside is human.

BURNS, *Address to the Unco Guid*.

17
It is the nature of every man to err, but only the fool perseveres in error. (Cujusvis hominis est errare; nullius nisi inspientis in errore perseverare.)

CICERO, *Philippicæ*. No. xii, sec. 2.

18
Forgive, son; men are men, they needs must err. (Σύγγνωθ'· ἁμαρτεῖν εἰκὸς ἀνθρώπους, τέκνον.)

EURIPIDES, *Hippolytus*, l. 615. According to Buchmann, Theognis (540 B.C.) had anticipated the saying.

19
While man's desires and aspirations stir,
He cannot choose but err.
(Es irrt der Mensch so lang er strebt.)

GOETHE, *Faust: Prolog im Himmel: Der Herr*, l. 77. (Bayard Taylor, tr.) Taylor remarks, "It has seemed to me impossible to give the full meaning of these words—that error is a natural accompaniment of the struggles and aspirations of man—in a single line."

20
All men are liable to error; and most men are,

in many points, by passion or interest, under temptation to it.

JOHN LOCKE, *Essay Concerning Human Understanding*. Bk. iv, ch. 20, sec. 17.

1
For to err in opinion, though it be not the part of wise men, is at least human.

PLUTARCH, *Morals: Against Colotes the Epicurean.*

Error of opinion may be tolerated where reason is left free to combat it.

THOMAS JEFFERSON, *First Inaugural.*

2
To err is human. (Humanum est errare.)

SENECA, *Naturales Questiones*. Bk. iv, sec. 2. Probably the first expression in this form of a sentiment proverbial in all languages. Used by COGNATUS, *Adagia;* ST. JEROME, *Epistles*, lvii, 12; POLIGNAC, *Anti-Lucretius*, v, 58, and by many others with slight variations.

Good nature and good sense must ever join;
To err is human, to forgive divine.

POPE, *Essay on Criticism*. Pt. ii, l. 324.

3
To err is common to all men, but the man who, having erred, hugs not his errors, but repents and seeks the cure, is not a wastrel.

SOPHOCLES, *Antigone*, l. 1023.

4
We are none of us infallible, not even the youngest.

WILLIAM HEPWORTH THOMPSON. (JAMES STUART, *Reminiscences*, 1912.)

III—Error and Truth

5
An error is the more dangerous in proportion to the degree of truth which it contains.

AMIEL, *Journal*, 26 Dec., 1852.

6
The truth is perilous never to the true,
Nor knowledge to the wise; and to the fool,
And to the false, error and truth alike.

P. J. BAILEY, *Festus: A Mountain Sunrise.*

7
Many . . . have too rashly charged the troops of Error, and remain as trophies unto the enemies of Truth.

SIR THOMAS BROWNE, *Religio Medici*. Pt. i, sec. 6.

8
Truth, crushed to earth, shall rise again;
  Th' eternal years of God are hers;
But Error, wounded, writhes in pain,
  And dies among his worshippers.

BRYANT, *The Battle-Field*. St. 9.

9
Error and mistake are infinite,
But truth has but one way to be i' th' right.

SAMUEL BUTLER, *Miscellaneous Thoughts*, l. 114.

10
A man protesting against error is on the way towards uniting himself with all men that believe in truth.

CARLYLE, *Heroes and Hero-Worship*. Lect. 4.

11
Truth is a good dog; but, beware of barking too close to the heels of an error, lest you get your brains kicked out.

S. T. COLERIDGE, *Table Talk*, 7 June, 1830.

12
Truth is immortal; error is mortal.

MARY BAKER EDDY, *Science and Health*, p. 466.

You conquer error by denying its verity.

MARY BAKER EDDY, *Science and Health*, p. 339.

13
Truth only smells sweet forever, and illusions, however innocent, are deadly as the cankerworm.

J. A. FROUDE, *Short Studies: Calvinism.*

14
Error belongs to libraries, truth to the human mind.

GOETHE, *Conversations with Eckermann.*

Truth belongs to the man, error to his age.

GOETHE, *Sprüche in Prosa.*

15
It is much easier to recognize error than to find truth; error is superficial and may be corrected; truth lies hidden in the depths.

GOETHE, *Sprüche in Prosa.*

16
Little by little we subtract
Faith and Fallacy from Fact,
The Illusory from the True,
And starve upon the Residue.

SAMUEL HOFFENSTEIN, *Observation.*

17
Dark Error's other hidden side is truth.

VICTOR HUGO, *La Légende des Siècles.*

18
Irrationally held truths may be more harmful than reasoned errors.

T. H. HUXLEY, *The Coming of Age of the Origin of Species.*

19
An error cannot be believed sincerely enough to make it a truth.

R. G. INGERSOLL, *The Great Infidels.*

20
Error cannot be defended but by error. Untruth cannot be shielded but by untruth.

JOHN JEWEL, *A Defence of the Apology for the Church of England.*

21
Truth does not do so much good in the world, as the appearance of it does evil. (La vérité ne fait pas tant de bien dans le monde que ses apparences y font de mal.)

LA ROCHEFOUCAULD, *Maximes*. No. 64.

22
It is one thing to show a man that he is in error, and another to put him in possession of truth.

JOHN LOCKE, *Essay Concerning Human Understanding*. Bk. iv, ch. 7, sec. 11.

Knowledge being to be had only of visible and certain truth, error is not a fault of our knowledge, but a mistake of our judgement, giving assent to that which is not true.

JOHN LOCKE, *Essay Concerning Human Understanding*. Bk. iv, ch. 20, sec. 1.

1
Nine times out of ten, in the arts as in life, there is actually no truth to be discovered; there is only error to be exposed.
H. L. MENCKEN, *Prejudices*. Ser. iii, p. 93.

2
Truth lies within a little and certain compass, but error is immense.
HENRY ST. JOHN, *Reflections Upon Exile*.

Plain truth will influence half a score men at most in a nation, or an age, while mystery will lead millions by the nose.
HENRY ST. JOHN, *Letter*, 28 July, 1721.

3
Shall Error in the round of time
Still father Truth?
TENNYSON, *Love and Duty*, l. 4.

4
Error is the force that welds men together; truth is communicated to men only by deeds of truth.
LEO TOLSTOY, *My Religion*. Ch. 12.

5
Love truth, but pardon error.
VOLTAIRE, *Discours sur l'Homme*. No. 3.

ETERNITY

For Eternity in the sense of eternal life see Immortality

6
Eternity! thou pleasing, dreadful thought!
Through what variety of untried being,
Through what new scenes and changes must we pass!
The wide, th' unbounded prospect lies before me,
But shadows, clouds, and darkness rest upon it.
ADDISON, *Cato*. Act v, sc. 1, l. 10.

7
For, Oh! eternity's too short
To utter all Thy praise.
ADDISON, *Hymn: When All Thy Mercies*.

Eternity, too short to speak Thy praise!
Or fathom Thy profound of love to man!
YOUNG, *Night Thoughts*. Night iv, l. 592.

8
'Tis time unfolds Eternity.
P. J. BAILEY, *Festus: A Ruined Temple*.

Eternity is in love with the productions of time.
WILLIAM BLAKE, *Proverbs of Hell*.

I saw the starry Tree, Eternity,
Put forth the blossom Time.
ROBERT BUCHANAN, *Proteus*.

9
Who can speak of Eternity without a solecism?
SIR THOMAS BROWNE, *Religio Medici*. Pt. i, sec. 11.

10
But there are wanderers o'er Eternity
Whose bark drives on and on, and anchor'd ne'er shall be.
BYRON, *Childe Harold*. Canto iii, st. 70.

Which makes life itself a lie,
Flattering dust with eternity.
BYRON, *Sardanapalus*. Act i, sc. 2.

11
Eternity! How know we but we stand
On the precipitous and crumbling verge
Of Time e'en now, Eternity below?
ABRAHAM COLES, *Eternity*.

Eternity is not something that begins after you are dead. It is going on all the time. We are in it now.
CHARLOTTE P. GILMAN, *The Forerunner*.

It is eternity now. I am in the midst of it. It is about me in the sunshine; I am in it, as the butterfly in the light-laden air. Nothing has to come; it is now. Now is eternity; now is the immortal life.
RICHARD JEFFERIES, *The Story of My Heart*.
See also PRESENT: THE EVERLASTING NOW.

12
Eternity is not an everlasting flux of time, but time is as a short parenthesis in a long period.
JOHN DONNE, *Devotions*. Meditation 14. (1624)

13
For ever and ever.
New Testament: Galatians, i, 5. (In sæcula sæculorum.—*Vulgate*.)

Yesterday, and to-day, and for-ever.
New Testament: Hebrews, xiii, 8.

Rosalind: Now tell me how long you would have her after you have possessed her.
Orlando: For ever and a day.
SHAKESPEARE, *As You Like It*. Act iv, sc. 1, l. 143.

14
Eternity's another word for change.
GERALD GOULD, *Monogamy*. Pt. ii, st. 5.

15
In the presence of eternity, the mountains are as transient as the clouds.
R. G. INGERSOLL, *The Christian Religion*.

16
Thou, silent form, dost tease us out of thought
As doth eternity: Cold Pastoral!
KEATS, *Ode on a Grecian Urn*. St. 5.

17
To have the sense of the eternal in life is a short flight for the soul. To have had it, is the soul's vitality.
GEORGE MEREDITH, *Diana of the Crossways*. Ch. 1.

18
That Golden Key,
That opes the Palace of Eternity.
MILTON, *Comus*, l. 13.

19
Then shall be shown, that but in name
Time and eternity were both the same;
A point which life nor death could sever,
A moment standing still for ever.
JAMES MONTGOMERY, *Time, A Rhapsody*.

20
Eternity is not, as men believe,

Before and after us an endless line.
JOSEPH JOHN MURPHY, *Eternity*.

What, will the line stretch out to the crack of doom?
SHAKESPEARE, *Macbeth*. Act iv, sc. 1, l. 117.

1

Those spacious regions where our fancies roam,
Pain'd by the past, expecting ills to come,
In some dread moment, by the fates assign'd,
Shall pass away, nor leave a rack behind;
And Time's revolving wheels shall lose at last
The speed that spins the future and the past:
And, sovereign of an undisputed throne,
Awful eternity shall reign alone.
PETRARCH, *The Triumph of Eternity*, l. 102.

2

I am the things that are, and those that are to be, and those that have been. No one ever lifted my skirts: the fruit which I bore was the sun.
PROCLUS, *On Plato's Timæus*. Inscription in the temple of Neith, at Saïs, Egypt.

3

My refuge is eternity. (Éternité deviens mon asile!)
ÉTIENNE PIVERT DE SENANCOUR, author of *Obermann*. The inscription he desired placed on his grave.

If Paris that brief flight allow,
My humble tomb explore;
It bears: "Eternity, be thou
My refuge!" and no more.
MATTHEW ARNOLD, *Obermann Once More*, l. 269.

Gout, hack-work, and Madame Senancour explain the inscription he desired to be placed on his tomb, *Éternité deviens mon asile!* though perhaps his meaning would have been even more clearly conveyed had he borrowed the subtitle of his youthful work, *Éternité, ou le Bonheur dans l'Obscurité*.
HUGH KINGSMILL, *Matthew Arnold*, p. 121.

4

Eternity consists of opposites. (Contrariis rerum æternitas constat.)
SENECA, *Epistulæ ad Lucilium*. Epis. cvii, 8.

5

And make us heirs of all eternity.
SHAKESPEARE, *Love's Labour's Lost*. Act i, sc. 1, l. 7.

I, the heir of all the ages, in the foremost files of time.
TENNYSON, *Locksley Hall*, l. 178.

6

Or sells eternity to get a toy.
SHAKESPEARE, *The Rape of Lucrece*. St. 31.

Eternity for bubbles proves at last
A senseless bargain.
COWPER, *The Task*. Bk. iii, l. 175.

7

The Pilgrim of Eternity, whose fame
Over his living head like Heaven is bent,
An early but enduring monument,
Came, veiling all the lightnings of his song
In sorrow.
SHELLEY, *Adonais*. St. 30. Referring to Byron.

Thetis, bright image of eternity.
SHELLEY, *Prometheus Unbound*. Act iii, sc. 1.

8

Till the sun grows cold,
And the stars are old,
And the leaves of the Judgment Book unfold.
BAYARD TAYLOR, *Bedouin Song*.

9

In time there is no present,
In eternity no future.
In eternity no past.
TENNYSON, *The "How" and the "Why."*

10

And in those weaker glories spy
Some shadows of eternity.
HENRY VAUGHAN, *The Retreat*.

11

Beyond the stars, and all this passing scene,
Where change shall cease, and Time shall be no more.
HENRY KIRKE WHITE, *Time*, l. 726.

12

The clock indicates the moment—but what does eternity indicate?
WALT WHITMAN, *Song of Myself*. Pt. xliv, l. 4.

The sidewalks of Eternity, they are the freckles of Jupiter.
WALT WHITMAN, *Dilation*. (*Uncollected Prose*. Vol. ii, p. 68.)

13

Eternity is written in the skies.
YOUNG, *Night Thoughts*. Night ix, l. 659.

ETHICS, see Right

EUPHEMISM

See also Hanging: Some Euphemisms

14

Those expressions are omitted which can not with propriety be read aloud in the family.
DR. THOMAS BOWDLER, *Preface* to his *Family Shakespeare*, 1818.

No profane hand shall dare, for me, to curtail my Chaucer, to Bowdlerize my Shakespeare, or mutilate my Milton.
UNKNOWN. (*Notes and Queries*. Ser. iv, vi, 41.)

15

This instinct of politeness in speech—euphemism, as it is called—which seeks to hint at an unpleasant or indelicate thing rather than name it directly, has had much to do with making words acquire new meanings and lose old ones.
ROBERT CHAMBERS, *Information for the People*.

It is good to find modest words to express immodest things.
UNKNOWN, *MS. Proverbs*, c. 1645.

16

The Chairman felt it his imperative duty to demand . . . whether he had used the expression . . . in a common sense. Mr. Blot-ton had no hesitation in saying that he had not—he had used the word in its Pickwickian sense.

DICKENS, *Pickwick Papers*. Ch. 1.

In every case it had only a political, perhaps I might say a Pickwickian meaning.

JOSEPH CHAMBERLAIN, *Speech,* at Birmingham, 17 Nov., 1902.

1
In calling a prostitute an "unfortunate" the Victorians wished to imply that a prostitute was someone who had invested in the wrong stock, in spite of the advice of more experienced investors.

HUGH KINGSMILL, *Matthew Arnold,* p. 12.

2
The ancient Athenians used to cover up the ugliness of things with auspicious and kindly terms, giving them polite and endearing names. Thus they called harlots "companions," taxes "contributions," and the prison a "chamber."

PLUTARCH, *Lives: Solon.* Sec. 15.

3
To rest, the cushion and soft dean invite,
Who never mentions hell to ears polite.

POPE, *Moral Essays*. Epis. iv, l. 149.

In the reign of Charles II, a certain worthy divine at Whitehall thus addressed himself to the auditory at the conclusion of his sermon: "In short, if you don't live up to the precepts of the gospel, but abandon yourselves to your irregular appetites, you must expect to receive your reward in a certain place which 'tis not good manners to mention here."

TOM BROWN, *Laconics.*

4
She [my mother] says, I am *too witty;* Anglicè, *too pert;* I, that she is *too wise;* that is to say, being likewise put into English, *not so young as she has been.*

RICHARDSON, *Clarissa.* Vol. ii, letter 13.

5
Marry, then, sweet wag, when thou art king, let not us, that are squires of the night's body, be called thieves of the day's beauty: let us be Diana's foresters, gentlemen of the shade, minions of the moon; and let men say we be men of good government, being governed, as the sea is, by our noble and chaste mistress the moon, under whose countenance we steal.

SHAKESPEARE, *I Henry IV.* Act i, sc. 2, l. 26.

6
If you have reason, be brief; 'tis not the time of the moon with me to make one in so skipping a dialogue.

SHAKESPEARE, *Twelfth Night.* Act i, sc. 5, l. 214.

7
I will but look upon the hedge and follow you.

SHAKESPEARE, *The Winter's Tale.* Act iv, sc. 4, l. 857.

A Shakespearean exit (I go to look upon a hedge).

E. A. ROBERTSON, *Four Frightened People,* p. 101.

The thoughtless wits shall frequent forfeits pay,
Who 'gainst the sentry's box discharge their tea:
Do thou some court or secret corner seek,
Nor flush with shame the passing virgin's cheek.

JOHN GAY, *Trivia.* Bk. ii, l. 297.

8
Life on life downstricken goes, swifter than the wild bird's flight, to the land of the western god. (πρὸς ἑσπέρου θεοῦ.)

SOPHOCLES, *Œdipus Tyrannus,* l. 176. The origin, perhaps of "Going West," a euphemism for dying, particularly in vogue during the World War.

When we say of the martyr St. Stephen that "he fell asleep," instead of "he died," the euphemism partakes of the nature of a metaphor, intimating a resemblance between a sleep and the death of such a person.

JAMES BEATTIE, *Elements of Moral Science.* Sec. 866.

9
I've heard that breeches, petticoats and smock
Give to the modest mind a grievous shock,
And that my brain (so lucky its device,)
Christ'neth them inexpressible, so nice.

JOHN WOLCOT (PETER PINDAR), *A Rowland for an Oliver,* ii, 154.

The knees of the unmentionables . . . soon began to get alarmingly white.

DICKENS, *Sketches by Boz.*

EUROPE

See also Names of European Countries

10
There is not a nation in Europe but labours
To toady itself and to humbug its neighbours.

R. H. BARHAM, *The Auto-da-Fé.* Canto ii, l. 1.

11
Europe is given a prey to sterner fates,
And writhes in shackles; strong the arms that chain
To earth her struggling multitude of states.

BRYANT, *The Ages.* St. 34.

12
Can we never extract the tapeworm of Europe from the brain of our countrymen?

EMERSON, *Conduct of Life: Culture.*

Forget Europe wholly, your veins throb with blood,
To which the dull current in hers is but mud;
Let her sneer, let her say your experiment fails,
In her voice there's a tremble e'en now while she rails. . . .
O my friends, thank your god, if you have one, that he
'Twixt the Old World and you set the gulf of a sea.

J. R. LOWELL, *A Fable for Critics,* l. 1115.

13
In settling an island, the first building erected by a Spaniard will be a church; by a French-

man, a fort; by a Dutchman, a warehouse; and by an Englishman. an alehouse.
GROSE, *Provincial Glossary.* (1790)

1
I will hold New Orleans in spite of Urop and all hell.
ANDREW JACKSON. (1812)

If that doesn't spell Europe, what does it spell?
THEODORE ROOSEVELT. (1906)

2
Man is the only animal which devours his own kind, for I can apply no milder term to the governments of Europe, and the general prey of the rich on the poor.
THOMAS JEFFERSON, *Writings.* Vol. vi, p. 56.

3
Roll up that map; it will not be wanted these ten years.
WILLIAM PITT, after the battle of Austerlitz, referring to the map of Europe. (STANHOPE, *Life of Pitt.* Ch. 43.)

4
Now Europe balanc'd, neither side prevails:
For nothing's left in either of the scales.
POPE, *The Balance of Europe.*

The Balance of Europe.
UNKNOWN. Sub-title of folio publication of 1653, entitled *A German Diet.*

The balance of power.
Phrase used by both Edmund Burke and Sir Robert Walpole in speeches delivered in 1741. Ascribed to the King of Sweden by John Wesley. (*Journal,* 20 Sept., 1790)

An untoward event, threatening to disturb the balance of power.
DUKE OF WELLINGTON, referring to the destruction of the Turkish navy at the battle of Navarino, 20 Oct., 1827.

5
Led by my hand, he saunter'd Europe round.
And gather'd ev'ry vice on Christian ground.
POPE, *The Dunciad.* Bk. iv, l. 311.

6
Europe. which in twenty years' time will be nothing but a mass of French slaves.
SYDNEY SMITH, *Peter Plymley Letters* No. 1.

7
Sharp the concert wrought of discord shrills the tune of shame and death,
Turk by Christian fenced and fostered, Mecca backed by Nazareth:
All the powerless powers tongue-valiant, breathe but greed's or terror's breath.
SWINBURNE, *The Concert of Europe.*

8
Better fifty years of Europe than a cycle of Cathay.
TENNYSON, *Locksley Hall,* l. 184. Tennyson's line is less clever than it appears, if it is true, as has been stated, that a Chinese cycle consists of sixty years.

9
And while she hid all England with a kiss,
Bright over Europe fell her golden hair.
CHARLES TENNYSON TURNER, *Letty's Globe.*

10
Nor red from Europe's old dynastic slaughter-house,
(Area of murder-plots of thrones, with scent left yet of wars and scaffolds everywhere).
WALT WHITMAN, *Song of the Redwood Tree.*

Without so much as pausing to wipe her feet, which are dipped in blood to the ankle, hasn't Europe always been willing to recommence hostilities?
HONORÉ DE BALZAC.

EVE, see Adam

EVENING

See also Day: Its End; Sun: Sunset; Twilight

11
The sunbeams dropped
Their gold, and, passing in porch and niche,
Softened to shadows, silvery, pale, and dim,
As if the very Day paused and grew Eve.
EDWIN ARNOLD, *Light of Asia.* Bk. ii, l. 466.

12
The death-bed of a day, how beautiful!
P. J. BAILEY, *Festus: A Library and Balcony.*

13
At the close of the day, when the hamlet is still,
And mortals the sweets of forgetfulness prove,
When nought but the torrent is heard on the hill,
And nought but the nightingale's song in the grove.
JAMES BEATTIE, *The Hermit,* l. 1.

14
And whiter grows the foam,
The small moon lightens more;
And as I turn me home,
My shadow walks before.
ROBERT BRIDGES, *The Clouds Have Left the Sky.*

15
To me at least was never ev ning yet
But seemed far beautifuller than its day.
ROBERT BROWNING, *The Ring and the Book: Pompilia,* l. 357.

16
Hath not thy heart within thee burned
At evening's calm and holy hour?
S. G. BULFINCH, *Meditation.*

17
It is the hour when from the boughs
The nightingale's high note is heard;
It is the hour when lovers' vows
Seem sweet in every whispered word;
And gentle winds and waters near,
Make music to the lonely ear.
BYRON, *Parisina.* St. 1.

18
When the Gloaming is, I never made the ghost of an endeavour

To discover—but whatever were the hour, it would be sweet.
C. S. CALVERLEY, *In the Gloaming.*

1
So let us welcome peaceful evening in.
COWPER, *The Task.* Bk. iii, l. 41.

2
Oh how grandly cometh Even,
Sitting on the mountain summit,
Purple-vestured, grave, and silent,
Watching o'er the dewy valleys,
Like a good king near his end.
DINAH M. M. CRAIK, *A Stream's Singing.*

3
When day is done, and clouds are low,
And flowers are honey-dew,
And Hesper's lamp begins to glow
Along the western blue;
And homeward wing the turtle-doves,
Then comes the hour the poet loves.
GEORGE CROLY, *The Poet's Hour.*

4
Now was the hour that wakens fond desire
In men at sea, and melts their thoughtful hearts, . . .
And pilgrim, newly on his road, with love
Thrills if he hear the vesper bell from far
That seems to mourn for the expiring day.
DANTE, *Purgatorio.* Canto viii, l. 1. (Cary, tr.)

5
Welcome sweet night! the evening crowns the day.
JOHN FORD, *'Tis Pity She's a Whore.* Act ii, 6.

Though the cares of the day be many,
And the fruits of the struggle few,
I know at the close comes evening—
Evening, my love, and you.
W. R. ANDERSON, *Evening and You.*

6
Now fades the glimmering landscape on the sight,
And all the air a solemn stillness holds.
THOMAS GRAY, *Elegy Written in a Country Church-yard,* l. 5.

And hie him home, at evening's close,
To sweet repast and calm repose.
THOMAS GRAY, *Ode on the Pleasure Arising from Vicissitude,* l. 87. Said to have been added by Gray's biographer and editor, Rev. William Mason.

7
Day, like a weary pilgrim, had reached the western gate of heaven, and Evening stooped down to unloose the latchets of his sandal shoon.
LONGFELLOW, *Hyperion.* Bk. iv, ch. 5.

8
When the gray-hooded Ev'n,
Like a sad votarist in palmer's weed,
Rose from the hindmost wheel of Phœbus' wain.
MILTON, *Comus,* l. 188.

9
Now came still evening on, and twilight gray
Had in her sober livery all things clad;
Silence accompany'd; for beast and bird,
They to their grassy couch, these to their nests,
Were slunk, all but the wakeful nightingale;
She all night long her amorous descant sung;
Silence was pleas'd: now glow'd the firmament
With living sapphires; Hesperus, that led
The starry host, rode brightest, till the moon,
Rising in clouded majesty, at length
Apparent queen unveil'd her peerless light,
And o'er the dark her silver mantle threw.
MILTON, *Paradise Lost.* Bk. iv, l. 598.

Sweet the coming on Of grateful evening mild.
MILTON, *Paradise Lost.* Bk. iv, l. 646.

Just then return'd at shut of evening flowers.
MILTON, *Paradise Lost.* Bk. ix, l. 278.

10
Adown the golden sunset way
The evening comes in wimple gray.
L. M. MONTGOMERY, *A Summer Day.*

11
Fly not yet, 'tis just the hour
When pleasure, like the midnight flower
That scorns the eye of vulgar light,
Begins to bloom for sons of night,
And maids who love the moon.
THOMAS MOORE, *Fly Not Yet.*

12
One by one the flowers close,
Lily and dewy rose
Shutting their tender petals from the moon.
CHRISTINA ROSSETTI, *Twilight Calm.*

13
The hills grow dark,
On purple peaks a deeper shade descending.
SCOTT, *The Lady of the Lake: Conclusion.*

14
The pale child, Eve, leading her mother, Night.
ALEXANDER SMITH, *A Life Drama.* Sc. 8.

15
I was heavy with the even,
When she lit her glimmering tapers
Round the day's dead sanctities.
FRANCIS THOMPSON, *Hound of Heaven,* l. 84.

16
The summer skies are darkly blue,
The days are still and bright,
And Evening trails her robes of gold
Through the dim halls of Night.
SARAH H. P. WHITMAN, *Summer's Call.*

17
It is a beauteous evening, calm and free;
The holy time is quiet as a Nun
Breathless with adoration.
WORDSWORTH, *It Is a Beauteous Evening.*

As pensive evening deepens into night.
WORDSWORTH, *To ——.*

EVIDENCE, see Proof

EVIL

See also Goodness: Good and Evil

1
Thou art in the gall of bitterness, and in the bond of iniquity.
New Testament: Acts, viii, 23.

2
As long as the evil deed does not bear fruit, the fool thinks it like honey; but when it ripens, then the fool suffers grief.
SUBHADRA BHIKSHU, *A Buddhist Catechism.*

3
Often the fear of one evil leads one into a worse. (Souvent la peur d'un mal nous conduit dans un pire.)
BOILEAU, *L'Art Poétique.* Canto i, l. 64.

4
I have wrought great use out of evil tools.
BULWER-LYTTON, *Richelieu.* Act iii, sc. 1, l. 49.

5
The counsels of pusillanimity very rarely put off, whilst they are always sure to aggravate, the evils from which they would fly.
EDMUND BURKE, *Letters on the Regicide Peace.* No. 1.

Evil, once manfully fronted, ceases to be evil.
CARLYLE, *Chartism.* Ch. 10.

6
The authors of great evils know best how to remove them.
CATO THE YOUNGER, when advising the Senate to place all power in Pompey's hands. (PLUTARCH, *Lives: Cato.* Ch. 47, sec. 3.)

7
Welcome, evil, if thou comest alone. (Bien vengas Mal, si vienes solo.)
CERVANTES, *Don Quixote.* Pt. ii, ch. 55.
See also MISFORTUNE: MISFORTUNES NEVER COME SINGLY.

8
Evil shall have that evil well deserves.
CHAUCER, *The Prioresses Tale,* l. 180.

9
In full, fair tide let information flow;
That evil is half-cured whose cause we know.
CHARLES CHURCHILL, *Gotham.* Bk. iii, l. 651.

10
Every evil in the bud is easily crushed; as it grows older, it becomes stronger. (Omne malum nascens facile opprimitur; inveteratum fit pleurumque robustius.)
CICERO, *Philippicæ.* No. v, sec. 11.

The resolution to avoid an evil is seldom framed till the evil is so far advanced as to make avoidance impossible.
THOMAS HARDY, *Far from the Madding Crowd.* Ch. 18.

11
All evils are equal when they are extreme.
CORNEILLE, *Horace.* Act iii, sc. 4.

12
The more of kindly strength is in the soil,
So much doth evil seed and lack of culture
Mar it the more, and make it run to wildness.
DANTE, *Purgatorio.* Canto xxxvi, l. 119. (Cary, tr.)

13
None but the base in baseness do delight.
MICHAEL DRAYTON, *Legend of Robert Duke of Normandy.*

14
I am overcome of evil. (Ἀλλὰ νικῶμαι κακοῖς.)
EURIPIDES, *Medea,* l. 1077.

15
Don't let us make imaginary evils, when you know we have so many real ones to encounter.
GOLDSMITH, *The Good-Natured Man.* Act i, 1.

16
Ah me! we believe in evil,
Where once we believed in good;
The world, the flesh, and the devil
Are easily understood.
ADAM LINDSAY GORDON, *Wormwood and Nightshade.* St. 8.

17
Evil no nature hath; the loss of good
Is that which gives to sin a livelihood.
ROBERT HERRICK, *Evil.*

18
Evil is here in the world, not because God wants it or uses it here, but because he knows not how at the moment to remove it. . . . Evil, therefore, is a fact not to be explained away, but to be accepted; and accepted not to be endured, but to be conquered. It is a challenge neither to our reason nor to our patience, but to our courage.
JOHN HAYNES HOLMES. (NEWTON, *My Idea of God,* p. 119.)

19
The melancholy joys of evils pass'd.
HOMER, *Odyssey.* Bk. xv, l. 435. (Pope, tr.)

20
Evil is wrought by want of Thought
As well as want of Heart.
THOMAS HOOD, *The Lady's Dream,* l. 95.

21
What does it avail you from many thorns to pluck out one? (Quid te exempta juvat spinis de pluribus una?)
HORACE, *Epistles.* Bk. ii, epis. 2, l. 212.

22
Their feet run to evil.
Old Testament: Isaiah, lix, 7.

23
Evils must be cured by their contraries.
JOHN JEWEL, *A Defence of the Apology for the Church of England.*

24
Every one that doeth evil hateth the light.
New Testament: John, iii, 20.

25
No one becomes at once completely vile (Nemo repente fuit turpissimus.)
JUVENAL, *Satires.* Sat. ii, l. 83.

26
No evil man is happy. (Nemo malus felix.)
JUVENAL, *Satires.* Sat. iv, l. 8.

Multitudes think they like to do evil; yet no

man really enjoyed doing evil since God made the world.
RUSKIN, *Stones of Venice*. Vol. i, ch. 2.

1
Earth now maintains none but evil men and cowards. (Terra malos homines nunc educat atque pusillos.)
JUVENAL, *Satires*. Sat. xv, l. 70.

2
We believe no evil till the evil's done. (Nous ne croyons le mal que quand il est venu.)
LA FONTAINE, *Fables*. Bk. i, fab. 8.

3
Evil is fittest to consort with evil. (Fere fit malum malo aptissimum.)
LIVY, *History*. Bk. i, ch. 46.

EVIL COMMUNICATIONS, *see under* COMPANIONS.

4
The best known evil is the most tolerable. (Notissimum quodque malum maxime tolerabile.)
LIVY, *History*. Bk. xxiii, sec. 3.

5
Evil springs up, and flowers, and bears no seed,
And feeds the green earth with its swift decay,
Leaving it richer for the growth of truth.
J. R. LOWELL, *Prometheus*, l. 263.

6
Sufficient unto the day is the evil thereof.
New Testament: Matthew, vi, 34.

7
Evil on itself shall back recoil.
MILTON, *Comus*, l. 593.

8
Evil into the mind of God or man
May come and go, so unapprov'd, and leave
No spot or blame behind.
MILTON, *Paradise Lost*. Bk. v, l. 117.

We are no more responsible for the evil thoughts that pass through our minds than a scarecrow for the birds which fly over the seedplot he has to guard. The sole responsibility in each case is to prevent them from settling.
CHURTON COLLINS, *Maxims and Reflections*.

9
If evils come not, then our fears are vain;
And if they do, fear but augments the pain.
SIR THOMAS MORE, *On Fear*; FRANKLIN, *Poor Richard*, 1741. *See also under* TROUBLE.

10
No evil is great which is the last. (Nullum magnum malum quod extremum est.)
CORNELIUS NEPOS, *De Viris Illustribus*.

No evil is great which is the last evil of all. (Nullum malum est magnum, quod extremum est.)
SENECA, *Epistulæ ad Lucilium*. Epis. iv, sec. 3.

11
Evil is easy and has infinite forms.
PASCAL, *Pensées*. Sec. vi, No. 408.

12
Submit to the present evil, lest a greater one befall you.
PHÆDRUS, *Fables*. Bk. i, fab. 2, l. 31.

Keep what you have got; the known evil is best. (Habeas ut nactus: nota mala res optima est.)
PLAUTUS, *Trinummus*. Act i, sc. 2.

The oldest and best known evil was ever more supportable than one that was new and untried
MONTAIGNE, *Essays*. Bk. iii, ch. 9.

And makes us rather bear the ills we have
Than fly to others that we know not of.
SHAKESPEARE, *Hamlet*. Act iii, sc. 1, l. 81.

13
Out of many evils the evil which is least is the least of evils. (E malis multis, malum, quod minimum est, id minimum est malum.)
PLAUTUS, *Stichus*. Act i, sc. 2.

OF TWO EVILS CHOOSE THE LEAST, *see under* CHOICE.

14
He who is bent on doing evil can never want occasion. (Male facere qui vult, numquam non causam invenit.)
PUBLILIUS SYRUS, *Sententiæ*. No. 459.

15
When evil is advantageous, he errs who does rightly. (Cum vita prosunt, peccat qui recte facit.)
PUBLILIUS SYRUS, *Sententiæ*. No. 110.

16
It is good to see in another's evil the things that we should flee from. (Bonum est fugienda aspicere in alieno malo.)
PUBLILIUS SYRUS, *Sententiæ*. No. 57.

17
Of evil grain no good seed can come.
JOHN RAY, *English Proverbs*, 8. (1670)

Of evil life cometh evil ending.
UNKNOWN, *King Alisaunder*, l. 754. (c. 1300)

18
Recompense to no man evil for evil.
New Testament: Romans, xii, 17.

19
Evil often triumphs, but never conquers.
JOSEPH ROUX, *Meditations of a Parish Priest*. Pt. v, No. 45.

20
There is no evil in the world without a remedy. (Al mondo mal non e senza rimedio.)
JACOPO SANNAZARO, *Ecloga Octava*.

For every evil under the sun,
There is a remedy, or there is none;
If there be one, try and find it,
If there be none, never mind it.
W. C. HAZLITT, *English Proverbs*, 135. Apparently an adaptation of the Spanish proverb: Si hay remedio porqui te apuras? Si no hay remedio porqui te apuras?

What's amiss I'll strive to mend,
And endure what can't be mended.
ISAAC WATTS, *Good Fellowship*.

21
For by excess of evil, evil dies.
GEORGE SANTAYANA, *Sorrow*.

22
There is no evil that does not offer inducements. Avarice promises money; luxury, a varied assortment of pleasures; ambition, a

purple robe and applause. Vices tempt you by the rewards which they offer.
SENECA, *Epistulæ ad Lucilium*. Epis. lxix, 4.

No time is too brief for the wicked to accomplish evil. (Nullum ad nocendum tempus angustum est malis.)
SENECA, *Medea*, l. 292.

1
Desperate evils generally make men calm. (Solent suprema facere securos mala.)
SENECA, *Œdipus*, l. 386.

2
Thou art as opposite to every good,
As the Antipodes are unto us,
Or as the south to the septentrion.
SHAKESPEARE, *III Henry VI*. Act i, sc. 4, l. 134.

3
Evils that take leave,
On their departure most of all show evil.
SHAKESPEARE, *King John*. Act iii, sc. 4, l. 114.

4
All spirits are enslaved which serve things evil.
SHELLEY, *Prometheus Unbound*. Act ii, sc. 4.

5
Man creates the evil he endures.
SOUTHEY, *Inscriptions*. No. 2, last line.

Evil has an appetite for falsity, and eagerly seizes upon it as truth.
SWEDENBORG, *Arcana Cœlesta*. Sec. 10648.

6
One evil rises out of another. (Aliud ex alio malum.)
TERENCE, *Eunuchus*, l. 987. (Act v, sc. 5.)

The curse of an evil deed is that it must always continue to engender evil.
SCHILLER, *Piccolomini*. Act v, sc. 1.

Blood will have blood, revenge beget revenge,
Evil must come of evil.
SOUTHEY, *Madoc in Wales*. Pt. i, sec. 7, l. 45.

7
Evil, like a rolling stone upon a mountain-top,
A child may first impel, a giant cannot stop.
RICHARD CHENEVIX TRENCH, *Evil*.

8
Evil to him who thinks evil. (Honi soit qui mal y pense.)
The motto of the Order of the Garter, originated by Edward III in 1349. He was in warm rivalry with Philip of France, and Sir Walter Scott (*Essay on Chivalry*) says that the motto seems to apply to possible misrepresentations which the King of France might seek to make concerning the order. The garter was probably selected as the badge of the order, because Edward had given his own as a signal of battle at Crecy. There is no historical authority for the tradition that the king picked up the garter of the Countess of Salisbury at a ball, and founded the order with it as a badge, and the French proverb as a motto. (HUME, *History of England*. Ch. 10.)

To who thinks evil, evil befalls him.
TORRIANO, *Piazza Universale*, 200. (1666)

"I like the Garter," said Lord Melbourne, "there is no damned merit in it."
AXEL MUNTHE, *Story of San Michele*, p. 409.

A man's star is not complete without a woman's garter.
BERNARD SHAW, *The Man of Destiny*, p. 214.

EVOLUTION

9
Men were first produced in fishes, and when they were grown and able to help themselves, were thrown up, and so lived upon the land.
ANAXIMANDER. (PLUTARCH, *Symposiacs*. Bk. viii, sec. 8.)

10
Therefore I summon age
To grant youth's heritage,
Life's struggle having so far reached its term:
Thence shall I pass, approved
A man, for aye removed
From the developed brute; a God though in the germ.
ROBERT BROWNING, *Rabbi Ben Ezra*. St. 13.

11
Still wond'ring how the Marvel came because two coupling mammals chose
To slake the thirst of fleshly love, and thus the "Immortal Being" rose.
SIR RICHARD BURTON, *Kasîdah*. Pt. iii, st. 3.

12
A fire-mist and a planet,
A crystal and a cell,
A jellyfish and a saurian,
And caves where the cavemen dwell;
Then a sense of law and beauty,
And a face turned from the clod—
Some call it Evolution,
And others call it God.
W. H. CARRUTH, *Each in His Own Tongue*.

13
The evolutionists seem to know everything about the missing link except the fact that it is missing.
G. K. CHESTERTON, *Evolution*.

14
There was an Ape in the days that were earlier;
Centuries passed and his hair became curlier;
Centuries more gave a thumb to his wrist,—
Then he was Man,—and a Positivist.
MORTIMER COLLINS, *The British Birds*. St. 5.

Cried this pretentious Ape one day,
"I'm going to be a Man!
And stand upright, and hunt, and fight,
And conquer all I can."
CHARLOTTE PERKINS GILMAN, *Similar Cases*.

15
The waves came shining up the sands,
As here today they shine;
And in my pre-pelasgian hands
The sand was warm and fine.
FRANCES CORNFORD, *Preëxistence*.

1
I have called this principle, by which each slight variation, if useful, is preserved, by the term of Natural Selection.
CHARLES DARWIN, *The Origin of Species*. Ch. 3.

The struggle for existence.
CHARLES DARWIN, *The Origin of Species*. Ch. 3.

2
The question is this: Is man an ape or an angel? I, my lord, am on the side of the angels.
BENJAMIN DISRAELI, *Speech*, at Oxford Diocesan Conference, 1864.

I have no patience with these gorilla damnifications of humanity.
THOMAS CARLYLE, referring to Darwinism.

3
How far off yet is the trilobite! how far the quadruped! how inconceivably remote is man! All duly arrive, and then race after race of men. It is a long way from granite to the oyster; farther yet to Plato and the preaching of the immortality of the soul.
EMERSON, *Essays, Second Series: Nature*.

Each animal or vegetable form remembers the next inferior and predicts the next higher.
EMERSON, *Poetry and Imagination*.

4
A subtle chain of countless rings
The next unto the farthest brings:
The eye reads omens where it goes,
And speaks all languages the rose;
And, striving to be Man, the worm
Mounts through all the spires of form.
EMERSON, *May-Day*.

5
Recall from Time's abysmal chasm
That piece of primal protoplasm
The First Amœba, strangely splendid,
From whom we're all of us descended.
ARTHUR GUITERMAN, *Ode to the Amœba*.

6
A mighty stream of tendency.
HAZLITT, *Essay: Why Distant Objects Please*. Used also by Matthew Arnold and Emerson.

And hear the mighty stream of tendency
Uttering, for elevation of our thought,
A clear sonorous voice, inaudible
To the vast multitude.
WORDSWORTH, *The Excursion*. Bk. ix, l. 87.

7
Children, behold the Chimpanzee;
He sits on the ancestral tree
From which we sprang in ages gone.
I'm glad we sprang: had we held on,
We might, for aught that I can say,
Be horrid Chimpanzees to-day.
OLIVER HERFORD, *The Chimpanzee*.

8
Arrested development.
JOHN HUNTER. (*See* EMERSON, *Journal*, 1868.)

9
We seem to exist in a hazardous time,
Driftin' along here through space;
Nobody knows just when we begun,
Or how fur we've gone in the race.
BEN KING, *Evolution*.

10
We are very slightly changed
From the semi-apes who ranged
India's prehistoric clay;
Whoso drew the longest bow
Ran his brother down, you know,
As we run men down to-day.
RUDYARD KIPLING, *A General Summary*.

11
From what flat wastes of cosmic slime,
And stung by what quick fire,
Sunward the restless races climb!—
Men risen out of mire!
DON MARQUIS, *Unrest*.

12
Man's nourishment, by gradual scale sublim'd,
To vital spirits aspire, to animal,
To intellectual; give both life and sense,
Fancy and understanding; whence the soul
Reason receives.
MILTON, *Paradise Lost*. Bk. v, l. 483.

13
Evolution is not a force but a process; not a cause but a law.
JOHN MORLEY, *On Compromise*.

14
Pouter, tumbler and fantail are from the same source;
The racer and hack may be traced to one horse;
So men were developed from monkeys of course,
Which nobody can deny.
LORD CHARLES NEAVES, *The Origin of Species*.

15
A man sat on a rock and sought
Refreshment from his thumb;
A dinotherium wandered by
And scared him some.
His name was Smith. The kind of rock
He sat upon was shale.
One feature quite distinguished him:
He had a tail.
DANIEL LAW PROUDFIT, *Prehistoric Smith*.

Nature abhors imperfect work
And on it lays her ban;
And all creation must despise
A tailless man.
DANIEL LAW PROUDFIT, *Prehistoric Smith*.

16
When you were a tadpole and I was a fish,
In the Paleozoic time,
And side by side on the ebbing tide,
We sprawled through the ooze and slime, . . .
My heart was rife with the joy of life,
For I loved you even then.
LANGDON SMITH, *Evolution*.

17
I am proud of those bright-eyed, furry, four-

footed or feathered progenitors, and not at all ashamed of my cousins, the Tigers and Apes and Peacocks.

LOGAN PEARSALL SMITH, *Trivia: Desires.*

1
If a single cell, under appropriate conditions, becomes a man in the space of a few years, there can surely be no difficulty in understanding how, under appropriate conditions, a cell may, in the course of untold millions of years, give origin to the human race.

HERBERT SPENCER, *Principles of Biology.* Pt. iii, ch. 3, sec. 118.

As nine months go to the shaping an infant ripe for his birth,
So many a million of ages have gone to the making of man.

TENNYSON, *Maud,* l. 135.

2
This survival of the fittest, which I have here sought to express in mechanical terms, is that which Mr. Darwin has called "natural selection, or the preservation of favoured races in the struggle for life."

HERBERT SPENCER, *Principles of Biology.* Pt. iii, ch. 12, sec. 165.

The expression often used by Mr. Herbert Spencer of the Survival of the Fittest is more accurate, and is sometimes equally convenient.

CHARLES DARWIN, *Origin of Species.* Ch. 3.

"The unfit die—the fit both live and thrive."
Alas, who say so? They who do survive.

SARAH N. CLEGHORN, *The Survival of the Fittest.*

This is the law of the Yukon, that only the Strong shall thrive;
That surely the Weak shall perish, and only the Fit survive.
Dissolute, damned and despairful, crippled and palsied and slain,
This is the Will of the Yukon,—Lo, how she makes it plain!

ROBERT W. SERVICE, *The Law of the Yukon.*

3
Out of the dusk a shadow,
Then, a spark;
Out of the cloud a silence,
Then, a lark;
Out of the heart a rapture,
Then, a pain;
Out of the dead, cold ashes,
Life again.

JOHN BANISTER TABB, *Evolution.*

4
The Lord let the house of a brute to the soul of a man,
And the man said, "Am I your debtor?"
And the Lord—"Not yet: but make it as clean as you can,
And then I will let you a better."

TENNYSON, *By an Evolutionist.*

Is there evil but on earth? or pain in every peopled sphere?
Well, be grateful for the sounding watchword "Evolution" here,
Evolution ever climbing after some ideal good,
And Reversion ever dragging Evolution in the mud.

TENNYSON, *Locksley Hall Sixty Years After,* l. 198.

5
The rise of every man he loved to trace,
Up to the very pod O!
And, in baboons, our parent race
Was found by old Monboddo.
Their A, B, C, he made them speak,
And learn their qui, quæ, quod, O!
Till Hebrew, Latin, Welsh, and Greek
They knew as well's Monboddo!

UNKNOWN, *Monboddo.* Published originally in *Blackwood's Magazine.* James Burnett, Lord Monboddo, was the person referred to.

EXAMPLE

I—Example: Apothegms

6
Every life is a profession of faith, and exercises an inevitable and silent propaganda.

AMIEL, *Journal,* 2 May, 1852.

7
Example is the school of mankind, and they will learn at no other.

EDMUND BURKE, *On a Regicide Peace.*

8
Why doth one man's yawning make another yawn?

ROBERT BURTON, *Anatomy of Melancholy.* Pt. i, sec. 2, mem. 3, subs. 2.

9
So our lives
In acts exemplary, not only win
Ourselves good names, but doth to others give
Matter for virtuous deeds, by which we live.

GEORGE CHAPMAN, *Bussy d'Ambois.* Act i, sc. 1.

10
They do more harm by their evil example than by their actual sin. (Plus exemplo quam peccato nocent.)

CICERO, *De Legibus.* Bk. iii, sec. 14. Cicero is speaking of rulers.

The people are fashioned by the example of their kings, and edicts are of less power than the life of the ruler. (Componitur orbis Regis ad exemplum, nec sic inflectere sensus Humanos edicta valent quam vita regentis.)

CLAUDIAN, *Panegyricus de Quarto Consulatu Honorii Augusti,* l. 299.

Examples lead us, and we likely see
Such as the prince is, will his people be.

ROBERT HERRICK, *Hesperides.* No. 761.

Princes that would their people should do well
Must at themselves begin, as at the head;
For men, by their example, pattern out
Their imitations, and regard of laws.

BEN JONSON, *Cynthia's Revels.* Act v, sc. 3.

1
What is shown by example, men think they may justly do. (Quod exemplo fit, id etiam jure fieri putant.)
CICERO, *Epistolæ ad Atticum* Bk. iv, epis. 3.

Nor knowest thou what argument
Thy life to thy neighbor's creed has lent.
EMERSON, *Each and All.*

2
How soon are those streets made clean, where every one sweeps against his own door.
THOMAS FULLER, *Pisgah Sight.* Bk. iii, ch. 1.

3
Since truth and constancy are vain,
Since neither love, nor sense of pain,
Nor force of reason, can persuade,
Then let example be obey'd.
GEORGE GRANVILLE, *To Myra.*

4
Example is the greatest of all the seducers. (L'exemple est le plus grand de tous les séducteurs.)
COLLIN D'HARLEVILLE, *Mœurs du Jour.* Bk. ii, 5.

5
For each man to be a standard to himself is most excellent for the good, but for the bad it is the worst of all things.
HOMER. (*Contest of Hesiod and Homer.* Sec. 320.)

6
The tender mind is oft deterred from vice by another's shame. (Teneros animos aliena opprobria sæpe Absterrent vitiis.)
HORACE, *Satires.* Bk. i, sat. 4, l. 128. *See also under* EXPERIENCE.

7
I have ever deemed it more honorable and more profitable, too, to set a good example than to follow a bad one.
THOMAS JEFFERSON, *Writings.* Vol. xiv, p. 222.

8
The salutary influence of example.
SAMUEL JOHNSON, *Lives of the Poets: Milton.*

9
I do not give you to posterity as a pattern to imitate, but as an example to deter.
JUNIUS, *Letters.* No. 12.

10
So nature ordains: evil examples in the household corrupt us more readily and promptly, since they insinuate themselves into our minds with the force of authority. (Sic natura jubet: velocius et citius nos Corrumpunt vitiorum exempla domestica, magnis cum subeant animos auctoribus.)
JUVENAL, *Satires.* Sat. xiv, l. 31.

11
Example is a dangerous lure:
Where the wasp got through the gnat sticks sure.
(L'exemple est un dangereux luerre:
Où la guêpe a passé, le moucheron demeure.)
LA FONTAINE, *Fables.* Bk. ii, fab. 16.

12
So, when a great man dies,
For years beyond our ken,
The light he leaves behind him lies
Upon the paths of men.
LONGFELLOW, *Charles Sumner.*

13
Lives of great men all remind us
We can make our lives sublime,
And, departing, leave behind us
Footprints on the sands of time.
LONGFELLOW, *A Psalm of Life.* (1838)

We should endeavor to do something so that we may say that we have not lived in vain, that we may leave some impress of ourselves on the sands of time.
NAPOLEON BONAPARTE, *Letter,* to his Minister of the Interior. (This alleged letter was published 1 Feb., 1868.)

Everything passes and vanishes;
Everything leaves its trace;
And often you see in a footstep
What you could not see in a face.
WILLIAM ALLINGHAM, *Blackberries.*

14
Let your light so shine before men, that they may see your good works, and glorify your Father which is in heaven.
New Testament: Matthew, v, 16.

15
I am myself tormented, see! by the fear of my own example. (Exemplique metu torqueor, ecce, mei.)
OVID, *Amores.* Bk. i, eleg. 4, l. 45.

Every one is bound to bear patiently the results of his own example. (Sua quisque exempla debet æquo animo pati.)
PHÆDRUS, *Fables.* Bk. i, fab. 26, l. 12.

16
Example does the whole. Whoever is foremost
Still leads the herd.
SCHILLER, *Wallenstein.* Act i, sc. 4.

17
Heaven doth with us as we with torches do,
Not light them for themselves; for if our virtues
Did not go forth of us, 'twere all alike
As if we had them not.
SHAKESPEARE, *Measure for Measure.* Act i, sc. 1, l. 33.

18
I bid him look into the lives of all men, as into a mirror, and to take example to himself from others. (Inspicere tanquam in speculum, in vitas omnium Jubeo; atque ex aliis sumere exemplum sibi.)
TERENCE, *Adelphi,* l. 415. (Act iii, sc. 3.)

19
I tread in the footsteps of illustrious men . . . in receiving from the people the sacred trust confided to my illustrious predecessor.
MARTIN VAN BUREN, *Inaugural Address.* 4 March, 1837, referring to Andrew Jackson.

Illustrious predecessor.
EDMUND BURKE, *Thoughts on the Cause of the Present Discontents.* Vol. i, p. 456.

Illustrious predecessors.
HENRY FIELDING, *Covent Garden Journal*, 11 Jan., 1752.

1
Example is a lesson that all men can read.
GILBERT WEST, *Education*. Canto i, st. 81.

II—Example and Precept

See also Preaching and Practice; Words and Deeds

2
Words but direct, example must allure.
SIR WILLIAM ALEXANDER, *Doomsday: The Ninth Hour*. St. 113.

Precepts may lead but examples draw.
H. G. BOHN, *Hand-Book of Proverbs*, p. 475.

3
One example is more valuable . . . than twenty precepts written in books.
ROGER ASCHAM, *The Scholemaster*, 61. (1570)

4
This noble example to his sheep he gave,
That first he wrought, and afterward he taught.
Out of the gospel he the wordes caught;
And this figure he added eke thereto,
That if gold rust, what shall iron do?
For if a priest be foul, on whom we trust,
No wonder is a lewd man to rust.
CHAUCER, *Canterbury Tales: Prologue*, l. 496.

But Cristes lore, and his Apostles twelve,
He taught, but first he followed it himselve.
CHAUCER, *Canterbury Tales: Prologue*, l. 527.

5
Himself a wand'rer from the narrow way,
His silly sheep, what wonder if they stray?
COWPER, *The Progress of Error*, l. 118.

6
Examples work more forcibly on the mind than precepts.
FIELDING, *Joseph Andrews*. Bk. i, ch. 1.

Example is always more efficacious than precept.
SAMUEL JOHNSON, *Rasselas*. Ch. 30.

Example prevails more than precept.
FRANCIS OSBORNE, *Advice to His Son*, 34. (1656)

7
Content to follow when we lead the way.
HOMER, *Iliad*. Bk. x, l. 141. (Pope, tr.)

Allur'd to brighter worlds, and led the way.
GOLDSMITH, *The Deserted Village*, l. 170.

8
Precept begins, example accomplishes. (Précepte commence, exemple achève.)
UNKNOWN. A French proverb.

9
The path of precept is long, that of example short and effectual. (Longum iter est per præcepta, breve et efficax per exempla.)
SENECA, *Epistulæ ad Lucilium*. Epis. vi, sec. 5.

10
For what his wisdom planned, and power enforced,
More potent still his great example showed.
THOMSON, *The Seasons: Winter*, l. 986.

EXCELLENCE

11
There has nothing been more without a definition than Excellency: although it be what we are most concerned with: yea, we are concerned with nothing else.
JONATHAN EDWARDS, *Works*. Vol. i, p. 693.

12
I assure you I had rather excel others in the knowledge of what is excellent, than in the extent of my power and dominion.
ALEXANDER THE GREAT. (PLUTARCH, *Lives: Alexander*.)

13
Excellence is the perfect excuse. Dot it well, and it matters little what.
R. W. EMERSON, *Journal*, 1862.

Everyone has more to hide than he has to show, or is lamed by his excellence.
EMERSON, *Society and Solitude: Works and Days*.

14
Consider first, that great
Or bright infers not excellence.
MILTON, *Paradise Lost*. Bk. viii, l. 90.

15
It takes a long time to bring excellence to maturity.
PUBLILIUS SYRUS, *Sententiæ*. No. 780.

16
It is the witness still of excellency
To put a strange face on his own perfection.
SHAKESPEARE, *Much Ado About Nothing*. Act ii, sc. 3, l. 48.

Still constant in a wondrous excellence.
SHAKESPEARE, *Sonnets*. No. cv.

EXCESS, see Moderation

EXCUSE

17
A pretty hypothesis which explains many things. (Jolie hypothèse elle explique tant de choses.)
HERBERT ASQUITH, *Speech*, House of Commons, 29 March, 1917. Quoting "a witty Frenchman."

I do loathe explanations.
J. M. BARRIE, *My Lady Nicotine*. Ch. 16.

I wish he would explain his explanation.
BYRON, *Don Juan:* Canto i, *Dedication*, l. 16.

Explanations explanatory of things explained.
ABRAHAM LINCOLN, referring to Stephen A. Douglas, *Lincoln-Douglas Debates*.

18
How easy a thing it is to find a staff if a man be minded to beat a dog.
THOMAS BECON, *Early Works: Preface*. (1563)

19
Better a bad excuse, tLan none at all.
WILLIAM CAMDEN, *Remains*, p. 293. (1605)

20
Never make a defence or apology before you be accused.
CHARLES I, *Letter to Lord Wentworth*.

1
Apologies only account for that which they do not alter.
BENJAMIN DISRAELI, *Speech*, 28 July, 1871.

2
Stoop not then to poor excuse;
Turn on the accuser roundly; say,
"Here am I, here will I abide
Forever to myself soothfast;
Go thou, sweet Heaven, or at thy pleasure stay!"
Already Heaven with thee its lot has cast.
EMERSON, *Sursum Corda*.

Let us never bow and apologize more.
EMERSON, *Essays, First Series: Self-Reliance*.

Don't make excuses—make good.
ELBERT HUBBARD, *Epigrams*.

3
Accusing the times is but excusing ourselves.
THOMAS FULLER, *Gnomologia*. No. 759.

4
For years I've longed for some
Excuse for this revulsion.
W. S. GILBERT, *The Rival Curates*.

5
No 'polligy ain't gwine ter make h'ar come back whar de biling water hit.
JOEL CHANDLER HARRIS, *Nights with Uncle Remus*. Ch. 45.

6
Apologizing—a very desperate habit—one that is rarely cured. Apology is only egotism wrong side out.
O. W. HOLMES, *The Professor at the Breakfast-Table*. Ch. 6.

7
I find excuses for myself. (Egomet mi ignosco.)
HORACE, *Satires*. Bk. i, sat. 3, l. 23.

How pitiable is he who cannot excuse himself! (Quam miser est qui excusare sibi se non potest.)
PUBLILIUS SYRUS, *Sententiæ*. No. 605.

8
He who excuses himself accuses himself. (Qui s'excuse, s'accuse.)
GABRIEL MEURIER, *Trésor des Sentences*, p. 63, note. (c. 1590)

When you would excuse, you are accusing. (Dum excusare velis, accusas.)
ST. JEROME, *Epistles*. No. 4.

Excuses are no better than accusations.
MONTAIGNE, *Essays*. Bk. iii, ch. 5.

9
To him she hasted, in her face excuse
Came prologue, and apology too prompt.
MILTON, *Paradise Lost*. Bk. ix, l. 853.

10
You may often make excuses for another, never for yourself. (Ignoscito sæpe alteri; nunquam tibi.)
PUBLILIUS SYRUS, *Sententiæ*. No. 208.

Never excuse.
SHAKESPEARE, *A Midsummer-Night's Dream*. Act v, sc. 1, l. 363.

11
An excuse is a lie guarded.
SWIFT, *Thoughts on Various Subjects*. Sometimes ascribed to Pope.

12
I do not trouble my spirit to vindicate itself or be understood,
I see that the elementary laws never apologize.
WALT WHITMAN, *Song of Myself*. Sec. 20.

EXERCISE

13
Th' athletic fool, to whom what heaven denied
Of soul, is well compensated in limbs.
JOHN ARMSTRONG, *Art of Preserving Health*. Bk. iii, l. 206.

14
Fxercise and temperance can preserve something of our early strength even in old age. (Potest igitur exercitatio et temperantia etiam in senectute conservare aliquid pristini roboris.)
CICERO, *De Senectute*. Ch. 10, sec. 34.

15
By constant exercise one develops freedom of movement—for virtuous deeds.
DIOGENES. (DIOGENES LAERTIUS. *Diogenes*. Sec. 70.)

16
The wise for cure on exercise depend.
DRYDEN, *Epistle to John Driden*, l. 94.

17
Health is the first muse. . . . The Arabs say that "Allah does not count from life the days spent in the chase," that is, those are thrown in. Plato thought "exercise would almost cure a guilty conscience." Sydney Smith said: "You will never break down in a speech on the day when you have walked twelve miles."
EMERSON, *Letters and Social Aims: Inspiration*.

18
If you will form the habit of taking such exercises, you will see what mighty shoulders you develop, what sinews, what vigor.
EPICTETUS, *Discourses*. Bk. ii, ch. 18, sec. 26.

19
Rosy-complexion'd Health thy steps attends,
And exercise thy lasting youth defends.
JOHN GAY, *Trivia*. Bk. i, l. 73.

20
To cure the mind's wrong bias, Spleen,
Some recommend the bowling green;
Some, hilly walks; all, exercise;
Fling but a stone, the giant dies.
MATTHEW GREEN, *The Spleen*, l. 89.

21
Games played with the ball, and others of that nature, are too violent for the body and stamp no character on the mind.
THOMAS JEFFERSON, *Writings*. Vol. v, p. 83.

22
Why do strong arms fatigue themselves with silly dumb-bells? Trenching a vineyard is

worthier exercise for men. (Quid pereunt stulto fortes haltere lacerti? Exercet melius vinea fossa viros.)
MARTIAL, *Epigrams*. Bk. xiv, epig. 49.

2
'T is the breathing time of day with me.
SHAKESPEARE, *Hamlet*. Act v, sc. 2, l. 181.

3
The rich advantage of good exercise.
SHAKESPEARE, *King John*. Act iv, sc. 2, l. 60.

4
Health is the vital principle of bliss,
And exercise of health.
THOMSON, *The Castle of Indolence*. Canto ii, st. 57. *See also under* HEALTH.

5
For bodily exercise profiteth little: but godliness is profitable unto all things.
New Testament: I Timothy, iv, 8.

EXILE

6
Myself I know that exiles feed on hope. (Οἶδ' ἐγὼ φεύγοντας ἄνδρας ἐλπίδας σιτουμένους.)
ÆSCHYLUS, *Agamemnon*, l. 1668.

7
They bore within their breasts the grief
That fame can never heal—
The deep, unutterable woe
Which none save exiles feel.
W. E. AYTOUN, *The Island of the Scots*, l. 241.

8
Adieu, adieu! my native shore
Fades o'er the waters blue;
The night-winds sigh, the breakers roar,
And shrieks the wild sea-mew.
Yon sun that sets upon the sea
We follow in his flight;
Farewell awhile to him and thee,
My native land—Good Night!
BYRON, *Childe Harold*. Canto i, st. 13.

I can't but say it is an awkward sight
To see one's native land receding through
The growing waters; it unmans one quite,
Especially when life is rather new.
BYRON, *Don Juan*. Canto ii, st. 12.

I take a long, last, lingering view;
Adieu! my native land, adieu!
JOHN LOGAN, *The Lovers*.

9
Exile is terrible to those who have, as it were, a circumscribed habitation; but not to those who look upon the whole globe as one city.
CICERO, *Paradoxa*. Sec. 2.

10
A homeless exile, to his country dead.
A wanderer who begs his daily bread.
("Απολις, ἄοικος, πατρίδος ἐστερημένος,
πτωχός, πλανήτης, βίον ἔχων τοὐφ' ἡμέραν.)
DIOGENES LAERTIUS, *Diogenes*. Sec. 38. Quoting an unknown poet and referring to Diogenes.

11
What exile from his country ever escaped from himself? (Patriæ quis exsul se quoque fugit?)
HORACE, *Odes*. Bk. ii, ode 16, l. 19.

What exile from himself can flee?
To zones, though more and more remote,
Still, still pursues, where'er I be,
The blight of life—the demon Thought.
BYRON, *Childe Harold*. Canto i, st. 84.

12
He came unto his own, and his own received him not.
New Testament: John, i, 11.

13
The world was all before them, where to choose
Their place of rest, and Providence their guide:
They, hand in hand, with wand'ring steps and slow,
Through Eden took their solitary way.
MILTON, *Paradise Lost*. Bk. xii, l. 646.

14
Each voter took an ostrakon (ὄστρακον), or potsherd, wrote on it the name of that citizen whom he wished to remove from the city, and brought it to a place in the agora.
PLUTARCH, *Lives: Aristides*. Ch. 7, sec. 4. Hence ostracism.

Ostracism was not a penalty, but a method of satisfying that jealousy which delights to humble the eminent.
PLUTARCH, *Lives: Themistocles*. Sec. 22.

15
He suffers exile who denies himself to his country. (Exsilium patitur, patriæ qui se denegat.)
PUBLILIUS SYRUS, *Sententiæ*. No. 182.

16
He that sweareth Till no man trust him;
He that lieth Till no man believe him;
He that borroweth Till no man will lend him;
Let him go where No man knoweth him.
HUGH RHODES, *Book of Nurture*, 107.

17
No, my good lord: banish Peto, banish Bardolph, banish Poins; but for sweet Jack Falstaff, kind Jack Falstaff, true Jack Falstaff, valiant Jack Falstaff, and therefore more valiant, being, as he is, old Jack Falstaff, banish not him thy Harry's company: banish plump Jack and banish all the world.
SHAKESPEARE, *I Henry IV*. Act ii, sc. 4, l. 520.

18
Thy sly slow hours shall not determinate
The dateless limit of thy dear exile;
The hopeless word of "never to return"
Breathe I against thee, upon pain of life.
SHAKESPEARE, *Richard II*. Act i, sc. 3, l. 150.

19
Have . . . sigh'd my English breath in for eign clouds,
Eating the bitter bread of banishment.
SHAKESPEARE, *Richard II*. Act iii, sc. 1, l. 19.

For exile hath more terror in his look,
Much more than death.
SHAKESPEARE, *Romeo and Juliet*. Act iii, 3, 13.

They are free men, but I am banished.
And say'st thou yet that exile is not death?
SHAKESPEARE, *Romeo and Juliet*. Act iii, 3, 42.

Banished?
O friar, the damned use that word in hell;
Howlings attend it: how hast thou the heart,
Being a divine, a ghostly confessor,
A sin-absolver, and my friend profess'd,
To mangle me with that word "banished"?
SHAKESPEARE, *Romeo and Juliet*. Act iii, 3, 46.

1
We leave our country's bounds and sweet fields. We are outcasts from our country. (Nos patriæ finis et dulcia linquimus arva; Nos patriam fugimus.)
VERGIL, *Eclogues*. No. i, l. 3.

2
And for exile they change their homes and pleasant thresholds, and seek a country lying beneath another sun (Excilioque domos et dulcia limina mutant Atque alio patriam quærunt sub sole jacentem.)
VERGIL, *Georgics*. Bk. ii, l. 511.

EXPECTATION

3
I would not anticipate the relish of any happiness, nor feel the weight of any misery, before it actually arrives.
ADDISON, *The Spectator*. No. 7. *See also under* TROUBLE.

4
I suppose, to use our national motto, *something will turn up*.
BENJAMIN DISRAELI, *Popanilla*. Ch. 7. (1828)

He was fash and full of faith that "something would turn up."
BENJAMIN DISRAELI, *Tancred*. Bk. iii, ch. 6. (1847)

I have known him [Micawber] come home to supper with a flood of tears, and a declaration that nothing was now left but a jail; and go to bed making a calculation of the expense of putting bow-windows to the house, "in case anything turned up," which was his favorite expression.
DICKENS, *David Copperfield*. Ch. 11. (1849)

5
Indeed it is good, though wronged by my over great expectations, as all things else are.
PEPYS, *Diary*, 1661.

6
Blessed is he who expects nothing, for he shall never be disappointed.
POPE, *Letter to John Gay*, 6 Oct., 1727. Pope characterizes the saying as "a ninth beatitude added to the eighth in the Scripture." (ROSCOE, *Life of Pope*. Vol. x, p. 184.)

Blessed are those that nought expect,
For they shall not be disappointed.
JOHN WOLCOT, *Ode to Pitt*, l. 1.

7
Oft expectation fails, and most oft there
Where most it promises; and oft it hits,
Where hope is coldest and despair most fits.
SHAKESPEARE, *All's Well that Ends Well*. Act ii, sc. 1, l. 145.

8
The expectancy and rose of the fair state.
SHAKESPEARE, *Hamlet*. Act iii, sc. 1, l. 160.

9
And now sits Expectation in the air.
SHAKESPEARE, *Henry V*. Act ii, prol. l. 8.

Expectation whirls me round.
The imaginary relish is so sweet
That it enchants my sense.
SHAKESPEARE, *Troilus and Cressida*. Act iii, sc. 2, l. 19.

10
'Tis expectation makes a blessing dear;
Heaven were not Heaven, if we knew what it were.
SIR JOHN SUCKLING, *Against Fruition*.

If 'twere not heaven if we knew what it were,
'Twould not be heaven to them that now are there.
EDMUND WALLER, *In Answer to Suckling's Verses*.

11
Whatever happens beyond expectation should be counted clear gain. (Quidquid præter spem eveniat, omne id deputare esse in lucro.)
TERENCE, *Phormio*, l. 246. (Act ii, sc. 1.)

He hath indeed better bettered expectation.
SHAKESPEARE, *Much Ado About Nothing*. Act i, sc. 1, l. 16.

12
'Tis silence all, And pleasing expectation.
THOMSON, *The Seasons: Spring*, l. 161.

13
We must expect everything and fear everything from time and from men. (Il faut tout attendre et tout craindre du temps et des hommes.)
VAUVENARGUES, *Réflexions*. No. 102.

14
It is a folly to expect men to do all that they may reasonably be expected to do.
RICHARD WHATELY, *Apothegms*.

EXPERIENCE

I—Experience: Definitions

15
All experience is an arch, to build upon.
HENRY ADAMS, *Education of*, p. 87.

I am a part of all that I have met;
Yet all experience is an arch wherethro'
Gleams that untravell'd world whose margin fades
For ever and for ever when I move.
TENNYSON, *Ulysses*, l. 18.

16
Experience is the mother of knowledge.
NICHOLAS BRETON, *Works*, ii, 8. (1637)

Experience is the mother of all things.
JOHN FLORIO, *First Fruites*. Fo. 32. (1578)

Experience is the father of wisdom, and memory the mother.
THOMAS FULLER, *Gnomologia*. No. 1480.

1
To most men, experience is like the stern lights of a ship, which illumine only the track it has passed.
S. T. Coleridge, *Table Talk*, p. 434.

2
Experience seems to be like the shining of a bright lantern. It suddenly makes clear in the mind what was already there, perhaps, but dim.
Walter de la Mare, *Come Hither: Introduction.*

3
This gave me that precarious gait
Some call experience.
Emily Dickinson, *Poems*. Pt. i, No. 136.

4
Experience is the child of Thought, and Thought is the child of Action.
Benjamin Disraeli, *Vivian Grey*. Bk. v, ch. 1.

5
Experience joined with common sense,
To mortals is a providence.
Matthew Green, *The Spleen*, l. 312.

Experience holds the cautious glass,
To shun the breakers, as I pass,
And frequent throws the wary lead,
To see what dangers may be hid.
Matthew Green, *The Spleen*, l. 820.

6
Experience is the only prophecy of wise men.
Lamartine, *Speech*, at Macon, 1847.

7
Experience is the teacher of fools. (Stultorum eventus magister est.)
Livy, *History*. Bk. xxii, sec. 39.

Experience is the mistress of fools.
John Lyly, *Euphues*, p. 123. (1579)

Experience is the mistress of knaves as well as of fools.
Sir Roger L'Estrange, *Æsop*, 185. (1692)

8
What is experience? A poor little hut constructed from the ruins of the palace of gold and marble called our illusions.
Joseph Roux, *Meditations of a Parish Priest*. Pt. iv, No. 15.

Our experience is composed rather of illusions lost than of wisdom acquired.
Joseph Roux, *Meditations of a Parish Priest*. Pt. iv, No. 28.

II—Experience: Apothegms

9
It takes longer to hard-boil a man or a woman than an egg.
F. L. Allen, *Only Yesterday*, p. 118.

10
It is costly wisdom that is bought by experience.
Roger Ascham, *The Scholemaster*.

He hazardeth sore that waxeth wise by experience.
Roger Ascham, *The Scholemaster*.

11
By far the best proof is experience. (Demonstratio longe optima est experientia.)
Bacon, *Novum Organum*. Bk. i, ch. 70.

12
Oh, who can tell, save he whose heart hath tried?
Byron, *The Corsair*. Canto i, st. 1.

He saw with his own eyes the moon was round,
Was also certain that the earth was square,
Because he had journeyed fifty miles, and found
No sign that it was circular anywhere.
Byron, *Don Juan*. Canto v, st. 150.

13
A sadder and a wiser man
He rose the morrow morn.
S. T. Coleridge, *The Ancient Mariner*, l. 624.

14
Though spirit without experience is dangerous, experience, without spirit, is languid and defective.
Lord Chesterfield, *Letters*, 15 Jan., 1753.

15
Only so much do I know, as I have lived.
Emerson, *Nature Addresses: The American Scholar*.

16
Experience sometimes is perilous.
John Florio, *First Fruites*. Fo. 30. (1578)

17
Experience is good, if not bought too dear.
Thomas Fuller, *Gnomologia*. No. 1479.

Experience teacheth fools, and he is a great one that will not learn by it.
Thomas Fuller, *Gnomologia*. No. 1484.

18
I have but one lamp by which my feet are guided, and that is the lamp of experience.
Patrick Henry, *Speech*, Virginia House of Delegates, 23 March, 1775. (Arranged by William Wirt, 1818.)

19
The spectacles of experience; through them you will see clearly a second time.
Henrik Ibsen, *The League of Youth*. Act ii.

20
No man's knowledge here can go beyond his experience.
John Locke, *Essay Concerning Human Understanding*. Bk. ii, ch. 1, sec. 19.

Man knows nothing but what he learns from his own experience. (Man weiss doch nichts, als was man selbst erfährt.)
Wieland, *Oberon*. Pt. ii, 24.

21
One thorn of experience is worth a whole wilderness of warning.
J. R. Lowell, *Among My Books: Shakespeare Once More*.

22
Experience is forever sowing the seed of one thing after another (Semper enim ex aliis alia proseminat usus.)
Manilius, *Astronomica*. Bk. i, ch. 90.

1
The true wisdom of nations is experience
NAPOLEON I. (FREDERICKS, *Maxims of Napoleon*).

2
Who heeds not experience, trust him not.
JOHN BOYLE O'REILLY, *Rules of the Road*.

3
Experience inspires this work. (Usus opus movet hoc.)
OVID, *Ars Amatoria*. Bk. i, l. 29.

4
Sad experience leaves no room for doubt.
POPE, *January and May*, l. 630.

5
In almost everything, experience is more valuable than precept. (Nam in omnibus fere minus valent præcepta quam experimenta.)
QUINTILIAN, *De Institutione Oratoria*. Bk. v, ch. 10.

6
Take physic, pomp;
Expose thyself to feel what wretches feel.
SHAKESPEARE, *King Lear*. Act iii, sc. 4, l. 33.

7
Unless experience be a jewel that I have purchased at an infinite rate.
SHAKESPEARE, *The Merry Wives of Windsor*. Act ii, sc. 2, l. 213.

8
Men are wise in proportion, not to their experience, but to their capacity for experience.
BERNARD SHAW, *Maxims for Revolutionists*.

9
The dirty nurse, Experience, in her kind
Hath foul'd me.
TENNYSON, *The Last Tournament*, l. 317.

10
You that woo the Voices—tell them "old experience is a fool."
TENNYSON, *Locksley Hall Sixty Years After*, l. 131.

11
You shall know by experience. (Experiundo scies.)
TERENCE, *Heauton Timorumenos*, l. 331.

12
Believe one who has proved it. Believe an expert. (Experto credite.)
VERGIL, *Æneid*. Bk. xi, l. 283.

Believe an expert; believe one who has had experience. (Experto crede.)
ST. BERNARD OF CLAIRVAUX, *Epistles*. No. 106.

Believe the experienced Robert. Believe Robert, who has tried it. (Experto crede Roberto.)
ROBERT BURTON, *Anatomy of Melancholy: Introduction*. Burton is quoting an anonymous medieval line: Quam subito, quam certo, experto crede Roberto, How suddenly and how certainly [it will come] believe the experienced Robert. It appears in *Le Jardin de Récréation*, edited by Gomès de Trier (1611)

13
There are not words enough in all Shakespeare to express the merest fraction of a man's experience in an hour.
R. L. STEVENSON, *Walt Whitman*.

14
Experience is of no ethical value. It is merely the name men give to their mistakes.
OSCAR WILDE, *Picture of Dorian Gray*. Ch. 4. *Lady Windermere's Fan*. Act iii.

III—Experience the Best Teacher

15
By experience we find out a shorter way by a long wandering. Learning teacheth more in one year than experience in twenty.
ROGER ASCHAM, *The Scholemaster*.

Experience teaches slowly, and at the cost of mistakes.
J. A. FROUDE, *Short Studies on Great Subjects: Party Politics*.

16
In gaining all that useful sort of knowledge
Which is acquired in Nature's good old college.
BYRON, *Don Juan*. Canto ii, st. 136.

17
Experience is the best of schoolmasters, only the school-fees are heavy.
CARLYLE, *Miscellaneous Essays*. Vol. i, p. 137.

Experience keeps a dear school, yet Fools will learn in no other.
BENJAMIN FRANKLIN, *Poor Richard*, 1743.

Experience is a good school, but the fees are high.
HEINE. (INGE, *Wit and Wisdom: Preface*.)

18
Experience, slow preceptress, teaching oft
The way to glory by miscarriage foul.
COWPER, *The Task*. Bk. iii, l. 505.

19
Experience is our only teacher, both in war and peace.
W. S. LANDOR, *Imaginary Conversations: Æschines and Phocion*.

20
What that superlative master, experience, has taught me. (Quod me docuit usus, magister egregius.)
PLINY THE YOUNGER, *Epistles*. Bk. i, epis. 20.

21
To wilful men
The injuries that they themselves procure
Must be their schoolmasters.
SHAKESPEARE, *King Lear*. Act ii, sc. 4, l. 305.

22
Experience teaches. (Experientia docet.)
TACITUS, *History*. Bk. v, ch. 6.

Experientia does it—as papa used to say.
DICKENS, *David Copperfield*. Ch. 11. Mrs. Micawber speaking.

IV—Experience: Its Acquisition

23
He who hath proved war, storm or woman's rage,
Whether his winters be eighteen or eighty,

Hath won the experience which is deem'd so weighty.
BYRON, *Don Juan*. Canto xii, st. 50.

1
To show the world what long experience gains,
Requires not courage, though it calls for pains;
But at life's outset to inform mankind
Is a bold effort of a valiant mind.
GEORGE CRABBE, *The Borough*. Letter vii, l. 47.

2
Thou shalt know by experience how salt the savor is of other's bread, and how sad a path it is to climb and descend another's stairs.
(Tu proverai si come sa di sale
Lo pane altrui, e com' è duro calle
Lo scendere e'l salir per l'altrui scale.)
DANTE, *Paradiso*. Canto xvii, l. 58.

3
Experience is no more transferable in morals than in art.
J. A. FROUDE, *Short Studies on Great Subjects: Education.*

4
His head was silver'd o'er with age,
And long experience made him sage.
JOHN GAY, *Fables: Introduction*, l. 3.

The natural crown that sage Experience wears.
WORDSWORTH, *The Excursion*. Bk. vi, l. 281.

5
Each believes naught but his experience. (*Αὐτὸ μόνον πεισθέντες ὅτῳ προσέκυρσεν ἕκαστος.*)
EMPEDOCLES, *Fragments*. No. 2, l. 5.

6
Nor deem the irrevocable Past,
As wholly wasted, wholly vain,
If, rising on its wrecks, at last
To something nobler we attain.
LONGFELLOW, *Ladder of St. Augustine*. St. 12.

7
Does not he return wisest that comes home whipt with his own follies?
THOMAS MIDDLETON, *A Trick to Catch the Old One*. Act ii, sc. 1.

8
Till old experience do attain
To something like prophetic strain.
MILTON, *Il Penseroso*, l. 173.

9
Experience, next, to thee I owe,
Best guide; not following thee, I had remain'd
In ignorance; thou open'st wisdom's way,
And giv'st access, though secret she retire.
MILTON, *Paradise Lost*. Bk. ix, l. 807.

10
What man would be wise, let him drink of the river
That bears on its bosom the record of time;
A message to him every wave can deliver
To teach him to creep till he knows how to climb.
JOHN BOYLE O'REILLY, *Rules of the Road.*

11
Jacques: Yes, I have gained my experience.
Rosalind: And your experience makes you sad. I had rather have a fool to make me merry than experience to make me sad; and to travel for it too!
SHAKESPEARE, *As You Like It*. Act iv, sc. 1, l. 26.

12
I shall the effect of this good lesson keep,
As watchman to my heart.
SHAKESPEARE, *Hamlet*. Act i, sc. 3, l. 45.

13
Experience is by industry achieved
And perfected by the swift course of time.
SHAKESPEARE, *The Two Gentlemen of Verona*. Act i, sc. 3, l. 22.

His years but young, but his experience old;
His head unmellow'd, but his judgement ripe.
SHAKESPEARE, *The Two Gentlemen of Verona*. Act ii, sc. 4, l. 69.

14
I know
The past, and thence I will essay to glean
A warning for the future, so that man
May profit by his errors, and derive
Experience from his folly.
SHELLEY, *Queen Mab*. Pt. iii, l. 6.

15
I shall not let a sorrow die
Until I find the heart of it,
Nor let a wordless joy go by
Until it talks to me a bit;
And the ache my body knows
Shall teach me more than to another,
I shall look deep at mire and rose
Until each one becomes my brother.
SARA TEASDALE, *Servitors.*

V—Experience: The Burnt Child

16
He who suffers, remembers. (Cui dolet, meminit.)
CICERO, *Pro L. Murena*. Sec. 42.

17
A shipwrecked man fears every sea. (Timeo naufragus omne fretum.)
OVID, *Epistulæ ex Ponto*. Bk. ii, epis. 2, l. 126.

18
What, would'st thou have a serpent sting thee twice?
SHAKESPEARE, *The Merchant of Venice*. Act iv, sc. 1, l. 69.

19
Brent child fire dreadeth.
UNKNOWN, *Reliq. Antiquæ*, i, 113. (c. 1300)

Brent child of fire hath much dread.
UNKNOWN, *Romaunt of the Rose*, l. 1820. (c. 1400)

A burnt child dreadeth the fire.
JOHN LYLY, *Euphues*, p. 319. (1580)

The burnt child dreads the fire.
BEN JONSON, *The Devil Is an Ass*. Act i, sc. 2. (1616) In frequent use thereafter.

A burnt child loves the fire.
OSCAR WILDE, *Picture of Dorian Gray*. Ch. 17.

VI—Experience of Others

1
In her experience all her friends relied,
Heaven was her help and nature was her guide.
GEORGE CRABBE, *Parish Register*. Pt. iii, l. 472.

2
Draw from other people's dangers the lesson that may profit yourself. (Periculum ex aliis facto tibi quod ex usu siet.)
TERENCE, *Heauton Timorumenos*, l. 221. (Act ii, sc. 1.)

3
The best plan is, as the common proverb has it, to profit by the folly of others.
PLINY THE ELDER, *Historia Naturalis*. Bk. xviii, sec. 31. *See also under* EVIL.

4
Happy is he who gains wisdom from another's mishap. (Feliciter sapit qui alieno periculo sapit.)
PUBLILIUS SYRUS, *Sententiæ*. No. 825.

Happy is he that by other men's harms takes heed.
SIR ROBERT FOSTER, *Charge*, at trial of Thomas Tonge, 1662. (*6 How. St. Tr.* 265.)

Fortunate thou who are taught by another's suffering to avoid thy own. (Felix, quicumque dolore Alterius disces posse cavere tuom.)
TIBULLUS, *Elegies*. Bk. iii, eleg. 6, l. 43.

He is wise that can beware by another's harms.
HILL, *Commonplace Book*, 132. (c. 1490)

Happy is he whom the horns of others have made cautious. (Felix quem faciunt aliorum cornua cautum.)
JOHANNES RAVISIUS-TEXTOR, *Dialogue*. (1525)

A happy man and wise is he
By others' harms can warnèd be.
JOHN FLORIO, *Second Frutes*, 103. (1591)

5
But, ah, who ever shunned by precedent
The destined ill she must herself assay?
SHAKESPEARE, *The Lover's Complaint*, l. 155.

Nor gives it satisfaction to our blood
That we must curb it upon others' proof.
SHAKESPEARE, *The Lover's Complaint*, l. 162.

6
And others' follies teach us not,
Nor much their wisdom teaches;
And most, of sterling worth, is what
Our own experience preaches.
TENNYSON, *Will Waterproof's Lyrical Monologue*, l. 173.

EXPLANATION, see Excuse

EXTREMES

7
Men are as much blinded by the extremes of misery as by the extremes of poverty.
EDMUND BURKE, *Letter to Member of the National Assembly*, 1791.

8
Th' extremes of glory and of shame,
Like east and west, became the same:
No Indian Prince has to his palace
More foll'wers than a thief to th' gallows.
BUTLER, *Hudibras*. Pt. ii. canto i, l. 271.

9
The fierce extremes of good and ill to brook.
CAMPBELL, *Gertrude of Wyoming*. Pt. i, st. 23.

10
Thus each extreme to equal danger tends,
Plenty, as well as Want, can sep'rate friends.
ABRAHAM COWLEY, *Davideis*. Bk. iii, l. 205.

11
Extremes of fortune are true wisdom's test.
And he's of men most wise who bears them best.
RICHARD CUMBERLAND, *Philemon*.

12
Extremes are faulty and proceed from men: compensation is just, and proceeds from God.
LA BRUYÈRE, *Les Caractères*. Ch. 17.

13
Heard so oft In worst extremes.
MILTON, *Paradise Lost*. Bk. i, l. 275.

And feel by turns the bitter change
Of fierce extremes, extremes by change more fierce.
MILTON, *Paradise Lost*. Bk. ii, l. 599.

14
Perfect good sense shuns all extremity,
Content to couple wisdom with sobriety.
(La parfaite raison fuit toute extrémité,
Et veut que l'on soit sage avec sobriété.)
MOLIÈRE, *Le Misanthrope*. Act i, sc. 1, l. 151.

15
Avoid extremes, and shun the fault of such,
Who still are pleas'd too little or too much.
POPE, *Essay on Criticism*. Pt. ii, l. 184. The motto of Cleobulus of Lindos, *μέτρον ἄριστον*, "Moderation is best," is sometimes translated "Avoid extremes." *See under* MODERATION.

16
Extremes in Nature equal ends produce;
In Man they join to some mysterious use.
POPE, *Essay on Man*. Epis. ii, l. 205.

Extremes in Nature equal good produce,
Extremes in Man concur to gen'ral use.
POPE, *Moral Essays*. Epis. iii, l. 161.

17
The fate of all extremes is such,
Men may be read, as well as books, too much.
POPE, *Moral Essays*. Epis. i, l. 9.

18
We always distrust too much or too little.
JOSEPH ROUX, *Meditations of a Parish Priest*. Pt. ix, No. 33.

19
Like to the time o' the year between the extremes
Of hot and cold, he was nor sad nor merry.
SHAKESPEARE, *Antony and Cleopatra*. Act i, sc. 5, l. 51.

Not fearing death, nor shrinking for distress,
But always resolute in most extremes.
SHAKESPEARE, *I Henry VI*. Act iv, sc. 1, l. 37.

Who can be patient in such extremes?
SHAKESPEARE, *III Henry VI*. Act i, sc. 1, l. 215.

1
Extremes meet.
WALPOLE, *Letter to the Countess of Upper Ossory*, 12 June, 1780.

Les extrêmes se touchent.
L. S. MERCIER, *Tableaux de Paris*. Vol. iv, title of chapter. (1782)

Extremes meet, and there is no better example than the haughtiness of humility.
EMERSON, *Letters and Social Aims: Greatness.*

Extremes meet, as the whiting said with its tail in its mouth.
THOMAS HOOD, *The Doves and the Crows.*

That dead time of the dawn, when (as extremes meet) the rake . . . and the hard-handed artisan . . . jostle . . . for the honours of the pavement.
LAMB, *Essays of Elia: Chimney-Sweepers.*

2
Turning to scorn with lips divine
The falsehood of extremes!
TENNYSON, *Of Old Sat Freedom on the Heights.*

EYES

See also Observation; Sight

I—Eyes: Apothegms

3
His mild and magnificent eye.
BROWNING, *The Lost Leader.*

A still-soliciting eye.
SHAKESPEARE, *King Lear*. Act i, sc. 1, l. 234.

In silent wonder of still-gazing eyes.
SHAKESPEARE, *The Rape of Lucrece*. St. 12.

Pity-pleading eyes.
SHAKESPEARE, *The Rape of Lucrece*. St. 81.

4
The Chinese say that we Europeans have one eye, they themselves two, all the world else is blind.
ROBERT BURTON, *Anatomy of Melancholy: Democritus to the Reader.*

5
In every object there is inexhaustible meaning; the eye sees in it what the eye brings means of seeing.
CARLYLE, *French Revolution*. Bk. i, ch. 2, par. 1. Quoted, "It is well said."

No most gifted eye can exhaust the significance of any object.
CARLYLE, *Heroes and Hero-Worship*. Lect. 3.

6
Till crows' feet be grown under your eyes.
CHAUCER, *Troilus and Criseyde*. Bk. ii, l. 403.

7
What I can see with my eyes, I point out with my finger.
CERVANTES, *Don Quixote*. Pt. ii, ch. 62.

8
The eyes, like sentinels, have the highest station, to give them the widest outlook for the performance of their function. (Oculi tamquam speculatores altissimum locum obtinent, ex quo plurima conspicientes fungantur suo munere.)
CICERO, *De Natura Deorum*. Bk. ii, ch. 56, sec. 140.

Our eyes are sentinels unto our judgements,
And should give certain judgement what they see;
But they are rash sometimes, and tell us wonders
Of common things, which when our judgements find,
They can then check the eyes, and call them blind.
MIDDLETON AND ROWLEY, *The Changeling.* Act i, sc. 1.

9
He holds him with his glittering eye.
COLERIDGE, *The Ancient Mariner*. Pt. i, st. 4.

10
In a moment, in the twinkling of an eye.
New Testament: I Corinthians, xv, 52. *See also under* HASTE.

11
What you get by him you may put e'en in your eye, and ne'er see the worse for it.
ABRAHAM COWLEY, *The Guardian*. Act i, sc. 1.

12
He kept him as the apple of his eye.
Old Testament: Deuteronomy, xxxii, 10.

Keep me as the apple of the eye, hide me under the shadow of thy wings.
Old Testament: Psalms, xvii, 8.

13
With affection beaming in one eye and calculation shining out of the other.
DICKENS, *Martin Chuzzlewit*. Ch. 8.

14
The eye is not satisfied with seeing.
Old Testament: Ecclesiastes, i, 8.

15
A suppressed resolve will betray itself in the eyes.
GEORGE ELIOT, *Mill on the Floss*. Bk. v, ch. 14.

How many furtive inclinations are avowed by the eye, though dissembled by the lips!
EMERSON, *Conduct of Life: Behavior.*

16
Eyes are bold as lions,—roving, running, leaping, here and there, far and near. They speak all languages. They wait for no introduction; they are no Englishmen. . . . What inundation of life and thought is discharged from one soul into another through them!
EMERSON, *Conduct of Life: Behavior.*

There are asking eyes, asserting eyes, prowling eyes; and eyes full of fate,—some of good, and some of sinister omen.
EMERSON, *Conduct of Life: Behavior.*

17
Take my receipt in full: I ask but this,—
To sun myself in Huncamunca's eyes.
FIELDING, *Tom Thumb the Great*. Act i, sc. 3.

18
The eyes of other people are the eyes that ruin us. If all but myself were blind, I should

want neither fine clothes, fine houses, nor fine furniture.
FRANKLIN, *Letter to Benjamin Vaughan.*

1
A small hurt in the eye is a great one.
THOMAS FULLER, *Gnomologia.* No. 406.

2
Never rub your eye but with your elbow.
THOMAS FULLER, *Gnomologia.* No. 3529. (1732)

Diseases of the eye are to be cured with the elbow.
GEORGE HERBERT, *Jacula Prudentum.* (1640)

3
The eye that sees all things else, sees not itself.
THOMAS FULLER, *Gnomologia.* No. 4507.
See also JUDGMENT: THE MOTE AND THE BEAM.

4
All that's the matter with me is the affliction called a multiplying eye.
THOMAS HARDY, *Far From the Madding Crowd.* Ch. 42.

5
Men of cold passions have quick eyes.
HAWTHORNE, *Journals,* 1837.

6
The eyes have one language everywhere.
GEORGE HERBERT, *Jacula Prudentum.*

The eyes of men converse as much as their tongues, with the advantage, that the ocular dialect needs no dictionary, but is understood all the world over.
EMERSON, *Conduct of Life: Behavior.*

7
What the eye sees not, the heart rues not.
JOHN HEYWOOD, *Proverbs.* Pt. ii, ch. 7. (1546)

If eyes don't see, heart doesn't break.
CERVANTES, *Don Quixote.* Pt. ii, ch. 67.

What the eye views not, the heart craves not, as well as rues not.
WILLIAM PENN, *No Cross, No Crown.* Pt. i, ch. 5, sec. 11.

The present eye praises the present object.
SHAKESPEARE, *Troilus and Cressida.* Act iii, sc. 3, l. 180.

8
I have neither eyes to see nor tongue to speak but as the constitution is pleased to direct me.
WILLIAM LENTHALL, Speaker of the Long Parliament, to Charles I. (WENDELL PHILLIPS, *Under the Flag,* Boston, 21 April, 1861.)

As President, I have no eyes but constitutional eyes; I cannot see you.
ABRAHAM LINCOLN, to the Confederate Commissioners from South Carolina.

9
Your eyes are so sharp that you cannot only look through a millstone, but clean through the mind.
JOHN LYLY, *Euphues,* p. 289. (1580)

"Yes, I have a pair of eyes," replied Sam, "and that's just it. If they wos a pair of patent double million magnifyin' gas microscopes of hextra power, p'raps I might be able to see through a flight o' stairs and a deal door; but being only eyes, you see, my wision's limited."
DICKENS, *Pickwick Papers.* Ch. 34.

10
The eye hath ever been thought the pearl of the face.
JOHN LYLY, *Euphues,* p. 406. (1580)

11
The light of the body is the eye.
New Testament: Matthew, vi, 22.

12
Towers and battlements it sees
Bosom'd high in tufted trees,
Where perhaps some beauty lies,
The cynosure of neighbouring eyes.
MILTON, *L'Allegro,* l. 77.

13
Nothing is lost on him who sees
With an eye that feeling gave;—
For him there's a story in every breeze,
And a picture in every wave.
THOMAS MOORE, *Boat Glee.*

14
There are often voice and words in a silent look.
OVID, *Ars Amatoria.* Bk. i, l. 574.

For eyes can speak and eyes can understand.
CHAPMAN, *The Gentleman Usher.* Act ii, sc. 1.

An eye can threaten like a loaded and levelled gun, or can insult like hissing or kicking; or, in its altered mood, by beams of kindness, it can make the heart dance with joy.
EMERSON, *Conduct of Life: Behavior.*

15
The eyes, in beholding the afflicted, sometimes suffer affliction. (Dum spectant læsos oculi, læduntur et ipsi.)
OVID, *Remediorum Amoris,* l. 615.

16
The eyes of a fool are in the ends of the earth.
Old Testament: Proverbs, xvii, 24.

17
All looks yellow to the jaundic'd eye.
POPE, *Essay on Criticism.* Pt. ii, p. 359.

18
Why has not man a microscopic eye?
For this plain reason, man is not a fly.
Say, what the use, were finer optics giv'n,
T' inspect a mite, not comprehend the Heav'n?
POPE, *Essay on Man.* Epis. i, l. 193. Locke uses the phrase "Microscopical eye" in his *Essay Concerning Human Understanding.* Bk. ii, ch. 23, sec. 12.

19
The eyes do not go wrong if the mind rules the eyes. (Nil peccant oculi, si animus oculis imperat.)
PUBLILIUS SYRUS, *Sententiæ.* No. 415.

The guiltless eye
Commits no wrong, nor wastes what it enjoys.
COWPER, *The Task.* Bk. i, l. 333.

1
Hard must he wink that shuts his eyes from heaven.
FRANCIS QUARLES, *A Feast of Worms*. Sec. 3, 3.

2
The eye is a shrew.
JOHN RAY, *English Proverbs*, 354. (1678)

3
Faster than his tongue
Did make offence his eye did heal it up.
SHAKESPEARE, *As You Like It*. Act iii, sc. 5, l. 116.

4
It is a basilisk unto mine eye,
Kills me to look on't.
SHAKESPEARE, *Cymbeline*. Act ii, sc. 4, l. 107.

5
An eye like Mars, to threaten and command.
SHAKESPEARE, *Hamlet*. Act iii, sc. 4, l. 57.

Thou hast no speculation in those eyes
Which thou dost glare with!
SHAKESPEARE, *Macbeth*. Act iii, sc. 4, l. 95.

6
I have a good eye, uncle; I can see a church by daylight.
SHAKESPEARE, *Much Ado About Nothing*. Act ii, sc. 1, l. 85.

7
The fringed curtains of thine eye advance,
And say what thou seest yond.
SHAKESPEARE, *The Tempest*. Act i, sc. 2, l. 407.

8
Make the abhorrent eye roll back and close.
SOUTHEY, *Curse of Kehama*. Canto viii, st. 9.

Or roll the lucid orbit of an eye.
YOUNG, *Love of Fame*. Sat. v, l. 7.

9
His smiling eyes with simple truth were stored.
SPENSER [?], *Britain's Ida*. Canto i.

10
She hath an eye behind her.
JOHN STILL, *Gammer Gurton's Needle*. Act ii, sc. 2. (c. 1565)

He hath an eye behind, a wary man.
WILLIAM ROBERTSON, *Phraseologia Generalis*, 1032. (1681)

She has eyes in the back of her head.
P. FITZGERALD, *Comediettas*, 111. (1869)

11
For any man with half an eye,
What stands before him may espy;
But optics sharp it needs, I ween,
To see what is not to be seen.
JOHN TRUMBULL, *McFingal*. Canto i, l. 67.

12
One unguarded look betrayed David.
THOMAS WILSON, *Sacra Privata*, p. 151.

13
The harvest of a quiet eye
That broods and sleeps on his own heart.
WORDSWORTH, *A Poet's Epitaph*. St. 13.

II—Eyes: Women's Eyes

14
I knew you by your eyes,
That rest on nothing long,
And have forgot surprise.
ROBERT BRIDGES, *I Love My Lady's Eyes*.

15
Such a blue inner light from her eyelids outbroke,
You looked at her silence and fancied she spoke.
E. B. BROWNING, *My Kate*.

16
Thine eyes are springs, in whose serene
And silent waters heaven is seen;
Their lashes are the herbs that look
On their young figures in the brook.
BRYANT, *Oh, Fairest of the Rural Maids*.

17
Heart on her lips and soul within her eyes,
Soft as her clime and sunny as her skies.
BYRON, *Beppo*. St. 45.

Her eye (I'm very fond of handsome eyes)
Was large and dark, suppressing half its fire
Until she spoke, then through its soft disguise
Flash'd an expression more of pride than ire,
And love than either; and there would arise,
A something in them which was not desire,
But would have been, perhaps, but for the soul,
Which struggled through and chasten'd down the whole.
BYRON, *Don Juan*. Canto i, st. 60.

18
Those eyes, affectionate and glad,
Which seemed to love whate'er they looked upon.
CAMPBELL, *Gertrude of Wyoming*. Pt. ii, st. 4.

19
Paradise stood formed in her eye.
CHAUCER, *Troilus and Criseyde*. Bk. v, l. 817.

Grace was in all her steps, Heav'n in her eye,
In every gesture dignity and love.
MILTON, *Paradise Lost*. Bk. viii, l. 488.

Within her tender eye
The heaven of April, with its changing light.
LONGFELLOW, *The Spirit of Poetry*, l. 45.

20
The joy of youth and health her eyes display'd,
And ease of heart her every look convey'd.
CRABBE, *The Parish Register*. Pt. ii.

21
With store of ladies, whose bright eyes
Rain influence, and judge the prize.
MILTON, *L'Allegro*, l. 121.

22
Man for his glory To ancestry flies,
While woman's bright story Is told in her eyes.
THOMAS MOORE, *Desmond's Song*. St. 4.

From Persia's eyes of full and fawn-like ray,
To the small, half-shut glances of Kathay.
THOMAS MOORE, *Lalla Rookh: The Veiled Prophet*.

23
Those eyes, whose light seem'd rather given
To be ador'd than to adore—
Such eyes as may have looked *from* heaven,

But ne'er were rais'd to it before!
THOMAS MOORE, *Loves of the Angels*, l. 1707.

1
Bright as the sun her eyes the gazers strike,
And, like the sun, they shine on all alike.
POPE, *The Rape of the Lock*. Canto ii, l. 13.

2
From women's eyes this doctrine I derive:
They are the ground, the books, the academes,
From whence doth spring the true Promethean fire.
SHAKESPEARE, *Love's Labour's Lost*. Act iv, sc. 3, l. 302.

A wither'd hermit, five-score winters worn,
Might shake off fifty, looking in her eye.
SHAKESPEARE, *Love's Labour's Lost*. Act iv, sc. 3, l. 242.

For where is any author in the world
Teaches such beauty as a woman's eye?
SHAKESPEARE, *Love's Labour's Lost*. Act iv, sc. 3, l. 312.

3
Iago: What an eye she has! methinks it sounds a parley of provocation.
Cassio: An inviting eye; and yet methinks right modest.
SHAKESPEARE, *Othello*. Act ii, sc. 3, l. 22.

There's language in her eye, her cheek, her lip.
SHAKESPEARE, *Troilus and Cressida*. Act iv, sc. 5, l. 55.

4
Her eyes, like marigolds, had sheath'd their light;
And, canopied in darkness, sweetly lay,
Till they might open to adorn the day.
SHAKESPEARE, *The Rape of Lucrece*, l. 397.

5
If I could write the beauty of your eyes,
And in fresh numbers number all your graces,
The age to come would say, "This poet lies;
Such heavenly touches ne'er touch'd earthly faces."
SHAKESPEARE, *Sonnets*. No. xvii.

6
Thine eyes are like the deep, blue, boundless heaven
Contracted to two circles underneath
Their long, fine lashes; dark, far, measureless,
Orb within orb, and line through line inwoven.
SHELLEY, *Prometheus Unbound*. Act ii, sc. 1.

7
Alas! how little can a moment show
Of an eye where feeling plays
In ten thousand dewy rays;
A face o'er which a thousand shadows go.
WORDSWORTH, *The Triad*, l. 128.

8
Some ladies' judgment in their features lies,
And all their genius sparkles from their eyes.
YOUNG, *Love of Fame*. Sat. v, l. 143.

III—Eyes and Love

9
A thousand hearts beat happily; and when
Music arose with its voluptuous swell,
Soft eyes look'd love to eyes which spake again,
And all went merry as a marriage-bell.
BYRON, *Childe Harold*. Canto iii, st. 21.

10
Love's special lesson is to please the eye.
CHAPMAN, *Hero and Leander*. Sestiad v.

11
The love light in her eye.
HARTLEY COLERIDGE, *She Is not Fair to Outward View*.

The love light in your eye.
LADY DUFFERIN, *The Irish Emigrant*.

12
Sweet, silent rhetoric of persuading eyes,
Dumb eloquence, whose power doth move the blood
More than the words or wisdom of the wise.
SAMUEL DANIEL, *Complaint of Rosamond*. St. 19.

Ah! 'tis the silent rhetoric of a look
That works the league betwixt the states of hearts.
SAMUEL DANIEL, *Queen's Arcadia*. Act v, sc. 2.

The heavenly rhetoric of thine eye.
SHAKESPEARE, *Love's Labour's Lost*. Act iv, sc. 3, l. 60.

13
Adding once more the music of the tongue
To the sweet music of her alluring eyes.
SIR JOHN DAVIES, *Orchestra*. St. 96.

14
Our eye-beams twisted, and did thread
Our eyes, upon one double string;
So to, engraft our hands, as yet
Was all the means to make us one,
And pictures in our eyes to get
Was all our propagation.
JOHN DONNE, *The Ecstasy*, l. 7.

Think ye by gazing on each other's eyes
To multiply your lovely selves?
SHELLEY, *Prometheus Unbound*. Act iii, sc. 4.

15
It does not hurt weak eyes to look into beautiful eyes never so long.
EMERSON, *Conduct of Life: Beauty*.

16
The greatest curse that man can labour under
Is the strong witchcraft of a woman's eyes.
JOHN FLETCHER, *Lover's Progress*. Act iv, sc. 1.

17
Love's tongue is in the eyes.
PHINEAS FLETCHER, *Piscatory Eclogues*. Canto v, st. 13.

18
On whom he many a sheepish eye did cast.
JOHN GRANGE, *Golden Aphroditis*, D 1. (1577)

On Cleopatra he has cast a sheep's eye.
WILLIAM D'AVENANT, *Playhouse to be Let*. Act v. (c. 1663)

1
From whose eyelids also as they gazed flowed limb-unnerving love. (Τῶν καὶ απὸ βλεφάρων ἔρος εἴβετο δερκομενάων λυσιμελής.)

HESIOD, *Theogony*, l. 910.

2
Why did you swear mine eyes were bright,
Yet leave those eyes to weep?

DAVID MALLET, *Margaret's Ghost*.

These poor eyes, you called, I ween,
"Sweetest eyes were ever seen."

E. B. BROWNING, *Catarina to Camoens*. St. 1.

3
If you wish to love them, it shall be, by my faith, for their beautiful eyes. (Si vous les voulez aimer, se sera, ma foi, pour leurs beaux yeux.)

MOLIÈRE, *Les Précieuses Ridicules*. Sc. 15, l. 17.

4
The light that lies In women's eyes,
Has been my heart's undoing.

THOMAS MOORE, *The Time I've Lost in Wooing*.

And the world's so rich in resplendent eyes,
'Twere a pity to limit one's love to a pair.

THOMAS MOORE, *'Tis Sweet to Think*.

5
Your eyes were not silent. (Non oculi tacuere tui.)

OVID, *Amores*. Bk. ii, eleg. 5, l. 17.

Sometimes from her eyes.
I did receive fair speechless messages.

SHAKESPEARE, *Merchant of Venice*, i, 1, 163.

6
Love is allured by gentle eyes. (Comibus est oculis alliciendus amor.)

OVID, *Ars Amatoria*. Bk. iii, l. 510.

O Love! for Sylvia let me gain the prize,
And make my tongue victorious as her eyes.

POPE, *Pastorals: Spring*, l. 49.

7
Drink to me with your eyes alone. . . . And if you will, take the cup to your lips and fill it with kisses, and give it so to me.

PHILOSTRATUS, *Epistles*. No. 24.

Drink to me only with thine eyes,
And I will pledge with mine;
Or leave a kiss but in the cup,
And I'll not look for wine.
The thirst that from the soul doth rise
Doth ask a drink divine;
But might I of Jove's nectar sup,
I would not change for thine.

BEN JONSON, *To Celia*. A paraphrase of Philostratus. "Sup" (generally misquoted "sip") to rhyme with "cup."

Drink to me only with thine eyes—
'Tis all the law allows.

ALAN T. WINFIELD, *A Revised Classic*.

8
She looked down to blush, and she looked up to sigh,
With a smile on her lips, and a tear in her eye.

SCOTT, *Lochinvar*. (*Marmion*. Canto v, st. 12.)

Now Rory, be aisy, sweet Kathleen would cry;
Reproof on her lip, but a smile in her eye.

SAMUEL LOVER, *Rory O'More*.

9
Thou tell'st me there is murder in mine eye;
'Tis pretty, sure, and very probable,
That eyes, that are the frail'st and softest things,
Who shut their coward gates on atomies,
Should be call'd tyrants, butchers, murderers!

SHAKESPEARE, *As You Like It*. Act iii, sc. 5, 10.

10
Those doves' eyes
Which can make gods forsworn.

SHAKESPEARE, *Coriolanus*. Act v, sc. 3. l. 27.

11
A lover's eyes will gaze an eagle blind.

SHAKESPEARE, *Lover's Labour's Lost*. Act iv, sc. 3, l. 334.

Reason becomes the marshal to my will
And leads me to your eyes, where I o'erlook
Love's stories written in love's richest book.

SHAKESPEARE, *A Midsummer-Night's Dream*. Act ii, sc. 2, l. 120.

Alack! there lies more peril in thine eye,
Than twenty of their swords.

SHAKESPEARE, *Romeo and Juliet*. Act ii, sc. 2, 71.

12
O, hell! to choose love by another's eyes.

SHAKESPEARE, *A Midsummer-Night's Dream*. Act i, sc. 1, l. 140.

13
Young men's love then lies
Not truly in their hearts, but in their eyes.

SHAKESPEARE, *Romeo and Juliet*. Act ii, sc. 2, l. 67.

14
I ne'er could any lustre see,
In eyes that would not look on me.

SHERIDAN, *The Duenna*. Act i, sc. 2.

15
Somebody loves me, how do I know?
Somebody's eyes have told me so!

HATTIE STARR, *Somebody Loves Me*.

16
So when thou saw'st, in Nature's cabinet,
Stella, thou straight'st lookt'st babies in her eyes.

SIR PHILIP SIDNEY, *Astrophel and Stella*. Sonnet xi. (1591)

Can ye look babies, sisters, in the young gallants' eyes?

JOHN FLETCHER, *The Loyal Subject*. Act iii, sc. 2. (1618)

Look babies in your eyes, my pretty sweet one.

FLETCHER, *The Loyal Subject*. Act iii, sc. 2.

Sweeten her again with ogling smiles, look babies in her eyes.

THOMAS BAKER, *Fine Lady's Airs*. Act i, sc. 1. (1709)

It is an active flame that flies
First to the babies in the eyes.

ROBERT HERRICK, *The Kiss*.

She clung about his neck, gave him ten kisses,
Toyed with his locks, looked babies in his eyes.

THOMAS HEYWOOD, *Love's Mistress*.

In each of her two crystal eyes
Smileth a naked boy.
HENRY HOWARD, EARL OF SURREY, *Cupid.*

1
My Uncle Toby . . . would have sat quietly upon a sofa from June to January (which, you know, takes in both the hot and cold months) with an eye as fine as the Thracian Rhodope's beside him, without being able to tell whether it was a black or a blue one.
STERNE, *Tristram Shandy.* Bk. iii, ch. 24.

An eye full of gentle salutations, and soft responses, . . . whispering soft, like the last low accents of an expiring saint. . . . It did my Uncle Toby's business.
STERNE, *Tristram Shandy.* Bk. vii, ch. 25.

2
My heart, the bird of the wilderness, has found its sky in your eyes.
RABINDRANATH TAGORE, *The Gardener.* No. 31.

Eyes of pure women, wholesome stars of love.
TENNYSON, *Gareth and Lynette,* l. 307.

IV—Eyes and the Soul

3
These lovely lamps, these windows of the soul.
DU BARTAS, *Devine Weekes and Workes.* Week i, day 6. (Sylvester, tr.)

Ere I let fall the windows of my eyes.
SHAKESPEARE, *Richard III.* Act v, sc. 3, l. 116.

Were never four such lamps together mix'd.
SHAKESPEARE, *Venus and Adonis,* l. 489.

4
Eyes so transparent that they permit your soul to be seen. (Ils sont si transparents qu'ils laissent voir votre âme.)
THÉOPHILE GAUTIER, *Two Beautiful Eyes.*

5
The heart's letter is read in the eyes.
GEORGE HERBERT, *Jacula Prudentum.*

For it is said by man expert
That the eye is traitor of the heart.
SIR THOMAS WYATT, *That the Eye Bewrayeth.*

6
Yet his look with the reach of past ages was wise,
And the soul of eternity thought through his eyes.
LEIGH HUNT, *The Feast of the Poets.* Referring to Apollo.

7
Through her expressive eyes her soul distinctly spoke.
GEORGE LYTTELTON, *Monody to the Memory of Lady Lyttelton.*

Those true eyes
Too pure and too honest in aught to disguise
The sweet soul shining through them.
OWEN MEREDITH, *Lucile.* Pt. ii, canto ii, st. 3.

8
And looks commercing with the skies,
Thy rapt soul sitting in thine eyes.
MILTON, *Il Penseroso,* l. 39.

The majesty
That from man's soul looks through his eager eyes.
WILLIAM MORRIS, *Life and Death of Jason.* Bk. xiii.

9
Whatever of goodness emanates from the soul, gathers its soft halo in the eyes: and if the heart be a lurking-place of crime, the eyes are sure to betray the secret. A beautiful eye makes silence eloquent, a kind eye makes contradiction assent, an enraged eye makes beauty a deformity.
JOHN SAUNDERS, *Stray Leaves of Literature: Physiognomy.*

10
His soul seemed hovering in his eyes.
SHELLEY, *Rosalind and Helen,* l. 799.

11
Her eyes are homes of silent prayer.
TENNYSON, *In Memoriam.* Pt. xxxii, st. 1.

V—Eyes: Their Color

12
A gray eye is a sly eye,
And roguish is a brown one;
Turn full upon me thy eye,—
Ah, how its wavelets drown one!
A blue eye is a true eye;
Mysterious is a dark one,
Which flashes like a spark-sun!
A black eye is the best one.
W. R. ALGER, *Poetry of the Orient: Mirtsa Schaffŷ on Eyes.*

13
An eye's an eye, and whether black or blue
Is no great matter, so 'tis in request.
'Tis nonsense to dispute about a hue,—
The kindest may be taken as a test.
BYRON, *Don Juan.* Canto xiii, st. 3.

14
There are eyes of blue,
There are eyes of brown, too;
There are eyes of every size,
And eyes of every hue.
But I surmise, that if you are wise,
You'll be careful of the maiden with the dreamy eyes.
JAMES WELDON JOHNSON, *The Maiden With the Dreamy Eyes.* (1901)

Black Eyes

15
With eyes that look'd into the very soul— . . .
Bright—and as black and burning as a coal.
BYRON, *Don Juan.* Canto iv, st. 94.

16
There are eyes half defiant,
Half meek and compliant;
Black eyes, with a wondrous, witching charm
To bring us good or to work us harm.
PHŒBE CARY, *Doves' Eyes.*

17
And yet the large black eyes, like night,

Have passion and have power;
Within their sleepv depths is light,
For some wild wakening hour.
LETITIA LANDON, *The Nizam's Daughter.*

1
The flash of his keen, black eyes
Forerunning the thunder.
LONGFELLOW, *The Golden Legend.* Pt. iv.

2
His large sloe-black eyes
Melt in soft blandishments and humble joy.
WILLIAM SOMERVILLE, *The Chase.* Bk. i.

3
Black brows they say
Become some women best, so that there be not
Too much hair there, but in a semicircle
Or a half-moon made with a pen.
SHAKESPEARE, *Winter's Tale.* Act ii, sc. 1, l. 8.

Blue Eyes

4
How blue were Ariadne's eyes
When, from the sea's horizcn line,
At eve, she raised them to the skies!
My Psyche, bluer far are thine.
AUBREY DE VERE, *Psyche.*

5
When blue eyes, more softly bright,
Diffuse divinely humid light,
We gaze, and see the smiling loves,
And Cytherea's gentle doves.
MATTHEW GREEN, *The Spleen,* l. 222.

6
And heaven's soft azure in her eye was seen.
WILLIAM HAYLEY, *The Afflicted Father.*

O lovely eyes of azure,
Clear as the waters of a brook that run
Limpid and laughing in the summer sun.
LONGFELLOW, *The Masque of Pandora.* Pt. i.

7
Those blue violets, her eyes. (Die blauen Veilchen der Aeugelein.)
HEINE, *Lyrisches Intermezzo.* No. 31.

And violets, transform'd to eyes,
Inshrin'd a soul within their blue.
MOORE, *Evenings in Greece: Second Evening.*

Blue eyes shimmer with angel glances,
Like spring violets over the lea.
CONSTANCE F. WOOLSON, *October's Song.*

8
Like a beauteous woman's large blue eyes
Gone mad through olden songs and poesies.
KEATS, *Familiar Verses,* l. 53.

9
Where did you get your eyes so blue?
Out of the sky as I came through.
GEORGE MACDONALD, *At the Back of the North Wind: Song.* Ch. 33.

10
Eyes of most unholy blue.
THOMAS MOORE, *By That Lake.*

11
Her two blue windows faintlv she upheaveth,
Like the fair sun, when in his fresh array
He cheers the morn, and all the earth relieveth;
And as the bright sun glorifies the sky,
So is her face illumin'd with her eye.
SHAKESPEARE, *Venus and Adonis,* l. 482.

Dark Eyes

12
Lovely in your strength, as is the light
Of a dark eye in women.
BYRON, *Childe Harold.* Canto iii, st. 92.

13
Maiden! with the meek brown eyes.
LONGFELLOW, *Maidenhood.*

14
Dark eyes are dearer far
Than those that mock the hyacinthine bell.
J. H. REYNOLDS, *Sonnet.*

15
And her dark eyes—how eloquent!
Ask what they would, 'twas granted.
SAMUEL ROGERS, *Jacqueline.* Pt. i, l. 82.

Gray Eyes

16
Eyes too expressive to be blue,
Too lovely to be grey.
MATTHEW ARNOLD, *On the Rhine.*

Those eyes the greenest of things blue,
The bluest of things grey.
SWINBURNE, *Félise.* St. 24.

17
Mine eyes are grey and bright and quick in turning.
SHAKESPEARE, *Venus and Adonis,* l. 140.

18
A noticeable man with large grey eyes.
WORDSWORTH, *Stanzas Written in Thomson's "Castle of Indolence."*

Green Eyes

19
The Girl with the Green Eyes.
CLYDE FITCH. Title of play.

20
Her eyes were green as leeks.
SHAKESPEARE, *A Midsummer-Night's Dream.* Act v, sc. 1, 342.

21
The sea-green mirrors of your eyes.
SWINBURNE, *Félise.* St. 35.

Eyes coloured like a water-flower,
And deeper than the green seas' glass.
SWINBURNE, *Félise.* St. 36.

22
Do you see any green in my eye?
UNKNOWN. London street saying, c. 1840.

VI—Eyes: Their Brilliancy

23
There are whole veins of diamonds in thine eyes,
Might furnish crowns for all the Queens of earth.
P. J. BAILEY, *Festus: A Drawing Room.*

Eyes, that displace
The neighbour diamond, and out-face
That sunshine by their own sweet grace.
RICHARD CRASHAW, *Wishes to His (Supposed) Mistress.* St. 15.

I see how thine eye would emulate the diamond: thou hast the right arched beauty of the brow.
SHAKESPEARE, *The Merry Wives of Windsor.* Act iii, sc. 3, l. 58.

1
On woman Nature did bestow two eyes,
Like Hemian's bright lamps, in matchless beauty shining,
Whose beams do soonest captivate the wise
And wary heads, made rare by art's refining.
ROBERT GREENE, *Philomela.*

2
Her eyes the glow-worm lend thee,
The shooting stars attend thee;
And the elves also,
Whose little eyes glow
Like the sparks of fire, befriend thee.
ROBERT HERRICK, *The Night-Piece, to Julia.*

3
The light of midnight's starry heaven
Is in those radiant eyes.
LETITIA LANDON, *Poetical Portraits.* No. 5.

4
And thy deep eyes, amid the gloom,
Shine like jewels in a shroud.
LONGFELLOW, *The Golden Legend.* Pt. iv.

5
When did morning ever break,
And find such beaming eyes awake?
THOMAS MOORE, *Fly Not Yet.*

6
Look out upon the stars, my love,
And shame them with thine eyes.
EDWARD COOTE PINKNEY, *A Serenade.*

Two starry eyes, hung in the gloom of thought.
SHELLEY, *Alastor,* l. 490.

Those eyes which burn through smiles that fade in tears,
Like stars half-quenched in mists of silver dew.
SHELLEY, *Prometheus Unbound.* Act ii, sc. 1.

Her eyes as stars of twilight fair.
WORDSWORTH, *She Was a Phantom of Delight,* l. 5.

I dislike an eye that twinkles like a star. Those only are beautiful which, like the planets, have a steady, lambent light,—are luminous, but not sparkling.
LONGFELLOW, *Hyperion.* Bk. iii, ch. 4.

7
The dew that on the violet lies
Mocks the dark lustre of thine eyes.
SCOTT, *The Lord of the Isles.* Canto i, st. 3.

The sparkle of his swarthy eye.
SCOTT, *Rokeby.* Canto iii, st. 4.

8
Her eyes in heaven
Would through the airy region stream so bright
That birds would sing and think it were not night.
SHAKESPEARE, *Romeo and Juliet.* Act ii, sc. 2, l. 20.

And as the bright sun glorifies the sky,
So is her face illumined with her eye.
SHAKESPEARE, *Venus and Adonis,* l. 485.

But hers, which through the crystal tears gave light,
Shone like the moon in water seen by night.
SHAKESPEARE, *Venus and Adonis,* l. 491.

9
Nor brighter was his eye, nor moister
Than a too-long opened oyster.
ROBERT BROWNING, *The Pied Piper.* Pt. 4.

10
Their eyes seem'd rings from whence the gems were gone. (Parean l'occhiaje anella senza gemme.)
DANTE, *Purgatorio.* Canto xxiii, l. 31.

11
Lack-lustre eye.
SHAKESPEARE, *As You Like It.* Act ii, sc. 7, l. 21.

A lack-lustre dead-blue eye.
TENNYSON, *A Character.*

VII—Eye and Ear

12
I sometimes almost think that eyes have ears: . . .
'Tis wonderful how oft the sex have heard
Long dialogues—which pass'd without a word!
BYRON, *Don Juan.* Canto xv, st. 76.

13
The eyes are as ignorant as the ears are knowing. (*Καὶ τόσον ὀφθαλμοὶ γὰρ ἀπευθέες ὅσσον ἀκουὴ εἰδυλίς.*)
CALLIMACHUS, *Fragmenta Incertæ.* No. 128.

14
But sooth is said, gone sithen many years
That field hath eyen, and the wood hath ears.
CHAUCER, *The Knightes Tale,* l. 664. (l. 1522)

For poets have ears, and walls have eyes to see.
SIR JOHN HARINGTON, *Orlando Furioso.* Canto xxii, st. 32.

Fields have eyes and woods have ears.
JOHN HEYWOOD, *Proverbs.* Pt. ii, ch. 5.

Walls have tongues and hedges ears.
SWIFT, *Pastoral Dialogue,* l. 7.

The fields have eyes, the bushes ears,
False birds can fetch the wind.
THOMAS TUSSER, *Five Hundred Points of Good Husbandry: To Light a Candle Before the Devil.*

Wood has ears, field has sight.
WRIGHT, *Essays on the Middle Ages.* Vol. i, p. 168. Quoted as of the thirteenth century.

15
The ear is a less trustworthy witness than the eye. (*Ὦτα τυγχάνει ἀνθρώποισι ἐόντα ἀπιστότερα ὀφθαλμῶν.*)
HERODOTUS, *History.* Bk. i, ch. 8.

We credit most our sight; one eye doth please
Our trust far more than ten ear-witnesses.
ROBERT HERRICK, *The Eyes Before the Ears.*

A thing when heard, remember, strikes less keen
On the spectator's mind than when 'tis seen.
(Segnius irritant animos demiss per aurem;
Quam quæ sunt oculis subjecta fidelibus.)
HORACE, *Ars Poetica*, l. 180.

One eye-witness is better than ten hearsay witnesses. Those who see know beyond a doubt. (Pluris est oculatus testis unus, quam auriti decem; Qui audiunt, audita dicunt: qui vident plane sciunt.)
PLAUTUS, *Truculentus*. Act ii, sc. 6, l. 8.

1
All pleasure has departed from the ear to the vain delights of the wandering eye. (Migravit ab aure voluptas Omnis ad incertos oculos, et gaudia vana.)
HORACE, *Epistles*. Bk. ii, epis. 1, l. 187.

2
I have heard of thee by the hearing of the ear; but now mine eye seeth thee.
Old Testament: Job, xlii, 5.

3
The hearing ear, and the seeing eye.
Old Testament: Proverbs, xx, 12.

4
The ears can endure an injury better than the eyes. (Injuriam aures quam oculi facilius ferunt.)
PUBLILIUS SYRUS, *Sententiæ*. No. 295.

5
A man may see how this world goes with no eyes. Look with thine ears.
SHAKESPEARE, *King Lear*. Act iv, sc. 6, l. 153.

6
Stabbed with a white wench's black eye; shot through the ear with a love-song.
SHAKESPEARE, *Romeo and Juliet*. Act ii, sc. 4, l. 13.

7
O, learn to read what silent love hath writ:
To hear with eyes belongs to love's fine wit.
SHAKESPEARE, *Sonnets*. No. xxiii.

F

FACE

I—Face: Definitions

8
A man shall see faces, that if you examine them, part by part, you shall find never a good; and yet all together do well.
FRANCIS BACON, *Essays: Of Beauty.*

9
It is the common wonder of all men how, among so many million of faces, there should be none alike.
SIR THOMAS BROWNE, *Religio Medici*. Pt. ii, sec. 2.

The human features and countenance, although composed of but some ten parts or little more, are so fashioned that among so many thousands of men there are no two in existence who cannot be distinguished from one another.
PLINY, *Historia Naturalis*. Bk. vii, ch. 1.

10
As from our beginning we run through variety of looks, before we come to consistent and settled faces, so before our end, by sick and languishing alterations, we put on new visages.
SIR THOMAS BROWNE, *To a Friend*. Sec. 3.

11
The countenance is the portrait of the mind, the eyes are its informers. (Imago animi vultus est, indices oculi.)
CICERO, *De Oratore*. Bk. iii, sec. 59.

12
Some can form an opinion from the countenance as to how much ability a man possesses. (Quidam ex vultu conjecturam faciunt, quantum quisque animi habere videatur.)
CICERO, *Pro L. Murena*. Sec. 21. (Adapted.)

Physiognomy is not a guide that has been given us by which to judge of the character of men: it may only serve us for conjecture.
LA BRUYÈRE, *Les Caractères*. Pt. xii.

There's no art
To find the mind's construction in the face.
SHAKESPEARE, *Macbeth*. Act i, sc. 4, l. 11.

13
There is in every human countenance either a history or a prophecy, which must sadden, or at least soften, every reflecting observer.
S. T. COLERIDGE, *Additional Table Talk.*

His face, The tablet of unutterable thoughts.
BYRON, *The Dream*. St. 6.

14
Contending Passions jostle and displace
And tilt and tourney mostly in the Face: . . .
Unmatched by Art, upon this wondrous scroll
Portrayed are all the secrets of the soul.
ABRAHAM COLES, *Man, The Microcosm*, l. 26.

15
Joy to the face its own expression sent,
And gave a likeness in the looks it lent.
CRABBE, *Tales of the Hall*. Bk. ii, l. 33.

16
Your face doth testify what you be inwardly.
LEWIS EVANS, *Withals Dictionary Revised*. Sig. L7. (1586)

Man is read in his face.
BEN JONSON, *Explorata: Deus in Creaturis.*

What a man is lies as certainly upon his countenance as in his heart.
GEORGE MACDONALD, *Weighed and Wanting*. Ch. 11.

In whose gay red-lettered face
We read good living more than grace.
MATTHEW GREENE, *The Spleen*, l. 330.

1
Of all the branches of political economy, the human face is perhaps the best criterion of value.

WILLIAM HAZLITT, *Trifles Light as Air*. No. 17.

2
The human face is the masterpiece of God. The eyes reveal the soul, the mouth the flesh, The chin stands for purpose, the nose means will; But over and behind all is that fleeting something we call "expression."

ELBERT HUBBARD, *Little Journeys: Leonardo*.

3
Men's faces are not to be trusted; does not every street abound in gloomy-visaged debauchees? (Frontis nulla fides; quis enim non vicus abundat Tristibus obscænis?)

JUVENAL, *Satires*. Sat. ii, l. 8.

Trust not to outward show!

JUVENAL, *Satires*, ii, 8. (Gifford, tr.)

See also under APPEARANCES.

4
The face, when we are born, is no less tender than any other part of the body: it is use alone hardens it, and makes it more able to endure the cold. And therefore the Scythian philosopher gave a very significant answer to the Athenian, who wondered how he could go naked in frost and snow. "How," said the Scythian, "can you endure your face exposed to the sharp winter?" "My face is used to it," said the Athenian. "Think me all face," replied the Scythian.

JOHN LOCKE, *On Education*. Sec. 5.

You have your face bare; I am all face. (Vous avez bien la face descouverte; moi je suis tout face.)

MONTAIGNE, *Essays*. Bk. i, ch. 35. The answer of a naked beggar, when asked if he was cold. Fuller (*Worthies of England: Berkshire*, p. 82) tells the same story, and it is also given as the reply of an Indian, wearing only a breech-cloth, skating on the river at Quebec.

5
A face that had a story to tell. How different faces are in this particular! Some of them speak not. They are books in which not a line is written, save perhaps a date.

LONGFELLOW, *Hyperion*. Bk. i, ch. 4.

6
He [the Deity] gave to man an uplifted face, and bade him contemplate the heavens. (Os homini sublime dedit, cœlumque videri.)

OVID, *Metamorphoses*. Bk. i, l. 85.

7
Alas, how hard it is not to betray a guilty conscience in the face! (Heu! quam difficile est crimen non prodere vultu!)

OVID, *Metamorphoses*. Bk. ii, l. 447.

A troubled countenance oft discloses much. (Multa sed trepidus solet Detegere vultus.)

SENECA, *Thyestes*, l. 330.

8
The face of man is the index to joy and mirth, to severity and sadness. (Frons homini lætitiæ et hilaritatis, seceritatis et tristiæ index.)

PLINY THE ELDER, *Historia Naturalis*. Bk. ii, sec. 37.

The face is oftentimes a true index of the heart.

JAMES HOWELL, *Familiar Letters*. Bk. i, sec. 3, epis. 15. (1645)

For what is form and what is face,
But the soul's index or its case?

NATHANIEL COTTON, *Visions in Verse: Pleasure*.

The face the index of a feeling mind.

CRABBE, *Tales of the Hall*. Bk. xvi, l. 113.

All is not well within; for still we find
The face the unerring index of the mind.

JUVENAL, *Satires*. Sat. ix, l. 18. (Gifford, tr.)

That old saying is untrue, "the face
Is index of the heart."

UNKNOWN, *Times Whistle*, 23. (c. 1615)

9
All men's faces are true, whatsome'er their hands are.

SHAKESPEARE, *Antony and Cleopatra*, ii, 6, 102.

10
Your face, my thane, is as a book, where men
May read strange matters.

SHAKESPEARE, *Macbeth*. Act i, sc. 5, l. 63.

I saw Othello's visage in his mind.

SHAKESPEARE, *Othello*. Act i, sc. 3, l. 253.

11
Though men can cover crimes with bold stern looks,
Poor women's faces are their own faults' books.

SHAKESPEARE, *The Rape of Lucrece*, l. 1252.

12
I trowe that countenance cannot lie
Whose thoughts are legible in the eye.

SPENSER, *An Elegie*, l. 106.

For in the face judicious eyes may find
The symptoms of a good or evil mind.

JOHN WARD, *History of the Grand Rebellion*, i, 8. (1713)

13
In the faces of men and women I see God.

WALT WHITMAN, *Song of Myself*. St. 48.

14
The face of every one
That passes by me is a mystery!

WORDSWORTH, *The Prelude*. Bk. vii, st. 24.

II—Face: Apothegms

15
It is good that a man's face gives his tongue leave to speak.

FRANCIS BACON, *Essays: Of Simulation and Dissimulation*.

16
May the man be damned and never grow fat
Who wears two faces under one hat.

H. G. BOHN, *Hand-Book of Proverbs*, 451.

Two faces under one hood.

THOMAS FULLER, *Gnomologia*.

1
And in the scowl of Heaven, each face
Grew dark as they were speaking.
THOMAS CAMPBELL, *Lord Ullin's Daughter.*

2
I will not lend my countenance to the enterprise.
GROVER CLEVELAND, to John Finley, who had urged him to have his portrait painted. (NEVINS, *Grover Cleveland*, p. 762.)

3
I have always considered my face a convenience rather than an ornament.
O. W. HOLMES, *Life and Letters.* Vol. ii, p. 103.

4
That saw the manners in the face.
SAMUEL JOHNSON, *On the Death of Hogarth.*

5
Your face betrays your years. (Facies tua conputat annos.)
JUVENAL, *Satires.* Sat. vi, l. 199.

And careful hours with time's deformed hand
Have written strange defeatures in my face.
SHAKESPEARE, *Comedy of Errors*, v, 1, 298.

6
These faces in the mirrors
Are but the shadows and phantoms of myself.
LONGFELLOW, *Masque of Pandora.* Pt. ii, l. 72.

7
And where thou hast most matter to complain,
Make the good face and glad in port thee feign.
JOHN LYDGATE, *Troy Book.* Bk. ii, l. 4366. (1412)

Though it be a foul lie, set upon it a good face.
JOHN BALE, *Kynge Johan*, l. 1991. (c. 1540)

Set a good face on a bad matter.
HUMPHREY GIFFORD, *A Posie of Gilloflowers*, 44. (1580)

God hath done his part: she hath a good face.
JOHN HEYWOOD, *Spider and Flie*, 4. (1556)

8
Often a silent face has voice and words. (Sæpe tacens vocem verbaque vultus habet.)
OVID, *Ars Amatoria.* Bk. i, l. 574.

But still her silent looks loudly reproached me. (Sed taciti fecere tamen convicia vultus.)
OVID, *Amores.* Bk. i, eleg. 7, l. 21.

9
When the disposition is friendly the face pleases. (Ingenio facies conciliante placet.)
OVID, *De Medicamine Faciei*, l. 44.

10
Make thy face to shine upon thy servant.
Old Testament: Psalms, xxxi, 16.

Show thy servant the light of thy countenance.
Book of Common Prayer: The Psalter.

11
A comely face is a silent recommendation. (Formosa facies muta commendatio est.)
PUBLILIUS SYRUS, *Sententiæ.* No. 207.

A fair face is half a portion.
JOHN RAY, *English Proverbs.*

A good face needs no band, and a pretty wench no land.
JOHN RAY, *English Proverbs.*
See also under APPEARANCE.

12
The human face is my landscape.
SIR JOSHUA REYNOLDS, remarking that he did not enjoy the scenery of Richmond.

13
I next strained my eyes, with equally bad success, to see if, among the sea of upturned faces which bent their eyes on the pulpit as a common center, I could discover the sober and business-like physiognomy of Owen.
SIR WALTER SCOTT, *Rob Roy.* Ch. 20. (1817)

In this sea of upturned faces there is something which excites me strangely, deeply, before I even begin to speak.
DANIEL WEBSTER, *Speech,* Faneuil Hall, 30 Sept., 1842. Opening sentence.

The slope of faces from the floor to th' roof,
(As if one master-spring controll'd them all)
Relax'd into a universal grin.
COWPER, *The Task.* Bk. iv, l. 202.

A press of gaping faces.
SHAKESPEARE, *The Rape of Lucrece*, l. 1408.

15
Your honour's face is made of a fiddle; every one that looks on you, loves you.
SMOLLETT, *Sir Launcelot Greaves.* Ch. 8.

16
Well, I will set a face of brass on it.
GEORGE WHETSTONE, *Promos and Cassandra.* Pt. ii, 3, 1. (1578)

"Say, boys! if you give me just another whiskey
I'll be glad,
And I'll draw right here a picture of the face that drove me mad.
Give me that piece of chalk with which you mark the baseball score,
You shall see the lovely Madeleine upon the barroom floor."
H. ANTOINE D'ARCY, *The Face Upon the Floor.*

III—Face: Its Beauty

See also Beauty

17
A face to lose youth for, to occupy age
With the dream of, meet death with.
ROBERT BROWNING, *A Likeness.*

18
Whose face is this, so musically fair?
ROBERT BUCHANAN, *The Syren.*

19
The Deil he could na skaith thee,
Or aught that wad belang thee:
He'd look into thy bonnie face,
And say:— "I canna wrang thee!"
BURNS, *Saw Ye Bonnie Lesley.*

20
His honest, sonsie, baws'nt face
Aye gat him friends in ilka place.
BURNS, *The Twa Dogs*, l. 31.

A picturesque countenance, rather than one that is esteemed of regular features.
WILLIAM SHENSTONE, *An Humourist.*

1
Yet even her tyranny had such a grace,
The women pardoned all, except her face.
BYRON, *Don Juan.* Canto v, st. 113.

2
And to his eye
There was but one beloved face on earth,
And that was shining on him.
BYRON, *The Dream.* St. 2.

3
There is a garden in her face,
Where roses and white lilies grow;
A heavenly paradise is that place,
Wherein all pleasant fruits do flow.
There cherries grow, which none may buy,
Till "Cherry ripe" themselves do cry.
THOMAS CAMPION, *Cherry Ripe.* These verses, which appeared originally in *An Hour's Recreation in Music,* in 1606, without ascription of authorship, were for a time attributed to Richard Alison, who set them to music. Campion claimed them in a note in *Fourth Book of Airs,* and there is no reason to doubt his authorship.

Flushing white and soften'd red;
Mingling tints, as when there glows
In snowy milk the bashful rose.
THOMAS MOORE, *Odes of Anacreon.* Ode xvi, l. 28.

4
The magic of a face.
THOMAS CAREW, *Epitaph on the Lady S——.*

5
He had a face like a benediction.
CERVANTES, *Don Quixote.* Pt. i, ch. 4.

6
Her face, oh call it fair, not pale!
S. T. COLERIDGE, *Christabel.* Pt. i, l. 289.

Her brow was fair, but *very* pale, and looked
Like stainless marble; a touch methought would soil
Its whiteness. O'er her temple one blue vein
Ran like a tendril.
BARRY CORNWALL, *The Magdalen.*

7
The fairest garden in her looks
And in her mind the wisest books.
ABRAHAM COWLEY, *The Garden.* Pt. i.

8
With faces like dead lovers who died true.
DINAH M. M. CRAIK, *Indian Summer.*

9
What cunning can express
The favour of her face?
EDWARD DE VERE, *What Cunning Can Express.*

Sweet grave aspect.
DU BARTAS, *Devine Weekes and Workes.* Week i, day 4.

10
Her face betokened all things dear and good.
JEAN INGELOW, *Margaret in the Xebec.* St. 57.

The light upon her face
Shines from the windows of another world.
Saints only have such faces.
LONGFELLOW, *Michael Angelo.* Pt. ii, sec. 6.

11
Oh! could you view the melody
Of ev'ry grace,
And music of her face,
You'd drop a tear,
Seeing more harmony
In her bright eye,
Than now you hear.
RICHARD LOVELACE, *Orpheus to Beasts.* St. 2.

12
Human face divine.
MILTON, *Paradise Lost.* Bk. iii, l. 44.

13
Thy face remembered is from other worlds,
It has been died for, though I know not when,
It has been sung of, though I know not where.
STEPHEN PHILLIPS, *Marpessa.*

14
If to her share some female errors fall
Look on her face, and you'll forget 'em all.
POPE, *The Rape of the Lock.* Canto ii, l. 17.

15
The sweet expression of that face,
For ever changing, yet the same.
SAMUEL ROGERS, *A Farewell.*

With every change his features play'd,
As aspens show the light and shade.
SCOTT, *Rokeby.* Canto iii, st. 5.

16
A face which is always serene possesses a mysterious and powerful attraction: sad hearts come to it, as to the sun, to warm themselves again.
JOSEPH ROUX, *Meditations of a Parish Priest. Love, Friendship, Friends.* No. 10.

A sweet attractive kind of grace,
A full assurance given by looks,
Continual comfort in a face
The lineaments of Gospel books.
MATTHEW ROYDON, *An Elegie.*

17
His face was as the heavens; and therein stuck
A sun and moon, which kept their course, and lighted
The little O, the earth.
SHAKESPEARE, *Antony and Cleopatra.* Act v, sc. 2, l. 79.

18
For thou hast given me in this beauteous face,
A world of earthly blessings to my soul,
If sympathy of love unite our thoughts.
SHAKESPEARE, *II Henry VI.* Act i, sc. 1, l. 21.

Fair ladies mask'd are roses in their bud:
Dismask'd, their damask sweet commixture shown,
Are angels veiling clouds, or roses blown.
SHAKESPEARE, *Love's Labour's Lost.* Act v, sc. 2, l. 295.

1
Viola: Good madam, let me see your face.
Olivia: Have you any commission from your lord to negotiate with my face? You are now out of your text: but we will draw the curtain and show you the picture . . . . 'tis in grain, sir; 'twill endure wind and weather.
Viola: 'Tis beauty truly blent, whose red and white
Nature's own sweet and cunning hand laid on.
SHAKESPEARE, *Twelfth Night*. Act i, sc. 5, 248.

2
If I should die to-night,
My friends would look upon my quiet face
Before they laid it in its resting-place,
And deem that death had left it almost fair.
ARABELLA EUGENIA SMITH, *If I Should Die To-night.*

3
Her angel's face
As the great eye of heaven, shined bright,
And made a sunshine in the shady place;
Did never mortal eye behold such heavenly grace.
SPENSER, *Faerie Queene*. Bk. i, canto 3, st. 4.

4
Her cheeks so rare a white was on,
No daisy makes comparison
(Who sees them is undone);
For streaks of red were mingled there,
Such as are on a Cath'rine pear
(The side that's next the Sun).
SIR JOHN SUCKLING, *A Ballad Upon a Wedding*. St. 10.

Her face is like the Milky Way i' the sky,—
A meeting of gentle lights without a name.
SIR JOHN SUCKLING, *Brennoralt*. Act iii.

5
White rose in red rose-garden
Is not so white;
Snowdrops that plead for pardon
And pine for fright . . .
Grow not as this face grows from pale to bright.
SWINBURNE, *Before the Mirror.*

6
Your sweet faces make good fellows fools
And traitors.
TENNYSON, *Geraint and Enid,* l. 399.

7
A countenance in which did meet
Sweet records, promises as sweet.
WORDSWORTH, *She Was a Phantom of Delight.*

A face with gladness overspread!
Soft smiles, by human kindness bred!
WORDSWORTH, *To a Highland Girl.*

IV--Face: Its Ugliness

8
Thou hast a serious face.
A betting, bargaining and saving face,
A rich face; pawn it to the usurer.
BEAUMONT AND FLETCHER, *The Scornful Lady*. Act iii.

9
Her nose and chin they threaten ither.
BURNS, *Sic a Wife as Willie Had.*

10
He's Judas to a tittle that man is,
Just such a face!
ROBERT BROWNING, *Fra Lippo Lippi.*

11
As a beauty I'm not a great star,
There are others more handsome by far;
But my face I don't mind it
Because I'm behind it—
'Tis the folks out in front that I jar.
ANTHONY EUWER, *Limeratomy*. This limerick has sometimes been ascribed to Woodrow Wilson because it was his favorite one, and he occasionally wrote it in an album.

My face. Is this long strip of skin
Which bears of worry many a trace,
Of sallow hue, of features thin,
This mass of seams and lines, my face?
EDMUND YATES, *Aged Forty.*

12
In my poor, lean, lank face nobody has ever seen that any cabbages were sprouting.
ABRAHAM LINCOLN, *Speech,* Lincoln-Douglas Debates.

13
She was a lady of incisive features bound in stale parchment.
GEORGE MEREDITH, *Diana of the Crossways.* Ch. 14.

14
His face so pale and skin transparent was,
It seemed a ghastly looking-glass of death.
FRANCIS ROUS, *Thule.*

15
His face was of that doubtful kind
That wins the eye, but not the mind.
SCOTT, *Rokeby*. Canto v, st. 16.

16
Thou hast a grim appearance, and thy face
Bears a command in 't.
SHAKESPEARE, *Coriolanus*. Act iv, sc. 5, l. 66.

You have such a February face,
So full of frost, of storm, of cloudiness.
SHAKESPEARE, *Much Ado About Nothing*. Act v, sc. 4, l. 41.

17
The tartness of his face sours ripe grapes.
SHAKESPEARE, *Coriolanus*. Act v, sc. 4, l. 18.

I have seen better faces in my time
Than stands on any shoulder that I see.
SHAKESPEARE, *King Lear*. Act ii, sc. 2, l. 99.

18
Compare her face with some that I shall show;
And I will make thee think thy swan a crow.
SHAKESPEARE, *Romeo and Juliet*. Act i, sc. 2, l. 91.

Mislike me not for my complexion,
The shadow'd livery of the burnish'd sun.
SHAKESPEARE, *The Merchant of Venice*. Act ii, sc. 1, l. 1.

Dusk faces with white silken turbans wreath'd.
MILTON, *Paradise Regained*. Bk. iv, l. 76.

1
His face was like a snake's—wrinkled and
loose
And withered.
SHELLEY, *Fragment: A Face.*

2
A damned disinheriting countenance.
SHERIDAN, *School for Scandal.* Act iv, sc. 1.

V—Face: Painted

See also under Whore

3
Ægle, beauty and poet, has two little crimes:
She makes her own face, and does not make
her rhymes.
BYRON, *From the French.*

4
Ancient Phillis has young graces,
'Tis a strange thing, but a true one;
Shall I tell you how?
She herself makes her own faces,
And each morning wears a new one;
Where's the wonder now?
CONGREVE, *The Double-Dealer.* Act iii, sc. 10.

5
A Face, made up
Out of no other shop
Than what Nature's white hand sets ope.
RICHARD CRASHAW, *Wishes to His (Supposed) Mistress.* St. 10.

6
The ladies of St. James's!
They're painted to the eyes;
Their white it stays for ever,
Their red it never dies;
But Phyllida, my Phyllida!
Her colour comes and goes;
It trembles to a lily,—
It wavers to a rose.
AUSTIN DOBSON, *The Ladies of St. James's.*

7
Thy flattering picture, Phryne, is like thee,
Only in this, that you both painted be.
JOHN DONNE, *Phryne.*

8
Men say y'are fair; and fair ye are, 'tis true;
But, hark! we praise the painter now, not
you.
ROBERT HERRICK, *On a Painted Gentlewoman.*

9
A good face needs no painting.
THOMAS HEYWOOD, *Somers Tracts,* iii, 575. (1612)

Where the countenance is fair, there need no colours.
JOHN LYLY, *Euphues,* p. 204. (1581)

10
Oh! if to dance all night, and dress all day,
Charm'd the small-pox, or chas'd old age
away; . . .
To patch, nay, ogle, might become a saint,
Nor could it sure be such a sin to paint.
POPE, *The Rape of the Lock.* Canto v, l. 19.

11
Even now, mad girl, dost ape the painted Briton and wanton with foreign dyes upon thy cheek? The face is ever best as nature made it; foul shows the Belgian rouge on Roman cheeks!
PROPERTIUS, *Elegies.* Bk. ii, eleg. 18, l. 23.

12
I have heard of your paintings too, well enough; God has given you one face, and you make yourselves another.
SHAKESPEARE, *Hamlet.* Act iii, sc. 1, l. 148.

He's a god or a painter, for he makes faces.
SHAKESPEARE, *Love's Labour's Lost.* Act v, sc. 2, l. 648.

13
The intoxication of rouge is an insidious vintage known to more girls than mere man can ever believe.
DOROTHY SPEARE, *Dancers in the Dark.*

FACTS

14
Facts, when combined with ideas, constitute the greatest force in the world. They are greater than armaments, greater than finance, greater than science, business and law because they are the common denominator of all of them.
CARL W. ACKERMAN, *Address,* 26 Sept., 1931.

15
This plain, plump fact.
ROBERT BROWNING, *Mr. Sludge "The Medium."*

16
Truth, fact, is the life of all things; falsity, "fiction," or whatever it may call itself, is certain to be the death.
THOMAS CARLYLE, *Latter-Day Pamphlets.* No. 8.

17
Now what I want is, Facts. Facts alone are wanted in life.
DICKENS, *Hard Times.* Bk. i, ch. 1.

In this life we want nothing but facts, Sir; nothing but facts.
DICKENS, *Hard Times.* Bk. i, ch. 1. A phrase put into the mouth of Thomas Gradgrind: "A man of realities. A man of facts and calculations." (Bk. i, ch. 2.)

18
You can't alter facts by filming them over with dead romances.
JOHN DRINKWATER, *Mary Stuart.*

19
No facts to me are sacred; none are profane.
EMERSON, *Essays, First Series: Circles.*

I distrust the facts and the inferences.
EMERSON, *Essays, Second Series: Experience.*

Time dissipates to shining ether the solid angularity of facts. No anchor, no cable, no fences avail to keep a fact a fact.
EMERSON, *Essays, First Series: History.*

20
Why covet a knowledge of new facts? Day and night, house and garden, a few books,

a few actions, serve us as well as would all trades and spectacles.

EMERSON, *Essays, Second Series: The Poet.*

1
A concept is stronger than a fact.

CHARLOTTE P. GILMAN, *Human Work.*

2
Thoughts come back; beliefs persist; facts pass by, never to return.

GOETHE, *Sprüche in Prosa.*

3
Facts do not cease to exist because they are ignored.

ALDOUS HUXLEY, *Proper Studies,* p. 247.

4
A world of facts lies outside and beyond the world of words.

T. H. HUXLEY, *Lay Sermons,* p. 57.

5
I will sing of facts; but some will say that I invented them. (Facta canam; sed erunt qui me finxisse loquantur.)

OVID, *Fasti.* Bk. vi, l. 3.

6
Facts are facts, as the saying is.

SMOLLETT, *Sir Launcelot Greaves.*

But facts are facts and flinch not.

ROBERT BROWNING, *The Ring and the Book.* Pt. ii, l. 1049.

7
Matters of fact, as Mr. Budgell somewhere observes, are very stubborn things.

MATTHEW TINDAL, *Will,* p. 23. (1733)

Facts are stubborn things.

EBENEZER ELLIOTT, *Field Husbandry,* p. 35. (1747) The phrase was also used by Smollett in his translation of Le Sage's *Gil Blas* (bk. x, ch. 1), which was published in 1755.

But facts are chiels that winna ding,
An' downa be disputed.

BURNS, *A Dream.* St. 4.

8
Facts, or what a man believes to be facts, are delightful. . . . Get your facts first, and then you can distort them as much as you please.

MARK TWAIN. (KIPLING, *From Sea to Sea.* Letter 37.)

FAILURE

See also Fall; Success and Failure; Victory and Defeat

9
They fail, and they alone, who have not striven.

THOMAS BAILEY ALDRICH, *Enamored Architect of Airy Rhyme.*

Straight from a mighty bow this truth is driven:
"They fail, and they alone, who have not striven."

CLARENCE URMY, *The Arrow.*

10
The fight is lost—and he knows it is lost—and yet he is fighting still!

E. J. APPLETON, *The Fighting Failure.*

11
Charge once more, then, and be dumb!
Let the victors, when they come,
When the forts of folly fall,
Find thy body by the wall!

MATTHEW ARNOLD, *The Last Word.*

To fear not sensible failure,
Nor covet the game at all,
But fighting, fighting, fighting,
Die, driven against the wall.

LOUISE IMOGEN GUINEY, *The Kings.*

Thy part is with broken saber
To rise on the last redoubt;

LOUISE IMOGEN GUINEY, *The Kings.*

12
In life let men learn not to know defeat. (Proinde ita parent se in vita, ut vinci nesciant.)

ATREUS, *Sententiæ.* (CICERO, *Tusculanarum Disputationum,* v, 18.)

13
There's no defeat, in truth, save from within;
Unless you're beaten there, you're bound to win!

HENRY AUSTIN, *Perseverance Conquers All.*

14
For he that is used to go forward, and findeth a stop, falleth out of his own favour, and is not the thing he was.

FRANCIS BACON, *Essays: Of Empire.*

15
Jove strikes the Titans down
Not when they set about their mountain-piling
But when another rock would crown the work.

ROBERT BROWNING, *Paracelsus.* Pt. v, l. 128.

16
I give the fight up: let there be an end,
A privacy, an obscure nook for me.
I want to be forgotten even by God.

ROBERT BROWNING, *Paracelsus.* Pt. v, l. 373.

17
When human power and failure
Are equalized for ever.

ROBERT BUCHANAN, *To David in Heaven.* St. 22.

18
In the lexicon of youth, which Fate reserves
For a bright manhood, there is no such word
As—*fail!* . . . Never say "*Fail*" again.

BULWER-LYTTON, *Richelieu.* Act ii, sc. 2.

There 's no such word as "*fail!*"

BULWER-LYTTON, *Richelieu.* Act iii, sc. 1.

19
Now a' is done that men can do,
And a' is done in vain.

BURNS, *It Was a' for Our Rightfu' King.*

20
We are the doubles of those whose way
Was festal with fruits and flowers;
Body and brain we were sound as they,
But the prizes were not ours.

RICHARD BURTON, *Song of the Unsuccessful.*

1
Better to sink beneath the shock
Than moulder piecemeal on the rock.
BYRON, *The Giaour*, l. 969.

E'en if he failed, he still delayed his fall.
BYRON, *Lara*. Canto ii, st. 9.

2
They never fail who die
In a great cause: the block may soak their gore;
Their heads may sodden in the sun; their limbs
Be strung to city gates and castle walls—
But still their spirit walks abroad.
BYRON, *Marino Faliero*. Act ii, sc. 2, l. 606.

3
This voice did on my spirit fall,
Peschiera, when thy bridge I crossed:
"'Tis better to have fought and lost,
Than never to have fought at all."
ARTHUR HUGH CLOUGH, *Peschiera*. St. 10.

Say not the struggle nought availeth,
The labour and the wounds are vain.
A. H. CLOUGH, *Say Not*, etc.

4
And though contending long dread Fate to master,
He failed at last her enmity to cheat,
He turned with such a smile to face disaster
That he sublimed defeat.
FLORENCE EARLE COATES, *The Hero*.

5
A fool often fails because he thinks what is difficult is easy, and a wise man because he thinks what is easy is difficult.
CHURTON COLLINS, *Aphorisms*.

6
Secure of nothing—but to lose the race.
COWPER, *The Progress of Error*, l. 563.

7
Thou art weighed in the balances, and art found wanting.
Old Testament: Daniel, v, 27.

8
He has gone to the demnition bow-wows.
DICKENS, *Nicholas Nickleby*. Ch. 64.

9
It might be easier
To fail with land in sight,
Than gain my blue peninsula
To perish of delight.
EMILY DICKINSON, *Poems*. Pt. i, No. 132.

'Tis double death to drown in ken of shore.
SHAKESPEARE, *The Rape of Lucrece*, l. 1114.

10
"So it will go on, worsening and worsening," thought Adam. "There's no slipping up hill again, and no standing still when you've begun to slip down."
GEORGE ELIOT, *Adam Bede*. Ch. 4.

And nothing to look backward to with pride,
And nothing to look forward to with hope.
ROBERT FROST, *The Death of the Hired Man*.

11
They win who never near the goal;
They run who halt on wounded feet;
Art hath its martyrs like the soul,
Its victors in defeat.
EDMUND GOSSE, *William Blake*.

12
Half the failures in life arise from pulling in one's horse as he is leaping.
J. C. AND A. W. HARE, *Guesses at Truth*. Pt. i.

13
Failed the bright promise of your early day?
BISHOP REGINALD HEBER, *Palestine*, l. 113.

14
In the world who does not know how to swim goes to the bottom.
GEORGE HERBERT, *Jacula Prudentum*.

15
Who would not rather founder in the fight
Than not have known the glory of the fray?
RICHARD HOVEY, *Two and Fate*.

16
There's dignity in suffering—
Nobility in pain—
But failure is a salted wound
That burns and burns again.
MARGERY HOWELL, *Wormwood*.

17
A failure is a man who has blundered, but is not able to cash in the experience.
ELBERT HUBBARD, *Epigrams*.

18
He that fails in his endeavours after wealth and power, will not long retain either honesty or courage.
SAMUEL JOHNSON, *The Adventurer*. No. 99.

19
Complaints are vain; we will try to do better another time. Tomorrow and tomorrow. A few designs and a few failures, and the time of designing is past.
SAMUEL JOHNSON, *Letters*. Vol. i, p. 53.

20
There is not a fiercer hell than the failure in a great object.
KEATS, *Endymion: Preface*.

21
The probability that we may fail in the struggle ought not to deter us from the support of a cause we believe to be just.
ABRAHAM LINCOLN, *Speech*, Springfield, Ill., Dec., 1839.

22
To fail at all is to fail utterly.
J. R. LOWELL, *Among My Books: Dryden*.

23
"All honor to him who shall win the prize,"
The world has cried for a thousand years;
But to him who tries and fails and dies,
I give great honor and glory and tears.
JOAQUIN MILLER, *For Those Who Fail*.

24
If this fail,
The pillar'd firmament is rottenness,
And earth's base built on stubble.
MILTON, *Comus*, l. 597.

1
Born to fail, A name without an echo.
HENRY NEWBOLT, *The Non-Combatant.*

2
Their wreaths are willows and their tribute, tears;
Their names are old sad stories in men's ears;
Yet they will scatter the red hordes of Hell,
Who went to battle forth and always fell.
SHAEMAS O'SHEEL, *They Went Forth to Battle, But They Always Fell.*

They went forth to battle, but they always fell.
OSSIAN, *Cath-loda.* Duan ii.

3
And though he greatly failed, more greatly dared.
(Quem si non tenuit magnis tamen excidit ausis.)
OVID, *Metamorphoses.* Bk. ii, l. 328. The epitaph of Phaëton.

If thou art a man, admire those who attempt great things, even though they fail. (Si vir es, suspice, etiam si decidunt, magna conantes.)
SENECA, *De Brevitate Vitæ.* Sec. 20.

4
Who, like the hindmost chariot wheels, art curst
Still to be near, but ne'er to reach the first.
(Nam quamvis prope te, quamvis temone sub uno
Vertentem sese frustra sectabere canthum,
Cum rota posterior curras et in axe secundo.)
PERSIUS, *Satires.* Sat. v, l. 70.

Never mind;
If some of us were not so far behind,
The rest of us were not so far ahead.
E. A. ROBINSON, *Inferential.*

5
The work perishes fruitlessly. (Opera nequidquam perit.)
PHÆDRUS, *Fables.* Bk. ii, fab. 5, l. 24.

6
Lonely antagonists of Destiny,
That went down scornful before many spears.
STEPHEN PHILLIPS, *Marpessa.*

Better go down in the stirring fight
Than drowse to death by the sheltering shore.
DAISY RINEHART, *The Call of the Open Sea.*

7
He is good that failed never.
JAMES KELLY, *Scottish Proverbs.*

8
And the last sleeping-place of Nebuchadnezzar—
When I arrive there I shall tell the wind:
"You ate grass: I have eaten crow—
Who is better off now or next year?"
CARL SANDBURG, *Losers.*

9
The man who can fight to Heaven's own height
Is the man who can fight when he's losing.
ROBERT W. SERVICE, *Carry On.*

And each forgets, as he strips and runs
With a brilliant, fitful pace,
It's the steady, quiet, plodding ones
Who win in the lifelong race.
And each forgets that his youth has fled,
Forgets that his prime is past,
Till he stands one day, with a hope that's dead,
In the glare of the truth at last.
ROBERT W. SERVICE, *The Men That Don't Fit In.*

10
I have been all things and it availed nothing. (Omnia fui et nihil expedit.)
EMPEROR SEPTIMIUS SEVERUS. (*History of Augustus,* x, 18.)

11
My cake is dough: but I'll be among the rest,
Out of hope of all, but my share of the feast.
SHAKESPEARE, *The Taming of the Shrew.* Act v, sc. 1, l. 143.

12
We said on that first day, we said and swore
That self should be no more;
That we were risen, that we would wholly be
For love and liberty;
And in the exhilaration of that oath
We cast off spite and sloth,
And laboured for an hour, till we began,
Man after piteous man,
To lose the splendour, to forget the dream.
E. B. SHANKS, *Meditation in June, 1917.*

13
A living failure is better than a dead masterpiece.
BERNARD SHAW, *The Adventures of the Black Girl in Her Search for God.*

14
With timid foot he touched each plan,
Sure that each plan would fail;
Behemoth's tread was his, it seemed,
And every bridge too frail.
E. R. SILL, *Roland.*

15
Yes, this is life; and everywhere we meet,
Not victor crowns, but wailings of defeat.
ELIZABETH OAKES SMITH, *The Unattained.*

16
He who never fails will never grow rich.
C. H. SPURGEON, *John Ploughman.* Ch. 12.

17
I sing the hymn of the conquered, who fell in the battle of life,
The hymn of the wounded, the beaten who died overwhelmed in the strife;
Not the jubilant song of the victors for whom the resounding acclaim
Of nations was lifted in chorus, whose brows wore the chaplet of fame,
But the hymn of the low and the humble, the weary, the broken in heart,
Who strove and who failed, acting bravely a silent and desperate part.
WILLIAM WETMORE STORY, *Io Victis.*

18
God, though this life is but a wraith,
Although we know not what we use.

Although we grope with little faith,
Give me the heart to fight—and lose.
LOUIS UNTERMEYER, *Prayer*.

1
Who shines in the second rank, is eclipsed in the first. (Qui brille au second rang, s'éclipse au premier.)
VOLTAIRE, *La Henriade*. Canto i, l. 31.

2
Great is the facile conqueror;
Yet happy he, who, wounded sore,
Breathless, unhorsed, all covered o'er
With blood and sweat,
Sinks foiled, but fighting evermore,
Is greater yet.
WILLIAM WATSON, *In Laleham Churchyard*. St. 14. The burial place of Matthew Arnold.

3
Have you heard that it was good to gain the day?
I also say it is good to fall, battles are lost in the same spirit in which they are won.
WALT WHITMAN, *Song of Myself*. Sec. 18.

To those who've fail'd, in aspiration vast,
To unnam'd soldiers fallen in front on the lead,
To calm, devoted engineers—to over-ardent travellers—to pilots on their ships,
To many a lofty song and picture without recognition—I'd rear a laurel-cover'd monument.
WALT WHITMAN, *To Those Who've Fail'd*.

4
Let the thick curtain fall;
I better know than all
How little I have gained,
How vast the unattained.
WHITTIER, *My Triumph*. St. 7.

Sweeter than any sung
My songs that found no tongue;
Nobler than any fact
My wish that failed of act.
WHITTIER, *My Triumph*. St. 9.

Others shall sing the song,
Others shall right the wrong,—
Finish what I begin,
And all I fail of win.
WHITTIER, *My Triumph*. St. 10.

FAIRIES

5
Up the airy mountain,
Down the rushy glen,
We daren't go a-hunting
For fear of little men;
Wee folk, good folk,
Trooping all together;
Green jacket, red cap,
And white owl's feather!
WILLIAM ALLINGHAM, *The Fairies*.

6
When the first baby laughed for the first time, his laugh broke into a million pieces, and they all went skipping about. That was the beginning of fairies.
J. M. BARRIE, *Little White Bird*. Ch. 16.

Whenever a child says "I don't believe in fairies" there's a little fairy somewhere that falls right down dead.
J. M. BARRIE, *Peter Pan*.

Do you believe in fairies? If you believe clap your hands. Don't let Tinker die.
J. M. BARRIE, *Peter Pan*. Tinker Bell, the fairy of the play, was desperately ill because she had drunk some poison which Captain Hook, the pirate, had mixed for Peter Pan, and she could be saved only if children still believed in fairies.

The weird "Never, Never Land," so called by the earliest pioneers from the small chance they anticipated, on reaching it, of ever being able to return to civilization.
A. J. VOGAN, *The Black Police*, 85. That portion of Queensland north or west of Cape Capricorn.

7
For when the stars are shining clear
And all the world is still,
They float across the silver moon
From hill to cloudy hill.
ROBERT BIRD, *The Fairy Folk*.

8
Where Little People live in nuts,
And ride on butterflies.
ABBIE FARWELL BROWN, *The Fairy Book*.

9
Bright Eyes, Light Eyes, Daughter of a Fay!
ROBERT BUCHANAN, *The Fairy Foster Mother*.

10
On gossamer nights when the moon is low,
And stars in the mist are hiding,
Over the hill where the foxgloves grow
You may see the fairies riding.
MARY C. G. BYRON, *The Fairy Thrall*.

11
They live 'neath the curtain
Of fir woods and heather,
And never take hurt in
The wildest of weather.
PATRICK R. CHALMERS, *Puk-Wudjies*.

12
Farewell, rewards and fairies!
Good housewives now may say;
For now foul sluts in dairies
Do fare as well as they.
And though they sweep their hearths no less
Than maids were wont to do,
Yet who of late, for cleanliness,
Finds sixpence in her shoe?
RICHARD CORBET, *Farewell to the Fairies*.

Rewards and Fairies.
RUDYARD KIPLING. Title of book for children.

13
Children born of fairy stock
Never need for shirt or frock,
Never want for food or fire,
Always get their heart's desire.
ROBERT GRAVES, *I'd Love to Be a Fairy's Child*.

14
Have ye left the greenwood lone,
Are your steps for ever gone?

Fairy King and Elfin Queen,
Come ye to the sylvan scene,
From your dim and distant shore,
Never more?

FELICIA DOROTHEA HEMANS, *Fairy Song.*

Oberon! Titania!
Did your starlight mirth
With the song of Avon
Quit this work-day earth?
Yet, while green leaves glisten,
And while bright stars burn,
By that magic memory,
Oh! return, return!

FELICIA DOROTHEA HEMANS, *Fairies' Call.*

1
A little fairy comes at night,
Her eyes are blue, her hair is brown,
With silver spots upon her wings,
And from the moon she flutters down.

THOMAS HOOD, *Queen Mab.* St. 1.

2
Then take me on your knee, mother;
And listen, mother of mine.
A hundred fairies danced last night,
And the harpers they were nine.

MARY HOWITT, *The Fairies of the Caldon Low.* St. 5.

3
Nothing can be truer than fairy wisdom. It is as true as sunbeams.

DOUGLAS JERROLD, *Specimens of Jerrold's Wit: Fairy Tales.*

'Tis as true as the fairy tales told in the books.

S. G. GOODRICH, *Birthright of the Humming Birds.*

4
It is not children only that one feeds with fairy tales. (Nicht die Kinder bloss speist man mit Märchen ab.)

LESSING, *Nathan der Weise.* Act iii, sc. 6.

5
I took it for a faëry vision
Of some gay creatures of the element,
That in the colours of the rainbow live,
And play i' th' plighted clouds.

MILTON, *Comus,* l. 298.

Faëry elves,
Whose midnight revels by a forest-side,
Or fountain, some belated peasant sees,
Or dreams he sees, while overhead the Moon
Sits arbitress, and nearer to the Earth
Wheels her pale course, they on their mirth and dance
Intent, with jocund music charm his ear;
At once with joy and fear his heart rebounds.

MILTON, *Paradise Lost.* Bk. i, l. 781.

6
The dances ended, all the fairy train
For pinks and daisies search'd the flow'ry plain.

POPE, *January and May,* l. 623.

7
The old fable-existences are no more;
The fascinating race has emigrated.

SCHILLER, *Wallenstein.* Pt. i, act ii, sc. 2. (Hayward, tr.)

The intelligible forms of ancient poets,
The fair humanities of old religion,
The power, the beauty, and the majesty
That had their haunts in dale or piny mountain,
Or forest by slow stream, or pebbly spring,
Or chasms and watery depths,—all these have vanished;
They live no longer in the faith of reason.

SCHILLER, *Wallenstein.* Pt. i, act ii, sc. 2. (Coleridge, tr.)

8
There never was a merry world since the fairies left dancing and the parson left conjuring.

JOHN SELDEN, *Table-Talk: Parson.*

9
This is the fairy land; O spite of spites!
We talk with goblins, owls and sprites.

SHAKESPEARE, *The Comedy of Errors.* Act ii, sc. 2, l. 191.

They are fairies; he that speaks to them shall die:
I'll wink and couch: no man their works must eye.

SHAKESPEARE, *The Merry Wives of Windsor.* Act v, sc. 5, l. 51.

Fairies, black, grey, green, and white,
You moonshine revellers, and shades of night.

SHAKESPEARE, *The Merry Wives of Windsor.* Act v, sc. 5, l. 41.

10
Over hill, over dale,
Through brush, through brier,
Over park, over pale,
Through flood, through fire.

SHAKESPEARE, *A Midsummer-Night's Dream.* Act ii, sc. 1, l. 2.

In silence sad,
Trip we after night's shade:
We the globe can compass soon.
Swifter than the wand'ring moon.

SHAKESPEARE, *A Midsummer-Night's Dream.* Act iv, sc. 1, l. 100.

11
O, then, I see Queen Mab hath been with you.
She is the fairies' midwife, and she comes
In shape no bigger than an agate-stone
On the forefinger of an alderman,
Drawn with a team of little atomies
Athwart men's noses as they lie asleep: . . .
Her chariot is an empty hazel-nut
Made by the joiner squirrel, or old grub,
Time out o' mind the fairies' coach-makers.

SHAKESPEARE, *Romeo and Juliet.* Act i, sc. 4, l. 53.

This is Mab, the Mistress-Fairy,
That doth nightly rob the dairy.

BEN JONSON, *The Satyr: Song.*

12
Where the bee sucks, there suck I:

In a cowslip's bell I lie;
There I couch when owls do cry.
On the bat's back I do fly
After summer merrily.

SHAKESPEARE, *The Tempest*. Act v, sc. 1, l. 88.

Or like a fairy trip upon the green.

SHAKESPEARE, *Venus and Adonis*, l. 146.

1
Here, in cool grot and mossy cell,
We rural fays and fairies dwell;
Though rarely seen by mortal eye,
When the pale moon, ascending high,
Darts through yon limes her quivering beams,
We frisk it near these crystal streams.

WILLIAM SHENSTONE, *Lines Inscribed on a Tablet in the Gardens at the Poet's Residence.*

2
Ye fairies, from all evil keep her!

WORDSWORTH, *Peter Bell: Prologue*, l. 65.

FAITH

See also Belief, Trust

I—Faith: Definitions

3
Faith is a certitude without proofs. . . . Faith is a sentiment, for it is a hope; it is an instinct, for it precedes all outward instruction.

AMIEL, *Journal*, 7 Feb., 1872.

4
For what is faith unless it is to believe what you do not see? (Quid est enim fides nisi credere quod non vides?)

ST. AUGUSTINE. (*Joannis Evangelical Tract.* Ch. 40, sec. 8.)

To believe only possibilities is not Faith, but mere Philosophy.

SIR THOMAS BROWNE, *Religio Medici*. Pt. i, sec. 48.

The faith that stands on authority is not faith. The reliance on authority measures the decline of religion.

EMERSON, *Essays, First Series: The Over-Soul.*

5
Faith is love taking the form of aspiration.

WILLIAM ELLERY CHANNING. *Note-Books: Faith.*

6
To take up half on trust, and half to try,
Name it not faith, but bungling bigotry.

DRYDEN, *The Hind and the Panther*. Pt. i, l. 141.

7
Faith is the substance of things hoped for, the evidence of things not seen.

New Testament: Hebrews, xi, 1.

8
Faith, as an intellectual state, is self-reliance.

O. W. HOLMES, *The Professor at the Breakfast-Table*. Ch. 4.

Faith always implies the disbelief of a lesser fact in favor of a greater. A little mind often sees the unbelief, without seeing the belief of large ones.

O. W. HOLMES, *The Professor at the Breakfast-Table*. Ch. 5.

9
Faith is an act of self-consecration, in which the will, the intellect, and the affections all have their place.

DEAN W. R. INGE. (MARCHANT, *Wit and Wisdom of Dean Inge*. No. 48.)

10
Faith is the cliff on which the weak wave breaks,
The tree around whose might frail tendrils twine,
In cloudy skies it sets a starry sign,
And in the sorrowing soul an altar makes.

THOMAS S. JONES, *Quatrains.*

11
And we shall be made truly wise if we be made content; content, too, not only with what we can understand, but content with what we do not understand—the habit of mind which theologians call—and rightly—faith in God.

CHARLES KINGSLEY, *Health and Education: On Bio-Geology.*

12
The only faith that wears well and holds its color in all weathers, is that which is woven of conviction and set with the sharp mordant of experience.

J. R. LOWELL, *My Study Windows: Abraham Lincoln.*

13
The principal part of faith is patience.

GEORGE MACDONALD, *Weighed and Wanting* Ch. 53.

14
Faith may be defined briefly as an illogical belief in the occurrence of the improbable.

H. L. MENCKEN, *Prejudices*. Series iii, p. 267.

15
Faith is a kind of winged intellect. The great workmen of history have been men who believed like giants.

DR. CHARLES H. PARKHURST, *Sermons: Walking by Faith.*

16
Faith is like a lily, lifted high and white.

CHRISTINA ROSSETTI, *Hope.*

17
There are no tricks in plain and simple faith.

SHAKESPEARE, *Julius Cæsar*. Act iv, sc. 2, l. 22.

18
Faith is the subtle chain
Which binds us to the infinite; the voice
Of a deep life within, that will remain
Until we crowd it thence.

ELIZABETH OAKES SMITH, *Faith.*

19
Faith is the force of life.

LEO TOLSTOY, *My Confession*. Ch. ii.

II—Faith: Apothegms

1
Give to faith the things which belong to faith. (Da fidei, quæ fidei sunt.)
BACON, *Advancement of Learning*. Bk. ii.

2
Inflexible in faith, invincible in arms.
JAMES BEATTIE, *The Minstrel*. Bk. i, l. 99.

3
A little faith all undisproved.
E. B. BROWNING, *The Sleep*.

4
You can do very little with faith, but you can do nothing without it.
SAMUEL BUTLER THE YOUNGER, *Note-Books*, p. 336.

5
We walk by faith, not by sight.
New Testament: II Corinthians, v, 7.

6
His faith, perhaps, in some nice tenets might
Be wrong; his life, I'm sure, was in the right.
ABRAHAM COWLEY, *On the Death of Crashaw*, l. 55. (1649)

For modes of faith let graceless zealots fight;
He can't be wrong whose life is in the right.
POPE, *Essay on Man*. Epis. iii, l. 305. (1733)

7
Faith needs her daily bread.
DINAH M. M. CRAIK, *Fortune's Marriage*. Ch. 10.

8
No longer by implicit faith we err,
Whilst every man's his own interpreter.
SIR JOHN DENHAM, *Progress of Human Learning*, l. 148.

Whose faith has centre everywhere,
Nor cares to fix itself to form.
TENNYSON, *In Memoriam*. Pt. xxxiii, st. 1.

9
Who breaks his faith, no faith is held with him.
DU BARTAS, *Devine Weekes and Workes*. Week ii. (Sylvester, tr.)

10
The shield of faith.
New Testament: Ephesians, vi, 16.

11
Faith sees by the ears.
THOMAS FULLER, *Gnomologia*.

12
Love asks faith and faith, firmness.
GEORGE HERBERT, *Jacula Prudentum*.

13
Mirror of constant faith, rever'd and mourn'd.
HOMER, *Odyssey*. Bk. iv, l. 229. (Pope, tr.)

14
Guided by faith and matchless fortitude.
MILTON, *Sonnets: To Cromwell*.

15
Beautiful Faith, surrendering unto Time.
STEPHEN PHILLIPS, *Marpessa*, l. 62.

16
Th' enormous faith of many made for one.
POPE, *Essay on Man*. Epis. iii, l. 242.

In Faith and Hope the world will disagree.
POPE, *Essay on Man*. Epis. iii, l. 307.

17
And cling to Faith beyond the forms of Faith!
TENNYSON, *The Ancient Sage*, l. 69.

To persecute
Makes a faith hated, and is furthermore
No perfect witness of a perfect faith
In him who persecutes.
TENNYSON, *Queen Mary*. Act iii, sc. 4, l. 72.

18
The coalheaver's faith. (Fides carbonaria.)
A medieval proverb, founded on the anecdote of the coalheaver who said that he believed what the Church believed. When asked what that was, he answered, "What I believe."

III—Faith: Its Power

19
The cruse of oil and the barrel of meal overflow because the widow has firm faith.
AGATHIAS SCHOLASTICUS, *On the Widow Who Fed Elijah*. (*Greek Anthology*. Bk. i, epig. 77.)

20
They never fail who light
Their lamp of faith at the unwavering flame
Burnt for the altar service of the Race
Since the beginning.
ELSA BARKER, *The Frozen Grail*.

21
But there's a dome of nobler span,
A temple given
Thy faith, that bigots dare not ban—
Its space is Heaven!
THOMAS CAMPBELL, *Hallowed Ground*.

22
Daughter of Faith, awake, arise, illume
The dread unknown, the chaos of the tomb!
CAMPBELL, *The Pleasures of Hope*. Pt. ii, l. 261.

23
Yet courage, soul! Nor hold thy strength in vain,
In hope o'ercome the steeps God sets for thee;
For past the Alpine summits of great pain
Lieth thine Italy.
ROSE TERRY COOKE, *Beyond*.

24
We lean on Faith; and some less wise have cried,
"Behold the butterfly, the seed that's cast!"
Vain hopes that fall like flowers before the blast!
R. W. GILDER, *Love and Death*. St. 2.

25
When false things are brought low,
And swift things have grown slow,
Feigning like froth shall go,
Faith be aye for aye.
THOMAS HARDY, *Between Us Now*.

26
What here we hope for, we shall once inherit:
By Faith we walk here, not by the Spirit.
ROBERT HERRICK, *Faith*.

1
Wake in our breast the living fires,
The holy faith that warmed our sires.
O. W. HOLMES, *Army Hymn.*

Faith of our fathers—holy faith,
We will be true to thee till death.
FREDERICK WILLIAM FABER, *Faith of Our Fathers.* Used by William Jennings Bryan for close of his undelivered speech at the Scopes trial.

2
I know that my redeemer liveth.
Old Testament: Job, xix, 25.

I . . . exhort you that ye should earnestly contend for the faith which was once delivered unto the saints.
New Testament: Jude, i, 3.

3
O Faith, that meets ten thousand cheats
Yet drops no jot of faith!
RUDYARD KIPLING, *To the True Romance.*

4
Our faith triumphant o'er our fears.
LONGFELLOW, *The Building of the Ship.*

Ye whose hearts are fresh and simple,
Who have faith in God and nature.
LONGFELLOW, *Hiawatha: Introduction.*

5
A perfect faith would lift us absolutely above fear.
GEORGE MACDONALD, *Sir Gibbie.* Ch. 11.

6
O welcome pure-eyed Faith, white-handed Hope,
Thou hovering angel, girt with golden wings!
MILTON, *Comus,* l. 213.

7
I argue not
Against Heav'n's hand or will, nor bate a jot
Of heart or hope, but still bear up and steer
Right onward.
MILTON, *To Cyriac Skinner.*

8
Call no faith false which e'er hath brought
Relief to any laden life,
Cessation to the pain of thought,
Refreshment mid the dust of strife.
SIR LEWIS MORRIS, *Tolerance.*

9
But give me, Lord, eyes to behold the truth;
A seeing sense that knows the eternal right;
A heart with pity filled, and gentlest ruth;
A manly faith that makes all darkness light.
THEODORE PARKER, *The Higher Good.*

10
Be thou faithful unto death, and I will give thee a crown of life.
New Testament: Revelation, ii, 10.

The just shall live by faith.
New Testament: Romans, i, 17.

11
I know no deeper doubt to make me mad,
I need no brighter love to keep me pure.
To me the faiths of old are daily bread;
I bless their hope, I bless their will to save.
GEORGE SANTAYANA, *What Riches Have You.*

12
Thy path is plain and straight,—that light is given:
Onward in faith,—and leave the rest to Heaven.
ROBERT SOUTHEY, *The Retrospect,* l. 175.

13
And all but their faith overthrown.
WILLIAM WETMORE STORY, *Io Victis.*

14
Strong Son of God, immortal Love,
Whom we, that have not seen thy face,
By faith, and faith alone, embrace,
Believing where we cannot prove.
TENNYSON, *In Memoriam: Introduction.* St. 1.

We have but faith: we cannot know,
For knowledge is of things we see;
And yet we trust it comes from Thee,
A beam in darkness: let it grow.
TENNYSON, *In Memoriam: Introduction.* St. 6.

15
The night is long and pain weighs heavily,
But God will hold His world above despair;
Look to the East, where up the lucid sky
The morning climbs! The day shall yet be fair.
CELIA THAXTER, *Faith.*

16
Faith is required of thee, and a sincere life, not loftiness of intellect, nor deepness in the mysteries of God.
THOMAS À KEMPIS, *De Imitatione Christi.* Pt. iv, ch. 18, sec. 3.

17
The mason asks but a narrow shelf to spring his brick from; man requires only an infinitely narrower one to spring his arch of faith from.
H. D. THOREAU, *Journal,* 31 Jan., 1852.

18
Fight the good fight of faith.
New Testament: I Timothy, vi, 12.

I have fought a good fight, I have finished my course, I have kept the faith.
New Testament: II Timothy, iv, 7.

19
Faith, mighty faith, the promise sees,
And looks to that alone;
Laughs at impossibilities,
And cries it shall be done.
CHARLES WESLEY, *Hymns.*

20
Through the dark and stormy night
Faith beholds a feeble light
Up the blackness streaking;
Knowing God's own time is best,
In a patient hope I rest
For the full day-breaking!
J. G. WHITTIER, *Barclay of Ury.* St. 16.

He worshipped as his fathers did,
And kept the faith of childish days,
And, howsoe'er he strayed or slid,
He loved the good old ways.
WHITTIER, *My Namesake.*

1
A bending staff I would not break,
A feeble faith I would not shake,
Nor even rashly pluck away
The error which some truth may stay,
Whose loss might leave the soul without
A shield against the shafts of doubt.
WHITTIER, *Questions of Life*. St. 1.

2
Of one in whom persuasion and belief
Had ripened into faith, and faith become
A passionate intuition.
WORDSWORTH, *The Excursion*. Bk. iv, l. 1293.

Through love, through hope, and faith's transcendent dower,
We feel that we are greater than we know.
WORDSWORTH, *The River Duddon: After-Thought*.

3
Faith builds a bridge across the gulf of death,
To break the shock blind nature cannot shun,
And lands thought smoothly on the farther shore.
YOUNG, *Night Thoughts*. Night iv, l. 721.

IV—Faith: Its Weakness

4
'Tis well averred,
A scientific faith's absurd.
ROBERT BROWNING, *Easter Day*. Pt. vi.

5
Half our daylight faith's a fable.
THOMAS CAMPBELL, *A Dream*, l. 5.

Ghost, kelpie, wraith,
And all the trumpery of vulgar faith.
THOMAS CAMPBELL, *The Pilgrim of Glencoe*, l. 188.

6
Morality was held a standing jest,
And faith a necessary fraud at best.
CHARLES CHURCHILL, *Gotham*. Bk. ii, l. 597.

7
Faith is a fine invention
For gentlemen who see;
But microscopes are prudent
In an emergency!
EMILY DICKINSON, *Poems*. Pt. i, No. 56.

8
Faith is a kind of parasitic plant,
That grasps the nearest plant with tendril-rings;
And as the climate and the soil may grant,
So is the sort of tree to which it clings.
THOMAS HOOD, *Ode to Rae Wilson*, l. 257.

9
Faith is often the boast of the man who is too lazy to investigate.
F. M. KNOWLES, *A Cheerful Year Book*.

10
Yes, faith is a goodly anchor;
When skies are sweet as a psalm,
At the bows it lolls so stalwart
In its bluff, broad-shouldered calm. . . .
But, after the shipwreck, tell me
What help in its iron thews,
Still true to the broken hawser,
Deep down among sea-weed and ooze?
J. R. LOWELL, *After the Burial*.

11
Unfaith clamouring to be coined
To faith by proof.
GEORGE MEREDITH, *Earth and Man*. St. 41.

12
How many things served us yesterday for articles of faith, which to-day are fables to us! (Combien de choses nous servoient hier d'articles de foy, qui nous sont fables aujourd'hui!)
MONTAIGNE, *Essays*. Bk. i, ch. 26.

13
Faith, fanatic faith, once wedded fast
To some dear falsehood, hugs it to the last.
THOMAS MOORE, *Lalla Rookh: The Veiled Prophet*.

14
It will profit me nothing, for I have no faith in it. (Elle ne me profitera de rien, car je n'y adjouste point de foi.)
RABELAIS, *Works*. Bk. i, ch. 42. The monk's remark when he says that he knows a prayer which guarantees immunity from all firearms.

15
The old faiths light their candles all about,
But burly Truth comes by and puts them out.
LIZETTE WOODWORTH REESE, *Truth*.

16
Men's faiths are wafer-cakes.
SHAKESPEARE, *Henry V*. Act ii, sc. 3, l. 53.

17
And bloody Faith, the foulest birth of Time.
SHELLEY, *Feelings of a Republican*.

Faith, haggard as Fear that had borne her, and dark as the sire that begat her, Despair.
SWINBURNE, *An Autumn Vision*. Sec. vii, l. 9.

18
Christian, what of the night?—
I cannot tell; I am blind.
I halt and hearken behind
If haply the hours will go back
And return to the dear dead light,
To the watchfires and stars that of old
Shone where the sky now is black,
Glowed where the earth now is cold.
SWINBURNE, *A Watch in the Night*. St. 10.

19
In our windy world
What's up is faith, what's down is heresy.
TENNYSON, *Harold*. Act i, sc. 1.

V—Faith and Reason

20
Faith is a higher faculty than reason.
P. J. BAILEY, *Festus: Proem*, l. 84.

21
Reason is our soul's left hand, Faith her right,
By these we reach divinity.
JOHN DONNE, *To the Countess of Bedford*.

Reason is the triumph of the intellect, faith of the heart.
JAMES SCHOULER, *History of the United States.* Vol. ii.

1
Reason saw not, till Faith sprung the light.
DRYDEN, *Religio Laici,* l. 69.

2
The way to see by Faith is to shut the Eye of Reason.
BENJAMIN FRANKLIN, *Poor Richard,* 1758.

3
Faith has no merit where human reason supplies the proof. (Fides non habet meritum ubi humana ratio præbet experimentum.)
ST. GREGORY, *Homilies.* No. 40.

4
It is not reason makes faith hard, but life.
JEAN INGELOW, *A Pastor's Letter to a Young Poet.* Pt. ii, l. 233.

5
Surely investigation is better than unthinking faith. Surely reason is a better guide than fear.
R. G. INGERSOLL, *The Liberty of Man, Woman and Child.*

6
And Wisdom cries, "I know not anything";
And only Faith beholds that all is well.
S. R. LYSAGHT, *A Ritual: A Lesson,* l. 102.

7
They live no longer in the faith of reason.
SCHILLER, *I Wallenstein.* Act ii, sc. 4.

8
It is always right that a man should be able to render a reason for the faith that is within him.
SYDNEY SMITH. (LADY HOLLAND, *Memoir.* Vol. i, p. 53.)

9
Such lapses from knowledge to faith are perhaps necessary that human heroism may be possible.
H. G. WELLS, *Mr. Britling Sees It Through.* Bk. ii, ch. 2, sec. 1.

10
We live by Faith; but Faith is not the slave
Of text and legend. Reason's voice and God's,
Nature's and Duty's, never are at odds.
WHITTIER, *Requirement.*

VI—Faith Without Works

11
Faith without works is dead.
New Testament: James, ii, 20.

12
Faith without works is nothing worth,
As dead as door-nail unless deeds follow.
LANGLAND, *Piers Plowman.* Pt. ii, l. 183.

13
If faith produce no works, I see
That faith is not a living tree.
Thus faith and works together grow;
No separate life they e'er can know:
They're soul and body, hand and heart:
What God hath joined, let no man part.
HANNAH MORE, *Dan and Jane.*

14
Faith is the root of works. A root that produceth nothing is dead.
BISHOP THOMAS WILSON, *Maxims of Piety and of Christianity.*

VII—Faith: Want of Faith

15
He that has lost faith, what has he left to live on? (Fidem qui perdit, quo se servat in reliquum?)
PUBLILIUS SYRUS, *Sententiæ.* No. 196.

16
Geology, ethnology, what not?
(Greek endings, each little passing bell
That signifies some faith's about to die.)
ROBERT BROWNING, *Bishop Blougram's Apology.*

And my faith is torn to a thousand scraps,
And my heart feels ice while my words breathe flame.
ROBERT BROWNING, *The Worst of It.*

17
The disease with which the human mind now labors is want of faith.
EMERSON, *Essays, Second Series: New England Reformers.*

18
In the affairs of this World, Men are saved, not by Faith, but by the Want of it.
BENJAMIN FRANKLIN, *Poor Richard,* 1754.

19
Much knowledge of things divine escapes us through want of faith. ('Αλλὰ τῶν μὲν θείων τα πολλά ἀπιστίῃ διαφυγγάνει μὴ γινώσκεσθαι.)
HERACLITUS, *Fragments.* No. 116.

Th' extremes of too much faith, and none.
THOMAS MOORE, *Fables.* No. 5, l. 64.

20
Tell faith it's fled the city.
SIR WALTER RALEIGH, *The Lie.* (Sometimes attributed to Joshua Sylvester and to Sir John Davies.)

21
Play fast and loose with faith.
SHAKESPEARE, *King John.* Act iii, sc. 1, l. 242.

He wears his faith but as the fashion of his hat; it ever changes with the next block.
SHAKESPEARE, *Much Ado About Nothing.* Act i, sc. 1, l. 75.

22
The saddest thing that can befall a soul
Is when it loses faith in God and woman.
ALEXANDER SMITH, *A Life Drama.* Sc. 12.

23
One by one, like leaves from a tree,
All my faiths have forsaken me.
SARA TEASDALE, *Leaves.*

24
Faith and unfaith can ne'er be equal powers:
Unfaith in aught is want of faith in all.
TENNYSON, *Merlin and Vivien,* l. 386.

25
What faith is there in the faithless? (Τίς δ' ἄρα πίστις ἀπίστῳ.)
THEOGNIS, *Sententiæ.* (SPENSER, *Shepheards Calender: May: Piers' Emblem.*)

1
He hath denied the faith, and is worse than an infidel.
New Testament: I Timothy, v, 8.

2
It may be that we can no longer share
The faith which from his fathers he received;
It may be that our doom is to despair,
Where he with joy believed.
WILLIAM WATSON, *To James Bromley: With Wordsworth's Grave.*

FALCON, see Hawk

FALL

See also Greatness: Its Penalties. For Fall, a season of the year, see Autumn

3
Who lies upon the ground has no whither to fall. (Qui jacet in terra non habe unde cadat.)
ALAIN DE LILLE, *Book of Parables*. Ch. 2. This line was quoted by Charles I to the French minister, M. de Bellièvre, when the latter was trying to persuade him to seek safety in flight. The minister replied, "Sire, on peut lui faire tomber la tête."

He that is down needs fear no fall,
He that is low, no pride.
JOHN BUNYAN, *The Pilgrim's Progress*. Pt. ii.

I am not now in fortune's power:
He that is down can fall no lower.
BUTLER, *Hudibras*. Pt. i, canto 3, l. 877.

A lowly man cannot have a high or heavy fall. (Humilis nec alte cadere nec graviter potest.)
PUBLILIUS SYRUS, *Sententiæ*. No. 259.

4
Who falls from all he knows of bliss,
Cares little into what abyss.
BYRON, *The Giaour*, l. 1091.

5
The oak grows silently in the forest a thousand years; only in the thousandth year, when the axeman arrives with his axe, is there heard an echoing through the solitudes; and the oak announces itself when, with far-sounding crash, it *falls*.
CARLYLE, *The French Revolution*. Vol. i, bk. ii, ch. 1.

6
He that falls to-day may be up again to-morrow.
CERVANTES, *Don Quixote*. Pt. ii, ch. 65.

We fall to rise, are baffled to fight better,
Sleep to wake.
ROBERT BROWNING, *Asolando: Epilogue*.

He falls low that cannot rise again.
GEORGE MERITON, *Praise of Yorkshire Ale*, 72. (1683)

Some falls are means the happier to arise.
SHAKESPEARE, *Cymbeline*. Act iv, sc. 2, l. 403.

7
Let him that thinketh he standeth take heed lest he fall.
New Testament: I Corinthians, x, 12.

8
Fallen, fallen, fallen, fallen,
Fallen from his high estate,
And welt'ring in his blood;
Deserted at his utmost need,
By those his former bounty fed;
On the bare earth expos'd he lies,
With not a friend to close his eyes.
DRYDEN, *Alexander's Feast*, l. 77.

So noble a master fallen! All gone! and not
One friend to take his fortune by the arm,
And go along with him.
SHAKESPEARE, *Timon of Athens*. Act iv sc. 2, 6.

9
For a man
Low-fallen from high estate more sharply feels
The strangeness of it than the long unblest.
("Οταν δ' ἀνὴρ
πράξῃ κακῶς ὑψηλός, εἰς ἀηθίαν
πίπτει κακίω τοῦ πάλαι δυσδαίμονος.)
EURIPIDES, *Helen*, l. 417. (Way, tr.)

Whoever has fallen from his former high estate is in his calamity the scorn even of the base. (Quicumque amisit dignitatem pristinam Ignavis etiam jocus est in casu gravi.)
PHÆDRUS, *Fables*. Bk. i, fab. 21, l. 1.

10
Every slip is not a fall.
THOMAS FULLER, *Gnomologia*.

11
He that is fallen cannot help him that is down.
GEORGE HERBERT, *Jacula Prudentum*.

12
It falls, all hope falls, and the fortune of our name. (Occidit, occidit Spes omnis et fortuna nostri Nominis.)
HORACE, *Odes*. Bk. iv, ode 4, l. 70.

13
How art thou fallen from heaven, O Lucifer, son of the morning!
Old Testament: Isaiah, xiv, 12.

From morn
To noon he fell, from noon to dewy eve,
A summer's day; and with the setting sun
Dropt from the zenith like a falling star.
MILTON, *Paradise Lost*. Bk. i, l. 742.

And when he falls, he falls like Lucifer,
Never to hope again.
SHAKESPEARE, *Henry VIII*. Act iii, sc. 2, l. 371.

14
Who falls for love of God shall rise a star.
BEN JONSON, *Underwoods: To Master Colby*.

15
The vulgar falls and none laments his fate;
Sorrow has hardly leisure for the great.
LUCAN, *De Bello Civili*. Bk. iv. (Rowe, tr.)

16
And great was the fall of it.
New Testament: Matthew, vii, 27.

17
That water which falls from some Alpine

height is dashed, broken, and will murmur loudly, but grows limpid by its fall.
(Quell' onda, che ruina
Dalla pendice alpina,
Balza, si frange, e mormora
Ma limpida si fa.)
METASTASIO, *Alcide al Bivio.*

1
Awake, arise, or be for ever fall'n.
MILTON, *Paradise Lost.* Bk. i, l. 330.

2
I made him just and right,
Sufficient to have stood, though free to fall.
Such I created all th' ethereal Powers
And Spirits, both them who stood, and them who fail'd;
Freely they stood who stood, and fell who fell.
MILTON, *Paradise Lost.* Bk. iii, l. 98.

3
Everything that shakes does not fall. (Tout ce qui bransle ne tombe pas.)
MONTAIGNE, *Essays.* Bk. iii, ch. 8.

4
Who falls in honourable strife,
Surrenders nothing but his life;
Who basely triumphs casts away
The glory of the well-won day.
MONTGOMERY, *Thoughts on Wheels.* No. 1.

5
Low though I am, I have not fallen so low that I am beneath you too, for beneath you there can be nothing. (Non adeo cecidi, quamvis abjectus, ut infra Te quoque sim, inferius quo nihil esse potest.)
OVID, *Tristia.* Bk. v, eleg. 8, l. 1.

6
As he rose like a rocket, he fell like a stick.
THOMAS PAINE, *Letter to His Addressers.* Referring to Edmund Burke. *See also under* DICKENS.

I stood beside the grave of him who blazed
The comet of a season.
BYRON, *Churchill's Grave,* l. 1.

7
Fain would I climb, yet fear I to fall.
SIR WALTER RALEIGH, scratched with a diamond on a window-pane, either in the presence of Queen Elizabeth or where she would be certain to see it.

If thy heart fails thee, do not climb at all.
QUEEN ELIZABETH, written by her under Raleigh's line. (FULLER, *Worthies of England.* Vol. i, p. 19.) Raleigh's line is usually given, "Fain would I climb, but that I fear to fall." (SCOTT, *Kenilworth,* ch. 17.)

Fain would I, but I dare not; I dare, and yet I may not;
I may, although I care not for pleasure when I play not.
SIR WALTER RALEIGH, *Fain Would I.* Written in later life than the line on the window-pane.

8
Hasty climbers have sudden falls.
JOHN RAY, *English Proverbs.*

9
All things that rise will fall. (Omniaque orta occidunt.)
SALLUST, *Jugurtha.* Ch. 2, sec. 3.

One may sooner fall than rise.
JOHN RAY, *English Proverbs.*

10
How are the mighty fallen!
Old Testament: II Samuel, i, 19.

How are the mighty fallen in the midst of the battle!
Old Testament: II Samuel, i, 25.

Prostrate on earth the bleeding warrior lies,
And Isr'el's beauty on the mountains dies.
How are the mighty fallen!
WILLIAM SOMERVILLE, *The Lamentation of David over Saul and Jonathan.*

11
O Hamlet, what a falling-off was there!
SHAKESPEARE, *Hamlet.* Act i, sc. 5, l. 47.

I shall fall,
Like a bright exhalation in the evening,
And no man see me more.
SHAKESPEARE, *Henry VIII.* Act iii, sc. 2, l. 225.

Press not a falling man too far!
SHAKESPEARE, *Henry VIII.* Act iii, sc. 2, l. 333.

12
Great Cæsar fell.
O, what a fall was there, my countrymen!
Then I, and you, and all of us fell down.
SHAKESPEARE, *Julius Cæsar.* Act iii, sc. 2, l. 193.

I see thy glory like a shooting star
Fall to the base earth from the firmament.
Thy sun sets weeping in the lowly west.
SHAKESPEARE, *Richard II.* Act ii, sec. 4, l. 19.

13
"Yea," quoth he, "dost thou fall upon thy face?
Thou wilt fall backward when thou hast more wit."
SHAKESPEARE, *Romeo and Juliet.* Act i, sc. 3, l. 41.

14
What though success will not attend on all?
Who bravely dares, must sometimes risk a fall.
SMOLLETT, *Advice,* l. 207.

15
Woe to my wretched self! from what a height of hope have I fallen.
(Væ misero mihi! quanta de spe decidi.)
TERENCE, *Heauton Timorumenos.* Act i, sc. 3, l. 9.

Alas, from what high hope to what relapse
Unlook'd for, are we fall'n!
MILTON, *Paradise Regained.* Bk. ii, l. 30.

16
A great villain, a great fall. (De grand vilain grande chute.)
J. DE LA VEPRIE, *Les Proverbes Communs.*

1
How many are raised to high posts by the instigation of the devil, that their fall may be more dismal!

THOMAS WILSON, *Maxims of Piety*.

2
Who, taking counsel of unbending truth,
By one example hath set forth to all
How they with dignity may stand; or fall,
If fall they must.

WORDSWORTH, *Poems Dedicated to National Independence*. Pt. i, No. 7.

FALSEHOOD, see Lies and Lying

FAME

See also Death and Fame; Name and Fame; Poetry and Fame; Reputation

I—Fame: Definitions

3
Renown is the mother of virtues. (Τὴν δόξαν ἀρετῶν μητέρα εἶναι.)

BION. (DIOGENES LAERTIUS, *Bion*. Bk. iv, sec. 48.)

4
Fame is the thirst of youth.

BYRON, *Childe Harold*. Canto iii, st. 112.

5
Fame, we may understand, is no sure test of merit, but only a probability of such: it is an accident, not a property of a man.

CARLYLE, *Essays: Goethe*.

Money will buy money's worth, but the thing men call fame, what is it?

CARLYLE, *Memoirs of the Life of Scott*.

6
Fame Is nothing but an empty name.

CHARLES CHURCHILL, *The Ghost*. Bk. i, l. 230.

What is fame? an empty bubble.

JAMES GRAINGER, *Ode to Solitude*.

7
Fame is but wind.

THOMAS CORYATE, *Crudities*. Bk. i, l. 60. (1611)

The splendors of earthly fame are but a wind,
That in the same direction lasts not long.
(Non è il mondan romore altro che un fiato
Di vento, che or vien quinci ed or vien quindi,
E muta nome, perchè muta lato.)

DANTE, *Purgatorio*. Canto xi, l. 100.

Fame they tell you is air; but without air there is no life for any; without fame there is none for the best.

W. S. LANDOR, *Imaginary Conversations: The Ciceros*.

8
Fame is a fickle food
Upon a shifting plate.

EMILY DICKINSON, *Poems*. Pt. v, No. 4.

Fame is a food that dead men eat,—
I have no stomach for such meat.

AUSTIN DOBSON, *Fame Is a Food*.

9
Fame is a magnifying glass.

THOMAS FULLER, *Gnomologia*.

Fame is the echo of actions, resounding them to the world, save that the echo repeats only the last part, but fame relates all, and often more than all.

THOMAS FULLER, *The Holy and Profane States: Of Fame*.

10
What is this fame, thus crowded round with slaves?
The breath of fools, the bait of flattering knaves.

GEORGE GRANVILLE, *Imitation of Second Chorus in Act ii of Seneca's Thyestes*.

11
Fame is the inheritance not of the dead, but of the living. It is we who look back with lofty pride to the great names of antiquity, who drink of that flood of glory as of a river, and refresh our wings in it for future flight.

WILLIAM HAZLITT, *Characteristics*. No. 389.

Fame is not popularity. . . . It is the spirit of a man surviving himself in the minds and thoughts of other men.

WILLIAM HAZLITT, *Lectures on the English Poets*, p. 283.

12
If that thy fame with ev'ry toy be pos'd,
'Tis a thin web, which poisonous fancies make;
But the great soldier's honour was compos'd
Of thicker stuff, which would endure a shake.

GEORGE HERBERT, *The Church-Porch*. St. 38.

13
Ah, pensive scholar, what is fame?
A fitful tongue of leaping flame;
A giddy whirlwind's fickle gust,
That lifts a pinch of mortal dust;
A few swift years, and who can show
Which dust was Bill, and which was Joe?

O. W. HOLMES, *Bill and Joe*. St. 7.

14
And what after all is everlasting fame? Altogether vanity. (Τί δὲ καὶ ἔστιν ὅλως τὸ ἀείμνηστον; ὅλον κενόν.)

MARCUS AURELIUS, *Meditations*. Bk. 4, sec. 33.

15
Fame lulls the fever of the soul, and makes
Us feel that we have grasp'd an immortality.

JOAQUIN MILLER, *Ina*. Sc. 4, l. 273.

16
Read but o'er the stories
Of men most fam'd for courage or for counsel,
And you shall find that the desire of glory
(That last infirmity of noble minds)
Was the last frailty wise men e'er put off.

JOHN FLETCHER(?), *Sir John van Olden Barnavelt*. Act i, sc. 1. First acted in 1619, then lost, and not re-discovered until 1883 among some old manuscripts in the British Museum.

Fame is the spur that the clear spirit doth raise
(That last infirmity of noble mind)
To scorn delights, and live laborious days

MILTON, *Lycidas*, l. 70. (1637) "The most astonishing coincidence in the whole range of literature," Swinburne called the lines in parenthesis.

1
Fame is no plant that grows on mortal soil.
MILTON, *Lycidas*, l. 78.

2
What's fame? a fancied life in others' breath;
A thing beyond us, ev'n before our death.
POPE, *Essay on Man*. Epis. iv, l. 237.

And what is Fame? the meanest have their day,
The greatest can but blaze, and pass away.
POPE, *Imitations of Horace: Epistles*, i, 6, 46.

3
Fame's but a hollow echo.
SIR WALTER RALEIGH, *A Farewell to the Vanities of the World*.

4
Fame is a bugle call
Blown past a crumbling wall.
LIZETTE WOODWORTH REESE, *Taps*.

5
Fame is something which must be won; honor only something which must not be lost.
SCHOPENHAUER, *Aphorisms on the Wisdom of Life*.

6
Fame is the shadow of virtue. It will attend virtue even against her will. (Gloria umbra virtutis est, etiam invitam comitabitur.)
SENECA, *Epistulæ ad Lucilium*. Epis. lxxix, 13.

Renown is the praise rendered to a good man by good men. (Claritas laus est a bonis bono reddita.)
SENECA, *Epistulæ ad Lucilium*. Epis. cii, sec. 9.

Fame is the perfume of heroic deeds.
SOCRATES.

7
There is this difference between renown and glory—the latter depends upon the judgments of the many, the former on the judgments of good men.
SENECA, *Epistulæ ad Lucilium*. Epis. cii, sec. 18.

Fame has no necessary conjunction with praise: it may exist without the breath of a word: it is a *recognition of excellence* which *must be felt* but need not be *spoken*. Even the envious must feel it: feel it, and hate it in silence.
MRS. ANNA JAMESON, *Memoirs and Essays: Washington Allston*.

Reputation being essentially contemporaneous, is always at the mercy of the Envious and the Ignorant. But Fame, whose very birth is *posthumous*, and which is only *known to exist by the echo of its footsteps through congenial minds*, can neither be increased nor diminished by any degree of wilfulness.
MRS. ANNA JAMESON, *Memoirs and Essays: Washington Allston*.

8
Fame is love disguised.
SHELLEY, *An Exhortation*.

9
And what is fame in life but half-disfame,
And counterchanged with darkness?
TENNYSON, *Merlin and Vivien*, l. 463.

10
Fame is but an inscription on a grave, and glory the melancholy blazon on a coffin-lid.
ALEXANDER SMITH, *Dreamthorp: On the Writing of Essays*.

Fame is but a slow decay—
Even this shall pass away.
THEODORE TILTON, *Even This Shall Pass Away*.

11
Fame is a public mistress, none enjoys,
But, more or less, his rival's peace destroys.
YOUNG, *Epistles to Pope*. Epis. i, l. 25.

Fame is the shade of immortality,
And in itself a shadow. Soon as caught,
Contemn'd; it shrinks to nothing in the grasp.
YOUNG, *Night Thoughts*. Night vii, l. 365.

II—Fame: Apothegms

12
Distinction is the consequence, never the object, of a great mind.
WASHINGTON ALLSTON, *Aphorisms Written on Walls of His Studio*.

13
Fame is like a river, that beareth up things light and swoln, and drowns things weighty and solid.
BACON, *Essays: Of Ceremonies and Respects*.

Fame, like water, bears up the lighter things,
And lets the weighty sink.
CALDERON, *Adventures of Five Hours*. Act ii.

14
Herostratus lives that burnt the temple of Diana; he is almost lost that built it.
SIR THOMAS BROWNE, *Hydriotaphia*. Ch. 5.

The aspiring youth that fired the *Ephesian* dome
Outlives, in fame, the pious fool that rais'd it.
COLLEY CIBBER, *Richard III* (alt.). Act iii, sc. 1.

15
I awoke one morning and found myself famous.
BYRON. (MOORE, *Memoranda from Life*. Ch. 14.) Said after the publication of the first two cantos of *Childe Harold's Pilgrimage*, March, 1812.

16
Only to myself do I owe my fame. (Je ne dois qu'à moi seul toute ma renommée.)
CORNEILLE, *L'Excuse à Ariste*.

17
Fame, like man, will grow white as it grows old.
ABRAHAM COWLEY. (SAMUEL JOHNSON, *Lives of the Poets: Cowley*.)

Thy fame, like men, the older it doth grow,
Will of itself turn whiter too.
THOMAS SPRAT, *To the Happy Memory of the Late Lord Protector*, l. 5.

18
Fame finds never tomb t' inclose it in.
SAMUEL DANIEL, *Complaint of Rosamond*. St. 1.

19
Unnam'd as yet, at least unknown to fame.
DRYDEN, *Britannia Rediviva*, l. 192.

20
Fame is proof that the people are gullible.
EMERSON.

1
Fame sometimes hath created something of nothing.

Thomas Fuller, *Holy and Profane States: Fame.*

Fiction may deck the truth with spurious rays,
And round the hero cast a borrow'd blaze.

Joseph Addison, *The Campaign*, l. 471.

There are names written in her immortal scroll at which Fame blushes.

William Hazlitt, *Characteristics*. No. 53.

How partial is the voice of Fame!

Matthew Prior, *Epigrams: Partial Fame.*

2
There are many ways to fame.

George Herbert, *Jacula Prudentum.*

3
Fame grows like a tree with hidden life. (Crescit occulto velut arbor ævo Fama.)

Horace, *Odes*. Bk. i, ode 12, l. 45.

4
Fame is delightful, but as collateral it does not rank high.

Elbert Hubbard, *Epigrams.*

5
Sir, if they should cease to talk of me I must starve.

Samuel Johnson. (Boswell, *Life*, 1784.)

6
Contempt of fame begets contempt of virtue.

Ben Jonson, *Sejanus*. Act i, sc. 2.

7
All is ephemeral,—fame as well as the famous. (Πᾶν ἐφήμερον, καὶ τὸ μνημονεῦον καὶ τὸ μνημονευόμενον.)

Marcus Aurelius, *Meditations*. Bk. iv, sec. 35. Literally, "The rememberer, as well as the remembered."

The longest wave is quickly lost in the sea.

Emerson, *Representative Men: Plato.*

8
Regardless whether good or evil fame.

Milton, *Paradise Lost*. Bk. xii, l. 47.

9
I have made noise enough in the world already.

Napoleon Bonaparte. (O'Meara, *Napoleon in Exile*, 1816.) Echoing Danton.

10
All crowd, who foremost shall be damn'd to
fame.

Pope, *The Dunciad*. Bk. iii, l. 158.

Damn'd to everlasting fame.

Pope, *Essay on Man*. Epis. iv, l. 284.

May see thee now, though late, redeem thy
name,
And glorify what else is damn'd to fame.

Richard Savage, *Character of the Rev. James Foster*, l. 43.

11
Let humble Allen, with an awkward shame,
Do good by stealth, and blush to find it fame.

Pope, *Epilogue to the Satires*. Dial. i, l. 135. The reference is to Ralph Allen, who in 1720 contracted with the British Postoffice to improve the system of "cross-posts."

12
Fame, impatient of extremes, decays
Not more by envy than excess of praise.

Pope, *The Temple of Fame*, l. 43.

13
What is the fame of men compared to their happiness?

Walpole, *Letter to Horace Mann*, 3 Oct., 1762.

III—Fame: Love of Fame

14
Passion for fame; a passion which is the instinct of all great souls.

Edmund Burke, *Speech on American Taxation.*

15
Folly loves the martyrdom of fame.

Byron, *On the Death of Sheridan*, l. 68.

16
Men the most infamous are fond of fame,
And those who fear not guilt, yet start at
shame.

Charles Churchill, *The Author*, l. 233.

Man from his sphere eccentric starts astray;
All hunt for fame, but most mistake the way.

Charles Churchill, *The Rosciad*, l. 587.

17
Upon the very books in which philosophers bid us scorn ambition, they inscribe their names. They seek publicity for themselves on the very page where they pour contempt upon publicity. (Ipsi illi philosophi etiam illis libellis, quos de contemnenda gloria scribunt, nomen suum inscribunt: in eo ipso, in quo prædicationem nobilitatemque despiciunt, prædicari de se ac nominari volunt.)

Cicero, *Pro Archia Poeta*. Ch. 11, sec. 26.

Though they [philosophers] write *contemptu gloriæ*, yet as Hieron observes, they will put their names to their books.

Robert Burton, *Anatomy of Melancholy*. Pt. i, sec. 2, mem. 3, subs. 14.

Even those who write against fame wish for the fame of having written well, and those who read their works desire the fame of having read them.

Pascal, *Pensées*. Sec. ii, No. 150.

The hater of property and of government takes care to have his warranty-deed recorded, and the book written against Fame and learning has the author's name on the title-page.

R. W. Emerson, *Journal*, 1857.

18
Who fears not to do ill yet fears the name,
And free from conscience, is a slave to fame.

Sir John Denham, *Cooper's Hill*, l. 129.

19
The love of fame is almost another name for the love of excellence.

William Hazlitt, *Round Table*. No. 25.

20
So much the greater is the thirst for fame than for virtue. For who indeed would embrace virtue if you removed its rewards? (Tanto major famæ sitis est, quam Virtutis.

Quis enim virtutem amplectitur ipsam,
Præmia si tollas?)

JUVENAL, *Satires*. Sat. x, l. 140.

1
My quest is for everlasting fame, that I may be celebrated forever throughout the whole earth. (Mihi fama perennis Quæritur, in toto semper ut orbe canar.)

OVID, *Amores*. Bk. i, eleg. 15, l. 7.

The desire of fame delights me, and has grown with my renown. (Nam juvat, et studium famæ mihi crevit honore.)

OVID, *Remediorum Amoris*, l. 393.

2
And boasting youth, and narrative old age;
Their pleas were diff'rent, their request the same;
For good and bad alike are fond of Fame.

POPE, *The Temple of Fame*, l. 291.

3
Let fame, that all hunt after in their lives,
Live register'd upon our brazen tombs.

SHAKESPEARE, *Love's Labour's Lost*. Act i, sc. 1, l. 1.

4
Love of fame is the last weakness which even the wise resign. (Etiam sapientibus cupido gloriæ novissima exuitur.)

TACITUS, *History*. Bk. iv, sec. 6.

Though the desire of fame be the last weakness
Wise men put off.

MASSINGER, *The Very Woman*. Act iii, sc. 4.

Of the unreasoning humors of mankind, it seems that fame is the one which even philosophers have rid themselves of last and with most reluctance.

MONTAIGNE, *Essays*. Bk. i, ch. 41.

5
Proud of his prize, but prouder of his fame.

VERGIL, *Æneid*. Bk. v, l. 619. (Dryden, tr.)

And fired his soul with love of future fame. (Incenditque animum famæ venientis amore.)

VERGIL, *Æneid*. Bk. vi, l. 889.

6
I must essay a path whereby I, too, may rise from earth and fly victorious on the lips of men. (Temptanda via est, qua me quoque possim Tollere humo victorque virum volitare per ora.)

VERGIL, *Georgics*. Bk. iii, l. 8.

7
What rage for fame attends both great and small!
Better be d—n'd than mentioned *not at all*.

JOHN WOLCOT, *To the Royal Academicians*.

I am no cormorant of fame, d'ye see;
I ask not all the laurel, but a sprig.

JOHN WOLCOT, *Epistle to the Reviewers*.

8
Others are fond of Fame, but Fame of you.

YOUNG, *Love of Fame*. Sat. i, l. 10.

IV—Fame: How It Is Won

9
And what at first had been an idle joy,
Became a sober serious work for fame.

ROBERT BUCHANAN, *Hugh Sutherland's Pansies*

10
Mortals, who sought and found, by dangerous roads,
A path to perpetuity of fame.

BYRON, *Childe Harold*. Canto iii, st. 105.

The first in danger, as the first in fame.

HOMER, *Iliad*. Bk. vi, l. 637. (Pope, tr.)

If it is for fame that men do brave actions, they are only silly fellows after all.

R. L. STEVENSON, *The English Admirals*.

11
My advice to a young man seeking deathless fame would be to espouse an unpopular cause and devote his life to it.

GEORGE WILLIAM CURTIS, *Wendell Phillips*.

12
For not on downy plumes, nor under shade
Of canopy reposing, fame is won.
(Chè, seggendo in piuma,
In fama non si vien, nè sotto coltre.)

DANTE, *Inferno*. Canto xxiv, l. 46. (Cary, tr.)

Sloth views the towers of fame with envious eyes,
Desirous still, still impotent to rise.

WILLIAM SHENSTONE, *The Judgement of Hercules*, l. 436.

13
Fame then was cheap, and the first comer sped;
And they have kept it since, by being dead.

DRYDEN, *The Conquest of Granada: Epilogue*.

14
Nothing is less selfish than a desire of fame, since its only sure acquisition is by labouring for others.

WALTER SAVAGE LANDOR, *Letter*, 1853.

No true and permanent Fame can be founded except in labors which promote the happiness of mankind.

CHARLES SUMNER, *Fame and Glory*. Address at Amherst, 11 Aug., 1847.

15
Fame comes only when deserved, and then is as inevitable as destiny, for it is destiny.

LONGFELLOW, *Hyperion*. Bk. i, ch. 8.

Building nests in Fame's great temple, as in spouts the swallows build.

LONGFELLOW, *Nuremberg*. St. 16.

16
Thus fame shall be achiev'd, renown on earth,
And what most merits fame in silence hid.

MILTON, *Paradise Lost*. Bk. xi, l. 694.

17
Nor Fame I slight, nor for her favours call;
She comes unlook'd for, if she comes at all.

POPE, *The Temple of Fame*, l. 513.

Fame usually comes to those who are thinking about something else,—very rarely to those who say to themselves, "Go to, now, let us be a celebrated individual!" The struggle for fame, as such, commonly ends in notoriety;—that ladder is easy to climb, but it leads to the pillory which is crowded with fools who could not hold

their tongues and rogues who could not hide their tricks.
O. W. HOLMES, *The Autocrat of the Breakfast-Table*. Ch. 12.

1
True fame will never be in Chance's gift. (Non erunt honores umquam fortuiti muneris.)
SOLON. (AUSONIUS [?], *Septem Sapientum Sententiæ*, l. 31.)

Renown's all hit or miss;
There's fortune even in fame.
BYRON, *Don Juan*. Canto vii, st. 33.

2
Fame's loudest trump upon the ear of Time
Leaves but a dying echo; they alone
Are held in everlasting memory
Whose deeds partake of heaven.
ROBERT SOUTHEY, *Verses Spoken at Oxford upon the Installation of Lord Grenville*, l. 92.

Wouldst thou be fam'd? have those high deeds in view,
Brave men would act, though scandal should ensue.
YOUNG, *Love of Fame*. Satire vii, l. 181.

3
His very depreciation of fame increased his fame. (Ipsa dissimulatione famæ faman auxit.)
TACITUS, *Agricola*. Sec. 18.

V—Fame: Its Rewards

4
Let us now praise famous men.
Apocrypha: Ecclesiasticus, xliv, 1.

"Let us now praise famous men"—
Men of little showing—
For their work continueth,
And their work continueth,
Broad and deep continueth,
Greater than their knowing!
KIPLING, *A School Song*.

5
Sure of the Fortieth spare Arm-chair
When gout and glory seat me there.
ROBERT BROWNING, *Dîs Aliter Visum*. St. 12.

6
O Fame!—if I e'er took delight in thy praises,
'Twas less for the sake of thy high-sounding phrases,
Than to see the bright eyes of the dear one discover
She thought that I was not unworthy to love her.
BYRON, *Stanzas Written on the Road Between Florence and Pisa*.

7
Humanely glorious! Men will weep for him
When many a guilty martial fame is dim.
THOMAS CAMPBELL, *Lines in a Blank Leaf of La Perouse's Voyages*, l. 19.

Lights of the world and demi-gods of Fame.
CAMPBELL, *The Pleasures of Hope*. Pt. ii, l. 316.

8
How shall I then begin, or where conclude,
To draw a fame so truly circular?
DRYDEN, *On the Death of Cromwell*. St. 5.

9
Short is my date, but deathless my renown.
HOMER, *Iliad*. Bk. ix, l. 535. (Pope, tr.)

Earth sounds my wisdom, and high Heav'n my fame.
HOMER, *Odyssey*. Bk. ix, l. 20. (Pope, tr.)

10
Oh, 'tis all of thy dear grace
That every finger points me out in going
Lyrist of the Roman race;
Breath, power to charm (if mine) are they bestowing.
(Totum muneris hoc tui est,
Quod monstror digito prætereuntium
Romanæ fidicen lyræ.
Quod spiro et placeo, si placeo, tuum est.)
HORACE, *Odes*. Bk. iv, ode 3, l. 21.

It's a fine thing to have a finger pointed at one, and to hear people say, "That's the man." (At pulchrum est digito monstrari et dicier, "Hic est.")
PERSIUS, *Satires*. Sat. i, l. 28.

11
The temple of fame is the shortest passage to riches and preferment.
JUNIUS, *Letters*. Letter 59.

12
His fame was great in all the land.
LONGFELLOW, *Tales of a Wayside Inn: The Student's Tale: Emma and Eginhard*, l. 50.

13
Fame has only the span of a day, they say.
But to live in the hearts of the people—that is worth something.
OUIDA, *Wisdom, Wit, and Pathos: Signa*.

Sleep on, O brave-hearted, O wise man that kindled the flame—
To live in mankind is far more than to live in a name.
VACHEL LINDSAY, *The Eagle That Is Forgotten*.

14
The lofty lucre of renown.
PINDAR, *Isthmian Odes*. Ode i, l. 62. (Moore, tr.)

15
If you will observe, it does n't take
A man of giant mould to make
A giant shadow on the wall;
And he who in our daily sight
Seems but a figure mean and small,
Outlined in Fame's illusive light,
May stalk, a silhouette sublime,
Across the canvas of his time.
J. T. TROWBRIDGE, *Authors' Night*. St. 17.

16
For him—who ascended Fame's ladder so high:
From the round at the top he has stepped to the sky!
N. P. WILLIS, *The Death of Harrison*.

VI—Fame: Its Penalties

See also Greatness: Its Penalties

1
Were not this desire of fame very strong, the difficulty of obtaining it, and the danger of losing it when obtained, would be sufficient to deter a man from so vain a pursuit.
ADDISON, *The Spectator*. No. 255.

2
Fame always brings loneliness. Success is as ice cold and lonely as the north pole.
VICKI BAUM, *Grand Hotel*, p. 134.

3
Ah! who can tell how hard it is to climb
The steep where Fame's proud temple shines afar;
Ah! who can tell how many a soul sublime
Has felt the influence of malignant star,
And waged with Fortune an eternal war;
Check'd by the scoff of Pride, by Envy's frown,
And Poverty's unconquerable bar.
JAMES BEATTIE, *The Minstrel*. Bk. i, l. 1.

4
The best-concerted schemes men lay for fame,
Die fast away: only themselves die faster.
The far-fam'd sculptor, and the laurell'd bard,
Those bold insurancers of deathless fame,
Supply their little feeble aids in vain.
ROBERT BLAIR, *The Grave*, l. 185.

5
The strongest poison ever known
Came from Cæsar's laurel crown.
WILLIAM BLAKE, *Auguries of Innocence*.

6
Could any sober man be proud to hold
A lease of common talk, or die consoled
For thinking that on lips of fools to come
He'll live with Pontius Pilate and Tom Thumb?
ROBERT BRIDGES, *La Gloire de Voltaire*.

7
Happy is the man who hath never known what it is to taste of fame—to have it is a purgatory, to want it is a Hell!
BULWER-LYTTON, *Last of the Barons*. Bk. v, ch. 1.

8
Persecution dragged them into fame
And chased them up to heaven.
COWPER, *The Task*. Bk. v, l. 730.

The village sleeps, a name unknown, till men
With life-blood stain its soil, and pay the due
That lifts it to eternal fame,—for then
'Tis grown a Gettysburg or Waterloo.
M. A. DEWOLFE HOWE, *Distinction*.

9
And all the fair examples of renown
Out of distress and misery are grown.
SAMUEL DANIEL, *On the Earl of Southampton*.

10
Your fame is like the summer flower
Which blooms and dies in one short hour;
The sunny warmth which brings it forth
Soon slays with parching power.
(La vostra nominanza é color d'erba,
Che viene e va; e quei la discolora
Per cui ell' esce della terra acerba.)
DANTE, *Purgatorio*. Canto xi, l. 115.

11
He pays too high a price
For knowledge and for fame
Who sells his sinews to be wise,
His teeth and bones to buy a name,
And crawls through life a paralytic
To earn the praise of bard and critic.
EMERSON, *Fame*.

12
All fame is dangerous; good bringeth envy, bad shame.
THOMAS FULLER, *Gnomologia*.

13
How patient Nature smiles at Fame!
The weeds, that strewed the victor's way,
Feed on his dust to shroud his name,
Green where his proudest towers decay.
O. W. HOLMES, *A Roman Aqueduct*.

14
Our fruitless labors mourn,
And only rich in barren fame return.
HOMER, *Odyssey*. Bk. x, l. 46. (Pope, tr.)

15
And early though the laurel grows
It withers quicker than the rose. . . .
Runners whom renown outran
And the name died before the man.
A. E. HOUSMAN, *To an Athlete Dying Young*.

16
It is a wretched thing to lean on the fame of others. (Miserum est aliorum incumbere famæ.)
JUVENAL, *Satires*. Sat. viii, l. 76.

17
Ten thousand flakes about my windows blow,
Some falling and some rising, but all snow.
Scribblers and statesmen! are ye not just so?
W. S. LANDOR, *Fame*.

18
Fame, if not double fac'd, is double mouth'd,
And with contrary blast proclaims most deeds;
On both his wings, one black, the other white,
Bears greatest names in his wild aery flight.
MILTON, *Samson Agonistes*, l. 971.

19
I court no renown, nor that fame which usually sets the spur to talent. (Nulla mihi captatur gloria, quaeque Ingeniis stimulos subdere fama solet.)
OVID, *Tristia*. Bk. v, eleg. 1, l. 75.

20
Who grasp'd at earthly fame,
Grasped wind: nay, worse, a serpent grasped that through
His hand slid smoothly, and was gone; but left

A sting behind which wrought him endless pain.
ROBERT POLLOK, *Course of Time*. Bk. iii, l. 533.

1
All fame is foreign but of true desert,
Plays round the head, but comes not to the heart:
One self-approving hour whole years outweighs
Of stupid starers, and of loud huzzas:
And more true joy Marcellus exiled feels,
Than Cæsar with a senate at his heels.
POPE, *An Essay on Man*. Epis. iv, l. 253.

2
How vain that second life in others' breath,
Th' estate which wits inherit after death!
Ease, health, and life, for this they must resign,
(Unsure the tenure, but how vast the fine!)
POPE, *The Temple of Fame*, l. 505.

Then teach me, Heav'n! to scorn the guilty bays;
Drive from my breast that wretched lust of praise;
Unblemish'd let me live, or die unknown:
Oh, grant an honest Fame, or grant me none!
POPE, *The Temple of Fame*. Last lines.

3
The renown which riches or beauty confer is fleeting and frail; mental excellence is a splendid and lasting possession. (Divitiarum et formæ gloria fluxa atque fragilis est, virtus clara æternaque habetur.)
SALLUST, *Catiline*. Sec. 1.

4
Laurel is green for a season, and love is sweet for a day;
But love grows bitter with treason, and laurel outlives not May.
SWINBURNE, *Hymn to Proserpine*.

5
The loud impertinence of fame.
WILLIAM WATSON, *Laleham Churchyard*. St. 3.

6
And what so foolish as the chance of Fame?
How vain the prize! how impotent our aim!
YOUNG, *Love of Fame*. Sat. ii, l. 283.

VII—Fame and Death

7
The waters were his winding-sheet, the sea was made his tomb,
Yet for his fame the Ocean sea was not sufficient room.
RICHARD BARNFIELD, *Epitaph on Hawkins*.

8
There's many a crown for who can reach.
Ten lines, a statesman's life in each!
The flag stuck on a heap of bones,
A soldier's doing! what atones?
They scratch his name on the Abbey-stones.
ROBERT BROWNING, *The Last Ride Together*.

9
What is the end of Fame? 'tis but to fill
A certain portion of uncertain paper:
Some liken it to climbing up a hill,
Whose summit, like all hills, is lost in vapour:
For this men write, speak, preach, and heroes kill,
And bards burn what they call their "midnight taper,"
To have, when the original is dust,
A name, a wretched picture, and worse bust.
BYRON, *Don Juan*. Canto i, st. 218.

We toil for fame,
We live on crusts,
We make a name,
Then we are busts.
L. H. ROBBINS, *Lines*, intended for delivery at the unveiling of the memorials to Monroe, Maury, Whitman and Whistler at the Hall of Fame.

10
Fame is an undertaker that pays but little attention to the living, but bedizens the dead, furnishes out their funerals, and follows them to the grave.
C. C. COLTON, *Lacon*. Pt. i.

11
The temple of fame stands upon the grave: the flame that burns upon its altars is kindled from the ashes of dead men.
WILLIAM HAZLITT, *Lectures on the English Poets*. Lecture 8.

12
The life which others pay, let us bestow,
And give to Fame what we to Nature owe.
HOMER, *Iliad*. Bk. xii, l. 393. (Pope, tr.)

The rest were vulgar deaths, unknown to fame.
HOMER, *Iliad*. Bk. xi, l. 394. (Pope, tr.)

13
Fame is a revenue payable only to our ghosts; and to deny ourselves all present satisfaction, or to expose ourselves to so much hazard for this, were as great madness as to starve ourselves or fight desperately for food to be laid on our tombs after our death.
SIR GEORGE MACKENZIE, *Essay on Preferring Solitude*. (1665)

14
No hero to me is the man who wins fame by the easy shedding of his blood; give me the man who can win praise without dying. (Nolo virum facili redemit qui sanguine famam; Hunc volo, laudari qui sine morte potest.)
MARTIAL, *Epigrams*. Bk. i, epig. 8.

15
Life is too short for any distant aim;
And cold the dull reward of future fame.
LADY MARY WORTLEY MONTAGUE, *Epistle to the Earl of Burlington*.

16
To the quick brow Fame grudges her best wreath
While the quick heart to enjoy it throbs beneath:
On the dead forehead's sculptured marble shown,

Lo, her choice crown—its flowers are also stone.

JOHN JAMES PIATT, *The Guerdon.*

1
He lives, and he will always live; and his fame will be spread further by the recollection and the tongues of men now that he is removed from their sight. (Vivit enim vivetque semper atque etiam latius in memoria hominum et sermone versabitur, postquam ab oculis recessit.)

PLINY THE YOUNGER, *Epistles.* Bk. ii, epis. 1, sec. 3. Referring to Virginius Rufus.

2
Time magnifies everything after death: after his burial, a man's fame increases as it passes from mouth to mouth. (Omnia post obitum fingit majora vetustas: Majus ab exsequiis nomen in ora venit.)

PROPERTIUS, *Elegies.* Bk. iii, eleg. 1, l. 23.

Immortal heirs of universal praise!
Whose honours with increase of ages grow,
As streams roll down, enlarging as they flow;
Nations unborn your mighty names shall sound,
And worlds applaud that must not yet be found.

POPE, *Essay on Criticism.* Pt. i, l. 190.

3
Fame's mantle a funereal pall
Seems to the grief-dimmed eye,
For ever where the bravest fall
The best beloved die.

THOMAS P. RODMAN, *The Battle of Bennington.*

4
Why do you ask, "How long did he live?" He still lives; at one step he has passed over into posterity and consigned himself to the guardianship of memory. (Quid quæris quamdiu vixerit? Vivit; ad posteros usque transiluit et se in memoriam dedit.)

SENECA, *Epistulæ ad Lucilium.* Epis. xciii, 5.

Die two months ago, and not forgotten yet! Then there's hope a great man's memory may outlive his life half a year: but, by'r lady, he must build churches, then.

SHAKESPEARE, *Hamlet.* Act iii, sc. 2, l. 139.

5
You still shall live (such virtue hath my pen)
Where breath most breathes,—even in the mouths of men.

SHAKESPEARE, *Sonnets.* No. lxxxi.

He lives in fame, that died in virtue's cause.

SHAKESPEARE, *Titus Andronicus.* Act i, sc. 1, l. 390.

6
"Life is not lost," said she, "for which is bought
Endless renown."

SPENSER, *Faerie Queene.* Bk. iii, canto xi, st. 19.

On Fame's eternal bead-roll worthy to be filed.

SPENSER, *Faerie Queene.* Bk. iv, canto 2, st. 32.

7
The melancholy ghosts of dead renown,
Whisp'ring faint echoes of the world's applause.

YOUNG, *Night Thoughts.* Night ix, l. 119.

VIII—Fame: The Mouse-trap

8
I trust a good deal to common fame, as we all must. If a man has good corn, or wood, or boards, or pigs, to sell, or can make better chairs or knives, crucibles, or church organs, than anybody else, you will find a broad, hard-beaten road to his house, though it be in the woods.

RALPH WALDO EMERSON, *Common Fame: Journals,* 1855. Vol. viii, p. 528.

There has been much inquiry in the newspapers, recently [1911], as to whether Mr. Emerson wrote a sentence very like the above, which has been attributed to him in print. The Editors do not find the latter in his works; but there can be little doubt that it was a memory-quotation by some hearer, or, quite probably, correctly reported from one of his lectures, the same image in differing words.

EDWARD WALDO EMERSON AND WALDO EMERSON FORBES, *Footnote,* to preceding quotation, in *Journals of Ralph Waldo Emerson.*

If a man can write a better book, preach a better sermon, or make a better mouse-trap, than his neighbor, though he builds his house in the woods, the world will make a beaten path to his door.

Almost certainly a verbal variation of the preceding quotation, made by Emerson while delivering a lecture either at San Francisco or at Oakland, Calif., April 23, 26, 29, May 1, 17, and 18, 1871. This version, credited to Emerson, appears on page 38 of a little anthology called *Borrowings,* "Compiled by Ladies of the First Unitarian Church of Oakland, California," and published in December, 1889. This specific contribution was made by Mrs. Sarah S. B. Yule, who asserted (*The Docket,* Feb., 1912) that "to the best of my knowledge and belief, I copied it in my handbook from an address delivered long years ago, it being my custom to write everything there that I thought particularly good, if expressed in concise form; and when we were compiling *Borrowings,* I drew from this old handbook freely." Mrs. Yule died at Oakland, 1 Nov., 1916, at the age of 60. She undoubtedly told the essential truth about the origin of the quotation. Since she used the word "copied," it is probable that she copied it from a newspaper report of one of the California lectures, but she might, of course, have heard it, since she was a girl of sixteen at the time, and her parents, presumably being Unitarians, would naturally take her to hear the Concord sage. "Mouse-trap" was no doubt a happy thought which came to Emerson at the moment of delivery, as there is no record of his ever using it anywhere else. The compiler has had a search made through the files of such San Francisco papers of the period as still exist, but without result. For further discussion see APPENDIX.

Mr. Emerson was in the habit of repeating on different occasions, what was nominally the same lecture, in reality often varied by the introduction of part of some other or of new matter.

J. E. CABOT, *Letters and Social Aims: Introduction.*

1
If a man write a better book, preach a better sermon or build a better mouse-trap than his neighbor, though he build his house in the woods, the world will make a beaten path to his door.

ELBERT HUBBARD, *A Thousand and One Epigrams*, p. 166. (1911) Mr. Hubbard had previously used this quotation, in slightly different form, in *The Philistine*, crediting it to Emerson, and when his authorship of it was challenged, published the following in *The Fra* for May, 1911: "Mr. Hubbard, like all writers of epigrams, has attributed some of his good Class A product to other writers. For instance, he was once writing about the Roycrofters, and, having in mind the number of visitors who came to see us, he wrote: 'If a man can write a better book,' etc. . . . It was a little strain of his ego to let this thing go under his own stamp, so he saved his modesty and at the same time gave his epigram specific gravity, by attributing it to one Ralph Waldo Emerson." A somewhat similar explanation was made in *The Philistine* for July, 1912. In spite of which, it is certain that Hubbard did not originate the quotation, for the first number of *The Philistine* did not appear until June, 1895, whereas the quotation was printed in *Borrowings* in 1889.

2
A man can't be hid. He may be a peddler in the mountains, but the world will find him out to make him a king of finance. He may be carrying cabbages from Long Island, when the world will demand that he run the railways of a continent. He may be a groceryman on a canal, when the country shall come to him and put him in his career of usefulness. So that there comes a time finally when all the green barrels of petroleum in the land suggest but two names and one great company.

DR. JOHN RANDOLPH PAXTON, *Sermon: He Could Not Be Hid*, 25 Aug., 1889. As reported in the New York *Sun*, 26 Aug., 1889. The similarity of this to the "mouse-trap" quotation has caused Dr. Paxton to be credited with the authorship of both, but it is evidently an adaptation of Emerson's *Common Fame*, as given below.

If a man knows the law, people find it out, tho' he live in a pine shanty, and resort to him. And if a man can pipe or sing, so as to wrap the prisoned soul in an elysium; or can paint landscape, and convey into oils and ochres all enchantments of Spring and Autumn; or can liberate and intoxicate all people who hear him with delicious songs and verses; it is certain that the secret cannot be kept: the first witness tells it to a second, and men go by fives and tens and fifties to his door.

EMERSON, *Common Fame: Journals*, 1855. Vol. viii, p. 528.

FAMILIARITY

I—Familiarity: Apothegms

3
That man that hails you Tom or Jack,
And proves by thumps upon your back
  How he esteems your merit,
Is such a friend, that one had need
Be very much his friend indeed
  To pardon or to bear it.

COWPER, *Friendship*. St. 29.

And friend receiv'd with thumps upon the back.

YOUNG, *Love of Fame*. Sat. i, l. 259.

4
He calleth you by your Christian name, to imply that his other is the same with your own. He is too familiar by half, yet you wish he had less diffidence. With half the familiarity, he might pass for a casual dependent; with more boldness, he would be in no danger of being taken for what he is.

LAMB, *Last Essays of Elia: Poor Relations.*

I hold he loves me best that calls me Tom.

THOMAS HEYWOOD, *Hierarchie of the Blessed Angells.*

5
A man does not wonder at what he sees frequently, even though he be ignorant of the cause. If anything happens which he has never seen before, he calls it a prodigy. (Quod crebro videt, non miratur, etiamsi cur fiat nescit; quod ante non vidit, id si evenit, ostentum esse censet.)

CICERO, *De Divinatione*. Bk. ii, sec. 22.

6
Give a clown your finger and he'll take your whole hand.

JOHN RAY, *English Proverbs.*

7
The terrible gift of familiarity. (Don terrible de la familiarité.)

MIRABEAU, *Letters.*

8
Be . . . rather sweet than familiar; familiar than intimate; and intimate with very few, and upon very good grounds.

JAMES PUCKLE, *The Club.*

9
Be thou familiar, but by no means vulgar.

SHAKESPEARE, *Hamlet*. Act i, sc. 3, l. 61.

10
The coach jumbled us insensibly into some sort of familiarity.

RICHARD STEELE, *The Spectator*. No. 132.

II—Familiarity Breeds Contempt

11
Frequent use breeds contempt. (Parit enim conversatio contemptum.)

APULEIUS, *De Deo Socratis;* ST. THOMAS AQUINAS, *Ad Joannem Fratrem Monitio;* LIVY, *History*. Bk. xxxv, ch. 10.

1
Over-great homeliness engendereth dispraising.
CHAUCER, *Melibeus*. Sec. 55. (c. 1386)

2
Truth begetteth hatred; Virtue, envy; Familiarity, contempt.
GABRIEL HARVEY, *Works*. Vol. i, p. 293. (1593)

3
Familiarity begets boldness.
SHACKERLEY MARMION, *The Antiquary*. Act. i. (1641)

4
Familiarity breeds contempt. (Nimia familiaritas parit contemptum.)
PUBLILIUS SYRUS, *Sententiæ*. No. 640. The earliest known use of the phrase in English is c. 1160, by Alanus de Insulis. (WRIGHT, *Minor Anglo-Latin Satirists*. Ser. ii, p. 454.)

I find my familiarity with thee has bred contempt.
CERVANTES, *Don Quixote*. Pt. i, ch. 6. (1605)

Familiarity breeds contempt—and children.
MARK TWAIN, *Unpublished Diaries*.

5
I hope upon familiarity will grow more contempt.
SHAKESPEARE, *The Merry Wives of Windsor*. Act i, sc. 1, l. 256. (1600)

Greater familiarity on his side might have bred contempt.
SMOLLETT, *Adventures of an Atom*, p. 148. (1769)

6
Contempt born of familiarity. (Vitato assiduitatis fastidio.)
SUETONIUS, *Twelve Cæsars: Tiberius*. Ch. x, 1.

7
And sweets grown common lose their dear
delight.
SHAKESPEARE, *Sonnets*. No. cii.

Beauty soon grows familiar to the lover,
Fades in his eye, and palls upon the sense.
ADDISON, *Cato*. Act i, sc. 4.

8
Near acquaintance doth diminish reverent fear.
SIR PHILIP SIDNEY, *Arcadia*. Bk. iii.

Near the temple insult the god. (Chin miao 'chi shên.)
UNKNOWN. A Chinese proverb.

9
Staled by frequence, shrunk by usage into
commonest commonplace!
TENNYSON, *Locksley Hall Sixty Years After*. St. 38.

FAMILY

See also Home

10
He that hath wife and children hath given hostages to fortune; for they are impediments to great enterprises, either of virtue or mischief.
BACON, *Essays: Of Marriage and Single Life*.

We have given so many hostages to fortune. (Dedimus tot pignora fatis.)
LUCIAN, *Dialogues*. No. vii, l. 662.

11
There are some other that account wife and children but as bills of charges.
BACON, *Essays: Of Marriage and Single Life*.

Certainly wife and children are a kind of disciplining of humanity.
BACON, *Essays: Of Marriage and Single Life*.

12
It would puzzle a convocation of casuists to resolve their degrees of consanguinity.
CERVANTES, *Don Quixote*. Pt. i, ch. 8.

13
I would not answer for myself if I could find an affectionate family with good shooting and first-rate claret.
BENJAMIN DISRAELI, *Lothair*. Ch. 30.

14
The security and elevation of the family and of family life are the prime objects of civilization, and the ultimate ends of all industry.
CHARLES W. ELIOT, *The Happy Life*.

15
Most of the persons whom I see in my own house I see across a gulf.
EMERSON, *Journals*. Vol. v, p. 324.

Happy will that house be in which the relations are formed from character.
EMERSON, *Society and Solitude: Domestic Life*.

16
And so do his sisters and his cousins and his
aunts!
His sisters and his cousins,
Whom he reckons up by dozens,
And his aunts!
W. S. GILBERT, *H. M. S. Pinafore*. Act i.

17
The building up of a family is a manufacture very little above the building a house of cards.
LORD HALIFAX, *Works*, p. 250.

18
I believe in the fireside. I believe in the democracy of home. I believe in the republicanism of the family.
INGERSOLL, *Liberty of Man, Woman and Child*.

19
A holy family, that make
Each meal a Supper of the Lord.
LONGFELLOW, *The Golden Legend*. Pt. i.

20
It is a piece of luck to have relations scarce. (Εὐτύχημα δ' ἐστὶν ὀλίγους τοὺς ἀναγκαίους ἔχειν.)
MENANDER, *Thupopos*. Frag.

The Emperor also has straw-sandaled relatives. ('Huang ti yeh yu 'tsao hsieh 'chin.)
UNKNOWN. A Chinese proverb.

It is a melancholy truth, that even great men have their poor relations.
DICKENS, *Bleak House*. Ch. 28.

God gives us relatives; thank God, we can choose our friends.
ADDISON MIZNER, *The Cynics' Calendar*, p. 1.

21
The State and the family are for ever at war.
GEORGE MOORE, *Bending of the Bough*. Act i.

1
He that flies from his own family has far to travel. (Longe fuit, quisquis suos fugit.)
PETRONIUS, *Satyricon*. Sec. 43.

2
He who joins in sport with his own family will never be dull to strangers. (Numquam erit alienis gravis, qui suis se concinnat levem.)
PLAUTUS, *Trinummus*. Act iii, sc. 2, l. 58.

3
A family is but too often a commonwealth of malignants.
POPE, *Thoughts on Various Subjects*.

Every large family has its angel and its demon.
JOSEPH ROUX, *Meditations of a Parish Priest*. Pt. ix, No. 56.

4
The family is one of nature's masterpieces.
GEORGE SANTAYANA, *The Life of Reason*. Vol. ii, p. 35.

5
When the black-lettered list to the gods was presented
(The list of what Fate for each mortal intends),
At the long string of ills a kind goddess relented,
And slipped in three blessings,—wife, children, and friends.
WILLIAM ROBERT SPENCER, *Wife, Children, and Friends*.

6
He that loves not his wife and children, feeds a lioness at home, and broods a nest of sorrow.
JEREMY TAYLOR, *Sermons*. Vol. i, p. 236.

7
Love for one's family is an animal instinct which is good only so long as kept within the limits of an instinct.
TOLSTOY, *The Christian Teaching*.

All happy families resemble one another; every unhappy family is unhappy in its own way.
TOLSTOY, *Anna Karénina*. Pt. i, ch. 1.

8
The race remains immortal, and the fortune of the house endures through many years. (Genus immortale manet, multosque per annos Stat fortuna domus.)
VERGIL, *Georgics*. Bk. iv, l. 209.

9
Next to no wife and children, your own wife and children are best pastime; another's wife and your children worse; your wife and another's children worst.
SIR HENRY WOTTON, *Table-Talk*.

FAMINE, see Hunger

FANATICISM

See also Reformers

10
Earth's fanatics make
Too frequently heaven's saints.
ELIZABETH BARRETT BROWNING, *Aurora Leigh*. Bk. ii, l. 449.

11
They were possessed with a spirit of proselytism in the most fanatical degree.
EDMUND BURKE, *Reflections on the Revolution in France*.

12
There is no strong performance without a little fanaticism in the performer.
EMERSON, *Journals*. Vol. ix, p. 203.

13
Defined in psychological terms, a fanatic is a man who consciously over-compensates a secret doubt.
ALDOUS HUXLEY, *Proper Studies*, p. 262.

14
Fanatics have their dreams, wherewith they weave
A paradise for a sect.
JOHN KEATS, *Hyperion*, l. 1. (Earlier version.)

15
Fanatic fools, that in those twilight times,
With wild religion cloaked the worst of crimes!
JOHN LANGHORNE, *The Country Justice*. Pt. iii, l. 122.

16
To talk nonsense, or poetry, or the dash between the two, in a tone of profound sincerity, and to enunciate solemn discordances with received opinion so seriously as to convey the impression of a spiritual insight, is the peculiar gift by which monomaniacs, having first persuaded themselves, contrive to influence their neighbours, and through them to make conquest of a good half of the world, for good or for ill.
GEORGE MEREDITH, *The Ordeal of Richard Feverel*. Ch. 12.

17
Fanaticism consists in redoubling your effort when you have forgotten your aim.
GEORGE SANTAYANA, *Life of Reason*. Vol. i, p. 13.

FANCY

See also Imagination

18
Then read my fancies; they will stick like burrs.
JOHN BUNYAN, *The Pilgrim's Progress: The Author's Apology*.

19
Can Fancy's fairy hands no veil create
To hide the sad realities of fate?
CAMPBELL, *The Pleasures of Hope*. Pt. ii, l. 391.

20
Ingenious Fancy, never better pleas'd
Than when employ'd to accommodate the fair,
Heard the sweet moan with pity, and devis'd
The soft settee; one elbow at each end,
And in the midst an elbow it receiv'd,
United yet divided, twain at once.
COWPER, *The Task*. Bk. i, l. 72.

21
While fancy, like the finger of a clock,
Runs the great circuit, and is still at home.
COWPER, *The Task*. Bk. iv, l. 118.

1
How Fancy loves about the world to stray,
While Judgement slowly picks his sober way.
George Crabbe, *The Library*, l. 294.

2
Men live in their fancy, like drunkards whose hands are too soft and tremulous for successful labor.
Emerson, *Essays, Second Series: Experience.*

3
Fancy may kill or cure.
Thomas Fuller, *Gnomologia*. No. 1500.

4
Gay Hope is theirs, by Fancy fed,
Less pleasing when possest;
The tear forgot as soon as shed,
The sunshine of the breast.
Thomas Gray, *On a Distant Prospect of Eton College*. St. 5.

Bright-eyed Fancy, hov'ring o'er,
Scatters from her pictured urn
Thoughts that breathe, and words that burn.
Thomas Gray, *The Progress of Poesy*, l. 108.

5
But lay on fancy's neck the reins.
Matthew Green, *The Spleen*, l. 187.

Fancy's telescope applies
With tinctured glass to cheat his eyes.
Matthew Green, *The Spleen*, l. 736.

6
Aggressive Fancy working spells
Upon a mind o'erwrought.
Thomas Hardy, *The Dynasts*. Act i, sc. 6.

7
Fancy may bolt bran and make ye take it flour.
John Heywood, *Proverbs*. Pt. ii, ch. 4.

8
We may take Fancy for a companion, but must follow Reason as our guide.
Samuel Johnson, *Letter to Boswell*, 1774.

All power of fancy over reason is a degree of insanity.
Samuel Johnson, *Rasselas*. Ch. 44.

If but a beam of sober Reason play,
Lo, Fancy's fairy frost-work melts away.
Samuel Rogers, *Pleasures of Memory*. Pt. ii.

Woe to the youth whom Fancy gains,
Winning from Reason's hand the reins,
Pity and woe! for such a mind
Is soft, contemplative, and kind.
Scott, *Rokeby*. Canto i, st. 31.

9
Ever let the Fancy roam,
Pleasure never is at home.
Keats, *Fancy*, l. 1.

A moonlight traveler in Fancy's land.
Madison Cawein, *Unqualified*.

The truant Fancy was a wanderer ever.
Charles Lamb, *Fancy Employed on Divine Subjects*.

10
And as the moon from some dark gate of cloud
Throws o'er the sea a floating bridge of light
Across whose trembling planks our fancies crowd
Into the realm of mystery and night.
Longfellow, *Haunted Houses*. St. 9.

11
Two meanings have our lightest fantasies,
One of the flesh, and of the spirit one.
J. R. Lowell, *Sonnets*. No. 34.

12
Fancy is the friend of woe.
William Mason, *Ode*. No. vii, st. 2.

13
A thousand fantasies
Begin to throng into my memory,
Of calling shapes, and beck'ning shadows dire,
And airy tongues that syllable men's names
On sands and shores and desert wildernesses.
Milton, *Comus*, l. 205.

14
At the close of each sad, sorrowing day,
Fancy restores what vengeance snatch'd away.
Pope, *Eloisa to Abelard*, l. 225.

15
Fancy surpasses beauty.
John Ray, *English Proverbs*.

16
All impediments in fancy's course
Are motives of more fancy.
Shakespeare, *All's Well that Ends Well*. Act v, sc. 3, l. 214.

17
Chewing the food of sweet and bitter fancy.
Shakespeare, *As You Like It*. Act iv, sc. 3, l. 102.

Chew on fair fancy's food, nor deem unmeet
I will not with a bitter chase the sweet.
Ariosto, *Orlando Furioso*. Canto iii, st. 62.

18
Is not this something more than fantasy?
Shakespeare, *Hamlet*. Act i, sc. 1, l. 54.

She is troubled with thick-coming fancies,
That keep her from her rest.
Shakespeare, *Macbeth*. Act v, sc. 3, l. 38.

So full of shapes is fancy,
That it alone is high fantastical.
Shakespeare, *Twelfth Night*. Act i, sc. 1, l. 14.

19
Tell me where is fancy bred,
Or in the heart or in the head?
How begot, how nourished?
Reply, reply.
It is engender'd in the eyes,
With gazing fed; and fancy dies
In the cradle where it lies.
Shakespeare, *The Merchant of Venice*. Act iii, sc. 2, l. 63.

20
For boy, however we do praise ourselves,
Our fancies are more giddy and unfirm,
More longing, wavering, sooner lost and worn,
Than women's are.
Shakespeare, *Twelfth Night*. Act ii, sc. 4, l. 33.

Fancies too weak for boys, too green and idle
For girls of nine.
SHAKESPEARE, *Winter's Tale*. Act iii, sc. 2, 182.

1
We figure to ourselves
The thing we like; and then we build it up,
As chance will have it, on the rock or sand,—
For thought is tired of wandering o'er the world,
And home-bound Fancy runs her bark ashore.
SIR HENRY TAYLOR, *Philip Van Artevelde*. Pt. i, act i, sc. 5.

Safe upon the solid rock the ugly houses stand:
Come and see my shining palace built upon the sand.
EDNA ST. VINCENT MILLAY, *A Few Figs From Thistles: Second Fig.*

2
Fancy light from Fancy caught.
TENNYSON, *In Memoriam*. Sec. xxiii, st. 4.

3
Full of pale fancies and chimeras huge.
THOMSON, *The Seasons: Autumn*, l. 1147.

4
But not for golden fancies iron truths make room.
WILLIAM WATSON, *The Hope of the World.*

5
Good-bye my Fancy!
Farewell dear mate, dear love!
I'm going away, I know not where,
Or to what fortune, or whether I may ever see you again,
So Good-bye my Fancy!
WALT WHITMAN, *Good-Bye My Fancy.*

6
Fancy, who leads the pastimes of the glad,
Full oft is pleased a wayward dart to throw,
Sending sad shadows after things not sad,
Peopling the harmless fields with signs of woe.
WORDSWORTH, *A Morning Exercise*, l. 1.

Sad fancies do we then affect,
In luxury of disrespect
To our own prodigal excess
Of too familiar happiness.
WORDSWORTH, *Ode to Lycoris*, l. 23.

FAREWELL

See also Parting

7
Once more, farewell!
If e'er we meet hereafter, we shall meet
In happier climes, and on a safer shore.
ADDISON, *Cato*. Act iv, sc. 6.

Farewell, my friends! farewell, my foes!
My peace with these, my love with those.
The bursting tears my heart declare;
Farewell, the bonnie banks of Ayr.
BURNS, *The Banks of Ayr.*

8
He turn'd him right and round about
Upon the Irish shore,
And gae his bridle reins a shake,
With Adieu, for evermore, My dear,—
And adieu for evermore!
BURNS, *It Was a' for Our Rightfu' King.*

Scott, under the impression that this stanza was part of an ancient ballad, used it both in *Rokeby* and in *The Monastery.*

9
Farewell! a word that must be, and hath been—
A sound which makes us linger;—yet—farewell!
BYRON, *Childe Harold*. Canto iv, st. 186.

Farewell!
For in that word, that fatal word—howe'er
We promise, hope, believe—there breathes despair.
BYRON, *The Corsair*. Canto i, st. 15.

Fare thee well! and if for ever,
Still for ever, fare thee well.
BYRON, *Fare Thee Well.*

I only know we loved in vain;
I only feel—Farewell!—Farewell!
BYRON, *Farewell! If Ever Fondest Prayer.*

"Farewell!" into the lover's soul
You see Fate plunge the fatal iron.
All poets use it. It's the whole
Of Byron.
"I only feel—farewell!" said he;
And always fearful was the telling—
Lord Byron was eternally
Farewelling.
BERT LESTON TAYLOR, *Farewell.*

10
All farewells should be sudden, when forever.
BYRON, *Sardanapalus*. Act v, sc. 1.

11
Life's joy for us a moment lingers,
And death seems in the word—farewell.
THOMAS CAMPBELL, *Song: Withdraw Not Yet.*

12
For ever, brother, hail and farewell. (In perpetuum, frater, ave atque vale.)
CATULLUS, *Odes*. Ode ci, l. 10.

Live and fare well; long life and good health to you. (Vive valeque.)
HORACE, *Satires*. Bk. ii, sat. v, l. 110.

For ever, and for ever, farewell, Cassius!
If we do meet again, why, we shall smile;
If not, why then this parting was well made.
SHAKESPEARE, *Julius Cæsar*. Act v, sc. 1, l. 117.

13
Then farewell, my trim-built wherry!
Oars, and coat, and badge, farewell!
CHARLES DIBDIN, *Poor Tom.*

14
But two are walking apart forever
And wave their hands for a mute farewell.
JEAN INGELOW, *Divided.*

"Adieu," she cried, and waved her lily hand.
JOHN GAY, *Sweet William's Farewell.*

15
Friend, ahoy! Farewell! farewell!
Grief unto grief, joy unto joy,
Greeting and help the echoes tell
Faint, but eternal—Friend, ahoy!
HELEN HUNT JACKSON, *Friend, Ahoy!*

1
The happy never say, and never hear said. farewell.

W. S. LANDOR, *Pericles and Aspasia:* Sec. 235, *Pericles to Aspasia.*

2
Kiss me, and say good-bye;
Good-bye, there is no word to say but this.

ANDREW LANG, *Good-bye.*

Well, good bye, Jim, Take keer of yourself.

JAMES WHITCOMB RILEY, *The Old Man and Jim.*

3
Farewell happy fields,
Where joy for ever dwells.

MILTON, *Paradise Lost.* Bk. i, l. 249.

4
Farewell, farewell to thee, Araby's daughter!
Thus warbled a Peri beneath the dark sea.

THOMAS MOORE, *Lalla Rookh: The Fire-Worshippers.*

5
The last farewell. (Supremumque vale.)

OVID, *Metamorphoses.* Bk. vi, l. 509; bk. x, l. 62.

6
Farewell to Lochaber, and farewell, my Jean,
Where heartsome wi' thee I hae mony day been:
For Lochaber no more, Lochaber no more,
We'll maybe return to Lochaber no more.

ALLAN RAMSAY, *Farewell to Lochaber.*

7
Farewell and be hanged!

SAMUEL ROWLEY, *The Noble Soldier.* Act iv, sc. 2. (1634) A proverb in frequent use.

8
Fare thee well;
The elements be kind to thee, and make
Thy spirits all of comfort!

SHAKESPEARE, *Antony and Cleopatra.* Act iii, sc. 2, l. 39.

9
Good night, ladies; good night, sweet ladies.

SHAKESPEARE, *Hamlet.* Act iv, sc. 5, l. 72.

Good night, ladies; we're going to leave you now.

UNKNOWN, *Good Night, Ladies.*

Gude nicht, and joy be wi' you a'.

CAROLINA NAIRNE, *Gude Nicht.*

10
Farewell, and stand fast.

SHAKESPEARE, *I Henry IV.* Act ii, sc. 2, l. 75.

Poor Jack; farewell!
I could have better spared a better man.

SHAKESPEARE, *I Henry IV.* Act v, sc. 4, l. 103.

Farewell, for I must leave you.

SHAKESPEARE, *Othello.* Act i, sc. 1, l. 145.

11
O, now, for ever
Farewell the tranquil mind! farewell content!
Farewell the plumed troop, and the big wars,
That make ambition virtue! O, farewell!
Farewell the neighing steed, and the shrill trump,
The spirit-stirring drum, the ear-piercing fife,
The royal banner and all quality,
Pride, pomp, and circumstance of glorious war!
And, O you mortal engines, whose rude throats
The immortal Jove's dread clamours counterfeit,
Farewell! Othello's occupation 's gone!

SHAKESPEARE, *Othello.* Act iii, sc. 3, l. 347.

12
Farewell! thou art too dear for my possessing.

SHAKESPEARE, *Sonnets.* No. lxxxvii.

13
Welcome ever smiles,
And farewell goes out sighing.

SHAKESPEARE, *Troilus and Cressida.* Act iii, sc. 3, l. 169.

Troilus, farewell! one eye yet looks on thee;
But with my heart the other eye doth see.

SHAKESPEARE, *Troilus and Cressida.* Act v, sc. 2, l. 107.

14
So sweetly she bade me adieu,
I thought that she bade me return.

WILLIAM SHENSTONE, *A Pastoral Ballad.* Pt. i.

15
I'm bidding you a long farewell,
My Mary, kind and true,
But I'll not forget you, darling,
In the land I'm going to.

HELEN SELINA SHERIDAN, *Lament of the Irish Emigrant.*

FARMING

I—Farming: Apothegms

16
A better farmer ne'er brush'd dew from lawn.

BYRON, *The Vision of Judgment.* St. 8.

17
The eyes and footsteps of the master are things most salutary to the land. (Oculos et vestigia domini, res agro saluberrimas.)

LUCIUS JUNIUS COLUMELLA, *De Re Rustica.* Bk. iv, sec. 18.

The master's eye is the best fertilizer. (Majores fertilieium in agro oculum domini.)

PLINY THE ELDER, *Historia Naturalis.* Bk. xviii, sec. 84.

The best compost for the lands
Is the wise master's feet and hands.

ROBERT HERRICK, *The Country Life.*

See also MASTER: THE EYE OF THE MASTER.

18
I have planted, Apollos watered; but God gave the increase.

New Testament: I Corinthians, iii, 6.

When all is done, learn this, my son,
Not friend, nor skill, nor wit at will,
Nor ship, nor clod, but only God
Doth all in all.

THOMAS TUSSER, *The Author's Life: Hundreth Good Pointes of Husbandrie.* (1557)

19
Our farmers round, well pleased with constant gain,

Like other farmers, flourish and complain.
GEORGE CRABBE, *The Parish Register:* Pt. i, *Baptisms*, l. 274.

None says his garner is full.
GEORGE HERBERT, *Jacula Prudentum.*

1
He that by the Plough would thrive,
Himself must either hold or drive.
BENJAMIN FRANKLIN, *Poor Richard,* 1747.

2
'Tis the farmer's care
That makes the field bear.
THOMAS FULLER, *Gnomologia.*

3
Under water, famine; under snow, bread.
GEORGE HERBERT, *Jacula Prudentum.* Referring to the comparative effect of snow and rain on crops.

4
Let it please thee to keep in order a moderate-sized farm, that thy garners may be full of fruits in their season.
HESIOD, *Works and Days*, l. 304.

Praise a great estate, but cultivate a small one. (Laudato ingentia rura, Exiguum colito.)
VERGIL, *Georgics.* Bk. ii, l. 412. An old adage which Vergil echoes from Cato.

We all know how old farm folk especially delight in aphorisms of this kind, and in this respect, at all events, show much real wit.
JOHN KEBLE, *Lectures on Poetry.* Lecture 37.

5
Let us seek bread with the plough. (Panem quæramus aratro.)
JUVENAL, *Satires.* Sat. xiv, l. 181.

6
Six years thou shalt sow thy field, and six years thou shalt prune thy vineyard, and gather in the fruit thereof; But in the seventh year shall be a sabbath of rest unto the land, a sabbath for the Lord; thou shalt neither sow thy field nor prune thy vineyard. That which groweth of its own accord of thy harvest thou shalt not reap, neither gather the grapes of thy vine undressed: for it is a year of rest unto the land.
Old Testament: Leviticus, xxv, 3–5.

7
When the land is cultivated entirely by the spade, and no horses are kept, a cow is kept for every three acres of land.
JOHN STUART MILL, *Political Economy.* Bk. ii, ch. 6, sec. 5. Referring to peasant-farming in Flanders.

Three acres and a cow.
Usually attributed to JESSE COLLINGS, a member of Parliament who carried the "small holdings amendment" against Lord Salisbury's government in 1886.

Ten acres and a mule.
A phrase originating in America in 1862, indicating what a slave expected to receive when he was emancipated.

8
Constant tillage exhausts a field. (Continua messe senescit ager.)
OVID, *Ars Amatoria.* Bk. iii, l. 82.

9
Peace is the nurse of Ceres, and Ceres is the foster-child of Peace. (Pax nutrit Cererem, pacis alumna Ceres.)
OVID, *Fasti.* Bk. i, l. 704.

10
Each man reaps his own farm. (Sibi quisque ruri metit.)
PLAUTUS, *Mostellaria*, l. 799. (Act iii, sc. 2.)

11
Look at your corn in May,
And you'll come weeping away;
Look at the same in June,
And you'll come home to another tune.
JOHN RAY, *English Proverbs.*

12
Ill husbandry braggeth to go with the best;
Good husbandry baggeth up gold in his chest.
Ill husbandry lieth in prison for debt;
Good husbandry spieth where profit to get.
THOMAS TUSSER, *Hundreth Good Pointes of Husbandrie.* Ch. 52.

13
I believe the first receipt to farm well is to be rich.
SYDNEY SMITH, *Letter to John Wishaw,* 13 April, 1818.

He was a very inferior farmer when he first began, . . . and he is now fast rising from affluence to poverty.
MARK TWAIN, *Rev. Henry Ward Beecher's Farm.*

14
Farming is not really a business; it is an occupation.
W. E. WOODWARD, *Money for Tomorrow*, p. 177.

II—Farming: Its Dignity

15
The agricultural population produces the bravest men, the most valiant soldiers, and a class of citizens the least given of all to evil designs.
CATO. (PLINY THE ELDER, *Historia Naturalis.* Bk. xviii, sec. 26.)

16
Far back in the ages,
The plough with wreaths was crowned;
The hands of kings and sages
Entwined the chaplet round.
BRYANT, *Ode for an Agricultural Celebration.*

17
Of all occupations from which gain is secured, there is none better than agriculture, nothing more productive, nothing sweeter, nothing more worthy of a free man. (Omnium autem rerum, ex quibus aliquid acquiritur, nihil est agri cultura melius, nihil uberius, nihil dulcius, nihil homine libero dignius.)
CICERO, *De Officiis.* Bk. i, sec. 42.

1
The first farmer was the first man, and all historic nobility rests on possession and use of land.

EMERSON, *Society and Solitude: Farming.*

The glory of the farmer is that, in the division of labors, it is his part to create. All trade rests at last on his primitive activity.

EMERSON, *Society and Solitude: Farming.*

2
A Plowman on his legs is higher than a Gentleman on his Knees.

BENJAMIN FRANKLIN, *Poor Richard*, 1746.

3
Agriculture is the foundation of manufactures; since the productions of nature are the materials of art.

EDWARD GIBBON, *Decline and Fall of the Roman Empire*. Ch. 2.

4
Not the Atlantic sweeps a flood
Potent as the ploughman's blood.
He, his horse, his ploughshare, these
Are the only verities.

LOUIS GOLDING, *Ploughman at the Plough.*

5
A time there was, ere England's griefs began,
When every rood of ground maintain'd its man;
For him light Labour spread her wholesome store,
Just gave what life requir'd, but gave no more:
His best companions, innocence and health;
And his best riches, ignorance of wealth.

OLIVER GOLDSMITH, *The Deserted Village*, l. 57.

But a bold peasantry, their country's pride,
When once destroy'd, can never be supplied.

GOLDSMITH, *The Deserted Village*, l. 55.

6
A peasant may believe as much
As a great clerk, and reach the highest stature.

GEORGE HERBERT, *The Temple: Faith.*

No one, after the priest, approaches nearer the divinity than the peasant.

JOSEPH ROUX, *Meditations of a Parish Priest: The Peasant*. No. 89.

7
Ye rigid Ploughmen! bear in mind
Your labour is for future hours.
Advance! spare not! nor look behind!
Plough deep and straight with all your powers!

RICHARD HENGIST HORNE, *The Plough.*

8
To plow is to pray—to plant is to prophesy, and the harvest answers and fulfills.

R. G. INGERSOLL, *About Farming in Illinois.*

9
Those who labor in the earth are the chosen people of God, if He ever had a chosen people, whose breasts He has made His peculiar deposit for substantial and genuine virtue.

THOMAS JEFFERSON, *Writings*. Vol. ii, p. 229.

Whenever there are in any country uncultivated lands and unemployed poor it is clear that the laws of property have been so far extended as to violate natural right. The earth is given as a common stock for men to labor and live on. . . . The small landowners are the most precious part of the State.

THOMAS JEFFERSON, *Writings*. Vol. xix, p. 17.

10
The first and most respectable of all the arts is agriculture. (Le premier et le plus respectable de tous les arts est l'agriculture.)

ROUSSEAU, *Émile*. Bk. iii.

Fair Queen of arts! from Heaven itself who came.

JAMES THOMSON, *The Castle of Indolence*. Canto ii, st. 19. Referring to agriculture.

11
O peasant, thou tillest the fields and fertilizest them, and sowest them. Thou makest the wheat to rise from the earth; through thee the "barren" is converted into grain; thou nourishest man, who is flesh. It is thanks to thy effort that we live here below. Glory to thee, O peasant!

JOSEPH ROUX, *Meditations of a Parish Priest: The Country, The Peasant*. No. 31.

12
Let me be no assistant for a state,
But keep a farm and carters.

SHAKESPEARE, *Hamlet*. Act ii, sc. 2, l. 166.

13
And he gave it for his opinion . . . that whoever could make two ears of corn, or two blades of grass, to grow upon a spot of ground where only one grew before, would deserve better of mankind, and do more essential service to his country, than the whole race of politicians put together.

SWIFT, *Gulliver's Travels: Voyage to Brobdingnag.*

14
In ancient times the sacred plough employed
The kings and awful fathers of mankind;
And some, with whom compared your insect-tribes
Are but the beings of a summer's day,
Have held the scale of empire, ruled the storm
Of mighty war; then, with victorious hand,
Disdaining little delicacies, seized
The plough, and greatly independent, scorned
All the vile stores corruption can bestow.

THOMSON, *The Seasons: Spring*, l. 58.

15
Let us never forget that the cultivation of the earth is the most important labor of man.

DANIEL WEBSTER, *Remarks on Agriculture*, Boston, 13 Jan., 1840.

When tillage begins, other arts follow. The farmers, therefore, are the founders of human civilization.

DANIEL WEBSTER, *Remarks on Agriculture*, Boston, 13 Jan., 1840.

16
Give fools their gold, and knaves their power;

Let fortune's bubbles rise and fall;
Who sows a field, or trains a flower,
Or plants a tree, is more than all.

WHITTIER, *A Song of Harvest*.

1
He who sows the ground with care and diligence acquires a greater stock of religious merit than he could gain by the repetition of ten thousand prayers.

ZOROASTER. (*Zend-Avesta*, vol. i; *Précis du Système de Zoroaster*, vol. iii.)

III—Farming: Its Rewards

2
If fields are prisons, where is Liberty?

ROBERT BLOOMFIELD, *The Farmer's Boy: Autumn*, l. 226.

3
Look up! the wide extended plain
Is billowy with its ripened grain,
And on the summer winds are rolled
Its waves of emerald and gold.

W. H. BURLEIGH, *The Harvest Call*.

4
Drop a grain of California gold into the ground, and there it will lie unchanged until the end of time; . . . drop a grain of our blessed gold into the ground and lo! a mystery.

EDWARD EVERETT, *Address on Agriculture*, Boston, Oct., 1855. Referring to wheat.

5
And farmers fatten most when famine reigns.

SAMUEL GARTH, *The Dispensary*. Canto ii, l. 64.

6
Oft did the harvest to their sickle yield:
Their furrow oft the stubborn glebe has broke:
How jocund did they drive their team a-field!
How bow'd the woods beneath their sturdy stroke!

THOMAS GRAY, *Elegy Written in a Country Church-yard*, l. 25.

7
Tradition said he feather'd his nest
Through an Agricultural Interest
In the Golden Age of farming;
When golden eggs were laid by the geese,
And Colchian sheep wore a golden fleece,
And golden pippins—the sterling kind
Of Hesperus—now so hard to find—
Made Horticulture charming!

THOMAS HOOD, *Miss Kilmansegg: Her Pedigree*.

8
Happy the man who, far from cares of business,
Like the primitive race of mortals,
Works his ancestral acres with his oxen.
(Beatus ille qui procul negotiis,
Ut prisca gens mortalium,
Paterna rura bobus exercet suis.)

HORACE, *Epodes*. Epode ii, l. 1.

9
The life of the husbandman,—a life fed by the bounty of earth and sweetened by the airs of heaven.

DOUGLAS JERROLD, *The Husbandman's Life*.

10
Earth is here so kind, that just tickle her with a hoe and she laughs with a harvest.

DOUGLAS JERROLD, *A Land of Plenty*. Referring to Australia.

There is nothing grateful but the earth; you cannot do too much for it: it will continue to repay tenfold the pains and labour bestowed upon it.

LORD RAVENSWORTH. (BEWICK, *Life*.)

11
Well may we labour, still to dress
This garden, still to tend plant, herb, and flower.

MILTON, *Paradise Lost*. Bk. ix, l. 205.

12
'Tis sweet to spend one's time in the cultivation of the fields. (Tempus in agrorum cultu consumere dulce est.)

OVID, *Epistulæ ex Ponto*. Bk. ii, epis. 7, l. 69.

13
Here Ceres' gifts in waving prospect stand,
And nodding tempt the joyful reaper's hand.

POPE, *Windsor Forest*, l. 39.

14
Let your strong oxen plough up the rich soil of the earth, from the earliest months of the year. (Pingue solun primis extemplo a mensibus anni Fortes invertant tauri.)

VERGIL, *Georgics*. Bk. i, l. 63.

Plough deep while sluggards sleep.

BENJAMIN FRANKLIN, *Poor Richard*, 1758.

15
Work returns to the husbandmen, moving in a circle, as the year rolls itself round in its former track. (Redit agricolis labor actus in orbem, Atque in se sua per vestigia volvitur annus.)

VERGIL, *Georgics*. Bk. ii, l. 401.

O how happy beyond measure would be the husbandmen if they knew their own good fortune. (O fortunatos nimium, sua si bona norint, Agricolas!)

VERGIL, *Georgics*. Bk. ii, l. 458.

O happy life! if that their good
The husbandmen but understood!

ROBERT HERRICK, *Hesperides: The Country Life*. Adapting Vergil. See also APPENDIX.

16
He [the husbandman] equalled the riches of kings in the happiness of his mind; and returning home in the late evening, loaded his board with feasts unbought. (Regum æquabat opes animis; seraque revertens Nocte domum, dapibus mensas onerabat inemptis.)

VERGIL, *Georgics*. Bk. iv, l. 132.

He brings out dainties unbought. (Dapes inemptas adparet.)

HORACE, *Epodes*. No. ii, l. 48.

1
Heap high the farmer's wintry hoard!
  Heap high the golden corn!
No richer gift has Autumn poured
  From out her lavish horn!
  WHITTIER, *The Corn-Song.*

IV—Farming: Its Penalties

2
Husbandry is not governed by judgment and labor, but by the most uncertain of things, winds and tempests.
  CICERO, *In Verram.* No. iii, sec. 98.

The diligent farmer plants trees of which he himself will never see the fruit. (Arbores seret diligens agricola, quarum aspiciet bacam ipse numquam.)
  CICERO, *Tusculanarum Disputationum.* Bk. i, sec. 14.

3
How can he get wisdom that holdeth the plough, and that glorieth in the goad, that driveth oxen, and is occupied in their labours, and whose talk is of bullocks?
  Apocrypha: Ecclesiasticus, xxxviii, 25.

4
All taxes must, at last, fall upon agriculture.
  EDWARD GIBBON, *Decline and Fall of the Roman Empire.* Ch. 8.

5
A man's soul may be buried and perish under a dungheap or in a furrow of the field, just as well as under a pile of money.
  HAWTHORNE, *Journals,* 1 June, 1841.

6
They [the farmers] say it is too hard to give fifty bushels of corn (an acre of corn) for a pair of boots, simply to satisfy tariff monopolists. They are down on railroads and rings, and conspiracies, and monopolies, and treason against the general welfare.
  WILLIAM HERNDON. (*Illinois State Register,* 19 Feb., 1873.)

The farmer is endeavoring to solve the problem of a livelihood by a formula more complicated than the problem itself. To get his shoestrings he speculates in herds of cattle. With consummate skill he has set his trap with a hair springe to catch comfort and independence, and then, as he turned away, got his own leg into it. This is the reason he is poor.
  H. D. THOREAU, *Walden.* Ch. 1.

7
Slave of the wheel of labor, what to him
Are Plato and the swing of Pleiades?
  EDWIN MARKHAM, *The Man With the Hoe.*

Serving the wheels or guiding straight the plow
Leaves little thought of frankincense and nard.
  SCUDDER MIDDLETON, *Jezebel.*

8
No one hates his job so heartily as a farmer.
  H. L. MENCKEN, *What Is Going on in the World.* (*American Mercury,* Nov., 1933, p. 259.)

9
The pious farmer, who ne'er misses pray'rs,
  With patience suffers unexpected rain;
He blesses Heav'n for what its bounty spares,
  And sees, resign'd, a crop of blighted grain.
But, spite of sermons, farmers would blaspheme
If a star fell to set their thatch in flame.
  MARY WORTLEY MONTAGU, *The Farmer.*

10
Where grows?—where grows it not? If vain our toil,
We ought to blame the culture, not the soil.
  POPE, *Essay on Man.* Epis. iv, l. 13.

11
He that counts all costs will never put plough in the earth.
  JOHN RAY, *English Proverbs.*

12
The peasant loves nothing and nobody, except for the use he can make of him.
  JOSEPH ROUX, *Meditations of a Parish Priest: The Country, The Peasant.* No. 2.

The peasant is a sullen payer, like the soil he tills.
  JOSEPH ROUX, *Meditations of a Parish Priest: The Country, The Peasant.* No. 8.

The countryman is too much of a child not to be a liar.
  JOSEPH ROUX, *Meditations of a Parish Priest: The Country, The Peasant.* No. 22.

13
Farming is a most senseless pursuit, a mere laboring in a circle. You sow that you may reap, and then you reap that you may sow. Nothing ever comes of it.
  STOBÆUS, *Florilegium.* Pt. xxxviii, l. 30.

14
God did not will that the way of cultivation should be easy. (Pater ipse colendi Haud facilem esse viam colendi.)
  VERGIL, *Georgics.* Bk. i, l. 121.

E'en in mid-harvest, while the jocund swain
Plucked from the brittle stalk the golden grain,
Oft have I seen the war of winds contend,
And prone on earth th' infuriate storm descend,
Waste far and wide, and by the roots uptorn,
The heavy harvest sweep through ether borne,
As the light straw and rapid stubble fly
In darkening whirlwinds round the wintry sky.
  VERGIL, *Georgics.* Bk. i, l. 351. (Sotheby, tr.)

15
Blessed be agriculture! if one does not have too much of it.
  CHARLES DUDLEY WARNER, *My Summer in a Garden: Preliminary.*

FASHION

See also Dress

16
Nothing is thought rare
Which is not new, and follow'd; yet we know
That what was worn some twenty years ago
Comes into grace again.
  BEAUMONT AND FLETCHER, *The Noble Gentleman: Prologue,* l. 4.

17
He is only fantastical that is not in fashion.
  ROBERT BURTON, *Anatomy of Melancholy.* Pt. iii, sec. ii, mem. 2, subs. 3.

If you are not in fashion, you are nobody.
LORD CHESTERFIELD, *Letters*. 30 April, 1750.

1
Fashion is like God; man cannot see into its holy of holies and live.
SAMUEL BUTLER THE YOUNGER, *Note-Books*, p. 226.

2
So many lands, so many fashions.
GEORGE CHAPMAN, *Alphonsus*. Act iii, sc. 1. (1634) *See also under* OPINION.

3
Fashion—a word which knaves and fools may use,
Their knavery and folly to excuse.
CHARLES CHURCHILL, *The Rosciad*, l. 455.

4
As good be out of the World as out of the Fashion.
COLLEY CIBBER, *Love's Last Shift*. Act ii.

5
The fashion of this world passeth away.
New Testament: I Corinthians, vii, 31.

6
Fashion, leader of a chattering train,
Whom man, for his own hurt, permits to reign.
COWPER, *Conversation*, l. 457.

7
Fashion, though Folly's child, and guide of fools,
Rules e'en the wisest, and in learning rules.
GEORGE CRABBE, *The Library*, l. 165.

Fashions are for fools.
ROBERT DODSLEY, *Sir John Cockle at Court*. Act i, sc. 1.

8
Fine clothes wear soonest out of fashion.
THOMAS FULLER, *Gnomologia*.

It is in vain to mislike the current fashion.
THOMAS FULLER, *Gnomologia*.

The present fashion is always handsome.
THOMAS FULLER, *Gnomologia*.

Tailors and writers must mind the fashion.
THOMAS FULLER, *Gnomologia*.

9
And e'en while fashion's brightest arts decoy,
The heart distrusting asks if this be joy.
GOLDSMITH, *The Deserted Village*, l. 263.

10
Fashion is gentility running away from vulgarity, and afraid of being overtaken.
WILLIAM HAZLITT, *Conversations of James Northcote*, p. 264.

Fashion constantly begins and ends in the two things it abhors most—singularity and vulgarity.
WILLIAM HAZLITT, *Sketches and Essays: On Fashion*.

The Highly Fashionable and the Absolutely Vulgar are but two faces of the common coin of humanity.
H. G. WELLS, *Select Conversations with an Uncle*.

11
As far as Paris to fetch over a fashion and come back again.
BEN JONSON, *Every Man Out of His Humour*. Act ii, sc. 2.

And as the French we conquer'd once,
Now give us laws for pantaloons,
The length of breeches and the gathers,
Port-cannons, periwigs, and feathers.
BUTLER, *Hudibras*. Pt. i, canto iii, l. 923.

Report of fashions in proud Italy,
Whose manners still our tardy apish nation
Limps after in base imitation.
SHAKESPEARE, *Richard II*. Act ii, sc. 1, l. 21.

12
Fashion ever is a wayward child.
WILLIAM MASON, *The English Garden*. Bk. iv, l. 430.

13
All our talk about the great happiness that my Lady Wright says there is in being in fashion, and in variety of fashions, in scorn of others that are not so, as citizens' wives and country gentlewomen.
SAMUEL PEPYS, *Diary*, 3 Dec., 1661.

14
For fashion's sake, as dogs go to church.
JOHN RAY, *English Proverbs*.

15
The glass of fashion, and the mould of form,
The observed of all observers.
SHAKESPEARE, *Hamlet*. Act iii, sc. 1, l. 161.

He was indeed the glass
Wherein the noble youth did dress themselves.
SHAKESPEARE, *II Henry IV*. Act ii, sc. 3, l. 21.

He was the mark and glass, copy and book
That fashion'd others.
SHAKESPEARE, *II Henry IV*. Act ii, sc. 3, l. 31.

16
Their clothes are after such a pagan cut too,
That, sure, they've worn out Christendom.
SHAKESPEARE, *Henry VIII*. Act i, sc. 3, l. 14.

17
The fashion wears out more apparel than the man.
SHAKESPEARE, *Much Ado About Nothing*. Act iii, sc. 3, l. 148.

18
I'll be at charges for a looking-glass,
And entertain some score or two of tailors,
To study fashions to adorn my body:
Since I am crept in favour with myself,
I will maintain it with some little cost.
SHAKESPEARE, *Richard III*. Act i, sc. 2, l. 256.

19
Old fashions please me best.
SHAKESPEARE, *The Taming of the Shrew*. Act iii, sc. 1, l. 80.

This doth fit the time.
SHAKESPEARE, *The Taming of the Shrew*. Act iv, sc. 3, l. 69.

20
You cannot be both fashionable and first-rate.
LOGAN PEARSALL SMITH, *Afterthoughts*.

21
Fashion, the arbiter and rule of right.
STEELE, *The Spectator*. No. 478.

22
Every generation laughs at the old fashions, but follows religiously the new.
H. D. THOREAU, *Walden*. Ch. 1.

1
It is better to leave the Mode to its own vagaries.
WALPOLE, *Letter to Sir Horace Mann*, 7 Sept., 1781.

2
Disguise it as you will,
To right or wrong 'tis fashion guides us still.
JOSEPH WARTON, *Fashion*, l. 1.

3
Fashion is what one wears oneself. What is unfashionable is what other people wear.
OSCAR WILDE, *An Ideal Husband*. Act iii.

After all, what is a fashion? From the artistic point of view, it is usually a form of ugliness so intolerable that we have to alter it every six months.
OSCAR WILDE, *Suitable Dress for Women Workers*.

4
Fashion too often makes a monstrous noise,
Bids us, a fickle jade, like fools adore
The poorest trash, the meanest toys.
JOHN WOLCOT, *Lyric Odes to the Royal Academicians*. No. 11.

5
Give feminine fashions time enough and they will starve all the moths to death.
UNKNOWN. (*Detroit Free Press*, June, 1925.)

FASTING

See also Hunger

6
Whoso will pray, he must fast and be clean,
And fat his soul, and make his body lean.
CHAUCER, *The Somnours Tale*, l. 171.

7
He fasts enough who eats with reason.
A. J. CRONIN, *Grand Canary*, p. 183.

8
Noah the first was (as Tradition says)
That did ordain the fast of forty days.
ROBERT HERRICK, *The Fast, or Lent*.

9
Is this a fast, to keep
The larder leane? And clean
From fat of veals and sheep?
Is it to quit the dish
Of flesh, yet still to fill
The platter high with fish?
ROBERT HERRICK, *To Keep a True Lent*.

10
And join with thee calm Peace and Quiet,
Spare Fast, that oft with gods doth diet.
MILTON, *Il Penseroso*, l. 45.

11
'Tis but a three years' fast:
The mind shall banquet, though the body pine.
SHAKESPEARE, *Love's Labour's Lost*. Act i, sc. 1, l. 24.

And therein fasting, hast thou made me gaunt.
SHAKESPEARE, *Richard II*. Act ii, sc. 1, l. 81.

12
Surfeit is the father of much fast.
SHAKESPEARE, *Measure for Measure*. Act i, sc. 2, l. 130.

FATE

See also Destiny, Fortune, Providence

I—Fate: Apothegms

13
Fate laughs at probabilities.
BULWER-LYTTON, *Eugene Aram*. Bk. i, ch. 10.

14
Tempted Fate will leave the loftiest star.
BYRON, *Childe Harold*. Canto iii, st. 38.

15
To feel the step-dame buffetings of fate.
THOMAS CAMPBELL, *On the Grave of a Suicide*.

16
Fate leads the willing, drags the unwilling. (Ducunt volentem fata, nolentem trahunt.)
CLEANTHES, *Fragments*. Frag. 527. (SENECA, *Epistulæ ad Lucilium*. Epis. cvii, sec. 11.)

Fate leads the willing but drives the stubborn.
THOMAS FULLER, *Gnomologia*. No. 1508.

Fate leads him who follows it, and drags him who resists.
PLUTARCH, *Lives: Camillus*. Quoted by Montaigne, *Essays*. Bk. ii, ch. 38.

17
Whatever limits us, we call Fate. . . . The limitations refine as the soul purifies, but the ring of necessity is always perched at the top.
EMERSON, *Conduct of Life: Fate*.

'Tis weak and vicious people who cast the blame on Fate.
EMERSON, *Conduct of Life: Fate*.

18
Fate is nothing but the deeds committed in a prior state of existence.
EMERSON, *Conduct of Life: Fate*. Quoted as a Hindoo proverb.

Fate, then, is a name for facts not yet passed under the fire of thought. . . . Fate is unpenetrated causes.
EMERSON, *Conduct of Life: Fate*.

19
Stranger! may fate a milder aspect show,
And spin thy future with a whiter clue!
HOMER, *Odyssey*. Bk. xx, l. 249. (Pope, tr.)

20
For some must follow, and some command
Though all are made of clay!
LONGFELLOW, *Keramos*, l. 6.

21
Whither the fates lead, Virtue will fearlessly follow. (Sed quo fata trahunt, virtus secura sequetur.)
LUCAN, *De Bello Civili*. Bk. ii, l. 287.

Whither the Fates call. (Ubi fata vocant.)
OVID, *Heroides*. Epis. vii, l. 1.

The fates call. (Fata vocant.)
VERGIL, *Georgics*. Bk. iv, l. 49.

22
'Twas fated so. (Sic erat in fatis.)
OVID, *Fasti*. Bk. i, l. 481.

23
Swearing and supperless the hero sate,
Blasphemed his gods, the dice, and damn'd his fate.
POPE, *The Dunciad*. Bk. i, l. 115.

Each cursed his fate that thus their project crossed;
How hard their lot who neither won nor lost!
RICHARD GRAVES, *An Incident in High Life.*

1 No one is made guilty by fate. (Nemo fit fato nocens.)
SENECA, *Œdipus*, l. 1019.

2 O God! that one might read the book of fate!
SHAKESPEARE, *II Henry IV*. Act iii, sc. 1, l. 45.

3 To spread the sails to fate. (Dare fatis vela.)
VERGIL, *Æneid*. Bk. iii, l. 9.

4 Wherever the Fates, in their ebb and flow, lead, let us follow. (Quo fata trahunt retrahuntque sequamur.)
VERGIL, *Æneid*. Bk. v, l. 709.

The Fates will find a way. (Fata viam invenient.)
VERGIL, *Æneid*. Bk. x, l. 113.

5 Fate is the endless chain of causation, whereby things are; the reason or formula by which the world goes on.
ZENO. (DIOGENES LAERTIUS, *Zeno*. Bk. vii, 149.)

II—Fate: Its Power

6 Things are where things are, and, as fate has willed,
So shall they be fulfilled.
("Εστι δ' ὅπῃ νῦν
ἔστι· τελεῖται δ' ἐς τὸ πεπρωμένον.)
ÆSCHYLUS, *Agamemnon*, l. 67. (Browning, tr.)

As the old hermit of Prague, that never saw pen and ink, very wittily said to a niece of King Gorboduc, "That that is is."
SHAKESPEARE, *Twelfth Night*. Act iv, sc. 2, l. 14. The "hermit of Prague" was perhaps Jerome, the hermit of Camaldoli, but more probably an invention of Shakespeare.

7 The bow is bent, the arrow flies,
The wingèd shaft of fate.
IRA ALDRIDGE, *On William Tell*. St. 12.

Fate has carried me
'Mid the thick arrows: I will keep my stand—
Not shrink and let the shaft pass by my breast
To pierce another.
GEORGE ELIOT, *The Spanish Gypsy*. Bk. iii.

8 All things are produced by fate. (Καθ' εἱμαρμένην δέ φασι τὰ πάντα.)
CHRYSIPPUS, *De Fato*. (DIOGENES LAERTIUS, *Zeno*. Bk. vii, sec. 149.)

9 Fate steals along with silent tread,
Found oft'nest in what least we dread;
Frowns in the storm with angry brow,
But in the sunshine strikes the blow.
COWPER, *A Fable: Moral.*

10 'Tis fate that flings the dice, and as she flings
Of kings makes peasants, and of peasants kings.
DRYDEN, *Jupiter Cannot Alter the Decrees of Fate.*

Eternal Deities.
Who rule the World with absolute decrees,
And write whatever Time shall bring to pass
With pens of adamant on plates of brass.
DRYDEN, *Palamon and Arcite*. Bk. i, l. 470.

11 If we are related we shall meet.
EMERSON, *Essays, Second Series: Character.*

And two shall walk some narrow way of life, . . .
And yet, with wistful eyes that never meet, . . .
They seek each other all their weary days
And die unsatisfied—and this is Fate!
SUSAN MARR SPALDING, *Fate.*

12 See how the Fates their gifts allot,
For A is happy—B is not.
Yet B is worthy, I dare say,
Of more prosperity than A.
W. S. GILBERT, *The Mikado*. Act ii.

13 Fate holds the strings, and men like children move
But as they're led; success is from above.
GEORGE GRANVILLE, *Heroic Love*. Act v, sc. 2.

14 Let bounteous Fate your spindles full
Fill, and wind up with whitest wool.
ROBERT HERRICK, *An Epithalamie.*

And turn the adamantine spindle round,
On which the fate of gods and men is wound.
MILTON, *Arcades*, l. 66.

15 Jove lifts the golden balances, that show
The fates of mortal men, and things below.
HOMER, *Iliad*. Bk. xxii, l. 271. (Pope, tr.)

16 The thousand strands of the web of fate are so wildly, so strangely entangled . . . that if a man searches into it, he sees right and the bloodiest wrong become as one.
HENRIK IBSEN, *Brand*. Act iv.

The outward wayward life we see,
The hidden springs we may not know. . . .
It is not ours to separate
The tangled skein of will and fate.
J. G. WHITTIER, *Snow-Bound*, l. 565.

17 Three were the fates—gaunt Poverty that chains,
Gray Drudgery that grinds the hope away,
And gaping Ignorance that starves the soul.
EDWIN MARKHAM, *Young Lincoln.*

Swift-limbed they move with even pace,
Together, these immortal three;
These three, that never quit the chase
Wherever souls of mortals be.
ROBERT BURNS WILSON, *The Immortal Three.* [Death, Memory, Remorse.]

18 It lies not in our power to love or hate,
For will in us is over-ruled by fate.
MARLOWE, *Hero and Leander*. Sestiad 1. (1598)

Oh no! 'tis only Destiny or Fate
Fashions our wills to either love or hate.
RICHARD LOVELACE, *Dialogue on a Lost Heart.* (1649)

1
Fate is the gunman that all gunmen dread;
Fate stings the Stinger for his roll of green;
Fate, Strong-arm Worker, on the bean
Of strong-arm workers bumps his pipe of lead.
DON MARQUIS, *Proverbs.*

2
From no place can you exclude the fates. (Nullo fata loco possis excludere)
MARTIAL, *Epigrams.* Bk. iv, ep. 60, l. 5.

Yet who shall shut out Fate?
EDWIN ARNOLD, *Light of Asia.* Bk. iii, l. 336.

3
All the great things of life are swiftly done,
Creation, death, and love the double gate.
However much we dawdle in the sun
We have to hurry at the touch of Fate.
JOHN MASEFIELD, *The Widow in the Bye Street.* Pt. ii.

4
The fates are not quite obdurate.
They have a grim, sardonic way
Of granting men who supplicate
The things they wanted—yesterday!
ROSELLE MERCIER MONTGOMERY, *The Fates.*

5
Fate sits on these dark battlements, and frowns;
And as the portals open to receive me,
Her voice, in sullen echoes, through the courts,
Tells of a nameless deed.
ANN RADCLIFFE, *The Mysteries of Udolpho: Motto.*

6
Many have come upon their fate while shunning fate. (Multi ad fatum Venere suum dum fata timent.)
SENECA, *Œdipus,* l. 993.

And every man in love or pride,
Of his fate is never wide.
EMERSON, *Nemesis.*

7
Our wills and fates do so contrary run
That our devices still are overthrown;
Our thoughts are ours, their ends none of our own.
SHAKESPEARE, *Hamlet.* Act iii, sc. 2, l. 221.

We direct our affairs at the beginning, . . . but being once undertaken, they guide and transport us, and we must follow them.
MONTAIGNE, *Essays.* Bk. iii, ch. 10.

8
What fates impose, that men must needs abide;
It boots not to resist both wind and tide.
SHAKESPEARE, *III Henry VI.* Act iv, sc. 3, l. 58.

Fate, show thy force: ourselves we do not owe;
What is decreed must be, and be this so.
SHAKESPEARE, *Twelfth Night.* Act i, sc. 5, l. 329.

9
By eternal doom of Fate's decree.
SPENSER, *Faerie Queene.* Bk. vii, canto 6, st. 33.

10
Following the fate assigned to him. (Data fata secutus.)
VERGIL, *Æneid.* Bk. i, l. 382.

11
The Fates say us nay. (Fata obstant.)
VERGIL, *Æneid.* Bk. iv, l. 440.

But wisest Fate says No,
This must not yet be so.
MILTON, *Hymn on the Morning of Christ's Nativity,* l. 149.

12
Man blindly works the will of fate. (Blindlings that er blos den Willen des Geschickes.)
WIELAND, *Oberon.* Pt. iv, l. 59.

The compulsion of fate is bitter. (Des Schiksals Zwang ist bitter.)
WIELAND, *Oberon.* Pt. v, l. 60.

III—Fate: Its Mastery

13
Yet they, believe me, who await
No gifts from Chance, have conquer'd Fate.
MATTHEW ARNOLD, *Resignation,* l. 245.

14
The heart is its own Fate.
P. J. BAILEY, *Festus: Wood and Water: Sunset.*

15
Let those deplore their doom,
Whose hope still grovels in this dark sojourn:
But lofty souls, who look beyond the tomb,
Can smile at Fate, and wonder how they mourn.
JAMES BEATTIE, *The Minstrel.* Bk. i, l. 226.

16
Here's a sigh to those who love me,
And a smile to those who hate;
And, whatever sky's above me,
Here's a heart for every fate.
BYRON, *To Thomas Moore.* St. 2.

Let us, then, be up and doing,
With a heart for any fate.
LONGFELLOW, *A Psalm of Life.*

17
To bear is to conquer our fate.
THOMAS CAMPBELL, *Lines Written on Visiting a Scene in Argyleshire,* l. 36.

18
'Tis writ on Paradise's gate,
"Woe to the dupe that yields to Fate!"
HAFIZ. (EMERSON, *Letters and Social Aims: Persian Poetry.*)

19
Arise, O Soul, and gird thee up anew,
Though the black camel Death kneel at thy gate;
No beggar thou that thou for alms shouldst sue:
Be the proud captain still of thine own fate.
JAMES B. KENYON, *The Black Camel.*

20
Lord, make my childish soul stand straight
To meet the kindly stranger, Fate;
Shake hands with elder brother, Doom,
Nor bawl, nor scurry from the room.
WILLIAM LAIRD, *A Prayer.*

1
All are architects of Fate,
  Working in these walls of Time;
Some with massive deeds and great,
  Some with ornaments of rhyme.
  LONGFELLOW, *The Builders*. St. 1.

2
Necessity and Chance
Approach not me, and what I will is Fate.
  MILTON, *Paradise Lost*. Bk. vii, l. 172.

3
The glory and the glow
Of the world's loveliness have passed away;
And Fate hath little to inflict today,
And nothing to bestow.
  W. M. PRAED, *Stanzas*.

4
My fate cries out,
And makes each petty artery in this body
As hardy as the Nemean lion's nerve.
  SHAKESPEARE, *Hamlet*. Act i, sc. 4, l. 81.

5
Men at some time are masters of their fates.
  SHAKESPEARE, *Julius Cæsar*. Act i, sc. 2, l. 139.

I am the mistress of my fate.
  SHAKESPEARE, *The Rape of Lucrece*, l. 1069.

We are, when we will it, masters of our own fate. (On est, quand on veut, maître de son sort.)
  FERRIER, *Adraste*.

It matters not how strait the gate,
  How charged with punishments the scroll,
I am the master of my fate:
  I am the captain of my soul.
  W. E. HENLEY, *Invictus*.

For man is man and master of his fate.
  TENNYSON, *The Marriage of Geraint*, l. 355.

6
But, O vain boast! Who can control his fate?
  SHAKESPEARE, *Othello*. Act v, sc. 2, l. 264.

FATHER

I—Father: Apothegms

7
The noblest works and foundations have proceeded from childless men.
  BACON, *Essays: Of Parents and Children*.

8
He that has his father for judge goes safe to the trial.
  CERVANTES, *Don Quixote*. Pt. ii, ch. 43.

For a great sin a slight punishment contents a father. (Pro peccato magno paulum supplici satis est patri.)
  TERENCE, *Andria*, l. 903. (Act v, sc. 3.)

9
He that honoureth his father shall have a long life.
  Apocrypha: Ecclesiasticus, iii, 6.

10
No love to a father's.
  GEORGE HERBERT, *Jacula Prudentum*.

One father is more than a hundred schoolmasters.
  GEORGE HERBERT, *Jacula Prudentum*.

11
Like to a father's was his gentle sway. (Πατὴρ δ' ὣς ἤπιος ἦεν.)
  HOMER, *Odyssey*. Bk. ii, l. 47.

12
Father of a family. (Pater familiæ.)
  PLINY THE YOUNGER, *Epistles*. Bk. v, epis. 19.

13
O heavens, this is my true-begotten father!
  SHAKESPEARE, *The Merchant of Venice*. Act ii, sc. 2, l. 37.

14
Who would be a father?
  SHAKESPEARE, *Othello*. Act i, sc. 1, l. 165.

15
No man is responsible for his father. That is entirely his mother's affair.
  MARGARET TURNBULL, *Alabaster Lamps*, p. 300

16
Father!—to God himself we cannot give
A holier name.
  WORDSWORTH, *The Borderers*. Act i. Also *Ecclesiastical Sonnets*. Pt. iii, No. 21.

II—Fathers and Sons

See also Son

17
'Tis said that Donna Julia's grandmamma
Produced her Don more heirs at love than law.
  BYRON, *Don Juan*. Canto i, st. 58.

18
Yet in my lineaments they trace
Some features of my father's face.
  BYRON, *Parisina*. St. 13, l. 63.

Some time before his death, he had stamped his likeness upon a little boy.
  DICKENS, *Pickwick Papers*. Ch. 34.

Ask the mother if the child be like his father.
  THOMAS FULLER, *Gnomologia*. No. 818.

19
I'll meet the raging of the skies,
But not an angry father.
  THOMAS CAMPBELL, *Lord Ullin's Daughter*.

20
As fathers commonly go, it is seldom a misfortune to be fatherless; and considering the general run of sons, as seldom a misfortune to be childless.
  LORD CHESTERFIELD, *Letters*, 15 July, 1751.

Few fathers care much for their sons, or at least, most of them care more for their money.
  LORD CHESTERFIELD, *Letters*, 27 May, 1752.

21
A little child, a limber elf,
Singing, dancing to itself, . . .
Makes such a vision to the sight
As fills a father's eyes with light.
  S. T. COLERIDGE, *Christabel*. Pt. ii, l. 656.

22
One father is enough to govern one hundred sons, but not a hundred sons one father.
  GEORGE HERBERT, *Jacula Prudentum*.

23
Never did any man know his own parentage. (Οὐ γάρ πώ τις ἑὸν γόνον αὐτὸς ἀνέγνω.)
  HOMER, *Odyssey*. Bk. i, l. 216.

No one knows his own father, but all of us have a conjecture or a belief. (Αὐτὸν γὰρ οὐδεὶς οἶδ' ὅτου ποτ' ἐγένετο, ἀλλ' ὑπονοοῦμεν πάντες ἢ πιστεύομεν.)

MENANDER, *The Carthaginian*. Frag. 261.

It is a wise father that knows his own child.

SHAKESPEARE, *The Merchant of Venice*. Act ii, sc. 2, l. 80.

1
The night my father got me
His mind was not on me;
He did not plague his fancy
To muse if I should be
The son you see.

A. E. HOUSMAN, *Last Poems*. No. xiv.

I wish either my father or my mother, or indeed both of them, as they were in duty both equally bound to it, had minded what they were about when they begot me.

STERNE, *Tristram Shandy*. Bk. i, ch. 1.

2
The regal and parental tyrant differ only in the extent of their dominions, and the number of their slaves.

SAMUEL JOHNSON, *The Rambler*. No. 148.

3
The father to the bough, the son to the plough.

WILLIAM LAMBARDE, *Perambulation of Kent*, 497. (1576)

4
Like father, like son: every good tree maketh good fruits.

WILLIAM LANGLAND, *Piers Plowman*. Pt. iii.

Thou art thy father's own son.

WALKER, *Parœmologia*, 30. (1672)

He that loves the tree loves the branch.

GEORGE HERBERT, *Jacula Prudentum*.

5
Dear Child, 'tis your poor lot to be
My little Son;
I'm glad, though I am old, you see,—
While you are One.

F. LOCKER-LAMPSON, *A Rhyme of One*.

6
It behooves a father to be blameless, if he expects his son to be more blameless than he was himself. (Probum patrem esse oportet qui gnatum suom Esse probiorem quam ipsus fuerit postulet.)

PLAUTUS, *Pseudolus*, l. 438. (Act i, sc. 5.)

7
And still tomorrow's wiser than today.
We think our fathers fools, so wise we grow;
Our wiser sons, no doubt, will think us so.

POPE, *Essay on Criticism*. Pt. ii, l. 237.

We admire our fathers quite too much. It shows that we have no energy in ourselves, when we rate it so prodigiously high. Rather let us shame the fathers by superior virtue in the sons.

EMERSON, *Journal*, 1861.

The commonest axiom of history is that every generation revolts against its fathers and makes friends with its grandfathers.

LEWIS MUMFORD, *The Brown Decades*.

While we criticise the fathers for being narrow, we should not forget that they were also deep. We are inclined to be so broad that people can see through us most any place.

WILLIAM HIRAM FOULKES, *Sermon*.

8
A wise son maketh a glad father.

Old Testament: Proverbs, x, 1.

9
Raw dads make fat lads.

JOHN RAY, *English Proverbs*.

10
The fundamental defect of fathers is that they want their children to be a credit to them.

BERTRAND RUSSELL, *Sceptical Essays*, p. 194.

11
It is not flesh and blood but the heart which makes us fathers and sons. (Nicht Fleisch und Blut; das Herz macht uns zu Vätern und Söhnen.)

SCHILLER, *Die Räuber*. Act i, sc. 1.

12
We are all bastards;
And that most venerable man which I
Did call my father, was I know not where
When I was stamp'd; some coiner with his tools
Made me a counterfeit.

SHAKESPEARE, *Cymbeline*. Act ii, sc. 5, l. 2.

13
Fathers that wear rags
Do make their children blind;
But fathers that bear bags
Shall see their children kind.

SHAKESPEARE, *King Lear*. Act ii, sc. 4, l. 48.

14
To you your father should be as a god;
One that composed your beauties, yea, and one
To whom you are but as a form in wax
By him imprinted and within his power
To leave the figure or disfigure it.

SHAKESPEARE, *A Midsummer-Night's Dream*. Act i, sc. 1, l. 47.

15
Behold, my lords,
Although the print be little, the whole matter
And copy of the father, eye, nose, lip,
The trick of's frown, his forehead, nay, the valley,
The pretty dimples of his chin and cheek, his smiles;
The very mould and frame of hand, nail, finger.

SHAKESPEARE, *Winter's Tale*. Act ii, sc. 3, l. 97.

16
'Tis happy for him that his father was born before him.

SWIFT, *Polite Conversation*. Dial. iii.

17
A dead father's counsel, a wise son heedeth.

TEGNER, *Fridthjof's Saga*. Canto viii.

18
He who has been in the habit of lying to or deceiving his father, or who will dare to do

so, will be all the more daring in attempting the same with others. (Qui mentiri aut fallere insuerit patrem, aut Audebit, tanto magis audebit ceteros.)

TERENCE, *Adelphi,* l. 55. (Act i, sc. 1.)

This is the duty of a father, to accustom his son to act rightly rather of his own accord than from unnatural fear. (Hoc patrium est, potius consuefacere filium Sua sponte recte facere, quam alieno metu.)

TERENCE, *Adelphi,* l. 74. (Act i, sc. 1.)

Whom should he bear with if not with his own father? (Quem ferret, si parentem non ferret suom?)

TERENCE, *Heauton Timorumenos,* l. 202.

1
What harsh judges fathers are to all young men! (Quam iniqui sunt patres in omnis adulescentis judices!)

TERENCE, *Heauton Timorumenos,* l. 213.

What unjust judges fathers are, when in regard to us they hold
That even in our boyish days we ought in conduct to be old,
Nor taste at all the very things that youth and only youth requires;
They rule us by their present wants, not by their past long-lost desires.

TERENCE, *Heauton Timorumenos,* l. 213. (F. W. Ricord, tr.)

2
O dearest, dearest boy! my heart
For better lore would seldom yearn,
Could I but teach the hundredth part
Of what from thee I learn.

WORDSWORTH, *Anecdote for Fathers.*

In deep and awful channel runs
This sympathy of Sire and Sons.

WORDSWORTH, *The White Doe of Rylstone.* Canto ii, l. 469.

3
The booby father craves a booby son,
And by heaven's blessing thinks himself undone.

YOUNG, *Love of Fame.* Sat. ii, l. 165.

III—Father of His Country

4
Free Rome hailed Cicero as the parent, as the father of his country. (Roma parentem, Roma patrem patriæ Ciceronem libera dixit.)

JUVENAL, *Satires.* Sat. viii, l. 243. This title was bestowed upon Cicero for his services in unmasking the conspiracy of Catiline, 64 B.C. The title, "Pater Patriæ," was also offered to Marius, who refused it. Julius and Augustus were also so called. So was Cosimo de' Medici. The title was conferred upon Peter the Great by the Russian Senate in 1721. (*Post-Boy,* 28 Dec., 1721.) Frequently applied to George Washington. (q.v.)

5
There are many different voices and languages; but there is but one voice of the peoples when you are declared to be the true "Father of your country." (Vox diversa sonat: populorum est vox tamen una, Cum verus *Patriæ* diceris esse *Pater.*)

MARTIAL, *De Spectaculis,* iii, 11.

6
Parent of his country. (Parens patriæ.)

PLINY THE ELDER, *History.* Bk. vii. Referring to Cicero.

7
To safeguard the citizens is the greatest (virtue) of a father of his country. (Servare cives major est [virtus] patriæ patri.)

SENECA, *Octavia,* l. 444.

8
He pleased the ladies round him,—with manners soft and bland;
With reason good, they named him,—the father of his land.

W. M. THACKERAY, *The King of Brentford.* (After Béranger.)

FATNESS

9
Nobody loves a fat man.

EDMUND DAY, *The Round-Up.* Made famous by Macklyn Arbuckle, as Sheriff "Slim" Hoover.

10
As fat as hens i' th' forehead.

BEAUMONT AND FLETCHER, *Bonduca.* Act i, sc. 2.

Fat! ay, fat as a hen in the forehead.

SWIFT, *Polite Conversation.* Dial. iii.

As fat as a fool.

JOHN LYLY, *Euphues,* p. 118. (1579)

He shall be fat as a pork hog.

SIR THOMAS MALORY, *Morte d'Arthur.* Bk. vii, ch. 1. (1485)

As fat as a pig. (Gras comme un cochon.)

JOHN COTGRAVE, *Wit's Interpreter.* (1611)

He will grow not only to be very large, but as fat as a hog.

IZAAK WALTON, *Compleat Angler.* Pt. i, ch. 10.

As fat as butter.

SHAKESPEARE, *I Henry IV,* ii, 4, 560. (1597)

I shall grow as fat as a porpoise.

SWIFT, *Polite Conversation.* Dial. ii.

11
Gross feeders, great sleepers;
Great sleepers, fat bodies;
Fat bodies, lean brains!

BEAUMONT AND FLETCHER, *Love's Cure.* Bk. ii, sc. 1.

Great eaters and great sleepers are incapable of anything else that is great. (Les grands mangeurs et les grands dormeurs sont incapables de rien faire de grand.)

HENRY IV of France, *Epigram.*

Fat paunches have lean pates, and dainty bits
Make rich the ribs, but bankrupt quite the wits.

SHAKESPEARE, *Love's Labour's Lost.* Act i, sc. 1, l. 26.

A fat belly does not produce a fine sense. (Pinguis ventor non gignit sensum tenuem.)

ST. JEROME, *De Viris Illustribus.*

Fat heads, lean brains. (Capo grasso, cervello magro.)

UNKNOWN. An Italian proverb.

1
I am not much in fear of these fat, sleek fellows, but rather of those pale, thin ones.

JULIUS CÆSAR, referring to Anthony and Dolabella as the fat ones, and Brutus and Cassius as the thin ones. (PLUTARCH, *Lives: Cæsar*. Ch. 62, sec. 5.)

Let me have men about me that are fat;
Sleek-headed men and such as sleep o' nights:
Yond Cassius hath a lean and hungry look;
He thinks too much: such men are dangerous. . . .
Would he were fatter! But I fear him not:
Yet if my name were liable to fear,
I do not know the man I should avoid
So soon as that spare Cassius.

SHAKESPEARE, *Julius Cæsar*. Act i, sc. 2, l. 192.

2
All the gruel is in the fire.

CHAUCER, *Troilus and Criseyde*. Bk. iii, st. 95. (c. 1374)

Or else . . . All your fat lie in the fire.

THOMAS BECON, *Prayers*, 277. (1559)

All the fat's in the fire.

JOHN MARSTON, *What You Will*. (1607)

The fat is in the fire.

BEN JONSON, *Love's Welcome*. (1633) In frequent use thereafter.

3
Jeshurun waxed fat, and kicked.

Old Testament: Deuteronomy, xxxii, 15.

4
A man must take the fat with the lean: that's what he must make up his mind to, in this life.

DICKENS, *David Copperfield*. Ch. 51.

5
I am resolved to grow fat and look young till forty, and then slip out of the world with the first wrinkle and the reputation of five-and-twenty.

DRYDEN, *The Maiden Queen*. Act iii, sc. 1.

Fat, fair, and forty was all the toast of the young men.

JOHN O'KEEFFE, *Irish Minnie*. Act ii, sc. 3.

Fat, fair, and forty.

SCOTT, *St. Ronan's Well*. Ch. 7. The Prince Regent's description of what a wife should be.

6
Fat old women, fat and five-and-fifty.

JOHN FLETCHER, *Women Pleased*. Act ii, sc. 1.

A fat, fair, and fifty card-playing resident of the Crescent.

MRS. MELISINA TRENCH, *Letter*, 18 Feb., 1816.

7
I see no objection to stoutness—in moderation.

W. S. GILBERT, *Iolanthe*. Act i.

8
The fat man knoweth not what the lean man thinketh.

GEORGE HERBERT, *Jacula Prudentum*. (1640)

9
You may see me fat and shining, . . . a hog from Epicurus' herd. (Me pinguem et nitidum . . . Epicuri de grege porcum.)

HORACE, *Epistles*. Bk. i, epis. 4, l. 15.

The fattest hog in Epicurus' sty.

WILLIAM MASON, *Heroic Epistle*.

10
Who drives fat oxen should himself be fat.

SAMUEL JOHNSON. (BOSWELL, *Life*, 1784.) A parody of Henry Brooke's line, "Who rules o'er freemen should himself be free," from *The Earl of Essex*.

11
A light heart in a fat body ravishes not only the world, but the philosopher.

GEORGE MEREDITH, *Sandra Belloni*. Ch. 19.

12
What she wants in up and down she hath in round about.

JOHN RAY, *English Proverbs*, 346.

13
No gentleman ever weighs more than two hundred pounds.

THOMAS B. REED, when his statement of his own weight as 199 pounds was questioned. (ROBINSON, *Life*.)

14
Sweep on, you fat and greasy citizens!

SHAKESPEARE, *As You Like It*. Act ii, sc. 1, l. 55.

15
He's fat, and scant of breath.

SHAKESPEARE, *Hamlet*. Act v, sc. 2, l. 298.

Falstaff sweats to death,
And lards the lean earth as he walks along.

SHAKESPEARE, *I Henry IV*. Act ii, sc. 2, l. 115.

16
There live not three good men unhanged in England; and one of them is fat and grows old.

SHAKESPEARE, *I Henry IV*. Act ii, sc. 4, l. 144.

Thou seest I have more flesh than another man, and therefore more frailty.

SHAKESPEARE, *I Henry IV*. Act iii, sc. 3, l. 188.

I think the devil will not have me damned, lest the oil that's in me should set hell on fire.

SHAKESPEARE, *The Merry Wives of Windsor*. Act v, sc. 5, l. 38.

17
Laugh and Be Fat.

JOHN TAYLOR. Title of tract. (1615)

Laugh, and be fat, sir, your penance is known.

BEN JONSON, *Entertainments: The Penates*.

Fat and merry, lean and sad.

THOMAS WRIGHT, *Passions of the Mind*. (1604)

FAULTS

I—Faults: Apothegms

18
Faults for which we are responsible are blamable, while those for which we are not responsible are not.

ARISTOTLE, *Nicomachean Ethics*. Bk. iii, ch. 5, sec. 16.

19
The sad rhyme of men who proudly clung
To their first fault, and withered in their pride.

ROBERT BROWNING, *Paracelsus*. Pt. iv.

20
He had twa fauts, or maybe three.

BURNS, *Tam Samson's Elegy*. St. 15.

1
Faults in the life breed errors in the brain.
COWPER, *The Progress of Error*, l. 564.

2
I like her with all her faults; nay, like her for her faults.
CONGREVE, *The Way of the World*. Act i, sc. 3.

With all thy faults, I love thee still!
COWPER, *The Task*. Bk. ii, l. 206.

With all her faults I love her still.
MONROE H. ROSENFELD. Title and refrain of song. (1888)

See also under ENGLAND: FAMILIAR PHRASES.

3
Happy the man when he has not the defects of his qualities. (Heureux l'homme quand il n'a pas les défauts de ses qualités.)
BISHOP FÉLIX ANTOINE DUPANLOUP, *Sermons*.

4
A benevolent man should allow a few faults in himself, to keep his friends in countenance.
BENJAMIN FRANKLIN, *Autobiography*. Ch. 1.

5
The first faults are theirs that commit them;
The second theirs that permit them.
THOMAS FULLER, *Gnomologia*. No. 4528.

6
A fault is sooner found than mended.
ULPIAN FULWELL, *Ars Adulandi*. (1580)

7
A fault once excused is twice committed.
GABRIEL HARVEY, *Marginalia*, 100. (1590)

A fault once denied is twice committed.
THOMAS FULLER, *Gnomologia*. No. 93. (1732)

8
A fault confessed is half redressed.
H. G. BOHN, *Hand-Book of Proverbs*, p. 285.

A fault confessed
Is a new virtue added to a man.
J. S. KNOWLES, *The Love-Chase*. Act i, sc. 2.

9
In a leopard, the spots are not observed.
GEORGE HERBERT, *Jacula Prudentum*.

10
Faults done by night will blush by day.
ROBERT HERRICK, *The Vision to Electra*.

11
Faults are thick where love is thin.
JAMES HOWELL, *Proverbs:* Brit.-Eng., p. 2.

Where love fails we espy all faults.
JOHN RAY, *English Proverbs*.

12
To maintain a fault known is a double fault.
JOHN JEWEL, *A Defence of the Apology for the Church of England*.

And he that does one fault at first
And lies to hide it, makes it two.
ISAAC WATTS, *Divine Songs*. No. 15.

13
Men do not suspect faults which they do not commit.
SAMUEL JOHNSON. (BOSWELL, *Life*, 1755.)

14
Bad men excuse their faults, good men will leave them.
BEN JONSON, *Catiline*. Act iii, sc. 2.

15
Only great men may have great faults. (Il n'appartient qu'aux grands hommes d'avoir de grands défauts.)
LA ROCHEFOUCAULD, *Maximes*. No. 190.

The fault is as great as he that is faulty.
GEORGE HERBERT, *Jacula Prudentum*.

See also GREATNESS: GREAT AND SMALL.

16
Dishonest people are those who disguise their faults to others and to themselves; the truly honest are those who know their faults perfectly, and who confess them. (Les faux honnêtes gens sont ceux qui déguisent leurs défauts aux autres et à eux-mêmes; les vrais honnêtes gens sont ceux qui les connaissent parfaitement, et les confessent.)
LA ROCHEFOUCAULD, *Maximes*. No. 202.

We never confess our faults except through vanity. (Nous n'avouons jamais nos défauts que par vanité.)
LA ROCHEFOUCAULD, *Maximes Supprimées*. No. 609.

17
When you know the faults of a man you want to please, you must be very clumsy if you do not succeed. (Quand on connoît le défaut d'un homme à qui l'on veut plaire, il faut être bien maladroit pour n'y pas réussir.)
LE SAGE, *Gil Blas*. Bk. viii, ch. 2.

18
One must survey his faults and study them, ere he be able to repeat them.
MONTAIGNE, *Essays*. Bk. iii, ch. 5.

19
Mistakes remember'd are not faults forgot.
R. H. NEWELL, *The Orpheus C. Kerr Papers: Columbia's Agony*. St. 9.

20
Let a fault be concealed by its nearness to a virtue. (Lateat vitiam proximitate boni.)
OVID, *Ars Amatoria*. Bk. ii, l. 662.

21
Pardon the fault. (Da veniam culpæ.)
OVID, *Heroides*. Epis. vii, l. 105.

The fault is not of the man but of the place. (Non hominis culpa, sed ista loci.)
OVID, *Tristia*. Bk. v, eleg. vii, l. 60.

22
He who overlooks a fault, invites the commission of another. (Invitat culpam qui delictum præterit.)
PUBLILIUS SYRUS, *Sententiæ*. No. 269.

23
I do not write to excuse my faults, but to prevent my readers from imitating them. (Je n'écris pas pour excuser mes fautes, mais pour empêcher mes lecteurs de leur imiter.)
ROUSSEAU, *Émile*. Bk. iii, footnote.

And oftentimes excusing of a fault
Doth make the fault the worse by the excuse,
As patches set upon a little breach,
Discredit more in hiding of the fault
Than did the fault before it was so patch'd.
SHAKESPEARE, *King John*. Act iv, sc. 2, l. 30.

1
If you would be stripped of your faults, leave far behind you the pattern of the faults. (Si velis vitiis exui, longe a vitiorum exemplis recedendum est.)
SENECA, *Epistulæ ad Lucilium*. Epis. civ, sec. 21.

Every one fault seeming monstrous till his fellow-fault came to match it.
SHAKESPEARE, *As You Like It*. Act iii, sc. 2, l. 372.

2
'T is a fault to Heaven,
A fault against the dead, a fault to nature,
To reason most absurd.
SHAKESPEARE, *Hamlet*. Act i, sc. 2, l. 101.

3
Chide him for faults, and do it reverently,
When you perceive his blood inclined to mirth.
SHAKESPEARE, *II Henry IV*. Act iv, sc. 4, l. 37.

His faults lie open to the laws; let them,
Not you, correct him.
SHAKESPEARE, *Henry VIII*. Act iii, sc. 2, l. 334.

So may he rest, his faults lie gently on him!
SHAKESPEARE, *Henry VIII*. Act iv, sc. 2, l. 31.

The image of a wicked heinous fault
Lives in his eye.
SHAKESPEARE, *King John*. Act iv, sc. 2, l. 71.

4
The fault, dear Brutus, is not in our stars,
But in ourselves, that we are underlings.
SHAKESPEARE, *Julius Cæsar*. Act i, sc. 2, l. 140.

5
Condemn the fault, and not the actor of it?
Why, every fault's condemn'd ere it be done;
Mine were the very cipher of a function,
To fine the faults whose fine stands in record,
And let go by the actor.
SHAKESPEARE, *Measure for Measure*. Act ii, sc. 2, l. 37.

That we were all, as some would seem to be,
From our faults, as faults from seeming, free.
SHAKESPEARE, *Measure for Measure*. Act iii, sc. 2, l. 40.

6
O, what a world of vile ill-favour'd faults
Looks handsome in three hundred pounds a year!
SHAKESPEARE, *The Merry Wives of Windsor*. Act iii, sc. 4, l. 32.

Faults that are rich are fair.
SHAKESPEARE, *Timon of Athens*. Act i, sc. 2, l. 13.

7
It hath pleased the devil drunkenness to give place to the devil wrath: one unperfectness shows me another, to make me frankly despise myself.
SHAKESPEARE, *Othello*. Act ii, sc. 3, l. 297.

8
The fault unknown is as a thought unacted.
SHAKESPEARE, *The Rape of Lucrece*, l. 527.

9
We cite our faults,
That they may hold excus'd our lawless lives.
SHAKESPEARE, *The Two Gentlemen of Verona*. Act iv, sc. 1, l. 53.

We do not confess little faults except to insinuate that we have no great ones. (Nous n'avouons de petits défauts que pour persuader que nous n'en avons pas de grands.)
LA ROCHEFOUCAULD, *Maximes*. No. 327.

II—Faults: Every Man Has His Faults

10
No one is born without faults; he is best who is beset by fewest. (Vitiis nemo sine nascitur; optimus ille est, Qui minimis urgetur.)
HORACE, *Satires*. Bk. i, sat. 3, l. 68.

In vain you avoid one fault if you, in your depravity, turn aside after another. (Frustra vitium vitaveris illud, Si te alio pravum detorseris.)
HORACE, *Satires*. Bk. ii, sat. 2, l. 54.

Then farewell, Horace; whom I hated so,
Not for thy faults, but mine.
BYRON, *Childe Harold*. Canto iv, st. 77.

11
If we had no faults, we should not take so much pleasure in remarking them in others. (Si nous n'avions point de défauts, nous ne prendrions pas tant de plaisir à en remarquer dans les autres.)
LA ROCHEFOUCAULD, *Maximes*. No. 31.

Those, who twit others with their faults, should look at home. (Quia, qui alterum incusat probi, eum, ipsum se intueri oportet.)
PLAUTUS, *Truculentus*. Act i, sc. 2, l. 58.

See also EYE: MOTE AND BEAM.

12
A man must have his faults. (Sed sibi quisque peccat.)
PETRONIUS, *Satyricon*. Sec. 45.

13
All men make faults.
SHAKESPEARE, *Sonnets*. No. xxxv.

14
The faults and follies of most men make their deaths a gain;
But thou also art a man, full of faults and follies.
MARTIN F. TUPPER, *Proverbial Philosophy: Of Tolerance*.

III—Faults: Their Virtues

See also Vice and Virtue: The Two Natures; Virtues: Their Faults

15
Every man in his lifetime needs to thank his faults. . . . Has he a defect of temper that unfits him to live in society? Thereby he is driven to entertain himself alone and acquire habits of self-help; and thus, like the wounded oyster, he mends his shell with pearl.
EMERSON, *Essays, First Series: Compensation*.

16
E'en his failings lean'd to Virtue's side.
GOLDSMITH, *The Deserted Village*, l. 164.

All his faults are such that one loves him still the better for them.
GOLDSMITH, *The Good-Natured Man*. Act i.

There are some faults so nearly allied to excellence

that we can scarce weed out the vice without eradicating the virtue.
GOLDSMITH, *The Good-Natured Man*. Act i.

AMIABLE WEAKNESS, *see under* WEAKNESS.

1
Who mix'd reason with pleasure and wisdom
with mirth;
If he had any faults he has left us in doubt.
GOLDSMITH, *Retaliation*, l. 24.

2
His very faults smack of the raciness of his good qualities.
WASHINGTON IRVING, *Sketch Book: John Bull*. Of the Englishman.

3
Most of his faults brought their excuse with them.
SAMUEL JOHNSON, *Lives of the Poets*. Referring to Matthew Prior.

4
He abounds in sweet faults.
QUINTILIAN, *Institutes of Oratory*.

5
You, gods, will give us
Some faults to make us men.
SHAKESPEARE, *Antony and Cleopatra*. Act v, sc. 1, l. 32.

They say, best men are moulded out of faults;
And, for the most, become much more the better
For being a little bad.
SHAKESPEARE, *Measure for Measure*. Act v, sc. 1, l. 444.

6
Countries, like people, are loved for their failings.
FRANCIS YEATS-BROWN, *Lives of a Bengal Lancer*, p. 45.

IV—Faults of Others

7
Every man has his faults; but we do not see the wallet on our own back. (Suus cuique attributus est error: sed non videmus manticæ quod in tergost.)
CATULLUS, *Odes*. No. xxii, l. 20.

Not a soul is there who seeks to search into himself—not one! But the wallet of the person in front is kept carefully in view.
(Ut nemo in sese temptat descendere, nemo;
Sed præcedenti spectatur mantica tergo!)
PERSIUS, *Satires*. Sat. iv, l. 23.

Jupiter has loaded us with two wallets: the one, filled with our own faults, he has placed at our backs; the other, heavy with the faults of others, he has hung before.
PHÆDRUS, *Fables*. Fable x, l. 1.

Other men's faults are before our eyes; our own behind our backs. (Aliena vitia in oculis habemus; a tergo nostra sunt.)
SENECA, *De Ira*. Bk. ii, sec. 28.

From our necks, when life's journey begins
Two sacks Jove the Father suspends,
The one holds our own proper sins,
The other the sins of our friends:
The first, man immediately throws
Out of sight, out of mind, at his back;
The last is so under his nose,
He sees every grain in the sack.
BULWER-LYTTON, *Paraphrase of Phædrus*.

8
It is the peculiar quality of a fool to perceive the faults of others, and to forget his own. (Est proprium stultitiæ aliorum vitia cernere, oblivisci suorum.)
CICERO, *Tusculanarum Disputationum*. Bk. iii, ch. 30, sec. 74. *See also* JUDGMENT: THE MOTE AND THE BEAM.

9
Black detraction
Will find faults where they are not.
MASSINGER, *The Guardian*. Act i, sc. 2.

10
When that thy neighbor's faults thou wouldst
arraign,
Think first upon thine own delinquencies.
MENANDER, *Fabulæ Incertæ*. Frag. 162.

11
I will chide no breather in the world but myself, against whom I know most faults.
SHAKESPEARE, *As You Like It*. Act iii, sc. 2, l. 298.

12
All his faults observed,
Set in a note-book, learn'd, and conn'd by
rote.
SHAKESPEARE, *Julius Cæsar*. Act iv, sc. 3, l. 97.

13
If he had been as you and you as he,
You would have slipt like him.
SHAKESPEARE, *Measure for Measure*. Act ii, sc. 2, l. 64.

Shame to him whose cruel striking
Kills for faults of his own liking!
SHAKESPEARE, *Measure for Measure*. Act iii, sc. 2, l. 281.

14
Men's faults do seldom to themselves appear.
SHAKESPEARE, *The Rape of Lucrece*, l. 633.

15
A man sooner finds out his own foibles in a stranger than any other foibles.
WILLIAM SHENSTONE, *Of Men and Manners*, 68.

Do you wish to find out a person's weak points? Note the failings he has the quickest eye for in others.
J. C. AND A. W. HARE, *Guesses at Truth*.

16
If you want a person's faults, go to those who love him. They will not tell you, but they know.
R. L. STEVENSON, *Familiar Studies of Men and Books*, p. 159.

17
We would willingly have others perfect, and yet we amend not our own faults. We would have others severely corrected, and will not be corrected ourselves. The large liberty of others displeaseth us, and yet we will not have our own desires denied us. We will have others kept under by strict laws, but in no

sort will ourselves be restrained. And thus it appeareth how seldom we weigh our neighbor in the same balance with ourselves.

THOMAS À KEMPIS, *De Imitatione Christi*. Pt. i, ch. 16, sec. 4.

1

But, by all thy nature's weakness,
Hidden faults and follies known,
Be thou, in rebuking evil,
Conscious of thine own.

WHITTIER, *What the Voice Said*. St. 15.

2

'Tis a meaner part of sense
To find a fault than taste an excellence.

JOHN WILMOT, *An Epilogue*, l. 6.

3

For as, by discipline of Time made wise,
We learn to tolerate the infirmities
And faults of others—gently as he may,
So with our own the mild Instructor deals,
Teaching us to forget them, or forgive.

WORDSWORTH, *Ecclesiastical Sonnets*. Pt. iii, No. 35.

4

We see Time's furrows on another's brow,
And Death entrench'd, preparing his assault;
How few themselves, in that just mirror, see!

YOUNG, *Night Thoughts*. Night v, l. 627.

V—Faults in Women

5

Thy faults, my Lesbia, have such charm for me,
So far in love of thee I've lost myself,
Wert thou a saint, I could not wish thee well,
Nor cease to worship thee, whate'er thy sins.
(Huc est mens deducta tua, mea Lesbia, culpa,
Atque ita se officio perdidit ipsa suo,
Ut jam nec bene velle queat tibi, si optima fias,
Nec desistere amare, omnia si facias.)

CATULLUS, *Odes*. No. lxxv.

6

Be to her virtues very kind,
Be to her faults a little blind.

MATTHEW PRIOR, *An English Padlock*, l. 78.

7

If she be made of white and red,
Her faults will ne'er be known.
For blushing cheeks by faults are bred,
And fears by pale white shown.

SHAKESPEARE, *Love's Labour's Lost*. Act i, sc. 2, l. 105.

8

For several virtues
Have I lik'd several women; never any
Was so full of soul, but some defect in her
Did quarrel with the noblest grace she owed,
And put it to the foil.

SHAKESPEARE, *The Tempest*. Act iii, sc. 1, l. 42.

9

Is she not a wilderness of faults and follies?

R. B. SHERIDAN, *The Duenna*. Act i, sc. 2.

VI—Faults: Faultlessness

See also Perfection

10

Faultless to a fault.

ROBERT BROWNING, *The Ring and the Book*. Pt. ix, l. 1177.

11

The greatest of faults, I should say, is to be conscious of none.

CARLYLE, *Heroes and Hero-Worship: The Hero as Prophet*.

12

Thou hast no faults, or I no faults can spy;
Thou art all beauty, or all blindness I.

CHRISTOPHER CODRINGTON, *Lines to Garth, On His Dispensary*. (1696) Leigh Hunt states that this epigram was written by Lord Chesterfield in praise of David Mallet's *Truth in Rhyme*, but it is now generally attributed as above.

13

Men still had faults, and men will have them still;
He that hath none, and lives as angels do,
Must be an angel.

WENTWORTH DILLON, *Miscellanies: On Mr. Dryden's Religio Laici*, l. 8.

14

It is well that there is no one without a fault, for he would not have a friend in the world.

WILLIAM HAZLITT, *Characteristics*. No. 46.

15

He has no fault except that he has no fault. (Nihil peccat, nisi quod nihil peccat.)

PLINY THE YOUNGER, *Epistles*. Bk. 9, epis. 26.

He is all fault who hath no fault at all.

TENNYSON, *Lancelot and Elaine*, l. 132.

16

He is lifeless that is faultless.

JOHN HEYWOOD, *Proverbs*. Pt. i, ch. 11. (1546)

The old saying is, "Lifeless, faultless."

C. H. SPURGEON, *John Ploughman*. Ch. 10.

17

There's no such thing in Nature; and you'll draw
A faultless monster which the world ne'er saw.

JOHN SHEFFIELD, DUKE OF BUCKINGHAM, *Essay on Poetry*.

18

Faultily faultless, icily regular, splendidly null,
Dead perfection, no more.

TENNYSON, *Maud*, l. 82.

Insipid as the queen upon a card.

TENNYSON, *Aylmer's Field*, l. 28.

At the best, my lord, she is a handsome picture,
And, that said, all is spoken.

PHILIP MASSINGER, *The Great Duke of Florence*. Act iii, sc. 1.

FAVOR

See also Benefits, Gifts, Kindness

19

The landlady and Tam grew gracious
Wi' favours secret, sweet and precious.

BURNS, *Tam o' Shanter*. St. 7.

1
The greater the favor, the greater the obligation. (Quin maximo cuique plurimum debeatur.)
CICERO, *De Officiis*. Bk. i, ch. 15, sec. 49.

2
To accept a favour from a friend is to confer one.
CHURTON COLLINS, *Aphorisms*, 98.

3
A favor bestowed by a hard man is bread made of stone.
FABIUS VERRUCOSUS. (SENECA, *De Beneficiis*, ii, 7.) *See also under* BREAD.

4
That which among men is called favor is the relaxing of strictness in time of need.
FAVORINUS, *Fragments*. No. 81.

5
The favor of the great is no inheritance.
BENJAMIN FRANKLIN, *Poor Richard*, 1733.

6
You had better refuse a favour gracefully, than to grant it clumsily.
LORD CHESTERFIELD, *Letters*, 18 March, 1751.

7
When rogues like these (a sparrow cries)
To honours and employment rise,
I court no favour, ask no place,
For such preferment is disgrace.
GAY, *Fables*. Pt. ii, fab. 2.

8
He only confers favours generously who appears, when they are once conferred, to remember them no more.
SAMUEL JOHNSON, *Works*. Vol. ix, p. 467.

9
They whom I favour thrive in wealth amain,
While virtue, valour, wisdom sit in want.
MILTON, *Paradise Regained*. Bk. ii, l. 430.

10
Doing a favour for a bad man is quite as dangerous as doing an injury to a good one. (Malo bene facere tantundemst periculum Quantum bono male facere.)
PLAUTUS, *Pœnulus*, l. 633. (Act iii, sc. 3.)

11
He who does not know how to grant a favor has no right to seek one. (Beneficium qui dare nescit injuste petit.)
PUBLILIUS SYRUS, *Sententiæ*. No. 56.

He has received a favor who has granted one to a deserving person. (Beneficium dando accepit qui digno dedit.)
PUBLILIUS SYRUS, *Sententiæ*. No. 65.

12
The favor of ignoble men can be won only by ignoble means. (Conciliari nisi turpi ratione amor turpium non potest.)
SENECA, *Epistulæ ad Lucilium*. Epis. xxix, 11.

13
Many dream not to find, neither deserve,
And yet are steep'd in favours.
SHAKESPEARE, *Cymbeline*. Act v, sc. 4, l. 130.

14
No gentleman will ask as a favor what is not due him as a reward. (Neutique officium liberi esse hominis puto, Quom is nil mereat.)
TERENCE, *Andria*, l. 331. (Act ii, sc. 1.)

Don't ask as a favor what you can take by force.
CERVANTES, *Don Quixote*. Pt. i, ch. 21.

Never claim as a right what you can ask as a favour.
CHURTON COLLINS, *Aphorisms*.

FEAR

See also Hate and Fear; Hope and Fear; Love and Fear

I—Fear: Definitions

15
Early and provident fear is the mother of safety.
EDMUND BURKE, *Speech*, on the Unitarian petition, 11 May, 1792.

Fear is the parent of cruelty.
J. A. FROUDE, *Short Studies: Party Politics*.

Fear is the father of courage and the mother of safety.
HENRY H. TWEEDY, *Sermon*, Princeton chapel.

16
Fear is an ague, that forsakes
And haunts, by fits, those whom it takes;
And they'll opine they feel the pain
And blows they felt, to-day again.
BUTLER, *Hudibras*. Pt. i, canto iii, l. 471.

17
Fear is not a lasting teacher of duty. (Timor non est diuturnus magister officii.)
CICERO, *Philippicæ*. No. ii, sec. 36.

18
Fear is the fire that melts Icarian wings:
Who fears nor Fate, nor Time, nor what Time brings,
May drive Apollo's steeds, or wield the thunderbolt!
FLORENCE EARLE COATES, *The Unconquered Air*.

19
Fear and Guilt
Are the same things, and when our actions are not,
Our fears are, crimes.
SIR JOHN DENHAM, *The Sophy*.

20
Fear is an instructor of great sagacity, and the herald of all revolutions.
EMERSON, *Essays, First Series: Compensation*.

Fear always springs from ignorance.
EMERSON, *Nature, Addresses, and Lectures: The American Scholar*.

21
Fear, the beadle of the law.
GEORGE HERBERT, *Jacula Prudentum*.

22
Fear is a hindrance to all virtue. (Virtutis omnis impedimentum est timor.)
PUBLILIUS SYRUS, *Sententiæ*. No. 717.

23
Fear, the very worst prophet in misfortune, anticipates many evils. (Plurima versat Pessimus in dubiis augur timor.)
STATIUS, *Thebais*. Bk. iii, l. 5.

It was fear that first made gods in the world. (Primus in orbe deos fecit timor.)
STATIUS, *Thebais*. Bk. iii, l. 664. *See also under* GODS: APOTHEGMS.

1

Fear, that is akin to Death;
He is Shame's friend, and always as Shame saith,
Fear answers him again.
SWINBURNE, *A Ballad of Life*. St. 4.

2

Fear is a slinking cat I find
Beneath the lilacs of my mind.
SOPHIE TUNNELL, *Fear*.

3

Fear follows crime and is its punishment. (La crainte suit le crime, et c'est son châtiment.)
VOLTAIRE, *Semiramis*. Act v, sc. 1.

All infractions of love and equity in our social relations are speedily punished. They are punished by fear.
EMERSON, *Essays, First Series: Compensation*.

4

Fear is like a cloak which old men huddle
About their love, as if to keep it warm.
WORDSWORTH, *The Borderers*. Act i, l. 22.

II—Fear: Apothegms

5

Fear, admitted into public councils,
Betrays like treason.
JOSEPH ADDISON, *Cato*. Act ii, sc. 1.

Keep your fears to yourself but share your courage.
R. L. STEVENSON.

6

It is torture to fear what you cannot overcome. (Crux est, si metuas, vincere quod nequeas.)
ANACHARSIS. (AUSONIUS [?], *Septem Sapientum Sententiæ*. Pt. vii, l. 4.)

7

The fearless man is his own salvation.
ROBERT BRIDGES, *The First Seven Divisions*.

8

In extreme danger fear feels no pity. (In summo periculo timor misericordiam non recipit.)
CÆSAR, *De Bello Gallico*. Bk. vii, sec. 26.

9

O praise not him who fears his God
But show me him who knows not fear!
JAMES FENIMORE COOPER, JR., *Fate*.

10

We are not apt to fear for the fearless, when we are companions in their danger.
GEORGE ELIOT, *Mill on the Floss*. Bk. vii, ch. 5.

11

He has not learned the lesson of life who does not every day surmount a fear.
EMERSON, *Society and Solitude: Courage*.

12

Whom they fear they hate. (Quem metuunt, oderunt.)
QUINTUS ENNIUS, *Thyestes*. (CICERO, *De Officiis*, ii, 7.) *See also* HATE AND FEAR.

13

All the weapons of London will not arm fear.
JOHN FLORIO, *First Fruites*. Fo. 32. (1578)

All the arms of England will not arm fear.
GEORGE HERBERT, *Jacula Prudentum*. (1640)

14

Fear is stronger than love.
THOMAS FULLER, *Gnomologia*. No. 1513.

'Twas fear that first put on arms.
THOMAS FULLER, *Gnomologia*. No. 5317.

15

Fear not.
Old Testament: Genesis, xlii, 23. (Nolite timere.—*Vulgate*.)

Dismiss your fear. (Pone metum.)
OVID, *Tristia*. Bk. v, eleg. 2, l. 3.

16

Fear kills more than disease.
GEORGE HERBERT, *Jacula Prudentum*.

17

More frayd than hurt.
JOHN HEYWOOD, *Proverbs*. Pt. i, ch. 4. (1546)

18

A good scare is worth more to a man than good advice.
E. W. HOWE, *Howe's Monthly*.

19

The thing we fear we bring to pass.
ELBERT HUBBARD, *Philistine*. Vol. xxv, p. 143.

20

Fear loves the idea of danger. (La peur aime l'idée du danger.)
JOUBERT, *Pensées*. No. 63.

21

The less there is of fear the less there is of danger. (Quo timoris minus est, eo minus ferme periculi est.)
LIVY, *History*. Bk. xxii, ch. 5.

22

Whom each man fears, he longs to see destroyed. (Quem metuit quisque, perisse cupit.)
OVID, *Amores*. Bk. ii, eleg. 2, l. 10.

23

Fear itself made her daring. (Audacem fecerat ipse timor.)
OVID, *Fasti*. Bk. iii, l. 644.

Despair and confidence both banish fear.
WILLIAM ALEXANDER, *Doomsday*. Hour ix, 55.

Courage is often caused by fear. (Le courage est souvent un effet de la peur.)
UNKNOWN. A French proverb.

24

The mind which knows how to fear, knows how to go safely. (Animus vereri qui scit, scit tuto aggredi.)
PUBLILIUS SYRUS, *Sententiæ*. No. 3.

25

Happy is the man that feareth always: but he that hardeneth his heart shall fall into mischief.
Old Testament: Proverbs, xxviii, 14.

26

Fear, not clemency, restrains the wicked. (Metus improbos compescit, non clementia.)
PUBLILIUS SYRUS, *Sententiæ*. No. 391.

Fear keeps the garden better than the Gardener.
GEORGE HERBERT, *Jacula Prudentum.*

Moralists realize that the highest fence is fear.
DUDLEY NICHOLS.

1
It is enough to fright you out of your seven senses.
RABELAIS, *Works.* Bk. v, ch. 15.

Scared out of his seven senses.
SCOTT, *Rob Roy.* Ch. 34.

Huzzaed out of my seven senses.
STEELE [?], *The Spectator.* No. 616.

You frighten me out of my seven senses!
SWIFT, *Polite Conversation.* Dial. i.

2
If you wish to fear nothing, consider that everything is to be feared. (Si vultis nihil timere, cogitate omnia esse timenda.)
SENECA, *Naturales Questiones.* Bk. vi, sec. 2.

3
For the effect of judgement
Is oft the cause of fear.
SHAKESPEARE, *Cymbeline.* Act iv, sc. 2, l. 111.
Some editors give "defect of judgement."

O horror, horror, horror! Tongue nor heart
Cannot conceive nor name thee!
SHAKESPEARE, *Macbeth.* Act ii, sc. 3, l. 68.

4
When our actions do not,
Our fears do make us traitors.
SHAKESPEARE, *Macbeth.* Act iv, sc. 2, l. 3.

5
Fear that makes faith may break faith.
SWINBURNE, *Bothwell.* Act i, sc. 3.

I have no remedy for fear; there grows
No herb of help to heal a coward's heart.
SWINBURNE, *Bothwell.* Act ii, sc. 12.

6
Even the bravest are frightened by sudden terrors. (Etiam fortes viros subitis terreri.)
TACITUS, *Annals.* Bk. xv, sec. 59.

7
Always it comes about that the beginning of wisdom is a fear.
MIGUEL DE UNAMUNO, *Tragic Sense of Life,* p. 107.

8
Fear argues ignoble minds. (Degeneres animos timor arguit.)
VERGIL, *Æneid.* Bk. iv, l. 13.

9
Fear gave wings to his feet. (Pedibus timor addidit alas.)
VERGIL, *Æneid.* Bk. viii, l. 224.

Thereto fear gave her wings.
SPENSER, *Faerie Queene.* Bk. iii, canto vii, st. 26.

O! see how fear gives him wings.
SIR PHILIP SIDNEY, *Arcadia.* Bk. ii.

III—Fear: Its Folly

10
Nothing is so rash as fear.
EDMUND BURKE, *Letters on the Regicide Peace.* No. 1.

His fear was greater than his haste:
For fear, though fleeter than the wind,
Believes 'tis always left behind.
BUTLER, *Hudibras.* Pt. iii, canto iii, l. 64.

11
Fear is sharp-sighted, and can see underground, and much more in the skies.
CERVANTES, *Don Quixote.* Bk. iii, ch. 6.

Fear hath a hundred eyes, that all agree
To plague her beating heart.
WORDSWORTH, *Ecclesiastical Sonnets.* Pt. i, 42.

12
Fear, instead of avoiding, invites danger; for concealed cowards will insult known ones.
LORD CHESTERFIELD, *Letters,* 21 Sept., 1747.

13
No power is strong enough to last, if it labors under the weight of fear. (Nec vero ulla vis imperii tanta est, quæ premente metu possit esse diuturna.)
CICERO, *De Officiis.* Bk. ii, ch. 7, sec. 23.

14
Fear of danger is ten thousand times more terrifying than danger itself.
DANIEL DEFOE, *Robinson Crusoe,* p. 161.

The direst foe of courage is the fear itself.
GEORGE MACDONALD, *Sir Gibbie.* Ch. 20.

The fear's as bad as falling.
SHAKESPEARE, *Cymbeline.* Act iii, sc. 3, l. 48.
See also TROUBLE: NEVER TROUBLE TROUBLE.

15
It is not death or hardship that is a fearful thing, but the fear of hardship and death. (*οὐ γὰρ θάνατος ἢ πόνος φοβερόν, ἀλλὰ τὸ φοβεῖσθαι πόνον ἢ θάνατον.*)
EPICTETUS, *Discourses.* Bk. ii, ch. 1, sec. 13. (C. A. D. 100).

The things of which I have most fear is fear. (C'est de quoy j'ay le plus de peur que la peur.)
MONTAIGNE, *Essays.* Bk. i, Ch. xvii, *De la Peur.* (1580).

Nothing is terrible except fear itself. (Nil terribile nisi ipse timor.)
FRANCIS BACON, *De Augmentis Scientiarum: Fortitudo.* (1623).

The only thing I am afraid of is fear.
DUKE OF WELLINGTON, referring to the effect on the public mind of the crisis resulting in the Reform Act of 1832.

Nothing is so much to be feared as fear.
H. D. THOREAU. Quoted as from Thoreau's unpublished manuscripts by Ralph Waldo Emerson, in his address at Thoreau's funeral, 8 May, 1862, later included in his *Lectures and Biographical Sketches.*

The only thing we have to fear is fear itself.
F. D. ROOSEVELT, *First Inaugural Address,* 4 March, 1933. *See* 2298i:7.

16
You crystal break, for fear of breaking it:
Careless and careful hands like faults commit.
(Frangere dum metuis, franges crystallina;
Peccant securæ nimium, sollicitæque manus.)
MARTIAL, *Epigrams.* Bk. xiv, epig. 111.

1
It is foolish to fear what cannot be avoided. (Stultum est timere quod vitari non potest.)
PUBLILIUS SYRUS, *Sententiæ*. No. 682.

All fearfulness is folly.
JOHN FLORIO, *First Fruites*. Fo. 32.

2
Fear makes men ready to believe the worst. (Ad deteriora credenda proni metu.)
QUINTUS CURTIUS RUFUS, *De Rebus Gesti Alexandri Magni*, iv, 3, 22.

It is good to fear the worst; the best will save itself.
DRAXE, *Biblio. Schol. Instr.*, 65. (1633)

In grief we know the worst of what we feel,
But who can tell the end of what we fear?
HANNAH MORE, *The Fatal Falsehood*. Act iv.

To fear the worst oft cures the worse.
SHAKESPEARE, *Troilus and Cressida*. Act iii, sc. 2, l. 76.

3
No fear is so ruinous and uncontrollable as panic fear. For other fears are groundless, but this fear is witless. (Nulli itaque tam perniciosi, tam inrevocabiles quam lymphatici metus sunt. Ceteri enim sine ratione, hi sine mente sunt.)
SENECA, *Epistulæ ad Lucilium*. Epis. xiii, sec. 9.

4
To fear the foe, since fear oppresseth strength,
Gives in your weakness strength unto your foe,
And so your follies fight against yourself.
Fear and be slain; no worse can come to fight:
And fight and die is death destroying death;
Where fearing dying pays death servile breath.
SHAKESPEARE, *Richard II*. Act iii, sc. 2, l. 180.

5
Fear will drive men to any extreme; and the fear inspired by a superior being is a mystery which cannot be reasoned away.
BERNARD SHAW, *Saint Joan: Preface*.

6
Desponding Fear, of feeble fancies full,
Weak and unmanly, loosens every power.
THOMSON, *The Seasons: Spring*, l. 286.

7
Fearful when all was safe. (Omnia tuta timens.)
VERGIL, *Æneid*. Bk. iv, l. 298.

8
The fear that kills.
WORDSWORTH, *Resolution and Independence*, l. 113.

IV—Fear: Unreasoning Fear

See also Imagination

9
The clouds dispell'd, the sky resum'd her light,
And Nature stood recover'd of her fright.
But fear, the last of ills, remain'd behind,
And horror heavy sat on ev'ry mind.
DRYDEN, *Theodore and Honoria*, l. 336.

10
The absent Danger greater still appears.
Less fears he who is near the thing he fears.
SAMUEL DANIEL, *Cleopatra*. Act iv, sc. 1.

11
If I quake, what matters it what I quake at?
EMERSON, *Essays, Second Series: Character*.

12
He returned with more fear of his shadow than true report of that he had in charge.
GEOFFREY FENTON, *Bandello*. Vol. ii, p. 285.

He is afraid of his own shadow.
JOHN BARET, *An Alvearie*, v, 92. (1574)

13
He that is afraid of every starting grass may not walk in a meadow.
GABRIEL HARVEY, *Marginalia*, p. 192. (1590)

He that's afraid of every grass must not sleep in a meadow.
SAMUEL PALMER, *Essays on Proverbs*, p. 195.

He that is afraid of leaves goes not to the wood.
GEORGE HERBERT, *Jacula Prudentum*. (1640)

He that feareth every bush must never go a-birding.
JOHN LYLY, *Euphues*, p. 354. (1580)

Or in the night, imagining some fear,
How easy is a bush supposed a bear.
SHAKESPEARE, *A Midsummer-Night's Dream*. Act v, sc. 1, l. 21. (1595)

14
The one permanent emotion of the inferior man is fear—fear of the unknown, the complex, the inexplicable. What he wants beyond everything else is safety.
H. L. MENCKEN, *Prejudices*. Ser. ii, p. 75.

15
The wounded body shrinks even from a gentle touch; an empty shadow fills the anxious with fear. (Membra reformidant mollem quoque saucia tactum; Vanaque sollicitis incutit umbra metum.)
OVID, *Epistulæ ex Ponto*. Bk. ii, epis. 7, l. 13.

What I am to fear, I know not—yet none the less I fear all things. (Quid timeam, ignoro—timeo tamen omnia.)
OVID, *Heroides*. Epis. i, l. 71.

The least rustle of a feather brings dread upon the dove that thy talons, O hawk, have wounded. (Terretur minimo pennæ stridore columba, Unguibus, accipiter, saucia facta tuis.)
OVID, *Tristia*. Bk. i, eleg. 1, l. 75.

16
Where truth cannot be determined, what is false is increased by fear. (Ubi explorari vera non possunt, falsa per metum augentur.)
QUINTUS CURTIUS RUFUS, *De Rebus Gestis Alexandri Magni*, iv, 10, 10.

17
Terror closes the ears of the mind. (Timor animi auribus officit.)
SALLUST, *Catilina*. Ch. 58, sec. 3.

18
The terror we fear is often empty, but nevertheless it causes real misery.
SCHILLER, *Piccolomini*. Act v, sc. 1, l. 105.

1
For I am sick and capable of fears,
Oppress'd with wrongs, and therefore full of fears,
A widow, husbandless, subject to fears,
A woman, naturally born to fears;
And though thou now confess thou didst but jest,
With my vex'd spirit I cannot take a truce.
SHAKESPEARE, *King John*. Act iii, sc. 1, l. 12.

2
Give me the daggers: the sleeping and the dead
Are but as pictures: 'tis the eye of childhood
That fears a painted devil.
SHAKESPEARE, *Macbeth*. Act ii, sc. 2, l. 53.

3
Extreme fear can neither fight nor fly,
But coward-like with trembling terror die.
SHAKESPEARE, *The Rape of Lucrece*, l. 230.

Blind fear, that seeing reason leads, finds safer footing than blind reason stumbling without fear.
SHAKESPEARE, *Troilus and Cressida*. Act iii, sc. 2, l. 74.

4
Do you think I was born in a wood to be afraid of an owl?
SWIFT, *Polite Conversation*. Dial. 1.

5
Things seen, or believed through fear. (Visa, sive ex metu.)
TACITUS, *Annales*. Bk. ii, sec. 24.

6
Horror itself in that fair scene looks gay,
And joy springs up e'en in the midst of fear.
(Bello in si bella vistà anco è l'orrore,
E di mezzo la tema esce il diletto.)
TASSO, *Gerusalemme*. Bk. xx, st. 30.

7
My apprehensions come in crowds;
I dread the rustling of the grass;
The very shadows of the clouds
Have power to shake me as they pass:
I question things and do not find
One that will answer to my mind,
And all the world appears unkind.
WORDSWORTH, *The Affliction of Margaret*. St. 10.

V—Fear: Feared and Fearing

8
If you are terrible to many, beware of many. (Multis terribilis caveto multos.)
PERIANDER. (AUSONIUS [?], *Septem Sapientum Sententiæ*. Sec. iv, l. 5.)

10
Whoso causes fear is himself more fearful. (Qui terret, plus ipse timet.)
CLAUDIAN, *De Quarto Consulatu Honorii Augusti*, l. 290.

11
He must fear many whom many fear. (Multos timere debet, quem multi timent.)
PUBLILIUS SYRUS, *Sententiæ*. No. 372. Quoted by BACON, *Ornamenta Rationalia*. No. 32.

He must necessarily fear many, whom many fear. (Necesse est multos timeat, quem multi timent.)
SENECA, *De Ira*. Bk. ii, l. 11.

12
Fear him who fears thee, though he be a fly and thou an elephant.
SADI, *Gulistan*. Ch. 1, No. 8.

13
The man who fears nothing is not less powerful than he who is feared by every one. (Wer nichts fürchtet ist nicht weniger mächtig, als der, den Alles fürchtet.)
SCHILLER, *Die Räuber*. Act i, sc. 1.

VI—Fear: Its Effects

14
Right as an aspes leaf she 'gan to shake.
CHAUCER, *Troilus*. Bk. iii, l. 1200.

A sudden tremor seized his limbs. (Subitus tremor occupat artus.)
VERGIL, *Æneid*. Bk. vii, l. 446.

15
We listened and looked sideways up!
Fear at my heart, as at a cup,
My life-blood seemed to sip!
COLERIDGE, *The Ancient Mariner*. Pt. iii.

Like one, that on a lonesome road
Doth walk in fear and dread,
And having once turned round, walks on,
And turns no more his head;
Because he knows a frightful fiend
Doth close behind him tread.
COLERIDGE, *The Ancient Mariner*. Pt. vi.

"I wants to make your flesh creep," replied the boy.
DICKENS, *Pickwick Papers*. Ch. 8.

16
His frown was full of terror, and his voice
Shook the delinquent with such fits of awe
As left him not, till penitence had won
Lost favour back again, and clos'd the breach.
COWPER, *The Task*. Bk. ii, l. 659.

17
Having their heart at their very mouth for fear.
ERASMUS, *Paraphrase of Luke*, xxiii. *See also under* HEART.

18
Distill'd
Almost to jelly with the act of fear.
SHAKESPEARE, *Hamlet*. Act i, sc. 2, l. 204.

Pale as his shirt, his knees knocking each other.
SHAKESPEARE, *Hamlet*. Act ii, sc. 1, l. 81.

19
Thou tremblest; and the whiteness in thy cheek
Is apter than thy tongue to tell thy errand.
SHAKESPEARE, *II Henry IV*. Act i, sc. 1, l. 68.

And make my seated heart knock at my ribs,
Against the use of nature.
SHAKESPEARE, *Macbeth*. Act i, sc. 3, l. 136.

20
Then comes my fit again: I had else been perfect,

Whole as the marble, founded as the rock,
As broad and general as the casing air:
But now I am cabin'd, cribb'd, confined, bound in
To saucy doubts and fears.
SHAKESPEARE, *Macbeth*. Act iii, sc. 4, l. 21.

I have almost forgot the taste of fears.
I have supp'd full with horrors;
Direness, familiar to my slaughterous thoughts,
Cannot once start me.
SHAKESPEARE, *Macbeth*. Act v, sc. 5, l. 13.

1
Sweating with guilty fear.
SHAKESPEARE, *The Rape of Lucrece*, l. 740.

I am surprised with an uncouth fear:
A chilling sweat o'er-runs my trembling joints.
SHAKESPEARE, *Titus Andronicus*. Act ii, sc. 3, l. 211.

2
Truly, the souls of men are full of dread:
Ye cannot reason almost with a man
That looks not heavily and full of fear.
SHAKESPEARE, *Richard III*. Act ii, sc. 3, l. 39.

3
I have a faint cold fear thrills through my veins,
That almost freezes up the heat of life.
SHAKESPEARE, *Romeo and Juliet*. Act iv, sc. 3, l. 15.

4
Fear
Stared in her eyes, and chalk'd her face.
TENNYSON, *The Princess*. Pt. iv, l. 357.

5
My hair stood on end, and my voice stuck in my throat. (Steteruntque comæ, et vox faucibus hæsit.)
VERGIL, *Æneid*. Bk. ii, l. 774; bk. iii, l. 48.

Fear came upon me, and trembling; . . . the hair of my flesh stood up.
Old Testament: Job, iv, 14, 15.

Anastasio having heard all this discourse his hair stood upright like porcupine's quills.
BOCCACCIO, *Decameron*. Day v, novel 8. (1358)

I could a tale unfold whose lightest word
Would harrow up thy soul, freeze thy young blood,
Make thy two eyes, like stars, start from their spheres,
Thy knotted and combined locks to part
And each particular hair to stand on end,
Like quills upon the fretful porpentine.
SHAKESPEARE, *Hamlet*. Act i, sc. 5, l. 15. (1600)

My fell of hair
Would at a dismal treatise rouse and stir
As life were in't.
SHAKESPEARE, *Macbeth*. Act v, sc. 5, l. 11.

6
Fear shakes the pencil; Fancy loves excess;
Dark Ignorance is lavish of her shades:
And these the formidable picture draw.
YOUNG, *Night Thoughts*. Night vi, l. 58.

FEAST and FESTIVAL

See also Dining, Eating

7
Some men are born to feast, and not to fight;
Whose sluggish minds, e'en in fair honour's field,
Still on their dinner turn—
Let such pot-boiling varlets stay at home,
And wield a flesh-hook rather than a sword.
JOANNA BAILLIE, *Basil*. Act i, sc. 1.

8
Hogmanay, like all festivals, being but a bank from which we can only draw what we put in.
J. M. BARRIE, *Sentimental Tommy*, p. 108.

9
Antipater, who had an anniversary feast every year upon his birthday, needed no astrological revelation to know what day he should die on.
SIR THOMAS BROWNE, *To a Friend*. Sec. 8.

10
On such an occasion as this,
All time and nonsense scorning,
Nothing shall come amiss,
And we won't go home till morning.
JOHN B. BUCKSTONE, *Billy Taylor*. Act i, sc. 2.

11
As much valour is to be found in feasting as in fighting, and some of our city captains and carpet knights will make this good, and prove it.
ROBERT BURTON, *Anatomy of Melancholy*. Pt. i, sec. i, mem. 2, subs. 2.

12
This feast is named the Carnival, which being
Interpreted, implies "farewell to flesh";
So call'd, because, the name and thing agreeing,
Through Lent they live on fish both salt and fresh.
BYRON, *Beppo*. St. vi.

13
There was a sound of revelry by night,
And Belgium's capital had gather'd then
Her Beauty and her Chivalry, and bright
The lamps shone o'er fair women and brave men.
BYRON, *Childe Harold*. Canto iii, st. 21.

The music, and the banquet, and the wine—
The garlands, the rose odours, and the flowers—
The sparkling eyes, and flashing ornaments—
The white arms and the raven hair—the braids
And bracelets; swan-like bosoms, and the necklace,
An India in itself; yet dazzling not.
BYRON, *Marino Faliero*. Act iv, sc. 1, l. 51.

14
The promised feast became a feast of the Lapithæ.
CARLYLE, *French Revolution*. Pt. ii, bk. i, ch. 5.
The chief of the Lapithæ gave a feast to celebrate the wedding of Pirithous and Hippodamia, which ended in blows and "very great slaughter," owing to the fact that the

Centaurs, who had mistakenly been invited, offered violence to the bride. (OVID, *Metamorphoses*. Bk. xii.)

1
Be not made a beggar by banqueting upon borrowing.
Apocrypha: Ecclesiasticus, xviii, 33.

2
A little dish oft furnishes enough,
And sure enough is equal to a feast.
FIELDING, *Covent Garden Tragedy*. Act ii, sc. 6.
See also MODERATION: ENOUGH IS AS GOOD AS A FEAST.

3
Fools make the banquets, and wise men enjoy them.
JOHN FLORIO, *First Fruites*. Fo. 30. (1578)

Fools make feasts and wise men eat them.
JOHN RAY, *English Proverbs*. As might be guessed, this proverb is of Scottish origin. It appealed to Benjamin Franklin, who inserted it in *Poor Richard's Almanac* for 1733.

4
Little difference between a feast and a belly-full.
THOMAS FULLER, *Gnomologia*. No. 3253.

5
Blest be those feasts with simple plenty crown'd,
Where all the ruddy family around
Laugh at the jests or pranks that never fail,
Or sigh with pity at some mournful tale,
Or press the bashful stranger to his food,
And learn the luxury of doing good.
GOLDSMITH, *The Traveller*, l. 17.

6
There is no great banquet but some fares ill.
GEORGE HERBERT, *Jacula Prudentum*.

7
The true essentials of a feast are only fun and feed.
O. W. HOLMES, *Nux Postcœnatica*. St. 11.

8
When mirth reigns throughout the town, and feasters about the house, sitting in order, listen to a minstrel; when the tables beside them are laden with bread and meat, and the wine-bearer draws sweet drink from the mixing-bowl and fills the cups; this I think in my heart to be the most delightsome of all to men.
HOMER. (*Contest of Homer and Hesiod*. Sec. 316.)

It is said that when Homer recited these verses, they were so admired by the Greeks as to be called golden by them, and that even now at public sacrifices all the guests solemnly recite them before feasts and libations.
ALCIDAMUS, *Contest of Homer and Hesiod*.

9
Here let us feast, and to the feast be join'd
Discourse, the sweeter banquet of the mind.
HOMER, *Odyssey*. Bk. xv, l. 432. (Pope, tr.)
See also under CONVERSATION.

10
A feast of fat things.
Old Testament: Isaiah, xxv, 6.

11
Hans Breitmann gife a barty—
Vhere ish dat barty now?
CHARLES G. LELAND, *Hans Breitmann's Party*.

12
One, bidding me to a banquet, killed me with silver hunger, serving famished dishes. And in wrath I spoke amid the silver sheen of famine: "Where is the plenty of my earthenware dishes?"
LUCILIUS. (*Greek Anthology*. Bk. xi, epig. 313.)

13
When your crowd of followers applaud you so loudly, Pomponius, it is not you, but your banquet, that is eloquent. (Quod tam grande sophos clamat tibi turba togata, Non tu, Pomponi, cena diserta tua est.)
MARTIAL, *Epigrams*. Bk. vi, epig. 48.

14
Midnight shout and revelry,
Tipsy dance and jollity.
MILTON, *Comus*, l. 103.

Drive far off the barb'rous dissonance
Of Bacchus and his revellers.
MILTON, *Paradise Lost*. Bk. vii, l. 32.

15
A feast not profuse but elegant; more of salt than of expense. (Non ampliter, sed munditer convivium; plus salis quam sumptus.)
MONTAIGNE, *Essays*. Bk. iii, ch. 9. Montaigne is quoting Cornelius Nepos (*Life of Atticus*, ch. 13) and by "salt" he means wit or refinement.

What neat repast shall feast us, light and choice
Of Attic taste?
MILTON, *Sonnet: To Mr. Lawrence*.

16
His wine and beasts supplied our feasts,
And his overthrow our chorus.
T. L. PEACOCK, *Misfortunes of Elphin*. Ch. 2.

17
Holiday feasting makes everyday fasting,
Unless you save while the money's lasting.
(Festo die si quid prodegeris,
Profesto egere liceat, nisi peperceris.)
PLAUTUS, *Aulularia*, l. 380. (Act ii, sc. 8.)

18
There St. John mingles with my friendly bowl
The feast of reason and the flow of soul.
POPE, *Imitations of Horace: Satires*. Bk. ii, sat. 1, l. 127.

19
The apples she had gather'd smelt most sweet,
The cake she kneaded was the savoury meat:
But fruits their odour lost, and meats their taste,
If gentle Abra had not deck'd the feast;
Dishonour'd did the sparkling goblet stand,
Unless receiv'd from gentle Abra's hand.
MATTHEW PRIOR, *Solomon*. Bk. ii, l. 493.

1
The feast is good, until the reck'ning come.
QUARLES, *A Feast for Worms*. Sec. vi, med. 6.

2
Feasting makes no friendship.
JOHN RAY, *English Proverbs*.

3
Small cheer and great welcome makes a merry feast.
SHAKESPEARE, *The Comedy of Errors*. Act iii, sc. 1, l. 26.

4
To the latter end of a fray and the beginning of a feast
Fits a dull fighter and a keen guest.
SHAKESPEARE, *I Henry IV*. Act iv, sc. 2, l. 85.

Our grandsires said, Haste to the beginning of a feast, but to the end of a fray.
MASSINGER, *The Bashful Lover*. Act iii.

I arrived just at the conclusion of the ceremony; but the latter end of a feast is better than the beginning of a fray.
GEORGE COLMAN THE ELDER, *Man and Wife*. Act iii, sc. 2.

5
This night I hold an old accustom'd feast,
Whereto I have invited many a guest,
Such as I love; and you, among the store,
One more, most welcome, makes my number more.
SHAKESPEARE, *Romeo and Juliet*. Act i, sc. 2, l. 20.

We have a trifling foolish banquet towards.
SHAKESPEARE, *Romeo and Juliet*. Act i, sc. 5, l. 124.

This night in banqueting must all be spent.
SHAKESPEARE, *Troilus and Cressida*. Act v, sc. 1, l. 51.

6
Our feasts
In every mess have folly, and the feeders
Digest it with a custom, I should blush
To see you so attir'd.
SHAKESPEARE, *Winter's Tale*. Act iv, sc. 4, l. 10.

7
"Fancy a party, all Mulligans!" thought I, with a secret terror.
THACKERAY, *Mrs. Perkins's Ball*.

8
Oh, leave the gay and festive scenes,
The halls of dazzling light.
H. S. VAN DYKE, *The Light Guitar*.

FEATHER

9
Who . . . fancy female ruin a feather in your caps of vanity.
GEORGE COLMAN THE YOUNGER, *John Bull*. Act i, sc. 1.

10
It hath been an ancient custom among them [the Hungarians] that none should wear a feather but he who had killed a Turk, to whom only it was lawful to show the number of his slain enemies by the number of feathers in his cap.
RICHARD HANSARD, *A Description of Hungary*, 1599. (Lansdowne MS., British Museum. Vol. 149, MS. 775.) Hence "a feather in his cap."

Men . . . then put fethers in their caps.
BERNARD MANDEVILLE, *The Fable of the Bees*. (1714)

11
Feather by feather, birds build nests.
MIDDLETON AND ROWLEY, *Spanish Gypsy*. Act ii, sc. 1. FEATHER MY NEST, see 1637:3.

12
I am a feather for each wind that blows.
SHAKESPEARE, *Winter's Tale*. Act ii, sc. 3, 154.

FEBRUARY

13
While the slant sun of February pours
Into the bowers a flood of light.
BRYANT, *A Winter Palace*.

14
All the months in the year curse a fair Februeer.
THOMAS FULLER, *Gnomologia*. No. 6151.

15
February makes a bridge and March breaks it.
GEORGE HERBERT, *Jacula Prudentum*.

16
February was filling the dykes to the very margin.
E. V. LUCAS, *Genevra's Money*, p. 4.

February, fill the dyke with what ye like.
THOMAS TUSSER, *Hundredth Good Pointes of Husbandrie*. Ch. 34.

17
Late February days; and now, at last,
Might you have thought that Winter's woe was past;
So fair the sky was and so soft the air.
WILLIAM MORRIS, *The Earthly Paradise: February*.

18
If foul-faced February keep true touch, . . .
By night, by day, by little and by much,
It fills the ditch with either black or white.
JOHN TAYLOR THE WATER-POET, *Works*, p. 257.

19
So, in a single night,
Fair February came,
Bidding my lips to sing
Or whisper their surprise,
With all the joys of spring
And morning in her eyes.
FRANCIS BRETT YOUNG, *February*.

FEELING

20
Below the surface-stream, shallow and light,
Of what we *say* we feel—below the stream,
As light, of what we *think* we feel—there flows
With noiseless current strong, obscure and deep,
The central stream of what we feel indeed.
MATTHEW ARNOLD, *St. Paul and Protestantism*, p. 70. (See Arnold's *Letters*, ii, 32.)

21
There are some feelings time cannot benumb.
BYRON, *Childe Harold*. Canto iv, st. 19.

The keenest pangs the wretched find
  Are rapture to the dreary void,
The leafless desert of the mind,
  The waste of feelings unemployed.
  BYRON, *The Giaour*, l. 957.

1
Thought is deeper than all speech,
Feeling deeper than all thought.
  CHRISTOPHER PEARSE CRANCH, *Thought*.

2
A nation with whom sentiment is nothing is on the way to cease to be a nation at all.
  J. A. FROUDE, *Oceana: The Premier*.

3
The fine emotions whence our lives we mold
Lie in the earthly tumult dumb and cold.
(Die uns das Leben gaben, herrliche Gefühle,
Erstarren in dem irdischen Gewühle.)
  GOETHE, *Faust*. Pt. i, sc. 1, l. 286.

4
I perfectly feel, even at my finger's end.
  JOHN HEYWOOD, *Proverbs*. Pt. i, ch. 6.

5
If you wish me to weep, you must first feel grief. (Si vis me flere, dolendum est Primum ipsi tibi.)
  HORACE, *Ars Poetica*, l. 102.

But, spite of all the criticising elves,
Those who would make us feel, must feel themselves.
  CHARLES CHURCHILL, *The Rosciad*, l. 961.

See also under SYMPATHY.

6
Some are more strongly affected by the facts of human life; others by the beauty of earth and sky.
  JOHN KEBLE, *Lectures on Poetry*. Lecture 31.

7
There are moments in life, when the heart is so full of emotion,
That if by chance it be shaken, or into its depths like a pebble
Drops some careless word, it overflows, and its secret,
Spilt on the ground like water, can never be gathered together.
  LONGFELLOW, *The Courtship of Miles Standish*. Pt. vi, l. 12.

8
Sentiment is intellectualized emotion, emotion precipitated, as it were, in pretty crystals by the fancy.
  J. R. LOWELL, *Among My Books: Rousseau and the Sentimentalists*.

9
      If he comes beneath a heel,
He shall be crushed until he cannot feel,
Or, being callous, haply till he can.
  GEORGE MEREDITH, *Modern Love*. St. 3.

10
Great thoughts, great feelings came to him,
Like instincts, unawares.
  R. M. MILNES, *The Men of Old*

The wealth of rich feelings—the deep—the pure;
With strength to meet sorrow, and faith to endure.
  FRANCES S. OSGOOD, *To F. D. Maurice*.

11
Feeling hath no fellow.
  JOHN RAY, *English Proverbs*.

Seeing is believing, but feeling 's the naked truth.
  JOHN RAY, *English Proverbs*.

12
Some feelings are to mortals given
With less of earth in them than heaven.
  SCOTT, *Lady of the Lake*. Canto ii, st. 22.

14
My feelings at that moment could only be expressed in camera.
  ALFRED SUTRO, *Mollentrave on Women*. Act i.

15
Too quick a sense of constant infelicity.
  JEREMY TAYLOR, *Sermon*.

16
Trust not to thy feeling, for whatever it be now, it will quickly be changed into another thing.
  THOMAS À KEMPIS, *De Imitatione Christi*. Pt. i, ch. 13.

And inasmuch as feeling, the East's gift,
Is quick and transient,—comes, and lo! is gone.
  ROBERT BROWNING, *Luria*. Act v.

17
The advantage of the emotions is that they lead us astray.
  OSCAR WILDE, *Picture of Dorian Gray*. Ch. 3.

18
      Sensations sweet,
Felt in the blood, and felt along the heart.
  WORDSWORTH, *Lines Composed a Few Miles Above Tintern Abbey*, l. 27.

Feelings and emanations—things that were
Light to the sun, and music to the wind.
  WORDSWORTH, *Michael*, l. 201.

FICTION

See also Truth and Fiction

19
The phantasmagorical world of novels and of opium.
  MATTHEW ARNOLD, *Literature and Dogma*. Ch. 11.

20
True fiction hath a higher end, and scope
Wider than fact; it is nature's possible,
Contrasted with life's actual mean.
  P. J. BAILEY, *Festus: Proem*, l. 135.

21
A novel, which, like a beggar, should always be kept "moving on." Nobody knew this better than Fielding, whose novels, like most good ones, are full of inns.
  AUGUSTINE BIRRELL, *Obiter Dicta: The Office of Literature*.

There is nothing better fitted to delight the reader than change of circumstances and varieties of fortune.
  CICERO, *Epistolæ ad Atticum*. Bk. v, epis. 12.

1
Scrofulous novels of the age.
ROBERT BUCHANAN, *Saint Abe and his Seven Wives: Dedication.*

2
Romances paint at full length people's woo-
ings,
But only give a bust of marriages:
For no one cares for matrimonial cooings.
BYRON, *Don Juan.* Canto iii, st. 8.

3
Fiction, while the feigner of it knows that he is feigning, partakes more than we suspect, of the nature of *lying.*
THOMAS CARLYLE, *Essays: Biography.*

We must remember, however, that fiction is not falsehood.
ARTHUR HELPS, *Friends in Council.* Bk. i, ch. 6.

4
Novels are to love as fairy tales to dreams.
S. T. COLERIDGE, *Lectures: Cervantes.*

5
O Richardson, I make bold to say that the truest history is full of falsehoods and that your romance is full of truths.
DIDEROT. (MORLEY, *Diderot and the Encyclopædists.*)

6
Novels are as useful as Bibles, if they teach you the secret that the best of life is conversation, and the greatest success is confidence.
EMERSON, *Conduct of Life: Behavior.*

How far off from life and manners and motives the novel still is! Life lies about us dumb; the day, as we know it, has not yet found a tongue.
EMERSON, *Society and Solitude: Books.*

Great is the poverty of their [novelists] inventions. She was beautiful and he fell in love.
EMERSON, *Society and Solitude: Books.*

7
Now as the Paradisiacal pleasures of the Mahometans consist in playing upon the flute and lying with Houris, be mine to read eternal new romances of Marivaux and Crebillon.
THOMAS GRAY, *Letter to Mr. West.* Ser. iii.

8
Novels (receipts to make a whore).
MATTHEW GREEN, *The Spleen,* l. 269.

9
Fictions meant to please should be close to the real. (Ficta voluptatis causa sint proxima veris.)
HORACE, *Ars Poetica,* l. 338.

10
A little attention to the nature of the human mind evinces that the entertainments of fiction are useful as well as pleasant. . . . Everything is useful which contributes to fix the principles and practices of virtue.
THOMAS JEFFERSON, *Writings.* Vol. iv, p. 237.

11
Where there is leisure for fiction there is little grief.
SAMUEL JOHNSON, *Works.* Vol. ii, p. 148.

12
Character in decay is the theme of the great bulk of superior fiction.
H. L. MENCKEN, *Prejudices.* Ser. i, p. 41.

13
The first thing will be to have a censorship of the writers of fiction, to accept the good and reject the bad.
PLATO, *The Republic.* Bk. ii, sec. 377.

14
A Novel was a book
Three-volumed, and once read, and oft
crammed full
Of poisonous error, blackening every page;
And oftener still, of trifling, second-hand
Remark, and old, diseasèd, putrid thought,
And miserable incident, at war
With nature, with itself and truth at war:
Yet charming still the greedy reader on,
Till, done, he tried to recollect his thoughts,
And nothing found but dreaming emptiness.
POLLOCK, *The Course of Time.* Bk. iv, l. 325.

Novels, remarkable only for their exaggerated pictures, impossible ideals, and specimens of depravity, fill our young readers with wrong tastes and sentiments.
MARY BAKER EDDY, *Science and Health,* p. 195.

15
Make them laugh, make them cry, make them wait.
CHARLES READE, *Recipe for Writing Novels.* (Given to a young novelist.)

16
The rest of the characters are simply the sweepings out of a Pentonville omnibus.
JOHN RUSKIN, *Fiction Fair and Foul,* referring to GEORGE ELIOT'S *Mill on the Floss.*

Mr. Ruskin once described the characters in George Eliot's novels as being like the sweepings of a Pentonville omnibus.
OSCAR WILDE, *The Decay of Lying.*

17
If this were played upon the stage now, I could condemn it as an improbable fiction.
SHAKESPEARE, *Twelfth Night.* Act iii, sc. 4, l. 140.

18
The most influential books, and the truest in their influence, are works of fiction. . . . They repeat, they re-arrange, they clarify the lessons of life; they disengage us from ourselves, they constrain us to the acquaintance of others; and they show us the web of experience, but with a singular change,—that monstrous, consuming *ego* of ours being, for the nonce, struck out.
R. L. STEVENSON. (*Books Which Have Influenced Me.*)

19
Novels are sweets. All people with healthy literary appetites love them—almost all women; a vast number of clever, hard-headed men.
THACKERAY, *Roundabout Papers: On a Lazy, Idle Boy.*

The novels I like best myself—novels without love or talking, or any of that sort of nonsense, but containing plenty of fighting, escaping, robbery, and rescuing.

THACKERAY.

Figs are sweet, but fictions are sweeter.

THACKERAY.

1
They [realistic novelists] find life crude and leave it raw.

OSCAR WILDE, *The Decay of Lying.*

The only real people are the people who never existed.

OSCAR WILDE, *The Decay of Lying.*

2
Lady Hunstanton: I don't know how he made his money originally.
Kelvil: I fancy in American dry goods.
Lady Hunstanton: What are American dry goods?
Lord Illingworth: American novels.

WILDE, *A Woman of No Importance.* Act i.

3
The Peerage . . . is the best thing in fiction the English have ever done.

WILDE, *A Woman of No Importance.* Act iii.

4
The wicked nobleman of the transpontine melodrama or of penny dreadfuls.

EDMUND YATES. (*World,* London, 20 Aug., 1884.)

FIDELITY

See also Constancy; Love: Constant

5
This thing Allegiance, as I suppose,
Is a ring fitted in the subject's nose,
Whereby that organ is kept rightly pointed
To smell the sweetness of the Lord's anointed.

AMBROSE BIERCE, *The Devil's Dictionary,* p. 22.

6
Piteous, sad, wise, and true as steel.

CHAUCER, *Legend of Good Women.* Pt. ix, l. 21. (1385)

My heart Is true as steel.

SHAKESPEARE, *A Midsummer-Night's Dream.* Act ii, sc. 1, l. 196.

My man's as true as steel.

SHAKESPEARE, *Romeo and Juliet.* Act ii, sc. 4, l. 210.

As true as steel, as plantage to the moon,
As sun to day, as turtle to her mate,
As iron to adamant.

SHAKESPEARE, *Troilus and Cressida.* Act iii, sc. 2, l. 184.

See also CONSTANCY: THE NEEDLE AND THE POLE.

7
Who loves me, follows me! (Qui m'aime me suivre!)

FRANCIS I of France, at the battle of Marignano, 13 Sept., 1515.

If the ensigns fail you, rally to my white plume: you will always find it in the path of honor and victory!

HENRY IV of France, at the battle of Ivry, 14 March, 1590.

Press where ye see my white plume shine, amidst the ranks of war,
And be your oriflamme to-day the helmet of Navarre!

MACAULAY, *Ivry.*

If I advance, follow me! if I retreat, kill me! if I die, avenge me!

LA ROCHEJAQUELIN, in La Vendée, 1793.

8
For this proverb is ever new
That strong locks maken true.

JOHN GOWER, *Confessio Amantis.* Pt. v.

9
Many free countries have lost their liberty, and ours may lose hers: but if she shall, be it my proudest plume, not that I was the last to desert, but that I never deserted her.

ABRAHAM LINCOLN, *Speech,* Springfield, Ill., Dec., 1839.

10
The fidelity of barbarians depends on fortune. (Barbaris ex fortuna pendet fides.)

LIVY, *Annals.* Bk. xxviii, ch. 42.

11
Fidelity's a virtue that ennobles
E'en servitude itself.

WILLIAM MASON, *Elfrida.*

12
So spake the seraph Abdiel, faithful found,
Among the faithless faithful only he.

MILTON, *Paradise Lost.* Bk. v, l. 893.

13
There are two kinds of fidelity, that of dogs and that of cats: you, gentlemen, have the fidelity of cats, who never leave the house.

NAPOLEON BONAPARTE, to de Ségur and others who met him at the Tuileries on his return from Elba and assured him of their fidelity.

14
Abra was ready ere I called her name;
And, though I called another, Abra came.

MATTHEW PRIOR, *Solomon.* Bk. ii, l. 362.

15
Be thou faithful unto death.

New Testament: Revelation, ii, 10.

Faithful unto death. (Fidelis ad urnam.)

UNKNOWN. A Latin proverb.

16
It is better to be faithful than famous.

THEODORE ROOSEVELT. (RIIS, *Theodore Roosevelt, the Citizen,* p. 403.)

17
Fidelity gained by bribes is overcome by bribes. (Pretio parata vincitur pretio fides.)

SENECA, *Agamemnon,* l. 287.

Prosperity asks for fidelity; adversity exacts it. (Fidem secunda poscunt, adversa exigunt.)

SENECA, *Agamemnon,* l. 934.

18
He who has been able to say, "Neptune, you shall never sink this ship except on an even keel," has fulfilled the requirements of his art.

SENECA, *Epistulæ ad Lucilium.* Epis. lxxxv, 33.

The ancient sailor said this to Neptune in a great

storm, "O God, thou shalt save me if thou please, if not, thou shalt lose me; yet will I keep my rudder true."

MONTAIGNE, *Essays*. Bk. ii, ch. 16.

1
Loyalty is the holiest good in the human heart. (Fides sanctissimum humani pectoris bonum est.)

SENECA, *Epistulæ ad Lucilium*. Epis. 88, 29.

2
The loyalty well held to fools does make
Our faith mere folly: yet he that can endure
To follow with allegiance a fall'n lord
Does conquer him that did his master conquer,
And earns a place i' the story.

SHAKESPEARE, *Antony and Cleopatra*. Act iii, sc. 13, l. 42.

O, where is loyalty?
If it be banish'd from the frosty head,
Where shall it find a harbour in the earth?

SHAKESPEARE, *II Henry VI*. Act v, sc. 1, l. 166.

3
Master, go on, and I will follow thee,
To the last gasp, with truth and loyalty.

SHAKESPEARE, *As You Like It*. Act ii, sc. 3, l. 69.

Set on your foot,
And with a heart new-fir'd I follow you,
To do I know not what.

SHAKESPEARE, *Julius Cæsar*. Act ii, sc. 1, l. 331.

And all my fortunes at thy foot I'll lay,
And follow thee my lord throughout the world.

SHAKESPEARE, *Romeo and Juliet*. Act ii, sc. 2, l. 147.

4
That, sire, is a question of dates.

TALLEYRAND, to Alexander of Russia, when the latter spoke to him of fidelity. (COOPER, *Talleyrand*.)

5
Faithful Achates. (Fidus Achates.)

VERGIL, *Æneid*. Bk. vi, l. 158, and elsewhere. Achates was the faithful companion of Æneas.

FIG

6
Train up a fig-tree in the way it should go, and when you are old sit under the shade of it.

DICKENS, *Dombey and Son*. Bk. i, ch. 19.

7
Full on its crown, a fig's green branches rise,
And shoot a leafy forest to the skies.

HOMER, *Odyssey*. Bk. xii, l. 125. (Pope, tr.)

8
And Judah and Israel dwelt safely, every man under his vine and under his fig tree.

Old Testament: I Kings, iv, 25.

9
So counsel'd he, and both together went
Into the thickest wood; there soon they chose
The fig-tree, not that kind for fruit renown'd,
But such as at this day to Indians known
In Malabar or Decan spreads her arms
Branching so broad and long, that in the ground
The bended twigs take root, and daughters grow
About the mother tree, a pillar'd shade
High overarch'd, and echoing walks between.

MILTON, *Paradise Lost*. Bk. ix, l. 1099.

10
All thy strongholds shall be like fig trees with the first ripe figs: if they be shaken, they shall even fall into the mouth of the eater.

Old Testament: Nahum, iii, 12.

11
Peel a fig for your friend, a peach for your enemy.

JOHN RAY, *English Proverbs*.

12
In the name of the Prophet—figs!

HORACE AND JAMES SMITH, *Johnson's Ghost*.

FIGHTING

See also War

13
Distrust yourself, and sleep before you fight.
'Tis not too late to-morrow to be brave.

JOHN ARMSTRONG, *Art of Preserving Health*. Bk. iv, l. 456.

14
No, when the fight begins within himself,
A man's worth something.

ROBERT BROWNING, *Bishop Blougram's Apology*.

15
With many a stiff thwack, many a bang,
Hard crab-tree and old iron rang.

BUTLER, *Hudibras*. Pt. i, canto ii, l. 831.

'Twas blow for blow, disputing inch by inch,
For one would not retreat, nor t'other flinch.

BYRON, *Don Juan*. Canto viii, st. 77.

16
What can alone ennoble fight? A noble cause!

THOMAS CAMPBELL, *Hallowed Ground*, l. 41.

17
Do not fight against two adversaries. (Noli pugnare duobus.)

CATULLUS, *Odes*. No. lxii, l. 64.

18
So fight I, not as one that beateth the air.

New Testament: I Corinthians, ix, 26.

Without were fightings, within were fears.

New Testament: II Corinthians, vii, 5.

19
And the combat ceased, for want of combatants. (Et le combat cessa, faute de combattants.)

CORNEILLE, *Le Cid*. Act iv, sc. 3.

20
'Tis easier far to flourish than to fight.

DRYDEN, *The Hind and the Panther*. Pt. iii, l. 202.

21
I, too, am fighting my campaign.

EMERSON, *Journal*, 1864.

22
Away he scours and lays about him,

Resolved no fray should be without him.
JOHN GAY, *Fables*. Pt. i, No. 34.

1
We fight to great disadvantage when we fight with those who have nothing to lose. (Con disavvantaggio grande si fa la guerra con chi non ha che perdere.)
GUICCIARDINI, *Storia d'Italia*.

2
He smote them hip and thigh with a great slaughter.
Old Testament: Judges, xv, 8.

Abner . . . smote him under the fifth rib.
Old Testament: II Samuel, ii, 23.

Gregory, remember thy swashing blow.
SHAKESPEARE, *Romeo and Juliet*. Act i, sc. 1, l. 69.

3
As we wax hot in faction,
In battle we wax cold;
Wherefore men fight not as they fought
In the brave days of old.
MACAULAY, *Horatius*. St. 33.

4
For of thy slaying nowise are we fain,
If we may pass unfoughten.
WILLIAM MORRIS, *Life and Death of Jason*. Bk. ix, l. 368.

5
The fight is over when the enemy is down. (Pugna suum finem, quum jacet hostia, habet.)
OVID, *Tristia*. Bk. iii, eleg. 5, l. 34.

7
To fight is a radical instinct; if men have nothing else to fight over they will fight over words, fancies, or women, or they will fight because they dislike each other's looks, or because they have met walking in opposite directions. To knock a thing down, especially if it is cocked at an arrogant angle, is a deep delight to the blood.
GEORGE SANTAYANA, *Soliloquies in England: On War*.

8
Hath his bellyful of fighting.
SHAKESPEARE, *Cymbeline*. Act ii, sc. 1, l. 21.

He which hath no stomach to this fight,
Let him depart; his passport shall be made.
SHAKESPEARE, *Henry V*. Act iv, sc. 3, l. 35.

9
We must have bloody noses and crack'd crowns,
And pass them current too. God's me, my horse!
SHAKESPEARE, *I Henry IV*. Act ii, sc. 3, l. 96.

10
They have tied me to a stake; I cannot fly,
But, bear-like, I must fight the course.
SHAKESPEARE, *Macbeth*. Act v, sc. 7, l. 1.

I am tied to the stake, and I must stand the course.
SHAKESPEARE, *King Lear*. Act iii, sc. 7, l. 54.

11
By a sudden and adroit movement I placed my left eye agin the Secesher's fist. . . . The ground flew up and hit me in the hed.
ARTEMUS WARD, *Thrilling Scenes in Dixie*.

12
There is such a thing as a man being too proud to fight.
WOODROW WILSON, *Address*, Philadelphia, 10 May, 1915. *See under* AMERICA: FAMILIAR PHRASES.

13
Fight on, my men, Sir Andrew says,
A little I'm hurt, but yet not slain;
I'll but lie down and bleed awhile,
And then I'll rise and fight again.
UNKNOWN. *Ballad of Sir Andrew Barton*.

FINANCE

See also Business, Dividends, Money

14
The plain high-road of finance.
EDMUND BURKE, *On American Taxation*.

15
The cohesive power of the vast surplus in the banks.
JOHN C. CALHOUN, *Speech*, U. S. Senate, 27 May, 1836. See 2048:8.

Cohesive power of public plunder.
GROVER CLEVELAND, paraphrasing Calhoun.

16
Great is Bankruptcy: the great bottomless gulf into which all Falsehoods, public and private, do sink, disappearing.
CARLYLE, *The French Revolution*. Vol. i, bk. 3, ch. 1.

17
They throw cats and dogs together and call them elephants.
ANDREW CARNEGIE, *Interview*. Referring to industrial promoters.

What are fantastically termed securities.
S. WEIR MITCHELL, *Characteristics*. Ch. 2.

18
The communism of combined wealth and capital, the outgrowth of overweening cupidity and selfishness which assiduously undermines the justice and integrity of free institutions, is not less dangerous than the communism of oppressed poverty and toil which, exasperated by injustice and discontent, attacks with wild disorder the citadel of misrule.
GROVER CLEVELAND, *Annual Message*. (1888)

19
What good, honest, generous men at home will be wolves and foxes on change!
EMERSON, *Conduct of Life: Fate*.

20
In saucy pride the griping broker sits,
And laughs at honesty and trudging wits.
JOHN GAY, *Trivia*. Bk. i, l. 117.

Where are the c-c-c-customers' yachts?
WILLIAM R. TRAVERS, on being shown a squadron of brokers' yachts in New York harbor. (HENRY CLEWS, *Fifty Years in Wall Street*, p. 416.)

2
This bank-note world.
FITZ-GREENE HALLECK, *Alnwick Castle.*

3
Should all the banks of Europe crash,
The bank of England smash,
Bring all your notes to Zion's bank,
You're sure to get your cash.
HENRY HOYT, *Zion's Bank, or Bible Promises: Secured to All Believers.* (Boston, 1857.)

4
I sincerely believe that banking establishments are more dangerous than standing armies, and that the principle of spending money to be paid by posterity, under the name of funding, is but swindling futurity on a large scale.
THOMAS JEFFERSON, *Letter to Elbridge Gerry*, 26 Jan., 1799.

5
One-third of the people in the United States promote, while the other two-thirds provide.
WILL ROGERS, *The Illiterate Digest*, p. 121.

6
Let him look to his bond.
SHAKESPEARE, *The Merchant of Venice*, iii, 1, 52.

7
Banks are failing all over the country, but not the sand banks, solid and warm and streaked with bloody blackberry vines. You may run on them as much as you please, even as the crickets do, and find their account in it. They are the stockholders in these banks, and I hear them creaking their content. In these banks, too, and such as these, are my funds deposited, funds of health and enjoyment. Invest in these country banks. Let your capital be simplicity and contentment.
H. D. THOREAU, *Journal*, 14 Oct., 1859.

8
The way to stop financial joy-riding is to arrest the chauffeur, not the automobile.
WOODROW WILSON. (LINTHICUM, *Wit and Wisdom of Woodrow Wilson.*)

FINGERS

8a
Why are the fingers tapered like pegs? So that when one hears improper language he may insert them in his ears.
Babylonian Talmud: Kethuboth, fo. 5b.

9
His fingers made of lime-twigs.
SIR JOHN HARINGTON, *Metamorphoses of Ajax.*

10
Do not put your finger in too tight a ring.
W. G. BENHAM, *Proverbs*, p. 752.

Between the tree and your finger do not put the bark. (Entre l'arbre et le doigt il ne faut point mettre l'écorce.)
MOLIÈRE, *Le Médicin Malgré Lui.* Act i, sc. 2.

11
To put my finger too far in the fire.
JOHN HEYWOOD, *Proverbs.* Pt. ii, ch. 2.

12
When he should get aught, each finger is a thumb.
JOHN HEYWOOD, *Proverbs.* Pt. ii, ch. 5. (1546)

When he should work, all his fingers are thumbs.
JAMES HOWELL, *Proverbs*, 5. (1659)

13
I will be the finger next thy thumb.
JOHN LYLY, *Euphues*, p. 68. (1579)

You two are finger and thumb.
JAMES HOWELL, *Proverbs*, 13. (1659)

14
By these ten bones, my lord.
SHAKESPEARE, *II Henry VI.* Act i, sc. 3, l. 193.

15
And he hath cut those pretty fingers off,
That could have better sew'd than Philomel.
SHAKESPEARE, *Titus Andronicus.* Act ii, sc. 4, l. 42.

16
I have them at my fingers' ends.
SHAKESPEARE, *Twelfth Night.* Act i, sc. 3, l. 82.

Every schoolboy hath that famous testament of Grunnius Corocotta Porcellus at his fingers' ends.
ROBERT BURTON, *Anatomy of Melancholy.* Pt. iii, sec. i, mem. 1, subs. 1.

17
She locks her lily fingers one in one.
SHAKESPEARE, *Venus and Adonis*, l. 228.

18
Or else her ten commandments
She fastens on his face.
UNKNOWN, *Philip and Mary.* (c. 1560)

Could I come near your dainty visage with my nails,
I'd set my ten commandments in your face.
UNKNOWN, *First Part Contention*, p. 16. (1594)

Could I come near your beauty with my nails,
I'ld set my ten commandments in your face.
SHAKESPEARE, *II Henry VI.* Act i, sc. 3, l. 144.

FIRE

19
If you light your fire at both ends, the middle will shift for itself.
ADDISON, *The Spectator.* No. 265. Called "the old kitchen proverb."

20
For men say oft that fire nor pride
But discovering, may no man hide.
JOHN BARBOUR, *Bruce.* Bk. iv, l. 119. (c. 1375)

21
Heap logs and let the blaze laugh out!
ROBERT BROWNING, *Paracelsus.* Pt. iii, l. 1.

No spectacle is nobler than a blaze.
SAMUEL JOHNSON, *Works.* Vol. ii, p. 228.

The garnered fervors of forgotten Junes
Flare forth again and waste away.
DON MARQUIS, *An Open Fire.*

A fair fire makes a room gay.
JOHN RAY, *English Proverbs.*

1
The hand that kindles cannot quench the flame.
BYRON, *Lara*. Canto ii, st. 11.

2
Yet in our asshen old is fire y-reke.
CHAUCER, *The Reeve's Prologue*, l. 28. "Y-reke" means "raked together."

E'en in our ashes live our wonted fires.
GRAY, *Elegy in a Country Churchyard*. St. 23.

The fire which seems extinguished often slumbers beneath the ashes. (Le feu qui semble éteint souvent dort sous la cendre.)
CORNEILLE, *Rodogune*. Act iii, sc. 4.

3
To take fire from fire. (Ab igne ignem capere.)
CICERO, *De Officiis*. Bk. i, ch. 16, sec. 52. Quoted as a proverb.

4
Bright-flaming, heat-full fire,
The source of motion.
DU BARTAS, *Devine Weekes and Workes*. Wk. i, day 2. (Sylvester, tr.)

Heat, Considered as a Mode of Motion.
JOHN TYNDALL. Title of treatise. (1863)

5
The nearer the fire, the hotter.
EGBERT OF LIÈGE, *Fecunda Ratis;* CHAUCER, *Troilus*, i, 449.

6
Who makes a fire of straw hath much smoke and naught else.
JOHN FLORIO, *First Fruites*. Fo. 28. (1578)

Those that with haste will make a mighty fire,
Begin it with weak straws.
SHAKESPEARE, *Julius Cæsar*. Act i, sc. 3, l. 107.

7
Fire and flax agree not.
JOHN FLORIO, *First Fruites*. Fo. 30. (1578)

For he is fire and flax.
BEAUMONT AND FLETCHER, *Elder Brother*, i, 2.

There's danger in assembling fire and tow.
POPE, *The Wife of Bath's Prologue*, l. 30.

8
[He] won't set fire to the Thames, though he lives near the Bridge.
SAMUEL FOOTE, *The Trip to Calais*. Act iii, sc. 3. (c. 1770) This is the first known appearance in literature of a saying which was in common use thereafter. It is alleged (and disputed, *N. & Q.*, vi, ix, 14) that it dates back to the fifteenth century and has nothing to do with the river Thames, but with "temse," a sieve made of horsehair, used for sifting grain. Good workers would sieve so vigorously that sometimes the friction would cause the horsehair to smoulder, but a lazy worker would never set the temse on fire.

9
Fire and People do in this agree,
They both good servants, both ill masters be.
FULKE GREVILLE, *Inquisition upon Fame*.

11
What ye cannot quench, pull down;
Spoil a house to save a town.
Better 'tis that one should fall
Then by one to hazard all.
ROBERT HERRICK, *The Scare-fire*.

12
Make no fire, raise no smoke.
JOHN HEYWOOD, *Proverbs*. Pt. ii, ch. 5.

Youk'n hide de fier, but w'at you gwine do wid de smoke?
JOEL CHANDLER HARRIS, *Plantation Proverbs*.

13
To throw oil on the fire. (Oleum adde camino.)
HORACE, *Satires*. Bk. ii, sat. 3, l. 21. To add fuel to the flames.

You add flames to flame, and waters to the sea. (In flammam flammas, in mare fundis aquas.)
OVID, *Amores*. Bk. iii, eleg. 2, l. 34.

14
Fire is put out by fire. (Incendium ignibus exstinguitur.)
MONTAIGNE, *Essays*. Bk. iii, ch. 5. Quoted.

15
The more the fire is covered up, the more it burns. (Quoque magis tegitur, tectus magis æstuat ignis.)
OVID, *Metamorphoses*. Bk. iv, l. 64.

Fire that's closest kept burns most of all.
SHAKESPEARE, *The Two Gentlemen of Verona*. Act i, sc. 2, l. 30.

16
Kneel always when you light a fire!
Kneel reverently and thankful be
For God's unfailing charity.
JOHN OXENHAM, *The Sacrament of Fire*.

17
While I was musing the fire burned.
Old Testament: Psalms, xxxix, 3.

18
Better a little fire that warms than a big one that burns.
JOHN RAY, *English Proverbs*.

19
By wind is a fire fostered, and by wind extinguished; a gentle breeze fans the flame, a strong breeze kills it. (Nutritur vento, vento restinguitur ignis: Lenis alit flammas, grandior aura necat.)
OVID, *Remediorum Amoris*, l. 807.

Small lights are soon blown out, huge fires abide,
And with the wind in greater fury fret.
SHAKESPEARE, *The Rape of Lucrece*, l. 647.

20
There is no smoke without fire. (Flamma fumo est proxima.)
PLAUTUS, *Curculio*, l. 53. (Act i, sc. 1.)

There can no great smoke arise, but there must be some fire, no great report without great suspicion.
JOHN LYLY, *Euphues*, p. 153. (1579)

21
A small spark neglected has often kindled a mighty conflagration. (Parva sæpe scintilla contemptu magnum excitavit incendium.)
QUINTUS CURTIUS RUFUS, *De Rebus Gestis Alexandri Magni*. Bk. vi, sec. 3, l. 11.

I rose, and shook my clothes, as knowing well
That from small fires comes oft no small mishap.
GEORGE HERBERT, *Artillerie*.

Behold, how great a matter a little fire kindleth!
New Testament: James, iii, 5.

A little fire is quickly trodden out,
Which, being suffer'd, rivers cannot quench.
SHAKESPEARE, *III Henry VI*. Act iv, sc. 8, l. 7.

1
Tut, man, one fire burns out another's burning.
SHAKESPEARE, *Romeo and Juliet*. Act i, sc. 2, l. 46.

Whose desire
Was all this while, by fire, to draw out fire.
FRANCIS QUARLES, *Works*. Vol. iii, p. 267.

Fire will fetch out fire.
SIR JOHN VANBRUGH, *The Mistake*. Act iii, sc. 1.

And where two raging fires meet together,
They do consume the thing that feeds their fury:
Though little fire grows great with little wind,
Yet extreme gusts will blow out fire and all.
SHAKESPEARE, *The Taming of the Shrew*. Act ii, sc. 1, l. 133.

2
The fire i' the flint
Shows not till it be struck.
SHAKESPEARE, *Timon of Athens*. Act i, sc. 1, l. 22.

An opal holds a fiery spark,
But a flint holds fire.
CHRISTINA ROSSETTI, *The Flint*.

3
Out of the frying-pan into the fire. (Pervenimus igitur de calcaria (quod dici solet) in carbonariam.)
TERTULLIAN, *De Carne Christi*. Ch. 6.

Leap they like a flounder out of a frying-pan into the fire.
SIR THOMAS MORE, *Works*, p. 179. (1528)

Some of the ditch shy are, yet can
Lie tumbling in the mire:
Some, though they shun the frying-pan,
Do leap into the fire.
JOHN BUNYAN, *The Pilgrim's Progress*. Pt. ii.

4
Fire is the most tolerable third party.
H. D. THOREAU, *Journal*. (EMERSON, *Thoreau*.)

Light-winged smoke, Icarian bird,
Melting thy pinions in thy upward flight;
Lark without song, and messenger of dawn . . .
Go thou, my incense, upward from this hearth,
And ask the gods to pardon this clear flame.
H. D. THOREAU, *Smoke*.

Burn, wood, burn—
Wood that once was a tree, and knew
Blossom and sheaf, and the Spring's return,
Nest, and singing, and rain, and dew—
Burn, wood, burn!
NANCY BYRD TURNER, *Flame Song*.

5
Man is the animal that has made friends with the fire.
HENRY VAN DYKE, *Fisherman's Luck*. Ch. 11.

6
In the stubble a great fire rages in vain. (In stipulis magnus sine viribus ignis, Incassum furit.)
VERGIL, *Georgics*. Bk. iii, l. 99.

7
We go through both fire and water.
UNKNOWN, *Vesp. Psalter*, lxv, 12. (c. 825)

He shall pass through fire and water or he get it.
JOHN PALSGRAVE, *L'Éclairs. Langue Française*, 653. (1530)

A woman would run through fire and water for such a kind heart.
SHAKESPEARE, *The Merry Wives of Windsor*. Act iii, sc. 4, l. 107. (1600)

FIREFLY

8
I saw, one sultry night above a swamp,
The darkness throbbing with their golden pomp.
EDGAR FAWCETT, *Fireflies*.

9
Little lamps of the dusk,
You fly low and gold
When the summer evening
Starts to unfold.
CAROLYN HALL, *Fireflies*.

10
Before, beside us, and above
The firefly lights his lamp of love.
REGINALD HEBER, *Tour Through Ceylon*.

11
The fireflies dance thro' the myrtle boughs.
FELICIA DOROTHEA HEMANS, *The Better Land*.

12
Tiny Salmoneus of the air,
His mimic bolts the firefly threw.
J. R. LOWELL, *The Lesson*.

FIRMAMENT, see Sky

FISH and FISHING

I—Fish: Apothegms

13
The whales, you see, eat up the little fish.
THOMAS CHURCHYARD, *Chippes*, 145. (1575)

Third Fisherman: Master, I marvel how the fishes live in the sea.
First Fisherman: Why, as men do a-land: the great ones eat up the little ones.
SHAKESPEARE, *Pericles*. Act ii, sc. 1, l. 29. (1608)

Men lived like fishes; the greater ones devoured the small.
ALGERNON SIDNEY, *Discourses on Government*. Ch. ii, sec. 18. (1698)

14
A sly old fish, too cunning for the hook.
GEORGE CRABBE, *The Parish Register*. Pt. ii.

15
All is fish that cometh to net.
JOHN HEYWOOD, *Proverbs*. Pt. i, ch. 2.

All's fish they get that cometh to net.
THOMAS TUSSER, *Hundreth Pointes of Good Husbandrie: February Abstract*.

But Death is sure to kill all he can get,
And all is fish with him that comes to net.
UNKNOWN. (*Witts Recreations*. Ep. 644.)

16
The fishermen could perhaps be bought for less than the fish. (Potuit fortasse minoris Piscator quam piscis emi.)
JUVENAL, *Satires*. Sat. iv, l. 26.

1
All fish are not caught with flies.
JOHN LYLY, *Euphues*, p. 350.

2
The fish, once wounded by the treacherous hook,
Fancies the barb concealed in every food.
(Qui semel est læsus fallaci piscis ab hamo,
Omnibus unca cibis aera subesse putat.)
OVID, *Epistulæ ex Ponto*. Bk. ii, epis. 7, l. 9.

The fish once caught, new bait will hardly bite.
SPENSER, *Faerie Queene*. Bk. ii, canto i, st. 4.

3
We have other fish to fry.
RABELAIS, *Works*. Bk. v, ch. 12. (1552)

I have other fish to fry.
CERVANTES, *Don Quixote*. Pt. ii, ch. 35. (1615)

He hath other fish to fry.
JOHN EVELYN, *Diary*. Vol. iii, p. 132. In frequent use thereafter.

4
No human being, however great, or powerful, was ever so free as a fish.
JOHN RUSKIN, *The Two Paths*. Lecture 5.

5
It's no fish ye're buying; it's men's lives.
SCOTT, *The Antiquary*. Ch. 11.

It is not linen you're wearing out,
But human creatures' lives.
HOOD, *The Song of the Shirt*.

Wha'll buy my caller herrin'?
They're no brought here without brave darin'. . . .
O you may ca' them vulgar farin',
Wives and mithers, maist despairin',
Ca' them lives o' men.
LADY CAROLINA NAIRNE, *Caller Herrin'*.

6
There are as good fish in the sea as ever came out of it.
SCOTT, *Fortunes of Nigel*. Ch. 35.

There's fish in the sea, no doubt of it,
As good as ever came out of it.
W. S. GILBERT, *Patience*. Act i.

Oh, you who've been a-fishing will endorse me when I say
That it always *is* the biggest fish you catch that gets away!
EUGENE FIELD, *Our Biggest Fish*.

7
Here comes the trout that must be caught with tickling.
SHAKESPEARE, *Twelfth Night*. Act ii, sc. 5, l. 24.

8
It was thought she was a woman and was turned into a cold fish.
SHAKESPEARE, *Winter's Tale*. Act iv, sc. 4, 284.

A strange fish!
SHAKESPEARE, *The Tempest*. Act ii, sc. 2, l. 28.

9
Like a fish out of water. (Sicut piscis sine aqua caret vita.)
SOZOMEN, *Ecclesiastical History*. Bk. i, ch. 13. Attributed to a Pope Eugenius. Also in *Life of St. Anthony*, attributed to St. Athanasius. (c. 85) See also PETRARCH, *Sonnet 58;* SHADWELL, *True Widow*, iii, 1; DEFOE, *Roxana;* READE, *Cloister and the Hearth*. Ch. 31.

10
They say fish should swim thrice . . . first it should swim in the sea (do you mind me?), then it should swim in butter, and at last, sirrah, it should swim in good claret.
SWIFT, *Polite Conversation*. Dial. ii.

II—Fish and Flesh

11
I will not make fish of one and flesh of another.
JOHN CLARKE, *Parœmiologia*, 182. (1639)

12
Fish marreth the water, and flesh doth dress it.
JOHN FLORIO, *First Fruites*. Fo. 29. (1578)

13
Why, she's neither fish nor flesh; a man knows not where to have her.
SHAKESPEARE, *I Henry IV*. Act iii, sc. 3, l. 144.

O flesh, flesh, how art thou fishified!
SHAKESPEARE, *Romeo and Juliet*. Act ii, sc. 4, l. 39.

14
One that is neither flesh nor fish.
UNKNOWN, *Rede Me and be Not Wrothe*, i, 3. (1528)

Neither fish, nor flesh, nor good red herring.
JOHN HEYWOOD, *Proverbs*. Pt. i, ch. 10. (1546)
In frequent use thereafter.

Damn'd neuters, in their middle way of steering,
Are neither fish, nor flesh, nor good red herring.
DRYDEN, *Duke of Guise: Epilogue*, l. 39.

III—Fish and Bait

15
That fish will soon be caught that nibbles at every bait.
THOMAS FULLER, *Gnomologia*. No. 4342.

The fish adores the bait.
GEORGE HERBERT, *Jacula Prudentum*.

The tender nibbler would not touch the bait.
SHAKESPEARE [?], *Passionate Pilgrim*, l. 53.

16
You must lose a fly to catch a trout.
GEORGE HERBERT, *Jacula Prudentum*.

For you catch your next fish with a piece of the last.
O. W. HOLMES, *Verses for After Dinner*.

17
Your bait of falsehood takes this carp of truth.
SHAKESPEARE. *Hamlet*, Act ii, sc. 1, l. 63.

Bait the hook well; this fish will bite.
SHAKESPEARE, *Much Ado About Nothing*. Act ii, sc. 3, l. 114.

19
But fish not, with this melancholy bait,
For this fool gudgeon, this opinion.
SHAKESPEARE, *The Merchant of Venice*. Act i, sc. 1, l. 101.

1
Sweet innocent, the mother cried,
And started from her nook,
That horrid fly is put to hide
The sharpness of the hook.
ANN AND JANE TAYLOR, *The Little Fish that Would Not Do as It Was Bid.*

IV—Fish: Description

2
God quickened in the Sea and in the Rivers,
So many fishes of so many features,
That in the waters we may see all Creatures;
Even all that on the earth is to be found,
As if the world were in deep waters drowned.
DU BARTAS, *Devine Weekes and Workes.* Wk. i, day 5.

3
Here when the labouring fish does at the foot arrive,
And finds that by his strength but vainly he doth strive;
His tail takes in his teeth, and bending like a bow,
That's to the compass drawn, aloft himself doth throw:
Then springing at his height, as doth a little wand,
That, bended end to end, and flirted from the hand,
Far off itself doth cast, so does the salmon vaut.
And if at first he fail, his second summer-saut
He instantly assays and from his nimble ring,
Still yarking never leaves, until himself he fling
Above the streamful top of the surrounded heap.
MICHAEL DRAYTON, *Poly-Olbion.* Song vi, l. 45.

4
Now at the close of the soft summer's day,
Inclined upon the river's flowery side,
I pause to see the sportive fishes play,
And cut with finny oars the sparkling tide.
THOMAS FOSTER, *Perennial Calendar.*

5
O scaly, slippery, wet, swift, staring wights,
What is 't ye do? what life lead? eh, dull goggles?
How do you vary your vile days and nights?
How pass your Sundays?
LEIGH HUNT, *Fish, the Man, and the Spirit.*

6
Ye monsters of the bubbling deep,
Your Maker's praises spout;
Up from the sands ye codlings peep,
And wag your tails about.
COTTON MATHER, *Hymn.*

7
Our plenteous streams a various race supply,
The bright-eyed perch with fins of Tyrian dye,
The silver eel, in shining volumes roll'd,
The yellow carp, in scales bedropp'd with gold,
Swift trouts, diversified with crimson stains,
And pikes, the tyrants of the wat'ry plains.
POPE, *Windsor Forest,* l. 141.

'Tis true, no turbots dignify my boards.
But gudgeons, flounders, what my Thames affords.
POPE, *Imitations of Horace: Satires,* ii, 2, 141.

Inch for inch and pound for pound, the gamest fish that swims.
JAMES A. HENSHALL, *Book of the Black Bass,* p. 380. (1881) Referring to the black bass. Sometimes wrongly ascribed to Henry Van Dyke.

V—Fishing: Apothegms

8
There's no taking trout with dry breeches.
CERVANTES, *Don Quixote.* Pt. ii, ch. 71.

9
Still he fishes that catches one.
THOMAS FULLER, *Gnomologia.* No. 4262.

The end of fishing is not angling, but catching.
THOMAS FULLER, *Gnomologia.* No. 4497.

The end of fishing is catching.
JOHN LYLY, *Euphues,* p. 396. (1580)

10
He has well fished and caught a frog.
JOHN HEYWOOD, *Proverbs.* Pt. i, ch. 11. (1546)

The man that weds for greedy wealth,
He goes a fishing fair,
But often times he gets a frog,
Or very little share.
UNKNOWN, *Pepysian Garland,* 318. (1629)

11
They may the better fish in the water when it is troubled.
RICHARD GRAFTON, *Chronicles,* i, 283. (1569)

Best fishing in troubled waters.
HARINGTON, *Orlando Furioso.* Bk. xli. (1591)

To fish in troubled waters.
MATTHEW HENRY, *Commentaries. Psalm lx.*

For trouts are tickled best in muddy water.
SAMUEL BUTLER, *On a Hypocritical Nonconformist.* St. 4.

12
See how he throws his baited lines about,
And plays his men as anglers play their trout.
O. W. HOLMES, *The Banker's Secret.*

13
Canst thou draw out leviathan with a hook?
Old Testament: Job, xli, 1.

For angling-rod he took a sturdy oak;
For line, a cable that in storm ne'er broke; . . .
The hook was baited with a dragon's tail,—
And then on rock he stood to bob for whale.
SIR WILLIAM D'AVENANT, *Britannia Triumphans,* p. 16. (1637) This quatrain appeared in *The Mock Romance,* a rhapsody attached to *The Loves of Hero and Leander* (London, 1677), without ascription of authorship. In CHALMERS, *British Poets,* it was ascribed to William King, under the title, *Upon a Giant's Angling.*

14
Simon Peter saith unto them, I go a fishing.

They say unto him, We also go with thee.
New Testament: John, xxi, 3. Used as motto on the title page of the first edition of Walton's *Compleat Angler*.

The apostolic occupation of trafficking in fish.
SYDNEY SMITH, *Third Letter to Archdeacon Singleton*.

The first men that our Saviour dear
Did choose to wait upon Him here,
Blest fishers were; and fish the last
Food was, that He on earth did taste:
I therefore strive to follow those,
Whom He to follow Him hath chose.
IZAAK WALTON, *The Compleat Angler: The Angler's Song*.

1
Can the fish love the fisherman? (Piscatorem piscis amare potest?)
MARTIAL, *Epigrams*. Bk. vi, epig. 63, l. 5.

2
He who holds the hook is aware in what waters many fish are swimming. (Qui sustinet hamos, Novit, quæ multo pisce natentur aquæ.)
OVID, *Ars Amatoria*. Bk. i, l. 47.

Ever let your hook be hanging; where you least believe it, there will be a fish in the stream. (Semper tibi pendeat hamus: Quo minime credas gurgite, piscis erit.)
OVID, *Ars Amatoria*. Bk. iii, l. 425.

3
Angling: incessant expectation, and perpetual disappointment.
ARTHUR YOUNG, *Travels in France*, 16 Sept., 1787.

Never a fisherman need there be
If fishes could hear as well as see.
UNKNOWN. (*Notes and Queries*. Ser. iv, ii, 94.)

4
When the wind is in the east,
Then the fishes bite the least;
When the wind is in the west,
Then the fishes bite the best;
When the wind is in the north,
Then the fishes do come forth;
When the wind is in the south,
It blows the bait in the fish's mouth.
UNKNOWN, *Old Rhyme*. (J. O. HALLIWELL, *Popular Rhymes*.)

I shall stay him no longer than to wish . . . that if he be an honest angler, the east wind may never blow when he goes a fishing.
IZAAK WALTON, *The Compleat Angler: To the Reader*.

VI—Fishing: Its Delights

5
A rod twelve feet long and a ring of wire,
A winder and barrel, will help thy desire
In killing a Pike; but the forked stick,
With a slit and a bladder,—and that other fine trick,
Which our artists call snap, with a goose or a duck,—
Will kill two for one, if you have any luck.
THOMAS BARKER, *The Art of Angling*.

6
Of all the world's enjoyments
That ever valued were,
There's none of our employments
With fishing can compare.
THOMAS D'URFEY, *Pills to Purge Melancholy: Massaniello: Fisherman's Song*.

7
When if or chance or hunger's powerful sway
Directs the roving trout this fatal way,
He greedily sucks in the twining bait,
And tugs and nibbles the fallacious meat.
Now, happy fisherman; now twitch the line!
How thy rod bends! behold, the prize is thine!
JOHN GAY, *Rural Sports*. Canto i, l. 150.

8
A fishing-rod is a stick with a hook at one end and a fool at the other.
SAMUEL JOHNSON. (HAZLITT, *Essays: On Egotism*.) Also ascribed to Dean Swift.

Fly fishing is a very pleasant amusement; but angling or float fishing, I can only compare to a stick and a string, with a worm at one end and a fool at the other.
SAMUEL JOHNSON. (HAWKER, *On Worm Fishing*.) Not found in Johnson's works. (See *Notes and Queries*, 11 Dec., 1915.)

The line with its rod is a long instrument whose lesser end holds a small reptile, while the other is held by a great fool.
(La ligne avec sa canne est un long instrument,
Dont le plus mince bout tient un petit reptile,
Et dont l'autre est tenu par un grand imbecile.)
Alleged to have been written by a French poet of the 17th century named Guyet.

9
Down and back at day dawn,
Tramp from lake to lake,
Washing brain and heart clean
Every step we take.
Leave to Robert Browning
Beggars, fleas, and vines;
Leave to mournful Ruskin
Popish Apennines,
Dirty stones of Venice,
And his gas lamps seven,
We've the stones of Snowdon
And the lamps of heaven.
CHARLES KINGSLEY, *Letters and Memories*, Aug., 1856.

10
In genial Spring, beneath the quiv'ring shade,
When cooling vapours breathe along the mead,
The patient fisher takes his silent stand,
Intent, his angle trembling in his hand:
With looks unmov'd, he hopes the scaly breed,
And eyes the dancing cork and bending reed.
POPE, *Windsor Forest*, l. 135.

11
Give me mine angle; we'll to the river: there,
My music playing far off, I will betray
Tawny-finn'd fishes; my bended hook shall pierce

Their slimy jaws.
SHAKESPEARE, *Antony and Cleopatra.* Act ii, sc. 5, l. 10.

'T was merry when
You wager'd on your angling; when your diver
Did hang a salt-fish on his hook, which he
With fervency drew up.
SHAKESPEARE, *Antony and Cleopatra.* Act ii, sc. 5, l. 15.

1
The pleasant'st angling is to see the fish
Cut with her golden oars the silver stream,
And greedily devour the treacherous bait.
SHAKESPEARE, *Much Ado About Nothing.* Act iii, sc. 1, l. 26.

2
But, should you lure
From his dark haunt beneath the tangled roots
Of pendent trees the monarch of the brook,
Behoves you then to ply your finest art.
THOMSON, *The Seasons: Spring,* l. 422.

3
Then come, my friend, forget your foes, and leave your fears behind,
And wander forth to try your luck, with cheerful, quiet mind.
HENRY VAN DYKE, *The Angler's Reveille.*

'Tis an affair of luck.
HENRY VAN DYKE, *Fisherman's Luck.*

Two honest and good-natured anglers have never met each other by the way without crying out, "What luck?"
HENRY VAN DYKE, *Fisherman's Luck.*

4
No man is born an Artist nor an Angler.
IZAAK WALTON, *The Compleat Angler: To the Reader.*

Angling may be said to be so like the mathematics that it can never be fully learnt.
IZAAK WALTON, *The Compleat Angler: To the Reader.*

Angling is somewhat like poetry, men are to be born so.
IZAAK WALTON, *The Compleat Angler.* Ch. 1.

It is an art worthy the knowledge and patience of a wise man.
IZAAK WALTON, *The Compleat Angler.* Ch. 1.

You will find angling to be like the virtue of humility, which has a calmness of spirit and a world of other blessings attending upon it.
IZAAK WALTON, *The Compleat Angler.* Ch. 1.

All that are lovers of virtue, and dare trust in His providence, and be quiet, and go a-angling.
IZAAK WALTON, *The Compleat Angler.* Ch. 21.

5
I am a Brother of the Angle.
IZAAK WALTON, *The Compleat Angler.* Ch. 1.

An excellent angler, and now with God.
IZAAK WALTON, *The Compleat Angler.* Ch. 4.

Meek Walton's heavenly memory.
WORDSWORTH, *Ecclesiastical Sonnets.* Pt. iii, No. 5.

And angling too, that solitary vice,
Whatever Izaak Walton sings or says:
The quaint, old, cruel coxcomb, in his gullet
Should have a hook, and a small trout to pull it.
BYRON, *Don Juan.* Canto xiii, st. 106.

6
We may say of angling, as Dr. Boteler said of strawberries: "Doubtless God could have made a better berry, but doubtless God never did"; and so, (if I might be judge), God never did make a more calm, quiet, innocent recreation than angling.
IZAAK WALTON, *The Compleat Angler.* Ch. 5. (Second edition.) Boteler was Dr. William Butler. *See under* STRAWBERRY.

7
Oh the brave Fisher's life,
It is the best of any,
'Tis full of pleasure, void of strife,
And 'tis belov'd of many:
Other joys Are but toys;
Only this Lawful is,
For our skill Breeds no ill,
But content and pleasure.
IZAAK WALTON, *The Compleat Angler.* Ch. 11. (First edition.)

8
Thus use your frog: put your hook—I mean the arming-wire—through his mouth and out at his gills, and then with a fine needle and silk sew the upper part of his leg with only one stitch to the arming-wire of your hook, or tie the frog's leg above the upper joint to the armed wire; and in so doing, use him as though you loved him.
IZAAK WALTON, *The Compleat Angler.* Ch. 8.

9
'Tis an employment for my idle time, which is then not idly spent; a rest to my mind, a cheerer of my spirits, a diverter of sadness, a calmer of unquiet thoughts, a moderator of passions, a procurer of contentedness.
SIR HENRY WOTTON. (IZAAK WALTON, *The Compleat Angler.* Ch. 1.)

FLAG

I—Flag: Apothegms

10
These are our realms, no limit to their sway,—
Our flag the sceptre all who meet obey.
BYRON, *The Corsair.* Canto i, st. 1.

For where'er our country's banner may be planted,
All other local banners are defied!
W. S. GILBERT, *The Mikado.* Act i.

11
See the power of national emblems. Some stars, lilies, leopards, a crescent, a lion, an eagle, or other figure which came into credit God knows how, on an old rag of bunting, blowing in the wind on a fort at the ends of the earth, shall make the blood tingle under the rudest or the most conventional exterior.
EMERSON, *Essays, Second Series: The Poet*

1
A banner need not do much thinking.
WEIGAND VON MILTENBURG. (*Living Age*, March, 1931, p. 15.) Referring to Hitler. An expression once applied to General Boulanger.

2
Under the sooty flag of Acheron.
MILTON, *Comus*, l. 604.

3
And the flags were all a-flutter, and the bells were all a-chime.
HENRY NEWBOLT, *San Stephano.*

This is the song of the wind as it came
Tossing the flags of the nations to flame.
ALFRED NOYES, *The Avenue of the Allies.*

4
Stood for his country's glory fast,
And nailed her colours to the mast!
SCOTT, *Marmion:* Canto i, *Introduction*, l. 160. (1808) The reference is to Fox.

We fight them with our colours nailed to the mast.
SCOTT, *The Pirate*. Ch. 21. (1821)

Nail to the mast her holy flag.
O. W. HOLMES, *Old Ironsides.* (1830)

5
Mocking the air with colours idly spread.
SHAKESPEARE, *King John*. Act v, sc. 1, l. 72.

Banners flout the sky.
SHAKESPEARE, *Macbeth*. Act i, sc. 2, l. 49.

Hang out our banners on the outward walls;
The cry is still "They come!"
SHAKESPEARE, *Macbeth*. Act v, sc. 5, l. 1.

Banners yellow, glorious, golden,
On its roof did float and flow.
E. A. POE, *The Haunted Palace*. One of the best examples of interior alliteration in English.

6
A garish flag,
To be the aim of every dangerous shot.
SHAKESPEARE, *Richard III*. Act iv, sc. 4, l. 89.

II—Flag: American

7
I pledge allegiance to the flag of the United States and to the Republic for which it stands, one Nation, indivisible, with Liberty and Justice for all.
JAMES B. UPHAM AND FRANCIS M. BELLAMY, *Pledge to the Flag*. (1892) For discussion of authorship see APPENDIX.

8
Off with your hat as the flag goes by!
And let the heart have its say;
You're man enough for a tear in your eye
That you will not wipe away.
HENRY CUYLER BUNNER, *The Old Flag*.

Uncover when the flag goes by, boys,
'Tis freedom's starry banner that you greet,
Flag famed in song and story
Long may it wave, Old Glory
The flag that has never known defeat.
CHARLES L. BENJAMIN AND GEORGE SUTTON, *The Flag That Has Never Known Defeat.*

Hats off!
Along the street there comes
A blare of bugles, a ruffle of drums.
A flash of color beneath the sky:
Hats off!
The flag is passing by.
H. H. BENNETT, *The Flag Goes By*.

9
Fling out, fling out, with cheer and shout,
To all the winds Our Country's Banner!
Be every bar, and every star,
Displayed in full and glorious manner!
ABRAHAM COLES, *Our Country's Banner.*

10
Here's to the red of it,
There's not a thread of it,
No, not a shred of it,
In all the spread of it,
From foot to head,
But heroes bled for it,
Faced steel and lead for it,
Precious blood shed for it,
Bathing in red.
JOHN DALY, *A Toast to the Flag.*

11
When Freedom from her mountain height
Unfurled her standard to the air,
She tore the azure robe of night,
And set the stars of glory there.
She mingled with its gorgeous dyes
The milky baldric of the skies,
And striped its pure celestial white
With streakings of the morning light.
Then from his mansion in the sun
She called her eagle bearer down,
And gave into his mighty hand
The symbol of her chosen land.
JOSEPH RODMAN DRAKE, *The American Flag.*

Flag of the free heart's hope and home!
By angel hands to valor given;
Thy stars have lit the welkin dome,
And all thy hues were born in heaven.
For ever float that standard sheet!
Where breathes the foe but falls before us,
With Freedom's soil beneath our feet,
And Freedom's banner streaming o'er us?
JOSEPH RODMAN DRAKE, *The American Flag*
The last four lines are said to have been written by Fitz-Greene Halleck.

12
I have seen the glories of art and architecture, and mountain and river; I have seen the sunset on the Jungfrau, and the full moon rise over Mont Blanc; but the fairest vision on which these eyes ever looked was the flag of my country in a foreign land. Beautiful as a flower to those who love it, terrible as a meteor to those who hate it, it is the symbol of the power and glory, and the honor, of fifty millions of Americans.
GEORGE FRISBIE HOAR, *Speech*, 1878.

13
What flower is this that greets the morn,
Its hues from Heaven so freshly born?
With burning star and flaming band
It kindles all the sunset land:
Oh tell us what the name may be,—

Is this the Flower of Liberty?
It is the banner of the free,
The starry Flower of Liberty!
O. W. HOLMES, *The Flower of Liberty.*

Ay, tear her tattered ensign down!
Long has it waved on high,
And many an eye has danced to see
That banner in the sky.
O. W. HOLMES, *Old Ironsides.*

1
The flag of our stately battles, not struggles of wrath and greed,
Its stripes were a holy lesson, its spangles a deathless creed:
'T was red with the blood of freemen and white with the fear of the foe;
And the stars that fight in their courses 'gainst tyrants its symbols know.
JULIA WARD HOWE, *The Flag.*

2
The simple stone of Betsy Ross
Is covered now with mold and moss,
But still her deathless banner flies,
And keeps the color of the skies.
A nation thrills, a nation bleeds,
A nation follows where it leads,
And every man is proud to yield
His life upon a crimson field
For Betsy's battle flag!
MINNA IRVING, *Betsy's Battle Flag.*

3
Oh! thus be it ever, when freemen shall stand
Between their loved homes and the war's desolation!
Blest with victory and peace, may the heaven-rescued land
Praise the Power that hath made and preserved us a nation.
Then conquer we must, for our cause it is just,
And this be our motto: "In God is our trust."
And the star-spangled banner in triumph shall wave
O'er the land of the free and the home of the brave.
FRANCIS SCOTT KEY, *The Star-Spangled Banner.* Originally entitled *Defence of Fort M'Henry,* and first printed in *The Baltimore Patriot,* 20 Sept., 1814. Designated the American national anthem by Congress in 1931.

4
I am not the flag; not at all. I am but its shadow. I am whatever you make me, nothing more. I am your belief in yourself, your dream of what a People may become. . . . I am the day's work of the weakest man, and the largest dream of the most daring. . . . I am the clutch of an idea, and the reasoned purpose of resolution. I am no more than you believe me to be and I am all that you believe I can be. I am whatever you make me, nothing more.
FRANKLIN K. LANE, *Makers of the Flag.*

5
Each red stripe has blazoned forth
Gospels writ in blood;
Every star has sung the birth
Of some deathless good.
LUCY LARCOM, *The Flag.*

6
Take thy banner! May it wave
Proudly o'er the good and brave.
LONGFELLOW, *Hymn of the Moravian Nuns of Bethlehem.*

7
Your flag and my flag,
And how it flies today
In your land and my land
And half a world away!
Rose-red and blood-red
The stripes forever gleam;
Snow-white and soul-white—
The good forefathers' dream;
Sky-blue and true-blue,
With stars to gleam aright—
The gloried guidon of the day,
A shelter through the night.
WILBUR D. NESBIT, *Your Flag and My Flag.*

8
What shall I say to you, Old Flag?
You are so grand in every fold,
So linked with mighty deeds of old,
So steeped in blood where heroes fell,
So torn and pierced by shot and shell,
So calm, so still, so firm, so true,
My throat swells at the sight of you,
Old Flag!
HUBBARD PARKER, *Old Flag.*

9
Yes, we'll rally round the flag, boys, we'll rally once again,
Shouting the battle-cry of Freedom,
We will rally from the hill-side, we'll gather from the plain,
Shouting the battle-cry of Freedom.
GEORGE F. ROOT, *The Battle-Cry of Freedom.*

10
She's up there—Old Glory—where lightnings are sped,
She dazzles the nations with ripples of red,
And she'll wave for us living, or droop o'er us dead—
The flag of our country forever.
F. L. STANTON, *Our Flag Forever.*

My name is as old as the glory of God,
So I came by the name of Old Glory.
J. W. RILEY, *The Name of Old Glory.*

There it is—Old Glory!
CAPTAIN WILLIAM DRIVER, as an American flag was run up to the masthead of a new ship of which he had just been appointed master, at Salem, Mass., Dec., 1831. The most probable of the legends accounting for the name.

11
Might his last glance behold the glorious ensign of the Republic still full high advanced, its arms and trophies streaming in all their original lustre.
WEBSTER, *Reply to Hayne: Peroration.*

1
O hasten flag of man—O with sure and steady step, passing highest flag of kings,
Walk supreme to the heavens mighty symbol —run up above them all,
Flag of stars! thick-sprinkled bunting!
WALT WHITMAN, *Thick-Sprinkled Bunting*.

Banner so broad advancing out of the night, I sing you haughty and resolute, . . .
Not houses of peace indeed are you, nor any nor all their prosperity, (if need be, you shall again have every one of those houses to destroy them,
You thought not to destroy those valuable houses, standing fast, full of comfort, built with money,
May they stand fast, then? not an hour except you above them and all stand fast.)
WHITMAN, *Song of the Banner at Daybreak*.

2
"Shoot, if you must, this old gray head,
But spare your country's flag," she said. . . .
"Who touches a hair of yon gray head
Dies like a dog! March on!" he said.
WHITTIER, *Barbara Frietchie*.

3
When I think of the flag, . . . I see alternate strips of parchment upon which are written the rights of liberty and justice, and stripes of blood to vindicate those rights, and then, in the corner, a prediction of the blue serene into which every nation may swim which stands for these great things.
WOODROW WILSON, *Address*, N. Y., 17 May, 1915.

The lines of red are lines of blood, nobly and unselfishly shed by men who loved the liberty of their fellowmen more than they loved their own lives and fortunes. God forbid that we should have to use the blood of America to freshen the color of the flag. But if it should ever be necessary, that flag will be colored once more, and in being colored will be glorified and purified.
WOODROW WILSON, *Address*, 17 May, 1915.

4
Its red for love, and its white for law;
And its blue for the hope that our fathers saw,
Of a larger liberty.
UNKNOWN, *The American Flag*.

5
Your banner's constellation types
White freedom with its stars,
But what's the meaning of the stripes?
They mean your negroes' scars.
THOMAS CAMPBELL, *To the United States of North America*. (1838)

England! Whence came each glowing hue
That tints your flag of meteor light,—
The streaming red, the deeper blue,
Crossed with the moonbeams' pearly white?
The blood, the bruise—the blue, the red—
Let Asia's groaning millions speak;
The white it tells of colour fled
From starving Erin's pallid cheek.
GEORGE LUNT, *Answer to Thomas Campbell*. Published in the Newburyport. Mass., *News*.

Where bastard Freedom waves
Her fustian flag in mockery over slaves.
THOMAS MOORE, *To the Lord Viscount Forbes*, l. 153. Written from the City of Washington.

III—Flag: British

See also under England

6
Freedom's lion-banner.
THOMAS CAMPBELL, *Ode to the Germans*, l. 11.

7
The meteor flag of England
Shall yet terrific burn,
Till danger's troubled night depart,
And the star of peace return.
THOMAS CAMPBELL, *Ye Mariners of England*.

Th' imperial ensign, which, full high advanc'd,
Shone like a meteor streaming to the wind.
MILTON, *Paradise Lost*. Bk. i, l. 536.

8
There's a flag that waves o'er every sea,
No matter when or where.
ELIZA COOK, *The Englishman*.

9
A moth-eaten rag on a worm-eaten pole,
It does not look likely to stir a man's soul.
'Tis the deeds that were done 'neath the moth-eaten rag,
When the pole was a staff, and the rag was a flag.
SIR EDWARD BRUCE HAMLEY, *The Flag*. Referring specifically to the colors of 43rd Monmouth Light Infantry.

10
The dead dumb fog hath wrapped it—the frozen dews have kissed—
The naked stars have seen it, a fellow-star in the mist.
What is the flag of England? Ye have but my breath to dare,
Ye have but my waves to conquer. Go forth, for it is there!
KIPLING, *The English Flag*.

11
Banner of England, not for a season, O Banner of Britain, hast thou
Floated in conquering battle or flapt to the battle-cry!
Never with mightier glory than when we had rear'd thee on high,
Flying at top of the roofs in the ghastly siege of Lucknow—
Shot thro' the staff or the halyard, but ever we raised thee anew,
And ever upon the topmost roof our banner of England blew.
TENNYSON, *The Defence of Lucknow*. St. 1.

FLATTERY

See also Compliment, Praise

I—Flattery: Definitions

12
Flattery is like Kolone water, tew be smelt of, not swallowed.
JOSH BILLINGS, *Philosophy*.

1
Flattery, the handmaid of the vices. (Assentatio vitiorum adjutrix.)
CICERO, *De Amicitia*. Ch. 24, sec. 89.

Learn to contemn all praise betimes;
For flattery's the nurse of crimes.
JOHN GAY, *Fables*. Pt. i, No. 1.

For flattery is the bellows blows up sin.
SHAKESPEARE, *Pericles*. Act i, sc. 2, l. 39.

2
Sweet reader! you know what a Toady is?—that agreeable animal which you meet every day in civilized society.
BENJAMIN DISRAELI, *Vivian Grey*. Bk. ii, ch. 15.

3
The coin most current among us is flattery.
THOMAS FULLER, *Gnomologia*. No. 4452.

4
Just praise is only a debt, but flattery is a present.
SAMUEL JOHNSON, *The Rambler*. No. 155.

5
Gallantry of mind consists in saying flattering things in an agreeable manner. (La galanterie de l'esprit est de dire des choses flatteuses d'une manière agréable.)
LA ROCHEFOUCAULD, *Maximes*. No. 100.

It is happy for you that you possess the talent of flattering with delicacy.
JANE AUSTEN, *Mansfield Park*. Ch. 14.

6
How closely flattery resembles friendship! (Adulatio quam similis est amicitiæ!)
SENECA, *Epistulæ ad Lucilium*. Epis. xlv, sec. 7.

Flatterers look like friends, as wolves, like dogs.
GEORGE CHAPMAN, *Byron's Conspiracie*. Act iii, sc. 1.

Flattery is monstrous in a true friend.
JOHN FORD, *Lovers' Melancholy*. Act i, sc. 1.

7
Fawning and flattery, the worst poison of true feeling. (Adulatio, blanditiæ, pessimum veri affectus venenum.)
TACITUS, *History*. Bk. i, sec. 15.

8
Flattery's the turnpike road to Fortune's door.
JOHN WOLCOT, *Lyric Odes*. No. 9.

II—Flattery: Apothegms

9
Some are so highly polish'd, they display
Only your own face when you turn that way.
WILLIAM ALLINGHAM, *Blackberries*.

10
Daub yourself with honey and you will never want flies. (Haceos miel, y paparos han moscas.)
CERVANTES, *Don Quixote*. Pt. ii, ch. 49.

One rich drop of honey sweet,
As an alluring, luscious treat,
Is known to tempt more flies, by far,
Than a whole tun of vinegar.
WILLIAM COMBE, *Dr. Syntax in Search of a Wife*. Canto xxxiv, l. 748.

One catches more flies with a spoonful of honey than with twenty casks of vinegar.
HENRY IV of France, *Maxim*. Also attributed to St. Francis de Sales.

He that hath no honey in his pot, let him have it in his mouth.
GEORGE HERBERT, *Jacula Prudentum*.

But for your words, they rob the Hybla bees,
And leave them honeyless.
SHAKESPEARE, *Julius Cæsar*. Act v, sc. 1, l. 34.

11
Not to think of men above that which is written, that no one of you be puffed up for one against another.
New Testament: I Corinthians, iv, 6.

Yes, sir, puffing is of various sorts; the principal are, the puff direct, the puff preliminary, the puff collateral, the puff collusive, and the puff oblique, or puff by implication.
SHERIDAN, *The Critic*. Act i, sc. 2.

12
Flattery sits in the parlour, when plain dealing is kicked out of doors.
THOMAS FULLER, *Gnomologia*. No. 1552.

13
Flatterers make cream cheese of chalk.
THOMAS HOOD, *Miss Kilmansegg: Her Education*.

14
Let those flatter who fear; it is not an American art.
THOMAS JEFFERSON, *Writings*. Vol. i, p. 185.

15
Of all wild beasts preserve me from a tyrant;
And of all tame, a flatterer.
BEN JONSON, *Fall of Sejanus*. Act i. *See also under* SLANDER.

16
Skilful flatterers praise the discourse of an ignorant friend and the face of a deformed one. (Adulandi gens prudentissima laudat Sermonem indocti, faciem deformis amici.)
JUVENAL, *Satires*. Sat. iii, l. 86.

17
Every flatterer lives at the expense of the person who listens to him. (Tout flatteur vît au dépens de celui qui l'écoute.)
LA FONTAINE, *Fables*. Bk. i, fab. 2.

18
A flatterer can risk everything with great personages. (Un flatteur peut tout risquer avec les grands.)
LE SAGE, *Gil Blas*. Bk. iv, ch. 7.

19
There is no more certain indication of a weak and ill-regulated intellect than that propensity which, for want of a better name, we will venture to christen Boswellian.
MACAULAY, *Essays: Milton*.

20
It is possible to be below flattery, as well as above it.
MACAULAY, *History of England*. Ch. 2.

21
I believe no one who is profuse with flattery.

(Nemini credo qui large blandus est.)
PLAUTUS, *Aulularia*, l. 196. (Act ii, sc. 2.)

1
Nothing but pure piffle. (Σαὶ δὲ κολλῦραι λῦραι.)
PLAUTUS, *Pœnulus*, l. 137. (Act i, sc. 1.)

2
The arch-flatterer with whom all the petty flatterers have intelligence is a man's self.
PLUTARCH, *De Adulatio et Amico*. As quoted by BACON, *Essays: Of Love*.

We should have but little pleasure, were we never to flatter ourselves. (On n'aurait guère de plaisir si on ne se flattait jamais.)
LA ROCHEFOUCAULD, *Maximes*. No. 123.

3
Their throat is an open sepulchre; they flatter with their tongue.
Old Testament: Psalms, v, 9.

A flatterer's throat is an open sepulchre.
GEORGE HERBERT, *Jacula Prudentum*.

The Lord shall cut off all flattering lips, and the tongue that speaketh proud things.
Old Testament: Psalms, xii, 3.

4
Flattery, formerly a vice, is now the fashion. (Vitium fuit, nunc mos est, adsentatio.)
PUBLILIUS SYRUS, *Sententiæ*. No. 723.

5
When flatterers meet, the devil goes to dinner.
JOHN RAY, *English Proverbs*, 139.

6
It is easier for men to flatter than to praise.
JEAN PAUL RICHTER, *Titan*. Zykel 34.

7
Minds,
By nature great, are conscious of their greatness,
And hold it mean to borrow aught from flattery.
NICHOLAS ROWE, *Royal Convert*. Act i, sc. 1.

8
'Tis the most pleasing flattery to like what other men like.
JOHN SELDEN, *Table-Talk: Pleasure*.

9
Well said: that was laid on with a trowel.
SHAKESPEARE, *As You Like It*. Act i, sc. 2, l. 112. (1599)

Paints, d'ye say? Why, she lays it on with a trowel.
CONGREVE, *Double-Dealer*. Act iii, sc. 10 (1693)

10
Why should the poor be flatter'd?
No, let the candied tongue lick absurd pomp,
And crook the pregnant hinges of the knee
Where thrift may follow fawning.
SHAKESPEARE, *Hamlet*. Act iii, sc. 2, l. 64.

Flatterers haunt not cottages.
C. H. SPURGEON, *John Ploughman*. Ch. 14.

11
Mother, for love of grace,
Lay not that flattering unction to your soul.
SHAKESPEARE, *Hamlet*. Act iii, sc. 4, l. 144.

12
Tell me all me faults as man to man. I can stand anything but flatthery.
BERNARD SHAW, *John Bull's Other Island*. Act i.

What really flatters a man is that you think him worth flattering.
BERNARD SHAW, *John Bull's Other Island*. Act iv.

III—Flattery: Love of Flattery

See also Praise: Love of Praise

13
You've supped full of flattery:
They say you like it too—'tis no great wonder.
BYRON, *Don Juan*. Canto ix, st. 5.

14
We love flattery even though we are not deceived by it, because it shows that we are of importance enough to be courted.
EMERSON, *Essays, Second Series: Gifts*.

15
He that rewards flattery begs it.
THOMAS FULLER, *Gnomologia*. No. 2269.

16
I know the value of a kindly chorus.
W. S. GILBERT, *Pinafore*. Act i.

17
You think I love flattery, and so I do; but a little too much always disgusts me. That fellow Richardson, on the contrary, could not be contented to sail quietly down the stream of his reputation, without longing to taste the froth from every stroke of the oar.
SAMUEL JOHNSON, *Miscellanies*. Vol. i, p. 273.

We sometimes think that we hate flattery, but we hate only the manner in which it is done. (On croit quelquefois haïr la flatterie, mais on ne hait que la manière de flatter.)
LA ROCHEFOUCAULD, *Maximes*. No. 329.

18
Is there a Parson much bemused in beer,
A maudlin Poetess, a rhyming Peer,
A clerk foredoom'd his father's soul to cross,
Who pens a stanza when he should engross?
Is there who, lock'd from ink and paper, scrawls
With desp'rate charcoal round his darken'd walls?
All fly to Twit'nam, and in humble strain
Apply to me to keep them mad or vain.
POPE, *Epistle to Dr. Arbuthnot*, l. 15.

19
What drink'st thou oft, instead of homage sweet,
But poison'd flattery?
SHAKESPEARE, *Henry V*. Act iv, sc. 1, l. 267.

But when I tell him he hates flatterers,
He says he does, being then most flattered.
SHAKESPEARE, *Julius Cæsar*. Act ii, sc. 1, l. 208.

He that loves to be flattered is worthy o' the flatterer.
SHAKESPEARE, *Timon of Athens*. Act i, sc. 1, l. 232.

20
O, flatter me, for love delights in praises.
SHAKESPEARE, *The Two Gentlemen of Verona*. Act ii, sc. 4, l. 148. *See also under* WOOING.

1
'Tis an old maxim in the schools,
That flattery's the food of fools;
Yet now and then your men of wit
Will condescend to take a bit.

SWIFT, *Cadenus and Vanessa,* l. 769.

The wisest of the wise
Listen to pretty lies
And love to hear 'em told.
Doubt not that Solomon
Listened to many a one,—
Some in his youth, and more when he grew old.

WALTER SAVAGE LANDOR, *The One White Hair.*

2
Love of flattery, in most men, proceeds from the mean opinion they have of themselves; in women, from the contrary.

SWIFT, *Thoughts on Various Subjects.*

Your panegyrics here provide;
You cannot err on flattery's side.

SWIFT, *On Poetry.*

3
Of folly, vice, disease, men proud we see;
And, (stranger still!) of blockheads' flattery;
Whose praise defames; as if a fool should mean,
By spitting on your face, to make it clean.

YOUNG, *Love of Fame.* Sat. i, l. 97.

IV—Flattery: Its Dangers

4
A man that flattereth his neighbour spreadeth a net for his feet.

JOHN BUNYAN, *The Pilgrim's Progress.* Pt. i.

5
Flattery corrupts both the receiver and giver.

EDMUND BURKE, *Reflections on the Revolution in France.*

6
Remember to beware of soft and flattering sayings. (Sermones blandos blæsosque cavere memento.)

DIONYSIUS CATO, *Disticha de Moribus.* Bk. iii, No. 6.

We must beware of giving ear to flatterers. (Cavendum est ne assentatoribus patefaciamus auris.)

CICERO, *De Officiis.* Bk. i, sec. 26.

7
He hurts me most who lavishly commends.

CHARLES CHURCHILL, *The Apology,* l. 20.

8
Nor in these consecrated bowers
Let painted Flatt'ry hide her serpent-train in flowers.

THOMAS GRAY, *Ode for Music,* l. 7.

9
Bring no more vain oblations; incense is an abomination unto me.

Old Testament: Isaiah, i, 13.

No adulation; 'tis the death of virtue;
Who flatters, is of all mankind the lowest
Save he who courts the flattery.

HANNAH MORE, *Daniel.*

10
They who delight to be flattered, pay for their folly by a late repentance. (Qui se laudari gaudent verbis subdolis, Sera dant pœnas turpes pœnitentia.)

PHÆDRUS, *Fables.* Bk. i, fab. 13, l. 1.

11
The flatteries of a bad man cover treachery. (Habent insidias hominis blanditiæ mali.)

PHÆDRUS, *Fables.* Bk. i, fab. 19, l. 1.

Your flattery is so much birdlime. (Viscus merus vestra est blanditia.)

PLAUTUS, *Bacchides,* l. 16. (Act i, sc. 1.)

12
Thou shalt not fear sharp words, but dread fair words.

HUGH RHODES, *Boke of Nurture.*

13
No vizor does become black villainy
So well as soft and tender flattery.

SHAKESPEARE, *Pericles.* Act iv, sc. 4, l. 44.

O, that men's ears should be
To counsel deaf, but not to flattery!

SHAKESPEARE, *Timon of Athens.* Act i, sc. 2, l. 256.

14
Those worst of enemies, flatterers. (Pessimum inimicorum genus, laudantes.)

TACITUS, *Agricola.* Sec. 41.

15
All panegyrics are mingled with an infusion of poppy.

SWIFT, *Thoughts on Various Subjects.*

16
Distrust mankind; with your own heart confer;
And dread even there to find a flatterer.

YOUNG, *Love of Fame.* Sat. vi, l. 233.

V—Flattery: Disdain of Flattery

See also Candor

17
Madam, before you flatter a man so grossly to his face, you should consider whether or not your flattery is worth his having.

SAMUEL JOHNSON, *Remark to Hannah More.* (FANNY BURNEY, *Diary,* 1778.)

18
He would not flatter Neptune for his trident,
Or Jove for 's power to thunder.

SHAKESPEARE, *Coriolanus.* Act iii, sc. 1, l. 256.

19
Nay, do not think I flatter:
For what advancement may I hope from thee,
That no revenue hast but thy good spirits?

SHAKESPEARE, *Hamlet.* Act iii, sc. 2, l. 61.

By God, I cannot flatter: I do defy
The tongues of soothers.

SHAKESPEARE, *I Henry IV.* Act iv, sc. 1, l. 6.

He cannot flatter, he,
An honest mind and plain, he must speak truth!
An they will take it, so; if not, he's plain:
These kind of knaves I know.

SHAKESPEARE, *King Lear.* Act ii, sc. 2, l. 104.

20
Because I cannot flatter and speak fair,
Smile in men's faces, smooth, deceive, and cog.

Duck with French nods and apish courtesy,
I must be held a rancorous enemy.
Cannot a plain man live and think no harm,
But thus his simple truth must be abused
By silken, sly, insinuating Jacks?

SHAKESPEARE, *Richard III*. Act i, sc. 3, l. 47.

FLEA

1
The flea, though he kill none, he does all the harm he can.

JOHN DONNE, *Devotions*.

2
He that lies with the dogs riseth with fleas.

GEORGE HERBERT, *Jacula Prudentum*. (1640) Quoted by BENJAMIN FRANKLIN, *Poor Richard*, 1733.

3
"I cannot raise my worth too high;
Of what vast consequence am I!"
"Not of th' importance you suppose,"
Replies a Flea upon his nose;
"Be humble, learn thyself to scan;
Know, pride was never made for man."

JOHN GAY, *Fables: The Man and the Flea*.

4
When eager bites the thirsty flea,
Clouds and rain you sure shall see.

INWARDS, *Weather Lore*, p. 148.

5
I do honour the very flea of his dog.

BEN JONSON, *Every Man in His Humour*. Act iv, sc. 2.

6
A blockhead, bit by fleas, put out the light,
And chuckling cried, "Now you can't see to bite!"

("Εσβεσε τόν λύχνον μῶρος, ψυλλῶν ὑπὸ πολλῶν δακνόμενος, λέξας· Οὐκέτι με βλέπετε.)

LUCIAN, *Epigram*. (*Greek Anthology*. Bk. xi, epig. 432.)

7
They'd skin a flea for his hide and tallow.

HENRY MAYHEW, *London Labour*. Vol. i, p. 134. *See also under* AVARICE.

8
That's a valiant flea that dare eat his breakfast on the lip of a lion.

SHAKESPEARE, *Henry V*. Act iii, sc. 7, l. 154.

9
So, Nat'ralists observe, a Flea
Hath smaller Fleas that on him prey;
And these have smaller fleas to bite 'em,
And so proceed *ad infinitum*.

SWIFT, *On Poetry: A Rhapsody*, l. 337. (1733)

Great fleas have little fleas upon their backs to bite 'em,
And little fleas have lesser fleas, and so *ad infinitum*.
And the great fleas themselves, in turn, have greater fleas to go on;
While these again have greater still, and greater still, and so on.

AUGUSTUS DE MORGAN, *A Budget of Paradoxes*, p. 377.

Big fleas have little fleas to plague, perplex and bite 'em,
Little fleas have lesser fleas, and so *ad infinitum*.

R. R. FIELDER, *Pulex Irritans*.

there is always some
little thing that is too
big for us every
goliath has his david and so on ad infinitum

DON MARQUIS, *the merry flea*.

10
Elephants are always drawn smaller than life, but a flea always larger.

SWIFT, *Thoughts on Various Subjects*.

11
And many other great wonders, which been fleas in mine ears.

UNKNOWN, *Pilgr. Lyf. Manhode*, ii, 39, 91. (c. 1430)

How Panurge had a flea in his ear. (Comment Panurge avoyt la pulce en l'oreille.)

RABELAIS, *Works*. Bk. iii, ch. 7. Heading. (1532)

Ferardo . . . whispering Philantus in the ear (who stood as though he had a flea in his ear), desired him to keep silence.

JOHN LYLY, *Euphues*. (1578) The phrase was widely used: TEUTON, *Tragicall Discourses* (1579); THOMAS NASHE, *Pierce Penniless* (1592); GREENE, *Quip for an Upstart Courier* (1592), etc.

I will send him hence with a flea in his ear.

THOMAS MIDDLETON, *Blurt, Master Constable*. Act ii, sc. 2.

FLESH

12
The world, the flesh, and the devil.

Book of Common Prayer: Litany.

13
The nearer the bone, the sweeter the flesh.

COOK, *City Gallant*. (1614) (HAZLITT, *Old Plays*, xi, 207.)

14
A thorn in the flesh.

New Testament: II Corinthians, xii, 7.

15
Flesh of my flesh.

Old Testament: Genesis, ii, 23.

Flesh of thy flesh, nor yet bone of thy bone.

DU BARTAS, *Devine Weekes and Workes*. Week iv, Day 2. (Sylvester, tr.)

Who did leave His Father's throne,
To assume thy flesh and bone?

GEORGE HERBERT, *The Church: Business*.

16
The frailë flesh, whose nature is
Ay ready for the sporne and fall,
The firstë foeman is of all.
It warreth night, it warreth day,
So that a man hath never rest.

JOHN GOWER, *Confessio Amantis*. Bk. v.

Frail as flesh is.

LAMAN BLANCHARD, *Nell Gwynne's Looking-Glass*.

17
That flesh is but the glass, which holds the dust
That measures all our time; which also shall

Be crumbled into dust.
GEORGE HERBERT, *Church Monuments.*

1
It is a dear collop that is cut out of thy own flesh.
JOHN HEYWOOD, *Proverbs.* Pt. i, ch. 10. (1546)

God knows thou art a collop of my flesh.
SHAKESPEARE, *I Henry VI.* Act v, sc. 4, l. 18. (1591)

2
All flesh is grass.
Old Testament: Isaiah, xl, 6. *See also under* MORTALITY.

3
Sir Launcelot smiled and said hard it is to take out of the flesh that is bred in the bone.
SIR THOMAS MALORY, *Morte d'Arthur.* Bk. ix, ch. 39. (1470)

It will not out of the flesh, that is bred in the bone.
JOHN HEYWOOD, *Proverbs.* Pt. ii, ch. 8. (1546)

It will never out o' the flesh that's bred i' the bone.
BEN JONSON, *Every Man in His Humour.* Act ii, sc. 1.

What is bred in the bone will never come out of the flesh.
PILPAY, *Fables: No. 14, The Two Fishermen.*
See also ANCESTRY: HEREDITY.

4
The spirit indeed is willing, but the flesh is weak.
New Testament: Matthew, xxvi, 41.

5
I am no dish for the village. (Non ego sum pollucta pago.)
PLAUTUS, *Rudens,* l. 424. (Act ii, sc. 4.)

I am meat for your master.
SHAKESPEARE, *II Henry IV.* Act ii, sc. 4, l. 135.

Let my doxy rest in peace, she's meat for thy master.
THOMAS OTWAY, *Soldier's Fortune.* Act ii, sc. 1.

6
The useless and fleeting flesh, fitted only for the reception of food.
POSIDONIUS. (SENECA, *Epistulæ ad Lucilium.* Epis. xcii, sec. 10.)

7
No man is free who is a slave to the flesh. (Nemo liber est, qui corpori servit.)
SENECA, *Epistulæ ad Lucilium.* Epis. xcii, 33.

8
Countess: Tell me thy reason why thou wilt marry.
Clown: My poor body, madam, requires it: I am driven on by the flesh.
SHAKESPEARE, *All's Well that Ends Well.* Act i, sc. 3, l. 29.

And this night he fleshes his will in the spoil of her honour.
SHAKESPEARE, *All's Well that Ends Well.* Act iv, sc. 3, l. 19.

Such is the simplicity of man to hearken after the flesh.
SHAKESPEARE, *Love's Labour's Lost.* Act i, sc. 1, l. 220.

9
O, that this too too solid flesh would melt,
Thaw and resolve itself into a dew!
SHAKESPEARE, *Hamlet.* Act i, sc. 2, l. 129.

10
Her fair and unpolluted flesh.
SHAKESPEARE, *Hamlet.* Act v, sc. 1, l. 262.

11
The words expressly are "a pound of flesh:"
Take then thy bond, take thou thy pound of flesh.
SHAKESPEARE, *The Merchant of Venice.* Act iv, sc. 1, l. 307.

12
As pretty a piece of flesh as any is in Messina.
SHAKESPEARE, *Much Ado About Nothing.* Act iv, sc. 2, l. 85.

As witty a piece of Eve's flesh as any in Illyria.
SHAKESPEARE, *Twelfth Night.* Act i, sc. 5, l. 30.

My flesh is soft and plump, my marrow burning.
SHAKESPEARE, *Venus and Adonis,* l. 142.

I am a pretty piece of flesh. 'Tis well thou art not fish.
SHAKESPEARE, *Romeo and Juliet.* Act i, sc. 1, l. 36. *See also* FISH AND FLESH.

13
Ah, yet would God this flesh of mine might be
Where air might wash and long leaves cover me,
Where tides of grass break into foam of flowers,
Or where the wind's feet shine along the sea.
SWINBURNE, *Laus Veneris.* St. 14.

14
The way of all flesh.
JOHN WEBSTER, *Westward Ho!* Act ii, sc. 2. (1603) Title of novel by SAMUEL BUTLER THE YOUNGER, published in 1903.

I go the way of all flesh.
THOMAS HEYWOOD, *Golden Age,* iii. (1611)

FLIGHT

15
He is gone, he has fled, he has eluded our vigilance, he has broken through our guards. (Abiit, excessit, evasit, erupit.)
CICERO, *In Catilinam.* No. ii, sec. 1.

He had taken the decamping powder. (Celui avait pris la poudre d'escampette.)
DUMAS, *The Three Musketeers.* Ch. 31. (1844) A French popular idiomatic phrase.

And brave men fled who never fled before.
GEORGE H. CALVERT, *Bunker Hill.*

16 To flee is to triumph. (Fugere est triumphans.) UNKNOWN. A Latin proverb.

17
The rascal takes to flight and leaves me under the knife. (Fugit improbus, ac me sub cultro linquit.)
HORACE, *Satires.* Bk. i, sat. 9, l. 73.

18
Man gives little thought to his destination,

so long as he can remain out of reach of his pursuer.
ELBERT HUBBARD, *Epigrams.*

1
By flight we often rush into the thick of our fate. (Fugiendo in media sæpe ruitur fata.)
LIVY, *History.* Bk. viii, sec. 24.

2
The wicked flee when no man pursueth: but the righteous are bold as a lion.
Old Testament: Proverbs, xxviii, 1.

3
What follows I flee; what flees I ever pursue. (Quod sequitur, fugio; quod fugit, ipse sequor.)
OVID, *Amores.* Bk. ii, eleg. 19, l. 36. *See also* WOOING: PURSUER AND PURSUED.

4
He who flees from trial confesses his guilt. (Fatetur facinus is, qui judicium fugit.)
PUBLILIUS SYRUS, *Sententiæ.* No. 199.

Running away from justice must always be considered as evidence of guilt.
JOHN CLERK, *Muir's Case.* (1793) (23 How. St. Tr. 230.)

Flight, in criminal cases, is itself a crime.
WILLIAM MURRAY, EARL OF MANSFIELD, *Rex v. Wilkes.* (4 Burr, pt. iv, p. 2549.)

Flight is an acknowledgment of guilt.
SIR JOHN CHARLES DAY, *Johnson's Case.* (29 How. St. Tr. 192.)

5
'Tis vain to flee; till gentle Mercy show
Her better eye, the farther off we go,
The swing of Justice deals the mightier blow.
FRANCIS QUARLES, *Emblems.* Bk. iii, emb. 16.

6
Let us fly and save our bacon.
RABELAIS, *Works.* Bk. iv, ch. 55. *See also under* DISCRETION.

7
And sidelong glanced, as to explore,
In meditated flight, the door.
SCOTT, *Rokeby.* Canto vi, st. 6.

8
I will be gone:
That pitiful rumour may report my flight,
To consolate thine ear.
SHAKESPEARE, *All's Well that Ends Well.* Act iii, sc. 2, l. 129.

9
Let us make an honourable retreat.
SHAKESPEARE, *As You Like It.* Act iii, sc. 2, l. 169.

Show it a fair pair of heels and run for it.
SHAKESPEARE, *I Henry IV.* Act ii, sc. 4, l. 53.

I took to my heels as fast as I could. (Ego me in pedes quantum queo.)
TERENCE, *Eunuchus,* l. 844. (Act v, sc. 2.)

10
To fly the boar before the boar pursues,
Were to incense the boar to follow us
And make pursuit where he did mean no chase.
SHAKESPEARE. *Richard III.* Act iii, sc. 2, l. 28.

11
As she fled fast thro' sun and shade,
The happy winds upon her play'd,
Blowing the ringlet from the braid.
TENNYSON, *Sir Launcelot and Queen Guinevere.*

12
To all swift things for swiftness did I sue;
Clung to the whistling mane of every wind.
FRANCIS THOMPSON, *The Hound of Heaven.*

13
I girded up my Lions and fled the Seen.
ARTEMUS WARD, *A Visit to Brigham Young.*

FLIRTATION, see Coquetry

FLOWERS

I—Flowers: Apothegms

14
To create a little flower is the labour of ages.
WILLIAM BLAKE, *Proverbs of Hell.*

15
The faintest streak that on a petal lies
May speak instruction to initiate eyes.
BRYANT, *The Mystery of Flowers.*

Not a flower
But shows some touch, in freckle, streak or stain,
Of his unrivall'd pencil.
COWPER, *The Task.* Bk. vi, l. 241.

16
The bud may have a bitter taste,
But sweet will be the flower.
COWPER, *Light Shining Out of Darkness.*

17
Flowers are words
Which even a babe may understand.
ARTHUR C. COXE, *The Singing of Birds.*

18
The fairest flower that ever saw the light.
SAMUEL DANIEL, *Sonnets to Delia.* No. xxxvii

19
The flowers of the forest are a' wede away.
JANE ELLIOT, *The Flowers of the Forest.*

20
Earth laughs in flowers.
EMERSON, *Hamatreya.*

21
Full many a flower is born to blush unseen,
And waste its sweetness on the desert air.
GRAY, *Elegy Written in a Country Churchyard.* St. 14.

The flower of sweetest smell is shy and lowly.
WORDSWORTH, *Miscellaneous Sonnets:* Pt. ii, *Not Love, Not War.*

22
One flower makes no garland.
GEORGE HERBERT, *Jacula Prudentum.* *See also under* SWALLOW.

23
The Amen! of Nature is always a flower.
O. W. HOLMES, *The Autocrat of the Breakfast-Table.* Ch. 10.

24
Only the flower sanctifies the vase.
ROBERT UNDERWOOD JOHNSON, *The Temple.*

25
You are as welcome as the flowers in May.
CHARLES MACKLIN, *Love à la Mode.* Act i, sc. 1

The flowers that bloom in the spring, Tra la,
Have nothing to do with the case.
W. S. GILBERT, *The Mikado*. Act ii.

1
Flowers that their gay wardrobe wear.
MILTON, *Lycidas*, l. 47.

Flowers worthy of paradise.
MILTON, *Paradise Lost*. Bk. iv, l. 241.

Flowers of all hue, and without thorn the rose.
MILTON, *Paradise Lost*. Bk. iv, l. 256.

A wilderness of sweets.
MILTON, *Paradise Lost*. Bk. v, l. 294.

2
So from the root
Springs lighter the green stalk, from thence the leaves
More ærie, last the bright consummate flower.
MILTON, *Paradise Lost*. Bk. v, l. 479.

3
"A milkweed, and a buttercup, and cowslip," said sweet Mary,
"Are growing in my garden-plot, and this I call my dairy."
PETER NEWELL, *Her Dairy*.

4
One thing is certain and the rest is lies;
The Flower that once has blown for ever dies.
OMAR KHAYYÁM, *Rubáiyát*. St. 63. (Fitzgerald, tr.)

5
Here blushing Flora paints th' enamell'd ground.
POPE, *Windsor Forest*, l. 38.

6
The devil has not any flower,
But only money in his power.
JAMES STEPHENS, *In the Poppy Field*.

7
Flowers of all heavens, and lovelier than their names.
TENNYSON, *The Princess: Prologue*, l. 12.

8
One of the attractive things about the flowers is their beautiful reserve.
H. D. THOREAU, *Journal*, 17 June, 1853.

9
So great is their love of flowers. (Tantus amor florum.)
VERGIL, *Georgics*. No. iv, l. 205.

10
And 'tis my faith that every flower
Enjoys the air it breathes.
WORDSWORTH, *Lines Written in Early Spring*.

II—Flowers: Their Beauty

11
And because the breath of flowers is far sweeter in the air (where it comes and goes, like the warbling of music) than in the hand, therefore nothing is more fit for that delight than to know what be the flowers and plants that do best perfume the air.
FRANCIS BACON, *Essays: Of Gardens*.

I love these beautiful and peaceful tribes and wish I was better acquainted with them.
W. S. LANDOR, *Letter to Southey*, 1811. Referring to flowers.

12
Sweet letters of the angel tongue,
I've loved ye long and well,
And never have failed in your fragrance sweet
To find some secret spell,—
A charm that has bound me with witching power,
For mine is the old belief,
That midst your sweets and midst your bloom,
There's a soul in every leaf!
MATURIN MURRAY BALLOU, *Flowers*.

13
Flowers are the sweetest things God ever made and forgot to put a soul into.
HENRY WARD BEECHER, *Life Thoughts*.

As for marigolds, poppies, hollyhocks, and valorous sunflowers, we shall never have a garden without them, both for their own sake, and for the sake of old-fashioned folks, who used to love them.
HENRY WARD BEECHER, *Star Papers: A Discourse of Flowers*.

Flowers have an expression of countenance as much as men or animals. Some seem to smile; some have a sad expression; some are pensive and diffident; others again are plain, honest and upright, like the broad-faced sunflower and the hollyhock.
HENRY WARD BEECHER, *Star Papers: A Discourse of Flowers*.

14
I love the gorse and heather,
And bluebells close beside—
I'll find my cap a feather,
And kiss a Highland bride!
CHARLES G. BLANDEN, *The Rose Is a Royal Lady*.

15
Thick on the woodland floor
Gay company shall be,
Primrose and Hyacinth
And frail Anemone,
Perennial Strawberry-bloom,
Woodsorrel's pencilled veil,
Dishevel'd Willow-weed
And Orchis purple and pale.
ROBERT BRIDGES, *The Idle Flowers*.

I have loved flowers that fade,
Within whose magic tents
Rich hues have marriage made
With sweet unmemoried scents.
ROBERT BRIDGES, *Shorter Poems*. Bk. ii, No. 13.

16
The pink laburnam lays her cheek
In married, matchless, lovely bliss,
Against her golden mate, to seek
His airy kiss.
Tulips, in faded splendor drest,
Brood o'er their beds, a slumbrous gloom,
Dame Peony, red and ripe with bloom,

Swells the silk housing of her breast.
ALICE BROWN, *A Benedictine Garden.*

1
Brazen helm of daffodillies,
With a glitter toward the light.
Purple violets for the mouth,
Breathing perfumes west and south;
And a sword of flashing lilies,
Holden ready for the fight.
E. B. BROWNING, *Hector in the Garden.* St. 10.

2
The south wind searches for the flowers whose fragrance late he bore,
And sighs to find them in the wood and by the stream no more.
BRYANT, *The Death of the Flowers.*

The windflower and the violet, they perished long ago,
And the brier-rose and the orchis died amid the summer glow;
But on the hill the golden-rod, and the aster in the wood,
And the yellow sunflower by the brook, in autumn beauty stood,
Till fell the frost from the clear cold heaven, as falls the plague on men,
And the brightness of their smile was gone from upland, glade, and glen.
BRYANT, *The Death of the Flowers.*

3
Mourn, little harebells o'er the lea;
Ye stately foxgloves, fair to see;
Ye woodbines, hanging bonnily
In scented bowers;
Ye roses on your thorny tree,
The first o' flow'rs!
BURNS, *Elegy on Captain Matthew Henderson.*

Now blooms the lily by the bank,
The primrose down the brae;
The hawthorn's budding in the glen,
And milkwhite is the slae.
BURNS, *Lament of Mary, Queen of Scots.*

The snawdrop and primrose our woodlands adorn,
And violets bathe in the weet o' the morn.
BURNS, *My Nannie's Awa.*

4
Ye field flowers! the gardens eclipse you, 'tis true;
Yet, wildings of nature! I dote upon you,
For ye waft me to summers of old,
When the earth teem'd around me with fairy delight,
And when daisies and buttercups gladden'd my sight,
Like treasures of silver and gold.
THOMAS CAMPBELL, *Field Flowers.*

"Of what are you afraid, my child?" inquired the kindly teacher.
"Oh, sir! the flowers they are wild," replied the timid creature.
PETER NEWELL, *Wild Flowers.*

5
The deep red cones of the sumach
And the woodbine's crimson sprays
Have bannered the common roadside
For the pageant of passing days.
BLISS CARMAN, *An Autumn Garden.*

We are the roadside flowers,
Straying from garden grounds;
Lovers of idle hours,
Breakers of ordered bounds. . . .
Who shall inquire of the season,
Or question the wind where it blows?
We blossom and ask no reason,
The Lord of the Garden knows.
BLISS CARMAN, *Roadside Flowers.*

6
I know not which I love the most,
Nor which the comeliest shows,
The timid, bashful violet
Or the royal-hearted rose:
The pansy in her purple dress,
The pink with cheek of red,
Or the faint, fair heliotrope, who hangs,
Like a bashful maid her head.
PHŒBE CARY, *Spring Flowers.*

7
O the green things growing, the green things growing,
The faint sweet smell of the green things growing!
I should like to live, whether I smile or grieve,
Just to watch the happy life of my green things growing.
DINAH M. M. CRAIK, *Green Things Growing.*

8
And all the meadows, wide unrolled,
Were green and silver, green and gold,
Where buttercups and daisies spun
Their shining tissues in the sun.
JULIA C. R. DORR, *Unanswered.*

9
Why does the rose her grateful fragrance yield,
And yellow cowslips paint the smiling field?
JOHN GAY, *Panthea,* l. 71.

10
Through the laburnum's dropping gold
Rose the light shaft of Orient mould,
And Europe's violets, faintly sweet,
Purpled the mossbeds at its feet.
FELICIA DOROTHEA HEMANS, *The Palm-tree.*

11
Farewell, dear flowers, sweetly your time ye spent,
Fit, while ye liv'd, for smell or ornament,
And after death for cures.
I follow straight without complaints or grief,
Since, if my scent be good, I care not if
It be as short as yours.
GEORGE HERBERT, *Life.*

12
Fair pledges of a fruitful tree
Why do ye fall so fast?
Your date is not so past
But you may stay yet here awhile
To blush and gently smile

And go at last.
ROBERT HERRICK, *To Blossoms.*

1
What are the flowers of Scotland,
All others that excel?
The lovely flowers of Scotland,
All others that excel!
The thistle's purple bonnet,
And bonny heather bell,
Oh, they're the flowers of Scotland.
All others that excel!
JAMES HOGG, *The Flowers of Scotland.*

2
Yellow japanned buttercups and star-disked dandelions,—just as we see them lying in the grass, like sparks that have leaped from the kindling sun of summer.
O. W. HOLMES, *The Professor at the Breakfast-Table.* Ch. 10.

3
The cowslip is a country wench,
The violet is a nun;—
But I will woo the dainty rose,
The queen of every one.
THOMAS HOOD, *Flowers.*

I remember, I remember
The roses, red and white,
The violets and the lily-cups,
Those flowers made of light!
The lilacs, where the robin built,
And where my brother set
The laburnam on his birthday,—
The tree is living yet.
THOMAS HOOD, *I Remember, I Remember.*

4
What to them is winter!
What are stormy showers!
Buttercups and daisies
Are these human flowers!
He who gave them hardships
And a life of care,
Gave them likewise hardy strength
And patient hearts to bear.
MARY HOWITT, *Buttercups and Daisies.*

5
And in his left he held a basket full
Of all sweet herbs that searching eye could cull:
Wild thyme, and valley-lilies whiter still
Than Leda's love, and cresses from the rill.
KEATS, *Endymion.* Bk. i, l. 155.

Young playmates of the rose and daffodil,
Be careful ere ye enter in, to fill
Your baskets high
With fennel green, and balm, and golden pines,
Savory, latter-mint, and columbines.
KEATS, *Endymion.* Bk. iv, l. 572.

The rose
Blendeth its odour with the violet,—
Solution sweet.
KEATS, *The Eve of St. Agnes.* St. 36.

And O and O
The daisies blow,
And the primroses are waken'd;
And the violets white
Sit in silver plight,
And the green bud's as long as the spike end.
KEATS, *Fragment*, in a letter to Haydon.

6
Shed no tear! O shed no tear!
The flower will bloom another year.
Weep no more! O weep no more!
Young buds sleep in the root's white core.
KEATS, *Faery Song.*

7
The loveliest flowers the closest cling to earth,
And they first feel the sun: so violets blue;
So the soft star-like primrose—drenched in a dew—
The happiest of Spring's happy, fragrant birth.
JOHN KEBLE, *Spring Showers.*

8
Brave flowers, that I could gallant it like you
And be as little vain!
HENRY KING, *A Contemplation Upon Flowers.*

9
Need any man be told what flowers are,
That hold a star?
ALFRED KREYMBORG, *Bloom.*

10
Spake full well, in language quaint and olden,
One who dwelleth by the castled Rhine,
When he called the flowers, so blue and golden,
Stars, that in earth's firmament do shine.
LONGFELLOW, *Flowers.* St. 1.

The root of a forget-me-not caught the drop of water by the hair and sucked her in, that she might become a floweret, and twinkle as brightly as a blue star on the green firmament of earth.
FREDERICK WILHELM CAROVÉ, *The Story Without an End.* Carové, a resident of Coblentz, is the poet referred to in Longfellow's stanza.

11
Gorgeous flowerets in the sunlight shining,
Blossoms flaunting in the eye of day,
Tremulous leaves, with soft and silver lining,
Buds that open only to decay.
LONGFELLOW, *Flowers.* St. 6.

12
See how the flowers, as at parade,
Under their colours stand displayed:
Each regiment in order grows,
That of the tulip, pink, and rose.
ANDREW MARVELL, *A Garden.*

13
Throw hither all your quaint enamell'd eyes
That on the green turf suck the honied showers,
And purple all the ground with vernal flowers.
Bring the rathe primrose that forsaken dies,
The tufted crow-toe, and pale jessamine,
The white pink, and the pansy freakt with jet,

The glowing violet.
The musk-rose, and the well-attir'd woodbine,
With cowslips wan that hang the pensive head,
And every flower that sad embroidery wears:
Bid amaranthus all his beauty shed,
And daffadillies fill their cups with tears,
To strew the laureate hearse where Lycid lies.
MILTON, *Lycidas*, l. 139.

On either side
Acanthus and each odourous bushy shrub
Fenc'd up the verdant wall; each beauteous flower,
Iris all hues, roses, and jessamin
Rear'd high their flourish'd heads between, and wrought
Mosaic; under foot the violet,
Crocus, and hyacinth with rich inlay
Broider'd the ground, more colour'd than with stone
Of costliest emblem.
MILTON, *Paradise Lost*. Bk. iv, l. 695.

Rose, and went forth among her fruits and flowers,
To visit how they prosper'd, bud and bloom,
Her nursery; they at her coming sprung
And touch'd by her fair tendance gladlier grew.
MILTON, *Paradise Lost*. Bk. viii, l. 44.

1
The foxglove, with its stately bells
Of purple, shall adorn thy dells;
The wallflower, on each rifted rock,
From liberal blossoms shall breathe down,
(Gold blossoms flecked with iron brown,)
Its fragrance; while the hollyhock,
The pink, and the carnation vie
With lupin and with lavender,
To decorate the fading year.
D. M. MOIR, *The Birth of the Flowers*. St. 14.

2
The Wreath's of brightest myrtle wove
With brilliant tears of bliss among it,
And many a rose leaf cull'd by Love
To heal his lips when bees have stung it.
THOMAS MOORE, *The Wreath and the Chain*.

3
Where fall the tears of love the rose appears,
And where the ground is bright with friendship's tears,
Forget-me-nots, and violets, heavenly blue,
Spring glittering with the cheerful drops like dew.
NICKLAS MÜLLER, *Paradise of Tears*. (Bryant, tr.)

4
Here's Black-Eyed Susan weeping
Into exotic air,
And Bouncing Bet comes creeping
Back to her old parterre.
ADA FOSTER MURRAY, *Unguarded*.

5
He bore a simple wild-flower wreath:
Narcissus, and the sweet-briar rose;
Vervain, and flexile thyme, that breathe
Rich fragrance; modest heath, that glows
With purple bells; the amaranth bright,
That no decay nor fading knows,
Like true love's holiest, rarest light;
And every purest flower, that blows
In that sweet time, when Love most blesses,
When Spring on Summer's confines presses.
T. L. PEACOCK, *Rhododaphne*. Canto i, l. 107.

6
Here eglantine embalmed the air,
Hawthorn and hazel mingled there;
The primrose pale and violet flower
Found in each clift a narrow bower;
Foxglove and nightshade, side by side,
Emblems of punishment and pride,
Grouped their dark hues with every stain
The weather-beaten crags retain.
SCOTT, *The Lady of the Lake*. Canto i, st. 12.

7
Thou shalt not lack
The flower that's like thy face, pale primrose, nor
The azur'd harebell, like thy veins.
SHAKESPEARE, *Cymbeline*. Act iv, sc. 2, l. 220.

8
When daisies pied and violets blue
And lady-smocks all silver-white
And cuckoo-buds of yellow hue
Do paint the meadows with delight.
SHAKESPEARE, *Love's Labour's Lost*. Act v, sc. 2, l. 904.

In emerald tufts, flowers purple, blue, and white;
Like sapphire, pearl and rich embroidery.
SHAKESPEARE, *The Merry Wives of Windsor*. Act v, sc. 5, l. 74.

To strew thy green with flowers: the yellows, blues,
The purple violets, and marigolds.
SHAKESPEARE, *Pericles*. Act iv, sc. 1, l. 15.

9
I know a bank where the wild thyme blows,
Where oxslips and the nodding violet grows,
Quite over-canopied with luscious woodbine,
With sweet musk-roses and with eglantine.
SHAKESPEARE, *A Midsummer-Night's Dream*. Act ii, sc. 1, l. 251.

Here's flowers for you:
Hot lavender, mints, savory, marjoram;
The marigold, that goes to bed wi' the sun
And with him rises weeping: . . . daffodils
That come before the swallow dares, and take
The winds of March with beauty; violets dim,
But sweeter than the lids of Juno's eyes
Or Cytherea's breath; pale primroses,
That die unmarried, ere they can behold
Bright Phœbus in his strength—a malady
Most incident to maids: bold oxlips and
The crown imperial; lilies of all kinds,
The flower-de-luce being one!
SHAKESPEARE, *Winter's Tale*. Act iv, sc. 4, l. 103.

10
And the Spring arose on the garden fair,
Like the Spirit of Love felt everywhere;

And each flower and herb on Earth's dark breast
Rose from the dreams of its wintry rest.
SHELLEY, *The Sensitive Plant*. Pt. i, st. 2.

1
The tufted basil, pun-provoking thyme,
Fresh baum, and marigold of cheerful hue.
WILLIAM SHENSTONE, *Schoolmistress*. St. 11.

2
Were I, O God, in churchless lands remaining,
Far from all voice of teachers or divines,
My soul would find, in flowers of thy ordaining,
Priests, sermons, shrines!
HORACE SMITH, *Hymn to the Flowers*.

3
No dainty flower or herb that grows on ground,
No arborett with painted blossoms drest,
And smelling sweet, but there it might be found
To bud out fair, and her sweet smells throw all around.
SPENSER, *Faerie Queene*. Bk. ii, canto vi, st. 12.

Roses red and violets blue,
And all the sweetest flowers that in the forest grew.
SPENSER, *Faerie Queene*. Bk. iii, canto vi, st. 6.

Strowe me the ground with daffadowndillies,
And cowslips, and kingcups, and loved lillies.
SPENSER, *Shepheardes Calender: April*, l. 140.

4
The violets ope their purple heads;
The roses blow, the cowslip springs.
SWIFT, *Answer to a Scandalous Poem*, l. 150.

5
With roses musky-breathed,
And drooping daffodilly,
And silver-leaved lily,
And ivy darkly-wreathed,
I wove a crown before her,
For her I love so dearly.
TENNYSON, *Anacreontics*.

6
The gold-eyed kingcups fine,
The frail bluebell peereth over
Rare broidery of the purple clover.
TENNYSON, *A Dirge*. St. 6.

Here are cool mosses deep,
And thro' the moss the ivies creep,
And in the stream the long-leaved flowers weep,
And from the craggy ledge the poppy hangs in sleep.
TENNYSON, *Lotos-Eaters: Choric Song*. Pt. i.

7
The rose is fragrant, but it fades in time:
The violet sweet, but quickly past the prime:
White lilies hang their heads, and soon decay,
And white snow in minutes melts away.
THEOCRITUS, *The Despairing Lover*, l. 57. (Dryden, tr.)

8
The daisy, primrose, violet darkly blue;
And polyanthus of unnumbered dyes.
THOMSON, *The Seasons: Spring*, l. 529.

9
But when they had unloosed the linen band
Which swathed the Egyptian's body,—lo! was found
Closed in the wasted hollow of her hand
A little seed, which sown in English ground
Did wondrous snow of starry blossoms bear,
And spread rich odours through our spring-tide air.
OSCAR WILDE, *Athanasia*. St. 2.

Flowers of remarkable size and hue,
Flowers such as Eden never knew.
R. H. BARHAM, *The Nurse's Story*.

10
Along the river's summer walk,
The withered tufts of asters nod;
And trembles on its arid stalk
The hoar plume of the golden-rod.
WHITTIER, *The Last Walk in Autumn*.

11
The mysteries that cups of flowers enfold
And all the gorgeous sights which fairies do behold.
WORDSWORTH, *Stanzas Written in Thomson's Castle of Indolence*, l. 62.

III—Flowers: Their Language

12
Flowers are Love's truest language; they betray,
Like the divining rods of Magi old,
Where precious wealth lies buried, not of gold,
But love—strong love, that never can decay!
PARK BENJAMIN, *Sonnet*.

13
Who that has loved knows not the tender tale
Which flowers reveal, when lips are coy to tell?
BULWER-LYTTON, *The First Violets*.

14
The delicate odor of mignonette,
The ghost of a dead and gone bouquet,
Is all that tells of her story, yet,
Could she think of a sweeter way?
BRET HARTE, *A Newport Romance*.

15
They speak of hope to the fainting heart,
With a voice of promise they come and part,
They sleep in dust through the wintry hours,
They break forth in glory—bring flowers, bright flowers!
FELICIA DOROTHEA HEMANS, *Bring Flowers*.

16
An exquisite invention this,
Worthy of Love's most honeyed kiss,—
This art of writing billet-doux
In buds, and odours, and bright hues!
In saying all one feels and thinks
In clever daffodils and pinks;
In puns of tulips, and in phrases,
Charming for their truth, of daisies!
LEIGH HUNT, *Love-Letters Made of Flowers*.

Growing one's own choice words and fancies
In orange tubs, and beds of pansies;
One's sighs and passionate declarations,
In odorous rhetoric of carnations; . . .
Taking due care one's flowers of speech
To guard from blight as well as bathos,
And watering, every day, one's pathos!
LEIGH HUNT, *Love-Letters Made of Flowers.*

1
Yet, no—not words, for they
But half can tell love's feeling;
Sweet flowers alone can say
What passion fears revealing.
A once bright rose's wither'd leaf,
A tow'ring lily broken,—
Oh, these may paint a grief
No words could e'er have spoken.
THOMAS MOORE, *The Language of Flowers.*

2
In Eastern lands they talk in flowers,
And they tell in a garland their loves and cares;
Each blossom that blooms in their garden bowers,
On its leaves a mystic language bears.
J. G. PERCIVAL, *The Language of Flowers.*

3
There's rosemary, that's for remembrance; pray, love, remember: and there is pansies, that's for thoughts. . . . There's fennel for you, and columbines: there's rue for you; and here's some for me. . . . O, you must wear your rue with a difference. There's a daisy: I would give you some violets, but they withered all when my father died.
SHAKESPEARE, *Hamlet.* Act iv, sc. 5, l. 175.

4
And ye talk together still,
In the language wherewith Spring
Letters cowslips on the hill.
TENNYSON, *Adeline.* St. 5.

5
Thanks to the human heart by which we live,
Thanks to its tenderness, its joys, and fears,
To me the meanest flower that blows can give
Thoughts that do often lie too deep for tears.
WORDSWORTH, *Intimations of Immortality,* l. 204.

6
Take the flower from my breast, I pray thee,
Take the flower, too, from out my tresses;
And then go hence; for, see, the night is fair,
The stars rejoice to watch thee on thy way.
UNKNOWN. (*Bard of the Dimbovitza.* No. 3. English by Carmen Sylva and Alma Strettell.)

Here's eglantine,
Here's ivy!—take them as I used to do
Thy flowers, and keep them where they shall not pine.
Instruct thine eyes to keep their colours true,
And tell thy soul their roots are left in mine.
E. B. BROWNING, *Sonnets from the Portuguese.* No. xliv.

IV—Flowers: Individual

Quotations relating to the more important flowers will be found under their respective names: Buttercup, Daffodil, Daisy, etc.

Acacia

7
A great acacia, with its slender trunk
And overpoise of multitudinous leaves
(In which a hundred fields might spill their dew
And intense verdure, yet find room enough)
Stood reconciling all the place with green.
E. B. BROWNING. *Aurora Leigh.* Bk. vi, l. 537.

8
Our rocks are rough, but smiling there
Th' acacia waves her yellow hair,
Lonely and sweet, nor loved the less
For flow'ring in a wilderness.
THOMAS MOORE, *Lalla Rookh: Light of the Harem.*

Almond

9
Almond blossom, sent to teach us
That the spring days soon will reach us,
Lest, with longing over-tried,
We die, as the violets died.
EDWIN ARNOLD, *Almond Blossom.*

10
White as the blossoms which the almond tree,
Above its bald and leafless branches bears.
MARGARET JUNKIN PRESTON, *Royal Preacher.*

Amaranth

11
Immortal amaranth, a flower which once
In Paradise, fast by the Tree of Life,
Began to bloom, but soon for man's offence
To Heav'n remov'd, where first it grew, there grows,
And flow'rs aloft shading the Fount of Life,
MILTON, *Paradise Lost.* Bk. iii, l. 353.

Anemone, see WINDFLOWER, *infra.*

Arbutus

12
Darlings of the forest!
Blossoming alone
When Earth's grief is sorest
For her jewels gone—
Ere the last snow-drift melts your tender buds have blown.
ROSE TERRY COOKE, *Trailing Arbutus.*

13
Pure and perfect, sweet arbutus
Twines her rosy-tinted wreath.
ELAINE GOODALE EASTMAN, *The First Flowers.*

14
The shy little Mayflower weaves her nest,
But the south wind sighs o'er the fragrant loam,
And betrays the path to her woodland home.
SARAH HELEN WHITMAN, *Waking of the Heart.*

Asphodel

1
With her ankles sunken in asphodel
She wept for the roses of earth which fell.
E. B. BROWNING, *Calls on the Heart*.

2
And rest at last where souls unbodied dwell,
In ever-flow'ring meads of asphodel.
HOMER, *Odyssey*. Bk. xxiv, l. 19. (Pope, tr.)

By those happy souls who dwell
In yellow meads of asphodel.
POPE, *Ode on St. Cecilia's Day*, l. 74.

Aster

3
Chide me not, laborious band!
For the idle flowers I brought;
Every aster in my hand
Goes home loaded with a thought.
EMERSON, *The Apology*.

4
The aster greets us as we pass
With her faint smile.
SARAH HELEN WHITMAN, *A Day of the Indian Summer*, l. 35.

Azalea

5
And in the woods a fragrance rare
Of wild azaleas fills the air,
And richly tangled overhead
We see their blossoms sweet and red.
DORA READ GOODALE, *Spring Scatters Far and Wide*.

6
A very rapture of white;
A wedlock of silence and light:
White, white as the wonder undefiled
Of Eve just wakened in Paradise.
HARRIET MCEWAN KIMBALL, *White Azaleas*.

7
The fair azalea bows
Beneath its snowy crest.
SARAH H. WHITMAN, *She Blooms No More*.

Barberries

8
Do you love barberries? . . .
There is something splendid about them:
They are not afraid of being warm and glad and bold;
They flush joyously like a cheek under a lover's kiss;
They bleed cruelly like a dagger-wound in the breast;
They flame up madly for their little hour,
Knowing they must die.
MARY ALDIS, *Barberries*.

Bluebells

9
To-night from deeps of loneliness I wake in wistful wonder
To a sudden sense of brightness, an immanence of blue—
O are there bluebells swaying in the shadowy coppice yonder,
Shriven with the dawning and the dew?
LUCIA CLARK MARKHAM, *Bluebells*.

Broom

10
Oh the Broom, the yellow Broom,
The ancient poet sung it,
And dear it is on summer days
To lie at rest among it.
MARY HOWITT, *The Broom Flower*.

Buttercup, see separate heading.

Camomile, see ADVERSITY.

Celandine

11
Long as there's a sun that sets,
Primroses will have their glory;
Long as there are violets,
They will have a place in story:
There's a flower that shall be mine,
'Tis the little Celandine.
WORDSWORTH, *To the Small Celandine*.

Eyes of some men travel far
For the finding of a star;
Up and down the heavens they go,
Men that keep a mighty rout!
I'm as great as they, I trow,
Since the day I found thee out,
Little Flower!—I'll make a stir,
Like a great astronomer.
WORDSWORTH, *To the Small Celandine*.

There is a flower, the lesser Celandine,
That shrinks, like many more, from cold and rain;
And, the first moment that the sun may shine.
Bright as the sun himself, 'tis out again!
WORDSWORTH, *The Small Celandine*.

Clover, see separate heading.

Compass Plant

12
Look at this vigorous plant that lifts its head from the meadow,
See how its leaves are turned to the north, as true as the magnet;
This is the compass-flower, that the finger of God has planted
Here in the houseless wild, to direct the traveller's journey.
LONGFELLOW, *Evangeline*. Pt. ii, sec. iv, l. 140.

Convolvulus

13
There is an herb named in Latin Convolvulus (*i.e.* with wind), growing among shrubs and bushes, which carrieth a flower not unlike to this Lilly, save that it yieldeth no smell nor hath those chives within; for whiteness they resemble one another very much, as if Nature in making this flower were a learning and trying her skill how to frame the Lilly indeed.
PLINY, *Historia Naturalis*. Bk. xxi, ch. 10.

Cowslip, Daffodil, Daisy, Dandelion, see separate headings.

Edelweiss

1
Ye living flowers that skirt the eternal frost!
S. T. COLERIDGE, *Hymn Before Sunrise in the Vale of Chamouni.*

Eglantine

2
The fresh eglantine exhal'd a breath,
Whose odours were of pow'r to raise from death.
DRYDEN, *The Flower and the Leaf*, l. 96.

3
Rain-scented eglantine
Gave temperate sweets to that well-wooing sun.
KEATS, *Endymion*. Bk. i, l. 100.

Its sides I'll plant with dew-sweet eglantine.
KEATS, *Endymion*. Bk. iv, l. 700.

Flower-de-Luce

4
Born in the purple, born to joy and pleasance,
Thou dost not toil nor spin,
But makest glad and radiant with thy presence
The meadow and the lin.
LONGFELLOW, *Flower-de-Luce*. St. 3.

Forget-me-not

5
The blue significant Forget-me-not.
THOMAS HOOD, *Ode to Rae Wilson.*

6
The sweet forget-me-nots,
That grow for happy lovers.
TENNYSON, *The Brook*, l. 172.

Gentian

7
Then doth thy sweet and quiet eye
Look through its fringes to the sky,
Blue—blue—as if that sky let fall
A flower from its cerulean wall.
BRYANT, *To the Fringed Gentian.*

And the blue gentian-flower, that, in the breeze,
Nods lonely, of her beauteous race the last.
BRYANT, *November.*

8
Blue thou art, intensely blue;
Flower, whence came thy dazzling hue?
JAMES MONTGOMERY, *The Gentianella.*

Goldenrod

9
Reaching up through bush and brier,
Sumptuous brow and heart of fire,
Flaunting high its wind-rocked plume,
Brave with wealth of native bloom,—
Goldenrod!
ELAINE GOODALE EASTMAN, *Goldenrod.*

10
I know the lands are lit
With all the autumn blaze of Goldenrod.
HELEN HUNT JACKSON, *Asters and Goldenrod.*

11
Welcome, dear Goldenrod, once more,
Thou mimic, flowering elm!
I always think that Summer's store
Hangs from thy laden stem.
HORACE SCUDDER, *To the Goldenrod at Midsummer.*

12
And in the evening, everywhere
Along the roadside, up and down,
I see the golden torches flare
Like lighted street-lamps in the town.
FRANK DEMPSTER SHERMAN, *Golden-Rod.*

Gorse

13
Mountain gorses, ever-golden,
Cankered not the whole year long!
Do ye teach us to be strong,
Howsoever pricked and holden
Like your thorny blooms, and so
Trodden on by rain and snow,
Up the hillside of this life, as bleak as where ye grow?
E. B. BROWNING, *Lessons from the Gorse.*

Mountain gorses, since Linnæus
Knelt beside you on the sod,
For your beauty thanking God,—
For your teaching, ye should see us
Bowing in prostration new!
E. B. BROWNING, *Lessons from the Gorse.*

14
Love you not, then, to list and hear
The crackling of the gorse-flower near,
Pouring an orange-scented tide
Of fragrance o'er the desert wide?
WILLIAM HOWITT, *A June Day.*

Harebell

15
With drooping bells of clearest blue
Thou didst attract my childish view,
Almost resembling
The azure butterflies that flew
Where on the heath thy blossoms grew
So lightly trembling.
REGINALD HEBER, *The Harebell.*

16
Simplest of blossoms! To mine eye
Thou bring'st the summer's painted sky;
The May-thorn greening in the nook;
The minnows sporting in the brook;
The bleat of flocks; the breath of flowers;
The song of birds amid the bowers;
The crystal of the azure seas;
The music of the southern breeze;
And, over all, the blessed sun,
Telling of halcyon days begun.
DAVID M. MOIR, *The Harebell.*

Hawthorn, see separate heading.

Grass, see separate heading.

Honeysuckle

17
And honeysuckle loved to crawl

Up the low crag and ruin'd wall.
SCOTT, *Marmion:* Canto iii, *Introduction.*

1
So doth the woodbine the sweet honeysuckle
Gentle entwist.
SHAKESPEARE, *A Midsummer-Night's Dream.* Act iv, sc. 1, l. 45.

2
And bid her steal into the pleached bower,
Where honeysuckles, ripen'd by the sun,
Forbid the sun to enter, like favorites,
Made proud by princes, that advance their pride
Against that power that bred it.
SHAKESPEARE, *Much Ado About Nothing.* Act iii, sc. 1, l. 7.

Hyacinth, Ivy, Jasmine, see separate headings.

Knapweed

3
By copse and hedgerow, waste and wall,
He thrusts his cushions red;
O'er burdock rank, o'er thistles tall,
He rears his hardy head:
Within, without, the strong leaves press,
He screens the mossy stone,
Lord of a narrow wilderness,
Self-centred and alone.
A. C. BENSON, *Knapweed.*

Lichen

4
Sharing the stillness of the unimpassioned rock, they share also its endurance; and while the winds of departing Spring scatter the white hawthorn blossom like drifted snow, and summer dims on the parched meadow the drooping of its cowslip-gold, far above, among the mountains, the silver lichen-spots rest, starlike, on the stone; and the gathering orange stain upon the edge of yonder Western peak reflects the sunsets of a thousand years.
RUSKIN, *Modern Painters.* Vol. v, pt. vi, ch. 10.

Lilac, Lily, Lotus, see separate headings.

Love-in-Idleness

5
Give me to live with Love alone
And let the world go dine and dress;
For Love hath lowly haunts. . . .
If life's a flower, I choose my own—
'Tis "love in Idleness."
LAMAN BLANCHARD, *Dolce far Niente.* St. 4.

6
Yet mark'd I where the bolt of Cupid fell:
It fell upon a little western flower,
Before milk-white, now purple with love's wound,
And maidens call it love-in-idleness.
Fetch me that flower; the herb I shew'd thee once:
The juice of it on sleeping eyelids laid
Will make or man or woman madly dote
Upon the next live creature that it sees.
SHAKESPEARE, *A Midsummer-Night's Dream.* Act ii, sc. 1, l. 165.

Marigold

7
No marigolds yet closed are,
No shadows great appear.
ROBERT HERRICK, *To Daisies, Not to Shut So Soon.*

8
The sun-observing marigold.
QUARLES, *School of the Heart.* Ode xxx, st. 5.

Mignonette

9
The Frenchman's darling.
COWPER, *The Task.* Bk. iv, l. 765. Cowper is referring to the mignonette. He is said to have been the one who gave this flower this now common name.

10
A pitcher of mignonette
In a tenement's highest casement,—
Queer sort of a flower-pot—yet
That pitcher of mignonette
Is a garden in heaven set
To the little sick child in the basement—
The pitcher of mignonette,
In the tenement's highest casement.
H. C. BUNNER, *A Pitcher of Mignonette.*

Mint

11
I am that flower,—That mint.—That columbine.
SHAKESPEARE, *Love's Labour's Lost.* Act v, sc. 2, l. 661.

Moly

12
That moly
That Hermes once to wise Ulysses gave.
MILTON, *Comus,* l. 637.

13
Traveler, pluck a stem of moly,
If thou touch at Circe's isle,—
Hermes' moly, growing solely
To undo enchanter's wile!
EDITH M. THOMAS, *Moly.*

The root is hard to loose
From hold of earth by mortals; but God's power
Can all things do. 'Tis black, but bears a flower
As white as milk.
HOMER, *Odyssey.* (Chapman, tr.)

Morning-Glory

14
Was it worth while to paint so fair
Thy every leaf—to vein with faultless art
Each petal, taking the book light and air
Of summer so to heart? . . .
Thy silence answers: "Life was mine!
And I, who pass without regret or grief,
Have cared the more to make my moment fine,
Because it was so brief."
FLORENCE EARLE COATES, *The Morning-Glory.*

1
A morning-glory at my window satisfies me
more than the metaphysics of books.
WALT WHITMAN, *Song of Myself*. Sec. 24.

Myrtle

2
The myrtle (ensign of supreme command,
Consign'd by Venus to Melissa's hand)
Not less capricious than a reigning fair,
Oft favours, oft rejects a lover's prayer;
In myrtle shades oft sings the happy swain,
In myrtle shades despairing ghosts complain.
SAMUEL JOHNSON, *Written at the Request of a Gentleman*, l. 3.

3
Once more,
Ye myrtles brown, with ivy never-sere,
I come to pluck your berries harsh and crude,
And with forc'd fingers rude,
Shatter your leaves before the mellowing year.
MILTON, *Lycidas*, l. 1.

4
While the myrtle, now idly entwin'd with his
crown,
Like the wreath of Harmodius, shall cover his
sword.
THOMAS MOORE, *O, Blame Not The Bard*.

Narcissus

See also Hyacinth, under separate heading.

5
And narcissi, the fairest among them all,
Who gaze on their eyes in the stream's recess,
Till they die of their own dear loveliness.
SHELLEY, *The Sensitive Plant*. Pt. i, st. 5.

Nettle

6
This corner of the farmyard I like most:
As well as any bloom upon a flower
I like the dust on the nettles, never lost
Except to prove the sweetness of a shower.
EDWARD THOMAS, *Tall Nettles*.

Pansy, see separate heading.

Pink

7
You take a pink,
You dig about its roots and water it,
And so improve it to a garden-pink,
But will not change it to a heliotrope.
E. B. BROWNING, *Aurora Leigh*. Bk. vi, l. 1044.

8
And I will pu' the pink, the emblem o' my
dear,
For she's the pink o' womankind, and blooms
without a peer.
BURNS, *O Luve Will Venture In*.

Poppy, Primrose, see separate headings.

Rhodora

9
In May, when sea-winds pierced our solitudes,
I found the fresh Rhodora in the woods,
Spreading its leafless blooms in a damp nook,
To please the desert and the sluggish brook.
The purple petals, fallen in the pool,
Made the black water with their beauty gay;
Here might the red-bird come his plumes to
cool,
And court the flower that cheapens his array.
Rhodora! if the sages ask thee why
This charm is wasted on the earth and sky,
Tell them, dear, that if eyes were made for
seeing,
Then Beauty is its own excuse for being:
Why thou wert there, O rival of the rose!
I never thought to ask, I never knew:
But, in my simple ignorance, suppose
The self-same Power that brought me there
brought you.
EMERSON, *The Rhodora*.

Rose, see separate heading.

Rosemary

10
Dreary rosmarye
That always mourns the dead.
THOMAS HOOD, *Flowers*.

11
The humble rosemary
Whose sweets so thanklessly are shed
To scent the desert and the dead.
THOMAS MOORE, *Lalla Rookh: Light of the Harem*.

Sensitive Plant

12
A Sensitive Plant in a garden grew,
And the young winds fed it with silver dew;
And it opened its fan-like leaves to the light,
And closed them beneath the kisses of Night.
SHELLEY, *The Sensitive Plant*. Pt. i, st. 1.

For the Sensitive Plant has no bright flower;
Radiance and odour are not its dower;
It loves, even like Love,—its deep heart is full;
It desires what it has not, the beautiful.
SHELLEY, *The Sensitive Plant*. Pt. i, st. 19.

Shamrock, see Ireland.

Snowdrop

13
Close to the sod there can be seen
A thought of God in white and green. . . .
It is so holy and yet so lowly.
ANNA BUNSTON DE BARY, *The Snowdrop*.

14
The morning star of flowers.
JAMES MONTGOMERY, *Snow-Drop*.

15
Chaste Snowdrop, venturous harbinger of
Spring,
And pensive monitor of fleeting years.
WORDSWORTH, *To a Snowdrop*.

Lone Flower, hemmed in with snows and white
as they
But hardier far, once more I see thee bend
Thy forehead, as if fearful to offend,

Like an unbidden guest. Though day by day,
Storms, sallying from the mountain tops, waylay
The rising sun, and on the plains descend;
Yet art thou welcome, welcome as a friend
Whose zeal outruns his promise!

WORDSWORTH, *To a Snowdrop.*

Sunflower, see separate heading.

Sweet Basil

1
I pray your Highness mark this curious herb:
Touch it but lightly, stroke it softly, Sir,
And it gives forth an odor sweet and rare;
But crush it harshly and you'll make a scent
Most disagreeable.

CHARLES GODFREY LELAND, *Sweet Basil.*

Sweet Pea

2
Here are sweet peas, on tiptoe for a flight;
With wings of gentle flush o'er delicate white,
And taper fingers catching at all things,
To bind them all about with tiny rings.

KEATS, *I Stood Tiptoe Upon a Little Hill*, l. 57.

Tuberose

3
The tuberose, with her silvery light,
That in the gardens of Malay
Is call'd the Mistress of the Night,
So like a bride, scented and bright;
She comes out when the sun's away.

THOMAS MOORE, *Lalla Rookh: Light of the Harem.*

Tulip

4
'Mid the sharp, short emerald wheat, scarce risen three fingers well,
The wild tulip, at end of its tube, blows out its great red bell,
Like a thin clear bubble of blood, for the children to pick and sell.

ROBERT BROWNING, *Up at a Villa: Down in the City*. St. 6.

5
The tulip is a courtly quean,
Whom, therefore, I will shun.

THOMAS HOOD, *Flowers.*

6
Not one of Flora's brilliant race
A form more perfect can display;
Art could not feign more simple grace
Nor Nature take a line away.

MONTGOMERY, *On Planting a Tulip-Root.*

7
Clean as a lady,
cool as glass,
fresh without fragrance
the tulip was.

HUMBERT WOLFE, *Tulip.*

Violet, see separate heading.

Wallflower

8
Flower in the crannied wall,
I pluck you out of the crannies,
I hold you here, root and all, in my hand,
Little flower—but *if* I could understand
What you are, root and all, and all in all,
I should know what God and man is.

TENNYSON, *Flower in the Crannied Wall.*

Wind-flower

9
Or, bide thou where the poppy blows,
With wind-flowers frail and fair.

BRYANT, *The Arctic Lover.*

10
Teach me the secret of thy loveliness,
That, being made wise, I may aspire to be
As beautiful in thought, and so express
Immortal truths to earth's mortality.

MADISON CAWEIN, *To a Wind-Flower.*

11
Anemone, so well
Named of the wind, to which thou art all free.

GEORGE MACDONALD, *Wild Flowers*, l. 9.

12
Thou lookest up with meek, confiding eye
Upon the clouded smile of April's face,
Unharmed though Winter stands uncertain by,
Eyeing with jealous glance each opening grace.

JONES VERY, *The Wind-flower.*

FLY

For Fly in Amber, see Amber

13
It was prettily devised of Æsop: The fly sat upon the axle-tree of the chariot-wheel, and said, What a dust do I raise!

FRANCIS BACON, *Essays: Of Vain-Glory.*

What a dust have I rais'd! quoth the fly upon the coach.

THOMAS FULLER, *Gnomologia.* No. 5476.

The fly, which sitting upon a cart that was driven in the way, said he had raised a very great dust.

GUAZZO, *Civil Conversations.* Fo. 71. (1586)

Yet these are no more than the fly on the wheel.

WILLIAM GURNALL, *The Christian in Complete Armour*, p. 299. (1679)

"Let us breathe now," said the fly at once [after the horses had dragged the coach up the hill]. "I have done so much that our passengers are at last on level ground." ("Respirons maintenant!" dit la mouche aussitôt. "J'ai tant fait que nos gens sont enfin dans la plaine.")

LA FONTAINE, *Fables.* Bk. vii, fab. 9.

And so we plough along, as the fly said to the ox.

LONGFELLOW, *The Spanish Student.* Act iii, sc. 5.

14
The wanton boy that kills a fly
Shall feel the spider's enmity.

WILLIAM BLAKE, *Auguries of Innocence.*

I killed a fly this morning—it buzzed, and I wouldn't have it!

W. S. GILBERT, *Ruddigore.* Act i.

As willingly as one would kill a fly.
SHAKESPEARE, *Titus Andronicus*. Act v, sc. 1, l. 142.

1
Dead flies cause the ointment of the apothecary to send forth a stinking savour: so doth a little folly him that is in reputation for wisdom and honour.
Old Testament: Ecclesiastes, x, 1. Hence, "A fly in the ointment."

2
A fly is as untamable as a hyena.
EMERSON, *Conduct of Life: Considerations by the Way*.

3
An actually existing fly is more important than a possibly existing angel.
EMERSON, *Letter to Moncure D. Conway*.

4
'Twould make even a fly laugh.
THOMAS FULLER, *Gnomologia*. No. 5340.

5
The fly that sips treacle is lost in the sweets.
JOHN GAY, *The Beggar's Opera*. Act ii, sc. 2. *See also under* FLATTERY.

6
Make not thy sport abuses; for the fly
That feeds on dung is coloured thereby.
GEORGE HERBERT, *The Church-Porch*. St. 39.

7
To a boiling pot flies come not.
GEORGE HERBERT, *Jacula Prudentum*.

Flies come to feasts unasked.
W. G. BENHAM, *Proverbs*, p. 761.

8
A fly on your nose, you slap, and it goes;
If it comes back again, it will bring a good rain.
INWARDS, *Weather Lore*, p. 148.

9
Low trees have their tops, . . . the fly his spleen.
JOHN LYLY, *Euphues*, p. 316. (1580)

Ants have bile and flies have spleen. (Formicæ sua bilis inest, habet et musca splenem.)
SIR THOMAS BROWNE, *Pseudodoxia Epidemica*. Bk. iii, ch. 3. (1646) Quoted as a proverb.

Even a fly hath its spleen.
THOMAS FULLER, *Gnomologia*. No. 1388.

10
Busy, curious, thirsty fly,
Drink with me, and drink as I;
Freely welcome to my cup,
Couldst thou sip and sip it up.
Make the most of life you may;
Life is short and wears away.
Both alike are mine and thine,
Hastening quick to their decline;
Thine's a summer, mine no more,
Though repeated to three-score;
Three-score summers, when they've gone,
Will appear as short as one.
WILLIAM OLDYS, *On a Fly Drinking Out of a Cup of Ale*.

Go, poor devil, get thee gone! Why should I hurt thee? This world is surely wide enough to hold both thee and me.
STERNE, *Tristram Shandy*. Vol. ii, ch. 12. Uncle Toby is addressing a fly.

11
King James said to the fly, Have I three kingdoms, and thou must needs fly into my eye?
JOHN SELDEN, *Table-Talk: Religion*.

12
Though he in a fertile climate dwell,
Plague him with flies.
SHAKESPEARE, *Othello*. Act i, sc. 1, l. 70.

13
Baby bye, Here's a fly,
Let us watch him, you and I,
How he crawls Up the walls
Yet he never falls.
THEODORE TILTON, *Baby Bye*.

FLYING

See also Lindbergh

14
Let brisker youths their active nerves prepare
Fit their light silken wings and skim the buxom air.
RICHARD OWEN CAMBRIDGE, *Scriblerad*. (1751)

15
To her hurt the ant got wings.
CERVANTES, *Don Quixote*. Pt. ii, ch. 33.

16
But you the pathways of the sky
Found first, and tasted heavenly springs,
Unfettered as the lark that sings,
And knew strange raptures,—though we sigh,
"Poor Icarus!"
FLORENCE EARLE COATES, *Poor Icarus*.

17
Bishop Wilkins prophesied that the time would come when gentlemen, when they were to go a journey, would call for their wings as regularly as they call for their boots.
MARIA EDGEWORTH, *Essay on Irish Bulls*. Ch. 2.

18
Fly and you will catch the swallow.
JAMES HOWELL, *Proverbs*, 13. (1659)

19
Flying without feathers is not easy; my wings have no feathers. (Sine pennis volare hau facilest; meæ alea pennas non habent.)
PLAUTUS, *Pœnulus*, l. 871. (Act v, sc. 2.)

He would fain fly but wanted feathers.
JOHN HEYWOOD, *Proverbs*. Pt. i, ch. 11.

20
He rode upon a cherub, and did fly: yea, he did fly upon the wings of the wind.
Old Testament: Psalms, xviii, 10.

On cherubs and on cherubims
Full royally he rode;
And on the wings of all the winds
Came flying all abroad.
THOMAS STERNHOLD, *A Metrical Version of Psalm xviii*.

On wings of winds came flying all abroad.
POPE, *Epistle to Dr. Arbuthnot*, l. 218.

1
For I dipt into the future, far as human eye could see,
Saw the Vision of the world, and all the wonder that would be;
Saw the heavens fill with commerce, argosies of magic sails,
Pilots of the purple twilight, dropping down with costly bales;
Heard the heavens fill with shouting, and there rain'd a ghastly dew
From the nations' airy navies grappling in the central blue.

TENNYSON, *Locksley Hall*, l. 119.

2
Darius was clearly of the opinion
That the air is also man's dominion
And that with paddle or fin or pinion,
We soon or late shall navigate
The azure as now we sail the sea.

J. T. TROWBRIDGE, *Darius Green and His Flying Machine.*

"The birds can fly, an' why can't I?
Must we give in," says he, with a grin,
" 'T the bluebird an' phœbe are smarter 'n we be?
Jest fold our hands, an' see the swaller
An' blackbird an' catbird beat us holler? . . .
Jest show me that! er prove 't the bat
Hez got more brains than's in my hat,
An' I'll back down, an' not till then!"

J. T. TROWBRIDGE, *Darius Green and His Flying Machine.*

"Wal, I like flyin' well enough,"
He said, "but the' ain't sich a thundern' sight
O' fun in't when ye come to light."

J. T. TROWBRIDGE, *Darius Green and His Flying Machine.*

3
I have seen so much on my pilgrimage through my three score years and ten,
That I wouldn't be surprised to see a railroad in the air,
Or a Yankee in a flyin' ship a-goin' most anywhere.

J. H. YATES, *The Old Ways and the New.*

FOE, see Enemy

FOG

4
Wrapped in a cloak
Of grey mystery,
Fog, the magician,
Steals tip-toe out of the sea.

MELVILLE CANE, *Fog, The Magician.*

5
A fog cannot be dispelled with a fan.

MICHAEL A. DENHAM, *Proverbs.*

6
This is a London particular—a fog, miss.

DICKENS, *Bleak House.* Ch. 3.

7
The yellow fog that rubs its back upon the window-panes,

T. S. ELIOT, *The Love Song of J. Alfred Prufrock.*

8
The fog comes
on little cat feet.
It sits looking
over the harbor and city
on silent haunches
and then, moves on.

CARL SANDBURG, *Fog.*

9
There must be something good in you, I know,
Or why does everyone abuse you so?

OWEN SEAMAN, *In Praise of Fog.*

10
To lose itself in a fog.

SHAKESPEARE, *Coriolanus.* Act ii, sc. 3, l. 34.

The starry welkin cover thou anon
With drooping fog as black as Acheron.

SHAKESPEARE, *A Midsummer-Night's Dream.* Act iii, sc. 2, l. 357.

11
The yellow fog came creeping down
The bridges, till the houses' walls
Seemed changed to shadows, and St. Paul's
Loomed like a bubble o'er the town.

OSCAR WILDE, *Impression du Matin.*

FOLLY

12
The folly of one man is the fortune of another.

FRANCIS BACON, *Essays: Of Fortune.*

13
If others had not been foolish, we should be so.

WILLIAM BLAKE, *Proverbs of Hell.*

14
This picture, placed these busts between,
Gives Satire its full strength;
Wisdom and Wit are little seen,
But Folly at full length.

JANE BRERETON, *On Beau Nash's Picture at Full Length between the Busts of Sir Isaac Newton and Mr. Pope, in the Pump Room at Bath.* (*Poems*, 1744; DYCE, *Specimens of British Poetesses.*) This epigram is often ascribed to Lord Chesterfield (CAMPBELL, *English Poets*, p. 521, note; MATTHEW MATY, *Memoirs of Chesterfield*, sec. 4), and was also included by Henry Norris in an edition of his own poems published in 1740. (See *Notes and Queries*, 10 Feb., 1917, p 119.)

15
And Folly loves the martyrdom of Fame.

BYRON, *Monody on the Death of Sheridan.*

16
Folly is wont to have more followers and comrades than discretion. (Mas acompañados y paniguados debe di tener la locura que la discrecion.)

CERVANTES, *Don Quixote.* Pt. ii, ch. 13.

17
Many count their chickens before they are hatched; and where they expect bacon, meet with broken bones.

CERVANTES, *Don Quixote.* Pt. ii, ch. 55.

To swallow gudgeons ere they're catch'd,

And count their chickens ere they're hatch'd.
BUTLER, *Hudibras*. Pt. ii, canto iii, l. 923.

You reckon your chickens before they are hatched.
ERASMUS, *Colloquies*, 39. (Bailey, tr.)

Take care we don't reckon our chickens before they are hatched.
JAMES HOWARD, *English Monsieur*. Act iii, sc. 3. (1674)

My chickings are not hatched; I nil to count of them as yet.
UNKNOWN, *Misogonus*. Act iv, sc. 1. (1577)

You are over hasty: your harvest is still in the blade. (Nimium properas: et adhuc tua messis in herba est.)
OVID, *Heroides*. Epis. xvii, l. 263.

1
The shortest follies are the best. (Les plus courtes folies sont les meilleures.)
CHARRON, *La Sagesse*. Bk. i, ch. 34.

The shortest folly is always the best. (La plus courte folie est toujours le meilleure.)
LA GIRANDIÈRE, *Le Recueil des Voyeux Epigrammes.*

2
His ambition is to sink,
To reach a depth profounder still, and still
Profounder, in the fathomless abyss
Of folly.
COWPER, *The Task*. Bk. v, l. 592.

3
Folly in youth is sin, in age 'tis madness.
SAMUEL DANIEL, *The Tragedy of Cleopatra.* Act iii, sc. 2.

Happy the man who knows his follies in his youth.
SAMUEL RICHARDSON, *Clarissa Harlowe*, iv, 121. Quoting a proverb.

4
All is laughter, all is dust, all is nothing, for all that is cometh from folly. (Πάντα γέλως, καὶ πάντα κόνις, καὶ πάντα τὸ μηδέν· πάντα γὰρ ἐξ ἀλόγων ἐστὶ τὰ γινόμενα.)
GLYCON. (*Greek Anthology*. Bk. x, epig. 124.)

5
The folly of others is ever most ridiculous to those who are themselves most foolish.
GOLDSMITH, *The Citizen of the World*. No. 43.

In my time the follies of the town crept slowly among us, but now they travel faster than a stage coach.
GOLDSMITH, *She Stoops to Conquer*. Act i.

6
Scared at thy frown terrific, fly
Self-pleasing Folly's idle brood.
THOMAS GRAY, *Hymn to Adversity*, l. 17.

7
Till follies become ruinous, the world is better with them than it would be without them.
LORD HALIFAX, *Works*, p. 236.

8
Folly grows without watering.
GEORGE HERBERT, *Jacula Prudentum.*

If folly were grief, every house would weep.
GEORGE HERBERT, *Jacula Prudentum.*

The chief disease that reigns this year is folly.
GEORGE HERBERT, *Jacula Prudentum.*

9
And Follies are miscalled the crimes of Fate.
HOMER, *Odyssey*. Bk. i, l. 44. (Pope, tr.)

10
The shame is not in having once been foolish, but in not cutting the folly short. (Nec lusisse pudet, sed non incidere ludum.)
HORACE, *Epistles*. Bk. i, epis. 14, l. 36.

Wealth excuses folly. (Stultitiam patiuntur opes.)
HORACE, *Epistles*. Bk. i, epis. 18, l. 29.

11
Who lives without folly is not so wise as he thinks. (Qui vit sans folie n'est pas si sage qu'il croit.)
LA ROCHEFOUCAULD, *Maximes*. No. 209.

12
And every one that heareth these sayings of mine, and doeth them not, shall be likened unto a foolish man, which built his house upon the sand: And the rain descended, and the floods came, and the winds blew, and beat upon that house; and it fell: and great was the fall of it.
New Testament: Matthew, vii, 26–27.

Oft would he say, Who builds his house on sands,
Pricks his blind horse across the fallow lands,
Or lets his wife abroad with pilgrims roam,
Deserves a fool's-cap and long ears at home.
POPE, *The Wife of Bath: Her Prologue*, l. 347.

13
Folly is for mortals a self-chosen misfortune. ("Ανοια θνητοῖς δυστύχημ' αὐθαίρετον.)
MENANDER, *Fragments*. No. 618.

14
All are pleas'd, by partial passion led,
To shift their follies on another's head.
THOMAS PARNELL, *Elysium*, l. 103.

15
How much folly there is in human affairs. (Quantum est in rebus inane!)
PERSIUS, *Satires*. Sat. i, l. 1.

16
Eye Nature's walks, shoot folly as it flies,
And catch the manners living as they rise.
POPE, *Essay on Man*. Epis. i, l. 13.

Thou comedy to men,
Whose serious folly is a butt for all
To shoot their wits at!
BEAUMONT AND FLETCHER, *Love's Cure*. Act iii, sc. 1.

17
In Folly's cup still laughs the bubble joy.
POPE, *Essay on Man*. Epis. ii, l. 288.

Leave such to trifle with more grace and ease,
Whom Folly pleases, and whose follies please.
POPE, *Imitations of Horace: Epistles*. Bk. ii, epis. 2, l. 326.

18
I saw a new world in my dream,
Where all the follies alike did seem.
W. B. RANDS, *I Saw a New World.*

19
Young gentlemen! pray recollect, if you please,

Not to make assignations near mulberry trees;
Should your mistress be missing, it shows a weak head
To be stabbing yourself till you know she is dead.
J. G. SAXE, *Pyramus and Thisbe: Moral.*

1
Folly always loathes itself. (Omnis stultitia laborat fastidio sui.)
SENECA, *Epistulæ ad Lucilium.* Epis. ix, sec. 22.

Folly is often sick of itself.
THOMAS FULLER, *Gnomologia.* No. 1559.

2
Folly is low, abject, mean, slavish, and exposed to many of the cruellest passions. (Humilis res est stultitia, abiecta, sordida, servilis, multis affectibus et sævissimis subiecta.)
SENECA, *Epistulæ ad Lucilium.* Epis. xxxvii, 4.

3
The common curse of mankind—folly and ignorance.
SHAKESPEARE, *Troilus and Cressida.* Act ii, sc. 3, l. 31.

Foolery, sir, does walk about the orb like the sun, it shines every where.
SHAKESPEARE, *Twelfth Night.* Act iii, sc. 1, l. 44.

4
You may as well
Forbid the sea for to obey the moon,
As or by oath remove or counsel shake
The fabric of his folly.
SHAKESPEARE, *Winter's Tale.* Act i, sc. 2, l. 426.

5
The word Folly is, perhaps, the prettiest word in the language.
WILLIAM SHENSTONE, *Of Men and Manners,* 5.

Folly is the direct pursuit of Happiness and Beauty.
BERNARD SHAW, *Maxims for Revolutionists.*

6
'Tis not by guilt the onward sweep
Of truth and right, O Lord, we stay;
'Tis by our follies that so long
We hold the earth from heaven away.
E. R. SILL, *The Fool's Prayer.*

7
Brutes find out where their talents lie:
A bear will not attempt to fly;
A founder'd horse will oft debate,
Before he tries a five-barr'd gate;
A dog by instinct turns aside,
Who sees the ditch too deep and wide;
But man we find the only creature
Who, led by Folly, combats Nature;
Who, when she loudly cries, Forbear
With obstinacy fixes there;
And, where his genius least inclines,
Absurdly bends his whole designs.
SWIFT, *On Poetry,* l. 13.

8
It is well to advise folly, not to punish it. (Monere non punire stultitiam decet.)
PUBLILIUS SYRUS, *Sententiæ.* No. 412.

9
I receive the reward of my folly. (Pretium ob stultitiam fero.)
TERENCE, *Andria,* l. 610. (Act iii, sc. 5.)

The ultimate effect of shielding men from the effects of folly is to fill the world with fools.
HERBERT SPENCER, *State Tamperings with Money Banks.*

10
Suff'ring more from folly, than from fate.
YOUNG, *Night Thoughts.* Night viii, l. 167.

FOOD, see Eating

FOOL

I—Fool: Apothegms

11
Verily a prosperous fool is a heavy load. (Ἦ βαρὺ φόρημ' ἄνθρωπος εὐτυχῶν ἄφρων.)
ÆSCHYLUS, *Fragments.* Frag. 220.

A poor fool indeed is a very scandalous thing.
SUSANNAH CENTLIVRE, *Wonder.* Act i, sc. 1.

12
Listen to the fool's reproach! It is a kingly title!
WILLIAM BLAKE, *Proverbs of Hell.*

13
A fool always finds a bigger fool to admire him. (Un sot trouve toujours un plus sot qui l'admire.)
BOILEAU, *L'Art Poétique.* Canto i, l. 232.

14
Fool me no fools.
BULWER-LYTTON, *The Last Days of Pompeii.* Bk. iii, ch. 6.

15
Fools are my theme, let satire be my song.
BYRON, *English Bards and Scotch Reviewers,* l. 6.

16
There is *a* greatest Fool, as superlative in every kind; and *the* most Foolish man in the Earth is now indubitably living and breathing, and did this morning or lately eat breakfast.
CARLYLE, *Essays: Biography.*

17
A fool can not be still.
CHAUCER, *The Parlement of Foules,* l. 574.

18
Fools never perceive where they are ill-timed or ill-placed.
LORD CHESTERFIELD, *Letters,* 20 July, 1749.

Fool beckons fool, and dunce awakens dunce.
CHARLES CHURCHILL, *The Apology,* l. 42.

19
O fate of fools! officious in contriving;
In executing puzzled, lame and lost.
CONGREVE, *The Mourning Bride.* Act v, sc. 1.

We speak of hardships, but the true hardship is to be a dull fool, and permitted to mismanage life in our own dull and foolish manner.
R. L. STEVENSON, *Travels with a Donkey.*

20
Painted fools Are caught with silken shows.
MICHAEL DRAYTON, *The Quest of Cynthia.*

1
The fool of nature stood with stupid eyes
And gaping mouth, that testified surprise.
DRYDEN, *Cymon and Iphigenia*, l. 107.

2
Fools are made for jests to men of sense.
FARQUHAR, *The Beaux' Stratagem: Prologue.*

3
Fools grow without watering.
THOMAS FULLER, *Gnomologia*. No. 1574.

A fool can dance without a fiddle.
THOMAS FULLER, *Gnomologia*. No. 99.

Every fool is a fiddle to the company.
EDWARD SHARPHAM, *Cupid's Whirligig*. Act iv.

4
Even a fool sometimes gives good counsel. (Πολλάκι τοι καὶ μωρὸς ἀνὴρ μάλα καίριον εἶπεν.)
AULUS GELLIUS, *Noctes Atticæ*. Bk. ii, ch. 6, sec. 9. Referred to as a "very ancient line."

Though syllogisms hang not on my tongue,
I am not surely always in the wrong!
'Tis hard if all is false that I advance,—
A fool must now and then be right, by chance.
COWPER, *Conversation*, l. 93.

A fool's bolt may sometimes hit the white.
THOMAS FULLER, *Gnomologia*. No. 107.

5
The old proverb, of fools have fortune.
HENRY GLAPTHORNE, *Wit in a Constable*. Act iii.

Call me not fool till heaven hath sent me fortune.
SHAKESPEARE, *As You Like It*. Act ii, sc. 7, l. 19.

See also FORTUNE: FORTUNE FAVORS FOOLS.

6
Fools are never uneasy. [Stupidity is without anxiety.]
GOETHE, *Conversations with Eckermann*.

7
Fools will still be fools.
ROBERT HEATH, *Satyrs*, 9. (1650)

8
To make a trade of laughing at a fool is the highway to become one.
THOMAS FULLER, *The Holy State*, p. 172.

One should no more laugh at a contemptible fool than at a dead fly.
LORD HALIFAX, *Works*, p. 235.

All fools have still an itching to deride,
And fain would be upon the laughing side.
POPE, *Essay on Criticism*. Pt. i, l. 32.

9
A man may be as much a fool from the want of sensibility as the want of sense.
ANNA JAMESON, *Detached Thoughts*, p. 122.

10
Clowns' fawnings are a horse's salutations.
BEN JONSON, *The Staple of News*. Act i, sc. 1.

11
No precepts will profit a fool.
BEN JONSON, *Explorata: Præcipiendi Modi*.

To be a fool born is a disease incurable.
BEN JONSON, *Volpone*. Act ii, sc. 1.

12
A fool is one whom simpletons believe to be a man of merit. (Un fat est celui que les sots croient un homme de mérite.)
LA BRUYÈRE, *Les Caractères*. Pt. xii.

13
Alas, how soon the hours are over
Counted us out to play the lover!
And how much narrower is the stage
Allotted us to play the sage!
But when we play the fool, how wide,
The theatre expands! beside,
How long the audience sits before us!
How many prompters! what a chorus!
WALTER SAVAGE LANDOR, *Plays*.

14
It needs brains to be a real fool.
GEORGE MACDONALD, *Weighed and Wanting*. Ch. 26.

15
A fool! a fool! my coxcomb for a fool!
JOHN MARSTON, *Parasitaster*. (1606)

16
The strong fool breasts the flood and dies,
The weak fool turns his back and flies.
JOAQUIN MILLER, *A Song of Creation*. Canto v, st. 2.

17
You are a fool in three letters. (Vous êtes un sot, en trois lettres.)
MOLIÈRE, *Le Tartuffe*. Act i, sc. 1, l. 16.

A man of three letters. (Trium litterarum homo.)
PLAUTUS, *Aulularia*, l. 325. (Act ii, sc. 4.) Three letters, i. e., "fur," a thief.

18
A fool gives counsel to others but is not himself on his guard. (Sibi non cavere, et aliis consilium dare, Stultum esse.)
PHÆDRUS, *Fables*. Bk. i, fab. 9, l. 1.

19
Whoever or wherever they are, have been, or ever shall be, fools, blockheads, imbeciles, idiots, dunderheads, dullards, blunderers, I alone far exceed them all in folly and want of sense. (Quicumque ubi ubi sunt, qui fuerunt quique futiri sunt posthac Stulti, stolidi, fatui, fungi, bardi, blenni, buccones, Solus ego omnis longe antideo stultitia et moribus indoctis.)
PLAUTUS, *Bacchides*, l. 1087. (Act v, sc. 1.)

You are a bigger fool than you look. (Præter speciem stultus es.)
PLAUTUS, *Mostellaria*. Act iv, sc. 2.

20
Or serve (like other fools) to fill a room.
POPE, *The Dunciad*. Bk. i, l. 136.

21
You think me cruel? take it for a rule,
No creature smarts so little as a fool.
POPE, *Epistle to Dr. Arbuthnot*, l. 83.

22
No place so sacred from such fops is barr'd.
Nor is Paul's church more safe than Paul's church-yard:
Nay, fly to altars; there they'll talk you dead;
For fools rush in where angels fear to tread.
POPE, *Essay on Criticism*. Pt. iii, l. 63.

23
A whip for the horse, a bridle for the ass, and a rod for the fool's back.
Old Testament: Proverbs, xxvi, 3.

1
As a dog returneth to his vomit, so a fool returneth to his folly.
Old Testament: Proverbs, xxvi, 11.

Let a bear robbed of her whelps meet a man, rather than a fool in his folly.
Old Testament: Proverbs, xvii, 12.

Though thou shouldest bray a fool in a mortar among wheat with a pestle, yet will not his foolishness depart from him.
Old Testament: Proverbs, xxvii, 22.

2
A way foolishness has of revenging itself is to excommunicate the world.
GEORGE SANTAYANA, *Little Essays,* p. 112.

3
It is the part of a fool to say, I should not have thought it. (Insipientis est dicere, Non putaram.)
SCIPIO AFRICANUS. *See* VALERIUS MAXIMUS, *Facta et Dicta Memorabilia,* vii, ii, 2.

The fool saith, who would have thought it?
THOMAS FULLER, *Gnomologia.* No. 4539.

The impenetrable stupidity of Prince George [son-in-law of James II] served his turn. It was his habit, when any news was told him to exclaim, "Est-il possible?"—"Is it possible?"
MACAULAY, *History of England.* Vol. i, ch. 9.

4
The dulness of the fool is the whetstone of the wits.
SHAKESPEARE, *As You Like It.* Act i, sc. 2, l. 58.

5
A fool, a fool! I met a fool i' the forest,
A motley fool; a miserable world!
As I do live by food, I met a fool,
Who laid him down and bask'd him in the sun.
SHAKESPEARE, *As You Like It.* Act ii, sc. 7, l. 12.

O noble fool!
A worthy fool! Motley's the only wear.
SHAKESPEARE, *As You Like It.* Act ii, sc. 7, l. 33.

Here comes a pair of very strange beasts, which in all tongues are called fools.
SHAKESPEARE, *As You Like It.* Act v, sc. 4, l. 36.

6
Fools are not mad folk.
SHAKESPEARE, *Cymbeline.* Act ii, sc. 3, l. 105.

A lunatic, lean-witted fool.
SHAKESPEARE, *Richard II.* Act ii, sc. 1, l. 115.

7
Let the doors be shut upon him, that he may play the fool nowhere but in's own house.
SHAKESPEARE, *Hamlet.* Act iii, sc. 1, l. 134.

8
To suckle fools and chronicle small beer.
SHAKESPEARE, *Othello.* Act ii, sc. 1, l. 161.

9
I am but a fool to reason with a fool.
TENNYSON, *The Last Tournament,* l. 271.

Fool is he that deals with fools.
UNKNOWN, *Parlement of Three Ages,* l. 264. (c. 1350)

10
A fool and his money be soon at debate.
THOMAS TUSSER, *Hundreth Good Pointes of Husbandrie,* 19. (1580)

A fool and his money are soon parted.
UNKNOWN. (*Roxburghe Ballads,* iii, 550.)

11
Let us be thankful for the fools. But for them the rest of us could not succeed.
MARK TWAIN, *Pudd'nhead Wilson's New Calendar.*

12
Fools are like people who think themselves rich with little. (Le sot est comme le peuple qui se croit riche de peu.)
VAUVENARGUES, *Réflexions.* No. 260.

13
Cross words and angry names require
To be chastised at school;
And he's in danger of hell-fire
That calls his brother fool.
ISAAC WATTS, *Against Scoffing.*

14
The best way to silence any friend of yours whom you know to be a fool is to induce him to hire a hall.
WOODROW WILSON, *Speech,* New York, 27 Jan., 1916.

15
Nothing exceeds in ridicule, no doubt,
A fool in fashion, but a fool that's out;
His passion for absurdity's so strong,
He cannot bear a rival in the wrong.
YOUNG, *Love of Fame.* Sat. iv, l. 105.

16
A sot's bolt is soon shot.
UNKNOWN, *Proverbs of Alfred,* 128. (c. 1270)

Sot's bolt is soon shot.
UNKNOWN, *Reliq. Antiquæ,* i, 111. (c. 1320)

A fool's bolt is soon shot.
UNKNOWN, *Good Wyfe Wold a Pylgrimage,* l. 95. (1460); SHAKESPEARE, *Henry V.* Act iii, sc. 7, l. 132. (1598)

A fool's bell is soon rung.
CHAUCER, *Romaunt of the Rose,* l. 5267. (c. 1365)

II—Fool: All Men Are Fools

17
No excellent soul is exempt from a mixture of folly.
ARISTOTLE. (MONTAIGNE, *Essays.* Bk. ii, ch. 2.)

18
But we are all the same—the fools of our own woes!
MATTHEW ARNOLD, *Empedocles on Etna,* l. 166.

19
There is in human nature, generally, more of the fool than of the wise.
FRANCIS BACON, *Essays: Of Boldness.*

20
All men are fools, and spite of all their pains, they differ from each other only more or less. (Tous les hommes sont fous, et malgré tous leurs soins, Ne différent entr'eux, que de plus ou du moins.)
BOILEAU, *L'Art Poétique.*

Beside, is he the only fool in the world?
ROBERT BROWNING, *Mr. Sludge "The Medium."* Last line.

1
Since Adam's time, fools have been in the majority. (Les sots depuis Adam sont en majorité.)
DELAVIGNE, *L'Étude Fait-elle le Bonheur?*

Hain't we got all the fools in town on our side? And ain't that a big enough majority in any town?
MARK TWAIN, *The Adventures of Huckleberry Finn*. Ch. 26.

2
If all fools wore white caps, we should seem a flock of geese.
GEORGE HERBERT, *Jacula Prudentum*.

Everyone hath a fool in his sleeve.
GEORGE HERBERT, *Jacula Prudentum*.

3
None is a fool always, everyone sometimes.
GEORGE HERBERT, *Jacula Prudentum*.

4
Almost all men are fools. (Stultique prope omnes.)
HORACE, *Satires*. Bk. ii, sat. 3, l. 32.

5
The right to be a cussed fool
Is safe from all devices human,
It's common (ez a gin'l rule)
To every critter born o' woman.
J. R. LOWELL, *The Biglow Papers*. Ser. ii, No. 7.

6
Men are so necessarily fools that it would be being a fool in a higher strain of folly not to be a fool.
PASCAL, *Pensées*. Sec. vi, No. 414.

7
What fools these mortals be! (Tanta stultitia mortalium est!)
SENECA, *Epistulæ ad Lucilium*. Epis. i, sec. 3.

What fools these mortals be!
SHAKESPEARE, *A Midsummer-Night's Dream*. Act iii, sc. 2, l. 115.

8
Come out, my lord, it is a world of fools.
TENNYSON, *Queen Mary*. Act iv, sc. 3.

9
Men may live fools, but fools they cannot die.
YOUNG, *Night Thoughts*. Night iv, l. 842. Quoted.

III—Fool: No Fool Like an Old Fool

10
He who at fifty is a fool,
Is far too stubborn grown for school.
CHARLES COTTON, *Visions*. No. 1.

Be wise with speed;
A fool at forty is a fool indeed.
YOUNG, *Love of Fame*. Sat. ii, l. 281.

11
There is no fool to the old fool.
JOHN HEYWOOD, *Proverbs*. Pt. ii, ch. 2. (1546)

There is no fool like an old fool.
JOHN LYLY, *Mother Bombie*. Act iv, sc. 2. (1592) In frequent use thereafter.

Ah! there's no fool like the old one.
TENNYSON, *The Grandmother*, l. 44.

12
Old fools are bigger fools than young ones. (Les vieux fous sont plus fous que les jeunes.)
LA ROCHEFOUCAULD, *Maximes*. No. 444.

13
How ill white hairs become a fool and jester.
SHAKESPEARE, *II Henry IV*. Act v, sc. 5, l. 52.

14
At thirty man suspects himself a fool;
Knows it at forty, and reforms his plan;
At fifty chides his infamous delay,
Pushes his prudent purpose to resolve;
In all the magnanimity of thought
Resolves; and re-resolves; then dies the same.
YOUNG, *Night Thoughts*. Night i, l. 417.

IV—Fool: The Fool's Tongue

15
The treasure of a fool is always in his tongue.
APULEIUS. (JONSON, *Explorata: Acutius Cernantur*.)

16
And fools cannot hold their tongue.
CHAUCER, *Romaunt of the Rose*, l. 5266.

A fool could never hold his peace; for too much talking is ever the indice of a fool.
DEMACATUS. (JONSON, *Explorata: Homeri Ulysses*, quoting Plutarch.)

But fools, to talking ever prone,
Are sure to make their follies known.
JOHN GAY, *Fables*. Pt. i, No. 44.
See also under SILENCE.

17
A blockhead is as ridiculous when he talketh, as is a goose when it flieth.
LORD HALIFAX, *Works*, p. 235.

18
By foolish words may men a foolë ken.
ROBERT MANNYNG, *Handlyng Synne*, l. 2970. (1303)

For by his tongue a fool is often known.
JOHN LYDGATE, *Troy Book*. Bk. ii, l. 7022. (1412)

A fool is known by speech negligent.
ALEXANDER BARCLAY, *Mirrour of Good Manners*, 73. (1550)

A fool, when he hath spoke, hath done all.
THOMAS FULLER, *Gnomologia*. No. 111. (1732)

19
A fool's mouth is his destruction.
Old Testament: Proverbs, xviii, 7.

V—Fools and Knaves

20
A fool and knave with different views
For Julia's hand apply;
The knave to mend his fortune sues,
The fool to please his eye.

Ask you how Julia will behave,
Depend on't for a rule,
If she's a fool she'll wed the knave—
If she's a knave, the fool.
SAMUEL BISHOP, *The Touchstone*.

21
O reader, behold the Philosopher's grave!

He was born quite a Fool, but he died quite a Knave.
WILLIAM BLAKE, *On Sir Joshua Reynolds.*

Folly is the cloak of knavery.
WILLIAM BLAKE, *Proverbs of Hell.*

1
Fools will prate o' right or wrang,
While knaves laugh in their sleeve.
BURNS, *The Five Carlins.* St. 20.

A knave and fool are plants of every soil.
BURNS, *Prologue for Mrs. Sutherland's Benefit.*

2
We live our lives with rogues and fools, dead and alive, alive and dead;
We die 'twixt one who feels the pulse and one who frets and clouds the head.
SIR RICHARD BURTON, *Kasîdah.* Pt. iii, st. 30.

3
Which made some take him for a tool
That knaves do work with, call'd a Fool.
BUTLER, *Hudibras.* Pt. i, canto i, l. 35.

4
There are more fools than knaves in the world, else the knaves would not have enough to live upon.
SAMUEL BUTLER, *Remains.* Vol. ii, p. 474.

5
More knave than fool.
CERVANTES, *Don Quixote.* Pt. ii, ch. 2.

6
After their [knaves and fools] friendship, there is nothing so dangerous as to have them for enemies.
LORD CHESTERFIELD, *Letters,* 17 Feb., 1754.

7
For one rogue still suspects another, . . .
Well knowing, by unerring rules,
Knaves starve not in the land of fools.
CHARLES CHURCHILL, *The Ghost.* Bk. ii, l. 292.

8
A rogue is a roundabout fool.
S. T. COLERIDGE, *Table Talk,* 4 Jan., 1823.

9
A knave, when tried on honesty's plain rule,
And, when by that of reason, a mere fool.
COWPER, *Hope,* l. 566.

For ev'ry inch that is not fool is rogue.
DRYDEN, *Absalom and Achitophel.* Pt. ii, l. 463.

10
None are so busy as the fool and knave.
DRYDEN, *The Medal,* l. 186.

11
You'll find at last this maxim true,
Fools are the game which knaves pursue.
JOHN GAY, *Fables.* Pt. ii, fab. 12, l. 61.

12
The eagerness of a knave maketh him often as catchable as ignorance maketh a fool.
LORD HALIFAX, *Works,* p. 232.

13
It might be argued, that to be a knave is the gift of fortune, but to play the fool to advantage it is necessary to be a learned man.
HAZLITT, *Table Talk: Intellectual Superiority.*

Better be a fool than a knave.
GEORGE HERBERT, *Jacula Prudentum.*

14
Now will I show myself to have more of the serpent than the dove; that is—more knave than fool.
MARLOWE, *The Jew of Malta.* Act ii, sc. 3.

15
Men never turn rogues without turning fools.
THOMAS PAINE, *The Crisis.* No. 3.

16
Lafeu: Whether dost thou profess thyself, a knave or a fool?
Clown: A fool, sir, at a woman's service, and a knave at a man's.
SHAKESPEARE, *All's Well that Ends Well.* Act iv, sc. 5, l. 24.

Thou art both knave and fool.
SHAKESPEARE, *All's Well that Ends Well.* Act iv, sc. 5, l. 35.

A knavish speech sleeps in a foolish ear.
SHAKESPEARE, *Hamlet.* Act iv, sc. 2, l. 25.

17
Earth bears no balsam for mistakes;
Men crown the knave, and scourge the tool
That did his will; but Thou, O Lord,
Be merciful to me, a fool!
E. R. SILL, *The Fool's Prayer.*

18
This is the sublime and refined point of felicity, called the possession of being well deceived; the serene peaceful state of being a fool among knaves.
SWIFT, *Tale of a Tub.* Sec. 9.

19
The world is made up for the most part of fools and knaves.
GEORGE VILLIERS, DUKE OF BUCKINGHAM, *To Mr. Clifford, On His Humane Reason.*

20
Very often, say what you will, a rogue is only a fool. (Bien souvent, quoi qu'on dise, un fripon n'est qu'un sot.)
VOLTAIRE, *Le Dépositaire.* Act ii, sc. 6.

VI—Fools and Wise Men

21
Either mere fools or good physicians all.
BARNABE BARNES, *Divils Charter.* Sig. L3. (1607)

No matter whether I be a fool or a physician.
THOMAS HEYWOOD, *Maiden-Head Well Lost.* Act iii. (1634)

See also under DOCTOR.

22
If the fool would persist in his folly he would become wise.
WILLIAM BLAKE, *Proverbs of Hell.*

23
The selfish, smiling fool, and the sullen, frowning fool, shall both be thought wise, that they may be a rod.
WILLIAM BLAKE, *Proverbs of Hell.*

24
A fool sees not the same tree that a wise man sees.
WILLIAM BLAKE, *Proverbs of Hell.*

1
Nothing can confound
A wise man more than laughter from a dunce.
BYRON, *Don Juan*. Canto xvi, st. 88.

In the vain laughter of folly wisdom hears half its applause.
GEORGE ELIOT, *Romola*. Bk. i, ch. 12.
See also under LAUGHTER.

2
Fools set stools for wise men to stumble at.
WILLIAM CAMDEN, *Remains*, p. 322. (1605)

A fool may throw a stone into a well which a hundred wise men cannot pull out.
GEORGE HERBERT, *Jacula Prudentum*.

3
Wise men profit more from fools than fools from wise men; for the wise shun the mistakes of fools, but fools do not imitate the successes of the wise.
MARCUS CATO. (PLUTARCH, *Lives: Marcus Cato*. Ch. ix, sec. 4.)

Cato Major would say: "That wise men learned more by fools than fools by wise men."
FRANCIS BACON, *Apothegms*. No. 167. MONTAIGNE, *Essays*. Bk. iii, ch. 8.

Wise men learn by others' harms, fools scarcely by their own.
BENJAMIN FRANKLIN, *Poor Richard*, 1758.
See also under EXPERIENCE.

4
A fool knows more in his own house than a wise man in another's.
CERVANTES, *Don Quixote*. Pt. ii, ch. 43.

5
A fool may eke a wise man often guide.
CHAUCER, *Troilus and Criseyde*. Bk. i, l. 630.

6
The strongest plume in wisdom's pinion
Is the memory of past folly.
S. T. COLERIDGE, *To an Unfortunate Woman*.

7
Any fool can carry on, but only the wise man knows how to shorten sail.
JOSEPH CONRAD, *Message to Tusitala*.

8
God hath chosen the foolish things of the world to confound the wise; and God hath chosen the weak things of the world to confound the things which are mighty.
New Testament: I Corinthians, i, 27.

9
The wise too jealous are, fools too secure.
CONGREVE, *The Way of the World*. Act iii, sc. 3.

10
Design'd by Nature wise, but self-made fools.
COWPER, *Tirocinium*, l. 837.

11
Who are a little wise, the best fools be.
JOHN DONNE, *The Triple Fool*.

Nae man can play the fule sae weel as the wise man.
JOHN RAY, *English Proverbs: Scottish*.

This fellow's wise enough to play the fool;
And to do that well craves a kind of wit.
SHAKESPEARE, *Twelfth Night*. Act iii, sc. 1, l. 67.

12
Then I saw that wisdom excelleth folly, as far as light excelleth darkness. The wise man's eyes are in his head; but the fool walketh in darkness.
Old Testament: Ecclesiastes, ii, 13, 14.

It is better to hear the rebuke of the wise, than for a man to hear the song of fools.
Old Testament: Ecclesiastes, vii, 5.

13
The wise through excess of wisdom is made a fool.
EMERSON, *Essays, Second Series: Experience*.

14
The wise man draws more advantage from his enemies, than the fool from his friends.
BENJAMIN FRANKLIN, *Poor Richard*, 1749.

15
Fools are wise men in the affairs of women.
THOMAS FULLER, *Gnomologia*. No. 1571.

16
A fool and a wise man are alike both in the starting-place—their birth, and at the post—their death; only they differ in the race of their lives.
THOMAS FULLER, *The Holy and Profane States: Of Natural Fools*. Maxim 4.

Solomon laid hold of folly, as well as wisdom, that he might see what was good for the Sons of Men.
FULLER, *Introductio ad Prudentiam*, 188.

17
The fools and the wise are equally harmless; it is the half-wise and the half-foolish who are the most to be feared.
GOETHE, *Sprüche in Prosa*.

18
The wisest fool in Christendom.
HENRY IV OF FRANCE, of James I of England, when the latter abandoned him for an alliance with Spain.

19
Better be foolish with all than wise by yourself. (Il vaut mieux être fou avec tous que sage tout seul.)
UNKNOWN. A French proverb.

None is so wise but the fool o'ertakes him.
GEORGE HERBERT, *Jacula Prudentum*. No. 730.

Fools bite one another, but wise men agree together.
GEORGE HERBERT, *Jacula Prudentum*. No. 448.

20
It is the folly of the world constantly which confounds its wisdom.
O. W HOLMES, *The Professor at the Breakfast-Table*. Ch. 1.

21
He dares to be a fool, and that is the first step in the direction of wisdom
JAMES HUNEKER, *Pathos of Distance*, p. 257.

22
Fears of the brave, and follies of the wise!
JOHNSON, *The Vanity of Human Wishes*, l. 314.

23
He who lives without folly is not so wise as he

thinks. (Qui vit sans folie n'est pas si sage qu'il croit.)

La Rochefoucauld, *Maximes*. No. 209.

He who hath not a dram of folly in his mixture hath pounds of much worse matter in his composition.

Charles Lamb, *Essays of Elia: All Fools' Day.*

1
And what, in a mean man, I should call folly,
Is in your majesty remarkable wisdom.

Massinger, *The Picture*. Act i, sc. 2.

2
At times discretion should be thrown aside,
And with the foolish we should play the fool.
(Οὐ πανταχοῦ τὸ φρόνιμον ἁρμόττει παρόν,
καὶ συμμανῆναι δ' ἔνια δεῖ.)

Menander, *Poloumenoi*. Frag. 2.

Mingle a short spell of folly with your studies; it is sweet on occasion to play the fool. (Misce stultitiam consiliis brevem; Dulce est desipere in loco.)

Horace, *Odes*. Bk. iv, ode 12, l. 27.

Then, Pallas, take away thine Owl,
And let us have a lark instead.

Thomas Hood, *To Minerva*.

A wise man holds himself in check,
But fools and poets run ahead.
One must be credulous or sit
Forever with the living dead.

The wise man shuts his door at night
And pulls the bolts and drops the bars.
One must go trustful through the dark
To earn the friendship of the stars.

Scudder Middleton, *Wisdom*.

3
He who has once been very foolish will at no other time be very wise. (Qui aura esté une fois bien fol ne sera nulle aultre fois bien sage.)

Montaigne, *Essays*. Bk. iii, ch. 6.

4
A little folly is desirable in him that will not be guilty of stupidity.

Montaigne, *Essays*. Bk. iii, ch. 9.

A little nonsense now and then, *see under* Nonsense.

5
To succeed in this world, one must have the appearance of a fool and be wise.

Montesquieu, *Maximes*.

6
He may be called a fool that . . . announced himself to be wise.

Sir Thomas North, *Dialogue of Princes*. Fo. 91. (1557)

The first chapter of fools is to count themselves wise.

John Florio, *First Fruites*. Fo. 29. (1578)

People are never so near playing the fool as when they think themselves wise.

Mary Wortley Montagu, *Letter to Lady Bute*, 1 March, 1755.

He who thinks himself wise, O heavens! is a great fool. (Qui se croit sage, ô ciel! est un grand fou.)

Voltaire, *Le Droit du Seigneur*. Act iv, sc. 1.

7
For fools admire, but men of sense approve.

Pope, *Essay on Criticism*. Pt. ii, l. 191.

8
The learn'd is happy Nature to explore,
The fool is happy that he knows no more.

Pope, *Essay on Man*. Epis. ii, l. 263.

Just as a blockhead rubs his thoughtless skull,
And thanks his stars he was not born a fool.

Pope, *Jane Shore: Epilogue*, l. 7.

9
And the first wisdom to be fool no more.

Pope, *Imitations of Horace: Epistles*. Bk. i, epis. 1, l. 66.

10
A single day in the life of a learned man is worth more than the lifetime of a fool. (Unus dies hominum eruditorum plus patet quam inperitis longissima ætas.)

Posidonius, *Exhortations*. (Seneca, *Epistulæ ad Lucilium*. Epis. lxxviii, sec. 28.)

11
Answer a fool according to his folly, lest he be wise in his own conceit.

Old Testament: Proverbs, xxvi, 5.

Seest thou a man wise in his own conceit? there is more hope of a fool than of him.

Old Testament: Proverbs, xxvi, 12.

See also under Conceit.

12
Those who wish to appear wise among fools, among the wise seem foolish. (Qui stultis videri eruditi volunt, stulti eruditis videntur.)

Quintilian, *De Institutione Oratoria*. Bk. x, ch. 7, sec. 22.

A fool with judges, among fools a judge.

Cowper, *Conversation*, l. 298.

13
A fool may ask more questions in an hour than a wise man can answer in seven years.

John Ray, *English Proverbs*, 91. (1670)

A fool will ask more questions than the wisest can answer.

Swift, *Polite Conversation*. Dial. ii.

Examinations are formidable even to the best prepared, for the greatest fool may ask more than the wise man can answer.

C. C. Colton, *Lacon: Reflections*. No. 322.

14
Professing themselves to be wise, they became fools.

New Testament: Romans, i, 22.

15
A little group of wise hearts is better than a wilderness of fools.

Ruskin, *Crown of Wild Olive: War*.

16
The Italian seems wise, and is wise; the Spaniard seems wise, and is a fool; the French seems a fool, and is wise; and the English seems a fool and is a fool.

Thomas Scot, *The Highwaies of God and the King*, p. 8. (1623) Quoted as a proverb.

1
Folly is pursued, and confronted, by peril. . . . But the wise man is fortified against all attacks. (Secuntur pericula et occurrunt. . . . Sapiens autem ad omnem incursum munitus.)
SENECA, *Epistulæ ad Lucilium*. Epis. lix, sec. 8.

Folly may creep upwards toward wisdom, but wisdom never slips back into folly. (Stultitia ad sapientiam erepit, sapientia in stultitiam non revolvitur.)
SENECA, *Epistulæ ad Lucilium*. Epis. lxxvi, 19.

2
Full oft we see
Cold wisdom waiting on superfluous folly.
SHAKESPEARE, *All's Well that Ends Well*. Act i, sc. 1, l. 115.

3
Touchstone: The more pity, that fools may not speak wisely, what wise men do foolishly.
Celia: By my troth, thou say'st true; for since the little wit that fools have was silenced, the little foolery that wise men have makes a great show.
SHAKESPEARE, *As You Like It*. Act i, sc. 2, l. 92.

The fool doth think he is wise, but the wise man knows himself to be a fool.
SHAKESPEARE, *As You Like It*. Act v, sc. 1, l. 34. Quoted as "a saying."

4
Well, thus we play the fools with the time, and the spirits of the wise sit in the clouds and mock us.
SHAKESPEARE, *II Henry IV*. Act ii, sc. 2, l. 153.

Powers above in clouds do sit,
Mocking our poor apish wit,
That so lamely, with such state
Their high glory imitate.
THOMAS CAMPION, *Life's Progress*.

5
Servant: Thou art not altogether a fool.
Fool: Nor thou altogether a wise man: as much foolery as I have, so much wit thou lackest.
SHAKESPEARE, *Timon of Athens*. Act ii, sc. 2, l. 122.

Well, God give them wisdom that have it; and those that are fools, let them use their talents.
SHAKESPEARE, *Twelfth Night*. Act i, sc. 5, l. 14.

6
Twenty wise men may easily add up into one fool.
J. A. SPENDER, *Comments of Bagshot*. Ch. 11.

7
Some people take more care to hide their wisdom than their folly.
SWIFT, *Thoughts on Various Subjects*.

8
Wise men may think, what hardly fools would say.
SWINBURNE, *Mary Stuart*. Act iv, sc. 2.

9
Immortal gods! how much does one man excel another! What a difference there is between a wise person and a fool! (Di immortales, homini homo quid præstat! Stulto intellegens quid interest!)
TERENCE, *Eunuchus*, l. 232. (Act ii, sc. 2.)

10
Nor is he the wisest man who never proved himself a fool.
TENNYSON, *Locksley Hall Sixty Years After*, l. 244.

If thou hast never been a fool, be sure thou wilt never be a wise man.
THACKERAY, *Lovel the Widower*.

And he is oft the wisest man
Who is not wise at all.
WORDSWORTH, *The Oak and the Broom*. St. 7.

11
A man of sense can artifice disdain,
As men of wealth may venture to go plain. . . .
I find the fool when I behold the screen,
For 'tis the wise man's interest to be seen.
YOUNG, *Love of Fame*. Sat. ii, l. 193.

VII—Fool's Paradise

12
I would not be in a fool's paradise.
UNKNOWN, *Paston Letters*. Vol. ii, p. 109. (1462)

Thou shouldst not bring me in a fool's paradise.
Mathew's Bible: II Kings, iv. (1549)

13
Thy fairest prospects, rightly viewed,
The Paradise of Fools.
THOMAS BLACKLOCK, *Ode on the Refinements in Metaphysical Philosophy*.

14
The fool shall not enter into heaven, let him be ever so holy.
WILLIAM BLAKE, *Why Men Enter Heaven*.

15
A fool's paradise is better than a wiseacre's purgatory.
GEORGE COLMAN THE ELDER, *The Deuce Is In Him*. Act i, sc. 1.

16
In this fool's paradise he drank delight.
GEORGE CRABBE, *The Borough*. Letter 12.

17
The joyous Paradise of Fools
Has space to spare for young and old.
ROBERT CREWE-MILNES, *Fool's Paradise*.

18
A fool's paradise is a wise man's hell.
THOMAS FULLER, *The Holy State*, p. 320.

19
Even the paradise of fools is not an unpleasant abode while it is habitable.
DEAN W. R. INGE. (MARCHANT, *Wit and Wisdom of Dean Inge*. No. 198.)

20
Into a Limbo large and broad, since call'd
The Paradise of Fools, to few unknown.
MILTON, *Paradise Lost*. Bk. iii, l. 495.

Limbus fatuorum is the name given by the old schoolmen to the intermediate region between heaven and hell, where dwelt what Dante calls "the praiseless and the blameless dead," or, in other words, fools, idiots and lunatics.

1
Hence the fool's paradise, the statesman's
scheme,
The air-built castle and the golden dream.
POPE, *The Dunciad*. Bk. iii, l. 9.

2
The fools we know have their own Paradise,
The wicked also have their proper Hell.
JAMES THOMSON, *The City of Dreadful Night*. Pt. xi.

3
Promise of matrimony by a young gallant, to bring a virgin lady into a fool's paradise.
WEBSTER AND MARSTON, *The Malcontent*. Act v, sc. 3.

FOOT

4
Make your feet your friend.
J. M. BARRIE, *Sentimental Tommy*, p. 137. In other words, "Get out!"

5
My feet, they haul me Round the House,
They Hoist me up the Stairs;
I only have to steer them, and
They Ride me Everywheres.
GELETT BURGESS, *My Feet*.

6
The many-twinkling feet so small and sylph-
like,
Suggesting the more perfect symmetry
Of the fair forms which terminate so well.
BYRON, *Marino Faliero*. Act iv. *See also under* DANCING.

7
This image's head was of fine gold, his breast and his arms of silver, his belly and his thighs of brass, His legs of iron, his feet part of iron and part of clay.
Old Testament: Daniel, ii, 32, 33.

It is the feet of clay that makes the gold of the image precious.
OSCAR WILDE, *Picture of Dorian Gray*. Ch. 15.

8
Be swift their feet as antelopes,
And as behemoth strong.
EMERSON, *Boston Hymn*.

9
Better a bare foot than none.
GEORGE HERBERT, *Jacula Prudentum*.

10
From the foot, Hercules. (Ex pede, Herculem.)
HERODOTUS, *Histories*. Bk. iv, sec. 82. Plutarch, as reported by Aulus Gellius (*Noctes Atticæ*, i, 1) tells how Pythagoras deduced the stature of Hercules from the length of his foot.

You shall not know the length of my foot.
JOHN LYLY, *Euphues*, p. 290. (1580)

Having now the full length of his foot, then shows she herself what she is.
THOMAS DEKKER, *Works*. Vol. i, p. 203.

Well, gossip, I know too the length of your foot.
D'AVENANT, *Play-House to be Let*. Act v.

11
It frightens me to see all the footprints directed towards thy den, and none returning. (Quia me vestigia terrent. Omnia te adversum spectantia, nulla retrorsum.)
HORACE, *Epistles*. Bk. i, epis. i, l. 74. The fox speaking to the lion. "Vestigia nulla retrorsum" is the motto of the Hampden family and others.

12
By the foot of Pharaoh!
BEN JONSON, *Every Man in His Humour*. Act i, sc. 3.

13
Her treading would not bend a blade of grass
Or shake the downy blue-ball from his stalk,
And where she went, the flowers took thickest
root,
As she had sow'd them with her odorous foot.
BEN JONSON, *The Sad Shepherd*. Act i, sc. 1.

Whilst from off the waters fleet
Thus I set my printless feet
O'er the cowslip's velvet head,
That bends not as I tread.
MILTON, *Comus*, l. 896.

A foot more light, a step more true,
Ne'er from the heath-flower dashed the dew;
E'en the slight harebell raised its head,
Elastic from her airy tread.
SCOTT, *The Lady of the Lake*. Canto i, st. 18.

The grass stoops not, she treads on it so light.
SHAKESPEARE, *Venus and Adonis*, l. 1028.

Steps with a tender foot, light as on air,
The lovely, lordly creature floated on.
TENNYSON, *The Princess*. Pt. vi, l. 72.

But light as any wind that blows
So fleetly did she stir,
The flower she touch'd on dipt and rose,
And turn'd to look at her.
TENNYSON, *The Talking Oak*, l. 129.

14
Feet that run on willing errands!
LONGFELLOW, *Hiawatha*. Pt. x, l. 33.

15
Whose feet are shod with silence.
LONGFELLOW, *Tegnér's Drapa*. St. 6.

16
He stood a spell on one foot fust,
Then stood a spell on t'other,
An' on which one he felt the wust
He couldn't ha' told ye nuther.
J. R. LOWELL, *The Courtin'*.

17
His very foot has music in't
As he comes up the stair.
WILLIAM JULIUS MICKLE, *The Sailor's Wife*. Sometimes attributed to Jean Adam.

18
It is the foulness of the peacock's feet which doth abate his pride, and stoop his gloating-eyed tail.
MONTAIGNE, *Essays*. Bk. iii, ch. 5.

19
Right foot first. (Dextro pede.)
PETRONIUS, *Satyricon*. Sec. 30.

20
Make haste; the better foot before.
SHAKESPEARE, *King John*. Act iv, sc. 2, l. 170.

Come on, my lords, the better foot before.
SHAKESPEARE, *Titus Andronicus*. Act ii, sc. 3, l. 192.

You should . . . put your best foot forward.
CONGREVE, *Way of the World*. Act iv, sc. 10.

1
Here comes the lady! O, so light a foot
Will ne'er wear out the everlasting flint.
SHAKESPEARE, *Romeo and Juliet*. Act ii, sc. 6, l. 16.

2
Nay, her foot speaks.
SHAKESPEARE, *Troilus and Cressida*. Act iv, sc. 5, l. 56.

3
O happy earth,
Whereon thy innocent feet do ever tread!
SPENSER, *Faerie Queene*. Bk. i, canto x, st. 9.

4
Her feet beneath her petticoat,
Like little mice, stole in and out,
As if they feared the light.
SIR JOHN SUCKLING, *A Ballad Upon a Wedding*. St. 8. (1637)

Her pretty feet like snails did creep
A little out, and then,
As if they playèd at Bo-peep,
Did soon draw in again.
ROBERT HERRICK, *Upon Mistress Susanna Southwell: Her Feet*. (1650)

The prettiest foot! Oh, if a man could but fasten his eyes to her feet, as they steal in and out and play at Bo-peep under her petticoats.
CONGREVE, *Love for Love*. Act i, sc. 2. (1695)

But from the hoop's bewitching round,
Her very shoe has power to wound.
EDWARD MOORE, *Fables: The Spider and the Bee*. (1744)

5
And feet like sunny gems on an English green.
TENNYSON, *Maud*, l. 175.

FOP

6
Curl'd minion, dancer, coiner of sweet words!
MATTHEW ARNOLD, *Sohrab and Rustum*, l. 458.

The wealthy curled darlings of our nation.
SHAKESPEARE, *Othello*. Act i, sc. 2, l. 68.

That dandy-despot, he,
That jewell'd mass of millinery,
That oil'd and curl'd Assyrian bull
Smelling of musk and of insolence.
TENNYSON, *Maud*, l. 231.

7
We've no accomplish'd blackguards, like Tom Jones,
But gentlemen in stays, as stiff as stones.
BYRON, *Don Juan*. Canto xiii, st. 110.

8
All affectation is bad. (Toda Afertacion es mala.)
CERVANTES, *Don Quixote*. Pt. ii, ch. 25.

They are the affectation of affectation.
FIELDING, *Joseph Andrews*. Bk. iii, ch. 3.

9
I marched the lobby, twirled my stick, . . .
The girls all cried, "He's quite the kick."
GEORGE COLMAN THE YOUNGER, *Broad Grins*.

10
The solemn fop; significant and budge;
A fool with judges, amongst fools a judge.
COWPER, *Conversation*, l. 299.

He cannot drink five bottles, bilk the score,
Then kill a constable, and drink five more;
But he can draw a pattern, make a tart,
And has the ladies' etiquette by heart.
COWPER, *The Progress of Error*, l. 193.

11
Foppery atones
For folly, gallantry for ev'ry vice.
COWPER, *The Task*. Bk. iv, l. 689.

12
True fops help nature's work, and go to school
To file and finish God Almighty's fool.
DRYDEN, *Man of Mode: Epilogue*.

13
Squinting upon the lustre
Of the rich Rings which on his fingers glistre;
And, snuffing with a wrythed nose the Amber,
The Musk and Civet that perfum'd the chamber.
DU BARTAS, *Devine Weekes and Workes*. Week ii, day 3. (Sylvester, tr.)

Soft carpet-knights all scenting musk and amber.
DU BARTAS, *Devine Weekes and Workes*. Week i, day 3.

Carpet knights are men who are by the prince's grace and favour made knights at home. . . . They are called carpet knights because they receive their honours in the court and upon carpets.
GERVASE MARKHAM, *Booke of Honour*. (1625)

14
Of all the fools that pride can boast,
A Coxcomb claims distinction most.
JOHN GAY, *Fables*. Pt. i, fab. 5.

15
A greenery-yallery, Grosvenor Gallery
Foot-in-the-grave young man!
W. S. GILBERT, *Patience*. Act ii.

16
There's Bardus, a six-foot column of fop,
A lighthouse without any light atop.
THOMAS HOOD, *Miss Kilmansegg: Her First Step*.

17
Fitted for girls; a ladies' man. (Puellis nuper idoneus.)
HORACE, *Odes*. Bk. iii, ode 26, l. 1.

18
He has thrown his spats away,
He is wearing spurs today,
And the world will please take notice that the Yankee dude'll do!
S. E. KISER, *The Yankee Dude'll Do*.

19
A beau is one who, with the nicest care,
In parted locks divides his curling hair;
One who with balm and cinnamon smells sweet,
Whose humming lips some Spanish air repeat;

Whose naked arms are smooth'd with pumice-stone,
And toss'd about with graces all their own:
A beau is one who takes his constant seat
From morn to evening, where the ladies meet;
And ever, on some sofa hovering near,
Whispers some nothing in some fair one's ear;
Who scribbles thousand billets-doux a day;
Still reads and scribbles, reads, and sends away: . . .
Who knows who flirts with whom, and still is found
At each good table in successive round.

MARTIAL, *Epigrams*. Bk. iii, ep. 63. (Elton, tr.)

He, Cotta, who is a pretty man is a paltry man. (Qui bellus homo, Cotta, pusillus homo est.)

MARTIAL, *Epigrams*. Bk. i, epig. 9.

1
Accustom him to everything, that he may not be a Sir Paris, a carpet-knight, but a sinewy, hardy, and vigorous young man.

MONTAIGNE, *Essays*. Bk. i, ch. 25.

Ye curious carpet knights, that spend the time in sport and play,
Abroad, and see new sights, your country's cause calls you away.

HUMPHREY GIFFORD, *For Soldiers*.

3
Nature made ev'ry fop to plague his brother,
Just as one beauty mortifies another.

POPE, *Satires of Dr. John Donne*. Sat. iv, l. 258.

Who knows a fool must know his brother;
One fop will recommend another.

JOHN GAY, *Fables*. Pt. i, fab. 9, l. 11.

4
Sir Plume, of amber snuff-box justly vain,
And the nice conduct of a clouded cane.

POPE, *The Rape of the Lock*. Canto iv, l. 123.

He was perfumed like a milliner;
And 'twixt his finger and his thumb he held
A pouncet-box, which ever and anon
He gave his nose, and too 't away again.

SHAKESPEARE, *I Henry IV*. Act i, sc. 3, l. 36.

5
A beardless boy, A cocker'd, silken wanton.

SHAKESPEARE, *King John*. Act v, sc. 1, l. 69.

He is too picked, too spruce, too affected, too odd, as it were; too peregrinate, as I may call it.

SHAKESPEARE, *Love's Labour's Lost*. Act v, sc. 1, l. 13.

6
I call'd him Crichton, for he seem'd
All-perfect, finish'd to the finger-nail.

TENNYSON, *Edwin Morris*, l. 22.

7
A fop? In this brave, licentious age
To bring his musty morals on the stage?

SAMUEL TUKE, *Adventures of Five Hours*. Act v.

8
A man who can dominate a London dinner-table can dominate the world. The future belongs to the dandy. It is the exquisites who are going to rule.

OSCAR WILDE, *A Woman of No Importance*. Act iii.

9
A lofty cane, a sword with silver hilt,
A ring, two watches, and a snuff box gilt.

UNKNOWN, *Recipe to Make a Modern Fop*. (c. 1770)

FORCE

See also Might, Power, Strength

10
Force is of brutes.

DRYDEN, *Palamon and Arcite*. Bk. iii, l. 742.

The blind wild-beast of force.

TENNYSON, *The Princess*. Pt. v, l. 256.

11
Force is not a remedy.

JOHN BRIGHT, *Speech*, Birmingham, 16 Nov., 1880.

Tries force because persuasion fails.

ROBERT BROWNING, *Prince Hohenstiel-Schwangau*. *See also* GENTLENESS.

12
Force overcome by force. (Vi victa vis.)

CICERO, *Pro Milone*. Sec. 11.

By force of arms. (Vi et armis.)

CICERO, *Ad Pontifices*. Sec. 24.

13
What force cannot effect, fraud shall devise.

RICHARD CRASHAW, *Sospetto d'Herode*. *See also under* DECEIT.

14
We love force and we care very little how it is exhibited.

EMERSON, *Journal*. Vol. v, p. 262.

15
Force without fore-cast is of little avail.

THOMAS FULLER, *Gnomologia*. No. 1589.

16
Force works on servile natures, not the free.

BEN JONSON, *Every Man in His Humour*. Act i, sc. 1.

17
Who overcomes
By force, hath overcome but half his foe.

MILTON, *Paradise Lost*. Bk. i, l. 648.

18
Men must reap the things they sow,
Force from force must ever flow.

SHELLEY, *Lines Written Among the Euganean Hills*, l. 232.

19
Force finds a way. (Fit via vi.)

VERGIL, *Æneid*. Bk. ii, l. 494.

20
And hence no force, however great,
Can stretch a cord, however fine,
Into a horizontal line
That shall be absolutely straight.

WILLIAM WHEWELL, *Elementary Treatise on Mechanics: The Equilibrium of Forces on a Point*. Vol. i, l. 44. (First edition, 1819) A famous instance of the accidental use of rhyme and meter, which so annoyed its author when he was chaffed about it by Professor Adam Sedgwick at a dinner in Hall at Cambridge, that he deleted it from all later editions of his book. Sedgwick, or some other wag, polished the sentence up a little, for it really read, "Hence no force however great can stretch a cord however fine into a horizontal line which is accurately straight."

FOREIGNERS

1
Wide open and unguarded stand our gates,
Named of the four winds, North, South, East, and West. . . .
O Liberty, white Goddess! is it well
To leave the gates unguarded? On thy breast
Fold Sorrow's children, soothe the hurts of Fate,
Lift the down-trodden but with hand of steel
Stay those who to thy sacred portals come
To waste the gifts of Freedom.

T. B. ALDRICH, *Unguarded Gates.*

2
Each breath
Of foreign air he draws seems a slow poison.

BYRON *The Two Foscari.* Act i, sc. 1.

3
The more I saw of foreign lands, the more I loved my own.

DE BELLOY, *Siège de Calais.*

What I gained by being in France was learning to be better satisfied with my own country.

SAMUEL JOHNSON. (BOSWELL, *Life.*)

4
An English lady on the Rhine hearing a German speaking of her party as foreigners, exclaimed, "No, we are not foreigners; we are English; it is you that are foreigners."

EMERSON, *English Traits,* p. 151.

Father, Mother and Me,
Sister and Auntie say
All the people like us are We,
And every one else is They.

RUDYARD KIPLING, *We and They.*

5
Here you would know, and enjoy, what posterity will say of Washington. For a thousand leagues have nearly the same effect with a thousand years.

BENJAMIN FRANKLIN, *Letter to Washington.* 5 March, 1780.

We are a kind of posterity in respect to them.

BENJAMIN FRANKLIN, *Letter to William Strahan,* 1745.

Foreigners are contemporary posterity. (Les étrangers sont la postérité contemporaine.)

MADAME DE STAËL. (CROKER, *Memoirs,* i, 326.)

Byron's European fame is the best earnest of his immortality, for a foreign nation is a kind of contemporaneous posterity.

HORACE BINNEY WALLACE, *Stanley, or the Recollections of a Man of the World.* Vol. ii, p. 89. (1838)

6
And I'll wager in their joy they kissed each other's cheek
(Which is what them furriners do).

W. S. GILBERT, *Ruddigore.* Act i.

7
People have prejudices against a nation in which they have no acquaintance.

PHILIP HAMERTON, *Modern Frenchmen: Henri Perreyve.*

8
Immoral money first brought in foreign manners. (Prima peregrinos obscœna Pecunia mores Intulit.)

JUVENAL, *Satires.* Sat. vi, l. 298.

9
Hope nothing from foreign governments. They will never be really willing to aid you until you have shown that you are strong enough to conquer without them.

MAZZINI, *Life and Writings: Young Italy.*

10
By foreign hands thy dying eyes were closed,
By foreign hands thy decent limbs composed,
By foreign hands thy humble grave adorn'd,
By strangers honour'd, and by strangers mourn'd.

POPE, *Elegy to the Memory of an Unfortunate Lady,* l. 51.

11
At the gate of the West I stand,
On the isle where the nations throng.
We call them "scum o' the earth."

R. H. SCHAUFFLER, *Scum o' the Earth.*

12
They spell it Vinci and pronounce it Vinchy; foreigners always spell better than they pronounce.

MARK TWAIN, *Innocents Abroad.*

13
A foreigner can photograph the exteriors of a nation, but I think that is as far as he can get. No foreigner can report its interior—its soul, its life, its speech, its thought.

MARK TWAIN, *What Paul Bourget Thinks of Us.*

He reports the American joke correctly. In Boston they ask, How much does he know? In New York, How much is he worth? In Philadelphia, Who were his parents? And when an alien observer turns his telescope upon us, a natural apprehension moves us to ask, What is the diameter of his reflector?

MARK TWAIN, *What Paul Bourget Thinks of Us.*

FORESIGHT, see Prudence

FOREST, see Woods

FORGETFULNESS

See also Forgive and Forget; Memory and Forgetfulness

14
But each day brings its petty dust
Our soon-chok'd souls to fill,
And we forget because we must,
And not because we will.

MATTHEW ARNOLD, *Absence.*

15
The sweets of forgetfulness.

JAMES BEATTIE, *The Hermit,* l. 2.

Life's best balm—forgetfulness.

FELICIA HEMANS, *The Caravan in the Desert.*

For gems of darkest jet may lie

Within a golden setting,
And he is wise who understands
The science of forgetting.
I. EDGAR JONES, *The Science of Forgetting.*

1
Oh, I have roamed o'er many lands,
And many friends I've met;
Not one fair scene or kindly smile
Can this fond heart forget.
T. H. BAYLY, *Oh, Steer My Bark.*

2
The only pang my bosom dare not brave
Must be to find forgetfulness in thine.
BYRON, *The Corsair.* Canto i, st. 14.

3
The world is turned memorial, crying, "Thou
Shalt not forget!"
MARY E. COLERIDGE, *Mandragora.*

4
I feel assured there is no such thing as ultimate forgetting; traces once impressed upon the memory are indestructible.
THOMAS DE QUINCEY, *Confessions of an English Opium Eater.* Pt. iii.

Forgotten? No, we never do forget:
We let the years go; wash them clean with tears, . . .
But we forget not, never can forget.
DINAH M. M. CRAIK, *A Flower of a Day.*

5
In a thousand years we shall all forget
The things that trouble us now.
ADAM LINDSAY GORDON, *After the Quarrel.*

6
A man must *get* a thing before he can *forget* it.
O. W. HOLMES, *Medical Essays,* p. 300.

7
Forgetting my people, and by them forgot. (Oblitusque meorum, obliviscendus et illis.)
HORACE, *Epistles.* Bk. i, epis. 11, l. 8.

The world forgetting, by the world forgot.
POPE, *Eloisa to Abelard,* l. 208.

9
There is no need to say "forget," I know,
For youth is youth, and time will have it so.
ANDREW LANG, *Good-Bye.*

10
You say, when I kissed you, you are sure I must quite
Have forgotten myself. So I did; you are right.
No, I'm not such an egotist, dear, it is true,
As to think of myself when I'm looking at you.
WALTER LEARNED, *Humility.*

In the middle of a moment
You and I forgot what "No" meant.
BILLY ROSE, *In the Middle of the Night.* The rhyme which is said to have fascinated Fannie Brice, who afterwards became Mrs. Rose.

11
I shook my head, perhaps,—but quite
Forgot to quite forget her.
F. LOCKER-LAMPSON, *St. James's Street.*

12
Darker grows the valley, more and more forgetting:
So were it with me if forgetting could be willed.
Tell the grassy hollow that holds the bubbling well-spring,
Tell it to forget the source that keeps it filled.
GEORGE MEREDITH, *Love in the Valley.*

13
There, held in holy passion still,
Forget thy self to Marble.
JOHN MILTON, *Il Penseroso,* l. 41.

14
But in that lovely land and still
Ye may remember what ye will,
And what ye will forget for aye.
WILLIAM MORRIS, *Life and Death of Jason.* Bk. xiv, l. 371.

15
"Forget thee?"—If to dream by night, and muse on thee by day,
If all the worship, deep and wild, a poet's heart can pay, . . .
If busy Fancy blending thee with all my future lot—
If this thou call'st "forgetting," thou indeed shalt be forgot!
JOHN MOULTRIE, *Forget Thee.*

16
O too, too forgetful of your own kin. (O nimium, nimiumque oblite tuorum.)
OVID, *Heroides.* Epis. i, l. 41.

Too forgetful of your own people. (Nimiumque oblite tuorum.)
STATIUS, *Thebais.* Bk. vii, l. 547.

17
Of all affliction taught a lover yet,
'Tis sure the hardest science to forget!
POPE, *Eloisa to Abelard,* l. 189.

18
Thou hast wounded the spirit that loved thee
And cherish'd thine image for years;
Thou hast taught me at last to forget thee,
In secret, in silence, and tears.
MRS. DAVID PORTER, *Thou Hast Wounded the Spirit.*

19
If I forget thee, O Jerusalem, let my right hand forget her cunning.
Old Testament: Psalms, cxxxvii, 5.

20
It is sometimes expedient to forget even what you know. (Etiam oblivisci quod scis, interdum expedit.)
PUBLILIUS SYRUS, *Sententiæ.* No. 234. Also printed *quid scis,* i.e., It is sometimes expedient to forget even who you are.

21
Men are men; the best sometimes forget.
SHAKESPEARE, *Othello.* Act ii, sc. 3, l. 241.

When I do forget
The least of these unspeakable deserts,
Romans, forget your fealty to me.
SHAKESPEARE, *Titus Andronicus.* Act i, sc. 1, l. 255.

22
We bury love,
Forgetfulness grows over it like grass;

That is a thing to weep for, not the dead.
ALEXANDER SMITH, *A Boy's Poem*. Pt. iii.

1
I remember the way we parted,
The day and the way we met;
You hoped we were both broken-hearted,
And knew we should both forget.
SWINBURNE, *An Interlude*. St. 11.

And the best and the worst of this is
That neither is most to blame,
If you've forgotten my kisses
And I've forgotten your name.
SWINBURNE, *An Interlude*. St. 14.

2
Forget thee . . . Never—
Till Nature, high and low, and great and small
Forgets herself, and all her loves and hates
Sink again into Chaos.
TENNYSON, *The Foresters*. Act i, sc. 3.

3
Of what significance the things you can forget? A little thought is sexton to all the world.
H. D. THOREAU, *Journal*. (EMERSON, *Thoreau*.)

4
And have you been to Borderland?
Its country lies on either hand
Beyond the river I-forget.
HERMAN KNICKERBOCKER VIELÉ, *Borderland*.

5
Go, forget me—why should sorrow
O'er that brow a shadow fling?
Go, forget me—and to-morrow
Brightly smile and sweetly sing.
CHARLES WOLFE, *Go, Forget Me!*

6
We bleed, we tremble; we forget, we smile—
The mind turns fool, before the cheek is dry.
YOUNG, *Night Thoughts*. Night v, l. 511.

FORGIVENESS

I—Forgive and Forgiven

7
They who forgive most shall be most forgiven.
P. J. BAILEY, *Festus: Home*.

8
And throughout all Eternity
I forgive you, you forgive me.
WILLIAM BLAKE, *Broken Love*.

9
Now may the good God pardon all good men!
E. B. BROWNING, *Aurora Leigh*. Bk. iv, l. 506.

10
But Thou art good; and Goodness still
Delighteth to forgive.
ROBERT BURNS, *A Prayer in the Prospect of Death*.

11
But to have power to forgive,
Is empire and prerogative:
And 'tis in crowns a nobler gem
To grant a pardon than condemn.
BUTLER, *An Heroical Epistle of Hudibras to His Lady*, l. 135.

12
He who forgives readily only invites offense. (Qui pardonne aisément invite à l'offenser.)
CORNEILLE, *Cinna*. Act iv, sc. 4.

To forgive everyone is as much cruelty as to forgive no one. (Tam ignoscere omnibus crudelitas est quam nulli.)
SENECA.

13
But I forgive you. . . . I do, and you can't help yourself.
DICKENS, *David Copperfield*. Ch. 42. Uriah Heep speaking.

14
God may forgive you, but I never can.
QUEEN ELIZABETH, to the Countess of Nottingham. (HUME, *History of England*. Ch. 44.)

And unforgiving, unforgiven dies.
UNKNOWN, *Lines on the Death of Queen Caroline*. (1821)

15
If anyone will take these two words to heart and use them for his own guidance and regulation, he will be almost without sin and will lead a very peaceful life. These two words are bear and forbear. (Ἀνέχου καὶ ἀπέχου.)
EPICTETUS. (AULUS GELLIUS, *Noctes Atticæ*. Bk. xvii, epis. 19, sec. 6.)

16
O Thou, who Man of baser Earth did make,
And ev'n with Paradise devise the Snake:
For all the sin wherewith the Face of Man
Is blackened—Man's forgiveness give,—and take!
FITZGERALD, *Rubáiyát of Omar Khayyám*. St. 81. This stanza is not in Omar, but is an interpolation by Fitzgerald.

17
The offender never pardons.
GEORGE HERBERT, *Jacula Prudentum*.

FORGIVENESS TO THE INJURED DOTH BELONG, *see under* INJURY.

18
It is just that he who asks forgiveness for his offenses should give it in turn. (Æquum est Peccatis veniam poscentem reddere rursus.)
HORACE, *Satires*. Bk. i, sat. 3, l. 74.

19
Nobuddy ever fergits where he buried a hatchet.
KIN HUBBARD, *Abe Martin's Broadcast*, p. 52.

20
One pardons in the degree that one loves. (On pardonne tant que l'on aime.)
LA ROCHEFOUCAULD, *Maximes*. No. 330.

21
Father, forgive them; for they know not what they do.
New Testament: Luke, xxiii, 34.

22
Forgive us our debts, as we forgive our debtors.
New Testament: Matthew, vi, 12.

Forgive us our trespasses, as we forgive those that trespass against us.
Book of Common Prayer: The Lord's Prayer.

This is the version generally in use in English and American churches, both Catholic and Protestant.

Forgive us our sins; for we also forgive every one that is indebted to us.
New Testament: Luke, xi, 4.

1
And I think, in the lives of most women and men,
There's a moment when all would go smooth and even,
If only the dead could find out when
To come back, and be forgiven.
OWEN MEREDITH, *Aux Italiens.*

2
Philosophy is toleration, and it is only one step from toleration to forgiveness.
PINERO, *The Second Mrs. Tanqueray.* Act ii.

3
Forgiveness is better than revenge. (Συγγνώμη τιμωρίας κρείσσων.)
PITTACUS, when he released Alcæus, after having him in his power. (DIOGENES LAERTIUS, *Pittacus.* Bk. i, sec. 76.)

Forgiveness is better than revenge; for forgiveness is the sign of a gentle nature, but revenge the sign of a savage nature.
EPICTETUS, *Fragments.* No. 68.

4
Only heaven
Means crowned, not conquered, when it says "Forgiven."
ADELAIDE ANN PROCTER, *A Legend of Provence.*

5
Forgive others often, yourself never. (Ignoscito sæpe alter, nunquam tibi.)
PUBLILIUS SYRUS, *Sententiæ.* No. 325.

Pardon all but thyself.
GEORGE HERBERT, *Jacula Prudentum.*

6
To forgive much makes the powerful more powerful. (Multa ignoscendo fit potens potentior.)
PUBLILIUS SYRUS, *Sententiæ.* No. 384.

To forgive is beautiful. (Pulchrum ignoscere.)
PUBLILIUS SYRUS, *Sententiæ.* No. 544.

7
Forgive that you may be forgiven. (Ut absolvaris, ignosce.)
SENECA, *De Beneficiis.* Bk. vii, sec. 28.

8
Pardon's the word to all.
SHAKESPEARE, *Cymbeline.* Act v, sc. 5, l. 422.

I pardon him, as God shall pardon me.
SHAKESPEARE, *Richard II.* Act v, sc. 3, l. 131.

A virtuous and a Christian-like conclusion,
To pray for them that have done scathe to us.
SHAKESPEARE, *Richard III.* Act i, sc. 3, l. 316.

Not to relent is beastly, savage, devilish.
SHAKESPEARE, *Richard III.* Act i, sc. 4, l. 265.

9
May one be pardoned, and retain the offence?
SHAKESPEARE, *Hamlet.* Act iii, sc. 3, l. 56.

10
God *never* pardons; his laws are irrevocable; the mind that deserts its better knowledge must suffer.
God *always* pardons; for remorse is penitence, and penitence is new life, and returning peace.
WILLIAM SMITH, *Thorndale.* Pt. ii, sec. 13.

11
To understand everything makes one very indulgent. (Tout comprendre rend très indulgent.)
MADAME DE STAËL, *Corinne.* Bk. xviii, ch. 5.

To understand is to pardon. To understand everything is to forgive everything. (Comprendre c'est pardonner. Tout comprendre c'est tout pardonner.)
Both these phrases have been attributed to Madame de Staël, but are not found in her works. They are probably misquotations of—as well as great improvements on—the sentence from *Corinne* cited above.

The more we know, the better we forgive;
Whoe'er feels deeply, feels for all who live.
Attributed to MADAME DE STAËL, but exact source not discovered.

Know all and you will pardon all.
THOMAS À KEMPIS, *De Imitatione Christi.* Pt. i.

He who understands everything understands nothing, and he who forgives everything forgives nothing.
MIGUEL DE UNAMUNO, *Essays and Soliloquies.* p. 93.

12
Only the brave know how to forgive. . . . A coward never forgave; it is not in his nature.
LAURENCE STERNE, *Sermons.* No. 12.

13
If the injured one could read your heart, you may be sure he would understand and pardon.
R. L. STEVENSON, *Truth of Intercourse.*

14
Sleep; and if life was bitter to thee, pardon;
If sweet, give thanks; thou hast no more to live,
And to give thanks is good, and to forgive.
SWINBURNE, *Ave atque Vale.* St. 17.

15
Forgive! How many will say, "forgive," and find
A sort of absolution in the sound
To hate a little longer!
TENNYSON, *Sea Dreams,* l. 60.

16
But to forgive our enemies their virtues—that is a greater miracle, and one which no longer happens.
(Mais à ses ennemis pardonner les vertus,
C'est un plus grand miracle, et qui ne se fait plus.)
VOLTAIRE, *Discours sur la Vraie Vertu.*

17
The best of what we do and are,
Just God, forgive!
WORDSWORTH, *Thoughts Suggested on the Banks of Nith.*

II—Forgive and Forget

1
"I can forgive, but I cannot forget," is only another way of saying, "I cannot forgive."
HENRY WARD BEECHER, *Life Thoughts.*

2
Good, to forgive; Best, to forget!
Living, we fret; Dying, we live.
ROBERT BROWNING, *La Saisiaz: Dedication.*

3
The memory and conscience never did, nor never will, agree about forgiving injuries.
LORD HALIFAX, *Works,* p. 252.

4
All our great fray . . . is forgiven and forgotten between us quite.
JOHN HEYWOOD, *Proverbs.* Pt. ii, ch. 3. (1546)

Pray you now, forget and forgive.
SHAKESPEARE, *King Lear.* Act iv, sc. 7, l. 84. (c. 1605) Usually misquoted, "Forgive and forget."

Endeavour to forget, sir, and forgive.
THOMAS SOUTHERNE, *Oroonoko.* Act v, sc. 2. (1696)

Yon little thatch is where she lives,
Yon spire is where she met me;—
I think that if she quite forgives,
She cannot quite forget me.
F. LOCKER-LAMPSON, *Mrs. Smith.*

FORTUNE

See also Chance, Destiny, Luck, Providence. For Fortune in the sense of wealth see Riches.

I—Fortune: Apothegms

5
Bear good fortune modestly. (Fortunam reverenter habe.)
AUSONIUS, *Epigrams.* No. ii, l. 8.

6
Fortune makes him a fool whom she makes her darling. (Fortuna nimium quem fovet, stultum facit.)
BACON, *Ornamenta Rationalia.* No. 13.

7
Fortune is not content to do a man but one ill turn. (Fortuna obesse nulli contenta est semel.)
FRANCIS BACON, *Ornamenta Rationalia.* No. 14.

Fortune rarely brings good or evil singly.
THOMAS FULLER, *Gnomologia.* No. 1605. (1732) *See also under* MISFORTUNE.

8
The fortune which nobody sees makes a man happy and unenvied. (Facit gratum fortuna, quam nemo videt.)
BACON, *Ornamenta Rationalia.* No. 15.

9
Good fortune is not known until it is lost.
CERVANTES, *Don Quixote.* Pt. ii, ch. 54.

10
Fortune hath somewhat the nature of a woman; if she be too much wooed, she is the farther off.
EMPEROR CHARLES V. (BACON, *Advancement of Learning.* Bk. ii.)

Fortune is a woman, and therefore friendly to the young, who with audacity command her.
MACHIAVELLI, *Il Principe.* Ch. 25. (Helps, tr.)

11
No one is satisfied with his fortune, nor dissatisfied with his intellect. (Nul n'est content de sa fortune; Ni mécontent de son esprit.)
DESHOULIÈRES, *Epigram.*

12
When fortune favours, none but fools will dally.
DRYDEN, *The Duke of Guise: Epilogue,* l. 20.

When Fortune smiles, embrace her!
THOMAS FULLER, *Gnomologia.* No. 5553.

The day of fortune is like a harvest day,
We must be busy when the corn is ripe.
(Ein Tag der Gunst ist wie ein Tag der Ernte,
Man muss geschäftig sein sobald sie reift.)
GOETHE, *Torquato Tasso.* Act iv, sc. 4.
See also under OPPORTUNITY.

13
Nature magically suits a man to his fortunes, by making them the fruit of his character.
EMERSON, *Conduct of Life: Fate.*

Fortunes are not exceptions, but fruits.
EMERSON, *Conduct of Life: Worship.*

14
Fortune seldom interferes with the wise man, for his highest interests are always directed by reason.
EPICURUS, *Sovran Maxims.* No. 16.

15
Fortune once in the course of our life doth put into our hands the offer of a good turn.
SIR GEOFFREY FENTON, *Bandello.* Vol. ii, p. 148. (1567)

There is a deep nick in time's restless wheel
For each man's good.
GEORGE CHAPMAN, *Bussy d'Ambois.* Act i, sc. 1.
See also under OPPORTUNITY.

16
He that waits upon fortune, is never sure of a dinner.
BENJAMIN FRANKLIN, *Poor Richard,* 1734.

17
It is the fortunate who should praise fortune. (Das Glück erhebe billig der Beglückte.)
GOETHE, *Torquato Tasso.* Act ii, sc. 3, l. 115.

18
Alas! till now I had not known
My guide and fortune's guide are one.
HAFIZ. (EMERSON, *Conduct of Life: Fate.*)

19
Fortune to one is mother, to another is stepmother.
GEORGE HERBERT, *Jacula Prudentum.*

20
Fortune's favorite. (Fortunæ filius.)
HORACE, *Satires.* Bk. ii, sat. 6, l. 49.

Fortune turns everything to the advantage of its favorites. (La fortune tourne tout à l'avantage de ceux qu'elle favorise.)
LA ROCHEFOUCAULD, *Maximes.* No. 60.

With a fortunate man, all things are fortunate.
THEOCRITUS, *Idyls.* No. 15, l. 24.

1
It is writ on the palace where luxury dwells,
That fortune, in seeming to give, really sells.
(Il lit au front de ceux qu'un vain luxe environne
Que la fortune vend ce qu'on croit qu'elle donne.)

LA FONTAINE, *Fables: Philemon et Baucis.*

Usually fortune sells very dearly that which we think she gives us. (Pour l'ordinaire la fortune nous vend bien chèrement, ce qu'on croit qu'elle nous donne.)

VOITURE, *Le Comte du Guiche.*

2
Greater qualities are necessary to bear good fortune than bad. (Il faut de plus grandes vertus pour soutenir la bonne fortune que la mauvaise.)

LA ROCHEFOUCAULD, *Maximes.* No. 25. *See also* PROSPERITY AND ADVERSITY.

3
Seldom are men blessed with good fortune and good sense at the same time. (Raro simul hominibus bonam fortunam bonamque mentem dari.)

LIVY, *History.* Bk. xxx, sec. 42.

4
Fortune comes well to all that comes not late.

LONGFELLOW, *The Spanish Student.* Act iii, sc. 5, l. 281.

5
Fortune gives too much to many, enough to none. (Fortuna multis dat nimis, satis nulli.)

MARTIAL, *Epigrams.* Bk. xii, epig. 10.

Fortune, men say, doth give too much to many:
But yet she never gave enough to any.

SIR JOHN HARINGTON, *Of Fortune.*

6
To Fortune I commit the rest. (Fortunæ cetera mando.)

OVID, *Metamorphoses.* Bk. ii, l. 140.

7
Fortune, indulgent Fortune. (Fortunam, atque Obsequentem.)

PLAUTUS, *Asinaria,* l. 716. (Act iii, sc. 3.)

8
When Fortune flatters, she does it to betray. (Fortuna cum blanditur, captatum venit.)

PUBLILIUS SYRUS, *Sententiæ.* No. 277.

9
It is more easy to get a favor from fortune than to keep it. (Fortunam citius reperias quam retineas.)

PUBLILIUS SYRUS, *Sententiæ.* No. 282.

10
Fortune runs to meet us not less often than we go to meet her. (Non minus sæpe fortuna in nos incurrit quam nos in illam.)

SENECA, *Epistulæ ad Lucilium.* Epis. xxxvii, 5.

11
That which Fortune has not given, she cannot take away. (Quod non dedit fortuna, non eripit.)

SENECA, *Epistulæ ad Lucilium.* Epis. lix, sec. 18.

What fortune has made yours is not really yours. (Non est tuum, fortuna quod fecit tuum.)

PUBLILIUS SYRUS, *Sententiæ.* (SENECA, *Epistulæ ad Lucilium.* Epis. viii, sec. 10.)

12
He who can bear fortune, can also beware of fortune. (Potest fortunam cavere, qui potest ferre.)

SENECA, *Epistulæ ad Lucilium.* Epis. xcviii, 7.

Amid the greatest disturbance of fortune, he was undisturbed. (Æqualis fuit in tanta inequalitate fortunæ.)

SENECA, *Epistulæ ad Lucilium.* Epis. civ, sec. 28. Referring to Socrates.

Fortune can take away riches, but not courage. (Fortuna opes auferre, non animum potest.)

SENECA, *Medea,* l. 176.

13
O giglot fortune!

SHAKESPEARE, *Cymbeline.* Act iii, sc. 1, l. 31.

Fortune brings in some boats, that are not steer'd.

SHAKESPEARE, *Cymbeline.* Act iv, sc. 3, l. 46.

14
Fortune is merry,
And in this mood will give us any thing.

SHAKESPEARE, *Julius Cæsar.* Act iii, sc. 2, l. 271.

For herein Fortune shows herself more kind
Than is her custom.

SHAKESPEARE, *The Merchant of Venice.* Act iv, sc. 1, l. 267.

15
And all the unsettled humours of the land . . .
Have sold their fortunes at their native homes . . .
To make a hazard of new fortunes here.

SHAKESPEARE, *King John.* Act ii, sc. 1, l. 66.

A Hazard of New Fortunes.

W. D. HOWELLS. Title of novel.

16
'Tis more by fortune, lady, than by merit.

SHAKESPEARE, *Pericles.* Act ii, sc. 3, l. 12.

17
'Tis pity bounty had not eyes behind,
That man might ne'er be wretched for his mind.

SHAKESPEARE, *Timon of Athens.* Act i, sc. 2, l. 169.

18
A just fortune awaits the deserving. (Fors æqua merentes Respicit.)

STATIUS, *Thebais.* Pt. i, l. 661.

19
We are corrupted by good fortune. (Felicitate corrumpimur.)

TACITUS, *History.* Bk. i, sec. 15.

20
And fortune smil'd, deceitful, on her birth.

THOMSON, *The Seasons: Autumn,* l. 178.

21
Fortune, who oft proves
The careless wanderer's friend.

WORDSWORTH, *The Excursion.* Bk. ii, l. 185.

Fortune's friend is mishap's foe.

SIR THOMAS WYATT, *The Lover Complaineth Himself Forsaken,* l. 8.

II—Fortune: Its Blindness

1
If a man look sharply and attentively, he shall see Fortune; for though she is blind, she is not invisible.
FRANCIS BACON, *Essays: Of Fortune.*

2
Not only is Fortune blind herself, but as a rule she blinds those whom she favors. (Non enim solum ipsa fortuna cæca est, sed eos etiam plerumque efficit cæcos, quos complexa est.)
CICERO, *De Amicitia.* Ch. xv, sec. 54.

3
Blind fortune pursues blind rashness. (Fortune aveugle suit aveugle hardiesse.)
LA FONTAINE, *Fables.* Bk. x, fab. 14.

4
Fortune never seems so blind as to those upon whom she has bestowed no favors. (La fortune ne paraît jamais si aveugle qu'à ceux à qui elle ne fait pas de bien.)
LA ROCHEFOUCAULD, *Maximes.* No. 391.

5
That goddess blind,
That stands upon the rolling restless stone.
SHAKESPEARE, *Henry V.* Act iii, sc. 6, l. 29.

Fortune is painted blind, with a muffler afore her eyes, to signify to you that Fortune is blind.
SHAKESPEARE, *Henry V.* Act iii, sc. 6, l. 32.

6
Fortune has often been blamed for her blindness; but Fortune is not so blind as men are.
SAMUEL SMILES, *Self-Help.* Ch. 3.

III—Fortune: Its Fickleness

7
Fortune ever hath an uncertain end.
ALEXANDER BARCLAY, *Shyp of Folys,* l. 126. (1509)

8
Fortune is full of fresh variety.
Constant in nothing but inconstancy.
RICHARD BARNFIELD, *The Shepherd's Content.* St. 11.

9
Gifts of fortune,
That pass as a shadow upon a wall.
CHAUCER, *The Marchantes Tale,* l. 70.

Fortune hath in her honey gall.
CHAUCER, *The Monkes Tale,* l. 557.

10
Variant Fortune was; aye in short space
Her wheel was ready to turn without let.
LYDGATE, *Assembly of Gods.* St. 46. (c. 1420)

11
She sings defiance to the giddy wheel of fortune.
SIR THOMAS OVERBURY, *A Fair and Happy Milkmaid.*

Let us sit and mock the good housewife Fortune from her wheel, that her gifts may henceforth be bestowed equally.
SHAKESPEARE, *As You Like It.* Act i, sc. 2, l. 34.

And railed on Lady Fortune in good terms,
In good set terms.
SHAKESPEARE, *As You Like it.* Act ii, sc. 7, l. 16.

12
Fortune knows neither reason or law. She is inclined to favor the wicked, and hates the just, as if to display her unreasoning force.
PALLADAS. (*Greek Anthology.* Bk. x, epig. 62.)

13
Fortune changes suddenly: life is changeable. (Actutum fortunæ solent mutarier: varia vita est.)
PLAUTUS, *Truculentus.* Act ii, sc. 1, l. 9.

14
The wheel goes round and round,
And some are up and some are on the down,
And still the wheel goes round.
JOSEPHINE POLLARD, *The Wheel of Fortune.*

For fortune's wheel is on the turn,
And some go up and some go down.
MARY F. TUCKER, *Going Up and Coming Down.*

15
Who thinks that Fortune cannot change her mind,
Prepares a dreadful jest for all mankind.
POPE, *Imitations of Horace: Satires.* Bk. ii, sat. ii, l. 123.

16
Dame Fortune is a fickle gipsy,
And always blind, and often tipsy;
Sometimes, for years and years together,
She'll bless you with the sunniest weather,
Bestowing honour, pudding, pence,
You can't imagine why or whence;—
Then in a moment—Presto, Pass!—
Your joys are withered like the grass.
W. M. PRAED, *The Legend of the Haunted Tree.*

17
Fortune is glass; just as it becomes bright it is broken. (Fortuna vitrea est; tum cum splendet frangitur.)
PUBLILIUS SYRUS, *Sententiæ.* No. 280. Said to be a maxim of Seneca.

18
On doubtful wings flies the inconstant hour, nor does swift Fortune keep faith with any. (Volat ambiguis mobilis alis Hora, nec ulli præstat velox Fortuna fidem.)
SENECA, *Hippolytus,* l. 1141.

19
And giddy Fortune's furious fickle wheel.
SHAKESPEARE, *Henry V.* Act iii, sc. 6, l. 29.

Fortune, good night: smile once more; turn thy wheel!
SHAKESPEARE, *King Lear.* Act ii, sc. 2, l. 180.

And turn the giddy round of Fortune's wheel.
SHAKESPEARE, *The Rape of Lucrece.* St. 136.

20
O fortune, fortune! all men call thee fickle.
SHAKESPEARE, *Romeo and Juliet.* Act iii, sc. 5, l. 60.

IV—Fortune: Its Ups and Downs

21
Though I was long in coming to the light,

Yet may I mount to fortune's highest height.
WILLIAM ALEXANDER, *Aurora*. Sonnet xcviii.

1
Fortune turns round like a mill-wheel, and he who was yesterday at the top, lies today at the bottom.
CERVANTES, *Don Quixote*. Pt. i, ch. 20.

2
Whenever Fortune wishes to jest, she lifts people from the gutter to the mighty places of the earth. (Ex humili magna ad fastigia rerum Extollit quotiens voluit Fortuna jocari.)
JUVENAL, *Satires*. Sat. iii, l. 39.

3
Fortune in men has some small diff'rence made;
One flaunts in rags, one flutters in brocade,
The cobbler apron'd, and the parson gown'd,
The friar hooded, and the monarch crown'd.
POPE, *Essay on Man*. Epis. iv, l. 195.

4
Fortune rules in all things; she raises to eminence or buries in oblivion from caprice rather than from principle. (Sed perfecta fortuna in omni re dominatur; ea res cunctas ex lubidine magis quam ex vero celebrat obscuratque.)
SALLUST, *Catilina*. Ch. 8, sec. 1.

5
Whatever Fortune has raised on high, she has raised but to bring low. (Quidquid in altum Fortuna tulit, Ruitura levat.)
SENECA, *Agamemnon*, l. 101.

6
I do but wait a time and fortune's chance;
Oft many things do happen in one hour.
SIR THOMAS WYATT, *Whether Liberty or Prison*.

7
Lo, thus Fortune can turn her dice,
Now up, now down; her wheel is unstable.
UNKNOWN, *Partonope*, l. 4389. (c. 1490)

V—Fortune: Its Power

8
Sovereign of all the gods is Fortune, and these other names are given her in vain; for she alone disposeth all things as she will.
ÆSCHYLUS [?], *Fragments*. Frag. 254.

9
Fortune, the great commandress of the world,
Hath divers ways to advance her followers:
To some she gives honour without deserving;
To other some, deserving without honour;
Some wit, some wealth; and some, wit without wealth;
Some wealth without wit; some nor wit nor wealth.
GEORGE CHAPMAN, *All Fools*. Act v, sc. 1.

10
Thou wouldst have no divinity, O Fortune, if we had but wisdom; it is we that make a goddess of thee, and place thee in the skies. (Nullum numen habes, si sit prudentia: nos te, nos facimus, Fortuna, deam cæloque locamus.)
JUVENAL, *Satires*. Sat. x, l. 365.

11
Fortune rules all.
MASSINGER, *The Bashful Lover*. Act iv, sc. 1.

12
If the gale of Fortune bear thee, bear with it and be borne; if thou rebellest, the gale bears thee just the same
PALLADAS. (*Greek Anthology*. Bk. x, epig. 73.)

13
Fortune moulds and limits human affairs as she pleases. (Fortuna humana fingit artatque ut lubet.)
PLAUTUS, *Captivi*, l. 304. (Act ii, sc. 2.)

The schemes of a hundred learned men are all inferior to one lone goddess, Fortune. (Centum doctum hominum consilia sola hæc devincit dea, Fortuna.)
PLAUTUS, *Pseudolus*, l. 678. (Act ii, sc. 1.)

14
Behold! if fortune or a mistress frowns,
Some plunge in business, others shave their crowns.
POPE, *Moral Essays*. Epis. i, l. 103.

15
Fortune is of more value to a man than judgment. (Fortuna plus homini quam consilium valet.)
PUBLILIUS SYRUS, *Sententiæ*. No. 283.

16
Against fortune the carter cracks his whip in vain. (Centre fortune, la diverse un chartier rompit nazardes son fouet.)
RABELAIS, *Works*. Bk. ii, ch. 11.

17
Fortune turns on her wheel the fate of kings. (Præcipites regum casus Fortuna rotat.)
SENECA, *Agamemnon*, l. 71.

18
Fortune has all power over one who lives, but no power over one who knows how to die.
SENECA, *Epistulæ ad Lucilium*. Epis. lxx, 7.

19
Fortune reigns in gifts of the world.
SHAKESPEARE, *As You Like It*. Act i, sc. 2, l. 44.

Under Heaven's high cope
Fortune is God: all you endure and do
Depends on circumstance as much as you.
SHELLEY, *Epigrams from the Greek Circumstance*.

20
The power of fortune is confessed only by the miserable; for the happy impute all their success to prudence and merit.
SWIFT, *Thoughts on Various Subjects*.

21
Fortune, not wisdom, rules the life of men. (Τύχη τὰ θνητῶν πράγματ' οὐκ εὐβουλία.)
THEOPHRASTUS, *Callisthenes*. (PLUTARCH, *De Fortuna*, 97.) Latined by CICERO (*Tusculanarum Disputationum*, v, 9): Vitam regit fortuna, non sapientia.

VI—Fortune: Good and Bad

22
Ah! who can tell how many a soul sublime

Has felt the influence of malignant star,
And waged with Fortune an eternal war.
JAMES BEATTIE, *The Minstrel*. Bk. i, l. 3.

1
Incapable of compromises,
Unable to forgive or spare,
The strange awarding of the prizes
He had no fortitude to bear.
WILLA CATHER, *A Likeness*.

2
For I deem that contrarious Fortune profiteth more to men than Fortune debonaire.
CHAUCER, *Boethius*. Bk. ii, prose 8.

In losing fortune, many a lucky elf
Has found himself.
HORACE SMITH, *Moral Alchemy*. St. 12.

3
Fortune came smiling to my youth and woo'd it,
And purple greatness met my ripened years.
DRYDEN, *All for Love*. Act i, sc. 1.

4
Vicissitudes of fortune, which spares neither man nor the proudest of his works, which buries empires and cities in a common grave.
GIBBON, *Decline and Fall of the Roman Empire*. Ch. 71.

5
The greatest reverses of fortune are the most easily borne, from a sort of dignity belonging to them.
WILLIAM HAZLITT, *Life of Napoleon Buonaparte*. Vol. iv, p. 267.

6
The bitter dregs of Fortune's cup to drain.
HOMER, *Iliad*. Bk. xxii, l. 85. (Pope, tr.)

7
You are sad, though fortunate. Take care that Fortune does not perceive this, or she will call you ungrateful. (Tristis es et felix. Sciat hoc Fortuna caveto Ingratum dicet te.)
MARTIAL, *Epigrams*. Bk. vi, epig. 79.

8
The most wretched fortune is safe, for it lacks fear of anything worse. (Fortuna miserrima tuta est, nam timor eventus deterioris abest.)
OVID, *Epistulæ ex Ponto*. Bk. ii, epis. 2, l. 31.

His only solace was, that now
His dog-bolt fortune was so low,
That either it must quickly end
Or turn about again, and mend.
BUTLER, *Hudibras*. Pt. ii, canto i, l. 39.

I wish thy lot, now bad, still worse, my friend,
For when at worst, they say, things always mend.
JOHN OWEN, *To a Friend in Distress*.

See also BUNYAN *under* FALL.

9
Even men of the noblest virtue are seldom spared by adverse fortune. (Iniqua raro maximis virtutibus Fortuna parcit.)
SENECA, *Hercules Furens*, l. 325.

O Fortune, jealous of the brave, in allotting thy favors, how unjust art thou unto the righteous! (O Fortuna viris invida fortibus, Quam non æqua bonis præmia dividis.)
SENECA, *Hercules Furens*, l. 524.

10
Fortune is gentle to the lowly. (Minor in parvis Fortuna furit.)
SENECA, *Hippolytus*, l. 1124.

Fortune, that arrant whore,
Ne'er turns the key to the poor.
SHAKESPEARE, *King Lear*. Act ii, sc. 4, l. 52.

11
I am now, sir, muddied in fortune's mood, and smell somewhat strong of her strong displeasure.
SHAKESPEARE, *All's Well that Ends Well*. Act v, sc. 2, l. 4.

One out of suits with fortune.
SHAKESPEARE, *As You Like It*. Act i, sc. 2, l. 258.

On Fortune's cap we are not the very button.
SHAKESPEARE, *Hamlet*. Act ii, sc. 2, l. 233.

A good man's fortune may grow out at heels.
SHAKESPEARE, *King Lear*. Act ii, sc. 2, l. 164.

12
Will Fortune never come with both hands full,
But write her fair words still in foulest letters?
She either gives a stomach and no food;
Such are the poor, in health: or else a feast
And takes away the stomach; such are the rich,
That have abundance, and enjoy it not.
SHAKESPEARE, *II Henry IV*. Act iv, sc. 4, l. 103.

13
When Fortune means to men most good,
She looks upon them with a threatening eye.
SHAKESPEARE, *King John*. Act iii, sc. 4, l. 119.

14
So was their fortune good, though wicked was their mind.
SPENSER, *Faerie Queene*. Bk. iii, canto ii, st. 43.

15
For ever, Fortune, wilt thou prove
An unrelenting foe to love.
JAMES THOMSON, *To Fortune*.

16
Where God and cruel fortune call, let us follow. (Quo Deus, et quo dura vocat Fortuna, sequamur.)
VERGIL, *Æneid*. Bk. xii, l. 677.

17
A man is never so on trial as in the moment of excessive good-fortune.
LEW WALLACE, *Ben Hur*. Bk. v, ch. 7.

VII—Fortune: Architects of Fortune

18
Every man is the architect of his own fortune. (Fabrum esse suæ quemque fortunæ.)
APPIUS CLAUDIUS CÆCUS, who held the office of censor in 312 B.C. His poems have not survived. (PSEUDO-SALLUST, *Duæ Epistulæ de Republica Ordinanda*. Epis. i, sec. 1. These letters were addressed to Cæsar, and are attributed to Sallust on doubtful authority. The entire sentence reads: "But these things teach us the truth of what Appius says in his verses, that everyone is the architect of his own fortune.")

It is a highway saying, that we are architects of our own fortune.

JOHN DUNTON, *Athenianism*, p. 454. (1707)

We have not a commoner saying among us than "Every man is the architect of his own fortune," and we have very few much older.

E. TEW. (*Notes and Queries*. Ser. iv, vol. xii, p. 515.)

1
It cannot be denied, but outward accidents conduce much to fortune: favour, opportunity, death of others, occasion fitting virtue. But chiefly the mould of a man's fortune is in his own hands: (Faber quisque fortunæ suæ.)

FRANCIS BACON, *Essays: On Fortune*.

2
Each person is the founder
Of his own fortune, good or bad.

BEAUMONT AND FLETCHER, *Love's Pilgrimage*. Act i, sc. 1.

3
The brave man carves out his fortune, and every man is the son of his own works.

CERVANTES, *Don Quixote*. Pt. i, ch. 4.

Each is the maker of his own fortune.

CERVANTES, *Don Quixote*. Pt. ii, ch. 66.

4
Every man's fortune is moulded by his character. (Mores cuique sui fingunt fortunam.)

CORNELIUS NEPOS, *Atticus*. Ch. 11.

A man's own character is the arbiter of his fortune.

PUBLILIUS SYRUS, *Sententiæ*. No. 141.

5
The wise man is the maker of his own fortune, and, unless he be a bungling workman, little can befall him which he would desire to change.

PLAUTUS, *Trinummus*. Act ii, sc. 2.

6
Every man is the maker of his own fortune.

RICHARD STEELE, *The Tatler*. No. 52.

7
A man's own manners do shape his fortune.

RICHARD TAVERNER, *Proverbs*. Fo. 37. (1539)

VIII—Fortune: Mastery of Fortune

9
All fortune is to be conquered by bearing it. (Vincenda est omnia fortuna ferendo.)

BACON, *Advancement of Learning*. Quoted as a maxim.

10
Let not one look of fortune cast you down;
She were not fortune, if she did not frown:
Such as do braveliest bear her scorns awhile,
Are those on whom, at last, she most will smile.

JOHN BOYLE, *Imitation of Horace*.

11
Let not Fortune, which hath no name in Scripture, have any in thy divinity.

SIR THOMAS BROWNE, *Christian Morals*. Pt. i, sec. 25.

12
My worthy friend, ne'er grudge an' carp,
Tho' Fortune use you hard and sharp;
Come, kittle up your moorland harp
Wi' gleesome touch!
Ne'er mind how Fortune waft an' warp;
She's but a bitch.

BURNS, *Second Epistle to J. Lapraik*.

Fortune! if thou'll but gie me still
Hale breeks, a scone, an' whisky-gill,
An' rowth o' rhyme to rave at will,
Tak a' the rest.

BURNS, *Scotch Drink*. St. 21.

Is Fortune's fickle Luna waning?
E'en let her gang!
Beneath what light she has remaining,
Let's sing our sang.

BURNS, *Epistle to James Smith*.

13
I can enjoy her while she's kind;
But when she dances in the wind,
And shakes the wings, and will not stay,
I puff the prostitute away.

DRYDEN, *Imitations of Horace*. Bk. iii, ode 29, l. 81.

14
Never think you Fortune can bear the sway,
Where Virtue's force can cause her to obey.

QUEEN ELIZABETH, *In Defiance of Fortune*. (PUTTENHAM, *Art of Poesie: Of Ornament*.)

15
A change of fortune hurts a wise man no more than a change of the moon.

BENJAMIN FRANKLIN, *Poor Richard*, 1756.

16
Learn to bear great fortune well. (Bene ferre magnam Disce fortunam.)

HORACE, *Odes*. Bk. iii, ode 27, l. 74.

17
Ill fortune never crushed that man whom good fortune deceived not.

BEN JONSON, *Explorata: Fortuna*.

18
Largesse! Largesse, Fortune!
Give or hold at your will.
If I've no care for Fortune
Fortune must follow me still.

RUDYARD KIPLING, *The Wishing-Caps*.

If fortune favour I may have her, for I go about her;
If fortune fail you may kiss her tail, and go without her.

JOHN RAY, *English Proverbs*, p. 212.

19
Fortune knows
We scorn her most when most she offers blows.

SHAKESPEARE, *Antony and Cleopatra*. Act iii, sc. 11, l. 73.

A man that fortune's buffets and rewards
Hast ta'en with equal thanks.

SHAKESPEARE, *Hamlet*. Act iii, sc. 2, l. 72.

20
Blest are those
Whose blood and judgement are so well commingled,

That they are not a pipe for fortune's finger
To sound what stop she please.
SHAKESPEARE, *Hamlet*. Act iii, sc. 2, l. 73.

1
We ready are to try our fortunes
To the last man.
SHAKESPEARE, *II Henry IV*. Act iv, sc. 2, l. 43.

Myself could else outfrown false fortune's frown.
SHAKESPEARE, *King Lear*. Act v, sc. 3, l. 6.

How some men creep in skittish Fortune's hall,
While others play the idiots in her eyes!
SHAKESPEARE, *Troilus and Cressida*. Act iii, sc. 3, l. 134.

2
They make their fortune who are stout and wise.
TASSO, *Jerusalem Delivered*. Bk. x, st. 20.

IX—Fortune Favors the Bold

3
Fortune favors the bold. (Audentis Fortuna juvat.)
VERGIL, *Æneid*. Bk. x, l. 284. Used in this form by many Latin writers. Sometimes written, "Fors juvat audentes," as by CLAUDIAN, *Ad Probinum*, l. 8.

4
Fortune favors the brave. (Fortis fortuna adjuvat.)
TERENCE, *Phormio*. Act i, sc. 4, l. 26. Used in this form by CICERO, *De Finibus*, bk. iii, ch. 4, sec. 116, and by many others.

5
Hap helpeth hardy man alday, quoth he.
CHAUCER, *The Legend of Good Women*. Pt. v, l. 94.

6
Fortune and Venus help the bold. (Audentem Forsque Venusque juvat.)
OVID, *Ars Amatoria*. Bk. i, l. 608.

Be bold: Venus herself aids the stout-hearted. (Audendum est: fortes adjuvat ipsa Venus.)
TIBULLUS, *Odes*. Bk. i, ode 2, l. 16.

7
Fortune is like a widow won,
And truckles to the bold alone.
WILLIAM SOMERVILLE, *The Fortune-Hunter*. Canto ii. *See also* WIDOW: WOOING.

8
Fortune is not on the side of the faint-hearted.
SOPHOCLES, *Phædra*. Frag. 842.

X—Fortune Favors Fools

9
Fortune makes Folly her peculiar care.
CHARLES CHURCHILL, *The Rosciad*, l. 604.

10
'Tis a gross error held in schools,
That Fortune always favours fools.
JOHN GAY, *Fables*. No. 12.

11
Fortune favours fools.
BARNABE GOOGE, *Eglogs*, l. 74. (1563)

Does my patron lose? fortune favours fools!
SIR CHARLES SEDLEY, *Bellamira*.

Fortune, that favours fools.
BEN JONSON, *The Alchemist: Prologue; Every Man Out of His Humour*. Act i, sc. 1.

12
When fortune favors a man too much, she makes him a fool. (Fortuna nimium quem fovet, stultum facit.)
PUBLILIUS SYRUS, *Sententiæ*. No. 198.

13
O, I am fortune's fool!
SHAKESPEARE, *Romeo and Juliet*. Act iii, sc l. 141.

FOURTH OF JULY, see Independence Day

FOX

14
Like Æsop's fox, when he had lost his tail, would have all his fellow foxes cut off theirs.
ROBERT BURTON, *Anatomy of Melancholy: Democritus to the Reader*. (ÆSOP, *Fables*. Bk. v, fab. 5.)

15
The fox has many tricks, and the hedgehog only one, but that is the best of all.
ERASMUS, *Adagia*.

The fox has many tricks, and the cat only one, but that the best of all. (i. e., climbing a tree.)
JOHN RAY, *English Proverbs*.

Though the fox run, the chicken hath wings.
GEORGE HERBERT, *Jacula Prudentum*.

16
A fox should not be of the jury at a goose's trial.
THOMAS FULLER, *Gnomologia*. No. 116.

An old fox needs not be taught tricks.
THOMAS FULLER, *Gnomologia*. No. 644.

He that will outwit the fox must rise betimes.
THOMAS FULLER, *Gnomologia*. No. 2357.

Old foxes want no tutors.
THOMAS FULLER, *Gnomologia*. No. 3712.

The fox may grow grey but never good.
THOMAS FULLER, *Gnomologia*. No. 4545.

With foxes we must play the fox.
THOMAS FULLER, *Gnomologia*. No. 5797.

17
The more the fox is cursed, the better he fares.
ROBERT GREENE, *Friar Bacon*. Sc. 11. (1594)

The cursed fox thrives the best.
CERVANTES, *Don Quixote*. Pt. ii, ch. 1.

18
At length the fox is brought to the furrier.
GEORGE HERBERT, *Jacula Prudentum*.

19
Where the lion's skin will not reach, a little of the fox's must be used. ("Οπου γὰρ ἡ λεοντῆ μὴ ἐφικνεῖται, προσραπτέον ἐκεῖ τὴν ἀλωπεκῆν.)
LYSANDER. (PLUTARCH, *Lives: Lysander*. Ch. 7, sec. 4.)

Craft, where strength doth fail,
And piece the lion with the fox's tail!
JOHN WILSON, *Andron. Commenius*, iv, 4.

The lion's skin too short, you know . . .
Was lengthened by the fox's tail;
And art supplies, where strength may fail.
UNKNOWN, *Agreeable Companion*, 182.

1
Assailant on the perched roosts
And nests in order rang'd
Of tame villatic fowl.
MILTON, *Samson Agonistes*, l. 1693.

2
The fox barks not when he would steal the lamb.
SHAKESPEARE, *II Henry VI*. Act iii, sc. 1, l. 55.

Thou hast entertain'd
A fox to be the shepherd of thy lambs.
SHAKESPEARE, *The Two Gentlemen of Verona*. Act iv, sc. 4, l. 97.

The fox which lives by subtlety.
SHAKESPEARE, *Venus and Adonis*, l. 675.

3
The little foxes, that spoil the vines.
Old Testament: Song of Solomon, ii, 15.

4
An old fox is shy of a trap.
C. H. SPURGEON, *Ploughman's Pictures*, p. 116.

5
The fox changes his fur, but not his habits. (Vulpem pilum mutare, non mores.)
SUETONIUS, *Twelve Cæsars: Vespasian*. Ch. 16, sec. 3. Suetonius says that this expression was used by an old herdsman in reference to Vespasian, who had promised him liberty, but refused to confer it without payment.

FRANCE AND THE FRENCH

I—France: Familiar Phrases

6
Nec Pluribus impar.
DOUVIER, *Motto*, of the device of the rising sun, adopted by Louis XIV of France. It has been variously translated, but "I shine on more worlds than one" is as good as any. Fournier says it was devised by an antiquarian named Douvier.

7
Liberty, equality, fraternity. (Liberté, égalité, fraternité.)
BENJAMIN FRANKLIN is said to have suggested this phrase, which became the watchword of the French revolution, and which is still placed upon the front of every public building in France.

Be my brother, or I will kill thee.
SEBASTIAN CHAMFORT, paraphrasing the revolutionary watchword, "Fraternity or death," which he called a "brotherhood of Cain." "We will have equality, should we descend for it to the tomb." (CARLYLE, *French Revolution*, ii, i, 12.)

The binding of the hands, the thrusting of the head out of the little national sash-window, the crash of the axe.
MACAULAY, *Essays: Memoirs of Barère*.

I have lived. (J'ai vécu.)
JOSEPH SIEYÈS, after the Reign of Terror, when asked what he had done. (MIGNET, *Notices Historiques*, i, 81.)

8
Nothing is changed in France: there is only one Frenchman the more. (Il n'y a rien de changé en France; il n'y a qu'un Français de plus.)
COMTE D'ARTOIS, afterwards CHARLES X OF FRANCE, in proclamation published in the *Moniteur* upon the restoration of Louis XVIII, April 12, 1814. Said to have been composed in his name by Comte Beugnot. (*Contemporary Review*, Feb., 1854. DE VAULABELLE, *Hist. Deux Restorations*, ii, 30.)

Nothing is changed: there is only one animal more. (Il n'y a qu'un bête de plus.)
Caricature circulated in Paris the day after the arrival of Comte d'Artois, celebrating the arrival of the first giraffe for the zoölogical gardens. (See LADY MORGAN, *Diary*, August, 1818.)

Nothing is altered: there is only one Austrian less.
Epigram on the death of Francis I, Emperor of Austria, 1835, when Metternich remained at the head of affairs.

9
Unhappy France! Unhappy king! (Malheureuse France! Malheureuse roi!)
ÉTIENNE BÉQUET, *Heading*, of an article in the *Journal des Débats*, when Charles X was driven from the French throne.

10
What is the Third Estate? Every thing. What part has it in government? Nothing. What does it want? To become something. (Qu'est-ce le Tiers État? Tout. Qu'a-t-il? Rien. Que veut-il? Y devenir quelque chose.)
SEBASTIAN CHAMFORT. Given to Sieyès as title for a pamphlet.

11
We will not cede either an inch of our territory or a stone of our fortresses.
JULES FAVRE, Minister of Foreign Affairs, in a circular to the diplomatic representatives of France abroad, 6 Sept., 1870, immediately after the fall of the empire.

We are so well equipped, that, if the war were to last ten years, we should not have to buy the button of a soldier's gaiter.
MARSHAL LEBŒUF, in June, 1870, speaking of the preparedness of the French forces.

We accept it with a light heart.
ÉMILE OLLIVIER, Prime Minister of France, on July 15, 1870, speaking of the declaration of war against Germany.

12
That will go, that will last. (Ça ira, ça tiendra.)
BENJAMIN FRANKLIN, according to Cassagnac (*History of the Girondists*, i, 373), who says that the *Ça Ira*, the revolutionary song of France, was composed by an itinerant musician who took the refrain from this *mot* of Franklin's on the revolution.

If a sparrow cannot fall without God's knowledge, how can an empire rise without His aid?
BENJAMIN FRANKLIN, proposing that the sessions of the Constitutional Convention, May, 1787, be opened with prayer.

1
Good! I need no sand!

MARSHAL ANDOCHE JUNOT, when a bursting shell threw some dirt on a dispatch he was writing from Bonaparte's dictation, Toulon, Dec., 1793.

2
Ye sons of freedom, wake to glory!
Hark! hark! what myriads bid you rise!
Your children, wives, and grandsires hoary,
Behold their tears and hear their cries!
(Allons, enfants de la patrie!
Le jour de gloire est arrivé!
Contre nous de la tyrannie
L'étendard sanglant est levé.)

ROUGET DE LISLE, *La Marseillaise*. (1792)

3
M. le Grand is about to pass a bad quarter of an hour. (Un mauvais quart d'heure.)

LOUIS XIII OF FRANCE, on the execution of Cinq-Mars, in 1642. (LADY JACKSON, *Old Paris*, i, 227.) Lady Jackson asserts that this French proverb was first used on this occasion.

4
The marquise has a very unpleasant day for her journey.

LOUIS XV, seeing that it was raining hard on the day when the body of Madame de Pompadour was taken from Versailles to Paris. (*Nouvelle Biog. Univ.*)

5
They sing, they will pay. (Ils chantent, ils payeront.)

CARDINAL MAZARIN, referring to the fact that the French received each new tax with satirical poems.

France is an absolute monarchy, tempered by songs.

CHAMFORT, *Characters and Anecdotes*, quoting an anonymous wit.

6
The empire, it is peace. (L'empire, c'est la paix.)

NAPOLEON III, *Address*, before the Chamber of Commerce at Toulouse, 9 Oct., 1852. (JERROLD, *Life of Louis Napoleon*.) In Germany this pronouncement was parodied, "L'empire, c'est l'épée"—The empire, it is the sword. (*Kladderdatsch*, 8 Nov., 1862.)

7
The King of France went up the hill
With twenty thousand men;
The King of France came down the hill,
And ne'er went up again.

UNKNOWN, *Old Tarleton's Song*. Quoted in a tract entitled *Pigges Corantoe, or Newes from the North*, London, 1642.

The king of France with twenty thousand men
Went up the hill, and then came down again;
The king of Spain with twenty thousand more,
Climbed the same hill the French had climbed before.

UNKNOWN, *The King of France*. (*Sloane MS.* No. 1489) An earlier version of *Old Tarleton's Song*. For other versions see Halliwell, *Nursery Rhymes*.

The song, "The King of France with Forty Thousand Men," has reference to the raising of 40,000 men by Henry IV, of France, in 1609–1610.

JAMES HOWELL, *Letter to James Crofts*, 12 May, 1620.

8
Adieu, pleasant land of France. Oh, my country, the dearest in the world! (Adieu, plaisant pays de France, O ma patrie la plus cherie!)

UNKNOWN. A song supposed to have been sung by Mary Stuart on leaving France to become Queen of Scotland, but really a forgery by De Querlon. Béranger gave the lines wide currency by taking them as the refrain for his song, *Les Adieux de Marie Stuart*.

9
Look at Marianne! (Voilà la Marianne!)

Shouted by the Royalists at Albi in 1830, when the Republicans were parading through the streets a painting of Minerva supposed to personify the Republic. Marianne, in the local slang, meant a prostitute.

II—France: Her Virtues

10
Gay lilied fields of France.

CAMPBELL, *Gertrude of Wyoming*. Pt. ii, st. 15.

11
The further off from England the nearer is to France.

LEWIS CARROLL, *Alice in Wonderland*. Ch. 10.

12
Is morning here? Then speak that we may know!
The sky seems lighter, but we are not sure.
Is morning here? . . . The whole world holds its breath
To hear the crimson Gallic rooster crow!

RALPH CHAPLIN, *To France*. (May Day, 1919.)

13
Gay sprightly land of mirth and social ease,
Pleas'd with thyself, whom all the world can please.

GOLDSMITH, *The Traveller*, l. 241.

14
France is a meadow that cuts thrice a year.

GEORGE HERBERT, *Jacula Prudentum*.

15
In a comparison of this with other countries we have the proof of primacy which was given to Themistocles after the battle of Salamis. Every general voted himself the first reward of valor, and the second to Themistocles. So, ask the travelled inhabitant of any nation, in what country on earth you would rather live? Certainly in my own. . . . Which would be your second choice? France.

THOMAS JEFFERSON, *Writings*. Vol. i, p. 159.

16
Half artist and half anchorite,
Part siren and part Socrates.

PERCY MACKAYE, *France*.

1
My thoughts and wishes bend again toward
France.
SHAKESPEARE, *Hamlet*. Act i, sc. 2, l. 55.

2
That sweet enemy, France.
SIR PHILIP SIDNEY, *Astrophel and Stella*. Sonnet xli.

3
And threat'ning France, plac'd like a painted
Jove,
Kept idle thunder in his lifted hand.
DRYDEN, *Annus Mirabilis*. St. 39.

4
"They order," said I, "this matter better in France."
LAURENCE STERNE, *A Sentimental Journey*. Ch. i, l. 1.

These things are managed so well in France.
BRET HARTE, *The Tale of a Pony*.

III—France: Her Faults

5
The thirst for truth is not a French passion. In everything appearance is preferred to reality, the outside to the inside, the fashion to the material, that which shines to that which profits, opinion to conscience. That is to say, the Frenchman's centre of gravity is always outside him,—he is always thinking of others, playing to the gallery.
AMIEL, *Journal*, 22 Jan., 1875.

6
France, fam'd in all great arts, in none
supreme.
MATTHEW ARNOLD, *To a Republican Friend*.

7
The most frivolous and fickle of civilised nations—they pass from the game of war to the game of peace, from the game of science to the game of art, from the game of liberty to the game of slavery, from the game of slavery to the game of licence.
WALTER BAGEHOT, *Literary Studies: Shakespeare*.

Fickle in everything else, the French have been faithful in one thing only,—their love of change.
SIR ARCHIBALD ALISON, *History of Europe*.

8
My scrofulous French novel.
ROBERT BROWNING, *Soliloquy in a Spanish Cloister*.

9
Never was there a country where the practice of governing too much had taken deeper root and done more mischief.
THOMAS JEFFERSON, *Writings*. Vol. vii, p. 445.

10
Have the French for friends, but not for neighbors.
EMPEROR NICEPHORUS, when treating with the ambassadors of Charlemagne in 803.

11
Others import yet nobler arts from France,
Teach kings to fiddle, and make senates dance.
POPE, *The Dunciad*. Bk. iv, l. 597.

12
'Tis better using France than trusting France.
SHAKESPEARE, *III Henry VI*. Act iv, sc. 1, l. 42.

13
The faithless vain disturber of mankind,
Insulting Gaul.
THOMSON, *The Seasons: Autumn*, l. 1076.

14
The cross of the Legion of Honor has been conferred upon me. However, few escape that distinction.
MARK TWAIN, *A Tramp Abroad*. Ch. 8.

We distribute tracts, the French distribute medals.
GEORGE MOORE, *Meissonier and the Salon Julian*.

IV—France: Her Language

15
Ther was also a Nonne, a Prioresse, . . .
And Frensh she spak ful faire and fetisly,
After the scole of Stratford atte Bowe,
For Frensh of Paris was to hir unknowe.
CHAUCER, *Canterbury Tales: Prologue*, l. 118. (c. 1386)

16
The Frenchman feels an easy mastery in speaking his mother tongue, and attributes it to some native superiority of parts that lifts him high above us barbarians of the West.
J. R. LOWELL, *On a Certain Condescension in Foreigners*.

17
The French tongue, which is the speech of the clear, the cheerful, or the august among men.
JOHN MORLEY, *Rousseau*, p. 436.

Speak in French when you can't think of the English for a thing.
LEWIS CARROLL, *Through the Looking-Glass*. Ch. 2.

18
It is the true and native language of insincerity.
ALFRED SUTRO, *A Marriage Has Been Arranged*. Referring to the French language.

V—France: The French

19
The French are wiser than they seem, and the Spaniards seem wiser than they are.
FRANCIS BACON, *Essays: Of Seeming Wise*.

20
Frenchmen are like gunpowder, each by itself smutty and contemptible; but mass them together, they are terrible indeed!
S. T. COLERIDGE, *Table Talk*.

21
The Frenchman, easy, debonair, and brisk,
Give him his lass, his fiddle, and his frisk,
Is always happy, reign whoever may,
And laughs the sense of mis'ry far away.
COWPER, *Table Talk*, l. 237.

22
Much like the French (or like ourselves,
their apes),
Who with strange habit do disguise their
shapes;

Who loving novels, full of affectation,
Receive the manners of each other nation.

Du Bartas, *Devine Weekes and Workes*. Week i, day 2. (Sylvester, tr.)

1
The French woman says, "I am a woman and a Parisienne, and nothing foreign to me appears altogether human."

Emerson, *Uncollected Lectures: Table-Talk*.

There is a quality in which no woman in the world can compete with her [the French woman], —it is the power of intellectual irritation. She will draw wit out of a fool.

Attributed to William Shenstone.

Every Frenchwoman, as I suppose, knows, well or ill, how to do a little cookery.
(Toute Française, à ce que j'imagine,
Sait, bien ou mal, faire un peu de cuisine.)

Voltaire, *Le Bégueule*.

She's only a darned Mounseer.

W. S. Gilbert, *Ruddigore*. Act i.

2
I hate the French because they are all slaves and wear wooden shoes.

Goldsmith, *Essays: The History of a Disabled Soldier*.

3
Fifty million Frenchmen can't be wrong.

Attributed to Texas Guinan. (*New York World-Telegram*, 21 March, 1931.)

4
The French are excellent in this, they have a book on every subject.

Samuel Johnson. (Boswell, *Life*, 1783.)

5
A Frenchman loves his mother—in the abstract.

Henry Seton Merriman, *The Sowers*. Ch. 3.

6
Why, is it not a lamentable thing, grandsire, that we should be thus afflicted with these strange flies, these fashion-mongers, these perdona-mi's.

Shakespeare, *Romeo and Juliet*. Act ii, sc. 4, l. 32.

7
A nation of monkeys with the throat of parrots.

Joseph Sieyès, referring to the French, *Letter to Mirabeau*.

Your nation is divided into two species: the one of idle monkeys who mock at everything; and the other of tigers who tear.

Voltaire, *Letter to Madame du Deffand*, 21 Nov., 1766.

Something of the monkey aspect inseparable from a little Frenchman.

Hawthorne, *Journals*, 5 July, 1837.

8
If they have a fault, they are too serious.

Laurence Sterne, *A Sentimental Journey: The Address: Versailles*.

9
I do not dislike the French from the vulgar antipathy between neighbouring nations, but for their insolent and unfounded airs of superiority.

Walpole, *Letter to Hannah More*, 14 Oct., 1787.

FRANKLIN, BENJAMIN

10
The body of Benjamin Franklin, Printer, (like the cover of an old book, its contents torn out and stripped of its lettering and gilding), lies here, food for worms; but the work shall not be lost, for it will (as he believed) appear once more in a new and more elegant edition, revised and corrected by the Author.

Benjamin Franklin, *Epitaph on Himself*. Composed in 1728, at the age of twenty-two. It was not placed on his monument. Franklin was admittedly familiar with Cotton Mather's *Magnalia Christi*. *See also* Epitaphs: Revised by the Author.

11
While Franklin's quiet memory climbs to heaven,
Calming the lightning which he thence hath riven.

Byron, *The Age of Bronze*, l. 245.

And stoic Franklin's energetic shade
Robed in lightnings which his hand allay'd.

Byron, *The Age of Bronze*, l. 386.

12
Benjamin Franklin, incarnation of the peddling, tuppenny Yankee.

Jefferson Davis. (Cairns, *History of American Literature*, p. 98.)

13
It is hardly necessary to state that Franklin did not originate all the "Sayings of Poor Richard." He himself tells us that they were "the wisdom of many ages and nations." Any one familiar with Bacon, Rochefoucauld, and Rabelais, as well as others, will recognize old friends in some of these sayings, while a study of the collections of Proverbs, made in the early part of the last century by Ray and Palmer, will reveal the probable source from which Poor Richard pilfered. Yet with but few exceptions these maxims and aphorisms had been filtered through Franklin's brain, and were tinged with that mother wit which so strongly and individually marks so much that he said and wrote.

Paul Leicester Ford, *The Sayings of Poor Richard: Introduction*.

14
But matchless Franklin! What a few
Can hope to rival such as you.
Who seized from kings their sceptred pride
And turned the lightning's darts aside.

Philip Freneau, *On the Death of Benjamin Franklin*.

15
I succeed him; no one could replace him.

Thomas Jefferson, to the Comte de Vergennes, when the latter remarked, "You replace Mr. Franklin," as envoy to France.

1
Nations should wear mourning only for their benefactors. . . . Antiquity would have raised altars to this mighty genius, who, to the advantage of mankind, compassing in his mind the heavens and the earth, was able to restrain alike thunderbolts and tyrants.

MIRABEAU, *Address,* moving that the French National Assembly should go into mourning, when Franklin's death was announced.

"Antiquity," said Mirabeau, "would raise
Altars to honor him!"

FLORENCE EARLE COATES, *Franklin.*

2
Prudence is a wooden Juggernaut, before whom Benjamin Franklin walks with the portly air of a high priest.

R. L. STEVENSON, *Crabbed Age and Youth.*

3
He snatched the thunderbolt from heaven, then the sceptre from tyrants. (Eripuit cœlo fulmen, mox sceptra tyrannis.)

A. R. J. TURGOT, *Inscription,* for the Houdon bust of Franklin, 1778. According to Condorcet (*Vie de Turgot,* p. 200) this is the phrase as Turgot wrote it, but it is frequently misquoted, "Eripuit cælo fulmen, sceptrumque tyrannis." Frederick von der Trenck, at his trial before the Revolutionary Tribunal of Paris, 9 July, 1794, asserted that he was the author of the line. (GARTENLAUBE, *Last Hours of Baron Trenck.*) Manilius (*Astronomica,* i, 104) has the line, "Eripuit Jovi fulmen viresque tonandi." Cardinal Melchior de Polignac (*Anti-Lucretius,* i, 96) published in 1745, has, "Eripuit fulmenque Jovi, Phœboque sagittas."

Notwithstanding my experiments with electricity the thunderbolt continues to fall under our noses and beards; and as for the tyrant, there are a million of us still engaged at snatching away his sceptre.

BENJAMIN FRANKLIN, *Letter to Felix Nogaret,* commenting on Turgot's inscription.

FRANKNESS, see Candor

FRATERNITY, see Brotherhood

FRAUD, see Deceit

FREEDOM

See also Liberty

I—Freedom: Definitions

4
Ah! freedom is a noble thing!
Freedom makes man to have liking!
Freedom all solace to man gives!
He lives at ease, that freely lives!

JOHN BARBOUR, *The Bruce.* Bk. i, l. 228.

5
Freedom is not caprice, but room to enlarge.

C. A. BARTOL, *Radical Problems: Open Questions.*

6
O Freedom! thou art not, as poets dream,
A fair young girl, with light and delicate limbs,
And wavy tresses. . . . A bearded man,
Armed to the teeth, art thou; one mailèd hand
Grasps the broad shield, and one the sword; thy brow
Glorious in beauty though it be, is scarred
With tokens of old wars; thy massive limbs
Are strong with struggling.

BRYANT, *The Antiquity of Freedom.*

7
Perfect freedom is reserved for the man who lives by his own work and in that work does what he wants to do.

R. G. COLLINGWOOD, *Speculum Mentis.*

8
Restraint from ill is freedom to the wise.

DANIEL DEFOE, *The True-Born Englishman.* Pt. ii, l. 206.

But what is Freedom? Rightly understood,
A universal license to be good.

HARTLEY COLERIDGE, *Liberty.*

Where justice reigns, 'tis freedom to obey.

MONTGOMERY, *Greenland.* Canto iv, l. 88.

That sweet bondage which is freedom's self.

SHELLEY, *Queen Mab.* Canto ix, l. 76.

Nought nobler is than to be free;
The stars of heaven are free because
In amplitude of liberty
Their joy is to obey the laws.

WILLIAM WATSON, *The Things that Are More Excellent.*

9
Is freedom anything but the right to live as we wish? Nothing else. (Ἄλλο τί ἐστιν ἐλευθερία ἢ τὸ ἐξεῖναι ὡς βουλόμεθα διεξάγειν· οὐδέν.)

EPICTETUS, *Discourses.* Bk. ii, ch. 1, sec. 23.

He is free who lives as he chooses. (Ἐλεύθερός ἐστιν ὁ ζῶν ὡς βούλεται.)

EPICTETUS, *Discourses.* Bk. iv, ch. 1, sec. 1,

Is any man free except the one who can live as he chooses? (An quisquam est alius liber, nisi ducere vitam Cui licet ut libuit?)

PERSIUS, *Satires.* Sat. v, l. 83.

The only freedom which deserves the name, is that of pursuing our own good in our own way, so long as we do not attempt to deprive others of theirs, or impede their efforts to obtain it.

JOHN STUART MILL, *On Liberty.* Ch. 1.

10
No man is free who is not master of himself. (Οὐδεὶς ἐλεύθερος ἑαυτοῦ μὴ κρατῶν.)

EPICTETUS [?], *Encheiridion.* Frag. 35. Stobæus ascribes this maxim to Pythagoras.

11
Who then is free? The wise man, who is lord over himself, whom neither poverty, nor death, nor bonds affright, who bravely defies his passions, and scorns ambition, who in himself is a whole, smoothed and rounded, so that nothing from outside can rest on

the polished surface, and against whom Fortune in her onset is ever defeated.

HORACE, *Satires*. Bk ii, sat. 7, l. 83.

1
There will be no true freedom without virtue, no true science without religion, no true industry without the fear of God and love to your fellow-citizens. Workers of England, be wise, and then you *must* be free, for you will be *fit* to be free.

CHARLES KINGSLEY, *Placard*, 1848.

2
Men are free when they are in a living homeland, not when they are straying and breaking away. . . . The most unfree souls go west, and shout of freedom. Men are freest when they are most unconscious of freedom.

D. H. LAWRENCE, *Studies in Classic American Literature*.

3
'Tis not a freedom that, where all command.

ANDREW MARVELL, *The First Anniversary*.

Inferior, who is free?

MILTON, *Paradise Lost*. Bk. ix, l. 825.

4
To be free is to live under a government by law.

WILLIAM MURRAY, EARL OF MANSFIELD, *King v. Shipley*. (3 *Douglas's Rep*. 170.)

Freedom is political power divided into small fragments.

THOMAS HOBBES. (MAINE, *Popular Government*, p. 70.)

That man is free who is protected from injury.

DANIEL WEBSTER, *Address to Charlestown Bar*, 10 May, 1847.

5
Oh! let me live my own, and die so too
(To live and die is all I have to do)!
Maintain a poet's dignity and ease,
And see what friends, and read what books
I please.

POPE, *Epistle to Dr. Arbuthnot*, l. 261.

6
Man is created free, and is free, even though born in chains. (Der Mensch ist frei geschaffen, ist frei Und würd' er in Ketten geboren.)

SCHILLER, *Die Worte des Glaubens*. St. 2.

7
What is freedom? It means not being a slave to any circumstance, to any constraint, to any chance; it means compelling Fortune to enter the lists on equal terms. (Quæ sit libertas? Nulli rei servire, nulli necessitati, nullis casibus, fortunam in æquum deducere.)

SENECA, *Epistulæ ad Lucilium*. Epis. li, sec. 9.

Freedom is re-created year by year,
In hearts wide open on the Godward side.

J. R. LOWELL, *Freedom*, l. 21.

8
What other liberty is there worth having, if we have not freedom and peace in our minds,—if our inmost and most private man is but a sour and turbid pool?

H. D. THOREAU, *Journal*, 26 Oct., 1853.

9
Freedom exists only where the people take care of the government.

WOODROW WILSON, *Speech*, N. Y., 4 Sept., 1912.

Those who expect to reap the blessings of freedom, must, like men, undergo the fatigue of supporting it.

THOMAS PAINE, *The Crisis*. No. iv.

II—Freedom: Apothegms

10
The cause of freedom is the cause of God.

W. L. BOWLES, *To Edmund Burke*.

11
Whilst freedom is true to itself, everything becomes subject to it.

EDMUND BURKE, *Speech*, at Bristol.

Depend upon it, the lovers of freedom will be free.

EDMUND BURKE, *Speech*, 1780.

12
Hereditary bondsmen! know ye not
Who would be free themselves must strike
the blow?

BYRON, *Childe Harold*. Canto ii, st. 76.

They can only set free men free . . .
And there is no need of that:
Free men set themselves free.

JAMES OPPENHEIM, *The Slave*.

13
Freedom suppressed and again regained bites with keener fangs than freedom never endangered. (Acriores autem morsus sunt intermissæ libertatis quam retentæ.)

CICERO, *De Officiis*. Bk. ii, ch. 7, sec. 24.

Regained my freedom with a sigh.

BYRON, *The Prisoner of Chillon*. St. 14.

14
Freedom our pain, and plenty our disease.

DRYDEN, *Absalom and Achitophel*. Pt. ii, l. 32.

16
Wherever snow falls, man is free. Where the orange blooms, man is the foe of man.

R. W. EMERSON, *Journals*, 1862.

Countries are well cultivated, not as they are fertile, but as they are free.

MONTESQUIEU.

17
No bad man is free. (Τοίνυν οὐδ' ἐλεύθερός ἐστιν.)

EPICTETUS, *Discourses*. Bk. iv, ch. 1, sec. 4. Usually quoted as the Stoic maxim, "All bad men are slaves." (Πάντες κακοὶ δοῦλοι.)

No man who is in fear, or sorrow, or turmoil is free, but whoever is rid of sorrows and fears and turmoils, that man is by the self-same course rid also of slavery.

EPICTETUS, *Discourses*. Bk. ii, ch. 1, sec. 24.

Let them fear bondage who are slaves to fear,
The sweetest freedom is an honest heart.

JOHN FORD, *The Lady's Trial*. Act i, sc. 3.

18
Bred in the lap of Republican Freedom.

WILLIAM GODWIN, *Enquiry*. Bk. ii, 12, 402.

19
We are not free; it was not intended we

should be. A book of rules is placed in our cradle, and we never get rid of it until we reach our graves. Then we are free, and only then.

E. W. HOWE, *Howe's Monthly.*

1
There is no freedom on earth or in any star for those who deny freedom to others.

ELBERT HUBBARD, *A Thousand and One Epigrams.*

No! true freedom is to share
All the chains our brothers wear.

JAMES RUSSELL LOWELL, *Stanzas on Freedom.*

2
A man should never put on his best trousers when he goes out to battle for freedom and truth.

HENRIK IBSEN, *An Enemy of the People.* Act v.

3
Pray you use your freedom,
And, so far as you please, allow me mine.

PHILIP MASSINGER, *Duke of Milan.* Act iv, sc. 3.

4
None can love freedom heartily but good men; the rest love not freedom, but licence.

MILTON, *Tenure of Kings and Magistrates.*

5
The path of freedom is blocked much more by those who wish to obey than by those who desire to command.

M. D. PETRE. (INGE, *Wit and Wisdom: Preface.*)

6
Freedom is only in the land of dreams. (Freiheit ist nur in dem Reich der Träume.)

SCHILLER, *The Beginning of the New Century.*

7
Freedom, near at hand, makes an old man brave. (Fortem facit vicina libertas senem.)

SENECA, *Hippolytus,* l. 139.

8
They wish to be free, and know not how to be just. (Ils veulent être libres et ne savent pas être justes.)

ABBÉ JOSEPH SIEYÈS, in the Constituent Assembly, 10 Aug., 1789. (DUMONT, *Recollections of Mirabeau.*)

9
O, lift your natures up;
Embrace our aims: work out your freedom.

TENNYSON, *The Princess.* Pt. ii, l. 74.

10
Ne'er yet by force was freedom overcome.

JAMES THOMSON, *Liberty.* Pt. ii, l. 494.

11
Man is free at the moment he wishes to be.

VOLTAIRE, *Brutus.* Act ii, sc. 1.

III—Freedom: Its Virtues

12
The time will come when men
Will be as free and equal as the waves,
That seem to jostle, but that never jar.

ALFRED AUSTIN, *Tower of Babel.* Act ii, sc. 1.

13
Yet, Freedom, yet thy banner, torn but flying,
Streams like the thunder-storm *against* the wind.

BYRON, *Childe Harold.* Canto iv, st. 98.

And Freedom hallows with her tread
The silent cities of the dead.

BYRON, *On the Star of "The Legion of Honour."*

14
No! Freedom has a thousand charms to show
That slaves, howe'er contented, never know. . . .
Religion, virtue, truth—whate'er we call
A blessing—freedom is the pledge of all.

WILLIAM COWPER, *Table Talk,* l. 260.

15
I want free life, and I want fresh air;
And I sigh for the canter after the cattle,
The crack of the whips like shots in a battle,
The mellay of hoofs, and horns, and heads
That wars, and wrangles, and scatters and spreads;
The green beneath and the blue above,
And dash, and danger, and life and love!

FRANK DESPREZ, *Lasca.*

16
I am as free as nature first made man,
Ere the base laws of servitude began,
When wild in woods the noble savage ran.

DRYDEN, *Conquest of Granada.* Act i, sc. 1.

17
My angel—his name is Freedom—
Choose him to be your king;
He shall cut pathways east and west,
And fend you with his wing.

EMERSON, *Boston Hymn.*

For what avail the plough or sail,
Or land or life, if freedom fail?

EMERSON, *Boston.*

18
Aye, call it holy ground,
The soil where first they trod!
They have left unstained what there they found—
Freedom to worship God!

FELICIA DOROTHEA HEMANS, *Landing of the Pilgrim Fathers.*

19
Oh, only a free soul will never grow old! (O, nur eine freie Seele wird nicht alt.)

JEAN PAUL RICHTER, *Titan.* Zykel 140.

20
All the arts of pleasure grow when suckled by freedom. (Von der Freiheit gesäugt wachsen die Künste der Lust.)

SCHILLER, *Der Spaziergang,* l. 122.

21
Of old sat Freedom on the heights,
The thunders breaking at her feet;
Above her shook the starry lights;
She heard the torrents meet.

TENNYSON, *Of Old Sat Freedom.*

And Freedom rear'd in that august sunrise
Her beautiful bold brow.

TENNYSON, *The Poet.*

1
Only free peoples can hold their purpose and their honor steady to a common end, and prefer the interests of mankind to any narrow interest of their own.
WOODROW WILSON, *War Address to Congress*, 2 April, 1917.

2
Me this unchartered freedom tires;
I feel the weight of chance-desires:
My hopes no more must change their name,
I long for a repose that ever is the same.
WORDSWORTH, *Ode to Duty*. St. 5.

IV—Freedom: Its Defense

3
This hand, to tyrants ever sworn the foe,
For Freedom only deals the deadly blow;
Then sheathes in calm repose the deadly blade,
For gentle Peace in Freedom's hallowed shade.
JOHN QUINCY ADAMS, *Inscription in an Album*, 1842. See 2065:1.

4
"Freedom!" their battle-cry,—
"Freedom! or leave to die!"
G. H. BOKER, *The Black Regiment*.

5
Righteous monarchs,
Justly to judge, with their own eyes should see;
To rule o'er freemen should themselves be free.
HENRY BROOKE, *The Earl of Essex*. Act i. The lines are spoken by Queen Elizabeth.

Johnson was present when a tragedy was read in which there occurred this line: Who rules o'er freemen should himself be free. The company admired it much.—"I cannot agree with you," said Johnson, "it might as well be said, Who drives fat oxen should himself be fat."
BOSWELL, *Life of Johnson*, June, 1784.

6
For he was Freedom's champion, one of those,
The few in number, who had not o'erstept
The charter to chastise which she bestows
On such as wield her weapons; he had kept
The whiteness of his soul, and thus men o'er him wept.
BYRON, *Childe Harold*. Canto iii, st. 57.

7
For Freedom's battle once begun,
Bequeath'd by bleeding sire to son,
Though baffled oft is ever won.
BYRON, *The Giaour*, l. 123.

The greatest glory of a freeborn people
Is to transmit that freedom to their children.
WILLIAM HAVARD, *Regulus*. Act v. sc. 4.

All we have of freedom, all we use or know—
This our fathers bought for us, long and long ago.
RUDYARD KIPLING, *The Old Issue*.

8
Hope, for a season, bade the world farewell,
And Freedom shrieked—as Kosciusko fell!
CAMPBELL, *The Pleasures of Hope*. Pt. i, l. 381.

O what a loud and fearful shriek was there! . . .
Ah me! they saw beneath a Hireling's sword
Their Koskiusko fall!
S. T. COLERIDGE, *Sonnet: Koskiusko*.

9
Yes! to this thought I hold with firm persistence;
The last result of wisdom stamps it true;
He only earns his freedom and existence
Who daily conquers them anew.
GOETHE, *Faust*. Act v, sc. 6, l. 63. (Bayard Taylor, tr.)

10
Off with the fetters
That chafe and restrain!
Off with the chain!
RICHARD HOVEY, *Vagabondia*.

11
In the beauty of the lilies Christ was born across the sea,
With a glory in his bosom that transfigures you and me;
As he died to make men holy, let us die to make men free,
While God is marching on.
JULIA WARD HOWE, *Battle Hymn of the Republic*.

12
Freedom needs all her poets: it is they
Who give her aspirations wings,
And to the wiser law of music sway
Her wild imaginings.
J. R. LOWELL, *To the Memory of Hood*. St. 4.

13
'Tis sweeter to bleed for an age at thy shrine
Than to sleep but a moment in chains!
THOMAS MOORE, *Remember the Glories of Brien the Brave*.

O Freedom! once thy flame hath fled,
It never lights again.
THOMAS MOORE, *Weep On, Weep On*.

14
Tyranny, like hell, is not easily conquered, yet we have this consolation within us, that the harder the conflict, the more glorious the triumph. What we obtain too cheap, we esteem too lightly. . . . It would be strange indeed if so celestial an article as freedom should not be highly rated.
THOMAS PAINE, *The Crisis: Introduction*.

15
Freedom and Arts together fall;
Fools grant whate'er Ambition craves,
And men, once ignorant, are slaves.
POPE, *Brutus: Chorus*, l. 26.

16
Blandishments will not fascinate us, nor will threats of a "halter" intimidate. For, under God, we are determined that wheresoever, whensoever, or howsoever we shall be called to make our exit, we will die free men.
JOSIAH QUINCY, *Observations on the Boston Port Bill*, 1774.

17
O Freedom! if to me belong

Nor mighty Milton's gift divine,
 Nor Marvell's wit and graceful song,
 Still with a love as deep and strong
As theirs, I lay, like them, my best gifts on thy shrine!

WHITTIER, *Proem.*

The nations lift their right hands up and swear
Their oath of freedom.

WHITTIER, *Garibaldi.*

V—Freedom of Speech

1
Liberty of speech inviteth and provoketh liberty to be used again, and so bringeth much to a man's knowledge.

BACON, *Advancement of Learning.* Bk. ii.

2
The most beautiful thing in the world is freedom of speech. (παρρησία.)

DIOGENES. (DIOGENES LAERTIUS, *Diogenes,* 69.)

3
To speak his thoughts is every freeman's right,
In peace and war, in council and in fight.

HOMER, *Iliad.* Bk. xii, l. 249. (Pope, tr.)

4
Such being the happiness of the times, that you may think as you wish, and speak as you think. (Rara temporum felicitate, ubi sentire quæ velis, et quæ sentias dicere licet.)

TACITUS, *History.* Bk. i, sec. 1. Tacitus is referring to the reigns of Nerva and Trajan.

 I may stand alone,
But would not change my free thoughts for a throne.

BYRON, *Don Juan.* Canto xi, st. 89.

5
I disapprove of what you say, but I will defend to the death your right to say it.

Attributed to VOLTAIRE by S. G. Tallentyre (E. Beatrice Hall), in her book, *The Friends of Voltaire* (p. 199), published in 1906, but later stated by her to be a summary of Voltaire's attitude toward *De l'Ésprit* by Claude Adrien Helvétius. For further discussion see APPENDIX.

FRIEND

I—Friend: Definitions

6
What is a friend? A single soul dwelling in two bodies. (Μία ψυχὴ δύο σώμασιν ἐνοικοῦσα.)

ARISTOTLE. (DIOGENES LAERTIUS, *Aristotle.* Bk. v, sec. 20.)

He ought not to pretend to friendship's name,
Who reckons not himself and friend the same.

SAMUEL TUKE, *The Adventures of Five Hours.*

Two friends, two bodies with one soul inspired.

HOMER, *Iliad.* Bk. xvi, l. 267. (Pope, tr.)

True friends are those seeking solitude together.

ABEL BONNARD, *The Art of Friendship.* Pt. ii.

7
A faithful friend is the medicine of life.

Apocrypha: Ecclesiasticus, vi, 16.

I do not remember to have met with any saying that has pleased me more than that of a friend's being the medicine of life.

UNKNOWN, *The Speaker.* No. 68.

8
A friend is a person with whom I may be sincere.

EMERSON, *Essays, First Series: Friendship.*

What is a Friend? I will tell you. It is a person with whom you dare to be yourself.

FRANK CRANE, *A Definition of Friendship.*

9
A friend may well be reckoned the masterpiece of Nature.

EMERSON, *Essays, First Series: Friendship.*

A divine person is the prophecy of the mind; a friend is the hope of the heart.

EMERSON, *Essays, Second Series: Character.*

A man's friends are his magnetisms.

EMERSON, *Conduct of Life: Fate.*

Friends are fictions founded on some single momentary experience.

EMERSON, *Journals.* Vol. x, p. 11.

11
There are three faithful friends—an old wife, an old dog, and ready money.

BENJAMIN FRANKLIN, *Poor Richard,* 1738.

A Father's a Treasure; a Brother's a Comfort; a Friend is both.

BENJAMIN FRANKLIN, *Poor Richard,* 1747.

12
O ev'ry sacred name in one! my Friend!

HOMER, *Odyssey.* Bk. xxii, l. 226. (Pope, tr.)

13
A faithful friend is a true image of the Deity.

NAPOLEON BONAPARTE, *Sayings of Napoleon.*

14
A friend is another I. (ἄλλος ἐγώ.)

ZENO. (DIOGENES LAERTIUS, *Zeno.* Bk. vii, sec. 23.) "Alter ego" is, of course, the Latin.

A friend is, as it were, a second self. (Amicus est tamquam alter idem.)

CICERO, *De Amicitia.* Ch. 21, sec. 80.

II—Friend: Apothegms

15
It is better to have one friend of great value than many friends who are good for nothing.

ANARCHARSIS. (LAERTIUS, *Anarcharsis.* Sec. 105.)

16
A friend to all is a friend to none. (Ὦ φίλοι, οὐδεὶς φίλος.)

ARISTOTLE. (LAERTIUS, *Aristotle,* Sec. 21.)

All men's friend, no man's friend.

WODROEPE, *Spared Houres,* 475.

17
Friends are like fiddle-strings, they must not be screwed too tight.

H. G. BOHN, *Hand-Book of Proverbs,* p. 358.

18
Let me have no good thing unknown to a friend. (Ἄγνωστον δὲ φίλῳ μηδὲν ἔχοιμι καλόν.)

CALLIMACHUS, *Fragmenta Incertæ.* No. 121.

19
O my friends, there is no friend. (Ὦ φίλοι οὐδεὶς φίλος.)

CHILO. (DIOGENES LAERTIUS, *Chilo.*)

20
Defendit numerus [there is safety in numbers] is the maxim of the foolish; *Deperdit numerus* [there is ruin in numbers] of the wise.

C. C. COLTON, *Lacon.* Vol. 1, No. 34. Referring to the number of one's friends.

She, that asks
Her dear five hundred friends, contemns them all,
And hates their coming.
COWPER, *The Task*. Bk. ii, l. 642.

He has friends, but no friend.
SAMUEL JOHNSON. (BOSWELL, *Life*, 1779.)

To the rare few, who, early in life, have rid themselves of the friendship of the many.
J. MCNEILL WHISTLER, *The Gentle Art of Making Enemies: Dedication.*

1
Codlin's your friend, not Short.
DICKENS, *The Old Curiosity Shop*. Ch. 19.

2
The wretched have no friends.
DRYDEN, *All for Love*. Act iii, sc. 1.

A fav'rite has no friend!
THOMAS GRAY, *On the Death of a Favourite Cat*.

The poor make no new friends.
HELEN SELINA SHERIDAN, *Lament of the Irish Emigrant*.

The vanquish'd have no friends.
ROBERT SOUTHEY, *The Vision of the Maid of Orleans*. Bk. vii, l. 465.

3
The only way to have a friend is to be one.
EMERSON, *Essays, First Series: Friendship*.

4
The ornament of a house is the friends who frequent it.
EMERSON, *Society and Solitude: Domestic Life*.

5
If you have one true friend, you have more than your share.
THOMAS FULLER, *Gnomologia*. No. 2760.

One friend in a lifetime is much; two are many; three are hardly possible.
HENRY ADAMS, *Education of*, p. 312.

6
Beware, I say, beware, how thou fallest in with indigent friends.
THOMAS FULLER, *Introductio ad Prudentiam*. Vol. i, p. 215.

I once had Money and a Friend;
Of either, thought I store.
I lent my Money to my Friend
And took his word therefor.
I sought my Money from my Friend,
Which I had wanted long.
I lost my Money and my Friend;
Now was not that a wrong?
UNKNOWN, *Money and a Friend*.

7
Those friends who are above interest are seldom above jealousy.
LORD HALIFAX, *Works*, p. 243.

8
I have begun to be a friend to myself. (Amicus esse mihi cœpi.)
HECATO, *Fragments*. Frag. 26.

That was indeed a great benefit; such a person can never be alone. You may be sure that such a man is a friend to all mankind.
SENECA, *Epistulæ ad Lucilium*. Epis. vi, sec. 7. Commenting on Hecato's declaration.

Be a friend to thyself, and others will be so too.
THOMAS FULLER, *Gnomologia*. No. 847.

He that is friend to himself, know, he is friend to all.
MONTAIGNE, *Essays*. Bk. iii, ch. 10.

9
When a friend asks there is no to-morrow.
GEORGE HERBERT, *Jacula Prudentum*.

10
Be friends with the friendly, and visit him who visits you.
HESIOD, *Works and Days*, l. 353.

A fresh, a free, a friendly man.
JOHN GOWER, *Confessio Amantis*. Bk. v.

11
Greater love hath no man than this, that a man lay down his life for his friends.
New Testament: John, xv, 13.

12
I lay it down as a fact that, if all men knew what others say of them, there would not be four friends in the world.
PASCAL, *Pensées*. Sec. ii, No. 101.

13
A constant friend is a thing rare and hard to find.
PLUTARCH, *Morals: On Abundance of Friends*.

Friends are rare, for the good reason that men are not common.
JOSEPH ROUX, *Meditations of a Parish Priest*. Pt. ix, No. 2.

14
Yea, mine own familiar friend, in whom I trusted, which did eat of my bread, hath lifted up his heel against me.
Old Testament: Psalms, xli, 9.

15
But it was thou, a man mine equal, my guide, and mine acquaintance.
Old Testament: Psalms, lv, 13.

But it was even thou, my companion, my guide, and mine own familiar friend.
Book of Common Prayer: The Psalter. Psalm lv, 6.

Thou wert my guide, philosopher, and friend.
POPE, *Essay on Man*. Epis. iv, l. 390.

Ah! were I sever'd from thy side,
Where were my friend—and who my guide?
BYRON, *The Bride of Abydos*. Canto i, st. 11.

16
Friends are not so easily made as kept.
GEORGE SAVILLE, *Maxims of State*. No. 12.

17
There is a fat friend at your master's house.
SHAKESPEARE, *The Comedy of Errors*. Act v, sc. 1, l. 414.

Who's your fat friend?
CLYDE FITCH, *Beau Brummell*. Brummell is referring to the Prince of Wales.

18
I would be friends with you and have your love.
SHAKESPEARE, *The Merchant of Venice*. Act i, sc. 3, l. 139.

1
It is better to make one's friendships at home. (Οἴκοι βελτιόν ἐστι ποιεῖσθαι φιλίας.)

SOLON. (PLUTARCH, *Lives: Solon*. Sec. 5.)

2
'Tis something to be willing to commend;
But my best praise is, that I am your friend.

THOMAS SOUTHERNE, *To Mr. Congreve*.

3
Such a good friend that she will throw all her acquaintances into the water for the pleasure of fishing them out again.

TALLEYRAND, of Madame de Staël. (COOPER, *Talleyrand*.)

4
I know the Table Round, my friends of old;
All brave, and many generous, and some chaste.

TENNYSON, *Merlin and Vivien*, l. 814.

5
A man cannot be said to succeed in this life who does not satisfy one friend.

THOREAU, *Winter: Journal*, 19 Feb., 1857.

6
Change your pleasure, but never change your friends. (Changez de volupté, ne changez point d'amis.)

VOLTAIRE, *Le Dépositaire*.

Be slow in choosing a friend, slower in changing.

BENJAMIN FRANKLIN, *Poor Richard*.

7
Friends should be preferred to kings.

VOLTAIRE, *Letter to Frederick, Crown Prince of Prussia*, 26 Aug., 1736.

8
An egg of one hour old, bread of one day, a goat of one month, wine of six months, flesh of a year, fish of ten years, a wife of twenty years, a friend among a hundred, are the best of all number.

WODROEPHE, *Spared Houres*, p. 253. (1623)

9
But since friends grow not thick on ev'ry bough,
Nor ev'ry friend unrotten at the core.

YOUNG, *Night Thoughts*. Night ii, l. 563.

10
The friends of my friends are my friends. (Les amis de mes amis sont mes amis.)

UNKNOWN. A French proverb.

III—Friend: Friends Share in Common

11
Friends share in common. (Κοινὰ τὰ φίλων.)

BION. (DIOGENES LAERTIUS, *Bion*. Bk. iv, 53.)

Friends share all things in common. (Κοινὰ δὲ τὰ τῶν φίλων.)

DIOGENES. (DIOGENES LAERTIUS, *Diogenes*. Sec. 72.)

Friends have all things in common. (Κοινὰ τὰ τῶν φίλων.)

PLATO, *Phædrus*. Conclusion. MENANDER, *Adelphoi*. Frag. 9.

Friends have all things in common. (Κοινὰ τὰ φίλων εἶναι.)

PYTHAGORAS. According to Timæus, Pythagoras was the first to say this. (DIOGENES LAERTIUS, *Pythagoras*. Sec. 10.)

12
With friends all things are in common. (Amicorum esse omnia communia.)

CICERO, *De Officiis*. Bk. i, sec. 16. Quoted as a Greek saying.

It is an old saying that friends have all things in common. (Communia esse amicorum inter se omnia.)

TERENCE, *Adelphi*, l. 803.

13
Common are the possessions of friends. (Ὁ κοινὰ ἀποφαίνων τὰ τῶν φίλων.)

DIO CHRYSOSTOM, *Third Discourse on Kingship*. Sec. 110. Quoted as a proverb.

14
Oh, how you wrong our friendship, valiant youth.
With friends there is not such a word as debt:
Where amity is tied with band of truth,
All benefits are there in common set.

ELIZABETH, LADY CAREY, *The Tragedy of Marian*.

15
The benefits of fortune are common among friends.

WILLIAM FULLWOOD, *Enemie of Idlenesse*, 91. (1593)

16
What is thine is mine, and all mine is thine. (Quod tuum'st meum'st: omne meum est autem tuum.)

PLAUTUS, *Trinummus*. Act ii, sc. 2, l. 47.

17
He that has much in common with his fellowmen will have much in common with a friend.

SENECA, *Epistulæ ad Lucilium*. Epis. xlviii, 3.

IV—Friends: Their Choice

19
He is like to be mistaken, who makes choice of a covetous man for a friend, or relieth upon the reed of narrow and poltroon friendship.

SIR THOMAS BROWNE, *Christian Morals*. Pt. i, sec. 36.

20
Friends should not be chosen to flatter. The quality we should prize is that rectitude which will shrink from no truth. Intimacies which increase vanity destroy friendship.

WILLIAM ELLERY CHANNING, *Note-Book: Friendship*.

21
Acquaintance I would have, but when 't depends
Not on the number, but the choice of friends.

ABRAHAM COWLEY, *Of Myself*.

True happiness
Consists not in the multitude of friends,
But in the worth and choice. Nor would I have
Virtue a popular regard pursue:
Let them be good that love me, though but few

BEN JONSON, *Cynthia's Revels*. Act iii, sc. 2.

1
I would not enter on my list of friends,
(Tho' grac'd with polish'd manners and fine sense
Yet wanting sensibility) the man
Who needlessly sets foot upon a worm.

COWPER, *The Task*. Bk. vi, l. 560.

2
Fate makes relatives, but choice makes friends. (Le sort fait les parents, le choix fait les amis.)

DELILE, *Pitié*.

Friends—those relatives that one makes for one's self. (Les amis—ces parents que l'on se fait soi-même.)

DESCHAMPS, *L'Ami*.

3
'Tis thus that on the choice of friends
Our good or evil name depends.

JOHN GAY, *Fables: Old Woman and Her Cats*.

4
Choose thy friends like thy books, few but choice.

JAMES HOWELL, *Proverbs*. (1659)

5
Friends are like melons. Shall I tell you why?
To find one good, you must a hundred try.

CLAUDE MERMET, *Epigram*.

6
Do not be rash to make friends and, when once they are made, do not drop them.

SOLON. (DIOGENES LAERTIUS, *Solon*. Sec. 16.)

7
Choose for your friend him that is wise and good, secret and just, ingenious and honest, and in those things which have a latitude, use your own liberty.

JEREMY TAYLOR, *Discourse of the Nature, Measures, and Offices of Friendship*.

When I choose my friend, I will not stay till I have received a kindness; but I will choose such a one that can do me many if I need them; but I mean such kindnesses which make me wiser, and which make me better.

JEREMY TAYLOR, *Discourse of the Nature, Measures, and Offices of Friendship*.

A good man is the best friend, and therefore soonest to be chosen, longer to be retained; and indeed, never to be parted with.

JEREMY TAYLOR, *A Discourse of the Nature, Measures, and Offices of Friendship*.

V—Friends: Their Value

8
Without friends no one would choose to live, even if he had all other goods. ("Ανευ γὰρ φίλων οὐδεὶς ἕλοιτ' ἂν ζῆν ἔχων τὰ λοιπὰ ἀγαθὰ πάντα.)

ARISTOTLE, *Nicomachean Ethics*. Bk. viii, sec. 1.

Friends are an aid to the young, to guard them from error; to the elderly, to attend to their wants; and to supplement their failing power of action; to those in the prime of life, to assist them to noble deeds.

ARISTOTLE, *Nicomachean Ethics*. Bk. viii, sec. 1.

9
No receipt openeth the heart but a true friend.

FRANCIS BACON, *Essays: Of Friendship*.

From quiet homes and first beginning,
Out to the undiscovered ends,
There's nothing worth the wear of winning
But laughter and the love of friends.

HILAIRE BELLOC, *Sonnets and Verse: Dedicatory Ode*.

10
I wish my deadly foe no worse
Than want of friends, and empty purse.

NICHOLAS BRETON, *A Farewell to Town*.

11
Hand Grasps at hand, eye lights eye in good friendship, and great hearts expand
And grow one in the sense of this world's life.

ROBERT BROWNING, *Saul*. St. 7.

12
Elysium is as far as to
The very nearest room,
If in that room a friend await
Felicity or doom.

EMILY DICKINSON, *Poems*. Pt. iii, No. 4.

13
Who is more indefatigable in toil, when there is occasion for toil, than a friend? Who is readier to rejoice in one's good fortune? Whose praise is sweeter? From whose lips does one learn the truth with less pain? What fortress, what bulwarks, what arms are more steadfast than loyal hearts?

DIO CHRYSOSTOM, *First Discourse on Kingship*. Sec. 31.

14
Best friend, my well-spring in the wilderness!

GEORGE ELIOT, *Spanish Gypsy*. Bk. iii, l. 486.

Friend more divine than all divinities.

GEORGE ELIOT, *The Spanish Gypsy*. Bk. iv, l. 8.

15
A day for toil, an hour for sport,
But for a friend is life too short.

EMERSON, *Conduct of Life: Considerations by the Way*.

We take care of our health; we lay up money; we make our roof tight, and our clothing sufficient; but who provides wisely that he shall not be wanting in the best property of all,—friends?

EMERSON, *Conduct of Life: Considerations by the Way*.

16
O friend, my bosom said,
Through thee alone the sky is arched,
Through thee the rose is red.

RALPH WALDO EMERSON, *Friendship*.

17
Of all the means to insure happiness throughout the whole of life, by far the most important is the acquisition of friends.

EPICURUS, *Sovran Maxims*. No. 27.

18
A friend in the market is better than money in the chest.

THOMAS FULLER, *Gnomologia*. No. 119.

1
Large was his bounty, and his soul sincere,
Heav'n did a recompense as largely send:
He gave to Mis'ry all he had, a tear,
He gain'd from Heav'n ('twas all he wish'd) a friend.

THOMAS GRAY, *Elegy Written in a Country Church-yard*, l. 121.

2
Of all the heavenly gifts that mortal men commend,
What trusty treasure in the world can countervail a friend?

NICHOLAS GRIMALD, *Of Friendship*.

3
Thy friend put in thy bosom: wear his eyes
Still in thy heart, that he may see what's there.

GEORGE HERBERT, *The Church-Porch*. St. 46.

Life without a friend is death without a witness.

GEORGE HERBERT, *Jacula Prudentum*.

4
We hae friends ane or twa that aft gie us a ca',
To laugh when we're happy or grieve when we're wa'.

JAMES HOGG, *Moggy and Me*.

5
Whilst in my senses I shall prefer nothing to a pleasant friend. (Nil ego contulerim jucundo sanus amico.)

HORACE, *Satires*. Bk. i, sat. 5, l. 44.

6
Without a horse and a dog and a friend, man would perish.

RUDYARD KIPLING, *Parnesius: On the Great Wall*.

7
A true friend is the greatest of all blessings, and the one which we take least thought to acquire. (Un veritable ami est le plus grand de tous les biens et celui de tous qu'on songe le moins à acquérir.)

LA ROCHEFOUCAULD, *Maximes Posthumes*. No. 544.

8
The thread of our life would be dark, Heaven knows!
If it were not with friendship and love intertwin'd.

THOMAS MOORE, *Oh! Think Not*.

9
This is the comfort of friends, that though they may be said to die, yet their friendship and society are, in the best sense, ever present, because immortal.

WILLIAM PENN, *Fruites of Solitude*.

A true friend unbosoms freely, advises justly, assists readily, adventures boldly, takes all patiently, defends courageously, and continues a friend unchangeably.

WILLIAM PENN, *Fruites of Solitude*.

10
Honest men esteem and value nothing so much in this world as a real friend. Such a one is, as it were, another self.

PILPAY, *Choice of Friends*. Ch. iv.

11
Nothing but heaven itself is better than a friend who is really a friend. (Homini amico, qui est amicus ita uti nomen possidet, Nisi deos ei nil præstare.

PLAUTUS, *Bacchides*, l. 385. (Act iii, sc. 2.)

Above our life we love a steadfast friend.

MARLOWE, *Hero and Leander*. Sestiad ii.

To have the greatest blessing, a true friend.

MASSINGER, *Parliament of Love*. Act iii, sc. 2.

12
Where there are friends, there is wealth. (Ubi amici, esse ibidem opes.)

PLAUTUS, *Truculentus*. Act ii, l. 14.

They are rich who have true friends.

THOMAS FULLER, *Gnomologia*. No. 4957.

I am wealthy in my friends.

SHAKESPEARE, *Timon of Athens*. Act ii, sc. 2, l. 193.

13
Friends given by God in mercy and in love;
My counsellors, my comforters, and guides;
My joy in grief, my second bliss in joy;
Companions of my young desires; in doubt
My oracles; my wings in high pursuit.
O, I remember, and will ne'er forget
Our meeting spots, our chosen sacred hours,
Our burning words, that utter'd all the soul,
Our faces beaming with unearthly love;
Sorrow with sorrow sighing, hope with hope
Exulting, heart embracing heart entire.

POLLOK, *The Course of Time*. Bk. v, l. 315.

14
Friend to my life (which did you not prolong,
The world had wanted many an idle song)!

POPE, *Epistle to Dr. Arbuthnot*, l. 27.

15
Neither armies nor treasures form the bulwarks of a throne, but friends. (Non exercitus, neque thesauri, præsidia regni sunt, verum amici.)

SALLUST, *Jugurtha*. Ch. 10, sec. 4.

16
Keep thy friend Under thy own life's key.

SHAKESPEARE, *All's Well that Ends Well*. Act i, sc. 1, l. 75.

Those friends thou hast, and their adoption tried,
Grapple them to thy soul with hoops of steel;
But do not dull thy palm with entertainment
Of each new-hatch'd, unfledged comrade.

SHAKESPEARE, *Hamlet*. Act i, sc. 3, l. 62.

I count myself in nothing else so happy
As in a soul remembering my good friends.

SHAKESPEARE, *Richard II*. Act ii, sc. 3, l. 46.

17
But every road is rough to me that has no friend to cheer it.

ELIZABETH SHANE, *Sheskinbeg*.

18
It is strange that a man can always tell how

many sheep he has, but he cannot tell how many friends he has, so slight is the value he puts upon them.
SOCRATES. (DIOGENES LAERTIUS, *Socrates*. Sec. 13.)

1
The best elixir is a friend.
WILLIAM SOMERVILLE, *The Hip*.

2
'Tis pleasant to have found and proved a friend;
For him who good for good returns I hold
A friend more precious than unnumbered gold.
SOPHOCLES, *Philoctetes*, l. 671.

3
Nothing can be purchased which is better than a firm friend. (Amico firmo nihil emi melius potest.)
TACITUS, *Annals*. Bk. i, sec. 12.

4
Nothing makes the earth seem so spacious as to have friends at a distance; they make the latitudes and longitudes.
THOREAU, *Letter to Mrs. E. Castleton*, 22 May, 1843.

5
A friend is worth all hazards we can run.
YOUNG, *Night Thoughts*. Night ii, l. 571.

6
There is no treasure which may be compared unto a faithful friend;
Gold soon decayeth, and worldly wealth consumeth, and wasteth in the wind;
But love once planted in a perfect and pure mind endureth weal and woe;
The frowns of fortune, come they never so unkind, cannot it overthrow.
UNKNOWN, *The Bride's Good-Morning*. (*Roxburghe Ballads*.)

VI—Friends: Their Loyalty

7
I have loved my friends as I do virtue, my soul, my God.
SIR THOMAS BROWNE, *Religio Medici*. Pt. ii, sec. 5.

8
Let us be friends, Cinna, it is I who invite you. (Soyons amis, Cinna, c'est moi qui t'en convie.)
CORNEILLE, *Cinna*. Act v, sc. 3.

9
Then come the wild weather, come sleet or come snow,
We will stand by each other, however it blow.
SIMON DACH, *Annie of Tharaw*, l. 7. (Longfellow, tr.)

10
"Wal'r, my boy," replied the captain; "in the Proverbs of Solomon you will find the following words: 'May we never want a friend in need, nor a bottle to give him!' When found, make a note of."
DICKENS, *Dombey and Son*. Vol. i, ch. 15.

What is the odds so long as the fire of souls is kindled at the taper of conwiviality, and the wing of friendship never moults a feather?
DICKENS, *Old Curiosity Shop*. Ch. 2.

11
Here's to the friends we can trust
When storms of adversity blaw;
May they live in our songs and be nearest our hearts,
Nor depart like the year that's awa'.
JOHN DUNLOP, *The Year That's Awa'*

12
A friend ought to shun no pain, to stand his friend in stead.
RICHARD EDWARDS, *Damon and Pithias*.

13
So, if I live or die to serve my friend,
'Tis for my love—'tis for my friend alone,
And not for any rate that friendship bears
In heaven or on earth.
GEORGE ELIOT, *Spanish Gypsy*. Bk. iii, l. 361.

14
Promises may get friends, but it is performance that must nurse and keep them.
OWEN FELLTHAM, *Resolves: Of Promises*.

15
Particular contentment of mind that I have such an odd friend in a corner.
GABRIEL HARVEY, *Letter-Book*, p. 80. (c. 1579)

And, Cæsar, you shall find—a friend in corner.
SIR WILLIAM D'AVENANT, *Play-House to Be Let*. Act v.

16
True friends appear less mov'd than counterfeit. (Derisor vero plus laudatore movetur.)
HORACE, *Ars Poetica*, l. 433. (Dillon, tr.)

17
A good friend never offends.
JAMES HOWELL, *Proverbs*, 23. (1659)

18
Friend of my bosom, thou more than a brother,
Why wert thou not born in my father's dwelling?
CHARLES LAMB, *The Old Familiar Faces*.

19
Yes, we must ever be friends; and of all who offer you friendship
Let me be ever the first, the truest, the nearest and dearest!
LONGFELLOW, *The Courtship of Miles Standish*. Pt. vi, l. 72.

20
A true friend is forever a friend.
GEORGE MACDONALD, *Marquis of Lossie*. Ch. 71.

21
A man that hath friends must shew himself friendly: and there is a friend that sticketh closer than a brother.
Old Testament: Proverbs, xviii, 24.

Neither make thy friend equal to a brother. (Μηδὲ κασιγνήτῳ ἴσον ποιεῖσθαι ἑταῖρον.)
HESIOD, *Works and Days*, l. 707.

22
But oh! if grief thy steps attend,
If want, if sickness be thy lot,

And thou require a soothing friend,
  Forget me not, forget me not!
  AMELIA OPIE, *Go, Youth Beloved.*

1
Convey thy love to thy friend, as an arrow to the mark, to stick there, not as a ball against the wall, to rebound back to thee.
  FRANCIS QUARLES, *Enchiridion.* Cent. iv, No. 100.

2
He is a good friend that doth thee good.
  RIVERS, *Dictes and Sayings,* 57. (1477)

But he is my friend
That helps me in the end.
  UNKNOWN, *Roxburghe Ballads,* iii, 288. (1640)

He is my friend that succoureth me, not he that pitieth me.
  THOMAS FULLER, *Gnomologia.* No. 1926.

3
He was my friend, faithful and just to me.
  SHAKESPEARE, *Julius Cæsar.* Act iii, sc. 2, l. 90.

4
If it be ne'er so false, a true gentleman may swear it in the behalf of his friend.
  SHAKESPEARE, *Winter's Tale.* Act v, sc. 2, l. 175.

5
Life hath no joy like his who fights with Fate
Shoulder to shoulder with a stricken friend.
  THEODORE WATTS-DUNTON, *Midshipman Lanyon.*

6
To God, thy country, and thy friend be true.
  HENRY VAUGHAN, *Rules and Lessons.* No. 8.

7
If you have a friend worth loving,
  Love him. Yes, and let him know
That you love him, ere life's evening
  Tinge his brow with sunset glow.
Why should good words ne'er be said
Of a friend—till he is dead?
  UNKNOWN, *Say It Now.*

VII—Friends: Their Faults

8
While friends we were, the hot debates
  That rose 'twixt you and me!
Now we are mere associates,
  And never disagree.
  WILLIAM ALLINGHAM, *Blackberries.*

9
In friendship I early was taught to believe; . . .
I have found that a friend may profess, yet deceive.
  BYRON, *Lines to the Rev. J. T. Becher.* St. 7.

A good friend, but bad acquaintance.
  BYRON, *Don Juan.* Canto iii, st. 54.

10
No discord should arise between friends, but if it does, then our care should be that the friendships appear to have been burned out rather than to have been stamped out.
  CICERO, *De Amicitia.* Ch. 21, sec. 78.

Never break off friendship, rather untie it, when those you become bound to appear cheats. Hall says, "I will use my friend as Moses did his rod: while it was a rod he held it familiarly in his hand: When once a serpent, he ran away from it."
  JAMES PUCKLE, *The Club.*

11
All are not friends that speak us fair.
  JOHN CLARKE, *Paræmiologia,* 128. (1639)

A slender acquaintance with the world must convince every man, that actions, not words, are the true criterion of the attachment of friends; and that the most liberal professions of good-will are very far from being the surest marks of it.
  GEORGE WASHINGTON, *Social Maxims. Friendship.*

12
There is a friend, which is only a friend in name.
  Apocrypha: Ecclesiasticus, xxxvii, 1.

13
Our best friends are the source of our greatest sorrow and bitterness.
  FÉNELON, *Letter to Destouches,* 13 Aug., 1714.

CANDID FRIEND, *see under* CANDOR.

14
A broken friendship may be soldered, but will never be sound.
  THOMAS FULLER, *Gnomologia.* No. 27.

15
He who betrays his friend, shall never be
Under one roof, or in one ship, with me.
  HORACE, *Odes.* Bk. iii, ode 2. (Swift, tr.)

16
A friend is long a-getting and soon lost.
  JOHN LYLY, *Euphues,* p. 324. (1580)

They that study man say of a friend, There's nothing in the world that's harder found, nor sooner lost.
  WEBSTER AND ROWLEY, *Cure for a Cuckold.* Act iii, sc. 1. (1661)

17
Here our long web of friendship I untwist.
  MASSINGER, *The Fatal Dowry.* Act. iii, sc. 1.

18
It is more shameful to mistrust one's friends than to be deceived by them. (Il est plus honteux de se défier de ses amis que d'en être trompé.)
  LA ROCHEFOUCAULD, *Maximes.* No. 84.

19
Nothing is more annoying than a tardy friend. (Tardo amico nihil est quidquam inæquius.)
  PLAUTUS, *Pœnulus,* l. 504. (Act iii, sc. 1.)

20
Oft our displeasures, to ourselves unjust,
Destroy our friends and after weep their dust.
  SHAKESPEARE, *All's Well that Ends Well.* Act v, sc. 3, l. 63.

21
Call you that backing of your friends? A plague upon such backing! give me them that will face me.
  SHAKESPEARE, *I Henry IV.* Act ii, sc. 4, l. 165.

1
I am weary of friends, and friendships are all monsters.
SWIFT, *Letter to Stella.* 23 Oct, 1710.

2
The path of social advancement is, and must be, strewn with broken friendships.
H. G. WELLS, *Kipps.* Bk. ii, ch. 5.

VIII—Friends and Enemies

3
If he draw aside from your proper end,
No enemy like a bosom friend.
WILLIAM ALLINGHAM, *Blackberries.*

4
For much better it is
To bide a friend's anger than a foe's kiss.
ALEXANDER BARCLAY, *Mirror of Good Manners,* 21. (1570)

A friend's frown is better than a foe's smile.
JAMES HOWELL, *Proverbs.* (1659)

5
Our friends, the enemy. (Nos amis, les ennemis.)
BÉRANGER, *L'Opinion de ces Demoiselles.* The French are said to have used the expression, "Nos amis, nos ennemis," when the Allies entered Paris after the abdication of Napoleon in 1814.

6
I have tried to make friends by corporeal gifts, but have only made enemies. I have never made friends but by spiritual gifts, by severe contentions of friendship, and the burning fire of thought.
WILLIAM BLAKE, *Jerusalem.*

7
Thy friendship oft has made my heart to ache:—
Do be my enemy, for friendship's sake.
WILLIAM BLAKE, *To Hayley.*

8
In life it is difficult to say who do you the most mischief, enemies with the worst intentions, or friends with the best.
BULWER-LYTTON, *What Will He Do With It?* Bk. iii, ch. 17, heading.

9
Angry friendship is sometimes as bad as calm enmity.
EDMUND BURKE, *An Appeal from the New to the Old Whigs.*

10
For what man that hath friends through fortune,
Mishap will make them enemies, I guess:
This proverb is full sooth.
CHAUCER, *The Monkes Tale,* l. 254.

I no doubt deserved my enemies, but I don't believe I deserved my friends.
WALT WHITMAN. (BRADFORD, *Biography and the Human Heart,* p. 75.)

11
Greatly his foes he dreads, but more his friends;
He hurts me most who lavishly commends.
CHARLES CHURCHILL, *The Apology,* l. 19.

Friends I have made, whom Envy must commend,
But not one foe whom I would wish a friend.
CHARLES CHURCHILL, *The Conference,* l. 297.

12
Our enmities mortal, our friendships eternal. (Mortalis inimicitias, sempiternas amicitias.)
CICERO, *Pro Rabirio Postumo.* Ch. 12, sec. 33.

13
We should render a service to a friend to bind him closer to us, and to an enemy to make a friend of him.
CLEOBULUS. (DIOGENES LAERTIUS, *Cleobulus,* 5.)

14
It is always safe to learn, even from our enemies; seldom safe to venture to instruct, even our friends.
C. C. COLTON, *Lacon.* No. 286.

15
We read that we ought to forgive our enemies; but we do not read that we ought to forgive our friends.
COSIMO DE' MEDICI, of perfidious friends. (BACON, *Apothegms.* No. 206.)

16
Friends are as dangerous as enemies.
THOMAS DE QUINCEY, *Essays: Schlosser's Literary History.*

17
He that can be a worthy enemy, will, when reconciled, be a worthier friend.
OWEN FELLTHAM, *Resolves: Of Reconciling Enemies.*

18
You and I were long friends; you are now my enemy, and I am
Yours, Benjamin Franklin.
BENJAMIN FRANKLIN, *Letter to William Strahan.* 5 July, 1775.

19
Do good to thy friend to keep him, to thy enemy to gain him.
BENJAMIN FRANKLIN, *Poor Richard's Almanac.*

20
An open foe may prove a curse,
But a pretended friend is worse.
JOHN GAY, *Fables.* Pt. i, No. 17.

21
He rose without a friend, and sat down without an enemy.
HENRY GRATTAN, of Dr. Lucas after a speech in the Irish Parliament.

22
It is a misfortune for a man not to have a friend in the world, but for that reason he shall have no enemy.
LORD HALIFAX, *Works,* p. 243.

He will never have true friends who is afraid of making enemies.
WILLIAM HAZLITT, *Characteristics.* No. 401.

No man's defects sought they to know;
So never made themselves a foe.
No man's good deeds did they commend;
So never rais'd themselves a friend.
MATTHEW PRIOR, *An Epitaph.*

He makes no friend who never made a foe.
TENNYSON, *Lancelot and Elaine*, l. 1082.

1
Save a man from his friends, and leave him struggle with his enemies.
W. C. HAZLITT, *English Proverbs*, 328.

2
Invite your friend to a feast, but leave your enemy alone. (Τὸν φιλέοντ' ἐπὶ δαῖτα καλεῖν, τὸν δ' ἐχθρὸν ἐᾶσαι.)
HESIOD, *Works and Days*, l. 342.

3
Not hate, but glory, made these chiefs contend;
And each brave foe was in his soul a friend.
HOMER, *Iliad*. Bk. vii, l. 364. (Pope, tr.)

4
I can defend myself from my enemies, but not from my friends.
HONEIN BEN ISAAK, *Moral Maxims*. (c. 870) Appears in various forms in all literatures.

A feigned friend God shield me from his danger,
For well I'll save myself from foe and stranger.
ANTHONY COPLEY, *Wits, Fits, and Fancies*.

From him whom I trust, God defend me; for from him whom I trust not I will defend myself.
JAMES HOWELL, *Familiar Letters*. Bk. ii, letter 75.

Against a foe I can myself defend,—
But Heaven protect me from a blundering friend!
D'ARCY WENTWORTH THOMPSON, *Sales Attici*.

Defend me from my friends; I can defend myself from my enemies.
MARÉCHAL DE VILLARS, when taking leave of Louis XIV. Also attributed in slightly different form to Voltaire: "May God defend me from my friends; I can defend myself from my enemies." The saying is, of course, much older. (See *Notes and Queries*, ser. vii, No. 10, p. 428.)

5
When fails our dearest friend,
There may be refuge with our direst foe.
J. S. KNOWLES, *The Wife*. Act v, sc. 2.

6
Nothing is so dangerous as an ignorant friend: better have a wise enemy. (Rien n'est si dangereux qu'un ami ignorant; Mieux vaudrait un sage ennemi.)
LA FONTAINE, *Fables*. Bk. viii, fab. 10.

Better to have a loving friend
Than ten admiring foes.
GEORGE MACDONALD, *After Thomas à Kempis*. St. 2.

7
Our best friend is a blundering enemy.
JOHN MACY, *About Women*, p. 82.

8
If you never tell your secret to your friend, you will never fear him when he becomes your enemy.
MENANDER, *Fragments*. No. 695.

9
Trust not yourself; but your defects to know,
Make use of ev'ry friend—and ev'ry foe.
POPE, *Essay on Criticism*. Pt. ii, l. 13.

10
What war could ravish, commerce could bestow,
And he return'd a friend who came a foe.
POPE, *Essay on Man*. Epis. iii, l. 205.

11
To lasting toils expos'd, and endless cares,
To open dangers, and to secret snares;
To malice which the vengeful foe intends,
And the more dangerous love of seeming friends.
MATTHEW PRIOR, *Solomon*. Bk. iii, l. 75.

12
Faithful are the wounds of a friend; but the kisses of an enemy are deceitful.
Old Testament: Proverbs, xxvii, 5.

One cried: "The wounds are faithful of a friend:
The wilderness shall blossom as the rose."
One answered: "Rend the veil, declare the end,
Strengthen her ere she goes."
CHRISTINA ROSSETTI, *From House to House*.

13
Treat your friend as if he might become an enemy.
PUBLILIUS SYRUS, *Sententiæ*. No. 401.

14
Inflict not on an enemy every injury in your power, for he may afterwards become your friend.
SADI, *The Gulistan: Rules for Conduct in Life*. No. 10.

15
It is better to break off a thousand friendships, than to endure the sight of a single enemy.
SADI, *The Gulistan: Of Youth and Love*. No. 15.

16
Dear is my friend—yet from my foe, as from my friend, comes good:
My friend shows what I can do, and my foe what I should.
SCHILLER, *Votive Tablets: Friend and Foe*.

17
The zeal of friends it is that razes me,
And not the hate of enemies.
(Der Freunde Eifer ist's, der mich
Zu Grunde richtet, nicht der Hass der Feinde.)
SCHILLER, *Wallenstein's Tod*. Act iii, sc. 18.

18
The angry prayers of our enemies make us falsely afraid, and the affection of our friends spoils us with kindly wishes.
SENECA, *Epistulæ ad Lucilium*. Epis. xciv, 54.

19
The great man down, you mark his favourite flies;
The poor advanced makes friends of enemies,
And hitherto doth love on fortune tend;
For who not needs shall never lack a friend,
And who in want a hollow friend doth try,
Directly seasons him his enemy.
SHAKESPEARE, *Hamlet*. Act iii, sc. 2, l. 214.

1
Give him all kindness: I had rather have
Such men my friends, than enemies.
SHAKESPEARE, *Julius Cæsar*. Act v, sc. 4, l. 28.

2
The private wound is deepest: O Time most accurst
'Mongst all foes that a friend should be the worst!
SHAKESPEARE, *The Two Gentlemen of Verona*. Act v, sc. 4, l. 71.

3
Having some friends whom he loves dearly,
And no lack of foes, whom he laughs at sincerely.
ROBERT SOUTHEY, *Robert the Rhymer's Account of Himself*.

4
Better new friend than an old foe.
SPENSER, *Faerie Queene*. Bk. i, canto ii, st. 27.

Faint friends when they fall out most cruel foemen be.
SPENSER, *Faerie Queene*. Bk. iv, canto ix, st. 27.

5
One enemy can do more hurt than ten friends can do good.
SWIFT, *Letter*, 30 May, 1710. (Quoted.)

6
He who has a thousand friends has not a friend to spare,
And he who has one enemy shall meet him everywhere.
ALI BEN ABU TALEB. (EMERSON, *Conduct of Life: Considerations by the Way*. Emerson ascribes the couplet to Omar Khayyám.)

Whatever the number of a man's friends, there will be times in his life when he has one too few; but if he has only one enemy, he is lucky indeed if he has not one too many.
BULWER-LYTTON, *What Will He Do With It?* Bk. ix, ch. 3.

The world is large when its weary leagues two loving hearts divide;
But the world is small when your enemy is loose on the other side.
JOHN BOYLE O'REILLY, *Distance*.

7
Some great misfortune to portend,
No enemy can match a friend.
SWIFT, *On the Death of Dr. Swift*, l. 119.

8
Foes in the forum in the field were friends,
By social danger bound.
JAMES THOMSON, *Liberty*. Pt. iii, l. 218.

9
It takes your enemy and your friend, working together, to hurt you to the heart: the one to slander you and the other to get the news to you.
MARK TWAIN, *Pudd'nhead Wilson's Calendar*.

10
If I have not a friend, God send me an enemy, that I may hear of my faults.
BENJAMIN WHICHCOTE, *Sermons*.

11
As good a foe that hurts not, as a friend that helps not.
LEONARD WRIGHT, *Display of Dutie*, p. 19.

12
A foe to God was ne'er true friend to man;
Some sinister intent taints all he does.
YOUNG, *Night Thoughts*. Night viii, l. 704.

13
Perish our friends, so foes may die withal.
(Ἐρρέτω φίλος σὺν ἐχθρῷ.)
UNKNOWN. Quoted by CICERO, *Pro Rege Diotaro*, ix, 25, who puts it into Latin: Pereant amici, dum inimici una intercidant. Cicero condemns the sentiment.

IX—Friends and Adversity

14
Faithful friends are hard to find:
Every man will be thy friend
Whilst thou hast wherewith to spend;
But if store of crowns be scant,
No man will supply thy want.
RICHARD BARNFIELD, *Passionate Pilgrim*, l. 407.

15
Let no man grumble when his friends fall off,
As they will do like leaves at the first breeze:
When your affairs come round, one way or t' other,
Go to the coffee-house, and take another.
BYRON, *Don Juan*. Canto xiv, st. 48.

16
If thou be poor, thy brother hateth thee,
And all thy friends do flee from thee, alas!
CHAUCER, *Man of Law's Tale: Prologue*, l. 22.

17
While the pot boils, friendship blooms.
A. B. CHEALES, *Proverbial Folk-Lore*, 95.

Pot friendship; cupboard love. (Ollæ amicitia.)
UNKNOWN. A Latin proverb.

18
Interiorly, most people enjoy the inferiority of their best friends.
LORD CHESTERFIELD, *Letters*, 9 July, 1750.

19
Be more ready to visit friends in adversity than in prosperity.
CHILON. (DIOGENES LAERTIUS, *Chilon*. Sec. 3.)

Come slowly to the banquets of thy friends, but swiftly to their misfortunes.
CHILON. (STOBÆUS, *Florilegium*, iii, 79, 7.)

20
The swallows are at hand in summer time, but in cold weather they are driven away. . . . So false friends are at hand in life's clear weather, but as soon as they see the winter of misfortune, they all fly away.
CICERO, *Ad Herennium*. Bk. iv, sec. 48.

Like summer friends,
Flies of estate and sunshine.
GEORGE HERBERT, *The Answer*.

When the sun shines on you, you see your friends.
Friends are the thermometers by which one may judge the temperature of our fortunes.
COUNTESS OF BLESSINGTON, *Commonplace Book*.

O summer-friendship,
Whose flattering leaves, that shadow'd us in our
Prosperity, with the least gust drop off
In the autumn of adversity!

MASSINGER, *The Maid of Honour*. Act iii, sc. 1.

For men, like butterflies,
Show not their mealy wings but to the summer.

SHAKESPEARE, *Troilus and Cressida*. Act iii, sc. 3, l. 78.

1
In prosperity our friends know us; in adversity we know our friends.

CHURTON COLLINS, *Aphorisms*.

2
Our very best friends have a tincture of jealousy even in their friendship.

C. C. COLTON, *Lacon*. No. 121.

3
For friendship, of itself a holy tie,
Is made more sacred by adversity.

DRYDEN, *Hind and the Panther*. Pt. iii, l. 47.

4
If we from wealth to poverty descend,
Want gives to know the flatterer from the friend.

DRYDEN, *The Wife of Bath: Her Tale*, l. 485.

5
When Fortune's fickle, the faithful friend is found. (Amicus certus in re incerta cernitur.)

ENNIUS. (CICERO, *De Amicitia*, xvii, 64.)

6
In prosperity it is very easy to find a friend; but in adversity it is the most difficult of all things.

EPICTETUS, *Fragments*. No. 127.

7
Friends disappear with the dregs from the empty wine casks. (Diffugiunt cadis Cum fæce siccatis, amici.)

HORACE, *Odes*. Bk. i, ode 35, l. 26.

So vanish friendships only made in wine.

TENNYSON, *Geraint and Enid*, l. 379.

8
In time of prosperity friends will be plenty;
In time of adversity not one among twenty.

JAMES HOWELL, *Proverbs*, 20. (1659)

9
In the adversity of our best friends we always find something which does not displease us. (Dans l'adversité de nos meilleurs amis nous trouvons toujours quelque chose qui ne nous déplaît pas.)

LA ROCHEFOUCAULD, *Maximes*. No. 99. This maxim was withdrawn from the third edition, probably because of the outcry it occasioned. (*Maximes Supprimées*. No. 583.)

This maxim more than all the rest
Is thought too base for human breast:
"In all distresses of our friends,
We first consult our private ends;
While nature, kindly bent to ease us,
Points out some circumstance to please us."

SWIFT, *On the Death of Dr. Swift*, l. 5. Swift defends the sentiment on the ground that good fortune is always sentimentally enhanced by contrast with the misfortunes of others.

Those who know the deception and wickedness of the human heart will not be either romantic or blind enough to deny what Rochefoucauld and Swift have affirmed as a general truth.

LORD CHESTERFIELD, *Letters*, 129.

See also MISFORTUNE: THE MISFORTUNES OF OTHERS.

10
The vulgar herd estimate friendship by its advantages. (Vulgus amicitias utilitate probat.)

OVID, *Epistulæ ex Ponto*. Bk. ii, epis. iii, p. 8.

There is love for none, save him whom fortune favors. (Diligitur nemo, nisi cui fortuna secunda est.)

OVID, *Epistulæ ex Ponto*. Bk. ii, epis. 3, l. 23.

The rest of the crowd were friends of my fortune, not of me. (Cætera Fortunæ, non mea, turba fuit.)

OVID, *Tristia*. Bk. i, eleg. v, l. 34.

11
Just as yellow gold is tested in the fire, so is friendship to be tested by adversity. (Scilicet ut fulvum spectatur in ignibus aurum, Tempore sic duro est inspicienda fides.)

OVID, *Tristia*. Bk. i, eleg. v, l. 25.

12
So long as you are secure you will count many friends; if your life becomes clouded you will be alone. (Donec eris sospes, multos numerabis amicos; Tempora si fuerint nubila, solus eris.)

OVID, *Tristia*. Bk. i, eleg. ix, l. 5.

Ants do not bend their ways to empty barns, so no friend will visit the place of departed wealth. (Horrea formicæ tendunt ad inania nunquam Nullus ad amissas ibit amicus opes.)

OVID, *Tristia*. Bk. i, eleg. 9, l. 9.

If wealth totters, friends begin to waver simultaneously with it. Wealth finds friends. (Si res labat Itidem amici collabascunt: res amicos invenit.)

PLAUTUS, *Stichus*. Act ii, sc. 4.

13
Be the same to your friends, whether in prosperity or adversity.

PERIANDER. (DIOGENES LAERTIUS, *Periander*. Sec. 4.)

14
Prosperity makes friends and adversity tries them. (Amicum an nomen habeas, aperit calamitas.)

PUBLILIUS SYRUS, *Sententiæ*. No. 872. Repeated in many Latin authors.

Prosperity gets followers, but adversity distinguishes them.

THOMAS FULLER, *Gnomologia*. No. 3962.

15
He who begins to be your friend because it pays will also cease because it pays.

SENECA, *Epistulæ ad Lucilium*. Epis. ix, sec. 9.

That friendship will not continue to the end that is begun for an end.

FRANCIS QUARLES, *Enchiridion*. Cent. iv, 100.

1
Where you are liberal of your loves and counsels
Be sure you be not loose; for those you make friends
And give your hearts to, when they once perceive
The least rub in your fortunes, fall away
Like water from ye, never found again
But where they mean to sink ye.
SHAKESPEARE, *Henry VIII*. Act ii, sc. 1, l. 126.

2
I have learned which friends of mine are true and which are false, now that I am no longer able to reward or punish either. (Tum se intellexisse, quos fidos amicos habuisset, quos infidos, cum jam neutris gratiam referre posset.)
TARQUIN, on going into exile. (CICERO, *De Amicitia*. Ch. xv, sec. 53.)

3
Many thy boon companions at the feast,
But few the friends who cleave to thee in trouble.
THEOGNIS, *Sententiæ*. No. 115.

Feast, and your halls are crowded;
Fast, and the world goes by.
ELLA WHEELER WILCOX, *Solitude*.

Now that I no longer need,
I can get full many a feed.
C. H. SPURGEON, *Salt-Cellars*.

4
There is an old time toast which is golden for its beauty. "When you ascend the hill of prosperity may you not meet a friend."
MARK TWAIN, *Pudd'nhead Wilson's New Calendar*.

X—Friend: A Friend in Need

5
A friend is known in necessity.
GEORGE ASHBY, *Poems*, p. 67. (c. 1470)

6
He that is thy friend indeed,
He will help thee in thy need:
If thou sorrow, he will weep;
If thou wake, he cannot sleep;
Thus of every grief in heart
He with thee doth bear a part.
These are certain signs to show
Faithful friend from faltering foe.
RICHARD BARNFIELD, *Passionate Pilgrim*, l. 423.

7
To be a strong hand in the dark to another in a time of need.
HUGH BLACK, *The Culture of Friendship*.

8
Three things are known only in three places: Valour, which knows itself only in war; Wisdom, only in anger; and Friendship, only in need.
EMERSON, *Journal*, 1863. Quoted as a Persian saying.

9
Behold how much it stands a man in steed,
To have a friend answer in time of need.
SIR JOHN HARINGTON, *Epigrams*. Bk. ii, No. 101. (1618)

10
But in deed,
A friend is never known till a man hath need.
JOHN HEYWOOD, *Proverbs*. Pt. i, ch. 9. (1546)

11
At need shall men prove their friends.
ROBERT MANNYNG (ROBERT DE BRUNNE), *Handlyng Synne*, l. 2251. (1303)

12
A friend is not known but in need.
GEORGE MERITON, *Praise of Yorkshire Ale*, 83. (1683)

13
A friend in a pinch is a friend in deed, when deeds are needed. (Is est amicus, qui in re dubia re juvat, ubi rest opus.)
PLAUTUS, *Epidicus*, l. 113. (Act i, sc. 1.)

Nothing is dearer to a man than a friend in need. (Nihil homini amicost opportuno amicius.)
PLAUTUS, *Epidicus*, l. 425. (Act iii, sc. 3.)

14
I am not of that feather to shake off
My friend when he must need me.
SHAKESPEARE, *Timon of Athens*. Act i, sc. 1, l. 100.

15
A safe companion is he that helps at need.
UNKNOWN, *Proverbs of Alfred*, 247. (c. 1270)

A friend thou art in deed,
That helps thy friend in time of nipping need.
THOMAS HOWELL, *Devises*, 58. (1581)

A friend in need is a friend indeed.
RICHARD GRAVES, *The Spiritual Quixote*. Bk. vii, ch. 22, heading. (1772)

16
It is good to have friends, but bad to need them.
UNKNOWN, *New Help to Discourse*, 15. (1669)

XI—Friends: Old and New

17
No friend's a friend until he prove a friend.
BEAUMONT AND FLETCHER, *The Faithful Friends*. Act iii, sc. 3, l. 50.

18
Are new friends who are worthy of friendship, to be preferred to old friends? The question is unworthy of a human being, for there should be no surfeit of friendships as there is of other things; and, as in the case of wines that improve with age, the oldest friendships ought to be the most delightful; moreover, the well-known adage is true: "Men must eat many a peck of salt together before the claims of friendship are fulfilled." (Multos modios salis simul edendos esse, ut amicitiæ munus expletum sit.)
CICERO, *De Amicitia*. Ch. 19, sec. 67. *See also under* SALT.

19
Old friends burn dim, like lamps in noisome air;

Love them for what they are; nor love them less,
Because to thee they are not what they were.
S. T. COLERIDGE, *Duty Surviving Self-Love.*

1
Forsake not an old friend; for the new is not comparable to him: a new friend is as new wine; when it is old, thou shalt drink it with pleasure.
Apocrypha: Ecclesiasticus, ix, 10.

As old wood is best to burn, old horse to ride, old books to read, and old wine to drink, so are old friends always most trusty to use.
LEONARD WRIGHT, *Display of Dutie,* 19. (1589) *For other quotations on old wine, old books, etc., see under* AGE: ITS COMPENSATIONS.

2
Old friendships are like meats served up repeatedly, cold, comfortless, and distasteful. The stomach turns against them.
WILLIAM HAZLITT, *The Plain Speaker: On the Pleasure of Hating.*

3
An old friend is a new house.
GEORGE HERBERT, *Jacula Prudentum.*

4
It is delightful to me to go mad over a friend restored to me. (Recepto Dulci mihi furere est amico.)
HORACE, *Odes.* Bk. ii, ode 7, l. 27.

They are twice as good friends as they were before [they quarrelled].
PLAUTUS, *Amphitruo.* Act iii, sc. 2, l. 62.

5
And newest friend is oldest friend in this:
That, waiting him, we longest grieved to miss
One thing we sought.
HELEN HUNT JACKSON, *My New Friend.*

6
I find friendship to be like wine, raw when new, ripened with age, the true old man's milk and restorative cordial.
THOMAS JEFFERSON, *Writings.* Vol. xiii, p. 77.

7
Ah, how good it feels!
The hand of an old friend.
LONGFELLOW, *John Endicott.* Act iv, sc. 1.

8
We have been friends together
In sunshine and in shade.
CAROLINE NORTON, *We Have Been Friends.*

9
How much the best of a man's friends is his oldest friend! (Quam veterrimus homini optimus est amicus!)
PLAUTUS, *Truculentus.* Act i, sc. 2, l. 71.

10
Old friends are best. King James used to call for his old shoes, for they were easiest for his feet.
JOHN SELDEN, *Table-Talk: Friends.*

11
Should auld acquaintance be forgot, and never thought upon?
FRANCIS SEMPILL, *Auld Lang Syne.* (JAMES WATSON, *Choice Collection of Scots Poems.* Pt. iii. 1711.) This is the earliest known version of *Auld Lang Syne,* and is sometimes attributed to Sir Robert Ayton.

Should auld acquaintance be forgot,
Though they return with scars?
ALLAN RAMSAY, *Auld Lang Syne.* 1721. (See FITZGERALD, *Stories of Famous Songs.*)

Should auld acquaintance be forgot,
And never brought to mind?
Should auld acquaintance be forgot,
And auld lang syne?
ROBERT BURNS, *Auld Lang Syne.* (1788) Burns himself in a letter to Mrs. Dunlop, speaks of *Auld Lang Syne* as an "old fragment," but, with the exception of the first stanza, the song is his. Allan Ramsay's song suggested nothing except the opening line and the title.

12
It's an owercome sooth for age an' youth,
And it brooks wi' nae denial,
That the dearest friends are the auldest friends,
And the young are just on trial.
R. L. STEVENSON, *It's an Owercome Sooth.*

13
Be courteous to all, but intimate with few, and let those few be well tried before you give them your confidence. True friendship is a plant of slow growth, and must undergo and withstand the shocks of adversity before it is entitled to the appellation.
GEORGE WASHINGTON, *Letter,* Newburgh, 15 Jan., 1783.

14
Friendship's the wine of life; but friendship new . . .
Is neither strong nor pure.
YOUNG, *Night Thoughts.* Night ii, l. 582.

XII—Friends: Behavior

15
We should behave to our friends as we would wish our friends to behave to us. (Ὡ ἂν εὐξαίμεθα αὐτοὺς ἡμῖν προσφέρεσθαι.)
ARISTOTLE. (DIOGENES LAERTIUS, *Aristotle.* Sec. 21.)

If men are friends, there is no need of justice between them; whereas when they are just, they still need friendship. The just possess friendliness in its highest form.
ARISTOTLE, *Nicomachean Ethics.* Bk. viii, ch. 1, sec. 5.

16
My son, keep well thy tongue, and keep thy friend.
CHAUCER, *The Maunciples Tale,* l. 215.

17
Between friends, frequent reproofs make the friendship distant.
CONFUCIUS, *Analects.* Bk. iv, ch. 26.

Reprove your friends in secret, praise them openly. (Secrete amicos admone, lauda palam.)
PUBLILIUS SYRUS, *Sententiæ.*

Alas! I then have chid away my friend!
SHAKESPEARE, *King John.* Act iv, sc. 1, l. 87.

1
Be kind to my remains· and O defend,
Against your judgment, your departed friend!
DRYDEN, *To Mr. Congreve,* l. 72.

2
To act the part of a true friend requires more conscientious feeling than to fill with credit and complacency any other station or capacity in social life.
SARAH STICKNEY ELLIS, *Pictures of Private Life*. Ser. ii, ch. 4.

3
There can never be deep peace between two spirits, never mutual respect, until, in their dialogue, each stands for the whole world.
EMERSON, *Essays, First Series: Friendship.*

4
Better be a nettle in the side of your friend than his echo.
EMERSON, *Essays, First Series: Friendship.*

If I mayn't tell you what I feel, what is the use of a friend?
THACKERAY, *Unpublished Letters.*

5
Do not expect friends to do for you what you can do for yourself. (Ne quid expectes amicos, quod tute agere possies.)
QUINTUS ENNIUS, *Saturæ*. (AULUS GELLIUS, *Noctes Atticæ*. Bk. ii, epis. 29, sec. 20.) The conclusion of a poetical rendering of Æsop's fable of the lark.

6
When our friends are present, we ought to treat them well; and when they are absent, to speak of them well.
EPICTETUS, *Fragments*. No. 155.

7
He does good to himself who does good to his friend. (Sibi benefacit qui benefacit amico.)
ERASMUS, *Familiar Colloquies.*

8
The discussing the characters and foibles of common friends is a great sweetener and cement of friendship.
WILLIAM HAZLITT, *Table Talk*. No. 20.

9
When my friends are one-eyed, I look at their profile. (Quand mes amis sont borgnes, je les regarde de profil.)
JOUBERT, *Pensées*. No. 4.

10
A judicious friend is better than a zealous.
J. S. KNOWLES, *The Love Chase*. Act ii, sc. 1.

11
The greatest endeavor of friendship is not to show our faults to a friend, but to make him see his own. (Le plus grand effort de l'amitié n'est pas de montrer nos défauts à un ami; c'est de lui faire voir les siens.)
LA ROCHEFOUCAULD, *Maximes*. No. 410.

12
Iron sharpeneth iron; so a man sharpeneth the countenance of his friend.
Old Testament: Proverbs, xxvii, 17.

13
Unless you bear with the faults of a friend, you betray your own. (Amici vitium ni feras, facis tua.)
PUBLILIUS SYRUS, *Sententiæ*. No. 10.

A friend should bear his friend's infirmities.
SHAKESPEARE, *Julius Cæsar*. Act iv, sc. 3, l. 86.

14
A friend must not be wounded, even in jest. (Amicum lædere ne joco quidem licet.)
PUBLILIUS SYRUS, *Sententiæ*. No. 54.

15
The inclination to lose a friend rather than a jest should be far from us. (Potius amicum quam dictum perdendi.)
QUINTILIAN, *De Institutione Oratoria,* vi, 3.

He that will lose his friend for a jest, deserves to die a beggar by the bargain.
THOMAS FULLER, *The Holy and Profane States: Of Jesting.*

It is better to lose a new jest than an old friend.
GABRIEL HARVEY, *Works*. Vol. ii, p. 125. (1593)

16
When friendship is settled, you must trust; before it is formed, you must pass judgment.
SENECA, *Epistulæ ad Lucilium*. Epis. iii, sec. 2.

17
The amity that wisdom knits not, folly
May easily untie.
SHAKESPEARE, *Troilus and Cressida,* ii, 3, 110.

18
If it is abuse, why one is always sure to hear of it from one damned good-natured friend or another.
R. B. SHERIDAN, *The Critic*. Act i, sc. 1.

19
Hast thou a friend, as heart may wish at will?
Then use him so, to have his friendship still.
THOMAS TUSSER, *Posies for a Parlour.*

20
The smoothest course of nature has its pains,
And truest friends, through error, wound our rest.
YOUNG, *Night Thoughts*. Night i, l. 278.

All like the purchase, few the price will pay,
And this makes friends such miracles below.
YOUNG, *Night Thoughts*. Night ii, l. 556.

XIII—Friends: Their Loss

See also Death: They Are All Gone

21
A man dies as often as he loses his friends. (Homo toties moritur quoties amittit suos.)
BACON, *Ornamenta Rationalia*. No. 17.

22
King Pandion he is dead,
All thy friends are lapp'd in lead.
RICHARD BARNFIELD, *Philomel.*

Friends depart, and memory takes them
To her caverns, pure and deep.
THOMAS HAYNES BAYLY, *Teach Me to Forget.*

23
Friends of my youth, a last adieu! haply some day we meet again;

Yet ne'er the self-same men shall meet; the
years shall make us other men.
SIR RICHARD BURTON, *The Kasîdah*. Pt. i, st. 16.

Farewell, dear friend, that smile, that harmless
mirth,
No more shall gladden our domestic hearth.
H. F. CARY, *Epitaph on Charles Lamb*.

1
As we sail through life towards death,
Bound unto the same port—heaven,—
Friend, what years could us divide?
DINAH M. M. CRAIK, *A Christmas Blessing*.

2
Let the soul be assured that somewhere in the universe it should rejoin its friend, and it would be content and cheerful alone for a thousand years.
EMERSON, *Essays, First Series: Friendship*.

3
Green be the turf above thee,
Friend of my better days!
None knew thee but to love thee,
Nor named thee but to praise.
FITZ-GREENE HALLECK, *On the Death of Joseph Rodman Drake*.

For my boyhood's friend hath fallen, the pillar of
my trust,
The true, the wise, the beautiful, is sleeping in
the dust.
G. S. HILLARD, *On The Death of Motley*.

4
I see no comfort in outliving one's friends, and remaining a mere monument of the times which are past.
THOMAS JEFFERSON, *Writings*. Vol. xviii, p. 297.

5
Friendship between mortals can be contracted on no other terms than that one must sometime mourn for the other's death.
SAMUEL JOHNSON, *The Rambler*. No. 17.

6
Thrice blessed are our friends:
They come, they stay—
And presently go away.
RICHARD R. KIRK, *Thrice Blessed*.

7
Let the loss of our friends be our only grief, and the apprehension of displeasing them our only fear.
W. S. LANDOR, *Imaginary Conversations: Epicurus, Leontion, and Ternissa*.

8
Come back! ye friends, whose lives are ended,
Come back, with all that light attended,
Which seemed to darken and decay
When ye arose and went away!
LONGFELLOW, *The Golden Legend*. Pt. i.

O friend! O best of friends! Thy absence more
Than the impending night darkens the landscape
o'er!
LONGFELLOW, *The Golden Legend*. Pt. i.

9
Friend after friend departs!
Who hath not lost a friend?
There is no union here of hearts
That finds not here an end.
JAMES MONTGOMERY, *Friends*.

10
When I remember all
The friends, so link'd together,
I've seen around me fall,
Like leaves in wintry weather,
I feel like one Who treads alone
Some banquet-hall deserted,
Whose lights are fled, Whose garlands dead,
And all but he departed!
THOMAS MOORE, *Oft in the Stilly Night*.

The friends, who in our sunshine live,
When winter comes, are flown;
And he who has but tears to give,
Must weep those tears alone.
THOMAS MOORE, *Oh, Thou! Who Dry'st the Mourner's Tear*.

11
Of all my many friends, scarcely two or three of you are left to me. (Vix duo tresve mihi de tot superestis amici.)
OVID, *Tristia*. Bk. i, eleg. 5, l. 33.

12
For all are friends in heaven, all faithful
friends;
And many friendships in the days of time
Begun, are lasting here, and growing still.
ROBERT POLLOK, *The Course of Time*. Bk. v, l. 336.

13
Saul and Jonathan were lovely and pleasant in their lives, and in their death they were not divided.
Old Testament: II Samuel, i, 23.

These are two friends whose lives were undi-
vided:
So let their memory be, now they have glided
Under the grave; let not their bones be parted,
For their two hearts in life were single-hearted.
SHELLEY, *Epitaph*.

14
To lose a friend is the greatest of all evils, but endeavour rather to rejoice that you possessed him than to mourn his loss.
SENECA, *Epistulæ ad Lucilium*. Epis. xcix, 3.

To wail friends lost
Is not by much so wholesome-profitable
As to rejoice at friends but newly found.
SHAKESPEARE, *Love's Labour's Lost*. Act v, sc. 2, l. 759.

15
This passion, and the death of a dear friend, would go near to make a man look sad.
SHAKESPEARE, *A Midsummer-Night's Dream*. Act v, sc. 1, l. 293.

16
Friends I have had both old and young,
And ale we drank and songs we sung:
Enough you know when this is said,
That, one and all, they died in bed.
In bed they died, and I'll not go

Where all my friends have perished so.
CHARLES HENRY WEBB, *Dum Vivamus Vigilamus.*

1
But Fate ordains the dearest friends must part.
YOUNG, *Love of Fame.* Sat. ii, l. 232.

For friends, you know, must part.
UNKNOWN, *Roxburghe Ballads,* i, 253. (1620)

2
Each friend by fate snatch'd from us is a plume
Pluck'd from the wing of human vanity,
Which makes us stoop from our aërial heights.
YOUNG, *Night Thoughts.* Night iii, l. 285.

FRIENDSHIP

I—Friendship: Definitions

3
It redoubleth joys and cutteth griefs in halfs.
FRANCIS BACON, *Essays: Of Friendship.*

4
Friendship is a word the very sight of which in print makes the heart warm.
AUGUSTINE BIRRELL, *Obiter Dicta, Second Series: Emerson.*

5
Friendship! mysterious cement of the soul!
Sweet'ner of life, and solder of society!
ROBERT BLAIR, *The Grave,* l. 88.

6
Friendship is a slow grower, and never thrives unless ingrafted upon a stock of known and reciprocal merit.
LORD CHESTERFIELD, *Letters,* 9 Oct., 1747.

7
Friendship is nothing else than an accord in all things, human and divine, conjoined with mutual good-will and affection. (Est enim amicitia nihil aliud nisi omnium divinarum humanarumque rerum cum benevolentia et caritate consensio.)
CICERO, *De Amicitia.* Ch. 6, sec. 20.

8
Friendship is a sheltering tree.
S. T. COLERIDGE, *Youth and Age.*

9
Friendship is the gift of the gods, and the most precious boon to man.
BENJAMIN DISRAELI, *Speech,* House of Commons, 16 July, 1855.

10
'Tis a French definition of friendship, rien que s'entendre, good understanding.
EMERSON, *Conduct of Life: Behavior.*

I hate the prostitution of the name of friendship to signify modish and worldly alliances.
EMERSON, *Essays, First Series: Friendship.*

11
Without confidence there is no friendship. (Εἰ δ' ἀπίστων οὐδὲ φίλων.)
EPICURUS. (DIOGENES LAERTIUS, *Epicurus.* Bk. x, sec. 11.)

12
Friendship is a disinterested commerce between equals.
GOLDSMITH, *The Good-Natured Man.* Act i, sc. 1.

Full of this maxim, often heard in trade,
Friendship with none but equals should be made.
THOMAS CHATTERTON, *Fragment.*

There is a maxim indeed which says—"Friendship can only subsist between equals."
THOMAS HOLCROFT, *The School for Arrogance.* Act iii, sc. 1.

Friendship is seldom lasting, but between equals, or where the superiority on one side is reduced by some equivalent advantage on the other.
SAMUEL JOHNSON, *The Rambler.* No. 64.

There is little friendship in the world, and least of all between equals.
BACON, *Essays: Of Followers and Friends.*

13
Fame is the scentless sunflower, with gaudy crown of gold;
But friendship is the breathing rose, with sweets in every fold.
O. W. HOLMES, *No Time Like the Old Time.*

14
Friendship is only a reciprocal conciliation of interests, and an exchange of good offices; it is a species of commerce out of which self-love always expects to gain something.
LA ROCHEFOUCAULD, *Maximes.* No. 83.

15
That sacred and venerable name of friendship. (Illud amicitiæ sanctum et venerabile nomen.)
OVID, *Tristia.* Bk. i, eleg. 8, l. 15.

16
Friendship is a union of spirits, a marriage of hearts, and the bond thereof virtue.
WILLIAM PENN, *Fruites of Solitude.* Pt. i.

There can be no Friendship where there is no *Freedom.* Friendship loves a *Free* Air, and will not be fenced up in straight and narrow Enclosures.
WILLIAM PENN, *Fruites of Solitude.* Pt. i.

The vital air of friendship is composed of confidence. Friendship perishes in proportion as this air diminishes.
JOSEPH ROUX, *Meditations of a Parish Priest.* Pt. ix, No. 3.

17
Nothing is meritorious but virtue and friendship, and, indeed, friendship is only a part of virtue.
ALEXANDER POPE, his last words. (JOHNSON, *Lives of the Poets: Pope.*)

18
Friendship is equality. (Φιλίαν ἰσότητα.)
PYTHAGORAS. (DIOGENES LAERTIUS, *Pythagoras.* Sec. 10.)

19
To desire the same things and to reject the same things, constitutes true friendship. (Idem velle atque idem nolle, ea demum firma amicitia est.)
SALLUST, *Catilina.* Ch. 20, sec. 4.

1
Ceremony was but devised at first
To set a gloss on faint deeds, hollow welcomes,
Recanting goodness, sorry ere 'tis shown;
But where there is true friendship, there
needs none.

SHAKESPEARE, *Timon of Athens*. Act i, sc. 2, l. 15.

Friendship should be surrounded with ceremonies and respects, and not crushed into corners. Friendship requires more time than poor, busy men can usually command.

EMERSON, *Conduct of Life: Behavior*.

Friendship cannot live with ceremony, nor without civility.

LORD HALIFAX, *Works*, p. 243.

2
Friendship is the bond of reason.

R. B. SHERIDAN, *The Duenna*. Act i, sc. 2.

3
Friendship's the privilege
Of private men; for wretched greatness
knows
No blessing so substantial.

NAHUM TATE, *The Loyal General*.

4
Some friendships are made by nature, some by contract, some by interest, and some by souls.

JEREMY TAYLOR, *A Discourse of the Nature, Measures, and Offices of Friendship*.

Nature and religion are the bands of friendship, excellence and usefulness are its great endearments.

JEREMY TAYLOR, *A Discourse of the Nature, Measures, and Offices of Friendship*.

5
Friendship is the marriage of the soul.

VOLTAIRE, *Philosophical Dictionary: Friendship*.

6
True friendship is of a royal lineage. It is of the same kith and breeding as loyalty and self-forgetting devotion and proceeds upon a higher principle even than they. For loyalty may be blind, and friendship must not be; devotion may sacrifice principles of right choice which friendship must guard with an excellent and watchful care. . . . The object of love is to serve, not to win.

WOODROW WILSON, *Baccalaureate Sermon*, Princeton, 9 May, 1907.

II—Friendship: Apothegms

7
Great souls by instinct to each other turn,
Demand alliance, and in friendship burn.

ADDISON, *The Campaign*, l. 101.

8
The bird a nest, the spider a web, man friendship.

WILLIAM BLAKE, *Proverbs of Hell*.

9
What a thing friendship is, world without
end!

ROBERT BROWNING, *The Flight of the Duchess*. Sec. 17.

10
Friendship is more than is catell.

CHAUCER, *The Romaunt of the Rose*, l. 5540.

11
The firmest friendships have been formed in mutual adversity, as iron is most strongly united by the fiercest flame.

C. C. COLTON, *Lacon*.

True friendship is like sound health, the value of it is seldom known until it be lost.

C. C. COLTON, *Lacon*.

12
We were the twins of friendship.

JOHN FLETCHER, *Wife for a Month*. Act v, 1.

13
A sudden thought strikes me,—let us swear an eternal friendship.

J. H. FRERE, *The Rovers*. Act i, sc. 1.

Madam, I have an inspiration! We will remain together!

GOETHE, *Stella*. Stella's paramour has shot himself in her presence and that of his wife, and makes the above remark to the latter. It is this scene which Frere parodies in *The Rovers*.

Let us embrace and from this moment vow an eternal misery together.

THOMAS OTWAY, *The Orphan*. Act iv, sc. 2.

My fair one, let us swear an eternal friendship.
(Entre lui, vous et moi, jurons, jurons, ma belle,
Une ardeur éternelle.)

MOLIÈRE, *Bourgeois Gentilhomme*. Act iv, sc. 1.

Madam, I have been looking for a person who disliked gravy all my life; let us swear eternal friendship.

SYDNEY SMITH. (LADY HOLLAND, *Memoir*, p. 257.)

14
Friendship is not to be bought at a fair.

THOMAS FULLER, *Gnomologia*. No. 1619.

15
Friendship closes its eye, rather than see the moon eclipst; while malice denies that it is ever at the full.

J. C. AND A. W. HARE, *Guesses at Truth*.

16
Sweet is the scene where genial friendship
plays
The pleasing game of interchanging praise.

O. W. HOLMES, *An After-Dinner Poem*.

17
If a man does not make new acquaintances, as he advances through life, he will soon find himself left alone. A man, Sir, should keep his friendship in constant repair.

SAMUEL JOHNSON. (BOSWELL, *Life*. 1755)

Keep your friendships in repair.

EMERSON, *Uncollected Lectures: Table-Talk*

18
The endearing elegance of female friendship.

SAMUEL JOHNSON, *Rasselas*. Ch. 46.

On firmer ties his joys depend
Who has a polished female friend!

CORNELIUS WHUR, *The Female Friend*.

1
Friendships renewed demand more care than those which have never been broken. (Les amitiés renouées demandent plus de soins que celles qui n'ont jamais été rompues.)

LA ROCHEFOUCAULD, *Maximes Posthumes,* 560.

2
The friendship between me and you I will not compare to a chain; for that the rains might rust, or the falling tree might break.

WILLIAM PENN, *Treaty With the Indians.* (BANCROFT, *History of the United States.*)

3
When did friendship take
A breed for barren metal of his friend?

SHAKESPEARE, *The Merchant of Venice.* Act i, sc. 3, l. 134.

If I do vow a friendship, I'll perform it
To the last article.

SHAKESPEARE, *Othello.* Act iii, sc. 1, l. 21.

4
No friendship can survive the gift of gold. The generous can indeed forget that they have given, but the grateful can never forget that they have received.

WILLIAM SMITH, *Thorndale.* Bk. ii, ch. 6.

5
Either friendship or death.

Babylonian Talmud: Taanith, p. 23a.

The virtue is no less to conserve friendship,gotten, than the wisdom was great to get and win the same.

WILLIAM PAINTER, *The Palace of Pleasure,* ii, 177. (1567)

6
Friendship is to be purchased only by friendship.

THOMAS WILSON, *Maxims of Piety,* p. 52.

III—Friendship: Its Virtues

7
The worst solitude is to have no true friendships.

FRANCIS BACON, *De Augmentis Scientiarum:* Pt. i, bk. 6, *Amicitia.*

8
Friendship can smooth the front of rude despair.

RICHARD CAMBRIDGE, *The Scribleraid.* Bk i, l. 196.

9
Friendship adds a brighter radiance to prosperity and lightens the burden of adversity by dividing and sharing it. (Nam et secundas res splendidiores facit amicitia, et adversas, partiens communicansque leviores.)

CICERO, *De Amicitia.* Ch. 6, sec. 22.

They seem to take the sun from the heavens who take friendship from life, for we receive from the immortal gods no better or more delightful boon. (Solem enim e mundo tollere videntur ei, qui amicitiam e vita tollunt, qua nihil a dis immortalibus melius habemus nihil jucundius.)

CICERO, *De Amicitia.* Ch. 13, sec. 47.

10
Complete unity of aim is the traditional condition of genuine and sincere friendship. (Neque est ullum certius amicitiæ vinculum quam consensus et societas consiliorum et voluntatum.)

CICERO, *Pro Cnæo Plancio.* Ch. ii, sec. 5.

11
There is a magic in the memory of schoolboy friendships; it softens the heart, and even affects the nervous system of those who have no heart.

BENJAMIN DISRAELI, *Endymion.* Ch. 52.

12
To friendship every burden's light.

JOHN GAY, *The Hare with Many Friends.*

13
A gen'rous friendship no cold medium knows,
Burns with one love, with one resentment glows;
One should our int'rests and our passions be:
My friend must hate the man that injures me.

HOMER, *Iliad.* Bk. ix, l. 725. (Pope, tr.)

14
Friendship, peculiar boon of Heav'n,
The noble mind's delight and pride,
To men and angels only giv'n,
To all the lower world denied.

SAMUEL JOHNSON, *Friendship: An Ode.*

15
Pure friendship is something which men of an inferior intellect can never taste.

LA BRUYÈRE, *Les Caractères.* Ch. 5.

16
Life is to be fortified by many friendships. To love, and to be loved, is the greatest happiness of existence.

SYDNEY SMITH. (LADY HOLLAND, *Memoir: Of Friendship.* Vol. i, ch. 6, p. 122.)

IV—Friendship: Its Faults

17
The friendships of the world are oft
Confederacies in vice, or leagues of pleasure.

ADDISON, *Cato.* Act iii, sc. 1.

18
The most fatal disease of friendship is gradual decay, or dislike hourly increased by causes too slender for complaint, and too numerous for removal.

SAMUEL JOHNSON, *The Idler.* No. 23.

The great effect of friendship is beneficence, yet by the first act of uncommon kindness it is endangered, like plants that bear their fruit and die.

SAMUEL JOHNSON, *The Rambler.* No. 64.

19
Safe and frequented is the path of deceit under the name of friendship. (Tuta frequensque via est per amici fallere nomen.)

OVID, *Ars Amatoria.* Bk. i, l. 585.

20
Friendship is but a name. (Nomen amicitia est.)

OVID, *Ars Amatoria.* Bk. i, l. 740.

Friendship, like love, is but a name,
Unless to one you stint the flame.
The child, whom many fathers share,
Hath seldom known a father's care.

'Tis thus in friendships; who depend
On many, rarely find a friend.
JOHN GAY, *The Hare with Many Friends.*

And what is friendship but a name,
A charm that lulls to sleep;
A shade that follows wealth or fame,
But leaves the wretch to weep?
GOLDSMITH, *A Ballad.* (*Vicar of Wakefield.* Ch. 8.)

Friendship's an empty name, made to deceive
Those whose good nature tempts them to believe:
There's no such thing on earth; the best that we
Can hope for here is faint neutrality.
SAMUEL TUKE, *Adventures of Five Hours.* Act v, sc. 3. (An adaptation from Calderon.)

Friendship is but a word.
PHILIP MASSINGER, *A New Way to Pay Old Debts.* Act ii, sc. 1.

1
The name of friend is common, but faith in friendship is rare. (Vulgare amici nomen, sed rara est fides.)
PHÆDRUS, *Fables.* Bk. iii, fab. 9, l. 1.

2
What ill-starr'd rage
Divides a friendship long confirm'd by age?
POPE, *The Dunciad.* Bk. iii, l. 173.

3
Friendship's full of dregs.
SHAKESPEARE, *Timon of Athens.* Act i, sc. 2, l. 240.

4
Trust not before you try,
For under cloak of great good-will
Doth feignèd friendship lie.
GEORGE TURBERVILLE, *Of Light Belief,* l. 1.

V—Friendship: Friendship and Love

5
In love one has need of being believed, in friendship of being understood.
ABEL BONNARD, *The Art of Friendship.* Pt. ii.

Love can die of a truth, as friendship of a lie.
ABEL BONNARD, *The Art of Friendship.* Pt. ii.

6
Yet I will but say what mere friends say,
Or only a thought stronger;
I will hold your hand just as long as all may,
Or so very little longer!
ROBERT BROWNING, *The Lost Mistress.*

No protesting, dearest!
Hardly kisses even!
Don't we both know how it ends?
How the greenest leaf turns serest,
Bluest outbreak—blankest heaven,
Lovers—friends?
ROBERT BROWNING, *St. Martin's Summer.*

One should master one's passions, (love. in chief)
And be loyal to one's friends.
ROBERT BROWNING, *A Light Woman.*

7
Love is only chatter,
Friends are all that matter.
GELETT BURGESS, *Willy and the Lady.*

8
Friendship is Love without his wings.
BYRON, *L'Amitié est l'Amour Sans Ailes.* The line is a translation of the title, which is a familiar French proverb.

If Cupid has wings, is it not that he may flutter hither and thither? (Si l'amour porte des ailes N'est-ce pas pour voltiger?)
BEAUMARCHAIS, *Mariage de Figaro.*

9
Friendship's a noble name, 'tis love refined.
SUSANNAH CENTLIVRE, *The Stolen Heiress,* ii, 2.

10
Friendship often ends in love; but love, in friendship—never.
C. C. COLTON, *Lacon.*

11
To be capable of steady friendship and lasting love, are the two greatest proofs, not only of goodness of heart, but of strength of mind.
WILLIAM HAZLITT, *Characteristics.* No. 235.

12
But love is lost; the art of friendship's gone;
Though David had his Jonathan, Christ his John.
GEORGE HERBERT, *The Church-Porch.* St. 46.

13
Love seeks a guerdon; friendship is as God,
Who gives and asks no payment.
RICHARD HOVEY, *The Marriage of Guenevere.* Act i, sc. 1.

14
It is a rule in friendship, when Distrust enters in at the foregate, Love goes out at the postern.
HOWELL, *Familiar Letters: To Dr. H. W.*

15
Friendship, like love, is destroyed by long absence, though it may be increased by short intermissions.
SAMUEL JOHNSON, *The Idler,* No. 23.

Time, which strengthens Friendship, weakens Love.
LA BRUYÈRE, *Les Caractères.* Ch. 4.

16
The feeling of friendship is like that of being comfortably filled with roast beef; love, like being enlivened with champagne.
SAMUEL JOHNSON, (BOSWELL, *Life,* 1775.)

17
Love and friendship exclude each other.
LA BRUYÈRE, *Les Caractères.* Ch. 5.

In Friendship we only see those faults which may be prejudicial to our friends. In love we see no faults but those by which we suffer ourselves.
LA BRUYÈRE, *Les Caractères.* Ch. 5.

18
However rare true love may be, it is still less rare than true friendship. (Quelque rare que soit le véritable amour, il l'est encore moins que la véritable amitié.)
LA ROCHEFOUCAULD, *Maximes.* No. 473.

19
A friendship that like love is warm;
A love like friendship, steady.
THOMAS MOORE, *How Shall I Woo?*

Oh call it by some better name,
  For friendship sounds too cold.
  THOMAS MOORE, *Oh Call It by Some Better Name.*

1
May the hinges of friendship never rust, or the wings of luve lose a feather.
  DEAN EDWARD BANNERMAN RAMSEY, *Reminiscences of Scottish Life: A Toast.*

2
Friendship is a prodigal, but love is a miser. (L'amitié est prodigue, mais l'amour est avare.)
  ROUSSEAU, *Julie.* Pt. vi, letter 14.

3
What is love? two souls and one flesh; friendship? two bodies and one soul.
  JOSEPH ROUX, *Meditations of a Parish Priest.* Pt. ix, No. 31.

4
He who is a friend, loves; he who loves is not therefore always a friend. So friendship profits always, but love sometimes is hurtful.
  SENECA, *Epistulæ ad Lucilium.* Epis. xxxv.

5
Most friendship is feigning, most loving mere
  folly.
  SHAKESPEARE, *As You Like It.* Act ii, sc. 7, l. 181.

6
Friendship is constant in all other things,
Save in the office and affairs of love.
  SHAKESPEARE, *Much Ado About Nothing.* Act ii, sc. 1, l. 182.

7
But, if at first her virgin fear
  Should start at love's suspected name,
With that of friendship soothe her ear—
  True love and friendship are the same.
  JAMES THOMSON, *Song: Hard Is the Fate.*

When Psyche's friend becomes her lover,
  How sweetly these conditions blend!
But, oh, what anguish to discover
  Her lover has become—her friend!
  MARY AINGE DE VERE, *Friend and Lover.*

8
Friendship, take heed; if woman interfere,
Be sure the hour of thy destruction's near.
  SIR JOHN VANBRUGH. (FIELDING, *Amelia.*)

When love puts in, friendship is gone.
  FLETCHER AND MASSINGER, *The Lovers' Progress.* Act i, sc. 1. Qouted as a proverb.

A friend married is a friend lost.
  HENRIK IBSEN, *Love's Comedy.* Act ii. (Quoted as proverb.)

FROG

9
Though boys throw stones at frogs in sport, the frogs do not die in sport, but in earnest.
  BION. (PLUTARCH, *Water and Land Animals.* Sec. 7.)

Though this be play to you, 'Tis death to us.
  ROGER L'ESTRANGE, *The Boys and the Frog.*

10
Can these, indeed, be voices, that so greet
  The twilight still? I seem to hear
Oboe and cymbal in a rhythmic beat
  With bass-drum and bassoon; their drear
  And droll crescendo louder growing,
  Then falling back, like waters ebbing, flowing,—
Back to the silence sweet!
  FLORENCE EARLE COATES, *The Frogs.*

11
Can I unmoved see thee dying
  On a log, expiring frog?
  DICKENS, *The Pickwick Papers.* Ch. xv.

12
There are not frogs wherever there is water; but wherever there are frogs, water will be found.
  GOETHE, *Sprüche in Prosa.*

13
The frog's own croak betrays him.
  W. G. BENHAM, *Proverbs,* p. 845.

14
I don't see no p'ints about that frog that's any better'n any other frog.
  MARK TWAIN, *The Celebrated Jumping Frog.*

FROST

15
These Winter nights against my window-pane
  Nature with busy pencil draws designs
Of ferns and blossoms and fine spray of pines,
  Oak-leaf and acorn and fantastic vines.
  T. B. ALDRICH, *Frost-Work.*

He went to the windows of those who slept,
And over each pane, like a fairy, crept;
Wherever he breathed, wherever he stepped,
  By the light of the morn, were seen
Most beautiful things; there were flowers and trees;
There were bevies of birds, and swarms of bees;
There were cities, with temples and towers; and these
  All pictured in silver sheen!
  HANNAH FLAGG GOULD, *The Frost.*

16
Frost and fraud have always foul ends.
  WILLIAM CAMDEN, *Remains,* p. 322. (1605)

Frost and fraud have dirty ends.
  WILLIAM GURNALL, *Christian in Complete Armour.* Pt. ii, ch. 17. (1657)

17
The frost performs its secret ministry,
Unhelped by any wind.
  S. T. COLERIDGE, *Frost at Midnight,* l. 1.

18
The frost which kills the harvest of a year, saves the harvests of a century, by destroying the weevil or the locust.
  EMERSON, *Conduct of Life: Considerations by the Way.*

19
On a lone winter evening, when the frost
Has wrought a silence.
  KEATS, *On the Grasshopper and Cricket.*

20
    An envious sneaping frost,

That bites the first-born infants of the spring.
SHAKESPEARE, *Love's Labour's Lost*. Act i, sc. 1, l. 100.

Hoary-headed frosts
Fall in the fresh lap of the crimson rose.
SHAKESPEARE, *A Midsummer-Night's Dream*. Act ii, sc. 1, l. 107.

The earth, When it is baked with frost.
SHAKESPEARE, *The Tempest*. Act i, sc, 2, l. 256.

1
Fine as ice-ferns on January panes
Made by a breath.
TENNYSON, *Aylmer's Field*, l. 222.

2
What miracle of weird transforming
Is this wild work of frost and light,
This glimpse of glory infinite?
WHITTIER, *The Pageant*. St. 8.

FRUGALITY, see Economy

FRUIT

3
Fruit is gold in the morning, silver in the afternoon and lead at night.
BISHOP SHUTE BARRINGTON, *Rules of Health*. (*See Notes and Queries*. Ser. x, i, 251.) *See also under* APPLE.

4
The kindly fruits of the earth.
Book of Common Prayer: Prayer for All Conditions of Men.

5
We cannot eat the fruit while the tree is in blossom.
BENJAMIN DISRAELI, *Alroy*. Ch. 4.

6
Fruit out of season, sorrow out of reason.
HENRY FRIEND, *Flowers and Fruit Lore*, 207.

7
He that would have the fruit must climb the tree.
THOMAS FULLER, *Gnomologia*. No. 2366.

Who will the fruit that harvest yields, must take the pain.
JOHN GRANGE, *Golden Aphroditis*. Sig. M1. (1577)

8
There is greater relish for the earliest fruit of the season.
MARTIAL, *Epigrams*. Bk. iv, epig. 29, l. 4.

What beautiful fruit! I love fruit, when it is expensive.
PINERO, *The Second Mrs. Tanqueray*. Act i.

9
You should go to a pear-tree for pears, not to an elm.
PUBLILIUS SYRUS, *Sententiæ*. No. 674.

He who hopes this, would hope
To gather apples from the tamarisk,
And search for honey in the flowing stream.
OVID, *Ars Amatoria*. Bk. i, l. 747.

You may as well expect pears from an elm.
CERVANTES, *Don Quixote*. Pt. ii, ch. 40.

10
Much bruit, little fruit. (Beaucoup de bruit, peu de fruit.)
JOHN RAY, *English Proverbs*.

11
Fruit unripe, sticks on the tree;
But fall, unshaken, when they mellow be.
SHAKESPEARE, *Hamlet*. Act iii, sc. 2, l. 200.

The weakest kind of fruit
Drops earliest to the ground.
SHAKESPEARE, *The Merchant of Venice*. Act iv, sc. 1, l. 115.

Fruits that blossom first will first be ripe.
SHAKESPEARE, *Othello*. Act iii, sc. 3, l. 383.

The ripest fruit first falls.
SHAKESPEARE, *Richard II*. Act ii, sc. 1, l. 153.

12
Before thee stands this fair Hesperides,
With golden fruit, but dangerous to be touched.
SHAKESPEARE, *Pericles*. Act i, sc. 1, l. 27.

13
Superfluous branches
We lop away, that bearing boughs may live.
SHAKESPEARE, *Richard II*. Act iii, sc. 4, l. 63.

When swelling buds their od'rous foliage shed,
And gently harden into fruit, the wise
Spare not the little offsprings, if they grow
Redundant.
JOHN PHILIPS, *Cider*. Bk. i.

14
Fair fruit in an unwholesome dish
Are like to rot untasted.
SHAKESPEARE, *Troilus and Cressida*. Act ii, sc. 3, l. 129.

15
A little fruit a little while is ours,
And the worm finds it soon.
SWINBURNE, *Atalanta in Calydon: Chorus*.

FUNERAL

16
The care of funeral, the manner of burial, the pomp of obsequies, are rather a consolation to the living than of any service to the dead.
ST. AUGUSTINE, *Civitas Dei*. Bk. i, sec. 12.

Funeral pomp is more for the vanity of the living than for the honor of the dead. (La pompe des enterrements regarde plus la vanité des vivants que l'honneur des morts.)
LA ROCHEFOUCAULD, *Maximes Supprimées*. No. 612.

Why is the hearse with scutcheons blazon'd round,
And with the nodding plume of ostrich crown'd?
No; the dead know it not, nor profit gain;
It only serves to prove the living vain.
JOHN GAY, *Trivia*. Bk. iii, l. 231.

17
Ye undertakers! tell us,
'Midst all the gorgeous figures you exhibit,
Why is the principal conceal'd, for which
You make this mighty stir?
ROBERT BLAIR, *The Grave*, l. 171.

18
Of all The fools who flocked to swell or see the show,

Who cared about the corpse? The funeral
Made the attraction, and the black the woe.
BYRON, *The Vision of Judgment*. St. 10.

1
As grand
And griefless as a rich man's funeral.
SIDNEY DOBELL, *A Musing on a Victory*.

2
I've a great fancy to see my own funeral afore I die.
MARIA EDGEWORTH, *Castle Rackrent: Continuation of Memoirs*.

3
Worldly faces never look so worldly as at a funeral.
GEORGE ELIOT, *Janet's Repentance*.

If a man will observe as he walks the streets, I believe he will find the merriest countenances in mourning-coaches.
JONATHAN SWIFT, *Works*. Vol. iii, p. 400.

For sometimes they contain a deal of fun,
Like mourning coaches when the funeral's done.
BYRON, *Beppo*. St. 20. Referring to gondolas.

4
When this solemn mockery is o'er.
W. H. IRELAND, *Vortigern*. Act iii.

What tho' no friends in sable weeds appear,
Grieve for an hour, perhaps, then mourn a year,
And bear about the mockery of woe
To midnight dances, and the public show?
POPE, *Elegy to the Memory of an Unfortunate Lady*, l. 55.

5
What men prize most is a privilege, even if it be that of chief mourner at a funeral.
J. R. LOWELL, *Democracy*.

6
There's a grim one-horse hearse in a jolly round trot;
To the churchyard a pauper is going I wot;
The road it is rough, and the hearse has no springs,
And hark to the dirge that the sad driver sings—
Rattle his bones over the stones,
He's only a pauper whom nobody owns.
THOMAS NOEL, *The Pauper's Drive*.

7
Run, someone, and fetch the undertaker. (Ecquis currit pollictorem accersere.)
PLAUTUS, *Asinaria*, l. 910. (Act v, sc. 2.)

Let me be his undertaker.
SHAKESPEARE, *Othello*. Act iv, sc. 1, l. 223.

Nay, if you be an undertaker, I am for you.
SHAKESPEARE, *Twelfth Night*. Act iii, sc. 4, 350.

8
After a funeral, a feast.
W. G. BENHAM, *Proverbs*, p. 731.

After a funeral, one drinks. (Après tout deuil, boit on.)
UNKNOWN. A French proverb.

The funeral baked meats
Did coldly furnish forth the marriage tables.
SHAKESPEARE, *Hamlet*. Act i, sc. 2, l. 180.

9
His obscure funeral,
No trophy, sword, nor hatchment o'er his bones,
No noble rite, nor formal ostentation.
SHAKESPEARE, *Hamlet*. Act iv, sc. 5, l. 213.

10
All things that we ordained festival,
Turn from their office to black funeral;
Our instruments to melancholy bells,
Our wedding cheer to a sad burial feast.
SHAKESPEARE, *Romeo and Juliet*, iv, 5, 84.

Hung be the heavens with black, yield day to night!
SHAKESPEARE, *I Henry VI*. Act i, sc. 1, l. 1.

11
But safer triumph is this funeral pomp,
That hath aspired to Solon's happiness
And triumphs over chance in honour's bed.
SHAKESPEARE, *Titus Andronicus*. Act i, sc. 1, 176.

12
We should have shone at a wake, but not at anything more festive.
MARK TWAIN, *The Innocents Abroad*. Ch. 2.

13
Fair youth, do you know what I'd do with you if you was my sun?—No, sez he —Wall, sez I, I'd appint your funeral to-morrow arternoon & the *korps should be ready!*
ARTEMUS WARD, *Artemus Ward, His Book: Edwin Forrest as Othello*.

14
When we attend a funeral, we are apt to comfort ourselves with the happy difference that is betwixt us and our dead friend.
THOMAS WILSON, *Maxims of Piety*. No. 34.

15
There was a young fellow of Clyde
Who went to a funeral and cried;
When they asked who was dead,
He stammered and said,
"I don't know—I just came for the ride."
UNKNOWN, *The Young Fellow of Clyde*.

FUTILITY

16
To attack windmills. (Acometer molinos de viento.)
CERVANTES, *Don Quixote*. Bk. i, ch. 8.

To go into the water and grasp the foam. (Lo shui 'chin shui pao.)
UNKNOWN. A Chinese proverb.

17
With Sisyphus thus do I roll the stone,
And turn the wheel with damnèd Ixion.
MICHAEL DRAYTON, *Idea*. Sonnet xl.

With useless endeavor,
Forever, forever,
Is Sisyphus rolling
His stone up the mountain!
LONGFELLOW, *The Masque of Pandora*. Pt. v.

18
It's but little good you'll do a-watering the last year's crop.
GEORGE ELIOT, *Adam Bede*. Ch. 18.

1
For none upon earth can achieve his scheme;
The best as the worst are futile here.
VICTOR HUGO, *Early Love Revisited.*

Inscribe all human effort with one word,
Artistry's haunting curse, the Incomplete!
ROBERT BROWNING, *The Ring and the Book.* Canto xi, l. 1560.

2
Still we persist; plough the light sand, and sow
Seed after seed, where none can ever grow.
(Nos tamen hoc agimus tenuique in pulvere sulcos
Ducimus et litus sterili versamus arato.)
JUVENAL, *Satires.* Sat. vii, l. 48. (Gifford, tr.)

You may boldly say, you did not plough,
Or trust the barren and ungrateful sands
With the fruitful grain of your religious counsels.
MASSINGER, *The Renegado.* Act iv, sc. 3.

Plough the sands. (Arenas arantes.)
HERBERT ASQUITH, *Speech,* 21 Nov., 1894.
See also WOMAN: HER INCONSTANCY.

3
Lyke Saint George, who is ever on horse backe yet never rideth.
JOHN LYLY, *Euphues.* Pt. ii, p. 260.

He is like St. George on the signs, always on horseback and never rides on.
BENJAMIN FRANKLIN, *Autobiography.*

Saint George, that swinged the dragon, and e'er since
Sits on his horse back at mine hostess' door.
SHAKESPEARE, *King John.* Act ii, sc. 1, l. 288.

4
Out of breath to no purpose, in doing much doing nothing. (Gratis anhelans, multa agendo nihil agens.)
PHÆDRUS, *Fables.* Bk. ii, fab. 5, l. 3.

5
You are wounding a Hydra. ("Ὕδραν τέμνεις.)
PLATO, *The Republic.* Sec. 426. The Hydra produced two heads for every one cut off.

'Tis a hydra's head contention; the more they strive the more they may: and as Praxiteles did by his glass, when he saw a scurvy face in it, brake it in pieces; but for that one he saw many more as bad in a moment.
ROBERT BURTON, *Anatomy of Melancholy.* Pt. ii, sec. iii, mem. 7.

6
That's a perilous shot out of an elder-gun.
SHAKESPEARE, *Henry V.* Act iv, sc. 1, l. 211.

7
He has spent all his life in letting down buckets into empty wells; and he is frittering away his age in trying to draw them up again.
SYDNEY SMITH. (LADY HOLLAND, *Memoir.* Vol. i, p. 259.)

Defend me, therefore, common sense, say I,
From reveries so airy, from the toil
Of dropping buckets into empty wells,
And growing old in drawing nothing up!
COWPER, *The Task.* Bk. iii, l. 187.

To climb life's worn, heavy wheel
Which draws up nothing new.
YOUNG, *Night Thoughts.* Night iii, l. 331.

8
But what am I?
An infant crying in the night:
An infant crying for the light,
And with no language but a cry.
TENNYSON, *In Memoriam.* Pt. liv, st. 5.

9
To wash bricks: to waste your labor. (Laterem lavem.)
TERENCE, *Phormio,* l. 87. (Act i, sc. 4.)

10
Great cry and little wool, as the Devil said when he sheared the hogs.
UNKNOWN, *David and Abigail.*

Thou wilt at best but suck a bull,
Or shear swine, all cry and no wool.
BUTLER, *Hudibras.* Pt. i, canto i, l. 851.

FUTURE

See also Past and Future; Present and Future; To-morrow

11
I never think of the future. It comes soon enough.
ALBERT EINSTEIN, *Interview,* on *Belgenland,* Dec., 1930.

12
When I am dead, let the earth be dissolved in fire. (Ἐμοῦ θανόντος γαῖα μειχθήτω πυρί.)
EURIPIDES, *Bellerophon.* Frag. 27. Put by Dio (58, 23) into the mouth of Tiberius. Quoted by Suetonius (*Twelve Cæsars: Nero,* 38, 1), who says that Nero rejoined, "Nay, rather while I live" (Ἐμου ζῶντος.)

After us the deluge. (Après nous le déluge.)
MADAME DE POMPADOUR, after the battle of Rossbach. (LAROUSSE, *Fleurs Historiques.* MADAME DE HAUSSET, *Mémoires,* p. 19.) This saying, an old French proverb, has also been attributed to Louis XV.

13
Remember this also, and be well persuaded of its truth: the future is not in the hands of Fate, but in ours.
JULES JUSSERAND, *Farewell Radio Talk to America,* 10 April, 1932.

14
We fight and die, but our hopes beat high,
In spite of the toil and tears,
For we catch the gleam of our vanished dream
Down the path of the untrod years.
WILMA KATE MCFARLAND, *The Untrod Years.*

15
The future is a world limited by ourselves; in it we discover only what concerns us and, sometimes, by chance, what interests those whom we love the most.
MAURICE MAETERLINCK, *Joyzelle.* Act i.

16
The never-ending flight Of future days.
MILTON, *Paradise Lost.* Bk. ii, l. 221.

17
The wise man guards against the future as

if it were the present. (Quod est venturum, sapiens quasi præsens cavet.)
PUBLILIUS SYRUS, *Sententiæ*. No. 615.

1
Fear of the future is worse than one's present fortune. (Præsente fortuna pejor est futuri metus.)
QUINTILIAN, *De Institutione Oratoria*. Bk. xii, sec. 5. *See also* TROUBLE: NEVER TROUBLE TROUBLE.

2
No one has any right to draw for himself upon the future. (Nihil sibi quisquam de futuro debet promittere.)
SENECA, *Epistulæ ad Lucilium*. Epis. ci, sec. 5.

He is only anxious about the future to whom the present is unprofitable. (Ille enim ex futuro suspenditur, cui inritum est præsens.)
SENECA, *Epistulæ ad Lucilium*. Epis. ci, sec. 9.

3
How many ages hence
Shall this our lofty scene be acted over
In states unborn and accents yet unknown!
SHAKESPEARE, *Julius Cæsar*. Act iii, sc. 1, l. 111.

4
Leave hereafter to the spirit and the wisdom of hereafter.
SYDNEY SMITH, *Peter Plymley Letters*. No. 2.

5
I dipt into the future far as human eye could see,
Saw the vision of the world and all the wonder that would be.
TENNYSON, *Locksley Hall*, l. 15.

6
We see by the glad light
And breathe the sweet air of futurity,
And so we live, or else we have no life.
WORDSWORTH, *The Excursion*. Bk. ix, l. 24.

To whom in vision clear
The aspiring heads of future things appear,
Like mountain-tops whose mists have rolled away.
WORDSWORTH, *Poems Dedicated to National Independence*. No. 43.

II—Future: Knowledge of the Future

7
For my part, I think that a knowledge of the future would be a disadvantage. (Atque ego ne utilem quidem arbitror esse nobis futuram rerum scientiam.)
CICERO, *De Divinatione*. Bk. ii, ch. 9, sec. 22.

Undoubtedly ignorance of future ills is more useful than knowledge of them. (Certe ignoratio futurorum malorum utilior est quam scientia.)
CICERO, *De Divinatione*. Bk. ii, ch. 9, sec. 23.

Seek not to know what must not be reveal'd;
Joys only flow where Fate is most conceal'd.
Too-busy man would find his sorrows more
If future fortunes he should know before;
For by that knowledge of his Destiny
He would not live at all, but always die.
DRYDEN, *The Indian Queen*. Act iii, sc. 2.

8
No means of predicting the future really exists, and if it did, we must regard what happens according to it as nothing to us.
EPICURUS. (DIOGENES LAERTIUS, *Epicurus*. Bk. x, sec. 135.)

No man can tell what the future may bring forth.
DEMOSTHENES, *Ad Leptinem*. Sec. 162.

What the evening may bring forth is uncertain. (Quid vesper ferat incertum est.)
LIVY, *History*. Bk. xlv, sec. 8.

The wise god covers with the darkness of night the issues of the future. (Prudens futuri temporis exitum, Caliginosa nocte premit Deus.)
HORACE, *Odes*. Bk. iii, ode 29, l. 30.

9
The mind of man is ignorant of fate, or of coming doom.
VERGIL, *Æneid*. Bk. x, l. 501.

10
Cease to inquire what the future has in store, and take as a gift whatever the day brings forth. (Quid sit futurum cras, fuge quærere: et Quem Fors dierum cumque dabit, lucro Appone.)
HORACE, *Odes*. Bk. i, ode 9, l. 13.

11
Oh, bless the law that veils the Future's face;
For who could smile into a baby's eyes,
Or bear the beauty of the evening skies,
If he could see what cometh on apace?
EUGENE LEE-HAMILTON, *Mimma Bella*.

12
Let the mind of man be blind as to future destiny. (Sit cæca futuri Mens hominum fati.)
LUCAN, *De Bello Civili*. Bk. ii, l. 14.

13
Heav'n from all creatures hides the Book of Fate,
All but the page prescribed, their present state:
From brutes what men, from men what spirits know;
Or who could suffer being here below?
POPE, *Essay on Man*. Epis. i, l. 77.

O blindness to the future! kindly giv'n,
That each may fill the circle mark'd by Heav'n;
Who sees with equal eye, as God of all,
A hero perish or a sparrow fall,
Atoms or systems into ruin hurl'd,
And now a bubble burst, and now a world.
POPE, *Essay on Man*. Epis. i, l. 85.

Not present good or ill the joy or curse,
But future views of better or of worse.
POPE, *Essay on Man*. Epis. iv, l. 71.

14
Out of our reach the gods have laid
Of time to come th' event,
And laugh to see the fools afraid
Of what the knaves invent.
SIR CHARLES SEDLEY, *Imitation of Lycophron*.

G

GAIETY, see Merriment, Mirth

GAIN

I—Gain: Apothegms

1
Light gains make heavy purses.
FRANCIS BACON, *Essays: Of Ceremonies and Respects;* GEORGE CHAPMAN, *Eastward Hoe.* Act i, sc. 1.

Lightly come, lightly go.
UNKNOWN, *Times Whistle,* l. 2828. (1614)

As extravagance and good luck, by long custom, go hand-in-hand, he spent as fast as he acquired.
FANNY BURNEY, *Camilla.* Bk. v, ch. 13.

2
He gains enough that misses an ill turn. (Assez gaigne qui malheur perd.)
COTGRAVE, *French-English Dictionary.* (1611)

3
No man should so act as to make a gain out of the ignorance of another. (Neminem id agere, ut ex alterius prædetur inscitia.)
CICERO, *De Officiis.* Bk. iii, ch. 17, sec. 72.

4
Some men make gain a fountain, whence proceeds
A stream of liberal and heroic deeds.
COWPER, *Charity,* l. 244.

5
To do nothing and get something formed a boy's ideal of a manly career.
BENJAMIN DISRAELI, *Sybil.* Bk. i, ch. 5. Hence, "Something for nothing."

6
A captive fetter'd to the oar of gain.
WILLIAM FALCONER, *The Shipwreck.* Canto i, sec. 1, l. 99.

A toiling man Intent on worldly gains.
ROBERT SOUTHEY, *Joan of Arc.* Bk. i, l. 199.

7
Remote from cities lived a swain,
Unvex'd with all the cares of gain.
JOHN GAY, *Fables.* Pt. i, No. 14.

8
He grows old with the love of gain. (Amore senescit habendi.)
HORACE, *Epistles.* Bk. i, epis. 7, l. 85.

9
Make no distinction between hides and unguents: good is the smell of gain from whatever source. (Neu credas ponendum aliquid discriminis inter Unguenta et corium; lucri bonus est odor ex re Qualibet.)
JUVENAL, *Satires.* Sat. xiv, l. 203. *See also* MONEY: MAKING MONEY.

10
Counts his sure gains, and hurries back for more.
MONTGOMERY, *The West Indies.* Pt. iii.

11
They struggle to gain in order that they may spend, and then to re-gain what they have spent. (Quærere, ut absumant, absumpta requirere certant.)
OVID, *Fasti.* Bk. i, l. 213.

To gain teacheth how to spend.
GEORGE HERBERT, *Jacula Prudentum.*

12
Nor do I esteem all gain useful to man. (Non ego omnino lucrum omne esse utile homini existimo.)
PLAUTUS, *Captivi,* l. 325. (Act ii, sc. 2.)

13
No gain is possible without attendant outlay, but there will be no profit if the outlay exceeds the receipts. (Non enim potis est quæstus fieri, ni sumptus sequitur, scio, Et tamen quæstus non consistet, si eum sumptus superat.)
PLAUTUS, *Pœnulus,* l. 286. (Act i, sc. 2.)

No gain without pain.
LEONARD WRIGHT, *Display of Dutie,* 4. (1589)

Little pains
In a due hour employ'd great profit yields.
JOHN PHILIPS, *Cider.* Bk. i, l. 126.

You have deeply ventured;
But all must do so who would greatly win.
BYRON, *Marino Faliero.* Act i, sc. 2.

See also under GAMBLING.

14
Every way makes my gain.
SHAKESPEARE, *Othello.* Act v, sc. 1, l. 14.

Despair to gain doth traffic oft for gaining.
SHAKESPEARE, *The Rape of Lucrece.* St. 19.

15
Desire of gain, the basest mind's delight.
"A. W.," *Sonnet I.* (DAVISON'S *Rhapsody.*)

16
Better it is to have more of profit and less honour.
UNKNOWN, *Melusine.* Ch. 34. (c. 1385)

Honour and profit lie not all in one sack.
GEORGE HERBERT, *Jacula Prudentum.*

No one was ever ruined by taking a profit.
UNKNOWN. A maxim of the stock exchange.

II—Gain: Ill-Gotten

17
Of good ill got The third heir joyeth not.
JOSEPH BURROUGHS, *Sermons: On Hosea.*

18
Prefer a loss to a dishonest gain: the one brings pain at the moment, the other for all time.
CHILON. (DIOGENES LAERTIUS, *Chilon.* Sec. 3.)

19
Ill gotten gains will be ill spent. (Mala parta, male dilabuntur.)
CICERO, *Philippicæ.* No. ii, sec. 27. Quoted.

Ill gotten is ill spent. (Male partum, male disperit.)
PLAUTUS, *Pœnulus,* l. 844. (Act iv, sc. 2.)

And that with guile was got, ungraciously be dispended.

WILLIAM LANGLAND, *Piers Plowman*. Passus xvii, l. 278. (1392)

Evil gotten goods are evil spent, said our curate upon Sunday.

WILLIAM BULLEIN, *A Dialogue Against the Fever Pestilence*. (1564)

1

Ill-gotten gain brings loss. (Κέρδη πονηρὰ ζημίαν ἠμείψατο.)

EURIPIDES, *The Cyclops*, l. 312.

Gain not evil gains; evil gains are the same as losses. (Μὴ κακὰ κερδαίνειν· κακὰ κέρδεα ἶσ' ἀάτῃσιν.)

HESIOD, *Works and Days*, l. 353.

An evil gain equals a loss. (Lucrum malum æquale dispendio.)

PUBLILIUS SYRUS, *Sententiæ*. No. 343.

2

Evil gain does not bring good luck. (Non habet eventus sordida præda bonos.)

OVID, *Amores*. Bk. i, eleg. 10, l. 48.

Ill gotten goods seldom prosper.

JOHN RAY, *English Proverbs*.

But, Clifford, tell me, didst thou never hear
That things ill-got had ever bad success?

SHAKESPEARE, *III Henry VI*. Act ii, sc. 2, l. 45.

3

Ill-gotten gains work evil. (Τὰ δειλὰ κέρδη πημονὰς ἐργάζεται.)

SOPHOCLES, *Antigone*, l. 326.

4

III—Gain and Loss

Whatsoever is somewhere gotten, is somewhere lost.

BACON, *Essays: Of Seditions and Troubles*.

What's lost upon the roundabouts we pulls up on the swings.

PATRICK CHALMERS, *Roundabouts and Swings*.

5

"God bless all our gains," say we;
But "May God bless all our losses,"
Better suits with our degree.

E. B. BROWNING, *The Lost Bower*. St. 1.

6

What I lost i' th' salt fish I gained i' th' red herrings.

JOHN CLARKE, *Paræmiologia*, 17. (1639)

7

I laugh not at another's loss;
I grudge not at another's gain.

SIR EDWARD DYER, *My Mind to Me a Kingdom Is*.

8

The loss will be outweighed by the greatness of your gain. (Esse solent magno damna minora bono.)

OVID, *Remediorum Amoris*, l. 672. Ovid is counselling the lover to permit the discarded mistress to retain his gifts.

9

There are times when it is undoubtedly better to incur loss than to make gain. (Est etiam ubi profecto damnum præstet facere quam lucrum.)

PLAUTUS, *Captivi*, l. 327. (Act ii, sc. 2.)

I would rather have lost honorably than gained basely. (Perdidisse honeste mallem quam accepisse turpiter.)

PUBLILIUS SYRUS, *Sententiæ*. No. 518.

10

To gain without another's loss is impossible. (Lucrum sine damno alterius fieri non potest.)

PUBLILIUS SYRUS, *Sententiæ*. No. 330.

11

Who loses and who wins; who's in, who's out.

SHAKESPEARE, *King Lear*. Act v, sc. 3, l. 15.

12

And all through life I see a cross
Where sons of God yield up their breath;
There is no gain except by loss;
There is no life except by death.

WALTER C. SMITH, *Otrig Grange*.

13

I have lost, you have won this hazard: yet perchance
My loss may shine yet goodlier than your gain,
When time and God give judgment.

SWINBURNE, *Marino Faliero*. Act v, sc. 2.

14

If it wasn't we had been robbed, dashed if I'd care a rap about losing that money. . . . I reely b'lieve, Ann, it'll prove a savin' in the end.

H. G. WELLS, *Kipps*. Bk. ii, ch. 3, sec. 3.

15

Then with the losers let it sympathise,
For nothing can seem foul to those that win.

SHAKESPEARE, *I Henry IV*. Act v, sc. 1, l. 7.

GAMBLING

See also Cards, Chance

I—Gambling: Apothegms

16

Gaming is a principle inherent in human nature.

EDMUND BURKE, *Speech*, House of Commons, 11 Feb., 1780.

Man is a gaming animal.

CHARLES LAMB, *Essays of Elia: Mrs. Battle's Opinions on Whist*.

Gambling is a disease of barbarians superficially civilized.

DEAN W. R. INGE. (MARCHANT, *Wit and Wisdom of Dean Inge*. No. 116.)

17

See the virtue of a wager, that new philosophical way, lately found out, of deciding all hard questions.

APHRA BEHN, *The Rover*. Act iii, sc. 1.

Fools for arguments use wagers.

BUTLER, *Hudibras*. Pt. ii, canto i, l. 298.

For most men (till by losing render'd sager)
Will back their own opinions with a wager.

BYRON, *Beppo*. St. 27.

18

Whose game was empires, and whose stakes were thrones;

Whose table earth—whose dice were human bones.
BYRON, *The Age of Bronze*. St. 3, l. 9.

Councillors of state sit plotting and playing their high chess-game whereof the pawns are men.
THOMAS CARLYLE, *Sartor Resartus*. Bk. i, ch. 3.

Knight nor Bishop can resist
The pawns of this Antagonist
Whose countenance is dark with mist.
The game goes on and will not wait,
Cæsar is gripped in a deadly strait—
What if the pawns should give checkmate,
Iscariot?
FRANK BETTS, *The Pawns*.

1
In play there are two pleasures for your choosing—
The one is winning, and the other losing.
BYRON, *Don Juan*. Canto xiv, st. 12.

2
Keep flax from fire, youth from gaming.
BENJAMIN FRANKLIN, *Poor Richard*.

3
Could fools to keep their own contrive,
On what, on whom could gamesters thrive?
JOHN GAY, *Fables: Pan and Fortune*.

And remember, dearie, never give a sucker an even break.
W. C. FIELDS(?), *Poppy*. Act ii. (1923) *Poppy* was written by Dorothy Donnelly, but:

Fields added this immortal line to American literature (and I'll bet the line was his own).
HELEN HAYES, *Collier's*, 22 Sept., 1951, p. 80.

4
The strength of Monaco is the weakness of the world.
H. A. GIBBONS, *Riviera Towns: Monte Carlo*.

You can hear them sigh and wish to die,
You can see them wink the other eye
At the man who broke the Bank at Monte Carlo.
FRED GILBERT, *The Man Who Broke the Bank at Monte Carlo*.

At play, anything may happen. (Dans le jeu, tout arrive.)
Maxim of a chef de partie at Monte Carlo.

5
Play not for gain but sport. Who plays for more
Than he can lose with pleasure, stakes his heart,—
Perhaps his wife's too, and whom she hath bore.
GEORGE HERBERT, *The Church-Porch*. St. 33.

If yet thou love game at so dear a rate,
Learn this, that hath old gamesters dearly cost:
Dost lose? rise up: dost win? rise in that state.
Who strive to sit out losing hands are lost.
GEORGE HERBERT, *The Church-Porch*. St. 34.

6
Gamesters and racehorses never last long.
GEORGE HERBERT, *Jacula Prudentum*.

7
He that plays his money ought not to value it.
GEORGE HERBERT, *Jacula Prudentum*.

8
Nought lay down, nought take up.
JOHN HEYWOOD, *Proverbs*. Pt. i, ch. 6. (1546)

Nothing stake, nothing draw.
JOHN RAY, *English Proverbs*, 206.

Nought won by the one, nought won by the other.
JOHN HEYWOOD, *Proverbs*. Pt. i, ch. 11.

Naught venture, naught have.
THOMAS TUSSER, *Five Hundred Points of Good Husbandry: October's Abstract*.

But boundless risk must pay for boundless gain.
WILLIAM MORRIS, *Earthly Paradise: The Wanderers*.

9
Why they call a feller that keeps losin' all the time a good sport gits me.
KIN HUBBARD, *Abe Martin's Broadcast*, p. 28.

10
We cannot expect to have an honest horse race until we have an honest human race.
Attributed to CHARLES EVANS HUGHES, but denied by him in a letter to the compiler.

11
He began to think . . . that he had betted too deep . . . and that it was time to hedge.
MACAULAY, *History of England*. Vol. iv, ch. 17.

12
Lest he should lose, the gambler ceases not to lose. (Sic, ne perdiderit, non cessat perdere lusor.)
OVID, *Ars Amatoria*. Bk. i, l. 451.

13
The better the gambler the worse the man. (Aleator quanto in arte est potior, tanto est nequior.)
PUBLILIUS SYRUS, *Sententiæ*. No. 33.

A gamester, the greater master he is in his art, the worse man is he.
FRANCIS BACON, *Apothegms*.

14
Gie o'er when the play is gude.
JOHN RAY, *English Proverbs: Scottish*.

15
The most patient man in loss, the most coldest that ever turned up ace.
SHAKESPEARE, *Cymbeline*. Act ii, sc. 3, l. 2.

16
Were it good
To set the exact wealth of all our states
All at one cast? to set so rich a main
On the nice hazard of one doubtful hour?
SHAKESPEARE, *I Henry IV*. Act iv, sc. 1, l. 46.

I have set my life upon a cast,
And I will stand the hazard of the die!
SHAKESPEARE, *Richard III*. Act v, sc. 4, l. 9.

By the hazard of the spotted die,
Let die the spotted.
SHAKESPEARE, *Timon of Athens*. Act v, sc. 4, l. 34.

I'll lay my head to any good man's hat.
SHAKESPEARE, *Love's Labour's Lost*. Act i, sc. 1, l. 310.

17
In my school-days, when I had lost one shaft,

I shot his fellow of the self-same flight
The self-same way with more advised watch,
To find the other forth, and by adventuring both
I oft found both.

SHAKESPEARE, *The Merchant of Venice*. Act i, sc. 1, l. 139.

1
If Hercules and Lichas play at dice,
Which is the better man? the greater throw
May turn by fortune from the weaker hand.

SHAKESPEARE, *The Merchant of Venice*. Act ii, sc. 1, l. 32.

2
A wise player ought to accept his throws and score them, not bewail his luck.

SOPHOCLES, *Phædra: Fragment*. No. 862.

3
If there were two birds sitting on a fence, he would bet you which one would fly first.

MARK TWAIN, *The Jumping Frog*.

4
There are two times in a man's life when he should not speculate: when he can't afford it, and when he can.

MARK TWAIN, *Pudd'nhead Wilson's New Calendar*.

II—Gambling a Vice

5
The devil invented dicing. (Aleam invenit Dæmon.)

ST. AUGUSTINE, *De Civitate Dei*. Bk. iv.

The devil goes share in gaming.

H. G. BOHN, *Hand-Book of Proverbs*.

The devil is in the dice.

JOHN RAY, *English Proverbs*, 70. (1678)

The very dice obey him.

SHAKESPEARE, *Antony and Cleopatra*. Act ii, sc. 3, l. 33.

However for real harmony, the sort that is divine,
I'll take the animated dominoes. [Dice.]

STEUART M. EMERY, *I'll Say It's Music*.

Cards and dice . . . the devil's books and the devil's bones.

UNKNOWN, *Poor Robin Almanack*. (1676)

6
The winner's shout, the loser's curse
Shall dance before dead England's hearse.

WILLIAM BLAKE, *Auguries of Innocence*.

7
A man may play with decency; but if he games, he is disgraced.

LORD CHESTERFIELD, *Letters*, 5 Feb., 1750.

8
Gambling is the child of avarice, but the parent of prodigality.

C. C. COLTON, *Lacon*.

It is the child of avarice, the brother of iniquity, and the father of mischief.

GEORGE WASHINGTON, *Letter to Bushrod Washington*. 15 Jan., 1783. Referring to gaming.

9
The gamester, if he die a martyr to his profession, is doubly ruined. He adds his soul to every other loss, and by the act of suicide, renounces earth to forfeit Heaven.

C. C. COLTON, *Lacon*.

10
Who games, is felon of his wealth,
His time, his liberty, his health.

NATHANIEL COTTON, *Pleasure*.

By gaming, we lose both our time and treasure,—two things most precious to the life of man.

OWEN FELLTHAM, *Resolves*.

11
One begins by being a dupe and ends by being a rascal. (On commence par être dupe, On finit par être fripon.)

DESCAMPS, *Réflexion sur le Jeu*. Also attributed to Madame Deshoulières.

12
Death and the dice level all distinctions.

SAMUEL FOOTE, *The Minor*. Act i, sc. 1.

13
Do not trust nor contend,
Nor lay wagers, nor lend,
And you'll have peace to your life's end.

THOMAS FULLER, *Gnomologia*. No. 6351.

14
Shake off the shackles of this tyrant vice;
Hear other calls than those of cards and dice;
Be learn'd in nobler arts than arts of play;
And other debts than those of honour pay.

DAVID GARRICK, *The Gamester: Prologue*.

Our Quixote bard sets out at monster-taming,
Arm'd at all points to fight that hydra, gaming.

DAVID GARRICK, *The Gamester: Prologue*.

15
Look round, the wrecks of play behold;
Estates dismember'd, mortgag'd, sold!
Their owners now to jails confin'd,
Show equal poverty of mind.

JOHN GAY, *Fables*. Pt. ii, fab. 12.

16
Gaming, women, and wine, while they laugh they make men pine.

GEORGE HERBERT, *Jacula Prudentum*.

Play, women, and wine undo men laughing.

JOHN RAY, *English Proverbs*.

Play, women, and wine, are enough to make a prince a pauper.

C. H. SPURGEON, *Ploughman's Pictures*, 11.

See also WINE AND WOMEN.

17
Gaming is the mother of lies and perjuries. (Mendaciorum et perjuriarum mater est alea.)

JOHN OF SALISBURY, Bishop of Chartres, *Polycraticus*. Bk. i. (1175)

Hazard is very mother of lyings
And of deceit, and cursed forswearings.

CHAUCER, *The Pardoners Tale*, l. 263.

18
Oh, this pernicious vice of gaming!

EDWARD MOORE, *The Gamester*. Act i, sc. 1.

I'll tell thee what it says: it calls me villain, a treacherous husband, a cruel father, a false brother; one lost to nature and her charities; or

to say all in one short word, it calls me—gamester.
EDWARD MOORE, *The Gamester*. Act ii, sc. 1.

Ay, rail at gaming—'tis a rich topic, and affords noble declamation. Go, preach against it in the city—you'll find a congregation in every tavern.
EDWARD MOORE, *The Gamester*. Act iv, sc. 1.

1
How, sir! not damn the sharper, but the dice?
POPE, *Epilogue to the Satires*. Dial. ii, l. 13.

2
Sir, for a *quart d'écu* he will sell the fee-simple of his salvation, the inheritance of it; and cut the entail from all remainders.
SHAKESPEARE, *All's Well that Ends Well*. Act iv, sc. 3, l. 311.

3
And once or twice to throw the dice
Is a gentlemanly game,
But he does not win who plays with Sin
In the secret House of Shame.
OSCAR WILDE, *The Ballad of Reading Gaol*. Pt. iii, st. 23.

GAME

See also Life: A Game

4
And who, 'mid e'en the Fools, but feels that half the joy is in the race.
SIR RICHARD BURTON, *Kasîdah*. Pt. viii, st. 18.

5
Life's too short for chess.
H. J. BYRON, *Our Boys*. Act i.

He hates chess. He says it is a foolish expedient for making idle people believe they are doing something very clever, when they are only wasting their time.
BERNARD SHAW, *The Irrational Knot*. Ch. 14.

6
He's up to these grand games, but one of these days I'll loore him on to skittles, and astonish him.
H. J. BYRON, *Our Boys*. Act ii.

7
Sine periculo friget lusus. [Without danger the game grows cold.]
GEORGE CHAPMAN, *All Fools*. Act iii. Quoting a Latin proverb.

No game was ever yet worth a rap
For a rational man to play,
Into which no accident, no mishap,
Could possibly find its way.
A. L. GORDON, *Ye Weary Wayfarer*. Fytte iv.

8
It is a silly game where nobody wins.
THOMAS FULLER, *Gnomologia*.

9
The twelve good rules, the royal game of goose.
GOLDSMITH, *The Deserted Village*, l. 232. The twelve good rules were ascribed to King Charles I: 1. Urge no healths. 2. Profane no divine ordinances. 3. Touch no state matters. 4. Reveal no secrets. 5. Pick no quarrels. 6. Make no comparisons. 7. Maintain no ill opinions. 8. Keep no bad company. 9. Encourage no vice. 10. Make no long meals. 11. Repeat no grievances. 12. Lay no wagers.

10
At the game's end we shall see who gains.
GEORGE HERBERT, *Jacula Prudentum*. No. 534.

11
Sport begets tumultuous strife and wrath, and wrath begets fierce quarrels and war to the death. (Ludus enim genuit trepidum certamen et iram, Ira truces inimicitias et funebre bellum.)
HORACE, *Epistles*. Bk. i, epis. 19, l. 48.

12
The only athletic sport I ever mastered was backgammon.
DOUGLAS JERROLD, *Douglas Jerrold's Wit*.

13
Then ye contented your souls
With the flannelled fools at the wicket or the muddied oafs at the goals.
RUDYARD KIPLING, *The Islanders*, l. 31.

Those athletic brutes whom undeservedly we call heroes.
DRYDEN, *Fables: Preface*.

You base foot-ball player.
SHAKESPEARE, *King Lear*. Act i, sc. 4, l. 94.

14
In all time of our distress,
And in our triumph too,
The game is more than the player of the game,
And the ship is more than the crew!
RUDYARD KIPLING, *A Song in Storm*.

To love the game beyond the prize.
HENRY NEWBOLT, *Clifton Chapel*.
See also under REWARD.

15
The game is not worth the candle. (Le jeu ne vaut pas la chandelle.)
MONTAIGNE, *Essays*. Bk. ii, ch. 27.

It is a poor sport that is not worth the candle.
GEORGE HERBERT, *Jacula Prudentum*. An adaptation of the French proverb.

Yet when the light of life is so near going out, and ought to be so precious, *Le jeu ne vaut pas la Chandelle*, The play is not worth the expence of the candle.
ABRAHAM COWLEY, *Essays*. No. 10.

16
This they all with a joyful mind
Bear through life like a torch in flame,
And falling, fling to the host behind—
"Play up! Play up! and play the game!"
HENRY NEWBOLT, *Vitaï Lampada*.

For when the One Great Scorer comes to write against your name,
He marks—not that you won or lost—but how you played the game.
GRANTLAND RICE, *Alumnus Football*.

17
The little pleasure of the game
Is from afar to view the flight.
MATTHEW PRIOR, *To the Hon. Charles Montague*.

1
He'll play a small game rather than stand out.
JOHN RAY, *English Proverbs.*

2
If thou dost play with him at any game,
Thou art sure to lose; and, of that natural luck,
He beats thee 'gainst the odds.
SHAKESPEARE, *Antony and Cleopatra,* ii, 3, 24.

3
Let's to billiards.
SHAKESPEARE, *Antony and Cleopatra,* ii, 5, 3.

To play billiards well is a sign of a misspent youth.
HERBERT SPENCER, perhaps quoting from *Noctes Ambrosianiæ,* March, 1827. (DUNCAN, *Life of Spencer.*)

A man who wants to play billiards must have no other ambition. Billiards is all.
E. V. LUCAS, *Character and Comedy.*

4
What work's, my countrymen, in hand? where go you
With bats and clubs?
SHAKESPEARE, *Coriolanus.* Act i, sc. 1, l. 56.

The faith they have in tennis, and tall stockings.
SHAKESPEARE, *Henry VIII.* Act i, sc. 3, l. 30.

5
There's no game
So desperate, that the wisest of the wise
Will not take freely up for love of power,
Or love of fame, or merely love of play.
SIR HENRY TAYLOR, *Philip von Artevelde.* Pt. i, act i, sc. 3.

6
The game's up. (Ilicet.)
TERENCE, *Phormio,* l. 208.

The game is up.
SHAKESPEARE, *Cymbeline.* Act iii, sc. 3, l. 107.

7
There was ease in Casey's manner as he stept into his place,
There was pride in Casey's bearing and a smile on Casey's face,
And when responding to the cheers he lightly doft his hat,
No stranger in the crowd could doubt, 't was Casey at the bat.
ERNEST LAWRENCE THAYER, *Casey at the Bat.*

And now the pitcher holds the ball, and now he lets it go,
And now the air is shattered by the force of Casey's blow.

Oh, somewhere in this favored land the sun is shining bright;
The band is playing somewhere, and somewhere hearts are light,
And somewhere men are laughing, and little children shout;
But there is no joy in Mudville—mighty Casey has struck out.
ERNEST LAWRENCE THAYER, *Casey at the Bat.* Erroneously ascribed to Joseph Quinlan Murphy and William Valentine; claimed, without foundation by George Whitefield D'Vys. (See STEVENSON, *Famous Single Poems.*)

These are the saddest of possible words:
"Tinker to Evers to Chance."
Trio of bear cubs, and fleeter than birds,
Tinker and Evers and Chance.
Ruthlessly pricking our gonfalon bubble,
Making a Giant hit into a double—
Words that are heavy with nothing but trouble:
"Tinker to Evers to Chance."
FRANKLIN P. ADAMS, *Baseball's Sad Lexicon.*

8
Which would you rather be,—a conqueror in the Olympic games, or the crier who proclaims the conquerors?
THEMISTOCLES, when asked whether he would rather be Achilles or Homer. (PLUTARCH, *Lives: Themistocles.*)

9
This is a sport which makes the body's very liver curl with enjoyment.
MARK TWAIN, *Life on the Mississippi.* Referring to piloting.

GARDEN

9a
Who loves a garden still his Eden keeps,
Perennial pleasures plants, and wholesome harvests reaps.
AMOS BRONSON ALCOTT, *Tablets: The Garden.* Bk. i, *Antiquity.* The lines are printed without quotation marks, and the assumption is that they are Alcott's.

10
God Almighty first planted a garden. And, indeed, it is the purest of human pleasures.
FRANCIS BACON, *Essays: Of Gardens.*

God the first garden made, and the first city Cain.
ABRAHAM COWLEY, *The Garden.* Essay v.

11
Men but make monuments of sin
Who walk the earth's ambitous round;
Thou hast the richer realm within
This garden ground.
ALICE BROWN, *A Benedictine Garden.*

12
A garden is a lovesome thing, God wot!
Rose plot, Fringed pool, Ferned grot—
The veriest school
Of peace; and yet the fool
Contends that God is not.
Not God! in gardens! when the eve is cool?
Nay, but I have a sign:
'Tis very sure God walks in mine.
THOMAS EDWARD BROWN, *My Garden.*

13
My tent stands in a garden
Of aster and golden-rod,
Tilled by the rain and the sunshine,
And sown by the hand of God.
BLISS CARMAN, *An Autumn Garden.*

14
Which May had painted with his softe showers
This garden full of leaves and of flowers.
CHAUCER, *The Frankeleyns Tale,* l. 179.

15
Who loves a garden loves a greenhouse too.
COWPER, *The Task.* Bk. iii, l. 566.

16
Speak not—whisper not;

Here bloweth thyme and bergamot; . . .
Dark-spiked rosemary and myrrh,
Lean-stalked, purple lavender. . . .
WALTER DE LA MARE, *The Sunken Garden.*

1
Here, in this sequestered close,
Bloom the hyacinth and rose;
Here beside the modest stock
Flaunts the flaring hollyhock;
Here, without a pang, one sees
Ranks, conditions, and degrees.
AUSTIN DOBSON, *A Garden Song.*

2
A garden is like those pernicious machineries which catch a man's coat-skirt or his hand, and draw in his arm, his leg, and his whole body to irresistible destruction.
EMERSON, *Conduct of Life: Wealth.*

3
My garden is a forest ledge
Which older forests bound;
The banks slope down to the blue lake-edge,
Then plunge to depths profound.
EMERSON, *My Garden.* St. 3.

4
In green old gardens, hidden away
From sight of revel and sound of strife, . . .
Here may I live what life I please,
Married and buried out of sight.
VIOLET FANE, *In Green Old Gardens.*

5
What makes a garden
And why do gardens grow?
Love lives in gardens—
God and lovers know!
CAROLYN GILTINAN, *The Garden.*

6
As is the gardener, so is the garden.
THOMAS FULLER, *Gnomologia.* No. 701.

7
The kiss of the sun for pardon,
The song of the birds for mirth;
One is nearer God's Heart in a garden
Than anywhere else on earth.
DOROTHY FRANCES GURNEY, *God's Garden.*

8
The market is the best garden.
GEORGE HERBERT, *Jacula Prudentum.* A London variant is, "Cheapside is the best garden."

9
Yes, in the poor man's garden grow
Far more than herbs and flowers—
Kind thoughts, contentment, peace of mind,
And joy for weary hours.
MARY HOWITT, *The Poor Man's Garden.*

10
I would be back in my own garden,
Watching my windy daffodils.
ALINE KILMER, *A Guest Speaks.*

11
I walk down the garden paths,
And all the daffodils
Are blowing, and the bright blue squills.
I walk down the patterned garden-paths
In my stiff, brocaded gown.
With my powdered hair, and jewelled fan,
I too am a rare
Pattern. As I wander down
The garden paths.
AMY LOWELL, *Patterns.*

12
Fair Quiet, have I found thee here,
And Innocence, thy sister dear?
ANDREW MARVELL, *The Garden.*

13
Jesus is in a garden, not of delight as the first Adam, where he lost himself and the whole human race, but in one of agony, where he saved himself and the whole human race.
PASCAL, *Pensées.* No. 553. Sometimes condensed to: "Man was lost and saved in a garden."

14
Grove nods at grove, each alley has a brother,
And half the platform just reflects the other.
The suff'ring eye inverted nature sees,
Trees cut to statues, statues thick as trees;
With here a fountain never to be play'd,
And there a summer-house that knows no shade.
POPE, *Moral Essays.* Epis. iv, l. 117.

15
This rule in gardening ne'er forget,
To sow dry and set wet.
JOHN RAY, *English Proverbs.*

16
There is no ancient gentlemen but gardeners.
SHAKESPEARE, *Hamlet.* Act v, sc. 1, l. 33. *See also under* ADAM.

17
The best place to seek God is in a garden. You can dig for Him there.
BERNARD SHAW, *The Adventures of the Black Girl in Her Search for God.*

Oh, Adam was a gardener, and God who made him sees
That half a proper gardener's work is done upon his knees.
So when your work is finished, you can wash your hands and pray
For the Glory of the Garden that it may not pass away!
And the glory of the Garden it shall never pass away!
RUDYARD KIPLING, *The Glory of the Garden.*

18
A little garden square and wall'd.
TENNYSON, *Enoch Arden,* l. 730.

19
Come into the garden, Maud,
For the black bat, night, has flown.
TENNYSON, *Maud.* Pt. i, sec. 22, st. 1.

The splash and stir
Of fountains spouted up and showering down
In meshes of the jasmine and the rose:
And all about us peal'd the nightingale,
Rapt in her song, and careless of the snare.
TENNYSON, *The Princess.* Pt. i, l. 214.

20
That is well said, replied Candide, but we

must cultivate our garden. (Cela est bien dit. répondit Candide, mais il faut cultiver notre jardin.)

VOLTAIRE, *Candide*. Ch. 30.

One should cultivate letters or his garden. (Il faut cultiver les lettres ou son jardin.)

VOLTAIRE, *Letter to D'Alembert*, July, 1773.

1
A little garden Little Jowett made,
And fenced it with a little palisade;
If you would know the mind of little Jowett,
This little garden don't a little show it.

FRANCIS WRANGHAM, *Jowett's Little Garden*. Referring to Dr. Joseph Jowett.

2
I used to love my garden,
But now my love is dead,
For I found a bachelor's button
In black-eyed Susan's bed.

UNKNOWN. (Printed by Christopher Morley in his column in N. Y. *Evening Post*, c. 1922.)

GARRICK, DAVID

3
If manly sense, if Nature link'd with art;
If thorough knowledge of the human heart;
If powers of acting vast and unconfined;
If fewest faults with greatest beauties join'd, . . .
Deserve the preference;—Garrick! take the chair,
Nor quit it—till thou place an equal there.

CHARLES CHURCHILL, *The Rosciad*. Conclusion.

4
Our Garrick's a salad; for in him we see
Oil, vinegar, sugar, and saltness agree.

GOLDSMITH, *Retaliation*, l. 11.

Here lies David Garrick: describe me, who can,
An abridgment of all that was pleasant in man;
As an actor, confess'd without rival to shine;
As a wit, if not first, in the very first line;
Yet, with talents like these, and an excellent heart,
The man had his failings—a dupe to his art.
Like an ill-judging beauty, his colours he spread,
And beplaster'd with rouge his own natural red.
On the stage he was natural, simple, affecting:
'Twas only that when he was off, he was acting.

GOLDSMITH, *Retaliation*, l. 93.

He cast off his friends as a huntsman his pack,
For he knew, when he pleas'd, he could whistle them back.
Of praise a mere glutton, he swallow'd what came,
And the puff of a dunce he mistook it for fame.

GOLDSMITH, *Retaliation*, l. 107.

5
But what are the hopes of man? I am disappointed by that stroke of death, which has eclipsed the gaiety of nations, and impoverished the public stock of harmless pleasure.

SAMUEL JOHNSON, *Lives of the Poets: Edmund Smith*. Alluding to Garrick's death.

6
Here lie together, waiting the Messiah
The little David and the great Goliath.

UNKNOWN, *Note in Thespian Dictionary*, appended to the life of Garrick. Garrick and Johnson are buried close together in Westminster Abbey.

GEESE, see Goose

GENEROSITY, see Gifts and Giving

GENIUS

I—Genius: Definitions

7
Genius is mainly an affair of energy.

MATTHEW ARNOLD, *Essays in Criticism: Literary Influence of Academies.*

Genius . . . that energy which collects, combines, amplifies, and animates.

SAMUEL JOHNSON, *Lives of the Poets: Pope.*

8
Genius, that power which dazzles mortal eyes,
Is oft but perseverance in disguise.

HENRY AUSTIN, *Perseverance Conquers All.*

9
What is genius? It is the power to be a boy again at will.

J. M. BARRIE, *Tommy and Grizel*, p. 249.

Genius has somewhat of the infantine:
But of the childish, not a touch nor taint.

ROBERT BROWNING, *Prince Hohenstiel-Schwangau.*

10
As diamond cuts diamond, and one hone smooths a second, all the parts of intellect are whetstones to each other; and genius, which is but the result of their mutual sharpening, is character too.

C. A. BARTOL, *Radical Problems: Individualism.*

11
Genius is patience. (Le Génie, c'est la patience.)

BUFFON. (STEVENS, *Study of the Life and Times of Madame de Staël*. Ch. iii, p. 61.) The sentence is not in Buffon's works, but Herault de Séchelles (*Voyage à Montbar*, p. 15) also ascribes the statement to Buffon in a slightly different form: "Le génie n'est qu'un plus grande aptitude à la patience," Genius is nothing but the greatest aptitude for patience.

Patience is a necessary ingredient of genius.

BENJAMIN DISRAELI, *Contarini Fleming*. Pt. iv, ch. 5.

12
Every man who observes vigilantly and resolves steadfastly, grows unconsciously into genius.

BULWER-LYTTON, *Caxtoniana*. Essay 21.

13
Genius, in one respect, is like gold,—numbers of persons are constantly writing about *both*, who have *neither*.

C. C. COLTON, *Lacon*. Vol. ii. No. 133.

1
Genius is fostered by industry. (Ingenium industria alitur.)
CICERO, *Pro Cælio*. Ch. xix, sec. 45.

No man's genius, however shining, can raise him from obscurity, unless he has industry, opportunity, and also a patron to recommend him. (Neque enim cuiquam tam clarum statim ingenium, ut possit emergere, nisi illi materia, occasio, fautor etiam commendatorque contingat.)
PLINY THE YOUNGER, *Epistles*. Bk. vi, epis. 23.

Genius is the father of a heavenly line; but the mortal mother, that is industry.
THEODORE PARKER, *Ten Sermons on Religion: Of the Culture of the Religious Powers.*

If you have genius, industry will improve it; if you have none, industry will supply its place.
SIR JOSHUA REYNOLDS, *Saying*. As quoted by John Graham to Edinburgh Art Students.

Genius can never despise labour.
MADAME DE STAËL. (STEVENS, *Life*. Ch. 38.)

Genius is nothing but labour and diligence.
WILLIAM HOGARTH.

2
To think, and to feel, constitute the two grand divisions of men of genius—the men of reasoning and the men of imagination.
ISAAC D'ISRAELI, *Literary Character of Men of Genius*. Ch. 2.

3
Time, place, and action may with pains be wrought,
But genius must be born, and never can be taught.
DRYDEN, *Epistle to Congreve*, l. 59.

4
Genius is one per cent inspiration and ninety-nine per cent perspiration.
THOMAS A. EDISON, *Newspaper Interview*. (Quoted in *Golden Book*, April, 1931.)

5
Genius is religious. It is a larger imbibing of the common heart.
EMERSON, *Essays, First Series: The Over-Soul.*

To believe your own thought, to believe that what is true for you in your private heart is true for all men—that is genius.
EMERSON, *Essays, First Series: Self-Reliance.*

In every work of genius we recognize our own rejected thoughts: they come back to us with a certain alienated majesty.
EMERSON, *Essays, First Series: Self-Reliance.*

The miracles of genius always rest on profound convictions which refuse to be analyzed.
EMERSON, *Letters and Social Aims: Progress of Culture.*

6
Great geniuses have the shortest biographies. Their cousins can tell you nothing about them. They lived in their writings, and so their house and street life was trivial and commonplace.
EMERSON, *Representative Men: Plato.*

That necessity of isolation which genius feels. Each must stand on his glass tripod if he would keep his electricity.
EMERSON, *Essays: Society and Solitude.*

Genius is lonely without the surrounding presence of people to inspire it.
T. W. HIGGINSON, *Atlantic Essays: A Plea for Culture.*

7
Genius even, as it is the greatest good, is the greatest harm.
EMERSON, *Society and Solitude: Farming.*

He is a blockhead; he is nothing but a genius.
EMERSON, *Uncollected Lectures: Table-Talk.* Quoted as a French proverb.

8
Genius is the talent of a man who is dead.
EDMOND AND JULES DE GONCOURT, *Journal.*

9
Rules and models destroy genius and art.
WILLIAM HAZLITT, *Sketches and Essays: On Taste.*

Genius is always impatient of its harness; its wild blood makes it hard to train.
O. W. HOLMES, *The Professor at the Breakfast-Table*. Ch. 10.

Genius can only breathe freely in an atmosphere of freedom.
JOHN STUART MILL, *On Liberty*. Ch. 3.

A genius in a reverend gown
Must ever keep its owner down;
'Tis an unnatural conjunction,
And spoils the credit of the function.
SWIFT, *To Dr. Delany.*

10
Perhaps, moreover, he whose genius appears deepest and truest excels his fellows in nothing save the knack of expression; he throws out occasionally a lucky hint at truths of which every human soul is profoundly though unutterably conscious.
HAWTHORNE, *Mosses from an Old Manse: The Procession of Life.*

11
Man's genius is a deity.
HERACLITUS. (PLUTARCH, *Platonic Questions*. Sec. 1.)

12
Gift, like genius, I often think only means an infinite capacity for taking pains.
JANE ELLICE HOPKINS, *Work Amongst Working Men*. (1870) (A correspondent in *Notes and Queries* for 13 Sept., 1879, p. 213, states that Miss Hopkins was the first to use the exact phrase, "Genius is an infinite capacity for taking pains." She was a social reformer, and her article referred to her work among the navvies at Cambridge.)

Charles Dickens in an after-dinner speech stated that genius was an infinite capacity for taking pains.
SOMERSET MAUGHAM, *Cakes and Ale*, p. 4.

Genius is an infinite love of taking pains.
J. M. BARRIE, *Chancellor's Address*, University of Edinburgh.

Genius . . . means the transcendent capacity of taking trouble.

CARLYLE, *Frederick the Great*. Bk. iv, ch. 3.

Genius has been defined as a supreme capacity for taking trouble. . . . It might be more fitly described as a supreme capacity for getting its possessors into trouble of all kinds.

SAMUEL BUTLER THE YOUNGER, *Note-Books*, p. 174.

1
Genius is the capacity of evading hard work.

ELBERT HUBBARD, *The Philistine*. Vol. xi, p. 114.

Genius, cried the commuter,
As he ran for the 8:13,
Consists of an infinite capacity
For catching trains.

CHRISTOPHER MORLEY, *An Ejaculation*.

2
Genius is the ability to act rightly without precedent—the power to do the right thing the first time.

ELBERT HUBBARD, *A Thousand and One Epigrams*, p. 39.

3
The true Genius is a mind of large general powers, accidentally determined to some particular direction.

SAMUEL JOHNSON, *Lives of the Poets: Cowley*.

4
Many a genius has been slow of growth. Oaks that flourish for a thousand years do not spring up into beauty like a reed.

G. H. LEWES, *Spanish Drama: Life of Lope De Vega*. Ch. 2.

5
All the means of action—
The shapeless masses, the materials—
Lie everywhere about us. What we need
Is the celestial fire to change the flint
Into transparent crystal, bright and clear.
That fire is genius!

LONGFELLOW, *The Spanish Student*. Act i, sc. 5.

6
I think it may as well be admitted that the disease of the endocrine glands called genius simply does not appear among women as frequently as it does among men. If one can find consolation in the thought, neither does idiocy.

ELSIE MCCORMICK, in *New York World*.

7
A good memory is an essential element of genius.

J. F. NISBET, *The Insanity of Genius*, p. 255.

8
Originality and genius must be largely fed and raised on the shoulders of some old tradition.

GEORGE SANTAYANA, *The Life of Reason*. Vol. ii, p. 101.

9
Genius consists in this, that the knowing faculty has received a considerably greater development than the service of the will demands. . . . The fundamental condition of genius is an abnormal predominance of sensibility over irritability and reproductive power.

ARTHUR SCHOPENHAUER, *The World as Will and Idea*. Sec. 20.

10
Only when genius is married to science, can the highest results be produced.

HERBERT SPENCER, *Education*. Ch. 1.

Genius without education is like silver in the mine.

BENJAMIN FRANKLIN, *Poor Richard*, 1750.

11
Genius is essentially creative; it bears the stamp of the individual who possesses it.

MADAME DE STAËL, *Corinne*. Bk. vii, ch. 1.

12
When a true genius appears in the world, you may know him by this sign, that the dunces are all in confederacy against him.

SWIFT, *Thoughts on Various Subjects*.

In the republic of mediocrity genius is dangerous.

R. G. INGERSOLL, *Liberty in Literature*.

13
There is a certain characteristic common to all those whom we call geniuses. Each of them has a consciousness of being a man apart.

MIGUEL DE UNAMUNO, *Essays and Soliloquies*, p. 44.

14
Of the three requisites of genius, the first is soul, and the second, soul, and the third, soul.

E. P. WHIPPLE, *Literature and Life: Genius*.

15
But on the whole, "genius is ever a secret to itself."

CARLYLE, *Characteristics*.

II—Genius: Apothegms

16
Improvement makes straight roads; but the crooked roads without improvement are the roads of Genius.

WILLIAM BLAKE, *Proverbs of Hell*.

17
Genius is of no country.

CHARLES CHURCHILL, *The Rosciad*, l. 207.

18
"Eccentricities of genius, Sam," said Mr. Pickwick.

DICKENS, *Pickwick Papers*. Ch. 30.

Eccentricity is not a proof of genius, and even an artist should remember that originality consists not only in doing things differently, but also in "doing things better."

E. C. STEDMAN, *Victorian Poets*. Ch. 9.

19
Fortune has rarely condescended to be the companion of genius.

ISAAC D'ISRAELI, *Curiosities of Literature: Poverty of the Learned*.

Genius and its rewards are briefly told:
A liberal nature and a niggard doom,
A difficult journey to a splendid tomb.

JOHN FORSTER, *Oliver Goldsmith: Dedication*.

1
Many men of genius must arise before a particular man of genius can appear.

ISAAC D'ISRAELI, *Literary Character of Men of Genius*. Ch. 12.

2
Nor mourn the unalterable Days
That Genius goes and Folly stays.

EMERSON, *In Memoriam.*

3
When Nature has work to be done, she creates a genius to do it.

EMERSON, *Nature Addresses and Lectures: The Method of Nature.*

In all great works of art . . . the Genius draws up the ladder after him.

EMERSON, *Representative Men: Shakspeare.*

4
The first and last thing required of genius is the love of truth. (Das erste und letzte, was vom Genie gefordert wird, ist Wahrheits-Liebe.)

GOETHE, *Sprüche in Prosa*. Pt. iii.

5
The freemasonry of genius.

WILLIAM HARVEY, *Lectures: Burke and Goldsmith.*

6
Genius, like humanity, rusts for want of use.

WILLIAM HAZLITT, *The Plain Speaker: On Application to Study.*

7
A person of genius should marry a person of character. Genius does not herd with genius.

O. W. HOLMES, *The Professor at the Breakfast-Table*. Ch. 12.

8
Unless one is a genius, it is best to aim at being intelligible.

ANTHONY HOPE, *The Dolly Dialogues*. No. 15.

9
Adversity reveals genius, prosperity hides it. (Ingenium res Adversæ nudare solent, celare secundæ.)

HORACE, *Satires*. Bk. ii, sat. 8, l. 73.

Ill fortune is often an incentive to genius. (Ingenium mala sæpe movent.)

OVID, *Ars Amatoria*. Bk. ii, l. 43.

The worship of genius never makes a man rich. (Amor ingenii neminem unquam divitem fecit.)

PETRONIUS ARBITER, *Satyricon*. Sec. 83.

Genius and virtue, like diamonds, are best plain-set—set in lead, set in poverty.

EMERSON, *Society and Solitude: Domestic Life.*

Hunger is the handmaid of genius.

MARK TWAIN, *Pudd'nhead Wilson's New Calendar.*

See also POETRY AND POVERTY.

10
Genius never drops from the skies.

JAMES HUNEKER, *Pathos of Distance*, p. 103.

11
A man of genius has been seldom ruined but by himself.

SAMUEL JOHNSON. (BOSWELL, *Life*, i, 381.)

12
Many have genius, but, wanting art, are forever dumb.

LONGFELLOW, *Kavanagh*. Ch. 20.

13
How often the greatest geniuses lie hidden in obscurity! (Ut sæpe summa ingenia in occulto latent!)

PLAUTUS, *Captivi*, l. 165. (Act i, sc. 2.)

14
For genius renown endures deathless. (Ingenio stat sine morte decus.)

PROPERTIUS, *Elegies*. Bk. iii, eleg. 2, l. 24.

The memory of genius is immortal. (Immortalis est ingenii memoria.)

SENECA, *Ad Polybium*. Sec. 37.

Genius survives: all else is claimed by death. (Vivitur ingenio: cætera mortis erunt.)

SPENSER, *The Shepheardes Calender: December: Colin's Emblem*. Quoted probably from *Consolatio ad Liviam,* written shortly after the death of Mæcenas by an anonymous author. (See *Notes and Queries,* Jan., 1918, p. 12.)

Vivitur ingenio: that damn'd motto there
Seduced me first to be a wicked player.

GEORGE FARQUHAR, *Love and a Bottle: Epilogue*. The motto, "Vivitur ingenio," (Genius survives), was probably displayed in Drury Lane Theatre.

15
Premature genius seldom arrives at maturity. (Illud ingenorum velut præcox genus, non temere unquam pervenit at frugem.)

QUINTILIAN, *De Institutione Oratoria*. Bk. i, ch. 3, sec. 10.

16
The lamp of genius burns more rapidly than the lamp of life. (Das Licht des Genie's bekam weniger Fett, als das Licht des Lebens.)

SCHILLER, *Fiesco*. Act ii, sc. 17.

17
If it were not for my respect for human opinion, I would not open my window to see the Bay of Naples for the first time; while I would go five hundred leagues to talk with a man of genius.

MADAME DE STAËL. (EMERSON, *Uncollected Lectures: Table-Talk.*)

18
When genius is punished, its fame is exalted. (Punitis ingeniis, gliscit auctoritas.)

TACITUS, *Annals*. Bk. iv, sec. 35. Tacitus is telling of the burning, by order of the Roman Senate, of the books written by Crematius Cordus, and derides the stupidity which thinks it can suppress books by burning them, an action which, Tacitus says, has never produced any effect except infamy to the persons who ordered the burning and glory to the sufferers.

19
I have nothing to declare except my genius.

OSCAR WILDE, to the revenue officers, when he

landed in America in January, 1882. (HARRIS, *Oscar Wilde*, p. 52.)

III—Genius: Its Virtues

1
Genius hath electric power
Which earth can never tame,
Bright suns may scorch and dark clouds lower,
Its flash is still the same.
LYDIA MARIA CHILD, *Marius Amid the Ruins of Carthage.*

2
Philosophy becomes poetry, and science imagination, in the enthusiasm of genius.
ISAAC D'ISRAELI, *Literary Character of Men of Genius.* Ch. 12.

3
To clothe the fiery thought
In simple words succeeds,
For still the craft of genius is
To mask a king in weeds.
EMERSON, *The Poet.*

We owe to genius always the same debt, of lifting the curtain from the common, and showing us that divinities are sitting disguised in the seeming gang of gypsies and peddlers.
EMERSON, *Society and Solitude: Works and Days.*

4
Genius, indeed, melts many ages into one, and thus effects something permanent, yet still with a similarity of office to that of the more ephemeral writer. A work of genius is but the newspaper of a century, or perchance of a hundred centuries.
HAWTHORNE, *Mosses from an Old Manse: The Old Manse.*

5
There is no work of genius which has not been the delight of mankind, no word of genius to which the human heart and soul have not, sooner or later, responded.
J. R. LOWELL, *Among My Books: Rousseau and the Sentimentalists.*

6
It is the privilege of genius that to it life never grows commonplace as to the rest of us.
J. R. LOWELL, *Democracy and Other Addresses: On Unveiling the Bust of Fielding.*

7
There are two kinds of genius. The first and highest may be said to speak out of the eternal to the present, and must compel its age to understand *it;* the second understands its age, and tells it what it wishes to be told.
J. R. LOWELL, *My Study Windows: Pope.*

8
This is the highest miracle of genius, that things which are not should be as though they were, that the imaginations of one mind should become the personal recollections of another.
MACAULAY, *Essays: The Pilgrim's Progress.*

9
Nature with Genius stands united in league everlasting;
What is promised by one, surely the other performs.
SCHILLER, *Steer, Bold Mariner, On.*

IV—Genius: Its Faults

10
There was never a great genius without a tincture of madness. (Nullam magnum ingenium sine mixtura dementiæ fuit.)
ARISTOTLE. (SENECA, *De Tranquilitate Animi.* Bk. i, sec. 15.) Also quoted by other writers.

Great wits are sure to madness near allied,
And thin partitions do their bounds divide.
DRYDEN, *Absalom and Achitophel.* Pt. i, l. 163.
See also under SENSE.

I have heard, madam, your greatest wits have ever a touch of madness and extravagance in them.
DRYDEN AND CAVENDISH, *Sir Martin Mar-All.* Act v, sc. 1.

The heart and soul of genius may be mad, but the mind of true genius is ever as clear as the heavens seen through pine trees.
GEORGE JEAN NATHAN, *Materia Critica.*

11
Men of genius are often dull and inert in society, as the blazing meteor when it descends to the earth is only a stone.
LONGFELLOW, *Kavanagh.* Ch. 13.

12
Strange power of Genius, that can throw
Round all that's vicious, weak, and low,
Such magic lights, such rainbow dyes
As dazzle ev'n the steadiest eyes.
THOMAS MOORE, *Rhymes on the Road.* Extract xvi, l. 1.

What an impostor Genius is;
How, with that strong, mimetic art,
Which forms its life and soul, it takes
All shapes of thought, all hues of heart,
Nor feels, itself, one throb it wakes;
How like a gem its light may smile
O'er the dark path, by mortals trod,
Itself as mean a worm, the while,
As crawls at midnight o'er the sod.
THOMAS MOORE, *Rhymes on the Road.* Extract xvi, l. 72.

13
It is the characteristic of a certain blunderer called genius to see things too far in advance.
CHARLES READE, *Recipe for Writing Novels.*

V—Genius and Talent

14
Doing easily what others find difficult is talent; doing what is impossible *for talent* is genius.
AMIEL, *Journal,* 17 Dec., 1856.

15
The eagle never lost so much time as when he submitted to learn of the crow.
WILLIAM BLAKE, *Proverbs of Hell.*

Men ov genius are like eagles, tha live on what

tha kill, while men ov talents is like crows, tha live on what has been killed for them.

JOSH BILLINGS, *Talent and Genius.*

1

Talent convinces—Genius but excites;
This tasks the reason, that the soul delights.
Talent from sober judgment takes its birth,
And reconciles the pinion to the earth;
Genius unsettles with desires the mind,
Contented not till earth be left behind;
Talent, the sunshine on a cultured soil,
Ripens the fruit, by slow degrees, for toil;
Genius, the sudden Iris of the skies,
On cloud itself reflects its wondrous dyes: . .
Talent gives all that vulgar critics need—
And frames a horn-book for the Dull to read;
Genius, the Pythian of the Beautiful,
Leaves its large truths a riddle to the Dull—
From eyes profane a veil the Isis screens,
And fools on fools still ask—"What Hamlet means?"

BULWER-LYTTON, *Talent and Genius.*

Talent repeats; Genius creates. Talent is a cistern; Genius a fountain. Talent deals with the actual, with discovered and realized truths, analyzing, arranging, combining, applying positive knowledge, and in action looking to precedents; Genius deals with the possible, creates new combinations, discovers new laws, and acts from an insight into principles. Talent jogs to conclusions to which Genius takes giant leaps. Talent accumulates knowledge, and has it packed up in the memory; Genius assimilates it with its own substance, grows with every new accession, and converts knowledge into *power*. Talent gives out what it has taken in; Genius what has risen from its unsounded wells of living thought. Talent, in difficult situations, strives to untie knots, which Genius instantly cuts with one swift decision. Talent is full of thoughts, Genius of thought; one has definite acquisitions, the other indefinite power.

E. P. WHIPPLE, *Literature and Life: Genius.*

2

Talent, lying in the understanding, is often inherited; genius, being the action of reason and imagination, rarely or never.

S. T. COLERIDGE, *Table Talk.*

3

We call partial half-lights, by courtesy, genius; talent which converts itself into money; talent which glitters to-day that it may dine and sleep well tomorrow.

EMERSON, *Essays, First Series: Prudence.*

When the will is absolutely surrendered to the moral sentiment, that is virtue; when the wit is surrendered to intellectual truth, that is genius. Talent for talent's sake is a bauble and a show. Talent working with joy in the cause of universal truth lifts the possessor to new power.

EMERSON, *Letters and Social Aims: Progress of Culture.*

4

Mediocrities sweat blood to produce rubbish. Geniuses create wonders without an effort.

ANATOLE FRANCE. (*Opinions of Anatole France*, p. 100.)

5

Nature is the master of talents; genius is the master of nature.

J. G. HOLLAND, *Plain Talk on Familiar Subjects: Art and Life.*

6

Unpretending mediocrity is good, and genius is glorious; but the weak flavor of genius in a person essentially common is detestable.

O. W. HOLMES, *The Autocrat of the Breakfast-Table.* Ch. 1.

7

There is the same difference between talent and genius that there is between a stone mason and a sculptor.

R. G. INGERSOLL, *Shakespeare.*

8

Genius begins great works; labor alone finishes them. (Le génie commence les beaux ouvrages, mais le travail seul les achève.)

JOUBERT, *Pensées.* No. 335.

9

Between talent and genius there is the same proportion as the whole to its part. (Entre esprit et talent il y a la proportion du tout à sa partie.)

LA BRUYÈRE, *Les Caractères.* No. 12.

10

Talent is that which is in a man's power; genius is that in whose power a man is.

J. R. LOWELL, *Among My Books: Rousseau and the Sentimentalists.*

11

Talk not of genius baffled. Genius is master of man.
Genius does what it must, and Talent does what it can.

OWEN MEREDITH, *Last Words of a Sensitive Second-rate Poet.*

12

Antony was not a genius; he was a gigantic commonplace.

ARTHUR WEIGALL, *Life and Times of Cleopatra.*

13

A genius bright, and base,
Of tow'ring talents, and terrestrial aims.

YOUNG, *Night Thoughts.* Night vi, l. 266.

GENTLEMAN

I—Gentleman: Definitions

14

He is a Gentleman, because his nature
Is kind and affable to every creature.

RICHARD BARNFIELD, *The Shepherd's Content.* St. 41.

Gentlemanliness, being another word for intense humanity.

RUSKIN, *Modern Painters.* Pt. ix, ch. 7, sec. 23.

We must be gentle, now we are gentlemen.

SHAKESPEARE, *Winter's Tale.* Act v, sc. 2, l. 164.

15

Look who that is most virtuous alway,

Prive and apart, and most intendeth aye
To do that gentle deedes that he can,
And take him for the greatest gentle man.

CHAUCER, *Tale of the Wyf of Bathe,* l. 257.

He is gentle that doth gentle deeds.

CHAUCER, *Tale of the Wyf of Bathe,* l. 314.

It is almost a definition of a gentleman to say he is one who never inflicts pain.

CARDINAL NEWMAN.

1
The character of gentleman . . . is frequent in England, rare in France, and found, where it is found, in age or the latest period of manhood; while in Germany the character is almost unknown. But the proper *antipode* of a gentleman is to be sought for among the Anglo-American democrats.

S. T. COLERIDGE, *Biographia Literaria: Satyrane's Letters.* No. 2.

2
Living blood and a passion of kindness does at last distinguish God's gentleman from Fashion's.

EMERSON, *Essays, Second Series: Manners.*

The flowering of civilization is the finished man, the man of sense, of grace, of accomplishment, of social power—the gentleman.

EMERSON, *Miscellanies: Fortune of the Republic.*

3
Manners and money make a gentleman.

THOMAS FULLER, *Gnomologia.*

It's not the gay coat makes the gentleman.

JOHN RAY, *English Proverbs.*

4
According to my mild way of thinking, it is not essential that a gentleman should be bright.

CORRA HARRIS. "I remember writing it, but have no idea where it occurs."—Letter to compiler.

5
What's a gentleman but his pleasure?

GABRIEL HARVEY, *Letter-Book,* 15. (1573)

6
A gentleman is one who understands and shows every mark of deference to the claims of self-love in others, and exacts it in return from them.

WILLIAM HAZLITT, *Table Talk: On the Look of a Gentleman.*

7
His ideal Gentleman is . . . the calculating adventurer who affects the supercilious aid of a shallow dandy and cherishes the heart of a frog.

OLIVER H. G. LEIGH, *Lord Chesterfield's Letters: Introduction.*

8
He would be the finer gentleman that should leave the world untainted with falsehood, or dissimulation, or wantonness, or conceit.

MARCUS AURELIUS, *Meditations.* Bk. ix, sec. 2.

9
A gentleman's first characteristic is that fineness of structure in the body, which renders it capable of the most delicate sensations; and of structure in the mind which renders it capable of the most delicate sympathies—one may say, simply, "fineness of nature."

RUSKIN, *Modern Painters.* Pt. ix, ch. 7, sec. 9.

10
A gentleman of our days is one who has money enough to do what every fool would do if he could afford it: that is, consume without producing.

BERNARD SHAW, *Maxims for Revolutionists.*

A gentleman ain't a man—leastways not a common man—the common man bein' but the slave wot feeds and clothes the gentleman beyond the common.

BERNARD SHAW, *An Unsocial Socialist.* Ch. 4.

II—Gentleman: Apothegms

11
I am a gentleman, though spoiled i' the breeding. The Buzzards are all gentlemen. We came in with the Conqueror.

RICHARD BROME, *English Moor.* Act ii, sc. 4.

See also under ANCESTRY.

12
His lockèd, letter'd, braw brass collar
Show'd him the gentleman an' scholar.

BURNS, *The Twa Dogs.* The phrase, "a gentleman and a scholar" dates from 1621.

A gentleman by nature, and a scholar by education.

C. C. COLTON, *Lacon.*

13
Like two single gentlemen rolled into one.

GEORGE COLMAN THE YOUNGER, *Broad Grins: Lodgings for Single Gentlemen.*

You are not like a Cerberus, three gentlemen at once, are you?

SHERIDAN, *The Rivals.* Act iv, sc. 2.

14
Gentleman is written legibly on his brow.

GEORGE COLMAN THE YOUNGER, *The Heir-at-Law.* Act iii, sc. 1. (1797)

Though modest, on his unembarrass'd brow
Nature had written "gentleman."

BYRON, *Don Juan.* Canto ix, st. 83. (1821)

15
Take one more disguise, and put thyself into the habit of a gentleman.

ABRAHAM COWLEY, *Cutter of Coleman Street.* Act i, sc. 5. (1641) Hence: "Disguised as a gentleman."

16
I had rather have a plain russet-coated Captain, that knows what he fights for, and loves what he knows, than that which you call a Gentleman and is nothing else. I honour a Gentleman that is so indeed.

OLIVER CROMWELL, *Letter to Sir W. Spring and Maurice Barrow,* Sept., 1643.

17
Wherever I go the world cries "that's a gentleman, my life on't a gentleman!" and when y'ave said a gentleman, you have said all.

JOHN CROWNE, *Sir Courtly Nice.* (1685)

1
Once a gentleman, and always a gentleman.
DICKENS, *Little Dorrit*. Bk. ii, ch. 28.

To be a gentleman is to be one all the world over, and in every relation and grade of society.
R. L. STEVENSON, *The American Emigrant.*

2
I shall be a gen'l'm'n myself one of these days, perhaps, with a pipe in my mouth, and a summer-house in the back garden.
DICKENS, *Pickwick Papers*. Ch. 16.

3
What fact more conspicuous in modern history than the creation of the gentleman?
EMERSON, *Essays, Second Series: Manners.*

4
The genteel thing is the genteel thing at any time. If so be that a gentleman bees in a concatenation accordingly.
GOLDSMITH, *She Stoops to Conquer*. Act i, sc. 2.

5
A gentleman may make a king, and a clerk may prove a pope.
SIR JOHN HARINGTON, *Orlando Furioso*. Bk. v.

6
He that would be a gentleman let him go to an assault.
GEORGE HERBERT, *Jacula Prudentum.*

Who would be a gentleman let him storm a town.
JOHN RAY, *English Proverbs.*

7
A fine-paced gentleman as you shall see walk
The middle aisle.
BEN JONSON, *The Staple of News*. Act i, sc. 1.

8
A man may learn from his Bible to be a more thorough gentleman than if he had been brought up in all the drawing-rooms in London.
CHARLES KINGSLEY, *The Water Babies*. Ch. 3.

9
A gentleman who lives ill is a monster in nature. (Un gentilhomme qui vit mal est un monstre dans la nature.)
MOLIÈRE, *Dom Juan*. Act iv, sc. 4, l. 50.

10
No continuance of time, no favor of Prince, no office, no virtue, nor any wealth can make a clown to become a gentleman.
MONTAIGNE, *Essays*. Bk. iii, ch. 5.

Somebody has said that a king may make a nobleman, but he cannot make a gentleman.
EDMUND BURKE, *Letter to William Smith*, 29 Jan., 1795.

Any king or queen may make a lord, but only the devil himself—and the graces—can make a Chesterfield.
DICKENS, *Barnaby Rudge*. Ch. 23.

I can make a lord, but only God Almighty can make a gentleman.
JAMES I, *Remark,* to his old nurse, when she begged him to make her son a gentleman.

The king cannot make a gentleman of blood, nor God Almighty, but he can make a gentleman by creation.
JOHN SELDEN, *Table-Talk: Gentlemen.*

Of seven peasants I can make as many lords; but of seven lords I could not make one Holbein.
HENRY VIII, when a nobleman complained of Holbein.

See also under TITLES.

11
Gentlemen and rich men are venison in heaven, very rare and dainty to have them come thither.
JOHN NORTHBROOKE, *Against Dicing,* 22. (1577)

12
"Excuse the liberty I take,"
Modestus said, with archness on his brow,
"Pray, why did not your father make
A gentleman of you?"
SELLECK OSBORN, *A Modest Wit.*

13
I am a gentleman of blood and breeding.
SHAKESPEARE, *King Lear*. Act iii, sc. 1, l. 40.

I freely told you, all the wealth I had
Ran in my veins, I was a gentleman.
SHAKESPEARE, *The Merchant of Venice*. Act iii, sc. 2, l. 257.

A gentleman born, master parson; who writes himself "Armigero," in any bill, warrant, quittance, or obligation, "Armigero."
SHAKESPEARE, *The Merry Wives of Windsor*. Act i, sc. 1, l. 8.

He bears him like a portly gentleman.
SHAKESPEARE, *Romeo and Juliet*. Act i, sc. 5, l. 68.

14
A gentleman . . . I'll be sworn thou art;
Thy tongue, thy face, thy limbs, actions and spirit,
Do give thee five-fold blazon.
SHAKESPEARE, *Twelfth Night*. Act i, sc. 5, l. 310.

He is complete in feature and in mind,
With all good grace to grace a gentleman.
SHAKESPEARE, *The Two Gentlemen of Verona*. Act ii, sc. 4, l. 73.

Well born, well dressed, and moderately learned. (Bene nati, bene vestiti, et modiocriter docti.)
Statutes of All Souls College, Oxford. The qualifications of a Fellow of the College.

15
There cannot be a greater reproach to a gentleman than to be accounted a liar.
SIR HENRY SIDNEY, *Letters to His Son.*

16
Notwithstanding he be a dunghill gentleman, or a gentleman of the first head, as they used to term them.
PHILIP STUBBS, *Anatomie of Abuses*, 122. (1583) Huloet (*Abced*, sig. N 5), in 1552, defined a "gentleman of the first head" as "ironice to be applied to such as would be esteemed a gentleman, having no point or quality of a gentleman." Robertson (*Phraseology Generalis*, 710) stated that it was equivalent to "Novus homo."

1
It don't cost nothin' to be a gentleman.
JOHN L. SULLIVAN, reproving a rowdy.

2
But if you fail, or if you rise,
Be each, pray God, a gentleman.
W. M. THACKERAY, *The End of the Play.*

The Pall Mall Gazette is written by gentlemen for gentlemen.
THACKERAY, *Pendennis.* Ch. 32.

3
If a man is a gentleman, he knows quite enough, and if he is not a gentleman, whatever he knows is bad for him.
OSCAR WILDE, *A Woman of No Importance* Act iii.

When Adam delved and Eve span,
Who was then the gentleman?
See under ANCESTRY.

III—Gentleman: His Virtues

4
With fascination in his very bow, . . .
A finished gentleman from top to toe.
BYRON, *Don Juan.* Canto xii, st. 84.

5
The gentleman of honor, ragged sooner than patched.
CERVANTES, *Don Quixote.* Pt. ii, ch. 2.

E'en as he trod that day to God, so walked he from his birth,
In simpleness and gentleness and honour and clean mirth.
RUDYARD KIPLING, *Barrack Room Ballads: Dedication.*

And they rise to their feet as He passes by, gentlemen unafraid.
KIPLING, *Barrack Room Ballads: Dedication.*

6
Old Crestien rightly says no language can
Express the worth of a true Gentleman.
J. R. LOWELL, *An Epistle to George William Curtis.*

7
My master hath been an honourable gentleman; tricks he hath had in him, which gentlemen have.
SHAKESPEARE, *All's Well that Ends Well.* Act v, sc. 3, l. 238.

An absolute gentleman, full of the most excellent differences.
SHAKESPEARE, *Hamlet.* Act v, sc. 2, l. 112.

8
I do not think a braver gentleman,
More active-valiant, or more valiant-young,
More daring or more bold, is now alive,
To grace this latter age with noble deeds.
SHAKESPEARE, *I Henry IV.* Act v, sc. 1, l. 89.

This earth that bears thee dead
Bears not alive so stout a gentleman.
SHAKESPEARE, *I Henry IV.* Act v, sc. 4, l. 92.

A kinder gentleman treads not the earth.
SHAKESPEARE, *The Merchant of Venice.* Act ii, sc. 8, l. 35.

A sweeter and a lovelier gentleman,
Framed in the prodigality of nature,
Young, valiant, wise, and, no doubt, right royal,
The spacious world cannot again afford.
SHAKESPEARE, *Richard III.* Act i, sc. 2, l. 243.

An affable and courteous gentleman.
SHAKESPEARE, *The Taming of the Shrew.* Act i, sc. 2, l. 98.

9
We are gentlemen,
That neither in our hearts nor outward eyes
Envy the great nor do the low despise.
SHAKESPEARE, *Pericles.* Act ii, sc. 3, l. 25.

10
And thus he bore without abuse
The grand old name of gentleman,
Defamed by every charlatan,
And soil'd with all ignoble use.
TENNYSON, *In Memoriam.* Pt. cxi, st. 6.

O selfless man and stainless gentleman!
TENNYSON, *Merlin and Vivien,* l. 790.

GENTLENESS

11
The great mind knows the power of gentleness,
Only tries force because persuasion fails.
ROBERT BROWNING, *Prince Hohenstiel-Schwangau.*

12
If there be any good in gentleness, I trowe it to be only this, that it seemeth a manner imposed to gentle men, that they should not disgrace or degenerate from the virtues of their noble kindred.
CHAUCER, *Boethius.* Bk. iii, prose 6.

13
Power can do by gentleness what violence fails to accomplish. (Peragit tranquilla potestas Quod violenta nequit.)
CLAUDIAN, *Panegyricus Dictus Manlio Theodoro Consuli,* l. 239.

Gentleness succeeds better than violence. (Plus fait douceur que violence.)
LA FONTAINE, *Fables.* Bk. vi, fab. 3.

Might there not be
Some power in gentleness we dream not of?
STEPHEN PHILLIPS, *Herod.* Act i.

What would you have? Your gentleness shall force
More than your force move us to gentleness.
SHAKESPEARE, *As You Like It.* Act ii, sc. 7, l. 102.

Let gentleness my strong enforcement be.
SHAKESPEARE, *As You Like It.* Act ii, sc. 7, l. 118.

14
Severity is allowable where gentleness is in vain. (La violence est juste où la douceur est vaine.)
CORNEILLE, *Héraclius.* Act i, sc. 2.

15
A gentle heart is tied with an easy thread.
GEORGE HERBERT, *Jacula Prudentum.*

1
Gentle of speech, beneficent of mind.
HOMER, *Odyssey*. Bk. iv, l. 917. (Pope, tr.)

But he whose inborn worth his acts commend,
Of gentle soul, to human race a friend.
HOMER, *Odyssey*. Bk. xix, l. 383. (Pope, tr.)

2
It is only people who possess firmness who can possess true gentleness. Those who appear gentle generally possess nothing but weakness, which is readily converted into harshness.
LA ROCHEFOUCAULD, *Maximes*. No. 479.

3
Speak gently! 'tis a little thing
Dropped in the heart's deep well;
The good, the joy that it may bring
Eternity shall tell.
G. W. LANGFORD, *Speak Gently*.

4
Gentle to others, to himself severe.
SAMUEL ROGERS, *The Voyage of Columbus*. Canto vi.

5
They are as gentle
As zephyrs blowing below the violet.
SHAKESPEARE, *Cymbeline*. Act iv, sc. 2, l. 171.

This milky gentleness.
SHAKESPEARE, *King Lear*. Act i, sc. 4, l. 364.

Touch'd with human gentleness and love.
SHAKESPEARE, *The Merchant of Venice*. Act iv, sc. 1, l. 25.

6
The gentleness of all the gods go with thee.
SHAKESPEARE, *Twelfth Night*. Act ii, sc. 1, l. 46.

7
Gentle is that gentle does.
J. W. WARTER, *Last of the Old Squires*, p. 43. Quoted as a proverb. *See also under* GENTLEMAN.

8
Gentle in manner, strong in performance. (Suaviter in modo, fortiter in re.)
A proverbial expression derived from a phrase of Claudio Aquaviva, "Fortes in fine consequendo, et suaves in modo." (*Industrie ad Curandos Animæ Morbos*, ii, 1.) Aquaviva was General of the Society of Jesus, and his treatise was published in Venice in 1606.

GEORGE

9
I sing the Georges Four,
For Providence could stand no more.
Some say that far the worst
Of all the Four was George the First.
But yet by some 'tis reckoned
That worser still was George the Second.
And what mortal ever heard
Any good of George the Third?
When George the Fourth from earth descended,
Thank God the line of Georges ended.
WALTER SAVAGE LANDOR, *Epigram*, after hearing Thackeray's lectures on the Four Georges.

The injured Stewart line is gone,
A race outlandish fills their throne:
An idiot race, to honour lost—
Who know them best despise them most.
BURNS, *On Seeing the Royal Palace at Stirling in Ruins*.

10
Here every virtue pleased thou mayst behold
Which raised a hero to a god of old;
To form this One, the mixed ideas draw
From Edward, Henry, and the loved Nassau.
LAURENCE EUSDEN, *Poet Laureate*, 1718, *Birthday Ode to George I*.

11
Great friend of Liberty! in Kings a name
Above all Greek, above all Roman fame.
POPE, *Imitations of Horace: Epistles*. Bk. ii, epis. 1, l. 25. Referring to George II.

12
In the first year of freedom's second dawn
Died George the Third; although no tyrant, one
Who shielded tyrants. . . .
A better farmer ne'er brush'd dew from lawn,
A worse king never left a realm undone!
BYRON, *The Vision of Judgment*. St. 8.

He ever warr'd with freedom and the free:
Nations as men, home subjects, foreign foes,
So that they utter'd the word "Liberty!"
Found George the Third their first opponent.
BYRON, *The Vision of Judgment*. St. 45.

Talk no more of the lucky escape of the head
From a flint so unhappily thrown;
I think very different from thousands; indeed
'Twas a lucky escape for the stone.
JOHN WOLCOT, *On a Stone Thrown at George III*.

13
And where is Fum the Fourth, our royal bird?
BYRON, *Don Juan*. Canto xi, st. 78. Referring to George IV.

How Monarchs die is easily explain'd,
And thus it might upon the Tomb be chisell'd,
"As long as George the Fourth could *reign* he *reign'd*,
And then he *mizzled*."
THOMAS HOOD, *On a Royal Demise*.

That he was the handsomest prince in the whole world was agreed by men, and, alas! by many women.
THACKERAY, *The Four Georges: George the Fourth*.

A corpulent Adonis of fifty.
LEIGH HUNT, who was imprisoned for thus referring to George IV, when Regent. (*Examiner*, 1813.)

14
Let George do it. (Laissez faire à Georges, il est l'homme d'age.)
LOUIS XII of France. A satirical reference to his prime minister, Cardinal Georges d'Amboise. (c. 1500.) (See SLAUGHTER, *Two Children in Old Paris*, p. 233.) Translated into modern slang as meaning, "Let the other fellow do it."

GERMANY AND THE GERMANS

I—National Songs

1
This is the German's Fatherland,
Where wrath pursues the foreign band,
Where every Frank is held a foe,
And Germans all as brothers glow;
That is the land!
All Germany's thy Fatherland!
(Das ist des Deutschen Vaterland,
Wo Zorn vertilgt den wälschen Tand,
Wo jeder Franzmann heisset Feind,
Wo jeder Deutsche heisset Freund—
Das soll es sein!
Das ganze Deutschland soll es sein!)

ERNST MORITZ ARNDT, *Des Deutschen Vaterland.* (c. 1808)

O Germany! bright Fatherland!
O German love so true!
Thou sacred land, thou beauteous land,
We swear to thee anew!
Outlawed, each knave and craven shall
The crow and raven feed!
But we will to the battle all—
Revenge shall be our meed.
(O Deutschland, heil'ges Vaterland!
A deutsche Lieb und Treue!
Du hohes Land! Du schönes Land!
Dir schwören wir aufs neue;
Dem Buben und dem Knecht die Acht!
Der füttre Krähn und Raben!
So ziehn wir aus zur Hermannschlact
Und wollen Rache haben.)

ERNST MORITZ ARNDT, *Vaterlandslied.* (c. 1808)

2
Germany [stands for me] above all, above all the world! (Deutschland, Deutschland über Alles, über Alles in der Welt.)

A. H. HOFFMAN VON FALLERSLEBEN, *Deutschlandlied.* (1841) The melody was composed by Joseph Haydn, and is that of the old Austrian Imperial Anthem, the *Kaiserhymne.* It was first played 12 Feb., 1797. Popular as a marching song during World War I, it is amusing to recall that they also marched to "Weit ist der weg zurueck ins Heimatland, Weit, weit, weit," exactly the same meter and tune as the British soldiers' "Pack your troubles in the old kit bag and smile, smile, smile." "Austria above all" (*Oesterrich über Alles*) was the title of a pamphlet written in 1684 by P. W. von Hornich, and "Prussia above all" (*Preussen über Alles*) came from an unknown author in 1817. The third stanza of the *Deutschlandlied,* beginning" "Einigkeit und Recht und Freiheil (Unity and Right and Freedom), was proclaimed the official Anthem of the Federal Republic of Germany by President Theodore Heuss, 2 May, 1952. It runs as follows:

Unity and Right and Freedom
For the German Fatherland!
For this let all fraternally
Strive each with heart and hand!
Unity and Right and Freedom
Are the pledge of happiness.
Bloom in splendor of this happiness,
Germany, our Fatherland.
(Einigkeit und Recht und Freiheit
Für das deutsche Vaterland!
Danach lasst uns alle streben
Brüderlich mit Herz und Hand!
Einigkeit und Recht und Freiheit
Sind des Glückes Unterpfand.
Blüh im Glanze dieses Glückes,
Blühe, deutsches Vaterland!)

3
French and Russian they matter not,
A blow for a blow and a shot for a shot! . . .
We have one foe and one alone, England!
(Wir haben nur einen einzigen Feind,
England!)

ERNST LISSAUER, *Hassgesang Gegen England.* (1914) *For fuller quotation see* 2299c:4.

3a
I had a faithful comrade,
None better could you find;
The battle drum beat gaily,
He marched beside me daily,
And never fell behind.
(Ich hatt einen Kameraden,
Einen bessern findst du nit.
Die Tromme schlug zum Streite,
Er ging an meiner Seite
In gleichem Schritt und Tritt.

LUDWIG UHLAND, *Der Gute Kamerad.* (1915)

4
Dear Fatherland, no danger thine,
Firm stand thy sons to watch the Rhine!
(Lieb Vaterland, magst ruhig sein,
Fest stet und treu die Wacht am Rhein.
(1840)

II—Germany: Some Familiar Phrases

6
Our next war will be fought for the highest interests of our country and of mankind. . . . "World power or downfall" will be our rallying cry. (Weltmacht oder Niedergang.)

FRIEDRICH VON BERNHARDI, *Germany and the Next War.* Ch. 3. (1914)

7
Just for the word "neutrality," a word which in wartime had so often been disregarded—just for a scrap of paper, Great Britain is going to make war on a kindred nation who desires nothing better than to be friends with her.

THEOBALD VON BETHMANN-HOLLWEG, German Foreign Minister to Sir Edward Goschen, British Ambassador, 4 Aug., 1914. (Despatch by Sir Edward Goschen to British Foreign Office. *War Encyclopedia,* Govt. Printing Office, Washington, 1918)

I will do my duty as I see it, without regard to scraps of paper called constitutions.

KING WILHELM I of Germany, *Speech*, to the Prussian Diet, which had refused to grant appropriations. (*Harper's Weekly*, 26 March, 1887.)

For what this whirlwind all aflame?
This thunderstroke of hellish ire,
Setting the universe afire?
While millions upon millions came
Into a very storm of war?
For a scrap of paper.
(Pourquoi cette trombe enflammée
Qui vient foudroyer l'univers?
Cet embrasement de l'enfer?
Ce tourbillonnement d'armées
Par mille milliers de milliers?
—C'est pour un chiffon de papier.)

PÈRE HYACINTHE LOYSON, *Pour un Chiffon de Papier*. (Edward Brabrook, tr.)

1
Let us put Germany, so to speak, in the saddle! you will see that she can ride. (Setzen wir Deutschland, so zu sagen, in den Sattel! Reiten wird es schon können.)

BISMARCK, *Speech*, in the Parliament of the Confederation, 11 March, 1867.

We are not going to Canossa. (Nach Canossa gehen wir nicht.)

BISMARCK, *Speech*, in the Reichstag, May 14, 1872. It was to Canossa that Emperor Henry IV went to do three days' penance, barefoot, bareheaded, in the snow, before Pope Gregory VII, in January, 1077. Bismarck used the phrase at the beginning of the "Kulturkampf" contest with the Pope in 1872, to indicate that the revived German Empire would not surrender to the Papal claims. In the end the Pope won.

We Germans fear God, but nothing else in the world. (Wir Deutschen fürchten Gott, sonst aber Nichts in der Welt.)

BISMARCK, *Speech*, in the Reichstag, 1887.

BLOOD AND IRON, *see* WAR: DEFINITIONS.

2
German fury. (Furor teutonicus.)

LUCAN, *De Bello Civili*. Bk. i, l. 255.

Destroyed by German fury, rebuilt by American generosity.

WHITNEY WARREN, *Inscription*, for library at Louvain, Belgium. Removed, c. 1926, as the result of German pressure.

3 I beg that the small steamers . . . be spared if possible, or else sunk without a trace being left. (Spurlos versenkt.)

COUNT KARL VON LUXBURG, Chargé d'Affaires at Buenos Aires, *Telegram*, to the Berlin Foreign Office, 19 May, 1917.

If neutrals were destroyed so that they disappeared without leaving any trace, terror would soon keep seamen and travelers away from the danger zones.

PROF. OSWALD FLAMM, Berlin *Woche*. (See New York *Times*, 15 May, 1917.)

4
Der Kaiser auf der Vaterland
Und Gott on high, all dings gommand,
Ve too, ach, don'd you understandt?
Meinself—und Gott.

ALEXANDER MACGREGOR ROSE, *Kaiser & Co.* St. 1. First published in the Toronto *Herald* in 1897; recited by Captain Joseph Bullock Coghlan at a banquet at the Union League Club, New York, 21 April, 1899, on his return from the battle of Manila. Usually called, "Hoch der Kaiser." (See Stevenson, *Famous Single Poems*, p. 32.)

5
Shout! Let it reach the startled Huns!
And roar with all thy festal guns!
It is the answer of thy sons,
Carolina!

HENRY TIMROD, *Carolina*. Written in 1865, referring to Sherman's army. "Huns" became the popular name for the Germans in 1914.

6
Our German Fatherland to which I hope will be granted . . . to become in the future as closely united, as powerful, and as authoritative as once the Roman world-empire was, and that, just as in the old times they said, "Civis romanus sum," hereafter, at some time in the future, they will say, "I am a German citizen."

WILHELM II, *Speech*, Oct., 1900.

What was the old formula of Pan-Germanism? From Bremen to Bagdad, wasn't it?

WOODROW WILSON, *Address*, St. Louis, Mo., 5 Sept., 1919.

7
The Emperor's will is law. (Des Kaisers Wille ist des Gesetz.)

WILHELM II of Germany. (DAVIDSON, *Imperialization of Germany. Forum*, xxiii, 252.)

If any man dares impugn our right, then drive in with your mailed fist! (Dann fahre darein mit gepanzerter Faust.)

WILHELM II of Germany, to his brother, Prince Henry of Prussia, at Kiel, on the eve of the latter's departure in 1897, in command of the German expedition against China. See *Wilhelm II*, vol. ii, p. 80.

It will now be my duty to see to it that this place in the sun shall remain our undisputed possession.

WILHELM II, *Speech*, on the acquisition of Kiaochow, China, 18 June, 1901. Lebensraum (living room or space) became the equivalent Hitler slogan.

"That dog is mine," said those poor children; "that place in the sun is mine." Such is the beginning and type of usurpation throughout the earth. ("Ce chien est à moi," disaient ces pauvres enfants; "c'est là ma place au soleil." Voilà le commencement et l'image de l'usurpation.)

PASCAL, *Pensées*. No. 295.

A German quarrel. (Querelle d'allemand.)

A French phrase for an unjust quarrel.

III—Germany: Praise and Criticism

8
Germany is the only country I have visited

where the hands of the men are better cared for than the hands of the women.

PRICE COLLIER, *Germany and the Germans*, p. 280.

The Germans since 1870 have taken the place of the English as the boors of Europe.

COLLIER, *England and the English*, p. 429.

1
The wee wee German Lairdie.

ALLAN CUNNINGHAM, *Jacobite Song*. Claimed by some authorities to be a traditional Scottish song long antedating Cunningham.

2
The Germans want to be governed. (Die Deutschen wollen regiert sein.)

THOMAS DAVIDSON, *The Imperialization of Germany*, quoting "the very patriotic rector of one of the chief German universities." (*Forum*, xxiii, 248.)

The German's wit is in his fingers.

GEORGE HERBERT, *Jacula Prudentum*.

3
They say ve for we, and wisy wersy.

THOMAS HOOD, *Up the Rhine*.

4
Think of the man who first tried German sausage.

J. K. JEROME, *Three Men in a Boat*. Ch. 14.

5
Little things make Germany a lovely place:
Small square fields where cabbages grow red,
Fire glowing golden on blue tiles,
Flowered cloth around a feather bed.

JOSEPHINE MILES, *Germany*.

6
If a man were drowning to-day he would have to shout for help in German.

SIR OSWALD MOSLEY, *Speech*, 1931. At a time when Germany was pleading for the cancellation of reparations.

7
It was a dictum of Porson, that "Life is too short to learn German"; meaning, I apprehend, not that it is too difficult to be acquired within the ordinary space of life, but that there is nothing in it to compensate for the portion of life bestowed on its acquirement.

THOMAS LOVE PEACOCK, *Gryll Grange*. Ch. 3.

8
Germans are honest men.

SHAKESPEARE, *Merry Wives of Windsor*, iv, 5, 73.

9
Ah, a German and a genius! a prodigy! Admit him.

SWIFT, his last words, referring to Handel.

10
Germany, the diseased world's bathhouse.

MARK TWAIN, *Autobiography*. Vol. i, p. 219.

GHOST

See also Spirits, Vision, Witch

11
Great Pompey's shade complains that we are slow,
And Scipio's ghost walks unaveng'd amongst us!

ADDISON, *Cato*. Act ii, sc. 1.

12
Then, like the last priest of a vanished nation,
The Shadow drew the cowl about its head,
And with a web-like hand made salutation,
And went back to the Dead

HERVEY ALLEN, *Shadow to Shadow*.

13
Ghosts, like ladies, never speak till spoke to.

R. H. BARHAM, *The Ghost*.

14
Horrid apparition, tall and ghastly,
That walks at dead of night, or takes his stand
O'er some new-open'd grave; and (strange to tell!)
Evanishes at crowing of the cock.

ROBERT BLAIR, *The Grave*, l. 67.

15
Where Entity and Quiddity,
The ghosts of defunct bodies, fly.

BUTLER, *Hudibras*. Pt. i, canto i, l. 145.

16
Are we not Spirits, that are shaped into a body, into an Appearance; and that fade away again into air and Invisibility? Oh, Heaven, it is mysterious, it is awful to consider that we not only carry a future Ghost within us; but are, in very deed, Ghosts!

THOMAS CARLYLE, *Sartor Resartus: Natural Supernaturalism*.

17
He flits across the stage a transient and embarrassed phantom.

BENJAMIN DISRAELI, *Endymion*. Ch. 3.

18
By midnight moons, o'er moistening dews,
In habit for the chase arrayed,
The hunter still the deer pursues,
The hunter and the deer—a shade!

PHILIP FRENEAU, *The Indian Burying-Ground*. (1787)

Now o'er the hills in chase he flits,
The hunter and the deer a shade!

THOMAS CAMPBELL, *O'Connor's Child*. St. 4. (1809) Campbell's appropriation of Freneau's line is one of the most barefaced in literary history.

Fond man! the vision of a moment made!
Dream of a dream! and shadow of a shade!

EDWARD YOUNG, *Paraphrase on Part of the Book of Job*, l. 187.

A hunter of shadows, himself a shade.

HOMER, *Odyssey*. Bk. xi, l. 574. Referring to Orion. *See also under* SHADOW.

19
At first cock-crow the ghosts must go
Back to their quiet graves below.

THEODOSIA GARRISON, *The Neighbors*.

20
O'er all there hung a shadow and a fear;
A sense of mystery the spirit daunted,
And said as plain as whisper in the ear,
The place is Haunted.

THOMAS HOOD, *The Haunted House*.

1
Thin, airy shoals of visionary ghosts.
HOMER, *Odyssey*. Bk. xi, l. 48. (Pope, tr.)

2
All argument is against it, but all belief is for it.
SAMUEL JOHNSON, referring to the appearance of men's spirits after death. (BOSWELL, *Life*, 1778.)

I look for ghosts; but none will force
Their way to me: 'tis falsely said
That there was ever intercourse
Between the living and the dead.
WORDSWORTH, *The Affliction of Margaret*, l. 57.

I don't believe in ghosts, but I've been afraid of them all my life.
CHARLES A. DANA. (Quoted by BERT LESTON TAYLOR, *The So-Called Human Race*, p. 156.)

I expressed just now my mistrust of what is called Spiritualism . . . I owe it a trifle for a message said to have come from Voltaire's Ghost. It was asked, "Are you now convinced of another world?" and rapped out, "There *is* no other world—Death is only an incident in Life."
WILLIAM DE MORGAN, *Joseph Vance*. Ch. 11.

3
What gentle ghost, besprent with April dew,
Hails me so solemnly to yonder yew?
BEN JONSON, *Elegy on Lady Jane Pawlet*, l. 1.

What beck'ning ghost along the moonlight shade
Invites my steps, and points to yonder glade?
POPE, *Elegy to the Memory of an Unfortunate Lady*, l. 1.

4
So many ghosts, and forms of fright,
Have started from their graves to-night,
They have driven sleep from mine eyes away;
I will go down to the chapel and pray.
LONGFELLOW, *The Golden Legend*. Pt. iv.

5
All houses wherein men have lived and died
Are haunted houses. Through the open doors
The harmless phantoms on their errands glide,
With feet that make no sound upon the floors.
LONGFELLOW, *Haunted Houses*. St. 1.

The stranger at my fireside cannot see
The forms I see, nor hear the sounds I hear;
He but perceives what is; while unto me
All that has been is visible and clear.
LONGFELLOW, *Haunted Houses*. St. 4.

6 A thousand fantasies
Begin to throng into my memory
Of calling shapes, and beck'ning shadows dire,
And airy tongues, that syllable men's names
On sands, and shores, and desert wildernesses.
MILTON, *Comus*, l. 205.

The other shape,
If shape it might be call'd that shape had none
Distinguishable in member, joint, or limb;
Or substance might be call'd that shadow seem'd.
MILTON, *Paradise Lost*. Bk. ii, l. 666.

Whence and what are thou, execrable shape?
MILTON, *Paradise Lost*. Bk. ii, l. 681.

7
But O as to embrace me she inclin'd,
I wak'd, she fled, and day brought back my night.
MILTON, *Sonnet on His Deceased Wife*.

With a slow and noiseless footstep
Comes that messenger divine,
Takes the vacant chair beside me,
Lays her gentle hand in mine.
LONGFELLOW, *Footsteps of Angels*.

8
Men say that in this midnight hour,
The disembodièd have power
To wander as it liketh them,
By wizard oak and fairy stream.
WILLIAM MOTHERWELL, *Midnight*.

9
Peace, break thee off; look, where it comes again!
SHAKESPEARE, *Hamlet*. Act i, sc. 1, l. 40.

A figure like your father,
Armed at point exactly, cap-a-pe.
SHAKESPEARE, *Hamlet*. Act i, sc. 2, l. 199.

10
Angels and ministers of grace defend us!
Be thou a spirit of health or goblin damn'd,
Bring with thee airs from heaven or blasts from hell,
Be thy intents wicked or charitable,
Thou comest in such questionable shape
That I will speak to thee.
SHAKESPEARE, *Hamlet*. Act i, sc. 4, l. 39.

Alas, poor ghost!
SHAKESPEARE, *Hamlet*. Act i, sc. 5, l. 4.

11 Unhand me, gentlemen.
By heaven, I'll make a ghost of him that lets me!
SHAKESPEARE, *Hamlet*. Act i, sc. 4, l. 84.

12 I am thy father's spirit,
Doom'd for a certain term to walk the night.
SHAKESPEARE, *Hamlet*. Act i, sc. 5, l. 9.

No ghost should be allowed to walk
And make such havoc with its talk:
When folks are dead, they should retire—
I have no patience with you, Sire!
CHARLES DALMON, *To the Ghost of Hamlet's Father*.

13
There needs no ghost, my lord, come from the grave
To tell us this.
SHAKESPEARE, *Hamlet*. Act i, sc. 5, l. 125.

It is an honest ghost, that let me tell you.
SHAKESPEARE, *Hamlet*. Act i, sc. 5, l. 138.

Art thou there, truepenny?
Come on,—you hear this fellow in the cellarage.
SHAKESPEARE, *Hamlet*. Act i, sc. 5, l. 150.

14 The time has been,
That, when the brains were out, the man would die,
And there an end; but now they rise again,

With twenty mortal murders on their crowns.
SHAKESPEARE, *Macbeth*. Act iii, sc. 4, l. 79.

Avaunt! and quit my sight! let the earth hide thee!
Thy bones are marrowless, thy blood is cold;
Thou hast no speculation in those eyes
Which thou dost glare with!
SHAKESPEARE, *Macbeth*. Act iii, sc. 4, l. 93.

Hence, horrible shadow! Unreal mockery, hence!
SHAKESPEARE, *Macbeth*. Act iii, sc. 4, l. 106.

1
Now it is the time of night,
That the graves, all gaping wide,
Every one lets forth his sprite,
In the church-way paths to glide.
SHAKESPEARE, *A Midsummer-Night's Dream*. Act v, sc. 1, l. 386.

2
For all that here on earth we dreadful hold,
Be but as bugs to fearen babes withall.
SPENSER, *Faerie Queene*. Bk. ii, canto xii, st. 25.

Warwick was a bug that fear'd us all.
SHAKESPEARE, *III Henry VI*. Act v, sc. 2, l. 2.

To the world no bugbear is so great
As want of figure and a small estate.
POPE, *Imitations of Horace: Epistles*. Bk. i, epis. 1, l. 67.

At desperate doings with a bauble-sword,
And other bugaboo-and-baby-work.
ROBERT BROWNING, *The Ring and the Book*. Pt. v, l. 949.

3
I seem'd to move among a world of ghosts,
And feel myself the shadow of a dream.
TENNYSON, *The Princess*. Pt. i, l. 17.

A footstep, a low throbbing in the walls,
A noise of falling weights that never fell,
Weird whispers, bells that rang without a hand,
Door-handles turn'd when none was at the door,
And bolted doors that open'd of themselves;
And one betwixt the dark and light had seen
Her, bending by the cradle of her babe.
TENNYSON, *The Ring*, l. 375.

4
There came a ghost to Marg'ret's door,
With many a grievous groan,
And aye he tirlèd at the pin,
But answer made she none.
UNKNOWN, *Sweet William and May Marg'ret*.

GIANT

5
The giant loves the dwarf.
R. D. BLACKMORE, *Lorna Doone*. Ch. 1. Quoted as a proverb.

6
Pigmies placed on the shoulders of giants see more than the giants themselves. (Pigmæi gigantum humeris imporiti plusquam ipsi gigantes vident.)
DIDACUS STELLA. (LUCAN, *De Bello Civili*, x, ii.) Quoted by Burton, *Anatomy of Melancholy: Democritus to the Reader*.

For as our modern wits behold,
Mounted a pick-back on the old,
Much farther off, much further he,
Rais'd on his aged beast, could see.
BUTLER, *Hudibras*. Pt. i, canto ii, l. 71.

A dwarf sees farther than the giant when he has the giant's shoulders to mount on.
S. T. COLERIDGE, *The Friend*. Vol. i, p. 8.

A dwarf on a giant's shoulders sees farther of the two.
GEORGE HERBERT, *Jacula Prudentum*.

7
A giant will starve with what will surfeit a dwarf.
THOMAS FULLER, *Gnomologia*. No. 209.

8
There were giants in the earth in those days.
Old Testament: Genesis, vi, 4.

Strong were our sires, and as they fought they writ,
Conqu'ring with force of arms and dint of wit:
Theirs was the giant race before the flood.
DRYDEN, *Epistle to Mr. Congreve*, l. 3.

A fellow thirteen cubits high. (τρισκαιδεκάπηχυς.)
THEOCRITUS, *Idyls*. No. xv, l. 17.

9
Great giants work great wrongs—but we are small,
For love goes lowly; but Oppression's tall.
THOMAS HOOD, *Plea of the Midsummer Fairies*.

You Stump-o'-the-Gutter, you Hop-o'-my-Thumb,
Your husband must from Lilliput come.
KANE O'HARA, *Midas*.

10
Far be it from me to tell them of the battles of the giants.
PLATO, *The Republic*. Sec. 378. (Jowett, tr.)

11
A dwarf is not tall, though he stand upon a mountain-top; a giant keeps his height, even though he stands in a well. (Non est magnus pumilio, licet in monte constiterit; colossus magnitudinem suam servabit, etiam si steterit in puteo.)
SENECA, *Epistulæ ad Lucilium*. Epis. lxxvi, 32.

Pigmies are pigmies still, though perch'd on alps,
And pyramids are pyramids in vales.
YOUNG, *Night Thoughts*. Night vi, l. 309.

12
A stirring dwarf we do allowance give
Before a sleeping giant.
SHAKESPEARE, *Troilus and Cressida*. Act ii, sc. 3, l. 146.

13
Shall a man go hang himself because he belongs to the race of pygmies, and not be the biggest pygmy that he can?
H. D. THOREAU, *Walden: Conclusion*.

GIFTS AND GIVING

I—Gifts: Apothegms

14
To treat a poor wretch with a bottle of Burgundy, and fill his snuff-box, is like giving a

pair of laced ruffles to a man that has never a shirt on his back.

Tom Brown, *Laconics.*

But hang it—to poets who seldom can eat,
Your very good mutton's a very good treat;
Such dainties to them, their health it might hurt:
It's like sending them ruffles, when wanting a
shirt.

Goldsmith, *The Haunch of Venison,* l. 33.

1
When they offer thee a heifer, run with a halter.

Cervantes, *Don Quixote.* Pt. ii, ch. 4.

When the pig's proffered, hold up the poke.

John Heywood, *Proverbs.*

2
Gifts break rocks. (Dadivas quebrantan peñas.)

Cervantes, *Don Quixote.* Pt. ii, ch. 35. Quoted by Fuller, *Gnomologia. See also under* Bribery.

3
Giving and keeping require brains.

Cervantes, *Don Quixote.* Pt. ii, ch. 43.

To give and keep there is need of wit.

John Ray, *English Proverbs.*

4
Be careful to whom you give. (Cui des videto.)

Dionysius Cato(?), *Disticha Moralia: Prologus,* l. 17.

He that's liberal
To all alike, may do a good by chance,
But never out of judgement.

Beaumont and Fletcher, *The Spanish Curate.* Act i, sc. 1.

Who gives to all denies all.

George Herbert, *Jacula Prudentum.*

5
One must be poor to know the luxury of giving.

George Eliot, *Middlemarch.* Bk. ii, ch. 17.

To give is the business of the rich. (Denn Geben ist Sache des Reichen.)

Goethe, *Hermann und Dorothea.* Canto i, l. 15.

Poor and liberal; rich and covetous.

George Herbert, *Jacula Prudentum.*

6
It is said that gifts persuade even the gods. (Πείθειν δῶρα καὶ Θεοὺς λόγος.)

Euripides, *Medea,* l. 964.

Gifts persuade the gods, gifts persuade noble kings. (Δῶρα θεοὺς πείθει δῶρ' αἰδοίους βασιλῆας.)

Plato, *De Republica.* Bk. iii. Quoted. Attributed to Hesiod by Suidas.

7
One gift well given recovereth many losses.

Thomas Fuller, *Gnomologia.*

8
Give a thing, take a thing,
That's an old man's plaything.

Unknown. (Halliwell, *Proverb-Rhymes.*)

Give a thing and take again,
And you shall ride in hell's wain.

John Ray, *English Proverbs.*

9
Steal the hog, and give the feet for alms.

George Herbert, *Jacula Prudentum.*

Steal the goose and give the giblets in alms.

John Ray, *English Proverbs.*

10
When I gave you an inch, you took an ell.

John Heywood, *Proverbs.* Pt. ii, ch. 9.

Give an inch, he'll take an ell.

John Webster, *Sir Thomas Wyatt.*

11
What shall I give? What shall I not give? (Quid dem? Quid non dem?)

Horace, *Epistles.* Bk. ii, epis. 2, l. 63.

12
The greatest grace of a gift, perhaps, is that it anticipates and admits of no return.

Longfellow, *Journals and Letters,* 28 Feb., 1871.

13
Giving calls for genius. (Res est ingeniosa dare.)

Ovid, *Amores.* Bk. i, eleg. 8, l. 62.

For what he has he gives, what thinks he shows;
Yet gives he not till judgement guide his bounty.

Shakespeare, *Troilus and Cressida.* Act iv, sc. 5, l. 101.

14
Let your portal be deaf to prayers, but wide to the giver. (Surda sit oranti tua janua, laxa ferenti.)

Ovid, *Amores.* Bk. i, eleg. 8, l. 77. Ovid's advice to a woman.

15
Blessed is he who gets the gift, not he for whom it is meant. (Cui datum est, non cui destinatum.)

Petronius, *Satyricon.* Sec. 43.

A gift is as a precious stone in the eyes of him that hath it.

Old Testament: Proverbs, xvii, 8.

16
Length of days is in her right hand; and in her left hand riches and honour.

Old Testament: Proverbs, iii, 16.

17
Giff-gaff makes gude friends.

John Ray, *English Proverbs: Scottish.* Giff-gaff means one gift for another.

Giff-gaff was a good man, but he is soon weary.

John Ray, *English Proverbs.*

18
I am not in the giving vein today.

Shakespeare, *Richard III.* Act iv, sc. 2, l. 119.

Sure the duke is In the giving vein.

Philip Massinger, *The Great Duke of Florence.* Act v, sc. 3.

19
The Gods themselves cannot recall their gifts.

Tennyson, *Tithonus,* l. 49. Quoted.

20
Only he can be trusted with gifts who can present a face of bronze to expectations.

H. D. Thoreau, *Journal.* (Emerson, *Thoreau.*)

II—Gifts: The Gift Horse

1
Never examine the teeth of a gift horse. (Noli equi dentes inspicere donati.)
St. Jerome (Hieronymus), *Epistulæ ad Ephesus: Proem.* Sometimes given: "Equi donati dentes non inspiciuntur." Referred to as "ut vulgare proverbium est." The expression was used by St. Jerome, according to Archbishop Trench (*Study of Words*), when he replied to certain critics that they ought not to find fault with his writings, since they were free-will offerings.

A given horse may not be looked in the teeth.
John Stanbridge, *Vulgaria*. Sig. C4. (c. 1520)

2
He always looked a given horse in the mouth.
Rabelais, *Works*. Bk. i, ch. 11. (1532)

3
A given horse (we say) may not be looked in the mouth.
Richard Taverner, *Proverbs*. Fo. 49. (1539)

No man ought to look a given horse in the mouth.
John Heywood, *Proverbs*. Pt. i, ch. 5. (1546)

4
I am resolved to ride this way [facing the tail], to make good the proverb, that I may not look a gift horse in the mouth.
Head and Kirkman, *English Rogue*, iii, 158. (1674)

5
He ne'er consider'd it, as loth
To look a gift-horse in the mouth,
And very wisely would lay forth
No more upon it than 'twas worth;
But as he got it freely, so
He spent it frank and freely too:
For saints themselves will sometimes be,
Of gifts that cost them nothing, free.
Butler, *Hudibras*. Pt. i, canto i, l. 489.

III—Giving and Receiving

6
It is more blessed to give than to receive.
New Testament: Acts, xx, 35.

It is more blissful to give than to take.
Unknown, *Dives and the Pauper*. Fo. 2. (1536)

It is better to give than to take.
John Heywood, *Proverbs*. Pt. i, ch. v. (1546)

7
A man there was, though some did count him mad,
The more he cast away the more he had.
Bunyan, *The Pilgrim's Progress*. Pt. ii.

So that the more she gave away,
The more, y-wis, she had alway.
Chaucer, *Romaunt of the Rose*, l. 1159. Referring to Largesse.

The only things we ever keep
Are what we give away.
Louis Ginsberg, *Song*.

8
That man may last, but never lives,
Who much receives, but nothing gives;
Whom none can love, whom none can thank,
Creation's blot, creation's blank.
Thomas Gibbons, *When Jesus Dwelt*.

9
To get by giving, and to lose by keeping,
Is to be sad in mirth, and glad in weeping.
Christopher Harvie, *The Synagogue: The Church Stile*.

10
Give is a good girl, but Take is bad and she brings death. (Δὼς ἀγαθή, ἅρπαξ δὲ κακή, θανάτοιο δότειρα.)
Hesiod, *Works and Days*, l. 356.

11
Who shuts his hand, hath lost his gold:
Who opens it, hath it twice told.
George Herbert, *Charms and Knots*.

Giving much to the poor
Doth enrich a man's store;
It takes much from the account
To which his sin doth amount.
George Herbert, *Jacula Prudentum*.

12
The truly generous is the truly wise.
John Home, *Douglas*. Act iii, sc. 1.

13
The wise man does not lay up treasure. The more he gives to others, the more he has for his own.
Lao-tsze, *The Simple Way*. No. 81.

14
Give, and it shall be given unto you; good measure, pressed down, and shaken together, and running over.
New Testament: Luke, vi, 38. (Date et dabitur vobis.—*Vulgate*.)

In giving, a man receives more than he gives, and the more is in proportion to the worth of the thing given.
George Macdonald, *Mary Marston*. Ch. 5.

15
Who gives to friends so much from Fate secures.
That is the only wealth forever yours.
(Extra fortunam est quidquid donatur amicis:
Quas dederis solas semper habebis opes.)
Martial, *Epigrams*. Bk. v, epig. 42.

16
Go and sell that thou hast, and give to the poor, and thou shalt have treasure in heaven.
New Testament: Matthew, xix, 21.

The poor work miracles every day: we give them, and they give us treasure in heaven.
Thomas Wilson, *Maxims of Piety*, 29.

17
For all you can hold in your cold, dead hand
Is what you have given away.
Joaquin Miller, *Peter Cooper*. A translation of an ancient Sanscrit proverb.

18
The liberal soul shall be made fat.
Old Testament: Proverbs, xi, 25.

19
The goods we spend we keep; and what we

save we lose; and only what we lose we have.

FRANCIS QUARLES, *Divine Fancies*. Bk. iv, sec. 70. An apothegm which occurs in various forms in many writers.

1
Whatever I have given I still possess. (Hoc habeo quodcunque dedi.)

C. RABIRIUS. (SENECA, *De Beneficiis*, vi, 3, 1.)

2
The hand that gives, gathers.

JOHN RAY, *English Proverbs*.

3
Back of the sound broods the silence, back of the gift stands the giving;
Back of the hand that receives thrill the sensitive nerves of receiving.

RICHARD REALF, *Indirection*.

4
What we give to the wretched is given to Fortune. (Misero datur quodcumque, fortunæ datur.)

SENECA, *Troades*, l. 697.

5
What we gave, we have;
What we spent, we had;
What we left, we lost.

UNKNOWN, *Epitaph* on Edward Courtenay, Earl of Devon. (1419) (CLEVELAND, *Genealogical History of the Family of Courtenay*, p. 142.) Similar inscriptions are found on many old tombstones.

Quod expendi habui;
Quod donavi habeo;
Quod servavi perdidi.

RAVENSHAW, *Antiente Epitaphes*, p. 5. Quoted as the epitaph under the effigy of a priest.

6
I have spent; I have given; I have kept; I have possessed; I do possess; I have lost; I am punished; what I spent, I had; what I gave away, I have.

UNKNOWN, *Gesta Romanorum*. Tale xvi. Quoted as the epitaph on a sarcophagus.

IV—Gift and Giver

7
If thou doest aught good, do it quickly. For what is done quickly will be acceptable. Favors slowly granted are unfavorably received. (Si bene quid facias, facias cito. Nam cito factum Gratum erit. Ingratum gratia tarda facit.)

AUSONIUS, *Epigrams*. No. xvii.

He gives by halves, who hesitates to give.

WILLIAM BROOME, *Letter to Lord Cornwallis*.

8
For whoso giveth a gift, or doth a grace,
Does it betimes, his thank is well the more.

CHAUCER, *Legend of Good Women: Prologue*, l. 451.

Whate'er you give, give ever at demand,
Nor let old age stretch long his palsied hand;
Those who give late are importun'd each day,
And still are teas'd because they still delay.

JOHN GAY, *Trivia*. Bk. ii, l. 457.

He that's long a-giving knows not how to give.

GEORGE HERBERT, *Jacula Prudentum*.

9
Give nobly to indigent merit, and do not refuse your charity even to those who have no merit but their misery.

LORD CHESTERFIELD, *Letters*. (Undated. To be delivered after his death.)

Shut not thy purse-strings always against painted distress. . . . Rake not into the bowels of unwelcome truth to save a half-penny.

LAMB, *Essays of Elia: The Decay of Beggars*.

10
The good received, the giver is forgot.

WILLIAM CONGREVE, *To Lord Halifax*, l. 39. *See also under* DEVIL.

11
Now there are diversities of gifts, but the same Spirit.

New Testament: I Corinthians, xii, 4.

It is not the weight of jewel or plate,
Or the fondle of silk or fur;
'Tis the spirit in which the gift is rich,
As the gifts of the Wise Ones were,
And we are not told whose gift was gold,
Or whose was the gift of myrrh.

EDMUND VANCE COOKE, *The Spirit of the Gift*.

12
God loveth a cheerful giver.

New Testament: II Corinthians, ix, 7.

13
He giveth oft who gives what's oft refused.

RICHARD CRASHAW, *Epigrammata Sacra*, l. 103.

14
We do not quite forgive a giver. The hand that feeds us is in some danger of being bitten.

EMERSON, *Essays, Second Series: Gifts*.

15
The gift, to be true, must be the flowing of the giver unto me, correspondent to my flowing unto him.

EMERSON, *Essays, Second Series: Gifts*.

Rings and jewels are not gifts, but apologies for gifts. The only gift is a portion of thyself. . . . Therefore the poet brings his poem; the shepherd, his lamb; the farmer, corn; the miner, a gem; the sailor, coral and shells; the painter, his picture; the girl, a handkerchief of her own sewing.

EMERSON, *Essays, Second Series: Gifts*.

For the will and not the gift makes the giver. (Denn der Wille und nicht die Gabe macht den Geber.)

LESSING, *Nathan der Weise*. Act i, sc. 5.

16
Give, if thou canst, an alms: if not, afford,
Instead of that, a sweet and gentle word.

ROBERT HERRICK, *Alms*.

Give unto all, lest he whom thou deny'st
May chance to be no other man but Christ.

ROBERT HERRICK, *Alms*.

17
From Zeus are all strangers and beggars. (Πρὸς γὰρ Διός εἰσιν ἅπαντες ξεῖνοί τε πτωχοί τε.)

HOMER, *Odyssey*. Bk. vi, l. 207.

By Jove the stranger and the poor are sent,
And what to those we give, to Jove is lent.
HOMER, *Odyssey*. Bk. vi, l. 207. (Pope, tr.)

1
To give awkwardly is churlishness. The most difficult part is to give, then why not add a smile?
LA BRUYÈRE, *Les Caractères: Of the Court.*

2
That is no true alms which the hand can hold;
He gives only the worthless gold
Who gives from a sense of duty.
J. R. LOWELL, *Vision of Sir Launfal*. Pt. i, st. 6.

Not what we give, but what we share,
For the gift without the giver is bare;
Who gives himself with his alms feeds three,
Himself, his hungering neighbor, and me.
J. R. LOWELL, *Vision of Sir Launfal*. Pt. ii, st. 8.

3
When you give, Give not by halves.
MASSINGER, *The Bashful Lover*. Act ii, sc. 3.

4
Take heed that ye do not your alms before men, to be seen of them. . . . But when thou doest alms, let not thy left hand know what thy right hand doeth.
New Testament: Matthew, vi, 1–3.

5
The obligation of a gift hath reference wholly unto the will of him that giveth.
MONTAIGNE, *Essays*. Bk. iii, ch. 5.

6
Thanks are not forthcoming for a service which has come late through delay. (Gratiaque officio, quod mora tardet, abest.)
OVID, *Epistulæ ex Ponto*. Bk. iii, epis. 4, l. 52.

The gift which stays too long in the hands of the donor is not thankfully received. (Ingratum est beneficium quod diu inter manus dantis hæsit.)
SENECA, *De Beneficiis*. Bk. ii, l. 1.

7
The gift derives its value from the rank of the giver (Majestatem res data dantis habet.)
OVID, *Epistulæ ex Ponto*. Bk. iv, epis. ix, l. 68.

While you look at what is given, look also at the giver. (Cum quod datur spectabis, et dantem adspice.)
SENECA, *Thyestes,* l. 416.

8
Gifts are scorned where givers are despised.
DRYDEN, *The Hind and the Panther*. Pt. iii, l. 64.

9
Gifts which the giver makes precious are always the most acceptable. (Acceptissima semper Munera sunt, auctor quæ pretiosa facit.)
OVID, *Heroides*. Epis. xvii, l. 71.

10
That which is desired becomes doubly acceptable if you offer it spontaneously. (Bis est gratum quod opus est, si ultro sit datum.)
PUBLILIUS SYRUS, *Sententiæ*. No. 54.

11
He gives a double favor to a poor man who gives quickly. (Inopi beneficium bis dat, qui dat celeriter.)
SENECA. (PUBLILIUS SYRUS, *Proverbs of Seneca*. No. 235.) Usually quoted, "Bis dat, qui cito dat," "He gives twice who gives quickly." Bacon quoted it in this form when he took his seat in Chancery, 7 May, 1617. It appears in some form in many of the classics, attributed to various authors. Langius (*Polyanth. Noviss,* p. 382) credits it to Publius Mimus. Erasmus (*Adagia,* p. 265) credits it to Seneca.

Who gives at once gives twice. (El que luego Da, da dos veces.)
CERVANTES, *Don Quixote*. Pt. i, ch. 34.

He gives doubly who gives quickly. (Duplex fit bonitas, simul accessit celeritas.)
PUBLILIUS SYRUS, *Sententiæ*. No. 161.

He giveth twice that gives in a trice.
JOHN RAY, *English Proverbs.*

12
Hamlet: I never gave you aught.
Ophelia: My honour'd lord, you know right well you did;
And, with them, words of so sweet breath composed,
As made the things more rich: their perfume lost,
Take these again; for to the noble mind,
Rich gifts wax poor when givers prove unkind.
SHAKESPEARE, *Hamlet*. Act iii, sc. 1, l. 96.

13
To loyal hearts the value of all gifts
Must vary as the giver's.
TENNYSON, *Lancelot and Elaine,* l. 1207.

14
Enhance our gift with words as much as you can. (Munus nostrum ornato verbis, quod poteris.)
TERENCE, *Eunuchus,* l. 214. (Act ii, sc. 1.)

15
It is not the shilling I give you that counts, but the warmth that it carries with it from my hand.
MIGUEL DE UNAMUNO, *Essays and Soliloquies,* p. 136.

16
Behold, I do not give lectures or a little charity,
When I give I give myself.
WALT WHITMAN, *Song of Myself*. Sec. 40.

V—Gifts: Great and Small

17
Silver and gold have I none; but such as I have give I thee.
New Testament: Acts, iii, 6.

'Twas all he gave, 'twas all he had to give.
SAMUEL ROGERS, *Pleasures of Memory*. Pt. i, l. 132.

18
I give thee sixpence! I'll see thee damned first.
GEORGE CANNING, *The Friend of Humanity and the Knife-Grinder.*

1
Give plenty of what is given to you,
Listen to pity's call;
Don't think the little you give is great,
And the much you get is small.
PHŒBE CARY, *A Legend of the Northland.*

2
But covet earnestly the best gifts.
New Testament: 1 Corinthians, xii, 31.

3
The great gifts are not got by analysis. . . . Nature hates calculators.
EMERSON, *Essays, Second Series: Experience.*

4
He that gives me small gifts would have me live.
GEORGE HERBERT, *Jacula Prudentum.*

A little given seasonably excuses a great gift.
GEORGE HERBERT, *Jacula Prudentum.*

5
A gift though small is welcome. (Δόσις δ' ὀλίγη τε, φίλη τε.)
HOMER, *Odyssey*. Bk. vi, l. 208.

6
Rare gift! but oh, what gift to fools avails!
HOMER, *Odyssey*. Bk. x, l. 29. (Pope, tr.)

A gift worthy of Apollo. (Munus Apolline dignum.)
HORACE, *Epistles*. Bk. ii, epis. 1, l. 216. Referring to a book or poem.

7
"Here it is," said Father Phil, "here it is, and no denying it—down in black and white; but if they who give are in black, how much blacker are those who have not given at all?"
SAMUEL LOVER, *Handy Andy*. Ch. 28.

8
Great gifts are for great men.
JOHN RAY, *English Proverbs.*

9
Seven hundred pounds and possibilities is good gifts.
SHAKESPEARE, *The Merry Wives of Windsor*. Act i, sc. 1, l. 66.

10
If thou hast abundance, give alms accordingly; if thou hast but a little, be not afraid to give according to that little.
Apocrypha: Tobit, iv, 8.

Give what you have. To some one, it may be better than you dare to think.
LONGFELLOW, *Kavanagh*. Ch. 30.

11
I have found out a gift for my fair;
I have found where the wood-pigeons breed.
(Parta meæ Veneri sunt munera: nam que notavi
Ipse locum, aëriæ quo congessere palumbes.)
VERGIL, *Eclogues*. No. iii, l. 68. (William Shenstone, tr.)

12
Give all thou canst: high Heaven rejects the lore
Of nicely-calculated less or more.
WORDSWORTH, *Ecclesiastical Sonnets*. Pt. iii, 43.

VI—Gifts: Their Danger

13
We must take care to indulge only in such generosity as will help our friends and hurt no one . . . for nothing is generous, if it is not at the same time just. (Nihil est liberale, quod non idem justum.)
CICERO, *De Officiis*. Bk. i, ch. 14, sec. 43.

14
A gift destroyeth the heart.
Old Testament: Ecclesiastes, vii, 7.

15
The gifts of a bad man bring no good with them. (Κακοῦ γὰρ ἀνδρὸς δῶρ' ὄνησιν οὐκ ἔχει.)
EURIPIDES, *Medea*, l. 618.

A wicked man's gift hath a touch of its master.
GEORGE HERBERT, *Jacula Prudentum.*

16
Thou shalt take no gift: for the gift blindeth the wise, and perverteth the words of the righteous.
Old Testament: Exodus, xxiii, 8.

17
The generous man pays for nothing so much as for what is given him.
THOMAS FULLER, *Gnomologia.*

I find nothing so dear as what is given me.
MONTAIGNE, *Essays*. Bk. iii, ch. 9.

18
He is very fond of making things which he doesn't want, and then giving them to people who have no use for them.
ANTHONY HOPE, *The Dolly Dialogues*. No. 17.

19
The prodigal and the fool give what they despise and hate, and this seed produces a crop of ingrates. (Prodigus et stultus donat quæ spernit et odit; Hæc seges ingratos tulit.)
HORACE, *Epistles*. Bk. i, epis. 7, l. 20.

20
He who has given this to-day, may, if he pleases, take it away to-morrow. (Qui dedit hoc hodie, cras, si volet, auferet.)
HORACE, *Epistles*. Bk. i, epis. 16, l. 33.

The good that can be given, can be removed. (Dari bonum quod potuit, auferri potest.)
LUCILIUS. (SENECA, *Epistulæ ad Lucilium*. Epis. viii, sec. 10.)

What can be given can also be taken away. (Quod dari posset, et eripi posse.)
SENECA, *Epistulæ ad Lucilium*. Epis. xcviii, 13.

21
"He sent out great gifts indeed." But he sent them on a hook, and is it possible that the fish can love the fisherman? ("Munera magna tamen misit." Sed misit in hamo; Et piscatorem piscis amare potest?)
MARTIAL, *Epigrams*. Bk. vi, ep. 63, l. 5.

Whoever makes great presents, expects great presents in return. (Quisquis magna dedit, voluit sibi magna remitti.)
MARTIAL, *Epigrams*. Bk. v, ep. lix, l. 3.

Take gifts with a sigh: most men give to be paid.
JOHN BOYLE O'REILLY, *Rules of the Road.*

1
I give that you may give. (Do ut des.)
BISMARCK, *Maxim.*

2
Thy pompous delicacies I contemn,
And count thy specious gifts no gifts but guiles.
MILTON, *Paradise Regained.* Bk. ii, l. 390.

Their offers should not charm us,
Their evil gifts would harm us.
CHRISTINA ROSSETTI, *Goblin Market.*

3
All the other gifts appertinent to man, as the malice of this age shapes them, are not worth a gooseberry.
SHAKESPEARE, *II Henry IV.* Act i, sc. 2, l. 194.

4
The gifts of a foe are not gifts, and have no value. (Ἐχθρῶν ἄδωρα δῶρα κοὐκ ὀνήσιμα.)
SOPHOCLES, *Ajax,* l. 665. A proverb.

The gifts of an enemy seemed to them much to be feared. (Les dons d'un ennemi leur semblainte trop à craindre.)
VOLTAIRE, *Henriade.* Ch. 2.

5
The deadly gift of Minerva. (Donum exitiale Minervæ.)
VERGIL, *Æneid.* Bk. ii, l. 31. Referring to the gift of the wooden horse which led to Troy's downfall. *See also under* GREECE.

VII—Gifts: Generosity

6
Our generosity should never exceed our means. (Ne benignitas major esset quam facultates.)
CICERO, *De Officiis.* Bk. i, ch. 14, sec. 44.

Bounty has no bottom. (Largitionem fundum non habere.)
CICERO, *De Officiis.* Bk ii, ch. 15, sec. 55. Quoted as "a common proverb."

7
A hand as liberal as the light of day.
COWPER, *Hope,* l. 410.

8
It is always so pleasant to be generous, though very vexatious to pay debts.
EMERSON, *Essays, Second Series: Gifts.*

9
A man being sometimes more generous when he has but a little money than when he has plenty, perhaps through fear of being thought to have but little.
BENJAMIN FRANKLIN, *Autobiography.* Ch. 1.

10
Generosity is the flower of justice.
HAWTHORNE, *American Note-Books,* 19 Dec., 1850.

11
I had rather be a beggar and spend my last dollar like a king, than be a king and spend my money like a beggar.
INGERSOLL, *Liberty of Man, Woman and Child.*

12
What is called liberality is often merely the vanity of giving. (Ce qu'on nomme libéralité n'est le plus souvent que la vanité de donner.)
LA ROCHEFOUCAULD, *Maximes.* No. 263.

13
The very name of Liberality sounds Liberty. (Le nom même de la Libéralité sonne Liberté.)
MONTAIGNE, *Essays.* Bk. iii, ch. 6.

14
He partly begs
To be desir'd to give. It much would please him,
That of his fortunes you should make a staff
To lean upon.
SHAKESPEARE, *Antony and Cleopatra.* Act iii, sc. 13, l. 66.

For his bounty,
There was no winter in 't; and autumn 'twas
That grew the more by reaping.
SHAKESPEARE, *Antony and Cleopatra.* Act v, sc. 2, l. 86.

My purse, my person, my extremest means
Lie all unlock'd to your occasions.
SHAKESPEARE, *The Merchant of Venice.* Act i, sc. 1, l. 138.

15
Good-humour and generosity carry the day with the popular heart all the world over.
ALEXANDER SMITH, *Dreamthorp: On Vagabonds.*

16
I have always been deeply impressed by an old Jewish proverb which says, "What you give for the cause of charity in health is gold; what you give in sickness is silver; what you give after death is lead."
NATHAN STRAUS. First paragraph of Will.

VIII—Gifts of the Gods

17
God's gifts put man's best dreams to shame.
E. B. BROWNING, *Sonnets from the Portuguese.* No. xxvi.

18
That gift of his, from God descended.
Ah! friend, what gift of man's does not?
ROBERT BROWNING, *Christmas Eve.* Canto xvi.

19
Gifts come from above in their own peculiar forms. (Die Gaben Kommen von oben herab, in ihren eignen Gestalten.)
GOETHE, *Hermann und Dorothea.* Canto v, l. 69.

20
Every good gift and every perfect gift is from above, and cometh down from the Father of lights, with whom is no variableness, neither shadow of turning.
New Testament: James, i, 17.

21
How blind men are to Heaven's gifts! (O munera nondum Intellecta deum!)
LUCAN, *De Bello Civili.* Bk. v, l. 528.

22
God has given some gifts to the whole human

race, from which no one is excluded. (Deus quædam munera universo humano generi dedit. a quibus excluditur nemo.)
SENECA, *De Beneficiis*. Bk. iv, sec. 28.

1
O you gods!
Why do you make us love your goodly gifts,
And snatch them straight away?
SHAKESPEARE, *Pericles*. Act iii, sc. 1, l. 23.

2
For whatever a man has, is in reality only a gift. (Denn was ein Mensch auch hat, so sind's am Ende Gaben.)
WIELAND, *Oberon*. Pt. ii, l. 19.

3
A gift of that which is not to be given
By all the blended powers of earth and heaven.
WORDSWORTH, *Poems Dedicated to National Independence*. Pt. ii, No. 1.

That every gift of noble origin
Is breathed upon by Hope's perpetual breath.
WORDSWORTH, *Poems Dedicated to National Independence*. No. 20.

GIRL

See also Maiden

4
Oh, you mysterious girls, when you are fifty-two we shall find you out. You must come into the open then.
J. M. BARRIE, *The Little White Bird*. Ch. 1.

5
Girls are so massive and complete,
The ponderous important feet . . .
These awe me so I half-way miss
The fact that girls are made to kiss.
ROBERT LOUIS BURGESS, *Girls*.

6
'Tis true, your budding Miss is very charming,
But shy and awkward at first coming out,
So much alarm'd that she is quite alarming,
All Giggle, Blush—half Pertness, and half Pout, . . .
The Nursery still lisps out in all they utter—
Besides, they always smell of bread and butter.
BYRON, *Beppo*. St. 39.

7
Let every girl attend to her spinning. (Cada puta hile.)
CERVANTES, *Don Quixote*. Pt. i, ch. 46.

8
I grudge no expense in your education, but I positively will not keep you a Flapper.
LORD CHESTERFIELD, *Letters*, 22 Sept., 1749. Chesterfield's reference is to Swift (*Gulliver's Travels: Voyage to Laputa*), who tells how the Laputans were so absent-minded that a "flapper" was necessary to brush their eyelids from time to time, to keep them from falling over precipices, etc.

See the three skirts in the back? That's the Missus and the two squabs. Young one's only a flapper.
HARRY LEON WILSON, *Bunker Bean*. (1912) "Flapper" was further popularized by Scott Fitzgerald in 1920.

If there's anything in a beauty nap most o' the flappers I see must suffer from insomnia.
KIN HUBBARD, *Abe Martin's Broadcast*, p. 119.

If a davenport is a sheik's workbench, a rumble seat is a flapper's showcase.
G. E. SAMS. (*Pathfinder*. No. 1866.)

9
One of those little prating girls,
Of whom fond parents tell such tedious stories.
DRYDEN, *The Rival Ladies*. Act i, sc. 1.

10
My gal is a high born lady,
She's black but none too shady,
Feather'd like a peacock, just as gay,
She is not colored. she was born that way.
BARNEY FAGAN, *My Gal Is a High Born Lady*.

11
They are not young ladies, they are young persons.
W. S. GILBERT, *The Mikado*. Act i.

12
Girls like to be played with, and rumpled a little, too, sometimes.
GOLDSMITH, *She Stoops to Conquer*. Act v, 1.

But lest, by frail desires misled,
The girls forbidden paths should tread,
Of ignorance raised the safe high wall;
We sink ha-has, and show them all.
Thus we at once solicit sense,
And charge them not to break the fence.
MATTHEW GREEN, *The Spleen*, l. 274.

Defiant love sonnets
demanding nude joys
lure girls to be naughty
and live like the boys.
ALFRED KREYMBORG, *E.S.V.M.—Authors in Epigram*.

You may tempt the upper classes
With your villainous demi-tasses,
But Heaven will protect the working-girl!
EDGAR SMITH, *Heaven Will Protect the Working-Girl*. Sung with great success by Marie Dressler in *Tillie's Nightmare*, 1909.

13
When she was a girl (forty summers ago)
Aunt Tabitha tells me they never did so.
O. W. HOLMES, *The Poet at the Breakfast-Table: Aunt Tabitha*.

14
Wretched, un-idea'd girls.
SAMUEL JOHNSON. (BOSWELL, *Life*, 1752.)

15
This all girls learn before their alphabet. (Hoc discunt omnes ante alpha et beta puellæ.)
JUVENAL, *Satires*. Sat. xiv, l. 209. Referring to love of money.

16
There was a little girl
Who had a little curl
Right in the middle of her forehead,
And when she was good

She was very, very good,
  But when she was bad she was horrid.

HENRY WADSWORTH LONGFELLOW (?). According to Longfellow's son (ERNEST W. LONGFELLOW, *Random Memories*, p. 15), this little chant was composed while the poet was walking up and down his garden, carrying his second daughter, "Edith with the golden hair," in his arms. (See also BLANCHE R. TUCKER-MACHETTA, *Home Life of Longfellow*, p. 90.)

1
Perhaps it is better so—this world is a hard place for girls.

MARTIN LUTHER, *Remark*, to his wife, as they stood beside the coffin of their only daughter.

There! little girl, don't cry!

JAMES WHITCOMB RILEY, *A Life-Lesson*.

2
Your Rome has as many girls as the sky has stars. (Quot cœlum stellas, tot habet tua Roma puellas.)

OVID, *Ars Amatoria*. Bk. i, l. 59.

3
Dear to the heart of girls is their own beauty. (Virginibus cordi grataque forma sua est.)

OVID, *De Medicamine Faciei*, l. 32.

4
Men seldom make passes
At girls who wear glasses.

DOROTHY PARKER, *News Item*.

5
The most impudent hussy I have ever seen. (Quam ego unam vidi mulierem audacissimam.)

PLAUTUS, *Asinaria*, l. 521. (Act iii, sc. 1.)

6
We yet call a wench that skippeth or leapeth like a boy, a tomboy.

RICHARD ROWLANDS, *Antiquities Concerning the English Nation*, p. 234. (1605)

7
You bring up your girls as if they were meant for sideboard ornaments; and then complain of their frivolity.

RUSKIN, *Sesame and Lilies: Queen's Gardens*. Sec. 80.

8
          But the full sum of me . . .
Is an unlesson'd girl, unschool'd, unpractis'd:
Happy in this, she is not yet so old
But she may learn; happier than this,
She is not bred so dull but she can learn.

SHAKESPEARE, *Merchant of Venice*, iii, 2, 159.

9
'Tis a *credit* to any good girl to be neat,
But quite a disgrace to be *fine*.

ANN AND JANE TAYLOR, *Neatness*.

For a good-natured girl is loved best in the main,
If her dress is but decent, though ever so plain.

ANN AND JANE TAYLOR, *Finery*.

10
Queen rose of the rosebud garden of girls.

TENNYSON, *Maud*. Pt. i, sec. 22, st. 9.

11
Sweet girl-graduates in their golden hair.

TENNYSON, *The Princess: Prologue*, l. 142

12
It is no sin to look at a nice girl.

LEO TOLSTOY, *The Cossacks*. Ch. 12.

Thir breeks o' mine, my only pair,
That ance were plush o' guid blue hair,
I wad hae gi'en them off my hurdies,
For ae blink o' the bonnie burdies!

BURNS, *Tam o' Shanter*.

A sight to make an old man young.

TENNYSON, *The Gardener's Daughter*, l. 140.

13
And after him a finikin lass,
  Did shine like glistering gold.

UNKNOWN, *Robin Hood and Allen-a-Dale*.

14
What man can calculate on what a girl will say or do.

UNKNOWN. Said of Fortunata, a Rajput Princess, 12th c. (*History's Most Famous Words*.)

GLADSTONE, W. E.

15
An almost spectral kind of phantasm of a man—nothing in him but forms and ceremonies and outside wrappings.

THOMAS CARLYLE, *Letter*, 23 March, 1873.

16
A sophistical rhetorician, inebriated with the exuberance of his own verbosity, and gifted with an egotistical imagination that can at all times command an interminable and inconsistent series of arguments to malign an opponent and glorify himself.

BENJAMIN DISRAELI, *Speech*, 27 July, 1878.

He has not a single redeeming defect.

BENJAMIN DISRAELI. Referring to Gladstone.

17
He has one gift most dangerous to a speculator, a vast command of a kind of language, grave and majestic, but of vague and uncertain import.

MACAULAY, *Essays: Gladstone on Church and State*.

The rising hope of those stern and unbending Tories.

MACAULAY, *Gladstone on Church and State*.

18
The faculty of concealing his thoughts in words, of separating conviction from argument, was not the least striking of the great statesman's talents.

AGNES REPPLIER. In *Life*.

GLORY

See also Fame, Renown

I—Glory: Definitions

19
True glory takes deep root and spreads its branches wide; but all pretences soon fall to the ground like fragile flowers, and nothing counterfeit can be lasting. (Vera gloria radices agit atque etiam propagatur, ficta omnia celeriter tamquam flosculi decidunt, nec simulatum potest quicquam esse diuturnum.)

CICERO, *De Officiis*. Bk. ii, ch. 12, sec. 43.

1
Glory follows virtue as if it were its shadow. (Gloria virtutem tanquam umbra sequitur.)
CICERO, *Tusculanarum Disputationum*. Bk. i, ch. 45, sec. 110.

Of all the rewards of virtue, if we are to take any account of rewards, the most splendid is glory; for it is glory alone that can offer us the memory of posterity as a consolation for the shortness of life, so that, though absent, we are present, though dead, we live; it is by the ladder of glory only that mere men appear to rise to the heavens.
CICERO, *Pro Milone*. Ch. 35, sec. 97.

Glory is never where virtue is not. (La gloire n'est jamais où la vertu n'est pas.)
LE FRANC, *Didon*.

He that would have his virtue published, is not the servant of virtue, but glory.
BEN JONSON, *Explorata: De Sibi Molestis.*

2
Glory, built
On selfish principles, is shame and guilt.
COWPER, *Table Talk*, l. 1.

The chequered spectacle of so much glory and so much shame.
MACAULAY, *Essays: Mackintosh's History of the Revolution.*

On Butler who can think without just rage,
The glory and the scandal of the age.
JOHN OLDHAM, *Satire Against Poetry.*

3
He will have true glory who despises glory. (Gloriam qui spreverit, veram habet.)
FABIUS MAXIMUS. (LIVY, *History*. Bk. xxii, 39.)

4
True glory dwells where glorious deeds are done,
Where great men rise whose names athwart the dusk
Of misty centuries gleam like the sun!
WILLIAM DUDLEY FOULKE, *The City's Crown.*

5
Popular glory is a perfect coquette; her lovers must toil, feel every inquietude, indulge every caprice, and perhaps at last be jilted into the bargain. True glory, on the other hand, resembles a woman of sense; her admirers must play no tricks. They feel no great anxiety, for they are sure in the end of being rewarded in proportion to their merit.
GOLDSMITH, *The Bee*. No. 6.

6
No flowery road leads to glory. (Aucun chemin de fleurs ne conduit à la gloire.)
LA FONTAINE, *Fables*. Bk. x, fab. 14.

I climb a difficult road, but glory gives me strength. (Magnum iter adscendo, sed dat mihi gloria vires.)
PROPERTIUS, *Elegies*. Bk. iv, eleg. 10, l. 3.

Great is the glory, for the strife is hard!
WORDSWORTH, *To B. R. Haydon*, l. 14.

7
The glory of great men should always be measured by the means which they have used to acquire it. (La gloire des grands hommes se doit toujours mesurer aux moyens dont ils se sont servis pour l'acquérir.)
LA ROCHEFOUCAULD, *Maximes*. No. 157.

8
Glory is the true and honorable recompense of gallant actions.
LE SAGE, *Gil Blas*. Bk. vii, ch. 12.

9
Military glory—the attractive rainbow that rises in showers of blood.
ABRAHAM LINCOLN, *Speech*, House of Representatives. (GROSS, *Lincoln's Own Stories*, p. 53.)

10
Glory the reward
That sole excites to high attempts the flame
Of most erected spirits.
MILTON, *Paradise Regained*. Bk. iii, l. 25.

11
Glory is a mighty spur. (Immensum gloria calcar habet.)
OVID, *Epistulæ ex Ponto*. Bk. iv, epis. ii, l. 36.

Glory and honour serve as goads and spurs to virtue.
FRANCIS BACON, *De Augmentis Scientiarum*. Pt. i, bk. vi, ch. 3.

12
The nearest way to glory—a short-cut, as it were,—is to strive to be what you wish to be thought to be. (Viam ad gloriam proximam et quasi compendiariam dicebat esse, si quis id ageret, ut, qualis haberi vellet, talis esset.)
SOCRATES. (CICERO, *De Officiis*. Bk. ii, 12, 43.)

13
The glory of good men is in their conscience and not in the mouths of men.
THOMAS À KEMPIS, *De Imitatione Christi*. Pt. ii, ch. 6.

II—Glory: Apothegms

14
So may a glory from defect arise.
ROBERT BROWNING, *Deaf and Dumb*.

15
The glory dies not, and the grief is past.
SIR SAMUEL BRYDGES, *On the Death of Scott.*

16
Who track the steps of Glory to the grave.
BYRON, *Monody on the Death of Sheridan.*

Their glory illumines the gloom of their grave.
BYRON, *To the Rev. J. T. Becher.*

The paths of glory lead but to the grave.
THOMAS GRAY, *Elegy in a Country Churchyard*. St. 9.

17
Go then, Patroclus, where thy glory calls.
GEORGE GRANVILLE, *Heroic Love*. Act iv, sc. 1.

Go where glory waits thee;
But, while fame elates thee,
O, still remember me!
THOMAS MOORE, *Go Where Glory Waits Thee.*

This goin' ware glory waits ye haint one agreeable feetur.
J. R. LOWELL, *Biglow Papers*. Ser. i, No. 2.

1
Weep for the voiceless, who have known
The cross without the crown of glory!
O. W. HOLMES, *The Voiceless.*

2
The first in glory, as the first in place.
HOMER, *Odyssey*. Bk. xi, l. 441. (Pope, tr.)

3
To please great men is not the lowest glory. (Principibus placuisse viris non ultima laus est.)
HORACE, *Epistles*. Bk. i, epis. 17, l. 35.

4
Sound, sound the clarion, fill the fife,
To all the sensual world proclaim
One crowded hour of glorious life
Is worth an age without a name.
MAJOR THOMAS OSBERT MORDAUNT, *A Poem, Written During the Last German War.* First published in *The Bee,* Edinburgh, 12 Oct., 1791. Used by Sir Walter Scott at the head of ch. 13, bk. ii, of *Old Mortality*. The "Last German War" referred to in the title of the poem was the Seven Years' War, 1756–1763, between Austria and Prussia. Major Mordaunt was with the 10th Dragoons, which was in Germany at the close of the war. (See *Literary Digest,* 11 Sept., 1920, p. 38.) BIRRELL, *More Obiter Dicta* (1924) ventures the opinion that Scott, glancing over the proof of Mordaunt's "vapid verses," caught fire at the tenth stanza, and sitting down, "in a fine frenzy dashed off the immortal lines. This is not proof positive," Birrell adds, "but it is good enough for me."

5
When the moon shone, we did not see the candle;
So doth the greater glory dim the less.
SHAKESPEARE, *The Merchant of Venice*. Act v, sc. 1, l. 92. *See also under* CANDLE.

III—Glory: The Thirst for Glory

6
Glory pursue, and generous shame,
Th' unconquerable mind, and freedom's holy flame.
THOMAS GRAY, *The Progress of Poesy,* l. 64.

8
Glory drags all men captive at the wheel of her glittering car. (Fulgente trahit constrictos Gloria curru.)
HORACE, *Satires*. Bk. i, sat. 6, l. 23.

9
When I rush on, sure none will dare to stay;
'Tis Beauty calls and Glory shows the way.
NATHANIEL LEE, *The Rival Queens*. Act iv, sc. 2. Usually quoted, "Glory leads the way," which is the text of the stage editions of the play.

10
Our aim is glory, and to leave our names
To aftertime.
MASSINGER, *The Roman Actor*. Act i, sc. 1.

11
Yet years, and to ripe years judgment mature,
Quench not the thirst of glory, but augment.
MILTON, *Paradise Regained*. Bk. iii, l. 37.

12
Higher, higher will we climb
Up the mount of glory,
That our names may live through time
In our country's story.
JAMES MONTGOMERY, *Aspirations of Youth.*

13
Here is her witness: this, her perfect son,
This delicate and proud New England soul
Who leads despisèd men, with just-unshackled feet,
Up the large ways where death and glory meet.
WILLIAM VAUGHN MOODY, *An Ode in Time of Hesitation.*

14
How shall we rank thee upon Glory's page?
Thou more than soldier and just less than sage!
THOMAS MOORE, *To Thomas Hume, Esq.*

15
Ye know right well, how meek soe'er he seem,
No keener hunter after glory breathes.
TENNYSON, *Lancelot and Elaine,* l. 154.

16
Slight is the field of toil, but not slight the glory. (In tenui labor; at tenuis non gloria.)
VERGIL, *Georgics*. Bk. iv, l. 6.

17
Of some for glory such the boundless rage,
That they're the blackest scandal of their age.
YOUNG, *Love of Fame*. Sat. iv, l. 65.

IV—Glory: Its Emptiness

18
Glory comes late to our ashes. (Cineri gloria sera venit.)
MARTIAL, *Epigrams*. Bk. i, ep. 25, last line.

Those glories come too late
That on our ashes wait.
A translation of Martial's epigram used on the title-page of the posthumous poems of Richard Lovelace, 1659.

Seldom comes Glory till a man be dead.
ROBERT HERRICK, *Hesperides*. No. 624.

19
If glory comes after death, I am in no hurry. (Si post fata venit gloria non propero.)
MARTIAL, *Epigrams*. Bk. v, ep. 10, l. 12.

20
Who pants for glory finds but short repose:
A breath revives him, or a breath o'erthrows.
POPE, *Imitations of Horace: Epistles*. Bk. ii, epis. 2, l. 300.

A breath can make them, as a breath has made.
GOLDSMITH, *The Deserted Village,* l. 54.

21
Alas! how difficult it is to retain glory! (Heu, quam difficilis gloriæ custodia est.)
PUBLILIUS SYRUS, *Sententiæ*. No. 233.

22
Glory is like a circle in the water,
Which never ceaseth to enlarge itself

Till by broad spreading it disperse to nought.
SHAKESPEARE, *I Henry VI*. Act i, sc. 2, l. 133.

1
I have ventured,
Like little wanton boys that swim on bladders,
This many summers in a sea of glory,
But far beyond my depth.
SHAKESPEARE, *Henry VIII*. Act iii, sc. 2, l. 358.

Like madness is the glory of this life.
SHAKESPEARE, *Timon of Athens*. Act i, sc. 2, l. 139.

Who would be so mock'd with glory?
SHAKESPEARE, *Timon of Athens*. Act iv, sc. 2, l. 33.

2
Avoid shame, but do not seek glory; nothing so expensive as glory.
SYDNEY SMITH. (LADY HOLLAND, *Memoir*. Ch. 4.)

3
How swiftly passes away the glory of the world! (O quam cito transit gloria mundi.)
THOMAS À KEMPIS, *De Imitatione Christi*. Pt. i, ch. 3.

So passes away the glory of the world. (Sic transit gloria mundi.)
The sentence used during the ceremony of enthroning a new Pope at the moment that flax is burned to indicate the transitoriness of earthly grandeur. Perhaps derived from the phrase by Thomas à Kempis. A similar rite is said to have been used in the triumphal processions of the Roman Republic. (ZONARA, *Annales*. Basle, 1553.)

4
Short is the glory that is given and taken by men; and sorrow followeth ever the glory of the world.
THOMAS À KEMPIS, *De Imitatione Christi*. Pt. ii, ch. 6.

5
We rise in glory as we sink in pride.
YOUNG, *Night Thoughts*. Night viii, l. 508.

GLOW-WORM

6
Tasteful illumination of the night,
Bright scattered, twinkling star of spangled earth.
JOHN CLARE, *To the Glowworm*.

7
While many a glowworm in the shade
Lights up her love torch.
COLERIDGE, *The Nightingale*.

8
Glow-worms on the ground are moving,
As if in the torch-dance circling.
HEINE, *Donna Clara*. St. 17.

9
Her eyes the glow-worm lend thee.
ROBERT HERRICK, *The Night-Piece, to Julia*.

10
Ye living lamps, by whose dear light
The nightingale does sit so late;
And studying all the summer night,
Her matchless songs does meditate.
ANDREW MARVELL, *The Mower to the Glow-worm*.

11
Here's a health to the glow-worm, Death's sober lamplighter.
OWEN MEREDITH, *Au Café*.

12
When evening closes Nature's eye,
The glow-worm lights her little spark
To captivate her favourite fly
And tempt the rover through the dark.
JAMES MONTGOMERY, *The Glow-worm*.

Shine, little glow-worm, glimmer.
LILLA CAYLEY ROBINSON, *The Glow-Worm*. The great song success of *The Girl Behind the Counter*. (1905)

13
The glow-worm shows the matin to be near,
And 'gins to pale his uneffectual fire.
SHAKESPEARE, *Hamlet*. Act i, sc. 5, l. 89.

Twenty glow-worms shall our lanterns be,
To guide our measure round about the tree.
SHAKESPEARE, *The Merry Wives of Windsor*. Act v, sc. 5, l. 82.

Like a glow-worm in the night,
The which hath fire in darkness, none in light.
SHAKESPEARE, *Pericles*. Act ii, sc. 3, l. 43.

14
Among the crooked lanes, on every hedge,
The glow-worm lights his gem; and, through the dark,
A moving radiance twinkles.
THOMSON, *The Seasons: Summer*, l. 1682.

15
There the glow-worms hang their lamps.
WORDSWORTH, *The Primrose of the Rock*.

GLUTTONY, see Eating

GOD

See also Nature and God

I—God: Definitions

16
God's wisdom and God's goodness!—Ay, but fools
Mis-define these till God knows them no more.
Wisdom and goodness, they are God!—what schools
Have yet so much as heard this simpler lore?
This no Saint preaches, and this no Church rules:
'Tis in the desert, now and heretofore.
MATTHEW ARNOLD, *The Divinity*. St. 3.

17
God is the poet, men are but the actors.
HONORÉ DE BALZAC, *Christian Socrates*.

God Himself is the best Poet,
And the Real is his song.
E. B. BROWNING, *The Dead Pan*. St. 36.

God is the perfect poet,
Who in his person acts his own creations.
ROBERT BROWNING, *Paracelsus*. Pt. ii, *ad fin*.

God on His throne is eldest of poets:
Unto His measures moveth the Whole.
WILLIAM WATSON, *England My Mother*. Pt. ii.

1
When we say God, we seem to denote a substance, but it is a substance that is supersubstantial. (Nam cum dicimus "deus," substantiam quidem significare videmur, sed eam quæ sit ultra substantiam.)
BOETHIUS, *De Trinitate*. Ch. 4, sec. 15.

The gods possess the form of man; yet their form is not corporeal, but only resembles bodily substance. (Homines esse specie deos contitendum est; nec tamen ea species corpus est, sed quasi corpus.)
GAIUS VELLEIUS, expounding the Epicurean doctrine. (CICERO, *De Natura Deorum*. Bk. i, ch. 18, sec. 49.)

"God has not body, but a semblance of body": what "a semblance of body" may mean, in the case of God, I cannot understand; nor can you either, Velleius, only you won't admit it. (Non corpus esse in deo sed quasi corpus: . . . in deo quid sit quasi corpus intellegere non possum. Ne tu quidem, Vellei, sed non vis fateri.)
COTTA, refuting Velleius. (CICERO, *De Natura Deorum*. Bk. i, ch. 24, sec. 68.)

2
God is not one thing because He is, and another thing because He is just; with Him to be just and to be God are one and the same. (Neque enim aliud est quod est, aliud est quod justus est, sed idem est esse deo quod justo.)
BOETHIUS, *De Trinitate*. Ch. 4, sec. 19.

3
No worldly thing
Can a continuance have
Unless love back again it bring
Unto the cause which first the essence gave.
(Quia non aliter durare queant,
Nisi converso rursus amore
Refluant causæ quæ dedit esse.)
BOETHIUS, *Philosophiæ Consolationis*. Bk. iv, ch. 6, l. 46.

From thee, great God, we spring, to thee we tend,
Path, motive, guide, original, and end.
SAMUEL JOHNSON, *The Rambler*. No. 7. Paraphrasing Boethius.

God shall be my hope,
My stay, my guide and lantern to my feet.
SHAKESPEARE, *II Henry VI*. Act ii, sc. 3, l. 24.

4
A picket frozen on duty—
A mother starved for her brood—
Socrates drinking the hemlock,
And Jesus on the rood;
And millions who, humble and nameless,
The straight, hard pathway trod—
Some call it Consecration,
And others call it God.
W. H. CARRUTH, *Each in His Own Tongue*.

5
God is to me that creative Force, behind and in the universe, who manifests Himself as energy, as life, as order, as beauty, as thought, as conscience, as love.
HENRY SLOANE COFFIN. (NEWTON, *My Idea of God*, p. 125.)

6
God is incorporeal, divine, supreme, infinite Mind, Spirit, Soul, Principle, Life, Truth, Love.
MARY BAKER EDDY, *Science and Health*, p. 465.

Every law of matter or the body, supposed to govern man, is rendered null and void by the law of Life, God.
MARY BAKER EDDY, *Science and Health*, p. 380.

7
God is not a cosmic bell-boy for whom we can press a button to get things.
HARRY EMERSON FOSDICK, *Prayer*.

8
Who believes that equal grace
God extends in every place,
Little difference he scans
'Twixt a rabbit's God and man's.
BRET HARTE, *Battle Bunny: Envoi*.

9
O thou, whose certain eye foresees
The fix'd event of fate's remote decrees.
HOMER, *Odyssey*. Bk. iv, l. 627. (Pope, tr.)

10
The God of many men is little more than their court of appeal against the damnatory judgment passed on their failures by the opinion of the world.
WILLIAM JAMES, *Varieties of Religious Experience*, p. 138.

11
God is a Spirit: and they that worship him must worship him in spirit and in truth.
New Testament: John, iv, 24.

There are three that bear record in heaven, the Father, the Word, and the Holy Ghost: and these three are one.
New Testament: I John, v, 7.

12
God, to be God, must transcend what is. He must be the maker of what ought to be.
RUFUS M. JONES. (NEWTON, *My Idea of God*, p. 63.)

13
One sole God; One sole ruler,—his Law;
One sole interpreter of that law—Humanity.
MAZZINI, *Young Europe: General Principles*.

14
God is a geometrician. (Ὁ Θεὸς γεωμετρεῖ.)
PLATO. (PLUTARCH, *Symposium*.) Quoted as a traditional saying of Plato, but not found in his works.

God is like a skillful geometrician.
SIR THOMAS BROWNE, *Religio Medici*. Pt. i, sec. 16.

Nature geometrizeth and observeth order in all things.
SIR THOMAS BROWNE, *Garden of Cyrus*. Ch. 3.

God acts the part of a Geometrician. . . . His

government of the world is no less exact than His creation of it.

JOHN NORRIS, *Practical Discourses*. Vol. ii, p. 228. Paraphrasing Plato.

By a carpenter mankind was created and made, and by a carpenter meet it was that man should be repaired.

ERASMUS, *Paraphrase of St. Mark*.

1
God is truth and light his shadow.

PLATO. Not Plato's exact words, but the essence of Secs. 506–510 of *The Republic*.

God is light
And never but in unapproached light
Dwelt from eternity.

MILTON, *Paradise Lost*. Bk. iii, l. 3.

The Lord is my light and my salvation.

Old Testament: Psalms, xxvii, 1. (Dominus illuminatio mea.—*Vulgate*.)

God is a light that is never darkened; an unwearied life that cannot die; a fountain always flowing; a garden of life; a seminary of wisdom; a radical beginning of all goodness.

FRANCIS QUARLES, *Emblems*. Bk. i.

2
God is our refuge and strength, a very present help in trouble.

Old Testament: Psalms, xlvi, 1.

I will say of the Lord, He is my refuge and my fortress: my God; in him will I trust.

Old Testament: Psalms, xci, 2.

A mighty fortress is our God,
A bulwark never failing.
(Ein feste Burg ist unser Gott
Ein gute Wehr und Waffen.)

MARTIN LUTHER, *Ein Feste Burg*. (Hedge, tr.)

God is our fortress, in whose conquering name
Let us resolve to scale their flinty bulwarks.

SHAKESPEARE, *I Henry VI*. Act ii, sc. 1, l. 26.

3
I am Alpha and Omega, the beginning and the end, the first and the last.

New Testament: Revelation, xxii, 13.

God is *alpha* and *omega* in the great world: endeavour to make Him so in the little world; make Him thy evening epilogue and thy morning prologue . . . so shall thy rest be peaceful, thy labours prosperous, thy life pious, and thy death glorious.

FRANCIS QUARLES, *Enchiridion*. Cent. ii, No. 28.

4
God is an unutterable sigh, planted in the depths of the soul. (Gott ist ein unaussprechlicher Seufzer, im Grunde der Seele gelegen.)

JEAN PAUL RICHTER.

God is an unutterable Sigh in the Human Heart, said the old German mystic. And therewith said the last word.

HAVELOCK ELLIS, *Impressions and Comments*. Ser. i, p. 190.

5
Tell them, I AM, Jehovah said
To Moses; while earth heard in dread,
And, smitten to the heart,
At once above, beneath, around,
All Nature, without voice or sound,
Replied, O LORD THOU ART.

CHRISTOPHER SMART, *Song to David*.

Thus saith Brahm—
Cast your life upon the deep And sleep: I AM.

E. W. STRATFORD, *India*.

6
Man is an organ of life, and God alone is life.

SWEDENBORG, *True Christian Religion*. Sec. 504.

We are, because God is.

SWEDENBORG, *Divine Providence*. Sec. 46.

7
God, the ruler of all. (Regnator omnium Deus.)

TACITUS, *Germania*. Sec. 39.

8
There is one evident, indubitable manifestation of the Divinity, and that is the laws of right which are made known to the world through Revelation.

TOLSTOY, *Anna Karénina*. Pt. viii, ch. 19.

II—God: Apothegms

9
God is no respecter of persons.

New Testament: Acts, x, 34.

There is no respect of persons with God.

New Testament: Romans, ii, 11.

With him is no respect of persons.

Apocrypha: Ecclesiasticus, xxxv, 12.

10
Naught but God Can satisfy the soul.

P. J. BAILEY, *Festus: Heaven*.

He testified this solemn truth, while phrenzy desolated,
—Nor man nor nature satisfies whom only God created.

E. B. BROWNING, *Cowper's Grave*. St. 8.

11
If thou knowest God, thou knowest that everything is possible for God to do. (Εἰ θεὸν οἶσθα, ἴσθ' ὅτι καὶ ῥέξαι δαίμονι πᾶν δυνατὸν.)

CALLIMACHUS, *Fragmenta Incertæ*. No. 27.

There is nothing which God cannot effect. (Nihil esse quod deus efficere non possit.)

CICERO, *De Natura Deorum*. Bk. iii, ch. 39, sec. 92.

My God commands, whose power no power resists.

ROBERT GREENE, *A Looking-Glass for London*.

12
When God dawns he dawns for all. (Quando Dios amanece, para todos amanece.)

CERVANTES, *Don Quixote*. Pt. ii, ch. 4.

13
We are Goddes stewardes all, noughte of our owne we bare.

THOMAS CHATTERTON, *Excellente Balade of Charitie*.

14
'Tis god-like God in his own coin to pay.

DRYDEN, *Britannia Rediviva*, l. 303.

1
Fear God, and where you go men will think they walk in hallowed cathedrals.
EMERSON, *Conduct of Life: Worship.*

2
The god of the cannibals will be a cannibal, of the crusaders a crusader, and of the merchant a merchant.
EMERSON, *Conduct of Life: Worship.*

The Ethiop gods have Ethiop lips,
Bronze cheeks, and woolly hair;
The Grecian gods are like the Greeks,
As keen-eyed, cold, and fair.
WALTER BAGEHOT, *Literary Studies: The Ignorance of Man.*

As a man is, so is his God; therefore was God so often an object of mockery. (Wie einer ist, so ist sein Gott, darum ward Gott so oft zu Spott.)
GOETHE, *Gedichte.*

3
God enters by a private door into every individual.
EMERSON, *Essays, First Series: Intellect.*

To Be is to live with God.
EMERSON, *Journals,* 1865.

4
As the bird alights on the bough, then plunges into the air again, so the thoughts of God pause but for a moment in any form.
EMERSON, *Letters and Social Aims: Poetry and Imagination.*

God only opened his hand to give flight to a thought that he had held imprisoned from eternity.
HOLLAND, *Gold-Foil: Patience.*

5
The way to God is by ourselves.
PHINEAS FLETCHER, *The Purple Island: To the Reader.*

6
Shall not the Judge of all the earth do right?
Old Testament: Genesis, xviii, 25.

7
No one against God, except God himself. (Nemo contra Deum nisi Deus ipse.)
GOETHE, *Autobiography.* Bk. xix. Quoted as "that strange but striking proverb."

8
The duchess thinking to have gotten God by the foot, when she had the devil by the tail.
EDWARD HALL, *Chronicles,* p. 462. (1548)

They think they have got God almighty by the toe.
SIR JOHN HARINGTON, *Orlando Furioso.* Bk. xliv. Notes. (1591) Quoted as a proverb.

9
Where there is peace, God is.
GEORGE HERBERT, *Jacula Prudentum.*

He loseth nothing that loseth not God.
GEORGE HERBERT, *Jacula Prudentum.*

God complains not, but doth what is fitting.
GEORGE HERBERT, *Jacula Prudentum.*

God, and parents, and our master, can never be requited.
GEORGE HERBERT, *Jacula Prudentum.*

10
The river passed and God forgotten.
GEORGE HERBERT, *Jacula Prudentum. See also under* DEVIL.

11
Where God is merry, there write down thy fears:
What He with laughter speaks, hear thou with tears.
ROBERT HERRICK, *God's Mirth, Man's Mourning.*

I have never understood why it should be considered derogatory to the Creator to suppose that He has a sense of humour.
DEAN W. R. INGE. (MARCHANT, *Wit and Wisdom of Dean Inge.* No. 235.)

Even the gods love jokes. (Jocos et Dii amant.)
PLATO, *Cratylus.*

12
Every man for himself and God for us all.
JOHN HEYWOOD, *Proverbs.* Pt. ii, ch. 9.

13
An honest God is the noblest work of man.
R. G. INGERSOLL, *The Gods.*

14
All growth that is not towards God
Is growing to decay.
GEORGE MACDONALD, *Within and Without.* Pt. i, sc. 3.

15
Every one is in a small way the image of God. (Exemplumque dei quisque est in imagine parva.)
MANILIUS, *Astronomica.* Pt. iv, l. 895.

In the faces of men and women I see God.
WALT WHITMAN, *Song of Myself.* Sec. 48.

16
As ever in my great Task-master's eye.
MILTON, *On His Being Arrived to the Age of Twenty-three.*

17
The eternal Being is forever if he is at all.
PASCAL, *Pensées.* No. 233.

18
God forbid!
New Testament: Romans, iii, 31.

God save the mark!
SHAKESPEARE, *I Henry IV.* Act i, sc. 3, l. 56.

19
Served the creature more than the Creator.
New Testament: Romans, i, 25.

There is no fear of God before their eyes.
New Testament: Romans, iii, 18.

A zeal of God, but not according to knowledge.
New Testament: Romans, x, 2.

20
If God be for us, who can be against us?
New Testament: Romans, viii, 31. (Si Deus pro nobis, quis contra nos?—*Vulgate.*)

If this counsel or this work be of men, it will come to nought: But if it be of God, ye cannot overthrow it.
New Testament: Acts, v, 38, 39.

Where God will helpen, nought can harm.
UNKNOWN, *Havelok,* l. 648. (c. 1300)

Whom that God will aid no man can hurt.
JOHN BOURCHIER, *Huon of Burdeux*, 480. (1534)

Whom God will help nae man can hinder.
JOHN RAY, *English Proverbs: Scottish.*

1
God never repents his first decision. (Nec unquam primi concilii deos pœnitet.)
SENECA, *De Beneficiis*. Bk. vi, ch. 23, sec. 2.

2
God ye good den, gentlewoman.
SHAKESPEARE, *Romeo and Juliet*. Act ii, sc. 4, l. 116. An abbreviation of "God give you good evening."

3
Beware of the man whose god is in the skies.
BERNARD SHAW, *Maxims for Revolutionists.*

4
No man doth well but God hath part in him.
SWINBURNE, *Atalanta in Calydon: Chorus.*

5
Whate'er we leave to God, God does
And blesses us.
H. D. THOREAU, *Inspiration.*

6
He who serves God hath a good master.
TORRIANO, *Piazza Universale*, 69. (1666)

7
When God is to be served, the cost we weigh
In anxious balance, grudging the expense.
RICHARD CHENEVIX TRENCH, *Sonnet.*

8
But God, who is able to prevail, wrestled with him, as the angel did with Jacob, and marked him; marked him for his own.
IZAAK WALTON, *Life of Donne.*

9
There is no God but God. (Lā illāh illā allāh.)
The Koran. Ch. 3. The first clause of the Mohammedan confession of faith.

God! there is no God but he, the living, the self-subsisting.
The Koran. Ch. ii.

"There is no god but God!—to prayer—lo! God is great!"
BYRON, *Childe Harold*. Canto ii, st. 59.

10
God is the best deviser of stratagems.
The Koran. Ch. 3.

An' you've gut to git up airly
Ef you want to take in God.
J. R. LOWELL, *The Biglow Papers*. Sec. i, No. 1.

God is clever, but not dishonest.
DR. ALBERT EINSTEIN. Engraved over a fireplace in Fine Hall, Princeton, N. J.

11
God is better pleased with adverbs than with nouns.
UNKNOWN, *Complete History of England*. Vol. ii, p. 502. (1570)

God loves adverbs, and cares not how good but how well.
BISHOP JOSEPH HALL, *Holy Observations*. Sec. 14. (1607)

God is the rewarder of adverbs, not of nouns.
JOHN FORD, *Line of Life*, 64. (1620)

12
There came one which said that God was a good man.
UNKNOWN, *Hundred Mery Tales*. No. 85. (1526)

Well, God's a good man.
SHAKESPEARE, *Much Ado About Nothing*. Act iii, sc. 5, l. 39.

13
God's grace is worth a new fair.
UNKNOWN, *Mirks Festival*, 86. (c. 1400) Referred to as a "common saying."

The grace of God is gear enough.
UNKNOWN, *Quarterly Review*. Vol. cxxv, p. 248. "Our old and beautiful adage."

14
To the greater glory of God. (Ad majorem Dei gloriam.)
Motto of the Society of Jesus.

Three things joined in one. (Tria juncta in uno.)
Motto of the Order of the Bath.

Lord, direct us. (Domine, dirige nos.)
Motto of the City of London.

God has breathed and they are dispersed. (Afflavit Deus et dissipantur.)
Motto on medal struck to commemorate the victory over the Spanish Armada.

III—God: Man Proposes but God Disposes

15
Man thinks, God directs. (Homo cogitat, Deus indicat.)
ALCUIN, *Epistles.*

Though men determine, the gods too dispose.
ROBERT GREENE, *Perimedes the Blacksmith.*

16
We, in some unknown Power's employ,
Move on a rigorous line:
Can neither, when we will, enjoy,
Nor, when we will, resign.
MATTHEW ARNOLD, *Stanzas in Memory of the Author of Obermann*, l. 133.

17
God may consent, but only for a time.
EMERSON, *Conduct of Life: Fate*. Quoted.

18
Man moves himself, but God leads him. (L'homme s'agite, mais Dieu le mène.)
FÉNELON, *Epiphany Sermon*, 1685.

19
I will cast, but the issue rests with Zeus. (Ἥσω γὰρ καὶ ἐγώ, τὰ δέ κεν Διὶ πάντα κεῖται.)
HOMER, *Iliad*. Bk. xvii, l. 515.

20
Zeus does not ratify all the designs of men. (Ἀλλ' οὐ Ζεὺς ἄνδρεσσι νοήματα πάντα τελευτᾷ.)
HOMER, *Iliad*. Bk. xviii, l. 328.

21
For that ye ought to say, If the Lord will, we shall live, and do this, or that.
New Testament: James, iv, 15. Hence, "If the Lord will" came to be known as St. James's reservation, and "Sub reservatione Jacobæo" became a Latin proverb.

I claim not to have controlled events, but confess plainly that events have controlled me.
ABRAHAM LINCOLN, *Speech*, 1864.

1
We do nothing without the leave of God. (Nil facimus non sponte Dei.)
LUCAN, *De Bello Civili*. Bk. ix, l. 574.

From God derived, to God by nature joined,
We act the dictates of His mighty mind;
And tho' the priests are mute, and temples still,
God never wants a voice to speak His will.
LUCAN, *De Bello Civili*. Bk. ix, l. 574.

2
The issue is in God's hands. ('Εν θεῷ γε μὰν τέλος.)
PINDAR, *Olympian Odes*. Ode xiii, l. 104.

The mind is hopeful; success is in God's hands. (Sperat quidem animus: quo evenat dis in manust.)
PLAUTUS, *Bacchides*, l. 144. (Act i, sc. 2.) Usually translated, "Man proposes, but God disposes."

3
A man's heart deviseth his way: but the Lord directeth his steps.
Old Testament: Proverbs, xvi, 9. (Cor hominis disponet viam suam, sed Domini est dirigere gressus ejus.—*Vulgate*.)

4
Man intends one thing, Fate another. (Homo semper aliud, Fortuna aliud cogitat.)
PUBLILIUS SYRUS, *Sententiæ*. No. 216.

5
Man doth what he can, and God what he will.
JOHN RAY, *English Proverbs*, 97.

6
God, under whose guidance everything proceeds. (Qui imperatorem gemens sequitur.)
SENECA, *Epistulæ ad Lucilium*. Epis. cvii, 10.

7
Man proposes, but God disposes. (Homo proponit, sed Deus disponit.)
THOMAS À KEMPIS, *De Imitatione Christi*. Pt. i, ch. 19.

Homo proponet at Deus disponit,
And governeth all good virtues.
WILLIAM LANGLAND, *Piers Plowman*, l. 13,994. Langland attributes this to Plato, but it has not been found in his works.

Man proposes, and God disposes. (Ordina l'uomo, e dio dispone.)
ARIOSTO, *Orlando Furioso*. Canto xlvi, st. 35.

Man proposes, God disposes. (El hombre pone y Dios dispone.)
CERVANTES, *Don Quixote*. Pt. ii, ch. 55.

8
God willing it. (Volento Deo.)
VERGIL, *Æneid*. Bk. i, l. 303.

The gods so willed it. (Sic dii voluistis.)
VERGIL, *Æneid*. Bk. v, l. 50.

Heaven decreed it otherwise. (Dis aliter visum est.)
VERGIL, *Æneid*. Bk. ii, l. 428.

9
Yield to God. (Cede Deo.)
VERGIL, *Æneid*. Bk. v, l. 467.

Where God and hard fortune call us, let us follow. (Quo Deus, et quo dura vocat fortuna sequamur.)
VERGIL, *Æneid*. Bk. xii, l. 677.

IV—God Helps Them Who Help Themselves

10
God loves to help him who strives to help himself. (Φιλεῖ δὲ τῷ κάμνοντι συσπεύδειν θεός.)
ÆSCHYLUS, *Fragments*. Frag. 223.

To the man who himself strives earnestly, God also lends a helping hand. ('Αλλ' ὅταν σπεύδῃ τις αὐτός, χὠ θεὸς συνάπτεται.)
ÆSCHYLUS, *Persæ*, l. 742.

11
God helps everyone with what is his own. (Ayude Dios con le suyo á cada uno.)
CERVANTES, *Don Quixote*. Pt. ii, ch. 26.

12
Try first thyself, and after call in God;
For to the worker God himself lends aid.
EURIPIDES, *Hippolytus*. Frag. 435.

13
Help yourself and Heaven will help you. (Aide toi, le ciel t'aidera.)
LA FONTAINE, *Fables*. Bk. vi, fab. 18.

14
To complete the design of the Gods we have to put a stitch here and there.
GEORGE MOORE, *Aphrodite in Aulis*, p. 28.

15
Heaven ne'er helps the men who will not act.
SOPHOCLES, *Fragments*. No. 288.

16
"Let God do it all," someone will say; but if man folds his arms, God will go to sleep.
MIGUEL DE UNAMUNO, *Tragic Sense of Life*, p. 286.

17
God helps them who help themselves. (Σὺν 'Αθηνᾷ καὶ χεῖρα κίνει.)
A proverb in all languages: Spanish, "Quien se muda, Dios le ayuda"; French, "À qui se lève matin, Dieu aide et prête sa main." An early use in English, ALGERNON SIDNEY, *Discourse Concerning Government*. (1698)

18
The whole trouble is that we won't let God help us.
GEORGE MACDONALD, *The Marquis of Lossie*. Ch. 27.

V—God: His Invention

19
He was a wise man who invented God. (Σοφὸς ἦν τις, ὃς τὸ θεῖον εἰσηγήσατο.)
PLATO, *Sisyphus*. This dialogue is included in editions of Plato, but is generally thought to be spurious. It has been attributed to Æschines and Euripides.

The being of God is so comfortable, so convenient, so necessary to the felicity of Mankind, that, (as Tully admirably says) Dii immortales ad usum hominum fabricati pene videantur, if God were not a necessary being of himself, he might almost seem to be made on purpose for the use and benefit of men.

ARCHBISHOP JOHN TILLOTSON, *Works*. Vol. i, p. 696. Sermon 93.

1
If God did not exist, it would be necessary to invent him. (Si Dieu n'existait pas, il faudrait l'inventer.)

VOLTAIRE, *Épître à l'Auteur du Livre des Trois Imposteurs,* 10 Nov., 1770.

Consulte Zoroastre, et Minos et Solon,
Et le grand Socrate, et le grand Ciceron,
Ils ont adoré tous un maître, un juge, un père.
Ce système sublime à l'homme est necessaire,
C'est le sacré lien de la société,
Le premier fondement de la sainte equité,
Le frein au scelerat, l'espérance du juste,
Si les cieux dépouillés de leur empreinte auguste
Pouvait cesser jamais de le manifester,
Si Dieu n'existait pas, il faudrait l'inventer.

VOLTAIRE, *Épître à l'Auteur du Livre des Trois Imposteurs.* Voltaire was very proud of this last line. "Though I am seldom satisfied with my lines," he wrote to Frederick the Great, "I must confess that I feel for this one the tenderness of a father." He perhaps did not know that the idea had been anticipated by Plato or Euripides, in *Sisyphus,* and by Archbishop Tillotson quoting Cicero. Tillotson died in 1694, the year of Voltaire's birth.

2
We had needs invent heaven if had not been revealed to us.

R. L. STEVENSON, *St. Ives.*

VI—God and the Watchmaker

3
In all the parts of Nature's spacious sphere
Of art ten thousand miracles appear;
And will you not the Author's skill adore
Because you think He might discover more?
You own a watch, the invention of the mind,
Though for a single motion 'tis designed,
As well as that which is with greater thought,
With various springs, for various motions wrought.

SIR RICHARD BLACKMORE, *The Creation.* Bk. iii. (1712)

4
Suppose I had found a watch upon the ground. . . . The mechanism being observed, . . . the inference we think is inevitable that the watch must have a maker; that there must have existed, at some time, and at some place or other, an artificer or artificers, who formed it for the purpose which we find it actually to answer; who comprehended its construction, and designed its use.

WILLIAM PALEY, *Natural Theology.* Ch. i. Probably derived from Nieuwentyt's *The Religious Philosopher,* translated into English from the Dutch in 1718. Paley's book was published in 1802. Hallam (*Literature of Europe,* ii, 385) traces the idea back to Cicero, *De Natura Deorum,* and it was used by Herbert of Cherbury (*De Religione Gentilium*) and by Sir Matthew Hale (*Primitive Origination of Mankind*).

5
Paley's simile of the watch . . . must be replaced by the simile of the flower. The universe is not a machine but an organism with an indwelling principle of life. It was not made, but it has grown.

JOHN FISKE. (NEWTON, *My Idea of God.*)

6
The reasoning by which Socrates in Xenophon's hearing confuted the little atheist Aristodemus, is exactly the reasoning of Paley's *Natural Theology.* Socrates makes precisely the same use of the statues of Polycletus and the pictures of Zeuxis which Paley makes of the watch.

MACAULAY, *Essays: Von Ranke.*

7
The world embarrasses me, and I cannot think
That this watch exists and has no Watchmaker.
(Le monde m'embarasse, et je ne puis pas songer
Que cette horloge existe et n'a pas d'Horloger.)

VOLTAIRE, *Epigram.*

VII—God: His Mercy

8
When all thy mercies, O my God,
My rising soul surveys,
Transported with the view I'm lost,
In wonder, love, and praise.

ADDISON, *Hymn: With All Thy Mercies.*

9
The mercy of God [may be found] between the bridge and the stream. (Misericordia Domine inter pontem et fontem.)

ST. AUGUSTINE, *Confessions.* Of a man falling into a river.

My friend, judge not me,
Thou seest I judge not thee.
Betwixt the stirrup and the ground
Mercy I asked, mercy I found.

WILLIAM CAMDEN, *Remains Concerning Britain,* p. 392. An epitaph for a man falling from his horse and breaking his neck. Quoted as "made by a good friend of the author."

Between the stirrup and the ground,
I mercy asked, I mercy found.

SAMUEL JOHNSON, misquoting Camden. (BOSWELL, *Life,* 28 April, 1783.)

Though a sharp sword be laid to thy throat, still pray to God for mercy.

Babylonian Talmud: Berachoth, p. 10a.

10
God never made mouth but he made meat.

THOMAS BECON, *Catechism,* 602. (c. 1560) Cited as a proverb "no less true than common."

Be sure that God
Ne'er dooms to waste the strength he deigns impart.

ROBERT BROWNING, *Paracelsus*. Pt. 1.

God who gives the wound gives the salve. (Dios que da la llaga da la medicina.)

CERVANTES, *Don Quixote*. Pt. ii, ch. 19.

To the bird's young ones he gives food. (Aux petits des oiseaux il donne la pâture.)

CORNEILLE, *Athalie*. Gozlan added a second line: "Et sa bonté s'arrête qu'à la littérature," And His bounty stops only with men-of-letters.

1
Oft have I heard, and now believe it true,
Whom man delights in, God delights in too.

PONS CAPDUEIL. (EMERSON, *Letters and Social Aims: Poetry and Imagination.*)

2
God tempers the cold to the shorn lamb. (Dieu mesure le froid à la brébis tondue.)

HENRI ESTIENNE, *Prémices*, p. 47. (1594) Quoted from an older collection.

To a close shorn sheep God gives wind by measure.

GEORGE HERBERT, *Jacula Prudentum*. No. 861. (1640)

She had travelled all over Lombardy without money, and through the flinty roads of Savoy without shoes: how she had borne it, she could not tell; but "God tempers the wind," said Maria, "to the shorn lamb." "Shorn, indeed! and to the quick," said I.

STERNE, *A Sentimental Journey: Maria*.

God sends men cold according to their cloth; viz. afflictions according to their faith.

JOHN HEYWOOD, *Proverbs*. Pt. i, ch. 4. (1546)

God moderates all at His pleasure. (Dieu modère tout à son plaisir.)

RABELAIS, *Works*. Bk. ii.

3
The greatest attribute of heaven is mercy;
And 'tis the crown of justice, and the glory,
Where it may kill with right, to save with pity.

JOHN FLETCHER, *Lover's Progress*. Act iii, sc. 3.

Mercy's indeed the attribute of heaven.

THOMAS OTWAY, *Windsor Castle*.

4
Whom the Lord loveth he chasteneth.

New Testament: Hebrews, xii, 6.

Whom the Lord loveth he correcteth.

Old Testament: Proverbs, iii, 12.

Heaven is not always angry when he strikes,
But most chastises those whom most he likes.

JOHN POMFRET, *Verses to a Friend Under Affliction*, l. 89.

5
God strikes not with both hands, for to the sea He made havens, and to rivers fords.

GEORGE HERBERT, *Jacula Prudentum*. No 311.

God strikes with his finger, and not with all his arm.

GEORGE HERBERT, *Jacula Prudentum*.

6
God gives his wrath by weight, and without weight his mercy.

GEORGE HERBERT, *Jacula Prudentum*.

7
God hath two wings, which He doth ever move,
The one is Mercy, and the next is Love:
Under the first the Sinners ever trust;
And with the last he still directs the Just.

ROBERT HERRICK, *Mercy and Love*.

8
And the publican, standing afar off, would not lift up so much as his eyes unto heaven, but smote upon his breast, saying, God be merciful to me a sinner.

New Testament: Luke, xviii, 13.

Have mercy upon us miserable sinners.

Book of Common Prayer: Litany.

For heathen heart that puts her trust
In reeking tube and iron shard,
All valiant dust that builds on dust,
And guarding, calls not Thee to guard,
For frantic boast and foolish word—
Thy mercy on Thy people, Lord!

KIPLING, *Recessional*.

A sentinel angel sitting high in glory
Heard this shrill wail ring out from Purgatory:
"Have mercy, mighty angel, hear my story!"

JOHN HAY, *A Woman's Love*.

9
Though God have iron hands which when they strike pay home, yet hath he leaden feet which are as slow to overtake a sinner.

JOHN LYLY, *Euphues*, p. 172. (1579)

God comes with leaden feet, but strikes with iron hands.

JOHN RAY, *English Proverbs*, 11. (1670)

10
Praise be to Allah, the Lord of creation,
The merciful, the compassionate
Ruler of the Day of Judgment
Help us, lead us in the path.

MAHOMET, *Sura*, i.

11
Whoever falls from God's right hand
Is caught into his left.

EDWIN MARKHAM, *The Divine Strategy*.

12
The corn that makes the holy bread
By which the soul of man is fed,
The holy bread, the food unpriced,
Thy everlasting mercy, Christ.

MASEFIELD, *The Everlasting Mercy*. St. 88.

13
Our father which art in heaven.

New Testament: Matthew, vi, 9. (Pater noster, qui es in cœlis.—*Vulgate*.)

For in him we live, and move, and have our being; as certain also of your own poets have said, For we are also his offspring.

New Testament: Acts, xvii, 28.

For we also are his offspring.

ARATUS, *Phænomena*.

1
The mercy of the Lord is from everlasting to everlasting upon them that fear Him.
Old Testament: Psalms, ciii, 17.

Who crowneth thee with lovingkindness and tender mercies.
Old Testament: Psalms, ciii, 4.

Marvelous mercies and infinite love.
SWINBURNE, *Les Noyades*.

2
Pardon, not wrath, is God's best attribute.
BAYARD TAYLOR, *The Temptation of Hassan Ben Khaled*. St. 11.

3
Forgive me if, midst all Thy works
No hint I see of damning;
And think there's faith among the Turks,
And hope for e'en the Brahmin.
THACKERAY, *Jolly Jack*.

4
A God all mercy is a God unjust.
YOUNG, *Night Thoughts*. Night iv, l. 233. *See also* JUSTICE: LET JUSTICE BE DONE.

VIII—God: His Love

See also Grace: Spiritual

5
The Lord my pasture shall prepare,
And feed me with a shepherd's care;
His presence shall my wants supply,
And guard me with a watchful eye.
ADDISON, *The Spectator*. No. 444.

6
By aspiring to a similitude of God in goodness, or love, neither man nor angel ever transgressed, or shall transgress.
BACON, *Advancement of Learning*. Bk. ii.

7
All love is lost but upon God alone.
WILLIAM DUNBAR, *The Merle and the Nightingale*.

Not God above gets all men's love.
THOMAS FULLER, *Gnomologia*. No. 6105.

8
Too wise to err, too good to be unkind,—
Are all the movements of the Eternal Mind.
REV. JOHN EAST, *Songs of My Pilgrimage*.

Too wise to be mistaken still
Too good to be unkind.
SAMUEL MEDLEY, *Hymn of God*.

9
A true love to God must begin with a delight in his holiness, and not with a delight in any other attribute; for no other attribute is truly lovely without this.
JONATHAN EDWARDS, *A Treatise Concerning Religious Affections: Works*. Vol. v, p. 143.

10
Love is God's essence; Power but his attribute; therefore is his love greater than his power.
RICHARD GARNETT, *De Flagello Myrteo*, iv.

11
God will provide.
Old Testament: Genesis, xxii, 8. (Dominus providebit.—*Vulgate*.)

12
Forgetful youth! but know, the Power above
With ease can save each object of his love;
Wide as his will, extends his boundless grace.
HOMER, *Odyssey*. Bk. iii, l. 285. (Pope, tr.)

13
In this stupendous manner, at which Reason stands aghast, and Faith herself is half confounded, was the grace of God to man at length manifested.
RICHARD HURD, *Sermons*. Vol. ii, p. 287.

14
God is love; and he that dwelleth in love dwelleth in God, and God in him.
New Testament: I John, iv, 16.

God! Thou art love! I build my faith on that.
ROBERT BROWNING, *Paracelsus*. Pt. v, l. 52.

One unquestioned text we read,
All doubt beyond, all fear above;
Nor crackling pile nor cursing creed
Can burn or blot it: GOD IS LOVE.
O. W. HOLMES, *What We All Think*.

Yes, if you're a tramp in tatters,
While the blue sky bends above
You've got nearly all that matters—
You've got God and God is Love.
ROBERT W. SERVICE, *Comfort*.

God, from a beautiful necessity, is Love.
M. F. TUPPER, *Of Immortality*.

And man is hate, but God is love!
WHITTIER, *The Chapel of the Hermits*. St. 75.

15
The sun and every vassal star,
All space, beyond the soar of angel wings,
Wait on His word: and yet He stays His car
For every sigh a contrite suppliant brings.
KEBLE, *The Christian Year: Ascension Day*.

16
Whom the heart of man shuts out,
Sometimes the heart of God takes in.
J. R. LOWELL, *The Forlorn*.

17
O unexampl'd love!
Love nowhere to be found less than Divine!
MILTON, *Paradise Lost*. Bk. iii, l. 410.

18
He maketh me to lie down in green pastures: he leadeth me beside the still waters. He restoreth my soul: he leadeth me in the paths of righteousness for his name's sake.
Old Testament: Psalms, xxiii, 2, 3.

19
We know that all things work together for good to them that love God.
New Testament: Romans, viii, 28.

20
But O! th' exceeding grace
Of highest God that loves his creatures so,
And all his works with mercy doth embrace.
SPENSER, *Faerie Queene*. Bk. ii, canto viii, st. 1.

21
As sure as ever God puts His children in the furnace, He will be in the furnace with them.
C. H. SPURGEON, *Privileges of Trial*.

1
The divine essence itself is love and wisdom.
SWEDENBORG, *Divine Love and Wisdom*. Sec. 28.

2
He is rich indeed whom God loves. (Celui est bien riche que Dieu aime.)
J. DE LA VEPRIE, *Les Proverbs Communs*.

He is poor that God hates.
JOHN RAY, *English Proverbs*.

3
Love divine, all love excelling,
Joy of heaven to earth come down.
CHARLES WESLEY, *Divine Love*.

4
Yet, in the maddening maze of things,
And tossed by storm and flood,
To one fixed trust my spirit clings;
I know that God is good! . . .

I know not where His islands lift
Their fronded palms in air;
I only know I cannot drift
Beyond His love and care.
J. G. WHITTIER, *The Eternal Goodness*.

5
Who worship God, shall find him. Humble love,
And not proud reason, keeps the door of heaven;
Love finds admission, where proud science fails.
YOUNG, *Night Thoughts*. Night ix, l. 1855.

6
Could we with ink the ocean fill,
And were the heavens of parchment made,
Were every stalk on earth a quill,
And every man a scribe by trade,
To write the love of God above
Would drain the ocean dry,
Nor could the scroll contain the whole,
Though stretch'd from sky to sky.
UNKNOWN, *Chaldee Ode*, sung in Jewish synagogues on the first day of the Feast of the Pentecost. (Rabbi Mayir ben Isaac, tr.) The Ode in the original Chaldee may be found in *Notes and Queries*, 31 Dec., 1853, p. 648.

But if the sky were paper and a scribe each star above,
And every scribe had seven hands, they could not write all my love.
UNKNOWN, *Dürsli und Bäbeli*. An old Swiss ditty, given in *Notes and Queries*, 10 Feb., 1872, p. 114.

IX—God: His Wrath

See also Punishment: Divine

7
God's mouth knows not to utter falsehood, but he will perform each word. (Ψευδηγορεῖν, γὰρ οὐκ ἐπίσταται στόμα τὸ Δῖον, ἀλλὰ πᾶν ἔπος τελεῖ.)
ÆSCHYLUS, *Prometheus Bound*, l. 1032.

8
Let us hear the conclusion of the whole matter: Fear God, and keep his commandments: for this is the whole duty of man.
Old Testament: Ecclesiastes, xii, 13.

Henceforth the majesty of God revere;
Fear Him, and you have nothing else to fear.
JAMES FORDYCE, *To a Gentleman Who Apologized for Swearing*.

9
It is highly convenient to believe in the infinite mercy of God when you feel the need of mercy, but remember also his infinite justice.
B. R. HAYDON, *Table Talk*.

The Lord had a job for me, but I had so much to do,
I said, "You get somebody else—or wait till I get through."
I don't know how the Lord came out, but He seemed to get along:
But I felt kinda sneakin' like, 'cause I knowed I'd done Him wrong.
One day I needed the Lord—needed Him right away,
And He never answered me at all, but I could hear Him say
Down in my accusin' heart, "Nigger, I'se got too much to do;
You get somebody else, or wait till I get through."
PAUL LAURENCE DUNBAR, *The Lord Had a Job*.

10
Throw away thy rod,
Throw away thy wrath;
O my God,
Take the gentle path.
GEORGE HERBERT, *Discipline*.

11
God has His whips here to a twofold end,
The bad to punish, and the good t' amend.
ROBERT HERRICK, *Whips*.

12
God is a being cruel and severe,
And man a wretch by his command placed here,
In sunshine for a while to take a turn,
Only to dry and make him fit to burn.
SOAME JENYNS, *An Essay on Virtue*.

13
The purple winepress of the wrath of God.
LIONEL JOHNSON, *Ireland*.

Mine eyes have seen the glory of the coming of the Lord:
He is trampling out the vintage where the grapes of wrath are stored:
He hath loosed the fateful lightning of his terrible swift sword:
His truth is marching on.
JULIA WARD HOWE, *Battle Hymn of the Republic*.

14
Fear not them which kill the body, but are not able to kill the soul: but rather fear him which is able to destroy both soul and body in hell.
New Testament: Matthew, x, 28.

15
Nothing is so lofty or so far above danger

that it is not below and in the power of God. (Nil ita sublime est supraque pericula tendit Non sit ut inferius suppositumque deo.)

Ovid, *Tristia*. Bk. iv, eleg. 8, l. 47.

1
If any man hopes, in whatever he does, to escape the eye of God, he is grievously wrong. (Εἰ δὲ θεὸν ἀνήρ τις ἔλπεταί τι λαθέμεν ἔρδων, ἁμαρτάνει.)

Pindar, *Olympian Odes*. Ode i, l. 64.

There is indeed a God that hears and sees whate'er we do. (Est profecto deus, qui, quæ nos gerimus, auditque et videt.)

Plautus, *Captivi*, l. 313. (Act ii, sc. 2.)

2
Fear God. Honour the King.

New Testament: I Peter, ii, 17.

The fear of the Lord is the beginning of knowledge.

Old Testament: Proverbs, i, 7. (Initium sapientiæ timor Domini.—*Vulgate*.)

I fear God, yet am not afraid of him.

Sir Thomas Browne, *Religio Medici*. Bk. i, sec. 52.

I fear God, my dear Abner, and I have no other fear. (Je crains Dieu, cher Abner, et n'ai point autre crainte.)

Racine, *Athalie*. Act i, sc. 1.

3
Out of the depths have I cried unto thee, O Lord. Lord, hear my voice.

Old Testament: Psalms, cxxx, 1, 2. (De profundis clamavi ad te, Domine. Domine exaude vocem meam.—*Vulgate*.)

4
And one of the four beasts gave unto the seven angels seven golden vials full of the wrath of God.

New Testament: Revelation, xv, 7.

And I heard a great voice out of the temple saying to the seven angels, Go your ways, and pour out the vials of the wrath of God upon the earth.

New Testament: Revelation, xvi, 1.

5
If ye despise the human race, and mortal arms, yet remember that there is a God who is mindful of right and wrong. (Si genus humanum et mortalia temnitis arma, At sperate deos memores fandi atque nefandi.)

Vergil, *Æneid*. Bk. i, l. 542.

There is a God to punish and avenge. (Es lebt ein Gott zu strafen und zu rächen.)

Schiller, *Wilhelm Tell*. Act iv, sc. 3, l. 37.

X—God: His Praise

6
He sendeth sun, he sendeth shower,
Alike they're needful to the flower;
And joys and tears alike are sent
To give the soul fit nourishment.
As comes to me or cloud or sun,
Father! thy will, not mine, be done.

Sarah Flower Adams, *He Sendeth Sun, He Sendeth Shower*.

7
Nearer, my God, to Thee,
Nearer to Thee!
E'en though it be a cross
That raiseth me.

Sarah Flower Adams, *Nearer to Thee*.

8
For oh! Eternity's too short
To utter all thy praise.

Addison, *Hymn: When All Thy Mercies*.

9
We praise thee, O God. (Te Deum laudamus.)

St. Ambrose, *Te Deum Laudamus*.

10
Thou hast made us for Thyself, and the heart of man is restless until it finds its rest in Thee. (Fecisti enim nos ad te, et cor inquietum donec requiescat in te.)

St. Augustine, *Confessions*. Bk. i, sec. 1.

11
Not when the sense is dim,
But now, from the heart of joy,
I would remember Him:
Take the thanks of a boy.

H. C. Beeching, *Prayers*.

12
God appears and God is light
To those poor souls who dwell in night;
But doth a human form display
To those who dwell in realms of day.

William Blake, *Auguries of Innocence*.

13
From Thee all human actions take their springs,
The rise of empires, and the fall of kings.

Samuel Boyse, *The Deity*.

14
O Rock of Israel, Rock of Salvation, Rock struck and cleft for me, let those two streams of blood and water which once gushed out of thy side . . . bring down with them salvation and holiness into my soul.

Daniel Brevint, *Works*, p. 17. (1679)

These waters are the Well of Life, and lo!
The Rock of Ages there, from whence they flow.

Robert Southey, *The Poet's Pilgrimage to Waterloo*. Pt. ii, canto iii, st. 39.

Rock of Ages, cleft for me,
Let me hide myself in Thee!

Augustus Montague Toplady, *Rock of Ages*.
"Rock of Ages" is a rendering of the Hebrew in Isaiah xxvi, 4, which in the accepted version is translated as "everlasting strength."

15
And I smiled to think God's greatness flowed around our incompleteness,—
Round our restlessness, His rest.

E. B. Browning, *Rhyme of the Duchess May*.

16
Whether therefore ye eat, or drink, or whatsoever ye do, do all to the glory of God.

New Testament: I Corinthians, x, 31.

17
O majesty unspeakable and dread!
Wert thou less mighty than Thou art,

Thou wert, O Lord, too great for our belief,
Too little for our heart.
FREDERICK WILLIAM FABER, *Greatness of God.*

1
Holy, Holy, Holy, Lord God Almighty!
Early in the morning our song shall rise to Thee;
Holy, Holy, Holy! Merciful and Mighty!
God in Three Persons, blessed Trinity!
REGINALD HEBER, *Holy, Holy, Holy.*

2
Sure, Lord, there is enough in thee to dry
Oceans of ink; for as the deluge did
Cover the earth, so doth thy majesty.
Each cloud distils thy praise, and doth forbid
Poets to turn it to another use.
GEORGE HERBERT. (IZAAK WALTON, *Life*, p. 325.)

3
Lord of the light unfading
From day to reborn day;
God of the worlds brocading
This planet's nightly way;
Master of Hope, and builder
Of life's immortal span,
Now, when the days bewilder,
Thunder again to man!
LEIGH MITCHELL HODGES, *Processional, 1933.*

5
Far better in its place the lowliest bird
Should sing aright to Him the lowliest song,
Than that a seraph strayed should take the word
And sing His glory wrong.
JEAN INGELOW, *Honours.* Pt. ii.

6
Trust ye in the Lord for ever: for in the Lord Jehovah is everlasting strength.
Old Testament: Isaiah, xxvi, 4.

In thee, O Lord, do I put my trust.
Old Testament: Psalms, xxxi, 1. (In te, Domine, speravi.—*Vulgate.*)

Though he slay me, yet will I trust in him.
Old Testament: Job, xiii, 15.

Passive to His Holy will,
Trust I in my Master still,
Even though He slay me.
WHITTIER, *Barclay of Ury.* St. 7.

7
Praise God from whom all Blessings flow;
Praise Him all creatures here below;
Praise Him above, ye Heavenly Host:
Praise Father, Son, and Holy Ghost.
THOMAS KEN, *Morning and Evening Hymn.* (1709) The original version of 1695 has "Angelic Host."

God be with you, till we meet again,
By his counsels guide, uphold you,
With his sheep securely fold you;
God be with you, till we meet again.
JEREMIAH EAMES RANKIN, *Mizpah.* First sung in 1882; popularized by Moody and Sankey.

All people that on earth do dwell,
Sing to the Lord with cheerful voice;
Him serve with fear, His praise forth tell,
Come ye before Him and rejoice.
WILLIAM KETHE, *Old Hundredth.* (1561) Usually (and wrongly) called "Old Hundred." A metrical rendering of the hundredth Psalm. Shakespeare refers to it in *The Merry Wives of Windsor*, ii, 1, 63.

8
All but God is changing day by day.
CHARLES KINGSLEY, *The Saint's Tragedy.*

Let nothing disturb thee,
Let nothing affright thee,
All things are passing,
God changeth never.
LONGFELLOW, *Santa Teresa's Bookmark.* (After Santa Teresa de Avila.)

Darkness is strong, and so is Sin,
But surely God endures forever!
J. R. LOWELL, *Villa Franca.* Conclusion.

All things change, creeds and philosophies and outward systems—but God remains.
MRS. HUMPHRY WARD, *Robert Elsmere.* Bk. iv, ch. 26.

9
And suddenly there was with the angel a multitude of the heavenly host praising God, and saying, Glory to God in the highest, and on earth peace, good will toward men.
New Testament: Luke, ii, 13, 14.

10
Abide with me: fast falls the even-tide;
The darkness deepens: Lord, with me abide:
When other helpers fail, and comforts flee,
Help of the helpless, O abide with me!
HENRY FRANCIS LYTE, *Abide with Me.*

I fear no foe with Thee at hand to bless;
Ills have no weight, and tears no bitterness.
HENRY FRANCIS LYTE, *Abide with Me.*

11
God doth not need
Either man's work or his own gifts; who best
Bear his mild yoke, they serve him best; his state
Is kingly. Thousands at his bidding speed
And post o'er land and ocean without rest:
They also serve who only stand and wait.
MILTON, *On His Blindness.*

God for His service needeth not proud work of human skill.
WORDSWORTH, *Poet's Dream*, l. 65. See 1473:14.

That we devote ourselves to God, is seen
In living just as though no God there were.
ROBERT BROWNING, *Paracelsus.* Pt. i.

12
What in me is dark,
Illumine; what is low, raise and support;
That to the height of this great argument
I may assert Eternal Providence,
And justify the ways of God to men.
MILTON, *Paradise Lost.* Bk. i, l. 22.

Just are the ways of God, And justifiable to men.
MILTON, *Samson Agonistes*, l. 293.

Vindicate the ways of God to man.
POPE, *Essay on Man.* Epis. i, l. 15. See 1251:13.

1
Steal from the throng to haunts untrod,
And commune there alone with God.
JAMES MONTGOMERY, *Night*. St. 8.

2
Trumpeter sound for the splendour of God!
ALFRED NOYES, *Trumpet Call*.

3
Father of all! in ev'ry age,
In ev'ry clime, ador'd
By saint, by savage, and by sage,
Jehovah, Jove, or Lord!
POPE, *Universal Prayer*.

If I am right, thy grace impart,
Still in the right to stay;
If I am wrong, O teach my heart
To find that better way!
POPE, *Universal Prayer*.

4
"A still small voice" comes through the wild,
Like a father consoling his fretful child,
Which banishes bitterness, wrath, and fear,
Saying—Man is distant, but God is near!
THOMAS PRINGLE, *Afar in the Desert*.

As thus we sat in darkness,
Each one busy in his prayers,—
"We are lost!" the captain shouted,
As he staggered down the stairs.

But his little daughter whispered,
As she took his icy hand,
"Isn't God upon the ocean,
Just the same as on the land?"
JAMES T. FIELDS, *Ballad of the Tempest*.

See also HEAVEN: ITS DISTANCE.

I would rather walk with God in the dark than go alone in the light.
MARY GARDINER BRAINARD, *Not Knowing*.

6
The Lord reigneth; let the earth rejoice.
Old Testament: Psalms, xcvii, 1.

Without Thy presence, wealth are bags of cares;
Wisdom, but folly; joy, disquiet, sadness:
Friendship is treason, and delights are snares;
Pleasure's but pain, and mirth but pleasing madness.
FRANCIS QUARLES, *Emblems*. Bk. v, emb. 6.

7
Give ear, my children, to my words,
Whom God hath dearly bought,
Lay up his laws within your heart,
And print them in your thought.
JOHN ROGERS. *Advice to His Children*, a few days before his martyrdom. (From *The New England Primer*.)

8
He who has known God reverences him. (Deum colit qui novit.)
SENECA, *Epistulæ ad Lucilium*. Epis. xcv, 48

God is not to be worshipped with sacrifices and blood, for what pleasure can he have in the slaughter of the innocent? but with a pure mind, a good and honest purpose. Temples are not to be built for him with stones piled on high, but he is to be consecrated in one's own breast.
SENECA, *Fragments*. No. 204.

9
Come ill or well, the cross, the crown,
The rainbow or the thunder.
I fling my soul and body down
For God to plough them under.
R. L. STEVENSON *Youth and Love*. No. 2.

10
Speak to Him, thou, for He hears, and Spirit with Spirit can meet—
Closer is He than breathing, and nearer than hands and feet.
TENNYSON, *The Higher Pantheism*, l. 11.

11
I fled Him, down the nights and down the days;
I fled Him, down the arches of the years;
I fled Him, down the labyrinthine ways
Of my own mind; and in the midst of tears
I hid from Him, and under running laughter.
FRANCIS THOMPSON, *The Hound of Heaven*.

Still with unhurrying chase,
And unperturbèd pace,
Deliberate speed, majestic instancy,
Came on the following Feet,
And a Voice above their beat—
"Naught shelters thee, who wilt not shelter Me."
FRANCIS THOMPSON, *The Hound of Heaven*.

12
None but God can satisfy the longings of an immortal soul; that as the heart was made for Him, so He only can fill it.
RICHARD CHENEVIX TRENCH, *Notes on the Parables: The Prodigal Son*.

13
A dear Companion here abides;
Close to my thrilling heart He hides;
The holy silence is His Voice:
I lie and listen, and rejoice.
J. T. TROWBRIDGE, *Midsummer*.

14
To God the Father, God the Son,
And God the Spirit, Three in One,
Be honour, praise, and glory given
By all on earth, and all in heaven.
ISAAC WATTS, *Doxology*.

15
Our God, our help in ages past,
Our hope for years to come,
Our shelter from the stormy blast,
And our eternal home.
ISAAC WATTS, *The Psalms of David*, p. 229. (1719) The first line was altered to "O God, our help in ages past" by John Wesley in his *Collection* of 1738.

16
"God . . . is the only King." . . . Then after a time he said: "Our sons who have shown us God."
H. G. WELLS, *Mr. Britling Sees It Through*. Bk. iii, ch. 2, sec. 11.

17
Our fathers' God! From out whose hand
The centuries fall like grains of sand,

We meet to-day, united, free,
And loyal to our land and Thee,
To thank Thee for the era done,
And trust Thee for the opening one.
WHITTIER, *Centennial Hymn.*

1

Thou, my all!
My theme! my inspiration! and my crown!
My strength in age! my rise in low estate!
My soul's ambition, pleasure, wealth!—my world!
My light in darkness! and my life in death!
My boast thro' time! bliss thro' eternity!
Eternity, too short to speak thy praise!
Or fathom thy profound of love to man!
YOUNG, *Night Thoughts.* Night iv, l. 586.

A deity believ'd, is joy begun;
A deity ador'd, is joy advanc'd;
A deity belov'd, is joy matur'd.
Each branch of piety delight inspires.
YOUNG, *Night Thoughts.* Night viii, l. 713.

2

God's might to direct me,
God's power to protect me,
God's wisdom for learning,
God's eye for discerning,
God's ear for my hearing,
God's word for my clearing.
The earliest Christian hymn written in Gælic, and attributed to ST. PATRICK. (Sigerson, tr.)

XI—God and the Universe

3

Set God apart from mortal men, and deem not that he, like them, is fashioned out of flesh. Thou knowest him not; now he appeareth as fire, now as water, now as gloom; and he is dimly seen in the likeness of wild beasts, of wind, of cloud, of lightning, thunder, and of rain. All power hath he; lo, this is the glory of the Most High God.
ÆSCHYLUS [?], *Fragments.* Frag. 239.

4

The celestial order and the beauty of the universe compel me to admit that there is some excellent and eternal Being, who deserves the respect and homage of men.
CICERO, *De Divinatione.* Bk. ii, ch. 72, sec. 148.

5

Face to face with the universe, man will be the sole evidence of his audacious dreams of divinity, since the God he vainly sought is himself.
GEORGES CLEMENCEAU, *In the Evening of My Thought,* p. 503.

6

Treading beneath their feet all visible things,
As steps that upwards to their Father's throne
Lead gradual.
S. T. COLERIDGE, *Religious Musings,* l. 51.

The great world's altar-stairs
That slope thro' darkness up to God.
TENNYSON, *In Memoriam.* Sec. 55.

Teach me, by this stupendous scaffolding,
Creation's golden steps, to climb to Thee.
YOUNG, *Night Thoughts.* Night ix, l. 592.

7

God moves in a mysterious way
His wonders to perform;
He plants his footsteps in the sea,
And rides upon the storm.
COWPER, *Light Shining Out of Darkness.*

Nor God alone in the still calm we find,
He mounts the storm, and walks upon the wind.
POPE, *Essay on Man.* Epis. ii, l. 109.

8

There is a God! the sky his presence shares,
His hand upheaves the billows in their mirth,
Destroys the mighty, yet the humble spares
And with contentment crowns the thought of worth.
CHARLOTTE CUSHMAN, *There Is a God.*

9

God of the granite and the rose,
Soul of the sparrow and the bee,
The mighty tide of being flows
Thro' countless channels, Lord, from Thee.
ELIZABETH DOTEN, *Reconciliation.*

10

By tracing Heav'n his footsteps may be found:
Behold! how awfully he walks the round!
God is abroad, and wondrous in his ways
The rise of empires, and their fall surveys.
DRYDEN, *Britannia Rediviva,* l. 75.

O God, I am thinking Thy thoughts after Thee.
JOHN KEPLER, *Remark,* when studying astronomy.

11

I believe in God the Father Almighty because wherever I have looked, through all that I see around me, I see the trace of an intelligent mind, and because in natural laws, and especially in the laws which govern the social relations of men, I see, not merely the proofs of intelligence, but the proofs of beneficence.
HENRY GEORGE, *Speech,* New York, 1887.

12

The great soul that sits on the throne of the universe is not, never was, and never will be, in a hurry.
J. G. HOLLAND, *Gold-Foil: Patience.*

13

The Glory of him who
Hung his masonry pendant on naught, when the world He created.
LONGFELLOW, *The Children of the Lord's Supper,* l. 177.

14

Has God any dwelling-place save earth and sea, the air of heaven and virtuous hearts? Why seek the Deity further? Whatever we see is God, and wherever we go. (Estque dei sedes, nisi terra et pontus et aer et Cælum et virtus? Superos quid quærimus ultra?

Juppiter est, quodcumque vides, quodcumque moveris.)

LUCAN, *De Bello Civili*. Bk. ix, l. 578. The last line sums up the doctrine of Pantheism.

Know first, the heaven, the earth, the main,
The moon's pale orb, the starry train,
  Are nourished by a soul,
A bright intelligence, whose flame
Glows in each member of the frame,
  And stirs the mighty whole.
(Principio cœlum ac terras camposque liquentis
Lucentemque globum Lunæ Titaniaque astra
Spiritus intus alit, totamque infusa per artus
Mens agitat molem et magno se corpore miscet.)

VERGIL, *Æneid*. Bk. vi, l. 724. (Conington, tr.)

What, but God?
Inspiring God! who, boundless Spirit all,
And unremitting Energy, pervades,
Adjusts, sustains, and agitates the whole.

THOMSON, *The Seasons: Spring*, l. 852.

1
God, I can push the grass apart
And lay my finger on Thy heart!

EDNA ST. VINCENT MILLAY, *Renascence*.

2
These are thy glorious works, Parent of good.

MILTON, *Paradise Lost*. Bk. v, l. 153.

3
Who coverest thyself with light as with a garment: who stretchest out the heavens like a curtain: Who layeth the beams of his chambers in the waters: who maketh the clouds his chariot: who walketh upon the wings of the wind: Who maketh his angels spirits; his ministers a flaming fire.

Old Testament: Psalms, civ, 2–4.

4
He bowed the heavens also, and came down: and darkness was under his feet.

Old Testament: Psalms, xviii, 9.

The Lord descended from above
  And bow'd the heavens high;
And underneath his feet he cast
  The darkness of the sky.

THOMAS STERNHOLD, *A Metrical Version of Psalm xviii*.

5
Nothing is void of God; He Himself fills His work. (Nihil ab illo vacat; opus suum ipse implet.)

SENECA, *De Beneficiis*. Bk. iv, l. 8.

6
Between the birthday and the grave,
Teaching the tender heart be brave,
He woos our better from our worse,
The Artist of the Universe.

PAUL SHIVELL, *The Studios Photographic*.

XII—God the Unknowable

7
God is more truly imagined than expressed, and he exists more truly than is imagined. (Verius cogitatur Deus quam dicitur, et verius est quam cogitatur.)

ST. AUGUSTINE, *De Trinitate*. Pt. vii, sec. 6.

8
It were better to have no opinion of God at all, than such an opinion as is unworthy of him: for the one is unbelief, the other is contumely.

FRANCIS BACON, *Essays: Of Superstition*.

It is better to have no belief in the gods than a dishonouring belief. (Præstat nullam habere de dis opinionem, quam contumeliosam.)

FRANCIS BACON, *De Augmentis Scientiarum: Superstitio*.

9
God never meant that man should scale the heav'ns
By strides of human wisdom. In his works,
Though wondrous, he commands us in his word
To seek him rather where his mercy shines.

COWPER, *The Task*. Bk. iii, l. 221.

'Tis revelation satisfies all doubts,
Explains all mysteries except her own,
And so illuminates the path of life,
That fools discover it, and stray no more.

COWPER, *The Task*. Bk. ii, l. 527.

10
'Tis hard to find God, but to comprehend
Him, as He is, is labour without end.

ROBERT HERRICK, *God Not to be Comprehended*.

God is above the sphere of our esteem,
And is the best known, not defining him.

ROBERT HERRICK, *What God Is*.

To seek of God more than we well can find,
Argues a strong distemper of the mind.

ROBERT HERRICK, *Sobriety in Search*.

11
I askt the seas and all the deeps below
  My God to know,
I askt the reptiles, and whatever is
  In the abyss;
Even from the shrimps to the leviathan
  Enquiry ran;
But in those deserts that no line can sound,
The God I sought for was not to be found.

THOMAS HEYWOOD, *Searching After God*.

Dangerous it were for the feeble brain of man to wade far into the doings of the Most High. . . . Our soundest knowledge is to know that we know him not as indeed he is, neither can know him; and our safest eloquence concerning him is our silence, when we confess without confession that his glory is inexplicable, his greatness above our capacity and reach.

RICHARD HOOKER, *Ecclesiastical Polity*. Bk. i, ch. 2, sec. 3.

12
Canst thou by searching find out God?

Old Testament: Job, xi, 7.

13
Who thou art I know not,
  But this much I know:
Thou hast set the Pleiades
  In a silver row.

HARRY KEMP, *God, the Architect*.

1
The very impossibility in which I find myself to prove that God is not, discloses to me His existence. (L'impossibilité où je suis de prouver que Dieu n'est pas, me découvre son existence.)

LA BRUYÈRE, *Les Caractères*. Sec. 16.

2
Who can know heaven save by the gifts of heaven,
Or search out God save as a part of God?
(Quis cœlum possit nisi cœli munera nosse?
Et reperire deum nisi qui pars ipse deorum est?)

MANILIUS, *Astronomica*. Pt. ii, l. 115.

3
Only God is permanently interesting. Other things we may fathom, but he out-tops our thought and can neither be demonstrated nor argued down.

J. F. NEWTON, *My Idea of God*, p. 5.

4
There is sufficient clearness to lighten the elect, and sufficient obscurity to humble them. There is sufficient obscurity to blind the reprobate, and sufficient clearness to condemn them.

PASCAL, *Pensées*. Sec. viii, No. 578. Quoting St. Augustine, and Montaigne.

5
We understand nothing of the works of God, if we do not assume that He has willed to blind some and enlighten others.

PASCAL, *Pensées*. Sec. lx, No. 566.

6
I am whatever was or is or will be, and my veil no mortal ever took up.

PLUTARCH, *Of Isis and Osiris*.

7
Say first, of God above or Man below
What can we reason but from what we know?

POPE, *Essay on Man*. Epis. i, l. 17.

Thou Great First Cause, least understood,
Who all my sense confin'd
To know but this, that thou art good,
And that myself am blind.

POPE, *Universal Prayer*.

9
Every conjecture we can form with regard to the works of God has as little probability as the conjectures of a child with regard to the works of a man.

THOMAS REID, *Intellectual Powers*. Vol. i.

9
It is more religious and more reverent to believe in the works of the Deity than to comprehend them. (Sanctiusque ac reverentius visum de actis deorum credere quam scire.)

TACITUS, *Germania*. Sec. 34.

10
Reason refuseth its homage to a God who can be fully understood.

M. F. TUPPER, *Proverbial Philosophy: Of a Trinity*.

11
God has made thee to love Him, and not to understand Him. (Dieu t'a fait pour l'aimer, et non pour le comprendre.)

VOLTAIRE, *La Henriade*.

12
And the infinite pathos of human trust
In a God whom no one knows.

WILLIAM WATSON, *Churchyard in the Wold*.

13
If God is not in us, He never existed. (Si Dieu n'est pas dans nous, il n'exista jamais.)

VOLTAIRE, *La Loi Naturelle: Exordium*.

The God I know of, I shall ne'er
Know, though he dwells exceeding nigh.
Raise thou the stone and find me there,
Cleave thou the wood and there am I.
Yea, in my flesh his spirit doth flow,
Too near, too far, for me to know.

WILLIAM WATSON, *The Unknown God*. The third and fourth lines are a translation of a Hebrew proverb.

We may scavenge the dross of the nation, we may shudder past bloody sod,
But we thrill to the new revelation that we are parts of God.

R. H. SCHAUFFLER, *New Gods for Old*.

14
The Somewhat which we name but cannot know,
Ev'n as we name a star and only see
Its quenchless flashings forth, which ever show
And ever hide him, and which are not he.

WILLIAM WATSON, *Wordsworth's Grave*. St. 6.

15
And I say to mankind, Be not curious about God,
For I who am curious about each am not curious about God,
(No array of terms can say how much I am at peace about God and about death.)

WALT WHITMAN, *Song of Myself*. Sec. 48.

Who fathoms the Eternal Thought?
Who talks of scheme and plan?
The Lord is God! He needeth not
The poor device of man.

J. G. WHITTIER, *The Eternal Goodness*. St. 4.

A God alone can comprehend a God.

YOUNG, *Night Thoughts*. Night ix, l. 835.

XIII—God: Some Questionings

16
I sometimes wish that God were back
In this dark world and wide;
For though some virtues he might lack,
He had his pleasant side.

GAMALIEL BRADFORD, *Exit God*.

17
There is no God, no man made God; a bigger, stronger, crueller man;
Black phantom of our baby-fears, ere Thought, the life of Life, began.

SIR RICHARD BURTON, *The Kasîdah*. Pt. iv, 2.

18
Some men treat the God of their fathers as

they treat their father's friend. They do not deny him; by no means: they only deny themselves to him, when he is good enough to call upon them.

J. C. AND A. W. HARE, *Guesses at Truth.*

God often visits us, but most of the time we are not at home.

JOSEPH ROUX, *Meditations of a Parish Priest: God.* No. 65.

1
God does not know everything and never has known everything.

MAURICE MAETERLINCK. (NEWTON, *My Idea of God,* p. 117.)

2
The Lord who gave us Earth and Heaven
Takes that as thanks for all He's given.
The book he lent is given back
All blotted red and smutted black.

MASEFIELD, *The Everlasting Mercy.* St. 27.

3
I see little evidence in this world of the so-called goodness of God. On the contrary, it seems to me that, on the strength of His daily acts, He must be set down a most stupid, cruel and villainous fellow.

H. L. MENCKEN. (DURANT, *On the Meaning of Life,* p. 34.)

4
As far remov'd from God and light of Heav'n,
As from the centre thrice to th' utmost pole.

MILTON, *Paradise Lost.* Bk. i, l. 73.

5
Give us a God—a living God,
One to wake the sleeping soul,
One to cleanse the tainted blood
Whose pulses in our bosoms roll.

C. G. ROSENBERG, *The Winged Horn.*

6
At last I heard a voice upon the slope
Cry to the summit, "Is there any hope?"
To which an answer peal'd from that high land,
But in a tongue no man could understand;
And on the glimmering limit far withdrawn,
God made Himself an awful rose of dawn.

TENNYSON, *The Vision of Sin,* l. 219.

7
When the universe began
God, they say, created man.
Later, with a mocking nod,
Man annihilated God.

MIRIAM VEDDER, *Warning.*

8
When whelmed are altar, priest, and creed;
When all the faiths have passed;
Perhaps, from darkening incense freed,
God may emerge at last.

WILLIAM WATSON, *Revelation.*

9
Devoutly, thus, Jehovah they depose,
The pure! the just! and set up, in his stead
A deity that's perfectly well-bred.

YOUNG, *Love of Fame.* Sat. vi, l. 444.

GODS AND GODDESSES

I—Gods: Definitions

10
Where man is met
The gods will come; or shall I say man's spirit
Hath operative faculties to mix
And make his gods at will?

ROBERT BRIDGES, *Achilles in Scyros,* l. 552.

To be a god First I must be a god-maker.
We are what we create.

JAMES OPPENHEIM, *Jottings: To Be a God.*

Man is certainly stark mad; he cannot make a flea, and yet he will be making gods by dozens.

MONTAIGNE, *Essays.* Bk. ii, ch. 12.

11
The belief in the gods has not been established by authority, custom or law, but rests upon the unanimous and abiding consensus of mankind. (Cum enim non instituto aliquo aut more aut lege sit opinio constituta maneatque ad unum omnium firma consensio.)

CICERO, *De Natura Deorum.* Bk. i, ch. 17, 44.

I do not know whether there are gods, but there ought to be.

DIOGENES. (TERTULLIAN, *Ad Nationes.* Bk. ii, ch. 2.)

12
The gods of fable are the shining moments of great men.

EMERSON, *Representative Men: Uses of Great Men.*

13
I have always said, and will say, that there is a race of gods,
But I fancy that what men do is to them but little odds.

ENNIUS, *Telamon.* (King, tr.) These lines were preserved by Cicero who used them in *De Inventione Rhetorica,* ii, 50, 104.

14
The gods we stand by are the gods we need and can use.

WILLIAM JAMES, *Varieties of Religious Experience,* p. 331.

15
The gods appear, and their serene abodes,
Which winds fret not, nor clouds bedew with showers.
(Apparet divum numen sedesque quietæ
Quas neque concutiunt venti nec nubila nimbis Aspergunt.)

LUCRETIUS, *De Rerum Natura.* Bk. iii, l. 18.

16
It is pleasant to die, if there be gods; and sad to live, if there be none.

MARCUS AURELIUS, *Meditations.* Bk. ii, sec. 11. (EMERSON, *Conduct of Life: Worship.*)

17
It is expedient there should be gods, and, since it is expedient, let us believe that gods exist. (Expedit esse deos, et, ut expedit, esse putemus.)

OVID, *Ars Amatoria.* Bk. i, l. 637.

1
A god is won by the humblest offering of incense, no less than by the outpoured blood of a hundred bulls. (Sed tamen, ut fuso taurorum sanguine centum, Sic capitur minimo turis honore deus.)
OVID, *Tristia*. Bk. ii, l. 75.

The gods despise enforced offerings.
When the heart brings its dearest and its last
Then only will they hear—if then, if then!
WILLAM VAUGHN MOODY, *Fire-Bringer*. Act ii.

2
The first way to worship the gods is to believe in the gods. (Primus est deorum cultus deos credere.)
SENECA, *Epistulæ ad Lucilium*. Epis. xcv, 50.

3
Gods fade; but God abides and in man's
heart
Speaks with the clear unconquerable cry
Of energies and hopes that can not die.
J. A. SYMONDS, *On the Sacro Monte*.

II—Gods: Apothegms

4
'Tis only of your own desire that you curse the gods. (Σύ θην ἃ χρήζεις, ταῦτ' επιγωσσᾶ Διός.)
ÆSCHYLUS, *Prometheus Bound*, l. 928.

Small praise man gets dispraising the high gods.
SWINBURNE, *Atalanta in Calydon: Chorus*.

5
He is to be feared who fears the gods. (Δεινὸς ὃς θεοὺς σέβει.)
ÆSCHYLUS, *The Seven Against Thebes*, l. 596.

6
Make not my path offensive to the Gods
By spreading it with carpets.
(Μηδ' εἵμασι στρώσασ' ἐπίφθονον πορον τίθει.)
ÆSCHYLUS, *Agamemnon*, l. 891.

7
The gods are careful about great things and neglect small ones. (Magna di curant, parva negligunt.)
CICERO, *De Natura Deorum*. Bk. ii, ch. 66, 167.

Ye immortal gods! where in the world are we? (O dii immortales! ubinam gentium sumus?)
CICERO, *In Catilinam*. No. i, sec. 4.

8
Human murmurs never touch the gods. (Humanæ superos numquam tetigere querellæ.)
CLAUDIAN, *Epigrams*. No. xxii, l. 9.

9
Never, believe me,
Appear the Immortals,
Never alone.
S. T. COLERIDGE, *The Visit of the Gods*. Imitating Schiller.

Heartily know,
When half-gods go,
The gods arrive.
EMERSON, *Give All to Love*.

10
The gods are athirst. (Les dieux ont soif.)
CAMILLE DESMOULINS, *Vieux Cordelier*, 3 Feb., 1794; closing words of last issue. Title of novel by Anatole France dealing with the French Revolution. See HATE AND THE GODS.

11
Gods meet gods, and justle in the dark.
DRYDEN AND LEE, *Œdipus*. Act iv, last line.

Birds met birds, and justled in the dark.
DRYDEN, *The Hind and the Panther*. Pt. iii, l. 604.

12
If we meet no gods, it is because we harbor none.
EMERSON, *Conduct of Life: Worship*.

13
Slowly but surely withal moveth the might of the gods. (Ὁρμᾶται μόλις, ἀλλ' ὅμως πιστόν τι τὸ θεῖον σθένος.)
EURIPIDES, *Bacchæ*, l. 882.

Let us beware the jealousy of the gods. (Μή τις θεῶν φθόνος ἔλθῃ.)
EURIPIDES, *Iphigeneia at Aulis*, l. 1098.

14
Shakes his ambrosial curls, and gives the nod,
The stamp of fate, and sanction of the god.
HOMER, *Iliad*. Bk. i, l. 684. (Pope, tr.)

He caused all Olympus to tremble with his nod. (Totum nutu tremefecit Olympum.)
VERGIL, *Æneid*. Bk. ix, l. 106.

With ravish'd ears The monarch hears;
Assumes the god, Affects to nod,
And seems to shake the spheres.
DRYDEN, *Alexander's Feast*, l. 37.

15
She moves a goddess, and she looks a queen. (Δῖα γυναικῶν.)
HOMER, *Iliad*. Bk iii, l. 228. (Pope, tr.)

Where'er he mov'd, the goddess shone before.
HOMER, *Iliad*. Bk. xx, l. 127. (Pope, tr.)

Oh! a goddess surely! (O dea certe!)
VERGIL, *Æneid*. Bk. i, l. 328.

By her gait one knew the goddess. (Incessu patuit dea.)
VERGIL, *Æneid*. Bk. i, l. 405.

16
For verily these things lie on the knees of the gods. (Ἀλλ' ἦ τοι μὲν ταῦτα θεῶν ἐν γούνασι κεῖται.)
HOMER, *Iliad*. Bk. xvii, l. 514; *Odyssey*, i, 267. Often misquoted "On the lap of the gods."

The rest leave to the gods. (Permitte divis cetera.)
HORACE, *Odes*. Bk. i, ode 9, l. 9.

The gods my protectors. (Di me tuentur.)
HORACE, *Odes*. Bk. i, ode 17, l. 13.

17
To that large utterance of the early gods!
KEATS, *Hyperion*. Bk. i, l. 51.

18
Much must he toil who serves the Immortal
Gods.
LONGFELLOW, *The Masque of Pandora*. Pt. ii.

19
The god from the machine. (Θεὸς ἐκ μηχανῆς.)
LUCIAN, *Hermotimus*. Sec. 86. Usually quoted in its Latin form, "Deus ex machina," as in-

dicating divine help from some contrivance unseen or unexpected. It was a reference to the way in which the gods appeared suddenly upon the Greek stage by the help of mechanism.

A god from the machine. (Ἀπὸ μηχανῆς θεός.)
MENANDER, *Theophoroumene*. Frag. 227.

Nor let a god intervene, unless the difficulty is worthy his intervention. (Nec deus intersit, nisi dignus vindice nodus.)
HORACE, *Ars Poetica*, l. 191.

1
Walk with the gods. (Συζῆν θεοῖς.)
MARCUS AURELIUS, *Meditations*. Bk. v, sec. 27.

2
Those whom the gods care for are gods. (Cura deum di sunt.)
OVID, *Metamorphoses*. Bk. viii, l. 724.

The gods profit the man to whom they are propitious. (Cui homini dii propitii sunt aliquid objicunt lucri.)
PLAUTUS, *Persa*. Act iv, sc. 3, l. 1.

The gods are with me and love me. (Di me servant atque amant.)
PLAUTUS, *Pseudolus*, l. 613. (Act ii, sc. 1.)

WHOM THE GODS LOVE DIES YOUNG, *see under* DEATH.

3
The gods are a law unto themselves. (Sunt superis sua jura!)
OVID, *Metamorphoses*. Bk. ix, l. 500.

4
It was fear first brought gods into the world, when the lightning fell from high heaven, and the ramparts of the world were rent with flame. (Primus in orbe deos fecit timor, ardua cælo Fulmina cum caderent discussaque mœnia flammis.)
PETRONIUS, *Poems*. Frag. 76 P.L.M. (c. A. D. 60) *See* Loeb ed., p. 342. Quoted by STATIUS, *Thebaid*. Bk. iii, l. 664.

'Twas only fear first in the world made gods.
BEN JONSON, *The Fall of Sejanus*. Act ii, sc. 2. (1603)

Fear made the gods; audacity has made kings.
PROSPER JOLYOT DE CRÉBILLON, *Catilina*.

As dreadful as the Manichean god,
Ador'd through fear, strong only to destroy.
COWPER, *The Task*. Bk. v, l. 444. The Manichean god was the Power of Evil.

5
The gods play games with men as balls. (Di nos quasi pilas homines habent.)
PLAUTUS, *Captivi: Prologue*, l. 22.

In wondrous ways do the gods make sport with men. (Miris modis di ludos faciunt hominibus.)
PLAUTUS, *Rudens*, l. 593. (Act iii, sc. 1.)

As flies to wanton boys, are we to the gods;
They kill us for their sport.
SHAKESPEARE, *King Lear*. Act iv, sc. 1, l. 38.

6
I have with me two gods, Persuasion and Compulsion. (Πειθὼ καὶ βιαν.)
THEMISTOCLES, to the Andrians, when demanding a tribute. To which the Andrians replied that they were protected by two great gods, Penury and Powerlessness. (Πενίαν καὶ Ἀπορίαν.) PLUTARCH, *Lives: Themistocles*. Sec. 21.

7
Would you placate the gods? Then be a good man. Whoever imitates them is worshipping them. (Vis deos propitiare? Bonus esto. Satis illos coluit, quisquis imitatus est.)
SENECA, *Epistulæ ad Lucilium*. Epis. xcv, 50.

8
For thou, if ever godlike foot there trod
These fields of ours, wert surely like a god.
SWINBURNE, *In the Bay*. St. 18.

9
Alas! it is not well to be confident when the gods are adverse. (Heu! nihil invitis fas quemquam fidere divis!)
VERGIL, *Æneid*. Bk. ii, l. 402.

10
Be warned: learn justice, and not to despise the gods. (Discite justitiam moniti et non temnere divos.)
VERGIL, *Æneid*. Bk. vi, l. 620.

First and foremost reverence the Gods. (Imprimis venerare Deos.)
VERGIL, *Georgics*. Bk. i, l. 338.

III—Gods and Goddesses: Individuals

For Venus, see under separate heading

11
Clio, singing of famous deeds, restores the past to life. Euterpe's breath fills the sweet-voiced flutes. Thalia rejoices in the careless speech of comedy. Melpomene cries aloud with the echoing voice of gloomy tragedy. Terpsichore with her lyre stirs and governs the emotions. Erato bearing the plectrum harmonizes foot and song in the dance. Urania examines the motions of the stars. Calliope commits heroic songs to writing. Polymnia expresses all things with her hands and speaks by gesture. The power of Apollo's will enlivens the whole circle of these muses: he sits in their midst and in himself possesses all their gifts.
AUSONIUS [?], *Nomina Musarum*.

12
Atlas, we read in ancient song,
Was so exceeding tall and strong,
He bore the skies upon his back,
Just as the pedler does his pack;
But, as the pedler overpress'd
Unloads upon a stall to rest,
Or, when he can no longer stand,
Desires a friend to lend a hand,
So Atlas, lest the ponderous spheres
Should sink, and fall about his ears,
Got Hercules to bear the pile,
That he might sit and rest awhile.
SWIFT, *Atlas; or, the Minister of State*.

1 Who knows not Circe,
The daughter of the Sun, whose charmed cup
Whoever tasted, lost his upright shape,
And downward fell into a groveling swine?
MILTON, *Comus*, l. 50.

2
Great is Diana of the Ephesians.
New Testament: Acts, xix, 28.

3
Sweet Europa's mantle blew unclasp'd,
From off her shoulder backward borne;
From one hand droop'd a crocus; one hand grasp'd
The mild bull's golden horn
TENNYSON, *The Palace of Art*, l. 117.

Or else flush'd Ganymede, his rosy thigh
Half buried in the eagle's down,
Sole as a flying star shot thro' the sky
Above the pillar'd town.
TENNYSON, *The Palace of Art*, l. 121.

4
Janus am I; oldest of potentates;
Forward I look, and backward, and below
I count, as god of avenues and gates,
The years that through my portals come and go.
I block the roads, and drift the fields with snow;
I chase the wild-fowl from the frozen fen;
My frosts congeal the rivers in their flow,
My fires light up the hearths and hearts of men.
LONGFELLOW, *The Poet's Calendar: January*

5
Or ask of yonder argent fields above
Why Jove's satellites are less than Jove.
POPE, *Essay on Man*. Epis. i, l. 41.

6
The ox-eyed awful Juno.
HOMER, *Iliad* Bk iii, l. 144; vii, 10; xviii, 40.

6a
Mumbo-jumbo, God of the Congo.
VACHEL LINDSAY, *The Congo*.

7
Great Pan is dead.
PLUTARCH, *De Defectu Oraculorum*. Sec. xvii.
See also under PAN.

8
Pluto, the grisly god, who never spares,
Who feels no mercy, and who hears no prayers.
HOMER, *Iliad* Bk. ix, l. 209. (Pope, tr.)

9
Ye men of Athens, I perceive that in all things ye are too superstitious. For as I passed by, and beheld your devotions, I found an altar with this inscription, TO THE UNKNOWN GOD
New Testament: Acts, xvii, 22, 23. (Ignoto Deo.—*Vulgate*.)

The presiding genius of the place. (Genius loci.)
VERGIL, *Æneid*. Bk. vii, l. 136. Genius signifies a divinity The Romans often raised monumental stones inscribed "Genio loci."

GOLD

See also Money, Riches

I—Gold: Apothegms

10
Gold is tried with the touchstone, and men with gold.
CHILO. (BACON, *Apothegms*. No. 225.)

As the touch-stone trieth gold, so gold trieth men.
THOMAS FULLER, *Gnomologia*. No. 736.

Men have a touchstone whereby to try gold; but gold is the touchstone whereby to try men.
FULLER, *The Holy State: The Good Judge*.

11
Gold is pale because it has so many thieves plotting against it.
DIOGENES. (DIOGENES LAERTIUS, *Diogenes*. Sec 51.)

12
That is gold which is worth gold.
GEORGE HERBERT, *Jacula Prudentum*.

The balance distinguisheth not between gold and lead.
GEORGE HERBERT, *Jacula Prudentum*.

13
If gold knew what gold is,
Gold would get gold, I wis.
GEORGE HERBERT, *Jacula Prudentum*.

Foul cankering rust the hidden treasure frets,
But gold that's put to use more gold begets.
SHAKESPEARE, *Venus and Adonis*, l. 767.

14
This is the famous stone
That turneth all to gold.
GEORGE HERBERT, *The Elixir*.

If by fire
Of sooty coal th' empiric alchymist
Can turn, or holds it possible to turn,
Metals of drossiest ore to perfect gold
MILTON, *Paradise Lost* Bk v, l. 439

You are an alchemist; make gold of that.
SHAKESPEARE, *Timon of Athens*. Act v, sc. 1, l. 117.

15
And gold but sent to keep the fools in play,
For some to heap, and some to throw away.
POPE, *Moral Essays*. Epis. iii, l. 5.

16
We live by the gold for which other men die.
PRIOR, *The Thief and the Cordelier*. St. 12.

17
When we have gold we are in fear; when we have none we are in danger.
JOHN RAY, *English Proverbs*, 12.

18
Thou gaudy gold, Hard food for Midas!
SHAKESPEARE, *The Merchant of Venice*. Act iii, sc. 2, l. 101.

19
Now do I play the touch,
To try if thou be current gold indeed.
SHAKESPEARE, *Richard III*. Act iv, sc. 2, l. 9.

Gold is proved by touch. (À la touche l'on epreuve l'or.)
J. DE LA VEPRIE, *Les Proverbes Communs.*

ALL IS NOT GOLD THAT GLITTERS, *see under* APPEARANCES.

II—Gold: The Lust for Gold

1
O cursed lust of gold! when, for thy sake,
The fool throws up his interest in both worlds;
First starved in this, then damned in that to come.
ROBERT BLAIR, *The Grave*, l. 347.

2
A thirst for gold,
The beggar's vice, which can but overwhelm
The meanest hearts.
BYRON, *The Vision of Judgment*. St. 43.

3
For gold in physic is a cordial;
Therefore he loved gold in special.
CHAUCER, *Canterbury Tales: Prologue*, l. 443.

4
The lust of gold succeeds the rage of conquest;
The lust of gold, unfeeling and remorseless!
The last corruption of degenerate man.
SAMUEL JOHNSON, *Irene*. Act i, sc. 1.

5
Men dig the earth for gold, seed of unnumbered ills. (Effodiuntur opes, inritamenta malorum.)
OVID, *Metamorphoses*. Bk. i, l. 140.

Where the pale children of the feeble sun
In search of gold through every climate run:
From burning heat to freezing torrents go,
And live in all vicissitudes of woe.
CHATTERTON, *Narva and Mored*, l. 55.

Days of old and days of gold,
And the days of Forty-nine.
UNKNOWN, *The Days of Forty-Nine.*

6
Gold is a child of Zeus; neither moth nor rust devoureth it; but the mind of man is devoured by this supreme possession.
PINDAR, *Fragments*. No. 222.

7
To what dost thou not drive the hearts of men, O accursed lust for gold! (Quid non mortalia pectora cogis, Auri sacra fames!)
VERGIL, *Æneid*. Bk. iii, l. 56.

O love of gold! thou meanest of amours!
YOUNG, *Night Thoughts*. Night iv, l. 350.

III—Gold: Its Power

8
Even to ugliness gold gives a look of beauty. (L'or même à la laideur donne un teint de beauté.)
BOILEAU, *Satires*. Sat. viii, l. 209.

Gold gives to the ugliest a certain pleasing charm. (L'or donne aux plus laids certain charme pour plaire.)
MOLIÈRE, *Sganarelle*. Sc. 1, l. 49.

9
Though wisdom cannot be gotten for gold, still less can it be gotten without it. . . No gold, no Holy Ghost.
SAMUEL BUTLER THE YOUNGER, *Note-Books*, p. 172.

10
Gold dust blinds all eyes.
A. B. CHEALES, *Proverbial Folk-Lore*, 98.

11
Now gold hath sway; we all obey
And a ruthless king is he.
H. F. CHORLEY, *The Brave Old Oak.*

12
Gold begets in brethren hate;
Gold in families debate;
Gold does friendship separate;
Gold does civil wars create.
ABRAHAM COWLEY, *Anacreontics: Gold*, l. 17.

13
Gold hath been the ruin of many.
Apocrypha: Ecclesiasticus, xxxi, 6.

Gold maketh an honest man an ill man.
JOHN LYLY, *Euphues*, p. 63. Cited as "a byword among us."

14
An ass loaded with gold climbs to the top of the castle.
THOMAS FULLER, *Gnomologia*. See also Ass.

15
Chains of gold are stronger than chains of iron.
THOMAS FULLER, *Gnomologia*. No. 1079.

16
The tongue hath no force when gold speaketh.
GUAZZO, *Civil Conversation*, p. 88.

Man prates, but gold speaks.
TORRIANO, *Piazza Universale*, p. 179.

17
Gold opens all locks, no lock will hold against the power of gold.
GEORGE HERBERT, *Jacula Prudentum.*

Every door is barred with gold, and opens but to golden keys.
TENNYSON, *Locksley Hall*. St. 50.

Gold! Gold! Gold! Gold!
Bright and yellow, hard and cold,
Molten, graven, hammer'd, and roll'd;
Heavy to get, and light to hold;
Hoarded, barter'd, bought, and sold,
Stolen, borrow'd, squander'd, doled:
Spurn'd by the young, but hugg'd by the old
To the very verge of the churchyard mould;
Price of many a crime untold:
Gold! Gold! Gold! Gold!
Good or bad a thousand-fold!
How widely its agencies vary—
To save—to ruin—to curse—to bless—
As even its minted coins express,
Now stamp'd with the image of Good Queen Bess,
And now of a Bloody Mary.
THOMAS HOOD, *Miss Kilmansegg: Her Moral.*

18
Gold can a path through hosts of warders clear,
And walls of stone more swiftly can displace
Than ever lightning could.

(Aurum per medios ire satellites
Et perrumpere amat saxa, potentius
Ictu fulmineo.)
HORACE, *Odes*. Bk. iii, ode 16, l. 9.

The cities of Greece were taken not by Philip but by Philip's gold. (Τὰς πόλεις αἱρεῖ τῶν Ἑλλήνων οὐ Φίλιππος, ἀλλὰ τὸ Φιλίππου χρυσίον.)
PLUTARCH, *Lives: Æmilius Paulus*. Ch. 12, sec. 6.

The strongest castle, tower, and town,
The golden bullet beats it down.
SHAKESPEARE, *The Passionate Pilgrim*, l. 327.

1 But brief to be, what can you crave,
That now for gold you may not have?
THOMAS HOWELL, *Howell His Devises*, 54.

3 Whilst that for which all virtue now is sold,
And almost every vice,—almighty gold.
BEN JONSON, *Epistle to Elizabeth, Countess of Rutland.*

Almighty gold.
FARQUHAR, *The Recruiting Officer*. Act iii, sc. 2.

No, let the monarch's bags and others hold
The flattering, mighty, nay, al-mighty gold.
JOHN WOLCOT, *To Kien Long*. Ode iv.

4 Truly now is the golden age; the highest honor comes by means of gold; by gold love is procured. (Aurea nunc vere sunt sæcula; plurimus auro Venit honos; auro conciliatur amor.)
OVID, *Ars Amatoria*. Bk ii, l. 277. *For other quotations relating to the Golden Age see under* AGE: THE GOLDEN AGE.

Piety is vanquished and all men worship gold. Gold has banished faith, gold has made judgment to be bought and sold, gold rules the law, and, law once gone, rules chastity as well. (Aures omnes victa jam pietate colunt. Auro pulsa fides, auro venalia jura, Aurum lex sequitur, mox sine lige pudor.)
PROPERTIUS, *Elegies*. Bk. iii, eleg. 13, l. 47.

Judges and senates have been bought for gold;
Esteem and love were never to be sold.
POPE, *Essay on Man*. Epis. iv, l. 187.

5 What nature wants, commodious gold bestows;
'Tis thus we eat the bread another sows.
POPE, *Moral Essays*. Epis. iii, l. 21.

6 Gold goes in at any gate, except Heaven's.
JOHN RAY, *English Proverbs.*

7 'Tis gold
Which buys admittance, . . . and 'tis gold
Which makes the true man kill'd and saves the thief.
SHAKESPEARE, *Cymbeline*. Act ii, sc. 3, l. 72.

8 Gold were as good as twenty orators.
SHAKESPEARE, *Richard III*. Act iv, sc. 2, l. 38. (1592)

Gold is a deep-persuading orator.
RICHARD BARNFIELD, *The Affectionate Shepherd*, 48. (1594)

Saint-seducing gold.
SHAKESPEARE, *Romeo and Juliet*. Act i, 1, 220.

9 Commerce has set the mark of Selfishness,
The signet of its all-enslaving power
Upon a shining ore, and called it gold;
Before whose image bow the vulgar great,
The vainly rich, the miserable proud,
The mob of peasants, nobles, priests, and kings,
And with blind feelings reverence the power
That grinds them to the dust of misery.
But in the temple of their hireling hearts
Gold is a living god, and rules in scorn
All earthly things but virtue.
SHELLEY, *Queen Mab*. Pt. v, l. 53.

10 What words won't do, gold will.
EDWARD WARD, *The London Spy*, p. 400.

IV—Gold: Its Worthlessness

11 All's alike at the latter day,
A bag of gold and a wisp of hay.
JOHN CLARKE, *Parœmiologia*, 215.

12 What is fame? an empty bubble;
Gold? a transient, shining trouble.
JAMES GRAINGER, *Ode to Solitude*.

Gold is the money of monarchs; kings covet it; the exchanges of the nations are effected by it. . . . It is the instrument of gamblers and speculators, and the idol of the miser and the thief. . . . No people in a great emergency ever found a faithful ally in gold. It is the most cowardly and treacherous of all metals. It makes no treaty that it does not break. It has no friend whom it does not sooner or later betray.
SENATOR JOHN J. INGALLS, *Speech on the Coinage of Silver Dollars*, U. S. Senate, 15 Feb., 1878. (*Cong. Record*, 45th Cong., 2d. sess., p. 1052.)

13 Gold is but muck.
BEN JONSON, *The Case Is Altered*. Act iv, sc. 4. Cited as "the old proverb."

14 O God! how poor a man may be
With nothing in this world but gold!
JOAQUIN MILLER, *A Song of the South*. Sec. vii.

15 When a ship sinks, gold weighs down its possessor. (Sic rate demersa fulvum deponderat aurum.)
PETRONIUS, *Fragments*. No. 80.

16 I despise gold; it has persuaded many a man into many an evil. (Odi ego aurum; multa multis sæpe suasit perperam.)
PLAUTUS, *Captivi*, l. 328. (Act ii, sc. 2.)

17 Gold is a chimera. (L'or est une chimère.)
SCRIBE AND DELAVIGNE, *Robert le Diable*. Act i, sc. 7.

1
Poison is drunk out of gold. (Venenum in auro bibitur.)
SENECA, *Thyestes*, l. 453.

There is thy gold, worse poison to men's souls,
Doing more murders in this loathsome world,
Than these poor compounds that thou mayst not sell.
SHAKESPEARE, *Romeo and Juliet*. Act v, sc. 1, 80.

2
All gold and silver rather turn to dirt!
As 'tis no better reckon'd, but of those
Who worship dirty gods.
SHAKESPEARE, *Cymbeline*. Act iii, sc. 6, l. 54.

GOLDEN RULE, THE

3
We should behave to friends as we would wish friends to behave to us. (Ὡς ἂν ευξαίμεθα αὐτοὺς ἡμῖν προσφέρεσθαι.)
ARISTOTLE. (DIOGENES LAERTIUS, *Aristotle*. Sec. 21.)

4
Do as you would be done by is the surest method that I know of pleasing.
LORD CHESTERFIELD, *Letters*, 16 Oct., 1747.

To do as you would be done by, is the plain, sure, and undisputed rule of morality and justice.
LORD CHESTERFIELD, *Letters*, 27 Sept., 1748.

5
Is there one word which may serve as a rule of practice for all one's life? The master said, Is not *reciprocity* such a word? What you do not want done to yourself, do not do to others.
CONFUCIUS, *Analects*. Bk. xv, ch. 23. A negative statement of the Golden Rule.

What is hateful to thyself do not unto thy neighbor.
Babylonian Talmud: Shabbath, p. 31a. The Talmudic formulation of the Golden Rule, also negative.

6
The Golden Rule works like gravitation.
C. F. DOLE, *Cleveland Address*.

7
Every man takes care that his neighbor does not cheat him. But a day comes when he begins to care that he do not cheat his neighbor. Then all goes well.
EMERSON, *Conduct of Life: Worship*.

8
Therefore if anyone would take these two words to heart and use them for his own guidance, he will be almost without sin. These two words are bear (ἀνέχου) and forbear (ἀπέχου).
EPICTETUS. (AULUS GELLIUS, *Noctes Atticæ*. Bk. xvii, ch. 19, sec. 6.)

9
The Golden Law, "do as ye would be done by."
ROBERT GODFREY, *Physics*. (1674)

Thence arises that Golden Rule of dealing with others as we would have others deal with us.
ISAAC WATTS, *Logick*. (1725)

Such is that golden principle of morality which our blessed Lord has given us.
ISAAC WATTS, *Improving the Mind*. (1741)

In our dealings with each other we should be guided by the Golden Rule.
W. D. HOWELLS, *The Rise of Silas Lapham*. Vol. ii, p. 26. (1885)

10
Therefore all things whatsoever ye would that men should do to you, do ye even so to them: for this is the law and the prophets.
New Testament: Matthew, vii, 12.

11
Men are used as they use others.
PILPAY, *The King Who Became Just*. Fable 9.

Look to be treated by others as you have treated others. (Ab alio exspectes alteri quod feceris.)
PUBLILIUS SYRUS, *Sententiæ*. No. 1.

You must expect to be treated by others as you yourself have treated them. (Ab alio exspectes, alteri quod feceris.)
SENECA, *Epistulæ ad Lucilium*. Epis. xciv, sec. 43. Quoted.

12
The rule of proportion which, for excellency, is called the Golden Rule.
ROBERT RECORDE, *The Grounde of Arts*, p. 240. (1540) The earliest known use of the words "Golden Rule." It refers to mathematics, not to the verse from Matthew.

The rule of three, or golden rule, as it is called in sacred algebray.
DANIEL FEATLEY, *Clavis Mystica*, p. 279. (c. 1635)

13
Treat your inferiors as you would be treated by your betters. (Sic cum inferiore vivas, quemadmodum tecum superiorem velis vivere.)
SENECA, *Epistulæ ad Lucilium*. Epis. xlvii, 11.

In your dealings with others, harm not that you be not harmed. (Alterum intuere, ne lædaris, alterum ne lædas.)
SENECA, *Epistulæ ad Lucilium*. Epis. ciii, 3.

14
Be as just and gracious unto me,
As I am confident and kind to thee.
SHAKESPEARE, *Titus Andronicus*. Act i, sc. 1, l. 60.

15
The golden rule is that there are no golden rules.
BERNARD SHAW, *Maxims for Revolutionists*.

Do not do unto others as you would they should do unto you. Their tastes may not be the same.
BERNARD SHAW, *Maxims for Revolutionists*.

16
If it be a duty to respect other men's claims, so also is it a duty to maintain our own.
SPENCER, *Social Statics*. Pt. iii, ch. 21, sec. 8.

17
Do unto the other feller the way he'd like to do unto you, an' do it fust.
EDWARD NOYES WESTCOTT, *David Harum*.

18
His statecraft was the Golden Rule,

His right of vote a sacred trust;
Clear, over threat and ridicule,
All heard his challenge: "Is it just?"
J. G. WHITTIER, *Sumner.*

1
Deal with another as you'd have
Another deal with you;
What you're unwilling to receive,
Be sure you never do.
UNKNOWN, *The New England Primer.*

GOLDSMITH, OLIVER

2
Here lies Nolly Goldsmith, for shortness called Noll,
Who wrote like an angel, and talk'd like poor Poll.
DAVID GARRICK, *Impromptu Epitaph.* Goldsmith resembled Addison in admitting that he wrote much better than he talked. "I always get the better when I argue alone," he said Of de Tréville, a fluent talker, he remarked, "He vanquishes me in the drawing-room, but surrenders to me at discretion on the stairs." For Addison's remark as recorded by Boswell see 313:2.

No man was more foolish when he had not a pen in his hand, or more wise when he had.
SAMUEL JOHNSON, referring to Goldsmith. (BOSWELL, *Life.* Vol. ii, ch. 10.)

While he talks he is great, but goes out like a taper,
If you shut him up closely with pen, ink, and paper.
J. R. LOWELL, *A Fable for Critics,* l. 649. Of Bronson Alcott.

Tom Birch is as brisk as a bee in conversation; but no sooner does he take a pen in his hand, than it becomes a torpedo to him, and benumbs all his faculties.
SAMUEL JOHNSON. (BOSWELL, *Life,* 1743.) The exact antithesis of Goldsmith.

3
Poet, Naturalist, Historian, who left scarcely any style of writing untouched, and touched nothing which he did not adorn. (Poetæ, Physici, Historici, Qui nullum fere scribendi genus non tetigit, Nullum quod tetigit non ornavit.)
SAMUEL JOHNSON, *Epitaph of Goldsmith.* (BOSWELL, *Life.* Vol. vii, ch. 3.) Dr. Johnson's Latin, it will be noted, is by no means above reproach. The antithesis had already been used by Lord Chesterfield in writing of Bolingbroke, and by Fénelon with reference to Cicero. *See also under* ELOQUENCE.

Goldsmith, however, was a man who, whatever he wrote, did it better than any other man could.
SAMUEL JOHNSON. (BOSWELL, *Life,* ii, 3.)

4
Goldsmith was a plant that flowered late.
SAMUEL JOHNSON. (BOSWELL, *Life,* ii, 3.)

5
Was ever poet so trusted before?
SAMUEL JOHNSON, *Letter to Boswell,* 4 July, 1774. Referring to Goldsmith's debts at his death.

GOODNESS

See also Beauty and Goodness; Character: Good; Greatness and Goodness; Nobility

I—Goodness: Definitions

6
True goodness springs from a man's own heart. All men are born good.
CONFUCIUS, *Analects.* (Giles, tr.)

If you wish to be good, first believe that you are bad.
EPICTETUS, *Fragments.* (Long, tr.)

7
That is good which commends to me my country, my climate, my means and materials, my associates.
EMERSON, *Society and Solitude: Works and Days.*

8
It is good to be zealously affected always in a good thing.
New Testament: Galatians, iv, 18.

9
Who is the "good man"? He who keeps the decrees of the Fathers, the laws and ordinances. (Vir bonus est quis? Qui consulta patrum, qui leges juraque servat.)
HORACE, *Epistles.* Bk. i, epis. 16, l. 40.

The good hate to sin through love of virtue. (Oderunt peccare boni virtutis amore.)
HORACE, *Epistles.* Bk. i, epis. 16, l. 52.

10
It is not growing like a tree
In bulk, doth make man better be;
Or standing long an oak, three hundred year,
To fall a log at last, dry, bald, and sere:
A lily of a day
Is fairer far in May,
Although it fall and die that night;
It was the plant and flower of light.
In small proportions we just beauties see;
And in short measures life may perfect be.
BEN JONSON, *A Pindaric Ode to the Immortal Memory and Friendship of that Noble Pair, Sir Lucius Cary and Sir H. Morison.* St. 7.

11
A good man doubles the length of his life, for to be able to enjoy in memory one's past life is to live twice. (Ampliat ætatis spatium sibi vir bonus. Hoc est Vivere bis vita posse priore frui.)
MARTIAL, *Epigrams.* Bk. x, epig. 23, l. 7.

Thus would I double my life's fading space;
For he, that runs it well, runs twice his race.
ABRAHAM COWLEY, *Of Myself.*

For he lives twice who can at once employ
The present well, and e'en the past enjoy.
POPE, *Imitation of Martial.*

The good live longest; to the good alone
The record of the past remains their own.
J. E. T. ROGERS, *Critics.*

1
There needs but thinking right, and meaning well.
POPE, *An Essay on Man*. Epis. iv, l. 32.

2
The good, as I conceive it, is happiness, happiness for each man after his own heart, and for each hour according to its inspiration.
GEORGE SANTAYANA, *Soliloquies in England.*

3
That which is good makes men good. (Quod bonum est, bonos facit.)
SENECA, *Epistulæ ad Lucilium*. Epis. lxxxvii, 12.

That's my good that does me good.
JOHN RAY, *English Proverbs.*

4
The larger part of goodness is the will to become good. (Itaque pars magna bonitatis est velle fieri bonum.)
SENECA, *Epistulæ ad Lucilium*. Epis. xxxiv, 3.

5
My meaning in saying he is a good man, is to have you understand me that he is sufficient.
SHAKESPEARE, *The Merchant of Venice*. Act i, sc. 3, l. 16.

6
Good is no good, but if it be spend:
God giveth good for none other end.
SPENSER, *The Shepheardes Calender: Maye*, l. 71.

7
Hold thou the good; define it well;
For fear divine Philosophy
Should push beyond her mark, and be
Procuress to the Lords of Hell.
TENNYSON, *In Memoriam*. Pt. liii, st. 4.

8
He can never be good that is not obstinate.
BISHOP THOMAS WILSON, *Maxims of Piety*, p. 126.

II—Goodness: Apothegms

9
Tread softly and circumspectl in this funambulatory track and narrow path of goodness.
SIR THOMAS BROWNE, *Christian Morals*. Sec. 1.

10
Our best is bad, nor bears Thy test;
Still, it should be our very best.
ROBERT BROWNING, *Christmas Eve*. Canto iv.

There's a further good conceivable
Beyond the utmost earth can realise.
ROBERT BROWNING, *Prince Hohenstiel-Schwangau.*

11
A good heart is better than all the heads in the world.
BULWER-LYTTON, *The Disowned*. Ch. 33.

12
It's guid to be merry and wise,
It's guid to be honest and true,
BURNS, *Here's a Health to Them That's Awa.*

That pure pride, which, lessening to her breast
Life's ills, gave all its joys a treble zest,
Before the mind completely understood
That mighty truth—how happy are the good!
THOMAS CAMPBELL, *Theodric*, l. 322.

Goodness does not more certainly make men happy than happiness makes them good.
W. S. LANDOR, *Imaginary Conversations: Lord Brooke and Sir Philip Sidney.*

For the good are always the merry,
Save by an evil chance.
W. B. YEATS, *The Fiddler of Dooney.*

13
He cannot long be good that knows not why he is good.
RICHARD CAREW, *Survey of Cornwall*, p. 219. (1602)

14
Be good and leave the rest to Heaven.
WILLIAM COMBE, *Dr. Syntax in Search of the Picturesque*. Canto vii.

15
Who soweth good seed shall surely reap.
JULIA C. R. DORR, *To the "Bouquet Club."*

16
If you wish any good thing, get it from yourself. (Εἴ τι ἀγαθὸν θέλεις, παρὰ σεαυτοῦ λάβε.)
EPICTETUS, *Discourses*. Bk. i, ch. 29, sec. 4.

Your good qualities should face inwards. (Introrsus bona tua spectent.)
SENECA, *Epistulæ ad Lucilium*. Epis. vii, sec. 12.

17
Hard was their lodging, homely was their food,
For all their luxury was doing good.
SAMUEL GARTH, *Claremont*, l. 149. (c. 1700)

Learn the luxury of doing good.
GOLDSMITH, *The Traveller*, l. 22. (1765)

Now, at a certain time, in pleasant mood,
He tried the luxury of doing good.
CRABBE, *Tales of the Hall*. Bk. iii. (1819)

18
Good is not good, where better is expected.
THOMAS FULLER, *Church History*. Bk. xi, 3.

Good is good, but better carries it.
GEORGE HERBERT, *Jacula Prudentum.*

Though good be good, yet better is better.
JOHN RAY, *English Proverbs*, 97.

Better is the enemy of good.
VOLTAIRE, *La Bégueule*, who ascribed the saying to "a wise Italian."

19
Let them be good that love me, though but few.
BEN JONSON, *Cynthia's Revels*. Act iii, sc. 2.

20
Look round the habitable world! How few
Know their own good, or knowing it, pursue!
(Omnibus in terris, . . . pauci dinoscere possunt
Vera bona atque illis multum diversa.)
JUVENAL, *Satires*. Sat. x, l. 1. (Dryden, tr.)

21
Every country can produce good men. (Alle Länder gute Menschen tragen.)
LESSING, *Nathan der Weise*. Act ii, sc. 5.

1
The common good. (Commune bonum.)
LUCRETIUS, *De Rerum Natura*. Bk. v, l. 956.

The highest good at which we all aim. (Bonum summum quo tendimus omnes.)
LUCRETIUS, *De Rerum Natura*. Bk. vi, l. 25.

2
Whatever anyone does or says, I must be good. ("Ο τι ἄν τις ποιῇ ἢ λέγῃ, ἐμὲ δεῖ ἀγαθὸν εἶναι.)
MARCUS AURELIUS, *Meditations*. Bk. vii, 15.

3
It is not enough to do good; one must do it the right way.
JOHN MORLEY, *On Compromise*.

4
It is hard to be good. (Χαλεπὸν ἐσθλὸν ἔμμεναι.)
PITTACUS. (DIOGENES LAERTIUS, *Pittacus*. Bk. i, sec. 76.)

5
I would far rather be called good than fortunate. (Bonam ego quam beatam me esse nimio dici mavolo.)
PLAUTUS, *Pœnulus*, l. 304. (Act i, sc. 2.)

6
Let us not weary in well-doing. (Μήτι παυσώμεσθα δρῶντες εὖ βροτοῖς.)
PLUTARCH. *An Seni Respublica Gerenda Sit*. Sec. xiv.

Let us not be weary in well-doing: for in due season we shall reap, if we faint not.
New Testament: Galatians, vi, 9.

7
All things work together for good to them that love God.
New Testament: Romans, viii, 28.

8
I never did repent for doing good,
Nor shall not now.
SHAKESPEARE, *The Merchant of Venice*. Act iii, sc. 4, l. 10.

9
Be good (if you can't be good, be careful).
HARRINGTON TATE. Refrain of popular song. (1907)

10
We do not love people so much for the good they have done us, as for the good we have done them.
TOLSTOY, *War and Peace*, Pt. i, *ad fin*. Tolstoy quoted this sentence, in Russian, as being from Laurence Sterne, but its source has not been identified.

11
Prove all things; hold fast that which is good.
New Testament: I Thessalonians, v, 21. (Omnia autem probate: quod bonum est tenete. —*Vulgate*.)

III—Goodness: Praise

12
So young, so fair,
Good without effort, great without a foe.
BYRON, *Childe Harold*. Canto iii, st. 172.

13
He wos wery good to me, he wos.
DICKENS, *Bleak House*. Ch. 11.

14
If whole in life, and free from sin,
Man needs no Moorish bow, nor dart,
Nor quiver, carrying death within
By poison's art.
(Integer vitæ scelerisque purus
Non eget Mauris jaculis neque arcu
Nec venenatis gravida sagittis,
Fusce, pharetra.)
HORACE, *Odes*. Bk. i, ode 22, l. 1. (Gladstone, tr.) Quoted by Shakespeare, *Titus Andronicus*, iv, 2, 21.

15
God whose gifts in gracious flood
Unto all who seek are sent,
Only asks you to be good
And is content.
VICTOR HUGO, *God Whose Gifts in Gracious Flood*.

16
Good men are the stars, the planets of the ages wherein they live, and illustrate the times.
BEN JONSON, *Explorata: De Piis et Probis*.

A good man happy is a common good.
CHAPMAN, *Bussy d'Ambois*. Act iv, sc. 1.

Good men are a public good.
THOMAS FULLER, *Gnomologia*.

17
Be good, sweet maid, and let who can be clever;
Do lovely things, not dream them, all day long;
And so make Life, and Death, and that For Ever,
One grand sweet song.
CHARLES KINGSLEY, *A Farewell*. This is the version given in the final edition of Kingsley's poems, in 1889.

Be good, sweet maid, and let who will be clever;
Do noble things, not dream them, all day long;
And so make life, death, and that vast for ever
One grand sweet song.
CHARLES KINGSLEY, *A Farewell*. Version in 1882 edition of Kingsley's poems. Mrs. Kingsley, in the *Life* (vol. i, p. 487, uses the third line as here given except that she capitalizes Life, Death, and For Ever.

18
Honest fame awaits the truly good. (Veris magna paratur fama bonis.)
LUCAN, *De Bello Civili*. Bk. ix, l. 593.

19
The good man makes others good. (Ὁ χρηστός καὶ χρηστοὺς ποεῖ.)
MENANDER, *The Charioteer: Fragment*.

You are not only good yourself, but the cause of goodness in others.
SOCRATES, to Protagoras. (PLATO, *Protagoras*.)

Good, the more
Communicated, more abundant grows.
MILTON, *Paradise Lost*. Bk. v, l. 71.

That good diffused may more abundant grow
COWPER, *Conversation*, l. 441.

1
Abash'd the devil stood,
And felt how awful goodness is, and saw
Virtue in her shape how lovely.
MILTON, *Paradise Lost*. Bk. iv, l. 846.

2
None
But such as are good men can give good things,
And that which is not good, is not delicious
To a well-govern'd and wise appetite.
MILTON, *Comus*, l. 702.

3
Let Joy or Ease, let Affluence or Content,
And the gay Conscience of a life well spent,
Calm ev'ry thought, inspire ev'ry grace,
Glow in thy heart, and smile upon thy face.
POPE, *To Mrs. M. B., on her Birthday*.

4
In every good man a god doth dwell. (In unoquoque virorum bonorum habitat deus.)
SENECA, *Epistulæ ad Lucilium*. Epis. xli, 2.

A good mind possesses a kingdom. (Mens regnum bona possidet.)
SENECA, *Thyestes*, l. 380.

IV—Goodness: Some Doubts

5
Good me no goods.
JOHN FLETCHER, *The Chances*. Act i, sc. 9.

Good critics who have stamped out poet's hope,
Good statesmen who pulled ruin on the state,
Good patriots who for a theory risked a cause,
Good kings who disembowelled for a tax,
Good popes who brought all good to jeopardy,
Good Christians who sat still in easy chairs
And damned the general world for standing up.—
Now may the good God pardon all good men!
E. B. BROWNING, *Aurora Leigh*. Bk. iv, l. 499.

6
Dubius is such a scrupulous good man.
COWPER, *Conversation*, l. 119.

He was so good he would pour rose-water on a toad.
DOUGLAS JERROLD, *A Charitable Man*.

So good that he is good for nothing. (Tanto buon che val niente.)
UNKNOWN. An Italian proverb. Quoted by BACON, *Essays; Of Goodness*.

7
The good we never miss we rarely prize.
COWPER, *Retirement*, l. 406.

8
If goodness lead him not, yet weariness
May toss him to my breast.
GEORGE HERBERT, *The Pulley*.

9
Can there any good thing come out of Nazareth?
New Testament: John, i, 46.

10
The good, alas, how few! scarcely as many
As gates of Thebes or mouths of fertile Nile.
(Rari quippe boni: numera, vix sunt totidem quot
Thebarum portæ vel divitis ostia Nili.)
JUVENAL, *Satires*. Sat. xiii, l. 26.

What is good is never plentiful. (Nunca lo Bueno fue mucho.)
CERVANTES, *Don Quixote*. Pt. i, ch. 6.

Good people are scarce.
UNKNOWN, *Poor Robin Almanac*. Sept., 1668.

Good folks are scarce.
SWIFT, *Polite Conversation*. Dial. i.

As good people's very scarce, what I says is, make the most on 'em.
DICKENS, *Sketches by Boz: Gin-Shops*.

11
None deserves praise for being good who has not spirit enough to be bad: goodness, for the most part, is nothing but indolence or weakness of will. (Nul ne mérite d'être loué de bonté, s'il n'a pas la force d'être méchant: toute autre bonté n'est le plus souvent qu'une paresse ou une impuissance de la volonté.)
LA ROCHEFOUCAULD, *Maximes*. No. 237.

There is a great difference whether one have no will or no wit to do amiss.
MONTAIGNE, *Essays*. Bk. i, ch. 25.

12
A good man is always a greenhorn. (Semper homo bonus tiro est.)
MARTIAL, *Epigrams*. Bk. xii, epig. 51.

13
There is no man so good, who, were he to submit all his thoughts and actions to the laws, would not deserve hanging ten times in his life.
MONTAIGNE, *Essays*. Bk. iii, ch. 9.

14
It is easy to be good when that which prevents it is far off. (Esse bonam facile est, ubi, quod vetet esse, remotum est.)
OVID, *Tristia*. Bk. v, eleg. 14, l. 25.

15
If there were *many* more like her, the stock of halos would give out.
A. W. PINERO, *Preserving Mr. Panmure*. Act i.

16
The good must merit God's peculiar care;
But who but God can tell us who they are?
POPE, *Essay on Man*. Epis. iv, l. 135.

17
There is none that doeth good, no, not one.
Old Testament: Psalms, xiv, 3.

No mere man since the Fall, is able in this life perfectly to keep the Commandments.
Book of Common Prayer: Shorter Catechism.

18
You're good for Madge or good for Cis
Or good for Kate, maybe:
But what's to me the good of this
While you're not good for me?
CHRISTINA ROSSETTI, *Jessie Cameron*. St. 3.

1
Ah! how much alone is a virtuous man!
JOSEPH ROUX, *Meditations of a Parish Priest*. Pt. iv, No. 27.

Be good and you will be lonesome.
MARK TWAIN, *Following the Equator*. Legend under frontispiece.

2
It is not, nor can it come to good.
SHAKESPEARE, *Hamlet*. Act i, sc. 2, l. 158.

For goodness, growing to a pleurisy,
Dies in his own too much.
SHAKESPEARE, *Hamlet*. Act iv, sc. 7, l. 118.

3
As for doing good, that is one of the professions that are full.
THOREAU, *Walden: Economy*.

4
The vacillating, inconsistent good.
WORDSWORTH, *The Excursion*. Bk. iv, l. 309.

V—Goodness and Death

5
Say not that the good are dead. (Θνάσκειν μὴ λέγε τοὺς αγαθους.)
CALLIMACHUS, *Epitaph*. (*Greek Anthology*. Bk. vii, epig. 451.)

6
The best of men cannot suspend their fate;
The good die early, and the bad die late.
DANIEL DEFOE, *Character of the Late Dr. S. Annesley*.

When good men die their goodness does not perish,
But lives though they are gone. As for the bad,
All that was theirs dies and is buried with them.
EURIPIDES, *Temenidæ*. Frag. 734.

Good deeds remain; all things else perish.
THOMAS FULLER, *Gnomologia*. No. 1710.

7
Great spirits never with their bodies die.
ROBERT HERRICK, *Great Spirits Supervive*.

Were a star quenched on high,
For ages would its light,
Still travelling downward from the sky,
Shine on our mortal sight.
So when a great man dies,
For years beyond our ken,
The light he leaves behind him lies
Upon the paths of men.
LONGFELLOW, *Charles Sumner*.

When the good man yields his breath
(For the good man never dies).
JAMES MONTGOMERY, *The Wanderer of Switzerland*. Pt. v.

8
Oh, Sir! the good die first,
And they whose hearts are dry as summer dust
Burn to the socket.
WORDSWORTH, *The Excursion*. Bk. i, l. 500. *See also* DEATH: DEATH AND YOUTH.

9
Do good whilst thou livest if thou wishest to live after death. (Fac bona dum vives, post mortem vivere si vis.)
UNKNOWN, *Medieval Inscription*, Tamworth church.

VI—Good and Evil

See also Vice and Virtue

10
Evil and good are God's right hand and left.
P. J. BAILEY, *Festus: Proem*.

11
Make good things from ill things, best from worst,
As men plant tulips upon dunghills when they wish them finest.
E. B. BROWNING, *Aurora Leigh*. Bk. ii, l. 284.

There shall never be one lost good! What was shall live as before;
The evil is null, is nought, is silence implying sound;
What was good shall be good, with, for evil, so much good more;
On the earth the broken arcs; in the heaven a perfect round.
ROBERT BROWNING, *Abt Vogler*. St. 9.

There is no Good, there is no Bad; these be the whims of mortal will:
What works me weal that call I "good," what harms and hurts I hold as "ill."
SIR RICHARD BURTON, *The Kasîdah*. Pt. v, st. 1.

12
O, why is the good of man with evil mixt?
Never were days yet called two
But one night went betwixt.
THOMAS CAMPION, *When We Submit to Women So*.

13
Inability to tell good from evil is the greatest worry of man's life. (Ignoratione rerum bonarum et malarum, maxime hominum vita vexetur.)
CICERO, *De Finibus*. Bk. i, ch. 13, sec. 43.

Few are able to distinguish true good from what is widely different from it. (Pauci dignoscere possunt, Vera bona atque illis multum diversa.)
JUVENAL, *Satires*. Sat. x, l. 1.

One that confounds good and evil is an enemy to good.
EDMUND BURKE, *Impeachment of Warren Hastings*, 16 Feb., 1788.

14
What we all love is good touched up with evil—
Religion's self must have a spice of devil.
A. H. CLOUGH, *Dipsychus*. Pt. i, sc. 3.

15
When you see a good man, think of emulating him; when you see a bad man, examine your own heart.
CONFUCIUS, *Analects*. (Giles, tr.)

16
By evil report and good report.
New Testament: II Corinthians, vi, 8.

17
The essence of good and evil is a certain kind

of moral purpose. (Οὐσία τοῦ ἀγαθοῦ . . . τοῦ κακοῦ προαίρεσις ποιά.)
EPICTETUS, *Discourses*. Bk. i, ch. 29, sec. 1.

1
Most good hath he to whom no ill befalls as days wear on. (Κεῖνος ὀλβιώτατος, ὅτῳ κατ' ἦμαρ τυγχάνει μηδὲν κακόν.)
EURIPIDES, *Hecuba*, l. 627.

Enough, and more, of good is his who hath no ill. (Nimium boni est cui nihil est mali.)
ENNIUS, *Hecuba*. (CICERO, *De Finibus*. Bk. ii, ch. 13, sec. 41.

2
There is no good without ill in the world,
But everything is mixed in due proportion.
(Οὐκ ἂν γένοιτο χωρὶς ἐσθλὰ καὶ κακὰ
Ἀλλ' ἐστί τις σύγκρασις, ὥστ' ἔχειν καλῶς.)
EURIPIDES. (PLUTARCH, *Morals: On Contentedness*. Sec. 15.)

There is no evil in human affairs that has not some good mingled with it. (Non è male alcuno nelle cose umane che non abbia congiunto seco qualche bene.)
FRANCESCO GUICCIARDINI, *Storia d'Italia*.
See also ROSE AND THORN.

3
Good and evil are chiefly in the imagination.
THOMAS FULLER, *Gnomologia*. No. 1699. *See also* THOUGHT: ITS POWER.

4
Do not grudge
To pick out treasures from an earthen pot.
The worst speak something good.
GEORGE HERBERT, *The Church-Porch*. St. 72.

5
How wicked we are, and how good they were then.
O. W. HOLMES, *The Poet at the Breakfast-Table: Aunt Tabitha*.

6
Two urns by Jove's high throne have ever stood,
The source of evil, one, and one of good.
HOMER, *Iliad*. Bk. xxiv, l. 663. (Pope, tr.)

Jove weighs affairs of earth in dubious scales,
And the good suffers while the bad prevails.
HOMER, *Odyssey*. Bk. vi, l. 229. (Pope, tr.)

7
And would'st thou evil for his good repay?
HOMER, *Odyssey*. Bk. xvi, l. 448.

Evil for good and good for evil. (Bene merenti mala es, male merenti bona es.)
PLAUTUS, *Asinaria*, l. 129. (Act i, sc. 2.)

But then I sigh; and, with a piece of Scripture,
Tell them that God bids us do good for evil.
SHAKESPEARE, *Richard III*. Act i, sc. 3, l. 334.

8
The Bad among the Good are here mixt ever:
The Good without the Bad are here plac'd never.
ROBERT HERRICK, *Good and Bad*.

The world in all doth but two nations bear,—
The good, the bad; and these mixed everywhere.
ANDREW MARVELL, *The Loyal Scot*.

All things are mixed, the usefu' with the vain,
The good with bad, the noble with the vile.
FRANCIS QUARLES, *Emblems*. Bk. ii, No. 7.

There are only two qualities in the world: efficiency and inefficiency; and only two sorts of people: the efficient and the inefficient.
G. B. SHAW, *John Bull's Other Island*. Act iv.

There are two kinds of people on earth to-day,
Just two kinds of people, no more, I say.
Not the good and the bad, for 'tis well understood
That the good are half bad and the bad are half good. . . .
No! the two kinds of people on earth I mean
Are the people who lift and the people who lean.
ELLA WHEELER WILCOX, *Lifting and Leaning*.

It is absurd to divide people into good and bad. People are either charming or tedious.
OSCAR WILDE, *Lady Windermere's Fan*. Act i.

9
Woe unto them that call evil good, and good evil; that put darkness for light, and light for darkness; and put bitter for sweet, and sweet for bitter!
Old Testament: Isaiah, v, 20.

10
As in this bad world below
Noblest things find vilest using.
KEBLE, *The Christian Year: Palm Sunday*.

11
To good and evil equal bent,
He's both a devil and a saint.
SHEPARD KOLLOCK, of Samuel Loudon. (A. J. WALL, *N. Y. Hist. Soc. Quart. Bull.*, Oct., 1922.) *See also* CHARACTER: GOOD AND BAD.

12
We often do good in order that we may do evil with impunity. (On fait souvent du bien pour pouvoir impunément faire du mal.)
LA ROCHEFOUCAULD, *Maximes*. No. 121.

13
The end of good is an evil, and the end of evil is a good. (La fin du bien est un mal, et la fin du mal est un bien.)
LA ROCHEFOUCAULD, *Maximes Posthumes*. No. 519.

14
Men have less lively perception of good than of evil. (Segnius homines bona quam mala sentiunt.)
LIVY, *History*. Bk. xxx, sec. 21.

In doing good we are generally cold, and languid, and sluggish; and of all things afraid of being too much in the right. But the works of malice and injustice are quite in another style. They are finished with a bold masterly hand.
EDMUND BURKE, *Speech*, at Bristol.

Good and quickly seldom meet.
GEORGE HERBERT, *Jacula Prudentum*.

15
Evil is only good perverted.
LONGFELLOW, *The Golden Legend*. Pt. ii.

16
From lower to the higher next,
Not to the top, is Nature's text;

And embryo Good, to reach full stature,
Absorbs the Evil in its nature.
J. R. LOWELL, *Festina Lente: Moral.*

1
Good and evil, we know, in the field of this world grow up together almost inseparably.
MILTON, *Areopagitica.*

If then his Providence
Out of our evil seek to bring forth good,
Our labour must be to pervert that end,
And out of good still to find means of evil.
MILTON, *Paradise Lost.* Bk. i, l. 162.

All good to me is lost; Evil, be thou my good.
MILTON, *Paradise Lost.* Bk. iv, l. 109.

Knowledge of good bought dear by knowing ill.
MILTON, *Paradise Lost.* Bk. iv, l. 222.

2
Where good and ill, together blent,
Wage an undying strife.
JOHN HENRY NEWMAN, *A Martyr Convert.*

3
Evil things are neighbors to good. (Et mala sunt vicina bonis.)
OVID, *Remediorum Amoris,* l. 323.

4
To a good man nothing that happens is evil. (Ὅτι οὐκ ἔστιν ἀνδρὶ ἀγαθῷ κακὸν.)
PLATO, *Apology of Socrates.* Ch. 33, sec. 41.

5
Good men make me poor, bad ones make me rich. (Boni me viri pauperant, improbi augent.)
PLAUTUS, *Pseudolus,* l. 1128. (Act iv, sc. 7.)

6
All partial evil, universal good.
POPE, *Essay on Man.* Epis. i, l. 292.

7
The good are better made by ill,
As odours crushed are sweeter still.
SAMUEL ROGERS, *Jacqueline.* Pt. iii, l. 16. *See also under* ADVERSITY.

8
Abhor that which is evil; cleave to that which is good.
New Testament: Romans, xii, 9.

Be not overcome of evil, but overcome evil with good.
New Testament: Romans, xii, 21.

9
He was always for ill, and never for good.
SCOTT, *The Lay of the Last Minstrel.* Canto iii, st. 12.

10
From lowest place when virtuous things proceed,
The place is dignified by the doer's deed:
Where great additions swell 's, and virtue none,
It is a dropsied honour. Good alone
Is good without a name. Vileness is so:
The property by what it is should go,
Not by the title.
SHAKESPEARE, *All's Well that Ends Well.* Act ii, sc. 3, l. 132.

In working well, if travail you sustain,
Into the wind shall lightly pass the pain;
But of the deed the glory shall remain,
And cause your name with worthy wights to reign.
In working wrong, if pleasure you attain,
The pleasure soon shall fade, and void as vain;
But of the deed throughout the life the shame
Endures, defacing you with foul defame.
NICHOLAS GRIMALD, *Musonius the Philosopher's Sayings.*

11
The web of our life is of a mingled yarn, good and ill together.
SHAKESPEARE, *All's Well that Ends Well.* Act iv, sc. 3, l. 83.

12
There is some soul of goodness in things evil,
Would men observingly distil it out; . . .
Thus may we gather honey from the weed,
And make a moral of the devil himself.
SHAKESPEARE, *Henry V.* Act iv, sc. 1, l. 4.

We too often forget that not only is there "a soul of goodness in things evil," but very generally also, a soul of truth in things erroneous.
HERBERT SPENCER, *First Principles.* Pt. i, ch. 1, sec. 1.

13
The evil that men do lives after them;
The good is oft interred with their bones.
SHAKESPEARE, *Julius Cæsar.* Act iii, sc. 2, l. 80.

14
Wisdom and goodness to the vile seem vile:
Filths savour but themselves.
SHAKESPEARE, *King Lear.* Act iv, sc. 2, l. 37.

15
I am in this earthly world; where to do harm
Is often laudable, to do good sometime
Accounted dangerous folly.
SHAKESPEARE, *Macbeth.* Act iv, sc. 2, l. 75.

16
Unruly blasts wait on the tender spring;
Unwholesome weeds take root with precious flowers;
The adder hisses where the sweet birds sing;
What virtue breeds, iniquity devours:
We have no good that we can say is ours.
SHAKESPEARE, *The Rape of Lucrece,* l. 869.

O, no! the apprehension of the good
Gives but the greater feeling to the worse.
SHAKESPEARE, *Richard II.* Act i, sc. 3, l. 300.

17
For nought so vile that on the earth doth live
But to the earth some special good doth give,
Nor aught so good but strain'd from that fair use
Revolts from true birth, stumbling on abuse.
SHAKESPEARE, *Romeo and Juliet.* Act ii, 3, 17.

Two such opposed kings encamp them still
In man as well as herbs, grace and rude will;
And where the worser is predominant,

Full soon the canker death eats up that plant.
SHAKESPEARE, *Romeo and Juliet*. Act ii, 3, 27.

1
Evil minds Change good to their own nature.
SHELLEY, *Prometheus Unbound*. Act i, l. 380.

2
There is no man suddenly either excellently good or extremely evil.
SIR PHILIP SIDNEY, *Arcadia*. Bk. i.

3
So far as any one shuns evils, so far he does good.
SWEDENBORG, *Doctrine of Life*. Sec. 21.

4
For good ye are and bad, and like to coins,
Some true, some light.
TENNYSON, *The Holy Grail*, l. 25.

5
O, yet we trust that somehow good
Will be the final goal of ill,
To pangs of nature, sins of will,
Defects of doubt, and taints of blood.
TENNYSON, *In Memoriam*. Pt. liv, st. 1. "Somehow Good" was used by William de Morgan as the title of a novel.

One may not doubt that, somehow Good
Shall come of Water and of Mud;
And sure, the reverent eye must see
A purpose in Liquidity.
RUPERT BROOKE, *Heaven*.

6
From seeming evil still educing good,
And better thence again, and better still,
In infinite progression.
JAMES THOMSON, *Hymn on the Seasons*, l. 114.

7
If not good, why then evil,
If not good god, good devil.
Goodness!—you hypocrite, come out of that,
Live your life, do your work, then take your hat.
H. D. THOREAU, *A Week on the Concord and Merrimack Rivers*.

The greater part of what my neighbors call good I believe in my soul to be bad, and if I repent of anything, it is very likely to be my good behavior.
H. D. THOREAU, *Walden*. Ch. 1.

8
Roaming in thought over the Universe, I saw the little that is Good steadily hastening towards immortality,
And the vast all that is call'd Evil I saw hastening to merge itself and become lost and dead.
WALT WHITMAN, *Roaming in Thought*.

Evil perpetually tends to disappear.
HERBERT SPENCER, *The Evanescence of Evil*.

9
The evil cannot brook delay,
The good can well afford to wait.
Give ermined knaves their hour of crime;
Ye have the future grand and great,
The safe appeal of Truth to Time!
WHITTIER, *For Righteousness' Sake*.

10
'Tis a habit of the foolish and the vulgar
To value equally the good and bad.
(Siempre acostumbra hacer el vulgo necio,
De la bueno y lo malo igual aprecio.)
YRIARTE, *Fables*. No. 28.

GOOSE

11
Let the long contention cease!
Geese are swans, and swans are geese,
Let them have it how they will!
MATTHEW ARNOLD, *The Last Word*.

For the goose of To-day still is Memory's swan.
J. R. LOWELL, *In the Half-Way House*. St. 6.

12
What meaneth he by blinking like a goose in the rain?
WILLIAM BULLEIN, *A Dialogue Against the Fever Pestilence*. (1564)

13
Goslins lead the geese to water.
THOMAS FULLER, *Gnomologia*. No. 1740.

Shall the goslins teach the goose to swim?
THOMAS FULLER, *Gnomologia*. No. 4115.

14
As is the gander, so is the goose.
THOMAS FULLER, *Gnomologia*. No. 700.

15
What was sauce for the goose was sauce for the gander.
HEAD AND KIRKMAN, *The English Rogue*. Pt. ii, l. 120. (1671)

Sauce for the goose is sauce for the gander.
SWIFT, *Journal to Stella*, 24 Jan., 1785.

Let Attius have the same rights as Tertius. (Attio idem, quod Tettio, jus esto.)
MARCUS VARRO, *The Will*. Frag. 543. A clause in Varro's will, providing that a son born to him eleven months after his death shall have the same rights as one born in ten months. (AULUS GELLIUS, *Noctes Atticæ*. Bk. iii, ch. 16, sec. 13.) Frequently quoted, "What is sauce for the goose is sauce for the gander."

16
As deep drinketh the goose as the gander.
JOHN HEYWOOD, *Proverbs*. Pt. ii, ch. 7.

When the goose drinks as deep as the gander, pots are soon empty, and the cupboard is bare.
C. H. SPURGEON, *Ploughman's Pictures*, 136.

17
It is thus that you silence the goose [huss], but a hundred years hence there will arise a swan whose singing you shall not be able to silence.
Attributed to JOHN HUSS, as he was being burned at the stake, 6 July, 1415. Luther is supposed to have fulfilled the prophecy.

18
Dark flying rune against the western glow—
It tells the sweep and loneliness of things,
Symbol of Autumns vanished long ago.
Symbol of coming Springs!
FREDERICK PETERSON, *Wild Geese*.

1
A goose is a silly bird, too much for one, not enough for two.

POOLE, *Archaic Words*, 25. Poole says the presumed foundation for the proverb is that it was the reply of a Walsall man when asked if he and his wife were going to have a goose for their Christmas dinner.

2
There swims no goose so grey.

POPE, *The Wife of Bath*, l. 98. See 2208:8.

3
Gae shoe the goose.

JOHN RAY, *English Proverbs*. To "shoe the goose" was to do something futile or silly.

4
Goose, gander, and gosling,
Are three sounds, but one thing.

JOHN RAY, *English Proverbs*.

5
Here you may roast your goose.

SHAKESPEARE, *Macbeth*. Act ii, sc. 3, l. 18.

Thou cream-faced loon,
Where got'st thou that goose look?

SHAKESPEARE, *Macbeth*. Act v, sc. 3, l. 11.

6
When the rain raineth and the goose winketh,
Little wots the gosling what the goose thinketh.

SKELTON, *Garland of Laurel*, l. 1430. (c. 1520)

7
In faith, else I had gone too long to school,
But if I could know a goose from a swan.

JOHN SKELTON, *Magnyfycence*, l. 302. (1529)

That by his art, can make a goose a swan.

JOHN ANDREWS, *Anatomy of Baseness*, p. 30. (1615)

All our geese are swans.

ROBERT BURTON, *Anatomy of Melancholy*. Pt. i, sec. ii, mem. 3, subs. 14.

8
The wild goose is more cosmopolite than we; he breaks his fast in Canada, takes a luncheon in the Susquehanna, and plumes himself for the night in a Louisiana bayou.

H. D. THOREAU, *Journal*, 21 March, 1840.

9
A goose is a goose still, dress it as you will.

H. D. THOREAU, *Walden: Conclusion*.

10
He gabbles like a goose among melodious swans. (Argutos inter strepere anser olores.)

VERGIL, *Eclogues*. No. ix, l. 36.

I dare not hope to please a Cinna's ear,
Or sing what Varus might vouchsafe to hear;
Harsh are the sweetest lays that I can bring,
So screams a goose where swans melodious sing.

VERGIL, *Eclogues*. No. 9, l. 34. (Beattie, tr.)

Shall I, like Curtius, desp'rate in my zeal,
O'er head and ears plunge for the Commonweal?
Or rob Rome's ancient geese of all their glories,
And cackling save the monarchies of Tories?

POPE, *The Dunciad*. Bk. i, l. 209.

11
He is not able to say bo to a goose.

UNKNOWN, *Mar-Prelate's Epistle*, 60. (1588)

He never durst say so much as boh to a mouse.

SAMUEL ROWLANDS, *Martin Mark-all*. (1610)

12
To kill the goose that laid the golden eggs.

The phrase originates from the second fable of Æsop, first translated into English in 1484 by William Caxton.

The goose hangs high.

An American colloquialism of unknown origin, meaning "prospects are bright, things are going well." *The Century Dictionary* suggests it may have come from "The goose honks high," because wild geese fly higher than usual in fine weather, but this is unsubstantiated.

GOSPEL, see Bible

GOSSIP, see Scandal

GOVERNMENT

See also Democracy, State

I—Government: Definitions

13
The essence of a free government consists in an effectual control of rivalries.

JOHN ADAMS, *Discourses on Davila*. (1789)

A government of laws and not of men.

JOHN ADAMS, *Constitution of Massachusetts: Declaration of Rights*. Art. 30. (1780) (See *American Bar Association Journal*, Dec., 1929, p. 747.)

14
If any ask me what a free government is, I answer, that, for any practical purpose, it is what the people think so.

EDMUND BURKE, *Letter to the Sheriffs of Bristol*.

In all forms of government the people is the true legislator.

EDMUND BURKE, *Tracts on the Popery Laws*. Ch. 3, pt. 1.

15
Government is a contrivance of human wisdom to provide for human wants. Men have a right that these wants should be provided by this wisdom.

EDMUND BURKE, *Reflections on the Revolution in France*.

The moment you abate anything from the full rights of men each to govern himself, and suffer any artificial positive limitation upon those rights, from that moment the whole organization of government becomes a consideration of convenience.

BURKE, *Reflections on the Revolution in France*.

Obedience is what makes government, and not the names by which it is called.

BURKE, *Speech on Conciliation with America*.

16
Government is emphatically a machine: to the discontented a "taxing machine," to the contented a "machine for securing property."

CARLYLE, *Signs of the Times*.

17
Of governments, that of the mob is most sanguinary, that of soldiers the most expensive, and that of civilians the most vexatious.

C. C. COLTON, *Lacon*. Pt. i.

1
The divine right of kings may have been a plea for feeble tyrants, but the divine right of government is the keystone of human progress, and without it government sinks into police and a nation into a mob.

BENJAMIN DISRAELI, *Lothair: Preface.*

2
Realms are households which the great must guide.

DRYDEN, *Annus Mirabilis,* l. 552.

For just experience tells, in every soil,
That those who think must govern those that toil;
And all that freedom's highest aims can reach,
Is but to lay proportion'd loads on each.

GOLDSMITH, *The Traveller,* l. 371.

3
A sober prince's government is best.

DRYDEN, *Epistle to Sir Robert Howard,* l. 54.

What government is the best? That which teaches us to govern ourselves. (Welche Regierung die beste sei? Diejenige die uns lehrt uns selbst zu regieren.)

GOETHE, *Sprüche in Prosa.* Pt. iii.

That is the best government which desires to make the people happy, and knows how to make them happy.

MACAULAY, *Essays: Mitford's History of Greece.*

For forms of government let fools contest;
Whate'er is best administer'd is best.

POPE, *Essay on Man.* Epis. iii, l. 303.

The best of human governments is the patriarchal rule.

TUPPER, *Proverbial Philosophy: Of Subjection.*

4
Government has been a fossil: it should be a plant.

EMERSON, *Miscellanies: To the Mercantile Library Association.*

5
All government is an evil, but of the two forms of that evil, democracy or monarchy, the sounder is monarchy; the more able to do its will, democracy.

B. R. HAYDON, *Table-Talk.*

6
Nothing appears more surprising to those who consider human affairs with a philosophical eye, than the easiness with which the many are governed by the few.

HUME, *Essays: First Principles of Government.*

7
The whole of government consists in the art of being honest.

THOMAS JEFFERSON, *Writings.* Vol. vi, p. 186.

After all, government is just a device to protect man so that he may earn his bread in the sweat of his labor.

HUGH S. JOHNSON, *Where Do We Go from Here?* (*The American,* July, 1935, p. 90.)

8
Freedom of men under government is to have a standing rule to live by, common to every one of that society, and made by the legislative power vested in it; a liberty to follow my own will in all things, when the rule prescribes not, and not to be subject to the inconstant, uncertain, unknown, arbitrary will of another man.

JOHN LOCKE, *On Government.* Bk. x, ch. 4.

9
It is a great error, in my opinion, to suppose that government founded on force has more weight or stability than that which is bound together by the tie of good-will. (Et errat longe mea quidem sententia, Qui imperium credat gravius esse aut stabilius Vi quod fit quam illud quod amicitia adjungitur.)

PLAUTUS, *Adelphi,* l. 65. (Act i, sc. 1.)

Unjust rule never endures perpetually. (Iniqua numquam regna perpetuo morant.)

SENECA, *Medea,* l. 196.

A hated government does not endure long. (Invisa numquam imperia retinentur diu.)

SENECA, *Phœnissæ,* l. 660.

No one has long maintained a violent government; temperate rule endures. (Violenta nemo imperia continuit diu; Moderata durant.)

SENECA, *Troades,* l. 258.

No government is safe unless buttressed by good-will. (Nullum imperium tutum nisi benevolentia munitum.)

CORNELIUS NEPOS. (DIONYSIUS CATO, *Lives: Cornelius Nepos.*)

No Government can be long secure without a formidable Opposition.

BENJAMIN DISRAELI, *Coningsby.* Bk. ii, ch. 1.

10
As in men's bodies, so in government, that disease is most dangerous which proceeds from the head. (Utque in corporibus sic in imperio gravissimus est morbus, qui a capite diffunditur.)

PLINY THE YOUNGER, *Epistles.* Bk. iv, epis. 22.

Every wand or staff of empire is forsooth curved at the top. (Adeo ut omnes imperii virga sive bacillum vere superius inflexum sit.)

FRANCIS BACON, *De Sapientia Veterum: Pan, Sive Natura.* Sometimes condensed to, "All sceptres are crooked at the top." Referring to the shepherd's crook of Pan.

The deterioration of a government begins almost always by the decay of its principles. (La corruption de chaque gouvernement commence presque toujours par celle des principes.)

MONTESQUIEU, *De l'Esprit des Lois.* Bk. viii, ch. 1.

11
The body politic, like the human body, begins to die from its birth, and bears in itself the causes of its destruction. (Le corps politique, aussi bien que le corps de l'homme, commence à mourir dès sa naissance, et porte en lui-même les causes de sa destruction.)

ROUSSEAU, *Contrat Social.* Bk. iii, ch. 11.

12
The very idea of the power and the right of the People to establish Government, presup-

poses the duty of every individual to obey the established Government.

GEORGE WASHINGTON, *Farewell Address*, 1796.

I believe every citizen should support the government when final action is taken, whether he approves of the action or not.

W. J. BRYAN, in N.Y. *Times*, 2 June, 1898.

While the people should patriotically and cheerfully support their Government its functions do not include the support of the people.

GROVER CLEVELAND, *Message*, vetoing the Texas Seed Bill, 16 Feb., 1887.

1
In general, the art of government consists in taking as much money as possible from one class of citizens to give it to the other.

VOLTAIRE, *Philosophical Dictionary: Money*.

1a
No man ever saw a government. I live in the midst of the Government of the United States, but I never saw the Government of the United States.

WOODROW WILSON, *Speech*, at Pittsburgh, Pa., 29 Jan., 1916.

II—Government: Apothegms

2
Nero could touch and tune the harp well; but in government, sometimes he used to wind the pins too high, sometimes to let them down too low.

APPOLONIUS, when Vespasian asked him the cause of Nero's overthrow. (BACON, *Essays: Of Empire*.)

Nothing destroyeth authority so much, as the unequal and untimely interchange of power pressed too far, and relaxed too much.

FRANCIS BACON, *Essays: Of Empire*.

3
The four pillars of government . . . religion, justice, counsel, treasure.

FRANCIS BACON, *Essays: Of Seditions*.

4
In government change is suspected, though to the better.

FRANCIS BACON, *Filum Labyrinthi*.

5
"Separa et impera," that same cunning maxim.

FRANCIS BACON, *Letter to James I*, 1615, quoting Machiavelli.

Divide et impera, that exploded adage.

SIR EDWARD COKE, *Institutes*. Pt. iv, ch. 1.

Divide and govern, a capital motto! Unite and lead, a better one! (Entzwei' und gebiete! Tüchtig Wort; Verein' und leite! Bess'rer Hort.)

GOETHE, *Sprüche in Reimen*, 516.

Divide and govern. (Divide et impera.)

LOUIS XI OF FRANCE, his motto when dealing with his nobles.

And yet they have learnt the chief Art of a Sov'reign,
As Machiavel taught 'em, *divide and ye govern*.

SWIFT, *On the Irish Bishops*, l. 47. (1732)

6
To govern mankind one must not over-rate them.

LORD CHESTERFIELD, *Letters*, 15 Feb., 1754.

You can only govern men by serving them. The rule is without exception. (On ne gouverne les hommes qu'en les servant. Le règle est sans exception.)

VICTOR COUSIN.

7
The good governor should have a broken leg and keep at home.

CERVANTES, *Don Quixote*. Pt. ii, ch. 34.

8
It were better to be a poor fisherman, than to meddle with the government of men!

GEORGES JACQUES DANTON. (CARLYLE, *French Revolution*. Vol. iii, bk. vi, ch. 2.)

9
I have been carried into the ministry by a cannon-ball.

GEORGES JACQUES DANTON, after the insurrection of August, 1792. (TAINE, *French Revolution*.)

10
An institution is the lengthened shadow of one man.

EMERSON, *Essays, First Series: Self-Reliance*.

No institution will be better than the institutor.

EMERSON, *Essays, Second Series: Character*.

11
He has erected the negation of God into a system of government.

W. E. GLADSTONE, referring to the King of Naples. (EMERSON, *Conduct of Life: Worship*.)

12
I will govern according to the commonweal, but not according to the common will.

JAMES I OF ENGLAND, *Address*, to the House of Commons, 1621.

13
I would not give half a guinea to live under one form of government rather than another It is of no moment to the happiness of an individual.

SAMUEL JOHNSON. (BOSWELL, *Life*, ii, 170.)

14
A wise man neither suffers himself to be governed, nor attempts to govern others.

LA BRUYÈRE, *Les Caractères*.

15
Every country has the government it deserves. (Toute nation a le gouvernement qu'elle mérite.)

JOSEPH DE MAISTRE, *Letter*, Aug., 1811.

16
He that would govern others, first should be
The master of himself.

PHILIP MASSINGER, *The Bondman*. Act i, sc. 3.

See also under SELF-CONTROL.

17
Republics end through luxury; monarchies through poverty. (Les républiques finissent

par le luxe; les monarchies, par la pauvreté.)

MONTESQUIEU, *De l'Esprit des Lois*. Bk. vii, ch. 4.

1
The vanity and presumption of governing beyond the grave is the most ridiculous and insolent of all tyrannies. Man has no property in the generations which are to follow.

THOMAS PAINE, *Reply to Burke*, 1791.

2
They that govern most make least noise.

JOHN SELDEN, *Table-Talk: Power*. STILL WATERS RUN DEEP, *see under* WATER.

3
May I govern so,
To heal Rome's harms, and wipe away her woe!

SHAKESPEARE, *Titus Andronicus*. Act v, sc. 3, l. 147.

4
Ill can he rule the great that cannot reach the small.

SPENSER, *Faerie Queene*. Bk. v, canto ii, st. 43.

5
By common consent, he would have been deemed capable of governing had he never governed. (Omnium consensu capax imperii, nisi imperasset.)

TACITUS, *Annals*. Bk. i, sec. 49. Said of Galba. A masterpiece of epigrammatic point as written in the Latin.

But who can penetrate man's secret thought,
The quality and temper of his soul,
Till by high office put to frequent proof,
And execution of the laws?

SOPHOCLES, *Antigone*.

Command shows the man. ('Αρχὰ ἄνδρα δείξει.)

BIAS. (ARISTOTLE, *Ethics*, v, i, 16.)

6
The Athenians govern the Greeks; I govern the Athenians; you, my wife, govern me; your son governs you.

THEMISTOCLES. (PLUTARCH, *Lives: Themistocles*. Ch. 18, sec. 5.)

7
Influence is not government.

GEORGE WASHINGTON, *Political Maxims*.

8
We have been taught to regard a representative of the people as a sentinel on the watchtower of liberty.

DANIEL WEBSTER, *Speech*, U. S. Senate, 7 May, 1834.

III—Government: Its Purpose

9
The principal business of government is to further and promote human strivings.

WILBUR L. CROSS, in *N. Y. Times*, 29 Mar., 1931.

10
The care of human life and happiness, and not their destruction, is the first and only legitimate object of good government.

THOMAS JEFFERSON, *Notes on Virginia: Writings*, Vol. iii, p. 263.

The only orthodox object of the institution of government is to secure the greatest degree of happiness possible to the general mass of those associated under it.

THOMAS JEFFERSON, *Writings*. Vol. xviii, p. 135.

The legitimate powers of government extend to such acts only as are injurious to others.

THOMAS JEFFERSON, *Writings*. Vol. i, p. 221.

11
A wise and frugal government, which shall restrain men from injuring one another, which shall leave them otherwise free to regulate their own pursuits of industry and improvement, and shall not take from the mouth of labor the bread it has earned—this is the sum of good government.

THOMAS JEFFERSON, *Writings*. Vol. iii, p. 320.

12
When a white man governs himself, that is self-government; but when he governs himself and also governs another man, that is despotism. . . . No man is good enough to govern another man without that other's consent.

ABRAHAM LINCOLN, *Speech*, Peoria, Ill., 16 Oct., 1854. Lincoln-Douglas Debates.

13
Our object in the construction of the state is the greatest happiness of the whole, and not that of any one class.

PLATO, *The Republic*. Bk. iv, sec. 1.

14
That wise Government, the general friend,
Might every where its eye and arm extend.

ROBERT SOUTHEY, *The Poet's Pilgrimage to Waterloo*. Pt. ii, canto iv, st. 47.

15
The aggregate happiness of society, which is best promoted by the practice of a virtuous policy, is, or ought to be, the end of all government.

GEORGE WASHINGTON, *Political Maxims*.

IV—Government: Its Faults

16
A Parliament is nothing less than a big meeting of more or less idle people.

WALTER BAGEHOT, *English Constitution*, p. 180.

To be acquainted with the merit of a ministry, we need only observe the condition of the people.

JUNIUS, *Letters*. Letter 1.

The Commons, faithful to their system, remained in a wise and masterly inactivity.

SIR JAMES MACKINTOSH, *Vindiciæ Gallicæ*. Sec. 1.

As though conduct could be made right or wrong by the votes of some men sitting in a room in Westminster!

HERBERT SPENCER, *Social Statics*. Pt. iv, ch. 30, sec. 7.

17
Law represents the effort of men to organ-

ize society; government, the efforts of selfishness to overthrow liberty.

HENRY WARD BEECHER, *Proverbs from Plymouth Pulpit.*

1
I have in general no very exalted opinion of the virtue of paper government.

EDMUND BURKE, *Speech on Conciliation with America.*

2
The quacks of government (who sate
At th' unregarded helm of State).

BUTLER, *Hudibras.* Pt. iii, canto ii, l. 333.

Nothing's more dull and negligent
Than an old, lazy government,
That knows no interest of state,
But such as serves a present strait.

BUTLER, *Miscellaneous Thoughts,* l. 159.

3
An oppressive government is more to be feared than a tiger.

CONFUCIUS, *Analects.*

4
A government of statesmen or of clerks? Of Humbug or of Humdrum?

BENJAMIN DISRAELI, *Coningsby.* Bk. ii, ch. 4.

5
The depositary of power is always unpopular.

BENJAMIN DISRAELI, *Coningsby.* Bk. iv, ch. 13.

Men are suspicious; prone to discontent:
Subjects still loathe the present government.

HERRICK, *Present Government Grievous.*

He that goeth about to persuade a multitude that they are not so well governed as they ought to be, shall never want attentive and favourable hearers.

RICHARD HOOKER, *Ecclesiastical Polity.*

6
No government has ever been, or ever can be, wherein time-servers and blockheads will not be uppermost.

DRYDEN, *Examen Poeticum: Dedication.*

The foul, corruption-gendered swarm of state.

ROBERT SOUTHEY, *Joan of Arc.* Bk. iv, l. 94.

Every actual State is corrupt.

EMERSON, *Essays, Second Series: Politics.*

7
The teaching of politics is that the Government, which was set for protection and comfort of all good citizens, becomes the principal obstruction and nuisance with which we have to contend. . . . The cheat and bully and malefactor we meet everywhere is the Government.

R. W. EMERSON, *Journal,* 1860.

8
I am convinced that those societies (as the Indians) which live without government, enjoy in their general mass an infinitely greater degree of happiness than those who live under the European governments. Among the former, public opinion is in the place of law, and restrains morals as powerfully as laws ever did anywhere. Among the latter, under pretense of governing, they have divided their nations into two classes, wolves and sheep.

THOMAS JEFFERSON, *Letter,* Paris, 16 Jan., 1787.

It is error alone which needs support of government. Truth can stand by itself.

THOMAS JEFFERSON, *Letter to Tyler,* 1804.

It is really more questionable than may at first be thought, whether Bonaparte's dumb legislature, which said nothing and did much, may not be preferable to one which talks much and does nothing.

THOMAS JEFFERSON, *Writings.* Vol. i, p. 86.

Were we directed from Washington when to sow and when to reap, we should soon want bread.

THOMAS JEFFERSON, *Papers,* vol. i, p. 66.

9
There is no state in Europe where the least wise have not governed the most wise.

W. S. LANDOR, *Imaginary Conversations: Rousseau and Malesherbes.*

10
Nothing is so galling to a people, not broken in from the birth, as a paternal or, in other words, a meddling government, a government which tells them what to read and say and eat and drink and wear.

MACAULAY, *Essays: Southey's Colloquies.*

11
Government, even in its best state, is but a necessary evil; in its worst state, an intolerable one.

THOMAS PAINE, *Common Sense.* Ch. 1.

12
Government arrogates to itself that it alone forms men. . . . Everybody knows that government never began anything. It is the whole world that thinks and governs.

WENDELL PHILLIPS, *Lecture: Idols,* Boston, 4 Oct., 1859.

13
The punishment which the wise suffer who refuse to take part in the government, is, to live under the government of worse men.

PLATO. (EMERSON, *Society and Solitude: Eloquence.*)

14
One of the greatest delusions in the world is the hope that the evils of this world can be cured by legislation. I am happy in the belief that the solution of the great difficulties of life and government are in better hands even than that of this body.

THOMAS B. REED. (W. A. ROBINSON, *Life.*)

15
The art of government is the organization of idolatry. The bureaucracy consists of functionaries; the aristocracy, of idols; the democracy, of idolaters. The populace cannot understand the bureaucracy: it can only worship the national idols.

BERNARD SHAW, *Maxims for Revolutionists.*

16
My reading of history convinces me that

most bad government has grown out of too much government.

JOHN SHARP WILLIAMS, *Thomas Jefferson*, p. 49.

The world is governed too much.

UNKNOWN, *Motto*, of the Boston *Globe*.

I confess the motto of the "Globe" newspaper is so attractive to me that I can seldom find much appetite to read what is below it in its columns.

EMERSON, *Essays, Second Series: New England Reformers.*

1
Let's be jovial, fill our glasses;
Madness 'tis for us to think
How the world is ruled by asses,
And the wise are swayed by chink.

UNKNOWN, *Let's Be Jovial.* (*Charms of Melody*, Dublin, c. 1810.)

V—Government: Its Lack of Wisdom

2
Learn, my son, with how little wisdom the world is governed. (Nescis, mi fili, quantilla sapientia regitur mundus.)

POPE JULIUS III, to a Portuguese monk who pitied him because he had the weight of the world on his shoulders. (BÜCHMANN, *Geflügelte Wörte.*) Also attributed to Count Axel von Oxenstierna, Chancellor of Sweden, when urging his son to accept an appointment to the Peace Congress of Westphalia in 1648. Told also in connection with Conrad von Benningen, the Dutch statesman.

It calls to my mind what some pope, Alexander VI or Leo, said to a son of his afraid to undertake governing,—i. e., confounding the Christian world: "Nescis, mi fili, quam parva sapientia his noster mundus regitur."

LORD CHATHAM, *Letter to Lord Shelburne*, 25 Jan., 1775.

He was a wise pope that, when one that used to be merry with him before he was advanced to the popedom refrained afterwards to come at him (presuming he was busy in governing the Christian world), sent for him and bade him come again, and (says he) we will be merry as we were before, for thou little thinkest what a little foolery governs the world.

JOHN SELDEN, *Table-Talk: Pope.*

3
With how little wisdom the world is governed. (Quam pauca sapientia mundus regitur.)

DR. JOHN ARBUTHNOT, *Letter to Swift*, 1732. Quoted.

4
Yet if thou didst but know how little wit governs this mighty universe.

APHRA BEHN, *The Round Heads.* Act i, sc. 2.

5
It is indeed astonishing with how little wisdom mankind can be governed, when that little wisdom is its own.

DEAN W. R. INGE. (MARCHANT, *Wit and Wisdom of Dean Inge.* No. 171.)

GRACE

I—Grace: Spiritual and Divine

6
Grace groweth after governance.

THOMAS BECON, *Early Works*, p. 395. (1566)

Sure 'tis an orthodox opinion,
That grace is founded in dominion.

BUTLER, *Hudibras.* Pt. i, canto 3, l. 1173.

7
There, but for the grace of God, goes John Bradford.

JOHN BRADFORD, *Works.* Vol. ii, p. 13, in biographical notice. (FARRAR, *Eternal Hope: Fourth Sermon.*) Bradford uttered the sentence on seeing a criminal pass by. It has been credited also to John Bunyan and John Wesley.

8
'Cause grace and virtue are within
Prohibited degrees of kin;
And therefore no true Saint allows
They shall be suffer'd to espouse.

BUTLER, *Hudibras.* Pt. iii, canto 1, l. 1293.

9
My grace is sufficient for thee: for my strength is made perfect in weakness.

New Testament: II Corinthians, xii, 9.

10
Thus all below is strength, and all above is grace.

DRYDEN, *Epistle to Congreve*, l. 19.

11
An outward and visible sign of an inward and spiritual grace.

Book of Common Prayer: Catechism.

12
Ye are fallen from grace.

New Testament: Galatians, v, 4.

13
So grace is a gift of God and kind wit a chance.

WILLIAM LANGLAND, *Piers Plowman.* Passus xv, l. 33.

14
Prevenient grace descending had remov'd
The stony from their hearts.

MILTON, *Paradise Lost.* Bk. xi, l. 3.

15
From vulgar bounds with brave disorder part,
And snatch a grace beyond the reach of Art.

POPE, *An Essay on Criticism.* Pt. i, l. 154.

16
In his own grace he doth exalt himself.

SHAKESPEARE, *King Lear.* Act v, sc. 3, l. 67.

Alack, when once our grace we have forgot,
Nothing goes right: we would, and we would not.

SHAKESPEARE, *Measure for Measure.* Act iv, sc. 4, l. 36.

Hail to thee, lady! and the grace of heaven,
Before, behind thee and on every hand,
Enwheel thee round!

SHAKESPEARE, *Othello.* Act ii, sc. 1, l. 85

God give him grace to groan!
SHAKESPEARE, *Love's Labour's Lost*. Act iv, sc. 3, l. 21.

1
Grace me no grace, nor uncle me no uncle.
SHAKESPEARE, *Richard II*. Act ii, sc. 3, l. 87.

2
He made it a part of his religion never to say grace to his meat.
SWIFT, *Tale of a Tub*. Sec. 11.

She ask'd him for stuffing, she ask'd him for gravy,
She ask'd him for gizzard;—but not for Grace.
R. H. BARHAM, *A Lay of St. Nicholas*.

II—Grace: Physical

3
Her gracious, graceful, graceless Grace.
BYRON, *Don Juan*. Canto xvi, st. 49.

4
Beauty without grace is the hook without the bait.
EMERSON, *Conduct of Life: Beauty*.

Grace is more beautiful than beauty.
EMERSON, *Letters and Social Aims: Social Aims*.

Grace will last, beauty will blast.
THOMAS FULLER, *Gnomologia*. No. 6292.

5
Stately and tall he moves in the hall
The chief of a thousand for grace.
KATE FRANKLIN, *Life at Olympus*.

6
Grace is to the body what judgment is to the mind. (La bonne grâce est au corps ce que le bon sens est à l'esprit.)
LA ROCHEFOUCAULD, *Maximes*. No. 67.

7
And grace that won who saw to wish her stay.
MILTON, *Paradise Lost*. Bk. viii, l. 43.

8
Absence of grace and inharmonious movement and discord are nearly allied to ill words and ill nature, as grace and harmony are the sisters and images of goodness and virtue.
PLATO, *The Republic*. Bk. iii, sec. 401.

9
See, what a grace was seated on this brow;
Hyperion's curls; the front of Jove himself;
An eye like Mars, to threaten and command;
A station like the herald Mercury
New-lighted on a heaven-kissing hill;
A combination and a form indeed,
Where every god did seem to set his seal,
To give the world assurance of a man.
SHAKESPEARE, *Hamlet*. Act iii, sc. 4, l. 55.

10
One woman is fair, yet I am well; another is wise, yet I am well: another virtuous, yet I am well; but till all graces be in one woman, one woman shall not come in my grace.
SHAKESPEARE, *Much Ado About Nothing*. Act ii, sc. 3, l. 28.

11
Whatever she does, wherever she goes, grace orders her actions and follows her movements. (Illam, quidquid agit, quoquo vestigia movit, componit furtim subsequiturque Decor.)
TIBULLUS, *De Sulpicia*. Bk. iii, eleg. 8, l. 7.

12
Narcissus is the glory of his race:
For who does nothing with a better grace?
YOUNG, *Love of Fame*. Sat. iv, l. 85.

He does it with a better grace, but I do it more natural.
SHAKESPEARE, *Twelfth Night*. Act ii, sc. 3, l. 88

III—Grace: The Graces

13
Take time enough: all other graces
Will soon fill up their proper places.
JOHN BYROM, *Advice to Preach Slow*.

Learn to read slow: all other graces
Will follow in their proper places.
WILLIAM WALKER, *The Art of Reading*.

14
There are Batavian graces in all he says.
BENJAMIN DISRAELI, *Speech*, House of Commons, retorting to Beresford Hope, who had referred to Disraeli as an "Asian mystery." Hope was descended from an Amsterdam family, and Disraeli's reference was to a sentence from Erasmus' *Naufragium:* "O crassum ingenium! Suspicor fuisse Batavum," "O dense intelligence! I suspect that it was Batavian," i. e. from the Netherlands, otherwise Batavia.

15
Alas! when all the gods assembled around his cradle to present their gifts, the graces were not there, and he to whom the favor of these fair powers is wanting may indeed possess much and be able to confer much, yet on his bosom we can never rest.
GOETHE, *Tasso*. Act ii, sc. 1, l. 197.

16
And joined with the Nymphs the lovely Graces. (Junctæque Nymphis Gratiæ decentes.)
HORACE, *Odes*. Bk. i, ode 4, l. 6.

Such stains there are—as when a Grace
Sprinkles another's laughing face
With nectar, and runs on.
W. S. LANDOR, *Catullus*.

17
Every man of any education would rather be called a rascal than accused of deficiency in the graces.
SAMUEL JOHNSON. (BOSWELL, *Life*, iii, 54.)

18
Around the child bend all the three
Sweet Graces—Faith, Hope, Charity.
Around the man bend other faces—
Pride, Envy, Malice, are his Graces.
WALTER SAVAGE LANDOR, *Epigram*.

The three black graces, Law, Physic, and Divinity.
HORACE AND JAMES SMITH, *Punch's Holiday*.

1
My good Xenocrates, sacrifice to the Graces. (Ὦ μακάριε Ξενόκρατες, θῦε ταῖς Χάρισιν.)

PLATO, his advice to Xenocrates, whom he considered too grave and dignified. (PLUTARCH, *Lives: Caius Marius*. Ch. 2, sec. 3. DIOGENES LAERTIUS, *Xenocrates*. Bk. iv, ch. 2, sec. 6.)

Dear Boy: I must from time to time remind you of what I have often recommended to you, and of what you cannot attend to too much: Sacrifice to the Graces.

LORD CHESTERFIELD, *Letters*, 9 March, 1748.

The Graces, the Graces; remember the Graces!

LORD CHESTERFIELD, *Letters*, 10 Jan., 1749.

Adorn yourself with all those graces and accomplishments, which, without solidity, are frivolous; but without which solidity is, to a great degree, useless.

LORD CHESTERFIELD, *Letters*, 18 Jan., 1750.

2
Four are the Graces, there are two Aphrodites and ten Muses. Dercylis is one of all, a Grace, an Aphrodite, and a Muse. (Τέσσαρες αἱ Χάριτες, Παφίαι δύο, και δέκα Μοῦσαι· Δερκυλὶς ἐν πάσαις Μοῦσα, Χάρις, Παφίη.)

UNKNOWN, *Greek Anthology*. Bk. v, no. 95. Sometimes attributed to Callimachus.

Two goddesses now must Cyprus adore;
The Muses are ten, and the Graces are four;
Stella's wit is so charming, so sweet her fair face,
She shines a new Venus, a Muse, and a Grace.

SWIFT's rendering of the above epigram from the *Greek Anthology*.

3
Some say the Muses are nine; but how carelessly! Look at the tenth, Sappho from Lesbos. (Ἐννέα τὰς Μούσας φασίν τινες· ὡς ὀλιγώρως· ἠνίδε καὶ Σαπφὼ Λεσβόθεν ἡ δεκάτη.)

PLATO, *Epigram*. (*Greek Anthology*. Bk. ix, No. 506.)

GRAMMAR

4
Idly curious race of grammarians, ye who dig up by the roots the poetry of others, . . . away with you, bugs that bite secretly the eloquent.

ANTIPHANES OF MACEDONIA. (*Greek Anthology*. Bk. xi, epig. 322.)

5
So hath man sought to come forth of the second general curse, which was the confusion of tongues, by the art of grammar.

BACON, *Advancement of Learning*. Bk. ii.

6
Heedless of grammar, they all cried, "That's him"!

R. H. BARHAM, *The Jackdaw of Rheims*.

7
More fault of those who had the hammering
Of prosody into me, and syntax,
And did it, not with hobnails but tintacks!

ROBERT BROWNING, *The Flight of the Duchess*. Sec. 15.

8
For all a rhetorician's rules
Teach nothing but to name his tools.

BUTLER, *Hudibras*. Pt. i, canto i, l. 89.

9
A heretic in grammar. (Hæreticus in Grammatica.)

ERASMUS, *Synodus Grammaticorum*.

10
The grammarians are at variance, and the matter is still undecided. (Grammatici certant, et adhuc sub judice lis est.)

HORACE, *Ars Poetica*, l. 78.

In all the mazes of metaphorical confusion.

JUNIUS, *Letters*. No. 7, 3 Mar., 1769.

11
Grammar is the grave of letters.

ELBERT HUBBARD, *A Thousand and One Epigrams*, p. 114.

12
Who climbs the Grammar-Tree, distinctly knows
Where Noun, and Verb, and Participle grows.

JUVENAL, *Satires*. Sat. vi, l. 583. (John Dryden, tr.)

13
Grammar, which knows how to lord it over kings, and with high hands makes them obey its laws. (La grammaire, qui sait régenter jusqu'aux rois, Et les fait, la main haute, obéir à ses lois.)

MOLIÈRE, *Les Femmes Savantes*. Act ii, sc. 6, l. 38.

14
The greater part of this world's troubles are due to questions of grammar. (La plus part des occasions des troubles du monde sont grammairiennes.)

MONTAIGNE, *Essays*. Bk. ii, ch. 12.

15
An aspersion upon my parts of speech!

SHERIDAN, *The Rivals*. Act iii, sc. 3.

16
I am king of the Romans, and above grammar. (Ego sum rex Romanus, et supra grammaticam.)

EMPEROR SIGISMUND, at the Council of Constance, 1414, to a prelate who called his attention to a grammatical error in his opening speech. (MENZEL, *History of the Romans*, p. 325.)

Cæsar is above grammar.

FREDERICK THE GREAT, to Voltaire, when the latter urged him to write better French than Louis XIV.

17
When I read some of the rules for speaking and writing the English language correctly, . . . I think—

Any fool can make a rule
And every fool will mind it.

H. D. THOREAU, *Journal*, 3 Feb., 1860.

18
Why care for grammar as long as we are good?

ARTEMUS WARD, *Natural History*. Pt. v.

GRANT, ULYSSES S.

1
Great Captain, glorious in our wars—
No meed of praise we hold from him;
About his brow we wreathe the stars
The coming ages shall not dim.

THOMAS BAILEY ALDRICH, *"Great Captain, Glorious in Our Wars."*

The cloud-sent man! Was it not he
That from the hand of adverse fate
Snatched the white flower of victory?
He spoke no word, but saved the State.

THOMAS BAILEY ALDRICH, *"Great Captain, Glorious in Our Wars."*

2
Let us have peace: our clouded eyes
Fill, Father, with another light,
That we may see with clearer sight
Thy servant's soul in Paradise.

AMBROSE BIERCE, *The Death of Grant.*

His was the heavy hand, and his
The service of the despot blade;
His the soft answer that allayed
War's giant animosities.

AMBROSE BIERCE, *The Death of Grant.*

3
The Conqueror of a hundred fields
To a mighty Conqueror yields;
No mortal foeman's blow
Laid the great Soldier low;
Victor in his latest breath—
Vanquished but by Death.

FRANCIS FISHER BROWNE, *Vanquished.*

4
And if asked what state he hails from,
This our sole reply shall be,
"From near Appomattox Court-house,
With its famous apple-tree."

CHARLES GRAHAM HALPINE, *A Bumper to Grant.* (Quoted by Roscoe Conkling in nominating Grant for the Presidency, June, 1880.)

5
Strong, simple, silent, such was he
Who helped us in our need. . . .
Nothing ideal, a plain people's man. . . .
Doer of hopeless tasks which praters shirk,
One of those still plain men that do the world's rough work.

J. R. LOWELL, *On a Bust of General Grant.*

6
The iron shackles which Lincoln declared should be loosed from the limbs and souls of the black slaves, Grant, with his matchless army, melted and destroyed in the burning glories of the war.

WILLIAM MCKINLEY, *Address,* on Grant's birthday, 1893.

7
How history repeats itself
You'll say when you remember Grant,
Who, in his boyhood days, once sought
Throughout the lexicon for "can't."

HARRIET PRESCOTT SPOFFORD, *Grant.*

GRAPES

8
The grapes are sour. (Ὄμφακές εἰσιν... ['Ρᾶγες ὀμφακίζουσι μάλα.])

ÆSOP, Fables: The Fox and the Grapes.

"They are too green," said he, "and only good for fools." ("Ils sont trop verts," dit-il, "et bons pour des goujats.")

LA FONTAINE, *Le Renard et les Raisins.* The fable is that the fox, seeing the lovely ripe grapes high on a trellis, and being unable to reach them, passed by with the above remark, and La Fontaine adds, "Wasn't that better than complaining?" (Fit-il pas mieux que de se plaindre?)

9
I see full well the fox will eat no grapes because he cannot reach them.

ULPIAN FULWELL, *Ars Adulandi.* Sig. E3. (1580)

10
There, economy was always "elegant," and money-spending always "vulgar" and ostentatious—a sort of sour grapeism, which made us very peaceful and satisfied.

MRS. GASKELL, *Cranford.* Ch. 1.

11
Winter grape sour, whedder you kin reach 'im or not.

JOEL CHANDLER HARRIS, *Plantation Proverbs*

12
The fox, when he cannot reach the grapes, says they are not ripe.

GEORGE HERBERT, *Jacula Prudentum.*

And like the fox, to cry the grapes are sour.

UNKNOWN, *Wit for Money.* Act iv. (1691)

13
Prudish clods of barren clay,
Who mope for heaven because earth's grapes are sour.

CHARLES KINGSLEY, *The Saint's Tragedy.* Act ii, sc. 3.

14
The fathers have eaten sour grapes, and the children's teeth are set on edge.

Old Testament: Ezekiel, xviii, 2.

The fathers have eaten a sour grape, and the children's teeth are set on edge.

Old Testament: Jeremiah, xxxi, 29.

15
And he looked that it should bring forth grapes, and it brought forth wild grapes.

Old Testament: Isaiah, v, 2.

16
Is not the gleaning of the grapes of Ephraim better than the vintage of Abi-ezer?

Old Testament: Judges, viii, 2.

17
Poor birds, deceived with painted grapes,
Do surfeit by the eye and pine the maw.

SHAKESPEARE, *Venus and Adonis,* l. 601.

GRASS

18
Go to grass.

BEAUMONT AND FLETCHER, *The Little French Lawyer.* Act iv, sc. 7.

1
Here I come creeping, creeping everywhere;
My humble song of praise
Most joyfully I raise
To Him at whose command
I beautify the land,
Creeping, silently creeping everywhere.
SARAH ROBERTS BOYLE, *The Voice of the Grass.*

2
Grass and hay, we are all mortal.
RICHARD BRATHWAIT, *Whimzies,* 73. (1631)
See also under MORTALITY.

3
The grey horse, while his grass groweth, may starve for hunger, thus saith the proverb.
JOHN CAPGRAVE, *Life of St. Katherine,* ii, 253. (c. 1440)

While the grass groweth the horse starveth.
JOHN HEYWOOD, *Proverbs.* Pt. i, ch. 11.

Yet the old proverb I would have them know,
The horse may starve whilst the grass doth grow.
JOHN TAYLOR THE WATER-POET, *A Kicksey-Winsey.* Pt. iv, last line.

Whilst grass doth grow, oft starves the silly steed.
GEORGE WHETSTONE, *Promos and Cassandry.*

While the grass grows—
The proverb is something musty.
SHAKESPEARE, *Hamlet.* Act iii, sc. 2, l. 358.

Live, horse! and thou shalt have grass.
SWIFT, *Polite Conversation.* Dial. i.

4
Grass grows at last above all graves.
JULIA C. R. DORR, *Grass-Grown.*

Pile the bodies high at Austerlitz and Waterloo.
Shovel them under and let me work—
I am the grass; I cover all.
CARL SANDBURG, *Grass.*

5
We say of the oak, "How grand of girth!"
Of the willow we say, "How slender!"
And yet to the soft grass clothing the earth
How slight is the praise we render.
EDGAR FAWCETT, *The Grass.*

6
Grass springeth not where the grand signior's horse setteth his foot.
THOMAS FULLER, *Holy War.* Bk. v, ch. 30. Referred to as "the old proverb." (1639)

Of whom you may say, as of the Great Sultan's horse, where he treads the grass grows no more.
JOHN CLEVELAND, *Works,* p. 77. (1658)

7
I am tired of four walls and a ceiling;
I have need of the grass.
RICHARD HOVEY, *Along the Trail: Spring.*

8
A blade of grass is always a blade of grass, whether in one country or another.
SAMUEL JOHNSON. (MRS. PIOZZI, *Anecdotes of Johnson,* p. 100.)

9
The green grass floweth like a stream
Into the ocean's blue.
J. R. LOWELL, *The Sirens,* l. 87.

10
The murmur that springs
From the growing of grass.
EDGAR ALLAN POE, *Al Aaraaf.* Pt. ii, l. 124.

The grass you almost hear it growing,
You hear it now, if e'er you can.
WORDSWORTH, *The Idiot Boy,* l. 285.

11
Grass grows not upon the highway.
JOHN RAY, *English Proverbs,* 149.

12
How lush and lusty the grass looks! how green!
SHAKESPEARE, *The Tempest.* Act ii, sc. 1, l. 52.

O'er the smooth enamell'd green
Where no print of step hath been.
MILTON, *Arcades,* l. 84.

The scented wild weeds and enamelled moss.
THOMAS CAMPBELL, *Theodric,* l. 15.

13
In the world's audience hall, the simple blade of grass sits on the same carpet with the sunbeam, and the stars of midnight.
RABINDRANATH TAGORE, *The Gardener.* No. 74.

14
There hath grown no grass on my heel since I went hence.
NICHOLAS UDALL, *Ralph Roister Doister.* Act iii, sc. 3.

I have not been idle—I have not let grass grow under my feet.
UNKNOWN, *The Spanish Bawd.* Act iv, sc. 3.

15
A child said *What is the grass?* fetching it to me with full hands;
How could I answer the child? I do not know what it is any more than he.
I guess it must be the flag of my disposition, out of hopeful green stuff woven.
Or I guess it is the handkerchief of the Lord,
A scented gift and remembrancer designedly dropt. . . .
And now it seems to me the beautiful uncut hair of graves.
WALT WHITMAN, *Song of Myself.* Sec. 6.

GRASSHOPPER

16
Because half a dozen grasshoppers under a fern make the field ring with their importunate chink, whilst thousands of great cattle, reposed beneath the shadow of the British oak, chew the cud and are silent, pray do not imagine that those who make the noise are the only inhabitants of the field; that, of course, they are many in number; or that, after all, they are other than the little, shrivelled, meagre, hopping, though loud and troublesome, insects of the hour.
EDMUND BURKE, *Reflections on the Revolution in France.*

17
Happy insect! what can be
In happiness compared to thee?

Fed with nourishment divine,
The dewy morning's gentle wine!
Nature waits upon thee still,
And thy verdant cup does fill;
'Tis fill'd wherever thou dost tread,
Nature's self's thy Ganymede.

COWLEY, *Anacreontiques: The Grasshopper.*

1
The grasshopper shall be a burden, and desire shall fail: because man goeth to his long home, and the mourners go about the streets.

Old Testament: Ecclesiastes, xii, 5.

2
Green little vaulter, in the sunny grass,
Catching your heart up at the feel of June,
Sole noise that's heard amidst the lazy noon.

LEIGH HUNT, *To the Grasshopper and the Cricket.*

Divine insect,
That sips of dew And sings!

WILLIAM GRIFFITH, *Grasshopper.*

3
When all the birds are faint with the hot sun,
And hide in cooling trees, a voice will run
From hedge to hedge about the new-mown mead;
That is the grasshopper's—he takes the lead
In summer luxury—he has never done
With his delights; for when tired out with fun,
He rests at ease beneath some pleasant weed.

KEATS, *On the Grasshopper and Cricket.*

4
The Grasshopper, the Grasshopper,
I will explain to you:—
He is the Brownies' Racehorse,
The Fairies' Kangaroo.

VACHEL LINDSAY, *The Grasshopper.*

GRATITUDE

I—Gratitude: Definitions

5
Gratitude is a burden upon our imperfect nature.

LORD CHESTERFIELD, *Letters,* 7 Nov., 1765.

Gratitude is a burden, and every burden is made to be shaken off. (La reconnaissance est un fardeau, et tout fardeau est fait pour être secoué.)

DIDEROT, *Encyclopédie.*

6
While I would fain have some tincture of all the virtues, there is no quality I would rather have, and be thought to have, than gratitude. For it is not only the greatest virtue, but even the mother of all the rest. (Hæc est enim una virtus non solum maxima, sed etiam mater virtutum omnium reliquarum.)

CICERO, *Pro Plancio.* Ch. 33, sec. 80.

7
Gratitude is one of those things that cannot be bought. It must be born with men, or else all the obligations in the world will not create it.

LORD HALIFAX, *Works,* p. 205.

8
Gratitude is a fruit of great cultivation; you do not find it among gross people.

SAMUEL JOHNSON, *Tour to the Hebrides,* 20 Sept., 1773.

9
Justice is often pale and melancholy; but Gratitude, her daughter, is constantly in the flow of spirits and the bloom of loveliness.

W. S. LANDOR, *Imaginary Conversations: Hume and Home.*

10
The gratitude of most men is nothing but a secret hope of receiving greater favors. (La reconnaissance de la plupart des hommes n'est qu'une secrète envie de recevoir de plus grands bienfaits.)

LA ROCHEFOUCAULD, *Maximes.* No. 298.

The gratitude of place-expectants is a lively sense of future favours.

SIR ROBERT WALPOLE. (HAZLITT, *Wit and Humour.*)

11
Gratitude is the memory of the heart. (La reconnaissance est la mémoire du cœur.)

JEAN BAPTISTE MASSIEU, *Letter to the Abbé Sicard.*

12
And name it gratitude, the word is poor.

GEORGE MEREDITH, *The Sage Enamoured.*

13
Gratitude is a nice touch of beauty added last of all to the countenance, giving a classic beauty, an angelic loveliness, to the character.

THEODORE PARKER, *Sermon: Of Moral Dangers Incident to Prosperity.*

14
If you do anything well, gratitude is lighter than a feather; if you give offense in anything, people's wrath is as heavy as lead. (Si quid bene facias, levior pluma est gratia: Si quid peccatumst, plumbeas iras gerunt.)

PLAUTUS, *Pœnulus,* l. 812. (Act iii, sc. 6.)

15
Evermore thanks, the exchequer of the poor.

SHAKESPEARE, *Richard II.* Act ii, sc. 3, l. 65.

16
Swift gratitude is sweetest; if it delays, all gratitude is empty and unworthy of the name. (Ὠκεῖαι χάριτες γλυκερώτεραι· ἢν δὲ βραδύνῃ, πᾶσα χάρις κενεή, μηδὲ λέγοιτο χάρις.)

UNKNOWN. (*Greek Anthology.* Bk. x, epig. 30.)

They say late thanks are ever best.

FRANCIS BACON, *Letter to Robert, Lord Cecil,* July 1603.

II—Gratitude: Apothegms

17
What soon grows old? Gratitude. (Τί γηράσκει ταχύ—χάρις.)

ARISTOTLE. (DIOG. LAERTIUS, *Aristotle.* Sec. 18.)

Gratitude is a charge upon the inheritance which the second generation is apt to repudiate.

HONORÉ DE BALZAC, *Gobseck,* p. 4. (1840)

1
Next to ingratitude, the most painful thing to bear is gratitude.
HENRY WARD BEECHER, *Proverbs from Plymouth Pulpit.*

2
Some people always sigh in thanking God.
E. B. BROWNING, *Aurora Leigh.* Bk. i, l. 445.

I am glad that he thanks God for anything.
SAMUEL JOHNSON. (BOSWELL, *Life,* 1775.)

3
In grateful looks,
Seraphs write lessons more divine than books.
BULWER-LYTTON, *New Timon.* Pt. i, sec. ii, l. 58.

4
I thank you for nothing, because I understand nothing.
JOHN LYLY, *Mother Bombie,* ii, 3. (1594)
SHADWELL, *Sullen Lovers,* v, 3. (1668)

5
Words are but empty thanks.
COLLEY CIBBER, *Woman's Wit.* Act v.

Accept my thoughts for thanks; I have no words.
HANNAH MORE, *Moses.*

Though my mouth be dumb, my heart shall thank you.
NICHOLAS ROWE, *Jane Shore.* Act ii, sc. 1.

6
Praise the bridge that carried you over.
GEORGE COLMAN THE YOUNGER, *The Heir-at-Law.* Act i, sc. 1.

It is strange men cannot praise the bridge they go over, or be thankful for favours they have had.
ROGER NORTH, *Examen,* p. 368.

When our perils are past, shall our gratitude sleep?
No,—here's to the pilot that weathered the storm!
GEORGE CANNING, *The Pilot.* Sung in honor of William Pitt at a public dinner, 28 May, 1802.

7
When I'm not thanked at all I'm thanked enough.
FIELDING, *Tom Thumb the Great.* Act i, sc. 2.

8
Sweet music's melting fall, but sweeter yet
The still small voice of Gratitude.
THOMAS GRAY, *Ode for Music,* l. 63.

9
Thanksgiving for a former doth invite
God to bestow a second benefit.
ROBERT HERRICK, *Thanksgiving.*

10
Lord, for the erring thought
Not into evil wrought:
Lord, for the wicked will
Betrayed and baffled still:
For the heart from itself kept,
Our thanksgiving accept.
WILLIAM DEAN HOWELLS, *Thanksgiving.*

11
To receive honestly is the best thanks for a good thing.
GEORGE MACDONALD, *Mary Marston.* Ch. 5.

12
A grateful mind
By owing owes not, but still pays, at once
Indebted and discharg'd.
MILTON, *Paradise Lost* Bk. iv, l. 55.

13
Thanks are justly due for boons unbought. (Gratia pro rebus merito debetur inemptis.)
OVID, *Amores.* Bk. i, eleg. 10, l. 43.

14
One good turn deserves another. (Manus manum lavat.)
PETRONIUS, *Satyricon.* Sec. 45.

Scratch my back, and I'll scratch yours. (Serva me, servabo te.)
PETRONIUS, *Satyricon.* Sec. 44.

15
Th' unwilling gratitude of base mankind!
POPE, *Imitations of Horace: Epistles.* Bk. ii, epis. i, l. 14.

16
Possessions gained by the sword are not lasting; gratitude for benefits is eternal. (Non est diuturna possessio in quam gladio ducimus; beneficiorum gratia sempiterna est.)
QUINTUS CURTIUS RUFUS, *De Rebus Gestis Alexandri Magni,* viii, 8, 11.

17
Let the man, who would be grateful, think of repaying a kindness, even while receiving it. (Qui gratus futurus est, statim, dum accipit, de reddendo cogitet.)
SENECA, *De Beneficiis.* Bk. ii, ch. 25, sec. 3.

18
Nothing is more honorable than a grateful heart. (Nihil esse grato animo honestius.)
SENECA, *Epistulæ ad Lucilium.* Epis. lxxxi, 30.

19
Thou thought'st to help me; and such thanks I give
As one near death to those that wish him live.
SHAKESPEARE, *All's Well that Ends Well.* Act ii, sc. 1, l. 135.

For this relief, much thanks.
SHAKESPEARE, *Hamlet.* Act i, sc. 1, l. 8.

Such thanks As fits a king's remembrance.
SHAKESPEARE, *Hamlet.* Act ii, sc. 2, l. 25.

20
Beggar that I am, I am even poor in thanks.
SHAKESPEARE, *Hamlet.* Act ii, sc. 2, l. 280.

21
Let never day nor night unhallow'd pass,
But still remember what the Lord hath done.
SHAKESPEARE, *II Henry VI.* Act ii, sc. 1, l. 85.

22
Let but the commons hear this testament—
Which, pardon me, I do not mean to read—
And they would go and kiss dead Cæsar's wounds
And dip their napkins in his sacred blood,
Yea, beg a hair of him for memory,
And, dying, mention it within their wills,
Bequeathing it as a rich legacy

Unto their issue.
SHAKESPEARE, *Julius Cæsar*. Act iii, sc. 2, l. 135.

1
Within this wall of flesh
There is a soul counts thee her creditor.
SHAKESPEARE, *King John*. Act iii, sc. 3, l. 20.

2
Thank me no thankings, nor proud me no prouds.
SHAKESPEARE, *Romeo and Juliet*. Act iii, sc. 5, l. 153.

3
Do you like gratitude? I don't. If pity is akin to love, gratitude is akin to the other thing.
BERNARD SHAW, *Arms and the Man*. Act iii.

4
And though I ebb in worth, I'll flow in thanks.
JOHN TAYLOR THE WATER-POET, *A Very Merry-Wherry-Ferry Voyage*, l. 520.

5
In everything give thanks. (Ἐν παντὶ εὐχαριστεῖτε.)
New Testament: I Thessalonians, v, 18.

6
I've heard of hearts unkind, kind deeds
With coldness still returning;
Alas! the gratitude of men
Hath oftener left me mourning.
WORDSWORTH, *Simon Lee*, l. 93.

7
But whether we have less or more,
Always thank we God therefor.
UNKNOWN, *Fabliau of Sir Cleyes*. (c. 1450)

Be thankful f'r what ye have not, Hinnissy—'tis the on'y safe rule.
FINLEY PETER DUNNE, *Thanksgiving*.

GRAVE

I—Grave: Definitions

8
The grave is Heaven's golden gate,
And rich and poor around it wait;
O Shepherdess of England's fold,
Behold this gate of pearl and gold!
WILLIAM BLAKE, *Dedication of the Designs to Blair's "Grave": To Queen Charlotte*.

9
Our noblest piles and stateliest rooms,
Are mere out-houses to our tombs;
Cities, tho' ere so great and brave,
But mere warehouses to the grave.
SAMUEL BUTLER, *The Weakness and Misery of Man*, l. 85.

The most magnificent and costly dome
Is but an upper chamber to the tomb.
YOUNG, *The Last Day*. Bk. ii, l. 87.

The gay assembly's gayest room
Is but the upper story of some tomb.
YOUNG, *Love of Fame*. Sat. vi, l. 481.

Build houses of five hundred by a hundred feet, forgetting that of six by two.
FIELDING, *Tom Jones*. Bk. ii, ch. 8.

10
A clayey tenement.
THOMAS CAREW, *Epitaphs: On the Lady Mary Villiers*.

A pick-axe and a spade,
And eke a shrouding-sheet,
A house of clay for to be made
For such a guest most meet.
THOMAS VAUX, *The Aged Lover Renounceth Love*.

11
Man goeth to his long home.
Old Testament: Ecclesiastes, xii, 5.

And thy travail shalt thou soon end,
For to thy long home soon shalt thou wend.
ROBERT MANNYNG (ROBERT DE BRUNNE), *Handlyng Synne*, l. 9195. (1303)

12
The grave is the general meeting-place.
THOMAS FULLER, *Gnomologia*. No. 4563.

13
If the heats of hate and lust
In the house of flesh are strong,
Let me mind the house of dust
Where my sojourn shall be long.
A. E. HOUSMAN, *A Shropshire Lad*, p. 19.

14
The house appointed for all living.
Old Testament: Job, xxx, 23.

15
The grave itself is but a covered bridge,
Leading from light to light, through a brief darkness!
LONGFELLOW, *The Golden Legend*. Pt. v.

16
He spake well who said that graves are the footprints of angels.
LONGFELLOW, *Hyperion*. Bk. iv, ch. 5.

17
Laid up in the wardrobe of the grave.
BISHOP JOHN PEARSON, *Exposition of the Creed*. Art. iv.

18
To that dark inn, the grave!
SCOTT, *The Lord of the Isles*. Canto vi, l. 717.

Inn of a traveller on his way to Jerusalem.
UNKNOWN, *Inscription*, on monument of Henry Alford, Dean of Canterbury, St. Martin's Churchyard, Canterbury.

19
The houses that he makes last till doomsday.
SHAKESPEARE, *Hamlet*. Act v, sc. 1, l. 66.

20
That small model of the barren earth
Which serves as paste and cover to our bones.
SHAKESPEARE, *Richard II*. Act iii, sc. 2, l. 148.

21
All roads end at the grave, which is the gate of nothingness.
BERNARD SHAW, *The Adventures of the Black Girl in Her Search for God*.

22
The lone couch of his everlasting sleep.
SHELLEY, *Alastor*, l. 57.

1

The grave
Is but the threshold of eternity.

SOUTHEY, *Vision of the Maid of Orleans*. Bk. ii, l. 20.

2

The low green tent
Whose curtain never outward swings.

WHITTIER, *Snow-Bound*. St. 13.

II—Grave: Apothegms

3

Measure not thyself by thy morning shadow, but by the extent of thy grave; and reckon thyself above the earth by the line thou must be contented with under it.

SIR THOMAS BROWNE, *Christian Morals*. Pt. i, sec. 19.

4

An untimely grave.

THOMAS CAREW, *On the Duke of Buckingham*.

5

Even if he had one foot in the grave. (Etsi alterum pedem in sepulchro haberem.)

POMPONIUS, speaking of Julian. (Quoted by Erasmus.) The original phrase was "One foot in the ferry boat," indicating Charon's boat. (LUCIAN, *Dialogues of the Dead*.)

An old doting fool, with one foot already in the grave. (Κρονόληρος καὶ σοροδαίμων.)

PLUTARCH, *Morals: On the Education of Children*. Sec. 13B.

One foot in the grave.

BEAUMONT AND FLETCHER, *The Little French Lawyer*. Act i, sc. 1.

In shepherd's phrase,
With one foot in the grave.

WORDSWORTH, *Michael*, l. 89.

6

Earth is the best shelter.

JOHN RAY, *English Proverbs*.

No sure dungeon but the grave.

SCOTT, *The Talisman*. Ch. 19.

7

Of all the pulpits from which human voice is ever sent forth there is none from which it reaches so far as from the grave.

RUSKIN, *Seven Lamps of Architecture*. Ch. vi, sec. 9.

Still from the grave their voice is heard.

SCOTT, *Marmion:* Canto iii, *Introduction*.

8

Renowned be thy grave!

SHAKESPEARE, *Cymbeline*. Act iv, sc. 2, l. 281.

The graves of those that cannot die.

BYRON, *The Giaour*, l. 140.

9

Taking the measure of an unmade grave.

SHAKESPEARE, *Romeo and Juliet*. Act iii, sc. 3, l. 70.

10

Cruel as death, and hungry as the grave!

THOMSON, *The Seasons: Winter*, l. 393.

III—Grave: Its Democracy

See also Death the Leveler

11

Earth to earth and dust to dust!
Here the evil and the just,
Here the youthful and the old,
Here the fearful and the bold,
Here the matron and the maid
In one silent bed are laid;
Here the sword and sceptre rust—
Earth to earth and dust to dust.

GEORGE CROLY, *A Dirge*.

12

Earth laughs in flowers, to see her boastful boys
Earth-proud, proud of the earth which is not theirs;
Who steer the plough, but can not steer their feet
Clear of the grave.

EMERSON, *Hamatreya*.

13

The boast of heraldry, the pomp of pow'r,
And all that beauty, all that wealth e'er gave,
Awaits alike th' inevitable hour.
The paths of glory lead but to the grave.

THOMAS GRAY, *Elegy Written in a Country Church-yard*, l. 33 (1751)

Ah me! what boots us all our boasted power,
Our golden treasure, and our purple state.
They cannot ward the inevitable hour,
Nor stay the fearful violence of fate.

RICHARD WEST, *Monody on Queen Caroline*. (1737)

14

Fond fool! six feet shall serve for all thy store,
And he that cares for most shall find no more.

JOSEPH HALL, *Satires*. Ser. ii, sat. 3.

15

And now he has no single plot of ground,
Excepting that in which he sleeps so sound!

HENRY HARRISON, *Epitaph for a Real-Estate Dealer*.

16

A piece of a Churchyard fits everybody.

GEORGE HERBERT, *Jacula Prudentum*. No. 1020.

Both, heirs to some six feet of sod,
Are equal in the earth at last.

J. R. LOWELL, *The Heritage*.

17

Now limb doth mingle with dissolvèd limb
In nature's busy old democracy

WILLIAM VAUGHN MOODY, *An Ode in Time of Hesitation*.

18

For who's a prince or beggar in the grave?

THOMAS OTWAY, *Windsor Castle*.

19

The grave unites; where ev'n the great find rest,
And blended lie th' oppressor and th' opprest!

POPE, *Windsor Forest*, l. 317.

20

And my large kingdom for a little grave,

A little little grave, an obscure grave.
SHAKESPEARE, *Richard II*. Act iii, sc. 3, l. 153.

1
I'll take a turn among the tombs,
And see whereto all glory comes.
ISAAC WATTS, *The Hero's School*.

IV—Grave: Its Comfort

2
Mine be the breezy hill that skirts the down;
Where a green grassy turf is all I crave,
With here and there a violet bestrown,
Fast by a brook, or fountain's murmuring wave;
And many an evening sun shine sweetly on my grave!
JAMES BEATTIE, *The Minstrel*. Bk. ii, st. 17.

3
I gazed upon the glorious sky
And the green mountains round,
And thought that when I came to lie
At rest within the ground,
'Twere pleasant, that in flowery June,
When brooks send up a cheerful tune,
And groves a joyous sound,
The sexton's hand, my grave to make,
The rich, green mountain turf should break.
WILLIAM CULLEN BRYANT, *June*, l. 1.

4
I would rather sleep in the southern corner of a little country churchyard than in the tomb of the Capulets.
EDMUND BURKE, *Letter to Matthew Smith*.

Family vault of "all the Capulets."
EDMUND BURKE, *Reflections on the Revolution in France*.

5
Soft sigh the winds of Heaven o'er their grave!
THOMAS CAMPBELL, *Battle of the Baltic*. St. 8.

6
Once there, one will not be bothered. (Oui, alors je serai sans souci.)
FREDERICK THE GREAT, looking at the royal tombs at Potsdam. The country house he built close by was called "Sans Souci."

7
Oh, the grave!—the grave!—It buries every error—covers every defect—extinguishes every resentment! From its peaceful bosom spring none but fond regrets and tender recollections. Who can look down upon the grave even of an enemy and not feel a compunctious throb, that he should ever have warred with the poor handful of earth that lies mouldering before him?
WASHINGTON IRVING, *The Sketch-book: Rural Funerals*.

8
A very worthless rogue may dig the grave,
But Hands unseen will dress the turf with daisies.
F. LOCKER-LAMPSON, *A Human Skull*.

9
For rain it hath a friendly sound
To one who's six feet underground;
And scarce the friendly voice or face:
A grave is such a quiet place.
EDNA ST. VINCENT MILLAY, *Renascence*.

10
There is a calm for those who weep,
A rest for weary pilgrims found,
They softly lie and sweetly sleep
Low in the ground.
JAMES MONTGOMERY, *The Grave*.

11
A grave seems only six feet deep
And three feet wide,
Viewed with the calculating eye
Of one outside.

But when fast bound in the chill loam
For that strange sleep,
Who knows how wide its realm may be?
Its depths, how deep?
JOHN RICHARD MORELAND, *A Grave*.

12
Let children play
And sit like flowers upon thy grave
And crown with bowers,—that hardly have
A briefer blooming-tide than they.
FRANCIS TURNER PALGRAVE, *A Danish Barrow*.

13
Yet shall thy grave with rising flowers be dress'd,
And the green turf lie lightly on thy breast;
There shall the morn her earliest tears bestow,
There the first roses of the year shall blow.
POPE, *Elegy to the Memory of an Unfortunate Lady*, l. 65.

14
But I must go before him; and, 'tis said,
The grave's good rest when women go first to bed.
WILLIAM ROWLEY, *A Woman Never Vexed*. Act v.

15
So be my grave my peace.
SHAKESPEARE, *King Lear*. Act i, sc. 1, l. 127.

16
This little life is all we must endure,
The grave's most holy peace is ever sure.
JAMES THOMSON, *City of Dreadful Night*, xiv.

17
All things have rest, and ripen towards the grave.
TENNYSON, *Lotos Eaters: Choric Song*, l. 51.

A quiet passage to a welcome grave.
IZAAK WALTON, *The Compleat Angler: The Angler's Wish*.

And gently slope our passage to the grave.
YOUNG, *Night Thoughts*. Night v, l. 689.

V—Grave: Its Terror

18
Far from famous sepulchres, toward a lonely cemetery, my heart, like a muffled drum, goes beating a funeral march. (Loin des

sépultures célèbres, Vers un cimitière isolé, Mon cœur, comme un tambour voilé, Va battant des marches funèbres.)
CHARLES BAUDELAIRE, *Le Guignon.*

Our lives are but our marches to the grave.
JOHN FLETCHER, *The Humorous Lieutenant.* Act iii, sc. 5, l. 76.

Our hearts, though stout and brave,
Still, like muffled drums, are beating
Funeral marches to the grave.
LONGFELLOW, *A Psalm of Life.*

1
But when shall spring visit the mouldering urn!
O when shall it dawn on the night of the grave!
JAMES BEATTIE, *The Hermit.* St. 4.

2
Here are sands, ignoble things,
Dropt from the ruined sides of kings.
FRANCIS BEAUMONT, *On the Tombs of Westminster Abbey.*

3
For in the silent grave, no conversation,
No joyful tread of friends, no voice of lovers!
No careful father's counsels, nothing's heard,
For nothing is, but all oblivion,
Dust and an endless darkness.
BEAUMONT AND FLETCHER, *Tragedy of Thierry and Theodoret.* Act iv, sc. 1.

The grave's a fine and private place,
But none, I think, do there embrace.
ANDREW MARVELL, *To His Coy Mistress.*

4
Done with the work of breathing; done
With all the world; the mad race run
Through to the end; the golden goal
Attained and found to be a hole!
AMBROSE BIERCE, *The Devil's Dictionary,* p. 63.

5
The grave, dread thing!
Men shiver when thou'rt named: Nature appalled,
Shakes off her wonted firmness.
ROBERT BLAIR, *The Grave,* l. 9.

6
There is no work, nor device, nor knowledge, nor wisdom, in the grave, whither thou goest.
Old Testament: Ecclesiastes, ix, 10.

7
Graves, they say, are warm'd by glory;
Foolish words and empty story.
HEINE, *Latest Poems: Epilogue,* l. 1.

8
Lost to the world, lost to myself, alone
Here now I rest under this marble stone,
In depth of silence, heard and seen of none.
ROBERT HERRICK, *On Himself.*

9
The eyes of the sage, and the heart of the brave,
Are hidden and lost in the depths of the grave.
WILLIAM KNOX, *Oh, Why Should the Spirit of Mortal Be Proud?*

10
She smiled; then drooping mute and broken-hearted
To the cold comfort of the grave departed.
H. H. MILMAN, *The Apollo Belvidere.*

11
There are three things that are never satisfied, yea, four things say not, It is enough: The grave; and the barren womb; the earth that is not filled with water; and the fire that saith not, It is enough.
Old Testament: Proverbs, xxx, 15, 16.

12
The sepulchre,
Wherein we saw thee quietly inurn'd,
Hath op'd his ponderous and marble jaws.
SHAKESPEARE, *Hamlet.* Act i, sc. 4, l. 48.

They bore him barefac'd on the bier; . . .
And in his grave rain'd many a tear.
SHAKESPEARE, *Hamlet.* Act iv, sc. 5, l. 164.

13
Gilded tombs do worms infold.
SHAKESPEARE, *The Merchant of Venice.* Act ii, sc. 7, l. 69.

14
O heart, and mind, and thoughts! what thing do you
Hope to inherit in the grave below?
SHELLEY, *Sonnet: Ye Hasten to the Grave!*

15
Hark from the tombs a doleful sound.
ISAAC WATTS, *Funeral Thoughts.*

16
The shadows of the grave.
YOUNG, *Night Thoughts.* Night v, l. 236.

GRAVEYARD

17
Here's an acre sown indeed,
With the richest royalest seed.
FRANCIS BEAUMONT, *On the Tombs in Westminster Abbey.*

There is an acre sown with royal seed.
JEREMY TAYLOR, *Holy Living and Dying.* Ch. 1.

18
What's hallow'd ground? Has earth a clod
Its Maker meant not should be trod
By man, the image of his God,
Erect and free,
Unscourged by Superstition's rod
To bow the knee?
THOMAS CAMPBELL, *Hallowed Ground.*

19
This passive place a Summer's nimble mansion,
Where Bloom and Bees
Fulfilled their Oriental Circuit,
Then ceased like these.
EMILY DICKINSON, *Poems.* Pt. v, No. 74.

1
The solitary, silent, solemn scene,
Where Cæsars, heroes, peasants, hermits lie,
Blended in dust together; where the slave
Rests from his labours; where th' insulting proud
Resigns his powers, the miser drops his hoard:
Where human folly sleeps.
JOHN DYER, *Ruins of Rome*, l. 540.

2
And in some little lone churchyard,
Beside the growing corn,
Lay gentle Nature's stern prose bard,
Her mightiest peasant-born.
EBENEZER ELLIOTT, *Elegy on William Cobbett.*

3
Beneath those rugged elms, that yew-tree's shade,
Where heaves the turf in many a moldering heap,
Each in his narrow cell for ever laid,
The rude forefathers of the hamlet sleep.
THOMAS GRAY, *Elegy Written in a Country Church-yard*, l. 13.

4
What corpse is curious on the longitude
And situation of his cemetery!
THOMAS HARDY, *The Dynasts.* Act vi, sc. 7.

5
Nowhere probably is there more true feeling, and nowhere worse taste, than in a churchyard.
BENJAMIN JOWETT, *Letters*, p. 244.

6
I like that ancient Saxon phrase, which calls
The burial-ground God's-Acre! It is just;
It consecrates each grave within its walls,
And breathes a benison o'er the sleeping dust.
LONGFELLOW, *God's-Acre.*

This is the field and Acre of our God,
This is the place where human harvests grow.
LONGFELLOW, *God's-Acre.*

7
We give to each a tender thought, and pass
Out of the graveyards with their tangled grass.
LONGFELLOW, *Morituri Salutamus*, l. 124.

There are slave-drivers quietly whipped underground,
There bookbinders, done up in boards, are fast bound,
There card-players wait till the last trump be played,
There all the choice spirits get finally laid,
There the babe that's unborn is supplied with a berth,
There men without legs get their six feet of earth,
There lawyers repose, each wrapped up in his case,
There seekers of office are sure of a place,
There defendant and plaintiff get equally cast,
There shoemakers quietly stick to the last.
J. R. LOWELL, *A Fable for Critics*, l. 1656.

8
The churchyard's peace. (Ruhe eines Kirchhofs!)
SCHILLER, *Don Carlos.* Act iii, sc. 10, l. 220.

9
From the bountiful infinite west, from the happy memorial places,
Full of the stately repose and the lordly delight of the dead.
A. C. SWINBURNE, *Hesperia.*

10
There is a certain frame of mind to which a cemetery is, if not an antidote, at least an alleviation. If you are in a fit of the blues, go nowhere else.
R. L. STEVENSON, *Immortelles.*

11
The country home I need is a cemetery.
MARK TWAIN. (PAINE, *Mark Twain.*)

12
The visible quiet of this holy ground.
WORDSWORTH, *The Excursion.* Bk. vi, l. 482.

GRAVITY

13
Gravity is only the bark of wisdom's tree, but it preserves it.
CONFUCIUS, *Analects.*

14
Never make people laugh. If you would succeed in life, you must be solemn, solemn as an ass. All the great monuments are built over solemn asses.
THOMAS CORWIN, advice to a young speaker, based upon his own experience.

15
His smile is sweetened by his gravity.
GEORGE ELIOT, *Spanish Gypsy.* Bk. i.

16
Gravity is the ballast of the soul, which keeps the mind steady.
THOMAS FULLER, *Holy and Profane States: Gravity.*

17
Gravity is a trick of the body devised to conceal deficiencies of the mind. (La gravité est un mystère du corps inventé pour cacher les défauts de l'esprit.)
LA ROCHEFOUCAULD, *Maximes.* No. 257.

18
Gravity is of the very essence of imposture.
LORD SHAFTESBURY, *Characteristics*, i, 11.

19
What doth gravity out of his bed at midnight?
SHAKESPEARE, *I Henry IV.* Act ii, sc. 4, l. 324.

'Tis not for gravity to play at cherry-pit with Satan.
SHAKESPEARE, *Twelfth Night.* Act iii, sc. 4, l. 129.

20
As grave as judge that's giving charge.
SAMUEL WESLEY, *Maggots.*

Grave as an owl in a barn.
GEORGE FARQUHAR, *Inconstant*. Act iii, sc. 2.

GREATNESS

I—Greatness: Definitions

1
Great men are the true men, the men in whom nature has succeeded.
AMIEL, *Journal*. 13 Aug., 1865.

2
Greatness is a spiritual condition worthy to excite love, interest, and admiration; and the outward proof of possessing greatness is, that we excite love, interest, and admiration.
MATTHEW ARNOLD, *Culture and Anarchy: Sweetness and Light*.

3
Greatness, after all, in spite of its name, appears to be not so much a certain size as a certain quality in human lives. It may be present in lives whose range is very small.
PHILLIPS BROOKS, *Sermons: Purpose and Use of Comfort*.

4
All things that we see standing accomplished in the world are properly the outer material result, the practical realization and embodiment of Thoughts that dwell in the Great Men sent into the world.
CARLYLE, *Heroes and Hero-Worship*. Lecture i, sec. 1.

5
For he seems to me to be the greatest man, who rises to a high position by his own merit, and not one who climbs up by the injury and disaster of another.
CICERO, *Pro Roscio Amerino*. Sec. 30.

6
Some must be great. Great offices will have
Great talents.
COWPER, *The Task*. Bk. iv, l. 788.

7
Man is only truly great when he acts from the passions.
BENJAMIN DISRAELI, *Coningsby*. Bk. iv, ch. 13.

8
The measure of a master is his success in bringing all men round to his opinion twenty years later.
EMERSON, *Conduct of Life: Culture*.

He is great who confers the most benefits.
EMERSON, *Essays, First Series: Compensation*.

It is easy in the world to live after the world's opinion; it is easy in solitude after our own; but the great man is he who in the midst of the crowd keeps with perfect sweetness the independence of solitude.
EMERSON, *Essays, First Series: Self-reliance*.

I count him a great man who inhabits a higher sphere of thought, into which other men rise with labor and difficulty.
EMERSON, *Representative Men: Uses of Great Men*.

He is great who is what he is from nature, and who never reminds us of others.
EMERSON, *Representative Men: Uses of Great Men*.

9
Nothing great comes into being all at once; not even the grape or the fig. If you say to me now, "I want a fig," I shall answer, "That requires time." Let the tree blossom first, then put forth its fruit, and finally let the fruit ripen.
EPICTETUS, *Discourses*. Bk. i, ch. 15, sec. 7.

The heights by great men reached and kept
Were not attained by sudden flight,
But they, while their companions slept,
Were toiling upward in the night.
H. W. LONGFELLOW, *The Ladder of St. Augustine*. Inscribed beneath Longfellow's bust in the Hall of Fame.

10
Great men are the gifts of kind Heaven to our poor world; instruments by which the Highest One works out his designs; light-radiators to give guidance and blessing to the travelers of time.
MOSES HARVEY, *Columbus*.

11
Great men are rarely isolated mountain-peaks; they are the summits of ranges.
T. W. HIGGINSON, *Atlantic Essays: Plea for Culture*.

12
To be a great man, one must know how to make the most of fortune. (Pour être un grand homme, il faut savoir profiter de toute sa fortune.)
LA ROCHEFOUCAULD, *Maximes*. No. 343.

It is not enough to have great qualities; one must make good use of them. (Ce n'est pas assez d'avoir de grandes qualités; il en faut avoir l'économie.)
LA ROCHEFOUCAULD, *Maximes*. No. 159.

13
Great spirits are not those who have fewer passions and greater virtue than ordinary men, but only those who have the greatest aims. (Les grandes âmes ne sont pas celles qui ont moins de passions et plus de vertu que les âmes communes, mais celles seulement qui ont de plus grands desseins.)
LA ROCHEFOUCAULD, *Maximes Supprimées*. No. 602.

Great hopes make great men.
THOMAS FULLER, *Gnomologia*. No. 1759.

14
The great man is the man who can get himself made and who will get himself made out of anything he finds at hand.
GERALD STANLEY LEE, *Crowds*. Bk. ii, ch. 15.

15
A great man is made up of qualities that meet or make great occasions.
J. R. LOWELL, *My Study Windows: Garfield*.

1
The great man is he who does not lose his child's heart.

MENCIUS, *Works*. Bk. iv, pt. 2, ch. 12.

2
That man is great, and he alone,
Who serves a greatness not his own,
For neither praise nor pelf:
Content to know and be unknown:
Whole in himself.

OWEN MEREDITH, *A Great Man.*

3
He alone is worthy of the appellation who either does great things, or teaches how they may be done, or describes them with a suitable majesty when they have been done; but those only are great things which tend to render life more happy, which increase the innocent enjoyments and comforts of existence, or which pave the way to a state of future bliss more permanent and more pure.

MILTON, *The Second Defence of the People of England.*

4
My formula for greatness in man is *amor fati:* that a man should wish to have nothing altered, either in the future, the past, nor for all eternity.

FRIEDRICH NIETZSCHE, *Ecce Homo.*

5
That man is great who can use the brains of others to carry on his work.

DONN PIATT, *Memories of Men Who Saved the Union: W. H. Seward.*

6
Look next on Greatness: say where Greatness lies:
"Where but among the heroes and the wise?"

POPE, *Essay on Man.* Epis. iv, l. 217.

Who wickedly is wise, or madly brave,
Is but the more a fool, the more a knave.
Who noble ends by noble means obtains,
Or failing, smiles in exile or in chains,
Like good Aurelius let him reign, or bleed
Like Socrates:—that man is great indeed!

POPE, *Essay on Man.* Epis. iv, l. 231.

7
It is true greatness to have the frailty of a man with the security of a god. (Vere magnum, habere fragilitatem hominis, securitatem dei.)

SENECA. (BACON, *Essays: Of Adversity.*)

8
He is a great man who uses earthenware dishes as if they were silver; but he is equally great who uses silver as if it were earthenware. (Magnus ille est, qui fictilibus sic utitur quemadmodum argento. Nec ille minor est. qui sic argento utitur quemadmodum fictilibus.)

SENECA, *Epistulæ ad Lucilium.* Epis. v, sec. 6.

Greatness is not absolute; comparison increases it or lessens it. A ship which looms large in the river seems tiny when on the ocean. (Nam magnitudo non habet modum certum; comparatio illam aut tollit aut deprimit. Navis, quæ in flumine magna est, in mari parvula est.)

SENECA, *Epistulæ ad Lucilium.* Epis. xliii, 2.

None of those who have been raised to a loftier height by riches and honors is really great. Why then does he seem great to you? It is because you are measuring the pedestal along with the man.

SENECA, *Epistulæ ad Lucilium.* Epis. lxxvi, 31.

Why, then, is a wise man great? Because he has a great soul. (Quare ergo sapiens magnus est? Quia magnum animum habet.)

SENECA, *Epistulæ ad Lucilium.* Epis. lxxxvii, sec. 18.

That man has shown himself great who has never grieved in evil days and never bewailed his destiny. (Magnus apparuit qui numquam malis ingemuit, numquam de fato suo questus est.)

SENECA, *Epistulæ ad Lucilium.* Epis. cxx, 13.

9
Rightly to be great
Is not to stir without great argument,
But greatly to find quarrel in a straw,
When honour's at the stake.

SHAKESPEARE, *Hamlet.* Act iv, sc. 4, l. 53.

10
He only is a great man who can neglect the applause of the multitude, and enjoy himself independent of its favour.

RICHARD STEELE, *The Spectator.* No. 172.

11
He is truly great that is little in himself, and that maketh no account of any height of honors.

THOMAS À KEMPIS, *De Imitatione Christi.* Bk. i, ch. 3.

Yea, all things good await
Him who cares not to be great,
But as he saves or serves the state.

TENNYSON, *Ode on the Death of the Duke of Wellington.* St. 3.

12
What is a great life? It is the dream of youth realized in old age. (Qu'est-ce qu'une grande vie? C'est un rêve de jeunesse réalisé dans l'âge mûr.)

ALFRED DE VIGNY. (LOUIS RATISBONNE, *Journal des Débats,* 4 Oct., 1863.)

II—Greatness: Apothegms

13
We have not the love of greatness, but the love of the love of greatness.

CARLYLE, *Essays: Characteristics.*

No sadder proof can be given by a man of his own littleness than disbelief in great men.

CARLYLE, *Heroes and Hero-Worship.* Lect. 1.

14
Great men are seldom over-scrupulous in the arrangement of their attire.

DICKENS, *Pickwick Papers.* Ch. 2.

The defects of great men are the consolation of dunces.

ISAAC D'ISRAELI, *Literary Character of Men of Genius: Preface.*

1

The great man who thinks greatly of himself, is not diminishing that greatness in heaping fuel on his fire.

ISAAC D'ISRAELI, *Literary Character of Men of Genius.* Ch. 15.

2

Great men have great faults.

THOMAS DRAXE, *Biblio. Scholas. Instruct.*, 127.

Only great men have a right to great faults. (Il n'appartient qu'aux grands hommes d'avoir des grands défauts.)

LA ROCHEFOUCAULD, *Maximes.* No. 190.

Great men too often have greater faults than little men can find room for.

W. S. LANDOR, *Imaginary Conversations: Diogenes and Plato.*

It is not by his faults, but by his excellences, that we must measure a great man.

G. H. LEWES, *On Actors and Acting.* Ch. 1.

3

To become a great man, it is necessary to be a great rascal.

CARDINAL GUILLAUME DUBOIS, preceptor to the Duc de Chartres, later the Regent Orleans. While he was archbishop of Cambrai, he was kicked five times by the regent, once each for the rogue, the pimp, the priest, the minister, and the archbishop. He stood waiting for another kick. "What are you waiting for?" the regent demanded. "I beg your pardon," answered Dubois, "I await the sixth as cardinal." The regent gave him both kick and red hat.

4

Every great man is a unique. The Scipionism of Scipio is precisely that part he could not borrow. Shakespeare will never be made by the study of Shakespeare. Do that which is assigned you, and you cannot hope too much or dare too much.

EMERSON, *Essays, First Series: Self-Reliance.*

5

The great man makes the great thing. Wherever Macdonald sits, there is the head of the table.

EMERSON, *Nature Addresses and Lectures: The American Scholar.* A misquotation from Sir Walter Scott. See 1504:13.

6

France has been considered thus far as the asylum of unfortunate monarchs: I wish that my capital should become the temple of great men.

FREDERICK THE GREAT, *Letter to Voltaire,* 7 Oct., 1743.

7

In short, whoever you may be,
To this conclusion you'll agree,
When everyone is somebodee,
Then no one's anybody!

W. S. GILBERT, *The Gondoliers.* Act ii.

8

No really great man ever thought himself so.

WILLIAM HAZLITT, *Table Talk.* Ser. ii, ch. 4.

On wind and wave the boy would toss,
Was great, nor knew how great he was.

S. T. COLERIDGE, *William Tell.*

9

He who comes up to his own idea of greatness, must always have had a very low standard of it in his mind.

WILLIAM HAZLITT, *The Plain Speaker: Whether Genius Is Conscious of Its Powers?*

10

Our grandeur lies in our illusions.

SAMUEL HOFFENSTEIN, *Grandeur.*

11

Great in the council, glorious in the field.

HOMER, *Iliad.* Bk. ii, l. 335. (Pope, tr.)

Great in glory, greater in arms. (O fama ingens, ingentior armis.)

VERGIL, *Æneid.* Bk. xi, l. 124.

Too huge for mortal tongue, or pen of scribe.

KEATS, *Hyperion.* Bk. i, l. 159.

Gallantly great.

SAMUEL PEPYS, *Diary,* 9 June, 1660.

12

The civilities of the great are never thrown away.

SAMUEL JOHNSON, *Works.* Vol. vi, p. 446.

13

Great men will always pay deference to greater.

W. S. LANDOR, *Imaginary Conversations: Southey and Porson.*

A great man knows the value of greatness; he does not hazard it, he will not squander it.

W. S. LANDOR, *Pericles and Aspasia: Aspasia to Cleone.*

14

He would be greater to posterity if he had been willing to be less great. (Major et apud posteros futuros, si minor esse voluisset.)

AUBROTUS MIRÆUS, *Elogia Belgica.* Of Erasmus.

15

And all the courses of my life do show
I am not in the roll of common men.

SHAKESPEARE, *I Henry IV.* Act iii, sc. 1, l. 42.

Greatness knows itself.

SHAKESPEARE, *I Henry IV.* Act iv, sc. 3, l. 74.

16

Yea, the elect o' the land.

SHAKESPEARE, *Henry VIII.* Act ii, sc. 4, l. 60.

The choice and master spirits of this age.

SHAKESPEARE, *Julius Cæsar.* Act iii, sc. 1, l. 163.

The foremost man of all this world.

SHAKESPEARE, *Julius Cæsar.* Act iv, sc. 3, l. 22.

17

But be not afraid of greatness: some are born great, some achieve greatness and some have greatness thrust upon 'em.

SHAKESPEARE, *Twelfth Night.* Act ii, sc. 5, l. 156.

18

In me there dwells
No greatness, save it be some far-off touch
Of greatness to know well I am not great.

TENNYSON, *Lancelot and Elaine,* l. 447.

III—Greatness: Praise
See also Name: Great Names

1
Great souls care only for what is great.
AMIEL, *Journal*, 17 Mar., 1868.

2
Burn to be great.
P. J. BAILEY, *Festus: Home.*

Desire of greatness is a godlike sin.
DRYDEN, *Absalom and Achitophel*. Pt. i, l. 372.

3
Great men are the guide-posts and landmarks in the State.
EDMUND BURKE, *Speech on American Taxation.*

Are not great Men the models of nations?
OWEN MEREDITH, *Lucile*. Pt. ii, canto vi, st. 29.

The names and memories of great men are the dowry of a nation.
VILLARI, *Savonarola and His Times.*

4
The heart ran o'er
With silent worship of the great of old!
The dead but sceptred sovereigns, who still rule
Our spirits from their urns.
BYRON, *Manfred*. Act iii, sc. 4.

5
I say great men are still admirable; I say there is, at bottom, nothing else admirable!
CARLYLE, *Heroes and Hero-Worship*. Lect. 1.

No great man lives in vain. The History of the world is but the Biography of great men.
CARLYLE, *Heroes and Hero-Worship*. Lect. 1.

Great lives never go out. They go on.
BENJAMIN HARRISON, *Address*, at cottage at Mt. McGregor where Grant died.

6
At whose sight, like the sun,
All others with diminished lustre shone.
CICERO, *Tusculanarum Quæstionum*. Bk. iii, ch. 18, sec. 39. (Yonge, tr.)

That constellation set, the world in vain
Must hope to look upon their like again.
COWPER, *Table Talk*, l. 660.

7
When the high heart we magnify,
And the clear vision celebrate,
And worship greatness passing by,
Ourselves are great.
JOHN DRINKWATER, *Abraham Lincoln.*

8
Fortune came smiling to my youth and wooed it,
And purple greatness met my ripened years.
DRYDEN, *All for Love*. Act i, sc. 1.

But thou art fair, and at thy birth, dear boy,
Nature and Fortune join'd to make thee great.
SHAKESPEARE, *King John*. Act iii, sc. 1, l. 51.

He was great ere fortune made him so.
DRYDEN, *Death of Oliver Cromwell*. St. 6.

9
Great men, great nations, have not been boasters and buffoons, but perceivers of the terror of life, and have manned themselves to face it.
EMERSON, *Conduct of Life: Fate.*

10
When divine souls appear, men are compelled by their own self-respect to distinguish them.
EMERSON, *Journals*, 1865.

Nature never sends a great man into the planet, without confiding the secret to another soul.
EMERSON, *Representative Men: Uses of Great Men.*

11
The greatest truths are the simplest; and so are the greatest men.
J. C. AND A. W. HARE, *Guesses at Truth.*

12
A great man, living for high ends, is the divinest thing that can be seen on earth.
G. S. HILLARD, *Life and Service of Webster.*

13
They would not be the great, were not the cause
They love so great that it must needs be lost.
MARY SINTON LEITCH, *Pity the Great.*

14
Great men stand like solitary towers in the city of God.
LONGFELLOW, *Kavanagh*. Ch. 1.

15
Great truths are portions of the soul of man;
Great souls are portions of eternity.
J. R. LOWELL, *Sonnets*. No. vi.

16
His the impartial vision of the great,
Who see not as they wish, but as they find.
J. R. LOWELL, *Under the Old Elm.*

17
A great man who neither sought nor shunned greatness, who found glory only because glory lay in the plain path of duty.
MACAULAY, *Essays: John Hampden.*

As long as he lived he was the guiding-star of a whole brave nation, and when he died the little children cried in the streets.
JOHN LOTHROP MOTLEY, *The Rise of the Dutch Republic*. Closing sentence, referring to William of Orange. A literal translation of the official report made by Greffier Corneille Aertsens to the magistracy of Brussels, 11 July, 1584: "Dont par toute la ville l'on est en si grand duil tellement que les petits enfants en pleurent par les rues."

18
No great intellectual thing was ever done by great effort; a great thing can only be done by a great man, and he does it without effort.
RUSKIN, *Pre-Raphaelitism.*

19
One can be helped by a great man, even when he is silent. (Et est aliquid, quod ex magno viro vel tacente.)
SENECA, *Epistulæ ad Lucilium*. Epis. xciv, 40.

20
He fought a thousand glorious wars,
And more than half the world was his,

And somewhere, now, in yonder stars,
Can tell, mayhap, what greatness is.
THACKERAY, *The Chronicle of the Drum.*

1
Dost thou look back on what hath been,
As some divinely gifted man,
Whose life in low estate began
And on a simple village green; . . .

And moving up from high to higher,
Becomes on Fortune's crowning slope
The pillar of a people's hope,
The centre of a world's desire?
TENNYSON, *In Memoriam.* Sec. lxiv.

2
Great let me call him, for he conquered me.
YOUNG, *The Revenge.* Act i, sc. 1.

IV—Greatness and Goodness

3
They're only truly great who are truly good.
GEORGE CHAPMAN, *Revenge for Honour.* Act v, sc. 2.

The essence of greatness is the perception that virtue is enough.
EMERSON, *Essays, First Series: Heroism.*

There was never yet a truly great man that was not at the same time truly virtuous.
BENJAMIN FRANKLIN, *The Busy-body.* No. 3.

4
He is at no end of his actions blest
Whose ends will make him greatest, and not best.
GEORGE CHAPMAN, *Tragedy of Charles, Duke of Byron.* Act v, sc. 1.

Greatness and goodness are not means, but ends!
Hath he not always treasures, always friends,
The good great man? three treasures, Love, and Light,
And Calm Thoughts, regular as infant's breath;
And three firm friends, more sure than day and night,
Himself, his Maker, and the Angel Death!
S. T. COLERIDGE, *The Good Great Man.*

5
Great and good are seldom the same man.
THOMAS FULLER, *Gnomologia.* No. 1752.

Too good for great things and too great for good.
THOMAS FULLER, *Worthies of England.*

6
Beyond the limits of a vulgar fate,
Beneath the Good how far—but far above the Great.
THOMAS GRAY, *The Progress of Poesy,* l. 122.

7
There have, undoubtedly, been bad great men; but inasmuch as they were bad, they were not great.
LEIGH HUNT, *Table Talk: Bad Great Men.*

8
For he that once is good, is ever great.
BEN JONSON, *The Forest: To Lady Aubigny.*

9
Goodness is not tied to greatness, but greatness to goodness.
THOMAS MOFFETT, *Healths Improvement,* 161. (1655) Quoted as a Greek proverb.

10
Ah God, for a man with heart, head, hand,
Like some of the simple great ones gone
For ever and ever by,
One still strong man in a blatant land,
Whatever they call him—what care I?—
Aristocrat, democrat, autocrat—one
Who can rule, and dare not lie!
TENNYSON, *Maud.* Pt. i, sec. 10, st. 5.

Dear Lord, but once before I pass away
Out of this Hell into the starry night
Where still my hopes are set in Death's despite,
Let one great man be good, let one pure ray
Shine through the gloom of this my earthly day
From one tall candle set upon a height.
ALFRED BRUCE DOUGLAS, *Lighten Our Darkness.*

11
The happy only are the truly great.
YOUNG, *Love of Fame.* Sat. vi, l. 300.

V—Greatness: Its Falsity

12
Great men are not always wise.
Old Testament: Job, xxxii, 9.

13
The more one approaches great men the more one finds that they are men. (Plus on approche les grands hommes, plus on trouve qu'ils sont hommes.)
LA BRUYÈRE, *Les Caractères.*

14
Dignity without pride was formerly the characteristic of greatness; the revolution in morals is completed, and it is now pride without dignity.
W. S. LANDOR, *Imaginary Conversations: Lopez Banos and Romero Alpuente.*

15
Great is advertisement! 'tis almost fate;
But, little mushroom men, of puff-ball fame,
Ah, do you dream to be mistaken great
And to be really great are just the same?
RICHARD LE GALLIENNE, *Alfred Tennyson.*

16
To those who walk beside them, great men seem
Mere common earth; but distance makes them stars.
GERALD MASSEY, *Hood,* l. 11.

The Great Man is a man who lives a long way off.
ELBERT HUBBARD, *The Philistine,* xii, 36.

17
Great men,
Till they have gain'd their ends, are giants in
Their promises, but, those obtain'd, weak pigmies
In their performance. And it is a maxim
Allow'd among them, so they may deceive,
They may swear any thing.
PHILIP MASSINGER, *The Great Duke of Florence.* Act ii, sc. 3.

18
Consider first, that great

Or bright infers not excellence.
MILTON, *Paradise Lost*. Bk. viii, l. 90.

1
But still the great have kindness in reserve:
He help'd to bury whom he help'd to starve.
POPE, *Epistle to Dr. Arbuthnot*, l. 247.

2
The great are only great because we are on our knees. Let us rise! (Les grands ne sont grands que parceque nous sommes à genoux; relevons nous.)
P. J. PROUDHON, *Révolutions de Paris: Motto*.

The great are only great because we carry them on our shoulders; when we throw them off they sprawl on the ground.
DUBOSCQ-MONTANDRÉ, *Point de l'Ovale*.

Great men have to be lifted upon the shoulders of the whole world, in order to conceive their great ideas, or perform their great deeds.
HAWTHORNE, *Journals*, 7 May, 1850.

3
He that of greatest works is finisher,
Oft does them by the weakest minister.
SHAKESPEARE, *All's Well that Ends Well*. Act ii, sc. 1, l. 139.

4
There is no such thing as a great man or a great woman. People believe in them, just as they used to believe in unicorns and dragons. The greatest man or woman is 99 per cent just like yourself.
BERNARD SHAW, *Radio Address*, 11 July, 1932.

Yet what are they, the learned and the great?
Awhile of longer wonderment the theme!
Who shall presume to prophesy *their* date,
Where nought is certain, save the uncertainty of fate?
HORACE AND JAMES SMITH, *Cui Bono?*

5
Ah vanity of vanities!
How wayward the decrees of fate are,
How very weak the very wise,
How very small the very great are!
THACKERAY, *Vanitas Vanitatum*. St. 9.

VI—Greatness: Great and Small

See also Man: Great and Small

6
I had seen the great, but I had not seen the small. (J'avais vu les grands, mais je n'avais pas vu les petits.)
ALFIERI, *Reason for Changing His Democratic Opinions*.

7
Pay not thy praise to lofty things alone.
The plains are everlasting as the hills.
P. J. BAILEY, *Festus: Home*.

8
"There's nothing great
Nor small," has said a poet of our day,
Whose voice will ring beyond the curfew of eve
And not be thrown out by the matin's bell.
E. B. BROWNING, *Aurora Leigh*. Bk. vii, l. 809.

There is no great and no small
To the soul that maketh all.
EMERSON, *History*.

To him no high, no low, no great, no small;
He fills, he bounds, connects and equals all!
POPE, *Essay on Man*. Epis. i, l. 279.

9
We find great things are made of little things
And little things go lessening, till at last
Comes God behind them.
BROWNING, *Mr. Sludge "The Medium."*

10
Squirrels for nuts contend, and, wrong or right,
For the world's empire kings ambitious fight.
What odds?—to us 'tis all the self-same thing,
A nut, a world, a squirrel, and a king.
CHARLES CHURCHILL, *Night*, l. 203.

If I cannot carry forests on my back,
Neither can you crack a nut.
EMERSON, *Fable*. The squirrel's retort to the mountain, which had called it, "Little Prig."

11
The big thieves lead away the little one. (Οἱ μεγάλοι κλέπται τὸν μικρὸν ἀπάγουσι.)
DIOGENES, when he saw the officials of a temple leading away a man who had stolen one of the sacred vessels. (DIOGENES LAERTIUS, *Diogenes*. Sec. 45.)

Alas! we see that, since the dawn of time,
The Small have suffered for the Great One's crime.
(Helas! on voit que de tout temps,
Les Petits ont pâti des sottises des Grands.)
LA FONTAINE, *Fables*. Bk. ii, fab. 4.

Small sacrileges are punished; great ones are celebrated by triumphs. (Nam sacrilegia minuta puniuntur, magna in triumphis feruntur.)
SENECA, *Epistulæ ad Lucilium*. Epis. lxxxvii, 24.

Great men may jest with saints: 'tis wit in them,
But in the less, foul profanation.
SHAKESPEARE, *Measure for Measure*. Act ii, sc. 2, l. 127.

Great men's vices are esteemed as virtues.
SHACKERLEY MARMION, *Holland's Leaguer*. Act i, sc. 1.

12
It is as easy to be great as to be small.
EMERSON, *Representative Men: Plato*.

13
The great and the little have need of one another.
THOMAS FULLER, *Gnomologia*. No. 4564.

There could be no great ones if there were no little ones.
THOMAS FULLER, *Gnomologia*. No. 4868.

14
The great would have none great and the little all little.
GEORGE HERBERT, *Jacula Prudentum*.

15
The "real, genuine, no-mistake Tom Thumbs"
Are little people fed on great men's crumbs.
O. W. HOLMES, *A Rhymed Lesson*, l. 310.

1
The use of great men is to serve the little men, to take care of the human race, and act as practical interpreters of justice and truth.
THEODORE PARKER, *Speeches: Death of John Quincy Adams.*

2
Those little creatures whom we are pleased to call the Great.
RICHARD SAVAGE, *Letter to a Friend.*

3
Why, man, he doth bestride the narrow world
Like a Colossus, and we petty men
Walk under his huge legs and peep about
To find ourselves dishonourable graves.
SHAKESPEARE, *Julius Cæsar.* Act i, sc. 2, l. 135.

4
Take physic, pomp;
Expose thyself to feel what wretches feel.
SHAKESPEARE, *King Lear.* Act iii, sc. 4, l. 33.

5
He that high growth on cedars did bestow,
Gave also lowly mushrumps leave to grow.
ROBERT SOUTHWELL, *Great and Small.*

6
Not that the heavens the little can make great,
But many a man has lived an age too late.
R. H. STODDARD, *To Edmund Clarence Stedman.*

7
So greatest and most glorious thing on ground
May often need the help of weaker hand.
SPENSER, *Faerie Queene.* Bk. ii, canto xi, st. 30.

VII—Greatness: Its Penalties

See also Fame: Its Penalties

8
Glory in excess is fraught with peril; 'tis the lofty peak which is smitten by heaven's thunderbolt. (Τὸ δ' ὑπερκότως κλύειν εὖ βαρύ· βάλλεται γὰρ ὄσσοις Διόθεν κάρανα.)
ÆSCHYLUS, *Agamemnon,* l. 468.

The god smites with his thunderbolt creatures of greatness more than common, nor suffers them to display their pride; but such as are little move him not to anger; and it is ever on the tallest buildings and trees that his bolts fall; for it is heaven's way to bring low all things of surpassing bigness.
ARTABANUS. (HERODOTUS, *History.* Bk. vii, sec. 10.)

'Tis the tall pine that is oftenest shaken by the wind; 'tis the lofty towers that fall with heaviest crash; 'tis the highest mountains that the lightning strikes.
(Sæpius ventis agitatur ingens
Pinus et celsæ graviore casu
Decidunt turres feriuntque summos
Fulgura montis.)
HORACE, *Odes.* Bk. ii, ode 10, l. 9.

What is highest is envy's mark; winds sweep the summits and thunderbolts sped by Jove's right hand seek out the heights. (Summa petit livor; perfluant altissima venti: Summa petunt dextra fulmina missa Jovis.)
OVID, *Remediorum Amoris,* l. 369.

Who are so high above,
Are near to lightning, that are near to Jove.
SAMUEL DANIEL, *Philotas.* Act iv, sc. 1.

9
Men in great place are thrice servants: servants of the sovereign or state, servants of fame, and servants of business. So as they have no freedom, neither in their persons, nor in their actions, nor in their times.
FRANCIS BACON, *Essays: Of Great Place.*

The rising unto place is laborious, and by pains men come to greater pains; and it is sometimes base; and by indignities, men come to dignities. The standing is slippery, and the regress is either a downfall, or at least an eclipse.
FRANCIS BACON, *Essays: Of Great Place.*

Glorious men are the scorn of wise men, the admiration of fools, the idols of parasites, and the slaves of their own vaunts.
FRANCIS BACON, *Essays: Of Vain-glory.*

10
Great heights are hazardous to the weak head.
ROBERT BLAIR, *The Grave,* l. 293.

11
None are completely wretched but the great,
Superior woes superior stations bring;
A peasant sleeps, while cares awake a king.
WILLIAM BROOME, *Epistle to Mr. Fenton.*

That pompous misery of being great.
WILLIAM BROOME, *On the War in Flanders.*

12
The fairest mark is easiest hit.
BUTLER, *Hudibras.* Pt. ii, canto i, l. 664.

Great marks are soonest hit.
THOMAS FULLER, *Gnomologia.* No. 1760.

13
Great men are too often unknown, or, what is worse, misknown.
CARLYLE, *Sartor Resartus.* Bk. i, ch. 3.

To be great is to be misunderstood.
EMERSON, *Essays, First Series: Self-Reliance.*

The world knows nothing of its greatest men.
HENRY TAYLOR, *Philip Van Artevelde.* Act i, sc. 5.

14
Man's Unhappiness, as I construe, comes of his Greatness; it is because there is an Infinite in him, which with all his cunning he cannot quite bury under the Finite.
CARLYLE, *Sartor Resartus.* Bk. ii, ch. 9.

15
They are raised on high that they may be dashed to pieces with a greater fall. (Tolluntur in altum Ut lapsu graviore ruant.)
CLAUDIAN, *In Rufinum.* Bk. i, l. 22.

Look high and fall low.
THOMAS FULLER, *Gnomologia.*

Who climbeth highest most dreadful is his fall.
JOHN LYDGATE, *Minor Poems,* p. 120. (c. 1430)

He that climbs highest has the greatest fall.
CYRIL TOURNEUR, *The Revenger's Tragedy*. Act v.

The bigger they come the harder they fall.
BOB FITZSIMMONS, just before his losing fight with James Jeffries, 25 July, 1902.

See also under FALL.

1
How dreary to be somebody!
How public, like a frog
To tell your name the livelong day
To an admiring bog!
EMILY DICKINSON, *Poems*. Pt. i, No. 27.

2
Glories
Of human greatness are but pleasing dreams,
And shadows soon decaying.
JOHN FORD, *The Broken Heart*. Act iii, sc. 5.

3
The mortal race is far too weak
Not to grow dizzy on unwonted heights.
(Das sterbliche Geschlecht ist viel zu schwach
In ungewohnter Höhe nicht zu schwindeln.)
GOETHE, *Iphigenia auf Tauris*. Act i, sc. 3.

4
How vain the ardour of the crowd,
How low, how little are the proud,
How indigent the great!
THOMAS GRAY, *An Ode on the Spring*.

5
Great men by small means oft are overthrown.
ROBERT HERRICK, *Hesperides*. No. 488. *See also under* TRIFLES.

6
To have a great man for a friend seems pleasant to those who have never tried it; those who have, fear it. (Dulcis inexpertis cultura potentis amici; Expertus metuit.)
HORACE, *Epistles*. Bk. i, epis. 18, l. 86.

Companionship with a powerful person is never to be trusted. (Nunquam est fidelis cum potente societas.)
PHÆDRUS, *Fables*. Bk. i, fab. 5, l. 1.

7
And seekest thou great things for thyself? seek them not.
Old Testament: Jeremiah, xlv, 5.

8
Greatness, with private men
Esteem'd a blessing, is to me a curse;
And we, whom, for our high births, they conclude
The only freemen, are the only slaves.
Happy the golden mean!
MASSINGER, *Great Duke of Florence*. Act i, sc. 1. *See also under* MODERATION.

9
If on the sudden he begin to rise:
No man that lives can count his enemies.
THOMAS MIDDLETON, *A Trick to Catch the Old One*. Act iii, sc. 1.

Whoso reaps above the rest,
With heaps of hate, shall surely be opprest.
SIR WALTER RALEIGH, *In Commendation of the Steele Glass*.

'Tis eminence makes envy rise,
As fairest fruits attract the flies.
SWIFT, *To Dr. Delany*.

With fame, in just proportion, envy grows;
The man that makes a character makes foes.
EDWARD YOUNG, *To Mr. Pope*. Epis. i, l. 28.

He who ascends to mountain-tops shall find
Their loftiest peaks most wrapt in clouds and snow;
He who surpasses or subdues mankind
Must look down on the hate of those below.
Though high *above* the sun of glory glow,
And far *beneath* the earth and ocean spread,
Round him are icy rocks, and loudly blow
Contending tempests on his naked head.
BYRON, *Childe Harold*. Canto iii, st. 45.

10
However exalted men are, they should fear those of low estate, because vengeance lies open to patient craft. (Quamvis sublimes debent humiles metuere, Vindicta docili quia patet sollertiæ.)
PHÆDRUS, *Fables*. Bk. i, fab. 28, l. 1.

11
Whatsoever people direful fate oppresses, the greatness of the chief men places them in danger, but the small folk escape notice in easy safety.
PHÆDRUS, *Fables*. Bk. iii, fab. 5, l. 11.

12
They who grasp the world,
The kingdom and the power and the glory,
Must pay with deepest misery of spirit,
Atoning unto God for a brief brightness.
STEPHEN PHILLIPS, *Herod*. Act iii.

13
Do you not know
When from the bottom of a well you've mounted
Up to the top, then there's the greatest danger,
Lest from the brink you topple back again?
PLAUTUS, *Miles Gloriosus*. Act iv, sc. 4, l. 14. (Thornton, tr.)

14
Painful preëminence! yourself to view
Above life's weakness, and its comforts too.
POPE, *Essay on Man*. Epis. iv, l. 267.

Ignobly vain and impotently great.
POPE, *Prologue to Addison's Cato*, l. 29.

15
Unless degree is preserved, the first place is safe for no one. (Ni gradus servetur, nulli tutus est summus locus.)
PUBLILIUS SYRUS, *Sententiæ*. No. 1042.

16
As if misfortune made the throne her seat,
And none could be unhappy but the great.
NICHOLAS ROWE, *The Fair Penitent: Prologue*.

17
The curse of greatness:
Ears ever open to the babbler's tale.

(Es ist der Fluch der Hohen, dass die Niedern Sich ihres offnen Ohrs bemächtigen.)
SCHILLER, *Die Braut von Messina*. Pt. i.

1
It is the practice of the multitude to bark at eminent men, as little dogs do at strangers.
SENECA, *De Vita Beata*. Sec. 19.

2
It is a rough road that leads to the heights of greatness. (Confragosa in fastigium dignitatis via est.)
SENECA, *Epistulæ ad Lucilium*. Epis. lxxxiv, 13.

3
There are various ways of falling, and the topmost point is the most slippery. (Varios casus et in sublimi maxime lubricos.)
SENECA, *Epistulæ ad Lucilium*. Epis. xciv, 74.

The top of honor is a slippery place.
JONATHAN MITCHEL, *Sermon: Of the Glory to Which God Hath Called Believers by Jesus Christ*. (1677)

4
I have touch'd the highest point of all my
greatness;
And, from that full meridian of my glory
I haste now to my setting.
SHAKESPEARE, *Henry VIII*. Act iii, sc. 2, l. 223.

Farewell! a long farewell, to all my greatness!
SHAKESPEARE, *Henry VIII*. Act iii, sc. 2, l. 351.

The soul and body rive not more in parting
Than greatness going off.
SHAKESPEARE, *Antony and Cleopatra*. Act iv, sc. 13, l. 5.

5
The mightier man, the mightier is the thing
That makes him honour'd, or begets him
hate;
For greatest scandal waits on greatest state.
SHAKESPEARE, *The Rape of Lucrece*, l. 1004.

When men of infamy to grandeur soar,
They light a torch to show their shame the more.
YOUNG, *Love of Fame*. Sat. i, l. 157.

6
They that stand high have many blasts to
shake them;
And if they fall, they dash themselves to
pieces.
SHAKESPEARE, *Richard III*. Act i, sc. 3, l. 259.

7
Grandeur has a heavy tax to pay.
ALEXANDER SMITH, *Dreamthorp: On the Writing of Essays*.

8
Censure is the tax a man pays to the public for being eminent.
SWIFT, *Thoughts on Various Subjects*.

Censure's to be understood
Th' authentic mark of the elect;
The public stamp Heav'n sets on all that's great
and good,
Our shallow search and judgment to direct.
SWIFT, *Ode to the Athenian Society*.

9
High stations tumult, but not bliss, create:
None think the great unhappy, but the great.
YOUNG, *Love of Fame*. Sat. i, l. 237.

GREECE AND THE GREEKS

See also Language: Greek

I—Greece: Apothegms

10
They will pay at the Greek Kalends. (Ad Kalendas Græcas soluturos.)
CÆSAR AUGUSTUS, of certain men who never paid their debts. (SUETONIUS, *Lives of the Cæsars: Augustus*. Ch. 87, sec. 1.) As the Greeks had no Kalends, the phrase was used of anything that could never take place.

It must be dated ad Græcas Kalendas.
NORTH, *Examen*, 477. (1740)

At the Greekish calends, or a day after doomsday.
JOHN PALSGRAVE, *Acolastus*. Sig. V1. (1540)

The judgment or decree shall be given out and pronounced at the next Greek Calends, that is, never.
RABELAIS, *Works*. Bk. i, ch. 20.

11
Most Greek among the Greeks, most Latin among the Latins. (Inter Græcos græcissimus inter Latinos latinissimus.)
ERASMUS, *Adagia: Dissimilitudo*. Of Rudolphus Agricola, i. e., Rœlof Huysmann.

12
Achilles' wrath, to Greece the direful spring
Of woes unnumber'd, heav'nly Goddess, sing!
HOMER, *Iliad*. Bk. i, l. 1. (Pope, tr.)

My faithful scene from true records shall tell,
How Trojan valour did the Greek excel;
Your great forefathers shall their fame regain,
And Homer's angry ghost repine in vain.
DRYDEN, *Troilus and Cressida: Prologue*.

13
He is a mad Greek, no less than a merry.
BEN JONSON. (CORYAT, *Crudities*, i, 17.)

14
When Greeks joyn'd Greeks, then was the tug
of war.
NATHANIEL LEE, *The Rival Queens*, Act iv, sc. 2. (1677) Constantly misquoted: "When Greek meets Greek, then comes the tug of war."

15
By trying the Greeks got into Troy. ('Ες Τρόιαν πειρώμενοι ἦλθον 'Αχαιοί.)
THEOCRITUS, *Idyls*. No. xv, l. 61.

16
I fear the Greeks, even when bringing gifts. (Timeo Danaos et dona ferentis.)
VERGIL, *Æneid*. Bk. ii, l. 49.

Learn now of the treachery of the Greeks, and from one know the wickedness of all. (Accipe nunc Danaum insidias et crimine ab uno.)
VERGIL, *Æneid*. Bk. ii, l. 65.

II—Greece: Her Glory

17
Cold is the heart, fair Greece, that looks on
thee,
Nor feels as lovers o'er the dust they loved;
Dull is the eye that will not weep to see

Thy walls defaced, thy mouldering shrines removed
By British hands.
BYRON, *Childe Harold.* Canto ii, st. 15.

Fair Greece, sad relic of departed worth!
Immortal, though no more; though fallen, great!
BYRON, *Childe Harold.* Canto ii, st. 73.

And yet how lovely in thine age of woe,
Land of lost gods and godlike men, art thou!
BYRON, *Childe Harold.* Canto ii, st. 85.

Where'er we tread 'tis haunted, holy ground.
BYRON, *Childe Harold.* Canto ii, st. 88.

1
The isles of Greece, the isles of Greece!
Where burning Sappho loved and sung,
Where grew the arts of war and peace,
Where Delos rose, and Phœbus sprung!
Eternal summer gilds them yet,
But all, except their sun, is set.
BYRON, *Don Juan.* Canto iii, st. 86.

The mountains look on Marathon—
And Marathon looks on the sea;
And musing there an hour alone,
I dream'd that Greece might still be free.
BYRON, *Don Juan.* Canto iii, st. 86.

Earth! render back from out thy breast
A remnant of our Spartan dead!
Of the three hundred grant but three,
To make a new Thermopylæ!
BYRON, *Don Juan.* Canto iii, st. 86.

You have the Pyrrhic dance as yet,
Where is the Pyrrhic phalanx gone?
Of two such lessons, why forget
The nobler and the manlier one?
You have the letters Cadmus gave—
Think ye he meant them for a slave?
BYRON, *Don Juan.* Canto iii, st. 86.

2
Such is the aspect of this shore;
'Tis Greece, but living Greece no more!
So coldly sweet, so deadly fair,
We start, for soul is wanting there.
BYRON, *The Giaour,* l. 90.

Clime of the unforgotten brave!
Whose land from plain to mountain-cave
Was Freedom's home or Glory's grave!
Shrine of the mighty! can it be
That this is all remains of thee?
BYRON, *The Giaour,* l. 103.

3
Again to the battle, Achaians!
Our hearts bid the tyrants defiance;
Our land, the first garden of Liberty's tree,
It has been, and shall yet be, the land of the free.
THOMAS CAMPBELL, *Song of the Greeks.*

4
Earth proudly wears the Parthenon,
As the best gem upon her zone.
RALPH WALDO EMERSON, *The Problem.*

5
Bozzaris! with the storied brave
Greece nurtured in her glory's time,
Rest thee—there is no prouder grave,
Even in her own proud clime.
FITZ-GREENE HALLECK, *Marco Bozzaris.*

6
Greece, taken captive, captured her savage conqueror, and carried her arts into clownish Latium. (Græcia capta ferum victorem cepit et artes Intulit agresti Latio.)
HORACE, *Epistles.* Bk. ii, epis. 1, l. 156.

7
The duration of the freedom and the glory of Greece was short. But a few such years are worth myriads of ages of monkish slumber, and one such victory as Salamis or Bannockburn is of more value than the innumerable triumphs of the vulgar herds of conquerors.
J. G. LOCKHART. (*Blackwood's Magazine.* Vol. i, No. 2.)

8
On desperate seas long wont to roam,
Thy hyacinth hair, thy classic face,
Thy Naiad airs, have brought me home
To the glory that was Greece
And the grandeur that was Rome.
EDGAR ALLAN POE, *To Helen.*

III—Greece: Athens

9
Ancient of days! august Athena! where,
Where are thy men of might? thy grand in soul?
Gone—glimmering through the dream of things that were:
First in the race that led to Glory's goal,
They won, and pass'd away—is this the whole?
BYRON, *Childe Harold.* Canto ii, st. 2.

10
I would rather live on a few grains of salt at Athens than dine like a prince at Craterus's table. (Ἀλλὰ βούλομαι ἐν Ἀθήναις ἅλα λείχειν ἢ παρὰ Κρατερῷ τῆς πολυτελοῦς τραπέζης ἀπολαύειν.)
DIOGENES, when Craterus invited him for a visit. (DIOGENES LAERTIUS, *Diogenes.* Bk. vi, sec. 57.) *See also under* NEW YORK.

11
Wherever literature consoles sorrow or assuages pain, wherever it brings gladness to eyes which fail with wakefulness and tears, and ache for the dark house and the long sleep, there is exhibited, in its noblest form, the immortal influence of Athens.
MACAULAY, *Essays: Mitford's History of Greece.*

This is the gift of Athens to man. . . . her intellectual empire is imperishable. And when those who have rivalled her greatness shall have shared her fate; . . . when the sceptre shall have passed away from England; when, perhaps, travellers from distant regions shall in vain labour to decipher on some mouldering pedestal the name of our proudest chief; shall hear savage hymns chanted to some misshapen idol over the ruined dome of our proudest temple; and shall see a single naked fisherman wash his nets in the river of the ten thousand masts; her influence and her glory will still survive, fresh in eternal youth, exempt from mutability and decay, immortal as the intellectual principle from which they derived their origin, and over which they exercise their control.

MACAULAY, *Essays: Mitford's History of Greece*. First published *Edinburgh Review*, Nov., 1824. *See also* ROME: HER CHURCH.

1
An Aristotle was but the rubbish of an Adam, and Athens but the rudiments of Paradise.

ROBERT SOUTH, *Sermons*. No. 2.

2
Athens, the eye of Greece, mother of arts
And eloquence.

MILTON, *Paradise Regained*. Bk. iv, l. 240.

GRIEF

See also Sorrow, Woe

I—Grief: Definitions

3
O brothers, let us leave the shame and sin
Of taking vainly, in a plaintive mood,
The holy name of *Grief!*—holy herein,
That, by the grief of One came all our good.

E. B. BROWNING, *Sonnets: Exaggeration*.

Grief may be joy misunderstood.

E. B. BROWNING, *De Profundis*. St. 21. *See also* JOY AND SORROW.

4
But grief should be the instructor of the wise.

BYRON, *Manfred*. Act i, sc. 1.

5
Grief is itself a medicine.

WILLIAM COWPER, *Charity*, l. 159.

Some griefs are medicinable.

SHAKESPEARE, *Cymbeline*. Act iii, sc. 2, l. 33.

Great griefs, I see, medicine the less.

SHAKESPEARE, *Cymbeline*. Act iv, sc. 2, l. 243.

6
Grief is the agony of an instant: the indulgence of grief the blunder of a life.

BENJAMIN DISRAELI, *Vivian Grey*. Bk. vi, ch. 7.

Why should I sorrow for what was pain?
A cherished grief is an iron chain.

STEPHEN VINCENT BENÉT, *King David*.

7
Things of greatest, so of meanest worth,
Conceiv'd with grief are, and with tears brought forth.

ROBERT HERRICK, *To Primroses Fill'd with Morning Dew*.

8
Grief is a species of idleness.

SAMUEL JOHNSON, *Letters*. Vol. i, p. 212.

9
Grief should not exceed proper bounds, but should be in proportion to the blow. (Flagrantior æquo Non debet dolor esse viri, nec vulnere major.)

JUVENAL, *Satires*. Sat. xiii, l. 11.

10
Of all the many evils common to all men, the greatest is grief. (Πολλῶν φύσει τοῖς πᾶσιν ἀνθρώποις κακῶν ὄντων μέγιστόν ἐστιν ἡ λύπη κακόν.)

MENANDER, *Fragments*. No. 668.

What philosophers can praise grief, the one thing most detestable of all? (Ægritudinem laudare, unam rem maxime detestabilem, quorum est tandem philosophorum?)

CICERO, *Tusculanarum Disputationum*. Bk. iv, ch. 25, sec. 55.

Grief is to man as certain as the grave:
Tempests and storms in life's whole progress rise,
And hope shines dimly through o'er-clouded skies;
Some drops of comfort on the favour'd fall,
But showers of sorrow are the lot of all.

GEORGE CRABBE, *The Library*, l. 641.

11
Nothing becomes offensive so quickly as grief. When fresh, it finds some one to console it, but when it becomes chronic, it is ridiculed, and rightly.

SENECA, *Epistulæ ad Lucilium*. Epis. lxviii, 13.

12
Oft have I heard that grief softens the mind
And makes it fearful and degenerate.

SHAKESPEARE, *II Henry VI*. Act iv, sc. 4, l. 1.

For Grief is proud, and makes his owner stoop.

SHAKESPEARE, *King John*. Act iii, sc. 1, l. 69.

13
Each substance of a grief hath twenty shadows,
Which shows like grief itself, but is not so;
For sorrow's eye, glazed with blinding tears,
Divides one thing entire to many objects.

SHAKESPEARE, *Richard II*. Act ii, sc. 2, l. 14.

14
Some grief shows much of love;
But much of grief shows still some want of wit.

SHAKESPEARE, *Romeo and Juliet*. Act iii, sc. 5, l 73.

15
Grief, that's beauty's canker.

SHAKESPEARE, *The Tempest*. Act i, sc. 2, l. 414.

II—Grief: Apothegms

16
Wherein is life sweet to him who suffers grief? (Τί γὰρ καλὸν ζῆν ᾧ βίος λύπας φερει.)

ÆSCHYLUS, *Oplæ Krisis*. Frag. 91.

17
Little griefs make us tender; great ones make us hard. (Les petits chagrins rendent tendre; les grands dur.)

ANDRÉ CHÈNIER.

18
Grief never mended no broken bones.

DICKENS, *Sketches by Boz: Gin-Shops*.

19
Those who have known grief seldom seem sad.

BENJAMIN DISRAELI, *Endymion*. Ch. 4.

1
The only thing grief has taught me is to know how shallow it is.
EMERSON, *Essays, Second Series: Experience.*

Some men are above grief and some below it.
EMERSON, *Natural History of Intellect: The Tragic.*

2
No blessed leisure for love or hope,
But only time for grief.
THOMAS HOOD, *The Song of the Shirt.*

3
The only cure for grief is action.
G. H. LEWES, *The Spanish Drama: Life of Lope De Vega.* Ch. 2.

4
If inward griefs were written on the brow, how many would be pitied who are now envied!
METASTASIO, *Giuseppe Riconosciuto.* Pt. i. See 220:20 for full quotation.

What private griefs they have, alas, I know not.
SHAKESPEARE, *Julius Cæsar.* Act iii, sc. 2, l. 216.

5
Alas, how easy it is, though sorrow has touched us all, to speak brave words in another's grief! (Ei mihi, quam facile est, quamvis hic contigit omnes, Alterius luctu fortia verba loqui.)
OVID, *Consolatio ad Liviam,* l. 9.

Every one can master a grief but he that has it.
SHAKESPEARE, *Much Ado About Nothing.* Act iii, sc. 2, l. 29.

Men
Can counsel and speak comfort to that grief
Which they themselves not feel; but, tasting it,
Their counsel turns to passion.
SHAKESPEARE, *Much Ado About Nothing.* Act v, sc. 1, l. 20.

6
I followed rest; rest fled and soon forsook me;
I ran from grief; grief ran and overtook me.
FRANCIS QUARLES, *Emblems.* Bk. ii, emb. 12.

7
Much is needed to bring us grief, little to console us.
JEAN ROSTAND, *Journal d'un Caractère.*

8
It is idle to grieve if you get no help from grief. (Supervacuum est dolore, si nihil dolendo proficias.)
SENECA, *Epistulæ ad Lucilium.* Epis. xcix, 6.

9
O, grief hath changed me since you saw me last.
SHAKESPEARE, *The Comedy of Errors.* Act v, sc. 1, l. 297.

His grief grew puissant and the strings of life
Began to crack.
SHAKESPEARE, *King Lear.* Act v, sc. 3, l. 216.

Alas, poor man! grief has so wrought on him,
He takes false shadows for true substances.
SHAKESPEARE, *Titus Andronicus.* Act iii, sc. 2, l. 79.

10
Grief makes one hour ten.
SHAKESPEARE, *Richard II.* Act i, sc. 3, l. 261.
See also under HOUR.

11
You may my glories and my state depose,
But not my griefs; still am I king of those.
SHAKESPEARE, *Richard II.* Act iv, sc. 1, l. 192.

Griefs of mine own lie heavy in my breast.
SHAKESPEARE, *Romeo and Juliet.* Act i, sc. 1, l. 192.

The grief is fine, full, perfect, that I taste,
And violenteth in a sense as strong
As that which causeth it.
SHAKESPEARE, *Troilus and Cressida.* Act iv, sc. 4, l. 3.

12
What's gone and what's past help,
Should be past grief.
SHAKESPEARE, *Winter's Tale.* Act iii, sc. 2, 223.

13
Winter is come and gone,
But grief returns with the revolving year.
SHELLEY, *Adonais.* St. 18.

14
Will was his guide, and grief led him astray.
SPENSER, *Faerie Queene.* Bk. i, canto i, st. 12.

Chawing the cud of grief and inward pain.
SPENSER, *Faerie Queene.* Bk. v, canto vi, st. 19.

15
You bid me, O queen, reopen unspeakable grief. (Infandum, regina, jubes renovare dolorem.)
VERGIL, *Æneid.* Bk. ii, l. 3.

New grief awakens the old.
THOMAS FULLER, *Gnomologia.* No. 3535.

III—Grief: Silent and Vocal

See also Mourning

16
It is dangerous to abandon one's self to the luxury of grief: it deprives one of courage, and even of the wish for recovery.
AMIEL, *Journal.* 29 Dec., 1871.

There is a solemn luxury in grief.
WILLIAM MASON, *The English Garden,* l. 25.

Weep on! and as thy sorrows flow,
I'll taste the luxury of woe.
THOMAS MOORE, *Anacreontic.*

17
We hear the rain fall, but not the snow.
Bitter grief is loud, calm grief is silent.
BERTHOLD AUERBACH, *On the Heights.*

18
I tell you, hopeless grief is passionless;
That only men incredulous of despair,
Half-taught in anguish, through the midnight air
Beat upward to God's throne in loud access
Of shrieking and reproach.
E. B. BROWNING, *Sonnets: Grief.*

Thank God, bless God, all ye who suffer not
More grief than ye can weep for. That is well—
That is light grieving!
E. B. BROWNING, *Tears.*

Oh, then indulge thy grief, nor fear to tell
The gentle source from whence thy sorrows flow!
Nor think it weakness when we love to feel,
Nor think it weakness what we feel to show.

WILLIAM COWPER, *To Delia: On Her Endeavouring to Conceal Her Grief at Parting.*

1
Nothing speaks our grief so well
As to speak nothing.

RICHARD CRASHAW, *Upon the Death of a Gentleman.*

2
Funeral grief loathes words.

THOMAS DEKKER, *The Honest Whore.* Pt. i, act i, sc. 1.

3
There is a sort of pleasure in indulging grief.

THOMAS FULLER, *Gnomologia.*

4
In all the silent manliness of grief.

GOLDSMITH, *The Deserted Village,* l. 384.

5
Small griefs find tongues: full casques are ever found
To give, if any, yet but little sound.
Deep waters noiseless are; and this we know,
That chiding streams betray small depth below.

ROBERT HERRICK, *To His Mistresse Objecting to Him Neither Toying or Talking.*

The saying is true "The empty vessel makes the greatest sound."

SHAKESPEARE, *Henry V.* Act iv, sc. 4, l. 73.

Vessels never give so great a sound as when they are empty.

BISHOP JOHN JEWEL, *Defense of the Apology for the Church of England.*

6
Words are less needful to sorrow than to joy.

HELEN HUNT JACKSON, *Ramona.* Ch. 17.

7
A solitary sorrow best befits
Thy lips, and antheming a lonely grief.

KEATS, *Hyperion.* Bk. iii, l. 5.

8
Oh, well has it been said, that there is no grief like the grief which does not speak!

LONGFELLOW, *Hyperion.* Bk. ii, ch. 2.

9
Suppressed grief suffocates. (Strangulat inclusus dolor.)

OVID, *Tristia.* Bk. v, eleg. 1, l. 63.

10
Great souls suffer in silence. (Doch grosse Seelen dulden still.)

SCHILLER, *Don Carlos.* Act i, sc. 4, l. 52.

11
Grief claimed his right, and tears their course.

SCOTT, *The Lady of the Lake.* Canto iii, st. 18.

12
The display of grief makes more demands than grief itself. How few men are sad in their own company. (Plus ostentatio doloris exigit quam dolor: quotus quisque sibi tristis est!)

SENECA, *Epistulæ ad Lucilium.* Epis. xcix, 16.

He grieves sincerely who grieves unseen. (Ille dolet vere qui sine teste dolet.)

MARTIAL, *Epigrams.* Bk. i, ep. 33, l. 4.

He grieves sore who grieves alone. (Il plaidoye beau qui plaidoye sans partie.)

J. DE LA VEPRIE, *Les Proverbes Communs.*

13
Light griefs can speak; but deeper ones are dumb. (Curæ leves loquuntur; ingentes stupent.)

SENECA, *Hippolytus,* l. 607.

Striving to tell his woes, words would not come;
For light cares speak, when mighty griefs are dumb.

SAMUEL DANIEL, *Complaint of Rosamond.* St. 114.

That grief is light which can take counsel. (Levis est dolor qui capere consilium potest.)

SENECA, *Medea,* l. 155.

14
The bravery of his grief did put me
Into a towering passion.

SHAKESPEARE, *Hamlet.* Act v, sc. 2, l. 79.

15
What, man! ne'er pull your hat upon your brows;
Give sorrow words: the grief that does not speak
Whispers the o'er-fraught heart and bids it break.

SHAKESPEARE, *Macbeth.* Act iv, sc. 3, l. 208.

True sorrow makes a silence in the heart.

ROBERT NATHAN, *A Cedar Box.*

16
Nor doth the general care
Take hold on me, for my particular grief
Is of so flood-gate and o'erbearing nature
That it engluts and swallows other sorrows
And it is still itself.

SHAKESPEARE, *Othello.* Act i, sc. 3, l. 54.

Let sorrow lend me words, and words express
The manner of my pity-wanting pain.

SHAKESPEARE, *Sonnets.* No. cxi.

I have
That honourable grief lodg'd here which burns
Worse than tears drown.

SHAKESPEARE, *Winter's Tale.* Act ii, sc. 1, l. 110.

17
Dark is the realm of grief: but human things
Those may not know of who cannot weep for them.

SHELLEY, *Otho: Fragment.*

18
To me so deep a silence portends some dread event; a clamorous sorrow wastes itself in sound.

SOPHOCLES, *Antigone,* l. 1251.

The silent man still suffers wrong.

UNKNOWN, *The Rock of Regard.* (1576)

See also under SORROW.

19
"Oh, but," quoth she, "great grief will not be told,

And can more easily be thought than said."
SPENSER, *Faerie Queene*. Bk. i, canto vii, st. 41.

1
People will pretend to grieve more than they really do, and that takes off from their true grief.
SWIFT, *Letter to Mrs. Dingley*, 14 Jan., 1712.

2
What shall be said? for words are thorns to grief.
SWINBURNE, *Atalanta in Calydon: Chorus.*

3
I sometimes hold it half a sin
To put in words the grief I feel;
For words, like Nature, half reveal
And half conceal the Soul within.
TENNYSON, *In Memoriam*. Pt. v, st. 1.

But, for the unquiet heart and brain,
A use in measured language lies;
The sad mechanic exercise,
Like dull narcotics, numbing pain.
TENNYSON, *In Memoriam*. Pt. v, st. 2.

IV—Grief: Companionship in

See also Misery Loves Company

4
It is only kindred griefs that draw forth our tears, and each weeps really for himself.
HEINE, *Wit, Wisdom, and Pathos: Italy.*

5
And of all the griefs that mortals share,
The one that seems the hardest to bear
Is the grief without community.
THOMAS HOOD, *Miss Kilmansegg: Her Misery.*

6
The sad relief
That misery loves—the fellowship of grief.
MONTGOMERY, *The West Indies*. Pt. iii.

7
For grief once told brings somewhat back of peace.
WILLIAM MORRIS, *The Earthly Paradise: Prologue: The Wanderers*, l. 72.

8
But then the mind much sufferance doth o'er-skip,
When grief hath mates.
SHAKESPEARE, *King Lear*. Act iii, sc. 6, l. 113.

9
Grief best is pleased with grief's society.
SHAKESPEARE, *The Rape of Lucrece*. St. 159.

One pain is lessen'd by another's anguish;
One desperate grief cures with another's languish.
SHAKESPEARE, *Romeo and Juliet*. Act i, sc. 2, l. 47.

10
No bond
In closer union knits two human hearts
Than fellowship in grief.
ROBERT SOUTHEY, *Joan of Arc*. Bk. i, l. 339.

11
Grief finds some ease by him that like doth bear.
SPENSER, *Daphnaida*, l. 67.

12
He oft finds med'cine who his grief imparts.
SPENSER, *Faerie Queene*. Bk. i, canto ii, st. 34.

V—Grief: Its Cure

13
The flood of grief decreaseth when it can swell no longer.
BACON, *Ornamenta Rationalia.*

The ocean has its ebbings—so has grief.
THOMAS CAMPBELL, *Theodric*, l. 510.

14
Since no grief ever born can ever die,
Thro' changeless change of seasons passing by.
WILLIAM MORRIS, *The Earthly Paradise: February*. St. 3.

15
See how time makes all grief decay.
ADELAIDE ANN PROCTER, *Life in Death.*

16
I shall grieve down this blow, of that I'm conscious:
What does man not grieve down?
SCHILLER, *Death of Wallenstein*. Act iii, sc. 9. (Coleridge, tr.)

17
Great grief does not of itself put an end to itself. (Magnus sibi ipse non facit finem dolor.)
SENECA, *Troades*, l. 786.

18
There is no grief which time does not lessen. (Nullus dolor est quem non longinquitas temporis minuat.)
SERVIUS SUPLICIUS. (CICERO, *Epistles*, iv, 5.)

19
This grief is crowned with consolation.
SHAKESPEARE, *Antony and Cleopatra*. Act i, sc. 2, 173.

O, if I could, what grief I should forget!
SHAKESPEARE, *King John*. Act iii, sc. 4, l. 50.

20
When remedies are past, the griefs are ended
By seeing the worst, which late on hopes depended.
SHAKESPEARE, *Othello*. Act i, sc. 3, l. 202.

GUILT

20a
It is better that ten guilty persons escape than that one innocent suffer.
BLACKSTONE, *Commentaries*. Vol. iv, ch. 27, p. 358.

21 God hath yoked to guilt
Her pale tormentor, misery.
BRYANT, *Inscription for the Entrance to a Wood. See also under* REMORSE.

22
Thank God, guilt was never a rational thing.
EDMUND BURKE, *Impeachment of Warren Hastings*, 17 Feb., 1788.

Men that are greatly guilty are never wise.
EDMUND BURKE, *Impeachment of Warren Hastings*, 30 May, 1794.

23
Guilt is present in the very hesitation, even though the deed be not committed. (In ipsa

dubitatione facinus inest, etiamsi ad id non pervenerint.)
CICERO, *De Officiis*. Bk. iii, ch. 8, sec. 37.

It is a great comfort to be free from guilt. (Vacare culpa magnum est solatium.)
CICERO, *Epistolæ ad Familiares*. Bk. vi, sec. 3.

1
Tell them the men that placed him here
Are friends unto the times;
But at a loss to find his guilt,
They can't commit his crimes.
DANIEL DEFOE, *A Hymn to the Pillory*.

2
Guilt has very quick ears to an accusation.
HENRY FIELDING, *Amelia*. Bk. iii, ch. 11.

3
There smiles no Paradise on earth so fair
But guilt will raise avenging phantoms there.
FELICIA HEMANS, *The Abencerrage*. Canto i, l. 133.

4
But Guilt was my grim Chamberlain
That lighted me to bed,
And drew my midnight curtains round,
With fingers bloody red!
THOMAS HOOD, *The Dream of Eugene Aram*.

5
How guilt, once harbour'd in the conscious breast,
Intimidates the brave, degrades the rest.
SAMUEL JOHNSON, *Irene*. Act iv, sc. 8.

6
The gods
Grow angry with your patience. 'Tis their care
And must be yours, that guilty men escape not.
BEN JONSON, *Catiline*. Act iii, sc. 5.

Let no guilty man escape.
ULYSSES S. GRANT, *Indorsement*, of letter concerning the Whiskey Ring, 29 July, 1875.

President Grant had just written across the back of a letter charging his own personal private secretary with colossal crookedness: "Let no guilty man escape"—and then proceeded to use all the mighty machinery of the Presidency to see that Orville E. Babcock did escape.
PAXTON HIBBEN, *The Peerless Leader*, p. 56.

7
It is so natural and easy to despise heavenly witnesses of our guilt, if only no mortal knows of it. (Tam facile et pronum est superos contemnere testes, Si mortalis idem nemo sciat!)
JUVENAL, *Satires*. Sat. xiii, l. 75.

8
Men's minds are too ready to excuse guilt in themselves. (Ingenia humana sunt ad suam cuique levandam culpam nimio plus facunda.)
LIVY, *History*. Bk. xxviii, ch. 25.

9
We mourn the guilty, while the guilt we blame.
DAVID MALLET, *The Siege of Damascus: Prologue. See also under* OFFENCE.

10
I am in,
And must go on; and since I have put off
From the shore of innocence, guilt be now my pilot.
PHILIP MASSINGER, *The Duke of Milan*. Act ii, sc. 1.

11
He that knows no guilt can know no fear.
MASSINGER, *The Great Duke of Florence*. Act iv, sc. 2.

12
These false pretexts and varnish'd colours failing,
Bare in thy guilt how foul must thou appear.
MILTON, *Samson Agonistes*, l. 901.

13
The informer vanishes when once she shares the guilt. (Tolliter index, Cum semel in partem criminis ipsa venit.)
OVID, *Ars Amatoria*. Bk. i, l. 389.

14
Guilt is always jealous.
JOHN RAY, *English Proverbs*.

So full of artless jealousy is guilt,
It spills itself in fearing to be spilt.
SHAKESPEARE, *Hamlet*. Act iv, sc. 5, l. 19.

15
Guilt is the source of sorrow, 'tis the fiend,
Th' avenging fiend, that follows us behind
With whips and stings.
NICHOLAS ROWE, *Fair Penitent*. Act iii, sc. 1.

16
Haste, holy Friar,
Haste, ere the sinner shall expire!
Of all his guilt let him be shriven,
And smooth his path from earth to heaven!
SCOTT, *The Lay of the Last Minstrel*. Canto v, st. 22.

17
And then it started like a guilty thing
Upon a fearful summons.
SHAKESPEARE, *Hamlet*. Act i, sc. 1, l. 148.

18
The lady doth protest too much, methinks.
SHAKESPEARE, *Hamlet*. Act iii, sc. 2, l. 240.

19
My stronger guilt defeats my strong intent.
SHAKESPEARE, *Hamlet*. Act iii, sc. 3, l. 40.

O wretched state! O bosom black as death!
O limed soul, that, struggling to be free,
Art more engaged!
SHAKESPEARE, *Hamlet*. Act iii, sc. 3, l. 67.

20
Suspicion always haunts the guilty mind.
SHAKESPEARE, *III Henry VI*. Act v, sc. 6, l. 11.

Terror haunts the guilty mind.
NATHANIEL LEE, *The Rival Queens*. Act v, sc. 1.

21
Guiltiness will speak
Though tongues were out of use.
SHAKESPEARE, *Othello*. Act v, sc. 1, l. 109. *See also under* MURDER.

1
What heavy guilt upon him lies!
How cursed is his name!
The ravens shall pick out his eyes,
And eagles eat the same.
Isaac Watts, *Obedience.*

GYPSIES, see Wanderlust

H

HABIT

See also Custom

I—Habit: Definitions

2
Men acquire a particular quality by constantly acting in a particular way.
Aristotle, *Nicomachean Ethics.* Bk. iii, ch. 5, sec. 10.

3
If you want to do something, make a habit of it; if you want not to do something, refrain from doing it.
Epictetus, *Discourses.* Bk. ii, ch. 18, sec. 4.

4
Habit is the approximation of the animal system to the organic. It is a confession of failure in the highest function of being, which involves a perpetual self-determination, in full view of all existing circumstances.
O. W. Holmes, *The Autocrat of the Breakfast-Table.* Ch. 7.

5
Habit is the enormous fly-wheel of society, its most precious conservative agent.
William James, *Psychology.* Vol. i, p. 121.

6
Habits change into character. (Abeunt studia in mores.)
Ovid, *Heroides.* Epis. xv, l. 83.

We sow our thoughts, and we reap our actions; we sow our actions, and we reap our habits; we sow our habits, and we reap our characters; we sow our characters, and we reap our destiny.
C. A. Hall.

Sow an act and you reap a habit. Sow a habit and you reap a character. Sow a character and you reap a destiny.
Charles Reade.

7
Habits are the daughters of action, but then they nurse their mother, and produce daughters after her image, but far more beautiful and prosperous.
Jeremy Taylor, *Sermons.* Vol. i, p. 181.

A thought,—good or evil,—an act, in time a habit,—so runs life's law.
Ralph Waldo Trine, *Life's Law.*

8
In ways and thoughts of weakness and of wrong,
Threads turn to cords, and cords to cables strong.
Isaac Williams, *The Baptistry.* Image 18.

9
Habit rules the unreflecting herd.
Wordsworth, *Ecclesiastical Sonnets.* Pt. ii, No. 28.

II—Habit: Apothegms

10
The old coachman likes to hear the whip.
George Borrow, *Lavengro.* Ch. 30.

11
Used to it, no doubt, as eels are to be flay'd.
Byron, *Don Juan.* Canto v, st. 7.

12
We are all, more or less, *des animaux d'habitude.*
Lord Chesterfield, *Letters,* 17 Sept., 1757.

Man is an animal of habits. (Der Mensch ist ein Gewohnheitsthier.)
Unknown. A German proverb.

13
Habit with him was all the test of truth;
"It must be right: I've done it from my youth."
George Crabbe, *The Borough.* Letter iii, l. 138.

14
A nail is driven out by another nail, habit is overcome by habit. (Clavus clavo pellitur, consuetudo consuetudine vincitur.)
Erasmus, *Diluculum.*

Habit is overcome by habit. (Consuetudo consuetudine vincitur.)
Thomas à Kempis, *De Imitatione Christi.* Bk. i, ch. 21, sec. 5.

15
Cultivate only the habits that you are willing should master you.
Elbert Hubbard, *The Philistine.* Vol. xxv, p. 62.

16
Fixed as a habit or some darling sin.
John Oldham, *A Letter from the Country to a Friend in Town.*

17
Use established habit. (Morem fecerat usus.)
Ovid, *Metamorphoses.* Bk. ii, l. 345.

18
Practice is everything. (Μελέτη τὸ παν.)
Periander. (Ausonius, *Ludus Septem Sapientum,* l. 215.)

Practice is the best of all instructors.
Publilius Syrus, *Sententiæ.* No. 439. The origin, perhaps, of the proverb: "Practice makes perfect."

19
The habit is not a trifle. ('Αλλὰ τό γ' ἔθος οὐ μικρόν.)
Plato, when a man whom he had rebuked for gambling protested that he played only for a trifle. (Diogenes Laertius, *Plato,* 38.)

Plato did once chide a child for playing with nuts, who answered him, "Thou chidest me for a small matter." "Habit" (replied Plato) "is no small matter."
Montaigne, *Essays.* Bk. i, ch. 22.

1
Evil habits, once settled, are more easily broken than mended. (Frangas enim citius quam corrigas quæ in parvum inducerunt.)
QUINTILIAN, *De Institutione Oratoria*. Bk. i, ch. 3, sec. 12.

2
For the ordinary business of life, an ounce of habit is worth a pound of intellect.
THOMAS B. REED. (W. A. ROBINSON, *Life*.)

3
But when the fox hath once got in his nose,
He'll soon find means to make the body follow.
SHAKESPEARE, *III Henry VI*. Act iv, sc. 7, l. 25.

To evil habit's earliest wile
Lend neither ear, nor glance, nor smile—
Choke the dark fountain ere it flows,
Nor e'en admit the camel's nose.
LYDIA H. SIGOURNEY, *The Camel's Nose*.

Lord! how they chided with themselves,
That they had let him in;
To see him grow so monstrous now,
That came so small and thin.
THOMAS HOOD, *The Wee Man*.

III—Habit: Its Power

4
That which has become habitual becomes, as it were, a part of our nature; in fact, habit is something like nature, for the difference between "often" and "always" is not great, and nature belongs to the idea of "always," habit to that of "often."
ARISTOTLE, *Rhetorica*. Bk. i, ch. 11, sec. 3.

Habit becomes a sort of second nature, which supplies a motive for many actions. (Consuetudine quasi alteram quandam naturam effici, qua impulsi multa faciant.)
CICERO, *De Finibus*. Bk. v, ch. 25, sec. 74.

Habit is second nature.
MONTAIGNE, *Essays*. Bk. iii, ch. 10.

For in physique this I find,
Usage is the second kind.
JOHN GOWER, *Confessio Amantis*. Bk. vi, l. 664. (c. 1390)

5
This restless world
Is full of chances, which by habit's power
To learn to bear is easier than to shun.
JOHN ARMSTRONG, *Art of Preserving Health*. Bk. ii, l. 474.

6
Great is the power of habit. (Consuetudinis magna vis est.)
CICERO, *Tusculanarum Disputationum*. Bk. ii, ch. 17, sec. 40.

7
Men's natures are alike; it is their habits that carry them far apart.
CONFUCIUS, *Analects*. Bk. xvii, ch. 2.

8
Nothing really pleasant or unpleasant subsists by nature, but all things become so by habit.
EPICTETUS, *Fragments*. No. 143.

9
There is nothing greater than habit. (Nil adsuetudine majus.)
OVID, *Ars Amatoria*. Bk. ii, l. 345.

10
Ill habits gather by unseen degrees,
As brooks make rivers, rivers run to seas.
OVID, *Metamorphoses*. Bk. xv, l. 155. (Dryden, tr.)

Small habits well pursued betimes
May reach the dignity of crimes.
HANNAH MORE, *Florio*. Pt. i.

11
Through habit you will be led into it again. (Consuetudine animus rursus te huc inducet.)
PLAUTUS, *Mercator*, l. 1001. (Act v, sc. 4.)

12
Habit is stronger than nature. (Consuetudo natura potentior est.)
QUINTUS CURTIUS RUFUS, *De Rebus Gestis Alexandri Magni*. Bk. v, sec. 5, l. 21.

For use almost can change the stamp of nature.
SHAKESPEARE, *Hamlet*. Act iii, sc. 4, l. 169.

Habit is ten times nature.
DUKE OF WELLINGTON, *Sayings*.

13
For me, who have spent my whole life in the practice of virtue, right conduct has become a habit. (Mihi, qui omnem ætatem in optumis artibus egi, bene facere jam ex consuetudine in naturam vortit.)
SALLUST, *Jugurtha*. Ch. 85, sec. 9.

14
How many unjust and wicked things are done from habit. (Quam multa injusta ac prava fiunt moribus!)
TERENCE, *Heauton Timoroumenos*, l. 839. (Act iv, sc. 7.)

15
To fall into a habit is to begin to cease to be.
MIGUEL DE UNAMUNO, *Tragic Sense of Life*, p. 206.

HAIR

I—Hair: Apothegms

16
And though it be a two-foot trout,
'Tis with a single hair pull'd out.
BUTLER, *Hudibras*. Pt. ii, canto iii, l. 13.

BEAUTY DRAWS WITH A SINGLE HAIR, *see* BEAUTY: Sec. vii.

17
Loose his beard, and hoary hair
Stream'd, like a meteor, to the troubled air.
THOMAS GRAY, *The Bard*. Pt. i, st. 2.

Like a red meteor in the troubled air.
THOMAS HEYWOOD, *Four Prentices of London*.

Shone like a meteor streaming to the wind.
MILTON, *Paradise Lost*. Bk. i, l. 537.

18
A hairy body, and arms stiff with bristles, give promise of a manly soul. (Hispida membra quidem et duræ per bracchia sætæ Promittunt atrocem animum.)
JUVENAL, *Satires*. Sat ii, l. 11.

1
Katterfelto, with his hair on end,
At his own wonders, wond'ring for his bread.
COWPER, *The Task*. Bk. iv, l. 86. *See also* FEAR: ITS EFFECTS.

2
When friends leave we're downhearted;
Hair knows what 'tis to be parted!
W. S. LAPSLEY, *Parting*.

3
A fine head of hair adds beauty to a good face, and terror to an ugly one.
LYCURGUS. (PLUTARCH, *Lives: Lycurgus*. Ch. 22, sec. 1.)

4
The very hairs of your head are all numbered.
New Testament: Matthew, x, 30.

5
Even a hair has its own shadow. (Vel capillus habet umbram suam.)
PUBLILIUS SYRUS, *Sententiæ*. No. 228.

Even a hair has its own shadow. (Etiam capillus unus habet umbram suam.)
BACON, *Ornamenta Rationalia*. No. 10.

I'll make a shadow for thee of my hairs.
SHAKESPEARE, *Venus and Adonis*, l. 191.

6
Long hair and short wit.
JOHN HEYWOOD, *Proverbs*. Pt. ii, ch. 7. The French form is: "Longues cheveux, courte cervelle."

TO SPLIT A HAIR, *see under* ARGUMENT.

7
Our heads are some brown, some black, some auburn, some bald.
SHAKESPEARE, *Coriolanus*. Act ii, sc. 3, l. 21.

8
Never shake Thy gory locks at me.
SHAKESPEARE, *Macbeth*. Act iii, sc. 4, l. 50.

II—Hair: Women's Hair

9
Those curious locks so aptly twin'd,
Whose every hair a soul doth bind.
THOMAS CAREW, *To A. L.: Persuasions to Love*.

10
Tresses, that wear
Jewels, but to declare
How much themselves more precious are.
RICHARD CRASHAW, *Wishes to His (Supposed) Mistress*.

11
For whom do you bind your hair, plain in your neatness? (Cui flavem religias comam Simplex munditiis?)
HORACE, *Odes*. Bk. i, ode 5, l. 4.

We are charmed by neatness: let not your locks be lawless. (Munditiis capimur: non sint sine lege capilli.)
OVID, *Ars Amatoria*. Bk. iii, l. 133.

Locks not wide-dispread,
Madonna-wise on either side her head.
TENNYSON, *Isabel*.

12
A chaste woman ought not to dye her hair yellow. (Τὴν γυναῖκα γὰρ τὴν σώφρον' οὐ δεῖ τὰς τρίχας ξανθὰς ποεῖν.)
MENANDER, *Fragments*. No. 610.

13
To sport with Amaryllis in the shade
Or with the tangles of Neæra's hair.
MILTON, *Lycidas*, l. 68.

14
She, as a veil, down to the slender waist
Her unadorned golden tresses wore
Dishevelled, but in wanton ringlets wav'd
As the vine curls her tendrils.
MILTON, *Paradise Lost*. Bk. iv, l. 304.

15
I warn you that no rude goat find his way beneath your arms, and that your legs be not rough with bristling hairs! (Admonui, ne trux caper iret in alas, Neve forent duris aspera crura pilis!)
OVID, *Ars Amatoria*. Bk. iii, l. 193.

16
Her head was bare,
But for her native ornament of hair;
Which in a simple knot was tied above,
Sweet negligence, unheeded bait of love!
OVID, *Metamorphoses: Meleager and Atalanta*, l. 68. (Dryden, tr.)

17
The meeting points the sacred hair dissever
From the fair head, for ever, and for ever.
POPE, *The Rape of the Lock*. Canto iii, l. 153.

18
Even nature herself abhors to see a woman shorn or polled; a woman with cut hair is a filthy spectacle, and much like a monster; . . . it being natural and comely to women to nourish their hair, which even God and nature have given them for a covering, a token of subjection, and a natural badge to distinguish them from men.
WILLIAM PRYNNE, *Histrio-Mastix*.

III—Hair: Blonde and Brunette

19
Dear, dead women, with such hair, too—what's become of all the gold
Used to hang and brush their bosoms?
ROBERT BROWNING, *A Toccata of Galuppi's*. St. 15.

20
When you see fair hair be pitiful.
GEORGE ELIOT, *The Spanish Gypsy*. Bk. iv, sc. ii, l. 107.

21
Beware of her fair hair, for she excels
All women in the magic of her locks;
And when she winds them round a young man's neck,
She will not ever set him free again.
GOETHE, *Faust: The Hartz Mountain*, l. 335. (Shelley, tr.)

22
It was brown with a golden gloss, Janette,
It was finer than silk of the floss, my pet;
'Twas a beautiful mist falling down to your wrist,
'Twas a thing to be braided, and jewelled, and kissed—

'Twas the loveliest hair in the world, my pet.
CHARLES GRAHAM HALPINE, *Janette's Hair.*

1
And yonder sits a maiden,
The fairest of the fair,
With gold in her garment glittering,
And she combs her golden hair.
HEINE, *The Lorelei.* St. 3.

2
The little wind that hardly shook
The silver of the sleeping brook
Blew the gold hair about her eyes,—
A mystery of mysteries.
So he must often pause, and stoop,
And all the wanton ringlets loop
Behind her dainty ear—emprise
Of slow event and many sighs.
W. D. HOWELLS, *Through the Meadow.*

3
Borgia, thou once wert almost too august
And high for adoration; now thou'rt dust.
All that remains of thee these plaits unfold,
Calm hair meandering in pellucid gold.
W. S. LANDOR, *On Lucretia Borgia's Hair.*

4
Sabrina fair,
Listen where thou art sitting,
Under the glassy, cool, translucent wave,
In twisted braids of lilies knitting
The loose train of thy amber-dropping hair.
JOHN MILTON, *Comus,* l. 859.

5
His . . . hyacinthine locks
Round from his parted forelock manly hung
Clust'ring, but not beneath his shoulders broad.
MILTON, *Paradise Lost.* Bk. iv, l. 300.

6
The red-gold cataract of her streaming hair.
STEPHEN PHILLIPS, *Herod.* Act i.

7
Golden hair, like sunlight streaming
On the marble of her shoulder.
J. G. SAXE, *The Lover's Vision.* St. 3.

8
Her hair is auburn, mine is perfect yellow:
If that be all the difference in his love,
I'll get me such a colour'd periwig.
SHAKESPEARE, *The Two Gentlemen of Verona.* Act iv, sc. 4, l. 194.

And her sunny locks
Hang on her temples like a golden fleece.
SHAKESPEARE, *The Merchant of Venice.* Act i, sc. 1, l. 169.

9
Thy fair hair my heart enchained.
SIR PHILIP SIDNEY, *Neapolitan Villanelle.*

10
Her long loose yellow locks like golden wire,
Sprinkled with pearl, and pearling flowers between,
Do like a golden mantle her attire.
SPENSER, *Epithalamion.* St. 9, l. 154.

Her golden hair was hanging down her back.
FELIX MCGLENNON. Title and refrain of popular song. (1884)

Gentlemen Prefer Blondes.
ANITA LOOS. Title of book. (1925).

11
Rosalind: His hair is of a good colour.
Celia: An excellent colour: your chestnut was ever the only colour.
SHAKESPEARE, *As You Like It,* iii, 4, 11.

12
But she is vanish'd to her shady home
Under the deep, inscrutable; and there
Weeps in a midnight made of her own hair.
THOMAS HOOD, *Hero and Leander.* St. 116.

13
Within the midnight of her hair,
Half-hidden in its deepest deeps.
BRYAN WALLER PROCTER, *The Pearl Weavers.*

14
Rising up,
Robed in the long night of her deep hair.
TENNYSON, *The Princess.* Pt. iv, l. 469.

IV—Hair: Gray

See also Age: Its Crown of Glory

15
My hair is gray, but not with years,
Nor grew it white
In a single night,
As men's have grown with sudden fears.
BYRON, *The Prisoner of Chillon,* l. 1.

Beauty, for confiding youth
Those shocks of passion can prepare
That kill the bloom before its time,
And blanch, without the owner's crime,
The most resplendent hair.
WORDSWORTH, *Lament of Mary Queen of Scots.* St. 6.

16
Then shall ye bring down my gray hairs with sorrow to the grave.
Old Testament: Genesis xlii, 38.

17
Since time a thousand cares
And griefs hath filed upon my silver hairs.
HERRICK, *Hesperides: The Parting Verse.*

18
'Tis not white hair that engenders wisdom.
(Οὐχ αἱ τρίχες ποιοῦσιν αἱ λευκαὶ φρονεῖν.)
MENANDER, *Fragments.* No. 639.

19
Bind up those tresses. O, what love I note
In the fair multitude of those her hairs!
Where but by chance a silver drop hath fallen.
SHAKESPEARE, *King John.* Act iii, sc. 4, l. 61.

V—Hair: Baldness

20
It is foolish to pluck out one's hair for sorrow, as if grief could be assuaged by baldness. (Stultissimum in luctu capillum sibi evellere quasi calvitio mæror levaretur.)
BION OF BORYSTHENES, *Sententiæ.* (CICERO, *Tusculanarum Disputationum.* Bk. iii, ch. 26, sec. 62.)

Oft tearing in his grief his unshorn hair. (Scindens dolore identidem intonsam comam.)
ACCIUS, *Fragment*. (Quoted by Cicero, *Tusculanarum Disputationum*. Bk. iii, ch. 26, sec. 62.)

Many were the hairs that he pulled from his head by the very roots. (Πολλὰς ἐκ κεφαλῆς προθελύμνους ἕλκετο χαίτας.)
HOMER, *Iliad*. Bk. x, l. 15.

1
A bald head is soon shaven.
THOMAS FULLER, *Gnomologia*. No. 836.

2
No stealth of time has thinned my flowing hair.
JAMES HAMMOND, *Elegies*. Elegy iv, st. 5.

3
He used to cut his hair, but now his hair has cut him.
THEODORE HOOK, of Planché. (THOMS, *Nineteenth Century*, Dec., 1881.)

4
He was as ballid as a cote.
LYDGATE, *Troy-Book*. Bk. ii, l. 4673. (1415)

Older than my father, more bald than a coot.
APULEIUS, *The Golden Ass*. Bk. v.

5
As incredulous as those who think none bald until they see his brains.
JOHN LYLY, *Euphues*, p. 267. (1580)

6
You manufacture, with the aid of unguents, a false head of hair, and your bald and dirty scalp is covered with painted locks. There is no need to call a hairdresser for your head. A sponge, Phœbus, would do the business better.
MARTIAL, *Epigrams*. Bk. vi, epig. 57.

You collect your straggling hairs on either side, Marinus, endeavoring to conceal the vast expanse of your shining bald pate by the locks which still grow on your temples. . . . Why not confess yourself an old man? . . . There is nothing more contemptible than a bald man who pretends to have hair.
MARTIAL, *Epigrams*. Bk. x, ep. 83.

7
Ugly is a field without grass, a plant without leaves, or a head without hair. (Turpis sine gramine campus, Et sine fronde frutex, et sine crine caput.)
OVID, *Ars Amatoria*. Bk. iii, l. 249.

8
There's no time for a man to recover his hair that grows bald by nature.
SHAKESPEARE, *The Comedy of Errors*. Act ii, sc. 2, l. 73.

Time himself is bald and therefore to the world's end will have bald followers.
SHAKESPEARE, *The Comedy of Errors*. Act ii, sc. 2, l. 108.

A curled pate will grow bald.
SHAKESPEARE, *Henry V*. Act v, sc. 2. l. 169.

HAND

I—Hand: Apothegms

9
Go—let thy less than woman's hand
Assume the distaff—not the brand.
BYRON, *The Bride of Abydos*. Canto i, st. 4.

10
This hand hath offended—this unworthy hand.
THOMAS CRANMER, putting into the fire his right hand, which had previously subscribed to the doctrines of Papal supremacy, as he was being burned at the stake, 1556.

11
Living from hand to mouth, soon satisfi'd.
DU BARTAS, *Devine Weekes and Workes*. Wk. ii, day 1, l. 122. (Sylvester, tr.) 1605.

All the means of his gettings is but from hand to mouth.
RICHARD BRATHWAITE, *Whimzies*, 143. (1631)

He lives from hand to mouth.
JOHN ARBUTHNOT, *History of John Bull*. Pt. i, ch. 3. (1712)

12
Let him value his hands and feet, he has but one pair.
EMERSON, *Conduct of Life: Fate*.

13
Help, Hands, for I have no Lands.
BENJAMIN FRANKLIN, *Poor Richard*, 1758.

No man can feel himself alone
The while he bravely stands
Between the best friends ever known
His two good, honest hands.
NIXON WATERMAN, *Interludes*.

14
With his red right hand. (Rubente dextera.)
HORACE, *Odes*. Bk. i, ode 2, l. 2.

His red right hand.
MILTON, *Paradise Lost*. Bk. ii, l. 174.

15
His hand will be against every man, and every man's hand against him.
Old Testament: Genesis, xvi, 12.

16
The voice is Jacob's voice, but the hands are the hands of Esau.
Old Testament: Genesis, xxvii, 22.

17
The wise hand doth not all that the foolish mouth speaks.
GEORGE HERBERT, *Jacula Prudentum*.

18
And then in the fulness of joy and hope,
Seem'd washing his hands with invisible soap
In imperceptible water.
THOMAS HOOD, *Miss Kilmansegg: Her Christening*.

19
Our hands have met, but not our hearts;
Our hands will never meet again.
THOMAS HOOD, *To a False Friend*.

20
And should not I spare Nineveh, that great city, wherein are more than six score thousand

persons that cannot discern between their right hand, and their left?
Old Testament: Jonah, iv, 11.

1
Hand-over-head, come who would.
HUGH LATIMER, *Sermons*, 284. (1555)

Hand over head pell mell upon them run.
MICHAEL DRAYTON, *Agincourt*. St. 204.

Hand-over-head: in a reckless, thoughtless manner.
ELWORTHY, *West Somerset Word-Book*, 316.

2
When Pilate saw that he could prevail nothing, but that rather a tumult was made, he took water, and washed his hands before the multitude, saying, I am innocent of the blood of this just person: see ye to it.
New Testament: Matthew, xxvii, 24.

3
Their fatal hands No second stroke intend.
MILTON, *Paradise Lost*. Bk. ii, l. 712.

4
They'll wondering ask how hands so vile
Could conquer hearts so brave.
THOMAS MOORE, *Weep On, Weep On.*

5
Every one with one of his hands wrought in the work, and with the other hand held a weapon.
Old Testament: Nehemiah, iv, 17.

6
What my right hand has dared to do, it does not dare to write. (Quod facere ausa mea est, non audet scribere, dextra.)
OVID, *Heroides*. Eleg. xii, l. 115.

7
It is the one nobility that a man's hands have shown no fear. (Una est nobilitas timidas non habuisse manus.)
PETRONIUS, *Fragments*. No. 98.

8
God looks with favor at pure, not full, hands. (Puras deus non plenas adspicit manus.)
PUBLILIUS SYRUS, *Sententiæ*. No. 544.

9
Put your hand quickly to your hat and slowly to your purse.
UNKNOWN. A Danish proverb.

10
They two are hand in glove.
JOHN RAY, *English Proverbs*, 347. (1678)

They both put their hands in one glove.
FULLER, *Gnomologia*. No. 4960. (1732)

As if the world and they were hand and glove.
COWPER, *Table Talk*, l. 174.

Connected as the hand and glove
Is, madam, poetry and love.
DAVID LLOYD, *Epistle to a Friend.*

11
One hand washeth the other. (Manus manum lavat.)
SENECA, *Apoclocyntosis*, ix, fin. A proverb found also in Petronius Arbiter, and derived from the Greek: *χεὶρ χεῖρα νίπτει, δάκτυλος τε δάκτυλον*, Hand washes hand, and finger finger.

One hand washeth the other, and both the face.
JOHN FLORIO, *First Fruites*. Fo. 34. (1578) Afterwards given in his Italian-English Dictionary, 1598, with the Italian: Una mano lava l'altra, ed ambedue lavano il volto.

This hand will rub the other.
THOMAS MIDDLETON, *The Phœnix*. Act i, sc. 1.

12
The hand which turns from the plough to the sword never objects to toil. (Nullum laborem recusant manus, quæ ad arma ab aratro transferuntur.)
SENECA, *Epistulæ ad Lucilium*. Epis. li, sec. 10.

13
My playfellow, your hand.
SHAKESPEARE, *Antony and Cleopatra*. Act iii, sc. 13, l. 125.

14
Let's go hand in hand, not one before another.
SHAKESPEARE, *The Comedy of Errors*. Act v, sc. 1, l. 425.

15
The hand of little employment hath the daintier sense.
SHAKESPEARE, *Hamlet*. Act v, sc. 1, l. 76.

16
A hand open as day.
SHAKESPEARE, *II Henry IV*. Act iv, sc. 4, l. 31.

Stout heart, and open hand.
SCOTT, *Marmion*. Canto i, st. 10.

17
There's no better sign of a brave mind than a hard hand.
SHAKESPEARE, *II Henry VI*. Act iv, sc. 2, l. 21.

His sweating palm
The precedent of pith and livelihood.
SHAKESPEARE, *Venus and Adonis*, l. 25.

And blessed are the horny hands of toil.
LOWELL, *A Glance Behind the Curtain*, l. 204.

She makes her hand hard with labour.
SIR THOMAS OVERBURY, *Characters: The Milkmaid.*

Hands were made for honest labour,
Not to plunder or to steal.
ISAAC WATTS, *The Thief.*

18
Let each man render me his bloody hand:
First, Marcus Brutus, will I shake with you.
SHAKESPEARE, *Julius Cæsar*. Act iii, sc. 1, l. 184.

Ferdinand: Here's my hand.
Miranda: And mine, with my heart in it.
SHAKESPEARE, *The Tempest*. Act iii, sc. 1, l. 39.

And there's a hand, my trusty fiere,
And gie's a hand o' thine.
ROBERT BURNS, *Auld Lang Syne.*

19
The hearts of old gave hands:
But our new heraldry is hands, not hearts.
SHAKESPEARE, *Othello*. Act iii, sc. 4, l. 46.

20
The gods hear men's hands before their lips.
SWINBURNE, *Atalanta in Calydon: Althea*. *See also* WORD AND DEED.

1
Let your left hand turn away what your right hand attracts.
Talmud. Sota, 47.

2
To join right hand to right hand. (Dextræ jungere dextram.)
VERGIL, *Æneid*. Bk. i, l. 408.

My right hand is to me as a god. (Dextra mihi deus.)
VERGIL, *Æneid*. Bk. x, l. 773.

3
Yet many hands together make light work.
WRIGHT, *Political Poems*, ii, 106. (1401)

Many hands make light work.
UNKNOWN, *How the Good Wife*. 1460. (HAZLITT, *Early Popular Poetry*, i, 188.) These are the earliest known uses in English of a proverb common to all languages.

II—Hand: Description

4
There is a hand that has no heart in it, there is a claw or paw, a flipper or fin, a bit of wet cloth to take hold of, a piece of unbaked dough on the cook's trencher, a cold clammy thing we recoil from, or greedy clutch with the heat of sin, which we drop as a burning coal. What a scale from the talon to the horn of plenty, is this human palm-leaf! Sometimes it is like a knife-shaped, thin-bladed tool we dare not grasp, or like a poisonous thing we shake off, or unclean member, which, white as it may look, we feel polluted by!
C. A. BARTOL, *The Rising Faith: Training*.

5
Your soft hand is a woman of itself,
And mine the man's bared breast she curls inside.
ROBERT BROWNING, *Andrea del Sarto*.

6
Even to the delicacy of their hand
There was resemblance, such as true blood wears.
BYRON, *Don Juan*. Canto iv, st. 45.

For through the South the custom still commands
The gentleman to kiss the lady's hands.
BYRON, *Don Juan*. Canto v, st. 105.

7
Her hand seemed milk in milk, it was so white.
WILLIAM DRUMMOND, *Of Phyllis*.

Twas a hand
White, delicate, dimpled, warm, languid, and bland.
The hand of a woman is often, in youth,
Somewhat rough, somewhat red, somewhat graceless, in truth;
Does its beauty refine, as its pulses grow calm,
Or as Sorrow has cross'd the life-line in the palm?
OWEN MEREDITH, *Lucile*. Pt. i, canto iii, sec. 14.

8
Hands, that the rod of empire might have sway'd,
Or wak'd to ecstasy the living lyre.
THOMAS GRAY, *Elegy Written in a Country Church-yard*, l. 47.

9
Pale hands I loved beside the Shalimar,
Where are you now? Who lies beneath your spell?
LAURENCE HOPE, *Kashmiri Song*.

Pale hands, pink-tipped, like lotus buds that float
On those cool waters where we used to dwell,
I would have rather felt you round my throat,
Crushing out life, than waving me farewell.
LAURENCE HOPE, *Kashmiri Song*.

10
Hands of invisible spirits touch the strings
Of that mysterious instrument, the soul,
And play the prelude of our fate.
LONGFELLOW, *The Spanish Student*. Act i, sc. 3.

11
His trembling hand had lost the ease,
Which marks security to please.
SCOTT, *The Lay of the Last Minstrel: Introduction*.

12
What if this cursed hand
Were thicker than itself with brother's blood,
Is there not rain enough in the sweet heavens
To wash it white as snow?
SHAKESPEARE, *Hamlet*. Act iii, sc. 3, l. 43.

Will all great Neptune's ocean wash this blood
Clean from my hand? No, this my hand will rather
The multitudinous seas incarnadine,
Making the green one red.
SHAKESPEARE, *Macbeth*. Act ii, sc. 2, l. 60.

All the perfumes of Arabia will not sweeten this little hand.
SHAKESPEARE, *Macbeth*. Act v, sc. 1, l. 58.

Worse than a bloody hand is a hard heart.
SHELLEY, *The Cenci*. Act v, sc. 2.

13
Without the bed her other fair hand was,
On the green coverlet; whose perfect white
Show'd like an April daisy on the grass,
With pearly sweat, resembling dew of night.
SHAKESPEARE, *The Rape of Lucrece*, l. 393.

14
See, how she leans her cheek upon her hand!
O, that I were a glove upon that hand,
That I might touch that cheek!
SHAKESPEARE, *Romeo and Juliet*. Act ii, 2, 23.

The white wonder of dear Juliet's hand.
SHAKESPEARE, *Romeo and Juliet*. Act iii, 3, 35.

O had the monster seen those lily hands
Tremble like aspen leaves, upon a lute.
SHAKESPEARE, *Titus Andronicus*. Act ii, 5, 45.

"Adieu," she cried, and waved her lily hand.
JOHN GAY, *Sweet William's Farewell*.

15
O, that her hand,
In whose comparison all whites are ink,
Writing their own reproach, to whose soft seizure

The cygnet's down is harsh and spirit of sense
Hard as the palm of ploughman.

SHAKESPEARE, *Troilus and Cressida*. Act i, sc. 1, l. 55.

1
She has certainly the finest hand of any woman in the world.

RICHARD STEELE, *The Spectator*. No. 113. Sir Roger is speaking of the widow.

HANGING

2
He who was knotting a halter for his neck, found gold and buried the halter in the treasure's place. But he who had hidden the gold, not finding it, fitted about his neck the halter which he had found.

AUSONIUS, *Epigrams*. No. xiv.

3
Three merry boys, and three merry boys,
And three merry boys are we,
As ever did sing in a hempen string
Under the gallows-tree.

BEAUMONT AND FLETCHER, *The Bloody Brother*. Act iii, sc. 2.

4
Hanging is too good for him, said Mr. Cruelty.

JOHN BUNYAN, *The Pilgrim's Progress*. Pt. i. (1678) *The Author's Apology*.

5
Were it not that they are loath to lay out money on a rope, they would be hanged forthwith, and sometimes die to save charges.

ROBERT BURTON, *Anatomy of Melancholy*. Pt. i, sec. ii, mem. 3, subs. 12.

6
No Indian prince has to his palace
More followers than a thief to the gallows.

BUTLER, *Hudibras*. Pt. ii, canto i, l. 273.

For next to that interesting job,
The hanging of Jack, or Bill, or Bob,
There's nothing so draws a London mob
As the noosing of very rich people.

THOMAS HOOD, *Miss Kilmansegg: Her Dream*.

7
The rope must not be mentioned in the house of a man who has been hanged.

CERVANTES, *Don Quixote*. Pt. i, ch. 25.

Mention not a halter in the house of him that was hanged.

GEORGE HERBERT, *Jacula Prudentum*. LORD CHESTERFIELD (*Letters*, 13 June, 1751) quotes the French original, "De ne jamais parler de cordes dans la maison d'un pendu."

8
A halter made of silk's a halter still.

COLLEY CIBBER, *Love in a Riddle*. Act ii, sc. 1.

9
See the hangman when it comes home to him!

DICKENS, *Barnaby Rudge*. Ch. 76.

Far better hang wrong fler than no fler.

DICKENS, *Bleak House*. Ch. 53.

10
They hanged a man today. . . . He died as game as if he was wan of th' Christyan martyrs instead iv a thief that'd hit his man wan crack too much. Saint or murdherer, 'tis little different whin death comes up face front.

FINLEY PETER DUNNE, *Mr. Dooley in the Hearts of his Countrymen: The Idle Apprentice*.

11
The humorous thief who drank a pot of beer at the gallows blew off the foam because he had heard it was unhealthy.

EMERSON, *Society and Solitude: Old Age*.

12
Yes, we must, indeed, all hang together, or, most assuredly, we shall all hang separately.

BENJAMIN FRANKLIN, *Retort*, to John Hancock, who, in his address to the Continental Congress, just previous to the signing of the Declaration of Independence, had said, "It is too late to pull different ways; the members of the Continental Congress must hang together."

13
They were suffered to have rope enough till they had haltered themselves.

FULLER, *Holy War*. Bk. v, ch. 7. (1639)

Give him rope enough and he'll hang himself.

CHARLOTTE BRONTË, *Shirley*. Ch. 3.

You shall never want rope enough.

RABELAIS, *Works*: Bk. v, *Prologue*.

14
He that's born to be hanged shall never be drowned.

THOMAS FULLER, *Gnomologia*. No. 2279.

He hath no drowning mark upon him; his complexion is perfect gallows.

SHAKESPEARE, *The Tempest*. Act i, sc. 1, l. 32.

15
And naked to the hangman's noose
The morning clocks will ring
A neck God made for other use
Than strangling in a string.

A. E. HOUSMAN, *A Shropshire Lad*. No. 9.

For they're hangin' Danny Deever, you can hear the Dead March play,
The regiment's in 'ollow square—they're hangin' him to-day;
They've taken of his buttons off an' cut his stripes away,
An' they're hangin' Danny Deever in the mornin'.

RUDYARD KIPLING, *Danny Deever*.

16
And folks are beginning to think it looks odd,
To choke a poor scamp for the glory of God.

J. R. LOWELL, *A Fable for Critics*, l. 492.

17
I will not leave you until I have seen you hanged. (Je ne te quitterai point que je ne t'aie vu pendu.)

MOLIÈRE, *Le Médecin Malgré Lui*. Act iii, sc. 9, l. 18.

18
I went out to Charing Cross to see Major-General Harrison hanged, drawn, and quar-

tered; which was done there, he looking as cheerful as any man could do in that condition.
SAMUEL PEPYS, *Diary*, 13 Oct., 1660.

1
Go and hang yourself. (Exige, ac suspende te.)
PLAUTUS, *Bacchides*, l. 903. (Act iv, sc. 8.)

Get yourself a fine thick rope and hang yourself. (Restim tu tibi cape crassam ac suspende te.)
PLAUTUS, *Persa*, l. 815. (Act v, sc. 2.)

Go, hang yourselves all!
SHAKESPEARE, *Twelfth Night*. Act iii, sc. 4, 136.

Hang yourself, brave Crillon: we have fought at Arques and you were not there; but I love you all the same. (Pends-toi, brave Crillon, nous avons combattu à Arques, et tu n'y étais pas.)
HENRY IV OF FRANCE, *Letter*, to his friend Crillon, the Ney of the sixteenth century. (VOLTAIRE, *Henriade*, viii, 109.) But Voltaire, that "inventor of history," changed the king's letter to suit himself, for it was written before Amiens, 20 Sept., 1597, not after Arques in 1589. Crillon had not joined Henry's party at that time. The sentence is engraved on a plaque at the Hotel de Crillon, Paris.

2
Now fitted the halter, now travers'd the cart,
And often took leave, but was loth to depart.
MATTHEW PRIOR, *The Thief and the Cordelier*.

Nay, stay, quoth Stringer, when his neck was in the halter.
JOHN RAY, *English Proverbs*, p. 82.

3
First Clown: What is he that builds stronger than either the mason, the shipwright, or the carpenter?
Second Clown: The gallows-maker; for that frame outlives a thousand tenants.
SHAKESPEARE, *Hamlet*. Act v, sc. 1, l. 47.

4
I'll see thee hanged first.
SHAKESPEARE, *I Henry IV*. Act ii, sc. 1, l. 44.

5
That would hang us, every mother's son.
SHAKESPEARE, *A Midsummer-Night's Dream*. Act i, sc. 2, l. 80.

6
A man is never undone till he be hanged.
SHAKESPEARE, *The Two Gentlemen of Verona*. Act ii, sc. 5, l. 5.

7
Light as a feather, hanging will ne'er kill him.
JAMES SHIRLEY, *The Wedding*. Act ii, sc. 3.

8
Hangman leads the dance.
JOHN STEPHENS, *Satyrical Essays*. Bk. ii, 28.

9
Nothing indeed remains for me but that I should hang myself. (Ad restim mihi quidem res redit planissume.)
TERENCE, *Phormio*, l. 686. (Act iv, sc. 4.)

10
I admire him, I frankly confess it; and when his time comes I shall buy a piece of the rope for a keepsake.
MARK TWAIN, *Following the Equator*. Of Cecil Rhodes.

11
Hanging was the worst use a man could be put to.
SIR HENRY WOTTON, *The Disparity Between Buckingham and Essex*.

12
Hanging and wiving go by destiny.
UNKNOWN, *School-House for Women* (1541); SHAKESPEARE, *The Merchant of Venice*, ii, 9. *See also under* MARRIAGE.

13
I fear hanging, whereto no man is hasty.
UNKNOWN, *Jack Juggeler*. (c. 1550)

There's no haste to hang true men.
HENRY PORTER, *Two Angry Women of Abington*. (1599)

II—Hanging: Some Euphemisms

14
As pretty a Tyburn blossom as ever was brought up to ride a horse foaled by an acorn.
BULWER-LYTTON, *Pelham*. Bk. iii, p. 296.

15
To be hang'd, to kick the wind. (Dar de' calci a Rouaio.)
JOHN FLORIO, *World of Words*. (1598)

16
You'll dance at the end of a rope without teaching.
THOMAS FULLER, *Gnomologia*. No. 6022.

17
At last he hath leaped at a daisy, with a halter about his neck.
ROBERT GREENE, *Black Book's Messenger: To the Reader*.

18
Your hap may be to wag upon a wooden nag.
HAZLITT, *Early Popular Poetry*, iii, 261. (c. 1550)

19
You'll hang on a cross to feed crows. (Non pasces in cruce corvos.)
HORACE, *Epistles*. Bk. i, epis. 16, l. 47.

20
You'll go up the ladder to bed.
JOHN RAY, *English Proverbs*. (1678)

21
I have been told by a fortune-teller that I should die in my shoes.
UNKNOWN, *Matchless Rogue*, 87. (1725)

Ye sharpers so rich, who can buy off the noose,
Ye honester poor rogues, who die in your shoes.
JOHN GAY, *Newgate's Garland*, l. 4.

22
If I swing by the string,
I shall hear the bell ring,
And then there's an end of poor Jenny.
UNKNOWN, *Newgate Song*.

HAPPINESS

See also Bliss; Delight; Joy; Pleasure; Virtue and Happiness

I—Happiness: Definitions

1
Happiness does away with ugliness, and even makes the beauty of beauty.
AMIEL, *Journal*, 3 April, 1865.

2
No one praises happiness as one praises justice, but we call it "a blessing," deeming it something higher and more divine than things we praise.
ARISTOTLE, *Nicomachean Ethics*. Bk. i, ch. 12, sec. 4.

Felicity is the perfect virtue in a perfect life.
ARISTOTLE. (TRAHERNE, *Centuries of Meditations*.)

3
Happiness is but a name.
ROBERT BURNS, *Lines Written in Friars-Carse Hermitage*.

4
A happy life consists in tranquillity of mind. (In animi securitate vitam beatam.)
CICERO, *De Natura Deorum*. Bk. i, sec. 20.

A happy life must be to a great extent a quiet life, for it is only in an atmosphere of quiet that true joy can live.
BERTRAND RUSSELL, *The Conquest of Happiness*, p. 67. *See also under* QUIET.

5
To fill the hour—that is happiness; to fill the hour, and leave no crevice for a repentance or an approval.
EMERSON, *Essays, Second Series: Experience*.

Just to fill the hour—that is happiness.
EMERSON, *Society and Solitude: Works and Days*.

6
I can find no meaning which I can attach to what is termed good, if I take away from it the pleasures obtained by taste, the pleasures which come from listening to music, the charm derived by the eyes from the sight of figures in movement, or other pleasures produced by any of the senses in the whole man.
EPICURUS, *Athens*, vii, 280. Quoted by Cicero, *Tusculanarum Disputationum*, iii, 18.

7
Whoever does not regard what he has as most ample wealth, is unhappy, though he be master of the world.
EPICURUS, *Fragments*. No. 474.

A man may rule the world and still be unhappy, if he does not feel that he is supremely happy.
SENECA, paraphrasing Epicurus. (*Epistulæ ad Lucilium*. Epis. ix, sec. 21.)

Unblest is he who thinks himself unblest. (Non est beatus, esse se qui non putat.)
SENECA, *Epistulæ ad Lucilium*. Epis., ix, sec. 21. Quoted from an unknown author.

He is not happy who does not think himself so.
PUBLILIUS SYRUS, *Sententiæ*. No. 984.

No man can enjoy happiness without thinking that he enjoys it.
SAMUEL JOHNSON, *The Rambler*. No. 150.

8
Now happiness consists in activity: such is the constitution of our nature: it is a running stream, and not a stagnant pool.
J. M. GOOD, *Book of Nature*. Ser. iii, lect. 7.

9
Happiness is a habit—cultivate it.
ELBERT HUBBARD, *Epigrams*.

The hardest habit of all to break
Is the terrible habit of happiness.
THEODOSIA GARRISON, *The Lake*.

10
Happiness is above all things the calm, glad certainty of innocence.
HENRIK IBSEN, *Rosmersholm*. Act iii.

It is only the spirit of rebellion which craves for happiness in this life. What right have we human beings to happiness?
HENRIK IBSEN, *Ghosts*. Act i.

Man is not born for happiness.
SAMUEL JOHNSON, *Works*. Vol. iv, p. 206.

We're born to be happy, all of us.
ALFRED SUTRO, *The Perfect Lover*. Act ii.

11
Happiness is the only good, reason the only torch, justice the only worship, humanity the only religion, and love the only priest.
R. G. INGERSOLL, *A Tribute to Eben Ingersoll*.

12
Happiness is not a reward—it is a consequence. Suffering is not a punishment—it is a result.
R. G. INGERSOLL, *The Christian Religion*.

Happiness is the legal tender of the soul.
INGERSOLL, *Liberty of Man, Woman and Child*.

13
Happiness consists in the multiplicity of agreeable consciousness.
SAMUEL JOHNSON. (BOSWELL, *Life*, 1766.)

Happiness is not found in self-contemplation; it is perceived only when it is reflected from another.
SAMUEL JOHNSON, *The Idler*. No. 41.

Happiness is nothing if it is not known, and very little if it is not envied.
SAMUEL JOHNSON, *The Idler*. No. 80.

14
We deem those happy who, from the experience of life, have learned to bear its ills, without being overcome by them.
JUVENAL, *Satires*. Sat. xiii, l. 20.

15
To be strong Is to be happy!
LONGFELLOW, *The Golden Legend*. Pt. ii, l. 731.

16
Happiness, to some elation;
Is to others, mere stagnation.
AMY LOWELL, *Happiness*.

1
Happiness is a by-product of an effort to make some one else happy.
GRETTA PALMER, *Permanent Marriage.*

Happiness and Beauty are by-products.
BERNARD SHAW, *Maxims for Revolutionists.*

2
Happiness is a way-station between too little and too much.
CHANNING POLLOCK, *Mr. Moneypenny.*

3
O happiness! our being's end and aim!
Good, Pleasure, Ease, Content! whate'er thy name,
That something still which prompts th' eternal sigh,
For which we bear to live, or dare to die.
POPE, *Essay on Man.* Epis. iv, l. 1.

Happiness is the goal of every normal human being. As it is given to few men to die happy, the best that man can hope and strive and pray for is momentary happiness during life, repeated as frequently as the cards allow.
G. J. NATHAN, *Testament of a Critic,* p. 6.

4
Happiness: a good bank account, a good cook, and a good digestion.
JEAN-JACQUES ROUSSEAU.

5
Happiness lies in the consciousness we have of it, and by no means in the way the future keeps its promises.
GEORGE SAND, *Handsome Lawrence.* Ch. 3.

6
Happiness is the only sanction of life; where happiness fails, existence remains a mad and lamentable experiment.
GEORGE SANTAYANA, *Little Essays,* p. 251.

7
Happiness is a wine of the rarest vintage, and seems insipid to the vulgar taste.
LOGAN PEARSALL SMITH, *Afterthoughts.*

8
Happiness is added Life, and the giver of Life.
HERBERT SPENCER, *Representative Government.*

9
He is not happy that knoweth not himself happy.
RICHARD TAVERNER, *Proverbs.* Fo. 51. (1539)

He is happy that knoweth not himself to be otherwise.
FULLER, *Gnomologia.* No. 1918. (1732)

10
The happiness of a man consisteth not in having temporal things in abundance, but a moderate competency sufficeth.
THOMAS À KEMPIS, *De Imitatione Christi.* Pt. i, ch. 22. *See also under* MODERATION.

11
What wisdom, what warning can prevail against gladness? There is no law so strong which a little gladness may not transgress.
H. D. THOREAU, *Journal,* 3 Jan., 1853.

12
The happiness of man consists in life, and life is in labor.
TOLSTOY, *What Is to Be Done?* Ch. 38.

13
Happiness is the shadow of things past,
Which fools shall take for that which is to be.
FRANCIS THOMPSON, *The Night of Forebeing.*

There is that in me—I do not know what it is—but I know it is in me. . . .
I do not know it—it is without name—it is a word unsaid;
It is not in any dictionary, utterance, symbol.
Something it swings on more than the earth I swing on.
To it the creation is the friend whose embracing awakes me. . . .
It is not chaos or death—it is form, union, plan—it is eternal life—it is Happiness.
WALT WHITMAN, *Song of Myself.* Sec. 50.

14
True happiness ne'er enter'd at an eye;
True happiness resides in things unseen.
YOUNG, *Night Thoughts.* Night viii, l. 1021.

II—Happiness: Apothegms

15
Happy, as it were, by report.
FRANCIS BACON, *Essays: Of Great Place.*

16
How soon a smile of God can change the world!
How we are made for happiness—how work
Grows play, adversity a winning fight!
ROBERT BROWNING, *In a Balcony.*

17
More happy, if less wise.
BYRON, *The Island.* Canto ii, st. 11.

Better to be happy than wise.
JOHN HEYWOOD, *Proverbs.* Pt. ii, ch. 6.

The days that make us happy make us wise.
JOHN MASEFIELD, *Biography.*

18
What is the worth of anything
But for the happiness 'twill bring?
RICHARD OWEN CAMBRIDGE, *Learning,* l. 23.

19
What is given by the gods more desirable than a happy hour? (Quid datur a divis felici optatius hora?)
CATULLUS, *Odes.* Ode lxii, l. 30.

20
Nature has given the opportunity of happiness to all, knew they but how to use it. (Natura beatis Omnibus esse dedit, si quis cognoverit uti.)
CLAUDIAN, *In Rufinum.* Bk. i, l. 215.

There is an hour wherein a man might be happy all his life, could he find it.
GEORGE HERBERT, *Jacula Prudentum.*

21
We ne'er can be Made happy by compulsion.
S. T. COLERIDGE, *The Three Graves.*

22
Gladness of the heart is the life of man, and

the joyfulness of a man prolongeth his days.
Apocrypha: Ecclesiasticus, xxx, 22.

As long liveth the merry man, they say,
As doth the sorry man—and longer by a day.
NICHOLAS UDALL, *Ralph Roister Doister*. Act i, sc. 1.

1
Happiness is not steadfast but transient. (Ὁ δ' ὄλβος οὐ βέβαιος, ἀλλ' ἐφήμερος.)
EURIPIDES, *Phœnissæ*, l. 558.

The highest happiness, the purest joys of life, wear out at last. (Das beste Glück, des Lebens schönste Kraft Ermattet endlich.)
GOETHE, *Iphigenia auf Tauris*. Act iv, sc. 5, l. 9.

Happiness too swiftly flies.
THOMAS GRAY, *Ode on a Distant Prospect of Eton College*.

2
Happy man, happy dole.
JOHN HEYWOOD, *Proverbs*. Pt. i, ch. 3. (1546)

Happy man be his dole.
SHAKESPEARE, *Merry Wives of Windsor*. Act iii, sc. 4, l. 67; BUTLER, *Hudibras*. Pt. i, canto iii.

3
One is never as happy or as unhappy as one thinks. (On n'est jamais si heureux ni si malheureux qu'on s'imagine.)
LA ROCHEFOUCAULD, *Maximes*. No. 49.

A man is never as unhappy as he thinks, nor as happy as he had hoped. (On n'est jamais si malheureux qu'on croit, ni si heureux qu'on avait espéré.)
LA ROCHEFOUCAULD, *Maximes Supprimées*, 572.

4
The rays of happiness, like those of light, are colorless when unbroken.
LONGFELLOW, *Kavanagh*. Ch. 13.

5
And feel that I am happier than I know.
MILTON, *Paradise Lost*. Bk. viii, l. 282.

6
The happiness of the blessed is no fugitive. (Δραπέτας οὐκ ἔστιν ὄλβος.)
PINDAR, *Fragments*. No. 134.

7
My cup runneth over.
Old Testament: Psalms, xxiii, 5.

8
I were but little happy, if I could say how much.
SHAKESPEARE, *Much Ado About Nothing*. Act ii, sc. 1, l. 318.

9
If it be my lot to crawl, I will crawl contentedly; if to fly, I will fly with alacrity; but, as long as I can avoid it, I will never be unhappy.
SYDNEY SMITH, *Table Talk*.

10
Be happy, but be happy through piety.
MADAME DE STAËL, *Corinne*. Bk. xx, ch. 3.

11
There is no duty we so much under-rate as the duty of being happy.
R. L. STEVENSON, *An Apology for Idlers*.

12
So long as we can lose any happiness, we possess some.
BOOTH TARKINGTON, *Looking Forward*, p. 172.

13
O thrice, four times happy they! (O terque quaterque beati.)
VERGIL, *Æneid*. Bk. i, l. 94.

Be happy ye, whose fortunes are already completed. (Vivite felices, quibus est fortuna peracta Jam sua.)
VERGIL, *Æneid*. Bk. iii, l. 493.

14
Happy days are here again,
The skies above are clear again.
Let us sing a song of cheer again,
Happy days are here again!
JACK YELLEN, *Happy Days Are Here Again*. Sung in a musical comedy, *Chasing Rainbows*. (1929) Roosevelt campaign song, 1936.

15
The spider's most attenuated thread
Is cord, is cable, to man's tender tie
On earthly bliss; it breaks at every breeze.
YOUNG, *Night Thoughts*. Night i, l. 178.

III—Happiness: How It Is Won

16
Inwardness, mildness, and self-renouncement do make for man's happiness.
MATTHEW ARNOLD, *Literature and Dogma*. Ch. 3.

The eternal *not ourselves* which makes for happiness.
MATTHEW ARNOLD, *Literature and Dogma*. Ch. 8.

17
Oh, make us happy and you make us good.
ROBERT BROWNING, *The Ring and the Book*. Pt. iv, l. 302

To be happy here is man's chief end,
For to be happy he must needs be good.
KIRKE WHITE, *To Contemplation*.

See also under GOODNESS.

18
Happiness seems made to be shared. (Le bonheur semble fait être partagé.)
CORNEILLE, *Notes par Rochefoucauld*. Also attributed to Racine.

All who joy would win
Must share it,—Happiness was born a twin.
BYRON, *Don Juan*. Canto ii, st. 172.

19
The best way to secure future happiness is to be as happy as is rightfully possible to-day.
CHARLES W. ELIOT, *The Happy Life*.

20
Human felicity is produced not so much by great pieces of good fortune that seldom happen, as by little advantages that occur every day.
BENJAMIN FRANKLIN, *Autobiography*. Ch. 1.

21
Who is the happiest of men? He who values the merits of others.

And in their pleasure takes joy, even as though 'twere his own.
GOETHE, *Distichs.*

1
Happiness in this world, when it comes, comes incidentally. Make it the object of pursuit, and it leads us a wild-goose chase, and is never attained.
HAWTHORNE, *Journals.* 21 Oct., 1852.

2
I stumbled upon happiness once
In a forgotten cove
Between impassable ranges.
DUBOSE HEYWARD, *I Stumbled Upon Happiness.*

3
Is it by riches or by virtue that men are made happy? (Utrumne Divitiis homines an sint virtute beati?)
HORACE, *Satires.* Bk. ii, sat. 6, l. 73.

It's pretty hard to tell what does bring happiness. Poverty an' wealth have both failed.
KIN HUBBARD, *Abe Martin's Broadcast,* p. 191.

4
The happy people are those who are producing something; the bored people are those who are consuming much and producing nothing.
DEAN W. R. INGE. (MARCHANT, *Wit and Wisdom of Dean Inge.* No. 76.)

The happiest people seem to be those who have no particular cause for being happy except that they are so.
DEAN W. R. INGE. (MARCHANT, *Wit and Wisdom of Dean Inge.* No. 223.)

5
Do you wish never to be sad? Live rightly! (Vis nunquam tristis esse? Recte vive!)
ISIDORUS, *Scriptura,* xiii, 223.

6
How to gain, how to keep, how to recover happiness is in fact for most men at all times the secret motive of all they do, and of all they are willing to endure.
WILLIAM JAMES, *Varieties of Religious Experience,* p. 78.

7
Happiness or misery usually go to those who have the most of the one or the other. (Le bonheur ou le malheur vont d'ordinaire à ceux qui ont le plus de l'un ou de l'autre.)
LA ROCHEFOUCAULD, *Maximes Posthumes.* No. 551.

8
You have to believe in happiness,
Or happiness never comes.
DOUGLAS MALLOCH, *You Have to Believe.*

9
A man's happiness is to do a man's true work. (Εὐφροσύνη ἀνθρώπου ποιεῖν τὰ ἴδια ἀνθρώπου.)
MARCUS AURELIUS, *Meditations.* Bk. viii, 26.

The happiness and unhappiness of the rational social animal depends not on what he feels, but on what he does.
MARCUS AURELIUS, *Meditations.* Bk. ix, sec. 16.

I sat there hard at work, happy as the day's long.
GEORGE BORROW, *Lavengro.* Bk. iii, ch. 12.

10
Fix'd to no spot is Happiness sincere;
'Tis nowhere to be found, or ev'rywhere;
'Tis never to be bought, but always free.
POPE, *Essay on Man.* Epis. iv, l. 15.

11
And if thou wouldst be happy, learn to please.
MATTHEW PRIOR, *Solomon.* Bk. ii, l. 266.

12
Obviously the right to be happy demands that people should in so far as is humanly possible learn what they wish to know, and exercise the talents and faculties which bring them the most pleasure.
DORA RUSSELL, *The Right to Be Happy,* p. 126.

13
You need never believe that a man can become happy through the unhappiness of another. (Non est quod credas quemquem fieri aliena infelicitate felicem.)
SENECA, *Epistulæ ad Lucilium.* Epis. xciv, 67.

14
We have no more right to consume happiness without producing it than to consume wealth without producing it.
BERNARD SHAW, *Candida.* Act i.

15
Ye seek for happiness—alas, the day!
Ye find it not in luxury nor in gold,
Nor in the fame, nor in the envied sway
For which, O willing slaves to Custom old,
Severe taskmistress! ye your hearts have sold.
SHELLEY, *The Revolt of Islam.* Canto xi, st. 17.

16
Happiness never lays its finger on its pulse. If we attempt to steal a glimpse of its features it disappears.
ALEXANDER SMITH, *Dreamthorp: On Death and the Fear of Dying.*

17
In every part and corner of our life, to lose oneself is to be gainer; to forget oneself is to be happy.
R. L. STEVENSON, *Memories and Portraits: Old Mortality.*

18
Be not glad but when thou hast done well.
THOMAS À KEMPIS, *De Imitatione Christi.* Pt. ii, ch. 6.

19
No man is bless'd by accident or guess;
True wisdom is the price of happiness.
YOUNG, *Love of Fame.* Sat. i, l. 191.

IV—Happiness: The Happy Man

20
'Twas a jolly old pedagogue, long ago,
Tall and slender, and sallow and dry;
His form was bent, and his gait was slow,
His long thin hair was white as snow,
But a wonderful twinkle shone in his eye.
And he sang every night as he went to bed,
"Let us be happy down here below;

The living should live, though the dead be dead,"
  Said the jolly old pedagogue long ago.

GEORGE ARNOLD, *The Jolly Old Pedagogue.*

1
She was a soft landscape of mild earth,
Where all was harmony, and calm, and quiet,
Luxuriant, budding; cheerful without mirth,
Which, if not happiness, is much more nigh it
Than are your mighty passions.

BYRON, *Don Juan.* Canto vi, st. 53.

2
There is in man a higher than love of happiness; he can do without happiness, and instead thereof find blessedness.

CARLYLE, *Sartor Resartus: The Everlasting Yea.*

3
The happiest heart that ever beat
Was in some quiet breast
That found the common daylight sweet,
And left to Heaven the rest.

JOHN VANCE CHENEY, *The Happiest Heart.*

The message from the hedge-leaves,
  Heed it, whoso thou art;
Under lowly eaves
  Lives the happy heart.

JOHN VANCE CHENEY, *The Hedge-bird's Message.*

4
I do not understand what the man who is happy wants in order to be happier. (Qui beatus est non intelligo quid requirat, ut sit beatior.)

CICERO, *Tusculanarum Disputationum.* Bk. v, ch. 8, sec. 23.

5
I've touched the height of human happiness,
And here I fix *nil ultra.*

JOHN FLETCHER, *The Prophetess.* Act iv, sc. 6.

6
Happy the man, who, innocent,
Grieves not at ills he can't prevent;
His skiff does with the current glide,
Not puffing pulled against the tide.
He, paddling by the scuffling crowd,
Sees unconcerned life's wager rowed,
And when he can't prevent foul play,
Enjoys the folly of the fray.

MATTHEW GREEN, *The Spleen,* l. 365.

7
The happy man is he that knows the world and cares not for it.

JOSEPH HALL. (INGE, *Wit and Wisdom: Preface.*)

8
Not him who possesses much, would one rightly call the happy man, but him who knows how to use with wisdom the blessings of the gods, and to endure hard poverty, who fears dishonor worse than death, and is not afraid to die for cherished friends or fatherland.

(Non possidentem multa vocaveris
Recte beatum; rectius occupat
Nomen beati, qui deorum
Muneribus sapienter uti

Duramque callet pauperiem pati
Peiusque leto flagitium timet,
Non ille pro caris amicis
Aut patria timidus perire.)

HORACE, *Odes.* Bk. iv, ode 9, l. 45.

9
Now the heart is so full that a drop overfills it,
We are happy now because God wills it.

LOWELL, *The Vision of Sir Launfal: Prelude.*

10
Some have much, and some have more,
Some are rich, and some are poor,
Some have little, some have less,
Some have not a cent to bless
Their empty pockets, yet possess
True riches in true happiness.

JOHN OXENHAM, *True Happiness.*

11
Happy the man, who, void of cares and strife,
In silken or in leathern purse retains
A Splendid Shilling.

JOHN PHILIPS, *The Splendid Shilling.*

12
The blest today is as completely so
As who began a thousand years ago.

POPE, *Essay on Man.* Epis. i, l. 75.

Heav'n to mankind impartial we confess,
If all are equal in their happiness:
But mutual wants this happiness increase;
All Nature's diff'rence keeps all Nature's peace.

POPE, *Essay on Man.* Epis. iv, l. 53.

13
That man is happy whom nothing makes less strong than he is; he keeps to the heights, leaning upon none but himself; for one who sustains himself by any prop may fall.

SENECA, *Epistulæ ad Lucilium.* Epis. xcii, sec. 2.

14
Mankind are always happy for having been happy; so that if you make them happy now, you make them happy twenty years hence by the memory of it.

SYDNEY SMITH, *Lectures: Benevolent Affections. See also under* REMEMBRANCE.

15
A happy man or woman is a better thing to find than a five-pound note.

R. L. STEVENSON, *An Apology for Idlers.*

16
If I have faltered more or less
In my great task of happiness;
If I have moved among my race
And shown no glorious morning face; . . .
Lord, thy most pointed pleasure take,
And stab my spirit broad awake;
Or, Lord, if too obdurate I,
Choose thou, before that spirit die,
A piercing pain, a killing sin,
And to my dead heart run them in!

R. L. STEVENSON, *The Celestial Surgeon.*

1
We think no greater bliss than such
To be as be we would,
When blessed none but such as be
The same as be they should.

WILLIAM WARNER, *Albion's England*. Bk. x, ch. 59, st. 68.

V—Happiness: The Greatest Happiness of the Greatest Number

2
That action is best which procures the greatest happiness for the greatest numbers; and that worst, which, in like manner, occasions misery.

FRANCIS HUTCHESON, *Inquiry into the Original of Our Ideas of Beauty and Virtue*: Pt. ii, sec. 3, *An Inquiry Concerning Moral Good and Evil*. (1720)

3
The greatest happiness of the greatest number. (La massima felicita divisa nel maggior numero.)

CESARE DI BONESANA BECCARIA, *Trattato dei Delitti e Delle Pene: Introduction*. (1764)

4
Priestley was the first (unless it was Beccaria) who taught my lips to pronounce this sacred truth—that the greatest happiness of the greatest number is the foundation of morals and legislation.

JEREMY BENTHAM, *Works*. Vol. x, p. 142. (1830) The real author of the phrase was Francis Hutcheson, as given above. Bentham was responsible for its general introduction into literature, never losing an opportunity to enforce it as the basic principle of legislation and morality.

It is the greatest good to the greatest number which is the measure of right and wrong.

JEREMY BENTHAM, *Works*. Vol. x, p. 142.

5
That truth once known, all else is worthless lumber;
The greatest pleasure of the greatest number.

BULWER-LYTTON, *King Arthur*. Bk. viii, l. 70.

6
No one can be perfectly happy till all are happy.

HERBERT SPENCER, *Social Statics*. Pt. iv, ch. 30, sec. 16. Last sentence.

The production of the greatest happiness . . . is the true end of morality.

HERBERT SPENCER, *Social Statics*. Ch. 31, sec. 2.

7
The greatest happiness of the greatest number is best secured by a prudent consideration for Number One.

BULWER-LYTTON, *Kenelm Chillingly*.

VI—Happiness: Near not Far

8
Wherefore, O mortal men, why seek you for your felicity abroad, which is placed within yourselves? (Quid igitur o mortales extra petitis intra uos positam felicitatem?)

BOETHIUS, *Philosophiæ Consolationis*. Bk. ii, sec. 4, l. 72.

9
To enjoy true happiness we must travel into a very far country, and even out of ourselves; for the pearl we seek for is not to be found in the Indian but in the Empyrean ocean.

SIR THOMAS BROWNE, *Christian Morals*. Pt. iii, sec. 11.

10
If happiness hae not her seat
An' centre in the breast,
We may be wise, or rich, or great,
But never can be blest.

ROBERT BURNS, *Epistle to Davie*. St. 5.

If solid happiness we prize,
Within our breast this jewel lies,
And they are fools who roam.

NATHANIEL COTTON, *The Fireside*.

Thus happiness depends, as Nature shows,
Less on exterior things than most suppose.

COWPER, *Table Talk*, l. 246.

11
Still to ourselves in every place consign'd,
Our own felicity we make or find.

GOLDSMITH, *The Traveller*, l. 431.

12
Happiness grows at our own firesides, and is not to be picked in strangers' gardens.

DOUGLAS JERROLD, *Jerrold's Wit: Happiness*.

13
The foolish man seeks happiness in the distance;
The wise grows it under his feet.

JAMES OPPENHEIM, *The Wise*.

14
The will of a man is his happiness. (Des Menschen Wille, das ist sein Glück.)

SCHILLER, *Wallenstein's Lager*, vii, 25.

15
Man is the artificer of his own happiness.

THOREAU, *Journal*, 21 Jan., 1838.

16
True happiness is to no spot confined.
If you preserve a firm and constant mind,
'Tis here, 'tis everywhere.

J. H. WYNNE, *History of Ireland*.

VII—Happiness: Its Dangers

17
What thing so good which not some harm may bring?
Even to be happy is a dangerous thing.

WILLIAM ALEXANDER, *Darius: Chorus*.

18
Real happiness is cheap enough, yet how dearly we pay for its counterfeit.

HOSEA BALLOU, *MS. Sermons*.

19
There comes
For ever something between us and what
We deem our happiness.

BYRON, *Sardanapalus*. Act i, sc. 2.

1
He who talks much of his happiness summons grief.
GEORGE HERBERT, *Jacula Prudentum.*

2
There is ev'n a happiness
That makes the heart afraid!
THOMAS HOOD, *Ode to Melancholy,* l. 90.

3
Nothing is happy in every way. (Nihil est ab omni Parte beatum.)
HORACE, *Odes.* Bk. ii, ode 16, l. 27.

4
You need never believe that anyone who depends upon happiness is happy. (Numquam credideris felicem quemquam ex felicitate suspensum.)
SENECA, *Epistulæ ad Lucilium.* Epis. xcviii, 1.

5
O, how bitter a thing it is to look into happiness through another man's eyes!
SHAKESPEARE, *As You Like It.* Act v, sc. 2, 48.

6
A lifetime of happiness! No man alive could bear it: it would be hell on earth.
BERNARD SHAW, *Man and Superman.* Act i.

7
Happy, alas! too happy. (Felix, heu! nimium felix.)
VERGIL, *Æneid.* Bk. iv, l. 657.

A man too happy for mortality.
WORDSWORTH, *Vaudracour and Julia,* l. 53.

8
Happiness is no laughing matter.
RICHARD WHATELY, *Apothegms.*

9
How sad a sight is human happiness,
To those whose thought can pierce beyond an hour!
YOUNG, *Night Thoughts.* Night i, l. 307.

With anxious care they labour to be glad.
YOUNG, *Love of Fame.* Sat. i, l. 226.

Beware what Earth calls happiness.
YOUNG, *Night Thoughts.* Night i, l. 341.

HARLOT, see Whore

HARMONY

See also Music

10
There are few such swains as he
Nowadays for harmonie.
WILLIAM BROWNE, *The Shepherd's Pipe.*

11
Where all was harmony, and calm and quiet.
BYRON, *Don Juan.* Canto vi, st. 53.

12
So in our life the different degrees
Render sweet harmony among these wheels.
DANTE, *Paradiso.* Canto vi, l. 127. (Cary, tr.)

13
Golden hours of vision come to us in this present life when . . . our faculties work together in harmony.
C. F. DOLE, *The Hope of Immortality.*

14
From Harmony, from heav'nly Harmony,
This universal Frame began:
From Harmony to Harmony
Through all the compass of the notes it ran,
The diapason closing full in Man.
DRYDEN, *A Song for St. Cecilia's Day.* St. 1.

15
By harmony our souls are swayed;
By harmony the world was made.
GEORGE GRANVILLE, *The British Enchanters.* Act i, sc. 1.

16
Many have held the soul to be
Nearly allied to harmony.
MATTHEW GREEN, *The Spleen,* l. 147.

17
I even think that sentimentally I am disposed to harmony. But organically I am incapable of a tune.
LAMB, *Essays of Elia: A Chapter on Ears.*

18
Seeing more harmony In her bright eye
Than now you hear.
RICHARD LOVELACE, *Orpheus to Beasts.*

19
The melting voice through mazes running,
Untwisting all the chains that tie
The hidden soul of harmony.
MILTON, *L'Allegro,* l. 142.

20
Ring out, ye crystal spheres! . . .
And with your ninefold harmony,
Make up full consort to th' angelic symphony.
MILTON, *Hymn on the Morning of Christ's Nativity.* St. 13.

And in their motions harmony divine
So smooths her charming tones, that God's own ear
Listens delighted.
MILTON, *Paradise Lost.* Bk. v, l. 625.

Sphere-born harmonious sisters, Voice and Verse.
MILTON, *At a Solemn Music.*

Just like the harmony of the spheres, that is to be admired and never heard.
DRYDEN, *Sir Martin Mar-All.* Act v, sc. 1.
See also MUSIC OF THE SPHERES.

This lesson teaching, which our souls may strike,
That harmonies may be in things unlike.
CHARLES LAMB, *Harmony in Unlikeness.*

21
Rest springs from strife, and dissonant chords beget
Divinest harmonies.
LEWIS MORRIS, *Love's Suicide. See also under* DISCORD.

22
The soft or drinking harmonies are the Ionian and the Lydian; they are termed "solute."
PLATO, *The Republic.* Bk. iii, sec. 399.

23
That air and harmony of shape express,
Fine by degrees, and beautifully less.
PRIOR, *Henry and Emma,* l. 432.

1
Harmony makes small things grow; lack of it makes great things decay. (Nam concordia parvæ res crescunt, discordia maximæ dilabuntur.)

SALLUST, *Jugurtha*. Ch. 10, sec. 6.

2
How irksome is this music to my heart!
When such strings jar, what hope of harmony?

SHAKESPEARE, *II Henry VI*. Act ii, sc. 1, l. 57.

3
Soft stillness and the night
Become the touches of sweet harmony.

SHAKESPEARE, *The Merchant of Venice*. Act v, sc. 1, l. 56.

4
Weave harmonies divine, yet ever new.

SHELLEY, *Prometheus Unbound*. Act iii, sc. 2.

5
No sound is uttered,—but a deep
And solemn harmony pervades
The hollow vale from steep to steep,
And penetrates the glades.

WORDSWORTH, *Composed Upon an Evening of Extraordinary Splendour and Beauty*, l. 21.

6
Rapt Cecilia, seraph-haunted Queen
Of Harmony.

WORDSWORTH, *Ecclesiastical Sonnets*. Pt. ii, 24.

HARP, see Music: Harp and Lute

HARVEST

See also Farming

7
Though placed in poorer soil, good seed can yet
Of its own nature bear a shining crop.
(Probæ etsi in segetem sunt deteriorem datæ
Fruges, tamen ipsæ suapte natura enitent.)

ACCIUS, *Annales*. Bk. i, sec. 105.

8
You mustn't spit on the harvest, as Papa Noah said.

BALZAC, *Les Paysans*. Ch. iv.

9
For now, the corn house filled, the harvest home,
Th' invited neighbors to the husking come;
A frolic scene, where work and mirth and play
Unite their charms to cheer the hours away.

JOEL BARLOW, *The Hasty Pudding*.

10
And the ripe harvest of the new-mown hay
Gives it a sweet and wholesome odour.

CIBBER, *Richard III* (altered). Act v, sc. 3.

11
He that observeth the wind shall not sow; and he that regardeth the clouds shall not reap.

Old Testament: Ecclesiastes, xi, 4.

In the morning sow thy seed, and in the evening withhold not thine hand.

Old Testament: Ecclesiastes, xi, 6.

12
Harvest comes not every day, though it comes every year.

THOMAS FULLER, *Gnomologia*. No. 1799.

Harvest will come, and then every farmer's rich.

THOMAS FULLER, *Gnomologia*. No. 1800.

13
Ye have . . . made a long harvest for a little corn.

JOHN HEYWOOD, *Proverbs*. Pt. i, ch. 12.

Ye two . . . have made a long harvest of a little corn, and have spent a great deal of money about a little matter.

NICHOLAS BRETON, *Works*, ii, 12.

But why . . . should I make so long a harvest of so little corn?

RICHARDSON, *Clarissa*. Bk. iv, 175. A proverb meaning to be tedious about trifles.

14
Fear not that I shall mar so fair an harvest
By putting in my sickle ere 'tis ripe.

JOHN HOME, *Douglas*. Act iii, sc. 1.

15
The harvest is past, the summer is ended, and we are not saved.

Old Testament: Jeremiah, viii, 20.

16
Lift up your eyes, and look on the fields; for they are white already to harvest.

New Testament: John, iv, 35.

17
The harvest truly is plenteous, but the labourers are few.

New Testament: Matthew, ix, 37.

18
Thou art a hard man, reaping where thou hast not sown, and gathering where thou hast not strewed.

New Testament: Matthew, xxv, 24; *Luke*, xix, 21.

19
That is a harvest unsatisfactory to the husbandman. (Illa est agricolæ messis iniqua suo.)

OVID, *Heroides*. Epis. xii, l. 48.

20
When corn is ripe 'tis time to reap.

MARTIN PARKER, *An Excellent New Medley*.

21
Live within your harvest. (Messe tenus propria vive.)

PERSIUS, *Satires*. Sat. vi, l. 25.

22
Autumn will heap the granaries high.
Whatever you reap, corn, wheat or clover,
Barley or rye, when autumn is over . . .
Whatever you reap you will be raising
Again and again.

ANNE PERSOV, *Whatever You Reap*.

Silver-tongued Hope promised another harvest.

POLLOK, *The Course of Time*. Bk. vii, l. 178.

23
He that hath a good harvest may be content with some thistles.

JOHN RAY, *English Proverbs*.

1
Who eat their corn while yet 'tis green,
At the true harvest can but glean.
SADI, *Gulistan: Introduction.* (Eastwick, tr.)

2
The seedsman
Upon the slime and ooze scatters his grain,
And shortly comes to harvest.
SHAKESPEARE, *Antony and Cleopatra.* Act ii, sc. 7, l. 26.

3
To glean the broken ears after the man
That the main harvest reaps.
SHAKESPEARE, *As You Like It.* Act iii, sc. 5, l. 102.

4
You sunburnt sicklemen, of August weary,
Come hither from the furrow and be merry.
SHAKESPEARE, *The Tempest.* Act iv, sc. 1, l. 134.

In harvest time, harvest-folk, servants and all,
Should make altogether good cheer in the hall.
THOMAS TUSSER, *Five Hundred Points of Good Husbandry: August's Husbandry.*

5
And thus of all my harvest-hope I have
Nought reaped but a weedy crop of care.
SPENSER, *The Shepheardes Calender: December,* l. 121.

6
Think, oh! grateful think
How good the God of Harvest is to you!
THOMSON, *The Seasons: Autumn,* l. 169.

7
Fancy with prophetic glance
Sees the teeming months advance; . . .
Sees the reddening orchard blow,
The harvest wave, the vintage flow.
THOMAS WARTON, *The First of April,* l. 97.

8
Once more the liberal year laughs out
O'er richer stores than gems of gold;
Once more with harvest song and shout
Is nature's boldest triumph told.
J. G. WHITTIER, *Harvest Hymn.*

HASTE

9
Haste is ever the parent of failure. (*'Επειχθῆναι μέν νῦν πᾶν πρῆγμα τίκτει σφάλματα.*)
ARTANABUS. (HERODOTUS, *History.* Bk. vii, 10.)

10
Make haste slowly. (Festina lente.)
CÆSAR AUGUSTUS. (SUETONIUS, *Twelve Cæsars: Augustus,* xxv, 4.) *See also under* PRUDENCE.

11
Quickly enough, if done well enough. (Sat cito, si sat bene.)
CATO. Quoted by ST. JEROME, *Epistles,* lxvi, 9.

Quickly enough if safely enough. (Sat cito si sat tuto.)
LORD ELDON, his favorite maxim. (TWISS, *Life of Eldon.* Vol. i, p. 46.)

12
There nis no workman, what-so-ever he be,
That may both worken well and hastily.
CHAUCER, *The Marchantes Tale,* l. 588.

13
He hasteth well that wisely can abide.
CHAUCER, *Troilus and Criseyde.* Bk. i, l. 956.

14
For hasty man ne wanteth never care.
CHAUCER, *Troilus and Criseyde.* Bk. iv, l. 1568. (c. 1374)

The hasty person never wants woe.
CHAPMAN, *Eastward Hoe.* Act v, sc. 1. (1605)

15
Whoever is in a hurry, shows that the thing he is about is too big for him. Haste and hurry are very different things.
LORD CHESTERFIELD, *Letters,* 20 Aug., 1749.

He is invariably in a hurry. Being in a hurry is one of the tributes he pays to life.
ELIZABETH BIBESCO, *Balloons.*

Let us leave hurry to slaves.
EMERSON, *Essays, Second Series: Manners.*

Though I am always in haste, I am never in a hurry.
JOHN WESLEY, *Letter,* 10 Dec., 1777.

16
He that mounts him on the swiftest hope,
Shall often run his courser to a stand.
COLLEY CIBBER, *Richard III* (altered). Act i, 1.

17
Sharp's the word!
COLLEY CIBBER, *The Rival Fools.* Act i.

18
With oars and sails. (Remis velisque.)
CICERO, *Tusculanarum Disputationum.* Bk. iii, ch. 11, sec. 25.

Add sails to your oars. (Remis adice vela tuis.)
OVID, *Remediorum Amoris,* l. 790.

19
In a moment, in the twinkling of an eye.
New Testament: I Corinthians, xv, 52.

I'll take my leave of the Jew in the twinkling of an eye.
SHAKESPEARE, *Merchant of Venice,* ii, 2, 170.

I'll be with you in the squeezing of a lemon.
GOLDSMITH, *She Stoops to Conquer.* Act i, sc. 2.

Instantly, in the twinkling of a bedstaff.
THOMAS SHADWELL, *Virtuoso.*

20
Nothing is more vulgar than haste.
EMERSON, *Conduct of Life: Behavior.*

Never lose your presence of mind, and never get hurried.
EMERSON, *Uncollected Lectures: Books.*

Nothing in haste but catching fleas. (Nichts mit Hast als Flöhe fangen.)
UNKNOWN. A German proverb.

21
Such persons as do make most haste in the beginning, have commonly worst speed toward the ending.
ERASMUS, *Apothegms.* (Udall, tr., 1542.)

The more haste the less speed.
JOHN HEYWOOD, *Proverbs.* Pt. i, ch. 2. (1546)

Her more than haste is mated with delays.
SHAKESPEARE, *Venus and Adonis,* l. 909. (1593)

The more haste, the worse speed.
SAMUEL ROWLEY, *Match at Midnight*. Act i. (1633)

The greater hurry the worst speed.
EDWARD WARD, *Hudibras Redivivus*. Pt. i, canto i, l. 23. (1705)

The more haste, ever the worst speed.
CHARLES CHURCHILL, *The Ghost*. Bk. iv, l. 1162. (1762)

1
I find this proverb true, that haste makes waste.
GEORGE GASCOIGNE, *Gascoigne's Memories*, iii, 7. (1575)

Haste makes waste.
JOHN HEYWOOD, *Proverbs*. Pt. i, ch. 2. (1546); GREENE, *Works*, ii, 28. (1583); BUTLER, *Hudibras*, i, iii, 1254. (1663); FRANKLIN, *Poor Richard*, May, 1753.

Haste makes waste, and waste makes want, and want makes strife between the good man and his wife.
JOHN RAY, *English Proverbs*, 151. (1678)

2
Haste and wisdom are things far odd.
JOHN HEYWOOD, *Proverbs*. Pt. i, ch. 2.

3
Ye make such tastings
As approve you to be none of the hastings.
JOHN HEYWOOD, *Proverbs*. Pt. i, ch. 11.

They are none of the hastings, who being slow and slack, go about business with no agility.
FULLER, *Worthies of England*. Vol. iii, p. 243.

4
Man is created of hastiness.
The Koran. Ch. 21.

Haste is of the devil.
Alleged to be from the *Koran*, but not to be found there.

5
Hasty and adventurous schemes are at first view flattering, in execution difficult, and in the issue disastrous.
LIVY, *History*. Bk. xxxv, ch. 32.

Nothing can be done at once hastily and prudently.
PUBLILIUS SYRUS, *Sententiæ*. No. 557.

6
Back to thy punishment,
False fugitive, and to thy speed add wings.
MILTON, *Paradise Lost*. Bk. ii, l. 699.

Stand not upon the order of your going,
But go at once.
SHAKESPEARE, *Macbeth*. Act iii, sc. 4, l. 118.

7
Too great haste leads us to error. (Le trop de promptitude à l'erreur nous expose.)
MOLIÈRE, *Sganarelle*. Sc. 12.

8
Stay a while, that we may make an end the sooner.
SIR AMYAS PAULET, when he saw too much haste in any matter. (FRANCIS BACON, *Apothegms*. No. 76.)

9
Ease and speed in doing a thing do not give the work lasting solidity or exactness of beauty.
PLUTARCH, *Lives: Pericles*.

10
Haste is slow. (Festinatio tarda est.)
QUINTUS CURTIUS RUFUS, *De Rebus Gestis Alexandri Magni*. Bk. ix, ch. 9, sec. 12.

11
Unless we hasten, we shall be left behind. (Nisi properamus, relinquemur.)
SENECA, *Epistulæ ad Lucilium*. Epis. cviii, 24.

12
Celerity is never more admired
Than by the negligent.
SHAKESPEARE, *Antony and Cleopatra*. Act iii, sc. 7, l. 25.

13
This sweaty haste
Doth make the night joint-labourer with the day.
SHAKESPEARE, *Hamlet*. Act i, sc. 1, l. 77.

14
Helter-skelter have I rode to thee,
And tidings do I bring.
SHAKESPEARE, *II Henry IV*. Act v, sc. 3, l. 99.

Then, horn for horn, they stretch an' strive;
Deil tak the hindmost, on they drive.
BURNS, *Address to a Haggis*. St. 4.

15
Be Mercury, set feathers to thy heels
And fly, like thought, from them to me again.
SHAKESPEARE, *King John*. Act iv, sc. 2, l. 174.

Swifter than arrow from the Tartar's bow.
SHAKESPEARE, *A Midsummer-Night's Dream*. Act iii, sc. 2, l. 101.

Bloody with spurring, fiery-red with haste.
SHAKESPEARE, *Richard II*. Act ii, sc. 3, l. 58.

As swift as swallow flies.
SHAKESPEARE, *Titus Andronicus*. Act iv. sc. 2, l. 172.

16
We must do something, and i' the heat.
SHAKESPEARE, *King Lear*. Act i, sc. 1, l. 312.

Not so hot.
SHAKESPEARE, *King Lear*. Act v, sc. 3, l. 66.

17
Haste still pays haste, and leisure answers leisure;
Like doth quit like, and measure still for measure.
SHAKESPEARE, *Measure for Measure*. Act v, sc. 1, l. 415.

18
Yea, marry, that's the eftest way.
SHAKESPEARE, *Much Ado About Nothing*. Act iv, sc. 2, l. 38.

The cause craves haste.
SHAKESPEARE, *The Rape of Lucrece*. St. 185.

19
He tires betimes that spurs too fast betimes.
SHAKESPEARE, *Richard II*. Act ii, sc. 1, l. 36.

Wisely and slow; they stumble that run fast.
SHAKESPEARE, *Romeo and Juliet*. Act ii, sc. 3, l. 94.

Too swift arrives as tardy as too slow.
SHAKESPEARE, *Romeo and Juliet*. Act ii, sc. 6, l. 15.

1
Yet, wilful man, he never would forecast
How many mischiefs should ensue his heedless haste.
SPENSER, *Faerie Queene*. Bk. i, canto iii, st. 34.

2
Allow time and moderate delay; haste manages all things badly. (Da spatium, tenuem moram; mala cuncta ministrat Impetus.)
STATIUS, *Thebais*. Bk. x, l. 704.

3
Hasty climbers quickly catch a fall.
UNKNOWN, *The Play of Stuckley*, l. 710.

4
And quickly hied he down the stair;
Of fifteen steps he made but three.
UNKNOWN, *Young Beichan and Susie Pye*.

HAT

5
"So," he said, "by the same hat
I can know if my wife be bad
To me by any other man;
If my flowers ever fade or fall,
Then doth my wife me wrong with all,
As many a woman can.
ADAM OF COBSHAM, *The Wright's Chaste Wife*.

6
So Britain's monarch once uncovered sat,
While Bradshaw bullied in a broad-brimmed hat.
JAMES BRAMSTON, *Man of Taste*. The reference is to John Bradshaw, who presided at the trial of Charles I.

It is the custom here for but one man to be allowed to stand covered.
CHARLES II, removing his hat when he saw that William Penn, during an audience, remained covered. Penn's reply is said to have been, "Friend Charles, keep thy hat on!"

7
Here's your hat, what's your hurry?
BARTLEY C. COSTELLO. Title and refrain of popular song. (1904)

8
A hat not much the worse for wear.
COWPER, *John Gilpin*. St. 46.

Far happier is thy head that wears
That hat without a crown.
THOMAS HOOD, *Ode: Clapham Academy*.

9
"If I knew as little of life as that, I'd eat my hat and swallow the buckle whole," said the clerical gentleman.
DICKENS, *Pickwick Papers*. Ch. 42.

10
Pull down thy hat on the windy side.
THOMAS FULLER, *Gnomologia*. No. 3978.

11
I live by pulling off the hat.
MATTHEW GREEN, *On Barclay's Apology*.

12
The hat is the *ultimatum moriens* of respectability.
O. W. HOLMES, *The Autocrat of the Breakfast-Table*. Ch. 8.

Virtue may flourish in an old cravat,
But man and nature scorn the shocking hat.
O. W. HOLMES, *A Rhymed Lesson*, l. 452.

13
It cannot be,—it is,—it is,—
A hat is going round.
O. W. HOLMES, *The Music-Grinders*.

14
Come, my old hat, my steps attend!
However wags may sneer and scoff,
My castor still shall be my friend,
For I'll not be a caster off. . . .
Black, rusty grey, devoid of pelt,
A shocking shape or beaten flat,
Still there are joys that may be felt
All round my hat, all round my hat
THOMAS HOOD, *All Round My Hat*. St. 1.

All round my hat I wore a green ribbon.
UNKNOWN, refrain of song, c. 1830. "Who's your hatter?" "What, the same old hat?" "What a shocking bad hat!" were English jokes of the same period.

15
The Quaker loves an ample brim
A hat that bows to no salaam;
And dear the beaver is to him
As if it never made a dam.
THOMAS HOOD, *All Round My Hat*. St. 3.

It's odd how hats expand their brims as riper years invade,
As if when life had reached its noon it wanted them for shade!
O. W. HOLMES, *Nux Postcœnatica*. St. 3.

16
A sermon on a hat: " 'The hat, my boy, the hat, whatever it may be, is in itself nothing—makes nothing, goes for nothing; but, be sure of it, everything in life depends upon the cock of the hat.' For how many men—we put it to your own experience, reader—have made their way through the thronging crowds that beset fortune, not by the innate worth and excellence of their hats, but simply, as Sampson Piebald has it, by 'the cock of their hats'? The cock's all."
DOUGLAS JERROLD, *The Romance of a Keyhole*. Ch. 3.

17
As with my hat upon my head
I walk'd along the Strand,
I there did meet another man
With his hat in his hand.
SAMUEL JOHNSON, *Johnsoniana*. A parody on Percy's *Hermit of Warkworth*.

18
bumped
off the running board of existence
to furnish plumage
for a lady's hat
DON MARQUIS, *unjust*.

1
Put your bonnet to its right use; 'tis for the head.

SHAKESPEARE, *Hamlet*. Act v, sc. 2, l. 95.

2
Their hats are pluck'd about their ears.

SHAKESPEARE, *Julius Cæsar*. Act ii, sc. 1, l. 73.

With your hat penthouse-like o'er the shop of your eyes.

SHAKESPEARE, *Love's Labour's Lost*. Act iii, sc. 1, l. 17.

3
If he be not in love with some woman, there is no believing old signs: a' brushes his hat o' mornings; what should that bode?

SHAKESPEARE, *Much Ado About Nothing*. Act iii, sc. 2, l. 40.

An old hat and "the humour of forty fancies" prick'd in 't for a feather.

SHAKESPEARE, *The Taming of the Shrew*. Act iii, sc. 2, l. 69.

4
Where did you get that hat, that collar and
that tie?

JOSEPH J. SULLIVAN, *Where Did You Get that Hat?* (1888)

5
I never saw so many shocking bad hats in my life.

DUKE OF WELLINGTON, on seeing the first Reformed Parliament. (WILLIAM FRASER, *Words on Wellington*, p. 12.) The saying is attributed to the Duke of York, second son of George III, about 1817, by Gronow, in his *Recollections*.

6
All good hats are made out of nothing.

OSCAR WILDE, *Picture of Dorian Gray*. Ch. 17.

HATRED

See also Love and Hate

I—Hatred: Definitions

7
Severity breedeth fear, but roughness breedeth hate.

FRANCIS BACON, *Essays: Of Great Place*.

8
Hatred is self-punishment.

HOSEA BALLOU, *MS. Sermons*.

9
The ruling principle of Hate,
Which for its pleasure doth create
The things it may annihilate.

BYRON, *Prometheus*. St. 2.

10
People hate those who make them feel their own inferiority.

LORD CHESTERFIELD, *Letters*, 30 April, 1750.

A little murder now and then,
A little bit of burglarizing,
Won't earn the hate of fellow-men
As much as being patronizing.

R. T. WOMBAT, *Quatrains*.

11
Hatred is a settled anger. (Odium ira inveterata.)

CICERO, *Tusculanarum Disputationum*. Bk. iv, ch. 9, sec. 21.

12
Hatred is like fire—it makes even light rubbish deadly.

GEORGE ELIOT, *Janet's Repentance*.

There are glances of hatred that stab and raise no cry of murder.

GEORGE ELIOT, *Felix Holt: Introduction*.

13
Hating people is like burning down your own house to get rid of a rat.

HARRY EMERSON FOSDICK, *The Wages of Hate*.

Hatred—ah yes, but what are little hates
But little deaths that wander on and on.

WALTER GREENOUGH, *The Vision*.

Hatreds are the cinders of affection.

SIR WALTER RALEIGH.

14
The greatest hatred, like the greatest virtue and the worst dogs, is silent. (Der grösste Hass ist, wie die grösste Tugend und die schlimmsten Hunde, still.)

JEAN PAUL RICHTER, *Hesperus*. Ch. 12.

15
Hatred is the coward's revenge for being intimidated.

BERNARD SHAW, *Major Barbara*. Act iii.

16
The hatred of relatives is the most violent. (Accerima proximorum odia.)

TACITUS, *History*. Bk. iv, sec. 70.

17
Love, friendship, respect, do not unite people as much as a common hatred for something.

ANTON PAVLOVITCH TCHEKHOV, *Note-Books*.

18
Hate and mistrust are the children of blindness.

WILLIAM WATSON, *England to Ireland*.

We hold our hate too choice a thing
For light and careless lavishing.

WILLIAM WATSON, *Hate*.

II—Hatred: Apothegms

19
It does not matter much what a man hates provided he hates something.

SAMUEL BUTLER THE YOUNGER, *Note-Books*, 217.

20
I do not hate him nearly as much as I fear I ought to.

THOMAS CARLYLE, *Remark*, referring to the Bishop of Oxford. (FROUDE, *Life*.)

A healthy hatred of scoundrels.

CARLYLE, *Latter-Day Pamphlets*. No 12.

21
He who is hated by all can not expect to live long. (Qui vit haï de tous ne saurait longtemps vivre.)

CORNEILLE, *Cinna*. Act i, sc. 2. *See* FEAR FEARED AND FEARING.

1
Not only hating David, but the king.
DRYDEN, *Absalom and Achitophel*. Pt. i, l. 512.

2
He most is hated when he most is praised.
DRYDEN, *The Rival Ladies*. Act iii, sc. 1.

3
Hate at first sight.
EMERSON, *Society and Solitude: Works and Days.*

4
Everybody hates me. (Πάντες με μισοῦσιν.)
EPICTETUS, *Discourses*. Bk. i, ch. 18, sec. 19.

5
High above hate I dwell, O storms! farewell.
LOUISE IMOGEN GUINEY, *The Sanctuary.*

Honey from silkworms who can gather,
Or silk from the yellow bee?
The grass may grow in winter weather
As soon as hate in me.
SHELLEY, *Lines to a Critic.*

6
We can scarcely hate any one that we know.
WILLIAM HAZLITT, *Table Talk: Why Distant Objects Please.*

7
It is to fast from strife,
From old debate And hate;
To circumcise thy life.
ROBERT HERRICK, *To Keep a True Lent.*

8
There are no eyes so sharp as the eyes of hatred.
G. S. HILLARD, *Life of G. B. McClellan*. Ch. 13.

9
They hated me without a cause.
New Testament: John, xv, 25.

10
He hated a fool, and he hated a rogue, and he hated a whig. He was a very good hater.
SAMUEL JOHNSON, referring to Earl Bathurst. (PIOZZI, *Anecdotes of Johnson*, p. 38.)

I like a good hater.
SAMUEL JOHNSON. (PIOZZI, *Anecdotes*, p. 89.)

11
The man that is once hated, both his good and his evil deeds oppress him.
BEN JONSON, *Explorata: Fama.*

12
He sowed doubtful speeches, and reaped plain, unequivocal hatred.
CHARLES LAMB, *Last Essays of Elia: Preface.*

13
Folks never understand the folks they hate.
J. R. LOWELL, *Biglow Papers*. Ser. ii, *Mason and Slidell.*

14
Intoxicated with animosity.
MACAULAY, *History of England*. Ch. 2.

15
A true man hates no one.
NAPOLEON BONAPARTE, *Sayings of Napoleon.*

16
Take care that no one hates you justly. (Id agas tuo te merito ne quis oderit.)
PUBLILIUS SYRUS, *Sententiæ*. No. 325.

17
Thou add'st but fuel to my hate.
SCOTT, *The Lady of the Lake*. Canto v, st. 14.

18
Hatred openly proclaimed loses its chance for vengeance. (Professa perdunt odia vindictæ locum.)
SENECA, *Medea*, l. 154.

19
Cherish those hearts that hate thee.
SHAKESPEARE, *Henry VIII*. Act iii, sc. 2, l. 443.

20
There are very few who would not rather be hated than laughed at.
SYDNEY SMITH, *Moral Philosophy*. Lect. 11.

21
One shriek of hate would jar all the hymns
of heaven.
TENNYSON, *Sea Dreams*, l. 251.

22
You shall never vanquish me by your hatred. (Nunquam tu odio tuo me vinces.)
TERENCE, *Phormio*. l. 849. (Act v, sc. 6.)

III—Hatred: Its Deadliness

23
Their ineffectual feuds and feeble hates—
Shadows of hates, but they distress them still.
MATTHEW ARNOLD, *Balder Dead*. Pt. iii, l. 472.

24
And where his frown of hatred darkly fell,
Hope withering fled—and Mercy sigh'd farewell.
BYRON, *The Corsair*. Canto i, st. 9.

Now rose the unleaven'd hatred of his heart.
BYRON, *Lara*. Canto ii, st. 4.

25
Then let him know that hatred without end
Or intermission is between us two.
HOMER, *Iliad*. Bk. xv, l. 270. (Bryant, tr.)

These two hated with a hate
Found only on the stage.
BYRON, *Don Juan*. Canto iv, st. 93.

26
Spleen to mankind his envious heart possess'd,
And much he hated all, but most the best.
HOMER, *Iliad*. Bk. ii, l. 267. (Pope, tr.)

27
The sad hate the merry; the merry hate the sad;
The swift hate the slow; the lazy hate the brisk.
(Oderunt hilarem tristes tristemque jocosi,
Sedatum celeres, agilem navumque remissi.)
HORACE, *Epistles*. Bk. i, epis. 18, l. 89.

28
I do hate him as I hate the devil.
BEN JONSON, *Every Man Out of his Humour*. Act i, sc. 1.

I do hate him as I do hell-pains.
SHAKESPEARE, *Othello*. Act i, sc. 1, l. 155.

More abhorr'd Than spotted livers in the sacrifice.
SHAKESPEARE, *Troilus and Cressida*. Act v, sc. 3, l. 17.

1
An undying hatred and a wound never to be cured. (Immortale odium et numquam sanabile vulnus.)
JUVENAL, *Satires*. Sat. xv, l. 34.

2
For him who fain would teach the world
The world holds hate in fee—
For Socrates, the hemlock cup;
For Christ, Gethsemane.
DON MARQUIS, *Wages*.

3
For never can true reconcilement grow,
Where wounds of deadly hate have pierc'd so deep.
MILTON, *Paradise Lost*. Bk. iv, l. 98.

4
Hate cannot wish thee worse
Than guilt and shame have made thee.
THOMAS MOORE, *When First I Met Thee*.

5
The malevolent have hidden teeth. (Malevolus animus abditos dentes habet.)
PUBLILIUS SYRUS, *Sententiæ*. No. 375.

6
It is droll and sad, but true, that Christendom is full of men in a hurry to hate.
CHARLES READE. (THOMPSON, *Presidents I've Known*, p. 32.)

7
To offend is my pleasure; I love to be hated. (Déplaire est mon plaisir; j'aime qu'on me haisse.)
EDMOND ROSTAND, *Cyrano de Bergerac*. Act ii, sc. 8.

8
Bassanio: Do all men kill the things they do not love?
Shylock: Hates any man the thing he would not kill?
Bassanio: Every offence is not a hate at first.
SHAKESPEARE, *The Merchant of Venice*. Act iv, sc. 1, l. 66.

9
Hated by fools, and fools to hate,
Be that my motto, and my fate.
SWIFT, *To Dr. Delany*. Last lines.

10
Planting hatreds of long duration in his mind, that he might store them up, and produce them grown by keeping.
TACITUS, *Annals*. Bk. i, sec. 69.

11
They attack this one man with their hate. (Uni odiisque viro.)
VERGIL, *Æneid*. Bk. x, l. 692.

The more he was with vulgar hate oppressed,
The more his fury boiled within his breast.
VERGIL, *Æneid*. Bk. xii, l. 5. (Dryden, tr.)

12
Press not thy hatred further. (Ulterius ne tende odiis.)
VERGIL *Æneid*. Bk. xii, l. 938.

IV—Hate and Fear

13
Let them hate me, so long as they fear me. (Oderint, dum metuant.)
ACCIUS, *Atreus*, l. 203. A favorite maxim of Caligula. (SUETONIUS, *Twelve Cæsars: Caligula*, 30.)

Let them hate me, so long as they fear me. (Oderint, dum metuant.)
CICERO, *Pro Sextio Roscio Amerino*, Sec. 48. *Philippicæ*. No. i, sec. 14; SENECA, *De Ira*. Bk. i, sec. 16. Quoted by Cicero as an ancient saying, and denounced by Seneca as a detestable sentiment.

14
Whom men fear they hate, and whom they hate, they wish dead. (Quem metuunt oderunt, quem quisque odit periisse expetit.)
QUINTUS ENNIUS, *Thyestes*. (CICERO, *De Officiis*, ii, 7, 23.)

15
In time we hate that which we often fear.
SHAKESPEARE, *Antony and Cleopatra*. Act i, sc. 3, l. 12.

The love of wicked men converts to fear;
That fear to hate, and hate turns one or both
To worthy danger and deserved death.
SHAKESPEARE, *Richard II*. Act v, sc. 1, l. 66.
See also HENRY VIII *under* MAN.

16
Let them hate me, provided they approve my conduct. (Oderint, dum probent.)
TIBERIUS. (SUETONIUS, *Twelve Cæsars: Tiberius*, 59.)

V—Hate and the Gods

17
Can so much gall find place in godly souls? (Tant de fiel entre-t-il dans l'âme des devôts?)
BOILEAU, *Le Lutrin*.

And hated, with the gall of gentle souls.
E. B. BROWNING, *Aurora Leigh*. Bk. i, l. 341.

18
For what so dreadful as celestial hate! (Χαλεπὴ δὲ θεοῦ ἔπι μῆνις.)
HOMER, *Iliad*. Bk. v, l. 178. (Pope, tr., l. 227.)

19
In heav'nly spirits could such perverseness dwell?
MILTON, *Paradise Lost*. Bk. vi, l. 788.

And is there then
Such rancour in the hearts of mighty men?
EDMUND SPENSER, *Muiopotmos*. St. 2.

20
And haughty Juno's unrelenting hate. (Sævæ memorem Junonis ob iram.)
VERGIL, *Æneid*. Bk. i, l. 4. (Dryden, tr.)

21
Can heavenly natures nourish hate,
So fierce, so blindly passionate?
(Tantæne animis cælestibus iræ?)
VERGIL, *Æneid*. Bk. i, l. 11. (Conington, tr.)

HAWK AND HAWKING

22
The falcon and the dove sit there together,

And th' one of them doth prune the other's
feather.
MICHAEL DRAYTON, *Noah's Flood.*

1
Pretty pastime, nephew! 'Tis royal sport.
PHILIP MASSINGER, *The Guardian.* Act i, sc. 1. Of hawking.

2
We hate the hawk because he always lives in arms. (Odimus accipitrem quia semper vivit in armis.)
OVID, *Ars Amatoria.* Bk. ii, l. 147.

3
As the hawk is wont to pursue the frightened doves. (Ut solet accipere trepidas urguere columbas.)
OVID, *Metamorphoses.* Bk. v, l. 606.

Say, will the falcon, stooping from above,
Smit with her varying plumage, spare the dove?
POPE, *Essay on Man.* Epis. iii, l. 53.

4
The first point of hawking is hold fast.
JOHN RAY, *English Proverbs.*

With empty hand nae man should hawks allure.
JOHN RAY, *Scottish Proverbs.*

5
My hawk is tired of perch and hood.
SCOTT, *The Lady of the Lake.* Canto vi, l. 24.

Let the wild falcon soar her swing,
She'll stoop when she has tired her wing.
SCOTT, *Marmion.* Canto i, st. 17.

6
When the wind is southerly, I know a hawk from a handsaw.
SHAKESPEARE, *Hamlet.* Act ii, sc. 2, l. 397.

7
No marvel, an it like your majesty,
My lord protector's hawks do tower so well;
They know their master loves to be aloft,
And bears his thoughts above his falcon's
pitch.
SHAKESPEARE, *II Henry VI.* Act ii, sc. 1, l. 9.

A falcon, tow'ring in her pride of place,
Was by a mousing owl hawk'd at and kill'd.
SHAKESPEARE, *Macbeth.* Act ii, sc. 4, l. 12.

8
I have a fine hawk for the bush.
SHAKESPEARE, *The Merry Wives of Windsor.* Act iii, sc. 3, l. 247.

Dost thou love hawking? thou hast hawks will
soar
Above the morning lark.
SHAKESPEARE, *The Taming of the Shrew: Induction.* Sc. 2, l. 45.

9
She rears her young on yonder tree;
She leaves her faithful mate to mind 'em;
Like us, for fish she sails to sea,
And, plunging, shows us where to find 'em.
Yo, ho, my hearts! let's seek the deep,
Ply every oar, and cheerly wish her,
While slow the bending net we sweep,
God bless the fish-hawk and the fisher.
ALEXANDER WILSON, *The Fisherman's Hymn.*

HAWTHORN

10
The hawthorn I will pu' wi' its lock o' siller
grey,
Where, like an aged man, it stands at break
o' day.
BURNS, *The Posie.*

Tho' large the forest's monarch throws
His army-shade,
Yet green the juicy hawthorn grows,
Adown the glade.
BURNS, *The Vision.* Duan ii, st. 21.

11
Yet walk with me where hawthorns hide
The wonders of the lane.
EBENEZER ELLIOTT, *The Wonders of the Lane.*

12
The hawthorn bush with seats beneath the
shade,
For talking age and whispering lovers made.
GOLDSMITH, *The Deserted Village,* l. 13.

13
And every shepherd tells his tale
Under the hawthorn in the dale.
MILTON, *L'Allegro,* l. 67.

Gives not the hawthorn-bush a sweeter shade
To shepherds looking on their silly sheep
Than doth a rich embroider'd canopy
To kings that fear their subjects' treachery?
SHAKESPEARE, *III Henry VI.* Act ii, sc. 5, l. 42.

14
In hawthorn-time the heart grows light.
SWINBURNE, *The Tale of Balen.* Pt. i.

HAWTHORNE, NATHANIEL

15
How paltry, how shrivelled and shrunken does the swallow-tail culture of the literary snob appear in contrast with the provinciality which invests the works of Hawthorne with the swift passion of New England summers.
JOEL CHANDLER HARRIS. (WIGGINS, *Life,* p. 148.)

16
There in seclusion and remote from men,
The wizard hand lies cold,
Which at its topmost speed let fall the pen,
And left the tale half told.

Ah, who shall lift that wand of magic power,
And the lost clew regain?
The unfinished window in Aladdin's tower
Unfinished must remain!
LONGFELLOW, *Hawthorne.* Hawthorne died with his last romance unfinished.

17
There is Hawthorne, with genius so shrinking
and rare
That you hardly at first see the strength that
is there;
A frame so robust, with a nature so sweet,
So earnest, so graceful, so lithe, and so fleet,
Is worth a descent from Olympus to meet.
J. R. LOWELL, *A Fable for Critics,* l. 997.

His strength is so tender, his wildness so meek,

That a suitable parallel sets one to seek,— . . .
When Nature was shaping him, clay was not granted
For making so full-sized a man as she wanted,
So, to fill out her model, a little she spared
From some finer-grained stuff for a woman prepared,
And she could not have hit a more excellent plan
For making him fully and perfectly man.

J. R. LOWELL, *A Fable for Critics*, l. 1006.

HEAD

See also Heart and Head

1
Such as take lodgings in a head
That's to be let unfurnished.

BUTLER, *Hudibras*. Pt. i, canto i, l. 161. *See also* MIND.

2
The dome of Thought, the palace of the Soul.

BYRON, *Childe Harold*. Canto ii, st. 6.

O human head! Majestic box! O wondrous can, from labels free! If man is craving fame or rocks, he'll get them if he uses thee!

WALT MASON, *The Human Head*.
See also SKULL.

3
Off with his head; so much for Buckingham!

CIBBER, *Richard III* (altered). Act iv, sc. 3.

The Queen . . . began screaming "Off with her head! Off with . . ." "Nonsense!" said Alice, very loudly and decidedly, and the Queen was silent.

LEWIS CARROLL, *Alice's Adventures in Wonderland*. Ch. 8.

Down from the tree with hollow scoff,
The raven cried: "Head-off! head-off!"

HEINE, *Youthful Sorrows*.

4
Without head or tail.

S. T. COLERIDGE, *To the Author of the Ancient Mariner*.

5
His head alone remain'd to tell
The cruel death he died.

COWPER, *On the Death of Mrs. Throckmorton's Bulfinch*, l. 65.

6
It's my old girl that advises. She has the head.

DICKENS, *Bleak House*. Ch. 27.

7
As the saying is, So many heads, so many wits.

QUEEN ELIZABETH, *Godly Meditation of the Christian Soul*. (1548) A proverb included in John Heywood's collection.

So many heads, so many wits—fie, fie!
Is't not a shame for Proverbs thus to lie?
Myself, though my acquaintance be but small,
Know many heads that have no wit at all.

WILLIAM CAMDEN, *Remains: Epitaphs*.

8
Scabby heads love not the comb.

THOMAS FULLER, *Gnomologia*. No. 4072.

9
Their heads sometimes so little that there is no room for wit; sometimes so long that there is no wit for so much room.

THOMAS FULLER, *Holy and Profane State: Of Natural Fools*.

10
Some men's heads are as easily blown away as their hats.

LORD HALIFAX, *Works*, p. 241.

11
He that hath a head of wax must not walk in the sun.

GEORGE HERBERT, *Jacula Prudentum*. No. 421.
FRANKLIN, *Poor Richard*.

12
It's better to be head of a lizard than the tail of a lion.

GEORGE HERBERT, *Jacula Prudentum*. No. 575.

13
Thy head is great . . . and without wit within.

JOHN HEYWOOD, *Epigrams*. Cent. vi, No. 56.

A great head and a little wit.

THOMAS FULLER, *Gnomologia*. No. 196.

14
Two heads are better than one. (Σύν τε δύ' ἐρχομένω.)

HOMER, *Iliad*. Bk. x, l. 225; HEYWOOD, *Proverbs*, i, 9. (1546)

Two have more wit than one.

JOHN GOWER, *Confessio Amantis*, l. 1020.

15
'Tis strange how like a very dunce,
Man, with his bumps upon his sconce,
Has lived so long, and yet no knowledge he
Has had, till lately, of Phrenology—
A science that by simple dint of
Head-combing, he should find a hint of,
When scratching o'er those little pole-hills,
The faculties throw up like mole-hills.

THOMAS HOOD, *Craniology*.

16
Be sure always that your head be not higher than your hat.

JOHN LYLY, *Euphues*, p. 284. (1580)

17
Hang the pensive head.

MILTON, *Lycidas*, l. 147.

Hide their diminished heads.

MILTON, *Paradise Lost*. Bk. iv, l. 35.

Hide their ignominious heads.

HOMER, *Iliad*. Bk. xiv, l. 170. (Pope tr.)

His comprehensive head.

POPE, *Moral Essays*. Epis. i, l. 84.

18
He is of the race of the mushroom; he covers himself altogether with his head. (Fungino genere est; capite se totum tegit.)

PLAUTUS, *Trinummus*. Act iv, sc. 2, l. 9.

19
Cover your head by day as much as you will, by night as much as you can.

JOHN RAY, *English Proverbs*, 41.

1
I never knew so young a body with so old a head.
SHAKESPEARE, *The Merchant of Venice*. Act iv, sc. 1, l. 164. *See also* AGE AND YOUTH.

2
Faith, thou hast some crotchets in thy head.
SHAKESPEARE, *The Merry Wives of Windsor*. Act ii, sc. 1, l. 157.

3
Thou hast a head, and so has a pin.
SWIFT, *Polite Conversation*. Dial. i.

4
I should like to see your head stroked down with a sandal. (Utinam tibi commitigari videam sandalio caput.)
TERENCE, *Eunuchus*, l. 1028. (Act v, sc. 7.)

Doubt not her care should be
To comb your noddle with a three-legg'd stool.
SHAKESPEARE, *The Taming of the Shrew*. Act i, sc. 1, l. 64. (1594)

She flew in my face and called me a fool,
And combed my head with a three-legg'd stool.
UNKNOWN, *Westminster Drollery*, 38. (1671)

5
One head will be given for many. (Unum pro multis dabitur caput.)
VERGIL, *Æneid*. Bk. v, l. 815.

6
When the head acheth all the body is the worse. (Cui caput infirmum cetera membra dolent.)
UNKNOWN. (WRIGHT, *Political Songs*, 31. c. 1230)

When the head aches, all the body is out of tune.
CERVANTES, *Don Quixote*. Pt. ii, ch. 2.

She sighs for ever on her pensive bed.
Pain at her side, and Megrim at her head.
POPE, *The Rape of the Lock*. Canto iv, l. 23.

HEALTH

See also Medicine

I—Health: Apothegms

7
Health and cheerfulness mutually beget each other.
ADDISON, *The Spectator*. No. 387.

Happiness lies, first of all, in health.
G. W. CURTIS, *Lotus-Eating: Trenton*.

8
A healthy body is the guest-chamber of the soul; a sick, its prison.
FRANCIS BACON, *Augmentis Scientiarum: Valetudo*.

9
He who hath good health is young.
H. G. BOHN, *Hand-Book of Proverbs*, 400.

Health and wealth create beauty.
H. G. BOHN, *Hand-Book of Proverbs*, 405.

10
The healthy know not of their health, but only the sick: this is the Physician's Aphorism.
THOMAS CARLYLE, *Characteristics*.

Health is not valued till sickness comes.
THOMAS FULLER, *Gnomologia*. No. 2478.

11
Health is not a condition of matter, but of Mind; nor can the material senses bear reliable testimony on the subject of health.
MARY BAKER EDDY, *Science and Health*, p. 120.

12
Give me health and a day, and I will make the pomp of emperors ridiculous.
EMERSON, *Nature, Addresses, and Lectures: Beauty*.

13
Health that snuffs the morning air.
JAMES GRAINGER, *Solitude: An Ode*, l. 35.

The "madness of superfluous health" I have never known.
EDWARD GIBBON, *Miscellaneous Works*. Vol. i, p. 183.

14
Health and money go far.
GEORGE HERBERT, *Jacula Prudentum*.

Health without money is half an ague.
GEORGE HERBERT, *Jacula Prudentum*.

15
I eat well, drink well, and sleep well, but that's all, Tom, that's all.
THOMAS MORTON, *A Rowland for an Oliver*.

16
I am as sound as a bell, fat, plump, and juicy.
SIR CHARLES SEDLEY, *Bellamira*. Act iii. (1687)

17
If you are well, it is well; I also am well. (Si vales bene est, ego valeo.)
SENECA, *Epistulæ ad Lucilium*. Epis. xv, sec. 1.

II—Health: Its Value

18
Health is indeed a precious thing, to recover and preserve which we undergo any misery, drink bitter potions, freely give our goods; restore a man to his health, his purse lies open to thee.
ROBERT BURTON, *Anatomy of Melancholy*. Pt. iii, sec. i, mem. 2, subs. 1.

19
The health of the people is really the foundation upon which all their happiness and all their powers as a State depend.
BENJAMIN DISRAELI, *Speech*, Battersea Park, 23 June, 1877. (London *Times*, 25 June, p. 10.)

Dread to the poor the least suspense of health,—
Their hands their friends, their labour all their wealth;
Let the wheel rest from toil a single sun,
And all the humble clock-work is undone.
BULWER-LYTTON, *New Timon*. Pt. i, sec. ii, l. 70.

20
My wealth is health and perfect ease;
My conscience clear my chief defense.
EDWARD DYER, *My Mind to Me a Kingdom Is*.

21
Health and good estate of body are above

all gold, and a strong body above infinite wealth.

Apocrypha: Ecclesiasticus, xxx, 15.

1

The first wealth is health. Sickness is poor-spirited, and cannot serve any one; it must husband its resources to live. But health or fulness answers its own ends, and has to spare, runs over, and inundates the neighborhoods and creeks of other men's necessities.

EMERSON, *Conduct of Life: Power.*

2

Nor love, nor honour, wealth nor pow'r,
Can give the heart a cheerful hour
When health is lost. Be timely wise;
With health all taste of pleasure flies.

JOHN GAY, *Fables.* Pt. i, fab. 31.

Rich, from the very want of wealth,
In Heaven's best treasures, Peace and Health.

THOMAS GRAY, *Ode on Vicissitude*, l. 95.

3

Health is the first good lent to men;
A gentle disposition then;
Next, to be rich by no by-ways;
Lastly, with friends t' enjoy our days.

ROBERT HERRICK, *Four Things Make Us Happy Here.*

4

A sound mind in a manly body. (Ὡς μὲν ἐμῇ γνώμῃ, φρένες ἐσθλαὶ σώμασιν ἀνδρῶν.)

HOMER, when asked the greatest blessing of man. (*Contest of Hesiod and Homer.* Sec. 320.)

A sound mind in a sound body is a thing to be prayed for. (Orandum est ut sit mens sana in corpore sano.)

JUVENAL, *Satires.* Sat. x, l. 356.

A sound mind in a sound body, is a short but full description of a happy state in this world. He that has these two, has little more to wish for; and he that wants either of them, will be little the better for anything else.

JOHN LOCKE, *Some Thoughts Concerning Education.*

Mens sana in corpore sano is a foolish saying. The sound body is a product of the sound mind.

BERNARD SHAW, *Maxims for Revolutionists.*

5

If all be well with belly, feet, and sides,
A king's estate no greater good provides.
(Si ventri bene, si lateri est pedibusque tuis, nil
Divitiæ poterunt regales addere majus.)

HORACE, *Epistles.* Bk. i, epis. 12, l. 5. Quoted by Montaigne, *Essays.* Bk. i, ch. 42.

6

O health! health! the blessing of the rich! the riches of the poor! who can buy thee at too dear a rate, since there is no enjoying this world without thee?

BEN JONSON, *Volpone.* Act ii, sc. 1.

7

Life is not merely to be alive, but to be well. (Non est vivere, sed valere, vita.)

MARTIAL, *Epigrams.* Bk. vi, ep. 70, l. 15.

Without health, life is not life; life is lifeless. (Χωρὶς ὑγιείας ἄβιος βίος, βίος ἀβίωτος.)

ARIPHON THE SICYONIAN.

8

Health and intellect are the two blessings of life. (Ὑγίεια καὶ νοῦς ἐσθλὰ τῷ βίῳ δύο.)

MENANDER, *Monostikoi.* No. 15.

Good health and good sense are two of life's greatest blessings.

PUBLILIUS SYRUS, *Sententiæ.* No. 827.

9

All health is better than wealth.

SCOTT, *Familiar Letters.* Vol. i, p. 255.

10

Good wife and health is a man's best wealth.

C. H. SPURGEON, *John Ploughman.* Ch. 16.
FRANKLIN, *Poor Richard*, 1746.

11

Grant me but health, thou great Bestower of it, and give me but this fair goddess as my companion—and shower down thy mitres, if it seem good unto thy Divine Providence, upon those heads which are aching for them.

STERNE, *A Sentimental Journey: The Passport: The Hotel at Paris.*

O blessed health! . . . thou art above all gold and treasure. . . . He that has thee, has little more to wish for; and he that is so wretched as to want thee, wants everything with thee.

STERNE, *Tristram Shandy.* Bk. v, ch. 33.

12

Let health my nerves and finer fibres brace,
And I their toys to the great children leave:
Of fancy, reason, virtue, nought can me bereave.

THOMSON, *Castle of Indolence.* Canto ii, st. 3.

But what avail the largest gifts of Heaven,
When drooping health and spirits go amiss?
How tasteless then whatever can be given!
Health is the vital principle of bliss.

THOMSON, *Castle of Indolence.* Canto ii, st. 57.

13

Look to your health; and if you have it, praise God, and value it next to a good conscience; for health is the second blessing that we mortals are capable of; a blessing that money cannot buy.

IZAAK WALTON, *Compleat Angler.* Pt. i, ch. 21.

14

Ask me no more which is the greatest wealth,
Our rich possessions, liberty, or health.

ROWLAND WATKYNS, *Flamma Sine Fumo: Sickness.*

15

Gold that buys health can never be ill spent
Nor hours laid out in harmless merriment.

JOHN WEBSTER, *Westward Hoe.* Act v, sc. 3, l. 345.

III—Health: Its Preservation

See also Eating: Abstemiousness

16

A man's own observation, what he finds good of and what he finds hurt of, is the best physic to preserve health.

BACON, *Essays: Of Regimen of Health.*

1
Men that look no further than their outsides, think health an appurtenance unto life, and quarrel with their constitutions for being sick; but I, that have examined the parts of man, and know upon what tender filaments that fabric hangs, do wonder that we are not always so.

SIR THOMAS BROWNE, *Religio Medici*. Pt. i, sec. 51.

2
The first was called Doctor Diet, the second Doctor Quiet, the third Doctor Merryman.

WILLIAM BULLEIN, *Government of Health*. Fo. 51. (1558)

After these two, Doctor Diet and Doctor Quiet, Doctor Merriman is requisite to preserve health.

JAMES HOWELL, *Parly of Beasts*, p. 23. (1660)

The best doctors in the world are Doctor Diet, Doctor Quiet, and Doctor Merryman.

SWIFT, *Polite Conversation*. Dial. ii.

Use three physicians still:
First, Dr. Quiet;
Next, Dr. Merryman;
Then, Dr. Diet.

UNKNOWN, *Regimen Sanitatis Salernitanum*. (1607)

If doctors fail you, let these three be your doctors: a cheerful mind, rest, and moderate diet. (Si tibi deficiant medici, medici tibi fiant Hæc tria: mens hilaris, requies, moderata diæta.)

UNKNOWN, *Regimen Sanitatis Salernitanum*. In a version given by Gabriel Harvey, "labor" is substituted for "requies" in the second line.

Diet cures more than doctors.

A. B. CHEALES, *Proverbial Folk-Lore*. No. 82.

Nature, time and patience are the three great physicians.

H. G. BOHN, *Hand-Book of Proverbs*, 457.

3
The surest road to health, say what they will,
Is never to suppose we shall be ill.
Most of those evils we poor mortals know
From doctors and imagination flow.

CHARLES CHURCHILL, *Night*, l. 69.

Say you are well, or all is well with you,
And God shall hear your words and make them true.

ELLA WHEELER WILCOX, *Speech*.

Every day, in every way, I am getting better and better. (Tous les jours, à tous points de vue, je vais de mieux en mieux.)

EMIL COUÉ, formula of auto-suggestion used at his clinic at Nancy.

4
That he may be healthy, happy, and wise, let him rise early. (Sanat, sanctificat, et ditat, surgere mane.)

JOHN CLARKE, *Parœmiologia*. (1639)

Early to bed and early to rise,
Makes a man healthy, wealthy, and wise.

BENJAMIN FRANKLIN, *Poor Richard*, 1758.

5
Unbought health, a deity presiding over the affairs of men. (Præsens numen, inempta salus.)

CLAUDIAN, *Idylls*. No. vi, l. 76.

Better to hunt in fields for health unbought,
Than fee the doctor for a nauseous draught.
The wise, for cure, on exercise depend;
God never made his work for man to mend.

DRYDEN, *To John Driden*, l. 92.

Ruddy Health the loftiest Muse.
Live in the sunshine, swim the sea,
Drink the wild air's salubrity.

EMERSON, *Conduct of Life: Considerations by the Way*.

See also under EXERCISE.

6
Safeguard the health both of body and soul. (Εὖ τὸ σῶμα ἔχειν καὶ τὴν ψυχήν.)

CLEOBULUS. (STOBÆUS, *Florilegium*. Pt. iii, 79.)

Guard your health. (Cura ut valeas.)

CICERO, *Epistolæ ad Diversos*. Bk. vii, epis. 5.

7
Before supper walk a little; after supper do the same. (Sub cœnam paulisper inambula; cœnatus idem facito.)

ERASMUS, *De Ratione Studii*.

After dinner sit awhile;
After supper walk a mile.

JOHN RAY, *English Proverbs*. A proverb with slight variations, in all languages: Latin, "Post epulas stabis vel passus mille meabis," After dinner stand or walk a mile; Italian, "Dopo pranza sta, dopo cena va," After dinner rest, after supper walk; German, "Nach dem Essen sollst du stehen, Oder tausend Schritte gehen," After dinner you must stand a while or walk a thousand paces.

After dinner sleep a while; after supper go to bed.

JOHN RAY, *English Proverbs*.

Some tell us after supper walk a mile,
But we say, after supper dance a measure.

J. R. PLANCHÉ, *Extravaganza*, iii, 135.

After lunch, rest; after dinner, walk. (Post prandium stabis, post cœnam ambulabis.)

UNKNOWN, *Maxim of School of Salerno*.

8
Health is the first muse, and sleep is the condition to produce it.

EMERSON, *Uncollected Lectures: Resources*.

9
Clothe warm, eat little, drink well, so shalt thou live.

JOHN FLORIO, *First Fruites*. Fo. 34.

Head and feet keep warm, the rest will take no harm.

THOMAS FULLER, *Gnomologia*. No. 6255.

A cool mouth, and warm feet, live long.

GEORGE HERBERT, *Jacula Prudentum*.

10
I always choose the plainest food
To mend viscidity of blood.
Hail! water-gruel, healing power,

Of easy access to the poor, . . .
To thee I fly, by thee dilute—
Through veins my blood doth quicker shoot.
MATTHEW GREEN, *The Spleen*, l. 53.

1
He that goes to bed thirsty rises healthy.
GEORGE HERBERT, *Jacula Prudentum.*

2
Till April's dead
Change not a thread.
INWARDS, *Weather Lore*, 23.

3
A courtier extraordinary, who by diet
Of meats and drinks, his temperate exercise,
Choice music, frequent bath, his horary shifts
Of shirts and waistcoats, means to immortalize
Mortality itself.
BEN JONSON, *The Magnetic Lady*. Act i, sc. 1.

4
Joy and Temperance and Repose
Slam the door on the doctor's nose.
H. W. LONGFELLOW, *The Best Medicines.*

5
Reason's whole pleasure, all the joys of sense,
Lie in three words—Health, Peace, and Competence.
But health consists with temperance alone,
And peace, O Virtue! peace is all thy own.
POPE, *Essay on Man*. Epis. iv, l. 79.

Temperance and labor are the two true physicians of man. (La tempérance et le travail sont les deux vrais médecins de l'homme.)
ROUSSEAU, *Émile*. Bk. i.

6
Rise at five, dine at nine; sup at five, to bed at nine. (Lever à cinq, diner à neuf; souper à cinq, coucher à neuf.)
RABELAIS, *Works*. Bk. iv, ch. 64. Rabelais, himself a doctor, says that these are the "canonical hours" for preserving health.

7
Wash your hands often, your feet seldom, and your head never.
JOHN RAY, *English Proverbs*, 38.

Our fathers who were wondrous wise,
Did wash their throats before their eyes.
JOHN RAY, *English Proverbs*, 212.

Prithee let me intreat thee now to drink before thou wash; our fathers that were wise, were wont to say 'twas wholesome for the eyes.
GEORGE WITHER, *Abuses Stript*. Bk. ii, sat. 1.

8
Hold fast, then, to this sound and wholesome rule of life: indulge the body only so far as is needful for health.
SENECA, *Epistulæ ad Lucilium*. Epis. viii, sec. 5.

9
The preservation of health is a duty. Few seem conscious that there is such a thing as physical morality.
HERBERT SPENCER, *Education*. Ch. 4.

10
He had had much experience of physicians, and said, "The only way to keep your health is to eat what you don't want, drink what you don't like, and do what you'd druther not."
MARK TWAIN, *Pudd'nhead Wilson's Neu Calendar.*

The doctor is sure that my health is poor, he says that I waste away; so bring me a can of the shredded bran, and a bale of the toasted hay.
WALT MASON, *Health Food.*

IV—Health: The Valetudinarian

11
The life of the valetudinarian: *Cf.* the Italian epitaph of a person of this description: I was well; I would be better; and here I am.
ADDISON, *The Spectator*. No. 25.

12
Who lives medically lives miserably. (Qui medice vivit misere vivit.)
ROBERT BURTON, *Anatomy of Melancholy*. Quoted.

He that liveth by physic liveth miserably.
THOMAS COGAN, *Haven of Health: Dedication.* (1588)

13
When Health, affrighted, spreads her rosy wing,
And flies with every changing gale of spring.
BYRON, *Childish Recollections*, l. 3.

14
Some men employ their health, an ugly trick,
In making known how oft they have been sick.
COWPER, *Conversation*, l. 311.

15
And each imbibes his rations from a Hygienic Cup—
The Bunny and the Baby and the Prophylactic Pup.
ARTHUR GUITERMAN, *Strictly Germ-Proof.*

Oh, powerful bacillus,
With wonder how you fill us,
Every day!
While medical detectives,
With powerful objectives,
Watch your play.
W. T. HELMUTH, *Ode to the Bacillus.*

16
The most uninformed mind with a healthy body is happier than the wisest valetudinarian.
THOMAS JEFFERSON, *Writings*. Vol. vi, p. 167.

17
It is a grievous illness to preserve one's health by a regimen too strict. (C'est une ennuyeuse maladie que de conserver sa santé par un trop grand régime.)
LA ROCHEFOUCAULD, *Maximes Supprimées.* No. 633.

'Tis an odious kind of remedy
To owe our health to a disease.
BEN JONSON, *The New Inn*. Act iv, sc. 3.

He dies every day who lives a lingering life. (Celuy meurt tous les jours, qui languit en vivant.)
Pierrard Poullet, *La Charité*.

1
No man can have a peaceful life who thinks too much about lengthening it. (Nulli potest secura vita contingere, qui de producenda nimis cogitat.)
Seneca, *Epistulæ ad Lucilium*. Epis. iv, sec. 4.

Drinking and sweating—'tis the life of a dyspeptic. (Bibere et suadere vita cardiaci est.)
Seneca, *Epistulæ ad Lucilium*. Epis. xv, sec. 3.

2
It is better to lose health like a spendthrift than to waste it like a miser.
R. L. Stevenson, *Æs Triplex*.

3
He destroys his health by laboring to preserve it. (Ægrescitque medendo.)
Vergil, *Æneid*. Bk. xii, l. 46.

4
Health—silliest word in our language, and one knows so well the popular idea of health. The English country gentleman galloping after a fox—the unspeakable in full pursuit of the uneatable.
Oscar Wilde, *A Woman of No Importance*. Act i.

She is very much interested in her own health.
Oscar Wilde, *A Woman of No Importance*. Act iii.

5
Some reckon he killed himself with purgations.
Charles Wriothesley, *Chronicle*. Vol. i, p. 16. (1560)

A valetudinarian, who quacked himself to death.
Jeremy Bentham.

HEARING, see Ears

HEART

I—Heart: Definitions

6
In each human heart are a tiger, a pig, an ass, and a nightingale. Diversity of character is due to their unequal activity.
Ambrose Bierce, *The Devil's Dictionary*.

7
The heart has such an influence over the understanding, that it is worth while to engage it in our interest. It is the whole of women, who are guided by nothing else: and it has so much to say, even with men, and the ablest men too, that it commonly triumphs in every struggle with the understanding.
Lord Chesterfield, *Letters*, 9 March, 1748.

8
The heart of the wise, like a mirror, should reflect all objects, without being sullied by any.
Confucius, *Analects*.

For the human heart is the mirror
Of the things that are near and far;
Like the wave that reflects in its bosom
The flower and the distant star.
Alice Cary, *The Time to Be*.

9
The heart of a man is of itself but little, yet great things cannot fill it.
Thomas Dekker, *Four Birds of Noah's Arke*. (1609)

The heart is a small thing, but desireth great matters. It is not sufficient for a kite's dinner, yet the whole world is not sufficient for it.
Francis Quarles, *Emblems:* Bk. i, *Hugo de Anima*. (1635)

10
The heart asks pleasure first,
And then, excuse from pain;
And then, those little anodynes
That deaden suffering.
And then, to go to sleep;
And then, if it should be
The will of its Inquisitor,
The liberty to die.
Emily Dickinson, *Poems*. Pt. i, No. 9.

11
Who hath sailed about the world of his own heart, sounded each creek, surveyed each corner, but that there still remains therein much terra incognita to himself?
Thomas Fuller, *The Holy State*, p. 34.

12
The alarum watch, your pulse.
Matthew Green, *The Spleen*, l. 36.

My pulse, as yours, doth temperately keep time,
And make as healthful music.
Shakespeare, *Hamlet*. Act iii, sc. 4, l. 140.

13
The heart of man is made to reconcile contradictions.
David Hume, *Essays: Parties of Great Britain*.

14
The heart hath its own memory, like the mind,
And in it are enshrined
The precious keepsakes, into which is wrought
The giver's loving thought.
Longfellow, *From My Arm-Chair*. St. 12.

15
For all earth's width of waters is a span,
And their convulsed existence mere repose,
Matched with the unstable heart of man,
Shoreless in wants, mist-girt in all it knows,
Open to every wind of sect or clan,
And sudden-passionate in ebbs and flows.
J. R. Lowell, *Ode for the Fourth of July, 1876*. Pt. iv, sec. 1.

The heart is like an instrument whose strings
Steal nobler music from Life's many frets:
The golden threads are spun thro' Suffering's fire,
Wherewith the marriage-robes for heaven are woven:
And all the rarest hues of human life

Take radiance, and are rainbow'd out in tears.
GERALD MASSEY, *Wedded Love.*

1
The human heart is like a millstone in a mill: when you put wheat under it, it turns and grinds and bruises the wheat to flour; if you put no wheat, it still grinds on, but then 'tis itself it grinds and wears away.
MARTIN LUTHER, *Table Talk: Of Temptation and Tribulation.*

A mill-stone and the human heart are driven ever round;
If they have nothing else to grind, they must themselves be ground.
FRIEDRICH VON LOGAU, *Sinnegedichte.* (Longfellow, tr.)

Something the heart must have to cherish,
Must love, and joy, and sorrow learn;
Something with passion clasp, or perish,
And in itself to ashes burn.
LONGFELLOW, *Hyperion: Motto.* Bk. ii. Longfellow states this to be a translation of a German poem, *Forsaken,* but does not give the author.

2
Two chambers hath the heart.
There dwelling, Live Joy and Pain apart.
(Zwei Kammern hat das Herz.
Drin wohnen, Die Freude und der Schmerz.)
HERMANN NEUMANN, *Das Herz.* (Robinson, tr.)

3
Hearts have as many fashions as the world has shapes. (Pectoribus mores tot sunt, quot in orbe figuræ.)
OVID, *Ars Amatoria.* Bk. i, l. 759.

4
The heart is a free and a fetterless thing—
A wave of the ocean, a bird on the wing.
JULIA PARDOE, *The Captive Greek Girl.*

5
By every light, in every pose,
In God's Eternal Studios,
The human heart, with frown and laugh,
Is posing for its photograph.
PAUL SHIVELL, *The Studios Photographic.*

6
The hearts of men, which fondly here admire
Fair seeming shows, and feed on vain delight,
Transported with celestial desire
Of those fair forms, may lift themselves up higher,
And learn to love, with zealous humble duty,
Th' Eternal Fountain of that heavenly beauty.
SPENSER, *Hymn in Honour of Beautie,* l. 16.

II—Heart: Apothegms

7
The same heart beats in every human breast.
MATTHEW ARNOLD, *The Buried Life,* l. 23.

We have hearts within,
Warm, live, improvident, indecent hearts.
E. B. BROWNING, *Aurora Leigh.* Bk. iii. l. 462.

Every human heart is human.
LONGFELLOW, *Hiawatha: Introduction,* l. 91.

World-wide apart, and yet akin,
As showing that the human heart
Beats on forever as of old.
LONGFELLOW, *Tales of a Wayside Inn:* Pt. iii, *The Theologian's Tale: Elizabeth: Interlude.*

He fashioneth their hearts alike.
Old Testament: Psalms, xxxiii, 15.

8
'Twas when young Eustace wore his heart in's breeches.
BEAUMONT AND FLETCHER, *Elder Brother.* Act v.

Thy heart is in thy hose!
UNKNOWN, *Towneley Plays,* 113. (c. 1410)

My heart's sunk down into my hose.
RABELAIS, *Works.* Bk. v, ch. 36. (1552)

My heart sank, as the saying is, into my boots.
R. L. STEVENSON, *Treasure Island.* Ch. 13.

9
It is now high time to take heart of grace.
THOMAS BECON, *Catechism,* 245. (1560)

Come, come, take heart of grace.
APHRA BEHN, *Emperor of the Moon.* Act ii, sc. 2. (1687)

10 One can't tear out one's heart,
And show it, how sincere a thing it is!
ROBERT BROWNING, *Strafford.* Act i, sc. 2.

I will pluck it from my bosom, tho' my heart be at the root.
TENNYSON, *Locksley Hall,* l. 66.

11
The heart ay's the part ay
That makes us right or wrang.
BURNS, *Epistle to Davie.* St. 5.

12
My heart is wax to be moulded as she pleases, but enduring as marble to retain.
CERVANTES, *La Gitanilla.*

His heart was one of those which most enamour us,
Wax to receive, and marble to retain.
BYRON, *Beppo.* St. 34.

13
There are strings in the human heart which had better not be wibrated.
DICKENS, *Barnaby Rudge.* Ch. 22.

14
Futile the winds To a heart in port.
EMILY DICKINSON, *Poems,* p. 141.

15
Their hearts are in the right place.
DISRAELI, *The Infernal Marriage.* Pt. i, ch. 1.

15a
We shut our heart up, nowadays,
Like some old music-box that plays
Unfashionable airs that raise
Derisive pity.
AUSTIN DOBSON, *A Gage d'Amour,* l. 33.

16
Some heart once pregnant with celestial fire.
THOMAS GRAY, *Elegy Written in a Country Church-yard,* l. 46.

17
The great conservative is the heart.
HAWTHORNE, *Journals,* 6 Jan., 1854.

1
Let us lift up our heart with our hands unto God in the heavens.
Old Testament: Lamentations, iii, 41. (Sursum corda.—*Vulgate*.)

2
Where your treasure is, there will your heart be also.
New Testament: Luke, xii, 34; *Matthew*, vi, 21.

Only where the heart is can the treasure be found.
J. M. BARRIE, *Tommy and Grizel*. Ch. 1.

For his heart was in his work, and the heart
Giveth grace unto every Art.
LONGFELLOW, *The Building of the Ship*, l. 7.

3
Did not our heart burn within us, while he talked with us by the way?
New Testament: Luke, xxiv, 32.

4
With most people the heart grows old with the body.
GUY DE MAUPASSANT, *Julie Romain*.

5
The beating of my own heart
Was all the sound I heard.
MILNES, *I Wandered by the Brookside*.

6
Would I were as happy as my heart is clean! (Tam felix utinam quam pectore candidus essem!)
OVID, *Epistulæ ex Ponto*. Bk. iv, epis. 14, l. 43.

Brave hearts and clean! and yet—God guide them!—young.
TENNYSON, *Merlin and Vivien*, l. 29.

7
My heart is not made of horn. (Neque enim mihi cornea fibra est.)
PERSIUS, *Satires*. Sat. i, l. 47.

8
My heart was in my mouth. (Mihi anima in naso esse.)
PETRONIUS, *Satyricon*. Sec. 62.

Having their heart at their very mouth for fear.
ERASMUS, *Paraphrase of Luke, xxiii*. (Udall, tr., 1548.)

My heart was almost at my mouth.
DRYDEN, *Love Triumphant*. Act i, sc. 1. (1694)

The heart of the fool is in his mouth, but the mouth of the wise man is in his heart.
BENJAMIN FRANKLIN, *Poor Richard*, 1733.

9
What takes our heart must merit our esteem.
MATTHEW PRIOR, *Solomon*. Bk. ii, l. 101.

10
My heart is fixed, O God, my heart is fixed.
Old Testament: Psalms, lvii, 7.

11
Even the very middle of my heart Is warm'd.
SHAKESPEARE, *Cymbeline*. Act i, sc. 6, l. 27.

In my heart's core, ay, in my heart of heart.
SHAKESPEARE, *Hamlet*. Act iii, sc. 2, l. 78.

The inmost cupboards of her heart.
THACKERAY, *The Virginians*. Ch. 33.

12
And let me wring your heart; for so I shall,
If it be made of penetrable stuff.
SHAKESPEARE, *Hamlet*. Act iii, sc. 4, l. 36.

13
But I will wear my heart upon my sleeve
For daws to peck at.
SHAKESPEARE, *Othello*. Act i, sc. 1, l. 64.

"Young Strephon wears his heart upon his sleeve,"
Thus Sardon spoke, with scoffing air;
Perhaps 'twas envy made the gray-beard grieve—
For Sardon never had a heart to wear.
R. W. GILDER, *Strephon and Sardon*.

14
My heart is ever at your service.
SHAKESPEARE, *Timon of Athens*. Act i, sc. 2, l. 76.

15
From the bottom of the heart. (Imo pectore.)
VERGIL, *Æneid*. Bk. xi, l. 377.

16
It terrifies the cockles of my heart.
SAMUEL WESLEY, *Maggots*, p. 126. (1685)

17
Heaven's sovereign saves all beings, but himself,
That hideous sight, a naked human heart.
YOUNG, *Night Thoughts*. Night iii, l. 226.

18
We'll wait on you with all our hearts, and with a piece of my liver, too.
UNKNOWN, *Mucedorus*. Sig. F 4. (1598)

With all my heart and a piece of my liver.
SWIFT, *Polite Conversation*. Dial. i.

III—Heart: Eating the Heart

19
To eat thy heart through comfortless dispairs.
SPENSER [?], *Mother Hubberds Tale*, l. 904.

In the desert
I saw a creature, naked, bestial,
Who, squatting upon the ground,
Held his heart in his hand
And ate of it.
I said, "Is it good, friend?"
"It is bitter—bitter," he answered;
"But I like it
Because it is bitter,
And because it is my heart."
STEPHEN CRANE, *The Heart*.

20
Spread yourself upon his bosom publicly, whose heart you would eat in private.
BEN JONSON, *Every Man Out of His Humour*. Act iii, sc. 1.

21
Eat not thy heart. (Καρδίην μὴ ἐσθίειν.)
PYTHAGORAS. (DIOGENES LAERTIUS, *Pythagoras*. Sec. 17.)

Eat not thy heart; which forbids to afflict our souls, and waste them with vexatious cares.
PLUTARCH, *Of the Training of Children*.

IV—Heart: The Merry Heart

1
I have a heart with room for every joy.
P. J. BAILEY, *Festus: A Mountain*

So simple is the heart of man,
So ready for new hope and joy:
Ten thousand years since it began
Have left it younger than a boy.
STOPFORD A. BROOKE, *The Earth and Man.*

2
No sky is heavy if the heart be light.
CHURCHILL, *The Prophecy of Famine*, l. 362.

Oh! timely happy, timely wise,
Hearts that with rising morn arise!
JOHN KEBLE, *The Christian Year: Morning.*

3
A light heart and thin pair of breeches,
Go thro' the world, brave boys!
CHARLES COFFEY, *Boarding-School.* Act i.

4
The joy of the heart fairly colours the face.
JOHN DAVIES, *The Scourge of Folly*, p. 46. (1611)

The heart's mirth doth make the face fair.
UNKNOWN, *Book of Merry Riddles.* Prov. 54. (1629)

5
He that is of a merry heart hath a continual feast.
Old Testament: Proverbs, xv, 15.

A merry heart doeth good like a medicine.
Old Testament: Proverbs, xvii, 22.

6
My heart is like a singing bird
Whose nest is in a water'd shoot;
My heart is like an apple-tree
Whose boughs are bent with thick-set fruit;
My heart is like a rainbow shell
That paddles in a halcyon sea;
My heart is gladder than all these,
Because my love is come to me.
CHRISTINA ROSSETTI, *A Birthday.*

7
My bosom's lord sits lightly in his throne.
SHAKESPEARE, *Romeo and Juliet.* Act v, sc. 1, 3.

8
Jog on, jog on, the foot-path way,
And merrily hent the stile-a:
A merry heart goes all the day,
Your sad tires in a mile-a.
SHAKESPEARE, *The Winter's Tale.* Act iv, sc. 3, l. 132.

V—Heart: The Sad Heart

9
My heart is sair, I daur na tell,
My heart is sair for Somebody.
BURNS, *My Heart is Sair for Somebody.*

10
No more—no more—Oh! never more on me
The freshness of the heart can fall like dew
BYRON, *Don Juan*, canto i, st. 214.

11
The heaviness of the heart breaketh strength. . . . Take no heaviness to heart.
Apocrypha: Ecclesiasticus, xxxviii, 18, 20.

Let not your heart be troubled.
New Testament: John, xiv, 1.

12
Every heart hath its own ache.
THOMAS FULLER, *Gnomologia.* No. 1418.

13
My heart is heavy. (Mein Herz ist schwer.)
GOETHE, *Faust.* Pt. i, sc. 16.

A wounded heart is hard to cure.
GOETHE, *Torquato Tasso.* Act iv, sc. 4, l. 24.

14
There is an evening twilight of the heart,
When its wild passion-waves are lulled to rest.
FITZ-GREENE HALLECK, *Twilight.*

15
Hearts, like apples, are hard and sour,
Till crushed by Pain's resistless power;
And yield their juices rich and bland
To none but Sorrow's heavy hand.
J. G. HOLLAND, *Bitter-Sweet.* Epis. i.

16
The whole head is sick, and the whole heart faint.
Old Testament: Isaiah, i, 5.

17
The long-lost ventures of the heart,
That send no answers back again.
LONGFELLOW, *The Fire of Driftwood.*

18
The heart knoweth its own bitterness.
Old Testament: Proverbs, xiv, 10.

19
This house is to be let for life or years,
Her rent is sorrow, and her income tears;
Cupid, 't has long stood void; her bills make known,
She must be dearly let, or let alone.
FRANCIS QUARLES, *Emblems.* Bk. ii, emb. 10.

20
My heart is turn'd to stone: and while 'tis mine,
It shall be stony.
SHAKESPEARE, *II Henry VI.* Act v, sc. 2, l. 50.

My heart is turned to stone; I strike it, and it hurts my hand.
SHAKESPEARE, *Othello.* Act iv, sc. 1, l. 193.

21
My heart hath one poor string to stay it by,
Which holds but till thy news be uttered.
SHAKESPEARE, *King John.* Act v, sc. 7, l. 55.

22
Hearts live by being wounded.
WILDE, *A Woman of No Importance.* Act iii.

23
Out-worn heart, in a time out-worn,
Come clear of the nets of wrong and right.
W. B. YEATS, *Into the Twilight.*

VI—Heart: The Broken Heart

24
An innocent heart is a brittle thing, and one false vow can break it.
BULWER-LYTTON, *Last of the Barons.* Bk. i, ch. 2.

1
And thus the heart will break, yet brokenly live on.
BYRON, *Childe Harold*. Canto iii, st. 32.

And long she pined—for broken hearts die slow!
THOMAS CAMPBELL, *Theodric*, l. 389.

As an egg, when broken, never
Can be mended, but must ever
Be the same crushed egg for ever—
So shall this dark heart of mine.
T. H. CHIVERS, *To Allegra Florence in Heaven.*

2
O hearts that break and give no sign
Save whitening lips and fading tresses.
O. W. HOLMES, *The Voiceless.*

3
No truer word, save God's, was ever spoken,
Than that the largest heart is soonest broken.
WALTER SAVAGE LANDOR, *Epigram.*

And the heart that is soonest awake to the flowers,
Is always the first to be touch'd by the thorns.
THOMAS MOORE, *Oh! Think Not My Spirits.*

4
And when she ceas'd, we sighing saw
The floor lay pav'd with broken hearts.
RICHARD LOVELACE, *Gratiana Dancing.*

5 Throw thy heart
Against the flint and hardness of my fault;
Which, being dried with grief, will break to powder.
SHAKESPEARE, *Antony and Cleopatra*, iv, 9, 14.

Queen: O Hamlet! thou hast cleft my heart in twain.
Hamlet: O, throw away the worser part of it,
And live the purer with the other half.
SHAKESPEARE, *Hamlet*. Act iii, sc. 4, l. 156.

6
Now cracks a noble heart. Good-night, sweet prince.
SHAKESPEARE, *Hamlet*. Act v, sc. 2, l. 370.

My old heart is crack'd, is crack'd!
SHAKESPEARE, *King Lear*. Act ii, sc. 1, l. 92.

His flaw'd heart,
Alack, too weak the conflict to support!
'Twixt two extremes of passion, joy and grief,
Burst smilingly.
SHAKESPEARE, *King Lear*. Act v, sc. 3, l. 196.

7 Never morning wore
To evening, but some heart did break.
TENNYSON, *In Memoriam*. Pt. vi, st. 2.

How else but through a broken heart
May Lord Christ enter in?
OSCAR WILDE, *The Ballad of Reading Gaol.*

VII—Heart: The Good Heart

8
To thee only God granted A heart ever new:
To all always open, To all always true.
MATTHEW ARNOLD, *Parting*, l. 79.

9
A heart at leisure from itself
To soothe and sympathise.
ANNA LETITIA WARING, *Father, I Know that All My Life.*

10
A heart to pity, and a hand to bless.
CHURCHILL, *The Prophecy of Famine*, l. 178.

11
What outward form and feature are
He guesseth but in part;
But that within is good and fair
He seeth with the heart.
S. T. COLERIDGE, *To a Lady Offended by a Sportive Observation.*

12
His heart was as great as the world, but there was no room in it to hold the memory of a wrong.
EMERSON, *Letters and Social Aims: Greatness.*

13
Thy heart above all envy and all pride,
Firm as man's sense, and soft as woman's love.
JAMES HAMMOND, *Elegies*. No. 14.

14
'Tis the heart's current lends the cup its glow,
Whate'er the fountain whence the draught may flow.
O. W. HOLMES, *A Sentiment.*

15
A gen'rous heart repairs a sland'rous tongue.
HOMER, *Odyssey*. Bk. viii, l. 432. (Pope, tr.)

16 The full heart's a Psalter,
Rich in deep hymns of gratitude and love.
THOMAS HOOD, *Ode to Rae Wilson.*

The incense of the heart may rise.
JOHN PIERPONT, *Every Place a Temple.*

17
Ye whose hearts are fresh and simple,
Who have faith in God and nature.
LONGFELLOW, *Hiawatha: Introduction.*

18
All that hath been majestical
In life or death, since time began,
Is native in the simple heart of all,
The angel heart of man.
J. R. LOWELL, *An Incident in a Railroad Car.*

Into the sunshine, Full of light,
Leaping and flashing From morn till night!
Glorious fountain! Let my heart be
Fresh, changeful, constant, Upward, like thee!
J. R. LOWELL, *The Fountain.*

19
Her heart is always doing lovely things,
Filling my wintry mind with simple flowers;
Playing sweet tunes on my untuned strings,
Delighting all my undelightful hours.
JOHN MASEFIELD, *Her Heart.*

20
Mine is a soft heart. (Molle cor esse mihi.)
OVID, *Epistulæ ex Ponto*. Bk. i, epis. 3, l. 32.

Bow, stubborn knees; and, heart with strings of steel,
Be soft as sinews of the new-born babe!
SHAKESPEARE, *Hamlet*. Act iii, sc. 3, l. 69.

1
A heart imbued with the noble sense of virtue. (Incoctum generoso pectus honesto.)
PERSIUS, *Satires*. Sat. ii, l. 74.

2
A good heart helps in misfortune. (In re mala, animo si bono utare, adjuvat.)
PLAUTUS, *Captivi*, l. 202. (Act ii, sc. 1.)

3
Create in me a clean heart, O God; and renew a right spirit within me.
Old Testament: Psalms, li, 10.

4
A man 'at stands
And jest holds out in his two hands
As warm a heart as ever beat
Betwixt here and the Mercy Seat!
J. W. RILEY, *Eugene Debs*.

Far may we search before we find
A heart so manly and so kind!
SCOTT, *Marmion:* Canto iv, *Introduction*, l. 136.

For his heart is like the sea,
Ever open, brave, and free.
F. E. WEATHERLY, *They All Love Jack*.

5
A good heart's worth gold.
SHAKESPEARE, *II Henry IV*. Act ii, sc. 4, l. 34.

Kind hearts are more than coronets,
And simple faith than Norman blood.
TENNYSON, *Lady Clara Vere de Vere*. St. 7.

6
What stronger breastplate than a heart untainted!
SHAKESPEARE, *II Henry VI*. Act iii, sc. 2, l. 232.

His heart as far from fraud as heaven from earth.
SHAKESPEARE, *The Two Gentlemen of Verona*. Act ii, sc. 7, l. 78.

7
My heart Is true as steel.
SHAKESPEARE, *A Midsummer-Night's Dream*. Act ii, sc. 1, l. 196. *See also under* CONSTANCY.

8
Thou shalt rest sweetly if thy heart reprehend thee not.
THOMAS À KEMPIS, *De Imitatione Christi*. Pt. ii, ch. 6.

Only the heart without a stain knows perfect ease (Ganz unbefleckt geniesst sich nur das Herz.)
GOETHE, *Iphigenia auf Tauris*. Act iv, sc. 4.

9
Enough of Science and of Art;
Close up those barren leaves;
Come forth, and bring with you a heart
That watches and receives.
WORDSWORTH, *The Tables Turned*. St. 8.

VIII—Heart: The Gallant Heart

10
Although my hap be hard, my heart is high.
WILLIAM ALEXANDER, *Aurora*. Sonnet 30.

11
I said to Heart, "How goes it?" Heart replied:
"Right as a Ribstone Pippin!" But it lied.
HILAIRE BELLOC, *For False Heart*.

12
Here's a heart for any fate!
BYRON, *To Thomas Moore*.

With a heart for any fate.
LONGFELLOW, *A Psalm of Life*.

13
Soul of fibre and heart of oak. (Alma de esparto y corazon de encina.)
CERVANTES, *Don Quixote*. Pt. ii, ch. 70. *See also* ENGLAND: HEARTS OF OAK.

14
For his heart was hot within him,
Like a living coal his heart was.
LONGFELLOW, *Hiawatha*. Pt. iv.

15
I account more strength in a true heart than in a walled city.
JOHN LYLY, *Endymion*.

16
My heart is a kicking horse
Shod with Kentucky steel!
VACHEL LINDSAY, *My Fathers Came from Kentucky*.

17
Steady of heart, and stout of hand.
SCOTT, *Lay of the Last Minstrel*. Canto i, st. 21.

Stout heart, and open hand.
SCOTT, *Marmion*. Canto i, st. 10.

The very firstlings of my heart shall be
The firstlings of my hand.
SHAKESPEARE, *Macbeth*. Act iv, sc. 1, l. 147.

18
Your hearts are mighty, your skins are whole.
SHAKESPEARE, *The Merry Wives of Windsor*. Act iii, sc. 1, l. 111.

19
The hearts that dare are quick to feel;
The hands that wound are soft to heal.
BAYARD TAYLOR, *Soldiers of Peace*.

20
One equal temper of heroic hearts,
Made weak by time and fate, but strong in will
To strive, to seek, to find, and not to yield.
TENNYSON, *Ulysses*, l. 68.

IX—Heart: The Humble Heart

21
My favoured temple is an humble heart.
P. J. BAILEY, *Festus: Colonnade and Lawn*.

22
A gentle heart is tied with an easy thread.
GEORGE HERBERT, *Jacula Prudentum*.

23
A small heart hath small desires.
GEORGE HERBERT, *Jacula Prudentum*.

24
The tumult and the shouting dies;
The Captains and the Kings depart:
Still stands Thine ancient sacrifice,
An humble and a contrite heart.
RUDYARD KIPLING, *Recessional*.

1
Th' Almighty, from his throne, on earth surveys
Nought greater, than an honest, humble heart.
YOUNG, *Night Thoughts*. Night viii, l. 475.

X—Heart: The Speaking Heart

See also Candor

2
That which cometh from the heart will go to the heart.
JEREMIAH BURROUGHES, *In Hosea*. (1652)

3
Where hearts are true, Few words will do.
A. B. CHEALES, *Proverbial Folk-Lore*, 86.

4
When the heart is a fire, some sparks will fly out of the mouth.
THOMAS FULLER, *Gnomologia*. No. 5589.

5
What the heart did think, the tongue would clink.
ROBERT GREENE, *Works*, ii, 116. (1583)

What the heart thinketh, the tongue speaketh.
JOHN RAY, *English Proverbs*, 13. (1670)

6
When the heart dares to speak, it needs no preparation. (Wo das Herz reden darf braucht es keiner Vorbereitung.)
LESSING, *Minna von Barnhelm*. Act v, sc. 4.

7
Out of the abundance of the heart the mouth speaketh.
New Testament: Matthew, xii, 34.

9
Unhappy that I am, I cannot heave
My heart into my mouth.
SHAKESPEARE, *King Lear*. Act i, sc. 1, l. 92.

A heavy heart bears not a humble tongue.
SHAKESPEARE, *Love's Labour's Lost*. Act v, sc. 2, l. 747.

10
A man who desires to soften another man's heart, should always abuse himself. In softening a woman's heart, he should abuse her.
ANTHONY TROLLOPE, *Last Chronicle of Barset*. Ch. 44.

11
The mouth obeys poorly when the heart murmurs. (La bouche obéit mal lorsque le cœur murmure.)
VOLTAIRE, *Tancrède*. Act i, sc. 4.

XI—Heart: The Lover's Heart

12
Her o'erflowing heart, which pants
With all it granted, and with all it grants.
BYRON, *Don Juan*. Canto ii, st. 195.

13
In sailing o'er life's ocean wide,
Your heart should be your only guide;
With summer sea and favouring wind
Yourself in port you'll surely find.
W. S. GILBERT, *Ruddigore*. Act i.

14
Bid me to live, and I will live
Thy Protestant to be:
Or bid me love, and I will give
A loving heart to thee.

A heart as soft, a heart as kind,
A heart as sound and free
As in the whole world thou canst find,
That heart I'll give to thee.
ROBERT HERRICK, *To Anthea, Who May Command Him Anything*.

When I was one-and-twenty
I heard a wise man say:
"Give crowns and pounds and guineas
But not your heart away."
A. E. HOUSMAN, *A Shropshire Lad*. No. 13.

15
A watchman's part compels my heart
To keep you off its beat,
THOMAS HOOD, *I'm Not a Single Man*.

16
My heart led me past and took me away;
And yet it was my heart that wanted to stay.
HELEN HOYT, *In the Park*.

17
But to her heart, her heart was voluble,
Paining with eloquence her balmy side;
JOHN KEATS, *The Eve of St. Agnes*. St. 23.

18
There's a girl in the heart of Maryland
With a heart that belongs to me.
BALLARD MACDONALD, *There's a Girl in the Heart of Maryland*. (1913)

19
Knit your hearts With an unslipping knot.
SHAKESPEARE, *Antony and Cleopatra*. Act ii, sc. 2, l. 128.

20
I'll warrant him heart-whole.
SHAKESPEARE, *As You Like It*. Act iv, sc. 1, l. 49.

21
My true-love hath my heart, and I have his,
By just exchange, one for the other given.
SIR PHILIP SIDNEY, *My True Love Hath my Heart*.

22
I prithee send me back my heart,
Since I cannot have thine:
For if from thine thou wilt not part,
Why then shouldst thou have mine?
SIR JOHN SUCKLING, *Song*.

Maid of Athens, ere we part,
Give, oh, give me back my heart!
Or, since that has left my breast,
Keep it now, and take the rest!
Hear my vow before I go,
Ζώη μοῦ, σάς ἀγαπῶ.
BYRON, *Maid of Athens, Ere we Part*.

23
I thought to undermine the heart
By whispering in the ear.
SIR JOHN SUCKLING, *The Siege of a Heart*.

24
Oh, ye gods, why should my poor, resistless heart

Stand to oppose thy might and power?
GEORGE WASHINGTON, *My Poor Resistless Heart*. (1748)

XII—Heart: The Wicked Heart

1
The heart of a man is the place the Devil's in.
SIR THOMAS BROWNE, *Religio Medici*. Pt. i, sec. 44.

2
A bitter heart that bides its time and bites.
ROBERT BROWNING, *Caliban Upon Setebos*.

3
His heart was form'd for softness, warp'd to wrong;
Betray'd too early, and beguiled too long.
BYRON, *The Corsair*. Canto iii, st. 23.

4
Thou hast a heart, though 'tis a savage one.
CONGREVE, *The Mourning Bride*. Act ii, sc. 3.

5
He withers at his heart, and looks as wan,
As the pale spectre of a murder'd man.
DRYDEN, *Palamon and Arcite*. Bk. i, l. 528.

6
Look into any man's heart you please, and you will always find, in every one, at least one black spot which he has to keep concealed.
HENRIK IBSEN, *Pillars of Society*. Act iii.

7
The heart is deceitful above all things, and desperately wicked.
Old Testament: Jeremiah, xvii, 9.

8
His heart is as firm as a stone; yea, as hard as a piece of the nether millstone.
Old Testament: Job, xli, 24.

My idol fell down and was utterly broken,
The fragments of stone lay all scattered apart;
And I picked up the hardest to keep as a token—
Her heart.
GORDON CAMPBELL, *My Idol*.

9
The heart is hardest in the softest climes;
The passions flourish, the affections die.
WALTER SAVAGE LANDOR, *Hellenics*.

Worse than a bloody hand is a hard heart.
SHELLEY, *The Cenci*. Act v, sc. 2.

Oh the dullness and hardness of the human heart. (O hebetudo et duritia cordis humani.)
THOMAS À KEMPIS, *De Imitatione Christi*. Bk. i, sec. 23.

10
His heart I know, how variable and vain.
MILTON, *Paradise Lost*. Bk. xi, l. 92.

11
Your hearts are steeped in gall and biting vinegar. (Corda in felle sunt sita atque acerbo aceto.)
PLAUTUS, *Truculentus*. Act i, sc. 2.

12
Bare the mean heart that lurks beneath a star.
POPE, *Imitations of Horace: Satires*. Bk. ii, sat. 1, l. 108.

13
But your heart
Is cramm'd with arrogancy, spleen, and pride.
SHAKESPEARE, *Henry VIII*. Act ii, sc. 4, l. 110.

14
Every heart, when sifted well,
Is a clot of warmer dust,
Mix'd with cunning sparks of hell.
TENNYSON, *The Vision of Sin*, l. 112.

15
The selfish heart deserves the pain it feels.
YOUNG, *Night Thoughts*. Night i, l. 300.

XIII—Heart: Want of Heart

16
Devotion's ev'ry grace, except the heart.
BURNS, *The Cotter's Saturday Night*. St. 17.

17
Some hearts are hidden, some have not a heart.
GEORGE CRABBE, *The Borough*. Letter 17, l. 73.

18
He hath the sore which no man healeth,
The which is known as lack of heart.
JOHN GOWER, *Confessio Amantis*. Bk. iv, l. 334.

19
"With every pleasing, ev'ry prudent part,
Say, what can Chloe want?"—She wants a heart.
POPE, *Moral Essays*. Epis. ii, l. 159.

20
Ward has no heart, they say; but I deny it;—
He has a heart, and gets his speeches by it.
SAMUEL ROGERS, *On John William Ward*.

21
Malebranche declares that not a soul is left;
We humbly think that there are still some hearts.
(Malebranche dirait qu'il n'y plus une âme;
Nous pensons humblement qu'il reste encor des cœurs.)
EDMOND ROSTAND, *Chanticler: Prelude*.

XIV—Heart and Head

22
Can art, alas! or genius, guide the head
Where truth and freedom from the heart are fled?
Can lesser wheels repeat their native stroke,
When the prime function of the soul is broke?
MARK AKENSIDE, *Epistle to Curio*, l. 265.

23
A faithless heart betrays the head unsound.
JOHN ARMSTRONG, *Art of Preserving Health*. Bk. iv, l. 284.

24
The brave impetuous heart yields everywhere
To the subtle, contriving head.
MATTHEW ARNOLD, *Empedocles on Etna*. Act ii, l. 90.

25
My heart beat in my brain.
E. B. BROWNING, *Aurora Leigh*. Bk. i, l. 961.

1
A good heart is better than all the heads in the world.
BULWER-LYTTON, *The Disowned*. Ch. 33.

2
What hand and brain went ever paired?
What heart alike conceived and dared?
ROBERT BROWNING, *The Last Ride Together*.

3
His madness was not of the head, but heart.
BYRON, *Lara*. Canto i, sec. 18.

For his was error of head, not heart.
THOMAS MOORE, *The Irish Slave*, l. 45.

4
Men, as well as women, are much oftener led by their hearts than by their understandings.
LORD CHESTERFIELD, *Letters*, 21 Jan., 1748.

Nine times in ten, the heart governs the understanding.
LORD CHESTERFIELD, *Letters*, 15 May, 1749.

5
And a man may still lift up his head,
But nevermore his heart.
G. K. CHESTERTON, *Ballad of the White Horse*.

6
His heart runs away with his head.
GEORGE COLMAN THE YOUNGER, *Who Wants a Guinea*. Act i, sc. 1.

7
Here the heart
May give a useful lesson to the head.
COWPER, *The Task*. Bk. vi, l. 85.

8
I love thee for a heart that's kind—
Not for the knowledge in thy mind.
W. H. DAVIES, *Sweet Stay-at-Home*.

9
Hearts may agree though heads differ.
THOMAS FULLER, *Gnomologia*. No. 2480.

10
The heart is wiser than the intellect.
J. G. HOLLAND, *Kathrina*. Pt. ii, st. 9.

11
Whatever comes from the brain carries the hue of the place it came from, and whatever comes from the heart carries the heat and color of its birthplace.
O. W. HOLMES, *The Professor at the Breakfast-Table*. Ch. vi.

12
Every one speaks well of his heart, but no one dares speak of his head. (Chacun dit du bien de son cœur, et personne n'en ose dire de son esprit.)
LA ROCHEFOUCAULD, *Maximes*. No. 98.

13
The head is always the dupe of the heart. (L'esprit est toujours la dupe de cœur.)
LA ROCHEFOUCAULD, *Maximes*. No. 102.

Monsieur de Rochefoucault, in his Maxims, says, that *l'esprit est souvent la dupe du cœur* If he had said, instead of *souvent*, *presque toujours* [almost always], I fear he would have been nearer the truth.
LORD CHESTERFIELD, *Letters*, 9 March, 1748.
Chesterfield had the maxim wrong, for La Rochefoucauld wrote "toujours."

14
It is the heart, and not the brain,
That to the highest doth attain.
LONGFELLOW, *The Building of the Ship*, l. 124.

15
Where the mind is past hope, the heart is past shame.
JOHN LYLY, *Euphues*, p. 341. (1580)

16
Better to have the poet's heart than brain,
Feeling than song.
GEORGE MACDONALD, *Within and Without*. Pt. iii, sc. 9, l. 30.

17
The heart has its reasons, which reason does not know. (Le cœur a ses raisons, que la raison connait pas.)
PASCAL, *Pensées*. Pt. ii, art. xvii, No. 5.

The heart has arguments with which the understanding is not acquainted.
EMERSON, *Conduct of Life: Worship*. Quoted.

The heart has eyes that the brain knows nothing of.
CHARLES H. PARKHURST, *Sermons: Coming to the Truth*.

18
A brain of feathers, and a heart of lead.
POPE, *The Dunciad*. Bk. ii, l. 44.

19
The head is not more native to the heart,
The hand more instrumental to the mouth,
Than is the throne of Denmark to thy father.
SHAKESPEARE, *Hamlet*. Act i, sc. 2, l. 47.

20
If wrong our hearts, our heads are right in vain.
YOUNG, *Night Thoughts*. Night vi, l. 281.

HEAVEN

See also Paradise. For Heaven in the sense of sky, see Sky

I—Heaven: Definition and Description

21
Where imperfection ceaseth, heaven begins.
P. J. BAILEY, *Festus: Wood and Water*.

Is Heaven a place where pearly streams
Glide over silver sand?
Like childhood's rosy dazzling dreams
Of some far faery land?
Is Heaven a clime where diamond dews
Glitter on fadeless flowers?
And mirth and music ring aloud
From amaranthine bowers?
P. J. BAILEY, *Festus: Alcove and Garden*. The next line is, "Ah no; not such, not such is Heaven!"

22
Spend in pure converse our eternal day;
Think each in each, immediately wise;
Learn all we lacked before; hear, know, and say
What this tumultuous body now denies;

And feel, who have laid our groping hands away;
And see, no longer blinded by our eyes.
RUPERT BROOKE, *Sonnet.*

1
Earth breaks up, time drops away,
In flows heaven, with its new day.
ROBERT BROWNING, *Christmas-Eve.* Sec. 10.

2
Heaven means to be one with God.
CONFUCIUS, *Analects.* (FARRAR, *What Heaven Is.*)

3
He showed me like a master
That one rose makes a gown;
That looking up to Heaven
Is merely looking down.
NATHALIA CRANE, *My Husbands.*

Hence, Heaven looks down on earth with all her eyes.
YOUNG, *Night Thoughts.* Night vii, l. 1094.

4
I never spoke with God,
Nor visited in heaven;
Yet certain am I of the spot
As if the chart were given.
EMILY DICKINSON, *Poems.* Pt. iv, No. 17.

5
Who has not found the heaven below
Will fail of it above.
God's residence is next to mine,
His furniture is love.
EMILY DICKINSON, *Poems.* Pt. i, No. 100.

The heaven of poetry and romance still lies around us and within us.
LONGFELLOW, *Drift-Wood: Twice-Told Tales.*

I know not where lies Eden-land;
I only know 'tis like unto
God's kingdom, ever right at hand—
Ever right here in reach of you.
JOAQUIN MILLER, *With Love to You and Yours.* Pt. iv, sec. 12.

6
And so upon this wise I prayed,—
Great Spirit, give to me
A heaven not so large as yours,
But large enough for me.
EMILY DICKINSON, *Poems.* Pt. i, No. 39.

How vast is heaven? lo it will fit
In any space you give to it. . . .
So broad—it takes in all things true;
So narrow—it can hold but you.
JOHN RICHARD MORELAND, *How Vast is Heaven.*

7
Where billows never break, nor tempests roar.
SAMUEL GARTH, *The Dispensary.* Canto iii, l. 226. (1699)

Where tempests never beat nor billows roar.
COWPER, *On the Receipt of My Mother's Picture.* (1798) Misquoting Garth.

8
I hear thee speak of the better land,
Thou callest its children a happy band;
Mother! oh, where is that radiant shore?
Shall we not seek it, and weep no more?
FELICIA DOROTHEA HEMANS, *The Better Land.*

9
Olympus, the abode of the gods, that stands fast forever. Neither is it shaken by winds nor ever wet with rain, nor does snow fall upon it, but the air is outspread clear and cloudless, and over it hovers a radiant whiteness.
HOMER, *Odyssey.* Bk. vi, l. 42.

10
Heaven is largely a matter of digestion, and digestion is mostly a matter of mind.
ELBERT HUBBARD, *A Thousand and One Epigrams,* p. 34.

11
There the wicked cease from troubling; and there the weary be at rest.
Old Testament: Job, iii, 17.

And the wicked cease from troubling, and the weary are at rest.
TENNYSON, *The May Queen.* Last line.

12
In my father's house are many mansions.
New Testament: John, xiv, 2.

Nearer my Father's house,
Where the many mansions be,
Nearer the great white throne,
Nearer the crystal sea.
PHŒBE CARY, *Nearer Home.*

Therefore will I wait patiently,
Trusting, where all God's mansions be,
There hath been one prepared for me.
PHŒBE CARY, *Many Mansions.* St. 46.

No, not cold beneath the grasses,
Not close-walled within the tomb;
Rather in our Father's mansion,
Living in another room.
ROBERT FREEMAN, *In My Father's House.*

When I can read my title clear
To mansions in the skies,
I'll bid farewell to every fear,
And wipe my weeping eyes.
ISAAC WATTS, *When I Can Read My Title Clear.*

13
Great is the idleness which prevails in heaven. (Magna otia cæli.)
JUVENAL, *Satires.* Sat. vi, l. 394.

14
And when Booth halted by the curb for prayer
He saw his Master through the flag-filled air.
Christ came gently with a robe and crown
For Booth the soldier, while the throng knelt down.
He saw King Jesus. They were face to face,
And he knelt a-weeping in that holy place.
Are you washed in the blood of the Lamb?
VACHEL LINDSAY, *General William Booth Enters into Heaven.*

15
We see but dimly through the mists and vapors;
Amid these earthly damps

What seem to us but sad, funereal tapers
May be heaven's distant lamps.
LONGFELLOW, *Resignation*. St. 4.

1
Heaven to me's a fair blue stretch of sky,
Earth's jest a dusty road.
JOHN MASEFIELD, *Vagabond*.

2
What if Earth
Be but the shadow of Heav'n, and things therein
Each to other like, more than on earth is thought?
MILTON, *Paradise Lost*. Bk. v, l. 574.

3
Heav'n open'd wide
Her ever-during gates, harmonious sound,
On golden hinges moving.
MILTON, *Paradise Lost*. Bk. vii, l. 205.

God said, "Be light"—and light was on the grave!
No more alone to sage and hero given,
Ope for all life the impartial gates of Heaven!
BULWER-LYTTON, *The NewTimon*. Pt. iv, sec. 2.

When Christ ascended
Triumphantly, from star to star,
He left the gates of heaven ajar.
LONGFELLOW, *The Golden Legend*. Pt. ii, sc. 2.

4
There *is* a world above,
Where parting is unknown;
A whole eternity of love,
Form'd for the good alone;
And faith beholds the dying here
Translated to that happier sphere.
JAMES MONTGOMERY, *Friends*.

5
A Persian's Heav'n is easily made,
'Tis but black eyes and lemonade.
THOMAS MOORE, *Intercepted Letters*. No. vi, l. 32.

6
There's nae sorrow there, John,
There's neither cauld nor care, John,
The day is aye fair,
In the land o' the leal.
CAROLINA NAIRNE, *The Land o' the Leal*.

7
A sea before
The Throne is spread;—its pure still glass
Pictures all earth-scenes as they pass.
We, on its shore,
Share, in the bosom of our rest,
God's knowledge, and are blest.
JOHN HENRY NEWMAN, *A Voice from Afar*.

8
To heaven's high city I direct my journey,
Whose spangled suburbs entertain mine eye.
FRANCIS QUARLES, *Emblems*. Bk. v, emb. 6.

10
Heaven . . . The treasury of everlasting joy.
SHAKESPEARE, *II Henry VI*. Act ii, sc. 1, l. 17.

11
And is there care in Heaven? And is there love
In heavenly spirits to these Creatures base?
SPENSER, *Faerie Queene*. Bk. ii, canto 8, st. 1.

12
Could we but know
The land that ends our dark, uncertain travel.
E. C. STEDMAN, *The Undiscovered Country*.

For if, beyond the shadow and the sleep,
A place there be for souls without a stain,
Where peace is perfect, and delight more deep
Than seas or skies that change and shine again,
There none of all unsullied souls that live
May hold a surer station.
SWINBURNE, *In Memory of John William Inchbold*. St. 24.

12a
Heaven is such that all who have lived well, of whatever religion, have a place there.
SWEDENBORG, *Divine Providence*. Sec. 330.

13
O world invisible, we view thee:
O world intangible, we touch thee,
O world unknowable, we know thee,
Inapprehensible, we clutch thee!
FRANCIS THOMPSON, *In No Strange Land*.

14
So all we know of what they do above
Is that they happy are, and that they love.
EDMUND WALLER, *Upon the Death of My Lady Rich*, l. 75.

For all we know
Of what the blessed do above
Is, that they sing, and that they love.
EDMUND WALLER, *While I Listen to Thy Voice*, l. 10.

What know we of the blest above
But that they sing and that they love?
WORDSWORTH, *Scene on the Lake of Brientz*, l. 1. Wordsworth puts this couplet in quotation marks as an acknowledgment of his indebtedness to Waller.

15
There is a land of pure delight,
Where saints immortal reign;
Infinite day excludes the night,
And pleasures banish pain.
ISAAC WATTS, *There Is a Land*.

16
As much of heaven is visible as we have eyes to see.
WILLIAM WINTER, *The Actor and His Duty: Address*, 4 June, 1889.

17
Heaven lies about us in our infancy.
WORDSWORTH, *Intimations of Immortality*. St. 5.

Infancy: The period of our lives when, according to Wordsworth, "Heaven lies about us." The world begins lying about us pretty soon afterward.
AMBROSE BIERCE, *The Devil's Dictionary*.

Not only around our infancy
Doth heaven with all its splendors lie;
Daily, with souls that cringe and plot,

We Sinais climb and know it not.
J. R. LOWELL, *The Vision of Sir Launfal*: Pt. i. *Prelude*.

The gates of heaven are so easily found when we are little, and they are always standing open to let children wander in.
J. M. BARRIE, *Sentimental Tommy*, p. 52.

It was a childish ignorance,
But now 'tis little joy,
To know I'm farther off from heaven
Than when I was a boy.
THOMAS HOOD, *I Remember*.

II—Heaven: Apothegms

1
The New Jerusalem, when it comes, will probably be found so far to resemble the old as to stone its prophets freely.
SAMUEL BUTLER THE YOUNGER, *Note-Books*, p. 175.

2
He who offends against Heaven has none to whom he can pray.
CONFUCIUS, *Analects*. Bk. iii, ch. 13.

3
The sword of heaven is not in haste to smite,
Nor yet doth linger.
DANTE, *Paradiso*. Canto xxii, l. 16.

4
Heav'n would no bargain for its blessings drive.
DRYDEN, *Astrea Redux*, l. 137.

Heaven is a cheap purchase, whatever it cost.
THOMAS FULLER, *Gnomologia*.

For a cap and bells our lives we pay,
Bubbles we buy with a whole soul's tasking:
'Tis heaven alone that is given away,
'Tis only God may be had for the asking.
J. R. LOWELL, *The Vision of Sir Launfal*: *Prelude*.

5
Heaven without good society cannot be heaven.
THOMAS FULLER, *Gnomologia*.

Heaven was not heaven if Phaon was not there.
R. M. MILNES, *A Dream of Sappho*.

6
Hello, Central! give me heaven,
For my mama's there.
CHARLES K. HARRIS, *Hello, Central! Give Me Heaven*. (1901)

7
All this, and Heaven too!
PHILIP HENRY. (MATTHEW HENRY, *Life of Philip Henry*, p. 70.)

8
The net of Heaven has large meshes and yet nothing escapes it.
LAO-TSZE, *The Simple Way*. No. 73.

9
Struggle against it as thou wilt,
Yet Heaven's ways are Heaven's ways.
(Sperre dich, so viel du willst!
Des Himmels Wege sind des Himmels Wege.)
LESSING, *Nathan der Weise*. Act iii, sc. 1.

10
Lay up for yourselves treasures in heaven, where neither moth nor rust doth corrupt and where thieves do not break through nor steal.
New Testament: *Matthew*, vi, 20.

11
A heaven on earth.
MILTON, *Paradise Lost*. Bk. iv, l. 208.

I have been there, and still would go;
'Tis like a little heaven below.
ISAAC WATTS, *For the Lord's Day Evening*.

12
No man can resolve himself into Heaven.
DWIGHT L. MOODY, *Heaven*.

13
That they may be considered wise, they rail at heaven. (Ut putentur sapere, cœlum vituperant.)
PHÆDRUS, *Fables*. Bk. iv, fab. 6, l. 26.

14
I shall see you in the next world. (Apud Orcum te videbo.)
PLAUTUS, *Asinaria*, l. 606. (Act iii, sc. 3.)

15
The blessed damozel leaned out
From the gold bar of Heaven.
D. G. ROSSETTI, *The Blessed Damozel*, l. 1.

16
Heaven wills our happiness, allows our doom.
YOUNG, *Night Thoughts*. Night vii, l. 1301.

III—Heaven: Its Distance

17
All places are distant from heaven alike.
ROBERT BURTON, *Anatomy of Melancholy*. Pt. ii, sec. ii, mem. 4.

The way to heaven out of all places is of like length and distance.
SIR THOMAS MORE, *Utopia*.

18
Nothing must part them whom God hath joined, and the way to Heaven is as near in the Holy Land (if not nearer) as in England or Spain.
QUEEN ELEANOR, wife of Edward I., insisting on accompanying her husband to the Holy Land. (CAMDEN, *Remains*, 283.)

19
The road to heaven lies as near by water as by land.
FRIAR ELSTOWE, when threatened with drowning by the Earl of Essex in 1532. (JOHN STOW, *Annales of England*, p. 562. 1580.)

We are as near to Heaven by sea as by land.
SIR HUMPHREY GILBERT. There is a legend that these words, uttered by Gilbert, were heard on board his companion ship, the *Hind*, just before his own ship, the *Squirrel*, disappeared among the icebergs off the Azores in 1583.

He sat upon the deck,
The Book was in his hand;
"Do not fear! Heaven is as near,"
He said, "by water as by land!"
LONGFELLOW, *Sir Humphrey Gilbert*.

1
Heaven is far, the world is nigh.
JOHN GOWER, *Confessio Amantis: Prologue*, l. 261.

2
God, to remove His Ways from human sense,
Plac'd Heav'n from earth so far, that earthly sight
If it presume, might err in things too high,
And no advantage gain.
MILTON, *Paradise Lost*. Bk. viii, l. 119.

Heav'n is for thee too high
To know what passes there; be lowly wise:
Think only what concerns thee and thy being;
Dream not of other worlds, what creatures there
Live, in what state, condition, or degree,
Contented that thus far hath been reveal'd
Not of earth only, but of highest Heav'n.
MILTON, *Paradise Lost*. Bk. viii, l. 172.

IV—Heaven: Abraham's Bosom

3
Now he lives in Abraham's bosom. . . . For what other place is there for such a soul?
ST. AUGUSTINE, *Confessions*. Bk. ix, sec. 3.

4
With whom there is no place of toil, no burning heat, no piercing cold, nor any briars there . . . this place we call the Bosom of Abraham.
JOSEPHUS, *Discourse to the Greeks concerning Hades*.

5
Nay, sure, he's not in hell: he's in Arthur's bosom, if ever man went to Arthur's bosom.
SHAKESPEARE, *Henry V*. Act ii, sc. 3, l. 10.

6
Sweet peace conduct his sweet soul to the bosom
Of good old Abraham!
SHAKESPEARE, *Richard II*. Act iv, sc. 1, l. 103.

The sons of Edward sleep in Abraham's bosom.
SHAKESPEARE, *Richard III*. Act iv, sc. 3, l. 38.

7
Thou liest in Abraham's bosom all the year.
WORDSWORTH, *Miscellaneous Sonnets*. Pt. i, No. 30.

8
Two or three old ladies, who are languishing to be in Abraham's bosom, as the only man's bosom to whom they can hope for admittance.
WALPOLE, *Letter to John Chute*, 3 Oct., 1765.

V—Heaven: Praise

9
Jerusalem the golden, with milk and honey blest,
Beneath thy contemplation sink heart and voice oppressed.
(Urbs Syon aurea, patria lactea, cive decora,
Omne cor obruis, omnibus obstruis et cor et ora.)
BERNARD OF CLUNY, *Hora Novissima: Urbs Syon Aurea*. (John Mason Neale, tr.)

Jerusalem the Golden!
I toil on day by day;
Heart-sore each night with longing,
I stretch my hands and pray,
That mid thy leaves of healing
My soul may find her nest;
Where the wicked cease from troubling,
And the weary are at rest!
GERALD MASSEY, *Jerusalem the Golden*.

10
Scatter the clouds that hide
The face of heaven, and show
Where sweet peace doth abide,
Where Truth and Beauty grow.
ROBERT BRIDGES, *Morning Hymn*.

11
But Heaven that brings out good from evil,
And loves to disappoint the Devil.
S. T. COLERIDGE, *Job's Luck*.

12
Like a bairn to his mither, a wee birdie to its nest,
I wud fain be ganging noo unto my Saviour's breast;
For he gathers in his bosom witless, worthless lambs like me,
An' he carries them himsel' to his ain countree.
MARY LEE DEMAREST, *My Ain Countree*.

13
Heaven is most fair, but fairer He
That made that fairest Canopy.
ROBERT HERRICK, *Heaven*.

14
Know from the bounteous heaven all riches flow.
HOMER, *Odyssey*. Bk. xviii, l. 26. (Broome, tr.)

Just are the ways of heaven.
HOMER, *Odyssey*. Bk. viii, l. 128. (Broome, tr.)

In man's most dark extremity
Oft succour dawns from Heaven.
SCOTT, *The Lord of the Isles*. Canto i, st. 20.

Heaven still guards the right.
SHAKESPEARE, *Richard II*. Act iii, sc. 2, l. 61.

15
Men have not heard, nor perceived by the ear, neither hath the eye seen, O God, besides thee, what he hath prepared for him that waiteth for him.
Old Testament: Isaiah, lxiv, 4.

Eye hath not seen, nor ear heard, neither have entered into the heart of man, the things which God hath prepared for them that love him.
New Testament: I Corinthians, ii, 9.

Eye hath not seen it, my gentle boy!
Ear hath not heard its deep songs of joy;
Dreams cannot picture a world so fair—
Sorrow and death may not enter there;
Time doth not breathe on its fadeless bloom,
For beyond the clouds, and beyond the tomb,
It is there, it is there, my child!
FELICIA DOROTHEA HEMANS, *The Better Land*.

16
Earth has no sorrow that Heaven cannot heal.
THOMAS MOORE, *Come, Ye Disconsolate*.

1
This world is all a fleeting show,
For man's illusion given;
The smiles of joy, the tears of woe,
Deceitful shine, deceitful flow,—
There's nothing true but Heaven!
THOMAS MOORE, *This World is All a Fleeting Show.*

2
A day in thy courts is better than a thousand. I had rather be a door-keeper in the house of my God than to dwell in the tents of wickedness.
Old Testament: Psalms, lxxxiv, 10.

Take all the pleasures of all the spheres,
And multiply each through endless years,—
One minute of heaven is worth them all.
THOMAS MOORE, *Lalla Rookh: Paradise and the Peri.*

3
All places that the eye of heaven visits,
Are to a wise man ports and happy havens.
SHAKESPEARE, *Richard II.* Act i, sc. 3, l. 275.

The selfsame heaven
That frowns on me looks sadly upon him.
SHAKESPEARE, *Richard III.* Act v, sc. 3, l. 285.

4
Heaven is lovelier than the stars,
The sea is fairer than the shore;
I've seen beyond the sunset bars
A color more.
TRUMBULL STICKNEY, *Driftwood.*

VI—Heaven: Winning Heaven

See also Aspiration

5
Lose who may—I still can say,
Those who win heaven, blest are they!
ROBERT BROWNING, *One Way of Love.*

6
Not scorned in heaven, though little noticed here.
COWPER, *On the Receipt of my Mother's Picture,* l. 73.

7
Nor can his blessed soul look down from heaven,
Or break the eternal Sabbath of his rest.
DRYDEN, *The Spanish Friar.* Act v, sc. 2.

Heaven's eternal year is thine.
DRYDEN, *To the Memory of Mrs. Anne Killigrew.*

While yet a young probationer
And candidate of heaven.
DRYDEN, *To the Memory of Mrs. Anne Killigrew.*

8
Our heart is in heaven, our home is not here.
REGINALD HEBER, *Hymns: Fourth Sunday in Advent.*

No foot of land do I possess,
No cottage in the wilderness,
A poor wayfaring man,
Awhile I dwell in tents below,
Or gladly wander to and fro,
Till I my Canaan gain.
Yonder 's my home and portion fair,
My kingdom and my heart are there,
And my eternal home.
CHARLES WESLEY, *A Pilgrim's Lot.* (*Methodist Hymnal,* No. 68. 1877.)

9
Undaunted by the clouds of fear,
Undazzled by a happy day,
She made a Heaven about her here,
And took how much! with her away.
RICHARD MONCKTON MILNES, *In Memoriam.*

10
It were a journey like the path to heaven.
MILTON, *Comus,* l. 303.

11
Here in the body pent,
Absent from Him I roam,
Yet nightly pitch my moving tent
A day's march nearer home.
JAMES MONTGOMERY, *At Home in Heaven.*

One sweetly solemn thought
Comes to me o'er and o'er;
I am nearer home to-day
Than I ever have been before.
PHŒBE CARY, *Nearer Home.*

12
Joy, joy for ever!—my task is done—
The gates are pass'd, and Heaven is won!
THOMAS MOORE, *Lalla Rookh: Paradise and the Peri.* Concluding lines.

13
The pleasing way is not the right:
He that would conquer Heaven must fight.
FRANCIS QUARLES, *Emblems.* Bk. ii, emb. 11.

14
Sir, fare you well:
Hereafter, in a better world than this,
I shall desire more love and knowledge of you.
SHAKESPEARE, *As You Like It.* Act i, sc. 2, l. 295.

My hopes in heaven do dwell.
SHAKESPEARE, *Henry VIII.* Act iii, sc. 2, l. 459.

Look for me in the nurseries of Heaven.
FRANCIS THOMPSON, *To My Godchild.*

16
What matter it *how* heaven we gain
If at the last we really get to heaven?
WILLIAM WETMORE STORY, *St. Peter's.*

17
Far from mortal cares retreating,
Sordid hopes and vain desires,
Here, our willing footsteps meeting,
Every heart to heaven aspires.
JANE TAYLOR, *Hymn.*

18
Short arm needs man to reach to Heaven,
So ready is Heaven to stoop to him.
FRANCIS THOMPSON, *Grace of the Way.*

19
But I account it worth
All pangs of fair hopes crost—
All loves and honors lost,—
To gain the heavens, at cost
Of losing earth.
THEODORE TILTON, *Sir Marmaduke's Musings.*

1
Of this blest man let this just praise be given,
Heaven was in him before he was in heaven.
IZAAK WALTON, *Written in Dr. Richard Sibbes' "Returning Backslider."*

Earth is less fragrant now and heaven more sweet.
SIR WILLIAM WATSON, *A Maiden's Epitaph.*

3
No man must go to heaven who hath not sent his heart thither before.
THOMAS WILSON, *Maxims of Piety*, 66.

4
One eye on death, and one full fix'd on heaven.
YOUNG, *Night Thoughts*. Night v, l. 838.

5
Jerusalem, my happy home,
Would God I were in thee!
Would God my woes were at an end,
Thy joys that I might see!
UNKNOWN, *Song of Mary Mother of Christ.*

VII—Heaven and Hell

6
As high as Heaven, as deep as Hell.
BEAUMONT AND FLETCHER, *Honest Man's Fortune*. Act iv, sc. 1.

7
There is no Heaven, there is no Hell; these be the dreams of baby minds;
Tools of the wily Fetisheer, to 'fright the fools his cunning blinds.
SIR RICHARD BURTON, *Kasidah*. Pt. viii, st. 1.

8
Deep in yon cave Honorius long did dwell,
In hope to merit heaven by making earth a hell.
BYRON, *Childe Harold*. Canto i, st. 20.

9
'Tis not where we lie, but whence we fell;
The loss of heaven's the greatest pain in hell.
CALDERON, *Adventures of Five Hours*. Act v. (Tuke, tr.)

To appreciate heaven well
'Tis good for a man to have some fifteen minutes of hell.
WILL CARLETON, *Gone With a Handsomer Man.*

10
Not less but more than Dante, we know for certain that there is a heaven and a hell—a heaven, when a good deed has been done, a hell, in the dark heart able no longer to live openly.
EDWARD DOWDEN, *Studies in Literature*, p. 117.

11
Here we may reign secure; and in my choice
To reign is worth ambition, though in Hell:
Better to reign in Hell, than serve in Heav'n.
MILTON, *Paradise Lost*. Bk. i, l. 261. (1663)

Now forasmuch as I was an Angel of Light, it was the Will of Wisdom to confine me to Darkness, and make me Prince thereof; so that I, that could not obey in Heaven, might command in Hell; and believe me, I had rather rule within my dark domain than to rehabit Cœlum Imperium, and there live in subjection under check, a slave of the Most High.
ANTHONY STAFFORD, *Niobe*. (1611)

12
Beholding heaven, and feeling hell.
THOMAS MOORE, *Lalla Rookh: The Fire-Worshippers.*

13
Men have fiendishly conceived a heaven only to find it insipid, and a hell to find it ridiculous.
GEORGE SANTAYANA, *Little Essays*, p. 278.

14
I'll follow thee, and make a heaven of hell,
To die upon the hand I love so well.
SHAKESPEARE, *A Midsummer-Night's Dream*. Act ii, sc. 1, l. 243.

14a
Heaven is doing good from good-will; hell is doing evil from ill-will.
SWEDENBORG, *Arcana Cœlesta*. Sec. 4776.

Hell and heaven are near man, yea, in him; and every man after death goes to that hell or that heaven in which he was, as to his spirit, during his abode in the world.
SWEDENBORG, *Arcana Cœlesta*. Sec. 8918.

15
The fear of hell, or aiming to be blest,
Savours too much of private interest.
This moved not Moses, nor the zealous Paul,
Who for their friends abandoned soul and all.
EDMUND WALLER, *Of Divine Love*. Canto ii.

16
How do I pity those that dwell
Where ignorance and darkness reign!
They know no heaven—they fear no hell—
That endless joy—that endless pain.
ISAAC WATTS, *Praise for Birth in a Christian Land.*

17
Time flies, death urges, knells call, Heaven invites,
Hell threatens.
YOUNG, *Night Thoughts*. Night ii, l. 292.

HEIR, see Inheritance

HELEN OF TROY

18
He flung the sword away,
And kissed her feet, and knelt before her there,
The perfect Knight before the perfect Queen.
RUPERT BROOKE, *Menelaus and Helen.*

So Menelaus nagged; and Helen cried;
And Paris slept on by Scamander side.
RUPERT BROOKE, *Menelaus and Helen.*

19
And, like another Helen, fired another Troy.
DRYDEN, *Alexander's Feast*, l. 150.

20
Helen's lips are drifting dust;
Ilion is consumed with rust.
F. L. KNOWLES, *Love Triumphant.*

1
Was this the face that launch'd a thousand ships,
And burnt the topless towers of Ilium?
Sweet Helen, make me immortal with a kiss.
CHRISTOPHER MARLOWE, *Doctor Faustus*, l. 1328.

2
Though Helen's lips are dust
The kisses of her lips
Must burn the towers, and must
Still launch the thousand ships. . . .
O passion of wisdom, this
(Helen held it for such):
You cannot unkiss that kiss,
You cannot untouch that touch.
FRANCIS MEYNELL, *Permanence*.

3
The fight for Helen still goes on;
There topple down to dust
A hundred Troys each day; that rose
Survives the gust.
LIZETTE WOODWORTH REESE, *Heredity*.

4
Helen's cheek, but not her heart.
SHAKESPEARE, *As You Like It*. Act iii, sc. 2, 153.

On Helen's cheek all art of beauty set.
SHAKESPEARE, *Sonnets*. No. liii.

5
The ravish'd Helen, Menelaus' queen,
With wanton Paris sleeps.
SHAKESPEARE, *Troilus and Cressida*: Prol., l. 8.

Is she worth keeping? why, she is a pearl,
Whose price hath launch'd above a thousand ships,
And turn'd crown'd kings to merchants.
SHAKESPEARE, *Troilus and Cressida*. Act ii, sc. 2, l. 81.

6
You will never know what Helen said to Paris,
You have lost Egypt though you saved your ships.
MURIEL STUART, *The Old Saint*.

7
A shudder in the loins engenders there
The broken wall, the burning roof and tower
And Agamemnon dead.
WILLIAM BUTLER YEATS, *Leda*. Helen was the daughter of Leda and Jupiter disguised as a swan.

HELL

See also Heaven and Hell

I—Hell: Definition and Description

8
Hell is the wrath of God—His hate of sin.
P. J. BAILEY, *Festus: Hell*, l. 194.

9
A vast, unbottom'd, boundless pit,
Fill'd fou o' lowin brunstane,
Wha's ragin' flame an' scorchin' heat,
Wad melt the hardest whunstane.
BURNS, *The Holy Fair*. St. 22.

When frae my mither's womb I fell,
Thou might hae plung'd me deep in Hell,
To gnash my gooms, and weep, and wail,
In burnin' lakes,
Whar damned devils roar and yell,
Chain'd to their stakes.
BURNS, *Holy Willie's Prayer*. St. 4.

10
There is in hell a place stone-built throughout,
Called Malebolge, of an iron hue,
Like to the wall that circles it about.
(Loco è inferno detto Malebolge,
Tutto di pietra e di color ferrigno,
Come la cerchia che d' intorno il volge.)
DANTE, *Inferno*. Canto xviii, l. 1.

11
Hell is no other but a soundless pit,
Where no one beam of comfort peeps in it.
ROBERT HERRICK, *Hell*.

Hell is the place where whipping-cheer abounds,
But no one jailor there to wash the wounds.
ROBERT HERRICK, *Hell*.

12
Hell is a circle about the unbelieving.
The Koran.

13
Into hell, into the fire that never shall be quenched: Where their worm dieth not.
New Testament: Mark, ix, 43, 44.

14
Hell hath no limits, nor is circumscrib'd
In one self-place; for where we are is hell;
And where hell is, there must we ever be;
And to conclude, when all the world dissolves,
And every creature shall be purified,
All places shall be hell that are not heaven.
CHRISTOPHER MARLOWE, *Faustus*, l. 553.

15
A dungeon horrible on all sides round
As one great furnace flam'd yet from those flames
No light, but rather darkness visible,
Serv'd only to discover sights of woe,
Regions of sorrow, doleful shades, where peace
And rest can never dwell, hope never comes
That comes to all, but torture without end.
MILTON, *Paradise Lost*. Bk. i, l. 61.

A gulf profound as that Serbonian bog
Betwixt Damiata and Mount Casius old,
Where armies whole have sunk: the parching air
Burns frore, and cold performs th' effect of fire.
Thither by harpy-footed Furies hal'd,
At certain revolutions, all the damn'd
Are brought, and feel by turns the bitter change
Of fierce extremes, extremes by change more fierce,
From beds of raging fire to starve in ice
Their soft ethereal warmth, and there to pine
Immovable, infix'd, and frozen round,
Periods of time, thence hurried back to fire.
MILTON, *Paradise Lost*. Bk. ii, l. 592.

O'er many a frozen, many a fiery Alp,

Rocks, caves, lakes, fens, bogs, dens, and shades of death.
MILTON, *Paradise Lost*. Bk. ii, l. 620.

On a sudden open fly
With impetuous recoil and jarring sound
Th' infernal doors, and on their hinges grate
Harsh thunder, that the lowest bottom shook
Of Erebus.
MILTON, *Paradise Lost*. Bk. ii, l. 879.

1
Hell is both sides of the tomb, and a devil may be respectable and wear good clothes.
CHARLES H. PARKHURST, *Sermons: The Pharisee's Prayer*.

2
I see a brimstone sea of boiling fire,
And fiends, with knotted whips of flaming wire
Torturing poor souls, that gnash their teeth in vain,
And gnaw their flame-tormented tongues for pain.
FRANCIS QUARLES, *Emblems*. Bk. iii, emb. 14.

3
It doesn't matter what they preach,
Of high or low degree;
The old Hell of the Bible
Is Hell enough for me.
FRANK L. STANTON, *Hell*.

4
Hell itself may be contained within the compass of a spark.
H. D. THOREAU, *Journal*, 19 Dec., 1838.

5
In the deepest pits of 'Ell,
Where the worst defaulters dwell
(Charcoal devils used as fuel as you require 'em),
There's some lovely coloured rays,
Pyrotechnical displays,
But you can't expect the burning to admire 'em!
EDGAR WALLACE, *Nature Fails: L'Envoi*.

6
There is a dreadful hell,
And everlasting pains;
Where sinners must with devils dwell
In darkness, fire, and chains.
ISAAC WATTS, *Heaven and Hell*.

7
Pale Disease dwells there, and sad Old Age, and Fear, and Famine persuading to evil, and hateful Want. (Pallentesque habitant Morbi, tristisque Senectus, Et Metus, et malesuada Fames, ac turpis Egestas.)
VERGIL, *Æneid*. Bk. vi, l. 275.

At Orcus' portal hold their lair
Wild Sorrow and avenging Care;
And pale Diseases cluster there,
And pleasureless Decay,
Dour Penury, and Fears that kill,
And Hunger, counsellor of ill.
VERGIL, *Æneid*, vi, 275. (Conington, tr.)

8
That's the greatest torture souls feel in hell:
In hell, that they must live, and cannot die.
WEBSTER, *Duchess of Malfi*. Act iv, sc. 1, l. 84.

9
For what, my small philosopher! is hell?
'Tis nothing but full knowledge of the truth,
When truth, resisted long, is sworn our foe,
And calls eternity to do her right.
YOUNG, *Night Thoughts*. Night ix, l. 2403.

10
Satan the envious said with a sigh:
Christians know more about their hell than I.
ALFRED KREYMBORG, *Envious Satan*.

II—Hell: Apothegms

11
Hell is more bearable than nothingness.
P. J. BAILEY, *Festus: Heaven*.

12
They order things so damnably in Hell.
HILAIRE BELLOC, *To Dives*.

13
The princess had all the virtues with which hell is filled.
JACQUES BOSSUET, *Sermon on the Death of the Princess Palatine*, 1684.

14
Now Hell has wholly boiled away
And God become a shade.
There is no place for him to stay
In all the world he made.
GAMALIEL BRADFORD, *Exit God*.

Hell's rather out of date.
ALFRED SUTRO, *The Perfect Lover*. Act i.

15
From Hell, Hull, and Halifax, good Lord deliver us.
ANTHONY COPLEY, *Wits, Fits, etc.*, 112. (1594)

Hell, Hull and Halifax all begin with one letter;
Brag is a good dog, but hold-fast is a better.
SAMUEL PEGGE, *Derbicisms*, 137.

There is a proverb, and a prayer withal,
That we may not to three strange places fall
From Hull, from Halifax, from Hell, 'tis thus,
From all these three, good Lord, deliver us!
JOHN TAYLOR THE WATER POET, *A Very Merry-Wherry-Ferry Voyage*, l. 575.

16
Hair-hung and breeze-shaken over hell.
EDWARD EGGLESTON, *The Circuit Rider*. Ch. 27.

17
Hell and Chancery are always open.
THOMAS FULLER, *Gnomologia*.

18
Give ample room, and verge enough
The characters of hell to trace.
THOMAS GRAY, *The Bard*. Canto ii.

19
Hell from beneath is moved for thee to meet thee at thy coming.
Old Testament: Isaiah, xiv, 9.

20
They should say, and swear, hell were broken loose, ere they went hence.
BEN JONSON, *Every Man in His Humour*. Act iv, sc. 1.

All hell is broken loose yonder!

THOMAS D'URFEY, *Comical History of Don Quixote*. Pt. ii, act ii, sc. 1.

All hell broke loose.

MILTON, *Paradise Lost*. Bk. iv, l. 918.

Hell Maria!

CHARLES GATES DAWES, at Congressional Committee hearing, 2 Feb., 1921, using an expletive said to be of Ohio origin. "Some meticulous but soulless editor tried to make sense by writing in the 'and.' Thus Dawes got his nickname and the great Dawes myth its start."—STANLEY FROST, *Hell an' Maria—Revised. The Outlook,* 27 Aug., 1924.

1

What you Kansas farmers ought to do is to raise less corn and raise more hell.

MRS. MARY ELIZABETH CLYENS LEASE, *Speech,* in campaign against J. J. Ingalls, 1890.

What's the matter with Kansas? . . . We have decided to send three or four harpies out lecturing, telling the people that Kansas is raising hell and letting the corn go to weeds.

WILLIAM ALLEN WHITE, *Editorial,* Emporia *Gazette,* 15 Aug., 1896.

2

Not even Hell can lay hand on the invincible. (Ἀνικήτων ἅπτεται οὐδ' Ἀΐδης.)

PARMENION, *Epitaph on Alexander*. (*Greek Anthology*. Bk. vii, epig. 239.)

3

There is no redemption from hell. (In inferno nulla est redemptio.)

POPE PAUL III, to Michelangelo, who had refused to alter a portrait introduced among the condemned in his painting of the Last Judgment.

In hell there is no retention. (Quien ha infierene nula es retencio.)

CERVANTES, *Don Quixote*. Pt. i, ch. 25. (Sancho's attempt to quote the Latin saying.)

O villain! thou wilt be condemned into everlasting redemption for this.

SHAKESPEARE, *Much Ado About Nothing*. Act iv, sc. 2, l. 58.

The most frightful idea that has ever corroded human nature—the idea of eternal punishment.

JOHN MORLEY, *Essays: Vauvenargues*.

4

You . . . have the office opposite to Saint
Peter,
And keep the gate of hell!

SHAKESPEARE, *Othello*. Act iv, sc. 2, l. 90.

5

Hell is empty And all the devils are here.

SHAKESPEARE, *The Tempest*. Act i, sc. 2, l. 214. Ariel is repeating the words of Ferdinand, as he leaped from the sinking ship into the sea.

6

If I owned Texas and Hell, I would rent out Texas and live in Hell.

GENERAL PHILIP H. SHERIDAN, at the officers' mess at Fort Clark, Texas, in 1855. (On the authority of Judge Richard B. Levy, of Texarkana.)

7

If I cannot influence the gods, I will move all hell. (Flectere si nequeo superos Acheronta movebo.)

VERGIL, *Æneid*. Bk. vii, l. 312. Juno says this as she turns to the Furies to stay Æneas.

All hell shall stir for this.

SHAKESPEARE, *Henry V*. Act v, sc. 1, l. 72.

8

I would send them to hell across lots if they meddled with me.

BRIGHAM YOUNG, *Speech,* 1857.

III—Hell: Its Pavement

9

Hell is full of good intentions or desires. (L'enfer est plein de bonnes volontés ou désirs.)

ST. BERNARD OF CLAIRVAUX. Attributed to him by St. Francis de Sales, *Letters,* Letter 74. (Blaise edition.) Bk. ii, letter 22. (Leonard edition.) The letter was written in 1605 to Madame de Chantal, and St. Francis says to her, "Do not be troubled by St. Bernard's saying that Hell is full of good intentions and desires."

Hell is full of good desires.

EDWARD HELLOWES, *Guevara's Epistles,* 205. (1574)

Hell is full of good meanings and wishings.

GEORGE HERBERT, *Jacula Prudentum*. No. 176.

10

Hell is paved with great granite blocks hewn from the hearts of those who said, "I can do no other."

HEYWOOD BROUN, *Syndicate Column,* 20 Jan., 1934. *See under* LUTHER.

11

Hell is paved with good intentions.

JOHN RAY, *English Proverbs*. (1670) Dr. Johnson used the proverb in this form. (BOSWELL, 1775.) Coleridge (*Notes Theological, Political and Miscellaneous,* p. 259) attributes the saying to Richard Baxter (1615–1691). TRENCH, *On the Lessons in Proverbs,* p. 65 (1851), refers to this as "perhaps the queen of all proverbs," and cites the modern form, "The road to hell is paved with good intentions."

Hell is paved with good intentions, not with bad ones.

BERNARD SHAW, *Maxims for Revolutionists*.

It has been more wittily than charitably said that hell is paved with good intentions; they have their place in heaven also.

ROBERT SOUTHEY, *Colloquies on Society*. Sec. v.

Hell is paved with good intentions and roofed with lost opportunities.

UNKNOWN. Proverb of Portuguese origin.

12

Hell is paved with infants' skulls.

RICHARD BAXTER, Non-conformist divine, was almost stoned to death by the women of

Kidderminster for quoting this from the pulpit. (HAZLITT, *Table Talk*.)

Hell is paved with priests' skulls.
ST. CHRYSOSTOM.

Hell is paved with the skulls of great scholars, and paled in with the bones of great men.
GILES FIRMIN, *The Real Christian*. (1670)

IV—Hell: The Road Thither

1
A single path leads to the house of Hades. ('Απλῆ οἶμος εἰς ''Αιδου φέρει.)
ÆSCHYLUS, *Telephus*. Frag. 131.

2
From every direction there is equally a way to the lower world. (Undique ad inferos tantundem viæ est.)
ANAXAGORAS. (CICERO, *Tusculanarum Disputationum*. Bk. i, ch. 43, sec. 104.)

3
Hearken, Lady Betty, hearken,
To the dismal news I tell,
How your friends are all embarking
For the fiery gulf of hell.
CHRISTOPHER ANSTEY, *New Bath Guide*, xiv, 1.

4
The road to Hell is easy to travel.
BION. (DIOGENES LAERTIUS, *Bion*. Bk. iv, 49.)

6
Here Rixus lies, a novice in the laws,
Who plains he came to hell without a cause.
WILLIAM DRUMMOND, *On Rixus*.

7
Christ, what a crowd are sent to Hell
Through love, and poverty, and beer!
DOUGLAS GOLDRING, *Newport Street, E.*

8
There is nobody will go to hell for company.
GEORGE HERBERT, *Jacula Prudentum*.

9
Wide is the gate and broad is the way that leadeth to destruction, and many there be which go in thereat: Because strait is the gate and narrow is the way which leadeth unto life, and few there be that find it.
New Testament: Matthew, vii, 13, 14.

10
Long is the way
And hard, that out of Hell leads up to Light.
MILTON, *Paradise Lost*. Bk. ii, l. 432.

A passage broad,
Smooth, easy, inoffensive, down to Hell.
MILTON, *Paradise Lost*. Bk. x, l. 304.

11
The way to Hell's a seeming Heav'n.
FRANCIS QUARLES, *Emblems*. Bk. ii, emblem 11.

12
Down, down to hell; and say I sent thee thither.
SHAKESPEARE, *III Henry VI*. Act v, sc. 6, l. 67.

13
The primrose way to the everlasting bonfire.
SHAKESPEARE, *Macbeth*. Act ii, sc. 3, l. 23.

The primrose path of dalliance.
SHAKESPEARE, *Hamlet*. Act i, sc. 3, l. 50.

The lovely way that led
To the slimepit and the mire
And the everlasting fire.
A. E. HOUSMAN, *Hell Gate*.

14
So, while their bodies moulder here,
Their souls with God himself shall dwell,—
But always recollect, my dear,
That wicked people go to hell.
ANN AND JANE TAYLOR, *About Dying*.

15
The descent to hell is easy; the gates stand open night and day; but to re-climb the slope, and escape to the outer air, this indeed is a task. (Facilis descensus Averno: Noctes atque dies patet atri janua Ditis; Sed revocare gradum, superasque evadere as auras, Hoc opus, hic labor est.)
VERGIL, *Æneid*. Bk. vi, l. 126.

Smooth the descent and easy is the way;
(The Gates of Hell stand open night and day):
But to return, and view the cheerful skies,
In this the task and mighty labour lies.
VERGIL, *Æneid*, vi, 126. (Dryden, tr.)

16
One Hades receives all mortals alike. (Πάντας ὁμῶς θνητοὺς εἰς 'Αΐδης δέχεται.)
UNKNOWN, *Epigram*. (*Greek Anthology*. Bk. vii, No. 342.)

V—Hell: The Fear of Hell

17
I thank God, and with joy I mention it, I was never afraid of Hell, nor never grew pale at the description of that place.
SIR THOMAS BROWNE, *Religio Medici*. Pt. i, sec. 59.

18
The fear o' Hell's a hangman's whip
To haud the wretch in order;
But where ye feel your honour grip,
Let that aye be your border.
BURNS, *Epistle to a Young Friend*. St. 8.

19
The devil is waiting for them, hell is gaping for them, the flames gather and flash about them. . . . When you come to be a firebrand of hell . . . you will appear as you are, a viper indeed. . . . Then will you as a serpent spit poison at God and vent your rage and malice in fearful blasphemies.
JONATHAN EDWARDS, *Men Naturally God's Enemies*. (*Works* vii, 168.)

20
No hell will frighten men away from sin.
THOMAS HAWEIS, *Speech in Season:* Bk. i, *Hell*.

Hell is given up *so* reluctantly by those who don't expect to go there.
HARRY LEON WILSON, *The Spenders*, p. 241.

21
The dreadful fear of hell, which disturbs the life of man and renders it miserable, is to be driven out.
LUCRETIUS, *De Rerum Natura*. Bk. iii, l. 37.

1
Lives there who loves his pain?
Who would not, finding way, break loose from Hell,
Though thither doom'd?
MILTON, *Paradise Lost*. Bk. iv, l. 888.

2
The infliction of cruelty with a good conscience is a delight to moralists. That is why they invented Hell.
BERTRAND RUSSELL, *Sceptical Essays*, p. 16.

VI—Hell: The Hell Within

3
The heart of man is the place the devils dwell in: I feel sometimes a hell within my self.
SIR THOMAS BROWNE, *Religio Medici*. Pt. i, sec. 51.

4
The Hell within him, for within him Hell
He brings, and round about him, nor from Hell
One step no more than from himself can fly
By change of place.
MILTON, *Paradise Lost*. Bk. iv, l. 20.

5
Which way I fly is Hell; myself am Hell;
And in the lowest deep a lower deep
Still threat'ning to devour me opens wide,
To which the Hell I suffer seems a Heav'n.
MILTON, *Paradise Lost*. Bk. iv, l. 75.

6
I sent my Soul through the Invisible,
Some letter of that After-life to spell:
And by and by my Soul return'd to me,
And answered, "I Myself am Heav'n and Hell."
OMAR KHAYYÁM, *Rubáiyát*. (Fitzgerald, tr.)

Heaven but the Vision of fulfill'd Desire,
And Hell the Shadow from a Soul on fire.
OMAR KHAYYÁM, *Rubáiyát*. (Fitzgerald, tr.)

HELP

See also Philanthropy

7
What is past my help is past my care.
BEAUMONT AND FLETCHER, *The Double Marriage*. Act i.

8
Sweet the help Of one we have helped!
E. B. BROWNING, *Aurora Leigh*. Bk. vii, l. 513.

9
Help refused Is hindrance sought and found.
ROBERT BROWNING, *Ferishtah's Fancies, Two Camels*.

10
I would help others, out of a fellow-feeling.
ROBERT BURTON, *Anatomy of Melancholy: Democritus to the Reader*.

11
This is our special duty, that if anyone specially needs our help, we should give him such help to the utmost of our power. (Hoc maxime officii est, ut quisque maxime opis indigeat, ita ei potissimum opitulari.)
CICERO, *De Officiis*. Bk. i, ch. 15, sec. 49.

12
Our chief want in life is, somebody who shall make us do what we can.
EMERSON, *Conduct of Life: Considerations by the Way*.

13
Help the lame dog over the stile.
THOMAS FULLER, *Gnomologia*.

Do the work that's nearest,
Though it's dull at whiles,
Helping, when we meet them,
Lame dogs over stiles.
CHARLES KINGSLEY, *Invitation to Thomas Hughes*. (*Memoirs of Kingsley*, by his wife. Ch. 15.)

Help your lame dog o'er a stile.
SWIFT, *Whig and Tory*.

14
He may not score, and yet he helps to Win
Who makes the Hit that brings the Runner in.
ARTHUR GUITERMAN, *A Poet's Proverbs*, p. 17.

15
One thing asks the help of another. (Alterius sic Altera poscit opem res.)
HORACE, *Ars Poetica*, l. 410.

Who helps a man against his will, does the same as murder him. (Invitum qui servat, idem facit occidenti.)
HORACE, *Ars Poetica*, l. 467.

16
I looked, and there was none to help.
Old Testament: Isaiah, lxiii, 5.

17
Aid the dawning, tongue and pen:
Aid it, hopes of honest men!
CHARLES MACKAY, *Clear the Way*.

18
I am known throughout the world as the Help-Bringer. (Opiferque per orbem Dicor.)
OVID, *Metamorphoses*. Bk. i, l. 521. Said of Apollo.

19
It is a kingly action, believe me, to help the fallen. (Regia crede mihi, res est sucurrere lapsis.)
OVID, *Epistulæ ex Ponto*. Bk. ii, epis. 9, l. 11.

20
Vain is the help of man.
Old Testament: Psalms, lx, 11; cviii, 12. (Vana salus hominis.—*Vulgate*.)

21
Now, ye familiar spirits, that are cull'd
Out of the powerful regions under earth,
Help me this once.
SHAKESPEARE, *I Henry VI*. Act v, sc. 3, l. 10.

Help me, Cassius, or I sink!
SHAKESPEARE, *Julius Cæsar*. Act i, sc. 2, l. 111.

I to your assistance do make love.
SHAKESPEARE, *Macbeth*. Act iii, sc. 1, l. 124.

Your breath of full consent bellied his sails.
SHAKESPEARE, *Troilus and Cressida*. Act ii, sc. 2, l. 74.

1
After the verb "To Love," "To Help" is the most beautiful verb in the world!
BARONESS VON SUTTNER, *Ground Arms.*

2
Something between a hindrance and a help.
WORDSWORTH, *Michael*, l. 189.

HEREDITY, see Ancestry

HERACLITUS

3
One told me, Heraclitus, of thy death, and brought me to tears, and I remembered how often we two in talking put the sun to rest. Thou, methinks, Halicarnassian friend, art ashes long and long ago; but thy nightingales live still, whereon Hades, snatcher of all things, shall not lay his hand.

(Εἶπέ τις, 'Ηράκλειτε, τεὸν μόρον, ἐς δέ με δάκρυ
ἤγαγεν, ἐμνήσθην δ' ὁσσάκις ἀμφότεροι
ἥλιον ἐν λέσχῃ κατεδύσαμεν· ἀλλὰ σὺ μέν που,
ξεῖν' 'Αλικαρνησεῦ, τετράπαλαι σποδιή·
αἱ δὲ τεαὶ ζώουσιν ἀηδόνες, ᾗσιν ὁ πάντων
ἁρπακτὴς 'Αίδης οὐκ ἐπὶ χεῖρα βαλεῖ.)

CALLIMACHUS, *Epigrams*. No. 2. Quoted by Diogenes Laertius, ix, 17, where he gives a list of the persons called Heraclitus.

They told me, Herakleitos, thou wast dead.
What tears I shed!
As I remembered how we two as one
Talked down the sun.
Well, Halicarnassian friend, long since thou must
Have turned to dust;
Yet live thy nightingales, and Hades, who
Doth all subdue,
Shall never until Time itself shall close
Lay hand on those.

CALLIMACHUS. (Basil L. Gildersleeve, tr., *American Journal of Philology*. Vol. xxxiii, p. 111.)

They told me, Heraclitus, they told me you were dead,
They brought me bitter news to hear and bitter tears to shed.
I wept as I remembered how often you and I
Had tired the sun with talking and sent him down the sky.
And now that thou art lying, my dear old Carian guest,
A handful of grey ashes, long, long ago at rest,
Still are thy pleasant voices, thy nightingales, awake;
For Death, he taketh all away, but them he cannot take.

CALLIMACHUS. (William Johnson-Cory, tr.)

One told me, Heraclitus, of thy fate;
He brought me tears, he brought me memories;
Alas, my Carian friend, how oft, how late,
We twain have talked the sun adown the skies,
And somewhere thou art dust without a date!
But of thy songs death maketh not his prize,
In death's despite, that stealeth all, they wait,
The new year's nightingale that never dies.

CALLIMACHUS. (Andrew Lang, tr.)

They tell me, Heraclitus, thou art dead,
And many are the tears for thee I shed,
With memories of those summer nights opprest
When we together talked the sun to rest.
Alas! my guest, my friend! no more art thou;
Long, long ago wert ashes, and yet now
Thy nightingales live on, I hear them sing,
E'en death spares them, who spares not anything.

CALLIMACHUS. (Lilla Cabot Perry, tr., *From the Garden of Hellas*, p. 80.) "Nightingales" was probably the title of a collection of poems left by Heraclitus, who died about 250 B.C.

HERESY

4
False doctrine, heresy, and schism.
Book of Common Prayer: Litany.

5
Heresy is the school of pride.
GEORGE HERBERT, *Jacula Prudentum.*

Heresy may be easier kept out than shook off.
GEORGE HERBERT, *Jacula Prudentum.*

6
They that approve a private opinion, call it opinion; but they that mislike it, heresy: and yet heresy signifies no more than private opinion.
THOMAS HOBBES, *Leviathan*. Pt. i, ch. 11.

7
Only heretics grow old gracefully.
ELBERT HUBBARD, *The Philistine*, xi, 89.

8
It is the customary fate of new truths to begin as heresies and to end as superstitions.
T. H. HUXLEY, *The Coming of Age of the Origin of Species.*

9
Heresy is what the minority believe; it is the name given by the powerful to the doctrine of the weak.
R. G. INGERSOLL, *Heretics and Heresies.*

In the history of the world, the man who is ahead has always been called a heretic.
R. G. INGERSOLL, *Liberty of Man, Woman and Child.*

10
A man may be a heretic in the truth; and if he believe things only because his pastor says so, or the assembly so determines, without knowing other reason, though his belief be true, yet the very truth he holds becomes his heresy.
MILTON, *Areopagitica.*

11
In our windy world
What's up is faith, what's down is heresy.
TENNYSON, *Harold*. Act i, sc. 1.

12
Better heresy of doctrine than heresy of heart.
WHITTIER, *Mary Garvin.*

HERITAGE, see Inheritance

HERMIT

1
The hermit thinks the sun shines nowhere but in his cell.

THOMAS FULLER, *Gnomologia.*

2
Hermit hoar, in solemn cell
Wearing out life's evening grey;
Smite thy bosom, Sage, and tell
What is bliss, and which the way.

Thus I spoke, and speaking sigh'd;—
Scarce repress'd the starting tear;—
When the smiling sage replied,
"Come, my lad, and drink some beer."

SAMUEL JOHNSON. (BOSWELL, *Life,* 18 Sept., 1777.)

3
Far in a wild, unknown to public view,
From youth to age a reverend hermit grew;
The moss his bed, the cave his humble cell,
His food the fruits, his drink the crystal well:
Remote from man, with God he pass'd the days,
Prayer all his business, all his pleasure praise.

THOMAS PARNELL, *The Hermit,* l. 1.

4
Shall I, like a hermit, dwell
On a rock or in a cell?

SIR WALTER RALEIGH, *Shall I, Like a Hermit, Dwell.*

HERO and HEROISM

See also Courage

I—Hero: Definitions

5
Heroism is the brilliant triumph of the soul over the flesh—that is to say, over fear. . . . Heroism is the dazzling and glorious concentration of courage.

AMIEL, *Journal,* 1 Oct., 1849.

6
The hero is the world-man, in whose heart
One passion stands for all, the most indulged.

P. J. BAILEY, *Festus: Proëm,* l. 114.

7
All actual heroes are essential men,
And all men possible heroes.

E. B. BROWNING, *Aurora Leigh.* Bk. v, l. 151.

8
The Hero is he who lives in the inward sphere of things, in the True, Divine and Eternal, which exists always, unseen to most, under the Temporary, Trivial: his being is in that.

CARLYLE, *Heroes and Hero-Worship: The Hero as Man of Letters.*

There needs not a great soul to make a hero; there needs a God-created soul which will be true to its origin; that will be a great soul.

CARLYLE, *Heroes and Hero-Worship: The Hero as Priest.*

The Hero can be a Poet, Prophet, King, Priest or what you will, according to the kind of world he finds himself born into.

CARLYLE, *Heroes and Hero-Worship: The Hero as Poet.*

9
If Hero mean *sincere man,* why may not every one of us be a Hero?

CARLYLE, *Heroes and Hero-Worship: The Hero as Priest.*

Thou and I, my friend, can, in the most flunky world, make, each of us, one non-flunky, one hero, if we like; that will be two heroes to begin with.

CARLYLE, *Past and Present.* Bk. i, ch. 6.

10
I am convinced that a light supper, a good night's sleep, and a fine morning, have sometimes made a hero of the same man, who, by an indigestion, a restless night, and rainy morning, would have proved a coward.

LORD CHESTERFIELD, *Letters,* 26 April, 1748.

11
He's of stature somewhat low—
Your hero always should be tall, you know.

CHARLES CHURCHILL, *The Rosciad,* l. 1029.

12
To believe in the heroic makes heroes.

BENJAMIN DISRAELI, *Coningsby.* Bk. iii, ch. 1.

13
There is no king nor sovereign state
That can fix a hero's rate.

R. W. EMERSON, *Astræa.*

The hero is not fed on sweets,
Daily his own heart he eats;
Chambers of the great are jails,
And head-winds right for royal sails.

R. W. EMERSON, *Heroism.*

The characteristic of genuine heroism is its persistency. All men have wandering impulses, fits and starts of generosity. But when you have resolved to be great, abide by yourself, and do not weakly try to reconcile yourself with the world. The heroic cannot be the common, nor the common the heroic.

EMERSON, *Essays, First Series: Heroism.*

14
It is fortune (or chance) chiefly that makes heroes.

THOMAS FULLER, *Gnomologia.*

Nor deem that acts heroic wait on chance,
Or easy were as in a boy's romance;
The man's whole life precludes the single deed
That shall decide if his inheritance
Be with the sifted few of matchless breed,
Our race's sap and sustenance,
Or with the unmotived herd that only sleep and feed.

J. R. LOWELL, *Under the Old Elm.*

15
Heroism is the self-devotion of genius manifesting itself in action.

J. C. AND A. W. HARE, *Guesses at Truth.*

16
The greatest obstacle to being heroic is the doubt whether one may not be going to prove

one's self a fool; the truest heroism is to resist the doubt, and the profoundest wisdom to know when it ought to be resisted, and when to be obeyed.

HAWTHORNE, *The Blithedale Romance*. Ch. 2.

1
In a truly heroic life there is no peradventure. It is always either doing or dying.

R. D. HITCHCOCK, *Eternal Atonement: Life Through Death*.

2
There are heroes in evil as well as in good. (Il y a des héros en mal comme en bien.)

LA ROCHEFOUCAULD, *Maximes*. No. 185.

3
Dost thou know what a hero is? Why, a hero is as much as one should say,—a hero.

LONGFELLOW, *Hyperion*. Bk. i, ch. 1.

4
Heroes are bred by lands where livelihood comes hard. (Τὸ κακῶς τρέφοντα χωρί' ἀνδρείους ποεῖ.)

MENANDER, *Anephioi*. Frag. 63.

5
Heroes are much the same, the point's agreed,
From Macedonia's madman to the Swede;
The whole strange purpose of their lives to find,
Or make, an enemy of all mankind!

POPE, *Essay on Man*. Epis. iv, l. 219.

6
Whoe'er excels in what we prize,
Appears a hero in our eyes.

SWIFT, *Cadenus and Vanessa*, l. 733.

7
But when religion does with virtue join,
It makes a hero like an angel shine.

EDMUND WALLER, *A Fragment on Ovid*.

8
One brave deed makes no hero.

WHITTIER, *The Hero*.

II—Hero: Apothegms

9
I want a hero: an uncommon want,
When every year and month sends forth a new one.

BYRON, *Don Juan*. Canto i, st. 1.

10
Pause, traveler, your foot is upon a hero. (Sta, viator, heroem calcas.)

CONDÉ, *Epitaph*, on his antagonist, Mercy.

Heroes have trod this spot—'tis on their dust ye tread.

BYRON, *Childe Harold*. Canto iv, st. 144.

11
Every hero becomes a bore at last.

EMERSON, *Representative Men: Uses of Great Men*.

12
A hero cannot be a hero unless in an heroic world.

HAWTHORNE, *Journals*, 7 May, 1850.

13
Heroes as great have died, and yet shall fall.

HOMER, *Iliad*. Bk. xv, l. 157. (Pope, tr.)

BRAVE MEN WERE LIVING BEFORE AGAMEMNON, *see* POETRY AND FAME.

14
The idol of to-day pushes the hero of yesterday out of our recollection; and will, in turn, be supplanted by his successor of to-morrow.

WASHINGTON IRVING, *The Sketch Book: Westminster Abbey*.

15
The one cruel fact about heroes is that they are made of flesh and blood.

HENRY ARTHUR JONES, *The Liars*. Act i.

16
Crowds speak in heroes.

GERALD STANLEY LEE, *Crowds*. Bk. iv, ch. 3.

17
'Tis as easy to be heroes as to sit the idle slaves
Of a legendary virtue carved upon our father's graves.

J. R. LOWELL, *The Present Crisis*. St. 15.

18
Nothing is more depressing than the conviction that one is not a hero.

GEORGE MOORE, *Ave*, p. 35.

19
See the conquering hero comes!
Sound the trumpets, beat the drums!

DR. THOMAS MORELL. Morell furnished the libretto for Handel's *Joshua*, in which these lines appear. Introduced later into Nathaniel Lee's *The Rival Queens*. Act ii, sc. 1.

20
You cannot be a hero without being a coward.

BERNARD SHAW, *John Bull's Other Island: Preface*.

21
What a hero one can be without moving a finger!

H. D. THOREAU, *Journal*, 13 July, 1838.

22
Such lapses from knowledge to faith are perhaps necessary that human heroism may be possible.

H. G. WELLS, *Mr Britling Sees It Through*. Bk. ii, ch. 2, sec. 1.

III—Heroes: Their Praise

23
A patriot hero or despotic chief,
To form a nation's glory or its grief.

BYRON, *The Island*. Canto ii, st. 9.

24
Strike home, and the world shall revere us
As heroes descended from heroes.

THOMAS CAMPBELL, *Song of the Greeks*.

25
That subject for an angel's song,
The hero and the saint!

COWPER, *Ode on Reading "Sir Charles Grandison."*

26
The memory of a great name and the inheritance of a great example is the legacy of heroes.

BENJAMIN DISRAELI, *Speech*, House of Commons, 1 Feb., 1849.

1
Heroes of old! I humbly lay
The laurel on your graves again;
Whatever men have done, men may,—
The deeds you wrought are not in vain!
AUSTIN DOBSON, *A Ballad of Heroes.*

2
Heroism feels and never reasons and therefore is always right.
EMERSON, *Essays, First Series: Heroism.*

3
In death a hero, as in life a friend.
HOMER, *Iliad.* Bk. xvii, l. 758. (Pope, tr.)

But to the hero, when his sword
Has won the battle for the free,
Thy voice sounds like a prophet's word;
And in its hollow tones are heard
The thanks of millions yet to be.
FITZ-GREENE HALLECK, *Marco Bozzaris.*

Like the day-star in the wave,
Sinks a hero in his grave,
'Midst the dew-fall of a nation's tears.
THOMAS MOORE, *Before the Battle. See also* SOLDIER: HOW SLEEP THE BRAVE.

4
Still the race of hero spirits pass the lamp from hand to hand.
CHARLES KINGSLEY, *The World's Age.*

5
In the world's broad field of battle,
In the bivouac of Life,
Be not like dumb, driven cattle!
Be a hero in the strife!
LONGFELLOW, *A Psalm of Life.*

6
Samson hath quit himself
Like Samson, and heroically hath finish'd
A life heroic.
MILTON, *Samson Agonistes,* l. 1709.

7
For Witherington needs must I wail,
As one in doleful dumps;
For when his legs were smitten off,
He fought upon his stumps.
RICHARD SHEALE, attr., *Ballad of Chevy Chase.* This is from a later version of the original ballad which was written c. 1475.

8
'Tis sweet to hear of heroes dead,
To know them still alive;
But sweeter if we earn their bread,
And in us they survive.
H. D. THOREAU, *The Great Adventure.*

9
Great-souled heroes, born in happier years.
(Magnanimi heroes, nati melioribus annis.)
VERGIL, *Æneid.* Bk. vi, l. 649.

10
Give honour to our heroes fall'n, how ill
Soe'er the cause that bade them forth to die.
WILLIAM WATSON, *The English Dead.*

11
There's not a breathing of the common wind
That will forget thee; thou hast great allies;
Thy friends are exultations, agonies,
And love, and man's unconquerable mind.
WORDSWORTH, *To Toussaint L'Ouverture.*

IV—Hero-Worship

12
Worship of a hero is transcendent admiration of a great man.
CARLYLE, *Heroes and Hero-Worship: The Hero as Divinity.*

Society is founded on hero-worship.
CARLYLE, *Heroes and Hero-Worship: The Hero as Divinity.*

In all times and places the Hero has been worshipped. It will ever be so. We all love great men. . . . Does not every true man feel that he is himself made higher by doing reverence to what is really above him? No nobler or more blessed feeling dwells in man's heart.
CARLYLE, *Heroes and Hero-Worship: The Hero as Divinity.*

13
Hero-worship exists, has existed, and will forever exist universally among mankind.
CARLYLE, *Sartor Resartus: Organic Filaments.*

14
Hero-worship is healthy. It stimulates the young to deeds of heroism, stirs the old to unselfish efforts, and gives the masses models of mankind that tend to lift humanity above the commonplace meanness of ordinary life.
DONN PIATT, *Memories of Men Who Saved the Union: Preface.*

15
Hero-worship is strongest where there is least regard for human freedom.
HERBERT SPENCER, *Social Statics.* Pt. iv, ch. 30, sec. 6.

V—Hero and Valet

16
He who attends my close-stool sings me no such song.
ANTIGONUS I, King of Sparta, when addressed by Hermodotus as "Son of the Sun." (PLUTARCH, *Apothegms of Kings and Great Commanders: Antigonus.*)

17
In short, he was a perfect cavaliero,
And to his very valet seemed a hero.
BYRON, *Beppo.* St. 33.

18
Heroes, it would seem, exist always, and a certain worship of them! We will also take the liberty to deny altogether that saying of the witty Frenchman, that no man is a hero to his valet-de-chambre. Or, if so, it is not the hero's blame, but the valet's: that his soul, namely, is a mean valet-soul.
CARLYLE, *Heroes and Hero-Worship: The Hero as Man of Letters.*

19
No man is a hero to his valet. (Il n'y a point de héros pour son valet de chambre.)
MADAME CORNUEL (d. 1694). See *Lettres de*

Mlle. Aissé, xii, 13 août, 1728. Attributed also to the Duke de Condé (d. 1686).

No man is a hero to his *valet de chambre.*
SAMUEL FOOTE, *The Patron.* Act ii, sc. 1.

1
Each man is a hero and an oracle to somebody.
EMERSON, *Letters and Social Aims: Quotation and Originality.*

2
To a valet no man is a hero. (Es gibt für den Kammerdiener keinen Helden.)
GOETHE, *Wahlverwandtschaften: Aus Ottilien's Tagebüche.*

It is said that no man is a hero to his valet. That is only because a hero can be recognized only by a hero. The valet will probably be able to appreciate his like,—that is, his fellow-valet.
GOETHE, *Sprüche in Prosa.* Vol. iii, p. 204.

3
The nearer we approach great men, the clearer we see that they are men. Rarely do they appear great before their valets.
LA BRUYÈRE, *Les Caractères.* *See also under* SERVANTS.

HESITATION, see Indecision

HILLS

See also Mountains

4
Live thou upon hill as thou would live in hall.
ALEXANDER BARCLAY, *Mirrour of Good Manners,* 25. (1570)

5
The hills, Rock-ribbed, and ancient as the sun.
BRYANT, *Thanatopsis.*

6
The hills are going somewhere;
They have been on the way a long time.
They are like camels in a line
But they move more slowly.
HILDA CONKLING, *Hills.*

7
The higher the hill the lower the grass.
THOMAS FULLER, *Gnomologia.* No. 4593.

8
Ah, happy hills! ah, pleasing shade!
Ah, fields belov'd in vain,
Where once my careless childhood stray'd,
A stranger yet to pain!
I feel the gales, that from ye blow,
A momentary bliss bestow.
THOMAS GRAY, *On a Distant Prospect of Eton College.*

9
Praise be to you, O hills, that you can breathe
Into our souls the secret of your power!
RICHARD HOVEY, *Comrades.*

10
Every hill hath his dale.
BRIAN MELBANCKE, *Philotinus.* Sig. U 2. (1583)

11
But on and up, where Nature's heart
Beats strong amid the hills.
MILNES, *Tragedy of the Lac de Gaube.* St. 2.

12
For we were nursed upon the self-same hill.
MILTON, *Lycidas,* l. 23.

13
Hills peep o'er hills, and Alps on Alps arise.
POPE, *Essay on Criticism.* Pt. ii, l. 32.

14
To climb steep hills
Requires slow pace at first.
SHAKESPEARE, *Henry VIII.* Act i, sc. 1, l. 131.

15
What if the bridge men built goes down,
What if the torrent sweeps the town,
The hills are safe, the hills remain,
And hills are happy in the rain.
SARA TEASDALE, *Even To-day.*

16
Men climb tall hills to suffer and die.
NANCY BYRD TURNER, *Hills.*

17
Fly like a youthful hart or roe
Over the hills where spices grow.
ISAAC WATTS, *Hymns and Spiritual Songs.* Bk. i, No. 79.

18
The hills are dearest which our childish feet
Have climbed the earliest; and the streams most sweet
Are ever those at which our young lips drank.
WHITTIER, *Bridal of Pennacook: At Pennacook.*

19
Come, heart, where hill is heaped upon hill:
For there the mystical brotherhood
Of sun and moon and hollow and wood
And river and stream work out their will.
W. B. YEATS, *Into the Twilight.*

II—Hills: Over the Hills and Far Away

20
Tom he was a piper's son,
He learned to play when he was young;
But all the tune that he could play
Was "Over the hills and far away."
UNKNOWN, *The Distracted Jockey's Lamentation.* (THOMAS D'URFEY, *Pills to Purge Melancholy.* 1661)

21
Our prentice Tom may now refuse
To wipe his scoundrel master's shoes;
For now he's free to sing and play—
Over the hills and far away.
GEORGE FARQUHAR, *The Recruiting Officer.* Act ii, sc. 3. (1706)

Over the hills, and over the main,
To Flanders, Portugal, or Spain:
The Queen commands, and we'll obey—
Over the hills and far away.
FARQUHAR, *The Recruiting Officer.* Act ii, sc. 3.

1
And I would love you all the day,
Every night would kiss and play,
If with me you'd fondly stray
Over the hills and far away.

JOHN GAY, *The Beggar's Opera*. Act i. (1728)

2
The gauger walked with willing foot,
And aye the gauger played the flute;
And what should Master Gauger play
But *Over the hills and far away*.

R. L. STEVENSON, *A Song of the Road*.

3
And o'er the hills, and far away,
Beyond their utmost purple rim,
Beyond the night, across the day,
Thro' all the world she follow'd him.

TENNYSON, *The Day-dream: The Departure*.

HISTORY

I—History: Definitions

4
History is a pageant and not a philosophy.

AUGUSTINE BIRRELL, *Obiter Dicta, Second Series: The Muse of History*.

That great dust-heap called "history."

AUGUSTINE BIRRELL, *Obiter Dicta: Carlyle*.

5
History after all is the true poetry.

CARLYLE, *Essays: Boswell's Life of Johnson*.

6
History is the essence of innumerable Biographies.

CARLYLE, *Essays: On History*.

There is properly no history, only biography.

EMERSON, *Essays, First Series: History*.

All history resolves itself very easily into the biography of a few stout and earnest persons.

EMERSON, *Essays, First Series: Self-Reliance*.
See also under BIOGRAPHY.

7
History, as it lies at the root of all science, is also the first distinct product of man's spiritual nature; his earliest expression of what can be called Thought.

CARLYLE, *Essays: On History*.

8
All history . . . is an inarticulate Bible.

CARLYLE, *Latter-Day Pamphlets*. No. 8.

All history is a Bible—a thing stated in words by me more than once.

CARLYLE. (FROUDE, *Early Life of Carlyle*.)

9
History is only a confused heap of facts.

LORD CHESTERFIELD, *Letters*, 5 Feb., 1750.

10
History is Philosophy learned from examples.
(Ἱστορία φιλοσοφία ἐστὶν ἐκ παραδειγμάτων.)

DIONYSIUS OF HALICARNASSUS, *Ars Rhetorica*, xi, 2. A paraphrase from Thucydides, *History*. Bk. i, sec. 22.

I have read somewhere or other, in Dionysius of Halicarnassus, I think, that history is philosophy teaching by examples.

LORD BOLINGBROKE, *On the Study and Use of History*. Letter 2.

11
History is bunk.

HENRY FORD, on the witness stand at Mt. Clemens, Mich., in his libel suit against the *Chicago Tribune*, July, 1919.

Long years in money-grubbing sunk,
Cried Poros: "History is bunk!"
Well, such a verdict holds no mystery;
When, where, and how learned Poros history?

GEORGE MEASON WHICHER, *Critique Manqué*.

12
History is but the unrolled scroll of prophecy.

JAMES A. GARFIELD, *The Province of History*.

13
History is the chart and compass for national endeavour.

HELPS, *Friends in Council*. Bk. i, ch. 11.

14
History, by apprising [men] of the past, will enable them to judge of the future.

THOMAS JEFFERSON, *Writings*. Vol. i, p. 207.

History, in general, only informs us what bad government is.

THOMAS JEFFERSON, *Writings*. Vol. xi, p. 223.

15
History teaches everything, even the future.

LAMARTINE, *Speech*, at Macon, 1847.

16
The history of the world is the record of a man in quest of his daily bread and butter.

H. W. VAN LOON, *The Story of Mankind*.

17
Old events have modern meanings; only that survives
Of past history which finds kindred in all hearts and lives.

J. R. LOWELL, *Mahmood*, l. 1.

18
The course of life is like the sea;
Men come and go; tides rise and fall;
And that is all of history.

JOAQUIN MILLER, *The Sea of Fire*. Canto iv.

19
History is the crystallisation of popular beliefs.

DONN PIATT, *Memories of Men Who Saved the Union: Abraham Lincoln*.

20
We may gather out of history a policy no less wise than eternal; by the comparison and application of other men's forepassed miseries with our own like errors and ill deservings.

SIR WALTER RALEIGH, *Hist. of World: Preface*.

21
History is a cyclic poem written by Time upon the memories of man.

SHELLEY. (BIRRELL, *Obiter Dicta*. Ser. ii, 203.)

II—History: Apothegms

22
You are called upon to remake history.

BERTRAND BARÈRE, to the Jacobins. (MARTIN, *History of France*, xvi.)

23
History, with all her volumes vast,
Hath but *one* page.

BYRON, *Childe Harold*. Canto iv, st. 108.

1
But that is ancient history. (Sed hæc et vetera.)
CICERO, *Tusculanarum Disputationum*. Bk. i, ch. 30, sec. 74.

2
While we read history we make history.
G. W. CURTIS, *The Call of Freedom*.

Every great crisis of human history is a pass of Thermopylæ, and there is always a Leonidas and his three hundred to die in it, if they can not conquer.
G. W. CURTIS, *The Call of Freedom*.

3
This human mind wrote history, and this must read it. The Sphinx must solve her own riddle.
EMERSON, *Essays, First Series: History*.

In analysing history do not be too profound, for often the causes are quite superficial.
EMERSON, *Journals*. Vol. iv, p. 160.

4
The use of history is to give value to the present hour and its duty.
EMERSON, *Society and Solitude: Works and Days*.

5
And read their history in a nation's eyes.
THOMAS GRAY, *Elegy Written in a Country Church-yard*. St. 16.

6
They who live in history only seemed to
walk the earth again.
LONGFELLOW, *The Belfry of Bruges*. St. 9.

History casts its shadow far into the land of song.
LONGFELLOW, *Outre-Mer: Ancient Spanish Ballads*.

7
History, however it is written, always pleases. (Historia quoquo modo scripta delectat.)
PLINY THE YOUNGER, *Epistles*. Bk. v, epis. 8.

8
[History] hath triumphed over Time, which besides it, nothing but Eternity hath triumphed over.
SIR WALTER RALEIGH, *The History of the World: Preface*.

9
The dignity of history.
HENRY SAINT-JOHN, LORD BOLINGBROKE, *On the Study and Use of History*. Letter 5. (1738)

The strange lady now laboured under a difficulty which appears almost below the dignity of history to mention.
FIELDING, *Tom Jones*. Bk. xi, ch. 2. (1749)

I shall cheerfully bear the reproach of having descended below the dignity of history.
MACAULAY, *History of England*. Vol. i, ch. 1. (1839)

10
The world's history is the world's judgment. (Die Weltgeschichte ist das Weltgericht.)
SCHILLER, *Resignation*.

11
Duke. And what's her history?
Viola. A blank, my lord.
SHAKESPEARE, *Twelfth Night*. Act ii, sc. 4, l. 112.

12
Must not a great history be always an epic?
W. C. SMITH, *Books Which Have Influenced Me*.

13
And this is exactly how history is written. (Et voilà justement comme on écrit l'histoire.)
VOLTAIRE, *Charlot*. Act i, sc. 7. Voltaire's contempt for history was frequently expressed in nearly the same words.

What more can you ask? He has invented history. (Que voulez-vous de plus? Il a inventé l'histoire!)
MADAME DU DEFFAND, of Voltaire, when some one remarked that he lacked invention. (FOURIER, *L'Esprit dans Histoire*, p. 141.)

14
How history makes one shudder and laugh by turns!
WALPOLE, *Letter to the Earl of Strafford*, 1786.

Don't you begin to think, Madam, that it is pleasanter to read history than to live it? Battles are fought and towns taken in every page, but a campaign takes six or seven months to hear, and achieves no great matter at last. I dare to say Alexander seemed to the coffee-houses of Pella a monstrous while about conquering the world.
WALPOLE, *Letter to the Countess of Ossory*, 8 Oct., 1777.

III—History: Its Truth

15
History indeed is the witness of the times, the light of truth. (Historia vero testis temporum, lux veritatis.)
CICERO, *De Oratore*. Bk. ii, sec. 9.

Who does not know that it is the first law of history that it shall not dare to state anything which is false, and consequently that it shall not shrink from stating anything that is true? (Quis nescit primam esse historiæ legem, ne quid falsi dicere audeat, deinde ne quid veri non audeat?)
CICERO, *De Oratore*. Bk. ii, sec. 15.

16
To be ignorant of what happened before you were born is to be ever a child. For what is man's lifetime unless the memory of past events is woven with those of earlier times?
CICERO, *Orator*. Sec. 34.

17
One may cover secret actions, but to be silent concerning what all the world knows and things which have had effects which are public and of so much consequence, is an inexcusable fault. (On peult couvrir les actions secrettes; mais de taire tout ce que tout le monde sçait, et les choses qui ont tiré des

effects publiques et de telle consequence, c'est un défault inexcusable.)

MONTAIGNE, *Essays*. Bk. ii, ch. 10. Of the duty of historians.

1
I hold it a noble task to rescue from oblivion those who deserve to be eternally remembered. (Quia mihi pulchrum in primis videtur non pati occidere.)

PLINY THE YOUNGER, *Epistles*. Bk. v, epis. 8.

History should be guided by strict truth, and worthy actions require nothing more.

PLINY THE YOUNGER, *Epistles*. Bk. vii, epis. 33.

2
It is no great wonder if, in long process of time, while fortune takes her course hither and thither, numerous coincidences should spontaneously occur. If the number and variety of subjects be infinite, it is all the more easy for fortune, with such abundance of material, to effect this similarity of results.

PLUTARCH, *Lives: Sertorius*. Sec. 1.

3
The principal office of history I take to be this: to prevent virtuous actions from being forgotten, and that evil words and deeds should fear an infamous reputation with posterity.

TACITUS, *Annals*. Bk. iii, sec. 65.

4
I shall be content if those shall pronounce my history useful who wish to be given a view of events as they really happened, and as they are very likely to repeat themselves.

THUCYDIDES, *Historia*. Bk. i, sec. 2. Hence the phrase, "History repeats itself."

History never repeats itself, but historians always repeat each other.

HUGH ROSS WILLIAMSON, *Historical Whodunits*, p. 17. Quoted as an epigram.

5 I will trace the outlines of the chief events. (Sed summa sequar fastigia rerum.)

VERGIL, *Æneid*. Bk. i, l. 342.

In due order I will describe the manners, the pursuits, the peoples, and the battles of the race. (Ordine gentis Mores et studia et populos, et prœlia dicam.)

VERGIL, *Georgics*. Bk. iv, l. 4.

6
In leaves, more durable than leaves of brass,
Writes our whole history.

YOUNG, *Night Thoughts*. Night ii, l. 275.

IV—History: Its Falsity

7
The vast Mississippi of falsehood.

MATTHEW ARNOLD, *Essays: History*.

8
She was ever a notable wag at history.

APHRA BEHN, *The Young King*. Act i, sc. 1. Referring to Fame.

9
History
With the supernatural element,—you know.

ROBERT BROWNING, *Mr. Sludge "The Medium."*

10
Where history's pen its praise or blame supplies,
And lies like truth, and still most truly lies.

BYRON, *Lara*. Canto i, st. 11.

11
History, a distillation of Rumour.

CARLYLE, *The French Revolution*. Pt. i, bk. vii, ch. 5.

12
How many histories are there filled with these marvels?

CERVANTES, *Don Quixote*. Pt. ii, ch. 1.

13
History shows you prospects by starlight, or, at best, by the waning moon.

RUFUS CHOATE, *New England History*.

14
Some write a narrative of wars, and feats
Of heroes little known, and call the rant
An history: describe the man, of whom
His own coevals took but little note,
And paint his person, character and views,
As they had known him from his mother's womb.

COWPER, *The Task*. Bk. iii, l. 139.

15
Gossip which is written down is no more veracious than gossip which flies current. . . . Gossip is none the less gossip because it comes from venerable antiquity.

MANDELL CREIGHTON, *Manuscript Notes*.

16
Historians relate, not so much what is done, as what they would have believed.

BENJAMIN FRANKLIN, *Poor Richard*, 1739.

17
History fades into fable; fact becomes clouded with doubt and controversy; the inscription moulders from the tablet: the statue falls from the pedestal. Columns, arches, pyramids, what are they but heaps of sand; and their epitaphs, but characters written in the dust?

WASHINGTON IRVING, *The Sketch-Book: Westminster Abbey*.

18
Seldom any splendid story is wholly true.

SAMUEL JOHNSON, *Works*. Vol. ii, p. 281.

19
Such bickerings to recount, met often in these our writers, what more worth is it than to chronicle the wars of kites or crows flocking and fighting in the air?

MILTON, *History of Britain*. Bk. iv.

By this time, like one who had set out on his way by night, and travelled through a region of smooth or idle dreams, our history now arrives on the confines, where daylight and truth meet us with a clear dawn, representing to our view, though at a far distance, true colours and shapes.

MILTON, *History of Britain*. Bk. i.

20
So difficult a matter is it to determine the truth of anything by history.

PLUTARCH, *Lives: Themistocles*.

1
Half-legend, half-historic.
TENNYSON, *The Princess: Prologue*, l. 30.

2
Ancient histories, as one of our wits has said, are but fables that have been agreed upon. (Toutes les histoires anciens, comme le disait un de nos beaux esprits, ne sont que des fables convenues.)
VOLTAIRE, *Jeannot et Colin.*

There are no other ancient histories except fables. (Il n'y a point d'autres histoires anciennes que les fables.)
VOLTAIRE, *Letter.*

What is history but a fable agreed upon?
NAPOLEON BONAPARTE, *Sayings.*

3
Anything but history, for history must be false.
ROBERT WALPOLE, when his secretary asked what he wished read to him as he lay on a sick-bed. (*Walpoliana.* No. 141.) *Notes and Queries,* No. 3, states that the correct version is, "Oh, do not read history, for that I know must be false."

4
Those old credulities, to nature dear,
Shall they no longer bloom upon the stock
Of History, stript naked as a rock
'Mid a dry desert?
WORDSWORTH, *Memorials of a Tour in Italy:* No. 4, *Regrets.* Alluding to Niebuhr and other modern historians.

V—History: A Record of Crime

5
I pore on musty chronicles,
And muse on usurpations long forgot,
And other historied dramas of high wrong!
THOMAS HARDY, *The Dynasts.* Pt. ii, act i, sc. 8.

6
Sin writes histories, goodness is silent.
GOETHE, *Table-Talk,* 1810.

7
The long historian of my country's woes.
HOMER, *Odyssey.* Bk. iii, l. 142. (Pope, tr.)

8
The history of the great events of this world is scarcely more than the history of crimes. (L'histoire des grands évènements de ce monde n'est guère que l'histoire des crimes.)
VOLTAIRE, *Essai sur les Mœurs.* (1753)

History is but a picture of crimes and misfortunes. (L'histoire n'est que le tableau des crimes et des malheurs.)
VOLTAIRE, *L'Ingénu.* Ch. 10. (1757)

On whatever side we regard the history of Europe, we shall perceive it to be a tissue of crimes, follies, and misfortunes.
OLIVER GOLDSMITH, *The Citizen of the World.* No. 42. (1762)

History is, indeed, little more than the register of the crimes, follies, and misfortunes of mankind.
GIBBON, *Decline and Fall of the Roman Empire.* Ch. 3. (1776)

VI—History: Happy the Nation Whose Annals Are Blank

9
Happy is the nation without a history.
BECCARIA, *Trattato dei Delitti e Delle Pene: Introduction.*

10
Blest is that Nation whose silent course of happiness furnishes nothing for history to say.
THOMAS JEFFERSON, *Writings.* Vol. xi, p. 180.

He is happiest of whom the world says least, good or bad.
THOMAS JEFFERSON, *Letter to John Adams,* 1786.

11
Happy the people whose annals are tiresome.
MONTESQUIEU, *Maximes.*

A paradoxical philosopher carrying to the utmost length that aphorism of Montesquieu's, "Happy the people whose annals are tiresome," has said "Happy the people whose annals are vacant."
CARLYLE, *The French Revolution.* Vol. i, bk. ii, ch. 1.

Happy the people whose annals are blank.
CARLYLE, *Frederick the Great.* Bk. xvi, ch. 1.

12
How the best state to know?—it is found out
Like the best woman;—that least talked about.
SCHILLER, *Votive Tablets: The Best Governed State.*

The happiest women, like the happiest nations, have no history.
GEORGE ELIOT, *The Mill on the Floss.* Bk. vi, ch. 3.

VII—History: The Historian

13
It is the true office of history to represent the events themselves, together with the counsels, and to leave the observations and conclusions thereupon to the liberty and faculty of every man's judgment.
BACON, *Advancement of Learning.* Bk. ii.

Cæsar, in modesty mixed with greatness, did for his pleasure apply the name of a Commentary to the best history of the world.
BACON, *Advancement of Learning.* Bk. ii.

14
These gentle historians, on the contrary, dip their pens in nothing but the milk of human kindness.
EDMUND BURKE, *A Letter to a Noble Lord.*

15
Histories are as perfect as the Historian is wise, and is gifted with an eye and a soul.
CARLYLE, *Cromwell's Letters and Speeches: Introduction.*

In a certain sense all men are historians.
CARLYLE, *Essays: On History.*

16
Historians ought to be precise, faithful, and unprejudiced; and neither interest nor fear,

hatred nor affection, should make them swerve from the way of truth.

CERVANTES, *Don Quixote*. Pt. i, ch. 9.

1
History owes its excellency more to the writer's manner than to the material of which it is composed.

GOLDSMITH, *Life of Richard Nash*.

2
The historian is a sort of talking ghost from out the past.

HOFFMAN, *Doge and Dogaressa*.

3
Every great writer is a writer of history, let him treat on almost any subject he may.

W. S. LANDOR, *Imaginary Conversations: Diogenes and Plato*.

4
To be a really good historian is perhaps the rarest of intellectual distinctions.

MACAULAY, *Essays: History*.

5
I regard the writing of history as one of the most difficult of tasks. (In primus arduum videtur res gestas scribere.)

SALLUST, *Catilina*. Sec. 3.

6
The historian is a prophet looking backwards. (Der Historiker ist ein rückwärts gekehrter Prophet.)

SCHLEGEL, *Athenæum: Berlin*, i, ii, 20.

7
Anybody can make history. Only a great man can write it.

OSCAR WILDE, *Aphorisms*, p. 52.

8
Deal not in history, often I have said;
'Twill prove a most unprofitable trade.

JOHN WOLCOT, *Benevolent Epistle*.

HOLIDAY

9
There were his young barbarians all at play,
There was their Dacian mother—he, their sire,
Butcher'd to make a Roman holiday.

BYRON, *Childe Harold*. Canto iv, st. 141.

10
Still thou playest:—short vacation
Fate grants each to stand aside;
Now must thou be man and artist,—
'Tis the turning of the tide.

EMERSON, *Holidays*.

11
The red-letter days now become, to all intents and purposes, dead-letter days.

LAMB, *Essays of Elia: Oxford in the Vacation*.

12
The holiest of all holidays are those
Kept by ourselves in silence and apart;
The secret anniversaries of the heart,
When the full river of feeling overflows;—
The happy days unclouded to their close;
The sudden joys that out of darkness start
As flames from ashes; swift desires that dart
Like swallows singing down each wind that blows!

LONGFELLOW, *Holidays*.

13
On a sunshine holiday.

MILTON, *L'Allegro*, l. 98.

14
For now I am in a holiday humour.

SHAKESPEARE, *As You Like It*. Act iv, sc. 1, l. 69.

15
If all the year was playing holidays,
To sport would be as tedious as to work.

SHAKESPEARE, *I Henry IV*. Act i, sc. 2, l. 227.

A perpetual holiday is a good working definition of hell.

BERNARD SHAW, *Parents and Children*.

16
Is this a holiday?

SHAKESPEARE, *Julius Cæsar*. Act i, sc. 1, l. 2.

The yearly course that brings this day about
Shall never see it but a holiday.

SHAKESPEARE, *King John*. Act iii, sc. 1, l. 82.

He speaks holiday.

SHAKESPEARE, *The Merry Wives of Windsor*. Act iii, sc. 2, l. 69.

17
Monday is parson's holiday.

SWIFT, *Letter to Stella*, 3 March, 1711.

18
Time for work,—yet take
Much holiday for art's and friendship's sake.

GEORGE JAMES DE WILDE, *On the Arrival of Spring*.

HOLINESS

See also Goodness

19
Things sacred should not only be untouched with the hands, but unviolated in thought. (Res sacros non modo manibus attingi, sed ne cogitatione quidem violari fas fuit.)

CICERO, *In Verrem*. No. ii, sec. 4.

20
Holiness appeared to me to be of a sweet, pleasant, charming, serene, calm nature; which brought an inexpressible purity, brightness, peacefulness, and ravishment to the soul. In other words, that it made the soul like a field or garden of God, with all manner of pleasant flowers.

JONATHAN EDWARDS, *Holiness*.

21
We believe that holiness confers a certain insight, because not by private, but by our public force can we share and know the nature of things.

EMERSON, *Conduct of Life: Worship*.

Ascending thorough just degrees
To a consummate holiness,
As angel blind to trespass done,
And bleaching all souls like the sun.

EMERSON, *Fragments: Life*. Frag. 29.

1
And many a holy text around she strews
That teach the rustic moralist to die.
THOMAS GRAY, *Elegy Written in a Country Church-yard*, l. 83.

2
In the beauties of holiness.
Old Testament: Psalms, cx, 3.

3
But all his mind is bent to holiness,
To number Ave-Maries on his beads;
His champions are the prophets and apostles,
His weapons holy saws of sacred writ,
His study is his tilt-yard, and his loves
Are brazen images of canonized saints.
SHAKESPEARE, *II Henry VI*. Act i, sc. 3, l. 58.

4
What thou wouldst highly
That wouldst thou holily.
SHAKESPEARE, *Macbeth*. Act i, sc. 5, l. 22.

Our holy lives must win a new world's crown.
SHAKESPEARE, *Richard II*. Act v, sc. 1, l. 24.

5
Holiness is the architectural plan upon which God buildeth up His living temple.
C. G. SPURGEON, *Holiness*.

HOLLAND AND THE HOLLANDERS

6
A country that draws fifty foot of water,
In which men live as in the hold of Nature,
And when the sea does in upon them break,
And drowns a province, does but spring a leak. . . .
That feed, like cannibals, on other fishes,
And serve their cousin-germans up in dishes:
A land that rides at anchor, and is moor'd,
In which they do not live, but go aboard.
SAMUEL BUTLER, *Description of Holland*.

7
That water-land of Dutchmen and of ditches.
BYRON, *Don Juan*. Canto x, st. 63.

8
Well may they boast themselves an ancient nation,
For they were bred ere manners were in fashion.
DRYDEN, *Satire on the Dutch*, l. 31.

9
Embosom'd in the deep where Holland lies,
Methinks her patient sons before me stand,
Where the broad ocean leans against the land.
GOLDSMITH, *The Traveller*, l. 282.

Then we upon our globe's last verge shall go
And see the ocean leaning on the sky.
DRYDEN, *On the Royal Society*.

10
The Scotch may be compared to a tulip planted in dung; but I never see a Dutchman in his own house but I think of a magnificent Egyptian temple dedicated to an ox.
OLIVER GOLDSMITH, *Letter to Thomas Contarine*, 1753.

11
Holland . . . lies so low, they're only saved by being dammed.
THOMAS HOOD, *Up the Rhine*.

12
Holland, that scarce deserves the name of land,
As but the off-scouring of the British sand;
And so much earth as was contributed
By English pilots, when they heaved the lead.
ANDREW MARVELL, *The Character of Holland*.

Who best could know to pump an earth so leak,
Him they their lord and country's father speak;
To make a bank was a great plot of state;—
Invent a shovel, and be a magistrate.
ANDREW MARVELL, *The Character of Holland*.

13
Adieu, canals, ducks, rabble! (Adieu, canaux, canards, canaille!)
VOLTAIRE, when leaving Holland, summing up his impressions of the country.

HOME

See also House

I—Home: Definitions

14
Home,—the nursery of the infinite.
W. E. CHANNING, *Note-Book: Children*.

Home interprets heaven. Home is heaven for beginners.
CHARLES PARKHURST, *Sermons: The Perfect Peace*.

15
My idea of a home is a house in which each member of the family can on the instant kindle a fire in his or her private room.
EMERSON, *Journals*.

16
Home is the place where, when you have to go there,
They have to take you in.
ROBERT FROST, *The Death of the Hired Man*.

16a
It takes a heap o' livin' in a house t' make it home.
EDGAR A. GUEST, *Home*.

But meanwhile I ask you to believe that
It takes a heap of other things besides
A heap o' livin' to make a home out of a house.
To begin with, it takes a heap o' payin'.
OGDEN NASH, *A Heap o' Livin'*.

17
Home, in one form or another, is the great object of life.
J. G. HOLLAND, *Gold-Foil: Home*.

No genuine observer can decide otherwise than that the homes of a nation are the bulwarks of personal and national safety.
J. G. HOLLAND, *Gold-Foil: Home*.

18
A house full of books and a garden of flowers.
ANDREW LANG, *Ballade of True Wisdom*.

19
Home is where the heart is.
Attributed to PLINY. Claimed by ELBERT HUBBARD, *Thousand and One Epigrams*, p. 73.

Where we love is home,
Home that our feet may leave, but not our hearts.

O. W. HOLMES, *Homesick in Heaven*. St. 5.

1
Home is the girl's prison and the woman's workhouse.

BERNARD SHAW, *Maxims for Revolutionists*.

2
The modern idea of home has been well expressed as the place one goes from the garage.

GEORGE W. WICKERSHAM. "I am sorry to say that sentence . . . is not original."—Letter to Compiler.

MY HOUSE MY CASTLE, *see under* HOUSE.

II—Home Sweet Home

3
Nor has the world a better thing,
Though one should search it round,
Than thus to live one's own sole king,
Upon one's own sole ground.

WILFRID SCAWEN BLUNT, *The Old Squire*.

4
But what on earth is half so dear—
So longed for—as the hearth of home?

EMILY BRONTË, *A Little While*.

5
Fare you well, old house! you're naught that can feel or see,
But you seem like a human bein'—a dear old friend to me;
And we never will have a better home, if *my* opinion stands,
Until we commence a-keepin' house in the house not made with hands.

WILL CARLETON, *Out of the Old House, Nancy*.

6
Old homes! old hearts! Upon my soul forever
Their peace and gladness lie like tears and laughter.

MADISON CAWEIN, *Old Homes*.

7
Whom God loves, his house is sweet to him.

CERVANTES, *Don Quixote*. Pt. ii, ch. 43.

8
Wherever smoke wreaths Heavenward curl—
Cave of a hermit, Hovel of churl,
Mansion of merchant, princely dome—
Out of the dreariness,
Into its cheeriness,
Come we in weariness
Home.

STEPHEN CHALMERS, *Home*.

9
No place is more delightful than one's own fireside. (Nullus est locus domestica sede jucúndior.)

CICERO, *Epistolæ ad Familiares*. Bk. iv, epis. 8.

10
When the flower is i' the bud and the leaf is on the tree,
The lark shall sing me hame in my ain countree;
Hame, hame, hame, hame fain wad I be,
O hame, hame, hame, to my ain countree!

ALLAN CUNNINGHAM, *Hame, Hame, Hame*.

11
Blest be that spot, where cheerful guests retire
To pause from toil, and trim their ev'ning fire;
Blest that abode, where want and pain repair,
And every stranger finds a ready chair.

GOLDSMITH, *The Traveller*, l. 13.

12
Of a' roads to happiness ever were tried,
There's nane half so sure as ane's ain fireside.

ELIZABETH HAMILTON, *My Ain Fireside*.

My ain fireside, my ain fireside,
O, there's naught to compare wi' ane's ain fireside.

ELIZABETH HAMILTON, *My Ain Fireside*.

Pleasant are one's own brands.

UNKNOWN, *Proverbs of Hending*, 14. (c. 1300)

13
Sweet is the smile of home; the mutual look
When hearts are of each other sure.

KEBLE, *Christian Year: First Sunday in Lent*.

14
His home, the spot of earth supremely blest,
A dearer, sweeter spot than all the rest.

MONTGOMERY, *West Indies*. Pt. iii, l. 67.

15
Round the hearth-stone of home, in the land of our birth,
The holiest spot on the face of the earth.

GEORGE POPE MORRIS, *Land Ho!*

A bleezing ingle, and clean hearth-stane.

ALLAN RAMSAY, *Gentle Shepherd*. Act i, sc. 2.

16
To fireside happiness, to hours of ease,
Blest with that charm, the certainty to please.

SAMUEL ROGERS, *Human Life*, l. 355.

17
A comfortable house is a great source of happiness. It ranks immediately after health and a good conscience.

SYDNEY SMITH, *Letter to Lord Murray*, 29 Sept., 1843.

18
I read within a poet's book
A word that starred the page,
"Stone walls do not a prison make,
Nor iron bars a cage."

Yes, that is true, and something more:
You'll find, where'er you roam,
That marble floors and gilded walls
Can never make a home.

But every house where Love abides
And Friendship is a guest,
Is surely home, and home, sweet home;
For there the heart can rest.

HENRY VAN DYKE, *Home Song*.

19
Type of the wise, who soar, but never roam—

True to the kindred points of Heaven and Home!
WORDSWORTH, *To a Skylark.*

1
Let us make resound the sweet song of "Home." (Dulce domum resonemus.)
UNKNOWN, *Concinamus, O sodales (Comrades, Let us Sing Together)*. Sung at Winchester and other English schools on the eve of the holidays. "Dulce domum" is sometimes improperly used for "sweet home."

III—Home: Be It Never so Homely

2
Hame's hame, be it never so hamely.
JOHN ARBUTHNOT, *Law a Bottomless Pit.* Pt. iii, ch. 4. (1712)

Home is home, be it never so homely.
DICKENS, *Dombey and Son.* Ch. 35. (1848)

3
For home, though homely 'twere, yet it is sweet.
ARIOSTO, *Orlando Furioso.* Canto xxxix, st. 61. (Harington, tr., 1591.)

Though home be homely, it is more delightful than finer things abroad.
SAMUEL BUTLER, *Remains.* Vol. ii, p. 285. (1680)

Home is homely, though it be poor in sight.
JOHN HEYWOOD, *Proverbs.* Pt. i, ch. 4. (1546)

4
Is not a small house best? Put a woman into a small house, and after five years she comes out large and healthy.
EMERSON, *Journals.* Vol. vii, p. 47.

5
My house, my house, though thou art small,
Thou art to me the Escurial.
GEORGE HERBERT, *Jacula Prudentum.*

God oft hath a great share in a little house.
GEORGE HERBERT, *Jacula Prudentum.* Perhaps from the French proverb, "En petite maison a Dieu grand part."

I've read in many a novel, that unless they've souls that grovel—
Folks *prefer* in fact a hovel to your dreary marble halls.
C. S. CALVERLEY, *In the Gloaming.*

6
Joy dwells beneath a humble roof;
Heaven is not built of country seats
But little queer suburban streets.
CHRISTOPHER MORLEY, *To the Little House.*

7
'Mid pleasures and palaces though we may roam,
Be it ever so humble, there's no place like home.
JOHN HOWARD PAYNE, *Home, Sweet Home.* From the first act of his opera, *Clari, The Maid of Milan,* produced at Covent Garden, London, 8 May, 1823.

The banishment was overlong,
But it will soon be past;
The man who wrote home's sweetest song
Is coming home at last.
WILL CARLETON, *Coming Home at Last.* John Howard Payne, the author of *Home, Sweet Home,* died in Tunis, 9 April, 1852, and was buried there. Thirty years later, the body was exhumed, shipped to the United States, and re-buried in the chapel of Oak Hill Cemetery, Washington, D. C., on the ninety-second anniversary of his birth, 9 June, 1883.

8
A little house well fill'd, a little land well till'd, and a little wife well will'd, are great riches.
JOHN RAY, *English Proverbs.*

9
Just the wee cot—the cricket's chirr—
Love and the smiling face of her.
JAMES WHITCOMB RILEY, *Ike Walton's Prayer.*

10
Though home be but homely, yet huswife is taught
That home hath no fellow to such as have aught.
THOMAS TUSSER, *Five Hundred Points of Good Husbandry: Housewifery.*

IV—Home: East, West, Hame's Best

11
Now will I to home and household hearth
Move on, and first give thanks unto the Gods,
Who led me forth and brought me back again.
ÆSCHYLUS, *Choëphori,* l. 824. (Plumptre, tr.)

He who is truly happy should bide at home (and he who fares ill, he too should bide at home.)
ÆSCHYLUS, *Fragments.* Frag. 177.

12
But wheresoe'er I'm doomed to roam,
I still shall say—that home is home.
WILLIAM COMBE, *Dr. Syntax in Search of the Picturesque.* Canto xxvi.

For the whole world, without a native home,
Is nothing but a prison of larger room.
ABRAHAM COWLEY, *To the Bishop of Lincoln.*

13
If solid happiness we prize,
Within our breast this jewel lies,
And they are fools who roam.
The world has nothing to bestow;
From our own selves our joys must flow,
And that dear hut, our home.
NATHANIEL COTTON, *The Fireside.* St. 3.

14
Cleave to thine acre; the round year
Will fetch all fruits and virtues here.
Fool and foe may harmless roam,
Loved and lovers bide at home.
EMERSON, *Conduct of Life: Considerations by the Way.*

Who bides at home, nor looks abroad,
Carries the eagles, and masters the sword.
EMERSON, *Destiny.*

That each should in his house abide,
Therefore was the world so wide.
EMERSON, *Fragments: Life.* Frag. 37.

Stay at home. The way to have large occasional views is to have large habitual views.
EMERSON, *Uncollected Lectures: Table-Talk.*

1
Oh, to be home again, home again, home again!
Under the apple-boughs, down by the mill!
J. T. FIELDS, *In a Strange Land.*

2
Way down upon de Swanee ribber,
Far, far away,
Dere's wha my heart is turning ebber,
Dere's wha de old folks stay.
All up and down de whole creation,
Sadly I roam,
Still longing for de old plantation,
And for de old folks at home.
STEPHEN COLLINS FOSTER, *Old Folks at Home.*

3
However we toil, or wherever we wander, our fatigued wishes still recur to home for tranquillity.
GOLDSMITH, *The Citizen of the World.* No. 103.

Such is the patriot's boast, where'er we roam,
His first, best country ever is at home.
GOLDSMITH, *The Traveller,* l. 73.

4
What strong, mysterious links enchain the heart
To regions where the morn of life was spent.
JAMES GRAHAME, *The Sabbath,* l. 404.

5
He that doth live at home, and learns to know
God and himself, needeth no farther go.
CHRISTOPHER HARVEY, *Travels at Home.*

6
And for their birthplace moan, as moans the ocean-shell.
FELICIA HEMANS, *The Forest Sanctuary.*

7
A man is always nearest to his good when at home, and farthest from it when away.
J. G. HOLLAND, *Gold-Foil: Home.*

8
His native home deep imag'd in his soul.
(*Δὴ γὰρ μενέαινε νέεσθαι.*)
HOMER, *Odyssey.* Bk. xiii, l. 30. (Pope, tr.)

9
Peace and rest at length have come,
All the day's long toil is past;
And each heart is whispering, "Home,
Home at last!"
THOMAS HOOD, *Home At Last.*

10
To be happy at home is the ultimate result of all ambition.
SAMUEL JOHNSON, *The Rambler.* No. 68.

Goethe once said, "He is happiest, king or peasant, who finds his happiness at home." And Goethe knew—because he never found it.
ELBERT HUBBARD, *Epigrams.*

11
And Judah and Israel dwelt safely, every man under his vine and under his fig tree.
Old Testament: I Kings, iv, 25.

And then eat ye every man of his own vine, and every one of his fig tree.
Old Testament: II Kings, xviii, 31.

They shall sit every man under his vine and under his fig tree.
Old Testament: Micah, iv, 4.

12
Cling to thy home! If there the meanest shed
Yield thee a hearth and shelter for thy head,
And some poor plot, with vegetables stored,
Be all that Heaven allots thee for thy board,
Unsavory bread, and herbs that scatter'd grow
Wild on the river-brink or mountain-brow;
Yet e'en this cheerless mansion shall provide
More heart's repose than all the world beside.
LEONIDAS, *Cling to Thy Home.*

13
Over the hills of home, laddie, over the hills of home.
LILLIAN LEVERIDGE, *A Cry from the Canadian Hills.*

14
Stay, stay at home, my heart, and rest;
Home-keeping hearts are happiest,
For those that wander they know not where
Are full of trouble and full of care;
To stay at home is best.
LONGFELLOW, *Song.* St. 1.

15
He never cares to wander from his own fireside,
He never cares to wander or to roam.
With his baby on his knee,
He's as happy as can be,
For there's no place like home, sweet home.
FELIX MCGLENNON, *He Never Cares to Wander from His Own Fireside.* (1892)

16
Far from all resort of mirth,
Save the cricket on the hearth.
MILTON, *Il Penseroso,* l. 81.

The Cricket on the Hearth.
CHARLES DICKENS. Title of a Christmas book.

17
Who has not felt how sadly sweet
The dream of home, the dream of home,
Steals o'er the heart, too soon to fleet,
When far o'er sea or land we roam?
THOMAS MOORE, *The Dream of Home.*

18
The bird, let loose in eastern skies,
When hast'ning fondly home,
Ne'er stoops to earth her wing, nor flies
Where idle warblers roam;
But high she shoots through air and light,
Above all low delay,
Where nothing earthly bounds her flight,
Nor shadow dims her way.
THOMAS MOORE, *The Bird, Let Loose.*

19
So sung he joyously, nor knew that they
Must wander yet for many an evil day
Or ever the dread gods should let them come
Back to the white walls of their long-left home.
WILLIAM MORRIS, *Life and Death of Jason.* Bk. ix, l. 330.

1
Happy the man, whose wish and care
A few paternal acres bound,
Content to breathe his native air
In his own ground.
POPE, *Ode on Solitude.*

2
Nor hell nor heaven shall that soul surprise,
Who loves the rain,
And loves his home,
And looks on life with quiet eyes.
FRANCES SHAW, *Who Loves the Rain.*

3
East and West, Home is best.
C. H. SPURGEON, *John Ploughman.* Ch. 13.

Seek home for rest, For home is best.
THOMAS TUSSER, *Five Hundred Points of Good Husbandry: Housewifery.*

4
Here is our home, here our country! (His domus, hæc patria est.)
VERGIL, *Æneid.* Bk. vii, l. 122.

None love their country, but who love their home.
S. T. COLERIDGE, *Il Zapolya.* Act iv, sc. 3.

V—Home, Wife, and Children

See also Family

5
As much as I converse with sages and heroes, they have very little of my love and admiration. I long for rural and domestic scenes, for the warbling of birds and the prattling of my children.
JOHN ADAMS, *Letter to His Wife,* 16 March, 1777.

6
At length his lonely cot appears in view
Beneath the shelter of an aged tree;
Th' expectant wee things, toddlin', stacher through
To meet their dad, wi' flictherin' noise an' glee.
BURNS, *The Cotter's Saturday Night.* St. 3.

To make a happy fireside clime
To weans and wife,
That's the true pathos and sublime
Of human life.
BURNS, *Epistle to Dr. Blacklock.*

7
'Tis sweet to hear the watch-dog's honest bark
Bay deep-mouth'd welcome as we draw near home;
'Tis sweet to know there is an eye will mark
Our coming, and look brighter when we come.
BYRON, *Don Juan.* Canto i, st. 123.

8
For altars and hearths; for hearth and home. (Pro aris et focis.)
CICERO, *Pro Roscio Amerino.* Sec. 5. A common saying, meaning the defense of one's nearest and dearest. Among the Romans, the family or household gods (Penates) had their altars (aræ) in the open court about which each house was built, and the tutelar deities of each dwelling (Lares) their niches round the hearth or ingle-nook (foci).

9
I love it—I love it, and who shall dare
To chide me for loving that old Arm-chair?
ELIZA COOK, *The Old Arm-Chair.*

10
Domestic Happiness, thou only bliss
Of Paradise that hast surviv'd the Fall!
COWPER, *The Task.* Bk. iii, l. 41.

11
"She made home happy!" these few words I read
Within a churchyard, written on a stone.
HENRY COYLE, *She Made Home Happy.*

12
Be not as a lion in thy house, nor frantic among thy servants.
Apocrypha: Ecclesiasticus, iv, 30.

Whatever brawls disturb the street,
There should be peace at home.
ISAAC WATTS, *Love.*

13
'Tis joy to him that toils, when toil is o'er,
To find home waiting, full of happy things.
(Εἰσιόντι δ' ἐργάτῃ
θύραθεν ἡδὺ τἄνδον εὑρίσκειν καλῶς.)
EURIPIDES, *Electra,* l. 76. (Murray, tr.)

14
A night-cap deck'd his brows instead of bay,
A cap by night,—a stocking all the day!
GOLDSMITH, *Description of an Author's Bed-chamber.* (*Citizen of World.* No. 30. 1760.)

The white-wash'd wall, the nicely sanded floor,
The varnish'd clock that click'd behind the door;
The chest contriv'd a double debt to pay,
A bed by night, a chest of drawers by day.
GOLDSMITH, *The Deserted Village,* l. 227. (1770)

What if in Scotland's wilds we veil'd our head,
Where tempests whistle round the sordid bed;
Where the rug's two-fold use we might display,
By night a blanket, and a plaid by day.
EDWARD BURNABY GREENE, *The Satires of Juvenal Paraphrastically Imitated.* (1764)

15
At night returning, every labour sped,
He sits him down, the monarch of a shed:
Smiles by his cheerful fire, and round surveys
His children's looks, that brighten at the blaze;
While his lov'd partner, boastful of her hoard,
Displays her cleanly platter on the board.
GOLDSMITH, *The Traveller,* l. 191.

Dark is the night, and fitful and drearily
Rushes the wind, like the waves of the sea!
Little care I, as here I sit cheerily,
Wife at my side and my baby on knee:
King, king, crown me the king:
Home is the kingdom and love is the king!
WILLIAM RANKIN DURYEA, *A Song for Hearth and Home.* Awarded a prize for the best poem on home, by the *Home Journal,* New York, in 1866.

1
How small, of all that human hearts endure,
That part which laws or kings can cause or cure!
Still to ourselves in every place consign'd,
Our own felicity we make or find:
With secret course, which no loud storms annoy,
Glides the smooth current of domestic joy.

OLIVER GOLDSMITH AND SAMUEL JOHNSON, *The Traveller*, l. 429. Johnson indicated to Boswell that he had written the last ten lines of the poem with the exception of the last couplet but one. (BOSWELL, *Life*, Feb., 1766.)

2
Home and a pleasing wife. (Domus et placens Uxor.)

HORACE, *Odes*. Bk. ii, ode 14, l. 21.

A house and a woman suit excellently.

GEORGE HERBERT, *Jacula Prudentum*.

3
The happiness of the domestic fireside is the first boon of mankind; and it is well it is so, since it is that which is the lot of the mass of mankind.

THOMAS JEFFERSON, *Writings*. Vol. xiii, p. 220.

4
The many make the household,
But only one the home.

J. R. LOWELL, *The Dead House*. St. 9.

It takes a hundred men to make an encampment, but one woman can make a home.

R. G. INGERSOLL, *Woman*.

What is the fireside if it warm but one?

R. U. JOHNSON, *O Made for Love*.

5
No more shall thy family welcome thee home
Nor around thee thy wife and sweet little ones come,
All clamoring joyous to snatch the first kiss,
Transporting thy bosom with exquisite bliss.
(Nam jam non domus accipiet te læta, neque uxor
Optima, nec dulces occurrent oscula nati
Præripere, et tacita pectus dulcedine tangent.)

LUCRETIUS, *De Rerum Natura*. Bk. iii, l. 907. (King, tr.)

For them no more the blazing hearth shall burn,
Or busy housewife ply her evening care;
No children run to lisp their sire's return,
Or climb his knees the envied kiss to share.

THOMAS GRAY, *Elegy Written in a Country Church-yard*, l. 21.

6
Subduing and subdued, the petty strife,
Which clouds the colour of domestic life;
The sober comfort, all the peace which springs
From the large aggregate of little things;
On these small cares of daughter, wife or friend,
The almost sacred joys of home depend.

HANNAH MORE, *Sensibility*.

7
The eagle nestles near the sun;
The dove's low nest for me!—
The eagle's on the crag; sweet one,
The dove's in our green tree!
For hearts that beat like thine and mine
Heaven blesses humble earth;—
The angels of our Heaven shall shine
The angels of our Hearth!

JOHN JAMES PIATT, *A Song of Content*.

8
We have wrought for glory and for beauty and for pleasure,
And have builded little houses for the women we hold dear.

VICTOR STARBUCK, *The Little Houses*.

9
God looks down well pleased to mark
In earth's dusk each rosy spark,
Lights of home and lights of love,
And the child the heart thereof.

KATHERINE TYNAN, *A Night Thought*.

10
Meantime his sweet children hang upon his kisses: his pure home preserves its sanctity. (Interea dulces pendent circum oscula nati: Casta pudicitiam servat domus.)

VERGIL, *Georgics*. Bk. ii, l. 523.

His little children, climbing for a kiss,
Welcome their father's late return at night;
His faithful bed is crowned with chaste delight.

VERGIL, *Georgics*. Bk. ii, l. 523. (Dryden, tr.)

VI—Home: Its Drawbacks

11
The largest part of mankind are nowhere greater strangers than at home.

S. T. COLERIDGE, *Table Talk*.

I am now no more than a mere lodger in my own house.

GOLDSMITH, *The Good-Natured Man*. Act i.

12
Be thou thine own home, and in thyself dwell;
Inn anywhere, continuance maketh hell.
And seeing the snail, which everywhere doth roam,
Carrying his own house still, still is at home,
Follow (for he is easy-paced) this snail,
Be thine own palace, or the world's thy jail.

JOHN DONNE, *To Sir Henry Wotton*, l. 47.

13
Every spirit makes its house, but afterwards the house confines the spirit.

EMERSON, *Conduct of Life: Fate*.

A man builds a fine house; and now he has a master, and a task for life: he is to furnish, watch, show it, and keep it in repair, the rest of his days.

EMERSON, *Society and Solitude: Works and Days*.

14
Who hath not met with home-made bread,
A heavy compound of putty and lead—
And home-made wines that rack the head,

And home-made liqueurs and waters?
Home-made pop that will not foam,
And home-made dishes that drive one from home, . . .
Home-made by the homely daughters?

Home-made physic that sickens the sick;
Thick for thin and thin for thick;—
In short each homogeneous trick
For poisoning domesticity?
And since our Parents, called the First,
A little family squabble nurst,
Of all our evils, the worst of the worst
Is home-made infelicity.

THOMAS HOOD, *Miss Kilmansegg: Her Misery.*

1
There's no place like home, and many a man is glad of it.

F. M. KNOWLES, *A Cheerful Year Book.*

2
Three things there be that doth a man by strength
For to flee his own house as Holy Writ sheweth,
That one is a wicked wife that will not be chasted;
Her husband fleeth from her for fear of her tongue.
And if his house be untiled and rain on his bed,
He seeketh and seeketh till he sleep dry.
And when smoke and smoulder smite in his sight,
It doth him worse than his wife or wet to sleep.

WILLIAM LANGLAND, *Piers Plowman.* xvii, 315. (1377) The Latin original of this saying, which is a combination of *Proverbs* x, 26, xix, 13, and xxvii, 15, will be found in *De Contemptu Mundi,* i, 18.

Three things drive a man out of his house: that is to say, smoke, dropping of rain, and wicked wives.

CHAUCER, *Tale of Melibeus.* Sec. 15. (c. 1386)

3
It is for homely features to keep home,
They had their name thence; coarse complexions
And cheeks of sorry grain will serve to ply
The sampler and to tease the huswife's wool.
What need a vermeil-tinctur'd lip for that,
Love-darting eyes, or tresses like the morn?

MILTON, *Comus,* l. 748.

4
I find by all you have been telling,
That 'tis a house, but not a dwelling.

POPE, *On the Duke of Marlborough's House.*

5
Such wind as scatters young men through the world
To seek their fortunes further than at home
Where small experience grows.

SHAKESPEARE, *The Taming of the Shrew.* Act i, sc. 2, l. 50.

6
Home-keeping youth have ever homely wits.
Were 't not affection chains thy tender days
To the sweet glances of thy honour'd love,
I rather would entreat thy company
To see the wonders of the world abroad,
Than, living dully sluggardized at home,
Wear out thy youth with shapeless idleness.

SHAKESPEARE, *The Two Gentlemen of Verona.* Act i, sc. 1, l. 2.

He that lives always at home, sees nothing but home.

NICHOLAS BRETON, *Works.* Vol. ii, ch. 7. (1618)

How much a dunce, that has been sent to roam,
Excels a dunce that has been kept at home.

COWPER, *The Progress of Error,* l. 415.

7
Our lives are domestic in more senses than we think. From the hearth, the field is a great distance. It would be well, perhaps, . . . if the poet did not speak so much from under a roof, or the saint dwell there so long. Birds do not sing in caves, nor do doves cherish their innocence in dovecotes.

H. D. THOREAU, *Walden.* Ch. 1.

8
One rubber plant can never make a home,
Not even when combined with brush and comb,
And spoon, and fork, and knife,
And graphophone, and wife—
No! Something more is needed for a home.

UNKNOWN, *Home.*

VII—Home: Homelessness

9
The earth is all the home I have,
The heavens my wide roof-tree.

W. E. AYTOUN, *The Wandering Jew,* l. 49.

Any old place I can hang my hat is home, sweet home to me.

JEROME-SCHWARTZ. Title of popular song. (1901)

10
Oh, it was pitiful!
Near a whole city full
Home she had none.

THOMAS HOOD, *The Bridge of Sighs.*

11
The foxes have holes, and the birds of the air have nests; but the Son of man hath not where to lay his head.

New Testament: Matthew, viii, 20.

12
Horses, oxen, have a home
When from daily toil they come;
Household dogs, when the wind roars,
Find a home within warm doors;

Asses, swine, have litter spread,
And with fitting food are fed;
All things have a home but one—
Thou, O Englishman, hast none!

SHELLEY, *The Masque of Anarchy.* St. 50.

1
And homeless near a thousand homes I stood.
WORDSWORTH, *Guilt and Sorrow*. St. 41.

HOMER

I—Homer: His Birthplace

2
As to Homer's native city, there is a very great divergence of opinion. Some say that he was from Colophon, some from Smyrna; others assert that he was an Athenian, still others, an Egyptian; and Aristotle declares that he was from the island of Ios.
AULUS GELLIUS, *Noctes Atticæ*. Bk. iii, epis. 11, sec. 6.

3
Colophon asserts that Homer is her citizen, Chios claims him for her own, Salamis appropriates him, while Smyrna is so confident that he belongs to her that she has dedicated a shrine to him. (Homerum Colophonii civem esse dicunt suum, Chii suum vindecant, Salaminii repetunt, Smyrnæi vero suum esse confirmant, itaque etiam delubrum ejus in oppido dedicaverunt.)
CICERO, *Pro Archia Poeta*. Ch. 8, sec. 19.

4
Seven cities warred for Homer, being dead,
Who, living, had no roof to shroud his head.
THOMAS HEYWOOD, *On Homer's Birthplace*. (1546)

5
Great Homer's birthplace seven rival cities claim,
Too mighty such monopoly of Fame.
THOMAS SEWARD, *On Shakespeare's Monument at Stratford-upon-Avon*.

Seven wealthy towns contend for Homer dead,
Through which the living Homer begged his bread.
THOMAS SEWARD, *On Homer*.

Homer himself must beg if he wants means, as by report he sometimes did "go from door to door and sing ballads, with a company of boys about him."
ROBERT BURTON, *Anatomy of Melancholy*. Pt. i, sec. ii, mem. 4, subs. 6.

6
Seven cities strive for the learned root of Homer:
Smyrna, Chios, Colophon, Ithaca, Pylos, Argos, Athens.
(Ἑπτὰ πόλεις μάρναντο σοφὴν διὰ ῥίζαν Ὁμήρου, Σμύρνα, Χίος, Κολοφών, Ἰθάκη, Πύλος, Ἄργος, Ἀθῆναι.)
UNKNOWN. (*Greek Anthology*. Bk. xvi, epig. 298. Epigrams 295–299 are concerned with Homer's birthplace.)

7
Thou askest me that which is unknown to thee, the parentage and country of the ambrosial Siren. A certain Ithaca was the seat of Homer, Telemachus was his father, and his mother Nestor's daughter, Polycaste.
Spoken by the Pythian oracle to the Emperor Hadrian. (*Greek Anthology*. Bk. xiv, epig. 102.)

II—Homer: His Greatness

8
O fortunate youth, who found a Homer to proclaim thy valor! (O fortunate adolescens, qui tuæ virtutis Homerum præconem invereris!)
ALEXANDER THE GREAT, at the tomb of Achilles, at Sigeum. (CICERO, *Pro Archia Poeta*. Ch. 10, sec. 24.) Plutarch tells the story in his life of Alexander, ch. 15, sec. 4.

9
After your song the world could say it possessed eleven Pierian sisters.
ANTIPHILUS OF BYZANTIUM, *Epigram*. (*Greek Anthology*. Bk. ix, epig. 192.)

10
A man who has not read Homer is like a man who has not seen the ocean. There is a great object of which he has no idea.
WALTER BAGEHOT, *Literary Studies*, i, 225.

11
Here Homer, with a broad suspense
Of thunderous brows, and lips intense
Of garrulous god-innocence.
E. B. BROWNING, *A Vision of Poets*, l. 295.

12
Or list'ning to the tide, with closèd sight,
Be that blind bard, who on the Chian strand
By those deep sounds possessed with inward light,
Beheld the Iliad and the Odyssee
Rise to the swelling of the voiceful sea.
S. T. COLERIDGE, *Fancy in Nubibus*.

The blind old man of Scio's rocky isle.
BYRON, *The Bride of Abydos*. Canto ii, st. 2.

13
Strongly it bears us along in swelling and limitless billows,
Nothing before and nothing behind but the sky and ocean.
S. T. COLERIDGE, *The Homeric Hexameter*. An adaptation of Schiller.

They hear like Ocean on a western beach
The surge and thunder of the Odyssey.
ANDREW LANG, *The Odyssey*.

14
I can no more believe old Homer blind,
Than those who say the sun hath never shin'd:
The age wherein he liv'd was dark, but he
Could not want sight who taught the world to see.
SIR JOHN DENHAM, *Progress of Learning*.

15
Every novel is a debtor to Homer.
EMERSON, *Representative Men: Uses of Great Men*.

16
I, too, am indignant when the worthy Homer nods, but in a long work it is allowable to snatch a little sleep. (Et idem Indignor quan-

doque bonus dormitat Homerus, verum operi longo fas est obrepere somnum.)
HORACE, *Ars Poetica,* l. 358.

While e'en good Homer may deserve a tap,
If, as he does, he drop his head and nap,
Yet, when a work is long, 'twere somewhat hard
To blame a drowsy moment in a bard.
HORACE, *Ars Poetica,* l. 358. (Conington, tr.)

In longer works sleep will sometimes surprise;
Homer himself hath been observed to nod.
WENTWORTH DILLON, *Art of Poetry.*

Homer himself, in a long work, may sleep.
ROBERT HERRICK, *Hesperides.* No. 95.

Those oft are stratagems which errors seem,
Nor is it Homer nods, but we that dream.
POPE, *Essay on Criticism.* Pt. i, l. 179.

1
[Homer tells] that which is excellent, that which is base, that which is useful, that which is not. (Quid sit pulchrum, quid turpe, quid utile, quid non.)
HORACE, *Epistles.* Bk. i, epis, 2, l. 3.

By his praises of wine Homer is proved a wine-bibber. (Laudibus arguitur vini vinosus Homerus.)
HORACE, *Epistles.* Bk. i, epis. 19, l. 6.

2
Much have I travell'd in the realms of gold,
And many goodly states and kingdoms seen;
Round many western islands have I been
Which bards in fealty to Apollo hold.
Oft of one wide expanse had I been told
That deep brow'd Homer ruled as his demesne:
Yet did I never breathe its pure serene
Till I heard Chapman speak out loud and bold:
Then felt I like some watcher of the skies
When a new planet swims into his ken;
Or like stout Cortez when with eagle eyes
He star'd at the Pacific—and all his men
Look'd at each other with a wild surmise—
Silent, upon a peak in Darien.
JOHN KEATS, *On First Looking Into Chapman's Homer.*

3
As he could speak of the rich and royal without envy, so he could deal with the poorest of the poor without a touch of slight or contempt.
JOHN KEBLE, *Lectures on Poetry.* Lecture 14. Referring to Homer.

4
As the burning sun, rolling his chariot-wheels. dims the stars and the holy circle of the moon, so Homer, holding on high the Muses' brightest torch, dims the glory of all the flock of singers.
LEONIDAS OF TARENTUM, *Epigram.* (*Greek Anthology.* Bk. ix, epig. 24.)

5
Envy belittles the genius even of the great Homer. (Ingenium magni livor detractat Homeri.)
OVID, *Remediorum Amoris,* l. 365.

6
Heaven shall sooner quench its stars and the sun make bright the face of night . . . than oblivion rob us of the gracious name of Homer.
PHILIPPUS, *Epigram.* (*Greek Anthology.* Bk. ix, epig. 575.)

7
Led by the light of the Mæonian star.
POPE, *Essay on Criticism.* Pt. iii, l. 89. Referring to Homer.

8
Old Homer's theme Was but a dream,
Himself a fiction too.
SCOTT, *The Monastery: Answer to Introductory Epistle.*

9
Read Homer once, and you can read no more,
For all books else appear so mean, so poor,
Verse will seem prose; but still persist to read,
And Homer will be all the books you need.
JOHN SHEFFIELD, DUKE OF BUCKINGHAMSHIRE, *An Essay on Poetry,* l. 323.

10
As learned commentators view
In Homer more than Homer knew.
SWIFT, *On Poetry.*

11
It was Homer who inspired the poet. It was Homer who gave laws to the artist.
FRANCIS WAYLAND, *The Iliad and the Bible.*

12
The song is divine, but divine Homer wrote it down.
UNKNOWN. (*Greek Anthology.* Bk. ix, epig. 455.)

I, Phœbus, sang those songs that gained so much renown;
I, Phœbus, sang them; Homer but wrote them down.
UNKNOWN. (*Greek Anthology.*)

13
By telling the burnt city's story, Homer, thou hast caused unsacked cities to envy her fate.
UNKNOWN. (*Greek Anthology.* Bk. xvi, epig. 304.)

III—Homer: Epitaphs

14
The poet whom not one country honors as its own, but all the lands of two countries.
ALPHEIUS OF MITYLENE, *Epitaph on Homer.* (*Greek Anthology.* Bk. ix, epig. 97.)

15
Here the earth covers the sacred head of divine Homer, the glorifier of hero-men. (Ἐνθάδε τὴν ἱερὴν κεφαλὴν κατὰ γαῖα καλύπτει, ἀνδρῶν ἡρώων κοσμήτορα, θεῖον Ὅμηρον.)
HOMER, his own epitaph. (*Contest of Homer and Hesiod,* fin.; *Greek Anthology,* bk. vii, epig. 3.) *See also under* RIDDLE.

1
This snow-white kid the tomb of Homer marks,
For such the Ietæ offer to the dead.
(Capélla Homeri candida hæc tumulus indicat,
Quod hæc Ietæ faciúnt sacra.)

MARCUS VARRO, *De Imaginibus*. Bk. i. (AULUS GELLIUS, *Noctes Atticæ*. Bk. iii, epis. 11, sec. 7.) The Ietæ were the inhabitants of Ios, which Aristotle (*Fragment* 76) declares to have been Homer's birthplace.

2
Wayfarer, though the tomb be small, pass me not by, but pour on me a libation, and venerate me as thou dost the gods. For I hold the divine Homer, the poet of the epic, honored exceedingly by the Pierian muses.

UNKNOWN, *Epitaph*. (*Greek Anthology*. Bk. vii, epig. 2b.)

3
O stranger, the sea-beat earth covers Homer, the herald of the heroes' valor, the spokesman of the gods, a second sun to the life of the Greeks, the light of the Muses, the one mouth of the whole world that groweth not old.

ANTIPATER OF SIDON, *Epitaph on Homer*. (*Greek Anthology*. Bk. vii, epig. 6.)

HONESTY

For Honest in the Sense of Chaste, see Chastity

I—Honesty: Apothegms

4
One deserves no praise for being honest when no one tries to corrupt. (Nulla est laus ibi esse integrum, ubi nemo est qui conetur rumpere.)

CICERO, *In Verrem*. No. ii, sec. 1.

5
Too much honesty did never man harm.

JOHN CLARKE, *Parœmiologia*. No. 213.

No honest man ever repented of his honesty.

THOMAS FULLER, *Gnomologia*.

A man never surfeits of too much honesty.

JOHN RAY, *English Proverbs*.

6
Honesty is not greater where elegance is less.

SAMUEL JOHNSON, *Works*. Vol. ix, p. 38.

Cottages have them [falsehood and dissimulation] as well as courts, only with worse manners.

LORD CHESTERFIELD, *Letters*, 15 April, 1748.

Hearts just as pure and fair,
May beat in Belgrave Square,
As in the lowly air
Of Seven Dials.

W. S. GILBERT, *Iolanthe*. Act i.

7
If he were
To be made honest by an act of parliament
I should not alter in my faith of him.

BEN JONSON, *The Devil Is an Ass*. Act iv, sc. 1.

8
He that loseth his honesty, hath nothing else to lose.

JOHN LYLY, *Euphues: Euphues and Eubulus*.

The measure of life is not length, but honesty.

JOHN LYLY, *Euphues: Euphues and Eubulus*.

9
Friends, if we be honest with ourselves, we shall be honest with each other.

GEORGE MACDONALD, *The Marquis of Lossie*. Ch. 71.

10
Never too late is trod the path to honesty. (Sera numquam est ad bonos mores via.)

SENECA, *Agamemnon*, l. 242.

11
No legacy is so rich as honesty.

SHAKESPEARE, *All's Well that Ends Well*. Act iii, sc. 5, l. 14.

II—Honesty the Best Policy

12
My policy was chosen from the proverb; I thought honesty the best.

GEORGE COLMAN THE YOUNGER, *Ways and Means*. Act i, sc. 2.

13
Honestie In shew, not deed, is policie.

PATRICK HANNAY, *Poetical Works*, 166. (1622)

14
Divine Providence has granted this gift to man, that those things which are honest are also the most advantageous. (Dedit hoc providentia hominibus munus, ut honesta magis juvarent.)

QUINTILIAN, *De Institutione Oratoria*. Bk. i, ch. 12, sec. 19.

15
Knavery may serve for a turn, but honesty is best in the long run.

JOHN RAY, *English Proverbs*.

16
Our gross conceits, who think honesty the best policy.

EDWIN SANDYS, *Europæ Speculum*, 102. (1599)

Honesty is the best policy.

DAVID TUVILL, *Vade Mecum*, 27. (1638)

17
I am afraid we must make the world honest before we can honestly say to our children that honesty is the best policy.

BERNARD SHAW, *Radio Address*, 11 July, 1932

Let none of us delude himself by supposing that honesty is always the best policy. It is not.

DEAN W. R. INGE. (MARCHANT, *Wit and Wisdom of Dean Inge*. No. 171.)

18
It should seem that indolence itself would incline a person to be honest; as it requires infinitely greater pains and contrivance to be a knave.

WILLIAM SHENSTONE, *Of Men and Manners*, 78

19
Integrity is better than charity. The gods approve of the depth and not of the tumult of the soul.

SOCRATES. (EMERSON, *Uncollected Lectures*: *Natural Religion*.)

1
"Honesty is the best policy," but he who acts on that principle is not an honest man.
ARCHBISHOP RICHARD WHATELY, *Thoughts and Apothegms*. Pt. ii, ch. 18.

III—Honesty: The Honest Man

2
As honest a man as any in the cards when the kings are out.
JOHN CLARKE, *Paræmiologia*, 286. (1639)

3
An honest man, close-button'd to the chin,
Broadcloth without, and a warm heart within.
COWPER, *Epistle to Joseph Hill*, l. 62.

4
A few honest men are better than numbers.
OLIVER CROMWELL, *Letter to Sir W. Spring*, Sept., 1643.

5
Honest men fear neither the light nor the dark.
THOMAS FULLER, *Gnomologia*. No. 2528.

Of all crafts to an honest man, downright is the only craft.
THOMAS FULLER, *Gnomologia*. No. 3696.

6
All his dealings are square, and above the board.
JOSEPH HALL, *Virtues and Vices*, 15. (1608)

Here's nothing but fair play, and all above board.
RICHARD BROME, *Antipodes*. Act iii, sc. 1. (1640)

All is fair; all is above-board.
SAMUEL RICHARDSON, *Sir Charles Grandison*. i, 185. (1753)

7
An honest plain man, without pleats.
JAMES HOWELL, *Proverbs*, 15. (1659)

Be plain without pleats.
JOHN HEYWOOD, *Proverbs*. Pt. ii, ch. 5. (1546)

8
Every honest man will suppose honest acts to flow from honest principles.
THOMAS JEFFERSON, *Writings*. Vol. x, p. 304.

9
But he couldn't lie if you paid him, and he'd
starve before he stole.
RUDYARD KIPLING, *The Seven Seas: The Mary Gloster*.

He never flunked, and he never lied,—
I reckon he never knowed how.
JOHN HAY, *Jim Bludso*.

10
Though I be poor, I'm honest.
THOMAS MIDDLETON, *The Witch*. Act iii, sc. 2.
See also under POVERTY.

11
As honest a man as the sun ever shone on.
GEORGE PARKER, *Life's Painter*, 26. (1789)

12
An honest man's the noblest work of God.
POPE, *Essay on Man*. Epis. iv, l. 248.

Princes and lords are but the breath of kings:
"An honest man's the noblest work of God."
BURNS, *The Cotter's Saturday Night*. St. 19.

An honest God is the noblest work of man.
R. G. INGERSOLL, *Epigram*.

13
An honest man is a citizen of the world.
JAMES PUCKLE, *England's Path to Wealth and Honour*. (1700)

14
As honest a man as ever trod on shoe leather.
JOHN RAY, *English Proverbs*, 181. (1670)

As good a man as ever went on neats leather.
HENRY PORTER, *Two Angry Women of Abington*. Sc. 11. (1599)

15
Yet Heav'n, that made me honest, made me
more
Than ever king did, when he made a lord.
NICHOLAS ROWE, *Jane Shore*. Act ii, sc. 1, l. 261.

A prince can mak a belted knight,
A marquis, duke, an' a' that;
But an honest man's aboon his might,
Guid faith, he mauna fa' that!
BURNS, *For a' That and a' That*.

16
An honest man, look you, . . . a marvellous good neighbour, faith, and a very good bowler.
SHAKESPEARE, *Love's Labour's Lost*. Act v, sc. 2, l. 587.

An old man, sir, and his wits are not so blunt, as, God help, I would desire they were; but, in faith, honest as the skin between his brows.
SHAKESPEARE, *Much Ado About Nothing*. Act iii, sc. 5, l. 11.

I am as true, I would thou knew, as the skin between thy brows.
JOHN STILL, *Gammer Gurton's Needle*. Act v, sc. 2.

17
I thank God I am as honest as any man living that is an old man and no honester than I.
SHAKESPEARE, *Much Ado About Nothing*. Act iii, sc. 5, l. 17.

18
An honest soul . . . as ever broke bread.
SHAKESPEARE, *Much Ado About Nothing*. Act iii, sc. 5, l. 42. (1600)

An honest maid as ever broke bread.
SHAKESPEARE, *The Merry Wives of Windsor*. Act i, sc. 4, l. 161.

As good a man . . . as ere broke bread.
HENRY PORTER, *Two Angry Women of Abington*. Sc. 11. (1599)

As good natur'd a man as ever broke bread.
JOHN O'KEEFFE, *World in a Village*. Act i, 1.

19
I do proclaim
One honest man—mistake me not—but one;
No more, I pray—and he's a steward.
SHAKESPEARE, *Timon of Athens*. Act iv, sc. 3, l. 504.

His heart as far from fraud as heaven from earth.
SHAKESPEARE, *The Two Gentlemen of Verona*. Act ii, sc. 7, l. 78.

1
Barring that natural expression of villainy which we all have, the man looked honest enough.
MARK TWAIN, *A Mysterious Visit.*

2
I hope I shall always possess firmness and virtue enough to maintain what I consider the most enviable of all titles, the character of an "Honest Man."
GEORGE WASHINGTON, *Moral Maxims.*

3
Were there nor heaven nor hell
I should be honest.
JOHN WEBSTER, *Duchess of Malfi.* Act i, sc. 1.

4
Such was our friend. Formed on the good old plan,
A true and brave and downright honest man!
WHITTIER, *Daniel Neall.*

An upright downright honest man.
UNKNOWN, *Epitaph on John James,* Ripon Cathedral, 1707.

IV—Honesty: Its Virtues

5
Wicked mirth never true pleasure brings,
But honest minds are pleased with honest things.
BEAUMONT AND FLETCHER, *The Knight of the Burning Pestle: Prologue.*

Man is his own star; and that soul that can
Be honest is the only perfect man.
BEAUMONT AND FLETCHER, *The Honest Man's Fortune: Epilogue.*

6
An honest man may like a glass,
An honest man may like a lass,
But mean revenge, an' malice fause,
He'll still disdain.
BURNS, *Epistle to the Rev. John M'Math.*

7
The modest front of this small floor,
Believe me, reader, can say more
Than many a braver marble can,—
"Here lies a truly honest man."
RICHARD CRASHAW, *Epitaph upon Mr. Ashton.*

9
Though honesty be no puritan, yet it will do no hurt; it will wear the surplice of humility over the black gown of a big heart.
SHAKESPEARE, *All's Well that Ends Well.* Act i, sc. 3, l. 97.

10
There is no terror, Cassius, in your threats;
For I am arm'd so strong in honesty
That they pass by me as the idle wind.
SHAKESPEARE, *Julius Cæsar.* Act iv, sc. 3, l. 66.

11
The man who consecrates his hours
By vig'rous effort and an honest aim,
At once he draws the sting of life and death;
He walks with nature; and her paths are peace.
YOUNG, *Night Thoughts.* Night ii, l. 185.

V—Honesty: Its Faults

12
'Tis my opinion every man cheats in his way, and he is only honest who is not discovered.
SUSANNAH CENTLIVRE, *The Artifice.* Act v.

13
Honesty is ill to thrive by.
JOHN CLARKE, *Parœmiologia,* 30. (1639)

The honester man the worse luck.
JOHN RAY, *English Proverbs,* 117. (1670)

14
Fools out of favour grudge at knaves in place,
And men are always honest in disgrace.
DANIEL DEFOE, *The True-Born Englishman: Introduction,* l. 7.

15
Honest men and knaves may possibly wear the same cloth.
THOMAS FULLER, *Gnomologia.* No. 2525.

He that resolves to deal with none but honest men must leave off dealing.
THOMAS FULLER, *Gnomologia.* No. 2530.

Honesty is a fine jewel but much out of fashion.
THOMAS FULLER, *Gnomologia.* No. 2533.

16
A man who only does what every one of the society to which he belongs would do, is not a dishonest man.
SAMUEL JOHNSON. (BOSWELL, *Life,* ii, 176.)

17
Integrity without knowledge is weak and useless, and knowledge without integrity is dangerous and dreadful.
SAMUEL JOHNSON, *Rasselas.* Ch. 41.

18
Integrity is praised and starves. (Probitas laudatur et alget.)
JUVENAL, *Satires.* Sat. i, l. 74.

19
To strictest justice many ills belong,
And honesty is often in the wrong.
LUCAN, *De Bello Civili.* Bk. viii, l. 657. (Rowe, tr.)

20
Honest men
Are the soft easy cushions on which knaves
Repose and fatten.
THOMAS OTWAY, *Venice Preserved.* Act i, sc. 1.

21
It is annoying to be honest to no purpose. (Gratis pænitet esse probum.)
OVID, *Epistulæ ex Ponto.* Bk. ii, epis. 3, l. 14.

22
Rich honesty dwells like a miser, sir, in a poor house; as your pearl in your foul oyster.
SHAKESPEARE, *As You Like It.* Act v, sc. 4, l. 62.

23
Ay, sir; to be honest, as this world goes, is to be one man picked out of ten thousand.
SHAKESPEARE, *Hamlet.* Act ii, sc. 2, l. 178.

Hamlet: What's the news?
Rosencrantz: None, my lord, but that the world's grown honest.

Hamlet: Then is doomsday near.
SHAKESPEARE, *Hamlet*. Act ii, sc. 2, l. 240.

1
I am myself indifferent honest.
SHAKESPEARE, *Hamlet*. Act iii, sc. 1, l. 124.

Though I am not naturally honest, I am so sometimes by chance.
SHAKESPEARE, *The Winter's Tale*. Act iv, sc. 4, l. 733.

There's neither honesty, manhood, nor good fellowship in thee.
SHAKESPEARE, *I Henry IV*. Act i, sc. 2, l. 155.

2
Take note, take note, O world,
To be direct and honest is not safe.
SHAKESPEARE, *Othello*. Act iii, sc. 3, l. 377.

Honesty's a fool. And loses that it works for.
SHAKESPEARE, *Othello*. Act iii, sc. 3, l. 382.

3
Every man has his fault, and honesty is his.
SHAKESPEARE, *Timon of Athens*. Act iii, sc. 1, l. 29.

4
Ha, ha! what a fool Honesty is! and Trust, his sworn brother, a very simple gentleman!
SHAKESPEARE, *The Winter's Tale*. Act iv, sc. 3, l. 606.

HONEY, see Bee

HONOR

I—Honor: Definitions

5
Honour's a fine imaginary notion,
That draws in raw and unexperienced men
To real mischiefs, while they hunt a shadow.
ADDISON, *Cato*. Act ii, sc. 5.

The sense of honour is of so fine and delicate a nature, that it is only to be met with in minds which are naturally noble, or in such as have been cultivated by good examples, or a refined education.
ADDISON, *The Guardian*. No. 161.

6
Honor is like an island, rugged and without a beach; once we have left it, we can never return.
(L'honneur est comme une île escarpée et
sans bords;
On n'y peut plus rentrer dès qu'on en est
dehors.)
BOILEAU, *Satires*. Sat. x, l. 167.

7
Honour was but ancient riches.
NICHOLAS BRETON, *Court and Country*, 190.

8
Honour's but a word
To swear by only in a Lord.
BUTLER, *Hudibras*. Pt. ii, canto ii, l. 389.

Honour's a lease for lives to come,
And cannot be extended from
The legal tenant.
BUTLER, *Hudibras*. Pt. i, canto iii, l. 1043.

HONOUR IS LIKE A WIDOW WON, *see* WIDOW: WOOING.

9
What is fitting is honorable, and what is honorable is fitting (Quod decet honestum est, et quod honestum est, decet.)
CICERO, *De Officiis* Bk. i, ch. 27, sec. 94.

It is beyond question that expediency can never conflict with honor. (Dubitandum non est, quin numquam possit utilitas cum honestate contendere.)
CICERO, *De Officiis*. Bk. iii, ch. 3, sec. 11.

10
Honor nourishes the arts, and all are incited to study by the desire of glory. (Honos alit artes, omnesque incenduntur ad studia gloria.)
CICERO, *Tusculanarum Disputationum*. Bk. i, ch. 2, sec. 4.

Sayeth not the proverb, Honours nourish arts?
FRANCIS THYNNE, *Pride and Lowliness*, 22. (1570)

11
Honour is a public enemy, and conscience a domestic; and he that would secure his pleasure, must pay a tribute to one, and go halves with t'other.
CONGREVE, *Love for Love*. Act iii, sc. 14.

12
As to honour—you know—it's a very fine medieval inheritance, which women never get hold of. It wasn't theirs.
JOSEPH CONRAD, *Chance*. Ch. 2.

13
Honour but an empty bubble.
DRYDEN, *Alexander's Feast*, l. 100.

Honour is a baby's rattle.
THOMAS RANDOLPH, *The Muses' Looking Glass*. Act iii, sc. 2.

14
Some things the honorable man cannot do, never does. He never wrongs or degrades a woman. He never oppresses or cheats a person weaker or poorer than himself. He never betrays a trust. He is honest, sincere, candid and generous.
CHARLES W. ELIOT, *The Durable Satisfactions of Life*, p. 6.

15
Purity is the feminine, truth the masculine of honor.
A. C. AND A. W. HARE, *Guesses at Truth*. *See also under* CHASTITY.

16
Honour is but an itch in youthful blood
Of doing acts extravagantly good.
SIR ROBERT HOWARD, *The Indian Queen*.

17
Honour is the very breath in our nostrils.
JEFFREY HUDSON, page to Queen Henrietta Maria, on the occasion of a duel.

18
What is most honorable is also safest. (Quod pulcherrimum idem tutissimum est.)
LIVY, *History*. Bk. xxxiv, ch. 14.

19
Honour is purchas'd by the deeds we do;
. . . Honour is not won

Until some honourable deed be done.
CHRISTOPHER MARLOWE, *Hero and Leander*. Ses. i, l. 276.

Nobody can acquire honor by doing what is wrong.
THOMAS JEFFERSON, *Writings*. Vol. xvi, p. 444.

1
Honour, the spur that pricks the princely mind.
GEORGE PEELE, *The Battle of Alcazar*. Act i.

2
Honour and shame from no condition rise;
Act well your part: there all the honour lies.
POPE, *An Essay on Man*. Epis. iv, l. 193.

3
Without money honor is nothing but a malady.
(Sans argent l'honneur n'est qu'une maladie.)
RACINE, *Les Plaideurs*. Act i, sc. 1.

4
Honour, the darling but of one short day.
SIR WALTER RALEIGH, *A Farewell to the Vanities of the World*.

5
Be noble-minded! Our own heart, and not other men's opinions Forms our true honor.
SCHILLER, *Wallenstein's Tod*. (Coleridge, tr.)

6
Abroad in arms, at home in studious kind,
Who seeks with painful toil, shall Honour soonest find.
SPENSER, *Faerie Queene*. Bk. ii, canto iii, st. 40.

7
I sent to know from whence, and where
These hopes and this relief?
A spy inform'd, Honour was there,
And did command in chief.

"March, march," quoth I; "the word straight give,
Let's lose no time, but leave her;
That giant upon air will live,
And hold it out for ever."
SIR JOHN SUCKLING, *The Siege of a Heart*.

8
Honour's a mistress all mankind pursue;
Yet most mistake the false one for the true:
Lured by the trappings, dazzled by the paint,
We worship oft the idol for the saint.
PAUL WHITEHEAD, *Honour*.

II—Honor: Apothegms

9
All honor's wounds are self-inflicted.
ANDREW CARNEGIE. (HENDRICK, *Life*.)

10
Seek Honour first, and Pleasure lies behind.
THOMAS CHATTERTON, *The Tournament*.

11
He that hath no honour hath no sorrow.
THOMAS DRAXE, *Biblio. Scholas. Instruc.*, 91.

Where there is no honour, there is no grief.
GEORGE HERBERT, *Jacula Prudentum*.

12
Leave not a stain in thine honour.
Apocrypha: Ecclesiasticus, xxxiii, 22.

13
The louder he talked of his honor, the faster we counted our spoons.
EMERSON, *Conduct of Life: Worship*.

14
Costar: Pray now, what may be that same bed of honour?
Kite: Oh, a mighty large bed! bigger by half than the great bed of Ware: ten thousand people may lie in it together and never feel one another.
FARQUHAR, *The Recruiting Officer*. Act i, sc. 1.

If he that in the field is slain,
Be in the bed of honour lain,
He that is beaten may be said
To lie in honour's truckle-bed.
BUTLER, *Hudibras*. Pt. i, canto iii, l. 1047.

Although the sheet were big enough for the bed of Ware.
SHAKESPEARE, *Twelfth Night*. Act iii, sc. 2, 49.

15
All is lost save honor. (Tout est perdu fors l'honneur.)
FRANCIS I OF FRANCE, in a letter to his mother, the morning after the disastrous battle of Pavia, accompanying a safe conduct given to the Viceroy of Naples for the Commander Penalosa. Tradition has altered Francis's words to the form given above, but what he really wrote was: "Nothing remains to me save honor and life." (De toutes choses ne m'est demeuré que l'honneur et la vie.) The letter is printed in Dulaure's *Histoire de Paris*. (See also Sismondi, xvi, 241.) Napoleon is said to have quoted this epigram to Caulaincourt after Waterloo; and Louis XVIII repeated it in reply to a proposal that he renounce his claim to the French throne. (BOURRIENNE, *Memoirs of Napoleon*, ii, 25.)

And all at Worcester but the honour lost.
DRYDEN, *Astræa Redux*, l. 74.

We have lost all, yet life is still left. (Omnia perdidimus, tantummodo vita relicta est.)
OVID, *Epistulæ ex Ponto*. Bk. iv, epis. 16, l. 49.

16
It is a worthier thing to deserve honour than to possess it.
THOMAS FULLER, *Gnomologia*.

17
To those whose god is honour, disgrace alone is sin.
J. C. AND A. W. HARE, *Guesses at Truth*.

18
I could not love thee, Dear, so much
Lov'd I not Honour more.
RICHARD LOVELACE, *To Lucasta, Going to the Wars*.

19
How many sacrifice honor, a necessity, to glory, a luxury!
JOSEPH ROUX, *Meditations of a Parish Priest*. Pt. iv, No. 38.

20
I am myself the guardian of my honour.
NICHOLAS ROWE, *Fair Penitent*. Act iii, sc. 1.

1
To few is honor dearer than gold. (Paucis carior fides quam pecunia fuit.)
SALLUST, *Jugurtha*. Ch. 16, sec. 5.

2
The depths and shoals of honour.
SHAKESPEARE, *Henry VIII*. Act iii, sc. 2, l. 436.

To plainness honour's bound,
When majesty stoops to folly.
SHAKESPEARE, *King Lear*. Act i, sc. 1, l. 150.

3
As the sun breaks through the darkest clouds,
So honour peereth in the meanest habit.
SHAKESPEARE, *The Taming of the Shrew*. Act iv, sc. 3, l. 176.

4
Honour should be concerned in honour's cause.
THOMAS SOUTHERNE, *Oroonoko*. Act v, sc. 3.

5
The shackles of an old love straiten'd him,
His honour rooted in dishonour stood,
And faith unfaithful kept him falsely true.
TENNYSON, *Lancelot and Elaine*, l. 870.

Upon this fatal quest
Of honour, where no honour can be gain'd.
TENNYSON, *Geraint and Enid*, l. 702.

III—Honor: Greater Than Life

6
Better to die ten thousand thousand deaths,
Than wound my honour.
ADDISON, *Cato*. Act i, sc. 4.

7
When honour's lost, 'tis a relief to die;
Death's but a sure retreat from infamy.
GARTH, *The Dispensary*. Canto v, l. 321.

8
Honour alone we cannot, must not lose;
Honour, that spark of the celestial fire,
That above nature makes mankind aspire;
Ennobles the rude passions of our fame
With thirst of glory, and desire of fame:
The richest treasure of a generous breast,
That gives the stamp and standard to the rest.
LORD HALIFAX, *The Man of Honour*.

9
Count it the greatest of infamies to prefer life to honor, and to lose, for the sake of living, all that makes life worth having. (Summum crede nefas animam præferre pudori, Et propter vitam vivendi perdere causas.)
JUVENAL, *Satires*. Sat. viii, l. 83.

10
This day beyond its term my fate extends,
For life is ended when our honour ends.
LABERIUS, *Prologue*. (Goldsmith, tr. from the Latin of Macrobius.)

11
Who loses honor can lose nothing else. (Fidem qui perdit, ultra perdere nil potest.)
PUBLILIUS SYRUS, *Sententiæ*. No. 265.

If I lose mine honour, I lose myself.
SHAKESPEARE, *Antony and Cleopatra*. Act iii, sc. 4. l. 22.

12
Set honour in one eye and death i' the other,
And I will look on both indifferently;
For let the gods so speed me as I love
The name of honour more than I fear death.
SHAKESPEARE, *Julius Cæsar*. Act i, sc. 2, l. 86.

Mine honour is my life; both grew in one;
Take honour from me, and my life is done.
Then, dear my liege, mine honour let me try:
In that I live, and for that will I die.
SHAKESPEARE, *Richard II*. Act i, sc. 1, l. 182.

For honour travels in a strait so narrow,
Where one but goes abreast.
SHAKESPEARE, *Troilus and Cressida*. Act iii, sc. 3, l. 154.

Life every man holds dear; but the brave man
Holds honour far more precious-dear than life.
SHAKESPEARE, *Troilus and Cressida*. Act v, sc. 3, l. 27.

13
When faith is lost, when honor dies,
The man is dead!
WHITTIER, *Ichabod*. St. 8.

IV—Honor: The Man of Honor

14
Lo, one who loved true honour more than fame.
WILLIAM ALEXANDER, EARL OF STIRLING, *Doomsday: The Eighth Hour*. St. 100.

15
There may be danger in the deed,
But there is honour too.
W. E. AYTOUN, *The Island of the Scots*.

He that is valiant and dares fight
Though drubbed, can lose no honour by't.
BUTLER, *Hudibras*. Pt. i, canto iii, l. 1041.

16
Thine is the self-approving glow
Of conscious honour's part.
BURNS, *To Chloris*.

17
If honour calls, where'er she points the way,
The sons of honour follow and obey.
CHARLES CHURCHILL, *The Farewell*, l. 67.

18
Here honor binds me, and I wish to satisfy it. (Ici l'honneur m'oblige, et j'y veux satisfaire.)
CORNEILLE, *Polyeucte*. Act iv, sc. 3.

19
Godlike erect, with native honour clad.
MILTON, *Paradise Lost*. Bk. iv, l. 289.

In native worth and honour clad.
BARON VAN SWIETEN. (HAYDN, *The Creation: Libretto*.)

20
Wronged me! in the nicest point—
The honour of my house.
THOMAS OTWAY, *Venice Preserved*. Act i, sc. 1.

21
A Quixotic sense of the honorable—of the chivalrous.
EDGAR ALLAN POE, *Letter to Mrs. Whitman*, 18 Oct., 1848.

1
Let us do what honor demands. (Faisons ce que l'honneur exige.)
RACINE, *Bérénice*. Act iv, sc. 4.

2
See that you come
Not to woo honour, but to wed it.
SHAKESPEARE, *All's Well that Ends Well*. Act ii, sc. 1, l. 14.

The heavens hold firm
The walls of thy dear honour.
SHAKESPEARE, *Cymbeline*. Act ii, sc. 1, l. 67.

3
By heaven, methinks it were an easy leap
To pluck bright honour from the pale-faced moon,
Or dive into the bottom of the deep,
Where fathom-line could never touch the ground,
And pluck up drowned honour by the locks.
SHAKESPEARE, *I Henry IV*. Act i, sc. 3, l. 201.

4
The fewer men, the greater share of honour.
SHAKESPEARE, *Henry V*. Act iv, sc. 3, l. 22.

By Jove, I am not covetous for gold,
Nor care I who doth feed upon my cost;
It yearns me not if men my garments wear;
Such outward things dwell not in my desires:
But if it be a sin to covet honour,
I am the most offending soul alive.
SHAKESPEARE, *Henry V*. Act iv, sc. 3, l. 24.

5
Thou art a fellow of a good respect;
Thy life hath had some smatch of honour in it.
SHAKESPEARE, *Julius Cæsar*. Act v, sc. 5, l. 45.

6
I had rather crack my sinews, break my back,
Than you should such dishonour undergo.
SHAKESPEARE, *The Tempest*. Act iii, sc. 1. l. 26.

7
Worth, courage, honor, these indeed
Your sustenance and birthright are.
E. C. STEDMAN, *Beyond the Portals*. Pt. x.

8
A true man, pure as faith's own vow,
Whose honour knows not rust.
SWINBURNE, *The Tale of Balen*. Pt. i, st. 1.

9
Thy honor, thy name and thy praises shall endure for ever. (Semper honos, nomenque tuum, laudesque manebunt.)
VERGIL, *Eclogues*. No. v, l. 78; *Æneid*. Bk. i, l. 609.

10
Thou great Commander! leading on
Through weakest darkness to strong light;
By any anguish, give us back
Our life's young standard, pure and bright.
O fair, lost Colors of the soul!
For your sake storm we any height.
ELIZABETH PHELPS WARD, *The Lost Colors*.

V—Honor: Its Faults

11
Honour and ease are seldom bedfellows.
THOMAS FULLER, *Gnomologia*. No. 2540.

Honour and profit lie not all in one sack.
GEORGE HERBERT, *Jacula Prudentum*.

Honour will buy no beef.
THOMAS SHADWELL, *Sullen Lovers*. Act v. sc. 3. Cited as "the excellent proverb."

12
Honour pricks me on. Yea, but how if honour prick me off when I come on? how then? Can honour set to a leg? no: or an arm? no: or take away the grief of a wound? no. Honour hath no skill in surgery, then? no. What is honour? a word. What is in that word honour? what is that honour? air. A trim reckoning! Who hath it? he that died o' Wednesday. Doth he feel it? no. Doth he hear it? no. 'Tis insensible, then? Yea, to the dead. But will it not live with the living? no. Why? detraction will not suffer it. Therefore I'll none of it. Honour is a mere scutcheon: and so ends my catechism.
SHAKESPEARE, *I Henry IV*. Act v, sc. 1, l. 130.

13
In whose cold blood no spark of honour bides.
SHAKESPEARE, *III Henry VI*. Act i, sc. 1, l. 184.

For Brutus is an honourable man;
So are they all, all honourable men.
SHAKESPEARE, *Julius Cæsar*. Act iii, sc. 2, l. 87.

14
Well, honour is the subject of my story.
I cannot tell what you and other men
Think of this life; but, for my single self,
I had as lief not be as live to be
In awe of such a thing as I myself.
SHAKESPEARE, *Julius Cæsar*. Act i, sc. 2, l. 92.

15
I, I myself sometimes, leaving the fear of God on the left hand and hiding mine honour in mine necessity, am fain to shuffle, to hedge and to lurch; and yet you, rogue, will ensconce your rags, your cat-a-mountain looks, your red-lattice phrases, and your bold-beating oaths, under the shelter of your honour!
SHAKESPEARE, *The Merry Wives of Windsor*. Act ii, sc. 2, l. 23.

But why should honour outlive honesty?
SHAKESPEARE, *Othello*. Act v, sc. 2, l. 245.

Honour sits smiling at the sale of truth.
SHELLEY, *Queen Mab*. Canto iv, l. 218.

16
Don't you think we may as well leave honour out of the argument?
SHERIDAN, *School for Scandal*. Act iv, sc. 3.

VI—Honors

See also Nobility, Titles

17
When vice prevails and impious men bear sway,
The post of honour is a private station.
ADDISON, *Cato*. Act iv, sc. 4.

Give me, kind heav'n, a private station,
A mind serene for contemplation,

Title and profit I resign;
The post of honour shall be mine.
JOHN GAY, *Fables: The Vulture and Sparrow.*

1
Patricius, the consul, stains the honors which he sells; still more he stains those which he himself bears. (Patricius consul maculat quos vendit honores; Plus maculat quos ipse gerit.)
CLAUDIAN, *In Eutropium.* Bk. ii, l. 561.

2
These were honoured in their generations, and were the glory of the times.
Apocrypha: Ecclesiasticus, xliv, 7.

3
Honours are shadows, which from seekers fly;
But follow after those who them deny.
RICHARD BAXTER, *Love Breathing Thanks.* Pt. ii.

4
To fish for honour with a silver hook.
NICHOLAS BRETON, *Honour of Valour.*

To exchange one's freedom for a little gain, . . . I count it fishing with a golden hook.
RICHARD FLECKNOE, *Miscellanies,* p. 126.

Be not with honour's gilded baits beguiled.
SIR WILLIAM D'AVENANT, *Gondibert.* Bk. i, canto v, st. 75.

5
Posts of honor are evermore posts of danger and of care.
J. G. HOLLAND, *Gold-Foil: Every Man Has His Place.*

6
With all its beauteous honours on its head.
HOMER, *Iliad.* Bk. iv, l. 557. (Pope, tr.)

7
Since all must life resign,
Those sweet rewards, which decorate the brave,
'Tis folly to decline,
And steal inglorious to the silent grave.
SAMUEL JOHNSON, *Lines Added to an Ode by Sir William Jones.*

8
Great honours are great burdens, but on whom
They are cast with envy, he doth bear two loads.
His cares must still be double to his joys,
In any dignity.
BEN JONSON, *Catiline.* Act iii, sc. 1, l. 1.

Honours and great employments are great burthens.
MASSINGER, *The Bondman.* Act i, sc. 3.

9
I am now past the craggy paths of study, and come to the flowery plains of honour and reputation.
BEN JONSON, *Volpone.* Act ii, sc. 1.

10
An honor won is surety for more. (L'honneur acquis est caution de celui qu'on doit acquérir.)
LA ROCHEFOUCAULD, *Maximes.* No. 270.

11
No honor shall make thee worthy of Cæsar's wrath. (Dignum te Cæsaris ira Nullus honor faciet.)
LUCAN, *De Bello Civili.* Bk. iii, l. 137.

12
The blind longing for honors. (Honorum cæca cupido.)
LUCRETIUS, *De Rerum Natura.* Bk. iii, l. 59.

13
When he counted up his honors, he fancied himself an old man. (Dum numerat palmas, credidit esse senem.)
MARTIAL, *Epigrams.* Bk. x, ep. 53.

14
Honours never fail to purchase silence.
MASSINGER, *The Duke of Milan.* Act ii, sc. 1.

15
When honor comes to you be ready to take it;
But reach not to seize it before it is near.
JOHN BOYLE O'REILLY, *Rules of the Road.*

16
It is the fashion to seek honor for disgraceful conduct. (Petere honorem pro flagitio more fit.)
PLAUTUS, *Trinummus.* Act iv, sc. 3, l. 28.

17
He died full of years and honors, as illustrious for those he refused as for those he accepted. (Et ille quidem plenus annis abiit, plenus honoribus, illis etiam, quos recusavit.)
PLINY THE YOUNGER, *Epistles.* Bk. ii, epis. 1.

A studious decliner of honours and titles.
JOHN EVELYN, *Diary: Introduction.*

18
Honours thrive,
When rather from our acts we them derive
Than our foregoers: the mere word's a slave
Debosh'd on every tomb; on every grave,
A lying trophy, and as oft is dumb
Where dust and damn'd oblivion is the tomb
Of honour'd bones indeed.
SHAKESPEARE, *All's Well that Ends Well.* Act ii, sc. 3, l. 142.

19
And all the budding honours on thy crest
I'll crop, to make a garland for my head.
SHAKESPEARE, *I Henry IV.* Act v, sc. 4, l. 72.

And bears his blushing honours thick upon him.
SHAKESPEARE, *Henry VIII.* Act iii, sc. 2, l. 354.

20
New honours come upon him,
Like our strange garments, cleave not to their mould,
But with the aid of use.
SHAKESPEARE, *Macbeth.* Act i, sc. 3, l. 144.

Now, while the honour thou hast got
Is spick and span new.
BUTLER, *Hudibras.* Pt. i, canto iii, l. 397.

21
Let none presume
To wear an undeserved dignity.
O, that estates, degrees and offices

Were not derived corruptly, and that clear honour
Were purchased by the merit of the wearer!
SHAKESPEARE, *The Merchant of Venice*. Act ii, sc. 9, l. 39.

An outward honour for an inward toil.
SHAKESPEARE, *Richard III*. Act i, sc. 4, l. 79.

1
Honors change manners. (Honores mutant mores.)
POLYDORE VERGIL, *Proverbiorum Libellus*. No. 202.

So they verify the saying, Honores mutant mores.
HUGH LATIMER, *Sermons*, p. 437. (1552)

Lord Rutland said to my father [Sir Thomas More], in his acute sneering way: "Ah, ah, Sir Thomas, Honores mutant *Mores;*" to which my father replied, "Not so, in faith, but have a care lest we translate the proverb and say, "Honours change *Manners*."
MARGARET MORE, *Diary, October*, 1524. The point of the jest will be better appreciated when it is remembered that Manners was Lord Rutland's family name.

This good creature is resolved to show the world, that great honour cannot at all change his manners; he is the same civil person he ever was.
ADDISON, *The Spectator*. No. 259.

HOPE

See also Optimism

I—Hope: Definitions

2
Hope is a waking dream. (Ἐλπίς, ἐγρηγορότος ἐνύπνιον.)
ARISTOTLE. (DIOGENES LAERTIUS, *Aristotle*. Sec. 18.) Ascribed to Plato by Ælian, and to Pindar by Stobæus.

The hopes of men have been justly called waking dreams.
BASIL, BISHOP OF CÆSAREA, *Letter to Gregory of Nazianzus*. (c. 370) Quoted in Humboldt's *Cosmos*.

For hope is but the dream of those that wake!
MATTHEW PRIOR, *Solomon on the Vanity of the World*. Bk. iii, l. 102.

The hopes that lost in some far distance seem,
May be the truer life, and this the dream.
ADELAIDE ANN PROCTER, *A Legend of Provence*.

Vain hopes, like certain dreams of those who wake. (Spes inanes, et velut somnia quædam, vigilantium.)
QUINTILIAN, *Institutione de Oratoria*. Bk. vi, ch. 2, sec. 30.

3
Hope is the parent of faith.
C. A. BARTOL, *Radical Problems: Hope*.

4
Hope! thou nurse of young desire.
BICKERSTAFFE, *Love in a Village*. Act i, sc. 1, 1.

5
Hope! of all ills that men endure,
The only cheap and universal cure.
ABRAHAM COWLEY, *For Hope*.

Hope, the patent medicine
For disease, disaster, sin.
WALLACE RICE, *Hope*.

The miserable have no other medicine
But only hope.
SHAKESPEARE, *Measure for Measure*. Act iii, sc. 1, l. 2.

I suppose it can be truthfully said that Hope is the only universal liar who never loses his reputation for veracity.
R. G. INGERSOLL, *Address*, Manhattan Liberal Club, at celebration of the 155th Paine Anniversary. (*Truth-Seeker*, 28 Feb., 1892.)

6
Hope is the thing with feathers
That perches in the soul.
EMILY DICKINSON, *Poems*. Pt. i, No. 32.

7
Hope is the second soul of the unhappy.
GOETHE, *Sprüche in Prosa*.

8
Hope is the poor man's bread.
GEORGE HERBERT, *Jacula Prudentum*.

9
Things past belong to memory alone;
Things future are the property of hope.
JOHN HOME, *Agis: Lysander*. Act ii.

10
Hope—that star of life's tremulous ocean.
PAUL MOON JAMES, *The Beacon*.

11
Hope is itself a species of happiness, and, perhaps, the chief happiness which this world affords.
SAMUEL JOHNSON. (BOSWELL, *Life*, i, 368.)

When there is no hope, there can be no endeavour.
SAMUEL JOHNSON, *The Rambler*. No. 110.

12
It is hope which maintains most of mankind. ("Εστ' ἐλπὶς ἡ βόσκουσα τοὺς πολλοὺς βροτῶν.)
SOPHOCLES, *Fragment*.

13
Hope in action is charity, and beauty in action is goodness.
MIGUEL DE UNAMUNO, *Tragic Sense of Life*, p. 203.

14
Hope, the paramount duty that Heaven lays,
For its own honour, on man's suffering heart.
WORDSWORTH, *Poems Dedicated to National Independence*. Pt. ii, No. 33.

II—Hope: Apothegms

15
Unhappy, hope; happy, be cautious (Sperate, miseri; cavete, felices.)
ROBERT BURTON, *Anatomy of Melancholy*, closing advice in final paragraph.

16
Better a good hope than a bad holding.
CERVANTES, *Don Quixote*. Pt. ii, ch. 7.

17
But now of hope the calends begin.
CHAUCER, *Troilus and Criseyde*. Bk. ii, l. 8.

1 And Hope enchanted smil'd, and wav'd her golden hair.

William Collins, *The Passions*, l. 38.

2 Abandon hope, all ye who enter here. (Lasciate ogni speranza, voi ch'entrate.)

Dante, *Inferno*. Canto iii, l. 9. (Cary, tr.) Dante states that he beheld these words "written in sombre colors," on the gate through which he entered Hell. Longfellow's translation of the line is: All hope abandon, ye who enter in.

Quick, open, open wide this gate of hell;
For I in truth can count it nothing less.
No one comes here who has not lost all hope
Of being good.
(Pandite atque aperite propere januam hanc Orci, obsecro!
Nam equidem haud aliter esse duco, quippe quo nemo advenit,
Nisi quem spes reliquere omnes, esse ut frugi possiet.)

Plautus, *Bacchides*, l. 368. (Act iii, sc. 1. Thornton, tr.)

3 We ought neither to fasten our ship to one small anchor nor our life to a single hope. (Οὔτε ναῦν ἐξ ἑνὸς ἀγκυρίου οὔτε βίον ἐκ μιᾶς ἐλπίδος ἁρμοστέον.)

Epictetus [?], *Fragments*. Frag. 30.

4 Hope never leaves a wretched man that seeks her.

John Fletcher, *The Captain*. Act ii, sc. 1.

5 He that wants hope is the poorest man alive.

Thomas Fuller, *Gnomologia*. No. 2342.

When our hopes break, let our patience hold.

Thomas Fuller, *The Holy State: Of Expecting Preferment*.

6 All men are guests where Hope doth hold the feast.

George Gascoigne, *The Fruits of War*, l. 88.

7 Men should do with their hopes as they do with tame fowl, cut their wings that they may not fly over the wall.

Lord Halifax, *Works*, p. 237.

8 The natural flights of the human mind are not from pleasure to pleasure, but from hope to hope.

Samuel Johnson, *The Rambler*. No. 2.

We all live upon the hope of pleasing somebody.

Samuel Johnson. (Boswell, *Life*, ii, 22.)

9 Hope well and have well.

Brian Melbancke, *Philotinus*. Sig. H 2. (1583)

Hope well and have well, quoth Hickwell.

Thomas Fuller, *Gnomologia*. No. 2545.

10 I hoped for better things. (Speravi melius.)

Ovid, *Heroides*. Epis. ii, l. 61.

My hopes are not always realized, but I always hope. (Et res non semper, spes mihi semper adest.)

Ovid, *Heroides*. Epis. xviii, l. 178.

11 Hope to the end.

New Testament: I Peter, i, 13.

12 With him liveth sweet Hope, the nurse of eld, the fosterer of his heart,—Hope, who chiefly ruleth the changeful mind of men.

Pindar, *Fragments*. No. 214.

13 The unhoped for happens much oftener than the hoped for. (Insperata accidunt magis sæpe quæ speres.)

Plautus, *Mostellaria*, l. 197. (Act i, sc. 3.)

14 Hope springs eternal in the human breast:
Man never is, but always to be, blest.
The soul, uneasy and confin'd from home,
Rests and expatiates in a life to come.

Pope, *Essay on Man*. Epis. i, l. 95.

Hope springs exulting on triumphant wing.

Burns, *The Cotter's Saturday Night*. St. 16.

15 Hope deferred maketh the heart sick.

Old Testament: Proverbs, xiii, 12.

Delayed hope afflicteth the heart.

John Mabbe, *Celestina*, 38. (1631)

Long hope is the fainting of the soul.

Thomas Draxe, *Bib. Sch. Instr.*, 42. (1633)

And felt what sort of sickness of the heart it was which arises from hope deferred.

Sterne, *Sentimental Journey: The Captive*.

The sickening pang of hope deferr'd.

Scott, *Lady of the Lake*. Canto iii, st. 1.

16 Hope is like a harebell, trembling from its birth.

Christina Rossetti, *Hope*.

17 Who against hope believed in hope.

New Testament: Romans, iv, 18.

Hope against hope, and ask till ye receive.

Montgomery, *The World Before the Flood*.

To hope till Hope creates
From its own wreck the thing it contemplates.

Shelley, *Prometheus Unbound*. Act iv, l. 573.

18 So long an interval has room for many a hope. (Tamquam multas spes tam longum tempus reciperet.)

Seneca, *Epistulæ ad Lucilium*. Epis. lxx, sec. 9.

19 A high hope for a low heaven.

Shakespeare, *Love's Labour's Lost*. Act i, sc. 1, l. 197.

20 I do not buy hope with money. (Ego spem pretio non emo.)

Terence, *Adelphi*, l. 219. (Act ii, sc. 2.)

1
Such hopes had I when fortune was kind. (Speravimus ista Dum fortuna fuit.)
VERGIL, *Æneid*. Bk. x, l. 42.

2
All the hopes of thy house rest centred in thee. (In te omnis domus inclinata recumbit.)
VERGIL, *Æneid*. Bk. xii, l. 59.

The hope of the flock. (Spes gregis.)
VERGIL, *Eclogues*. No. i, l. 15.

3
So lives inveterate Hope, on her own hardihood.
WILLIAM WATSON, *The Hope of the World*.

4
Prisoners of hope.
Old Testament: Zechariah, ix, 12. Title of novel by Mary Johnston.

III—Hope: While There's Life There's Hope

5
While there's life, there's hope. (Dum anima est, spes est.)
CICERO, *Epistolæ ad Atticum*. Bk. ix, epis. 10. Quoted as a saying referring to the sick: Ægroto, dum anima est, spes est, dicitur.

While there's life, there's hope. (Modo liceat vivere, est spes.)
TERENCE, *Heauton Timorumenos*, l. 981.

6
Until death all is life; i.e., while there's life there's hope. (Hasta la Muerte todo es vida.)
CERVANTES, *Don Quixote*. Pt. ii, ch. 59.

7
Though hope be dying yet it is not dead.
DRYDEN, *The Rival Ladies*. Act iv, sc. 1.

8
No one is to be despaired of as long as he breathes. (Nulli desperandum, quam diu spirat.)
ERASMUS, *Colloquies: Epicurus*.

9
While there is life there's hope (he cried,)
Then why such haste?—so groan'd and died.
JOHN GAY, *The Sick Man and the Angel*.

10
To the last moment of his breath,
On hope the wretch relies;
And ev'n the pang preceding death
Bids expectation rise.
GOLDSMITH, *The Captivity*. Act ii, l. 33.

11
The hope of life returns with the sun. (Spes vitæ cum sole redit.)
JUVENAL, *Satires*. Sat. xii, l. 70.

12
All is well, if my life remains. (Vita dum superest, bene est.)
MÆCENAS, *Fragments*. No. 1. (SENECA, *Epistulæ ad Lucilium*. Epis. ci, sec. 11.)

13
All things, said an ancient saw, may be hoped for by a man as long as he lives. (Toutes choses, disoit un mot ancien, sont esperables à un homme, pendant qu'il vit.)
MONTAIGNE, *Essays*. Bk. ii, ch. 3.

14
Hope travels thro', nor quits us when we die.
POPE, *Essay on Man*. Epis. ii, l. 274.

15
A man may hope for anything while he has life. (Homini, dum vivit, speranda sunt.)
TELESPHORUS OF RHODES. (SENECA, *Epistulæ ad Lucilium*. Epis. lxx, sec. 7. Seneca adds that he considers these words as most unmanly: "effeminatissimam.")

16
There is hope for the living, but none for the dead. (Ἐλπίδες ἐν ζωοῖσιν, ἀνέλπιστοι δὲ θανόντες.)
THEOCRITUS, *Idylls*. No. iv, l. 42.

17
Ere now I would have ended my miseries in death, but fond Hope keeps the spark alive, whispering ever that tomorrow will be better than today.
TIBULLUS, *Elegies*. Bk. ii, eleg. 6, l. 19.

18
Hope, and reserve yourself for better times. (Sperate, et vosmet rebus servate secundis.)
VERGIL, *Æneid*. Bk. i, l. 207.

IV—Hope: Living on Hope

19
Hope is a good breakfast, but an ill supper.
FRANCIS BACON, *Apothegms*. No. 95.

Ah! he was a wise man who said Hope is a good breakfast but a bad dinner. It shall be my supper, however, when all's said and done.
HESTER LYNCH PIOZZI. (HAYWARD, *Autobiography*, Vol. ii, p. 188.)

20
Hope is a poor salad To dine and sup with.
BEAUMONT AND FLETCHER, *The Custom of the Country*. Act ii, sc. 1.

21
I live on hope and that I think do all
Who come into this world.
ROBERT BRIDGES, *Sonnets*. No. 83.

22
He that lives upon hope will die fasting.
BENJAMIN FRANKLIN, *Poor Richard*, 1758.

He that lives on hope has but a slender diet.
THOMAS FULLER, *Gnomologia*. No. 2220.

He that liveth in hope danceth without a fiddle.
THOMAS FULLER, *Gnomologia*. No. 2224.

He who lives on hope makes a thin belly.
WODROEPHE, *Spared Houres*, 302. (1623)

V—Hope: Its Virtues

23
Know then, whatever cheerful and serene
Supports the mind, supports the body too:
Hence, the most vital movement mortals feel
Is hope, the balm and lifeblood of the soul.
JOHN ARMSTRONG, *Art of Preserving Health*. Bk. iv, l. 310.

24
Hope keeps the heart whole.
ANTONY BREWER, *The Love-Sick King*. Act ii.

Hope—the only tie which keeps the heart from breaking.
FULLER, *Worthies of England*. Vol. i, p. 40.

If hope were not, heart would break.
UNKNOWN, *Gesta Romanorum*. Tale 51. (c. 1375)

1
Sweet Hope,
Bearer of dreams, enchantress fond and kind.
ROBERT BRIDGES, *Prometheus*, l. 75.

2
Hope and patience are two sovereign remedies for all, the surest reposals, the sofest cushions to lean on in adversity.
ROBERT BURTON, *Anatomy of Melancholy*. Pt. ii, sec. iii, mem. 3.

3
When Peace and Mercy, banish'd from the plain,
Sprung on the viewless winds to Heaven again;
All, all forsook the friendless guilty mind,
But Hope, the charmer, linger'd still behind.
CAMPBELL, *The Pleasures of Hope*. Pt. i, l. 37.

Auspicious Hope! in thy sweet garden grow
Wreaths for each toil, a charm for every woe.
CAMPBELL, *The Pleasures of Hope*. Pt. i, l. 45.

Congenial Hope! thy passion-kindling power,
How bright, how strong, in youth's untroubled hour!
On yon proud height, with Genius hand in hand,
I see thee light, and wave thy golden wand.
CAMPBELL, *The Pleasures of Hope*. Pt. i, l. 121.

Cease, every joy, to glimmer on my mind,
But leave, oh! leave the light of Hope behind.
CAMPBELL, *The Pleasures of Hope*. Pt. ii, l. 375.

4
Hope, like the short-lived ray that gleams awhile, . . .
Cheers e'en the face of misery to a smile.
WILLIAM COWPER, *Despair at His Separation*.

5
Hope is worth any money.
THOMAS FULLER, *Gnomologia*.

A good hope is better than a bad possession.
THOMAS FULLER, *Gnomologia*.

6
Great hopes make great men.
THOMAS FULLER, *Gnomologia*.

The mighty hopes that make us men.
TENNYSON, *In Memoriam*. Pt. lxxxv, st. 15.

7
Hope, like the glimmering taper's light,
Adorns and cheers our way;
And still, as darker grows the night,
Emits a brighter ray.
GOLDSMITH, *The Captivity*. Act ii, sc. 1.

8
'Tis hope supports each noble flame,
'Tis hope inspires poetic lays;
Our heroes fight in hopes of fame,
And poets write in hopes of praise.
She sings sweet songs of future years,
And dries the tears of present sorrow;
Bids doubting mortals cease their fears,
And tells them of a bright to morrow.
THOMAS JEFFERSON, *To Ellen*. In his *Literary Bible*.

9
In all the wedding cake, hope is the sweetest of the plums.
DOUGLAS JERROLD, *Jerrold's Wit: The Catspaw*.

10
Hope, that with honey blends the cup of pain.
SIR WILLIAM JONES, *Hymn to Sereswaty*, l. 19.

11
So, when dark thoughts my boding spirit shroud,
Sweet Hope, celestial influence round me shed,
Waving thy silver pinions o'er my head.
KEATS, *To Hope*. Concluding lines.

12
Who bids me hope, and in that charming word
Has peace and transport to my soul restor'd.
GEORGE LYTTELTON, *Progress of Love: Hope*.

13
Hope elevates, and joy Brightens his crest.
MILTON, *Paradise Lost*. Bk. ix, l. 633.

Hope swells my sail.
JAMES MONTGOMERY, *The West Indies*.

The Gods are kind, and hope to men they give.
WILLIAM MORRIS, *The Earthly Paradise: Bellerophon at Argos*, l. 1617.

14
Take hope from the heart of man, and you make him a beast of prey.
OUIDA, *Wisdom, Wit, and Pathos: A Village Commune*.

15
It is hope which makes even the fettered miner live.
OVID, *Epistulæ ex Ponto*. Bk. i, epis. 6, l. 31.

It is hope which makes the shipwrecked sailor strike out with his arms in the midst of the sea, though no land is in sight.
OVID, *Epistulæ ex Ponto*. Bk. i, epis. 6, l. 35.

16
Hope maketh not ashamed.
New Testament: Romans, v, 5.

17
Who in Life's battle firm doth stand
Shall bear Hope's tender blossoms
Into the Silent Land.
J. G. VON SALIS-SEEWIS, *Ins Stille Land*. (Longfellow, tr.)

18
True hope is swift, and flies with swallow's wings:
Kings it makes gods, and meaner creatures kings.
SHAKESPEARE, *Richard III*. Act v, sc. 2, l. 23.

Hope is a lover's staff; walk hence with that
And manage it against despairing thoughts.
SHAKESPEARE, *The Two Gentlemen of Verona*. Act iii, sc. 1, l. 246.

19
Through the sunset of hope,
Like the shapes of a dream,
What Paradise islands of glory gleam!
SHELLEY, *Hellas*, l. 1050.

But hope will make thee young, for Hope and Youth
Are children of one mother, even Love.
SHELLEY, *Revolt of Islam*. Canto viii, st. 27.

1
Hope is like the sun, which, as we journey towards it, casts the shadow of our burden behind us.
SAMUEL SMILES, *Self-Help*. Ch. 3.

2
The most universal thing is hope, for hope stays with those who have nothing else.
THALES. (EPICTETUS, *Fragment*, xci.)

3
Alone 'mongst mortals dwelleth kindly Hope;
The other gods are to Olympus fled.
(*Ἐλπὶς ἐν ἀνθρώποις μούνη θεὸς ἐσθλὴ ἔνεστιν,*
ἄλλοι δ' Οὔλυμπόνδ' ἐκπρολιπόντες ἔβαν.)
THEOGNIS, *Sententiæ*.

4
Behind the cloud the starlight lurks,
Through showers the sunbeams fall;
For God, who loveth all His works,
Has left His hope with all!
WHITTIER, *A Dream of Summer*. *See also under* COMPENSATION.

5
Every gift of noble origin
Is breathed upon by Hope's perpetual breath.
WORDSWORTH, *Poems Dedicated to National Independence*. Pt. i, No. 20.

Hope rules a land for ever green:
All powers that serve the bright-eyed Queen
Are confident and gay;
Clouds at her bidding disappear;
Points she to aught?—the bliss draws near,
And Fancy smooths the way.
WORDSWORTH, *The Wishing-Gate*. St. 1.

6
Hope, of all passions, most befriends us here.
YOUNG, *Night Thoughts*. Night vii, l. 1461.

Hope, like a cordial, innocent, tho' strong,
Man's heart, at once, inspirits, and serenes;
Nor makes him pay his wisdom for his joys.
YOUNG, *Night Thoughts*. Night vii, l. 1464.

VI—Hope: Its Illusions

7
The Promised Land is the land where one is not.
AMIEL, *Journal*, 10 Feb., 1853.

8
If things then from their end we happy call,
'Tis Hope is the most hopeless thing of all.
ABRAHAM COWLEY, *Against Hope*.

9
That very popular trust in flat things coming round!
DICKENS, *Bleak House*. Ch. 20.

10
Too much hope deceiveth.
JOHN FLORIO, *First Fruites*. Fo. 33.

Hope deceives, enjoyment undeceives.
JOSEPH ROUX, *Meditations of a Parish Priest: Joy*. No. 9.

And thus Hope me deceived, as she deceiveth all.
SCOTT, *Harold the Dauntless*. Canto iii, st. 1.

11
Hope is a kind of cheat: in the minute of our disappointment we are angry; but upon the whole matter there is no pleasure without it.
LORD HALIFAX, *Works*, p. 236.

12
Reflected on the lake, I love
To see the stars of evening glow;
So tranquil in the heavens above,
So restless in the wave below.
Thus heavenly hope is all serene,
But earthly hope, how bright soe'er,
Still fluctuates o'er this changing scene,
As false and fleeting as 'tis fair.
REGINALD HEBER, *On Heavenly and Earthly Hope*.

13
It is natural to man to indulge in the illusions of hope. We are apt to shut our eyes against a painful truth, and listen to the song of that siren, till she transforms us into beasts.
PATRICK HENRY, *Speech*, Virginia House of Delegates, 23 March, 1775. (Arranged by William Wirt, 1818.)

14
Put aside trifling hopes. (Mitte levis spes.)
HORACE, *Epistles*. Bk. i, epis. 5, l. 8.

15
He that raises false hopes to serve a present purpose, only makes a way for disappointment and discontent.
SAMUEL JOHNSON, *The Patriot*.

Ye who listen with credulity to the whispers of fancy, and pursue with eagerness the phantoms of hope; who expect that age will perform the promises of youth, and that the deficiencies of the present day will be supplied by the morrow, —attend to the history of Rasselas, Prince of Abyssinia.
SAMUEL JOHNSON, *Rasselas*. Ch. 1.

16
Hopers go to hell.
JAMES KELLY, *Scottish Proverbs*.

17
I write *nil ultra* to my proudest hopes.
PHILIP MASSINGER, *a New Way to Pay Old Debts*. Act iv, sc. 1.

18
Where peace
And rest can never dwell, hope never comes,
That comes to all.
MILTON, *Paradise Lost*. Bk. i, l. 65.

Vain hopes, vain aims, inordinate desires.
MILTON, *Paradise Lost*. Bk. iv, l. 808.

19
Hope, once conceived, is long-lived; a treacherous goddess is she, but a timely one. (Spes tenet in tempus, semel est si credita, longum: Illa quidem fallax, sed tamen apta dea est.)
OVID, *Ars Amatoria*. Bk. i, l. 445.

Hope, great deceiver as she is, at least serves to carry us to the end of life by a pleasant road.

(L'espérance, toute trompeuse qu'elle est, sert au moins à nous mener à la fin de la vie par un chemin agréable.)
LA ROCHEFOUCAULD, *Maximes*. No. 168.

Hope is generally a wrong guide, though it is very good company by the way.
LORD HALIFAX, *Works*, p. 236.

1
Careless of things which are near, we pursue eagerly things which are far away. (Proximorum incuriosi, longinqua sectamur.)
PLINY THE YOUNGER, *Epistles*. Bk. viii. ep. 20.

2
Many a hopeful man has hope beguiled. (Qui speraverint spem decepisse multos.)
PLAUTUS, *Rudens*, l. 401. (Act ii, sc. 3.)

3
Our hopes, like towering falcons, aim
At objects in an airy height.
MATTHEW PRIOR, *To Charles Montague*.

4
I cultivated hope, and see it wither day by day. What serves it, alas! to water the leaves when the tree is severed at the root? (Je cultivais l'espérance, et la vois flétrir tous les jours. Que sert, helas! d'arroser le feuillage quand l'arbre est coupé par le pied?)
ROUSSEAU, *La Nouvelle Héloïse*. Pt. i. Letter 25.

5
The hour when you too learn that all is vain,
And that Hope sows what Love shall never reap.
D. G. ROSSETTI, *The House of Life*. Sonnet xliv.

6
The Worldly Hope men set their Hearts upon
Turns Ashes—or it prospers; and anon,
Like Snow upon the Desert's dusty Face,
Lighting a little hour or two—is gone.
OMAR KHAYYÁM, *Rubáiyát*. St. 16. (Fitzgerald, tr.)

7
What madness to plot out far-reaching hopes! (Quanta dementia est spes longas inchoantium!)
SENECA, *Epistulæ ad Lucilium*. Epis. ci, sec. 4.

8
Lined himself with hope,
Eating the air on promise of supply.
SHAKESPEARE, *II Henry IV*. Act i, sc. 3, l. 27.

Cozening hope: he is a flatterer,
A parasite, a keeper back of death,
Who gently would dissolve the bands of life,
Which false hope lingers in extremity.
SHAKESPEARE, *Richard II*. Act ii, sc. 2, l. 69.

9
Hope is the fawning traitor of the mind, while, under colour of friendship, it robs it of its chief force of resolution.
SIR PHILIP SIDNEY, *Arcadia*. Bk. iii.

10
When we have discovered a continent, or crossed a chain of mountains, it is only to find another ocean or another plain upon the further side. . . O toiling hands of mortals! O wearied feet, travelling ye know not whither! Soon, soon, it seems to you, you must come forth on some conspicuous hilltop, and but a little way further, against the setting sun, descry the spires of El Dorado.
R. L. STEVENSON, *Virginibus Puerisque: El Dorado*.

11
Races, better than we, have leaned on her wavering promise,
Having naught else but Hope.
ESAÍAS TEGNÉR, *The Children of the Lord's Supper*, l. 230. (Longfellow, tr.)

12
Hope doubtful of the future. (Spes incerta futuri.)
VERGIL, *Æneid*. Bk. viii, l. 580.

You feed an idle hope. (Spes pascis inanes.)
VERGIL, *Æneid*. Bk. x, l. 627.

13
Is Man
A child of hope? Do generations press
On generations, without progress made?
WORDSWORTH, *The Excursion*. Bk. v, l. 465.

Confiding tho' confounded; hoping on,
Untaught by trial, unconvinc'd by proof,
And ever looking for the never-seen.
YOUNG, *Night Thoughts*. Night viii, l. 126.

14
Hopes, what are they?—Beads of morning
Strung on slender blades of grass;
Or a spider's web adorning
In a strait and treacherous pass.
WORDSWORTH, *Inscriptions*. No. 10.

15
Restless hope, for ever on the wing.
YOUNG, *Night Thoughts*. Night vii, l. 133.

16
Hope told a flattering tale
That joy would soon return;
Ah, naught my sighs avail
For love is doomed to mourn.
UNKNOWN, *Hope Told a Flattering Tale*. (*Universal Songster*. Vol. i, p. 320.) The song was introduced by John Wolcot into the opera *Artaxerxes*.

Hope tells a flattering tale,
Delusive, vain and hollow.
Ah! let not hope prevail,
Lest disappointment follow.
MARY WROTHER, *Hope*. (*Universal Songster*. Vol. ii, p. 86.)

Hope told a flattering tale,
Much longer than my arm,
That love and pots of ale
In peace would keep me warm.
WILLIAM BARNES RHODES, *Bombastes Furioso*.

VII—Hope and Fear

17
Our greatest good, and what we least can spare,
Is hope: the last of all our evils, fear.
JOHN ARMSTRONG, *Art of Preserving Health*. Bk. iv, l. 318.

Entertaining hope Means recognising fear.

ROBERT BROWNING, *Two Poets of Croisic*, l. 158.

1
Far greater numbers have been lost by hopes,
Than all the magazines of daggers, ropes,
And other ammunitions of despair,
Were ever able to dispatch by fear.

SAMUEL BUTLER, *Miscellaneous Thoughts*, l. 483.

2
If hopes were dupes, fears may be liars;
It may be, in yon smoke concealed,
Your comrades chase e'en now the fliers,
And, but for you, possess the field.

ARTHUR HUGH CLOUGH, *Say Not the Struggle Nought Availeth.*

3
He has no hope who never had a fear.

COWPER, *Truth*, l. 299.

For where no hope is left, is left no fear.

MILTON, *Paradise Regained*. Bk. iii, l. 206.

But I strode on austere;
No hope could have no fear.

JAMES THOMSON, *City of Dreadful Night*. Pt. iv.

So farewell hope, and with hope farewell fear.

MILTON, *Paradise Lost*. Bk. iv, l. 108.

4
Cease to hope and you will cease to fear. (Desines timere, si sperare desieris.)

HECATO, *Fragments*. Frag. 25. (SENECA, *Epistulæ ad Lucilium*. Epis. v, sec. 7.)

5
Hope and fear are inseparable; there is no fear without hope, no hope without fear. (L'espérance et la crainte sont inséparables, et il n'y a point de crainte sans espérance, ni d'espérance sans crainte.)

LA ROCHEFOUCAULD, *Maximes Posthumes*. No. 515.

6
Let the fearful be allowed to hope. (Liceat sperare timenti.)

LUCAN, *De Bello Civili*. Bk. ii, l. 14.

7
Yet, where an equal poise of hope and fear
Does arbitrate th' event, my nature is
That I incline to hope, rather than fear.

MILTON, *Comus*, l. 410.

8
Hope and fear bring trust and mistrust by turns. (Alternant spesque timorque fidem.)

OVID, *Heroides*. Epis. vi, l. 38.

9
Fear made her devils, and weak hope her gods.

POPE, *Essay on Man*. Epis. iii, l. 256.

10
Hope is brightest when it dawns from fears.

SCOTT, *The Lady of the Lake*. Canto iv, st. 1.

Her hopes, her fears, her joys were all
Bounded within the cloister wall.

SCOTT, *Marmion*. Canto ii, st. 3.

As hope and fear alternate chase
Our course through life's uncertain race.

SCOTT, *Rokeby*. Canto vi, st. 2.

11
Just as the same chain fastens the prisoner and the soldier who guards him, so hope and fear keep step together: fear follows hope.

SENECA, *Epistulæ ad Lucilium*. Epis. v, sec. 8.

12
Most wretched 'tis to fear when you can hope for naught. (Miserrimum est timere, cum speres nihil.)

SENECA, *Troades*, l. 425.

13
And other hopes and other fears
Effaced the thoughts of happier years.

ROBERT SOUTHEY, *To Mary*.

14
The kind wise word that falls from years that fall—
"Hope thou not much, and fear thou not at all."

A. C. SWINBURNE, *Hope and Fear*.

VIII—Hope and Despair

15
It is to hope, though hope were lost.

ANNA LETITIA BARBAULD, *Song: Come Here, Fond Youth*.

16
The heart bowed down by weight of woe
To weakest hope will cling.

ALFRED BUNN, *The Bohemian Girl: Song*.

17
Work without Hope draws nectar in a sieve,
And Hope without an object cannot live.

S. T. COLERIDGE, *Work Without Hope*.

18
Still desiring, we live without hope. (Senza speme vivemo in desio.)

DANTE, *Inferno*. Canto iv, l. 42.

19
Hope is cheap as despair.

THOMAS FULLER, *Gnomologia*. No. 2542.

It is better to hope than to despair. (Ist besser hoffen als verzweifeln.)

GOETHE, *Torquato Tasso*. Act iii, sc. 4, l. 197.

Like strength is felt from hope and from despair.

HOMER, *Iliad*. Bk. xv, l. 852. (Pope, tr.)

20
Homely phrases, but each letter
Full of hope and yet of heart-break.

LONGFELLOW, *Hiawatha: Introduction*.

21
The setting of a great hope is like the setting of the sun. The brightness of our life is gone.

LONGFELLOW, *Hyperion*. Bk. i, ch. 1.

22
Our dearest hopes in pangs are born,
The kingliest Kings are crown'd with thorn

GERALD MASSEY, *The Kingliest Kings*.

23
What re-inforcement we may gain from hope,
If not, what resolution from despair.

MILTON, *Paradise Lost*. Bk. i, l. 190.

24
Do not hope without despair, nor despair without hope. (Nec speraveris sine desperatione nec desperaveris sine spe.)

SENECA, *Epistulæ ad Lucilium*. Epis. civ, 12.

He who can hope for nothing, let him despair of nothing. (Qui nil potest sperare, desperet nihil.)
SENECA, *Medea*, l. 163.

1
Our hap is loss, our hope but sad despair.
SHAKESPEARE, *III Henry VI*. Act ii, sc. 3, l. 9.

2
Worse than despair,
Worse than the bitterness of death, is hope.
SHELLEY, *The Cenci*. Act v, sc. 4.

3
It's best to hope the best, though of the worst affrayd.
SPENSER, *Faerie Queene*. Bk. iv, canto 6, st. 37.

4
Though sick with weighty cares, he feigns hope in his face. (Curisque ingentibus æger Spem voltu simulat.)
VERGIL, *Æneid*. Bk. i, l. 208.

5
We did not dare to breathe a prayer
Or to give our anguish scope!
Something was dead in each of us,
And what was dead was Hope.
OSCAR WILDE, *The Ballad of Reading Gaol*. Pt. iii, st. 31.

6
Hope, eager hope, th' assassin of our joy,
All present blessings treading under foot,
Is scarce a milder tyrant than despair.
YOUNG, *Night Thoughts*. Night vii, l. 107.

HORACE

7
Then farewell, Horace; whom I hated so,
Not for thy faults, but mine.
BYRON, *Childe Harold*. Canto iv, st. 77.

8
Serene and clear, harmonious Horace flows,
With sweetness not to be expressed in prose.
WENTWORTH DILLON, *Essay on Translated Verse*, l. 41.

9
But, oh, the echoes of those songs
That soothed our cares and lulled our hearts!
Not to that age nor this belongs
The glory of what heaven-born arts
Speak with the old distinctive charm
From yonder humble Sabine farm!
EUGENE FIELD, *Epilogue*.

10
Then finish, dear Chloe, this pastoral war;
And let us, like Horace and Lydia, agree:
For thou art a girl as much brighter than her,
As he was a poet sublimer than me.
MATTHEW PRIOR, *To Chloe Jealous*.

HORSE

I—Horse: Apothegms

11
That man has the horse of Sejanus. (Ille homo habet equum Sejanum.)
AULUS GELLIUS, *Noctes Atticæ*. Bk. iii, ch. 9, sec. 6. Referred to as a proverb, which originated from the misfortunes which befel the owners of a famous horse which had belonged originally to Gnæus Sejanus.

12
They are manifest asses, but you, good Leech, you are a horse of another colour.
R. H. BARHAM, *Leech of Folkestone*.

Farmer Gripper thinks we can live upon nothing, which is a horse of another colour.
C. H. SPURGEON, *Ploughman's Pictures*, 51.

13
A horse misused upon the road
Calls to Heaven for human blood.
WILLIAM BLAKE, *Auguries of Innocence*.

14
A true Philip, a lover of horses.
JOHN BROWN, *Horæ Subsecivæ: Presence of Mind*. A reference to the Greek meaning of Philip, or Phil-hippos.

15
The seat on a horse makes gentlemen of some and grooms of others.
CERVANTES, *Don Quixote*. Pt. ii, ch. 43.

16
Ride not a free horse to death.
CERVANTES, *Don Quixote*. Pt. ii, ch. 71.

Spur a free horse, he'll run himself to death.
BEN JONSON, *Tale of a Tub*, iii, 4.

A pair of good spurs to a borrowed horse is better than a peck of haver [oats].
GEORGE MERITON, *Praise of Yorkshire Ale*, 83.

LOOK NOT A GIFT HORSE IN THE MOUTH, *see under* GIFT.

17
Noblest of the train
That wait on man, the flight-performing horse.
COWPER, *The Task*. Bk. vi, l. 425.

18
'Orses and dorgs is some men's fancy. They're wittles and drink to me.
CHARLES DICKENS, *David Copperfield*. Ch. 19.

19
I know the gall'd horse will soonest wince.
RICHARD EDWARDS, *Damon and Pithias*.

There is a common saying that when a horse is rubbed on the gall, he will kick.
HUGH LATIMER, *Sermon on St. Andrew's Day*, 1552.

Let the galled jade wince, our withers are unwrung.
SHAKESPEARE, *Hamlet*. Act iii, sc. 2, l. 253.

20
A good horse should be seldom spurred.
THOMAS FULLER, *Gnomologia*. No. 156.

A good horse oft needs a good spur.
JOHN CLARKE, *Parœmiologia*, p. 93.

It is the bridle and spur that makes a good horse.
THOMAS FULLER, *Gnomologia*. No. 3021.

21
Altogether upon the high horse.
DAVID GARRICK, *Correspondence*. Vol. i, p. 205

1
O barbarous Men! your cruel breasts assuage;
Why vent ye on the generous steed your rage?
Does not his service earn your daily bread?
Your wives, your children, by his labours fed!
JOHN GAY, *Trivia*. Bk. ii. l. 233.

2
Yet if man, of all the Creator planned,
His noblest work is reckoned,
Of the works of His hand, by sea or by land,
The horse may at least rank second.
A. L. GORDON, *Hippodromania*. Pt. i, st. 3.

3
Good horses make short miles.
GEORGE HERBERT, *Jacula Prudentum*.

4
A short horse is soon curried.
JOHN HEYWOOD, *Proverbs*. Pt. i, ch 10. (1546); JOHN FLETCHER, *Valentinian*. Act ii, sc. 1.

When the steed is stolen, shut the stable door.
JOHN HEYWOOD, *Proverbs* Pt. i, ch. 10. *See also* WISDOM: AFTER THE EVENT.

All lay the load on the willing horse.
THOMAS FULLER, *Gnomologia*. No. 532.

6
Saddle-leather is in some respects even preferable to sole-leather. . . . One's hepar, or, in vulgar language, liver, . . . goes up and down like the dasher of a churn in the midst of the other vital arrangements, at every step of a trotting horse. The brains also are shaken up like coppers in a money-box.
O. W. HOLMES, *The Autocrat of the Breakfast-Table*. Ch. 7, p. 166.

The Squire will wind up . . . with an apocryphal saying which he attributes to Lord Palmerston—'There's nothing so good for the inside of a man as the outside of a horse.'
G. W. E. RUSSELL, *Social Silhouettes*. Ch. 32. Attributed also to Dr John Abernethy and to Oliver Wendell Holmes.

7
Be wise in time, and turn loose the ageing horse, lest at the last he stumble amid jeers and break his wind. (Solve senescentem mature sanus equum, ne Peccet ad extremum ridendus et ilia ducat.)
HORACE, *Epistles*. Bk. i, epis. 1, l. 8.

8
The ear of a bridled horse is in his mouth. (Equi frenato est auris in ore.)
HORACE, *Epistles*. Bk. i, epis 15, l. 13.

9
A four white-foot horse is a horse for a fool;
A three white-foot horse is a horse for a king;
And if he hath but one, I'll give him to none.
JAMES HOWELL, *Proverbs*, 13. (1659)

One white foot, buy a horse;
Two white feet, try a horse;
Three white feet, look well about him,
Four white feet, do without him.
UNKNOWN, *Old Rhyme*. (*Notes and Queries*. Ser. 5, vol. vii, p. 64.)

10
Hast thou given the horse strength? hast thou clothed his neck with thunder?
Old Testament: Job, xxxix, 19.

11
They say Princes learn no art truly, but the art of horsemanship. The reason is, the brave beast is no flatterer. He will throw a Prince as soon as his groom.
BEN JONSON, *Explorata: Illiteratus Princeps*.

12
Eaten up by horses. (Præda caballorum.)
JUVENAL, *Satires*. Sat. xi, l. 193. By the expense of keeping horses.

13
Here were we fallen in a great question of the law, whether the grey mare may be the better horse or not.
SIR THOMAS MORE, *Dialogue*. Bk. ii, ch. 5. (1528)

The grey mare is the better horse.
JOHN HEYWOOD, *Proverbs*. Pt. ii, ch. 4. (1546) Used by Butler, Fielding, Prior, Steele, and many others.

The vulgar proverb, that the grey mare is the better horse, originated, I suspect, in the preference generally given to the grey mares of Flanders over the finest coach horses of England.
MACAULAY, *History of England*. Bk. i, ch. 3, note.

14
The valiant horse races best, at the barrier's fall, when he has others to follow and o'erpass. (Tum bene fortis equus reserato carcere currit, Cum quos prætereat, quosque sequatur, habet.)
OVID, *Ars Amatoria*. Bk. iii, l. 595.

Competition makes a horse-race.
OVID, *Ars Amatoria*, iii, 595. (Young, tr.)

The spirited horse, which will of its own accord strive to win the race, will run still more swiftly if encouraged.
OVID, *Epistulæ ex Ponto*. Bk. ii, epis. 2, l. 21.

15
You have set spurs to a willing horse. (Addidisti calcaria sponte currenti.)
PLINY THE YOUNGER, *Epistles*. Bk. i, epis. 8.

16
An horse is a vain thing for safety.
Old Testament: Psalms, xxxiii, 17.

18
The blind horse is hardiest.
JOHN RAY, *Proverbs: Scottish*.

The blind horse is fittest for the mill.
THOMAS SOUTHERNE, *Maid's Last Prayer*. Act iii, sc. 1.

19
Woe worth the chase, woe worth the day,
That costs thy life, my gallant grey.
SCOTT, *The Lady of the Lake*. Canto i, st. 9

Dear to me is my bonny white steed;
Oft has he helped me at pinch of need.
SCOTT, *The Lay of the Last Minstrel*, iv, 10.

20
Spur not an unbroken horse.
SCOTT, *The Monastery*. Ch. 25.

21
O for a horse with wings!
SHAKESPEARE, *Cymbeline*. Act iii, sc. 2, l. 49

Give me another horse: bind up my wounds.
SHAKESPEARE, *Richard III*. Act v, sc. 3, l. 177

A horse! a horse! my kingdom for a horse!
SHAKESPEARE, *Richard III*. Act v, sc. 4, l. 7.

Villain, a horse—
Villain, I say, give me a horse to fly,
To swim the river, villain, and to fly.
GEORGE PEELE, *Battle of Alcazar*. Act v, l. 104.

1
I wish your horses swift and sure of foot;
And so I do command you to their backs.
SHAKESPEARE, *Macbeth*. Act iii, sc. 1, l. 39.

2
He doth nothing but talk of his horse.
SHAKESPEARE, *Merchant of Venice*, i, 2, 44.

Whose only fit companion is his horse.
WILLIAM COWPER, *Conversation*, l. 412.

Whose laughs are hearty, tho' his jests are coarse,
And loves you best of all things—but his horse.
POPE, *Epistle to Mrs. Teresa Blount on Her Leaving Town*, l. 29.

He will hold thee, when his passion shall have spent its novel force,
Something better than his dog, a little dearer than his horse.
TENNYSON, *Locksley Hall*, l. 49.

3
Go anywhere in England where there are natural, wholesome, contented, and really nice English people; and what do you always find? That the stables are the real centre of the household.
BERNARD SHAW, *Heartbreak House*. Act iii.

4
It is a good horse that never stumbles.
C. H. SPURGEON, *John Ploughman*. Ch. 10.

5
A horse thou knowest, a man thou dost not know.
TENNYSON, *Gareth and Lynette*, l. 453.

6
Trust not the horse, ye Trojans. (Equo ne credite, Teucri.)
VERGIL, *Æneid*. Bk. ii. l. 48. Meaning the wooden horse, by which the Greeks got into Troy.

7
And the hoofs of the horses as they run shake the crumbling field. (Quadrupedumque putrem cursu quatit ungula campum.)
VERGIL, *Æneid*. Bk. xi, l. 875. A famous example of onomatopœia.

8
There is no good horse of a bad color.
IZAAK WALTON, *The Compleat Angler*. Pt. i, ch. 5. Quoted as a proverb.

9
Who is he that may water the horse and not drink himself?
UNKNOWN, *Old English Homilies*. Ser. i, p. 9. (c. 1175.)

A man may lead a horse to the water, but he'll choose to drink.
UNKNOWN, *Jack Drum*. Act i. (1616)

A man may well bring a horse to the water,
But he cannot make him drink without he will.
JOHN HEYWOOD, *Proverbs*. Pt. i, ch. 11. (1546)

One man may lead a horse to the water, but twenty cannot make him drink.
SAMUEL JOHNSON. BOSWELL, *Life*, 14 July, 1763.

II—Horse: Descriptions

10
This horse was of extraordinary size, with a lofty neck, bay in color, with a thick, glossy mane; but that same horse was of such a fate or fortune that whoever possessed it came to utter ruin, as well as his whole house and all his possessions.
AULUS GELLIUS, *Noctes Atticæ*. Bk. iii, ch. 9.

11
Cob was the strongest, Mob was the wrongest,
Chittabob's tail was the finest and longest!
R. H. BARHAM, *The Truants*.

12
She was iron-sinew'd and satin-skinn'd,
Ribb'd like a drum and limb'd like a deer,
Fierce as the fire and fleet as the wind—
There was nothing she couldn't climb or clear.
A. L. GORDON, *Romance of Britomarte*. St. 6.

13
Gamarra is a dainty steed,
Strong, black, and of a noble breed,
Full of fire, and full of bone,
With all his line of fathers known;
Fine his nose, his nostrils thin,
But blown abroad by the pride within!
His mane is like a river flowing,
And his eyes like embers glowing
In the darkness of the night,
And his pace as swift as light.
BRYAN WALLER PROCTER, *The Blood Horse*.

14
Hurrah, hurrah for Sheridan!
Hurrah, hurrah for horse and man!
And when their statues are placed on high,
Under the dome of the Union sky,—
The American soldier's Temple of Fame,—
There with the glorious General's name
Be it said in letters both bold and bright:
"Here is the steed that saved the day
By carrying Sheridan into the fight,
From Winchester,—twenty miles away!"
THOMAS BUCHANAN READ, *Sheridan's Ride*.

15
I will not change my horse with any that treads but on four pasterns. Ça, ha! he bounds from the earth, as if his entrails were hairs, le cheval volant, the Pegasus, chez les narines de feu! When I bestride him, I soar, I am a hawk: he trots the air; the earth sings when he touches it; the basest horn of his hoof is more musical than the pipe of Hermes. . . . He is pure air and fire . . . the prince of palfreys; his neigh is like the bidding of a monarch and his countenance enforces homage.
SHAKESPEARE, *Henry V*. Act iii, sc. 7, l. 11.

It is a most absolute and excellent horse.
SHAKESPEARE, *Henry V*. Act iii, sc. 7, l. 28.

1
Round-hoof'd, short-jointed, fetlocks shag and long,
Broad breast, full eye, small head and nostril wide,
High crest, short ears, straight legs and passing strong,
Thin mane, thick tail, broad buttock, tender hide:
Look, what a horse should have he did not lack,
Save a proud rider on so proud a back.
SHAKESPEARE, *Venus and Adonis*, l. 295.

2
I saw them go; one horse was blind,
The tails of both hung down behind,
Their shoes were on their feet.
HORACE AND JAMES SMITH, *The Baby's Début*. Parody of Wordsworth.

3
Steeds decked with purple and with tapestry,
With golden harness hanging from their necks,
Champing their yellow bits, all clothed in gold.
VERGIL, *Æneid*. Bk. vii, l. 277. Describing the gifts sent by King Latinus to Æneas.

4
His neck is high and erect, his head replete with intelligence, his belly short, his back full, and his proud chest swells with hard muscle. (Ardua cervix, Argumtumque caput, brevis alvos, obesaque terga, Luxuriatque toris animosum pectus.)
VERGIL, *Georgics*. Bk. iii, l. 79.

HORSEMANSHIP

5
Men will keep going on their nerve or their head,
But you cannot ride a horse when he's dead.
LEONARD BACON, *Colorado Morton's Ride*.

6
So that his horse, or charger, hunter, hack,
Knew that he had a rider on his back.
BYRON, *Don Juan*. Canto xiv, st. 32.

7
A canter is the cure for every evil.
BENJAMIN DISRAELI, *The Young Duke*. Bk. ii, ch. 11.

8
If you ride a horse, sit close and tight,
If you ride a man, sit easy and light.
BENJAMIN FRANKLIN, *Poor Richard*, 1734.

9
A jolly wight there was, that rode
Upon a sorry mare.
THOMAS HOOD, *The Epping Hunt*.

10
A horseman better than Bellerophon himself. (Eques ipso melior Bellerophonte.)
HORACE, *Odes*. Bk. iii, ode 12, l. 7. Bellerophon was the rider of Pegasus.

11
The driving is like the driving of Jehu the son of Nimshi; for he driveth furiously.
Old Testament: II Kings, ix, 20. Hence "Jehu" for a fast driver; used especially of drivers of hansom cabs and other public vehicles.

I like, my dear Lord, the road you are travelling, but I don't like the pace you are driving; too similar to that of the son of Nimshi. I always feel myself inclined to cry out, Gently, John—gently down hill. Put on the drag.
SYDNEY SMITH, *Letter to Lord John Russell*.

Spark the lash, my boy, and hold the reins more firmly! (Parce, puer, stimulis, et fortius utere loris!)
OVID, *Metamorphoses*. Bk. ii, l. 127.

12
Lord Ronald said nothing; he flung himself from the room, flung himself upon his horse and rode madly off in all directions.
STEPHEN LEACOCK, *Nonsense Novels: Gertrude the Governess*.

13
He grew unto his seat;
And to such wondrous doing brought his horse,
As he had been incorpsed and demi-natured
With the brave beast.
SHAKESPEARE, *Hamlet*. Act iv, sc. 7, l. 86.

I saw young Harry, with his beaver on,
His cuisses on his thighs, gallantly arm'd,
Rise from the ground like feather'd Mercury,
And vaulted with such ease into his seat
As if an angel dropp'd down from the clouds,
To turn and wind a fiery Pegasus
And witch the world with noble horsemanship.
SHAKESPEARE, *I Henry IV*. Act iv, sc. 1, l. 104.

Well could he ride, and often men would say
"That horse his mettle from his rider takes."
SHAKESPEARE, *A Lover's Complaint*, l. 106.

14
A rider unequalled—a sportsman complete,
A rum one to follow, a bad one to beat.
G. J. WHYTE-MELVILLE, *Hunting Song*.

HOSPITALITY

See also Inn

I—Hospitality: Apothegms

15
The merry, but unlook'd for guest,
Full often proves to be the best.
WILLIAM COMBE, *Dr. Syntax's Tour in Search of Consolation*. Canto xxix.

16
Hospitality consists in a little fire, a little food, and an immense quiet.
R. W. EMERSON, *Journal*, 1856.

17
For whom he means to make an often guest,
One dish shall serve; and welcome make the rest.
JOSEPH HALL, *Come Dine with Me*.

1
Be not forgetful to entertain strangers: for thereby some have entertained angels unawares.
Old Testament: Hebrews, xiii, 2.

2
'Tis equal wrong if a man speed on a guest who is loath to go, and if he keep back one that is eager to be gone. One should make welcome the present guest, and send forth him that would go.
(Ἶσόν τοι κακόν ἐσθ', ὅς τ' οὐκ ἐθέλοντα νέεσθαι ξεῖνον ἐποτρύνει καὶ ὃς ἐσσύμενον κατερύκει. χρὴ ξεῖνον παρεόντα φιλεῖν, ἐθέλοντα δὲ πέμπειν.)
HOMER, *Odyssey*. Bk. xv, l. 72.

Alike he thwarts the hospitable end
Who drives the free, or stays the hasty friend:
True friendship's laws are by this rule express'd,
Welcome the coming, speed the parting guest.
HOMER, *Odyssey*. Bk. xv, l. 81. (Pope, tr.)

For I, who hold sage Homer's rule the best,
Welcome the coming, speed the going guest.
POPE, *Imitations of Horace: Satires*. Bk. ii, sat. 2, l. 159.

To the guests that must go, bid God's speed and brush away all traces of their steps.
RABINDRANATH TAGORE, *The Gardener*. No. 45.

3
Wherever the storm carries me, I go a willing guest. (Quo me cumque rapit tempestas, deferor hospes.)
HORACE, *Epistles*. Bk. i, epis. i, l. 15.

As drives the storm, at any door I knock,
And house with Montaigne now, or now with Locke.
POPE, *Imitations of Horace: Epistles,* i, 1, 25.

4
There is room for several uninvited guests. (Locus est et pluribus umbris.)
HORACE, *Epistles*. Bk. i, epis. 5, l. 28. The "umbræ" were the uninvited guests who came with a man of high station.

Unbidden guests
Are often welcomest when they are gone.
SHAKESPEARE, *I Henry VI*. Act ii, sc. 2, l. 55.

5
A host is like a general: mishaps oft reveal his genius. (Sed convivatoris, uti ducis, ingenium res adversæ nudare solent.)
HORACE, *Satires*. Bk. ii, sat. 8, l. 73.

6
As welcome as flowers in May.
JAMES HOWELL, *Letters*. Bk. i, No. 60. (1645)

You are as welcome as the flowers in May.
SCOTT, *Rob Roy*. Ch. 8.

7
In good company you need not ask who is the master of the feast. The man who sits in the lowest place, and who is always industrious in helping every one, is certainly the man.
DAVID HUME, *Essays: Rise and Progress of Arts.*

Sometimes, when guests have gone, the host remembers
Sweet courteous things unsaid.
JOHN MASEFIELD, *The Faithful*.

8
Oh that I had in the wilderness a lodging place of wayfaring men!
Old Testament: Jeremiah, ix, 2.

HOUSE BY THE SIDE OF THE ROAD, *see under* PHILANTHROPY.

9
It is more disgraceful to turn out a guest than not to admit him. (Turpius ejicitur, quam non admittitur hospes.)
OVID, *Tristia*. Bk. v, eleg. 6, l. 13.

10
Given to hospitality.
New Testament: Romans, xii, 13.

A lover of hospitality, a lover of good men, sober, just, holy, temperate.
New Testament: Titus, i, 8.

He kept no Christmas-house for once a year,
Each day his boards were fill'd with Lordly fare:
He fed a rout of yeomen with his cheer,
Nor was his bread and beef kept in with care;
His wine and beer to strangers were not spare,
And yet beside to all that hunger grieved,
His gates were ope, and they were there relieved.
ROBERT GREENE, *A Maiden's Dream,* l. 232.

11
No guest is so welcome that he will not become a nuisance after three days in a friend's house. (Nam hospes nullus tam in amici hospitium devorti potest, Quin, ubi triduom continuom fuerit, jam odiosus siet.)
PLAUTUS, *Miles Gloriosus,* l. 741. (Act iii, sc. 1.)

The first day a man is a guest, the second a burden, the third a pest.
LABOULAYE, *Abdallah*. Ch. 9.

Fish and guests in three days are stale.
JOHN LYLY, *Euphues,* p. 307. (1580)

Like some poor nigh-related guest,
That may not rudely be dismissed;
He hath out-stayed his welcome while,
And tells the jest without the smile.
S. T. COLERIDGE, *Youth and Age.*

12
My master is of churlish disposition
And little recks to find the way to heaven
By doing deeds of hospitality.
SHAKESPEARE, *As You Like It*. Act ii, sc. 4, l. 80.

13
I am your host;
With robbers' hands my hospitable favours
You should not ruffle thus.
SHAKESPEARE, *King Lear*. Act iii, sc. 7, l. 39.

Reward not hospitality
With such black payment as thou hast pretended.
SHAKESPEARE, *The Rape of Lucrece*, l. 575.

14
Bear Welcome in your eye,
Your hand, your tongue.
SHAKESPEARE. *Macbeth*. Act i, sc. 5, l. 65.

Be bright and jovial among your guests to-night.
SHAKESPEARE, *Macbeth*. Act iii, sc. 2, l. 28.

You do not give the cheer: the feast is sold
That is not often vouch'd, while 'tis a-making,
'Tis given with welcome.
SHAKESPEARE, *Macbeth*. Act iii, sc. 4, l. 33.

See, your guests approach:
Address yourself to entertain them sprightly,
And let's be red with mirth.
SHAKESPEARE, *Winter's Tale*. Act iv, sc. 4, l. 52.

A woeful hostess brooks not merry guests.
SHAKESPEARE, *The Rape of Lucrece*, l. 1125.

1
Macbeth: Here's our chief guest.
Lady Macbeth: If he had been forgotten,
It had been as a gap in our great feast.
SHAKESPEARE, *Macbeth*. Act iii, sc. 1, l. 11.

His worth is warrant for his welcome.
SHAKESPEARE, *The Two Gentlemen of Verona*. Act ii, sc. 4, l. 102.

2
Hospitality sitting with Gladness.
TEGNÉR, BISHOP OF WEXIÖ, *Fritiof's Saga*. Pt. i. (Longfellow, tr.)

II—Hospitality: Its Praise

3
Stay is a charming word in a friend's vocabulary.
A. B. ALCOTT, *Concord Days: June*.

The courteous host, and all-approving guest.
BYRON, *Lara*. Canto i, st. 29.

4
When friends are at your hearthside met,
Sweet courtesy has done its most
If you have made each guest forget
That he himself is not the host.
T. B. ALDRICH, *Hospitality*.

If my best wines mislike thy taste,
And my best service win thy frown,
Then tarry not, I bid thee haste;
There's many another Inn in town.
T. B. ALDRICH, *Quits*.

5
Come in the evening, or come in the morning,
Come when you're looked for, or come without warning,
Kisses and welcome you'll find here before you,
And the oftener you come here the more I'll adore you.
THOMAS O. DAVIS, *The Welcome*.

There's an organ in the parlor, to give the house a tone,
And you're welcome every evening at Maggie Murphy's home.
EDWARD HARRIGAN, *Maggie Murphy's Home*. The song hit of *Reilly and the 400*, which opened at Harrigan and Hart's Theatre, December, 1890.

6
"God save all here!" my comrade cries,
And rattles on the raised latch-pin;
"God save you kindly!" quick replies
A clear sweet voice, and asks us in.
SAMUEL FERGUSON, *The Pretty Girl of Loch Dan*.

7
Hail Guest! We ask not what thou art:
If Friend, we greet thee, hand and heart;
If Stranger such no longer be;
If Foe, our love shall conquer thee.
ARTHUR GUITERMAN, *Old Welsh Door Verse*

8
A stone jug and a pewter mug,
And a table set for three!
A jug and a mug at every place,
And a biscuit or two with Brie!
Three stone jugs of Cruiskeen Lawn,
And a cheese like crusted foam!
The Kavanagh receives to-night!
McMurrough is at home!
RICHARD HOVEY, *The Kavanagh*.

For it's always fair weather
When good fellows get together,
With a stein on the table and a good song ringing clear.
RICHARD HOVEY, *A Stein Song*.

9
So saying, with despatchful looks in haste
She turns, on hospitable thoughts intent.
MILTON, *Paradise Lost*. Bk. v, l. 331.

10
A hundred thousand welcomes: I could weep,
And I could laugh; I am light and heavy:
Welcome.
SHAKESPEARE, *Coriolanus*. Act ii, sc. 1, l. 200.

Ladies, a general welcome from his grace
Salutes ye all: . . . he would have all as merry
As first good company, good wine, good welcome
Can make good people.
SHAKESPEARE, *Henry VIII*. Act i, sc. 4, l. 1.

Sir, you are very welcome to our house:
It must appear in other ways than words,
Therefore I scant this breathing courtesy.
SHAKESPEARE, *The Merchant of Venice*. Act v, sc. 1, l. 139.

From heart of very heart, great Hector, welcome!
SHAKESPEARE, *Troilus and Cressida*. Act iv, sc. 5, l. 171.

11
I charge thee, invite them all: let in the tide
Of knaves once more; my cook and I'll provide.
SHAKESPEARE, *Timon of Athens*. Act iii, sc. 4, l. 118.

12
You must come home with me and be my guest;
You will give joy to me, and I will do
All that is in my power to honour you.
SHELLEY, *Hymn to Mercury*. St. 5.

13
The lintel low enough to keep out pomp and pride;
The threshold high enough to turn deceit aside;
The doorband strong enough from robbers to defend;

This door will open at a touch to welcome every friend.
HENRY VAN DYKE, *Inscription for a Friend's House.*

1
A genial hearth, a hospitable board,
And a refined rusticity.
WORDSWORTH, *Ecclesiastical Sonnets.* Pt. iii, No. 18.

HOURS

See also Sundial, Time

I—Hours: Their Flight

See also Time: Its Flight

2
The auld kirk-hammer strak the bell
Some wee short hour ayont the twal.
BURNS, *Death and Dr. Hornbook,* l. 182.

The bell strikes one. We take no note of time
But from its loss.
YOUNG, *Night Thoughts.* Night i, l. 55.

3
An hour of pain is as long as a day of pleasure.
THOMAS FULLER, *Gnomologia.* No. 614.

O, in one hour what years of anguish crowd!
BULWER-LYTTON, *Richelieu.* Act iii, sc. 1.

The hours are passing slow,
I hear their weary tread.
ANDREW LANG, *Ballade of Sleep.*

For the unhappy how slowly pass the hours! (Que pour les malheureux l'heure lentement fuit!)
SAURIN, *Blanche et Guiscard,* v, 5.

The wingless, crawling hours.
SHELLEY, *Prometheus Unbound.* Act i, l. 48.

Pleasure and action make the hours seem short.
SHAKESPEARE, *Othello.* Act ii, sc. 3, l. 385.

4
To me, perhaps, the passing hour will grant what it denies to you. (Mihi forsan, tibi quod negarit, Porriget hora.)
HORACE, *Odes.* Bk. ii, ode 16, l. 31. *See also under* TO-DAY.

5
The hours fly around in a circle. (Volat hora per orbem.)
MANILIUS, *Astronomica.* Bk. iii, l. 641.

So runs the round of life from hour to hour.
TENNYSON, *Circumstance,* l. 9.

6
Lost, yesterday, somewhere between Sunrise and sunset, two golden hours, each set with sixty diamond minutes. No reward is offered for they are gone forever.
HORACE MANN, *Lost, Two Golden Hours.*

7
They [the hours] pass by and are put to our account. (Pereunt et inputantur.)
MARTIAL, *Epigrams.* Bk. v, epig. 20, l. 13.

8
'Tis but an hour ago since it was nine,
And after one hour more 'twill be eleven.
And so, from hour to hour, we ripe and ripe,
And then, from hour to hour, we rot and rot;
And thereby hangs a tale.
SHAKESPEARE, *As You Like It.* Act ii, sc. 7, l. 24.

II—Hours: Their Employment

See also Industry

9
This hour's the very crisis of your fate,
Your good or ill, your infamy or fame,
And the whole colour of your life depends
On this important now.
DRYDEN, *The Spanish Friar.* Act iv, sc. 2. *See also under* PRESENT.

10
Too busied with the crowded hour to fear to live or die.
EMERSON, *Quatrains: Nature.*

11
These hours that I throw away—
What would I give for one
If you were lying newly dead,
Eternity begun?
CAROLINE GILTINAN, *Unarmoured.*

12
It happeth in one hour that happeth not in seven year.
JOHN HEYWOOD, *Proverbs.* Pt. i, ch. 11. (1546)

It happens in an hour that comes not in an age.
THOMAS FULLER, *Gnomologia.* No. 2836.

An hour's cold will suck out seven years' heat.
MICHAEL DENHAM, *Proverbs,* p. 3.

An hour may destroy what an age was a building.
THOMAS FULLER, *Gnomologia.* No. 613.

13
An hour in the morning before breakfast is worth two all the rest of the day.
WILLIAM HONE, *Every-Day Book,* ii, 477. Cited as "an old and true saying."

14
Hours are golden links, God's token,
Reaching heaven; but, one by one,
Take them, lest the chain be broken
Ere the pilgrimage be done.
ADELAIDE ANN PROCTER, *One By One.*

15
I never tie myself to hours, for the hours are made for man, and not man for the hours. (Les heures sont faictes pour l'homme, et non l'homme pour les heures.)
RABELAIS, *Works.* Bk. i, ch. 41. The monk is arguing against punctuality.

16
The hour is come, but not the man.
SCOTT, *Heart of Midlothian:* Ch. 4, *Heading.*

17
This was an hour
That sweeten'd life, repaid and recompensed
All losses; and although it could not heal
All griefs, yet laid them for awhile to rest.
ROBERT SOUTHEY, *Roderick.* Pt. xviii, l. 39.

18
Let each as likes him best his hours employ.
THOMSON, *Castle of Indolence.* Canto i, st. 28.

1
Six hours to sleep, as many to righteous law;
Four to your prayers, and two to fill your maw;
The rest bestow upon the sacred Muses.
(Sex horas somno, totidem des legibus æquis,
Quatuor orabis, des epulisque duas;
Quod superest ultra sacris largire Camoenis.)
UNKNOWN. These "ancient verses" were introduced by Sir Edward Coke into his *Institutes of the Laws of England.* Bk. ii, ch. 1, sec. 85.

Six hours in sleep, in law's grave study six,
Four spend in prayer, the rest on nature fix.
SIR EDWARD COKE, *Paraphrase,* of the "ancient verses" given above.

Seven hours to law, to soothing slumber seven,
Ten to the world allot, and all to heaven.
SIR WILLIAM JONES, *An Ode in Imitation of Alcæus.* (See TEIGNMOUTH, *Memoirs of the Life of Sir William Jones,* p. 251.)

Six hours in sleep is enough for youth and age;
Seven for the lazy, but eight are allowed to none.
(Sex horis dormire sat est juvenique senique;
Septem vix pigro; nulli concedimus octo.)
UNKNOWN, *Collectio Salernitans.* Vol. ii, l. 130.

The four eights, that ideal of operative felicity, are here a realized fact.
JAMES ANTHONY FROUDE, *Oceana.* Ch. 14. Referring to New Zealand. A footnote explains that the "four eights" are, "Eight hours to work, eight to play, eight to sleep, and eight shillings a day."

So many hours must I take my rest;
So many hours must I contemplate.
SHAKESPEARE, *III Henry VI.* Act ii, sc. 5, l. 32.

HOUSE

See also Architecture: Home

2
God planteth in mortal men the cause of sin whensoever he wills utterly to destroy a house.
ÆSCHYLUS, *Niobe.* Frag. 77.

3
Cast the house out at the window.
WILLIAM BULLEIN, *Bulwarke of Defence.* Fo. 28.

I'll have a virtuous wife, or I'll throw the house out o' th' window.
JOHN OZELL, *Molière,* i, 180.

4
A man's dignity may be enhanced by the house he lives in, but not wholly secured by it; the owner should bring honor to the house, not the house to its owner.
CICERO, *De Officiis.* Bk. i, ch. 39, sec. 139.

The house shows the owner.
GEORGE HERBERT, *Jacula Prudentum.*

5
He that in a neat house will dwell
Must priest and pigeon thence expel.
COTGRAVE, *Dictionary: Pigeon.* (1611)

6
He that buys a house ready wrought
Hath many a pin and nail for nought.
WILLIAM CAMDEN, *Remains,* p. 324.

A house ready made, but a wife to make.
THOMAS FULLER, *Gnomologia.* No. 222.

7
Better one's house be too little one day, than too big all the year after.
THOMAS FULLER, *Gnomologia.* No. 919.

8
Choose not a house near an inn [for noise] or in a corner [for filth].
GEORGE HERBERT, *Jacula Prudentum.*

9
He that hath no house must lie in a yard.
JOHN LYLY, *Endymion,* iv, 2. (1591)

10
And the rain descended, and the floods came, and the winds blew, and beat upon that house; and it fell not: for it was founded upon a rock.
New Testament: Matthew, vii, 25.

And the rain descended, and the floods came, and the winds blew, and beat upon that house; and it fell: and great was the fall of it.
New Testament: Matthew, vii, 27.

11
A house built by the wayside is either too high or too low.
JOHN RAY, *English Proverbs,* 106. (1670)

12
He that has a house to put 's head in has a good head-piece.
SHAKESPEARE, *King Lear.* Act iii, sc. 2, l. 25.

13
You take my house when you do take the prop
That doth sustain my house; you take my life
When you do take the means whereby I live.
SHAKESPEARE, *The Merchant of Venice.* Act iv, sc. 1, l. 375.

14
Like a fair house, built on another man's ground.
SHAKESPEARE, *The Merry Wives of Windsor.* Act ii, sc. 2, l. 224.

II—House: My House Is My Castle

15
No outward doors of a man's house can in general be broken open to execute any civil process; though in criminal cases the public safety supersedes the private.
SIR WILLIAM BLACKSTONE, *Commentaries on the Laws of England.* Vol. iv, p. 108. (ed. 1880)

16
My whinstone house my castle is,
I have my own four walls.
CARLYLE, *My Own Four Walls.*

17
The house is a castle which the King cannot enter.
EMERSON, *English Traits: Wealth.*

1
Public laws protect the privacies of a house. (Jura publica favent privata domus.)

JOHN RAY, *English Proverbs*, p. 106. (1670) Ray comments, "this is a kind of law proverb."

2
I in my own house am an emperor,
And will defend what's mine.

MASSINGER, *The Roman Actor*. Act i, sc. 2.

3
The poorest man may in his cottage bid defiance to all the force of the Crown. It may be frail, its roof may shake; the wind may blow through it; the storms may enter, the rain may enter,—but the King of England cannot enter; all his forces dare not cross the threshold of the ruined tenement!

WILLIAM PITT, EARL OF CHATHAM, *Speech*, on the Excise Bill.

I think some orator said that though the winds of heaven might whistle around an Englishman's cottage, the King of England could not.

JOHN J INGALLS, *Speech*, U. S. Senate. 10 May. 1880.

4
My house is to me as my castle, from which the law does not compel me to flee. (Ma meason est a moy come mon castel, hors de quel le ley ne moy arta a fuer.)

SIR WILLIAM STAUNFORD, *Plees del Coron*. (1567)

Our law calleth a man's house his castle, meaning that he may defend himself therein.

WILLIAM LAMBARDE, *Eirenarcha*. Bk. ii, ch. 7. (1581)

His house . . . is his castle.

JOHN MANNINGHAM, *Diary*, 21. (1602)

The house of every one is to him his castle and fortress, as well for his defence against injury and violence, as for his repose.

SIR EDWARD COKE, *Semayne's Case*, 1605. (3 Rep. 186.)

A man's house is his castle.

SIR EDWARD COKE, *Institutes* Pt. iii, p 162.

My lodging, as long as I rent it, is my castle.

DRYDEN, *Wild Gallant*. Act i, sc. 1. (1663)

Masters of families are much favoured in our law, for their houses are termed their castles.

DUDLEY NORTH, *Observation and Advice*, 72. (1669)

My house is my castle, gentlemen, and nobody must offer violence here.

ARTHUR MURPHY, *School for Guardians*. Act iii, sc. 5. (1767)

Mrs. MacStinger immediately demanded whether an Englishwoman's house was her castle or not.

DICKENS, *Dombey and Son*. Ch. 9. (1848)

HUMANITY, see Man

HUMILITY

See also Heart: The Humble Heart

5
True humility is contentment.

AMIEL, *Journal*, 17 Dec., 1854.

6
Lowliness is the base of every virtue.

P. J. BAILEY, *Festus: Home*.

7
Owe not thy humility unto humiliation from adversity, but look humbly down in that state when others look upwards upon thee.

SIR THOMAS BROWNE, *Christian Morals*. Pt. i, sec. 14.

8
Mountain gorses, do ye teach us . . .
That the wisest word man reaches
Is the humblest he can speak?

E. B. BROWNING, *Lessons from the Gorse*.

9
For it is a hard matter for a man to go down into the Valley of Humiliation, and to catch no slip by the way.

JOHN BUNYAN, *The Pilgrim's Progress*. Pt. i.

He that is humble, ever shall
Have God to be his guide.

JOHN BUNYAN, *The Pilgrim's Progress*. Pt. ii.

10
Humility may clothe an English dean.

WILLIAM COWPER, *Truth*, l. 118.

11
The higher we are placed, the more humbly should we walk. (Quanto superiores simus, tanto nos geramus summissius.)

CICERO, *De Officiis*. Ch. 26, sec. 90.

12
I am well aware that I am the 'umblest person going. . . . 'umble we are, 'umble we have been, 'umble we shall ever be.

DICKENS, *David Copperfield*. Ch. 17. (Uriah Heep speaking.)

13
None shall rule but the humble,
And none but Toil shall have.

EMERSON, *Boston Hymn*.

14
You've no idea what a poor opinion I have of myself, and how little I deserve it.

W. S. GILBERT, *Ruddigore*. Act i.

15
Humility is the true cure for many a needless heartache.

ARTHUR HELPS, *Friends in Council*. Bk. i, ch. 9.

16
That very thing so many Christians want—
Humility!

THOMAS HOOD, *Ode to Rae Wilson*, l. 218.

17
Humble things become the humble. (Parvum parva decent.)

HORACE, *Epistles*. Bk. i, epis. 7, l. 44.

18
God hath sworn to lift on high
Who sinks himself by true humility.

JOHN KEBLE, *At Hooker's Tomb*.

19
Humble because of knowledge, mighty by sacrifice.

RUDYARD KIPLING, *The Islanders*.

20
Humility is often only a pretended submis-

sion, an artifice of pride, which abases itself in order to exalt itself. (L'humilité n'est souvent qu'une feinte soumission, . . . un artifice de l'orgueil qui s'abaisse pour s'élever.)

La Rochefoucauld, *Maximes*. No. 254. *See also* Pride: Apothegms.

Humility is the altar upon which God wishes us to offer him sacrifices. (L'humilité est l'autel sur lequel Dieu veut qu'on lui offre des sacrifices.)

La Rochefoucauld, *Maximes Posthumes*, 537.

1
Whosoever exalteth himself shall be abased; and he that humbleth himself shall be exalted.

New Testament: Luke, xiv, 11; *Matthew*, xxiii, 12.

2
Courage, brother! do not stumble,
Though thy path be dark as night;
There's a star to guide the humble,
Trust in God and do the Right.

Norman Macleod, *Trust in God*.

Let me be a little meeker
With the brother that is weaker,
Let me think more of my neighbor
And a little less of me.

Edgar A. Guest, *A Creed*.

3
Whosoever shall smite thee on thy right cheek, turn to him the other also.

New Testament: Matthew, v, 39; *Luke*, vi, 29.

Wisdom has taught us to be calm and meek,
To take one blow, and turn the other cheek;
It is not written what a man shall do,
If the rude caitiff smite the other too!

O. W. Holmes, *Non-Resistance*.

Turning the other cheek is a kind of moral jiu-jitsu.

Gerald Stanley Lee, *Crowds*. Bk. iv, ch. 9.

4 No man will learn anything at all,
Unless he first will learn humility.

Owen Meredith, *Vanini*, l. 328.

5
Nearest the throne itself must be
The footstool of humility.

James Montgomery, *Humility*.

Fairest and best adorned is she
Whose clothing is humility.

James Montgomery, *Humility*.

Humility, that low, sweet root,
From which all heavenly virtues shoot.

Thomas Moore, *Loves of the Angels: Third Angel's Story*.

6
No more lessen or dissemble thy merit, than overrate it; for though humility be a virtue, an affected one is not.

William Penn, *Fruits of Solitude*.

Humility is to make a right estimate of one's self. It is no humility for a man to think less of himself than he ought, though it might rather puzzle him to do that.

C. H. Spurgeon, *Gleanings: Humility*.

7
Let not this weak unknowing hand
Presume thy bolts to throw,
And deal damnation round the land
On each I judge thy foe.

If I am right, thy grace impart
Still in the right to stay;
If I am wrong, oh teach my heart
To find that better way!

Pope, *Universal Prayer*. Sts. 7, 8.

8
She should be humble, who would please,
And she must suffer, who can love.

Matthew Prior, *Chloe Jealous*. St. 5.

9
There is no humiliation for humility.

Joseph Roux, *Meditations of a Parish Priest*. Pt. iv, No. 5.

10
Humility is a virtue all men preach, none practise, and yet everybody is content to hear. The master thinks it good doctrine for his servants, the laity for the clergy, and the clergy for the laity.

John Selden, *Table-Talk: Humility*.

11
And bow'd his eminent top to their low ranks,
Making them proud of his humility.

Shakespeare, *All's Well that Ends Well*. Act i, sc. 2, l. 43.

As if Olympus to a molehill should
In supplication nod.

Shakespeare, *Coriolanus*. Act v, sc. 3, v, 3, l. 30.

12
In peace there's nothing so becomes a man
As modest stillness and humility.

Shakespeare, *Henry V*. Act iii, sc. 1, l. 3.

An humble gait.

Shakespeare, *The Rape of Lucrece*. St. 215.

I thank my God for my humility.

Shakespeare, *Richard III*. Act ii, sc. 1, l. 72.

13 The virtuous man,
Who, great in his humility, as kings
Are little in their grandeur.

Shelley, *Queen Mab*. Canto iii, l. 150.

14
The higher a man is in grace, the lower he will be in his own esteem.

C. H. Spurgeon, *Gleanings Among the Sheaves: The Right Estimate*.

15 True humility,
The highest virtue, mother of them all.

Tennyson, *The Holy Grail*, l. 445.

16
Make way for your betters. (Da locum melioribus.)

Terence, *Phormio*, l. 522.

17
Humble thyself in all things. (Humilia te in omnibus.)

Thomas à Kempis, *De Imitatione Christi*. Bk. iii, ch. 24.

1
Humility like darkness reveals the heavenly lights.
H. D. THOREAU, *Walden: Conclusion.*

2
The lowly heart doth win the love of all.
GEORGE TURBERVILLE, *To Piero: Of Pride.*

3
A fault which humbles a man is of more use to him than a good action which puffs him up.
THOMAS WILSON, *Maxims of Piety.*

4
Rather to bow than break is profitable;
Humility is a thing commendable.
UNKNOWN, *The Moral Proverbes of Cristyne,* translated from the French by Richard Woodville, Earl Rivers. (1390)

5
To kiss the rod.
UNKNOWN, *Roman de Renart.* (c. 1200) (William Caxton, tr.)

HUMMINGBIRD

6
And all it lends to the eye is this—
A sunbeam giving the air a kiss.
HARRY KEMP, *The Hummingbird.*

7
Jewelled coryphée
With quivering wings like shielding gauze outspread.
EDNAH DEAN PROCTOR, *Humming-Bird.*

8
And the humming-bird that hung
Like a jewel up among
The tilted honeysuckle horns.
JAMES WHITCOMB RILEY, *The South Wind and the Sun.*

9
A flash of harmless lightning,
A mist of rainbow dyes,
The burnished sunbeams brightening
From flower to flower he flies.
J. B. TABB, *Humming Bird.*

HUMOR

See also Jesting

10
Guess his humor ain't refined
Quite enough to suit my mind.
ELLIS PARKER BUTLER, *Jabed Meeker, Humorist.* Referring to Mark Twain.

11
Unconscious humour.
SAMUEL BUTLER THE YOUNGER, *Life and Habit.* (1877) Butler claims to have coined this phrase.

A sense of humour keen enough to show a man his own absurdities will keep him from the commission of all sins, or nearly all, save those that are worth committing.
SAMUEL BUTLER THE YOUNGER, *Life and Habit.*

12
The essence of humour is sensibility; warm tender fellow-feeling with all forms of existence.
CARLYLE, *Essays: Richter.*

True humour springs not more from the head than from the heart; it is not contempt, its essence is love; it issues not in laughter, but in still smiles, which lie far deeper. It is a sort of inverse sublimity, exalting as it were, into our affections what is below us, while sublimity draws down into our affections what is above us.
CARLYLE, *Essays: Richter.*

Humour has justly been regarded as the finest perfection of poetic genius.
CARLYLE, *Essays: Schiller.*

13
Joking and humor are pleasant, and often of extreme utility. (Suavis autem est, et vehementer sæpe utilis jocus et facetiæ.)
CICERO, *De Oratore.* Bk. ii, sec. 54.

14
No mind is thoroughly well organized that is deficient in a sense of humour.
S. T. COLERIDGE, *Table Talk.*

15
I never dare to write As funny as I can.
O. W. HOLMES, *The Height of the Ridiculous.*

16
Humor's the true democracy.
R. U. JOHNSON, *Divided Honors.*

17
Humor is the only test of gravity, and gravity of humor, for a subject which will not bear raillery is suspicious, and a jest which will not bear serious examination is false wit.
GORGIAS LEONTINUS. (ARISTOTLE, *Rhetoric.* Bk. iii, ch. 18. As quoted by Shaftesbury, *Essay on the Freedom of Wit and Humour.* Sec. 5.) *See also under* JESTING.

Humor is gravity concealed behind the jest.
JOHAN WEISS, *Wit, Humor, and Shakespeare.*

18
Reader who art too seriously disposed, depart whither you will: I wrote these verses for the man of wit. (Qui gravis es nimium, potes hinc jam, lector, abire Quo libet: urbanæ scripsimus ista togæ.)
MARTIAL, *Epigrams.* Bk. xi, epig. 16.

19
It [a sense of humor] always withers in the presence of the messianic delusion, like justice and truth in front of patriotic passion.
H. L. MENCKEN, *Prejudices.* Ser. i, p. 32

20
Everything is funny as long as it is happening to somebody else.
WILL ROGERS, *The Illiterate Digest,* p. 131.

21
What an ornament and safeguard is humour! Far better than wit for a poet and writer. It is a genius itself, and so defends from the insanities.
SIR WALTER SCOTT, *Miscellanies: Emerson.*

22
For the love of laughter, hinder not the humour of his design.
SHAKESPEARE, *All's Well that Ends Well.* Act iii, sc. 6, l. 44.

1
I love not the humour of bread and cheese, and there's the humour of it.
SHAKESPEARE, *The Merry Wives of Windsor*. Act ii, sc. 1, l. 140.

2
Humour is the mistress of tears.
THACKERAY, *Charity and Humour*.

3
Humour is odd, grotesque, and wild,
Only by affectation spoiled;
'Tis never by invention got;
Men have it when they know it not.
SWIFT, *To Mr. Delany*.

HUNGER

See also Fasting

I—Hunger: Apothegms

4
Hunger is sharper than the sword.
BEAUMONT AND FLETCHER, *The Honest Man's Fortune*. Act ii, sc. 2, l. 1.

Hunger is sharper than thorn.
THOMAS BECON, *Catechism*, 601. (c. 1560)

5
This ravening fellow has a wolf in his belly.
BEAUMONT AND FLETCHER, *Women Pleased*. Act i, sc. 2.

6
Before breakfast, a man feels but queasily,
And a sinking at the lower abdomen
Begins the day with indifferent omen.
ROBERT BROWNING, *Flight of the Duchess*. Sec. 12.

He learns the look of things, and none the less
For admonition from the hunger-pinch.
ROBERT BROWNING, *Fra Lippo Lippi*.

7
Oliver Twist has asked for more.
DICKENS, *Oliver Twist*. Ch. 2.

8
The stomach sets us to work.
GEORGE ELIOT, *Felix Holt*. Ch. 30. *See also under* BELLY.

9
There is no reason that the senseless Temples of God should abound in riches, and the living Temples of the Holy Ghost starve for hunger.
ETHELWOLD, Bishop of Winchester, when selling the gold and silver vessels of his church during a famine, c. 980. (CAMDEN, *Remains*, p. 257.)

10
A hungry man smells meat afar off.
THOMAS FULLER, *Gnomologia*. No. 224.

11
Hungry rooster don't cackle w'en he fine a wum.
JOEL CHANDLER HARRIS, *Plantation Proverbs*.

12
Hunger pierceth stone wall.
JOHN HEYWOOD, *Proverbs*. Pt. i, ch. 12. (1546)

"Hunger," they say, "breaks stone walls."
GEORGE CHAPMAN, *Eastward Hoe*. Act v, sc. 1.

Hunger, by you know whom, 'tis said,
Will break through walls to get its bread.
WILLIAM COMBE, *Doctor Syntax in Search of a Wife*. Canto xxxiv, st. 53.

13
Hunger maketh hard bones soft.
HILL, *Commonplace-Book*, p. 133. (1500)

Hunger makes hard beans sweet.
JOHN HEYWOOD, *Proverbs*. Pt. i, ch. 10. (1546)

14
Hunger is insolent, and will be fed.
HOMER, *Odyssey*. Bk. vii, l. 300. (Pope, tr.)

15
The hungry stomach rarely despises common food. (Jejunus raro stomachus vulgaria temnit.)
HORACE, *Satires*. Bk. ii, sat. 2, l. 38.

Hunger is not dainty.
THOMAS FULLER, *Gnomologia*. No. 2567.

Our stomachs
Will make what's homely savoury.
SHAKESPEARE, *Cymbeline*. Act iii, sc. 6, l. 32.

Hunger finds no fault with the cook.
C. H. SPURGEON, *John Ploughman*. Ch. 5.

16
Any of us would kill a cow rather than not have beef.
SAMUEL JOHNSON. (BOSWELL, *Life*, v, 247.)

17
Bid the hungry Greek go to heaven, he will go. (Græculus esuriens in cœlum, jusseris ibit.)
JUVENAL, *Satires*. Sat. iii, l. 78.

All arts his own, the hungry Greekling counts;
And bid him mount the skies, the skies he mounts.
JUVENAL, *Satires*, iii, 78. (Gifford, tr.)

No nice extreme a true Italian knows;
But bid him go to hell, to hell he goes.
JUVENAL, iii. Paraphrased by Thomas Phillips. in a letter to George III, with reference to the trial of the king's sister, Caroline of Denmark.

All sciences a fasting Monsieur knows,
And bid him go to hell, to hell he goes!
SAMUEL JOHNSON, *London*, l. 115.

18
Hunger forceth the wolf out of her den.
WILLIAM PAINTER, *Palace of Pleasure*, iii, 216. (1567)

Hunger, thou knowest, brings the wolf out of the wood.
LE SAGE, *Gil Blas*, iv, 245. (Smollett, tr. 1750)

19
I am more hungry than any wolf.
JOHN PALSGRAVE, *Acolastus*. Sig. L 1. (1540)

As hungry as a kite.
UNKNOWN, *Philip and Mary*, 17. (c. 1555)

I and my men were as hungry as hawks.
JOHN TAYLOR THE WATER-POET, *Christmas In and Out*. (1652)

Hungry as the grave.
THOMSON, *The Seasons: Winter*, l. 393. (1730)

I came home . . . hungry as a hunter.
CHARLES LAMB, *Letters*. Vol. i, p. 162. (1800)

1
I suspect that hunger was my mother. (Famem ego fuisse suspicor matrem mihi.)
PLAUTUS, *Stichus*, l. 155. Act i, sc. 3, l. 1.

2
Obliged by hunger and request of friends.
POPE, *Epistle to Dr. Arbuthnot*, l. 44.

3
So if unprejudiced you scan
The goings of this clock-work, man,
You find a hundred movements made
By fine devices in his head;
But 'tis the stomach's solid stroke
That tells his being what's o'clock.
MATTHEW PRIOR, *Alma*. Pt. iii, l. 272.

My stomach serves me instead of a clock.
SWIFT, *Polite Conversation*. Dial. i.

My belly began to cry cupboard.
SWIFT, *Polite Conversation*. Dial. ii.

4
Hunger and cold deliver a man up to his enemy.
JOHN RAY, *English Proverbs*, 126.

5
A hungry people listens not to reason, nor cares for justice, nor is bent by any prayers. (Nec rationem patitur, nec æquitate mitigatur nec ulla prece flectitur, populus esuriens.)
SENECA, *De Brevitate Vitæ*, i, 18.

An empty stomach is not a good political adviser.
ALBERT EINSTEIN, *Cosmic Religion*, p. 107.

A hungry man is an angry man.
JAMES HOWELL, *Proverbs*, 13. (1659)

If thou be hungry, I am angry; let us go fight.
JOHN RAY, *English Proverbs*. No. 65.

6
Oppress'd by two weak evils, age and hunger.
SHAKESPEARE, *As You Like It*. Act ii, sc. 7, l. 32.

They said they were an-hungry; sigh'd forth proverbs,
That hunger broke stone walls, that dogs must eat,
That meat was made for mouths, that the gods sent not
Corn for rich men only: with these shreds
They vented their complainings.
SHAKESPEARE, *Coriolanus*. Act i, sc. 1, l. 209.

7
Hunger that persuades to evil. (Malesuada fames.)
VERGIL, *Æneid*. Bk. vi, l. 276.

8
Because of body's hunger are we born,
And by contriving hunger are we fed;
Because of hunger is our work well done,
As so are songs well sung, and things well said.
Desire and longing are the whips of God.
ANNA WICKHAM, *Sehnsucht*.

II—Hunger: The Best Sauce

See also Appetite

9
Hunger is the best sauce in the world. (La mejor salsa del mundo es la hambre.)
CERVANTES, *Don Quixote*. Pt. ii, ch. 5.

Hunger is the best Pickle.
BENJAMIN FRANKLIN, *Poor Richard*, 1750.

Nor do you Find fault with the sauce, keen hunger being the best.
PHILIP MASSINGER, *Unnatural Combat*. Act iii, sc. 1. (1639)

10
My more-having would be a sauce
To make me hunger more.
SHAKESPEARE, *Macbeth*. Act iv, sc. 3, l. 81.

11
The best sauce for food is hunger and the best flavoring for drink thirst. (Cibi condimentum esse famen, potionis sitim.)
SOCRATES. (CICERO, *De Finibus*. Bk. ii, sec. 90.)

Socrates said, the best sauce in the world for meats is to be hungry.
ERASMUS, *Apothegms*, 2. (Udall, tr., 1542.)

12
Make hunger thy sauce as a medicine for health.
THOMAS TUSSER, *Five Hundred Points of Good Husbandry: Good Husbandry Lessons*.

III—Hunger: Famine

13
All's good in a famine.
THOMAS FULLER, *Gnomologia*.

14
They that die by famine die by inches.
MATTHEW HENRY, *Commentaries*. Psalm lix.

15
Famine ends famine.
BEN JONSON, *Explorata: Amor Nummi*.

16
Famine is in thy cheeks,
Need and oppression starveth in thine eyes,
Contempt and beggary hangs upon thy back.
SHAKESPEARE, *Romeo and Juliet*. Act v, sc. 1, l. 69.

17
Famine can smile
On him who brings it food, and pass, with guile
Of thankful falsehood, like a courtier grey,
The house-dog of the throne; but many a mile
Comes Plague, a wingèd wolf, who loathes alway
The garbage and the scum that strangers make her prey.
SHELLEY, *The Revolt of Islam*. Canto x, st. 24.

18
Our stern foe
Had made a league with Famine.
ROBERT SOUTHEY, *Joan of Arc*. Bk. ii l. 182.

HUNTING

I—Hunting: Apothegms

1
There is a passion *for hunting something* deeply implanted in the human breast.
DICKENS, *Oliver Twist*. Ch. 10.

2
Don't think to hunt two hares with one dog.
BENJAMIN FRANKLIN, *Poor Richard*, 1734.

3
He was a mighty hunter before the Lord; wherefore it is said, Even as Nimrod the mighty hunter before the Lord.
Old Testament: Genesis, x, 9.

Proud Nimrod first the bloody chase began,
A mighty hunter, and his prey was man.
POPE, *Windsor Forest*, l. 61.

4
What he hit is history,
What he missed is mystery.
THOMAS HOOD, *Impromptu*. In reference to a guest's shooting stories.

5
It is folly to take unwilling dogs out to hunt. (Stultitia est venatum ducere invitos canes.)
PLAUTUS, *Stichus*. Act i, sc. 2, l. 83.

6
Huntsman, rest! thy chase is done.
SCOTT, *The Lady of the Lake*. Canto i, st. 32.

Back limped with slow and crippled pace,
The sulky leaders of the chase.
SCOTT, *The Lady of the Lake*. Canto i, st. 10.

7
Hold, Warwick, seek thee out some other
chase,
For I myself must hunt this deer to death.
SHAKESPEARE, *II Henry VI*. Act v, sc. 2, l. 14.

A buck of the first head.
SHAKESPEARE, *Love's Labour's Lost*. Act iv, sc. 2, l. 10.

8
Like a dog, he hunts in dreams.
TENNYSON, *Locksley Hall*, l. 79.

9
Oh, Sir Thomas Lucy,
Your venison's juicy.
Juicy is your venison;
Hence I apply my benison.
UNKNOWN. Old bit of doggerel, sometimes humorously attributed to Shakespeare, referring to Sir Thomas Lucy, who prosecuted Shakespeare for poaching.

II—Hunting: Its Pleasures

10
The mellow autumn came, and with it came
The promised party, to enjoy its sweets.
The corn is cut, the manor full of game;
The pointer ranges, and the sportsman
beats
In russet jacket;—lynx-like is his aim;
Full grows his bag, and wonder*ful* his feats.
Ah, nut-brown partridges! Ah, brilliant pheas-
ants!
And ah, ye poachers!—'Tis no sport for peas-
ants.
BYRON, *Don Juan*. Canto xiii, st. 75.

11
By perilous paths in coomb and dell,
The heather, the rocks, and the river-bed,
The pace grew hot, for the scent lay well,
And a runnable stag goes right ahead,
The quarry went right ahead—
Ahead, ahead, and fast and far;
His antlered crest, his cloven hoof,
Brow, bay and tray and three aloof,
The stag, the runnable stag.
JOHN DAVIDSON, *A Runnable Stag*.

A stag of warrant, a stag, a stag,
A runnable stag, a kingly crop,
Brow, bay and tray the three on top,
A stag, a runnable stag.
JOHN DAVIDSON, *A Runnable Stag*.

12
The dusky night rides down the sky
And ushers in the morn:
The hounds all join in glorious cry,
The huntsman winds his horn;
And a-hunting we will go.
HENRY FIELDING, *A-Hunting We Will Go*.

13
Soon as Aurora drives away the night,
And edges eastern clouds with rosy light,
The healthy huntsman, with the cheerful
horn,
Summons the dogs, and greets the dappled
Morn.
JOHN GAY, *Rural Sports*. Canto ii, l. 93.

14
Yet if once we efface the joys of the chase
From the land, and outroot the Stud,
Good-bye to the Anglo-Saxon race,
Farewell to the Norman blood!
A. L. GORDON, *Ye Wearie Wayfarer*. Fytte 7.

15
Hunting I reckon very good
To brace the nerves, and stir the blood: . . .
Hygeia's sons with hound and horn,
And jovial cry awake the Morn.
MATTHEW GREEN, *The Spleen*, l. 67.

16
Oh, who will stay indoor, indoor,
When the horn is on the hill?
With the crisp air stinging, and the huntsmen
singing,
And a ten-tined buck to kill!
RICHARD HOVEY, *King Arthur: Hunting-Song*.

17
A wild bear chase didst never see?
Then thou hast lived in vain.
Thy richest bump of glorious glee
Lies desert in thy brain.
ABRAHAM LINCOLN, *The Bear Hunt*. (1844)

18
With a hey, ho, chevy!
Hark forward, hark forward, tantivy!
This day a stag must die!
JOHN O'KEEFFE, *Czar Peter: Song*. Act i, sc. 4.

1
Good and much company, and a good dinner; most of their discourse was about hunting, in a dialect I understand very little.
SAMUEL PEPYS, *Diary,* 22 Nov., 1663.

2
The chase I follow far,
'Tis mimicry of noble war.
SCOTT, *The Lady of the Lake.* Canto ii, st. 26.

3
The horn, the horn, the lusty horn
Is not a thing to laugh to scorn.
SHAKESPEARE, *As You Like It.* Act iv, sc. 2, l. 18.

4
Theseus: We will, fair queen, up to the mountain's top
And mark the musical confusion
Of hounds and echo in conjunction.
Hippolyta: I was with Hercules and Cadmus once,
When in a wood of Crete they bay'd the bear
With hounds of Sparta: never did I hear . . .
So musical a discord, such sweet thunder.
SHAKESPEARE, *A Midsummer-Night's Dream.* Act iv, sc. 1, l. 113.

5
Rose-cheeked Adonis hied him to the chase;
Hunting he loved, but love he laughed to scorn.
SHAKESPEARE, *Venus and Adonis,* l. 3.

6
My hoarse-sounding horn
Invites thee to the chase, the sport of kings,
Image of war, without its guilt.
WILLIAM SOMERVILLE, *The Chase.* Bk. i.

7
Come out, 'tis now September,
The hunter's moon's begun,
And through the wheaten stubble
Is heard the frequent gun.
UNKNOWN, *All Among the Barley.*

8
D'ye ken John Peel with his coat so gay?
D'ye ken John Peel at the break of the day?
D'ye ken John Peel when he's far, far away,
With his hounds and his horn in the morning?
UNKNOWN, *John Peel.* Old hunting song.

III—Hunting: Its Cruelty and Stupidity

9
Assassins find accomplices. Man's merit
Has found him three, the hawk, the hound, the ferret.
WILFRID SCAWEN BLUNT, *Assassins.*

10
For what were all these country patriots born?
To hunt, and vote, and raise the price of corn?
BYRON, *The Age of Bronze.* St. 14.

He thought at heart like courtly Chesterfield,
Who, after a long chase o'er hills, dales, bushes,
And what not, though he rode beyond all price,
Ask'd next day, "If men ever hunted *twice?*"
BYRON, *Don Juan.* Canto xiv, st. 35.

11
And though the fox he follows may be tam'd,
A mere fox-follower never is reclaim'd.
COWPER, *Conversation,* l. 409.

Detested sport,
That owes its pleasures to another's pain.
COWPER, *The Task.* Bk. iii, l. 326.

12
Hunting has now an idea of quality joined to it and is become the most important business in the life of a gentleman. Anciently it was quite otherways. M. Fleury has severely remarked that this extravagant passion for hunting is a strong proof of our Gothic extraction, and shows an affinity of humour with the savage Americans.
DRYDEN, *Preface to the Pastorals of Vergil.* Sometimes attributed to William Walsh.

13
The woods are made for the hunters of dreams,
The brooks for the fishers of song;
To the hunters who hunt for the gunless game
The streams and the woods belong.
SAM WALTER FOSS, *Bloodless Sportsmen.*

14
Wild animals never kill for sport. Man is the only one to whom the torture and death of his fellow creatures is amusing in itself.
J. A. FROUDE, *Oceana: Passengers' Amusements.*

15
Of horn and morn, and hark and bark,
And echo's answering sounds,
All poets' wit hath ever writ
In dog-rel verse of hounds.
THOMAS HOOD, *The Epping Hunt,* l. 37.

Where folks that ride a bit of blood
May break a bit of bone.
THOMAS HOOD, *The Epping Hunt,* l. 99.

The field kept getting more select;
Each thicket served to thin it.
THOMAS HOOD, *The Epping Hunt,* l. 303.

16
Soe that courageous Hart doth fight
With Fate, and calleth up his might,
And standeth stout that he maye fall
Bravelye, and be avenged of all,
Nor like a Craven yeeld his Breath
Under the Jawes of Dogges and Death!
THOMAS HOOD, *The Fall of the Deer.*

17
It is very strange, and very melancholy, that the paucity of human pleasures should persuade us ever to call hunting one of them.
SAMUEL JOHNSON, *Miscellanies.* Vol. i, p. 288.

Hunting was the labour of the savages of North America, but the amusement of the gentlemen of England.
SAMUEL JOHNSON. (KEARSLEY, *Johnsoniana,* 606.)

1
He did not know that a keeper is only a poacher turned inside out and a poacher a keeper turned outside in.

CHARLES KINGSLEY, *The Water Babies*. Ch. 1.

2
To the which place a poor sequester'd stag,
That from the hunter's aim had ta'en a hurt,
Did come to languish, and indeed, my lord,
The wretched animal heaved forth such groans,
That their discharge did stretch his leathern coat
Almost to bursting, and the big round tears
Coursed one another down his innocent nose
In piteous chase.

SHAKESPEARE, *As You Like It*. Act ii, sc. 1, l. 33.

I was a stricken deer that left the herd
Long since: with many an arrow deep infix'd
My panting side was charg'd, when I withdrew
To seek a tranquil death in distant shades.

COWPER, *The Task*. Bk. iii, l. 108.

A herd-abandoned deer, struck by the hunter's dart.

SHELLEY, *Adonais*. St. 33.

Fainting, breathless toil,
Sick seizes on his heart: he stands at bay, . . .
The big round tears run down his dappled face;
He groans in anguish.

THOMSON, *The Seasons: Autumn*, l. 451.

3
Everybody can see that the people who hunt are the right people, and the people who don't are the wrong ones.

BERNARD SHAW, *Heartbreak House*. Act iii.

4
When a man wants to murder a tiger he calls it sport: when the tiger wants to murder him he calls it ferocity.

BERNARD SHAW, *Maxims for Revolutionists*.

5
Hunting their sport, and plundering was their trade;
In arms they ploughed, to battle still prepared:
Their soil was barren and their hearts were hard.

VERGIL, *Æneid*. Bk. vii, *ad fin*. (Dryden, tr.)

HURRY: See Haste

HUSBAND

See also Marriage, Wife

6
Being a husband is a whole-time job. That is why so many husbands fail. They cannot give their entire attention to it.

ARNOLD BENNETT, *The Title*.

7
And yet thou art the nobler of us two:
What dare I dream of that thou canst not do?

ROBERT BROWNING, *Any Wife to Any Husband*.

8
So bent on self-sanctifying,
That she never thought of trying
To save her poor husband as well.

ROBERT BUCHANAN, *Fra Giacomo*.

9
Ah, gentle dames! it gars me greet,
To think how monie counsels sweet,
How monie lengthened, sage advices,
The husband frae the wife despises!

ROBERT BURNS, *Tam o' Shanter*.

10
A good husband makes a good wife.

ROBERT BURTON, *Anatomy of Melancholy*. Pt. iii, sec. iii, mem. 3, subs. 1.

As the husband is, the wife is.

TENNYSON, *Locksley Hall*, l. 47.

11
But—Oh! ye lords of ladies intellectual,
Inform us truly, have they not hen-peck'd you all?

BYRON, *Don Juan*. Canto i, st. 22.

12
And then this best and weakest woman bore
With such serenity her husband's woes,
Just as the Spartan ladies did of yore,
Who saw their spouses kill'd, and nobly chose
Never to say a word about them more.

BYRON, *Don Juan*. Canto i, st. 29.

Wedded she was some years, and to a man
Of fifty, and such husbands are in plenty;
And yet, I think, instead of such a ONE,
'Twere better to have TWO of five-and-twenty, . . .
Ladies, even of the most uneasy virtue,
Prefer a spouse whose age is short of thirty.

BYRON, *Don Juan*. Canto i, st. 62.

13
Until the hours of absence should run through,
And truant husband should return, and say,
"My dear, I was the first who came away."

BYRON, *Don Juan*. Canto i, st. 141.

14
Emperors are only husbands in wives' eyes.

BYRON, *Don Juan*. Canto v, st. 115.

15
We wedded men live in sorrow and care.

CHAUCER, *Marchantes Tale: Prologue*, l. 17.

16
Husbands, love your wives, and be not bitter against them.

New Testament: Colossians, iii, 19.

17
She's been thinking of the old 'un.

DICKENS, *David Copperfield*. Ch. 3.

18
The calmest husbands make the stormiest wives.

ISAAC D'ISRAELI, *Curiosities of Literature*. Ser. ii, pt. i, p. 423. Quoting a proverb.

19
Feed the brute.

GEORGE DU MAURIER, in *Punch*, vol. lxxxix, p. 206. (1886) His famous prescription for keeping a husband's love.

1
There's no form of prayer in the liturgy against bad husbands.
FARQUHAR, *Beaux' Stratagem*. Act ii, sc. 1, l. 3.

3
She commandeth her husband, in any equal matter, by constant obeying him.
THOMAS FULLER, *Holy and Profane State: The Good Wife.*

4
A wife is to thank God her husband hath faults. . . . A husband without faults is a dangerous observer.
LORD HALIFAX, *Works*, p. 12.

5
Husbands are in heaven whose wives scold not.
JOHN HEYWOOD, *Proverbs*. Pt. ii, ch. 7.

6
I should like to see any kind of a man, distinguishable from a gorilla, that some good and even pretty woman could not shape a husband out of.
O. W. HOLMES, *The Professor at the Breakfast-Table*. Ch. 7.

7
Already, with unblushing face. Lalage seeks for a husband. (Jam proterva Fronte petet Lalage maritum.)
HORACE, *Odes*. Bk. ii, ode 5, l. 15.

8
The husband is the last to know the dishonor of his house. (Dedecus ille domus sciet ultimus.)
JUVENAL, *Satires*. Sat. x, l. 342.

9
Father to me thou art, and mother dear,
And brother too, kind husband of my heart.
JOHN KEBLE, *The Christian Year: Monday before Easter.*

Think you I am no stronger than my sex,
Being so father'd and so husbanded?
SHAKESPEARE, *Julius Cæsar*. Act ii, sc. 1, l. 296.

There is only one real tragedy in a woman's life. The fact that her past is always her lover, and her future invariably her husband.
OSCAR WILDE, *An Ideal Husband*. Act iii.

11
If you want a man's money, you should be willing to put up with his company.
JOHN COLE MCKIM, *Husbands and Wives.*

12
God is thy law, thou mine.
MILTON, *Paradise Lost*. Bk. iv, l. 637.

And to thy husband's will
Thine shall submit; he over thee shall rule.
MILTON, *Paradise Lost*. Bk. x, l. 195.

With thee goes
Thy husband, him to follow thou art bound;
Where he abides, think there thy native soil.
MILTON, *Paradise Lost*. Bk. xi, l. 290.

Her husband the relater she preferr'd
Before the angel, and of him to ask
Chose rather: he, she knew would intermix
Grateful digressions, and solve high dispute
With conjugal caresses, from his lip
Not words alone pleas'd her.
MILTON, *Paradise Lost*. Bk. viii, l. 52.

A woman never forgets her sex. She would rather talk with a man than an angel, any day.
O. W. HOLMES, *The Poet at the Breakfast-Table*. Ch. 4.

13
Serve your husband as your master, and beware of him as a traitor. (Sers ton mari comme ton maître, Et t'en garde comme d'un traître.)
MONTAIGNE, *Essays*. Bk. iii, ch. 5. Quoted.

14
Married men are viler than bachelors.
A. W. PINERO, *Preserving Mr. Panmure*. Act ii.

15
Well, if our author in the Wife offends,
He has a Husband that will make amends:
He draws him gentle, tender, and forgiving,
And sure such kind good creatures may be living.
POPE, *Epilogue to Jane Shore*, l. 25.

No worse a husband than the best of men.
SHAKESPEARE, *Antony and Cleopatra*, ii, 2, 131.

16
Men, more divine, the masters of all these,
Lords of the wide world and wild watery seas,
Indued with intellectual sense and souls,
Of more pre-eminence than fish and fowls,
Are masters to their females, and their lords.
SHAKESPEARE, *The Comedy of Errors*, ii, 1, 20.

I will attend my husband, be his nurse,
Diet his sickness, for it is my office.
SHAKESPEARE, *The Comedy of Errors*, v, 1, 98.

That lord whose hand must take my plight shall carry
Half my love with him, half my care and duty.
SHAKESPEARE, *King Lear*. Act i, sc. 1, l. 103.

17
If I should marry him, I should marry twenty husbands.
SHAKESPEARE, *The Merchant of Venice*. Act i, sc. 2, l. 67.

18
What a taking was he in when your husband asked who was in the basket!
SHAKESPEARE, *The Merry Wives of Windsor*. Act iii, sc. 3, l. 192.

Your husband is in his old lunes again.
SHAKESPEARE, *The Merry Wives of Windsor*. Act iv, sc. 2, l. 21.

19
Benedick the married man.
SHAKESPEARE, *Much Ado About Nothing*. Act i, sc. 1, l. 270.

20
Hero: My heart is exceeding heavy.
Margaret: 'Twill be heavier soon by the weight of a man.
Hero: Fie upon thee! art not ashamed?
Margaret: Of what, lady? of speaking hon-

ourably? . . . Is there any harm in "the heavier for a husband"?

SHAKESPEARE, *Much Ado About Nothing*. Act iii, sc. 4, l. 26.

1
Thy husband is thy lord, thy life, thy keeper,
Thy head, thy sovereign; one that cares for thee,
And for thy maintenance commits his body
To painful labour both by sea and land,
To watch the night in storms, the day in cold,
Whilst thou liest warm at home, secure and safe;
And craves no other tribute at thy hands
But love, fair looks and true obedience;
Too little payment for so great a debt.
Such duty as the subject owes the prince
Even such a woman oweth to her husband; . . .
I am ashamed that women are so simple
To offer war where they should kneel for peace,
Or seek for rule, supremacy and sway,
When they are bound to serve, love, and obey.

SHAKESPEARE, *Taming of the Shrew*, v, 2, 146.

2
I am thine husband—not a smaller soul,
Nor Lancelot, nor another.

TENNYSON, *Guinevere*, l. 563.

3
The husband who desires to surprise is often very much surprised himself. (Mari qui veut surprendre est souvent fort surpris.)

VOLTAIRE, *La Femme Qui a Raison*. Act ii, sc. 2.

If he [the husband] takes a chance and returns home suddenly, he is the master, but it is imprudent and in bad taste, for he exposes himself to unhappy surprises.

(Si, par mégarde, Il se hazarde,
À rentrer chez lui tout à coup,
Il est le maître, Mais c'est peut-être
Imprudent et de mauvais goût;
Car il s'expose À . . . triste chose!)

HENRY MEILHAC AND LUDOVIC HALÉVY, *La Belle Hélène*. Act ii.

3a
Husband! thou Dull unpitied miscreant,
Wedded to Noise, to Misery, and Want;
Sold an eternal Vassal for thy life,
Oblig'd to Cherish and to Heat a Wife:
Repeat thy loath'd embraces every Night,
Prompted to Act by Duty, not delight. . . .
The wretch is marry'd, and has known the worst,
And now his Blessing is, he can't be Curst.

UNKNOWN, *Against Marriage*. (c. 1690)

HYACINTH

4
If of thy mortal goods thou art bereft,
And from thy slender store two loaves alone to thee are left,
Sell one, and with the dole
Buy hyacinths to feed thy soul.

SADI, *Gulistan: Garden of Roses*.

If thou of fortune be bereft
And in thy store there be but left
Two loaves—sell one, and with the dole
Buy hyacinths to feed thy soul.

JAMES TERRY WHITE, *Not by Bread Alone: After Hippocrates*. (*Century Magazine*, Aug., 1907.)

If thou hast a loaf of bread, sell half and buy the flowers of the narcissus; for bread nourisheth the body, but the narcissus the soul.

MOHAMMED. (OSWALD CRAWFURD, *Round the Calendar in Portugal*, p. 114.)

Hearts starve as well as bodies: give us Bread, but give us Roses!

JAMES OPPENHEIM, *Bread and Roses*.

5
The hyacinth's for constancy wi' its unchanging blue.

BURNS, *The Posie*. St. 3.

6
Come, evening gale! the crimsonne rose
Is drooping for thy sighe of dewe;
The hyacinthe wooes thy kisse to close
In slumberre sweete its eye of blue.

GEORGE CROLY, *Inscription for a Grotto*.

7
Here hyacinths of heavenly blue
Shook their rich tresses to the morn.

JAMES MONTGOMERY, *The Adventure of a Star*.

8
And the hyacinth purple, and white, and blue,
Which flung from its bells a sweet peal anew
Of music so delicate, soft, and intense,
It was felt like an odour within the sense.

SHELLEY, *The Sensitive Plant*. Pt. i, l. 25.

HYPOCRISY

See also Appearance, Cunning, Deceit

I—Hypocrisy: Definitions

9
Your cold hypocrisy's a stale device,
A worn-out trick; would'st thou be thought in earnest,
Clothe thy feign'd zeal in rage, in fire, in fury!

ADDISON, *Cato*. Act i, sc. 3.

10
The veil
Spun from the cobweb fashion of the times,
To hide the feeling heart.

MARK AKENSIDE, *Pleasures of Imagination*. Bk. ii, l. 147.

11
Of all villainy, there is none more base than that of the hypocrite, who, at the moment he is most false, takes care to appear most virtuous.

CICERO, *De Officiis*. Bk. i, ch. 13, sec. 41.

12
A hypocrite is in himself both the archer and the mark, in all actions shooting at his own praise or profit.

THOMAS FULLER, *The Holy and Profane States: The Hypocrite*.

13
The only vice that cannot be forgiven is

hypocrisy. The repentance of a hypocrite is itself hypocrisy.

WILLIAM HAZLITT, *Characteristics*. No. 256.

There is some virtue in almost every vice, except hypocrisy; and even that, while it is a mockery of virtue, is at the same time a compliment to it.

WILLIAM HAZLITT, *Characteristics*. No. 274.

A hypocrite despises those whom he deceives, but has no respect for himself. He would make a dupe of himself, too, if he could.

WILLIAM HAZLITT, *Characteristics*. No. 398.

1
He never used his arms against the stream, nor uttered the unfettered thoughts of his mind, nor devoted his life to the cause of truth.

JUVENAL, *Satires*. Sat. iv, l. 89.

2
When a man puts on a Character he is a stranger to, there's as much difference between what he appears, and what he really is, as there is between a Vizor and a Face.

LA BRUYÈRE, *Les Caractères*. Ch. 11.

One is never so ridiculous for the qualities he has as for those he pretends to have. (On n'est jamais si ridicule par les qualités que l'on a que par celles que l'on affecte d'avoir.)

LA ROCHEFOUCAULD, *Maximes*. No. 134.

3
Hypocrisy is a homage which vice pays to virtue. (L'hypocrisie est un hommage que le vice rend à la vertu.

LA ROCHEFOUCAULD, *Maximes*. No. 218.

4
Affectation is an awkward and forced imitation of what should be genuine and easy, wanting the beauty that accompanies what is natural.

LOCKE, *On Education*. Sec. 66.

5
Thou hypocrite, first cast out the beam out of thine own eye; and then shalt thou see clearly to cast out the mote out of thy brother's eye.

New Testament: Matthew, vii, 5.

Woe unto you, scribes and Pharisees, hypocrites! for ye make clean the outside of the cup and of the platter, but within they are full of extortion and excess.

New Testament: Matthew, xxiii, 25.

6
For neither man nor angel can discern
Hypocrisy, the only evil that walks
Invisible, except to God alone.

MILTON, *Paradise Lost*. Bk. iii, l. 682.

7
Those who daub both sides of the wall. (Qui utrosque parietes linunt.)

PETRONIUS, *Satyricon*. Sec. 39. The equivalent of being on both sides of the fence.

8
Your tongues are steeped in honey and milk, your hearts in gall and biting vinegar.

PLAUTUS, *Truculentus*. Act i, sc. 2.

9
I want that glib and oily art
To speak and purpose not.

SHAKESPEARE, *King Lear*. Act i, sc. 1, l. 227.

To beguile the time,
Look like the time; . . . look like the innocent flower,
But be the serpent under 't.

SHAKESPEARE, *Macbeth*. Act i, sc. 5, l. 63.

Away, and mock the time with fairest show;
False face must hide what the false heart doth know.

SHAKESPEARE, *Macbeth*. Act i, sc. 7, l. 81.

10
I am a woman of the world, Hector, and I can assure you that if you will only take the trouble always to say the perfectly correct thing, you can do just what you like.

BERNARD SHAW, *Heartbreak House*. Act i.

11
Face-flatterer and back-biter are the same.
And they, sweet soul, that most impute a crime
Are pronest to it.

TENNYSON, *Merlin and Vivien*, l. 822.

12
How inexpressible is the meanness of being a hypocrite! how horrible is it to be a mischievous and malignant hypocrite.

VOLTAIRE, *A Philosophical Dictionary: Philosopher*. Sec. i.

13
I hope you have not been leading a double life, pretending to be wicked, and being really good all the time. That would be hypocrisy.

OSCAR WILDE, *The Importance of Being Earnest*. Act ii.

II—Hypocrisy: Apothegms

15
There be many wise men that have secret hearts, and transparent countenances.

FRANCIS BACON, *Essays: Of Cunning*.

16
A sheep without, a wolf within.

BUTLER, *Hudibras*. Pt. i, canto iii, l. 1232.

17
Oh, for a *forty-parson power* to chant
Thy praise, Hypocrisy!

BYRON, *Don Juan*. Canto x, st. 34.

Be hypocritical, be cautious, be
Not what you *seem* but always what you *see*.

BYRON, *Don Juan*. Canto xi, st. 86.

18
Till Cant cease, nothing else can begin.

CARLYLE, *The French Revolution*. Pt. ii, bk. iii, ch. 7.

It is now almost my sole rule of life to clear myself of cants and formulas, as of poisonous Nessus shirts.

CARLYLE, *Letter to His Wife*, 2 Nov., 1835.

My dear friend, clear your *mind* of cant. You may *talk* as other people do, . . . but don't *think* foolishly.

SAMUEL JOHNSON. (BOSWELL, *Life*, 15 May, 1783.)

Sworn foe of Cant, he smote it down
With trenchant wit unsparing,
And, mocking, rent with ruthless hand
The robe Pretence was wearing.

J. G. WHITTIER, *Randolph of Roanoke.*

Great King of Cant!

AMBROSE BIERCE, *An Impostor.* Referring to Andrew Carnegie.

1
How cheerfully he seems to grin,
How neatly spreads his claws,
And welcomes little fishes in
With gently smiling jaws!

LEWIS CARROLL, *Alice in Wonderland.* Ch. 2.

2
Musical as the chime of tinkling rills,
Weak to perform, though mighty to pretend.

COWPER, *The Progress of Error,* l. 14.

3
Mr. Podsnap settled that whatever he put behind him he put out of existence. . . . Mr. Podsnap had even acquired a peculiar flourish of his right arm in often clearing the world of its most difficult problems, by sweeping them behind him.

DICKENS, *Our Mutual Friend.* Bk. i, ch. 11. Hence "Podsnappery."

4
She looketh as butter would not melt in her mouth.

JOHN HEYWOOD, *Proverbs.* Pt. i, ch. 10. (1546); SWIFT, *Polite Conversation.* Dial. i.

5
No man is a hypocrite in his pleasures.

SAMUEL JOHNSON. (BOSWELL, *Life,* 1783.)

6
Who could endure the Gracchi railing at sedition? (Quis tulerit Gracchos de seditione querentes?)

JUVENAL, *Satires.* Sat. ii, l. 24. That is: Who could listen to a man denouncing things which he does shamelessly himself?

7
It is more difficult to disguise feelings which one has than to feign those which one has not. (Il est plus difficile de dissimuler les sentiments que l'on a que de feindre ceux que l'on n'a pas.)

LA ROCHEFOUCAULD, *Maximes Supprimées.* No. 559.

8
He passed by on the other side.

New Testament: Luke, x, 31.

9
Ye blind guides, which strain at a gnat, and swallow a camel.

New Testament: Matthew, xxiii, 24. The correct reading, used in the revised version is "strain out a gnat," the allusion being to straining wine lest insects should be inadvertently swallowed.

10
I hate a bad man saying what is good. (Μισῶ πονηρόν, χρηστὸν ὅταν εἴπῃ λόγον.)

MENANDER, *Fragments.* No. 767.

11
Act as if I did not know it. (Faites comme si je ne le savois pas.)

MOLIÈRE, *Le Bourgeois Gentilhomme.* Act ii, sc. 4, l. 19. The teacher of philosophy has remarked that of course M. Jourdain knows Latin, and the latter answers, "Of course; but explain it just as if I didn't."

12
Who point, like finger-posts, the way
They never go.

THOMAS MOORE, *Song: For the Poco-Curante Society.*

13
He is an extremely hypocritical man; a Greek of the lower empire.

NAPOLEON BONAPARTE, referring to Alexander I of Russia. (O'MEARA, *Napoleon in Exile,* 5 Dec., 1816.)

He has the smartness of an attorney's clerk, and the intrigues of a Greek of the lower empire.

BENJAMIN DISRAELI, referring to Lord Palmerston. (*Runnymede Letters,* 1836.)

14
The foolish, fashionable air
Of knowing all and feeling nought.

COVENTRY PATMORE, *The Angel in the House: Sahara.* Pt. iv.

15
There Affectation, with a sickly mien,
Shows in her cheek the roses of eighteen.

POPE, *The Rape of the Lock.* Canto iv, l. 31.

16
He knows how much of what men paint themselves
Would blister in the light of what they are.

EDWIN ARLINGTON ROBINSON, *Ben Jonson Entertains a Man from Stratford.*

17
There are people who laugh to show their fine teeth; and there are those who cry to show their good hearts.

JOSEPH ROUX, *Meditations of a Parish Priest.* Pt. ix, No. 51.

18
At home he is a savage; abroad a saint. (Intra domum sævus est; foris mitis.)

SENECA, *De Ira.* Bk. iii, sec. 10.

A saint abroad, and a devil at home.

JOHN BUNYAN, *The Pilgrim's Progress.* Pt. i.

See also WOMEN: SAINTS ABROAD.

19
Why, I can smile, and murder whiles I smile,
And cry "Content" to that which grieves my heart;
And wet my cheeks with artificial tears,
And frame my face to all occasions.

SHAKESPEARE, *III Henry VI.* Act iii, sc. 2, l. 182. *See also* SMILE: DECEITFUL SMILES.

'Tis too much prov'd—that with devotion's visage
And pious action, we do sugar o'er
The devil himself.

SHAKESPEARE, *Hamlet.* Act iii, sc. 1, l. 46.

1
Now step I forth to whip hypocrisy.
SHAKESPEARE, *Love's Labour's Lost*. Act iv, sc. 3, l. 151.

III—Hypocrisy: The Whited Sepulchre

2
An ill man is always ill, but he is worst of all when he pretends to be a saint. (Malus ubi bonum se simulat, tunc est pessimus.)
FRANCIS BACON, *Ornamenta Rationalia*. No. 28.

3
God knows, I'm no the thing I should be,
Nor am I even the thing I could be,
But twenty times I rather would be
An atheist clean,
Than under gospel colours hid be
Just for a screen.
BURNS, *Epistle to the Rev. John M'Math.*

4
There's nothing so absurd, or vain,
Or barbarous, or inhumane,
But if it lay the least pretence
To piety and godliness,
Or tender-hearted conscience,
And zeal for gospel-truths profess
Does sacred instantly commence.
SAMUEL BUTLER, *On a Hypocritical Nonconformist*. Pt. i, l. 1.

5
He blam'd and protested, but join'd in the plan;
He shar'd in the plunder, but pitied the man.
COWPER, *Pity for Poor Africans*, l. 43.

6
Built God a church, and laugh'd his word to scorn.
COWPER, *Retirement*, l. 688.

The cross on the breast and the devil in the heart.
THOMAS FULLER, *Gnomologia*. No. 4462.

Not he who scorns the Saviour's yoke
Should wear his cross upon the heart.
SCHILLER, *The Fight with the Dragon*. St. 24.

They set the sign of the cross over their outer doors, and sacrifice to their gut and their groin in their inner closets.
BEN JONSON, *Explorata: Impostura.*

He hailed the power of Jesus' name
An' soaked 'em twelve per cent.
DOUGLAS MALLOCH, *Behind a Spire.*

7
You, too, take cobweb attitudes
Upon a plane of gauze!
EMILY DICKINSON, *Poems*. Pt. i, No. 125.

8
Thus 'tis with all: their chief and constant care
Is to seem everything but what they are.
GOLDSMITH, *Epilogue to "The Sister,"* l. 25.

9
A man may cry Church! Church! at ev'ry word,
With no more piety than other people—
A daw's not reckoned a religious bird
Because it keeps a-cawing from a steeple.
THOMAS HOOD, *Ode to Rae Wilson*, l. 171.

That little simile exactly paints
How sinners are despis'd by saints.
By saints!—the Hypocrites that ope heav'n's door
Obsequious to the sinful man of riches—
But put the wicked, naked, barelegg'd poor
In parish stocks instead of breeches.
THOMAS HOOD, *Ode to Rae Wilson*, l. 347.

10
Inwardly base, but with an outward appearance of virtue. (Introrsum turpem, speciosum pelle decora.)
HORACE, *Epistles*. Bk. i, epis. 16, l. 45.

11
Who pretend to be men of the austere pattern of Curius, and who live the life of Bacchanals. (Qui Curios simulant, et Bacchanalia vivunt.)
JUVENAL, *Satires*. Sat. ii, l. 3.

Far worse are those who denounce evil ways in the language of a Hercules; and after discoursing upon virtue, prepare to practise vice. (Sed peiores, qui talia verbis Herculis invadunt et de virtute locuti Clunem agitant.)
JUVENAL, *Satires*. Sat. ii, l. 19.

For vice deceives, under the appearance of virtue, when sad in mien and austere in countenance and dress. (Fallit enim vitium, specie virtutis et umbra, Cum sit triste habitu vultuque et veste severum.)
JUVENAL, *Satires*. Sat. xiv, l. 109.

12
Some hypocrites and seeming mortified men, that held down their heads, were like the little images that they place in the very bowing of the vaults of churches, that look as if they held up the church, but are but puppets.
WILLIAM LAUD, Archbishop of Canterbury. (FRANCIS BACON, *Apothegms*. No. 273.)

13
Woe unto you, scribes and Pharisees, hypocrites! for ye are like unto whited sepulchres, which indeed appear beautiful outward, but are within full of dead men's bones, and of all uncleanness.
New Testament: Matthew, xxiii, 27.

After the most straitest sect of our religion I lived a Pharisee.
New Testament: Acts, xxvi, 5.

Publicans and sinners on the one side; Scribes and Pharisees on the other.
WILLIAM CHILLINGWORTH, *Sermon.*

Our academical Pharisees.
MACAULAY, *Critical Essays: Milton.*

14
I, under fair pretence of friendly ends,
And well-plac'd words of glozing courtesy
Baited with reasons not unplausible,
Wind me into the easy-hearted man,
And hug him into snares.
MILTON, *Comus*, l. 160.

The first
That practis'd falsehood under saintly show,
Deep malice to conceal, couch'd with revenge.
MILTON, *Paradise Lost*. Bk. iv, l. 121.

1
With pious fraud. (Pia mendacia fraude.)
OVID, *Metamorphoses*. Bk. ix, l. 711.

Madam, 'twas a pious fraud, if it were one.
APHRA BEHN, *Lucky Chance*. Act v, sc. 7.

When pious frauds and holy shifts
Are dispensations and gifts.
BUTLER, *Hudibras*. Pt. i, canto iii, l. 1145.

It is with a pious fraud as with a bad action; it begets a calamitous necessity of going on.
THOMAS PAINE, *Age of Reason*. Pt. i.

The outworn rite, the old abuse,
The pious fraud transparent grown.
J. G. WHITTIER, *The Reformer*.

2
The hypocrite had left his mask, and stood
In naked ugliness. He was a man
Who stole the livery of the court of heaven
To serve the devil in; in virtue's guise,
Devoured the widow's house and orphan's bread;
In holy phrase, transacted villanies
That common sinners durst not meddle with.
ROBERT POLLOK, *The Course of Time*. Bk. viii, l. 615.

3
With one hand he put
A penny in the urn of poverty,
And with the other took a shilling out.
ROBERT POLLOK, *The Course of Time*. Bk. viii, l. 632.

If you cannot make a speech,
Because you are a flat,
Go very quietly and drop
A button in the hat!
O. W. HOLMES, *The Music-Grinders*.

4
Constant at Church and 'Change; his gains were sure;
His givings rare, save farthings to the poor.
POPE, *Moral Essays*. Epis. iii, l. 347.

5
Apparel vice like virtue's harbinger;
Bear a fair presence, though your heart be tainted;
Teach sin the carriage of a holy saint.
SHAKESPEARE, *The Comedy of Errors*. Act iii, sc. 2, l. 12.

With an auspicious and a dropping eye,
With mirth in funeral, and with dirge in marriage,
In equal scale weighing delight and dole.
SHAKESPEARE, *Hamlet*. Act i, sc. 2, l. 11.

6
Thou simular man of virtue
That art incestuous.
SHAKESPEARE, *King Lear*. Act iii, sc. 2, l. 54.

Thou rascal beadle, hold thy bloody hand!
Why dost thou lash that whore? Strip thine own back;
Thou hotly lust'st to use her in that kind
For which thou whipp'st her.
SHAKESPEARE, *King Lear*. Act iv, sc. 6, l. 164.

Behold yond simpering dame, . . .
That minces virtue, and does shake the head
To hear of pleasure's name;
The fitchew, nor the soiled horse, goes to 't
With a more riotous appetite.
SHAKESPEARE, *King Lear*. Act iv, sc. 6, l. 120.

7
O, 'tis the cunning livery of hell,
The damned'st body to invest and cover
In phrenzie guards!
SHAKESPEARE, *Measure for Measure*. Act iii, sc. 1, l. 95.

O, what may man within him hide,
Though angel on the outward side!
SHAKESPEARE, *Measure for Measure*. Act iii, sc. 2, l. 285.

8
The devil can cite Scripture for his purpose.
An evil soul, producing holy witness,
Is like a villain with a smiling cheek,
A goodly apple rotten at the heart:
O, what a goodly outside falsehood hath!
SHAKESPEARE, *The Merchant of Venice*. Act i, sc. 3, l. 99.

But then I sigh; and, with a piece of Scripture,
Tell them that God bids us do good for evil:
And thus I clothe my naked villainy
With old odd ends, stolen out of holy writ;
And seem a saint, when most I play the devil.
SHAKESPEARE, *Richard III*. Act i, sc. 3, l. 334.

9
He is no less than a stuffed man.
SHAKESPEARE, *Much Ado About Nothing*. Act i, sc. 1, l. 58.

10
O, what authority and show of truth
Can cunning sin cover itself withal!
SHAKESPEARE, *Much Ado About Nothing*. Act iv, sc. 1, l. 36.

When devils will the blackest sins put on,
They do suggest at first with heavenly shows.
SHAKESPEARE, *Othello*. Act ii, sc. 3, l. 357.

11
So smooth he daub'd his vice with show of virtue, . . .
He liv'd from all attainder of suspect.
SHAKESPEARE, *Richard III*. Act iii, sc. 5, l. 29.
See also VICE AND VIRTUE.

12
Knaves are men
That lute and flute fantastic tenderness,
And dress the victim to the offering up,
And paint the gates of Hell with Paradise,
And play the slave to gain the tyranny.
TENNYSON, *The Princess*. Pt. iv, l. 113.

13
A man I knew who liv'd upon a smile,
And well it fed him; he look'd plump and fair,
While rankest venom foam'd thro every vein.
Living, he fawn'd on every fool alive;
And, dying, curs'd the friend on whom he liv'd.
YOUNG, *Night Thoughts*. Night viii, l. 336.

I

ICE

1
In things that are tender and unpleasing, it is good to break the ice, by some whose words are of less weight, and to reserve the more weighty voice, to come in, as by chance.
FRANCIS BACON, *Essays: Of Cunning.*

When I had but broke the ice of my affection, she fell over head and ears in love with me.
JAMES SHIRLEY, *Love Tricks.* Act iii, sc. 1.

To break the ice in making the first overture.
ALEMAN, *Guzman,* i, 173.

"If he would have the goodness to break the—in point of fact, the ice," said Cousin Feenix.
DICKENS, *Dombey and Son.* Ch. 61.

2
Yet all how beautiful! Pillars of pearl
Propping the cliffs above, stalactites bright
From the ice roof depending; and beneath,
Grottoes and temples with their crystal spires
And gleaming columns radiant in the sun.
WILLIAM HENRY BURLEIGH, *Winter.*

3
Motionless torrents! silent cataracts!
S. T. COLERIDGE, *Hymn Before Sunrise in the Vale of Chamouni.*

4
And ice, mast-high, came floating by
As green as emerald.
S. T. COLERIDGE, *The Ancient Mariner.* Pt. i.

5
In skating over thin ice our safety is in our speed.
EMERSON, *Essays, First Series: Prudence.*

6
Some say the world will end in fire,
Some say in ice.
From what I've tasted of desire,
I hold with those who favor fire.
But if it had to perish twice,
I think I know enough of hate
To say that for destruction ice
Is also great
And would suffice.
ROBERT FROST, *Fire and Ice.*

7
When it cracks, it bears; when it bends, it breaks.
UNKNOWN. An old proverb, referring to ice.

8
Trust not one night's ice.
GEORGE HERBERT, *Jacula Prudentum.*

9
What a sea Of melting ice I walk on!
MASSINGER, *Maid of Honour.* Act iii, sc. 3.

10
O'er the ice the rapid skater flies,
With sport above and death below,
Where mischief lurks in gay disguise
Thus lightly touch and quickly go.
(Sur un mince cristal l'hiver conduit leurs pas,
Telle est de nos plaisirs la legère surface,
Glissez, mortels; n'appuyez pas!)
PIERRE CHARLES ROY, *Lines,* beneath a print of a picture by Lancret. (Samuel Johnson, tr.)

Three children sliding on the ice,
Upon a summer's day,
As it fell out, they all fell in,
The rest they ran away.
UNKNOWN, *The Lamentation of a Bad Market.* (1653)

IDEA

See also Mind, Thought

11
If the ancients left us ideas, to our credit be it spoken that we moderns are building houses for them.
A. B. ALCOTT, *Table Talk: Enterprise.*

12
One of the greatest pains to human nature is the pain of a new idea.
WALTER BAGEHOT, *Physics and Politics,* p. 163.

13
Only the wise possess ideas; the greater part of mankind are possessed by them.
S. T. COLERIDGE, *Miscellanies,* p. 154.

14
The moment of finding a fellow-creature is often as full of mingled doubt and exultation as the moment of finding an idea.
GEORGE ELIOT, *Daniel Deronda.* Ch. 17.

15
God screens us evermore from premature ideas.
EMERSON, *Essays, First Series: Spiritual Laws.*

16
The party of virility rules the hour, the party of ideas and sentiments rules the age.
EMERSON, *Journal,* 1864.

17
Ideas must work through the brains and the arms of good and brave men, or they are no better than dreams.
EMERSON, *Miscellanies: American Civilization.*

It is a lesson which all history teaches wise men to put trust in ideas, and not in circumstances.
EMERSON, *Miscellanies: War.*

18
Olympian bards who sung
Divine ideas below,
Which always find us young
And always keep us so.
EMERSON, *Ode to Beauty.*

19
When we are exalted by ideas, we do not owe this to Plato. but to the idea, to which also Plato was debtor.
EMERSON, *Representative Men: Uses of Great Men.*

1
Almost everyone knows this, but it has not occurred to everyone. (Sciunt plerique omnes, sed non omnibus hoc venit in mentem.)
ERASMUS, *Epicureus.*

2
A favourite theory is a possession for life.
WILLIAM HAZLITT, *Characteristics.* No. 117.

3
Ideas are, in truth, forces. Infinite, too, is the power of personality. A union of the two always makes history.
HENRY JAMES, *Charles W. Eliot,* i, 235

4
An idea, to be suggestive, must come to the individual with the force of a revelation.
WILLIAM JAMES, *Varieties of Religious Experience,* p. 113.

5
He who receives an idea from me, receives instruction himself without lessening mine; as he who lights his taper at mine receives light without darkening me.
THOMAS JEFFERSON, *Writings.* Vol. xiii, p. 334.

6
That fellow seems to possess but one idea, and that is a wrong one.
SAMUEL JOHNSON. (BOSWELL, *Life,* 1770.)

Mr. Kremlin himself was distinguished for ignorance, for he had only one idea, and that was wrong.
BENJAMIN DISRAELI, *Sybil.* Bk. iv, ch. 5.

7
To die for an idea: it is unquestionably noble. But how much nobler it would be if men died for ideas that were true!
H. L. MENCKEN, *Prejudices.* Ser. v, p. 283.

8
General notions are generally wrong.
MARY WORTLEY MONTAGU, *Letter to Wortley Montagu,* 28 March, 1710.

General and abstract ideas are the source of the greatest errors of mankind. (Les idées générales et abstraites sont la source des plus grandes erreurs des hommes.
ROUSSEAU, *Émile.* Bk. iv.

9
There is no squabbling so violent as that between people who accepted an idea yesterday and those who will accept the same idea tomorrow.
CHRISTOPHER MORLEY, *Religio Journalistici.*

10
For an idea ever to be fashionable is ominous, since it must afterwards be always old-fashioned.
GEORGE SANTAYANA, *Words of Doctrine,* 55.

11
This creature man, who in his own selfish affairs is a coward to the backbone, will fight for an idea like a hero.
BERNARD SHAW, *Man and Superman.* Act iii.

12
Early ideas are not usually true ideas.
HERBERT SPENCER, *Principles of Biology.* Pt. iii, ch. 2, sec. 110.

13
It's bad form to think, feel, or have an idea.
ALFRED SUTRO, *The Walls of Jericho.* Act i.

14
A nice man is a man of nasty ideas.
SWIFT, *Thoughts on Various Subjects.*

15
Ten thousand great ideas filled his mind;
But with the clouds they fled, and left no trace behind.
THOMSON, *Castle of Indolence.* Canto i, st. 59.

16
He had ideas about everything. He could no more help having ideas about everything than a dog can resist smelling at your heels.
H. G. WELLS, *Mr. Britling Sees It Through.* Bk. i, sec. 2.

17
Through thy idea, lo, the immortal reality!
Through thy reality, lo, the immortal idea!
WALT WHITMAN, *Thou Mother With Thy Equal Brood.* Sec. 2.

18
Ideas are free. But when the author confines them to his study, they are like birds in a cage, which none but he can have a right to let fly.
SIR JOSEPH YATES, *Judgment,* Miller v. Taylor. (*4 Burr.* Pt. iv, p. 2379.)

IDEALS

19
Our ideals are our better selves.
A. B. ALCOTT, *Table Talk: Habits.*

20
Still bent to make some port he knows not where,
Still standing for some false impossible shore.
MATTHEW ARNOLD, *A Summer Night,* l. 68.

21
Egeria! sweet creation of some heart
Which found no mortal resting-place so fair
As thine ideal breast!
BYRON, *Childe Harold.* Canto iv, st. 115.

22
Ah! would but one might lay his lance in rest,
And charge in earnest—were it but a mill.
AUSTIN DOBSON, *Don Quixote.*

23
An idealist is a person who helps other people to be prosperous.
HENRY FORD, on the witness stand at Mt. Clemens, Mich., in his libel suit against the *Chicago Tribune,* July, 1919.

24
Ideals are the world's masters.
J. G. HOLLAND, *Gold-Foil: The Ideal Christ.*

25
Every man has at times in his mind the ideal of what he should be, but is not. . . . Man never falls so low that he can see nothing higher than himself.
THEODORE PARKER, *A Lesson for the Day.*

1
The ideal should never touch the real. (Der Schein soll nie die Wirklichkeit erreichen.)
SCHILLER. *To Goethe,* when the latter produced Voltaire's *Mahomet.*

2
We have two lives about us,
Two worlds in which we dwell,
Within us and without us,
Alternate Heaven and Hell:—
Without, the somber Real,
Within, our heart of hearts,
The beautiful Ideal.
R. H. STODDARD, *The Castle in the Air.*

3
To nurse a blind ideal like a girl.
TENNYSON, *The Princess.* Pt. iii, l. 201.

IDLENESS

I—Idleness: Definitions

4
Idleness is emptiness; the tree in which the sap is stagnant, remains fruitless.
HOSEA BALLOU, *MS. Sermons.*

5
Idleness, which is the well-spring and root of all vice.
THOMAS BECON, *Early Works,* p. 444. (1566)

Men must not be poor; idleness is the root of all evil; the world's wide enough, let 'em bustle.
FARQUHAR, *The Beaux' Stratagem.* Act i, sc. 1.

Idleness is the root of all mischief.
UNKNOWN, *Servingman's Comfort.* (HAZLITT, *Inedited Tracts,* 158.)

6
Idleness is the canker of the mind.
JOHN BODENHAM, *Belvedere,* p. 131.

Idleness makes the wit rust.
THOMAS FULLER, *Gnomologia.* No. 3061.

Indolence is the sleep of the mind. (L'indolence est le sommeil des esprits.)
VAUVENARGUES, *Réflexions.* No. 392.

7
Idleness is an appendix to nobility.
ROBERT BURTON, *Anatomy of Melancholy.* Pt. i, sec. ii, mem. 2, subs. 6.

8
Idleness is only the refuge of weak minds, and the holiday of fools.
LORD CHESTERFIELD, *Letters,* 20 July, 1749.

I look upon indolence as a sort of suicide; for the man is effectually destroyed, though the appetites of the brute may survive.
LORD CHESTERFIELD, *Letters,* 26 Feb., 1754.

9
An idler is a watch that wants both hands;
As useless if it goes as when it stands.
COWPER, *Retirement,* l. 681.

10
He is idle that might be better employed.
THOMAS FULLER, *Gnomologia.* No. 1919.

That man is idle who can do something better.
EMERSON.

11
Idleness is the sepulchre of a living man.
J. G. HOLLAND, *Gold-Foil: Indolence.*

12
Idleness is ever the root of indecision. (Variam semper dant otia mentem.)
LUCAN, *De Bello Civili.* Bk. iv, l. 704.

13
Mother of vices, called idleness.
JOHN LYDGATE, *The Fall of Princes.* Bk. ii, l. 2249. (c. 1440)

Sluggish idleness, the nurse of sin.
SPENSER, *Faerie Queene.* Bk. i, canto iv, st. 18.

Idleness the parent of all vice.
WILLIAM WAGER, *The Longer Thou Livest.*

14
In lazy apathy let Stoics boast
Their virtue fix'd: 'tis fix'd as in a frost;
Contracted all, retiring to the breast;
But strength of mind is Exercise, not Rest.
POPE, *Essay on Man.* Epis. ii, l. 101.

15
Nothing is so certain as that the evils of idleness can be shaken off by hard work. (Nihilque tam certum est quam otii vitia negotio discuti.)
SENECA, *Epistulæ ad Lucilium.* Epis. lvi, sec. 9.

16
That ghostliest of all unrealities, the non-working man.
BERNARD SHAW, *The Irrational Knot.* Ch. 17.

17
Idleness is the greatest prodigality in the world; it throws away that which is invaluable in respect of its present use, and irreparable when it is past, being to be recovered by no power of art or nature.
JEREMY TAYLOR, *Holy Living and Dying.* Ch. i, sec. 1.

II—Idleness: Apothegms

18
Be not solitary, be not idle.
ROBERT BURTON, *Anatomy of Melancholy,* his closing prescription for health of body and mind.

If you are idle, be not solitary; if you are solitary, be not idle.
JOHNSON. (BOSWELL, *Life,* 1779.)

19
Idlers, game-preservers and mere human clothes-horses.
CARLYLE, *Latter-Day Pamphlets.* No. 3.

20
As idle as a painted ship
Upon a painted ocean.
S. T. COLERIDGE, *The Ancient Mariner.* Pt. ii.

21
Says little, thinks less, and does—nothing at all, faith!
FARQUHAR, *The Beaux' Stratagem.* Act i, sc. 1.

22
I live an idle burden to the ground.
HOMER, *Iliad.* Bk. xviii, l. 134. (Pope, tr.)

23
Masterly inactivity. (Strenua inertia.)
HORACE, *Epistles.* Bk. i, epis. 11, l. 28. The

English phrase is by Sir James Mackintosh, *Vindiciæ Gallicæ*.

Disciplined inaction.
SIR JAMES MACKINTOSH, *Causes of the Revolution of 1688*. Ch. 7.

The frivolous work of polished idleness.
SIR JAMES MACKINTOSH, *Dissertation on Ethical Philosophy: Remarks on Thomas Brown.*

1
Perhaps man is the only being that can properly be called idle.
SAMUEL JOHNSON, *The Idler*. No. 1.

To do nothing is in every man's power.
SAMUEL JOHNSON, *The Rambler*. No. 155.

2
Of all our faults, that which we excuse the most easily is idleness. (De tous nos défauts, celui dont nous demeurons le plus aisément d'accord, c'est de la paresse.)
LA ROCHEFOUCAULD, *Maximes*. No. 398.

We have more idleness of mind than of body. (Nous avons plus de paresse dans l'esprit que dans le corps.)
LA ROCHEFOUCAULD, *Maximes*. No. 487.

3
As good to be an addled egg as an idle bird.
JOHN LYLY, *Euphues*, p. 207.

4
Why stand ye here all the day idle?
New Testament: Matthew, xx, 6.

5
Fight off your indolence, banish your sloth. (Abige abs te lassitudinem, cave pigritiæ præverteris.)
PLAUTUS, *Mercator*, l. 113. (Act ii, sc. 2.)

6
The unyok'd humour of your idleness.
SHAKESPEARE, *I Henry IV*. Act i, sc. 2, l. 219.

When on my three-foot stool I sit.
SHAKESPEARE, *Cymbeline*. Act iii, sc. 3, l. 89.

7
Their only labour was to kill the time;
And labour dire it is, and weary woe.
THOMSON, *Castle of Indolence*. Canto i, st. 72.

8
I trow he was infect certeyn
With the faitour, or the fever lordeyn.
UNKNOWN. (HAZLITT, *Early English Poetry*, i, 93. c. 1500) Fever lurden: laziness.

You have the palsy or eke the fever lurden.
WILLIAM FULWOOD, *Enemies of Idleness*, 132.

Sick of the idles.
JOHN RAY, *English Proverbs*, 182.

III—Idleness: Busy Idleness

9
It is better to do nothing, than to be doing of nothing. (Otiosum esse quam nihil agere.)
ATILIUS. (PLINY, *Epistles*. Bk. i, epis. 9.)

10
Wretched estate of men by fortune blest,
That being ever idle never rest.
GEORGE CHAPMAN, *The Tears of Peace*, l. 341.

11
Admirals, extoll'd for standing still,
Or doing nothing with a deal of skill.
COWPER, *Table Talk*, l. 192.

12
I have spent my life laboriously doing nothing. (Vitam perdidi laboricose agendo.)
GROTIUS. Quoted by him on his death-bed.

My life is lost in laboriously doing nothing. (Vitam perdidi operse nihil agendo.)
JOSIAH WOODWARD, *Fair Warnings to a Careless World*, p. 97.

13
They'll do little
That shall offend you, for their chief desire
Is to do nothing at all, sir.
MASSINGER, *A Very Woman*. Act ii, sc. 1.

14
A nation rushing hastily to and fro, busily employed in idleness. (Trepide concursans, occupata in otio.)
PHÆDRUS, *Fables*. Bk. v, fab. 2.

Thus idly busy rolls their world away.
GOLDSMITH, *The Traveller*, l. 256.

She went from opera, park, assembly, play,
To morning walks, and prayers three times a day;
To part her time 'twixt reading and bohea,
To muse, and spill her solitary tea,
Or o'er cold coffee trifle with the spoon,
Count the slow clock, and dine exact at noon.
POPE, *Epistle to Mrs. Teresa Blount*, l. 13.

15
They do nothing laboriously. (Operose nihil agunt.)
SENECA, *De Brevitate Vitæ*. Bk. i, sec. 13.

16
Idle folk have the least leisure.
C. H. SPURGEON, *John Ploughman*. Ch. 1.

17
In the diligence of his idleness.
Apocrypha: The Wisdom of Solomon, xiii, 13. (Diligenter per vacuitatem suam.—*Vulgate*.)

18
Worldlings revelling in the fields
Of strenuous idleness.
WORDSWORTH, *This Lawn, a Carpet All Alive.*

IV—Idleness: Sloth

19
Sloth is the tempter that beguiles, and expels from paradise.
A. B. ALCOTT, *Table Talk: Pursuits*.

20
The foul sluggard's comfort: "It will last my time."
THOMAS CARLYLE, *Count Cagliostro: Flight Last.*

21
Ever sick of the slothful guise,
Loath to bed and loath to rise.
JOHN CLARKE, *Paræmiologia*, 292. (1639)

'Tis the voice of the sluggard, I heard him complain,
"You have waked me too soon, I must slumber again".

As the door on its hinges, so he on his bed,
Turns his sides, and his shoulders, and his heavy
head.
ISAAC WATTS, *The Sluggard.*

1
Sloth, like rust, consumes faster than labor wears.
BENJAMIN FRANKLIN, *Poor Richard.* (1744)

All things are easy to industry, all things difficult to sloth.
BENJAMIN FRANKLIN, *Poor Richard.* (1734)

2
Sloth brings in all woe.
GOWER, *Confessio Amantis.* Bk. iv, l. 424.

3
Sloth must breed a scab.
JOHN HEYWOOD, *Proverbs.* Pt. i, ch. 3. (1546)

Sloth turns the edge of wit.
JOHN LYLY, *Euphues,* p. 126. (1579)

Sloth is a foe unto all virtuous deeds.
ANTHONY MUNDAY, *Sloth.*

Hog in sloth.
SHAKESPEARE, *King Lear.* Act iii, sc. 4, l. 95.

4
That shameful Siren, sloth, is ever to be avoided. (Vitanda est improba Siren Desidia.)
HORACE, *Satires.* Bk. ii, sat. 3, l. 14.

5
Go to the ant, thou sluggard; consider her ways, and be wise.
Old Testament: Proverbs, vi, 6.

6
The slothful man saith, There is a lion in the way.
Old Testament: Proverbs, xxvi, 13.

The sluggard is wiser in his own conceit than seven men that can render a reason.
Old Testament: Proverbs, xxvi, 16.

We excuse our sloth under the pretext of difficulty. (Difficultas patrocinia prætextimus segnitiæ.)
QUINTILIAN, *De Institutione Oratoria.* Bk. i, ch. 12.

7
No one has become immortal by sloth. (Ignavia nemo immortalis factus.)
SALLUST, *Jugurtha.* Ch. lxxxv, sec. 49.

For sluggard's brow the laurel never grows;
Renown is not the child of indolent repose.
JAMES THOMSON, *The Castle of Indolence.* Canto ii, st. 50.

See also under BOLDNESS.

8
Many faint with toil,
That few may know the cares and woe of
sloth.
SHELLEY, *Queen Mab.* Canto iii, l. 116.

9
But when dread Sloth, the Mother of Doom,
steals in,
And reigns where Labour's glory was to
serve,
Then is the day of crumbling not far off.
WILLIAM WATSON, *The Mother of Doom.*

10
Sloth is the devil's pillow.
UNKNOWN, *Politeuphuia,* 306. (1669)

V—Idleness and Satan

11
Find some work for your hands to do, so that Satan may never find you idle. (Facito aliquid operis, ut semper te diabolus inveniat occupatum.)
ST. JEROME, *Letters.* No. 125. (MIGNE, *Patrologiæ Cursus.* Vol. xxii, p. 939.)

12
An idle person tempts the devil to tempt him.
RICHARD KINGSTON, *Apoph. Curiosa,* 57. (1709)

13
An idle brain is the devil's shop.
JOHN RAY, *English Proverbs,* p. 161.

14
Eschew the idle life,
Flee, flee from doing nought:
For never was there idle brain
But bred an idle thought.
GEORGE TURBERVILLE, *The Lover to Cupid for Mercy,* l. 109.

15
In works of labour or of skill
I would be busy too;
For Satan finds some mischief still
For idle hands to do.
ISAAC WATTS, *Against Idleness.*

VI—Idleness: Its Pleasures

16
With ecstacies so sweet
As none can even guess,
Who walk not with the feet
Of joy in idleness.
ROBERT BRIDGES, *Spring.* Ode i, st. 10.

17
You should do nothing that did not absolutely *please* you. Be idle, be very idle! The habits of your mind are such that you will necessarily do much; but be as idle as you can.
S. T. COLERIDGE, *Letter to Southey,* 1799.

18
How various his employments whom the
world
Calls idle; and who justly, in return,
Esteems that busy world an idler too!
COWPER, *The Task.* Bk. iii, l. 352.

19
God loves an idle rainbow,
No less than labouring seas.
RALPH HODGSON, *A Wood Song.*

20
It is impossible to enjoy idling thoroughly unless one has plenty of work to do.
JEROME K. JEROME, *Idle Thoughts of an Idle Fellow: On Being Idle.*

21
Every man is, or hopes to be, an Idler.
SAMUEL JOHNSON, *The Idler.* No. 1.

As peace is the end of war, so to be idle is the ultimate purpose of the busy.
SAMUEL JOHNSON, *The Idler.* No. 1.

We would all be idle if we could.
SAMUEL JOHNSON. (BOSWELL, *Life*, iii, 13.)

1
I am sure that indolence—indefeasible indolence—is the true state of man, and business the invention of the old Teazer.
CHARLES LAMB, *Letter to Wordsworth*, 28 Sept., 1805.

2
I have ever loved to repose myself, whether sitting or lying, with my heels as high or higher than my seat.
MONTAIGNE, *Essays*. Bk. iii, ch. 13.

3
That indolent but delightful condition of doing nothing. (Illud iners quidem, jucundum tamen nihil agere.)
PLINY THE YOUNGER, *Epistles*. Bk. viii, epis. 9.

4
But see, while idly I stood looking on,
I found the effect of love in idleness.
SHAKESPEARE, *The Taming of the Shrew*. Act i, sc. 1, l. 155.

5
There is one piece of advice, in a life of study, which I think no one will object to; and that is, every now and then to be completely idle,—to do nothing at all.
SYDNEY SMITH, *Sketches of Moral Philosophy*. Lecture 19.

6
Extreme *busyness*, whether at school or college, kirk or market, is a symptom of deficient vitality; and a faculty for idleness implies a catholic appetite and a strong sense of personal identity.
R. L. STEVENSON, *An Apology for Idlers*.

7
The more characteristic American hero in the earlier day, and the more beloved type at all times, was not the hustler but the whittler.
MARK SULLIVAN, *Our Times*. Vol. iii, p. 297.

8
The sweetness of being idle. (Inertiæ dulcedo.)
TACITUS, *Agricola*. Sec. 3. The origin, perhaps, of the pseudo-Italian phrase, "Dolce far niente."

9
Other men have acquired fame by industry, but this man by indolence. (Utque alios industria, ita hunc ignavia ad famam protulerat.)
TACITUS, *Annals*. Bk. xvi, sec. 18. Referring to Caius Petronius.

So that what was indolence was called wisdom. (Ut quod segnitia erat, sapienta vocaretur.)
TACITUS, *History*. Bk. i, sec. 49.

10
Life does not agree with philosophy: there is no happiness without idleness, and only the useless is pleasurable.
TCHEKHOV, *Note-Books*.

11
It is well to lie fallow for a while.
M. F. TUPPER, *Proverbial Philosophy: Of Recreation*.

12
I am happiest when I am idle. I could live for months without performing any kind of labour, and at the expiration of that time I should feel fresh and vigorous enough to go right on in the same way for numerous more months.
ARTEMUS WARD, *Natural History*. Ch. 3.

13
I loafe and invite my soul,
I lean and loafe at my ease observing a spear of summer grass.
WALT WHITMAN, *Song of Myself*. Sec. 1.

14
The lazy man gets round the sun
As quickly as the busy one.
R. T. WOMBAT, *Quatrains*.

VII—Idleness: Its Penalties

15
He slept beneath the moon,
He basked beneath the sun;
He lived a life of going-to-do,
And died with nothing done.
JAMES ALBERY, *Epitaph Written for Himself*.

16
Expect poison from the standing water.
WILLIAM BLAKE, *Proverbs of Hell*.

17
There is no greater cause of melancholy than idleness; "no better cure than business," as Rhasis holds.
ROBERT BURTON, *Anatomy of Melancholy: Democritus to the Reader*.

Idleness overthrows all.
ROBERT BURTON, *Anatomy of Melancholy*. Pt. iii, sec. ii, mem. 2, subs. 1.

18
Perpetual repose is unendurable. (Quietem sempiternam possit pati.)
CICERO, *De Finibus*. Bk. v, ch. 20, sec. 55.

A life of ease a difficult pursuit.
COWPER, *Retirement*, l. 634.

The sad fatigue of idleness.
MATTHEW GREEN, *The Spleen*, l. 601.

The insupportable labour of doing nothing.
RICHARD STEELE, *Spectator*. No. 54.

The tedium of fastidious idleness.
WORDSWORTH, *The Excursion*. Bk. v, l. 430.
See also under HOLIDAY.

19
All Nature seems at work. Slugs leave their lair—
The bees are stirring—birds are on the wing— . . .
And I the while, the sole unbusy thing,
Nor honey make, nor pair, nor build, nor sing.
S. T. COLERIDGE, *Work Without Hope*. St. 1.

20
A lazy man is necessarily a bad man; an

idle is necessarily a demoralized population
J. W DRAPER, *Thoughts on Future Civil Policy.*

1
The idle mind knows not what 'tis it wants. (Otioso in otio animus nescit quid velit.)
QUINTUS ENNIUS, *Iphigenia: Chorus.* (AULUS GELLIUS, *Noctes Atticæ.* Bk. xix, ch. 10, sec. 12.)

2
Idleness and pride tax with a heavier hand than kings and parliaments.
BENJAMIN FRANKLIN, *Letter on the Stamp Act,* 11 July, 1765.

Trouble springs from idleness, and grievous toil from needless ease.
BENJAMIN FRANKLIN, *Poor Richard,* 1758.

3
Pastime, like wine, is poison in the morning.
THOMAS FULLER, *The Holy State.* Bk. ii, ch. 13.

4
Woe to the idol shepherd that leaveth the flock!
Old Testament: Zechariah, xi, 17.

Alas! what boots it with incessant care
To tend the homely, slighted shepherd's trade,
And strictly meditate the thankless Muse?
Were it not better done, as others use,
To sport with Amaryllis in the shade,
Or with the tangles of Neæra's hair?
JOHN MILTON, *Lycidas,* l. 64.

5
Both gods and men are angry with a man who lives in idleness, for in nature he is like the stingless drones who waste the labor of the bees, eating without working.
HESIOD, *Works and Days,* l. 303.

Not, like a cloistered drone, to read and doze,
In undeserving, undeserved repose.
GEORGE LYTTELTON, *To the Rev. Dr. Ayscough.*

A glorious lazy drone, grown fat with feeding
On others' toil.
PHILIP MASSINGER, *The Great Duke of Florence.* Act i, sc. 2.

6
What heart can think, or tongue express,
The harm that groweth of idleness?
JOHN HEYWOOD, *Idleness.*

7
To do nothing is the way to be nothing.
NATHIEL HOWE, *A Chapter of Proverbs.*

8
To be idle and to be poor have always been reproaches, and therefore every man endeavours with his utmost care to hide his poverty from others, and his idleness from himself.
SAMUEL JOHNSON, *The Idler.* No. 17.

Time, with all its celerity, moves slowly to him whose whole employment is to watch its flight.
SAMUEL JOHNSON, *The Idler.* No. 21.

Money and time are the heaviest burdens of life, and . . . the unhappiest of all mortals are those who have more of either than they know how to use.
SAMUEL JOHNSON, *The Idler.* No. 30.

Gloomy calm of idle vacancy.
SAMUEL JOHNSON. (BOSWELL, *Life,* 8 Dec., 1763.)

9
The Camel's hump is an ugly lump
Which well you may see at the Zoo;
But uglier yet is the hump we get
From having too little to do.
RUDYARD KIPLING, *Just-So Stories: The Camel's Hump.*

Kiddies and grown ups too-oo-oo,
If we haven't enough to do-oo-oo,
We get the hump,
Cameelious hump,
The hump that is black and blue!
RUDYARD KIPLING, *Just-So Stories: The Camel's Hump.*

10
Drowsiness shall clothe a man with rags.
Old Testament: Proverbs, xxiii, 21.

Laziness travels so slowly that poverty soon overtakes him.
BENJAMIN FRANKLIN, *Way to Wealth.* Pt. i.

Idleness is the mother of poverty.
UNKNOWN, *Rich Cabinet,* p. 73. (1616)

11
Of other tyrants short the strife,
But Indolence is King for life.
HANNAH MORE, *Florio.* Pt. i.

12
Idleness wastes the sluggish body, as water is corrupted unless it moves. (Cernis ut ignavum corrumpant otia corpus, Ut capiant vitium, ni moveantur, aquæ.)
OVID, *Epistulæ ex Ponto.* Bk. i, epis. 5, l. 5.

13
Thee, too, my Paridel! she mark'd thee there,
Stretch'd on the rack of a too easy chair,
And heard thy everlasting yawn confess
The pains and penalties of Idleness.
POPE, *The Dunciad.* Bk. iv, l. 341.

14
A man who has no office to go to—I don't care who he is—is a trial of which you can have no conception.
BERNARD SHAW, *The Irrational Knot.* Ch. 18.

15
Indolent ability hardly ever raises itself out of narrow fortunes. (Pigra extulit arctis Haud umquam sese virtus.)
SILIUS, *Punica.* Bk. xiii, l. 733.

16
How dull it is to pause, to make an end,
To rust unburnish'd, not to shine in use,—
As tho' to breathe were life!
TENNYSON, *Ulysses,* l. 22.

17
There is no remedy for time misspent;
No healing for the waste of idleness,
Whose very languor is a punishment
Heavier than active souls can feel or guess.
AUBREY DE VERE, *A Song of Faith.*

18
But how can he expect that others should
Build for him, sow for him, and at his call

Love him, who for himself will take no heed
at all?
WORDSWORTH, *Resolution and Independence*. St. 6.

IDOLATRY

1
Four species of idols beset the human mind: idols of the tribe; idols of the den; idols of the market; and idols of the theatre.
FRANCIS BACON, *Novum Organum: Summary of the Second Part*. Aphorism 39.

Mankind are an incorrigible race. Give them but bugbears and idols—it is all that they ask.
WILLIAM HAZLITT, *Commonplaces*. No. 76.

2
God keeps a niche
In Heaven to hold our idols; and albeit
He brake them to our faces, and denied
That our close kisses should impair their white,
I know we shall behold them raised, complete,
The dust swept from their beauty,—glorified,
New Memnons singing in the great God-light.
E. B. BROWNING, *Sonnet: Futurity*.

3
Spurn every idol others raise: before thine own Ideal bow.
SIR RICHARD BURTON, *The Kasîdah*. Pt. ix, st. 20.

4
Her overpowering presence made you feel
It would not be idolatry to kneel.
BYRON, *Don Juan*. Canto iii, st. 74.

Her spirit is devout, and burns
With thoughts averse to bigotry;
Yet she herself, the idol, turns
Our thoughts into idolatry.
THOMAS CAMPBELL, *Verses on Our Queen*.

5
Ah, spare your idol! think him human still.
Charms he may have, but he has frailties too!
Dote not too much, nor spoil what ye admire.
COWPER, *The Task*. Bk. ii, l. 496.

6
There's a one-eyed yellow idol to the north of Khatmandu,
There's a little marble cross below the town,
There's a broken-hearted woman tends the grave of Mad Carew,
And the yellow god forever gazes down.
J. MILTON HAYES, *The Green Eye of the Yellow God*.

7
What though the spicy breezes
Blow soft o'er Ceylon's isle;
Though every prospect pleases,
And only man is vile:
In vain with lavish kindness
The gifts of God are strown;
The heathen, in his blindness,
Bows down to wood and stone.
REGINALD HEBER, *From Greenland's Icy Mountains*.

The 'eathen in 'is blindness bows down to wood an' stone;
'E don't obey no orders unless they is 'is own.
RUDYARD KIPLING, *The 'Eathen*.

Ev'n them who kept thy truth so pure of old,
When all our fathers worshipt stocks and stones.
MILTON, *On the Late Massacre in Piedmont*.

8
In that day a man shall cast his idols . . . to the moles and to the bats.
Old Testament: Isaiah, ii, 20.

9
Yet, if he would, man cannot live all to this world. If not religious, he will be superstitious. If he worship not the true God, he will have his idols.
THEODORE PARKER, *Critical and Miscellaneous Writings: A Lesson for the Day*.

10
Idolatry is in a man's own thought, not in the opinion of another.
JOHN SELDEN, *Table-Talk: Idolatry*.

11
The god of my idolatry.
SHAKESPEARE, *Romeo and Juliet*. Act ii, sc. 2, l. 114.

She is the goddess of my idolatry.
FANNY BURNEY, *Letter to Miss S. Burney*, 5 July, 1778.

Was this the idol that you worship so?
SHAKESPEARE, *The Two Gentlemen of Verona*. Act ii, sc. 4, l. 144.

12
An idiot holds his bauble for a god.
SHAKESPEARE, *Titus Andronicus*. Act v, sc. 1, l. 79.

'Tis mad idolatry
To make the service greater than the god.
SHAKESPEARE, *Troilus and Cressida*. Act ii, sc. 2, l. 56.

13
He who slays a king and he who dies for him are alike idolaters.
BERNARD SHAW, *Maxims for Revolutionists*.

14
And taking . . . a crooked piece of wood, and full of knots, hath carved it diligently, . . . and fashioned it to the image of a man; Or made it like some vile beast, laying it over with vermilion; . . . and when he had made a convenient room for it, set it in a wall. . . . Then maketh he prayer for his goods, for his wife and children, and is not ashamed to speak to that which hath no life.
Apocrypha: Wisdom of Solomon, xiii, 13–17.

IGNORANCE

See also Knowledge and Ignorance; Wisdom and Ignorance

I—Ignorance: Definitions

15
Ignorance is not innocence, but sin.
ROBERT BROWNING, *The Inn Album*. Canto v.

1
By ignorance we know not things necessary; by error we know them falsely.
ROBERT BURTON, *Anatomy of Melancholy: Democritus to the Reader.*

2
The truest characters of ignorance
Are vanity, and pride, and arrogance.
SAMUEL BUTLER, *Miscellaneous Thoughts,* l. 88.

3
Ignorance is the mother of admiration.
CHAPMAN, *The Widow's Tears.* Act ii, sc. 4.

Ignorance is the mother of impudence.
C. H. SPURGEON, *John Ploughman.* Ch. 2.

Impudence is the bastard of ignorance.
SAMUEL BUTLER, *Remains,* ii, 213. (1680)

4
Ignorance is the mother of devotion.
HENRY COLE, Dean of St. Paul's, *Disputation with the Papists at Westminster,* 31 March, 1559. (JEWEL, *Works,* Vol. iii, p. 1202.) Cole was one of the eight Romanist disputants at Westminster Abbey; BURTON, *Anatomy of Melancholy,* iii, 4, 1. (1621); JEREMY TAYLOR, *To a Person Newly Converted to the Church of England,* 1657.

Your ignorance is the mother of your devotion to me.
DRYDEN, *The Maiden Queen.* Act i, sc. 2.

5
Ignorance and superstition ever bear a close, and even a mathematical, relation to each other.
J. FENIMORE COOPER, *Jack Tier.* Ch. 13. *See also under* SUPERSTITION.

6
If there are two things not to be hidden—love and a cough—I say there is a third, and that is ignorance, when once a man is obliged to do something besides wagging his head.
GEORGE ELIOT, *Romola.*

7
Ignorance is the dominion of absurdity.
J. A. FROUDE, *Short Studies on Great Subjects: Party Politics.*

8
The recipe for perpetual ignorance is: be satisfied with your opinions and content with your knowledge.
ELBERT HUBBARD, *The Philistine.* Vol. v, p. 23.

The tragedy of ignorance is its complacency.
ROBERT QUILLEN, in syndicated editorial, 1932.

Or the dull sneer of self-loved ignorance.
SHELLEY, *Prometheus Unbound.* Act iii, sc. 4.

Ignorance and conceit go hand in hand.
The Talmud.

9
He that voluntarily continues in ignorance, is guilty of all the crimes which ignorance produces.
SAMUEL JOHNSON, *Letter to Mr. W. Drummond,* 13 Aug., 1766.

Ignorance is a voluntary misfortune.
UNKNOWN, *Politeuphuia,* 63. (1669)

10
I know no disease of the soul but ignorance: . . . a pernicious evil, the darkener of man's life, the disturber of his reason, and common confounder of truth.
BEN JONSON, *Explorata: Ignorantia Animæ.*

11
A man may live long, and die at last in ignorance of many truths which his mind was capable of knowing, and that with certainty.
JOHN LOCKE, *An Essay Concerning Human Understanding.* Bk. i, ch. 2.

But let a man know that there are things to be known, of which he is ignorant, and it is so much carved out of his domain of universal knowledge.
HORACE MANN, *Lectures on Education.* No. 6.

12
The living man who does not learn, is dark, dark, like one walking in the night.
UNKNOWN, *Ming-hsin pao-chien.* (William Milne, tr., in the *Indo-Chinese Gleaner,* Aug., 1818.)

13
The common curse of mankind—folly and ignorance.
SHAKESPEARE, *Troilus and Cressida.* Act ii, sc. 3, l. 30.

14
There is no darkness but ignorance.
SHAKESPEARE, *Twelfth Night.* Act iv, sc. 2, l. 47.

There is no slavery but ignorance.
R. G. INGERSOLL, *Liberty of Man, Woman and Child.*

15
Blind and naked Ignorance
Delivers brawling judgments, unashamed,
On all things all day long.
TENNYSON, *Merlin and Vivien,* l. 662.

16
For thus the saying goes, and I hold so:
Ignorance only is true wisdom's foe.
GEORGE WITHER, *Abuses Stript and Whipt.* Bk. ii, sat. 1. (1613)

17
I know that the multitude walk in darkness. I would put into each man's hand a lantern, to guide him; and not have him set out upon his journey depending for illumination on abortive flashes of lightning, or the coruscations of transitory meteors.
WORDSWORTH, *Letter to Matthew.*

II—Ignorance: Apothegms

18
The ignorant arise and seize heaven itself. (Surgunt indocti et cœlum repiunt.)
ST. AUGUSTINE, *Confessions.* Bk. viii, sec. 8. *See also under* BOLDNESS.

19
Whatever is unknown is magnified. (Omne ignotum pro magnifico est.)
CALGACUS, leader of the Britons, to his men before the battle of the Grampian Hills. (TACITUS, *Agricola.* Sec. 30.) *See also under* TROUBLE.

1
Ignorance never settles a question.
BENJAMIN DISRAELI, *Speech*, House of Commons, 14 May, 1866.

2
Be not ignorant of anything in a great matter or a small.
Apocrypha: Ecclesiasticus, v, 15.

3
Oh, more than Gothic ignorance!
FIELDING, *Tom Jones*. Bk. vii, ch. 3.

4
To learning and law there's no greater foe
Than they that nothing know.
ROBERT GREENE, *Works*. xii, 103. (1592)

5
The ignorant hath an eagle's wings and an owl's eyes.
GEORGE HERBERT, *Jacula Prudentum*.

6
He that knows nothing doubts nothing.
GEORGE HERBERT, *Jacula Prudentum*.

He who knows nothing is confident in everything.
C. H. SPURGEON, *John Ploughman*. Ch. 2.

7
Better unborn than untaught.
JOHN HEYWOOD, *Proverbs*. Bk. i, ch. 10. (1546)

A man without knowledge, and I have read,
May well be compared to one that is dead.
THOMAS INGELEND, *The Disobedient Child*.

Better unfed than untaught.
FRANCIS SEGAR, *School of Virtue*, 348. (1557)

A child were better to be unborn, than to be untaught.
SYMON SIMEONIS, *Lessons of Wysedome for All Maner Chyldryn*. (c. 1322)

Unborn is better than untaught.
UNKNOWN, *Reign of Philip and Mary*, 6. (1555)

8
Why, through false shame, do I prefer to be ignorant rather than to learn? (Cur nescire, pudens prave, quam discere malo?)
HORACE, *Ars Poetica*, l. 88.

9
Ignorance, madam, pure ignorance.
SAMUEL JOHNSON, in reply to the lady who asked why "pastern" was defined in his dictionary as "the knee of the horse." (BOSWELL, *Life*. 1755.)

10
Oh ye gods! what darkness of night there is in mortal minds! (Pro superi! quantum mortalia pectora cæcæ Noctis habent!)
OVID, *Metamorphoses*. Bk. vi, l. 472.

11
You know, Percy, everybody is ignorant, only on different subjects.
WILL ROGERS, *The Illiterate Digest*, p. 64.

12
Ignorance is a feeble remedy for our ills. (Iners malorum remedium ignorantia est.)
SENECA, *Œdipus*, l. 515.

13
Let me not burst in ignorance.
SHAKESPEARE, *Hamlet*. Act i, sc. 4, l. 46.

That unletter'd small-knowing soul.
SHAKESPEARE, *Love's Labour's Lost*. Act i, sc. 1, l. 253.

14
O thou monster, Ignorance, how deformed dost thou look!
SHAKESPEARE, *Love's Labour's Lost*. Act iv, sc. 2, l. 24.

15
Our lives are universally shortened by our ignorance.
HERBERT SPENCER, *Principles of Biology*. Pt. vi, ch. 12, sec. 372.

Drink to heavy Ignorance!
Hob-and-nob with brother Death!
TENNYSON, *The Vision of Sin*, l. 193.

16
As God loves me, I know not where I am! (Ita me di ament, ubi sim nescio.)
TERENCE, *Heauton Timoroumenos*, l. 308.

Nor do I know what is become
Of him, more than the Pope of Rome.
BUTLER, *Hudibras*. Pt. i, canto iii, l. 263.

17
Miraculously ignorant.
MARK TWAIN, *The Innocents at Home*. Ch. 1.

III—Ignorance: Where Ignorance is Bliss

18
Be ignorance thy choice, where knowledge
leads to woe.
JAMES BEATTIE, *The Minstrel*. Bk. ii, st. 30.

19
I honestly believe it iz better tew know nothing than tew know what ain't so.
JOSH BILLINGS, *Encyclopedia of Proverbial Philosophy*, p. 286.

20
Ignorance of better things makes man,
Who cannot much, rejoice in what he can.
COWPER, *Retirement*, l. 503.

21
Ignorance of one's misfortunes is clear gain.
EURIPIDES, *Antiope*. Frag. 204. *See also under* TROUBLE.

22
Where ignorance is bliss,
'Tis folly to be wise.
THOMAS GRAY, *Ode on a Distant Prospect of Eton College*, last lines.

23
Hys was the Blisse of Ignorance, but We, being born to bee learned, and unhappye withal, have noght but the Ignorance of Blisse.
THOMAS HOOD, *Sentimental Journey from Islington to Waterloo Bridge*.

24
It is well for men to be in ignorance of many things. (Multa viros nescire decet.)
OVID, *Ars Amatoria*. Bk. iii, l. 229.

1
If we see right, we see our woes:
Then what avails it to have eyes?
From ignorance our comfort flows.
The only wretched are the wise.
MATTHEW PRIOR, *To the Hon. Charles Montague.*

2
I had been happy, if the general camp,
Pioneers and all, had tasted her sweet body,
So I had nothing known.
SHAKESPEARE, *Othello.* Act iii, sc. 3, l. 345.

3
In knowing nothing is the sweetest life. (Ἐν τῷ φρονεῖν γὰρ μηδὲν ἥδιστος βίος.)
SOPHOCLES, *Ajax,* l. 554.

4
Stay here, fond youth, and ask no more, be wise;
Knowing too much long since lost paradise.
SIR JOHN SUCKLING, *Against Fruition.*

IV—Ignorance of Ignorance

5
To be ignorant of one's ignorance is the malady of the ignorant.
A. B. ALCOTT, *Table Talk: Discourse.*
See also KNOWLEDGE: ITS LIMITATIONS.

With Ignorance wage eternal war, to know thyself for ever strain,
Thine ignorance of thine ignorance is thy fiercest foe, thy deadliest bane;
That blunts thy sense, and dulls thy taste; that deafs thine ears, and blinds thine eyes;
Creates the thing that never was, the Thing that ever is defies.
SIR RICHARD BURTON, *The Kasîdah.* Pt. ix, st. 14.

6
I am not ashamed to confess that I am ignorant of what I do not know. (Nec me pudet fateri nescire quod nesciam.)
CICERO, *Tusculanarum Disputationum.* Bk. i, ch. 25, sec. 60.

7
We have become increasingly and painfully aware of our abysmal ignorance. No scientist, fifty years ago, could have realized that he was as ignorant as all first-rate scientists now know themselves to be.
ABRAHAM FLEXNER, *Universities,* p. 17.

8
Content, if hence th' unlearn'd their wants may view,
The learn'd reflect on what before they knew.
POPE, *Essay on Criticism.* Pt. iii, l. 180.

Indocti discant, et ament meminisse periti.
HÉNAULT, *Abrégé Chronologique.* Hénault was President of the French Academy, and his Latin verse was a very neat rendering of Pope's couplet.

ILLNESS, see Disease

ILLUSION

See also Hope: Its Illusions; Youth: Illusion and Disillusion

9
We strip illusion of her veil;
We vivisect the nightingale
To probe the secret of his note.
THOMAS BAILEY ALDRICH, *Realism.*

10
But time strips our illusions of their hue,
And one by one in turn, some grand mistake
Casts off its bright skin yearly, like a snake.
BYRON, *Don Juan.* Canto v, st. 21.

11
I drink the wine of aspiration and the drug of illusion. Thus I am never dull.
JOHN GALSWORTHY, *The White Horn Mountain.*

12
Impell'd with steps unceasing to pursue
Some fleeting good, that mocks me with the view;
That, like the circle bounding earth and skies,
Allures from far, yet, as I follow, flies.
GOLDSMITH, *The Traveller,* l. 25.

13
Death only grasps; to live is to pursue,—
Dream on! there's nothing but illusion true!
O. W. HOLMES, *The Old Player.*

Feeling is deep and still; and the word that floats on the surface
Is as the tossing buoy, that betrays where the anchor is hidden.
Therefore trust to thy heart, and to what the world calls illusions.
LONGFELLOW, *Evangeline.* Pt. ii, sec. 2, l. 112.

14
Rob the average man of his life-illusion, and you rob him also of his happiness.
HENRIK IBSEN, *The Wild Duck.* Act v.

15
Better a dish of illusion and a hearty appetite for life, than a feast of reality and indigestion therewith.
H. A. OVERSTREET, *The Enduring Quest,* p. 197.

16
Nothing can justly be called an illusion which is a permanent and universal human experience.
J. C. POWYS, *The Complex Vision,* p. 352.

17
And here we wander in illusions;
Some blessed power deliver us from hence!
SHAKESPEARE, *The Comedy of Errors,* iv, 3, 42.

18
I have, alas, only one illusion left, and that is the Archbishop of Canterbury.
SYDNEY SMITH. (LADY HOLLAND, *Memoir.* Vol. i, ch. 9, p. 231.)

19
Don't part with your illusions. When they are gone, you may still exist, but you have ceased to live.
MARK TWAIN, *Pudd'nhead Wilson's Calendar.*

IMAGINATION

See also Fancy

I—Imagination: Definitions

1
Imagination is the air of mind.
P. J. BAILEY, *Festus: Another and a Better World.*

2
Imagination, the real and eternal World of which this Vegetable Universe is but a faint shadow. What is the life of Man but Art and Science?
WILLIAM BLAKE, *Jerusalem.*

3
Imagination is not a talent of some men but is the health of every man.
EMERSON, *Letters and Social Aims: Poetry and Imagination.*

4
Imagination and memory are but one thing, which for divers considerations hath divers names.
THOMAS HOBBES, *Leviathan.* Pt. i, ch. 2.

5
Imagination is the eye of the soul. (L'imagination est l'œil de l'âme.)
JOUBERT, *Pensées.* No. 42.

Imagination is the first faculty wanting in those that do harm to their kind.
MRS. MARGARET OLIPHANT, *Innocent.*

We sin against our dearest, not because we do not love, but because we do not imagine.
IAN MACLAREN, *Afterwards.* Pt. i. Conclusion.

6
To one it is a mighty, heavenly Goddess;
To another, a cow that furnishes his butter.
(Einem ist sie die hohe, die himmlische Göttin, dem andern
Eine tüchtige Kuh, die ihn mit Butter versorgt.)
SCHILLER, *Wissenschaft.*

7
This is a gift that I have, simple, simple; a foolish extravagant spirit, full of forms, figures, shapes, objects, ideas, apprehensions, motions, revolutions: these are begot in the ventricle of memory, nourished in the womb of pia mater; and delivered upon the mellowing of occasion. But the gift is good in those in whom it is acute, and I am thankful for it.
SHAKESPEARE, *Love's Labour's Lost.* Act iv, sc. 2, l. 67.

8
The great instrument of moral good is the imagination.
SHELLEY, *The Defence of Poetry.*

9
The mightiest lever
Known to the moral world, Imagination.
WORDSWORTH, *Ecclesiastical Sonnets.* Pt. i, No. 34.

II—Imagination: Apothegms

10
Imagination droops her pinion.
BYRON, *Don Juan.* Canto iv, st. 3.

11
He wants imagination, that's what he wants.
DICKENS, *Barnaby Rudge.* Ch. 10.

12
Imagination is more important than knowledge.
ALBERT EINSTEIN, *On Science.*

Imagination is a poor substitute for experience.
HAVELOCK ELLIS, *The New Spirit,* p. 179.

13
He who has imagination without learning has wings and no feet. (Celui qui a de l'imagination sans érudition a des ailes et n'a pas des pieds.)
JOUBERT, *Pensées.* No. 53.

His imagination resembled the wings of an ostrich. It enabled him to run, though not to soar.
MACAULAY, *Essays: John Dryden.*

Has your imagination the gout, that it limps so?
EDMOND ROSTAND, *Cyrano de Bergerac.* Act iii, sc. 6.

14
"I am imaginative," quoth he, "idle was I never."
WILLIAM LANGLAND, *Piers the Plowman.* Passus xv, l. 1.

15
The faculty of degrading God's works which man calls his "imagination."
JOHN RUSKIN, *Modern Painters: Preface.*

16
In my mind's eye, Horatio.
SHAKESPEARE, *Hamlet.* Act i, sc. 2, l. 185.

17
My imaginations are as foul As Vulcan's stithy.
SHAKESPEARE, *Hamlet.* Act iii, sc. 2, l. 88.

How abhorred in my imagination it is!
SHAKESPEARE, *Hamlet.* Act v, sc. 1, l. 206.

The black utterances of a depraved imagination.
W. S. GILBERT, *H. M. S. Pinafore.* Act i.

18
Give me an ounce of civet, good apothecary, to sweeten my imagination.
SHAKESPEARE, *King Lear.* Act iv, sc. 6, l. 132.

19
Them that build castles in the air.
SIR PHILIP SIDNEY, *Apology for Poetry.* Par. 12. CASTLE IN THE AIR, CASTLE IN SPAIN, *see under* CASTLE.

20
Imagination wanders far afield.
YOUNG, *Night Thoughts.* Night viii, l. 901.

III—Imagination: Its Power

21
That minister of ministers,
Imagination, gathers up
The undiscovered Universe,
Like jewels in a jasper cup.
JOHN DAVIDSON, *There is a Dish to Hold the Sea.*

22
To make a prairie it takes a clover and one bee,—
And revery.

The revery alone will do
If bees are few.
EMILY DICKINSON, *Poems*. Pt. ii, No. 97.

1
Whene'er my maiden kisses me,
I'll think that I the Sultan be;
And when my cheery glass I tope,
I'll fancy then I am the Pope.
CHARLES LEVER, *Harry Lorrequer*. Ch. 43.

2
So every person by his dread gives strength to rumour, and with no foundation for the existence of evils, they fear the things which they have imagined. (Sic quisque pavendo Dat vires famæ, nulloque auctore malorum, Quæ finxere timent.)
LUCAN, *De Bello Civili*. Bk. i, l. 480.

Never yet was shape so dread,
But Fancy, thus in darkness thrown,
And by such sounds of horror fed,
Could frame more dreadful of her own.
THOMAS MOORE, *Lalla Rookh: The Fire-Worshippers*. Pt. iii, l. 374.

Imagination frames events unknown,
In wild, fantastic shapes of hideous ruin,
And what it fears creates.
HANNAH MORE, *Belshazzar*. Pt. ii.

3
The human race is governed by its imagination. (C'est l'imagination qui gouverne le genre humain.)
NAPOLEON BONAPARTE. (BOURRIENNE, *Life*, ii, 2.)

4
This is the very coinage of your brain:
This bodiless creation ecstasy
Is very cunning in.
SHAKESPEARE, *Hamlet*. Act iii, sc. 4, l. 137.

5
The lunatic, the lover, and the poet
Are of imagination all compact: . . .
Such tricks hath strong imagination,
That, if it would but apprehend some joy,
It comprehends some bringer of that joy;
Or in the night, imagining some fear,
How easy is a bush supposed a bear!
SHAKESPEARE, *A Midsummer-Night's Dream*. Act v, sc. 1, l. 7.

6
The best in this kind are but shadows; and the worst are no worse, if imagination amend them.
SHAKESPEARE, *A Midsummer-Night's Dream*. Act v, sc. 1, l. 213.

7
The idea of her life shall sweetly creep
Into his study of imagination,
And every lovely organ of her life,
Shall come apparell'd in more precious habit,
More moving-delicate and full of life
Into the eye and prospect of his soul.
SHAKESPEARE, *Much Ado About Nothing*. Act iv, sc. 1, l. 226.

Look, what thy soul holds dear, imagine it
To lie that way thou go'st, not whence thou com'st:
Suppose the singing birds musicians;
The grass whereon thou tread'st the presence strew'd,
The flowers fair ladies, and thy steps no more
Than a delightful measure or a dance.
SHAKESPEARE, *Richard II*. Act i, sc. 3, l. 286.

8
O, who can hold a fire in his hand,
By thinking on the frosty Caucasus?
Or cloy the hungry edge of appetite
By bare imagination of a feast?
Or wallow naked in December snow
By thinking on fantastic summer's heat?
SHAKESPEARE, *Richard II*. Act i, sc. 3, l. 294.

And twenty more such names and men as these
Which never were nor no man ever saw.
SHAKESPEARE, *The Taming of the Shrew: Induction*. Sc. 1.

9
But thou, that didst appear so fair
To fond imagination,
Dost rival in the light of day
Her delicate creation.
WORDSWORTH, *Yarrow Visited*.

10
In mid-way flight imagination tires;
Yet soon re-prunes her wing to soar anew.
YOUNG, *Night Thoughts*. Night ix, l. 1217.

IMITATION

See also Plagiarism, Quotation

11
We are, in truth, more than half what we are by imitation. The great point is, to choose good models and to study them with care.
LORD CHESTERFIELD, *Letters*, 18 Jan., 1750.

12
Imitation is the sincerest of flattery.
C. C. COLTON, *Lacon: Reflections*. Vol. i, No. 217. (1820)

Imitation is the sincerest form of flattery.
BARRY PAIN, *Playthings and Parodies*. Sec. 1.

13
But imitative strokes can do no more
Than please the eye.
COWPER, *The Task*. Bk. i, l. 426.

14
Imitation is suicide.
EMERSON, *Essays, First Series: Self-Reliance*.

15
There is a difference between imitating a good man and counterfeiting him.
BENJAMIN FRANKLIN, *Poor Richard*, 1738.

16
I would advise one who wishes to imitate well, to look closely into life and manners, and thereby to learn to express them with living words. (Respicere exemplar vitæ morumque jubebo Doctum imitatorem, et vivas hinc ducere voces.)
HORACE, *Ars Poetica*, l. 317.

1
O imitators, slavish herd! (O imitatores, servum pecus.)

Horace, *Epistles*. Bk. i, epis. 19, l. 19.

A slavish herd and stupid, to my mind,
These imitators.
(C'est un bétail servile et sot à mon avis
Que les imitateurs.)

La Fontaine, *Clymène*, v. 54.

2
No man was ever great by imitation.

Samuel Johnson, *Lines added to Goldsmith's Deserted Village*.

Almost all absurdity of conduct arises from the imitation of those whom we cannot resemble.

Samuel Johnson, *The Rambler*. No. 135.

3
The grape gains its purple tinge by looking at another grape. (Uvaque conspecta livorem ducit ab uva.)

Juvenal, *Satires*. Sat. ii, l. 81.

If they tell you, Sir Artist, your light and your shade
Are simply "adapted" from other men's lore;
That—plainly to speak of a "spade" as a "spade"—
You've "stolen" your grouping from three or from four;
That (however the writer the truth may deplore),
'Twas Gainsborough painted *your* "Little Boy Blue";
Smile only serenely—though cut to the core—
For the man who plants cabbages imitates, too!

Austin Dobson, *Ballade of Imitation*.

4
We are all easily taught to imitate what is base and depraved. (Dociles imitandis Turpibus ac pravis omnes sumus.)

Juvenal, *Satires*. Sat. xiv, l. 40.

He who imitates what is evil always goes beyond the example that is set; on the contrary, he who imitates what is good always falls short. (L'imitazione del male supera sempre l'esempio; comme per il contrario, l'imitazione del bene è sempre inferiore.)

Guicciardini, *Storia d' Italia*.

5
The only good copies are those which make us see the absurdity of bad originals. (Les seules bonnes copies sont celles qui nous font voir le ridicule des méchants originaux.)

La Rochefoucauld, *Maximes*. No. 133. The first version was "des excellents originaux," and Meré asked, "Is not one version as true as the other? There are none of M. de la Rochefoucauld's maxims of which the opposite is not equally true."

6
Go, and do thou likewise.

New Testament: Luke, x, 37.

7
Oh injurious and death-killing imitation!

Montaigne, *Essays*. Bk. iii, ch. 5.

8
A needy man is lost when he wishes to imitate a powerful man. (Inops, potentem dum vult imitari, perit.)

Phædrus, *Fables*. Bk. i, fab. 24, l. 1.

9
I have heard the bird himself. (Αὐτᾶς ἄκουκα τήνας.)

Plutarch, *Lives: Lycurgus*. Ch. 20, sec. 5. Relating the reply of a Spartan who had been invited to hear a man imitate a nightingale. Elsewhere credited to Agesilaus II.

10
He who resolves never to ransack any mind but his own will be soon reduced from mere barrenness to the poorest of all imitations; he will be obliged to imitate himself, and to repeat what he has before repeated.

Sir Joshua Reynolds, *Discourses on Painting*. No. 3.

11
Man is an imitative creature. (Der Mensch ist ein nachahmendes Geschöpf.)

Schiller, *Wallenstein's Tod*. Act iii, sc. 4, l. 9.

12
A substitute shines brightly as a king,
Until a king be by, and then his state
Empties itself, as doth an inland brook
Into the main of waters.

Shakespeare, *The Merchant of Venice*. Act v, sc. 1, l. 94.

IMMORALITY, see Morality

IMMORTALITY

See also Death and Immortality; Eternity; Virtue and Immortality

I—Immortality: Definitions

13
Immortality is the bravest gesture of our humanity toward the unknown. It is always a faith, never a demonstration.

Gaius Glenn Atkins. (*Greatest Thoughts on Immortality*, p. 47.)

14
Immortality is a great affirmation of the soul of man.

Hugh Black. (*Greatest Thoughts on Immortality*, p. 45.)

15
There is nothing strictly immortal, but immortality.

Sir Thomas Browne, *Hydriotaphia*. Ch. v, sec. 12.

16
That which is the foundation of all our hopes and of all our fears; all our hopes and fears which are of any consideration: I mean a Future Life.

Joseph Butler, *Analogy of Religion*.

17
Immortality is the glorious discovery of Christianity.

William Ellery Channing, *Immortality*.

18
Immortality—twin sister of Eternity.

J. G. Holland, *Gold-Foil: The Way to Grow Old*.

1
The idea of immortality . . . will continue to ebb and flow beneath the mists and clouds of doubt and darkness as long as love kisses the lips of death. It is the rainbow—Hope, shining upon the tears of grief.

ROBERT G. INGERSOLL, *The Ghosts*.

2
Belief in the future life is the appetite of reason.

W. S. LANDOR, *Imaginary Conversations: Marcus Tullius and Quinctus Cicero*.

3
There is no more mystery or miracle or supernaturalness . . . in the wholly unproved fact of immortality than there is in the wholly unexplainable fact of life or in the unimaginable fact of the universe.

HOWARD LEE MCBAIN, *Address*, Columbia University, 7 Jan., 1934.

II—Immortality: Apothegms

4
Thus God's children are immortal whiles their Father hath anything for them to do on earth.

THOMAS FULLER, *Church History*. Bk. ii, cen. 8.

Men are immortal till their work is done.

DAVID LIVINGSTONE, *Letter*, March, 1862, describing the death of Bishop Mackenzie.

Man is immortal till his work is done.

JAMES WILLIAMS, *Sonnet: Ethandune*. (See *The Guardian*, 17 Nov., 1911.)

5
They had finished her own crown in glory, and she couldn't stay away from the coronation.

THOMAS GRAY, *Enigmas of Life*.

6
Work for immortality if you will; then wait for it.

J. G. HOLLAND, *Gold-Foil: Patience*.

7
From the voiceless lips of the unreplying dead, there comes no word; but in the night of death Hope sees a star, and listening Love can hear the rustle of a wing.

R. G. INGERSOLL, *Tribute to Eben C. Ingersoll*.

8
He ne'er is crowned
With immortality, who fears to follow
Where airy voices lead.

KEATS, *Endymion*. Bk. ii, l. 211.

9
All men deserve to be saved, but he above all deserves immortality who desires it passionately and even in the face of reason.

MIGUEL DE UNAMUNO, *Tragic Sense of Life*, p. 265.

10
The universe is a stairway leading nowhere unless man is immortal.

E. Y. MULLINS. (NEWTON, *My Idea of God*, p. 199.)

11
All men desire to be immortal.

THEODORE PARKER, *Sermon on the Immortal Life*, 20 Sept., 1846.

13
The cry of the human for a life beyond the grave comes from that which is noblest in the soul of man.

HENRY VAN DYKE. (*Greatest Thoughts on Immortality*, p. 68.)

14
He saw wan Woman toil with famished eyes;
He saw her bound, and strove to sing her free.
He saw her fall'n; and wrote "The Bridge of Sighs";
And on it crossed to immortality.

WILLIAM WATSON, *Hood*.

15
He sins against this life, who slights the next.

YOUNG, *Night Thoughts*. Night iii, l. 399.

But if man loses all, when life is lost,
He lives a coward, or a fool expires.

YOUNG, *Night Thoughts*. Night vii, l. 199.

III—Immortality: Belief

16
My flesh shall rest in hope.

New Testament: Acts, ii, 26.

Immortal Hope dispels the gloom!
An angel sits beside the tomb.

SARAH FLOWER ADAMS, *The Mourners Came at Break of Day*.

On the cold cheek of Death smiles and roses are blending,
And Beauty immortal awakes from the tomb.

JAMES BEATTIE, *The Hermit*. Last lines.

It must be so,—Plato, thou reason'st well!—
Else whence this pleasing hope, this fond desire,
This longing after immortality?
Or whence this secret dread, and inward horror,
Of falling into nought? Why shrinks the soul
Back on herself, and startles at destruction?
'T is the divinity that stirs within us;
'T is Heav'n itself that points out an hereafter,
And intimates eternity to man.

ADDISON, *Cato*. Act v, sc. 1.

17
Singly they are mortal, collectively they are immortal. (Singillatim mortales; cunctim perpetui.)

APULEIUS, *De Deo Socratis*.

18
No, no! The energy of life may be
Kept on after the grave, but not begun;
And he who flagg'd not in the earthly strife,
From strength to strength advancing—only he,
His soul well-knit, and all his battles won,
Mounts, and that hardly, to eternal life.

MATTHEW ARNOLD, *Immortality*.

19
Earth to earth, ashes to ashes, dust to dust, in sure and certain hope of the resurrection.

Book of Common Prayer: Burial of the Dead.

Dust thou art, to dust returnest,
Was not spoken of the soul.
LONGFELLOW, *A Psalm of Life.*

1
As to immortality, my conviction stands thus: If there be anything in me that is of permanent worth and service to the universe, the universe will know how to preserve it. Whatsoever in me is not of permanent worth and service, neither can nor should be preserved.
HORACE JAMES BRIDGES. (NEWTON, *My Idea of God,* p. 176.)

2
There is surely a piece of Divinity in us, something that was before the elements, and owes no homage to the sun.
SIR THOMAS BROWNE, *Religio Medici.* Pt. ii, sec. 11.

3
I go to prove my soul!
I see my way as birds their trackless way.
I shall arrive! what time, what circuit first,
I ask not: but unless God send his hail
Or blinding fireballs, sleet or stifling snow,
In some time, his good time, I shall arrive.
ROBERT BROWNING, *Paracelsus.* Pt. i.

If I stoop
Into a dark tremendous sea of cloud,
It is but for a time; I press God's lamp
Close to my breast; its splendour, soon or late,
Will pierce the gloom: I shall emerge one day.
ROBERT BROWNING, *Paracelsus.* Pt. v.

Unfettered to the secrets of the stars
In thy good time.
JOHN DRINKWATER, *A Prayer.*

4
Fool! All that is, at all,
Lasts ever, past recall;
Earth changes, but thy soul and God stand sure:
What entered into thee,
That was, is, and shall be:
Time's wheel runs back or stops; Potter and clay endure.
ROBERT BROWNING, *Rabbi Ben Ezra.* St. 27.

And I shall thereupon
Take rest, ere I be gone
Once more on my adventure brave and new.
ROBERT BROWNING, *Rabbi Ben Ezra.* St. 14.

5
When mortal man resigns his breath,
And falls, a clod of clay,
The soul immortal wings its flight
To never-setting day.
MICHAEL BRUCE, *The Complaint of Nature.*

6
Cold in the dust this perished heart may lie,
But that which warmed it once shall never die!
That spark unburied in its mortal frame,
With living light, eternal, and the same.
THOMAS CAMPBELL, *The Pleasures of Hope.* Canto ii, l. 429.

7
I laugh, for hope hath happy place with me,
If my bark sinks, 'tis to another sea.
WILLIAM ELLERY CHANNING, *A Poet's Hope.*

8
If I err in my belief that the souls of men are immortal, I gladly err, nor do I wish this error, in which I find delight, to be wrested from me. (Si in hoc erro, qui animos hominum immortales esse credam, libenter erro, nec mihi hunc errorem, quo delector, dum vivo, extorqueri volo.)
CICERO, *De Senectute.* Ch. xxiii, sec. 85.

Whatever that may be which feels, which has knowledge, which wills, which has the power of growth, it is celestial and divine, and for that reason it must of necessity be eternal. (Quicquid est illud, quod sentit, quod sapit, quod vult, quod viget, cœleste et divinum, ob eamque rem æternum sit necesse est.)
CICERO, *Tusculanarum Disputationum.* Bk. i, ch. 27, sec. 66.

9
For this corruptible must put on incorruption, and this mortal must put on immortality.
New Testament: I Corinthians, xv, 53.

They do it to obtain a corruptible crown; but we an incorruptible.
New Testament: I Corinthians, ix, 25.

10
Though life's valley be a vale of tears,
A brighter scene beyond that vale appears.
COWPER, *Conversation,* l. 881.

11
Believing as I do that man in the distant future will be a far more perfect creature than he now is, it is an intolerable thought that he and all other sentient beings are doomed to complete annihilation after such long-continued slow progress. To those who fully admit the immortality of the human soul, the destruction of our world will not appear so dreadful.
CHARLES DARWIN, *Life and Letters.*

12
If then all souls, both good and bad do teach
With general voice, that souls can never die;
'Tis not man's flattering gloss, but Nature's speech,
Which, like God's oracles can never lie.
SIR JOHN DAVIES, *Nosce Teipsum.* Sec. 30, st. 81.

13
For I never have seen, and never shall see, that the cessation of the evidence of existence is necessarily evidence of the cessation of existence.
WILLIAM DE MORGAN, *Joseph Vance.* Ch. 40.

14
Or ever the silver cord be loosed or the golden bowl be broken, or the pitcher be broken at the fountain, or the wheel broken at the

cistern. Then shall the dust return to the earth as it was: and the spirit shall return unto God who gave it.

Old Testament: Ecclesiastes, xii, 6, 7.

1
I believe in immortality fundamentally, not because I vehemently crave it for myself as an individual, but because its denial seems to me to land the entire race in a hopeless situation and to reduce philosophy to a counsel of despair.

HARRY EMERSON FOSDICK. (*Greatest Thoughts on Immortality*, p. 12.)

2
Here is my Creed. I believe in one God, Creator of the Universe. That he governs it by his Providence. That he ought to be worshipped. That the most acceptable service we render him is doing good to his other children. That the soul of Man is immortal, and will be treated with justice in another life respecting its conduct in this.

BENJAMIN FRANKLIN, *Letter to Ezra Stiles*, 9 March, 1790.

3
I am immortal! I know it! I feel it!
Hope floods my heart with delight!
Running on air, mad with life, dizzy, reeling,
Upward I mount—faith is sight, life is feeling,
Hope is the day-star of might!

MARGARET WITTER FULLER, *Dryad Song*.

4
I shall not wholly die; large residue
Shall 'scape the queen of death.
(Non omnis moriar multaque pars mei
Vitabit Libitinam.)

HORACE, *Odes*. Bk. iii, ode 30, l. 6.

5
Let us not be uneasy then about the different roads we may pursue, as believing them the shortest, to that our last abode, but following the guidance of a good conscience, let us be happy in the hope that by these different paths we shall all meet in the end.

THOMAS JEFFERSON, *Writings*. Vol. xiv, p. 198.

6
And though after my skin worms destroy this body, yet in my flesh shall I see God.

Old Testament: Job, xix, 26.

This is the promise that He hath promised us, even eternal life.

New Testament: I John, ii, 25.

Our Saviour Jesus Christ, who hath abolished death, and hath brought life and immortality to light through the gospel.

New Testament: II Timothy, i, 10.

7
I long to believe in immortality. . . . If I am destined to be happy with you here—how short is the longest life. I wish to believe in immortality—I wish to live with you forever.

KEATS, *Letters to Fanny Brawne*. No. 36.

8
Then to the grave I turned me to see what therein lay;
'Twas the garment of the Christian, worn out and thrown away.

F. A. KRUMMACHER, *Death and the Christian*.

9
The great world of light, that lies
Behind all human destinies.

LONGFELLOW, *To a Child*.

10
The few little years we spend on earth are only the first scene in a Divine Drama that extends on into Eternity.

EDWIN MARKHAM, *Address*, at the funeral of Adam Willis Wagnalls.

11
We call this life, that is life's preparation,
We call this life, a little time of tears;
But think you God for this designed creation,
A few short years?

DOUGLAS MALLOCH, *We Call This Life*.

12
For who would lose,
Though full of pain, this intellectual being,
Those thoughts that wander through eternity,
To perish rather, swallow'd up and lost
In the wide womb of uncreated night,
Devoid of sense and motion?

MILTON, *Paradise Lost*. Bk. ii, l. 146.

13
Beyond this vale of tears
There is a life above,
Unmeasured by the flight of years;
And all that life is love.

MONTGOMERY, *The Issues of Life and Death*.

14
I shall take flight as a bird wings
Into the infinite blue—
What if my song comes ringing
Down through the stars and the dew?

CHARLES L. O'DONNELL, *Immortality*.

15
In my better part I shall be raised to immortality above the lofty stars. (Parte tamen meliore mei super alta perinnis Astra ferar.)

OVID, *Metamorphoses*. Bk. xv, l. 875.

Thus all things are but altered; nothing dies:
And here and there th' unbodied spirit flies.

OVID, *Metamorphoses*. Bk. xv, l. 158. (Dryden, tr.)

16
There is something beyond the grave; death does not end all, and the pale ghost escapes from the vanquished pyre. (Sunt aliquid Manes: letum non omnia finit, Luridaque evictos effugit umbra rogos.)

PROPERTIUS, *Elegies*. Bk. iv, eleg. 7, l. 1.

17
This life is but the passage of a day,
This life is but a pang and all is over;
But in the life to come which fades not away
Every love shall abide and every lover.

CHRISTINA ROSSETTI, *Saints and Angels*.

1
As the mother's womb holds us for ten months, making us ready, not for the womb itself, but for life, just so, through our lives, we are making ourselves ready for another birth. . . . Therefore look forward without fear to that appointed hour—the last hour of the body, but not of the soul. . . . That day, which you fear as being the end of all things, is the birthday of your eternity.
SENECA, *Epistulæ ad Lucilium*. Epis. cii, sec. 23.

2
We have passed Age's icy caves,
And Manhood's dark and tossing waves,
And Youth's smooth ocean, smiling to betray:
Beyond the glassy gulfs we flee
Of shadow-peopled Infancy,
Through Death and Birth, to a diviner day.
SHELLEY, *Prometheus Unbound*. Act ii, sc. 5, l. 98.

3
For tho' from out our bourne of Time and Place
The flood may bear me far,
I hope to see my Pilot face to face
When I have crost the bar.
TENNYSON, *Crossing the Bar*.

My own dim life should teach me this,
That life shall live for evermore.
TENNYSON, *In Memoriam*. Pt. xxxiv, st. 1.

4
If there is a Universal and Supreme Consciousness, I am an idea in it; and is it possible for any idea in this Supreme Consciousness to be completely blotted out? After I have died, God will go on remembering me, and to be remembered by God, to have my consciousness sustained by the Supreme Consciousness, is not that, perhaps, to be?
MIGUEL DE UNAMUNO, *Tragic Sense of Life*, p. 149.

5
But felt through all this fleshly dress
Bright shoots of everlastingness.
HENRY VAUGHAN, *The Retreat*.

6
There is another, and a better world.
AUGUST F. F. VON KOTZEBUE, *The Stranger*. Act i, sc. 1.

7
All, all for immortality,
Love like the light silently wrapping all.
WALT WHITMAN, *Song of the Universal*. Sec. 4.

I swear I think there is nothing but immortality.
WALT WHITMAN, *To Think of Time*.

8
Happy he whose inward ear
Angel comfortings can hear,
O'er the rabble's laughter;
And while Hatred's fagots burn,
Glimpses through the smoke discern
Of the good hereafter.
WHITTIER, *Barclay of Ury*. St. 19.

Alas for him who never sees
The stars shine through his cypress-trees!
Who, hopeless, lays his dead away,
Nor looks to see the breaking day
Across the mournful marbles play!
Who hath not learned, in hours of faith,
The truth to flesh and sense unknown,
That Life is ever lord of Death,
And Love can never lose its own!
J. G. WHITTIER, *Snow-Bound*, l. 203.

9
God created man to be immortal, and made him to be an image of his own eternity.
Apocrypha: Wisdom of Solomon, ii, 23.

10
O joy! that in our embers
Is something that doth live.
WORDSWORTH, *Intimations of Immortality*, l. 133.

11
Though inland far we be,
Our Souls have sight of that immortal sea
Which brought us hither.
WORDSWORTH, *Intimations of Immortality*, l. 166.

We see by the glad light
And breathe the sweet air of futurity;
And so we live, or else we have no life.
WORDSWORTH, *The Excursion*. Bk. ix, l. 24.

High sacrifice, and labour without pause,
Even to the death:—else wherefore should the eye
Of man converse with immortality?
WORDSWORTH, *Poems Dedicated to National Independence*. Pt. ii, No. 14.

12
Immortal! ages past, yet nothing gone!
Morn without eve! a race without a goal!
Unshorten'd by progression infinite!
Futurity for ever future! Life
Beginning still, where computation ends!
'Tis the description of a Deity!
YOUNG, *Night Thoughts*. Night vi, l. 542.

Still seems it strange, that thou shouldst live forever?
Is it less strange, that thou shouldst live at all?
This is a miracle; and that no more.
YOUNG, *Night Thoughts*. Night vii, l. 1407.

IV—Immortality: Doubt

13
And then he thinks he knows
The Hills where his life rose,
And the Sea where it goes.
MATTHEW ARNOLD, *The Buried Life*, l. 96.

Stern law of every mortal lot!
Which man, proud man, finds hard to bear,
And builds himself I know not what
Of second life, I know not where.
MATTHEW ARNOLD, *Geist's Grave*.

14
Fish say, they have their Stream and Pond;
But is there anything Beyond?
RUPERT BROOKE, *Heaven*.

1
As for a future life, every man must judge for himself between conflicting vague probabilities.

CHARLES DARWIN, *Life and Letters.*

While Reason sternly bids us die, Love longs for life beyond the grave:
Our hearts, affections, hopes and fears for Life-to-be shall ever crave.

SIR RICHARD BURTON, *The Kasîdah.* Pt. viii, st. 5.

When I go to sleep, it would be no pleasure to think I might be awakened in the middle of the night.

GEORGES CLEMENCEAU, when asked why he did not desire immortality.

2
But ask not bodies (doomed to die),
To what abode they go;
Since knowledge is but sorrow's spy,
It is not safe to know.

SIR WILLIAM D'AVENANT, *The Just Italian.* Act v, sc. 1.

3
Personal immortality may be a fact, but we have no shred of evidence, one way or another.

FRANKLIN H. GIDDINGS. (*Greatest Thoughts on Immortality,* p. 114.)

Thou canst not prove thou art immortal—no,
Nor yet that thou art mortal.

TENNYSON, *The Ancient Sage,* l. 62.

4
Is there beyond the silent night
An endless day?
Is death a door that leads to light?
We cannot say.

R. G. INGERSOLL, *Declaration of the Free.*

5
If a man die, shall he live again?

Old Testament: Job, xiv, 14.

6
But blind to former as to future fate,
What mortal knows his pre-existent state?

POPE, *The Dunciad.* Bk. iii, l. 47.

7
A future life is a matter of faith or presumption; it is a prophetic hypothesis regarding occult existences.

GEORGE SANTAYANA, *Reason in Religion.* Vol. iii, p. 13.

8
What shall become of man so wise,
When he dies?
None can tell
Whether he goes to heaven or hell.

SIR CHARLES SEDLEY, *Lycophron.*

9
Man's ignorance as to what will become of him after he dies never disturbs a noble, a truly religious soul.

W. M. SLATER, *Ethical Religion,* p. 40.

10
Until that immortality of the individual is irrefragably demonstrated, the sweet, the immeasurably precious hope of ending, with this life, the ache and languor of existence, remains open to burdened human personalities.

J. A. SYMONDS, *Letter to Henry Sidgwick.*

12
And can eternity belong to me,
Poor pensioner on the bounties of an hour?

YOUNG, *Night Thoughts.* Night i, l. 66.

13
Shall man alone, for whom all else revives,
No resurrection know? shall man alone,
Imperial man! be sown in barren ground,
Less privileg'd than grain, on which he feeds?

YOUNG, *Night Thoughts.* Night vi, l. 704.

V—Immortality: Unbelief

14
It seems nobler to me to hide one's self and one's nudity, than to ask for anything more.

BJÖRNSTJERNE BJÖRNSON. (*Greatest Thoughts on Immortality,* p. 115.)

15
Whitman once said to me that he would as soon hope to argue a man into good health as to argue him into a belief in immortality. He said he *knew* it was so without proof; but I never could light my candle at his great torch.

JOHN BURROUGHS. (BARRUS, *Life and Letters of John Burroughs.*)

16
Suns may rise and set; we, when our short day has closed, must sleep on during one perpetual night.
(Soles occidere et redire possunt;
Nobis' cum semel occidit brevis lux,
Nox est perpetua una dormienda.)

CATULLUS, *Ode.* Ode v, l. 4.

17
The origin of the absurd idea of immortal life is easy to discover; it is kept alive by hope and fear, by childish faith, and by cowardice.

CLARENCE DARROW. (*Greatest Thoughts on Immortality,* p. 111.)

I do not believe in immortality and have no desire for it. The belief in it issues from the puerile egos of inferior men.

H. L. MENCKEN. (DURANT, *On the Meaning of Life,* p. 35.)

Life is pleasant and I have enjoyed it, but I have no yearning to clutter up the Universe after it is over.

H. L. MENCKEN. (*Greatest Thoughts on Immortality,* p. 114.)

18
Human society may most wisely seek justice and right in this world without depending on any other world to redress the wrongs of this.

CHARLES W. ELIOT. (*Greatest Thoughts on Immortality,* p. 108.)

Other world! There is no other world! Here or nowhere is the whole fact.
EMERSON, *Uncollected Lectures: Natural Religion.*

1
Lo, in my heart I hear, as in a shell,
The murmur of the world beyond the grave.
Distinct, distinct, though faint and far it be.
Thou fool; this echo is a cheat as well,—
The hum of earthly instincts; and we crave
A world unreal as the shell-heard sea.
EUGENE LEE-HAMILTON, *Sea-Shell Murmurs.*

2
The thought of life that ne'er shall cease
Has something in it like despair.
LONGFELLOW, *The Golden Legend.* Pt. i, l. 42.

3
His last day places man in the same state as before he was born; nor after death has the body or soul any more feeling than they had before birth.
PLINY THE ELDER, *Historia Naturalis.* Bk. lvi, sec. 1.

4
To desire immortality is to desire the eternal perpetuation of a great mistake.
SCHOPENHAUER, *The World as Will.* Vol. ii, p. 561.

5
After death there is nothing and death itself is nothing, the final goal of a course full swiftly run. (Post mortem nihil est ipsaque mors nihil, Velocis spatii meta novissima.)
SENECA, *Troades,* l. 397.

Dost ask where thou shalt lie when death has claimed thee? Where the unborn lie. (Quæris quo jaceas post obitum loco? Quo non nata jacent.)
SENECA, *Troades,* l. 407.

6
If you wish to live forever you must be wicked enough to be irretrievably damned, since the saved are no longer what they were, and in hell alone do people retain their sinful nature: that is to say, their individuality.
BERNARD SHAW, *Parents and Children.*

If some devil were to convince us that our dream of perpetual immortality is no dream but a hard fact, such a shriek of despair would go up from the human race as no other conceivable horror could provoke. . . . What man is capable of the insane self-conceit of believing that an eternity of himself would be tolerable even to himself?
BERNARD SHAW, *Parents and Children.*

7
This little life is all we must endure,
The grave's most holy peace is ever sure,
We fall asleep, and never wake again;
Nothing is of us but the mouldering flesh,
Whose elements dissolve and merge afresh
In earth, air, water, plants, and other men.
JAMES THOMSON, *The City of Dreadful Night.* Pt. xiv.

8
I am a temporary enclosure for a temporary purpose; that served, my skull and teeth, my idiosyncrasy and desire, will disperse, I believe, like the timbers of a booth after a fair.
H. G. WELLS, *First and Last Things.*

VI—Immortality and the Soul

9
The soul secur'd in her existence, smiles
At the drawn dagger, and defies its point.
The stars shall fade away, the sun himself
Grow dim with age, and Nature sink in years,
But thou shalt flourish in immortal youth,
Unhurt amidst the war of elements,
The wreck of matter, and the crush of worlds.
ADDISON, *Cato.* Act v, sc. 1.

10
Awake, my soul! stretch every nerve,
And press with vigour on;
A heavenly race demands thy zeal,
And an immortal crown.
PHILIP DODDRIDGE, *Zeal and Vigour in the Christian Race.*

11
Calm on the bosom of thy God,
Fair spirit! rest thee now!
FELICIA DOROTHEA HEMANS, *Dirge.*

Dust, to its narrow house beneath!
Soul, to its place on high!
They that have seen thy look in death
No more may fear to die.
FELICIA DOROTHEA HEMANS, *Dirge.*

12
Crocus and cowslip from earth's riven tomb
Flower in the sun; but thou, O soul, shalt bloom,
Waked by the Star of that perpetual Spring,
Beyond the seed-time and the harvesting.
THOMAS S. JONES, JR., *Quatrains.*

13
No, no, I'm sure,
My restless spirit never could endure
To brood so long upon one luxury,
Unless it did, though fearfully, espy
A hope beyond the shadow of a dream.
KEATS, *Endymion.* Bk. i, l. 853.

14
Either the soul is immortal and we shall not die, or it perishes with the flesh, and we shall not know that we are dead. Live, then, as if you were eternal.
ANDRÉ MAUROIS. (DURANT, *On the Meaning of Life,* p. 53.)

15
Who, as they sung, would take the prison'd soul
And lap it in Elysium.
MILTON, *Comus,* l. 256.

16
The soul, uneasy and confin'd from home,
Rests and expatiates in a life to come.
POPE, *Essay on Man.* Epis. i, l. 97.

1
Where souls do couch on flowers, we'll hand in hand,
And with our sprightly port make the ghosts gaze.
SHAKESPEARE, *Antony and Cleopatra*. Act iv, sc. 14, l. 51.

2
I do not set my life at a pin's fee;
And, for my soul, what can it do to that,
Being a thing immortal as itself?
SHAKESPEARE, *Hamlet*. Act i, sc. 4, l. 67.

3
I swear I think now that everything without exception has an eternal soul!
The trees have, rooted in the ground! the weeds of the sea have! the animals!
WALT WHITMAN, *To Think of Time*.

IMPERIALISM

4
The burning issue of imperialism growing out of the Spanish War involves the very existence of the Republic and the destruction of our free institutions. We regard it as the paramount issue of the campaign.
WILLIAM JENNINGS BRYAN, *Platform*, adopted at Democratic National Convention, 5 July, 1900.

5
Learn to think imperially.
JOSEPH CHAMBERLAIN, *Speech*, at Guildhall, London, 19 Jan., 1904.

6
So that Lancashire merchants whenever they like
Can water the beer of a man in Klondike,
Or poison the beer of a man in Bombay;
And that is the meaning of Empire Day.
G. K. CHESTERTON, *Songs of Education*.

7
My idea of anti-imperialism is opposition to the fashion of shooting everybody who doesn't speak English.
RICHARD CROKER, *Interview*, during 1900 campaign.

8
I do not share in the apprehension held by many as to the danger of governments becoming weakened and destroyed by reason of their extension of territory . . . Rather do I believe that our Great Maker is preparing the world, in His own good time, to become one nation, speaking one language, and when armies and navies will no longer be required.
U. S. GRANT, *Second Inaugural*, 4 March, 1873.

9
Nursed by stern men with empires in their brains.
J. R. LOWELL, *The Biglow Papers: Mason and Slidell*.

10
The mission of the United States is one of benevolent assimilation, substituting the mild sway of justice and right for arbitrary rule.
WILLIAM MCKINLEY, *Letter to General Otis*, 21 Dec., 1898.

11
We have bought ten million Malays at two dollars a head unpicked, and nobody knows what it will cost to pick them.
THOMAS B. REED, referring to the purchase of the Philippines. (ROBINSON, *Life*.)

12
With a hero at head, and a nation
Well gagged and well drilled and well cowed,
And a gospel of war and damnation,
Has not Empire a right to be proud?
SWINBURNE, *A Word for the Country*. St. 14.

13
Nerva has united two things long incompatible, Empire and liberty. (Nerva Cæsar res olim dissociabilis miscuerit, principatum ac libertatem.)
TACITUS, *Agricola*. Sec. 3. Cicero has "Libertatem imperiumque." (*Philippicæ*, iv, 4.)

Here the two great principles, Imperium et libertas, res olim insociabiles (saith Tacitus), began to encounter each other.
SIR WINSTON CHURCHILL, *Divi Britannici*, p. 349. (1675)

One of the greatest Romans, when asked what were his politics replied, "Imperium et libertas." That would not make a bad program for a British Ministry.
BENJAMIN DISRAELI, *Speech*, Mansion House, London, 10 Nov., 1879.

IMPOSSIBILITY

14
You cannot make a crab walk straight. (Οὔποτε ποιήσεις τὸν καρκίνον ὀρθὰ βαδίζειν.)
ARISTOPHANES, *The Peace*, l. 1083.

15
It is a disease of the soul to be enamoured of things impossible of attainment.
BIAS. (DIOGENES LAERTIUS, *Bias*. Bk. i, 86.)

16
It is not a lucky word, this same *impossible*; no good comes of those that have it so often in their mouth.
CARLYLE, *French Revolution*. Pt. iii, bk. 3, ch. 10.

17
There is no obligation to attempt the impossible. (Impossibilium nulla obligatio est.)
CELSUS, *Alethes Logos*.

A wise man never Attempts impossibilities.
MASSINGER, *The Renegado*. Act i, sc. 1.

18
This might possibly happen to Hercules, sprung from the seed of Jove, but not in like manner to us. (Hoc Herculi, Jovis satu edito, potuit fortasse contingere, nobis non item.)
CICERO, *De Officiis*. Bk. i, ch. 32, sec. 118.

19
Consider nothing, before it has come to pass,

as impossible. (Nihil, ante quam evenerit, non evenire posse arbitrari.)
CICERO, *Tusculanarum Disputationum*. Bk. iii, ch. 14, sec. 30.

And what's impossible, can't be,
And never, never comes to pass.
GEORGE COLMAN THE YOUNGER, *The Maid of the Moor*.

Apparently there is nothing that cannot happen.
MARK TWAIN, *Autobiography*. Vol. 1, p. 91.

1
I think, and think on things impossible,
Yet love to wander in that Golden Maze.
DRYDEN, *The Rival Ladies*. Act iii, sc. 1.

2
Hope not for impossibilities.
THOMAS FULLER, *The Holy and Profane States: Of Expecting Preferment*.

3
To believe a business impossible is the way to make it so.
THOMAS FULLER, *Gnomologia*.

To the timid and hesitating everything is impossible because it seems so.
SCOTT, *Rob Roy*. Ch. 16.

4
Impossible is a word which I never say. (Impossible est un mot que je ne dis jamais.)
COLLIN D'HARLEVILLE, *Malice pour Malice*. (1793)

"It is not possible," you write me? That is not French. ("Ce n'est pas possible," m'écrivez-vous? Cela n'est pas français.)
NAPOLEON BONAPARTE, *Letter to Lemarois*, 9 July, 1813. Usually quoted, "Le mot 'impossible' n'est pas français."

5
Impossibilities recede as experience advances.
HELPS, *Friends in Council*. Bk. iii, ch. 5.

6
Nothing is impossible to a willing heart.
JOHN HEYWOOD, *Proverbs*. Pt. i, ch. 4.

Few things are impossible to diligence and skill.
SAMUEL JOHNSON, *Rasselas*. Ch. 12.

Nothing is impossible to the man who can will.
MIRABEAU. (EMERSON, *Considerations by the Way*.)

Nothing is impossible to a valiant heart. (À cœur vaillant rien d'impossible.)
Motto of JEANNE D'ALBRET of Navarre, mother of Henry IV, and adopted by him as his own device.

7
Do not think that what is difficult for thee to master is impossible for man; but if a thing is possible and proper to man, deem it attainable by thee.
MARCUS AURELIUS, *Meditations*. Bk. vi, sec. 19.

8
You bid me to number the waves of the sea. (Oceani fluctus me numerare jubes.)
MARTIAL, *Epigrams*. Bk. vi, ep. 34, l. 2.

You tell me to strip the clothes off a naked man. (Nudo detrahere vestimenta me jubes.)
PLAUTUS, *Asinaria*, l. 92. (Act i, sc. 1.)

Alas, poor duke! the task he undertakes
Is numbering sands and drinking oceans dry.
SHAKESPEARE, *Richard II*. Act ii, sc. 2, l. 145.

9
Everything will be accomplished which I once believed impossible. (Omnia jam fient, fieri quæ posse negabam.)
OVID, *Tristia*. Bk. i, eleg. 8, l. 7.

10
To blow and to swallow at the same time is not easy; I cannot at the same time be here and also there. (Simul flare sorbereque haud factu facilest. Ego hic esse et illic simitu hau potui.)
PLAUTUS, *Mostellaria*, l. 791. (Act iii, sc. 2.)

We cannot be here and there too.
SHAKESPEARE, *Romeo and Juliet*. Act i, sc. 5, l. 15.

11
I will strive with things impossible.
SHAKESPEARE, *Julius Cæsar*. Act ii, sc. 1, l. 325.

I cannot draw a cart, nor eat dried oats.
SHAKESPEARE, *King Lear*. Act v, sc. 3, l. 38.

Who can be wise, amazed, temperate and furious,
Loyal and neutral, in a moment? No man.
SHAKESPEARE, *Macbeth*. Act ii, sc. 3, l. 113.

Make not impossible
That which but seems unlike.
SHAKESPEARE, *Measure for Measure*. Act v, sc. 1, l. 51.

12
Nothing is unnatural that is not physically impossible.
SHERIDAN, *The Critic*. Act ii, sc. 1.

13
Only he who attempts the absurd is capable of achieving the impossible.
MIGUEL DE UNAMUNO, *Essays and Soliloquies*, p. 104.

14
Th' inverted pyramid can never stand.
YOUNG, *Night Thoughts*. Night viii, l. 1302.

IMPULSE

15
A thing of impulse and a child of song.
BYRON, *Don Juan*. Canto viii, st. 24.

I am the very slave of circumstance
And impulse,—borne away with every breath!
BYRON, *Sardanapalus*. Act iv, sc. 1.

16
The pupil of impulse.
OLIVER GOLDSMITH, *Retaliation*, l. 45.

17
What is now reason was formerly impulse. (Quod nunc ratio est, impetus ante fuit.)
OVID, *Remediorum Amoris*, l. 10.

18
Impulse manages all things badly. (Male cuncta ministrat Impetus.)
STATIUS, *Thebais*. Bk. x, l. 704.

19
Mistrust first impulses, they are always good.
TALLEYRAND. (*Biographie Universelle*.)

INCONSISTENCY, see Consistency

INCONSTANCY, see Constancy

INDECISION

See also Timidity

1
The sin I impute to each frustrate ghost
Is—the unlit lamp and the ungirt loin,
Though the end in sight was a vice, I say.
ROBERT BROWNING, *The Statue and the Bust.*

2
The stream runs on,—why tarry at the brink?
BULWER-LYTTON, *The New Timon.* Pt. iii, sec. iii, l. 2.

3
In such a strait the wisest may well be perplexed, and the boldest staggered.
EDMUND BURKE, *Thoughts on the Cause of the Present Discontents.*

4
The shill I, shall I, of Congreve becomes shilly shally.
FANNY BURNEY, *Cecilia,* v, 119.

5
In indecision itself grief is present. (In ipsa dubitatione facinus inest.)
CICERO, *De Officiis.* Bk. iii, ch. 8, sec. 37.

6
Ares hates those who hesitate. ("Ἄρης στυγεῖ μέλλοντας.)
EURIPIDES, *Heraclidæ,* l. 722. Ares, the War-god.

7
Lose this day loitering 'twill be the same story
Tomorrow, and the next, more dilatory;
Each indecision brings its own delays,
And days are lost lamenting o'er lost days.
GOETHE, *Faust: Prelude at the Theater.* (Auster, tr.)

8
And while I at length debate and beat the bush,
There shall step in other men and catch the birds.
JOHN HEYWOOD, *Proverbs.* Pt. i, ch. 3.

9
How long halt ye between two opinions.
Old Testament: I Kings, xviii, 21.

10
I mean a kin' o' hangin' roun' an' settin' on a fence.
J. R. LOWELL, *The Biglow Papers.* Ser. ii, No. 3.

11
And Jesus said unto him, No man, having put his hand to the plough, and looking back, is fit for the kingdom of God.
New Testament: Luke, ix, 62.

12
Time was, I shrank from what was right
From fear of what was wrong;
I would not brave the sacred fight,
Because the foe was strong.

But now I cast that finer sense
And sorer shame aside:
Such dread of sin was indolence,
Such aim at Heaven was pride.
JOHN HENRY NEWMAN, *Sensitiveness.*

13
Now this, now that way torn, Quintus, in doubt
And fear of doing ill, does nothing well.
ETIENNE PASQUIER, *Epigrammata,* ii, 63.

14
Through indecision opportunity is often lost. (Deliberando sæpe perit occasio.)
PUBLILIUS SYRUS, *Sententiæ.* No. 185.

15
While we consider when to begin, it becomes too late to do so. (Dum deliberamus quando incipiendum, incipere jam serum fit.)
QUINTILIAN, *De Institutione Oratoria.* Bk. xii, ch. 6, sec. 3.

He who considers too much will perform little. (Wer gar zu viel bedenkt wird wenig leisten.)
SCHILLER, *Wilhelm Tell.* Act iii, sc. 1.

The man that cries Consider is our foe.
BEAUMONT AND FLETCHER, *The Scornful Lady.* Act ii.

16
Fain would I but dare not; I dare, and yet I may not;
I may, although I care not for pleasure when I play not.
SIR WALTER RALEIGH, *A Lover's Verses. See also under* OPPORTUNITY.

17
Like a man to double business bound,
I stand in pause where I shall first begin,
And both neglect.
SHAKESPEARE, *Hamlet.* Act iii, sc. 3, l. 41.

Now, whether it be
Bestial oblivion, or some craven scruple
Of thinking too precisely on the event,
A thought which, quarter'd, hath but one part wisdom,
And ever three parts coward, I do not know
Why yet I live to say "This thing's to do";
Sith I have cause and will and strength and means
To do't.
SHAKESPEARE, *Hamlet.* Act iv, sc. 4, l. 39.

18
That we would do,
We should do when we would.
SHAKESPEARE, *Hamlet.* Act iv, sc. 7, l. 119.

What thou wouldst highly,
That wouldst thou holily; wouldst not play false,
And yet wouldst wrongly win.
SHAKESPEARE, *Macbeth.* Act i, sc. 5, l. 21.

19
I am At war 'twixt will and will not.
SHAKESPEARE, *Measure for Measure.* Act ii, sc. 2, l. 32.

We would, and we would not.
SHAKESPEARE, *Measure for Measure*. Act iv, sc. 4, l. 37.

INDEPENDENCE

1
Let every vat stand upon its own bottom.
WILLIAM BULLEIN, *Dialogue*, 65. (1564)

Sloth said, Yet a little more sleep; and Presumption said, Every vat must stand upon his own bottom.
JOHN BUNYAN, *The Pilgrim's Progress*. Pt. i.

Every tub must stand upon its bottom.
CHARLES MACKLIN, *The Man of the World*. Act i, sc. 2.

2
To catch Dame Fortune's golden smile,
Assiduous wait upon her;
And gather gear by ev'ry wile
That's justified by honour;
Not for to hide it in a hedge,
Nor for a train-attendant,
But for the glorious privilege
Of being independent.
ROBERT BURNS, *Epistle to a Young Friend*.

A little in one's own pocket is better than much in another man's purse.
CERVANTES, *Don Quixote*. Pt. ii, ch. 7.

3
I came hither [to Craigenputtoch] solely with the design to simplify my way of life and to secure the independence through which I could be enabled to remain true to myself.
THOMAS CARLYLE, *Letter to Goethe*, 1828.

4
Every man for himself, and God for us all.
CERVANTES, *Don Quixote*. Pt. ii, ch. 7. *See also* SELFISHNESS: APOTHEGMS.

5
Whoso would be a man, must be a Non-conformist.
EMERSON, *Essays, First Series: Self-Reliance*.

6
That independence Britons prize too high,
Keeps man from man, and breaks the social tie.
GOLDSMITH, *The Traveller*, l. 339.

7
The strongest man in the world is he who stands most alone.
HENRIK IBSEN, *An Enemy of the People*. Act v.

He travels fastest who travels alone.
RUDYARD KIPLING, *The Winners*. *See* MARRIAGE AND CELIBACY.

8
We've a war, an' a debt, an' a flag; an' ef this
Ain't to be inderpendunt, why, wut on airth is?
J. R. LOWELL, *Biglow Papers*. Ser. ii, No. 4.

9
Paddle your own canoe.
FREDERICK MARRYAT, *Settlers in Canada*. Ch. 8. (1840)

Voyager upon life's sea,
To yourself be true,
And whate'er your lot may be,
Paddle your own canoe.
UNKNOWN, *Paddle Your Own Canoe*. Published anonymously in the *Editor's Drawer* of *Harper's Monthly* for May, 1854, with this prefatory note: "They have a very expressive term at the West, in speaking of a young man who would be the architect of his own fortune, that he must 'paddle his own canoe.' A lady of Indiana has expanded the curt advice into a piece of original and sparkling verse." The poem consisted of seven eight-line stanzas, each closing with the same refrain. It has been attributed to Sarah K. Bolton, Sarah Tittle and Edward P. Philpots. Mrs. Bolton was only thirteen years old at the time, and it is difficult to see how Philpots could qualify as "a lady from Indiana." The probability is that all three wrote verses with this refrain. (See *Notes and Queries*, 25 May, 1901, p. 414.)

Leave to heaven, in humble trust,
All you will to do;
But if you succeed, you must
Paddle your own canoe.
UNKNOWN, *Paddle Your Own Canoe*.

If you want to get rich, you son of a bitch,
I'll tell you what to do:
Never sit down with a tear or a frown,
And paddle your own canoe!
UNKNOWN, *Paddle Your Own Canoe*. (Heard by the compiler about 1882.)

10
Follow your own bent no matter what people say.
KARL MARX, *Capital: Preface*.

11
Independence, like honor, is a rocky island without a beach.
NAPOLEON BONAPARTE, *Sayings of Napoleon*.

12
Let each man have the wit to go his own way
(Unus quisque sua noverit ire via.)
PROPERTIUS, *Elegies*. Bk. ii, eleg. 25, l. 38.

13
You would play upon me; you would seem to know my stops; you would pluck out the heart of my mystery; you would sound me from my lowest note to the top of my compass: and there is much music, excellent voice, in this little organ; yet cannot you make it speak. 'Sblood, do you think that I am easier to be played on than a pipe? Call me what instrument you will, though you can fret me, yet you cannot play upon me.
SHAKESPEARE, *Hamlet*. Act iii, sc. 2, l. 379.

14
Speak then to me, who neither beg nor fear
Your favours nor your hate.
SHAKESPEARE, *Macbeth*. Act i, sc. 3, l. 60.

15
Thy spirit, Independence, let me share!
Lord of the lion-heart and eagle-eye,
Thy steps I follow with my bosom bare,

Nor heed the storm that howls along the sky.

TOBIAS SMOLLETT, *Ode to Independence,* l. 1.

1

To know what you prefer, instead of humbly saying Amen to what the world tells you you ought to prefer, is to have kept your soul alive.

R. L. STEVENSON, *An Inland Voyage.*

2

Hail! Independence, hail! heaven's next best gift
To that of life and an immortal soul!
The life of life! that to the banquet high
And sober meal gives taste; to the bow'd roof
Fair-dream'd repose, and to the cottage charms.

JAMES THOMSON, *Liberty.* Pt. v, l. 124.

3

I would rather sit on a pumpkin and have it all to myself than be crowded on a velvet cushion.

H. D. THOREAU, *Walden.* Ch. 1.

4

A nihilist is a man who does not bow down before any authority; who does not take any principle on faith, whatever reverence that principle may be enshrined in.

TURGENEV, *Fathers and Children.* Ch. v.

5

How happy is he born and taught,
That serveth not another's will;
Whose armour is his honest thought,
And simple truth his utmost skill.

SIR HENRY WOTTON, *The Character of a Happy Life.*

6

So live that you can look any man in the eye and tell him to go to hell.

UNKNOWN. First given currency by one of the engineers of the Panama canal, a gentleman later retired, it would seem, for attempting to execute his own counsel.—MENCKEN, *American Language,* p. 434. Used by John D. Rockefeller, jr., in an address before senior class at Dartmouth, June, 1930.

INDEPENDENCE DAY

7

Independence forever!

JOHN ADAMS. Adams died July 4, 1826. He had been aroused on the morning of that day by a discharge of cannon, and asked the cause. On being told it was Independence Day, he murmured "Independence forever!" Four days previously he had given those words in answer to a request for a toast to be offered in his name on the Fourth.

It is my living sentiment, and by the blessing of God it shall be my dying sentiment,—Independence now and Independence forever!

DANIEL WEBSTER. The closing words of the imaginary speech attributed to John Adams, in a eulogy pronounced 2 August, 1826. The eulogy was in memory of both Adams and Jefferson, who had died on the same day, 4 July, 1826.

8

Yesterday the greatest question was decided which ever was debated in America; and a greater perhaps never was, nor will be, decided among men. A resolution was passed without one dissenting colony, that those United Colonies are, and of right ought to be, free and independent States.

JOHN ADAMS, *Letter to Mrs. Adams.* 3 July, 1776.

The second day of July, 1776, will be the most memorable epoch in the history of America. I am apt to believe that it will be celebrated by succeeding generations as the great anniversary festival. It ought to be commemorated as the day of deliverance, by solemn acts of devotion to God Almighty. It ought to be solemnized with pomp and parade, with shows, games, sports, guns, bells, bonfires, and illuminations, from one end of this continent to the other, from this time forward forevermore.

JOHN ADAMS, *Letter to Mrs. Adams.* 3 July, 1776.

While Gen'l Howe with a Large Armament is advancing towards N. York, our Congress resolved to Declare the United Colonies Free and Independent States. A Declaration for this Purpose, I expect, will this day pass Congress. . . . It is gone so far that we must now be a free independent State, or a Conquered Country.

ABRAHAM CLARK, *Letter to Elias Dayton,* Phila., July 4, 1776. Clark was a member of the Continental Congress from New Jersey.

9

The United States is the only country with a known birthday.

JAMES G. BLAINE, *America's Natal Day.*

10

That which distinguishes this day from all others is that then both orators and artillerymen shoot blank cartridges.

JOHN BURROUGHS, *Journal,* July 4, 1859.

11

The glittering and sounding generalities of natural right which make up the Declaration of Independence.

RUFUS CHOATE, *Letter to Maine Whig Convention,* 9 Aug., 1856.

We fear that the glittering generalities of the speaker have left an impression more delightful than permanent.

F. J. DICKMAN, *Review of Lecture by Rufus Choate.* (*Providence Journal,* 14 Dec., 1849.)

"Glittering generalities!" They are blazing ubiquities.

EMERSON, *Uncollected Lectures: Books.* Referring to Choate's remark.

12

The flippant mistaking for freedom of some paper preamble like a "Declaration of Independence."

EMERSON, *Conduct of Life: Fate.*

Declarations of Independence make nobody really independent.
George Santayana. (Inge, *Wit and Wisdom.*)

1
The cannon booms from town to town,
Our pulses beat not less,
The joy-bells chime their tidings down,
Which children's voices bless.
Emerson, *Ode,* July 4, 1857.

2
Let independence be our boast,
Ever mindful what it cost;
Ever grateful for the prize,
Let its altar reach the skies!
Joseph Hopkinson, *Hail, Columbia!*

3
When in the course of human events, it becomes necessary for one people to dissolve the political bonds which have connected them with another, and to assume among the powers of the earth the separate and equal station to which the laws of nature and of nature's God entitle them, a decent respect to the opinions of mankind requires that they should declare the causes which impel them to the separation.
Thomas Jefferson, *Declaration of Independence: Preamble.*

4
We hold these truths to be self-evident: that all men are created equal; that they are endowed by their Creator with inherent and inalienable rights; that among these are life, liberty, and the pursuit of happiness.
Thomas Jefferson, *First Draft of Declaration of Independence.* (*Writings,* xix, 278.)

We hold these truths to be self-evident, that all men are created equal, that they are endowed by their Creator with certain unalienable Rights, that among these are Life, Liberty and the pursuit of Happiness. That to secure these rights, Governments are instituted among Men, deriving their just powers from the consent of the governed. That whenever any Form of Government becomes destructive of these ends, it is the Right of the People to alter or to abolish it, and to institute new Government, laying its foundation on such principles and organizing its powers in such form, as to them shall seem most likely to effect their Safety and Happiness. . . . We, therefore, . . . do . . . solemnly publish and declare, That these United Colonies are, and of Right ought to be free and independent States. . . . And for the support of this Declaration, with a firm reliance on the protection of Divine Providence, We mutually pledge to each other our Lives, our Fortunes, and our sacred Honor.
Thomas Jefferson, *Declaration of Independence,* as adopted by the Continental Congress, in session at Philadelphia, on the evening of July 4, 1776. Printed as a broadside and sent to the colonies 6 July, 1776.

Among the natural rights of the colonists are these: First a right to life, secondly to liberty, thirdly to property; together with the right to defend them in the best manner they can.
Samuel Adams, *Statement of the Rights of the Colonists,* etc., 20 Nov., 1772. (Wells, *Life of Samuel Adams,* i, 496.)

All men are born free and equal, and have certain natural, essential, and unalienable rights.
John Adams, *Constitution of Massachusetts.* 1779. (*Works,* vi, 465.)

5
To-day her thanks shall fly on every wind,
Unstinted, unrebuked, from shore to shore,
One love, one hope, and not a doubt behind!
Cannon to cannon shall repeat her praise,
Banner to banner flap it forth in flame;
Her children shall rise up to bless her name,
And wish her harmless length of days,
The mighty mother of a mighty brood,
Blessed in all tongues and dear to every blood,
The beautiful, the strong, and, best of all, the good.
J. R. Lowell, *Ode for the Fourth of July, 1876,* l. 43.

A safe and sane Fourth.
Tom Masson, *Editorial,* in *Life.* (1896)

6
Day of glory! Welcome day!
Freedom's banners greet thy ray.
John Pierpont, *The Fourth of July.*

7
Jefferson's Declaration of Independence is a practical document for the use of practical men. It is not a thesis for philosophers, but a whip for tyrants; it is not a theory of government, but a program of action.
Woodrow Wilson, *Speech,* Indianapolis, 13 April, 1911.

8
Sink or swim, live or die, survive or perish,
I give my heart and my hand to this vote.
Daniel Webster. In a eulogy upon John Adams and Thomas Jefferson, 2 August, 1826, Webster introduced a speech supposed to have been made by Adams in favor of the adoption of the Declaration of Independence. The phrase was derived from the record of a conversation between Adams and Jonathan Sewall in 1774: "I answered that the die was now cast; I had passed the Rubicon. Sink or swim, live or die, survive or perish with my country, was my unalterable determination."

9
"Ring!" he shouts; "ring, grandpapa,
Ring! oh, ring for liberty!"
Unknown, *Independence Bell.*

INDEX

10
I certainly think that the best book in the world would owe the most to a good index, and the worst book, if it had but a single good thought in it, might be kept alive by it.
Horace Binney, *Letter to S. A. Allibone,* 8 April, 1868.

1
So essential did I consider an index to be to every book, that I proposed to bring a bill into Parliament to deprive an author who publishes a book without an index of the privilege of copyright, and, moreover, to subject him for his offence to a pecuniary penalty.

LORD JOHN CAMPBELL, *Lives of the Chief Justices of England:* Vol. iii, *Preface.*

An index is a necessary *implement,* and no *impediment,* of a book, except in the same sense wherein the carriages of an army are termed *impediments.* Without this a large author is but a labyrinth without a clew to direct the reader therein.

THOMAS FULLER, *History of the Worthies of England: Norfolk Writers: Alan of Llyn.*

2
One writer, for instance, excels at a plan or a title-page, another works away at the body of the book, and a third is a dab at an index.

GOLDSMITH, *The Bee.* No. 1.

He writes indexes to perfection.

GOLDSMITH, *The Citizen of the World.* Letter No. 7.

3
The index tells us the contents of stories and directs us to the particular chapters.

MASSINGER AND FIELD, *The Fatal Dowry.* Act iv, sc. 1.

4
Index-learning turns no student pale,
Yet holds the eel of science by the tail.

POPE, *The Dunciad.* Bk. i, l. 279.

A mere index hunter, who held the eel of science by the tail.

SMOLLETT, *Peregrine Pickle.* Ch. 43.

The most accomplished way of using books at present is twofold: either, first to serve them as men do lords,—learn their titles exactly and then brag of their acquaintance; or, secondly, which is, indeed, the choicer, the profounder and politer method, to get a thorough insight into the index, by which the whole book is governed and turned, like fishes by the tail. For to enter the palace of learning at the great gate requires an expense of time and forms, therefore men of much haste and little ceremony are content to get in by the back door. . . . For this great blessing we are wholly indebted to systems and abstracts, in which the modern fathers of learning, like prudent usurers, spent their sweat for the ease of us their children. For labour is the seed of idleness, and it is the peculiar happiness of our noble age to gather the fruit.

SWIFT, *A Tale of a Tub: A Digression in Praise of Digressions.*

5
And in such indexes, although small pricks
To their subsequent volumes, there is seen
The baby figure of the giant mass
Of things to come at large.

SHAKESPEARE, *Troilus and Cressida.* Act i, sc. 3, l. 343.

INDIAN (AMERICAN)

6
But don't you go and make mistakes, like many derned fools I've known,
For dirt is dirt, and snakes is snakes, but an Injin's flesh and bone!

ROBERT BUCHANAN, *Phil Blood's Leap.*

7
As monumental bronze unchanged his look;
A soul that pity touched, but never shook;
Trained from his tree-rocked cradle to his bier
The fierce extremes of good and ill to brook
Impassive—fearing but the shame of fear—
A stoic of the woods—a man without a tear.

CAMPBELL, *Gertrude of Wyoming.* Pt. i, st. 23.

8
His erect and perfect form, though disclosing some irregular virtues, was found joined to a dwindled soul. Master of all sorts of woodcraft, he seemed a part of the forest and the lake, and the secret of his amazing skill seemed to be that he partook of the nature and fierce instincts of the beasts he slew. . . . Thomas Hooker anticipated the opinion of Humboldt, and called them "the ruins of mankind."

EMERSON, *Miscellanies: Historical Discourse.*

The interest of the Puritans in the natives was heightened by a suspicion at that time prevailing that these were the lost ten tribes of Israel.

EMERSON, *Miscellanies: Historical Discourse.*

9
Savages we call them, because their manners differ from ours.

BENJAMIN FRANKLIN, *Remarks Concerning the Savages of North America.*

10
Lo, the poor Indian! whose untutor'd mind
Sees God in clouds, or hears him in the wind;
His soul proud Science never taught to stray
Far as the solar walk or milky way;
Yet simple nature to his hope has giv'n,
Behind the cloud-topt hill, an humbler Heav'n; . . .
To be, contents his natural desire;
He asks no Angel's wing, no Seraph's fire;
But thinks, admitted to that equal sky,
His faithful dog shall bear him company.

POPE, *Essay on Man.* Epis. i, l. 99.

11
The only good Indian is a dead Indian.

GENERAL PHILIP HENRY SHERIDAN. On the authority of Edward M. Ellis, who stated that he was present at old Fort Cobb, Indian Territory, in January, 1869, when, after a fight with the Indians, a Chief named Old Toch-a-way was presented to General Sheridan as "a good Indian," and Sheridan remarked, "The only good Indian I ever saw was a dead Indian."

12
You can make an Injun of a white man but you can never make a white man of an Injun.

GENERAL WILLIAM T. SHERMAN.

1
Ye say they all have passed away,
That noble race and brave;
That their light canoes have vanished
From off the crested wave;
That mid the forests where they roamed
There rings no hunter's shout;
But their name is on your waters;
Ye may not wash it out.
LYDIA HUNTLY SIGOURNEY, *Indian Names.*

The memory of the red man
How can it pass away,
While their names of music linger
On each mount and stream and bay?
RICHARD HUNTINGTON, *The Indian Names of Acadia.*

INDIANA

2
Oh the moonlight's fair to-night along the Wabash,
From the fields there comes the breath of new-mown hay;
Thro' the sycamores the candle lights are gleaming,
On the banks of the Wabash far away.
PAUL DRESSER, *On the Banks of the Wabash.* (1897)

When an Eastern man is cheated by a Hoosier he is said to be *Wabashed.*
R. W. EMERSON, *Journal,* 1860.

3
Blest Indiana! in whose soil
Men seek the sure rewards of toil,
And honest poverty and worth
Find here the best retreat on earth,
While hosts of Preachers, Doctors, Lawyers,
All independent as wood-sawyers,
With men of every hue and fashion,
Flock to the rising "Hoosier" nation.
JOHN FINLEY, *The Hoosier's Nest,* published as the *Address of the Carrier of the Indianapolis Journal,* 1 January, 1833. (The first recorded use of "hoosier.")

The Hoosier State of Indiana!
JOHN W. DAVIS, *Toast,* at the Jackson dinner at Indianapolis, 8 Jan., 1933.

4
I come from Indiana, the home of more first-rate second-class men than any State in the Union.
THOMAS R. MARSHALL, *Recollections.*

The brighter they were the sooner they came.
GEORGE ADE, referring to the "bright" men who came from Indiana.

5
I was born in Indiany—an' I'm pinin' to git back.
EZRA B. NEWCOMB, *Homesick.*

INDIFFERENCE

6
The earth revolves with me, yet makes no motion,
The stars pale silently in a coral sky.
In a whistling void I stand before my mirror,
Unconcerned, and tie my tie.
CONRAD AIKEN, *Morning Song of Senlin.*

7
Moral indifference is the malady of the cultivated classes.
AMIEL, *Journal,* 26 Oct., 1870.

A mild indifferentism.
ROBERT BROWNING, *Christmas-Eve.* Sec. 19.

Full of a sweet indifference.
ROBERT BUCHANAN, *Charmian.*

8
However, 'tis expedient to be wary:
Indifference certes don't produce distress.
BYRON, *Don Juan.* Canto xiii, st. 35.

9
I care not two-pence.
BEAUMONT AND FLETCHER, *The Coxcomb.* Act v, sc. 1.

Not worth two-pence. (Ne vaut pas deux sous.)
MARSHAL FERDINAND FOCH, a favorite expression of his, which caused him to be nicknamed "General Deux Sous."

Not worth a two-penny dam.
DUKE OF WELLINGTON, *Letter to His Brother.* (*Dispatches.* Vol. i.)

10
I care for nobody, no, not I,
If no one cares for me.
ISAAC BICKERSTAFFE, *Love in a Village.* Act i, sc. 5.

11
A wise and salutary neglect.
EDMUND BURKE, *Speech on Conciliation With America.*

Whose most tender mercy is neglect.
GEORGE CRABBE, *The Village.* Bk. i.

12
The whole frame of things preaches indifferency.
EMERSON, *Essays, First Series: Experience.*

13
O haste to shed the sovereign balm—
My shattered nerves new string:
And for my guest serenely calm,
The nymph Indifference bring.
FRANCES MACARTNEY FULKE-GREVILLE, *Prayer for Indifference.*

14
I could do without your face and your neck, and your hands, and your limbs, and your bosom, and other of your charms. Indeed, not to fatigue myself with enumerating each of them, I could do without you, Chloe, altogether.
MARTIAL, *Epigrams.* Bk. iii, ep. 53.

15
Happy are the men whom nature has buttressed with indifference and cased in stoicism.
GUY DE MAUPASSANT, *After.*

16
She, while her lover pants upon her breast,
Can mark the figures in an Indian chest;

And when she sees her friend in deep despair,
Observes how much a chintz exceeds mohair.

POPE, *Moral Essays*. Epis. ii, l. 167.

"Pray, my dear," quoth my mother, "have you not forgot to wind up the clock?" "Good God!" cried my father. "Did ever woman, since the creation of the world, interrupt a man with such a silly question?"

STERNE, *Tristram Shandy*. Bk. i, ch. 1. The incident which, so Tristram believed, gave a peculiar quirk to his disposition.

2
I know thy works, that thou art neither cold nor hot: I would thou wert cold or hot.

New Testament: Revelation, iii, 15.

Out of the same mouth you blow hot and cold.

AESOP, *Fables: The Man and the Satyr*. The satyr's remark to the man who blew first on his hands to warm them, and then on his soup to cool it.

3
At length the morn and cold indifference came.

NICHOLAS ROWE, *The Fair Penitent*. Act i, sc. 1.

4
Harvard indifference. "A cult of cleverness, exquisiteness and boredom."

ARTHUR RUHL. (See COOKE, under LIFE: A BUBBLE.)

5
'Tis lack of kindly warmth.

SHAKESPEARE, *Timon of Athens*, ii, 2, 226.

We are cold to others only when we are dull in ourselves.

HAZLITT, *Literary Remains*. Vol. ii, p. 197.

6
Adieu, ball, pleasure, love! They only said, "Poor Constance!" And they danced until day at the house of the French ambassador.

(Adieu, bal, plaisir, amour!
On disait, Pauvre Constance!
Et on dansait, jusqu'au jour,
Chez l'ambassadeur de France.)

CASIMIR DE LA VIGNE, *La Toilette de Constance*.

A lovely young lady I mourn in my rhymes:
She was pleasant, good-natured, and civil sometimes.
Her figure was good, she had very fine eyes,
And her talk was a mixture of foolish and wise.
Her adorers were many, and one of them said,
"She waltzed rather well! It's a pity she's dead!"

GEORGE JOHN CAYLEY [?], *An Epitaph*.

7
Indifference and hypocrisy between them keep orthodoxy alive.

ISRAEL ZANGWILL, *Children of the Ghetto*. Bk. ii, ch. 15.

8
Whatever turn the matter takes,
I deem it all but ducks and drakes.

JOHN BYROM, *Careless Content*.

The cat is in the parlor, the dog is in the lake;
The cow is in the hammock—what difference does it make?

UNKNOWN, *Indifference*.

INDIGESTION

See also Dreams: Their Cause

9
Confirmed dyspepsia is the apparatus of illusions.

GEORGE MEREDITH, *Richard Feverel*. Ch. 34.

10
What boots the calm of this whole shop
If my inside is going pop? (Quid prodest totius regionis silentium, si adfectus fremunt?)

SENECA, *Epistles*. (Arthur Gordon Webster, tr.)

11
He sows hurry and reaps indigestion.

R. L. STEVENSON, *An Apology for Idlers*.

INDIGNATION, See Anger

INDIVIDUALITY

See also Character, Personality

12
The individual is always mistaken.

EMERSON, *Essays, Second Series: Experience*.

13
Each man . . . is justified in his individuality, as his nature is found to be immense.

EMERSON, *Essays, Second Series: Nominalist and Realist*.

If the single man plant himself indomitably on his instincts, and there abide, the huge world will come round to him.

EMERSON, *Nature, Addresses, and Lectures: The American Scholar*.

Everything that tends to insulate the individual . . . tends to true union as well as greatness.

EMERSON, *The American Scholar*.

14
The universal does not attract us until housed in an individual.

EMERSON, *Nature, Addresses, and Lectures: The Method of Nature*.

Every individual strives to grow and exclude and to exclude and grow, to the extremities of the universe, and to impose the law of its being on every other creature.

EMERSON, *Representative Men: Uses of Great Men*.

To clap copyright on the world: this is the ambition of individualism.

EMERSON, *Representative Men: Plato*.

15 Rugged individualism.

HERBERT HOOVER, *The New Day*, p. 154. (1928)

16
The man whom God wills to slay in the struggle of life He first individualizes.

HENRIK IBSEN, *Brand*. Act v.

17
A people, it appears, may be progressive for a certain length of time, and then stop. When does it stop? When it ceases to possess individuality.

JOHN STUART MILL, *On Liberty*, Ch. 3.

Whatever crushes individuality is despotism, by whatever name it may be called.
JOHN STUART MILL, *On Liberty*. Ch. 3.

1
The history of every individual should be a Bible.
NOVALIS, *Christianity of Europe*. (Carlyle, tr.)

2
The individual is the end of the Universe.
MIGUEL DE UNAMUNO, *Tragic Sense of Life*, p. 312.

3
Individualism is a fatal poison. But individuality is the salt of common life. You may have to live in a crowd, but you do not have to live like it, nor subsist on its food. You may have your own orchard. You may drink at a hidden spring. Be yourself if you would serve others.
HENRY VAN DYKE, *The School of Life*, p. 33.

4
I announce the great individual, fluid as Nature, chaste, affectionate, compassionate, fully arm'd.
WALT WHITMAN, *So Long!*

Underneath all, individuals,
I swear nothing is good to me now that ignores individuals. . . .
The only government is that which makes minute of individuals,
The whole theory of the universe is directed unerringly to one single individual—namely to You.
WALT WHITMAN, *By Blue Ontario's Shore*. Sec. 15.

5
I celebrate myself, and sing myself,
And what I assume you shall assume,
For every atom belonging to me as good belongs to you.
WALT WHITMAN, *Song of Myself*. Sec. 1.

I pass death with the dying and birth with the new-wash'd babe, and am not contain'd between my hat and my boots.
WALT WHITMAN, *Song of Myself*. Sec. 7.

I wear my hat as I please indoors or out.
Why should I pray? why should I venerate and be ceremonious?
Having pried through the strata, analyzed to a hair, counsel'd with doctors and calculated close,
I find no sweeter fat than sticks to my own bones.
WALT WHITMAN, *Song of Myself*. Sec. 20.

I know I am solid and sound,
To me the converging objects of the universe perpetually flow,
All are written to me.
WALT WHITMAN, *Song of Myself*. Sec. 20.

INDOLENCE, see Idleness

INDUSTRY

6
In the ordinary business of life, industry can do anything which genius can do, and very many things which it cannot.
HENRY WARD BEECHER, *Proverbs from Plymouth Pulpit*.

7
The dog that trots about finds a bone.
GEORGE BORROW, *The Bible in Spain*. Ch. 47. Quoted as a gypsy saying.

The sleeping fox catches no poultry.
BENJAMIN FRANKLIN, *Poor Richard*, 1758.

8
Industry is a loadstone to draw all good things.
ROBERT BURTON, *Anatomy of Melancholy: Democritus to the Reader*.

9
To be busy at something is a modest maid's holiday.
CERVANTES, *Don Quixote*. Pt. ii, ch. 5.

10
Pray to God and ply the hammer.
CERVANTES, *Don Quixote*. Pt. ii, ch. 35.

The sound of your hammer at five in the morning, or nine at night, heard by a creditor, makes him easy six months longer.
BENJAMIN FRANKLIN, *Letter to My Friend, A.B.*

11
Diligence is the mother of good fortune. (La diligencia es madre de la buena ventura.)
CERVANTES, *Don Quixote*. Pt. i, ch. 46.

Diligence is the mother of good luck.
BENJAMIN FRANKLIN, *Poor Richard's Almanack*, 1736.

12
She is so diligent, withouten slowth
To serve and plesen evrich in that place,
That all her loven that loken on her face.
CHAUCER, *Tale of the Man of Lawe*, l. 432.

13
Industry is the soul of business and the keystone of prosperity.
DICKENS, *Barnaby Rudge*. Ch. 27.

14
My constant attendance, I never making a St. Monday, recommended me to the master.
BENJAMIN FRANKLIN, *Autobiography*. Ch. 1. Never turning a Monday into a holiday by drinking too much Saturday night and Sunday.

15
At the working man's house hunger looks in, but dares not enter.
BENJAMIN FRANKLIN, *Poor Richard*, 1737.

16
Plough deep while Sluggards sleep,
And you shall have Corn to sell and to keep.
BENJAMIN FRANKLIN, *Poor Richard*, 1756.

A diligent Spinner has a large Shift.
BENJAMIN FRANKLIN, *Poor Richard*, 1756.

Industry need not wish.
BENJAMIN FRANKLIN, *Poor Richard*, 1739.

The used key is always bright.
BENJAMIN FRANKLIN, *Poor Richard*, 1744.

1
In every rank, or great or small,
'Tis industry supports us all.
JOHN GAY, *Fables*. Pt. ii, No. 8, l. 65.

2
Never idle a moment, but thrifty and thoughtful of others.
LONGFELLOW, *Courtship of Miles Standish*. Pt. viii, l. 46.

Let us, then, be up and doing.
LONGFELLOW, *A Psalm of Life*.

3
All things are won by diligence. (Πάντα ταῖς ἐνδελεχείαις καταπονεῖται πράγματα.)
MENANDER, *Fragments*. No. 742.

God gives all things to industry.
THOMAS FULLER, *Gnomologia*.

4
Push on—keep moving.
THOMAS MORTON, *A Cure for the Heart-Ache*. Act iii, sc. 1.

Watch your step.
THEODORE SHONTS, when manager of the New York subway.

5
Genius is the father of a heavenly line but the mortal mother, that is industry.
THEODORE PARKER, *Ten Sermons: Culture of Religious Powers*. *See also under* GENIUS.

6
Much industry and little conscience make a man rich.
W. G. BENHAM, *Proverbs*, p. 812.

Industry is fortune's right hand, and frugality her left.
JOHN RAY, *English Proverbs*.

7
If you have great talents, industry will improve them; if you have but moderate abilities, industry will supply their deficiencies.
SIR JOSHUA REYNOLDS, *Discourses on Painting*. No. 2.

8
The best of me is diligence.
SHAKESPEARE, *King Lear*. Act i, sc. 4, l. 37.

9
Nothing is achieved before it be thoroughly attempted.
SIR PHILIP SIDNEY, *Arcadia*. Bk. ii.

10
The hope, and not the fact, of advancement, is the spur to industry.
SIR HENRY TAYLOR, *The Statesman*, p. 187.

11
Thanks to my friends for their care in my breeding,
Who taught me betimes to love working and reading.
ISAAC WATTS, *The Sluggard*.

12
In books, or work, or healthful play,
Let my first years be past,
That I may give for every day
Some good account at last.
ISAAC WATTS, *Against Idleness*.

HOW DOTH THE LITTLE BUSY BEE, *see under* BEE.

INFLUENCE

I—Influence: Apothegms

13
Every life is a profession of faith, and exercises an inevitable and silent influence.
AMIEL, *Journal*, 2 May, 1852.

14
A little leaven leaveneth the whole lump.
New Testament: I Corinthians, v, 6; *Galatians*, v, 9.

15
He raised a mortal to the skies;
She drew an angel down.
DRYDEN, *Alexander's Feast*, l. 169.

I thank God that if I am gifted with little of the spirit which is said to be able to raise mortals to the skies, I have yet none, as I trust, of that other spirit, which would drag angels down.
DANIEL WEBSTER, *Second Speech on Foote's Resolution*, 26 Jan., 1830.

16
It has been said that "common souls pay with what they do, nobler souls with that which they are."
EMERSON, *Essays, First Series: History*.

17
Every man who speaks out loud and clear is tinting the "Zeitgeist." Every man who expresses what he honestly thinks is changing the Spirit of the Times.
ELBERT HUBBARD, *Pig-Pen Pete: The Bee*.

18
Canst thou bind the sweet influences of Pleiades, or loose the bands of Orion?
Old Testament: Job, xxxviii, 31.

19
The salutary influence of example.
SAMUEL JOHNSON, *Lives of the Poets: Milton*. *See also under* EXAMPLE.

20
The finest edge is made with the blunt whetstone.
JOHN LYLY, *Euphues*, p. 47.

21
A cock has great influence on his own dunghill.
PUBLILIUS SYRUS, *Sententiæ*. No. 357. *See also under* CHANTICLEER.

22
Influence, like the wreath of radiant fire
On flickering Phœbus' front.
SHAKESPEARE, *King Lear*. Act ii, sc. 2, l. 113. *See also* STARS: THEIR INFLUENCE.

23
They'll take suggestion as a cat laps milk.
SHAKESPEARE, *The Tempest*. Act ii, sc. 1, l. 288.

24
It is your human environment that makes climate.
MARK TWAIN, *Pudd'nhead Wilson's New Calendar*.

II—Influence: Its Power

25
The sexton tolling his bell at noon,
Deems not that great Napoleon

Stops his horse, and lists with delight,
Whilst his files sweep round yon Alpine height;
Nor knowest thou what argument
Thy life to thy neighbor's creed has lent.
EMERSON, *Each and All.*

1
This learned I from the shadow of a tree,
That to and fro did sway against a wall:
Our shadow-selves, our influence, may fall
Where we ourselves can never be.
ANNA E. HAMILTON, *Influence.*

2
Thou canst mould him into any shape like soft clay. (Argilla quidvis imitaberis uda.)
HORACE, *Epistles.* Bk. ii, epis. 2, l. 8.

His soul is so enfetter'd to her love,
That she may make, unmake, do what she list,
Even as her appetite shall play the god
With his weak function.
SHAKESPEARE, *Othello.* Act ii, sc. 3, l. 351.

3
I shot an arrow into the air,
It fell to earth, I knew not where;
For, so swiftly it flew, the sight
Could not follow it in its flight.

I breathed a song into the air,
It fell to earth, I knew not where;
For who has sight so keen and strong,
That it can follow the flight of song?

Long, long afterward, in an oak
I found the arrow, still unbroke;
And the song, from beginning to end,
I found again in the heart of a friend.
LONGFELLOW, *The Arrow and the Song.*

You never can tell when you send a word
Like an arrow shot from a bow
By an archer blind, be it cruel or kind,
Just where it may chance to go.
ELLA WHEELER WILCOX, *You Never Can Tell.*

4
Pluck one thread, and the web ye mar;
Break but one
Of a thousand keys, and the paining jar
Through all will run.
WHITTIER, *My Soul and I.* St. 38.

III—Influence for Good

5
The weak and the gentle, the ribald and rude,
She took as she found them, and did them all good.
E. B. BROWNING, *My Kate.*

None knelt at her feet confessed lovers in thrall;
They knelt more to God than they used—that was all.
E. B. BROWNING, *My Kate.*

6
Even so he turned
The saddest things to beauty. With his face
Came calm and consecration.
ROBERT BUCHANAN, *Balder the Beautiful.* Pt. iii.

7
The work an unknown good man has done is like a vein of water flowing hidden underground, secretly making the ground green.
CARLYLE, *Essays: Varnhagen von Ense's Memoirs.*

8
So our lives In acts exemplary, not only win
Ourselves good names, but doth to others give
Matter for virtuous deeds, by which we live.
CHAPMAN, *Bussy D'Ambois.* Act i, sc. 1.

9
Thou art the framer of my nobler being;
Nor does there live one virtue in my soul,
One honourable hope, but calls thee father.
S. T. COLERIDGE, *Zapolya.* Act i, sc. 1.

10
Blessed influence of one true loving human soul on another.
GEORGE ELIOT, *Janet's Repentance.* Ch. 19.

11
O may I join the choir invisible
Of those immortal dead who live again
In minds made better by their presence: live
In pulses stirred to generosity,
In deeds of daring rectitude, in scorn
For miserable aims that end with self,
In thoughts sublime that pierce the night like stars,
And with their mild persistence urge man's search
To vaster issues.
GEORGE ELIOT, *O May I Join the Choir Invisible.*

12
It costs a beautiful person no effort to paint her image on our eyes; yet how splendid is that benefit! It costs no more for a wise soul to convey his quality to other men.
EMERSON, *Representative Men: Uses of Great Men.*

It is for man to tame the chaos; on every side, whilst he lives, to scatter the seeds of science and of song, that climate, corn, animals, men, may be milder, and the germs of love and benefit may be multiplied.
EMERSON, *Representative Men: Uses of Great Men.*

13
The very room, coz she was in,
Seemed warm f'om floor to ceilin'.
J. R. LOWELL, *The Courtin'.* St. 6.

Before her ran an influence fleet,
That bowed my heart like barley bending.
J. R. LOWELL, *Hebe.*

14
No life
Can be pure in its purpose or strong in its strife
And all life not be purer and stronger thereby.
OWEN MEREDITH, *Lucile.* Pt. ii, canto vi, sec. 40.

15
So it often happens that more good is done

without our knowledge than by us intended.
PLAUTUS, *Captivi: Prologue*, l. 44.

1
To dazzle let the vain design,
To raise the thought and touch the heart be thine!
POPE, *Moral Essays*. Ep. ii, l. 249.

2
O, he sits high in all the people's hearts:
And that which would appear offence in us,
His countenance, like richest alchemy,
Will change to virtue and to worthiness.
SHAKESPEARE, *Julius Cæsar*. Act i, sc. 3, l. 157.

He makes a July's day short as December,
And with his varying childness cures in me
Thoughts that would thick my blood.
SHAKESPEARE, *Winter's Tale*. Act i, sc. 2, l. 169.

3
For, when the power of imparting joy
Is equal to the will, the human soul
Requires no other heaven.
SHELLEY, *Queen Mab*. Pt. iii, l. 11.

4
Though her mien carries much more invitation than command, to behold her is an immediate check to loose behaviour; to love her is a liberal education.
RICHARD STEELE, *The Tatler*. No. 49. Of Lady Elizabeth Hastings. Swinburne called this passage "the most exquisite tribute ever paid to the memory of a noble woman," and Augustine Birrell, in *Obiter Dicta*, echoes the opinion.

5
Such souls,
Whose sudden visitations daze the world,
Vanish like lightning, but they leave behind
A voice that in the distance far away
Wakens the slumbering ages.
HENRY TAYLOR, *Philip Van Artevelde*. Pt. i, act i, sc. 7.

6
Whose powers shed round him in the common strife,
Or mild concerns of ordinary life,
A constant influence, a peculiar grace.
WORDSWORTH, *Character of the Happy Warrior*, l. 45.

Controls them and subdues, transmutes, bereaves
Of their bad influence, and their good receives.
WORDSWORTH, *Character of the Happy Warrior*, l. 17.

An instinct call it, a blind sense;
A happy, genial influence,
Coming one knows not how, nor whence,
Nor whither going.
WORDSWORTH, *To the Daisy*.

IV—Influence for Evil

7
Corrupt influence, which is in itself the perennial spring of all prodigality, and of all disorder; which loads us, more than millions of debt; which takes away vigour from our arms, wisdom from our councils.
EDMUND BURKE, *Speech on Economical Reform*, House of Commons, 11 Feb., 1780.

8
You made me what I am to-day,
I hope you're satisfied. . . .
And though you're not true,
May God bless you,
That's the curse of an aching heart.
HENRY FINK, *The Curse of an Aching Heart*. (1913)

I was once a step above her,
But she brought me to her level,
So I drink the *death* of Daisy—
Little angel—little devil!
E. J. APPLETON, *Little Angel, Little Devil*.

9
Each man, in corrupting others, corrupts himself; he imbibes, and then imparts, badness.
SENECA, *Epistulæ ad Lucilium*. Epis. xciv, 54.

10
Like a mildewed ear,
Blasting his wholesome brother.
SHAKESPEARE, *Hamlet*. Act iii, sc. 4, l. 64.

The rotten apple spoils his companions.
BENJAMIN FRANKLIN, *Poor Richard*, 1736.

See also under SHEEP.

V—Influence: In Battle

11
We must have your name. There will be more efficacy in it than in many an army.
JOHN ADAMS, *Letter to George Washington*, 1798, when war with France seemed imminent.

12
But how many ships do you reckon my presence to be worth?
ANTIGONUS, when told by his pilot that the enemy outnumbered him in ships. (PLUTARCH, *Apothegms of Kings and Great Commanders: Antigonus II.*)

The saying of old Antigonus, who when he was to fight at Andros, and one told him, "The enemy's ships are more than ours," replied, "For how many then wilt thou reckon me?"
PLUTARCH, *Lives: Pelopidas*.

13
As that great captain, Ziska, would have a drum made of his skin when he was dead, because he thought the very noise of it would put his enemies to flight.
ROBERT BURTON, *Anatomy of Melancholy: Democritus to the Reader*.

14
Oh, for one hour of blind old Dandolo,
The octogenarian chief, Byzantium's conquering foe!
BYRON, *Childe Harold*. Canto iv, st. 12.

15
Napoleon was called by his men Cent Mille.
EMERSON, *Conduct of Life: Considerations by the Way*. Because his presence was worth a hundred thousand men.

It is very true that I have said that I considered Napoleon's presence in the field equal to forty thousand men in the balance. This is a very loose way of talking; but the idea is a very different one from that of his presence at a battle being equal to a reinforcement of forty thousand men.

DUKE OF WELLINGTON, *Memorandum*, 18 Sept., 1836. (STANHOPE, *Conversations with the Duke of Wellington*, p. 81.)

1
The great, himself a host. (Πελώριος, ἕρκος Ἀχαιῶν.)

HOMER, *Iliad*, Bk. iii, l. 219. (Pope, tr., l. 293.) Referring to Ajax.

2
Whenever I stamp my foot in any part of Italy, there will rise up forces enough in an instant.

POMPEY, when asked where the forces were to come from to resist Cæsar. (PLUTARCH, *Lives: Pompey.*)

3
Where, where was Roderick then?
One blast upon his bugle horn
Were worth a thousand men.

SCOTT, *The Lady of the Lake*. Canto vi, st. 18

Oh for a blast of that dread horn
On Fontarabian echoes borne!

SCOTT, *Marmion*. Canto vi, st. 33.

O for the voice of that wild horn.

SCOTT, *Rob Roy*. Ch. 2.

4
Your eye in Scotland
Would create soldiers, make our women fight,
To doff their dire distresses.

SHAKESPEARE, *Macbeth*. Act iv, sc. 3, l. 186.

5
Is not the king's name twenty thousand names?

SHAKESPEARE, *Richard II*. Act iii, sc. 2, l. 85.

The King's name is a tower of strength.

SHAKESPEARE, *Richard III*. Act v, sc. 3, l. 12.

6
Lord John is a host in himself.

DUKE OF WELLINGTON, to Samuel Rogers, 1839, referring to Lord John Russell.

7
Oh for a single hour of that Dundee
Who on that day the word of onset gave!

WORDSWORTH, *Sonnet in the Pass of Killicrankie*. "Oh, for an hour of Dundee," was the cry of Gordon of Glenbucket, at the battle of Sheriffmuir, 13 Nov., 1715. "Dundee" was the terrible Grahame of Claverhouse, Viscount Dundee. (MAHON, *History of England*, i, 184.)

VI—Influence: Homer's Golden Chain

8
Make ye fast from heaven a chain of gold. (Σειρὴν χρυσείην ἐξ οὐρανόθεν.)

HOMER, *Iliad*. Bk. viii, l. 19.

Lay ye down the golden chain
From Heaven, and pull at its inferior links
Both Goddesses and Gods.

HOMER, *Iliad*. Bk. viii. (Cowley, tr.)

By the golden chain Homer meant nothing else than the sun.

PLATO. (KIRCHER, *Magnes Sive de Arte Magnetica*.)

9
And this is that Homer's golden chain, which reacheth down from heaven to earth, by which every creature is annexed, and depends on his Creator.

ROBERT BURTON, *Anatomy of Melancholy*. Pt. iii, sec. i, mem. 1, subs. 2. Referring to God's love for the world.

10
Now lately heaven and earth, another world
Hung o'er my realm, link'd in a golden chain.

MILTON, *Paradise Lost*. Bk. ii, l. 1004.

And fast by, hanging in a golden chain,
This pendent world, in bigness as a star
Of smallest magnitude close by the moon.

MILTON, *Paradise Lost*. Bk. ii, l. 1051.

11
This gift which you have . . . is not an art, but an inspiration; there is a divinity moving you, like that in the stone which Euripides calls a magnet, but which is commonly known as the stone of Heraclea. For that stone not only attracts iron rings, but also imparts to them a similar power of attracting other rings; and sometimes you may see a number of pieces of iron and rings suspended from one another so as to form a long chain: and all of them derive their power of suspension from the original stone. Now this is like the Muse, who first gives to men inspiration herself: and from these inspired persons a chain of other persons is suspended, who take the inspiration from them.

PLATO, *Ion*. Sec. 533. This simile has come to be known as "Plato's rings."

12
To be imprisoned in the viewless winds
And blown with restless violence around about
The pendent world.

SHAKESPEARE, *Measure for Measure*. Act iii, sc. 1, l. 124.

13
Together linkt with adamantine chains.

SPENSER, *An Hymn in Honour of Love*, l. 89.

I gnawed my brazen chain, and sought to sever
Its adamantine links.

SHELLEY, *The Revolt of Islam*. Canto iii, st. 19.

14
For so the whole round earth is every way
Bound by gold chains about the feet of God.

TENNYSON, *Morte D'Arthur*, l. 305.

15
The chain that's fixed to the throne of Jove,
On which the fabric of our world depends,
One link dissolved, the whole creation ends.

EDMUND WALLER, *Of the Danger His Majesty Escaped*, l. 68.

INGRATITUDE

1
Earth produces nothing worse than an ungrateful man. (Nil homine terra pejus ingrato creat.)

AUSONIUS, *Epigrams*. No. 140, l. 1.

2
And having looked to Government for bread, on the very first scarcity they will turn and bite the hand that fed them.

EDMUND BURKE, *Thoughts and Details on Scarcity*.

We set ourselves to bite the hand that feeds us.

BURKE, *Cause of the Present Discontents*.

3
The wicked are always ungrateful.

CERVANTES, *Don Quixote*. Pt. i, ch. 23.

Hell is full of the ungrateful.

THOMAS FULLER, *Gnomologia*.

4
Ingratitude is the daughter of pride.

CERVANTES, *Don Quixote*. Pt. ii, ch. 51.

6
Ingratitude's a weed of every clime,
It thrives too fast at first, but fades in time.

SAMUEL GARTH, *Epistle to the Earl of Godolphin*, l. 27.

7
A man is very apt to complain of the ingratitude of those who have risen far above him.

SAMUEL JOHNSON. (BOSWELL, *Life*, 1776.)

8
An ingrate is sometimes less to blame for his ingratitude than the one who did him the favor. (Tel homme est ingrat, qui est moins coupable de son ingratitude que celui qui lui a fait du bien.)

LA ROCHEFOUCAULD, *Maximes*. No. 96.

Too great haste in repaying an obligation is a species of ingratitude. (Le trop grand empressement qu'on a de s'acquitter d'une obligation est une espèce d'ingratitude.)

LA ROCHEFOUCAULD, *Maximes*, No. 226.

One finds few ingrates as long as one is capable of bestowing favors. (On ne trouve guère d'ingrats tant qu'on est en état de faire du bien.)

LA ROCHEFOUCAULD, *Maximes*. No. 306.

9
Ah, how have I deserved, inhuman maid,
To have my faithful service thus repaid?

GEORGE LYTTELTON, *Progress of Love*.

10
Besotted base ingratitude.

MILTON, *Comus*, l. 778.

11
You love a nothing when you love an ingrate. (Nihil amas, quom ingratum amas.)

PLAUTUS, *Persa*, l. 228. (Act ii, sc. 2.)

12
We should not treat living creatures like shoes, or pots and pans, casting them aside when they are bruised and worn out with service.

PLUTARCH, *Lives: Marcus Cato*. Ch. v, sec. 5.

13
One ungrateful man does an injury to all who are in suffering. (Ingratus unus miseris omnibus nocet.)

PUBLILIUS SYRUS, *Sententiæ*. No. 274.

13a
They whom I benefit injure me most.

SAPPHO. (*The Songs of Sappho*, MARION MILLS MILLER, tr., p. 204.)

They whom I most have helped
Were 'neath the Dog-Star whelped
By Shamelessness and Spite:
The hand that feeds they bite.

MARION MILLS MILLER, *Ingratitude*. An amplification of the fragment from Sappho given above.

14
He is ungrateful who denies that he has received a kindness; he is ungrateful who conceals it; he is ungrateful who makes no return for it; most ungrateful of all is he who forgets it.

SENECA, *De Beneficiis*. Bk. iii, sec. 1. *See also* BENEFITS: BENEFITS AND INJURIES.

15
Blow, blow, thou winter wind,
Thou art not so unkind
As man's ingratitude:
Thy tooth is not so keen,
Because thou art not seen,
Although thy breath be rude.

SHAKESPEARE, *As You Like It*. Act ii, sc. 7, l. 174.

Freeze, freeze, thou bitter sky,
Thou dost not bite so nigh
As benefits forgot:
Though thou the waters warp,
Thy sting is not so sharp
As friend remember'd not.

SHAKESPEARE, *As You Like It*. Act ii, 7, 184.

16
This was the most unkindest cut of all;
For when the noble Cæsar saw him stab,
Ingratitude, more strong than traitors' arms,
Quite vanquish'd him; then burst his mighty heart.

SHAKESPEARE, *Julius Cæsar*. Act iii, sc. 2, l. 187.

You also, O Brutus, my son. (Et tu, Brute fili.)

JULIUS CÆSAR, on being stabbed by Brutus. (SUETONIUS, *Lives of the Cæsars: Julius*.)

Et tu Brute! Then fall, Cæsar!

SHAKESPEARE, *Julius Cæsar*. Act iii, sc. 1, l. 77.

See what a rent the envious Casca made.

SHAKESPEARE, *Julius Cæsar*. Act iii, sc. 2, l. 179.

17
Ingratitude! thou marble-hearted fiend!

SHAKESPEARE, *King Lear*. Act i, sc. 4, l. 281.

Monster ingratitude!

SHAKESPEARE, *King Lear*. Act i, sc. 5, l. 43.

18
How sharper than a serpent's tooth it is
To have a thankless child!

SHAKESPEARE, *King Lear*. Act i, sc. 4, l. 310.

All the stor'd vengeances of heaven fall
On her ingrateful top!

SHAKESPEARE, *King Lear*. Act ii, sc. 4, l. 164.

Filial ingratitude!
Is it not as this mouth should tear this hand
For lifting food to 't?
SHAKESPEARE, *King Lear*. Act iii, sc. 4, l. 14.

He gives his daughters his estate:
The daughters give him—what? The gate.
UNKNOWN, *Our Book Review Department: King Lear*.

1
I hate ingratitude more in a man,
Than lying, vainness, babbling, drunkenness,
Or any taint of vice.
SHAKESPEARE, *Twelfth Night*. Act iii, sc. 4, l. 388.

2
When ingratitude barbs the dart of injury, the wound has double danger in it.
R. B. SHERIDAN, *The Critic*. Act iv, sc. 3.

3
He that's ungrateful, has no guilt but one;
And other crimes may pass for virtues in him.
EDWARD YOUNG, *Busiris*.

INHERITANCE

See also Ancestry

4
"Yet doth he live!" exclaims the impatient heir,
And sighs for sables which he must not wear.
BYRON, *Lara*. Canto i, st. 3.

5
The fool inherits, but the wise must get
WILLIAM CARTWRIGHT, *The Ordinary*. Act iii, sc. 6.

6
My inheritance, how lordly wide and fair:
Time is my fair seed-field; to Time I'm heir.
(Mein Vermächtniss, wie herrlich weit und breit:
Die Zeit ist mein Vermächtniss, mein Acker ist die Zeit.)
GOETHE, *Wilhelm Meister's Travels*. (Carlyle, tr., in *Chartism*, ch. 10. Carlyle has another version of the same lines in *Sartor Resartus*.)

7
Let an ill man lie in thy straw and he looks to be thy heir.
GEORGE HERBERT, *Jacula Prudentum*.

Who wait for dead men's shoes shall go long barefoot.
JOHN HEYWOOD, *Proverbs*. Pt. i, ch. 11.

8
Heir follows heir as wave succeeds on wave. (Heres Heredem alterius velut unda supervenit undam.)
HORACE, *Epistles*. Bk. ii, epis. 2, l. 175.

9
A son could bear complacently the death of his father, while the loss of his inheritance might drive him to despair.
MACHIAVELLI, *Il Principe*. Ch. xvii.

10
Never think of leaving perfumes or wine to your heir. Let him have your money, but give these to yourself. (Unguentum heredi numquam nec vina relinquas. Ille habeat nummos, hæc tibi toto dato.)
MARTIAL, *Epigrams*. Bk. xiii, epig. 126.

11
Atossa, curs'd with every granted prayer,
Childless with all her children, wants an heir;
To heirs unknown descends th' unguarded store,
Or wanders, Heav'n-directed, to the poor.
POPE, *Moral Essays*. Epis. ii, l. 147.

Pulling his beard because he had no heir.
THOMAS HOOD, *The Stag-Eyed Lady*.

12
The lines are fallen unto me in pleasant places; yea, I have a goodly heritage.
Old Testament: Psalms, xvi, 6.

13
The tears of an heir are laughter under a mask. (Heredis fletus sub persona risus est.)
PUBLILIUS SYRUS, *Sententiæ*. No. 221. Quoted by BACON, *Ornamenta Rationalia*. No. 18.

The weeping of an heir is laughter in disguise.
MONTAIGNE, *Essays*. Bk. i, ch. 37.

14
I owe much; I have nothing; the rest I leave to the poor.
RABELAIS, *His Will*. (MOTTEUX, *Life*.)

To Messire Noël, named the neat,
By those who love him, I bequeath
A helmless ship, a houseless street,
A wordless book, a swordless sheath.
J. H. MCCARTHY, *If I Were King*. (After Villon.)

Thou left'st me nothing in thy will.
SHAKESPEARE [?], *The Passionate Pilgrim*, l. 138.

Left her his all—his blessing and a name unstained.
M. F. TUPPER, *Of Estimating Character*.

15
The next heir is always suspected and hated. (Suspectum semper invisumque qui proximus destinaretur.)
TACITUS, *History*. Bk. i, sec. 21.

16
To inherit property is not to be born—is to be still-born, rather.
H. D. THOREAU, *Journal*, 13 March, 1853.

17
Great use did he take, and for me did rake,
What now with the fork I will scatter.
UNKNOWN, *Roxburghe Ballads*, i, 134.

The fork is commonly the rake's heir.
THOMAS FULLER, *Gnomologia*. No. 4536.

INHUMANITY, see Cruelty

INJURY

See also Insult, Wrong

I—Injury: Apothegms

18
The injuries we do and those we suffer are seldom weighed in the same scales.
ÆSOP, *Fables: The Partial Judge*.

1
Injuries come from them that hath the upper hand. (Injuriæ potentiorum sunt.)
BACON, *Of Church Controversies.*

2
He that injures one threatens an hundred. (Multis minatur, qui uni facit injuriam.)
BACON, *Ornamenta Rationalia.* No. 25.

He threatens many that hath injured one.
BEN JONSON, *Fall of Sejanus.* Act ii.

3
Patient meekness takes injuries like pills, not chewing, but swallowing them down, laconically suffering, and silently passing them over, while angered pride makes a noise . . . at every scratch.
SIR THOMAS BROWNE, *Christian Morals.* Pt. iii, sec. 12.

To ruminate upon evils, to make critical notes upon injuries, and be too acute in their apprehension, is to add unto our own tortures, to feather the arrows of our enemies, and to resolve to sleep no more.
SIR THOMAS BROWNE, *Christian Morals.* Pt. iii, sec. 12.

4
Injury may be done by two methods, by fraud or by force. (Duobus modis, id est aut vi, aut fraude, fiat injuria.)
CICERO, *De Officiis.* Bk. i, ch. 13, sec. 41.

5
It is better to receive than to do an injury. (Accipere quam facere injuriam præstat.)
CICERO, *Tusculanarum Disputationum.* Bk. v, ch. 19, sec. 56.

It is more wretched to commit than to suffer an injury. (Miserius est nocere quam lædi.)
SENECA, *Epistulæ ad Lucilium.* Epis. xcv, 52.

6
What a fool
An injury may make of a staid man.
KEATS, *Otho the Great.* Act iii, sc. 1.

7
No one should be injured. (Nulli nocendum.)
PHÆDRUS, *Fables.* Bk. i, fab. 26.

8
A strong sense of injury often gives point to the expression of our feelings. (Plerumque dolor etiam venustos facit.)
PLINY THE YOUNGER, *Epistles.* Bk. iii, epis. 9.

9
It is the mark of a good man not to know how to do an injury. (Vivi boni est nescire facere injuriam.)
PUBLILIUS SYRUS, *Sententiæ.* No. 711.

10
Whom they have injured they also hate. (Quos læserunt, et oderunt.)
SENECA, *De Ira.* Bk. ii, sec. 33.

It is a principle of human nature to hate those whom you have injured. (Proprium humani ingenii est odisse quem læseris.)
TACITUS, *Agricola.* Sec. 42.

11
To wilful men
The injuries that they themselves procure
Must be their schoolmasters.
SHAKESPEARE, *King Lear.* Act ii, sc. 4, l. 306.

His heart-struck injuries.
SHAKESPEARE, *King Lear.* Act iii, sc. 1, l. 17.

12
A readiness to resent injuries is a virtue only in those who are slow to injure.
SHERIDAN, *A Trip to Scarborough.* Act v, sc. 1.

13
The injury is long to relate. (Longa est injuria.)
VERGIL, *Æneid.* Bk. i, l. 341.

14
It costs more to revenge injuries than to bear them.
THOMAS WILSON, *Maxims.* No. 303.

15
No one is injured except by himself. (Nemo læditur nisi a seipso.)
UNKNOWN. *Latin Proverb.*

II—Injuries: Their Forgiveness

16
The fairest action of our human life
Is scorning to revenge an injury;
For who forgives without a further strife,
His adversary's heart to him doth tie:
And 'tis a firmer conquest, truly said,
To win the heart than overthrow the head.
LADY ELIZABETH CAREY, *The Tragedie of Marian: Chorus.* (1613) This attribution of authorship has been disputed.

17
Forgiveness to the injured doth belong,
But they ne'er pardon who have done the wrong.
DRYDEN, *Conquest of Granada.* Pt. ii, act i, sc. 2.

18
A worthy man forgets past injuries. (Νείκεων παλαιῶν χεηστὸς ἀμνήμων ἀνήρ.)
EURIPIDES, *Andromache,* l. 1164.

19
Christianity commands us to pass by injuries; policy, to let them pass by us.
BENJAMIN FRANKLIN, *Poor Richard,* 1741.

20
A brave man thinks no one is superior who does him an injury; for he has it then in his power to make himself superior to the other by forgiving it.
POPE, *Thoughts on Various Subjects.*

21
The remedy for injuries is to forget them. (Injuriarum remedium est oblivio.)
PUBLILIUS SYRUS, *Sententiæ.* No. 250. Quoted by SENECA, *Epistulæ ad Lucilium,* xciv, 28.

22
He who has injured thee was either stronger or weaker. If weaker, spare him; if stronger, spare thyself. (Aut potentior te, aut imbecillior læsit: si imbecillior, parce illi; si potentior, tibi.)
SENECA, *De Ira.* Bk. iii, sec. 5.

III—Injuries and Benefits

1
An injury graves itself in metal, but a benefit writes itself on the wave. (L'injure se grave en metal, et le bienfait s'escrit en l'onde.)
JEAN BERTAUT, *Maximes.* (c. 1611)

On adamant our wrongs we all engrave,
But write our benefits upon the wave.
WILLIAM KING, *The Art of Love,* l. 971.

All your better deeds
Shall be in water writ, but this in marble.
BEAUMONT AND FLETCHER, *Philaster.* Act v, sc. 3.

Men's evil manners live in brass; their virtues
We write in water.
SHAKESPEARE, *Henry VIII.* Act iv, sc. 2, l. 45.

Here lies one whose name was writ in water.
JOHN KEATS, his epitaph dictated by himself for his monument in Rome.

2
Some write their wrongs in marble: he, more just,
Stoop'd down serene and wrote them in the dust,
Trod under foot, the sport of every wind,
Swept from the earth and blotted from his mind.
There, secret in the grave, he bade them lie,
And grieved they could not 'scape the Almighty eye.
SAMUEL MADDEN, *Boulter's Monument.*

For men use, if they have an evil turn, to write it in marble; and who doth us a good turn, we write it in dust.
SIR THOMAS MORE, *Richard III and His Miserable End.*

Write injuries in the sand, but benefits in marble. (Écrives les injures sur le sable, Mais les bienfaits sur le marbre.)
UNKNOWN. A French proverb.

Write injuries in dust, benefits in marble.
BENJAMIN FRANKLIN, *Poor Richard,* 1747.

3
Injuries are writ in brass, kind Graccho,
And not to be forgotten.
MASSINGER, *The Duke of Milan.* Act v, sc. 1.

4
How bitter it is, when you have sown benefits to reap injuries! (Sed ut acerbum est, pro bene factis cum mali messim metas.)
PLAUTUS, *Epidicus,* l. 718. (Act v, sc. 2.)

5
A benefit cited by way of reproach is equivalent to an injury. (Un bienfait reproché tint toujours lieu d'offense.)
RACINE, *Iphigénie.* Act iv, sc. 5.

6
What is more wretched than the man who forgets his benefits and clings to his injuries? (Quid autem eo miserius, cui beneficia excidunt hærent injuriæ?)
SENECA, *Epistulæ ad Lucilium.* Epis. lxxxi, 23.

7
Kindnesses are easily forgotten; but injuries?—what worthy man does not keep *those* in mind?
THACKERAY, *Lovel the Widower.*

INJUSTICE

See also Justice and Injustice

8
Let twenty pass, and stone the twenty-first.
ROBERT BROWNING, *Caliban Upon Setebos.*

9
No man can mortgage his injustice as a pawn for his fidelity.
EDMUND BURKE, *Reflections on the Revolution in France.*

10
But when I observed the affairs of men plunged in such darkness, the guilty flourishing in continuous happiness, and the righteous tormented, my religion, tottering, began once more to fall. (Sed cum res hominum tanta caligine volvi Adspicerem lætosque diu florere nocentes, Vexarique pios, rursus labefacta cadebat Relligio.)
CLAUDIAN, *In Rufinum.* Bk. i, l. 12.

It's hardly in a body's pow'r
To keep at times frae being sour,
To see how things are shar'd;
How best o' chiels are whiles in want,
While coofs on countless thousands rant,
And ken na how to wair't.
BURNS, *Epistle to Davie.* St. 2.

11
National injustice is the surest road to national downfall.
W. E. GLADSTONE, *Speech,* Plumstead, 1878.

12
Injustice, swift, erect, and unconfin'd,
Sweeps the wide earth, and tramples o'er mankind,
While prayers, to heal her wrongs, move slow behind.
HOMER, *Iliad.* Bk. ix, l. 628. (Pope, tr.)

13
It is too common for those who have unjustly suffered pain to inflict it likewise in their turn with the same injustice.
SAMUEL JOHNSON, *Works.* Vol. iii, p. 294.

14
A good man should and must
Sit rather down with loss, than rise unjust.
BEN JONSON, *Sejanus.* Act iv, sc. 3.

15
To do injustice is more disgraceful than to suffer it.
PLATO, *Gorgias.* Sec. 489.

It is better to suffer injustice than to do it.
EMERSON, *Representative Men: Plato.*

I swear 't is better to be much abused
Than but to know 't a little.
SHAKESPEARE, *Othello.* Act iii, sc. 3, l. 336.

16
My comfort is that heaven will take our souls
And plague injustice with the pains of hell.
SHAKESPEARE, *Richard II.* Act iii, sc. 1. l 33.

1
Injustice in the end produces independence. (L'injustice à la fin produit l'indépendance.)
VOLTAIRE, *Tancrède*. Act iii, sc. 2.

The injustice done to an individual is sometimes of service to the public.
JUNIUS, *Letters*. No. 41.

2
Condemn you me for that the duke did love me?
So may you blame some fair and crystal river
For that some melancholic, distracted man
Hath drown'd himself in 't.
JOHN WEBSTER, *The White Devil*. Act iii, sc. 1.

INN and INNKEEPER

See also Life: An Inn

I—Inn: Apothegms

3
Whosoever reckoneth without his host, he reckoneth twice.
WILLIAM CAXTON, *Blanchardyn*, 202. (c. 1489)

Do not reckon without your host.
RABELAIS, *Works*. Bk. ii, ch. 11.

He reckoneth without his hostess.
JOHN LYLY, *Euphues*, p. 84. (1579)

A handsome hostess makes a dear reckoning.
BISHOP RICHARD CORBET, *Iter Boreale*. (1635)

Half-a-crown in the bill, if you look at the waiter.
DICKENS, *Pickwick Papers*. Ch. 2.

4
Though I am an innkeeper, thank Heaven I am a Christian.
CERVANTES, *Don Quixote*. Pt. i, ch. 32.

5
He knew the taverns well in every town.
CHAUCER, *Canterbury Tales: Prologue*, l. 240.

6
All hosts are of an evil kind.
DRYDEN, *The Cock and the Fox*, l. 264.

7
He goes not out of his way that goes to a good inn.
GEORGE HERBERT, *Jacula Prudentum*.

8
To let the world wag and take mine ease in mine inn.
JOHN HEYWOOD, *Proverbs*. Pt. i, ch. 5. (1546)
In this proverbial saying, inn does not mean a tavern or public house, but one's own home. The original meaning of inn was a private house or dwelling-place.

Thou most beauteous inn,
Why should hard-favour'd grief be lodged in thee,
When triumph is become an alehouse guest?
SHAKESPEARE, *Richard II*. Act v, sc. 1, l. 13.
Here "inn," a private house, is contrasted with tavern.

Shall I not take mine ease in mine inn?
SHAKESPEARE, *I Henry IV*. Act iii, sc. 3, l. 92.

These great rich men take their ease i' their inn.
THOMAS MIDDLETON, *The World at Tennis*.

9
But I'm for toleration and for drinking at an inn.
Says the old bold mate of Henry Morgan.
JOHN MASEFIELD, *Captain Stratton's Fancy*. St. 6.

10
Servant: Where dwell'st thou?
Coriolanus: Under the canopy. . . . I' the city of kites and crows.
SHAKESPEARE, *Coriolanus*. Act iv, sc. 5, l. 40.

And there's naught to pay
For a couch of hay
At the Inn of the Silver Moon.
H. K. VIELÉ, *The Inn of the Silver Moon*.

When you sleep in your cloak there's no lodging to pay.
G. J. WHYTE-MELVILLE, *Boots and Saddles*.

11
Falstaff: And is not my hostess of the tavern a most sweet wench?
Prince: As the honey of Hybla, my old lad of the castle.
SHAKESPEARE, *I Henry IV*. Act i, sc. 2, l. 45.

12
The red-nose innkeeper of Daventry.
SHAKESPEARE, *I Henry IV*. Act iv, sc. 2, l. 51.

How like a fawning publican he looks!
SHAKESPEARE, *The Merchant of Venice*. Act i, sc. 3, l. 42.

Lastly and finally, mine host of the Garter.
SHAKESPEARE, *The Merry Wives of Windsor*. Act i, sc. 1, l. 143.

13
I reckon this always, that a man is never undone till he be hanged, nor never welcome to a place till some certain shot be paid and the hostess say "Welcome!"
SHAKESPEARE, *The Two Gentlemen of Verona*. Act ii, sc. 5, l. 3.

II—Inns: Their Praise

14
You may go to Carlisle's and to Almack's too,
And I'll give you my head if you find such a host,
For coffee, tea, chocolate, butter, or toast;
How he welcomes at once all the world and his wife,
And how civil to folks he ne'er saw in his life.
CHRISTOPHER ANSTEY, *New Bath Guide*, p. 130. (1767)

15
He who has not been at a tavern knows not what a paradise it is. O holy tavern! O miraculous tavern!—holy, because no carking cares are there, nor weariness, nor pain; and miraculous, because of the spits, which of themselves turn round and round!
ARETINO. (LONGFELLOW, *Hyperion*. Bk. iii, ch. 2.)

16
Now musing o'er the changing scene
Farmers behind the tavern screen

Collect; with elbows idly press'd
On hob, reclines the corner's guest,
Reading the news to mark again
The bankrupt lists or price of grain.
Puffing the while his red-tipt pipe
He dreams o'er troubles nearly ripe,
Yet, winter's leisure to regale,
Hopes better times, and sips his ale.
John Clare, *The Shepherd's Calendar.*

1
Along the varying road of Life,
In calm content, in toil or strife,
At morn or noon, by night or day,
As time conducts him on his way,
How oft doth man, by Care oppressed,
Find in an Inn a place of rest.
William Combe, *Dr. Syntax in Search of the Picturesque.* Canto ix, l. 1. (1809)

Where'er his fancy bids him roam,
In ev'ry Inn he finds a home. . . .
Will not an Inn his cares beguile,
Where on each face he sees a smile?
William Combe, *Dr. Syntax in Search of the Picturesque.* Canto ix, l. 13.

2
Would you have each blessing full,
Hither fly and live with Bull,
Feast for body, feast for mind,
Best of welcome, taste refin'd.
Bull does nothing here by halves,
All other landlords are but calves.
Lord Thomas Erskine. (*Notes and Queries,* 8 Sept., 1866.)

3
There is no private house in which people can enjoy themselves so well as at a capital tavern. Let there be ever so great plenty of good things, ever so much grandeur, ever so much elegance, ever so much desire that everybody should be easy, in the nature of things, it cannot be: there must always be some degree of care and anxiety. . . . There is nothing which has yet been contrived by man by which so much happiness is produced as by a good tavern or inn.
Samuel Johnson. (Boswell, *Life,* 21 March, 1776.)

4
Souls of Poets dead and gone,
What Elysium have ye known,
Happy field or mossy cavern,
Choicer than the Mermaid Tavern?
Keats, *Lines on the Mermaid Tavern,* l. 1.

5
The atmosphere
Breathes rest and comfort, and the many chambers
Seem full of welcomes.
Longfellow, *Masque of Pandora.* Pt. v, l. 33.

6
Whoe'er has travelled life's dull round,
Where'er his stages may have been,
May sigh to think he still has found
The warmest welcome at an inn.
William Shenstone, *Written at an Inn at Henley.* (c. 1738)

INNOCENCE

7
For what is that which innocence dares not?
Beaumont and Fletcher, *The Little French Lawyer.* Act i, sc. 1.

8
E'en drunken Andrew felt the blow
That innocence can give,
When its resistless accents flow
To bid affection live.
Robert Bloomfield, *The Drunken Father.* St. 18.

The love of higher things and better days;
The unbounded hope, and heavenly ignorance
Of what is call'd the world, and the world's ways.
Byron, *Don Juan.* Canto xvi, st. 108.

9
Folly and Innocence are so alike,
The diff'rence, though essential, fails to strike.
Cowper, *The Progress of Error,* l. 203.

10
The innocent are gay.
Cowper, *The Task.* Bk. i, l. 493.

Oh, Mirth and Innocence! Oh, Milk and Water!
Ye happy mixtures of more happy days.
Byron, *Beppo.* St. 80.

11
Without unspotted, innocent within,
She fear'd no danger, for she knew no sin.
Dryden, *The Hind and the Panther.* Pt. i, l. 3.

12
However few of the other good things of life are thy lot, the best of all things, which is innocence, is always within thy power.
Fielding, *Amelia.* Bk. viii, ch. 3.

13
Innocence is no protection.
Thomas Fuller, *Gnomologia.* No. 3100.

Innocence itself hath need of a mask.
Thomas Fuller, *Gnomologia.* No. 3101.

14
He saw, he lov'd; for yet he ne'er had known
Sweet innocence and beauty meet in one.
John Gay, *Trivia.* Bk. i, l. 243.

15
Dear lovely bowers of innocence and ease.
Goldsmith, *The Deserted Village,* l. 5.

His best companions, innocence and health.
Goldsmith, *The Deserted Village,* l. 61.

16
Be this our wall of bronze, to have no guilt at heart, no wrongdoing to turn us pale. (Hic murus æneus esto, Nil conscire sibi, nulla pallescere culpa.)
Horace, *Epistles.* Bk. i, epis. 1, l. 60.

True, conscious Honour is to feel no sin;
He's arm'd without that's innocent within:
Be this thy screen, and this thy wall of brass.
Horace, *Epistles,* i, 1. (Pope, tr., l. 93.)

Innocency beareth her defence with her.
John Florio, *First Fruites.* Fo. 31. (1578)

Innocence has nothing to dread. (L'innocence enfin n'a rien à redouter.)
RACINE, *Phèdre*. Act iii, sc. 6.

For unstain'd thoughts do seldom dream on evil;
Birds never lim'd no secret bushes fear.
SHAKESPEARE, *The Rape of Lucrece*, l. 87.

1
Often has outraged Jupiter involved the innocent with the guilty. (Sæpe Diespiter Neglectus incesto addidit integrum.)
HORACE, *Odes*. Bk. iii, ode 2, l. 29.

Jupiter hurls chance thunderbolts at many who have not deserved to suffer the penalty of guilt. (Juppiter in multos temeraria fulmina torquet, Qui pœnam culpa non meruere pati.)
OVID, *Epistulæ ex Ponto*. Bk. iii, epis. 6, l. 27.

2
The exactest vigilance and caution can never maintain a single day of unmingled innocence.
SAMUEL JOHNSON, *The Rambler*. No. 14.

3
To dread no eye, and to suspect no tongue, is the greatest prerogative of innocence.
SAMUEL JOHNSON, *The Rambler*. No. 68.

Calmness is not Always the attribute of innocence.
BYRON, *Werner*. Act iv, sc. 1.

4
The sweet converse of an innocent mind.
KEATS, *Sonnet to Solitude*.

5
We become innocent when we are unfortunate. (On devient innocent quand on est malheureux.)
LA FONTAINE, *Nymphes de Vaux*.

6
Innocence and youth should ever be unsuspicious.
W. S. LANDOR, *Imaginary Conversations: Beniowski and Aphanasia*.

7
What can innocence hope for,
When such as sit her judges are corrupted!
MASSINGER, *The Maid of Honour*. Act v, sc. 2.

8
O God, keep me innocent; make others great! (O mon dieu, conserve-moi innocente, donne la grandeur aux autres!)
CAROLINE MATILDA, QUEEN OF DENMARK. Scratched with a diamond on a window of the castle of Frederiksborg, Denmark.

9
To vice, innocence must always seem only a superior kind of chicanery.
OUIDA, *Two Little Wooden Shoes*.

10
A mind conscious of innocence laughs at the falsehoods of rumor. (Conscia mens recti famæ mendacia risit.)
OVID, *Fasti*. Bk. iv, l. 311.

11
Of all the forms of innocence, mere ignorance is the least admirable.
PINERO, *The Second Mrs. Tanqueray*. Act ii.

12
True innocence is ashamed of nothing.
ROUSSEAU, *Émile*. Bk. iv.

13
What narrow innocence it is for one to be good only according to the law. (Quam angusta innocentia est, ad legem bonum esse.)
SENECA, *De Ira*. Bk. ii, sec. 27.

14
Be innocent of the knowledge, dearest chuck,
Till thou applaud the deed.
SHAKESPEARE, *Macbeth*. Act iii, sc. 2, l. 45.

15
O, take the sense, sweet, of my innocence!
Love takes the meaning in love's conference.
SHAKESPEARE, *A Midsummer-Night's Dream*. Act ii, sc. 2, l. 45.

Hence, bashful cunning!
And prompt me, plain and holy innocence!
SHAKESPEARE, *The Tempest*. Act iii, sc. 1, l. 81.

16
We were as twinn'd lambs that did frisk i' the sun,
And bleat the one at the other; what we chang'd
Was innocence for innocence.
SHAKESPEARE, *Winter's Tale*. Act i, sc. 2, l. 67.

17
I doubt not then but innocence shall make
False accusation blush, and tyranny Tremble.
SHAKESPEARE, *Winter's Tale*. Act iii, sc. 2, l. 31.

Our innocence is as an armèd heel
To trample accusation.
SHELLEY, *The Cenci*. Act iv, sc. 4, l. 154.

18
O white Innocence,
That thou shouldst wear the mask of guilt to hide
Thine awful and serenest countenance!
SHELLEY, *The Cenci*. Act v, sc. 3, l. 24.

19
There is no courage but in innocence;
No constancy but in an honest cause.
THOMAS SOUTHERNE, *The Fate of Capua*.

20
I preserve my safety better by innocence than by eloquence. (Securitatem melius innocentia tueor, quam eloquentia.)
TACITUS, *Dialogus de Oratoribus*. Sec. 11.

21
The hills look over on the South,
And southward dreams the sea;
And, with the sea-breeze hand in hand,
Came innocence and she.
FRANCIS THOMPSON, *Daisy*.

22
This shall be a test of innocence—if I can hear a taunt, and look out on this friendly moon, pacing the heavens in queen-like majesty, with the accustomed yearning.
H. D. THOREAU, *Journal*, 13 Nov., 1838.

23
A man had better starve at once than lose his innocence in the process of getting his bread.
H. D. THOREAU, *Journal*, 26 Oct., 1853.

1
Nothing looks so like innocence as an indiscretion.
OSCAR WILDE, *Lady Windermere's Fan.* Act ii.

2
Innocence is strong,
And an entire simplicity of mind
A thing most sacred in the eye of Heaven.
WORDSWORTH, *The Excursion.* Bk. vi, l. 177.

Who swerves from innocence, who makes divorce
Of that serene companion—a good name,
Recovers not his loss; but walks with shame,
With doubt, with fear, and haply with remorse.
WORDSWORTH, *The River Duddon.* Sonnet xxx.

3
As innocent as the child unborn.
UNKNOWN. (*Somers Tracts,* viii, 131. 1679.)

She was innocent as the child unborn.
SWIFT, *Directions to Servants.*

You are as innocent as a devil of two years old.
SWIFT, *Polite Conversation.* Dial. i.

As innocent as a new-laid egg.
W. S. GILBERT, *Engaged.* Act i.

INSANITY, see Madness

INSPIRATION

4
Midnight filled my slumbers with song;
Music haunted my dreams by day.
Now I listen and wait and long,
But the Delphian airs have died away.
T. B. ALDRICH, *The Flight of the Goddess.*

And the woman I loved was now my bride,
And the house I wanted was my own;
I turned to the Goddess satisfied—
But the Goddess had somehow flown.
T. B. ALDRICH, *The Flight of the Goddess.*

5
'Tis inspiration expounds experience.
P. J. BAILEY, *Festus: A Ruined Temple.*

6
To see a world in a grain of sand,
And a heaven in a wild flower,
Hold infinity in the palm of your hand,
And eternity in an hour.
WILLIAM BLAKE, *Auguries of Innocence.*

7
Gie me ae spark o' Nature's fire,
That's a' the learning I desire;
Then, tho' I trudge thro' dub an' mire
At pleugh or cart,
My Muse, tho' hamely in attire,
May touch the heart.
BURNS, *Epistle to John Lapraik.* Epis. i, st. 13.

8
No man was ever great without some portion of divine inspiration. (Nemo vir magnus sine aliquo adflatu divino umquam fuit.)
CICERO, *De Natura Deorum.* Bk. ii, ch. 66, sec. 167. Hence, "divine afflatus."

9
Fill'd with fury, rapt, inspired.
WILLIAM COLLINS, *The Passions,* l. 10.

10
Inebriate of air am I
And debauchee of dew,
Reeling, through endless summer days,
From inns of moulten blue. . . .

Till seraphs swing their snowy hats,
And saints to windows run,
To see the little tippler
Leaning against the sun!
EMILY DICKINSON, *Poems.* Pt. i, No. 20.

11
The text inspires not them, but they the text inspire.
DRYDEN, *The Medal,* l. 166.

12
We cannot carry on inspiration and make it consecutive. One day there is no electricity in the air, and the next the world bristles with sparks like a cat's back.
EMERSON, *Uncollected Lectures: Resources.*

13
If there be good in that I wrought,
Thy hand compelled it, Master, Thine—
Where I have failed to meet Thy Thought
I know, through Thee, the blame was mine.
RUDYARD KIPLING, *"My New-Cut Ashlar."*

14
Earth's fiery core alone can feed the bough
That blooms between Orion and the Plough.
EDNA ST. VINCENT MILLAY, *Sonnet: Grow Not Too High.*

15
The heart desires, The hand refrains,
The godhead fires, The soul attains.
WILLIAM MORRIS, *Inscription* on Burne-Jones's painting, Pygmalion and Galatea, in the Grosvenor Gallery, London.

16
Fair are the flowers and the children, but their subtle suggestion is fairer;
Rare is the roseburst of dawn, but the secret that clasps it is rarer;
Sweet the exultance of song, but the strain that precedes it is sweeter
And never was poem yet writ, but the meaning outmastered the meter.
RICHARD REALF, *Indirection.*

I wonder if ever a song was sung but the singer's heart sang sweeter!
I wonder if ever a rhyme was rung but the thought surpassed the meter!
I wonder if ever a sculptor wrought till the cold stone echoed his ardent thought!
Or, if ever a painter with light and shade the dream of his inmost heart portrayed!
JAMES C. HARVEY, *Incompleteness.*

17
No more inspiration in her than in a plate of muffins.
BERNARD SHAW, *Man and Superman.* Act ii.

18
All around him Patmos lies
Who hath spirit-gifted eyes.
EDITH M. THOMAS, *Patmos.*

1
She with one breath attunes the spheres,
And also my poor human heart.
HENRY DAVID THOREAU, *Inspiration.*

2
But if with bended neck I grope,
Listening behind me for my wit, . . .
Then will the verse forever wear,—
Time cannot bend the line which God hath writ.
HENRY DAVID THOREAU, *Inspiration.*

3
She comes not when Noon is on the roses—
Too bright is Day.
She comes not to the Soul till it reposes
From work and play.

But when Night is on the hills, and the great Voices
Roll in from Sea,
By starlight and by candle-light and dreamlight
She comes to me.
HERBERT TRENCH, *She Comes Not When Noon Is on the Roses.*

4
Immured in sense, with fivefold bonds confined,
Rest we content if whispers from the stars.
In waftings of the incalculable wind
Come blown at midnight through our prison-bars.
WILLIAM WATSON, *Epigrams.*

5
Great God! I'd rather be
A Pagan suckled in a creed outworn;
So might I, standing on this pleasant lea,
Have glimpses that would make me less forlorn;
Have sight of Proteus rising from the sea,
Or hear old Triton blow his wreathèd horn.
WORDSWORTH, *Miscellaneous Sonnets.* Pt. i, No. 33.

INSTINCT

I—Instinct: Definitions and Apothegms

6
The *not ourselves,* which is in us and all around us. . . . The enduring power, not ourselves, which makes for righteousness.
MATTHEW ARNOLD, *Literature and Dogma.*

An unfathomable Somewhat, which is *Not we.*
CARLYLE, *French Revolution.* Pt. i, bk. i, ch. 2.

7
That which is imprinted upon the spirit of man by an inward instinct.
BACON, *Advancement of Learning.* Bk. ii.

8
Instinct is untaught ability.
BAIN, *Senses and Intellect,* p. 256.

Instinct is intelligence incapable of self-consciousness.
JOHN STERLING, *Thoughts and Images.*

9
My natural instinct teaches me
(And instinct is important O!)
You're everything you ought to be,
And nothing that you oughtn't O!
W. S. GILBERT, *Princess Ida.* Act ii.

10
A good man, through obscurest aspirations,
Has still an instinct of the one true way.
GOETHE, *Faust: Prolog in Himmel: Der Herr,* l. 88.

11
We heed no instincts but our own. (Nous n'écoutons d'instincts que ceux qui sont les nôtres.)
LA FONTAINE, *Fables.* Bk. i, fab. 8.

12
Man's natural instinct is never toward what is sound and true; it is toward what is specious and false.
H. L. MENCKEN, *Prejudices.* Ser. iii, p. 126.

13
By a divine instinct men's minds mistrust
Ensuing dangers.
SHAKESPEARE, *Richard III.* Act ii, sc. 3, l. 42.

14
I'll never
Be such a gosling to obey instinct.
SHAKESPEARE, *Coriolanus.* Act v, sc. 3, l. 34.

Beware instinct.
SHAKESPEARE, *I Henry IV* Act ii, sc. 4, l. 299.

15
Instinct is a great matter; I was now a coward on instinct.
SHAKESPEARE, *I Henry IV.* Act ii, sc. 4, l. 300.

You ran away upon instinct.
SHAKESPEARE, *I Henry IV.* Act ii, sc. 4, l. 331.

Upon instinct.—I grant ye, upon instinct.
SHAKESPEARE, *I Henry IV.* Act ii, sc. 4, l. 389.

16
A few strong instincts and a few plain rules.
WORDSWORTH, *Poems Dedicated to National Independence* Pt. ii, No. 12.

High instincts before which our mortal nature
Did tremble like a guilty thing surprised.
WORDSWORTH, *Intimations of Immortality.* St. 9.

II—Instinct and Reason

17
Reas'ning at every step he treads,
Man yet mistakes his way,
Whilst meaner things, whom instinct leads,
Are rarely known to stray.
COWPER, *The Doves.*

18
A moment's insight is sometimes worth a life's experience.
O. W. HOLMES, *The Professor at the Breakfast-Table.* Ch. 10

19
It is the instinct of understanding to contradict reason
JACOBI THE ELDER. (CARLYLE, *Novalis.*)

20
Instinct preceded wisdom
Even in the wisest men, and may sometimes
Be much the better guide.
GEORGE LILLO, *Fatal Curiosity.* Act i, sc. 3.

1
How instinct varies in the grovelling swine,
Compared, half-reas'ning elephant, with thine!
'Twixt that and reason what a nice barrier!
For ever separate, yet for ever near!
POPE, *Essay on Man*. Epis. i, l. 221.

2
Reason, however able, cool at best,
Cares not for service, or but serves when prest,
Stays till we call, and then not often near;
But honest instinct comes a volunteer;
Sure never to o'er-shoot, but just to hit,
While still too wide or short in human wit.
POPE, *Essay on Man*. Epis. iii, l. 85.

And reason raise o'er instinct as you can,
In this 'tis God directs, in that 'tis man.
POPE, *Essay on Man*. Epis. iii, l. 97.

3
Instinct and reason how can we divide?
'Tis the fool's ignorance, and the pedant's pride.
MATTHEW PRIOR, *Solomon on the Vices of the World*. Bk. i, l. 231.

Let him make use of instinct who cannot make use of reason. (Utatur motu animi, qui uti ratione non potest.)
UNKNOWN. A Latin proverb.

5
They live no longer in the faith of reason;
But still the heart doth need a language, still
Doth the old instinct bring back the old names.
SCHILLER, *Piccolomini*. Act ii, sc. 4.

6
Reason progressive, instinct is complete;
Swift instinct leaps; slow reason feebly climbs.
YOUNG, *Night Thoughts*. Night vii, l. 81.

INSULT

7
Let those who have betrayed him by their adulation, insult him with their malevolence.
EDMUND BURKE, *American Taxation*. Referring to Chatham.

8
An injury is much sooner forgotten than an insult.
LORD CHESTERFIELD, *Letters*, 9 Oct., 1746.

An old affront will stir the heart
Through years of rankling pain.
JEAN INGELOW, *Strife and Peace*.

9
He who allows himself to be insulted deserves to be. (Qui se laisse outrager, mérite qu'on l'outrage.)
CORNEILLE, *Héraclius*. Act i, sc. 2.

10
Am I to set my life upon a throw
Because a bear is rude and surly? No—
A moral, sensible, and well-bred man
Will not affront me, and no other can.
COWPER, *Conversation*, l. 191.

11
To one well-born the affront is worse and more,
When he's abused and baffled by a boor.
DRYDEN, *Satire on the Dutch*, l. 27.

Fate never wounds more deep the gen'rous heart,
Than when a blockhead's insult points the dart.
SAMUEL JOHNSON, *London*, l. 168.

12
If he is insulted, he can be insulted; all his affair is not to insult.
EMERSON, *Conduct of Life: Worship*.

13
No sacred fane requires us to submit to insult. (Kein Heiligthum heisst uns den Schimpf ertragen.)
GOETHE, *Torquato Tasso*. Act iii, sc. 3, l. 191.

The way to procure insults is to submit to them.
WILLIAM HAZLITT, *Characteristics*. No. 402.

14
Ashamed am I that such an insult could have been uttered and yet could not be answered. (Pudet hæc opprobria nobis Et dici potuisse et non potuisse refelli.)
OVID, *Metamorphoses*. Bk. i, l. 758.

15
To add insult to injury. (Injuriæ qui addideris contumeliam.)
PHÆDRUS, *Fables*. Bk. v, fab. 3, l. 5.

This is adding insult to injuries.
EDWARD MOORE, *The Foundling*. Act v, sc. 2. (1748)

16
If you speak insults, you shall also hear them. (Contumeliam si dices, audies.)
PLAUTUS, *Pseudolus*, l. 1173. (Act iv, sc. 7.)

17
Noble-mindedness does not receive an insult. (Ingenuitas non recipit contumeliam.)
PUBLILIUS SYRUS, *Sententiæ*. No. 271.

18
It is often better not to see an insult than to avenge it. (Sæpe satius fuit dissimulare quam ulcisci.)
SENECA, *De Ira*. Bk. ii, sec. 32.

19
Insults are like bad coins; we cannot help their being offered to us, but we need not take them.
C. H. SPURGEON, *Salt-Cellars*.

20
They accept everything as an insult. (Ad contumeliam omnia accipiunt magis.)
TERENCE, *Adelphi*, l. 606. (Act iv, sc. 3.)

INTELLIGENCE

See also Cleverness, Mind

21
Instinct perfected is a faculty of using and even constructing organized instruments; intelligence perfected is the faculty of making and using unorganized instruments.
HENRI BERGSON, *Creative Evolution*. Ch. 2.

Intelligence is the faculty of manufacturing artificial objects.

HENRI BERGSON, *Creative Evolution*. Ch. 2.

1
I can look sharp as well as another, and let me alone to keep the cobwebs out of my eyes.

CERVANTES, *Don Quixote*. Pt. ii, ch. 33.

2
'Tis good-will makes intelligence.

EMERSON, *The Titmouse*, l. 65; *Letters and Social Aims: Immortality*.

The intelligent have a right over the ignorant; namely, the right of instructing them.

EMERSON, *Representative Men: Plato: New Readings*.

3
On the whole we are Not intelligent.

W. S. GILBERT, *Princess Ida*. Act i.

4
To perceive things in the germ is intelligence.

LAO-TSZE, *The Simple Way*. No. 52.

5
To educate the intelligence is to enlarge the horizon of its desires and wants.

J. R. LOWELL, *Democracy and Other Addresses: Democracy*.

It is not the insurrections of ignorance that are daı.gerous, but the revolts of intelligence.

J. R. LOWELL, *Democracy*.

6
All things are slaves to intelligence. (Ἅπαντα δοῦλα τοῦ φρονεῖν καθίσταται.)

MENANDER, *Fragments*. No. 769.

7
You will more easily stamp out intelligence and learning than recall them. (Sic ingenia studiaque oppresseris facilius quam revocaveris.)

TACITUS, *Agricola*. Sec. 3.

8
He's very knowing.

SHAKESPEARE, *Antony and Cleopatra*. Act iii, sc. 3, l. 26.

9
She had no more intelligence than a banjo. (Νοῦν δ' εἶχεν ἐλάσσονα κινδαψοῖο.)

TIMON, *Silli*. Frag. 38.

10
All men see the same objects, but do not equally understand them. Intelligence is the tongue that discerns and tastes them.

THOMAS TRAHERNE, *Centuries of Meditations*.

INTEMPERANCE, see Drunkenness

INTENTION

See also Purpose

11
Of every noble action, the intent
Is to give worth reward—vice punishment.

BEAUMONT AND FLETCHER, *The Captain*. Act v, sc. 5.

12
Stain not fair acts with foul intentions.

SIR THOMAS BROWNE, *Christian Morals*. Pt. i, sec. 1.

13
The consciousness of good intentions is the greatest solace in misfortune. (Conscientia rectæ voluntatis maxima est rerum incommodarum.)

CICERO, *Epistolæ ad Atticum*. Bk. v, epis. 4.

14
A good intention clothes itself with sudden power.

EMERSON, *Conduct of Life: Fate*.

15
One often sees good intentions, if pushed beyond moderation, bring about very vicious results.

MONTAIGNE, *Essays*. Bk. ii, ch. 19.

For there's nothing we read of in torture's inventions,
Like a well-meaning dunce, with the best of intentions.

J. R. LOWELL, *A Fable for Critics*, l. 250.

16
Forgive my deeds, since you know that crime was absent from my intent. (Factis ignoscite nostris, Si scelus ingenio scitis abesse meo.)

OVID, *Fasti*. Bk. iii, eleg. 3, l. 309.

17
"He means well" is useless unless he does well. (Bene vult, nisi qui bene facit.)

PLAUTUS, *Trinummus*. Act ii, sc. 4, l. 37.

18
A good intender needs nothing but a voice. (À bon entendeur ne faut qu'un parole.)

RABELAIS, *Works*. Bk. v, ch. 7.

19
Oft has good nature been the fool's defence,
And honest meaning gilded want of sense.

WILLIAM SHENSTONE, *Ode to a Lady*.

20
All men mean well.

BERNARD SHAW, *Maxims for Revolutionists*.

See also HELL: ITS PAVEMENT.

INTOLERANCE, see Tolerance

INVENTION

21
The industry of artificers maketh some small improvement of things invented; and chance sometimes in experimenting maketh us to stumble upon somewhat which is new; but all the disputation of the learned never brought to light one effect of nature before unknown.

FRANCIS BACON, *In Praise of Knowledge*.

The art of invention grows young with the things invented. (Ars inveniendi adolescit cum inventis.)

FRANCIS BACON. Quoted as a maxim.

22
A tool is but the extension of a man's hand, and a machine is but a complex tool. And he that invents a machine augments the power of a man and the well-being of mankind.

HENRY WARD BEECHER, *Proverbs from Plymouth Pulpit: Business*.

1
A fond thing vainly invented.
Book of Common Prayer: Articles. No. 22.

2
If it is not true, it is very well invented. (Se non è vero, è molto ben trovato.)
GIORDANO BRUNO, *Degli Eroici Furori.* (1585). The "molto" is frequently omitted in quotation, which is rendered, "If not true, it is a happy invention." Antonio Doni (*Marmi,* 1552) said the same thing thirty years earlier, in slightly different form: "Se non è vero, egli è stato un bel trovato." Pasquier (*Recherches,* 1600) turns it into French: "Si cela n'est vrai, il est bien trouvé."

If it is not true, it is certainly well invented. (Se non è vero, è ben trovato.)
CARDINAL IPPOLITO D'ESTE, speaking of the *Orlando Furioso,* which Ariosto dedicated to him. (*Grosse Leute, Kleine Schwächen.*) Büchmann questions the authorship.

It's my own invention.
LEWIS CARROLL, *Through the Looking-Glass,* Ch. 8.

3
A weak invention of the enemy.
CIBBER, *Richard III* (altered). Act v, sc. 3.

Invented by the lying enemy. (Inventé par le calomniateur ennemi.)
RABELAIS, *Works.* Bk. iii, ch. 11.

4
Beggars invention and makes fancy tame.
COWPER, *Retirement,* l. 709.

5
Countless ages will beget many new inventions, but my own is mine. (Μυρίος αἰὼν πολλα προσευρήσει χἄτερα· τἀμὰ δ' ἐμα.)
DIOSCORIDES, *Epigram on Thespis.* (*Greek Anthology.* Bk. vii, No. 410.)

6
God hath made man upright; but they have sought out many inventions.
Old Testament: Ecclesiastes, vii, 29.

Many Inventions.
RUDYARD KIPLING. Title of book of short stories.

7
'Tis frivolous to fix pedantically the date of particular inventions. They have all been invented over and over fifty times. Man is the arch machine, of which all these shifts drawn from himself are toy models.
EMERSON, *Conduct of Life: Fate.*

8
Only an inventor knows how to borrow, and every man is or should be an inventor.
EMERSON, *Letters and Social Aims: Quotation and Originality.*

Invention breeds invention.
EMERSON, *Society and Solitude: Works and Days.*

9
Take the advice of a faithful friend, and submit thy inventions to his censure.
THOMAS FULLER, *The Holy and Profane States: Of Fancy.*

10
What doth Invention but together place
The blocks of a child's game to make it whole?
R. U. JOHNSON, *Psalm of Happiness in Nature.*

11
Electric telegraphs, printing, gas,
Tobacco, balloons, and steam,
Are little events that have come to pass
Since the days of the old *régime.*
And, spite of Lemprière's dazzling page,
I'd give—though it might seem bold—
A hundred years of the Golden Age
For a year of the Age of Gold.
H. S. LEIGH, *The Two Ages.*

12
Th' invention all admir'd, and each, how he
To be th' inventor miss'd, so easy it seem'd,
Once found, which yet unfound most would have thought
Impossible.
MILTON, *Paradise Lost.* Bk. vi, l. 498.

13
Nothing is invented and perfected at the same time. (Nihil simul inventum est et perfectum.)
UNKNOWN. A Latin proverb.

14
False things may be imagined, and false things composed; but only truth can be invented.
RUSKIN, *Modern Painters.* Pt. viii, ch. 4, sec. 23.

15
This is a man's invention and his hand.
SHAKESPEARE, *As You Like It.* Act iv, sc. 3, l. 29.

16
I am not so nice
To change true rules for old inventions.
SHAKESPEARE, *The Taming of the Shrew.* Act iii, sc. 1, l. 80.

17
The greatest inventions were produced in times of ignorance; as the use of the compass, gunpowder, and printing; and by the dullest nation, as the Germans.
SWIFT, *Thoughts on Various Subjects.*

He had been eight years upon a project for extracting sunbeams out of cucumbers, which were to be put into phials hermetically sealed, and let out to warm the air in raw inclement summers.
SWIFT, *Gulliver's Travels: Voyage to Laputa.*

IRELAND AND THE IRISH

See also Patrick, Saint

I—Ireland: Apothegms

18
Mr. Speaker, I smell a rat; I see him forming in the air and darkening the sky; but I'll nip him in the bud.
SIR BOYLE ROCHE. (BARRINGTON, *Personal Sketches.*) See 1671:7

There is one distinguishing peculiarity of the

Irish bull—its horns are tipped with brass [*i.e.*, with impudence or assurance].
MARIA EDGEWORTH, *Irish Bulls*. Ch. 7.

It was Whewell who asserted that all the Irish bulls had been calves in Greece; and it was Professor Tyrrell who neatly explained that the Irish bull differed from the bull of all other islands in that "it was always pregnant."
BRANDER MATTHEWS, *Recreations of an Anthologist*, p. 20.

1
There came to the beach a poor exile of Erin. . .
He sang the bold anthem of Erin go bragh.
THOMAS CAMPBELL, *Exile of Erin*. Erin go bragh: Ireland for ever.

Erin go bragh! A far better anthem would be, Erin go bread and cheese.
SYDNEY SMITH, *Fragment on the Irish Roman Catholic Church*.

2
That domestic Irish giant, named of Despair.
CARLYLE, *Latter-Day Pamphlets*. No. 3.

Nought was said of the years of pain,
The starving stomach, the maddened brain,
The years of sorrow and want and toil,
And the murdering rent for the bit of soil.
ROBERT BUCHANAN, *O'Murtogh*.

And the niggardness of Nature makes the misery of man.
WILLIAM WATSON, *Ireland*. 1 Dec., 1890.

3
Ireland is in a state of social decomposition.
BENJAMIN DISRAELI, *Speech*, 2 July, 1849.

4
Arm of Erin! prove strong, but be gentle as brave,
And, uplifted to strike, still be ready to save,
Nor one feeling of vengeance presume to defile
The cause, or the men of the Emerald Isle.
WILLIAM DRENNAN, *Erin*. (c. 1800) This has sometimes been stated to be the first use of the phrase, "Emerald Isle," but Dr. Drennan, in an introduction to the poem written in 1815, expressly states that the phrase was first used in *Erin, To Her Own Tune*, a "party song written without the rancour of party in the year 1795."

For dear is the Emerald Isle of the ocean,
Whose daughters are fair as the foam of the wave,
Whose sons unaccustom'd to rebel commotion,
Tho' joyous, are sober—tho' peaceful, are brave.
HORACE AND JAMES SMITH, *Rejected Addresses*. (1812)

5
Our Irish blunders are never blunders of the heart.
MARIA EDGEWORTH, *Irish Bulls*. Ch. 4.

6
Ah, sweet is Tipperary in the springtime of the year.
D. A. MCCARTHY, *Ah, Sweet Is Tipperary*.

It's a long way to Tipperary, it's a long way to go;
It's a long way to Tipperary, to the sweetest girl I know!
Good-bye, Piccadilly, farewell, Leicester Square;
It's a long, long way to Tipperary, but my heart's right there!
JACK JUDGE, *Tipperary*. Written in 1908, and popular with both British and American soldiers during the World War. Judge was a mediocre actor, who ran a fish-shop by day. A man named Harry Williams lent him money to finance the shop, and shared in the returns from Judge's song, his name appearing on it as co-author. His family claimed that he wrote it, and after his death in 1924, repeated the claim on his tombstone; but it was probably Judge's alone.

7
Nothing in Ireland lasts long except the miles.
GEORGE MOORE, *Ave*, p. 11. An Irish mile is 2,240 yards—a little more than an English mile and a quarter.

Ireland is a little Russia in which the longest way round is the shortest way home, and the means more important than the end.
GEORGE MOORE, *Ave*, p. 116.

It is not a question of race; it is the land itself that makes the Celt.
GEORGE MOORE, *The Bending of the Bough*. Act iii.

8
The western isles Of kerns and gallowglasses.
SHAKESPEARE, *Macbeth*. Act i, sc. 2, l. 12.

9
If you want to interest him [the Irishman] in Ireland, you've got to call the unfortunate island Kathleen ni Hoolihan and pretend she's a little old woman.
BERNARD SHAW, *John Bull's Other Island*. Act i.

10
Daughter of all the implacable ages.
WILLIAM WATSON, *England to Ireland*.

II—Ireland: Her Praise

11
Will my soul pass through old Ireland,
Past my dear old Irish home?
VINCENT P. BRYAN AND HENRY W ARMSTRONG, *Will My Soul Pass Through Old Ireland?*

12
Dear Erin, how sweetly thy green bosom rises!
An emerald set in the ring of the sea.
Each blade of thy meadows my faithful heart prizes,
Thou queen of the west, the world's cushla ma-chree.
JOHN PHILPOT CURRAN, *Cushla-ma-Chree* (Cushla-ma-Chree: Darling of My Heart.)

The great waves of the Atlantic sweep storming on their way,
Shining green and silver with the hidden herring shoal;

But the little waves of Breffny have drenched my heart in spray,
And the little waves of Breffny go stumbling through my soul.
EVA GORE-BOOTH, *The Little Waves of Breffny.*

1
Who fears to speak of Ninety-eight?
Who blushes at the name?
When cowards mock the patriot's fate,
Who hangs his head for shame?
JOHN KELLS INGRAM, *The Memory of the Dead.* (*Dublin Nation*, 1 Apr., 1843.)

2
Th' an'am an Dhia, but there it is—
The dawn on the hills of Ireland.
God's angels lifting the night's black veil
From the fair sweet face of my sireland!
O Ireland, isn't it grand, you look,
Like a bride in her rich adornin',
And with all the pent up love of my heart
I bid you the top of the mornin'.
JOHN LOCKE, *The Exile's Return.* (Th' an'am an Dhia: My Soul to God.)

3
The groves of Blarney
They look so charming
Down by the purling
Of sweet, silent brooks.
R. A. MILLIKEN, *The Groves of Blarney.*

There is a stone there,
That whoever kisses,
Oh! he never misses
To grow eloquent.
'Tis he may clamber
To a lady's chamber
Or become a member
Of Parliament.
FRANCIS SYLVESTER MAHONY, (FATHER PROUT), *The Groves of Blarney.* Additional lines to Milliken's poem.

4
Sweet Innisfallen, long shall dwell
In memory's dream that sunny smile,
Which o'er thee on that evening fell,
When first I saw thy fairy isle.
THOMAS MOORE, *Sweet Innisfallen.*

5
And blest for ever is she who relied
Upon Erin's honour and Erin's pride.
THOMAS MOORE, *Rich and Rare.*

6
And the Land of Youth lies gleaming, flushed with rainbow light and mirth,
And the old enchantment lingers in the honey-heart of earth.
GEORGE WILLIAM RUSSELL, *Carrowmore.*

7
After the spiritual powers, there is nothing in the world more unconquerable than the spirit of nationality. . . . The spirit of nationality in Ireland will persist even though the mightiest of material powers be its neighbour.
GEORGE WILLIAM RUSSELL, *The Economics of Ireland*, p. 23.

8
They say there's bread and work for all,
And the sun shines always there;
But I'll not forget old Ireland,
Were it fifty times as fair.
HELEN SELINA SHERIDAN, *Lament of the Irish Emigrant.*

9
Whether on the scaffold high
Or on the battle-field we die,
Oh, what matter, when for Erin dear we fall!
T. D. SULLIVAN, *God Save Ireland.*

10
Lovelier than thy seas are strong,
Glorious Ireland, sword and song
Gird and crown thee: none may wrong,
Save thy sons alone.
The sea that laughs around us
Hath sundered not but bound us:
The sun's first rising found us
Throned on its equal throne.
SWINBURNE, *The Union.* St. 3.

11
Och, Dublin City, there is no doubtin',
Bates every city upon the say;
'Tis there you'll see O'Connell spoutin',
An' Lady Morgan makin' tay;
For 'tis the capital of the finest nation,
Wid charmin' pisintry on a fruitful sod,
Fightin' like divils for conciliation,
An' hatin' each other for the love of God.
UNKNOWN, *Dublin City.* (Lady Morgan, in her *Memoirs*, ii, 232, tells of this compliment paid her by a street ballad-singer, 30 Oct., 1826.) Sometimes attributed to Charles Lever, who perhaps rewrote the old song.

III—Ireland: Her Sorrows

12
There came to the beach a poor Exile of Erin—
The dew on his thin robe was heavy and chill:
For his country he sigh'd when at twilight repairing
To wander alone by the wind-beaten hill.
THOMAS CAMPBELL, *Exile of Erin.*

Green be thy fields, sweetest isle of the ocean!
And thy harp-striking bards sing aloud with devotion,—
"Erin mavournin—Erin go bragh!"
THOMAS CAMPBELL, *Exile of Erin.*

13
The dust of some is Irish earth,
Among their own they rest.
JOHN KELLS INGRAM, *The Memory of the Dead.*

Many and many a son of Conn the Hundred-Fighter
In the red earth lies at rest;
Many a blue eye of Clan Colman the turf covers,
Many a swan-like breast.
T. W. ROLLESTON, *The Dead at Clonmacnois.*

1
Thy sorrow, and the sorrow of the sea,
Are sisters; the sad winds are of thy race:
The heart of melancholy beats in thee,
And the lamenting spirit haunts thy face,
Mournful and mighty Mother!
LIONEL JOHNSON, *Ireland.*

2
The Judgment Hour must first be nigh,
Ere you shall fade, ere you can die,
My dark Rosaleen!
JAMES CLARENCE MANGAN, *Dark Rosaleen.*

3
Down thy valleys, Ireland, Ireland,
Still thy spirit wanders mad;
All too late they love that wronged thee,
Ireland, Ireland, green and sad.
HENRY NEWBOLT, *Ireland, Ireland.*

4
"Oh! rise up, Willy Reilly, and come along with me,
I mean for to go with you and leave this counterie,
To leave my father's dwelling, his houses and free land;"
And away goes Willy Reilly and his dear Coolen Ban.
UNKNOWN, *Willy Reilly.*

IV—Ireland: The Shamrock

5
There's a dear little plant that grows in our isle,
'Twas St. Patrick himself sure that set it;
And the sun on his labour with pleasure did smile,
And with dew from his eye often wet it.
It thrives through the bog, through the brake, and the mireland;
And he called it the dear little shamrock of Ireland—
The sweet little shamrock, the dear little shamrock,
The sweet little, green little, shamrock of Ireland!
ANDREW CHERRY, *The Green Little Shamrock of Ireland.*

O, the Shamrock, the green, immortal Shamrock!
Chosen leaf Of Bard and Chief,
Old Erin's native Shamrock.
THOMAS MOORE, *Oh, the Shamrock.*

6
Oh, Paddy dear, an' did ye hear the news that's goin' round?
The shamrock is by law forbid to grow on Irish ground!
No more Saint Patrick's Day we'll keep, his colour can't be seen,
For there's a cruel law agin the wearin' o' the green!
UNKNOWN, *The Shan-van-Voght.* This old Irish song is quoted in Trench, *Realities of Irish Life.*

When law can stop the blades of grass from growing as they grow;
And when the leaves in Summer-time their colour dare not show;
Then will I change the colour too, I wear in my caubeen;
But till that day, plaze God, I'll stick to wearin' o' the Green.
DION BOUCICAULT, *The Wearin' o' the Green.* An expansion of the old song written for Boucicault's *Arrah-na-Pogue.*

V—Ireland and England

7
England and Ireland may flourish together. The world is large enough for us both. Let it be our care not to make ourselves too little for it.
EDMUND BURKE, *Letter to Samuel Span, Esq.*

8
The bane of England, and the opprobrium of Europe.
BENJAMIN DISRAELI, *Speech,* 9 Aug., 1843, referring to Ireland.

9
To apply, in all their unmitigated authority, the principles of abstract political economy to the people and circumstances of Ireland, exactly as if he had been proposing to legislate for the inhabitants of Saturn or Jupiter.
W. E. GLADSTONE, *Speech,* House of Commons, 7 April, 1881.

10
'Tis Ireland gives England her soldiers, her generals too.
GEORGE MEREDITH, *Diana of the Crossways.* Ch. 2.

11
A mirror faced a mirror: ire and hate
Opposite ire and hate.
ALICE MEYNELL, *Reflexions in Ireland.*

12
Mr. Butler was now all full of his high discourse in praise of Ireland. . . . But so many lies I never heard in praise of anything as he told of Ireland.
SAMUEL PEPYS, *Diary,* 28 July, 1660.

13
He that would England win,
Must with Ireland first begin.
H. G. BOHN, *Hand-Book of Proverbs,* p. 396. Quoted by FROUDE, *History of England,* x, 480.

14
The uncivil kerns of Ireland.
SHAKESPEARE, *II Henry VI.* Act iii, sc. 1, l. 310.

Now for the rebels which stand out in Ireland.
SHAKESPEARE, *Richard II.* Act i, sc. 4, l. 38.

Now for our Irish wars:
We must supplant those rough rug-headed kerns,
Which live like venom where no venom else
But only they have privilege to live.
SHAKESPEARE, *Richard II.* Act ii, sc. 1, l. 156.

15
The moment the very name of Ireland is mentioned, the English seem to bid adieu to

common feeling, common prudence and common sense, and to act with the barbarity of tyrants and the fatuity of idiots.

SYDNEY SMITH, *Peter Plymley Letters*. No. 2.

1
The lovely and the lonely bride,
Whom we have wedded but have never won.

WILLIAM WATSON, *Ode on the Coronation of Edward VII*, l. 79. Referring to Ireland.

2
As the northern men loveth fight, also the southern, falseness; they strutteth to strength, these to sleights; they to stalwartness, these to treason.

UNKNOWN, *Of Ireland*. (c. 1425) (MS. Trinity College, Dublin, relating to the conquest of Ireland by the British.)

VI—Ireland: The Irish

3
For the great Gaels of Ireland
Are the men that God made mad,
For all their wars are merry
And all their songs are sad.

G. K. CHESTERTON, *The Ballad of the White Horse*.

4
"Well, here's thank God for the race and the sod!"
Said Kelly and Burke and Shea.

J. I. C. CLARKE, *The Fighting Race*.

"Oh, the fighting races don't die out,
If they seldom die in bed,
For love is first in their hearts, no doubt,"
Said Burke.

J. I. C. CLARKE, *The Fighting Race*.

5
Every Irishman has a potato in his head.

J. C. AND A. W. HARE, *Guesses at Truth*.

6
The Irish are a fair people; they never speak well of one another.

SAMUEL JOHNSON. (BOSWELL, *Life*, 1775.)

7
And now the Irish are ashamed
To see themselves in one year tamed:
So much one man can do,
That does both act and know.

ANDREW MARVELL, *Horatian Ode upon Cromwell's Return from Ireland*, l. 75.

8
An Irishman, a very valiant gentleman, i' faith.

SHAKESPEARE, *Henry V*. Act iii, sc. 2, l. 71.

9
An Irishman's heart is nothing but his imagination.

BERNARD SHAW, *John Bull's Other Island*. Act i.

10
A servile race in folly nursed,
Who truckle most when treated worst.

SWIFT, *On the Death of Dr. Swift*, l. 461.

11
O, love is the soul of a true Irishman;
He loves all that's lovely, loves all that he can,
With his sprig of shillelagh and shamrock so green.

UNKNOWN, *The Sprig of Shillelagh*. Sometimes attributed to Edward Lysaght.

12
More Irish than the Irish. (Hibernicis ipsis Hibernior.)

UNKNOWN. A proverbial expression.

IRON

I—Iron: Apothegms

13
"Gold is for the mistress—silver for the maid—
Copper for the craftsman cunning at his trade."
"Good!" said the Baron, sitting in his hall,
"But Iron—Cold Iron—is master of them all."

RUDYARD KIPLING, *Cold Iron*.

Ay me! what perils do environ
The man that meddles with cold iron!

BUTLER, *Hudibras*. Pt. i, canto iii, l. 1.

Put up your iron.

SHAKESPEARE, *Twelfth Night*. Act iv, sc. 1, l. 42.

14
Iron sharpeneth iron; so a man sharpeneth the countenance of his friend.

Old Testament: Proverbs, xxvii, 17.

15
He was laid in iron.

Old Testament: Psalms, cv, 18. The meaning being that Joseph was bound with fetters or chains, but in the *Vulgate* the phrase was mistranslated, "Ferrum pertransiit animam ejus" (The iron entered into his soul), a perversion carried into the *Psalter*, cv, 18, and into the *Great Bible* of 1539.

I saw the iron enter into his soul.

STERNE, *Sentimental Journey: The Captive*.

16
He is teaching iron to swim.

JOHN RAY, *English Proverbs*, 75.

17
I'll make thee eat iron like an ostrich.

SHAKESPEARE, *II Henry VI*. Act iv, sc. 10, l. 30.

18
This extraordinary metal, the soul of every manufacture, and the mainspring perhaps, of civilised society.

SAMUEL SMILES, *Invention and Industry*. Ch. 4.

II—Iron: Strike While the Iron Is Hot

19
Strike while the iron is hot. (Εὐθὺς τὸ πρῆγμα κροτείσθω.)

ADDÆUS, *Epigram*. (*Greek Anthology*. Bk. x, epig. 20.)

The iron hot, time is for to smite.

LYDGATE, *Troy Book*. Bk. ii, l. 6110. (1412)

Strike the iron whilst it is hot.

RABELAIS, *Works*. Bk. ii, ch. 31. (1534)

When thy iron is hot, strike.

JOHN HEYWOOD, *Proverbs*. Pt. i, ch. 3. (1546)

Strike while the iron is hot.

SIR EDWARD HOBY, *To Cecil*. 14 Oct., 1587; DEKKER, *Works*, i, 100. (1603) Etc., etc.

1
When the iron is well hot, it worketh the better.
WILLIAM CAXTON, *Sonnes of Aymon*, 136. (c. 1489)

2
Pandare, which that stood her fast by,
Felt iron hot, and he began to smite.
CHAUCER, *Troilus and Criseyde*. Bk. ii, l. 1276. (c. 1374)

3
We must beat the iron while it is hot; but we may polish it at leisure.
JOHN DRYDEN, *Dedication of the Æneis.*

4
Strike now, or else the iron cools.
SHAKESPEARE, *III Henry VI*. Act v, sc. 1, l. 49.

And with new notions,—let me change the rule,—
Don't strike the iron till it's slightly cool.
O. W. HOLMES, *A Rhymed Lesson*, l. 302.

IRONY

See also Satire

5
Irony is the foundation of the character of Providence. (L'ironie est le fond du caractère de la Providence.)
BALZAC, *Eugénie Grandet.*

6
Calmness and irony are the only weapons worthy of the strong.
ÉMILE GABORIAU, *Monsieur Lecoq*. Pt. ii, ch. 4.

7
Life's Little Ironies.
THOMAS HARDY. Title of collection of short stories.

8
Irony is jesting hidden behind gravity.
JOHN WEISS, *Wit, Humor and Shakespeare.*

9
Irony is an insult conveyed in the form of a compliment.
E. P. WHIPPLE, *Literature and Life: Wit.*

ISLAND

10
Some isle With the sea's silence on it, . . .
Some unsuspected isle in the far seas,—
Some unsuspected isle in far-off seas!
ROBERT BROWNING, *Pippa Passes*. Pt. ii.

11 From the sprinkled isles,
Lily on lily, that o'erlace the sea.
ROBERT BROWNING, *Cleon.*

12
Beautiful isle of the sea,
Smile on the brow of the waters.
GEORGE COOPER, *Song.*

13
O, it's a snug little island!
A right little, tight little island!
THOMAS DIBDIN, *The Snug Little Island*. *See also* ENGLAND: FAST-ANCHORED ISLE.

14
Sprinkled along the waste of years
Full many a soft green isle appears:
Pause where we may upon the desert road,
Some shelter is in sight, some sacred safe abode.
JOHN KEBLE, *The Christian Year: The First Sunday in Advent.*

15
Many a green isle needs must be
In the deep wide sea of Misery,
Or the mariner, worn and wan,
Never thus could voyage on.
SHELLEY, *Lines Written Amongst the Euganean Hills*, l. 1.

Ay, many flowering islands lie
In the waters of wide Agony.
SHELLEY, *Lines Written Among the Euganean Hills*, l. 66.

16
Summer isles of Eden lying in dark-purple spheres of sea.
TENNYSON, *Locksley Hall*, l. 164.

ITALY AND THE ITALIANS

I—Italy

17
How has kind heaven adorn'd the happy land,
And scatter'd blessings with a wasteful hand!
JOSEPH ADDISON, *A Letter from Italy*, l. 105.

For wheresoe'er I turn my ravish'd eyes,
Gay gilded scenes and shining prospects rise;
Poetic fields encompass me around,
And still I seem to tread on classic ground.
JOSEPH ADDISON, *A Letter from Italy*, l. 9.

18
Naples, the Paradise of Italy,
As that is of earth.
BEAUMONT AND FLETCHER, *The Double Marriage*. Act i.

Naples sitteth by the sea, keystone of an arch of azure.
TUPPER, *Proverbial Philosophy: Of Death.*

My soul to-day Is far away
Sailing the Vesuvian Bay.
THOMAS BUCHANAN READ, *Drifting.*

See Naples and die. (Vedi Napoli, e poi muori.)
UNKNOWN. An Italian proverb.

19
Oh, woman-country, wooed, not wed,
Loved all the more by earth's male-lands
Laid to their hearts instead!
ROBERT BROWNING, *By the Fireside.*

Queen Mary's saying serves for me—
(When fortune's malice
Lost her Calais)
Open my heart and you will see
Graved inside of it, "Italy."
ROBERT BROWNING, *"De Gustibus—"*

20
Italy a paradise for horses, hell for women, as the proverb goes.
BURTON, *Anatomy of Melancholy*. Pt. iii, sec. iii, mem. 1, subs. 2. *See also under* ENGLAND.

21
I love the language, that soft bastard Latin,

Which melts like kisses from a female mouth,
And sounds as if it had been writ on satin,
With syllables which breathe of the sweet South.
BYRON, *Beppo*. St. 44.

The Tuscan's siren tongue,
That music in itself, whose sounds are song,
The poetry of speech.
BYRON, *Childe Harold*. Canto iv, l. 58.

The story is extant, and writ in choice Italian.
SHAKESPEARE, *Hamlet*. Act iii, sc. 2, l. 273.

1
O Italy! thy sabbaths will be soon
Our sabbaths, clos'd with mumm'ry and buffoon.
COWPER, *The Progress of Error*, l. 152.

2
Ah, slavish Italy! thou inn of grief!
Vessel without a pilot in loud storm!
Lady no longer of fair provinces,
But brothel-house impure!
(Ahi serva Italia, di dolore ostello,
Nave senza nocchiere in gran tempesta,
Non donna di provincie, ma bordello!)
DANTE, *Purgatorio*. Canto vi, l. 46. (Cary, tr.)

Italy! Italy! thou who'rt doomed to wear
The fatal gift of beauty, and possess
The dower funest of infinite wretchedness
Written upon thy forehead by despair.
(Italia, Italia, O tu cui feo la sorte,
Dono infelice di bellezza, ond' hai
Funesta dote d'infinita guai
Che in fronte scritti per gran doglia porte.)
VICENZO DA FILICAJA, *Italia*. (Longfellow, tr.)

Italia! oh Italia! thou who hast
The fatal gift of beauty, which became
A funeral dower of present woes and past,
On thy sweet brow is sorrow plough'd by shame,
And annals graved in characters of flame.
BYRON, *Childe Harold*. Canto iv, st. 42. A free rendering of Filicaja's sonnet, *Italia*, which Byron appropriated without credit.

O Italy, how beautiful thou art!
Yet I could weep—for thou art lying, alas!
Low in the dust. . .
Thine was a dangerous gift, the gift of Beauty.
SAMUEL ROGERS, *Italy*. Pt. i, sec. 9, l. 9.

3
Know'st thou the land where the lemon-trees bloom,
Where the gold orange glows in the deep thicket's gloom,
Where a wind ever soft from the blue heaven blows,
And the groves are of laurel and myrtle and rose?
(Kennst du das Land wo die Citronen blühen,
Im dunkeln Laub die Gold-Orangen glühn,
Ein sanfter Wind vom blauen Himmel weht,
Die Myrthe still und hoch der Lorbeer steht?)
GOETHE, *Wilhelm Meister:* Bk. iii, ch. 1, *Mignon's Song* (Carlyle, tr.)

Knowest thou the land where bloom the lemon trees?
And darkly gleam the golden oranges?
A gentle wind blows down from that blue sky;
Calm stands the myrtle and the laurel high.
Knowest thou the land? So far and fair!
Thou, whom I love, and I will wander there.
GOETHE, *Kennst Du das Land*. (Flecker, tr.)

4
Home of the Arts! where glory's faded smile
Sheds lingering light o'er many a mouldering pile.
FELICIA DOROTHEA HEMANS, *Restoration of the Works of Art to Italy*.

5
Dear Italy! The sound of thy soft name
Soothes me with balm of Memory and Hope.
R. U. JOHNSON, *Italian Rhapsody*.

6
A man who has not been in Italy is always conscious of an inferiority.
SAMUEL JOHNSON. (BOSWELL, *Life*, 1776.)

7
Beyond the Alps lies Italy. (In conspectu Alpes habeant, quarum alterum latus Italiæ sit.)
LIVY, *History*. Bk. xxi, ch. 30, l. 17.

Yet courage, soul! nor hold thy strength in vain,
In hope o'er come the steeps God set for thee,
For past the Alpine summits of great pain
Lieth thine Italy.
ROSE TERRY COOKE, *Beyond*.

8
Italy is only a geographical expression.
PRINCE METTERNICH, *Memorandum to the Great Powers*, 2 Aug., 1814.

9
Can this be Italy, or but a dream
Emerging from the broken waves of sleep? . . .
This world of beauty, color, and perfume,
Hoary with age, yet of unaging bloom.
ADA FOSTER MURRAY, *Above Salerno*.

10
By many a temple half as old as Time.
SAMUEL ROGERS, *Italy*.

11
There is a pool on Garda,
You'll see it in your dreams;
'Tis shaped of silvery glamor,
'Tis fused of golden beams.
CLINTON SCOLLARD, *There Is a Pool on Garda*.

12
Keats and Shelley sleep at Rome,
She in well-loved Tuscan earth;
Finding all their death's long home
Far from their old home of birth.
Italy, you hold in trust
Very sacred English dust.
JAMES THOMSON, *Elizabeth Barrett Browning*

13
Hail, land of Saturn! great mother of earth's fruits, great mother of men! (Salve, magna parens frugum, Saturnia tellus, Magna virum!)
VERGIL, *Georgics*. Bk. ii, l. 173.

1
Lump the whole thing! Say that the Creator made Italy from designs by Michael Angelo!

Mark Twain, *The Innocents Abroad.* Ch. 3.

2
A paradise inhabited with devils.

Sir Henry Wotton, *Letters from Italy.*

II—The Italians

3
The Italians are wise before the deed; the Germans in the deed; the French after the deed.

George Herbert, *Jacula Prudentum.*

4
All Italians are plunderers. (Gli Italiani tutti ladroni.)

Napoleon Bonaparte, *Remark,* in a loud voice in public company. To which a lady replied, "Non tutti, ma buona parte," "Not all, but a good part," a play upon Napoleon's name. (Coleridge, *Biographia Literaria: Satyrane's Letters.* No. 2.) Pasquin made the same pun when the French were in possession of Rome: "I Francesi son tutti ladri; non tutti, ma buona parte." (Catherine Taylor, *Letters from Italy.* Vol. i, p. 239.)

5
Salad, and eggs, and lighter fare,
Tune the Italian spark's guitar.

Matthew Prior, *Alma.* Canto iii, l. 246.

6
Subtle, discerning, eloquent, the slave
Of Love, of Hate, for ever in extremes;
Gentle when unprovoked, easily won,
But quick in quarrel—through a thousand shades
His spirit flits, chameleon-like; and mocks
The eye of the observer.

Samuel Rogers, *Italy: Venice.*

7
Thy locks jet-black, and clustering round a face
Open as day and full of manly daring.
Thou hadst a hand, a heart for all that came,
Herdsman or pedlar, monk or muleteer;
And few there were that met thee not with smiles.
Mishap pass'd o'er thee like a summer-cloud.
Cares thou hadst none; and they, who stood to hear thee,
Caught the infection and forgot their own.
Nature conceived thee in her merriest mood,
. . . And at thy birth the cricket chirp'd.

Samuel Rogers, *Italy: Luigi.*

IVY

8
For ivy climbs the crumbling hall
To decorate decay.

P. J. Bailey, *Festus: A Large Party.*

As creeping ivy clings to wood or stone,
And hides the ruin that it feeds upon.

Cowper, *The Progress of Error,* l. 285.

Where round some mould'ring tow'r pale ivy creeps,
And low-brow'd rocks hang nodding o'er the deeps.

Pope, *Eloisa to Abelard,* l. 243.

Round broken columns clasping ivy twin'd.

Pope, *Windsor Forest,* l. 69.

From a tower in an ivy-green jacket.

Thomas Hood, *Miss Kilmansegg: Her Marriage.*

9
That headlong ivy! . . . bold to leap a height
'Twas strong to climb; as good to grow on graves
As twist about a thyrsus; pretty too
(And that's not ill) when twisted round a comb.

E. B. Browning, *Aurora Leigh.* Bk. ii, l. 47.

10
Oh, a dainty plant is the Ivy green,
That creepeth o'er ruins old!
Of right choice food are his meals I ween,
In his cell so lone and cold. . . .
Creeping where no life is seen,
A rare old plant is the Ivy green.

Dickens, *The Ivy Green.* (*Pickwick Papers.* Ch. 6.)

For the stateliest building man can raise
Is the Ivy's food at last.
Creeping on, where time has been,
A rare old plant is the Ivy Green.

Charles Dickens, *The Ivy Green.*

11
Oh! how could Fancy crown with *thee,*
In ancient days, the God of Wine,
And bid thee at the banquet be
Companion of the Vine?
Ivy! *thy* home is where each sound
Of revelry hath long been o'er;
Where song and beaker once went round,
But now are known no more.

Felicia Dorothea Hemans, *Ivy Song.*

12
Direct The clasping ivy where to climb.

Milton, *Paradise Lost.* Bk. ix, l. 216.

Yet once more, O ye laurels, and once more,
Ye myrtles brown, with ivy never-sere,
I come to pluck your berries harsh and crude,
And with forc'd fingers rude,
Shatter your leaves before the mellowing year.

Milton, *Lycidas,* l. 1.

13
On my velvet couch reclining,
Ivy leaves my brow entwining,
While my soul expands with glee,
What are kings and crowns to me?

Thomas Moore, *Odes of Anacreon.* Ode 48.

14
Bring, bring the madding Bay, the drunken vine;
The creeping, dirty, courtly Ivy join.

Pope, *The Dunciad.* Bk. i, l. 303.

J

JACK

I—Jack

1
When there was need of any service, . . . I was Jack at a pinch.
MATEO ALEMAN, *Guzman de Alfarache*, l. 130. (1622)

Jack-at-a-pinch, a sudden, unexpected call to do anything.
HALLIWELL, *Dictionary*.

2
I'd do it as soon as say Jack Robinson.
FANNY BURNEY, *Evelina*. Let. 82. (1778)

Before you could say Jack Robinson.
MARIA EDGEWORTH, *The Absentee*. Ch. 2. (1812)

A work it is as easy to be done
As 'tis to say Jacke! Robys on.
HALLIWELL, *Archaic Dictionary*, gives this as from an "old play," but the play has never been identified, and the couplet is palpably *ben trovato*. Many tales have been invented to explain the origin of the phrase, but none convincing.

3
As cunningly . . . as ever poor cuckoo could commend his Jack in a box.
HENRY CHETTLE, *Kind-Hart's Dreame*, 45. (1592)

No other Jack i' the box but he.
BEAUMONT AND FLETCHER, *Love's Cure*. Act iii, sc. 1. (1623)

4
Jack Sprat will eat no fat,
And Jill doth love no lean,
Yet betwixt them both,
They lick the dishes clean.
JOHN CLARKE, *Parœmiologia*, 17. (1639)

Jack Sprat he loved no fat,
And his wife she loved no lean:
And yet betwixt them both,
They lick't the platters clean.
JOHN RAY, *English Proverbs*, 211. (1670)

Jack Sprat could eat no fat,
His wife could eat no lean;
And so, betwixt them both, you see,
They lick'd the platter clean.
HALLIWELL, *Nursery Rhymes*, 34. (1843)

5
'Twas all one to Jack.
CHARLES DIBDIN, *All's One to Jack*. Jack Tar, the popular name for a sailor. *See also under* SEA.

6
"He calls the knaves Jacks, this boy," said Estella with disdain, before our first game was out.
DICKENS, *Great Expectations*. Ch. 8.

7
What is vulgarly called Jack of both sides. (Ut vulgo dici solet Joannem ad oppositum.)
EDMUND GRINDAL, *Letter to John Foxe*, 28 Dec., 1557.

Who played jacks on both sides, and were indeed Neuters.
THOMAS DEKKER, *Works*, iv, 158. (1609)

Reader, John Newter, who erst played
The Jack on both sides, here is laid.
UNKNOWN, *Wits' Recreations*. (1654)

How often have those men of honour . . . play'd
Jack a both sides, to-day for and to-morrow against.
DANIEL DEFOE, *Complete Gentleman*. Pt. i, ch. 1. (1729)

8
Small jacks we have in many ale-houses, tipped with silver.
JOHN HEYWOOD, *Philocothonista*. (1635) A pitcher of waxed leather, sometimes called a black-jack.

Body of me, I'm dry still; give me the jack, boy;
This wooden skilt holds nothing.
JOHN FLETCHER, *Bloody Brother*. Act ii, sc. 2.

9
All work and no play makes Jack a dull boy.
JAMES HOWELL, *Proverbs*, 12. (1659) THOMAS FULLER, *Gnomologia*. No. 6372. (1732)

All work and no play makes Jack a dull boy,
All play and no work makes Jack a mere toy.
MARIA EDGEWORTH, *Harry and Lucy*.

All work and no play may make Peter a dull boy as well as Jack.
CHARLES DICKENS, *Letters*. Vol. i, p. 313.

And all labour without any play, boys,
Makes Jack a dull boy in the end.
H. A. PAGE, *Vers de Société*.

10
There are giants to slay, and they call for their Jack.
GEORGE MEREDITH, *The Empty Purse*.

11
Some broken citizen who hath played Jack-of-all-trades.
GEFFRAY MINSHULL, *Essays*, 50. (1618)

You mongrel, you John-of-all-trades!
JASPER MAYNE, *City Match*. Act ii, sc. 5. (1639)

Yet I am still in my vocation; for you know I am a Jack of all trades.
DRYDEN, *Amphitryon*. Act i, sc. 1. (1690)

He is a bit of Jack of all trades, or to use his own words, "a regular Robinson Crusoe."
DICKENS, *Sketches by Boz*. Ch. 2. (1836)

12
To be Jack in an office.
JOHN RAY, *English Proverbs*, 214. (1670)

Jack in an office is a great man.
THOMAS FULLER, *Gnomologia*. No. 3050. (1732)

A type of Jacks-in-office insolence and absurdity.
DICKENS, *Little Dorrit*. Bk. i, ch. 2. (1857)

And Jack out of office she may bid me walk.
JOHN HEYWOOD, *Proverbs*. Pt. ii, ch. 3. (1546)

But long I will not be Jack out of office.
SHAKESPEARE, *I Henry VI*. Act i, sc. 1, l. 175.

1
I am no proud Jack, like Falstaff; but a Corinthian, a lad of mettle, a good boy.
SHAKESPEARE, *I Henry IV*. Act ii, sc. 4, l. 12.

2
He speak for a jack-an-ape to Anne Page.
SHAKESPEARE, *The Merry Wives of Windsor*. Act ii, sc. 3, l. 87. (1600)

Can Jack an apes be merry when his clog is at his heels?
WILLIAM CAMDEN, *Remains*, p. 321. (1605)

There is more ado with one Jack an apes than all the bears.
THOMAS D'URFEY, *Comical History of Don Quixote*. Pt. ii, act i, sc. 2. (1694)

3
Silken, sly, insinuating Jacks.
SHAKESPEARE, *Richard III*. Act i, sc. 3, l. 53.

4
I stand fooling here, his Jack o' the clock.
SHAKESPEARE, *Richard II*. Act v, sc. 5, l. 60. A "Jack o' the clock" was a mechanical figure which struck the bell.

This is the night, nine the hour, and I the jack that gives warning.
THOMAS MIDDLETON, *Blurt*. Act ii, sc. 2.

5
Lo, Jack would be a gentleman!
JOHN SKELTON, *Works*, i, 15. (1529)

Jack would be a gentleman, if he could speak French.
JOHN HEYWOOD, *Proverbs*. Pt. i, ch. 11. (1546)

We ape the French chiefly in two particulars: First, in their language ("which if Jack could speak, he would be a gentleman").
THOMAS FULLER, *Worthies of England*, i, 118. (1662)

Since every Jack became a gentleman,
There's many a gentle person made a Jack.
SHAKESPEARE, *Richard III*. Act i, sc. 3, l. 170. (1592)

6
Then Jack-a-lent comes justling in,
With the head-piece of a herring.
UNKNOWN, *Philip and Mary*, 191. (c. 1560)

He was dressed up like a Jack a Lent.
THOMAS CHURCHYARD, *Chippes*, 50. (1575)

You little Jack-a-Lent, have you been true to us?
SHAKESPEARE, *Merry Wives of Windsor*. Act iii, sc. 3, l. 27. (1600) A Jack-a-Lent was a puppet thrown at during the Lenten fairs.

II—Jack and Jill

7
There is not so bad a Jack but there is as bad a Jill.
BERTHELSON, *English-Danish Dictionary*. (1754) There are many variations of this proverb: "A good Jack makes a good Jill." "Jack's as good as Jill." "If Jack were better, Jill would not be so bad," Jack being a sort of generic name for a young fellow and Jill for a young woman.

8
For not a Jack among them but must have his Jill.
DANIEL DEFOE, *Everybody's Business*. (1725)

9
If Jack's in love, he's no judge of Jill's Beauty.
BENJAMIN FRANKLIN, *Poor Richard*, 1748.

10
What availeth lordship, yourself for to kill
With care and with thought how Jack shall have Jill?
JOHN SKELTON, *Magnyfycence*, l. 290. (c. 1520)

Jack shall have Jill, Nought shall go ill.
SHAKESPEARE, *A Midsummer-Night's Dream*. Act iii, sc. 2, l. 461. (1595)

Every Jack will find a Jill, gang the world as it may.
SCOTT, *St. Ronan's Well*. Ch. 2.

11
While the ancient law fulfills,
Myriad moons shall wane and wax.
Jack must have his pair of Jills,
Jill must have her pair of Jacks.
BERT LESTON TAYLOR, *Old Stuff*.

12
Jack shall pipe and Jill shall dance.
GEORGE WITHER, *Christmas*.

13
Jack and Jill went up the hill,
To fetch a pail of water;
Jack fell down and broke his crown
And Jill came tumbling after.
UNKNOWN, *Jack and Jill*.

JACKSON, ANDREW

14
In answer to our shouting, fire lit his eye of gray;
Erect, but thin and pallid, he passed upon his bay. . . .
But spite of fever and fasting, and hours of sleepless care,
The soul of Andrew Jackson shone forth in glory there.
THOMAS DUNN ENGLISH, *The Battle of New Orleans*.

15
Old turkey-cock on a forest rock,
Old faithful heart who could boast and strut;
I will think of you when the woods are cut—
Old, old Andrew Jackson. . . .

He broke the bones of all cattle who horned him,
He broke the bones of all who scorned him,— . . .
The finest hope from the Cave of Adullam,
Since Davis ascended the throne;—
Old Andrew Jackson, the old, old raven, lean as a bone!
VACHEL LINDSAY, *Old Old Old Andrew Jackson.*

1
This is the day that we honor "Old Hickory,"
Honor him, aye, for the name that he bore!
Fierce as a fighter, and yet above trickery,
Virile and valiant and leal to the core!
CLINTON SCOLLARD, *Old Hickory.*

How General Andrew Jackson got the title of "Old Hickory" is told by Captain William Allen, who messed with him during the Creek War. Allen's story is that Jackson caught a severe cold during the advance. There were no tents, but Allen and his brother cut down a stout hickory tree, peeled off the bark and persuaded Jackson to use it as a covering. A drunken citizen fell over it next morning, and as Jackson crawled out, greeted him with, "Hello, Old Hickory! come out of your bark and jine us in a drink." This seems a tall yarn, and the sobriquet more probably referred to Jackson's strong and wiry build.

JACKSON, THOMAS JONATHAN (STONEWALL)

2
There is Jackson standing like a stone wall!
BRIG.-GEN. BARNARD E. BEE, at battle of Bull Run, 21 July, 1861, referring to the Confederate general, Thomas Jonathan Jackson. General Jackson always insisted that Bee had referred to his brigade and not to himself personally, but the sobriquet "Stonewall" stuck to him the rest of his life. (POORE, *Reminiscences of Metropolis*, ii, 85.)

3
Says he, "That's Banks, he's fond of shell,
Lord save his soul! we'll give him—;" well
That's Stonewall Jackson's way.
JOHN WILLIAMSON PALMER, *Stonewall Jackson's Way.*

4
Yes, it was noblest for him—it was best
(Questioning naught of our Father's decrees),
There to pass over the river and rest
Under the shade of the trees!
MARGARET JUNKIN PRESTON, *Under the Shade of the Trees.* General Jackson's last words were, "Let us cross the river and rest in the shade."

5
Whom have we here—shrouded in martial manner,
Crowned with a martyr's charm?
A grand dead hero, in a living banner,
Born of his heart and arm.
UNKNOWN, *The Brigade Must Not Know, Sir.*

JASMINE

6
Jasmine is sweet and has many loves.
THOMAS HOOD, *Flowers.*

7
Jas in the Arab language is despair,
And *Min* the darkest meaning of a lie.
Thus cried the Jessamine among the flowers,
How justly doth a lie
Draw on its head despair!
Among the fragrant spirits of the bowers
The boldest and the strongest still was I.
Although so fair,
Therefore from Heaven
A stronger perfume unto me was given
Than any blossom of the summer hours.
CHARLES GODFREY LELAND, *Jessamine.*

Among the flowers no perfume is like mine:
That which is best in me comes from within.
So those in this world who would rise and shine,
Should seek internal excellence to win.
And though 'tis true that falsehood and despair
Meet in my name, yet bear it still in mind
That where they meet they perish. All is fair
When they are gone and nought remains behind.
CHARLES GODFREY LELAND, *Jessamine.*

8
And the jasmine flower in her fair young breast,
(O the faint, sweet smell of that jasmine flower!)
And the one bird singing alone to his nest.
And the one star over the tower.
OWEN MEREDITH, *Aux Italiens.*

It smelt so faint, and it smelt so sweet,
It made me creep and it made me cold.
Like the scent that steals from the crumbling sheet
Where a mummy is half unroll'd.
OWEN MEREDITH, *Aux Italiens.*

9
And the jessamine faint, and the sweet tuberose,
The sweetest flower for scent that blows.
SHELLEY, *The Sensitive Plant.* St. 10.

10
Out in the lonely woods the jasmine burns
Its fragrant lamps, and turns
Into a royal court with green festoons
The banks of dark lagoons.
HENRY TIMROD, *Spring.*

11
As climbing jasmine pure.
WORDSWORTH, *Elegiac Stanzas.*

JEALOUSY

I—Jealousy: Definitions

12
Thou tyrant, tyrant Jealousy,
Thou tyrant of the mind!
DRYDEN, *Song of Jealousy.*

1
Jealousy is the bellows of the mind;
Touch it but gently, and it warms desire,
If handled roughly, you are all on fire.
DAVID GARRICK, *Epilogue to Horne's Alonzo.*

2
Jealousy is said to be the offspring of Love. Yet, unless the parent makes haste to strangle the child, the child will not rest till it has poisoned the parent.
J. C. AND A. W. HARE, *Guesses at Truth.*

3
Jealousy is nourished by doubt, and becomes madness or ends when it passes from doubt to certainty. (La jalousie se nourrit dans les doutes, et elle devient fureur, ou elle finit, sitôt qu'on passe du doute à la certitude.)
LA ROCHEFOUCAULD, *Maximes.* No. 32.

Jealousy is always born with love, but does not always die with it. (La jalousie naît toujours avec l'amour, mais elle ne meurt pas toujours avec lui.)
LA ROCHEFOUCAULD, *Maximes.* No. 361.

Jealousy is the greatest evil of all, and the one which excites the least pity in the persons who occasion it. (La jalousie est le plus grand de tous les maux, et celui qui fait le moins de pitié aux personnes qui le causent.)
LA ROCHEFOUCAULD, *Maximes.* No. 503.

4
No true love there can be without
Its dread penalty—jealousy.
OWEN MEREDITH, *Lucile.* Pt. ii, canto i, st. 24, l. 8.

5
Nor jealousy
Was understood, the injur'd lover's hell.
MILTON, *Paradise Lost.* Bk. v, l. 449.

6
O jealousy thou magnifier of trifles!
SCHILLER, *Fiesco.* Act i, sc. 1. (Bohn, tr.)

7
Jealous souls will not be answer'd so;
They are not jealous for the cause,
But jealous for they are jealous: 'tis a monster
Begot upon itself, born on itself.
SHAKESPEARE, *Othello.* Act iii, sc. 4, l. 159.

8
Jealousy, at any rate, is one of the consequences of love; you may like it or not, at pleasure; but there it is.
R. L. STEVENSON, *On Falling in Love.*

9
Jealousy's a city passion; 'tis a thing unknown among people of quality.
SIR JOHN VANBRUGH, *The Confederacy.*

10
Moral indignation is jealousy with a halo.
H. G. WELLS, *The Wife of Sir Isaac Harman.* Ch. ix, sec. 2.

11
It is the hydra of calamities,
The sevenfold death.
YOUNG, *The Revenge.* Act ii, sc. 1.

II—Jealousy: Apothegms

12
That is ever the way. 'Tis all jealousy to the bride, and good wishes to the corpse.
J. M. BARRIE, *Quality Street.* Act i.

13
Jealousy be so bred in the bone that it will never out of the flesh.
WILLIAM BULLEIN, *Bulwark of Defence.* Fo. 75.

14
Yet he was jealous, though he did not show it,
For jealousy dislikes the world to know it.
BYRON, *Don Juan.* Canto i, st. 65.

15
Our very best friends have a tincture of jealousy even in their friendship; and when they hear us praised by others, will ascribe it to sinister and interested motives if they can.
C. C. COLTON, *Lacon,* p. 80. *See also under* FRIEND.

16
Anger and jealousy can no more bear to lose sight of their objects than love.
GEORGE ELIOT, *Mill on the Floss.* Bk. i, ch. 10.

Jealousy is never satisfied with anything short of an omniscience that would detect the subtlest fold of the heart.
GEORGE ELIOT, *Mill on the Floss.* Bk. vi, ch. 10.

17
He that a white horse and a fair wife keepeth,
For fear, for care, for jealousy scarce sleepeth.
JOHN FLORIO, *Second Frutes,* 191.

'Tis not to make me jealous
To say my wife is fair, feeds well, loves company,
Is free of speech, sings, plays and dances well.
SHAKESPEARE, *Othello.* Act iii, sc. 3, l. 183.

18
Man's of a jealous and mistaking kind.
HOMER, *Odyssey.* Bk. vii, l. 394. (Pope, tr.)

19
There is more self-love than love in jealousy. (Il y a dans la jalousie plus d'amour-propre que d'amour.)
LA ROCHEFOUCAULD, *Maximes.* No. 324.

20
Jealousy will be the ruin of you. (Perdet te dolor hic.)
MARTIAL, *Epigrams.* Bk. x, ep. 98, l. 11.

21
Build on your own deserts, and ever be
A stranger to love's enemy, jealousy.
MASSINGER, *A Very Woman.* Act iv, sc. 2.

22
Jealousy shuts one door and opens two.
SAMUEL PALMER, *Moral Essays,* p. 370.

23
Love being jealous makes a good eye look asquint.
JOHN RAY, *English Proverbs.*

24
One not easily jealous, but, being wrought,
Perplexed in the extreme.
SHAKESPEARE, *Othello.* Act v, sc. 2, l. 345.

1
Jealousy in love . . . That is love's curse.
TENNYSON, *Lancelot and Elaine*, l. 1340.

2
The ear of jealousy heareth all things.
Apocrypha: Wisdom of Solomon, i, 10.

This carry-tale, dissentious Jealousy,
That sometime true news, sometime false doth bring.
SHAKESPEARE, *Venus and Adonis*, l. 657.

III—Jealousy: Its Torments

3
A jealous love lights his torch from the firebrands of the furies.
EDMUND BURKE, *Speech*, 11 Feb., 1780.

4
Then wherefore should we sigh and whine,
With groundless jealousy repine,
With silly whims and fancies frantic,
Merely to make our love romantic?
BYRON, *To a Lady*.

5
But whither am I strayed? I need not raise
Trophies to thee from other men's dispraise;
Nor is thy fame on lesser ruins built;
Nor needs thy juster title the foul guilt
Of Eastern kings, who, to secure their reign,
Must have their brothers, sons, and kindred slain.
SIR JOHN DENHAM, *On Mr. John Fletcher's Works*.

Should such a man, too fond to rule alone,
Bear, like the Turk, no brother near the throne;
View him with scornful, yet with jealous eyes,
And hate for arts that caus'd himself to rise.
POPE, *Epistle to Dr. Arbuthnot*, l. 197.

6
Then grew a wrinkle on fair Venus' brow,
The amber sweet of love is turn'd to gall!
Gloomy was Heaven; bright Phœbus did avow
He would be coy, and would not love at all:
Swearing no greater mischief could be wrought,
Than love united to a jealous thought.
ROBERT GREENE, *Jealousy*.

7
O jealousy,
Thou ugliest fiend of hell! thy deadly venom
Preys on my vitals, turns the healthful hue
Of my fresh cheek to haggard sallowness,
And drinks my spirit up!
HANNAH MORE, *David and Goliath*. Pt. v.

8
Self-harming jealousy. . . .
How many fond fools serve mad jealousy!
SHAKESPEARE, *The Comedy of Errors*. Act ii, sc. 1, l. 102; l. 116.

A jealousy so strong
That judgement cannot cure.
SHAKESPEARE, *Othello*. Act ii, sc. 1, l. 310.

9
Though I perchance am vicious in my guess,
As, I confess, it is my nature's plague
To spy into abuses, and oft my jealousy
Shapes faults that are not.
SHAKESPEARE, *Othello*. Act iii, sc. 3, l. 146.

10
Green-eyed jealousy.
SHAKESPEARE, *The Merchant of Venice*. Act iii, sc. 2, l. 110.

O, beware, my lord, of jealousy;
It is the green-eyed monster which doth mock
The meat it feeds on: that cuckold lives in bliss
Who, certain of his fate, loves not his wronger;
But, O, what damned minutes tells he o'er
Who dotes, yet doubts, suspects, yet strongly loves!
SHAKESPEARE, *Othello*. Act iii, sc. 3, l. 165.

Trifles light as air
Are to the jealous confirmations strong
As proofs of holy writ.
SHAKESPEARE, *Othello*. Act iii, sc. 3, l. 322.

11
Think'st thou I'ld make of life a jealousy
To follow still the changes of the moon
With fresh suspicions?
SHAKESPEARE, *Othello*. Act iii, sc. 3, l. 177.

For where Love reigns, disturbing Jealousy
Doth call himself Affection's sentinel;
Gives false alarms, suggesteth mutiny.
SHAKESPEARE, *Venus and Adonis*, l. 649.

12
What heart-breaking torments from jealousy flow,
Ah! none but the jealous—the jealous can know!
R. B. SHERIDAN, *The Duenna*. Act i, sc. 2.

13
Jealousy is cruel as the grave: the coals thereof are coals of fire, which hath a most vehement flame.
Old Testament: Song of Solomon, viii, 6.

But through the heart
Should Jealousy its venom once diffuse,
'Tis then delightful misery no more,
But agony unmix'd, incessant gall,
Corroding every thought, and blasting all
Love's Paradise.
THOMSON, *The Seasons: Spring*, l. 1075.

14
How great so e'er your rigours are,
With them alone I'll cope;
I can endure my own despair,
But not another's hope.
WILLIAM WALSH, *Song*.

The damning thought stuck in my throat and cut me like a knife,
That she, whom all my life I'd loved, should be another's wife.
H. G. BELL, *The Uncle*.

15
Hunger, Revenge, to sleep are petty foes,
But only Death the jealous eyes can close.
WYCHERLEY, *Love in a Wood*. Act ii, sc. 4.

Inquisitiveness as seldom cures jealousy, as drinking in a fever quenches the thirst.
WYCHERLEY, *Love in a Wood*. Act iv, sc. 5.

1
It is jealousy's peculiar nature,
To swell small things to great, nay, out of nought,
To conjure much; and then to lose its reason
Amid the hideous phantoms it has form'd.
YOUNG, *The Revenge*. Act iii, sc. 1.

IV—Jealousy and Women

2
She'd have you spew up what you've drunk abroad. (Ut devomas vult, quod foris potaveris.)
CÆCILIUS, *Plocium*, l. 162.

3
In jealousy I rede eek thou him bind,
And thou shalt make him crouch as doth a quail.
CHAUCER, *The Clerkes Tale*, l. 1149. Advice to a wife on the way to treat a husband. "Rede" means to advise.

4
Jealousy is inborn in women's hearts. (Ἐπίφθονόν τι χρῆμα θηλείας φρενός.)
EURIPIDES, *Andromache*, l. 181.

5
A jealous woman believes everything her passion suggests.
JOHN GAY, *The Beggar's Opera*. Act ii, sc. 2.

What frenzy dictates, jealousy believes.
JOHN GAY, *Dione*.

6
Can't I another's face commend,
And to her virtues be a friend,
But instantly your forehead lowers,
As if her merit lessen'd *yours?*
EDWARD MOORE, *Fables: The Farmer, the Spaniel and the Cat*.

7
All jealous women are mad.
PINERO, *The Second Mrs. Tanqueray*. Act ii.

8
For story and experience tell us
That man grows old and woman jealous.
MATTHEW PRIOR, *Alma*. Canto ii, l. 65.

9
A jealous woman sets the whole house afire. (Incendit omnem feminae zelus domum.)
PUBLILIUS SYRUS, *Sententiæ*.

10
I will be more jealous of thee than a Barbery cock-pigeon over his hen.
SHAKESPEARE, *As You Like It*. Act iv, sc. 1, l. 151.

11
The venom clamours of a jealous woman
Poisons more deadly than a mad dog's tooth.
SHAKESPEARE, *The Comedy of Errors*. Act v, sc. 1, l. 69.

Each jealous of the other, as the stung are of the adder.
SHAKESPEARE, *King Lear*. Act v, sc. 1, l. 55.

12
Plain women are always jealous of their husbands, beautiful women never are!
OSCAR WILDE, *A Woman of No Importance*. Act i.

JEFFERSON, THOMAS

13
Here was buried Thomas Jefferson, author of the Declaration of American Independence, of the statute of Virginia for religious freedom, and father of the University of Virginia.
JEFFERSON, *Epitaph*, written for himself.

14
I have the consolation to reflect that during the period of my administration not a drop of the blood of a single fellow citizen was shed by the sword of war or of the law.
THOMAS JEFFERSON, *Writings*. Vol. xix, p. 256.

15
Thomas Jefferson still lives.
JOHN ADAMS. Last words. As a matter of fact, Jefferson had died on the morning of that very day, 4 July, 1826. However, Adams's words were a prophecy, for he does still live.

16
He had a steadfast and abiding faith in justice, righteousness and liberty as the prevailing and abiding forces in the conduct of States, and that justice and righteousness were sure to prevail where any people bear rule in perfect liberty.
GEORGE F. HOAR, *Thomas Jefferson*.

17
Since the days when Jefferson expounded his code of political philosophy, the whole world has become his pupil.
MICHAEL MACWHITE, *Address*, at University of Virginia, 13 April, 1931.

18
A gentleman of thirty-two who could calculate an eclipse, survey an estate, tie an artery, plan an edifice, try a cause, break a horse, dance a minuet and play the violin.
JAMES PARTON, *Life of Jefferson*, p. 164.

19
The immortality of Thomas Jefferson does not lie in any one of his achievements, but in his attitude toward mankind.
WOODROW WILSON, *Speech*, Washington, 13 April, 1916.

JERUSALEM, see Heaven

JESTING

See also Laughter, Mirth

I—Jesting: Apothegms

20
Intermingle . . . jest with earnest.
FRANCIS BACON, *Essays: Of Discourse*.

A joke's a very serious thing.
CHURCHILL, *The Ghost*. Bk. iv, l. 1373.

And tells the jest without the smile.
S. T. COLERIDGE, *Youth and Age*.

21
He'd rather lose his dinner than his jest.
BEAUMONT AND FLETCHER, *Wit at Several Weapons*. Act i.

A joke never gains over an enemy, but often loses a friend.
THOMAS FULLER, *Gnomologia*. No. 228.

Some had rather lose their friend than their jest.
GEORGE HERBERT, *Jacula Prudentum*.
See also under FRIEND.

1
The ordinary and over-worn trade of jesting.
BEAUMONT AND FLETCHER, *The Woman Hater: Prologue*.

Vivacity and wit make a man shine in company; but trite jokes and loud laughter reduce him to a buffoon.
LORD CHESTERFIELD, *Letters*, 5 Feb., 1750.

A threadbare jester's threadbare jest.
CHARLES CHURCHILL, *The Ghost*. Bk. iv, l. 529.

2
Jesting lies bring serious sorrows.
H. G. BOHN, *Hand-Book of Proverbs*, 436.

3
The manner of jesting ought not to be extravagant or immoderate, but refined and witty. . . . There are, generally speaking, two sorts of jests: the one, coarse, rude, vicious, indecent; the other polite, refined, clever, witty. . . . The first, if well timed, is becoming to the most dignified person; the other is unfit for any gentleman.
CICERO, *De Officiis*. Bk. i, ch. 19, sec. 103.

4
O happy mortal! he never failed to have his jest. (O mortalem beatum! cui certo scio ludum numquam defuisse.)
CICERO, *De Divinatione*. Bk. ii, ch. 13, sec. 30.

I love my jest, an the ship were sinking, as we say'n at sea.
CONGREVE, *Love for Love*. Act iii, sc. 3.

5
Joking and humor are pleasant, and often of extreme utility. (Suavis autem est, et vehementer sæpe utilis jocus et facetiæ.)
CICERO, *De Oratore*. Bk. ii, sec. 24.

Moderation should be observed in joking. (Adhibenda est in jocando moderatio.)
CICERO, *De Oratore*. Bk. ii, sec. 59.

6
And the sign of the true-hearted sailor
Is to give and to take a good joke.
CHARLES DIBDIN, *Jack at the Windlass*.

7
A chestnut. I have heard you tell the joke twenty-seven times, and I am sure it was a chestnut.
WILLIAM DIMOND, *The Broken Sword*. A forgotten melodrama first produced in 1816. Captain Xavier, the principal character, is always repeating the same yarns, and is telling about one of his exploits connected with a cork-tree, when Pablo corrects him, "A chestnut-tree, you mean, captain," and the discussion continues as to whether it was a cork or a chestnut.

8
As men aim rightest when they shoot in jest.
DRYDEN, *Essay upon Satire*, l. 20.

9
Beware of jokes; . . . we go away hollow and ashamed.
EMERSON, *Letters and Social Aims: Social Aims*.

10
Jest not with the two-edged sword of God's word.
FULLER, *Holy and Profane States: Of Jesting*.

11
Cease your funning.
JOHN GAY, *Beggar's Opera*. Song, l. 1.

12
When thou dost tell another's jest, therein
Omit the oaths, which true wit cannot need;
Pick out of tales the mirth, but not the sin.
GEORGE HERBERT, *The Church-Porch*. St. 11.

13
Less at thine own things laugh; lest in the jest
Thy person share, and the conceit advance.
GEORGE HERBERT, *The Church-Porch*. St. 39.

He must not laugh at his own wheeze:
A snuff-box has no right to sneeze.
KEITH PRESTON, *The Humorist*.

A jest loses its point when the jester laughs himself. (Der Spass verliert Alles, wenn der Spassmacher selber lacht.)
SCHILLER, *Fiesco*. Act i, sc. 7.

He does not only find the jest, but the laugh too.
COLLEY CIBBER, *The Refusal*. Act i.

14
All things are big with jest: nothing that's plain
But may be witty, if thou hast the vein.
GEORGE HERBERT, *The Church-Porch*. St. 40.

15
Putting jesting aside, let us turn to serious thoughts. (Sed tamen amoto quæramus seria ludo.)
HORACE, *Satires*. Bk. i, sat. 1, l. 27.

Jesting apart. (Omissis jocis.)
PLINY THE YOUNGER, *Epistles*. Bk. i, epis. 21.

Leave jesting whiles it pleaseth, lest it turn to earnest.
GEORGE HERBERT, *Jacula Prudentum*.

16
Jesting often cuts hard knots more effectively than gravity. (Ridiculum acri Fortius et melius magnas plerumque secat res.)
HORACE, *Satires*. Bk. i, sat. 10, l. 14.

Joking decides great things,
Stronglier, and better oft than earnest can.
MILTON, *Imitation of Horace*. Bk. i, sat. 10, l. 14. (*Apology for Smectymnuus*.)

17
I gleaned jests at home from obsolete farces.
SAMUEL JOHNSON, *The Rambler*. No. 141.

A jest breaks no bones.
SAMUEL JOHNSON. (BOSWELL, *Life*, 1781.)

18
Suppress me if you can! I am a Merry Jest!
ANDREW LANG, *Ballade of the Primitive Jest*.

1
The saddest ones are those that wear
The jester's motley garb.
DON MARQUIS, *The Tavern of Despair.*

2
Haste thee, Nymph, and bring with thee
Jest and youthful Jollity,
Quips and Cranks, and wanton Wiles,
Nods, and Becks, and wreathèd Smiles.
MILTON, *L'Allegro,* l. 25.

3
A jester, a bad character. (Discur de bons mots, mauvais caractère.)
PASCAL, *Pensées.* ch. 29, No. 26.

4
If a thing be spoken in jest, it is not fair to take it seriously. (Si quid dictum est per jocum, Non æquum est id te serio prævortier.)
PLAUTUS, *Amphitruo,* l. 920. (Act iii, sc. 2.)

5
And gentle dulness ever loves a joke.
POPE, *The Dunciad.* Bk. ii, l. 34.

6
When Whistler's strongest colors fade,
When inks and canvas rot,
Those jokes on Oscar Wilde he made
Will dog him unforgot.
For gags still set the world agog,
When fame begins to flag,
And, like the tail that wagged the dog,
The smart tale dogs the wag.
KEITH PRESTON, *The Durable Bon Mot.*

7
That's the cream of the jest.
JOHN RAY, *English Proverbs,* 69. (1678)

The Cream of the Jest.
JAMES BRANCH CABELL. Title of novel.

8
Many a true word is spoken in jest.
H. G. BOHN, *Hand-Book of Proverbs,* p. 449.

Jesters do oft prove prophets.
SHAKESPEARE, *King Lear.* Act v, sc. 3, l. 71.

9
The wise make jests and fools repeat them.
JOHN RAY, *English Proverbs. See also under* FEASTS.

10
Alas, poor Yorick! I knew him, Horatio: a fellow of infinite jest, of most excellent fancy. . . . Here hung those lips that I have kissed I know not how oft. Where be your gibes now? your gambols? your songs? your flashes of merriment, that were wont to set the table on a roar? Not one now, to mock your own grinning? quite chap-fallen?
SHAKESPEARE, *Hamlet.* Act v, sc. 1, l. 203.

11
Thy quips and thy quiddities.
SHAKESPEARE, *I Henry IV.* Act i, sc. 2, l. 51.

It would be argument for a week, laughter for a month, and a good jest for ever.
SHAKESPEARE, *I Henry IV.* Act ii, sc. 2, l. 100.

Though Nestor swear the jest be laughable.
SHAKESPEARE, *The Merchant of Venice.* Act i, sc. 1, l. 56.

12
A jest's prosperity lies in the ear
Of him that hears it, never in the tongue
Of him that makes it.
SHAKESPEARE, *Love's Labour's Lost.* Act v, sc. 2, l. 871.

13
'Tis my familiar sin
With maids to seem the lapwing and to jest.
SHAKESPEARE, *Measure for Measure.* Act i, sc. 4, l. 32.

14
These are old fond paradoxes to make fools laugh i' the alehouse.
SHAKESPEARE, *Othello.* Act ii, sc. 1, l. 139.

A dry jest, sir. . . . I have them at my fingers' end.
SHAKESPEARE, *Twelfth Night.* Act i, sc. 3, l. 80.

O jest unseen, inscrutable, invisible,
As a nose on a man's face, or a weather-cock on a steeple.
SHAKESPEARE, *The Two Gentlemen of Verona.* Act ii, sc. 1, l. 141.

15
The right honourable gentleman is indebted to his memory for his jests, and to his imagination for his facts.
R. B. SHERIDAN, *Speech,* in reply to Mr. Dundas. (*Sheridaniana.* See MOORE, *Life,* for an account of the origin of this phrase.)

One may say that his wit shines at the expense of his memory. (On peut dire que son esprit brille aux dépens de sa mémoire.)
LE SAGE, *Gil Blas.* Bk. iii, ch. 11.

How hard soe'er it be to bridle wit,
Yet memory oft no less requires the bit.
How many, hurried by its force away,
Forever in the land of gossips stray.
BENJAMIN STILLINGFLEET, *Essay on Conversation.*

16
The jester and jestee.
STERNE, *Tristram Shandy.* Vol. i, ch. 12.

You could read Kant by yourself, if you wanted; but you must share a joke with some one else.
R. L. STEVENSON, *Virginibus Puerisque.* Pt. i.

17
A college joke to cure the dumps.
SWIFT, *Cassinus and Peter.*

The simple joke that takes the shepherd's heart.
THOMSON, *The Seasons: Winter,* l. 623.

18
It is difficult to fashion a jest with a sad mind. (Difficile est tristi fingere mente locum.)
TIBULLUS, *Elegies.* Bk. iii, eleg. 6, l. 34.

No time to break jests when the heartstrings are about to be broken.
THOMAS FULLER, *The Holy and Profane States: Of Jesting.*

19
I tried him with mild jokes, then with severe ones.
MARK TWAIN, *A Deception.*

Guides cannot master the subtleties of the American joke.
MARK TWAIN, *Innocents Abroad*. Ch. 27.

1
If any clerk or monk utters jocular words causing laughter, let him be excommunicated. (Si quis clericus, aut monachus, verba joculatoria risum moventia serat anathemata esto.)
UNKNOWN, *Ordinance, Second Council of Carthage.*

II—Jesting: The Bitter Jest

2
Jests that give pain are no jests.
CERVANTES, *Don Quixote*. Pt. ii, ch. 62.

3
What is this savage jesting of thine? (Quænam ista jocandi Sævita?)
CLAUDIAN, *In Eutropium*. Bk. i, l. 24.

4
The cruel jest. (Sævus jocus.)
HORACE, *Epistles*. Bk. ii, epis. 1, l. 148.

5
Of all the griefs that harass the distress'd,
Sure the most bitter is a scornful jest.
SAMUEL JOHNSON, *London*, l. 166.

6
Let there be jesting without bitterness. (Accedent sine felle joci.)
MARTIAL, *Epigrams*. Bk. x, epig. 48, l. 21.

May there be no ill-natured interpreter to put false constructions on the honest intention of my jests. (Absit a jocorum nostrorum simplicitate malignus interpres.)
MARTIAL, *Epigrams*. Bk. i, *Preface*.

7
Not a letter of mine is dipped in poisoned jest. (Nulla venenato littera mixta joco est.)
OVID, *Tristia*. Bk. ii, l. 566.

No, no, they do but jest, poison in jest; no offence i' the world.
SHAKESPEARE, *Hamlet*. Act iii, sc. 2, l. 244.

8
Bitter jests, whereof the memory is of long duration. (Acerbis facitiis . . . quarum . . . in longum memoria est.)
TACITUS, *Annals*. Bk. v, sec. 2.

A bitter jest that comes too near the truth leaves a sharp sting behind. (Asperæ facetiæ, ubi nimis ex vero taxere, acram sui memoriam relinquunt.)
TACITUS, *Annals*. Bk. xv, sec. 68.

9
You jest: ill jesting with edge-tools!
TENNYSON, *The Princess*. Pt. ii, l. 184.

JESUS CHRIST, see Christ

JEW

10
The unbelieving Jews.
New Testament: Acts, xiv, 2.

11
To be a Jew is a destiny.
VICKI BAUM, *And Life Goes On*, p. 193.

12
Have mercy upon all Jews, Turks, Infidels, and Heretics.
Book of Common Prayer: Good Friday.

13
A people still, whose common ties are gone;
Who, mixed with every race, are lost in none.
GEORGE CRABBE, *The Borough*. Letter 4.

14
Yes, I am a Jew, and when the ancestors of the right honourable gentleman were brutal savages in an unknown island, mine were priests in the temple of Solomon.
BENJAMIN DISRAELI, reputed reply to Daniel O'Connell.

The gentleman will please remember that when his half-civilized ancestors were hunting the wild boar in Silesia, mine were princes of the earth.
JUDAH BENJAMIN, in reply to a taunt by a Senator of German descent. (MOORE, *Reminiscences of Sixty Years in the National Metropolis*.)

You call me a damned Jew. My race was old when you were all savages. I am proud to be a Jew.
JOHN GALSWORTHY, *Loyalties*. Act ii.

15
The Jews are among the aristocracy of every land; if a literature is called rich in the possession of a few classic tragedies, what shall we say to a national tragedy lasting for fifteen hundred years, in which the poets and the actors were also the heroes.
GEORGE ELIOT, *Daniel Deronda*. Bk. vi, ch. 42.

16
The sufferance, which is the badge of the Jew, has made him, in these days, the ruler of the rulers of the earth.
EMERSON, *Conduct of Life: Fate.*

17
Suavity toward the Jews! Although you have lived among them, it is evident that you little understand those enemies of the human race. Haughty and at the same time base, combining an invincible obstinacy with a spirit despicably mean, they weary alike your love and your hatred.
ANATOLE FRANCE, *The Procurator of Judea.*

18
As dear as a Jew's eye.
GABRIEL HARVEY, *Works*, ii, 146. (1593)

There will come a Christian by
Will be worth a Jewess' eye.
SHAKESPEARE, *The Merchant of Venice*. Act ii, sc. 5, l. 43.

19
Triumphant race! and did your power decay?
Failed the bright promise of your early day?
REGINALD HEBER, *Palestine.*

20
When people talk about a wealthy man of my creed, they call him an Israelite; but if he is poor they call him a Jew.
HEINRICH HEINE, *MS. papers.*

If my theory of relativity is proven successful, Germany will claim me as a German and France will declare that I am a citizen of the world. Should my theory prove untrue, France will say that I am a German and Germany will declare that I am a Jew.

ALBERT EINSTEIN, *Address*, Sorbonne, Paris.

1

The Jews spend at Easter.

GEORGE HERBERT, *Jacula Prudentum*. No. 244.

2

Behold an Israelite indeed, in whom is no guile!

New Testament: John, i, 47. Jesus, referring to Nathanael.

3 A hopeless faith, a homeless race,
Yet seeking the most holy place,
And owning the true bliss. . . .
Or like pale ghosts that darkling roam,
Hovering around their ancient home,
But find no refuge there.

JOHN KEBLE, *The Christian Year: Fifth Sunday in Lent*.

4

And Israel shall be a proverb and a by-word among all people.

Old Testament: I Kings, ix, 7.

5

It is curious to see a superstition dying out. The idea of a Jew (which our pious ancestors held in horror) has nothing in it now revolting. We have found the claws of the beast, and pared its nails, and now we take it to our arms, fondle it, write plays to flatter it: it is visited by princes, affects a taste, patronizes the arts, and is the only liberal and gentleman-like thing in Christendom.

CHARLES LAMB, *Specimens of the English Dramatic Poets: Marlowe's Rich Jew of Malta*.

6

Still on Israel's head forlorn,
Every nation heaps its scorn.

EMMA LAZARUS, *The World's Justice*.

His cup is gall, his meat is tears,
His passion lasts a thousand years.

EMMA LAZARUS, *Crowing of the Red Cock*.

7

Who hateth me but for my happiness?
Or who is honoured now but for his wealth?
Rather had I, a Jew, be hated thus,
Than pitied in a Christian poverty.

MARLOWE, *The Jew of Malta*. Act i, sc. 1.

To undo a Jew is charity, and not sin.

MARLOWE, *The Jew of Malta*. Act iv, sc. 6.

8

Sound the loud timbrel o'er Egypt's dark sea!
Jehovah has triumph'd—His people are free.

THOMAS MOORE, *Sound the Loud Timbrel*.

9

This is the Jew
That Shakespeare drew.

Attributed to POPE, after a performance of Shylock by Charles Macklin, 14 Feb., 1741. (*Biographica Dramatica*. Vol. i, pt. 2, p. 469.)

I believe there are few
But have heard of a Jew
Named Shylock, of Venice, as arrant a screw
In money transactions as ever you knew.

R. H. BARHAM, *The Merchant of Venice*.

10

Salvation is from the Jews.

Old Testament: Proverbs, xi, 14. (Salus ex Judæis.—*Vulgate*.)

11

When Israel, of the Lord belov'd,
Out of the land of bondage came,
Her fathers' God before her mov'd,
An awful guide in smoke and flame.

SCOTT, *Ivanhoe*. Ch. 39.

12

I am a Jew else, an Ebrew Jew.

SHAKESPEARE, *I Henry IV*. Act ii, sc. 4, l. 198.

Still have I borne it with a patient shrug,
For sufferance is the badge of all our tribe.
You call me misbeliever, cut-throat dog,
And spit upon my Jewish gabardine.

SHAKESPEARE, *The Merchant of Venice*. Act i, sc. 3, l. 110.

13

He hath . . . laughed at my losses, mocked at my gains, scorned my nation, thwarted my bargains, cooled my friends, heated mine enemies; and what's his reason? I am a Jew.

SHAKESPEARE, *The Merchant of Venice*. Act iii, sc. 1, l. 58.

Hath not a Jew eyes? hath not a Jew hands, organs, dimensions, senses, affections, passions? fed with the same food, hurt with the same weapons, subject to the same diseases, healed by the same means, warmed and cooled by the same winter and summer, as a Christian is? If you prick us, do we not bleed? if you tickle us, do we not laugh? if you poison us, do we not die? and if you wrong us, shall we not revenge?

SHAKESPEARE, *The Merchant of Venice*. Act iii, sc. 1, l. 60.

I pray you, think you question with the Jew:
You may as well go stand upon the beach
And bid the main flood bate his usual height;
You may as well use question with the wolf
Why he hath made the ewe bleat for the lamb;
You may as well forbid the mountain pines
To wag their high tops, and to make no noise,
When they are fretten with the gusts of heaven;
You may as well do any thing most hard,
As seek to soften that—than which what's harder?—
His Jewish heart.

SHAKESPEARE, *The Merchant of Venice*. Act iv, sc. 1, l. 70.

14

I took by the throat the circumcised dog,
And smote him, thus.

SHAKESPEARE, *Othello*. Act v, sc. 2, l. 355.

15

The Jews generally give value. They make you pay; but they deliver the goods. In my

experience the men who want something for nothing are invariably Christians.
BERNARD SHAW, *Saint Joan*. Sc. 4.

1
A race prone to superstition, opposed to religion. (Gens superstitioni obnoxia, religionibus adversa.)
TACITUS, *Annals*. Bk. v, sec. 13.

JEWEL

See also Diamond, Pearl

2
Have you ever noticed, Harry, that many jewels make women either incredibly fat or incredibly thin?
J. M. BARRIE, *The Twelve-pound Look*.

3
Nay, tarry a moment, my charming girl:
Here is a jewel of gold and pearl;
A beautiful cross it is, I ween,
As ever on beauty's breast was seen.
There's nothing at all but love to pay;
Take it, and wear it, but only stay!
Ah! Sir Hunter, what excellent taste!
I'm not—in such—particular—haste!
BÉRANGER, *Le Chasseur et la Laitière*. (Saxe, tr.)

Jewels pawned for loss of game,
And then redeemed by loss of fame.
MATTHEW GREEN, *The Spleen*, l. 192.

4
Stones of small worth may lie unseen by day,
But night itself does the rich gem betray.
ABRAHAM COWLEY, *Davideis*. Bk. iii, l. 37.

5
Jewels, orators of Love,
Which, ah! too well men know, do women move.
SAMUEL DANIEL, *Complaint of Rosamond*. St. 52.

Dumb jewels often, in their silent kind,
More quick than words do move a woman's mind.
SHAKESPEARE, *The Two Gentlemen of Verona*. Act iii, sc. 1, l. 90.

6
These gems have life in them: their colours speak,
Say what words fail of.
GEORGE ELIOT, *The Spanish Gypsy*. Bk. i, sc. 2, l. 528.

7
The rarest things in the world, next to a spirit of discernment, are diamonds and pearls. (Après l'esprit de discernement, ce qu'il y a au monde de plus rare, ce sont les diamants et les perles.)
LA BRUYÈRE, *Les Caractères*. Sec. 12.

8
Bags of fiery opals, sapphires, amethysts,
Jacinths, hard topaz, grass-green emeralds,
Beauteous rubies, sparkling diamonds,
And seld-seen costly stones of so great price. . .
This is the ware wherein consists my wealth;
And thus, methinks, should men of judgement frame
Their means of traffic from the vulgar trade
And, as their wealth increaseth, so inclose
Infinite riches in a little room.
MARLOWE, *The Jew of Malta*. Act i, l. 60.

'Tis plate of rare device, and jewels
Of rich and exquisite form; their value's great.
SHAKESPEARE, *Cymbeline*. Act i, sc. 6, l. 189.

One entire and perfect chrysolite.
SHAKESPEARE, *Othello*. Act v, sc. 2, l. 145.

9
How many a thing which we cast to the ground,
When others pick it up, becomes a gem!
GEORGE MEREDITH, *Modern Love*. St. 41.

10
On her white breast a sparkling cross she bore,
Which Jews might kiss, and infidels adore.
POPE, *Rape of the Lock*. Canto ii, l. 7.

11
From the east to western Ind,
No jewel is like Rosalind.
SHAKESPEARE, *As You Like It*. Act iii, sc. 2, l. 94.

She hangs upon the cheek of night
Like a rich jewel in an Ethiope's ear.
SHAKESPEARE, *Romeo and Juliet*. Act i, sc. 5, l. 48.

12
I see the jewel best enameled
Will lose his beauty.
SHAKESPEARE, *The Comedy of Errors*. Act ii, sc. 1, l. 109.

13
Your ring first;
And here the bracelet of the truest princess
That ever swore her faith.
SHAKESPEARE, *Cymbeline*. Act v, sc. 5, l. 416.

A hoop of gold, a paltry ring.
SHAKESPEARE, *The Merchant of Venice*. Act v, sc. 1, l. 147.

Rich and rare were the gems she wore,
And a bright gold ring on her hand she bore.
THOMAS MOORE, *Rich and Rare*.

14
I took a costly jewel from my neck,
A heart it was, bound in with diamonds.
SHAKESPEARE, *II Henry VI*. Act iii, sc. 2, l. 106.

15
I'll give my jewels for a set of beads.
SHAKESPEARE, *Richard II*. Act iii, sc. 3, l. 147.

16
Like stones of worth, they thinly placed are,
Or captain jewels in the carcanet.
SHAKESPEARE, *Sonnets*. No. lii.

17
The tip no jewel needs to wear:
The tip is jewel of the ear.
SIR PHILIP SIDNEY, *What Tongue Can Her Perfection Tell?*

18
Have I caught my heavenly jewel?
SIR PHILIP SIDNEY, *Astrophel and Stella*. Son-

net ii. From earliest times it has been the custom to call any shining excellence, or precious thing, a "jewel," as in the examples which follow:

Plain dealing's a jewel, but they that use it die beggars.
JOHN RAY, *English Proverbs.*

My chastity's the jewel of our house.
SHAKESPEARE, *All's Well that Ends Well.* Act iv, sc. 2, l. 46.

The jewel of life
By some damn'd hand was robb'd and ta'en away.
SHAKESPEARE, *King John.* Act v, sc. 1, l. 40.

My modesty, the jewel in my dower.
SHAKESPEARE, *The Tempest.* Act iii, sc. 1, l. 54.

O discretion, thou art a jewel.
UNKNOWN. From a song included in a collection called *The Skylark,* London, 1772.

Consistency, thou art a jewel.
UNKNOWN. A proverbial expression.

1
The best of us has our weaknesses, & if a man has gewelry let him show it.
ARTEMUS WARD, *Edwin Forrest as Othello.*

JOB

2
There was a man named Job lived in the land of Uz,
He had a good gift of the gab, the same thing happen us.
ZACHARY BOYD (?), *The Book of Job.* (1650)

3
All bare was his tower as Job was poor man.
ROBERT MANNYNG (DE BRUNNE), *Chronicles,* 323. (c. 1300)

To be forever till I die As poor as Job.
JOHN GOWER, *Confessio Amantis.* Bk. v, l. 2505. (c. 1390)

I am as poor as Job, my lord, but not so patient.
SHAKESPEARE, *II Henry IV.* Act i, sc. 2, l. 144.

Ford: And one that is as slanderous as Satan?
Page: And as poor as Job?
Ford: And as wicked as his wife?
SHAKESPEARE, *The Merry Wives of Windsor.* Act v, sc. 5, l. 163.

Who are all as proud as Lucifer and as poor as Job.
SCOTT, *Fortunes of Nigel.* Ch. 8.

4
Miserable comforters are ye all.
Old Testament: Job, xvi, 2.

Job called his friends miserable comforters.
BRATHWAIT, *English Gentleman,* p. 132. (1630)

They sat down, like Job's three comforters, and said not a word to me for a great while.
DANIEL DEFOE, *Roxana.* (*Works,* xii, 20.)

He called her Small Hopes, and Job's comforter.
RICHARDSON, *Clarissa Harlowe,* vii, 230.

5
Poor as Job's turkey.
UNKNOWN. In Thomas C. Haliburton's *Sam Slick* a turkey gobbler is described as being so poor that he had only one feather in his tail, and so weak he had to lean against a fence to gobble. This is the probable origin of the phrase. Job, of course, had no turkey, since the turkey was a native of America.

JOHNSON, SAMUEL

6
All the nodosities of the oak without its strength; all the contortions of the sibyl without the inspiration.
EDMUND BURKE, of Croft's style in his *Life of Young,* which some one had compared to that of Dr. Johnson. (PRIOR, *Life of Burke.*)

A sort of broken Johnsonese.
MACAULAY, *Essays: Madame d'Arblay.*

7
Indeed, the freedom with which Dr. Johnson condemns whatever he disapproves, is astonishing.
FANNY BURNEY, *Diary,* 23 Aug., 1778.

You must not mind me, madam; I say strange things, but I mean no harm.
SAMUEL JOHNSON. (FANNY BURNEY, *Diary,* 23 Aug., 1778.)

8
Rough Johnson, the great moralist.
BYRON, *Don Juan.* Canto xiii, st. 7.

9
Would that every Johnson in the world had his veridical Boswell, or leash of Boswells.
CARLYLE, *Essays: Voltaire.*

10
Who wit with jealous eye surveys,
And sickens at another's praise.
CHARLES CHURCHILL, *The Ghost.* Bk. ii, l. 663. Referring to Dr. Johnson.

11
Here Johnson lies—a sage, by all allow'd,
Whom to have bred may well make England proud;
Whose prose was eloquence by wisdom taught,
The graceful vehicle of virtuous thought;
Whose verse may claim—grave, masculine, and strong,
Superior praise to the mere poet's song;
Who many a noble gift from heav'n possess'd
And faith at last—alone worth all the rest.
Oh man immortal by a double prize!
By Fame on earth—by Glory in the skies!
COWPER, *Epitaph on Dr. Johnson.*

Here lies poor Johnson; reader have a care;
Tread lightly, lest you rouse a sleeping bear.
Religious, moral, generous, and humane
He was; but self-sufficient, rude, and vain;
Ill-bred, and overbearing in dispute,
A scholar and a Christian and a brute.
SOAME JENYNS, *Epitaph on Samuel Johnson.*

12
If you were to make little fishes talk, they would talk like whales.
GOLDSMITH, to Dr. Johnson. (BOSWELL, *Life,* 1773.)

13
The great English moralist. Never was a

descriptive epithet more nicely appropriate than that! Dr. Johnson's morality was as English an article as a beefsteak.

HAWTHORNE, *Our Old Home: Lichfield and Uttoxeter.*

1
What a singular destiny has been that of this remarkable man! To be regarded in his own age as a classic, and in ours as a companion! To receive from his contemporaries that full homage which men of genius have in general received from posterity; to be more intimately known to posterity than other men are known to their contemporaries.

MACAULAY, *Essays: Boswell's Life of Johnson.*

2
O rough, pure, stubborn, troubled soul: for whom
A smile of special tenderness men keep—
Who prayed for strength "to regulate my room,"
And "preservation from immoderate sleep."

CHRISTOPHER MORLEY, *On a Portrait of Dr. Samuel Johnson, LL.D.*

3
His bow-wow way.

LORD PEMBROKE, referring to Dr. Johnson. (BOSWELL, *Life*, 1775.)

4
The conversation of Johnson is strong and clear, and may be compared to an antique statue, where every vein and muscle is distinct and bold. Ordinary conversation resembles an inferior cast.

THOMAS PERCY, Bishop of Dromore and editor of the *Reliques*. (BOSWELL, *Life of Johnson*, 1778.)

5
This last and long enduring passion for Mrs. Thrale was, however, composed of cupboard love, Platonic love, and vanity tickled and gratified.

ANNA SEWARD, *Letters*, ii, 103. Referring to Dr. Johnson.

6
I have not wasted my life trifling with literary fools in taverns as Johnson did when he should have been shaking England with the thunder of his spirit.

BERNARD SHAW, *Parents and Children.*

Garrick, had he called Dr. Johnson Punch, would have spoken profoundly and wittily, whereas Dr. Johnson, in hurling that epithet at him, was but picking up the cheapest sneer an actor is subject to.

BERNARD SHAW, *Plays, Pleasant and Unpleasant: Preface.*

7
That great Cham of literature.

SMOLLETT, *Letter to Wilkes*, 16 March, 1759.

8
Of those who have thus survived themselves most completely, left a sort of personal seduction behind them in the world, and retained, after death, the art of making friends, Montaigne and Samuel Johnson certainly stand first.

R. L. STEVENSON, *Familiar Studies of Men and Books: Charles of Orleans.*

9
I own I like not Johnson's turgid style,
That gives an inch the importance of a mile,
Casts of manure a wagon-load around
To raise a simple daisy from the ground;
Uplifts the club of Hercules, for what?
To crush a butterfly or brain a gnat! . . .
Alike in every theme his pompous art
Heaven's awful thunder, or a rumbling cart!

JOHN WOLCOT, *On Dr. Samuel Johnson.*

JONSON, BEN

10
Too nicely Jonson knew the critic's part;
Nature in him was almost lost in Art.

WILLIAM COLLINS, *An Epistle to Sir Thomas Hammer, on His Edition of Shakespeare*, l. 55.

11
Next these learn'd Jonson in this list I bring
Who had drunk deep of the Pierian Spring.

MICHAEL DRAYTON, *Of Poets and Poesy.*

12
Let Hebron, nay let Hell produce a Man
So made for Mischief as Ben Jochanan.
A Jew of humble Parentage was He,
By Trade a Levite, though of low Degree:
His Pride no higher than the Desk aspir'd. . . .
He could not live by God, but chang'd his Master:
Inspir'd by Want, was made a Factious Tool,
They got a Villain, and we lost a Fool.

JOHN DRYDEN, *Absalom and Achitophel*. Pt. ii, l. 352.

13
Here lies Jonson with the rest
Of the Poets; but the Best.
Reader, would'st thou more have known?
Ask his Story, not this Stone.
That will speak what this can't tell
Of his glory. So farewell.

ROBERT HERRICK, *Upon Ben Jonson.*

Ah Ben! Say how, or when
Shall we thy guests Meet at those Lyric Feasts,
Made at the Sun, The Dog, the Triple Tun?
Where we such clusters had
As made us nobly wild, not mad;
And yet each Verse of thine
Out-did the meat, out-did the frolic wine!

ROBERT HERRICK, *An Ode for Ben Jonson.*

14
Then Jonson came, instructed from the school,
To please in method, and invent by rule.

SAMUEL JOHNSON, *Prologue on the Opening of the Drury Lane Theatre*, l. 10.

15
Ben Jonson, his best piece of poetry.

BEN JONSON, *Epitaph on His Son.*

2
O rare Ben Jonson!

SIR JOHN YOUNG, *Epitaph,* cut on the stone covering Jonson's grave in Westminster Abbey.

Which was donne at the charge of Jack Young. who, walking there when the grave was covering, gave the fellow 18 pence to cutt it.

JOHN AUBREY, *Brief Lives: Ben Jonson.*

JOURNALISM, see Press

JOY

See also Bliss, Delight, Happiness, Pleasure

I—Joy: Definitions

3
Every joy is gain
And gain is gain, however small.

ROBERT BROWNING, *Paracelsus.* Pt. iv.

4
An infant when it gazes on a light,
A child the moment when it drains the breast,
A devotee when soars the Host in sight,
An Arab with a stranger for a guest,
A sailor when the prize has struck in fight,
A miser filling his most hoarded chest,
Feel rapture; but not such true joy are reaping
As they who watch o'er what they love while sleeping.

BYRON, *Don Juan.* Canto ii, st. 196.

5
Joy is the sweet voice, joy the luminous cloud.
We in ourselves rejoice!
And thence flows all that charms or ear or sight,
All melodies the echoes of that voice,
All colours a suffusion from that light.

S. T. COLERIDGE, *Dejection.* St. 5.

6
For present joys are more to flesh and blood
Than a dull prospect of a distant good.

DRYDEN, *The Hind and Panther.* Pt. iii, l. 364.

7
Not by appointment do we meet Delight
And Joy; they heed not our expectancy;
But round some corner in the streets of life,
They, on a sudden, clasp us with a smile.

GERALD MASSEY, *The Bridegroom of Beauty.*

8
Joy, in Nature's wide dominion,
Mightiest cause of all is found;
And 'tis joy that moves the pinion
When the wheel of time goes round.

SCHILLER, *Hymn to Joy.* (Bowring, tr.)

9
Joy is an elation of spirit—of a spirit which trusts in the goodness and truth of its own possessions. (Est enim animi elatio suis bonis verisque fidentis.)

SENECA, *Epistulæ ad Lucilium.* Epis. lix, sec. 2.

Real joy, believe me, is a serious matter. (Mihi crede, verum gaudium res severa est.)

SENECA, *Epistulæ ad Lucilium.* Epis. xxiii, 4.

Deemest thou labour only is earnest?
Grave is all beauty, solemn is joy.

WILLIAM WATSON, *England, My Mother.* Pt. iv.

10
For, when the power of imparting joy
Is equal to the will, the human soul
Requires no other Heaven.

SHELLEY, *Queen Mab.* Canto iii, l. 11.

II—Joy: Apothegms

11
The joy late coming late departs.

LEWIS J. BATES, *Some Sweet Day.*

12
Weak is the joy which is never wearied.

WILLIAM BLAKE. (GILCHRIST, *Life,* i, 62.)

13
Capacity for joy Admits temptation.

E. B. BROWNING, *Aurora Leigh.* Bk. i, l. 703.

14
There's sic parade, sic pomp an' art,
The joy can scarcely reach the heart.

BURNS, *The Twa Dogs.*

15
Oh, frabjous day! Callooh! Callay!
He chortled in his joy.

LEWIS CARROLL, *Through the Looking-Glass.* Ch. 1.

16
One universal smile it seemed of all things;
Joy past compare.

DANTE, *Inferno.* Canto xxvii, l. 6. (Cary, tr.)

17
Joy rul'd the day, and Love the night.

DRYDEN, *The Secular Masque,* l. 82.

18
Who baths in worldly joys, swims in a world of fears.

PHINEAS FLETCHER, *The Purple Island.* Canto viii, st. 7.

They hear a voice in every wind,
And snatch a fearful joy.

THOMAS GRAY, *On a Distant Prospect of Eton College.* St. 4.

Joy, but with fear yet link'd.

MILTON, *Paradise Lost.* Bk. xi, l. 139.

19
And, e'en while fashion's brightest arts decoy,
The heart, distrusting, asks if this be joy.

GOLDSMITH, *The Deserted Village,* l. 263.

20
All creatures have their joy and man hath his.

GEORGE HERBERT, *Man's Medley.*

21
Joy makes us giddy, dizzy. (Die Freude macht drehend, wirblicht.)

LESSING, *Minna von Barnhelm.* Act ii, sc. 3.

22
Hence, vain deluding joys,
The brood of Folly, without father bred.

MILTON, *Il Penseroso,* l. 1.

23
I will not be cheated—nor will I employ long years of repentance for moments of joy.

MARY WORTLEY MONTAGU, to Pope. (COLLIER, *Hist. Eng. Lit.,* p. 293.)

1
For bonny sweet Robin is all my joy.
SHAKESPEARE, *Hamlet*. Act iv, sc. 5, l. 186.

2
A foutre for the world and worldlings base!
I speak of Africa and golden joys.
SHAKESPEARE, *II Henry IV*. Act v, sc. 3, l. 102.

3
'Tis safer to be that which we destroy
Than by destruction dwell in doubtful joy.
SHAKESPEARE, *Macbeth*. Act iii, sc. 2, l. 6.

4
I wish you all the joy that you can wish.
SHAKESPEARE, *The Merchant of Venice*. Act iii, sc. 2, l. 192.

Sweets with sweets war not, joy delights in joy.
SHAKESPEARE, *Sonnets*. No. viii.

5
They send their shout to the stars. (Clamorem ad sidera mittunt.)
STATIUS, *Thebais*. Bk. xii, l. 521.

6
Beauty for ashes and oil of joy!
WHITTIER, *The Preacher*, l. 385.

Beauty for ashes, the oil of joy for mourning.
Old Testament: Isaiah, lxi, 3.

7
Joys season'd high, and tasting strong of guilt.
YOUNG, *Night Thoughts*. Night viii, l. 837.

8
Joy is a fruit that Americans eat green.
AMANDO ZEGRI. (*Golden Book*, May, 1931.)

III—Joy: Its Praise

9
To-day, whatever may annoy,
The word for me is Joy, just simple Joy.
JOHN KENDRICK BANGS, *The Word*.

10
Joy rises in me like a summer's morn.
S. T. COLERIDGE, *Christmas Carol*.

11
Sing out my soul, thy songs of joy;
Such as a happy bird will sing,
Beneath a rainbow's lovely arch,
In early spring.
W. H. DAVIES, *Songs of Joy*.

12
Gladness in every face express'd,
Their eyes before their tongues confess'd.
Men met each other with erected look,
The steps were higher that they took.
DRYDEN, *Threnodia Augustalis*, l. 122.

13
O close my hand upon Beatitude!
Not on her toys.
LOUISE IMOGEN GUINEY, *Deo Optimo Maximo*.

14
At Earth's great market where Joy is trafficked in,
Buy while thy purse yet swells with golden Youth.
ALAN SEEGER, *Ode to Antares*.

15
Make the coming hour o'erflow with joy,
And pleasure drown the brim.
SHAKESPEARE, *All's Well that Ends Well*. Act ii, sc. 4, l. 47.

Every humour hath his adjunct pleasure,
Wherein it finds a joy above the rest.
SHAKESPEARE, *Sonnets*. No. xci.

16
I have drunken deep of joy,
And I will taste no other wine to-night.
SHELLEY, *The Cenci*. Act i, sc. 3, l. 92.

IV—Joy: Its Evanescence

17
Seeks painted trifles and fantastic toys,
And eagerly pursues imaginary joys.
MARK AKENSIDE, *The Virtuoso*.

18
Joys Are bubble-like—what makes them bursts them too.
P. J. BAILEY, *Festus: A Library and Balcony*, l. 62.

In Folly's cup still laughs the bubble joy.
POPE, *Essay on Man*. Epistle ii, l. 288.

19
He who bends to himself a Joy
Does the wingèd life destroy;
But he who kisses the Joy as it flies
Lives in Eternity's sunrise.
WILLIAM BLAKE, *Eternity*.

20
There's not a joy the world can give like that it takes away.
BYRON, *Stanzas for Music*.

21
Joy of this world, for time will not abide;
From day to night it changeth as the tide.
CHAUCER, *Tale of the Man of Lawe*, l. 1035

22
All human joys are swift of wing,
For heaven doth so allot it,
That when you get an easy thing,
You find you haven't got it.
EUGENE FIELD, *Ways of Life*.

23
There's a hope for every woe,
And a balm for every pain,
But the first joys o' our heart
Come never back again.
ROBERT GILFILLAN, *The Exile's Song*.

24
And Joy, whose hand is ever at his lips,
Bidding adieu.
KEATS, *Ode on Melancholy*. St. 3.

25
Joys do not abide, but take wing and fly away. (Gaudia non remanent, sed fugitiva volant.)
MARTIAL, *Epigrams*. Bk. i, epig. 15.

But headlong joy is ever on the wing.
MILTON, *The Passion*, l. 5.

26
Joys too exquisite to last,
—And yet *more* exquisite when past.
JAMES MONTGOMERY, *The Little Cloud*, l. 159.

Bliss in possession will not last;
Remember'd joys are never past;
At once the fountain, stream, and sea,
They were,—they are,—they yet shall be.
MONTGOMERY, *The Little Cloud.* Conclusion.

1
Oh stay! oh stay!
Joy so seldom weaves a chain
Like this to-night, that oh 'tis pain
To break its links so soon.
THOMAS MOORE, *Fly Not Yet.*

2
How fading are the joys we dote upon!
Like apparitions seen and gone;
But those which soonest take their flight
Are the most exquisite and strong;
Like angels' visits, short and bright,
Mortality's too weak to bear them long.
JOHN NORRIS, *The Parting.*

3
Oh, had I but Aladdin's lamp
Tho' only for a day,
I'd try to find a link to bind
The joys that pass away.
CHARLES SWAIN, *Oh, Had I.*

4
But we are pressed by heavy laws;
And often, glad no more,
We wear a face of joy, because
We have been glad of yore.
WORDSWORTH, *The Fountain,* l. 45.

V—Joy and Sorrow

See also Laughter and Tears; Smile and Tear

5
Whate'er there be of Sorrow
I'll put off till To-morrow,
And when To-morrow comes, why then
'Twill be To-day and Joy again.
JOHN KENDRICK BANGS, *The Word.*

6
Man was made for joy and woe;
And when this we rightly know,
Thro' the world we safely go.
WILLIAM BLAKE, *Auguries of Innocence.*

7
Joys impregnate. Sorrows bring forth.
WILLIAM BLAKE, *Proverbs of Hell.*

Excess of sorrow laughs; excess of joy weeps.
WILLIAM BLAKE, *Proverbs of Hell.*

Great joys weep, great sorrows laugh.
JOSEPH ROUX, *Meditations of a Parish Priest.* Pt. v, No. 3.

To weep for joy is a kind of manna.
GEORGE HERBERT, *Jacula Prudentum.*

8
Joy which is crystallised for ever,
Or grief, an eternal petrifaction.
ROBERT BROWNING, *Old Pictures in Florence.*

9
For ever the latter end of joy is woe.
God wot that worldly joy is soon ago.
CHAUCER, *The Nonne Preests Tale,* l. 385.

Momentary joy breeds months of pain.
SHAKESPEARE, *The Rape of Lucrece.* St. 99.

10
Poor human nature, so richly endowed with nerves of anguish, so splendidly organized for pain and sorrow, is but slenderly equipped for joy.
GEORGE DU MAURIER, *Peter Ibbetson.*

11
We pick our own sorrows out of the joys of other men and from their sorrows likewise we derive our joys.
OWEN FELLTHAM, *Resolves.* Pt. i.

12
Our present joys are sweeter for past pain;
To Love and Heaven by suffering we attain.
GEORGE GRANVILLE, *The British Enchanters.* Act v, sc. 2.

Sorrows remembered sweeten present joy.
POLLOK, *The Course of Time.* Bk. i, l. 464.
See also MEMORY: SWEET AND BITTER.

13
Full from the fount of joy's delicious springs
Some bitter o'er the flowers its bubbling venom flings.
(Medio de fonte leporum
Surgit amari aliquid, quod in ipsis floribus angat.)
LUCRETIUS, *De Rerum Natura.* Bk. iv, l. 1129. (Byron, tr., *Childe Harold.* Canto i, st. 82.)

14
The fairest day must set in night;
Summer in winter ends;
So anguish still succeeds delight,
And grief our joy attends.
GEORGE LILLO, *Song from "Sylvia."*

Joy comes, grief goes, we know not how.
J. R. LOWELL, *The Vision of Sir Launfal:* Pt. i, *Prelude.*

Grief suages grief, and joy does joy enhance;
Nature is generous to her children so.
GEORGE MACDONALD, *A Book of Sonnets: To S. F. S. See also under* COMPENSATION.

15
Great joys, like griefs, are silent.
SHACKERLEY MARMION, *Holland's Leaguer* Act i, sc. 1. *See also* GRIEF: VOCAL AND SILENT.

16
Sorrow that bides, and joy that fleets away.
WILLIAM MORRIS, *Life and Death of Jason.* Bk. ix, l. 436.

17
It is heaven's will for sorrow to follow joy.
(Ita divis est placitum, voluptatem ut mæror comes consequator.)
PLAUTUS, *Amphitruo,* l. 635. (Act ii, sc. 2.)

18
Weeping may endure for a night, but joy cometh in the morning.
Old Testament: Psalms, xxx, 5.

19
One inch of joy surmounts of grief a span,
Because to laugh is proper to the man.
RABELAIS, *Works: To the Reader*

Every inch of joy has an ell of annoy.
W. G. BENHAM, *Proverbs*, p. 755.

1
A sorrow that's shared is but half a trouble,
But a joy that's shared is a joy made double.
JOHN RAY, *English Proverbs*.

Grief can take care of itself, but to get the full value from joy you must have somebody to divide it with.
MARK TWAIN, *Pudd'nhead Wilson's New Calendar*.

One can endure sorrow alone, but it takes two to be glad.
ELBERT HUBBARD, *One Thousand and One Epigrams*, p. 36.

2
The rose and thorn, the treasure and dragon, joy and sorrow, all mingle into one.
SADI, *The Gulistan*. Ch. vii, Apologue 21.

3
Brief is sorrow, and endless is joy. (Kurz ist der Schmerz, und ewig ist die Freude!)
SCHILLER, *Die Jungfrau von Orleans*. Act v, sc. 14.

4
'Tis cruel to prolong a pain and to defer a joy.
SIR CHARLES SEDLEY, *Love Still Has Something of the Sea*.

5
My plenteous joys,
Wanton in fulness, seek to hide themselves
In drops of sorrow.
SHAKESPEARE, *Macbeth*. Act i, sc. 4, l. 33.

Joy, being altogether wanting,
It doth remember me the more of sorrow.
SHAKESPEARE, *Richard II*. Act iii, sc. 4, l. 13.

Eighty odd years of sorrow have I seen,
And each hour's joy wrecked with a week of teen.
SHAKESPEARE, *Richard III*. Act iv, sc. 1, l. 96.

My grief lies onward and my joy behind.
SHAKESPEARE, *Sonnets*. No. 50.

6
There is a sweet joy which comes to us through sorrow.
C. H. SPURGEON, *Gleanings Among the Sheaves: Sweetness in Sorrow*.

7
Joy may be a miser,
But Sorrow's purse is free.
RICHARD HENRY STODDARD, *Persian Song*.

8
I found more joy in sorrow
Than you could find in joy.
SARA TEASDALE, *The Answer*.

9
The sweetest joys a heart can hold
Grow up between its crosses.
NIXON WATERMAN, *Recompense*.

JUDAS

10
A false Judas kiss he hath given and is gone.
JOHN BALE, *Kynge Johan*, l. 2109. (c. 1540)

Of a flattering foe to have a Judas kiss.
WILLIAM BARCLAY, *Mirrour of Good Manners*, 75. (1570)

12
Judas he japed with Jewen silver,
And sithen on an elder hanged himself.
WILLIAM LANGLAND, *Piers Plowman*. Passus i.

Fast by is the elder-tree on which Judas hanged himself.
SIR JOHN MANDEVILLE, *Travels: Pool of Siloe*.

Judas was hanged on an elder.
SHAKESPEARE, *Love's Labour's Lost*, v, 2, 610.

13
And while he yet spake, lo, Judas, one of the twelve, came. . . . And forthwith he came to Jesus, and said, Hail, Master; and kissed him.
New Testament: Matthew, xxvi, 47, 49.

To say the truth, so Judas kiss'd his master,
And cried "all hail!" whereas he meant all harm.
SHAKESPEARE, *III Henry VI*. Act v, sc. 7, l. 33.

14
Marry, his kisses are Judas's own children.
SHAKESPEARE, *As You Like It*. Act iii, sc. 4, l. 10.

Holofernes: Judas I am, . . . Not Iscariot, sir.
Judas I am, ycliped Maccabæus. . . .
Biron: A kissing traitor.
SHAKESPEARE, *Love's Labour's Lost*, v, 2, 599.

JUDGE

14a
Ordained of God to be the Judge of quick and dead.
New Testament: Acts, x, 42.

Ready to judge the quick and the dead.
New Testament: I Peter, iv, 5.

Shall judge the quick and the dead.
New Testament: II Timothy, iv, 1.

The Quick or the Dead.
AMÉLIE RIVES. Title of her first novel. (1888)

15
Two parties are here present: he hears but half who hears one party only. (Δυοῖν παρόντοιν ἥμισυς λόγου πάρα.)
ÆSCHYLUS, *Eumenides*, l. 428.

He who decides a case with the other side unheard,
Though he decide justly, is himself unjust.
(Qui statuit aliquid parte inaudita altera,
Æquum licet statuerit, haud æquus fuit.)
SENECA, *Medea*, l. 199.

Hear the other side. (Audi alteram partem.)
ST. AUGUSTINE, *De Duabus Animabus*. Ch. xiv, sec. 22.

16
The arbitrator has regard to equity and the judge to law. (Ὁ γὰρ διαιτητὴς τὸ ἐπιεικὲς ὁρᾷ, ὁ δὲ δικαστὴς τὸν νόμον.)
ARISTOTLE, *Rhetoric*. Bk. i, ch. 13, sec. 19.

17
A judge were better a briber than a respecter of persons; for a corrupt judge offendeth not so highly as a facile. (Qui cognoscit in judicio famiem, non bene facit.)
FRANCIS BACON, *Advancement of Learning: Civil Knowledge*. Sec. 16.

Judges ought to be more learned than witty, more reverend than plausible, and more advised than confident. Above all things, integrity is their portion and proper virtue.
FRANCIS BACON, *Essays: Of Judicature.*

When he departs from the letter of the law, the judge becomes a law-maker. (Cum receditur a litera, judex transit in legislatorem.)
FRANCIS BACON, *De Augmentis Scientiarum: Verba Legis.*

Slavish fidelity is out of date;
When exposition fails, interpolate.
UNKNOWN. A metrical version of Bacon's maxim.

1
He who will have no judge but himself condemns himself.
H. G. BOHN, *Hand-Book of Proverbs*, 401.

2
The cold neutrality of an impartial judge.
EDMUND BURKE, *Preface to Brissot's Address.*

3
He who has the judge for his father, goes into court with an easy mind.
CERVANTES, *Don Quixote*. Pt. ii, ch. 43.

4
It is better that a judge should lean on the side of compassion than severity.
CERVANTES, *Don Quixote*. Pt. ii, ch. 43.

Be this, ye rural magistrates, your plan,
Firm be your justice, but be friends to man.
JOHN LANGHORNE, *The Country Justice*, l. 133.
See also JUSTICE AND MERCY.

5
The magistrate is a speaking law, but the law is a silent magistrate. (Magistratum legem esse loquentem, legem autem mutum magistratum.)
CICERO, *De Legibus*. Bk. iii, ch. 1, sec. 2.

It is always the business of a judge in a trial to find out the truth. (Judicis est semper in causis verum sequi.)
CICERO, *De Officiis*. Bk. ii, ch. 14, sec. 51.

6
The judge weighs the arguments, and puts a brave face on the matter, and, since there must be a decision, decides as he can, and hopes he has done justice.
EMERSON, *Conduct of Life: Considerations by the Way.*

7
When the judges shall be obliged to go armed, it will be time for the courts to be closed.
JUDGE S. J. FIELD, of California, in 1889, when advised to arm himself.

8
I am as sober as a judge.
HENRY FIELDING, *Don Quixote in England.* Act iii, sc. 14.

Half as sober as a judge.
CHARLES LAMB, *Letter to Mr. and Mrs. Moxon,* August, 1833.

9
When a judge puts on his robes, he puts off his relations to any, and like Melchisedech, becomes without pedigree.
THOMAS FULLER, *Holy and Profane State.*

10
A justice with grave justices shall sit;
He praise their wisdom, they admire his wit.
JOHN GAY, *The Birth of the Squire*, l. 77.

11
Art thou a magistrate? then be severe:
If studious, copy fair what time hath blurr'd,
Redeem truth from his jaws.
GEORGE HERBERT, *The Church-Porch.* St. 15.

12
A great judge, and a little judge,
The judges of a-size.
THOMAS HOOD, *Tim Turpin.*

13
A good and faithful judge prefers what is right to what is expedient. (Bonus atque fides Judex honestum prætulit utili.)
HORACE, *Odes*. Bk. iv, ode 9, l. 40.

A corrupt judge weighs truth badly. (Male verum examinat omnis Corruptus judex.)
HORACE, *Satires*. Bk. ii, sat. 2, l. 8.

14
He was knighted and made a Judge; but, his constitution being too weak for business, he retired before any disreputable compliances became necessary.
SAMUEL JOHNSON, *Lives of the Poets: Milton.* Referring to Milton's brother.

15
The duty of a judge is to administer justice, but his practice is to delay it. (Le devoir des Juges est de rendre la justice; leur métier de la différer.)
LA BRUYÈRE, *Les Caractères*. Sec. 14.

16
He that judges without informing himself to the utmost that he is capable, cannot acquit himself of judging amiss.
JOHN LOCKE, *An Essay Concerning Human Understanding*. Bk. ii, ch. 21.

17
Neither side is guiltless if its adversary is the judge. (Nulla manus, belli mutato judice, pura est.)
LUCAN, *De Bello Civili*. Bk. vii, l. 263.

18
There should be many judges, for a few will always be ruled by the few. (Bisogna che i giudici siano assai, perchè pochi sempre fanno a modo de' pochi.)
MACHIAVELLI, *Dei Discorsi*, i, 7.

19
Give your decisions, never your reasons; your decisions may be right, your reasons are sure to be wrong.
WILLIAM MURRAY, EARL OF MANSFIELD, *Advice*, to Judges.

20
It is a judge's duty to investigate both the circumstances and time of an act. (Judiciis

officium est ut res, ita tempora rerum quærere.)

OVID, *Tristia*. Bk. i, eleg. i, l. 37.

'Tis but half a judge's task to know.

POPE, *Essay on Criticism*. Pt. iii, l. 2.

1
The discretion of a Judge is the law of tyrants: it is always unknown. It is different in different men. It is casual, and depends upon constitution, temper, passion. In the best it is oftentimes caprice; in the worst it is every vice, folly and passion to which human nature is liable.

SIR CHARLES PRATT, EARL CAMDEN, *Case of Hindson and Kersey*, 1780. (*8 How. St. Tr.*, 57)

2
That money is well lost which the guilty man gives to the judge. (Bene perdit nummos judici cum dat nocens.)

PUBLILIUS SYRUS, *Sententiæ*. No. 82.

He that buyeth magistracy must sell justice.

JOHN RAY, *English Proverbs*.

And the chief-justice was rich, quiet, and infamous.

MACAULAY, *Essays: Warren Hastings*.

3
No one should be judge in his own cause.

PUBLILIUS SYRUS, *Sententiæ*. No. 545.

No man's a faithful judge in his own cause.

MASSINGER, *The Bashful Lover*. Act ii, sc. 7.

It is not permitted to the most equitable of men to be a judge on his own cause.

PASCAL, *Pensées*. Ch. iv, No. 1.

4
The law is loosened when the judge grows tender-hearted. (Dissolvitur lex cum fit judex misericors.)

PUBLILIUS SYRUS, *Sententiæ*. No. 406.

The judge is condemned when the guilty is acquitted. (Judex damnatur cum nocens absolvitur.)

PUBLILIUS SYRUS, *Sententiæ*. No. 407.

When by a pardon'd murd'rer blood is spilt,
The judge that pardon'd hath the greatest guilt.

SIR JOHN DENHAM, *On Justice*, l. 81.

5
All men who deliberate upon difficult questions should be free from hatred and friendship, anger and pity. (Omnis homines qui de rebus dubiis consultant, ab odio, amicitia, ira atque misericordia vacuos esse decet.)

SALLUST, *Catilina*. Ch. li, sec. 1.

6
The upright judge condemns the crime, but does not hate the criminal. (Bonus judex damnat improbanda, non odit.)

SENECA, *De Ira*. Bk. i, ch. 16, sec. 7.

7
If you judge, investigate; if you reign, command. (Si judicas, cognosce; si regnas, jube.)

SENECA, *Medea*, l. 194.

8
And then the justice
In fair round belly with good capon lined.

SHAKESPEARE, *As You Like It*. Act ii, sc. 7, l. 153.

9
A man may see how this world goes with no eyes. Look with thine ears: see how yond justice rails upon yond simple thief. Hark, in thine ear: change places; and, handy-dandy, which is the justice, which is the thief?

SHAKESPEARE, *King Lear*. Act iv, sc. 6, l. 153.

Thieves for their robbery have authority
When judges steal themselves.

SHAKESPEARE, *Measure for Measure*. Act ii, sc. 2, l. 176.

10
He who the sword of heaven will bear
Should be as holy as severe;
Pattern in himself to know,
Grace to stand, and virtue go.

SHAKESPEARE, *Measure for Measure*. Act iii, sc. 2, l. 275.

11
To offend, and judge, are distinct offices
And of opposed natures.

SHAKESPEARE, *The Merchant of Venice*. Act ii, sc. 9, l. 61.

12
A Daniel come to judgement! yea, a Daniel!
O, wise young judge, how I do honour thee!

SHAKESPEARE, *The Merchant of Venice*. Act iv, sc. 1, l. 223.

It doth appear you are a worthy judge;
You know the law; your exposition
Hath been most sound.

SHAKESPEARE, *The Merchant of Venice*. Act iv, sc. 1, l. 236.

The law,
Whereof you are a well deserving pillar.

SHAKESPEARE, *The Merchant of Venice*. Act iv, sc. 1, l. 238.

An upright judge, a learned judge!

SHAKESPEARE, *The Merchant of Venice*. Act iv, sc. 1, l. 323.

13
Judges are best at the beginning, and deteriorate toward the end. (Initia magistratuum nostrorum meliora, ferme finis inclinat.)

TACITUS, *Annals*. Bk. xv, sec. 21.

14
Fill the seats of justice
With good men, not so absolute in goodness
As to forget what human frailty is.

SIR THOMAS NOON TALFOURD, *Ion*. Act v.

15
If thou be a severe, sour-complexioned man, then I here disallow thee to be a competent judge.

IZAAK WALTON, *The Compleat Angler: Preface.*

16
He only judges right, who weighs, compares,
And, in the sternest sentence which his voice
Pronounces, ne'er abandons charity.

WORDSWORTH, *Ecclesiastical Sonnets*. Pt. ii, No. 1.

JUDGMENT

I—Judgment: Definitions

1
Fortune is for all; judgment is theirs who have won it for themselves. (Κοινὸν τύχη, γνώμη δὲ τῶν κεκτημενων.)

Æschylus, *Fragments*. Frag. 217.

2
"Mature" means neither "too soon" nor "too late." (Mature est, quod neque citius est neque serius.)

Aulus Gellius, *Noctes Atticæ*. Bk. x, ch. 11, sec. 2.

3
Till, from its summit,
Judgment drops her damning plummet,
Pronouncing such a fatal space
Departed from the founder's base.

Robert Browning, *Christmas-Eve*. Pt. ii.

4
We judge others according to results; how else?—not knowing the process by which results are arrived at.

George Eliot, *Mill on the Floss*. Bk. vii, ch. 2.

And purge me from all heresies of thought and speech and pen
That bid me judge him otherwise than I am judged. Amen!

Rudyard Kipling, *A Pilgrim's Way*.

5
What of me when my judgment wars with itself, when it despises what it sought, and seeks what it lately cast aside? (Quid, mea cum pugnat sententia secum, Quod petiit spernit, repetit quod nuper omisit?)

Horace, *Epistles*. Bk. i, epis. 1, l. 97.

6
All wholesale judgments are loose and imperfect. (Touts jugements en gros sont lâches et imparfaits.)

Montaigne, *Essays*. Bk. iii, ch. 8.

7
We shall be judged, not by what we might have been, but what we have been.

Rev. William Sewell, *Passing Thoughts on Religion: Sympathy in Gladness*.

I judge people by what they might be—not are, nor will be.

Robert Browning, *A Soul's Tragedy*. Act ii.

8
Men's judgements are
A parcel of their fortunes; and things outward
Do draw the inward quality after them,
To suffer all alike.

Shakespeare, *Antony and Cleopatra*. Act iii, sc. 13, l. 31.

9
Men see and judge the affairs of other men better than their own. (Aliena ut melius videant et dijudicent, Quam sua.)

Terence, *Heauton Timoroumenos*, l. 504. (Act iii, l. 94.)

II—Judgment: Apothegms

10
I bear no enmity to any human being; but, alas! as Mrs. Placid said to her friend, by which of thy good works wouldst thou be willing to be judged?

Abigail Adams, *Letters*, p. 411.

11
Judge me by myself. (Σκόπει δέ με ἐξ ἐμαυτοῦ.)

Bion. (Diogenes Laertius, *Bion*. Bk. iv, sec. 47.)

12
Woe to him . . . who has no court of appeal against the world's judgment.

Thomas Carlyle, *Essays: Mirabeau*.

13
Men's judgments sway on that side fortune leans.

George Chapman, *Widow's Tears*. Act ii, sc. 2.

14
Where men of judgment creep and feel their way,
The positive pronounce without dismay.

Cowper, *Conversation*, l. 145.

15
Thou art weighed in the balances, and art found wanting.

Old Testament: Daniel, v, 27.

16
Who reproves the lame must go upright.

Samuel Daniel, *History of the Civil War*. Bk. iii, st. 10.

17
The chief good is the suspension of judgment, which tranquillity of mind follows like a shadow.

Diogenes Laertius, *Pyrrho*. Bk. ix, sec. 107. Referring to the Sceptics.

18
Rawness of judgment.

John Ford, *The Broken Heart*. Act ii, sc. 2.

19
Where the fault springs, there let the judgment fall.

Robert Herrick, *Hesperides*. No. 608.

20
In my judgment. (Me judice.)

Horace, *Ars Poetica*, l. 244.

21
Judge righteous judgment.

New Testament: John, vii, 24. (Justum judicium judicate.—*Vulgate*.)

22
With thumb turned. (Verso pollice.)

Juvenal, *Satires*. Sat. iii, l. 36. The sign of condemnation in the Roman arena. Prudentius (*Contra Symmachum*. Bk. ii, l. 1098) has, "Converso pollice."

23
We sometimes see a fool possessed of talent, but never of judgment. (On est quelquefois un sot avec de l'esprit; mais on ne l'est jamais avec du jugement.)

La Rochefoucauld, *Maximes*. No. 456.

1
Still mark if vice or nature prompts the deed;
Still mark the strong temptation and the need.
JOHN LANGHORNE, *The Country Justice*, l. 143.

2
Out of thine own mouth will I judge thee.
New Testament: Luke, xix, 22.

3
Judge not, that ye be not judged.
New Testament: Matthew, vii, 1; *Luke*, vi, 37. (Nolite judicare.—*Vulgate*.)

O mortal men, be wary how ye judge.
DANTE, *Paradiso*. Canto xx, l. 125. (Henry Francis Cary, tr.)

Forbear to judge, for we are sinners all.
Close up his eyes.
SHAKESPEARE, *II Henry VI*. Act iii, sc. 3, l. 32.

4
Remember. when the judgment's weak the prejudice is strong.
KANE O'HARA, *Midas*. Act i, sc. 4.

5
They have a right to censure, that have a heart to help.
WILLIAM PENN, *Some Fruits of Solitude*, p. 15.

6
You must stand afar off to judge St. Peter's.
WENDELL PHILLIPS, *Speech*, 17 Feb., 1861.

7
None judge so wrong as those who think amiss.
POPE, *Wife of Bath: Prologue*, l. 810.

8
'Tis with our judgments as our watches, none
Go just alike, yet each believes his own.
POPE, *Essay on Criticism*. Pt. i, l. 9.

But as when an authentic watch is shown,
Each man winds up and rectifies his own,
So in our very judgments.
SIR JOHN SUCKLING, *Aglaura: Epilogue*.

9
Haste in giving judgment is criminal. (In judicando criminosa est celeritas.)
PUBLILIUS SYRUS, *Sententiæ*. No. 285.

Whoso giveth hasty judgement
Must be the first that shall repent.
UNKNOWN, *Partonope*, l. 9975. (c. 1450)

10
Weigh, not merely count, men's judgments. (*Æstimes judicia, non numeres.*)
SENECA, *Epistulæ ad Lucilium*. Epis. xxix, sec. 12.

11
Give every man thy ear, but few thy voice;
Take each man's censure, but reserve thy judgement.
SHAKESPEARE, *Hamlet*. Act i, sc. 3, l. 68.

12
Blest are those
Whose blood and judgement are so well commingled
That they are not a pipe for fortune's finger
To sound what stop she please.
SHAKESPEARE, *Hamlet*. Act iii, sc. 2, l. 73.

13
Answer my life my judgement.
SHAKESPEARE, *King Lear*. Act i, sc. 1, l. 153.

What judgement shall I dread, doing no wrong?
SHAKESPEARE, *The Merchant of Venice*. Act iv, sc. 1, l. 89.

14
Though our works
Find righteous or unrighteous judgment, this
At least is ours, to make them righteous.
SWINBURNE, *Marino Faliero*. Act iii, sc. 1.

15
From one crime judge them all. (Crimine ab uno Disce omnes.)
VERGIL, *Æneid*. Bk. ii, l. 65.

16
One cool judgment is worth a thousand hasty councils.
WOODROW WILSON, *Speech*, Pittsburgh, 29 Jan., 1916.

III—Judgment: Its Fallibility

17
If I was as bad as they say I am,
And you were as good as you look,
I wonder which one would feel the worse
If each for the other was took?
GEORGE BARR BAKER, *Good and Bad*.

18
Cruel and cold is the judgment of man,
Cruel as winter, and cold as the snow;
But by-and-by will the deed and the plan
Be judged by the motive that lieth below.
LEWIS J. BATES, *By-and-By*.

19
No man can justly censure or condemn another, because indeed no man truly knows another.
SIR THOMAS BROWNE, *Religio Medici*. Pt. ii, sec. 4.

Meanwhile "Black sheep, black sheep!" we cry,
Safe in the inner fold;
And maybe they hear, and wonder why,
And marvel, out in the cold.
RICHARD BURTON, *Black Sheep*.

20
Mad in the vulgar judgment, sane, perhaps, in yours. (Demens Judicio vulgi, sanus fortasse tuo.)
HORACE, *Satires*. Bk. i, sat. 6, l. 97.

21
In men whom men condemn as ill
I find so much of goodness still,
In men whom men pronounce divine
I find so much of sin and blot,
I do not dare to draw a line
Between the two, where God has not.
JOAQUIN MILLER, *Byron*.

There is so much good in the worst of us,
And so much bad in the best of us,
That it hardly becomes any of us
To talk about the rest of us.
UNKNOWN, *Good and Bad*. Attributed to Edward Wallis Hoch, ex-Governor of Kansas, because first printed in the *Record*, of Marion, Kansas, of which he was editor. (Boston *Transcript*, 24 Apr., 1915. *The Reader*, 7

Sept., 1907.) Governor Hoch, however, disclaimed the verses in a letter to W. S. Close, 15 Feb., 1916. Attributed to Robert Louis Stevenson, but disclaimed by Lloyd Osbourne; ascribed to Ellen Thorneycroft Fowler, but denied by her; also to Joaquin Miller, probably because of the somewhat similar stanza in his *Byron*. Has appeared in slightly differing versions. *See also* GOODNESS: GOOD AND EVIL.

1
The judgment of man is fallible. (Hominum sententia fallax.)

OVID, *Fasti*. Bk. v, l. 191.

2
He makes speed to repentance who judges hastily. (Ad pœnitendum properat, cito qui judicat.)

PUBLILIUS SYRUS, *Sententiæ*. No. 32.

3
We should hesitate to pronounce judgment on the conduct of such eminent men, lest we fall into the common error of condemning what we do not understand. (Damnant quod non intelligunt.)

QUINTILIAN, *De Institutione Oratoria*. Bk. x, ch. 1, sec. 26.

4
Commonly we say a Judgment falls upon a Man for something in him we cannot abide.

JOHN SELDEN, *Table-Talk: Judgments*.

5
O judgement! thou art fled to brutish beasts,
And men have lost their reason!

SHAKESPEARE, *Julius Cæsar*. Act iii, sc. 2, l. 109.

6
It's the bad that's in the best of us
Leaves the saint so like the rest of us!
It's the good in the darkest-curst of us
Redeems and saves the worst of us!
It's the muddle of hope and madness;
It's the tangle of good and badness;
It's the lunacy linked with sanity
Makes up, and mocks, humanity!

ARTHUR STRINGER, *Humanity*.

7
Crime has its heroes, error has its martyrs:
Of true zeal and false, what vain judges we
are!
(Le crime a ses héros; l'erreur a ses martyrs:
Du vrai zèle et du faux vains juges que nous
sommes!)

VOLTAIRE, *Henriade*. Chant v, l. 200.

8
Man judges from a partial view,
None ever yet his brother knew;
The Eternal Eye that sees the whole
May better read the darkened soul,
And find, to outward sense denied,
The flower upon its inmost side!

J. G. WHITTIER, *The Pressed Gentian*.

IV—Judgment: The Mote and the Beam
See also Faults: Faults of Others

9
We all are wise when others we'd admonish,
And yet we know not when we trip ourselves.

EURIPIDES, *Fragments*. No. 862.

10
E'er you remark another's sin,
Bid your own conscience look within.

BENJAMIN FRANKLIN, *Poor Richard*, 1741.

11
In other men we faults can spy,
And blame the mote that dims their eye;
Each little speck and blemish find:
To our own stronger errors blind.

JOHN GAY, *Fables*. Pt. i, fab. 38.

12
The same vices which are huge and insupportable in others we do not feel in ourselves.

LA BRUYÈRE, *Caractères: Des Jugements*.

13
Lynx-eyed toward our equals, and moles to ourselves. (Lynx envers nos pareils, et taupes envers nous.)

LA FONTAINE, *Fables*. Bk. i, fab. 7.

14
We judge ourselves by what we feel capable of doing, while others judge us by what we have already done.

LONGFELLOW, *Kavanagh*. Ch. 1.

15
Why beholdest thou the mote that is in thy brother's eye, but considerest not the beam that is in thine own eye? Or how wilt thou say to thy brother, Let me pull out the mote out of thine eye, and, behold, a beam is in thine own eye? Thou hypocrite, first cast out the beam out of thine own eye; and then shalt thou see clearly to cast out the mote out of thy brother's eye.

New Testament: Matthew, vii, 3; *Luke*, vi, 41.

16
Do you never look at yourself when you abuse another person? (Non soles respicere te, quom dicas injuste alteri?)

PLAUTUS, *Pseudolus*, l. 612. (Act ii, sc. 2.)

17
Why, all the souls that were, were forfeit
once;
And He that might the vantage best have
took
Found out the remedy. How would you be,
If He, which is the top of judgement, should
But judge you as you are?

SHAKESPEARE, *Measure for Measure*. Act ii, sc. 2, l. 73.

JUDGMENT DAY

18
At the piping of all hands,
When the judgment-signal's spread—
When the islands and the lands
And the seas give up their dead,
And the South and North shall come;
When the sinner is dismayed,
And the just man is afraid,

Then Heaven be thy aid,
Poor Tom.
JOHN G. C. BRAINARD, *Lament for Long Tom.*

The trumpet! the trumpet! the dead have all heard:
Lo, the depths of the stone-cover'd charnels are stirr'd;
From the sea, from the land, from the south and the north,
The vast generations of man are come forth.
H. H. MILMAN, *Second Sunday in Advent.*

1
So, I think, God hides some souls away,
Sweetly to surprise us, the last day.
MARY BOLLES BRANCH, *The Petrified Fern.*

2
The last loud trumpet's wondrous sound,
Shall thro' the rending tombs rebound,
And wake the nations under ground.
WENTWORTH DILLON, *On the Day of Judgment.* St. 3.

3
When rattling bones together fly
From the four corners of the sky.
JOHN DRYDEN, *To the Pious Memory of Mrs. Anne Killigrew,* l. 184.

4
God will not look you over for medals, degrees or diplomas, but for scars.
ELBERT HUBBARD, *Epigrams.*

5
That fellow would vulgarize the day of judgement.
DOUGLAS JERROLD, *A Comic Author.*

6
The deeds we do, the words we say,
Into still air they seem to fleet,
We count them ever past;
But they shall last,—
In the dread judgement they
And we shall meet.
JOHN KEBLE, *The Effect of Example.*

7
I hope there is a resurrection day
For bodies, as the ancient prophets say,
When Helen's naked limbs again will gleam
Regathered from the dust of death's long dream.—
When those who thrilled the ages, being fair,
Will take the singing angels unaware
And make God's perfect meadows doubly sweet
With rosy vagrancy of little feet.
HARRY KEMP, *Resurrection.*

8
Flee from the wrath to come.
New Testament: Matthew, iii, 7.

Be ye also ready; for in such an hour as ye think not, the Son of man cometh.
New Testament: Matthew, xxiv, 44.

9
Day of wrath, that day of burning,
Seer and Sibyl speak concerning,
All the world to ashes turning.
(Dies iræ, dies illa!
Solvet sæclum in favilla,
Teste David cum Sybilla.)
TOMMASO DI CELANO, *Dies Iræ.* (DANIEL, *Thesaurus Hymnology,* ii, 103.) This, called the greatest of all hymns, has been attributed also to St. Gregory and St. Bernard.

Day of wrath, that day whose knelling
Gives to flames this earthly dwelling;
Psalm and Sibyl thus foretelling.
TOMMASO DI CELANO, *Dies Iræ.* (O'Hagan, tr.)

That day of wrath, that dreadful day,
When heaven and earth shall pass away.
SCOTT, *The Lay of the Last Minstrel.* Canto vi, l. 542.

10
If after death, love, comes a waking,
And in their camp so dark and still
The men of dust hear bugles, breaking
Their halt upon the hill,

To me the slow and silver pealing
That then the last high trumpet pours
Shall softer than the dawn come stealing,
For, with its call, comes yours!
HERBERT TRENCH, *I Heard a Soldier.*

11
I see the judge enthron'd! the flaming guard!
The volume open'd!—open'd ev'ry heart!
YOUNG, *Night Thoughts.* Night ix, l. 268.

The Book was opened! Men in wonder stood!
No record kept of wrong! It told of good!
Each deed of love! A Soul crept up in fright,
Then passed into the dark—his page was white!
CLARENCE URMY, *The Judgment-Book.* *See also* ANGEL: RECORDING ANGEL.

JUNE

12
Knee-deep in June.
ALFRED AUSTIN, *A Wild Rose.*

Tell you what I like the best—
'Long about knee-deep in June,
'Bout the time strawberries melts
On the vine,—some afternoon
Like to jes' git out and rest,
And not work at nothin' else!
JAMES WHITCOMB RILEY, *Knee-Deep in June.*

13
Flame-flowered, yellow-petalled June.
DON BLANDING, *Hawaiian June.*

14
June's twice June since she breathed it with me.
ROBERT BROWNING, *The Flower's Name.*

15
The leafy month of June.
S. T. COLERIDGE, *The Ancient Mariner.* Pt. v.

16
What joy have I in June's return?
My feet are parched—my eyeballs burn,
I scent no flowery gust;
But faint the flagging Zephyr springs,
With dry Macadam on its wings,
And turns me "dust to dust."
THOMAS HOOD, *Town and Country.*

1
The fair
Tanned face of June, the nomad gipsy, laughs
Above her widespread wares, the while she
tells
The farmers' fortunes in the fields, and quaffs
The water from the spider-peopled wells.
FRANCIS LEDWIDGE, *June.*

2
And what is so rare as a day in June?
Then, if ever, come perfect days;
Then Heaven tries the earth if it be in tune,
And over it softly her warm ear lays.
J. R. LOWELL, *The Vision of Sir Launfal:* Pt. i, *Prelude.*

No price is set on the lavish summer;
June may be had by the poorest comer.
J. R. LOWELL, *The Vision of Sir Launfal:* Pt. i. *Prelude.*

3
The roses make the world so sweet,
The bees, the birds have such a tune,
There's such a light and such a heat
And such a joy in June.
GEORGE MACDONALD, *To* ——.

4
How softly runs the afternoon
Beneath the billowy clouds of June!
CHARLES HANSON TOWNE, *How Softly Runs.*

5
O you poor folk in cities,
A thousand, thousand pities!
Heaping the fairy gold that withers and dies;
One field in the June weather
Is worth all the gold ye gather,
One field in June weather—one Paradise.
KATHERINE TYNAN, *June Song.*

6
It is the month of June,
The month of leaves and roses,
When pleasant sights salute the eyes
And pleasant scents the noses.
N. P. WILLIS, *The Month of June.*

JURY

7
Wise men plead causes, but fools decide them. (Λέγουσι μὲν οἱ σοφοί, κρίνουσι δὲ οἱ ἀμαθεῖς.)
ANACHARSIS. (PLUTARCH, *Lives: Solon.* Sec. 5.)

8
In my mind, he was guilty of no error, he was chargeable with no exaggeration, he was betrayed by his fancy into no metaphor, who once said that all we see about us, kings, lords, and Commons, the whole machinery of the State, all the apparatus of the system, and its varied workings, end in simply bringing twelve good men into a box.
LORD BROUGHAM, *Present State of the Law.* 7 Feb., 1828.

9
Trial by jury itself, instead of being a security to persons who are accused, shall be a delusion, a mockery, and a snare.
THOMAS, LORD DENMAN, *Judgment,* O'Connell vs. Queen, 4 Sept., 1894.

10
The high-minded and intelligent dozen of men whom he now saw in that box before him.
DICKENS, *Pickwick Papers.* Ch. 34.

11
A man should be tried by a jury of his peers.
GOETHE, *Die Aufgeregten,* iii, 1.

12
As harsh as a prejudiced jury.
THOMAS HOOD, *For the New Year.*

13
Since twelve honest men have decided the
cause,
And were judges of fact, though not judges
of laws.
SIR WILLIAM PULTENEY, *The Honest Jury.* (See *The Craftsman,* v, 337.)

14
The jury, passing on the prisoner's life,
May in the sworn twelve have a thief or two
Guiltier than him they try.
SHAKESPEARE, *Measure for Measure.* Act ii, sc. 1, l. 19.

15
They have been grand-jurymen since before Noah was a sailor.
SHAKESPEARE, *Twelfth Night.* Act iii, sc. 2, l. 16.

16
The hungry judges soon the sentence sign,
And wretches hang that jurymen may dine.
POPE, *Rape of the Lock.* Canto iii, l. 21.

If it's near dinner time, the foreman takes out his watch when the jury have retired, and says: "Dear me, gentlemen, ten minutes to five, I declare! I dine at five, gentlemen." "So do I," says everybody else except two men who ought to have dined at three, and seem more than half disposed to stand out in consequence.
DICKENS, *Pickwick Papers.* Vol. ii, ch. 6.

Whin the case is all over, the jury'll pitch th' tistimony out iv the window, an' consider three questions: "Did Lootgert look as though he'd kill his wife? Did his wife look as though she ought to be kilt? Isn't it time we wint to supper?"
FINLEY PETER DUNNE, *On Expert Testimony.*

Thou that goest upon Middlesex juries, and wilt make haste to give up thy verdict because thou wilt not lose thy dinner.
THOMAS MIDDLETON, *A Trick to Catch the Old One.* Act iv, sc. 5.

17
Let the judges answer to the question of law, and the jurors to the matter of the fact. (Ad quæstionem juris respondeant judices ad quæstionem facti respondeant juratores.)
UNKNOWN. A law maxim.

JUSTICE

I—Justice: Definitions

18
Liberty, equality,—bad principles! The true principle of humanity is justice. (Le vrai principe humain, c'est la justice.)
HENRI FRÉDÉRIC AMIEL, *Journal Intime,* 4 Dec., 1863.

1
Justice is that virtue of the soul which is distributive according to desert.
ARISTOTLE, *Metaphysics: On the Virtues and Vices: Justice.*

2
There are in nature certain fountains of justice, whence all civil laws are derived.
BACON, *Advancement of Learning.* Bk. ii.

3
Justice is itself the great standing policy of civil society; and any eminent departure from it, under any circumstances, lies under the suspicion of being no policy at all.
EDMUND BURKE, *Reflections on the Revolution in France.*

Those eternal laws of justice, which are our rule and our birthright.
EDMUND BURKE, *Impeachment of Warren Hastings,* 15 Feb., 1788.

A good parson once said that where mystery begins religion ends. Cannot I say, as truly at least, of human laws, that where mystery begins, justice ends?
EDMUND BURKE, *A Vindication of Natural Society.*

4
Justice is one; it binds all human society, and is based on one law, which is right reason applied to command and prohibition.
CICERO, *De Legibus.* Bk. i, ch. 15, sec. 42.

Justice is compliance with the written laws. (Justitia est obtemperatio scriptis legibus.)
CICERO, *De Legibus.* Bk. i, ch. 15, sec. 42. This is stated by Cicero only for the purpose of refutation.

5
Justice, in which is the crowning glory of the virtues. (Justitia, in qua virtutis est splendor maximus.)
CICERO, *De Officiis.* Bk. i, ch. 7, sec. 20.

Good faith is the foundation of justice. (Fundamentum autem est justitiæ fides.)
CICERO, *De Officiis.* Bk. i, ch. 7, sec. 23.

Justice shines by its own light. (Æquitas enim lucet ipsa per se.)
CICERO, *De Officiis.* Bk. i, ch. 9, sec. 30.

Let us remember that justice must be observed even to the lowest. (Meminerimus etiam adversus infimos justitiam esse servandam.)
CICERO, *De Officiis.* Bk. i, ch. 13, sec. 41.

Nothing that lacks justice can be morally right. (Nihil honestum esse potest, quod justitia vacat.)
CICERO, *De Officiis.* Bk. i, ch. 19, sec. 62.

It is the function of justice not to wrong one's fellow men. (Justitiæ partes sunt non violare homines.)
CICERO, *De Officiis.* Bk. i, ch. 28, sec. 99.

Justice is indispensable for the conduct of business. Its importance is so great, that not even those who live by wickedness and crime can get on without some small share of justice.
CICERO, *De Officiis.* Bk. ii, ch. 11, sec. 40.

6
Justice is the end of government.
DANIEL DEFOE, *The True-born Englishman.* Pt. ii, l. 368.

Justice is always violent to the party offending, for every man is innocent in his own eyes.
DANIEL DEFOE, *Shortest Way with Dissenters.*

7
Justice is truth in action.
BENJAMIN DISRAELI, *Speech,* House of Commons, 11 Feb., 1851. Referring to the saying, "Peace is beauty in action."

Justice is truth in action. (La justice est la vérité en action.)
JOUBERT, *Pensées.* No. 203. (1838)

8
Justice without wisdom is impossible.
J. A. FROUDE, *Short Studies on Great Subjects: Party Politics.*

9
That justice is the highest quality in the moral hierarchy I do not say, but that it is the first. That which is above justice must be based on justice, and include justice, and be reached through justice.
HENRY GEORGE, *Social Problems.* Ch. 9.

10
Justice is the virtue that innocence rejoiceth in.
BEN JONSON, *Explorata: Religio.*

11
Justice is the firm and continuous desire to render to everyone that which is his due. (Justitia est constans et perpetua voluntas jus suum cuique tribuendi.)
JUSTINIAN, *Institutiones.* Bk. i, sec. 1.

12
A man's vanity tells him what is honour; a man's conscience what is justice.
W. S. LANDOR, *Imaginary Conversations: Peter Leopold and President Du Paty.*

13
Justice indeed
Should ever be close-eared and open mouthed;
That is to hear a little, and speak much.
THOMAS MIDDLETON, *The Old Law.* Act v, sc. 1.

14
Justice is what is established; and thus all our established laws will be regarded as just, without being examined, since they are established.
PASCAL, *Pensées.* Ch. vii, No. 6.

15
A just man is not one who does no ill,
But he, who with the power, has not the will.
PHILEMON, *Sententiæ.*

16
Things which partake of justice are just; things which partake of beauty are beautiful.
PLATO. (DIOGENES LAERTIUS, *Plato.* Bk. iii, 13.)

All knowledge that is divorced from justice must be called cunning rather than wisdom.
PLATO. (CICERO, *De Officiis.* Bk. i, ch. 19, sec. 63.)

1
Poetic Justice, with her lifted scale,
Where, in nice balance, truth with gold she weighs,
And solid pudding against empty praise.
POPE, *The Dunciad*. Bk. i, l. 52.

2
Truth is its [justice's] handmaid, freedom is its child, peace is its companion, safety walks in its steps, victory follows in its train; it is the brightest emanation from the gospel; it is the attribute of God.
SYDNEY SMITH, (LADY HOLLAND, *Memoir*. Vol. i, p. 29.)

3
The administration of justice is the firmest pillar of government.
GEORGE WASHINGTON, *Letter to Edmund Randolph*, 27 Sept., 1789. (WASHINGTON, *Writings*, ii, 432.) Inscribed on New York County courthouse.

Justice, sir, is the great interest of man on earth.
DANIEL WEBSTER, *On Mr. Justice Story*.

4
The hope of all who suffer,
The dread of all who wrong.
WHITTIER, *Mantle of St. John De Matha*. St. 21.

5
Justice has nothing to do with expediency. Justice has nothing to do with any temporary standard whatever. It is rooted and grounded in the fundamental instincts of humanity.
WOODROW WILSON, *Speech*, Washington, 26 Feb., 1916.

II—Justice: Apothegms

6
Justice discards party, friendship, kindred, and is therefore always represented as blind.
JOSEPH ADDISON, *The Guardian*. No. 99.

For justice, though she's painted blind,
Is to the weaker side inclined.
BUTLER, *Hudibras*. Pt. iii, canto iii, l. 709.

Justice is blind, he knows nobody.
DRYDEN, *The Wild Gallant*. Act v, sc. 1.

Justice is lame as well as blind, amongst us.
THOMAS OTWAY, *Venice Preserved*. Act i, sc. 1.

Justice is blind. Blind she is, an' deef an' dumb an' has a wooden leg.
FINLEY PETER DUNNE, *Cross-Examinations*.

7
So justice while she winks at crimes,
Stumbles on innocence sometimes.
BUTLER, *Hudibras*. Pt. i, canto ii, l. 1177.

Justice may wink a while, but see at last.
THOMAS MIDDLETON, *The Mayor of Queenborough*. Act v, sc. 1.

8
Justice is too good for some people and not good enough for the rest.
NORMAN DOUGLAS, *Good-bye to Western Culture*.

9
Justice again our guide. (Astræa redux.)
DRYDEN. Title of poem. Astræa was the goddess of justice.

10
Every place is safe to him who lives in justice.
EPICTETUS, *Fragments*. No. 102.

11
Only the just man enjoys peace of mind.
EPICURUS, *Sovran Maxims*. No. 17.

12
All that is needed to remedy the evils of our time is to do justice and give freedom.
HENRY GEORGE, *The Condition of Labor*.

13
As crimes do grow, justice should rouse itself.
BEN JONSON, *Catiline*. Act iii, sc. 5.

14
There should be no sword in the hand of Justice. (Tractanda putabat inermi justicia.)
JUVENAL, *Satires*. Sat. iv, l. 80.

15
Live and let live is the rule of common justice.
SIR ROGER L'ESTRANGE, *Fables of Æsop*, 127.

16
He reminds me of the man who murdered both his parents, and then, when sentence was about to be pronounced, pleaded for mercy on the grounds that he was an orphan.
ABRAHAM LINCOLN. (GROSS, *Lincoln's Own Stories*, p. 179.)

17
He who refuses justice surrenders everything to him who is armed. (Arma tenati Omnia dat qui justa negat.)
LUCAN, *De Bello Civili*. Bk. i, l. 348.

18
Render therefore unto Cæsar the things which are Cæsar's; and unto God the things that are God's.
New Testament: Matthew, xxii, 21.

Render therefore to all their dues: tribute to whom tribute is due; custom to whom custom; fear to whom fear; honour to whom honour.
New Testament: Romans, xiii, 7.

Render unto all men their due, but remember thou art also a man.
MARTIN F. TUPPER, *Proverbial Philosophy: Of Humility*.

19
Where justice reigns, 'tis freedom to obey.
JAMES MONTGOMERY, *Greenland*.

20
There is no debt with so much prejudice put off as that of justice.
PLUTARCH, *Of Those Whom God Is Slow to Punish*.

21
If elected, I shall see to it that every man has a square deal, no less and no more.
THEODORE ROOSEVELT, *Address*, 4 Nov., 1904.

I stand for the square deal.
THEODORE ROOSEVELT, *Speech*, Ossawatomie, 31 Aug., 1910.

22
We love justice greatly, and just men but little.
JOSEPH ROUX, *Meditations of a Parish Priest*. Pt. iv, No. 10.

He that is void of fear, may soon be just.
BEN JONSON, *Catiline*. Act iii, sc. 2.

1
Liberty plucks justice by the nose.
SHAKESPEARE, *Measure for Measure*. Act i, sc. 3, l. 29.

Through tatter'd clothes small vices do appear;
Robes and furr'd gowns hide all. Plate sin with gold,
And the strong lance of justice hurtless breaks;
Arm it in rags, a pigmy's straw does pierce it.
SHAKESPEARE, *King Lear*. Act iv, sc. 6, l. 168.

See also LAW: THE NET OF LAW.

2
Justice is pleasant, even when she destroys.
SYDNEY SMITH, *Sketches of Moral Philosophy: On Taste.*

3
A sense of justice is a noble fancy.
TEGNÉR, *Frithjof's Saga*. Canto viii.

4
As soon as Justice returns, the golden age returns. (Jam redit et Virgo, redeunt Saturnia regna.)
VERGIL, *Eclogues*. No. iv, l. 6.

Learn justice. (Discite justitiam.)
VERGIL, *Æneid*. Bk. vi, l. 620.

5
To no one will we deny justice, to no one will we delay it. (Nulli negabimus, nulli differemus justitiam.)
UNKNOWN, *Magna Carta*, 12 June, 1215.

6
One hour in doing justice is worth a hundred in prayer.
UNKNOWN. A Mahometan proverb.

III—Justice: Its Virtues

7
There is no virtue so truly great and godlike as justice.
JOSEPH ADDISON, *The Guardian*. No. 99.

8
Justice is the first of the virtues, for, unsupported by justice, valor is good for nothing; and if all men were just, there would be no need of valor.
AGESILAÜS II. (PLUTARCH, *Lives: Agesilaüs*. Ch. 22, sec. 5.)

9
It is due to Justice that man is a God to man and not a wolf. (Justitiæ debetur, quod homo homini sit Deus, non lupus.)
FRANCIS BACON, *De Augmentis Scientiarum: Justitia.*

The place of justice is a hallowed place.
FRANCIS BACON, *Essays: Of Judicature.*

10
Justice does not descend from its pinnacle. (Cima di giudizio non s'avvalla.
DANTE, *Purgatorio*. Canto vi, l. 37.

11
A prince's favours but on few can fall,
But justice is a virtue shar'd by all.
DRYDEN, *Britannia Rediviva*, l. 337.

12
Justice is like the kingdom of God—it is not without us as a fact, it is within us as a great yearning.
GEORGE ELIOT, *Romola*. Bk. iii, ch. 67.

13
Whoever fights, whoever falls,
Justice conquers evermore, . . .
And he who battles on her side,
God, though he were ten times slain,
Crowns him victor glorified,
Victor over death and pain.
R. W. EMERSON, *Voluntaries*. Pt. iv.

Fear not, then, thou child infirm,
There's no god dare wrong a worm;
Laurel crowns cleave to deserts,
And power to him who power exerts.
R. W. EMERSON, *Essays: Compensation*. Motto.

14
Above all other things is justice: success is a good thing; wealth is good also; honor is better, but justice excels them all.
D. D. FIELD, *Speeches: Law Reform*, 18 March, 1876.

15
And Heav'n, that ev'ry virtue bears in mind,
Ev'n to the ashes of the just is kind.
HOMER, *Iliad*. Bk. xxiv, l. 523. (Pope, tr.)

The bad man's death is horror: but the just
Keeps something of his glory in the dust.
WILLIAM HABINGTON, *Elegie*. (c. 1650)

The memory of the just is blessed; but the name of the wicked shall rot.
Old Testament: Proverbs, x, 7.

16
But the sunshine aye shall light the sky,
As round and round we run;
And the Truth shall ever come uppermost,
And Justice shall be done.
CHARLES MACKAY, *Eternal Justice*.

17
Prompt sense of equity! to thee belongs
The swift redress of unexamined wrongs!
Eager to serve, the cause perhaps untried,
But always apt to choose the suffering side!
HANNAH MORE, *Sensibility*, l. 243.

18
The bright actions of the just
Survive unburied in the kindred dust.
(Κατακρύπτει δ' οὐ κόνις
συγγόνων κεδνὰν χάριν.)
PINDAR, *Olympian Odes*. Ode viii, l. 103. (Wheelwright, tr.)

Only the actions of the just
Smell sweet and blossom in their dust.
JAMES SHIRLEY, *Contention of Ajax and Ulysses*. Sec iii, l. 23. (1659)

The sweet remembrance of the just
Shall flourish when he sleeps in dust.
NAHUM TATE AND NICHOLAS BRADY, *New Version of the Psalms*, cxii, 6. (1696)

The memory of the just survives in Heaven.
WORDSWORTH, *The Excursion*. Bk. vii, l. 388.

1
That most kingly and godlike surname, The Just. (Τὴν βασιλικωτάτην καὶ θειοτάτην προσηγορίαν τὸν Δίκαιον.)

PLUTARCH, *Lives: Aristides*. Ch. 5, sec. 7. Referring to Aristides.

I don't know the fellow, but I am tired of hearing him everywhere called The Just.

The reply of a citizen to Aristides, when the latter asked why he was voting against him. (PLUTARCH, *Lives: Aristides*, 7, 6.)

2
The path of the just is as the shining light, that shineth more and more unto the perfect day.

Old Testament: Proverbs, iv, 18.

The spirits of just men made perfect.

New Testament: Hebrews, xii, 23.

IV—Justice: Its Certainty

See also Punishment: Its Certainty

3
Justice, voiceless, unseen, seeth thee when thou sleepest and when thou goest forth and when thou liest down. Continually doth she attend thee, now athwart thy course, now at a later time.

ÆSCHYLUS [?], *Fragments*. Frag. 253.

4
God's justice, tardy though it prove perchance,
Rests never on the track until it reach
Delinquency.

ROBERT BROWNING, *Cenciaja*.

5
Murder may pass unpunish'd for a time,
But tardy justice will o'ertake the crime.

DRYDEN, *The Cock and the Fox*, l. 285.

6
Justice, though moving slowly, seldom fails to overtake the wicked. (Raro antecedentem scelestum Deseruit pede pœna claudo.)

HORACE, *Odes*. Bk. iii, ode 2, l. 31.

7
Man is unjust, but God is just; and finally justice Triumphs.

LONGFELLOW, *Evangeline*. Pt. i, sec. 3, l. 34.

8
For though usurpers sway the rule a while,
Yet heavens are just, and time suppresseth wrongs.

SHAKESPEARE, *III Henry VI*. Act iii, sc. 3, l. 76.

9
As thou urgest justice, be assur'd
Thou shalt have justice more than thou desir'st.

SHAKESPEARE, *The Merchant of Venice*. Act iv, sc. 1, l. 315.

10
Justice, even if slow, is sure. (Πάντως ὕστερον ἦλθε δίκη.)

SOLON. (PLUTARCH, *Lives: Solon*. Sec. 2.)

V—Justice: Its Power

11
Where might and justice are yoke-fellows—what pair is stronger than this?

ÆSCHYLUS, *Fragments*. Frag. 209. *See also* MIGHT AND RIGHT.

12
The humblest citizen of all the land, when clad in the armor of a righteous cause is stronger than all the hosts of Error.

W. J. BRYAN, *Speech at the National Democratic Convention*, Chicago, 1896.

13
Let laurels, drench'd in pure Parnassian dews,
Reward his mem'ry, dear to ev'ry muse,
Who, with a courage of unshaken root,
In honour's field advancing his firm foot,
Plants it upon the line that justice draws,
And will prevail or perish in her cause.

COWPER, *Table Talk*, l. 13.

14
I'm armed with more than complete steel,—
The justice of my quarrel.

MARLOWE (?), *Lust's Dominion*. Act iv, sc. 3.

Thrice is he arm'd that hath his quarrel just,
And he but naked, though lock'd up in steel,
Whose conscience with injustice is corrupted.

SHAKESPEARE, *II Henry VI*. Act iii, sc. 2, l. 233.

"Thrice is he armed that hath his quarrel just"—
And four times he who gets his fist in fust.

ARTEMUS WARD, *Shakespeare Up-to-Date*.

15
The weakest arm is strong enough that strikes
With the sword of justice.

JOHN WEBSTER, *Duchess of Malfi*. Act v, sc. 2.

VI—Justice: Let Justice Be Done

16
Let justice be done, though the heavens fall. (Fiat justitia et ruant cœli.)

WILLIAM WATSON, *Ten Quodlibeticall Questions Concerning Religion and State*. (1601) The whole quotation is: "You go against that general maxim in the laws, which is, 'Fiat justitia et ruant cœli.'" This is the first appearance in English literature, so far as known, of what was apparently a maxim even in 1600. It was used by William Prynne (*Fresh Discovery of Prodigious Wandering New-Blazing Stars*, 1646), by Nathaniel Ward (*Simple Cobbler of Agawam*, 1647), and frequently thereafter, but was given its widest celebrity in 1768 when it was quoted by Lord Mansfield in *Rex vs. Wilkes*. The maxim is given in various forms: "Fiat justitia et ruant cœli" (William Watson); "Fiat justitia et cœlum ruat" (Manningham, *Diary*, 11 April, 1603); "Justitia fiat, ruat cœlum" (Lord Mansfield).

The constitution does not allow reasons of state to influence our judgement. God forbid it should! We must not regard political consequences, however formidable they might be; if rebellion was the certain consequence, we are bound to say, 'Justitia fiat, ruat cœlum.'"

WILLIAM MURRAY, EARL OF MANSFIELD, *Judg-*

ment, Rex vs. Wilkes. (BURROWS, *Reports.* Vol. iv, p. 2562.) In this judgment, Lord Mansfield reversed the sentence of outlawry passed upon John Wilkes for the publication of the *North Briton.*

1
Let justice reign though the heaven fall. (Regnet justicia et ruat cœlum.)
DUKE OF RICHMOND, *Speech,* House of Lords, 31 Jan., 1642. (*Old Parliamentary History,* Vol. x, p. 28.)

2
Let justice be done though the world perish. (Fiat justitia et ruat mundus.)
UNKNOWN, *Egerton Papers,* p. 52. (1552) (AIKIN, *Court and Times of James I,* ii, 500. 1625.) Said to be the motto of Ferdinand I, Emperor of Germany. (JOHANNES MANLIUS, *Loci Communes,* ii.)

Let justice be done though the world perish. (Fiat jus et pereat mundus.)
ST. AUGUSTINE. (Attributed to him by Jeremy Taylor.)

Though the heaven falls, let thy will be done. (Ruat cœlum, fiat voluntas tua.)
SIR THOMAS BROWNE, *Religio Medici.* Pt. ii, sec. 12.

3
Do well and right, and let the world sink..
GEORGE HERBERT, *Country Parson.* Ch. 29.

4
Where the offence is, let the great axe fall.
SHAKESPEARE, *Hamlet.* Act iv, sc. 5, l. 218.

This even-handed justice
Commends the ingredients of our poison'd chalice
To our own lips.
SHAKESPEARE, *Macbeth.* Act i, sc. 7, l. 10.

VII—Justice and Mercy

5
Hard is the task of justice, where distress
Excites our mercy, yet demands redress.
COLLEY CIBBER, *The Heroic Daughter.* Act iii.

6
He who spares the bad seeks to corrupt the good. (Parcit quisque malis, perdere vult bonos.)
CLEOBULUS (AUSONIUS [?], *Septem Sapientum Sententiæ,* l. 19.)

7
When justice on offenders is not done,
Law, government, and commerce are o'erthrown.
SIR JOHN DENHAM, *Of Justice,* l. 85.

Our mercy is become our crime.
DRYDEN, *Absalom and Achitophel.* Pt. ii, l. 734.

There is a mercy which is weakness, and even treason against the common good.
GEORGE ELIOT, *Romola.* Bk. iii, ch. 59.

8
Mercy and justice, marching cheek by jowl.
DU BARTAS, *Devine Weekes and Workes.* Week i, day 1. (Sylvester, tr.)

9
Thwackum was for doing justice, and leaving mercy to Heaven.
FIELDING, *Tom Jones.* Bk. iii, ch. 10.

10
Ah, to be just, as well as kind,—
It costs so little and so much!
RICHARD HOVEY, *Contemporaries.*

11
It is easier to be beneficent than to be just.
SAMUEL JOHNSON. (EMERSON, *Uncollected Lectures: Natural Religion.*)

12
Justice, that in the rigid paths of law,
Would still some drops from Pity's fountain draw.
JOHN LANGHORNE, *The Country Justice: Introduction,* l. 125.

13
Exact justice is commonly more merciful in the long run than pity, for it tends to foster in men those stronger qualities which make them good citizens.
J. R. LOWELL, *Among My Books: Dante.*

14
I may mitigate their doom
On me deriv'd, yet I shall temper so
Justice with mercy, as may illustrate most
Them fully satisfied, and thee appease.
MILTON, *Paradise Lost.* Bk. x, l. 77.

15
You yourself are guilty of a crime when you do not punish crime. (Injuriam ipse facias ubi non vindices.)
PUBLILIUS SYRUS, *Sententiæ.* No. 410.

Mercy as judge loosens the law. (Dissolvit legem judex misericordia.)
PUBLILIUS SYRUS, *Sententiæ.* No. 168.

16
Pardon one offense and you encourage the commission of many. (Qui culpæ ignoscit uni, suadet pluribus.)
PUBLILIUS SYRUS, *Sententiæ,* No. 578.

Every unpunished delinquency has a family of delinquencies.
HERBERT SPENCER, *The Study of Sociology: Postscript.*

Every unpunished murder takes away something from the security of every man's life.
DANIEL WEBSTER, *Argument,* Salem, Mass., 3 Aug., 1830. *The Murder of Capt. Joseph White.*

17
He hurts the good who spares the bad. (Bonis nocet quisquis pepercerit malis.)
PUBLILIUS SYRUS, *Sententiæ.* No. 412.

He that's merciful
Unto the bad, is cruel to the good.
THOMAS RANDOLPH, *The Muses' Looking Glass.*

He harms the good that doth the evil spare.
UNKNOWN, *The Times Whistle,* l. 1350. (c. 1614)

1
It is impossible to be just if one is not generous.
JOSEPH ROUX, *Meditations of a Parish Priest*. Pt. iv, No. 109.

Be just before you are generous.
SHERIDAN, *The School for Scandal*. Act iv, sc. 1.

2
Justice must tame, whom mercy cannot win.
GEORGE SAVILE, *On the Death of Charles II*.

3
And earthly power doth then show likest God's
When mercy seasons justice.
SHAKESPEARE, *The Merchant of Venice*. Act iv, sc. 1, l. 196.

4
Sparing justice feeds iniquity.
SHAKESPEARE, *The Rape of Lucrece*, l. 1687.

Mercy but murders, pardoning those that kill.
SHAKESPEARE, *Romeo and Juliet*. Act iii, sc. 1, l. 202.

Nothing emboldens sin so much as mercy.
SHAKESPEARE, *Timon of Athens*. Act iii, sc. 5, l. 3.

5
One can not be just if one is not humane. (On ne peut être juste si on n'est pas humain.)
VAUVENARGUES, *Réflexions*. No. 28.

6
He who is merely just is severe. (Qui n'est que juste est dur.)
VOLTAIRE, *Letter to the King of Prussia*, 1740.

VIII—Justice and Injustice

7
He's just, your cousin, ay, abhorrently;
He'd wash his hands in blood, to keep them clean.
E. B. BROWNING, *Aurora Leigh*. Bk. ix, l. 118.

8
One man's justice is another's injustice; one man's beauty another's ugliness; one man's wisdom another's folly.
EMERSON, *Essays, First Series: Circles*.

9
That which is unjust can really profit no one; that which is just can really harm no one.
HENRY GEORGE, *The Land Question*. Ch. 14.

10
I have loved justice and hated iniquity; therefore I die in exile. (Dilexi justitiam et odi iniquitatem, propterea morior in exilio.)
POPE GREGORY VII, HILDEBRAND. (BOWDEN, *Life*. Bk. iii, ch. 20.)

11
"A book," I observed, "might be written on the injustice of the just."
ANTHONY HOPE, *Dolly Dialogues*. No. 14.

12
Love of justice, with most men, is nothing but the fear of suffering injustice. (L'amour de la justice n'est, en la plupart des hommes, que la crainte de souffrir l'injustice.)
LA ROCHEFOUCAULD, *Maximes*. No. 78.

13
Delay of justice is injustice.
W. S. LANDOR, *Imaginary Conversations: Peter Leopold and President Du Paty*.

14
The hour of justice does not strike
On the dials of this world.
(L'heure de la justice ne sonne pas
Aux cadrans de ce monde.)
MAETERLINCK, *Measure of the Hours*.

15
Injustice is relatively easy to bear; what stings is justice.
H. L. MENCKEN, *Prejudices*. Ser. iii, p. 101.

16
To entreat what is unjust from the just is wrong; but to seek what is just from the unjust is folly. (Injusta a justis impetrare non decet; Justa autem ab injustis petere, insipientia est.)
PLAUTUS, *Amphitruo: Prologue*, l. 31.

17
O, I were damn'd beneath all depth in hell,
But that I did proceed upon just grounds
To this extremity.
SHAKESPEARE, *Othello*. Act v, sc. 2, l. 137.

18
There is a point at which even justice is unjust. (Ἔστιν ἔνθα χἠ δίκη βλάβην φέρει.)
SOPHOCLES, *Electra*, l. 1042.

Injustice often arises through chicanery, that is, through an over-subtle and even fraudulent construction of the law. This it is that gave rise to the now familiar saw, "The more law, the less justice." (Summum jus, summa injuria.)
CICERO, *De Officiis*. Bk. i, ch. 10, sec. 33. The "tritum proverbium" is quoted by Cicero again in *De Republica*, v, 3, and may also be found in Columella (*De Re Rustica*, i, 7), Racine (*La Thébiade*, iv, 3), and many other writers.

The strictest law is sometimes the greatest injustice. (Jus summum sæpe summast malitia.)
TERENCE, *Heauton Timoroumenos*, l. 796.

The extremity of justice is extreme injustice.
RICHARD GRAFTON, *Chronicles*. Vol. ii, p. 228.

There is one motto that ought to be put at the head of our penal code, "Summum jus, summa injuria."
C. C. COLTON, *Lacon*. Pt. ii, No. 139.

K

KATYDID

1
I love to hear thine earnest voice,
Wherever thou art hid,
Thou testy little dogmatist,
Thou pretty Katydid!
Thou mindest me of gentlefolks,—
Old gentlefolks are they,—
Thou say'st an undisputed thing
In such a solemn way.
O. W. HOLMES, *To an Insect.*

2
Where the katydid works her chromatic reed on the walnut-tree over the well.
WALT WHITMAN, *Song of Myself.* Sec. 33.

KEATS, JOHN

3
And Keats the real
Adonis with the hymeneal
Fresh vernal buds half sunk between
His youthful curls, kissed straight and sheen
In his Rome-grave, by Venus queen.
E. B. BROWNING, *A Vision of Poets,* l. 407.

4
Stand still, true poet that you are!
I know you; let me try and draw you.
Some night you'll fail us: when afar
You rise, remember one man saw you,
Knew you, and named a star!
ROBERT BROWNING, *Popularity.*

Who fished the murex up?
What porridge had John Keats?
ROBERT BROWNING, *Popularity.*

Dumb to Keats—him, even!
ROBERT BROWNING, *One Word More.*

5
If you still behave in dancing rooms and other societies as I have seen you—I do not want to live—if you have done so, I wish this coming night may be my last. I cannot live without you, and not only you but *chaste you; virtuous you.*
JOHN KEATS, *Letter to Fanny Brawne,* 1820.

6
It is a better and a wiser thing to be a starved apothecary than a starved poet; so back to the shop, Mr. John, back to "plasters, pills, and ointment boxes."
JOHN GIBSON LOCKHART [?], *Review,* of *Endymion* in *Blackwood.*

A Mr. John Keats, a young man who had left a decent calling for the melancholy trade of Cockney-poetry, has lately died of a consumption, after having written two or three little books of verse, much neglected by the public.
LOCKHART or WILSON, *Review,* of *Adonais* in *Blackwood.*

The savage criticism on his Endymion, which appeared in the *Quarterly Review,* produced the most violent agitation on his susceptible mind; the agitation thus originated ended in the rupture of a blood-vessel in the lungs; a rapid consumption ensued.
SHELLEY, *Adonais: Preface.* See also 343:6.

John Keats, who was kill'd off by one critique,
Just as he really promised something great. . .
Poor fellow! his was an untoward fate:
'Tis strange the mind, that very fiery particle,
Should let itself be snuff'd out by an article.
BYRON, *Don Juan.* Canto xi, st. 59.

That dirty little blackguard Keats.
BYRON. (MOORE, *Life of Byron,* 1820.)

7
But now thy youngest, dearest one has perished,
The nursling of thy widowhood, who grew
Like a pale flower by some sad maiden cherished,
And fed with true love tears instead of dew,
Most musical of mourners, weep anew!
SHELLEY, *Adonais.* St. 6.

He has outsoared the shadow of our night;
Envy and calumny, and hate and pain,
And that unrest which men miscall delight,
Can touch him not and torture not again.
SHELLEY, *Adonais.* St. 40. The first line was inscribed by direction of Theodore Roosevelt on the slab over the grave of his son, Quentin, shot down near Chambry, France, 14 July, 1918.

I am borne darkly, fearfully afar;
Whilst, burning through the inmost veil of Heaven,
The soul of Adonais, like a star,
Beacons from the abode where the Eternal are.
SHELLEY, *Adonais.* St. 55.

8
Yet thou hast won the gift Tithonus missed:
Never to feel the pain of growing old,
Nor lose the blissful sight of beauty's truth,
But with the ardent lips Urania kissed
To breathe thy song, and, ere thy heart grew cold,
Become the Poet of Immortal Youth.
HENRY VAN DYKE, *Keats.*

9
This grave contains all that was mortal of a young English poet, who, on his death bed, in the bitterness of his heart at the malicious power of his enemies, desired these words to be graven on his tomb-stone, "Here lies one whose name was writ in water."
Epitaph, on tombstone of Keats at Rome.

Among the many things he has requested of me tonight, this is the principal,—that on his gravestone shall be this inscription: Here lies one whose name was writ in water.
RICHARD MONCKTON MILNES, *Life of Keats: Letter to Severn.* Vol. ii, p. 91.

"Whose name was writ in water!" What large laughter

Among the immortals when that word was brought!
RICHARD WATSON GILDER, *Keats.*

Lo! in the moonlight gleams a marble white,
On which I read: "Here lieth one whose name
Was writ in water." And was this the meed
Of his sweet singing? Rather let me write:
"The smoking flax before it burst to flame
Was quenched by death, and broken the bruised reed."
LONGFELLOW, *Keats.*

1
Below lies one whose name was traced in sand.
DAVID GRAY, *His Own Epitaph.*

Even Keats's epitaph—*Here lies one whose name was writ in water*—finds an echo in David Gray's *Below lies one whose name was traced in sand.* Poor Gray was at least the better prophet.
T. B. ALDRICH, *Ponkapog Papers*, p. 121.

2
Your fame shall (spite of proverbs) make it plain
To write in water's not to write in vain.
UNKNOWN, *Lines.* (SIR WILLIAM SANDERSON, *Art of Painting in Water Colours: Preface.*)

KENTUCKY

3
There are children lucky from dawn till dusk,
But never a child so lucky!
For I cut my teeth on "Money Musk"
In the Bloody Ground of Kentucky!
S. V. BENÉT, *The Ballad of William Sycamore.*

4
She was bred in old Kentucky,
Where the meadow grass is blue,
There's the sunshine of the country
In her face and manner, too;
She was bred in old Kentucky,
Take her, boy, you're mighty lucky,
When you marry a girl like Sue.
HARRY BRAISTED, *She Was Bred in Old Kentucky.* (1898)

5
Yo' is mighty lucky, babe of old Kentucky.
RICHARD HENRY BUCK, *Kentucky Babe.*

6
Weep no more, my lady,
Oh! weep no more to-day!
We will sing one song for the old Kentucky Home,
For the old Kentucky Home far away.
STEPHEN COLLINS FOSTER, *My Old Kentucky Home.*

7
But I ran in Kentucky hills
Last week. They were hearth and home.
VACHEL LINDSAY, *My Fathers Came from Kentucky.*

8
The moonlight is the softest, in Kentucky;
Summer days come oftest, in Kentucky;
Friendship is the strongest,
Love's fires glow the longest,
Yet a wrong is always wrongest,
In Kentucky.
JAMES H. MULLIGAN, *In Kentucky.*

Here's a health to old Kentucky,
Where the fathers, through the years,
Hand down the courtly graces
To the sons of cavaliers;
Where the golden age is regnant,
And each succeeding morn
Finds "the corn is full of kernels,
And the Colonels full of corn."
WILLIAM J. LAMPTON, *To Old Kentucky.* St. 7.

Here's to old Kentucky,
The State where I was born,
Where the corn is full of kernels,
And the Colonels full of "corn."
UNKNOWN, *A Kentucky Toast.* (COMBS, *All That's Kentucky.*)

9
Sons of the Dark and Bloody Ground.
THEODORE O'HARA, *The Bivouac of the Dead.*

That beautiful region which was soon to verify its Indian appellation of the dark and bloody ground.
C. J. LATROBE, *Rambles in North America*, i, 90. The Cherokee word "kentucke" meant simply a meadow or prairie.

KICK

10
It is hard for thee to kick against the pricks.
New Testament: Acts, ix, 5; xxvi, 14.

If you beat goads with your fists, your hands suffer most. (Si stimulos pugnis cædis, manibus plus dolet.)
PLAUTUS, *Truculentus.* Act iv, sc. 2, l. 55.
See also under RESIGNATION.

11
It is human nature to kick a fallen man. ("Ωστε σύγγονον βροτοῖσι τὸν πεσόντα λακτίσαι πλέον.)
ÆSCHYLUS, *Agamemnon*, l. 884.

12
And out of the window he flew like a shot,
For the foot went up with a terrible thwack,
And caught the foul demon about the spot
Where his tail joins on to the small of his back.
R. H. BARHAM, *A Lay of St Nicholas.*

13
But Hudibras gave him a twitch
As quick as lightning in the breech,
Just in the place where honour's lodg'd,
As wise philosophers have judg'd;
Because a kick in that part more
Hurts honour than deep wounds before.
BUTLER, *Hudibras.* Pt. ii, canto iii, l. 1065.

14
A kick that scarce would move a horse,
May kill a sound divine.
COWPER, *Yearly Distress.* St. 16.

15
I am going to be an absolute wreck astern. (Puppis pereunda est probe.)
PLAUTUS, *Epidicus*, l. 74. (Act i, sc. 1.)

1
I should kick. being kick'd.
SHAKESPEARE, *The Comedy of Errors*. Act iii, sc. 1, l. 17.

2
Pitt kicked the bucket.
JOHN WOLCOT, *Works*, v, 242. (1796)

To kick the bucket, an unfeeling phrase for to die.
CARR, *Craven Dialect*, i, 55.

Despondency may make you kick the beam and the bucket both at once.
THOMAS HOOD, *Hood's Own*. Ser. i, No. 5. (1838)

3
When late I attempted your pity to move,
Why seemed you so deaf to my prayers?
Perhaps it was right to dissemble your love,
But—why should you kick me downstairs?
UNKNOWN. Published anonymously in *An Asylum for Fugitive Pieces*. Vol. i, p. 15. (1785) Quoted by John Philip Kemble, in his play, *The Panel*. Act i, sc. 1. (1788) He is sometimes credited with the authorship of the lines.

KINDNESS

I—Kindness: Apothegms

4
Kindness is wisdom. There is none in life
But needs it and may learn.
P. J. BAILEY, *Festus: Home*.

Both man and womankind belie their nature
When they are not kind.
P. J. BAILEY, *Festus: Home*.

5
'Twas her thinking of others made you think of her.
E. B. BROWNING, *My Kate*.

6
'Twas a thief said the last kind word to Christ:
Christ took the kindness and forgave the theft.
ROBERT BROWNING, *The Ring and the Book*. Pt. vi, l. 869.

7
With the sweet milk of human kindness bless'd.
CHARLES CHURCHILL, *Epistle to William Hogarth*, l. 57. (1762)

Feels the same comfort while his acrid words
Turn the sweet milk of kindness into curds.
O. W. HOLMES, *The Moral Bully*.

But what the better are their pious saws
To ailing souls, than dry hee-haws,
Without the milk of human kindness?
THOMAS HOOD, *Ode to Rae Wilson*, l. 494.

To rankling poison hast thou turned in me the milk of human kindness. (In gährend Drachengift hast du Die Milch der frommen Denkart mir verwandelt.)
SCHILLER, *Wilhelm Tell*. Act iv, sc. 3.

Yet I do fear thy nature;
It is too full o' the milk of human kindness
To catch the nearest way.
SHAKESPEARE, *Macbeth*. Act i, sc. 5, l. 17. (1606)

8
Nothing is so popular as kindness. (Nihil est tam populare quam bonitas.)
CICERO, *Pro Ligario*. Sec. 12.

9
A kind heart loseth nought at last.
JOHN CLARKE, *Parœmiologia*, 45.

10
O wouldst thou be less killing, soft or kind.
CONGREVE, *The Mourning Bride*. Act iii, sc. 6.

11
Good Will is the mightiest practical force in the universe.
C. F. DOLE, *Cleveland Address*.

12
Are you tender and scrupulous,—you must eat more mince-pie.
EMERSON, *Representative Men: Montaigne*.

13
Enough, and more than enough, has your kindness enriched me. (Satis superque me benignitas tua Ditavit.)
HORACE, *Epodes*. No. i, l. 31.

For tho' the faults were thick as dust
In vacant chambers, I could trust
Your kindness.
TENNYSON, *To the Queen*. St. 5.

14
Kindness is the sunshine in which virtue grows.
R. G. INGERSOLL, *A Lay Sermon*.

15
Kindness consists in loving people more than they deserve. (Une partie de la bonté consiste peut-être à estimer et à aimer les gens plus qu'ils ne le méritent.)
JOUBERT, *Pensées*. No. 71.

16
Though he was rough, he was kindly.
LONGFELLOW, *Courtship of Miles Standish*. Pt. iii.

17
I would resemble the ape, and kill it by cullyng it.
JOHN LYLY, *Euphues*, p. 215. (1579)

With kindness, lo, the ape doth kill her whelp.
GEOFFREY WHITNEY, *Choice of Emblems*, 188.

She killeth what she loveth by pressing it too hard.
EDWARD TOPSELL, *Four-footed Beasts*.

This is the way to kill a wife with kindness.
SHAKESPEARE, *The Taming of the Shrew*. Act iv, sc. 1, l. 211.

18
The greater the kindred is, the less the kindness.
JOHN LYLY, *Mother Bombie*. Act iii, sc. 1.

A little more than kin, and less than kind.
SHAKESPEARE, *Hamlet*. Act i, sc. 2, l. 65.

19
Then within my bosom
Softly this I heard:
"Each heart holds the secret;
Kindness is the word."
JOHN BOYLE O'REILLY, *What Is Good?*

1
Not always actions show the man: we find
Who does a kindness is not therefore kind.
Pope, *Moral Essays*. Epis. i, l. 109.

2
In her tongue is the law of kindness.
Old Testament: Proverbs, xxxi, 26.

3
That tender education which we call kindness, destroys all the vigor of both mind and body. (Mollis illa educatio quam indulgentiam vocamus, nervos omnes et mentis et corporis frangit.)
Quintilian, *Institutione de Oratoria*. Bk. i, ch. 2, sec. 6.

4
For your kindness I owe you a good turn.
Shakespeare, *Measure for Measure*, iv, 2, 62.

A kind overflow of kindness.
Shakespeare, *Much Ado About Nothing*, i, 1, 26.

5
Timon will to the woods; where he shall find
The unkindest beast more kinder than mankind.
Shakespeare, *Timon of Athens*, iv, 1, 35.

Ah yet, we cannot be kind to each other here for an hour.
Tennyson, *Maud*. Pt. i, sec. 4, st. 5.

6
Kindness is ever the begetter of kindness. (Χάρις χάριν γάρ ἐστιν ἡ τίκτουσ' ἀεί.)
Sophocles, *Ajax*, l. 522.

Kindness is produced by kindness. (Benignitate benignitas tollitur.)
Cicero, *De Officiis*. Bk. ii, ch. 15, sec. 52.

7
And loving-kindness, that is pity's kin
And is most pitiless.
Swinburne, *A Ballad of Life*. St. 2.

8
Kindness is very indigestible. It disagrees with very proud stomachs.
Thackeray, *Adventures of Philip*. Bk. ii, ch. 6.

9
Animosities are mortal, but the Humanities live for ever.
John Wilson, *Noctes Ambrosianæ*. No. 35.

II—Kindness: Its Virtues

10
Life is short, and we have never too much time for gladdening the hearts of those who are travelling the dark journey with us. Oh, be swift to love, make haste to be kind!
Amiel, *Journal*, 16 Dec., 1868.

11
The heart benevolent and kind
The most resembles God.
Robert Burns, *A Winter Night*.

12
Have you had a kindness shown?
Pass it on;
'Twas not given for thee alone,
Pass it on;
Let it travel down the years,
Let it wipe another's tears,
'Till in Heaven the deed appears—
Pass it on.
Henry Burton, *Pass It On*.

13
Set not thy foot to make the blind to fall;
Nor wilfully offend thy weaker brother:
Nor wound the dead with thy tongue's bitter gall,
Neither rejoice thou in the fall of other.
Robert Burton, *Anatomy of Melancholy*. Pt. i, sec. ii, mem. 4, subs. 4. A footnote states this is from "Pybrac in his Quadrant 37."

14
Thy Godlike crime was to be kind,
To render with thy precepts less
The sum of human wretchedness.
Byron, *Prometheus*, l. 35.

15
Little deeds of kindness,
Little words of love,
Help to make earth happy
Like the Heaven above.
Julia Fletcher Carney, *Little Things*.

16
It is difficult to say how much men's minds are conciliated by a kind manner and gentle speech. (Sed tamen difficile dictu est, quantopere conciliet animos comitas affabilitasque sermonis.)
Cicero, *De Officiis*. Bk. ii, ch. 14, sec. 48.

Kindness to the good is a better investment than kindness to the rich. (Quam ob rem melius apud bonos quam apud fortunatos beneficium collocari puto.)
Cicero, *De Officiis*. Bk. ii, ch. xx, sec. 71.

17
If I can stop one heart from breaking,
I shall not live in vain;
If I can ease one life the aching,
Or cool one pain,
Or help one fainting robin
Unto his nest again,
I shall not live in vain.
Emily Dickinson, *Poems*. Pt. i, No. 6.

Let me be a little kinder,
Let me be a little blinder
To the faults of those around me.
Edgar A. Guest, *A Creed*.

18
Yet still he fills affection's eye,
Obscurely wise, and coarsely kind.
Samuel Johnson, *On the Death of Dr. Robert Levet*.

19
There's no dearth of kindness
In this world of ours;
Only in our blindness
We gather thorns for flowers.
Gerald Massey, *No Dearth of Kindness*.

20
Persistent kindness conquers the ill-disposed. (Vincit malos pertinax bonitas.)
Seneca, *De Beneficiis*. Bk. vii, sec. 31.

1
Kindness, nobler ever than revenge.
SHAKESPEARE, *As You Like It*. Act iv, sc. 3, 129.

When your head did but ache,
I knit my handkerchief about your brows,
The best I had, a princess wrought it me,
And I did never ask it you again;
And with my hand at midnight held your head,
And like the watchful minutes to the hour,
Still and anon cheer'd up the heavy time,
Saying "What lack you?" and "Where lies your grief?"
SHAKESPEARE, *King John*. Act iv, sc. 1, l. 41.

2
The kindest man,
The best-condition'd and unwearied spirit
In doing courtesies.
SHAKESPEARE, *Merchant of Venice*, iii, 2, 295.

O do not slander him, for he is kind.
SHAKESPEARE, *Richard III*. Act i, sc. 4, l. 247.

3
Kindness in women, not their beauteous looks,
Shall win my love.
SHAKESPEARE, *Taming of the Shrew*, iv, 2, 41.

And thy despised disdain too late shall find
That none are fair but who are kind.
THOMAS STANLEY, *The Deposition*.

4
For he was kind and she was kind,
And who so blest as they?
SOUTHEY, *Rudiger*, l. 47.

4a
So many gods, so many creeds,
So many paths that wind and wind,
While just the art of being kind
Is all the sad world needs.
ELLA WHEELER WILCOX, *The World's Need*.

5
Fierce for the right, he bore his part
In strife with many a valiant foe;
But Laughter winged his polished dart,
And kindness tempered every blow.
WILLIAM WINTER, *I. H. Bromley*.

Surely never did there live on earth
A man of kindlier nature.
WORDSWORTH, *The Excursion*, Bk. i, l. 414.

6
That best portion of a good man's life,
His little, nameless, unremembered acts
Of kindness and of love.
WORDSWORTH, *Lines Composed a Few Miles Above Tintern Abbey*, l. 33.

Nor greetings where no kindness is, nor all
The dreary intercourse of daily life.
WORDSWORTH, *Tintern Abbey*, l. 130.

KINGS

See also Crown, Prince, Throne

I—Kings: Apothegms

7
Our converse with kings should be either as rare, or as pleasing, as possible.
ÆSOP, to Solon, who had been banished by Crœsus. To which Solon replied, "No, indeed! as rare or as *beneficial* as possible." (PLUTARCH, *Lives: Solon*. Sec. 28.)

8
For commonly it is said that a king without letter or cunning is compared to an ass crowned.
BERNERS, *Huon*, 730. (c. 1534)

An unlettered king is a crowned ass.
EDWARD FREEMAN, *Norman Conquest*. Vol. ii, p. 277.

9
God bless the King, I mean the faith's defender,
God bless (no harm in blessing) the Pretender,
But who pretender is or who is king,
God bless us all—that's quite another thing.
JOHN BYROM, *Extempore to an Officer in the Army*.

10
King is Kön-ning, Kan-ning, Man that knows or cans.
CARLYLE, *Heroes and Hero-Worship: The Hero as Divinity*.

11
The king's leavings are better than the lord's bounty.
CERVANTES, *Don Quixote*. Pt. i, ch. 39.

Better to die a king than to live a prince.
NAPOLEON BONAPARTE, to his brother, Louis, when the latter urged his ill health against taking the crown of Holland.

For a King, death is better than dethronement and exile.
Attributed to THEODORA, wife of Justinian I.

12
To be a kingdom's bulwark, a king's glory,
Yet loved by both, and trusted and trustworthy,
Is more than to be king.
S. T. COLERIDGE, *Zapolya*. Sc. i.

13
One who has given you more kingdoms than you had towns before.
CORTEZ, to Charles V., when the latter demanded who he was. (VOLTAIRE, *Essai sur les Mœurs*. Ch. 147.) Prescott calls it a "most improbable story." (*Conquest of Mexico*, vii, 5, note.)

14
I would not be a king to be belov'd
Causeless, and daub'd with undiscerning praise.
COWPER, *The Task*. Bk. v, l. 359.

15
Royalty is but a feather in a man's cap: let children enjoy their rattle.
OLIVER CROMWELL, when rejecting the offer of the title of king, in 1658.

What shall we do with the bauble? Take it away!
OLIVER CROMWELL, picking up the mace, when dissolving the Long Parliament, 20 April, 1653. (CARLYLE, *Cromwell*.)

A prince, the moment he is crown'd,
Inherits every virtue sound,
As emblems of the sovereign power,
Like other baubles in the Tower:

Is generous, valiant, just, and wise,
And so continues till he dies.
SWIFT, *On Poetry*, l. 191.

1
A King's a King, do Fortune what she can.
MICHAEL DRAYTON, *Barons' War*. Bk. v, st. 36.

2
Kind as kings upon their coronation day.
DRYDEN, *The Hind and the Panther*. Pt. i, l. 271.

3
A man's a man,
But when you see a king, you see the work
Of many thousand men.
GEORGE ELIOT, *Spanish Gypsy*. Bk. i.

4
If the king is in the palace, nobody looks at the walls.
EMERSON, *Essays, Second Series: Nature*.

5
They are not kings who sit on thrones, but they who know how to govern.
EMERSON, *Society and Solitude: Eloquence*.

This 'tis to be a monarch when alone
He can command all, but is awed by none.
MASSINGER, *The Roman Actor*. Act i, sc. 4.

6
A king's favour is no inheritance.
THOMAS FULLER, *Gnomologia*. No. 4618.

7
The sun has set; no night has followed. (Sol occubuit; nox nulla secuta est.)
GIRALDUS DE BARRI, in 1189, referring to the accession of Richard I, Cœur-de-Lion, to the throne of England on the death of Henry II.

8
Beware, for dreadful is the wrath of kings.
HOMER, *Iliad*. Bk. ii, l. 234. (Pope, tr.)

The wrath of kings is always heavy. (Gravis ira regum est semper.)
SENECA, *Medea*, l. 494.

9
There is no king who has not had a slave among his ancestors, and no slave who has not had a king among his.
HELEN KELLER, *Story of My Life*, p. 4.

10
Who knows not that the king is a name of dignity and office, not of person?
MILTON, *Tenure of Kings and Magistrates*.

11
King David and King Solomon
Led merry, merry lives,
With many, many lady friends,
And many, many wives;
But when old age crept over them,
With many, many qualms,
King Solomon wrote the Proverbs
And King David wrote the Psalms.
JAMES BALL NAYLOR, *David and Solomon*.

12
For the Island's sons the word still runs,
"The King, and the King's Highway."
HENRY NEWBOLT, *The King's Highway*.

13
Know you not that kings have long hands? (An nescis longos regibus esse manus?)
OVID, *Heroides*. Epis. xvii, l. 166.

Kings are commonly said to have long hands; I wish they had as long ears.
SWIFT, *Thoughts on Various Subjects*.

14
Honour the king.
New Testament: I Peter, ii, 17.

15
The more regal king of kings. (Regum rex reglior.)
PLAUTUS, *Captivi*, l. 825.

16
He that eats the king's goose shall be choked with his feathers.
RICHARDSON, *Clarissa Harlowe*, iv, 243.

17
The king is not the nation's representative, but its clerk.
ROBESPIERRE, *Speech*, National Assembly, 17 May, 1790.

I am indeed the clerk (*commis*) and the explorer (*voyageur*) of democracy.
GAMBETTA, *Speech*, Havre, 18 April, 1872, accepting the nickname of "Commercial Traveler" (*Commis-voyageur*), which had been given him because of the rapidity of his movements during the war.

18
O Richard! O my king, the universe forsakes thee!
On earth there is none but I who cares for thy welfare.
(O Richard! O mon roy, l'univers t'abandonne!
Sur la terre il n'est que moy qui s'interesse de tes affaires.)
MICHEL JEAN SEDAINE, *Richard Cœur-de-Lion: Blondel's Song*. The singing of this song at the dinner given at Versailles, 1 Oct., 1789, by the King and Marie Antoinette was a famous episode in French history. (See CARLYLE, *French Revolution*. Pt. i, bk. vii, ch. 2.)

19
It is superior to all, monarch of all it surveys. (Dominus omnium est, supra omnia est.)
SENECA, *Epistulæ ad Lucilium*. Epis. civ, 24.

I am monarch of all I survey,
My right there is none to dispute;
From the center all round to the sea,
I am lord of the fowl and the brute.
COWPER, *Verses Supposed to be Written by Alexander Selkirk*.

20
On alien soil, kingship stands not sure. (Alieno in loco Haut stabile regnum est.)
SENECA, *Hercules Furens*, l. 344.

Stolen sceptres are held in anxious hands. (Rapta sed trepidu manu Sceptre obtinentur.)
SENECA, *Hercules Furens*, l. 341.

21
The king's a beggar, now the play is done.
SHAKESPEARE, *All's Well that Ends Well: Epilogue*, l. 335.

1
A king of shreds and patches.
SHAKESPEARE, *Hamlet*. Act iii, sc. 4, l. 102.

The theory of the world is a thing of shreds and patches.
EMERSON, *Representative Men: Plato*. (1850) The phrase, "A thing of shreds and patches," was echoed many years later by W. S. GILBERT in the first act of *The Mikado*. See 1879:3.

2
Proud setter up and puller down of kings!
SHAKESPEARE, *III Henry VI*. Act iii, sc. 3, 157.

3
Ay, every inch a king.
SHAKESPEARE, *King Lear*. Act iv, sc. 6, l. 109.

4
O that I were a mockery king of snow,
Standing before the sun of Bolingbroke,
To melt myself away in water-drops!
SHAKESPEARE, *Richard II*. Act iv, sc. 1, l. 260.

5
Hail, glorious edifice, stupendous work!
God bless the Regent, and the Duke of York!
HORACE AND JAMES SMITH, *Loyal Effusion*.

6
Kinquering Congs their titles take.
WILLIAM A. SPOONER, Warden of New College, Oxford, announcing the hymn, "Conquering Kings their titles take," early in 1879. Hence, "spoonerisms," most of which were the inventions of Dr. Spooner's friends.

7
A brave man, were he seven times king,
Is but a brave man's peer.
A. C. SWINBURNE, *Marino Faliero*. Act ii, sc. 2.

8
He who knows not how to dissimulate knows not how to reign. (Qui nescit dissimulare, nescit regnare.)
VINCENTIUS LUPANUS. (JUSTUS LIPSIUS, *Politica Sive Civilis Doctrina*. Bk. iv, ch. 14.) Sometimes given as a saying of Emperor Frederick I (Barbarossa), Louis XII and Philip II of Spain. Tacitus (*Annals*. Bk. iv, ch. 71), speaking of Tiberius, says, "He was prouder of his dissimulation than of all his other virtues; for such he considered it." One of the favorite maxims of Louis IX of France, and all the Latin he thought the Dauphin needed to learn. (DE THOU, *Hist. Univ.*, iii, 293.)

He who knows not how to dissimulate, knows not how to reign.
LOUIS XI OF FRANCE. (ROCHE ET CHASLES, *Histoire de France*. Vol. ii, p. 30.)

To know how to dissimulate is the knowledge of kings. (Savoir dissimuler est le savoir des rois.)
CARDINAL RICHELIEU, *Miranne*.

9
The first king was a successful soldier. (Le premier qui fut roi, fut un soldat heureux.)
VOLTAIRE, *Mérope*. Act i, sc. 3.

What can they see in the longest kingly line in Europe, save that it runs back to a successful soldier?
SCOTT, *Woodstock*. Ch. 37.

10
Every one is born a king, and most people die in exile.
OSCAR WILDE, *A Woman of No Importance*. Act iii.

11
The king reigns but does not govern. (Rex regnat sed non gubernat.)
JAN ZAMOISKA, *Speech*, at the Diet of 1605, alluding to King Sigismund III.

The king reigns but does not govern. (Der König herrscht aber regiert nicht.)
BISMARCK, *Debate*, Reichstag, 24 Jan., 1882. Bismarck quoted this proverb in order to deny its application to Germany.

She governed but she did not reign. (Elle gouvernait, mais elle ne régnait pas.)
HÉNAULT, *Memoirs*, p. 161, referring to Madame des Ursins, the favorite of Philip V of Spain.

The king reigns, but does not govern. (Le roi régne, il ne gouverne pas.)
LOUIS ADOLPHE THIERS, *Editorial Article*, in *Le Nationale*, a newspaper of which he was editor, Paris, 18 January, 1830.

II—Kings: The Good King

12
'Tis clemency which is the surest mark
By which the world may know a true monarch.
(La clémence est la plus belle marque
Qui fasse à l'univers connaître un vrai monarcque.)
CORNEILLE, *Cinna*. Act iv, sc. 4.

13
We, too, are friends to loyalty. We love
The king who loves the law, respects his bounds,
And reigns content within them. Him we serve
Freely and with delight, who leaves us free.
COWPER, *The Task*. Bk. v, l. 331.

14
The clearest mark of a true king is that he is one whom all good men can praise without compunction not only during his life, but even afterwards.
DIO CHRYSOSTOM, *First Discourse on Kingship*. Sec. 33.

15
A king so good, so just, so great,
That at his birth the heavenly council paused
And then at last cried out, This is a man!
DRYDEN, *The Duke of Guise*. Act i, sc. 1. *See also under* MAN.

16
A good king is a public servant.
BEN JONSON, *Explorata*.

17
For therein stands the office of a king,
His honour, virtue, merit, and chief praise,
That for the public all this weight he bears.
MILTON, *Paradise Regained*. Bk. ii, l. 463.

18
It is something to hold the scepter with a firm

hand. (Est aliquid valida sceptra tenere manu.)
OVID, *Remediorum Amoris*, l. 480.

1
Nothing becomes a king so much as the administration of justice. War is a tyrant, as Timotheus expresses it, but Pindar says, Justice is the rightful sovereign of the world.
PLUTARCH, *Lives: Demetrius*. Ch. 42, sec. 5.

2
'Twere good That kings should think withal,
When peace and wealth their land has blessed,
'Tis better to sit still at rest,
Than rise, perchance to fall.
SCOTT, *Marmion*. Canto iv, st. 29.

3
A king is he who has no fear; a king is he who desires naught. (Rex est qui metuit nihil; Rex est qui cupiet nihil.)
SENECA, *Thyestes*, l. 388.

4
I made them lay their hands in mine and swear
To reverence the King, as if he were
Their conscience, and their conscience as their King.
TENNYSON, *Guinevere*, l. 463.

III—Kings: Their Virtues

5
These unhappy kings, of whom so much evil is said, have their good points sometimes. (Ces malheureux rois Dont on dit tant de mal, ont du bon quelquefois.)
ANDRIEUX, *Meunier de Sans Souci*.

6
To do well and be ill spoken of—'tis the lot of kings. (Βασιλικὸν μὲν εὖ πράττειν, κακῶς δὲ ἀκούειν.)
ANTISTHENES. (MARCUS AURELIUS, *Meditations*. Bk. vii, sec. 36; DIOGENES LAERTIUS, *Antisthenes*. Sec. 3.) Sometimes translated: 'It is a royal privilege to do well and be ill-spoken of." Alexander the Great quoted this apothegm. (PLUTARCH, *Lives: Alexander*. Ch. 41, sec. 1.) Carlyle saw it written in Latin on the town-hall of Zittau, Germany: "Bene facere et male audire regium est." (CARLYLE, *Frederick the Great*, xv, 13.)

'Tis the first art of kings, the power to suffer hate. (Ars prima regni est posse invidiam pati.)
SENECA, *Hercules Furens*, l. 353.

7
He is the fountain of honour.
FRANCIS BACON, *Of a King*.

8
And in the years he reigned, through all the country wide,
There was no cause for weeping, save when the good man died.
(Ce n'est que lorsqu'il expira
Que le peuple, qui l'enterra, pleura.)
BÉRANGER, *Le Roi Yvetot*. (Thackeray, tr., *The King of Brentford*.)

So sit two kings of Brentford on one throne;
And so two citizens who take the air,
Close pack'd, and smiling, in a chaise and one.
COWPER, *The Task*. Bk. i, l. 78.

9
He errs who thinks that life under a noble prince is slavery; never does liberty appear more fair than under a righteous king. (Fallitur egregio quisquis sub principe credit Servitium. Numquam libertas gratior extat Quam sub rege pio.)
CLAUDIAN, *De Consulatu Stilichonis*. Bk. iii, l. 113.

10
Whoever is king, is also the father of his country.
CONGREVE, *Love for Love: Dedication*. *See also under* PATRIOTISM.

11
The king's word is more than another man's oath.
PRINCESS ELIZABETH. (ELLIS, *Original Letters*, Ser. ii, p. 255. 1554.) Cited as "this old saying."

A king's word must stand. (Verbum regis stet oportet.)
BISHOP JOHN FISHER, *English Works*, p. 230. (1509) Cited as "a common proverb."

A King's word should be a King's bond.
UNKNOWN, *Sir Lancelot du Lake*, l. 1673. (c. 1490)

12
If fidelity were lost, it should be found in the heart of a king.
FRANCIS I OF FRANCE. (*L'Esprit dans l'Histoire*, 113.)

Though good faith should be banished from the rest of the world, it should be found in the mouths of kings. (Si la bonne foi était bannie du reste du monde, il faudrait qu'on la trouvât dans la bouche des rois.)
JEAN II OF FRANCE, speaking to his council. (*Biographie Universelle*.)

13
There was a king of Thule,
Was faithful till the grave,
To whom his mistress dying,
A golden goblet gave.
(Es war ein König in Tule
Gar treu bis an das Grab,
Dem sterbend seine Buhle
Einen gold'nen Becher gab.)
GOETHE, *Faust: The King of Thule*. (Bayard Taylor, tr.)

14
The virtue of kings seems to consist chiefly in justice. (La vertu royale semble consister le plus en la justice.)
MONTAIGNE, *Essays*. Bk. iii, ch. 6.

15
The Monarch drank, that happy hour,
The sweetest, holiest draught of Power.
SCOTT, *Lady of the Lake*. Canto vi, st. 28.

16
Pre-eminence, and all the large effects

That troop with majesty.
SHAKESPEARE, *King Lear*. Act i, sc. 1, l. 133.

The king-becoming graces,
As justice, verity, temperance, stableness,
Bounty, perseverance, mercy, lowliness,
Devotion, patience, courage, fortitude.
SHAKESPEARE, *Macbeth*. Act iv, sc. 3, l. 91.

Yet looks he like a king; behold, his eye,
As bright as is the eagle's, lightens forth
Controlling majesty.
SHAKESPEARE, *Richard II*. Act iii, sc. 3, l. 68.

1
Not making his high place the lawless perch
Of wing'd ambitions, nor a vantage-ground
For pleasure; but thro' all this tract of years
Wearing the white flower of a blameless life,
Before a thousand peering littlenesses.
TENNYSON, *Idylls of the King: Dedication*, l. 21.

IV—Kings: Their Faults

2
For this is the true strength of guilty kings,
When they corrupt the souls of those they rule.
MATTHEW ARNOLD, *Merope*, l. 1451.

3
Kings, that made laws, first broke them.
APHRA BEHN, *The Golden Age*. St. 4.

A king promises, but observes only when he pleases.
H. G. BOHN, *Hand-Book of Proverbs*, 292.

4
Kings are naturally lovers of low company.
EDMUND BURKE, *Speech*, House of Commons, 11 Feb., 1780.

5
The animal known as king is by nature carnivorous. ('Αλλὰ φύσει τοῦτο τὸ ζῷον ὁ βασιλεὺς σαρκοφάγον ἐστίν.)
MARCUS CATO. (PLUTARCH, *Lives: Marcus Cato*. Ch. viii, sec. 8.)

6
Kings climb to eminence
Over men's graves.
AUSTIN DOBSON, *Before Sedan*.

7
But though each court a jester lacks,
To laugh at monarchs to their face;
All mankind do behind their backs
Supply the honest jester's place.
ROBERT DODSLEY, *The Kings of Europe*.

8
Kings fight for kingdoms, madmen for applause.
DRYDEN, *Palamon and Arcite*. Bk. ii, l. 322.

And Tom the second reigns like Tom the first.
DRYDEN, *To Mr. Congreve*, l. 48.

9
God said, "I am tired of kings,
I suffer them no more;
Up to my ear the morning brings
The outrage of the poor."
EMERSON, *Boston Hymn*.

The world is growing weary of that most costly of all luxuries, hereditary kings.
GEORGE BANCROFT, *Letter*, London, March, 1848.

And when Reason's voice,
Loud as the voice of Nature, shall have waked
The nations, . . . kingly glare
Will lose its power to dazzle; . . . whilst falsehood's trade
Shall be as hateful and unprofitable
As that of truth is now.
SHELLEY, *Queen Mab*. Pt. iii, l. 126.

The passing poor magnificence of kings.
JAMES THOMSON, *Liberty*. Pt. iii, l. 555.

10
Kingship is passing down the yellow road,
And crowns are dangling from the willow tree;
Royalty flees to seek a last abode
With the other outcasts of eternity.
DONALD EVANS, *Bonfire of Kings*.

11
Kings govern by means of popular assemblies only when they cannot do without them.
CHARLES JAMES FOX, *Speech*, House of Commons, 31 Oct., 1776.

12
Ruin seize thee, ruthless king!
Confusion on thy banners wait;
Tho' fann'd by Conquest's crimson wing,
They mock the air with idle state.
THOMAS GRAY, *The Bard*, l. 1.

As yourselves your empires fall,
And every kingdom hath a grave.
WILLIAM HABINGTON, *Night*.

13
Deceived for once, I trust not kings again.
HOMER, *Iliad*. Bk. ix, l. 455. (Pope, tr.)

14
Whatever folly kings commit, the people suffer. (Quidquid delirant reges, plectuntur Atriden.)
HORACE, *Epistles*. Bk. i, epis. 2, l. 14.

15
Presently the kingly pile will leave but few acres to the plough. (Jam pauca aratro jugera regiæ Moles relinquent.)
HORACE, *Odes*. Bk. ii, ode 15, l. 1.

When kings are building, draymen have something to do. (Wenn die Könige bau'n, haben die Kärrner zu thun.)
SCHILLER, *Kant und Seine Ausleger*.

16
If any of our countrymen wish for a king, give them Æsop's fable of the frogs who asked a King; if this does not cure them, send them to Europe. They will go back republicans.
THOMAS JEFFERSON, *Writings*. Vol. vi, p. 225.

17
The trappings of a monarchy would set up an ordinary republic.
SAMUEL JOHNSON, *Lives of the Poets: Milton*. Johnson places this sentence in quotation marks, but it is not found in Milton's works. It is, perhaps, a paraphrase of Milton's arguments in *A Ready and Easy Way*.

1
Step by step and word by word: who is ruled may read.
Suffer not the old Kings: for we know the breed.
RUDYARD KIPLING, *The Old Issue.*

2
Ah! vainest of all things
Is the gratitude of kings.
LONGFELLOW, *Belisarius.* St. 8.

3
We hardly know any instance of the strength and weakness of human nature so striking and so grotesque as the character of this haughty, vigilant, resolute, sagacious blue-stocking, half Mithridates and half Trissotin, bearing up against a world in arms, with an ounce of poison in one pocket and a quire of bad verses in the other.
MACAULAY, *Essays: Frederick the Great.*

4
First Moloch, horrid King, besmear'd with blood.
MILTON, *Paradise Lost.* Bk. i, l. 392.

5
Kings most commonly, though strong in legions, are but weak in arguments.
MILTON, *Tenure of Kings and Magistrates.*

6
Scratch a king and find a fool!
DOROTHY PARKER, *Salome's Dancing Lesson.*

7
Good men are always more suspected by kings than bad; and virtue in other men is always to them a terrible thing. (Regibus boni quam mali suspectiores sunt; semperque eis aliena virtus formidulosa est.)
SALLUST, *Catilina.* Ch. vii, sec. 2.

8
No more pleasing blood has stained the altars . . . than that of an unjust king. (Gratior nullus liquor Tinxisset aras . . . Quam rex iniquus.)
SENECA, *Hercules Furens,* l. 921.

It is impossible to reign innocently. (On ne peut régner innocemment.)
ANTOINE SAINT-JUST, beginning his speech on the sentence of Louis XVI.

A dead king is not a man less.
CAMILLE DESMOULINS, voting for the death of Louis XVI.

9
By blood a king, at heart a clown.
TENNYSON, *In Memoriam.* Pt. cxi, st. 1.

10
All kings is mostly rapscallions.
MARK TWAIN, *Huckleberry Finn.* Ch. 23.

V—Kings: Their Trials

11
Ten poor men sleep in peace on one straw heap, as Saadi sings,
But the immensest empire is too narrow for two kings.
W. R. ALGER, *Oriental Poetry: Elbow Room.*

12
It is a miserable state of mind, to have few things to desire and many things to fear: and yet that commonly is the case of Kings.
FRANCIS BACON, *Essays: Of Empire.*

13
Ah, monarchs! could ye taste the mirth ye mar,
Not in the toils of Glory would ye fret;
The hoarse dull drum would sleep, and man be happy yet.
BYRON, *Childe Harold.* Canto i, st. 47.

For a king
'Tis sometimes better to be fear'd than loved.
BYRON, *Sardanapalus.* Act i, sc. 3.

14
Whilst doubts assailed him o'er and o'er again,
If men were made for kings, or kings for men.
CAMPBELL, *The Pilgrim of Glencoe,* l. 164.

15
The vices of kings cannot remain hid, for the splendor of their lofty station permits naught to be concealed. (Nec posse dari regalibus usquam Secretum vitiis; nam lux altissima fati Occultum nihil est sinit.)
CLAUDIAN, *Panegyricus de Quarto Consulatu Honorii Augusti,* l, 272.

Kings' misdeeds cannot be hid in clay.
SHAKESPEARE, *The Rape of Lucrece,* l. 609.

'Tis so much to be a king, that he only is so by being so. The strange lustre that surrounds him conceals and shrouds him from us; our sight is there broken and dissipated, being stopped and filled by the prevailing light.
MONTAIGNE, *Essays.* Bk. iii, ch. 7.

In that fierce light which beats upon a throne
And blackens every blot.
TENNYSON, *Idylls of the King: Dedication,* 26.

16
If monarchy consists in such base things,
Sighing, I say again, I pity kings!
COWPER, *Table Talk,* l. 139.

God's pity on poor kings,
They know no gentle rest;
The North and South cry out,
Cries come from East and West—

"Come, open this new Dock,
Building, Bazaar, or Fair."
Lord, what a wretched life
Such men must bear.
WILLIAM H. DAVIES, *Poor Kings.*

When in green lanes I muse,
Alone, and hear birds sing,
God's pity then, say I,
On some poor king.
WILLIAM H. DAVIES, *Poor Kings.*

If happy I and wretched he,
Perhaps the king would change with me.
CHARLES MACKAY, *Differences.*

17
The king is the least independent man in his dominions; the beggar the most so.
J. C. AND A. W. HARE, *Guesses at Truth.*

1
The King's cheese goes three parts away in parings.

JAMES HOWELL, *Parley of Beasts,* 19. Referred to as a proverb.

I see it is impossible for the King to have things done as cheap as other men.

SAMUEL PEPYS, *Diary,* 21 July, 1662.

2
On the king's gate the moss grew gray;
The king came not. They called him dead
And made his eldest son one day
Slave in his father's stead.

HELEN HUNT JACKSON, *Coronation.*

3
The fortune which made you a king, forbade you to have a friend. It is a law of nature, which cannot be violated with impunity.

JUNIUS, *Letters.* Letter 35.

The halls of kings are full of men, but void of friends. (Atria regum hominibus plena sunt, amicis vacua.)

SENECA, *Epistulæ ad Lucilium.*

4
Few kings and tyrants descend to Pluto without violence or bloodshed, or by a natural death.

JUVENAL, *Satires.* Sat. x, l. 112.

It is one of the incidents of my profession. (E un incidente del mertiere.)

UMBERTO I OF ITALY, after escaping assassination. Sometimes quoted: "Assassination is the perquisite of kings."

An accident of my trade.

ALFONSO XIII OF SPAIN, to his bride, as a bomb was hurled at their carriage on their wedding day, 31 May, 1906.

5
The kingliest kings are crowned with thorn.

GERALD MASSEY, *The Kingliest Kings. See also under* CROWN.

6
What is a king? a man condemn'd to bear
The public burthen of the nation's care.

MATTHEW PRIOR, *Solomon.* Bk. iii, l. 275.

7
And haggard men will clamber to be kings
As long as Glory weighs itself in dust.

E. A. ROBINSON, *Three Quatrains.*

8
The gates of monarchs
Are arch'd so high that giants may jet through
And keep their impious turbans on.

SHAKESPEARE, *Cymbeline.* Act iii, sc. 3, l. 4.

9
What infinite heart's ease
Must kings neglect, that private men enjoy!
And what have kings, that privates have not too,
Save ceremony, save general ceremony?

SHAKESPEARE, *Henry V.* Act iv, sc. 1, l. 253.

What art thou, thou idol ceremony?
What kind of god art thou, that suffer'st more
Of mortal griefs than do thy worshippers? . . .
Art thou aught else but place, degree and form,
Creating awe and fear in other men?

SHAKESPEARE, *Henry V.* Act iv, sc. 1, l. 256.

Ceremony keeps up all things.

JOHN SELDEN, *Table Talk: Ceremony.*

10
It is the curse of kings to be attended
By slaves that take their humours for a warrant
To break within the bloody house of life.

SHAKESPEARE, *King John.* Act iv, sc. 2, l. 208.

For God's sake, let us sit upon the ground
And tell sad stories of the death of kings:
How some have been depos'd, some slain in war;
Some haunted by the ghosts they have depos'd;
Some poison'd by their wives, some sleeping kill'd;
All murder'd.

SHAKESPEARE, *Richard II.* Act iii, sc. 2, l. 155.

I give this heavy weight from off my head,
And this unwieldy sceptre from my hand,
The pride of kingly sway from out my heart.

SHAKESPEARE, *Richard II.* Act iv, sc. 1, l. 204.

Who knows
What racking cares disease a monarch's bed?

CONGREVE, *The Mourning Bride.* Act iii, sc. 4.

11
Authority forgets a dying king.

TENNYSON, *The Passing of Arthur,* l. 289.

VI—Kings: Divine Right

12
Injury to majesty, *i.e.,* high treason. (Læsæ majestatis.)

AMMIANUS, *Rerum Gestarum.* Bk. xvi, ch. 8, sec. 4. The French form, lèse-majesté, is the one usually used.

13
The Prussian Sovereigns are in possession of a crown not by the grace of the people, but by God's grace.

BISMARCK, *Speech,* in the Prussian Parliament, 1847. *See also under* GERMANY.

14
That the king can do no wrong is a necessary and fundamental principle of the English constitution.

BLACKSTONE, *Commentaries.* Bk. iii, ch. 17.

The King can do no wrong?

R. H. BARHAM, *New-made Honour,* l. 9.

15
The king never dies.

BLACKSTONE, *Commentaries.* Bk. iv, p. 249.

The King is dead. Long live the King! (Le Roi est mort. Vive le Roi!)

The French form of proclamation, last used at the death of Louis XVIII.

The death of Louis XIV was announced by the captain of the body-guard from a window of the state apartment. Raising his truncheon above his head, he broke it in the centre, and throwing the pieces among the crowd, exclaimed in a loud voice, "Le Roi est mort!" Then seizing another staff, he flourished it in the air as he shouted, "Vive le Roi!"

JULIA PARDOE, *Life of Louis XIV.* Vol. iii, 457.

16
Such is our good pleasure. (Tel est nôtre bon plaisir.)

FRANCIS I OF FRANCE, his form of assent.

(SULLY, *Memoirs.*) The formula by which his successors indicated their approval of legislative enactments.

The King wills it. (Le Roi le veut.)
Formula of royal assent as signified by the King to the British Parliament.

1
I am the State! (L'état, c'est moi!)
LOUIS XIV OF FRANCE, to the President of Parliament, 22 Dec., 1655, at the age of seventeen. (DULAURE, *Histoire de Paris*, p. 387.) Other historians dispute the authenticity of the utterance. Years later, however, the first sentence of a course in public law which he caused to have written for his grandson was, "The nation is not corporate in France: it lives entirely in the person of the king." And Bossuet declared of the sovereign, "Tout l'état est en lui": "All the state is in him." (CHÉRUEL, *Histoire de l'Administration Monarchique en France*, ii, 32.)

Homage is due to kings; they do what they like.
LOUIS XIV OF FRANCE, when a boy. (MARTIN, *History of France*, xv, 95.)

It was said of Louis the Fourteenth that his gait was becoming enough in a king, but in a private man would have been an insufferable strut.
EMERSON, *Uncollected Lectures: Public and Private Education.*

2
When the King speaks, every one else should be silent.
FRANZ LISZT, explaining why he had suddenly stopped playing before the Russian Emperor, when Alexander began whispering to his friends.

3
His fair large front and eye sublime declar'd
Absolute rule.
MILTON, *Paradise Lost.* Bk. iv, l. 300.

4
But methought it lessened my esteem of a king, that he should not be able to command the rain.
SAMUEL PEPYS, *Diary*, 19 July, 1662.

5
For sure if Dulness sees a grateful day,
'Tis in the shade of arbitrary sway.
O! if my sons may learn one earthly thing,
Teach but that one, sufficient for a King;
That which my priests, and mine alone, maintain,
Which, as it dies or lives, we fall or reign:
May you, may Cam and Isis, preach it long!
"The right divine of Kings to govern wrong."
POPE, *The Dunciad.* Bk. iv, l. 181. Cam and Isis, the universities of Cambridge and Oxford. Though Pope encloses the last line in quotation marks, it is probably his own.

Divine right of kings means the divine right of anyone who can get uppermost.
HERBERT SPENCER, *Social Statics.* Pt. ii, ch. 6, sec. 3.

6
Monarchs seldom sigh in vain.
WALTER SCOTT, *Marmion.* Canto v, st. 9.

7
Never king dropped out of the clouds.
JOHN SELDEN, *Table-Talk: Power.*

8
Every monarch is subject to a mightier one.
(Omne sub regno graviore regnum est.)
SENECA, *Thyestes*, l. 612.

9
There's such divinity doth hedge a king,
That treason can but peep to what it would.
SHAKESPEARE, *Hamlet.* Act iv, sc. 5, l. 123.

Kings are earth's gods, in vice their law's their will;
And if Jove stray, who dares say Jove doth ill?
SHAKESPEARE, *Pericles.* Act i, sc. 1, l. 103.

10
Not all the water in the rough rude sea
Can wash the balm from an anointed King;
The breath of worldly men cannot depose
The deputy elected by the Lord.
SHAKESPEARE, *Richard II.* Act iii, sc. 2, l. 54.

Let not the heavens hear these tell-tale women
Rail on the Lord's anointed.
SHAKESPEARE, *Richard III.* Act iv, sc. 4, l. 149.

11
Kings are not born: they are made by universal hallucination.
BERNARD SHAW, *Maxims for Revolutionists.*

12
The power of kings (if rightly understood)
Is but a grant from Heaven of doing good.
WILLIAM SOMERVILLE, *Fables.* No. 12.

13
An emperor should die standing. (Decet imperatorem stantem mori.)
VESPASIAN. (SUETONIUS, *Twelve Cæsars: Vespasian.*)

A king of France dies, but ought never to be ill.
LOUIS XVIII, 25 August, 1824, when urged not to hold his usual reception to celebrate the anniversary of St. Louis.

Name me an emperor who was ever struck by a cannon-ball.
CHARLES V OF SPAIN, when urged not to expose himself in action.

I never heard of a king being drowned. Make haste, loose your cables, you will see the elements join to obey me.
WILLIAM RUFUS, in 1099. (FREEMAN, *Life of William Rufus*, ii, 284.)

Queens of England are never drowned.
HENRIETTA MARIA, wife of Charles I, during a storm at sea, Feb., 1642.

VII—Kings: King and Subject

14
Kings will be tyrants from policy, when subjects are rebels from principle.
EDMUND BURKE, *Reflections on the Revolution in France.*

15
A sovereign's ear ill brooks a subject's questioning.
S. T. COLERIDGE, *Zapolya.* Sc. 1.

1
He is ours,
T' administer, to guard, t' adorn the state,
But not to warp or change it. We are his,
To serve him nobly in the common cause,
True to the death, but not to be his slaves.
COWPER, *The Task*. Bk. v, l. 341.

2
When kings the sword of justice first lay down,
They are no kings, though they possess the crown;
Titles are shadows, crowns are empty things:
The good of subjects is the end of kings.
DANIEL DEFOE, *The True-born Englishman*. Pt. ii, l. 313.

3
Minions too great argue a King too weak.
SAMUEL DANIEL, *The History of the Civil War*. Bk. i, st. 38.

4
Happy when both to the same centre move,
When Kings give liberty, and subjects love.
SIR JOHN DENHAM, *Cooper's Hill*, l. 333.

Thus Kings, by grasping more than they could hold,
First made their subjects by oppression bold;
And popular sway, by forcing Kings to give
More than was fit for subjects to receive,
Ran to the same extremes; and one excess
Made both, by striving to be greater, less.
SIR JOHN DENHAM, *Cooper's Hill*, l. 343.

5
Subjects may grieve, but Monarchs must redress.
DRYDEN, *Annus Mirabilis*. St. 242.

6
Every citizen is king under a citizen king. (Tout citoyen est roi sous un roi citoyen.)
FAVART, *Les Trois Sultanes*. Act ii, sc. 3.

7
A bad King but a good Subject.
W. S. GILBERT, *Utopia, Limited*. Act i.

8
The obligation of subjects to the sovereign is understood to last as long, and no longer, than the power lasteth by which he is able to protect them.
THOMAS HOBBES, *Leviathan*. Pt. ii, ch. 21.

9
God gives not kings the style of Gods in vain.
For on his throne his sceptre do they sway;
And as their subjects ought them to obey,
So kings should fear and serve their God again.
JAMES I OF SCOTLAND, *Sonnet Addressed to His Son, Prince Henry*.

10
When King and People understand each other past a doubt,
It takes a foe and more than a foe to knock that country out.
RUDYARD KIPLING, *"Together."*

11
I recommend my son, if he has the misfortune to become king, to remember that he owes himself to the happiness of his people.
LOUIS XIV OF FRANCE, in the testament which he made 25 Dec., 1792.

12
Entire and sure the monarch's rule must prove,
Who founds her greatness on her subjects' love.
MATTHEW PRIOR, *Prologue Spoken on Her Majesty's Birthday*, 1704.

13
He that is hated of his subjects cannot be counted a king.
JOHN RAY, *English Proverbs*.

14
Every subject's duty is the king's; but every subject's soul is his own.
SHAKESPEARE, *Henry V*. Act iv, sc. 1, l. 186.

15
Was never subject longed to be a king,
As I do long and wish to be a subject.
SHAKESPEARE, *II Henry VI*. Act iv, sc. 9, l. 5.

16
Vulgarity in a king flatters the majority of the nation.
BERNARD SHAW, *Maxims for Revolutionists*.

17
The king who fights his people fights himself.
TENNYSON, *The Passing of Arthur*, l. 72.

18
The greatest king is he who is the king
Of greatest subjects.
GILBERT WEST, *Institution of the Garter*, l. 302.

KISS AND KISSING

I—Kiss: Definitions

19
Something made of nothing, tasting very sweet,
A most delicious compound, with ingredients complete;
But if, as on occasion, the heart and mind are sour,
It has no great significance, and loses half its power.
MARY E. BUELL, *The Kiss*.

20
The anatomical juxtaposition of two orbicularis oris muscles in a state of contraction.
DR. HENRY GIBBONS, *Definition of a Kiss*.

21
What is a kiss? Why this, as some approve:
The sure sweet cement, glue, and lime of love.
ROBERT HERRICK, *A Kiss*.

22
What is a kiss? Alacke! at worst,
A single Dropp to quenche a Thirst,
Tho' oft it prooves, in happie Hour,
The first swete Dropp of our long Showre.
CHARLES GODFREY LELAND, *In the Old Time*.

23
What's in a kiss?
Oh, when for love the kiss is given, this:
Truth, purity, abiding trust, the seal
Of loyalty to love, come woe, come weal,

Unspoken promise of a soul's allegiance—this,
All this, and more, ah more! is in a kiss.
MARION PHELPS, *What's in a Kiss?*

1
A kiss, when all is said, what is it?
. . . a rosy dot
Placed on the "i" in loving; 'tis a secret
Told to the mouth instead of to the ear.
EDMOND ROSTAND, *Cyrano de Bergerac*. Act iii. sc. 10. *For full quotation see* 2298s:7.

II—Kiss: Apothegms

2
I wonder who's kissing her now?
FRANK R. ADAMS AND WILL M. HOUGH. Title and refrain of a lyric set to music by Joseph E. Howard in 1912.

3
Isn't it strange how one man's kiss can grow
To be like any other's . . . or a woman's
To be like any woman's?
MAXWELL ANDERSON, *Elizabeth the Queen*. Act i.

4
Kiss till the cows come home.
BEAUMONT AND FLETCHER, *The Scornful Lady*. Act ii, sc. 2.

5
A paroxysmal kiss.
HENRY WARD BEECHER, his description of the kiss he had given Mrs. Henry C. Bowen. It gained wide currency in the '70's. (*Tilton vs. Beecher*. Vol. i, p. 66.)

6
A kiss of the mouth often touches not the heart.
H. G. BOHN, *Hand-Book of Proverbs*, 292.

7
There's nothing wrong in a connubial kiss.
BYRON, *Don Juan*. Canto iii, st. 8.

8
Many a miss would not be a missus
If liquor did not add a spark to her kisses.
E. L. C., *Listen*. (*Life*, March, 1933.)

9
Kissing goes by favour.
WILLIAM CAMDEN, *Remains*, p. 327. (1605); FRANCIS QUARLES, *The Virgin Widow*. Act i. (1649) A proverb of great antiquity.

Ere they hewed the Sphinx's visage,
Favouritism governed kissage,
Even as it does in this age.
RUDYARD KIPLING, *General Summary*.

10
Sweetest the kiss that's stolen from weeping maid. (Primus titubans audacia furtis.)
CLAUDIAN, *De Nuptiis Honorii Augusti*, l. 81.

I do not care for kisses, unless I have snatched them in spite of resistance. (Basia dum nolo, nisi quæ luctantia carpsi.)
MARTIAL, *Epigrams*. Bk. v, ep. 46.

Stolen kisses are always sweeter.
LEIGH HUNT, *The Indicator*.

A legal kiss is never as good as a stolen one.
GUY DE MAUPASSANT, *A Wife's Confession*.

To kiss in private. An unauthorized kiss.
SHAKESPEARE, *Othello*. Act iv, sc. 1, l. 2.

The kiss, snatch'd hasty from the sidelong maid.
THOMSON, *The Seasons: Winter*, l. 625.

See also under PROHIBITION.

11
Kisses honeyed by oblivion.
GEORGE ELIOT, *The Spanish Gypsy*. Bk. iii.

12
She had rather kiss than spin.
THOMAS FULLER, *Gnomologia*. No. 4123.

13
The kiss you take is paid by that you give:
The joy is mutual, and I'm still in debt.
GEORGE GRANVILLE, *Heroic Love*. Act v, sc. 1

And if you'll blow to me a kiss,
I'll blow a kiss to you.
HORACE AND JAMES SMITH, *The Baby's Debut*

14
No man can *print* a kiss; lines may deceive.
FULKE GREVILLE, *Another to Myra*.

"May I print a kiss on your lips?" I said,
And she nodded her full permission;
So we went to press and I rather guess
We printed a full edition.
JOSEPH LILIENTHAL, *A Full Edition*.

15
The sound of a kiss is not so loud as that of a cannon, but its echo lasts a great deal longer.
O. W. HOLMES, *The Professor at the Breakfast-Table*. Ch. 11.

16
To kiss with the maid when the mistress is kind
A gentleman ought to be loth, sir.
WILLIAM HONE, *Every-Day Book*, ii, 377.

17
'Tis no sin love's fruit to steal,
But the sweet theft to reveal.
BEN JONSON, *Song: To Celia*.

And if he needs must kiss and tell,
I'll kick him headlong into hell.
COTTON, *Burlesque upon Burlesque*, 200.

Oh, fie, Miss, you must not kiss and tell.
CONGREVE, *Love for Love*. Act ii, sc. 10.

18
They are pecked on the ear and the chin and the nose who are lacking in lore.
RUDYARD KIPLING, *Certain Maxims of Hafiz*.

19
My lips the sextons are of thy slain kisses.
G. E. LANCASTER, *Pygmalion in Cyprus*, p. 18.

20
Kiss and be friends.
PETER LANGTOFT, *Chronicles*, 64. (c. 1300) In common use thereafter.

Let's see you buss and be friends.
SAMUEL RICHARDSON, *Pamela*, ii, 73.

21
Cupid and my Campaspe played
At cards for kisses; Cupid paid.
JOHN LYLY, *Alexander and Campaspe*.

My love and I for kisses play'd;
She would keep stakes; I was content;
But when I won, she would be paid;
This made me ask her what she meant.
Pray, since I see (quoth she) your wrangling vain,

Take your own kisses; give me mine again.
WILLIAM STRODE, *My Love and I for Kisses Play'd.* (c. 1640) Dryden added three lines to this stanza, and it is included in his *Miscellany.* (1716)

1
Sweet Helen, make me immortal with a kiss!
Her lips suck forth my soul: see, where it flies!
CHRISTOPHER MARLOWE, *Faustus*, l. 1330.

It was thy kiss, Love, that made me immortal.
MARGARET FULLER, *Dryad Song.*

O love! O fire! once he drew
With one long kiss my whole soul thro'
My lips, as sunlight drinketh dew.
TENNYSON, *Fatima.* St. 3.

2
Why do I not kiss you, Philænis? You are bald, you are carrotty, you are one-eyed. He who kisses you sins against nature.
MARTIAL, *Epigrams.* Bk. ii, epig. 33.

3
Let my hand have the honour
To convey a kiss from my lips to the cover of
Your foot, dear signior.
PHILIP MASSINGER, *The Great Duke of Florence.* Act iv, sc. 1.

4
When a man's hose be down, it is easy to kiss him where he sat on Saturday.
BRIAN MELBANCKE, *Philotinus.* (1583)

5
Kissing don't last: cookery do.
GEORGE MEREDITH, *Richard Feverel.* Ch. 28.

6
If you kiss me you hate me, and if you hate me you kiss me. But if you don't hate me, dear friend, don't kiss me! (Εἴ με φιλεῖς, μισεῖς με· καὶ εἰ μισεῖς, σὺ φιλεῖς με· εἰ δέ με μὴ μισεῖς, φίλτατε, μή με φίλει.)
NICARCHUS. (*Greek Anthology.* Bk. xi, epig. 252.)

7
And I will have a lover's fee; they say, unkiss'd unkind.
GEORGE PEELE, *Arraignement of Paris.* Act i, sc. 2 (1584)

8
The kisses of an enemy are deceitful.
Old Testament: Proverbs, xxvii, 6.

Many kiss the hand they wish cut off.
GEORGE HERBERT, *Jacula Prudentum.*

9
A lisping lass is good to kiss.
JOHN RAY, *English Proverbs.*

10
An horse-kiss: a rude kiss, able to beat one's teeth out.
JOHN RAY, *English Proverbs.*

11
Thou knowest the maiden who ventures to kiss a sleeping man, wins of him a pair of gloves.
SCOTT, *The Fair Maid of Perth.* Ch. 5.

12
Strangers and foes do sunder, and not kiss.
SHAKESPEARE, *All's Well that Ends Well.* Act ii, sc. 5, l. 91.

Ae fond kiss and then we sever.
BURNS, *Farewell to Nancy.*

One kiss more, and so farewell.
UNKNOWN, *Loyal Garland.* Song 22. (1686)

One fond kiss before we part,
Drop a tear and bid adieu.
ROBERT DODSLEY, *The Parting Kiss.*

13
I understand thy kisses and thou mine.
SHAKESPEARE, *I Henry IV.* Act iii, sc. 1, l. 205.

The kiss you take is better than you give;
Therefore no kiss.
SHAKESPEARE, *Henry VIII.* Act iv, sc. 5, l. 38.

Upon thy cheek lay I this zealous kiss,
As seal to this indenture of my love.
SHAKESPEARE, *King John.* Act ii, sc. 1, l. 19.

14
Speak, cousin, or, if you cannot, stop his mouth with a kiss.
SHAKESPEARE, *Much Ado About Nothing.* Act ii, sc. 1, l. 321.

15
Till thy wound be thoroughly heal'd;
And thus I search it with a sovereign kiss.
SHAKESPEARE, *The Two Gentlemen of Verona.* Act i, sc. 2, l. 116.

Kiss the place to make it well.
ANN TAYLOR, *My Mother.*

16
Bachelor's fare: bread and cheese and kisses.
SWIFT, *Polite Conversation.* Dial. i.

17
Lord! I wonder what fool it was that first invented kissing.
SWIFT, *Polite Conversation.* Dial. ii.

Tell me who first did kisses suggest?
It was a mouth all glowing and blest;
It kissed and it thought of nothing beside.
HEINE, *Book of Songs.* No. 25.

May his soul be in heaven—he deserves it I'm sure—
Who was first the inventor of kissing.
UNKNOWN, *The Inventor of Kissing.*

18
Dear as remember'd kisses after death,
And sweet as those by hopeless fancy feign'd
On lips that are for others.
TENNYSON, *The Princess.* Pt. iv, l. 36.

19
Many kiss the child for love of the nurse.
(Osculor hunc ore natum nutricis amore.)
THOMAS WRIGHT, *Essays on the Middle Ages.* Vol. i, p. 150. Quoting a medieval proverb.

Many kiss the child for the nurse's sake.
JOHN HEYWOOD, *Proverbs.* Pt. ii, ch. 7. (1546)

For love of the nurse the bairn gets mony a cuss.
GEORGE MERITON, *Praise of Yorkshire Ale,* 83.

20
You must kiss the rod.
UNKNOWN, *History of Reynard the Fox.* Ch. 12 (c. 1200) This is a series of fables first

collected in France under the title, *Roman de Renart*. The first English version was printed by Caxton in 1481.

Take thy correction mildly, kiss the rod.
SHAKESPEARE, *Richard II*. Act v, sc. 1, l. 32.

A testy babe will scratch the nurse
And presently all humble kiss the rod!
SHAKESPEARE, *The Two Gentlemen of Verona*. Act i, sc. 2, l. 58.

1
Make them kiss the book.
UNKNOWN, *The Manner of Keeping a Court Baron*. Printed by the widow of Robert Redman, c. 1539.

III—Kissing: Its Delights

2
Blush, happy maiden, when you feel
The lips which press love's glowing seal;
But as the slow years darklier roll,
Grown wiser, the experienced soul
Will own as dearer far than they
The lips which kiss the tears away.
ELIZABETH AKERS ALLEN, *Kisses*.

3
But is there nothing else,
That we may do but only walk? Methinks,
Brothers and sisters lawfully may kiss.
BEAUMONT AND FLETCHER, *A King and No King*. Act iv, sc. 4.

4
Remember the Viper:—'twas close at your feet,
How you started and threw yourself into my arms;
Not a strawberry there was so ripe nor so sweet
As the lips which I kiss'd to subdue your alarms.
ROBERT BLOOMFIELD, *Nancy*. St. 4.

5
And when my lips meet thine,
Thy very soul is wedded unto mine.
H. H. BOYESEN, *Thy Gracious Face I Greet with Glad Surprise*.

6
A winning kiss she gave,
A long one, with a free and yielding lip.
WILLIAM BROWNE, *Britannia's Pastorals*. Bk. iii, song 2, l. 193.

7
I was betrothed that day;
I wore a troth-kiss on my lips I could not give away.
E. B. BROWNING, *Lay of the Brown Rosary*. Pt. ii, l. 168.

First time he kissed me, he but only kissed
The fingers of this hand wherewith I write;
And ever since, it grew more clean and white,
. . . The second passed in height
The first, and sought the forehead, and half missed,
Half falling on the hair. O beyond meed! . . .
The third upon my lips was folded down
In perfect, purple state; since when, indeed,
I have been proud and said, "My love, my own."
E. B. BROWNING, *Sonnets from the Portuguese*. No. xxxviii.

The moth's kiss, first!
Kiss me as if you made believe
You were not sure, this eve,
How my face, your flower, had pursed
Its petals up.
ROBERT BROWNING, *In a Gondola*.

8
All the breath and the bloom of the year in the bag of one bee:
All the wonder and wealth of the mine in the heart of one gem:
In the core of one pearl all the shade and the shine of the sea:
Breath and bloom, shade and shine,—wonder, wealth, and—how far above them—
Truth, that's brighter than gem,
Trust, that's purer than pearl—
Brightest truth, purest trust in the universe—all were for me
In the kiss of one girl.
ROBERT BROWNING, *Summum Bonum*.

Her lips, whose kisses pout to leave their nest,
Bid man be valiant ere he merit such.
BYRON, *Childe Harold*. Canto i, st. 58.

9
Their lips drew near, and clung into a kiss;
A long, long kiss, a kiss of youth and love. . . .
Each kiss a heart-quake,—for a kiss's strength,
I think, it must be reckon'd by its length.
BYRON, *Don Juan*. Canto ii, st. 185–6.

10
I love the sex, and sometimes would reverse
The tyrant's wish "that mankind only had
One neck, which he with one fell stroke might pierce:"
My wish is quite as wide, but not so bad, . . .
That womankind had but one rosy mouth,
To kiss them all at once from North to South.
BYRON, *Don Juan*. Canto vi, st. 27.

"Kiss" rhymes to "bliss" in fact as well as verse.
BYRON, *Don Juan*. Canto vi, st. 59.

11
How delicious is the winning
Of a kiss at Love's beginning.
THOMAS CAMPBELL, *Song*.

When age chills the blood, when our pleasures are past—
For years fleet away with the wings of the dove—
The dearest remembrance will still be the last,
Our sweetest memorial the first kiss of love.
BYRON, *The First Kiss of Love*.

And in that first flame
Is all the nectar of the kiss.
(Et c'est dans la première flamme
Qu'est tout le nectar du baiser.)
LEBRUN, *Mes Souvenirs*.

12
Kisses kept are wasted;
Love is to be tasted.
There are some you love, I know;

Be not loath to tell them so.
Lips go dry and eyes grow wet
Waiting to be warmly met,
Keep them not in waiting yet;
Kisses kept are wasted.
EDMUND VANCE COOKE, *Kisses Kept Are Wasted.*

1
Rose kissed me today.
Will she kiss me tomorrow?
Let it be as it may,
Rose kissed me today.
AUSTIN DOBSON, *A Kiss.*

2
Never a lip is curved with pain
That can't be kissed into smiles again.
BRET HARTE, *The Lost Galleon.*

3
Give me a kiss and to that kiss a score;
Then to that twenty, add a hundred more;
A thousand to that hundred; so kiss on,
To make that thousand up a million;
Treble that million, and when that is done,
Let's kiss afresh, as when we first begun.
ROBERT HERRICK, *To Anthea.*

4
Jenny kissed me when we met,
Jumping from the chair she sat in;
Time, you thief, who love to get
Sweets into your list, put that in!
Say I'm weary, say I'm sad,
Say that health and wealth have missed me:
Say I'm growing old, but add
Jenny kissed me.
LEIGH HUNT, *Jenny Kissed Me.* "Jenny" was Jane Welsh Carlyle.

Only he felt he could no more dissemble,
And kissed her, mouth to mouth, all in a tremble.
LEIGH HUNT, *Story of Rimini.*

You kissed me! My head drooped low on your breast
With a feeling of shelter and infinite rest,
While the holy emotions my tongue dared not speak
Flashed up as a flame from my heart to my cheek.
JOSEPHINE SLOCUM HUNT, *You Kissed Me.*

I kissed you, I own, but I did not suppose
That you, through the papers, the deed would disclose,
Like free-loving cats, when on ridge-poles they meet,
And their squalls of "You kissed me!" disturb the whole street.
UNKNOWN, *You Kissed me.*

5
A soft lip,
Would tempt you to eternity of kissing!
BEN JONSON, *Volpone.* Act i, sc. 1.

Leave a kiss but in the cup,
And I'll not look for wine.
BEN JONSON, *To Celia. See also under* EYES AND LOVE.

6
And our lips found ways of speaking
What words cannot say,
Till a hundred nests gave music,
And the East was gray.
FREDERIC LAWRENCE KNOWLES, *A Memory.*

7
When she kissed me once in play,
Rubies were less bright than they;
And less bright were those which shone
In the palace of the Sun.
Will they be as bright again?
Not if kiss'd by other men.
WALTER SAVAGE LANDOR, *Rubies.*

8
Says he, "I'd better call agin;"
Says she, "Think likely, mister!"
Thet last word pricked him like a pin,
An' . . Wal, he up an' kist her.
J. R. LOWELL, *The Courtin'.*

9
The kiss, in which he half forgets even such a yoke as yours.
MACAULAY, *Virginia,* l. 138.

10
I rest content; I kiss your eyes,
I kiss your hair in my delight:
I kiss my hand and say "Good-night."
JOAQUIN MILLER, *Isles of the Amazons:* Pt. v, *Introduction.*

11
One kiss the maiden gives, one last,
Long kiss, which she expires in giving.
THOMAS MOORE, *Lalla Rookh: Paradise and the Peri,* l. 200.

I kiss'd thee ere I kill'd thee; no way but this;
Killing myself, to die upon a kiss.
SHAKESPEARE, *Othello.* Act v, sc. 2, l. 358.

12
How should great Jove himself do else than miss
To win the woman he forgets to kiss.
COVENTRY PATMORE, *De Natura Deorum.*

The lips he must briskly invade
That would possess the heart.
THOMAS YALDEN, *Song.*

13
Give me kisses! Nay, 'tis true
I am just as rich as you;
And for every kiss I owe,
I can pay you back, you know.
Kiss me, then,
Every moment—and again!
J. G. SAXE, *To Lesbia.*

Do thou snatch treasures from my lips,
And I'll take kingdoms back from thine!
SHERIDAN, *The Duenna.* Act iii, sc. 3.

14
Quicken with kissing: had my lips that power,
Thus would I wear them out.
SHAKESPEARE, *Antony and Cleopatra.* Act iv, sc. 15, l. 39.

15
His kissing is as full of sanctity as the touch of holy bread.
SHAKESPEARE, *As You Like It.* Act iii, sc. 4, l. 14.

1

O, a kiss,
Long as my exile, sweet as my revenge!
Now, by the jealous queen of heaven, that kiss
I carried from thee, dear.
SHAKESPEARE, *Coriolanus*. Act v, sc. 3, l. 44.

Falstaff: Thou dost give me flattering busses.
Doll Tearsheet: By my troth, I kiss thee with a most constant heart.
SHAKESPEARE, *II Henry IV*. Act ii, sc. 4, l. 291.

2

Take, O, take those lips away,
That so sweetly were forsworn;
And those eyes, the break of day,
Lights that do mislead the morn:
But my kisses bring again, bring again;
Seals of love, but seal'd in vain.
SHAKESPEARE, *Measure for Measure*. Act iv, sc. 1, l. 1.

Hide, O hide those hills of snow,
Which thy frozen bosom bears,
On whose tips the pinks that grow
Are of those that April wears!
But first set my poor heart free
Bound in icy chains by thee!
BEAUMONT AND FLETCHER, *The Bloody Brother*. Act v, sc. 2. This stanza, with the one above, attributed to Shakespeare, may have been a current song of anonymous authorship; or perhaps Shakespeare wrote the first stanza, and Fletcher appropriated it and added another.

3

And then, sir, would he gripe and wring my hand,
Cry "O sweet creature!" and then kiss me hard,
As if he pluck'd up kisses by the roots
That grew upon my lips.
SHAKESPEARE, *Othello*. Act iii, sc. 3, l. 421.

4

Then come kiss me, sweet and twenty.
SHAKESPEARE, *Twelfth Night*. Act ii, sc. 3, l. 52.

Ten kisses short as one, one long as twenty.
SHAKESPEARE, *Venus and Adonis*, l. 22.

She kissed his brow, his cheek, his chin,
And where she ends she doth anew begin.
SHAKESPEARE, *Venus and Adonis*, l. 59.

You may ride 's
With one soft kiss a thousand furlongs ere
With spur we heat an acre.
SHAKESPEARE, *Winter's Tale*. Act i, sc. 2, l. 94.

I think there is not half a kiss to choose
Who loves another best.
SHAKESPEARE, *Winter's Tale*. Act iv, sc. 4, l. 175.

5

See the mountains kiss high heaven,
And the waves clasp one another;
No sister flower would be forgiven
If it disdained its brother;
And the sunlight clasps the earth,
And the moonbeams kiss the sea:
What are all these kissings worth,
If thou kiss not me?
SHELLEY, *Love's Philosophy*. St. 2.

As in the soft and sweet eclipse,
When soul meets soul on lover's lips.
SHELLEY, *Prometheus Unbound*. Act iv, l. 450.

6

Her ambrosial kiss,
That sweeter far than any nectar is.
SPENSER, *An Hymn in Honour of Love*, l. 25.

I ne'er saw nectar on a lip,
But where my own did hope to sip.
SHERIDAN, *The Duenna*. Act i, sc. 2.

7

My lips till then had only known
The kiss of mother and of sister,
But somehow, full upon her own
Sweet, rosy, darling mouth,—I kissed her.
E. C. STEDMAN, *The Door-Step*.

8

We vulgar take it to be a sign of love. We servants, we poor people, that have nothing but our persons to bestow or treat for, are forced to deal and bargain by way of sample, and therefore as we have no parchments, or wax necessary in our agreements, we squeeze with our hands and seal with our lips, to ratify vows and promises.
RICHARD STEELE, *The Conscious Lovers*. Act iii, sc 1.

9

One rose, but one, by those fair fingers cull'd,
Were worth a hundred kisses press'd on lips
Less exquisite than thine.
TENNYSON, *The Gardener's Daughter*, l. 148.

A man had given all other bliss,
And all his worldly worth for this,
To waste his whole heart in one kiss
Upon her perfect lips.
TENNYSON, *Sir Launcelot and Queen Guinevere*.

And sweet red splendid kissing mouth.
VILLON, *Complaint of the Fair Armouress*. (Swinburne, tr.)

10

Many an evening by the waters did we watch the stately ships,
And our spirits rush'd together at the touching of the lips.
TENNYSON, *Locksley Hall*, l. 37.

That glance of theirs, but for the street, had been
A clinging kiss.
TENNYSON, *Merlin and Vivien*, l. 103.

Kisses balmier than half-opening buds Of April.
TENNYSON, *Tithonus*, l. 59.

11

Girl, when he gives you kisses twain,
Use one, and let the other stay;
And hoard it, for moons may die, red fades,
And you may need a kiss—some day.
RIDGELY TORRENCE, *The House of a Hundred Lights*.

12

If only in dreams may Man be fully blest,
Is heaven a dream? Is she I claspt a dream?
Or stood she here even now where dew-drops gleam

And miles of furze shine yellow down the
West? . . .
Can this be Earth? Can these be banks of
furze?
Like burning bushes fired of God they shine!
I seem to know them, though this body of
mine
Passed into spirit at the touch of hers!

THEODORE WATTS-DUNTON, *The Coming of Love: Rhona's First Kiss.*

1
When Youth and Beauty dwelt in Love's own
palace,
And life flowed on in one eternal kiss.

ELLA WHEELER WILCOX, *The Farewell of Clarimonde.*

IV—Kissing: Its Perils

2
Wanton kissings with the tongue. (Καταγλωττισμάτων.)

ARISTOPHANES, *The Clouds*, l. 51.

Give me another naughty, naughty kiss before we part. (Da savium etiam prius quam abis.)

PLAUTUS, *Asinaria*, l. 940. (Act v, sc. 2.)

Take me by the earlaps and match my little lips to your little lips. (Prehende auriculis, compara labella cum labella.)

PLAUTUS, *Asinaria*, l. 668. (Act iii, sc. 3.)

Kissing with inside lip? stopping the career
Of laughter with a sigh?

SHAKESPEARE, *Winter's Tale*. Act i, sc. 2, l. 286.

Do not make me kiss, and you will not make me sin.

H. G. BOHN, *Hand-Book of Proverbs*, 345.

3
You should not take a fellow eight years old
And make him swear to never kiss the girls.

ROBERT BROWNING, *Fra Lippo Lippi.*

4
Gin a body meet a body
Comin' thro' the rye,
Gin a body kiss a body,
Need a body cry?
Gin a body meet a body
Comin' thro' the glen,
Gin a body kiss a body,
Need the warld ken?

BURNS, *Comin' Thro' the Rye.* As was often his custom, Burns built this song upon the refrain of an older one, in this case a song of unknown authorship called *The Bob-Tailed Lass.* (JOHNSON, *Scots' Musical Museum.* Vol. v, p. 430.)

If a body meet a body going to the Fair,
If a body kiss a body need a body care?

JAMES C. CROSS, *The Harlequin Mariner: Song.* (1796)

5
A man may drink and no be drunk;
A man may fight and no be slain;
A man may kiss a bonnie lass,
And ay be welcome back again!

BURNS, *Duncan Davison.*

6
Kissing is nigh parent and cousin unto the foul feat or deed.

WILLIAM CAXTON, *La Tour-Landry.* Ch. 33. (1484)

After kissing comes more kindness.

JOHN CLARKE, *Parœmiologia*, p. 28.

She that will kiss, they say, will do worse.

ROBERT DAVENPORT, *City Night Cap.* Act i.

7
Kisses are keys; wanton kisses are keys of sin.

JOHN CLARKE, *Parœmiologia*, 28.

Kissin' is the key o' love,
An' clappin' is the lock.

BURNS, *O Can Ye Labour Lea, Young Man?*

8
Kisses and favours are sweet things,
But those have thorns and these have stings.

ROBERT HERRICK, *The Shower of Blossoms.*

9
He that doth kiss and do no more
May kiss behind and not before.

JAMES HOWELL, *Proverbs*, 9.

10
Mayhem, death and arson
Have followed many a thoughtless kiss
Not sanctioned by a parson.

DON MARQUIS, *On Kissing.*

11
For love or lust, for good or ill,
Behold the kiss is potent still.

JOHN RICHARD MORELAND, *The Kiss.*

12
Kiss—kiss—thou hast won me,
Bright, beautiful sin.

WILLIAM MOTHERWELL, *The Demon Lady.*

13
He who has taken kisses, if he take not the rest beside, deserves to lose even what was granted. (Oscula qui sumpsit, si non et cetera sumet, Hæc quoque, quæ data sunt, perdere dignus erit.)

OVID, *Ars Amatoria.* Bk. i, l. 669.

14
"I saw you take his kiss!" " 'Tis true."
"Oh, modesty!" " 'Twas strictly kept:
He thought I slept; at least, I knew
He thought I thought he thought I slept."

COVENTRY PATMORE, *Epigram.*

15
And secrecy made their courting the sweeter,
While Peter kissed Thisbe, and Thisbe kissed
Peter,—
For kisses, like folks with diminutive souls,
Will manage to creep through the smallest of
holes!

J. G. SAXE, *Pyramus and Thisbe.*

Young ladies: You shouldn't go strolling about
When your anxious mammas don't know you are
out;
And remember that accidents often befall
From kissing young fellows through holes in the
wall.

J. G. SAXE, *Pyramus and Thisbe: Moral.*

O kiss me through the hole of this vile wall!
SHAKESPEARE, *Midsummer-Night's Dream*. Act v, sc. 1, l. 202.

1
Yet whoop, Jack! kiss Gillian the quicker,
Till she bloom like a rose, and a fig for the vicar!
SCOTT, *The Lady of the Lake*. Canto vi, st. 5.

2
We have kiss'd away Kingdoms and provinces.
SHAKESPEARE, *Antony and Cleopatra*. Act iii, sc. 10, l. 7.

Or ere I could
Give him that parting kiss which I had set
Betwixt two charming words, comes in my father
And like the tyrannous breathing of the north
Shakes all our buds from growing.
SHAKESPEARE, *Cymbeline*. Act i, sc. 3, l. 33.

It is not a fashion for the maids in France to kiss before they are married.
SHAKESPEARE, *Henry V*. Act v, sc. 2, l. 286.

3
Were kisses all the joys in bed,
One woman would another wed.
SHAKESPEARE [?], *Passionate Pilgrim*, l. 345.

As well a woman with an eunuch play'd
As with a woman.
SHAKESPEARE, *Antony and Cleopatra*. Act ii, sc. 5, l. 5.

4
The woman that cries hush bids kiss: I learnt
So much of her that taught me kissing.
SWINBURNE, *Marino Faliero*. Act i, sc. 1.

Alas! that women do not know
Kisses make men loath to go.
UNKNOWN, *Kisses Make Men*.

5
'Twas ever thus with misses,
They leave the ancient home
To plant their Judas kisses
Upon some manly dome.
UNKNOWN. (*Punch*, 2 Sept., 1925.)

6
And hug and kiss and are so great
As the devil and witch of Endor.
UNKNOWN, *Political Merriment*. Pt. iii, p. 20.

I've seen her hug you as the devil hugged the witch.
SWIFT, *Polite Conversation*. Dial. i.

KNAVE AND KNAVERY

See also Fools and Knaves

7
Successful rascals are insufferable. (Κακοὶ εὖ πράσσοντες οὐκ ἀνασχετοί.)
ÆSCHYLUS, *Fragments*. Frag. 226.

8
The fox condemns the trap, not himself.
WILLIAM BLAKE, *Proverbs of Hell*.

9
Glasgow thuggery, Glasgow thugs; it is a witty nickname.
THOMAS CARLYLE, *Chartism*, i, 4.

10
He's tough, ma'am, tough is J. B. Tough and de-vilish sly.
DICKENS, *Dombey and Son*. Book i, ch. 7.

11
As there is a use in medicine for poison, so the world cannot move without rogues.
EMERSON, *Conduct of Life: Power*.

12
A more præternotorious rogue than himself.
JOHN FLETCHER, *Fair Maid of the Inn*. Act iv.

13
Who friendship with a knave has made
Is judged a partner in the trade.
JOHN GAY, *Fables*. Pt. i, No. 24.

14
The most necessary thing in the world, and yet the least usual, is to reflect that those we deal with may know how to be as arrant knaves as ourselves.
LORD HALIFAX, *Works*, p. 232.

If knaves had not foolish memories, they would never trust one another as often as they do.
LORD HALIFAX, *Works*, p. 233.

15
Clever men are the tools with which bad men work.
WILLIAM HAZLITT, *Works*. Vol. xi, p. 340.

16
One rogue is usher to another still.
HOMER, *Odyssey*. Bk. xvii, l. 251. (Pope, tr.)

17
To you, who distinguish between a knave and an honest man. (Tibi, qui turpi secernis honestum).
HORACE, *Satires*. Bk. i, sat. 6, l. 63.

18
One of the four and twenty policies of a knave is to stay long at his errand.
JAMES HOWELL, *Proverbs*, 2.

19
Knaves sore with conscience of their own defects.
J. R. LOWELL, *Epistle to George William Curtis*.

20
The biggest rascal that walks upon two legs. (Omnium bipedum nequissimus.)
MODESTUS, speaking of Regulus. (PLINY THE YOUNGER, *Letters*. Bk. i, epis. 5.)

It's my opinion you are a damned rascal. (Scelestissimum te arbitror.)
PLAUTUS, *Amphitruo*, l. 552. (Act ii, sc. 1.)

21
When knaves in grain meet.
JOHN PALSGRAVE, *Acolastus*. Sig. S 2. (1540)

Knave in grain, a knave of the first rate.
GROSE, *Classical Dict. of the Vulgar Tongue*.

A rogue in grain is a rogue amain.
H. G. BOHN, *Hand-Book of Proverbs*, 299.

22
Whether the fellow do this out of kindness or knavery, I cannot tell, but it is pretty to observe.
SAMUEL PEPYS, *Diary*, 7 Oct., 1665.

KNAVE AND KNAVERY

1 The success of knaves entices many. (Successus improborum plures adlicit.)
PHÆDRUS, *Fables*. Bk. ii, fab. 3, l. 7.

The more knave, the better luck.
JOHN RAY, *English Proverbs*.

2 When knaves fall out, true men come by their own.
JOHN RAY, *English Proverbs*.

3 He that sweareth till no man trust him,
He that lieth till no man believe him,
He that borroweth till no man will lend him,
Let him go where no man knoweth him.
HUGH RHODES, *Book of Nurture*, 107. (c. 1530)

4 Wilt thou ever be a foul-mouthed and calumnious knave?
SHAKESPEARE, *All's Well that Ends Well*. Act i, sc. 3, l. 61.

A poor, decayed, ingenious, foolish, rascally knave.
SHAKESPEARE, *All's Well that Ends Well*. Act iv, sc. 2, l. 25.

Hamlet: There's ne'er a villain dwelling in all Denmark
But he's an arrant knave.
Horatio: There needs no ghost, my lord, come from the grave
To tell us this.
SHAKESPEARE, *Hamlet*. Act i, sc. 5, l. 124.

We are arrant knaves all.
SHAKESPEARE, *Hamlet*. Act iii, sc. 1, l. 125.

How absolute the knave is!
SHAKESPEARE, *Hamlet*. Act v, sc. 1, l. 148.

O royal knavery!
SHAKESPEARE, *Hamlet*. Act v, sc. 2, l. 19.

5 Ah! whoreson caterpillars! bacon-fed knaves!
SHAKESPEARE, *I Henry IV*. Act ii, sc. 2, l. 89.

What a frosty-spirited rogue is this!
SHAKESPEARE, *I Henry IV*. Act ii, sc. 3, l. 21.

Three misbegotten knaves in Kendal green.
SHAKESPEARE, *I Henry IV*. Act ii, sc. 4, l. 246.

A rascally yea-forsooth knave.
SHAKESPEARE, *II Henry IV*. Act i, sc. 2, l. 41.

What an arrant, rascally, beggarly, lousy knave it is!
SHAKESPEARE, *Henry V*. Act iv, sc. 8, l. 37.

The rascally, scauld, beggarly, lousy, pragging knave.
SHAKESPEARE, *Henry V*. Act v, sc. 1, l. 6.

A knave; a rascal; an eater of broken meats; a base, proud, shallow, beggarly, three-suited, hundred pound, filthy, worsted-stocking knave.
SHAKESPEARE, *King Lear*. Act ii, sc. 2, l. 14.

Such smiling rogues as these,
Like rats, oft bite the holy cords a-twain
Which are too intrinse t' unloose.
SHAKESPEARE, *King Lear*. Act ii, sc. 2, l. 79.

Filthy, worsted-stocking knave; a lily-livered, action-taking knave.
SHAKESPEARE, *King Lear*. Act ii, sc. 2, l. 18.

Poor cuckoldy knave.
SHAKESPEARE, *The Merry Wives of Windsor*. Act ii, sc. 2, l. 281.

An arrant knave.
SHAKESPEARE, *Much Ado About Nothing*. Act v, sc. 1, l. 330.

6 A crafty knave does need no broker.
SHAKESPEARE, *II Henry VI*. Act i, sc. 2, l. 100.

7 Though this knave came something saucily into the world before he was sent for, yet was his mother fair; there was good sport at his making.
SHAKESPEARE, *King Lear*. Act i, sc. 1, l. 20.

8 *Second Watchman:* How if a' will not stand?
Dogberry: Why, then, take no note of him, but let him go; and presently call the rest of the watch together, and thank God you are rid of a knave.
SHAKESPEARE, *Much Ado About Nothing*. Act iii, sc. 3, l. 28.

Masters, it is proved already that you are little better than false knaves; and it will go near to be thought so shortly.
SHAKESPEARE, *Much Ado About Nothing*. Act iv, sc. 2, l. 30.

9 Whip me such honest knaves.
SHAKESPEARE, *Othello*. Act i, sc. 1, l. 49.

A slipper and subtle knave, a finder of occasions.
SHAKESPEARE, *Othello*. Act ii, sc. 1, l. 246.

10 Knavery's plain face is never seen till used.
SHAKESPEARE, *Othello*. Act ii, sc. 1, l. 321.

A knave teach me my duty! I'll beat the knave into a twiggen bottle!
SHAKESPEARE, *Othello*. Act ii, sc. 3, l. 151.

Some most villainous knave,
Some base notorious knave, some scurvy fellow.
O heaven, that such companions thou 'ldst unfold,
And put in every honest hand a whip
To lash the rascals naked through the world
Even from the east to the west!
SHAKESPEARE, *Othello*. Act iv, sc. 2, l. 139.

11 'Tis the base knave that jars.
SHAKESPEARE, *The Taming of the Shrew*. Act iii, sc. 1, l. 47.

A whoreson, beetle-headed, flap-ear'd knave!
SHAKESPEARE, *The Taming of the Shrew*. Act iv, sc. 1, l. 160.

12 'Gainst knaves and thieves men shut their gate.
SHAKESPEARE, *Twelfth Night*. Act v, sc. 1, l. 404.

13 Ay, knave, because thou strikest as a knight,
Being but knave, I hate thee all the more.
TENNYSON, *Gareth and Lynette*, l. 994.

14 Knavery nowadays is its own reward. (Eis nunc praemiumst, qui recta prava faciunt.)
TERENCE, *Phormio*, l. 771.

1
Knavery is the best defence against a knave.
ZENO. (PLUTARCH, *Life.*)

KNOWLEDGE

See also Learning; Wisdom

I—Knowledge: Definitions

2
For all knowledge and wonder (which is the seed of knowledge) is an impression of pleasure in itself.
BACON, *Advancement of Learning*. Bk. i.

A rich storehouse, for the glory of the Creator, and the relief of man's estate.
BACON, *Advancement of Learning*. Bk. i.

3
What is all Knowledge too but recorded Experience, and a product of History; of which, therefore, Reasoning and Belief, no less than Action and Passion, are essential materials?
THOMAS CARLYLE, *Essays: On History.*

Integrity without knowledge is weak and useless. . . . Knowledge without integrity is dangerous and dreadful.
SAMUEL JOHNSON, *Rasselas*. Ch. 41.

4
Knowledge is the only instrument of production that is not subject to diminishing returns.
J. M. CLARK, *Overhead Costs in Modern Industry*. (*Jour. Pol. Econ.*, Oct., 1927.)

An investment in knowledge pays the best interest.
BENJAMIN FRANKLIN, *Poor Richard.*

5
The fruits of the tree of knowledge are various; he must be strong indeed who can digest all of them.
MARY COLERIDGE, *Gathered Leaves*, p. 8.

6
Knowledge comes
Of learning well retain'd, unfruitful else.
DANTE, *Paradiso*. Canto v, l. 41.

7
All our progress is an unfolding, like the vegetable bud. You have first an instinct, then an opinion, then a knowledge.
EMERSON, *Essays, First Series: Intellect.*

Knowledge is the only elegance.
EMERSON, *Journal*, 1856.

Our knowledge is the amassed thought and experience of innumerable minds.
EMERSON, *Letters and Social Aims: Quotation and Originality.*

Knowledge is the antidote to fear,—Knowledge, Use and Reason, with its higher aids.
EMERSON, *Society and Solitude: Courage.*

8
Knowledge is a treasure, but practice is the key to it.
THOMAS FULLER, *Gnomologia*. No. 3139.

Knowledge without practice makes but half the artist.
THOMAS FULLER, *Gnomologia*. No. 3141.

9
All our knowledge is symbolic.
GOETHE, *Table-Talk*. 1805.

In the world the important thing is not to know more than all men, but to know more at each moment than any particular man.
GOETHE, *Table-Talk*, 1808.

10
The tree of knowledge in your garden grows,
Not single, but at every humble door.
O. W. HOLMES, *Wind-Clouds and Star-Drifts:* Pt. viii, *Manhood*, l. 46.

11
Knowledge and timber shouldn't be much used till they are seasoned.
O. W. HOLMES, *The Autocrat of the Breakfast-Table*. Ch. 6.

12
It is the peculiarity of knowledge that those who really thirst for it always get it.
RICHARD JEFFERIES, *Country Literature.*

13
Knowledge is of two kinds. We know a subject ourselves or we know where we can find information upon it.
SAMUEL JOHNSON. (BOSWELL, *Life*, 1775.)

14
A desire of knowledge is the natural feeling of mankind; and every human being whose mind is not debauched, will be willing to give all that he has to get knowledge.
SAMUEL JOHNSON. (BOSWELL, *Life*, 30 July, 1763.)

15
Knowledge is the action of the soul.
BEN JONSON, *Explorata: Scientia.*

16
History tells what man has done; art, what man has made; literature, what man has felt; religion, what man has believed; philosophy, what man has thought.
BENJAMIN C. LEEMING, *Imagination.*

17
What can give us more sure knowledge than our senses? How else can we distinguish between the true and the false? (Quid nobis certius ipsis Sensibus esse potest? qui vera ac falsa notemus?)
LUCRETIUS, *De Rerum Natura*. Bk. i, l. 700.

18
Knowledge advances by steps, and not by leaps.
MACAULAY, *Essays: History.*

19
Knowledge apart from justice is rather to be described as cunning than as knowledge. (Scientia, quæ est remota ab justitia, calliditas potius quam sapientia est appellanda.)
PLATO. (CICERO, *De Officiis*. Bk. i, ch. 19, sec. 63.)

20
It is one thing to remember, another to know. Remembering is merely safeguarding something entrusted to the memory; knowing means making everything your own. (Aliud autem est meminisse, aliud scire. Meminisse

est rem commissam memoriæ custodire. At contra, scire est et sua facere.)

SENECA, *Epistulæ ad Lucilium*. Epis. xxxiii, 8.

Nature has given us the seeds of knowledge, but not knowledge itself. (Natura . . . semina nobis scientiæ dedit, scientiam non dedit.)

SENECA, *Epistulæ ad Lucilium*. Epis. cxx, sec. 4.

1

The desire of knowledge, like the thirst of riches, increases ever with the acquisition of it.

STERNE, *Tristram Shandy*. Vol. ii, ch. 3.

Let knowledge grow from more to more,
But more of reverence in us dwell;
That mind and soul, according well,
May make one music as before.

TENNYSON, *In Memoriam: Introduction*. St. 7.

Who loves not Knowledge? Who shall rail
Against her beauty? May she mix
With men and prosper! Who shall fix
Her pillars? Let her work prevail.

TENNYSON, *In Memoriam*. Pt. cxiv, st. 1.

2

Knowledge is now no more a fountain seal'd:
Drink deep, until the habits of the slave,
The sins of emptiness, gossip and spite
And slander, die.

TENNYSON, *The Princess*. Pt. ii, l. 76.

A Fountain Sealed.

ANNE DOUGLAS SEDGWICK. Title of novel.

Knowledge is the only fountain, both of the love and the principles of human liberty.

DANIEL WEBSTER, *Address*, at dedication of Bunker Hill Monument, 17 June, 1843.

3

Knowledge, in truth, is the great sun in the firmament. Life and power are scattered with all its beams.

DANIEL WEBSTER, *Address*, at laying of the corner-stone of Bunker Hill Monument, 1825.

II—Knowledge: Apothegms

4

They know enough who know how to learn.

HENRY ADAMS, *Education of*, p. 314.

5

A man is but what he knoweth.

FRANCIS BACON, *Miscellaneous Tracts: In Praise of Knowledge*. Sec. 1.

I have taken all knowledge to be my province.

FRANCIS BACON, *Letter to Lord Burghley*, 1592.

He said it that knew it best.

FRANCIS BACON, *Essays: Of Boldness*.

We speak that we do know, and testify that we have seen.

New Testament: John, iii, 11. (Quod scimus loquimur, et quod vidimus testamur.—*Vulgate*.)

6

It is better not to know so much than to know so many things that ain't so.

JOSH BILLINGS. (JEROME A. HART, *In Our Second Century*, p. 307.) The form of the saying was varied by its author from time to time. On 13 Oct., 1885, he wrote it for a friend: "It is better to know less than to know so much that ain't so." The original wording (*Josh Billings's Encyclopedia of Wit and Wisdom*, p. 286, 1874) was: "It is better to know nothing than to know what ain't so."

A man of vast and varied misinformation.

WILLIAM GAYNOR. When Mayor of New York, referring to Rabbi Stephen S. Wise.

7

He knew whats'ever 's to be known,
But much more than he knew would own.

BUTLER, *Hudibras*. Pt. ii, canto iii, l. 297.

8

I am greedy of getting information. (Λίχνος εἰμὶ καὶ τὸ πεύθεσθαι.)

CALLIMACHUS, *Iambi*. No. 18.

9

Let him who knows how ring the bells. (Quien las sabe las tañe.)

CERVANTES, *Don Quixote*. Pt. ii, ch. 59.

10

Knowledge must be adorned, it must have lustre as well as weight, or it will be oftener taken for lead than for gold.

LORD CHESTERFIELD, *Letters*, 24 Nov., 1749.

Knowledge may give weight, but accomplishments give lustre, and many more people see than weigh.

LORD CHESTERFIELD, *Letters*, 8 May, 1750.

Grace is given of God, but knowledge is bought in the market.

ARTHUR HUGH CLOUGH, *The Bothie of Tober-na-Vuolich*. Pt. iv. *See also under* GRACE.

11

The Pursuit of Knowledge Under Difficulties.

GEORGE LILLIE CRAIK. Title of book published 1830–31 under the auspices of the Society for the Diffusion of Useful Knowledge. Craik had originally intended to call his book, *The Love of Knowledge Overcoming Difficulties in Its Pursuit*, and the shorter form is said to have been suggested by Lord Henry Peter Brougham.

But wot's that you're a doin' of? Pursuit of knowledge under difficulties, Sammy?

DICKENS, *Pickwick Papers*. Ch. 33. (1836)

12

Many shall run to and fro, and knowledge shall be increased.

Old Testament: Daniel, xii, 4.

13

Look here. Upon my soul you mustn't come into the place saying you want to know, you know.

DICKENS, *Little Dorrit*. Pt. i, ch. 10.

14

And let in knowledge by another sense.

DRYDEN, *King Arthur*. Act iii, sc. 2.

15

For lust of knowing what should not be known
We make the Golden Journey to Samarkand.

J. E. FLECKER, *The Golden Journey to Samarkand*.

1
He knoweth enough that knoweth nothing, if he know how to hold his peace.
GUAZZO, *Civil Conversation*. Fo. 55. (1586)
See also under SILENCE.

2
It is not permitted us to know everything. (Nec scire fas est omnia.)
HORACE, *Odes*. Bk. iv, ode 4, l. 22.

Ole man Know-All died las' year.
JOEL CHANDLER HARRIS, *Plantation Proverbs*.

3
A man without knowledge, an' I have read,
May well be compared to one that is dead.
THOMAS INGELEND, *The Disobedient Child*.
See IGNORANCE: BETTER UNBORN THAN UNTAUGHT.

4
Banish me from Eden when you will, but first let me eat of the fruit of the tree of knowledge.
ROBERT G. INGERSOLL, *The Gods*.

5
All wish to know, but none to pay the fee. (Nosse volunt omnes, mercedem solvere nemo.)
JUVENAL, *Satires*. Sat. vii, l. 157.

6
What man knows is everywhere at war with what he wants.
JOSEPH W. KRUTCH, *The Modern Temper*, p. 14.

7
To know is not to know, unless someone else has known that I know. (Scire est nescire, nisi id me scire alius scierit.)
LUCILIUS, *Fragment*.

Your knowing is nothing unless some other person knows that you know. (Scire tuum nihil est, nisi te scire hoc sciat alter.)
PERSIUS, *Satires*. Sat. i, l. 27.

To have a thing is nothing if you've not the chance to show it,
And to know a thing is nothing, unless others know you know it.
LORD NANCY, *Epigram*.

This you know I know.
SHAKESPEARE, *A Midsummer-Night's Dream*. Act iii, sc. 2, l. 163.

8
I have not the Chancellor's encyclopedic mind. He is indeed a kind of semi-Solomon. He *half* knows everything, from the cedar to the hyssop.
MACAULAY, *Letter to Macvey Napier*, 17 Dec., 1830. Referring to Lord Brougham.

What a wonderful versatile mind has Brougham! he knows politics, Greek, history, science; if he only knew a little law, he would know a little of everything.
DANIEL O'CONNELL, when Lord Brougham became Lord Chancellor. Attributed to SIR EDWARD ALDERSON by Emerson, in *Quotation and Originality*.

If the abbé had spoken a little of religion, he would have spoken of everything.
LOUIS XVI. After a sermon by the Abbé Maury. (See GRIMM, *Mémoires*.)

9
I know all that better than my own name. (Et teneo melius ista quam meum nomen.)
MARTIAL, *Epigrams*. Bk. iv, ep. xxxvii, l. 7.

I know you even under the skin. (Ego te intus ei in cute novi.)
PERSIUS, *Satires*. Sat. iii, l. 30.

I know him as well as if I had gone through him with a lighted candle.
C. H. SPURGEON, *Ploughman's Pictures*, 97.

You know me Al.
RING LARDNER. Title and refrain of a book of of baseball stories.

10
You speak before a man to whom all Naples is known. (Vous parlez devant un homme à qui tout Naples est connu.)
MOLIÈRE, *L'Avare*. Act v, sc. 5, l. 47.

11
It is far better to know something about everything than to know all about one thing. Universality is the best.
PASCAL, *Pensées*. Sec. i, No. 37.

Diffused knowledge immortalizes itself.
JAMES MACKINTOSH, *Vindiciæ Gallicæ*.

12
In vain sedate reflections we would make,
When half our knowledge we must snatch, not take.
POPE, *Moral Essays*. Epis. i, l. 39.

13
What harm in getting knowledge even from a sot, a pot, a fool, a mitten, or a slipper?
RABELAIS, *Works*. Bk. iii, ch. 16.

14
How haughtily he cocks his nose,
To tell what every schoolboy knows.
SWIFT, *The Country Life*.

Every school-boy knows it.
JEREMY TAYLOR, *On the Real Presence*. Sec. v. The phrase, "As every schoolboy knows," was used frequently by Macaulay and is often attributed to him.

Of an old tale which every schoolboy knows.
WILLIAM WHITEHEAD, *The Roman Father: Prologue*.

15
My name it is Benjamin Jowett,
I'm Master of Balliol College;
Whatever is knowledge I know it,
And what I don't know isn't knowledge.
UNKNOWN, *Epigram*, on Dr. Jowett, of Balliol, Oxford.

16
For wa I wist not what was what.
UNKNOWN, *Ywaine and Gavin*, l. 432. (c. 1400)

And else wot I never what is what.
THOMAS HOCCLEVE, *Dialogue*, l. 138. (c. 1420)

He said he knew what was what.
JOHN SKELTON, *Why Come Ye Not to Court*, l. 1107. (c. 1520)

He knew what's what, and that's as high
As metaphysic wit can fly.
BUTLER, *Hudibras*. Pt. i, canto i, l. 149. (1663)

That 're young lady . . . knows wot's wot, she does.

DICKENS, *Pickwick Papers*. Ch. 37. (1837)

III—Knowledge: Its Value

1
Knowledge is, indeed, that which, next to virtue, truly and essentially raises one man above another.

ADDISON, *The Guardian*. No. 111.

2
There is no power on earth which setteth up a throne, or chair of state, in the spirits and souls of men, and in their cogitations, imaginations, opinions, and beliefs, but knowledge and learning.

BACON, *Advancement of Learning*. Bk. i.

The knowledge of man is as the waters, some descending from above, and some springing up from beneath; the one informed by the light of nature, the other inspired by divine revelation.

BACON, *Advancement of Learning*. Bk. ii.

3
The sovereignty of man lieth hid in knowledge; wherein many things are reserved that kings with their treasure cannot buy, nor with their force command.

BACON, *Cogitationes de Scientia Humana*.

It is no less true in this human kingdom of knowledge, than in God's kingdom of heaven, that no man shall enter into it, "except he become first as a little child."

BACON, *Of the Interpretation of Nature*. Ch. 1.

4
There is no knowledge which is not valuable.

EDMUND BURKE, *American Taxation*.

5
Knowledge is a comfortable and necessary retreat and shelter for us in an advanced age; and if we do not plant it while young, it will give us no shade when we grow old.

LORD CHESTERFIELD, *Letters*, 11 Dec., 1747.

One of the most agreeable consequences of knowledge is the respect and importance which it communicates to old age.

SYDNEY SMITH, *Female Education*.

6
Let the fools talk, knowledge has its value. (Laissez dire les sots, le savoir a son prix.)

LA FONTAINE, *Fables*. Bk. viii, fab. 19.

Let fools the studious despise,
There's nothing lost by being wise.

LA FONTAINE, *Fables*. Bk. viii, fab. 19.

7
Deeper, deeper let us toil
In the mines of knowledge.

JAMES MONTGOMERY, *Aspirations of Youth*.

8
A learned man has always riches in himself. (Homo doctus in se semper divitias habet.)

PHÆDRUS, *Fables*. Bk. iv, fab. 21.

Knowledge of itself is riches.

SADI, *Gulistan*. Ch. 7, tale 2. *Of the Effects of Education*.

9
O what a brave thing it is, in every case and circumstance of a matter, to be thoroughly well informed!

RABELAIS, *Works*. Bk. iii, ch. 7.

10
For the more a man knows, the more worthy he is.

ROBERT OF GLOUCESTER, *Rhyming Chronicle of the History of England*. (1270)

Crowns have their compass—length of days their date—
Triumphs their tomb—felicity, her fate—
Of nought but earth can earth make us partaker,
But knowledge makes a king most like his Maker.

SHAKESPEARE, *Epigram on King James I*. (PAYNE COLLIER, *Life of Shakespeare*.)

11
Sweet food of sweetly uttered knowledge.

SIR PHILIP SIDNEY, *Defence of Poesy*.

12
A life of knowledge is not often a life of injury and crime.

SYDNEY SMITH, *Pleasures of Knowledge*.

A man who dedicates his life to knowledge becomes habituated to pleasure which carries with it no reproach.

SYDNEY SMITH, *Sketches of Moral Philosophy*. Lecture 19.

13
He who binds
His soul to knowledge, steals the key of heaven.

N. P. WILLIS, *The Scholar of Thibèt Ben Khorat*. Pt. ii, l. 6 fr. end.

14
Oh, be wiser, Thou!
Instructed that true knowledge leads to love.

WORDSWORTH, *Lines Left upon a seat in a Yew-tree*. l. 59.

IV—Knowledge and Power

15
For knowledge, too, is itself a power. (Nam et ipsa scientia potestas est.)

FRANCIS BACON, *De Hæresibus*.

Knowledge and human power are synonymous, since the ignorance of the cause frustrates the effect.

BACON, *Novum Organum: Summary*. Pt. ii, aph. 3.

If materialistic knowledge is power, it is not wisdom. It is but a blind force.

MARY BAKER EDDY, *Science and Health*, p. 196.

16
There is no knowledge that is not power.

EMERSON, *Society and Solitude: Old Age*.

17
Knowledge is power.

THOMAS HOBBES, *Leviathan*. Ch. 9.

They say that "Knowledge is power." I used to think so.

BYRON, *Letter to Prothero*.

18
Knowledge is more than equivalent to force.

SAMUEL JOHNSON, *Rasselas*. Ch. 13.

19
Simple as it seems, it was a great discovery that the key of knowledge could turn both

ways, that it could open, as well as lock, the door of power to the many.
J. R. LOWELL, *Among My Books: New England Two Centuries Ago.*

1
Every addition to true knowledge is an addition to human power.
HORACE MANN, *Lectures on Education.* No. 1.

2
A wise man is strong; yea, a man of knowledge increaseth strength.
Old Testament: Proverbs, xxiv, 5.

V—Knowledge and Wisdom

3
There is no great concurrence between learning and wisdom.
FRANCIS BACON, *Advancement of Learning: Civil Knowledge.* Sec. 4.

Knowledge and Wisdom, far from being one,
Have ofttimes no connexion. Knowledge dwells
In heads replete with thoughts of other men;
Wisdom in minds attentive to their own.
Knowledge, a rude unprofitable mass,
The mere materials with which Wisdom builds; . . .
Knowledge is proud that he has learn'd so much;
Wisdom is humble that he knows no more.
COWPER, *The Task.* Bk. vi, l. 88.

4
The greatest clerks be not the wisest men.
CHAUCER, *The Reves Tale,* l. 4051.

I counsel all creatures no clerk to despise.
LANGLAND, *Piers Plowman.* Passus xv, l. 64.

5
I've studied now Philosophy
And Jurisprudence, Medicine
And even, alas, Theology
From end to end with labor keen;
And here, poor fool, with all my lore
I stand no wiser than before.
GOETHE, *Faust: Night.* (Bayard Taylor, tr.)

6
It is the province of knowledge to speak, and it is the privilege of wisdom to listen.
O. W. HOLMES, *The Poet at the Breakfast-Table.* Ch. 10.

7
Deign on the passing world to turn thine eyes,
And pause awhile from letters, to be wise.
SAMUEL JOHNSON, *The Vanity of Human Wishes,* l. 155.

8
Knowledge is as food, and needs no less
Her temperance over appetite, to know
In measure what the mind may well contain,
Oppresses else with surfeit, and soon turns
Wisdom to folly, as nourishment to wind.
MILTON, *Paradise Lost.* Bk. vii, l. 126.

9
We live and learn, but not the wiser grow.
JOHN POMFRET, *Reason,* l. 112.

10
Knowledge, when wisdom is too weak to guide her,
Is like a headstrong horse, that throws the rider.
FRANCIS QUARLES, *Miscellanies.* Sometimes attributed to Robert Robinson, Vicar of Harlow. (c. 1580) See *Notes and Queries,* 25 June, 1910.

11
No man is the wiser for his learning.
JOHN SELDEN, *Table-Talk: Wit.*

12
Knowledge comes, but wisdom lingers.
TENNYSON, *Locksley Hall,* l. 141.

13
But you are learn'd; in volumes, deep you sit;
In wisdom, shallow: Pompous ignorance!
YOUNG, *Night Thoughts.* Night v, l. 735.

VI—Knowledge: Its Limitations

14
Our knowledge, compared with Thine, is ignorance. (Scientia nostra, scientiæ tuæ comparata, ignorantia est.)
ST. AUGUSTINE, *Confessions.* Bk. xi, sec. 4.

Before God we are all equally wise—equally foolish.
ALBERT EINSTEIN, *Cosmic Religion,* p. 105.

15
There's lots of people—this town wouldn't hold them—
Who don't know much excepting what's told them.
WILL CARLETON, *City Ballads,* p. 143.

All I know is what I read in the papers.
WILL ROGERS.

16
And yet, alas! when all our lamps are burned,
Our bodies wasted, and our spirits spent,
When we have all the learned volumes turned,
Which yield men's wits both help and ornament,
What can we know or what can we discern?
SIR JOHN DAVIES, *Nosce Teipsum: Introduction.* Sec. i, st. 14.

17
We know accurately only when we know little; with knowledge doubt increases. (Eigentlich weiss man nur wenn man wenig weiss; mit dem Wissen wächst der Zweifel.)
GOETHE, *Sprüche in Prosa.*

18
Knowledge is folly except grace guide it.
GEORGE HERBERT, *Jacula Prudentum.*

19
This world, where much is to be done and little to be known.
SAMUEL JOHNSON, *Prayers and Meditations.*

20
Now learn too late
How few sometimes may know, when thousands err.
MILTON, *Paradise Lost.* Bk. vi, l. 148.

21
Do they not show by too much knowledge that they know nothing? (Faciuntne intellegendo ut nihil intellegant?)
TERENCE, *Andria: Prologue,* l. 17.

Too much to know is to know nought but fame.
SHAKESPEARE, *Love's Labour's Lost*. Act i, sc. 1, l. 92.

1
The more we study, we the more discover our ignorance.
SHELLEY, *Scenes from the Magico Prodigioso of Calderon*. Sc. 1.

2
And no man knows distinctly anything, and no man ever will. (Καὶ τὸ μὲν οὖν σαφὲς οὔτις ἀνὴρ ἴδεν οὐδέ τις ἔσται εἰδώς.)
XENOPHANES, *Fragment*. No. 34. (DIOGENES LAERTIUS, *Pyrrho*. Sec. 12.)

We know nothing rightly, for want of perspective.
EMERSON, *Essays, Second Series: Nature*.

We don't know one millionth of one per cent about anything.
THOMAS A. EDISON. (*Golden Book*, April, 1931.)

We can do interesting mechanical things . . . but we know nothing important. In the essentials we are still as wholly a mystery to ourselves as Adam was to himself.
BOOTH TARKINGTON, *Looking Forward*, p. 34.

3
Still we say as we go,—
"Strange to think by the way
Whatever there is to know,
That shall we know one day."
D. G. ROSSETTI, *The Cloud Confines*.

VII—Knowledge: Its Futility

4
What is all our knowledge? We do not even know what weather it will be tomorrow.
BERTHOLD AUERBACH, *On the Heights*.

5
The desire of power in excess caused the angels to fall; the desire of knowledge in excess caused man to fall.
FRANCIS BACON, *Essays: Of Goodness*.

6
Men are called fools in one age for not knowing what they were called fools for averring in the age before.
HENRY WARD BEECHER, *Life Thoughts*.

7
They who know the most
Must mourn the deepest o'er the fatal truth,
The Tree of Knowledge is not that of life.
BYRON, *Manfred*. Act i, sc. 1.

8
Knowledge puffeth up, but charity edifieth.
New Testament: I Corinthians, viii, 1.

Knowledge bloweth up, but charity buildeth up.
BACON, *Rendering of I Corinthians*, viii, 1.

9
He that increaseth knowledge increaseth sorrow.
Old Testament: Ecclesiastes, i, 18.

10
Metaphysics may be, after all, only the art of being sure of something that is not so, and logic only the art of going wrong with confidence.
J. W. KRUTCH, *The Modern Temper*, p. 228.

11
He who knows has many cares. (Wer viel weiss Hat viel zu sorgen.)
LESSING, *Nathan der Weise*. Act iv, sc. 2.

12
Our knowledge is a torch of smoky pine
That lights the pathway but one step ahead
Across a void of mystery and dread.
GEORGE SANTAYANA, *O World*.

13
We know what we are, but know not what we may be.
SHAKESPEARE, *Hamlet*. Act iv, sc. 5, l. 42.

14
When a man's knowledge is not in order, the more of it he has the greater will be his confusion.
HERBERT SPENCER, *The Study of Sociology*. Ch. 15.

15
There are many things, the knowledge of which is of little or no profit to the soul.
THOMAS À KEMPIS, *De Imitatione Christi*. Ch. 2.

VIII—Knowledge and Ignorance

16
A seeming ignorance is often a most necessary part of worldly knowledge.
LORD CHESTERFIELD, *Letters*, 15 Jan., 1753.

17
Ignorance seldom vaults into knowledge, but passes into it through an intermediate state of obscurity, even as night into day through twilight.
S. T. COLERIDGE, *Essays*. No. 16.

18
True knowledge is modest and wary; 'tis ignorance that is bold and presuming.
JOSEPH GLANVIL, *Scepsis Scientifica*.

19
But Knowledge to their eyes her ample page,
Rich with the spoils of time, did ne'er unroll.
THOMAS GRAY, *Elegy Written in a Country Church-yard*. St. 13.

20
Better be ignorant of a matter than half know it.
PUBLILIUS SYRUS, *Sententiæ*. No. 865.

He that knows little often repeats it.
THOMAS FULLER, *Gnomologia*. No. 2209.

Not well understood, as good not known.
MILTON, *Paradise Regained*. Bk. i, l. 437.

I wish I had not known so much of this affair, added my Uncle Toby, or that I had known more of it.
STERNE, *Tristram Shandy*. Vol. vi, ch. 7.

21
It is better, of course, to know useless things than to know nothing. (Satius est supervacua scire quam nihil.)
SENECA, *Epistulæ ad Lucilium*. Epis. 88, sec. 45.

1
Ignorance is the curse of God,
Knowledge the wing wherewith we fly to heaven.
SHAKESPEARE, *II Henry VI*. Act iv, sc. 7, l. 78

2
There is only one good, that is knowledge; there is only one evil, that is ignorance. (Μόνον ἀγαθὸν ἔιναν, τὴν ἐπιστήμην, καὶ ἓν μόνον κακόν, τὴν ἀμαθίαν.)
SOCRATES. (DIOGENES LAERTIUS, *Socrates*. Sec. 14.)

3
It is necessary to fathom one's ignorance on one subject to discover how little one knows on other subjects.
J. A. SPENDER, *The Comments of Bagshot*. Ch. 11.

4
Knowledge is sympathy, charity, kindness,
Ignorance only is maker of hell.
WILLIAM WATSON, *England to Ireland*.

IX—Knowledge: Knowing One's Knowledge

See also Ignorance of Ignorance

5
There are four sorts of men:
He who knows not and knows not he knows not: he is a fool—shun him;
He who knows not and knows he knows not: he is simple—teach him;
He who knows and knows not he knows: he is asleep—wake him;
He who knows and knows he knows: he is wise—follow him.
LADY BURTON, *Life of Sir Richard Burton*. Quoted as an Arabian proverb. (See *Spectator*, 11 Aug., 1894, p. 176.) Sometimes attributed to Darius the Persian.

We think so because other people all think so;
Or because—or because—after all, we do think so;
Or because we were told so, and think we must think so;
Or because we once thought so, and think we still think so;
Or because, having thought so, we think we will think so.
HENRY SIDGWICK, *Lines Composed in His Sleep*. (WILLIAM OSLER, *Harveian Oration*, in *South Place Magazine*, Feb., 1907.)

Sæpe ego audivi, milites, eum primum esse virum, qui ipse consultat quid in rem sit; secundum eum, qui bene monenti oboediat; qui nec ipse consulere nec alteri parere sciat, eum extremi ingenii esse.
LIVY, *History*. Bk. xxii, ch. 29. *See also* CICERO, *Pro Cluentio*, 31; HESIOD, *Works and Days*, 293; ARISTOTLE, *Nicomachean Ethics*, i, 4.

6
The wisest saying of all was that the only true wisdom lay in not thinking that one knew what one did not know.
CICERO, *Academicarum Quæstionum*. Bk. i, ch. 4, sec. 16.

7
When you know a thing, to hold that you know it; and when you do not know a thing, to allow that you do not know it: this is knowledge.
CONFUCIUS, *Analects*. Bk. ii, ch. 17. (Legge, tr.)

To know that we know what we know, and that we do not know what we do not know, that is true knowledge.
H. D. THOREAU, *Walden*. Ch. 1. Quoting Confucius.

To be conscious that you are ignorant is a great step to knowledge.
BENJAMIN DISRAELI, *Sybil*. Bk. i, ch. 5.

8
Knowledge is the knowing that we cannot know.
EMERSON, *Representative Men: Montaigne*.

9
To know one's ignorance is the best part of knowledge.
LAO-TSZE, *The Simple Way*. No. 71.

10
All things I thought I knew; but now confess
The more I know I know, I know the less.
ROBERT OWEN, *Works*. Bk. vi, ch. 39.

11
What I do not know I do not think I know. (Ὅτι ἃ μὴ οἶδα, οὐδὲ οἴομαι εἰδέναι.)
PLATO, *Apologia of Socrates*. Sec. 21.

12
The only thing that we never know is to ignore what we cannot know. (La seule chose que nous ne savons point, est d'ignorer ce que nous ne pouvons savoir.)
ROUSSEAU, *Émile*. Bk. iv.

13
As for me, all I know is that I know nothing. (Συνειδὼς ἐμαυτῷ ἀμαθίαν.)
SOCRATES. (PLATO, *Phædrus*. Sec. 235.)

I know nothing except the fact of my ignorance. (Εἰδέναι μὲν μηδὲν πλὴν αὐτὸ τοῦτο [εἰδέναι].)
SOCRATES. (DIOGENES LAERTIUS, *Socrates*. Bk. ii, sec. 32.)

Well didst thou speak, Athena's wisest son!
"All that we know is, nothing can be known."
BYRON, *Childe Harold*. Canto ii, st. 7.

L

LABOR

See also Industry, Work

I—Labor: Definitions

1
Labor is discovered to be the grand conqueror, enriching and building up nations more surely than the proudest battles.
WILLIAM ELLERY CHANNING, *War*.

2
American labor, which is the capital of our workingmen.
GROVER CLEVELAND, *First Annual Message*, Dec., 1885.

3
Toil, says the proverb. is the sire of fame.
EURIPIDES, *Licymnius*. Frag. 477.

4
Labour and love! there are no other laws
To rule the liberal action of that soul
Which fate hath set beneath thy brief control.
EDMUND GOSSE, *Labour and Love*.

Labour we must, and labour hard,
In th' Forum here, or the Vineyard.
ROBERT HERRICK, *Labour*.

5
Toil is the true knight's pastime.
KINGSLEY, *The Saint's Tragedy*. Act i, sc. 2.

6
Labour is but refreshment from repose.
JAMES MONTGOMERY, *Greenland*. Canto ii.

For this of old is sure,
That change of toil is toil's sufficient cure.
LEWIS MORRIS, *Love in Death*.

7
Toil is the law of life and its best fruit.
LEWIS MORRIS, *The Ode of Perfect Years*.

8
Labor is the handmaid of religion.
C. H. PARKHURST, *Sermons: Pattern in Mount*.

9
Labor is the law of happiness.
ABEL STEVENS, *Life of Mme. de Staël*. Ch. 16.

10
Nature is inexhaustible and untiring labor is a god which rejuvenates her. (La nature est inépuisable, Et le travail infatigable Est un dieu qui la rajeunit.)
VOLTAIRE, *Sur l'Ingratitude*.

II—Labor: Apothegms

11
To him that toileth God oweth glory, child of his toil. (Τῷ πονοῦντι δ' ἐκ θεῶν ὀφείλεται τέκνωμα τοῦ πόνου κλέος.)
ÆSCHYLUS, *Fragments*. Frag. 175.

12
I laboured more abundantly than they all.
New Testament: I Corinthians, xv, 10.

Consider that I laboured not for myself only, but for all them that seek learning.
Apocrypha: Ecclesiasticus, xxxiii, 17.

13
Honest labour bears a lovely face.
THOMAS DEKKER, *Patient Grissell*. Act i, sc. 1.

14
Who does not teach his child a trade or profession brings him up to steal, say the Persians.
R. W. EMERSON, *Journals*, 1863.

Each one to his own trade. (Chacun son métier.)
FLORIAN, *Le Vacher et le Garde-chasse*.

He that hath a trade hath an estate; he that hath a calling hath an office of profit and honor.
BENJAMIN FRANKLIN, *Poor Richard*, 1758.

15
The gods demand of us toil as the price of all good things. (Τῶν πόνων πωλοῦσιν ἡμῖν πάντα τἀγάθ' οἱ θεοί.)
EPICHARMUS. (XENOPHON, *Memorabilia*. Bk. ii, ch. 1, sec. 20.) Sometimes translated, "The gods sell us all good things at the price of labor."

Life grants no boon to man without much toil. (Nil sine magno Vita labore dedit mortalibus.)
HORACE, *Satires*. Bk. i, sat. 9, l. 59. Probably a quotation from an unknown poet.

There is nothing truly valuable which can be purchased without pains and labour.
ADDISON, *The Tatler*. No. 97.

16
Sweet is the memory of past labor. (Ἀλλ' ἡδύ τοι σωθέντα μεμνῆσθαι πόνων.)
EURIPIDES, *Andromeda*. (CICERO, *De Finibus*. Bk. ii, ch. 32, sec. 105.) Cicero's Latin is: Suavis laborum est præteritorum memoria.

Toil is pleasant when it is done. (Jucundi acti labores.)
CICERO, *De Finibus*. Bk. ii, ch. 32, sec. 105. Cited as a popular saying.

But now my task is smoothly done.
I can fly, or I can run.
MILTON, *Comus*, l. 1012.

17
Virtue proceeds through toil. (Ἁ δ' ἀρετὰ βαίνει διὰ μόχθων.)
EURIPIDES, *Heraclidæ*, l. 625.

Honor lies in honest toil.
GROVER CLEVELAND, *Letter*, accepting nomination for President, 18 Aug., 1884. (STODDARD, *Life of Cleveland*. Ch. 15.)

The nobility of labor—the long pedigree of toil.
LONGFELLOW, *Nuremberg*.

There's a dignity in labour
Truer than e'er pomp arrayed.
CHARLES SWAIN, *What Is Noble?*

18
Handle your tools without mittens.
BENJAMIN FRANKLIN, *Poor Richard*, 1758.

19
Bodily labour earns not much.
THOMAS FULLER, *Gnomologia*.

If little labour, little are our gains:
Man's fortunes are according to his pains.
ROBERT HERRICK, *Hesperides*. No. 754.

1
Daring is the labor, lordly the reward. (Kühn ist das Mühen, herrlich der Lohn.)
GOETHE, *Faust:* Pt. vi, *Soldiers' Chorus.*

2
Better owe
A yard of land to labour, than to chance
Be debtor for a rood!
SHERIDAN KNOWLES, *The Hunchback.* Act i, sc. 1.

3
Labour for labour's sake is against nature.
JOHN LOCKE, *Conduct of the Understanding.* Sec. 16.

Be sure it is of vanities most vain,
To toil for what you here untoiling may obtain.
JAMES THOMSON, *The Castle of Indolence.* Canto i, st. 19.

4
Come unto me, all ye that labour and are heavy laden.
New Testament: Matthew, xi, 28.

5
This was a good week's labour.
THOMAS MIDDLETON, *Anything for a Quiet Life.* Act v, sc. 3.

6
He who would eat the kernel must crack the shell. (Qui e nuce nucleum esse vult, frangit nucem.)
PLAUTUS, *Curculio,* l. 55. (Act i, sc. 1.)

If any would not work, neither should he eat.
New Testament: II Thessalonians, iii, 10. (Si quis non vult operari, nec manducet.—*Vulgate.*)

He that will not live by toil
Has no right on English soil!
CHARLES KINGSLEY, *Alton Locke's Song.* Under the title, *My Last Words,* it forms conclusion of novel *Alton Locke.*

7
In all labour there is profit.
Old Testament: Proverbs, xiv, 23.

He that labours and thrives spins gold.
JOHN RAY, *English Proverbs.*

8
O Athenians, what toil do I undergo to please you!
ALEXANDER THE GREAT. (PLUTARCH, *Lives: Alexander.* Ch. 60, sec. 3.) Quoted by CARLYLE, *Essays: Voltaire.*

9
It is not the part of a man to fear sweat. (Non est viri timere sudorem.)
SENECA, *Epistulæ ad Lucilium.* Epis. xxxi, 8.

10
Why, Hal, 'tis my vocation. Hal: 'tis no sin for a man to labour in his vocation.
SHAKESPEARE, *I Henry IV.* Act i, sc. 2, l. 116.

Labour in thy vocation.
SHAKESPEARE, *II Henry VI.* Act iv, sc. 2, l. 17.

The test of a vocation is the love of the drudgery it involves.
LOGAN PEARSALL SMITH, *Afterthoughts.*

11
Winding up days with toil and nights with sleep.
SHAKESPEARE, *Henry V.* Act iv, sc. 1, l. 296.

12
We'll set thee to school to an ant, to teach thee there's no labouring i' the winter.
SHAKESPEARE, *King Lear.* Act ii, sc. 4, l. 68.

13
Labour of love.
New Testament: I Thessalonians, i, 3.

14
What region of the earth is not full of our labors? (Quæ regio in terris nostri non plena laboris?)
VERGIL, *Æneid.* Bk. i, l. 460.

This is the task, this is the labor. (Hoc opus, hic labor est.)
VERGIL, *Æneid.* Bk. vi, l. 129. Quoted by OVID, *Ars Amatoria.* Bk. i, l. 453.

15
Labor conquers everything. (Labor omnia vincit.)
VERGIL, *Georgics.* Bk. i, l. 145.

16
For all there is one season of rest and one of toil. (Omnibus una quies operum, labor omnibus unus.)
VERGIL, *Georgics.* Bk. iv, l. 184.

17
Six hours are most suitable for labor, and the four that follow, when set forth in letters, say to men, "Live!" (ΖΗΘΙ)
UNKNOWN. (*Greek Anthology.* Bk. x, epig. 43.) The letters of the Greek alphabet were used as figures, and ΖΗΘΙ, meaning "live," is 7, 8, 9, 10.

Six hours are enough for work; the others say to men, "Live!"
LUCIAN, *Sententiæ.* No. 17.

III—Labor: Labor Lost

18
I have bestowed upon you labour in vain.
New Testament: Galatians, iv, 11.

19
I have lost my oil and my labor. (Oleum et operam perdidi.)
PLAUTUS, *Pœnulus,* l. 332. (Act i, sc. 2.)

I have altogether lost my time and my labour. (Je tout perdu mon temps et mon labor.)
CHAUCER, *The Persones Tale.* Sec. 11. Quoted as the title of a new French song.

20
They have nought but their toil for their heat, their pains for their sweat, and (to bring it to our English proverb) their labour for their travail.
THOMAS NASH, *To the Gentlemen Students of Both Universities.* Introductory to Robert Greene's *Menaphon.* (1589)

21
They can expect nothing but their labor for their pains.
CERVANTES, *Don Quixote: Preface.* (1605)

I have had my labour for my travail; . . . small thanks for my labour.
SHAKESPEARE, *Troilus and Cressida*. Act i, sc. 1, l. 70. (1609)

And all that I by that should gain
Would be my labour for my pain.
CHARLES COTTON, *Burlesque upon Burlesque*, 186. (1675)

His labour for his pains.
EDWARD MOORE, *Boy and the Rainbow*. (1744)

I'm glad the villain got nothing but his labour for his pains.
FANNY BURNEY, *Evelina*. Let. 33. (1778)

1
Whence all his labor was wasted. (Ibi omnis Effusus labor.)
VERGIL, *Georgics*. Bk. iv, l. 491.

IV—Labor: To Labor is to Pray

2
To labor is to pray. (Laborare est orare.)
The ancient motto of the Benedictine monks. A variation of this, "Qui laborat, orat," "Who labors, prays," is attributed to St. Augustine.

3
Who prays and works lifts up to God his heart with his hands. (Qui orat et laborat, cor levat ad Deus cum manibus.)
ST. BERNARD, *Works*. Vol. ii, p. 866. A version of *Lamentations*, iii, 41: "Let us lift up our heart with our hands unto God in the heavens."

4
Even in the meanest sorts of Labour, the whole soul of a man is composed into a kind of real harmony the instant he sets himself to work.
CARLYLE, *Past and Present*. Ch. 15.

What worship, for example, is there not in mere washing!
CARLYLE, *Past and Present*. Ch. 15. Referring to "Work is prayer."

God walks among the pots and pipkins.
SAINT TERESA. See APPENDIX.

5
Lo! all life this truth declares,
Laborare est orare;
And the whole earth rings with prayers.
DINAH M. M. CRAIK, *Labour is Prayer*.

6
Labour as long lived· pray as ever dying.
GEORGE HERBERT, *Jacula Prudentum*.

7
To labor rightly and earnestly is to walk in the golden track that leads to God.
J. G. HOLLAND, *Plain Talks: Work and Play*.

8
For he that is true of his tongue, and of his two hands,
And doth his work therewith, and willeth no man ill,
He is a god by the gospel.
WILLIAM LANGLAND, *Piers Plowman*. Passus ii, l. 82.

Work as though work alone thine end could gain;
But pray to God as though all work were vain.
D'ARCY W. THOMPSON, *Sales Attici*.

9
Great thoughts hallow any labor. . . . If the ditcher muse the while how he may live uprightly, the ditching spade and turf knife may be engraved on the coat-of-arms of his posterity.
H. D. THOREAU, *Journal*, 20 April, 1841.

10
Ah, little recks the laborer,
How near his work is holding him to God,
The loving Laborer through space and time.
WALT WHITMAN, *Song of the Exposition*, l. 1.

V—Labor: A Blessing

See also Work: A Blessing

11
And yet without labour there were no ease, no rest, so much as conceivable.
THOMAS CARLYLE, *Essays: Characteristics*.

Labour, wide as the earth, has its summit in heaven.
THOMAS CARLYLE, *Essays: Work*.

12
The habit of toil renders the endurance of pain easier. . . . Toil of itself brings a certain callousness to pain. (Consuetudo enim laborum perpessionem dolorum efficit faciliorum. . . . Ipse labor callum quoddam obducit dolori.)
CICERO, *Tusculanarum Disputationum*. Bk. ii, ch. 15, sec. 36.

The labour we delight in physics pain.
SHAKESPEARE, *Macbeth*. Act ii, sc. 3, l. 55.

13
The sleep of a labouring man is sweet.
Old Testament: Ecclesiastes, v, 12.

From toil he wins his spirits light,
From busy day the peaceful night.
THOMAS GRAY, *Ode on the Pleasure Arising from Vicissitude*, l. 87.

Toiling—rejoicing—sorrowing,
Onward through life he goes;
Each morning sees some task begin,
Each evening sees it close,
Something attempted, something done,
Has earned a night's repose.
LONGFELLOW, *The Village Blacksmith*.

14
A little labour, much health.
GEORGE HERBERT, *Jacula Prudentum*.

15
O sweet solace of labor. (O laborum Dulce lenimen.)
HORACE, *Odes*. Bk. i, ode 32, l. 14.

By his eagerness gently beguiling the unpleasing labor. (Molliter austerum studio fallente laborem.)
HORACE, *Satires*. Bk. ii, sat. 2, l. 12.

16
The modest wants of every day
The toil of every day supplied.
SAMUEL JOHNSON, *On the Death of Dr. Robert Levet*.

1
Labor and pleasure, two things most unlike in their nature, are joined together by a certain natural association. (Labor, voluptasque. dissimillima natura, societate quadam inter se naturali sunt juncta.)
LIVY, *History*. Bk. v, sec. 4.

Labor is itself a pleasure. (Labor est etiam ipsa voluptas.)
MANILIUS, *Astronomica*, iv, 155.

Labor is often the father of pleasure. (Le travail est souvent le père du plaisir.)
VOLTAIRE, *Discours*. No. 4.

Thou, O God, dost sell unto us all good things at the price of labor.
LEONARDO DA VINCI.

2
Taste the joy That springs from labor.
LONGFELLOW, *Masque of Pandora:* Pt. vi, *In the Garden*.

From labor there shall come forth rest.
LONGFELLOW, *To a Child*, l. 162.

The labor itself is a delight. (Juvat ipso labor.)
MARTIAL, *Epigrams*. Bk. i, epig. 107.

3
Labor is life! 'Tis the still water faileth;
Idleness ever despaireth, bewaileth;
Keep the watch wound, for the dark rust assaileth.
FRANCES S. OSGOOD, *To Labor Is to Pray*.

Labor is rest—from the sorrows that greet us;
Rest from all petty vexations that meet us,
Rest from sin-promptings that ever entreat us,
Rest from world-sirens that lure us to ill.
Work—and pure slumbers shall wait on thy pillow;
Work—thou shalt ride over Care's coming billow;
Lie not down wearied 'neath Woe's weeping willow!
Work with a stout heart and resolute will!
FRANCES S. OSGOOD, *To Labor Is to Pray*.

4
The man who by his labour gets
His bread, in independent state,
Who never begs, and seldom eats,
Himself can fix or change his fate.
MATTHEW PRIOR, *The Old Gentry*.

His brow is wet with honest sweat,
He earns whate'er he can,
And looks the whole world in the face,
For he owes not any man.
LONGFELLOW, *The Village Blacksmith*.

5
No man needs sympathy because he has to work. . . . Far and away the best prize that life offers is the chance to work hard at work worth doing.
THEODORE ROOSEVELT, *Address*, Syracuse, Labor Day, 1903.

6
The happiness of men consists in life. And life is in labor.
TOLSTOY, *What Is to Be Done?* Ch. 38.

7
Heaven is blessed with perfect rest but the blessing of earth is toil.
HENRY VAN DYKE, *The Toiling of Felix*.

8
The fruit of toil is the sweetest of pleasures. (Le fruit du travail est le plus doux des plaisirs.)
VAUVENARGUES, *Réflexions*. No. 200.

VI—Labor: A Curse

See also Work: A Curse

9
Do ye hear the children weeping, O my brothers,
Ere the sorrow comes with years?
They are leaning their young heads against their mothers,
And that cannot stop their tears.
E. B. BROWNING, *The Cry of the Children*.

But the young, young children, O my brothers,
They are weeping bitterly!
They are weeping in the playtime of the others,
In the country of the free.
E. B. BROWNING, *The Cry of the Children*.

The child's sob in the silence curses deeper
Than the strong man in his wrath.
E. B. BROWNING, *The Cry of the Children*.

The golf links lie so near the mill
That almost every day
The laboring children can look out
And see the men at play.
SARAH N. CLEGHORN, *The Golf Links*.

Age after age the children give
Their lives that Herod still may live—
WINIFRED M. LETTS, *The Children's Ghosts*.

10
They who always labour can have no true judgment. . . These are amongst the effects of unremitted labour, when men exhaust their attention, burn out their candles, and are left in the dark.
EDMUND BURKE, *Letter*, to a member of the National Assembly, 1791.

11
What profit hath a man of all his labour which he taketh under the sun?
Old Testament: Ecclesiastes, i, 3.

All things are full of labour; man cannot utter it: the eye is not satisfied with seeing, nor the ear filled with hearing.
Old Testament: Ecclesiastes, i, 8.

12
Labour itself is but a sorrowful song,
The protest of the weak against the strong.
F. W. FABER, *The Sorrowful World*.

13
The path that leads to a loaf of bread
Winds through the swamps of toil,
And the path that leads to a suit of clothes
Goes through a flowerless soil,
And the paths that lead to the loaf of bread
And the suit of clothes are hard to tread.
SAM WALTER FOSS, *Paths*.

1
A toiling dog comes halting home.
THOMAS FULLER, *Gnomologia.*

2
Labor is the curse of the world, and nobody can meddle with it without becoming proportionately brutified.
HAWTHORNE, *American Note-Books.* 12 Aug., 1841.

3
To labour is the lot of man below;
And when Jove gave us life, he gave us woe.
HOMER, *Iliad.* Bk. x, l. 78. (Pope, tr.)

Toil is the lot of all, and bitter woe
The fate of many.
HOMER, *Iliad.* Bk. xxi, l. 646. (Bryant, tr.)

He toiled and toiled, of toil no end to know,
But endless toil and never-ending woe.
SOUTHEY, *Vision of the Maid of Orleans.* Bk. ii.

4
With fingers weary and worn,
With eyelids heavy and red,
A woman sat in unwomanly rags,
Plying her needle and thread. . . .

O men with sisters dear,
O men with mothers and wives,
It is not linen you're wearing out,
But human creatures' lives!
THOMAS HOOD, *Song of the Shirt.*

Not all the labor of the earth
Is done by hardened hands.
WILL CARLETON, *A Working Woman.*

5
No period of rest releases me from my labor. (Nullum ab labore me reclinat otium.)
HORACE, *Epodes.* No. xvii, l. 25.

Whose sore task
Does not divide the Sunday from the week.
SHAKESPEARE, *Hamlet.* Act i, sc. 1, l. 75.

Our ardent labours for the toys we seek
Join night to day, and Sunday to the week.
YOUNG, *Love of Fame.* Sat. v, l. 101.

6
Meshed within this smoky net
Of unrejoicing labour.
MORRIS, *Life and Death of Jason.* Bk. xvii, l. 10.

7
Coal-black, and grizzled here and there,
But more through toil than age.
SCOTT, *Marmion.* Canto i, st. 5.

8
Ah, why Should life all labour be?
TENNYSON, *Lotos-Eaters: Choric Song,* l. 41.

9
Why seekest thou rest, since thou art born to labor? (Cur quæris quietem, cum natus sis ad laborem?)
THOMAS À KEMPIS, *De Imitatione Christi.* Bk. ii, ch. 10, sec. 1.

Man is born unto labor. (Homo nascitur ad laborem.)
Vulgate: Job, v, 7. The revised version is: "Man is born to trouble."

10
O mortal man! who livest here by toil,
Do not complain of this thy hard estate.
THOMSON, *Castle of Indolence.* Canto i, st. 1.

VII—Labor: The Laborer

11
The rights and interests of the laboring man will be protected and cared for—not by labor agitators, but by the Christian men to whom God in His infinite wisdom has given the control of the property interests of the country.
GEORGE F. BAER, President, Philadelphia and Reading Railway, *Letter to W. Y. Clark,* 17 July, 1902.

The doctrine of the divine right of kings was bad enough, but not so intolerable as the doctrine of the divine right of plutocrats.
UNKNOWN, *Editorial,* Boston *Watchman,* July, 1902.

And so it was all saved for us, the spot with the sign: "Beware!
This plant is run by the earth and sun and is making coal for Baer!"
WILBUR D. NESBIT, *The Reserved Section.*

12
The labouring people are only poor because they are numerous.
EDMUND BURKE, *Thoughts and Details on Scarcity.*

13
Till toil grows cheaper than the trodden weed,
And man competes with man, like foe with foe.
THOMAS CAMPBELL, *Lines on Revisiting a Scottish River.*

14
The glory of a workman, still more of a master-workman, that he does his work well, ought to be his most precious possession; like the "honour of a soldier," dearer to him than life.
CARLYLE, *Essays: Shooting Niagara.*

15
There is no right to strike against the public safety by anybody, anywhere, anytime.
CALVIN COOLIDGE, *Telegram to Samuel Gompers,* 14 Sept., 1919, referring to the strike of the Boston, Mass., police. This sentence made Coolidge famous and did much to win him the Republican nomination for Vice-President in 1920.

16
So every carpenter and workmaster, that laboureth night and day: and they that cut and grave seals, . . . the smith also, sitting by the anvil, . . . the potter sitting at his work, . . . all these trust to their hands: and every one is wise in his work. Without these cannot a city be inhabited. . . . They shall not be sought for in public council, nor sit high in the congregation, . . . but they will maintain the state of the world, and [all] their desire is in the work of their craft.
Apocrypha: Ecclesiasticus, xxxviii, 27-34.

17
The German and Irish millions, like the Negro, have a great deal of guano in their

destiny. They are ferried over the Atlantic, and carted over America, to ditch and to drudge, to make corn cheap, and then to lie down prematurely to make a spot of green grass on the prairie.
EMERSON, *Conduct of Life: Fate.*

The American workman who strikes ten blows with his hammer, while the foreign workman only strikes one, is really vanquishing that foreigner, as if the blows were aimed at and told on his person.
EMERSON, *Conduct of Life: Worship.*

1
For as labor cannot produce without the use of land, the denial of the equal right to the use of land is necessarily the denial of the right of labor to its own produce.
HENRY GEORGE, *Progress and Poverty.* Bk. vii, ch. 1.

2
I looked up at Nye,
And he gazed upon me;
And he rose with a sigh,
And said, "Can this be?
We are ruined by Chinese cheap labor,"—
And he went for that heathen Chinee.
BRET HARTE, *Plain Language from Truthful James.*

3
Labor is the foundation of all, and those that labor are the Caryatides that support the structure and glittering dome of civilization and progress.
R. G. INGERSOLL, *How to Reform Mankind.*

4
Horny-handed sons of toil.
DENIS KEARNEY (BIG DENNY), *Speech,* on the "sand lot" at San Francisco. (c. 1878)

And blessed are the horny hands of toil.
J. R. LOWELL, *A Glance Behind the Curtain,* l. 205.

The callous palms of the laborer are conversant with finer tissues of self-respect and heroism, whose touch thrills the heart, than the languid fingers of idleness.
H. D. THOREAU, *Walking.*

5
Long sleeps Delilah; but at Gaza still
The shorn deluded Samsons sweat and grind
Amid the dust and clangor of the mill,
Treading their sordid round, forever blind.
JAMES B. KENYON, *Væ Victis.*

6
By some it is assumed that labor is available only in connection with capital—that nobody labors unless somebody else owning capital, somehow, by the use of it, induces him to do it. . . . But another class of reasoners . . . hold that labor is prior to, and independent of, capital; that, in fact, capital is the fruit of labor, and could never have existed if labor had not first existed.
ABRAHAM LINCOLN, *Address,* Milwaukee, Wis., 30 Sept., 1859. For MUD-SILL *see* p. 1841, No. 8.

7
Laborin' man an' laborin' woman
Hev one glory an' one shame.
Ev'y thin' thet's done inhuman
Injers all on 'em the same.
J. R. LOWELL, *The Biglow Papers.* Ser. i, No. 1, st. 10.

8
The labourer is worthy of his hire.
New Testament: Luke: x, 7.

The labourer is worthy of his reward.
New Testament: I Timothy, v, 18.

9
Bowed by the weight of centuries he leans
Upon his hoe and gazes on the ground,
The emptiness of ages in his face,
And on his back the burden of the world.
EDWIN MARKHAM, *The Man with the Hoe.*

10
Thou hast made them equal unto us, which have borne the burden and heat of the day.
New Testament: Matthew, xx, 12.

11
The bad workmen, who form the majority of the operatives in many branches of industry, are decidedly of opinion that bad workmen ought to receive the same wages as good.
JOHN STUART MILL, *On Liberty.* Ch. 4.

12
Mechanic slaves
With greasy aprons, rules, and hammers.
SHAKESPEARE, *Antony and Cleopatra.* Act v, sc. 2, l. 209.

He was an honest man and a good bricklayer.
SHAKESPEARE, *II Henry VI.* Act iv, sc. 2, l. 42.

Another lean, unwashed artificer.
SHAKESPEARE, *King John.* Act iv, sc. 2, l. 201.

He talks of wood; it is some carpenter.
SHAKESPEARE, *I Henry VI.* Act v, sc. 3, l. 90.

A carpenter's known by his chips.
SWIFT, *Polite Conversation.* Dialogue ii.

13
Men, my brothers, men the workers, ever reaping something new.
TENNYSON, *Locksley Hall,* l. 117.

14
Labor in this country is independent and proud. It has not to ask the patronage of capital, but capital solicits the aid of labor.
DANIEL WEBSTER, *Speech,* April, 1824.

15
Labouring men Count the clock oftenest.
WEBSTER, *The Duchess of Malfi.* Act iii, sc. 2.

16
The hours are long, the pay is small,
So take your time and buck them all.
UNKNOWN. An I. W. W. poster.

17
Arise, ye prisoners of starvation,
Arise, ye wretched of the earth,
For justice thunders condemnation—
A better world's in birth.
UNKNOWN, *The Internationale.*

VIII—Labor: Drivers and Driven

1
We labour soon, we labour late,
To feed the titled knave, man;
And a' the comfort we're to get
Is that ayont the grave, man.

BURNS, *The Tree of Liberty*. St. 9.

Such hath it been—shall be—beneath the sun
The many still must labour for the one.

BYRON, *The Corsair*. Canto i, st. 8.

2
I hold that if the Almighty had ever made a set of men that should do all the eating and none of the work, He would have made them with mouths only and no hands; and if He had ever made another class that He intended should do all the work and no eating, He would have made them with hands only and no mouths.

ABRAHAM LINCOLN, *Mud-sill Theory of Labor*.

3
One half of the world must sweat and groan that the other half may dream.

LONGFELLOW, *Hyperion*. Bk. i, ch. 4.

4
What is there to say
When idlers feast and toilers lack for bread?

E. E. MILLER, *The Riddle of All Times*.

5
I never could believe that Providence had sent a few men into the world, ready booted and spurred to ride, and millions ready saddled and bridled to be ridden.

RICHARD RUMBOLD, on the scaffold, 1685. (MACAULAY, *Hist. of England*. Vol. i, ch. 5.)

All eyes are opened or opening to the rights of man. The general spread of the light of science has already laid open to every view the palpable truth that the mass of mankind has not been born with saddles on their backs nor a few favored few booted and spurred, ready to ride them legitimately, by the grace of God.

THOMAS JEFFERSON, *Letter to Roger Weightman*, 24 June, 1826. His last letter. He died ten days later on July 4.

Some are born to be bullied and chidden,
Born to be bridled, born to be ridden,
Born to be harried or whipped or hidden;
Others born booted and spurred to ride.

VACHEL LINDSAY, *Old Old Andrew Jackson*.

Aristotle has said it in the *Politica*: . . . how, "from the hour of their birth, some human beings are marked for subjection, others for rule."

REGINALD WRIGHT KAUFFMAN, *Front Porch*.

6
Many faint with toil,
That few may know the cares and woe of sloth.

SHELLEY, *Queen Mab*. Canto iii, l. 116.

7
And besides, the problem of land, at its worst, is a by one; distribute the earth as you will, the principal question remains inexorable—Who is to dig it? Which of us, in brief word, is to do the hard and dirty work for the rest, and for what pay? Who is to do the pleasant and clean work, and for what pay? Who is to do no work, and for what pay?

RUSKIN, *Sesame and Lilies: King's Treasuries*.

Men of England, wherefore plough
For the lords who lay ye low?
Wherefore weave with toil and care
The rich robes your tyrants wear?

SHELLEY, *Song: To the Men of England*. St. 1.

To tear at pleasure the dejected land,
With starving labour pampering idle waste.

JAMES THOMSON, *Liberty*. Pt. iv, l. 1159.

8
Clamorous pauperism feasteth,
While honest labour, pining, hideth his sharp ribs.

TUPPER, *Proverbial Philosophy: Of Discretion*.

9
Too long that some may rest
Tired millions toil unblest.

WILLIAM WATSON, *New National Anthem*.

10
We have fed you all for a thousand years,
And you hail us still unfed,
Though there's never a dollar of all your wealth
But marks the worker's dead.

UNKNOWN, *We Have Fed You All*.

LAMB

11
Mary had a little lamb,
Its fleece was white as snow,
And every where that Mary went
The lamb was sure to go. . . .
"What makes the lamb love Mary so?"
The eager children cry.
"Oh, Mary loves the lamb, you know,"
The teacher did reply.

SARAH JOSEPHA HALE, *Mary's Lamb*. The poem has been claimed for one John Roulstone, of Sterling, Mass., but is undoubtedly Mrs. Hale's. It was first printed over her initials in the *Juvenile Miscellany*, Sept., 1830, and was included in her *Poems for Our Children*, published in Nov., 1830. (See FINLEY, *The Lady of Godey's*. Ch. 17.)

12
I was like a lamb or an ox that is brought to the slaughter.

Old Testament: Jeremiah, xi, 19.

13
Behold the Lamb of God.

New Testament: John, i, 29. (Agnus Dei.—*Vulgate*.)

14
The lamb thy riot dooms to bleed today,
Had he thy reason, would he skip and play?
Pleas'd to the last, he crops the flowery food,
And licks the hand just rais'd to shed his blood.

POPE, *Essay on Man*. Epis. i, l. 81.

15
But the poor man had nothing, save one little ewe lamb, which he had bought and nourished up . . . and was unto him as a daughter.

Old Testament: II Samuel, xii, 3.

1
The ewe that will not hear her lamb when it baes will never answer a calf when he bleats.
SHAKESPEARE, *Much Ado About Nothing*. Act iii, sc. 3, l. 75.

2
In peace was never gentle lamb more mild.
SHAKESPEARE, *Richard II*. Act ii, sc. 1, l. 174.

3
Lions in the field and lambs in chamber.
THOMAS USK, *Testament of Love*. (c. 1387)

We say it is comely for a man to be a lamb in the house, and a lion in the field.
GEORGE PUTTENHAM, *English Poesie*, 299. (1589)

Though lions to their enemies they were lambs to their friends.
BENJAMIN DISRAELI, *The Infernal Marriage*. Pt. ii, ch. 4.

4
Abroad in the meadows to see the young lambs
Run sporting about by the side of their dams
With fleeces so clean and so white.
ISAAC WATTS, *Innocent Play*.

LAMENTATION, see Mourning

LANGUAGE

See also Grammar, Speech, Words

I—Language: Definitions

5
Examine Language; what, if you except some few primitive elements (of natural sound), what is it all but Metaphors, recognized as such, or no longer recognized?
CARLYLE, *Sartor Resartus*. Bk. i, ch. 11.

All slang is metaphor, and all metaphor is poetry.
G. K. CHESTERTON, *A Defence of Slang*.

I hate to hunt down a tired metaphor.
BYRON, *Don Juan*. Canto xiii, st. 36.

6
Language is the archives of history. . . . Language is fossil poetry.
EMERSON, *Essays, Second Series: The Poet*.

Language is a city to the building of which every human being brought a stone.
EMERSON, *Letters and Social Aims: Quotation and Originality*.

7
Language,—human language,—after all is but little better than the croak and cackle of fowls, and other utterances of brute nature,—sometimes not so adequate.
HAWTHORNE, *American Note-Books*, 14 July, 1850.

8
Every language is a temple, in which the soul of those who speak it is enshrined.
O. W. HOLMES, *The Professor at the Breakfast-Table*. Ch. 2.

9
Languages are the pedigrees of nations.
SAMUEL JOHNSON. (BOSWELL, *Life*, v, 224.)

Language is the only instrument of science, and words are but the signs of ideas.
SAMUEL JOHNSON, *Preface to His Dictionary*.

Languages are no more than the keys of Sciences. He who despises one, slights the other.
LA BRUYÈRE, *Les Caractères*. Ch. 12.

10
Language is the dress of thought.
SAMUEL JOHNSON, *Lives of the Poets: Cowley*.
See also CHESTERFIELD *under* WORD.

Language is called the Garment of Thought: however, it should rather be, Language is the Flesh-Garment, the Body, of Thought.
CARLYLE, *Sartor Resartus*. Bk. i, ch. 11.

Language is the picture and counterpart of thought.
MARK HOPKINS, *Address*, 1 Dec., 1841.

11
Accent is the soul of a language; it gives the feeling and truth to it. (L'accent est l'âme du discours, il lui donne le sentiment et la vérité.)
ROUSSEAU, *Émile*. Bk. i.

The accent of one's country dwells in the mind and the heart, as well as on the tongue. (L'accent du pays où l'on est né demeure dans l'esprit et dans le cœur, comme dans le langage.)
LA ROCHEFOUCAULD, *Maximes*. No. 342.

My dialect, which you discommend so much.
SHAKESPEARE, *King Lear*. Act ii, sc. 2, l. 115.

12
Language is the memory of the human race. It is as a thread or nerve of life running through all the ages, connecting them into one common, prolonged and advancing existence.
WILLIAM SMITH, *Thorndale*. Pt. i, sec. 11.

13
Language is but a poor bull's-eye lantern wherewith to show off the vast cathedral of the world.
R. L. STEVENSON, *Walt Whitman*.

14
Language is the amber in which a thousand precious and subtle thoughts have been safely imbedded and preserved.
R. C. TRENCH, *The Study of Words: Introductory Lecture*.

15
Language, as well as the faculty of speech, was the immediate gift of God.
NOAH WEBSTER, *Preface to His Dictionary*.

Language is the expression of ideas, and if the people of one country cannot preserve an identity of ideas they cannot retain an identity of language.
NOAH WEBSTER, *Preface to His Dictionary*.

II—Language: Apothegms

16
Speak the language of the company that you are in; speak it purely, and unlarded with any other.
LORD CHESTERFIELD, *Letters*, 22 Feb., 1748.

What progress do you make in the language

[Italian] in which Charles the Fifth said that he would choose to speak to his mistress? . . . You already possess, and, I hope, take care not to forget, that language [English] which he reserved for his horse. You are absolutely master, too, of that language [French] in which he said he would converse with men.
LORD CHESTERFIELD, *Letters,* 25 Jan., 1750.

1
The language of the street is always strong. What can describe the folly and emptiness of scolding like the word jawing?
EMERSON, *Journals,* 1840.

His language is painful and free.
BRET HARTE, *His Answer.*

2
We shall never understand one another until we reduce the language to seven words.
KAHLIL GIBRAN, *Sand and Foam.*

That is not good language that all understand not.
GEORGE HERBERT, *Jacula Prudentum.*

3
Custom is the most certain mistress of language, as the public stamp makes the current money.
BEN JONSON, *Explorata: Consuetudo.*

He strikes no coin, 'tis true, but coins new phrases,
And vends them forth as knaves vend gilded counters,
Which wise men scorn and fools accept in payment.
UNKNOWN. (Quoted by SCOTT, *The Monastery,* as from an old play.)

4
The Turkish language is like that: it says a lot in few words. (La langue turque est comme cela, elle dit beaucoup en peu de paroles.)
MOLIÈRE, *Le Bourgeois Gentilhomme.* Act iv, sc. 4.

5
I find sufficient store of stuff in our language, but some defect of fashion.
MONTAIGNE, *Essays.* Bk. iii, ch. 5.

6
I am a barbarian here, because I am understood by no one. (Barbarus hic ego sum, quia non intelligor ulli.)
OVID, *Tristia.* Bk. v, eleg. 10, l. 37.

7
Similes are like songs in love:
They much describe; they nothing prove.
MATTHEW PRIOR, *Alma.* Canto iii, l. 314.

Thou hast the most unsavoury similes.
SHAKESPEARE, *I Henry IV.* Act i, sc. 2, l. 88.

Oft on the dappled turf at ease
I sit, and play with similes,
Loose type of things through all degrees.
WORDSWORTH, *To the Daisy.* No. 2.

No simile runs on all fours. (Nullum simile quatuor pedibus currit.)
UNKNOWN. A Latin proverb, quoted by SIR EDWARD COKE, *Institutes.*

Allegory dwells in a transparent palace. (L' allégorie habite un palais diaphane.)
LEMIERRE, *Peinture.* Sec. 3.

8
Moth: They have been at a great feast of languages, and have stolen the scraps.
Costard: O, they have lived long in the alms-basket of words.
SHAKESPEARE, *Love's Labour's Lost.* Act v, sc. 1, l. 40.

9
There is not chastity enough in language
Without offence to utter them.
SHAKESPEARE, *Much Ado About Nothing.* Act iv, sc. i, l. 98.

Language was not powerful enough to describe the infant phenomenon.
DICKENS, *Nicholas Nickleby.* Ch. 23.

10
Sure, if I reprehend anything in this world, it is the use of my oracular tongue, and a nice derangement of epitaphs!
SHERIDAN, *The Rivals.* Act iii, sc. 3.

III—Language: Greek and Latin

11
Beside 'tis known he could speak Greek
As naturally as pigs squeak;
That Latin was no more difficile
Than to a blackbird 'tis to whistle.
BUTLER, *Hudibras.* Pt. i, canto i, l. 51.

A Babylonish dialect
Which learned pedants much affect.
BUTLER, *Hudibras.* Pt. i, canto i, l. 93.

He that is but able to express
No sense at all in several languages,
Will pass for learneder than he that's known
To speak the strongest reason in his own.
BUTLER, *Satire Upon the Abuse of Learning.* Pt. i, l. 65.

For though to smatter ends of Greek
Or Latin be the rhetoric
Of pedants counted, and vain-glorious,
To smatter French is meritorious.
BUTLER, *Satire Upon Our Ridiculous Imitation of the French,* l. 127.

12
He Greek and Latin speaks with greater ease
Than hogs eat acorns, and tame pigeons peas.
LIONEL CRANFIELD, *Panegyric on Tom Coriate.*

13
The ancient languages are the scabbard which holds the mind's sword.
GOETHE, *Table-Talk,* 1814. A paraphrase from Luther.

He who is ignorant of foreign languages knows not his own.
GOETHE, *Kunst und Alterthum.*

The knowledge of the ancient languages is mainly a luxury.
JOHN BRIGHT, *Letter to J. Churton Collins,* 1886.

1
And though thou hadst small Latin and less Greek.
BEN JONSON, *To the Memory of My Beloved Master, William Shakespeare.*

Small skill in Latin, and still less in Greek,
Is more than adequate to all I seek.
COWPER, *Tirocinium*, l. 385.

2
Everything is Greek, when it is more shameful to be ignorant of Latin. (Omnia Græce! Cum sit turpe magis nostris nescire Latine.)
JUVENAL, *Satires*. Sat. vi, l. 187. The concluding phrase is said to be spurious.

3
A laudation in Greek is of marvelous efficacy at the beginning of a book. (Une louange en grec est d'une merveilleuse efficace à la tête d'un livre.)
MOLIÈRE, *Les Précieuses Ridicules: Préface.*

4
This is your devoted friend, sir, the manifold linguist.
SHAKESPEARE, *All's Well that Ends Well.* Act iv, sc. 3, l. 264.

Speaks three or four languages word for word without book.
SHAKESPEARE, *Twelfth Night.* Act i, sc. 3, l. 27.

5
Cassius: Did Cicero say anything?
Casca: Ay, he spoke Greek.
Cassius: To what effect?
Casca: Nay, an I tell you that I'll ne'er look you i' the face again: but those that understood him smiled at one another and shook their heads; but, for mine own part, it was Greek to me.
SHAKESPEARE, *Julius Cæsar.* Act i, sc. 2, l. 281.

Hum, I think this is heathen Greek; I'm sure 'tis so to me.
APHRA BEHN, *The False Count.* Act iv, sc. 1.

All this to the husbandman was heathen Greek.
CERVANTES, *Don Quixote.* Pt. ii, ch. 19.

It is Greek, it cannot be read. (Græcum est, non potest legi.)
FRANCIS ACCURSIUS. There is a fable that a scholar of Queen's College, Oxon, strolling in Bagley Wood some centuries ago, encountered a wild boar, which attacked him. The student thrust the volume of Aristotle he was reading into the boar's jaws, crying out, "Græcum est," and so choked the brute. In commemoration of this exploit, a boar's head is still served every Christmas at the college.

It is Hebrew to me. (C'est de l'hebreu pour moi.)
MOLIÈRE, *L'Étourdi.* Act iii, sc. 3.

6
Learn Greek; it is the language of wisdom.
BERNARD SHAW, *The Adventures of the Black Girl in Her Search for God.*

7
Lord, they'd have taught me Latin in pure waste!
Lash'd into Latin by the tingling rod.
ROBERT BROWNING, *Fra Lippo Lippi.*

Lash'd into Latin by the tingling rod.
JOHN GAY, *The Birth of the Squire*, l. 46.

8
Away with him, away with him! he speaks Latin.
SHAKESPEARE, *II Henry VI.* Act iv, sc. 7, l. 62.

O! good my lord, no Latin;
I'm not such a truant since my coming,
As not to know the language I have liv'd in.
SHAKESPEARE, *Henry VIII.* Act iii, sc. 1, l. 42.

9
Egad, I think the interpreter is the hardest to be understood of the two!
SHERIDAN, *The Critic.* Act i, sc. 2.

IV—Language: English

10
God save the king, that is lord of this language.
CHAUCER, *The Astrolabe: Prologue*, l. 63. (c. 1380)

My dear ma'am how do you clack away,
King George's English hack away.
JOHN O'KEEFFE, *The Farmer.* Act i, sc. 3. (1787)

Here will be an old abusing of God's patience and the king's English.
SHAKESPEARE, *The Merry Wives of Windsor.* Act i, sc. 4, l. 5. (1600)

If a man should charge them for counterfeiting the king's English.
THOMAS WILSON, *Rhetorique*, 162. (1560)

11
Praise enough
To fill th' ambition of a private man,
That Chatham's language was his mother-tongue.
COWPER, *The Task.* Bk. ii, l. 235. (1783)

12
Sydneian showers
Of sweet discourse, whose powers
Can crown old Winter's head with flowers.
RICHARD CRASHAW, *Wishes to His (Supposed) Mistress.*

13
And who in time knows whither we may vent
The treasure of our tongue? To what strange shores
This gain of our best glory shall be sent,
T' enrich unknowing nations with our stores?
What worlds in th' yet unformed Occident
May come refin'd with th' accents that are ours?
SAMUEL DANIEL, *Musophilus.*

Well-languag'd Daniel.
WILLIAM BROWNE, *Britannia's Pastorals.* Bk. ii, song 2, l. 303. Referring to Samuel Daniel.

14
I trade both with the living and the dead for the enrichment of our native language.
DRYDEN, *Æneid: Dedication to Translation.*

15
I like to be beholden to the great metropolitan English speech, the sea which receives

tributaries from every region under heaven. I should as soon think of swimming across Charles River when I wish to go to Boston, as of reading all my books in originals, when I have them rendered for me in my mother tongue.

EMERSON, *Society and Solitude: Books.*

There is no more welcome gift to men than a new symbol. . . . Greek mythology called the sea "the tear of Saturn." The return of the soul to God was described as "a flask of water broken into the sea." St. John gave us the Christian figure of "souls washed in the blood of Christ." The aged Michel Angelo indicates his perpetual study as in boyhood,—"I carry my satchel still." Machiavel described the papacy as "a stone inserted in the body of Italy to keep the wound open." To the Parliament debating how to tax America, Burke exclaimed, "Shear the wolf." Our Kentuckian orator said of his dissent from his companion, "I showed him the back of my hand."

EMERSON, *Letters and Social Aims: Poetry and Imagination.*

1

Let foreign nations of their language boast,
What fine variety each tongue affords;
I like our language, as our men and coast;
Who cannot dress it well, want wit, not words.

GEORGE HERBERT, *The Sun.*

2

The American language differs from English in that it seeks the top of expression while English seeks its lowly valleys.

SALVADOR DE MADARIAGA, *Americans Are Boys.*

3

Thou whoreson Zed! thou unnecessary letter!

SHAKESPEARE, *King Lear.* Act ii, sc. 2, l. 69.

4

Dan Chaucer, well of English undefiled.

SPENSER, *Faerie Queene.* Bk. iv, canto ii, st. 32.

From purest wells of English undefiled
None deeper drank than he, the New World's Child.

WHITTIER, *James Russell Lowell.*

5

Oh, but the heavenly grammar did I hold
Of that high speech which angels' tongues turn gold! . . .
Or if that language yet with us abode
Which Adam in the garden talked with God!
But our untempered speech descends—poor heirs!
Grimy and rough-cast still from Babel's bricklayers:
Curse on the brutish jargon we inherit,
Strong but to damn, not memorise, a spirit!

FRANCIS THOMPSON, *Her Portrait.*

6

English as She is Spoke.

ANDREW WHITE TUER. Title of a reprint (1883) of the English part of a book first issued in 1855 at Paris, entitled *O novo guia da conversacao en Portuguez e Inglez* (*A Guide to English Conversation for the Use of Portuguese Students*). "English as she is spoke" does not occur in the original, but the specimens of English given there were so grotesque as to suggest the title to the English publisher, Mr. Tuer.

Under the tropic is our language spoke.

EDMUND WALLER, *Upon the Death of the Lord Protector.*

LARK

I—Lark: Apothegms

7

A skylark wounded on the wing
Doth make a cherub cease to sing.

WILLIAM BLAKE, *Auguries of Innocence.*

8

To rise with the lark, and go to bed with the lamb.

NICHOLAS BRETON, *Court and County,* p. 183.

Rise with the lark, and with the lark to bed.

JAMES HURDIS, *The Village Curate.*

Goe to bed with the Lamb, and rise with the Lark.

JOHN LYLY, *Euphues,* p. 229.

9

Near all the birds
Will sing at dawn—and yet we do not take
The chaffering swallow for the holy lark.

E. B. BROWNING, *Aurora Leigh.* Bk. i, l. 951.

10

The busy lark, the messenger of day.

CHAUCER, *The Knightes Tale,* l. 1493.

It was the lark, the herald of the morn.

SHAKESPEARE, *Romeo and Juliet.* Act iii, sc. 5, l. 6.

Up springs the lark,
Shrill-voic'd, and loud, the messenger of morn.

THOMSON, *The Seasons: Spring,* l. 590.

11

When the sky falleth we shall have Larks.

JOHN HEYWOOD, *Proverbs.* Pt. i, ch. 4.

By robbing Peter he paid Paul . . . and hoped to catch larks if ever the heavens should fall. (Si les nues tomboyent esperoyt prendre les alouettes tous rousties.)

RABELAIS, *Works.* Bk. i, ch. 11.

12

He thinks that roasted larks will fall into his mouth.

JAMES HOWELL, *Proverbs,* 3. Of a sluggard.

13

The sunrise wakes the lark to sing.

CHRISTINA ROSSETTI, *Bird Raptures.*

14

Hark, hark! the lark at heaven's gate sings,
And Phœbus 'gins arise.

SHAKESPEARE, *Cymbeline.* Act ii, sc. 3, l. 21.

How at heaven's gates she claps her wings,
The morn not waking till she sings.

JOHN LYLY, *Alexander and Campaspe.* Act v, sc. i.

15

Merry larks are ploughmen's clocks.

SHAKESPEARE, *Love's Labour's Lost.* Act v, sc. 2, l. 914.

Then my dial goes not true; I took this lark for a bunting.
SHAKESPEARE, *All's Well that Ends Well,* ii, 5, 5.

1
It is the lark that sings so out of tune,
Straining harsh discords and unpleasing sharps.
SHAKESPEARE, *Romeo and Juliet.* Act iii, 5, 27.

2
Larikie, Larikie lee!
Wha'll gang up the heaven wi' me?
No the lout that lies in his bed,
No the doolfu' that dreeps his head.
UNKNOWN, *The Lark's Song.*

II—Lark: Its Loveliness

3
The music soars within the little lark,
And the lark soars.
E. B. BROWNING, *Aurora Leigh.* Bk. iii, l. 155.

4
Who loves not music, still may pause to hark
Nature's free gladness hymning in the lark.
BULWER-LYTTON, *The New Timon.* Pt. iii, canto ii, l. 13.

5
Oh, stay, sweet warbling woodlark, stay,
Nor quit for me the trembling spray!
A hapless lover courts thy lay,
Thy soothing, fond complaining.
BURNS, *Address to the Woodlark.*

6
'Tis sweet to hear the merry lark,
That bids a blithe good-morrow.
HARTLEY COLERIDGE, *Song.*

The merry lark he soars on high,
No worldly thought o'ertakes him.
He sings aloud to the clear blue sky,
And the daylight that awakes him.
HARTLEY COLERIDGE, *Song.*

7
But the Lark is so brimful of gladness and love,
The green fields below him, the blue sky above,
That he sings, and he sings, and for ever sings he—
"I love my Love, and my Love loves me!"
S. T. COLERIDGE, *Answer to a Child's Question.*

And so, his senses gradually wrapt
In a half sleep, he dreams of better worlds,
And dreaming, hears thee still, O singing lark,
That singest like an angel in the clouds.
S. T. COLERIDGE, *Fears in Solitude,* l. 25.

8
I said to the sky-poised Lark:
"Hark—hark!
Thy note is more loud and free
Because there lies safe for thee
A little nest on the ground."
DINAH M. M. CRAIK, *A Rhyme About Birds.*

9
The lark now leaves his watery nest,
And climbing, shakes his dewy wings.
SIR WILLIAM D'AVENANT, *Morning Song.*

10
The pretty Lark, climbing the welkin clear,
Chants with a cheer, Heer peer, I near my Dear;
Then stooping thence (seeming her fall to rue)
Adieu, she saith, adieu, dear Dear, adieu.
DU BARTAS, *Devine Weekes and Workes.* Week i, day 5. (Sylvester, tr.)

11
Over the cloudlet dim,
Over the rainbow's rim,
Musical cherub, soar, singing, away!
Then, when the gloaming comes,
Low in the heather blooms
Sweet will thy welcome and bed of love be!
Emblem of happiness,
Blest is thy dwelling-place—
O, to abide in the desert with thee!
JAMES HOGG, *The Skylark.*

The shrill sweet lark.
THOMAS HOOD, *Plea of the Midsummer Fairies.*

12
For singing till his heaven fills,
'Tis love of earth that he instils.
GEORGE MEREDITH, *The Lark Ascending.*

13
To hear the lark begin his flight,
And singing, startle the dull night,
From his watch-tower in the skies,
Till the dappled Dawn doth rise;
Then to come, in spite of sorrow,
And at my window bid good morrow.
MILTON, *L'Allegro,* l. 41.

And now the herald lark
Left his ground-nest, high tow'ring to descry
The morn's approach, and greet her with his song.
MILTON, *Paradise Regained.* Bk. ii, l. 279.

14
No more the mounting larks, while Daphne sings,
Shall, list'ning, in mid-air suspend their wings.
POPE, *Pastorals: Winter,* l. 53.

15
Oh, far, far, far,
As any spire or star,
Beyond the cloistered wall!
Oh, high, high, high,
A heart-throb in the sky—
Then not at all!
LIZETTE WOODWORTH REESE, *The Lark.*

16
The lark whose notes do beat
The vaulty heaven, so high above our heads.
SHAKESPEARE, *Romeo and Juliet.* Act iii, sc. 5, l. 21.

Lo, here the gentle lark, weary of rest,
From his moist cabinet mounts up on high,
And wakes the morning, from whose silver breast
The sun ariseth in his majesty.
SHAKESPEARE, *Venus and Adonis,* l. 853.

The lark, that tirra-lyra chants.
SHAKESPEARE, *Winter's Tale.* Act iv, sc. 3, l. 9

1
Hail to thee, blithe Spirit!—
  Bird thou never wert!—
That from Heaven, or near it,
  Pourest thy full heart
In profuse strains of unpremeditated art.
  SHELLEY, *To a Skylark*. St. 1.

All the earth and air
  With thy voice is loud,
As, when Night is bare,
  From one lonely cloud,
The moon rains out her beams, and Heaven is overflowed.
  SHELLEY, *To a Skylark*. St. 6.

Like a glow-worm golden
  In a dell of dew,
Scattering unbeholden
  Its aërial hue
Among the flowers and grass which screen it from the view.
  SHELLEY, *To a Skylark*. St. 10.

Teach us, Sprite or Bird,
  What sweet thoughts are thine;
I have never heard
  Praise of love or wine
That panted forth a flood of rapture so divine.
  SHELLEY, *To a Skylark*. St. 13.

Better than all measures
  Of delightful sound—
Better than all treasures
  That in books are found,
Thy skill to poet were, thou scorner of the ground!
  SHELLEY, *To a Skylark*. St. 20.

Teach me half the gladness
  That thy brain must know,
Such harmonious madness
  From my lips would flow,
The world should listen then—as I am listening now.
  SHELLEY, *To a Skylark*. St. 21.

2
Now rings the woodland loud and long,
  The distance takes a lovelier hue,
  And drown'd in yonder living blue
The lark becomes a sightless song.
  TENNYSON, *In Memoriam*. Pt. cxv.

3
How the blithe Lark runs up the golden stair
That leans through cloudy gates from Heaven to Earth.
  FREDERICK TENNYSON, *The Skylark*.

4
Not loftiest bard of mightiest mind
  Shall ever chant a note so pure,
Till he can cast the earth behind,
  And breathe in heaven secure.
  WILLIAM WATSON, *The First Skylark of Spring*.

5
But *He* is risen, a later star of dawn,
Glittering and twinkling near yon rosy cloud;
Bright gem instinct with music, vocal spark;
The happiest bird that sprang out of the Ark!
  WORDSWORTH, *A Morning Exercise*, l. 27.

Ethereal minstrel! pilgrim of the sky!
Dost thou despise the earth where cares abound?
Or, while the wings aspire, are heart and eye
Both with thy nest upon the dewy ground?
Thy nest which thou canst drop into at will,
Those quivering wings composed, that music still!
  WORDSWORTH, *To a Skylark*.

Leave to the nightingale her shady wood;
A privacy of glorious light is thine:
Whence thou dost pour upon the world a flood
Of harmony, with instinct more divine:
Type of the wise who soar, but never roam:
True to the kindred points of Heaven and Home!
  WORDSWORTH, *To a Skylark*.

The bird that soars on highest wing,
  Builds on the ground her lowly nest;
And she that doth most sweetly sing,
  Sings in the shade when all things rest:
—In lark and nightingale we see
What honour hath humility.
  JAMES MONTGOMERY, *Humility*.

The lark, that shuns on lofty boughs to build
Her humble nest, lies silent in the field.
  EDMUND WALLER, *Of the Queen*.

LATENESS

See also Delay

6
Five minutes—Zounds! I have been five minutes too late all my lifetime.
  HANNAH COWLEY, *Belle's Stratagem*. Act i, sc. 1.

7
Better late than never. (Potius sero, quam nunquam.)
  LIVY, *History*. Bk. iv, sec. 23. The French form of the proverb is, "Il vaut mieux tard que jamais." (VÉPRIE, *Les Proverbes Communs.*) HEYWOOD, *Proverbs*, i, 10; MATTHEW HENRY, *Commentaries: Matthew*, xxi; BUNYAN, *Pilgrim's Progress*, pt. i; etc.

For better than never is late.
  CHAUCER, *The Chanouns Yemannes Tale*, l. 857. (c. 1386)

Better late than never, but better never late.
  C. H. SPURGEON, *Salt-Cellars*.

Better now than never.
  PEPYS, *Diary*, 17 March, 1667.

Better late than never, as Noah remarked to the Zebra, which had understood that passengers arrived in alphabetical order.
  BERT LESTON TAYLOR, *The So-Called Human Race*, p. 265.

NEVER TOO LATE TO MEND, *see* REFORMATION.

8
Often that which has come latest on the scene seems to have accomplished the whole matter. (Semper enim quod postremum adjectum sit, id rem totam, videtur traxisse.)
  LIVY, *History*. Bk. xxvii, ch. 45.

9
Ah! nothing is too late
Till the tired heart shall cease to palpitate.
  LONGFELLOW, *Morituri Salutamus*. St. 24.

1
Too late you look back to the land when, the rope being loosed, the curved keel rushes into the deep. (Sero respicitur tellus, ubi fune soluto, Currit in immensum panda carina salum.)
OVID, *Amores*. Bk. ii, eleg. 11, l. 23.

Too late I grasp my shield after my wounds. (Sero clypeum post vulnera sumo.)
OVID, *Tristia*. Bk. i, eleg. 3, l. 35.

There is an old adage about gladiators, that they plan their fight in the ring. (Vetus proverbium est gladiatorem in harena capere consilium.)
SENECA, *Epistulæ ad Lucilium*. Epis. xxii, 1.

To call a counsel when the enemy is under the very walls. (Cogere consilium, cum muros obsidet hostis.)
VERGIL, *Æneid*. Bk. xi, l. 304.

It is nae time to stoop when the head's aff.
JOHN RAY, *Proverbs: Scottish*.

The bird cries out too late when it is taken. (A tard crie l'oiseau quant il est pris.)
J. DE LA VEPRIE, *Les Proverbes Communs*.

2
My name is Might-have-been;
I am also called No-more, Too-late,
Farewell.
D. G. ROSSETTI, *Sonnets*. No. 97.

3
You come late, yet you come! (Spät kommt ihr—doch ihr kommt!)
SCHILLER, *Piccolomini*. Act i, sc. 1, l. 1.

4
And all too late the advantage came.
SCOTT, *The Lady of the Lake*. Canto v, st. 16.

5
Too early seen unknown, and known too late!
SHAKESPEARE, *Romeo and Juliet*. Act i, sc. 5, l. 141.

6
Ah, "all things come to those who wait,"
(I say these words to make me glad),
But something answers soft and sad,
"They come, but often come too late."
MARY MONTGOMERY SINGLETON, *Tout Vient à Qui Sait Attendre*.

While we send for the napkin the soup gets cold,
While the bonnet is trimming the face grows old,
When we've matched our buttons the pattern is sold,
And everything comes too late—too late.
FITZ HUGH LUDLOW, *Too Late*.

7
Late, late, so late! but we can enter still.
Too late, too late! ye cannot enter now.
TENNYSON, *Guinevere*, l. 167.

8
He was always late on principle, his principle being that punctuality is the thief of time.
OSCAR WILDE, *Picture of Dorian Gray*. Ch. 3.

If you're there before it's over, you're on time.
JAMES J. WALKER, *Remark*, to reporters, on arriving late at a dinner, Oct., 1931.

LAUGHTER

See also Smile

I—Laughter: Apothegms

9
Where is the laughter that shook the rafter?
Where is the rafter, by the way?
T. B. ALDRICH, *An Old Castle*.

10
Laffing iz the sensation ov pheeling good all over, and showing it principally in one spot.
JOSH BILLINGS, *Laffing*.

11
Laughter's never an end, it's a by-product.
STRUTHERS BURT, *Festival*. Ch. 13.

12
How much lies in Laughter: the cipher-key, wherewith we decipher the whole man.
CARLYLE, *Sartor Resartus*. Bk. i, ch. 4.

Men show their characters in nothing more clearly than in what they think laughable.
GOETHE, *Maxims*.

Men have been wise in very different modes. but they have always laughed the same way.
SAMUEL JOHNSON, *Works*, ii, 45.

13
'Tis fair lie down and laugh.
ANTHONY COPLEY, *A Fig for Fortune*, l. 24. (1596)

14
Laugh and be fat.
SIR JOHN HARINGTON, *Metamorphosis of Ajax*, 68. (1596)

Laugh and be fat, sir, your penance is known.
BEN JONSON, *The Penates*. (1604)

I'll laugh and be fat, for care kills a cat.
UNKNOWN. (*Roxburghe Ballads*, i, 476. 1610)

Laugh and be well.
MATTHEW GREEN, *The Spleen*, l. 93. (1737)

Laugh and be fat all the world over.
DAVID GARRICK, *Letters*. Vol. i, p. 201. (1765)

15
He laugheth that winneth.
JOHN HEYWOOD, *Proverbs*. Pt. i, ch. 4. (1546)

So, so, so, so. They laugh that win.
SHAKESPEARE, *Othello*. Act iv, sc. 1, l. 125.

Let them laugh that win.
DAVID GARRICK, *Epilogue* to Colman's *English Merchant*.

16
You laugh, and you are quite right,
For yours is the dawn of the morning,
For me is the solemn good night.
THEODORE EDWARD HOOK, *Impromptu at Fulham*. There are other versions of this famous impromptu in allusion to young Stopford, who had laughed heartily at the previous verse, but this is the best. J. R. Planché, who was present, asserts that the last line should be, "And God send you a good night."

17
Laughter holding both his sides.
MILTON, *L'Allegro*, l. 31.

1
He laugheth but from the lips forward.
SIR THOMAS MORE, *Confutation of Tyndale's Answer*, p. 148.

2
To laugh, if but for an instant only, has never been granted to man before the fortieth day from his birth, and then it is looked upon as a miracle of precocity.
PLINY THE ELDER, *Historia Naturalis*. Bk. vii, ch. 1.

3
Is he gone to a land of no laughter,
The man who made mirth for us all?
JAMES RHOADES, *On the Death of Artemus Ward*.

4
My lungs began to crow like chanticleer, . . .
And I did laugh sans intermission
An hour by his dial.
SHAKESPEARE, *As You Like It*. Act ii, sc. 7, l. 30.

I will laugh like a hyen.
SHAKESPEARE, *As You Like It*. Act iv, sc. 1, l. 158.

With his eyes in flood with laughter.
SHAKESPEARE, *Cymbeline*. Act i, sc. 6, l. 74.

O, I am stabb'd with laughter.
SHAKESPEARE, *Love's Labour's Lost*. Act v, sc. 2, l. 79.

Laugh when I am merry, and claw no man in his humour.
SHAKESPEARE, *Much Ado About Nothing*. Act i, sc. 3, l. 18.

5
A sight to shake
The midriff of despair with laughter.
TENNYSON, *The Princess*. Pt. i, l. 197.

6
Now you can laugh but on one side of your mouth, friend.
TORRIANO, *Piazza Universale*, p. 173. (1666)

If you provoke me, I'll make you laugh on the wrong side o' your mouth.
JOHN OZELL, *Molière*, iv, 36. (1714)

7
He laughs best that laughs last.
SIR JOHN VANBRUGH, *The Country House*. Act ii, sc. 5. (1706) Vanbrugh is quoting an old proverb, common to all languages.

Your Grace knows the French proverb, "He laughs best who laughs last."
SCOTT, *Peveril of the Peak*. Ch. 38.

Better the last smile than the first laughter.
JOHN RAY, *English Proverbs*.

8
The laughter of man is the contentment of God.
JOHN WEISS, *Wit, Humor, and Shakspeare*.

9
I canna be angry for lauchin.
JOHN WILSON, *Noctes Ambrosianæ*. No. 35.

II—Laughter: Its Virtue

10
When the green woods laugh with the voice of joy,
And the dimpling stream runs laughing by;
When the air does laugh with our merry wit,
And the green hill laughs with the noise of it.
WILLIAM BLAKE, *Laughing Song*.

11
And yet methinks the older that one grows
Inclines us more to laugh than scold, though laughter
Leaves us so doubly serious shortly after.
BYRON, *Beppo*. St. 79.

12
The man who cannot laugh is not only fit for treasons, stratagems, and spoils, but his whole life is already a treason and a stratagem.
CARLYLE, *Sartor Resartus*. Bk. i, ch. 4.

13
The most completely lost of all days is that on which one has not laughed. (La plus perdue de toutes les journées est celle où l'on n'a pas rit.)
CHAMFORT, *Maximes*.

14
'Tis a good thing to laugh at any rate; and if a straw can tickle a man, it is an instrument of happiness.
JOHN DRYDEN, *Essays*. Vol. ii, p. 133.

15
I am the laughter of the new-born child
On whose soft-breathing sleep an angel smiled.
R. W. GILDER, *Ode*.

Very sound of very light,
Heard from morning's rosiest height,
When the soul of all delight,
Fills a child's clear laughter.
SWINBURNE, *A Child's Laughter*.

16
I can't say whether we had more wit amongst us than usual, but I am certain we had more laughing, which answered the end as well.
GOLDSMITH, *The Vicar of Wakefield*. Ch. 32.

17
I'd rather laugh, a bright-haired boy,
Than reign, a gray-beard king.
O. W. HOLMES, *The Old Man Dreams*.

You hear that boy laughing?—You think he's all fun;
But the angels laugh, too, at the good he has done;
The children laugh loud as they troop to his call,
And the poor man that knows him laughs loudest of all!
O. W. HOLMES, *The Boys*.

18
Without love and laughter there is no joy; live amid love and laughter. (Sine amore jocisque Nil est jucundum; vivas in amore jocisque.)
HORACE, *Epistles*. Bk. i, epis. 6, l. 65.

1
Laugh, if you are wise. (Ride, si sapis.)
MARTIAL, *Epigrams*. Bk. ii, epig. 41.

One inch of joy surmounts of grief a span,
Because to laugh is proper to the man.
RABELAIS, *Works: To the Reader*.

2
To be born with the gift of laughter and a sense that the world is mad.
RAFAEL SABATINI, *Scaramouche*. Ch. 1. Prize-winning answer to the question, "What makes life worth living?"

3
A good laugh is sunshine in a house.
THACKERAY, *Sketches: Love, Marriage*.

4
Earnest, sombre-browed, we follow after
You, who fly a-mocking from the ruck;
O we have a desperate need of laughter!
Give us laughter, Puck!
BEATRICE LLEWELLYN THOMAS, *To Puck*.

III—Laughter: Its Folly

5
Nothing is more silly than a silly laugh. (Nam risu inepto res ineptior nullast.)
CATULLUS, *Odes*. Ode 39, l. 16.

And the loud laugh that spoke the vacant mind.
GOLDSMITH, *The Deserted Village*, l. 122.

The Horse-Laugh is a distinguishing characteristic of the rural hoyden.
RICHARD STEELE, *The Guardian*, No. 29.

The landlord's laugh was ready chorus.
BURNS, *Tam o' Shanter*.

6
Having mentioned laughing, I must particularly warn you against it; and I could heartily wish that you may often be seen to smile, but never heard to laugh, while you live. Frequent and loud laughter is the characteristic of folly and ill manners: it is the manner in which the mob express their silly joy at silly things, and they call it being merry. In my mind there is nothing so illiberal and so ill-bred as audible laughter.
LORD CHESTERFIELD, *Letters*, 9 March, 1748.

How low and unbecoming a thing laughter is, not to mention the disagreeable noise that it makes, and the shocking distortion of the face that it occasions. . . . I am neither of a melancholy nor a cynical disposition, and am as willing and as apt to be pleased as anybody; but I am sure that, since I have had the full use of my reason, nobody has ever heard me laugh.
LORD CHESTERFIELD, *Letters*, 9 March, 1748.

The vulgar often laugh, but never smile; whereas well-bred people often smile, but seldom laugh.
LORD CHESTERFIELD, *Letters*, 17 Feb., 1754.

I hate scarce smiles; I love laughing.
WILLIAM BLAKE. (GILCHRIST, *Life*, i, 62.)

7
There is nothing more unbecoming a man of quality than to laugh.
CONGREVE, *The Double-Dealer*. Act i, sc. 2.

8
If in these hallow'd times, when sober, sad,
All gentlemen are melancholy mad,
When 'tis not deem'd so great a crime by half
To violate a vestal as to laugh.
CHARLES CHURCHILL, *The Rosciad*, l. 461.

9
As the crackling of thorns under a pot, so is the laughter of the fool.
Old Testament: Ecclesiastes, vii, 6.

The more one is a fool, the more one laughs. (Plus on est de fous, plus on rit.)
DANCOURT, *Maison de Campagne*. Sc. 11.

10
Beware you don't laugh, for then you show all your faults.
EMERSON, *Conduct of Life: Behavior*.

11
Do not laugh much, nor at many things, nor boisterously. (Γέλως μὴ πολὺς ἔστω μηδὲ ἐπὶ πολλοῖς μηδὲ ἀνειμένος.)
EPICTETUS [?], *Encheiridion*, Sec. 33.

12
I believe they talked of me, for they laughed consumedly.
FARQUHAR, *The Beaux' Stratagem*. Act iii, sc. 1.

13
He who laugheth too much hath the nature of a fool; he that laugheth not at all hath the nature of an old cat.
THOMAS FULLER, *Gnomologia*.

14
Laugh not too much; the witty man laughs least.
GEORGE HERBERT, *The Church-Porch*. St. 39.

The giggler is a milk-maid.
GEORGE HERBERT, *The Church-Porch*. St. 42.

Besides, my prospects—don't you know that people won't employ
A man that wrongs his manliness by laughing like a boy,
And suspect the azure blossom that unfolds upon a shoot,
As if wisdom's old potato could not flourish at its root?
O. W. HOLMES, *Nux Postcœnatica*. St. 7.

15
Ill-timed laughter is a dangerous evil. (Γέλως ἄκαιρος ἐν βροτοῖς δεινὸν κακόν.)
MENANDER, *Monostikoi*. No. 88.

The fool will laugh though there be nought tc laugh at.
MENANDER, *Monostikoi*. No. 108. *See also under* FOOL.

16
The sense of humour has other things to do than to make itself conspicuous in the act of laughter.
ALICE MEYNELL, *Laughter*.

17
The price of a laugh is too high, if it is raised at the expense of propriety. (Nimium risus pretium est, si probitatis impendio constat.)
QUINTILIAN, *De Institutione Oratoria*. Bk. vi, ch. 3, sec. 34.

1
Theirs was the glee of martial breast,
And laughter theirs at little jest.
SCOTT, *Marmion*. Canto iii, st. 4.

2
Some that will evermore peep through their eyes,
And laugh, like parrots, at a bagpiper.
SHAKESPEARE, *The Merchant of Venice*. Act i, sc. 1, l. 52.

3
Laughter almost ever cometh of things most disproportioned to ourselves and nature: delight hath a joy in it either permanent or present; laughter hath only a scornful tickling.
SIR PHILIP SIDNEY, *The Defence of Poesie*.

4
There are not many things cheaper than supposing and laughing.
SWIFT, *On Sleeping in Church*.

IV—Laughter and Tears

See also Joy and Sorrow; Smile and Tear

5
I hasten to laugh at everything, for fear of being obliged to weep. (Je me presse de rire de tout, de peur d'être obligé d'en pleurer.)
BEAUMARCHAIS, *Le Barbier de Sèville*. Act i, sc. 2. (1775)

And if I laugh at any mortal thing,
'Tis that I may not weep.
BYRON, *Don Juan*. Canto iv, st. 4.

I struggle and struggle, and try to buffet down my cruel reflections as they rise; and when I cannot, *I am forced to try to make myself laugh that I may not cry;* for one or other I must do; and is it not philosophy carried to the highest pitch for a man to conquer such tumults of soul as I am sometimes agitated by, and in the very height of the storm to quaver out a horse-laugh?
RICHARDSON, *Clarissa Harlowe*. Letter 84.

6
Some things are of that nature as to make
One's fancy chuckle, while his heart doth ache.
BUNYAN, *The Author's Way of Sending Forth His Second Part of the Pilgrim*, l. 126.

7
For God hath not granted to woeful mortals even laughter without tears. (Ἐπεὶ θεὸς οὐδὲ γελάσσαι ἀκλαυτὶ μερόπεσσιν διζυροῖσιν ἔδωκε.)
CALLIMACHUS, *Fragmenta Incertæ*. No. 117.

8
Ill may a sad mind forge a merry face;
Nor hath constrained laughter any grace.
CHAPMAN, *Hero and Leander*. Sestiad v, l. 57.

9
On this hapless earth
There's small sincerity of mirth,
And laughter oft is but an art
To drown the outcry of the heart.
HARTLEY COLERIDGE, *Address to Certain Goldfishes*.

10
She can laugh and cry both in a wind.
THOMAS FULLER, *Gnomologia*. No. 4120.

Learn weeping and then thou shalt laugh gaining.
GEORGE HERBERT, *Jacula Prudentum*.

12
Laughter and tears are meant to turn the wheels of the same sensibility; one is wind-power and the other water-power, that is all.
O. W. HOLMES, *The Autocrat of the Breakfast-Table*. Ch. 4.

13
As men's faces smile on those who smile, so they respond to those who weep. (Ut ridentibus arrident, ita flentibus adsunt Humani voltus.)
HORACE, *Ars Poetica*, l. 101.

If you smile, he splits his sides with laughter; if he sees a friend drop a tear, he weeps; if you call for a bit of fire in winter-time, he puts on his cloak; if you say, "I am hot," he breaks into a sweat. (Si dixeris "æstuo," sudat.)
JUVENAL, *Satires*. Sat. iii, l. 100.

Joy has its friends, but grief its loneliness.
ROBERT NATHAN, *A Cedar Box*.

Laugh and the world laughs with you,
Weep and you weep alone,
For the sad old earth must borrow its mirth,
But has trouble enough of its own.
ELLA WHEELER WILCOX, *Solitude*. First printed in the N. Y. *Sun*, 25 Feb., 1883. Fraudulently claimed by John A. Joyce. (See STEVENSON, *Famous Single Poems*.)

It takes two for a kiss
Only one for a sigh,
Twain by twain we marry
One by one we die.

Joy is a partnership,
Grief weeps alone,
Many guests had Cana;
Gethsemane but one.
FREDERIC LAWRENCE KNOWLES, *Grief and Joy*.

14
We must laugh before we are happy, for fear we die before we laugh at all.
LA BRUYÈRE, *Les Caractères*. Ch. 4.

15
Take it, girl! And fear no after,
Take your fill of all this laughter,
Laugh or not, the tears will fall,
Take the laughter first of all.
RICHARD LE GALLIENNE, *Song*.

16
Even in laughter the heart is sorrowful; and the end of mirth is heaviness.
Old Testament: Proverbs, xiv, 13. Extrema gaudii luctus occupat.—*Vulgate*.

17
Better to write of laughter than of tears,
Because to laugh is proper to the man.
(Mieulx est de ris que de larmes escrire,
Pour ce que rire est le propre de l'homme.)
RABELAIS, *Works: To the Reader*.

To make the weeper laugh, the laugher weep,
He had the dialect and different skill.
SHAKESPEARE, *A Lover's Complaint*, l. 124.

1
He who laughs on Friday will weep on Sunday. (Tel qui rit vendredi, dimanche pleurera.)
RACINE, *Les Plaideurs*. Act i, sc. 1.

2
No one is more profoundly sad than he who laughs too much.
JEAN PAUL RICHTER, *Hesperus*.

3
I have asked to be left a few tears
And some laughter.
CARL SANDBURG, *Bundles*.

4
When laughter is humble, when it is not based on self-esteem, it is wiser than tears. . . . There is no cure for birth and death save to enjoy the interval. The dark background which death supplies brings out the tender colours of life in all their purity.
GEORGE SANTAYANA, *Soliloquies in England*.

5
All things are cause for either laughter or weeping. (Aut ridenda omnia aut flenda sunt.)
SENECA, *De Ira*. Bk. ii, sec. 10.

6
I am not merry; but I do beguile
The thing I am by seeming otherwise.
SHAKESPEARE, *Othello*. Act ii, sc. 1, l. 123.

7
Our sincerest laughter
With some pain is fraught.
SHELLEY, *To a Skylark*. St. 18.

8
If life were always merry,
Our souls would seek relief
And rest from weary laughter
In the quiet arms of grief.
HENRY VAN DYKE, *If All the Skies Were Sunshine*.

9
The house of laughter makes a house of woe.
YOUNG, *Night Thoughts*. Night viii, l. 757.

10
An onion can make people cry, but there has never been a vegetable invented to make them laugh.
UNKNOWN. May Irwin's favorite quotation. (*Sat. Eve. Post*, 25 Apr., 1931.)

V—Laughter and Scorn

See also Ridicule, Scorn

11
Truth's sacred fort th' exploded laugh shall win,
And coxcombs vanquish Berkeley by a grin.
JOHN BROWN, *Essay on Satire*. Pt. ii, l. 224.

Let people laugh, as long as I am warm. (Andeme yo Caliente, Y riase la gente.)
CERVANTES, *Don Quixote*. Bk. ii, ch. 50.

12
What is viler than to be laughed at? (Quid turpius quam illudi?)
CICERO, *De Amicitia*. Ch. 26, sec. 99.

13
You no doubt laugh in your sleeve. (Tu videlicet tecum ipse rides.)
CICERO, *De Finibus*. Bk. ii, ch. 23, sec. 76.

He laughed in his sleeve.
THOMAS HARMAN, *A Caveat*, 46. (1567)

Now did Oranda laugh within her sleeve.
JOHN CHALKHILL, *Thealma and Clarchus*, 2090. (1683)

14
He will laugh thee to scorn.
Apocrypha: Ecclesiasticus, xiii, 7.

15
He is not laughed at that laughs at himself first.
THOMAS FULLER, *Gnomologia*. No. 1936.

16
And a crook is in his back,
And a melancholy crack
In his laugh.
O. W. HOLMES, *The Last Leaf*.

17
And unextinguishable laughter rose among the gods. (*Ἄσβεστος δ' ἄρ' ἐνῶρτο γέλως μακάρεσσι θεοῖσιν.*)
HOMER, *Iliad*. Bk. i, l. 599; *Odyssey*, viii, 366.

Laugh with a vast and inextinguishable laughter.
SHELLEY, *Prometheus Unbound*. Act iv.

18
Can you withhold your laughter, my friends? (Risum teneatis, amici?)
HORACE, *Ars Poetica*, l. 5.

Were Democritus still on earth, he would laugh. (Si foret in terris, rideret Democritus.)
HORACE, *Epistles*. Bk. ii, epis. 1, l. 194. Democritus was the laughing philosopher. The name of Heraclitus, "the weeping philosopher," is sometimes substituted.

19
The case will be dismissed with laughter. (Solventur risu tabulæ.)
HORACE, *Satires*. Bk. ii, sat. 1, l. 86. Said of any question which only succeeds in raising general laughter, and is so dismissed, or "laughed out of court."

20
To condemn by a cutting laugh comes readily to us all. (Facilis cuivis rigidi censura cachinni.)
JUVENAL, *Satires*. Sat. x, l. 31.

21
The mocking laughter of Hell. (Das Hohngelächter der Hölle.)
LESSING, *Emilia Galotti*. Act v, sc. 2.

22
Laugh away, you fine laugher. (Riez donc, beau rieur.)
MOLIÈRE, *L'École des Maris*. Act i, sc. 2, l. 165.

23
To laugh were want of goodness and of grace,
And to be grave exceeds all power of face.
POPE, *Epistle to Dr. Arbuthnot*, l. 35.

Laugh at your friends, and if your friends are sore,
So much the better, you may laugh the more.

POPE, *Epilogue to Satires*. Dial. i, l. 55.

1
He chastises manners with a laugh. (Castigat ridendo mores.)

JEAN BAPTISTE DE SANTEUL, *Motto*, of the Opéra-Comique, Paris.

Fight Virtue's cause, stand up in Wit's defence,
Win us from vice and laugh us into sense.

THOMAS TICKELL, *On the Prospect of Peace*. St. 38.

2
Let us not be laughing-stocks to other men's humours.

SHAKESPEARE, *The Merry Wives of Windsor* Act iii, sc. 1, l. 88.

3
There are few who would not rather be hated than laughed at.

SYDNEY SMITH, *Sketches of Moral Philosophy*. Lecture 11.

4
For still the world prevail'd, and its dread laugh,
Which scarce the firm philosopher can scorn.

THOMSON, *The Seasons: Autumn*, l. 233.

LAW

I—Law: Definitions

5
Law is a form of order, and good law must necessarily mean good order.

ARISTOTLE, *Politica*. Bk. vii, ch. 4, sec. 5.

6
There are two, and only two, foundations of law, . . . equity and utility.

EDMUND BURKE, *Tracts on the Popery Laws*. Pt. i, ch. 3.

Laws, like houses, lean on one another.

EDMUND BURKE, *Tracts on the Popery Laws*. Pt. i, ch. 3.

7
Law is whatever is boldly asserted and plausibly maintained.

AARON BURR. (PARTON, *Life and Times of Aaron Burr*. Vol. i, p. 149.)

8
The absolute justice of the State, enlightened by the perfect reason of the State: that is law.

RUFUS CHOATE, *Conservative Force of the American Bar*.

9
The laws place the safety of all before the safety of individuals. (Leges omnium salutem singulorum saluti anteponunt.)

CICERO, *De Finibus*. Bk. iii, ch. 19, sec. 64.

The safety of the people shall be the highest law. (Salus populi suprema lex esto.)

CICERO, *De Legibus*. Bk. iii, sec. 3. Derived by tradition from the Twelve Tables of Roman law.

Judges ought above all to remember the Conclusion of the Roman Twelve Tables: Salus populi suprema lex; and to know that laws, except they be in order to that end, are but things captious, and oracles not well inspired.

FRANCIS BACON, *Essays: Of Judicature*.

10
Law is founded not on theory but upon nature. (Neque opinione sed natura constitutum esse jus.)

CICERO, *De Legibus*. Bk. i, ch. 10, sec. 28.

Law is nothing but a correct principle drawn from the inspiration of the gods, commanding what is honest, and forbidding the contrary.

CICERO, *Philippicæ*. No. xi, sec. 12.

11
Reason is the life of the law; nay, the common law itself is nothing but reason. . . . The law, which is perfection of reason.

SIR EDWARD COKE, *Institutes*. Pt. i.

How long soever it hath continued, if it be against reason, it is of no force in law.

SIR EDWARD COKE, *Institutes*. Pt. i.

Law governs man and reason the law.

THOMAS FULLER, *Gnomologia*. No. 3149.

Let us consider the reason of the case. For nothing is law that is not reason.

Sir JOHN POWELL, *Coggs vs. Bernard* (*2 Ld. Raym. Rep.* p. 911.)

12
The law is for the protection of the weak more than the strong.

SIR WILLIAM ERLE, *Reg. v. Woolley*. (4 Cox, C.C. 196)

13
The law groweth of sin, and doth punish it.

JOHN FLORIO, *First Fruites*. Fo. 32. (1578)

The law's made to take care of raskills.

GEORGE ELIOT, *Mill on the Floss*. Bk. iii, ch. 4.

14
The law, in its majestic equality, forbids the rich as well as the poor to sleep under bridges, to beg in the streets, and to steal bread.

ANATOLE FRANCE. (COURNOS, *Modern Plutarch*, p. 27.)

15
The Law is what it is—a majestic edifice, sheltering all of us, each stone of which rests on another.

JOHN GALSWORTHY, *Justice*. Act ii. It is the Judge speaking.

16
Law, licensed breaking of the peace.

MATTHEW GREEN, *The Spleen*, l. 286.

Law, grown a forest, where perplex
The mazes, and the brambles vex.

MATTHEW GREEN, *The Spleen*, l. 292.

17
Laws spring from the instinct of self-preservation.

R. G. INGERSOLL, *Some Mistakes of Moses*.

18
The law is the last result of human wisdom acting upon human experience for the benefit of the public.

SAMUEL JOHNSON, *Miscellanies*, i, 223.

Laws are not made for particular cases, but for men in general.
SAMUEL JOHNSON. (BOSWELL, *Life*, 1776.)

1
No law can possibly meet the convenience of every one: we must be satisfied if it be beneficial on the whole and to the majority.
LIVY, *History*. Bk. xxxiv, sec. 3.

The law is blind, and speaks in general terms;
She cannot pity where occasion serves.
THOMAS MAY, *The Heir*. Act iv. (1620)

2
The Habeas Corpus Act . . . the most stringent curb that ever legislation imposed on tyranny.
MACAULAY, *History of England*. Ch. 6.

3
The man who does no wrong needs no law. (Ὁ μηδὲν ἀδικῶν οὐδενὸς δεῖται νόμου.)
MENANDER, *Fragments*. No. 845.

All laws are useless, for good men do not need them and bad men are made no better by them.
DEMONAX. (PLUTARCH, *Apothegms*.)

When men are pure, laws are useless; when men are corrupt, laws are broken.
BENJAMIN DISRAELI, *Contarini Fleming*.

Just laws are no restraint upon the freedom of the good, for the good man desires nothing which a just law will interfere with.
J. A. FROUDE, *Short Studies on Great Subjects: Reciprocal Duties of State and Subject*.

It is only rogues who feel the restraint of law.
J. G. HOLLAND, *Gold-Foil: Perfect Liberty*.

The good needs fear no law,
It is his safety and the bad man's awe.
MASSINGER, *The Old Law*. Act v, sc. 1.

4
Virtue alone is not sufficient for the exercise of government; laws alone carry themselves into practice.
MENCIUS, *Works*. Bk. iv, pt. i, ch. 1, sec. 3.

5
Law can discover sin, but not remove,
Save by those shadowy expiations weak.
MILTON, *Paradise Lost*. Bk. xii, l. 290.

So many laws argue so many sins.
MILTON, *Paradise Lost*. Bk. xii, l. 283.

6
Laws were made that the stronger might not in all things have his way. (Inde datæ leges, ne firmior omnia posset.)
OVID, *Fasti*. Bk. iii, l. 279.

7
The laws obey custom. (Leges mori serviunt.)
PLAUTUS, *Trinummus*. Act iv, sc. 3, l. 36.

With customs we live well, but laws undo us.
GEORGE HERBERT, *Jacula Prudentum*.

8
A law should be a voice, as it were, sent down from heaven; it should command, not discuss. (Velut emissa divinitus vox sit; jubeat, non disputet.)
POSIDONIUS. (SENECA, *Epistulæ ad Lucilium*. Epis. xciv, sec. 38.)

A law should be brief in order that the unlearned may grasp it more easily. (Legem enim brevem esse oportet, quo facilius ab imperitis teneatur.)
POSIDONIUS. (SENECA, *Epistulæ ad Lucilium*. Epis. xciv, sec. 38.)

9
Law, in a free country, is, or ought to be, the determination of the majority of those who have property in land.
SWIFT, *Thoughts on Various Subjects*.

10
Law is the crystallization of the habit and thought of society.
WOODROW WILSON, *Lecture*, Princeton, 1893.

II—Law: Apothegms

11
The law is open.
New Testament: Acts, xix, 38.

12
The devil hath eleven points of the law against you, that is, possession.
THOMAS ADAMS, *Works*, p. 97. (1630)

Possession is nine points of the law.
THOMAS FULLER, *Holy War*. Bk. v, ch. 29.
Both these proverbs were in frequent use.

Possession is eleven points of the law and there are but twelve.
JOHN RAY, *English Proverbs*.

That possession was the strongest tenure of the law.
PILPAY, *Fables: The Cat and the Two Birds*.

Eight points of the law: 1. A good cause; 2. A good purse; 3. An honest and skilful attorney; 4. Good evidence; 5. Able counsel; 6. An upright judge; 7. An intelligent jury; 8. Good luck.
Attributed to GEORGE AUGUSTUS SELWYN, when a candidate for Chamberlain of the City of London, c. 1750.

13
Law Is a Bottomless Pit.
JOHN ARBUTHNOT, *Title of Pamphlet*, 1712.

He that goes to law (as the proverb is) holds a wolf by the ears.
ROBERT BURTON, *Anatomy of Melancholy: Democritus to the Reader*.

The worst of law is that one suit breeds twenty.
GEORGE HERBERT, *Jacula Prudentum*.

Lawsuits consume time, and money, and rest and friends.
GEORGE HERBERT, *Jacula Prudentum*.

Whoso loves law dies either mad or poor.
THOMAS MIDDLETON, *The Phœnix*.

14
There is no magic in parchment or in wax.
WILLIAM HENRY ASHURST, *Master v. Miller*, 1763. (4 T. R. 320.)

The mysterious virtue of wax and parchment.
EDMUND BURKE, *Speech on Conciliation with America*.

Is not this a lamentable thing, that of the skin of an innocent lamb should be made parchment; that parchment, being scribbled o'er, should undo a man?
SHAKESPEARE, *II Henry VI*. Act iv, sc. 2, l. 86.

1
Nowadays the law is ended as a man is friended.
HENRY BRINKELOW, *Complaint of Roderick Mors*. Ch. 11. (c. 1542)

Matters be ended as they be friended.
THOMAS STARKEY, *England in the Reign of Henry VIII*. Bk. i, ch. 3.

A friend in court is worth a penny in a man's purse.
JOHN RAY, *English Proverbs.*

Bon fait avoir ami en cour,
Car le procès en est plus court.
A French variant of the proverb.

See also under COURT.

2
Law and arbitrary power are in eternal enmity.
EDMUND BURKE, *Impeachment of Warren Hastings*, 16 Feb., 1788.

3
That which is a law to-day is none to-morrow.
ROBERT BURTON, *Anatomy of Melancholy: Democritus to the Reader.*

The law is not the same at morning and at night.
GEORGE HERBERT, *Jacula Prudentum.*

New lords, new laws.
JOHN RAY, *English Proverbs.*

And he that gives us in these days
New Lords may give us new laws.
GEORGE WITHER, *Contented Man's Morrice.*

4
Arms and laws do not flourish together. (Τὸν αὐτὸν ὅπλων καὶ νόμων καιρὸν εἶναι.)
JULIUS CÆSAR. (PLUTARCH, *Lives: Julius Cæsar*. Ch. 35, sec. 3.)

The law speaks too softly to be heard amid the din of arms. (Τοῦ νόμου διὰ τὸν τῶν ὅπλων ψόφον οὐ κατακούσειεν.)
GAIUS MARIUS. (PLUTARCH, *Lives: Gaius Marius*. Ch. 28, sec. 2.)

Laws are dumb in the midst of arms. (Silent enim leges inter arma.)
CICERO, *Pro Milone*. Ch. 4, sec. 11.

The clatter of arms drowns the voice of the law.
MONTAIGNE, *Essays*. Bk. iii, ch. 1.

5
Agree, for the law is costly.
WILLIAM CAMDEN, *Remains*, p. 316. (1605)

Agree, agree, says the old saw, the law is costly.
ROGER L'ESTRANGE, *Fables of Æsop*. (1692)

Come, agree, the law's costly.
SWIFT, *Polite Conversation*. Dial. i. (1738)

6
Who stood to gain? (Cui bono fuerit?)
LUCIUS CASSIUS LONGINUS, the judge, who used it as a maxim in instructing a jury to seek for the motive of a crime. (CICERO, *Pro Milone*. Ch. xii, sec. 32.)

For whose good? (Cui bono?)
CICERO, quoting from Lucius Cassius in the *Second Philippic*. "These two words," says Forsyth (*Life*), "have perhaps been oftener misapplied than any in the Latin language. They are constantly translated or used in the sense of, 'What good is it?' 'To what end does it serve?' Their real meaning is, 'Who gains by it?' 'To whom is it an advantage?' " Forsyth goes on to explain that in a trial for murder Lucius Cassius instructed the jury to inquire who had a motive for the crime, who would gain by the death, in other words, "cui bono fuerit?"

There was an ancient Roman lawyer, of great fame in the history of Roman jurisprudence, whom they called Cui Bono, from his having first introduced into judicial proceedings the argument, "What end or object could the party have had in the act with which he is accused."
EDMUND BURKE, *Impeachment of Warren Hastings.*

7
Laws go as kings like. (Allá van leyes do quieren Reyes.)
CERVANTES, *Don Quixote*. Pt. i, ch. 45.

She made what pleased her lawful. (Che libito fe' licito in sua legge.)
DANTE, *Inferno*. Canto v, l. 56. From the Latin, "Si libet, licet."

8
Who to himself is law, no law doth need,
Offends no law, and is a king indeed.
GEORGE CHAPMAN, *Bussy d'Ambois*. Act ii, sc. 1.

9
After an existence of nearly twenty years of almost innocuous desuetude these laws are brought forth.
GROVER CLEVELAND, *Message*, 1 March, 1886.

I used those words and thought they would please the Western taxpayers, who are fond of such things.
GROVER CLEVELAND, referring to "innocuous desuetude." (*Interview, New York Herald*, 9 June, 1886.)

The law hath not been dead, though it hath slept.
SHAKESPEARE, *Measure for Measure*. Act ii, sc. 2, l. 90.

10
The gladsome light of jurisprudence.
SIR EDWARD COKE, *Institutes*. Pt. i.

11
Law is the safest helmet. (Lex est tutissima cassis.)
SIR EDWARD COKE, *Inscription*, on rings which he gave to friends.

12
All things by Law. (Πάντα νομιστί.)
DEMOCRITUS. (MARCUS AURELIUS, *Meditations*. Bk. vii, sec. 31.)

13
A delusion, a mockery, and a snare.
SIR THOMAS DENMAN, an English judge, in his judgment in O'Connell vs. the Queen (11 *Clarke and Finnelly*, 351): "If it is possible that such a practice as that which has taken place in the present instance should be allowed to pass without a remedy, trial by

jury itself, instead of being a security to persons who are accused, will be a delusion, a mockery, and a snare." (4 Sept., 1894)

1
"If the law supposes that," said Mr. Bumble, "the law is a ass."
DICKENS, *Oliver Twist*. Ch. 51.

2
Any laws but those we make for ourselves are laughable.
EMERSON, *Essays, Second Series: Politics*.

3
Law makes long spokes of the short stakes of men.
EMPSON, *Legal Fiction*.

4
Laws too gentle are seldom obeyed; too severe, seldom executed.
BENJAMIN FRANKLIN, *Poor Richard*, 1756.

5
A penny-weight of love is worth a pound of law.
THOMAS FULLER, *Gnomologia*. No. 343.

In a thousand pounds of law there is not an ounce of love.
JOHN RAY, *English Proverbs*.

6
Much law but little justice.
THOMAS FULLER, *Gnomologia*.

Law cannot persuade where it cannot punish.
THOMAS FULLER, *Gnomologia*.

The more laws the more offenders.
THOMAS FULLER, *Gnomologia*.

7
Thou knowest a barley straw
Will make a parish parson go to law.
WILLIAM GODDARD, *Nest of Wasps*. No. 16. (1615)

8
Do law away, what is a king?
Where is the right of any thing?
JOHN GOWER, *Confessio Amantis*. Bk. vii.

9
Taken in flagrant violation of the law. (In flagranti crimine comprehensi.)
JUSTINIAN, *Corpus Juris Civilis Romani*. Codex ix, tit. 13, sec. 1. Usually quoted, "In flagrante delicto." Its English equivalent, "Caught red-handed," referred originally only to murderers.

10
The law is a sort of hocus-pocus science, that smiles in yer face while it picks yer pocket; and the glorious uncertainty of it is of mair use to the professors than the justice of it.
CHARLES MACKLIN, *Love à la Mode*. Act ii, sc. 1. (1759) This is probably the origin of the phrase, "The glorious uncertainty of the law," though there is a legend that it was used as a toast by a lawyer named Wilbraham at a dinner given to Lord Mansfield in London, in 1756. (See *Gentleman's Magazine*, August, 1830.)

11
Good laws are produced by bad manners. (Bonae leges ex malis moribus procreantur.)
MACROBIUS, *Saturnalia*. Bk. iii, l. 17.

Ill manners produce good laws.
CHARLES CAHIER, *Six Mille Proverbes*, p. 195.

As manners make laws, manners likewise repeal them.
SAMUEL JOHNSON. (BOSWELL, *Life*, ii, 419.)

12
As the case stands.
MIDDLETON AND MASSINGER, *The Old Law*. Act ii, sc. 1. (1626); MATTHEW HENRY, *Commentaries: Psalm* cxix.

Every case stands upon its own bottom.
SIR FRANCIS PEMBERTON, *Judgment*, Fitzharris case. (*8 How. St. Tr.*, 280)

13
No customer brings so much grist to the mill
As the wealthy old woman who makes her own Will.
CHARLES NEAVES, *The Jolly Testator*.

14
A famous case. (Cause célèbre.)
FRANÇOIS DE PETEVAL. Title of a work in 20 vols., Paris, 1734. The full title is *Causes Célèbres et Intéressantes*.

15
Where law ends, there tyranny begins.
WILLIAM PITT, *Case of Wilkes: Speech*, 9 Jan., 1770.

16
You little know how hazardous it is to go to law. (Nescis quam meticulosa res sit ire ad judicem.)
PLAUTUS, *Mostellaria*, l. 1101.

17
I will drive a coach and six through the Act of Settlement.
STEPHEN RICE, Chief Baron of the Irish Exchequer, 1686. (MACAULAY, *History of England*. Ch. 12; BURNET, *History of My Own Times*.)

I can drive a coach-and-six through any act of Parliament.
DANIEL O'CONNELL, *Speech*.

18
The law often allows what honor forbids. (La loi permet souvent ce que défend l'honneur.)
SAURIN, *Spartacus*. Act iii, sc. 3.

19
Ignorance of the law excuses no man: not that all men know the law, but because 'tis an excuse every man will plead, and no man can tell how to confute him.
JOHN SELDEN, *Table-Talk: Law*.

Ignorance of the law excuses no one. (Ignorantia legis excusat neminem.)
UNKNOWN. A legal maxim.

'Tis a sluggard's part not to know what he may lawfully do. (Inertis est nescire quid liceat sibi.)
SENECA, *Octavia*, l. 453.

20
The rusty curb of old father antic, the law.
SHAKESPEARE, *I Henry IV*. Act i, sc. 2, l. 69.

A rotten case abides no handling.
SHAKESPEARE, *II Henry IV*. Act iv, sc. 1, l. 161.

1 Has he affections in him,
That thus can make him bite the law by the nose?
SHAKESPEARE, *Measure for Measure,* iii, 1, 108.

2
The laws, your curb and whip, in their rough power
Have uncheck'd theft.
SHAKESPEARE, *Timon of Athens,* iv, 3, 446.

3
Still you keep o' the windy side of the law.
SHAKESPEARE, *Twelfth Night,* iii, 4, 181.

Just to the windward of the law.
CHARLES CHURCHILL, *The Ghost.* Bk. iii, l. 56.

4
Abraham: Do you bite your thumb at us, sir?
Sampson: Is the law of our side, if I say ay?
SHAKESPEARE, *Romeo and Juliet,* i, 1, 54.

The laws are with us, and God on our side.
ROBERT SOUTHEY, *Essays: On the Rise and Progress of Popular Disaffection.*

4a
I will not say with Lord Hale, that "The law will admit of no rival," . . . but I will say that it is a jealous mistress, and requires a long and constant courtship. It is not to be won by trifling favors, but by lavish homage.
JOSEPH STORY, *The Value and Importance of Legal Studies.* (*Miscellaneous Writings,* p. 523.) This was Justice Story's address at his inauguration, 15 Aug., 1829, as Dane Professor of Law at Harvard University. See *Dicta,* Nov., 1945. Often attributed to Blackstone. See *Illinois Law Review,* xxvii, 329.

5
A man must not go to law because the musician keeps false time with his foot.
JEREMY TAYLOR, *Worthy Communicant.* Ch. iv, sec. 4. Quoted from Schott, *Adagia.*

6
No man e'er felt the halter draw,
With good opinion of the law.
JOHN TRUMBULL, *MacFingal.* Canto iii, l. 489.

7
The Law: It has honored us, may we honor it.
DANIEL WEBSTER, *Toast,* at the Charleston Bar dinner, 10 May, 1847.

8
What we seek is the reign of law, based upon the consent of the governed and sustained by the organized opinion of mankind.
WOODROW WILSON, *Speech,* Mount Vernon, 4 July, 1918, referring to League of Nations.

The Reign of Law.
JAMES LANE ALLEN. Title of novel.

9
When the law shows her teeth, but dares not bite.
YOUNG, *Love of Fame.* Sat. i, l. 17.

III—Law: Varieties

10
For thus men say each country has its laws.
CHAUCER, *Troilus and Criseyde.* Bk. ii, st. 6. (c. 1374)

So many countries, so many laws.
UNKNOWN, *Politeuphuia,* 224. (1669) *See also under* OPINION.

Divine Law

11
There is but one law for all, namely, that law which governs all law, the law of our Creator, the law of humanity, justice, equity—the law of nature and of nations.
EDMUND BURKE, *Impeachment of Warren Hastings,* 28 May, 1794.

12 The ultimate, angels' law,
Indulging every instinct of the soul
There where law, life, joy, impulse are one thing!
ROBERT BROWNING, *A Death in the Desert.*

13
Our human laws are but the copies, more or less imperfect, of the eternal laws, so far as we can read them.
J. A. FROUDE, *Short Studies: Calvinism.*

The law of heaven and earth is life for life.
BYRON, *The Curse of Minerva.* St. 15.

EYE FOR EYE, *see under* RETRIBUTION.

14
Of Law there can be no less acknowledged, than that her seat is the bosom of God, her voice the harmony of the world.
RICHARD HOOKER, *Ecclesiastical Polity.* Bk. i.

15
All things obey fixed laws. (Legibus omnia parent.)
MANILIUS, *Astronomica,* i, 479.

In all things there is a kind of law of cycles. (Rebus cunctis inest quidam velut orbis.)
TACITUS, *Annals.* Bk. iii, sec. 55.

Things have their laws as well as men, and things refuse to be trifled with.
EMERSON, *Essays, Second Series: Politics.*

16
The first Almighty Cause
Acts not by partial but by gen'ral laws.
POPE, *Essay on Man.* Epis. i, l. 145.

Mark what unvaried laws preserve each state,
Laws wise as Nature, and as fix'd as Fate.
POPE, *Essay on Man.* Epis. iii, l. 189.

17
That very law which moulds a tear
And bids it trickle from its source,—
That law preserves the earth a sphere,
And guides the planets in their course.
SAMUEL ROGERS, *On a Tear.* Rogers is referring to the law of gravitation.

18
On a divine law divination rests.
SCHILLER, *Wallenstein.* Act i, sc. 9.

19
In the corrupted currents of this world
Offence's gilded hand may shove by justice,
And oft 'tis seen the wicked prize itself
Buys out the law: but 'tis not so above;
There is no shuffling, there the action lies
In his true nature; and we ourselves compell'd,
Even to the teeth and forehead of our faults,
To give in evidence.
SHAKESPEARE, *Hamlet.* Act iii, sc. 3, l. 57.

20
God is law, say the wise; O Soul, and let us rejoice,

For if He thunder by law the thunder is yet
His voice.
TENNYSON, *The Higher Pantheism*. St. 7.

1
Foul shame and scorn be on ye all
Who turn the good to evil,
And steal the Bible from the Lord,
To give it to the Devil!

Than garbled text or parchment law
I own a statute higher;
And God is true, though every book
And every man's a liar!
WHITTIER, *A Sabbath Scene*. St. 18.

The Law of Nations

2
The law of human society. (Jus humanæ societatis.)
CICERO, *De Officiis*. Bk. i, ch. 7, sec. 21.

3
Natural law; the law of mankind. (Jus hominum.)
CICERO, *Tusculanarum Disputationum*. Bk. i, ch. 26, sec. 64.

4
The bond of union is closer between those who belong to the same nation, and closer still between those who are citizens of the same state. It is for this reason that our forefathers chose to understand one thing by the law of nations (jus gentium), and another by the civil or common law (jus civile).
CICERO, *De Officiis*. Bk. iii, ch. 17, sec. 69.

In every matter the consensus of opinion among all nations is to be regarded as the law of nature. (Omni autem in re consensio omnium gentium lex naturae putanda est.)
CICERO, *Tusculanarum Disputationum*. Bk. i, ch. 13, sec. 30.

That which natural reason has established amongst all men is called the law of nations. (Quod naturalis ratio inter omnes homines constituit . . . vocatur jus gentium.)
GAIUS, *Institutione Juris Civilis*. Bk. i, sec. 1.

Against the law of nature, law of nations.
MILTON, *Samson Agonistes*, l. 889.

Miscellaneous Laws

5
I oft have heard of Lydford Law,
How in the morn they hang and draw,
And sit in judgement after.
SIR THOMAS BROWNE, *Lydford Journey*. St. 1. (1644)

First hang and draw,
Then hear the cause by Lidford law.
THOMAS FULLER, *Worthies of England*, i. 399. (1662)

I have had Halifax law—to be condemned first and inquired upon afterwards.
LEICESTER. (MOTLEY, *United Netherlands*. Vol. i, p. 444.)

Are you going to hang him *anyhow*—and try him afterwards?
MARK TWAIN, *Innocents at Home*. Ch. 5.

6
O king, establish the decree, and sign the writing, that it be not changed, according to the law of the Medes and Persians, which altereth not.
Old Testament: Daniel, vi, 8.

The thing is true, according to the law of Medes and Persians, which altereth not.
Old Testament: Daniel, vi, 12.

Let it be written among the laws of the Persians and the Medes, that it be not altered.
Old Testament: Esther, i. 19.

7
Draco made his laws not with ink, but with blood.
DEMADES. Draco had made the least theft punishable with death. (PLUTARCH, *Lives: Solon*.) Hence "Draconian," in the sense of severe.

8
Connecticut in her blue-laws, laying it down as a principle, that the laws of God should be the law of the land.
THOMAS JEFFERSON, *Letter to John Adams*, 24 Jan., 1814.

9
There is a written and an unwritten law. Written law is that under which we live in different cities, but that which has arisen from custom is called unwritten law. (Νόμου διαιρέσεις δύο, ὁ μὲν γὰρ αὐτοῦ γεγραμμένος, ὁ δὲ ἄγραφος.)
PLATO. (DIOGENES LAERTIUS, *Plato*. Sec. 86.)

Dementia Americana; the unwritten law.
DELPHIN MICHAEL DELMAS. At the trial of Harry Thaw for the murder of Stanford White, in 1907.

Brain-storm, the paranoia of the millionaire.
WILLIAM TRAVERS JEROME. The district attorney who prosecuted Thaw.

The silver-tongued spell-binder of the Pacific Coast.
Sobriquet of Delphin Michael Delmas.

10
First Clown: Argal, he that is not guilty of his own death shortens not his own life.
Second Clown: But is this law?
First Clown: Ay, marry is't; crowner's quest law.
SHAKESPEARE, *Hamlet*. Act v, sc. 1, l. 21.

11
A sumptuary law. (Lex sumptuaria.)
TACITUS, *Annals*. Bk. iii, sec. 52.

12
For this is the law of the feudal days,
The law for one and all,
That whoso lives on the baron's land,
May feed as he will at the baron's hand,
But whoso feeds at the baron's hand,
Must answer the baron's call.
THOMAS F. WOODLOCK, *The Law*.

IV—Law: The Net of Law

13
Laws are like spiders' webs; they hold the

weak and delicate who are caught in their meshes, but are torn in pieces by the rich and powerful.

ANACHARSIS, to Solon, when the latter was compiling his laws. (PLUTARCH, *Lives: Solon*. Ch. 5, sec. 2.)

Men keep their engagements when it is to the advantage of both parties not to break them.

SOLON, Answering Anacharsis. (PLUTARCH, *Lives: Solon.*) See also No. 7, below.

1
Laws grind the poor, and rich men rule the law.

GOLDSMITH, *The Traveller*, l. 386.

2
The verdict acquits the raven, but condemns the dove. (Dat veniam corvis, vexat censura columbas.)

JUVENAL, *Satires*. Sat. ii, l. 63.

3
In vain thy reason finer webs will draw,
Entangle justice in her net of law,
And right, too rigid, harden into wrong,
Still for the strong too weak, the weak too strong.

POPE, *Essay on Man*. Epis. iii, l. 191.

4
The net of law is spread so wide,
No sinner from its sweep may hide.
Its meshes are so fine and strong,
They take in every child of wrong.
O wondrous web of mystery!
Big fish alone escape from thee!

JAMES JEFFREY ROCHE, *The Net of Law*.

5
Petty sacrilege is punished, but sacrilege on a grand scale is honored by a triumphal procession. (Nam sacrilegia minuta puniuntur, magna in triumphis feruntur.)

SENECA, *Epistulæ ad Lucilium*. Epis. lxxxvii, sec. 24.

All, look up with reverential awe,
At crimes that 'scape, or triumph o'er the law.

POPE, *Epilogue to Satires*. Dial. i, l. 167.

6
Laws are generally found to be nets of such a texture, as the little creep through, the great break through, and the middle-sized are alone entangled in.

WILLIAM SHENSTONE, *On Politics*.

7
Laws are spiders' webs, which stand firm when any light and yielding object falls upon them, while a larger thing breaks through them and escapes.

SOLON. (DIOGENES LAERTIUS, *Solon*. Sec. 14.)

One of the Seven [Wise Men of Greece] was wont to say: "That laws were like cobwebs; where the small flies were caught, and the great brake through."

FRANCIS BACON, *Apothegms*. No. 181.

Should I sigh, because I see
Laws like spider-webs to be?
Lesser flies are quickly ta'en
While the great break out again.

RICHARD BRATHWAITE, *Care's Cure*.

Laws like to cobwebs, catch small flies,
Great ones break them before your eyes.

BENJAMIN FRANKLIN, *Poor Richard*, 1734.

For the most part, laws are but like spiders' webs, taking the small gnats, or perhaps sometimes the fat flesh flies, but hornets that have sharp stings and greater strength, break through them.

SIR JOHN HARINGTON, *Orlando Furioso*. Bk. 32.

Laws are like cobwebs, which may catch small flies, but let wasps and hornets break through.

SWIFT, *Essay on the Faculties of the Mind*.

8
The net's not spread to catch the hawk or kite
Who do us wrong, but for the innocent birds
Who do us none at all.
(Quia non rete accipitri tennitur neque milvo,
Qui male faciunt nobis: illis qui nihil faciunt tennitur.)

TERENCE, *Phormio*, l. 330. (Act iii, sc. 1.)

9
The law doth punish man or woman
That steals the goose from off the common,
But lets the greater felon loose,
That steals the common from the goose.

UNKNOWN. An 18th century epigram. (See *Notes and Queries*. Ser. vii, 6, 469; 7, 98. Ser. viii, 10, 273.) There are various versions, all prompted by the Enclosure Acts. The version given above was written when Sir Charles Pratt, First Earl of Camden, enclosed a common strip of land in front of Camden House, 7 Oct., 1764.

10
There is no law without a loophole for him who can find it. (Es giebt kein Gesetz was hat nicht ein Loch, wer's finden kann.)

UNKNOWN. A German proverb.

V—Law: Its Tyranny

11
Law is king of all.

HENRY ALFORD, *School of the Heart*. Lesson 6.

Law is King. (Lex Rex.)

SAMUEL RUTHERFORD. Title of book published 1644.

12
There is no worse torture than the torture of laws.

FRANCIS BACON, *Essays: Of Judicature*.

It is a hard thing to torture the laws so that they torture men.

FRANCIS BACON, *De Augmentis Scientiarum*. Pt. i, bk. viii, aph. 13.

13
We, like the eagles, were born to be free. Yet we are obliged, in order to live at all, to make a cage of laws for ourselves and to stand on the perch.

WILLIAM BOLITHO, *Twelve Against the Gods: Introduction*.

As soon as laws are necessary for men, men are no longer fit for freedom.
PYTHAGORAS.

1
People crushed by law have no hopes but from power. If laws are their enemies, they will be enemies to laws; and those who have much to hope and nothing to lose will always be dangerous.
EDMUND BURKE, *Letter,* to the Hon. C. J. Fox, 8 Oct., 1777.

Bad laws are the worst sort of tyranny.
EDMUND BURKE, *Speech,* Bristol.

2
Extreme law, extreme injustice. (Summum jus, summa injuria.)
CICERO, *De Officiis.* Bk. i, sec. 10. *See under* JUSTICE AND INJUSTICE.

3
Our sense of private dignity can survive the most oppressive man-despot, but the despotism of law corrodes it.
NORMAN DOUGLAS, *Good-bye to Western Culture.*

4
Shall free-born men, in humble awe,
Submit to servile shame;
Who from consent and custom draw
The same right to be ruled by law,
Which kings pretend to reign?
DRYDEN, *On the Young Statesman.*

5
All rights and laws are still transmitted,
Like an eternal sickness to the race.
(Es erben sich Gesetz und Rechte
Wie eine ew'ge Krankheit fort.)
GOETHE, *Faust.* Pt. i, sc. 4, l. 449.

6
O wearisome condition of humanity!
Born under one law, to another bound.
FULKE GREVILLE, *Mustapha.* Act v, sc. 4.

7
Law is the tyrant of mankind, and often compels us to do many things which are against nature.
HIPPIAS. (PLATO, *Protagoras.* Sec. 337.)

8
The law is laid down to you. (Dicta tibi est lex.)
HORACE, *Epistles.* Bk. ii, epis. 2, l. 18.

9
Then too [in law] there are a thousand causes of disgust, a thousand delays to be endured. (Tunc quoque mille ferenda Tædia, mille moræ.)
JUVENAL, *Satires.* Sat. xvi, l. 43.

10
The law is so lordly and loth to maken end.
LANGLAND, *Piers Plowman.* Passus iv, l. 199.

11
We have strict statutes and most biting laws.
SHAKESPEARE, *Measure for Measure.* Act i, sc. 3, l. 19.

12
God's blood! is law for man's sake made, or man
For law's sake only, to be held in bonds?
SWINBURNE, *Mary Stuart.* Act i, sc. 1.

VI—Law: Letter and Spirit

13
No man has ever yet been hanged for breaking the spirit of a law.
GROVER CLEVELAND. (RHODES, *History of the United States,* viii, 403; HIBBEN, *Peerless Leader,* p. 155.)

14
The letter killeth, but the spirit giveth life.
New Testament: II Corinthians, iii, 6. (Litera enim occidit, Spiritus autem vivificat. —*Vulgate.*)

Legality kills us. (La légalité nous tue.)
VIENNET, *Épîtres.*

15
We are lost by what is lawful. (Perimus licitis.)
SIR MATTHEW HALE, quoted from St. Gregory, *Morals.* Bk. v, homily 35, meaning, "We are demoralised by indulgence in things which are not contrary to law."

16
To the law and to the testimony.
Old Testament: Isaiah, viii, 20.

17
Exact laws, like all the other ultimates and absolutes, are as fabulous as the crock of gold at the rainbow's end.
G. N. LEWIS, *The Anatomy of Science,* p. 154.

18
But now we are delivered from the law, that being dead wherein we were held; that we should serve in newness of spirit, and not in the oldness of the letter.
New Testament: Romans, vii, 6.

19
Let him have all the rigour of the law.
SHAKESPEARE, *II Henry VI.* Act i, sc. 3, l. 199.

He . . . follows close the rigour of the statute,
To make him an example.
SHAKESPEARE, *Measure for Measure.* Act i, sc. 4, l. 66.

Is it so nominated in the bond?
SHAKESPEARE, *The Merchant of Venice.* Act iv, sc. 1, l. 259.

20
The bloody book of law
You shall yourself read in the bitter letter.
SHAKESPEARE, *Othello.* Act i, sc. 3, l. 67.

21
In bondage to the letter still,
We give it power to cramp and kill,—
To tax God's fulness with a scheme
Narrower than Peter's house-top dream,
His wisdom and his love with plans
Poor and inadequate as man's.
WHITTIER, *Miriam,* l. 97.

VII—Law: Precedent

See also Precedent

22
An argument derived from authority is of

the greatest force in law. (Argumentum ab auctoritate fortissimum est in lege.)

Sir Edward Coke, *On Littleton*, 144.

1
The mere repetition of the *Cantilena* of the lawyers cannot make it law.

Sir Thomas Denman, *O'Connell v. The Queen.*

2
The acts of today may become the precedents of tomorrow.

Farrer Herschell, Lord Chancellor, *Speech*, 23 May, 1878.

3
All the sentences of precedent judges that have ever been cannot altogether make a law contrary to natural equity.

Thomas Hobbes, *Leviathan*. Pt. ii, ch. 26.

4
One precedent creates another. They soon accumulate and become law.

Junius, *Letters: Dedication.*

5
A precedent embalms a principle.

William Scott, Baron Stowell, *Opinion*, while Advocate-General, 1788. (William Scott, *Lord Stowell.*) Benjamin Disraeli, *Speech*, House of Commons, 22 Feb., 1848; *Endymion*. Ch. 9.

6
It must not be; there is no power in Venice
Can alter a decree established:
'Twill be recorded for a precedent,
And many an error by the same example
Will rush into the state.

Shakespeare, *The Merchant of Venice*. Act iv, sc. 1, l. 218.

7
Every law which originated in ignorance and malice, and gratifies the passions from which it sprang, we call the wisdom of our ancestors.

Sydney Smith, *Peter Plymley Letters*. No. 5.

8
Mastering the lawless science of our law,
That codeless myriad of precedent,
That wilderness of single instances,
Through which a few, by wit or fortune led,
May beat a pathway out to wealth and fame.

Tennyson, *Aylmer's Field*, l. 436.

VIII—Law: Obedience to Law

9
Where there are laws, he who has not broken them need not tremble. (Ove son leggi, Tremar non dee chi leggi non infranse.)

Alfieri, *Virginia*. Sc. 2.

Who breaks no law is subject to no king.

Chapman, *Bussy d'Ambois*. Act iv, sc. 1.

Fear God, and offend not the Prince nor his laws,
And keep thyself out of the magistrate's claws.

Thomas Tusser, *Five Hundred Points of Good Husbandry.*

10
Laws are not masters but servants, and he rules them who obeys them.

Henry Ward Beecher, *Proverbs from Plymouth Pulpit: Political.*

11
Law will never be strong or respected unless it has the sentiment of the people behind it. If the people of a State make bad laws, they will suffer for it. They will be the first to suffer. Let them suffer. Suffering, and nothing else, will implant that sentiment of responsibility which is the first step to reform.

James Bryce, *American Commonwealth*. Vol. i, p. 352.

I know no method to secure the repeal of bad or obnoxious laws so effective as their stringent execution.

U. S. Grant, *Inaugural Address*, 4 March, 1869.

12
He who holds no laws in awe,
He must perish by the law.

Byron, *A Very Mournful Ballad on the Siege and Conquest of Alhama*. St. 12.

13
Let a man keep the law,—any law,—and his way will be strewn with satisfactions.

Emerson, *Essays, First Series: Prudence.*

14
Good men must not obey the laws too well.

Emerson, *Essays, Second Series: Politics.*

No law can be sacred to me but that of my nature. Good and bad are but names very readily transferable to that or this; the only right is what is after my own constitution; the only wrong what is against it.

Emerson, *Essays, First Series: Self-Reliance.*

15
For the bond of all men's states is this,
When they with honor hold by law.
(Τὸ γάρ τοι συνέχον ἀνθρώπων πόλεις
τοῦτ' ἔσθ', ὅταν τις τοὺς νόμους σῴζῃ καλῶς.)

Euripides, *Suppliants*, l. 313.

16
The laws of God, the laws of man,
He may keep that will and can;
Not I: let God and man decree
Laws for themselves and not for me.

A. E. Housman, *Laws.*

17
A strict observance of the written laws is doubtless one of the high virtues of a good citizen, but it is not the highest. The laws of necessity, of self-preservation, of saving our country when in danger, are of higher obligation.

Thomas Jefferson, *Writings*. Vol. xii, p. 418.

18
Without a notion of a law-maker, it is impossible to have a notion of a law, and an obligation to observe it.

John Locke, *An Essay Concerning Human Understanding*. Bk. i, ch. iv, sec. 8.

1
A law observed is merely law; broken, it is law and executioner.

MENANDER, *Fragments*. No. 700.

2
It is the rule of rules and the general law of laws that everyone should observe that of the place where he is. (C'est la règle des règles, et générale loi des loix, que chacun observe celle du lieu où il est.)

MONTAIGNE, *Essays*. Bk. i, ch. 22. *See also under* ROME.

3
The atrocity of the laws prevents their execution. (L'atrocité des lois en empêche l'exécution.)

MONTESQUIEU, *Esprit des Lois*.

Whenever the offence inspires less horror than the punishment, the rigour of penal law is obliged to give way to the common feelings of mankind.

GIBBON, *Decline and Fall*. Vol. i, ch. 14.

Laws that do not embody public opinion can never be enforced.

ELBERT HUBBARD, *Epigrams*.

4
For you'll ne'er mend your fortunes, nor help the just cause,
By breaking of windows, or breaking of laws.

HANNAH MORE, *Address to the Meeting in Spa Fields*.

5
The parish makes the Constable, and when the Constable is made he governs the Parish.

JOHN SELDEN, *Table-Talk: People*.

6
Laws do not persuade just because they threaten. (Ob hoc illæ non persuadent, quia minantur.)

SENECA, *Epistulæ ad Lucilium*. Epis. xciv, 37.

7
He hath resisted law,
And therefore law shall scorn him further trial.

SHAKESPEARE, *Coriolanus*. Act iii, sc. 1, l. 267.

Faith, I have been a truant in the law,
And never yet could frame my will to it;
And therefore frame the law unto my will.

SHAKESPEARE, *I Henry VI*. Act ii, sc. 4, l. 7.

8
We must not make a scarecrow of the law,
Setting it up to fear the birds of prey,
And let it keep one shape, till custom make it
Their perch and not their terror.

SHAKESPEARE, *Measure for Measure*. Act ii, sc. 1, l. 1.

9
The brain may devise laws for the blood, but a hot temper leaps o'er a cold decree.

SHAKESPEARE, *The Merchant of Venice*. Act i, sc. 2, l. 19.

10
Laws were made to be broken.

JOHN WILSON, *Noctes Ambrosianæ*. No. 24.

To the States or any one of them, or any city of the States, *Resist much, obey little*,
Once unquestioning obedience, once fully enslaved,
Once fully enslaved, no nation, state, city of this earth, ever afterward resumes its liberty.

WALT WHITMAN, *To the States*.

IX—Law: Law-makers and Law-breakers

11
What is a law, if those who make it
Become the forwardest to break it?

JAMES BEATTIE, *The Wolf and the Shepherds*, l. 71.

It becometh a law-maker not to be a law-breaker.

UNKNOWN, *Politeuphuia*, 95. (1669)

I impeach Warren Hastings of high crimes and misdemeanours. I impeach him in the name of the Commons House of Parliament, whose trust he has betrayed. I impeach him in the name of the English nation, whose ancient honor he has sullied. I impeach him in the name of the people of India, whose rights he has trodden underfoot, and whose country he has turned into a desert. Lastly, in the name of human nature itself, in the name of both sexes, in the name of every age, in the name of every rank, I impeach the common enemy and oppressor of all.

EDMUND BURKE, *Trial of Warren Hastings*, conclusion of speech, as condensed by Macaulay.

12
No power should be above the laws. (Nulla potentia supra leges esse debet.)

CICERO. (See *Pro Domo Sua*, xvii, 43.)

Be you never so high the law is above you.

THOMAS FULLER, *Gnomologia*.

13
A people shows more respect for justice, nor refuses submission, when it has seen their author obedient to his own laws. (Tunc observantior æqui Fit populus nec ferre negat, cum viderit ipsum Auctorem parere sibi.)

CLAUDIAN, *Panegyricus de Quarto Consulatu Honorii Augusti*, l. 297.

14
Magna Charta is such a fellow that he will have no sovereign.

SIR EDWARD COKE, *Debate*, House of Commons, 17 May, 1628.

15
Laws are vain, by which we right enjoy,
If kings unquestion'd can those laws destroy.

DRYDEN, *Absalom and Achitophel*. Pt. i, l. 763

16
For such law as man giveth other wight,
He should him-selven usen it by right.

CHAUCER, *Man of Law's Prologue*, l. 43.

17
And sovereign Law, that State's collected will,
O'er thrones and globes elate,
Sits Empress, crowning good, repressing ill.

SIR WILLIAM JONES, *Ode in Imitation of Alcæus*.

1
Obey the law, whoever you be that made the law. (Pareto legi, quisque legem sanxeris.)

PITTACUS. (AUSONIUS [?], *Septem Sapientum Sententiæ*, l. 12.)

2
The prince is not above the laws, but the laws above the prince. (Non est princeps super leges, sed leges supra principem.)

PLINY THE YOUNGER, *Panegyricus Trajanus*, 67.

3
No man is above the law and no man is below it; nor do we ask any man's permission when we require him to obey it.

THEODORE ROOSEVELT, *Message*, Jan., 1904.

Him, the same laws, the same protection yields,
Who ploughs the furrow, or who owns the field.

RICHARD SAVAGE, *Of Public Spirit*, l. 41.

4
He gives laws to the peoples, and makes for himself a way to the heavens. (Per populos dat jura, viamque affectat Olympo.)

VERGIL, *Georgics*. Bk. iv, l. 562.

X—Laws, Good and Bad

5
I am of his mind that said, "Better it is to live where nothing is lawful, than where all things are lawful."

FRANCIS BACON, *Apothegms*. No. 69.

6
Laws and institutions are constantly tending to gravitate. Like clocks, they must be occasionally cleansed, and wound up, and set to true time.

HENRY WARD BEECHER, *Life Thoughts*.

7
"Whatever is, is not," is the maxim of the anarchist, as often as anything comes across him in the shape of a law which he happens not to like.

RICHARD BENTLEY, *Declaration of Rights*.

8
It was the boast of Augustus . . . that he found Rome of brick and left it of marble; . . . but how much nobler will be the sovereign's boast when he shall have it to say that he found law dear, and left it cheap; found it a sealed book, left it a living letter; found it the patrimony of the rich, left it the inheritance of the poor; found it the two-edged sword of craft and oppression, left it the staff of honesty and the shield of innocence!

LORD BROUGHAM, *Speech on Law Reform*, House of Commons, Feb., 1828.

9
The law of England is the greatest grievance of the nation, very expensive and dilatory.

BISHOP GILBERT BURNET, *History of His Own Times*. (1723)

The law can take a purse in open court,
Whilst it condemns a less delinquent for 't. . . .
Old laws have not been suffer'd to be pointed,
To leave the sense at large the more disjointed,
And furnish lawyers, with the greater ease,
To turn and wind them any way they please.

SAMUEL BUTLER, *Miscellaneous Thoughts*, l. 535.

10
Men would be great criminals did they need as many laws as they make.

CHARLES JOHN DARLING, *Scintillæ Juris*.

11
No written laws can be so plain, so pure,
But wit may gloss, and malice may obscure.

DRYDEN, *Hind and the Panther*. Pt. ii, l. 318.

12
The wise know that foolish legislation is a rope of sand which perishes in the twisting. . . . The law is only a memorandum. . . . Our statute is a currency which we stamp with our own portrait.

EMERSON, *Essays, Second Series: Politics*.

13
The Law is the true embodiment
Of everything that's excellent.
It has no kind of fault or flaw,
And I, my Lords, embody the Law.

W. S. GILBERT, *Iolanthe*. Act i.

14
You cannot imagine the beauty of an intricate, mazy law process, embodying the doubts and subtleties of generations of men.

ARTHUR HELPS, *Friends in Council*. Bk. iii, ch. 1.

15
Unnecessary laws are not good laws, but traps for money.

THOMAS HOBBES, *Leviathan*. Pt. ii, ch. 30.

16
He who can stand within that holy door,
With soul unbowed by that pure spirit-level,
And frame unequal laws for rich and poor,—
Might sit for Hell and represent the Devil!

THOMAS HOOD, *Ode to Rae Wilson*, l. 144.

17
Of what use are laws nullified by immorality? (Quid leges sine moribus Vanæ proficiunt?)

HORACE, *Odes*. Bk. iii, ode 24, l. 35.

18
How lightly do we sanction a law unjust to ourselves. (Quam temere in nosmet legem sancimus iniquam!)

HORACE, *Satires*. Bk. i, sat. 3, l. 67.

19
It is safer that a bad man should not be accused, than that he should be acquitted. (Hominem improbum non accusari tutius est quam absolvi.)

LIVY, *History*. Bk. xxxiv, sec. 4.

20
I am further of opinion that it would be better for us to have [no laws] at all than to have them in such prodigious numbers.

MONTAIGNE, *Essays*. Bk. iii, ch. 13.

Were it made a question whether no law, as among the savage Americans, or too much law, as among the civilized Europeans, submits man to the greatest evil, one who has seen both conditions of existence would pronounce it to be the last; and that the sheep are happier of themselves, than under the care of wolves.

THOMAS JEFFERSON, *Writings*. Vol. ii, p. 128.

1
Petty laws breed great crimes.

OUIDA, *Wisdom, Wit and Pathos: Pipistrello.*

2
The best use of good laws is to teach men to trample bad laws under their feet.

WENDELL PHILLIPS, *Speech,* 12 April, 1852.

3
Laws are always useful to those who possess and vexatious to those who have nothing. (Les lois sont toujours utiles à ceux qui possèdent, et nuisibles à ceux qui n'ont rien.)

ROUSSEAU, *Contrat Social*. Bk. i, ch. 9, note.

4
"That sounds like nonsense, my dear." "Maybe so, my dear; but it may be very good law for all that."

SCOTT, *Guy Mannering*. Ch. 9.

5
Equity, in law, is the same that the spirit is in religion: what everyone pleases to make it.

JOHN SELDEN, *Table-Talk: Equity*.

Equity is a roguish thing: for law we have a measure, know what to trust to; equity is according to the conscience of him that is chancellor, and as that is larger or narrower, so is equity. 'Tis all one as if they should make the standard for the measure we call a foot, a chancellor's foot; what an uncertain measure would this be! One chancellor has a long foot, another a short foot, a third an indifferent foot. 'Tis the same thing in the chancellor's conscience.

JOHN SELDEN, *Table-Talk: Equity*.

Law and equity are two things which God hath joined, but which man hath put asunder.

C. C. COLTON, *Lacon*. Vol. i, No. 381.

6
A state with defective laws will have defective morals. (Itaque malis moribus uti videbis civitates usas malis legibus.)

SENECA, *Epistulæ ad Lucilium*. Epis. xciv, 39.

The more corrupt the state, the more numerous the laws. (Corruptissima republica, plurimæ leges.)

TACITUS, *Annals*. Bk. iii, sec. 27.

7
Between two hawks, which flies the higher pitch;
Between two dogs, which hath the deeper mouth;
Between two blades, which bears the better temper;
Between two horses, which doth bear him best;
Between two girls, which hath the merriest eye,—
I have perhaps some shallow spirit of judgement;
But in these nice sharp quillets of the law,
Good faith, I am no wiser than a daw.

SHAKESPEARE, *I Henry VI*. Act. ii, sc. 4, l. 11.

8
When law can do no right,
Let it be lawful that law bar no wrong.

SHAKESPEARE, *King John*. Act iii, sc. 1, l. 185.

9
No laws, however stringent, can make the idle industrious, the thriftless provident, or the drunken sober.

SAMUEL SMILES, *Self-Help*. Ch. 1.

10
Who ever knew an honest brute,
At law his neighbour prosecute?

SWIFT, *The Logicians Refuted*.

O great and sane and simple race of brutes
That own no lust because they have no law.

TENNYSON, *Pelleas and Ettarre*, l. 471.

11
The best laws, the noblest examples, are produced for the benefit of the good from the crimes of other men. (Leges egregias, exempla honesta, apud bonos ex delictis aliorum gigni.)

TACITUS, *Annals*. Bk. xv, sec. 20.

12
The law is good, if a man use it lawfully.

New Testament: I Timothy, i, 8.

13
Where is there any book of the law so clear to each man as that written in his heart?

LEO TOLSTOY, *The Chinese Pilot*.

14
When a people lose respect for one bad law, it is but a short step before they include the good laws with the bad and are shortly in rebellion against all law.

OSCAR W. UNDERWOOD, *Drifting Sands of Party Politics*, p. 42.

15
He it was that first gave to the law the air of a science. He found it a skeleton, and clothed it with life, colour, and complexion; he embraced the cold statue, and by his touch it grew into youth, health and beauty.

BARRY YELVERTON, LORD AVONMORE, *On Blackstone*.

LAWYERS

I—Lawyers: Apothegms

16
Lawyers' gowns are lined with the wilfulness of their clients.

H. G. BOHN, *Hand-Book of Proverbs*, 439.

Lawyers' houses are built on the heads of fools.

GEORGE HERBERT, *Jacula Prudentum*.

Court fool: the plaintiff.

AMBROSE BIERCE, *The Devil's Dictionary*.

17
No use pounding on the log. The coon's out.

SILAS BRYAN. To lawyers pleading their cases before him on the Circuit Bench. (HIBBEN, *The Peerless Leader*, p. 6.)

18
But what his common sense came short,
He eked out wi' law, man.

BURNS, *Extempore in the Court of Session*.

1
When you have no basis for an argument, abuse the plaintiff. (In hominem dicendum est igitur, quum oratio argumentationem non habet.)

CICERO, *Pro Flacco*. Sec. 10.

When facts were weak, his native cheek
Brought him serenely through.

C. H. SPURGEON. Quoted as being said of an "eminent lawyer."

Bluster, sputter, question, cavil; but be sure your argument be intricate enough to confound the court.

WYCHERLEY, *The Plain-Dealer*. Act iii, sc. 1.

2
If there were no bad people, there would be no good lawyers.

DICKENS, *The Old Curiosity Shop*. Ch. 56.

3
Battledore and shuttlecock's a wery good game, vhen you a'n't the shuttlecock and two lawyers the battledores, in which case it gets too excitin' to be pleasant.

DICKENS, *Pickwick Papers*. Ch. 20.

4
Oh Sammy, Sammy, vy worn't there a alleybi?

DICKENS, *Pickwick Papers*. Ch. 34.

5
This house, where once a lawyer dwelt,
Is now a smith's. Alas!
How rapidly the iron age
Succeeds the age of brass!

WILLIAM ERSKINE, *Epigram*.

6
Of three things the devil makes his mess:
Of lawyers' tongues, of scriveners' fingers,
you the third may guess.

JOHN FLORIO, *Second Frutes*, 179. (1591)

7
Necessity has no law; I know some attorneys of the same.

BENJAMIN FRANKLIN, *Poor Richard*, 1734. *See also under* NECESSITY.

8
A good lawyer, a bad neighbor.

BENJAMIN FRANKLIN, *Poor Richard*, 1737.
Franklin was quoting the French maxim, "Bon avocat, mauvais voisin."

9
God works wonders now and then;
Behold! a lawyer, an honest man.

BENJAMIN FRANKLIN, *Poor Richard*, 1733.

"An Honest Lawyer"—book just out—
What can the author have to say?
Reprint perhaps of ancient tome—
A work of fiction any way.

GRACE HIBBARD, *Books Received*.

10
Commonly physicians, like beer, are best when they are old; and lawyers, like bread, when they are young and new.

THOMAS FULLER, *The Holy State*. Bk. ii, ch. 1.

11
The charge is prepar'd, the lawyers are met,
The judges all ranged,—a terrible show!

JOHN GAY, *The Beggar's Opera*. Act iii, sc. 11.

12
And many a burglar I've restored
To his friends and his relations.

W. S. GILBERT, *Trial by Jury*.

And whether you're an honest man or whether you're a thief
Depends on whose solicitor has given me my brief.

W. S. GILBERT, *Utopia, Limited*. Act i.

13
If the laws could speak for themselves, they would complain of the lawyers in the first place.

LORD HALIFAX, *Works*, 224.

14
When lawyers take what they would give
And doctors give what they would take.

O. W. HOLMES, *Latter-Day Warnings*.

15
Clergymen can marry you, but if you find you have made a mistake, in order to get unmarried, you have to hire a lawyer.

ELBERT HUBBARD, *The Philistine*. Vol. xxv, 158.

16
I would be loath to speak ill of any person who I do not know deserves it, but I am afraid he is an *attorney*.

SAMUEL JOHNSON. (MRS. PIOZZI, *Johnsoniana*.)

17
Law, Logic, and Switzers may be hired to fight for anybody.

THOMAS NASH, *Christ's Tears*.

18
The good have no need of an advocate. (Μὴ δεῖσθαι βοηθείας.)

PHOCION, when criticized for appearing in behalf of an unworthy client. (PLUTARCH, *Lives: Phocion*. Ch. 10, sec. 5.)

19
Fair and softly, as lawyers go to heaven.

JOHN RAY, *English Proverbs*.

20
A lawyer without history or literature is a mechanic, a mere working mason; if he possesses some knowledge of these, he may venture to call himself an architect.

SCOTT, *Guy Mannering*. Ch. 37.

21
Why may not that be the skull of a lawyer? Where be his quiddities now, his quillets, his cases, his tenures, and his tricks?

SHAKESPEARE, *Hamlet*. Act v, sc. 1, l. 107.

The first thing we do, let's kill all the lawyers.

SHAKESPEARE, *II Henry VI*. Act iv, sc. 2, l. 83.

23
That litigious she pettifogger.

WYCHERLEY, *The Plain-Dealer*. Act i, sc. 1.

24
The New England folks have a saying that three Philadelphia lawyers are a match for the very devil himself.

UNKNOWN, *Salem Observer*, 13 March, 1824.
See APPENDIX.

1
For lawyers and their pleading,
They 'steem it not a straw;
They think that honest meaning
Is of itself a law.

UNKNOWN, *The Herdman's Happy Life.* (*Sonnets and Pastorals,* 1588.)

II—Lawyers: Their Fees

2
With books and money plac'd, for show,
Like nest-eggs, to make clients lay,
And for his false opinion pay.

BUTLER, *Hudibras.* Pt. iii, canto iii, l. 624.

3
Asebia: We never valued right and wrong
But as they serve our cause.
Zelota: Our business was to please the throng
And court their wild applause.
Asebia: For this we brib'd the lawyer's tongue
And then destroy'd the laws.

DRYDEN, *Albion and Anbanias.* Act iii, sc. 1.

4
My learned profession I'll never disgrace,
By taking a fee with a grin on my face,
When I haven't been there to attend to the case.

W. S. GILBERT, *Iolanthe.* Act i.

5
A man may as well open an oyster without a knife, as a lawyer's mouth without a fee.

BARTEN HOLYDAY, *Technogamia,* ii, 5.

Once (says an author, where I need not say)
Two travellers found an Oyster in their way:
Both fierce, both hungry, the dispute grew strong,
While, scale in hand, Dame Justice pass'd along.
Before her each with clamour pleads the laws,
Explain'd the matter, and would win the cause.
Dame Justice, weighing long the doubtful right,
Takes, opens, swallows it before their sight.
The cause of strife remov'd so rarely well,
"There take (says Justice), take ye each a shell.
We thrive at Westminster on fools like you:
'Twas a fat Oyster—Live in peace—Adieu."

POPE, *Verbatim from Boileau.*

6
So wise, so grave, of so perplex'd a tongue,
And loud withal, that would not wag, nor scarce
Lie still without a fee.

BEN JONSON, *Volpone.* Act i, sc. 1.

7
What is the price of your voice? (Quod vocis pretium?)

JUVENAL, *Satires.* Sat. vii, l. 119. Referring to a lawyer's fee.

8
They put off hearings wilfully,
To finger the refreshing fee.

BERNARD MANDEVILLE, *Fable of the Bees.*

9
There is no law for restitution of fees, sir.

MASSINGER, *The Old Law.* Act i, sc. 1. (1656)

10
Litigious terms, fat contentions, and flowing fees.

MILTON, *Tractate on Education.*

11
Law has bread and butter in it. (Aliquid de jure gustare. Habet hæc res panem.)

PETRONIUS, *Satyricon.* Sec. 46.

12
Trafficking in the mad wrangles of the noisy court, he lets out for hire his anger and his speech. (Clamosi rabiosa fori Jurgia vendens improbus iras Et verba locat.)

SENECA, *Hercules Furens,* l. 172. Referring to a lawyer.

13
'Tis like the breath of an unfee'd lawyer; you gave me nothing for it.

SHAKESPEARE, *King Lear.* Act i, sc. 4, l. 142.

III—Lawyers: Their Virtues

14
The good lawyer is not the man who has an eye to every side and angle of contingency, and qualifies all his qualifications, but who throws himself on your part so heartily, that he can get you out of a scrape.

EMERSON, *Conduct of Life: Power.*

15
He is one that will not plead that cause wherein his tongue must be confuted by his conscience.

THOMAS FULLER, *Holy and Profane States: The Good Advocate.* Bk. ii, ch. 1.

16
The study of the law is useful in a variety of points of view. It qualifies a man to be useful to himself, to his neighbors and to the public. It is the most certain stepping-stone in a political line.

THOMAS JEFFERSON, *Writings.* Vol. viii, p. 17.

The only road to the highest stations in this country is that of the law.

SIR WILLIAM JONES, *Letter to C. Revicski,* 17 March, 1771.

All lawyers, be they knaves or fools,
Know that a seat is worth the earning,
Since Parliament's astounding rules
Vouch for their honour and their learning.

J. E. T. ROGERS, *On the Eagerness of Lawyers to Obtain Seats in the House.*

17
The best and most blameless interpreter of the laws. (Optimus atque Interpres legum sanctissimus.)

JUVENAL, *Satires.* Sat. iv, l. 78. Referring to Pegasus.

18
Discourage litigation. Persuade your neighbors to compromise whenever you can. . . . As a peace-maker the lawyer has a superior opportunity of being a good man. There will still be business enough.

ABRAHAM LINCOLN, *Notes for Law Lecture,* 1 July, 1850. STERN, *Writings of Lincoln,* p. 328.

1
I went into the temple, there to hear
The teachers of our law, and to propose
What might improve my knowledge or their own.
MILTON, *Paradise Regained*. Bk. i, l. 211.

2
The man of law who never saw
The ways to buy and sell,
Weening to rise by merchandise,
I pray God speed him well!
SIR THOMAS MORE, *A Merry Jest*. (c. 1500) Lines to similar effect, but concluding, "God never speeds him well," are attributed to Sir John Fortescue, Chief Justice (1422–1476).

3
Bold of your worthiness, we single you
As our best-moving fair solicitor.
SHAKESPEARE, *Love's Labour's Lost*. Act ii, sc. 1, l. 28.

4
The profession of the law is the only aristocratic element which can be amalgamated without violence with the natural elements of democracy. . . . I cannot believe that a republic could subsist if the influence of lawyers in public business did not increase in proportion to the power of the people.
DE TOCQUEVILLE, *Democracy in America*. Vol. i, ch. 16.

IV—Lawyers: Their Faults

5
Our wrangling lawyers . . . are so litigious and busy here on earth, that I think they will plead their clients' causes hereafter, some of them in hell.
ROBERT BURTON, *Anatomy of Melancholy: Democritus to the Reader*.

6
Your pettifoggers damn their souls,
To share with knaves in cheating fools.
BUTLER, *Hudibras*. Pt. ii, canto i, l. 515.

Is not the winding up witnesses,
And nicking, more than half the bus'ness?
For witnesses, like watches, go
Just as they're set, too fast or slow;
And where in Conscience they're strait-lac'd,
'Tis ten to one that side is cast.
BUTLER, *Hudibras*. Pt. ii, canto ii, l. 359.

Make law and equity as dear
As plunder and free-quarter were;
And fierce encounters at the bar
Undo as fast as those in war;
Enrich bawds, whores, and usurers,
Pimps, scriv'ners, silenc'd ministers,
That get estates by being undone
For tender conscience, and have none.
BUTLER, *Satire upon the Weakness and Misery of Man*, l. 127.

7
He saw a lawyer killing a viper
On a dunghill hard by his own stable;
And the Devil smiled, for it put him in mind
Of Cain and his brother Abel.
S. T. COLERIDGE, *The Devil's Thoughts*. St. 4.

He saw a lawyer killing a viper
On a dunghill beside his stable;
Ho! quoth he, thou put'st me in mind
Of the story of Cain and Abel.
ROBERT SOUTHEY, *The Devil's Walk*. St. 6. An expansion of Coleridge's poem.

8
Then shifting his side (as a lawyer knows how).
COWPER, *Report of an Adjudged Case*.

9
Next bring some lawyers to thy bar,
By innuendo they might all stand there;
There let them expiate that guilt,
And pay for all that blood their tongues have spilt.
These are the mountebanks of state,
Who by the sleight of tongues can crimes create,
And dress up trifles in the robes of fate,
The mastiffs of a Government,
To worry and run down the innocent.
DANIEL DEFOE, *A Hymn to the Pillory*. St. 16.

10
The lawyer has spoiled the statesman.
BENJAMIN DISRAELI, *The Young Duke*. Bk. v, ch. 6. Referring to Lord Brougham.

11
I know you lawyers can, with ease,
Twist words and meanings as you please.
JOHN GAY, *Fables*. Pt. ii, No. 1.

12
Lawyers are always more ready to get a man into troubles than out of them.
GOLDSMITH, *The Good-Natured Man*. Act iii.

13
Come, you of the law, who can talk, if you please,
Till the man in the moon will allow it's a cheese.
O. W. HOLMES. *Lines Recited at the Berkshire Jubilee*.

14
That one hundred and fifty lawyers should do business together is not to be expected.
THOMAS JEFFERSON, *Writings*. Vol. i, p. 86. Referring to Congress.

How can expedition be expected from a body which we have saddled with an hundred lawyers, whose trade is talking?
THOMAS JEFFERSON, *Writings*. Vol. xiv, p. 310.

15
I oft have heard him say how he admir'd
Men of your large profession, that could speak
To every cause, and things mere contraries,
Till they were hoarse again, yet all be law.
BEN JONSON, *Volpone*. Act i, sc. 1.

16
Ye who plead for the poor, and take money at their hands, Ye lawyers, ye advocates, be sure of this:

When ye draw near to death, and pray for pardon,
Your pardon at your parting hence will be but small.
Saint Matthew bids me tell you this, and if I lie, blame him.

WILLIAM LANGLAND, *Piers Plowman: God's Bull of Pardon.*

And he said, Woe unto you also, *ye* lawyers, for ye lade men with burdens grievous to be borne, and ye yourselves touch not the burdens with one of your fingers.

New Testament: Luke, xi, 46.

1
My suit has nothing to do with the assault, or battery, or poisoning, but is about three goats, which, I complain, have been stolen by my neighbor. This the judge desires to have proved to him; but you, with swelling words and extravagant gestures, dilate on the Battle of Cannæ, the Mithridatic war, and the perjuries of the insensate Carthaginians, the Syllæ, the Marii, and the Mucii. It is time, Postumus, to say something about my three goats.

MARTIAL, *Epigrams*. Bk. vi, epig. 19.

You wear out a good wholesome forenoon in hearing a cause between an orange-wife and a fosset-seller; and then rejourn the controversy of three pence to a second day of audience.

SHAKESPEARE, *Coriolanus*. Act ii, sc. 1, l. 77.

2
The law the lawyers know about
Is property and land, . . .
Why Faith is more than what one sees,
And Hope survives the worst disease,
And Charity is more than these,
They do not understand.

H. D. C. PEPLER, *The Law the Lawyers Know.*

3
Piecemeal they win this acre first, then that,
Glean on, and gather up the whole estate;
Then strongly fencing ill-got wealth by law,
Indentures, cov'nants, articles, they draw,
Large as the fields themselves, and larger far
Than civil codes, with all their glosses, are.

POPE, *Satires of Dr. Donne*. Sat. ii, l. 91.

4
Why is there always a secret singing
When a lawyer cashes in?
Why does a hearse horse snicker
Hauling a lawyer away?

CARL SANDBURG, *The Lawyers Know Too Much.*

5
O perilous mouths,
That bear in them one and the self-same tongue,
Either of condemnation or approof;
Bidding the law make court'sy to their will;
Hooking both right and wrong to the appetite,
To follow as it draws.

SHAKESPEARE, *Measure for Measure*, ii, 4, 172.

In law, what plea so tainted and corrupt,
But, being season'd with a gracious voice,
Obscures the show of evil?

SHAKESPEARE, *Merchant of Venice*, iii, 2, 75.

6
And do as adversaries do in law,
Strive mightily, but eat and drink as friends.

SHAKESPEARE, *Taming of the Shrew*, i, 2, 277.

7
You have clearly proved that ignorance, idleness, and vice, are the proper ingredients for qualifying a legislator; that laws are best explained, interpreted and applied, by those whose interest and abilities lie in perverting, confounding and eluding them.

JONATHAN SWIFT, *Gulliver's Travels: Voyage to Brobdingnag.*

8
These
Insnare the wretched in the toils of law,
Fomenting discord, and perplexing right;
An iron race!

THOMSON, *The Seasons: Autumn*, l. 1291.

The toils of law—what dark insidious men
Have cumbrous added to perplex the truth,
And lengthen simple justice into trade.

THOMSON, *The Seasons: Winter*, l. 384.

Attorneys and rogues are vermin not easily rooted out of a rich soil.

WALPOLE, *Letter to Sir Horace Mann*, 11 Aug., 1777.

9
A Lawyer art thou?—draw not nigh!
Go, carry to some fitter place
The keenness of that practised eye,
The hardness of that sallow face.

WILLIAM WORDSWORTH, *A Poet's Epitaph.*

LEADER

10
And when we think we lead we most are led.

BYRON, *The Two Foscari*. Act ii, sc. 1.

11
An uninforming piece of wood;
Like other guides, as some folks say;
Who neither lead, nor tell the way.

WILLIAM COMBE, *Dr. Syntax in Search of the Picturesque*. Canto ii.

12
For if the trumpet give an uncertain sound, who shall prepare himself to the battle?

New Testament: I Corinthians, xiv, 8.

13
Lights of the world and stars of human race.

COWPER, *The Progress of Error*, l. 97.

14
Either I am
The foremost horse in the team, or I am none.

JOHN FLETCHER, *Two Noble Kinsmen*. Act i, sc. 2.

An two men ride of a horse, one must ride behind.

SHAKESPEARE, *Much Ado About Nothing*. Act iii, sc. 5, l. 40.

He that rides behind another must not think to guide.

THOMAS FULLER, *Gnomologia*. The forerunner of "back-seat driver."

1
There is no reason to despair with Teucer as our leader. (Nil desperandum Teucro duce.)
HORACE, *Odes*. Bk. i, ode 7.

Be it your care to follow; you shall be safe with me as your leader. (Sit tua cura sequi; me duce tutus eris.)
OVID, *Ars Amatoria*. Bk. ii, l. 58.

With me as leader, ye men, control your anxieties; under my guidance, let ship and crew run straight. (Me duce damnosas, homines, conpescite curas; Rectaque cum sociis me duce navis est.)
OVID, *Remediorum Amoris*, l. 69.

2
O wretched madness of the leader! (O rabies miseranda ducis!)
LUCAN, *De Bello Civili*. Bk. ii, l. 544.

What pilot so expert but needs must wreck,
Embark'd with such a steers-mate at the helm?
MILTON, *Samson Agonistes*, l. 1044.

3
They say that in his love affairs he was petted by the beauties, who always followed him as long as he walked before them.
(On dit que dans ses amours
Il fut caressé des belles,
Qui le suivrent toujours,
Tant qu'il marcha devant elles.)
BERNARD DE LA MONNOYE, *Chanson sur le Fameux Palisse*.

The king himself has follow'd her
When she has walk'd before.
GOLDSMITH, *Elegy on Madam Blaize*.

Pandarus: Do not you follow the young Lord Paris?
Servant: Ay, sir, when he goes before me.
SHAKESPEARE, *Troilus and Cressida*, iii, 1, 1.

4
The deeds of the leader shall live, and the hard-won glory of his exploits; this endures, this alone escapes the greedy destruction of death. (Facta ducis vivent, operosaque gloria rerum; Hæc manet, hæc avidos effugit una rogos.)
OVID, *Consolatio ad Liviam*, l. 265.

He was leader of leaders. (Dux erat ille ducum.)
OVID, *Heroides*. Epis. viii, l. 46.

The fire of God
Fills him. I never saw his like; there lives
No greater leader.
TENNYSON, *Lancelot and Elaine*, l. 314.

5
O for a living man to lead!
That will not babble when we bleed;
O for the silent doer of the deed!
One that is happy in his height,
And one that in a nation's night
Hath solitary certitude of light.
STEPHEN PHILLIPS, *A Man*.

6
Whoever is foremost, leads the herd. (Und wer der Vorderste ist, führt die Heerde.)
SCHILLER, *Wallenstein's Tod*. Act iii, sc. 4, l. 10.

7
Thou marshall'st me the way that I was going.
SHAKESPEARE, *Macbeth*. Act ii, sc. 1, l. 42.

8
Reason and calm judgment, the qualities specially belonging to a leader. (Ratione et consilio, propriis ducis artibus.)
TACITUS, *History*. Bk. iii, sec. 20.

8a
As I stand aloof and look there is to me something profoundly affecting in large masses of men following the lead of those who do not believe in men.
WALT WHITMAN, *Thought*.

LEARNING

See also Education, Knowledge, Scholar, Wisdom

I—Learning: Definitions

9
Learning hath his infancy, when it is but beginning and almost childish; then his youth, when it is luxuriant and juvenile; then his strength of years, when it is solid and reduced; and lastly his old age, when it waxeth dry and exhaust.
FRANCIS BACON, *Essays: Of Vicissitude of Things*.

10
The languages, especially the dead,
The sciences, and most of all the abstruse,
The arts, at least all such as could be said
To be the most remote from common use,
In all these he was much and deeply read.
BYRON, *Don Juan*. Canto i, st. 40.

11
Learning is the eye of the mind.
THOMAS DRAXE, *Bibliotheca Scholastica Instructissima*, p. 111. (1633)

12
Learning by study must be won;
'Twas ne'er entail'd from son to son.
JOHN GAY, *Fables: The Pack Horse and Carrier*, l. 41.

13
This is the highest learning,
The hardest and the best:
From self to keep still turning,
And honour all the rest.
GEORGE MACDONALD, *After Thomas à Kempis*.

14
Learned men are the cisterns of knowledge, not the fountain-heads.
JAMES NORTHCOTE, *Table-Talk*.

15
Learning is but an adjunct to ourself
And where we are our learning likewise is.
SHAKESPEARE, *Love's Labour's Lost*. Act iv, sc. 3, l. 314.

II—Learning: Apothegms

16
To unlearn what is nought.
ANTISTHENES, when asked what learning was

most necessary for man's life. (BACON, *Apothegms*. No. 177.)

Child of Nature, learn to unlearn.
BENJAMIN DISRAELI, *Contarini Fleming*. Pt. i, ch. 1.

It is the worst of madness to learn what has to be unlearnt. (Extremæ est dementiæ discere dediscenda.)
ERASMUS, *De Ratione Studii*.

The mind is slow in unlearning what it has been long in learning. (Dediscit animus sero qui didicit diu.)
SENECA, *Troades*, l. 633.

1
Learning will be cast into the mire and trodden down under the hoofs of a swinish multitude.
EDMUND BURKE, *Reflections on the Revolution in France*.

2
Wear your learning like your watch, in a private pocket; and do not pull it out, and strike it, merely to show that you have one.
LORD CHESTERFIELD, *Letters*, 22 Feb., 1748.

Swallow all your learning in the morning, but digest it in company in the evenings.
LORD CHESTERFIELD, *Letters*, 10 May, 1751.

3
The food of study and learning. (Pabulum studii atque doctrinæ.)
CICERO, *De Senectute*. Ch. 14, sec. 49.

4
When a great learned man (who is long in making) dieth, much learning dieth with him.
SIR EDWARD COKE, *The Institutes: Preface*.

5
All learned and all drunk!
COWPER, *The Task*. Bk. iv, l. 478.

6
In the shady walks of the divine Hecademus. (Ἐν εὐσκίοις δρόμοισιν Ἑκαδήμου θεοῦ.)
EUPOLIS, *Shirkers*. Act ii, l. 437. Diogenes Laertius explains (*Plato*, sec. 7) that Plato lived in the Academy, "which is a gymnasium outside the walls, in a grove named after a certain hero, Hecademus."

The green retreats Of Academus.
MARK AKENSIDE, *Pleasures of the Imagination*. Canto i, l. 591.

7
Learning makes a good man better and an ill man worse.
THOMAS FULLER, *Gnomologia*. No. 3162.

8
And still they gaz'd, and still the wonder grew,
That one small head could carry all he knew.
GOLDSMITH, *The Deserted Village*, l. 215.

9
Learn not and know not.
JAMES HOWELL, *Proverbs*, 26. (1659) *See also under* IGNORANCE.

10
Few men make themselves Masters of the things they write or speak. (Delle belle eruditissima, delle erudite bellissima.)
JOHN SELDEN, *Table-Talk: Learning*.

11
Find time to be learning somewhat good, and give up being desultory.
MARCUS AURELIUS, *Meditations*. Bk. ii, sec. 7.

12
Hated not learning worse than toad or asp.
MILTON, *Sonnets: On the Detraction*, etc.

13
Learn of the mole to plough, the worm to weave.
POPE, *Essay on Man*. Epis. iii, l. 176.

14
Some people will never learn anything, for this reason, because they understand everything too soon.
POPE, *Thoughts on Various Subjects*.

15
Learning makes the wise wiser, and the fool more foolish.
JOHN RAY, *English Proverbs*. *See also* KNOWLEDGE AND WISDOM.

16
Take away from our learned men the pleasure of making themselves heard, learning would then be nothing to them. (Otez à nos savants le plaisir de se faire écouter, le savoir ne sera rien pour eux.)
ROUSSEAU, *Julie*. Pt. i, letter 12.

17
All the learned and authentic fellows.
SHAKESPEARE, *All's Well that Ends Well*. Act ii, sc. 3, l. 14.

O this learning, what a thing it is!
SHAKESPEARE, *The Taming of the Shrew*. Act i, sc. 2, l. 160.

18
A prodigy in learning.
SMOLLETT, *Roderick Random*. Ch. 45.

I would by no means wish a daughter of mine to be a progeny of learning.
SHERIDAN, *The Rivals*. Act i, sc. 2.

19
He has more learning than appears
On the scroll of twice three thousand years.
E. C. STEDMAN, *The Discoverer*.

20
Intelligence and learning are more easily stamped out than revived. (Ingenia studiaque oppresseris facilius quam revocaveris.)
TACITUS, *Agricola*. Sec. 3.

21
Wearing all that weight
Of learning lightly like a flower.
TENNYSON, *In Memoriam: Conclusion*. St. 10.

III—Learning: Its Value

22
Learning teacheth more in one year than experience in twenty.
ROGER ASCHAM, *The Scholemaster*.

23
The learned eye is still the loving one.
ROBERT BROWNING, *Red Cotton Night-cap Country*. Bk. i.

1
In mathematics he was greater
Than Tycho Brahe, or Erra Pater;
For he, by geometric scale,
Could take the size of pots of ale.
BUTLER, *Hudibras*. Pt. i, canto i, l. 119.

And wisely tell what hour o' th' day
The clock does strike by Algebra.
BUTLER, *Hudibras*. Pt. i, canto i, l. 125.

2
As a field, however fertile, cannot be fruitful without cultivation, neither can a mind without learning. (Ut ager, quamvis fertilis, sine cultura fructuosus esse non potest, sic sine doctrina animus.)
CICERO, *Tusculanarum Disputationum*. Bk. ii, ch. 5, sec. 13.

3
When Honour's sun declines, and Wealth takes wings,
Then Learning shines, the best of precious things.
EDWARD COCKER, *Urania*. (1670)

When house and land are gone and spent,
Then learning is most excellent.
SAMUEL FOOTE, *Taste*.

When ign'rance enters, folly is at hand;
Learning is better far than house and land.
DAVID GARRICK, *She Stoops to Conquer: Prologue*.

4
Yet, he was kind; or if severe in aught,
The love he bore to learning was in fault;
The village all declar'd how much he knew,
'Twas certain he could write and cipher too.
GOLDSMITH, *The Deserted Village*, l. 205.

5
The true knight of Learning, the world holds him dear—
Love bless him, Joy crown him, God speed his career.
O. W. HOLMES, *A Parting Health: To J. L. Motley*.

6
Let ignorance talk as it will, learning has its value.
LA FONTAINE, *The Use of Knowledge*. Bk. viii, fab. 19. *See also under* KNOWLEDGE.

7
The Lord of Learning who upraised mankind
From being silent brutes to singing men.
C. G. LELAND, *The Music-lesson of Confucius*.

8
Thou art an heir to fair living, but that is nothing if thou be disinherited of learning. . . . Far more seemly were it for thee to have thy study full of books than thy purse full of money.
JOHN LYLY, *Euphues: Letter to Alcius*.

9
A learned man has always wealth in himself. (Homo doctus in se semper divitias habet.)
PHÆDRUS, *Fables*. Bk. vi, fab. 21.

10
A single day among the learned lasts longer than the longest life of the ignorant.
POSIDONIUS. (SENECA, *Epistulæ ad Lucilium*, lxxviii, 29.)

11
As the rough diamond from the mine,
In breakings only shews its light,
Till polishing has made it shine:
Thus learning makes the genius bright.
ALLAN RAMSAY, *The Gentle Shepherd*.

IV—Learning: Its Emptiness

12
Much learning doth make thee mad.
New Testament: Acts, xxvi, 24.

Out of too much learning become mad.
ROBERT BURTON, *Anatomy of Melancholy*. Pt. iii, sec. iv, mem. 1, subs. 2.

We know that you are mad with much learning. (Scimus te præ litteras fatuum esse.)
PETRONIUS, *Satyricon*. Sec. 45.

13
Then grew the learning of the schoolmen to be utterly despised as barbarous.
BACON, *Advancement of Learning*. Bk. i.

14
Learning, that cobweb of the brain,
Profane, erroneous, and vain.
BUTLER, *Hudibras*. Pt. i, canto iii, l. 1339.

15
Learning without thought is labor lost; thought without learning is perilous.
CONFUCIUS, *Analects*. Bk. ii, ch. 15.

There is the love of knowing without the love of learning—a beclouding which leads to dissipation of mind.
CONFUCIUS, *Analects*. Bk. xvii, ch. 8.

16
Learning itself, receiv'd into a mind
By nature weak, or viciously inclin'd,
Serves but to lead philosophers astray,
Where children would with ease discern the way.
COWPER, *The Progress of Error*, l. 431.

Learning unrefin'd,
That oft enlightens to corrupt the mind.
WILLIAM FALCONER, *Shipwreck*. Canto i, l. 166.

17
A learned blockhead is a greater blockhead than an ignorant one.
BENJAMIN FRANKLIN, *Poor Richard*, 1734.

18
Whence is thy learning? Hath thy toil
O'er books consum'd the midnight oil?
JOHN GAY, *Fables: Shepherd and Philosopher*, l. 15. *See also* STUDY: THE MIDNIGHT OIL.

19
My foolish parents taught me to read and write. (Me litterulas stulti docuere parentes.)
MARTIAL, *Epigrams*. Bk. ix, ep. 73, l. 7.

Well, for your favour, sir, why, give God thanks, and make no boast of it; and for your writing

and reading, let that appear when there is no need of such vanity.
SHAKESPEARE, *Much Ado About Nothing*. Act iii, sc. 3, l. 17.

1
A little learning is a dangerous thing;
Drink deep, or taste not the Pierian spring:
There shallow draughts intoxicate the brain,
And drinking largely sobers us again.
POPE, *Essay on Criticism*. Pt. ii, l. 15.

Next these learn'd Jonson in this list I bring
Who had drunk deep of the Pierian Spring.
MICHAEL DRAYTON, *Of Poets and Poesie*.

If a little knowledge is dangerous, where is the man who has so much as to be out of danger?
T. H. HUXLEY, *Science and Culture: On Elementary Instruction in Physiology*.

One must give the mind, not a slight tincture, but a thorough and perfect dye. (Il ne l'en faut pas arroser, il l'en faut teindre.)
MONTAIGNE, *Essays*. Bk. ii, ch. 6.

2
Ask of the Learn'd the way? The Learn'd are blind;
This bids to serve, and that to shun mankind:
Some place the bliss in Action, some in Ease,
Those call it Pleasure, and Contentment these.
POPE, *Essay on Man*. Epis. iv, l. 19.

So by false learning is good sense defaced:
Some are bewilder'd in the maze of schools,
And some made coxcombs Nature meant but fools.
POPE, *Essay on Criticism*. Pt. i, l. 25.

3
How vain is learning unless intelligence go with it! (Ὡς οὐδὲν ἡ μάθησις, ἂν μὴ νοῦς παρῇ.)
STOBÆUS, *Florilegium*.

Whereto serveth learning, if understanding be not joined to it?
MONTAIGNE, *Essays*. Bk. i, ch. 24.

4
How many perish in the world through vain learning.
THOMAS À KEMPIS, *De Imitatione Christi*. Pt. i, ch. 3.

5
A learned man is an idler who kills time with study. Beware of his false knowledge: it is more dangerous than ignorance.
BERNARD SHAW, *Maxims for Revolutionists*.

6
Much learning shows how little mortals know;
Much wealth, how little worldlings can enjoy.
YOUNG, *Night Thoughts*. Night vi, l. 520.

V—Learning: Never too Late to Learn

7
Learning is ever in the freshness of its youth, even for the old. (Ἀεὶ γὰρ ἥβη τοῖς γέρουσιν εὖ μαθεῖν.)
ÆSCHYLUS, *Agamemnon*, l. 584.

If I should not be learning now, when should I be?
LACYDES, when asked, in extreme age, why he was studying geometry. (DIOGENES LAERTIUS, *Lacydes*. Sec. 5.)

8
It is well to live that one may learn. (Bueno es Vivir para ver.)
CERVANTES, *Don Quixote*. Pt. ii, ch. 32.

A man may live and learn.
UNKNOWN, *Roxburghe Ballads*, i, 80. (c. 1620)

I was innocent myself once, but live and learn.
GARRICK, *Miss in Her Teens*. Act i, sc. 2. (1747)

The longer one lives the more he learns.
THOMAS MOORE, *Dream of Hindoostan*.

Learn to live, and live to learn,
Ignorance like a fire doth burn,
Little tasks make large return.
BAYARD TAYLOR, *To My Daughter*.

9
A zeal for learning, which, in the case of wise and well-trained men, advances in even pace with age. (Studia doctrinæ, quæ quidem prudentibus et bene institutis pariter cum ætate crescunt.)
CICERO, *De Senectute*. Ch. 14, sec. 50.

10
Better learn late than never. (Ὀψιμαθῆ ἢ ἀμαθῆ.)
CLEOBULUS. (STOBÆUS, *Florilegium*. Pt. iii, l. 79.)

11
Cease not to learn until thou cease to live;
Think that day lost wherein thou draw'st no letter
To make thyself more learned, wiser, better.
(Jusqu'au cercuil (mon fils) veuilles apprendre,
Et tien perdu le jour qui s'est passe,
Si tu n'y as quelque chose ammasse,
Pour plus scavant et plus sage te rendre.)
GUY DE FAUR PIBRAC, *Collection of Quatrains*. (Joshua Sylvester, tr., c. 1608.)

It is better to learn late than never.
PUBLILIUS SYRUS, *Sententiæ*. No. 864.

Learn young, learn fair; learn auld, learn mair.
W. G. BENHAM, *Quotations*, p. 799.

12
I grow old learning something new every day. (Γηράσκω δ' ἀεὶ πολλὰ διδασκόμενος.)
SOLON. (VALERIUS MAXIMUS. Bk. viii, ch. 7, sec. 14.) Valerius translates the phrase into Latin: "Quotidie aliquid addiscentem senescere."

Still I am learning. (Ancora imparo.)
The favorite maxim of Michelangelo.

13
Were man to live coeval with the sun,
The patriarch-pupil would be learning still.
YOUNG, *Night Thoughts*. Night vii, l. 86.

LEG

14
Stop where I may, the snake Sensualism spits its venom upon me. . . . It has penetrated into the very sweetshops; and there, among the commoner sorts of confectionery, may be

seen this year models of the female Leg, the whole definite and elegant article as far as the thigh, with a fringe of paper cut in imitation of the female drawers and embroidered in the female fashion!

ROBERT BUCHANAN, *The Fleshly School of Poetry.*

1
Down flow'd her robe, a tartan sheen,
Till half a leg was scrimply seen;
And such a leg! my bonny Jean
Could only peer it;
Sae straught, sae taper, tight an' clean,
Nane else cam near it.

ROBERT BURNS, *The Vision.* Duan i, st. 11.

2
A leg and foot, to speak more plain,
Rests here of one commanding;
Who though his wits he might retain,
Lost half his understanding.

GEORGE CANNING, *Epitaph for the Tombstone Erected over the Marquis of Anglesea's Leg, Lost at Waterloo.*

The leg wounded in his country's service should be embalmed in memory, while the dishonored body rots, forgotten, in the dust.

UNKNOWN, *Epigram on Benedict Arnold.* His monument on the battlefield of Saratoga shows the leg which was wounded there.

Lose a leg rather than life.

THOMAS FULLER, *Gnomologia.* No. 3278.

3
Then I shall be able to pull the leg of that chap Mike. He is always trying to do me.

WILLIAM BROWN CHURCHWARD, *Blackbirding in the South Pacific,* p. 215. (1888) See APPENDIX, p. 2296.

4
They took leg-bail and ran awa.

ROBERT FERGUSSON, *Poems,* p. 234. (1774)

I'll give him leg-bail for my honesty.

JOHN O'KEEFFE, *Positive Man.* Act ii, sc. 2.

5
The human knee is a joint and not an entertainment.

PERCY HAMMOND *Review of a Play.* (1930) (SULLIVAN, *Our Times.* Vol. iii, p. 338.)

6
Legs are staple articles and will never go out of fashion while the world lasts.

JARRETT AND PALMER, referring to their "spectacular drama," *The Black Crook.* (1866)

7
Since your legs resemble the horns of the moon, you could bathe your feet, Phœbus, in a drinking-horn. (Cum sint crura tibi simulent quæ cornua lunæ, In rhytio poteras, Phœbe, lavare pedes.)

MARTIAL, *Epigrams.* Bk. ii, epig. 35.

8
On his last legs.

MIDDLETON AND MASSINGER, *The Old Law.* Act v, sc. 1. (1656)

9
Though his face be better than any man's, yet his leg excels all men's.

SHAKESPEARE, *Romeo and Juliet.* Act ii, sc. 5, l. 40.

10
Horses are tied by the heads, dogs and bears by the neck, monkeys by the loins, and men by the legs: when a man's over-lusty at legs, then he wears wooden nether-stocks.

SHAKESPEARE, *King Lear.* Act ii, sc. 4, l. 7.

11
Taste your legs, sir; put them in motion.

SHAKESPEARE, *Twelfth Night.* Act iii, sc. 1, l. 87.

LEGACY, see Inheritance

LEISURE

See also Idleness

12
When a man's busy, why, leisure
Strikes him as wonderful pleasure;
'Faith, and at leisure once is he?
Straightway he wants to be busy.

ROBERT BROWNING, *The Glove,* l. 3.

13
He was never less at leisure than when at leisure. (Numquam se minus otiosum esse quam cum otiosus.)

CICERO, *De Officiis.* Bk. iii, ch. 1, sec. 1. Quoted as a saying of Scipio Africanus.

14
Ease (or leisure), with dignity. (Cum dignitate otium.)

CICERO, *Pro Publio Sestio.* Sec. 45. Usually quoted, "Otium cum dignitate." Described by Cicero as the supremely desirable object to all sane and good men.

What is more delightful than lettered ease? (Quid est enim dulcius otio litterato?)

CICERO, *Tusculanarum Disputationum.* Bk. v, ch. 36, sec. 105.

O Granta! sweet Granta! where studious of ease,
I slumbered seven years, and then lost my degrees.

CHRISTOPHER ANSTEY, *New Bath Guide: Epilogue.*

15
Is there no road now to Leisurely Lane? We traveled it long ago!
A place for the lagging of leisurely steps, sweet and shady and slow.

VIRGINIA WOODWARD CLOUD, *Leisurely Lane.*

16
Like a coy maiden, Ease, when courted most,
Farthest retires.

COWPER, *The Task.* Bk. i, l. 409.

17
Me, therefore, studious of laborious ease.

COWPER, *The Task.* Bk. iii, l. 361.

Studious of elegance and ease.

JOHN GAY, *Fables.* Pt. ii, No. 8.

Studious of ease, and fond of humble things.

AMBROSE PHILIPS, *Epistles from Holland, to a Friend in England,* l. 21.

18
A poor life this if, full of care,
We have no time to stand and stare.

WILLIAM H. DAVIES, *Leisure.*

1
Increased means and increased leisure are the two civilisers of man.
BENJAMIN DISRAELI, *Speech, to the Conservatives of Manchester*, 3 April, 1872.

To be able to fill leisure intelligently is the last product of civilization.
BERTRAND RUSSELL, *Conquest of Happiness*, p. 210.

2
Bankrupt of life, yet prodigal of ease.
DRYDEN, *Absalom and Achitophel*. Pt. i, l. 168.

3
Sweet is the pleasure itself cannot spoil.
Is not true leisure one with true toil?
JOHN S. DWIGHT, *True Rest*.

4
The wisdom of a learned man cometh by opportunity of leisure; and he that hath little business shall become wise.
Apocrypha: Ecclesiasticus, xxxviii, 24.

5
That man, in truth, who knows not leisure's use,
More trouble has than one by tasks pursued.
(Otio qui nescit uti
Plus negoti habet quam cum negotium in negotio.)
QUINTUS ENNIUS, *Iphigenia*. (Quoted by Aulus Gellius, *Noctes Atticæ*. Bk. xix, ch. 10, sec. 12.)

6
How came he to have the leisure to die, when there is so much stirring?
EPAMINONDAS, of a man who died at the time of the battle of Leuctra. (PLUTARCH, *Rules for the Preservation of Health*.)

Zounds! how has he leisure to be sick,
In such a justling time?
SHAKESPEARE, *I Henry IV*. Act iv, sc. 1, l. 17.

7
A life of leisure and a life of laziness are two things.
BENJAMIN FRANKLIN, *Poor Richard*, 1746.

Employ thy time well if thou meanest to gain leisure.
BENJAMIN FRANKLIN, *Poor Richard*, 1758.

Idle folks have the least leisure.
JOHN RAY, *English Proverbs*.

8
Leisure is the mother of Philosophy.
THOMAS HOBBES, *Leviathan*. Pt. iv, ch. 46.

9
No blessed leisure for love or hope,
But only time for grief.
THOMAS HOOD, *The Song of the Shirt*. St. 10.

10
Leisure is the time for doing something useful.
NATHIEL HOWE, *A Chapter of Proverbs*.

11
For Solomon, he liv'd at ease, and full
Of honour, wealth, high fare, aim'd not beyond
Higher design than to enjoy his state.
MILTON, *Paradise Regained*. Bk. ii, l. 201.

12
Leisure nourishes the body and the mind. (Otia corpus alunt, animus quoque pascitur illis.)
OVID, *Epistulæ ex Ponto*. Bk. i, epis. 4, l. 21.

13
Give time to your friends, leisure to your wife, relax your mind, give rest to your body, so that you may the better fulfil your accustomed occupation.
PHÆDRUS, *Fables:* Bk. iii, *Prol.*, l. 12.

14
You will soon break the bow if you keep it always stretched. (Cito rumpes arcum, semper si tensum habueris.)
PHÆDRUS, *Fables*. Bk. iii, fab. 14, l. 10; PUBLILIUS SYRUS, *Sententiæ*. No. 388.

15
Leisure is the reward of labour.
JOHN RAY, *English Proverbs*.

16
There's no music in a rest, Katie, that I know of; but there's the making of music in it. And people are always missing that part of the life melody; and scrambling on without counting—not that it's easy to count; but nothing on which so much depends ever is easy.
JOHN RUSKIN, *Ethics of the Dust*. Lecture 4,

17
Leisure without study is death; it is a tomb for the living man. (Otium sine litteris mors est et hominis vivi sepultura.)
SENECA, *Epistulæ ad Lucilium*. Epis. lxxxii, 3.

Nor should I regard leisure and freedom from trouble as a good; for what has more leisure than a worm? (Ne quietem quidem et molestia vacare bonum dicam; quid est otiosius verme?)
SENECA, *Epistulæ ad Lucilium*. Epis. lxxxvii, 19.

18
His life was . . . an illustration of the truth of the saying that those who have most to do, and are willing to work, will find the most time.
SAMUEL SMILES, *Self-Help*. Ch. 1.

19
Leisure is the best of all possessions. (Ἐπῄνει σχολὴν ὡς κάλλιστον κτημάτων.)
SOCRATES. (DIOGENES LAERTIUS, *Socrates*. Bk. ii, sec. 30.)

20
He enjoys true leisure who has time to improve his soul's estate.
H. D. THOREAU, *Journal*, 11 Feb., 1840.

A broad margin of leisure is as beautiful in a man's life as in a book.
H. D. THOREAU, *Journal*, 28 Dec., 1852.

21
Rejoicing in the pursuits of an inglorious ease. (Studiis florentem ignobilis oti.)
VERGIL, *Georgics*. Bk. iv, l. 564.

Thus Belial, with words cloth'd in reason's garb,
Counsel'd ignoble ease, and peaceful sloth.
MILTON, *Paradise Lost*. Bk. ii, l. 226.

1
Leisure is pain; takes off our chariot wheels;
How heavily we drag the load of life!
Blest leisure is our curse; like that of Cain,
It makes us wander, wander earth around
To fly that tyrant, thought.

YOUNG, *Night Thoughts*. Night ii, l. 125.

LENDING, see Borrowing

LETTERS

2
I knew one, that when he wrote a letter, he would put that which was most material, in the Post-script, as if it had been a by-matter.

FRANCIS BACON, *Essays: Of Cunning*.

His sayings are usually like women's letters: all the pith is in the postscript.

WILLIAM HAZLITT, *Boswell Redivivus*. Referring to Charles Lamb.

Jove and my stars be praised! Here is yet a postcript.

SHAKESPEARE, *Twelfth Night*. Act ii, sc. 5, l. 187.

A woman seldom writes her Mind, but in her Postscript.

RICHARD STEELE, *The Spectator*. No. 79.

3
The earth has nothing like a she epistle.

BYRON, *Don Juan*. Canto xiii, st. 105.

4
A letter does not blush. (Epistola enim non erubescit.)

CICERO, *Epistolæ ad Atticum*. Bk. v, epis. 12.

5
For his letters, say they, are weighty and powerful; but his bodily presence is weak, and his speech contemptible.

New Testament: II Corinthians, x, 10.

6
He whistles as he goes, light-hearted wretch,
Cold and yet cheerful; messenger of grief
Perhaps to thousands, and of joy to some.

COWPER, *The Task*. Bk. iv, l. 12. Referring to the postman.

7
She'll vish there wos more, and that's the great art o' letter-writin'.

DICKENS, *Pickwick Papers*. Ch. 33.

8
Belshazzar had a letter,—
He never had but one;
Belshazzar's correspondent
Concluded and begun
In that immortal copy
The conscience of us all
Can read without its glasses
On revelation's wall.

EMILY DICKINSON, *Poems*. Pt. i, No. 25.

9
More than kisses, letters mingle souls;
For, thus friends absent speak.

JOHN DONNE, *To Sir Henry Wotton*.

10
The welcome news is in the letter found;
The carrier's not commission'd to expound;
It speaks itself, and what it does contain,
In all things needful to be known, is plain.

DRYDEN, *Religio Laici*, l. 366.

11
Carrier of news and knowledge,
Instrument of trade and industry,
Promoter of mutual acquaintance,
Of peace and good-will
Among men and nations.

CHARLES W. ELIOT, *Inscription*, on south-east corner of post-office, Washington, D. C.

Messenger of sympathy and love,
Servant of parted friends,
Consoler of the lonely,
Bond of the scattered family,
Enlarger of the common life.

CHARLES W. ELIOT, *Inscription*, on south-west corner of post-office, Washington, D. C.

Neither snow, nor rain, nor heat, nor gloom of night stays these couriers from the swift completion of their appointed rounds.

HERODOTUS, *History*. Bk. viii, sec. 98. Inscribed on New York City postoffice.

12
Every day brings a ship,
Every ship brings a word;
Well for those who have no fear,
Looking seaward well assured
That the word the vessel brings
Is the word they wish to hear.

EMERSON, *Letters*.

13
The tongue is prone to lose the way,
Not so the pen, for in a letter
We have not better things to say,
But surely say them better.

R. W. EMERSON, *Life*.

In writing a letter to a friend we may find that we rise to thought and to a cordial power of expression that costs no effort.

EMERSON, *Letters and Social Aims: Inspiration*.

The power of a wafer or a drop of wax or gluten to guard a letter, as it flies over sea, over land, and comes to its address as if a battalion of artillery brought it, I look upon as a fine meter of civilization.

EMERSON, *Society and Solitude: Civilization*.

14
Sent letters by posts.

Old Testament: Esther, viii, 10.

15
Letters, from absent friends, extinguish fear
Unite division, and draw distance near;
Their magic force each silent wish conveys,
And wafts embodied thought, a thousand ways:
Could souls to bodies write, death's pow'r were mean,
For minds could then meet minds with heav'n between.

AARON HILL, *Verses Written on a Window in a Journey to Scotland*.

1
Friendship is the great chain of human society, and intercourse of letters is one of the chiefest links of that chain.
JAMES HOWELL, *Familiar Letters: To Dr. Pritchard.*

As keys do open chests,
So letters open breasts.
JAMES HOWELL, *To the Sagacious Reader.*

They [letters] are the soul of trade.
JAMES HOWELL, *Touching the Vertue and Use of Familiar Letters,* l. 41.

2
A strange volume of real life in the daily packet of the postman. Eternal love and instant payment!
DOUGLAS JERROLD, *The Postman's Budget.*

A piece of simple goodness—a letter gushing from the heart; a beautiful unstudied vindication of the worth and untiring sweetness of human nature—a record of the invulnerability of man, armed with high purpose, sanctified by truth.
DOUGLAS JERROLD, *The Postman's Budget.*

3
A wordy and grandiloquent letter. (Verbosa et grandis epistola.)
JUVENAL, *Satires.* Sat. x, l. 71.

I have made this letter rather long only because I have not had time to make it shorter. (Je n'ai fait celle-ci plus longue que parceque je n'ai pas eu le loisir de la faire plus courte.)
PASCAL, *Lettres Provinciales,* 14 Dec., 1656.

Thy letter sent to prove me,
Inflicts no sense of wrong;
No longer wilt thou love me,—
Thy letter, though, is long.
HEINE, *Book of Songs.* No. 34.

The letter is too long by half a mile.
SHAKESPEARE, *Love's Labour's Lost.* Act v, sc. 2, l. 54.

4
Kind messages, that pass from land to land;
Kind letters, that betray the heart's deep history,
In which we feel the pressure of a hand,—
One touch of fire,—and all the rest is mystery!
LONGFELLOW, *The Seaside and Fireside: Dedication.* St. 5.

5
Never read over your old letters.
GUY DE MAUPASSANT, *Suicides.*

6
Good-bye—my paper's out so nearly,
I've only room for, Yours sincerely.
MOORE, *The Fudge Family in Paris.* Letter 6.

7
Letter-writing, that most delightful way of wasting time.
JOHN MORLEY, *Life of George Eliot.*

8
Letters of Bellerophon. (Bellorophontem . . . tabellas.)
PLAUTUS, *Bacchides,* l. 810. Bellerophon carried a letter to the king of Lycia, which, unknown to the bearer, contained a request that the king should put him to death.

9
I write many letters, but letters, alas, of the most unlettered kind! (Scribo plurimas, sed inliteratissimas litteras.)
PLINY THE YOUNGER, *Epistles.* Bk. i, epis. 10.

There is nothing to write about, you say. Well, then, write and let me know just this—that there *is* nothing to write about. ("Nihil est," inquis, "quod scribam." At hoc ipse scribe, nihil est, quod scribas, vel solum illud.)
PLINY THE YOUNGER, *Epistles.* Bk. i, epis. 11.

You will say you had no news to write me; and that probably may be true; but, without news, one has always something to say to those with whom one desires to have anything to do.
LORD CHESTERFIELD, *Letters,* 12 Jan., 1757.

Let me hear from thee by letters.
SHAKESPEARE, *The Two Gentlemen of Verona.* Act i, sc. 1, l. 57.

10
Tell him there's a post come from my master, with his horn full of good news.
SHAKESPEARE, *The Merchant of Venice.* Act v, sc. 1, l. 46.

11
Thou bringest . . . letters into trembling hands.
TENNYSON, *In Memoriam.* Pt. x.

12
For my part, I could easily do without the post-office. . . . I never received more than one or two letters in my life that were worth the postage.
H. D. THOREAU, *Walden.* Ch. 2.

II—Letters: Love-Letters

13
Lay it by in some sacred deposit
For relics—we all have a few!
Love, some day they'll print it, because it
Was written to You.
F. LOCKER-LAMPSON, *A Nice Correspondent.*

If She have written a letter, delay not an instant, but burn it.
Tear it in pieces, O Fool, and the wind to her mate shall return it!
RUDYARD KIPLING, *Certain Maxims of Hafiz.*

14
Love is the marrow of friendship, and letters are the elixir of love.
JAMES HOWELL, *Familiar Letters.* Bk. i, sec. 1.

Love is the life of friendship; letters are
The life of love.
JAMES HOWELL, *Touching the Vertue and Use of Familiar Letters,* l. 1.

15
Great love-letters are written only to great women.
ELBERT HUBBARD, *Epigrams.*

16
Soon as thy letters trembling I unclose,
That well-known name awakens all my woes.
POPE, *Eloisa to Abelard,* l. 29.

Line after line my gushing eyes o'erflow,
Led thro' a safe variety of woe:
Now warm in love, now with'ring in my bloom,
Lost in a convent's solitary gloom!
POPE, *Eloisa to Abelard*, l. 35.

1
Heav'n first taught letters for some wretch's aid,
Some banish'd lover, or some captive maid;
They live, they speak, they breathe what love inspires,
Warm from the soul, and faithful to its fires;
The virgin's wish without her fears impart,
Excuse the blush, and pour out all the heart,
Speed the soft intercourse from soul to soul,
And waft a sigh from Indus to the Pole.
POPE, *Eloisa to Abelard*, l. 51.

And oft the pangs of absence to remove
By letters, soft interpreters of love.
MATTHEW PRIOR, *Henry and Emma*, l. 147.

2
What! have I 'scaped love-letters in the holiday-time of my beauty, and am I now a subject for them?
SHAKESPEARE, *The Merry Wives of Windsor*. Act ii, sc. 1, l. 1.

LIBERALITY, see Gifts and Giving

LIBERTY

See also Freedom

I—Liberty: Definitions

3
Among a people generally corrupt, liberty cannot long exist.
EDMUND BURKE, *Letter*, to the Sheriffs of Bristol.

Liberty, too, must be limited in order to be possessed.
EDMUND BURKE, *Letter*, to the Sheriffs of Bristol.

The only liberty I mean, is a liberty connected with order; that not only exists along with order and virtue, but which cannot exist at all without them.
EDMUND BURKE, *Speech*, at Bristol, 13 Oct., 1774.

Abstract liberty, like other mere abstractions, is not to be found.
EDMUND BURKE, *Speech on Conciliation with America*.

4
Where the Spirit of the Lord is, there is liberty.
New Testament: II Corinthians, iii, 17.

5
Man's liberty ends, and it ought to end, when that liberty becomes the curse of his neighbours.
FREDERIC WILLIAM FARRAR, *Ideals of Nations*.

6
Liberty is always dangerous, but it is the safest thing we have.
HARRY EMERSON FOSDICK, *Liberty*.

7
Only in fetters is liberty:
Without its banks could a river be?
LOUIS GINSBERG, *Fetters*.

8
The love of liberty is the love of others; the love of power is the love of ourselves.
WILLIAM HAZLITT, *Political Essays: On the Connection Between Toad-Eaters and Tyrants*.

9
Liberty is the breath of progress.
R. G. INGERSOLL, *How to Reform Mankind*.

10
The God who gave us life, gave us liberty at the same time.
THOMAS JEFFERSON, *Summary View of the Rights of British America*.

There can be no prescription old enough to supersede the Law of Nature and the grant of God Almighty, who has given to all men a natural right to be free, and they have it ordinarily in their power to make themselves so, if they please.
JAMES OTIS, *Rights of the British Colonies*, p. 14.

11
Liberty in the lowest rank of every nation is little more than the choice of working or starving.
SAMUEL JOHNSON. (*Works*, vi, 151.)

Ask this man what country and liberty mean, and he will reply that he wants money, and nothing to do. (Demandez à cet homme ce que c'est que la patrie et la liberté, il vous répondra qu'il veut de l'argent et ne rien faire.)
PAUL DE KOCK, *L'Homme aux Trois Culottes*. Ch. 4.

12
The world has never had a good definition of the word liberty.
ABRAHAM LINCOLN, *Address*, Baltimore, 18 April, 1864. For full quotation see APPENDIX.

13
All that makes existence valuable to anyone depends on the enforcement of restraints upon the actions of other people.
J. S. MILL, *On Liberty*. Ch. 1.

The liberty of the individual must be thus far limited; he must not make himself a nuisance to other people.
J. S. MILL, *On Liberty*. Ch. 3.

14
The Mountain Nymph, sweet Liberty.
MILTON, *L'Allegro*, l. 36.

15
God makes no man a slave, no doubter free;
Abiding faith alone wins liberty.
JAMES JEFFREY ROCHE, *Washington*.

16
That treacherous phantom which men call Liberty.
RUSKIN, *Seven Lamps of Architecture*. Ch. viii, sec. 10.

17
Liberty means responsibility. That is why most men dread it.
BERNARD SHAW, *Maxims for Revolutionists*.

1
The supremacy of the people tends to liberty. (Populi imperium juxta libertatem.)
TACITUS, *Annals*. Bk. vi, sec. 42.

Liberty is given by nature even to mute animals. (Libertatem natura etiam mutis animalibus datam.)
TACITUS, *History*. Bk. iv, sec. 17.

2
Liberty, when it begins to take root, is a plant of rapid growth.
GEORGE WASHINGTON, *Letter to James Madison*, 2 March, 1788.

If the true spark of religious and civil liberty be kindled, it will burn. Human agency cannot extinguish it. Like the earth's central fire, it may be smothered for a time; the ocean may overwhelm it; mountains may press it down; but its inherent and unconquerable force will heave both the ocean and the land, and at some time or other, in some place or other, the volcano will break out and flame up to heaven.
DANIEL WEBSTER, *Address*, 17 June, 1825, at Bunker Hill Monument.

3
Liberty exists in proportion to wholesome restraint; the more restraint on others to keep off from us, the more liberty we have.
DANIEL WEBSTER, *Speech*. 10 May, 1847.

A liberty to do that only which is good, just, and honest.
JOHN WINTHROP, *Life and Letters*, ii, 341.

4
Liberty has never come from the government. Liberty has always come from the subjects of it. The history of liberty is a history of resistance. The history of liberty is a history of limitations of governmental power, not the increase of it.
WOODROW WILSON, *Speech*, New York Press Club, 9 Sept., 1912.

II—Liberty: Apothegms

5
The tree of liberty grows only when watered by the blood of tyrants. (L'arbre de la liberté ne croît qu'arrosé par le sang des tyrans.)
BERTRAND BARÈRE, *Speech*, French National Assembly, 1792.

The tree of liberty must be refreshed from time to time with the blood of patriots and tyrants. It is its natural manure.
THOMAS JEFFERSON, *Letter to William S. Smith*, Paris, 13 Nov., 1787. (*Writings*, iv, 467.)

6
I pardon something to the spirit of liberty.
EDMUND BURKE, *Speech on Conciliation with America*, 22 March, 1775.

The people never give up their liberties except under some delusion.
EDMUND BURKE, *Speech*, Bucks, 1784.

7
Liberty's in every blow! Let us do or die.
BURNS, *Bruce to His Men at Bannockburn*.

"Make way for liberty!" he cried,
Made way for liberty, and died.
MONTGOMERY, *The Patriot's Pass-Word*, l. 1

Fair Liberty was all his cry;
For her he stood prepared to die.
SWIFT, *On the Death of Dr. Swift*, l. 411.

This hand, the tyrant smiting, ne'er will sword release,
Till liberty assure the quietude of peace.
A translation by John D. Long, formerly governor of Massachusetts, of the Latin lines by Algernon Sidney, the last of which, "Ense petit placidam sub libertate quietam," is the motto on the arms of Massachusetts.

8
O sweet name of liberty! (O nomen dulce libertatis!)
CICERO, *In Verrem*. No. v, sec. 63.

O liberty! how many crimes are committed in thy name! (O liberté! que de crimes on commêt dans ton nom!)
MADAME ROLAND, *Mémoires: Appendix*. LAMARTINE, *Histoire des Girondins*, ch. li, p. 8, states that Madame Roland said this on the scaffold a moment before her execution, addressing a large statue of Liberty which had been erected beside the guillotine, but others allege that what she really said was, "O Liberté, comme on t'a jouée!" (O Liberty, how you have been trifled with).

9
Strangers to liberty, 'tis true;
But that delight they never knew
And therefore never missed.
COWPER, *The Caged Linnets*.

10
To those the truth makes free,
Sacred as truth itself is lawful liberty.
AUBREY DE VERE, *Liberty*.

11
The sun of liberty is set; you must light up the candle of industry and economy.
BENJAMIN FRANKLIN (attr.). Said to be in his correspondence.

12
Where liberty dwells there is my country. (Ubi libertas, ibi patria.)
A Latin phrase whose author is unknown, but which Algernon Sidney (c. 1640) adopted as his motto. A similar sentiment is attributed to Thomas Jefferson and Thomas Paine.

13
Liberty, thy thousand tongues
None silence, who design no wrongs.
MATTHEW GREEN, *The Spleen*, l. 418.

14
The boisterous sea of liberty is never without a wave.
THOMAS JEFFERSON, *Writings*. Vol. xv, p. 283.

15
Proclaim liberty throughout all the land unto all the inhabitants thereof.
Old Testament: Leviticus, xxv, 10. By an odd coincidence, in a letter written by a committee of the Pennsylvania Provincial Assembly, 1 Nov., 1751, ordering a bell for the tower of the new State House, it was directed that this quotation from the Bible

should be inscribed around it "well-shaped in large letters." It was this bell, so tradition says, which announced the signing of the Declaration of Independence, 4 July, 1776, and it is still preserved in Independence Hall, Philadelphia.

1
He that would make his own liberty secure must guard even his enemy from oppression.
THOMAS PAINE, *Dissertation on First Principles of Government*, p. 242.

Whether in chains or in laurels, liberty knows nothing but victories.
WENDELL PHILLIPS, *Speech on John Brown*, 1 Nov., 1859.

2
I must have liberty
Withal, as large a charter as the wind
To blow on whom I please.
SHAKESPEARE, *As You Like It*. Act ii, sc. 7, l. 47.

So loving-jealous of his liberty.
SHAKESPEARE, *Romeo and Juliet*. Act ii, sc. 2, l. 182.

A fig for those by law protected!
Liberty's a glorious feast!
Courts for cowards were erected,
Churches built to please the priest.
ROBERT BURNS, *The Jolly Beggars*, line 292. Air, *Jolly Mortals, Fill Your Glasses*.

3
With empty praise of liberty. (Inani jactatione libertatis.)
TACITUS, *Agricola*. Sec. 42.

4
Liberty . . . came after a long time. (Libertas . . longo post tempore venit.)
VERGIL, *Eclogues*. No. i, l. 27.

5
I shall defer my visit to Faneuil Hall, the cradle of American liberty, until its doors shall fly open, on golden hinges, to lovers of Union as well as of Liberty.
DANIEL WEBSTER, *Letter*, April, 1851.

III—Liberty: Its Virtues

6
When Liberty is gone,
Life grows insipid, and has lost its relish.
ADDISON, *Cato*. Act ii, sc. 3.

'Tis liberty alone that gives the flower
Of fleeting life its lustre and perfume.
COWPER, *The Task*. Bk. v, l. 446.

Oh! remember life can be
No charm for him who lives not free.
THOMAS MOORE, *Before the Battle*.

7
But little do or can the best of us:
That little is achieved through Liberty.
ROBERT BROWNING, *Why I Am a Liberal*.

8
Liberty . . . is one of the greatest blessings that Heaven has bestowed upon mankind.
CERVANTES, *Don Quixote*. Pt. ii, ch. 58.

9
Thou rising Sun! thou blue rejoicing Sky!
Yea, every thing that is and will be free!
Bear witness for me, wheresoe'er ye be,
With what deep worship I have still adored
The spirit of divinest Liberty.
S. T. COLERIDGE, *France: An Ode*. St. 1.

Yes, while I stood and gazed, my temples bare,
And shot my being through earth, sea, and air,
Possessing all things with intensest love,
O Liberty! my spirit felt thee there.
S. T. COLERIDGE, *France: An Ode*. St. 5.

Liberty, like day,
Breaks on the soul, and by a flash from Heav'n
Fires all the faculties with glorious joy.
COWPER, *The Task*. Bk. v, l. 883.

10
The love of liberty with life is giv'n,
And life itself th' inferior gift of Heav'n.
JOHN DRYDEN, *Palamon and Arcite*. Bk. ii, l. 291.

11
Liberty is worth whatever the best civilization is worth.
HENRY GILES, *The Worth of Liberty*.

12
For ever in thine eyes, O Liberty,
Shines that high light whereby the world is saved,
And though thou slay us, we will trust to thee!
JOHN HAY, *Liberty*.

13
What light is to the eyes—what air is to the lungs—what love is to the heart, liberty is to the soul of man. Without liberty, the brain is a dungeon, where the chained thoughts die with their pinions pressed against the hingeless doors.
R. G. INGERSOLL, *Progress*.

15
Deep in the frozen regions of the north,
A goddess violated brought thee forth,
Immortal Liberty!
SMOLLETT, *Ode to Independence*, l. 5.

16
Behold in Liberty's unclouded blaze
We lift our heads, a race of other days.
CHARLES SPRAGUE, *Centennial Ode*. St. 22.

17
I tell you, liberty is the best of all things; never live beneath the noose of a servile halter. (Dico tibi verum, libertas optima rerum; Nunquam servili sub nexa vivito fili.)
SIR WILLIAM WALLACE, quoting a medieval proverb.

18
And, best beloved of best men, liberty,
Free lives and lips, free hands of men freeborn.
SWINBURNE, *Atalanta in Calydon: Althæa*.

19
If but the least and frailest, let me be
Evermore numbered with the truly free
Who find Thy service perfect liberty!
WHITTIER, *What of the Day?* l. 13.

1
I would rather belong to a poor nation that was free than to a rich nation that had ceased to be in love with liberty. We shall not be poor if we love liberty.

WOODROW WILSON, *Speech,* Mobile, Ala., 27 Oct., 1912.

IV—Liberty: Its Defense

2
It is the common fate of the indolent to see their rights become a prey to the active. The condition upon which God hath given liberty to man is eternal vigilance.

JOHN PHILPOT CURRAN, *Speech upon the Right of Election,* 10 July, 1790.

Eternal vigilance is the price of liberty.

WENDELL PHILLIPS, *Public Opinion.* This was an address delivered before the Massachusetts Antislavery Society, 28 Jan., 1852. The phrase is not in quotation marks. It has been said that Mr. Phillips was quoting Thomas Jefferson, but in a letter dated 14 April, 1879, Mr. Phillips wrote: "'Eternal vigilance is the price of liberty' has been attributed to Jefferson, but no one has yet found it in his works or elsewhere." It has also been attributed to Patrick Henry.

3
Liberty can neither be got, nor kept, but by so much care, that mankind are generally unwilling to give the price for it.

LORD HALIFAX, *Works,* p. 62.

4
The ground of liberty must be gained by inches.

THOMAS JEFFERSON, *Writings.* Vol. viii, p. 3.

We are not to expect to be translated from despotism to liberty in a feather bed.

THOMAS JEFFERSON, *Writings.* Vol. viii, p. 13.

5
By no sword save her own falls Liberty.

R. U. JOHNSON, *Hands Across Sea.*

6
Unless that liberty, which is of such a kind as arms can neither procure nor take away, which alone is the fruit of piety, of justice, of temperance, and unadulterated virtue, shall have taken deep root in your minds and hearts, there will not long be wanting one who will snatch from you by treachery what you have acquired by arms.

MILTON, *Second Defence of People of England.*

7
The manna of popular liberty must be gathered each day, or it is rotten. . . . Only by uninterrupted agitation can a people be kept sufficiently awake to principle not to let liberty be smothered by material prosperity. Republics exist only on tenure of being agitated.

WENDELL PHILLIPS, *Address: Public Opinion,* Boston, 28 Jan., 1852.

8
Our liberties and our lives are in danger. (Libertas et anima nostra in dubio est.)

SALLUST, *Catilina.* Sec. 52.

9
God grants liberty only to those who love it, and are always ready to guard and defend it.

WEBSTER, *Speech,* U. S. Senate, 3 June, 1834.

V—Liberty and Bondage

10
A day, an hour, of virtuous liberty
Is worth a whole eternity in bondage.

ADDISON, *Cato.* Act ii, sc. 1.

11
Chains or conquest, liberty or death.

ADDISON, *Cato.* Act ii, sc. 4, last line.

Is life so dear or peace so sweet as to be purchased at the price of chains and slavery? Forbid it, Almighty God! I know not what course others may take; but as for me, give me liberty, or give me death!

PATRICK HENRY, *Speech,* Virginia House of Delegates, 23 March, 1775. (Arranged by William Wirt, 1817.)

12
The Athenians will not sell their liberties for all the gold either above or under ground.

ARISTIDES, to the Lacedæmonians. (PLUTARCH, *Lives: Aristides.* Sec. 10.)

We sell our birthright whenever we sell our liberty for any price of gold or honor.

E. P. WHIPPLE, *Outlooks on Society: Literature and Politics.*

13
Eternal Spirit of the chainless Mind!
Brightest in dungeons, Liberty! thou art,
For there thy habitation is the heart—
The heart which love of thee alone can bind.

BYRON, *The Prisoner of Chillon: Introductory.*

14
He who, through fear of poverty, forfeits liberty, which is better than mines of wealth, will . . . be a slave forever. (Sic qui pauperiem veritus potiore metallis libertate caret, . . . serviet æternum.)

CICERO, *Epistles.* Bk. i, epis. 10, l. 39.

Those, who would give up essential liberty to purchase a little temporary safety, deserve neither liberty nor safety.

BENJAMIN FRANKLIN(?), *Historical Review of Pennsylvania.* (1759)

This sentence was much used in the Revolutionary period. It occurs even so early as November, 1755, in an answer by the Assembly of Pennsylvania to the Governor.

FROTHINGHAM, *Rise of the Republic of the United States.*

15
Stand fast therefore in the liberty wherewith Christ hath made us free, and be not entangled again with the yoke of bondage.

New Testament: Galatians, v, 1.

16
A bean in liberty is better than a comfit in prison.

GEORGE HERBERT, *Jacula Prudentum.*

Lean liberty is better than fat slavery.

THOMAS FULLER, *Gnomologia.* No. 3158.

1 Preferring
Hard liberty before the easy yoke
Of servile pomp.
MILTON, *Paradise Lost*. Bk. ii, l. 255.

2
Oh! if there be, on this earthly sphere,
A boon, an offering Heaven holds dear,
'Tis the last libation Liberty draws
From the heart that bleeds and breaks in her cause!
THOMAS MOORE, *Lalla Rookh: Paradise and the Peri*. St. 11.

The tribute most high to a head that is royal,
Is love from a heart that loves liberty too.
THOMAS MOORE, *The Prince's Day*.

3
"An 't please Your Honour," quoth the peasant,
"This same dessert is not so pleasant:
Give me again my hollow tree,
A crust of bread and Liberty!"
POPE, *Imitations of Horace: Satires*. Bk. ii, sat. 6, l. 218.

No use have I for such a life, and so farewell: my wood and hole, secure from alarms, will solace me with homely vetch. (Haud mihi vita Est opus hac, et valeas: me silva cavusque Tutus ab insidiis tenui solabitur, ervo.)
HORACE, *Satires*. Bk. ii, sat. 6, l. 115. Horace is telling the story of a peasant who tried to live in a palace.

I had rather munch a crust of brown bread and an onion in a corner, without ado or ceremony, than feed upon a turkey at another man's table, where I am forced to chew slowly, drink little, wipe my mouth every minute, and cannot sneeze or cough, or do other things that are the privileges of liberty and solitude.
CERVANTES, *Don Quixote*. Pt. i, ch. 11.

4
He that roars for liberty
Faster binds a tyrant's power,
And the tyrant's cruel glee
Forces on the freer hour.
TENNYSON, *The Vision of Sin*. Pt. iv, st. 17.

VI—Liberty and Licence

5
What is liberty without wisdom and without virtue? It is the greatest of all possible evils; for it is folly, vice, and madness, without tuition or restraint.
EDMUND BURKE, *Reflections on the Revolution in France*.

More liberty begets desire of more;
The hunger still increases with the store.
DRYDEN, *Hind and the Panther*. Pt. i, l. 519.

6
Liberty in the wild and freakish hands of fanatics has once more, as frequently in the past, proved the effective helpmate of autocracy and the twin-brother of tyranny.
OTTO KAHN, *Speech*, University of Wisconsin, 14 Jan., 1918.

The deadliest foe of democracy is not autocracy but liberty frenzied. Liberty is not fool-proof. For its beneficent working it demands self-restraint.
OTTO KAHN, *Speech*, University of Wisconsin, 14 Jan., 1918.

7
It is not good to have too much liberty. It is not good to have all one wants.
BLAISE PASCAL, *Pensées*. No. 379.

8
What in some is called liberty, in others is called licence. (Quæ in aliis libertas est, in aliis licentia vocatur.)
QUINTILIAN, *De Institutione Oratoria*. Bk. iii, ch. 8, sec. 48.

Foster-child of licence, which fools call liberty. (Alumna licentiæ, quam stulti libertatem vocabant.)
TACITUS, *Dialogus de Oratoribus*. Sec. 40.

License they mean when they cry, Liberty!
For who loves that, must first be wise and good.
MILTON, *On the Detraction Which Followed upon My Writing Certain Treatises*.

9
Why, headstrong liberty is lash'd with woe;
There's nothing situate under heaven's eye
But hath his bound, in earth, in sea, in sky.
SHAKESPEARE, *The Comedy of Errors*, ii, 1, 15.

And liberty plucks justice by the nose.
SHAKESPEARE, *Measure for Measure*, i, 3, 29.

10
Liberty, guest amiable,
Plants both elbows on the table.
(La liberté, convive aimable,
Met les deux coudes sur la table.)
VOLTAIRE.

11
The weight of too much liberty.
WORDSWORTH, *Miscellaneous Sonnets*. Pt. i, 1.

LIBRARY

See also Books, Reading

I—Libraries: Their Virtues

12
Libraries, which are as the shrines where all the relics of the ancient saints, full of true virtue, and that without delusion or imposture, are preserved and reposed.
BACON, *Advancement of Learning*. Bk. ii.

13
These are the tombs of such as cannot die.
GEORGE CRABBE, *The Library*.

Shelved around us lie The mummied authors.
BAYARD TAYLOR, *The Poet's Journal: Third Evening*.

Thou can'st not die. Here thou art more than safe
Where every book is thy epitaph.
VAUGHAN, *On Sir Thomas Bodley's Library*.

14
The true University of these days is a Collection of Books.
CARLYLE, *Heroes and Hero-Worship*. Lect. v.

1
A great library contains the diary of the human race.

REV. GEORGE DAWSON, *Address on Opening the Birmingham Free Library*, 26 Oct., 1866.

2
A sanatorium for the mind. (Ψυχῆς ἰατρεῖον.)

DIODORUS SICULUS, *History*. Bk. i, ch. 49. The inscription on the portal of the library at Alexandria, Egypt. The phrase is usually translated as "Medicine for the mind," or "Nourishment for the soul," but ἰατρεῖον means a surgery, or hospital, or sanatorium —a place which one visits to be cured—and the reference is plainly to the library as a whole.

Food for the soul. (Nutrimentum spiritus.)

UNKNOWN, *Inscription*, on the Royal Library, Berlin.

Let no profane person enter! (Μή τις βέβηλος εἰσίτω.)

UNKNOWN, *Inscription*, on the old library at Berne.

3
Consider what you have in the smallest chosen library. A company of the wisest and wittiest men that could be picked out of all civil countries, in a thousand years, have set in best order the results of their learning and wisdom. The men themselves were hid and inaccessible, solitary, impatient of interruption, fenced by etiquette; but the thought which they did not uncover to their bosom friend is here written out in transparent words to us, the strangers of another age.

EMERSON, *Society and Solitude: Books*.

4
He that revels in a well-chosen library, has innumerable dishes, and all of admirable flavour.

WILLIAM GODWIN, *The Enquirer: Early Taste for Reading*.

5
This is my world! within these narrow walls,
I own a princely service.

PAUL HAMILTON HAYNE, *My Study*.

6
Every library should try to be complete on something, if it were only the history of pinheads.

O. W. HOLMES, *The Poet at the Breakfast-Table*. Ch. 8.

7
I have often thought that nothing would do more extensive good at small expense than the establishment of a small circulating library in every county, to consist of a few well-chosen books, to be lent to the people of the county, under such regulations as would secure their safe return in due time.

THOMAS JEFFERSON, *Writings*. Vol. xii, p. 282.

8
What a place to be in is an old library! It seems as though all the souls of all the writers, that have bequeathed their labours to these Bodleians, were reposing here, as in some dormitory, or middle state. I do not want to handle, to profane the leaves, their winding-sheets. I could as soon dislodge a shade. I seem to inhale learning, walking amid their foliage; and the odour of their old moth-scented coverings is fragrant as the first bloom of those sciential apples which grew amid the happy orchard.

CHARLES LAMB, *Essays of Elia: Oxford in the Vacation*.

9
My library Was dukedom large enough.

SHAKESPEARE, *The Tempest*. Act i, sc. 2, l. 109.

Come, and take choice of all my library,
And so beguile thy sorrow.

SHAKESPEARE, *Titus Andronicus*. Act iv, sc. 1, l. 34.

10
I go into my library, and all history rolls before me. I breathe the morning air of the world while the scent of Eden's roses yet lingered in it. . . . I see the pyramids building; I hear the shoutings of the armies of Alexander. . . . I sit as in a theatre—the stage is time, the play is the play of the world.

ALEXANDER SMITH, *Dreamthorp: Books and Gardens*.

II—Libraries: Their Faults

11
The richest minds need not large libraries.

AMOS BRONSON ALCOTT, *Table Talk: Learning-Books*.

12
A library is but the soul's burial-ground. It is the land of shadows.

HENRY WARD BEECHER, *Star Papers: Oxford: The Bodleian Library*.

13
Meek young men grow up in libraries.

EMERSON, *Nature Addresses and Lectures: The American Scholar*.

14
It is a vanity to persuade the world one hath much learning, by getting a great library.

THOMAS FULLER, *Holy and Profane State: Of Books*.

15
The dust and silence of the upper shelf.

MACAULAY, *Essays: On Milton*.

16
Burn the libraries, for their value is in this book.

OMAR. Referring to the *Koran*.

17
I love vast libraries; yet there is a doubt
If one be better with them or without,—
Unless he use them wisely, and, indeed,
Knows the high art of what and how to read.
At Learning's fountain it is sweet to drink,
But 'tis a nobler privilege to think;
And oft, from books apart, the thirsting mind

May make the nectar which it cannot find.
'Tis well to borrow from the good and great;
'Tis wise to learn; 'tis godlike to create!

J. G. SAXE, *The Library*.

1
Since you cannot read all the books which you may possess, it is enough to possess only as many books as you can read. (Cum legere non possis, quantum habueris, satis est habere, quantum legas.)

SENECA, *Epistulæ ad Lucilium*. Epis. ii, sec. 4.

2
A circulating library in a town is as an evergreen tree of diabolical knowledge.

SHERIDAN, *The Rivals*. Act i, sc. 2.

3
Unlearned men of books assume the care,
As eunuchs are the guardians of the fair.

YOUNG, *Love of Fame*. Sat. ii, l. 83.

It is not observed that . . . librarians are wiser men than others.

RALPH WALDO EMERSON, *Spiritual Laws*.

LIES AND LYING

See also Truth and Falsehood

I—Lies: Apothegms

4
But Peter said, Ananias . . . thou hast not lied unto men, but unto God. And Ananias hearing these words fell down, and gave up the ghost.

New Testament: Acts, v, 3–5.

Ananias Club.

A name given by the irreverent press to an imaginary association whose membership consisted of the persons whom Theodore Roosevelt called liars, beginning with Senator Tillman in 1906.

5
Falsehood and fraud shoot up in every soil,
The product of all climes.

ADDISON, *Cato*. Act iv, sc. 4.

6
Husband a lie, and trump it up in some extraordinary emergency.

ADDISON, *The Spectator*, No. 507.

7
Resolved to die in the last dyke of prevarication.

EDMUND BURKE, *Impeachment of Warren Hastings*, 7 May, 1789.

Falsehood has a perennial spring.

EDMUND BURKE, *Speech on American Taxation*.

8
The talent of lying in a way that cannot be laid hold of.

CARLYLE, *Latter-Day Pamphlets*. No. 7.

9
Almost and wellnigh Saves many a lie.

JOHN CLARKE, *Parœmiologia*, 106.

10
No lie ever grows old.

EURIPIDES. (JONSON, *Explorata: Veritas*.)

A lie never lives to be old.

SOPHOCLES, *Acrisius*. Frag. 59.

Though a lie be well drest, it is ever overcome.

GEORGE HERBERT, *Jacula Prudentum*.

No falsehood can endure
Touch of celestial temper, but returns
Of force to its own likeness.

MILTON, *Paradise Lost*. Bk. iv, l. 811.

11
Sure men were born to lie, and women to believe them!

JOHN GAY, *The Beggar's Opera*. Act ii, sc. 2.

12
When I err every one can see it, but not when I lie. (Wenn ich irre kann es jeder bemerken; wenn ich lüge, nicht.)

GOETHE, *Sprüche in Prosa*, iii.

13
Ask me no questions, and I'll tell you no fibs.

GOLDSMITH, *She Stoops to Conquer*. Act iii, sc. 1.

I know where little girls are sent
For telling taradiddles.

HENRY SAMBROOKE LEIGH, *Only Seven*.

14
All is not Gospel that thou dost speak.

JOHN HEYWOOD, *Proverbs*. Pt. ii, ch. 2.

You do not speak Gospel. (Vous ne dictes l'euangile.)

RABELAIS, *Gargantua*. Bk. i, ch. 12. (1535)

15
Children and fools cannot lie.

JOHN HEYWOOD, *Proverbs*. Pt. i, ch. 11.

A beltless bairn canna lie.

JOHN RAY, *Proverbs: Scottish*.

16
More lying than the Parthians.

HORACE, *Epistles*. Bk. ii, epis. 1, l. 112.

Playing the Cretan with the Cretans, *i. e.* lying to liars. ("Ελαθε κρητίζων πρὸς Κρῆτας.)

PLUTARCH, *Lives: Æmilius Paulus*. Ch. 23, sec. 6. Quoting a Greek proverb.

17
A lie, turned topsy-turvy, can be prinked and tinselled out, decked in plumage new and fine, till none knows its lean old carcass.

HENRIK IBSEN, *Peer Gynt*. Act i.

18
It is an art to have so much judgment as to apparel a lie well, to give it a good dressing.

BEN JONSON, *Explorata: Mali Choragi Fuere*.

And fittest for to forge true-seeming lies.

SPENSER, *The Faerie Queene*. Bk. i, canto i, st. 38.

19
We're clean out o' money an' 'most out o' lyin'.

J. R. LOWELL, *The Biglow Papers*. Ser. ii, No. 4.

20
No bone, unhelped of brain, creates a lie.

DON MARQUIS, *Savage Portraits*.

21
A lie grows in size [as it is repeated]. (Mensuraque ficti crescit.)

OVID, *Metamorphoses*. Bk. xii, l. 57.

1
What you tell me is not true, never was true, never will be true. (Id quod neque est neque fuit neque futurum est Mihi prædicas.)
PLAUTUS, *Amphitruo*, l. 553. (Act ii, sc. 1.)

2
There is no lie so reckless as to be without some proof. (Nullam tam imprudens mendacium est ut teste careat.)
PLINY THE ELDER, *History*. Bk. viii, ch. 22.

3
The only thing that ever came back from the grave that we know of was a lie.
MARILLA M. RICKER, *The Philistine*. Vol. 25, p. 101.

4
'Tis as easy as lying.
SHAKESPEARE, *Hamlet*. Act iii, sc. 2, l. 372.

For my part, getting up seems not so easy
By half as *lying*.
THOMAS HOOD, *Morning Meditations*.

Which to me seemed as easy and natural as lying.
SCOTT, *St. Ronan's Well*, ch. 26.

5
Your bait of falsehood takes this carp of truth.
SHAKESPEARE, *Hamlet*. Act ii, sc. 1, l. 63.

If I tell thee a lie, spit in my face, call me horse.
SHAKESPEARE, *I Henry IV*. Act ii, sc. 4, l. 214..

6
Whose tongue soe'er speaks false,
Not truly speaks; who speaks not truly, lies.
SHAKESPEARE, *King John*. Act iv, sc. 3, l. 91.

7
Never tell a lie. (Μὴ ψεύδου.)
SOLON. (DIOGENES LAERTIUS, *Solon*. Bk. i, sec. 60.)

8
All is not false that seems at first a lie.
ROBERT SOUTHEY, *St. Gualberto*. St. 28. *See also under* APPEARANCE.

9
The cruelest lies are often told in silence.
R. L. STEVENSON, *Virginibus Puerisque: Truth of Intercourse*.

10
One of the striking differences between a cat and a lie is that a cat has only nine lives.
MARK TWAIN, *Pudd'nhead Wilson's Calendar*.

11
The only form of lying that is absolutely beyond reproach is lying for its own sake.
OSCAR WILDE, *The Decay of Lying*.

12
I give him joy that's awkward at a lie.
YOUNG, *Night Thoughts*. Night viii, l. 361.

13
In speaking thus I do not lie. (Οὐ ψεύδομαι ὧδ' ἀγορεύων.)
UNKNOWN, *On Pherecydes*. (*Greek Anthology*. Bk. vii, epig. 93.)

II—Lies: Their Variety

14
You lie—under a mistake,—
For this is the most civil sort of lie
That can be given to a man's face.
CALDERON, *Magico Prodigioso*. Sc. 1. (Shelley, tr.)

If, after all, there should be some so blind
To their own good this warning to despise, . . .
I tell him, if a clergyman, he lies—
Should captains the remark, or critics, make,
They also lie too—under a mistake.
BYRON, *Don Juan*. Canto i, st. 208.

I mean you lie—under a mistake.
SWIFT, *Polite Conversation*. Dial. i.

15
The best kind of lie, so I've heard, is a red-hot one. (Calidum esse audivi optimum mendacium.)
PLAUTUS, *Mostellaria*, l. 666.

That's a lie with a latchet;
All the dogs in town cannot match it.
THOMAS FULLER, *Gnomologia*. No. 6157.

That's a loud one!
JOHN RAY, *English Proverbs*, p. 89.

That's a lie with a lid on.
C. H. SPURGEON, *Ploughman's Pictures*, p. 99.

16
There is a difference between telling a falsehood and lying. One who lies is not himself deceived, but tries to deceive another; he who tells a falsehood is himself deceived. One who lies deceives, as far as he is able; but one who tells a falsehood does not himself deceive, any more than he can help. A good man ought to take pains not to lie; a wise man, not to tell what is false.
PUBLIUS NIGIDIUS, *Fragments*. No. 49. (AULUS GELLIUS, *Noctes Atticæ*. Bk. xi, ch. 11.)

17
That immortal lie. (Ce mensonge immortel.)
PÈRE DE RAVIGNAN. (POUJOULAT, *Sa Vie, Ses Œuvres*.)

18
She looked him frankly in the face,
And told a wicked, wicked lie.
OWEN SEAMAN, *A Vigo Street Eclogue*.

19
The Retort Courteous; . . . the Quip Modest; . . . the Reply Churlish; . . . the Reproof Valiant; . . . the Countercheck Quarrelsome; . . . the Lie with Circumstance; . . . the Lie Direct.
SHAKESPEARE, *As You Like It*. Act v, sc. 4, l. 76.

20
If a man had the art of the second sight for seeing lies, as they have in Scotland for seeing spirits, how admirably he might entertain himself in this town by observing the different shapes, sizes and colours of those swarms of lies which buzz about the heads of some people.
SWIFT, *The Examiner*. No. 15.

21
Magnanimous lie! and when was truth so beautiful that it could be preferred to thee?

(Magnanima menzogna! or quando è il vero
Si bello che si possa a te preporre?)

Tasso, *Jerusalem Delivered*. Bk. ii, st. 22. Sophronisba, a Christian virgin, falsely took upon herself the guilt of having secreted a statue of the Virgin from heathen profanation.

1
There are 869 different forms of lying, but only one of them has been squarely forbidden. Thou shalt not bear false witness against thy neighbor.

Mark Twain, *Pudd'nhead Wilson's New Calendar*.

III—Lies: Condemnation

2
It is not the lie that passeth through the mind, but the lie that sinketh in, and settleth in it, that doth the hurt.

Francis Bacon, *Essays: Of Truth*.

3
The beginning of all is to have done with Falsity; to eschew Falsity as Death Eternal.

Thomas Carlyle, *Journal*, 23 June, 1870.

Man everywhere is the born enemy of lies.

Carlyle, *Heroes and Hero-Worship*. Lect. 1.

4
It is the nature of a scoundrel to deceive by lying. (Improbi hominis est mendacio fallere.)

Cicero, *Pro Murena*. Ch. 39, sec. 62.

5
He neither uttered falsehood nor could endure it. (Mendacium neque dicebat, neque pati poterat.)

Cornelius Nepos, *Lives: Atticus*.

6
Every violation of truth is not only a sort of suicide in the liar, but is a stab at the health of human society.

Emerson, *Essays, First Series: Prudence*.

7
As ten millions of circles can never make a square, so the united voice of myriads cannot lend the smallest foundation to falsehood.

Goldsmith, *The Vicar of Wakefield*. Ch. 8.

8
Dare to be true: nothing can need a lie;
A fault which needs it most, grows two thereby.

George Herbert, *The Church-Porch*.

9
Sin has many tools, but a lie is the handle which fits them all.

O. W. Holmes, *The Autocrat of the Breakfast-Table*. Ch. 6, l. 1.

10
It is better to be lied about than to lie.

Elbert Hubbard, *The Philistine*. Vol. xi, p. 48.

11
There is no vice so mean, so pitiful, so contemptible; and he who permits himself to tell a lie once, finds it much easier to do it a second and third time, till at length it becomes habitual.

Thomas Jefferson, *Writings*. Vol. v, p. 83.

12
Men lie, who lack courage to tell truth.

Joaquin Miller, *Ina*. Sc. 3.

13
Equivocation is half-way to lying, as lying the whole way to hell.

William Penn, *Fruits of Solitude*, p. 36.

The mouth that lies slays the soul.

John Ray, *English Proverbs: Scottish*.

14
To lapse in fulness
Is sorer than to lie for need, and falsehood
Is worse in kings than beggars.

Shakespeare, *Cymbeline*. Act iii, sc. 6, l. 12.

15
You told a lie, an odious, damned lie:
Upon my soul, a lie, a wicked lie.

Shakespeare, *Othello*. Act v, sc. 2, l. 180.

Let me have no lying: it becomes none but tradesmen.

Shakespeare, *Winter's Tale*. Act iv, sc. 4, l. 743.

16
One falsehood treads on the heels of another. (Fallacia Alia aliam trudit.)

Terence, *Andria*, l. 779.

It is a true saying that one falsehood leads easily to another.

Cicero, *De Oratore*. Bk. i, sec. 33.

17
The silent colossal National Lie that is the support and confederate of all the tyrannies and shams and inequalities and unfairnesses that afflict the peoples—that is the one to throw bricks and sermons at.

Mark Twain, *My First Lie*.

18
He shall not prosper who deviseth lies.

The Koran. Ch. 20.

IV—Lies: Condonation

19
A little inaccuracy saves a world of explanation.

C. E. Ayres, *Science, the False Messiah*.

20
A mixture of a lie doth ever add pleasure.

Francis Bacon, *Essays: Of Truth*.

Untruths . . . such as are wittily contrived, and are not merely gross and palpable.

Francis Bacon, *Observations on a Libel*.

21
For breaking of an oath, and lying,
Is but a kind of self-denying,
A saint-like virtue; and from hence
Some have broke oaths by Providence.

Butler, *Hudibras*. Pt. ii, canto ii, l. 133.

22
A good portion of speaking well consists in knowing how to lie. (Bona pars bene dicendi est scite mentiri.)

Erasmus, *Philetymus et Pseudocheus*.

23
Merely corroborative detail, intended to give artistic verisimilitude to a bald and unconvincing narrative.

W. S. Gilbert, *The Mikado*. Act ii.

No mere veracity robs your sagacity
Or perspicacity, Barney McGee.
RICHARD HOVEY, *Barney McGee.*

1
Yet to so gentle lies, pardon is due.
A lie, well told, to some tastes is restoritie;
Besides, we Poets lie by good authoritie.
SIR JOHN HARINGTON, *Epigrams.* Bk. ii, No. 184. *See also* POETRY: POETIC LICENSE.

2
A good lie for its own sake is ever pleasing to honest men, but a patched up record never.
ELBERT HUBBARD, *The Philistine.* Vol. i, p. 88.

3
What you do not know, relate as if you knew it well. (Quæ nescieris, ut bene nota refer.)
OVID, *Ars Amatoria.* Bk. i, l. 98.

4
Parables are not lies because they describe events which never happened.
BERNARD SHAW, *Saint Joan.* Sc. ii.

V—Lies and Statistics

5
You may prove anything by figures.
THOMAS CARLYLE, *Chartism.* No. 2. Quoted as the saying of "a witty statesman."

6
Figures won't lie, but liars will figure.
GENERAL CHARLES H. GROSVENOR, Representative from Ohio, who for many years was famous for his prognostications of the vote at Presidential elections.

7
Round numbers are always false.
SAMUEL JOHNSON. (HAWKINS, *Johnsoniana,* 235.)

8
Statistics are like alienists—they will testify for either side.
F. H. LA GUARDIA, *The Banking Investigations.* (*Liberty,* 13 May, 1933.)

9
Figures often beguile me, particularly when I have the arranging of them myself; in which case the remark attributed to Disraeli would often apply with justice and force: "There are three kinds of lies: lies, damned lies, and statistics."
MARK TWAIN, *Autobiography.* Vol. i, p. 246. This phrase has also been attributed to Henry Labouchère, Abraham Hewitt and Commander Holloway R. Frost.

VI—Lies and the Memory

10
A good memory is needed after one has lied. (Il faut bonne mémoire après qu'on a menti.)
CORNEILLE, *Le Menteur.* Act iv, sc. 5.

11
There is nothing so pathetic as a forgetful liar.
F. M. KNOWLES, *A Cheerful Year Book.*

12
He who is not sure of his memory should not undertake the trade of lying. (Qui ne sent point assez ferme de mémoire, ne se doit pas mêler d'être menteur.)
MONTAIGNE, *Essays.* Bk. i, ch. 9.

13
He who tells a lie is not sensible how great a task he undertakes; for he must be forced to invent twenty more to maintain that one.
POPE, *Thoughts on Various Subjects.*

14
A liar needs a good memory. (Mendacem memorem esse oportere.)
QUINTILIAN, *De Institutione Oratoria.* Bk. iv, ch. 2, sec. 91.

This shows that liars ought to have good memories.
ALGERNON SIDNEY, *Discourses on Government.* Ch. ii, sec. 15.

Indeed, a very rational saying, that a liar ought to have a good memory.
ROBERT SOUTH, *Sermon: Concealment of Sin.*

VII—Liars

15
Liars are always most disposed to swear. (A giurar presti i mentitor son sempre.)
ALFIERI, *Virginia.* Act ii, sc. 3.

A liar is always lavish of oaths. (Un menteur est toujours prodigue de serments.)
CORNEILLE, *Le Menteur.* Act iii, sc. 5.

16
When they speak truth they are not believed.
ARISTOTLE, when asked what liars lose by lying. (DIOGENES LAERTIUS, *Aristotle.* Sec. 17.)

This is the punishment of a liar: He is not believed, even when he speaks the truth.
Babylonian Talmud: Sanhedrin, fo. 89b.

A liar is not believed even when he tells the truth. (Mendaci homini ne verum quidem dicenti credere solemus.)
CICERO, *De Divinatione.* Bk. ii, ch. 71, sec. 146.

But liars we can never trust,
Though they should speak the thing that's true.
ISAAC WATTS, *Against Lying.*

17
None speaks false, where there is none to hear.
JAMES BEATTIE, *The Minstrel.* Bk. ii, st. 24.

18
The greater fool, the greater liar.
WILLIAM BLAKE, *Miscellaneous Epigrams.* No. 6.

Do not tell everything, but never lie. . . . You may always observe that the greatest fools are the greatest liars.
LORD CHESTERFIELD, *Letters,* 17 Feb., 1754.

19
It isn't every fool that's fit
To make a real good lie, that 'll sit
On her keel, and answer the helm.
THOMAS EDWARD BROWN, *The Doctor.*

20
There's a real love of a lie,
Liars find ready made for lies they make.
ROBERT BROWNING, *Mr. Sludge "The Medium."*

1
He lied with such a fervour of intention,
There was no doubt he earned his laureate pension.
BYRON, *Don Juan*. Canto iii, st. 80.

2
With death doomed to grapple
Beneath this cold slab, he
Who lied in the Chapel
Now lies in the Abbey.
BYRON, *Epitaph for William Pitt*.

Some lie beneath the churchyard stone,
And some before the Speaker.
W. M. PRAED, *School and School-fellows*. St. 5.

3
It is the man who tells and who acts the lie who is guilty, and not he who honestly and sincerely believes the lie.
LORD CHESTERFIELD, *Letters*, 21 Sept., 1747.

4
Thou liar of the first magnitude!
CONGREVE, *Love for Love*. Act ii, sc. 1.

You licked not your lips since you lied last.
THOMAS FULLER, *Gnomologia*. No. 5931.

5
Even then the liar in you woke,
The traitor grew!
JOHN ERSKINE, *Dialogue*.

6
Show me a liar, and I will show you a thief.
GEORGE HERBERT, *Jacula Prudentum*.

7
A splendid liar. (Splendide mendax.)
HORACE, *Odes*. Bk. iii, ode. 11, l. 34. Hypermnestra alone, of all the fifty daughters of Danaus who had sworn to them to kill their husbands, broke her oath and was imprisoned, but declared innocent by the people.

One only, true to Hymen's flame,
Was traitress to her sire forsworn:
That splendid falsehood lights her name
Through times unborn.
HORACE, *Odes*. Bk. iii, ode 11, l. 33.

To lie magnificently. (Mentiri splendide.)
ERASMUS, *Familiar Colloquies*.

8
He is a liar, and the father of it.
New Testament: John, viii, 44.

These lies are like the father that begets them: gross as a mountain, open, palpable.
SHAKESPEARE, *I Henry IV*. Act ii, sc. 4, l. 249.

9
A man who has never been within the tropics does not know what a thunderstorm means; a man who has never looked on Niagara has but a faint idea of a cataract; and he who has not read Barère's Memoirs may be said not to know what it is to lie.
MACAULAY, *Review*, of *Mémoires de Bertrand Barère*.

10
Talkin' tall an' tactless, as saints hadn't orter.
DON MARQUIS, *Noah an' Jonah an' Cap'n John Smith*.

11
The thing that is not, Bassa's wont to say. (Istud quod non est. dicere Bassa solet.)
MARTIAL, *Epigrams*. Bk. v, ep. 45.

12
Thou liest in thy throat. (Mentiris in gutture.)
TITUS OATES, *On Jude*, p. 247.

He strode to Gauthier, in his throat
Gave him the lie. . . . The lie was dead,
And damned, and truth stood up instead.
ROBERT BROWNING, *Count Gismond*. St. 13.

But thou liest in thy throat.
SHAKESPEARE, *Twelfth Night*. Act iii, sc. 4, l. 172.

13
I said in my haste, All men are liars.
Old Testament: Psalms, cxvi, 11. (Omnis homo mendax.—*Vulgate*.)

Whosoever loveth and maketh a lie.
New Testament: Revelation, xxii, 15.

14
I have no use for liars, national, international, or those found in private life.
THEODORE ROOSEVELT, *Speech*, Arlington Cemetery.

15
He will lie, sir, with such volubility, that you would think truth were a fool.
SHAKESPEARE, *All's Well that Ends Well*. Act iv, sc. 3, l. 283.

He will lie as fast as a dog will trot.
JOHN PALSGRAVE, *Lesclarissement de la Langue Françoyse*, 610. (1530)

Thou canst cog, face and lie as fast as a dog can trot.
UNKNOWN, *Hay Any Worke for Cooper*, 65. (1589)

She will lie as fast as a dog will lick a dish.
JOHN HEYWOOD, *Proverbs*. Pt. ii, ch. 7. (1546)

16
Measureless liar, thou hast made my heart
Too great for what contains it.
SHAKESPEARE, *Coriolanus*. Act v, sc. 6, l. 103.

A heart for falsehood framed.
SHERIDAN, *The Duenna*. Act i, sc. 5.

17
Lord, Lord, how subject we old men are to the vice of lying!
SHAKESPEARE, *II Henry IV* Act iii, sc. 2, l. 325.

Lord, Lord, how this world is given to lying!
SHAKESPEARE, *I Henry IV* Act v, sc. 4, l. 149.

How you delight, my lords, I know not, I;
But, I protest, I love to hear him lie.
SHAKESPEARE, *Love's Labour's Lost*. Act i, sc. 1, l. 175.

18
If thou deny'st it, twenty times thou liest;
And I will turn thy falsehood to thy heart,
Where it was forged, with my rapier's point.
SHAKESPEARE, *Richard II*. Act iv, sc. 1, l. 38.

19
Like one
Who having into truth, by telling of it,

Made such a sinner of his memory,
To credit his own lie.

SHAKESPEARE, *The Tempest*. Act i, sc. 2, l. 99. A phrase which has puzzled the commentators. Boswell explains it: "Who having made his memory such a sinner as to credit his own lie by telling of it."

It was generally believed that he was indeed Duke Richard. Nay, himself with long and continual counterfeiting and with oft telling a lie, was turned by habit almost into the thing he seemed to be, and from a liar into a believer.

FRANCIS BACON, *History of Henry VII.*

1
An egg is not so full of meat as she is full of lies.

JOHN STILL, *Gammer Gurton's Needle*. Act v, sc. 2. (1565)

Thy head is as full of quarrels as an egg is full of meat.

SHAKESPEARE, *Romeo and Juliet*, iii, 1, 24.

2
An experienced, industrious, ambitious, and often quite picturesque liar.

MARK TWAIN, *My Military Campaign.*

LIFE

See also Love and Life.

I—Life: Definitions: The Optimists

3
Life's but a means unto an end—that end,
Beginning, mean and end to all things—God.

P. J. BAILEY, *Festus: A Country Town.*

4
I am convinced that the world is not a mere bog in which men and women trample themselves in the mire and die. Something magnificent is taking place here amid the cruelties and tragedies, and the supreme challenge to intelligence is that of making the noblest and best in our curious heritage prevail.

C. A. BEARD. (DURANT, *Meaning of Life*, p. 43.)

5
For life is the mirror of king and slave,
'Tis just what we are and do;
Then give to the world the best you have,
And the best will come back to you.

MADELEINE BRIDGES, *Life's Mirror.*

6
Life is a pure flame, and we live by an invisible sun within us.

SIR THOMAS BROWNE, *Hydriotaphia*. Ch. 5.

7
I count life just a stuff
To try the soul's strength on.

ROBERT BROWNING, *In a Balcony.*

Life is probation, and the earth no goal
But starting-point of man.

ROBERT BROWNING, *Ring and Book*. Pt. x, l. 1436.

8
Life is a ladder infinite-stepped, that hides its rungs from human eyes;
Planted its foot in chaos gloom, its head soars high above the skies.

SIR RICHARD BURTON, *Kasîdah*. Pt. vii, st. 7.

9
Life is but thought.

S. T. COLERIDGE, *Youth and Age. See also* THOUGHT AND LIFE.

Life consists in what man is thinking of all day.

EMERSON, *Journals*. Vol. vii, p. 319.

10
Life is a boundless privilege, and when you pay for your ticket, and get into the car, you have no guess what good company you will find there.

EMERSON, *Conduct of Life: Considerations by the Way.*

Life is an ecstasy.

EMERSON, *Conduct of Life: Fate.*

Life is a series of surprises, and would not be worth taking or keeping if it were not.

EMERSON, *Essays, Second Series: Experience.*

All life is an experiment. The more experiments you make the better.

EMERSON, *Journals.*

Life is a perpetual instruction in cause and effect.

EMERSON, *Uncollected Lectures: Natural Religion.*

11
Life seems to me like a Japanese picture which our imagination does not allow to end with the margin.

JUSTICE O. W. HOLMES, *Message to the Federal Bar Association*, 1932.

Life is a preparation for the future; and the best preparation for the future is to live as if there were none.

ELBERT HUBBARD, *The Philistine*. Vol. xx, p. 46.

12
Life is a loom, weaving illusion.

VACHEL LINDSAY, *The Chinese Nightingale.*

Life is the west-going dream-storms' breath,
Life is a dream, the sigh of the skies,
The breath of the stars, that nod on their pillows
With their golden hair mussed over their eyes.

VACHEL LINDSAY, *The Ghost of the Buffaloes.*

13
Life is a mission. Every other definition of life is false, and leads all who accept it astray. Religion, science, philosophy, though still at variance upon many points, all agree in this, that every existence is an aim.

MAZZINI, *Life and Writings*. Ch. 5.

14
Life is a flame that is always burning itself out, but it catches fire again every time a child is born.

BERNARD SHAW, *The Adventures of the Black Girl in Her Search for God.*

Life is a flame whose splendor hides its base.

GEORGE TUFTS, in letter to Emerson. (See *Journal*, 1868.)

15
Life is an arrow—therefore you must know
What mark to aim at, how to use the bow—
Then draw it to the head, and let it go!

HENRY VAN DYKE, *The Arrow.*

Life is an archer, fashioning an arrow

With anxious care, for in it life must trust;
A single flash across the earthly spaces
Straight to the throat of death—one conquering thrust!
CATHERINE CATE COBLENTZ, *Life.*

1
Yet I know that I dwell in the midst of the roar of the Cosmic Wheel
In the hot collision of Forces, and the clangour of boundless Strife,
Mid the sound of the speed of worlds, the rushing worlds, and the peal
Of the thunder of Life.
WILLIAM WATSON, *Dawn on the Headland.*

2
Our lives are albums written through
With good or ill, with false or true;
And as the blessed angels turn
The pages of our years,
God grant they read the good with smiles,
And blot the ill with tears!
WHITTIER, *Written in a Lady's Album.*

3
Our lives are songs; God writes the words
And we set them to music at pleasure;
And the song grows glad, or sweet or sad,
As we choose to fashion the measure.
ELLA WHEELER WILCOX, *Our Lives.* Wrongfully claimed for Rev. Thomas Gibbons. (See *Notes and Queries*, 1 April, 1905, p. 249.)

II—Life: Definitions: The Pessimists

4
Life is the apprenticeship to progressive renunciation, to the steady diminution of our claims, of our hopes, of our powers, of our liberty.
AMIEL, *Journal*, 22 Oct., 1856.

Life is only a document to be interpreted.
AMIEL, *Journal*, 9 Sept., 1880.

5
Life is a school of probability.
BAGEHOT, *Literary Studies.* Vol. ii, p. 257.

6
Life, Crichton, is like a cup of tea; the more heartily we drink the sooner we reach the dregs.
J. M. BARRIE, *The Admirable Crichton.* Act i.

Life is a long lesson in humility.
J. M. BARRIE, *The Little Minister.* Ch. 3.

The life of every man is a diary in which he means to write one story, and writes another, and his humblest hour is when he compares the volume as it is with what he vowed to make it.
J. M. BARRIE. (*Golden Book*, Jan., 1931.)

7
Life is a bumper filled by fate.
THOMAS BLACKLOCK, *Epigram on Punch.*

8
Do what you will, this life's a fiction,
And is made up of contradiction.
WILLIAM BLAKE, *Gnomic Verses.* No. 23.

9
Life is all a variorum.
BURNS, *The Jolly Beggars.*

10
Life is like playing a violin solo in public and learning the instrument as one goes on.
SAMUEL BUTLER THE YOUNGER, *Collected Essays.* Vol. ii, p. 93.

Life is the art of drawing sufficient conclusions from insufficient premises.
SAMUEL BUTLER THE YOUNGER, *Note-books*, p. 10.

Life is one long process of getting tired.
SAMUEL BUTLER THE YOUNGER, *Note-books*, p. 11.

To live is like to love—all reason is against it, and all healthy instinct for it.
SAMUEL BUTLER THE YOUNGER, *Note-books*, p. 227.

11
Life is a dusty corridor, I say,
Shut at both ends.
ROY CAMPBELL, *The Flaming Terrapin.* Pt. i.

How could life annoy me Any more?
Life: a lighted window And a closed door.
CLEMENT WOOD, *I Pass a Lighted Window.*

12
Ask what is human life—the sage replies,
With disappointment low'ring in his eyes,
"A painful passage o'er a restless flood,
A vain pursuit of fugitive false good,
A sense of fancied bliss and heartfelt care,
Closing at last in darkness and despair."
COWPER, *Hope*, l. 1.

To most, man's life but showed
A bridge of groans across a stream of tears.
P. J. BAILEY, *Festus.* Sc. 15.

13
Life is one demd horrid grind!
DICKENS, *Nicholas Nickleby.* Ch. 64. Mr. Mantalini speaking.

14
Life's a tumble-about thing of ups and downs.
BENJAMIN DISRAELI, *Sybil.* Bk. i, ch. 8.

The teeter-board of life goes up,
The teeter-board of life goes down,
The sweetest face must learn to frown;
The biggest dog has been a pup.
JOAQUIN MILLER, *William Brown of Oregon.*

15
Life is a jest, and all things show it:
I thought so once, but now I know it.
JOHN GAY, *My Own Epitaph.*

Ah! Matt, old age has brought to me
Thy wisdom, less thy certainty;
The world's a jest, and joy's a trinket;
I knew that once, but now I think it.
J. K. STEPHEN, *Senex to Matt Prior.*

16
Life is made up of interruptions.
W. S. GILBERT, *Patience.* Act i.

17
Who but knows How it goes!—
Life's a last year's Nightingale,
Love a last year's Rose.
W. E. HENLEY, *Echoes.* No. 45.

Life is (I think) a blunder and a shame.
W. E. HENLEY, *In Hospital: Waiting.*

Life is a smoke that curls—
  Curls in a flickering skein,
That winds and whisks and whirls,
  A figment thin and vain,
  Into the vast inane.
  W. E. HENLEY, *Of the Nothingness of Things.*

1
Life is made up of sobs, sniffles, and smiles, with sniffles predominating.
  O. HENRY, *Gifts of the Magi.*

2
Life is a great bundle of little things.
  O. W. HOLMES, *The Professor at the Breakfast-Table.* Ch. 1.

3
Life is not to be bought with heaps of gold;
Not all Apollo's Pythian treasures hold,
Or Troy once held, in peace and pride of sway,
Can bribe the poor possession of a day!
  HOMER, *Iliad.* Bk. ix, l. 524. (Pope, tr.)

Life is not to be purchased at any price. (Non omni pretio vita emenda est.)
  SENECA, *Epistulæ ad Lucilium.* Epis. lxx, sec. 7.

4
Life is just one damned thing after another.
  Claimed by ELBERT HUBBARD, *A Thousand and One Epigrams*, p. 137. (1911) Attributed, probably correctly, to Frank Ward O'Malley, in *United Press* story of his death, 19 Oct., 1932, and in *Literary Digest*, 5 Nov., 1932.

As I allays says to my brother,
If it isn't one thing it's the tother.
  H. L. C. PEMBERTON, *Geese: A Dialogue.*

"I expect," he said, "I was thinking jest what a Rum Go everything is. I expect it was something like that."
  H. G. WELLS, *Kipps.* Bk. iii, ch. 3, sec. 8.

5
Life is a progress from want to want, not from enjoyment to enjoyment.
  SAMUEL JOHNSON. (BOSWELL, *Life.* Vol. iii, p. 53.)

6
Life is a leaf of paper white
Whereon each one of us may write
His word or two, and then comes night.
  J. R. LOWELL, *For an Autograph.* St. 2.

7
Life is like a scrambled egg.
  DON MARQUIS, *Frustration.*

8
Life's a long headache in a noisy street.
  JOHN MASEFIELD, *The Widow in the Bye Street.*

9
Life is a waste of wearisome hours,
  Which seldom the rose of enjoyment adorns.
And the heart that is soonest awake to the flowers,
  Is always the first to be touch'd by the thorns.
  THOMAS MOORE, *Oh! Think Not My Spirits.*

This life is all chequer'd with pleasures and woes.
  THOMAS MOORE, *This Life Is All Chequer'd.*

10
Our life is but a pilgrimage of blasts,
And every blast brings forth a fear;
  And every fear. a death.
  FRANCIS QUARLES, *Hieroglyph,* iii, 4.

11
Real life is. to most men, a long second-best, a perpetual compromise between the ideal and the possible.
  BERTRAND RUSSELL, *Study of Mathematics.*

12
Life is not a spectacle or a feast; it is a predicament.
  GEORGE SANTAYANA, *Articles and Essays.*

13
Life is a sorry *mélange* of gold and silver and stubble,
Of roses and wormwood and weeds, of rubies and rubble.
  R. H. SCHAUFFLER, *Nonsense.*

14
Life is a shuttle.
  SHAKESPEARE, *The Merry Wives of Windsor.* Act v, sc. 1, l. 25. Quoting a proverb.

Does not our life consist of the four elements?
  SHAKESPEARE, *Twelfth Night.* Act ii, sc. 3, l. 10. Referring to fire, water, earth, and air.

15
What is the life of man! Is it not to shift from side to side?—from sorrow to sorrow?—to button up one cause of vexation, and unbutton another?
  STERNE, *Tristram Shandy.* Bk. iv, ch. 31.

16
When all is done, human life is, at the greatest and best, but like a froward child, that must be played with and humoured a little to keep it quiet till it falls asleep, and then the care is over.
  SIR WILLIAM TEMPLE, *Discourse of Poetry.* Last sentence. (1680)

Life at the greatest and best is but a froward child, that must be humoured and coaxed a little till it falls asleep, and then all the care is over.
  GOLDSMITH, *The Good-Natured Man.* Act i. (1768) Goldsmith gives no indication that he is quoting.

17
Life is simply a *mauvais quart d'heure* made up of exquisite moments.
  OSCAR WILDE, *A Woman of No Importance.* Act ii.

III—Life: Definitions: The Philosophers

18
Life does not proceed by the association and addition of elements, but by dissociation and division.
  HENRI BERGSON, *Creative Evolution.* Ch. 1.

For life is tendency, and the essence of a tendency is to develop in the form of a sheaf, creating, by its very growth, divergent directions among which its impetus is divided.
  HENRI BERGSON, *Creative Evolution.* Ch. 2.

Life appears as a wave which rises, and which is opposed by the descending movement of matter. At one point alone it passes freely, dragging with it the obstacle which will weigh on its progress but will not stop it. At this point is humanity.

HENRI BERGSON. (NEWTON, *My Idea of God*, p. 117.)

1
Life is like a library owned by an author. In it are a few books which he wrote himself, but most of them were written for him.

HARRY EMERSON FOSDICK, *Sermon: Life*.

2
This Being of mine, whatever it really is, consists of a little flesh, a little breath, and the ruling Reason.

MARCUS AURELIUS, *Meditations*. Bk. ii, sec. 2.

Deem not life a thing of consequence; look at the infinite void of the future, and the limitless space of the past.

MARCUS AURELIUS, *Meditations*. Bk. iv, sec. 50.

3
Our life consisteth partly in folly, and partly in wisdom.

MONTAIGNE, *Essays*. Bk. iii, ch. 5.

4
Life is a fortress which neither you nor I know anything about.

NAPOLEON, *Remark*, to Dr. Antonomarchi, at St. Helena.

5
Life is that which holds matter together.

PORPHYRY. (EMERSON, *Considerations by the Way*.)

6
Life is neither a good nor an evil; it is simply the place where good and evil exist. (Vita nec bonum nec malum est; boni ac mali locus est.)

SENECA, *Epistulæ ad Lucilium*. Epis. xcix, 12.

7
Life is the co-ordination of actions.

HERBERT SPENCER, *A Theory of Population*. (*Westminster Review*, April, 1852.) Repeated in *Principles of Biology*. Pt. i, ch. 4, sec. 24.

A living thing is distinguished from a dead thing by the multiplicity of the changes at any moment taking place in it.

HERBERT SPENCER, *Principles of Biology*, i, 4, 25.

8
Then, what is life? I cried.

PERCY BYSSHE SHELLEY, *The Triumph of Life*, l. 544. The first line of the last stanza written by Shelley the day before his death.

No power of genius has ever yet had the smallest success in explaining existence. The perfect enigma remains.

EMERSON, *Representative Men: Plato*.

The mystery of life is not a problem to be solved, it is a reality to be experienced.

VAN DER LEEUW, *The Conquest of Illusion*, 11.

9
Life's a very funny proposition you can bet,
And no one's solved the problem properly as yet;
Young for a day, then old and gray, . . .
Life's a very funny proposition after all.

GEORGE M. COHAN, *Life's a Funny Proposition*. (From *Little Johnny Jones*, 1907.)

IV—Life: Apothegms

10
The less of routine, the more of life.

A. B. ALCOTT, *Table Talk: Habits*.

Who but the learned and dull moral fool
Could gravely have foreseen man ought to live by rule?

APHRA BEHN, *The Golden Age*. St. 7.

11
Life is short to the fortunate, long to the unfortunate. (*Βραχὺς ὁ βίος ἀνθρώπῳ εὐ πράσσοντι, δυστυχοῦντι δὲ μακρός*.)

APOLLONIUS. (STOBÆUS, *Florilegium*. Pt. cxxi, l. 34.)

O life! an age to the miserable, a moment to the happy. (O vita! misero longa, felici brevis.)

BACON, *Ornamenta Rationalia*. No. 36.

How short this Life, how long withal; how false its weal, how true its woes;
This fever-fit with paroxysms to mark its opening and its close.

SIR RICHARD BURTON, *The Kasîdah*. Pt. iii, st. 23.

For men who are fortunate all life is short, but for the unfortunate one night is infinite time.

LUCIAN. (*Greek Anthology*. Bk. x, epig. 28.)

12
Who saw life steadily and saw it whole.

MATTHEW ARNOLD, *To a Friend*. Referring to Sophocles.

13
Weariness of life. (Tædium vitæ.)

AULUS GELLIUS, *Noctes Atticæ*. Bk. vi, ch. 18, sec. 11.

14
Life, like poverty, makes strange bedfellows.

BULWER-LYTTON, *The Caxtons*. Pt. iv, ch. 4.

15
On the Rampage, Pip, and off the Rampage, Pip; such is life.

DICKENS, *Great Expectations*. Ch. 15.

"Sairey," said Mrs. Harris, "sech is life. Vich likewise is the hend of all things."

DICKENS, *Martin Chuzzlewit*. Ch. 29. Mrs. Gamp speaking.

16
"A porochial life, ma'am," continued Mr. Bumble, "is a life of worrit."

DICKENS, *Oliver Twist*. Ch. 17.

17
Man's life is but seventy salads long.

EMERSON, *Essays, Second Series: Nature*.

Life is eating us up. We shall be fables presently.

EMERSON, *Representative Men: Montaigne*.

Life's well enough, but we shall be glad to get out of it, and they will all be glad to have us.

EMERSON, *Representative Men: Montaigne*.

We live ruins amid ruins.

EMERSON, *Society and Solitude: Domestic Life*.

1
The life worth living. (Vita vitalis.)
Ennius. (Cicero, *De Amicitia*. Ch. vi, sec. 20.)

Is life worth living? Yes, so long
As there is wrong to right.
Alfred Austin, *Is Life Worth Living?*

So long as faith in freedom reigns
And loyal hope survives,
And gracious charity remains
To leaven lowly lives;
While there is one untrodden tract
For intellect or will,
And men are free to think and act,
Life is worth living still.
Alfred Austin, *Is Life Worth Living?*

Is life worth living?
Aye, with the best of us—
Heights of us, depths of us—
Life is the test of us!
Corinne Roosevelt Robinson, *Life, A Question.*

Life is an end in itself, and the only question as to whether it is worth living is whether you have had enough of it.
Justice O. W. Holmes, in a Supreme Court decision.

Is life worth living? That depends on the liver!
Unknown, *Is Life Worth Living?*

2
We live merely on the crust or rind of things.
J. A. Froude, *Short Studies on Great Subjects: Lucian.*

We live amid surfaces, and the true art of life is to skate well on them.
Emerson, *Essays, Second Series: Experience.*

You cannot learn to skate without being ridiculous. . . . The ice of life is slippery.
Bernard Shaw, *Fanny's First Play: Induction.*

3
A merry life and a short.
Edmund Gayton, *Festivous Notes on Don Quixote*, 101. (1654)

A short life and a merry life, I cry. Happy man be his dole.
John Tatham, *The Rump*. Act i. (1660)

4
Yes, my love, whosoever lives, loses, . . . but he also wins. (Ja, meine Liebe, wer lebt, verliert . . . aber er gewinnt auch.)
Goethe, *Stella*. Act i.

5
There is more to life than increasing its speed.
Mahatma Gandhi.

6
Life is short and the art is long. (Ὁ βίος βραχὺς, ἡ δὲ τέχνη μακρή.)
Hippocrates, *Aphorisms*. No. 1. Referring to the art of healing. *See* Art: Art is Long.

7
Life isn't all beer and skittles.
Thomas Hughes, *Tom Brown's Schooldays*. Ch. 2. (1857)

Life is with such all beer and skittles;
They are not difficult to please about their victuals.
C. S. Calverley, *Contentment.*

They don't mind it: it's a reg'lar holiday to them—all porter and skittles.
Dickens, *Pickwick Papers*. Ch. 40.

Life ain't all beer and skittles, and more's the pity; but what's the odds, so long as you're happy?
George Du Maurier, *Trilby*, p. 25.

8
We now demand to be personally conducted through life, all risks to be taken by someone else.
Dean W. R. Inge. (Marchant, *Wit and Wisdom of Dean Inge*. No. 109.)

9
All that a man hath will he give for his life.
Old Testament: Job, ii, 4.

10
The land of the living.
Old Testament: Job, xxviii, 13.

There is ay life for a living man.
John Ray, *Scottish Proverbs.*

11
The business of life is to go forward.
Samuel Johnson, *The Idler*. No. 72.

Life, to be worthy of a rational being, must always be in progression.
Samuel Johnson, *Letter to Mrs. Piozzi.*

Life can only be understood backwards; but it must be lived forwards.
Sören Kierkegaard, *Life.*

12
The hope of life returns with the sun. (Spes vitæ cum sole redit.)
Juvenal, *Satires*. Sat. xii, l. 70. While there's life there's hope: *see under* Hope.

13
There is nothing of which men are so fond, and withal so careless, as life.
La Bruyère, *Les Caractères*. Sec. 10.

Most men employ the earlier part of life to make the other part miserable. (La plupart des hommes emploient la meilleure partie de leur vie à rendre l'autre misérable.)
La Bruyère, *Les Caractères*. Sec. 11.

14
Love is sunshine, hate is shadow,
Life is checkered shade and sunshine.
Longfellow, *Hiawatha's Wooing*, l. 265.

Oh thou child of many prayers!
Life hath quicksands,—life hath snares!
Longfellow, *Maidenhood.*

15
We live, not as we wish, but as we can. (Ζῶμεν γὰρ οὐχ ὡς θέλομεν, ἀλλ' ὡς δυνάμεθα.)
Menander, *Andria*. Frag. 50.

16
To destroy life is a power which the vilest of earth possess;
To bestow it belongs to gods and kings alone.
(Il torre altrui la vita È facoltà commune
Al più vil della terra; il darla è solo
De Numi, e de' Regnanti.)
Metastasio, *La Clemenza di Tito*. Act iii, sc. 7.

1
The great business of life is, to be, to do, to do without, and to depart.
JOHN MORLEY, *Address on Aphorisms*, Edinburgh, 1887.

2
Nor on one string are all life's jewels strung.
WILLIAM MORRIS, *The Life and Death of Jason*. Bk. xvii, l. 1170.

3
How light the touches are that kiss
The music from the chords of life!
COVENTRY PATMORE, *By the Sea*.

4
Twenty years a boy, twenty years a youth, twenty years a man, twenty years an old man.
PYTHAGORAS, the four quarters of life. (DIOGENES LAERTIUS, *Pythagoras*. Sec. 10.)

5
And there I began to think, that it is very true which is commonly said, that one half of the world knoweth not how the other half liveth. (Et là commençay à penser, qu'il est bien vray ce que l'on dit, que la moitié du monde ne sçait comment l'aultre vit.)
RABELAIS, *Works*. Bk. ii, ch. 32. (1532)

One half of the world knows not how the other half lives.
GEORGE HERBERT, *Jacula Prudentum*. (1640)

How the Other Half Lives.
JACOB A. RIIS. Title of book.

6
We must not look for a golden life in an iron age.
JOHN RAY, *English Proverbs*.

7
I wish to preach, not the doctrine of ignoble ease, but the doctrine of the strenuous life.
THEODORE ROOSEVELT, *Speech*, Hamilton Club, Chicago, 10 April, 1899.

The poorest way to face life is to face it with a sneer.
THEODORE ROOSEVELT, *Speech*, University of Paris.

In life as in a football game, the principle to follow is: Hit the line hard.
THEODORE ROOSEVELT, *The Strenuous Life: The American Boy*.

8
How many illustrious and noble heroes have lived too long by one day! (Combien de héros, glorieux, magnanimes, ont vécu trop d'un jour!)
JEAN-JACQUES ROUSSEAU.

9
Live and let live. (Leben und leben lassen.)
SCHILLER, *Wallenstein's Lager*. Act vi, l. 106.

10
He who lives for no one does not necessarily live for himself. (Non continuo sibi vivit, qui nemini.)
SENECA, *Epistulæ ad Lucilium*. Epis. lv, sec. 5.

It gives proof of a great heart to return to life for the sake of others, and noble men have often done this. (Ingentis animi est aliena causa ad vitam reverti, quod magni viri sæpe fecerunt.)
SENECA, *Epistulæ ad Lucilium*. Epis. civ, sec. 4.

11
There is one reason why we cannot complain of life: it keeps no one against his will. (Hoc est unum, cur de vita non possimus queri: neminem tenet.)
SENECA, *Epistulæ ad Lucilium*. Epis. lxx, 15.

12
The greatest flaw in life is that it is always imperfect. (Maximum vitæ vitium est, quod imperfecta semper est.)
SENECA, *Epistulæ ad Lucilium*. Epis. ci, sec. 8.

13
The web of our life is of a mingled yarn, good and ill together.
SHAKESPEARE, *All's Well that Ends Well*. Act i, sc. 3, l. 83.

14
I bear a charmed life.
SHAKESPEARE, *Macbeth*. Act v, sc. 8, l. 12.

15
If you choose to represent the various parts in life by holes upon a table, of different shapes,—some circular, some triangular, some square, some oblong,—and the persons acting these parts by bits of wood of similar shapes, we shall generally find that the triangular person has got into the square hole, the oblong into the triangular, and a square person has squeezed himself into the round hole. The officer and the office, the doer and the thing done, seldom fit so exactly that we can say they were almost made for each other.
SYDNEY SMITH, *Sketches of Moral Philosophy*.

The world is like a board with holes in it, and the square men have got into the round holes, and the round into the square.
BISHOP GEORGE BERKELEY. (*Punch* is responsible for the attribution. The quotation has not been found in Berkeley's works.)

A round man cannot be expected to fit a square hole right away. He must have time to modify his shape.
MARK TWAIN, *More Tramps Abroad*. Ch. 71.

16
One's real life is so often the life that one does not lead.
OSCAR WILDE, *Rose-Leaf and Apple-Leaf: Envoi*.

17
Life is far too important a thing ever to talk seriously about.
OSCAR WILDE, *Lady Windermere's Fan*. Act i.

Lord Illingworth: The Book of Life begins with a man and a woman in a garden.
Mrs. Allonby: It ends with Revelations.
OSCAR WILDE, *A Woman of No Importance*. Act i.

The secret of life is never to have an emotion that is unbecoming.
OSCAR WILDE, *A Woman of No Importance*. Act iii.

1
Life is most enjoy'd,
When courted least; most worth, when disesteem'd.
YOUNG, *Night Thoughts*. Night iii, l. 410.

V—Life: A Battle

2
Life is a battle, sojourning in a strange land; and the fame that comes after is oblivion. (Ὁ δὲ βίος πόλεμος καὶ ξένου ἐπιδημία.)
MARCUS AURELIUS, *Meditations*. Bk. ii, sec. 17.

3
Life, Lucilius, is a battle. (Vivere, Lucili, militare est.)
SENECA, *Epistulæ ad Lucilium*. Epis. xcvi, 5.

My life is a battle. (Ma vie est un combat.)
VOLTAIRE, *Mahomet*. Act ii, sc. 4. Adopted by Beaumarchais as his motto.

4
Who in Life's battle firm doth stand
Shall bear Hope's tender blossoms
Into the Silent Land!
J. G. VON SALIS-SEEWIS, *Song of the Silent Land*. (Longfellow, tr.)

5
Man's life on earth is a warfare. (Militia est vita hominis super terram.)
Vulgate: Job, vii, 1.

6
Life is war;
Eternal war with woe; who bears it best,
Deserves it least.
YOUNG, *Night Thoughts*. Night ii, l. 9.

VI—Life, A Bubble

See also Man: A Bubble; World: A Bubble

7
The world's a bubble, and the life of man
less than a span;
In his conception wretched, from the womb
so to the tomb:
Curst from his cradle, and brought up to years
with cares and fears.
Who then to frail mortality shall trust,
But limns on water, or but writes in dust.
SIR FRANCIS BACON, *The World*. A paraphrase of a Greek epigram by Posidippus. Sometimes wrongly attributed to Sir Henry Wotton. Izaak Walton, a friend of Wotton, definitely ascribed it to Bacon. (*Reliquæ Wottonianæ*, p. 513. 1651.) Positively ascribed to Bacon by Thomas Farnaby, a contemporary and a scholar. (*Florilegium Epigrammatum*. 1629.)

What life shall a man choose? In court and mart
Are quarrels and hard dealing; cares at home;
Labors by land; terrors at sea; abroad,
Either the fear of losing what thou hast,
Or worse, nought left to lose; if wedded, much
Discomfort; comfortless unwed; a life
With children troubled, incomplete without:
Youth foolish, age outworn. Of these two choose
then;
Or never to be born, or straight to die.
POSIDIPPUS (or PLATO, the Comic Poet). (*Greek Anthology*. Bk. ix, epig. 359.)

8
How little do we know that which we are!
How less what we may be! The eternal
surge
Of time and tide rolls on, and bears afar
Our bubbles.
BYRON, *Don Juan*. Canto xv, st. 99.

9
This life's a hollow bubble,
Don't you know?
Just a painted piece of trouble,
Don't you know?
We come to earth to cwy,
We grow oldeh and we sigh,
Oldeh still and then we die,
Don't you know?
EDMUND VANCE COOKE, *Fin de Siècle*. Referring to "Harvard indifference." *See under* INDIFFERENCE.

10
Life is mostly froth and bubble;
Two things stand like stone:
KINDNESS in another's trouble,
COURAGE in your own.
A. L. GORDON, *Ye Weary Wayfarer*. Fytte viii.

11
If Life an empty bubble be,
How sad for those who cannot see
The rainbow in the bubble!
F. LOCKER-LAMPSON, *Bramble-Rise*.

12
And fear not lest Existence closing your
Account and mine, should know the like no
more:
The Eternal Sáki from that Bowl has
poured
Millions of Bubbles like us. and will pour.
OMAR KHAYYÁM, *Rubáiyát*. St. 46. (Fitzgerald, tr.)

13
Man's life is but a jest,
A dream, a shadow, bubble, air, a vapour at
the best.
G. W. THORNBURY, *The Jester's Sermon*.

For what are men who grasp at praise sublime,
But bubbles on the rapid stream of time,
That rise, and fall, that swell, and are no more,
Born, and forgot, ten thousand in an hour?
YOUNG, *Love of Fame*. Sat. ii, l. 285.

VII—Life: A Disease

14
This strange disease of modern life,
With its sick hurry, its divided aims.
MATTHEW ARNOLD, *The Scholar Gipsy*. St. 21.

15
Why do not you look at this miserable little life, with all its ups and downs, as I do? At the very worst, 'tis but a scratch, a temporary

ill, to be soon cured by that dear old doctor, Death.

Edwin Booth, *Letter to William Winter*, 1886.

1
Let Nature and let Art do what they please,
When all is done, Life's an incurable disease.

Abraham Cowley, *Ode to Dr. Scarborough.*

That long and cruel malady which one calls life. (Cette longue et cruelle maladie qu'on appele la vie.)

Deschamps.

2
Life is a fatal complaint, and an eminently contagious one.

O. W. Holmes, *The Poet at the Breakfast-Table.* Ch. 12.

3
This long disease, my life.

Pope, *Epistle to Dr. Arbuthnot*, l. 132.

4
Own riches gather'd trouble, fame a breath,
And life an ill whose only cure is death.

Prior, *Epistle to Dr. Sherlock*, l. 26.

All covet life, yet call it pain:
All feel the ill, yet shun the cure.

Matthew Prior, *Epigram Written in Mezeray's History of France.*

5
It is silliness to live when to live is torment; and then have we a prescription to die when death is our physician.

Shakespeare, *Othello.* Act i, sc. 3, l. 309.

VIII—Life: A Dream

6
Now that I've come
To this place—alone—
Life is a spent dream
And a gray stone.

Verne Bright, *Gray Stone.*

7
We shall start up, at last awake
From Life, that insane dream we take
For waking now, because it seems.

Robert Browning, *Easter-Day.* Sec. 14.

Life is an empty dream.

Robert Browning, *Paracelsus.* Pt. ii.

Life and love are all a dream.

Burns, *Lament.*

Life is a dream. (La vida es sueño.)

Calderon. Title of Comedy.

8
Now the summer prime is her blithest rhyme
In the being and the seeming,
And they that have heard the overword
Know life's a dream worth dreaming.

W. E. Henley, *Echoes.* No. 33.

9
Life is a kind of Sleep. old men sleep longest, nor begin to wake but when they are to die.

La Bruyère, *Les Caractères.* Ch. 11.

Love to his soul gave eyes; he knew things are not as they seem.
The dream is his real life: the world around him is the dream.

F. T. Palgrave, *Dream of Maxim Wledig.*

10
To treat the whole spectacle as a dream within a dream, from which it is still possible that death may awaken us.

John Cowper Powys. (Durant, *On the Meaning of Life*, p. 47.)

11
Waking life is a dream controlled.

George Santayana, *Little Essays*, p. 146.

12
Peace, peace! he is not dead, he doth not sleep—
He hath awakened from the dream of life.

Shelley, *Adonais.* St. 39.

13
For life is but a dream whose shapes return,
Some frequently, some seldom.

James Thomson, *The City of Dreadful Night.* Pt. i, st. 3.

Life a dream in Death's eternal sleep.

James Thomson, *Philosophy.*

14
Life, believe, is not a dream,
So dark as sages say;
Oft a little morning rain
Foretells a pleasant day!

Charlotte Brontë, *Life.*

Tell me not, in mournful numbers,
Life is but an empty dream!—
For the soul is dead that slumbers,
And things are not what they seem.

Longfellow, *A Psalm of Life.* St. 1.

Sing it not in mournful numbers. (Singet nicht in Trauertonen.)

Goethe, *Wilhelm Meister: Philine.*

IX—Life: A Game

15
The heroes of ancient and modern fame . . . have treated life and fortune as a game to be well and skilfully played, but the stake not to be so valued but that any time it could be held a trifle light as air, and thrown up.

Emerson, *Essays, Second Series: New England Reformers.*

As a rule, the game of life is worth playing, but the struggle is the prize.

Dean W. R. Inge. (Marchant, *Wit and Wisdom of Dean Inge.* No. 199.)

16
But helpless Pieces of the Game He plays
Upon this Chequer-board of Nights and Days;
Hither and thither moves, and checks, and slays,
And one by one back in the Closet lays.

Omar Khayyám, *Rubáiyát.* St. 69. (Fitzgerald. tr.)

The chess-board is the world, the pieces are the phenomena of the universe, the rules of the game are what we call the laws of Nature. The player on the other side is hidden from us. We

know that his play is always fair, just, and patient. But also we know, to our cost, that he never overlooks a mistake, or makes the smallest allowance for ignorance.
HUXLEY, *Lay Sermons, Addresses, and Reviews: A Liberal Education.*

While we least think it he prepares his Mate.
Mate, and the King's pawn played, it never ceases,
Though all the earth is dust of taken pieces.
JOHN MASEFIELD, *The Widow in the Bye Street*. Pt. i, last lines.

We are puppets, Man in his pride, and Beauty fair in her flower;
Do we move ourselves, or are moved by an unseen hand at a game
That pushes us off from the board, and others ever succeed?
TENNYSON, *Maud,* l. 126.

1
I have set my life upon a cast,
And I will stand the hazard of the die.
SHAKESPEARE, *Richard III*. Act v, sc. 4, l. 9.

Life will always remain a gamble, with prizes sometimes for the imprudent, and blanks so often to the wise.
JEROME K. JEROME.

2
We are in the world like men playing at tables; the chance is not in our power, but to play it is; and when it is fallen, we must manage it as we can.
JEREMY TAYLOR, *Holy Living and Dying: Of Contentedness*. Sec. 2.

3
The life of man is like a game with dice: if you don't get the throw you want, you must show your skill in making the best of the throw you do get. (Ita vitast hominum quasi quom ludas tesseris: Si illud quod maxume opus est jacta non cadit, Illud quod cecidit forte, id arte ut corrigas.)
TERENCE, *Adelphi,* l. 739.

Life is a game of whist. From unseen sources
The cards are shuffled, and the hands are dealt.
Blind are our efforts to control the forces
That, though unseen, are no less strongly felt.

I do not like the way the cards are shuffled,
But yet I like the game and want to play;
And through the long, long night will I, unruffled,
Play what I get, until the break of day.
EUGENE F. WARE, *Whist.*

Life is a game of whist
Between Man and Nature
In which Nature knows all Man's cards.
CHRISTOPHER MORLEY, *Handicapped.*

X—Life: An Inn

4
We are all but Fellow-Travelers,
Along Life's weary way;
If any man can play the pipes,
In God's name, let him play.
JOHN BENNETT, *Fellow-Travelers.*

Away with funeral music—set
The pipe to powerful lips—
The cup of life's for him that drinks
And not for him that sips.
R. L. STEVENSON, *The Cup of Life.*

5
A fair, where thousands meet, but none can stay;
An inn, where travellers bait, then post away.
ISAAC HAWKINS BROWNE, *Immortality of the Soul.* (Tr. from the Latin by Soame Jenyns.)

6
For the world I count it not an inn, but an hospital, and a place not to live, but to die in.
SIR THOMAS BROWNE, *Religio Medici.* Pt. ii, sec. 11.

Archbishop Leighton used often to say that if he were to choose a place to die in, it should be an inn; it looking like a pilgrim's going home, to whom this world was all as an inn, and who was weary with the noise and confusion in it. . . . And he obtained what he desired, for he died at the Bell Inn in Warwick Lane.
GILBERT BURNET, *History of My Own Times.*

7
This world is but a thoroughfare full of woe,
And we but pilgrims passing to and fro.
Death is an end of every worldly sore.
CHAUCER, *The Knightes Tale,* l. 1989.

Like pilgrims to th' appointed place we tend;
The world's an inn, and death the journey's end.
DRYDEN, *Palamon and Arcite.* Bk. iii, l. 887.

8
I depart from life as from an inn, and not as from my home. (Ex vita discedo, tamquam ex hospitio, non tamquam e domo.)
CICERO, *De Senectute.* Ch. 23, sec. 84.

9
We are in this life as it were in another man's house. . . . In heaven is our home, in the world is our Inn: do not so entertain thyself in the Inn of this world for a day as to have thy mind withdrawn from longing after thy heavenly home.
PAUL GERHARDT, *Meditations.* No. 38. (1630)

10
One doth but breakfast here, another dine; he that lives longest does but sup; we must all go to bed in another World.
JOSEPH HENSHAW, BISHOP OF PETERBOROUGH, *Horæ Succissivæ*, p. 80. (1631)

Man's life is like unto a winter's day,—
Some break their fast and so depart away;
Others stay dinner, then depart full fed;
The longest age but sups and goes to bed.
O reader, then behold and see
As we are now, so must you be.
Attributed to Bishop Henshawe, but probably an elaboration by an unknown hand of the quotation from *Horæ Succissivæ* given above. Variations of the stanza were used frequently as epitaphs.

Our Life is nothing but a Winter's day;
Some only break their Fast, and so away:
Others stay to Dinner, and depart full fed:
The deepest Age but Sups, and goes to Bed:
He's most in debt that lingers out the Day:
Who dies betime, has less, and less to pay.

FRANCIS QUARLES, *Divine Fancies: On the Life of Man.* (1633)

The life of man is a winter's day, and a winter's way.

JOHN RAY, *English Proverbs.*

Man's life is like a Winter's day:
Some only breakfast and away;
Others to dinner stay and are full fed,
The oldest man but sups and goes to bed.
Long is his life who lingers out the day,
Who goes the soonest has the least to pay;
Death is the Waiter, some few run on tick,
And some alas! must pay the bill to Nick!
Tho' I owed much, I hope long trust is given,
And truly mean to pay all bills in Heaven.

UNKNOWN, *Epitaph,* Barnwell Churchyard, near Cambridge, England.

1 This life at best is but an inn,
And we the passengers.

JAMES HOWELL, *A Fit of Mortification.*

Nor is this lower world but a huge inn,
And men the rambling passengers.

JAMES HOWELL, *The Vote.* (Prefixed to his *Familiar Letters.*)

2 I came at morn; 'twas spring, I smiled,
The fields with green were clad;
I walked abroad at noon, and lo!
'Twas summer—I was glad;
I sate me down; 'twas autumn eve,
And I with sadness wept;
I laid me down at night, and then
'Twas winter, and I slept.

MARY PYPER, *Epitaph: A Life.*

3 Many mortals given up to the belly and to sleep, uninstructed and uncultured, have passed through life like sojourners in strange lands; whose bodies indeed have been given up to pleasure, and their souls to a heavy burden. (Multi mortales dediti ventri atque somno, indocti, incultique vitam sicuti peregrinantes transiere; quibus profecto contra naturam corpus voluptati, anima oneri.)

SALLUST, *Catilina.* Ch. 2, sec. 8.

4 This body is not a home but an inn, and that only for a short time. (Nec domum esse hoc corpus, sed hospitium, et quidem breve hospitium.)

SENECA, *Epistulæ ad Lucilium.* Epis. cxx, 14.

Born for a very brief space of time, we regard this life as an inn which we are soon to quit that it may be made ready for the coming guest.

SENECA, *Ad Polybium de Consolatione.* Sec. 21.

Making a perpetual mansion of this poor baiting-place.

SIR PHILIP SIDNEY, *Arcadia.*

XI—Life: An Isthmus

5 Many witty authors compare the present time to an isthmus, or narrow neck of land, that rises in the midst of an ocean, immeasurably diffused on either side of it.

ADDISON, *The Spectator.* No. 590.

There is an eternity behind and an eternity before, and this little speck in the center, however long, is comparatively but a minute.

JOHN BROWN, after his arrest at Harper's Ferry, in October, 1859.

6 The poorest day that passes over us is the conflux of two Eternities; it is made up of currents that issue from the remotest Past and flow onwards into the remotest Future.

CARLYLE, *Essays: Signs of the Times.*

One life;—a little gleam of Time between two Eternities.

CARLYLE, *Heroes and Hero-Worship.* Lect. 5.

7 As stand we percht on point of Time, betwixt the two Eternities,
Whose awful secrets gathering round with black profound oppress our eyes.

SIR RICHARD BURTON, *The Kasîdah.* Pt. ii, st. 4.

8 Life is a fragment, a moment between two eternities, influenced by all that has preceded, and to influence all that follows. The only way to illumine it is by extent of view.

WILLIAM ELLERY CHANNING, *Note-book: Life.*

9 Vain, weak-built isthmus, which dost proudly rise
Up between two eternities!

ABRAHAM COWLEY, *Life and Fame,* l. 18.

10 Life is a narrow vale between the cold and barren peaks of two eternities. We strive in vain to look beyond the heights.

R. G. INGERSOLL, *At His Brother's Grave.*

11 What shall we call this undetermin'd state,
This narrow isthmus 'twixt two boundless oceans,
That whence we came, and that to which we tend?

GEORGE LILLO, *Arden of Feversham.* Act iii, sc. 2.

Life, as we call it, is nothing but the edge of the boundless ocean of existence where it comes on soundings.

O. W. HOLMES, *The Professor at the Breakfast-Table.* Ch. 5.

12 Remember that man's life lies all within this present, as 't were but a hair's breadth of time; as for the rest, the past is gone, the future may never be. Short, therefore, is man's life, and narrow is the corner of the earth wherein he dwells.

MARCUS AURELIUS, *Meditations.* Bk. iii, sec. 10.

1
This speck of life in time's great wilderness
This narrow isthmus 'twixt two boundless seas,
The past, the future, two eternities!
THOMAS MOORE, *Lalla Rookh: The Veiled Prophet of Khorassan*. St. 42.

Placed on this isthmus of a middle state.
POPE, *Essay on Man*. Epis. ii, l. 3.

3
Amid two seas, on one small point of land,
Wearied, uncertain, and amaz'd we stand.
MATTHEW PRIOR, *Solomon on the Vanity of Human Wishes*. Pt. iii, l. 616.

Lo! on a narrow neck of land,
'Twixt two unbounded seas, I stand.
CHARLES WESLEY, *O God Mine Inmost Soul Convert*.

4
I desire to have both heaven and hell ever in my eye, while I stand on this isthmus of life, between two boundless oceans.
JOHN WESLEY, *Letter to Charles Wesley*, 1747.

XII—Life: A Medley

5
From fibers of pain and hope and trouble
And toil and happiness,—one by one,—
Twisted together, or single or double,
The varying thread of our life is spun.
Hope shall cheer though the chain be galling;
Light shall come though the gloom be falling;
Faith will list for the Master calling
Our hearts to his rest,—when the day is done.
A. B. BRAGDON, *When the Day Is Done*.

Life is patchwork—here and there,
Scraps of pleasure and despair
Join together, hit or miss.
ANNE BRONAUGH, *Patchwork*.

6
He fixed thee 'mid this dance
Of plastic circumstance.
ROBERT BROWNING, *Rabbi Ben Ezra*.

7
How many lives we live in one,
And how much less than one, in all!
ALICE CARY, *Life's Mysteries*.

8
What is it but a map of busy life,
Its fluctuations, and its vast concerns?
COWPER, *The Task*. Bk. iv, l. 55.

9
In real life serious things and mere trifles, laughable things and things that cause pain, are wont to be mixed in strangest medley. It is necessary, then, that Tragedy, as being a mirror of life, must leave room for an element of comic humour.
JOHN KEBLE, *Lectures on Poetry*.

10
Half my life is full of sorrow,
Half of joy, still fresh and new;
One of these lives is a fancy,
But the other one is true.
ADELAIDE ANN PROCTER, *Dream-Life*.

11
The Fates and Furies, as well as the Graces and Sirens, glide with linked hands over life. (Die Parzen und Furien ziehen auch mit verbundnen Händen um das Leben, wie die Grazien und die Sirenen.)
JEAN PAUL RICHTER, *Titan*. Zykel 140.

12
Twist ye, twine ye! even so
Mingle shades of joy and woe,
Hope and fear, and peace, and strife,
In the thread of human life.
SCOTT, *Guy Mannering*. Ch. 4.

We have two lives:
13
The soul of man is like the rolling world,
One half in day, the other dipt in night;
The one has music and the flying cloud,
The other, silence and the wakeful stars.
ALEXANDER SMITH, *Horton*, l 76.

14
Emblem of man, who, after all his moaning
And strain of dire immeasurable strife,
Has yet this consolation, all atoning—
Life, as a windmill, grinds the bread of Life.
LORD DE TABLEY, *The Windmill*.

15
Through all the changing scenes of life,
In trouble and in joy.
TATE AND BRADY, *Psalm xxxiv*.

16
Our life contains a thousand springs,
And dies if one be gone.
Strange! that a harp of thousand strings
Should keep in tune so long.
ISAAC WATTS, *Hymns*. Bk. ii, No. 19.

XIII—Life: A Play

See also World: A Stage

17
Since well I've played my part, all clap your hands
And from the stage dismiss me with applause.
('Επεὶ δὲ πάνυ καλῶς πέπαισται, δότε κρότον
Καὶ πάντες ἡμᾶς μετὰ χαρᾶς προπέμψατε.)
CÆSAR AUGUSTUS, *Epigram*, as he lay dying. The Emperor had called in his friends, and asked them whether it seemed to them that he had played the comedy of life fitly (ecquid iis videretur mimum vitæ commode transegisse), and then spoke the epigram given above, sent them away, and died shortly afterwards. (SUETONIUS. *Twelve Cæsars: Augustus*. Ch. 99, sec. 1.)

18
The human comedy (La comédie humaine)
HONORÉ DE BALZAC. The general title of his novels, adopted in 1842

Sit the comedy out, and that done,
When the Play's at an end, let the Curtain fall down.
THOMAS FLATMAN, *The Whim*

19
Remember that you are an actor in a play, the character of which is determined by the Playwright: if He wishes the play to be short,

it is short; if long, it is long; if He wishes you to play the part of a beggar, remember to act even this role adroitly. For this is your business: to play admirably the role assigned to you; but the selection of that role is Another's.

EPICTETUS [?], *Encheiridion*. Sec. 17.

1
So likewise all this life of mortal man, what is it but a kind of stage play, where men come forth, disguised one in one array, and another in another, each playing his part?

ERASMUS, *Praise of Folly*.

For though the most be players, some must be spectators.

BEN JONSON, *Explorata: De Piis et Probis*.

Life is a tragedy wherein we sit as spectators for a while, and then act out our part in it.

SWIFT, *Thoughts on Various Subjects*.

2
The endless mime goes on; new faces come,
New mummers babble in each other's ears;
And some wear masks of woe, of laughter some,
Nor know they play Life's Comedy of Tears.

JAMES B. KENYON, *The Play*.

3
Life has its heroes and its villains, its soubrettes and its ingenues, and all roles may be acted well.

J. W. KRUTCH, *The Modern Temper*.

4
Life is a stage, so learn to play your part,
Laying gravity aside, or learn to bear its griefs.
(Σκηνὴ πᾶς ὁ βίος καὶ παίγνιον· ἢ μάθε παίζειν, τὴν σπουδὴν μεταθείς, ἢ φέρε τὰς ὀδύνας.)

PALLADAS. (*Greek Anthology*. Bk. x, epig. 72.)

This life a theatre we well may call,
Where every actor must perform with art,
Or laugh it through, and make a farce of all,
Or learn to bear with grace his tragic part.

PALLADAS. (*Greek Anthology*, x, 72. Bland, tr.)

If character be fate, no need to ask
Who set the stage, who cast you for the role;
Put on what man you are, put off the mask,
Put on the tragic pattern of your soul. . . .
Let him who plays the monarch be a king,
Who plays the rogue, be perfect in his part.

JOHN ERSKINE, *At the Front*. Sonnet iv.

5
My soul, sit thou a patient looker-on;
Judge not the play before the play is done:
Her plot hath many changes; every day
Speaks a new scene; the last act crowns the play.

FRANCIS QUARLES, *Respice Finem*.

6
Draw the curtain, the farce is played out. (Tirez le rideau, la farce est jouée.)

RABELAIS, dying words, as he expired in a fit of laughter. (*Works*. Vol, i, p. 17. Dupont, ed., Paris, 1865.)

7
There is no incidental music to the dramas of real life.

SAX ROHMER, *Insidious Dr. Fu Manchu*. Ch. 9.

8
It is with life as with a play—it matters not how long the action is spun out, but how good the acting is. (Quomodo fabula, sic vita non quam diu, sed quam bene acta sit, refert.)

SENECA, *Epistulæ ad Lucilium*. Epis. lxxvii, 20.

'Tis not the mere stage of life but the part we play thereon that gives the value. (Nicht der Tummelplatz des Lebens—sein Gehalt bestimmt seinen Werth.)

SCHILLER, *Fiesco*. Act iii, sc. 2.

9
Life's but a walking shadow; a poor player
That struts and frets his hour upon the stage,
And then is heard no more.

SHAKESPEARE, *Macbeth*. Act v, sc. 5, l. 23.

10
Life's a long tragedy; this globe the stage,
Well fix'd and well adorn'd with strong machines,
Gay fields, and skies, and seas; the actors many:
The plot immense.

ISAAC WATTS, *Epistle to Mitio*. Pt. i, l. 1.

For they are blest that have not much to rue—
That have not oft misheard the prompter's cue,
Stammered and stumbled, and the wrong parts played,
And life a Tragedy of Errors made.

WILLIAM WATSON, *To a Friend*.

Fate has written a tragedy; its name is "The Human Heart,"
The Theatre is the House of Life, Woman the mummer's part;
The Devil enters the prompter's box and the play is ready to start.

ROBERT W. SERVICE, *The Harpy*.

XIV—Life: A Tale

11
Every man's life is a fairy-tale written by God's fingers.

HANS CHRISTIAN ANDERSEN, *Works: Preface*.

12
Life is as tedious as a twice-told tale,
Vexing the dull ear of a drowsy man.

SHAKESPEARE, *King John*. Act iii, sc. 4, l. 109.

13
Life . . . is a tale
Told by an idiot, full of sound and fury,
Signifying nothing.

SHAKESPEARE, *Macbeth*. Act v, sc. 5, l. 26.

14
Life's but a span, or a tale, or a word,
That in a trice, or sudden, is rehearsed.

UNKNOWN, *A Friend's Advice*. (*Roxburghe Ballads*, ii.)

XV—Life: A Voyage

15
We mortals cross the ocean of this world
Each in his average cabin of a life;

The best's not big, the worst yields elbow-room.
ROBERT BROWNING, *Bishop Blougram's Apology*.

Most men make the voyage of life as if they carried sealed orders which they were not to open till they were fairly in mid-ocean.
J. R. LOWELL, *Among My Books: Dante*.

Life hath set No landmarks before us.
OWEN MEREDITH, *Lucile*. Pt. ii, canto v, sec. 14.

1
Life's a voyage that's homeward bound.
HERMAN MELVILLE. (COURNOS, *Modern Plutarch*, p. 87.)

2
Life is a perilous voyage. (Πλοῦς σφαλερὸς τὸ ζῆν.)
PALLADAS. (*Greek Anthology*. Bk. x, No. 65.)

3
Humble voyagers are we,
O'er Life's dim, unsounded sea,
Seeking only some calm clime;—
Touch us gently, gentle Time.
BRYAN WALLER PROCTER, *Middle Age*.

O'er Ocean, with a thousand masts, sails forth the stripling bold—
One boat, hard rescued from the deep, draws into port the old!
SCHILLER, *Votive Tablets: Expectation and Fulfilment*.

4
Life's uncertain voyage.
SHAKESPEARE, *Timon of Athens*. Act v, sc. 1, l. 205.

Life is a voyage. The winds of life come strong
From every point; yet each will speed thy course along,
If thou with steady hand when tempests blow
Canst keep thy course aright and never once let go.
THEODORE WILLIAMS, *The Voyage of Life*.

5
Old and young we are all on our last cruise.
R. L. STEVENSON, *Crabbed Age and Youth*.

XVI—Life: The Conduct of Life

6
Whilst I yet live, let me not live in vain.
ADDISON, *Cato*. Act iv, sc. 4.

7
One must have lived greatly whose record would bear the full light of day from beginning to its close.
A. B. ALCOTT, *Table Talk: Learning*.

8
From fields of sense, and mines of thought,
Threads of life are twisted and wrought:
We are weaving Character, weaving Fate,
And Human History, little and great.
WILLIAM ALLINGHAM, *Blackberries*.

9
Let us be patient, tender, wise, forgiving,
In this strange task of living;
For if we fail each other, each will be
Grey driftwood lapsing to the bitter sea.
MARTIN ARMSTRONG, *Body and Spirit*.

For like a child, sent with a fluttering light
To feel his way along a gusty night,
Man walks the world. Again, and yet again,
The lamp shall be by fits of passion slain;
But shall not He who sent him from the door
Relight the lamp once more, and yet once more?
ATTAR, *Mantik-ut-Tair*. (Fitzgerald, tr.) See *Letters and Literary Remains of Edward Fitzgerald*. Vol. ii, p. 457.

10
I live for those who love me, for those who know me true;
For the heaven that smiles above me, and awaits my spirit too;
For the cause that lacks assistance, for the wrong that needs resistance,
For the future in the distance, and the good that I can do.
G. LINNÆUS BANKS, *My Aim*.

Only a life lived for others is a life worth while.
ALBERT EINSTEIN, defining success. (*Youth*, June, 1932)

11
Man always knows his life will shortly cease,
Yet madly lives as if he knew it not.
RICHARD BAXTER, *Hypocrisy*.

For yet I lived like one not born to die;
A thriftless prodigal of smiles and tears,
HARTLEY COLERIDGE, *Long Time a Child*.

Men deal with life as children with their play,
Who first misuse, then cast their toys away.
COWPER, *Hope*, l. 127.

12
God asks no man whether he will accept life. That is not the choice. You *must* take it. The only choice is *how*.
HENRY WARD BEECHER, *Life Thoughts*.

13
Live truly, and thy life shall be
A great and noble creed.
HORATIUS BONAR, *Be True*.

Do what thy manhood bids thee do, from none but self expect applause;
He noblest lives and noblest dies who makes and keeps his self-made laws.
All other Life is living Death, a world where none but Phantoms dwell,
A breath, a wind, a sound, a voice, a tinkling of the camel-bell.
SIR RICHARD BURTON, *The Kasîdah*. Pt. viii, sts. 37–8.

To seek the True, to glad the heart, such is of life the Higher Law.
SIR RICHARD BURTON, *The Kasîdah*. Pt. ix, st. 28.

14
All is concentred in a life intense,
Where not a beam, nor air, nor leaf is lost,
But hath a part of being.
BYRON, *Childe Harold*. Canto iii, st. 89.

15
To live content with small means; to seek elegance rather than luxury, and refinement rather than fashion; to be worthy, not respectable, and wealthy, not rich; to study

hard, think quietly, talk frankly; to listen to stars and birds, to babes and sages, with open heart; to bear all cheerfully, do all bravely, await occasion, hurry never; in a word, to let the spiritual, unbidden and unconscious grow up through the common: this is to be my symphony.

WILLIAM HENRY CHANNING, *My Symphony*.

1
Nature has granted the use of life like a loan, without fixing any day for repayment. (Natura . . . dedit usuram vitæ tamquam pecuniæ nulla præstituta die.)

CICERO, *Tusculanarum Disputationum*. Bk. i, ch. 19, sec. 93.

Life is given to all, not to be disposed of, but to be used. (Vitaque mancipio nulli datur, omnibus usu.)

LUCRETIUS, *De Rerum Natura*. Bk. iii, l. 971.

Man has been lent, not given, to life. (Homo vitæ commodatus, non donatus est.)

PUBLILIUS SYRUS, *Sententiæ*. No. 257.

2
For the conduct of life, we need right reason or a halter.

DIOGENES. (DIOGENES LAERTIUS, *Diogenes*, 24.)

3
Children of life are we, as we stand
With our lives uncarved before us.

GEORGE WASHINGTON DOANE, *Life-Sculpture*.

To each is given a bag of tools,
A shapeless mass and a book of rules,
And each must make, ere life is flown,
A stumbling-block or a stepping-stone.

R. L. SHARPE, *Stumbling-Block or Stepping-Stone*.

4
Trust flattering life no more, redeem time past,
And live each day as if it were thy last.

WILLIAM DRUMMOND, *Death's Last Will*.

To execute great things, one should live as though one would never die. (Pour exécuter de grandes choses, il faut vivre comme si on ne devait jamais mourir.)

VAUVENARGUES, *Réflexions*. No. 142.

Study as if you were to live forever. Live as if you were to die tomorrow.

ISIDORE OF SEVILLE.

5
Aimless we drift, we live but more or less. (Incerte errat animus, præterpropter vitam vivitur.)

QUINTUS ENNIUS, *Iphigenia*. (Aulus Gellius, *Noctes Atticæ*. Bk. xix, ch. 10, sec. 12.) Aulus Gellius is recording a discussion of the meaning of præterpropter, more or less.

Life without a plan,
As useless as the moment it began,
Serves merely as a soil for discontent
To thrive in.

COWPER, *Hope*, l. 95.

6
Choose the best life, habit will make it pleasant.

EPICTETUS, *Fragments*. No. 144.

7
Though we sometimes speak of a primrose path, we all know that a bad life is just as difficult, just as full of obstacles and hardships, as a good one. . . . The only choice is in the kind of life one would care to spend one's efforts on.

JOHN ERSKINE. (DURANT, *On the Meaning of Life*, p. 41.)

8
A noble life, crowned with heroic death, rises above and outlives the pride and pomp and glory of the mightiest empire of the earth.

JAMES A. GARFIELD, *Speech*, House of Representatives, 9 Dec., 1858.

9
He lives who lives to virtue; men who cast
Their ends for pleasure, do not live, but last.

ROBERT HERRICK, *On Himself*.

10
In the morning of life, work, in the midday give counsel, in the evening pray. (Ἔργα νέων, βουλαὶ δὲ μέσων, εὐχαὶ δε γερόντων.)

HESIOD, *Harpocration*. Frag. 19.

In seed time learn, in harvest teach, in winter enjoy.

WILLIAM BLAKE, *Proverbs of Hell*.

11
Do you wish to live well? Who does not? (Vis recte vivere: quis non?)

HORACE, *Epistles*. Bk. i, epis. 6, l. 29.

If live you cannot as befits a man,
Make room, at least you may, for those who can.
(Vivere si rectis nescis, decede peritis.)

HORACE, *Epistles*. Bk. ii, epis. 2, l. 213. (Conington, tr.)

Learn to live well, or fairly make your will;
You've play'd, and lov'd, and ate and drank, your fill.
Walk sober off, before a sprightlier age
Comes titt'ring on, and shoves you from the stage.

POPE, *Imitations of Horace Epistles*. Bk. ii, epis. 2, l. 322.

12
The rules for a happy life. (Vitæ præcepta beatæ.)

HORACE, *Satires*. Bk. ii, sat. 4, l. 95.

Amid hopes and cares, amid fears and passions, believe every day that dawns to be your last. Welcome will come to you another hour unhoped for. (Inter spem curamque, timores inter et iras, Omnem crede diem tibi diluxisse supremum. Grata superveniet, quæ non sperabitur hora.)

HORACE, *Epistles*. Bk. i, epis. 4, l. 12.

13
You'll see that, since our fate is ruled by chance,
Each man, unknowing, great,
Should frame life so that at some future hour
Fact and his dreamings meet.

VICTOR HUGO, *To His Orphan Grandchildren*.

14
Life must be filled up, and the man who is

not capable of intellectual pleasures must content himself with such as his senses can afford.
SAMUEL JOHNSON. (MRS. PIOZZI, *Johnsoniana.*)

That kind of life is most happy which affords us the most opportunities of gaining our own esteem.
SAMUEL JOHNSON, *Works.* Vol. ix, p. 114.

1
What a deal of cold business doth a man misspend the better part of life in! in scattering compliments, tendering visits, gathering and venting news, following feasts and plays, making a little winter-love in a dark corner.
BEN JONSON, *Explorata: Jactura Vitæ.*

2
A sacred burden is this life ye bear:
Look on it, lift it, bear it solemnly,
Stand up and walk beneath it steadfastly.
Fail not for sorrow, falter not for sin,
But onward, upward, till the goal ye win.
FRANCES ANNE KEMBLE, *Lines Addressed to the Young Gentlemen Leaving the Lenox Academy, Mass.*

3
Who laughs in motley to the crowded court,
And makes for idle days an idle sport,
May teach us yet, in life's impartial school,
'Tis *we* wear asses' ears and play the fool.
JAMES B. KENYON, *The Harlequin.*

4
Measure thy life by loss instead of gain;
Not by the wine drunk, but by the wine poured forth;
For love's strength standeth in love's sacrifice;
And whoso suffers most hath most to give.
HARRIET ELEANOR KING, *The Disciples.*

5
Life's all getting and giving,
I've only myself to give.
What shall I do for a living?
I've only one life to live.
End it? I'll not find another.
Spend it? But how shall I best?
Sure the wise plan is to live like a man
And Luck may look after the rest!
RUDYARD KIPLING, *The Wishing-Caps.*

6
Children of yesterday, heirs of tomorrow,
What are you weaving? Labor and sorrow?
Look to your looms again. Faster and faster
Fly the great shuttles prepared by the Master.
Life's in the loom! Room for it, room!
MARY A. LATHBURY, *Song of Hope.*

The years of men are the looms of God, let down from the place of the sun
Wherein we are weaving alway, till the mystic web is done—
Weaving blindly, but weaving surely, each for himself his fate.
We may not see how the right side looks: we can only weave and wait.
ANTON G. CHESTER, *The Tapestry Weavers.*

7
And in the wreck of noble lives
Something immortal still survives.
LONGFELLOW, *Building of the Ship*, l 375.

What else remains for me?
Youth, hope and love;
To build a new life on a ruined life.
LONGFELLOW, *The Masque of Pandora: In the Garden.* Pt. viii.

Thus at the flaming forge of life
Our fortunes must be wrought;
Thus on its sounding anvil shaped
Each burning deed and thought.
LONGFELLOW, *The Village Blacksmith.* St. 8.

8
The freer step, the fuller breath,
The wide horizon's grander view,
The sense of life that knows no death—
The life that maketh all things new.
SAMUEL LONGFELLOW, *The Horizon's View.*

9
Life may be given in many ways,
And loyalty to Truth be sealed
As bravely in the closet as the field,
So bountiful is fate.
J. R. LOWELL, *Commemoration Ode.*

10
Wanton is my page, but my life is right.
(Lasciva est nobis pagina, vita proba.)
MARTIAL, *Epigrams.* Bk. i, epig. 4. *See also* COWLEY *under* FAITH.

11
We spend our lives in learning pilotage,
And grow good steersmen when the vessel's crank!
GEORGE MEREDITH, *The Wisdom of Eld.*

12
To measure life, learn thou betimes, and know,
Toward solid good what leads the nearest way;
For other things mild Heav'n a time ordains,
And disapproves that care, though wise in show,
That with superfluous burden loads the day,
And when God sends a cheerful hour, refrains.
MILTON, *Sonnets: To Cyriac Skinner.*

13
My business and my art is to live. (Mon métier et mon art, c'est vivre.)
MONTAIGNE, *Essays.* Bk. ii, ch. 6.

Life and good living—what do we want beside? (Le vivre et le couvert, que faut-il davantage?)
LA FONTAINE, *Fables.*

Living is an art; and, to practise it well, men need, not only acquired skill, but also a native tact and taste.
ALDOUS HUXLEY, *Texts and Pretexts*, p. 129.

The finest art, the most difficult to learn, is the art of living.
JOHN MACY, *About Women*, p. 122.

The art of life is to be so well known at a good restaurant that you can pay with a cheque.
E. V. LUCAS, *Over Bemerton's.*

1
It is "to live happily" and not, as Antisthenes declares, "to die happily," which makes human felicity. (C'est "le vivre heureusement," non, comme disoit Antisthenes, "le mourir heureusement," qui fait l'humaine félicité.)
MONTAIGNE, *Essays.* Bk. iii, ch. 2.

2
How mean we seem when we look back into our lives!
GEORGE MOORE, *Ave,* p. 81.

3
To live as fully, as completely as possible, to be happy, and again to be happy is the true aim and end of life. "Ripeness is all."
LLEWELYN POWYS, *Impassioned Clay,* p. 94.

It is better to live recklessly and dangerously and even disastrously than not to live at all.
LLEWELYN POWYS, *Impassioned Clay,* p. 95.

Make no doubt of it, to have had an unhappy life is to have failed in life. It is the one consummate error, and around the death-bed of such a one the very angels weep.
LLEWELYN POWYS, *Impassioned Clay,* p. 98.

The essential thing is that in this brief interval between darkness and darkness, we should be thrillingly and passionately amused.
JOHN COWPER POWYS.

4
Since the span of life which we enjoy is short, let us make the memory of our lives as long as possible. (Quoniam vita ipsa qua fruimur brevis est, memoriam nostri quam maxume longam efficere.)
SALLUST, *Catiline.* Sec. 1.

That man alone lives and makes the most of life who devotes himself to some occupation, courting the fame of a glorious deed or a noble career.
SALLUST, *Catiline.* Sec. 2.

5
Nothing can be meaner than the anxiety to live on, to live on anyhow and in any shape; a spirit with any honour is not willing to live except in its own way, and a spirit with any wisdom is not over-eager to live at all.
GEORGE SANTAYANA, *Little Essays,* p. 164.

6
The largest portion of life passes while we are doing ill, a goodly share while we are doing nothing, and the whole while we are doing that which is not to the purpose.
SENECA, *Epistulæ ad Lucilium.* Epis. i, sec. 1.

We break up life into little bits and fritter it away. (Diducimus illam in particulas ac lancinamus.)
SENECA, *Epistulæ ad Lucilium.* Epis. xxxii, 2.

7
O gentlemen, the time of life is short!
To spend that shortness basely were too long,
If life did ride upon a dial's point,
Still ending at the arrival of an hour.
And if we live, we live to tread on kings;
If die, brave death, when princes die with us!
SHAKESPEARE, *I Henry IV.* Act v, sc. 2, l. 82.

Life is too short to waste
In critic peep or cynic bark,
Quarrel or reprimand;
'Twill soon be dark;
Up! mind thine own aim and
God save the mark!
EMERSON, *To J. W.*

Life is too short for mean anxieties.
CHARLES KINGSLEY, *The Saint's Tragedy.* Act ii, sc. 9.

8
Reason thus with life:
If I do lose thee, I do lose a thing
That none but fools would keep.
SHAKESPEARE, *Measure for Measure.* Act iii, sc. 1, l. 6.

9
To suffer woes which Hope thinks infinite;
To forgive wrongs darker than death or night;
To defy Power, which seems omnipotent;
To love, and bear, to hope till Hope creates
From its own wreck the thing it contemplates;
Neither to change, nor falter, nor repent;
This, this thy glory, Titan, is to be
Good, great and joyous, beautiful and free;
This is alone Life, Joy, Empire, Victory!
SHELLEY, *Prometheus Unbound.* Act iv, l. 570.

10
There are two things to aim at in life: first, to get what you want; and, after that, to enjoy it. Only the wisest of mankind achieve the second.
LOGAN PEARSALL SMITH, *Afterthoughts.*

11
To be honest, to be kind—to earn a little and to spend a little less, to make upon the whole a family happier for his presence, to renounce when that shall be necessary and not be embittered, to keep a few friends but these without capitulation—above all, on the same grim condition to keep friends with himself—here is a task for all that a man has of fortitude and delicacy.
R. L. STEVENSON, *A Christmas Sermon.*

To love playthings well as a child, to lead an adventurous and honourable youth, and to settle, when the time arrives, into a green and smiling age, is to be a good artist in life and deserve well of yourself and your neighbour.
R. L. STEVENSON, *Crabbed Age and Youth.*

12
Not what we would but what we must
Makes up the sum of living;
Heaven is both more and less than just
In taking and in giving.
R. H. STODDARD, *The Country Life.*

The secret of life is not to do what one likes, but to try to like that which one has to do.
DINAH MARIA MULOCK CRAIK.

See also GOD: MAN PROPOSES, GOD DISPOSES.

1
But this thing is God, to be man with thy
might,
To grow straight in the strength of thy spirit,
and live out thy life as the light.
SWINBURNE, *Hertha*. St. 15.

2
He regulated his life wisely. (Sapienter vitam instituit.)
TERENCE, *Andria*, l. 67. (Act i, sc. 1.)

3
The true pleasure of life is to live with your inferiors.
THACKERAY, *The Newcomes*. Bk. i, ch. 9.

4
The art of life, of a poet's life, is, not having anything to do, to do something.
H. D. THOREAU, *Journal*, 29 April, 1852.

5
I'll take life's hazards, rue not hours well
wasted,
Hide my heart's wounds, ask no miraculous
balm;
And ere I die, perhaps I shall have tasted
At last a little calm.
WILLIAM WATSON, *Just a Possibility*.

XVII—Life and Living

See also Eating: Eat, Drink and Be Merry; Opportunity; Time: Gather Ye Rosebuds

6
"Learn while you're young," he often said,
"There is much to enjoy, down here below;
Life for the living, and rest for the dead!"
Said the jolly old pedagogue, long ago.
GEORGE ARNOLD, *The Jolly Old Pedagogue*.

Cease, Man, to mourn, to weep, to wail; enjoy
thy shining hour of sun;
We dance along Death's icy brink, but is the
dance less full of fun?
SIR RICHARD BURTON, *The Kasidah*. Pt. iii, st. 45.

7
Each life's unfulfilled, you see;
It hangs still, patchy and scrappy:
We have not sighed deep, laughed free,
Starved, feasted, despaired,—been happy.
ROBERT BROWNING, *Youth and Art*.

8
All of the animals excepting man know that the principal business of life is to enjoy it.
SAMUEL BUTLER THE YOUNGER, *Note-Books*.

9
Let us make hay while the sun shines.
CERVANTES, *Don Quixote*. Pt. i, ch. 11.

10
Where we live or how we live is of little consequence. What is all-important is to live.
ERNEST DIMNET, *What We Live By*.

11
Learn to make the most of life,
Lose no happy day,
Time will never bring thee back
Chances swept away!
Leave no tender word unsaid,
Love while love shall last;
"The mill cannot grind
With the water that is past."
SARAH DOUDNEY, *The Lesson of the Water-Mill*.

12
The fool, with all his other faults, has this also: he is always getting ready to live. (Inter cetera mala hoc quoque habet stultitia: semper incipit vivere.)
EPICURUS, *Fragments*. No. 494. (SENECA, *Epistulæ ad Lucilium*, xiii, 16.)

They live ill who are always beginning to live. (Male vivunt, qui semper vivere incipiunt.)
EPICURUS, *Fragments*. No. 493. (SENECA, *Epistulæ ad Lucilium*, xxiii, 10.)

We are always beginning to live, but are never living. (Victuros agimus semper, nec vivimus unquam.)
MANILIUS, *Astronomica*. Pt. iv, l. 899.

We are always getting ready to live, but never living.
EMERSON, *Journals*. Vol. iii, p. 276.

Very few men, properly speaking, live at present, but are providing to live another time.
SWIFT, *Thoughts on Various Subjects*.

13
Live to-day, forgetting the anxieties of the past. (Hodie vivendum, amissa præteritorum cura.)
EPICURUS. The Maxim of the Epicureans.

14
Drink wine, and live here blitheful while ye
may;
The morrow's life too late is, live to-day.
ROBERT HERRICK, *To Youth*.

15
What is life where living is extinct?
JOHN HEYWOOD, *Proverbs*. Pt. ii, ch. 9.

16
For this is wisdom: to love, to live,
To take what Fate or the gods may give.
LAURENCE HOPE, *The Teak Forest*.

17
Dare to be wise: begin! He who postpones the hour of living rightly is like the rustic who waits for the river to run out before he crosses, yet on it glides, and will glide on forever. (Sapere aude;
Incipe! Qui recte vivendi prorogat horam,
Rusticus exspectat dum defluat amnis; at ille
Labitur et labetur in omne volubilis ævum.)
HORACE, *Epistles*. Bk. i, epis. 2, l. 40.

Whatever hour God has blessed you with, take it with grateful hand, nor postpone your joys from year to year, so that, in whatever place you have been, you may say that you have lived happily.
HORACE, *Epistles*. Bk. i, epis. ii, l. 22.

While you may, live happy in the midst of pleasures; live mindful also that your time is short. (Dum licet, in rebus jucundis vive beatus; Vive memor, quam sis ævi brevis.)
HORACE, *Satires*. Bk. ii, sat. 6, l. 96.

1
Fear not the menace of the bye-and-bye.
To-day is ours; to-morrow Fate must give.
Stretch out your hands and eat, although ye die!
Better to die than never once to live.

RICHARD HOVEY, *Fear Not the Menace.*

2
Live all you can; it's a mistake not to. It doesn't so much matter what you do in particular so long as you have your life.

HENRY JAMES, *The Ambassadors,* p. 149.

3
Reflect that life, like every other blessing,
Derives its value from its use alone.

SAMUEL JOHNSON, *Irene.* Act iii, sc. 8, l. 28.

To him that lives well every form of life is good.

SAMUEL JOHNSON, *Rasselas.* Ch. 21.

Catch, then, oh! catch the transient hour;
Improve each moment as it flies;
Life's a short Summer—man a flower;
He dies—alas! how soon he dies!

SAMUEL JOHNSON, *Winter: An Ode,* l. 33.

4
No man, remember, can lose another life than that which he now loses. The present is the same for all; what we now lose or win is just the flying moment.

MARCUS AURELIUS, *Meditations.* Bk. ii, sec. 14.

5
It is not wise, believe me, to say, "I shall live." Too late is tomorrow's life: live thou today. (Non est, crede mihi, sapientis dicere "Vivam"; Sera nimis vita est crastina: vive hodie.)

MARTIAL, *Epigrams.* Bk. i, epig. 15.

Life for delays and doubts no time does give,
None ever yet made haste enough to live.
(Properat vivere nemo satis.)

MARTIAL, *Epigrams.* Bk. ii, 90. (Cowley, tr.)

Tomorrow I will live, the fool does say;
Today itself's too late; the wise lived yesterday.
(Cras vives? hodie jam vivere, Postume, serum est. Ille sapit quisquis, Posthume, vixit heri.)

MARTIAL, *Epigrams.* Bk. v, 58. (Cowley, tr.)

6
Live while ye may, Yet happy pair.

MILTON, *Paradise Lost.* Bk. iv, l. 533.

7
Rejoice, lest pleasureless ye die.
Within a little time must ye go by.
Stretch forth your open hands, and while ye live
Take all the gifts that Death and Life may give!

WILLIAM MORRIS, *The Earthly Paradise: March.*

8
Make the most of life you may—
Life is short and wears away.

WILLIAM OLDYS, *Busy, Curious, Thirsty Fly.*

9
Ah, make the most of what we yet may spend,
Before we too into the Dust descend;
Dust into Dust, and under Dust, to lie,
Sans Wine, sans Song, sans Singer, and—sans End!

OMAR KHAYYÁM, *Rubáiyát.* St. 24. (Fitzgerald, tr.)

10
While you can, and still are in your springtime, have your fun; for the years pass like flowing water. (Dum licet, et vernos etiamnum educitis annos, Ludite: eunt anni more fluentis aquæ.)

OVID, *Ars Amatoria.* Bk. iii, l. 61.

Ay, and make haste, nor wait the coming hours; he who is not ready today will be less so tomorrow. (Sed propera, nec te venturas differ in horas; Qui est non hodie, cras minus aptus erit.)

OVID, *Remediorum Amoris,* l. 93.

11
Today let me live well; none knows what may be tomorrow. (Σήμερον ἐσθλὰ παθω; τὸ γαρ αὔριον οὐδενὶ δῆλον.)

PALLADAS. (*Greek Anthology.* Bk. v, epig. 72.)

Let us live then while it goes well with us. (Ergo vivamus, dum licet esse bene.)

PETRONIUS, *Satyricon.* Sec. 34.

The whole life of man is but a point of time; let us enjoy it, therefore, while it lasts, and not spend it to no purpose.

PLUTARCH, *Of the Training of Children.*

12
Flavia's a wit, has too much sense to pray;
To toast our wants and wishes is her way;
Nor asks of God, but of her stars, to give
The mighty blessing "while we live to live."

POPE, *Moral Essays.* Epis. ii, l. 87.

With too much quickness ever to be taught;
With too much thinking to have common thought:
You purchase pain with all that joy can give,
And die of nothing but a rage to live.

POPE, *Moral Essays.* Epis. ii, l. 97.

13
We, we live! ours are the hours,
And the living have their claims.
(Wir, wir leben! Unser sind die Stunden
Und der Lebende hat Recht.)

SCHILLER, *An die Freude.* St. 1.

14
As long as you live, keep learning how to live.
(Quemadmodum vivas, quamdiu vivas.)

SENECA, *Epistulæ ad Lucilium.* Epis. lxxvi, sec. 3. Quoted as a proverb.

Even in the longest life real living is the least portion thereof. (Etiam in longissima vita minimum esse, quod vivitur.)

SENECA, *Epistulæ ad Lucilium.* Epis. xcix, 12.

Let us balance life's account every day. (Cotidie cum vita paria faciamus.)

SENECA, *Epistulæ ad Lucilium.* Epis. ci, sec. 8.

Begin at once to live, and count each separate day as a separate life. (Ideo propera vivere et singulos dies singulas vitas puta.)

SENECA, *Epistulæ ad Lucilium.* Epis. ci, sec. 10.

1
Gonzalo: Here is everything advantageous to life.
Antonio: True; save means to live.
SHAKESPEARE, *The Tempest*. Act ii, sc. 1, l. 49.

2
May you live all the days of your life.
SWIFT, *Polite Conversation*. Dial. ii.

3
A short life and a merry life, I cry.
JOHN TATHAM, *The Rump*. Act i. (1660)

4
I cannot rest from travel: I will drink
Life to the lees.
TENNYSON, *Ulysses*, l. 6.

5
We live not in our moments or our years:
The present we fling from us like the rind
Of some sweet future, which we after find
Bitter to taste.
RICHARD CHENEVIX TRENCH, *To ——*.

6
Enjoy your own lot. (Utere sorte tua.)
VERGIL, *Æneid*. Bk. xii, l. 932.

Somehow the grace, the bloom of things has flown,
And of all men we are most wretched, who
Must live each other's lives and not our own.
OSCAR WILDE, *Humanitad*. St. 68.

7
Set forth the wine and the dice, and perish who thinks of tomorrow!
Here's Death twitching my ear, "Live," says he, "for I'm coming!"
(Pone merum et talos. Pereat, qui crastina curat!
Mors aurem vellens, "vivite," ait, "venio.")
VERGIL, *Copa*, l. 37. (Helen Waddell, tr.) Quoted by Justice O. W. Holmes in radio address on his 90th birthday, 8 March, 1931: "Death plucks my ear and says, 'Live—I am coming.'"

8
Since the bounty of Providence is new every day,
As we journey through life let us live by the way.
WALTER WATSON, *Sit Down, My Crony.*

9
Let us live, then, and be glad,
While young life's before us;
After youthful pastime had,
After old age, hard and sad,
Earth will slumber o'er us.
(Gaudeamus igitur dum juvenes sumus;
Post jucundam juventutem,
Post molestam senectutem,
Nos habebit humus.)
UNKNOWN, *Gaudeamus Igitur*. (Symonds, tr.)

10
While we live, let us live. (Dum vivimus, vivamus.)
UNKNOWN. The earliest known appearance of this familiar Latin phrase is in *Inscriptiones Grutuli*, a medieval collection of proverbs.

Live while you live, the epicure would say,
And seize the pleasures of the present day;
Live while you live, the sacred preacher cries,
And give to God each moment as it flies.
Lord, in my view let both united be;
I live in pleasure when I live to Thee.
DR. PHILIP DODDRIDGE, *Epigram on His Family Arms*. The motto attached to the arms was "Dum Vivimus, Vivamus."

Others mistrust and say, "But time escapes:
Live now or never!"
He said, "What's time? Leave Now for dogs and apes!
Man has Forever."
ROBERT BROWNING, *A Grammarian's Funeral.*

11
The pleasures of youth are flowers but of May;
Our Life's but a Vapour, our body's but clay.
Oh, let me live well though I live but one day.
UNKNOWN, *The Old Woman's Wishes*. (D'URFEY, *Pills to Purge Melancholy*. 1661.)

XVIII—Life: I Have Lived!

12
I die,—but first I have possess'd,
And come what may, I *have been* bless'd.
BYRON, *The Giaour*, l. 1114.

13
However, as far as I am concerned, I have lived my time. (Sed mihi quidem βεβιῶται.)
CICERO, *Epistulæ ad Atticum*. Bk. xiv, epis. 21.

To-morrow let my sun his beams display,
Or in clouds hide them: I have lived to-day.
ABRAHAM COWLEY, *A Vote.*

14
Fill my hour, ye gods, so that I may not say, whilst I have done this, "Behold, also, an hour of my life is gone,"—but rather, "I have lived an hour."
EMERSON, *Society and Solitude: Works and Days.*

15
We are the masters of the days that were:
We have lived, we have loved, we have suffered . . . even so.
W. E. HENLEY, *What Is to Come.*

16
That man lives happy and in command of himself, who from day to day can say, "I have lived!" (Ille potens sui Lætusque deget, cui licet in diem Dixisse Vixi!)
HORACE, *Odes*. Bk. iii, ode 29, l. 41.

Happy the man, and happy he alone,
He, who can call to-day his own:
He who, secure within, can say:
"To-morrow do thy worst, for I have liv'd to-day."
HORACE, *Odes*, iii, 29. (Dryden, tr., l. 65.)

Not Heav'n itself upon the past has pow'r;
But what has been, has been, and I have had my hour.
HORACE, *Odes*, iii, 29. (Dryden, tr., l. 71.)

17
I have fought my fight, I have lived my life,
I have drunk my share of wine;

From Trier to Coln there was never a knight
Led a merrier life than mine.

CHARLES KINGSLEY, *The Knight's Leap*. A similar inscription appears under the painting by Frans Hals, "The Laughing Cavalier."

1
I have lived; nor shall maligner fortune ever
Take from me what an earlier hour once gave.
(Pervixi: neque enim fortuna malignior unquam
Erepiet nobis quod prior hora dedit.)

PETRONIUS, *Fragments*. No. 84.

2
I have enjoyed earthly happiness,
I have lived and loved.
(Ich habe genossen das irdische Glück,
Ich habe gelebt und geliebet.)

SCHILLER, *Piccolomini*. Act iii, sc. 7, l. 9.

I have lived and I have loved;
I have waked and I have slept;
I have sung and I have danced;
I have smiled and I have wept.

CHARLES MACKAY, *Vixi*.

3
When a man has said, "I have lived," every morning he arises he receives a bonus. (Quisquis dixit "vixi," cotidie ad lucrum surgit.)

SENECA, *Epistulæ ad Lucilium*. Epis. xii, sec. 9.

4
What expiating agony
May for him, damned to poesy,
Shut in that little sentence be—
What deep austerities of strife—
He "lived his life." "He lived *his* life."

FRANCIS THOMPSON, *A Judgement in Heaven: Epilogue*.

5
I have lived; I have run the course Fortune allotted me;
Now my shade shall descend illustrious to the grave.
(Vixi, et quem dederat cursum Fortuna, peregi:
Et nunc magna mei sub terras currit imago.)

VERGIL, *Æneid*. Bk. iv, l. 653.

XIX—Life: Living Life Over

6
Yet for my own part I would not live over my hours past, or begin again the thread of my days, not upon Cicero's ground, because I have lived them well, but for fear I should live them worse.

SIR THOMAS BROWNE, *Religio Medici*. Pt. i, sec. 49.

Few men would be content to cradle it once again; except a man can lead his second life better than the first, a man may be doubly condemned for living evilly twice.

SIR THOMAS BROWNE, *To a Friend*. Sec. 13.

7
If I were to live my life over again, I would do all that I have done. (Si je recommençais ma carrière, je ferai tout ce que j'ai fait.)

FONTANELLE, *Dialogues des Morts*.

Were I to live my life over again, I should live it just as I have done. I neither complain of the past, nor fear the future.

MONTAIGNE, *Essays*. Bk. iii, ch. 2.

Vain was the man, and false as vain,
Who said, were he ordained to run
His long career of life again
He would do all that he *had* done.

THOMAS MOORE, *My Birthday*.

8
I should have no objection to a repetition of the same life from its beginning, only asking the advantages authors have in a second edition to correct some faults of the first.

BENJAMIN FRANKLIN, *Autobiography*. Ch. 1. *See also under* FRANKLIN.

9
I would live the same life over if I had to live again.

ADAM LINDSAY GORDON, *The Sick Stockrider*.

10
Who that hath ever been
Could bear to be no more?
Yet who would tread again the scene
He trod through life before?

MONTGOMERY, *The Falling Leaf*. St. 7.

XX—Life: Quality, Not Quantity

11
It matters not how long we live, but how.

P. J. BAILEY, *Festus: Wood and Water*.

12
A short space of life is long enough for living well and honorably. (Breve tempus ætatis satis longum est ad bene honesteque vivendum.)

CICERO, *De Senectute*. Ch. xix, sec. 70.

Who well lives, long lives; for this age of ours
Should not be numbered by years, days, and hours.

DU BARTAS, *Devine Weekes and Workes*. Week ii, day 4. (Sylvester, tr.)

13
The life given us by nature is short; but the memory of a well-spent life is eternal. (Brevis a natura nobis vita data est; at memoria bene reditæ vitæ sempiterna.)

CICERO, *Philippicæ*. No. xiv, sec. 12.

No one has lived too short a life who has performed its duties with unblemished character. (Nemo parum diu vixit, qui virtutis perfectæ perfecto functus est munere.)

CICERO, *Tusculanarum Disputationum*. Bk. i, ch. 45, sec. 109.

14
Life is not measured by the time we live.

GEORGE CRABBE, *The Village*. Bk. ii.

Life is not dated merely by years. Events are sometimes the best calendars.

BENJAMIN DISRAELI, *Venetia*. Bk. ii, ch. 1.

15
So that my life be brave, what though not long?

WILLIAM DRUMMOND, *Sonnets*. No. xii.

I have lived enough, for I die unconquered. (Satis vixi, invictus enim morior.)

EPAMINONDAS. (CORNELIUS NEPOS, *Lives: Epaminondas.*)

1
It is the depth at which we live and not at all the surface extension that imports.

EMERSON, *Society and Solitude: Works and Days.*

2
To live long is almost everyone's wish, but to live well is the ambition of a few.

JOHN HUGHES, *The Lay Monk.* No. 18.

3
It is not a great thing to have been to Jerusalem, but to have lived well is a great thing. (Non magnum est Hierosolymis fuisse, sed bene vixisse magnum est.)

ST. JEROME. (ERASMUS, *De Colloquiorum Utilitate.*)

4
Nor love thy life, nor hate; but what thou livest
Live well; how long or short permit to heaven.

MILTON, *Paradise Lost.* Bk. xi, l. 549.

5
I have lived to a riper age than years can show. 'Tis deeds make old: these must thou number: with these was my life fulfilled, not with idle years.

OVID, *Consolatio ad Liviam,* l. 448.

We live in deeds, not years; in thoughts, not breaths;
In feelings, not in figures on a dial.
We should count time by heart-throbs. He most lives
Who thinks most, feels the noblest, acts the best.

P. J. BAILEY, *Festus: A Country Town.*

He, who grown aged in this world of woe,
In deeds, not years, piercing the depths of life,
So that no wonder waits him.

BYRON, *Childe Harold.* Canto iii, st. 5.

A life spent worthily should be measured by a nobler line,—by deeds, not years.

SHERIDAN, *Pizarro.* Act iv, sc. 1.

Think'st thou existence doth depend on time?
It doth; but actions are our epochs.

BYRON, *Manfred.* Act ii, sc. 1, l. 54.

6
It is no happiness to live long, nor unhappiness to die soon; happy is he that hath lived long enough to die well.

FRANCIS QUARLES, *Enchiridion.* Cent. ii, No. 84.

7
The measure of a man's life is the well-spending of it, and not the length.

PLUTARCH, *Consolatio ad Apollonium.*

8
No parent would wish for his children that they might live forever, but rather that their lives might be noble and honored. (Neque quisquam parens liberis uti æterni forent optavit, magis uti boni honestique vitam exigerent.)

SALLUST, *Jugurtha.* Ch. 85, sec. 50.

9
Life, if thou knowest how to use it, is long enough. (Vita, si scias uti, longa est.)

SENECA, *De Brevitate Vitæ.* Sec. ii.

10
Mere living is not a good, but living well. (Non enim vivere bonum est, sed bene vivere.)

SENECA, *Epistulæ ad Lucilium.* Epis. lxx, 4.

We should strive, not to live long, but to live rightly. (Non ut diu vivamus curandum est, sed ut satis.)

SENECA, *Epistulæ ad Lucilium.* Epis. xciii, 2.

The point is, not how long you live, but how nobly you live. (Quam bene vivas refert, non quam diu.)

SENECA, *Epistulæ ad Lucilium.* Epis. ci, sec. 15.

He liveth long who liveth well!
All other life is short and vain;
He liveth longest who can tell
Of living most for heavenly gain.

HORATIUS BONAR, *He Liveth Long Who Liveth Well.*

Wish not so much to live long as to live well.

BENJAMIN FRANKLIN, *Poor Richard,* 1738.

They only have lived long who have lived virtuously.

SHERIDAN, *Pizarro.* Act iv, sc. 1.

Desire not to live long, but to live well;
How long we live not years, but actions, tell.

ROWLAND WATKYNS, *Flamma sine Fumo: The Hour Glass.*

For they lived long enough, that have lived well enough.

THOMAS WILSON, *Arte of Rhetorique,* 83. (1560)

11
The wise man will live as long as he ought, not as long as he can. . . . He always reflects concerning the quality, and not the quantity, of his life. (Itaque sapiens vivit, quantum debet, non quantum potest. . . . Cogitat semper, qualis vita, non quanta sit.)

SENECA, *Epistulæ ad Lucilium.* Epis. lxx, 4. Quoted by MONTAIGNE, *Essays.* Bk. ii, ch. 3.

The good man should not live as long as it pleases him, but as long as he ought. (Cum bono viro vivendum sit non quamdiu juvat sed quamdiu oportet.)

SENECA, *Epistulæ ad Lucilium.* Epis. civ, 3.

It is with life as with a play: what matters is not how long it is, but how good it is. (Quomodo fabula, sic vita: non quam diu, sed quam bene acta sit, refert.)

SENECA, *Epistulæ ad Lucilium.* Epis. lxxvii, 20.

Life is long if it is full. (Longa est vita, si plena est.)

SENECA, *Epistulæ ad Lucilium.* Epis. xciii, 2.

Let us see to it that our lives, like jewels of great price, be noteworthy not because of their width, but because of their weight.

SENECA, *Epistulæ ad Lucilium.* Epis. xciii, 4.

Just as one of small stature can be a perfect

man, so a life of small compass can be a perfect life.

SENECA, *Epistulæ ad Lucilium*. Epis. xciii, 7.

Circles are praised, not that abound
In largeness, but the exactly round:
So life we praise that does excel
Not in much time, but acting well.

EDMUND WALLER, *Long and Short Life*.

1
The measure of a happy life is not from the fewer or more suns we behold, the fewer or more breaths we draw, or meals we repeat, but from the having once lived well, acted our part handsomely, and made our exit cheerfully.

LORD SHAFTESBURY, *Characteristics*. Vol. i, p. 316.

2
The life of a man of virtue and talent, who should die in his thirtieth year, is, with regard to his own feelings, longer than that of a miserable priest-ridden slave who dreams out a century of goodness.

SHELLEY, *Queen Mab: Notes*.

Perhaps the perishing ephemeron enjoys a longer life than the tortoise.

SHELLEY, *Queen Mab: Notes*.

3
That life is long, which answers life's great end.
The time that bears no fruit, deserves no name;
The man of wisdom is the man of years.

YOUNG, *Night Thoughts*. Night v, l. 773.

XXI—Life: The Simple Life: Its Virtues

See also Simplicity

4
Remote from busy life's bewildered way.

CAMPBELL, *The Pleasures of Hope*. Pt. 2, l. 91.

Far from the madding crowd's ignoble strife,
Their sober wishes never learn'd to stray;
Along the cool, sequester'd vale of life
They kept the noiseless tenor of their way.

THOMAS GRAY, *Elegy Written in a Country Church-yard*, l. 73. (1751) Last line often misquoted "even tenor." "Far From the Madding Crowd" used by Thomas Hardy as the title of a novel.

Through the sequester'd vale of rural life
The venerable patriarch guileless held
The tenor of his way.

BEILBY PORTEUS, *Death*, l. 109. (c. 1775)

5
The supreme Good they believed to be the thing which . . . they expressed by the formula, "Life according to nature." (Secundum naturam vivere.)

CICERO, *De Finibus*. Bk. iv, ch. 10, sec. 26. CICERO is speaking of the Stoics.

I sought the simple life that Nature yields.

GEORGE CRABBE, *The Village*. Bk. i.

A child has beaten me in simplicity of living. (Παιδίον με νενίκηκεν εὐτελείᾳ.)

DIOGENES, throwing away his only utensil, a shell from which to drink, when he saw a boy drinking from his hands. (DIOGENES LAERTIUS, *Diogenes* Bk. vi, sec. 37.)

6
If you live according to nature, you will never be poor; if according to the world's opinion, you will never be rich. (Si ad naturam vives, numquam eris pauper; si ad opiniones, numquam eris dives.)

EPICURUS, *Fragments*. No. 201. (SENECA, *Epistulæ ad Lucilium*. Epis. xvi, sec. 7.)

7
We have learned the lesson of Time, and we know three things of worth;
Only to sow and sing and reap in the land of our birth.

RICHARD LE GALLIENNE, *The Cry of the Little Peoples*.

8
Anything for a quiet life!

THOMAS HEYWOOD, *The Captives*. Act iii, sc. 3. (1624) MIDDLETON; Title of play. (1662) SWIFT, *Polite Conversation*. Dial. 1, etc., etc.

Anythin' for a quiet life, as the man said wen he took the sitivation at the lighthouse.

DICKENS, *Pickwick Papers*. Ch. 43.

9
Taught to live
The easiest way, nor with perplexing thoughts
To interrupt the sweet of life.

MILTON, *Paradise Lost*. Bk. viii, l. 182.

His life
Private, unactive, calm, contemplative.

MILTON, *Paradise Regained*. Bk. ii, l. 80.

His life is neither tossed in boisterous seas
Of troublous world, nor lost in slothful ease.

PHINEAS FLETCHER, *The Happiness of the Shepherd's Life*.

10
Among good things, I prove and find
The quiet life doth most abound.

JOHN RAY, *English Proverbs*.

What sweet delight a quiet life affords.

WILLIAM DRUMMOND, *Sonnet*.

11
The happy life, which flows along with steady course, completely under the soul's control. (Beata vita, secundo defluens cursu, arbitrii sui tota.)

SENECA, *Epistulæ ad Lucilium*. Epis. cxx, 11.

12
A loving little life of sweet small works.

SWINBURNE, *Bothwell*. Act i, sc. 1.

13
So passed their life, a clear united stream,
By care unruffled.

THOMSON, *The Seasons: Summer*, l. 1189.

So his life has flowed
From its mysterious urn a sacred stream,
In whose calm depth the beautiful and pure
Alone are mirrored.

THOMAS N. TALFOURD, *Ion*. Act i, sc. 1, l. 138.

A life that leads melodious days.

TENNYSON, *In Memoriam*. Sec. xxxiii, st. 2.

Whose life was like the violet sweet,

As climbing jasmine pure.
WORDSWORTH, *Elegiac Stanzas.*

1
An elegant sufficiency, content,
Retirement, rural quiet, friendship, books,
Ease and alternate labour, useful life,
Progressive virtue, and approving Heaven!
THOMSON, *The Seasons: Spring*, l. 1161.

2
I love a life whose plot is simple,
And does not thicken with every pimple.
H. D. THOREAU, *Conscience.*

My life is like a stroll upon the beach,
As near the ocean's edge as I can go.
H. D. THOREAU, *The Fisher's Boy.*

3
What is the simple life? . . . It is a form of life described by pastoral poets, or the New Testament, but not livable today.
CHARLES WAGNER, *The Simple Life.* Ch. 7.

Humanity lives and always has lived on certain elemental provisions.
CHARLES WAGNER, *The Simple Life.* Ch. 3.

4
For all her quiet life flowed on
As meadow streamlets flow,
Where fresher green reveals alone
The noiseless ways they go.
J. G. WHITTIER, *The Friend's Burial.* St. 9.

So didst thou travel on life's common way
In cheerful godliness.
WORDSWORTH, *Poems Dedicated to National Independence.* Pt. i, No. 14.

5
Plain living and high thinking are no more:
The homely beauty of the good old cause
Is gone; our peace, our fearful innocence,
And pure religion breathing household laws.
WORDSWORTH, *Poems Dedicated to National Independence.* Pt. i, No. 13.

A conspicuous example of plain living and high thinking.
THOMAS HAWEIS, *Evenings for the People: George Herbert.*

I will show myself highly fed and lowly taught.
SHAKESPEARE, *All's Well that Ends Well.* Act ii, sc. 2, l. 3.

6
Who God doth late and early pray
More of his grace than gifts to lend;
And entertains the harmless day
With a religious book or friend.
SIR HENRY WOTTON, *The Character of a Happy Life.*

7
Oh, for the simple life,
For tents and starry skies!
ISRAEL ZANGWILL, *Aspiration.*

XXII—Life: The Simple Life: Its Faults

8
They do not live but linger.
ROBERT BURTON, *Anatomy of Melancholy.* Pt. i, sec. ii, mem. 3, subs. 10.

A quiet life, which was not life at all.
E. B. BROWNING, *Aurora Leigh.* Bk. i, l. 289.

To live a life half dead, a living death.
MILTON, *Samson Agonistes,* l. 100.

A life both dull and dignified.
SCOTT, *Marmion.* Canto vi, st. 1.

9
Born with a monocle he stares at life,
And sends his soul on pensive promenades.
DONALD EVANS, *En Monocle.*

10
Was it for this I uttered prayers,
And sobbed and cursed and kicked the stairs,
That now, domestic as a plate,
I should retire at half-past eight?
EDNA ST. VINCENT MILLAY, *Grown-Up.*

11
For to live at ease is not to live.
PERSIUS, *Satires.* Sat. v, l. 226. (Dryden, tr.)

12
Fix'd like a plant on his peculiar spot,
To draw nutrition, propagate, and rot.
POPE, *Essay on Man.* Epis. ii, l. 63.

See dying vegetables life sustain,
See life dissolving vegetate again.
POPE, *Essay on Man.* Epis. iii, l. 15.

One really lives nowhere; one does but vegetate and wish it all at an end.
FANNY BURNEY, *Cecilia.* Bk. iv, ch. 7.

13
Degenerate sons and daughters,
Life is too strong for you—
It takes life to love Life.
EDGAR LEE MASTERS, *Lucinda Matlock.*

XXIII—Life: A Little Work, A Little Play

14
We are the voices of the wandering wind,
Which moan for rest and rest can never find;
Lo! as the wind is so is mortal life,
A moan, a sigh, a sob, a storm, a strife.
EDWIN ARNOLD, *Light of Asia.* Bk. iii, l. 23.

15
I've played a little, And I've worked a lot,
I've loved and I've hated, As who would not?
I've had some fun And I've had some sorrow,
I've had to steal And I've had to borrow,
I've sinned a little, But all in all
I've hardly tasted Life at all.
But Death just smiled as he beckoned ahead—
"That was life," He gently said.
MILT BRONSTON, *Merry-Go-'Round.*

16
A little sun, a little rain,
A soft wind blowing from the west,
And woods and fields are sweet again,
And warmth within the mountain's breast.

A little love, a little trust,
A soft impulse, a sudden dream,
And life as dry as desert dust,
Is fresher than a mountain stream.
STOPFORD A. BROOKE, *Earth and Man.*

1
The king commands us, and the doctor quacks us,
The priest instructs, and so our life exhales,
A little breath, love, wine, ambition, fame,
Fighting, devotion, dust—perhaps a name.
BYRON, *Don Juan*. Canto ii, st. 4.

2
We come, we cry, and that is life;
We yawn, we go, and that is death.
(On entre, on crie, et c'est la vie!
On bâille, on sort, et c'est la mort!)
AUSONE DE CHANCEL, *Lines in an Album*. (1836)

We are born, then cry, We know not for why,
And all our lives long Still but the same song.
NATHANIEL CROUCH, attr., *Life*. (Appeared originally in *Bristol Drollery*, 1674.)

3
That he was born, it cannot be denied,
He ate, drank, slept, talked politics, and died.
JOHN CUNNINGHAM, *On an Alderman*.

4
They are not long, the weeping and the laughter,
Love and desire and hate:
I think they have no portion in us after
We pass the gate.
ERNEST DOWSON, *Vitæ Summa Brevis*.

They are not long, the days of wine and roses:
Out of a misty dream
Our path emerges for a while, then closes
Within a dream.
ERNEST DOWSON, *Vitæ Summa Brevis*.

4a
A crust of bread and a corner to sleep in,
A minute to smile and an hour to weep in,
A pint of joy to a peck of trouble,
And never a laugh but the moans come double;
And that is life!
PAUL LAURENCE DUNBAR, *Life*.

5
A little rule, a little sway,
A sunbeam in a winter's day,
Is all the proud and mighty have
Between the cradle and the grave.
JOHN DYER, *Grongar Hill*, l. 89.

6
He lives not who can refuse me;
All my force saith, Come and use me:
A gleam of sun, a summer rain,
And all the zone is green again.
EMERSON, *Fragments: Nature*. Frag. 28.

A train of gay and clouded days
Dappled with joy and grief and praise,
Beauty to fire us, saints to save,
Escort us to a little grave.
EMERSON, *Fragments: Life*. Frag. 1.

7
A little season of love and laughter,
Of light and life, and pleasure and pain,
And a horror of outer darkness after,
And the dust returneth to dust again.
Then the lesser life shall be as the greater,
And the lover of life shall join the hater,
And the one thing cometh, sooner or later,
And no one knoweth the loss or gain.
ADAM LINDSAY GORDON, *The Swimmer*. St. 10.

8
Life has given me of its best—
Laughter and weeping, labour and rest,
Little of gold, but lots of fun;
Shall I then sigh that all is done?
No, not I; while the new road lies
All untrodden, before my eyes.
NORAH M. HOLLAND, *Life*.

9
None knoweth a better thing than this:
The Sword, Love, Song, Honour, Sleep.
None knoweth a surer thing than this:
Birth, Sorrow, Pain, Weariness, Death.
WILLIAM SHARP, *Chant of Ardan the Pict*.

10
A little while the tears and laughter,
The willow and the rose;
A little while, and what comes after
No man knows.

An hour to sing, to love and linger,
Then lutanist and lute
Will fall on silence, song and singer
Both be mute.
DON MARQUIS, *A Little While*.

11
A little time for laughter,
A little time to sing,
A little time to kiss and cling,
And no more kissing after.
PHILIP BOURKE MARSTON, *After*.

12
A little work, a little sweating, a few brief, flying years; a little joy, a little fretting, some smiles and then some tears; a little resting in the shadow, a struggle to the height, a futile search for El Dorado, and then we say Good Night.
WALT MASON, *The Journey*.

13
Life is vain; a little love, a little hate, and then—Good-day! Life is short; a little hoping, a little dreaming, and then—Good-night! Life is whatever God wills it; and, such as it is, it's enough!
(La vie est vaine: Un peu d'amour,
Un peu de haine . . . Et puis—bon jour!
La vie est brève: Un peu d'espoir,
Un peu de rêve . . . Et puis—bon soir!
La vie est telle Que dieu la fit;
Et, telle qu'elle, Elle suffit!)
LÉON VON MONTENÆKEN, *Peu de Chose et Presque Trop*.

Life is but jest: a dream, a doom,
A gleam, a gloom—and then, good rest!
Life is but play; a throb, a tear,
A sob, a sneer—and then, good day.
LÉON VON MONTENÆKEN, *Nothing and Too Much*. His English version of *Peu de Chose*.

A little work, a little play
To keep us going—and so, good-day!
A little warmth, a little light
Of love's bestowing—and so, good-night!
A little fun, to match the sorrow
Of each day's gowing—and so, good-morrow!
A little trust that when we die
We reap our sowing—and so, good-bye!
GEORGE DU MAURIER. Paraphrase of *Peu de Chose* by Montenæken, used as conclusion for *Trilby*. Last couplet inscribed on Du Maurier memorial tablet, Hampstead churchyard.

Enough! or Too much.
WILLIAM BLAKE, *Proverbs of Hell.*

1
A little pain, a little pleasure,
A little heaping up of treasure;
Then no more gazing upon the sun.
All things must end that have begun.
JOHN PAYNE, *Kyrielle.*

2
A sudden wakin', a sudden weepin',
A li'l suckin', a li'l sleepin';
A cheel's full joys an' a cheel's short sorrows,
Wi' a power o' faith in gert tomorrows.
EDEN PHILLPOTTS, *Man's Days.*

3
One wakes, rises, dresses, goes out;
One comes home, dines, sups, goes to bed, sleeps.
(On s'éveille, on se lève, on s'habille, et on sort;
On rentre, on dine, on soupe, on se couche, on dort.)
DE PIIS, *C'Est la Vie!*

What trifling coil do we poor mortals keep;
Wake, eat and drink, evacuate, and sleep.
MATTHEW PRIOR, *Human Life.*

To get the whole world out of bed
And washed, and dressed, and warmed, and fed,
To work, and back to bed again,
Believe me, Saul, costs worlds of pain.
JOHN MASEFIELD, *The Everlasting Mercy.*

4
Man has here two and a half minutes—one to smile, one to sigh, and a half to love: for in the midst of this minute he dies. (Der Mensch hat hier dritthalb Minuten, eine zu lächeln—eine zu seufzen—und eine halbe zu lieben: denn mitten in dieser Minute stirbt er.)
JEAN PAUL RICHTER, *Hesperus.* Ch. 4.

5
Say, what is life? 'Tis to be born,
A helpless Babe, to greet the light
With a sharp wail, as if the morn
Foretold a cloudy noon and night;
To weep, to sleep, and weep again,
With sunny smiles between; and then?
J. G. SAXE, *The Story of Life.*

6
A little gain, a little pain,
A laugh, lest you may moan;
A little blame, a little fame,
A star-gleam on a stone.
ROBERT W. SERVICE, *Just Think.*

7
Forenoon and afternoon and night—Forenoon
And afternoon and night—forenoon, and what!
The empty song repeats itself. No more?
Yea, that is life: Make this forenoon sublime,
This afternoon a psalm, this night a prayer,
And time is conquered and thy crown is won.
E. R. SILL, *Life.*

8
A little fruit a little while is ours,
And the worm finds it soon.
SWINBURNE, *Atalanta in Calydon: Chorus.*

A little sorrow, a little pleasure,
Fate metes us from the dusty measure
That holds the date of all of us;
We are born with travail and strong crying,
And from the birth-day to the dying
The likeness of our life is thus.
SWINBURNE, *Ilicet.* St. 18.

9
What is this passing scene?
A peevish April day!
A little sun—a little rain,
And then night sweeps along the plain,
And all things fade away.
HENRY KIRKE WHITE, *On Disappointment.*

10
This is the height of our deserts:
A little pity for life's hurts;
A little rain, a little sun,
A little sleep when work is done.
UNKNOWN, *Deservings.*

XXIV—Life: Whence and Whither

11
I was born some time ago, but I know not why:
I have lived—I hardly know either how or where:
Some time or another, I suppose, I shall die;
But where, how, or when, I neither know nor care!
GEORGE ARNOLD, *An Autobiography.*

12
What endless questions vex the thought, of
Whence and Whither, When and How.
SIR RICHARD BURTON, *Kasîdah.* Pt. ii, st. 3.

Between two worlds, life hovers like a star
'Twixt night and morn, upon the horizon's verge.
How little do we know that which we are!
How less what we may be!
BYRON, *Don Juan.* Canto xv, st. 99.

13
Seek not the wherefore, race of human kind.
DANTE, *Purgatorio.* Canto iii, l. 35.

14
You hail from Dream-land, Dragon-fly?
A stranger hither? So am I,
And (sooth to say) I wonder why
We either of us came!
AGNES M. DARMESTETER, *To a Dragonfly.*

15
A man's ingress into the world is naked and bare,

His progress through the world is trouble and care;
And lastly, his egress out of the world, is nobody knows where.
If we do well here, we shall do well there;
I can tell you no more if I preach a whole year.
JOHN EDWIN, *The Eccentricities of John Edwin*. Vol. i, p. 74.

Our ingress into the world
Was naked and bare;
Our progress through the world
Is trouble and care;
Our egress from the world
Will be nobody knows where:
But if we do well here,
We shall do well there.
LONGFELLOW, *Tales of a Wayside Inn:* Pt. ii, *The Cobbler of Hagenau*. Quoted as "a familiar tune."

1
Not whence, but why and whither are the vital questions.
A. W. GREELY, *Reminiscences*, p. 338.

2
I think, ofttimes, that lives of men may be
Likened to wandering winds that come and go
Not knowing whence they rise, whither they blow
O'er the vast globe, voiceful of grief or glee.
PAUL HAMILTON HAYNE, *A Comparison*.

Our life is but a dark and stormy night,
To which sense yields a weak and glimmering light,
While wandering man thinks he discerneth all
By that which makes him but mistake, and fall.
EDWARD HERBERT, *To His Mistress, For Her Picture*.

3
Every cradle asks us "Whence?" and every coffin "Whither?"
R. G. INGERSOLL, *Oration at a Child's Grave*.

4
For men to tell how human life began
Is hard; for who himself beginning knew?
MILTON, *Paradise Lost*. Bk. viii, l. 250.

5
Life have we loved, through green leaf and through sere,
Though still the less we knew of its intent.
WILLIAM MORRIS, *The Earthly Paradise: L'Envoi*.

6
Into this Universe, and *Why* not knowing
Nor *Whence*, like Water willy-nilly flowing;
And out of it, as Wind along the Waste,
I know not *Whither*, willy-nilly blowing.
OMAR KHAYYÁM, *Rubáiyát*. St. 29. (Fitzgerald, tr.)

7
Like following life thro' creatures you dissect,
You lose it in the moment you detect.
POPE, *Moral Essays*. Epis. i, l. 29.

8
Our past is clean forgot,
Our present is and is not,
Our future's a sealed seedplot,
And what betwixt them are we?
D. G. ROSSETTI, *The Cloud Confines*. St. 5.

9
If we could push ajar the gates of life,
And stand within, and all God's workings see,
We could interpret all this doubt and strife,
And for each mystery could find a key.
MARY LOUISE SMITH, *Sometime*.

10
What use to brood? This life of mingled pains
And joys to me
Despite of every Faith and Creed, remains
The Mystery.
TENNYSON, *To Mary Boyle*.

11
Never had anyone so correct an estimate of life but that circumstances, time and experience ever bring him something new and ever instruct him. (Numquam ita quisquam bene subducta ratione ad vitam fuit, Quin res, ætas usus semper aliquid apportet novi, Aliquid moneat.)
TERENCE, *Adelphi*, l. 855. (Act v, sc. 4.)

12
Life is arched with changing skies:
Rarely are they what they seem:
Children we of smiles and sighs—
Much we know, but more we dream.
WILLIAM WINTER, *Light and Shadow*.

13
Here are we, in a bright and breathing world:
Our origin, what matters it?
WORDSWORTH, *The Excursion*. Bk. iii, l. 237.

XXV—Life: Its Shortness and Uncertainty

See also Man: His Life a Span

14
Why should there be such turmoil and such strife,
To spin in length this feeble line of life?
FRANCIS BACON, *Translation of Certain Psalms*. Psalm 90.

15
The changes and chances of this mortal life.
Book of Common Prayer, Communion: Collect.

16
Life is short and time is swift;
Roses fade and shadows shift.
EBENEZER ELLIOTT, *Epigrams*.

17
The King in a carriage may ride,
And the Beggar may crawl at his side;
But in the general race,
They are travelling all the same pace.
EDWARD FITZGERALD, *Chrononoros*.

18
How short is life! how frail is human trust!
JOHN GAY, *Trivia*. Bk. iii, l. 235

Our life is short, and our days run
As fast away as does the sun.
ROBERT HERRICK, *Corinna's Going a-Maying.*

Those who complain of the shortness of life, let it slide by them without wishing to seize and make the most of its golden minutes.
WILLIAM HAZLITT, *Spirit of the Age*, p. 336.

1
It is pleasant to know that if one is now and then ingenious and fifty per cent lucky, he may hope to live out his three score years and ten although intellectually honest and self-respecting.
FRANKLIN H. GIDDINGS, *The Mighty Medicine.*

2
There are three wicks, you know, to the lamp of a man's life: brain, blood, and breath. Press the brain a little, its light goes out, followed by both the others. Stop the heart a minute, and out go all three of the wicks. Choke the air out of the lungs, and presently the fluid ceases to supply the other centers of flame, and all is soon stagnation, cold, and darkness.
O. W. HOLMES, *The Professor at the Breakfast-Table.* Ch. 11.

3
As leaves on the trees, such is the life of man. (Οἵη περ φύλλων γενεή, τοίη δὲ καὶ ἀνδρῶν.)
HOMER, *Iliad.* Bk. vi, l. 146.

Like leaves on trees the race of man is found,
Now green in youth, now with'ring on the ground:
Another race the foll'wing spring supplies,
They fall successive, and successive rise.
HOMER, *The Iliad.* Bk. vi, l. 181. (Pope, tr.)

Like phantoms painted on the magic slide,
Forth from the darkness of the past we glide,
As living shadows for a moment seen
In airy pageant on the eternal screen,
Traced by a ray from one unchanging flame,
Then seek the dust and stillness whence we came.
O. W. HOLMES, *A Rhymed Lesson*, l. 73.

There, like the wind through woods in riot,
Through him the gale of life blew high;
The tree of man was never quiet:
Then 'twas the Roman, now 'tis I.
A. E. HOUSMAN, *On Wenlock Edge.*

4
Who knows whether the gods will add tomorrow to the present hour? (Quis scit, an adjiciant hodiernæ crastina summæ Tempora di superbi?)
HORACE, *Odes.* Bk. iv, ode 7, l. 17.

How foolish it is to set out one's life, when one is not even owner of the morrow!
SENECA, *Epistulæ ad Lucilium.* Epis. ci, sec. 4.

No man has been so favored of the gods
That he could pledge himself another day.
(Nemo tam divos habuit faventes,
Crastinum ut posset sibi polliceri.)
SENECA, *Thyestes*, l. 619.

Learn that the present hour alone is man's.
SAMUEL JOHNSON, *Irene.* Act iii, sc. 2, l. 33.

5
For what is your life? It is even a vapour, that appeareth for a little time, and then vanisheth away.
New Testament: James, iv, 14.

6
I would not live alway: let me alone; for my days are vanity.
Old Testament: Job, vii, 16.

I would not live alway; I ask not to stay
Where storm after storm rises dark o'er the way.
WILLIAM A. MUHLENBERG, *I Would Not Live Alway.* St. 2.

They live ill who think they will live for ever. (Male vivunt qui se semper victuros putant.)
PUBLILIUS SYRUS, *Sententiæ.* No. 364.

He that lives longest lives but a little while.
SAMUEL JOHNSON, *The Rambler*, No. 71.

7
The short bloom of our brief and narrow life flies fast away. While we are calling for flowers and wine and women, age is upon us.
(Festinat enim decurrere velox
Flosculus angustæ miseræque brevissima vitæ
Portio; dum bibimus, dum serta unguenta puellas
Poscimus, obrepit non intellecta senectus.)
JUVENAL, *Satires.* Sat. ix, l. 126.

See how the autumn leaves float by decaying,
Down the wild swirls of the rain-swollen stream;
So fleet the works of men, back to their earth again;
Ancient and holy things fade like a dream.

Nay! see the spring-blossoms steal forth a-maying,
Clothing with tender hues orchard and glen;
So, though old *forms* pass by, ne'er shall their *spirit* die.
Look! England's bare boughs show green leaf again.
CHARLES KINGSLEY, *Old and New: A Parable.* Kingsley's only poetical contribution to *Politics for the People*, published 13 May, 1848, signed "Parson Lot." Omitted from many editions of his poems. The third and fourth lines were on the curtain of the famous opera house of Senator Tabor, Denver, Colorado, 1880.

8
Time fleeteth on, youth soon is gone,
Naught earthly may abide;
Life seemeth fast, but may not last—
It runs as runs the tide.
C. G. LELAND, *Many in One.* Pt. ii, st. 21.

Ah! love, the world is fading,
Flower by flower,
Each has his little house,
And each his hour.
RICHARD LE GALLIENNE, *A Ballad of Kind Little Creatures.*

9
Take them, O great Eternity!
Our little life is but a gust
That bends the branches of thy tree,

And trails its blossoms in the dust!
Longfellow, *Suspira.*

1
There's nothing certain in man's life but this:
That he must lose it.
Owen Meredith, *Clytemnestra.* Pt. xx.

2
From golden dawn to purple dusk,
Piled high with bales of smiles and tears,
The caravans are dropping down
Across the desert-sands of years.
J. Corson Miller, *The March of Humanity.*

3
Life is too short for any distant aim;
And cold the dull reward of future fame.
Lady Mary Wortley Montagu, *Epistle to the Earl of Burlington.*

4
How short is human life! the very breath
Which frames my words accelerates my death.
Hannah More, *King Hezekiah.*

5
Between us and hell or heaven there is nothing but life, which of all things is the frailest.
Pascal, *Thoughts.* Sec. iii, No. 213.

6
Nature has given man no better thing than shortness of life. (Natura vero nihil hominibus brevitate vitæ præstitit melius.)
Pliny the Elder, *Historia Naturalis.* Bk. vii, ch. 51, sec. 3.

7
Creatures of such an extempore being that the whole term of their life is confined within the space of a day; for they are brought forth in the morning, are in the prime of their existence at noon, grow old at night, and then die.
Plutarch, *Consolatio ad Apollonium.*

Life is but a day at most.
Burns, *Lines Written in Friars' Carse Hermitage.*

Alas, the moral brings a tear!
'Tis all a transient hour below;
And we that would detain thee here,
Ourselves as fleetly go!
Thomas Campbell, *Stanzas to J. P. Kemble.*

Even so our life like to this fading flower
Doth spring, bud, blossom, wither in an hour.
Each stealing moment on it makes a prey,
Steals away part, till all is stole away.
Unknown, *Poor Robin's Almanack,* 1664.

8
Lord, make me to know mine end, and the measure of my days, what it is; that I may know how frail I am.
Old Testament: Psalms, xxxix, 4.

The days of our years are three-score years and ten; and if by reason of strength they be four-score years, yet is their strength labour and sorrow; for it is soon cut off and we fly away.
Old Testament: Psalms, xc, 10.

As for man his days are as grass: as a flower of the field, so he flourisheth.
Old Testament: Psalms, ciii, 15.

The wind passeth over it, and it is gone; and the place thereof shall know it no more.
Old Testament: Psalms, ciii, 16.

You know how little while we have to stay,
And, once departed, may return no more.
Omar Khayyám, *Rubáiyát.* St. 3. (Fitzgerald, tr.)

9
The Wine of Life keeps oozing drop by drop,
The Leaves of Life keep falling one by one.
Omar Khayyám, *Rubáiyát.* St. 8. (Fitzgerald, tr.)

Think, in this batter'd Caravanserai
Whose Portals are alternate Night and Day,
How Sultán after Sultán with his Pomp
Abode his destin'd Hour and went his way.
Omar Khayyám, *Rubáiyát.* St. 17. (Fitzgerald, tr.)

I came like Water, and like Wind I go.
Omar Khayyám, *Rubáiyát.* St. 28. (Fitzgerald, tr.)

A Moment's Halt—a momentary taste
Of Being from the Well amid the Waste—
And Lo! the phantom Caravan has reach'd
The Nothing it set out from. Oh, make haste!
Omar Khayyám, *Rubáiyát.* St. 48. (Fitzgerald, tr.)

10
The very life which we enjoy is short. (Vita ipsa qua fruimur brevis est.)
Sallust, *Catilina.* Ch. i, sec. 3.

The part of life which we really live is short. (Exigua pars est vitæ quam nos vivimus.)
Seneca, *De Brevitate Vitæ.* Sec. ii.

Life speeds on with hurried step. (Properat cursu Vita citato.)
Seneca, *Hercules Furens,* l. 178.

11
And so, from hour to hour, we ripe and ripe,
And then, from hour to hour, we rot and rot;
And thereby hangs a tale.
Shakespeare, *As You Like It.* Act ii, sc. 7, l. 26.

And a man's life's no more than to say "One."
Shakespeare, *Hamlet.* Act v, sc. 2, l. 74.

We are such stuff
As dreams are made on, and our little life
Is rounded with a sleep.
Shakespeare, *The Tempest.* Act iv, sc. 1, l. 156.

12
The sands are number'd that make up my life;
Here must I stay, and here my life must end.
Shakespeare, *III Henry VI.* Act i, sc. 4, l. 25.

Like as the waves make towards the pebbled shore,
So do our minutes hasten to their end.
Shakespeare, *Sonnets,* No. lx.

The wise man warns me that life is but a dewdrop on the lotus leaf.
Rabindranath Tagore, *The Gardener.* No. 46.

Our life is scarce the twinkle of a star
In God's eternal day.
BAYARD TAYLOR, *Autumnal Vespers.*

1
Poor little life that toddles half an hour
Crown'd with a flower or two, and there an end.
TENNYSON, *Lucretius,* l. 228.

2
My life is like a summer rose
That opens to the morning sky,
But ere the shades of evening close,
Is scattered on the ground—to die.
RICHARD HENRY WILDE, *My Life.* Fraudulently claimed by Patrick O'Kelly.

My life is like the autumn leaf
That trembles in the moon's pale ray;
Its hold is frail—its date is brief,
Restless,—and soon to pass away.
RICHARD HENRY WILDE, *My Life.*

XXVI—Life: Its Sweetness

3
"Life is sweet, brother." "Do you think so?" "Think so!—There's night and day, brother, both sweet things; sun, moon, and stars, brother, all sweet things; there's likewise a wind on the heath. Life is very sweet, brother; who would wish to die?"
GEORGE BORROW, *Lavengro.* Ch. 25.

So precious life is! Even to the old
The hours are as a miser's coins!
T. B. ALDRICH, *Broken Music.*

4
Have you found your life distasteful?
My life did, and does, smack sweet.
Was your youth of pleasure wasteful?
Mine I saved and hold complete.
Do your joys with age diminish?
When mine fail me, I'll complain.
Must in death your daylight finish?
My sun sets to rise again.
ROBERT BROWNING, *At the "Mermaid."* St. 10.

How good is man's life, the mere living! how fit to employ
All the heart and the soul and the senses forever in joy.
ROBERT BROWNING, *Saul.* Sec. 9.

5
The life of man, says our friend Herr Sauerteig, the life even of the meanest man, it were good to remember, is a Poem.
CARLYLE, *Count Cagliostro: Flight First.*

6
Life is not void or stuff for scorners:
We have laughed loud and kept our love,
We have heard singers in tavern corners
And not forgotten the birds above:
We have known smiters and sons of thunder
And not unworthily walked with them,
We have grown wiser and lost not wonder;
And we have seen Jerusalem.
G. K. CHESTERTON, *To F. C.*

7
Life to the last enjoy'd, here Churchill lies.
CHARLES CHURCHILL, *The Candidate,* l. 152.

8
Of divers voices is sweet music made:
So in our life the different degrees
Render sweet harmony among these wheels.
DANTE, *Paradiso.* Canto vi, l. 127. (Cary, tr.)

9
By the Lord of Ludgate it's a mad life to be lord mayor; it's a stirring life, a fine life, a velvet life, a careful life.
DEKKER, *The Shoemaker's Holiday.* Act v, sc. 1.

10
'Tis not for nothing that we life pursue;
It pays our hopes with something still that's new.
DRYDEN, *Aureng-Zebe.* Act iv, sc. 1.

11
The life of man is the true romance, which, when it is valiantly conducted, will yield the imagination a higher joy than any fiction.
EMERSON, *Essays, First Series: New England Reformers.*

Life is a festival only to the wise. Seen from the nook and chimney-side of prudence, it wears a ragged and dangerous front.
EMERSON, *Essays, First Series: Heroism.*

Life is good only when it is magical and musical, a perfect timing and consent, and when we do not anatomize it. . . . You must hear the bird's song without attempting to render it into nouns and verbs.
EMERSON, *Society and Solitude: Works and Days.*

12
When life is true to the poles of nature, the streams of truth will roll through us in song.
EMERSON, *Letters and Social Aims: Poetry and Imagination.*

Sooner or later that which is now life shall be poetry, and every fair and manly trait shall add a richer strain to the song.
EMERSON, *Letters and Social Aims: Poetry and Imagination.*

13
Chance cannot touch me! Time cannot hush me!
Fear, hope, and longing, at strife,
Sink as I rise, on, on, upward forever,
Gathering strength, gaining breath—naught can sever
Me from the Spirit of Life!
MARGARET FULLER, *Dryad Song.* St. 4.

When life leaps in the veins, when it beats in the heart,
When it thrills as it fills every animate part,
Where lurks it? how works it? . . . we scarcely detect it.
OWEN MEREDITH, *Lucile.* Pt. ii, canto i, sec. 5.

14
Life's a pudding full of plums,
Care's a canker than benumbs,
Wherefore waste our elocution
On impossible solution?

Life's a pleasant institution,
Let us take it as it comes!
W. S. GILBERT, *The Gondoliers*. Act i.

1
My worthy friend, all theories are gray,
And green alone Life's golden tree.
(Grau, theurer Freund, ist alle Theorie
Und grün des Lebens goldner Baum.)
GOETHE, *Faust*. Pt. i, sc. 4, l. 515.

2
Late may you return to the skies, and long may you be happily present to your people. (Serus in cœlum redeas, diuque Lætus intersis populo.)
HORACE, *Odes*. Bk. i, ode 2, l. 45. To Cæsar Augustus.

Happy long life, with honor at the close,
Friends' painless tears, the softened thought of foes!
J. R. LOWELL, *Memoriæ Positum: R. G. S.*

Just Fate, prolong his life, well spent,
Whose indefatigable hours
Have been as gayly innocent
And fragrant as his flowers.
J. R. LOWELL, *To Asa Gray, on His Seventy-Fifth Birthday.*

May he live, fife, pipe, drink. (Vivat, fifat, pipat, bibat.)
RABELAIS, *Works*. Bk. iv, ch. 53.

3
Like thee, noble river, like thee,
Let our lives in beginning and ending,
Fair in their gathering be,
And great in the time of their spending.
ISA CRAIG KNOX, *The Thames.*

4
But life is sweet, though all that makes it sweet
Lessen like sound of friends' departing feet.
J. R. LOWELL, *Epistle to George William Curtis: Postscript*, l. 49.

5
It is good for us to be here.
New Testament: Matthew, xvii, 4.

6
When I fail to cherish it [life] in every fibre the fires within are waning.
GEORGE MEREDITH, *Diana of the Crossways*. Ch. 1.

They may rail at this life—from the hour I began it,
I found it a life full of kindness and bliss;
And until they can show me some happier planet,
More social and bright, I'll content me with this.
THOMAS MOORE, *They May Rail.*

7
This also, that I live, I consider a gift of God. (Id quoque, quod vivam, munus habere dei.)
OVID, *Tristia*. Bk. i, eleg. 1, l. 20.

8
Life is delight; away, dull care. (Τρυφὴ βίος, ἔρρετ' ἀνίαι.)
PALLADAS. (*Greek Anthology*. Bk. v, No. 72.)

For be man's load never so heavy, the life is aye sweet.
UNKNOWN, *Patience*, l. 156. (c. 1350)

But now our fearful prelate saith, The life is sweet.
JOHN GOWER, *Confessio Amantis*, v, 1861. (1390)

Life is sweet to everyone.
GEORGE PETTIE, *Petite Pallace*, ii, 45. (1576)

How good it is to live, even at the worst!
STEPHEN PHILLIPS, *Christ in Hades*, l. 103.

And I thought to myself, How nice it is
For me to live in a world like this,
Where things can happen, and clocks can strike,
And none of the people are made alike.
W. B. RANDS, *I Saw a New World.*

9
And up from the pits when these shiver, and up from the heights when those shine,
Twin voices and shadows swim starward, and the essence of life is divine.
RICHARD REALF, *Indirection.*

10
From a boy
I gloated on existence. Earth to me
Seemed all-sufficient and my sojourn there
One trembling opportunity for joy.
ALAN SEEGER, *Sonnet: I Loved.*

11
O excellent! I love long life better than figs.
SHAKESPEARE, *Antony and Cleopatra*. Act i, sc. 2, l. 32.

O, our lives' sweetness!
That we the pain of death would hourly die
Rather than die at once!
SHAKESPEARE, *King Lear*. Act v, sc. 3, l. 184.

12
The One remains, the many change and pass;
Heaven's light forever shines, Earth's shadows fly;
Life, like a dome of many-coloured glass,
Stains the white radiance of Eternity.
SHELLEY, *Adonais.*

A Dome of Many-Coloured Glass.
AMY LOWELL. Title of book of poems.

13
I know I am—that simplest bliss
That millions of my brothers miss.
BAYARD TAYLOR, *Prince Deukalion*. Act iv.

14
Life is a sweet and joyful thing for one who has some one to love and a pure conscience.
LEO TOLSTOY, *Two Hussars*. Ch. 9.

15
Ah! somehow life is bigger after all
Than any painted Angel could we see
The God that is within us!
OSCAR WILDE, *Humanitad*. St. 60.

16
The pleasure which there is in life itself.
WORDSWORTH, *Michael*. l. 77.

XXVII—Life: Its Bitterness

17
Gosh! I feel like a real good cry!

Life, he says, is a cheat, a fake.
Well, I agree with the grouchy guy—
The best you get is an even break.

F. P. Adams, *Ballade of Schopenhauer's Philosophy*.

1
When life ceases to be a promise it does not cease to be a task; its true name even is trial.

Amiel, *Journal*, 29 Jan., 1866.

2
Ah, love, let us be true
To one another! for the world, which seems
To lie before us like a land of dreams,
So various, so beautiful, so new,
Hath really neither joy, nor love, nor light,
Nor certitude, nor peace, nor help for pain;
And we are here as on a darkling plain
Swept with confused alarms of struggle and flight,
Where ignorant armies clash by night.

Matthew Arnold, *Dover Beach*. l. 29.

Wandering between two worlds, one dead,
The other powerless to be born,
With nowhere yet to rest my head,
Like these, on earth I wait forlorn.

Matthew Arnold, *Grande Chartreuse*, l. 85.

What shelter to grow ripe is ours?
What leisure to grow wise? . . .
Too fast we live, too much are tried,
Too harass'd, to attain
Wordsworth's sweet calm, or Goethe's wide
And luminous view to gain.

Matthew Arnold, *In Memory of the Author of Obermann*, l. 71.

How many noble thoughts,
How many precious feelings of man's heart,
How many loves, how many gratitudes,
Do twenty years wear out, and see expire!

Matthew Arnold, *Merope*, l. 177.

3
With aching hands and bleeding feet
We dig and heap, lay stone on stone;
We bear the burden and the heat
Of the long day, and wish 'twere done.
Not till the hours of light return,
All we have built do we discern.

Matthew Arnold, *Morality*. St. 2.

For most men in a brazen prison live,
Where, in the sun's hot eye,
With heads bent o'er their toil, they languidly
Their lives to some unmeaning taskwork give.

Matthew Arnold, *A Summer Night*, l. 37.

4
Every life, even the most selfish and the most frivolous, is a tragedy at last, because it ends with death.

Alfred Austin, *Savonarola: Preface*.

I love the doubt, the dark, the fear,
That still surroundeth all things here.

Alfred Austin, *Hymn to Death*.

5
It is a misery to be born, a pain to live, a trouble to die. (Nasci miserum, vivere pœna, angustia mori.)

St. Bernard, *De Consideratione*. Ch. 3.

6
There is so much trouble in coming into the world, and so much more, as well as meanness, in going out of it, that 'tis hardly worth while to be here at all.

Lord Bolingbroke. (Emerson, *Representative Men: Montaigne*.)

7
My life is read all backward, and the charm of life undone.

E. B. Browning, *Lady Geraldine's Courtship*.

Life treads on life, and heart on heart;
We press too close in church and mart
To keep a dream or grave apart.

E. B. Browning, *A Vision of Poets*; l. 820.

8
O Life! thou art a galling load,
Along a rough, a weary road.

Burns, *Despondency*.

9
Desolate—Life is so dreary and desolate—
Women and men in the crowd meet and mingle,
Yet with itself every soul standeth single,
. . . Fighting its terrible conflicts alone.

Alice Cary, *Life*. St. 2.

10
Tell me, all-judging Jove, if this be fair,
To make so short a life so full of care?

Richard Cumberland, *On Human Life*.

11
I took one draught of life,
I'll tell you what I paid,
Precisely an existence—
The market-price, they said.

Emily Dickinson, *Further Poems*, cxx.

12
Ah, life could be so beautiful, Yet never is.

Carleton Drewry, *Father and Son*.

13
When I consider life, 'tis all a cheat.
Yet fool'd with hope, men favour the deceit;
Trust on, and think tomorrow will repay.
Tomorrow's falser than the former day; . . .
Strange cozenage! none would live past years again,
Yet all hope pleasure in what yet remain;
And from the dregs of life think to receive
What the first sprightly running could not give.

Dryden, *Aureng-Zebe*. Act iv, sc. 1.

When I consider Life and its few years—
A wisp of fog betwixt us and the sun;
A call to battle, and the battle done
Ere the last echo dies within our ears;
A rose choked in the grass; an hour of fears;
The gusts that past a darkening shore do beat;
The burst of music down an unlistening street—
I wonder at the idleness of tears.

Lizette Woodworth Reese, *Life*.

14
Once I supposed that only my manner of

living was superficial; that all other men's was solid. Now I find we are all alike shallow.
EMERSON, *Journals*. Vol. v, p. 198.

1
All the bloomy flush of life is fled.
GOLDSMITH, *Deserted Village*, l. 128. (1770)

Life's bloomy flush was lost.
GEORGE CRABBE, *The Parish Register*. Pt. ii, l. 453. (1807)

2
Nothing can exceed the vanity of our existence but the folly of our pursuits.
GOLDSMITH, *The Good-Natured Man*. Act i, sc. 1.

As a desolate bird that through darkness its lost way is winging,
As a hand that is helplessly raised when Death's sickle is swinging,
So is life! Ay, the life that lends passion and breath to my singing.
H. RIDER HAGGARD, *Sorais's Song*. (*Allan Quartermain*. Ch. 15.)

3
For Life I had never cared greatly,
As worth a man's while.
THOMAS HARDY, *For Life I Had Never Cared Greatly*.

4
To what a point of insignificance may not human life dwindle! To what fine, agonizing threads will it not cling!
WILLIAM HAZLITT, *Literary Remains*. Vol. ii, p. 246.

For Fate has wove the thread of life with pain!
And twins, ev'n from the birth, are Misery and Man!
HOMER, *Odyssey*. Bk. vii, l. 263. (Pope, tr.)

I say that I am myself, but what is this Self of mine
But a knot in the tangled skein of things where chance and chance combine?
DON MARQUIS, *Heir and Serf*.

5
Oh! take, young seraph, take thy harp,
And play to me so cheerily;
For grief is dark, and care is sharp,
And life wears on so wearily.
THOMAS HOOD, *To Hope*.

6
When I meet the morning beam,
Or lay me down at night to dream,
I hear my bones within me say,
"Another night, another day."
A. E. HOUSMAN, *The Immortal Part*.

7
Life is a pill which none of us can bear to swallow without gilding.
SAMUEL JOHNSON. (PIOZZI, *Johnsoniana*.)

Life is to most a nauseous pill,
A treat for which they dearly pay:
Let's take the good, avoid the ill,
Discharge the debt, and walk away.
PHILIP FRENEAU, *Human Frailty*.

8
Life is barren enough surely with all her trappings; let us therefore be cautious how we strip her.
SAMUEL JOHNSON, *Miscellanies*. Vol. i, p. 345.

Human life is everywhere a state in which much is to be endured, and little to be enjoyed.
SAMUEL JOHNSON, *Rasselas*. Ch. 11.

Condemn'd to Hope's delusive mine,
As on we toil from day to day,
By sudden blasts, or slow decline,
Our social comforts drop away.
SAMUEL JOHNSON, *On the Death of Dr. Robert Levet*.

9
"Enlarge my life with multitude of days!"
In health, in sickness, thus the suppliant prays:
Hides from himself his state, and shuns to know
That life protracted is protracted woe.
SAMUEL JOHNSON, *The Vanity of Human Wishes*, l. 253.

The weariness, the fever, and the fret
Here, where men sit and hear each other groan.
KEATS, *Ode to a Nightingale*. St. 3.

10
For men must work, and women must weep,
And the sooner it's over, the sooner to sleep;
And good-bye to the bar and its moaning.
CHARLES KINGSLEY, *The Three Fishers*.

11
Life can be bitter to the very bone
When one is poor, and woman, and alone.
JOHN MASEFIELD, *The Widow in the Bye Street*.

12
The basic fact about human existence is not that it is a tragedy, but that it is a bore.
H. L. MENCKEN, *Prejudices*.

Our civilization promises to make the question of a living easier and easier; and meanwhile living becomes emptier and emptier.
FRANK K. NOTCH, *King Mob*, p. 224.

13
In tragic life, God wot,
No villain need be! Passions spin the plot:
We are betrayed by what is false within.
GEORGE MEREDITH, *Modern Love*. St. 43.

Passions Spin the Plot.
VARDIS FISHER. Title of novel.

14
Life is a parting and not a meeting,
A comradeship of the lonely mile,
Only an hour for a passing greeting,
Only a friendship for a while.
DOUGLAS MALLOCH, *A Day*.

15
A bitter life 'twixt pain and nothing tost.
WILLIAM MORRIS, *The Earthly Paradise: The Hill of Venus*.

16
Moan, moan, ye dying gales!
The saddest of your tales

Is not so sad as life.
HENRY NEELE, *Moan, Moan, Ye Dying Gales.*

1
The life of man is the plaything of Fortune, a wretched life and a vagrant, tossed between riches and poverty.
PALLADAS. (*Greek Anthology.* Bk. x, epig. 80.)

The wretch, at summing up his misspent days,
Found nothing left, but poverty and praise.
JOHN OLDHAM, *A Satire: Spenser Dissuading the Author,* l. 182.

The life of man, solitary, poor, nasty, brutish, and short.
THOMAS HOBBES, *Leviathan: Of Man.*

2
O life! is *all* thy song, "Endure and—die?"
BRYAN WALLER PROCTER, *Life.*

3
Does the road wind up-hill all the way?
Yes, to the very end.
Will the day's journey take the whole long day?
From morn to night, my friend.
CHRISTINA ROSSETTI, *Up-Hill.*

4
Life did not present its sunny side to thee. (Nicht seine Freudenseite kehrte dir Das Leben zu.)
SCHILLER, *Marie Stuart.* Act ii, sc. 3, l. 136.

5
This is the state of man: today he puts forth
The tender leaves of hopes; tomorrow blossoms,
And bears his blushing honours thick upon him:
The third day comes a frost, a killing frost,
And, when he thinks, good easy man, full surely
His greatness is a-ripening, nips his root,
And then he falls, as I do.
SHAKESPEARE, *Henry VIII.* Act iii, sc. 2, l. 352.

The wine of life is drawn, and the mere lees
Is left this vault to brag of.
SHAKESPEARE, *Macbeth.* Act ii, sc. 3, l. 100.

6
To live I find it deadly dolorous,
For life draws care, and care continual woe.
EDMUND SPENSER, *Daphnaida,* l. 450.

7
The long mechanic pacings to and fro,
The set, grey life, and apathetic end.
TENNYSON, *Love and Duty,* l. 17.

8
Life holds more disappointment than satisfaction. (Τὸ δὲ κενὸν τοῦ βίου πλέον τοῦ συμφέροντος.)
THEOPHRASTUS. (DIOGENES LAERTIUS, *Theophrastus.* Bk. v, sec. 41.)

9
It is truly a misery to live upon earth. . . . For to eat, drink, watch, sleep, rest, labor, and to be subject to other necessities of nature, is truly a great misery and affliction. . . . And therefore the prophet devoutly prays to be freed from them, saying, "From my necessities, deliver me, O Lord."
THOMAS À KEMPIS, *De Imitatione Christi.* Ch. 22.

10
I tell you we're in a blessed drain-pipe, and we've got to crawl along it till we die.
H. G. WELLS, *Kipps.* Bk. i, ch. 2.

To climb life's worn, heavy wheel,
Which draws up nothing new.
YOUNG, *Night Thoughts.* Night iii, l. 331.

11
Not life itself, but living ill, is evil. (Οὐ τὸ ζῆν, ἀλλὰ τὸ κακῶς ζῆν.)
DIOGENES. (DIOGENES LAERTIUS, *Diogenes.* Bk. vi, sec. 55.)

XXVIII—Life and Death

See also Death: The Good Death

12
The Angel of Death is the invisible Angel of Life.
HENRY MILLS ALDEN, *A Study of Death.*

13
Ofttimes the test of courage becomes rather to live than to die. (Spesso è da forte, Più che il morire, il vivere.)
ALFIERI, *Oreste.* Act iv, sc. 2.

But where life is more terrible than death, it is then the truest valour to dare to live.
SIR THOMAS BROWNE, *Religio Medici.* Sec. 51.

'Tis more brave To live, than to die.
OWEN MEREDITH, *Lucile.* Pt. ii, canto vi, st. 11.

14
I strain too much this string of life, belike,
Meaning to make such music as shall save. . . .
Would that I had such help as man must have,
For I shall die, whose life was all men's hope.
EDWIN ARNOLD, *The Light of Asia.* Bk. vi, l. 107.

15
Life hath more awe than death.
P. J. BAILEY, *Festus: Wood and Water.*

16
Life! we've been long together
Through pleasant and through cloudy weather;
'Tis hard to part when friends are dear,—
Perhaps 't will cost a sigh, a tear;
Then steal away, give little warning,
Choose thine own time;
Say not "Good-night," but in some brighter clime
Bid me "Good-morning."
ANNA LETITIA BARBAULD, *Life.* St. 2. Wordsworth said of this stanza: "I am not in the habit of grudging people their good things, but I wish I had written those lines."

1
They that yet never learn'd to live and die,
Will scarcely teach it others feelingly.
RICHARD BAXTER, *Love Breathing Thanks and Praise*. Pt. ii. (c. 1650)

2
The mere habit of living makes mere men more hardly to part with life.
SIR THOMAS BROWNE, *To a Friend*. Sec. 28.

Mr. Wopsle's great-aunt conquered a confirmed habit of living into which she had fallen.
DICKENS, *Great Expectations*. Ch. 16.

While some no other cause for life can give
But a dull habitude to live.
JOHN OLDHAM, *To the Memory of Norwent*.

No particular motive for living, except the custom and habit of it.
THACKERAY. (Quoted in an article in *Blackwood's Magazine*, Jan., 1854.)

3
Knowledge by suffering entereth;
And Life is perfected by Death.
E. B. BROWNING, *A Vision of Poets*, l. 1004.

4
A man can have but one life, and one death,
One heaven, one hell.
ROBERT BROWNING, *In a Balcony*.

You never know what life means till you die:
Even throughout life, 'tis death that makes life live.
ROBERT BROWNING, *The Ring and the Book*. Pt. xi, l. 2375.

5
We live and die,
But which is best, you know no more than I.
BYRON, *Don Juan*. Canto vii, st. 4.

6
The dead to the grave and the living to the loaf. (El Muerto á la sepultura y el vivo á la hogaza.)
CERVANTES, *Don Quixote*. Pt. i, ch. 19.

Until death, it is all life. (Hasta la Muerte todo es vida.)
CERVANTES, *Don Quixote*. Pt. ii, ch. 59.

See also HOPE: WHILE THERE'S LIFE THERE'S HOPE.

7
I cannot but believe that we shall come to accept death as we do life—as we find it.
GEORGES CLEMENCEAU, *In the Evening of My Thought*, p. 503.

8
Her lips were red, her looks were free,
Her locks were yellow as gold:
Her skin was as white as leprosy,
The Nightmare Life-in-Death was she,
Who thicks man's blood with cold.
S. T. COLERIDGE, *The Ancient Mariner*. Pt. iii.

9
Few greatly live in Wisdom's eye—
But oh! how few who greatly die!
NATHANIEL COTTON, *The Last Scene*.

That man greatly lives,
Whate'er his fate, or fame, who greatly dies.
YOUNG, *Night Thoughts*. Night viii, l. 470.

10
Let's learn to live, for we must die alone.
GEORGE CRABBE, *The Borough*. Letter 10.

Live your own life, for you will die your own death. (Vive tibi, nam moriere tibi.)
UNKNOWN. A Latin proverb.

11
She'll bargain with them, and will give
Them God; teach them how to live
In Him; or, if they this deny,
For Him she'll teach them how to die.
RICHARD CRASHAW, *Hymn to the Name and Honour of St. Theresa*, l. 51. (1646)

He who should teach men to die, would at the same time teach them to live.
MONTAIGNE, *Essays*. Bk. i, ch. 19.

There taught us how to live; and (oh, too high
The price for knowledge!) taught us how to die.
THOMAS TICKELL, *To the Earl of Warwick, On the Death of Mr. Addison*, l. 81. (1719)

Thou,
Whom soft-eyed Pity once led down from Heaven
To bleed for Man, to teach him how to live,
And oh! still harder lesson, how to die!
BISHOP BEILBY PORTEUS, *Death*, l. 316. (c. 1770)

12
One should never think of death. One should think of life. That is real piety.
BENJAMIN DISRAELI, *Endymion*. Ch. 27.

13
Thales said there was no difference between life and death. "Why, then," said some one to him, "do you not die?" "Because," said he, "it *does* make no difference."
DIOGENES LAERTIUS, *Lives: Thales*. Sec. ix.

14
As life is to the living, so death is to the dead.
MARY MAPES DODGE, *The Two Mysteries*.

Life is a mystery as deep as ever death can be;
Yet oh, how dear it is to us, this life we live and see!
MARY MAPES DODGE, *The Two Mysteries*.

15
Who knoweth if to die be but to live,
And that called life by mortals be but death?
(*Τίς δ' οἶδεν εἰ τὸ ζῆν μέν ἐστι κατθανεῖν,
τὸ κατθανεῖν δὲ ζῆν νομίζεται βροτοῖς.*)
EURIPIDES, *Fragments*. No. 638.

Man, foolish man! no more thy soul deceive,
To die, is but the surest way to live.
WILLIAM BROOME, *Death*, l. 89.

There are daily sounds to tell us that Life
Is dying, and Death is living.
HOOD, *Miss Kilmansegg: Her Last Will*.

Passed from death unto life.
New Testament: John, v, 24.

Sleeping are men, and when they die, they wake.
The Koran.

In some circumstances, to die is to live.
ARCHBISHOP JOHN TILLOTSON, *Letter to Lady Russell*, 21 Nov., 1685.

1
Quick with the quick, and dead with the dead.
JOHN FLORIO, *First Fruites*, Fo. 34. (1578)

2
A useless life is an early death. (Ein unnütz Leben ist ein früher Tod.)
GOETHE, *Iphigenia auf Tauris*. Act i. sc. 2, l. 63.

Life is her [Nature's] most beautiful invention, and death her artifice to have much life. (Leben ist ihre schoenste Erfindung, und der Tod ist ihr Kunstgriff, viel Leben zu haben.)
GOETHE, *Aphorisms on Nature*. (*Edition Cotta*, vol. xxxiii, p. 164.)

3
Thy thoughts to nobler meditations give,
And study how to die, not how to live.
GEORGE GRANVILLE, *Meditations on Death*.

4
A stranger into life I'm come,
Dying may be our going home.
MATTHEW GREEN, *The Spleen*, l. 788.

5
I have subdued at last the will to live,
Expelling nature from my weary heart;
And now my life, so calm, contemplative,
No longer selfish, freely may depart.
The vital flame is burning less and less;
And memory fuses to forgetfulness.
P. G. HAMERTON, *The Sanyassi*.

6
Yet saw he something in the lives
Of those who ceased to live
That rounded them with majesty,
Which living failed to give.
THOMAS HARDY, *The Casterbridge Captains*.

7
For all may have,
If they dare try, a glorious life, or grave.
GEORGE HERBERT, *The Church-Porch*. St. 15.

8
Life evermore is fed by death,
In earth and sea and sky;
And, that a rose may breathe its breath,
Something must die.
J. G. HOLLAND, *Bitter-Sweet*. Epis. i.

9
Content with his past life, let him take leave of life like a satiated guest. (Exacto contentus tempore vita cedat uti conviva satur.)
HORACE, *Satires*. Bk. i, sat. 1, l. 118.

10
It matters not how a man dies, but how he lives.
SAMUEL JOHNSON. (BOSWELL, *Life*, iii, 4.)

11
The lordliest of all things,—
Life only lends us feet, Death gives us wings!
FREDERIC LAWRENCE KNOWLES, *Laus Mortis*.

12
There are but three general events that happen to mankind: birth, life, and death. Of their birth they are insensible, they suffer when they die, and neglect to live.
LA BRUYÈRE, *Les Caractères: De l'Homme*.

13
What is our life but a succession of preludes to that unknown song whose first solemn note is sounded by death? (Notre vie est-elle autre chose qu'une série de Préludes à ce chant inconnu dont la mort entonne la première et solennelle note?)
FRANZ LISZT, *Préface: Les Préludes*: Poème Symphonique. (D'après LAMARTINE, *Nouvelles méditations poétiques*. 1828.)

14
Various the roads of life; in one
All terminate, one lonely way.
We go; and "Is he gone?"
Is all our best friends say.
W. S. LANDOR, *Various the Roads of Life*.

15
Is Love a lie, and fame indeed a breath;
And is there no sure thing in life—but death?
RICHARD LE GALLIENNE, *R. L. S.*, l. 76.

16
Live I, so live I,
To my Lord heartily,
To my Prince faithfully,
To my Neighbor honestly,
Die I, so die I.
FRIEDRICH VON LOGAU, *Sinngedichte*. (Longfellow, tr.)

17
Our life must once have end; in vain we fly
From following Fate; e'en now, e'en now, we die.
LUCRETIUS, *De Rerum Natura*. Bk. iii, l. 1081. (Creech, tr.)

18
Why seek ye the living among the dead?
New Testament: Luke, xxiv, 5.

The earth belongs to the living, not the dead.
THOMAS JEFFERSON, *Writings*. Vol. xiii, p. 269.

Mem.—To think more of the living and less of the dead, for the dead have a world of their own.
THOMAS TYERS, *Resolutions*.

19
'Tis not the whole of life to live,
Nor all of death to die.
MONTGOMERY, *Issues of Life and Death*. St. 1.

20
This life is a fleeting breath,
And whither and how shall I go,
When I wander away with Death
By a path that I do not know?
LOUISE CHANDLER MOULTON, *When I Wander Away with Death*.

21
Life should never cease to unfold, and it will be time enough for Death to lower the banner when the last stitch of canvas is reached.
GEORGE MOORE, *Ave*, p. 178.

22
Live righteously; you shall die righteously. (Vive pius; moriere pius.)
OVID, *Amores*. Bk. iii, eleg. 9, l. 37.

No one has died miserably who has lived well (Nec misere quisquam, qui bene vixit obit.)
ERASMUS, *Apotheosis Capnionis*. Quoted.

The name of death was never terrible
To him that knew to live.
EMERSON, *Letters and Social Aims: Immortality*. Quoted.

Whoso lives the holiest life
Is fittest far to die.
MARGARET JUNKIN PRESTON, *Ready.*

1
A good death does honor to a whole life.
PETRARCH, *To Laura in Death.* Canz. xvi, st. 5.

2
To live is Christ, and to die is gain.
New Testament: Philippians, i, 21.

3
To me 'twas given to die: to thee 'tis given
To live: alas! one moment sets us even.
Mark! how impartial is the will of Heaven!
MATTHEW PRIOR, *For His Own Tomb-stone.*

So vanishes our state; so pass our days;
So life but opens now, and now decays;
The cradle and the tomb, alas! how nigh,
To live is scarce distinguish'd from to die.
MATTHEW PRIOR, *Solomon on the Vanity of the World.* Bk. iii, l. 527.

4
He rightly lives, That nobly dies: . . .
He that (in case) despises
Life, earns it best; but he that overprizes
His dearest blood, when honour bids him die,
Steals but a life, and lives by robbery.
FRANCIS QUARLES, *Esther.* Sec. xv, 15.

5
As a man lives, so shall he die;
As a tree falls, so shall it lie.
JOHN RAY, *English Proverbs.*

As the life is, so is the end. (Qualis vita, finis ita.)
UNKNOWN. A Latin proverb.

6
The long sleep of death closes our scars, and the short sleep of life our wounds. (Der lange Schlaf des Todes schliesst unsere Narben zu, und der kutze des Lebens unsere Wunden.)
JEAN PAUL RICHTER, *Hesperus.* Ch. 20.

7
They will not live, and do not know how to die. (Vivere nolunt, mori nesciunt.)
SENECA, *Epistulæ ad Lucilium.* Epis. iv, sec. 6.

If anything forbids you to live nobly, nothing forbids you to die nobly. (Si quid te vetat bene vivere, bene mori non vetat.)
SENECA, *Epistulæ ad Lucilium.* Epis. xvii, sec. 6.

He who does not wish to die cannot have wished to live. (Vivere noluit qui mori non vult.)
SENECA, *Epistulæ ad Lucilium.* Epis. xxx, 10.

Before I was old, I tried to live well; now that I am old, I shall try to die well; but dying well means dying gladly. (Ante senectutem curavi, ut bene viverem; in senectute, ut bene moriar; bene autem mori est libenter mori.)
SENECA, *Epistulæ ad Lucilium.* Epis. lxi, sec. 2.

8
Every man should make his life acceptable to others, but his death to himself alone. The best form of death is the one we like.
SENECA, *Epistulæ ad Lucilium.* Epis. lxx, 12.

9
What's yet in this
That bears the name of life? Yet in this life
Lie hid moe thousand deaths: yet death we fear.
SHAKESPEARE, *Measure for Measure.* Act iii, sc. 1, l. 38.

10
Let life burn down, and dream it is not death.
SWINBURNE, *Anactoria.*

From too much love of living,
From hope and fear set free,
We thank with brief thanksgiving
Whatever gods may be,
That no life lives forever;
That dead men rise up never;
That even the weariest river
Winds somewhere safe to sea.
SWINBURNE, *The Garden of Proserpine.* St. 11.

For if we live, we die not,
And if we die, we live.
SWINBURNE, *Jacobite Song.* St. 9.

11
Some come, some go; This life is so.
THOMAS TUSSER, *Hundred Points of Good Husbandry: August's Abstract.*

Some laugh, while others mourn;
Some toil, while others pray;
One dies, and one is born:
So runs the world away.
SAMUEL WESLEY, *The Way of the World.*

12
All say, "How hard it is to die"—a strange complaint from people who have had to live. Pity is for the living, envy for the dead.
MARK TWAIN, *Pudd'nhead Wilson's Calendar.*

A myriad of men are born; they labor and sweat and struggle for bread; they squabble and scold and fight; they scramble for little mean advantages over each other. Age creeps upon them; . . . ambition is dead; pride is dead; vanity is dead; longing for release is in their place. It comes at last—the only unpoisoned gift earth ever had for them—and they vanish from a world where they were of no consequence.
MARK TWAIN, *Autobiography.* Vol. ii, p. 37.

13
Many people are so afraid to die that they never begin to live.
HENRY VAN DYKE, *Counsels by the Way: Courage.*

14
Who die of having lived too much
In their large hours.
WILLIAM WATSON, *The Tomb of Burns.*

15
Why do we then shun Death with anxious strife?
If Light can thus deceive, wherefore not Life?
BLANCO WHITE, *Sonnet: Night.*

16
O I see now that life cannot exhibit all to me, as day cannot,
I see that I am to wait for what will be exhibited by death.
WALT WHITMAN, *Night on the Prairies.*

17
And the wild regrets and the bloody sweats

None knew so well as I:
For he who lives more lives than one
More deaths than one must die.
OSCAR WILDE, *Ballad of Reading Gaol*, iii, 37.

1
Life is much flatter'd, Death is much traduc'd.
YOUNG, *Night Thoughts*. Night iii, l. 444.

Life makes the soul dependent on the dust;
Death gives her wings to mount above the spheres. . . .
Death but entombs the body; life the soul.
YOUNG, *Night Thoughts*. Night iii, l. 448.

2
Be happy while ye'er leevin,
For y'er a lang time deid.
UNKNOWN, *Motto for a House*. (*Notes and Queries*, 7 Dec., 1901.)

XXIX—Life: A Journey to Death

3
And I still onward haste to my last night;
Time's fatal wings do ever forward fly:
So every day we live, a day we die.
CAMPION, *Divine and Moral Songs*. No. 17.

4
We do not die wholly at our deaths: we have mouldered away gradually long before. . . . Death only consigns the last fragment of what we were to the grave.
WILLIAM HAZLITT, *Winterslow: On the Feeling of Immortality in Youth*.

5
For life is nearer every day to death. (Nam vita morti propior est quotidie.)
PHÆDRUS, *Fables*. Bk. iv, fab. 25, l. 10.

Every moment of life is a step toward the grave. (Chaque instant de la vie est un pas vers la mort.)
CRÉBILLON, *Tite et Bérénice*. Act i, sc. 5.

6
He that begins to live begins to die.
FRANCIS QUARLES, *Hieroglyphics*. Epig. 1.

Our life's a clock, and every gasp of breath
Breathes forth a warning grief, till Time shall strike a death.
FRANCIS QUARLES, *Hieroglyphics*, ix, 6.

7
What new thing then is it for a man to die, whose whole life is nothing but a journey to death? (Quid est enim novi hominem mori. cujus tota vita nihil aliud quam ad mortem iter est?)
SENECA, *Ad Polybium de Consolatione*. Sec. 30.

What man can you show me who places any value on his time, who reckons the worth of every day, who understands that he is dying daily?
SENECA, *Epistulæ ad Lucilium*. Epis. i, sec. 2.

The hour which gives us life begins to take it away (Prima quæ vitam dedit hora, carpit.)
SENECA, *Hercules Furens*, l. 874.

8
While man is growing, life is in decrease;
And cradles rock us nearer to the tomb.
Our birth is nothing but our death begun;
As tapers waste, that instant they take fire.
YOUNG, *Night Thoughts*. Night v, l. 717.

Our life is but a chain of many deaths.
YOUNG, *The Revenge*. Act iv, sc. 1.

9
Life is real! Life is earnest!
And the grave is not its goal.
LONGFELLOW, *A Psalm of Life*.

XXX—Life: A Preparation for Death

10
May we so live we dread not here to die;
So die, we dread not afterward to live.
P. J. BAILEY, *Festus: Wood and Waters*.

So live, that when thy summons comes to join
The innumerable caravan, which moves
To that mysterious realm, where each shall take
His chamber in the silent halls of death,
Thou go not, like the quarry-slave at night,
Scourged to his dungeon, but, sustained and soothed
By an unfaltering trust, approach thy grave
Like one who wraps the drapery of his couch
About him, and lies down to pleasant dreams.
WILLIAM CULLEN BRYANT, *Thanatopsis*.

11
Made ev'ry day he had to live
To his last minute a preparative.
SAMUEL BUTLER, *To the Memory of Duval*. Sec. 2.

12
Learn to live well, that thou may'st die so too;
To live and die is all we have to do.
SIR JOHN DENHAM, *Of Prudence*, l. 93.

13
Live so, that, when you come to die,
You will have wished to live.
(Lebe, wie Du, wenn du stirbst,
Wünschen wirst, gelebt zu haben.)
C. F. GELLERT, *Geistliche Oden und Lieder: Vom Tode*.

14
Let all live as they would die.
GEORGE HERBERT, *Jacula Prudentum*.

15
Teach me to live that I may dread
The grave as little as my bed.
BISHOP THOMAS KEN, *Evening Hymn*.

16
Then, like a thankful guest,
Rise cheerfully from life's abundant feast
And with a quiet mind go take thy rest.
LUCRETIUS, *De Rerum Natura*. Bk. iii, l. 95. (Creech, tr.)

17
So may'st thou live, till like ripe fruit thou drop
Into thy mother's lap, or be with ease
Gather'd, not harshly pluck'd, for death mature.
MILTON, *Paradise Lost*. Bk. xi, l. 532.

LIGHT

18
Light, even though it passes through pollu-

tion, is not polluted. (Lux, etsi per immunda transeat. non inquinatur.)
St. Augustine, *Johannis Evang.* Ch. i, tr. 5, sec. 15. *See also* Sun: Unpolluted.

1
The first creature of God, in the works of the days, was the light of the sense, the last was the light of reason.
Francis Bacon, *Essays: Of Truth.*

God's first creature, which was light.
Francis Bacon, *New Atlantis.* Sec. 14. Quoted by Ruskin, *Crown of Wild Olive.* Lecture 4.

Light,—God's eldest daughter.
Thomas Fuller, *The Holy State: Building.*

Hail, holy light, offspring of Heav'n firstborn!
Milton, *Paradise Lost.* Bk. iii, l. 1.

Light, the prime work of God.
Milton, *Samson Agonistes,* l. 70.

2
Light that makes things seen, makes some things invisible; were it not for darkness and the shadow of the earth the noblest part of the creation had remained unseen and the stars in heaven as invisible as on the fourth day when they were created above the horizon with the sun and there was not an eye to behold them.
Sir Thomas Browne, *Garden of Cyrus.* Ch. 4.

The rising sun to mortal sight reveals
This earthly globe, but yet the stars conceals.
So may the sense discover natural things,
Divine above the reach of human wings.
C. B., *To the Memory of Sir Thomas Overbury.*

Then sorrow, touch'd by Thee, grows bright
With more than rapture's ray;
As darkness shows us worlds of light
We never saw by day.
Thomas Moore, *Oh, Thou Who Dry'st the Mourner's Tear.*

'Twas a light that made
Darkness itself appear A thing of comfort.
Southey, *The Curse of Kehama.* Pt. 23, l. 28.

3
I feel and seek the light I cannot see.
S. T. Coleridge, *Il Zapolya.* Act i, sc. 1.

4
I saw myself the lambent easy light
Gild the brown horror, and dispel the night.
Dryden, *Hind and Panther.* Pt. ii, l. 658.

5
Truly the light is sweet, and a pleasant thing it is for the eyes to behold the sun.
Old Testament: Ecclesiastes, xi, 7.

6
Light is the first of painters. There is no object so foul that intense light will not make it beautiful.
Emerson, *Nature.* Ch. 3, par. 2.

7
And God said, Let there be light: and there was light.
Old Testament: Genesis, i, 3.

Let there be Light, said God, and forthwith Light
Ethereal, first of things, quintessence pure,
Sprung from the deep; and, from her native east,
To journey through the aery gloom began,
Spher'd in a radiant cloud.
Milton, *Paradise Lost.* Bk. vii, l. 243.

If the light is,
It is because God said, Let there be light.
D. G. Rossetti, *At the Sunrise in 1848.*

8
Through love to light! O wonderful the way
That leads from darkness to the perfect day!
R. W. Gilder, *After-song.*

Against the darkness outer
God's light his likeness takes,
And he from the mighty doubter
The great believer makes.
R. W. Gilder, *The New Day.* Pt. iv. Song 15.

9
Where there is much light, the shadows are deepest. (Wo viel Licht ist, ist starker Schatten.)
Goethe, *Götz von Berlichingen,* i, 24.

Every light has its shadow.
H. G. Bohn, *Handbook of Proverbs,* p. 349.

10
Lamps make oil-spots, and candles need snuffing; it is only the light of heaven that shines pure and leaves no stain.
Goethe, *Sprüche in Prosa.*

11
Blasted with excess of light.
Thomas Gray, *The Progress of Poesy,* l. 101.

He's blind with too much light.
Philip Massinger, *The Great Duke of Florence.* Act ii, sc 1.

After light's term, a term of cecity.
Matthew Arnold, *Westminster Abbey.*

The Light that Failed.
Rudyard Kipling. Title of novel.

12
You stand in your own light.
John Heywood, *Proverbs.* Pt. ii, ch. 4. (1546)

Do we stand in our own light, wherever we go,
And fight our own shadows forever?
Owen Meredith, *Lucile.* Pt. ii, canto ii, sec. 5.

13
The light of Heav'n restore;
Give me to see, and Ajax asks no more.
Homer, *Iliad.* Bk. xvii, l. 729. (Pope, tr.)

The prayer of Ajax was for light;
Through all that dark and desperate fight,
The blackness of that noonday night.
Longfellow, *The Goblet of Life.* St. 9.

Father Zeus, deliver thou from darkness the sons of the Achæans, and make clear sky, and grant us to see with our eyes. In the light do thou e'en slay us, seeing such is thy good pleasure. ('Εν δὲ φάει καὶ ὄλεσσον, ἐπεί νύ τοι εὔαδεν οὕτως.)
Homer, *Iliad.* Bk. xvii, l. 645. The prayer of Ajax.

Thy prayer was "Light—more Light—while Time shall last!"
Thou sawest a glory growing on the night,
But not the shadows which that light would cast,

Till shadows vanish in the Light of Light.
TENNYSON, *Inscription on the Window in Memory of Caxton*. St. Margaret's Church, Westminster, London. Caxton's motto was "Fiat Lux."

More light! (Mehr Licht!)
GOETHE. Last words.

1
He seeks to produce not smoke from light, but light from smoke. (Non fumum ex fulgore, sed ex fumo dare lucem.)
HORACE, *Ars Poetica*, l. 143.

2
Like our dawn, merely a sob of light.
VICTOR HUGO, *La Légende des Siècles.*

3
And the light shineth in darkness; and the darkness comprehended it not.
New Testament: John, i, 5. (Lux in tenebris. —*Vulgate.*)

The true light, which lighteth every man that cometh into the world.
New Testament: John, i, 9.

And this is the condemnation, that light is come into the world, and men loved darkness rather than light, because their deeds were evil.
New Testament: John, iii, 19.

The shining light, that shineth more and more unto the perfect day.
Old Testament: Proverbs, iv, 18.

4
He was a burning and a shining light.
New Testament: John, v, 35.

I am the light of the world.
New Testament: John, viii, 12. (Lux mundi.—*Vulgate.*)

Ye are the light of the world.
New Testament: Matthew, v, 14.

5
Walk while ye have the light, lest darkness come upon you.
New Testament: John, xii, 35.

6
The great world of light, that lies
Behind all human destinies.
LONGFELLOW, *To a Child.*

7
Medicinal as light.
J. R. LOWELL, *Commemoration Ode.*

8
To give light to them that sit in darkness and in the shadow of death, to guide our feet into the way of peace.
New Testament: Luke, i, 79.

9
The tolerance and equity of light
That gives as freely to the shrinking flower
As to the great oak flaring to the wind.
EDWIN MARKHAM, *Lincoln, The Man of the People.*

10
In the dark a glimmering light often suffices for the pilot to find the pole star and set his course.
METASTASIO, *Achille.* Act i, sc. 6.

11
With thy long levell'd rule of streaming light.
MILTON, *Comus*, l. 340.

Where glowing embers through the room
Teach light to counterfeit a gloom.
MILTON, *Il Penseroso*, l. 79.

12
He that has light within his own clear breast
May sit i' the center and enjoy bright day;
But he that hides a dark soul and foul thoughts
Benighted walks under the mid-day sun.
MILTON, *Comus*, l. 381.

Not always right in all men's eyes,
But faithful to the light within.
O. W. HOLMES, *A Birthday Tribute.*

13
Dark with excessive bright thy skirts appear.
MILTON, *Paradise Lost*. Bk. iii, l. 380. Often misquoted "dark with excessive light."

14
Shut the windows that the house may be lighted. (Claude fenestras, ut luceat domus.)
DR. HENRY MORE, his motto. (WARD, *Life*. Ch. 12.)

15
Lead, Kindly Light, amid the encircling gloom,
Lead Thou me on!
JOHN HENRY NEWMAN, *Pillar of the Cloud.*

16
And this I know: whether the one True Light
Kindle to Love, or Wrath consume me quite,
One flash of It within the Tavern caught
Better than in the Temple lost outright.
OMAR KHAYYÁM, *Rubáiyát*. St. 77. (Fitzgerald, tr.)

17
Where art thou, beam of light? Hunters from the mossy rock, saw ye the blue-eyed fair?
OSSIAN, *Temora*. Bk. vi.

18
Out of light a little profit. (Ex luce lucellum.)
WILLIAM PITT, referring to the tax on windows. Suggested by Robert Lowe, Chancellor of the Exchequer, as a motto for match-boxes, in 1871, when a match tax was recommended by the government.

19
Light is sown for the righteous.
Old Testament: Psalms, xcvii, 11. (Lux orta est.—*Vulgate.*)

A lamp unto my feet, and a light unto my path.
Old Testament: Psalms, cxix, 105.

20
Lucus, a grove, is so called because. from the dense shade. there is very little light there. (Lucus, quia, umbra opacus, parum luceat.)
QUINTILIAN, *De Institutione Oratoria*. Bk. i, ch. 6, sec. 34. Hence the proverb, "Lucus a non lucendo," a grove (*lucus*) from not being lucent.

As by the way of innuendo,
Lucus is made *a non lucerdo.*
CHARLES CHURCHILL, *The Ghost*. Bk. ii, l. 257.

Having entirely banished the letter A from his first book, which was called Alpha (as *Lucus a non Lucendo*) because there was not an Alpha in it.
ADDISON, *The Spectator*. No. 59.

1
Light seeking light doth light of light beguile.
SHAKESPEARE, *Love's Labour's Lost*. Act i, sc. 1, l. 77.

2
Put out the light, and then put out the light:
If I quench thee, thou flaming minister,
I can again thy former light restore,
Should I repent me: but once put out thy light,
Thou cunning'st pattern of excelling nature,
I know not where is that Promethean heat
That can thy light relume.
SHAKESPEARE, *Othello*. Act v, sc. 2, l. 7.

3
The two noblest things, which are sweetness and light.
SWIFT, *The Battle of the Books. See also under* CULTURE.

4
Where God and Nature met in light.
TENNYSON, *In Memoriam*. Pt. cxi, st. 5.

5
The thing to do is to supply light and not heat.
WOODROW WILSON, *Speech*, Pittsburgh, 29 Jan., 1916.

6
The light that never was, on sea or land,
The consecration, and the Poet's dream.
WORDSWORTH, *Elegiac Stanzas, Suggested by a Picture of Peele Castle in a Storm*, l. 15.

But ne'er to a seductive lay
Let faith be given;
Nor deem that "light which leads astray
Is light from Heaven."
WORDSWORTH, *To the Sons of Burns*, l. 39.

LIGHTNING

See also Thunder

7
The lightning flies, the thunder roars,
And big waves lash the frightened shores.
JOHN GAY, *The Lady's Looking-Glass*.

8
It must be done like lightning.
BEN JONSON, *Every Man in His Humour*. Act iv, sc. 5.

As quick as lightning.
MRS. FRANCES SHERIDAN, *Discovery*. Act i, sc. 2.

9
I saw the lightning's gleaming rod
Reach forth and write upon the sky
The awful autograph of God.
JOAQUIN MILLER, *The Ship in the Desert*.

As lightning does the will of God.
JOHN PIERPONT, *A Word from a Petitioner*.

10
When you can use the lightning, it is better than cannon.
NAPOLEON BONAPARTE, *Sayings of Napoleon*.

11
Though the thunderbolts strike but one man, it is not one only whom they fill with terror. (Cum feriant unum, non unum fulmina terrent.)
OVID, *Epistulæ ex Ponto*. Bk. iii, epis. 2, l. 9.

12
It is vain to look for a defence against lightning.
PUBLILIUS SYRUS, *Sententiæ*. No. 835.

13
Lightnings, that show the vast and foamy deep,
The rending thunders, as they onward roll.
MRS. ANN RADCLIFFE, *Mysteries of Udolpho: The Mariner*. St. 9.

14
Loud o'er my head, though awful thunders roll,
And vivid lightnings flash from pole to pole,
Yet 'tis Thy voice, my God, that bids them fly,
Thy arm directs those lightnings through the sky.
SCOTT, *On a Thunderstorm*. (LOCKHART, *Life of Scott*. Vol. i, ch. 3.) Written at the age of twelve.

15
If I had a thunderbolt in mine eye, I can tell who should down.
SHAKESPEARE, *As You Like It*. Act i, sc. 2, l. 226.

Then flash'd the living lightning from her eyes.
POPE, *The Rape of the Lock*. Canto iii, l. 155.

16
Be thou as lightning in the eyes of France;
For ere thou canst report I will be there,
The thunder of my cannon shall be heard:
So hence! Be thou the trumpet of our wrath.
SHAKESPEARE, *King John*. Act i, sc. 1, l. 24.

Sulphurous and thought-executing fires,
Vaunt-couriers to oak-cleaving thunderbolts.
SHAKESPEARE, *King Lear*. Act iii, sc. 2, l. 4.

17
You nimble lightnings, dart your blinding flames
Into her scornful eyes!
SHAKESPEARE, *King Lear*. Act ii, sc. 4, l. 167.

The most terrible and nimble stroke
Of quick, cross lightning!
SHAKESPEARE, *King Lear*. Act iv, sc. 7, l. 34.

18
Merciful Heaven,
Thou rather with thy sharp and sulphurous bolt
Split'st the unwedgeable and gnarled oak
Than the soft myrtle.
SHAKESPEARE, *Measure for Measure*. Act ii, sc. 2, l. 114.

19
Brief as the lightning in the collied night,

That, in a spleen, unfolds both heaven and
earth,
And ere a man hath power to say "Behold!"
The jaws of darkness do devour it up:
So quick bright things come to confusion.
SHAKESPEARE, *A Midsummer-Night's Dream.* Act i, sc. 1, l. 145.

It is too rash, too unadvised, too sudden;
Too like the lightning, which does cease to be
Ere one can say "It lightens."
SHAKESPEARE, *Romeo and Juliet.* Act ii, sc. 2, l. 118.

1
Thunder crumples the sky,
Lightning tears at it.
LEONORA SPEYER, *The Squall.*

2
We saw the large white stars rise one by
one,
Or, from the darken'd glen,
Saw God divide the night with flying flame,
And thunder on the everlasting hills.
TENNYSON, *A Dream of Fair Women,* l. 223.

The lightnings flash a larger curve, and more
The noise astounds; till overhead a sheet
Of livid flame discloses wide, then shuts
And opens wider; shuts and opens still
Expansive, wrapping ether in a blaze.
Follows the loosen'd aggravated roar,
Enlarging, deepening, mingling, peal on peal,
Crush'd horrible, convulsing heaven and earth.
THOMSON, *The Seasons: Summer,* l. 1136.

3
Knowledge hath clipped the lightning's wings, and mewed it up for a purpose.
M. F. TUPPER, *Proverbial Philosophy: Of Hidden Uses. See also under* FRANKLIN.

4
The heavens thundered and the air shone with frequent fire; and all things threatened men with instant death. (Intonuere poli, et crebris micat ignibus æther; Præsentemque viris intentant omnia mortem.)
VERGIL, *Æneid.* Bk. i, l. 90.

5
Never from a cloudless sky fell more lightnings. (Non alias cælo ceciderunt plura sereno Fulgura.)
VERGIL, *Georgics.* Bk. i, l. 487.

For though it is the clouds that Jove is wont to cleave with his flashing bolts, this time he drove his thundering steeds through a cloudless sky. (Per purum tonantes.)
HORACE, *Odes.* Bk. i, ode 34, l. 7.

Arrestment, sudden really as a bolt out of the blue has hit strange victims.
THOMAS CARLYLE, *The French Revolution.* Vol. iii, p. 347.

6
Reach the bays—
I'll tie a garland here about his head;
'Twill keep my boy from lightning.
JOHN WEBSTER, *The White Devil,* v, 4. The bay was supposed by the Romans to protect against lightning because it was the tree of Apollo; hence, according to Pliny, Tiberius and other Roman emperors wore a wreath of bay as an amulet, especially in thunder storms.

LIKENESS

7
Our houses . . . are so like to another, that ye can less discern an egg from an egg.
THOMAS BECON, *Early Works,* p. 90. (1542)

They say we are Almost as like as eggs.
SHAKESPEARE, *The Winter's Tale.* Act i, sc. 2, l. 129. (1610)

He is as like one, as one egg is like another.
CERVANTES, *Don Quixote.* Pt. ii, ch. 27. (1615)

Not eggs to eggs are liker.
EDMUND GAYTON, *Festivous Notes on Don Quixote,* 23. (1654)

8
Likeness causeth liking.
JOHN CLARKE, *Parœmiologia,* 27. (1639)

9
As is the mother, so is her daughter.
Old Testament: Ezekiel, xvi, 44.

Like cow like calf.
WILLIAM BULLEIN, *Dialogue,* 21. (1573)

10
He answered the description the page gave to a T, sir.
GEORGE FARQUHAR, *Love and a Bottle.* Act iv, sc. 3. (1699)

They'd have fitted him to a T.
SAMUEL JOHNSON, referring to Bishop Warburton, and quoting the following lines:
Here Learning, blinded first, and then beguil'd,
Looks dark as Ignorance, as Frenzy wild.
RICHARD SAVAGE, *The Wanderer.* (BOSWELL, *Life,* 1784.)

Which was performed to a T.
RABELAIS, *Works.* Bk. iv, ch. 41.

11
Like to like.
GEORGE GASCOIGNE, *Complaynt of Philomene. See also* COMPANIONS: LIKE TO LIKE.

12
Like lips, like lettuce. (Similem habent labra lactucam.)
HEIRONYMUS, *Epistles,* vii, 5. A saying of Marcus Crassus when he saw an ass eating thistles.

Such lips, such lettuce.
JOHN HEYWOOD, *Proverbs.* Pt. ii, ch. 7. (1546)

There's other lettuce for your coarse lips.
PHILIP MASSINGER, *The Guardian.* Act ii, sc. 3.

13
As like as fig to fig. (Σῦκον εἰκάσαι σύκῳ.)
HERODAS, *Sententiæ,* vi, 60. (c. 250 B.C.)

14
As alike to compare in taste, chalk and cheese.
JOHN HEYWOOD, *Proverbs.* Pt. ii, ch. 4. (1546)

Differ as much as chalk and cheese.
SHERLOCKE, *Hatcher of Heresies.* (1565)

They take chalk for cheese.
NICHOLAS GRIMALD, *Cicero: Preface.*

No more like together than is chalk to coals.
SIR THOMAS MORE, *English Works*, p. 674.

1
Like father, like son. (Qualis pater, talis filius.)
LANGLAND, *Piers Plowman*. Passus ii, 28. (1377)

Oft the son in manner like will be unto the father.
ALEXANDER BARCLAY, *Shyp of Folys*, i, 236. (1509)

Such a father, such a son.
WILLIAM CAMDEN, *Remains*, p. 331. (1605)

Yet in my lineaments they trace
Some features of my father's face.
BYRON, *Parisina*. St. 13.

2
No more like than an apple to an oyster.
SIR THOMAS MORE, *English Works*, p. 724.

Tranio: He is my father, sir; and, sooth to say,
In countenance somewhat doth resemble you.
Biondello: As much as an apple doth an oyster.
SHAKESPEARE, *The Taming of the Shrew*. Act iv, sc. 2, l. 99.

She's as like this as a crab's like an apple.
SHAKESPEARE, *King Lear*. Act i, sc. 5, l. 15.

3
Like people like priest.
THOMAS NASHE, *Works*, i, 121. (1589)

4
Not altogether the same features, nor yet different; but such as would be natural in sisters. (Facies non omnibus una, Non diversa tamen, qualem decet esse sororum.)
OVID, *Metamorphoses*. Bk. ii, l. 13.

5
Like master, like man. (Plane qualis dominus, talis est servus.)
PETRONIUS, *Satyricon*. Sec. 58. *See also* MASTER: LIKE MASTER, LIKE MAN.

6
One drop of milk is no more like another than I is like me. (Neque lac lactis magis est simile quam ille ego similest mei.)
PLAUTUS, *Amphitruo*, l. 601. (Act ii, sc. 1.)

As much alike as two drops of milk. (Tam similem, quam lacte lacti est.)
PLAUTUS, *Miles Gloriosus*, l. 240. (Act ii, sc. 2.)

7
Looking as like . . . as one pea does like another.
RABELAIS, *Works*. Bk. v, ch. 2. (1532)

As like as one pea is to another.
JOHN LYLY, *Euphues*, p. 215. (1580)

8
The one so like the other
As could not be distinguish'd but by names.
SHAKESPEARE, *The Comedy of Errors*. Act i, sc. 1, l. 52.

These hands are not more like.
SHAKESPEARE, *Hamlet*. Act i, sc. 2, l. 212.

To show virtue her own feature, scorn her own image, and the very age and body of the time his form and pressure.
SHAKESPEARE, *Hamlet*. Act iii, sc. 2, l. 25.

Blood hath bought blood and blows have answer'd blows;
Strength match'd with strength, and power confronted power:
Both are alike; and both alike we like.
SHAKESPEARE, *King John*. Act ii, sc. 1, l. 329.

9
When you know one, you know all. (Unum quam noris, omnes noris.)
TERENCE, *Phormio*. Act i, sc. 5, l. 35.

LILAC

10
O lilac, whiter than swan's down,
Among your soft-green leaves,
Purer than snow new-fallen on the boughs.
F. S. FLINT, *Lilac*.

11
Lilacs, False blue, White, Purple,
Colour of lilac,
Your great puffs of flowers
Are everywhere in this my New England. . . .
Lilacs in dooryards
Holding quiet conversation with an early moon;
Lilacs watching a deserted house; . . .
Lilacs, wind-beaten, staggering under a lopsided shock of bloom, . . .
You are everywhere.
AMY LOWELL, *Lilacs*.

Now you are a very decent flower,
A reticent flower,
A curiously clear-cut, candid flower,
Standing beside clean doorways,
Friendly to a house-cat and a pair of spectacles,
Making poetry out of a bit of moonlight
And a hundred or two sharp blossoms.
AMY LOWELL, *Lilacs*.

12
Go down to Kew in lilac-time, in lilac-time, in lilac-time;
Go down to Kew in lilac-time (it isn't far from London!)
And you shall wander hand in hand with love in summer's wonderland;
Go down to Kew in lilac-time (it isn't far from London!)
ALFRED NOYES, *The Barrel-Organ*.

13
The purple clusters load the lilac-bushes.
AMELIA C. WELBY, *Hopeless Love*.

14
Warble me now for joy of lilac-time.
WALT WHITMAN, *Warble for Lilac-Time*.

When lilacs last in the dooryard bloom'd,
And the great star early droop'd in the western sky in the night,
I mourn'd, and yet shall mourn with ever-returning spring.
WALT WHITMAN, *When Lilacs Last in the Dooryard Bloom'd*. St. 1.

The lilac-bush tall-growing with heart-shaped leaves of rich green,
With many a pointed blossom rising delicate, with the perfume strong I love,

With every leaf a miracle.
WALT WHITMAN, *When Lilacs Last in the Dooryard Bloom'd*. St. 3.

1
Who thought of the lilac? "I," dew said,
"I made the lilac out of my head."
"She made the lilac? Pooh!" trilled a linnet,
And each dew-note had a lilac in it.
HUMBERT WOLFE, *The Lilac*.

LILY

2
I like the chaliced lilies,
The heavy Eastern lilies,
The gorgeous tiger-lilies,
That in our garden grow.
T. B. ALDRICH, *Tiger-Lilies*.

3
And lilies are still lilies, pulled
By smutty hands, though spotted from their white.
E. B. BROWNING, *Aurora Leigh*. Bk. iii, l. 741.

And lilies white, prepared to touch
The whitest thought, nor soil it much.
E. B. BROWNING, *A Flower in a Letter*.

4
Dante's purple lilies, which he blew
To a larger bubble with his prophet breath.
E. B. BROWNING, *Aurora Leigh*. Bk. vii, l. 935.

5
Very whitely still
The lilies of our lives may reassure
Their blossoms from their roots, accessible
Alone to heavenly dews that drop not fewer,
Growing straight, out of man's reach, on the hill.
E. B. BROWNING, *Sonnets from the Portuguese*. No. xxiv.

6
And every rose and lily there did stand
Better attired by Nature's hand.
ABRAHAM COWLEY, *The Garden*.

The lilies
Contending with the roses in her cheeks,
Who shall most set them off.
PHILIP MASSINGER, *The Great Duke of Florence*. Act v, sc. 3.

7
And the stately lilies stand
Fair in the silvery light,
Like saintly vestals, pale in prayer;
Their pure breath sanctifies the air,
As its fragrance fills the night.
JULIA C. R. DORR, *A Red Rose*.

8
Lilies are whitest in a blackamoor's hand.
THOMAS FULLER, *Gnomologia*. No. 3244.

9
By cool Siloam's shady rill
How sweet the lily grows!
REGINALD HEBER, *First Sunday After Epiphany*.

10
The lily is all in white, like a saint,
And so is no mate for me.
THOMAS HOOD, *Flowers*.

11
We are Lilies fair,
The flower of virgin light;
Nature held us forth, and said,
"Lo! my thoughts of white."
LEIGH HUNT, *Lilies*.

12
Like these cool lilies may our loves remain,
Perfect and pure, and know not any stain.
ANDREW LANG, *A Vow to Heavenly Venus*.

13
Go bow thy head in gentle spite,
Thou lily white,
For she who spies thee waving here,
With thee in beauty can compare
As day with night.
J. M. LEGARÉ, *To a Lily*.

14
O lovely lily clean,
O lily springing green,
O lily bursting white,
Dear lily of delight,
Spring in my heart agen
That I may flower to men.
JOHN MASEFIELD, *The Everlasting Mercy*. Last st.

15
Consider the lilies of the field, how they grow; they toil not, neither do they spin: And yet I say unto you, That even Solomon in all his glory was not arrayed like one of these.
New Testament: Matthew, vi, 28, 29; *Luke*, xii, 27.

Yet neither spins nor cards, nor cares nor frets,
But to her mother Nature all her care she lets.
SPENSER, *Faerie Queene*. Bk. ii, canto vi, st. 16.

"Look to the lilies how they grow!"
'Twas thus the Saviour said, that we,
Even in the simplest flowers that blow,
God's ever-watchful care might see.
DAVID MOIR, *Lilies*.

"Thou wert not, Solomon! in all thy glory
Array'd," the lilies cry, "in robes like ours;
How vain your grandeur! Ah, how transitory
Are human flowers!"
HORACE SMITH, *Hymn to the Flowers*. St. 10.

16
Is not this lily pure?
What fuller can procure
A white so perfect, spotless clear
As in this flower, doth appear?
FRANCIS QUARLES, *School of the Heart*. Ode 30.

17
How bravely thou becomest thy bed, fresh lily.
SHAKESPEARE, *Cymbeline*. Act ii, sc. 2, l. 15.

Like the lily,
That once was mistress of the field and flourish'd,
I'll hang my head and perish.
SHAKESPEARE, *Henry VIII*. Act iii, sc. 1, l. 151.

18
And the wand-like lily, which lifted up,
As a Mænad, its moonlight-coloured cup,

Till the fiery star, which is its eye,
Gazed through clear dew on the tender sky.
SHELLEY, *The Sensitive Plant*. Pt. i, l. 33.

1
Now folds the lily all her sweetness up,
And slips into the bosom of the lake.
TENNYSON, *The Princess*. Pt. vii, l. 171.

2
But lilies, stolen from grassy mold,
No more curlèd state unfold,
Translated to a vase of gold;
In burning throne though they keep still
Serenities unthawed and chill.
FRANCIS THOMPSON, *Gilded Gold*.

3
White as any lily flower.
UNKNOWN, *King Horn*, l. 15. (c. 1310)

Her cheekes round, white as the flour de lys.
WILLIAM CAXTON, *Charles the Great*. (1485)

II—Lily-of-the-Valley

4
The lily of the vale, of flowers the queen,
Puts on the robe she neither sew'd nor spun.
MICHAEL BRUCE, *Elegy*.

5
White bud! that in meek beauty dost lean
Thy cloistered cheek as pale as moonlight snow,
Thou seem'st, beneath thy huge, high leaf of green,
An Eremite beneath his mountain's brow.
GEORGE CROLY, *The Lily of the Valley*.

6
And the Naiad-like lily of the vale,
Whom youth makes so fair and passion so pale,
That the light of its tremulous bells is seen,
Through their pavilions of tender green.
SHELLEY, *The Sensitive Plant*. Pt. i, l. 21.

7
Where scattered wild the Lily of the Vale
Its balmy essence breathes.
THOMSON, *The Seasons: Spring*, l. 445.

8
That shy plant . . . the lily of the vale,
That loves the ground, and from the sun withholds
Her pensive beauty.
WORDSWORTH, *The Excursion*. Bk. ix, l. 540.

LIMERICKS

A few famous ones; see also Appendix

9
Un marin naufragé (de Doncastre)
Pour prière, au milieu du désastre,
Repetait à genoux
Ces mots simples et doux:—
"Scintellez, scintellez, petits astres!"
GEORGE DU MAURIER, *Vers Nonsensiques*.

10
There was a small boy of Quebec
Who was buried in snow to the neck;
When they said, "Are you friz?"
He replied, "Yes, I is—
But we don't call this cold in Quebec."
RUDYARD KIPLING, *The Boy of Quebec*.

11
There was an Old Man with a beard,
Who said, "It is just what I feared!
Two Owls and a Hen,
Four Larks and a Wren,
Have all built their nests in my beard!"
EDWARD LEAR, *Nonsense Verses*.

12
There was a young lady of Niger
Who smiled as she rode on a tiger;
They returned from the ride
With the lady inside,
And the smile on the face of the tiger.
UNKNOWN, *The Young Lady of Niger*.

13
There once was a guy named Othello,
A dark, disagreeable fellow;
After croaking his wife,
Then he took his own life—
That bird wasn't black, he was yellow!
E. M. ROBINSON, *Limericised Classics*.

14
A canner, exceedingly canny,
One morning remarked to his granny,
"A canner can can
Anything that he can,
But a canner can't can a can, can he?"
CAROLYN WELLS, *The Canner*.

15
A Tutor who tooted the flute
Tried to teach two young tooters to toot.
Said the two to the Tutor,
"Is it harder to toot, or
To tutor two tooters to toot?"
CAROLYN WELLS, *The Tutor*.

16
There's a Portuguese person called Howell
Who lays on his lies with a trowel;
Should he get over lying
'Twill be when he's done dying
For living is lying to Howell.
J. MCNEILL WHISTLER. Referring to Charles Augustus Howell, an adventurer of the period. It was Howell who, in 1869, exhumed the body of D G. Rossetti's first wife, in order to recover the manuscripts which Rossetti had impulsively placed in the coffin nine years previously.

17
There was an old man of Nantucket
Who kept all his cash in a bucket;
But his daughter, named Nan,
Ran away with a man—
And as for the bucket, Nantucket.
DAYTON VOORHEES, *The Old Man of Nantucket*. First published in the Princeton *Tiger* in 1902.

18
A fly and a flea in a flue
Were imprisoned, so what could they do?
Said the fly, "Let us flee!"
"Let us fly!" said the flea,

So they flew through a flaw in the flue.
UNKNOWN, *Flight.*

1
Oh, won't you come up, come all the way up,
Come all the way up to Limerick?
UNKNOWN, *Won't You Come Up to Limerick?* The chorus following the singing of an extemporized nonsense verse at convivial parties, the reference being to the town of Limerick, Ireland. The first instance of a limerick occurs in the anonymous *History of Sixteen Wonderful Old Women,* published in 1820.

LINCOLN, ABRAHAM

2
Abraham wore a stovepipe hat
That brushed the stars down where he walked;
His eyes were terrible to look at,
His eyes were black pools when he talked.
JOSEPH AUSLANDER, *Abraham Lincoln.*

3
Some opulent force of genius, soul, and race,
Some deep life-current from far centuries
Flowed to his mind and lighted his sad eyes,
And gave his name, among great names, high place.
JOEL BENTON, *Another Washington.*

4
Into his heart's great jar Truth's brother poured
Strong love for men and freedom—fatal deed!
Some liked the wine, and some its making scored;
One broke the jar that held his own life's need.
CHARLES GRANGER BLANDEN, *Lincoln.*

5
No king this man, by grace of God's intent;
No, something better, freeman,—President!
A nature, modeled on a higher plan,
Lord of himself, an inborn gentleman!
GEORGE HENRY BOKER, *Our Heroic Themes.* Read before Phi Beta Kappa at Harvard, 20 July, 1865, one of the earliest and most discriminating tributes to Lincoln.

Great in his goodness, humble in his state,
Firm in his purpose, yet not passionate,
He led his people with a tender hand,
And won by love a sway beyond command.
GEORGE HENRY BOKER, *Our Heroic Themes.*

6
Oh, slow to smite and swift to spare,
Gentle and merciful and just!
Who, in the fear of God, didst bear
The sword of power, a nation's trust!
W. C. BRYANT, *Abraham Lincoln.*

7
Our pastoral captain, skilled to crook
The spear into the pruning hook,
The simple, kindly man,
Lincoln, American.
JOHN VANCE CHENEY, *Lincoln.*

To set the stones back in the wall
Lest the divided house should fall.
The beams of peace he laid,
While kings looked on, afraid.
JOHN VANCE CHENEY, *Lincoln.*

Unheralded, God's captain came
As one that answers to his name;
Nor dreamed how high his charge,
His privilege how large.
JOHN VANCE CHENEY, *Lincoln.*

If so men's memories not a monument be,
None shalt thou have. Warm hearts, and not cold stone,
Must mark thy grave, or thou shalt lie, unknown.
Marbles keep not themselves; how then, keep thee?
JOHN VANCE CHENEY, *Thy Monument.*

8
O Uncommon Commoner! may your name
Forever lead like a living flame!
Unschooled scholar! how did you learn
The wisdom a lifetime may not earn?
EDMUND VANCE COOKE, *The Uncommon Commoner.*

9
Great Nature's forces, unrestrained and free,
Produced, by chance, this giant of mankind,
And challenged man to solve his mystery.
REMBRANDT W. B. DITMARS, *Lincoln.*

Spontaneous! Inspired! The perfect flower
Of chance, he was by liberal Nature sent
To lead men nobly with unconscious power,
And justify the law of accident.
REMBRANDT W. B. DITMARS, *Lincoln.*

10
Hail, Lincoln! As the swift years lengthen
Still more majestic grows thy fame;
The ties that bind us to thee strengthen;
Starlike-immortal shines thy name.
NATHAN HASKELL DOLE, *Lincoln's Birthday.*

11
His heart was as great as the world, but there was no room in it to hold the memory of a wrong.
EMERSON, *Letters and Social Aims: Greatness.*

12
We are coming, Father Abraham, three hundred thousand more.
J. S. GIBBONS, *We Are Coming, Father Abraham.* (New York *Evening Post,* 16 July, 1862.)

13
A martyr to the cause of man,
His blood is freedom's eucharist,
And in the world's great hero list
His name shall lead the van.
CHARLES G. HALPIN, *The Death of Lincoln.*

14
Lincoln had faith in time, and time has justified his faith.
BENJAMIN HARRISON, *Lincoln Day Address,* Chicago, 1898.

15
Strange mingling of mirth and tears, of the tragic and grotesque, of cap and crown, of

Socrates and Rabelais, of Æsop and Marcus Aurelius—Lincoln, the gentlest memory of the world.

R. G. INGERSOLL, *Lincoln.*

Lincoln was not a type. He stands alone—no ancestors, no fellows, no successors.

ROBERT G. INGERSOLL, *Lincoln.*

1 Hundreds of people are now engaged in smoothing out the lines on Lincoln's face—forcing all features to the common mold—so that he may be known, not as he really was, but, according to their poor standard, as he should have been.

R. G. INGERSOLL, *Lincoln.*

Another expense we didn' used to have wuz buyin' an entirely new life of Lincoln ever' month or so.

KIN HUBBARD, *Abe Martin's Broadcast*, p. 21.

2 If the good people in their wisdom shall see fit to keep me in the background, I have been too familiar with disappointment to be much chagrined.

ABRAHAM LINCOLN, *Communication*, Sangamon *Journal*, when first a candidate for the Illinois State Legislature, 1832.

3 Nobody ever expected me to be President. In my poor, lean, lank face nobody has ever seen that any cabbages were sprouting.

ABRAHAM LINCOLN, *Speech*, against Douglas, in campaign of 1860.

They have seen in his [Douglas's] round, jolly, fruitful face, post-offices, land-offices, marshalships and cabinet-appointments, chargé-ships and foreign missions, bursting out in wonderful exuberance.

ABRAHAM LINCOLN, *Speech*, against Douglas, in campaign of 1860.

4 His head is bowed. He thinks of men and kings.
Yea, when the sick world cries, how can he sleep?
Too many peasants fight, they know not why;
Too many homesteads in black terror weep.

VACHEL LINDSAY, *Abraham Lincoln Walks at Midnight.*

5 That nation has not lived in vain which has given the world Washington and Lincoln, the best great men and the greatest good men whom history can show.

HENRY CABOT LODGE, *Lincoln*. Address before Massachusetts Legislature, 12 Feb., 1909.

6 Great captains, with their guns and drums,
Disturb our judgment for the hour,
But at last silence comes;
These are all gone, and, standing like a tower,
Our children shall behold his fame,
The kindly-earnest, brave, foreseeing man,
Sagacious, patient, dreading praise, not blame,
New birth of our new soil, the first American.

J. R. LOWELL, *Commemoration Ode.*

Nature, they say, doth dote,
And cannot make a man
Save on some worn-out plan
Repeating us by rote:
For him her Old World moulds aside she threw
And, choosing sweet clay from the breast
Of the unexhausted West,
With stuff untainted shaped a hero new.

J. R. LOWELL, *Commemoration Ode.*

7 A blend of mirth and sadness, smiles and tears;
A quaint knight-errant of the pioneers;
A homely hero, born of star and sod;
A Peasant-Prince; a Masterpiece of God.

WALTER MALONE, *Abraham Lincoln.*

8 When the Norn Mother saw the Whirlwind Hour
Greatening and darkening as it hurried on,
She left the Heaven of Heroes and came down
To make a man to meet the mortal need.
She took the tried clay of the common road—
Clay warm yet with the genial heat of earth.
Dashed through it all a strain of prophecy,
Tempered the heap with thrill of human tears
Then mixed a laughter with the serious stuff.

EDWIN MARKHAM, *Lincoln, The Man of the People.*

Here was a man to hold against the world,
A man to match the mountains and the sea.

EDWIN MARKHAM, *Lincoln, The Man of the People.*

The color of the ground was in him, the red earth,
The smack and tang of elemental things:
The rectitude and patience of the cliff,
The goodwill of the rain that loves all leaves,
The friendly welcome of the wayside well,
The courage of the bird that dares the sea,
The gladness of the wind that shakes the corn,
The pity of the snow that hides all scars, . . .
The tolerance and equity of light.

EDWIN MARKHAM, *Lincoln, The Man of the People.*

One fire was on his spirit, one resolve—
To send the keen axe to the root of wrong,
Clearing a free way for the feet of God,
The eyes of conscience testing every stroke.

EDWIN MARKHAM, *Lincoln, The Man of the People.*

So came the Captain with the mighty heart;
And when the judgment thunders split the house,
Wrenching the rafters from their ancient rest,
He held the ridgepole up, and spiked again
The rafters of the house.

EDWIN MARKHAM, *Lincoln, The Man of the People.*

And when he fell in whirlwind, he went down
As when a lordly cedar, green with boughs,
Goes down with a great shout upon the hills,
And leaves a lonesome place against the sky.
EDWIN MARKHAM, *Lincoln, The Man of the People.*

1
His grave a nation's heart shall be,
His monument a people free!
CAROLINE ATHERTON MASON, *President Lincoln's Grave.*

2
I am Ann Rutledge who sleeps beneath these weeds,
Beloved of Abraham Lincoln,
Wedded to him, not through union,
But through separation.
Bloom forever, O Republic,
From the dust of my bosom.
EDGAR LEE MASTERS, *Ann Rutledge.* Engraved on her tombstone at Petersburg, Ill.

But from her beauty and her doom
A man rose merciful and just;
And a great People still can feel
The passion of her dust.
EDWIN MARKHAM, *Ann Rutledge.*

3
When Abraham Lincoln was murdered
The one thing that interested Matthew Arnold
Was that the assassin Shouted in Latin
As he leapt on the stage.
This convinced Matthew
There was still hope for America.
CHRISTOPHER MORLEY, *Point of View.* The Latin phrase was "Sic semper tyrannis."

4
Riding the storm-column in the lightning-stroke,
Calm at the peak, while down below worlds rage,
And Earth goes out in blood and battle-smoke,
And leaves him with the sun—an epoch and an age!
JAMES OPPENHEIM, *The Lincoln-Child.*

Our big, gaunt, homely brother—
Our huge Atlantic coast-storm in a shawl,
Our cyclone in a smile—our President.
JAMES OPPENHEIM, *The Lincoln-Child.*

Oh, to pour love through deeds—
To be as Lincoln was!—
That all the land might fill its daily needs,
Glorified by a human Cause!
JAMES OPPENHEIM, *The Lincoln-Child.*

5
Mr. Lincoln was deficient in those little links which make up the path of a woman's happiness.
MARY OWENS, explaining her refusal to marry Lincoln.

I have now come to the conclusion never again to think of marrying, and for this reason: I can never be satisfied with anyone who would be blockhead enough to have me.
ABRAHAM LINCOLN, *Letter to Mrs. Browning,* 1 April, 1838, after being rejected by Mary Owens.

6
For he, to whom we had applied
Our shopman's test of age and worth,
Was elemental when he died,
As he was ancient at his birth:
The saddest among kings of earth,
Bowed with a galling crown, this man
Met rancor with a cryptic mirth,
Laconic—and Olympian.
E. A. ROBINSON, *The Master.*

7
When Abraham Lincoln was shoveled into the tombs, he forgot the copperheads and the assassin . . . in the dust, in the cool tombs.
CARL SANDBURG, *Cool Tombs.*

8
There is Lincoln on the other side of the street. Just look at Old Abe.
LESLIE SMITH, at a River and Harbor Convention, in July, 1847. (WASHBURNE, *Reminiscences of Lincoln,* 16.) So far as known, the first use of the nickname.

9
Now he belongs to the ages.
EDWIN M. STANTON, at death of Abraham Lincoln, 15 April, 1865. (TARBELL, *Life,* p. 244.)

10
Look on this cast, and know the hand
That bore a nation in its hold;
From this mute witness understand
What Lincoln was—how large of mould.
E. C. STEDMAN, *The Hand of Lincoln.*

Lo, as I gaze, the statured man,
Built up from yon large hand appears:
A type that nature wills to plan
But once in all a people's years.
E. C. STEDMAN, *The Hand of Lincoln.*

11
No Cæsar he whom we lament,
A Man without a precedent,
Sent, it would seem, to do
His work, and perish, too.
R. H. STODDARD, *Abraham Lincoln.*

One of the people! born to be
Their curious epitome;
To share yet rise above
Their shifting hate and love.
R. H. STODDARD, *Abraham Lincoln.*

12
His love shone as impartial as the sun.
MAURICE THOMPSON, *At Lincoln's Grave.*

13
Heroic soul, in homely garb half-hid,
Sincere, sagacious, melancholy, quaint;
What he endured, no less than what he did,
Has reared his monument, and crowned him saint.
J. T. TROWBRIDGE, *Lincoln.*

1
A. Linkin, adoo! A. Ward.
ARTEMUS WARD, *Interview With Lincoln.*

2
O Captain! my Captain! our fearful trip is done,
The ship has weather'd every rack, the prize we sought is won,
The port is near, the bells I hear, the people all exulting,
While follow eyes the steady keel, the vessel grim and daring;
But O heart! heart! heart!
O the bleeding drops of red,
Where on the deck my Captain lies,
Fallen cold and dead.
WALT WHITMAN, *O Captain! My Captain!*

The ship is anchor'd safe and sound, its voyage closed and done.
From fearful trip the victor ship comes in with object won;
Exult, O shores, and ring, O bells!
But I with mournful tread,
Walk the deck my Captain lies,
Fallen cold and dead.
WALT WHITMAN, *O Captain! My Captain!*

This dust was once the man,
Gentle, plain, just and resolute, under whose cautious hand,
Against the foulest crime in history known in any land or age,
Was saved the Union of these States.
WALT WHITMAN, *This Dust Was Once the Man.*

3
There is no name in all our country's story
So loved as his today:
No name which so unites the things of glory
With life's plain, common way.
ROBERT WHITAKER, *Abraham Lincoln.*

4
Lincoln was a very normal man with very normal gifts, but all upon a great scale, all knit together in loose and natural form, like the great frame in which he moved and dwelt.
WOODROW WILSON, *Address,* Chicago, 12 Feb., 1909.

5
You lay a wreath on murdered Lincoln's bier,
You, who with mocking pencil wont to trace,
Broad for the self-complacent British sneer,
His length of shambling limb, his furrowed face.
TOM TAYLOR, *Abraham Lincoln.* This poem appeared in *Punch,* 6 May, 1865, accompanying a full-page cartoon with the caption, "Britannia Sympathises with Columbia," representing Punch among the mourners at Lincoln's bier, upon which Britannia is laying a wreath. It was *Punch's* apology for its scurrilous abuse and caricature of Lincoln during the whole period of the war. The poem has often been ascribed to Shirley Brooks, but an entry in his diary, under date of 10 May, 1865, is conclusive evidence that the verses were written by Taylor. Brooks wrote: "Dined *Punch,* all there. Let out my views about some verses on Lincoln in which T. T. had not only made P. eat 'umble pie, but swallow dish and all." So far from being the writer of the verses, he condemned their publication. At the time the poem appeared, it was also ascribed to Tennyson.

Beside this corpse, that bears for winding sheet
The Stars and Stripes he lived to rear anew,
Between the mourners at his head and feet,
Say, scurril jester, is there room for you?

Yes, he had lived to shame me from my sneer,
To lame my pencil and confute my pen—
To make me own this hind of Princes peer,
This rail-splitter a true-born king of men.
TOM TAYLOR, *Abraham Lincoln.*

Sore heart, so stopped when it at last beat high!
Sad life, cut short just as its triumph came!
TOM TAYLOR, *Abraham Lincoln.*

Vile hand, that brandest murder on a strife,
Whate'er its grounds, stoutly and nobly striven,
And with the martyr's crown, crownest a life
With much to praise, little to be forgiven.
TOM TAYLOR, *Abraham Lincoln.*

LINDBERGH, CHARLES AUGUSTUS

6
O it's Flying Charlie for you and me,
It's him that's the king of air and sea,
For Charlie *go bragh* from the Land of the Free,
The whole world's Flying Charlie.
LOUISE AYRES GARNETT, *Flying Charlie.*

7
If Ambassador Morrow's daughter had married a trapeze artist she would have had at least her forenoons on the ground.
KIN HUBBARD, *Abe Martin's Broadcast.*

There's no use talkin', Lindbergh gits all the breaks. He taught his wife to fly an' they're still speakin'.
KIN HUBBARD, *Abe Martin's Broadcast,* p. 69.

8
Wings and the Boy! Companions linked as one,
Prince of the Air, Columbia's bravest son,
Modest as brave—the glory of the deed
Joyously sharing with his wingèd steed,
Named for a gallant Knight—by happy chance,
The Spirit of Saint Louis, King of France.
OLIVER HERFORD, *Our Boy.*

9
Alone, yet never lonely,
Serene, beyond mischance,
The world was his, his only,
When Lindbergh flew to France!
ALINE MICHAELIS, *Lindbergh.*

10
Lad, you took the soul of me
That long had lain despairing,
Sent me Heaven-faring.

Gave me wings again.
Lad, you took the world's soul,
Thrilled it by your daring,
Lifted the uncaring
And made them joyous men.
ANGELA MORGAN, *Lindbergh.*

1
Of common earth men wrought it, and of wonder;
With lightning have men bitted it and shod;
The throat of it is clothed with singing thunder—
And Lindbergh rides with God!
JOHN G. NEIHARDT, *The Lyric Deed.*

2
Soul attuned to a magic summons,
Pulse attuned to a motor's song,
Cutting a path through sun and darkness,
Mile after conquering mile along.
BLANCHE W. SCHOONMAKER, *Wings.*

3
Lone eagle of the wild Atlantic plain,
Tall, laughing boy, with sun-glints in your eyes,
Playfellow of the lightning and the rain,
Co-sentry with old watchers of the skies.
WENDELL PHILLIPS STAFFORD, *Lindbergh.*

4
Not Galileo, with his dreaming power,
Not great Columbus, master of the gale,
Chartered for Time such harbors for man's flight.
HAROLD VINAL, *Flight.*

5
Now from the flowing bowl
Spoke forth a nation's soul:
"Skoal! Charles Lindbergh, skoal!
New York to Paris!"
UNKNOWN, *Skoal, Lindbergh, Skoal!*

LION

6
One, but that one a lion. ("Ενα . . . ἀλλὰ λέοντα.)
ÆSOP, *Fables.*

7
If the lion was advised by the fox, he would be cunning.
WILLIAM BLAKE, *Proverbs of Hell.*

The fox provides for himself, but God provides for the lion.
WILLIAM BLAKE, *Proverbs of Hell.*
See also under FOX.

Choose rather to be the tail of lions than the head of foxes.
UNKNOWN. A Hebrew proverb.

8
Lions are kings of beasts, and yet their pow'r
Is not to rule and govern, but devour.
SAMUEL BUTLER, *Miscellaneous Thoughts,* l. 155

9
A lion may be beholden to a mouse.
THOMAS FULLER, *Gnomologia.* No. 264.

10
The lion is not so fierce as they paint him.
GEORGE HERBERT, *Jacula Prudentum.* (1640)

The lion is not so fierce as painted.
THOMAS FULLER, *Of Preferment.* (1655)

The lion is not so fierce as they paint him.
SAMUEL PEPYS, *Diary,* 9 Aug., 1661.

The lion (sure) is not so fierce or stout
As foolish men do paint or set him out.
RICHARD WATKYNS, *Epigram.* (1662)

11
The lion is, beyond dispute,
Allow'd the most majestic brute;
His valour and his generous mind
Prove him superior of his kind.
JOHN GAY, *Fables.* Pt. ii, fab. 9.

12
This country, Francesco . . . had scarce seen the lions.
ROBERT GREENE, *Works.* Vol viii, p. 68. (1590)
The reference was originally to the lions in the Tower of London, but was soon extended to mean any unusual sight.

This is not the right season of the year to show the lions.
MRS. CIBBER. (*Garrick Correspondence,* i, 200.)

13
Who nourisheth a lion must obey him.
BEN JONSON, *Sejanus.* Act iii, sc. 3.

14
What weapons has the lion but himself?
KEATS, *King Stephen.* Act i, sc. 3, l. 20.

15
The African lions rush to attack bulls; they do not attack butterflies. (In tauros Libyci ruunt leones, Non sunt papilionibus molesti.)
MARTIAL, *Epigrams.* Bk. xii, epig. 61.

Bombastes: So have I heard on Afric's burning shore
A hungry lion give a grievous roar;
The grievous roar echoed along the shore.
Artax: So have I heard on Afric's burning shore
Another lion give a grievous roar
And the first lion thought the last a bore.
W. B. RHODES, *Bombastes Furioso.* Act i, sc. 4.

16
Do not pluck the beard of a dead lion. (Noli Barbam vellere mortuo leoni.)
MARTIAL, *Epigrams.* Bk. x, epig. 90.

17
Now half appear'd
The tawny lion, pawing to get free
His hinder parts.
MILTON, *Paradise Lost.* Bk. vii, l. 463.

18
I carry off the chief share because I am called the Lion. (Ego primam tollo, nominor quia Leo.)
PHÆDRUS, *Fables.* Bk. i, fab. 5, l. 7. Hence, the lion's share.

19
To attempt to shave a lion. (Ξυρεῖν ἐπιχειρεῖν λέοντα.)
PLATO, *The Republic.* Bk. i, sec. 15.

1
They gaped upon me with their mouths, as a ravening and a roaring lion.
Old Testament: Psalms, xxii, 13.

2
A lion among sheep and a sheep among lions.
PUTTENHAM. (ARBER, *English Poesie,* p. 299.) 1589. *See also under* LAMB.

3
The lion is the beast to fight:
He leaps along the plain,
And if you run with all your might,
He runs with all his mane.
I'm glad I'm not a Hottentot,
But if I were, with outwarm cal-lum
I'd either faint upon the spot
Or hie me up a leafy pal-lum.
A. T. QUILLER-COUCH, *Sage Counsel.*

4
Even the lion must defend itself against the flies. (Auch der Löwe muss sich vor der Mucke wehren.)
UNKNOWN. A German proverb.

5
Thy mirth refrain,
Thy hand is on a lion's mane.
SCOTT, *The Lady of the Lake.* Canto ii, st. 12.

Dar'st thou, then,
To beard the lion in his den?
SCOTT, *Marmion.* Canto vi, st. 14.

Rouse the lion from his lair.
SCOTT, *The Talisman.* Ch. 6.

6
'Tis better playing with a lion's whelp
Than with an old one dying.
SHAKESPEARE, *Antony and Cleopatra.* Act iii, sc. 13, l. 94.

7
The blood more stirs
To rouse a lion than to start a hare!
SHAKESPEARE, *I Henry IV.* Act i, sc. 3, l. 197.

8
The man that once did sell the lion's skin,
While the beast lived, was killed with hunting him.
SHAKESPEARE, *Henry V.* Act iv, sc. 3, l. 93.

The lion's skin is never cheap.
JOHN RAY, *English Proverbs.*

9
Small curs are not regarded when they grin;
But great men tremble when the lion roars.
SHAKESPEARE, *II Henry VI.* Act iii, sc. 1, l. 18.

Talks as familiarly of roaring lions
As maids of thirteen do of puppy-dogs!
SHAKESPEARE, *King John.* Act ii, sc. 1, l. 459.

10
Against the Capitol I met a lion,
Who glared upon me, and went surly by,
Without annoying me.
SHAKESPEARE, *Julius Cæsar.* Act i, sc. 3, l. 20.

11
Thou wear a lion's hide! doff it for shame,
And hang a calf's-skin on those recreant limbs.
SHAKESPEARE, *King John.* Act iii, sc. 1, l. 128.

12
God shield us!—a lion among ladies is a most dreadful thing; for there is not a more fearful wild-fowl than your lion living.
SHAKESPEARE, *A Midsummer-Night's Dream.* Act iii, sc. 1, l. 31.

Demetrius: Well roared, Lion.
Theseus: Well run, Thisbe.
Hippolyta: Well shone, Moon. Truly, the moon shines with a good grace.
Theseus: Well moused, Lion.
Lysander: And so the lion vanished.
SHAKESPEARE, *A Midsummer-Night's Dream.* Act v, sc. 1, l. 270.

13
The grim lion fawneth o'er his prey,
Sharp hunger by the conquest satisfied.
SHAKESPEARE, *The Rape of Lucrece.* St. 61.

14
Thou shalt hunt a lion, that will fly
With his face backward.
SHAKESPEARE, *Troilus and Cressida,* iv, 1, 19.

15
It is not good to wake a sleeping lion.
SIR PHILIP SIDNEY, *Arcadia.* Bk. iv. (1580)

Wake not a sleeping lion.
UNKNOWN, *The Countryman's New Commonwealth.* (1647) *See also under* DOG.

16
Lion and stoat have isled together, knave,
In time of flood.
TENNYSON, *Gareth and Lynette,* l. 871.

17
I hope we shall not be as wise as the frogs to whom Jupiter gave the stork as their king. To trust expedients with such a king on the throne would be just as wise as if there were a lion in the lobby, and we should vote to let him in and chain him, instead of fastening the door to keep him out.
COLONEL SILIUS TITUS, *Speech,* on the Exclusion Bill, House of Commons, 7 Jan., 1680. This, Titus's most famous speech, was delivered against the limitation which Charles offered to impose upon a Catholic sovereign rather than pass the bill excluding his brother from the throne. "A lion in the lobby" passed into a proverb.

But Titus said, with his uncommon sense,
When the Exclusion Bill was in suspense:
"I hear a lion in the lobby roar;
Say, Mr. Speaker, shall we shut the door
And keep him there, or shall we let him in
To try if we can turn him out again?"
JAMES BRAMSTON, *Art of Politics.*

18
I girdid up my Lions & fled the Seen.
ARTEMUS WARD, *A Visit to Brigham Young.*

19
The very hares insult the body of a dead lion. (Ὅττι καὶ αὐτοὶ νεκροῦ σῶμα λέοντος ἐφυβρίζουσι λαγωοί.)
UNKNOWN. (*Greek Anthology.* Bk. xvi, epig. 4.)

You are the hare of whom the proverb goes,
Whose valour plucks dead lions by the beard.
SHAKESPEARE, *King John.* Act ii, sc. 1, l. 137.

Do not, live hare, pull the dead lion's beard.
RANDOLPH, *The Jealous Lovers*. Act iv, sc. 3.

Little birds may pick a dead lion.
THOMAS FULLER, *Gnomologia*. No. 3250.

LIP

See also Kiss, Mouth

1
And though hard be the task,
"Keep a stiff upper lip."
PHŒBE CARY, *Keep a Stiff Upper Lip*.

2
Lips, however rosy, must be fed.
A. B. CHEALES, *Proverbial Folk-Lore*, 29.

3
My Lady's presence makes the Roses red,
Because to see her lips they blush for shame.
HENRY CONSTABLE, *Diana*. Sonnet ix.

Her lips are roses over-wash'd with dew,
Or like the purple of Narcissus' flower;
No frost their fair, no wind doth waste their power,
But by her breath her beauties do renew.
ROBERT GREENE, *Eclogue*.

4
Oh that those lips had language!
COWPER, *On the Receipt of My Mother's Picture*, l. 1.

5
Cherry-ripe, ripe, ripe, I cry,
Full and fair ones; come and buy:
If so be, you ask me where
They do grow, I answer, There,
Where my Julia's lips do smile;
There's the land, or cherry-isle.
ROBERT HERRICK, *Cherry-Ripe*.

O, how ripe in show
Thy lips, those kissing cherries, tempting grow!
SHAKESPEARE, *A Midsummer-Night's Dream*. Act iii sc. 2, l. 139.

6
Some ask'd me where the rubies grew?
And nothing did I say:
But with my finger pointed to
The lips of Julia.
ROBERT HERRICK, *The Rock of Rubies*.

7
I am a man of unclean lips.
Old Testament: Isaiah, vi, 5.

8
Lips are no part of the head, only made for a double-leaf door for the mouth.
JOHN LYLY, *Midas*.

Divers philosophers hold that the lips is parcel of the mouth.
SHAKESPEARE, *The Merry Wives of Windsor*. Act i, sc. 1, l. 236.

9
Love, how he melts! I cannot blame my lady's
Unwillingness to part with such marmalade lips.
PHILIP MASSINGER, *The Picture*. Act i, sc. 1.

10
His coward lips did from their colour fly.
SHAKESPEARE, *Julius Cæsar*. Act i, sc. 2, l. 122.

11
Take, O, take those lips away,
That so sweetly were forsworn.
SHAKESPEARE, *Measure for Measure*. Act iv, sc. 1, l. 1. This song appears also in Beaumont and Fletcher's *The Bloody Brother*, act v, sc. 2, with an additional stanza written by Beaumont.

12
Teach not thy lips such scorn, for they were made
For kissing, lady, not for such contempt.
SHAKESPEARE, *Richard III*. Act i, sc. 2. l. 172.

Oh, what a deal of scorn looks beautiful
In the contempt and anger of his lip!
SHAKESPEARE, *Twelfth Night*. Act iii, sc. 1, l. 157.

13
Their lips were four red roses on a stalk,
Which in their summer beauty kiss'd each other.
SHAKESPEARE, *Richard III*. Act iv, sc. 3, l. 12.

And steal immortal blessing from her lips,
Who, even in pure and vestal modesty,
Still blush, as thinking their own kisses sin.
SHAKESPEARE, *Romeo and Juliet*. Act iii, sc. 3, l. 37.

I'll take that winter from your lips.
SHAKESPEARE, *Troilus and Cressida*. Act iv, sc. 5, l. 23.

14
Romeo: Have not saints lips, and holy palmers too?
Juliet: Ay, pilgrim, lips that they must use in prayer.
SHAKESPEARE, *Romeo and Juliet*. Act i, sc. 5, l. 103.

15
I ne'er saw nectar on a lip,
But where my own could hope to sip.
SHERIDAN, *The Duenna*. Act i, sc. 2.

16
Her lips were red, and one was thin,
Compar'd to that was next her chin,
Some bee had stung it newly.
SIR JOHN SUCKLING, *A Ballad Upon a Wedding*. St. 11.

17
With that she dasht her on the lips,
So dyed double red:
Hard was the heart that gave the blow,
Soft were those lips that bled.
WILLIAM WARNER, *Albion's England*. Bk. viii, ch. xli, st. 53.

18
You are coming to woo me, but not as of yore,
When I hastened to welcome your ring at the door;
For I trusted that he who stood waiting me then,
Was the brightest, the truest, the noblest of men;
Your lips, on my own, when they printed "Farewell,"

Had never been soiled by the "beverage of hell;"
But they come to me now with the baccanal sign,
And the lips that touch liquor must never touch mine.

George W. Young, *The Lips that Touch Liquor Must Never Touch Mine.* (c. 1870)

LISTENING

See also Ears

1

But yet she listen'd—'tis enough—
Who listens once will listen twice.

Byron, *Mazeppa*. St. 6.

In short, there never was a better hearer.

Byron, *Don Juan*. Canto xiv, st. 37.

And listens like a three years' child.

S. T. Coleridge, *The Ancient Mariner*. Pt. i.

It takes a great man to make a good listener.

Sir Arthur Helps, *Brevia*.

Give us grace to listen well.

John Keble, *Christian Year: Palm Sunday*.

To listen well is a second inheritance. (Bene audire alterum patrimonium est.)

Publilius Syrus, *Sententiæ*. No. 93.

2

Were we as eloquent as angels, yet we should please some men, some women, and some children much more by listening, than by talking.

C. C. Colton, *Lacon*. No. 13.

3

He listens to good purpose who takes note. (Bene ascolta chi la nota.)

Dante, *Inferno*. Canto xv, l. 100.

4

The grace of listening is lost if the listener's attention is demanded, not as a favor, but as a right. (In audiendi officio perit gratia, si reposcatur.)

Pliny the Younger, *Epistles*. Bk. i, epis. 13.

5

Listeners seldom hear good of themselves.

John Ray, *English Proverbs*.

Hearkeners, we say, seldom hear good of themselves.

Mathew Henry, *Commentaries: Ecclesiastes*, vii.

6

Take care what you say before a wall, as you cannot tell who may be behind it.

Sadi, *Gulistan: Rules for Conduct*. No. 12.

7

In listening mood, sh seemed to stand,
The guardian Naiad of the strand.

Scott, *The Lady of the Lake*. Canto i, st. 17.

8

And this cuff was but to knock at your ear, and beseech listening.

Shakespeare, *The Taming of the Shrew*. Act iv, sc. 1, l. 66.

9

No syren did ever so charm the ear of the listener, as the listening ear has charmed the soul of the syren.

Sir Henry Taylor, *The Statesman*, p. 239.

LITERATURE

See also Writers and Writing

I—Literature: Definitions

10

Literature is the thought of thinking Souls.

Carlyle, *Essays: Memoirs of the Life of Scott*.

11

Literature is "The expression of a nation's mind in writing."

Channing, *Remarks on American Literature*.

12

Literature . . . is an art, a science, a profession, a trade, and an accident. The literature that is of lasting value is an accident. It is something that happens.

S. McC. Crothers, *Free Trade vs. Protection in Literature*.

13

There is first the literature of *knowledge*, and secondly, the literature of *power*. The function of the first is—to *teach;* the function of the second is—to *move;* the first is a rudder, the second an oar or a sail. The first speaks to the *mere* discursive understanding; the second speaks ultimately, it may happen, to the higher understanding of reason.

De Quincey, *Essays on the Poets: Pope*.

Books, we are told, propose to *instruct* or to *amuse*. Indeed! . . . The true antithesis to knowledge, in this case, is not pleasure but power. All that is literature seeks to communicate power: all that is not literature seeks to communicate knowledge.

Thomas De Quincey, *Letters to a Young Man*. No. 3. De Quincey adds that he is indebted for this distinction to "many years' conversation with Mr. Wordsworth."

Literature exists to please—to lighten the burden of men's lives; to make them for a short while forget their sorrows and their sins, their silenced hearths, their disappointed hopes, their grim futures—and those men of letters are the best loved who have best performed literature's truest office.

Birrell, *Obiter Dicta: Office of Literature*.

Literature does not please by moralizing us; it moralizes us because it pleases.

H. W. Garrod, *The Profession of Poetry*, p. 264.

14

Literature is an avenue to glory, ever open for those ingenious men who are deprived of honours or of wealth.

Isaac D'Israeli, *Literary Character of Men of Genius*. Ch. 24.

Literature—the most seductive, the most deceiving, the most dangerous of professions.

John Morley, *Life of Burke*, p. 9.

15

Literature is the effort of man to indemnify himself for the wrongs of his condition.

Emerson, *Natural History of Intellect: Landor*.

16

Literature, taken in all its bearings, forms the

grand line of demarcation between the human and the animal kingdoms.

William Godwin, *The Enquirer: Early Taste for Reading.*

1
Literature flourishes best when it is half a trade and half an art.

William Ralph Inge, *The Victorian Age.*

Literature was formerly an art and finance a trade: to-day it is the reverse.

Joseph Roux, *Meditations of a Parish Priest.* Pt. i, No. 65.

2
The classics are only primitive literature. They belong to the same class as primitive machinery and primitive music and primitive medicine.

Stephen Leacock, *Behind the Beyond: Homer and the Humbug.*

The fashion of liking Racine will pass like that of coffee. (La mode d'aimer Racine passera comme la mode du café.)

Madame de Sévigné, as quoted by Voltaire. (*Lettres,* 29 Jan., 1690.) La Harpe compressed the epigram to, "Racine passera comme le café." Since neither Racine nor coffee has passed, the prophecy may, from one angle, be considered a good one.

3
Language put to its best purpose, used at its utmost power and with the greatest skill, and recorded that it may not pass away, evaporate and be forgotten, is what we call, for want of a better word, literature.

J. W. Mackail, *Classical Studies,* p. 214.

4
American literature is English literature made in this country. . . . The American spirit in literature is a myth.

John Macy, *Spirit of American Literature.* Ch. 1.

Alas for the South! Her books have grown fewer—
She was never much given to literature.

J. Gordon Coogler. An immortal rhyme by a southern bard.

5
Take the whole range of imaginative literature, and we are all wholesale borrowers. In every matter that relates to invention, to use, or beauty, or form, we are borrowers.

Wendell Phillips, *The Lost Arts.*

Literature is a succession of books from books. . . . Every novel was suckled at the breasts of older novels, and great mothers are often prolific of anemic offspring.

John Macy, *Spirit of American Literature.* Ch. 1.

6
Great literature is simply language charged with meaning to the utmost possible degree.

Ezra Pound, *How to Read.* Pt. ii.

7
To turn events into ideas is the function of literature.

George Santayana, *Little Essays,* p. 138.

8
Just as we suffer from excess in all things, so we suffer from excess in literature. (Quemadmodum omnium rerum, sic litterarum quoque intemperantia laboramus.)

Seneca, *Epistulæ ad Lucilium.* Epis. cvi, 12.

Unhealthy literature. (Nihil sanantibus litteris.)

Seneca, *Epistulæ ad Lucilium.* Epis. lix, sec. 15.

9
Literature in many of its branches is no other than the shadow of good talk.

R. L. Stevenson, *Memories and Portraits: Talk and Talkers.*

10
Literature must be an analysis of experience and a synthesis of the findings into a unity.

Rebecca West, *Ending in Earnest.*

11
Literature always anticipates life. It does not copy it, but moulds it to its purpose.

Oscar Wilde, *The Decay of Lying.*

12
Literature is the orchestration of platitudes.

Thornton Wilder, *Literature.*

II—Literature: Apothegms

13
Life comes before literature, as the material always comes before the work. The hills are full of marble before the world blooms with statues.

Phillips Brooks, *Literature and Life.*

14
There is no such thing as either literature or poetry for the masses.

Jean Cocteau, *Le Rappel à l'Ordre,* p. 136.

15
I made a compact with myself that in my person literature should stand by itself, of itself, and for itself.

Dickens, *Speech,* at Liverpool, 1869.

16
Time, the great destroyer of other men's happiness, only enlarges the patrimony of literature to its possessor.

Isaac D'Israeli, *Literary Character of Men of Genius.* Ch. 22.

17
Our high respect for a well-read man is praise enough of literature.

Emerson, *Letters and Social Aims: Quotation.*

18
It is life that shakes and rocks us; it is literature which stabilizes and confirms.

H. W. Garrod, *Profession of Poetry,* p. 257.

19
Literature, like a gypsy, to be picturesque, should be a little ragged.

Douglas Jerrold, *Literary Men.*

20
One of the evils of our literature is that our learned men are without wit, and our witty men without learning. (Un des maux de notre littérature, c'est que nos savants ont peu

d'esprit, et que nos hommes d'esprit ne sont pas savants.)

JOUBERT, *Pensées*. No. 258.

1
National literature begins with fables and ends with novels. (La littérature des peuples commence par les fables et finit par les romans.)

JOUBERT, *Pensées*. No. 383.

Literature and fiction are two entirely different things. Literature is a luxury; fiction is a necessity.

G. K. CHESTERTON, *A Defence of Penny Dreadfuls*. *See also under* FICTION.

2
Literature is a very bad crutch, but a very good walking-stick.

CHARLES LAMB, *Letter to Bernard Barton*.

3
Break your worthless pens, Thalia, and tear up your books. (Frange leves calamos et scinde, Thalia, libellos.)

MARTIAL, *Epigrams*. Bk. ix, epig. 73. Written in indignation at the neglect of literature.

4
The republic of letters. (La république des lettres.)

MOLIÈRE, *Le Mariage Forcé*. Sc. 4, l. 2. (1664)

A pamphlet . . . which should make a great noise in the republic of letters. (Une brochure . . . qui doit faire grand bruit dans la république des lettres.)

LE SAGE, *Gil Blas*. Bk. xii, ch. 7. (1715)

The death of Dr. Hudson is a loss to the republic of letters.

WILLIAM KING, *Letter*, 7 Jan., 1719; FIELDING, *Tom Jones*. Bk. xiv, ch. 1. (1749)

"The Republic of Letters" is a very common expression among the Europeans.

GOLDSMITH, *Citizen of the World*. Letter 20.

The Commonwealth of Letters.

ADDISON, *The Spectator*. No. 529. (1712)

5
Literary fame is the only fame of which a wise man ought to be ambitious, because it is the only lasting and living fame.

ROBERT SOUTHEY, as quoted by Landor. (FORSTER, *Life of Landor*. Bk. vii, ch. 13.)

6
Literature is full of perfumes.

WALT WHITMAN, *Uncollected Prose*. Vol. ii, p. 74.

LONDON

I—London: Praise

7
As I came down the Highgate Hill,
  The Highgate Hill, the Highgate Hill,
As I came down the Highgate Hill
  I met the sun's bravado,
And saw below me, fold on fold,
Grey to pearl and pearl to gold,
This London like a land of old,
  The land of Eldorado.

HENRY BASHFORD, *Romances*.

8
What a place to plunder! (Was für Plunder!)

FIELD MARSHALL VON BLÜCHER, on viewing London from St. Paul's, after the peace banquet at Oxford, 1814. But the correct translation of "Was für Plunder" is "What trash! what rubbish!" What Blücher must have said was "Was für Plünder," to plunder, to sack. The Umlaut makes all the difference. Thackeray also forgot it:

The bold old Reiter looked down from St. Paul's
and sighed out, "Was für Plunder!"

THACKERAY, *The Four Georges: George I*.

9
London is the clearing-house of the world.

JOSEPH CHAMBERLAIN, *Speech*, Guildhall, London, 19 Jan., 1904.

The centre of a thousand trades.

COWPER, *Hope*, l. 248.

10
Oh, London is a fine town,
  A very famous city,
Where all the streets are paved with gold,
  And all the maidens pretty.

GEORGE COLMAN THE YOUNGER, *The Heir-at-Law*. Act i, sc. 2.

11
  Where has commerce such a mart,
So rich, so throng'd, so drain'd, and so supplied
As London, opulent, enlarg'd, and still
Increasing, London?

COWPER, *The Task*. Bk. i, l. 719.

Oh thou, resort and mart of all the earth,
Chequer'd with all complexions of mankind,
And spotted with all crimes; in which I see
Much that I love, and more that I admire,
And all that I abhor; thou freckl'd fair,
That pleasest and yet shock'st me.

COWPER, *The Task*. Bk. iii, l. 835.

12
London—a nation, not a city.

BENJAMIN DISRAELI, *Lothair*. Ch. 27.

13
London is the epitome of our times, and the Rome of to-day.

EMERSON, *English Traits: Result*.

14
He was born within the sound of Bow-bell.

THOMAS FULLER, *Gnomologia*.

15
The Old Lady in Threadneedle Street in Danger.

JAMES GILLRAY. Title of caricature dated 22 May, 1797, referring to the Bank of England, which is situated in Threadneedle Street, London, and which had suspended cash payments 26 Feb., 1797. The directors of the Bank were so-called by William Cobbett, because, like Mrs. Partington, they tried with their broom to sweep back the Atlantic flood of national progress.

A silver curl-paper that I myself took off the shining locks of the ever-beautiful old lady of Threadneedle Street.

DICKENS, *Dr. Marigold*. Referring to a banknote.

1
London is the only place in which the child grows completely up into the man.
WILLIAM HAZLITT, *Essays: On Londoners and Country People.*

I do not think there is anything deserving the name of society to be found out of London. . . . You can pick your society nowhere but in London.
WILLIAM HAZLITT, *Table Talk: On Coffee-House Politicians.*

2
When a man is tired of London he is tired of life; for there is in London all that life can afford.
SAMUEL JOHNSON. (BOSWELL, *Life,* 1777.)

3
The noble spirit of the metropolis is the life-blood of the state, collected at the heart.
JUNIUS, *Letters.* No. 37.

4
Ah London! London! our delight,
Great flower that opens but at night,
Great City of the midnight sun,
Whose day begins when day is done.
RICHARD LE GALLIENNE, *A Ballad of London.*

Paris, half Angel, half Grisette,
I would that I were with thee yet;
But London waits me, like a wife,
London, the love of my whole life.
RICHARD LE GALLIENNE, *Paris Day by Day.*

5
I love the haunts of old Cockaigne,
Where wit and wealth were squandered.
F. LOCKER-LAMPSON, *St. James's Street.*

6
In that temple of silence and reconciliation where the enmities of twenty generations lie buried, in the Great Abbey which has during many ages afforded a quiet resting-place to those whose minds and bodies have been shattered by the contentions of the Great Hall.
MACAULAY, *Essays: Warren Hastings.*

7
Go where we may, rest where we will,
Eternal London haunts us still.
THOMAS MOORE, *Rhymes on the Road.* No. 9.

8
In town let me live then, in town let me die
For in truth I can't relish the country, not I.
If one *must* have a villa in summer to dwell,
Oh give me the sweet shady side of Pall Mall.
CHARLES MORRIS, *The Contrast.*

9
Dear, damn'd, distracting town.
POPE, *A Farewell to London,* l. 1.

10
I hope to see London once ere I die.
SHAKESPEARE, *II Henry IV.* Act v, sc. 3, l. 64.

11
The way was long and weary,
But gallantly they strode,
A country lad and lassie,
Along the heavy road.
The night was dark and stormy,
But blithe of heart were they,
For shining in the distance
The lights of London lay.
O gleaming lights of London,
That gem of the city's crown;
What fortunes be within you,
O Lights of London Town!
GEORGE R. SIMS, *Lights of London: Song.*

12
To merry London, my most kindly nurse,
That to me gave this life's first native source.
EDMUND SPENSER, *Prothalamion,* l. 128.

13
Oh, mine in snows and summer heats,
These good old Tory brick-built streets!
My eye is pleased with all it meets
In Bloomsbury.
WILFRED WHITTEN, *Bloomsbury.*

And as sure as London is built of bricks.
THOMAS HOOD, *Miss Kilmansegg: Her Education.*

14
Earth has not anything to show more fair:
Dull would he be of soul who could pass by
A sight so touching in its majesty.
WORDSWORTH, *Miscellaneous Sonnets.* Pt. ii, No. 36. Composed upon Westminster Bridge.

Ne'er saw I, never felt, a calm so deep!
The river glideth at his own sweet will:
Dear God! the very houses seem asleep;
And all that mighty heart is lying still!
WORDSWORTH, *Miscellaneous Sonnets.* Pt. ii, No. 36.

II—London: Criticism

15
Lo, where huge London, huger day by day,
O'er six fair counties spreads it hideous sway!
ALFRED AUSTIN, *The Golden Age.*

16
I came to Gotham, where many, if not all,
I saw were fools. (Veni Gotham, ubi multos,
Si non omnes, vidi stultos.)
RICHARD BRATHWAITE, *Barnabæ Itinerarium.* (1638)

A mighty mass of brick, and smoke, and shipping,
Dirty and dusty, but as wide as eye
Could reach, with here and there a sail just skipping
In sight, then lost amidst the forestry
Of masts; a wilderness of steeples peeping
On tiptoe through their sea-coal canopy;
A huge, dun cupola, like a foolscap crown
On a fool's head—and there is London Town!
BYRON, *Don Juan.* Canto x, st. 82.

Thou art in London—in that pleasant place,
Where every kind of mischief's daily brewing.
BYRON, *Don Juan.* Canto xii, st. 23.

17
That monstrous tuberosity of civilised life, the capital of England.
CARLYLE, *Sartor Resartus.* Bk. iii, ch. 6.

There is a Stupidest of London men, actually resident, with bed and board of some kind, in London.
CARLYLE, *Essays: Biography.*

1
London Bridge was made for wise men to go over and fools to go under.
JOHN CLARKE, *Parœmiologia,* 249. (1639) A reference to the danger incurred by boats in shooting the rapids of the old bridge, where Anne Killigrew, to whose memory Dryden wrote a famous ode, was drowned in 1685.

There is a saying also that London Bridge was built upon wool-packs.
JOHN AUBREY, *Natural History of Wiltshire,* p. 98. (c. 1685)

2
Let but thy wicked men from out thee go,
And all the fools that crowd thee so,
Even thou, who dost thy millions boast,
A village less than Islington will grow,
A solitude almost.
ABRAHAM COWLEY, *Of Solitude.*

Methinks I see
The monster London laugh at me.
ABRAHAM COWLEY, *Of Solitude.*

3
A stony-hearted step-mother.
THOMAS DE QUINCEY, *Confessions of an English Opium Eater.* Pt. i. Referring to Oxford Street.

4
Mr. Weller's knowledge of London was extensive and peculiar.
DICKENS, *The Pickwick Papers.* Ch. 20.

5
London is a roost for every bird.
BENJAMIN DISRAELI, *Lothair.* Ch. 11.

London is a modern Babylon.
BENJAMIN DISRAELI, *Tancred.* Bk. v, ch. 5.

6
Beyond Hyde Park all is a desert.
ETHEREGE, *Man of Mode.* Act v, sc. 2. (1676)

London-over-the-Border.
A term applied to the Metropolitan district in Essex, derived from an article on that area in *Household Words* (12 Sept., 1857) entitled *Londoners-over-the-Border.* The article has been attributed without authority to Charles Dickens.

7
Ye towers of Julius, London's lasting shame,
With many a foul and midnight murder fed.
THOMAS GRAY, *The Bard.* Pt. ii, st. 3. Referring to the Tower of London.

Purg'd by the sword, and purified by fire,
Then had we seen proud London's hated walls;
Owls would have hooted in St. Peter's choir,
And foxes stunk and litter'd in St. Paul's.
THOMAS GRAY, *Impromptu on Lord Holland's Seat at Kingsgate.*

8
People-pestered London.
NICHOLAS GRIMALD, *The Lover to His Dear.*

9
London has a great belly but no palate.
THOMAS HOBBES, *History of Civil Wars,* p. 169.

London's the dining-room of Christendom.
THOMAS MIDDLETON, *City Pageant.*

10
London! the needy villain's gen'ral home,
The common shore of Paris, and of Rome;
With eager thirst, by folly or by fate,
Sucks in the dregs of each corrupted state.
SAMUEL JOHNSON, *London,* l. 93.

For who would leave, unbrib'd, Hibernia's land,
Or change the rocks of Scotland for the Strand? . . .
Here malice, rapine, accident, conspire,
And now a rabble rages, now a fire;
Their ambush here relentless ruffians lay,
And here the fell attorney prowls for prey;
Here falling houses thunder on your head,
And here a female atheist talks you dead.
SAMUEL JOHNSON, *London,* l. 9.

11
Where London's column, pointing at the skies,
Like a tall bully, lifts the head and lies.
POPE, *Moral Essays.* Epis. iii, l. 339.

12
Londoner-like ask as much more as you will take.
JOHN RAY, *English Proverbs,* 349. (1678)

13
You are now
In London, that great sea, whose ebb and flow
At once is deaf and loud, and on the shore
Vomits its wrecks, and still howls on for more.
SHELLEY, *Letter to Maria Gisborne,* l. 192.

14
We looked o'er London, where men wither and choke,
Roofed in, poor souls, renouncing stars and skies.
THEODORE WATTS-DUNTON, *A Talk on Waterloo Bridge.*

LONELINESS, see Solitude

LONGFELLOW, HENRY WADSWORTH

15
O gracious Poet and benign,
Belovèd presence! now as then
Thou standest by the hearths of men.
THOMAS BAILEY ALDRICH, *Longfellow.*

16
The New World's sweetest singer! Time may lay
Rude touch on some, thy betters; yet for thee
Thy seat is where the throned immortals be.
CRAVEN L. BETTS, *Longfellow.*

17
Whose Muse, benignant and serene,
Still keeps his Autumn chaplet green
Because his verse is pure!
AUSTIN DOBSON, *Longfellow.*

Ah! gentlest soul! how gracious, how benign
Breathes through our troubled life that voice of thine,

Filled with a sweetness born of happier spheres,
That wins and warms, that kindles, softens, cheers,
That calms the wildest woe and stays the bitterest tears!
O. W. Holmes, *To H. W. Longfellow.*

1
You may say that he's smooth and all that till you're hoarse,
But remember that elegance also is force;
After polishing granite as much as you will,
The heart keeps its tough old persistency still.
J. R. Lowell, *A Fable for Critics,* l. 1311.

2
The winds have talked with him confidingly;
The trees have whispered to him; and the night
Hath held him gently as a mother might,
And taught him all sad tones of melody.
James Whitcomb Riley, *Longfellow.*

3
A pure sweet spirit, generous and large
Was thine, dear poet. Calm, unturbulent,
Its course along Life's various ways it went,
Like some broad river. . . . Ever to the sea . . .
Thy life flowed on, from all low passions free,
Filled with high thoughts, charmed into Poesy
To all the world a solace and delight.
W. W. Story, *Henry Wadsworth Longfellow.*

The gentleman was a sweet, beautiful soul, but I have entirely forgotten his name.
Ralph Waldo Emerson, *Remark,* as he stood by the coffin of the dead poet.

4
Threadbare his songs seem now, to lettered ken:
They were worn threadbare next the hearts of men.
William Watson, *Longfellow.*

LOSS

See also Gain and Loss

5
I have lost my all. (Τάμὰ διοίχεται.)
Æschylus, *Myrmidones.* Frag. 62.

I have lost all and found myself.
John Clarke, *Parœmiologia,* 198. (1639)

In losing fortune, many a lucky elf
Has found himself.
Horace Smith, *Moral Alchemy.* St. 12.

6
If you have not lost a thing, you have it.
Chrysippus. (Diogenes Laertius, *Chrysippus.* Sec. 10.)

7
Losers must have leave to speak.
Colley Cibber, *The Rival Fools.* Act 1, l. 17.

8
For 'tis a truth well known to most,
That whatsoever thing is lost,
We seek it, ere it come to light,
In every cranny but the right.
Cowper, *The Retired Cat,* l. 95.

9
The cheerful loser is a winner.
Elbert Hubbard, *One Thousand and One Epigrams.* (1911)

10
It is madness, after losing all, to lose even your passage-money. (Furor est post omnia perdere naulum.)
Juvenal, *Satires.* Sat. viii, l. 97.

Let us not throw the rope after the bucket.
Cervantes, *Don Quixote.* Bk. ii, ch. 9.

For better is a little loss than a long sorrow.
Langland, *Piers Plowman.* Passus i, l. 195.

11
The losing horse blames the saddle.
Samuel Lover, *Handy Andy.* Ch. 34.

12
'Tis easier far to lose than to resign.
George Lyttelton, *Elegy.*

13
Things that are not at all, are never lost.
Christopher Marlowe, *Hero and Leander.* Sestiad i, l. 276.

No man can lose what he never had.
Izaak Walton, *Compleat Angler.* Pt. i, ch. v.

14
A wise man loses nothing, if he but save himself.
Montaigne, *Essays.* Bk. i, ch. 38.

He loseth nothing that loseth not God.
George Herbert, *Jacula Prudentum.*

15
All that's bright must fade,—
The brightest still the fleetest;
All that's sweet was made
But to be lost when sweetest.
Thomas Moore, *All That's Bright Must Fade.*

16
It is ignoble to renounce the acquisition of what we want for fear of losing it.
Plutarch, *Lives: Solon.* Sec. 7.

There is no difference between grief for something lost and the fear of losing it. (In æquo est autem amissæ rei miseratio et timor amittendæ.)
Seneca, *Epistulæ ad Lucilium.* Epis. xcviii, 6.

17
Whatever you can lose, you should reckon of no account.
Publilius Syrus, *Sententiæ.* No. 191.

The loss which is unknown is no loss at all.
Publilius Syrus, *Sententiæ.* No. 38.

18
No man can lose very much when but a driblet remains. (Nemo multum ex stilicidio potest perdere.)
Seneca, *Epistulæ ad Lucilium.* Epis. lxx, 5.

He has not lost all who has one cast left.
Thomas Fuller, *Gnomologia.* No. 1876.

19
And laughed and shouted, "Lost! Lost! Lost!"
Scott, *The Lay of the Last Minstrel.* Canto iii, st. 13.

Lost, lost! one moment knelled the woe of years.
Robert Browning, *Childe Rowland to the Dark Tower Came.*

1
Wise men ne'er sit and wail their loss,
But cheerly seek how to redress their harms.
SHAKESPEARE, *III Henry VI*. Act v, sc. 4, l. 1.

2
Losses,
That have of late so huddled on his back,
Enow to press a royal merchant down
And pluck commiseration of his state
From brassy bosoms and rough hearts of flint.
SHAKESPEARE, *The Merchant of Venice*. Act iv, sc. 1, l. 27.

A fellow that hath had losses.
SHAKESPEARE, *Much Ado About Nothing*. Act iv, sc. 2, l. 87.

3
Loss is no shame.
SPENSER, *Faerie Queene*. Bk. ii, canto v, st. 15.

Loss embraceth shame.
GEORGE HERBERT, *Jacula Prudentum*.

4
But over all things brooding slept
The quiet sense of something lost.
TENNYSON, *In Memoriam*. Pt. lxxviii, st. 2.

5
That which we lose we mourn, but must rejoice
That we have ever had.
C. J. WELLS, *Joseph and His Brethren*. Act iii, sc. 1.

LOTUS

6
Where drooping lotos-flowers, distilling balm,
Dream by the drowsy streamlets sleep hath crowned,
While Care forgets to sigh, and Peace hath balsamed Pain.
PAUL HAMILTON HAYNE, *Sonnet*.

7
Lotos the name: divine, nectareous juice!
HOMER, *Odyssey*. Bk. ix, l. 106. (Pope, tr.)

8
Stone lotus cups, with petals dipped in sand.
JEAN INGELOW, *Gladys and Her Island*, l. 460.

9
They wove the lotus band to deck
And fan with pensile wreath their neck.
THOMAS MOORE, *Odes of Anacreon*. Ode lxx.

Whose flowers have a soul in every leaf.
THOMAS MOORE, *Lalla Rookh: Paradise and the Peri*.

10
A spring there is, whose silver waters show,
Clear as a glass, the shining sands below:
A flowery lotos spreads its arms above,
Shades all the banks, and seems itself a grove.
POPE, *Sappho to Phaon*, l. 179.

11
The lotos bowed above the tide and dreamed.
MARGARET J. PRESTON, *Rhodope's Sandal*.

12
Thro' every hollow cave and alley lone,
Round and round the spicy downs the yellow
Lotos-dust is blown.
TENNYSON, *The Lotos-Eaters: Choric Song*.

13
In that dark land of mystic dream
Where dark Osiris sprung,
It bloomed beside his sacred stream
While yet the world was young;
And every secret Nature told,
Of golden wisdom's power,
Is nestled still in every fold,
Within the Lotos flower.
WILLIAM WINTER, *A Lotos Flower*.

LOUSE

14
Ha! Wha're ye gaun, ye crowlin' ferlie!
Your impudence protects you sairly;
I canna say but ye strunt rarely
Owre gauze an' lace;
Tho' faith! I fear ye dine but sparely
On sic a place.
BURNS, *To a Louse*.

Ye ugly, creepin', blastit wonner,
Detested, shunn'd by saunt an' sinner!
How dare ye set your fit upon her,
Sae fine a lady?
Gae somewhere else, and seek your dinner
On some poor body.
BURNS, *To a Louse*.

15
Better a louse in the pot than no flesh at all.
JOHN CLARKE, *Paræmiologia*, 241. (1639)

16
I care not I, sir, not three skips of a louse.
BEN JONSON, *Tale of a Tub*, ii, 1. (1633)

Lady Montague told me, and in her own house,
"I do not care for you three skips of a louse."
I forgive her, for women, however well-bred,
Will still talk of that which runs most in their head.
HENRY FOX, *Impromptu Retort*, to Lady Montague.

17
It is a familiar beast to man, and signifies —love.
SHAKESPEARE, *The Merry Wives of Windsor*. Act i, sc. 1, l. 21.

LOVE

See also Ambition and Love; Beauty and Love; Eyes and Love; Friendship and Love; Song and Love; Spring and Love; Venus; Woman and Love; Youth and Love

I—Love: Definitions

18
Nuptial love maketh mankind; friendly love perfecteth it; wanton love corrupteth and debaseth it.
FRANCIS BACON, *Essays: Of Love*.

If divine Plato's tenets they be true,
Two Venuses, two loves there be;
The one from heaven, unbegotten still,
Which knits our souls in unity;
The other famous over all the world,

Binding the hearts of gods and men,
Dishonest, wanton, and seducing she,
Rules whom she will, both where and when.
BEROALDUS, *Epigram*. (BURTON, *Anatomy of Melancholy*. Pt. iii, sec. i, mem. 1, subs. 2.)

1
Ask not of me, love, what is love?
Ask what is good of God above—
Ask of the great sun what is light—
Ask what is darkness of the night—
Ask sin of what may be forgiven—
Ask what is happiness of Heaven—
Ask what is folly of the crowd—
Ask what is fashion of the shroud—
Ask what is sweetness of thy kiss—
Ask of thyself what beauty is.
P. J. BAILEY, *Festus: A Large Party and Entertainment. See also* BEAUTY AND LOVE.

2
Love is a fiend, a fire, a heaven, a hell,
Where pleasure, pain, and sad repentance dwell.
RICHARD BARNFIELD, *The Shepherd's Content*. St. 38.

3
Love is that orbit of the restless soul
Whose circle grazes the confines of space,
Bounding within the limits of its race
Utmost extremes.
GEORGE HENRY BOKER, *Sonnet: Love*.

4
Unless you can think, when the song is done,
No other is soft in the rhythm;
Unless you can feel, when left by One,
That all men else go with him;
Unless you can know, when unpraised by his breath,
That your beauty itself wants proving;
Unless you can swear "For life, for death!"—
Oh, fear to call it loving!
E. B. BROWNING, *A Woman's Shortcomings*.

Unless you can muse in a crowd all day
On the absent face that fixed you;
Unless you can love, as the angels may,
With the breadth of heaven betwixt you;
Unless you can dream that his faith is fast,
Through behoving and unbehoving;
Unless you can *die* when the dream is past—
Oh, never call it loving!
E. B. BROWNING, *A Woman's Shortcomings*.

5
Love is the business of the idle, but the idleness of the busy.
BULWER-LYTTON, *Rienzi*. Ch. 4.

Love has no thought of self!
Love buys not with the ruthless usurer's gold
The loathsome prostitution of a hand
Without a heart! Love sacrifices all things
To bless the thing it loves!
BULWER-LYTTON, *The Lady of Lyons*. Act v, sc. 2, l. 23.

6
All love, at first, like generous wine,
Ferments and frets until 'tis fine;
But, when 'tis settled on the lee,
And from th' impurer matter free,
Becomes the richer still the older,
And proves the pleasanter the colder.
SAMUEL BUTLER, *Miscellaneous Thoughts*, l. 361.

7
Yes, Love indeed is light from heaven;
A spark of that immortal fire
With angels shared, by Allah given,
To lift from earth our low desire.
BYRON, *The Giaour*, l. 1131.

Love! the surviving gift of Heaven,
The choicest sweet of Paradise,
In life's else bitter cup distilled.
THOMAS CAMPBELL, *Ode to the Memory of Burns*, l. 16.

8
Love is ever the beginning of Knowledge as fire is of light.
CARLYLE, *Essays: Death of Goethe*.

A loving heart is the beginning of all knowledge.
CARLYLE, *Essays: Biography*.

Knowledge is the parent of love; wisdom, love itself.
J. C. AND A. W. HARE, *Guesses at Truth*.

9
What is love? 'tis nature's treasure,
'Tis the storehouse of her joys;
'Tis the highest heaven of pleasure,
'Tis a bliss which never cloys.
THOMAS CHATTERTON, *The Revenge*. Act i, 2.

Ah, what is love? It is a pretty thing,
As sweet unto a shepherd as a king,
And sweeter too,
For kings have cares that wait upon a crown,
And cares can make the sweetest love to frown.
ROBERT GREENE, *The Shepherd'. Wife's Song*.

What thing is love?—for (well I wot) love is a thing.
It is a prick, it is a sting.
It is a pretty, pretty thing;
It is a fire, it is a coal,
Whose flame creeps in at every hole!
GEORGE PEELE, *The Hunting of Cupid*.

10
Love's but the frailty of the mind,
When 'tis not with ambition join'd.
CONGREVE, *The Way of the World*. Act iii, sc. 12

And love's the noblest frailty of the mind.
DRYDEN, *The Indian Emperor*. Act ii, sc. 2.

That reason of all unreasonable actions.
DRYDEN, *The Assignation*. Act iii, sc. 1.

11
When too much zeal doth fire devotion,
Love is not love, but superstition.
RICHARD CORBET, *R. C.*

12
Our love is principle, and has its root
In reason, is judicious, manly, free.
COWPER, *The Task*. Bk. v, l. 353.

13
Love is a sickness full of woes,
All remedies refusing;

A plant that with most cutting grows,
Most barren with best using.
SAMUEL DANIEL, *Hymen's Triumph.*

1
Many are the names applied to friendship; but where youth and beauty enter in, there friendship is rightly called love and is held to be the fairest of the gods.
DIO CHRYSOSTOM, *Third Discourse on Kingship.* Sec. 99.

2
Knightly love is blent with reverence
As heavenly air is blent with heavenly blue.
GEORGE ELIOT, *The Spanish Gypsy.* Bk. i.

3
In the last analysis, love is only the reflection of a man's own worthiness from other men.
EMERSON, *Essays, First Series: Friendship.*

Love, which is the essence of God, is not for levity, but for the total worth of man.
EMERSON, *Essays, First Series: Friendship.*

4
Love is the blossom where there blows
Every thing that lives or grows.
GILES FLETCHER, *Christ's Victory.*

Love is life's end (an end, but never ending);
All joys, all sweets, all happiness, awarding;
Love is life's wealth (ne'er spent, but ever spending);
More rich by giving, taking by discarding;
Love 's life's reward, rewarded in rewarding.
GILES FLETCHER, *Britain's Ida.* Canto ii, st. 8.

Love is the tyrant of the heart; it darkens
Reason, confounds discretion; deaf to counsel,
It runs a headlong course to desperate madness.
JOHN FORD, *The Lover's Melancholy.* Act iii, sc. 3, l. 105.

5
Love is God's essence; Power but his attribute: therefore is his love greater than his power.
RICHARD GARNETT, *De Flagello Myrteo.* Pt. iv.

Thou canst not pray to God without praying to Love, but mayest pray to Love without praying to God.
RICHARD GARNETT, *De Flagello Myrteo.* Pt. xiii.

6
It is the special quality of love not to be able to remain stationary, to be obliged to increase under pain of diminishing.
ANDRÉ GIDE, *The Counterfeiters.* Pt. iii, ch. 5.

7
Love is a platform upon which all ranks meet.
W S. GILBERT, *H. M. S. Pinafore.* Act ii.

8
Love and desire are the spirit's wings to great deeds. (Lust und Liebe sind die Fittige zu grossen Thaten.)
GOETHE, *Iphigenia auf Tauris.* Act ii, sc. 1.

9
Love is a lock that linketh noble minds,
Faith is the key that shuts the spring of love.
ROBERT GREENE, *Alcida.*

10
Love is a circle, that doth restless move
In the same sweet eternity of love.
ROBERT HERRICK, *Love, What It Is.*

11
To love is to know the sacrifices which eternity exacts from life.
JOHN OLIVER HOBBES, *School for Saints.* Ch. 25.

12
In love inhere these evils—first war, then peace. (In amore hæc sunt mala, bellum, Pax rursum.)
HORACE, *Satires.* Bk. ii, sat. 3, l. 267.

13
Love 's like the flies, and, drawing-room or garden, goes all over a house.
DOUGLAS JERROLD, *Jerrold's Wit: Love.*

14
Love is only one of many passions . . . and has no great influence on the sum of life.
SAMUEL JOHNSON, *Works.* Vol. ix, p. 244.

15
Love is the leech of life, next to our Lord,
It is the graft of peace, the nearest road to heaven.
LANGLAND, *Piers Plowman.* Passus ii, l. 201.

16
Love keeps the cold out better than a cloak.
It serves for food and raiment.
LONGFELLOW, *The Spanish Student.* Act i, sc. 5, l. 52.

17
True Love is but a humble, low-born thing,
And hath its food served up in earthen ware;
It is a thing to walk with, hand in hand,
Through the everydayness of this workday world.
J. R. LOWELL, *Love,* l. 1.

18
Love is a beautiful dream.
WILLIAM SHARP, *Cor Cordium.*

19
Therefore the love which us doth bind,
But Fate so enviously debars,
Is the conjunction of the mind,
And opposition of the stars.
ANDREW MARVELL, *The Definition of Love.*

20
Love is a flame to burn out human wills,
Love is a flame to set the will on fire,
Love is a flame to cheat men into mire. . . .
Love puts such bitter poison on Fate's arrow.
JOHN MASEFIELD, *The Widow in the Bye Street.* Pt. ii.

21
Love is all in fire, and yet is ever freezing;
Love is much in winning, yet is more in leesing:
Love is ever sick, and yet is never dying;
Love is ever true, and yet is ever lying;
Love does doat in liking, and is mad in loathing;
Love indeed is anything, yet indeed is nothing.
THOMAS MIDDLETON, *Blurt.* Act ii, sc. 2.

Love is the mind's strong physic, and the pill
That leaves the heart sick and o'erturns the will.
THOMAS MIDDLETON, *Blurt.* Act iii, sc. 1.

1
This have I known always: Love is no more
Than the wide blossom which the wind assails,
Than the great tide that treads the shifting shore,
Strewing fresh wreckage gathered in the gales;
Pity me that the heart is slow to learn
What the swift mind beholds at every turn.
EDNA ST. VINCENT MILLAY, *Sonnets.* No. vi. (*The Harp-Weaver and Other Poems.*)

As God's my judge, I do cry Holy! Holy!
Upon the name of Love, however brief.
EDNA ST. VINCENT MILLAY, *Love Sonnet.*

2
Love is nothing else but an insatiate thirst of enjoying a greedily desired object.
MONTAIGNE, *Essays.* Bk. iii, ch. 5.

3
One of the glories of society is to have created woman where Nature made a female, to have created a continuity of desire where Nature only thought of perpetuating the species; in fine, to have invented love.
GEORGE MOORE, *Impressions.*

Love is based upon a view of women that is impossible to any man who has had any experience of them.
H. L. MENCKEN, *Prejudices.* Ser. iv, p. 67.

4
"Tell me, what's Love?" said Youth, one day,
To drooping Age, who crost his way.—
"It is a sunny hour of play,
For which repentance dear doth pay,
Repentance! Repentance!
And this is Love, as wise men say."
THOMAS MOORE, *Youth and Age.*

5
Romantic love is the privilege of emperors, kings, soldiers and artists; it is the butt of democrats, traveling salesmen, magazine poets and the writers of American novels.
G. J. NATHAN, *Testament of a Critic,* p. 14.

Romance cannot be put into quantity production—the moment love becomes casual, it becomes commonplace.
F. L. ALLEN, *Only Yesterday,* p. 239.

6
Youth's for an hour, beauty's a flower,
But love is the jewel that wins the world.
MOIRA O'NEILL, *Beauty's a Flower.*

7
Love is a kind of warfare. (Militiæ species amor est.)
OVID, *Ars Amatoria.* Bk. ii, l. 233.

Every lover is a soldier, and Cupid has a camp of his own. The age that is meet for the wars is also suited to Venus. (Militat omnis amans, et habet sua castra Cupido; Quæ bello est habilis, Veneri quoque convenit ætas.)
OVID, *Amores.* Bk. i, epis. 9, l. 1.

Love, an' please your Honour, is exactly like war, in this, that a soldier, though he has escaped three weeks complete o' Saturday night, may, nevertheless, be shot through his heart on Sunday morning.
STERNE, *Tristram Shandy.* Vol. vii, ch. 21.

Who sell their laurel for a myrtle wreath,
And love when they should fight.
COWPER, *The Task.* Bk. ii, l. 229.

8
'Tis that delightsome transport we can feel
Which painters cannot paint, nor words reveal,
Nor any art we know of can conceal.
THOMAS PAINE, *What Is Love?*

9
We may, without undue tension of speech, speak of Goodness as Love in conduct; of Truth as Love in thought; of Beauty as Love in self-expression, in whatever medium.
RICHARD ROBERTS. (NEWTON, *My Idea of God,* p. 81.)

10
Love is the fulfilling of the law.
New Testament: Romans, xiii, 10.

11
Love indeed is a light burden, not cumbering but lightening the bearer; and maketh glad both young and old. . . . Love is the fairest and most profitable guest that a reasonable creature can entertain. . . . In the light and warmth of love our life grows strong and comely: a better dwelling, nor a sweeter, never I found.
RICHARD ROLLE, *Incendium Amoris.*

12
To love is to choose.
JOSEPH ROUX, *Meditations of a Parish Priest.* Pt. ix, No. 1.

13
Love is an egotism of two. (L'amour est un égoïsme à deux.)
ANTOINE DE SALLE.

Many people when they fall in love look for a little haven of refuge from the world, where they can be sure of being admired when they are not admirable, and praised when they are not praiseworthy.
BERTRAND RUSSELL, *The Conquest of Happiness,* p. 180.

14
True love's the gift which God has given
To man alone beneath the heaven: . . .
It is the secret sympathy,
The silver link, the silken tie,
Which heart to heart, and mind to mind,
In body and in soul can bind.
SCOTT, *Lay of the Last Minstrel.* Can. v, st. 13

15
Good shepherd, tell this youth what 'tis to love.
It is to be all made of sighs and tears; . . .
It is to be all made of faith and service; . . .

It is to be all made of fantasy.
SHAKESPEARE, *As You Like It*. Act v, sc. 2, l. 89.

Love is merely a madness, and, I tell you, deserves as well a dark house and a whip as madmen do.
SHAKESPEARE, *As You Like It*. Act iii, sc. 2, l. 420.

Love is a familiar; Love is a devil: there is no evil angel but Love.
SHAKESPEARE, *Love's Labour's Lost*. Act i, sc. 2, l. 177.

It adds a precious seeing to the eye.
SHAKESPEARE, *Love's Labour's Lost*. Act iv, sc. 3, l. 333.

And when Love speaks, the voice of all the gods
Make heaven drowsy with the harmony.
SHAKESPEARE, *Love's Labour's Lost*. Act iv, sc. 3, l. 344.

1
Love is a smoke raised with the fume of sighs;
Being purged, a fire sparkling in lovers' eyes;
Being vex'd, a sea nourish'd with lovers' tears:
What is it else? a madness most discreet,
A choking gall and a preserving sweet.
SHAKESPEARE, *Romeo and Juliet*. Act i, sc. 1, l. 196. (1595)

Love is a sour delight, a sugar'd grief,
A living death, an ever-dying life;
A breach of Reason's law, a secret thief,
A sea of tears, an everlasting strife;
A bait for fools, a scourge of noble wits,
A deadly wound, a shot which ever hits.
THOMAS WATSON, *The Passionate Centurie of Love*. Sonnet xviii. (1582) Watson's eighteen-line "sonnets" were closely studied by Shakespeare, whose own sonnets appeared in 1600.

2 Love's heralds should be thoughts,
Which ten times faster glide than the sun's beams,
Driving back shadows over louring hills:
Therefore do nimble-pinion'd doves draw love,
And therefore hath the wind-swift Cupid wings.
SHAKESPEARE, *Romeo and Juliet*. Act ii, sc. 5, l. 4.

3 Love is not love
Which alters when it alteration finds,
Or bends with the remover to remove:
O, no! it is an ever-fixed mark
That looks on tempests and is never shaken;
It is a star to every wandering bark,
Whose worth's unknown, although his height be taken.
Love's not Time's fool, though rosy lips and cheeks
Within his bending sickle's compass come;
Love alters not with his brief hours and weeks,
But bears it out even to the edge of doom.
If this be error and upon me proved,
I never writ, nor no man ever loved.
SHAKESPEARE, *Sonnets*. No. cxvi.

Love's not love
When it is mingled with regards that stand
Aloof from the entire point.
SHAKESPEARE, *King Lear*. Act i, sc. 1, l. 241.

4
Love is the salt of life.
JOHN SHEFFIELD, *Ode on Love*. Canto v.

5
Love is a pleasing but a various clime.
WILLIAM SHENSTONE, *Elegy*, v.

Love is an April's doubtful day:
Awhile we see the tempest lour;
Anon the radiant heav'n survey,
And quite forget the flitting show'r.
WILLIAM SHENSTONE, *Song*, vii.

6
Love is an appetite of generation by the mediation of beauty.
SOCRATES. (MONTAIGNE, *Essays*. Bk. iii, ch. 5.)

7
Love is the emblem of eternity: it confounds all notion of time: effaces all memory of a beginning, all fear of an end.
MADAME DE STAËL, *Corinne*. Bk. viii, ch. 2.

8
Love in its essence is spiritual fire.
SWEDENBORG, *True Christian Religion*. Sec. 31.

Love consists in desiring to give what is our own to another and feeling his delight as our own.
SWEDENBORG, *Divine Love and Wisdom*. Sec. 47.

9
A reality in the domain of the imagination.
TALLEYRAND, defining love. (COOPER, *Talleyrand*.)

10
Love is swift, sincere, pious, pleasant, gentle, strong, patient, faithful, prudent, long-suffering, manly and never seeking her own; for wheresoever a man seeketh his own, there he falleth from love.
THOMAS À KEMPIS, *De Imitatione Christi*. Bk. iii, ch. 5.

11
Love is the strange bewilderment which overtakes one person on account of another person.
JAMES THURBER AND E. B. WHITE, *Is Sex Necessary?*

12
You are as prone to love as the sun is to shine; it being the most delightful and natural employment of the Soul of Man: without which you are dark and miserable. For certainly he that delights not in Love makes vain the universe, and is of necessity to himself the greatest burden.
THOMAS TRAHERNE, *Centuries of Meditations*.

13
The bodies of lovers are the forms of ineffable Desire,
Male and female serpents of the Holy Spirit
Breathing out its essence in individual outline.
W. J. TURNER, *The Pursuit of Psyche*.

14
Love is the child of illusion and the parent

of disillusion; love is consolation in desolation; it is the sole medicine against death, for it is death's brother.

UNAMUNO, *The Tragic Sense of Life*, p. 132.

1
For love is but the heart's immortal thirst
To be completely known and all forgiven.

HENRY VAN DYKE, *Love.*

Love is not getting, but giving; not a wild dream of pleasure, and a madness of desire—oh, no, love is not that—it is goodness, and honor, and peace and pure living.

HENRY VAN DYKE, *Little Rivers: A Handful of Heather.*

2
To love is to believe, to hope, to know;
'Tis an essay, a taste of Heaven below!

EDMUND WALLER, *Divine Love*. Canto iii, l. 17.

Life's one joy is this,
To love, to taste the soul's divine delight
Of loving some most lovely soul or sight—
To worship still, though never an answering sign
Should come from Love asleep within the shrine.

THEODORE WATTS-DUNTON, *The Coming of Love*. Pt. x, l. 12.

And I know that the hand of God is the promise of my own,
And I know that the spirit of God is the brother of my own,
And that all the men ever born are also my brothers, and the women my sisters and lovers,
And that a kelson of the creation is love.

WALT WHITMAN, *Song of Myself*. Sec. 5.

3
Say not you *love* a roasted fowl,
But you may love a screaming owl,
And, if you can, the unwieldy toad.

WORDSWORTH, *Loving and Liking.*

4
Love is the god who gives safety to the city.

ZENO. (DENIS, *Théories Morales*. Vol. i, p. 346.)

5
Now I know what love is. (Nunc scio quid sit Amor.)

VERGIL, *Eclogues*. No. viii, l. 43.

6
Tell me, my heart, if this be love.

GEORGE LYTTELTON, *Song: When Delia.*

But love is such a mystery
I cannot find it out:
For when I think I'm best resolved,
I then am most in doubt.

SIR JOHN SUCKLING, *Song: I Prithee Send Me Back My Heart.*

II—Love: Apothegms

7
Love spends his all, and still hath store.

P. J. BAILEY, *Festus: A Large Party and Entertainment.*

Where love is, there's no lack.

RICHARD BROME, *A Jovial Crew*. Act iii.

Love is liberal.

JOHN CLARKE, *Parœmiologia*, 28.

8
In love-making, as in the other arts, those do it best who cannot tell how it is done.

J. M. BARRIE, *Tommy and Grizel*, p. 17.

9
All stratagems
In love, and that the sharpest war, are lawful.

BEAUMONT AND FLETCHER, *The Lovers' Progress*. Act v, sc. 2. (c. 1630)

Advantages are lawful in love and war.

APHRA BEHN, *Emperor of the Moon*. Act i, sc. 3. (1687)

Stratagems ever were allow'd of in love and war.

SUSANNAH CENTLIVRE, *The Man's Bewitch'd*. Act v, sc. 1.

All's fair in love and war.

F. E. SMEDLEY, *Frank Fairlegh*. Ch. 50. (1850)

10
The shortest ladies love the longest men.

BEAUMONT AND FLETCHER, *Love's Cure*. Act iii, sc. 3.

The fairest ladies like the blackest men.

BEAUMONT AND FLETCHER, *Love's Cure*. Act iii, sc. 4.

Black men are pearls in beauteous ladies' eyes.

SHAKESPEARE, *The Two Gentlemen of Verona*. Act v, sc. 2, l. 12.

Two of one trade ne'er love.

DEKKER, *The Honest Whore*. Act ii, sc. iv.

Every theory of love, from Plato down, teaches that each individual loves in the other sex what he lacks in himself.

G. STANLEY HALL.

11
Love is more just than justice.

HENRY WARD BEECHER, *Proverbs from Plymouth Pulpit.*

12
There is no love lost between us.

CERVANTES, *Don Quixote*. Bk. iv, ch. 23; GOLDSMITH, *She Stoops to Conquer*. Act iv; FIELDING, *Grub Street Opera*. Act i, sc. 4.

There is no love lost.

LE SAGE, *Gil Blas*. Bk. ix, ch. 7.

There shall be no love lost.

BEN JONSON, *Every Man Out of His Humour*. Act ii, sc. 1.

There is no hate lost between us.

THOMAS MIDDLETON, *The Witch*. Act iv, sc. 3.

13
In love, a man may lose his heart with dignity; but if he loses his nose, he loses his character into the bargain.

LORD CHESTERFIELD, *Letters*, 5 Feb., 1750.

14
Let love have his way. (Vincat amor.)

CLAUDIAN, *Epigrams*. No. xli, l. 8.

15
All for Love, and the World Well Lost.

DRYDEN. Title of play on the same theme as Shakespeare's *Antony and Cleopatra.*

And Antony, who lost the world for love.

DRYDEN, *Palamon and Arcite*. Bk. ii, l. 607.

Did you ever hear of Captain Wattle?
He was all for love, and a little for the bottle.
CHARLES DIBDIN, *Captain Wattle and Miss Roe.*

And when my own Mark Antony
Against young Cæsar strove,
And Rome's whole world was set in arms,
The cause was,—all for love.
SOUTHEY, *All for Love.* Pt. ii, st. 26.

And all for love, and nothing for reward.
SPENSER, *Faerie Queene.* Bk. ii, canto viii, st. 2.

1
The first condition of human goodness is something to love; the second, something to reverence.
GEORGE ELIOT, *Janet's Repentance.*

2
All mankind love a lover.
EMERSON, *Essays, First Series: Of Love.*

3
Love teaches letters to a man unlearn'd.
EURIPIDES, *Sthenebœa.* Fragment.

We learn only from those we love.
GOETHE, *Conversations with Eckermann.*

4
Religion has done love a great service by making it a sin.
ANATOLE FRANCE.

5
Love and pride stock Bedlam.
THOMAS FULLER, *Gnomologia.* No. 3284.

6
Where true love is, there is little need of prim formality.
W. S. GILBERT, *Ruddigore.* Act i.

7
You know the old proverb, that sad are the effects of love and pease porridge.
HEAD AND KIRKMAN, *English Rogue,* iii, 176.

Love and pease porridge are two dangerous things; one breaks the heart, and the other the belly
SWIFT, *Polite Conversation.* Dial. i.

8
Love and a cough cannot be hid.
GEORGE HERBERT, *Jacula Prudentum.*

Love and a red nose cannot be hid.
THOMAS HOLCROFT, *Duplicity.* Act ii, sc. 1.

Love and murder will out.
CONGREVE, *The Double-Dealer.* Act iv, sc. 2.

9
Hot love soon cold.
JOHN HEYWOOD, *Proverbs.* Pt. i, ch. 2. (1546)

Gay love, God save it; so soon hot, so soon cold.
NICHOLAS UDALL, *Ralph Roister Doister.* Act iv, sc. 8. (1566)

Love that's soonest hot, is ever soonest cold.
GEORGE WITHER, *Fidelia,* l. 4.

Love in extremes can never long endure.
ROBERT HERRICK, *A Caution.*

10
Men say, kind will creep where it may not go.
JOHN HEYWOOD, *Proverbs.* Pt. i, ch. 11. (1546)

You know that love
Will creep in service where it cannot go.
SHAKESPEARE, *The Two Gentlemen of Verona.* Act iv, sc. 2, l. 19.

11
Lovers are fools. but nature makes them so.
ELBERT HUBBARD, *Epigrams.*

12
Good-nature is the cheapest commodity in the world, and love is the only thing that will pay ten per cent to both borrower and lender.
R. G. INGERSOLL, *The Liberty of Man, Woman and Child.*

13
Love is like the measles—all the worse when it comes late in life.
DOUGLAS JERROLD, *Table Talk.*

Love is like the measles; we all have to go through it.
JEROME K. JEROME, *Idle Thoughts of an Idle Fellow: On Being in Love.*

14
The shepherd in Virgil grew at last acquainted with Love, and found him a native of the rocks.
SAMUEL JOHNSON, *Letter to Lord Chesterfield.*

We must not ridicule a passion which he who never felt never was happy, and he who laughs at never deserves to feel.
SAMUEL JOHNSON, *Miscellanies.* Vol. i, p. 290.

15
Young men make great mistakes in life; for one thing, they idealize love too much.
BENJAMIN JOWETT, *Letters,* p. 252.

16
There is only one kind of love, but there are a thousand imitations. (Il n'y a que d'une sorte d'amour, mais il y en a mille différentes copies.)
LA ROCHEFOUCAULD, *Maximes.* No. 74.

It is difficult to love those whom we do not esteem, but it is no less difficult to love those whom we esteem much more than ourselves. (Il est difficile d'aimer ceux que nous n'estimons point; mais il ne l'est pas moins d'aimer ceux que nous estimons beaucoup plus que nous.)
LA ROCHEFOUCAULD, *Maximes.* No. 296.

The reason why lovers and their mistresses never tire of being together is because they are always talking of themselves. (Ce qui fait que les amants et les maitresses ne s'ennuient point d'être ensemble, c'est qu'ils parlent toujours d'eux-mêmes.)
LA ROCHEFOUCAULD, *Maximes.* No. 312.

17
It is good to love the unknown.
CHARLES LAMB, *Essays of Elia: Valentine's Day.*

18
Delicacy is to love what grace is to beauty.
MADAME DE MAINTENON, *Maximes.*

19
A caress is better than a career.
ELISABETH MARBURY, *Interview on Careers for Women.*

20
Our love is like our life;

There is no man blest in either till his end.
SHACKERLEY MARMION, *A Fine Companion*. Act i, sc. 1. *See also* DEATH: COUNT NO MAN HAPPY.

1
Until I truly loved, I was alone.
CAROLINE NORTON, *The Lady of La Garaye*. Pt. ii, l. 381.

2
Value each lover according to the gifts he brings. (Quantum quisque ferat, respiciendus erit.)
OVID, *Amores*. Bk i, eleg. viii, l. 38.

No lover's useful, except the kind that is a perpetual endowment. He should give and keep on giving: when everything's gone, he should give up loving. (Non est usu quisquam amator nisi qui perpetuat data; Det det usque: quando nil sit, simul amare desinat.)
PLAUTUS, *Pseudolus*, l. 306. (Act i, sc. 3.)

Alas! for the love that's linked with gold.
THOMAS HOOD, *Miss Kilmansegg: Her Courtship*.

3
Majesty and love do not go well together, nor tarry long in the same dwelling. (Non bene conveniunt nec in una sede morantur Majestas et amor.)
OVID, *Metamorphoses*. Bk. ii, l. 846.

Full sooth is said that love nor lordship
Will not, his thankës, have no fellowship.
CHAUCER, *The Knightes Tale*, l. 767. (c. 1386)

Love and ambition (I have heard men say) admit no fellowship.
RICHARD BROME, *Love-sick Court*. Act i, sc. 2.

4
Love is a credulous thing. (Credula res amor est.)
OVID, *Metamorphoses*. Bk. vii, l. 826; *Heroides*. Epis. vi, l. 21.

We are easily duped by what we love. (On est aisément dupé par ce qu'on aime.)
MOLIÈRE, *Le Tartuffe*. Act iv, sc. 3, l. 82.

Whoso loves believes the impossible.
E. B. BROWNING, *Aurora Leigh*. Bk. v, l. 408.

Love is always in the mood of believing in miracles.
J. C. POWYS, *The Meaning of Culture*, p. 144.

5
Spice a dish with love and it pleases every palate. (Ubi amor condimentum inerit, cuivis placituram escam.)
PLAUTUS, *Casina*, l. 221.

A man in love may be famishing, and yet want no food at all. (Qui amat, si esurit, nullum esurit.)
PLAUTUS, *Casina*, l. 795.

6
A great lover of the ladies. (Magnus amator mulierum.)
PLAUTUS, *Menæchmi*, l. 268. (Act ii, sc. 1.)

Says he, "I am a handsome man, but I'm a gay deceiver."
GEORGE COLMAN THE YOUNGER, *Unfortunate Miss Bailey*.

'A said once, the devil would have him about women.
SHAKESPEARE, *Henry V*. Act ii, sc. 3, l. 37.

He was formed for the ruin of our sex.
SMOLLETT, *Roderick Random*. Ch. 22.

7
To love is human; to be indulgent is human, too. (Humanun amarest; humanum autem ignoscerest.)
PLAUTUS, *Mercator*, l. 320. (Act ii, sc. 2.)

8
The man that loves and laughs must sure do well.
POPE, *Imitations of Horace: Epistles*. Bk. i, epis. 6, l. 129.

9
Whom we love best, to them we can say least.
JOHN RAY, *English Proverbs*, 47.

10
I love thee like pudding; if thou wert pie I'd eat thee.
JOHN RAY, *English Proverbs*, 349. (1678)

I love you so that I could eat ye.
SAMUEL WESLEY, *Maggots*, 24. (1685)

I love him like pie.
SWIFT, *Polite Conversation*. Dial. ii.

11
I do not always admire what I love, neither do I always love what I admire.
JOSEPH ROUX, *Meditations of a Parish Priest*. Pt. ix, No. 12.

12
It is as easy to count atomies as to resolve the propositions of a lover.
SHAKESPEARE, *As You Like It*. Act iii, sc. 2, l. 245.

13
No more of that, Hal, an thou lovest me!
SHAKESPEARE, *I Henry IV*. Act ii, sc. 4, l. 312.

14
Love is too young to know what conscience is;
Yet who knows not conscience is born of love?
SHAKESPEARE, *Sonnets*. No. cli.

15
Love sought is good, but given unsought is better.
SHAKESPEARE, *Twelfth Night*. Act iii, sc. 1, l. 168.

16
Were beauty under twenty locks kept fast,
Yet love breaks through and picks them all at last.
SHAKESPEARE, *Venus and Adonis*, l. 575.

Love Laughs at Locksmiths.
GEORGE COLMAN THE YOUNGER. Title of comedy. (1803)

17
Begot of Plenty and of Penury.
SPENSER, *An Hymn in Honour of Love*, l. 53.

18
Love better is than Fame.
BAYARD TAYLOR, *To J. L. G.*

For love's humility is Love's true pride.
BAYARD TAYLOR, *Poet's Journal: Third Evening: The Mother*.

They sang of love, and not of fame;
Forgot was Britain's glory;
Each heart recalled a different name,
But all sang Annie Laurie.
BAYARD TAYLOR, *Song of the Camp.*

1
Love's too precious to be lost.
TENNYSON, *In Memoriam.* Pt. lxv.

Love lieth deep; Love dwells not in lip-depths.
TENNYSON, *The Lover's Tale,* l. 456.

2
You must get your living by loving.
H. D. THOREAU, *Journal,* 13 March, 1853.

3
My weapons were love, and nest-hiding.
ELIZABETH RICHARDS TILTON, *Letter to Henry Ward Beecher, Tilton vs Beecher,* i, 84. "Nest-hiding" came to be a popular phrase, and was perhaps the origin of "love-nest." The letter was written in 1871.

4
Who can deceive a lover? (Quis fallere possit amantem?)
VERGIL, *Æneid.* Bk. iv, l. 296.

There is no hiding from lovers' eyes.
JOHN CROWNE, *I The Destruction of Jerusalem.* Act iv, sc. 1.

5
For what may we lovers not hope! (Quid non speramus amantes!)
VERGIL, *Eclogues.* No. viii, l. 26.

6
Love is the same in everyone. (Amor omnibus idem.)
VERGIL, *Georgics.* Bk. iii, l. 244.

Seas have their source, and so have shallow springs;
And love is love in beggars and in kings.
EDWARD DYER, *The Lowest Trees Have Tops.*

7
Love *stoops* as fondly as he soars.
WORDSWORTH, *On Seeing a Needle Case in the Form of a Harp.*

Such ever was love's way: to rise, it stoops.
ROBERT BROWNING, *A Death in the Desert.*

She Stoops to Conquer.
GOLDSMITH. Title of a comedy.

8
Who carved Love and placed him by the fountain, thinking to still this fire with water?
ZENODOTUS. (*Greek Anthology.* Bk. xvi, epig. 14.)

9
Tomorrow shall be love for the loveless, and for the lover tomorrow shall be love. (Cras amet qui nunquam amavit quique amavit cras amet.)
UNKNOWN. *Pervigilium Veneris,* l. 1, and refrain of succeeding stanzas. (J. W. Mackail, tr.) *Pervigilium Veneris, The Eve of St. Venus,* a Latin poem of unknown authorship, dating from about A. D. 350.

Let those love now, who never lov'd before;
Let those who always lov'd, now love the more.
THOMAS PARNELL, *Pervigilium Veneris*; ROBERT BURTON, *Anatomy of Melancholy,* iii, ii, 5, 5; ARTHUR MURPHY, *Know Your Own Mind,* iii, 1.

10
Love of lads and fire of chips is soon in and soon out.
UNKNOWN. *Good Wyfe Wold a Pylgrimage,* l. 83. (1460)

Lad's love's a busk of broom,
Hot awhile and soon done.
JOHN RAY, *English Proverbs,* p. 46.

Lads' love is lassies' delight,
And if lads don't love, lassies will flite.
CARR, *Craven Dialect.* Vol. i, p. 273.

11
Neither for love nor money.
UNKNOWN, *Pedlar's Prophecy,* l. 578. (1595)

If it were to be had for love or money.
THOMAS SHADWELL, *Royal Shepherd: Prologue.* (1669)

It can't be had for love nor money.
SMOLLETT, *Humphrey Clinker,* vi, 45. (1771)

III—Love: Its Blindness

12
If things were seen as they truly are, the beauty of bodies would be much abridged.
SIR THOMAS BROWNE, *Christian Morals.* Pt. ii, sec. 9.

13
For love is blind all day and may not see.
CHAUCER, *The Marchantes Tale,* l. 354.

14
I have heard of reasons manifold
Why Love must needs be blind,
But this the best of all I hold—
His eyes are in his mind.
What outward form and feature are
He guesseth but in part;
But that within is good and fair
He seeth with the heart.
S. T. COLERIDGE, *Reason for Love's Blindness.*

15
Never was owl more blind than a lover.
DINAH M. M. CRAIK, *Magnus and Morna.*

16
Love is not a hood, but an eye-water.
EMERSON, *Essays, First Series: Prudence.*

17
Every one is blind when maddened by love. (Scilicet insano nemo in amore videt.)
PROPERTIUS, *Elegies.* Bk. ii, eleg. 14, l. 18.

18
But love is blind, and lovers cannot see
The pretty follies that themselves commit.
SHAKESPEARE, *The Merchant of Venice.* Act ii, sc. 6, l. 36.

Things base and vile, holding no quality,
Love can transpose to form and dignity:
Love looks not with the eyes, but with the mind;
And therefore is wing'd Cupid painted blind:
Nor hath Love's mind of any judgement taste;
Wings and no eyes figure unheedy haste:
And therefore is Love said to be a child,

Because in choice he is so oft beguil'd.
SHAKESPEARE, *A Midsummer-Night's Dream.* Act i, sc. 1, l. 232.

The lover . . .
Sees Helen's beauty in a brow of Egypt.
SHAKESPEARE, *A Midsummer-Night's Dream.* Act v, sc. 1, l. 10.

Thou blind fool, Love, what dost thou to mine eyes,
That they behold, and see not what they see?
SHAKESPEARE, *Sonnets.* No. cxxxvii.

Love doth to her eyes repair,
To help him of his blindness.
SHAKESPEARE, *The Two Gentlemen of Verona.* Act iv, sc. 2, l. 46.

1
I joyed; but straight thus water'd was my wine.—
That love she did, but loved a love not blind.
SIR PHILIP SIDNEY, *Astrophel and Stella.* Sonnet lxii.

IV—Love and Pity

2
Of all the paths that lead to a woman's love
Pity's the straightest.
BEAUMONT AND FLETCHER, *The Knight of Malta.* Act i, sc. 1, l. 73.

Pity, some say, is the parent of future love.
BEAUMONT AND FLETCHER, *The Spanish Curate.* Act v, sc. 1.

3
'Tis pity makes a Deity;
Ah, Silvia, deign to pity me,
And I will worship none but thee.
APHRA BEHN, *Dialogue for Entertainment at Court.*

4
Love gains the shrine when pity opes the door.
BULWER-LYTTON, *The New Timon.* Pt. iii.

5
Anon her heart hath pity of his woe,
And with that pity love came in also.
CHAUCER, *The Legend of Good Women: Dido,* l. 155.

6
In women pity begets love, in men love begets pity.
CHURTON COLLINS, *Aphorisms.*

7
Pity is sworn servant unto love;
And thus be sure, wherever it begin
To make the way, it lets the master in.
SAMUEL DANIEL, *The Queen's Arcadia.* Act iii, sc. 1.

8
'Twas but a kindred sound to move,
For pity melts the mind to love.
DRYDEN, *Alexander's Feast.* St. 5.

Can you pretend to love
And have no pity? Love and that are twins.
DRYDEN, *Don Sebastian.* Act iii, sc. 1.

9
Pity is love when grown into excess.
ROBERT HOWARD, *The Vestal Virgin.*

10
Love's pale sister, Pity.
SIR WILLIAM JONES, *Hymn to Darga.*

11
He kin' o' l'itered on the mat,
Some doubtfle o' the sekle,
His heart kep' goin' pity-pat,
But hern went pity Zekle.
J. R. LOWELL, *The Courtin'.*

12
For trust me, they who never melt
With pity, never melt with love.
THOMAS MOORE, *To a Lady, With Some Manuscript Poems.*

13
Pity is but one remove from love.
RICHARDSON, *Sir Charles Grandison.* Bk. i, 34.

14
Soft pity never leaves the gentle breast
Where love has been received a welcome guest.
SHERIDAN, *The Duenna.* Act ii, sc. 4.

15
Pity's akin to love; and every thought
Of that soft kind is welcome to my soul.
THOMAS SOUTHERNE, *Oroonoko.* Act ii, sc. 2.

16
Pity swells the tide of love.
YOUNG, *Night Thoughts.* Night iii, l. 106.

V—Love and Wisdom

17
'Tis impossible to love and to be wise.
FRANCIS BACON, *Essays: Of Love.* Quoted.

Away with doubts, all scruples hence remove;
No man at one time can be wise, and love.
ROBERT HERRICK, *To Silvia to Wed.*

'Tis hard to be in love and to be wise.
NATHANIEL LEE, *Princess of Cleve.* Act i, sc. 3.

18
Men loved wholly beyond wisdom
Have the staff without the banner.
LOUISE BOGAN, *Men Loved Wholly.*

19
The first sigh of love is the last of wisdom.
(Le premier soupir de l'amour Est le dernier de la sagesse.)
ANTOINE BRET, *École Amoureuse.* Sc. 7.

20
The wisest man the warl' e'er saw,
He dearly lov'd the lasses, O.
BURNS, *Green Grow the Rashes, O.*

21
How wise are they that are but fools in love!
JO. COOKE, *How a Man May Choose a Good Wife.* Act i, sc. 1. (c. 1610) First name uncertain.

22
O tyrant love, when held by you,
We may to prudence bid adieu.
(Amour! Amour! quand tu nous tiens
On peut bien dire, Adieu, prudence.)
LA FONTAINE, *Fables.* Bk. iv, fab. 1.

Prudence and love are not made for each other: as love increases, prudence diminishes. (La prudence et l'amour ne sont pas faits l'un pour l'autre: à mesure que l'amour croît, la prudence diminue.)

LA ROCHEFOUCAULD, *Maximes Posthumes*. No. 546.

1
It is not reason that governs love. (La raison n'est pas ce qui règle l'amour.)

MOLIÈRE, *Le Misanthrope*. Act i, sc. 1, l. 248.

I have heard you say,
Love's reason's without reason.

SHAKESPEARE, *Cymbeline*. Act iv, sc. 2, l. 21.

To say the truth, reason and love keep little company together now-a-days.

SHAKESPEARE, *A Midsummer-Night's Dream*. Act iii, sc. 1, l. 146.

Love draws me one way, reason another. (Aliudque cupido, mens aliud suadet.)

OVID, *Metamorphoses*. Bk. vii, l. 18.

2
A little sane love is all right, but not the insane sort. (Bonum est pauxillum amare sane, insane non bonum est.)

PLAUTUS, *Curculio*, l. 176.

Find me a reasonable lover, and I'll give you his weight in gold. (Auro contra cedo modestum amatorem, a me aurem accipe.)

PLAUTUS, *Curculio*, l. 201.

3
Lover, lunatic. (Amans amens.)

PLAUTUS, *Mercator*, l. 82.

Of lunatics rather than of lovers. (Amentium, haud amantium.)

TERENCE, *Andria*, l. 218.

4
To love and to be wise is scarcely given to a god. (Amare et sapere vix deo conceditur.)

PUBLILIUS SYRUS, *Sententiæ*. No. 22.

The proverb holds, that to be wise and love,
Is hardly granted to the gods above.

DRYDEN, *Palamon and Arcite*. Bk. ii, l. 364.

To be wise and love,
Exceeds man's might; that dwells with gods above.

SHAKESPEARE, *Troilus and Cressida*. Act iii, sc. 2, l. 163.

To be wise and eke to love
Is granted scarce to god above.

SPENSER, *The Shepheardes Calender: March: Willye's Emblem*.

5
Only a wise man knows how to love. (Solus sapiens scit amare.)

SENECA, *Epistulæ ad Lucilium*. Epis. lxxxi, 12.

6
If thou remember'st not the slightest folly
That ever love did make thee run into,
Thou hast not lov'd.

SHAKESPEARE, *As You Like It*. Act ii, sc. 4, l. 34.

We that are true lovers, run into strange capers.

SHAKESPEARE, *As You Like It*. Act ii, sc. 4, l. 55.

7
Love is your master, for he masters you:
And he that is so yoked by a fool,
Methinks, should not be chronicled for wise.

SHAKESPEARE, *The Two Gentlemen of Verona*. Act i, sc. 1, l. 39.

8
In all I wish, how happy should I be,
Thou grand Deluder, were it not for thee?
So weak thou art that fools thy power despise;
And yet so strong, thou triumph'st o'er the wise.

SWIFT, *To Love*.

Love is master of the wisest. It is only fools who defy him.

THACKERAY, *Men's Wives: Dennis Haggarty's Wife*.

9
Knowledge and love, altogether cotton not.

TORRIANO, *Piazza Universale*, 7. (1666)

VI—Love: Two Souls With But a Single Thought

10
My heart, I fain would ask thee
What then is Love? say on.
"Two souls with one thought only,
Two hearts that beat as one."
(Mein Herz ich will dich fragen,
Was ist denn Liebe, sag?
"Zwei Seelen und ein Gedanke,
Zwei Herzen und ein Schlag.")

VON MÜNCH BELLINGHAUSEN (FRIEDRICH HALM), *Der Sohn der Wildniss*. Act ii. (W. H. Charlton, tr.) Charlton's translation was the one preferred by the author.

Two souls with but a single thought,
Two hearts that beat as one.

VON MÜNCH BELLINGHAUSEN, *Ingomar the Barbarian*. Last lines. (Maria Anne Lovell, tr.) This is the popular translation of the play, which was a favorite in the American theater for many years.

Trooly it is with us as it was with Mr. & Mrs. Ingomer in the Play, to whit—
2 soles with but a single thawt
2 harts which beet as 1.

ARTEMUS WARD, *Among the Spirits*.

11
As for the lover, his soul dwells in the body of another. (Τοῦ δ' ἐρῶντος την ψυχὴν ἐν ἀλλοτρίῳ σώματι ζῆν.)

MARCUS CATO. (PLUTARCH, *Lives: Marcus Cato*. Ch. ix, sec. 5.)

Love is a spiritual coupling of two souls,
So much more excellent, as it least relates
Unto the body.

BEN JONSON, *The New Inn*. Act iii, sc. 2.

12
Two souls in one, two hearts into one heart.

DU BARTAS, *Devine Weekes and Workes*. Week i, day 6, l. 1057. (Sylvester, tr.)

What is love? Two souls and one flesh. Friendship? Two bodies and one soul.

JOSEPH ROUX, *Meditations of a Parish Priest: Love, Friendship, Friends*. (Hapgood, tr.)

Bianca: Canst tell me what love is?
Guido: It is consent. The union of two minds, two souls, two hearts
In all they think, and hope, and feel.
OSCAR WILDE, *A Florentine Tragedy.*

1
Naught can restrain consent of twain. (Non caret effectu, quod voluere duo.)
OVID, *Amores.* Bk. ii, eleg. 3, l. 16.

Love keeps his revels where there are but twain.
SHAKESPEARE, *Venus and Adonis,* l. 123.

2
One turf shall serve as pillow for us both;
One heart, one bed, two bosoms and one troth
SHAKESPEARE, *A Midsummer-Night's Dream.* Act ii, sc. 2, l. 41.

3
Love, that two hearts makes one, makes eke one will.
SPENSER, *Faerie Queene.* Bk. ii, canto 4, st. 19.

We were two and had but one heart. (Deux etions et n'avions qu'un cœur.)
FRANÇOIS VILLON, *Rondeau.*

The world has little to bestow
Where two fond hearts in equal love are joined.
ANNA LETITIA BARBAULD, *Delia.*

Two human loves make one divine.
E. B. BROWNING, *Isobel's Child.* St. 16.

VII—Love: With All Your Faults

4
Affection should not be too sharp-eyed, and love is not to be made by magnifying glasses.
SIR THOMAS BROWNE, *Christian Morals,* p. 70.

Analysis kills love, as well as other things.
JOHN BROWN, *Horæ Subsecivæ.*

5
Never love unless you can
Bear with all the faults of man!
THOMAS CAMPION, *Advice to a Girl.*

6
With all thy faults, I love thee still.
COWPER, *The Task.* Bk. ii, l. 206.

7
But love can every fault forgive,
Or with a tender look reprove;
And now let naught in memory live
But that we meet, and that we love.
GEORGE CRABBE, *Tales of the Hall: The Elder Brother: Song.*

8
Love sees no faults.
THOMAS FULLER, *Gnomologia.* No. 3297.

9
For Love can beauties spy
In what seem faults to every common eye.
JOHN GAY, *Trivia.* Bk. ii, l. 121.

10
When we love, it is the heart that judges. (Quand on aime, c'est le cœur qui juge.)
JOUBERT, *Pensées.* No. 66.

11
If lovers should mark everything a fault,
Affection would be like an ill-set book,
Whose faults might prove as big as half the volume.
MIDDLETON AND ROWLEY, *The Changeling,* ii, 1.

12
The woman we love will always be in the right. (La femme qu'on aime aura toujours raison.)
ALFRED DE MUSSET, *Idylle.*

13
Could I her faults remember,
Forgetting every charm,
Soon would impartial reason
The tyrant love disarm.
SHERIDAN, *The Duenna.* Act i, sc. 2.

14
We love the things we love in spite
Of what they are.
LOUIS UNTERMEYER, *Love.*

VIII—Love and Life

15
One hour of right-down love
Is worth an age of dully living on.
APHRA BEHN, *II The Rover.* Act v, sc. 1.

Each moment of a happy lover's hour
Is worth an age of dull and common life.
APHRA BEHN, *Younger Brother.* Act iii, sc. 3.

16
For life, with all it yields of joy and woe, . . .
Is just a chance o' the prize of learning love.
ROBERT BROWNING, *A Death in the Desert,* l. 245.

17
What is life when wanting love?
Night without a morning!
Love's the cloudless summer sun,
Nature gay adorning.
BURNS, *Thine Am I.*

18
Love's the weightier business of mankind.
COLLEY CIBBER, *She Wou'd and She Wou'd Not.* Act i, last line.

We are all born for love; it is the principle of existence and its only end.
BENJAMIN DISRAELI, *Sibyl.* Bk. v, ch. 4.

Th' important business of your life is love.
GEORGE LYTTELTON, *Advice to a Lady.*

19
Life, without love, is load; and time stands still:
What we refuse to him, to death we give;
And then, then only, when we love, we live.
WILLIAM CONGREVE, *The Mourning Bride.* Act ii. Concluding lines.

Love, then, hath every bliss in store;
'Tis friendship, and 'tis something more.
Each other every wish they give;
Not to know love is not to live.
JOHN GAY, *Plutus, Cupid and Time,* l. 135.

She who has never loved has never lived.
JOHN GAY, *The Captives.* Act ii, sc. 1.

See also LIFE AND LIVING.

20
Canst thou not wait for Love one flying hour
O heart of little faith?
EDMUND GOSSE, *Sonnet: Dejection and Delay.*

Ye gods! annihilate but space and time,
And make two lovers happy.
POPE, *The Art of Sinking in Poetry*. Ch. 9. Quoted as "Anon."

1
Among the holy bookes wise,
I finde writ in such wise,
Who loveth nought is here as dead.
JOHN GOWER, *Confessio Amantis*. Bk. iv.

And he that liveth to himself is dead,
And he that lives for love lives evermore;
Only in love can life's true path be trod;
Love is self-giving; therefore love is God.
MORTON LUCE, *Thysia*. Sonnet xxxvi.

2
To live without loving is not really to live. (Vivre sans aimer n'est pas proprement vivre.)
MOLIÈRE, *La Princesse d'Élide*. Act ii, sc. 1, l. 40.

Take love away from life and you take away its pleasures. (Ôtez l'amour de la vie, Vous en ôtez les plaisirs.)
MOLIÈRE, *Le Bourgeois Gentilhomme*. Dialogue between Acts i and ii.

Life! what art thou without love?
EDWARD MOORE, *Fables*. Fable xiv.

3
Were it not for love,
Poor life would be a ship not worth the launching.
EDWIN ARLINGTON ROBINSON, *Tristram*.

4
Life's richest cup is Love's to fill—
Who drinks, if deep the draught shall be,
Knows all the rapture of the hill
Blent with the heart-break of the sea.
ROBERT CAMERON ROGERS, *Love's Cup*.

5
To love it is and love alone
That life or luxury is known.
J. B. TABB, *The Test*.

6
Love took up the harp of Life, and smote on all the chords with might;
Smote the chord of Self, that, trembling, pass'd in music out of sight.
TENNYSON, *Locksley Hall*, l. 33.

IX—Love in Man and Woman

See also Woman and Love

7
Love is so different with us men.
ROBERT BROWNING, *In a Year*.

8
Alas; the love of women! it is known
To be a lovely and a fearful thing.
BYRON, *Don Juan*. Canto ii, st. 199.

9
Man's love is of man's life a thing apart,
'Tis woman's whole existence: man may range
The court, camp, church, the vessel, and the mart,
Sword, gown, gain, glory, offer in exchange
Pride, fame, ambition, to fill up his heart,
And few there are whom these cannot estrange;
Men have all these resources, we but one,
To love again, and be again undone.
BYRON, *Don Juan*. Canto i, st. 194.

A woman's whole life is a history of the affections.
WASHINGTON IRVING, *The Sketch Book: The Broken Heart*.

To a man the disappointment of love may occasion some bitter pangs: it wounds some feelings of tenderness—it blasts some prospects of felicity; but he is an active being—he may dissipate his thoughts in the whirl of varied occupation. . . . But woman's is comparatively a fixed, a secluded, and meditative life. . . . Her lot is to be wooed and won; and if unhappy in her love, her heart is like some fortress that has been captured, and sacked, and abandoned, and left desolate.
WASHINGTON IRVING, *The Sketch Book: The Broken Heart*.

Love, that of every woman's heart
Will have the whole, and not a part,
That is to her, in Nature's plan,
More than ambition is to man,
Her light, her life, her very breath,
With no alternative but death.
LONGFELLOW, *The Golden Legend*. Pt. iv, sec. 7.

Howe'er man rules in science and in art,
The sphere of woman's glories is the heart.
THOMAS MOORE, *Epilogue to the Tragedy of Ina*, l. 53.

Man dreams of fame, while woman wakes to love.
TENNYSON, *Merlin and Vivien*, l. 458.

10
The love of man? Exotic flower,
Broken, crushed, within an hour.
The love of woman? Storm-swept sea
Surging into eternity.
ELLEN M. CARROLL, *Man and Woman*.

11
Poor love is lost in men's capacious minds,
In ours, it fills up all the room it finds.
JOHN CROWNE, *Thyestes*.

12
Oh! a man's love is strong
When fain he comes a-mating.
But a woman's love is long
And grows when it is waiting.
LAURENCE HOUSMAN, *The Two Loves*.

13
I know a woman's portion when she loves,
It's hers to give, my darling, not to take;
It isn't lockets, dear, nor pairs of gloves,
It isn't marriage bells nor wedding cake,
It's up and cook, although the belly ache;
And bear the child, and up and work again,
And count a sick man's grumble worth the pain.
JOHN MASEFIELD, *The Widow in the Bye Street*.

14
Women know no perfect love;
Loving the strong, they can forsake the strong:

Man clings because the being whom he loves
Is weak and needs him.
GEORGE ELIOT, *The Spanish Gypsy*. Bk. iii.

1
Love lessens woman's delicacy and increases man's. (Die Liebe vermindert die weibliche Feinheit und verstärkt die männliche.)
JEAN PAUL RICHTER, *Titan*. Zykel 34.

A loving maiden grows unconsciously more bold. (Ein liebendes Mädchen wird unbewust kühner.)
JEAN PAUL RICHTER, *Titan*. Zykel 71.

2
Love is the history of a woman's life; it is an episode in man's. (L'amour est l'histoire de la vie des femmes; c'est un épisode dans celle des hommes.)
MADAME DE STAËL, *De L'Influence des Passions*.

3
Thy love to me was wonderful, passing the love of women.
Old Testament: II Samuel, i, 26.

4
A man can be happy with any woman as long as he does not love her.
OSCAR WILDE, *Picture of Dorian Gray*. Ch. 15.

X—Love for Love

5
To be beloved, love. (Ut ameris, ama.)
AUSONIUS, *Epigrams*. No. xxii, l. 6; MARTIAL, *Epigrams*. Bk. vi, epig. 11.

If you would be loved, love. (Si vis amari, ama.)
HECATO, *Fragments*. No. 27. (SENECA, *Epistulæ ad Lucilium*. Epis. ix, sec. 6.)

That you may be loved, be lovable. (Ut ameris, amabilis esto.)
OVID, *Ars Amatoria*. Bk. ii, l. 107.

If you would be loved, love and be lovable.
BENJAMIN FRANKLIN, *Poor Richard*, 1755.

6
Show thou love to win love.
ALEXANDER BARCLAY, *Mirrour of Good Manners*, p. 74. (c. 1510)

7
But I love you, sir:
And when a woman says she loves a man,
The man must hear her, though he love her not.
E. B. BROWNING, *Aurora Leigh*. Bk. ix, l. 613.

Behold me! I am worthy
Of thy loving, for I love thee!
E. B. BROWNING, *Lady Geraldine's Courtship*. St. 79.

If thou must love me, let it be for nought
Except for love's sake only.
E. B. BROWNING, *Sonnets from the Portuguese*. No. xiv.

8
And because my heart I proffered,
With true love trembling at the brim,
He suffers me to follow him.
ROBERT BROWNING, *Christmas-Eve*. Canto ix.

Love like mine must have return.
ROBERT BROWNING, *A Soul's Tragedy*. Act i.

9
I cannot love where I'm beloved.
BUTLER, *Hudibras*. Pt. ii, canto i, l. 304.

I cannot love thee as I ought,
For love reflects the thing beloved.
TENNYSON, *In Memoriam*. Pt. lii, st. 1.

10
Love looks for love again.
JOHN CLARKE, *Parœmiologia*, 27. (1639)

Love is the loadstone of love.
THOMAS FULLER, *Gnomologia*. No. 3288.

The only present love demands is love.
JOHN GAY, *The Espousal*, l. 56.

And sure love craveth love, like asketh like.
SIR JOHN HARINGTON, *Orlando Furioso*. Bk. xxviii, st. 80. (1591)

Love prays devoutly when it prays for love.
THOMAS HOOD, *Hero and Leander*, l. 120.

11
If there's delight in love, 'tis when I see
That heart which others bleed for, bleed for me.
CONGREVE, *Way of the World*. Act iii, sc. 12.

Johnson: "True. When he whom everybody else flatters, flatters me, I then am truly happy." *Mrs. Thrale*: "The sentiment is in Congreve, I think." *Johnson*: "Yes, madam, in *The Way of the World*."
SAMUEL JOHNSON. (BOSWELL, *Life*.)

12
Love, which insists that love shall mutual be. (Amor che a nullo amato amar perdona.)
DANTE, *Inferno*. Canto v, l. 103.

13
The sense of the world is short,—
Long and various the report,—
To love and be beloved;
Men and gods have not outlearned it;
And, how oft soe'er they've turned it,
'Tis not to be improved.
RALPH WALDO EMERSON, *Eros*.

14
Let no man think he is loved by any when he loves none.
EPICTETUS, *Fragments*. No. 156.

Let him love no one, and be beloved by none. (Nec amet quemquam, nec ametur ab ullo.)
JUVENAL, *Satires*. Sat. xii, l. 130.

15
The devil take me, if I think anything but love to be the object of love.
FIELDING, *Amelia*. Bk. v, ch. 9. (1751)

16
Only in love they happy prove
Who love what most deserves their love.
PHINEAS FLETCHER, *Sicelides*. Act iii, sc. 6.

17
If I love you, what business is that of yours? (Wenn ich dich lieb habe, was geht's dich an?)
GOETHE, *Wilhelm Meister*. Bk. iv, ch. 9.

18
There is no heaven like mutual love.
GEORGE GRANVILLE, *Peleus and Thetis*.

19
Love is kindest, and hath most length,

The kisses are most sweet,
When it's enjoyed in heat of strength,
Where like affections meet.
PATRICK HANNAY, *Songs and Sonnets*. Sonnet iv.

1
That bliss no wealth can bribe, no pow'r bestow,
That bliss of angels, love by love repaid.
DAVID MALLETT, *Amyntas and Theodora*. Canto i, l. 367.

2
Divine is Love and scorneth worldly pelf,
And can be bought with nothing but with self.
SIR WALTER RALEIGH, *Love the Only Price of Love*

Like Dian's kiss, unasked, unsought,
Love gives itself, but is not bought.
LONGFELLOW, *Endymion*. St. 4.

3
Lovers live by love as larks live by leeks.
JOHN HEYWOOD, *Proverbs*. Pt. i, ch. 10.

4
Love begins with love.
LA BRUYÈRE, *Les Caractères*. Ch. 4.

5
The pleasure of love is in loving; and we are much happier in the passion we feel than in that which we inspire. (Le plaisir de l'amour est d'aimer, et l'on est plus heureux par la passion que l'on a que par celle que l'on donne.)
LA ROCHEFOUCAULD, *Maximes*. No. 259.

To love for the sake of being loved is human, but to love for the sake of loving is angelic.
LAMARTINE, *Graziella*. Pt. iv, ch. 5.

Or rather let me love than be in love.
SIR THOMAS OVERBURY, *A Wife*.

All love is sweet Given or returned. . . .
They who inspire it most are fortunate,
As I am now: but those who feel it most
Are happier still.
SHELLEY, *Prometheus Unbound*. Act ii, sc. 5, l. 39.

We love being in love, that's the truth on't.
THACKERAY, *Henry Esmond*. Bk. ii, ch 15

6
Love goes toward love, as schoolboys from their books.
But love from love, toward school with heavy looks
SHAKESPEARE, *Romeo and Juliet*. Act ii, sc. 2, l. 156.

7
Yet leave me not; yet, if thou wilt, be free,
Love me no more, but love my love of thee.
SWINBURNE, *Erotion*.

I that have love and no more
Give you but love of you, sweet:
He that hath more, let him give;
He that hath wings, let him soar;
Mine is the heart at your feet
Here, that must love you to live.
SWINBURNE, *The Oblation*

And he that shuts Love out, in turn shall be
Shut out from Love, and on her threshold lie
Howling in outer darkness.
TENNYSON, *The Palace of Art: Introduction*.

8
And you must love him, ere to you
He will seem worthy of your love.
WORDSWORTH, *A Poet's Epitaph*. St. 11.

A woman despises a man for loving her, unless she happens to return his love.
ELIZABETH STODDARD, *Two Men*. Ch. 32.

9
Love for love is evenest bought.
UNKNOWN, *Love for Love*. (c. 1420)

Love, which cannot be paid but with love.
EDWARD FENTON, *Certain Secret Wonders of Nature*. (1569)

Love is never paid but with pure love.
JAMES MAB, *Celestina*, 138. (1631)

What can pay love but love?
MRS. MARY MANLEY, *The Lost Lover*. Act v, sc. 3. (1696)

Love is love's reward.
DRYDEN, *Palamon and Arcite*, ii, 373. (1700)

XI—Love: Its Cause

10
Loving comes by looking.
JOHN CLARKE, *Parœmiologia*, 28. (1639)

I saw and loved.
EDWARD GIBBON, *Autobiographic Memoirs*, p. 48.

But looking liked, and liking loved.
SCOTT, *Marmion:* Canto v, *Introduction*, l. 78.

11
'Tisn't beauty, so to speak, nor good talk necessarily It's just It. Some women'll stay in a man's memory if they once walked down a street
RUDYARD KIPLING, *Mrs. Bathurst*. (1904) The creation of "It" has been erroneously credited to Elinor Glyn.

12
To love but little is in love an infallible means of being beloved. (N'aimer guère en amour est un moyen assuré pour être aimé.)
LA ROCHEFOUCAULD, *Maximes Supprimées*. No. 636.

13
Habit causes love. (Consuetudo concinnat amorem.)
LUCRETIUS, *De Rerum Natura*. Bk. iv, l. 1278.

By habit love enters the mind; by habit is love unlearnt (Intrat amor mentes usu, dediscitur usu.)
OVID, *Remediorum Amoris*, l. 503.

14
There is one genuine love philtre—consideration. By this the woman is able to sway her man.
MENANDER, *Fragments*. No. 646.

15
It is not virtue, wisdom, valour, wit,
Strength, comeliness of shape, or amplest merit,

That woman's love can win, or long inherit;
But what it is, hard is to say,
Harder to hit.
MILTON, *Samson Agonistes*, l. 1010.

1
Often the pretender begins to love truly and ends by becoming what he feigned to be. (Sæpe tamen vere coepit simulator amare, Sæpe. quod incipiens finxerat esse, fuit.)
OVID, *Ars Amatoria*. Bk. i, l. 615.

I have laughed at the foolish man who feigned to love and fell like a fowler into his own snare. (Deceptum risi, qui se simulabat amare, In laqueos auceps decideratque suos.)
OVID, *Remediorum Amoris*, l. 501.

2
Love must be fostered with soft words. (Dulcibus est verbis mollis alendus amor.)
OVID, *Ars Amatoria*. Bk. ii, l. 152.

Insidious love glides into defenseless hearts. (Adfluit incautis insidiosus Amor.)
OVID, *Remediorum Amoris*, l. 148.

He who says over-much, "I love not," is in love. (Qui nimium multis "non amo" dicit, amat.)
OVID, *Remediorum Amoris*, l. 648.

3
Love is commenced at the mind's bidding, but is not cast off by it. (Amor animi arbitrio sumitur, non ponitur.)
PUBLILIUS SYRUS, *Sententiæ*. No. 5.

4
Talking of love is making it.
W. G. BENHAM, *Proverbs*, p. 839.

There are many people who would never have been in love if they had never heard love spoken of. (Il y a des gens qui n'auraient jamais été amoureux, s'ils n'avaient jamais entendu parler de l'amour.)
LA ROCHEFOUCAULD, *Maximes*. No. 136.

5
The sight of lovers feedeth those in love.
SHAKESPEARE, *As You Like It*. Act iii, sc. 4, l. 60.

6
If the rascal have not given me medicines to make me love him, I'll be hanged.
SHAKESPEARE, *I Henry IV*. Act ii, sc. 2, l. 19.

I'll be damned if the dog ha'n't given me some stuff to make me love him.
SMOLLETT, *Peregrine Pickle*. Ch. 15.

7
She loved me for the dangers I had pass'd,
And I loved her that she did pity them.
SHAKESPEARE, *Othello*. Act i, sc. 3, l. 167.

8
A mastiff dog
May love a puppy cur for no more reason
Than that the twain have been tied up together.
TENNYSON, *Queen Mary*. Act i, sc. 4, l. 109.

9
The less my hope the hotter my love. (Quanto minus spei est tanto magis amo.)
TERENCE, *Eunuchus*, l. 1053. (Act v, sc. 4.)

10
Women are well aware that what is commonly called sublime and poetical love depends not upon moral qualities, but on frequent meetings, and on the style in which the hair is done up, and on the color and cut of the dress.
LEO TOLSTOY, *The Kreutzer Sonata*. Ch. 6.

XII—Love: Its Cure

11
Who loves, raves—'tis youth's frenzy; but the cure
Is bitterer still.
BYRON, *Childe Harold*. Canto iv, st. 123.

12
Then fly betimes, for only they
Conquer love, that run away.
THOMAS CAREW, *Conquest by Flight*.

In love's wars, he who flyeth is conqueror.
THOMAS FULLER, *Gnomologia*. No. 2819.

The only victory over love is flight.
NAPOLEON BONAPARTE. (O'MEARA, *Napoleon in Exile*.)

13
Hunger, perhaps, may cure your love,
Or time your passion greatly alter;
If both should unsuccessful prove,
I strongly recommend a halter.
(Ἔρωτα παύει λιμός· εἰ δὲ μή, χρόνος.
ἐὰν δὲ μηδὲ ταῦτα τὴν φλόγα σβέσῃ,
θεραπεία σοι τὸ λοιπὸν ἠρτήσθω βρόχος.)
CRATES, *Cures for Love*. (*Greek Anthology*. Bk. ix, epig. 497.)

Why has some lover cast the noose about his neck, and hung, a sad burden, from a lofty beam? (Cur aliquis laqueo collum nodatus amator A trabe sublimi triste pependit onus?)
OVID, *Remediorum Amoris*, l. 17.

But ah! should she false-hearted prove,
Suspended, I'll dangle in air;
A victim to delicate love,
In Dyot Street, Bloomsbury Square.
WILLIAM B. RHODES, *Bombastes Furioso*.

They love too much that die for love.
COTGRAVE, *Dictionary: Mourir*. (1611)

A lover forsaken a new love may get,
But a neck, when once broken, can never be set.
WILLIAM WALSH, *The Despairing Lover*. (1692) Quoted by Scott, *Peveril of the Peak*. Ch. 39.

14
Love's a malady without a cure.
DRYDEN, *Palamon and Arcite*. Bk. ii, l. 110.

O ye Gods, have ye ordained for every malady a medicine, for every sore a salve, for every pain a plaster, leaving only love remedyless?
JOHN LYLY, *Euphues*.

Love, the sole disease thou canst not cure.
POPE, *Pastorals: Summer*, l. 12.

15
Alas, wretched me, that love may not be cured by herbs! (Me miserum, quod amor non est medicabilis herbis!)
OVID, *Heroides*. Epis. v, l. 149.

Ah me! love can not be cured by herbs. (Ei mihi! quod nullis amor est sanabilis herbis.)
OVID, *Metamorphoses*. Bk. i, l. 523.

1
Take away leisure and Cupid's bow is broken. (Otia si tollas, Periere Cupidinus arcus.)
OVID, *Remediorum Amoris*, l. 139.

You who seek an end to love, be busy, and you will be safe. (Qui finem quæris amoris, res age, tutus eris.)
OVID, *Remediorum Amoris*, l. 143.

The lover too shuns business.
COWPER, *Retirement*, l. 219.

2
All love is vanquished by a succeeding love. (Successore novo vincitur omnis amor.)
OVID, *Remediorum Amoris*, l. 462.

The new drives out the old. (Cura cura repulsa nova.)
OVID, *Remediorum Amoris*, l. 484.

And love may be expelled by other love,
As poisons are by poisons.
DRYDEN, *All for Love*. Act iv, sc. 1.

Diamonds cut diamonds; they who will prove
To thrive in cunning, must cure love with love.
JOHN FORD, *Lover's Melancholy*. Act i, sc. 3.

In all cases of heart-ache, the application of another man's disappointment draws out the pain and allays the irritation.
BULWER-LYTTON, *The Lady of Lyons*. Act i, sc. 2.

There is no remedy for love but to love more.
H. D. THOREAU, *Journal*, 25 July, 1839.

3
The disease has a thousand forms, I have a thousand remedies. (Mille mali species, mille salutis erunt.)
OVID, *Remediorum Amoris*, l. 526.

Plenty destroys passion. (Copia tollat amorem.)
OVID, *Remediorum Amoris*, l. 541.

4
I loved her then, but now, another love overhangs my heart. (Illam amabam olim, nunc jam alia cura impendet pectora.)
PLAUTUS, *Epidicus*, l. 135. (Act i, sc. 1.)

Even as one heat another heat expels,
Or as one nail by strength drives out another,
So the remembrance of my former love
Is by a newer object quite forgotten.
SHAKESPEARE, *The Two Gentlemen of Verona*. Act ii, sc. 4, l. 192.

For one heat, all know, doth drive out another;
One passion doth expel another still.
CHAPMAN, *Monsieur d'Olive*. Act v, sc. 1.

5
But he who stems a stream with sand,
And fetters flame with flaxen band,
Has yet a harder task to prove—
By firm resolve to conquer love!
SCOTT, *The Lady of the Lake*. Canto iii, st. 28.

XIII—Love: Its Power

6
Love is not to be reason'd down, or lost
In high ambition or a thirst of greatness;
'Tis second life, it grows into the soul,
Warms every vein, and beats in every pulse.
ADDISON, *Cato*. Act i, sc. 1.

When love's well-tim'd, 'tis not a fault to love;
The strong, the brave, the virtuous, and the wise,
Sink in the soft captivity together.
ADDISON, *Cato*. Act iii, sc. 1.

When love once pleads admission to our hearts,
In spite of all the virtue we can boast,
The woman that deliberates is lost.
ADDISON, *Cato*. Act iv, sc. 1. Often misquoted, "She who hesitates is lost."

7
If two stand shoulder to shoulder against the gods,
Happy together, the gods themselves are helpless
Against them, while they stand so.
MAXWELL ANDERSON, *Elizabeth the Queen*, ii.

8
Somewhere there waiteth in this world of ours
For one lone soul another lonely soul,
Each choosing each through all the weary hours,
And meeting strangely at one sudden goal,
Then blend they, like green leaves with golden flowers,
Into one beautiful perfect whole;
And life's long night is ended, and the way
Lies open onward to eternal day.
EDWIN ARNOLD, *Somewhere There Waiteth*.

I know not when the day shall be,
I know not when our eyes may meet;
What welcome you may give to me,
Or will your words be sad or sweet,
It may not be 'till years have passed,
'Till eyes are dim and tresses gray;
The world is wide, but, love, at last,
Our hands, our hearts, must meet some day.
HUGH CONWAY, *Some Day*.

Two shall be born, the whole wide world apart, . . .
And bend each wandering step to this one end—
That, one day, out of darkness, they shall meet
And read life's meaning in each other's eyes.
And two shall walk some narrow way of life, . . .
And yet, with wistful eyes that never meet . . .
They seek each other all their weary days
And die unsatisfied—and this is Fate!
SUSAN MARR SPALDING, *Fate*.

9
Love can find entrance, not only into an open heart, but also into a heart well fortified, if watch be not well kept.
FRANCIS BACON, *Essays: Of Love*.

10
For love is of sae mickle might,
That it all paines makis light.
JOHN BARBOUR, *The Bruce*. Bk. ii, l. 520.

11
The night has a thousand eyes,
And the day but one;
Yet the light of the bright world dies
With the dying sun.

The mind has a thousand eyes,
And the heart but one;
Yet the light of a whole life dies
When love is done.
FRANCIS WILLIAM BOURDILLON, *Light.*

1
When first we met we did not guess
That Love would prove so hard a master.
ROBERT BRIDGES, *Triolet.*

Love, the mild servant, makes a drunken master.
JOHN MASEFIELD, *Widow in the Bye Street.*

2
Love Is something awful which one dare not touch
So early o' mornings.
E. B. BROWNING, *Aurora Leigh.* Bk. ii, l. 40.

3
God be thanked, the meanest of his creatures
Boasts two soul-sides, one to face the world with,
One to show a woman when he loves her.
ROBERT BROWNING, *One Word More.* St. 17.

Oh, their Rafael of the dear Madonnas,
Oh, their Dante of the dread Inferno,
Wrote one song—and in my brain I sing it,
Drew one angel—borne, see, on my bosom!
ROBERT BROWNING, *One Word More.* Conclusion.

Is she poor?—What costs it to be styled a donor?
Merely an earth to cleave, a sea to part.
ROBERT BROWNING, *Pippa Passes.* Pt. ii.

4
Love, thou art not a king alone,
Both slave and king thou art!
Who seeks to sway, must stoop to own
The kingdom of a heart.
BULWER-LYTTON, *The New Timon.* Pt. iii.

5
The man in arms 'gainst female charms,
Even he her willing slave is.
BURNS, *Lovely Davies.*

6
The law of love threads every heart
And knits it to its utmost kin,
Nor can our lives flow long apart
From souls our secret souls would win.
JOHN BURROUGHS, *Waiting.* Unpublished concluding stanza.

7
No cord nor cable can so forcibly draw, or hold so fast, as love can do with a twined thread.
ROBERT BURTON, *Anatomy of Melancholy.* Pt. iii, sec. 2, mem. 1, subs. 2.

See also BEAUTY: BEAUTY DRAWS WITH A SINGLE HAIR.

8
Love makes those young whom age doth chill.
And whom he finds young keeps young still.
WILLIAM CARTWRIGHT, *To Chloe.*

Those who love deeply cannot age.
PINERO, *The Princess and the Butterfly.* Act v.

I tell thee Love is Nature's second sun,
Causing a spring of virtues where he shines.
GEORGE CHAPMAN, *All Fools.* Act i, sc. 1, l. 98.

9
The god of love, a! *benedicite,*
How mighty and how great a lord is he!
CHAUCER, *The Knightes Tale,* l. 927.

For ever it was, and ever it shall befal,
That Love is he that alle thing may bind.
CHAUCER, *Troilus and Criseyde.* Bk. i, l. 236.

Love has a thousand varied notes to move
The human heart.
GEORGE CRABBE, *The Frank Courtship,* l. 433.

Duty's a slave that keeps the keys,
But Love, the master goes in and out
Of his goodly chambers with song and shout,
Just as he please—just as he please.
DINAH MARIA MULOCK CRAIK, *Plighted.*

10
All thoughts, all passions, all delights,
Whatever stirs this mortal frame,
All are but ministers of Love,
And feed his sacred flame.
S. T. COLERIDGE, *Love.* St. 1.

11
Love's great artillery.
RICHARD CRASHAW, *Prayer,* l. 18.

Mighty Love's artillery.
CRASHAW, *Wounds of the Lord Jesus,* l. 2.

12
The warrior for the True, the Right,
Fights in love's name;
The love that lures thee from that fight
Lures thee to shame:
That love which lifts the heart, yet leaves
The spirit free.—
That love, or none, is fit for one
Man-shaped like thee.
AUBREY DE VERE, *Song.*

13
Love maketh a wit of a fool.
CHARLES DIBDIN, *The Quaker.* Act i, sc. 8.

It hath been a saying more common than true that love makes all men orators.
ROBERT GREENE, *Works,* ii, 57. (1583)

Love makes a good eye squint.
GEORGE HERBERT, *Jacula Prudentum.*

Love makes people inventive. (L'amour rend inventif.)
MOLIÈRE, *L'École des Maris.* Act i, sc. 4, l. 31.

But love the sense of right and wrong confounds,
Strong love and proud ambition have no bounds
DRYDEN, *Palamon and Arcite.* Bk. iii, l. 808
See also AMBITION AND LOVE.

14
To infinite, ever present Love, all is Love, and there is no error, no sin, sickness, nor death.
MARY BAKER EDDY, *Science and Health,* p. 567.

15
The solid, solid universe
Is pervious to Love;
With bandaged eyes he never errs,

Around below. above.
His blinding light He flingeth white
On God's and Satan's brood,
And reconciles By mystic wiles
The evil and the good.
EMERSON, *Cupido.*

A ruddy drop of manly blood
The surging sea outweighs;
The world uncertain comes and goes,
The lover rooted stays.
EMERSON, *Friendship.*

1
No man ever forgot the visitation of that power to his heart and brain, which created all things anew; which was the dawn in him of music, poetry and art; which made the face of nature radiant with purple light, the morning and the night varied enchantments; . . . when he became all eye when one was present, and all memory when one was gone.
EMERSON, *Essays, First Series: Love.*

There is a power in love to divine another's destiny better than that other can, and, by heroic encouragements, hold him to his task.
EMERSON, *Representative Men: Uses of Great Men.*

2
Oh love! oh love! whose shafts of fire
Invade the soul with sweet surprise,
Through the soft dews of young desire
Trembling in beauty's azure eyes!
("Ερως "Ερως, ὁ κατ' ὀμμάτων
στάζεις πόθον, εισάγων γλυκεῖαν
ψυχᾷ χάριν οὓς ἐπιστρατεύσῃ.)
EURIPIDES, *Hippolytus*, l. 525. (Peacock, tr.)

3
Were Love exempt from the militations of Necessity, he were greater than God and the World.
RICHARD GARNETT, *De Flagello Myrteo*, ccxxv.

4
Love grants in a moment
What toil can hardly achieve in an age.
(In einem Augenblick gewährt die Liebe
Was Mühe kaum in langer Zeit erreicht.)
GOETHE, *Torquato Tasso.* Act ii, sc. 3, l. 76.

5
It hath and shall be evermore
That Love is master where he will.
JOHN GOWER, *Confessio Amantis.* Bk. i, l. 33.

And netheles there is no man
In all this world so wise, that can
Of Love temper the measure.
JOHN GOWER, *Confessio Amantis.* Bk. i, l. 21.

6
But ah! in vain from Fate I fly,
For first, or last, as all must die,
So 'tis as much decreed above,
That first, or last, we all must love.
GEORGE GRANVILLE, *To Myra.*

And Love, that watched us ever from afar,
Came fluttering to our side, and cried, "O ye
Who think to fly, ye cannot fly from me;
Lo! I am with you always where you are."
EDMUND GOSSE, *Reconciliation.*

7
Love is above King or Kaiser, lord or laws.
ROBERT GREENE. *Works.* Vol. ii, p. 122. (1583)

For love will still be lord of all.
SCOTT, *The Lay of the Last Minstrel.* Canto vi, st. 11.

8
By Love was consummated what Diplomacy begun.
BRET HARTE, *Concepcion de Arguello.*

9
Scorn no man's love, though of a mean degree;
Love is a present for a mighty king.
GEORGE HERBERT, *The Church-Porch.* St. 59.

Love is swift of foot, Love's a man of war,
And can shoot, And can hit from far.
GEORGE HERBERT, *Discipline.*

Thy fatal shafts unerring move,
I bow before thine altar, Love!
SMOLLETT, *Roderick Random.* Ch. 40.

10
Love rules his kingdom without a sword.
GEORGE HERBERT, *Jacula Prudentum.*

Love rules without a sword,
Love binds without a cord.
UNKNOWN. A proverbial jingle.

11
He that hath love in his breast, hath spurs in his sides.
GEORGE HERBERT, *Jacula Prudentum.*

12
O, love, love, love! Love is like a dizziness;
It winna let a poor body Gang about his business!
JAMES HOGG, *Love Is Like a Dizziness.*

13
One can't choose when one is going to love.
HENRIK IBSEN, *The Master Builder.* Act ii.

14
Love is the magician, the enchanter, that changes worthless things to joy, and makes right-royal kings and queens of common clay. It is the perfume of that wondrous flower, the heart, and without that sacred passion, that divine swoon, we are less than beasts: but with it, earth is heaven and we are gods.
R. G. INGERSOLL, *Works,* p. 363. (1930 ed.)

15
Love extinguish'd, earth and heav'n must fail.
SIR WILLIAM JONES, *Hymn to Durga.*

16
You have ravish'd me away by a Power I cannot resist; and yet I could resist till I saw you; and even since I have seen you I have endeavored often "to reason against the reasons of my Love."
KEATS, *Letter to Fanny Brawne,* 13 Oct., 1819.

17
By the accident of fortune a man may rule the world for a time, but by virtue of love he may rule the world forever.
LAO-TSZE, *The Simple Way.* No. 13.

Waters are lost, and fires will die;
But love alone can fate defy.
NATHANIEL LEE, *Theodosius.*

1
Ah, how skillful grows the hand
That obeyeth Love's command!
LONGFELLOW, *The Building of the Ship*, l. 122.

2
What does not love compel us to do? (Quid non cogit amor?)
MARTIAL, *Epigrams*. Bk. v, ep. 48.

O tyrant Love, to what do you not drive the hearts of men! (Improbe Amor, quid non mortalia pectora cogis!)
VERGIL, *Æneid*. Bk. iv, l. 412.

3
The might of one fair face sublimes my love,
That it hath weaned my soul from low desires.
MICHELANGELO, *Sonnet: Vittoria Colonna.* (Hartley Coleridge, tr.)

4
Whatsoever love commands, it is not safe to despise. (Quidquid Amor jussit, non est contemnere tutum.)
OVID, *Heroides*. Epis. iv, l. 11.

5
Love will make men dare to die for their beloved—love alone; and women as well as men.
PLATO, *The Symposium*. Sec. 179.

6
Look round our world; behold the chain of love
Combining all below and all above.
POPE, *Essay on Man*. Epis. iii, l. 7.

7
In peace, Love tunes the shepherd's reed;
In war, he mounts the warrior's steed;
In halls, in gay attire is seen;
In hamlets, dances on the green.
Love rules the court, the camp, the grove,
And men below, and saints above;
For love is heaven, and heaven is love.
SCOTT, *The Lay of the Last Minstrel*. Canto iii, st. 2.

"Love rules the camp, the court, the grove,"—
"for love
Is heaven, and heaven is love:"—so sings the bard.
BYRON, *Don Juan*. Canto xii, st. 13.

8
Whoever at the outset has resisted and routed love, has been safe and conqueror; but whoso by dalliance has fed the sweet torment, too late refused to bear the accepted yoke. (Quisquis in primo obstitit Pepulitque amorem, tutus ac victor fuit; Qui blandiendo dulce nutrivit malum, Sero recusat ferre quod subiit jugum.)
SENECA, *Hippolytus*, l. 132.

9
For valour, is not Love a Hercules,
Still climbing trees in the Hesperides?
SHAKESPEARE, *Love's Labour's Lost*. Act iv, sc. 3, l. 340.

O powerful love! that in some respects, makes a beast a man, in some other, a man a beast.
SHAKESPEARE, *The Merry Wives of Windsor.* Act v, sc. 5, l. 5.

10
With love's light wings did I o'erperch these walls,
For stony limits cannot hold love out,
And what love can do that dares love attempt.
SHAKESPEARE, *Romeo and Juliet*. Act ii, sc. 2, l. 66.

Time, force, and death,
Do to this body what extremes you can;
But the strong base and building of my love
Is as the very centre of the earth,
Drawing all things to it.
SHAKESPEARE, *Troilus and Cressida*. Act iv, sc. 2, l. 107.

11
I have done penance for contemning Love,
Whose high imperious thoughts have punish'd me
With bitter fasts, with penitential groans,
With nightly tears and daily heart-sore sighs.
SHAKESPEARE, *The Two Gentlemen of Verona.* Act ii, sc. 4, l. 129.

Love's a mighty lord;
And hath so humbled me, as, I confess
This is no woe to his correction,
Nor to his service no such joy on earth.
Now no discourse, except it be of love;
Now can I break my fast, dine, sup, and sleep,
Upon the very naked name of love.
SHAKESPEARE, *The Two Gentlemen of Verona.* Act ii, sc. 4, l. 136.

12
Through all the drama—whether damn'd or not—
Love gilds the scene, and women guide the plot.
SHERIDAN, *The Rivals: Epilogue*, l. 5.

13
Many waters cannot quench love, neither can the floods drown it.
Old Testament: Song of Solomon, viii, 7.

14
Love, resistless in battle. (Ἔρως ἀνίκατε μάχαν.)
SOPHOCLES, *Antigone*, l. 781.

15
For Love is lord of truth and loyalty,
Lifting himself out of the lowly dust
On golden plumes up to the purest sky,
Above the reach of loathly sinful lust.
SPENSER, *An Hymn in Honour of Love*, l. 176.

Such is the power of that sweet passion,
That it all sordid baseness doth expel,
And the refined mind doth newly fashion
Unto a fairer form.
SPENSER, *An Hymn in Honour of Love*, l. 190.

16
Why should we kill the best of passions, love?
It aids the hero, bids ambition rise
To nobler heights, inspires immortal deeds,

Even softens brutes, and adds a grace to virtue.
JAMES THOMSON, *Sophonisba*. Act v, sc. 2.

1
Yet Love consumes me; for what bounds are there to love? (Me tamen urit amor: quis enim modus adsit amori?)
VERGIL, *Eclogues*. No. ii, l. 68.

Love conquers all; let us too yield to Love. (Omnia vincit Amor: et nos cedamus Amori.)
VERGIL, *Eclogues*. No. x, l. 69.

Love will conquer at the last.
TENNYSON, *Locksley Hall Sixty Years After*, l. 280.

2
Whoe'er thou art, thy master see;
He was, or is, or is to be.
(Qui que tu soit, Voici ton maître;
Il l'est, le fut, Ou le doit être.)
VOLTAIRE, *Inscription for a Statue of Cupid*.

3
Mightier far
Than strength of nerve or sinew, or the sway
Of magic potent over sun and star,
Is Love, though oft to agony distrest,
And though his favourite seat be feeble woman's breast.
WORDSWORTH, *Laodamia*. St. 15.

4
It's love, it's love that makes the world go round.
UNKNOWN. (*Chansons Nationales et Populaires de France*, ii, 180.)

Love makes the time pass. (L'amour fait passer le temps.) Time makes love pass. (Le temps fait passer l'amour.)
UNKNOWN. Proverbial phrases.

5
Under floods that are deepest,
Which Neptune obey;
Over rocks that are steepest,
Love will find out the way.
UNKNOWN, *Love Will Find Out the Way*. (PERCY, *Reliques*.)

Love will find its way
Through paths where wolves would fear to prey.
BYRON, *The Giaour*, l. 1047.

Thus love, you see, can find a way
To make both man and maids obey.
THOMAS DELONEY, *Gentle Craft*. Ch. 15. (c. 1597)

'Tis love that makes me bold and resolute,
Love that can find a way where path there's none,
Of all the gods the most invincible.
EURIPIDES, *Hippolytus*. Frag. 2.

Tho' the sun in heaven desert you,
"Love will find out the way."
ALFRED NOYES, *Love Will Find Out the Way*.

Ah, to that far distant strand
Bridge there was not to convey,
Not a bark was near at hand,
Yet true love soon found the way.
SCHILLER, *Hero and Leander*. (Bowring, tr.)

6
Zeus came as an eagle to god-like Ganymede, as a swan came he to the fair-haired mother of Helen.
UNKNOWN, *Greek Anthology*. Bk. v, No. 65.

Jupiter himself was turned into a satyr, a shepherd, a bull, a swan, a golden shower, and what not for love.
ROBERT BURTON, *Anatomy of Melancholy*. Pt. iii, sec. ii, mem. 1, subs. 1.

Did not Jupiter transform himself into the shape of Amphitrio to embrace Alcmæna; into the form of a swan to enjoy Leda; into a bull to beguile Io; into a shower of gold to win Danaë?
JOHN LYLY, *Euphues*, p. 93.

Leda, sailing on the stream
To deceive the hopes of man,
Love accounting but a dream,
Doted on a silver swan;
Danaë, in a brazen tower,
Where no love was, loved a shower.
JOHN FLETCHER, *Valentinian*.

7
To enlarge or illustrate this power and effect of love is to set a candle in the sun.
ROBERT BURTON, *Anatomy of Melancholy*. Pt. iii, sec. ii, mem. 1, subs. 2.

XIV—Love: Its Lawlessness

See also Marriage and Love

8
Who can give law to lovers? Love is a greater law to itself. (Quis legem det amantibus? Major lex amor est sibi.)
BOËTHIUS, *De Consolatione Philosophiæ*. Bk. iii, meter 12, l. 47.

Wist thou not well the old clerks' saw,
That who shall give a lover any law?
CHAUCER, *The Knightes Tale*, l. 306. (c. 1380)

9
Love will not be constrained by mastery;
When mastery cometh, the god of love anon
Beateth his wings, and farewell! he is gone!
Love is a thing as any spirit free.
CHAUCER, *The Frankeleyns Tale*, l. 36.

Nor may love be compelled by mastery;
For soon as mastery comes, sweet love anon
Taketh his nimble wings, and soon away is gone.
SPENSER, *Faerie Queene*. Bk. iii, canto i, st. 25.

10
Love knows no mean or measure.
PHINEAS FLETCHER, *Piscatory Eclogues*.

11
Love's law is out of rule.
JOHN GOWER, *Confessio Amantis*. Bk. i, l. 18.

Love knows no rule. (Amor ordinem nescit.)
ST. JEROME, *Letter to Chromatius*.

He loves little who loves by rule. (Celuy ayme peu qui ayme à la mésure.)
MONTAIGNE, *Essays*. Bk. i, ch. 28.

12
As love knoweth no laws, so it regardeth no conditions.
JOHN LYLY, *Euphues*, p. 84.

1
Love knows no order. (Amor ordinem nescit.)
MONTAIGNE, *Essays*. Bk. iii, ch. 5.

2
Love is without law.
BARNABE RICH, *Farewell*, 191. (1581)

Love is lawless.
JOHN CLARKE, *Parœmiologia*, 27. (1639)

No law is made for love.
DRYDEN, *Palamon and Arcite*, i, 326. (1700)

3
For love will not be drawn, but must be led.
SPENSER, *Colin Clout*, l. 129.

4
Let love be free; free love is for the best.
And, after heaven, on our dull side of death,
What should be best, if not so pure a love
Clothed in so pure a loveliness?
TENNYSON, *Lancelot and Elaine*, l. 1370.

5
Oh, rank is good, and gold is fair,
And high and low mate ill;
But love has never known a law
Beyond its own sweet will!
WHITTIER, *Amy Wentworth*.

XV—Love: Love's Young Dream

6
I've pacèd much this weary, mortal round,
And sage experience bids me this declare:—
"If Heaven a draught of heavenly pleasure spare,
One cordial in this melancholy vale
'Tis when a youthful, loving, modest pair,
In other's arms breathe out the tender tale,
Beneath the milk white thorn that scents the ev'ning gale."
BURNS, *The Cotter's Saturday Night*. St. 9.

Oh Love! young Love! bound in thy rosy band,
Let sage or cynic prattle as he will,
These hours, and only these, redeem Life's years of ill.
BYRON, *Childe Harold*. Canto ii, st. 81.

Oh! there's nothing in life like making love.
THOMAS HOOD, *Miss Kilmansegg: Her Courtship*.

7
What a sweet reverence is that when a young man deems his mistress a little more than mortal and almost chides himself for longing to bring her close to his heart.
HAWTHORNE, *The Marble Faun*. Vol. ii, ch. 15.

8
Pillow'd upon my fair love's ripening breast,
To feel for ever its soft fall and swell;
Awake for ever in a sweet unrest;
Still, still to hear her tender-taken breath;
And so live ever—or else swoon to death.
KEATS, *Last Sonnet*.

Wishing forever in that state to lie,—
Forever to be dying so, yet never die.
CONGREVE, *On Arabella Hunt, Singing*.

9
And, happy melodist, unwearied,
For ever piping songs for ever new;
More happy love! more happy, happy love!
For ever warm and still to be enjoy'd,
For ever panting and for ever young.
KEATS, *Ode on a Grecian Urn*. St. 3.

10
There's nothing half so sweet in life
As love's young dream.
THOMAS MOORE, *Love's Young Dream*.

Is there on earth a space so dear
As that within the blessed sphere
Two loving arms entwine?
THOMAS MOORE, *To Fanny*.

11
One pulse of passion—youth's first fiery glow,—
Is worth the hoarded proverbs of the sage:
Vex not thy soul with dead philosophy;
Have we not lips to kiss with, hearts to love, and eyes to see?
OSCAR WILDE, *Panthea*. St. 2.

12
Love in thy youth, fair maid; be wise,
Old Time will make thee colder,
And though each morning new arise
Yet we each day grow older.
UNKNOWN. *Madrigal*. (PORTER, *Madrigals and Airs*, 1632.)

Take it, girl! And fear no after,
Take your fill of all this laughter,
Laugh or not the tears will fall,
Take the laughter first of all.
RICHARD LE GALLIENNE, *Song*.

XVI—Love: Its Sweetness

13
To love and be beloved, this is the good,
Which for most sovereign all the world will prove.
WILLIAM ALEXANDER, *Aurora*. Sonnet xliv.

14
The crowning glory of loving and being loved is that the pair make no real progress; however far they have advanced into the enchanted land during the day they must start again from the frontier next morning.
J. M. BARRIE, *Tommy and Grizel*, p. 189.

15
O happy race of men, if love, which rules heaven, rule your minds! (O felix hominum genus, Si vestros animos amor Quo cælum regitur regat.)
BOËTHIUS, *Philosophiæ Consolationis*. Bk ii, meter 8, l. 28.

16
"Oh! Love," they said, "is King of Kings,
And Triumph is his crown.
Earth fades in flame before his wings,
And Sun and Moon bow down."
RUPERT BROOKE, *Song*.

17
There is music even in the beauty, and the silent note which Cupid strikes, far sweeter than the sound of an instrument.
SIR THOMAS BROWNE, *Religio Medici*. Pt. ii, sec. 10.

1

Shut them in,
With their triumphs and their glories and the rest!
Love is best!

ROBERT BROWNING, *Love Among the Ruins*.

O lyric Love, half angel and half bird,
And all a wonder and a wild desire!

ROBERT BROWNING, *The Ring and the Book*. Pt. i, l. 1391.

What's the earth
With all its art, verse, music, worth—
Compared with love, found, gained, and kept?

ROBERT BROWNING, *Dis Aliter Visum*.

2

Devotion wafts the mind above,
But Heaven itself descends in love;
A feeling from the Godhead caught,
To wean from self each sordid thought;
A Ray of him who form'd the whole;
A Glory circling round the soul!

BYRON, *The Giaour*, l. 1135.

3

For soft the hours repeat one story,
Sings the sea one strain divine,
My clouds arise all flushed with glory;
I love, and the world is mine!

FLORENCE EARLE COATES, *The World Is Mine*.

4

Power and gold and fame denied,
Love laughs glad in the paths aside.

LOUISE DRISCOLL, *The Highway*.

Love has in store for me one happy minute.

DRYDEN, *No, No, Poor Suffering Heart*.

5

The person love does to us fit,
Like manna, has the taste of all of it.

EMERSON, *Essays, First Series: Love*. Quoted.

6

Earth's the right place for love:
I don't know where it's likely to go better.

ROBERT FROST, *Birches*.

7

If, as Mimnermus holds, without love and jests there is no joy, live amid love and jests. (Si, Mimnermus uti censet, sine amore jocisque Nil est jucundum, vivas in amore jocisque.)

HORACE, *Epistles*. Bk. i, epis. 6, l. 65.

9

I sing of little loves that glow
Like tapers shining in the rain,
Of little loves that break themselves
Like moths against the window-pane.

ALINE KILMER, *Prelude*.

10

Love is more than great richesse.

JOHN LYDGATE, *The Story of Thebes*. Pt. iii.

Though poor in gear, we're rich in love.

BURNS, *The Sodger's Return*.

11

Love's own hand the nectar pours,
Which never fails nor ever sours.

DAVID MALLETT, *Cupid and Hymen*.

12

The world is filled with folly and sin,
And Love must cling, where it can, I say:
For Beauty is easy enough to win;
But one isn't loved every day.

OWEN MEREDITH, *Changes*.

13

For what is knowledge duly weighed?
Knowledge is strong, but love is sweet;
Yea all the progress he had made
Was but to learn that all is small
Save love, for love is all in all.

CHRISTINA ROSSETTI, *The Convent Threshold*.

Love is like a rose, the joy of all the earth, . . .
Love is like a lovely rose, the world's delight.

CHRISTINA ROSSETTI, *Hope*.

14

Mortals, while through the world you go,
Hope may succor and faith befriend,
Yet happy your hearts if you can but know,
Love awaits at the journey's end!

CLINTON SCOLLARD, *The Journey's End: Envoy*.

15

But, mistress, know yourself: down on your knees,
And thank heaven, fasting, for a good man's love.

SHAKESPEARE, *As You Like It*. Act iii, sc. 5, l. 57.

16

This is the very ecstasy of love.

SHAKESPEARE, *Hamlet*. Act ii, sc. 1, l. 102.

Nature is fine in love, and where 't is fine,
It sends some precious instance of itself
After the thing it loves.

SHAKESPEARE, *Hamlet*. Act iv, sc. 5, l. 161.

Love's arms are peace, 'gainst rule, 'gainst sense, 'gainst shame,
And sweetens, in the suffering pangs it bears,
The aloes of all forces, shocks, and fears.

SHAKESPEARE, *A Lover's Complaint*, l. 271.

17

O spirit of love! how quick and fresh art thou,
That, notwithstanding thy capacity
Receiveth as the sea, nought enters there,
Of what validity and pitch soe'er,
But falls into abatement and low price,
Even in a minute!

SHAKESPEARE, *Twelfth Night*. Act i, sc. 1, l. 9.

18

Love, as is told by the seers of old,
Comes as a butterfly tipped with gold,
Flutters and flies in sunlit skies,
Weaving round hearts that were one time cold.

SWINBURNE, *Song*.

A lover looked. She dropped her eyes
That glowed like pansies wet with dew;
And lo, there came from out the skies
Butterflies all blue.

JOHN DAVIDSON, *Butterflies*.

1
O Love, what hours were thine and mine,
In lands of palm and southern pine;
In lands of palm, of orange-blossom,
Of olive, aloe, and maize and vine.
TENNYSON, *The Daisy*. St. 1.

Sweet is true love tho' given in vain, in vain.
TENNYSON, *Lancelot and Elaine,* l. 1000.

2
The wine of Love is music,
And the feast of Love is song:
And when Love sits down to the banquet,
Love sits long: . . .
Sits long and rises drunken,
But not with the feast and the wine;
He reeleth with his own heart,
That great, rich Vine.
JAMES THOMSON, *The Vine*.

3
The worlds in which we live are two—
The world "I am," and the world "I do."
LYMAN W. DENTON, *Two Worlds*. (*Harper's Magazine*, May, 1900, p. 946.)

The worlds in which we live at heart are one,
The world "I am," the fruit of "I have done";
And underneath these worlds of flower and fruit,
The world "I love," the only living root.
HENRY VAN DYKE, *One World*. Dr. Van Dyke's lines were a reply to Mr. Denton's, which he quoted.

Self is the only prison that can ever bind the soul;
Love is the only angel who can bid the gates unroll;
And when he comes to call thee, arise and follow fast;
His way may lie through darkness, but it leads to light at last.
HENRY VAN DYKE, *The Prison and the Angel*.

Who seeks for heaven alone to save his soul,
May keep the path, but will not reach the goal;
While he who walks in love may wander far,
But God will bring him where the Blessed are.
HENRY VAN DYKE, *The Way*.

4
Vain is the glory of the sky,
The beauty vain of field and grove,
Unless, while with admiring eye
We gaze, we also learn to love.
WORDSWORTH, *Poems of the Fancy*. No. 20.

5
He spake of love, such love as Spirits feel
In worlds whose course is equable and pure;
No fears to beat away—no strife to heal—
The past unsighed for, and the future sure.
WORDSWORTH, *Laodamia*. St. 16.

6
'Tis sense, unbridled will, and not true love,
That kills the soul: love betters what is best,
Even here below, but more in heaven above.
WORDSWORTH, *Miscellaneous Sonnets*. Pt. i, No. 25. After Michelangelo.

All these I better in one general best.
SHAKESPEARE, *Sonnets*. No. xci.

XVII—Love: Its Bitterness

7
Could I love less, I should be happier now.
P. J. BAILEY, *Festus: Garden and Bower*.

8
Love and sorrow twins were born
On a shining showery morn.
THOMAS BLACKLOCK, *The Graham*.

9
Love is like fire. . . . Wounds of fire are hard to bear; harder still are those of love.
HJALMAR HJORTH BOYESEN, *Gunnar*. Ch. 4.

10
Was it something said,
Something done,
Vexed him? Was it touch of hand,
Turn of head?
Strange! that very way
Love begun:
I as little understand
Love's decay.
ROBERT BROWNING, *In a Year*.

11
Ah woe is me, through all my days
Wisdom and wealth I both have got,
And fame and name and great men's praise;
But Love, ah! Love I have it not.
H. C. BUNNER, *The Way to Arcady*.

12
Had we never lov'd sae kindly,
Had we never lov'd sae blindly,
Never met, or never parted,
We had ne'er been broken-hearted!
BURNS, *Ae Fond Kiss*.

13
O Love! thou art the very god of evil,
For, after all, we cannot call thee devil.
BYRON, *Don Juan*. Canto ii, st. 205.

O love! what is it in this world of ours
Which makes it fatal to be loved? Ah, why
With cypress branches hast thou wreathed thy bowers,
And made thy best interpreter a sigh!
BYRON, *Don Juan*. Canto iii, st. 2.

Soon or late Love is his own avenger.
BYRON, *Don Juan*. Canto iv, st. 73.

14
Just like Love is yonder rose,
Heavenly fragrance round it throws,
Yet tears its dewy leaves disclose,
And in the midst of briars it blows
Just like Love.
CAMOËNS, *Rose and Thorn*. (Strangford, tr.)

15
My love-lies-bleeding.
THOMAS CAMPBELL, *O'Connor's Child*. St. 5.

16
O pang all pangs above,
Is kindness counterfeiting absent Love.
S. T. COLERIDGE, *Pang More Sharp than All*.

Love's despair is but Hope's pining ghost!
S. T. COLERIDGE, *The Visionary Hope*.

17
So, lovers dream a rich and long delight,

But get a winter-seeming summer's night.
JOHN DONNE, *Love's Alchemy*. See also DREAMS: DREAMS OF LOVE.

2
For winning love, we run the risk of losing.
THOMAS HARDY, *Revulsion*. St. 2.

3
A love that took an early root
And had an early doom.
T. K. HERVEY, *The Devil's Progress*.

4
O night of love and beauty, all the years
Shall pay for thy brief ecstasy with tears.
ROBERT HILLYER, *Sonnets*.

5
There are as many pangs in love as shells upon the shore. (Littore quot conchæ, tot sunt in amore dolores.)
OVID, *Ars Amatoria*. Bk. ii, l. 519.

There is love for none except him whom fortune favors. (Diligitur nemo, nisi cui fortuna secunda est.)
OVID, *Epistulæ ex Ponto*. Bk. ii, epis. 3, l. 23.

6
How wretched is the man who loves! (Uti miser est homo qui amat.)
PLAUTUS, *Asinaria*, l. 616. (Act iii, sc. 3.)

He who falls in love meets a worse fate than he who leaps from a rock. (Qui in amore Præcipitavit, pejus perit quam si saxo saliat.)
PLAUTUS, *Trinummus*. Act ii, sc. 1, l. 30.

Love not! love not! ye hopeless sons of clay;
Hope's gayest wreaths are made of earthly flowers—
Things that are made to fade and fall away,
Ere they have blossomed for a few short hours.
CAROLINE NORTON, *Love Not*.

The hour when you too learn that all is vain,
And that Hope sows what Love shall never reap.
D. G. ROSSETTI, *Sonnets*. No. 44.

7
The hind that would be mated by the lion
Must die for love.
SHAKESPEARE, *All's Well that Ends Well*. Act i, sc. 1, l. 102.

8
Say that you love me not, but say not so
In bitterness.
SHAKESPEARE, *As You Like It*. Act iii, sc. 5, l. 2.

9
The pangs of despised love.
SHAKESPEARE, *Hamlet*. Act i, sc. 3, l. 72.

The unconquerable pang of despised love.
WORDSWORTH, *The Excursion*. Bk. vi, l. 905.

Slighted love is sair to bide.
BURNS, *Duncan Gray*.

10
Ay me! for aught that I could ever read,
Could ever hear by tale or history,
The course of true love never did run smooth.
SHAKESPEARE, *A Midsummer-Night's Dream*. Act i, sc. 1, l. 132.

I never heard
Of any true affection but 'twas nipped.
THOMAS MIDDLETON, *Blurt*. Act iii, sc. 2.

11
There is no creature loves me,
And if I die, no soul shall pity me.
SHAKESPEARE, *Richard III*. Act v, sc. 3, l. 200.

Nobody loves me; I'm going into the garden and eat worms.
UNKNOWN, *A Valentine Greeting*.

12
To be in love, where scorn is bought with groans;
Coy looks with heart-sore sighs.
SHAKESPEARE, *The Two Gentlemen of Verona*. Act i, sc. 1, l. 29.

And writers say, as the most forward bud
Is eaten by the canker ere it blow,
Even so by love the young and tender wit
Is turn'd to folly, blasting in the bud,
Losing his verdure even in the prime.
SHAKESPEARE, *The Two Gentlemen of Verona*. Act i, sc. 1, l. 45.

What 'tis to love? how want of love tormenteth?
SHAKESPEARE, *Venus and Adonis*, l. 202.

13
Love's Pestilence, and her slow dogs of war.
SHELLEY, *Hellas*, l. 321.

14
Let Love clasp Grief lest both be drown'd.
TENNYSON, *In Memoriam*. Sec. 1, st. 3.

Of love that never found his earthly close,
What sequel? Streaming eyes and breaking hearts;
Or all the same as if he had not been?
TENNYSON, *Love and Duty*, l. 1.

There is no living in love without suffering. (Sine dolore non vivitur in amore.)
THOMAS À KEMPIS, *De Imitatione Christi*. Bk. iii, ch. 5, sec. 7.

15
Yet each man kills the thing he loves,
By each let this be heard,
Some do it with a bitter look,
Some with a flattering word,
The coward does it with a kiss,
The brave man with a sword!
OSCAR WILDE, *Ballad of Reading Gaol*. St. 7.

16
Love's Martyr, when his heat is past,
Proves Care's Confessor at the last.
UNKNOWN, *Advice to a Lover*.

XVIII—Love: Pain or Pleasure

17
Mysterious love, uncertain treasure,
Hast thou more of pain or pleasure. . . .
Endless torments dwell about thee:
Yet who would live, and live without thee!
ADDISON, *Rosamond*. Act iii, sc. 2.

18
Yes, loving is a painful thrill,
And not to love more painful still;
But oh, it is the worst of pain,

To love and not be lov'd again.
ANACREON, *Odes*. No. 29. (Moore, tr.)

A mighty pain to love it is,
And 'tis a pain that pain to miss;
But of all pains, the greatest pain
It is to love, but love in vain.
ABRAHAM COWLEY, *Anacreontiques: Gold.*

The sweetest joy, the wildest woe is love.
P. J. BAILEY, *Festus: Alcove and Garden.*

Love's alternate joy and woe.
BYRON, *Maid of Athens.*

I have tasted the sweets and the bitters of love.
BYRON, *Lines to the Rev. J. T. Becher.*

1
O Love, all other pleasures
Are not worth thy pains.
(Amour, tout les autres plaisirs
Ne valent pas tes peines.)
CHARLEVAL, *Ballade.*

All other pleasures are not worth its pains.
EMERSON, *Essays, First Series: Love.* Quoted.

2
What a recreation it is to be in love! It sets the heart aching so delicately, there's no taking a wink of sleep for the pleasure of the pain.
GEORGE COLMAN THE YOUNGER, *The Mountaineers.* Act i, sc. 1.

3
Lovers derive their pleasures from their misfortunes.
DIOGENES. (DIOGENES LAERTIUS, *Diogenes.* Sec. 67.)

4
Love has a thousand ways to please,
But more to rob us of our ease.
DRYDEN, *King Arthur.* Act v, sc. 1.

5
Pains of love be sweeter far
Than all other pleasures are.
DRYDEN, *Tyrannic Love.* Act iv, sc. 1.

The jolif woe.
JOHN GOWER, *Confessio Amantis.* Bk. vi, l. 84.

6
Oh Love! thou bane of the most generous souls!
Thou doubtful pleasure, and thou certain pain.
GEORGE GRANVILLE, *Heroic Love.*

7
Love's of itself too sweet; the best of all
Is when love's honey has a dash of gall.
ROBERT HERRICK, *Another of Love.*

The sweets of love are mixed with tears.
ROBERT HERRICK, *The Primrose.*

8
'Tis the pest
Of love that fairest joys give most unrest.
KEATS, *Endymion.* Bk. ii, l. 366.

But, for the general award of love,
The little sweet doth kill much bitterness.
KEATS, *Isabella.* St. 13.

9
Love leads to present rapture,—then to pain;
But all through Love in time is healed again.
CHARLES GODFREY LELAND, *Sweet Marjoram.*

10
O what a heaven is love! O what a hell!
MIDDLETON AND DEKKER, *I The Honest Whore.* Act i, sc. 1.

O, then, what graces in my love do dwell,
That he hath turn'd a heaven unto a hell!
SHAKESPEARE, *A Midsummer-Night's Dream.* Act i, sc. 1, l. 206.

11
Forgetfulness of grief I yet may gain;
In some wise may come ending to my pain;
It may be yet the Gods will have me glad!
Yet, love. I would that thee and pain I had!
WILLIAM MORRIS, *The Earthly Paradise: The Death of Paris.*

12
Love overflows with both honey and gall. It gives you a taste of sweetness, and then heaps bitterness before you to satiety. (Amor et melle et felle est fecundissimus; Gustui dat dulce, amarum ad satietatem usque oggerit.)
PLAUTUS, *Cistellaria,* l. 69.

She has more of aloes (bitterness) than of honey. (Plus aloes quam mellis habet.)
JUVENAL, *Satires.* Sat. vi, l. 181.

True he it said, whatever man it said,
That love with gall and honey doth abound,
But if the one be with the other weighed,
For every dram of honey therein found,
A pound of gall doth over it redound.
SPENSER, *Faerie Queene.* Bk. iv, canto x, l. 1.

Of honey and of gall in love there is store:
The honey is much, but the gall is more.
SPENSER, *The Shepheardes Calender: March: Thomalin's Emblem.*

13
There is no pleasure like the pain
Of being loved. and loving.
W. M. PRAED, *Legend of the Haunted Tree.*

14
In love, pain and pleasure are always at strife. (In venere semper certant dolor et gaudium.)
PUBLILIUS SYRUS, *Sententiæ.* No. 298.

15
Yet what is Love, good shepherd, sain?
It is a sunshine mixed with rain.
SIR WALTER RALEIGH, *Now What Is Love?*

16
Whether love be pain or pain be love I do not know; but I know one thing: that pain is pleasure if pain be love (An amor dolor sit, An dolor amor sit. Utrumque nescio. Hoc unum sentio: Jocundus dolor est Si dolor amor est.)
GEORGE SAINTSBURY, *Scrap Books.* Vol i, p. 185. Quoted, as a medieval Latin poem.

17
And love is loveliest when embalm'd in tears.
SCOTT, *The Lady of the Lake.* Canto iv, st. 1.

1
Love's very pain is sweet,
But its reward is in the world divine,
Which, if not here, it builds beyond the grave.
SHELLEY, *Epipsychidion,* l. 596.

2
"I thought *love* had been a joyous thing," quoth my Uncle Toby.—" 'Tis the most serious thing, an' please your Honour (sometimes) that is in the world."
STERNE, *Tristram Shandy*. Vol. vii, ch. 20.

3
Love kills happiness, happiness kills love.
MIGUEL DE UNAMUNO, *Essays and Soliloquies,* p. 57.

4
Whoever shall fear the sweets or taste the bitters of love. (Quisquis amores Aut metuet dulcis aut experietur amaros.)
VERGIL, *Eclogues*. No. iii, l. 109.

XIX—Love: Lovers' Quarrels

5
Little quarrels often prove
To be but new recruits of love;
When those who're always kind of coy,
In time must either tire or cloy.
BUTLER, *Hudibras*. Pt. iii, canto i, l. 905.

And to be wroth with one we love
Doth work like madness in the brain.
S. T. COLERIDGE, *Christabel*. Pt. ii, l. 101.

6
In love there are these evils: first war, and then peace. (In amore hæc sunt mala: bellum, Pax rursum.)
HORACE, *Satires*. Bk. ii, sat. 3, l. 267.

7
A lovers' quarrel is short-lived. ('Ὀργὴ φιλούντων ὀλίγον ἰσχύει χρόνον.)
MENANDER, *Fragments*. No. 797.

Lovers' quarrels are soon adjusted.
APHRA BEHN, *Emperor of the Moon*. Act ii, sc. 1.

Love-quarrels oft in pleasing concord end.
MILTON, *Samson Agonistes*, l. 1008.

8
Loving spite. (Dépit amoureux.)
MOLIÈRE. Title of comedy, 1654.

9
Alas! how light a cause may move
Dissension between hearts that love!
THOMAS MOORE, *Lalla Rookh: The Light of the Harem*, l. 183.

10
They are twice as much friends as they were before quarrelling. (Bis tanto amici sunt inter se quam prius.)
PLAUTUS, *Amphitruo*, l. 943. (Act iii, sc. 2.)

11
You must anger a lover if you wish him to love. (Cogas amantem irasci, amare si velis.)
PUBLILIUS SYRUS, *Sententiæ*. No. 118.

12
The difference is wide that the sheets will not decide.
JOHN RAY, *English Proverbs*.

13
Love is hurt with jar and fret;
Love is made a vague regret.
TENNYSON, *The Miller's Daughter*, l. 209.

14
The quarrels of lovers are the renewal of love. (Amantium iræ amoris integratiost.)
TERENCE, *Andria*, l. 555. (Act iii, sc. 3.)

Old Terence has taken notice of that; and observes upon it, That lovers falling-out occasions lovers falling in.
RICHARDSON, *Clarissa Harlowe*, iv, 48.

Then did she say, "Now have I found this proverb true to prove,
The falling out of faithful friends, renewing is of love.
RICHARD EDWARDS, *The Paradise of Dainty Devices*. No. 42, st. 1. (1560)

Let the falling out of friends be a renewing of affection.
JOHN LYLY, *Euphues*. (1579)

The falling out of lovers is the renewing of love.
ROBERT BURTON, *Anatomy of Melancholy*. Pt. iii, sec. 2. (1621)

And blessings on the falling out
That all the more endears,
When we fall out with those we love,
And kiss again with tears!
TENNYSON, *The Princess*. Pt. i, l. 251.

15
And how can curses keep him yours
When kisses could not make him so?
ANNE GOODWIN WINSLOW, *The Beaten Path*.

16
Love scarce is love that never knows
The sweetness of forgiving.
WHITTIER, *Among the Hills*. St. 77.

17
Apart
Must dwell those angels known as Peace and Love,
For only Death can reconcile the two.
ELLA WHEELER WILCOX, *Peace and Love*.

XX—Love: Constant

See also Constancy, Fidelity

18
We who alone are wise
Seeing we have the sign to exorcize
This ghost of desolation, let us tend
Love's fire till the end.
MARTIN ARMSTRONG, *Body and Spirit*.

19
Whoever lives true life, will love true love.
E. B. BROWNING, *Aurora Leigh*. Bk. i, l. 1096.

20
Chance cannot change my love, nor time impair.
ROBERT BROWNING. *Any Wife to Any Husband*.

1
With love that scorns the lapse of time,
And ties that stretch beyond the deep.
THOMAS CAMPBELL, *Ode to the Memory of Burns*, l. 47.

For time makes all but true love old;
The burning thoughts that then were told
Run molten still in memory's mould.
THOMAS CAMPBELL, *Hallowed Ground*, l. 19.

2
Banish that fear; my flame can never waste,
For love sincere refines upon the taste.
CIBBER, *The Double Gallant*. Act v, sc. 1.

3
Last night, ah, yesternight, betwixt her lips and mine
There fell thy shadow, Cynara! thy breath was shed
Upon my soul between the kisses and the wine;
And I was desolate and sick of an old passion,
Yea, I was desolate and bowed my head:
I have been faithful to thee, Cynara! in my fashion.
ERNEST DOWSON, *Non Sum Qualis Eram Bonæ Sub Regno Cynaræ*.

I cried for madder music and for stronger wine,
And when the feast is finished and the lamps expire,
Then falls thy shadow, Cynara! The night is thine;
And I am desolate and sick of an old passion,
Yea, hungry for the lips of my desire:
I have been faithful to thee, Cynara! in my fashion.
ERNEST DOWSON, *Non Sum Qualis*.

It's no matter what you do,
If your heart be only true:
And his heart *was* true to Poll.
F. C. BURNAND, *His Heart was True to Poll*.

4
I will never desert Mr. Micawber.
DICKENS, *David Copperfield*. Ch. 12.

For he was a man of unwearied and prolific conjugal fidelity.
BLASCO IBÁÑEZ, *Blood and Sand*, p. 82.

5
He is not a lover who does not love for ever.
(Οὐκ ἔστ' ἐραστὴς ὅστις οὐκ ἀεὶ φιλεῖ.)
EURIPIDES, *Troades*, l. 1051.

6
What makes love's dawning glow
Changeless through joy and woe?
Only the constant know!—
Eileen aroon!
GERALD GRIFFIN, *Eileen Aroon*.

7
So let our love As endless prove,
And pure as gold for ever.
ROBERT HERRICK, *A Ring Presented to Julia*.

8
Love me little, love me long.
JOHN HEYWOOD, *Proverbs*. Pt. ii, ch. 2. (1546)

You say to me-wards your affection 's strong;
Pray love me little, so you love me long.
ROBERT HERRICK, *Love Me Little, Love Me Long*.

Love moderately; long love doth so.
SHAKESPEARE, *Romeo and Juliet*. Act ii, sc. 6, l. 14.

Love me little, love me long,
Is the burden of my song.
UNKNOWN, *Old Ballad*.

9
Of all my loves the last, for hereafter I shall glow with passion for no other woman. (Meorum Finis amorum, Non enim posthac alia calebo Femina.)
HORACE, *Odes*. Bk. iv, ode. 11, l. 31.

10
Bold Lover, never, never canst thou kiss,
Though winning near the goal—yet, do not grieve;
She cannot fade, though thou hast not thy bliss,
For ever wilt thou love, and she be fair!
KEATS, *Ode on a Grecian Urn*, l. 17.

11
Sing the Lovers' Litany;
"Love like ours can never die!"
RUDYARD KIPLING, *The Lovers' Litany*.

12
True love is the ripe fruit of a lifetime.
LAMARTINE, *Graziella*. Pt. iv, ch. 30.

13
It is with true love as it is with ghosts; everyone talks of it, but few have seen it. (Il est du véritable amour comme de l'apparition des esprits: tout le monde en parle, mais peu de gens en ont vu.)
LA ROCHEFOUCAULD, *Maximes*. No. 76.

14
Like these cool lilies may our loves remain,
Perfect and pure, and know not any stain.
ANDREW LANG, *A Vow to Heavenly Venus*.

15
With all thy sober charms possest,
Whose wishes never learnt to stray.
WILLIAM LANGHORNE, *Poems*. Vol. ii, p. 123.

16
Age enricheth true love, Like noble wine.
GERALD MASSEY, *O, Lay Thy Hand in Mine*.

17
Great loves live on.
You need not die and dare the skies
In forms that poor creeds hinge upon
To pass the gates of Paradise.
JOAQUIN MILLER, *With Love to You and Yours*. Pt. iv, sec. 12.

18
The naturalists tell us that the flower called heliotrope turns without ceasing toward that star of day, and just so will my heart hereafter turn toward the resplendent stars of your adorable eyes. (Et comme les naturalistes remarquent que la fleur nommée hélio-

trope tourne sans cesse vers cet astre du jour, aussi mon cœur d'ores en avant tournera-t-il toujours vers les astres resplendissants de vos yeux adorables.)

MOLIÈRE, *Le Malade Imaginaire*. Act ii, sc. 5.

No, the heart that has truly lov'd never forgets,
But as truly loves on to the close,
As the sunflower turns on her god, when he sets,
The same look which she turn'd when he rose.

THOMAS MOORE, *Believe Me, If All Those Endearing Young Charms*. St. 2.

See also under SUNFLOWER.

1
But never a Circe has snared one yet,
In a green, cool cavern beside the sea,
Who could make the heart of him quite forget
A patiently waiting Penelope!

ROSELLE MERCIER MONTGOMERY, *Ulysses Returns*.

2
Think of my loyal love, my last adieu;
Absence and love are naught if we are true.

ALFRED DE MUSSET, *Rappelle-toi*. (Van Dyke, tr.)

3
A thousand girls do not charm me; I am not inconstant in love. (Non mihi mille placent; non sum desultor amoris.)

OVID, *Amores*. Bk. i, eleg. 3, l. 15.

Love fostered by diffidence is long-lasting. (Fit quoque longus amor, quem diffidentia nutrit.)

OVID, *Remediorum Amoris*, l. 543.

4
Lovers remember all things. (Meminerunt omnia amantes.)

OVID, *Heroides*. Epis. xv, l. 43.

When love is at its best, one loves
So much that he cannot forget.

HELEN HUNT JACKSON, *Two Truths*.

Of all affliction taught a lover yet,
'Tis sure the hardest science to forget!

POPE, *Eloisa to Abelard*, l. 189.

5
Whither thou goest, I will go; and where thou lodgest, I will lodge: thy people shall be my people, and thy God my God: Where thou diest, will I die, and there will I be buried: the Lord do so to me, and more also, if aught but death part thee and me.

Old Testament: Ruth, i, 16, 17.

And on her lover's arm she leant,
And round her waist she felt it fold,
And far across the hills they went
In that new world which is the old. . . .
And o'er the hills and far away
Beyond their utmost purple rim,
Beyond the night, across the day,
Thro' all the world she follow'd him.

TENNYSON, *The Day-dream: The Departure*.

Through thick and thin she followed him.

BUTLER, *Hudibras*. Pt. i, canto ii, l. 370.

See also under PROVERBS

6
As I am true to thee and thine,
Do thou be true to me and mine!

SCOTT, *The Lay of the Last Minstrel*. Canto v, st. 26.

7
Why then should I seek further store,
And still make love anew?
When change itself can give no more,
'Tis easy to be true!

SIR CHARLES SEDLEY, *To Celia*.

But, to the charms which I adore,
'Tis religion to be true.

SHERIDAN, *The Duenna*. Act i, sc. 3

8
Like to a pair of loving turtle-doves,
That could not live asunder day or night.

SHAKESPEARE, *I Henry VI*. Act ii, sc. 2, l. 30.

9
Her, that loves him with that excellence
That angels love good men with.

SHAKESPEARE, *Henry VIII*. Act ii, sc. 2, l. 34.

Except I be by Silvia in the night,
There is no music in the nightingale;
Unless I look on Silvia in the day,
There is no day for me to look upon.

SHAKESPEARE, *The Two Gentlemen of Verona*. Act iii, sc. 1, l. 178.

What are the fields, or flow'rs, or all I see?
Ah! tasteless all, if not enjoy'd with thee.

THOMAS PARNELL, *Health: An Eclogue*.

10
True love in this differs from gold and clay,
That to divide is not to take away.

SHELLEY, *Epipsychidion*, l. 160.

They sin who tell us Love can die.
With life all other passions fly,
All others are but vanity. . . .
But Love is indestructible.
Its holy flame for ever burneth,
From Heaven it came, to Heaven returneth; . . .
It soweth here with toil and care,
But the harvest time of Love is there.

SOUTHEY, *The Curse of Kehama*. Pt. x, st. 10.

11
To love one maiden only, cleave to her,
And worship her by years of noble deeds,
Until they won her.

TENNYSON, *Guinevere*, l. 472.

No lapse of moons can canker Love,
Whatever fickle tongues may say.

TENNYSON, *In Memoriam*. Pt. xxvi.

I know not if I know what true love is,
But if I know, then, if I love not him,
I know there is none other I can love.

TENNYSON, *Lancelot and Elaine*, l. 672.

12
Love is love for evermore.

TENNYSON, *Locksley Hall*, l. 74.

O tell her, brief is life but love is long.

TENNYSON, *The Princess*. Pt. iv, l. 93.

To be true to each other, let 'appen what maäy
Till the end o' the daäy

An the last loäd hoäm.
TENNYSON, *The Promise of May*. Act ii, l. 190.

1
For Truth makes holy Love's illusive dreams,
And their best promise constantly redeems.
H. T. TUCKERMAN, *Sonnets*. No. 22.

2
Change everything, except your loves.
(Changez tout, hors vos amours.)
VOLTAIRE, *Sur l'Usage de la Vie*.

XXI—Love: Inconstant

See also Woman: Her Inconstancy

3
I loved thee once, I'll love no more:
Thine be the grief as is the blame:
Thou art not what thou wast before—
What reason I should be the same?
ROBERT AYTON, *I Do Confess*.

I loved thee beautiful and kind,
And plighted an eternal vow:
So altered are thy face and mind,
'Twere perjury to love thee now!
ROBERT NUGENT, *Epigram*.

4
I cannot love as I have loved,
And yet I know not why;
It is the one great woe of life
To feel all feeling die.
P. J. BAILEY, *Festus: A Party*.

But they know love grows colder,
Grows false and dull, that was sweet lies at most.
Astonishment is no more in hand or shoulder,
But darkens, and dies out from kiss to kiss.
All this is love; and all love is but this.
RUPERT BROOKE, *Love*.

Dear, we know only that we sigh, kiss, smile;
Each kiss lasts but the kissing; and grief goes over;
Love has no habitation but the heart.
RUPERT BROOKE, *Mutability*.

Now, God be thanked Who has matched us with His hour,
And caught our youth, and wakened us from sleeping, . . .
And all the little emptiness of love!
RUPERT BROOKE, *1914, Peace*.

5
The glory dropped from their youth and love,
And both perceived they had dreamed a dream.
ROBERT BROWNING, *Statue and the Bust*, l. 152.

6
Love in your heart as idly burns
As fire in antique Roman urns.
BUTLER, *Hudibras*. Pt. ii, canto i, l. 309.

7
He that loves a rosy cheek,
Or a coral lip admires,
Or from star-like eyes doth seek
Fuel to maintain his fires,
As Old Time makes these decay,
So his flames must waste away.
THOMAS CAREW, *Disdain Returned*.

Time can but cloy love, And use destroy love.
BYRON, *Stanzas*.

8
What have I done? What horrid crime committed?
To me the worst of crimes—outliv'd my liking.
CIBBER, *Richard III* (altered). Act iii, sc. 2.

'Tis an unhappy circumstance that . . . the man so often should outlive the lover.
CONGREVE, *The Way of the World*. Act ii, sc. 1.

9
The miracle to-day is that we find
A lover true: not that a woman's kind.
CONGREVE, *Love for Love*. Act v, sc. 2.

10
Him, who loves always one, why should they call
More constant, than the man loves always all.
ABRAHAM COWLEY, *The Inconstant*.

11
Lukewarmness I account a sin,
As great in love as in religion.
ABRAHAM COWLEY, *The Request*.

12
Men and women call one another inconstant, and accuse one another of having changed their minds, when, God knows, they have but changed the object of their eye, and seen a better white or red.
JOHN DONNE, *Sermons*, p. 483.

13
Love is like linen, often chang'd, the sweeter.
PHINEAS FLETCHER, *Sicelides*. Act iii, sc. 5.

14
Pretty Polly say, When I was away,
Did your fancy never stray
To some newer lover?
JOHN GAY, *The Beggar's Opera*. Act ii, sc. 2.

15
Wisely a woman prefers to a lover a man who neglects her.
This one may love her some day, some day the lover will not.
JOHN HAY, *Distichs*.

16
I do love I know not what;
Sometimes this and sometimes that.
ROBERT HERRICK, *No Luck in Love*.

17
Love has a tide!
HELEN HUNT JACKSON, *Tides*.

18
In their first passions women love the lover, and in the others, they love love. (Dans les premières passions, les femmes aiment l'amant, et dans les autres, elles aiment l'amour.)
LA ROCHEFOUCAULD, *Maximes*. No. 471. (1665)

In her first passion woman loves her lover;
In all the others, all she loves is love.
BYRON, *Don Juan*. Canto iii, st. 3. Undoubtedly

a translation of La Rochefoucauld, to whom, however, Byron gave no credit.

The man's desire is for the woman; but the woman's desire is rarely other than for the desire of the man.
S. T. COLERIDGE, *Table Talk*, p. 75.

1
The beginning and the end of love are both marked by embarrassment when the two find themselves alone. (Le commencement et le déclin de l'amour se font sentir par l'embarras où l'on est de se trouver seul.)
LA BRUYÈRE, *Les Caractères*. Sec. 4.

There are few people who would not be ashamed of being loved when they love no longer. (Il n'y a guère de gens qui ne soient honteux de s'être aimés, quand ils ne s'aiment plus.)
LA ROCHEFOUCAULD, *Maximes*. No. 71.

2
Love never dies of starvation, but often of indigestion.
NINON DE L'ENCLOS. (*L'Esprit des Autres*, 3.)

But joy incessant palls the sense;
And love, unchanged, will cloy,
And she became a bore intense
Unto her love-sick boy!
W. S. GILBERT, *Trial by Jury*.

3
For as by basil the scorpion is engendered, and by means of the same herb destroyed: so love which by time and fancy is bred in an idle head, is by time and fancy banished from the heart: or, as the salamander, which being a long space nourished in the fire, at the last quencheth it, so affection having taken hold of the fancy, and living, as it were, in the mind of the lover, in tract of time altereth and changeth the heat, and turneth it to chilliness.
JOHN LYLY, *Euphues and His England*, p. 298.

4
Thanks be to God, the world is wide,
And I am going far from home!
And I forgot in Camelot
The man I loved in Rome.
EDNA ST. VINCENT MILLAY, *Fugitive*.

And in my heart there stirs a quiet pain
For unremembered lads that not again
Will turn to me at midnight with a cry.
EDNA ST. VINCENT MILLAY, *Sonnet*.

5
I know I am but summer to your heart,
And not the full four seasons of the year;
And you must welcome from another part
Such noble moods as are not mine, my dear.
EDNA ST. VINCENT MILLAY, *Sonnet*.

6
Some love is light and fleets away,
Heigho! the wind and rain;
Some love is deep and scorns decay,
Ah, well-a-day! in vain.
WILLIAM MOTHERWELL, *True Love's Dirge*.

The moods of love are like the wind,
And none knows whence or why they rise.
COVENTRY PATMORE, *The Angel in the House: Sarum Plain*.

7
Fickle is he, and he has two wings, wherewith to fly away. (Et levis est, et habit geminas, quibus avolet, alas.)
OVID, *Ars Amatoria*. Bk. ii, l. 19.

And lately had he learn'd with truth to deem
Love has no gift so grateful as his wings.
BYRON, *Childe Harold*. Canto i, st. 82.

Love, like a bird, hath perch'd upon a spray
For thee and me to hearken what he sings.
Contented, he forgets to fly away;
But hush! . . . remind not Eros of his wings.
WILLIAM WATSON, *Four Epigrams*.

8
What is the love of men that women seek it?
In its beginning pale with cruelty,
But having sipped of beauty, negligent,
And full of languor and distaste: for they
Seeking that perfect face beyond the world
Approach in vision earthly semblances,
And touch, and at the shadows flee away.
STEPHEN PHILLIPS, *Marpessa*.

9
Our love was like most other loves—
A little glow, a little shiver,
A rosebud, and a pair of gloves,
And "Fly not yet" upon the river.
W. M. PRAED, *The Belle of the Ball*.

10
Even the inconstant flame may burn brightly, if the soul is naturally combustible.
GEORGE SANTAYANA, *Life of Reason*. Vol. ii, p. 25.

11
Love still has something of the sea,
From whence his Mother rose;
No time his slaves from doubt can free,
Nor give their thoughts repose.
SIR CHARLES SEDLEY, *Song*.

12
Some jay of Italy,
Whose mother was her painting, hath betray'd him:
Poor I am stale, a garment out of fashion.
SHAKESPEARE, *Cymbeline*. Act iii, sc. 4, l. 51.

13
This world is not for aye, nor 'tis not strange
That even our loves should with our fortunes change.
SHAKESPEARE, *Hamlet*. Act iii, sc. 2, l. 210.

There lives within the very flame of love
A kind of wick or snuff that will abate it.
SHAKESPEARE, *Hamlet*. Act iv, sc. 7, l. 115.

14
When love begins to sicken and decay,
It useth an enforced ceremony.
SHAKESPEARE, *Julius Cæsar*. Act iv, sc. 2, l. 20.

He was a lover of the good old school,
Who still become more constant as they cool.
BYRON, *Beppo*. St. 34.

15
Sigh no more, ladies, sigh no more,

Men were deceivers ever,
One foot in sea and one on shore,
To one thing constant never.
SHAKESPEARE, *Much Ado About Nothing*. Act ii, sc. 3, l. 64.

Sigh no more, lady, sigh no more,
Men were deceivers ever:
One foot on sea and one on land,
To one thing constant never.
THOMAS PERCY, *The Friar of Orders Gray*. (*Reliques*. Vol. i, bk. ii, No. 18.) Percy says that his poem is a collection of the "fragments of ancient ballads dispersed through Shakespeare's plays," which he connected together by some stanzas of his own, to "form them into a little tale."

1
Fair is my love, but not so fair as fickle;
Mild as a dove, but neither true nor trusty.
SHAKESPEARE [?], *The Passionate Pilgrim*. St. 7.

2
O, how this spring of love resembleth
Th' uncertain glory of an April day,
Which now shows all the beauty of the sun,
And by and by a cloud takes all away!
SHAKESPEARE, *The Two Gentlemen of Verona*. Act i, sc. 3, l. 84.

3
Plough not the seas, sow not the sands,
Leave off your idle pain;
Seek other mistress for your minds;
Love's service is in vain.
ROBERT SOUTHWELL, *Love's Servile Lot*.

4
The last link is broken
That bound me to thee,
And the words thou hast spoken
Have render'd me free.
FANNY STEERS, *Song*.

5
Out upon it! I have lov'd
Three whole days together;
And am like to love three more,
If it prove fair weather.
SIR JOHN SUCKLING, *The Constant Lover*.

And Love, grown faint and fretful
With lips but half regretful
Sighs, and with eyes forgetful
Weeps that no loves endure.
SWINBURNE, *The Garden of Proserpine*.

6
I have lived long enough, having seen one thing, that love hath an end.
SWINBURNE, *Hymn to Proserpine*, l. 1.

7
To say that you can love one person all your life is just like saying that one candle will continue burning as long as you live.
LEO TOLSTOY, *The Kreutzer Sonata*. Ch. 2.

8
Love, like fortune, turns upon a wheel, and is very much given to rising and falling.
SIR JOHN VANBRUGH, *The False Friend*. Act i, sc. 1.

9
For surely it is something to have been
The best beloved for a little while,
To have walked hand in hand with Love, and seen
His scarlet wings flit once across thy smile.
OSCAR WILDE, *Apologie*.

10
Those who are faithful know only the trivial side of love: it is the faithless who know love's tragedies.
OSCAR WILDE, *Picture of Dorian Gray*. Ch. 1.

11
Give me, I ask it, nay I know no pride—
The love that's left when you
Have spent the greater part.
I have a beggar heart.
ANNE ELIZABETH WILSON, *The Beggar Heart*.

12
I loved a lass, a fair one,
As fair as e'er was seen;
She was indeed a rare one,
Another Sheba queen:
But, fool as then I was,
I thought she loved me too:
But now, alas! she's left me,
Falero, lero, loo!
GEORGE WITHER, *I Loved a Lass*.

Shall I, wasting in despair,
Die because a woman's fair?
GEORGE WITHER, *The Lover's Resolution*.

13
Oh, waly, waly, gin love be bonny,
A little while, when it is new;
But when it's auld it waxeth cauld,
And fades awa' like morning dew.
UNKNOWN, *Gin Love be Bonny*.

14
My love he loves another love:
Alas, sweetheart, why does he so?
UNKNOWN, *The Mourning Maiden*. (c. 1550)

XXII—Love: Its Caprice

15
Then crown my joys, or cure my pain:
Give me more love, or more disdain.
THOMAS CAREW, *Mediocrity in Love Rejected*

Give hopes of bliss or dig my grave:
More love or more disdain I crave.
CHARLES WEBBE, *Against Indifference*.

Or love me less, or love me more;
And play not with my liberty:
Either take all, or all restore;
Bind me at least, or set me free!
SIDNEY GODOLPHIN, *Song*.

I'll be this abject thing no more;
Love, give me back my heart again.
GEORGE GRANVILLE, *Adieu l'Amour*.

16
Would I were free from this restraint,
Or else had hopes to win her:
Would she could make of me a saint,
Or I of her a sinner.
WILLIAM CONGREVE, *Pious Selinda*.

1
Saith he, "Yet are you too unkind,
If in your heart you cannot find
To love us now and then."
MICHAEL DRAYTON, *Eclogue.*

2
Thou art to me a delicious torment.
EMERSON, *Essays, First Series: Friendship.*

3
One common fate we both must prove;
You die with envy, I with love.
JOHN GAY, *Fables: The Poet and Rose,* l. 29.

4
Time was when Love and I were well acquainted.
W. S. GILBERT, *The Sorcerer.* Act i.

5
And love is still an emptier sound,
The modern fair one's jest;
On earth unseen, or only found
To warm the turtle's nest.
GOLDSMITH, *A Ballad.* (*Vicar of Wakefield.* Ch. 8.)

6
As if to show that love had made him smart
All over—and not merely round his heart.
THOMAS HOOD, *Bianca's Dream.*

His love was great though his wit was small.
THOMAS HOOD, *Equestrian Courtship.*

7
Roses red and roses white
Plucked I for my love's delight.
She would none of all my posies,—
Bade me gather her blue roses.
RUDYARD KIPLING, *Blue Roses.*

8
None without hope e'er loved the brightest fair,
But love can hope where reason would despair.
GEORGE LYTTELTON, *Epigram.*

9
And how should I know your true love
From many another one?
Oh, by his cockle hat and staff,
And by his sandal shoon.
THOMAS PERCY, *The Friar of Orders Gray.*

10
Tying her bonnet under her chin,
She tied her raven ringlets in;
But not alone in the silken snare
Did she catch her lovely floating hair,
For, tying her bonnet under her chin,
She tied a young man's heart within.
NORA PERRY, *The Love-Knot.*

11
Ah! what avails it me the flocks to keep,
Who lost my heart while I preserv'd my sheep!
POPE, *Pastorals: Autumn,* l. 79.

12
For, as our different ages move,
'Tis so ordained (would Fate but mend it!),
That I shall be past making love
When she begins to comprehend it.
MATTHEW PRIOR, *To a Child of Quality.*

13
And then the lover,
Sighing like furnace, with a woeful ballad
Made to his mistress' eyebrow.
SHAKESPEARE, *As You Like It.* Act ii, sc. 7, l. 147.

By heaven, I do love; and it hath taught me to rhyme, and to be melancholy.
SHAKESPEARE, *Love's Labour's Lost.* Act iv, sc. 3, l. 14.

And frame love-ditties passing rare,
And sing them to a lady fair.
SCOTT, *Marmion.* Canto i, st. 7.

All that a man has to say or do that can possibly concern mankind, is in some shape or other to tell the story of his love,—to sing, and, if he is fortunate and keeps alive, he will be forever in love.
H. D. THOREAU, *Journal,* 6 May, 1854.

14
He is far gone, far gone: and truly in my youth I suffered much extremity for love; very near this.
SHAKESPEARE, *Hamlet.* Act ii, sc. 2, l. 190.

He was more than over shoes in love.
SHAKESPEARE, *The Two Gentlemen of Verona.* Act i, sc. 1, l. 24.

Gone already!
Inch-thick, knee-deep, o'er head and ears a fork'd one!
SHAKESPEARE, *The Winter's Tale.* Act i, sc. 2, l. 185.

15
I hold him but a fool that will endanger
His body for a girl that loves him not.
SHAKESPEARE, *The Two Gentlemen of Verona.* Act v., sc. 4, l. 133.

And though she saw all heaven in flower above,
She would not love.
SWINBURNE, *A Leave-taking.*

16
How wayward is this foolish love,
That, like a testy babe, will scratch the nurse
And presently, all humble, kiss the rod!
SHAKESPEARE, *The Two Gentlemen of Verona.* Act i, sc. 2, l. 57.

17
I think there is not half a kiss to choose
Who loves another best.
SHAKESPEARE, *The Winter's Tale.* Act iv, sc. 4, l. 175.

18
Love still a boy and oft a wanton is,
School'd only by his mother's tender eye.
SIR PHILIP SIDNEY, *Astrophel and Stella.* Sonnet lxxiii.

But a bevy of Eroses apple-cheek'd
In a shallop of crystal ivory-beak'd.
TENNYSON, *The Islet.*

Love is a boy by poets styl'd;

Then spare the rod and spoil the child.
BUTLER, *Hudibras*. Pt. ii, canto 1, l. 843.
See also CHILDREN: THEIR TRAINING.

1
Why so pale and wan, fond lover?
Prithee, why so pale?
Will, when looking well can't move her,
Looking ill prevail?
Prithee, why so pale?
SIR JOHN SUCKLING, *Aglaura: Song.*

2
You lovers are such clumsy summer-flies,
Forever buzzing at your lady's face.
TENNYSON, *The Foresters.* Act iv, sc. 1.

3
Werther had a love for Charlotte
Such as words could never utter;
Would you know how first he met her?
She was cutting bread and butter.
THACKERAY, *The Sorrows of Werther.*

Charlotte, having seen his body
Borne before her on a shutter,
Like a well-conducted person,
Went on cutting bread and butter.
THACKERAY, *The Sorrows of Werther.*

4
The only difference between a caprice and a life-long passion is that the caprice lasts a little longer.
OSCAR WILDE, *Picture of Dorian Gray.* Ch. 2.

5
When Madelon comes out to serve us drinks,
We always know she's coming by her song.
And every man he tells his little tale,
And Madelon, she listens all day long.
Our Madelon is never too severe—
A kiss or two is nothing much to her—
She laughs us up to love and life and God—
Madelon, Madelon, Madelon.
UNKNOWN, *Madelon.* Popular song during the World War.

XXIII—Love: Its Perjuries

6
Vows! dost think the gods regard the vows of lovers? They are things made in necessity and ought not to be kept, nor punished when broken.
APHRA BEHN, *The Dutch Lover.* Act v, sc. 1.

7
Lovers' oaths enter not the ears of the gods. ("Ερωτι ὅρκους μὴ δύνειν οὔατ' ἐς ἀθανάτων.)
CALLIMACHUS, *Epigrams.* No. 27.

8
Let no woman believe a man's oath, let none believe that a man's speeches can be trustworthy. They, while their mind desires something and longs eagerly to gain it, nothing fear to swear, nothing spare to promise; but as soon as the lust of their greedy mind is satisfied, they fear not then their words, they heed not their perjuries.
CATULLUS, *Odes.* Ode lxiv, l. 143.

What a woman says to her lover should be written in wind and running water. (Mulier cupido quod dicit amanti In vento et rapida scribere oportet aqua.)
CATULLUS, *Odes.* Ode lxx, l. 3.

9
Lovers' oaths, the sport of every lightest breeze. (Lasciva volant levibus perjuria ventis.)
CLAUDIAN, *Epithalamium De Nuptiis Honorii Augusti*, l. 83.

10
The old, yet still successful, cheat of love.
HOMER, *Iliad.* Bk. xiv, l. 188. (Pope, tr.)

11
No longer could I doubt him true—
All other men may use deceit;
He always said my eyes were blue,
And often swore my lips were sweet.
WALTER SAVAGE LANDOR, *Mother, I cannot Mind My Wheel.*

12
For the queen of love,
As they hold constantly, does never punish,
But smile at, lovers' perjuries.
PHILIP MASSINGER, *The Great Duke of Florence.* Act ii, sc. 3.

13
When a man talks of love, with caution trust him;
But if he swears, he'll certainly deceive thee.
THOMAS OTWAY, *The Orphan.* Act ii, sc. 1.

14
Venus lends deaf ears to love's deceits. (Commodat in lusus numina surda Venus.)
OVID, *Amores.* Bk. i, eleg, 8. l. 86.

15
Jupiter from on high laughs at the perjuries of lovers. (Juppiter ex alto perjuria ridet amantum.)
OVID, *Ars Amatoria.* Bk. i, l. 633.

For Jove himself sits in the azure skies
And laughs below at lovers' perjuries.
OVID, *Ars Amatoria,* l. 633. (Marlowe, tr.)

Jove laughs at lovers' perjuries, and bids the winds carry them away without fulfillment. (Perjuria ridet amantum Juppiter et ventos inrita ferre jubet.)
TIBULLUS, *Elegies.* Bk. iii, eleg. vi, l. 49.

Fool, not to know that love endures no tie,
And Jove but laughs at lovers' perjury.
DRYDEN, *Palamon and Arcite.* Bk. ii, l. 148.

At lovers' perjuries, They say, Jove laughs.
SHAKESPEARE, *Romeo and Juliet.* Act ii, sc. 2. l. 92.

16
Hell's afloat in lovers' tears.
DOROTHY PARKER.

17
Love is faithless. (Perfidiosus est amor.)
PLAUTUS, *Cistellaria*, l. 72. (Act i, sc. 1.)

18
Credit me, friend, it hath been ever thus,
Since the ark rested on Mount Ararat:
False man hath sworn, and woman hath believed—

Repented and reproached, and then believed once more.
SCOTT, *The Fortunes of Nigel:* Ch. 20, *Motto.* Quoted as from *The New World.*

She deceiving, I believing,
What can lovers wish for more?
SIR CHARLES SEDLEY, *Song.*

1
Men's vows are women's traitors! . . . A bait for ladies.
SHAKESPEARE, *Cymbeline.* Act iii, sc. 4, l. 56.

2
You would for paradise break faith and troth;
And Jove, for your love, would infringe an oath.
SHAKESPEARE, *Love's Labour's Lost.* Act iv, sc. 3, l. 143.

And swearing till my very roof was dry
With oaths of love.
SHAKESPEARE, *The Merchant of Venice.* Act iii, sc. 2, l. 206.

3
When my love swears that she is made of truth,
I do believe her, though I know she lies.
SHAKESPEARE, *Sonnets.* No. cxxxviii. Also *The Passionate Pilgrim,* l. 1.

4
All lovers swear more performance than they are able, and yet reserve an ability that they never perform; vowing more than the perfection of ten, and discharging less than the tenth part of one.
SHAKESPEARE, *Troilus and Cressida.* Act iii, sc. 2, l. 91.

We men may say more, swear more; but, indeed,
Our shows are more than will; for still we prove
Much in our vows, but little in our love.
SHAKESPEARE, *Twelfth Night.* Act ii, sc. 4, l. 119.

5
No oath too binding for a lover.
SOPHOCLES, *Phædra.* Frag. 848.

6
For kings and lovers are alike in this,
That their chief art in reign dissembling is.
SIR JOHN SUCKLING, *Loving and Beloved.*

7
Fear not to swear; void are the perjuries of love, which, thanks to Jove, the winds carry away over land and sea. (Nec jurare time: veneris perjuria venti Inrita per terras et freta summa ferunt, Gratia magna Jovi.)
TIBULLUS, *Elegies.* Bk. i, eleg. 4, l. 21.

8
When one is in love one begins to deceive oneself. And one ends by deceiving others.
OSCAR WILDE, *A Woman of No Importance.* Act iii.

XXIV—Love: Love at First Sight

9
None ever loved, but at first sight they loved.
GEORGE CHAPMAN, *The Blind Beggar of Alexandria.* (1596)

Who ever lov'd. that lov'd not at first sight?
CHRISTOPHER MARLOWE, *Hero and Leander.* First Sestiad, l. 176. (1598)

Dead shepherd, now I find thy saw of might,
"Who ever loved that loved not at first sight?"
SHAKESPEARE, *As You Like It.* Act iii, sc. 5, l. 82. (1599)

10
Love, that all gentle hearts so quickly know.
(Amor, ch'al cor gentil ratto s'apprende.)
DANTE, *Inferno.* Canto v, l. 100.

11
Amid the gloom and travail of existence suddenly to behold a beautiful being, and as instantaneously to feel an overwhelming conviction that with that fair form for ever our destiny must be entwined . . . this is love!
BENJAMIN DISRAELI, *Henrietta Temple.*

If thou hast loved, re-ope the magic book;
Say, do its annals date not from a look?
In which two hearts, unguess'd perchance before,
Rush'd each to each, and were as two no more;
While all thy being—by some Power above
Its will constrain'd—sigh'd, trembling, "This is Love."
BULWER-LYTTON, *The New Timon.* Pt. iii, l. 57.

12
That old miracle—Love-at-first-sight—
Needs no explanations.
OWEN MEREDITH, *Lucile.* Pt. ii, canto vi, sec. 16.

13
Your brother and my sister no sooner met but they looked, no sooner looked but they loved, no sooner loved but they sighed, no sooner sighed but they asked one another the reason, no sooner knew the reason but they sought the remedy: and in these degrees have they made a pair of stairs to marriage which they will climb incontinent, or else be incontinent before marriage: they are in the very wrath of love, and they will together; clubs cannot part them.
SHAKESPEARE, *As You Like It.* Act v, sc. 2, l. 36.

14
Not at first sight, nor with a dribbed shot,
Love gave the wound, which, while I breathe, will bleed.
SIR PHILIP SIDNEY, *Astrophel and Stella.* Sonnet ii.

15
The only true love is love at first sight; second sight dispels it.
ISRAEL ZANGWILL.

XXV—Love: First Love

16
As in the bosom o' the stream,
The moonbeam dwells at dewy e'en,
So trembling, pure, was tender love
Within the breast o' bonnie Jean.
BURNS, *Bonnie Jean.*

1
Nature's oracle—first love,—that all
Which Eve has left her daughters since her
fall.
BYRON, *Don Juan*. Canto ii, st. 189.

Love is so very timid when 'tis new.
BYRON, *Don Juan*. Canto i, st. 112.

2
The spot where love's first links were wound,
That ne'er are riven,
Is hallowed down to earth's profound,
And up to Heaven!
THOMAS CAMPBELL, *Hallowed Ground*.

3
The magic of first love is our ignorance that it can ever end.
BENJAMIN DISRAELI, *Henrietta Temple*, iv, 1.

4
Lovers should guard their strangeness.
EMERSON, *Essays, Second Series: Manners*.

The accepted and betrothed lover has lost the wildest charm of his maiden in her acceptance of him.
EMERSON, *Essays, Second Series: Nature*.

5
But one always returns to one's first loves. (Mais on revient toujours À ses premières amours.)
ÉTIENNE, *La Joconde*. Act iii, sc. 1.

6
The bashful virgin's side-long looks of love.
GOLDSMITH, *The Deserted Village*, l. 29.

7
Yet with low words she greeted me,
With smiles divinely tender;
Upon her cheek the red rose dawned,—
The white rose meant surrender.
JOHN HAY, *The White Flag*.

8
It is an ancient story Yet is it ever new. (Es ist eine alte Geschichte, Doch bleibt sie immer neu.)
HEINE, *Lyrisches Intermezzo*.

9
Soft is the breath of a maiden's Yes:
Not the light gossamer stirs with less;
But never a cable that holds so fast
Through all the battles of wave and blast.
O. W. HOLMES, *Dorothy Q*. St. 7.

10
A warrior so bold, and a virgin so bright,
Conversed as they sat on the green.
They gazed on each other with tender delight,
Alonzo the Brave was the name of the knight—
The maiden's the Fair Imogene.
M. G. LEWIS, *Alonzo the Brave and the Fair Imogene*. From his novel, *Ambrosio*.

11
O, there is nothing holier, in this life of ours, than the first consciousness of love,—the first fluttering of its silken wings.
LONGFELLOW, *Hyperion*. Bk. iii, ch. 6.

12
That was the first sound in the song of love!
Scarce more than silence is, and yet a sound.
LONGFELLOW, *The Spanish Student*. Act i, sc. 3, l. 109.

How can I tell the signals and the signs
By which one heart another heart divines?
How can I tell the many thousand ways
By which it keeps the secret it betrays?
LONGFELLOW, *Tales of a Wayside Inn*: Pt. iii, *Student's Tale: Emma and Eginhard*, l. 75.

13
I've wandered east, I've wandered west,
I've bourne a weary lot;
But in my wanderings far or near
Ye never were forgot.
The fount that first burst frae this heart
Still travels on its way
And channels deeper as it rins
The luve o' life's young day.
WILLIAM MOTHERWELL, *Jeanie Morrison*.

14
It was many and many a year ago,
In a kingdom by the sea,
That a maiden there lived whom you may know
By the name of Annabel Lee;
And this maiden she lived with no other thought
Than to love and be loved by me.
She was a child and I was a child,
In this kingdom by the sea,
But we loved with a love that was more than love,—
I and my Annabel Lee;
With a love that the winged seraphs of heaven
Coveted her and me.
EDGAR ALLAN POE, *Annabel Lee*.

And neither the angels in heaven above,
Nor the demons down under the sea,
Can ever dissever my soul from the soul
Of the beautiful Annabel Lee.
EDGAR ALLAN POE, *Annabel Lee*.

15
I have somewhat against thee, because thou hast left thy first love.
New Testament: Revelation, ii, 4.

16
All fancy-sick she is, and pale of cheer.
SHAKESPEARE, *A Midsummer-Night's Dream*. Act iii, sc. 2, l. 96.

For sometimes she would laugh, and sometimes cry,
Then sudden waxèd wroth, and all she knew not why.
JAMES THOMSON, *The Castle of Indolence*. Canto i, st. 76.

17
First love is only a little foolishness and a lot of curiosity.
BERNARD SHAW, *John Bull's Other Island*, iv.

18
For indeed I knew
Of no more subtle master under heaven
Than is the maiden passion for a maid,
Not only to keep down the base in man,
But teach high thought, and amiable words

And courtliness, and the desire of fame,
And love of truth, and all that makes a man.
TENNYSON, *Guinevere*, l. 475.

1
Men always want to be a woman's first love. That is their clumsy vanity. We women have a more subtle instinct about things. What we like is to be a man's last romance.
OSCAR WILDE, *A Woman of No Importance*. Act ii.

XXVI—Love: Old and New

2
Dawn love is silver,
Wait for the west:
Old love is gold love—
Old love is best.
KATHARINE LEE BATES, *For a Golden Wedding*.

3
'Tis well to be merry and wise,
'Tis well to be honest and true;
'Tis well to be off with the old love,
Before you are on with the new.
C. R. MATURIN, *Bertram: Motto*. A play produced at Drury Lane theatre in 1816.

It is best to be off wi' the old love,
Before you be on wi' the new.
SCOTT, *The Bride of Lammermoor*. Ch. 29. (1819) Quoted as "the end of an old song."

It is good to be merry and wise,
It is good to be honest and true,
It is best to be off with the old love
Before you go on with the new.
Version of the old song published in *Songs of England and Scotland*, London, 1835. Vol. ii, p. 73.

And afore you're off wi' the auld love
It's best to be on wi' the new.
UNKNOWN, *It's Gude to be Merry and Wise*. The Scotch version, showing characteristic Scotch caution.

There is an old song which gives us some very good advice about courting:—
"It's gude to be off with the auld luve
Before ye be on wi' the new."
ANTHONY TROLLOPE, *Barchester Towers*. Ch. 27. (1857)

It is better to love two too many than one too few.
SIR JOHN HARINGTON, *Epigrams*.

4
My merry, merry, merry roundelay
Concludes with Cupid's curse:
They that do change old love for new,
Pray gods, they change for worse!
GEORGE PEELE, *Fair and Fair*.

5
As one who cons at evening o'er an album all alone,
And muses on the faces of the friends that he has known,
So I turn the leaves of Fancy till, in shadowy design,
I find the smiling features of an old sweetheart of mine.
JAMES WHITCOMB RILEY, *An Old Sweetheart of Mine*.

6
Old love is little worth when new is more preferred.
SPENSER, *Faerie Queene*. Bk. vi, canto ix, st. 40.

7
I who all the Winter through,
Cherished other loves than you
And kept hands with hoary policy in marriage-bed and pew;
Now I know the false and true,
For the earnest sun looks through,
And my old love comes to meet me in the dawning and the dew.
R. L. STEVENSON, *My Old Love*. (1876)

8
The woods are hush'd, their music is no more;
The leaf is dead, the yearning past away;
New leaf, new life—the days of frost are o'er;
New life, new love, to suit the newer day:
New loves are sweet as those that went before:
Free love—free field—we love but while we may.
TENNYSON, *The Last Tournament*, l. 276.

At last she sought out Memory, and they trod
The same old paths where Love had walk'd with Hope,
And Memory fed the soul of Love with tears.
TENNYSON, *The Lover's Tale*. Pt. i, l. 808.

9
Other loves may come to us and will,
And may hold us in their spell until
With a half regretful sigh,
We discover by and by,
There's a charm about the old love still.
F. W. VANDERSLOOT, *There's a Charm About the Old Love Still*. (1901)

XXVII—Love: Unreturning

10
Love, like Reputation, once fled, never returns more.
APHRA BEHN, *History of the Nun*.

The moon returns, and the spring; birds warble, trees burst into leaf,
But Love once gone, goes for ever, and all that endures is the grief.
MATHILDE BLIND, *Love Trilogy*. No. 3.

And sigh to bethink me how vain is my sighing,
For love, once extinguished, is kindled no more.
REGINALD HEBER, *Song to a Welsh Air*.

11
Love, like Ulysses, is a wanderer,
For new fields always and new faces yearning. . . .
Put by, O waiting ones, put by your weaving,
Unlike Ulysses, love is unreturning.
ROSELLE MERCIER MONTGOMERY, *Counsel*.

12
For the man's love once gone never returns.
TENNYSON, *Geraint and Enid*, l. 333.

1
Nothing grows again more easily than love. (Nihil enim facilius quam amor recrudescit.)
SENECA, *Epistulæ ad Lucilium*. Epis. lxix, 3.

XXVIII—Love in a Cottage

2
Love lasteth as long as the money endureth.
WILLIAM CAXTON, *The Game of Chesse*, iii, 3. (1474) Cited as "a common proverb in England."

3
Love comes in at the window and goes out at the door.
WILLIAM CAMDEN, *Remains*, p. 327. (1605)

When poverty comes in at the door, love creeps out at the window.
THOMAS FULLER, *Gnomologia*. No. 5565.

4
When the glowing of passion's over, and pinching winter comes, will amorous sighs supply the want of fire, or kind looks and kisses keep off hunger?
SUSANNAH CENTLIVRE, *Artifice*. (1724)

Nobody wants to kiss when they are hungry.
DOROTHY DIX.

5
Love is maintained by wealth; when all is spent
Adversity then breeds the discontent.
ROBERT HERRICK, *Hesperides*. No. 144.

6
Love in a hut, with water and a crust,
Is—Love, forgive us!—cinders, ashes, dust;
Love in a palace is perhaps at last
More grievous torment than a hermit's fast.
KEATS, *Lamia*. Pt. ii, l. 1.

7
Love lurks as soon about a sheepcote as a palace.
THOMAS LODGE, *Rosalynde*, l. 95. (1590)

Love lives in cottages as well as in courts.
JOHN RAY, *English Proverbs*.

8
In the very smallest cot
There is room enough for a loving pair.
(Raum ist in der kleinsten Hütte
Für ein glücklich liebend Paar.)
SCHILLER, *Der Jüngling am Bache*. St. 4.

'Tis better far to love and be poor, than be rich with an empty heart.
SIR LEWIS MORRIS, *Songs of Two Worlds: Love in Death*.

Ah, better to love in the lowliest cot
Than pine in a palace alone.
G. J. WHYTE-MELVILLE, *Chastelar*.

9
Love in a cottage, with a broken window to let in the rain, is not my idea of comfort.
ALEXANDER SMITH, *Dreamthorp: On the Writing of Essays*.

10
Without Ceres (bread) and Liber (wine) Venus will starve. (Sine Cerere et Libero friget Venus.)
TERENCE, *Eunuchus*, l. 732.

Then the little maid she said, "Your fire may warm the bed,
But what shall we do for to eat?
Will the flames you're only rich in make a fire in the kitchen,
And the little God of Love turn the spit?"
UNKNOWN, *Old Nursery Rhyme*, from an 18th century broadside.

11
They may talk of love in a cottage,
And bowers of trellised vine—
Of nature bewitchingly simple,
And milkmaids half divine, . . .
But give me a sly flirtation,
By the light of a chandelier—
With music to play in the pauses,
And nobody very near.
N. P. WILLIS, *Love in a Cottage*.

Your love in a cottage is hungry,
Your vine is a nest for flies—
Your milkmaid shocks the Graces,
And simplicity talks of pies!
You lie down to your shady slumber
And wake with a bug in your ear,
And your damsel that walks in the morning
Is shod like a mountaineer.
N. P. WILLIS, *Love in a Cottage*.

True love is at home on a carpet,
And mightily likes his ease—
And true love has an eye for a dinner,
And starves beneath shady trees.
His wing is the fan of a lady,
His foot's an invisible thing,
And his arrow is tipp'd with a jewel,
And shot from a silver string.
N. P. WILLIS, *Love in a Cottage*.

XXIX—Love: Spoken and Silent

12
Love ceases to be a pleasure when it ceases to be a secret.
MRS. APHRA BEHN, *The Lover's Watch*.

13
Say thou dost love me, love me, love me—toll
The silver iterance!—only minding, Dear,
To love me also in silence, with thy soul.
E. B. BROWNING, *Sonnets from the Portuguese*. No. xxi.

14
In many ways doth the full heart reveal
The presence of the love it would conceal.
S. T. COLERIDGE, *Motto*.

Love most concealed, does most itself discover.
WALTER DAVISON, *Sonnets*. No. xiv.

A murderous guilt shows not itself more soon
Than love that would seem hid: love's night is noon.
SHAKESPEARE, *Twelfth Night*. Act iii, sc. 1, l. 159.

15
Words are the weak support of cold indifference; love has no language to be heard.
CONGREVE, *The Double-Dealer*. Act iv, sc. 17.

16
For God sake hold your tongue, and let me love.
JOHN DONNE, *The Canonization*.

1
Sweet are the words of Love, sweeter his thoughts:
Sweetest of all what Love nor says nor thinks.
RICHARD GARNETT, *De Flagello Myrteo*, clxv.

When Silence speaks for Love she has much to say.
RICHARD GARNETT, *De Flagello Myrteo*, lxxiii.

2
All the heart was full of feeling: love had ripened into speech,
Like the sap that turns to nectar, in the velvet of the peach.
WILLIAM WALLACE HARNEY, *Adonais*.

3
Love understands love; it needs no talk.
FRANCES RIDLEY HAVERGAL, *Loving Allegiance*.

4
They do not love that do not show their love.
JOHN HEYWOOD, *Proverbs*. Pt. ii, ch. 9.

5
Love is sparingly soluble in the words of men, therefore they speak much of it; but one syllable of woman's speech can dissolve more of it than a man's heart can hold.
O. W. HOLMES, *The Autocrat of the Breakfast-Table*. Ch. 11.

No love so true as love that dies untold.
O. W. HOLMES, *The Mysterious Illness*.

6
Listlessness and silence denote the lover. (Amantem languor et silentium arguit.)
HORACE, *Epodes*. No. xi, l. 9.

7
But oft the words come forth awrye of him that loveth well.
HENRY HOWARD, *Pangs and Sleights of Love*.

8
'Tis no sin love's fruits to steal;
But the sweet thefts to reveal;
To be taken, to be seen,
These have crimes accounted been.
BEN JONSON, *Volpone*. Act iii, sc. 6. *See also under* KISS.

9
Love contending with friendship, and self with each generous impulse,
To and fro in his breast his thoughts were heaving and dashing.
LONGFELLOW, *The Courtship of Miles Standish*. Pt. iii, l. 7.

Archly the maiden smiled, and, with eyes over-running with laughter,
Said, in a tremulous voice, "Why don't you speak for yourself, John?"
LONGFELLOW, *The Courtship of Miles Standish*. Pt. iii, concluding lines.

In the way of love and glory,
Each tongue best tells his own story.
SIR THOMAS OVERBURY, *Of the Choice of a Wife*.

Therefore all hearts in love use their own tongues;
Let every eye negotiate for itself
And trust no agent.
SHAKESPEARE, *Much Ado About Nothing*. Act ii, sc. 1, l. 184.

A day in April never came so sweet,
To show how costly summer was at hand,
As this fore-spurrer comes before his lord.
SHAKESPEARE, *The Merchant of Venice*. Act ii, sc. 9, l. 93.

10
[The passion wherewith] we lash ourselves into the persuasive speech distinguishing us from the animals.
GEORGE MEREDITH, *Diana of the Crossways*. Ch. 1.

11
All love gives words, and finds sustenance in delay. (Verba dat omnis amor, reperitque alimenta morando.)
OVID, *Remediorum Amoris*, l. 95.

12
To be able to say how much you love is to love but little. (Chi può dir com' egli arde, è in picciol fusco.)
PETRARCH, *Sonnets*. No. cxxxvii.

O, they love least that let men know their love.
SHAKESPEARE, *The Two Gentlemen of Verona*. Act i, sc. 2, l. 32.

13
But I. in love, was mute and still.
PUSHKIN, *Eugene Onyegin*. Canto i, st. 52.

14
Silence in love bewrays more woe
Than words, though ne'er so witty:
A beggar that is dumb, you know,
May challenge double pity.
SIR WALTER RALEIGH, *The Silent Lover*. St. 9.

15
There's beggary in the love that can be reckoned.
SHAKESPEARE, *Antony and Cleopatra*. Act i, sc. 1, l. 15.

16
Speak low, if you speak love.
SHAKESPEARE, *Much Ado About Nothing*. Act ii, sc. 1, l. 102.

O, love's best habit is a soothing tongue.
SHAKESPEARE, *The Passionate Pilgrim*, l. 11.

How silver-sweet sound lovers' tongues by night,
Like softest music to attending ears!
SHAKESPEARE, *Romeo and Juliet*. Act ii, sc. 2, l. 166.

17
She never told her love,
But let concealment, like a worm i' the bud,
Feed on her damask cheek.
SHAKESPEARE, *Twelfth Night*. Act ii, sc. 4, l. 113.

18
What, gone without a word?
Ay, so true love should do: it cannot speak;
For truth hath better deeds than words to grace it.
SHAKESPEARE, *The Two Gentlemen of Verona*. Act ii, sc. 2, l. 16.

Didst thou but know the inly touch of love,
Thou wouldst as soon go kindle fire with snow,

As seek to quench the fire of love with words.
SHAKESPEARE, *The Two Gentlemen of Verona*. Act ii, sc. 7, l. 18.

1
They love indeed who quake to say they love.
SIR PHILIP SIDNEY, *Astrophel and Stella*. Sonnet liv.

2
The wretched man gan them avise too late,
That love is not where most it is profest.
SPENSER, *Faerie Queene*. Bk. ii, canto 10, st. 31.

3
Silence, uttering love that all things understand.
SWINBURNE, *The Cliffside Path*. St. 2.

4
Who are wise in love, Love most, say least.
TENNYSON, *Merlin and Vivien*, l. 245.

5
Love is a talkative passion.
THOMAS WILSON, *Sacra Privata*, p. 194.

XXX—Love: Protestations

6
Mary kept the belt o' love, and O but she was gay!
She danced a jig, she sung a song that took my heart away.
WILLIAM ALLINGHAM, *Lovely Mary Donnelly*.

7
One sweet, sad secret holds my heart in thrall;
A mighty love within my breast has grown,
Unseen, unspoken, and of no one known;
And of my sweet, who gave it, least of all.
(Ma vie a son secret, mon âme a son mystère:
Un amour éternel en un moment concu.
La mal est sans remède, aussi j'ai dû le taire,
Et elle qui l'a fait n'en a jamais rien su.)
FELIX ARVERS, *Sonnet*. (Knight, tr.) In *Mes Heures Perdues*, Arvers states that it was taken from the Italian.

8
Heaven would not be Heaven were thy soul not with mine, nor would Hell be Hell were our souls together.
(Sive ad felices vadam post funera campos,
Seu ferar ardentem rapidi Phlegethontis ad undam,
Nec sine te felix ero, nec tecum miser unquam.)
BAPTISTA MANTUANUS, *Eclogues*. No. iii, l. 108.

O mother, mother, what is bliss?
O mother, what is bale?
Without my William what were heaven,
Or with him what were hell?
GOTTFRIED AUGUSTUS BÜRGER, *Lenoré*. (Walter Scott, tr., *William and Helen*. This was Scott's first publication.)

Would I were with him, wheresome'er he is, either in heaven or in hell!
SHAKESPEARE, *Henry V*. Act ii, sc. 3, l. 6.

9
And what am I but love of you made flesh,
Quickened by every longing love may bring,
A pilgrim fire, homeless and wandering.
KATHERINE BOWDITCH, *Reincarnation*.

10
"Honeypot" he called her,
Hurling words like javelins—
Stern John Knox with the flame in his eyes.
Steeled against shocks
Was great John Knox!
Target for surprise
From those side-glancing eyes?
Nay, I trow not—"Honeypot."
LOUISE MOREY BOWMAN, *John Knox and Mary Queen*.

11
In your arms was still delight,
Quiet as a street at night;
And thoughts of you, I do remember,
Were green leaves in a darkened chamber,
Were dark clouds in a moonless sky.
RUPERT BROOKE, *Retrospect*.

12
Beloved, let us love so well,
Our work shall still be better for our love,
And still our love be sweeter for our work,
And both commended, for the sake of each,
By all true workers and true lovers born.
E. B. BROWNING, *Aurora Leigh*. Bk. ix, l. 924.

How do I love thee? Let me count the ways.
I love thee to the depth and breadth and height
My soul can reach, when feeling out of sight
For the ends of Being and ideal Grace.
I love thee to the level of everyday's
Most quiet need, by sun and candle-light.
I love thee freely, as men strive for Right;
I love thee purely, as they turn from Praise.
E. B. BROWNING, *Sonnets from the Portuguese*. No. xliii.

13
For the lake, its swan;
For the dell, its dove;
And for thee—(oh, haste!)
Me, to bend above,
Me, to hold embraced.
ROBERT BROWNING, *James Lee's Wife*. Pt. i.

14
Flower o' the broom,
Take away love, and our earth is a tomb! . . .
Flower o' the clove,
All the Latin I construe is "amo," I love!
ROBERT BROWNING, *Fra Lippo Lippi*.

Be a god and hold me With a charm!
Be a man and fold me With thine arm!
ROBERT BROWNING, *A Woman's Last Word*

15
I canna tell, I mauna tell,
I darena for your anger;
But secret love will break my heart,
If I conceal it langer.
BURNS, *Craigie-burn Wood*.

The golden hours on angel wings
Flew o'er me and my dearie,
For dear to me as light and life

Was my sweet Highland Mary.
BURNS, *Highland Mary.*

To see her is to love her,
And love but her for ever;
For nature made her what she is,
And ne'er made sic anither!
BURNS, *O, Saw Ye Bonnie Lesley.* (1792)

Oh! she was good as she was fair,
None—none on earth above her!
As pure in thought as angels are,
To know her was to love her.
SAMUEL ROGERS, *Jacqueline.* Pt. i, l. 69. (1814)

1
Tho' father an' mither an' a' should gae mad,
O whistle, an' I'll come to ye, my lad.
BURNS, *O Whistle, an' I'll Come to Ye.*

Whistle, and she'll come to you.
JOHN FLETCHER, *Wit Without Money.* Act iv, sc. 4.

2
O, my luve is like a red, red rose
That's newly sprung in June.
O, my luve is like the melodie
That's sweetly play'd in tune.
BURNS, *A Red, Red Rose.*

3
The cold in clime are cold in blood,
Their love can scarce deserve the name;
But mine was like the lava flood
That boils in Ætna's breast of flame.
BYRON, *The Giaour,* l. 1099.

4
She was his life,
The ocean to the river of his thoughts,
Which terminated all.
BYRON, *The Dream.* Sec. 2.

She floats upon the river of his thoughts!
LONGFELLOW, *Spanish Student.* Act ii, sc. 3.

5
Of all the girls that are so smart
There's none like pretty Sally;
She is the darling of my heart,
And she lives in our alley.
HENRY CAREY, *Sally in Our Alley.*

6
Let Time and Chance combine, combine!
Let Time and Chance combine!
The fairest love from heaven above,
That love of yours was mine, My Dear!
That love of yours was mine.
THOMAS CARLYLE, *Adieu.*

7
Blest as the immortal gods is he,
The youth who fondly sits by thee,
And hears and sees thee all the while
Softly speak and sweetly smile.
(Ille mi par esse deo videtur,
Ille, si fas est, superare divos,
Qui sedens adversus identidem te
Spectat et audit Dulce ridentem.)
CATULLUS, *Odes.* Ode li, l. 1. An almost literal version of a stanza by Sappho.

8
He kissed the ground her feet did kiss.
JOHN DAVIDSON, *A New Ballad of Tannhäuser.*

9
Daisy, Daisy, give me your answer, do!
I'm half crazy all for the love of you!
It won't be a stylish marriage,
I can't afford a carriage,
But you'll look sweet upon the seat
Of a bicycle built for two.
HARRY DACRE, *Daisy Bell.* (1892)

10
Never will you hold me
With puddings and cake
Or even the threat
Of a heart to break. . . .

A song within a song
And eyes upon the door—
And you will always hold me
One day more.
CHARLES DIVINE, *Never Will You Hold Me.*

11
And for bonnie Annie Laurie
I'd lay me doun and dee.
WILLIAM DOUGLAS, *Annie Laurie.* Anne or Anna Laurie was the youngest daughter of Sir Robert Laurie (or Lawrie), of Maxwelton, b. 1682, d. 1761.

12
Not from the whole wide world I chose thee,
Sweetheart, light of the land and the sea!
The wide, wide world could not enclose thee,
For thou art the whole wide world to me.
R. W. GILDER, *Song.*

13
Thus let me hold thee to my heart,
And every care resign.
And we shall never, never part,
My life—my all that's mine!
GOLDSMITH, *The Hermit.* St. 39. (*The Vicar of Wakefield.* Ch. 8.)

14
There is a lady sweet and kind,
Was never face so pleased my mind;
I did but see her passing by,
And yet I love her till I die.
BARNABE GOOGE, *There is a Lady.* An English version of a Latin stanza by Thomas Naogeorgus. (*Popish Kingdome or Reigne of Antichrist,* 1570. Stanza written on back of leaf 53.) Wrongfully ascribed to Robert Herrick in *Scottish Student's Song-Book.* (See *Notes and Queries,* ix, x, 427.)

Thou art my love, my life, my heart,
The very eyes of me:
And hast command of every part
To live and die for thee.
ROBERT HERRICK, *To Althea Who May Command Him Anything.*

15
When the swallows homeward fly,
When the roses scattered lie,
When from neither hill or dale,
Chants the silvery nightingale:
In these words my bleeding heart
Would to thee its grief impart;
When I thus thy image lose,

Can I, ah! can I, e'er know repose?
KARL HERRLOSSOHN, *When the Swallows Homeward Fly.*

1
Heart of my heart, O come with me
To walk the ways of Arcadie.
NORAH M. HOLLAND, *Grasshopper's Song.*

Heart of my heart, the world is young;
Love lies hidden in every rose.
ALFRED NOYES, *Unity.*

2
I love thee—I love thee!
'Tis all that I can say;
It is my vision in the night,
My dreaming in the day.
THOMAS HOOD, *I Love Thee.*

I love thee, I love but thee,
With a love that shall not die
Till the sun grows cold,
And the stars are old,
And the leaves of the Judgment Book unfold!
BAYARD TAYLOR, *Bedouin Song.*

3
With thee I fain would live, with thee I'd gladly die! (Tecum vivere amem, tecum obeam libens!)
HORACE, *Odes.* Bk. iii, ode 9, l. 24.

4
If you become a Nun, dear,
The bishop Love will be;
The Cupids every one, dear!
Will chant—"We trust in thee!"
LEIGH HUNT, *The Nun.*

5
We have lived and loved together
Through many changing years;
We have shared each other's gladness,
And wept each other's tears.
CHARLES JEFFERYS, *We Have Lived and Loved Together.*

We twa hae run about the braes,
And pu'd the gowans fine.
ROBERT BURNS, *Auld Lang Syne.*

To stray together down Life's slope,
While Age came on like gentle rain.
R. U. JOHNSON, *The Winter Hour.* Pt. viii.

By the waters of Life we sat together,
Hand in hand, in the golden days
Of the beautiful early summer weather,
When skies were purple and breath was praise.
THOMAS NOEL, *An Old Man's Idyll.*

See also LIFE: I HAVE LIVED.

6
By the old Moulmein Pagoda, lookin' eastward to the sea,
There's a Burma girl a-settin', and I know she thinks o' me;
For the wind is in the palm-trees, and the temple-bells they say:
"Come you back, you British soldier; come you back to Mandalay!"
RUDYARD KIPLING, *Mandalay.*

Though I walks with fifty 'ousemaids outer Chelsea to the Strand,
An' they talks a lot o' lovin', but wot do they understand?
RUDYARD KIPLING, *Mandalay.*

7
I love a lassie, a bonnie, bonnie lassie,
She's as pure as the lily in the dell.
She's as sweet as the heather,
The bonnie, bloomin' heather,
Mary, ma Scotch Blue-bell.
HARRY LAUDER AND GERALD GRAFTON, *I Love a Lassie.*

8
The charms, alas! that won me,
I never can forget:
Although thou hast undone me,
I own I love thee yet.
WILLIAM LEGGETT, *Song.*

I love thee, as the good love heaven.
LONGFELLOW, *The Spanish Student.* Act i, sc. 3, l. 146.

If you lak-a me lak I lak-a you.
ROSAMOND JOHNSON, *Under the Bamboo Tree.* (1902)

I'd leave my happy home for you.
WILL A. HEELAN. Title and refrain of popular song, with music by Harry von Tilzer. (1899)

9
Not as all other women are
Is she that to my soul is dear;
Her glorious fancies come from far,
Beneath the silver evening-star,
And yet her heart is ever near.
J. R. LOWELL, *My Love.*

10
This lass so neat, with smile so sweet,
Has won my right good will,
I'd crowns resign to call her mine,
Sweet lass of Richmond Hill.
LEONARD MCNALLY, *The Lass of Richmond Hill.* Published anonymously in London *Public Advertiser*, 3 Aug., 1789. Sometimes attributed to William Upton.

11
Come live with me and be my Love,
And we will all the pleasures prove
That hills and valleys, dales and fields,
Or woods, or steepy mountain yields.
CHRISTOPHER MARLOWE, *The Passionate Shepherd to His Love.* Included by Walton in *The Compleat Angler*, ch. 2, as "that smooth song which was made by Kit Ma lowe, now at least fifty years ago." Sometimes wrongly attributed to Shakespeare, because fragments of the second and third stanzas are quoted in *The Merry Wives of Windsor* (Act iii, sc. 1, l. 16), and the entire poem included in *The Passionate Pilgrim* (Pt. xx). The versions vary slightly.

If all the world and love were young,
And truth in every shepherd's tongue,
These pretty pleasures might me move
To live with thee and be thy love.
SIR WALTER RALEIGH, *The Nymph's Reply to the Passionate Shepherd.* Walton included this poem in *The Compleat Angler*, ch. 2,

calling it *The Milkmaid's Mother's Answer,* saying that "it was made by Sir Walter Raleigh in his younger days." The first stanza was also included in *The Passionate Pilgrim,* immediately following Marlowe's poem.

Come live with me, and be my love,
And we will some new pleasures prove
Of golden sands, and crystal brooks,
With silken lines, and silver hooks.

JOHN DONNE, *The Bait.* Included by Walton in *The Compleat Angler,* ch. 9, as "made by Dr. Donne, and made to shew the world that he could make soft and smooth verses, when he thought them fit and worth his labour."

1
My love is of a birth as rare
As 'tis for object strange and high;
It was begotten by despair
Upon impossibility.

ANDREW MARVELL, *My Love.*

2
She whom I love is hard to catch and conquer,
Hard, but O the glory of the winning were she won!

GEORGE MEREDITH, *Love in the Valley.* St. 2.

Give me purity to be worthy the good in her, and grant her patience to reach the good in me.

GEORGE MEREDITH, *Richard Feverel,* Ch. 34.

3
I loved you ere I knew you; know you now,
And having known you, love you better still.

OWEN MEREDITH, *Vanini.*

4
With the first dream that comes with the first sleep
I run, I run, I am gathered to thy heart.

ALICE MEYNELL, *Renouncement.*

5
Sae true his heart, sae smooth his speech,
His breath like caller air,
His very foot has music in't,
As he comes up the stair.

WILLIAM JULIUS MICKLE, *The Sailor's Wife.* Also attributed to Jean Adam.

6
So dear I love him, that with him all deaths
I could endure, without him live no life.

MILTON, *Paradise Lost.* Bk. ix, l. 832.

7
Come, rest in this bosom, my own stricken deer,
Though the herd have fled from thee, thy home is still here.

THOMAS MOORE, *Come, Rest in This Bosom.*

I know not, I ask not, if guilt's in that heart,
I but know that I love thee, whatever thou art.

THOMAS MOORE, *Come, Rest in This Bosom.*

8
Wert thou more fickle than the restless sea,
Still should I love thee, knowing thee for such.

WILLIAM MORRIS, *Life and Death of Jason.* Bk. ix, l. 22.

9
A Book of Verses underneath the Bough,
A Jug of Wine, a Loaf of Bread—and Thou
Beside me singing in the Wilderness—
Oh, Wilderness were Paradise enow!

OMAR KHAYYÁM, *Rubáiyát.* St. 12. (Fitzgerald, tr.)

Or were I in the wildest waste,
Sae black and bare, sae black and bare,
The desert were a Paradise,
If thou wert there, if thou wert there.

BURNS, *Oh! Wert Thou in the Cold Blast.*

Oh that the desert were my dwelling-place,
With one fair spirit for my minister,
That I might all forget the human race,
And, hating no one, love but only her!

BYRON, *Childe Harold.* Canto iv, st. 177.

O Love! in such a wilderness as this,
Where transport and security entwine,
Here is the empire of thy perfect bliss,
And here thou art a god indeed divine.

THOMAS CAMPBELL, *Gertrude of Wyoming.* Pt. iii, st. 1.

"A jug and a book and a dame,
And a nice shady nook for the same,"
Said Omar Khayyám,
"And I don't give a darn
What you say, it's a great little game!"

E. M. ROBINSON, *Limericised Classics.*

10
Quick as a humming bird is my love,
Dipping into the hearts of flowers—
She darts so eagerly, swiftly, sweetly
Dipping into the flowers of my heart.

JAMES OPPENHEIM, *Quick as a Humming Bird.*

11
Dear as the vital warmth that feeds my life,
Dear as these eyes, that weep in fondness o'er thee.

THOMAS OTWAY, *Venice Preserved.* Act v, sc. 1.

12
I love thee then
Not only for thy body packed with sweet
Of all this world, that cup of brimming June, . . .
Not for this only do I love thee, but
Because Infinity upon thee broods;
And thou art full of whispers and of shadows.

STEPHEN PHILLIPS, *Marpessa.*

13
Thou wast all that to me, love,
For which my soul did pine:
A green isle in the sea, love,
A fountain and a shrine.

EDGAR ALLAN POE, *To One in Paradise.*

14
Love me if I live!
Love me if I die!
What to me is life or death,
So that thou be nigh?

BRYAN WALLER PROCTER, *Song.*

15
We are prepared, my love and I,
For winter on a hill:

I stored a theme of song, and she
A root of daffodil.
EDWIN QUARLES, *Stronghold.*

1
Love me and the world is mine.
DAVID REED, jr., Title of popular song, 1906.

2
The hours I spent with thee, dear heart,
Are as a string of pearls to me;
I count them over, every one apart,
My rosary, my rosary.
ROBERT CAMERON ROGERS, *My Rosary.*

3
Her voice, whate'er she said, enchanted;
Like music to the heart it went.
And her dark eyes—how eloquent!
Ask what they would, 'twas granted.
SAMUEL ROGERS, *Jacqueline.* Pt. i, l. 80.

4
Still so gently o'er me stealing,
Mem'ry will bring back the feeling,
Spite of all my grief revealing
That I love thee, love thee still.
(Ah! perchè non posso odiarti
Infedel, com' io vorrei!
Cancellata dal mio cor.)
FELICE ROMANI, *La Sonnambula.* Act ii.

5
For one man is my world of all the men
This wide world holds; O love, my world is you.
CHRISTINA ROSSETTI, *Come Back to Me.*

And in his heart my heart is locked,
And in his life my life.
CHRISTINA ROSSETTI, *Noble Sisters.*

6
Love, all the hours are long
That once so fleetly flew;
I am bereft of song
Being bereft of you.
But when you come again
How nimbly Time will run
To such a jocund strain,
For you and song are one.
CLINTON SCOLLARD, *Love and Song Are One.*

7
O coz, coz, coz, my pretty little coz, that thou didst know how many fathom deep I am in love! But it cannot be sounded; my affection hath an unknown bottom, like the bay of Portugal.
SHAKESPEARE, *As You Like It.* Act iv, sc. 1, l. 209.

8
The fair, the chaste and unexpressive she.
SHAKESPEARE, *As You Like It.* Act iii, sc. 2, l. 10.

That not impossible she.
RICHARD CRASHAW, *Wishes to His (Supposed) Mistress.*

9
Doubt thou the stars are fire;
Doubt that the sun doth move;
Doubt truth to be a liar;
But never doubt I love.
SHAKESPEARE, *Hamlet.* Act ii, sc. 2, l. 116.

Forty thousand brothers
Could not, with all their quantity of love,
Make up my sum.
SHAKESPEARE, *Hamlet.* Act v, sc. 1, l. 292.

From my heart-string I love the lovely bully.
SHAKESPEARE, *Henry V.* Act iv, sc. 1, l. 47.

10
Adieu, valour! rust, rapier! be still, drum! for your manager is in love; yea, he loveth. Assist me, some extemporal god of rhyme, for I am sure I shall turn sonnet. Devise, wit; write, pen; for I am for whole volumes in folio!
SHAKESPEARE, *Love's Labour's Lost.* Act i, sc. 2, l. 187.

11
Perdition catch my soul,
But I do love thee! and when I love thee not,
Chaos is come again.
SHAKESPEARE, *Othello.* Act iii, sc. 3, l. 90.

If heaven would make me such another world
Of one entire and perfect chrysolite,
I'ld not have sold her for it.
SHAKESPEARE, *Othello.* Act v, sc. 2, l. 144.

12
Speak but one rhyme, and I am satisfied;
Cry but "Ay me!" pronounce but "love" and "dove."
SHAKESPEARE, *Romeo and Juliet.* Act ii, sc. 1, l. 9.

In truth, fair Montague, I am too fond.
SHAKESPEARE, *Romeo and Juliet.* Act ii, sc. 2, l. 98.

13
This bud of love, by summer's ripening breath,
May prove a beauteous flower when next we meet.
SHAKESPEARE, *Romeo and Juliet.* Act ii, sc. 2, l 121.

You'll love me yet!—and I can tarry
Your love's protracted growing:
June reared that bunch of flowers you carry,
From seeds of April's sowing.
ROBERT BROWNING, *Pippa Passes.* Pt. iii.

14
My bounty is as boundless as the sea,
My love as deep; the more I give to thee
The more I have, for both are infinite.
SHAKESPEARE, *Romeo and Juliet.* Act ii, sc. 2, l. 133.

15
Give me my Romeo; and, when he shall die,
Take him and cut him out in little stars,
And he will make the face of heaven so fine
That all the world will be in love with night
And pay no worship to the garish sun.
SHAKESPEARE, *Romeo and Juliet.* Act iii, sc. 2, l 21.

Romeo, if dead, should be cut up into little stars to make the heavens fine.
EMERSON, *Essays, First Series: Love.*

1
Shall I compare thee to a summer's day?
Thou art more lovely and more temperate.
SHAKESPEARE, *Sonnets*. No. xviii.

Thy love is better than high birth to me,
Richer than wealth, prouder than garments' cost,
Of more delight than hawks or horses be.
SHAKESPEARE, *Sonnets*. No. xci.

2
If ever thou shalt love,
In the sweet pangs of it remember me;
For such as I am all true lovers are,
Unstaid and skittish in all motions else,
Save in the constant image of the creature
That is beloved.
SHAKESPEARE, *Twelfth Night*. Act ii, sc. 4, l. 15.

3
O, but I love his lady too too much!
SHAKESPEARE, *The Two Gentlemen of Verona*. Act ii, sc. 4, l. 205.

And notwithstanding all her sudden quips,
The least whereof would quell a lover's hope,
Yet, spaniel-like, the more she spurns my love,
The more it grows and fawneth on her still.
SHAKESPEARE, *The Two Gentlemen of Verona*. Act iv, sc. 2, l. 12.

4
Art thou a woman's son, and canst not feel
What 'tis to love?
SHAKESPEARE, *Venus and Adonis*, l. 201.

5
When you loved me I gave you the whole sun and stars to play with. I gave you eternity in a single moment . . . a moment only; but was it not enough? Were you not paid then for all the rest of your struggle on earth? . . . We spent eternity together; and you ask me for a little lifetime more. . . . I gave you your own soul: you ask me for my body as a plaything. Was it not enough? Was it not enough?
BERNARD SHAW, *Getting Married*.

6
The fountains mingle with the river,
And the rivers with the ocean;
The winds of heaven mix for ever
With a sweet emotion;
Nothing in the world is single;
All things, by a law divine,
In one another's being mingle—
Why not I with thine?
SHELLEY, *Love's Philosophy*.

7
I loved him for himself alone.
SHERIDAN, *The Duenna*. Act i, sc. 2.

But thou, through good and evil, praise and blame,
Wilt not thou love me for myself alone?
MACAULAY, *Lines Written 30 July, 1847*.

I love you because you're a sweet little fool.
J. H. BONER, *The Sweet Little Fool*.

8
As the lily among thorns, so is my love among the daughters.
Old Testament: Song of Solomon, ii, 2.

9
Our way lies where God knows
And Love knows where:
We are in Love's hand to-day.
SWINBURNE, *Love at Sea*.

Land me, she says, where love
Shows but one shaft, one dove,
One heart, one hand.—
A shore like that, my dear,
Lies where no man will steer,
No maiden land.
SWINBURNE, *Love at Sea*. Imitated from Théophile Gautier.

10
If love were what the rose is,
And I were like the leaf,
Our lives would grow together
In sad or singing weather.
SWINBURNE, *A Match*.

Were you the earth, dear love, and I the skies,
My love would shine on you like to the sun
And look upon you with ten thousand eyes
Till heaven waxed blind and till the world were done.
JOSHUA SYLVESTER, *Love's Omnipotence*.

11
There has fallen a splendid tear
From the passion-flower at the gate.
She is coming, my dove, my dear;
She is coming, my life, my fate;
The red rose cries, "She is near, she is near;"
And the white rose weeps, "She is late;"
The larkspur listens, "I hear, I hear;"
And the lily whispers, "I wait."
TENNYSON, *Maud*. Pt. i, sec. 22, st. 10.

She is coming, my own, my sweet;
Were it ever so airy a tread,
My heart would hear her and beat,
Were it earth in an earthy bed;
My dust would hear her and beat,
Had I lain for a century dead;
Would start and tremble under her feet,
And blossom in purple and red.
TENNYSON, *Maud*. Pt. i, sec. 22, st. 11.

12
I confess that I love this woman; if that is a sin, I confess that also. (Ego me amare hanc fateor; si id peccare est, fateor id quoque.)
TERENCE, *Andria*, l. 896.

13
How could I, blest with thee, long nights employ,
And how with thee the longest day enjoy!
(Quam vellem tecum longas requiescere noctes
Et tecum longos pervigilare dies!)
TIBULLUS, *Elegies*. Bk. iii, eleg. 6, l. 53.

14
The seamen on the wave, love,
When storm and tempest rave, love,
Look to one star to save, love,
Thou art that star to me!
JOHN TYLER, *To Julia Gardiner Tyler*. Written 1 Jan., 1855, at the age of 65.

1
Will you love me in December as you do in May,
Will you love me in the good old fashioned way?
When my hair has all turned gray,
Will you kiss me then and say,
That you love me in December as you do in May?
JAMES J. WALKER, *Will You Love Me in December as You Do in May?* Set to music by Ernest R. Ball in 1905.

2
A narrow compass, and yet there
Dwelt all that's good, and all that's fair:
Give me but what this riband bound,
Take all the rest the sun goes round.
EDMUND WALLER, *On a Girdle.*

3
No lance have I, in joust or fight,
To splinter in my lady's sight;
But, at her feet, how blest were I
For any need of hers to die!
WHITTIER, *The Henchman.*

The love that no return doth crave
To knightly levels lifts the slave.
WHITTIER, *The Henchman.*

4
Serene will be our days and bright,
And happy will our nature be,
When love is an unerring light,
And joy its own security.
WORDSWORTH, *Ode to Duty.* St. 3.

She who dwells with me, whom I have loved
With such communion, that no place on earth
Can ever be a solitude to me.
WORDSWORTH, *There Is an Eminence.*

5
O dearer far than light and life are dear.
WORDSWORTH, *To ——.* (To Mrs. W.)

Ah, dearer than my soul . . .
Dearer than light, or life, or fame.
JOHN OLDHAM, *Lament for Saul and Jonathan.*

Art thou not dearer to my eyes than light?
Dost thou not circulate through all my veins?
Mingle with life, and form my very soul?
EDWARD YOUNG, *Busiris.* Act v, sc. 1.

6
Tho' near the gates of Paradise,
Gladly I'd turn away,
Just to hear you say, "I love you!"
Sometime, somewhere, some day.
RIDA JOHNSON YOUNG, *Sometime.* (1919)

7
I seek for one as fair and gay,
But find none to remind me,
How blest the hours pass'd away
With the girl I left behind me.
UNKNOWN, *The Girl I Left Behind Me.* (1759) (*Charms of Melody*, Dublin, 1810.)

8
Greensleeves was all my joy,
Greensleeves was my delight,
Greensleeves was my heart of gold,
And who but Lady Greensleeves?
UNKNOWN, *A New Courtly Sonnet of the Lady Greensleeves.* (*A Handful of Pleasant Ditties*, 1584.) The tune of *Greensleeves* is referred to by Shakespeare, *Merry Wives of Windsor*, ii, l, and v, 5.

9
While roses deck the garden,
While yet the sun is high,
Doff sorry pride for pardon,
Or ever love go by.
ERNEST DOWSON, *Amantium Irae.*

XXXI—Love and Fear

10
Love is a thing aye full of busy dread.
CHAUCER, *Troilus and Criseyde.* Bk. iv, l. 1645. (c. 1374)

This proverb that I the lere . . .
Love goeth never without fear.
ALEXANDER BARCLAY, *Castle of Labour.* Sig. D 2. (1506)

11
There is no fear in love; but perfect love casteth out fear.
New Testament: I John, iv, 18.

Love cannot be mixed with fear. (Non potest amor cum timore misceri.)
SENECA, *Epistulæ ad Lucilium.* Epis. xlvii, sec. 19.

Perfect love casteth out prudery together with fear.
RICHARD GARNETT, *De Flagello Myrteo*, lix. (1905)

12
For there is only sorrow in my heart;
There is no room for fear.
But how I wish I were afraid again,
My dear, my dear!
ALINE KILMER, *I Shall Not Be Afraid.*

13
Love is a thing full of anxious fears. (Res est solliciti plena timoris amor.)
OVID, *Heroides.* Epis. i, l. 12.

14
I do not wish to be feared; I prefer to be loved. (Nolo ego metui: amari mavolo.)
PLAUTUS, *Asinaria*, l. 835.

15
To fear love is to fear life, and those who fear life are already three parts dead.
BERTRAND RUSSELL, *Marriage and Morals*, p. 287.

Of all forms of caution, caution in love is perhaps most fatal to true happiness.
BERTRAND RUSSELL, *Conquest of Happiness*, p. 186.

16
Where love is great, the littlest doubts are fear;
When little fears grow great, great love grows there.
SHAKESPEARE, *Hamlet.* Act iii, sc. 2, l. 181.

XXXII—Love and Hate

1
For those who love, the world is wide,
But not for those who hate.
THOMAS BAILEY ALDRICH, *Rencontre.*

2
For 'tis impossible hate to return with love.
(Che amar chi t'odia, ell'è impossibil cosa.)
ALFIERI, *Polinice.* Act ii, sc. 4.

3
I love you:
I'll cut your throat for your own sake.
BEAUMONT AND FLETCHER, *The Little French Lawyer.* Act iv, sc. 1.

4
When I love most, Love is disguised
In Hate; and when Hate is surprised
In Love, then I hate most.
ROBERT BROWNING, *Pippa Passes.* Pt. ii, l. 227.

Once, when I loved, I would enlace
Breast, eyelids, hands, feet, form and face
Of her I loved in one embrace—
As if by mere love I could love immensely!
Once, when I hated, I would plunge
My sword and wipe with the first lunge
My foe's whole life out like a sponge—
As if by mere hate I could hate intensely!
But now I am wiser, know better the fashion
How passion seeks aid from its opposite passion.
ROBERT BROWNING, *Pippa Passes.* Pt. ii, l. 207.

Our hatreds are beautiful when they mark the loftiness of our loves.
ABEL BONNARD, *The Art of Friendship:* Pt. ii, *Reflections.*

5
The self-same thing they will abhor
One way, and long another for.
BUTLER, *Hudibras.* Pt. i, canto i, l. 219.

6
Now hatred is by far the longest pleasure;
Men love in haste, but they detest at leisure.
BYRON, *Don Juan.* Canto xiii, st. 6.

7
I hate and I love. Perhaps you ask why I do so. I do not know, but I feel it, and I am in torment. (Odi et amo. Quare id faciam, fortasse requiris. Nescio, sed fieri sentio et excrucior.)
CATULLUS, *Odes.* Ode lxxxv.

One loves without reason, and without reason one hates. (On aime sans raison, et sans raison l'on haït.)
REGNARD, *Les Folies Amoureuses.*

8
Love as though some day you would have to hate; hate as though some day you would have to love.
CHILON. (DIOGENES LAERTIUS, *Chilon.*)

9
Few (especially young) people know how to love, or how to hate; their love is an unbounded weakness, fatal to the person they love; their hate is a hot, rash, and imprudent violence, always fatal to themselves.
LORD CHESTERFIELD, *Letters,* 29 Sept., 1752.

10
Dissembled hate or varnished love.
DRYDEN, *Threnodia Augustalis.* St. 4.

11
The doctrine of hatred must be preached, as the counteraction of the doctrine of love, when that pules and whines.
EMERSON, *Essays, First Series: Self-Reliance.*

12
I hate all that don't love me, and slight all that do.
FARQUHAR, *The Constant Couple.* Act i, sc. 1.

13
If you hate a man, eat his bread; if you love him, do the same.
THOMAS FULLER, *Gnomologia.* No. 2756.

14
Violent antipathies are always suspicious, and betray a secret affinity.
WILLIAM HAZLITT, *Table Talk.* Vol. i, p. 377.

15
He loos me for little that hates me for nought.
H. G. BOHN, *Handbook of Proverbs,* p. 379.

16
We've practiced loving long enough,
Let's come at last to hate.
(Wir haben lang genug geliebt,
Und wollen endlich hassen.)
GEORG HERWEGH, *Lied vom Hasse.*

17
Who love too much, hate in the like extreme.
HOMER, *Odyssey.* Bk. xv, l. 79. (Pope, tr.)

18
If one judges love by its effects, it resembles hate more than affection. (Si on juge de l'amour par la plupart de ses effets, il ressemble plus à la haine qu'à l'amitié.)
LA ROCHEFOUCAULD, *Maximes.* No. 72.

The more one loves a mistress, the more one is ready to hate her. (Plus on aime une maîtresse, et plus on est prêt de la haïr.)
LA ROCHEFOUCAULD, *Maximes.* No. 111.

19
There's nothing in this world so sweet as love,
And next to love the sweetest thing is hate.
LONGFELLOW, *The Spanish Student.* Act ii, sc. 5.

20
Nothing is more hateful than love.
JOHN LYLY, *Euphues and His England,* p. 325.

The noblest hateful love that e'er I heard of.
SHAKESPEARE, *Troilus and Cressida,* iv, 1, 33.

21
Where I love, I profess it; where I hate,
In every circumstance I dare proclaim it.
PHILIP MASSINGER, *A Very Woman.* Act i, sc. 1.

22
To love you was pleasant enough,
And, oh! 'tis delicious to hate you!
THOMAS MOORE, *To ——.*

Any kiddie in school can love like a fool,
But hating, my boy, is an art.
OGDEN NASH, *Plea for Less Malice Toward None.*

23
Thy sweet obligingness could supple hate,

And out of it, its contrary create.
JOHN OLDHAM, *To Charles Morwent*. St. 17.

1
I will hate, if I can: if not, I will unwillingly love. (Odero, si potero: si non, invitus amabo.)
OVID, *Amores*. Bk. iii, eleg. 11, l. 35.

What will you do in your hatred, when you are so cruel in your love? (Quid facies odio sic ubi amore noces?)
OVID, *Heroides*. Epis. xxi, l. 56.

2
Years of love have been forgot
In the hatred of a minute.
EDGAR ALLAN POE, *To ——*.

3
A woman either loves or hates; there is no third course. (Aut amat aut odit mulier; nihil est tertium.)
PUBLILIUS SYRUS, *Sententiæ*. No. 6.

4
Hatreds are the cinders of affection.
SIR WALTER RALEIGH, *Letter to Sir Robert Cecil*, 10 May, 1593.

5
Arise, black vengeance, from thy hollow cell!
Yield up, O love, thy crown and hearted throne
To tyrannous hate! Swell, bosom, with thy fraught,
For 'tis of aspics' tongues.
SHAKESPEARE, *Othello*. Act iii, sc. 3, l. 447.

6
Sweet love, I see, changing his property,
Turns to the sourest and most deadly hate.
SHAKESPEARE, *Richard II*. Act iii, sc. 2, l. 135.

Here's much to do with hate, but more with love.
SHAKESPEARE, *Romeo and Juliet*, i, 1, 181.

My only love sprung from my only hate!
Too early seen unknown, and known too late!
SHAKESPEARE, *Romeo and Juliet*, i, 5, 140.

It is a greater grief
To bear love's wrong than hate's known injury.
SHAKESPEARE, *Sonnets*. No. xl.

7
What medicine then can such disease remove,
Where love draws hate, and hate engendereth love?
SIR PHILIP SIDNEY, *Arcadia*. Bk. iii.

8
Let me arise and open the gate,
To breathe the wild warm air of the heath,
And to let in Love, and to let out Hate,
And anger at living, and scorn of Fate,
To let in Life, and to let out Death.
MARY M. SINGLETON, *A Reverie*.

9
Who cannot hate, can love not.
SWINBURNE, *In the Bay*. St. 31.

10
Dower'd with the hate of hate, the scorn of scorn,
The love of love.
TENNYSON, *The Poet*.

In a wink the false love turns to hate.
TENNYSON, *Merlin and Vivien*, l. 850.

11
Here love returns with love to the lover,
And beauty unto the heart thereof,
And hatred unto the heart of the hater.
JOHN HALL WHEELOCK, *The Triumph of Love*.

12
She may strike the pouncing eagle, but she dares not harm the dove;
And every gate she bars to Hate shall open wide to Love!
J. G. WHITTIER, *Brown of Osawatomie*.

13
Love lights more fire than hate extinguishes,
And men grow better as the world grows old.
ELLA WHEELER WILCOX, *Optimism*.

14
I've played the traitor Over and over;
I'm a good hater But a bad lover.
ELINOR WYLIE, *Peregrine*.

XXXIII—Love and Loss

15
Say what you will, 'tis better to be left than never to have been loved.
WILLIAM CONGREVE, *The Way of the World*. Act ii, sc. 1.

Better be cheated to the last
Than lose the blessed hope of truth.
FRANCES ANNE KEMBLE, *Faith*.

16
Better to love amiss than nothing to have loved.
GEORGE CRABBE, *Tales: The Struggles of Conscience*, l. 46.

17
Far worse it is
To lose than never to have tasted bliss.
(Che mai
Non v'avere ò provate, ò possedute.)
GUARINI, *Pastor Fido*.

18
Methinks it is better that I should have pined away seven of my goldenest years, when I was thrall to the fair hair, and fairer eyes, of Alice W——n, than that so passionate a love adventure should be lost.
CHARLES LAMB, *Essays of Elia: New Year's Eve*.

19
He who for love hath undergone
The worst that can befall,
Is happier thousandfold than one
Who never loved at all.
RICHARD MONCKTON MILNES, *To Myrzha: On Returning*.

20
I hold it true, whate'er befall;
I feel it, when I sorrow most;
'Tis better to have loved and lost
Than never to have loved at all.
TENNYSON, *In Memoriam*. Pt. xxvii, st. 4.

'Tis better to have loved and lost than never to have lost at all.
SAMUEL BUTLER THE YOUNGER, *The Way of*

All Flesh. Ch. 77. Usually misprinted "loved at all."

1
It is best to love wisely, no doubt; but to love foolishly is better than not to be able to love at all.
THACKERAY, *Pendennis*. Ch. 6.

To love and win is the best thing; to love and lose the next best.
THACKERAY, *Pendennis*. Ch. 6.

2
I fear to love thee, Sweet, because
Love's the ambassador of loss.
FRANCIS THOMPSON, *To Olivia*.

XXXIV—Love and Death

3
Scarcely a tear to shed;
Hardly a word to say;
The end of a summer day;
Sweet Love dead.
WILLIAM ALLINGHAM, *An Evening*.

4
Oh, listen! Love lasts! Love will never die.
I am only your Angel, who was your Bride;
And I know, that though dead, I have never died.
EDWIN ARNOLD, *She and He*.

Though I am dead my soul shall love thee still.
JAMES HAMMOND, *Elegies*. No. xiii.

5
And a voice said in mastery, while I strove,—
"Guess now who holds thee?"—"Death," I said. But, there,
The silver answer rang,—"Not Death, but Love."
E. B. BROWNING, *Sonnets from the Portuguese*. No. i.

6
Can we love but on condition that the thing we love must die?
ROBERT BROWNING, *La Saisiaz*.

7
Cold in the dust this perished heart may lie,
But that which warmed it once shall never die!
CAMPBELL, *The Pleasures of Hope*. Pt. ii, l. 429.

8
So blind is life, so long at last is sleep,
And none but Love to bid us laugh or weep.
WILLA CATHER, *Evening Song*.

9
A death for love's no death, but martyrdom.
GEORGE CHAPMAN, *Revenge for Honour*. Act iv, sc. 2.

10
My love is dead, Gone to his death-bed,
All under the willow-tree!
CHATTERTON, *Ælla: The Minstrel's Song*.

11
Love, like death, a universal leveller of mankind.
CONGREVE, *The Double-Dealer*. Act ii, sc. 8.

Love either finds equality or makes it;
Like death, he knows no difference in degrees,
But planes and levels all.
DRYDEN, *Marriage à la Mode*. Act iii, sc. 1.

12
Given thee back
To earth, to light and life, to love and me.
CONGREVE, *The Mourning Bride*. Act ii, sc. 2.

13
Life bears Love's cross, death brings Love's crown.
DINAH MARIA MULOCK CRAIK, *Lettice*.

14
As I lay my heart on your dead heart, Douglas,
Douglas, Douglas, tender and true!
DINAH MARIA MULOCK CRAIK, *Too Late*.

O Dowglas, O Dowglas, Tendir and trewe.
SIR RICHARD HOLLAND, *Buke of the Howlat*. St. 31. (c. 1450) (PINKERTON, *Collection of Scottish Poems*. Vol. iii, p. 146.)

15
Love is anterior to life,
Posterior to death.
EMILY DICKINSON, *Poems*. Pt. iii, No. 37.

16
He who dares love, and for that love must die,
And, knowing this, dares yet love on, am I.
DRYDEN, *II Conquest of Granada*. Act iv, sc. 3.

He that dares drink, and for that drink dares die,
And, knowing this, dares yet drink on, am I.
GEORGE VILLIERS, DUKE OF BUCKINGHAM, *Rehearsal*. Act iv, sc. 1. Drawcansir, the burlesque tyrant in Buckingham's play, was a burlesque of Dryden's Almanzor in the *Conquest of Granada*.

17
I know not if it rains, my love,
In the land where you do lie;
And oh, so sound you sleep, my love,
You know no more than I.
A. E. HOUSMAN, *The Half-Moon Westers Low*.

18
I had rather live and love where death is king, than have eternal life where love is not.
R. G. INGERSOLL, *Oration at a Child's Grave*.

19
But great loves, to the last, have pulses red;
All great loves that have ever died dropped dead.
HELEN HUNT JACKSON, *Dropped Dead*.

20
The grey-haired saint may fail at last,
The surest guide a wanderer prove;
Death only binds us fast
To the bright shore of love.
JOHN KEBLE, *The Christian Year: 8th Sunday after Trinity*.

21
If Love were jester at the court of Death,
And Death the king of all, still would I pray,
"For me the motley and the bauble, yea,
Though all be vanity, as the Preacher saith,

The mirth of love be mine for one brief breath!"
FREDERICK LAWRENCE KNOWLES, *If Love Were Jester at the Court of Death.*

1
No rest but the grave for the Pilgrim of Love.
AMELIA OPIE, *The Pilgrim of Love*, l. 6.

2
They that love beyond the world cannot be separated by it. Death cannot kill what never dies.
WILLIAM PENN, *Fruits of Solitude.*

3
O Death, all-eloquent! you only prove
What dust we dote on, when 'tis man we love.
POPE, *Eloisa to Abelard*, l. 335.

4
Love is Life, and Death at last
Crowns it eternal and divine.
ADELAIDE ANN PROCTER, *Life in Death.*

5
Methought I saw the grave where Laura lay.
SIR WALTER RALEIGH, *Verses to Edmund Spenser.*

6
If there be any one can take my place
And make you happy whom I grieve to grieve,
Think not that I can grudge it, but believe
I do command you to that nobler grace,
That readier wit than mine, that sweeter face.
CHRISTINA ROSSETTI, *Monna Innominata*. Sonnet xii.

7
Tell me if the lovers are losers . . . tell me if any get more than the lovers . . . in the dust . . . in the cool tombs.
CARL SANDBURG, *Cool Tombs.*

8
Men have died from time to time and worms have eaten them, but not for love.
SHAKESPEARE, *As You Like It*. Act iv, sc. 1, l. 107.

What mad lover ever dy'd,
To gain a soft and gentle bride?
Or for a lady tender-hearted,
In purling streams or hemp departed?
BUTLER, *Hudibras*. Pt. iii, canto i, l. 23.

I thought when love for you died, I should die.
It's dead. Alone, most strangely, I live on.
RUPERT BROOKE, *The Life Beyond.*

For, heaven be thank'd, we live in such an age,
When no man dies for love, but on the stage.
DRYDEN, *Epilogue: Mithridates.*

9
Eyes, look your last!
Arms, take your last embrace! and lips, O you
The doors of breath, seal with a righteous kiss
A dateless bargain to engrossing death.
SHAKESPEARE, *Romeo and Juliet*. Act v, sc. 3, l. 113.

10
Come away, come away, death,
And in sad cypress let me be laid;
Fly away, fly away, breath:
I am slain by a fair cruel maid.
My shroud of white, stuck all with yew,
O, prepare it!
My part of death, no one so true
Did share it.
SHAKESPEARE, *Twelfth Night*. Act ii, sc. 4, l. 52.

11
Love is strong as death.
Old Testament: Song of Solomon, viii, 6.

Love is greater than illusion, and as strong as death.
ALBERTO CASELLA, *Death Takes a Holiday*. Act iii.

Love, strong as death, the poet led.
POPE, *Ode on St. Cecilia's Day*. St. 4.

She is more strong than death,
Being strong as love.
SWINBURNE, *Madonna Mia.*

Love can vanquish Death.
TENNYSON, *A Dream of Fair Women*, l. 269.

12
I loved you, and my love had no return,
And therefore my true love has been my death.
TENNYSON, *Lancelot and Elaine*, l. 1268.

13
O that 'twere possible
After long grief and pain
To find the arms of my true love
Round me once again! . . .
Ah, Christ, that it were possible
For one short hour to see
The souls we loved, that they might tell us
What and where they be!
TENNYSON, *Maud*. Pt. ii, sec. 4, l. 1.

14
I believe if I should die,
And you should kiss my eyelids where I lie
Cold, dead, and dumb to all the world contains,
The folded orbs would open at thy breath,
And from its exile in the Isles of Death
Life would come gladly back along my veins.
MARY ASHLEY TOWNSEND, *Love's Belief.*

15
My love lies in the gates of foam,
The last dear wreck of shore;
The naked sea-marsh binds her home,
The sand her chamber-door.
JOHN BYRNE LEICESTER WARREN (LORD DE TABLEY), *The Churchyard on the Sands.*

16
Love still is Nature's truth, and Death her lie.
THEODORE WATTS-DUNTON, *The Coming of Love: The Spirit of the Sunrise.*

1
Where indeed the greatest and most honorable love exists, it is much better to be joined by death than separated by life. (Ubi idem et maximus et honestissimus amor est, aliquanto præstat morte jungi, quam vita distrahi.)
VALERIUS MAXIMUS, *De Factis Dictisque*. Bk. iv, ch. 6, sec. 3.

2
Life is ever lord of Death
And Love can never lose its own.
J. G. WHITTIER, *Snow-Bound*, l. 211.

And yet, dear heart, remembering thee,
Am I not richer than of old?
Safe in thy immortality,
What change can reach the wealth I hold?
What chance can mar the pearl and gold
Thy love hath left in trust with me?
J. G. WHITTIER, *Snow-Bound*, l. 422.

See also DEATH: THEY ARE ALL GONE.

3
I wish I were where Helen lies,
Nicht and day on me she cries;
Oh, that I were where Helen lies,
On fair Kirkconnel lee!
UNKNOWN, *Helen of Kirkconnel Lee*.

XXXV—Love: Its Fruition

4
Let us live, my Lesbia, and love, and value at a penny all the talk of crabbed old men. (Vivamus, mea Lesbia, atque amemus, Rumoresque senum severiorum Omnes unius æstimemus assis.)
CATULLUS, *Odes*. Ode v, l. 1.

Live we, Lesbia, and love!
What though the greybeards disapprove!
Let them wag their toothless jaws!
Who cares a copper for their saws?
RICHARD HOVEY, *To Lesbia*.

5
When love is satisfied, all its charm is gone. (À l'amour satisfait, tout son charme est ôté.)
CORNEILLE, *Don Juan*. Act i, sc. 2.

As soon as women belong to us, we no longer belong to them. (Soudain qu'elles sont à nous, nous ne sommes plus à elles.)
MONTAIGNE, *Essays*. Bk. iii, ch. 5.

Women enjoy'd (whate'er before they've been)
Are like romances read, or sights once seen.
SIR JOHN SUCKLING, *Against Fruition*.

Plays and romances read and seen, do fall
In our opinions; yet not seen at all,
Whom would they please? To an heroic tale
Would you not listen, lest it should grow stale?
EDMUND WALLER, *In Answer of Sir John Suckling's Verses*.

6
Perfect love implies Love in all capacities.
ABRAHAM COWLEY, *Platonic Love*.

7
Love's mysteries in souls do grow,
But yet the body is his book.
JOHN DONNE, *The Ecstasy*.

8
But she ne'er loved who durst not venture all.
DRYDEN, *Aureng-Zebe*. Act v, sc. 1.

Give all to love;
Obey thy heart;
Friends, kindred, days,
Estate, good-fame,
Plans, credit, and the Muse,—
Nothing refuse.
R. W. EMERSON, *Give All to Love*.

9
Love, while you are able to love. (O lieb, so lang du lieben kannst.)
FREILIGRATH, *Der Liebe Dauer*.

10
O'er her warm cheek and rising bosom move
The bloom of young Desire, and purple light
of Love.
THOMAS GRAY, *The Progress of Poesy*. Pt. i, sec. 3. (Λάμπει δ' ἐπὶ πορφυρέῃσι Παρείῃσι φῶς ἔρωτος.—PHRYNICHUS, *Apud Athenæum*.)

How beautiful she look'd! her conscious heart
Glow'd in her cheek, and yet she felt no wrong:
Oh love! how perfect is thy mystic art,
Strengthening the weak and trampling on the strong.
BYRON, *Don Juan*. Canto i, st. 106.

The light of love, the purity of grace,
The mind, the Music breathing from her face,
The heart whose softness harmonized the whole:
And, oh! that eye was in itself a Soul!
BYRON, *The Bride of Abydos*. Canto i, l. 178.

11
There is no sorrow like a love denied
Nor any joy like love that has its will.
RICHARD HOVEY, *The Marriage of Guenevere*. Act i, sc. 3.

12
When thou hast heard his name upon
The bugles of the cherubim,
Begin thou softly to unzone
Thy girlish bosom unto him,
And softly to undo the snood
That is the sign of maidenhood.
JAMES JOYCE, *Bid Adieu to Girlish Days*.

Did the harebell loose her girdle
To the lover bee,
Would the bee the harebell hallow
Much as formerly?

Did the paradise, persuaded,
Yield her moat of pearl,
Would the Eden be an Eden,
Or the earl an earl?
EMILY DICKINSON, *Poems*. Pt. iii, No. 28.

13
The reproduction of mankind is a great marvel and mystery. Had God consulted me in the matter, I should have advised him to continue the generation of the species by fashioning them of clay.
MARTIN LUTHER, *Table-Talk*. No. 752.

1
Perchance she thought my love was passionless,
Wanted what I withheld, yet longed to give.
PHILIP BOURKE MARSTON, *Estranged.*

2
Yielded with coy submission, modest pride,
And sweet, reluctant, amorous delay.
MILTON, *Paradise Lost.* Bk. iv, l. 310.

Imparadis'd in one another's arms.
MILTON, *Paradise Lost.* Bk. iv, l. 506.

Tangl'd in amorous nets.
MILTON, *Paradise Regained.* Bk. ii, l. 162.

3
Whoso would not lose all his spirit, let him love! (Qui nolet fieri desidiosus, amet!)
OVID, *Amores.* Bk. i, epis. 9, l. 46.

4
Let Wealth, let Honour, wait the wedded dame,
August her deed, and sacred be her fame;
Before true passion all those views remove;
Fame, Wealth, and Honour! what are you to Love?
POPE, *Eloisa to Abelard,* l. 77.

O happy state! when souls each other draw,
When Love is liberty, and Nature law.
POPE, *Eloisa to Abelard,* l. 91.

One thought of thee puts all the pomp to flight,
Priests, tapers, temples, swim before my sight.
POPE, *Eloisa to Abelard,* l. 273.

5
He plough'd her, and she cropp'd.
SHAKESPEARE, *Antony and Cleopatra,* ii, 2, 233.

The world must be peopled.
SHAKESPEARE, *Much Ado About Nothing.* Act ii, sc. 3, l. 251.

6
Love stops at nothing but possession.
THOMAS SOUTHERNE, *Oroonoko.* Act ii, sc. 2.

XXXVI—Love: Not Wisely But Too Well

See also Chastity; Woman: Her Virtue

7
Love shut our eyes, and all seemed right.
True, the world's eyes are open now:
—Less need for me to disallow
Some few that keep Love's zone unbuckled,
Peevish as ever to be suckled,
Lulled by the same old baby-prattle,
With intermixture of the rattle.
ROBERT BROWNING, *Christmas-Eve.* Sec. xi.

So down the flowery path of love we went.
ROBERT BUCHANAN, *Sigurd of Saxony.*

8
Now what could artless Jeanie do?
She had nae will to say him na:
At length she blushed a sweet consent,
And love was aye between them twa.
BURNS, *Bonnie Jean.*

The sweetest flower that decked the mead,
Now trodden like the vilest weed;
Let simple maid the lesson read!
The weird may be her ain, jo.
BURNS, *O, Let Me In This Ae Night.*

9
When love's delirium haunts the glowing mind,
Limping Decorum lingers far behind.
BYRON, *Answer to Some Elegant Verses Sent by a Friend.*

10
She for him had given
Her all on earth, and more than all in Heaven.
BYRON, *The Corsair.* Canto iii, st. 17.

And they were happy, for to their young eyes
Each was an angel, and earth paradise.
BYRON, *Don Juan.* Canto ii, st. 204.

Great is their love who love in sin and fear.
BYRON, *Heaven and Earth.* Pt. i, l. 67.

11
Inexperienced tears, Pallor that lovers ever prize,
Boldness trembling at his first thefts, happy Fears.
CLAUDIAN, *De Nuptiis Honorii Augusti,* l. 80.

12
Now, no doubt, my friend and I
Will proceed to lie and lie
To ourselves, till we begin
To act the truth and call it sin.
But I wish that life were made
So that lovers, unafraid
Of heaven, hell, and gossip, could
Go their way and call it good.
GRACE STONE COATES, *As It Is.*

13
She that gives all to the false one pursuing her
Makes but a penitent and loses a lover.
GOLDSMITH, *Song.* Intended for *She Stoops to Conquer.*

14
The old, old story,—fair, and young,
And fond,—and not too wise,—
That matrons tell, with sharpened tongue,
To maids with downcast eyes.
O. W. HOLMES, *Agnes.* Pt. i, st. 2.

15
A little, sorrowful, deserted thing,
Begot of love, and yet no love begetting.
HOOD, *Plea of the Midsummer Fairies,* l. 712.

A fair and sinless child of sin.
BYRON, *Don Juan.* Canto iv, st. 70.

16
I loved him too as woman loves—
Reckless of sorrow, sin, or scorn.
LETITIA ELIZABETH LANDON, *The Indian Bride.*

17
But once when love's betrayed,
Its sweet life blooms no more!
THOMAS MOORE, *Anacreontic: Friend of My Soul.*

18
I have loved not wisely. (Non sapienter amavi.)
OVID, *Heroides.* Epis. ii, l. 27.

Then must you speak
Of one that loved not wisely but too well.
SHAKESPEARE, *Othello.* Act v, sc. 2, l. 343.

And I, what is my crime I cannot tell,
Unless it be a crime t' have lov'd too well.
RICHARD CRASHAW, *Alexias.* Eleg. iii, l. 19.

Sorry her lot who loves too well,
Heavy the heart that hopes but vainly.
W. S. GILBERT, *H. M. S. Pinafore*. Act i.

Is it, in Heav'n, a crime to love too well?
POPE. *Elegy to the Memory of an Unfortunate Lady*, l. 6.

1
To deceive a trusting maid is glory but cheaply won. (Fallere credentem non est operosa puellam.)
OVID, *Heroides*. Epis. ii, l. 63.

For love deceives the best of womankind.
HOMER, *Odyssey*. Bk. xv, l. 463. (Pope, tr.)

For when success a lover's toil attends,
Few ask if fraud or force attain'd his ends.
POPE, *The Rape of the Lock*. Canto ii, l. 33.

But the thing that fills me with wonder, the thing that's most strange to me,
Is, why do the moths and the butterflies always fall for the son of a bee?
GEORGE L. NORTH, *A Tale of Two Bugs*.

2
Love, to her ear, was but a name
Combined with vanity and shame.
SCOTT, *Marmion*. Canto ii, st. 3.

3
The moonlight filled them both with sundry glamors,
Filtered silver in between white birches,
Blood whispered, like the stream, with urgent clamors,
And bells were struck that never rang in churches.
A. B. STEVENSON, *Et Sa Pauvre Chair*.

4
The World whips frank, gay love with rods,
But frankly, gayly shall we get the gods.
ANNA WICKHAM, *Meditation at Kew*.

XXXVII—Love and Lust

See also Wantonness, Whore

5
Money gets women, cards and dice
Get money, and ill-luck gets just
That copper couch and one clear nice
Cool squirt of water o'er your bust,
The right thing to extinguish lust!
ROBERT BROWNING, *Apparent Failure*.

6
A dear-lov'd lad, convenience snug,
A treach'rous inclination—
But, let me whisper i' your lug,
Ye're aiblins nae temptation.
BURNS, *Address to the Unco Guid*. St. 6.

The caird prevail'd—th' unblushing fair
In his embraces sunk,
Partly wi' love o'ercome sae sair,
An' partly she was drunk.
BURNS, *The Jolly Beggars: Recitativo*.

7
Love indeed (I may not deny) first united provinces, built cities, and by a perpetual generation makes and preserves mankind; but if it rage it is no more love, but burning lust, a disease, frenzy, madness, hell. . . . It subverts kingdoms, overthrows cities, towns, families; mars, corrupts, and makes a massacre of men; thunder and lightning, wars, fires, plagues, have not done that mischief to mankind, as this burning lust, this brutish passion.
ROBERT BURTON, *Anatomy of Melancholy*. Pt. iii, sec. 2, mem. 1, subs. 2.

8
For glances beget ogles, ogles sighs,
Sighs wishes, wishes words, and words a letter, . . .
And then, God knows what mischief may arise,
When love links two young people in one fetter,
Vile assignations, and adulterous beds,
Elopements, broken vows and hearts and heads.
BYRON, *Beppo*. St. 16.

For gentlemen must sometimes risk their skin
For that sad tempter, a forbidden woman:
Sultans too much abhor this sort of sin,
And don't agree at all with the wise Roman,
Heroic, stoic Cato, the sententious,
Who lent his lady to his friend Hortensius.
BYRON, *Don Juan*. Canto vi, st. 7.

The stoic husband was the glorious thing.
The man had courage, was a sage, 'tis true,
And lov'd his country.
POPE, *Jane Shore: Epilogue*, l. 38.

9
For men have ever a likerous appetite
On lower thing to pérform their delight
Than on their wives, be they never so fair,
Nor never so true, nor so debonair.
Flesh is so newfangel, with mischaunce,
That we can in no thing have plesaunce
That tendeth unto virtue any while.
CHAUCER, *The Maunciples Tale*, l. 85.

10
He was, I trow, a twenty winter old,
And I was forty, if I shall say sooth;
But yet I had alway a coltes tooth.
Gat-toothed I was, and that became me well.
CHAUCER, *The Wife of Bath's Prologue*, l. 600.

Your colt's-tooth is not cast yet.
SHAKESPEARE, *Henry VIII*. Act i, sc. 3, l. 48.

Her merry dancing-days are done;
She has a colt's tooth still, I warrant.
WILLIAM KING, *Orpheus and Eurydice*.

11
"Why do
You thus devise
Evil against her?" "For that
She is beautiful, delicate.
Therefore."
ADELAIDE CRAPSEY, *Susanna and the Elders*.

12
It is as safe to play with fire, as it is to dally

with gallantry Love is a passion that hath friends in the garrison.
Lord Halifax, *Works*, p. 31.

If anyone complains of not succeeding in affairs of gallantry, we will venture to say, it is because he is not gallant. He has mistaken his talent.
William Hazlitt, *Round Table*, Vol. i, p. 116.

1
To set your neighbor's bed a-shaking is now an ancient and long-established custom. It was the silver age that saw the first adulterers.
Juvenal, *Satires*. Sat. vi, l. 21.

2
I've taken my fun where I've found it;
I've rogued an' I've ranged in my time;
I've 'ad my pickin' o' sweethearts,
An' four o' the lot was prime.
Rudyard Kipling, *The Ladies*.

There's times when you'll think that you mightn't,
There's times when you'll know that you might;
But the things you will learn from the Yellow an' Brown,
They'll 'elp you a lot with the White!
Rudyard Kipling, *The Ladies*.

3
The new lust gives the lecher the new thrill.
John Masefield, *Widow in the Bye Street*.

4
The actors are, it seems, the usual three:
Husband, and wife, and lover.
George Meredith, *Modern Love*. St. 25.

Now, when I see an extra light,
Flaming, flickering on the night
From my neighbor's casement opposite,
I know as well as I know to pray,
I know as well as a tongue can say,
That the innocent Sultan Shah-Zaman
Has gone to the city Ispahan.
T. B. Aldrich, *When the Sultan Goes to Ispahan*.

5
When Lust
By unchaste looks, loose gestures, and foul talk,
But most by lewd and lavish act of sin,
Lets in defilement to the inward parts,
The soul grows clotted by contagion,
Imbodies and imbrutes.
John Milton, *Comus*, l. 463.

6
Blemishes are hid by night and every fault forgiven; darkness makes any woman fair. (Nocte latent mendæ, vitioque ignoscitur omni, Horaque formosam quamlibet illa facit.)
Ovid, *Ars Amatoria*. Bk. i, l. 249.

Under the blanket the black one is as good as the white.
Thomas Fuller, *Gnomologia*. No. 5396.

Joan is as good as my lady in the dark.
Duchess of Newcastle, *Sociable Companions*, ii, 4; Charles Shadwell, *Irish Hospitality*, i, 1.

Well, I will love, write, sigh, pray, sue and groan:
Some men must love my lady and some Joan.
Shakespeare, *Love's Labour's Lost*. Act iii, sc. 1, l. 206.

Were it not for imagination, Sir, a man would be as happy in the arms of a chambermaid as of a Duchess.
Samuel Johnson. (Boswell, *Life*, iii, 341.)

Mr. Pickle himself . . . was a mere dragon among the chambermaids.
Smollett, *Peregrine Pickle*. Ch. 82.

Neither let the love of a servant-maid be regarded as a disgrace. (Ne sit ancillæ amor pudori.)
Thackeray, *Fitz-Boodle's Confessions*. Quoted as from "a notorious poet": *i.e.*, Ovid, *Ars Amatoria*, ii, 251.

7
As stolen love is pleasant to a man, so is it also to a woman; the man dissembles badly: she conceals desire more cleverly. (Utque viro furtiva venus, sic grata puellæ: Vir male dissimulat: tectius illa cupit.)
Ovid, *Ars Amatoria*. Bk. i, l. 274.

Let every lover be pale; that is the color which suits him. (Palleat omnis amans: his est color aptus amanti.)
Ovid, *Ars Amatoria*. Bk. i, l. 729.

Skill makes love unending. (Arte perennat amor.)
Ovid, *Ars Amatoria*. Bk. iii, l. 42.

8
The pleasure of the act of love is gross and brief, and brings loathing after it. (Fœda est in coitu et brevis voluptas et tædet Veneris statim peractæ.)
Petronius, *Fragments*. No. 101.

There is no greater nor keener pleasure than that of bodily love—and none which is more irrational.
Plato, *The Republic*. Bk. iii, sec. 403.

9
A secret love is bad; 'tis sheer ruin. (Malus clandestinus est amor; damnum 'st merum.)
Plautus, *Curculio*, l. 49.

10
Love finds an altar for forbidden fires.
Pope, *Eloisa to Abelard*, l. 182.

Lust, thro' some certain strainers well refin'd,
Is gentle love, and charms all womankind.
Pope, *Essay on Man*. Epis. ii, l. 189.

11
There goes a saying, and 'twas shrewdly said,
Old fish at table, but young flesh in bed.
My soul abhors the tasteless dry embrace
Of a stale virgin with a winter face.
Pope, *January and May*, l. 101.

Give me a willing nymph! 'tis all I care,
Extremely clean, and tolerably fair,
Her shape her own, whatever shape she have,
And just that white and red which nature gave.
Pope, *A Sermon Against Adultery*, l. 161.

12
To be carnally minded is death.
New Testament: Romans, viii, 6.

1
Take back your gold, for gold can never buy me.
Take back your bribe, and promise you'll be true;
Give me the love, the love that you'd deny me;
Make me your wife, that's all I ask of you.
MONROE H. ROSENFELD, *Take Back Your Gold.* (1897)

2
Though Argus hundred eyes in watch doth keep,
Yet lust at length will lull them all asleep.
FRANCIS ROUS, *Thule.*

3
There are no instincts less harmful or more productive of delight in the whole range of human instinct and emotion than the desire for sex-love and the desire for children.
DORA RUSSELL, *The Right to Be Happy,* p. 126.

4
Lust is the oldest lion of them all.
MARJORIE ALLEN SEIFFERT, *An Italian Chest.*

5
I'll canvass thee between a pair of sheets.
SHAKESPEARE, *II Henry IV.* Act ii, sc. 4, l. 242.

6
Do not give dalliance Too much the rein.
SHAKESPEARE, *The Tempest.* Act iv, sc. 1, l. 53.

7
Love comforteth like sunshine after rain,
But Lust's effect is tempest after sun;
Love's gentle spring doth always fresh remain,
Lust's winter comes ere summer half be done:
Love surfeits not. Lust like a glutton dies;
Love is all truth, Lust full of forged lies.
SHAKESPEARE, *Venus and Adonis,* l. 799.

8
The lusts and greeds of the Body scandalize the Soul; but it has to come to heel.
LOGAN PEARSALL SMITH, *Afterthoughts.*

9
Herodotus tells us, that in cold countries beasts very seldom have horns, but in hot they have very large ones. This might bear a pleasant application.
SWIFT, *Thoughts on Various Subjects.*

What men call gallantry, and gods adultery,
Is much more common where the climate's sultry.
BYRON, *Don Juan.* Canto i, st. 63.

10
The way of the adulterer is hedged with thorns; full of fears and jealousies, burning desires and impatient waitings, tediousness of delay, and sufferance of affronts, and amazements of discovery.
JEREMY TAYLOR, *Holy Living.* Ch. ii, sec. 3.

11
Our bond is not the bond of man and wife.
TENNYSON, *Lancelot and Elaine,* l. 1198.

There must be now no passages of love
Betwixt us twain henceforward evermore.
TENNYSON, *Merlin and Vivien,* l. 901.

12
To couple is a custom,
All things thereto agree:
Why should not I then love,
Since love to all is free?
UNKNOWN, *Famous History of Friar Bacon.*

For everything created
In the bounds of earth and sky,
Hath such longing to be mated,
It must couple or must die.
G. J. WHYTE-MELVILLE, *Like to Like.*

LOYALTY, see Fidelity

LUCK

See also Chance, Fortune

I—Luck: Good Luck

13
Luck for fools and chance for the ugly.
BERTHELSON, *Dictionary: Luck.*

The more knave the better luck.
JOHN RAY, *English Proverbs.*

14
He forc'd his neck into a noose,
To show his play at fast and loose;
And, when he chanc'd t' escape, mistook
For art and subtlety, his luck.
BUTLER, *Hudibras.* Pt. iii, canto ii, l. 391.

15
When good luck comes to thee, take it in.
CERVANTES, *Don Quixote.* Pt. ii, ch. 4.

16
Give me hap and cast me in the sea.
THOMAS CHURCHYARD, *Charge,* 28. (1580) Cited as an old proverb.

Give a woman luck and throw her in the sea.
WILLIAM ROWLEY, *Woman Never Vexed.* Act i. (1632)

17
Good luck never comes too late.
MICHAEL DRAYTON, *Mooncalf.* (*Works,* ii, 511.)

18
Luck is a lord.
OSWALD DYKES, *English Proverbs,* p. 272.

19
Shallow men believe in luck. . . . Strong men believe in cause and effect.
EMERSON, *Conduct of Life: Worship.*

20
Good luck reaches farther than long arms.
THOMAS FULLER, *Gnomologia.* No. 1717.

Good luck comes by cuffing.
JOHN RAY, *English Proverbs,* p. 136.

21
Luck, mere luck, may make even madness wisdom.
DOUGLAS JERROLD, *Jerrold's Wit: Luck.*

22
A lucky man is rarer than a white crow.
(Felix ille tamen corvo quoque rarior albo.)
JUVENAL, *Satires.* Sat. vii, l. 202.

By wondrous accident perchance one may
Grope out a needle in a load of hay;

And though a white crow be exceedingly rare,
A blind man may, by fortune, catch a hare.
JOHN TAYLOR, *A Kicksey Winsey*. Pt. vii.

1
Good Luck she is never a lady
But the cursedest quean alive!
Tricksey, wincing and jady,
Kittle to lead or drive.
Greet her—she's hailing a stranger!
Meet her—she's busking to leave.
Let her alone for a shrew to the bone,
And the hussy comes plucking your sleeve!
RUDYARD KIPLING, *The Wishing-Caps*.

2
Good luck befriend thee, Son; for at thy birth
The fairy ladies danced upon the hearth.
MILTON, *At a Vacation Exercise in the College*.

And good luck go with thee.
SHAKESPEARE, *Henry V*. Act iv, sc. 3, l. 11.

3
Many a stroke of luck has come to many a hopeless man. (Multa præter spem scio multis bona evenisse.)
PLAUTUS, *Rudens*, l. 400. (Act ii, sc. 3.)

4
Against a lucky man even a god has little power. (Contra felicem vix deus vires habet.)
PUBLILIUS SYRUS, *Sententiæ*. No. 135.

5
It is better to be lucky than wise.
W. G BENHAM, *Proverbs*. From the Italian, "È megiio esser fortunato che savio."

An ounce of luck is better than a pound of wisdom. (Mieux vaut une once de fortune qu'une livre de sagesse.)
UNKNOWN. A French proverb.

That weigheth, as thou mayst see, a chip of chance more than a pound of wit.
SIR THOMAS WYATT, *Of the Courtier's Life*.

6
By the luckiest stars.
SHAKESPEARE, *All's Well that Ends Well*. Act i, sc. 3, l. 252.

If it be my luck, so; if not, happy man be his dole!
SHAKESPEARE, *The Merry Wives of Windsor*. Act iii, sc. 4, l. 67.

As good luck would have it.
SHAKESPEARE, *The Merry Wives of Windsor*. Act iii, sc. 5, l. 84.

II—Luck: Bad Luck

7
Just like my luck! If I had been bred a hatter, little boys would have come into the world without heads.
BULWER-LYTTON, *Money*. Act ii, sc. 4. Quoting a "poor Italian poet."

8
As ill-luck would have it.
CERVANTES, *Don Quixote*. Pt. i, ch. 2.

9
What's worse than ill-luck?
JOHN CLARKE, *Paræmiologia*, p. 166.

The proverb says, What's worse than ill luck?
UNKNOWN, *Roxburghe Ballads*, vii, 613. (1641)

10
Bad luck often brings good luck.
THOMAS FULLER, *Gnomologia*. No. 834.

11
What evil luck soever
For me remains in store,
'Tis sure much finer fellows
Have fared much worse before.
A. E. HOUSMAN, *Last Poems*, p. 14.

Little is the luck I've had,
And oh, 'tis comfort small
To think that many another lad
Has had no luck at all.
A. E. HOUSMAN, *Last Poems*, p. 54.

12
Some people are so fond of ill-luck that they run half-way to meet it.
DOUGLAS JERROLD, *Jerrold's Wit: Meeting Trouble Half-Way. See also under* TROUBLE.

13
Bad Luck, she is never a lady
But the commonest wench on the street,
Shuffling, shabby and shady,
Shameless to pass or meet.
Walk with her once—it's a weakness!
Talk to her twice—it's a crime!
Thrust her away when she gives you "good day"
And the besom won't board you next time.
RUDYARD KIPLING, *The Wishing-Caps*.

III—Luck: Mascots

14
These messengers from Paradise are Mascots, my friends; happy the man to whom Heaven gives a Mascot.
(Ces envoyés du paradis,
Sont des Mascottes, mes amis,
Heureux celui que le ciel dote
D'un Mascotte.)
DURU AND CHIVOT, *La Mascotte*. Act i. Music by Edmond Audran.

15
See a pin and pick it up,
All the day you'll have good luck;
See a pin and let it lay,
Bad luck you'll have all the day!
HALLIWELL, *Nursery Rhymes*, p. 120.

16
Dish yer rabbit foot'll gin you good luck. De man w'at tote it mighty ap'fer ter come out right en' up wen devs any racket gwine on in de neighborhoods, let 'er be whar she will en w'en she may; mo' espeshually ef de man w'at got it know 'zactly w'at he got ter do.
JOEL CHANDLER HARRIS, *Brother Rabbit and His Famous Foot*.

17
Now for good luck, cast an old shoe after me.
JOHN HEYWOOD, *Proverbs*. Pt. i, ch. 9. (1546)

And wheresoe'er thou move, good luck
Shall fling her old shoe after.
TENNYSON, *Will Waterproof's Lyrical Monologue*. St. 27.

1
A farmer travelling with his load
Picked up a horseshoe on the road,
And nailed it fast to his barn door,
That luck might down upon him pour.
JAMES T. FIELDS, *The Lucky Horseshoe.*

Happy art thou, as if every day thou hadst picked up a horseshoe.
LONGFELLOW, *Evangeline.* Pt. i, st. 2.

2
One leaf is for hope, and one is for faith,
And one is for love, you know,
And God put another in for luck.
ELLA HIGGINSON, *Four-Leaf Clover.*

3
The god delights in odd numbers. (Numero deus impare gaudet.)
VERGIL, *Eclogues.* No. viii, l. 75.

Why is it that we entertain the belief that for every purpose odd numbers are the most effectual?
PLINY, *Historia Naturalis.* Bk. xxviii, sec. 23.

This is the third time; I hope good luck lies in odd numbers. . . . There is divinity in odd numbers, either in nativity, chance, or death.
SHAKESPEARE, *The Merry Wives of Windsor.* Act v, sc. 1, l. 2.

"Now, Rory, leave off, sir; you'll hug me no more;
That's eight times to-day that you've kissed me before."
"Then here goes another," says he, "to make sure,
For there's luck in odd numbers," says Rory O'More.
SAMUEL LOVER, *Rory O'More or Good Omens.*

Number three is always fortunate.
SMOLLETT, *Peregrine Pickle.* Quoted as a proverb.

4
My right eye itches, some good luck is near.
THEOCRITUS, *Idylls.* No. iii, l. 86. (Dryden, tr.)

LUST, see Love and Lust

LUTE, see Music: Harp and Lute

LUTHER, MARTIN

5
I can do no other. (Ich kann nicht anders.)
MARTIN LUTHER, *Speech.* Diet of Worms, 18 April, 1521. Concluding sentence. Inscribed on his monument at Worms.

God helping her, she [America] can do no other.
WOODROW WILSON, *War Speech,* to Congress, 2 Apr., 1917. Concluding sentence.

6
I will go, though as many devils aim at me as there are tiles on the roofs of the houses.
MARTIN LUTHER. (RANKE, *History of the Reformation.* Vol. i, p. 533.)

On the 16th of April, 1521, Luther entered the imperial city [of Worms]. . . . On his approach, . . . the Elector's chancellor entreated him . . . not to enter a town where his death was decided. The answer which Luther returned was simply this: "Tell your master that if there were as many devils at Worms as tiles on its roofs, I would enter."
BUNSEN, *Life of Luther.*

7
Grand rough old Martin Luther
Bloomed fables—flowers on furze,
The better the uncouther:
Do roses stick like burrs?
ROBERT BROWNING, *The Twins.*

8
Luther was guilty of two great crimes,—he struck the Pope in his crown, and the monks in their belly.
ERASMUS, *Colloquies.*

9
What! shall one monk, scarce known beyond his cell,
Front Rome's far-reaching bolts, and scorn her frown?
Brave Luther answered YES; that thunder's swell
Rocked Europe, and discharmed the triple crown.
J. R. LOWELL, *To W. L. Garrison.* St. 5.

10
The solitary monk who shook the world,
From pagan slumber, when the gospel trump
Thunder'd its challenge from his dauntless lips
In peals of truth.
ROBERT MONTGOMERY, *Luther: Man's Need and God's Supply.*

11
His words are half battles.
RICHTER, of Martin Luther. (CARLYLE, *Heroes and Hero-Worship: The Hero as Priest.*)

12
They [Luther and Calvin] condemned the Pope and desired to imitate him.
VOLTAIRE, *To the Author of "Les Trois Imposteurs."*

Luther and Calvin, who, whate'er they taught,
Led folk from superstition to free thought.
ROBERT BRIDGES, *La Gloire de Voltaire.*

LUXURY

13
And if, the following day, he chance to find
A new repast, or an untasted spring,
Blesses his stars, and thinks it luxury.
ADDISON, *Cato.* Act i, sc. 4.

No wish profan'd my overwhelmèd heart.
Blest hour! it was a luxury,—to be!
S. T. COLERIDGE, *Reflections on Having Left a Place of Retirement,* l. 41.

14
Superfluities do not hurt. (Superflua non nocent.)
ST. AUGUSTINE, *De Civitate Dei.* Quoted as a saying of "those skilled in the law."

A rich man's superfluities are often a poor man's redemption.
GEORGE COLMAN THE YOUNGER, *Who Wants a Guinea?* Act i, sc. 1.

1
And ye sall walk in silk attire,
And siller hae to spare.

SUSANNA BLAMIRE, *The Siller Crown*. Quoted by Dickens, *Old Curiosity Shop*. Ch. 66.

Silks and satins, scarlets and velvets, put out the kitchen fire.

BENJAMIN FRANKLIN, *Poor Richard*, 1758.

2
Thus first necessity invented stools,
Convenience next suggested elbow-chairs,
And Luxury the accomplish'd Sofa last.

COWPER, *The Task*. Bk. i, l. 86.

3
Too much plenty makes mouth dainty.

BENJAMIN FRANKLIN, *Poor Richard*, 1749.

4
What will not Luxury taste? Earth, sea, and air,
Are daily ransacked for the bill of fare!

JOHN GAY, *Trivia*. Bk. iii, l. 199.

5
O Luxury! thou curs'd by heaven's decree,
How ill-exchang'd are things like these for thee!
How do thy potions, with insidious joy,
Diffuse their pleasures only to destroy!

GOLDSMITH, *The Deserted Village*, l. 395.

6
We can do without any article of luxury we have never had; but when once obtained, it is not in human natur' to surrender it voluntarily.

THOMAS CHANDLER HALIBURTON, *The Clockmaker*.

Them as ha' never had a cushion don't miss it.

GEORGE ELIOT, *Adam Bede*. Ch. 49.

7
Nature is free to all; and none were foes,
Till partial luxury began the strife.

JAMES HAMMOND, *Elegies*. No. 11.

8
Persian elegance, my lad, I hate. (Persicos odi, puer, apparatus.)

HORACE, *Odes*. Bk. i, ode 38, l. 1.

Dear Lucy, you know what my wish is,—
I hate all your Frenchified fuss.

W. M. THACKERAY, *Ad Ministram*.

The pomp of the Persian I hold in Aversion,
I loathe all those gingerbread tricks.

FRANKLIN P. ADAMS, *Persicos Odi*.

9
There is a limit to luxury.

ELBERT HUBBARD, *The Philistine*, xx, 186.

You can only drink thirty or forty glasses of beer a day, no matter how rich you are.

COL. ADOLPHUS BUSCH, *Newspaper Interview*.

10
Wherever luxury ceases to be innocent, it also ceases to be beneficial.

DAVID HUME, *Essays: Of Refinement*.

11
We read on the forehead of those who are surrounded by a foolish luxury, that Fortune sells what she is thought to give. (Il lit au front de ceux qu'un vain luxe environne, Que la fortune vend ce qu'on croit qu'elle donne.)

LA FONTAINE, *Philémon et Baucis*.

12
Luxury is like a wild beast, first made fiercer with tying and then let loose.

MONTAIGNE, *Essays*. Bk. iii, ch. 5.

13
Impatient of a scene whose luxuries stole,
Spite of himself, too deep into his soul.

THOMAS MOORE, *Lalla Rookh: The Veiled Prophet*.

14
Fell luxury! more perilous to youth
Than storms or quicksands, poverty or chains.

HANNAH MORE, *Belshazzar*.

Luxury and dissipation, soft and gentle as their approaches are, and silently as they throw their silken chains about the heart, enslave it more than the most active and turbulent vices.

HANNAH MORE, *Essays: Dissipation*.

15
Give us the luxuries of life, and we will dispense with its necessaries.

J. L. MOTLEY. (HOLMES, *The Autocrat of the Breakfast-Table*. Ch. 6.)

The superfluous, a very necessary thing. (Le superflu, chose très necessaire.)

VOLTAIRE, *Le Mondain*, l. 21.

16
Luxury is an enticing pleasure, a bastard mirth, which hath honey in her mouth, gall in her heart, and a sting in her tail.

FRANCIS QUARLES, *Emblems*: Bk. i, *Hugo*.

17
We rich men count our felicity and happiness to lie in these superfluities, and not in those necessities.

SCOPAS OF THESSALY. (PLUTARCH, *Morals: Of the Love of Wealth*. PASCAL, *Pensées*, v, 1.)

18
It is the superfluous things for which men sweat. (Ad supervacua sudatur.)

SENECA, *Epistulæ ad Lucilium*. Epis. iv, 11.

Superfluous things like these: doubtless the man who first called them "hindrances" had a prophetic foresight. (Quæ sine dubio talia divinavit futura, qualia nunc sunt, qui primus appellavit "inpedimenta.")

SENECA, *Epistulæ ad Lucilium*. Epis. lxxxvii, 11.

19
The want of necessaries is always . . . accompanied by the envious longing for superfluities.

SOLON. (ORELLI, *Opuscula Græcorum Veterum*, i, 168.)

20
Falsely luxurious! will not man awake?

THOMSON, *The Seasons: Summer*, l. 67.

21
Most of the luxuries, and many of the so-called comforts of life, are not only not indispensable, but positive hindrances to the elevation of mankind.

HENRY DAVID THOREAU, *Walden*. Ch. 1.

M

MACAULAY, THOMAS BABINGTON

1
As soon as I had time to look at my neighbour, . . . I settled that he was some obscure man of letters or of medicine, perhaps a cholera doctor. . . . Having thus settled my opinion, I went on eating my dinner, when Auckland. who was sitting opposite to me, addressed my neighbour, "Mr. Macaulay, will you drink a glass of wine?" I thought I should have dropped off my chair. It was MACAULAY, the man I had been so long most curious to see and to hear, whose genius, eloquence, astonishing knowledge, and diversified talents have excited my wonder and admiration, . . . and here I had been sitting next to him, hearing him talk, and setting him down for a dull fellow.

CHARLES C. F. GREVILLE, *Memoirs*. Pt. i, 6 Feb., 1832.

I never was more struck than upon this occasion by the inexhaustible variety and extent of his [Macaulay] information. . . . It is impossible to mention any book in any language with which he is not familiar; to touch upon any subject, whether relating to persons or things, on which he does not know everything that is to be known.

GREVILLE, *Memoirs*. Pt. ii, 21 Jan., 1841.

2
Macaulay is like a book in breeches. . . . He has occasional flashes of silence, that make his conversation perfectly delightful.

SYDNEY SMITH. (LADY HOLLAND, *Memoir*. Vol. i, p. 363.)

To take Macaulay out of literature and society and put him in the House of Commons, is like taking the chief physician out of London during a pestilence.

SYDNEY SMITH. (LADY HOLLAND, *Memoir*. Vol. i, p. 265.)

3
I wish I was as sure of anything as Macaulay is of everything.

WILLIAM WINDHAM.

MACHINERY

4
It is the Age of Machinery, in every outward and inward sense of that word.

CARLYLE, *Signs of the Times*.

5
The mystery of mysteries is to view machines making machines.

BENJAMIN DISRAELI, *Coningsby* Bk. iv, ch. 2.

6
Things are in the saddle and ride mankind.

EMERSON, *Ode*.

7
The machine unmakes the man. Now that the machine is so perfect, the engineer is nobody.

EMERSON, *Society and Solitude: Works and Days*.

What I ha' seen since ocean steam began
Leaves me na doot for the machine: but what about the man?

RUDYARD KIPLING, *McAndrew's Hymn*.

8
Armed with his machinery man can dive, can fly, can see atoms like a gnat; he can peer into Uranus with his telescope, or knock down cities with his fists of gunpowder.

EMERSON, *Uncollected Lectures: Resources*.

9
One machine can do the work of fifty ordinary men. No machine can do the work of one extraordinary man.

ELBERT HUBBARD, *The Philistine*. Vol. xviii, p. 26.

10
Don't throw a monkey-wrench into the machinery.

PHILANDER JOHNSON. (*Everybody's Magazine*, May, 1920, p. 36.)

11
It is never the machines that are dead. It is only the mechanically-minded men that are dead.

GERALD STANLEY LEE, *Crowds*. Pt. ii, ch. 5.

Machinery is the sub-conscious mind of the world.

GERALD STANLEY LEE, *Crowds*. Pt. ii, ch. 8.

12
It is questionable if all the mechanical inventions yet made have lightened the day's toil of any human being.

J. S. MILL, *Principles of Political Economy*.

Without doubt machinery has greatly increased the number of well-to-do idlers.

KARL MARX, *Capital*.

13
Machines are worshipped because they are beautiful, and valued because they confer power; they are hated because they are hideous, and loathed because they impose slavery.

BERTRAND RUSSELL, *Sceptical Essays*, p. 83.

14
You're not a man, you're a machine.

BERNARD SHAW, *Arms and the Man*. Act iii.

15
There will be little drudgery in this better ordered world. Natural power harnessed in machines will be the general drudge.

H. G. WELLS, *Outline of History*. Ch. xli, par. 4.

All their devices for cheapening labour simply resulted in increasing the burden of labour.

WILLIAM MORRIS, *News from Nowhere*, p. 131.

McKINLEY, WILLIAM

16
The bullet that pierced Goebel's breast
Cannot be found in all the West;
Good reason; it is speeding here [to Washington]

To stretch McKinley on his bier.
AMBROSE BIERCE, *New York Journal,* February 4, 1901. Basis of Roosevelt's denunciation of William Randolph Hearst as instigator of McKinley's assassination. (See SULLIVAN, *"Our Times,"* iii, 280.)

If bad institutions and bad men can be got rid of only by killing, then the killing must be done.
Editorial in N. Y. *Evening Journal,* April 10, 1901, attacking President McKinley.

1 Where is McKinley, Mark Hanna's McKinley,
His slave, his echo, his suit of clothes?
VACHEL LINDSAY, *Bryan, Bryan, Bryan.*

2 In his [McKinley's] photographs he is always the same. He would never consent to be photographed in a negligent pose, and always took the most meticulous care about every detail of his appearance and his posture. He embalmed himself, so far as posterity is concerned.
C. W. THOMPSON, *Presidents I've Known,* p. 16.

MADNESS

See also Mind: The Mind Diseased

I—Madness: Definitions and Apothegms

3 If only men would be mad in the same fashion and conformably, they might manage to agree fairly well together.
BACON, *De Augmentis Scientiarum.* Pt. ii, bk. 1, aphor. 27.

4 Lucid intervals and happy pauses.
FRANCIS BACON, *History of King Henry VII.* Sec. 3. (1622)

Some beams of wit on other souls may fall,
Strike through and make a lucid interval.
DRYDEN, *MacFlecknoe,* l. 21. (1682) Used also by SIDNEY, *On Government,* i, 2, 24; FULLER, *Pisgah Sight,* iv, 2; SOUTH, *Sermons,* viii, 403; HENRY, *Commentaries, Psalm* 88.

5 Like men condemned to thunderbolts,
Who, ere the blow, become mere dolts.
BUTLER, *Hudibras.* Pt. iii, canto ii, l. 565.

6 His madness was not of the head, but heart.
BYRON, *Lara.* Canto i, st. 18.

DEMENTIA AMERICANA; BRAIN-STORM. *See* LAW: VARIETIES.

7 Mad were as an hare.
CHAUCER, *The Freres Tale,* l. 29. (c. 1386)

There he runneth wild as any hare.
UNKNOWN, *Partonope,* l. 7934. (1450)

And be as brainless as a March hare.
UNKNOWN. (HAZLITT, *Early Popular Poetry,* i, 105.) (c. 1500)

As mad as a March hare.
JOHN HEYWOOD, *Proverbs.* Pt. ii, ch. 5. (1546)

They are all, all mad: I came from a world of mad women, mad as March hares.
JOHN FLETCHER, *The Wild Goose Chase.* Act iv, sc. 3. (1621)

8 And run as mad as Ajax.
CHAPMAN, *Bussy d'Ambois.* Act iii. (1607)

Mad as a hatter.
THACKERAY, *Pendennis.* Ch. 10.

As mad as a weaver.
UNKNOWN, *Every Woman in Humour.* Act i. (1609)

9 E'en Bacchanalian Madness has its charms.
COWPER, *The Progress of Error,* l. 56.

10 Queer street is full of lodgers just at present.
DICKENS, *Our Mutual Friend.* Bk. iii, ch. 1.

11 Blest madman, who could every hour employ,
With something New to wish, or to enjoy.
DRYDEN, *Absalom and Achitophel,* l. 553.

12 The alleged power to charm down insanity, or ferocity in beasts, is a power behind the eye.
EMERSON, *Conduct of Life: Of Behavior.*

13 Have not you maggots in your brain?
JOHN FLETCHER, *Woman Pleased.* Act iii, sc. 4.

His father's sister had bats in the belfry and was put away.
EDEN PHILLPOTTS, *Peacock House,* p. 219.

14 Ah! for that reckless fire men had
When it was witty to be mad.
EMUND GOSSE, *Impression.*

15 A pleasant madness. (Amabilis insania.)
HORACE, *Odes.* Bk. iii, ode 4, l. 5.

It is pleasant to go mad. (Insanire juvat.)
HORACE, *Odes.* Bk. iii, ode 19, l. 18.

There is a pleasure sure
In being mad, which none but madmen know.
DRYDEN, *The Spanish Friar.* Act ii, sc. 1.

16 O thou who art greatly mad, spare the lesser madman! (O major tandem parcas, insane, minori!)
HORACE, *Satires.* Bk. ii, sat. 3, l. 326.

17 He prepares to go mad with fixed rule and method. (Insanire paret certa ratione modoque.)
HORACE, *Satires.* Bk. ii, sat. 3, l. 271.

Though this be madness, yet there is method in 't.
SHAKESPEARE, *Hamlet.* Act ii, sc. 2, l. 208.

If she be mad,—as I believe no other,—
Her madness hath the oddest frame of sense . . .
As e'er I heard in madness.
SHAKESPEARE, *Measure for Measure.* Act v, sc. 1, l. 60.

O, matter and impertinancy mix'd!
Reason in madness!
SHAKESPEARE, *King Lear*. Act iv, sc. 6, l. 179.

1 All power of fancy over reason is a degree of insanity.
SAMUEL JOHNSON, *Rasselas*. Ch. 44.

2 With the mad it is necessary to be mad. (Necesse est cum insanientibus furere.)
PETRONIUS ARBITER, *Satyricon*.

3 The different sorts of madness are innumerable. (Maniæ infinitæ sunt species.)
RABELAIS, *Works:* Bk. v, *Prologue*. Quoted as a saying of Avicenna, an Arabic physician (980–1037), author of many treatises on medicine.

4 I am but mad north-north-west: when the wind is southerly I know a hawk from a handsaw.
SHAKESPEARE, *Hamlet*. Act ii, sc. 2, l. 396.

I am not mad; I would to heaven I were!
SHAKESPEARE, *King John*. Act iii, sc. 4, l. 48.

5 Though I am mad, I will not bite him.
SHAKESPEARE, *Antony and Cleopatra*. Act ii, sc. 3, l. 80.

6 Madness in great ones must not unwatch'd go.
SHAKESPEARE, *Hamlet*. Act iii, sc. 1, l. 197.

7 My wits begin to turn.
SHAKESPEARE, *King Lear*. Act iii, sc. 2, l. 67.

His wits begin to unsettle. . . . His wits are gone.
SHAKESPEARE, *King Lear*. Act iii, sc. 6, l. 67.

8 That way madness lies.
SHAKESPEARE, *King Lear*. Act iii, sc. 4, l. 21.

9 You will never run mad, niece;
No, not till a hot January.
SHAKESPEARE, *Much Ado About Nothing*. Act i, sc. 1, l. 93.

You'll never be mad, you are of so many minds.
SWIFT, *Polite Conversation*. Dial. i.

10 Fetter strong madness in a silken thread.
SHAKESPEARE, *Much Ado About Nothing*. Act v, sc. 1, l. 25.

11 Have we eaten on the insane root
That takes the reason prisoner?
SHAKESPEARE, *Macbeth*. Act i, sc. 3, l. 84.

12 I have heard my grandsire say full oft,
Extremity of griefs would make men mad;
And I have read that Hecuba of Troy
Ran mad for sorrow.
SHAKESPEARE, *Titus Andronicus*. Act iv, sc. 1, l. 18.

13 This is very midsummer madness.
SHAKESPEARE, *Twelfth Night*. Act iii, sc. 4, l. 61.

14 A little while, and the event will show
To all the world if I be mad or no.
SOLON, *Fragments*. No. 10. (DIOGENES LAERTIUS, *Solon*. Sec. 5.)

15 What madness has seized you? (Quæ te dementia cepit?)
VERGIL, *Eclogues*. No. vi, l. 47.

II—Madness: All Men Are Mad

16 You yourself are mad, and so are all fools. (Insanis et tu stultique prope omnes.)
HORACE, *Satires*. Bk. ii, sat. 3, l. 32.

Come hither, nearer to me, whilst I show you all that you are mad. (Huc propius me, Dum doceo insanire omnis, vos ordine, adite.)
HORACE, *Satires*. Bk. ii, sat. 3, l. 80.

He appears mad indeed but to a few, because the majority is infected with the same disease. (Nimirum insanus paucis videatur, eo quod Maxima pars hominum morbo jactatur eodem.)
HORACE, *Satires*. Bk. ii, sat. 3, l. 120.

17 It is a common calamity; we are all mad at some time or other. (Id commune malum; semel insanivimus omnes.)
JOHANNES BAPTISTA MANTUANUS, *Eclogues*. No. 1. *See* BOSWELL, *Johnson*, 30 March, 1783.

18 Men are mad so unavoidably that not to be mad would constitute one a madman of another order of madness.
PASCAL, *Pensées*. Pt. ii, art. xvii, No. 88.

19 My dear Sir, take any road, you can't go amiss. The whole state is one vast insane asylum.
JAMES L. PETIGRU, in 1860, when asked the way to the Charleston, S. C., insane asylum. The state was preparing for secession from the Union.

20 Can it be that they are mad themselves, since they call me mad? (An ille perperam insanire me aiunt, ipsi insaniunt?)
PLAUTUS, *Menæchmi*, l. 962.

Every madman thinks all other men mad. (Insanus omnis furere credit ceteros.)
PUBLILIUS SYRUS, *Sententiæ*.

21 Man's state implies a necessary curse;
When not himself, he's mad; when most himself, he's worse.
FRANCIS QUARLES, *Emblems*. Bk. ii, emblem 14.

22 I think for my part one-half of the nation is mad—and the other not very sound.
SMOLLETT, *The Adventures of Sir Launcelot Greaves*. Ch. 6.

III—Madness and the Gods

23 Reckless madness from the gods. (Εἶτ' οὖν ἀσαλῆς θεόθεν μανία.)
ÆSCHYLUS. *Fragments*. Frag. 179.

Whom the gods destroy, they first make mad. (Ὃν θεὸς θέλει ἀπόλεσαι, πρῶτ' ἀπόφρεναι.)

EURIPIDES, *Fragment*. (BOSWELL, *Life of Johnson*, 1783. Note.)

Whom God would destroy, he first makes mad. (Quem deus vult perdere, prius dementat.)

The Latin version of the Greek maxim, based probably on Euripides, though Plutarch (*De Audiend. Poet.*, 106) has preserved the adage as a fragment of Æschylus.

Though rashness can hope for but one result,
We are heedless, when fate draws nigh us;
And the maxim holds good, *Quem perdere vult*
Deus, dementat prius.

ADAM LINDSAY GORDON, *Ye Wearie Wayfarer*. Fytte 2.

Whom the Gods would destroy they first make mad.

LONGFELLOW, *Masque of Pandora*. Pt. vi, l. 58.

1
For those whom God to ruin has design'd,
He fits for Fate, and first destroys their mind.

DRYDEN, *Hind and Panther*. Pt. iii, l. 1093.

2
Zeus has robbed him of his wits. (Ἐκ γάρ οἱ φρένας εἵλετο μητίετα Ζεύς.)

HOMER, *Iliad*. Bk. ix, l. 377.

3
When falls on man the anger of the gods,
First from his mind they banish understanding.

LYCURGUS, *In Leocratem*. Ch. xxi, sec. 92. Quoted as "from one of the old poets."

4
Whom fate wishes to ruin she first makes mad. (Stultum facit fortuna quem vult perdere.)

PUBLILIUS SYRUS, *Sententiæ*. No. 479.

5
Whom the gods intend to make miserable, they lead to error. (Τὸ κακὸν δοκεῖν ποτ' ἐσθλὸν τῷδ' ἔμμεν ὅτῳ φρένας θεὸς ἄγει πρὸς ἄταν.)

SOPHOCLES, *Antigone*, l. 621. Quoted as a saying.

Whom Jupiter would destroy, he first drives mad. (Quem Juppiter vult perdere, dementat primus.)

SOPHOCLES, *Antigone*. (Johnson, tr.)

IV—Madness: Its Terrors

6
Babylon in ruins is not so melancholy a spectacle.

ADDISON, *The Spectator*. No. 421.

Babylon in all its desolation is a sight not so awful as that of the human mind in ruins.

S. B. DAVIES, *Letter to Thomas Raikes*, 25 May, 1835.

7
Today I had a strange warning. I felt the wing of insanity brush my mind.

CHARLES BAUDELAIRE, *Journal*, 23 Jan., 1862.

8
No skill in swordsmanship, however just,
Can be secure against a madman's thrust.

COWPER, *Charity*, l. 509.

9
I stept into Bedlam, where I saw several poor miserable creatures in chains; one of them was mad with making verses.

JOHN EVELYN, *Diary*, 21 April, 1657.

The present state of insane persons, confined within this commonwealth, in cages, closets, cellars, stalls, pens! Chained, naked, beaten with rods, and lashed into obedience.

DOROTHEA LYNDE DIX, Memorial to the Legislature of Massachusetts, 1843, p. 4.

I have myself seen more than nine thousand idiots, epileptics and insane in the United States . . . bound with galling chains, bowed beneath fetters, lacerated with ropes, scourged with rods.

DOROTHEA LYNDE DIX, First petition to Congress. (*Senate Misc. Doc.*, No. 150, 30 Cong. 1st Sess.)

O hark! what mean these yells and cries?
His chain some furious madman breaks;
He comes—I see his glaring eyes;
Now, now, my dungeon grate he shakes.
Help! help!—He's gone! O fearful woe,
Such screams to hear, such sights to see!
My brain, my brain!—I know, I know
I am *not* mad, but soon *shall* be.

MATTHEW GREGORY LEWIS, *The Maniac*.

10
Mad in the judgment of the mob, sane, perhaps, in yours. (Demens Judicio vulgi, sanus fortasse tuo.)

HORACE, *Satires*. Bk. i, sat. 6, l. 97.

Much madness is divinest sense
To a discerning eye;
Much sense the starkest madness.
'Tis the majority
In this, as all, prevails
Assent, and you are sane;
Demur,—you're straightway dangerous,
And handled with a chain.

EMILY DICKINSON, *Poems*. Pt. i, No. 11.

11
Not so much of thee is left among us
As the hum outliving the hushed bell.

J. R. LOWELL, *The Darkened Mind*. Referring to his mother, who had become insane.

12
Demoniac frenzy, moping melancholy,
And moon-struck madness.

MILTON, *Paradise Lost*. Bk. xi, l. 485.

13
Of all mad creatures, if the learn'd are right,
It is the slaver kills, and not the bite.

POPE, *Epistle to Dr. Arbuthnot*, l. 105.

14
That he is mad, 't is true: 't is true 't is pity;
And pity 't is 't is true.

SHAKESPEARE, *Hamlet*. Act ii, sc. 2, l. 97.

15
O, let me not be mad, not mad, sweet heaven!
Keep me in temper: I would not be mad!

SHAKESPEARE, *King Lear*. Act i, sc. 5, l. 50.

V—Madness and Sanity

16
Who then is sane? He who is not a fool

(Quisnam igitur sanus? Qui non stultus.)
HORACE, *Satires*. Bk. ii, sat. 3, l. 158.

1
Sanity consists in not being subdued by your means.
EMERSON, *Conduct of Life: Considerations by the Way*.

Sanity is a madness put to good uses.
GEORGE SANTAYANA, *Little Essays*, p. 146.

2
He who can simulate sanity will be sane. (Qui poterit sanum fingere, sanus erit.)
OVID, *Remediorum Amoris*, l. 504.

3
It is not madness
That I have utter'd: bring me to the test,
And I the matter will re-word; which madness
Would gambol from.
SHAKESPEARE, *Hamlet*. Act iii, sc. 4, l. 141.

4
Every man has a sane spot somewhere.
R. L. STEVENSON AND LLOYD OSBOURNE, *The Wrecker*.

MAID

See also Chastity, Girl, Virgin

5
Maidens' hearts are always soft:
Would that men's were truer!
BRYANT, *Song*.

6
I once was a maid, though I cannot tell when,
And still my delight is in proper young men.
BURNS, *The Jolly Beggars*.

7
The cloistered maiden. (Ἡ παῖς ἡ κατάκλειστος.)
CALLIMACHUS, *Fragmenta Incertæ*. No. 14.

8
A maid and a virgin is not all one.
JOHN CLARKE, *Paræmiologia*, p. 152.

All are not maidens that wear fair hair.
JOHN RAY, *English Proverbs*.

9
A tender, timid maid, who knew not how
To pass a pig-sty, or to face a cow.
GEORGE CRABBE, *Tales: The Widow's Tale*, l. 3.

10
The desire to please everything having eyes seems inborn in maidens.
SALOMON GESSNER, *Evander and Alcina*, iii, 1.

11
Is a maiden all the better when she's tough?
W. S. GILBERT, *The Mikado*. Act ii.

12
Tell me, pretty maiden, are there any more at home like you?
LESLIE STUART, *Tell Me, Pretty Maiden*. The beginning of the famous sextet from *Florodora*, which opened in New York, October, 1900.

Tell me, are there any more at home like you?
Disposition shady, But a perfect lady,
A beginner but a winner, Mamie!
WILL D. COBB, *Mamie*. (1901)

13
Maids' nays are nothing; they are shy
But do desire what they deny.
ROBERT HERRICK, *Maids' Nays Are Nothing*.
See also WOMAN: A WOMAN'S NO.

14
Ye have no more merit in mass nor in hours
Than Malkin of her maidenhead that no man desireth.
LANGLAND, *Piers Plowman*, i, 181. (c. 1377)

There be more maids than Mawkin, more men than Hodge, and more fools than Firk.
THOMAS DEKKER, *Shoemaker's Holiday*. Act iii, sc. 1. (1600)

15
And, when once the young heart of a maiden is stolen,
The maiden herself will steal after it soon.
THOMAS MOORE, *Ill Omens*.

16
Men often deceive; but tender maids not often. (Sæpe viri fallunt; teneræ non sæpe puellæ.)
OVID, *Ars Amatoria*. Bk. iii, l. 31.

I know a maiden fair to see,
Take care!
She can both false and friendly be,
Beware! Beware!
Trust her not, She is fooling thee!
LONGFELLOW, *Beware! (Hüt du Dich!)*

17
What tender maid but must a victim fall
To one man's treat, but for another's ball?
POPE, *The Rape of the Lock*. Canto i, l. 95

For what sad maiden can endure to seem
Set in for singleness?
THOMAS HOOD, *Bianca's Dream*.

18
Warn'd by the Sylph, O pious maid, beware!
This to disclose is all thy guardian can:
Beware of all, but most beware of man!
POPE, *The Rape of the Lock*. Canto i, l. 112.

And she who scorns a man must die a maid.
POPE, *The Rape of the Lock*. Canto v, l. 28.

19
A maid that laughs is half taken.
JOHN RAY, *English Proverbs*.

A maid that taketh yieldeth.
JOHN RAY, *English Proverbs*.

20
A maid often seen, a gown often worn,
Are disesteemed and held in scorn.
JOHN RAY, *English Proverbs*.

Be somewhat scanter of your maiden presence.
SHAKESPEARE, *Hamlet*. Act i, sc. 3, l. 121.

21
What shall be the maiden's fate?
Who shall be the maiden's mate?
SCOTT, *Lay of the Last Minstrel*. Canto i, st. 16

22
I am a simple maid, and therein wealthiest,
That I protest I simply am a maid.
SHAKESPEARE, *All's Well that Ends Well*. Act ii, sc. 3, l. 72.

1
The chariest maid is prodigal enough,
If she unmask her beauty to the moon.
SHAKESPEARE, *Hamlet*. Act i, sc. 3, l. 36.

The maid who modestly conceals
Her beauties, while she hides, reveals:
Gives but a glimpse, and fancy draws
Whate'er the Grecian Venus was.
EDWARD MOORE, *The Spider and the Bee*. Fable 10.

2
A maid yet rosed over with the virgin crimson of modesty.
SHAKESPEARE, *Henry V*. Act v, sc. 2, l. 323.

A most unspotted lily shall she pass
To the ground, and all the world shall mourn her.
SHAKESPEARE, *Henry VIII*. Act v, sc. 5, l. 62.

A maid of grace and complete majesty.
SHAKESPEARE, *Love's Labour's Lost*. Act i, sc. 1, l. 137.

An honest maid as ever broke bread.
SHAKESPEARE, *The Merry Wives of Windsor*. Act i, sc. 4, l. 161.

No maiden is more worthy of your choir. (Dignior est vestro nulla puella choro.)
TIBULLUS, *Elegies*. Bk. iii, eleg. 8, l. 24.

3
Not all the dukes of waterish Burgundy
Can buy this unprized precious maid of me.
SHAKESPEARE, *King Lear*. Act i, sc. 1, l. 261.

Here by God's rood is the one maid for me.
TENNYSON, *Geraint and Enid*, l. 368.

4
She that's a maid now, and laughs at my departure,
Shall not be a maid long, unless things be cut shorter.
SHAKESPEARE, *King Lear*. Act i, sc. 5, l. 55.

How go maidenheads?
SHAKESPEARE, *Troilus and Cressida*. Act iv, sc. 2, l. 24.

5
And let him learn to know, when maidens sue,
Men give like gods.
SHAKESPEARE, *Measure for Measure*. Act i, sc. 4, l. 80.

6
Neither maid, widow, nor wife.
SHAKESPEARE, *Measure for Measure*. Act v, sc. 1, l. 178.

Widowed wife, and wedded maid,
Betrothed, betrayer, and betrayed.
SCOTT, *The Betrothed*. Ch. 15.

7
And the imperial votaress passed on,
In maiden meditation, fancy-free.
SHAKESPEARE, *A Midsummer-Night's Dream*. Act ii, sc. 1, l. 163.

8
A maiden never bold;
Of spirit so still and quiet, that her motion
Blush'd at itself.
SHAKESPEARE, *Othello*. Act i, sc. 3, l. 94.

A maid
That paragons description and wild fame;
One that excels the quirks of blazoning pens,
And in the essential vesture of creation
Does tire the ingener.
SHAKESPEARE, *Othello*. Act ii, sc. 1, l. 61.

9
The spinsters and the knitters in the sun
And the free maids that weave their thread with bones.
SHAKESPEARE, *Twelfth Night*. Act ii, sc. 4, l. 45.

Maidens withering on the stalk.
WORDSWORTH, *Personal Talk*. St. 1.

Women, dying maids, lead apes in hell.
UNKNOWN, *The London Prodigal*. Act i, sc. 2.
See also under APE.

10
She's pretty to walk with:
And witty to talk with:
And pleasant too to think on.
SIR JOHN SUCKLING, *Brennoralt*. Act ii, sc. 1.

11
A simple maiden in her flower
Is worth a hundred coats-of-arms.
TENNYSON, *Lady Clara Vere de Vere*.

Mother, a maiden is a tender thing,
And best by her that bore her understood.
TENNYSON, *The Marriage of Geraint*, l. 510.

12
The sweetest garland to the sweetest maid.
THOMAS TICKELL, *To a Lady with a Present of Flowers*.

13
Glass and a maid are ever in danger.
TORRIANO, *Piazza Universale*, 304.

Glasses and lasses are brittle ware.
A. B. CHEALES, *Proverbial Folk-Lore*, 4.

14
And never maiden stoops to him
Who lifts himself to her.
WHITTIER, *Amy Wentworth*.

15
A maid should be seen but not heard.
UNKNOWN, *Mirk's Festival*, 230. (c. 1400)

Little gells must be seen and not heard.
GEORGE ELIOT, *Janet's Repentance*. Ch. 8.

Maidens must be mild and meek,
Swift to hear and slow to speak.
THOMAS FULLER, *Gnomologia*. No. 6410.

Maidens should be mim till they're married.
BRIDGE, *Cheshire Proverbs*, p. 93.

A maiden hath no tongue but thought.
SHAKESPEARE, *The Merchant of Venice*. Act iii, sc. 2, l. 8.

16
My son, I've travelled round the world
And many maids I've met:
There are two kinds you should avoid—
The blonde and the brunette.
UNKNOWN, *A Warning*.

MAIDENHOOD

17
A damsel with a dulcimer
In a vision once I saw:

It was an Abyssinian maid,
And on her dulcimer she played,
Singing of Mount Abora.
S. T. COLERIDGE, *Kubla Khan*, l. 37.

1
She's neither proud nor saucy yet,
She's neither plump nor gaucy yet;
But just a jinking,
Bonny blinking,
Hilty-skilty lassie yet.
JAMES HOGG, *My Love She's but a Lassie Yet.*

2
She stood breast-high amid the corn,
Clasp'd by the golden light of morn,
Like the sweetheart of the sun,
Who many a glowing kiss had won.
HOOD, *Ruth.*

3
Maiden! with the meek, brown eyes,
In whose orbs a shadow lies
Like the dusk in evening skies!

Thou whose locks outshine the sun,
Golden tresses, wreathed in one,
As the braided streamlets run!

Standing, with reluctant feet,
Where the brook and river meet,
Womanhood and childhood fleet!
LONGFELLOW, *Maidenhood.*

Bear a lily in thy hand;
Gates of brass cannot withstand
One touch of that magic wand.
LONGFELLOW, *Maidenhood.*

4
She walks—the lady of my delight—
A shepherdess of sheep.
Her flocks are thoughts. She keeps them white;
She guards them from the steep.
She feeds them on the fragrant height,
And folds them in for sleep.
ALICE MEYNELL, *The Shepherdess.*

5
The rare and radiant maiden, whom the angels name Lenore—
Nameless here for evermore.
EDGAR ALLAN POE, *The Raven.*

6
She dwelt among the untrodden ways
Beside the springs of Dove,
A maid whom there were none to praise
And very few to love.
WORDSWORTH, *Lucy*. Pt. ii.

MAJORITY AND MINORITY

7
When bad men combine, the good must associate; else they will fall one by one, an unpitied sacrifice in a contemptible struggle.
EDMUND BURKE, *Thoughts on the Cause of the Present Discontents.*

8
To be in the weakest camp is to be in the strongest school.
G. K. CHESTERTON, *Heretics.*

9
A majority is always the best repartee.
BENJAMIN DISRAELI, *Tancred.* Bk. ii, ch. 14.

10
Shall we judge a country by the majority, or by the minority? By the minority, surely.
EMERSON, *Conduct of Life: Considerations by the Way.*

11
All history is a record of the power of minorities, and of minorities of one.
EMERSON, *Letters and Social Aims: Progress of Culture.*

That cause is strong which has not a multitude, but one strong man behind it.
J. R. LOWELL, *Address*, Chelsea, Mass., 22 Dec., 1885.

12
Decision by majorities is as much an expedient as lighting by gas.
W. E. GLADSTONE, *Speech*, House of Commons, 21 Jan., 1858.

13
The oppression of a majority is detestable and odious: the oppression of a minority is only by one degree less detestable and odious.
GLADSTONE, *Speech*, House of Commons, 1870. on Irish Land Bill.

The most dangerous foe to truth and freedom in our midst is the compact majority. Yes, the damned, compact, liberal majority.
HENRIK IBSEN, *An Enemy of the People.* Act iv.

The only tyrannies from which men, women and children are suffering in real life are the tyrannies of minorities.
THEODORE ROOSEVELT, *Speech*, New York City, 20 March, 1912.

The great mass of the people are in more danger of having their rights invaded and their liberties destroyed by the overweening influence of organized minorities, who have fanatical or selfish interests to serve, than by the force of an unthinking or cruel majority.
OSCAR W. UNDERWOOD, *Drifting Sands of Party Politics*, p. 6.

14
Minority is no disproof:
Wisdom is not so strong and fleet
As never to have known defeat.
LAURENCE HOUSMAN, *Advocatus Diaboli.*

15
The minority is always in the right.
HENRIK IBSEN, *An Enemy of the People.* Act iv.

The majority never has right on its side.
HENRIK IBSEN, *An Enemy of the People.* Act iv.

The opinion of the majority is not the final proof of what is right. (Nicht Stimmenmehrheit ist des Rechtes Probe.)
SCHILLER. (Quoted by H. D. SEDGWICK, *In Praise of Gentlemen.* Title page.)

When great changes occur in history, when great principles are involved, as a rule the majority are wrong.
EUGENE V. DEBS, *Speech*, at trial, Cleveland, O., 12 Sept., 1918.

The fact disclosed by a survey of the past that majorities have been wrong, must not blind us to the complementary fact that majorities have usually not been entirely wrong.

HERBERT SPENCER, *First Principles*. Ch. 1, sec. 1.

1
If by the mere force of numbers a majority should deprive a minority of any clearly written constitutional right, it might, in a moral point of view, justify revolution—certainly would if such a right were a vital one.

ABRAHAM LINCOLN, *First Inaugural Address*, 4 March, 1861.

2
Safer with multitudes to stray,
Than tread alone a fairer way:
To mingle with the erring throng,
Than boldly speak ten millions wrong.

ROBERT NUGENT, *Epistle to a Lady*. *See also* PEOPLE: APOTHEGMS.

3
One, of God's side, is a majority.

WENDELL PHILLIPS, *Speech on John Brown*, Harper's Ferry, 1 Nov., 1859.

One, with God, is always a majority, but many a martyr has been burned at the stake while the votes were being counted.

THOMAS B. REED. (W. A. ROBINSON, *Life*.)

4
Governments exist to protect the rights of minorities. The loved and the rich need no protection,—they have many friends and few enemies.

WENDELL PHILLIPS, *Address*, Boston, 21 Dec., 1860.

5
How a minority,
Reaching majority,
Seizing authority,
Hates a minority!

LEONARD H. ROBBINS, *Minorities*.

6
A majority, with a good cause, are negligent and supine.

SWIFT, *Letter to a Member of Parliament in Ireland*, 1708.

THE SILENT MAJORITY, *see under* DEATH.

MALICE

See also Slander

7
In charity to all, bearing no malice or ill-will to any human being.

J. Q. ADAMS, *Letter to A. Bronson*, 30 July, 1838.

With malice toward none, with charity for all, with firmness in the right, as God gives us to see the right.

ABRAHAM LINCOLN, *Second Inaugural Address*, 4 March, 1865.

8
Malice seldom wants a mark to shoot at

H. G. BOHN, *Hand-Book of Proverbs*.

9
Vengeful malice, unrepenting.

BURNS, *A Winter Night*.

10
Malice never spoke well.

WILLIAM CAMDEN, *Remains*, p. 328.

11
Malice is cunning. (Est malitia versuta.)

CICERO, *De Natura Deorum*. Bk. iii, sec. 30.

Malice is pleasure derived from another's evil which brings no advantage to oneself. (Malevolentia sit voluptas ex malo alterius sine emolumento suo.)

CICERO, *Tusculanarum Disputationum*. Bk. iv, ch. 9, sec. 20.

12
Malice hath a strong memory.

THOMAS FULLER, *Pisgah Sight*. Bk. ii, ch. 3.

Malice is mindful.

THOMAS FULLER, *Gnomologia*. No. 3329.

Malice drinketh up the greatest part of its own poison.

THOMAS FULLER, *Gnomologia*. No. 3327.

13
Malice is blind. (Cæca invidia est.)

LIVY, *History*. Bk. xxxviii, sec. 49.

14
Malice feeds on the living. (Pascitur in vivis livor.)

OVID, *Amores*. Bk. i, eleg. 15, l. 39.

15
Biting malice. (Invidia mordax.)

PHÆDRUS, *Fables*: Bk. v, fab. 2, *Prologue*.

Venomous malice.

SHAKESPEARE, *Titus Andronicus*. Act v, sc. 3, l. 13.

The very fangs of malice.

SHAKESPEARE, *Twelfth Night*. Act i, sc. 5, l. 196.

16
Malice tells that which it sees, but not the causes. (Invidia loquitur quod videt, non quod subest.)

PUBLILIUS SYRUS, *Sententiæ*. No. 294.

The malice of one man quickly becomes the ill word of all. (Malitia unius cito fit maledictum omnium.)

PUBLILIUS SYRUS, *Sententiæ*. No. 397.

17
He who digs out malicious talk disturbs his own peace. (Qui malignos sermones inquirit se ipse inquietat.)

SENECA, *De Ira*. Bk. iii, sec. 11.

18
The malice of this age.

SHAKESPEARE, *II Henry IV*. Act i, sc. 2, l. 195.

The malice of mankind.

SHAKESPEARE, *Timon of Athens*. Act iv, sc. 3, l. 456.

19
Men that make
Envy and crooked malice nourishment,
Dare bite the best.

SHAKESPEARE, *Henry VIII*. Act v, sc. 3, l. 43.

Malice bears down truth.

SHAKESPEARE, *The Merchant of Venice*. Act iv, sc. 1, l. 214.

1
Speak of me as I am; nothing extenuate,
Nor set down aught in malice.
SHAKESPEARE, *Othello*. Act v, sc. 2, l. 342.

No levell'd malice
Infects one comma in the course I hold.
SHAKESPEARE, *Timon of Athens*. Act i, sc. 1, l. 47.

2
Wit larded with malice, and malice forced with wit.
SHAKESPEARE, *Troilus and Cressida*. Act v, sc. 1, l. 63.

Much malice mingl'd with a little wit.
DRYDEN, *The Hind and the Panther*. Pt. iii, l. 1.

3
The malice of a good thing is the barb that makes it stick.
SHERIDAN, *The School for Scandal*. Act i, sc. 1.

4
Yet malice never was his aim;
He lashed the vice, but spared the name.
No individual could resent,
Where thousands equally were meant.
SWIFT, *On the Death of Dr. Swift*, l. 523.

To spare the persons, but to publish the crimes. (Parcere personis, dicere de vitiis.)
MARTIAL, *Epigrams*. Bk. x, ep. xxxiii, l. 10.

5
There is such malice in men as to rejoice in misfortunes, and from another's woes to draw delight.
TERENCE, *Andria*. Act iv, sc. 1, l. 1.

Ah yet, we cannot be kind to each other here for an hour;
We whisper and hint, and chuckle, and grin at a brother's shame.
TENNYSON, *Maud*. Pt. i, sec. 4, st. 5.

6
Malice . . . the basest of all instincts, passions, vices—the most hateful.
MARK TWAIN, *The Character of Man*.

MAMMON

See also Gold, Riches

7
Pray'st thou for riches? Away, away!
This is the throne of Mammon grey.
WILLIAM BLAKE, *I Rose Up at the Dawn of Day*.

8
Midas-eared Mammonism, double-barrelled Dilettantism, and their thousand adjuncts and corollaries, are *not* the Law by which God Almighty has appointed this His universe to go.
CARLYLE, *Past and Present*. Ch. 6.

9
Cursed Mammon be, when he with treasures
To restless action spurs our fate!
Cursed when for soft, indulgent leisures,
He lays for us the pillows straight.
GOETHE, *Faust*. (Taylor, tr.)

10
Ye cannot serve God and mammon.
New Testament: Matthew, vi, 24; *Luke*, xvi, 13.

Poor souls! whose God is Mammon.
THOMAS EDWARD BROWN, *Per Omnia Deus*.

A slave unto Mammon makes no servant unto God.
SIR THOMAS BROWNE, *Christian Morals*. Pt. i, sec. 8.

Those who set out to serve both God and Mammon soon discover that there is no God.
LOGAN PEARSALL SMITH, *Afterthoughts*.

11
Mammon led them on,
Mammon, the least erected Spirit that fell
From heav'n; for ev'n in heav'n his looks and thoughts
Were always downward bent, admiring more
The riches of heav'n's pavement, trodden gold,
Than aught divine or holy else enjoy'd
In vision beatific.
MILTON, *Paradise Lost*. Bk. i, l. 678.

"Mammon leads me on"—Milton—Hem!
GEORGE COLMAN THE YOUNGER, *The Heir-at-Law*. Act iii, sc. 2.

12
Who sees pale Mammon pine amidst his store,
Sees but a backward steward for the poor.
POPE, *Moral Essays*. Epis. iii, l. 171.

13
What treasures here do Mammon's sons behold!
Yet know that all that which glitters is not gold.
FRANCIS QUARLES, *Emblems*. Bk. ii, emb. 5. *See also under* APPEARANCE.

MAN

I—Man: Definitions

14
Good Lord, what is man? for as simple he looks,
Do but try to develop his hooks and his crooks!
With his depths and his shallows, his good and his evil;
All in all he's a problem must puzzle the devil.
BURNS, *Inscribed to the Hon. C. J. Fox*.

Are we a piece of machinery that, like the Æolian harp, passive, takes the impression of the passing accident? Or do these workings argue something within us above the trodden clod?
BURNS, *Letter to Mrs. Dunlop*, 1 Jan., 1789.

15
Admire, exult—despise—laugh, weep,—for here
There is such matter for all feeling:—Man!
Thou pendulum betwixt a smile and tear.
BYRON, *Childe Harold*. Canto iv, st. 109.

For ours is a most fictile world, and man is the most fingent plastic of creatures.
CARLYLE, *French Revolution*. Pt. i, bk. i, ch. 2.

1
Man is an embodied paradox, a bundle of contradictions.
C. C. COLTON, *Lacon*. No. 408.

2
Man is the genuine offspring of revolt.
COWPER, *Hope*, l. 183.

3
A Being, erect upon two legs, and bearing all the outward semblance of a man, and not of a monster.
DICKENS, *Pickwick Papers*. Ch. 34.

A wonderful fact to reflect upon that every human creature is constituted to be that profound secret and mystery to every other.
DICKENS, *A Tale of Two Cities*. Ch. 3.

The subtle man is immeasurably easier to understand than the natural man.
G. K. CHESTERTON, *Robert Browning*. Ch. 1.

4
Man is not order of nature, sack and sack, belly and members, link in a chain, nor any ignominious baggage, but a stupendous antagonism, a dragging together of the poles of the Universe.
EMERSON, *Conduct of Life: Fate*.

A man is the whole encyclopedia of facts. The creation of a thousand forests is in one acorn, and Egypt, Greece, Rome, Gaul, Britain, America, lie folded already in the first man.
EMERSON, *Essays, First Series: History*.

A man is a bundle of relations, a knot of roots, whose flower and fruitage is the world.
EMERSON, *Essays, First Series: History*.

Every man of us has all the centuries in him.
JOHN MORLEY, *Life of Gladstone*. Vol. i, p. 201.

5
Every man is an impossibility until he is born.
EMERSON, *Essays, Second Series: Experience*.

A man is a golden impossibility. The line he must walk is a hair's breadth.
EMERSON, *Essays, Second Series: Experience*.

A man is like a bit of Labrador spar, which has no lustre as you turn it in your hand until you come to a particular angle; then it shows deep and beautiful colors.
EMERSON, *Essays, Second Series: Experience*.

6
A man is a god in ruins.
EMERSON, *Nature, Addresses, and Lectures: Nature*. Ch. 8, *Prospects*. Quoted.

One definition of man is "an intelligence served by organs."
EMERSON, *Society and Solitude: Works and Days*.

Men are all inventors sailing forth on a voyage of discovery.
EMERSON, *Uncollected Lectures: Resources*.

7
Man is a little soul carrying around a corpse (Ψυχάριον εἶ βαστάζον νεκρόν.)
EPICTETUS, *Fragments*. No. 26. Quoted by Marcus Aurelius. (*Meditations*. iv, 41.)

A little soul for a little bears up this corpse which is man.
SWINBURNE, *Hymn to Proserpine*.

8
Man is Nature's sole mistake.
W. S. GILBERT, *Princess Ida*. Act i.

9
Man is one world, and hath
Another to attend him.
GEORGE HERBERT, *The Church Man*.

10
The fool of fate—thy manufacture, man.
HOMER, *Odyssey*. Bk. xx, l. 254. (Pope, tr.)

11
Man is the miracle in nature. God
Is the One Miracle to man.
JEAN INGELOW, *The Story of Doom*. Bk. vii, l. 271.

12
Man is a machine into which we put what we call food and produce what we call thought.
R. G. INGERSOLL, *The Gods*.

13
Limited in his nature, infinite in his desires, man is a fallen god who remembers the heavens.
LAMARTINE, *Méditations*. Ser. ii.

14
Man is a torch, then ashes soon,
May and June, then dead December,
Dead December, then again June.
VACHEL LINDSAY, *The Chinese Nightingale*.

15
This Being of mine, whatever it be, consists of a little flesh, a little breath, and the part which governs. (Ὅ τί ποτε τουτό εἰμι, σαρκία ἐστὶ καὶ πνευμάτιον καὶ τὸ ἡγεμονικόν.)
MARCUS AURELIUS, *Meditations*. Bk. ii, sec. 2.

16
This many-headed, divers-armed, and furiously-raging monster is man; wretched, weak and miserable man: whom, if you consider well, what is he, but a crawling, and ever-moving ants'-nest?
MONTAIGNE, *Essays*. Bk. ii, ch. 12.

What a chimera, then, is man! What a novelty! What a monster, what a chaos, what a contradiction, what a prodigy! Judge of all things, feeble worm of the earth, depositary of truth, a sink of uncertainty and error, the glory and the shame of the universe.
PASCAL, *Pensées*. Sec. vii, No. 434.

17
A pilgrim panting for the rest to come;
An exile, anxious for his native home;
A drop dissevered from the boundless sea;
A moment parted from eternity.
HANNAH MORE, *Reflections of King Hezekiah*, l. 129.

O man, strange composite of heaven and earth!
Majesty dwarf'd to baseness! fragrant flower
Running to poisonous seed! and seeming worth
Cloaking corruption! weakness mastering power!
Who never art so near to crime and shame,
As when thou hast achieved some deed of name!
JOHN HENRY NEWMAN, *The Dream of Gerontius*, l. 291.

1
Man is a rope connecting animal and superman,—a rope over a precipice. . . . What is great in man is that he is a bridge and not a goal.
NIETZSCHE, *Thus Spake Zarathustra*. Sec. 4.

2
Man's the bad child of the universe.
JAMES OPPENHEIM, *Laughter*.

3
Placed on this isthmus of a middle state,
A being darkly wise and rudely great:
With too much knowledge for the Sceptic side,
With too much weakness for the Stoic's pride, . . .
Alike in ignorance, his reason such,
Whether he thinks too little or too much;
Chaos of thought and passion, all confused;
Still by himself abused or disabused;
Created half to rise, and half to fall;
Great lord of all things, yet a prey to all;
Sole judge of truth, in endless error hurl'd;
The glory, jest, and riddle of the world!
POPE, *Essay on Man*. Epis. ii, l. 3.

A feeble unit in the middle of a threatening Infinitude.
THOMAS CARLYLE, *Sartor Resartus*. Bk. ii, ch. 7.
See also LIFE: AN ISTHMUS.

4
Man is the measure of all things. (Πάντων χρημάτων μέτρον ανθρωπος.)
PROTAGORAS. (DIOGENES LAERTIUS, *Protagoras*. Bk. ix, sec. 51.)

5
I am fearfully and wonderfully made.
Old Testament: Psalms, cxxxix, 14.

What a piece of work is a man! how noble in reason! how infinite in faculty! in form and moving how express and admirable! in action how like an angel! in apprehension how like a god! the beauty of the world! the paragon of animals! And yet, to me, what is this quintessence of dust? man delights not me: no, nor woman neither.
SHAKESPEARE, *Hamlet*. Act ii, sc. 2, l. 316.

6
Man is Heaven's masterpiece.
FRANCIS QUARLES, *Emblems*. Bk. ii, emb. 6.

Man is Creation's master-piece. But who says so?
—Man!
GAVARNI, *Apothegms*.

7
A fanged but handless spider that sucks indeed and stings, but cannot spin.
JOHN RUSKIN. (As quoted by J. M. Bruce, in *The Century Magazine*.)

8
Man is a reasoning animal. (Rationale animal est homo.)
SENECA, *Epistulæ ad Lucilium*. Epis. xli, sec. 8.

Man is but a reed, the weakest thing in nature, but he is a thinking reed. (C'est un roseau pensant.)
PASCAL, *Pensées*. Pt. i, art. iv, No. 6.

9
We are weak watery beings, standing in the midst of unrealities. (Imbecilli fluvidique inter vana constitimus.)
SENECA, *Epistulæ ad Lucilium*. Epis. lviii, 27.

10
When I beheld this I sighed, and said within myself, Surely man is a Broomstick!
SWIFT, *A Meditation upon a Broomstick*.

11
Before the beginning of years,
There came to the making of man
Time, with a gift of tears;
Grief, with a glass that ran;
Pleasure, with pain for leaven;
Summer, with flowers that fell;
Remembrance fallen from heaven,
And madness risen from hell;
Strength without hands to smite;
Love that endures for a breath;
Night, the shadow of light,
And Life, the shadow of death.
SWINBURNE, *Atalanta in Calydon: Chorus*.

12
The piebald miscellany, man.
TENNYSON, *The Princess*. Pt. v, l. 190.

An ingenious assembly of portable plumbing.
CHRISTOPHER MORLEY.

13
Of all created creatures man is the most detestable. Of the entire brood he is the only one . . . that possesses malice. . . . Also . . . he is the only creature that has a nasty mind.
MARK TWAIN, *The Character of Man*.

A nice man is a man of nasty ideas.
SWIFT, *Thoughts on Various Subjects*.

14
Man is a summer's day, whose youth and fire
Cool to a glorious evening and expire.
HENRY VAUGHAN, *Silex Scintillans: Rules and Lessons*.

15
I am an acme of things accomplished, and I am encloser of things to be.
WALT WHITMAN, *Song of Myself*. Sec. 44.

16
The Ideal Man! Oh, the Ideal Man should talk to us as if we were goddesses, and treat us as if we were children. He should refuse all our serious requests, and gratify every one of our whims. He should encourage us to have caprices, and forbid us to have missions. He should always say much more than he means,

and always mean much more than he says.
OSCAR WILDE, *A Woman of No Importance.* Act ii.

1
What then is man? The smallest part of nothing.
EDWARD YOUNG, *The Revenge.* Act iv, sc. 1.

2
To Contemplation's sober eye
Such is the race of Man:
And they that creep, and they that fly,
Shall end where they began.
Alike the Busy and the Gay
But flutter thro' life's little day.
THOMAS GRAY, *An Ode on the Spring.* St. 4.

The bloom of a rose passes quickly away,
And the pride of a Butterfly dies in a day.
JOHN CUNNINGHAM, *The Rose and the Butterfly.*

3
Is man no more than this?
SHAKESPEARE, *King Lear.* Act iii, sc. 4, l. 107.

II—Man: Apothegms

4
No one blames a man for being ugly.
ARISTOTLE, *Nicomachean Ethics.* Bk. iii, ch. 5, sec. 15.

It is a misfortune to be too handsome a man. (Nimia est miseria nimis pulchrum esse hominem.)
PLAUTUS, *Miles Gloriosus.* Act i, sc. 1, l. 68.

5
All sorts and conditions of men.
Book of Common Prayer: Prayer for all Conditions of Men; WALTER BESANT. Title of novel.

6
A man's a man for a' that!
BURNS, *For A' That and A' That.*

7
A man is the child of his works.
CERVANTES, *Don Quixote.* Bk i, ch. 20.

8
Human nature is the same all over the world; but its operations are so varied by education and habit, that one must see it in all its dresses.
LORD CHESTERFIELD, *Letters,* 2 Oct., 1747.

Modes and customs vary often, but human nature is always the same.
LORD CHESTERFIELD, *Letters,* 7 Feb., 1749.

I have seen human nature in all its forms; it is everywhere the same, but the wilder it is, the more virtuous.
EMERSON, *Conduct of Life: Worship.* Quoting a traveller.

9
A new man; an upstart. (Homo novus.)
CICERO, *De Officiis.* Bk. i, ch. 39, sec. 138.

10
One man means as much to me as a multitude, and a multitude only as much as one man.
DEMOCRITUS, *Fragments.* No. 302.

11
A man ought to compare advantageously with a river, an oak, a mountain.
EMERSON, *Conduct of Life: Fate.*

12
Nature never rhymes her children, nor makes two men alike.
EMERSON, *Essays, Second Series: Character.*

Countless the various species of mankind,
Countless the shades which sep'rate mind from mind;
No general object of desire is known,
Each has his will, and each pursues his own.
WILLIAM GIFFORD, *Perseus.*

13
Of course everybody likes and respects self-made men. It is a great deal better to be made in that way than not to be made at all.
O. W. HOLMES, *The Autocrat of the Breakfast-Table.* Ch. 1.

A self-made man; who worships his creator.
JOHN BRIGHT, of Benjamin Disraeli. Attributed also to Henry Clapp.

Our self-made men are the glory of our institutions.
WENDELL PHILLIPS, *Speech,* at Boston, 21 Dec., 1860.

14
Every man should measure himself by his own standard. (Metiri se quemque suo modulo ac pede verum est.)
HORACE, *Epistles.* Bk. i, epis. vii, l. 98.

The only competition worthy a wise man is with himself.
MRS. ANNA JAMESON, *Memoirs and Essays: Washington Allston.*

15
Man is dearer to the gods than he is to himself. (Carior est illis homo quam sibi.)
JUVENAL, *Satires.* Sat. x, l. 350.

Man was made by the Gods for them to toy and play withal.
PLATO. (MONTAIGNE, *Essays.* Bk. iii, ch. 5.)

16
After all there is but one race—humanity.
GEORGE MOORE, *The Bending of the Bough.* Act iii.

17
I teach you the Superman. Man is something which shall be surpassed. (Ich lehre euch den Übermenschen!)
NIETZSCHE, *Also Sprach Zarathustra: Intro.* Sec. 3.

Nietzsche . . . he was a confirmed Life Force worshipper. It was he who raked up the Superman, who is as old as Prometheus.
BERNARD SHAW, *Man and Superman.* Act. iii.

Surpassing in strength; super-men. (Super vires.)
TACITUS, *Germania.* Sec. 43.

18
I'm as much of a man as you are! (Tam ego homo sum quam tu.)
PLAUTUS, *Asinaria,* l. 490. (Act ii, sc. 4.)

19
You are not wood, you are not stones, but men.
SHAKESPEARE, *Julius Cæsar.* Act iii, sc. 2, l. 147.

O, the difference of man and man!
SHAKESPEARE, *King Lear*. Act iv, sc. 2, l. 26.

Ay, in the catalogue ye go for men.
SHAKESPEARE, *Macbeth*. Act iii, sc. 1, l. 92.

The human mortals.
SHAKESPEARE, *A Midsummer-Night's Dream*. Act ii, sc. 1, l. 101.

The most senseless and fit man.
SHAKESPEARE, *Much Ado About Nothing*. Act iii, sc. 3, l. 23.

III—Man: An Animal

1
Man is a noble animal, splendid in ashes, and pompous in the grave, solemnizing nativities and deaths with equal lustre, not omitting ceremonies of bravery, in the infamy of his nature.
SIR THOMAS BROWNE, *Hydriotaphia*. Ch. 5.

In brief, we all are monsters, that is, a composition of man and beast.
SIR THOMAS BROWNE, *Religio Medici*. Pt. i, sec. 55.

2
Man is a tool-using animal.
THOMAS CARLYLE, *Sartor Resartus*. Bk. i, ch. 5.

Man is a tool-making animal.
BENJAMIN FRANKLIN. (BOSWELL, *Life of Johnson*.)

3
But what a thoughtless animal is man!
WENTWORTH DILLON, *Essay on Translated Verse*, l. 252.

4
Man is the most intelligent of animals—and the most silly.
DIOGENES. (DIOGENES LAERTIUS, *Diogenes*. Bk. vi, sec. 24.)

5
How dull, and how insensible a beast
Is man, who yet would lord it o'er the rest!
DRYDEN, *Essay upon Satire*, l. 1.

Man is a brute, without the brute's rough tongue
And woodland death that kills without a sound.
None can be sure from what the race is sprung:
Its virtue is, it must go underground.
ARTHUR FIELD, *War*.

6
Every man has a wild beast within him.
FREDERICK THE GREAT, *Letter to Voltaire*, 1759.

7
Man is a *make-believe* animal—he is never so truly himself as when he is acting a part.
WILLIAM HAZLITT, *Notes of a Journey through France and Italy*, p. 246.

8
Man is a toad-eating animal.
WILLIAM HAZLITT, *Political Essays: On the Connection between Toad-Eaters and Tyrants*.

9
Man,—the aristocrat amongst the animals.
HEINE, *Wit, Wisdom, and Pathos: Italy*.

10
Man is an imitative animal. This quality is the germ of all education in him. From his cradle to his grave he is learning to do what he sees others do.
THOMAS JEFFERSON, *Writings*. Vol. ii, p. 225.

11
Man is the only animal which spits.
DONALD A. LAIRD, *There Is a Lot to Just Sitting or Standing*. (*Scientific American*, Nov., 1928.)

12
Man is a gaming animal.
CHARLES LAMB, *Essays of Elia: Mrs. Battle's Opinions on Whist*.

13
Man is the plumeless genus of bipeds, birds are the plumed.
PLATO, *Politicus*. Sec. 266.

Plato had defined man as an animal, biped and featherless, and w. s applauded. Diogenes plucked a fowl, and brought it into the lecture room with the words, "Here is Plato's man." In consequence of which there was added to the definition, "having broad nails."
DIOGENES LAERTIUS, *Diogenes*. Sec. 40.

That unfeather'd two-legged thing, a son.
DRYDEN, *Absalom and Achitophel*. Pt. i, l. 170.

14
What is a man
If his chief good, and market of his time,
Be but to sleep and feed? A beast, no more.
SHAKESPEARE, *Hamlet*. Act iv, sc. 4, l. 33.

15
Man is the only animal that esteems itself rich in proportion to the number and voracity of its parasites.
BERNARD SHAW, *Maxims for Revolutionists*.

16
Man, an animal which makes bargains.
ADAM SMITH, *The Wealth of Nations*.

17
Man is a beast when shame stands off from him.
SWINBURNE, *Phædra: Hippolytus*.

18
Man is the only animal that blushes. Or needs to.
MARK TWAIN, *Pudd'nhead Wilson's New Calendar*.

19
The only laughing animal is man.
WILLIAM WHITEHEAD, *On Ridicule*, l. 2.

For smiles from reason flow, To brute denied.
MILTON, *Paradise Lost*. Bk. ix, l. 239.

Man is the only animal that laughs and weeps; for he is the only animal that is struck with the difference between what things are, and what they ought to be.
WILLIAM HAZLITT, *Lectures on the English Comic Writers*. Lect. 1.

Aye, think! since time and life began,
Your mind has only feared and slept;
Of all the beasts they called you man
Only because you toiled and wept.
ARTURO GIOVANNITTI, *The Thinker: The Statue by Rodin*.

1
Man is the only animal that eats when he is not hungry, drinks when he is not thirsty, and makes love at all seasons.

UNKNOWN. (*Bookman,* April, 1932, p. 137.)

IV—Man: A Bubble

See also Life: A Bubble; World: A Bubble

2
What's he, born to be sick, so always dying,
That's guided by inevitable fate;
That comes in weeping, and that goes out crying;
Whose calendar of woes is still in date;
Whose life's a bubble, and in length a span;
A concert still in discords? 'Tis a man.

WILLIAM BROWNE, *Britannia's Pastorals.* Bk. i, song 2, l. 192.

3
The not-incurious in God's handiwork
(This man's-flesh he hath admirably made,
Blown like a bubble, kneaded like a paste,
To coop up and keep down on earth a space
That puff of vapour from his mouth, man's soul).

ROBERT BROWNING, *An Epistle: Karshish,* l. 2.

A drop in Ocean's boundless tide, unfathom'd waste of agony;
Where millions live their horrid lives by making other millions die.

SIR RICHARD BURTON, *Kasîdah.* Pt. iii, st. 20.

4
The bubble winked at me, and said,
"You'll miss me, brother, when you're dead."

OLIVER HERFORD, *Toast: The Bubble Winked.*

5
Like to the falling of a Star;
Or as the flights of Eagles are;
Or like the fresh Spring's gaudy hue;
Or silver drops of morning Dew;
Or like a Wind that chafes the flood;
Or Bubbles which on water stood;
Even such is Man, whose borrow'd light
Is straight call'd in, and paid to night.

The Wing blows out; the Bubble dies;
The Spring entomb'd in Autumn lies;
The Dew dries up; the Star is shot;
The Flight is past; and Man forgot.

HENRY KING (?), *Sic Vita* (*Poems,* 1657). These lines were included in Francis Beaumont's *Poems,* published in 1640; nevertheless the evidence as to their authorship favors Bishop King, whose verses were circulated in manuscript form long before they were collected and printed. For further discussion of authorship, and examples of imitations, see APPENDIX.

Like the dew on the mountain,
  Like the foam on the river,
Like the bubble on the fountain,
  Thou art gone, and for ever!

SCOTT, *The Lady of the Lake.* Canto iii, st. 16.

6
A man is a bubble, said the Greek proverb (Πομφόλυξ ὁ ἄνθρωπος) . . . descending from God and the dew of heaven, from a tear and a drop of rain.

JEREMY TAYLOR, *Holy Dying.* Ch. i, sec. 1.

How we bladders of wind strut about. We are meaner than flies; flies have their virtues, but we are nothing but bubbles. (Utres inflati ambulamus. Minoris quam muscæ sumus, muscæ tamen aliquam virtutem habent, nos non pluris sumus quam bullæ.)

PETRONIUS, *Satyricon.* Sec. 42. The last phrase is a proverb used by many writers, among them: VARRO, *De Re Rustica: Preface;* SENECA, *Apocogyntosis;* LUCAN, *Charron;* and ERASMUS, *Adagia.*

Like bubbles on the sea of matter borne,
They rise, they break, and to that sea return.

POPE, *Essay on Man.* Epis. iii, l. 19.

7
For what are men who grasp at praise sublime,
But bubbles on the rapid stream of time,
That rise, and fall, that swell, and are no more,
Born, and forgot, ten thousand in an hour?

YOUNG, *Love of Fame.* Sat. ii, l. 285.

V—Man: A Child

8
What is man? A foolish baby;
Vainly strives, and fights, and frets:
Demanding all, deserving nothing,
One small grave is all he gets.

THOMAS CARLYLE, *Cui Bono.*

9
Men are but children of a larger growth;
Our appetites are apt to change as theirs,
And full as craving too, and full as vain.

DRYDEN, *All for Love.* Act iv, sc. 1.

10
Man to the last is but a froward child;
So eager for the future, come what may,
And to the present so insensible!

SAMUEL ROGERS, *Reflections.*

11
They are but children, too; though they have gray hairs, they are, indeed, children of a larger size.

SENECA, *De Ira.* Sec. 8.

12
Man is a restless thing: still vain and wild,
Lives beyond sixty, nor outgrows the child.

ISAAC WATTS, *To the Memory of T. Gunston, Esq.,* l. 189.

VI—Man: A Shadow

13
Dark fluxion, all unfixable by thought,
A phantom dim of past and future wrought,
Vain sister of the worm—life, death, soul, clod—
Ignore thyself, and strive to know thy God!

S. T. COLERIDGE, *Self-Knowledge.*

14
We are spirits clad in veils;
  Man by man was never seen;
All our deep communing fails
  To remove the shadowy screen.

CHRISTOPHER PEARSE CRANCH, *Gnosis.*

1
We are dust and shadow. (Pulvis et umbra sumus.)
HORACE, *Odes*. Bk. iv, ode 7, l. 16.

2
Cease ye from man, whose breath is in his nostrils.
Old Testament: Isaiah, ii, 22.

3
We are none other than a moving row
Of Magic Shadow-shapes that come and go
Round with the Sun-illumined Lantern held
In Midnight by the Master of the Show.
OMAR KHAYYÁM, *Rubáiyát*. St. 68. (Fitzgerald, tr.)

4
Man is but breath and shadow, nothing more. ('Ανθρωπός ἐστι πνεῦμα καὶ σκιὰ μόνον.)
SOPHOCLES, *Fragment: Ajax Locrus*. No. 13.

5
Man is a substance clad in shadows.
JOHN STERLING, *Essays and Tales: Thoughts*.

6
Fond man! the vision of a moment made!
Dream of a dream! and shadow of a shade!
YOUNG, *Paraphrase of Job xxxviii*, l. 187.

VII—Man: The Image of God

7
God in making man intended by him to reduce all His Works back again to Himself.
MATTHEW BARKER, *Natural Theology*, p. 85.

God made man merely to hear some praise
Of what He'd done on those Five Days.
CHRISTOPHER MORLEY, *Fons et Origo*.

8
It is not fit that men should be compared with gods. (Nec divis homines componier æqumst.)
CATULLUS, *Odes*. Ode lxviii, l. 141.

Thou hast made him a little lower than the angels.
Old Testament: Psalms, viii, 5.

Men are not angels, neither are they brutes.
BROWNING, *Bishop Blougram's Apology*.

Every man is as God made him, ay, and often worse.
CERVANTES, *Don Quixote*. Pt. ii, ch. 4.

God made him, and therefore let him pass for a man.
SHAKESPEARE, *The Merchant of Venice*. Act i, sc. 2, l. 60.

9
'Twas much, that man was made like God before,
But, that God should be made like man, much more.
JOHN DONNE, *Holy Sonnets*. No. xv.

10
So God created man in his own image, in the image of God created he him.
Old Testament: Genesis, i, 27.

Man is God's image; but a poor man is
Christ's stamp to boot.
GEORGE HERBERT, *The Church-Porch*. St. 64.

11
And first the golden race of speaking men
Were by the dwellers in Olympus made;
They under Cronos lived, when he was king
In heaven. Like gods were they, with careless mind,
From toil and sorrow free, and nought they knew
Of dread old age.
HESIOD, *Works and Days*, l. 109.

12
There wanted yet the master work, the end
Of all yet done; a creature who, not prone
And brute as other creatures, but endued
With sanctity of reason, might erect
His stature, and upright with front serene
Govern the rest, self-knowing, and from thence
Magnanimous to correspond with Heav'n.
MILTON, *Paradise Lost*. Bk. vii, l. 505.

Thus while the mute creation downward bend
Their sight, and to their earthy mother tend,
Man looks aloft, and with erected eyes
Beholds his own hereditary skies.
(Pronaque quum spectent animalia cætera terram,
Os homini sublime dedit, cælumque tueri
Jussit, et erectos ad sidera tollere vultus.)
OVID, *Metamorphoses*. Bk. i, l. 84. (Dryden, tr., l. 106.)

13
What a wonderful privilege to have the weakness of a man and the serenity of a god! (Ecca res magna, habere inbecillitatem hominis, securitatem dei.)
SENECA, *Epistulæ ad Lucilium*. Epis. liii, sec. 12.

Let each man think himself an act of God,
His mind a thought, his life a breath of God.
P. J. BAILEY, *Festus: Proëm*, l. 163.

14
For a man is not as God,
But then most Godlike being most a man.
TENNYSON, *Love and Duty*, l. 30.

15
The noble man is only God's image. (Der edle Mensch ist nur ein Bild von Gott.)
LUDWIG TIECK, *Genoveva*.

VIII—Man and the Potter

See also Potter

16
This is the porcelain clay of human kind,
And therefore cast into these noble moulds.
DRYDEN, *Don Sebastian*. Act i, sc. 1.

The precious porcelain of human clay.
BYRON, *Don Juan*. Canto iv, st. 11.

17
Mankind are earthen jugs with spirits in them.
HAWTHORNE, *American Note-Books*, 1842.

18
A vase is begun; why, as the wheel goes round, does it turn out a pitcher? (Amphora

cœpit Institui: currente rota cur urceus exit?)

HORACE, *Ars Poetica*, l. 21.

1
Shall the clay say to him that fashioneth it,
What makest thou?

Old Testament: Isaiah, xlv, 9.

2
Upon the potter's flying wheel the clay
Knows not the purpose of its plasmic day;
So we upon the blindly-whirling sphere
Are shaped to ends which do not yet appear.

JAMES B. KENYON, *The Potter's Clay*.

3
For I remember stopping by the way
To watch a Potter thumbing his wet Clay:
And with its all-obliterated Tongue
It murmured—"Gently, Brother, gently, pray!"

OMAR KHAYYÁM, *Rubáiyát*. St. 37. (Fitzgerald, tr.)

Said one among them—"Surely not in vain
My substance of the common Earth was ta'en
And to this Figure moulded, to be broke,
Or trampled back to shapeless Earth again."

OMAR KHAYYÁM, *Rubáiyát*. St. 84. (Fitzgerald, tr.)

The shatter'd bowl shall know repair; the riven lute shall sound once more;
But who shall mend the clay of man, the stolen breath to man restore?

SIR RICHARD BURTON, *The Kasîdah*. Pt. ix, st. 40.

4
Hath not the potter power over the clay, of the same lump to make one vessel unto honour, and another unto dishonour?

New Testament: Romans, ix, 21.

After a momentary silence spake
Some Vessel of a more ungainly make:
"They sneer at me for leaning all awry:
What! did the Hand then of the Potter shake?"

OMAR KHAYYÁM, *Rubáiyát*. St. 86. (Fitzgerald, tr.)

All this of Pot and Potter—Tell me then,
Who is the Potter, pray, and who the Pot?

OMAR KHAYYÁM, *Rubáiyát*. St. 87. (Fitzgerald, tr.)

5
I have thought some of Nature's journeymen had made men and not made them well, they imitated humanity so abominably.

SHAKESPEARE, *Hamlet*. Act iii, sc. 2, l. 38.

6
Not for this
Was common clay ta'en from the common earth,
Moulded by God, and temper'd with the tears
Of angels to the perfect shape of man.

TENNYSON, *The Palace of Art: Introduction*.

IX—Man: His Growth

7
What? Was man made a wheel-work to wind up.
And be discharged, and straight wound up anew?
No! grown, his growth lasts; taught, he ne'er forgets;
May learn a thousand things, not twice the same.

ROBERT BROWNING, *A Death in the Desert*, l. 447.

8
Though his beginnings be but poor and low,
Thank God, a man can grow!

FLORENCE EARLE COATES, *Per Aspera*.

9
Human improvement is from within outwards.

FROUDE, *Short Studies on Great Subjects: Divus Cæsar*.

10
Men never amount to much until they outgrow their fathers' notions, sir.

LANDON CABELL GARLAND, *Response*, while Chancellor of Vanderbilt University in 1891, to a student protesting against the agnostic tendencies of a professor.

11
Man seems the only growth that dwindles here.

GOLDSMITH, *The Traveller*, l. 126.

12
In the twentieth century war will be dead, the scaffold will be dead, hatred will be dead, frontier boundaries will be dead, dogmas will be dead; man will live. He will possess something higher than all these—a great country, the whole earth, and a great hope, the whole heaven.

VICTOR HUGO, *The Future of Man*.

13
And step by step, since time began,
I see the steady gain of man.

WHITTIER, *The Chapel of the Hermits*.

14
Nature revolves, but man advances.

YOUNG, *Night Thoughts*. Night vi, l. 691.

15
Though man sits still and takes his ease,
God is at work on man;
No means, no method unemploy'd,
To bless him, if he can.

YOUNG, *Resignation*. Pt. i, st. 119.

X—Man: His Virtues

16
Man is his own star; and the soul that can
Render an honest and a perfect man,
Commands all light, all influence, all fate;
Nothing to him falls early or too late.

BEAUMONT AND FLETCHER, *The Honest Man's Fortune: Epilogue*.

17
Love, hope, fear, faith—these make humanity;
These are its sign and note and character

ROBERT BROWNING, *Paracelsus*. Pt. iii

1
Precious is man to man.
THOMAS CARLYLE, *Journal*, 26 July, 1834.

O what a miracle to man is man.
YOUNG, *Night Thoughts*. Night i, l. 85.

2
Man is a name of honour for a king.
GEORGE CHAPMAN, *Bussy d'Ambois*. Act iv, sc. 1.

3
'Tis the sublime of man,
Our noontide majesty, to know ourselves
Parts and proportions of one wondrous whole!
SAMUEL TAYLOR COLERIDGE, *Religious Musings*, l. 127.

4
The way of the superior man is threefold. but I am not equal to it. Virtuous he is free from anxieties; wise, he is free from perplexities; bold, he is free from fear.
CONFUCIUS, *Analects*. Bk. xiv, ch. 30.

5
Men in all ways are better than they seem.
EMERSON, *Essays, Second Series: New England Reformers*.

Good and bad men are each less so than they seem.
SAMUEL TAYLOR COLERIDGE, *Table Talk*. 19 April, 1830.

Few persons have courage enough to appear as good as they really are.
J. C. AND A. W. HARE, *Guesses at Truth*.

6
Every person is a bundle of possibilities and he is worth what life may get out of him before it is through.
HARRY EMERSON FOSDICK, *The Rebirth of Self*.

7
On earth there is nothing great but man; in man there is nothing great but mind.
SIR WILLIAM HAMILTON, *Lectures on Metaphysics*.

8
There was a manhood in his look,
That murder could not kill!
THOMAS HOOD, *The Dream of Eugene Aram*. St. 16.

9
Down with your pride of birth
And your golden gods of trade!
A man is worth to his mother, Earth,
All that a man has made!
JOHN G. NEIHARDT, *Cry of the People*.

10
Man never falls so low that he can see nothing higher than himself.
THEODORE PARKER, *A Lesson for the Day*.

11
How beauteous mankind is! O brave new world
That has such people in 't!
SHAKESPEARE, *The Tempest*. Act v, sc. 1, l. 183.

12
Of Life immense in passion, pulse, and power,
Cheerful, for freest action form'd under the laws divine,
The Modern Man I sing.
WALT WHITMAN, *One's-Self I Sing*.

Each of us inevitable;
Each of us limitless—each of us with his or her right upon the earth.
WALT WHITMAN, *Salut au Monde*. Sec. 11.

In thy lone and long night-watches, sky above and sea below,
Thou didst learn a higher wisdom than the babbling schoolmen know;
God's stars and silence taught thee, as His angels only can,
That the one sole sacred thing beneath the cope of heaven is Man!
WHITTIER, *The Branded Hand*. St. 9.

13
There's not a man
That lives, who hath not known his godlike hours,
And feels not what an empire we inherit
As natural beings in the strength of nature.
WORDSWORTH, *The Prelude*. Bk. iii, l. 190.

14
To none man seems ignoble, but to man.
YOUNG, *Night Thoughts*. Night iv, l. 485.

15
To you I declare the holy mystery: There is nothing nobler than humanity.
Mahābhārata, 12, 300, 20.

XI—Man: His Faults

16
It is hard for a pure and thoughtful man to live in a state of rapture at the spectacle afforded him by his fellow-creatures.
MATTHEW ARNOLD, *Essays in Criticism: Marcus Aurelius*.

17
But oh, man, man, unconstant, careless man,
Oh, subtle man, how many are thy mischiefs!
BEAUMONT AND FLETCHER, *Love's Pilgrimage*. Act iii, sc. 2.

18
Mere man.
Book of Common Prayer: Shorter Catechism.

19
A spectacle unto the world, and to angels
New Testament: I Corinthians, iv, 9.

But man, proud man,
Drest in a little brief authority,
Most ignorant of what he's most assur'd,
His glassy essence, like an angry ape,
Plays such fantastic tricks before high heaven,
As make the angels weep.
SHAKESPEARE, *Measure for Measure*. Act ii, sc. 2, l. 117.

20
The first man is of the earth, earthy.
New Testament: I Corinthians, xv, 47.

21
A man said to the universe:
"Sir, I exist!"
"However," replied the universe,

"The fact has not created in me
A sense of obligation."
STEPHEN CRANE, *War Is Kind*. Pt. iv.

1
Man's not worth a moment's pain,
Base, ungrateful, fickle, vain.
JAMES GRAINGER, *Ode to Solitude*.

2
Though every prospect pleases,
And only man is vile.
REGINALD HEBER, *From Greenland's Icy Mountains*.

Where the virgins are soft as the roses they twine,
And all, save the spirit of man, is divine.
BYRON, *The Bride of Abydos*. Canto i, st. 1.

3
There is only one grade of men; they are all contemptible.
E. W. HOWE, *A Letter from Mr. Biggs*.

4
I despise mankind in all its strata. (Ich verachte die Menschheit in allen ihren Schichten.)
ALEXANDER VON HUMBOLDT, *Conversation*, with Arago in 1812.

I hate mankind, for I think myself one of the best of them, and I know how bad I am.
SAMUEL JOHNSON. (MRS. PIOZZI, *Johnsoniana*.)

I wish I loved the Human Race;
I wish I loved its silly face;
I wish I liked the way it walks,
I wish I liked the way it talks;
And when I'm introduced to one
I wish I thought What Jolly Fun!
WALTER RALEIGH THE YOUNGER, *Impromptu*.

5
The ant herself cannot philosophize—
While man does that, and sees, and keeps a wife,
And flies, and talks, and is extremely wise.
JULIAN HUXLEY, *For a Book of Essays*.

6
Mankind has honoured its destroyers and persecuted its benefactors, building palaces for living brigands, and tombs for long-dead prophets.
DEAN W. R. INGE. (MARCHANT, *Wit and Wisdom of Dean Inge*. No. 180.)

7
Man; false man, smiling destructive man.
NATHANIEL LEE, *Theodosius*. Act iii, sc. 2, l. 50.

Trust not a man; we are by nature false,
Dissembling, subtle, cruel, and unconstant.
THOMAS OTWAY, *The Orphan*. Act ii, sc. 1.

There's no trust,
No faith, no honesty in men; all perjured,
All forsworn, all naught, all dissemblers.
SHAKESPEARE, *Romeo and Juliet*. Act iii, sc. 2, l. 85.

8
What dwarfs men are. (Homunculi quanti sunt.)
PLAUTUS, *Captivi: Prologue*, l. 51.

However we brave it out, we men are a little breed.
TENNYSON, *Maud*, l. 131.

Man that is born of woman is small potatoes and few in a hill.
RUDYARD KIPLING, *Life's Handicap: The Head of the District*. (1891)

9 Man is the only one that knows nothing, that can learn nothing without being taught.
PLINY THE ELDER, *Historia Naturalis*. Bk. vii, sec. 4.

10
O how contemptible a thing is man unless he can raise himself above humanity. (O quam contempta res est homo nisi supra humana se erexerit.)
SENECA, *Naturales Quæstiones*: Bk. i, *Preface*.

"Oh, what a vile and abject thing is man, unless he can erect himself above humanity." Here is a bon mot and a useful desire, but equally absurd. For to make the handful bigger than the hand, the armful bigger than the arm, and to hope to stride further than the stretch of our legs, is impossible and monstrous.
MONTAIGNE, *Essays*. Bk. ii, ch. 12.

Unless above himself he can
Erect himself, how poor a thing is man.
SAMUEL DANIEL, *To the Lady Margaret, Countess of Cumberland*. St. 12. Quoted by Wordsworth, *The Excursion*. Bk. iv, l. 330.

"How poor a thing is man!" alas 'tis true,
I'd half forgot it when I chanced on you.
SCHILLER, *The Moral Poet*.

11
Like a man made after supper of a cheese-paring: when a' was naked, he was, for all the world, like a forked radish, with a head fantastically carved upon it with a knife.
SHAKESPEARE, *II Henry IV*. Act iii, sc. 2, l. 332.

Defused infection of a man.
SHAKESPEARE, *Richard III*. Act i, sc. 2, l. 78.

Why, he's a man of wax.
SHAKESPEARE, *Romeo and Juliet*. Act i, sc. 3, l. 76.

12
How weak and yet how vain a thing is man,
Mean what he will, endeavour what he can!
JOHN SHEFFIELD, *An Essay on Satire*.

13
Man and his affairs, church and state and school, trade and commerce, and manufactures and agriculture, even politics, the most alarming of them all—I am pleased to see how little space they occupy in the landscape.
H. D. THOREAU, *Walking*.

14
All that I care to know is that a man is a human being—that is enough for me; he can't be any worse.
MARK TWAIN, *Concerning the Jews*.

1
Mankind, when left to themselves, are unfit for their own government.

George Washington, *Letter to Lee*, 31 Oct., 1786.

The mass of men are neither wise nor good.

John Jay, *Letter to Washington*, 27 June, 1786.

2
Man only,—rash, refined, presumptuous Man—
Starts from his rank, and mars Creation's plan!
Born the free heir of nature's wide domain,
To art's strict limits bounds his narrow'd reign;
Resigns his native rights for meaner things,
For Faith and Fetters, Laws and Priests and Kings.

Unknown, *The Progress of Man*, l. 55. (*Poetry of the Anti-Jacobin.*)

XII—Men: Most Men Are Bad

3
Most men are bad. (Οἱ πλεῖστοι κακοί.)

Bias of Priene, one of the seven wise men of Greece, who lived about 566 B.C. The phrase is said to have been inscribed on the wall of the temple at Delphi. (Diogenes Laertius, *Bias*. Sec. 88. Ausonius, *Ludus Septem Sapientum*, l. 189.) Ausonius Latinizes it: Plures mali.

By "bad" I meant uncultured men and savages, who disregard right and equity and hallowed customs.

Ausonius, *Ludus Septem Sapientum*, l. 192.

4
Bad's the best of us.

John Fletcher, *Rollo*. Act iv, sc. 2.

Bad in the best, though excellent in neither.

Shakespeare [?], *The Passionate Pilgrim*, l. 102.

5
I'm no better than the best,
And whether worse than the rest
Of my fellow-men, who knows?

Longfellow, *The Divine Tragedy: The Third Passover*. Pt. vii, l. 4.

I am as bad as the worst, but thank God I am as good as the best.

Walt Whitman.

See also Judgment: Its Fallibility.

6
Some are good, some are middling, the most are bad. (Sunt bona, sunt quædam mediocria, sunt mala plura.)

Martial, *Epigrams*. Bk. i, epig. 17, l. 1.

7
All men are bad, and in their badness reign.

Shakespeare, *Sonnets*. No. cxxi.

8
A bold bad man.

Spenser, *Faerie Queene*. Bk. i, canto i, st. 37.

9
Men might be better if we better deemed
Of them. The worst way to improve the world
Is to condemn it.

P. J. Bailey, *Festus: A Mountain Sunrise*.

10
Bad as you please,
You've felt they were God's men and women still.

Robert Browning, *A Blot in the 'Scutcheon*. Act ii.

XIII—Man: Great and Small

See also Greatness: Great and Small

11
There is a cropping-time in the generations of men, as in the fruits of the field; and sometimes, if the stock be good, there springs up for a time a succession of splendid men; and then comes a period of barrenness.

Aristotle, *Rhetoric*. Bk. ii, ch. 15, sec. 3.

12
Why each is striving, from of old,
To love more deeply than he can?
Still would be true, yet still grows cold?
—Ask of the Powers that sport with man!

They yok'd in him, for endless strife,
A heart of ice, a soul of fire;
And hurl'd him on the Field of Life,
An aimless unallay'd Desire.

Matthew Arnold, *Destiny*.

13
A man's nature runs either to herbs or weeds; therefore let him seasonably water the one, and destroy the other.

Francis Bacon, *Essays: Of Nature in Men*.

Where soil is, men grow,
Whether to weeds or flowers.

Keats, *Endymion*. Bk. ii, l. 159.

14
Tallest of boys, or shortest of men,
He stood in his stockings just four foot ten.

R. H. Barham, *Mr. Sucklethumbkin's Story*.

15
But we, who name ourselves its sovereigns, we,
Half dust, half deity, alike unfit
To sink or soar.

Byron, *Manfred*. Act i, sc. 2.

With knowledge so vast, and with judgment so strong,
No man with the half of 'em e'er went far wrong;
With passions so potent, and fancies so bright,
No man with the half of 'em e'er went quite right.

Burns, *Inscribed to the Hon. C. J. Fox*.

16
Oh we are querulous creatures! Little less
Than all things can suffice to make us happy;
And little more than nothing is enough
To discontent us.

S. T. Coleridge, *Il Zapolya*. Act i, sc. 1.

1
What the superior man seeks is in himself: what the small man seeks is in others.
CONFUCIUS, *Analects*. Bk. xv, ch. 20.

2
A man so various that he seem'd to be
Not one, but all mankind's epitome.
DRYDEN, *Absalom and Achitophel*. Pt. i, l. 545.

Man is but man; unconstant still, and various;
There's no to-morrow in him, like to-day.
DRYDEN, *Cleomenes*. Act iii, sc. 1.

3
Too good for banning, and too bad for blessing.
EMERSON, *Essays, Second Series: Manners*.

4
We are the creatures of imagination, passion and self-will, more than of reason or even of self-interest. . . . The falling of a teacup puts us out of temper for the day; and a quarrel that commenced about the pattern of a gown may end only with our lives.
WILLIAM HAZLITT, *Winterslow*. Essay No. 7.

5
I've studied men from my topsy-turvy
Close, and, I reckon, rather true.
Some are fine fellows: some, right scurvy:
Most, a dash between the two.
GEORGE MEREDITH, *Juggling Jerry*. St. 7.

6
Then say not man's imperfect, Heav'n in fault;
Say rather man's as perfect as he ought;
His knowledge measured to his state and place,
His time a moment, and a point his space.
POPE, *Essay on Man*. Epis. i, l. 69.

Virtuous and vicious ev'ry man must be,
Few in th' extreme, but all in the degree.
POPE, *Essay on Man*. Epis. ii, l. 231.

7
But men are men; the best sometimes forget.
SHAKESPEARE, *Othello*. Act ii, sc. 3, l. 241.

8
Every man is odd.
SHAKESPEARE, *Troilus and Cressida*. Act iv, sc. 5, l. 42.

9
O God, that I had loved a smaller man!
I should have found in him a greater heart.
TENNYSON, *Merlin and Vivien*, l. 860

10
We are children of splendour and fame,
Of shuddering, also, and tears;
Magnificent out of the dust we came,
And abject from the Spheres.
WILLIAM WATSON, *Ode in May*.

Man and his littleness perish, erased like an error and cancelled;
Man and his greatness survive, lost in the greatness of God.
WILLIAM WATSON, *Hymn to the Sea*. Pt. iv, l. 17.

11
Part mortal clay, and part ethereal fire,
Too proud to creep, too humble to aspire.
RICHARD WEST, *Ad Amicos*.

A spirit all compact of fire
Not gross to sink, but light, and will aspire.
SHAKESPEARE, *Venus and Adonis*, l. 149.

12
How poor, how rich, how abject, how august,
How complicate, how wonderful, is man!
How passing wonder He, who made him such!
YOUNG, *Night Thoughts*. Night i, l. 68.

So great, so mean, is man!
YOUNG, *Night Thoughts*. Night vi, l. 441.

13
He hath made the small and the great, and careth for all alike.
Apocrypha: Wisdom of Solomon, vi, 7.

XIV—Man: His Inhumanity

14
What is man's greatest bane? His brother man alone. (Pernicies homini quæ maxima? Solus homo alter.)
BIAS. (AUSONIUS [?], *Septem Sapientum Sententiæ*, l. 2.)

In the evening, when we drink together, we are men, but when daybreak comes, we arise wild beasts, preying upon each other.
AUTOMEDON (*Greek Anthology* Bk xi, epig 46.)

15
Can spirit from the tomb, or fiend from Hell,
More hateful, more malignant be than man?
JOANNA BAILLIE, *Orra* Act iii, sc. 2.

16
Of all beasts the man-beast is the worst:
To others, and himself, the cruellest foe.
RICHARD BAXTER, *Hypocrisy*.

17
And Man, whose heav'n-erected face
The smiles of love adorn—
Man's inhumanity to man
Makes countless thousands mourn.
BURNS, *Man Was Made to Mourn*. St. 7.

But why should ae man better fare,
And a' men brithers?
BURNS, *Epistle to Dr Blacklock*.

18
Blow, blow, ye winds, with heavier gust!
And freeze, thou bitter-biting frost!
Descend, ye chilly, smothering snows!
Not all your rage, as now united, shows
More hard unkindness, unrelenting,
Vengeful malice, unrepenting,
Than heaven-illumin'd Man on brother Man bestows.
BURNS, *A Winter Night* St. 7.

Freeze, freeze, thou bitter sky,
Thou dost not bite so nigh
As benefits forgot
SHAKESPEARE, *As You Like It*. Act ii, sc. 7, 186.

19
The greatest enemy to man is man.
ROBERT BURTON, *Anatomy of Melancholy*. Pt. i, sec. i, mem. 1, subs 1

1
Man's that savage beast, whose mind,
From reason to self-love declin'd,
Delights to prey upon his kind.
SIR JOHN DENHAM, *Friendship and Single Life.*

2
Man, biologically considered, . . . is the most formidable of all the beasts of prey, and, indeed, the only one that preys systematically on its own species.
WILLIAM JAMES, *Memories and Studies,* p. 301.

We are the wisest, strongest race:
Long may our praise be sung—
The only animal alive
That lives upon its young!
CHARLOTTE P. S. GILMAN, *Child Labor.*

3
Tiger with tiger, bear with bear, you'll find
In leagues offensive and defensive joined;
But lawless man the anvil dares profane,
And forge that steel by which a man is slain.
JUVENAL, *Satires,* xv, 163. (Tate, tr.)

The hunting tribes of air and earth,
Respect the brethren of their birth; . . .
Even tiger fell, and sullen bear,
Their likeness and their lineage spare,
Man, only, mars kind Nature's plan,
And turns the fierce pursuit on man.
SCOTT, *Rokeby.* Canto iii, st. 1.

Each animal,
By nat'ral instinct taught, spares his own kind;
But man, the tyrant man! revels at large,
Free-booter unrestrain'd, destroys at will
The whole creation, men and beasts his prey,
These for his pleasure, for his glory those.
WILLIAM SOMERVILLE, *Field Sports,* l. 94.

4
O shame to men! devil with devil damn'd
Firm concord holds, men only disagree
Of creatures rational.
MILTON, *Paradise Lost.* Bk. ii, l. 496.

5
Man is no man, but a wolf. (Lupus est homo, non homo.)
PLAUTUS, *Asinaria,* l. 495. (Act ii, sc. 4.) Usually quoted, "Lupus est homo homini": Man is a wolf to man. So used by Erasmus (*Adagia*), Burton (*Anatomy of Melancholy,* i, 1), and many others.

A man is a wolf to a man, that is, a devourer one of another.
JOHN NORTHBROOKE, *Dicing,* 57. (c. 1577)

We are (by our own censures) judged wolves one to another.
SIR EDWARD DYER, *Writings,* p. 90. (1585)

6
With man, most of his misfortunes are occasioned by man.
PLINY THE ELDER, *Historia Naturalis.* Bk. vii, sec. 5.

7
But just disease to luxury succeeds,
And ev'ry death its own avenger breeds;
The fury-passions from that blood began,
And turn'd on man a fiercer savage, man.
POPE, *Essay on Man.* Epis. iii, l. 165.

I wonder men dare trust themselves with men.
SHAKESPEARE, *Timon of Athens.* Act i, sc. 2, l. 44.

8
It is from his fellow man that man's everyday danger comes. . . . Man delights to ruin man. (Ab homine homini cotidianum periculum. . . . Homini perdere hominem libet.)
SENECA, *Epistulæ ad Lucilium.* Epis. ciii, sec. 2.

9
Humanity must perforce prey on itself
Like monsters of the deep.
SHAKESPEARE, *King Lear.* Act iv, sc. 2, l. 49.

10
No greater shame to man than inhumanity.
SPENSER, *Faerie Queene.* Bk. vi, canto i, st. 26.

11
And much it grieved my heart to think
What Man has made of Man.
WORDSWORTH, *Lines Written in Early Spring.*

12
Ah, how unjust to Nature and himself
Is thoughtless, thankless, inconsistent man!
YOUNG, *Night Thoughts.* Night ii, l. 112.

Man is to man, the sorest, surest ill.
YOUNG, *Night Thoughts.* Night iii, l. 217.

Inhumanity is caught from man,
From smiling man.
YOUNG, *Night Thoughts.* Night v, l. 158.

Man's revenge,
And endless inhumanities on man.
YOUNG, *Night Thoughts.* Night viii, l. 104.

13
He only fears men who does not avoid them. (Die Menschen fürchtet nur, wer sie nicht kennt.)
GOETHE, *Torquato Tasso.* Act i, sc. 2, l. 72.

XV—Man: His Life a Span

See also Life: Its Shortness

14
Ye children of man! whose life is a span
Protracted with sorrow from day to day,
Naked and featherless, feeble and querulous,
Sickly, calam'tous creatures of clay.
ARISTOPHANES, *The Birds.* (Frere, tr.)

The world is old, and thou art young; the world is large, and thou art small;
Cease, atom of a moment's span, to hold thyself an All-in-All!
SIR RICHARD BURTON, *Kasîdah.* Pt. ii, st. 21.

15
As of the green leaves on a thick tree, some fall, and some grow.
Apocrypha: Ecclesiasticus, xiv, 18.

16
The short span of life forbids us to spin out hope to any length. (Vitæ summa brevis spem nos vetat inchoare longam.)
HORACE, *Odes.* Bk. i, ode 4, l. 15.

Our days begin with trouble here,
Our life is but a span,

And cruel death is always near,
So frail a thing is man.
UNKNOWN, *The New England Primer*

Her waist is ampler than her life,
For life is but a span.
O. W. HOLMES, *My Aunt.*

1
Man passes away; his name perishes from record and recollection; his history is as a tale that is told, and his very monument becomes a ruin.
WASHINGTON IRVING, *The Sketch Book: Westminster Abbey*. Conclusion.

2
Man being in honour abideth not: he is like the beasts that perish.
Old Testament: Psalms, xlix, 12, 20.

Mark how fleeting and paltry is the estate of man,—yesterday in embryo, to-morrow a mummy or ashes. So for the hair's-breadth of time assigned to thee live rationally, and part with life cheerfully, as drops the ripe olive, extolling the season that bore it and the tree that matured it.
MARCUS AURELIUS, *Meditations*. Bk. iv, sec. 48.

3
He weaves, and is clothed with derision;
Sows, and he shall not reap;
His life is a watch or a vision
Between a sleep and a sleep.
SWINBURNE, *Atalanta in Calydon: Chorus.*

4
Man is born in vanity and sin; he comes into the world like morning mushrooms, soon thrusting up their heads into the air, . . . and as soon they turn into dust and forgetfulness.
JEREMY TAYLOR, *Holy Dying*. Ch. i, sec. 1.

All the windy ways of men
Are but dust that rises up,
And is lightly laid again.
TENNYSON, *The Vision of Sin*. Pt. iv, st. 18.

5
The feathers in a fan
are not so frail as man;
the green embossèd leaf
than man is no more brief.
HUMBERT WOLFE, *Man.*

6
Nothing in life is certain for men, children of a day. (Οὐδὲν γὰρ βιότου πιστὸν ἐφημερίοις.)
UNKNOWN, *Epitaph on Cassandra.* (*Greek Anthology*. Bk. vii, epig. 327.)

XVI—Man: His Misery

See also Misery, Tears of Men

7
Lord of himself;—that heritage of woe.
BYRON, *Lara.* Canto i, st. 2.

8
Oh, wearisome condition of humanity!
Born under one law, to another bound,
Vainly begot and yet forbidden vanity.
Created sick, commanded to be sound.
What meaneth Nature by these diverse laws?
Passion and reason, self-division's cause.
FULKE GREVILLE, *Mustapha.* Act v, sc. 4.

O suffering, sad humanity!
O ye afflicted ones, who lie
Steeped to the lips in misery,
Longing, and yet afraid to die,
Patient, though sorely tried!
LONGFELLOW, *The Goblet of Life.*

9
For men on earth 'tis best never to be born at all; or being born, to pass through the gates of Hades with all speed.
HOMER. (*Contest of Homer and Hesiod*. Sec. 316.)

A still small voice spake unto me,
"Thou art so full of misery,
Were it not better not to be?"
TENNYSON, *The Two Voices,* l. 1.

10
The lot of man: to suffer, and to die.
HOMER, *Odyssey*. Bk. iii, l. 117. (Pope, tr.)

For Fate has wove the thread of life with pain,
And twins ev'n from the birth are Misery and Man!
HOMER, *Odyssey*. Bk. vii, l. 263. (Pope, tr.)

11
Man that is born of a woman is of few days, and full of trouble. He cometh forth like a flower, and is cut down: he fleeth also as a shadow, and continueth not.
Old Testament: Job, xiv, 1, 2.

12
Where is the bottom of the misery of man?
SAMUEL JOHNSON, *The Idler*. No. 41.

Must helpless man, in ignorance sedate,
Roll darkling down the torrent of his fate?
SAMUEL JOHNSON, *Vanity of Human Wishes,* l. 345.

13
The history of mankind is little else than a narrative of designs which have failed, and hopes that have been disappointed.
SAMUEL JOHNSON, *Works*. Vol. ix, p. 398.

14
The last state of that man is worse than the first.
New Testament: Matthew, xii, 45; *Luke,* xi, 26.

The state of man: inconstancy, weariness, unrest. (Condition de l'homme: inconstance, ennui, inquiétude.)
PASCAL, *Pensées*. Sec. ii, No. 127.

15
Nothing is more wretched or more proud than man. (Homine nihil miserius, aut superbius.)
PLINY THE ELDER, *Historia Naturalis*. Bk. ii, sec. 7.

And, to conclude, I know myself a man—
Which is a proud and yet a wretched thing.
SIR JOHN DAVIES, *Nosce Teipsum.*

16
Whome'er thou shalt see wretched, know him man. (Quemcumque miserum videris, hominem scias.)
SENECA, *Hercules Furens,* l. 463.

1
But hearing oftentimes
The still, sad music of humanity.
WORDSWORTH, *Tintern Abbey*, l. 91.

XVII—Man: The Study of Man

2
It needs a man to perceive a man.
A. B. ALCOTT, *Table Talk: Creeds.*

3
He studied from the life,
And in the original perused mankind.
JOHN ARMSTRONG, *Art of Preserving Health*. Bk. iv, l. 231.

He took the suffering human race,
He read each wound, each weakness clear;
And struck his finger on the place,
And said, "Thou ailest here and here!"
MATTHEW ARNOLD, *Memorial Verses*, l. 19. Referring to Goethe.

For he pursued a lonely road,
His eyes on Nature's plan;
Neither made man too much a God,
Nor God too much a man.
MATTHEW ARNOLD, *In Memory of the Author of "Obermann."* Referring to Goethe.

4
There is a book into which some of us are happily led to look, and to look again, and never tire of looking. It is the Book of Man. You may open that book whenever and wherever you find another human voice to answer yours, and another human hand to take in your own.
WALTER BESANT, *Books Which Have Influenced Me.*

It is more necessary to study men than books. (Il est plus nécessaire d'étudier les hommes que les livres.)
LA ROCHEFOUCAULD, *Maximes Posthumes*. No. 550.

The hearts of men are their books; events are their tutors; great actions are their eloquence.
MACAULAY, *Essays: A Conversation Touching the Great Civil War.*
See also BOOKS AND MEN.

5
My favourite, I might say my only study, is man.
GEORGE BORROW, *The Bible in Spain*. Ch. 5.

6
The proper Science and Subject for Man's Contemplation is *Man* himself. (La vraie science et le vrai étude de l'homme c'est l'homme.)
CHARRON, *Of Wisdom*. Bk. i, ch. 1.

I thought that I should find plenty of companions in the study of man, and that this was the study which in truth was fit for him.
PASCAL, *Pensées*. Ch. ii, No. 144.

7
There is no Theme more plentiful to scan
Than is the glorious goodly Frame of Man.
DU BARTAS, *Devine Weekes and Workes*. Week i, day 6, l. 421. (Sylvester, tr.)

8
Human documents. (Documents humains.)
EDMOND DE GONCOURT, first used by him in 1876. (*See* GONCOURT, *La Faustin: Preface.*)

9
Let observation with extensive view,
Survey mankind from China to Peru.
SAMUEL JOHNSON, *Vanity of Human Wishes*, l. 1.

10
Whatever men do, wishes, fears, angers, pleasures, joys and different pursuits, of these is the hotch-potch of our book. (Quicquid agunt homines, votum, timor, ira, voluptas, Gaudia discursus, nostri farrago libelli est.)
JUVENAL, *Satires*. Sat. i, l. 85.

11
It is easier to know mankind in general than man individually. (Il est plus aisé de connaître l'homme en général, que de connaître un homme en particulier.)
LA ROCHEFOUCAULD, *Maximes*. No. 436.

12
Unspeakable desire to see, and know
All these his wondrous works, but chiefly Man.
MILTON, *Paradise Lost*. Bk. iii, l. 663.

A Spirit, zealous, as he seem'd, to know
More of th' Almighty's works, and chiefly Man,
God's latest image.
MILTON, *Paradise Lost*. Bk. iv, l. 565.

13
Let us, since life can little more supply
Than just to look about us and to die,
Expatiate free o'er all this scene of man;
A mighty maze! but not without a plan; . . .
Eye Nature's walks, shoot folly as it flies,
And catch the manners living as they rise;
Laugh where we must, be candid where we can,
But vindicate the ways of God to man.
POPE, *Essay on Man*. Epis. i, l. 3.

In human works, tho' labour'd on with pain,
A thousand movements scarce one purpose gain;
In God's, one single can its end produce,
Yet serve to second too some other use:
So man, who here seems principal alone,
Perhaps acts second to some sphere unknown,
Touches some wheel, or verges to some goal:
'Tis but a part we see, and not a whole.
POPE, *Essay on Man*. Epis. i, l. 53.

14
Know then thyself, presume not God to scan;
The proper study of mankind is Man.
POPE, *Essay on Man*. Epis. ii, l. 1.

Man is man's A, B, C. There's none that can
Read God aright unless he first spell man.
FRANCIS QUARLES, *Hieroglyphics of the Life of Man.*

15
I have sedulously endeavored not to laugh at human actions, not to lament them, nor to detest them, but to understand them. (Sedulo curavi humanas actiones non ridere non

lugere, neque destestari, sed intelligere.)
SPINOZA, *Tractatus Politicus*. Ch. i, sec. 4.

XVIII—Man: Seeking and Finding

1
The man forget not, though in rags he lies,
And know the mortal through a crown's disguise.
MARK AKENSIDE, *An Epistle to Curio*, l. 197.

2
I am a man, and you are another.
BLACK HAWK, to Andrew Jackson, April, 1833, at their first interview.

Every inch a man.
JOHN CLARKE, *Parœmiologia*, p. 247. (1639)

3
Thus we are men, and we know not how: there is something in us that can be without us, and will be after us; though it is strange that it hath no history what it was before us.
SIR THOMAS BROWNE, *Religio Medici*. Pt. i, sec. 36.

4
I am seeking a man. (Ἄνθρωπον ζητῶ.)
DIOGENES, after lighting a lamp in broad daylight, and going about with it through the streets of Athens. (DIOGENES LAERTIUS, *Diogenes*. Bk. vi, sec. 41.)

I am in search of a man. (Hominem quæro.)
PHÆDRUS, *Fables*. Bk. iii, fab. 19, l. 9.

I came to seek an honest man. (Ἀγαθὸν ἄνδρα ζητεῖν.)
PLATO, when asked by Dionysius what business he had in Sicily. (PLUTARCH, *Lives: Dion*. Ch. 5, sec. 2.)

A man! A man! My kingdom for a man!
JOHN MARSTON, *Scourge of Villainy*.

I am more fortunate than Diogenes, for I have found the man for whom he searched so long.
FREDERICK THE GREAT, *Letter to d'Alembert*.

5
He of a temper was so absolute,
As that it seem'd, when Nature him began,
She meant to show all that might be in man.
MICHAEL DRAYTON, *The Barons' Wars*. Bk. iii.

6
Men's men: gentle or simple, they're much of a muchness.
GEORGE ELIOT, *Daniel Deronda*. Ch. 31.

7
We are coming we, the young men,
Strong of heart and millions strong;
We shall work where you have trifled,
Cleanse the temple, right the wrong,
Till the land our fathers visioned
Shall be spread before our ken,
We are through with politicians;
Give us Men! Give us Men!
ARTHUR GUITERMAN, *Challenge of the Young Men*.

God give us men. A time like this demands
Strong minds, great hearts, true faith and ready hands!
Men whom the lust of office does not kill,
Men whom the spoils of office cannot buy,
Men who possess opinions and a will,
Men who love honor, men who cannot lie.
J. G. HOLLAND, *Wanted*.

Give us a man of God's own mould,
Born to marshal his fellow-men;
One whose fame is not bought and sold
At the stroke of a politician's pen.
Give us the man of thousands ten,
Fit to do as well as to plan;
Give us a rallying-cry, and then,
Abraham Lincoln, give us a MAN!
E. C. STEDMAN, *Wanted—A Man*.

8
When shall we look upon his like again? (Quando ullum inveniet parem?)
HORACE, *Odes*. Bk. i, ode 24, l. 8.

He was a man, take him for all in all,
I shall not look upon his like again.
SHAKESPEARE, *Hamlet*. Act i, sc. 2, l. 187.

9
Though I've belted you and flayed you,
By the livin' Gawd that made you,
You're a better man than I am, Gunga Din!
KIPLING, *Gunga Din*.

10
A man of mark.
LONGFELLOW, *Tales of a Wayside Inn: The Saga of King Olaf*. Pt. ix, st. 2.

11
The surest plan to make a Man
Is, think him so.
J. R. LOWELL, *Jonathan to John*. St. 9.

12
Before Man made us citizens, great Nature made us men.
J. R. LOWELL, *On the Capture of Certain Fugitive Slaves Near Washington*.

13
A man after his own heart.
Old Testament: I Samuel, xiii, 14.

And Nathan said to David: "Thou art the man."
Old Testament: II Samuel, xii, 7.

14
O, such another sleep, that I might see
But such another man!
SHAKESPEARE, *Antony and Cleopatra*. Act v, sc. 2, l. 78.

15
He was the mark and glass, copy and book,
That fashion'd others. And him, O wondrous him!
O miracle of men!
SHAKESPEARE, *II Henry IV*. Act ii, sc. 3, l. 31.

As proper men as ever trod upon neat's leather.
SHAKESPEARE, *Julius Cæsar*. Act i, sc. 1, l. 29.

A proper man as one shall see in a summer's day.
SHAKESPEARE, *A Midsummer-Night's Dream*. Act i, sc. 2, l. 88.

His life was gentle, and the elements
So mix'd in him that Nature might stand up,
And say to all the world "This was a man!"
SHAKESPEARE, *Julius Cæsar*. Act v, sc. 5, l. 73

A man beloved, a man elect of men.
SWINBURNE, *In Memory of John William Inchbold*.

A princelier-looking man never stept thro' a prince's hall.

TENNYSON, *The Wreck*, l. 16.

1
Are you good men and true?

SHAKESPEARE, *Much Ado About Nothing*. Act iii, sc. 3, l. 1.

2
A man to match his mountains.

J. G. WHITTIER, *Among the Hills*.

Bring me men to match my mountains.

SAM WALTER FOSS, *The Coming American*.

Here was a man to hold against the world,
A man to match the mountains and the sea.

EDWIN MARKHAM, *Lincoln, the Man of the People*.

3
Render unto all men their due, but remember thou art also a man.

M. F. TUPPER, *Proverbial Philosophy: Of Humility. See also under* PHILANTHROPY.

XIX—Man and Woman

See also Sexes

4
If men are always more or less deceived on the subject of women, it is because they forget that they and women do not speak altogether the same language.

AMIEL, *Journal*, 26 Dec., 1868.

5
There is nothing enduring in life for a woman except what she builds in a man's heart.

JUDITH ANDERSON, *Newspaper Interview*, 8 March, 1931.

6
The vast mass of men have to depend on themselves alone; the vast mass of women hope or expect to get their life given to them.

WILLIAM BOLITHO, *Twelve Against the Gods: Isadora Duncan*, p. 310.

7
The whole world was made for man, but the twelfth part of man for woman; man is the whole world and the breath of God; woman the rib and crooked piece of man.

SIR THOMAS BROWNE, *Religio Medici*. Pt. ii, sec. 10.

8
Thou large-brain'd woman and large-hearted man.

E. B. BROWNING, *To George Sand: A Desire*.

9
Preach as we will, in this wrong world of ours,
Man's fate and woman's are contending powers;
Each strives to dupe the other in the game,—
Guilt to the victor—to the vanquish'd shame!

BULWER-LYTTON, *The New Timon*. Pt. ii, sec. 2.

10
What a strange thing is man! and what a stranger
Is woman! What a whirlwind is her head,
And what a whirlpool full of depth and danger
Is all the rest about her.

BYRON, *Don Juan*. Canto ix, st. 64.

11
There can no man in humbless him acquit
As woman can, nor can be half so true,
As woman been.

CHAUCER, *The Clerkes Tale*, l. 880.

12
I love men, not because they are men, but because they are not women.

QUEEN CHRISTINA of Sweden.

I am glad that I am not a man, as I should be obliged to marry a woman.

MADAME DE STAËL.

13
We should regard loveliness as the attribute of woman, and dignity as the attribute of man. (Venustatem muliebrem ducere debemus, dignitatem virilem.)

CICERO, *De Officiis*. Bk. i, ch. 36, sec. 130.

14
We were young, we were merry, we were very, very wise,
And the door stood open at our feast,
When there passed us a woman with the West in her eyes,
And a man with his back to the East.

MARY E. COLERIDGE, *Unwelcome*.

15
If men were as unselfish as women, women would very soon become more selfish than men.

CHURTON COLLINS, *Aphorisms*. No. 90.

16
Were there no women, men might live like gods.

THOMAS DEKKER, *II The Honest Whore*. Act iii, sc. 1.

17
One man among a thousand have I found; but a woman among all those have I not found.

Old Testament: Ecclesiastes, vii, 28.

18
I'm not denyin' the women are foolish: God Almighty made 'em to match the men.

GEORGE ELIOT, *Adam Bede*.

19
Most men and most women are merely one couple more.

EMERSON, *Conduct of Life: Fate*.

Let us treat men and women well; treat them as if they were real; perhaps they are.

EMERSON, *Essays, Second Series: Experience*.

20
Man's conclusions are reached by toil. Woman arrives at the same by sympathy.

EMERSON, *Journal*, 1866.

Man is the will, and woman the sentiment. In this ship of humanity, Will is the rudder, and Sentiment the sail; when woman affects to steer, the rudder is only a masked sail.

EMERSON, *Miscellanies: Woman*.

1
A man of straw is more worth than a woman of gold. (Un homme de paille vaut une femme d'or.)
JOHN FLORIO, *Second Frutes*, p. 173. (1591)

2
Man is fire and woman tow; the devil comes and sets them in a blaze.
THOMAS FULLER, *Gnomologia*. No. 5800.

Women commend a modest man but like him not.
THOMAS FULLER, *Gnomologia*. No. 5805.

Women's jars breed men's wars.
THOMAS FULLER, *The Holy and the Profane State: The Wise Statesman*.

3
Woman submits to her fate; man makes his.
ÉMILE GABORIAU, *Other People's Money*. Ch. 27.

4
Men are odd creatures. Women have to wait. It's always been that way.
WARREN GILBERT, *The Joy Ride*.

5
Men make laws, women make manners. (Les hommes font les lois, les femmes font les mœurs.)
GUIBERT.

6
Time and Circumstance, which enlarge the views of most men, narrow the views of women almost invariably.
THOMAS HARDY, *Jude the Obscure*. Ch. 6.

Directly domineering ceases in the man, snubbing begins in the woman.
THOMAS HARDY, *A Pair of Blue Eyes*. Ch. 27.

7
De wimmin, dey does de talkin' en de flyin', en de mens, dey does de walkin' en de pryin', en betwixt en betweenst um, dey ain't much dat don't come out.
JOEL CHANDLER HARRIS, *Brother Rabbit and His Famous Foot*.

8
Married men laugh at
Single men. Single men laugh
At the married men.
Wan Lo tells me that women
Laugh up their sleeves at both.
HENRY HARRISON, *Wan Lo Tanka*.

9
A man is as good as he has to be, and a woman as bad as she dares.
ELBERT HUBBARD, *Epigrams*.

When rewards are distributed, the woman gets one half the pay that a man does, and if disgrace is given out she bears it all.
ELBERT HUBBARD, *The Philistine*. Vol. iv, p. 179.

10
I had rather live with the woman I love in a world full of trouble, than to live in heaven with nobody but men.
R. G. INGERSOLL, *Liberty of Man, Woman and Child*.

11
A look of intelligence in men is what regularity of features is in women: it is a style of beauty to which the most vain may aspire.
LA BRUYÈRE, *Les Caractères*. Sec. 12.

12
It is because of men that women dislike each other. (Les hommes sont cause que les femmes ne s'aiment point.)
LA BRUYÈRE, *Les Caractères*. Sec. 3.

13
As unto the bow the cord is,
So unto the man is woman;
Though she bends him, she obeys him,
Though she draws him, yet she follows;
Useless each without the other!
LONGFELLOW, *Hiawatha*. Pt. x, l. 1.

Sure the shovel and tongs
To each other belongs.
SAMUEL LOVER, *Widow Machree*.

14
Laborin' man an' laborin' woman
Hev one glory an' one shame;
Ev'ythin' thet's done inhuman
Injers all on 'em the same.
J. R. LOWELL, *Biglow Papers*. Ser. i, No. 1, st. 10.

15
Campaspe: Were women never so fair, men would be false.
Apelles: Were women never so false, men would be fond.
JOHN LYLY, *Alexander and Campaspe*. Act iii, sc. 3.

16
Men may have rounded Seraglio Point: they have not yet doubled Cape Turk.
GEORGE MEREDITH, *Diana of the Crossways*. Ch. 1. Meaning that, though man has perhaps passed the stage of keeping harems, he has not yet learned to treat woman as an equal.

17
Two of far nobler shape, erect and tall,
Godlike erect, with native honour clad
In naked majesty seem'd lords of all,
And worthy seem'd. . . .
For contemplation he and valour form'd,
For softness she, and sweet attractive grace;
He for God only, she for God in him.
MILTON, *Paradise Lost*. Bk. iv, l. 288.

Female and male God made the man,
His image is the whole, not half.
COVENTRY PATMORE, *The Angel in the House: Sarum Plain: Preludes*. Pt. iv.

Male and female created he them.
Old Testament: Genesis, i, 27.

18
In argument with men, a woman ever
Goes by the worse, whatever be her cause.
MILTON, *Samson Agonistes*, l. 903.

Men are more eloquent than women made;
But women are more powerful to persuade.
THOMAS RANDOLPH, *Amyntas: Prologue*.

1
All the pursuits of men are the pursuits of women also, and in all of them a woman is only a lesser man.
PLATO, *The Republic*. Bk. iv, sec. 455.

2
Wretched women live under a hard law, and one much more unjust than men live under. (Lege dura vivont mulieres, multoque iniquiore miseræ, quam viri.)
PLAUTUS, *Mercator*, l. 817. (Act iv, sc. 6.)

3
Men some to bus'ness, some to pleasure take;
But ev'ry woman is at heart a rake:
Men some to quiet, some to public strife;
But ev'ry lady would be queen for life.
POPE, *Moral Essays*. Epis. ii, l. 215.

For story and experience tell us,
That man grows old and woman jealous;
Both would their little ends secure:
He sighs for freedom, she for power.
MATTHEW PRIOR, *Alma*. Canto ii, l. 65.

4
There's not so bad a Jill
But there's as bad a Will.
JOHN RAY, *English Proverbs*, 146. (1678) *See also under* JACK.

5
Men work and think, but women feel.
CHRISTINA ROSSETTI, *An "Immurata" Sister*.

Once it came into my heart, and whelmed me like a flood,
That these too are men and women, human flesh and blood;
Men with hearts and men with souls, though trodden down like mud.
CHRISTINA ROSSETTI, *A Royal Princess*. St. 12.

6
'Tis not a year or two shows us a man:
They are all but stomachs, and we all but food;
They eat us hungerly, and when they are full,
They belch us.
SHAKESPEARE, *Othello*. Act iii, sc. 4, l. 103. Desdemona's maid is speaking.

7
Men have marble, women waxen, minds.
SHAKESPEARE, *The Rape of Lucrece*. St. 178.

8
Pronounce this sentence, then,
Women may fall, when there's no strength in men.
SHAKESPEARE, *Romeo and Juliet*. Act ii, sc. 3, l. 79.

9
The only way for a woman to provide for herself decently is for her to be good to some man that can afford to be good to her.
BERNARD SHAW, *Mrs. Warren's Profession*. Act ii.

10
Woman's dearest delight is to wound Man's self-conceit, though Man's dearest delight is to gratify hers.
BERNARD SHAW, *An Unsocial Socialist*. Ch. 5.

11
Can man be free if woman be a slave?
SHELLEY, *The Revolt of Islam*. Canto ii, st. 43.

12
Woman is the lesser man, and all thy passions, match'd with mine,
Are as moonlight unto sunlight, and as water unto wine.
TENNYSON, *Locksley Hall*, l. 151.

She with all the charm of woman, she with all the breadth of man.
TENNYSON, *Locksley Hall Sixty Years After*, l. 48.

13
Lo now, what hearts have men! they never mount
As high as woman in her selfless mood.
TENNYSON, *Merlin and Vivien*, l. 440.

For men at most differ as Heaven and Earth.
But women, worst and best, as Heaven and Hell.
TENNYSON, *Merlin and Vivien*, l. 812.

A shameless woman is the worst of men.
YOUNG, *Love of Fame*. Sat. v, l. 468.

14
Man is the hunter; woman is his game:
The sleek and shining creatures of the chase,
We hunt them for the beauty of their skins;
They love us for it, and we ride them down.
TENNYSON, *The Princess*. Pt. v, l. 147.

And that one hunting, which the devil design'd
For one fair female, lost him half the kind.
DRYDEN, *Theodore and Honoria*, l. 427.

15
Man for the field and woman for the hearth;
Man for the sword, and for the needle she;
Man with the head, and woman with the heart;
Man to command, and woman to obey;
All else confusion.
TENNYSON, *The Princess*. Pt. v, l. 437.

The woman's cause is man's; they rise or sink
Together, dwarf'd or godlike, bond or free. .
TENNYSON, *The Princess*. Pt. vii, l. 243.

For woman is not undevelopt man,
But diverse. Could we make her as the man,
Sweet Love were slain; his dearest bond is this,
Not like to like, but like in difference.
Yet in the long years liker must they grow;
The man be more of woman, she of man;
He gain in sweetness and in moral height,
Nor lose the wrestling thews that throw the world;
She mental breadth, nor fail in childward care,
Nor lose the childlike in the larger mind;
Till at the last she set herself to man,
Like perfect music unto noble words.
TENNYSON, *The Princess*. Pt. vii, l. 259.

Either sex alone
Is half itself, and in true marriage lies
Nor equal, nor unequal: each fulfils
Defect in each, and always thought in thought,
Purpose in purpose, will in will, they grow,
The single pure and perfect animal.
TENNYSON, *The Princess*. Pt. vii, l. 283.

1
'Tis strange what a man may do and a woman yet think him an angel.
THACKERAY, *Henry Esmond*. Bk. i, ch. 7.

2
Woman is more impressionable than man. Therefore in the Golden Age they were better than men. Now they are worse.
LEO TOLSTOY, *Diary*.

3
When a man fronts catastrophe on the road, he looks in his purse—but a woman looks in her mirror.
MARGARET TURNBULL, *The Left Lady*, p. 44.

4
If women were humbler, men would be honester.
SIR JOHN VANBRUGH, *Æsop*. Act iv, sc. 2.

5
All the reasoning of men is not worth one sentiment of women.
VOLTAIRE, *Maximes*.

6
Silver is the king's stamp; man God's stamp, and a woman is man's stamp; we are not current till we pass from one man to another.
JOHN WEBSTER, *Northward Hoe*. *See also under* TITLES.

7
Women are never disarmed by compliments. Men always are.
OSCAR WILDE, *An Ideal Husband*. Act iii.

8
Women represent the triumph of matter over mind, just as men represent the triumph of mind over morals.
OSCAR WILDE, *The Picture of Dorian Gray*. Ch. 4.

9
I like men who have a future, and women who have a past.
OSCAR WILDE, *The Picture of Dorian Gray*. Ch. 15.

MANNERS

See also Behavior, Courtesy

I—Manners: Definitions

10
Manners must adorn knowledge, and smooth its way through the world. Like a great rough diamond, it may do very well in a closet by way of curiosity, and also for its intrinsic value; but it will never be worn, nor shine, if it is not polished.
LORD CHESTERFIELD, *Letters*, 1 July, 1748.

Virtue and learning, like gold, have their intrinsic value; but if they are not polished, they certainly lose a great deal of their lustre; and even polished brass will pass upon more people than rough gold.
LORD CHESTERFIELD, *Letters*, 6 March, 1747.

It is not sufficient to deserve well, one must please well too. Awkward, disagreeable merit will never carry anybody far.
LORD CHESTERFIELD, *Letters*, 22 Sept., 1749.

What's a fine person, or a beauteous face,
Unless deportment gives them decent grace?
Bless'd with all other requisites to please,
Some want the striking elegance of ease;
The curious eye their awkward movement tires:
They seem like puppets led about by wires.
CHARLES CHURCHILL, *The Rosciad*, l. 741.

11
Different manners belong to different pursuits (Disparis mores disparia studia sequuntur.)
CICERO, *De Amicitia*. Ch. xx, sec. 74.

12
Contact with manners is education.
DIONYSIUS OF HALICARNASSUS, *Ars Rhetorica*. Ch. xi, sec. 2.

13
Manners are the happy ways of doing things. . . . If they are superficial, so are the dewdrops which give such a depth to the morning meadows.
EMERSON, *Conduct of Life: Behavior*.

Manners have been somewhat cynically defined to be a contrivance of wise men to keep fools at a distance.
EMERSON, *Conduct of Life: Behavior*.

There is nothing settled in manners, but the laws of behavior yield to the energy of the individual.
EMERSON, *Essays, Second Series: Manners*.

Manners are greater than laws; by their delicate nature they fortify themselves with an impassible wall of defence.
EMERSON, *Uncollected Lectures: Public and Private Education*.

14
Perhaps, if we could examine the manners of different nations with impartiality, we should find no people so rude, as to be without any rules of politeness; nor any so polite, as not to have some remains of rudeness.
BENJAMIN FRANKLIN, *Remarks Concerning the Savages of North America*.

The mainners o' a' nations are equally bad.
JOHN WILSON, *Noctes Ambrosianæ*. No. 39.

15
The society of women is the foundation of good manners. (Der Umgang mit Frauen ist das Element guter Sitten.)
JOHANN WOLFGANG VON GOETHE, *Wahlverwandtschaften*. Bk. ii, ch. 5.

What better school for manners than the company of virtuous women?
DAVID HUME, *Essays: The Rise of Arts and Sciences*.

16
The difference between a well-bred and an ill-bred man is this: One immediately attracts your liking, and the other your aversion. You love the one till you find reason to hate him; you hate the other till you find reason to love him.
SAMUEL JOHNSON. (BOSWELL, *Life*, iv, 319.)

17
Too great refinement is false delicacy, and true delicacy is solid refinement. (La trop

grande subtilité est une fausse délicatesse, et la véritable délicatesse est une solide subtilité.)

La Rochefoucauld, *Maximes*. No. 128.

1
For as laws are necessary that good manners may be preserved, so there is need of good manners that laws may be maintained.

Machiavelli, *Dei Discorsi*. Pt. i, sec. 18.

2
Self-respect is at the bottom of all good manners. They are the expression of discipline, of good-will, of respect for other people's rights and comfort and feelings.

E. S. Martin, *A Father to His Freshman Son.*

3
You must practise
The manners of the time, if you intend
To have favour from it.

Massinger, *The Unnatural Combat*. Act i, sc. 1.

4
Good manners are the technic of expressing consideration for the feelings of others.

Alice Duer Miller, *I Like American Manners.* (*Saturday Evening Post,* 13 Aug., 1932.)

5
The most delightful of companions is he who combines the mind of a gentleman with the emotions of a bum. . . . Toward men, ever an aristocrat; toward women, ever a commoner—that way lies success.

G. J. Nathan, *The Autobiography of an Attitude.*

6
All Manners take a tincture from our own,
Or come discolour'd thro' our Passions shown;
Or Fancy's beam enlarges, multiplies,
Contracts, inverts, and gives ten thousand dyes.

Pope, *Moral Essays*. Epis. i, l. 33.

7
Our manners, like our faces, though ever so beautiful, must differ in their beauty.

Shaftesbury, *Characteristics*. Vol. iii, p. 262.

8
Those that are good manners at the court are as ridiculous in the country as the behaviour of the country is most mockable at the court.

Shakespeare, *As You Like It*. Act iii, sc. 2, l. 46.

9
The great secret is not having bad manners or good manners or any other particular sort of manners, but having the same manners for all human souls.

Bernard Shaw, *Pygmalion*. Act v.

10
For manners are not idle, but the fruit
Of loyal nature and of noble mind.

Tennyson, *Guinevere*, l. 333.

11
Manners,—the final and perfect flower of noble character.

William Winter, *The Actor and his Duty.*

12
Good-breeding is the blossom of good-sense.

Young, *Love of Fame*. Sat. v, l. 470.

13
Training is everything. The peach was once a bitter almond; cauliflower is nothing but cabbage with a college education.

Mark Twain, *Pudd'nhead Wilson's Calendar.*

Good breeding consists in concealing how much we think of ourselves and how little we think of the other person.

Mark Twain, *Unpublished Diaries.*

14
Men are polished, through act and speech,
Each by each,
As pebbles are smoothed on the rolling beach.

J. T. Trowbridge, *A Home Idyl.*

II—Manners: Apothegms

15
Office changes manners. (Oficion mudan las costumbres.)

Cervantes, *Don Quixote*. Pt. ii, ch. 4.

Honors change manners. (Honores mutant mores.)

Polydore Vergil, *Adagia*. No. 202.

See also Honor: Honors.

16
Not with whom you are born, but with whom you are bred. (No con quien naces, sino con quien paces.)

Cervantes, *Don Quixote*. Pt. ii, ch. 10.

17
What times! what manners! (O tempora! O mores!)

Cicero, *In Catilinam*. No. i, sec. 2. "Mores" may also be translated as morals, behavior.

What were once vices are now the manners of the day. (Quæ fuerant vitia mores sunt.)

Seneca, *Epistulæ ad Lucilium*. Epis. xxxix, 6.

How many injustices are due to the manners of the age. (Quam multa injusta ac prava fiunt moribus.)

Terence, *Heauton Timorumenos*, l. 839.

18
I felt myself extremely awkward about going away, not choosing, as it was my first visit, to take French leave.

Madame D'Arblay, *Diary*, 8 Dec., 1782.

You'd have taken leave without asking—French leave—if I had not been there.

George Colman the Younger, *Ways and Means*. Act iii, sc. 2. (1788)

What is called French leave was introduced that one person leaving might not disturb the company.

John Trusler, *Chesterfield's Principles and Politeness.* (1760)

19
He that hath more manners than he ought,
Is more a fool than he thought.

Thomas D'Urfey, *Quixote*. Act ii, sc. 1.

Unmannerly a little is better than troublesome a great deal.

Thomas Fuller, *Gnomologia*. No. 5404.

20
Fine manners need the support of fine manners in others.

Emerson, *The Conduct of Life: Behavior.*

1
I don't recall your name, but your manners are familiar.
OLIVER HERFORD, to a back-slapping person who descended upon him one afternoon at the Players, with a confident, "You remember me?"

1a
The manners of every age should be observed by you. (Ætatis cujusque notandi sunt tibi mores.)
HORACE, *Ars Poetica*, l. 156.

I describe not men, but manners; not an individual, but a species.
FIELDING, *Joseph Andrews*. Bk. iii, ch. 1.

Nor is it my wish to find fault with individuals, but truly to show forth the very life and the manners of mankind. (Neque enim notare singulos mens est mihi, Verum ipsam vitam et mores hominum ostendere.)
PHÆDRUS, *Fables*. Bk. iii, *Prologue*, l. 49.

2
A man polished to the nail. (Ad unguem factus homo.)
HORACE, *Satires*. Bk. i, sat. 5, l. 32. The phrase involves a metaphor from sculpture, for the Latin artist would pass his finger-nail over the marble to test its smoothness.

3
The attentive eyes
That saw the manners in the face.
SAMUEL JOHNSON, *On the Death of Hogarth*.

4
Evil communications corrupt good manners. (Φθείρουσιν ἤθη χρήσθ' ὁμιλίαι κακαί.)
MENANDER, *Thaïs*. Frag. 2; EURIPIDES, *Fragments*. Frag. 962; *New Testament: I Corinthians*, xv, 33. *See also* COMPANIONS: EVIL COMMUNICATIONS.

Evil words corrupt good manners, saith both Paul and Menander.
SIR JOHN HARINGTON, *Ulysses Upon Ajax*, 23.

5
Everyone's manners make his fortune. (Mores cuique sui fingunt fortunam.)
CORNELIUS NEPOS, *Lives: Atticus*. Ch. 14.

6
And all that's madly wild, or oddly gay,
We call it only pretty Fanny's way.
THOMAS PARNELL, *Elegy to an Old Beauty*.

Nobody ought to have been able to resist her coaxing manner; and nobody had any business to try. Yet she never seemed to know it was her manner at all. That was the best of it.
DICKENS, *Martin Chuzzlewit*. Vol. ii, ch. 14.

7
Well showed the elder lady's mien
That courts and cities she had seen.
SCOTT, *The Lady of the Lake*. Canto i, st. 30.

8
Everyone thinks himself well-bred.
LORD SHAFTESBURY, *Characteristics*. Vol. i, p. 65.

9
To the manner born.
SHAKESPEARE, *Hamlet*. Act i, sc. 4, l. 15.

10
Let us not be dainty of leave-taking,
But shift away.
SHAKESPEARE, *Macbeth*. Act ii, sc. 3, l. 150.

He wants the natural touch.
SHAKESPEARE, *Macbeth*. Act iv, sc. 2, l. 9.

11
Here's a million of manners.
SHAKESPEARE, *The Two Gentlemen of Verona*. Act ii, sc. 1, l. 105.

12
Oh! madam; after you is good manners.
SWIFT, *Polite Conversation*. Dial. 2.

Stop, friend! after me is manners.
JOHN O'KEEFFE, *Czar Peter*. Act iii, sc. 2.

13
Few are qualified to shine in company, but it is in most men's power to be agreeable.
SWIFT, *Thoughts on Various Subjects*.

14
Things which are unbecoming are unsafe. (Intuta quæ indecora.)
TACITUS, *History*. Bk. i, sec. 33.

15
Suit your manner to the man. (Ut homo est, ita morem geras.)
TERENCE, *Adelphi*, l. 431. *Also* PLAUTUS, *Mostellaria*, l. 724.

16
It is not learning, it is not virtue, about which people inquire in society. It's manners.
THACKERAY, *Sketches in London: On Tailoring*.

17
Good manners and soft words have brought many a difficult thing to pass.
SIR JOHN VANBRUGH, *I Æsop*. Act iv, sc. 2.

18
Manners before morals!
OSCAR WILDE, *Lady Windermere's Fan*. Act iv.

One should be sure of his own manners before attacking another's morals.
MRS. JACK GARDNER, referring to Josiah Royce's attack on Francis E. Abbot, in *International Journal of Ethics*, Oct., 1890.

More tears have been shed over men's lack of manners than their lack of morals.
HELEN HATHAWAY, *Manners for Men*.

They teach the morals of a harlot and the manners of a dancing-master.
SAMUEL JOHNSON, of Chesterfield's letters.

19
Manners makyth man.
WILLIAM OF WYKEHAM, *Motto*, on New College, Oxford, founded by him in 1380.

Nurture and good manners maketh man.
UNKNOWN, *Babees Book*, p. 14. (c. 1460)

Good manners and knowledge maketh a man.
HENRY BRADSHAW, *Life of St. Werburge*: Pt. ii, *Prologue*, l. 7. (1513)

Manners make the man.
DEFOE, *Complete Gentleman*. Pt. 1, ch. 1. (1729)

The difference is, that in the days of old
Men made the manners; manners now make men.
BYRON, *Don Juan*. Canto xv, st. 26.

III—Manners: Good Manners

1
Such easy greatness, such a graceful port,
So turn'd and finish'd for the camp or court!
ADDISON, *The Campaign,* l. 417.

We should lose something of the stately manners
Of the old school.
LONGFELLOW, *Michael Angelo.* Pt. i, sec. 2.

2
She puts off her patched petticoat today
And puts on Mayfair manners.
E. B. BROWNING, *Aurora Leigh.* Bk. iv, l. 658.

3
Genteel in personage,
Conduct, and equipage;
Noble by heritage,
Generous and free.
HENRY CAREY, *The Contrivances.* Act i, sc. 2.

4
Never seem wiser or more learned than the people you are with.
LORD CHESTERFIELD, *Letters,* 22 Feb., 1748.

Abhor a knave and pity a fool in your heart, but let neither of them unnecessarily see that you do so.
LORD CHESTERFIELD, *Letters,* 20 Dec., 1748.

A man's own good-breeding is his best security against other people's ill manners.
LORD CHESTERFIELD, *Letters,* 9 Feb., 1750.

You must embrace the man you hate, if you cannot be justified in knocking him down.
LORD CHESTERFIELD, *Letters,* 15 Jan., 1753.

5
Who fears t' offend takes the first step to please.
COLLEY CIBBER, *Love in a Riddle.* Act i.

6
Come when you're called,
And do as you're bid;
Shut the door after you,
And you'll never be chid.
MARIA EDGEWORTH, *The Contrast.* Ch. 1.

7
Good manners are made up of petty sacrifices.
EMERSON, *Letters and Social Aims: Social Aims.*

All that fashion demands is composure and self-content.
EMERSON, *Essays, Second Series: Manners.*

8
The mildest manners, and the gentlest heart.
HOMER, *Iliad.* Bk. xvii, l. 756. (Pope, tr.)

The mildest manners with the bravest mind.
HOMER, *Iliad.* Bk. xxiv, l. 963. (Pope, tr.)

He was the mildest mannered man
That ever scuttled a ship or cut a throat;
With such true breeding of a gentleman,
You never could divine his real thought.
BYRON, *Don Juan.* Canto iii, st. 41.

9
You may observe that I am well-bred to a degree of needless scrupulosity.
SAMUEL JOHNSON, *Miscellanies.* Vol. i, p. 169.

No dancing bear was s
Or half so *dégagé.*
COWPER, *Of Himself.*

10
Such high-bred mann
wit.
J. R. LOWELL, *Ep*
Curtis.

11
Teach me, like thee, in
To fall with dignity, w
Form'd by thy conver
From grave to gay, fr
Correct with spirit, el
Intent to reason, or p
POPE, *Essay on Man.*

12
Don't shake hands t
δεξιὰν ἐμβάλλειν.)
PYTHAGORAS. (DIOGEN
Bk. viii, sec. 17.)

13
Good manners be your
SHAKESPEARE, *I Henr*

14
Gentle blood will gentl
SPENSER, *Faerie Queen*

True is, that whilom tha
The gentle mind by gent
For a man by nothing is
As by his manners.
SPENSER, *Faerie Queene.* B
The reference is to Chau
GENTLEMAN.

IV—Manners: Bad M

15
You have the gift of impudence;
Every man has not the like talent.
BEAUMONT AND FLETCHER, *The*
Chase. Act i, sc. 2.

I am privileged to be very impertinent,
Oxonian.
FARQUHAR, *Sir Harry Wildair.* Act ii, s

With that dull, rooted, callous impudence
Which, dead to shame and every nicer sense,
Ne'er blush'd, unless, in spreading vice's snare
She blunder'd on some virtue unawares.
CHARLES CHURCHILL, *The Rosciad,* l. 135.

16
No manners at all—no more breeding than a bum-bailey.
CONGREVE, *The Way of the World.* Act i, sc. 6.

17
Though I be rude in speech.
New Testament: II Corinthians, xi, 6.

18
God may forgive sins, he said, but awkwardness has no forgiveness in heaven or earth.
EMERSON, *Essays: Society and Solitude.*

19
I suppose this is a spice of your foreign breeding, to let your uncle kick his heels in your hall.
SAMUEL FOOTE, *The Minor.* Act ii.

1 Mr. Burchell ... the conclusion of every sentence w... ut "*Fudge!*"—an expression which ... d us all.
GOLDS... *Vicar of Wakefield*. Ch. 11.

2 Unru... or ill-timed applause
W... peaker or the justest cause.
...x. xix, l. 86. (Pope, tr.)

... ss, awkward and loutish. (As... et inconcinna gravisque.)
... *es*. Bk. i, epis. 18, l. 6.

... s beyond her bounds; but Im... s none.
..., *Explorata: Scitum Hispanicum*.

... gues that heaven has sent,
... st impertinent.
... *Fables*. Pt. i, No. 8.

... s not a Vice of the Soul, but the ... everal Vices; of Vanity, Ignorance ... Laziness, Stupidity, Distraction, ... of others, and Jealousy.
... YÈRE, *Les Caractères*. Ch. 11.

... vers and masters of our souls have ... right to throw out their limbs as care... as they please, on the world that be... o them, and before the creatures they ... animated.
... S. LANDOR, *Imaginary Conversations: Per... cles and Aspasia*.

... enerate manners grow apace. (Mores de... ores increbescunt.)
PLAUTUS, *Mercator*, l. 838. (Act v, sc. 1.)

... il manners will, like watered grass, grow up ... ry quickly. (Mores mali, Quasi herba irrigua ... ccreverunt uberrime.)
PLAUTUS, *Trinummus*. Act i, sc. 1, l. 8.

8
Rude, and scant of courtesy.
SCOTT, *Lay of the Last Minstrel*. Can. v, st. 28.

But by and rade the Black Douglas,
And wow but he was rough!
UNKNOWN, *The Douglas Tragedy*.

9 I am much sorry, sir,
You put me to forget a lady's manners,
By being so verbal.
SHAKESPEARE, *Cymbeline*. Act ii, sc. 3, l. 110.

10
This rudeness is a sauce to his good wit,
Which gives men stomach to digest his words
With better appetite.
SHAKESPEARE, *Julius Cæsar*. Act i, sc. 2, l. 304.

He answered me in the roundest manner.
SHAKESPEARE, *King Lear*. Act i, sc. 4, l. 59.

This is some fellow,
Who, having been prais'd for bluntness, doth affect
A saucy roughness.
SHAKESPEARE, *King Lear*. Act ii, sc. 2, l. 101.

Fit for the mountains and the barb'rous caves,
Where manners ne'er were preach'd.
SHAKESPEARE, *Twelfth Night*. Act iv, sc. 1, l. 52.

11
One ugly trick has often spoiled
The sweetest and the best.
ANN TAYLOR, *Meddlesome Matty*.

12
Her manners had not that repose
Which stamps the caste of Vere de Vere.
TENNYSON, *Lady Clara Vere de Vere*. St. 5.

13
His trick of doing nothing with an air,
His *salon* manners and society smile
Were but skin deep.
WILLIAM WATSON, *Study in Contrasts*. Pt. i, l. 17.

13a
For rudeness none shall rightly blame thee
If soon thy bed thou seekest.
UNKNOWN, *The Elder Edda: Hovamol*. Sec. 19. (HENRY ADAMS BELLOWS, tr., *Poetic Edda*.)

MARCH

14
The stormy March has come at last,
With winds and clouds and changing skies;
I hear the rushing of the blast
That through the snowy valley flies.
WILLIAM CULLEN BRYANT, *March*.

15
March winds and April showers
Bring forth May flowers.
ELWORTHY, *West Somersetshire Word-Book*, 461.

March wind and May sun
Makes clothes white and maids dun.
JOHN RAY, *English Proverbs*, 41.

16
Men.: I would choose March, for I would come in like a lion.
Tony: But you'd go out like a lamb.
JOHN FLETCHER, *Wife for a Month*. Act ii, sc. 1. (1624)

Like the month of March, in like a lion and out like a lamb.
ROGER NORTH, *Lives of the Norths*, i, 259.

Like March, having come in like a lion, he purposed to go out like a lamb.
CHARLOTTE BRONTË, *Shirley*. Ch. 15.

March comes in with an adder's head, and goes out with a peacock's tail.
R. L. GALES, *Old-World Essays*, p. 250.

17
Blossom on the plum,
Wild wind and merry;
Leaves upon the cherry,
And one swallow come.
NORA HOPPER, *March*.

18 Ah, March! we know thou art
Kind hearted, spite of ugly looks and threats,
And, out of sight, art nursing April's violets!
HELEN HUNT JACKSON, *March*.

19
Slayer of the winter, art thou here again?
O welcome, thou that bring'st the summer nigh!

The bitter wind makes not thy victory vain,
Nor will we mock thee for thy faint blue sky.
WILLIAM MORRIS, *Earthly Paradise: March*. St. 1.

1
Now are the winds about us in their glee,
Tossing the slender tree;
Whirling the sands about his furious car,
March cometh from afar.
WILLIAM GILMORE SIMMS, *Song in March*.

2
With rushing winds and gloomy skies,
The dark and stubborn Winter dies:
Far-off, unseen, Spring faintly cries,
Bidding her earliest child arise: March!
BAYARD TAYLOR, *March*.

3
Up from the sea the wild north wind is blowing
Under the sky's gray arch;
Smiling, I watch the shaken elm boughs, knowing
It is the wind of March.
J. G. WHITTIER, *March*.

4
The braggart March stood in the season's door
With his broad shoulders blocking up the way.
ROBERT BURNS WILSON, *The Passing of March*.

5
Like an army defeated
The snow hath retreated, . . .
The Ploughboy is whooping—anon—anon!
There's joy in the mountains:
There's life in the fountains; . . .
The rain is over and gone.
WORDSWORTH, *Written in March*.

6
Its tree, Juniper; its stone, Bloodstone; its motto, "Courage and strength in time of danger."
UNKNOWN, *Old Saying*. Referring to March.

MARIGOLD

7
The marigold, whose courtier's face
Echoes the sun.
JOHN CLEVELAND, *Upon Phillis Walking in a Morning before Breakfast*.

8
The marigold abroad her leaves doth spread,
Because the sun's and her power is the same.
HENRY CONSTABLE, *Diana*.

9
Fair is the marygold, for pottage meet.
JOHN GAY, *The Shepherd's Week: Monday*.

10
Open afresh your round of starry folds,
Ye ardent marigolds!
KEATS, *I Stood Tiptoe upon a Little Hill*, l. 47.

11
The sun-observing marigold.
FRANCIS QUARLES, *School of the Heart*. Ode 30.

12
Nor shall the marigold unmentioned die,
Which Acis once found out in Sicily;
She Phœbus loves, and from him draws his hue,
And ever keeps his golden beams in view.
RENÉ RAPIN, *On Gardens*. (Gardiner, tr.)

13
And winking Mary-buds begin
To ope their golden eyes.
SHAKESPEARE, *Cymbeline*. Act ii, sc. 3, l. 25.

The marigold that goes to bed wi' the sun,
And with him rises weeping.
SHAKESPEARE, *Winter's Tale*. Act iv, sc. 4, l. 105.

14
The graceful and obsequious marigold,
How duly every morning she displays
Her open breast when Titan spreads his rays.
GEORGE WITHER, *The Marigold*.

MARLOWE, CHRISTOPHER

15
Neat Marlowe, bathèd in the Thespian springs,
Had in him those brave translunary things
That the first poets had; his raptures were
All air and fire, which made his verses clear,
For that fine madness still he did retain
Which rightly should possess a poet's brain.
MICHAEL DRAYTON, *Of Poets and Poesie*.

[Marlowe] had in him those brave translunary things that the first poets had.
JOHN DRINKWATER, *To Harry Reynolds: Of Poets and Poetry*.

16
Marlowe's mighty line.
BEN JONSON, *To the Memory of Shakespeare*.

17
For thou, if ever godlike foot there trod
These fields of ours, wert surely like a god.
Who knows what splendour of strange dreams was shed
With sacred shadow and glimmer of gold and red
From hallowed windows, over stone and sod
On thine unbowed, bright, insubmissive head?
The shadow stayed not, but the splendour stays,
Our brother, till the last of English days.
SWINBURNE, *In the Bay*. St. 18.

18
Marlowe was happy in his buskin Muse—
Alas, unhappy in his life and end:
Pity it is that wit so ill should dwell,
Wit lent from heaven, but vices sent from hell.
Our theatre hath lost, Pluto hath got,
A tragic penman for a dreary plot.
UNKNOWN, *The Return from Parnassus*. (1606)

MARRIAGE

I—Marriage: Definitions

19
Marriage always demands the greatest understanding of the art of insincerity possible between two human beings.
VICKI BAUM, *And Life Goes On*, p. 141.

The one charm of marriage is that it makes a life of deception absolutely necessary for both parties.
OSCAR WILDE, *Picture of Dorian Gray*. Ch. 1.

1
Marriage: The state or condition of a community consisting of a master, a mistress, and two slaves, making in all, two.
AMBROSE BIERCE, *Devil's Dictionary*, p. 213.

2
The mere idea of marriage, existing to weaken the will by distracting its straight aim in the life of practically every young girl, is the simple secret of their confessed inferiority in men's pursuits and professions today.
WILLIAM BOLITHO, *Twelve Against the Gods: Isadora Duncan*, p. 310.

3
In the married state, the world must own,
Divided happiness was never known.
To make it mutual, nature points the way:
Let husbands govern: gentle wives obey.
COLLEY CIBBER, *The Provok'd Husband*. Act v, sc. 2. *See also* WIFE: THE CROWING HEN.

4
The first bond of society is marriage. (Prima societas in ipso conjugio est.)
CICERO, *De Officiis*. Bk. i, ch. 17, sec. 54.

5
Wedlock's a lane where there is no turning.
DINAH M. M. CRAIK, *Magnus and Morna*. Sc. 3.

6
Marriage must be a relation either of sympathy or of conquest.
GEORGE ELIOT, *Romola*. Bk. iii, ch. 48.

7
Bone of my bones, and flesh of my flesh.
Old Testament: Genesis, ii, 23.

Therefore shall a man leave his father and his mother, and shall cleave unto his wife: and they shall be one flesh.
Old Testament: Genesis, ii, 24.

And they two shall be one flesh.
New Testament: Ephesians, v, 31.

And they twain shall be one flesh.
New Testament: Matthew, xix, 5; *Mark*, x, 8.

Our state cannot be sever'd; we are one,
One flesh; to lose thee were to lose myself.
MILTON, *Paradise Lost*. Bk. ix, l. 958.

8
The torment of one, the felicity of two, the strife and enmity of three.
WASHINGTON IRVING.

9
Matrimony is something that the bachelor misses and the widower escapes.
F. M. KNOWLES, *A Cheerful Year Book*.

9a
Death itself to the reflecting mind is less serious than marriage. . . . Death is not a blow, it is not even a pulsation; it is a pause. But marriage unrolls the awful lot of numberless generations. Health, genius, honour are the words inscribed on some; on others are disease, fatuity, and infamy.
WALTER SAVAGE LANDOR. (Quoted by SARAH GRAND, *The Heavenly Twins*. Motto to Bk. ii.)

10
Marrying cannot be without women, nor can the world subsist without them. To marry is physic against incontinence.
MARTIN LUTHER, *Table-Talk*. No. 726.

On what pretense can man have interdicted marriage, which is a law of nature? It is as though we were forbidden to eat, to drink, to sleep.
MARTIN LUTHER, *Table-Talk*. No. 728.

11
Marriage, if one will face the truth, is an evil, but a necessary evil. (Τὸ γαμεῖν, ἐάν τις τὴν ἀλήθειαν σκοπῇ, κακὸν μέν ἐστιν, ἀλλ' ἀναγκαῖον κακόν.)
MENANDER, *Fragments*. No. 651.

12
Wedlock is a padlock.
JOHN RAY, *English Proverbs*, 56. (1678)

13
Marriage is the Keeley cure for love's intoxication.
HELEN ROWLAND, *Love Letters of a Cynic*.

14
Marriage is nothing but a civil contract.
JOHN SELDEN, *Table-Talk: Marriage*.

15
A world-without-end bargain.
SHAKESPEARE, *Love's Labour's Lost*, v, 2, 799

16
Is it not the most horrible of all the means which the world has had recourse to, to bind the noble to itself?
SHELLEY, *Letter to T. J. Hogg*, 21 June, 1811.

17
Marriage is a lottery.
SAMUEL SMILES, *Thrift*, p. 252.

Marriage is a lottery in which men stake their liberty and women their happiness.
MADAME DE RIEUX, *Epigram*.

Marriage is a lottery, but you can't tear up your ticket if you lose.
F. M. KNOWLES, *A Cheerful Year Book*.

18
Marriage is one long conversation, chequered by disputes.
R. L. STEVENSON, *Memories and Portraits*, p. 189.

19
Marriage is a step so grave and decisive that it attracts light-headed variable men by its very awfulness.
R. L. STEVENSON, *Virginibus Puerisque*. Pt. i.

But marriage, if comfortable, is not at all heroic. It certainly narrows and dampens the spirits of generous men. In marriage, a man becomes slack and selfish, and undergoes a fatty degeneration of his moral being. . . . The air of the fireside withers out all the fine wildings of the husband's heart.
R. L. STEVENSON, *Virginibus Puerisque*. Pt. i.

Marriage is like life in this—that it is a field of battle, and not a bed of roses.
R. L. STEVENSON, *Virginibus Puerisque*. Pt. i.

20
Two lives bound fast in one with golden ease;
Two graves grass-green beside a grey church tower.
TENNYSON, *Circumstance*.

1
Marriage is the only adventure open to the cowardly.
VOLTAIRE, *Pensées d'un Philosophe.*

2
Marriage is a status of antagonistic coöperation. In such a status, necessarily, centripetal and centrifugal forces are continuously at work, and the measure of its success obviously depends on the extent to which the centripetal forces are predominant.
JOHN M. WOOLSEY, Federal Judge, *Decision*, rendered 6 April, 1931, holding that Marie Stopes's *Married Love* is not obscene.

3
But marriage is a fetter, is a snare,
A hell, no lady so polite can bear.
YOUNG, *Love of Fame.* Satire vi, l. 65.

4
Marriage with peace is this world's Paradise;
With strife, this life's Purgatory.
UNKNOWN, *Politeuphuia*, p. 227. (1669)

Where there is strife betwixt a man and wife, 'tis hell,
And mutual love may be compar'd to heaven.
JOSHUA COOKE, *How a Man May Choose a Good Wife.* Act i, sc. 1.

The marriage state, with and without the affection suitable to it, is the completest image of Heaven and Hell we are capable of receiving in this life.
RICHARD STEELE, *The Spectator.* No. 480.

Well-married, a man is winged: ill-matched, he is shackled.
HENRY WARD BEECHER, *Proverbs from Plymouth Pulpit.*

II—Marriage: Apothegms

5
Alfred and I intended to be married in this way almost from the first; we never meant to be spliced in the humdrum way of other people.
CHARLOTTE BRONTË, *Villette.* Ch. 42. (1853)

If you mean gettin' hitched, I'm in!
ARTEMUS WARD, *Artemus Ward, His Book: The Showman's Courtship.*

6
Won 1880. One 1884.
WILLIAM JENNINGS BRYAN, *Inscription,* in wedding ring given to his wife. (PAXTON HIBBEN, *Life.*)

7
Things at home are crossways, and Betsy and I are out.
WILL CARLETON, *Betsy and I Are Out.*

Launcelot and I are out.
SHAKESPEARE, *The Merchant of Venice.* Act iii, sc. 5, l. 34.

8
The road to success is filled with women pushing their husbands along.
LORD THOMAS ROBERT DEWAR, *Epigram.*

9
I am to be married within these three days: married past redemption.
DRYDEN, *Marriage à la Mode.* Act i, sc. 1.

10
One fool at least in every married couple.
FIELDING, *Amelia.* Bk. ix, ch. 4.

11
You are of the society of wits and railleurs; . . . the surest sign is you are an enemy to marriage, the common butt of every railleur.
DAVID GARRICK, *The Country Girl.* Act ii, sc. 1. An adaptation of Wycherley's *Country Wife.*

12
Ah me! when shall I marry me?
GOLDSMITH, *Song.* Intended for *She Stoops to Conquer.*

Beauty, youth, and fortune meeting in you,
I will vouchsafe to marry you.
MASSINGER, *The Maid of Honour.* Act ii, sc. 2.

13
Divorce is the sacrament of adultery. (Le divorce est le sacrement de l'adultère.)
JEAN FRANÇOIS GUICHARD, *Maximes.*

Divorce, the public brand of shameful life.
THOMAS PARNELL, *Hesiod*, l. 206.

14
We might knit that knot with our tongues, that we shall never undo with our teeth.
JOHN LYLY, *Euphues,* p. 468.

To get married is to tie a knot with the tongue that you cannot undo with your teeth.
E. M. WRIGHT, *Rustic Speech,* p. 272.

15
It is not marriage that fails; it is people that fail. All that marriage does is to show people up.
HARRY EMERSON FOSDICK, *Marriage.*

16
Women marry because they don't want to work.
MARY GARDEN, *Newspaper Interview.*

17
It is not good that the man should be alone.
Old Testament: Genesis, ii, 18.

He that said it was not good for man to be alone, placed the celibate amongst the inferior states of perfection.
ROBERT BOYLE, *Letter from Mr. Evelyn.* (*Works,* vi, 292.)

18
Marriage is honourable in all.
New Testament: Hebrews, xiii, 4.

Marriage is honourable, but housekeeping's a shrew.
JOHN RAY, *English Proverbs.*

19
Girls engaged write Sonnets from the Portuguese—married women never.
ELBERT HUBBARD, *The Philistine.* Vol. v, p. 91.

20
Marriages would in general be as happy, and often more so, if they were all made by the Lord Chancellor.
SAMUEL JOHNSON. (BOSWELL, *Life,* 1776.)

Notwithstanding all that wit, or malice, or pride, or prudence will be able to suggest, men and women must at last pass their lives together.

SAMUEL JOHNSON, *The Rambler*. No. 119.

1
I have met with women whom I really think would like to be married to a Poem, and to be given away by a Novel.

KEATS, *Letters to Fanny Brawne*. Letter 2.

2
Here you may see Benedick the married man.

SHAKESPEARE, *Much Ado About Nothing*. Act i, sc. 1, l. 269. (1598) It was from this use of the word that "Benedick" or "Benedict," as a synonym for a married man, originated, especially for a supposedly confirmed bachelor who falls victim to Cupid's arrow.

How dost thou, Benedick, the married man?

SHAKESPEARE, *Much Ado About Nothing*. Act v, sc. 4, l. 100.

Wish the veteran joy of his entrance into the band of Benedicts.

WALTER SCOTT. In LOCKHART, *Life* (1839), Vol. vi, p 313. (1821) In frequent use thereafter, usually in a jocular sense.

3
He married off his daughter, giving her, as he said himself, for a trial marriage of thirty days. ('Επὶ πεῖρᾳ δοὺς τριάκονθ' ἡμέρας.)

MENANDER, *Didymai*. Frag. 118.

4
Women when they marry buy a cat in the bag.

MONTAIGNE, *Essays*. Bk. iii, ch. 5.

5
Mind, not body, makes marriage lasting. (Perenne conjugium animus non corpus facit.)

PUBLILIUS SYRUS, *Sententiæ*. No. 520.

The wedlock of minds will be greater than that of bodies. (Magis erit animorum quam corporum conjugium.)

ERASMUS, *Procus et Puella*.

Let me not to the marriage of true minds
Admit impediments.

SHAKESPEARE, *Sonnets*. No. cxvi.

More things belong [to marriage] than four bare legs in a bed.

JOHN HEYWOOD, *Proverbs*. Pt. i, ch. 8.

6
She who is born handsome is born married.

JOHN RAY, *English Proverbs*.

Such as marry but to a fair face, tie themselves oft to a foul bargain.

ROBERT GREENE, *Works*. Vol. viii, p. 36.

Some ladies are too beauteous to be wed,
For where's the man that's worthy of their bed?

YOUNG, *Love of Fame*. Satire vi, l. 83.

7
It takes patience to appreciate domestic bliss; volatile spirits prefer unhappiness.

GEORGE SANTAYANA, *The Life of Reason*. Vol. ii, p. 4.

8
"Whenever I marry," says masculine Ann,
"I must really insist upon wedding a man!"
But what if the man (for men are but human)
Should be equally nice about wedding a woman?

J. G. SAXE, *Dilemma*.

9
Of all actions of a man's life, his marriage does least concern other people; yet of all actions of our life, 'tis most meddled with by other people.

JOHN SELDEN, *Table-Talk: Marriage*.

10
I say, we will have no more marriages. Those that are married already, all but one, shall live; the rest shall keep as they are. To a nunnery, go.

SHAKESPEARE, *Hamlet*. Act iii, sc. 1, l. 155.

11
Makes marriage vows
As false as dicers' oaths.

SHAKESPEARE, *Hamlet*. Act iii, sc. 4, l. 44. *See also* LOVE: LOVE'S PERJURIES.

12
The whole world is strewn with snares, traps, gins and pitfalls for the capture of men by women.

BERNARD SHAW, *Man and Superman: Introduction*.

13
Marriage is popular because it combines the maximum of temptation with the maximum of opportunity.

BERNARD SHAW, *Maxims for Revolutionists*.

Marriage is unpopular because it combines the minimum of temptation with the maximum of opportunity.

UNKNOWN, *Shaw Revised*.

14
Married women are kept women and they are beginning to find it out.

LOGAN PEARSALL SMITH, *Afterthoughts*.

15
What they do in heaven we are ignorant of; but what they do not we are told expressly, that they neither marry nor are given in marriage.

SWIFT, *Thoughts on Various Subjects*.

They which shall be accounted worthy to obtain that world; . . . neither marry, nor are given in marriage.

New Testament: Luke, xx, 35.

16
Wedded persons may thus pass over their lives quietly . . . if the husband becomes deaf and the wife blind.

RICHARD TAVERNER, *Garden of Wisdom*, ii, 4. (1539)

A good marriage would be between a blind wife and a deaf husband. (Un bon mariage se dressoit d'une femme aveugle, avecques un mary sourd.)

MONTAIGNE, *Essays*. Bk. iii, ch. 5. Quoted as a saying.

A husband must be deaf, and his wife blind, to have quietness.

TORRIANO, *Piazza Universale: Wife*.

1
She calls it wedlock, and with that name veils her sin. (Conjugium vocat; hoc prætexit nomine culpam.)

VERGIL, *Æneid*. Bk. iv, l. 172.

I have never laid claim to wedlock, nor entered into such a compact. (Nec conjugis umquam prætendi tædas, aut hæc in fœdera veni.)

VERGIL, *Æneid*. Bk. iv, l. 338.

2
He is dreadfully married. He's the most married man I ever saw in my life.

ARTEMUS WARD, *A Mormon Romance.*

3
In married life three is company and two none.

OSCAR WILDE, *The Importance of Being Earnest.* Act i.

4
There's nothing in the world like the devotion of a married woman. It's a thing no married man knows anything about.

OSCAR WILDE, *Lady Windermere's Fan.* Act iii.

5
Twenty years of romance make a woman look like a ruin; but twenty years of marriage make her something like a public building.

OSCAR WILDE, *A Woman of No Importance.* Act i.

6
Men marry because they are tired; women because they are curious. Both are disappointed.

OSCAR WILDE, *A Woman of No Importance.* Act iii.

7
Hanging and wiving go by destiny.

UNKNOWN, *School-House for Women.* (1541)

Wedding is destiny, And hanging likewise.

JOHN HEYWOOD, *English Proverbs*. Pt. i, ch. 3. (1546)

The ancient saying is no heresy,
Hanging and wiving go by destiny.

SHAKESPEARE, *The Merchant of Venice.* Act ii, sc. 9, l. 82. The proverb is used by many writers, among them: BURTON, *Anatomy of Melancholy,* iii, ii, 5, 5; CHAPMAN, *All Fools,* v, 1; FARQUHAR, *Recruiting Officer,* iii, 2; SWIFT, *Polite Conversation,* i.

8
Truly some men there be
That live always in great horrour,
And say it goeth by destiny
To hang or wed: both hath one hour;
And whether it be, I am well sure,
Hanging is better of the twain;
Sooner done, and shorter pain.

UNKNOWN, *The School-house.* (c. 1542)

If matrimony and hanging go
By dest'ny, why not whipping too?

BUTLER, *Hudibras.* Pt. ii, canto i, l. 839.

I spake to him of Garlic, he answered Asparagus: consulted him of marriage, he tells me of hanging, as if they went by one and the same destiny.

BEN JONSON, *Explorata: Impertinens.*

9
It is said full ryfe [often],
A man may not wive And also thrive,
And all in a year.

UNKNOWN. (*Towneley Plays.* No. 12. c. 1388.)

It is too much, we daily hear,
To wive and thrive both in one year.

THOMAS TUSSER, *Hundred Points of Good Husbandry: Wiving and Thriving.*

III—Marriage, Advice and Admonition

See also Wife: Her Choice

10
A woman seldom asks advice before she has bought her wedding clothes.

ADDISON, *The Spectator*. No. 475.

11
Therefore it is fitting for the women to be married at about the age of eighteen, and the men at thirty-seven, or a little before.

ARISTOTLE, *Politics*. Bk. vii, ch. 14, sec. 6.

Let still the woman take
An elder than herself; so wears she to him,
So sways she level in her husband's heart:
For, boy, however we do praise ourselves,
Our fancies are more giddy and unfirm,
More longing, wavering, sooner lost and worn,
Than women's are.

SHAKESPEARE, *Twelfth Night*. Act ii, sc. 4, l. 30.

Then let thy love be younger than thyself,
Or thy affection cannot hold the bent:
For women are as roses, whose fair flower
Being once display'd, doth fall that very hour.

SHAKESPEARE, *Twelfth Night*. Act ii, sc. 4, l. 37.

12
We should marry to please ourselves, not other people.

ISAAC BICKERSTAFFE, *The Maid of the Mill.* Act iii, sc. 4.

13
If you marry an ugly wife, she will be your bane; if a beautiful one, you will not keep her to yourself.

BION. (DIOGENES LAERTIUS, *Bion.* Bk. iv, 48.)

14
To change the name and not the letter
Is a change for the worse and not for the better.

CHAMBERS, *Book of Days.* Vol. i, p. 723.

15
It is better to marry than to burn.

New Testament: I Corinthians, vii, 9.

16
Misses! the tale that I relate
This lesson seems to carry—
Choose not alone a proper mate,
But proper time to marry.

COWPER, *Pairing Time Anticipated: Moral.*

17
For a young man not yet; for an old man never at all. (Τοὺς μὲν νέους μηδέπω, τοὺς δὲ πρεσβυτέρους μηδεπώποτε.)

DIOGENES, when asked the proper time to marry. (DIOGENES LAERTIUS, *Diogenes.* Sec. 54.)

He was reputed one of the wise men that made answer to the question when a man should marry? "A young man not yet, an elder man not at all."

FRANCIS BACON, *Essays: Of Marriage and Single Life*. Also *Apothegms*, No. 220.

Honest men marry quickly, but wise men not at all.

CERVANTES, *Don Quixote*. Pt. ii, ch. 2.

1
A woman needs a stronger head than her own for counsel—she should marry. (Una mujer no tiene. Valor para el consejo, y la conviene Casarse.)

CALDERON, *El Purgatorio de Sans Patricio*. Act iii, sc. 4.

2
I have always thought that every woman should marry, and no man.

BENJAMIN DISRAELI, *Lothair*. Ch. 30.

Men in single state should tarry,
While women, I suggest, should marry.

SAMUEL HOFFENSTEIN, *Advice on Marriage*.

It is a woman's business to get married as soon as possible, and a man's to keep unmarried as long as he can.

BERNARD SHAW, *Man and Superman*. Act ii.

Marriage is of so much use to a woman, opens out to her so much more of life, and puts her in the way of so much more freedom and usefulness, that, whether she marry well or ill, she can hardly miss some benefit.

R. L. STEVENSON, *Virginibus Puerisque*. Pt. i.

3
Keep thy eyes wide open before marriage, and half shut afterwards.

BENJAMIN FRANKLIN, *Poor Richard*, 1738.

4
Wholly abstain, or wed. Thy bounteous Lord
Allows thee choice of paths; take no by-ways. . . .
Continence hath his joy; weigh both, and so
If rottenness have more, let Heaven go.

GEORGE HERBERT, *The Church-Porch*. St. 3.

5
Marry your son when you will, your daughter when you can.

GEORGE HERBERT, *Jacula Prudentum*.

6
Be careful to marry a woman who lives near to you. (Τὴν δὲ μάλιστα γαμεῖν, ἥ τις σέθεν ἔγγθι ναίει.)

HESIOD, *Works and Days*, l. 700.

7
Who marries does well, who marries not does better.

JAMES HOWELL, *Familiar Letters*, ii, 666. (1659)

8
Marriage is the best state for man in general; and every man is the worse man, in proportion as he is unfit for the married state.

SAMUEL JOHNSON. (BOSWELL, *Life*, 1776.)

9
If you are honestly devoted to one woman, then bow your head and submit your neck to the yoke. (Si tibi simplicitas uxoria, deditus uni Est animus, summitte caput cervice parata Ferre jugum.)

JUVENAL, *Satires*. Sat. vi, l. 206.

10
To rise betimes, and to marry young, are what no man ever repents of doing.

MARTIN LUTHER, *Table-Talk: Marriage*.

11
Take heed, Camilla, that seeking all the Wood for a straight stick, you choose not at the last a crooked staff.

JOHN LYLY, *Euphues*.

12
Ev'n in the happiest choice, where fav'ring heaven
Has equal love and easy fortune giv'n,—
Think not, the husband gain'd, that all is done;
The prize of happiness must still be won:
And, oft, the careless find it to their cost,
The lover in the husband may be lost;
The graces might alone his heart allure;
They and the virtues, meeting, must secure.

GEORGE LYTTELTON, *Advice to a Lady*.

13
And, to all married men, be this a caution,
Which they should duly tender as their life,
Neither to doat too much, nor doubt a wife.

PHILIP MASSINGER, *The Picture*. Act v, sc. 3.

14
Advice to persons about to marry—Don't.

HENRY MAYHEW, in *Punch*, vol. viii, p. 1. (1845) This, the most famous joke that *Punch* ever made, is stated by Spielman, in his *History of Punch*, to have been written by Mayhew, one of the three co-editors under whose direction *Punch* was first published.

15
'Tis unlucky to marry in the month of May. (Mense malum Maio nubere.)

OVID, *Fasti*. Eleg. v, l. 490.

Marry in May, repent alway.

JOHN RAY, *English Proverbs*.

Marry in Lent, live to repent.

JOHN RAY, *English Proverbs*.

16
It does not much signify whom one marries, as one is sure to find next morning that it is some one else.

SAMUEL ROGERS, *Table-Talk*.

Maidens! why should you worry in choosing whom you should marry?
Choose whom you may, you will find you have got somebody else.

JOHN HAY, *Distiches*. No. 10.

17
If thou wilt needs marry, marry a fool; for wise men know well enough what monsters you make of them.

SHAKESPEARE, *Hamlet*. Act iii, sc. 1, l. 142.

'Tis my maxim, he's a fool that marries; but he's a greater that does not marry a fool.

WYCHERLEY, *Country Wife*. Act i, sc. 1, l. 502.

Intelligent women always marry fools.
ANATOLE FRANCE.

1
Whichever you do you will repent it. (Ὃ ἂν αὐτῶν ποιήσῃς, μεταγνώσῃ.)
SOCRATES, when asked whether or not a man should marry. (DIOGENES LAERTIUS, *Socrates*. Sec. 16.)

2
No woman should marry a teetotaller or a man who does not smoke.
R. L. STEVENSON, *Virginibus Puerisque*. Pt. i.

I see . . . men . . . taking into their lives acidulous vestals.
R. L. STEVENSON, *Virginibus Puerisque*. Pt. i.

3
Better to sit up all night than to go to bed with a dragon.
JEREMY TAYLOR, *Holy Living*, p. 213.

4
Monday for wealth, Tuesday for health,
Wednesday the best day of all:
Thursday for crosses, Friday for losses,
Saturday no luck at all.
UNKNOWN. (BRAND, *Popular Antiquities*.) Days lucky or unlucky for marriage.

Marry Monday, marry for wealth;
Marry Tuesday, marry for health;
Marry Wednesday, the best day of all;
Marry Thursday, marry for crosses:
Marry Friday, marry for losses;
Marry Saturday, no luck at all.
UNKNOWN. (HALLIWELL, *Nursery Rhymes*.)

IV—Marriage: Like with Like

5
Ah, wise was he who first pondered this truth and gave it utterance: that to marry in one's own degree is far the best, and that neither among the rich nor the high-born should marriage be desired by a man who toileth with his hands.
ÆSCHYLUS, *Prometheus Bound*, l. 887.

Oh! wise was he, the first who taught
This lesson of observant thought,
That equal fates alone may bless
The bowers of nuptial happiness;
That never where ancestral pride
Inflames, or affluence rolls its tide,
Should love's ill-omened bonds entwine
The offspring of an humbler line.
THOMAS LOVE PEACOCK, *Connubial Equality*. An adaptation of Æschylus, *Prometheus Bound*, l. 887. (ἦ σοφὸς ἦ σοφὸς, etc.)

6
Like blood, like goods, and like age,
Make the happiest marriage.
JOHN CLARKE, *Parœmiologia*, 28. (1639)

7
For any man to match above his rank
Is but to sell his liberty.
MASSINGER, *The Virgin Martyr*. Act i, sc. 1.

8
Among unequals what society
Can sort, what harmony, or true delight?
MILTON, *Paradise Lost*. Bk. viii, l. 383.

9
As the ill-mated steer yoked miserably at the plough, so fares the wife who is less than her mighty lord. (Quam male inæquales veniunt ad aratra juvenci, Tam premitur magno conjuge nupta minor.)
OVID, *Heroides*. Epis. ix, l. 29.

If you would marry wisely, marry your equal. (Siqua voles apte nubere, nube pari.)
OVID, *Heroides*. Epis. ix, l. 32.

10
Whip your own top. (Τὴν κατὰ σαυτὸν ἔλα.)
PITTACUS, when asked by a stranger whether he should marry his equal or his superior. Pittacus led him to a group of boys who were spinning tops, and bade him listen to them. The boys were crying to each other, "Whip your own top." The words also mean, "Keep to your own sphere," and the stranger led home the humbler bride. (CALLIMACHUS, *Epigrams: Anth. Pal.*, vii, 89.)

12
Let like mate with like; the ill-matched never agree. (Par pari jugator conjunx; quidquid impar, dissidet.)
SOLON. (AUSONIUS [?], *Septem Sapientum Sententiæ*, l. 30.)

V—Marriage and Money

See also Dowry

13
A poor man who marries a wealthy woman gets a ruler and not a wife.
ANAXANDRIDES. (STOBÆUS, *Florilegium*.)

14
There are but two objects in marriage, love or money. If you marry for love, you will certainly have some very happy days, and probably many very uneasy ones; if for money, you will have no happy days and probably no uneasy ones.
LORD CHESTERFIELD, *Letters*. (To be delivered posthumously.)

15
His designs were strictly honourable, as the phrase is, that is to rob a lady of her fortune by way of marriage.
FIELDING, *Tom Jones*. Bk. xi, ch. 4.

16
He that marries for wealth sells his liberty.
THOMAS FULLER, *Gnomologia*. No. 2238.

Who wives for a dower resigns his own power.
JOHN RAY, *English Proverbs*.

17
The woes of wedlock with the joys, we mix;
'Tis best repenting in a coach and six.
SAMUEL GARTH, *Cato: Prologue*.

18
'Tis sad when you think of her wasted life,
For youth cannot mate with age,
And her beauty was sold for an old man's gold—
She's a bird in a gilded cage.
ARTHUR J. LAMB, *A Bird in a Gilded Cage*. (1900) Music by HARRY VON TILZER.

1
Mark was a Pill. His little Dame had
Class . . .
One of those Unions that neglect to Une . . .
She was a Saint! He was a Hound! Alas,
That such a Peach should marry such a
Prune!
Why did she stick? Who knows the tune
To which these women march? We know, at
least,
Mark had a Wad, and bought her gowns and
shoon. . . .
Mayhap it was a case of Booty and the Beast!
DON MARQUIS, *Tristram and Isolt.*

Oh, you prune, you've been my ruin!
EVERETT SHINN, *Lucy Moore, The Prune-Hater's Daughter.* Last line.

2
O thrice ill-starred is he who marries when he is poor! (Ὦ τρὶς κακοδαίμων, ὅστις ὢν πένης γαμεῖ.)
MENANDER, *Plocius.*

3
Let all mankind this certain maxim hold:
Marry who will, our sex is to be sold.
With empty hands no tassels you can lure,
But fulsome love for gain we can endure;
For gold we love the impotent and old,
And heave, and pant, and kiss, and cling, for
gold.
Yet with embraces curses oft I mixt,
Then kiss'd again, and chid, and rail'd betwixt.
POPE, *Wife of Bath: Prologue,* l. 170.

But honored well are charms to sell
If priests the selling do.
NATHANIEL PARKER WILLIS, *Unseen Spirits.*

4
I asked of Echo, 't other day
(Whose words are few and often funny),
What to a novice she could say
Of courtship, love, and matrimony.
Quoth Echo, plainly,—"Matter-o'-money."
J. G. SAXE, *Echo.*

5
I come to wive it wealthily.
SHAKESPEARE, *The Taming of the Shrew.* Act i, sc. 2, l. 75.

6
Doänt thou marry for munny, but goä wheer
munny is!
TENNYSON, *Northern Farmer,* New Style. St. 5.

Remember, it is as easy to marry a rich woman as a poor woman.
THACKERAY, *Pendennis.* Bk. i, ch. 28.

7
I prefer a man without money, to money without a man. (Ego vero malo virum, qui pecunia egeat, quam pecuniam, quæ viro.)
THEMISTOCLES, when someone asked his advice as to whether he should give his daughter to a man who was poor but honest or to one who was rich but less esteemed. (PLUTARCH, *Lives: Themistocles.* Sec. 18; CICERO, *De Officiis.* Bk. ii, ch. 20, sec. 71.)

8
My Lord Denbigh is going to marry a fortune, I forget her name; my Lord Gower asked him how long the honey-moon would last? He replied, "Don't tell me of the honey-moon; it is harvest moon with me."
HORACE WALPOLE, *Letter to George Montagu,* 19 May, 1756.

VI—Marriage: December and May

9
What woes must such unequal union bring,
When hoary Winter weds the youthful
Spring?
You, like Mezentius, in the nuptial bed,
Once more unite the living and the dead.
WILLIAM BROOME, *On a Gentleman of Seventy Who Married a Lady of Sixteen.*

The living and the dead, at his [Mezentius']
command,
Were coupled face to face and hand to hand.
VERGIL, *Æneid.* Bk. viii.

10
What can a young lassie, what shall a young
lassie,
What can a young lassie do wi' an auld man?
BURNS, *What Can a Young Lassie.*

11
That she, this maiden, which that May us
highte . . .
Should wedded be unto this January.
CHAUCER, *The Marchantes Tale,* l. 449.

When asthmatic January weds buxom May.
ROBERT BUCHANAN, *Coming Terror,* 267.

12
Men should wedden after their estate,
For youth and eld are often at debate.
CHAUCER, *The Milleres Tale,* l. 43.

13
Husband twice as old as wife,
Argues ill for married life.
W. S. GILBERT, *Princess Ida.* Act. i.

14
Better be an old man's darling than a young man's warling.
JOHN HEYWOOD, *Proverbs.* Pt. ii, ch. 7. (1546) "Warling" was apparently coined for this proverb, which will be found also in CAMDEN, *Remains,* 293; SWIFT, *Polite Conversation,* i; AINSWORTH, *Miser's Daughter,* iii, 15, and elsewhere.

Better be an old man's darling
Than become a young man's slave.
J. R. PLANCHÉ, *Extravaganza,* v, 206.

15
For it ne sits not unto fresh May
Forto be coupled to cold January.
JOHN LYDGATE, *Temple of Glas.* (c. 1400)

Lustful he was, at forty must be wed,
Old January will have May in bed.
UNKNOWN, *Musarum Deliciæ,* i, 103.

16
Since thou wouldst needs (bewitched with
some ill charms!)
Be buried in those monumental arms,

All we can wish is, may that earth lie light
Upon thy tender limbs! and so good night.

EDMUND WALLER, *To One Married to an Old Man.*

1
For every marriage then is best in tune,
When that the wife is May, the husband June.

ROWLAND WATKYNS, *To the Most Courteous and Fair Gentlewoman, Mrs. Ellinor Williams.*

2
Take a doe in the month of May,
And a forester's courage she soon will allay.

UNKNOWN. (*Roxburghe Ballads*, vii, 558.)

VII—Marriage and Repentance

3
Be not hasty to marry; it's better to have one plough going than two cradles; and more profit to have a barn filled than a bed.

THOMAS FULLER, *Introductio ad Prudentiam.*

4
You should indeed have longer tarried
By the roadside before you married.

W. S. LANDOR, *To One Ill-mated.*

5
In hasty recklessness men often marry,
And afterwards repent it all their lives.
(Par un prompt désespoir souvent on se marie,
Qu'on s'en repent après tout le temps de sa vie.)

MOLIÈRE, *Les Femmes Savantes.* Act v, sc. 4, l. 89.

6
Lest in making hasty choice, leisure for repentance should follow.

WILLIAM PAINTER, *Palace of Pleasure*, l. 115. (1566)

She was afraid to match in haste lest she might repent at leisure.

ROBERT GREENE, *Works*, xi, 86. (1592)

Marry too soon, and you'll repent too late.

THOMAS RANDOLPH, *Jealous Lovers.* Act v, sc. 2. (1632)

Marry in haste, repent at leisure.

CONGREVE, *Old Batchelor.* Act v, sc. 8. (1692)

7
Hasty marriage seldom proveth well.

SHAKESPEARE, *III Henry VI.* Act iv, sc. 1, l. 18.

Wooing, wedding, and repenting, is as a Scotch jig, a measure, and a cinque pace.

SHAKESPEARE, *Much Ado About Nothing.* Act ii, sc. 1, l. 76.

Who woo'd in haste, and means to wed at leisure.

SHAKESPEARE, *The Taming of the Shrew.* Act iii, sc. 2, l. 11.

8
Marriage leapeth up upon the saddle, and repentance upon the crupper.

UNKNOWN, *Politeuphuia*, 35. (1669)

And sure all marriage in repentance ends.

DRYDEN, *Don Sebastian: Epilogue.*

VIII—Marriage and Love

9
The angry tyrant lays his yoke on all,
Yet in his fiercest rage is charming still;
Officious Hymen comes whene'er we call,
But haughty Love comes only when he will.

APHRA BEHN, *Love and Marriage.*

'Tis Love alone can make our fetters please.

APHRA BEHN, *Love and Marriage.*

10
Love-matches are made by people who are content, for a month of honey, to condemn themselves to a life of vinegar.

COUNTESS OF BLESSINGTON, *Commonplace Book.*

Marriage, from love, like vinegar from wine—
A sad, sour, sober beverage—by time
Is sharpen'd from its high celestial flavour
Down to a very homely household savour.

BYRON, *Don Juan.* Canto iii, st. 5.

11
For Wedlock without love, some say,
Is but a lock without a key.
It is a kind of rape to marry
One that neglects or cares not for ye.

BUTLER, *Hudibras.* Pt. ii, canto i, l. 321.

12
'Tis melancholy, and a fearful sign
Of human frailty, folly, also crime,
That love and marriage rarely can combine,
Although they both are born in the same clime.

BYRON, *Don Juan.* Canto iii, st. 5.

13
People marry through a variety of other reasons, and with varying results; but to marry for love is to invite inevitable tragedy.

J. B. CABELL, *The Cream of the Jest*, p. 235.

14
Can you keep the bee from ranging,
Or the ringdove's neck from changing?
No! nor fettered Love from dying
In the knot there's no untying.

THOMAS CAMPBELL, *Song.* St. 6.

15
There as my heart is set, there will I wive.

CHAUCER, *The Clerkes Tale*, l. 117.

16
Marriage has, as you say, no *natural* relation to love. Marriage belongs to society; it is a social contract.

S. T. COLERIDGE, *Table Talk*, p. 450.

17
And all the young ladies said . . . that to be sure a love-match was the only thing for happiness, where the parties could anyway afford it.

MARIA EDGEWORTH, *Castle Rackrent: Continuation of Memoirs.*

18
Where there's marriage without love, there will be love without marriage.

BENJAMIN FRANKLIN, *Poor Richard*, 1734.

There can be only one end to marriage without love, and that is love without marriage.
CHURTON COLLINS, *Aphorisms*.

Where love is there is marriage; where love is not, there is prostitution.
JOHN HAYNES HOLMES, *Where Love Is*.

1
'Tis highly rational, we can't dispute,
That Love, being naked, should promote a suit:
But doth not oddity to him attach
Whose fire's so oft extinguished by a match?
RICHARD GARNETT, *On Love and Marriage*.

2
Marriage the happiest bond of love might be,
If hands were only joined where hearts agree.
GEORGE GRANVILLE, *The British Enchanters*. Act v, sc. 1.

Union of hearts, not hands, does marriage make,
And sympathy of mind keeps love awake.
AARON HILL, *Alzira*.

3
If a man really loves a woman, of course he wouldn't marry her for the world if he were not quite sure that he was the best person she could by any possibility marry.
O. W. HOLMES, *The Autocrat of the Breakfast-Table*. Ch. 10.

4
It is commonly a weak man who marries for love.
SAMUEL JOHNSON. (BOSWELL, *Life*. 1776.)

5
It is love that is sacred. . . . Marriage and love have nothing in common. . . . We marry only once . . . but we may love twenty times. . . . Marriage is law, and love is instinct.
GUY DE MAUPASSANT, *The Love of Long Ago*.

6
Hail wedded love, mysterious law, true source
Of human offspring, sole propriety
In Paradise of all things common else.
By thee adulterous lust was driv'n from men
Among the bestial herds to range; by thee,
Founded in reason, loyal, just, and pure,
Relations dear, and all the charities
Of father, son, and brother, first were known.
MILTON, *Paradise Lost*. Bk. iv, l. 750.

7
Love is often a fruit of marriage. (L'amour est souvent un fruit de mariage.)
MOLIÈRE, *Sganarelle*. Sc. 1, l. 54.

The old family maxim, that "if she marries first, love will come after."
EUSTACE BUDGELL, *The Spectator*. No. 605.

Marry first and love will follow.
HANNAH COWLEY, *The Belle's Stratagem*. Act iii, sc. 1. Quoted as "the good old maxim."

The woman that marries to love better will be as much mistaken as the wencher that marries to live better. Marrying to increase love is like gaming to become rich; you only lose what little stock you had before.
WYCHERLEY, *The Country Wife*. Act iv.

8
A good marriage (if any there be) refuses the company and conditions of love; it endeavors to present those of amity.
MONTAIGNE, *Essays*. Bk. iii, ch. 5.

I see no marriages fail sooner, or more troubled, than such as are concluded for beauty's sake, and huddled up for amorous desires.
MONTAIGNE, *Essays*. Bk. iii, ch. 5.

You cannot pluck roses without fear of thorns,
Nor enjoy a fair wife without danger of horns.
BENJAMIN FRANKLIN, *Poor Richard*, 1734.

9
Where I love I must not marry,
Where I marry, cannot love.
THOMAS MOORE, *Love and Marriage*.

They gied him my hand, tho' my heart was at sea.
ANNE BARNARD, *Auld Robin Gray*.

10
The garlands fade, the vows are worn away;
So dies her love, and so my hopes decay.
POPE, *Pastorals: Autumn*, l. 69.

11
How oft, when press'd to marriage, have I said,
Curse on all laws but those which Love has made!
Love, free as air, at sight of human ties,
Spreads his light wings, and in a moment flies.
POPE, *Eloisa to Abelard*, l. 73.

12
Marry for love and work for siller.
JOHN RAY, *English Proverbs*.

Who marries for love without money, hath merry nights and sorry days.
JOHN RAY, *English Proverbs*.

13
Love as a relation between men and women was ruined by the desire to make sure of the legitimacy of children.
BERTRAND RUSSELL, *Marriage and Morals*, p. 27.

14
I will marry her, sir, at your request; but if there be no great love in the beginning, yet heaven may decrease it upon better acquaintance. . . . I hope, upon familiarity will grow more contempt: I will marry her; that I am freely dissolved, and dissolutely.
SHAKESPEARE, *The Merry Wives of Windsor*. Act i, sc. 1, l. 253.

15
'Tis safest in matrimony to begin with a little aversion.
SHERIDAN, *The Rivals*. Act ii, sc. 2.

16
If they only married when they fell in love, most people would die unwed.
R. L. STEVENSON, *Virginibus Puerisque*. Ch. 1

The Lion is the King of Beasts, but he is scarcely suitable for a domestic pet. In the same way, I suspect love is rather too violent a passion to make a good domestic sentiment.

R. L. STEVENSON, *Virginibus Puerisque*. Ch. 1.

1
Venus, a beautiful, good-natured lady, was the goddess of love; Juno, a terrible shrew, the goddess of marriage: and they were always mortal enemies.

SWIFT, *Thoughts on Various Subjects.*

2
The only thing that can hallow marriage is love, and the only genuine marriage is that which is hallowed by love.

LEO TOLSTOY, *The Kreutzer Sonata*. Ch. 2.

3
All true love is grounded on esteem.

GEORGE VILLIERS, DUKE OF BUCKINGHAM, *True Love.*

Wedded love is founded on esteem.

ELIJAH FENTON, *Mariamne.*

4
One should always be in love. That is the reason one should never marry.

OSCAR WILDE, *A Woman of No Importance.* Act iii.

IX—Marriage: Made in Heaven

5
True it is that marriages be done in heaven and performed on earth.

WM. PAINTER, *Palace of Pleasure*. iii, 24. (1567)

Marriages are made in heaven and consummated on earth:

JOHN LYLY, *Mother Bombie.* Act iv, sc. 1. (1590) The French have the same proverb, "Les mariages se font au ciel, et se consomment sur la terre."

6
Marriage is destiny, made in heaven.

JOHN LYLY, *Mother Bombie.* (1590)

7
Matches are made in heaven.

ROBERT BURTON, *Anatomy of Melancholy*. Pt. iii, sec. ii, mem. 5, subs. 5. (1621) In frequent use thereafter.

8
If marriages
Are made in Heaven, they should be happier.

THOMAS SOUTHERNE, *Isabella; or, The Fatal Marriage.* Act iv, sc. 2.

X—Marriage: The Wedding

9
They stood before the altar and supplied
The fire themselves in which their fat was fried.

AMBROSE BIERCE, *The Devil's Dictionary*, p. 23.

10
To have and to hold from this day forward, for better, for worse, for richer, for poorer, in sickness, and in health, to love and to cherish, till death us do part.

Book of Common Prayer: Solemnization of Matrimony.

With this ring I thee wed, with my body I thee worship, and with all my worldly goods I thee endow.

Book of Common Prayer: Solemnization of Matrimony. In America, the second clause is omitted.

She is mine to have and to hold!
She has chosen between love and gold!
All the joys life can give
Shall be hers, while I live,
For she's mine to have and to hold.

WILL A. HEELAN, *She Is Mine to Have and to Hold.*

To Have and to Hold.

MARY JOHNSTON. Title of novel.

11
The business of a poor waiting-woman, here upon earth, is to be scraping up something against a rainy day, called the day of marriage.

DRYDEN, *Amphitryon*. Act i, sc. 2.

12
Happiness untold awaits them
When the parson consecrates them.

W. S. GILBERT, *Ruddigore*. Act i.

13
So, with decorum all things carried;
Miss frown'd, and blush'd, and then was—married.

GOLDSMITH, *The Double Transformation*, l. 19.

14
For next to that interesting job,
The hanging of Jack, or Bill, or Bob,
There's nothing so draws a London mob
As the noosing of very rich people.

THOMAS HOOD, *Miss Kilmansegg: Her Courtship.*

15
There is something about a wedding-gown prettier than in any other gown in the world.

DOUGLAS JERROLD. (*Douglas Jerrold's Wit: A Wedding-Gown.*)

For talk six times with the same single lady,
And you may get the wedding dresses ready.

BYRON, *Don Juan*. Canto xii, st. 59.

16
The voice that breathed o'er Eden,
That earliest wedding-day,
The primal marriage blessing,
It hath not passed away.

JOHN KEBLE, *Holy Matrimony.*

17
Nothing is to me more distasteful than that entire complacency and satisfaction which beam in the faces of a new-married couple,—in that of the lady particularly.

CHARLES LAMB, *Essays of Elia: A Bachelor's Complaint.*

18
Fair Concord, ever abide by their couch, and to so well matched a pair may Venus ever be propitious. (Candida perpetuo reside, Concordia, lecto, Tamque pari semper sit Venus æqua jugo.)

MARTIAL, *Epigrams*. Bk. iv, epig. 13.

God the best maker of all marriages
Combine your hearts in one.
SHAKESPEARE, *Henry V*. Act v, sc. 2, l. 386.

1
What therefore God hath joined together, let not man put asunder.
New Testament: Matthew, xix, 6.

What God hath joined together no man shall ever put asunder: God will take care of that.
BERNARD SHAW, *Getting Married*.

Under this window in stormy weather
I marry this man and woman together;
Let none but Him who rules the thunder
Put this man and woman asunder.
SWIFT, *Marriage Service from His Chamber Window*.

Yet 'tis "so nominated in the bond,"
That both are tied till one shall have expired.
BYRON, *Don Juan*. Canto iii, st. 7.

2
To church in the morning, and there saw a wedding in the church, which I have not seen many a day; and the young people so merry one with another! and strange to see what delight we married people have to see these poor fools decoyed into our condition, every man and woman gazing and smiling at them.
SAMUEL PEPYS, *Diary*, 25 Dec., 1665.

To church the parties went,
At once with carnal and devout intent.
POPE, *January and May*, l. 309.

3
You've picked an unlucky day for changing your name. (Ne hodie malo cum auspicio nomen commutaveria.)
PLAUTUS, *Asinaria*, l. 373. (Act ii, sc. 2.)

4
Wooed. and married, and a',
Married, and wooed, and a'!
And was she nae very weel off
That was wooed, and married, and a'?
ALEXANDER ROSS, *Song*.

5
But who ever heard of a marriage deterred
Or even deferred
By any contrivance so very absurd
As scolding the boy, and caging his bird?
J. G. SAXE, *Pyramus and Thisbe*.

6
A man may weep upon his wedding day.
SHAKESPEARE, *Henry VIII: Prologue*, l. 32.

7
Till holy church incorporate two in one.
SHAKESPEARE, *Romeo and Juliet*. Act ii, sc. 6, l. 37.

Since first he called her his before the holy man.
CAMPBELL, *The Pleasures of Hope*. Pt. ii, l. 130.

8
I must marry the girl first, and ask his consent afterwards.
R. B. SHERIDAN, *St. Patrick's Day*. Act i, sc. 1.

9
Behold, whiles she before the altar stands,
Hearing the holy priest that to her speaks,
And blesseth her with his two happy hands,
How the red roses flush up in her cheeks,
And the pure snow with goodly vermeil stain,
Like crimson dyed in grain:
That even th' angels, which continually
About the sacred altar do remain,
Forget their service and about her fly,
Oft peeping in her face, that seems more fair.
The more they on it stare.
SPENSER, *Epithalamion*, l. 223.

Against their bridal day, which is not long:
Sweet Thames, run softly, till I end my song.
SPENSER, *Prothalamion*, l. 35.

10
Now when they sever wedded hands,
Joy trembles in their bosom-strands,
And lovely laughter leaps and falls
Upon their lips in madrigals.
R. L. STEVENSON, *Underwoods*. No. 4.

11
What woman, however old, has not the bridal-favours and raiment stowed away, and packed in lavender, in the inmost cupboards of her heart?
THACKERAY, *The Virginians*. Ch. 33.

12
Design, or chance makes others wive,
But nature did this match contrive.
EDMUND WALLER, *Marriage of the Dwarfs*.

13
A manly form at her side she saw,
And joy was duty, and love was law.
WHITTIER, *Maud Muller*.

XI—Marriage: Bride and Bridegroom

14
The bride hath paced into the hall,
Red as a rose is she.
S. T. COLERIDGE, *The Ancient Mariner*. Pt. i.

Holy and pure are the drops that fall
When the young bride goes from her father's hall.
FELICIA HEMANS, *The Bride of the Greek Isle*.

15
Blest is the Bride on whom the sun doth shine.
ROBERT HERRICK, *A Nuptial Song*.

Blessed is the corpse that the rain falls on;
Blessed is the bride that the sun shines on.
WILLIAM HONE, *Table-Book*, 667.

Fair weather weddings make fair weather lives.
RICHARD HOVEY, *The Marriage of Guenevere*. Act i, sc. 3.

16
As the bridegroom rejoiceth over the bride.
Old Testament: Isaiah, lxii, 5.

As are those dulcet sounds in break of day
That creep into the dreaming bridegroom's ear
And summon him to marriage.
SHAKESPEARE, *The Merchant of Venice*. Act iii, sc. 2, l. 51.

17
A bonny bride is soon buskit.
JOHN RAY, *Proverbs: Scottish*.

1
And you, brides and bridegrooms all,
With measure heap'd in joy to the measures fall.

SHAKESPEARE, *As You Like It*. Act v, sc. 4, l. 184.

2
A happy bridesmaid makes a happy bride.

TENNYSON, *The Bridesmaid.*

Bridesmaids may soon be brides; one wedding brings on another.

C. H. SPURGEON, *Salt-Cellars.*

XII—Marriage: the Honeymoon

3
Is Venus odious to brides? Or do they mock their parents with false tears, which they shed plentifully within their virgin bowers?

CATULLUS, *Odes*. Ode lxvi, l. 15.

4
More anxious than ever bride was on her wedding night, when wishes, hopes, fears, and doubts, tumultuously agitate, please, and terrify her.

LORD CHESTERFIELD, *Letters*, 26 June, 1752.

5
'Tis not beauty that witcheth bridegrooms, but nobleness. (Οὐ τὸ κάλλος ἀλλ' ἀρεταὶ τέρπουσι τοὺς ξυνευνέτας.)

EURIPIDES, *Andromache*, l. 208.

O lady, nobility is thine, and thy form is the reflection of thy nature!

EURIPIDES, *Ion*, l. 238.

Solon bade the bride eat a quince the first night of marriage, intimating thereby, it seems, that the bridegroom was to expect his first pleasure from the bride's mouth and conversation.

PLUTARCH, *Morals: Conjugal Precepts*. Sec. 2.

6
Need we expose to vulgar sight
The raptures of the bridal night? . . .
Let it suffice, that each had charms;
He clasp'd a goddess in his arms;
And, though she felt his usage rough,
Yet in a man 'twas well enough.

GOLDSMITH, *The Double Transformation*, l. 21.

7
The moon, the moon, so silver and cold,
Her fickle temper has oft been told,
Now shady—now bright and sunny—
But of all the lunar things that change,
The one that shows most fickle and strange,
And takes the most eccentric range,
Is the moon—so called—of honey!

THOMAS HOOD, *Miss Kilmansegg: Her Honeymoon.*

8
Other rites
Observing none, but adoration pure
Which God likes best, into their inmost bower
Handed they went; and eas'd the putting off
These troublesome disguises which we wear,
Straight side by side were laid; nor turn'd, I ween,
Adam from his fair spouse, nor Eve the rites
Mysterious of connubial love refus'd:
Whatever hypocrites austerely talk
Of purity and place and innocence,
Defaming as impure what God declares
Pure, and commands to some, leaves free to all.
Our Maker bids increase; who bids abstain
But our destroyer, foe to God and Man?

MILTON, *Paradise Lost*. Bk. iv, l. 736.

She what was honour knew,
And with obsequious majesty approv'd
My pleaded reason. To the nuptial bow'r
I led her blushing like the morn: all Heav'n
And happy constellations on that hour
Shed their selectest influence; the earth
Gave sign of gratulation, and each hill;
Joyous the birds; fresh gales and gentle airs
Whisper'd it to the woods, and from their wings
Flung rose, flung odours from the spicy shrub.

MILTON, *Paradise Lost*. Bk. viii, l. 508.

9
When a couple are newly-married, the first month is honey-moon or smick-smack;
The second is hither and thither: the third is thwick thwack:
The fourth, the Devil take them that brought thee and I together.

JOHN RAY, *English Proverbs*, p. 53.

10
To-night,
When I should take possession of the bride.

SHAKESPEARE, *All's Well that Ends Well*. Act ii, sc. 5, l. 28.

Surfeiting in joys of love, With his new bride.

SHAKESPEARE, *II Henry VI*. Act i, sc. 1, l. 252.

11
Put off your shame with your clothes when you go in to your husband, and put it on again when you come out.

THEANO, wife of Pythagoras, advising a woman. (DIOGENES LAERTIUS, *Pythagoras*. Bk. viii, sec. 43.)

12
All the women we need are inside, said the bridegroom, and closed the door on the bride.

THEOCRITUS, *Idyls*. No. xv, l. 77.

XIII—Marriage: Man and Wife

13
Thus in the East they are extremely strict,
And wedlock and a padlock mean the same; . . .
But then their own polygamy's to blame;
Why don't they knead two virtuous souls for life
Into that moral centaur, man and wife?

BYRON, *Don Juan*. Canto v, st. 158. This stanza, which Byron composed in bed, 27 Feb., 1821, was omitted by his publisher from the first edition of the poem, but replaced in subsequent editions when Byron protested in a fury "that I will not permit any human being to take such liberties with my writings."

1
Valentine: The two greatest monsters in the world are a man and a woman.
Sir Sampson Legend: Why my opinion is that those two monsters, joined together, make a yet greater, that's a man and his wife.
CONGREVE, *Love for Love*. Act iv, sc. 2.

Composed that monstrous animal, a husband and wife.
FIELDING, *Tom Jones*. Bk. xv, ch. 9.

2
The reason that husbands and wives do not understand each other is because they belong to different sexes.
DOROTHY DIX, in her syndicated column.

3
Pure, as the charities above,
Rise the sweet sympathies of love;
And closer chords than those of life
Unite the husband to the wife.
JOHN LOGAN, *The Lovers*.

4
There is no such cosy combination as man and wife. (Οἰκεῖον οὕτως οὐδέν ἐστιν ὡς ἀνήρ τε καὶ γυνή.)
MENANDER, *Fragments*. No. 647.

Husband and wife come to look alike at last.
O. W. HOLMES, *The Professor at the Breakfast-Table*. Ch. 7.

5
Men are April when they woo, December when they wed: maids are May when they are maids, but the sky changes when they are wives.
SHAKESPEARE, *As You Like It*. Act iv, sc. 1, l. 147.

They dream in courtship, but in wedlock wake.
POPE, *The Wife of Bath*, l. 103.

You must not contrast too strongly the hours of courtship with the years of possession.
BENJAMIN DISRAELI, *Speech*, 17 March, 1845.

6
He is the half part of a blessed man
Left to be finished by such as she;
And she a fair divided excellence,
Whose fulness of perfection lies in him.
O, two such silver currents, when they join,
Do glorify the banks that bound them in!
SHAKESPEARE, *King John*. Act ii, sc. 1, l. 437.

XIV—Marriage: Its Pleasures

7
And such a bliss is there betwixt them two
That, save the joy that lasteth evermo',
There is none like, that any creature
Hath seen or shall, while that the world may dure.
CHAUCER, *Man of Law's Tale*, l. 1075.

The joys of marriage are the heaven on earth,
Life's paradise, great princess, the soul's quiet,
Sinews of concord, earthly immortality,
Eternity of pleasures.
JOHN FORD, *The Broken Heart*. Act ii, sc. 2, l. 102.

8
Thus hand in hand through life we'll go;
Its checkered paths of joy and woe
With cautious steps we'll tread.
NATHANIEL COTTON, *The Fireside*. St. 31.

9
As your wedding ring wears,
You'll wear off your cares.
THOMAS FULLER, *Gnomologia*. No. 6146.

10
Remember the nightingales which sing only some months in the spring, but commonly are silent when they have hatched their eggs, as if their mirth were turned into care for their young ones. Yet all the molestations of Marriage are abundantly recompensed with other comforts which God bestoweth on them who make a wise choice of a wife.
THOMAS FULLER, *The Holy State*.

As the birds do, so do we,
Bill our mate, and choose our tree.
GEORGE MEREDITH, *The Three Singers to Young Blood*.

11
Thrice happy they whom an unbroken bond unites,
And whom no quarrel shall sunder before life's final day.
(Felices ter et amplius,
Quos inrupta tenet copula nec malis
Divulsus querimoniis
Suprema citius solvet amor die.)
HORACE, *Odes*. Bk. i, ode 13, l. 17.

12
There is, indeed, nothing that so much seduces reason from vigilance, as the thought of passing life with an amiable woman.
SAMUEL JOHNSON. (BOSWELL, *Life*, i, 381.)

13
Ay, marriage is the life-long miracle,
The self-begetting wonder, daily fresh.
CHARLES KINGSLEY, *The Saint's Tragedy*. Act ii, sc. 9.

14
Not caged, my bird, my shy, sweet bird,
But nested—nested!
HABBERTON LULHAM, *Nested*.

15
Let nothing break our bond but Death,
For in the world above
'Tis the breaker Death that soldereth
Our ring of Wedded Love.
GERALD MASSEY, *On a Wedding Day*. St. 11.

16
Blest pair; and O yet happiest if ye seek
No happier state, and know to know no more.
MILTON, *Paradise Lost*. Bk. iv, l. 774.

1
Grave authors say, and witty poets sing,
That honest wedlock is a glorious thing.
POPE, *January and May*, l. 21.

The married man may bear his yoke with ease,
Secure at once himself and Heav'n to please;
And pass his inoffensive hours away,
In bliss all night, and innocence all day:
Tho' fortune change, his constant spouse remains,
Augments his joys, or mitigates his pains.
POPE, *January and May*, l. 37.

2
Purest Love's unwasting treasure,
Constant faith, fair hope, long leisure,
Days of ease, and nights of pleasure,
Sacred Hymen! these are thine.
POPE, *Tragedy of Brutus: Chorus.*

3
The sacred academy of man's life,
Is holy wedlock in a happy wife.
FRANCIS QUARLES, *History of Queen Esther*. Sec. iii, med. 3.

4
One year of joy, another of comfort, and all the rest of content.
JOHN RAY, *English Proverbs*, p. 63. A marriage wish.

5
But happy they! the happiest of their kind!
Whom gentler stars unite, and in one fate
Their hearts, their fortunes, and their beings blend.
THOMSON, *The Seasons: Spring*, l. 1113.

6
Thrice happy is that humble pair,
Beneath the level of all care,
Over whose heads those arrows fly
Of sad distrust and jealousy.
EDMUND WALLER, *The Marriage of the Dwarfs*, l. 7.

XV—Marriage: Its Pains

7
Though women are angels, yet wedlock's the devil.
BYRON, *To Eliza*. Quoted.

8
Here's a happy new year! but with reason
I beg you'll permit me to say—
Wish me *many* returns of the *season*,
But as *few* as you please of the *day*.
BYRON, *On My Wedding-Day*.

This day, of all our days, has done
The worst for me and you:—
'Tis just *six* years since we were *one*,
And *five* since we were *two*.
BYRON, *To Penelope*, 2 Jan., 1821.

9
We wedded men live in sorrow and care.
CHAUCER, *The Merchant's Prologue*, l. 16.

10
Man and wife,
Coupled together for the sake of strife.
CHARLES CHURCHILL, *The Rosciad*, l. 1005.

War is no strife,
To the dark house and the detested wife.
SHAKESPEARE, *All's Well that Ends Well*. Act ii, sc. 3, l. 308.

Body and soul, like peevish man and wife,
United jar, and yet are loath to part.
YOUNG, *Night Thoughts*. Night ii, l. 175.

11
Oh! how many torments lie in the small circle of a wedding-ring!
COLLEY CIBBER, *Double Gallant*. Act. i, sc. 2.

12
The kindest and the happiest pair
Will find occasion to forbear,
And something every day they live
To pity, and, perhaps, forgive.
COWPER, *Mutual Forbearance Necessary to the Happiness of the Married State*.

13
If a man stay away from his wife for seven years, the law presumes the separation to have killed him; yet, according to our daily experience, it might well prolong his life.
CHARLES JOHN DARLING, *Scintilæ Juris*.

14
The wictim o' connubiality.
DICKENS, *Pickwick Papers*. Ch. 20.

Wen you're a married man, Samivel, you'll understand a good many things as you don't understand now; but vether it's worth while goin' through so much to learn so little, as the charity boy said ven he got to the end of the alphabet, is a matter o' taste.
DICKENS, *Pickwick Papers*. Ch. 27.

15
Falsely your Church seven sacraments does frame:
Penance and Matrimony are the same.
RICHARD DUKE, *To a Roman Catholic Friend upon Marriage*.

16
I don't think matrimony consistent with the liberty of the subject.
FARQUHAR, *The Twin Rivals*. Act v, sc. 3.

'Tis a kind of bilboes to be married.
FLETCHER, *The Wild Goose Chase*. Act i, sc. 2.

The married man turns his staff into a stake.
GEORGE HERBERT, *Jacula Prudentum*.

But married once,
A man is staked or poun'd, and cannot graze
Beyond his own hedge.
MASSINGER, *The Fatal Dowry*. Act iv, sc. 1.

No man with such a faithful true intelligence at his side would ever stray far from his reservation.
DAN QUIN, *Scrapbook*, 29 Jan., 1892, p. 32, referring to William Jennings Bryan.

17
When the husband is fire and the wife tow, the devil easily sets all in a flame.
THOMAS FULLER, *Gnomologia*. No. 5594.

18
They that marry ancient people, merely in expectation to bury them, hang themselves,

in hope that one will come and cut the halter.

THOMAS FULLER, *Holy and Profane States: Of Marriage.*

1
The husband's sullen, dogged, shy,
The wife grows flippant in reply;
He loves command and due restriction,
And she as well likes contradiction.
She never slavishly submits,
She'll have her will, or have her fits;
He his way tugs, she t'other draws;
The man grows jealous, and with cause.

JOHN GAY, *Cupid, Hymen, and Plutus.*

2
Yet Wedlock's a very awful thing!
'Tis something like that feat in the ring,
Which requires good nerve to do it—
When one of a "Grand Equestrian Troop"
Makes a jump at a gilded hoop,
Not certain at all
Of what may befall
After his getting through it!

THOMAS HOOD, *Miss Kilmansegg: Her Marriage.* St. 19.

3
It is so far from natural for a man and a woman to live in the state of marriage, that we find all the motives which they have for remaining in that connection, and the restraints which civilized society imposes to prevent separation, are hardly sufficient to keep them together.

SAMUEL JOHNSON. (BOSWELL, *Life,* 1772.)

4
No man likes to live under the eye of perpetual disapprobation.

SAMUEL JOHNSON. (BOSWELL, *Life,* 1772.)

You may think you had a conscience, but what is a conscience to a wife? . . . To marry is to domesticate the Recording Angel.

R. L. STEVENSON, *Virginibus Puerisque.* Pt. ii.

5
What! Posthumus, are you, who once had your wits, taking to yourself a wife? What snakes are driving you mad? Can you submit to a she-tyrant when there is so much rope to be had, so many dizzy heights of windows standing open?

JUVENAL, *Satires.* Sat. vi, l. 28.

At length he stretches out his foolish head to the conjugal halter. (Stulta maritali jam porrigit ora capistro.)

JUVENAL, *Satires.* Sat. vi, l. 43.

If you marry, it will be that the lyrist Echion or the flute player Ambrosius may become a father.

JUVENAL, *Satires.* Sat. vi, l. 76.

We, led by the impulse of our minds and by blind passion, desire marriage. (Nos, animorum Impulsu et cæca magnaque cupidine ducti, Conjugium petimus.)

JUVENAL, *Satires.* Sat. x, l. 350.

6
Pleasant the snaffle of Courtship, improving the manners and carriage;
But the colt who is wise will abstain from the terrible thornbit of Marriage.

RUDYARD KIPLING, *Certain Maxims of Hafiz.*

7
There are convenient marriages, but no delightful ones. (Il y a de bons mariages, mais il n'y en a point de délicieux.)

LA ROCHEFOUCAULD, *Maximes.* No. 113. Quoted by Bernard Shaw, *Candida.* Act i.

8
Who are happy in marriage? Those with so little imagination that they cannot picture a better state, and those so shrewd that they prefer quiet slavery to hopeless rebellion.

H. L. MENCKEN, *Prejudices.* Ser. ii, p. 245.

9
Like sculptured effigies they might be seen
Upon their marriage-tomb, the sword between;
Each wishing for the sword that severs all.

GEORGE MEREDITH, *Modern Love.* St. 1.

10
The Furies spread that wedding couch. (Eumenides stravere torum.)

OVID, *Metamorphoses.* Bk. vi, l. 431.

11
Accursed from their birth they be
Who seek to find monogamy,
Pursuing it from bed to bed—
I think they would be better dead.

DOROTHY PARKER, *Monogamy.*

Bigamy is having one wife too many. Monogamy in certain instances is the same thing.

UNKNOWN. (London *Opinion.*)

12
Some dish more sharply spiced than this
Milk-soup men call domestic bliss.

COVENTRY PATMORE, *Olympus.*

13
Good Heav'n, no doubt, the nuptial state approves,
Since it chastises still what best it loves.

POPE, *January and May,* l. 282.

14
The honest farmer and his wife,
To years declin'd from prime of life,
Had struggled with the marriage noose,
As almost every couple does, . . .
Jointly submitting to endure
That evil, which admits no cure.

MATTHEW PRIOR, *The Ladle.*

15
"A different cause," says Parson Sly,
"The same effect may give:
Poor Lubin fears that he may die;
His wife, that he may live."

MATTHEW PRIOR, *A Reasonable Affliction.*

16
Marriage is worse than cross I win, pile you lose.

THOMAS SHADWELL, *Epsom Wells.*

1
A young man married is a man that's marr'd.
SHAKESPEARE, *All's Well that Ends Well*. Act ii, sc. 3, l. 315.

2
O curse of marriage,
That we can call these delicate creatures ours,
And not their appetites! I had rather be a toad,
And live upon the vapour of a dungeon,
Than keep a corner in the thing I love
For others' uses.
SHAKESPEARE, *Othello*. Act iii, sc. 3, l. 268.

3
She's not well married that lives married long:
But she's best married that dies married young.
SHAKESPEARE, *Romeo and Juliet*. Act iv, sc. 5, l. 77.

4
When a man marries, dies, or turns Hindoo,
His best friends hear no more of him.
SHELLEY, *Letter to Maria Gisborne*.

When a man's friend marries, all is over between them.
GUY DE MAUPASSANT, *The Log*.

5
When a wife or mistress lives as in a jail, the person who confines her lives the life of a jailer.
WILLIAM SHENSTONE, *On Men and Manners*.

6
The best of men and the best of women may sometimes live together all their lives, and . . . hold each other lost spirits to the end.
R. L. STEVENSON, *Virginibus Puerisque*. Pt. i.

Even if we take matrimony at its lowest, even if we regard it as no more than a sort of friendship recognised by the police.
R. L. STEVENSON, *Virginibus Puerisque*. Pt. i.

Once you are married, there is nothing left for you, not even suicide, but to be good.
R. L. STEVENSON, *Virginibus Puerisque*. Pt. i.

7
As the husband is, the wife is; thou art mated with a clown,
And the grossness of his nature will have weight to drag thee down.

He will hold thee, when his passion shall have spent its novel force,
Something better than his dog, a little dearer than his horse.
TENNYSON, *Locksley Hall*, l. 47.

Alas! for all the pretty women who marry dull men,
Go into the suburbs and never come out again. . . .
What do these pretty women suffer when they marry?
They bear a boy who is like Uncle Harry.
ANNA WICKHAM, *Meditation at Kew*.

8
It is he who has broken the bond of marriage—not I. I only break its bondage.
OSCAR WILDE, *Lady Windermere's Fan*. Act ii.

9
The real drawback to marriage is that it makes one unselfish. Unselfish people are colorless.
OSCAR WILDE, *Picture of Dorian Gray*. Ch. 6.

10
"No married man but is tempest-tossed," they all say, and marry knowing it. ("Οὐκ ἔστι γήμας, ὅστις οὐ χειμάζεται," λέγουσι πάντες, καὶ γαμοῦσιν εἰδότες.)
UNKNOWN. (*Greek Anthology*. Bk x, epig. 116.)

11
Needles and pins, needles and pins,
When a man marries his trouble begins.
UNKNOWN. (HALLIWELL, *Nursery Rhymes*, p. 122.)

XVI—Marriage and Celibacy

12
Certainly, the best works and of greatest merit for the public, have proceeded from the unmarried or childless men.
FRANCIS BACON, *Essays: Of Marriage and Single Life*.

13
One was never married, and that's his hell; another is. and that's his plague.
ROBERT BURTON, *Anatomy of Melancholy*. Pt. i, sec. ii, mem. 4, subs. 7.

14
Single gentlemen who would be double.
BYRON, *Don Juan*. Canto xv, st. 48.

15
I would not answer for myself if I could find an affectionate family, with good shooting and first rate claret.
BENJAMIN DISRAELI, *Lothair*. Ch. 30.

16
Space is ample, east and west,
But two cannot go abreast.
RALPH WALDO EMERSON, *The Over-Soul*.

Though we called your friend from his bed this night, he could not speak for you,
For the race is run by one and one and never by two and two.
RUDYARD KIPLING, *Tomlinson*.

Down to Gehenna or up to the Throne,
He travels the fastest who travels alone.
RUDYARD KIPLING, *The Winners*.

Who travels alone, without lover or friend,
But hurries from nothing, to nought at the end.
ELLA WHEELER WILCOX, *Reply to Rudyard Kipling's Poem*.

Swift and sure go the lonely feet,
And the single eye sees cold and true,
And the road that has room and to spare for one
May be sorely narrow for two.
AMELIA JOSEPHINE BURR, *To Lovers*.

17
Bachelor's Hall! what a quare-lookin' place it is!

Kape me from sich all the days of my life!
JOHN FINLEY, *Bachelor's Hall.*

1
A bachelor
May thrive by observation on a little,
A single life's no burthen: but to draw
In yokes is chargeable, and will require
A double maintenance.
JOHN FORD, *The Fancies Chaste and Noble.* Act i, sc. 3, l. 82.

2
We bachelors laugh and show our teeth, but you married men laugh till your hearts ache.
GEORGE HERBERT, *Jacula Prudentum.*

3
Nothing is finer or better than a single life. (Melius nil cælibe vita.)
HORACE, *Epistles.* Bk. i, epis. 1, l. 88.

4
Marriage has many pains, but celibacy has no pleasures.
SAMUEL JOHNSON, *Works,* xi, 74.

5
Celibates replace sentiment by habits.
GEORGE MOORE, *Impressions.* Paraphrasing Balzac.

6
Marriage may often be a stormy lake, but celibacy is almost always a muddy horse-pond.
T. L. PEACOCK, *Melincourt.* Ch. 7.

7
Let sinful bachelors their woes deplore,
Full well they merit all they feel, and more.
POPE, *January and May,* l. 29.

8
Thrice-blessed they that master so their blood,
To undergo such maiden pilgrimage;
But earthlier happy is the rose distill'd,
Than that which, withering on the virgin thorn,
Grows, lives and dies in single blessedness.
SHAKESPEARE, *A Midsummer-Night's Dream.* Act i, sc. 1, l. 74.

9
Shall I never see a bachelor of threescore again?
SHAKESPEARE, *Much Ado About Nothing.* Act i, sc. 1, l. 201.

The world must be peopled. When I said, I would die a bachelor, I did not think I should live till I were married.
SHAKESPEARE, *Much Ado About Nothing.* Act ii, sc. 3, l. 251.

10
If you wish the pick of men and women, take a good bachelor and a good wife.
R. L. STEVENSON, *Virginibus Puerisque.* Pt. i.

It is not for nothing that Don Quixote was a bachelor and Marcus Aurelius married ill.
R. L. STEVENSON, *Virginibus Puerisque.* Pt. i.

11
Celibate, like the fly in the heart of an apple, dwells in a perpetual sweetness, but sits alone, and is confined and dies in singularity.
JEREMY TAYLOR, *Sermons: The Marriage Ring.*

12
The happy marrid man dies in good stile at home, surrounded by his weeping wife and children. The old bachelor don't die at all—he sort of rots away, like a pollywog's tail.
ARTEMUS WARD, *The Draft in Baldinsville.*

13
Nowadays all the married men live like bachelors, and all the bachelors like married men.
OSCAR WILDE, *Picture of Dorian Gray.* Ch. 15.

Married men are viler than bachelors.
A. W. PINERO, *Preserving Mr. Panmure.* Act ii.

14
I never married, and I wish my father never had. (Μὴ γήμας· αἴθε δὲ μηδ' ὁ πατήρ.)
UNKNOWN, *Epigram.* (*Greek Anthology.* Bk. vii, No. 309.)

I'm Smith of Stoke, aged sixty-odd,
I've lived without a dame
From youth-time on; and would to God
My dad had done the same.
THOMAS HARDY, *Epitaph on a Pessimist.*

XVII—Marriage: The Ins and the Outs

15
Wedlock, indeed, hath oft compared been
To public feasts, where meet a public rout,
Where they that are without would fain go in,
And they that are within would fain go out.
SIR JOHN DAVIES, *The Married State.* (1612)

Wedlock, as old men note, hath likened been
Unto a public crowd or common rout;
Where those that are without would fain get in,
And those that are within would fain get out.
Grief oft treads upon the heels of pleasure,
Marry'd in haste, we oft repent at leisure;
Some by experience find these words misplaced,
Marry'd at leisure, they repent in haste.
BENJAMIN FRANKLIN, *Poor Richard,* 1734.

Oh, could he have my share of din,
And I his quiet!—past a doubt
'Twould still be one man bored within,
And just another bored without.
J. R. LOWELL, *Without and Within.*

16
It happens as with cages: the birds without despair to get in, and those within despair of getting out.
MONTAIGNE, *Essays.* Bk. iii, ch. 5.

Is not marriage an open question, when it is alleged, from the beginning of the world, that such as are in the institution wish to get out, and such as are out wish to get in.
EMERSON, *Representative Men: Montaigne.*

'Tis just like a summer bird cage in a garden; the birds that are without despair to get in, and the birds that are within despair, and are in a consumption, for fear they shall never get out.
JOHN WEBSTER, *The White Devil.* Act i, sc. 2.

1
Marriage is like a beleaguered fortress; those who are without want to get in, and those within want to get out. (Le mariage est comme une forteresse assiégée; ceux qui sont dehors veulent y entrer et ceux qui sont dedans en sortir.)

QUITARD, *Études sur Proverbes Français*, p. 102.

I'd rather be outside a-looking in than on the inside a-looking out.

TED SNYDER. Title and refrain of popular song. (1906)

2
Marriage is a desperate thing: the frogs in Æsop were extreme wise; they had a great mind to some water, but they would not leap into the well, because they could not get out again.

JOHN SELDEN, *Table-Talk: Marriage*.

3
People who share a cell in the Bastile, or are thrown together on an uninhabited isle, if they do not immediately fall to fisticuffs, will find some possible ground of compromise.

R. L. STEVENSON, *Virginibus Puerisque*. Pt. i.

4
The reason why so few marriages are happy is because young ladies spend their time in making nets, not in making cages.

SWIFT, *Thoughts on Various Subjects*.

XVIII—Marriage: Second Marriage

5
Women who have been happy in a first marriage, are the most apt to venture upon a second.

ADDISON, *The Drummer*. Act ii, sc. 1.

6
When widows exclaim loudly against second marriages, I would always lay a wager that the man, if not the wedding-day, is absolutely fixed on.

FIELDING, *Amelia*. Bk. vi, ch. 8.

7
For I'm not so old, and I'm not so plain,
And I'm quite prepared to marry again.

W. S. GILBERT, *Iolanthe*. Act i.

8
He loves his bonds, who, when the first are broke,
Submits his neck unto a second yoke.

ROBERT HERRICK, *Hesperides*. No. 42.

9
Alas! another instance of the triumph of hope over experience.

SAMUEL JOHNSON, referring to the second marriage of a friend who had been unhappy with his first wife. (BOSWELL, *Life*, 1770, quoting from the *Collectanea* of Dr. William Maxwell.)

10
Christ saw a wedding once, the Scripture says,
And saw but one, 'twas thought, in all his days;
Whence some infer, whose conscience is too nice,
No pious Christian ought to marry twice.

POPE, *The Wife of Bath*, l. 9.

11
Disagreeable suspicions are usually the fruits of a second marriage. (Les soupcons importuns Sont d'un second hymen les fruits les plus communs.)

RACINE, *Phèdre*. Act ii, sc. 5.

12
In second husband let me be accurst!
None wed the second but who killed the first.

SHAKESPEARE, *Hamlet*. Act iii, sc. 2, l. 189.

The instances that second marriage move
Are base respects of thrift, but none of love:
A second time I kill my husband dead
When second husband kisses me in bed.

SHAKESPEARE, *Hamlet*. Act iii, sc. 2, l. 192.

13
I think you are happy in this second match,
For it excels your first.

SHAKESPEARE, *Romeo and Juliet*. Act iii, sc. 5, l. 224.

14
Alas, she married another. They frequently do. I hope she is happy—because I am.

ARTEMUS WARD, *Lecture*.

15
When a man marries again it is because he adored his first wife.

OSCAR WILDE, *Picture of Dorian Gray*. Ch. 15.

MARTYR AND MARTYRDOM

16
A tear is an intellectual thing,
And a sigh is the sword of an Angel King,
And the bitter groan of the martyr's woe
Is an arrow from the Almighty's bow.

WILLIAM BLAKE, *The Grey Monk*.

17
Commend me to the king, and tell him he is constant in his course of advancing me; from a private gentlewoman he made me a marquise, and from a marquise a queen; and now, as he had left no higher degree of earthly honour, he hath made me a martyr.

ANNE BOLEYN, on the way to execution. (FRANCIS BACON, *Apothegms*, No. 9.)

18
The noble army of martyrs.

Book of Common Prayer: Morning Prayer.

19
Plaintive martyrs, worthy of the name.

BURNS, *The Cotter's Saturday Night*.

20
To know how to say what others only know how to think is what makes men poets or sages; and to dare to say what others only dare to think makes men martyrs or reformers—or both.

ELIZABETH RUNDLE CHARLES, *Chronicle of the Schönberg-Cotta Family*.

1
They liv'd unknown
Till persecution dragg'd them into fame,
And chas'd them up to heav'n.
COWPER, *The Task*. Bk. v, l. 724.

2
I came from martyrdom unto this peace.
(E venni dal martiro a questa pace.)
DANTE, *Paradiso*. Canto xv, l. 148. Used by Longfellow as last line of his sonnet on President Garfield.

Tortured for the Republic. (Strangulatus pro republica.)
JAMES A. GARFIELD, *Last Words*. Written as he was dying, 17 July, 1882.

3
For all have not the gift of martyrdom.
DRYDEN, *Hind and the Panther*. Pt. ii, l. 59.

4
The martyr cannot be dishonored.
EMERSON, *Essays, First Series: Compensation*.

5
Pain is superficial and therefore fear is. The torments of martyrdom are probably most keenly felt by the bystanders.
EMERSON, *Society and Solitude: Courage*.

6
A little bread and wine in a dungeon sufficed for the liturgy of the martyrs.
P. G. HAMERTON, *Modern Frenchmen: Henri Perreyre*.

7
For one the dew, the hare-bell and the song;
For one the mire, the hurry and the thong.
AMORY HARE, *Life*.

8
Who falls for love of God, shall rise a star.
BEN JONSON, *An Epistle to a Friend*.

9
The dungeon oped its hungry door
To give the truth one martyr more.
J. R. LOWELL, *On the Death of C. T. Torrey*.

10
I look on martyrs as mistakes,
But still they burned for it at stakes.
JOHN MASEFIELD, *Everlasting Mercy*, l. 933.

11
Martyrs! who left for our reaping,
Truths you have sown in your blood!
THOMAS MOORE, *Where Is Your Dwelling?*

12
It is the cause, not the death, that makes the martyr.
NAPOLEON BONAPARTE. (O'MEARA, *Napoleon in Exile*.)

13
Every step of progress the world has made has been from scaffold to scaffold, and from stake to stake.
WENDELL PHILLIPS, *Woman's Rights*.

14
Who perisheth in needless danger is the devil's martyr.
JOHN RAY, *English Proverbs*.

15
From many a garnished niche around,
Stern saints and tortured martyrs frowned
SCOTT, *The Lay of the Last Minstrel*. Canto vi, st. 29.

16
Of one, whose naked soul stood clad in love,
Like a pale martyr in his shirt of fire.
ALEXANDER SMITH, *A Life Drama*. Sc. ii, l. 225. Pycroft (*Ways and Means of Men of Letters*) reports Smith's printer as saying, "We utterly ruined one poet through a ridiculous misprint of 'shirt' for 'sheet,'" but there is no foundation for the story, as the line is not a misprint.

17
And martyrs, when the joyful crown is given,
Forget the pain by which they purchased heaven.
GEORGE STEPNEY, *To King James II*.

Martyrs by the pang without the palm.
E. B. BROWNING.

18
The more ye mow us down, the more quickly we grow; the blood of Christians is fresh seed. (Plures efficimur quoties metimur a vobis; semen est sanguis Christianorum.)
TERTULLIAN, *Apologeticus*. Ch. 50. Generally quoted, "The blood of martyrs is the seed of the Church."

The blood of martyrs is the seed of Christians. (Sanguis martyrum semen Christianorum.)
BEYERLINCK, *Magnum Theatrum Vitæ Humanorum*. (1665)

The seed of the Church, I mean the blood of primitive Martyrs.
THOMAS FULLER, *Church History of Britain*. Pt. iv, bk. 1. (1665)

19
It is martyrs who create faith rather than faith that creates martyrs.
MIGUEL DE UNAMUNO, *Essays and Soliloquies*, p. 103.

There have been quite as many martyrs for bad causes as for good ones.
H. W. VAN LOON, *America*.

20
I am very fond of truth, but not at all of martyrdom.
VOLTAIRE, *Letter to D'Alembert*, Feb., 1776.

21
These Christs that die upon the barricades,
God knows it I am with them, in some things.
OSCAR WILDE, *Sonnet to Liberty*.

22
The world would use us just as it did the martyrs, if we loved God as they did.
THOMAS WILSON, *Maxims of Piety*, 90.

23
How, like a Roman, Sidney bowed his head,
And Russell's milder blood the scaffold wet.
WORDSWORTH, *Ecclesiastical Sonnets*. Pt. iii, No. 10.

MASTER

See also Servant

I—Master: Apothegms

1
Wealth without stint we have, yet for our eye we tremble;
For as the eye of home I deem a master's presence.
ÆSCHYLUS, *The Persians*, l. 170. (Plumptre, tr.)

The master absent and the house dead.
GEORGE HERBERT, *Jacula Prudentum*.

2
The master should bring honor to his house, not the house to its master. (Nec domo dominus, sed domino domus honestanda est.)
CICERO, *De Officiis*. Bk. i, ch. 39, sec. 139.

3
In mastery there is bondage, in bondage there is mastery. (Fit in dominatu servitus, in servitute dominatus.)
CICERO, *Pro Rege Deiotaro*. Ch. 11, sec. 30.

4
He can ill be master that never was scholar.
JOHN CLARKE, *Parœmiologia*, 149. (1639)

He that is a master must serve.
GEORGE HERBERT, *Jacula Prudentum*.

5
The measure of a master is his success in bringing all men round to his opinion twenty years later.
EMERSON, *Conduct of Life: Culture*.

6
He that is master of himself will soon be master of others.
THOMAS FULLER, *Gnomologia*. No. 2182.

7
Masters should be sometimes blind and sometimes deaf.
THOMAS FULLER, *Gnomologia*. No. 3376.

8
The man who gives me employment, which I must have or suffer, that man is my master, let me call him what I will.
HENRY GEORGE, *Social Problems*. Ch. 5.

9
Masters, to tell the truth, are queerly fashioned. They are full of faults and they wish us to be perfect. (Les maîtres, sans mentir, sont étrangement faits! Ils sont pleins de défauts, et nous veulent parfaits.)
COLLIN D'HARLEVILLE, *L'Inconstant*. Act ii, sc. 2.

10
In every art it is good to have a master.
GEORGE HERBERT, *Jacula Prudentum*.

11
No man can serve two masters.
New Testament: Matthew, vi, 24.

For no man may well serve two masters.
WILLIAM CAXTON, *Jason*, 57. (c. 1477)

We cannot serve two masters with a single heart.
THOMAS FORDE, *Lusus Fortunæ, Epistle*.

Men cannot serve two masters.
BERNARD SHAW, *Saint Joan*. Act iv.

He that will not serve one master, will have to serve many.
JOHN RAY, *English Proverbs*.

12
The master looks sharpest to his own business. (Dominum videre plurimum in rebus suis.)
PHÆDRUS, *Fables*. Bk. ii, fab. 8, l. 28.

13
We cannot all be masters, nor all masters
Cannot be truly followed.
SHAKESPEARE, *Othello*. Act i, sc. 1, l. 42.

14
He is master and lord of his brothers
Who is worthier and wiser than they.
SWINBURNE, *A Word for the Country*. St. 18.

II—Master: Like Master, Like Man

15
And it shall be, as with the people, so with the priest; as with the servant, so with his master; as with the maid, so with her mistress.
Old Testament: Isaiah, xxiv, 2.

Such master, such man, and such mistress, such maid,
Such husband and huswife, such houses arrayed.
THOMAS TUSSER. *Five Hundred Points of Good Husbandry: April's Abstract*. (1557)

Such mistress, such Nan;
Such master, such man.
THOMAS TUSSER, *Five Hundred Points of Good Husbandry: April's Abstract*.

Like mistress like maid.
SAMUEL ROWLANDS, *Night Raven*, 17. (1620)

Such captain, such retinue.
JOHN GOWER, *Confessio Amantis*. Bk. iii, l. 2421. (c. 1390)

Like lord like chaplain, neither barrel better herring.
JOHN BALE, *Kynge Johan*, 73. (c. 1540)

She call me a damned nigger, and say like massa like man.
FREDERICK MARRYAT, *King's Own*. Ch. 19.

Like master, like man. (Tel maître, tel valet.)
Attributed to CHEVALIER BAYARD by Ciniber.
See also under HERO.

16
If the abbot sings well, the novice is not far behind him. (Si bien canta el abad, no le va zaga el monacillo.)
CERVANTES, *Don Quixote*. Pt. ii, ch. 25.

17
As the master is, so is the servant. (Qualis dominus, talis est servus.)
PETRONIUS, *Satyricon*. Sec. 58.

18
As servants wish their masters to be, so is he wont to be. If they are good, he is good; if they are bad, he gets bad too. (Ut servi volunt esse erum, ita solet. Boni sunt, bonust; improbi sunt, malus fit.)
PLAUTUS. *Mostellaria*, l. 872

1
'Ban, 'Ban, Cacaliban
Has a new master: get a new man.
SHAKESPEARE, *The Tempest*. Act ii, sc. 2, l. 188.

2
Hail, fellow, well met,
All dirty and wet:
Find out, if you can,
Who's master, who's man.
SWIFT, *My Lady's Lamentation.*

III—Master: The Eye of the Master

See also Farming: Apothegms

3
Wherever the eyes of the master, himself upon the spot, have been frequently cast, in that part the fruit will ripen in greater profusion. (Quocunque domini præsentis oculi frequenter accessere, in ea parte majorem in modum fructus exuberat.)
COLUMELLA, *De Re Rustica*. Bk. iii.

4
The eye of a master will do more work than both his hands.
BENJAMIN FRANKLIN, *Poor Richard*, 1758.

5
The master's eye fattens the horse, and his foot the ground.
GEORGE HERBERT, *Jacula Prudentum.*

The master's eye, as it is always found,
Doth fat the horse; his foot doth fat the ground.
R. WATKYNS, *Epigram*. (1662)

6
One eye of the master's sees more than ten of the servant's.
GEORGE HERBERT, *Jacula Prudentum.*

7
Nothing fattens the horse so much as the eye of its master. (Δεσπότου ὀφθαλμός.)
XENOPHON, *Œconomicus*. Ch. 12, sec. 20. Also PLUTARCH, *Education of Children*. Sec. 9D.

8
The master's countenance avails more than the back of his head. (Frons domini plus prodest quam occipitium.)
PLINY THE ELDER, *History*. Bk. xviii, ch. 5, sec. 6. Quoted as a proverb.

MAXIMS, see Proverbs

MAY

9
Hebe's here, May is here!
The air is fresh and sunny;
And the miser-bees are busy
Hoarding golden honey.
THOMAS BAILEY ALDRICH, *May.*

10
As it fell upon a day
In the merry month of May,
Sitting in a pleasant shade
Which a grove of myrtles made.
RICHARD BARNFIELD, *Address to the Nightingale*. This song, often attributed to Shakespeare, is now assigned to Barnfield. It is found in his collection of *Poems in Divers Humours*, published in 1598.

11
Here's to the day when it is May
And care as light as a feather,
When your little shoes and my big boots
Go tramping over the heather.
BLISS CARMAN, *A Toast.*

12
He was as fresh as is the month of May.
CHAUCER, *Canterbury Tales: Prologue*, l. 92.

As full of spirit as the month of May.
SHAKESPEARE, *I Henry IV*. Act iv, sc. 1, l. 101.

In beauty as the first of May.
SHAKESPEARE, *Much Ado About Nothing*. Act i, sc. 1, l. 194.

13
Which May had painted with his softe showers
This garden full of leaves and of flowers.
CHAUCER, *The Frankeleyns Tale*, l. 180.

For May will have no slogardye a-night.
The season pricketh every gentle heart.
CHAUCER, *The Knightes Tale*, l. 184.

May, that mother is of monthes glad.
CHAUCER, *Troilus and Criseyde*. Bk. ii, l. 50.

14
For this is May! who with a daisy chain
Leads on the laughing Hours. . . .
And the glad earth, caressed by murmuring showers,
Wakes like a bride, to deck herself with flowers.
HENRY SYLVESTER CORNWELL, *May.*

15
Use May, while that you may,
For May hath but his time;
When all the fruit is gone, it is
Too late the tree to climb.
RICHARD EDWARDS, *May.*

16
What potent blood hath modest May!
EMERSON, *May-Day.*

17
Welcome May with his flowers.
JOHN FLORIO, *Second Frutes*, 55. (1620)

'Twas as welcome to me as flowers in May.
JAMES HOWELL, *Letters*, i, 6. (1645)

18
There was no month but May.
GEORGE HERBERT, *Affliction.*

19
May, queen of blossoms,
And fulfilling flowers,
With what pretty music
Shall we charm the hours?
Wilt thou have pipe and reed,
Blown in the open mead?
Or to the lute give heed
In the green bowers?
EDWARD HOVELL-THURLOW, *May.*

20
The voice of one who goes before, to make

The paths of June more beautiful, is thine
Sweet May!
HELEN HUNT JACKSON, *May.*

1
Worship, ye that lovers be, this May!
For of your bliss the calends are begun;
And sing with us, "Away! winter, away!
Come, summer, come, the sweet season and sun!"
JAMES I OF SCOTLAND, *The King's Quair.* St. 15.

2
Oh! that we two were Maying
Down the stream of the soft spring breeze;
Like children with violets playing,
In the shade of the whispering trees.
CHARLES KINGSLEY, *The Saint's Tragedy.* Act ii, sc. 9.

3
All flowers of Spring are not May's own;
The crocus cannot often kiss her;
The snow-drop, ere she comes, has flown—
The earliest violets always miss her.
LUCY LARCOM, *The Sister Months.*

4
May is a pious fraud of the almanac.
J. R. LOWELL, *Under the Willows.*

5
And May was come, the month of gladness.
JOHN LYDGATE, *Troy Book.* Bk. i, l. 1293.

It might be the merry month of May.
JOHN GRANGE, *Golden Aphroditis,* K 4.

6
Ah! my heart is weary waiting,
Waiting for the May:
Waiting for the pleasant rambles
Where the fragrant hawthorn brambles,
With the woodbine alternating,
Scent the dewy way;
Ah! my heart is weary, waiting,
Waiting for the May.
D. F. MCCARTHY, *Summer Longings.*

7
The hawthorne-scented dusks of May.
DON MARQUIS, *An Open Fire.*

8
Now the bright morning star, day's harbinger,
Comes dancing from the East, and leads with her
The flow'ry May, who from her green lap throws
The yellow cowslip, and the pale primrose.
Hail, bounteous May, that dost inspire
Mirth, and youth, and warm desire!
Woods and groves are of thy dressing,
Hill and dale doth boast thy blessing.
Thus we salute thee with our early song,
And welcome thee, and wish thee long.
MILTON, *Song: On May Morning.*

As Jupiter
On Juno smiles, when he impregns the clouds
That shed May flowers.
MILTON, *Paradise Lost.* Bk. iv, l. 499.

9
In the under-wood and the over-wood
There is murmur and trill this day,
For every bird is in lyric mood,
And the wind will have its way.
CLINTON SCOLLARD, *May Magic.*

10
January grey is here,
Like a sexton by her grave;
February bears the bier;
March with grief doth howl and rave,
And April weeps—but, O, ye hours,
Follow with May's fairest flowers.
SHELLEY, *Dirge for the Year.*

11
Another May new buds and flowers shall bring:
Ah! why has happiness no second Spring?
CHARLOTTE SMITH, *Elegiac Sonnets.* No. ii.

12
When May, with cowslip-braided locks,
Walks through the land in green attire.
BAYARD TAYLOR, *The Lost May.*

13
God ripes the wines and corn, I say,
And wenches for the marriage-day,
And boys to teach love's comely play.
By Goddes fay, by Goddes fay!
It is the month, the jolly month,
It is the jolly month of May.
FRANCIS THOMPSON, *A May Burden.*

Thy brow-garland pushed all aslant
Tells—but I tell not, wanton May!
FRANCIS THOMPSON, *A May Burden.*

14
Among the changing months, May stands confest
The sweetest, and in fairest colours drest.
JAMES THOMSON, *The Month of May.*

15
What is so sweet and dear
As a prosperous morn in May,
The confident prime of the day,
And the dauntless youth of the year,
When nothing that asks for bliss,
Asking aright, is denied,
And half of the world a bridegroom is
And half of the world a bride?
WILLIAM WATSON, *Ode in May.*

16
He has a very hard heart who does not love in May. (Moult a dur cuer qui en Mai n'aime.)
UNKNOWN, *Roman de la Rose.*

O month when they who love must love and wed.
HELEN HUNT JACKSON, *May.*

17
If you would the doctor pay,
Leave your flannels off in May.
UNKNOWN. (*West Somersetshire Word-Book,* 467.)

Change not a clout Till May be out.
UNKNOWN. (INWARDS, *Weather Lore,* 26.)

II—May-Day

1 Come, let us go, while we are in our prime,
And take the harmless folly of the time. . . .
Then while time serves, and we are but decaying,
Come, my Corinna, come, let's go a Maying.
ROBERT HERRICK, *Corinna's Going a Maying.*

Each flower has wept, and bowed toward the east,
Above an hour since: yet you not drest; . . .
Whenas a thousand virgins on this day,
Spring, sooner than the lark, to fetch in May.
ROBERT HERRICK, *Corinna's Going a Maying.*

2 To do observance to a morn of May.
SHAKESPEARE, *A Midsummer-Night's Dream.* Act i, sc. 1, l. 167.

No doubt they rose up early to observe
The rite of May.
SHAKESPEARE, *A Midsummer-Night's Dream.* Act iv, sc. 1, l. 136.

More matter for a May morning.
SHAKESPEARE, *Twelfth Night.* Act iii, sc. 4, l. 156.

3 You must wake and call me early, call me early, mother dear;
To-morrow 'ill be the happiest time of all the glad New-year;
Of all the glad New-year, mother, the maddest merriest day;
For I'm to be Queen o' the May, mother, I'm to be Queen o' the May.
TENNYSON, *The May Queen.*

MEDDLER

4 He that is too much in anything, so that he giveth another occasion of satiety, maketh himself cheap.
BACON, *Essays: Of Ceremonies and Respects.*

5 Thus everybody meddled with what they had nothing to do.
APHRA BEHN, *The Fair Jilt.*

6 We had among us, not so much a spy,
As a recording chief-inquisitor,
The town's true master, if the town but knew!
We merely kept a governor for form.
ROBERT BROWNING, *How It Strikes a Contemporary.*

7 I never thrust my nose into other men's porridge. It is no bread and butter of mine.
CERVANTES, *Don Quixote.* Pt. i, ch. 11.

He has an oar in every man's boat, and a finger in every pie.
CERVANTES, *Don Quixote.* Pt. ii, ch. 22.

No man's pie is freed
From his ambitious finger.
SHAKESPEARE, *Henry VIII.* Act i, sc. 1, l. 52.

You will have a finger in everybody's pie.
SOUTHERNE, *Fatal Marriage.* Act i, sc. 3.

Their law thrusteth its nose into every platter, and its finger into every pie.
CHARLES READE, *Cloister and Hearth.* Ch. 56.

8 Meddle with what you have to do.
JOHN CLARKE, *Paræmiologia,* 18. (1639)

9 You stir what should not be stirred. ('Ακίνητα κινεῖς.)
HERODOTUS, *History.* Bk. vi, sec. 134.

10 Whoso meddles of what men do,
Let him come here and shoe the goose.
JOHN HEYWOOD, *Proverbs.* Cited as an inscription in Whalley Church, c. 1434.

Who meddleth in all things may shoe the gosling.
JOHN HEYWOOD, *Proverbs.* Pt. ii, ch. 3. (1546)

11 'Tis said that people ought to guard their noses
Who thrust them into matters none of theirs.
THOMAS HOOD, *Ode to Rae Wilson,* l. 67.

12 Every fool will be meddling.
Old Testament: Proverbs, xx, 3.

13 Be no busybodies: meddle not with other folks' matter but when in conscience and duty prest; for it procures troubles and ill-manners, and is very unseemly to wise men.
WILLIAM PENN, *Letters to Wife and Children.*

14 Never thrust your sickle into another's corn.
PUBLILIUS SYRUS, *Sententiæ.* No. 593.

Did thrust (as now) in others' corn his sickle.
DU BARTAS, *Devine Weekes and Workes.* Week ii, day 2. (Sylvester, tr.)

Not presuming to put my sickle in another man's corn.
NICHOLAS YONGE, *Musica Transalpina: Epistle Dedicatory.* (1588)

15 Thou find'st to be too busy is some danger.
SHAKESPEARE, *Hamlet.* Act iii, sc. 4, l. 33.

For my part, I'll not meddle.
SHAKESPEARE, *Troilus and Cressida.* Act i, sc. 1.

16 Have you so much time to spare from your own affairs that you can attend to another man's with which you have no concern? (Tantumne ab re tuast oti tibi Aliena ut cures ea quæ nil ad te attinent?)
TERENCE, *Heauton Timorumenos,* l. 75.

The kiebitz is no song-bird. (Der Kiebitz ist kein Singvogel.)
UNKNOWN, a German proverb, referring to a bird similar to the plover, and of a very inquisitive nature. Hence, "kibitzer."

MEDICINE

See also Disease; Doctors; Health: Its Preservation

I—Medicine: Definitions

17 Medicine is a science which hath been, as

we have said, more professed than laboured, and yet more laboured than advanced: the labour having been, in my judgment, rather in circle than in progression.

BACON, *Advancement of Learning*. Bk. ii.

1
Surely every medicine is an innovation; and he that will not apply new remedies, must expect new evils.

BACON, *Essays: Of Innovations.*

2
Then comes the question, how do drugs, hygiene and animal magnetism heal? It may be affirmed that they do not heal, but only relieve suffering temporarily, exchanging one disease for another.

MARY BAKER EDDY, *Science and Health*, p. 483.

3
Dr. Bigelow's formula was, that fevers are self-limiting; afterwards that all disease is so; therefore no use in treatment. Dr. Holmes said, No use in drugs. Dr. Samuel Jackson said, Rest, absolute rest, is the panacea.

R. W. EMERSON, *Journal*, 1860.

Our foster nurse of nature is repose.

SHAKESPEARE, *King Lear*. Act iv, sc. 4, l. 12.

4
By opposites opposites are cured. (Τὰ ἐναντία τῶν ἐναντιῶν ἐστὶν ἰήματα.)

HIPPOCRATES, *De Flatibus*. Vol. i, p. 570.

In diseases, less [of everything]. (In morbis minus.)

HIPPOCRATES. Quoted by Bacon as "a good, profound aphorism."

Like cures like. (Similia similibus curantur.)

HAHNEMANN, *Motto*, for the homœopathic school of medicine which he founded, and which he attributed to Hippocrates, quoting: "By similar things disease is produced, and by similar things administered to the sick, they are healed of their diseases," a sentence derived from Περὶ τόπων τῶν κατ' ἄνθρωπον, attributed to Hippocrates.

Take a little rum
The less you take the better,
Pour it in the lakes
Of Wener or of Wetter.
Dip a spoonful out
And mind you don't get groggy,
Pour it in the lake
Of Winnipissiogie.
Stir the mixture well
Lest it prove inferior,
Then put half a drop
Into Lake Superior.
Every other day
Take a drop in water,
You'll be better soon
Or at least you oughter.

GEORGE WASHINGTON DOANE, *Lines on Homœopathy*.

5
I firmly believe that if the whole *materia medica* could be sunk to the bottom of the sea, it would be all the better for mankind and all the worse for the fishes.

O. W. HOLMES, *Lecture*, Harvard Medical School.

6
In physic things of melancholic hue and quality are used against melancholy, sour against sour, salt to remove salt humours.

MILTON, *Samson Agonistes: Preface.*

7
Medicine is a collection of uncertain prescriptions, the results of which, taken collectively, are more fatal than useful to mankind. Water, air, and cleanliness are the chief articles in my pharmacopœia.

NAPOLEON BONAPARTE, *Remark*, to Dr. Antommarchi at St. Helena.

8
Oft has a bitter medicine brought help to the languishing. (Sæpe tulit lassis sucus amarus opem.)

OVID, *Amores*. Bk. iii, eleg. 11, l. 8

We cannot endure sweets; a bitter potion strengthens us. (Dulcia non ferimus: suco renovemur amaro.)

OVID, *Ars Amatoria*. Bk. iii, l. 583.

For 'tis a physic That's bitter to sweet end.

SHAKESPEARE, *Measure for Measure*. Act iv, sc. 6, l. 7.

9
The art of medicine is a question of timeliness: wine timely given helps, untimely, harms. (Temporis ars medicina fere est: data tempore prosunt, Et data non apto tempore vina nocent.)

OVID, *Remediorum Amoris*, l. 131.

Medicine sometimes injures, sometimes restores health; showing which plant is healthful and which harmful. (Eripit interdum, modo dat medicina salutem, Quæque juvet, monstrat, quæque sit herba nocens.)

OVID, *Tristia*. Bk. ii, l. 269.

There is no medicine to remove the knotty gout, or relieve the fearful dropsy. (Tollere nodosam nescit medicina podagram, Nec formaditis auxiliatur aquis.)

OVID, *Epistulæ ex Ponto*. Bk. i, epis. 3, l. 23.

10
Nothing hinders a cure so much as frequent change of medicine. (Nihil æque sanitatem impedit quam remediorum crebra mutatio.)

SENECA, *Epistulæ ad Lucilium*. Epis. ii, sec. 3.

Remedies do not avail unless they remain in the system. (Remedia non prosunt, nisi inmorantur.)

SENECA, *Epistulæ ad Lucilium*. Epis. xl, sec. 4.

Not even medicines can master incurable diseases. (Ne medicina quidem morbos insanabiles vincit.)

SENECA, *Epistulæ ad Lucilium* Epis. xciv, 24

11
From the nature of human frailty, remedies operate more slowly than disease, and the body itself is slow to grow and quick to decay. (Natura tamen infirmitatis humanæ tar-

diora sunt remedia quam mala; et ut corpora nostra lente augescunt, cito extinguuntur.)
TACITUS, *Agricola*. Sec. 3.

II—Medicine: Apothegms

1
Dogs with their tongues their wounds do heal,
But men with hands, as thou shalt feel.
BUTLER, *Hudibras*. Pt. i, canto ii, l. 773.

2
Because all the sick do not recover does not prove that there is no art of medicine. (Ne ægri quidem quia non omnes convalescunt idcirco ars nulla medicina est.)
CICERO, *De Natura Deorum*. Bk. ii, ch. 4, 12.

3
When taken To be well shaken.
GEORGE COLMAN THE YOUNGER, *Newcastle Apothecary*.

4
Though I have patches on me pantaloons, I've ne'er a wan on me intestines.
FINLEY PETER DUNNE, *Thanksgiving*.

5
For of the most High cometh healing.
Aprocrypha: Ecclesiasticus, xxxviii, 2.

God who sends the wound sends the medicine. (Dios que dá la llaga, dá la medicina.)
CERVANTES, *Don Quixote*. Pt. ii, ch. 19.

A salve there is for every sore.
UNKNOWN, *School-House of Women*, l. 401. (1542) *See also* GOD: HIS MERCY.

6
Many dishes, many diseases. Many medicines, few cures.
BENJAMIN FRANKLIN, *Poor Richard*, 1734.

7
Different sores must have different salves.
THOMAS FULLER, *Gnomologia*. No. 1283.

For to strange sores strangely they strain the cure.
SHAKESPEARE, *Much Ado About Nothing*. Act iv, sc. 1, l. 254.

Is this the poultice for my aching bones?
SHAKESPEARE, *Romeo and Juliet*. Act ii, sc. 5, l. 66.

You rub the sore,
When you should bring the plaster.
SHAKESPEARE, *The Tempest*. Act ii, sc. 1, l. 138.

8
Some fell by laudanum, and some by steel,
And death in ambush lay in every pill.
GARTH, *The Dispensary*. Canto iv, l. 62.

9
Strange and rare escapes there happen sometimes in physic. (Monstra contingunt in medicina.)
HIPPOCRATES, *Adagia*.

Many men have been cured of diseases by accidents; but they were not remedies.
BEN JONSON, *Explorata: Beneficia*.

10
The worst about medicine is that one kind makes another necessary.
ELBERT HUBBARD, *Philistine*. Vol. xxvii, p. 61.

11
It is the sick who need medicine and not the well.
THOMAS JEFFERSON, *Writings*. Vol. x, p. 103.

12
My lord Jupiter knows how to gild the pill. (Le seigneur Jupiter sait dorer la pilule.)
MOLIÈRE, *Amphitryon*. Act iii, sc. 10, l. 24.

If the pills were pleasant, they would not want gilding.
THOMAS FULLER, *Gnomologia*. No. 2711.

A pill that the present moment is daily bread to thousands.
DOUGLAS JERROLD, *The Catspaw*. Act i, sc. 1.

When I was sick, you gave me bitter pills.
SHAKESPEARE, *The Two Gentlemen of Verona*. Act ii, sc. 4, l. 149.

13
The same medicine will both harm and cure me. (Res eadem vulnus opemque feret.)
OVID, *Tristia*. Bk. ii, l. 20.

14
Too late is the medicine prepared, when the disease has gained strength by long delay. (Sero medicina paratur, Cum mala per longas convaluere moras.)
OVID, *Remediorum Amoris*, l. 91.

For want of timely care,
Millions have died of medicable wounds.
JOHN ARMSTRONG, *The Art of Preserving Health*. Bk. iii, l. 519.

15
Meet the malady on its way. (Veniente occurrite morbo.)
PERSIUS, *Satires*. Sat. iii, l. 64.

Prevention is so much better than healing.
THOMAS ADAMS, *Works*, p. 598. (1630)

Prevention is better than cure.
DICKENS, *Martin Chuzzlewit*. Ch. 51.

'Twas a dangerous cliff, as they freely confessed,
Though to walk near its crest was so pleasant,
But over its terrible edge there had slipped
A Duke and full many a peasant;
So the people said something would have to be done,
But their projects did not at all tally.
Some said: "Put a fence round the edge of the cliff."
Some: "An ambulance down in the valley."
JOSEPH MALINES, *Prevention and Cure*. (*Virginia Health Bulletin*.)

16
If physic do not work, prepare for the kirk.
JOHN RAY, *English Proverbs*, 189. (1768)

17
It is medicine, not scenery, for which a sick man must go a-searching. (Medicina ægro, non regio, quærenda est.)
SENECA, *Epistulæ ad Lucilium*. Epis. civ, 18.

18
It is part of the cure to wish to be cured (Pars sanitatis velle sanari fuit.)
SENECA, *Hippolytus*, l. 249.

Our remedies oft in ourselves do lie,

Which we ascribe to heaven.
SHAKESPEARE, *All's Well that Ends Well*. Act i, sc. 1, l. 231.

1
Throw physic to the dogs; I'll none of it.
SHAKESPEARE, *Macbeth*. Act v, sc. 3, l. 47.

Out, loathed medicine! hated potion, hence!
SHAKESPEARE, *A Midsummer-Night's Dream*. Act iii, sc. 2, l. 264.

Trust not the physician;
His antidotes are poison, and he slays
More than you rob.
SHAKESPEARE, *Timon of Athens*. Act iv, sc. 3, l. 434.

2
Will toys amuse, when med'cines cannot cure?
YOUNG, *Night Thoughts*. Night ii, l. 67.

III—Medicine: Worse Than the Disease

3
I find the medicine worse than the malady.
BEAUMONT AND FLETCHER, *Love's Cure*. Act iii, sc. 2.

4
The cure is not worth the pain. (Τὸ ἐπανόρθωμα τῆς ἀλγηδόνος οὐκ ἄξιον.)
GAIUS MARIUS, after having had a varicose vein cut from his leg. (PLUTARCH, *Lives: Gaius Marius*. Ch. 6, sec. 3.)

The cure is worse than the disease.
PHILIP MASSINGER, *The Bondman*. Act i, sc. 1.

5
There are some remedies worse than the disease. (Graviora quædam sunt remedia periculis.)
PUBLILIUS SYRUS, *Sententiæ*. No. 301.

The remedy is worse than the disease.
FRANCIS BACON, *Essays: Of Seditions*; JUVENAL, *Satires*, xvi, 31; LE SAGE, *Gil Blas*, bk. xii, ch. 8, and many others.

6
His remedies were more grievous than the offence. (Gravior remediis quam delicta erant.)
TACITUS, *Annals*. Bk. iii, sec. 28.

7
The medicine increases the disease. (Ægrescitque medendo.)
VERGIL, *Æneid*. Bk. xii, l. 46.

IV—Medicine: Desperate Remedies

8
No remedies cause so much pain as those which are efficacious. (Nulla remedia tam faciunt dolorem quam quæ sunt salutaria.)
BACON, *Letter to Lord Henry Howard*. Quoted.

9
'Tis not amiss, ere ye're giv'n o'er,
To try one desp'rate med'cine more;
For where your case can be no worse,
The desp'rat'st is the wisest course.
BUTLER, *Epistle of Hudibras to Sidrophel*, l. 5.

And ill it therefore suits
The mood of one of my high temperature
To pause inactive while await me means
Of desperate cure for these so desperate ills.
THOMAS HARDY, *The Dynasts*. Act iv, sc. 3

10
Extreme remedies are very appropriate for extreme diseases.
HIPPOCRATES, *Adagia*.

11
When desperate ills demand a speedy cure,
Distrust is cowardice, and prudence folly.
SAMUEL JOHNSON, *Irene*. Act iv, sc. 1, l. 87.

12
For the strongest maladies the strongest remedies. (Aux plus fortes maladies les plus forts remèdes.)
MONTAIGNE, *Essays*. Bk. ii, ch. 3.

13
No one tries desperate remedies at first. (Extrema primo nemo tentavit loco.)
SENECA, *Agamemnon*, l. 153.

14
Diseases desperate grown
By desperate appliance are relieved,
Or not at all.
SHAKESPEARE, *Hamlet*. Act iv, sc. 3, l. 9. (1602)

A desperate disease must have a desperate cure.
THOMAS SHADWELL, *Humourists*, iv. (1670)

Strong disease requires a strong medicine.
TAVERNER, *Proverbs*. Fo. iv. (1539)

V—Medicine: Herbs as Medicine

15
The Lord hath created medicines out of the earth; and he that is wise will not abhor them.
Aprocrypha: Ecclesiasticus, xxxviii, 4.

16
And in requital ope his leathern scrip,
And show me simples of a thousand names,
Telling their strange and vigorous faculties.
MILTON, *Comus*, l. 626.

17
No cataplasm so rare,
Collected from all simples that have virtue
Under the moon, can save the thing from death.
SHAKESPEARE, *Hamlet*. Act iv, sc. 7, l. 144.

In such a night
Medea gather'd the enchanted herbs
That did renew old Æson.
SHAKESPEARE, *The Merchant of Venice*. Act v, sc. 1, l. 12.

18
O, mickle is the powerful grace that lies
In herbs, plants, stones, and their true qualities.
SHAKESPEARE, *Romeo and Juliet*. Act ii, sc. 3, l. 15.

19
He preferred to know the power of herbs and their value for curing purposes, and, heedless of glory, to exercise that quiet art. (Scire potestates herbarum usumque medendi Maluit et mutas agitare inglorius artis.)
VERGIL, *Æneid*. Bk. xii, l. 396.

Learn from the beasts the physic of the field.
POPE, *Essay on Man*. Epis. iii, l. 174.

1
Why should a man die who has sage in his garden? (Cur moriatur homo, cui salvia crescit in horto?)
UNKNOWN, *Regimen Sanitatis Salernitanum*, l. 177.

Of all the garden herbs none is of greater virtue than sage.
THOMAS COGAN, *The Haven of Health*. (1596)

MEDIOCRITY

2
Mediocrity is safest. (In medio spatio mediocria firma locantur.)
NICHOLAS BACON. Quoted by Chief-Justice Sir John Popham in sentencing Raleigh.

3
Commonplace and cringing, one gets everywhere. (Médiocre et rampant, et l'on arrive à tout.)
BEAUMARCHAIS, *Barbier de Séville*. Act iii, sc. 7.

4
This miserable fate
Suffer the wretched souls of those who lived
Without or praise or blame.
(Questo misero modo
Tengon l'anime triste di coloro,
Che visser senza infamia e senza lodo.)
DANTE, *Inferno*. Canto iii, l. 34. (Cary, tr.) They are being goaded along by swarms of wasps and hornets.

5
The secret of ugliness consists not in irregularity, but in being uninteresting.
EMERSON, *Conduct of Life: Beauty*.

6
Oh, mediocrity,
Thou priceless jewel, only mean men have,
But cannot value.
JOHN FLETCHER, *Queen of Corinth*. Act iii, sc. 1.

7
The universal subjugator, the commonplace. (Was uns alle bändigt, das Gemeine.)
GOETHE, *Taschenbuch für Damen auf das Jahr 1806*.

8
Not below mediocrity, nor above it.
SAMUEL JOHNSON, *Lives of the Poets: Phillips*.

9
Mediocre minds generally condemn everything which passes their understanding. (Les esprits médiocres condamnent d'ordinaire tout ce qui passe leur portée.)
LA ROCHEFOUCAULD, *Maximes*. No. 375.

To mediocrity genius is unforgivable.
ELBERT HUBBARD, *Epigrams*.

10
Mediocrity is praised in all cases. (Médiocrité est en tous cas louée.)
RABELAIS, *Works*. Bk. iii, ch. 13.

Wish then for mediocrity. (Souhaitez donc médiocrité.)
RABELAIS, *Works*. Bk. iv, *Prologue*.

11
Who shines in the second rank is eclipsed in the first. (Qui brille au second rang, s'éclipse au premier.)
VOLTAIRE, *La Henriade*. Canto i, l. 31.

Who, like the hindmost chariot wheels, art curst,
Still to be near, but ne'er to reach the first.
PERSIUS, *Satires*. Sat. v, l. 98. (Dryden, tr.)

MEDITATION, see Thought

MEDITATION, see Thought

MEEKNESS

See also Moses

12
Keep quiet by the fire
And never say "no" when the world says "ay."
E. B. BROWNING, *Aurora Leigh*. Bk. i, l. 436.

13
And of his port as meek as is a maid.
CHAUCER, *Canterbury Tales: Prologue*, l. 69.

14
Wisdom has taught us to be calm and meek,
To take one blow, and turn the other cheek.
O. W. HOLMES, *Non-Resistance*.

15
Blessed are the meek: for they shall inherit the earth.
New Testament: Matthew, v, 5.

It's goin' t' be fun t' watch an' see how long th' meek kin keep the earth after they inherit it.
KIN HUBBARD, *Sayings*.

16
Ornament of a meek and quiet spirit.
New Testament: I Peter, iii, 4.

17
Meekness is not weakness.
W. G. BENHAM, *Proverbs*, p. 809.

18
They can be meek that have no other cause.
SHAKESPEARE, *The Comedy of Errors*. Act ii, sc. 1, l. 33.

Put meekness in thy mind.
SHAKESPEARE, *Richard III*. Act ii, sc. 2, l. 107.

MEETING

19
If e'er we meet hereafter, we shall meet
In happier climes, and on a safer shore.
ADDISON, *Cato*. Act iv, sc. 4.

20
We met—'twas in a crowd—and I thought he would shun me.
T. H. BAYLY, *Song: We Met*.

21
We loved, sir—used to meet:
How sad and bad and mad it was—
But then, how it was sweet!
ROBERT BROWNING, *Confessions*. St. 9.

22
It lightens, it brightens
The tenebrific scene,
To meet with, and greet with
My Davie or my Jean!
ROBERT BURNS, *Epistle to Davie*.

1
For alday meeteth man at unset stevene (*i. e.*, unexpectedly).
CHAUCER, *The Knightes Tale*, l. 666.

It is sooth said, by God of heaven,
Many meeteth at on-sett stevyn.
UNKNOWN, *Sir Eglamour of Artoys*, l. 1282.

2
Between cultivated minds the first interview is the best.
EMERSON, *Journals*. Vol. iii, p. 496.

3
By the merest chance, in the twilight gloom,
In the orchard path he met me.
HOMER GREENE, *What My Lover Said*. Erroneously attributed to Horace Greeley, because, when the poem was first printed in the New York *Evening Post*, it was signed "H. G." Fraudulently claimed by Mrs. O. C. Jones. (*See* STEVENSON, *Famous Single Poems*.)

4
The joy of meeting not unmixed with pain.
LONGFELLOW, *Morituri Salutamus*, l. 113.

5
In whatever place you meet me, Postumus, you cry out immediately, and your first words are, "How do you do?" You say this, even if you meet me ten times in one single hour: you, Postumus, have nothing, I suppose, to do.
MARTIAL, *Epigrams*. Bk. ii, ep. 67.

6
In life there are meetings which seem
Like a fate.
OWEN MEREDITH, *Lucile*. Pt. ii, canto iii, sec. 8.

7
And we meet, with champagne and a chicken, at last.
MARY WORTLEY MONTAGU, *The Lover*. Quoted by Scott, *St. Ronan's Well*. Ch. 7.

8
Some day, some day of days, threading the street
With idle, heedless pace,
Unlooking for such grace,
I shall behold your face!
Some day, some day of days, thus may we meet.
NORA PERRY, *Some Day of Days*.

9
The joys of meeting pay the pangs of absence;
Else who could bear it?
NICHOLAS ROWE, *Tamerlane*. Act ii, sc. 1.

And doth not a meeting like this make amends
For all the long years I've been wand'ring away?
THOMAS MOORE, *And Doth Not a Meeting?*

10
The meeting of these champions proud
Seemed like the bursting thunder-cloud.
SCOTT, *The Lay of the Last Minstrel*. Canto iii, st. 5.

11
1st Witch: When shall we three meet again,
In thunder, lightning, or in rain?
2nd Witch: When the hurlyburly's done,
When the battle's lost and won.
SHAKESPEARE, *Macbeth*. Act i, sc. 1, l. 1.

I pray you know me when we meet again.
SHAKESPEARE, *The Merchant of Venice*. Act iv, sc. 1, l. 419.

12
Journeys end in lovers meeting,
Every wise man's son doth know.
SHAKESPEARE, *Twelfth Night*. Act ii, sc. 3, l. 44.

When gloaming treads the heels of day
And birds sit cowering in the spray,
Along the flowery hedge I stray,
To meet mine ain dear somebody.
ROBERT TANNAHILL, *Love's Fear*.

Like torrents from a mountain source
We rush'd into each other's arms.
TENNYSON, *The Letters*. St. 5.

13
Although I enter not,
Yet round about the spot
Ofttimes I hover,
And at the sacred gate
With longing eyes I wait,
Expectant of her.
THACKERAY, *At the Church Gate*. (*Pendennis*. Ch. 31.)

14
Meet me by moonlight alone,
And then I will tell you a tale
Must be told by the moonlight alone,
In the grove at the end of the vale!
J. AUGUSTINE WADE, *Meet Me by Moonlight*.

II—Meeting and Parting

15
Like a plank of driftwood
Tossed on the watery main,
Another plank encountered,
Meets, touches, parts again;
So tossed, and drifting ever,
On life's unresting sea,
Men meet, and greet, and sever,
Parting eternally.
EDWIN ARNOLD, *Book of Good Counsel*. A free translation from the Sanskrit of the *Hitopadêsa*. See *Fortnightly Review*, July, 1898, for literal translation by Max Müller.

As two floating planks meet and part on the sea,
O friend! so I met and then drifted from thee.
WILLIAM R. ALGER, *Poetry of the Orient: The Brief Chance Encounter*.

16
Like driftwood spars which meet and pass
Upon the boundless ocean-plain,
So on the sea of life, alas!
Man nears man, meets, and leaves again.
MATTHEW ARNOLD, *The Terrace at Berne*, l. 45.

Two lives that once part, are as ships that divide
When, moment on moment, there rushes between
The one and the other, a sea;—
Ah, never can fall from the days that have been
A gleam on the years that shall be!
BULWER-LYTTON, *A Lament*, l. 10.

1
Why meet we on the bridge of Time to 'change one greeting and to part?
SIR RICHARD BURTON, *The Kasîdah*. Pt. i, st. 11.

Weep not, she says, at Nature's transient pain,
Congenial spirits part to meet again!
CAMPBELL, *The Pleasures of Hope*. Pt. ii, l. 405.

We only part to meet again.
JOHN GAY, *Sweet William's Farewell*.

2
As vessels starting from ports thousands of miles apart pass close to each other in the naked breadth of the ocean, nay, sometimes even touch in the dark.
O. W. HOLMES, *The Professor at the Breakfast-Table*. Ch. 3.

Ships that pass in the night, and speak each other in passing,
Only a signal shown and a distant voice in the darkness;
So on the ocean of life, we pass and speak one another,
Only a look and a voice, then darkness again and a silence.
LONGFELLOW, *Tales of a Wayside Inn: The Theologian's Tale: Elizabeth*. Pt. iv. The first phrase was used by Beatrice Harradan as the title of a novel.

We twain have met like the ships upon the sea,
Who hold an hour's converse, so short, so sweet;
One little hour! and then, away they speed
On lonely paths, through mist, and cloud, and foam,
To meet no more.
ALEXANDER SMITH, *A Life Drama*. Sc. 4.

Alas, by what rude fate
Our lives, like ships at sea, an instant meet,
Then part forever on their courses fleet!
E. C. STEDMAN, *The Blameless Prince*. St. 51.

3
Sing, minstrel, sing us now a tender song
Of meeting and parting, with the moon in it.
STEPHEN PHILLIPS, *Ulysses*. Act i, sc. 1.

4
Our parting was all sob and sigh,
Our meeting was all mirth and laughter.
W. M. PRAED, *The Belle of the Ball*.

5
Say good-bye er howdy-do—
What's the odds betwixt the two?
Comin'—goin'—every day—
Best friends first to go away—
Grasp of hands you'd ruther hold
Than their weight in solid gold,
Slips their grip while greetin' you,—
Say good-bye er howdy-do?
JAMES WHITCOMB RILEY, *Good-Bye er Howdy-Do*.

6
Their meetings made December June.
Their every parting was to die.
TENNYSON, *In Memoriam*. Pt. xcvii.

7
We live to love; we meet to part;
And part to meet on earth no more.
BRYON FORCEYTHE WILLSON, *No More*.

MELANCHOLY

See also Sorrow

8
Melancholy is a kind of demon that haunts our island, and often conveys herself to us in an easterly wind.
ADDISON, *The Spectator*. No. 387. *See also* DICKENS, *under* WIND: APOTHEGMS.

9
Melancholy men of all others are most witty.
ARISTOTLE. (Quoted by Burton, *Anatomy of Melancholy*. Pt. i, sec. iii, mem. 1, subs. 3.)

10
It is the heaviest stone that melancholy can throw at a man, to tell him he is at the end of his nature; or that there is no further state to come.
SIR THOMAS BROWNE, *Hydriotaphia*. Ch. 4.

11
He hated nought but—to be sad.
BURNS, *The Jolly Beggars*.

12
There is no greater cause of melancholy than idleness; "no better cure than business," as Rhasis holds.
ROBERT BURTON, *Anatomy of Melancholy: Democritus to the Reader*.

Employment, sir, and hardships, prevent melancholy.
SAMUEL JOHNSON. (BOSWELL, *Life*, 1777.)

13
If there be a hell upon earth it is to be found in a melancholy man's heart.
ROBERT BURTON, *Anatomy of Melancholy*. Pt. i, sec. 4, mem. 1, subs. 2.

That feral melancholy which crucifies the soul.
ROBERT BURTON, *Anatomy of Melancholy*. Pt. iii, sec. 2, mem. 1, subs. 2.

14
As melancholy as an unbraced drum.
SUSANNAH CENTLIVRE, *Wonder*. Act ii, sc. 1.

15
Melancholy was made, not for beasts, but for men; but if men give way to it overmuch they turn to beasts.
CERVANTES, *Don Quixote*. Pt. ii, ch. 11.

16
With eyes up-rais'd, as one inspir'd,
Pale Melancholy sate retir'd;
And, from her wild, sequester'd seat,
In notes by distance made more sweet,
Pour'd thro' the mellow horn her pensive soul.
WILLIAM COLLINS, *The Passions*, l. 57.

17
There is a kindly mood of melancholy
That wings the soul, and points her to the skies.
JOHN DYER, *The Ruins of Rome*, l. 346.

18
There's naught in this life sweet,
If man were wise to see 't,
But only melancholy;

O sweetest Melancholy!
JOHN FLETCHER, *The Nice Valour*. Act iii, sc. 3. (c. 1620) Written probably in conjunction with Thomas Middleton. This song has also been attributed to Dr. William Strode, and appears in his play *The Floating Island*. (1636)

All my joys to this are folly,
Naught so sweet as melancholy.
ROBERT BURTON, *Anatomy of Melancholy: The Author's Abstract*.

All my griefs to this are jolly,
Naught so damn'd as melancholy.
ROBERT BURTON, *Anatomy of Melancholy: The Author's Abstract*.

1
Tell us, pray, what devil
This melancholy is, which can transform
Men into monsters.
JOHN FORD, *The Lover's Melancholy*. Act iii, sc. 1, l. 107.

Melancholy
Is not, as you conceive, indisposition
Of body, but the mind's disease.
JOHN FORD, *The Lover's Melancholy*. Act iii, sc. 1, l. 111.

2
Here rests his head upon the lap of Earth,
A Youth, to Fortune and to Fame unknown.
Fair Science frown'd not on his humble birth,
And Melancholy mark'd him for her own.
THOMAS GRAY, *Elegy Written in a Country Church-yard: The Epitaph*.

3
All things are touch'd with Melancholy,
Born of the secret soul's mistrust.
THOMAS HOOD, *Ode to Melancholy*, l. 109.

There's not a string attun'd to mirth
But has its chord in Melancholy.
THOMAS HOOD, *Ode to Melancholy*, l. 121.

4
Melancholy is the pleasure of being sad.
VICTOR HUGO, *Toilers of the Sea*. Pt. iii, bk. i, ch. 1.

Go! you may call it madness, folly;
You shall not chase my gloom away!
There's such a charm in melancholy
I would not if I could be gay.
SAMUEL ROGERS, *To* ——.

And yet I cannot tell thee why,
I'm pleased and yet I'm sad.
H. K. WHITE, *I'm Pleased and Yet I'm Sad*.

5
Sit melancholy and pick your teeth when you cannot speak.
BEN JONSON, *Every Man Out of His Humour*. Act i, sc. 2.

6
She dwells with Beauty—Beauty that must die;
And Joy, whose hand is ever at his lips
Bidding adieu; and aching Pleasure nigh,
Turning to Poison while the bee-mouth sips:
Aye, in the very temple of Delight
Veil'd Melancholy has her sovran shrine,
Though seen of none save him whose strenuous tongue
Can burst Joy's grape against his palate fine;
His soul shall taste the sadness of her might,
And be among her cloudy trophies hung.
KEATS, *Ode on Melancholy*. St. 3.

7
It is a kind of happiness to know just how unhappy one should be. (C'est une espèce de bonheur de connaître jusqu'a quel point on doit être malheureux.)
LA ROCHEFOUCAULD, *Maximes Supprimées*, 570.

8
A feeling of sadness and longing
That is not akin to pain,
And resembles sorrow only
As the mist resembles the rain.
LONGFELLOW, *The Day Is Done*. St. 3.

9
But hail, thou Goddess, sage and holy,
Hail, divinest Melancholy,
Whose Saintly visage is too bright
To hit the Sense of human sight.
MILTON, *Il Penseroso*, l. 11.

These pleasures, Melancholy, give;
And I with thee will choose to live.
MILTON, *Il Penseroso*, l. 175.

10
Hence, loathed Melancholy,
Of Cerberus, and blackest midnight born,
In Stygian cave forlorn,
'Mongst horrid shapes, and shrieks and sights unholy!
MILTON, *L'Allegro*, l. 1.

Moping melancholy, And moon-struck madness.
MILTON, *Paradise Lost*. Bk. xi, l. 485.

11
Oh! when a cheek is to be dried,
All pharmacy is folly; . . .
There's nothing like a rattling ride
For curing melancholy!
W. M. PRAED, *The Troubadour*.

12
He has a cloud in 's face.
SHAKESPEARE, *Antony and Cleopatra*. Act iii, sc. 2, l. 51.

Love, I am full of lead.
SHAKESPEARE, *Antony and Cleopatra*. Act iii, sc. 11, l. 72.

13
I can suck melancholy out of a song, as a weasel sucks eggs.
SHAKESPEARE, *As You Like It*. Act ii, sc. 5, l. 13.

I have neither the scholar's melancholy, which is emulation; nor the musician's, which is fantastical; nor the courtier's, which is proud; nor the soldier's, which is ambitious; nor the lawyer's, which is politic; nor the lady's, which is nice; nor the lover's, which is all these: but it is a melancholy of mine own, compounded of many simples, extracted from many objects, and in-

deed the sundry contemplation of my travels, in which my often rumination wraps me in a most humorous sadness.
SHAKESPEARE, *As You Like It*. Act iv, sc. 1, l. 10.

1
O melancholy!
Who ever yet could sound thy bottom? find
The ooze, to show what coast thy sluggish crare
Might easiliest harbour in?
SHAKESPEARE, *Cymbeline*. Act iv, sc. 2, l. 203.

2
There's something in his soul,
O'er which his melancholy sits on brood.
SHAKESPEARE, *Hamlet*. Act iii, sc. 1, l. 174.

3
I am as melancholy as a gib cat.
SHAKESPEARE, *I Henry IV*. Act i, sc. 2, l. 83.

As melancholy as a sick monkey.
MARRYAT, *Midshipman Easy*. Ch. 21.

As melancholy as a sick parrot.
APHRA BEHN, *False Count*. Act i, sc. 2.

4
Methinks no body should be sad but I.
SHAKESPEARE, *King John*. Act iv, sc. 1, l. 13.

My cue is villainous melancholy, with a sigh like Tom o' Bedlam.
SHAKESPEARE, *King Lear*. Act i, sc. 2, l. 147.

And such a want-wit sadness makes of me,
That I have much ado to know myself.
SHAKESPEARE, *The Merchant of Venice*. Act i, sc. 1, l. 6.

5
Turn melancholy forth to funerals.
SHAKESPEARE, *A Midsummer-Night's Dream*. Act i, sc. 1, l. 14.

6
He is of a very melancholy disposition.
SHAKESPEARE, *Much Ado About Nothing*. Act ii, sc. 1, l. 6.

The greatest note of it is his melancholy.
SHAKESPEARE, *Much Ado About Nothing*. Act iii, sc. 2, l. 53.

Melancholy is the nurse of frenzy.
SHAKESPEARE, *The Taming of the Shrew: Induction*. Sc. 2, l. 135.

Like a melancholy malcontent.
SHAKESPEARE, *Venus and Adonis*, l. 313.

Musing full sadly in his sullen mind.
SPENSER, *Faerie Queene*. Bk. i, canto ix, st. 35.

7
'Tis impious in a good man to be sad.
YOUNG, *Night Thoughts*. Night iv, l. 675.

MEMORIAL DAY, see Soldiers: How Sleep the Brave

MEMORY

See also Past, Yesterday

I—Memory: Definitions

8
Memory is the treasury and guardian of all things. (Memoria est thesaurus omnium rerum e custos.)
CICERO, *De Oratore*. Bk. i, sec. 5.

9
The memory strengthens as you lay burdens upon it, and becomes trustworthy as you trust it.
THOMAS DE QUINCEY, *Confessions of an English Opium-Eater*. Pt. i.

10
Some call her Memory,
And some Tradition; and her voice is sweet,
With deep mysterious accords.
GEORGE ELIOT, *The Spanish Gypsy*. Bk. ii.

11
Memory [is] like a purse,—if it be overfull that it cannot shut, all will drop out of it. Take heed of a gluttonous curiosity to feed on many things, lest the greediness of the appetite of thy memory spoil the digestion thereof.
THOMAS FULLER, *Holy and Profane States: Of Memory*.

12
Imagination and memory are but one thing which for divers considerations hath divers names.
THOMAS HOBBES, *Leviathan*. Pt. i, ch. 2.

13
The true art of memory is the art of attention.
SAMUEL JOHNSON, *The Idler*. No. 74.

Method is the mother of memory.
THOMAS FULLER, *History of the Worthies of England*, p. 166.

14
Memory, of all the powers of the mind, is the most delicate and frail.
BEN JONSON, *Explorata: Memoria*.

15
Memory is to us the hearing of deaf actions, and the seeing of blind.
PLUTARCH, *Morals: On the Cessation of Oracles*. Sec. 39.

Memory: what wonders it performs in preserving and storing up things gone by, or rather, things that are!
PLUTARCH, *Morals: On the Cessation of Oracles*. Sec. 39.

16
Hail, Memory, hail! in thy exhaustless mine
From age to age unnumber'd treasures shine!
Thought and her shadowy brood thy call obey,
And Place and Time are subjects to thy sway!
ROGERS, *Pleasures of Memory*. Pt. ii, l. 430.

17
Memory, the warder of the brain.
SHAKESPEARE, *Macbeth*. Act i, sc. 7, l. 65.

Storehouse of the mind, garner of facts and fancies.
M. F. TUPPER, *Proverbial Philosophy: Of Memory*.

Memory called the treasure of the mind.
THOMAS WILSON, *Arte of Rhetorique*. (1560)

1
A man's real possession is his memory. In nothing else is he rich, in nothing else is he poor.

ALEXANDER SMITH, *Dreamthorp: On Death and the Fear of Dying.*

II—Memory: Apothegms

2
Memory, no less than hope, owes its charm to "the far away."

BULWER-LYTTON, *A Lament. See also under* DISTANCE.

3
Memory, in widow's weeds, with naked feet
stands on a tombstone.

AUBREY DE VERE, *Widowhood.*

4
A man of great memory without learning hath a rock and a spindle and no staff to spin.

GEORGE HERBERT, *Jacula Prudentum.*

5
Better a little well kept, than a great deal forgotten.

BISHOP HUGH LATIMER, *Fifth Sermon Preached Before King Edward.*

6
Memory and Oblivion, all hail! Memory for goodness, Oblivion for evil.

MACEDONIUS THE CONSUL. (*Greek Anthology.* Bk. x, epig. 67.)

7
Experience teaches that a good memory is generally joined to a weak judgment.

MONTAIGNE, *Essays.* Bk. i, ch. 9.

A great memory does not make a philosopher, any more than a dictionary can be called a grammar.

JOHN HENRY NEWMAN, *Knowledge in Relation to Culture.*

8
Many a man fails to become a thinker for the sole reason that his memory is too good.

NIETZSCHE, *Maxims.*

9
The jar will long retain the fragrance with which it was steeped when new. (Quo semel est imbuta recens, servabit odorem Testa diu.)

HORACE, *Epistles.* Bk. i, epis. 2, l. 69.

Long, long be my heart with such memories fill'd!
Like the vase in which roses have once been distill'd:
You may break, you may shatter the vase if you will,
But the scent of the roses will hang round it still.

THOMAS MOORE, *Farewell! But Whenever.*

Rose-leaves, when the rose is dead,
Are heaped for the beloved's bed;
And so thy thoughts, when thou art gone,
Love itself shall slumber on.

SHELLEY, *To ——: Music When Soft Voices.*

10
Everyone complains of his lack of memory, but nobody of his want of judgment. (Tout le monde se plaint de sa mémoire, et personne ne se plaint de son jugement.)

LA ROCHEFOUCAULD, *Maximes.* No. 89.

11
Remarkable memory, yours! (Memor es probe!)

PLAUTUS, *Asinaria,* l. 343. (Act ii, sc. 2.)

12
If I do not remember thee, let my tongue cleave to the roof of my mouth.

Old Testament: Psalms, cxxxvii, 6.

13
Though yet of Hamlet . . . The memory be
green.

SHAKESPEARE, *Hamlet.* Act i, sc. 2, l. 2.

Lord, keep my Memory Green.

DICKENS, *The Haunted Man.* Ch. 3.

And the tear that we shed, though in secret it rolls,
Shall long keep his memory green in our souls.

THOMAS MOORE, *Oh, Breathe Not His Name.*

14
'Tis in my memory lock'd,
And you yourself shall keep the key of it.

SHAKESPEARE, *Hamlet.* Act i, sc. 3, l. 85.

15
Purpose is but the slave to memory.

SHAKESPEARE, *Hamlet.* Act iii, sc. 2, l. 197.

16
Illiterate him, I say, quite from your memory.

SHERIDAN, *The Rivals.* Act i, sc. 2.

17
Left behind as a memory for us. (Nobis meminisse relictum.)

STATIUS, *Silvæ.* Bk. ii, l. 55.

Nothing now is left But a majestic memory.

LONGFELLOW, *Three Friends of Mine,* l. 10.

III—Memory: Its Sweetness

18
The safe relation of past trouble possesses its delight. (Habet enim præteriti doloris secura recordatio delectionem.)

CICERO, *Ad Familiares.* Bk. v, epis. 12, sec. 5.

How sweet to remember the trouble that is past.

EURIPIDES. (PLUTARCH, *Morals.*)

That which is bitter to endure may be sweet to remember.

THOMAS FULLER, *Gnomologia.* No. 4385.

Sorrows remembered sweeten present joy.

ROBERT POLLOK, *Course of Time.* Bk. i, l. 464.

Things that were hard to bear are sweet to remember. (Quæ fuit durum pati, Meminisse dulce est.)

SENECA, *Hercules Furens,* l. 656.

Perchance some day the memory of this sorrow
Will even bring delight.
(Forsan et hæc olim meminisse juvabit.)

VERGIL, *Æneid.* Bk. i, l. 203.

19
What peaceful hours I once enjoy'd!
How sweet their mem'ry still!

WILLIAM COWPER, *Walking with God.*

When Time, who steals our years away
  Shall steal our pleasures, too,
The mem'ry of the past will stay,
  And half our joys renew.
  THOMAS MOORE, *Song*.

Oft, in the stilly night,
  Ere Slumber's chain has bound me,
Fond Memory brings the light
  Of other days around me.
  THOMAS MOORE, *The Light of Other Days*.

The light of other days is faded.
And all their glories past.
  ALFRED BUNN, *The Bohemian Girl: Song*.

1
Oh! the good times when we were so unhappy. (Oh le bon temps où étions si malheureux.)
  DUMAS, *Le Chevalier d'Harmental*. Bk. ii, p. 318.

Oh! that was the good time; I was very unhappy. (Oh! c'était le bon temps; j'étais bien malheureuse.)
  SOPHIE ARNOULD, *Remark*, to Rulhière.

One day, a famous actress was telling me of the rages of her first lover, and, half-dreaming, half-laughing, she added this charming word: Oh, that was the good time—I was very unhappy.
(Un jour, une actrice fameuse
  Me contait les fureurs de son premier amant;
Moitié rêvant, moitié rieuse,
  Elle ajouta ce mot charmant:
Oh! c'était le bon temps, j'était bien malheureuse.)
  CLAUDE RULHIÈRE, *Épître à Monsieur de Cha——*.

2
So may it be: that so dead Yesterday,
No sad-eyed ghost but generous and gay,
May serve you memories like almighty wine,
  When you are old!
  W. E. HENLEY, *When You Are Old*.

3
This memory brightens o'er the past,
  As when the sun, concealed
Behind some cloud that near us hangs,
  Shines on a distant field.
  LONGFELLOW, *A Gleam of Sunshine*. St. 14.

4
Only stay quiet while my mind remembers
The beauty of fire from the beauty of embers.
  JOHN MASEFIELD, *On Growing Old*.

5
  A thousand fantasies
Begin to throng into my memory.
  MILTON, *Comus*, l. 205.

6
And memories vague of half-forgotten things,
Not true nor false, but sweet to think upon.
  WILLIAM MORRIS, *The Earthly Paradise: March*, l. 63.

7
Then, when the world is born again
  And the sweet year before thee lies,
Shall thy heart think of coming pain,
  Or vex itself with memories?
  WILLIAM MORRIS, *Life and Death of Jason*. Bk. xiv, l. 213.

8
For it is a pleasure, too, to remember. (Namque est meminisse voluptas.)
  OVID, *Heroides*. Epis. xviii, l. 55.

9
Sweet Memory, wafted by thy gentle gale
Oft up the stream of Time I turn my sail.
  ROGERS, *The Pleasures of Memory*. Pt. ii, l. 1.

Lull'd in the countless chambers of the brain,
Our thoughts are link'd by many a hidden chain.
  ROGERS, *The Pleasures of Memory*. Pt. i, l. 171.

10
Thou fill'st from the winged chalice of the soul
Thy lamp, O Memory, fire-winged to its goal.
  D. G. ROSSETTI, *Mnemosyne*.

11
O Memory! thou soul of joy and pain!
  RICHARD SAVAGE, *The Bastard*, l. 57.

12
  Praising what is lost
Makes the remembrance dear.
  SHAKESPEARE, *All's Well that Ends Well*. Act v, sc. 3, l. 19.

13
Mankind are always happier for having been happy; so that, if you make them happy now, you make them happy twenty years hence by the memory of it.
  SYDNEY SMITH, *Sketches of Moral Philosophy: Lecture 22, On Benevolent Affections*.

14
A land of promise, a land of memory,
A land of promise flowing with the milk
And honey of delicious memories!
  TENNYSON, *The Lover's Tale*, l. 326.

15
Out of the cradle endlessly rocking,
Out of the mocking-bird's throat, the musical shuttle, . . .
A reminiscence sing.
  WALT WHITMAN, *Out of the Cradle*.

16
  And, when the stream
Which overflowed the soul was passed away,
A consciousness remained that it had left,
Deposited upon the silent shore
Of memory, images and precious thoughts,
That shall not die, and cannot be destroyed.
  WORDSWORTH, *The Excursion*. Bk. vii, l. 25.

If there be a joy that slights the claim
Of grateful memory, let that joy depart!
  WORDSWORTH, *Miscellaneous Sonnets*. Pt. ii, No. 5.

17
For oft, when on my couch I lie
In vacant or in pensive mood,
They flash upon that inward eye
Which is the bliss of solitude;

And then my heart with pleasure fills,
And dances with the daffodils.
WORDSWORTH, *I Wandered Lonely as a Cloud.* Wordsworth stated that this stanza was suggested by his wife.

The thought of our past years in me doth breed
Perpetual benediction.
WORDSWORTH, *Intimations of Immortality.* St. 9.

Where'er I go,
Thy genuine image, Yarrow!
Will dwell with me,—to heighten joy,
And cheer my mind in sorrow.
WORDSWORTH, *Yarrow Visited,* l. 85.

IV—Memory: Its Bitterness

1
For of fortune's sharp adversity
The worst kind of infortune is this,
A man to have been in prosperity,
And it remember, when it passed is.
CHAUCER, *Troilus and Criseyde.* Bk. iii, l. 1625.

Of joys departed,
Not to return, how painful the remembrance!
ROBERT BLAIR, *The Grave,* l. 109.

No traces left of all the busy scene,
But that remembrance says: The things have been.
SAMUEL BOYSE, *The Deity.*

2
There is no greater sorrow than to recall, in misery, the time when we were happy. (Nessun maggior dolore Che ricordarsi del tempo felice Nella miseria.)
DANTE, *Inferno.* Canto v, l. 121.

There is no worse sorrow than remembering happiness in the day of sorrow. (Il n'est pire douleur Qu'un souvenir heureux dans le jour de malheur.)
ALFRED DE MUSSET, *La Saule.*

But woe to him, who left to moan,
Reviews the hours of brightness gone.
EURIPIDES, *Iphigenia in Taurus,* l. 1121. (Anstice, tr.)

Memory of happiness makes misery woeful.
THOMAS FULLER, *Gnomologia.* No. 4650.

But were there ever any
Writh'd not at passèd joy?
KEATS, *Stanzas: In a Drear-Nighted December.*

Nor nothing more may heartes disavaunce
Than of old joy new remembrance.
LYDGATE, *Fall of Princes.* Bk. i, l. 650. (c. 1440)

3
O Memory! thou fond deceiver!
Still importunate and vain;
To former joys recurring ever,
And turning all the past to pain.
GOLDSMITH, *The Captivity.* Act i, sc. 1.

Remembrance wakes with all her busy train,
Swells at my breast, and turns the past to pain.
GOLDSMITH, *The Deserted Village,* l. 81.

4
The bitter memory
Of what he was, what is, and what must be.
MILTON, *Paradise Lost.* Bk. iv, l. 24.

5
O dear, dear Jeanie Morrison,
The thochts o' bygane years
Still fling their shadows ower my path,
And blind my een wi' tears.
WILLIAM MOTHERWELL, *Jeanie Morrison.*

6
When time has assuaged the wounds of the mind, he who unseasonably reminds us of them, opens them afresh.
(At cum longa dies sedavit vulnera mentis,
Intempestive qui movet illa, novat.)
OVID, *Epistulæ ex Ponto.* Bk. iv, epis. 11, l. 19.

7
Yet hath my night of life some memory,
My wasting lamps some fading glimmer left.
SHAKESPEARE, *The Comedy of Errors.* Act v, sc. 1, l. 314.

8
Remember thee!
Ay, thou poor ghost, while memory holds a seat
In this distracted globe. Remember thee!
Yea, from the table of my memory
I'll wipe away all trivial fond records.
SHAKESPEARE, *Hamlet.* Act i, sc. 5, l. 95.

I cannot but remember such things were,
That were most precious to me.
SHAKESPEARE, *Macbeth.* Act iv, sc. 3, l. 222.

It presses to my memory,
Like damned, guilty deeds to sinners' minds.
SHAKESPEARE, *Romeo and Juliet.* Act iii, sc. 2, l. 110.

9
Here did she fall a tear; here in this place
I'll set a bank of rue, sour herb of grace:
Rue, even for ruth, here shortly shall be seen,
In the remembrance of a weeping queen.
SHAKESPEARE, *Richard II.* Act iii, sc. 4, l. 104.

There's rosemary, that's for remembrance.
SHAKESPEARE, *Hamlet.* Act iv, sc. 5, l. 175.

10
When to the sessions of sweet silent thought
I summon up remembrance of things past,
I sigh the lack of many a thing I sought,
And with old woes new wail my dear time's waste.
SHAKESPEARE, *Sonnets.* No. xxx.

How sharp the point of this remembrance is!
SHAKESPEARE, *The Tempest.* Act v, sc. 1, l. 138.

Let us not burden our remembrance with
A heaviness that's gone.
SHAKESPEARE, *The Tempest.* Act v, sc. 1, l. 199.

11
This is truth the poet sings
That a sorrow's crown of sorrow is remembering happier things.
TENNYSON, *Locksley Hall.* St. 38.

The saddest lot of all is to know the good, and yet, perforce, to be debarred therefrom.
PINDAR, *Pythian Odes.* No. iv, l. 510. Said by

Churton Collins (*Illustrations of Tennyson*, p. 62) to have inspired Tennyson's line.

1
So joys, remembered without wish or will,
Sharpen the keenest edge of present ill.
WORDSWORTH, *Sonnet: Captivity*.

V—Memory: Tender Memories

2
Oh, I have roamed o'er many lands,
And many friends I've met;
Not one fair scene or kindly smile
Can this fond heart forget.
T. H. BAYLY, *Song: Oh, Steer My Bark*.

3
Ah, we fondly cherish
Faded things
That had better perish.
Memory clings
To each leaf it saves.
J. H. BONER, *Gather Leaves and Grasses*.

'T is but a little faded flower,
But oh, how fondly dear!
'T will bring me back one golden hour,
Through many a weary year.
ELLEN CLEMENTINE HOWARTH, *'Tis But a Little Faded Flower*.

Where is the heart that doth not keep,
Within its inmost core,
Some fond remembrance hidden deep,
Of days that are no more?
ELLEN CLEMENTINE HOWARTH, *'Tis But a Little Faded Flower*.

Who hath not saved some trifling thing
More prized than jewels rare,
A faded flower, a broken ring,
A tress of golden hair.
ELLEN CLEMENTINE HOWARTH, *'Tis But a Little Faded Flower*.

Yet for old sake's sake she is still, dears,
The prettiest doll in the world.
CHARLES KINGSLEY, *My Little Doll*.

4
When other lips and other hearts
Their tales of love shall tell,
In language whose excess imparts
The power they feel so well,
There may, perhaps, in such a scene,
Some recollection be
Of days that have as happy been,
And you'll remember me.
ALFRED BUNN, *Then You'll Remember Me*. (*The Bohemian Girl*. Act iii.)

5
Oh! scenes in strong remembrance set!
Scenes never, never to return!
ROBERT BURNS, *The Lament*. St. 10.

Still o'er these scenes my mem'ry wakes,
And fondly broods with miser care;
Time but th' impression stronger makes,
As streams their channels deeper wear.
ROBERT BURNS, *To Mary in Heaven*.

6
While Memory watches o'er the sad review
Of joys that faded like the morning dew.
CAMPBELL, *The Pleasures of Hope*. Pt. ii, l. 45.

7
How cruelly sweet are the echoes that start
When memory plays an old tune on the heart!
ELIZA COOK, *Old Dobbin*. St. 16.

8
O Genevieve, sweet Genevieve,
The days may come, the days may go,
But still the hands of mem'ry weave
The blissful dreams of long ago.
GEORGE COOPER, *Sweet Genevieve*. A popular song the music of which was written about 1877 by Henry Tucker.

9
Don't you remember sweet Alice, Ben Bolt,—
Sweet Alice, whose hair was so brown,
Who wept with delight when you gave her a smile,
And trembled with fear at your frown?
THOMAS DUNN ENGLISH, *Ben Bolt*. First published in *The New Mirror* (N. Y.), 2 Sept., 1843.

10
A place in thy memory, Dearest!
Is all that I claim:
To pause and look back when thou hearest
The sound of my name.
GERALD GRIFFIN, *A Place in Thy Memory*.

11
Only a dream, and yet I hear you singing,
Singing in the shadows, while gently falls the dew.
Roses may fade, but each returning twilight
Brings the fragrant memory of you.
BERNARD HAMBLEN, *The Memory of You*.

12
I recollect a nurse called Ann,
Who carried me about the grass,
And one fine day a fine young man
Came up and kissed the pretty lass.
She did not make the least objection.
Thinks I, "*Aha,*
When I can talk I'll tell Mama,"
And that's my earliest recollection.
F. LOCKER-LAMPSON, *A Terrible Infant*.

13
The leaves of memory seemed to make
A mournful rustling in the dark.
LONGFELLOW, *The Fire of Driftwood*.

There comes to me out of the Past
A voice, whose tones are sweet and wild,
Singing a song almost divine,
And with a tear in every line.
LONGFELLOW, *Tales of a Wayside Inn:* Pt. iii, *Interlude*.

14
To live with them is far less sweet
Than to remember thee.
THOMAS MOORE, *I Saw Thy Form*.

So turn our hearts, as on we rove,
To those we've left behind us!
THOMAS MOORE, *The Journey Onwards*.

15
All to myself I think of you,
Think of the things we used to do,

Think of the things we used to say,
Think of each happy bygone day.
Sometimes I sigh, and sometimes I smile,
But I keep each olden, golden while
All to myself.

WILBUR D. NESBIT, *All to Myself.*

1
My home, the city, and the image of well-known places pass before my eyes. (Ante oculos errant domus, urbsque et forma locorum.)

OVID, *Tristia*. Bk. iii, eleg. 4, l. 57.

I remember, I remember
The house where I was born,
The little window where the sun
Came peeping in at morn.

THOMAS HOOD, *I Remember, I Remember*.

2
I wept for memory.

CHRISTINA ROSSETTI, *She Sat and Sang Always.*

3
Still are the thoughts to memory dear.

SCOTT, *Rokeby*. Canto i, st. 33.

4
The idea of her life shall sweetly creep
Into his study of imagination,
And every lovely organ of her life
Shall come apparell'd in more precious habit,
More moving-delicate and full of life,
Into the eye and prospect of his soul.

SHAKESPEARE, *Much Ado About Nothing*. Act iv, sc. 1, l. 226.

5
Ah, how much less all living loves to me,
Than that one rapture of remembering thee.
(Heu quanto minus est cum reliquis versari,
quam tui meminisse.)

WILLIAM SHENSTONE, *Epitaph to the Memory of Mary Doleman.* (Munby, tr.)

6
I am with you,
Wandering through Memory Lane.

B. G. DE SILVA, *Memory Lane.* (1924)

7
As the dew to the blossom, the bud to the bee,
As the scent to the rose, are those memories to me.

AMELIA C. WELBY, *Pulpit Eloquence.*

8
Passing sweet
Are the domains of tender memory!

WORDSWORTH, *Ode to Lycoris*. No. ii, l. 50.

VI—Memory and Forgetfulness

See also Forgetfulness

9
I sit beside my lonely fire
And pray for wisdom yet:
For calmness to remember
Or courage to forget.

CHARLES HAMILTON AIDÉ, *Remember or Forget.*

Forget that I remember,
And dream that I forget.

A. C. SWINBURNE, *Rococo.*

10
Remembrances embellish life but forgetfulness alone makes it possible. (Les souvenirs embellissent la vie, l'oubli seul la rend possible.)

GENERAL CIALDINI, *Written in an Album.*

11
We have all forgot more than we remember.

THOMAS FULLER, *Gnomologia*. No. 5442.

12
A retentive memory is a good thing, but the ability to forget is the true token of greatness.

ELBERT HUBBARD, *Epigrams.*

13
Ah, tell me not that memory
Sheds gladness o'er the past;
What is recalled by faded flowers,
Save that they did not last?
Were it not better to forget,
Than but remember and regret?

LETITIA ELIZABETH LANDON, *Despondency.*

14
Better by far you should forget and smile,
Than that you should remember and be sad.

CHRISTINA ROSSETTI, *Remember.*

15
Though varying wishes, hopes, and fears
Fever'd the progress of these years,
Yet now, days, weeks, and months but seem
The recollection of a dream.

SCOTT, *Marmion:* Canto iv, *Introduction*, l. 21.

16
I shall remember while the light lives yet.
And in the night-time I shall not forget.

SWINBURNE, *Erotion.*

17
Teach me not the art of remembering, but the art of forgetting, for I remember things I do not wish to remember, but I cannot forget things I wish to forget.

THEMISTOCLES, when Simonides offered to teach him the art of memory. (CICERO, *De Finibus*. Bk. ii, ch. 32, sec. 104.)

18
Mem: To remember to forget to ask
Old Whitbred to my house one day.

JOHN WOLCOT, *Whitbread's Brewery Visited by Their Majesties.*

MERCY

19
For Mercy, Courage, Kindness, Mirth,
There is no measure upon earth;
Nay, they wither, root and stem,
If an end be set to them.

LAURENCE BINYON, *A Song.*

For Mercy has a human heart,
Pity a human face,
And Love, the human form divine,
And Peace, the human dress.

Then every man, of every clime,
That prays in his distress,

Prays to the human form divine,
Love, Mercy, Pity, Peace.
WILLIAM BLAKE, *The Divine Image.*

1
Mercy is for the merciful.
BYRON, *Lines on Hearing Lady Byron Was Ill.*

Mercy to him that shows it, is the rule.
COWPER, *The Task*. Bk. vi, l. 595.

Mercy of mercy needs must arise.
LANGLAND, *Piers Plowman*. Passus xii, l. 233.

2
Bowels of mercies, kindness, humbleness of mind, meekness, long-suffering.
New Testament: Colossians, iii, 12.

Open thy bowels of compassion.
CONGREVE, *The Mourning Bride*. Act iv, sc. 7.

3
We hand folks over to God's mercy, and show none ourselves.
GEORGE ELIOT, *Adam Bede*. Ch. 42. *See also* GOD: HIS MERCY.

4
Cowards are cruel, but the brave
Love mercy and delight to save.
JOHN GAY, *Fables*. Pt. i, fab. 1.

5
And shut the gates of mercy on mankind.
THOMAS GRAY, *Elegy Written in a Country Church-yard*. St. 17.

6
Mercy the wise Athenians held to be
Not an affection, but a Deity.
ROBERT HERRICK, *Mercy.*

7
Blessed are the merciful: for they shall obtain mercy.
New Testament: Matthew, v, 7.

Who will not mercy unto others show,
How can he mercy ever hope to have?
SPENSER, *Faerie Queene*. Bk. vi, canto i, st. 42.

8
Mercy is better than vengeance. (Συγγνώμη τιμωρίας κρείσσων.)
PITTACUS. (DIOGENES LAERTIUS, *Pittacus*. Bk. i, sec. 76.)

9
Mercy stood in the cloud, with eye that wept
Essential love.
POLLOK, *The Course of Time*. Bk iii, l. 658.

10
Teach me to feel another's woe,
To hide the fault I see;
That mercy I to others show,
That mercy show to me.
POPE, *Universal Prayer*. St. 10.

11
So much his courage and his mercy strive,
He wounds to cure, and conquers to forgive.
PRIOR, *Ode in Imitation of Horace*. Bk. iii, ode 2.

12
Mercy and truth are met together; righteousness and peace have kissed each other.
Old Testament: Psalms, lxxxv, 10.

13
It is a bad cause which asks for mercy. (Mala causa est quæ requirit misericordiam.)
PUBLILIUS SYRUS, *Sententiæ*. No. 346. *See also* JUSTICE AND MERCY.

14
It is impossible to imagine anything which better becomes a ruler than mercy. (Excogitare nemo quicquam poterit quod magis decorum regenti sit quam clementia.)
SENECA, *De Clementia*. Bk. i, ch. 19, sec. 1.

Humanity always becomes a conqueror.
SHERIDAN, *Pizarro*. Act i, sc. 1.

It is noble to grant life to the vanquished. (Pulchrum est vitam donare minori.)
STATIUS, *Thebais*. Bk. vi, l. 816.

Tigers have courage and the rugged bear,
But man alone can, whom he conquers, spare.
WALLER, *Epistle to My Lord Protector.*

15
Mercy often gives death instead of life. (Mortem misericors sæpe pro vita dabit.)
SENECA, *Troades*, l. 329.

16
Whereto serves mercy
But to confront the visage of offence?
SHAKESPEARE, *Hamlet*. Act iii, sc. 3, l. 46.

You must not dare, for shame, to talk of mercy;
For your own reasons turn into your bosoms,
As dogs upon their masters, worrying you.
SHAKESPEARE, *Henry V*. Act ii, sc. 2, l. 81.

I cry you, mercy, 'tis but Quid for Quo.
SHAKESPEARE, *I Henry VI*. Act v, sc. 3, l. 109.

17
Mercy is not itself, that oft looks so;
Pardon is still the nurse of second woe.
SHAKESPEARE, *Measure for Measure*. Act ii, sc. 1, l. 297. *See also* JUSTICE: LET JUSTICE BE DONE.

18
No ceremony that to great ones 'longs,
Not the king's crown, nor the deputed sword,
The marshal's truncheon, nor the judge's robe,
Become them with one half so good a grace
As mercy does.
SHAKESPEARE, *Measure for Measure*. Act ii, sc. 2, l. 59.

19
The quality of mercy is not strain'd;
It droppeth as the gentle rain from heaven
Upon the place beneath: it is twice blest;
It blesseth him that gives and him that takes:
'Tis mightiest in the mightiest: it becomes
The throned monarch better than his crown;
His sceptre shows the force of temporal power,
The attribute to awe and majesty,
Wherein doth sit the dread and fear of kings;
But mercy is above this sceptred sway;
It is enthroned in the hearts of kings,
It is an attribute to God himself;
And earthly power doth then show likest God's

When mercy seasons justice.
SHAKESPEARE, *The Merchant of Venice.* Act iv, sc. 1, l. 184.

We do pray for mercy;
And that same prayer doth teach us all to render
The deeds of mercy.
SHAKESPEARE, *The Merchant of Venice.* Act iv, sc. 1, l. 200.

1
Brother, you have a vice of mercy in you,
Which better fits a lion than a man.
SHAKESPEARE, *Troilus and Cressida.* Act v, sc. 3, l. 37.

2
Wilt thou draw near the nature of the gods?
Draw near them then in being merciful:
Sweet mercy is nobility's true badge.
SHAKESPEARE, *Titus Andronicus.* Act i, sc. 1, l. 117.

3
For mercy will soon pardon the meanest: but mighty men shall be mightily tormented.
Apocrypha: Wisdom of Solomon, vi, 6.

4
Sweet Mercy! to the gates of Heaven
This Minstrel lead, his sins forgiven;
The rueful conflict, the heart riven
With vain endeavour,
And memory of Earth's bitter leaven
Effaced for ever.
WORDSWORTH, *Thoughts Suggested on the Banks of the Nith,* l. 55.

MERIT

See also Deserving, Worth

5
Merit is worthier than fame.
BACON, *Letter to Lord Essex.* No. 48.

6
Merit and good-breeding will make their way everywhere.
LORD CHESTERFIELD, *Letters,* 9 Oct., 1747.

The force of his own merit makes his way.
SHAKESPEARE, *Henry VIII.* Act i, sc. 1, l. 64.

7
Amongst the sons of men how few are known
Who dare be just to merit not their own.
CHARLES CHURCHILL, *Epistle to Hogarth,* l. 1.

8
The little merit man can plead
In doing well, dependeth still
Upon his power of doing ill.
CHARLES CHURCHILL, *The Ghost.* Bk. iv, l. 248.

View the whole scene, with critic judgement scan,
And then deny him merit if you can.
Where he falls short, 'tis Nature's fault alone;
Where he succeeds, the merit's all his own.
CHARLES CHURCHILL, *The Rosciad,* l. 1023. Referring to Thomas Sheridan, the actor.

9
It sounds like stories from the land of spirits
If any man obtain that which he merits
Or any merit that which he obtains.
S. T. COLERIDGE, *The Good Great Man.*

10
No farther seek his merits to disclose,
Or draw his frailties from their dread abode,
(There they alike in trembling hope repose)
The bosom of his Father and his God.
THOMAS GRAY, *Elegy Written in a Country Church-yard: The Epitaph.*

11
Distinguish between baseness and merit, not by descent, but by purity of life and heart. (Turpi secernis honestum Non patre præclaro, sed vita et pectore puro.)
HORACE, *Satires.* Bk. i, sat. vi, l. 63.

12
Man's chief merit consists in resisting the impulses of his nature.
SAMUEL JOHNSON, *Miscellanies.* Vol. ii, p. 285.

13
What merit to be dropped on fortune's hill?
The honour is to mount it!
J. S. KNOWLES, *The Hunchback.* Act i, sc. 1.

14
The same principle leads us to neglect a man of merit that induces us to admire a fool. (Du même fonds dont on néglige un homme de mérite, l'on sait encore admirer un sot.)
LA BRUYÈRE, *Les Caractères.* Ch. 12.

15
Nature makes merit and fortune uses it. (La nature fait le mérite, et la fortune le met en œuvre.)
LA ROCHEFOUCAULD, *Maximes.* No. 153.

There are people who disgust with merit, and others who please with faults. (Il y a des gens dégoûtants avec du mérite, et d'autres qui plaisent avec des défauts.)
LA ROCHEFOUCAULD, *Maximes.* No. 155.

Our merit wins the esteem of honest men, and our lucky star that of the public. (Notre mérite nous attire l'estime des honnêtes gens, et notre étoile celle du public.)
LA ROCHEFOUCAULD, *Maximes.* No. 165.

The world more often rewards the appearance of merit than merit itself. (Le monde récompense plus souvent les apparences du mérite que le mérite même.)
LA ROCHEFOUCAULD, *Maximes.* No. 166.

16
There is merit without eminence, but there is no eminence without some merit. (Il y a du mérite sans élévation, mais il n'y a point d'élévation sans quelque mérite.)
LA ROCHEFOUCAULD, *Maximes.* No. 400.

Eminence is to merit what dress is to beauty. (L'élévation est au mérite ce que la parure est aux belles personnes.)
LA ROCHEFOUCAULD, *Maximes.* No. 401.

By merit rais'd To that bad eminence.
MILTON, *Paradise Lost.* Bk. ii, l. 5.

17
What is merit? The opinion one man entertains of another.
HENRY JOHN PALMERSTON, *Speeches.* Quoted by Carlyle in *Shooting Niagara.*

1
We should try to succeed by merit, not by favor. (Virtute ambire oportet, non favitoribus.)
PLAUTUS, *Amphitruo: Prologue*, l. 78.

2
Beauties in vain their pretty eyes may roll;
Charms strike the sight, but merit wins the soul.
POPE, *The Rape of the Lock*. Canto v, l. 33.

3
The sufficiency of merit is to know that my merit is not sufficient.
FRANCIS QUARLES, *Emblems*. Bk. ii, emb. 1.

4
O, if men were to be saved by merit, what hole in hell were hot enough for him?
SHAKESPEARE, *I Henry IV*. Act i, sc. 2, l. 119.

5
For merit lives from man to man,
And not from man, O Lord, to thee.
TENNYSON, *In Memoriam: Prelude*. St. 9.

6
In the use,
Not in the bare possession lies the merit.
GILBERT WEST, *Institution of the Garter*, l. 461.

MERMAID

7
According to the constitution of mermaids, so much of a mermaid as is not a woman must be a fish.
DICKENS, *Barnaby Rudge*. Ch. 1.

8
What at top is a lovely woman, ends below in a black and ugly fish. (Desinat in piscem mulier formosa superne.)
HORACE, *Ars Poetica*, l. 4.

9
O, train me not, sweet mermaid, with thy note.
SHAKESPEARE, *The Comedy of Errors*. Act iii, sc. 2, l. 45.

But, lest myself be guilty to self-wrong,
I'll stop mine ears against the mermaid's song.
SHAKESPEARE, *The Comedy of Errors*. Act iii, sc. 2, l. 168.

As if some mermaid did their ears entice.
SHAKESPEARE, *The Rape of Lucrece*. St. 202.

10
Once I sat upon a promontory,
And heard a mermaid on a dolphin's back
Uttering such dulcet and harmonious breath
That the rude sea grew civil at her song:
And certain stars shot madly from their spheres,
To hear the sea-maid's music.
SHAKESPEARE, *A Midsummer-Night's Dream*. Act ii, sc. 1, l. 149.

11
Who would be A mermaid fair,
Singing alone, Combing her hair?
TENNYSON, *The Mermaid*.

Slow sail'd the weary mariners and saw,
Betwixt the green brink and the running foam,
Sweet faces, rounded arms, and bosoms prest
To little harps of gold; and while they mused,
Whispering to each other half in fear,
Shrill music reach'd them on the middle sea.
TENNYSON, *The Sea Fairies*.

MERRIMENT

See also Mirth

I—Merriment: Apothegms

12
'Tis merry when gentle-folks meet.
ANTONY BREWER, *Countrie Girl*. Sig. H3. (1647)

It's merry when friends meet.
JOHN CLARKE, *Parœmiologia*, 26. (1639)

It is merry when gossips meet.
BEN JONSON, *Staple of News: Induction*. (1625)

Merry it is when knaves done meet.
UNKNOWN, *Cock Lorells Bote*, 14. (c. 1520)

13
Flower o' the rose,
If I've been merry, what matter who knows?
ROBERT BROWNING, *Fra Lippo Lippi*.

14
Go then merrily to Heaven.
ROBERT BURTON, *Anatomy of Melancholy*. Pt. ii, sec. iii, mem. 1.

I am of Ben's mind, madam; resolve to be merry though the ship were sinking.
SUSANNAH CENTLIVRE, *The Artifice*. Act v.

15
Your heart hangeth on a joly pin.
CHAUCER, *The Marchantes Tale*, l. 272. (1386)

Faith I was never on a merrier pin.
ROBERT DAVENPORT, *A New Trick to Cheat the Divell*. Act i, sc. 2. (1639)

16
"Let us be merry," said Mr. Pecksniff.
DICKENS, *Martin Chuzzlewit*. Ch. 5.

Some credit in being jolly.
DICKENS, *Martin Chuzzlewit*. Ch. 5.

17
A very merry, dancing, drinking,
Laughing, quaffing, and unthinking time.
JOHN DRYDEN, *Secular Masque*, l. 40.

So many, and so many, and such glee.
KEATS, *Endymion*. Bk. iv, l. 219.

Forward and frolic glee was there,
The will to do, the soul to dare.
SCOTT, *The Lady of the Lake*. Canto i, st. 21.

When every room
Hath blaz'd with lights and bray'd with minstrelsy.
SHAKESPEARE, *Timon of Athens*. Act ii, sc. 2, l. 169.

18
Be merry, man, and tak not sair in mind
The wavering of this wretchit warld of sorrow.
WILLIAM DUNBAR, *No Treasure Without Gladness*.

Be jolly, lords.
SHAKESPEARE, *Antony and Cleopatra*. Act ii sc. 7, l. 65.

1
The gift of gaiety may itself be the greatest good fortune, and the most serious step toward maturity.
IRWIN EDMAN. (*The Bookman*, May, 1926.)

2
Is any merry? let him sing psalms.
New Testament: James, v, 13.

3
Nothing is more hopeless than a scheme of merriment.
SAMUEL JOHNSON, *The Idler*. No. 58.

4
Haste thee, Nymph, and bring with thee
Jest and youthful Jollity,
Quips and Cranks, and wanton Wiles,
Nods, and Becks, and Wreathed Smiles.
JOHN MILTON, *L'Allegro*.

5
The more the merrier, the fewer the better fare.
JOHN PALSGRAVE, *Lesclarissement de la Langue Françoyse*. (1530) This is the first known appearance of the proverb in English. It is included in John Heywood's *Proverbs*, pt. ii, ch. 7, which was published in 1546, and was used frequently thereafter. It has been ascribed to King James I.

And mo the merrier is a proverb eke.
GEORGE GASCOIGNE, *Roses: Works*. Vol. i, p. 64. (1570)

6
A merry heart maketh a cheerful countenance.
Old Testament: Proverbs, xv, 13. *See also* HEART: THE MERRY HEART.

7
What should a man do but be merry?
SHAKESPEARE, *Hamlet*. Act iii, sc. 2, l. 131.

Hostess, clap to the doors: watch to-night, pray to-morrow. Gallants, lads, boys, hearts of gold, all the titles of good fellowship come to you! What, shall we be merry?
SHAKESPEARE, *I Henry IV*. Act ii, sc. 4, l. 305.

As merry,
As, first, good company, good wine, good welcome,
Can make good people.
SHAKESPEARE, *Henry VIII*. Act i, sc. 4, l. 5.

Put on
Your boldest suit of mirth, for we have friends
That purpose merriment.
SHAKESPEARE, *The Merchant of Venice*. Act ii, sc. 2, l. 210.

Merrily, merrily, shall I live now
Under the blossom that hangs on the bough.
SHAKESPEARE, *The Tempest*. Act v, sc. 1, l. 93.

8
Gaiety without eclipse,
Wearieth me, May Lilian.
ALFRED TENNYSON, *Lilian*.

9
Longer liveth a glad man than a sorry.
UNKNOWN. (Vernon MS., 347. c. 1300.)

As long liveth the merry man (they say),
As doth the sorry man, and longer by a day.
NICHOLAS UDALL, *Ralph Roister Doister*, i, 1. (c. 1550)

Had she been light, like you,
Of such a merry, nimble, stirring spirit,
She might ha' been a grandam ere she died:
And so may you; for a light heart lives long.
SHAKESPEARE, *Love's Labour's Lost*. Act v, sc. 2, l. 15.

II—Merriment: Merry and Wise

10
Be merry and be wise.
SIR WILLIAM D'AVENANT, *Man's the Master: Prologue*. (1668)

11
It's guid to be merry and wise,
It's guid to be honest and true.
BURNS, *Here's a Health to Them That's Awa*.

'Tis good to be merry and wise.
GEORGE CHAPMAN, *Eastward Hoe*. Act i, sc. 1.

Good to be merry and wise, they think and feel.
JOHN HEYWOOD, *Proverbs*. Pt. i, ch. 2. (1546)

12
Old Times have bequeathed us a precept, to be merry and wise, but who has been able to observe it?
SAMUEL JOHNSON, *Letters*. Vol. ii, p. 114.

13
Be merry if you are wise. (Ride si sapis.)
MARTIAL, *Epigrams*. Bk. ii, epig. 41, l. 1.

III—Merriment: Comparisons

14
As merry as grigs.
THOMAS BROWN, *Works*. Vol. ii, p. 188. (1700)

Ah, friend, we were merry as grigs in time past.
JOHN GAY, *Wife of Bath*, v, 3. (1713)

15
And all went merry as a marriage bell.
BYRON, *Childe Harold*. Canto iii, st. 21.

16
And forth she goeth, as jolif as a pye.
CHAUCER, *Shipmannes Tale*, l. 209. (1386)

I'll be as merry as a pie.
THOMAS DEKKER, *Shoemaker's Holiday*, v, 5. (1600)

17
Merry as a cricket.
JOHN HEYWOOD, *Proverbs*. Pt. i, ch. 11. (1546)

As merry as crickets.
SHAKESPEARE, *I Henry IV*. Act ii, sc. 4, l. 100. (1597)

Send them home as merry as crickets.
RABELAIS, *Works*. Bk. i, ch. 29. (1653)

18
As merry as forty beggars.
JAMES HOWELL, *Proverbs*, 11. (1659)

We should live together as merry and sociable as beggars.
SWIFT, *Drapier Letters*. Letter 4. (1724)

Who so merry as he who has nought to lose?
WALKER, *Paræmiologia*, 39. (1672)

19
As merry as the day is long.
SHAKESPEARE, *Much Ado About Nothing*. Act ii, sc. 1, l. 52. (1598)

1
As merry as mice in malt.
C. H. SPURGEON, *John Ploughman*. Ch. 16.

IV—Merriment: Some Merry Men

2
In Paris a queer little man you may see,
A little man all in gray;
Rosy and round as an apple is he,
Content with the present whate'er it may be,
While from care and from cash he is equally free,
And merry both night and day!
"Ma foi! I laugh at the world," says he,
"I laugh at the world, and the world laughs at me!"
What a gay little man in gray.
BÉRANGER, *The Little Man all in Gray*. (Amelia Edwards, tr.)

3
I'll be merry and free,
I'll be sad for naebody;
Naebody cares for me,
I care for naebody.
ROBERT BURNS, *I Hae a Wife*.

There was a jolly miller once,
Lived on the river Dee;
He work'd, and sung, from morn till night,
No lark more blythe than he.
And this the burthen of his song,
For ever us'd to be,
"I care for nobody, not I,
If no one cares for me."
ISAAC BICKERSTAFFE, *Love in a Village*. Act i, 5.

4
He was a care-defying blade
As ever Bacchus listed!
Tho' Fortune sair upon him laid,
His heart, she ever miss'd it.
He had nae wish but—to be glad,
Nor want but—when he thirsted;
He hated naught but—to be sad.
ROBERT BURNS, *The Jolly Beggars*.

5
A merrier man,
Within the limit of becoming mirth,
I never spent an hour's talk withal:
His eye begets occasion for his wit;
For every object that the one doth catch,
The other turns to a mirth-moving jest,
Which his fair tongue, conceit's expositor,
Delivers in such apt and gracious words
That aged ears play truant at his tales,
And younger hearings are quite ravished;
So sweet and voluble is his discourse.
SHAKESPEARE, *Love's Labour's Lost*. Act ii, sc. 1, l. 65.

6
Don Pedro: In faith, lady, you have a merry heart.
Beatrice: Yea, my lord: I thank it, poor fool, it keeps on the windy side of care.
SHAKESPEARE, *Much Ado About Nothing*. Act ii, sc. 1, l. 323.

Don Pedro: To be merry best becomes you: for, out of question, you were born in a merry hour
Beatrice: No, sure, my lord, my mother cried; but then there was a star danced, and under that was I born.
SHAKESPEARE, *Much Ado About Nothing*. Act ii, sc. 1, l. 346.

MIDNIGHT

7
This dead of midnight is the noon of thought,
And Wisdom mounts her zenith with the stars.
ANNA LETITIA BARBAULD, *A Summer's Evening Meditation*, l. 51.

8
That hour, o' night's black arch the keystane.
BURNS, *Tam o' Shanter*.

9
Is it for work? There comes no fool to bore us.
Midnight intoxicates the human swine;
I, pen in hand, with all the gods for chorus,
Write then my clearest thought, my noblest line.
Midnight is mine.
MORTIMER COLLINS, *Midnight Is Mine*.

But wouldst thou hear the melodies of Time,
Listen when sleep and drowsy darkness roll
Over hush'd cities, and the midnight chime
Sounds from their hundred clocks, and deep bells toll,
Like a last knell over the dead world's soul.
THOMAS HOOD, *The Plea of the Midsummer Fairies*, l. 298.

10
It was evening there,
But here the very noon of night.
(Vespero là, e qui mezza notte era.)
DANTE, *Purgatorio*. Canto xv, l. 6.

11
Comus and his midnight crew.
THOMAS GRAY, *Ode for Music*, l. 2.

12
There is a budding morrow in midnight.
KEATS, *To Homer*.

13
I stood on the bridge at midnight,
As the clocks were striking the hour,
And the moon rose o'er the city,
Behind the dark church-tower.
LONGFELLOW, *The Bridge*.

From the cool cisterns of the midnight air
My spirit drank repose;
The fountain of perpetual peace flows there,—
From those deep cisterns flows.
LONGFELLOW, *Hymn to the Night*.

Midnight! the outpost of advancing day!
The frontier town and citadel of night!
LONGFELLOW, *The Two Rivers*. Pt. i.

14
O wild and wondrous midnight,
There is a might in thee
To make the charmèd body
Almost like spirit be,

And give it some faint glimpses
  Of immortality!
J. R. LOWELL, *Midnight*.

1
Midnight brought on the dusky hour
Friendliest to sleep and silence.
MILTON, *Paradise Lost*. Bk. v, l. 667.

2
Once upon a midnight dreary, while I pondered, weak and weary.
EDGAR ALLAN POE, *The Raven*.

3
Let's mock the midnight bell.
SHAKESPEARE, *Antony and Cleopatra*. Act iii, sc. 13, l. 185.

4
In the dead vast and middle of the night.
SHAKESPEARE, *Hamlet*. Act i, sc. 2, l. 198.

The dreadful dead of dark midnight.
SHAKESPEARE, *The Rape of Lucrece*. St. 232.

5
'Tis now the very witching time of night,
When churchyards yawn and hell itself breathes out
Contagion to this world.
SHAKESPEARE, *Hamlet*. Act iii, sc. 2, l. 406.

When it draws near to witching time of night.
BLAIR, *The Grave*, l. 55.

'Tis the witching hour of night.
KEATS, *A Prophecy*, l. 1.

6
We have heard the chimes at midnight, Master Shallow.
SHAKESPEARE, *II Henry IV*. Act iii, sc. 2, l. 228.

7
The iron tongue of midnight hath told twelve;
Lovers, to bed; 'tis almost fairy time.
SHAKESPEARE, *A Midsummer-Night's Dream*. Act v, sc. 1, l. 370.

8
Pale Midnight on her starry throne.
SHELLEY, *Queen Mab*. Canto iv, l. 40.

9
  Midnight, and yet no eye
Through all the Imperial City closed in sleep!
ROBERT SOUTHEY, *Curse of Kehama*. Pt. i, l. 1.

Midnight, yet not a nose
From Tower Hill to Piccadilly snored!
HORACE AND JAMES SMITH, *Rejected Addresses: The Rebuilding*.

10
And thy dark pencil, midnight! darker still
In melancholy dipt, embrowns the whole.
YOUNG, *Night Thoughts*. Night v, l. 78.

MIGHT

See also Force, Power, Strength

11
  May Might and Right,
And sovran Zeus, as third, my helpers be!
(*Κράτος τε καὶ Δίκη σὺν τῷ τρίτῳ*
πάντων μεγίστῳ Ζηνὶ συγγένοιτό σοι.)
ÆSCHYLUS, *Cœphoræ*, l. 244. (Plumptre, tr.)

12
And much, and oft, he warn'd him to eschew
Falsehood and guile, and aye maintain the right,
By pleasure unseduc'd, unaw'd by lawless might.
JAMES BEATTIE, *The Minstrel*. Bk. i, st. 28.

Either by might or sleight.
JOHN CLARKE, *Parœmiologia*, 127. (1639)

13
  Might
That makes a Title, where there is no Right.
SAMUEL DANIEL, *Civil War*. Bk. ii, st. 36.

14
For who can be secure of private right,
If sovereign sway may be dissolv'd by might?
DRYDEN, *Absalom and Achitophel*. Pt. i, l. 779.

15
Useless is the dolphin's might upon the ground. (*Κακὴ γάρ ἡ δελφῖνος ἐν χέρσῳ βία.*)
ION. (PLUTARCH, *Lives: Demosthenes*. Sec. 3.)

16
Might and right govern everything in this world; might till right is ready. (C'est la force et le droit qui règlent toutes choses dans le monde; la force, en attendant le droit.)
JOUBERT, *Pensées*. Ch. 15, No. 2.

17
The reason of the strongest is always the best. (La raison du plus fort est toujours la meilleure.)
LA FONTAINE, *Fables*. Bk. i, fab. 10.

We have unmistakable proof that throughout all past time, there has been a ceaseless devouring of the weak by the strong.
HERBERT SPENCER, *First Principles*.

18
Let us have faith that right makes might, and in that faith let us to the end dare to do our duty as we understand it.
ABRAHAM LINCOLN, *Address*, Cooper Institute, N. Y., 27 Feb., 1860.

It has been said of the world's history hitherto that might makes right. It is for us and for our time to reverse the maxim, and to say that right makes might.
ABRAHAM LINCOLN.

19
Might was the measure of right. (Mensuraque juris Vis erat.)
LUCAN, *De Bello Civili*. Bk. i, l. 175.

20
Old Tubal Cain was a man of might
In the days when earth was young.
CHARLES MACKAY, *Tubal Cain*.

21
I proclaim that might is right, justice the interest of the stronger. (*Θημὶ γὰρ ἐγὼ εἶναι τὸ δίκαιον οὐκ ἄλλο τι ἤ τὸ τοῦ κρεὶττονος ξυμφέρον.*)
PLATO, *The Republic*. Bk. i, sec. 338. (Jowett, tr.)

Might is right. (Plus potest, qui plus valet.)
PLAUTUS, *Truculentus*. Act iv, sc. 3, l. 30.

Might makes right. (Jus est in armis.)
SENECA, *Hercules Furens*, l. 253.

For might is right.
UNKNOWN, *John to Edward II.* (WRIGHT, *Political Songs,* p. 254.) c. 1311.

Might overcometh right.
JOHN HEYWOOD, *English Proverbs.* Pt. ii, ch. 5.

Right is overcome by might. (Vi verum vincitur.)
PLAUTUS, *Amphitruo,* l. 591. (Act ii, sc. 1.)

1
O God, that right should thus overcome might!
SHAKESPEARE, *II Henry IV.* Act v, sc. 4, l. 27.

2
Where might is, the right is:
Long purses make strong swords.
Let weakness learn meekness:
God save the House of Lords.
SWINBURNE, *A Word for the Country.* St. 1.

3
But let the free-winged angel Truth their guarded passes scale,
To teach that right is more than might, and justice more than mail!
J. G. WHITTIER, *Brown of Ossawatomie.*

So let it be. In God's own might
We gird us for the coming fight,
And, strong in Him whose cause is ours
In conflict with unholy powers,
We grasp the weapons He has given,—
The Light, and Truth, and Love of Heaven.
WHITTIER, *The Moral Warfare.*

MILK

See also Cow

4
Such as have need of milk, and not of strong meat.
New Testament: Hebrews, v, 12.

Every one that useth milk is unskilful in the word of righteousness: for he is a babe.
New Testament: Hebrews, v, 13.

5
If you would live forever,
You must wash milk from your liver.
JOHN RAY, *English Proverbs. See also under* DRINKING.

6
Come to my woman's breasts,
And take my milk for gall.
SHAKESPEARE, *Macbeth.* Act i, sc. 5, l. 48.

7
Sir, there is no crying for shed milk, that which is past cannot be recall'd.
ANDREW YARRANTON, *England's Improvement.* Pt. ii, p. 107. (1681)

However, it's no use crying over spilt milk.
W. S. GILBERT, *Foggarty's Fairy.* Act i.

It's no good crying over spilt milk, because all the forces of the universe were bent on spilling it.
W. S. MAUGHAM, *Of Human Bondage,* p. 343.

Gospel of spilt milk.
THEODORE ROOSEVELT, *The Great Adventure.* Chapter heading.

MILL and MILLER

8
Two millers thin, called Bone and Skin,
Would starve us all, or near it;
But be it known to Skin and Bone
That Flesh and Blood can't bear it.
JOHN BYROM, *On Two Millers, Bone and Skin, Who Wished a Monopoly of Corn.*

9
Well could be stealen corn and tollen thrice,
And yet he had a thumb of gold, pardee.
CHAUCER, *Canterbury Tales: Prologue,* l. 563.

Every honest miller has a golden thumb.
CHAUCER, *Canterbury Tales.* An old saying, referring to a merchant keeping his thumb on the scales when weighing anything.

Honest millers have golden thumbs.
THOMAS FULLER, *Gnomologia.* No. 2531. Ray states that the miller's reply was, "None but a cuckold can see it"; or, "True, but it takes a thief to see it."

The miller—the prosperous fellow with the golden thumb.
DOUGLAS JERROLD, *Chronicles of Clovernook,* p. 94.

10
The water that is past cannot make the mill go.
THOMAS DRAXE, *Bib. Scho. Instruct.,* p. 151. (1633)

The mill cannot grind with water that's past.
GEORGE HERBERT, *Jacula Prudentum.* (1640)

Oh seize the instant time; you never will
With waters once passed by impel the mill.
RICHARD CHENEVIX TRENCH, *Proverbs.* (*Poems,* p. 303.)

Listen to the Water-Mill:
Through the live-long day
How the clicking of its wheel
Wears the hours away!
Languidly the Autumn wind
Stirs the forest leaves,
From the field the reapers sing
Binding up their sheaves:
And a proverb haunts my mind
As a spell is cast,
"The mill cannot grind
With the water that is past."
SARAH DOUDNEY, *The Lesson of the Water-Mill.* Fraudulently claimed by General D. C. McCallum. (See STEVENSON, *Famous Single Poems.*)

11
The mill goes toiling slowly around
With steady and solemn creak,
And my little one hears in the kindly sound
The voice of the old mill speak.
EUGENE FIELD, *Nightfall in Dordrecht.*

12
As good water goes by the mill as drives it.
THOMAS FULLER, *Gnomologia.* No. 691.

13
There is no likelihood that those things will bring grist to the mill.
GOLDING, *Calvin on Deuteronomy,* 755. (1583)

'Tis a pick-purse doctrine, contrived to bring grist to the Pope's mill.
WILLIAM GURNALL, *Christian in Complete Armour.* Pt. iii, ch. 5. (1661)

Some people make fat, some blood, and some bile; and whatever they take is a sort of grist to the mill.
George Eliot, *Middlemarch*. Ch. 10.

1
The same water that drives the mill, decayeth it.
Stephen Gosson, *The Schoole of Abuse*.

2 Much water goeth by the mill
That the miller knoweth not of.
John Heywood, *Proverbs*. Pt. ii, ch. 5. (1546)

More water glideth by the mill
Than wots the miller of.
Shakespeare, *Titus Andronicus*. Act ii, sc. 1, l 86. (1593)

The miller sees not all the water that goeth by his mill.
Robert Burton, *Anatomy of Melancholy*. Pt. iii, sec. iii, mem. 4, subs. 1. (1621)

3
The miller grinds more men's corn than one.
Thomas Nashe, *Works*. Vol. iii, p. 25.

Mills of The Gods, *see under* Retribution.

4
Here lies an Israelite indeed;
Match him if you can:
A neighbour good, a miller too,
And yet an honest man.
Unknown, *Epitaph*, Longbridge Deverill, Wiltshire, England.

MILTON, JOHN

5
Milton's golden lyre.
Mark Akenside, *Ode on a Sermon Against Glory*. St. 2.

6
On his anointed eyes, God set his seal
And gave him—blindness and the inward light,
That he, repining not at lack of sight,
Might see as never man saw.
Richard Rogers Bowker, *Milton*.

7
Milton's the prince of poets—so we say;
A little heavy, but no less divine;
An independent being in his day—
Learn'd, pious, temperate in love and wine.
Byron, *Don Juan*. Canto iii, st. 91.

8
The words of Milton are true in all things, and were never truer than in this: "He who would write heroic poems must make his whole life a heroic poem."
Carlyle, *Essays: Burns*.

9
Ages elaps'd ere Homer's lamp appear'd,
And ages ere the Mantuan swan was heard:
To carry nature lengths unknown before,
To give a Milton birth, ask'd ages more.
Thus genius rose and set at order'd times,
And shot a day-spring into distant climes,
Ennobling ev'ry region that he chose;
He sunk in Greece, in Italy he rose;
And, tedious years of Gothic darkness pass'd,
Emerg'd all splendour in our isle at last.
Cowper, *Table Talk*, l. 556.

Greece boasts her Homer, Rome can Virgil claim;
England can either match in Milton's fame.
(Græcia Mæonidam, jactet sibi Roma Maronem
Anglia Miltonum jactat utrique parem.)
Salvaggi, *Ad Joannem Miltonum*.

10
Three Poets, in three distant Ages born,
Greece, Italy, and England did adorn.
The first in loftiness of thought surpass'd,
The next in majesty, in both the last:
The force of nature could no farther go;
To make the third she join'd the former two.
Dryden, *Lines under the Portrait of Milton*.
Referring to Homer, Vergil, and Milton.

11
Nor second He, that rode sublime
Upon the seraph-wings of Ecstasy,
The secrets of th' Abyss to spy.
He pass'd the flaming bounds of Place and Time:
The living Throne, the sapphire blaze,
Where Angels tremble, while they gaze,
He saw; but blasted with excess of light,
Closed his eyes in endless night.
Thomas Gray, *Progress of Poesy*. Pt. iii, st. 2.

12
He was a Phidias that could cut a Colossus out of a rock, but could not cut heads out of cherry stones.
Samuel Johnson, referring to Milton. (Hannah More, *Johnsoniana*.)

13 I am old and blind!
Men point at me as smitten by God's frown.
Elizabeth Lloyd, *Milton on His Blindness*.
Sometimes attributed to Milton himself. Miss Lloyd was a member of the Society of Friends of Philadelphia, Pa.

14
Milton's strong pinion now not Heav'n can bound,
Now, serpent-like, in prose he sweeps the ground,
In quibbles, Angel and Archangel join,
And God the Father turns a School-divine.
Pope, *Imitations of Horace: Epistles*. Bk. ii, epis. 1, l. 99.

15
O mighty-mouth'd inventor of harmonies,
O skill'd to sing of Time or Eternity,
God-gifted organ-voice of England,
Milton, a name to resound for ages.
Tennyson, *Milton*.

16
Lover of Liberty at heart wast thou,
Above all beauty bright, all music clear:
To thee she bared her bosom and her brow,
Breathing her virgin promise in thine ear,
And bound thee to her with a double vow,—
Exquisite Puritan, grave Cavalier!
Henry van Dyke, *Milton*.

1
The ancients advised us to sacrifice to the Graces, but Milton sacrificed to the Devil.
VOLTAIRE, *Epigram.*

2
We who are Milton's kindred, Shakespeare's heirs.
WILLIAM WATSON, *An Exaggerated Deference to Foreign Literary Opinion.*

3
The New World honors him whose lofty plea
For England's freedom made her own more sure,
Whose song, immortal as its theme, shall be
Their common freehold while both worlds endure.
WHITTIER, *On the Milton Window, in St. Margaret's, Westminster.*

4
That mighty orb of song, The divine Milton.
WORDSWORTH, *The Excursion.* Bk. i, l. 249.

The sightless Milton, with his hair
Around his placid temples curled.
WORDSWORTH, *The Italian Itinerant.* Pt. i, l. 12.

Thy soul was like a Star, and dwelt apart;
Thou hadst a voice whose sound was like the sea:
Pure as the naked heavens, majestic, free,
So didst thou travel on life's common way,
In cheerful godliness; and yet thy heart
The lowliest duties on herself did lay.
WORDSWORTH, *Sonnet: London, 1802.*

MIND

See also Absence: Absence of Mind; Content: Mind Content; Thought

I—Mind: Definitions

5
A man's felicity consists not in the outward and visible blessings of fortune, but in the inward and unseen perfections and riches of the mind.
ANARCHARSIS. (PLUTARCH, *The Banquet of the Seven Wise Men.* Sec. 11.)

6
The mind of man is far from the nature of a clear and equal glass, . . . nay, it is rather like an enchanted glass, full of superstition and imposture.
BACON, *Advancement of Learning: Of the Understanding.*

7
I had rather believe all the fables in the Legend and the Talmud and the Alcoran, than that this universal frame is without a mind.
BACON, *Essays: Of Atheism.*

The mind is the man, and the knowledge of the mind.
BACON, *Miscellaneous Tracts Upon Human Philosophy: In Praise of Knowledge.* Sec. 1.

8
The forehead is the gate of the mind. (Frons est animi janua.)
CICERO, *De Provinciis Consularibus.* Sec. 11.

9
Nature's first great title—mind.
GEORGE CROLY, *Pericles and Aspasia.*

10
The growth of the intellect is spontaneous in every expansion.
EMERSON, *Essays, First Series: Intellect.*

11
Thou living ray of intellectual fire.
WILLIAM FALCONER, *The Shipwreck.* Canto i, l. 104.

12
The mind is like a sheet of white paper in this, that the impressions it receives the oftenest, and retains the longest, are black ones.
J. C. AND A. W. HARE, *Guesses at Truth.*

13
The mind of man is like a clock that is always running down, and requires to be as constantly wound up.
WILLIAM HAZLITT, *Sketches: On Cant and Hypocrisy.*

14
The most perfect mind is a dry light. (Lumen siccum optima anima.)
HERACLITUS. Quoted by Bacon, who explains it to mean, a mind "not steeped and infused in the humours of the affections."

15
The mind is the atmosphere of the soul. (L'esprit est atmosphère de l'âme.)
JOUBERT, *Pensées.* No. 40.

16
Our mind is God.
MENANDER. (PLUTARCH, *Platonic Questions.* Sec. 1.)

God is Mind, and God is infinite; hence all is Mind.
MARY BAKER EDDY, *Science and Health,* p. 492, l. 25. *See also under* DISEASE.

17
The brain is the citadel of the senses. (Habet cerebrum sensus arcem.)
PLINY THE ELDER, *Historia Naturalis.* Bk. xi, sec. 49.

Our brains are seventy-year clocks. The Angel of Life winds them up once for all, then closes the case, and gives the key into the hand of the Angel of the Resurrection.
O. W. HOLMES, *The Autocrat of the Breakfast-Table.* Ch. 8.

18
Our minds, like our stomachs, are whetted by change of food, and variety supplies both with fresh appetite. (Mens mutatione recreabitur, sicut in cibis, quorum diversitate reficitur stomachus, et pluribus minore fastidio alitur.)
QUINTILIAN, *De Institutione Oratoria.* Bk. i, ch. 11, sec. 1.

19
That little world, the human mind.
SAMUEL ROGERS, *Ode to Superstition.*

1
A man is not a wall, whose stones are crushed upon the road; or a pipe, whose fragments are thrown away at a street corner. The fragments of an intellect are always good.

GEORGE SAND, *Handsome Lawrence*. Ch. 2.

2
Keep unshak'd That temple, thy fair mind.

SHAKESPEARE, *Cymbeline*. Act ii, sc. 1, l. 67.

Thy mind is a very opal.

SHAKESPEARE, *Twelfth Night*. Act ii, sc. 4, l. 72.

3
Man's mind a mirror is of heavenly sights,
A brief wherein all marvels summèd lie,
Of fairest forms and sweetest shapes the store,
Most graceful all, yet thought may grace them more.

ROBERT SOUTHWELL, *Content and Rich*.

4
The human mind always makes progress, but it is a progress in spirals. (L'esprit humain fait progrès toujours, mais c'est progrès en spirale.)

MADAME DE STAËL.

"Spiral" the memorable Lady terms
Our mind's ascent.

GEORGE MEREDITH, *The World's Advance*. Trevelyan, in his notes to Meredith's *Poetical Works,* says that the "memorable lady" was Mrs. Browning (*see* quotation from *Aurora Leigh* under ART: DEFINITIONS), but the resemblance is much closer to the preceding quotation from Madame de Staël.

5
Were I so tall to reach the Pole,
Or grasp the ocean in my span,
I must be measured by my soul;
The mind's the standard of the man.

ISAAC WATTS, *False Greatness*.

6
Mind is the great lever of all things.

DANIEL WEBSTER, *Address,* on laying the corner-stone of the Bunker Hill Monument.

II—Mind: Apothegms

7
You will turn it over once more in what you are pleased to call your mind.

RICHARD BETHELL, LORD WESTBURY, to a solicitor who, after hearing one of Westbury's opinions, remarked that he had turned it over in his mind, and thought that something might be said on the other side. (NASH, *Life of Westbury*. Vol. ii, p. 292.)

8
So sat I talking with my mind.

ROBERT BROWNING, *Christmas-Eve*. Sec. 18.

9
The march of the human mind is slow.

EDMUND BURKE, *Conciliation with America*.

The march of intellect.

SOUTHEY, *Progress and Prospects of Society*.

10
The eye of the intellect "sees in all objects what it brought with it the means of seeing."

CARLYLE, *Essays: Varnhagen Von Ense's Memoirs*.

The mind does not create what it perceives, any more than the eye creates the rose.

EMERSON, *Representative Men: Plato: New Readings*.

11
The mind is free, whate'er afflict the man.

DRAYTON, *The Barons' War*. Bk. v, st. 36.

Intellect annuls Fate. So far as a man thinks he is free.

EMERSON, *Conduct of Life: Fate*.

12
Nothing is at last sacred but the integrity of your own mind.

EMERSON, *Essays, First Series: Self-Reliance*.

Nature is good, but intellect is better.

EMERSON, *Representative Men: Plato*.

Nothing is old but the mind.

EMERSON, *Letters and Social Aims: Progress of Culture*.

13
Other men are lenses through which we read our own minds.

EMERSON, *Representative Men: Uses of Great Men*.

14
Vain, very vain, my weary search to find
That bliss which only centres in the mind.

GOLDSMITH, *The Traveller*, l. 423.

15
He who endeavors to control the mind by force is a tyrant, and he who submits is a slave.

R. G. INGERSOLL, *Some Mistakes of Moses*.

16
I abhor brains
As I do tools: they're things mechanical.

J. S. KNOWLES, *The Hunchback*. Act iii, sc. 1.

17
Man's mind is larger than his crown of tears.

WILLIAM ELLERY LEONARD, *To the Victor*.

18
Clothed, and in his right mind.

New Testament: Mark, v, 15; *Luke,* viii, 35.

For God hath not given us the spirit of fear; but of power, and of love, and of a sound mind.

New Testament: II Timothy, i, 7.

19
Be ye all of one mind.

New Testament: I Peter, iii, 8.

Let every man be fully persuaded in his own mind

New Testament: Romans, xiv, 5.

20
Each man has his own peculiar cast of mind. (Sua cuique quum sit animi cogitatio.)

PHÆDRUS, *Fables:* Bk. v, *Prologue,* l. 7.

Each mind has its own method.

EMERSON, *Essays, First Series: Intellect*.

21
Alas! in truth, the man but chang'd his mind.

POPE, *Moral Essays*. Ep. i, pt. 2. *See also under* CONSTANCY.

1
The mind celebrates a little triumph whenever it can formulate a truth.
GEORGE SANTAYANA, *The Life of Reason*, p. 65.

2
A noble mind is free to all men; according to this test we may all gain distinction. (Bona mens omnibus patet, omnes ad hoc sumus nobiles.)
SENECA, *Epistulæ ad Lucilium*. Epis. xliv, 2.

The mind ennobles, not the blood. (Edel macht das Gemüth, nicht das Geblüt.)
UNKNOWN. A German proverb.

3
I do not distinguish men by the eye, but by the mind, which is the proper judge.
SENECA, *Epistulæ ad Lucilium*. Epis xcii.

4
Hamlet: Methinks I see my father.
Horatio: Where, my lord?
Hamlet: In my mind's eye, Horatio.
SHAKESPEARE, *Hamlet*. Act i, sc. 2, l. 184.

Within the book and volume of my brain.
SHAKESPEARE, *Hamlet*. Act i, sc. 5, l. 103.

5
Cudgel thy brains no more about it.
SHAKESPEARE, *Hamlet*. Act v, sc. 1, l. 63.

Who rack their brains.
BYRON, *English Bards, Scotch Reviewers*, l. 178.

The daily, nightly racking of the brains.
CHARLES CHURCHILL, *Gotham*. Bk. ii, l. 12.

6
It is impossible to find out what passes in the interior of any man's mind.
SYDNEY SMITH, *Peter Plymley Letters*. No. 2.

7
Bad mind, bad heart. (Mala mens, malus animus.)
TERENCE, *Andria*. Act i, l. 164. *See also under* HEART AND HEAD.

8
I have found that no exertion of the legs can bring two minds much nearer to one another.
H. D. THOREAU.

9
The guilty joys of the mind. (Et mala mentis gaudia.)
VERGIL, *Æneid*. Bk. vi, l. 278.

An improper mind is a perpetual feast.
LOGAN PEARSALL SMITH, *Afterthoughts*.

10
I have a single-track mind.
WOODROW WILSON, *Speech*, National Press Club, Washington.

He has a bungalow mind.
WOODROW WILSON, referring to President Harding. (THOMPSON, *Presidents I've Known*, p. 334.)

11
A man of hope and forward-looking mind.
WORDSWORTH, *The Excursion*. Bk. vii, l. 276.

In years that bring the philosophic mind.
WORDSWORTH, *Intimations of Immortality*.

12
Intellect obscures more than it illumines.
ISRAEL ZANGWILL, *Children of the Ghetto*. Bk. ii, ch. 15.

III—Mind: Little and Great

13
The mind soars to the lofty: it is at home in the grovelling, the disagreeable, and the little.
WILLIAM HAZLITT, *Winterslow*. Essay No. 4.

14
One-story intellects, two-story intellects, three-story intellects with skylights. All fact-collectors . . . are one-story men. Two-story men compare, reason, generalize. . . . Three-story men idealize, imagine, predict; their best illumination comes from above, through the skylight.
O. W. HOLMES, *The Poet at the Breakfast-Table*. Ch. 2.

Little minds are interested in the extraordinary; great minds in the commonplace.
ELBERT HUBBARD, *Epigrams*.

Great minds discuss ideas, average minds discuss events, small minds discuss people.
UNKNOWN, *Minds*.

15
Little minds are wounded too much by little things; great minds see all, and are not even hurt. (Les petits esprits sont trop blessés des petites choses; les grands esprits les voient toutes, et n'en sont point blessés.)
LA ROCHEFOUCAULD, *Maximes*. No. 357.

16
Nobody, I believe, will deny, that we are to form our judgement of the true nature of the human mind, not from sloth and stupidity of the most degenerate and vilest of men, but from the sentiments and fervent desires of the best and wisest.
ARCHBISHOP LEIGHTON, *Theological Lectures:* No. 5, *Of the Immortality of the Soul*.

17
It is good to be often reminded of the inconsistency of human nature, and to learn to look without wonder or disgust on the weaknesses which are found in the strongest minds.
MACAULAY, *Essays: Warren Hastings*.

It is not given to the human intellect to expand itself widely in all directions at once, and to be at the same time gigantic and well-proportioned.
MACAULAY, *Essays: Madame d'Arblay*.

18
The conformation of his mind was such, that whatever was little seemed to him great, and whatever was great seemed to him little.
MACAULAY, *Essays: Horace Walpole*.

IV—Mind: The Great Mind

20
Measure your mind's height by the shade it casts.
ROBERT BROWNING, *Paracelsus*. Pt. iii.

1
No beauty's like the beauty of the mind.
JOSHUA COOKE, *How a Man May Choose a Good Wife*. Act v, sc. 3.

2
It is the mind's for ever bright attire,
The mind's embroidery, that the wise admire.
That which looks rich to the gross vulgar eyes
Is the fop's tinsel which the grave despise.
JOHN DYER, *To Mr. Savage*.

3
A great mind is a good sailor, as a great heart is.
EMERSON, *English Traits*. Ch. 2.

Works of the intellect are great only by comparison with each other.
EMERSON, *Nature, Addresses, and Lectures: Literary Ethics*.

4
A noble mind disdains to hide his head,
And let his foes triumph in his overthrow.
ROBERT GREENE, *Alphonso, King of Arragon* Act i.

5
Whose well-taught mind the present age surpast.
HOMER, *Odyssey*. Bk. vii, l. 210. (Pope, tr.)

6
A mind thou hast, experienced in affairs, well-poised in weal or woe. (Est animus tibi Rerumque prudens et secundis Temporibus dubiisque rectus.)
HORACE, *Odes*. Bk. iv, ode 9, l. 34.

7
Such is the delight of mental superiority, that none on whom nature or study have conferred it, would purchase the gifts of fortune by its loss.
SAMUEL JOHNSON, *The Rambler*. No. 150.

8
The true, strong, and sound mind is the mind that can embrace equally great things and small.
SAMUEL JOHNSON. (BOSWELL, *Life*, 1778.)

A great mind conceives the greatest things; it sees and understands the smallest ones. (Un grand esprit . . . imagine les plus grandes choses; il voit et connaît les plus petites.)
LA ROCHEFOUCAULD, *Réflexions Diverses:* Ch. xvi, *De la Différence des Esprits*.

Greatness of mind is not shown by admitting small things, but by making small things great under its influence. He who can take no interest in what is small, will take false interest in what is great.
RUSKIN, *Modern Painters*. Pt. ii, sec. 4, ch. 4.

9
By a tranquil mind I mean nothing else than a mind well ordered.
MARCUS AURELIUS, *Meditations*. Bk. iv, sec. 3. *See also* CONTENT: THE MIND CONTENT.

10
That understanding is the noblest which knows not the most but the best things. (Ille intellectus qui plura intelligit non est noblior, sed qui digniora.)
DR. HENRY MORE. (WARD, *Life*. Ch. 12.) *See also under* KNOWLEDGE.

11
An undisturbed mind is the best sauce for affliction. (Animus æquos optimum est ærumnæ condimentum.)
PLAUTUS, *Rudens*, l. 402. (Act ii, sc. 3.)

A mind conscious of its own rectitude. (Mens sibi conscia recti.)
VERGIL, *Æneid*. Bk. i, l. 604.

The sweet converse of an innocent mind.
KEATS, *Sonnet: To Solitude*.

12
A mind undaunted by death. (Mens interrita leti.)
OVID, *Metamorphoses*. Bk. x, l. 616.

13
Minds,
By nature great, are conscious of their greatness.
NICHOLAS ROWE, *The Royal Convert*.

14
A great mind becomes a great fortune. (Magnam fortunam magnus animus decet.)
SENECA, *De Clementia*. Bk. i, sec. 5.

15
A golden mind stoops not to shows of dross.
SHAKESPEARE, *The Merchant of Venice*. Act ii, sc. 7, l. 20.

16
The mind that would be happy, must be great.
YOUNG, *Night Thoughts*, Night ix, l. 1378.

V—Mind: The Little Mind

17
Nature did never put her precious jewels into a garret four stories high, and therefore exceeding tall men have ever very empty heads.
FRANCIS BACON, *Apothegms*. No. 17.

Often the cockloft is empty in those whom nature hath built many stories high.
THOMAS FULLER, *Andronicus*. Pt. xviii, sec. 6.

Tall men are like houses of four stories, wherein commonly the uppermost room is worst furnished.
JAMES HOWELL, *Letters*. Bk. i, sec. 2, letter 1.

Whose cockloft is unfurnished.
RABELAIS, *Works:* Bk. v, *Prologue*.

18
The natural fog of the good man's mind.
ROBERT BROWNING, *Christmas-Eve*. Sec. 4.

19
His brains were only candle-grease, and wasted down like tallow.
ROBERT BUCHANAN, *City of the Saints*. Pt. i.

20
Such as take lodgings in a head
That's to be let, unfurnished.
BUTLER, *Hudibras*. Pt. i, canto i, l. 161.

21
The petrifactions of a plodding brain.
BYRON, *English Bards and Scotch Reviewers*, l. 416.

1
Could it be worth thy wondrous waste of pains
To publish to the world thy lack of brains?
CHARLES CHURCHILL, *The Rosciad*, l. 599.

3
Feels himself spent, and fumbles for his brains.
COWPER, *Table Talk*, l. 537.

4
here is little Effie's head
whose brains are made of gingerbread
when the judgment day comes
God will find six crumbs.
E. E. CUMMINGS, *Portrait*.

Your little voice, so soft and kind;
Your little soul, your little mind!
SAMUEL HOFFENSTEIN, *Love Song*.

5
To be bored by essentials is characteristic of small minds.
R. U. JOHNSON, *Poems of Fifty Years: Preface*.

6
Most brains reflect but the crown of a hat.
J. R. LOWELL, *A Fable for Critics*, l. 704.

The defect in his brain was just absence of mind.
J. R. LOWELL, *A Fable for Critics*, l. 228. *See also* ABSENCE: ABSENCE OF MIND.

7
How wretched are the minds of men, and how blind their understandings. (O miseras hominum mentes! oh, pectora cæca!)
LUCRETIUS, *De Rerum Natura*. Bk. ii, l. 14.

What darkness rules the minds of men! (Quantum mortalia pectora cæcæ Noctis habent!)
OVID, *Metamorphoses*. Bk. vi, l. 472.

8
Anxious minds quake with both hope and fear. (Sollicitæ mentes speque metuque pavent.)
OVID, *Fasti*. Bk. iii, l. 361.

10
O heavy burden of a doubtful mind!
FRANCIS QUARLES, *A Feast of Worms*. Sec. 1.

11
'Tis but a base, ignoble mind
That mounts no higher than a bird can soar.
SHAKESPEARE, *II Henry VI*. Act ii, sc. 1, l. 13.

12
In nature there's no blemish but the mind.
SHAKESPEARE, *Twelfth Night*. Act iii, sc. 4, l. 401.

13
Mental power cannot be got from ill-fed brains.
HERBERT SPENCER, *Principles of Ethics*. Sec. 238.

14
Let Gryll be Gryll, and have his hoggish mind.
EDMUND SPENSER, *The Faerie Queene*. Bk. ii, canto xii, st. 87. Gryll, or Grillus, was one of the companions of Ulysses, and was changed into a hog by the enchantments of Circe.

15
Now hither, now thither, he turns his wavering mind. (Animum nunc huc celerem, nunc dividit illuc.)
VERGIL, *Æneid*. Bk. iv, l. 285.

16
O mind of man, ignorant of fate and impending doom, unable to keep within due bounds when uplifted by favoring fortune! (Nescis mens hominum fati sortisque futuræ Et servare modum, rebus sublata secundis!)
VERGIL, *Æneid*. Bk. x, l. 501.

16a
The lightning-bug is brilliant, but he hasn't any mind;
He stumbles through existence with his headlight on behind.
EUGENE F. WARE, *The Lightning-Bug*. (Quoted by BERT LESTON TAYLOR, *The So-Called Human Race*, p. 301.)

17
Minds that have nothing to confer
Find little to perceive.
WORDSWORTH, *Yes! Thou Art Fair*.

VI—Mind: A Kingdom

18
Dame Nature doubtless has designed
A man the monarch of his mind.
JOHN BYROM, *Careless Content*. *See also* HENLEY, *under* SOUL.

19
His mind his kingdom, and his will his law.
COWPER, *Truth*, l. 405.

20
My mind to me a kingdom is;
Such present joys therein I find,
That it excels all other bliss
That earth affords or grows by kind:
Though much I want which most would have,
Yet still my mind forbids to crave.
EDWARD DYER, *My Mind to Me a Kingdom Is*.

My mind to me a kingdom is;
Such perfect joy therein I find
As far exceeds all earthly bliss,
That God or Nature hath assigned:
Though much I want, that most would have,
Yet still my mind forbids to crave
EDWARD DYER, *My Mind to Me a Kingdom Is*. As altered by William Byrd, in *Psalmes, Sonets, and Songs of Sadnes*. London, 1588. (PERCY, *Reliques*. Ser. i, bk. 3.)

I am no such pil'd cynic to believe
That beggary is the only happiness,
Or, with a number of these patient fools,
To sing, "My mind to me a kingdom is,"
When the lank hungry belly barks for food.
BEN JONSON, *Every Man Out of His Humour*. Act i, sc. 1.

My mind's my kingdom.
FRANCIS QUARLES, *School of the Heart*. Ode iv, st. 3.

21
A good mind possesses a kingdom. (Mens regnum bona possidet.)
SENECA, *Thyestes*, l. 380.

22
I feel no care of coin;
Well-doing is my wealth;
My mind to me an empire is,

While grace affordeth health.
ROBERT SOUTHWELL, *Content and Rich.*

VII—Mind: Its Power

1
The human understanding is naturally right, and has within itself a strength sufficient to arrive at the knowledge of truth, and to distinguish it from error.
BURLAMAQUI, *Principles of Natural Law.*

2
The brute-tamer stands by the brutes, a head's breadth only above them.
A head's breadth? Ay, but therein is hell's depth, and the height up to heaven,
And the thrones of the gods and their halls, their chariots, purples, and splendors.
PADRAIC COLUM, *The Plougher.*

3
How fleet is a glance of the mind!
Compar'd with the speed of its flight,
The tempest itself lags behind,
And the swift-wing'd arrows of light.
COWPER, *Verses Supposed to be Written by Alexander Selkirk.*

4
Thy mind reverting still to things of earth,
Strikes darkness from true light.
DANTE, *Purgatorio.* Canto xv, l. 62. (Cary, tr.)

5
'Tis true, 'tis certain; man, tho' dead, retains
Part of himself; th' immortal mind remains.
HOMER, *Iliad.* Bk. xxiii, l. 122. (Pope, tr.) *See also under* IMMORTALITY.

6
The mind can weave itself warmly in the cocoon of its own thoughts, and dwell a hermit anywhere.
J. R. LOWELL, *My Study Windows: On a Certain Condescension in Foreigners.*

7
The lively force of his mind has broken down all barriers, and has made its way far beyond the glittering walls of the Universe. (Vivida vis animi pervicit, et extra Processit longe flammantia mœnia Mundi.)
LUCRETIUS, *De Rerum Natura.* Bk. i, l. 73.

His vigorous and active mind was hurl'd
Beyond the flaming limits of this world
Into the mighty space, and there did see
How things began, what can, what cannot be.
LUCRETIUS, *De Rerum Natura.* Bk. i, l. 75. (Creech, tr.) The reference is to Epicurus.

Three sleepless nights I passed in sounding on,
Through words and things, a dim and perilous way.
WORDSWORTH, *The Borderers.* Act iv, sc. 2, l. 1774. (Written eighteen years before *The Excursion.*)

The intellectual power, through words and things,
Went sounding on, a dim and perilous way!
WORDSWORTH, *The Excursion.* Bk. iii, l. 700.

A mind forever
Voyaging through strange seas of thought alone.
WORDSWORTH, *The Prelude.* Bk. iii, l. 62.

8
Nothing can withstand the powers of the mind. Barriers, enormous masses of matter, the remotest recesses are conquered; all things succumb; the very heaven itself is laid open. (Rationi nulla resistunt. Claustra nec immensæ moles, ceduntque recessus: Omnia succumbunt; ipsum est penetrabile cœlum.)
MANILIUS, *Astronomica.* Bk. i, 541.

9
The mind, unmastered by passions, is a very citadel, for a man has no fortress more impregnable wherein to find refuge and be untaken forever.
MARCUS AURELIUS, *Meditations.* Bk. viii, sec. 48.

10
The mind, that ocean where each kind
Does straight its own resemblance find;
Yet it creates, transcending these,
Far other worlds, and other seas;
Annihilating all that's made
To a green thought in a green shade.
ANDREW MARVELL, *The Garden.*

11
The social states of human kinds
Are made by multitudes of minds,
And after multitudes of years
A little human growth appears
Worth having, even to the soul
Who sees most plain it's not the whole.
JOHN MASEFIELD, *The Everlasting Mercy.* St. 60.

12
The hand that follows intellect can achieve.
MICHELANGELO, *The Artist.* (Longfellow, tr.)

13
The mind is its own place, and in itself
Can make a Heav'n of Hell, a hell of Heav'n.
MILTON, *Paradise Lost.* Bk. i, l. 254.

14
The mind hath no horizon,
It looks beyond the eye, and seeks for mind
In all it sees, or all it sees o'erruling.
MONTGOMERY, *The Pelican Island.* Canto i, l. 78.

15
There are but two powers in the world, the sword and the mind. In the long run the sword is always beaten by the mind.
NAPOLEON. (FREDERIKS, *Maxims of Napoleon.*)

16
The joy of the mind marks its strength.
NINON DE L'ENCLOS, *Letter to St. Evremond.*

17
The mind alone cannot be exiled. (Mente tamen, quæ sola loco non exulat.)
OVID, *Epistulæ ex Ponto.* Bk. iv, epis. 9, l. 41.

The human mind cannot be burned nor bayonetted, nor wounded, nor missing.
R. W. EMERSON, *Journal,* 1863.

1
Mind is ever the ruler of the universe.
PLATO, *Philebus*. Sec. 30.

2
The flash and outbreak of a fiery mind,
A savageness in unreclaimed blood.
SHAKESPEARE, *Hamlet*. Act ii, sc. 1, l. 33.

3
It is the mind that maketh good or ill,
That maketh wretch or happy, rich or poor.
SPENSER, *Faerie Queene*. Bk. vi, canto 9, st. 30. *See also* THOUGHT: ITS POWER.

VIII—Mind: Its Cultivation

4
Constant attention wears the active mind,
Blots out our pow'rs, and leaves a blank behind.
CHARLES CHURCHILL, *Epistle to Hogarth*, l. 647.

5
He found a sort of food for the soul in cultivating his mind. (Animi cultus ille erat ei quasi quidam humanitatis cibus.)
CICERO, *De Finibus*. Bk. v, ch. 19, sec. 54.

We strive to improve the heart and mind. (Cor et mentem colere nititur.)
UNKNOWN, *Motto*, over a school at Marquise, France.

6
If the brain sows not corn, it plants thistles.
GEORGE HERBERT, *Jacula Prudentum*.

7
Rule your mind, which, if it is not your servant, is your master. Curb it with a bit; bind it with a chain. (Animum rege; qui nisi paret Imperat; hunc frenis, hunc tu compesce catena.)
HORACE, *Epistles*. Bk. i, epis. 2, l. 62.

Restrain your mind. (Compesce mentem.)
HORACE, *Odes*. Bk. i, ode 16, l. 22.

A wise man will be master of his mind, a fool will be its slave. (Animo imperabit sapiens, stultus serviet.)
PUBLILIUS SYRUS, *Sententiæ*. No. 40.

8
We must view with profound respect the infinite capacity of the human mind to resist the introduction of useful knowledge.
THOMAS R. LOUNSBURY. (LOCKWOOD, The *Freshman and His College*, p. 44.)

9
It is good to rub and polish our brain against that of others. (Il est bon de frotter et limer notre cervelle contre celle d'autrui.)
MONTAIGNE, *Essays*. Bk. i, ch. 24.

10
To relax the mind is to lose it. (Remittere animum quasi amittere est.)
MUSONIUS. (AULUS GELLIUS, *Noctes Atticæ*. Bk. xviii, ch. 2.)

Straining breaks the bow, relaxation the mind. (Arcum intensio frangit, animum remissio.)
PUBLILIUS SYRUS, *Sententiæ*. No. 53. Quoted by Bacon, *Ornamenta Rationalia*. No. 2.

The mind is like a bow, the stronger by being unbent.
BEN JONSON, *Explorata: Otium*.

11
A sick mind cannot endure any harshness. (Mensque pati durum sustinet ægra nihil.)
OVID, *Epistulæ ex Ponto*. Bk. i, epis. 5, l. 18.

We must spare the mind which has received a grievous wound. (Parcendum est animo miserabile vulnus habenti.)
OVID, *Epistulæ ex Ponto*. Bk. i, epis. 5, l. 23.

12
Recreation should sometimes be given to the mind that it may be restored to you in better condition for thinking. (Ludus animo debet aliquando dari Ad cogitandum melior ut redeat tibi.)
PHÆDRUS, *Fables*. Bk. iii, fab. 14, l. 12.

13
Strength of mind is exercise, not rest.
POPE, *Essay on Man*. Epis. ii, l. 104.

14
Love, Hope, and Joy, fair Pleasure's smiling train,
Hate, Fear, and Grief, the family of Pain,
These mix'd with art, and to due bounds confin'd
Make and maintain the balance of the mind.
POPE, *Essay on Man*. Epis. ii, l. 117.

15
We should toughen our minds. (Indurandus est animus.)
SENECA, *Epistulæ ad Lucilium*. Epis. li, sec. 5.

16
I, thus neglecting worldly ends, all dedicated
To closeness and the bettering of my mind.
SHAKESPEARE, *The Tempest*. Act i, sc. 2, l. 89.

17
He who seeks the mind's improvement,
Aids the world, in aiding mind.
CHARLES SWAIN, *What Is Noble?*

18
Nor less I deem that there are Powers
Which of themselves our minds impress;
That we can feed this mind of ours
In a wise passiveness.
WORDSWORTH, *Expostulation and Reply*.

19
If we work upon marble, it will perish. If we work upon brass, time will efface it. If we rear temples, they will crumble to dust. But if we work upon men's immortal minds, if we imbue them with high principles, with the just fear of God and love of their fellow men, we engrave on those tablets something which no time can efface, and which will brighten and brighten to all eternity.
DANIEL WEBSTER, *Speech*, Faneuil Hall, 1852

IX—Mind: The Mind Diseased

See also Madness

20
With curious art the brain, too finely wrought,

Preys on herself, and is destroy'd by thought.
CHARLES CHURCHILL, *Epistle to Hogarth*, l. 645.

1
A mental stain can neither be blotted out by the passage of time nor washed away by any waters. (Animi labes nec diuturnitate evanescere nec amnibus ullis elui potest.)
CICERO, *De Legibus*. Bk. ii, ch. 10, sec. 24.

2
In a disordered mind, as in a disordered body, soundness of health is impossible. (In perturbato animo sicut in corpore sanitas esse non posset.)
CICERO, *Tusculanarum Disputationum*. Bk. iii, ch. 4, sec. 9.

Not of sound mind. (Non compos mentis.)
CICERO, *In Pisonem*. Ch. 20, sec. 48.

See also under MADNESS.

3
All things can corrupt perverted minds. (Omnia perversas possunt corrumpere mentes.)
OVID, *Tristia*. Bk. ii, l. 301.

In sickness the mind reflects upon itself. (In morbo recolligit se animus.)
PLINY THE ELDER, *Historia Naturalis*. Bk. vii.

4
The incessant care and labour of his mind
Hath wrought the mure that should confine it in
So thin that life looks through and will break out.
SHAKESPEARE, *II Henry IV*. Act iv, sc. 4, l. 118.

As that the walls worn thin, permit the mind
To look out through, and his Frailty find.
SAMUEL DANIEL, *History of the Civil War*. Bk. iv, st. 84.

See also AGE: FACING THE SUNSET.

5
O, what a noble mind is here o'erthrown!
The courtier's, soldier's, scholar's, eye, tongue, sword;
The expectancy and rose of the fair state,
The glass of fashion and the mould of form,
The observed of all observers, quite, quite, down!
And I, of ladies most deject and wretched,
That suck'd the honey of his music vows,
Now see that noble and most sovereign reason,
Like sweet bells jangled, out of tune and harsh.
SHAKESPEARE, *Hamlet*. Act iii, sc. 1, l. 158.

6
Canst thou not minister to a mind diseased,
Pluck from the memory a rooted sorrow,
Raze out the written troubles of the brain,
And with some sweet oblivious antidote
Cleanse the stuff'd bosom of that perilous matter
Which weighs upon the heart?
SHAKESPEARE, *Macbeth*. Act v, sc. 3, l. 40.

Nature, too unkind,
That made no medicine for a troubled mind!
BEAUMONT AND FLETCHER, *Philaster*. Act iii, 1.

7
That is not a common chance
That takes away a noble mind.
TENNYSON, *To J. S.* St. 12.

X—Mind: Mind and Body

8
The shape alone let others prize,
The features of the fair:
I look for spirit in her eyes,
And meaning in her air.
MARK AKENSIDE, *Song*.

9
Fat bodies, lean brains!
BEAUMONT AND FLETCHER, *Love's Cure*. Act ii, sc. 1.

He has more guts than brains.
JOHN RAY, *English Proverbs*.

10
Certain it is that minds, like bodies, will often fall into a pimpled, ill-conditioned state from mere excess of comfort.
DICKENS, *Barnaby Rudge*. Ch. 7.

11
Bodies devoid of mind are as statues in the market place. (Αἱ δὲ σάρκες αἱ κεναὶ φρενῶν ἀγάλματ' ἀγορᾶς εἰσιν.)
EURIPIDES, *Electra*, l. 386.

12
A faultless body and a blameless mind.
HOMER, *Odyssey*. Bk. iii, l. 138. (Pope, tr.)

Whose little body lodg'd a mighty mind.
HOMER, *Iliad*. Bk. v, l. 999. (Pope, tr.)

13
A strong body makes the mind strong.
THOMAS JEFFERSON, *Writings*. Vol. v, p. 83.

14
A sound mind in a sound body is a thing to be prayed for. (Orandum est ut sit mens sana in corpore sano.)
JUVENAL, *Satires*. Sat. x, l. 356. *See also under* HEALTH.

15
We perceive that the mind strengthens and decays with the body. (Cum corpore ut una Crescere sentimus pariterque senescere mentem.)
LUCRETIUS, *De Rerum Natura*. Bk. iii, l. 446.

16
In these bodies of ours, the mind is of more value than the hand; all our vigor is in that. (In corpore nostro Pectora sunt potiora manu: vigor omnis in illis.)
OVID, *Metamorphoses*. Bk. xiii, l. 368.

17
The body must be repaired and supported, if we would preserve the mind in all its vigor. (Cujus fulturis animus sustinetur.)
PLINY THE YOUNGER, *Epistles*. Bk. i, epis. 9.

Hold fast to this sound and wholesome rule of life: that you indulge the body only so far as is needful for good health. The body should be treated rigorously, that it may not be disobedient to the mind. (Hanc ergo sanam ac salubrem formam vitæ tenete, ut corpori tantum indulgeatis, quantum bonæ valitudini satis est. Durius tractandum est, ne animo male pareat.)

SENECA, *Epistulæ ad Lucilium*. Epis. viii, sec. 5.

1
The contagion of a sick mind affects the body. (Vitiant artus ægræ contagia mentis.)

OVID, *Tristia*. Bk. iii, eleg. 8, l. 25.

The mind grows sicker than the body in contemplation of its sufferings. (Corpore sed mens est ægro magis ægra, malique In circumspectu stat sine fine sui.)

OVID, *Tristia*. Bk. iv, eleg. 6, l. 43. *See also under* DISEASE.

A feeble body enfeebles the mind. (Un corps débile affaiblit l'âme.)

ROUSSEAU, *Émile*. Ch. 1.

2
Pain of mind is worse than pain of body. (Dolor animi gravior est quam corporis.)

PUBLILIUS SYRUS, *Sententiæ*. No. 164.

3
We employ the mind to rule, the body to serve. (Animi imperio, corporis servitio magis utimur.)

SALLUST, *Catilina*. Ch. 1. sec. 2.

4
And when the mind is quicken'd, out of doubt,
The organs, though defunct and dead before,
Break up their drowsy grave and newly move
With casted slough and fresh legerity.

SHAKESPEARE, *Henry V*. Act iv, sc. 1, l. 20.

We are not ourselves
When nature, being oppress'd, commands the mind
To suffer with the body.

SHAKESPEARE, *King Lear*. Act ii, sc. 4, l. 108.

When the mind's free, The body's delicate.

SHAKESPEARE, *King Lear*. Act iii, sc. 4, l. 11.

5
Our purses shall be proud, our garments poor;
For 'tis the mind that makes the body rich.

SHAKESPEARE, *The Taming of the Shrew*. Act iv, sc. 3, l. 174.

6
Not body enough to cover his mind decently with; his intellect is improperly exposed.

SYDNEY SMITH. (LADY HOLLAND, *Memoir*. Vol. i, p. 258.)

There is an unseemly exposure of the mind, as well as of the body.

WILLIAM HAZLITT, *Sketches*, p. 165.

7
The clothing of our minds certainly ought to be regarded before that of our bodies.

RICHARD STEELE, *The Spectator*. No. 75.

8
A man's body and his mind, with the utmost reverence to both I speak it, are exactly like a jerkin and a jerkin's lining;—rumple the one,—you rumple the other.

STERNE, *Tristram Shandy*. Bk. iii, ch. 4.

9
The earthy tabernacle weigheth down the mind that museth upon many things.

Apocrypha: Wisdom of Solomon, ix, 15.

10
And, as her mind grew worse and worse,
Her body—it grew better.

WORDSWORTH, *The Idiot Boy*, l. 415.

XI—Mind: Mind and Matter

11
All the choir of heaven and furniture of earth—in a word, all those bodies which compose the mighty frame of the world—have not any subsistence without a mind.

BISHOP GEORGE BERKELEY, *Principles of Human Knowledge*.

12
Mind and Matter.

BISHOP GEORGE BERKELEY, title of dissertation.

Berkeley, in the early part of his life, wrote a dissertation against the existence of material beings and external objects, with such subtlety that Whiston acknowledged himself unable to confute it.

DR. JOHN HAWKESWORTH, *Note to Swift's Letters*, 1769.

13
When Bishop Berkeley said "there was no matter,"
And proved it—'twas no matter what he said.

BYRON, *Don Juan*. Canto xi, st. 1.

What is mind? No matter. What is matter? Never mind.

THOMAS HEWITT KEY. (On the authority of F. J. Furnivall.)

14
Doctor Berkeley, Bishop of Cloyne, a very worthy, ingenious, and learned man, has written a book to prove that there is no such thing as matter, and that nothing exists but in idea. . . . His arguments, strictly speaking, are unanswerable; but yet I am so far from being convinced by them, that I am determined to go on to eat and drink, and walk and ride, in order to keep that Matter, which I so mistakenly imagine my body at present to consist of, in as good plight as possible.

LORD CHESTERFIELD, *Letters*, 27 Sept., 1748.

15
Bishop Berkeley destroyed this world in one volume octavo; and nothing remained, after his time, but mind; which experienced a similar fate from the hand of Mr. Hume in 1737.

SYDNEY SMITH, *Sketches of Moral Philosophy: Introductory Lecture*.

16
Mind moves matter. (Mens agitat molem.)

VERGIL, *Æneid*. Bk. vi, l. 727.

17
I believe that there is no God, but that matter is God and God is matter; and that it is no matter whether there is any God or no.

UNKNOWN, *The Unbeliever's Creed*. (*Connoisseur*. No. 9, 28 March, 1754.)

MINORITY, see Majority

MINUTE

See also Time

1
The present moment is our ain,
The neist we never saw.
JAMES BEATTIE, *Stanza,* added to Mickle's song, *The Sailor's Wife.*

He who governed the world before I was born shall take care of it likewise when I am dead. My part is to improve the present moment.
JOHN WESLEY.

2
But yet what minutes! Moments like to these
Rend men's lives into immortalities.
BYRON, *The Island.* Canto iii, st. 4.

But what minutes! Count them by sensation, and not by calendars, and each moment is a day, and the race a life.
BENJAMIN DISRAELI, *Sybil.* Bk. i, ch. 2.

There are moments in life worth purchasing with worlds.
FIELDING, *Amelia.* Bk. iii, ch. 2.

Oh! what a crowded world one moment may contain.
FELICIA HEMANS, *The Last Constantine.*

O moments big as years!
JOHN KEATS, *Hyperion.*

3
Myself and the lucky moment.
CHARLES V OF SPAIN. (PRESCOTT, *Philip II.* Bk. i, ch. 9.)

4
I recommend you to take care of the minutes, for the hours will take care of themselves.
LORD CHESTERFIELD, *Letters,* 9 Oct., 1746.

Take care of the pence, and the pounds will take care of themselves.
WILLIAM LOWNDES, as quoted by Chesterfield. *See under* THRIFT.

5
Since our office is with moments, let us husband them. Five minutes of today are worth as much to me as five minutes in the next millennium.
EMERSON, *Essays, Second Series: Experience.*

This shining moment is an edifice
Which the Omnipotent cannot rebuild.
EMERSON, *Fragment.*

6
An old French sentence says, "God works in moments." We ask for long life, but 'tis deep life, or grand moments, that signify.
EMERSON, *Society and Solitude: Works and Days.* Emerson is translating an old French proverb, "En peu d'heure Dieu labeure."

7
His best things are done in the flash of a moment.
J. R. LOWELL, *A Fable for Critics,* l. 836.

8
Still work for the minute and not for the year.
JOHN BOYLE O'REILLY, *Rules of the Road.*

Eternity gives back nothing of what one leaves out of the minutes.
SCHILLER, *Resignation.* St. 18.
See also under OPPORTUNITY.

9
Like as the waves make toward the pebbled shore,
So do our minutes hasten to their end.
SHAKESPEARE, *Sonnets.* No. lx.

One by one the sands are flowing,
One by one the moments fall;
Some are coming, some are going;
Do not strive to grasp them all.
ADELAIDE ANN PROCTER, *One by One. See also* LIFE: ITS SHORTNESS.

10
Alas! how little can a moment show
Of an eye where feeling plays
In ten thousand dewy rays;
A face o'er which a thousand shadows go!
WORDWORTH, *The Triad,* l. 128.

MIRACLE

11
I should not be a Christian but for the miracles.
ST. AUGUSTINE. (PASCAL, *Pensées.* No. 812.)

12
Every believer is God's miracle.
BAILEY, *Festus: Home.*

13
The Age of Miracles, as it ever was, now is.
CARLYLE, *Essays: Characteristics.*

14
When Christ, at Cana's feast, by pow'r divine,
Inspir'd cold water with the warmth of wine,
See! cry'd they while, in red'ning tide, it gush'd,
The bashful stream hath seen its God, and blush'd.
(Unde rubor vestris, et non sua purpura, lymphis?
Quæ rosa mirantes tam nova mutat aquas?
Numen (convivæ) præsens agnoscite Numen;
Nympha pudica Deum vidit, et erubuit.)
RICHARD CRASHAW, *Epigrammationa Sacra.* No. 96. (Aaron Hill, tr.)

The conscious water saw its God, and blushed.
(Vidit et erubuit lympha pudica Deum.)
RICHARD CRASHAW, *Upon the Water Made Wine.* His own translation of his Latin line.

Thou water turn'st to wine (fair friend of life);
Thy foe, to cross the sweet arts of Thy reign,
Distils from thence the tears of wrath and strife,
And so turns wine to water back again.
RICHARD CRASHAW, *Steps to the Temple: To Our Lord, Upon the Water Made Wine.*

The water owns a power Divine,
And conscious blushes into wine;
Its very nature changed displays
The power divine that it obeys.
SEDULIUS, *Hymn.* Sedulius (Scotus Hybernicus) was a biblical commentator of Irish

birth who died in 828. His poem was written in Latin and translated into English by Canon MacIlwaine. (*Lyra Hibernica Sacra.*)

1
We must not sit down, and look for miracles. Up, and be doing, and the Lord will be with thee. Prayer and pains, through faith in Christ Jesus, will do anything.

JOHN ELIOT, *Indian Grammar Begun: Postscript.*

2
Miracles exist as ancient history merely; they are not in the belief, nor in the aspiration of society.

EMERSON, *Nature, Addresses, and Lectures: Address.*

The word Miracle, as pronounced by Christian churches, gives a false impression; it is Monster.

EMERSON, *Nature, Addresses, and Lectures: Address.*

I have never seen a greater monster or miracle in the world than myself.

MONTAIGNE, *Essays.* Bk. iii, ch. 11.

3
Miracles are the swaddling-clothes of infant churches.

THOMAS FULLER, *Church History.* Vol. ii, p. 239.

Religion seems to have grown an infant with age, and requires miracles to nurse it, as it had in its infancy.

SWIFT, *Thoughts on Various Subjects.*

4
The dearest child of Faith is Miracle. (Das Wunder ist des Glaubens liebstes Kind.)

GOETHE, *Faust.* Part i, sc. 1, l. 413.

Things that are mysterious are not necessarily miracles.

GOETHE, *Sprüche in Prosa.*

5
A Miracle: An event described by those to whom it was told by men who did not see it.

ELBERT HUBBARD, *Epigrams.*

6
The question before the human race is, whether the God of Nature shall govern the world by His own laws, or whether priests and kings shall rule it by fictitious miracles.

THOMAS JEFFERSON, *Letter to John Adams,* 1815.

7
Miracles and truth are necessary, because it is necessary to convince the entire man, in body and soul.

PASCAL, *Pensées.* No. 806.

Had it not been for the miracles, there would have been no sin in not believing in Christ.

PASCAL, *Pensées.* No. 811.

8
Miracles serve not to convert, but to condemn.

PASCAL, *Pensées.* No. 825.

To aim to convert a man by miracles is a profanation of the soul.

EMERSON, *Nature, Addresses, and Lectures: Address.*

9
Accept a miracle: instead of wit,
See two dull lines by Stanhope's pencil writ.

ALEXANDER POPE to Lord Chesterfield, on using the latter's pencil. (JOHN TAYLOR, *Records of My Life.* Vol. i, p. 161; NEWBERRY, *Art of Poetry on a New Plan.* Vol. i, p. 57.)

10
Miracles are to those who believe in them.

W. G. BENHAM, *Proverbs,* p. 810.

Miracle comes to the miraculous, not to the arithmetician.

EMERSON, *Conduct of Life: Worship.*

11
Great seas have dried
When miracles have by the greatest been denied.

SHAKESPEARE, *All's Well that Ends Well.* Act ii, sc. 1, l. 143.

12
They say miracles are past.

SHAKESPEARE, *All's Well that Ends Well.* Act ii, sc. 3, l. 1.

It must be so; for miracles are ceased.

SHAKESPEARE, *Henry V.* Act i, sc. 1, l. 67.

Alas! there are no longer any miracles! (Ach! es geschehen keine Wunder mehr.)

SCHILLER, *Jungfrau von Orleans.* Act i, sc. 1.

13
A miracle is an event which creates faith. . . . Frauds deceive. An event which creates faith does not deceive; therefore it is not a fraud, but a miracle.

BERNARD SHAW, *Saint Joan.* Sc. ii.

14
To me every hour of the light and dark is a miracle,
Every cubic inch of space is a miracle.

WALT WHITMAN, *Miracles,* l. 17.

15
What is a miracle?—'Tis a reproach,
'Tis an implicit satire, on mankind;
And while it satisfies, it censures too.

YOUNG, *Night Thoughts.* Night ix, l. 1241.

16
By order of the King: "It is forbidden for God to work miracles here." (De par de roi: Defense à Dieu De faire des miracles en ce lieu.)

Epigram, written by an unknown wit upon the gates of the cemetery of St. Médard, when closed by Louis XV, because of the reputed miracles worked by the relics of Le Diacre Paris, a Jansenist interred there.

MIRROR

17
Glass antique! 'twixt thee and Nell
Draw we here a parallel!
She, like thee, was forced to bear
All reflections, foul or fair.
Thou art deep and bright within,
Depths as bright belong'd to Gwynne;
Thou art very frail as well,

Frail as flesh is —so was Nell.
LAMON BLANCHARD, *Nell Gwynne's Looking Glass.*

1
The mirror reflects all objects without being sullied.
CONFUCIUS, *Analects.*

2
What your glass tells you will not be told by counsel.
GEORGE HERBERT, *Jacula Prudentum.*

The best mirror is an old friend.
GEORGE HERBERT, *Jacula Prudentum.*

3
When her mother tends her, before the
laughing mirror.
GEORGE MEREDITH, *Love in the Valley.*

4
Pride grows, forsooth, by the reflection in the mirror. (Scilicet a speculi sumuntur imagine fastus.)
OVID, *Amores.* Bk. ii, eleg. 17, l. 9.

5
When such a spacious mirror's set before
him,
He needs must see himself.
SHAKESPEARE, *Antony and Cleopatra.* Act v, sc. 1, l. 34.

'Tis not her glass, but you, that flatters her.
SHAKESPEARE, *As You Like It.* Act iii, sc. 5, l. 54.

Thy glass will show thee how thy beauties wear.
SHAKESPEARE, *Sonnets.* No. lxxvii.

6
To hold as 'twere, the mirror up to nature.
SHAKESPEARE, *Hamlet.* Act iii, sc. 2, l. 24.

7
You have no such mirrors as will turn
Your hidden worthiness into your eye.
SHAKESPEARE, *Julius Cæsar.* Act i, sc. 2, l. 56.

8
Go some of you and fetch a looking-glass.
SHAKESPEARE, *Richard II.* Act iv, sc. 1, l. 268.

An if my word be sterling yet in England,
Let it command a mirror hither straight,
That it may show me what a face I have.
SHAKESPEARE, *Richard II.* Act iv, sc. 1, l. 265.

I'll be at charges for a looking-glass.
SHAKESPEARE, *Richard III.* Act i, sc. 2, l. 256.

Shine out, fair sun, till I have bought a glass,
That I may see my shadow as I pass.
SHAKESPEARE, *Richard III.* Act i, sc. 2, l. 263.

9
The devil's behind the glass.
J. C. WALL, *Devils,* p. 128.

10
I change, and so do women too;
But I reflect, which women never do.
UNKNOWN, *Written on a Looking-Glass.*

11
As in a looking-glass. (Veluti in speculum.)
UNKNOWN. A Latin proverbial phrase of unknown origin

MIRTH

See also Merriment

12
An ounce of mirth is worth a pound of sorrow.
RICHARD BAXTER, *Self-Denial. See also* JOY AND SORROW.

13
For wicked mirth never true pleasure brings,
But honest minds are pleased with honest
things.
BEAUMONT AND FLETCHER, *The Knight of the Burning Pestle: Prologue.*

Unseasonable mirth always turns to sorrow.
CERVANTES, *Don Quixote.*

14
The mirth and fun grew fast and furious.
BURNS, *Tam o' Shanter.*

And vexed with mirth the drowsy ear of night.
BYRON, *Childe Harold.* Canto i, st. 2.

15
Mirth makes the banquet sweet.
GEORGE CHAPMAN, *The Blind Beggar of Alexandria.*

Be large in mirth; anon we'll drink a measure
The table round.
SHAKESPEARE, *Macbeth.* Act iii, sc. 4, l. 11.

16
Love fram'd with Mirth, a gay fantastic
round:
Loose were her tresses seen, her zone unbound.
WILLIAM COLLINS, *Ode: The Passions,* l. 90.

17
True mirth resides not in the smiling skin:
The truest solace is to act no sin.
ROBERT HERRICK, *Mirth.*

18
Mirth's concussions rip the outward case,
And plant the stitches in a tenderer place.
O. W. HOLMES, *A Rhymed Lesson,* l. 35.

19
Dance and Provençal song and sunburnt
mirth!
KEATS, *Ode to a Nightingale.*

20
Come, thou Goddess fair and free,
In heav'n yclept Euphrosyne,
And by men, heart-easing Mirth.
MILTON, *L'Allegro,* l. 11.

And if I give thee honour due,
Mirth, admit me of thy crew,
To live with her, and live with thee,
In unreproved pleasures free.
MILTON, *L'Allegro,* l. 37.

21
To hear the addled citizens at their mirth—
Their lewd and lackwit innocent noble mirth!
CHRISTOPHER MORLEY, *Good Theatre.*

22
Where lives the man that has not tried,
How mirth can into folly glide,
And folly into sin.
SCOTT, *The Bridal of Triermain.* Canto i, st. 21

1
I'll use you for my mirth, yea, for my laughter,
When you are waspish.
SHAKESPEARE, *Julius Cæsar*. Act iv, sc. 3, l. 49.

You have displaced the mirth, broke the good meeting.
With most admired disorder.
SHAKESPEARE, *Macbeth*. Act iii, sc. 4, l. 109.

2
Let me play the fool:
With mirth and laughter let old wrinkles come,
And let my liver rather heat with wine
Than my heart cool with mortifying groans.
Why should a man, whose blood is warm within,
Sit like his grandsire cut in alabaster?
SHAKESPEARE, *The Merchant of Venice*. Act 1, sc. 1, l. 79.

And let's be red with mirth.
SHAKESPEARE, *Winter's Tale*. Act iv, sc. 4, l. 54.

3
From the crown of his head to the sole of his foot. he is all mirth.
SHAKESPEARE, *Much Ado About Nothing*. Act iii, sc. 2, l. 9.

4
Let your mirth be ever void of scurrility and biting words to any man, for a wound given by a word is oftentimes harder to be cured than that which is given with the sword.
SIR HENRY SIDNEY, *Letter to His Son, Sir Philip Sidney*.

5
The glad circle round them yield their souls
To festive mirth, and wit that knows no gall.
THOMSON, *The Seasons: Summer*, l. 403.

6
Mirth is hard to feign when the mind is sad. (Difficile est tristi fingere mente jocum.)
TIBULLUS, *Elegies*. Bk. iii, eleg. 6, l. 33.

Mirth cannot move a soul in agony.
SHAKESPEARE, *Love's Labour's Lost*. Act v, sc. 2, l. 867.

Very tragical mirth.
SHAKESPEARE, *A Midsummer-Night's Dream*. Act v, sc. 1, l. 57.

7
Mirth prolongeth life, and causeth health.
NICHOLAS UDALL, *Ralph Roister Doister: Prologue*.

And frame your mind to mirth and merriment,
Which bars a thousand harms and lengthens life.
SHAKESPEARE, *The Taming of the Shrew: Induction*. Sc. 2, l. 137.

8
I love such mirth as does not make friends ashamed to look upon one another next morning.
IZAAK WALTON, *The Compleat Angler*. Ch. 5.

In mirth, that after no repenting draws.
JOHN MILTON, *To Cyriac Skinner*.

9
The mirth of the world dureth but a while.
UNKNOWN, *Book of Merry Riddles*. No. 11. (1629)

MISANTHROPY

10
The misanthropic idea, as in Byron, is not a truth, but it is one of the immortal lies. As long as humanity lasts it can be hated.
G. K. CHESTERTON, *Uses of Adversity*.

11
Lean, hungry, savage anti-everythings.
O. W. HOLMES, *A Modest Request*.

12
Spleen to mankind his envious heart possess'd,
And much he hated all, but most the best.
HOMER, *Iliad*. Bk. ii, l. 267. (Pope, tr.)

Spleen, which only seizes on the lazy, the luxurious, and the rich.
SWIFT, *Gulliver's Travels: A Voyage to the Houyhnhnms*.

13
I consider him an unhappy man whom no one pleases. (Miserum credo, cui placet nemo.)
MARTIAL, *Epigrams*. Bk. v, ep. 29, l. 9.

He who is pleased with nobody is much more unhappy than he with whom nobody is pleased. (Un homme à qui personne ne plaît est bien plus malheureux que celui qui ne plaît à personne.)
LA ROCHEFOUCAULD, *Maximes Posthumes*. No. 561.

14
Oh, the nothingness of one who loves nothing! (Certo is quidem nihilist, Qui nil amat.)
PLAUTUS, *Persa*, l. 179.

15
A misanthrope I can understand—a womanthrope never.
OSCAR WILDE, *The Importance of Being Earnest*. Act ii.

MISCHIEF

See also Evil

16
He that mischief hatcheth, mischief catcheth.
WILLIAM CAMDEN, *Remains*, p. 324.

17
What plaguy mischief and mishaps
Do dog him still with after-claps!
BUTLER, *Hudibras*. Pt. i, canto iii, l. 3.

18
He'll find money for mischief, when he can find none for corn.
THOMAS FULLER, *Gnomologia*. No. 2425.

19
Mischief comes by the pound and goes away by the ounce.
THOMAS FULLER, *Gnomologia*. No. 3417.

Mischief is well said to have swift wings.
JOHN MELTON, *Six-fold Politician*, p. 13.

20
Let them call it mischief:
When it is past and prospered 'twill be virtue.
BEN JONSON, *Catiline*. Act iii, sc. 3.

1
But when to mischief mortals bend their will,
How soon they find fit instruments of ill!
POPE, *Rape of the Lock*. Canto iii, l. 125.

2
Marry, this is miching mallecho; it means mischief.
SHAKESPEARE, *Hamlet*. Act iii, sc. 2, l. 149.

Mischief, thou art afoot,
Take thou what course thou wilt.
SHAKESPEARE, *Julius Cæsar*. Act iii, sc. 2, l. 265.

O mischief, thou art swift
To enter in the thoughts of desperate men!
SHAKESPEARE, *Romeo and Juliet*. Act v, sc. 1, l. 35.

3
To mourn a mischief that is past and gone,
Is the next way to draw new mischief on.
SHAKESPEARE, *Othello*. Act i, sc. 3, l. 204.

4
Better a mischief than an inconvenience.
RICHARD STEELE, *The Spectator*. No. 564.

MISER, see Avarice

MISERY

See also Despair; Man: His Misery; Suffering; Woe

I—Misery: Definitions

5
It is a miserable state of mind to have few things to desire, and many things to fear.
FRANCIS BACON, *Essays: Of Empire*.

6
Nothing is a misery,
Unless our weakness apprehend it so.
BEAUMONT AND FLETCHER, *Honest Man's Fortune*. Act i, sc. 1. *See also* MIND: ITS POWER.

7
To have a stomach and lack meat, to have meat and lack a stomach, to lie in bed and cannot rest are great miseries.
WILLIAM CAMDEN, *Remains*, p. 333. (1605)

8
Misery of any kind is not the *cause* of Immorality, but the effect thereof.
CARLYLE, *Count Cagliostro: Flight Last*.

And all the fair examples of renown
Out of distress and misery are grown.
SAMUEL DANIEL, *On the Earl of Southampton*.

9
O Misery! where once thou art possessed,
See but how quickly thou canst alter kind,
And, like a Circe, metamorphosest
The man that hath not a most godlike mind.
DRAYTON, *The Barons' Wars*. Bk. vi, st. 77.

10
Nay, misery's blackest night may chance,
By Fortune's turn, to show a happy dawn.
(Ἀλλ' ἔστιν ἔστιν ἡ λίαν δυσπραξία
λίαν διδοῦσα μεταβολάς, ὅταν τύχῃ.)
EURIPIDES, *Iphigenia in Tauris*, l. 721.

Better days, perhaps, await the wretched. (Forsan miseros meliora sequentur.)
VERGIL, *Æneid*. Bk. xii, l. 153.

My desolation does begin to make
A better life.
SHAKESPEARE, *Antony and Cleopatra*. Act v, sc. 2, l. 1.

11
Never did any public misery
Rise of itself: God's plagues still grounded are
On common stains of our humanity;
And, to the flame which ruineth mankind,
Man gives the matter, or at least gives wind.
FULKE GREVILLE, *Treatie of Warres*.

The chief cause of our misery is less the violence of our passions than the feebleness of our virtues.
JOSEPH ROUX, *Meditations of a Parish Priest*. Pt. v, No. 25.

12
Misery is but the shadow of happiness. Happiness is but the cloak of misery.
LAO-TSZE, *The Simple Way*. No. 58.

13
The secret of being miserable is to have leisure to bother about whether you are happy or not. The cure for it is occupation.
BERNARD SHAW, *Parents and Children*.

II—Misery: Apothegms

14
None would be wretched and none would not be blessed. (Οὐδεὶς ἑκὼν πονηρὸς οὐδ' ἄκων μάκαρ.)
SOLON [?]. (ARISTOTLE, *Nicomachean Ethics*. Bk. iii, ch. 5, sec. 4.)

15
Afflictions induce callosities, miseries are slippery, or fall like snow upon us.
SIR THOMAS BROWNE, *Hydriotaphia*. Ch. 5.

16
It is misery enough to have once been happy.
JOHN CLARKE, *Parœmiologia*, p. 166. *See also* MEMORY: ITS BITTERNESS.

17
Horatio looked handsomely miserable, like Hamlet slipping on a piece of orange-peel.
DICKENS, *Sketches by Boz: Horatio Sparkins*.

18
It would be far better to work at the prevention of misery, than to multiply places of refuge for the miserable.
DIDEROT, *The Encyclopedia*. Vol. i, p. 182.

19
He beareth his misery best that hideth it most.
GABRIEL HARVEY, *Marginalia*, p. 95.

20
There are a good many real miseries in life that we cannot help smiling at, but they are the smiles that make wrinkles and not dimples.
O. W. HOLMES, *The Poet at the Breakfast-Table*. Ch. 3.

21
It is easy to mock the miserable. (Facile est miserum irridere.)
PLAUTUS, *Curculio*, l. 239. (Act ii, sc. 1.)

One should never mock the miserable, for who can be sure of continued happiness?
(Il ne faut jamais moquer des misérables,
Car qui peut s'assurer d'être toujours heureux?)
LA FONTAINE, *Fables*. Bk. v, fab. 17.

Misery makes sport to mock itself.
SHAKESPEARE, *Richard II*. Act ii, sc. 1, l. 85.

1
Press anything you will, a groan will issue forth.
JOSEPH ROUX, *Meditations of a Parish Priest*. Pt. v, No. 12.

2
Nothing almost sees miracles But misery.
SHAKESPEARE, *King Lear*. Act ii, sc. 2, l. 172.

3
Misery acquaints a man with strange bedfellows.
SHAKESPEARE, *The Tempest*. Act ii, sc. 2, l. 40.

III—Misery Loves Company

See also Grief: Companionship in

4
Men say, "To a wretch is consolation
To have another fellow in his pain."
CHAUCER, *Troilus and Criseyde*. Bk. i, l. 708. (c. 1374)

It is good to have companions in misery.
JOHN GOWER, *Confessio Amantis*. Bk. ii, l. 261. (c. 1390)

In misery, Euphues, it is great comfort to have a companion.
JOHN LYLY, *Euphues*, p. 96. (1579)

It is a consolation to the wretched to have companions in misery. (Solamen miseris socios habuisse doloris.)
PUBLILIUS SYRUS, *Sententiæ*. No. 995; THOMAS À KEMPIS, *De Valle Liliorum*. Ch. 16. Quoted. The probable origin of the proverb, "Misery loves company."

Misery loves company.
JOHN RAY, *English Proverbs*. (1670)

5
Misery still delights to trace
Its semblance in another's case.
COWPER, *The Castaway*. St. 10.

6
Let us embrace, and from this very moment
Vow an eternal misery together.
THOMAS OTWAY, *The Orphan*. Act iv, sc. 2.

7
A crowd of fellow sufferers is a kind of comfort in misery. (Male voli solatii genus est turbu miserorum.)
SENECA, *Ad Marciam de Consolatione*. Ch. 12, sec. 5.

Slight is the pleasure derived from the misery of others. (Levis est consolatio ex miseria aliorum.)
CICERO, *Ad Familiares*. Bk. vi, epis. 3.

Fellowship in pain divides not smart,
Nor lightens aught each man's peculiar load.
MILTON, *Paradise Regained*. Bk. i, l. 401.

8
'Tis sweet to mingle tears with tears;
Griefs, where they wound in solitude,
Wound more deeply.
(Lacrimas lacrimis miscere juvat;
Magis exurunt quos secretæ
Lacerant curæ.)
SENECA, *Agamemnon*, l. 664.

9
Who alone suffers suffers most i' the mind,
Leaving free things and happy shows behind:
But then the mind much sufferance doth o'erskip,
When grief hath mates, and bearing fellowship.
SHAKESPEARE, *King Lear*. Act iii, sc. 6, l. 111.

10
If misery loves company, misery has company enough.
H. D. THOREAU, *Journal*, 1 Sept., 1851.

11
A fellowship in misfortune having nevertheless to a certain extent a certain alleviation.
THUCYDIDES, *History*. Bk. vii, sec. 75.

12
Thy hard hap doth mine appease,
Company doth sorrow ease.
UNKNOWN, *The Willow Tree*. (PERCY, *Reliques*. Ser. iii, bk. ii, No. 9.)

IV—Misery: The Miserable

13
The world goes whispering to its own,
"This anguish pierces to the bone;"
And tender friends go sighing round,
"What love can ever cure this wound?"
My days go on, my days go on.
E. B. BROWNING, *De Profundis*. St. 5.

14
I stood in unimaginable trance
And agony that cannot be remembered.
S. T. COLERIDGE, *Remorse*. Act iv, sc. 3.

15
This, this is misery! the last, the worst,
That man can feel.
HOMER, *Iliad*. Bk. xxii, l. 106. (Pope, tr.)

Heav'n hears and pities hapless men like me,
Far sacred ev'n to gods is misery.
HOMER, *Odyssey*. Bk. v, l. 572. (Pope, tr.)

16
He that wanders about the world sees new forms of human misery, and if he chances to meet an old friend, meets a face darkened with troubles.
SAMUEL JOHNSON, *Letters*. Vol. i, p. 227.

17
Remembering mine affliction and my misery, the wormwood and the gall.
Old Testament: Lamentations, iii, 19.

I perceive that thou art in the gall of bitterness, and in the bond of iniquity.
New Testament: Acts, viii, 23.

18
The child of misery, baptized in tears!
JOHN LANGHORNE, *The Country Justice*. Pt. i, l. 166.

Listless and sad, without complaint,

Like dead men in a dream.
GEORGE MACDONALD, *The Disciple*. Pt. xi, st. 8.

1
Me miserable! which way shall I fly
Infinite wrath and infinite despair?
MILTON, *Paradise Lost*. Bk. iv, l. 73.

But O yet more miserable!
Myself my sepulchre, a moving grave.
MILTON, *Samson Agonistes*, l. 101.

2
Mountains of misery toppling down on you. (In te inruont montes mali.)
PLAUTUS, *Epidicus*, l. 84. (Act i, sc. 1.)

3
The wretched are in haste to hear their wretchedness. (Miserias properant suas Audire miseri.)
SENECA, *Hercules Œtæus*, l. 754.

4
Poor naked wretches, whereso'er you are,
That bide the pelting of this pitiless storm,
How shall your houseless heads and unfed sides,
Your loop'd and window'd raggedness, defend you
From seasons such as this.
SHAKESPEARE, *King Lear*. Act iii, sc. 4, l. 28.

First Murderer: I am one, my liege,
Whom the vile blows and buffets of the world
Have so incensed that I am reckless what
I do to spite the world.
Second Murderer: And I another
So weary with disasters, tugg'd with fortune,
That I would set my life on any chance,
To mend it, or be rid on 't.
SHAKESPEARE, *Macbeth*. Act iii, sc. 1, l. 109.

5
Sharp misery had worn him to the bones.
SHAKESPEARE, *Romeo and Juliet*. Act v, sc. 1, l. 41.

6
All of which misery I saw, and a great part of which I was. (Quæque ipse miserrima vidi, Et quorum pars magna fui.)
VERGIL, *Æneid*. Bk. ii, l. 5.

7
Preach to the storm, and reason with despair,
But tell not Misery's son that life is fair.
HENRY KIRKE WHITE, *Lines on Reading Capel Lofft's Preface to Bloomfield's Poems.*

MISFORTUNE

See also Adversity, Trouble

I—Misfortune: Apothegms

8
In every adversity of fortune, to have been happy is the most unhappy kind of misfortune. (In omni adversitate fortunæ, infelicissimum est genus infortunii fuisse felicem.)
BOËTHIUS, *De Consolatione Philosophiæ*. Bk. ii, pt. 4, l. 4.

To have been happy, madame, adds to calamity.
BEAUMONT AND FLETCHER, *The Fair Maid of the Inn*. Act i, sc. 1, l. 250.

See also MEMORY: SWEET AND BITTER.

9
Misfortunes come on wings and depart on foot.
H. G. BOHN, *Hand-Book of Proverbs*, 452.

10
And ne'er misfortune's eastern blast
Did nip a fairer flower.
BURNS, *To Chloris.*

11
O Miss Bailey; Unfortunate Miss Bailey!
GEORGE COLMAN THE YOUNGER, *Love Laughs at Locksmiths.*

12
Misfortunes, like the owl, avoid the light;
The sons of Care are always sons of Night.
CHARLES CHURCHILL, *Night*, l. 17.

13
Misfortune ever claimed the pity of the brave.
CHARLES DIBDIN, *The Veterans.*

14
Misfortune is friendless. (Ἄφιλον τὸ δυστυχές.)
EURIPIDES, *Hercules Furens*, l. 561. *See also* PROSPERITY AND ADVERSITY.

15
When Misfortune sleeps, let no one wake her. (Quando la mala ventura se duerme, nadie la despierte.)
UNKNOWN. A Spanish proverb.

Misfortunes tell us what fortune is.
THOMAS FULLER, *Gnomologia*. No. 3420.

16
And from the top of all my trust,
Mishap hath thrown me in the dust.
JOHN HARINGTON, *The Lover That Once Disdained Love*. (TOTTLE, *Miscellany*, 1557.) Mary Queen of Scots is said to have written these lines with a diamond on a window in Fotheringay Castle.

17
Strong of limb
And swift of foot misfortune is, and, far
Outstripping all, comes first to every land,
And there wreaks evil on mankind.
HOMER, *Iliad*. Bk. ix, l. 625. (Bryant, tr.)

For there is none misfortune cannot reach. (Κακῶν γὰρ δυσάλωτος οὐδείς.)
SOPHOCLES, *Œdipus Coloneus*, l. 1722.

Misfortune had conquered her. How true it is, that, sooner or later, the most rebellious must bow beneath the same yoke.
MADAME DE STAËL, *Corinne*. Bk. xvii, ch. 2.

18
Philosophy triumphs easily over misfortunes past and to come, but present misfortunes triumph over philosophy. (La philosophie triomphe aisément des maux passés et des maux à venir, mais les maux présents triomphent d'elle.)
LA ROCHEFOUCAULD, *Maximes*. No. 22.

19
Whatever we may pretend, interest and vanity are the usual sources of our misfortunes. (Quelque prétexte que nous donnions à nos

afflictions, ce n'est souvent que l'intérêt et la vanité qui les causent.)

La Rochefoucauld, *Maximes*. No. 232.

1
Little minds are tamed and subdued by misfortune, but great minds rise above it.

Washington Irving, *Sketch Book: Philip of Pokanoket*.

2
There is no one more unfortunate than the man who has never been unfortunate, for it has never been in his power to try himself. (Nihil infelicius eo, cui nihil unquam evenit adversi, non licuit enim illi se experiri.)

Seneca, *De Providentia*. Sec. 3.

3
I am that he, that unfortunate he.

Shakespeare, *As You Like It*. Act iii, 2, 417.

What a case am I in.

Shakespeare, *As You Like It: Epilogue*, l. 7.

One writ with me in sour misfortune's book.

Shakespeare, *Romeo and Juliet*. Act v, 3, 82.

4
There are vicissitudes in all things. (Omnium rerum vicissitudost.)

Terence, *Eunuchus*, l. 276. (Act ii, sc. 2.)

II—Misfortune: Misfortunes Never Come Singly

See also under Woe

5
Misfortunes never come singly. (Sequitur vara bibiam.)

Ausonius, *Technopægnion*. Pt. iv, l. 1. Literally, "The trestle follows the plank."

Misfortunes, you know, seldom come singly.

Cervantes, *Don Quixote*. Pt. i, ch. 6.

Ill fortune seldom comes alone.

Dryden, *Cymon and Iphigenia*, l. 392.

One misfortune never comes alone.

Fielding, *Jonathan Wild*. Bk. i, ch. 8.

6
One misfortune is generally followed closely by another. (Fere fit malum malo aptissimum.)

Livy, *History*. Bk. i, sec. 46.

7
Fate is not satisfied with inflicting one calamity.

Publilius Syrus, *Sententiæ*. No. 274.

8
Welcome, misfortune, if thou comest alone.

John Ray, *English Proverbs*.

9
When sorrows come, they come not single spies.
But in battalions.

Shakespeare, *Hamlet*. Act iv, sc. 5, l. 78.

One sorrow never comes but brings an heir,
That may succeed as his inheritor.

Shakespeare, *Pericles*. Act i, sc. 4, l. 63.

10
Men tellen, in oldë mone [remembrance],
Misfortune cometh nowhere alone.

Unknown, *King Alisaundre*, l. 1281. (c. 1300)

For after one evil cometh many more.

Unknown, *Partonope*, l. 5542. (c. 1490)

For wise men sayeth . . . that one mishap fortuneth never alone.

Alex. Barclay, *Ship of Fools*. Pt. ii, l. 251.

III—Misfortune: The Misfortunes of Others

See also Friends and Adversity

11
It is the nature of mortals to kick a man when he is down. (Ὥστε σύγγονον βροτοῖσι τὸν πεσόντα λακτίσαι πλέον.)

Æschylus, *Agamemnon*, l. 884.

What! Ben, my old hero, is this your renown?
Is *this* the new go?—kick a man when he's down?
When the foe has knock'd under, to tread on him then—
By the fist of my father, I blush for thee, Ben!

Thomas Moore, *Epistle from Tom Crib to Big Ben*, l. 1. Written soon after Bonaparte's exile to St. Helena. "Big Ben" was a nickname for the Prince Regent.

12
I am convinced that we have a degree of delight, and that no small one, in the real misfortunes and pains of others.

Edmund Burke, *On the Sublime and Beautiful*. Pt. i, sec. 14.

13
O ye who, sunk in beds of down,
Feel not a want but what yourselves create,
Think for a moment on his wretched fate,
Whom friends and fortune quite disown!

Burns, *A Winter Night*. St. 8.

14
A person seldom falls sick, but the bystanders are animated with a faint hope that he will die.

Emerson, *Conduct of Life: Considerations by the Way*.

15
To bear other people's afflictions, every one has courage and enough to spare.

Benjamin Franklin, *Poor Richard*, 1740.

We all have sufficient strength to bear other people's misfortunes. (Nous avons tous assez de force pour supporter les maux d'autrui.)

La Rochefoucauld, *Maximes*. No. 19.

16
When we describe our sensations of another's sorrows, either in friendly or ceremonious condolence, the customs of the world seldom admit of rigid veracity.

Samuel Johnson, *The Idler*. No. 50.

17
It is pleasant, when the sea runs high, to view from land the distress of another. (Suave, mari magno, turbantibus æquora ventis, E terra magnum alterius spectare laborem.)

Lucretius, *De Rerum Natura*. Bk. ii, l. 1.

How sweet to stand, when tempests tear the main,
On the firm cliff and mark the seaman's toil!
Not that another's danger soothes the soul,

But from such toil how sweet to feel secure!
LUCRETIUS, *De Rerum Natura*. Bk. ii, l. 1.

I wander not to seek for more:
In greatest storm I sit on shore,
And laugh at those that toil in vain
To get what must be lost again.
BEN JONSON, *Every Man Out of His Humour*. Quoting an old song.

1
In the midst of compassion, we feel within us a kind of bitter-sweet pricking of malicious delight in the misfortunes of others.
MONTAIGNE, *Essays*. Bk. iii, ch. 1.

2
I never knew any man who could not bear another's misfortunes perfectly like a Christian.
POPE, *Thoughts on Various Subjects*. In October, 1706, Pope and Swift, being together in the country, agreed to write down such involuntary thoughts as occurred to them during their walks, and this quotation is often ascribed to Swift's *Thoughts on Various Subjects*. It does not appear there, however, and really belongs to Pope.

3
Learn to see in another's misfortune the ills which you should avoid.
PUBLILIUS SYRUS, *Sententiæ*. No. 120. *See also under* EXAMPLE.

4
What each feared for himself, he bore with patience when turned to another's ruin. (Etiam quæ sibi quisque timebat Unius in miseri exitium conversa tulere.)
VERGIL, *Æneid*. Bk. ii, l. 130.

5
Is this to be believed or to be told?
Can such inbred malice live in man,
To joy in ill, and from another's woes
To draw his own delight?
(Hocine credibile aut memorabile,
Tanta vecordia innate quoiquam ut siet
Ut malis gaudeant atque ex incommodis
Alterius sua ut comparent commoda?)
TERENCE, *Andria*, l. 625. (Colman, tr.)

6
Anyone can stand his own misfortunes; but when I read in the papers all about the rascalities and outrages going on I realize what a creature the human animal is.
MARK TWAIN. (PAINE, *Mark Twain*.)

IV—Misfortune: How to Bear It

7
He who cannot bear misfortune is truly unfortunate.
BIAS. (DIOGENES LAERTIUS, *Bias*. Bk. i, sec. 86.)

8
"For all that let me tell thee, brother Panza," said Don Quixote, "that there is no recollection which time does not put an end to, and no pain which death does not remove."
"And what greater misfortune can there be," replied Panza, "than the one that waits for time to put an end to it and death to remove it?"
CERVANTES, *Don Quixote*. Pt. ii, ch. 15.

9
Most of our misfortunes are more supportable than the comments of our friends upon them.
C. C. COLTON, *Lacon*. Vol. i, No. 517.

10
By speaking of our misfortunes we often relieve them. (À raconter ses maux souvent on les soulage.)
CORNEILLE, *Polyeucte*. Act i, sc. 3. *See also* GRIEF: SILENT AND VOCAL.

11
The misfortunes hardest to bear are those which never come.
J. R. LOWELL, *Democracy: Address*, Birmingham, 6 Oct., 1884. *See also* TROUBLE: NEVER TROUBLE TROUBLE.

12
There is no misfortune but to bear it nobly is good fortune. (Οὐχ ὅτι τοῦτο ἀτύχημα, ἀλλὰ τὸ φέρειν αὐτὸ γενναίως εὐτύχημα.)
MARCUS AURELIUS, *Meditations*. Bk. iv, sec. 49.

13
In misfortune, if you muster a brave spirit, it helps. (In re mala animo si bono utare, adjuvat.)
PLAUTUS, *Captivi*, l. 202. (Act ii, sc. 1.)

14
To bear misfortune is a light thing; to endure it to the end is a heavy thing. (Leve est miserias ferre, perferre est grave.)
SENECA, *Thyestes*, l. 307.

15
From good to bad, and from bad to worse,
From worse unto that is worst of all,
And then return to his former fall.
SPENSER, *The Shepheardes Calender: February*.

The worst is not
So long as we can say, "This is the worst."
SHAKESPEARE, *King Lear*. Act iv, sc. 1, l. 29.

Things at the worst will cease, or else climb upward
To what they were before.
SHAKESPEARE, *Macbeth*. Act iv, sc. 2, l. 24.

16
Yield not to misfortunes, but go all the more boldly to face them. (Tu ne cede malis, sed contra audentior ito.)
VERGIL, *Æneid*. Bk. vi, l. 95. *See* BEHAVIOR.

MISSIONARY

17
A machine for converting the heathen.
CARLYLE, *Signs of the Times*. Referring to the Bible Society.

18
Our noble society for providing the infant negroes in the West Indies with flannel waistcoats and moral pocket-handkerchiefs.
DICKENS, *Pickwick Papers*. Ch. 27.

Never have a mission, my dear child.
DICKENS, *Bleak House*. Ch. 30.

1
Things are saturated with moral law. . . . Every cause in Nature is nothing but a disguised missionary.

EMERSON, *Lectures: Perpetual Forces.*

I won't give you a damned cent. There don't half enough of them go there now.

HORACE GREELEY, to a man soliciting money for missionary work, "to save millions of your fellow creatures from going to hell." (*Unpublished Diaries of Mark Twain.*)

2
From Greenland's icy mountains,
From India's coral strand,
Where Afric's sunny fountains
Roll down their golden sand;
From many an ancient river,
From many a palmy plain,
They call us to deliver
Their land from error's chain.

REGINALD HEBER, *Missionary Hymn.*

3
Or hand his tracts to the untractable.

THOMAS HOOD, *A Recipe.*

4
Men go to the East to convert the infidels. And the infidels pervert them.

BERNARD SHAW, *Saint Joan.* Act iv.

5
God sifted a whole nation that he might send choice grain over into this wilderness.

WILLIAM STOUGHTON, *Election Sermon,* Boston, 29 Apr., 1669.

6
If I were a Cassowary
On the plains of Timbuctoo,
I would eat a missionary,
Coat and bands and hymn-book too.

BISHOP SAMUEL WILBERFORCE, *Epigram.*

MISTAKE

See also Error

7
And one by one in turn, some grand mistake
Casts off its bright skin yearly like the snake.

BYRON, *Don Juan.* Canto v, st. 21.

8
I can pardon everybody's mistakes except my own. (*Συγγνώμην διδόναι πᾶσι τοῖς ἁμαρτάνουσι πλὴν αὑτου.*)

MARCUS CATO. (PLUTARCH, *Lives: Marcus Cato.* Ch. viii, sec. 9.)

9
Any man may make a mistake; none but a fool will persist in it. (Cujusvis hominis est errare; nullius, nisi insipientis, in errore perseverare.)

CICERO, *Philippicæ.* No. xii, ch. 2, sec. 5.

10
Half our mistakes in life arise from feeling where we ought to think, and thinking where we ought to feel.

CHURTON COLLINS, *Aphorisms.*

11
To avoid all mistakes in the conduct of great enterprises is beyond man's powers. (*Τὸ μὲν ἁμαρτεῖν μηδὲν ἐν πράγμασι μεγάοις μεῖζον ἢ κατ' ἄνθρωπόν ἐστι.*)

FABIUS MAXIMUS. (PLUTARCH, *Lives: Fabius.* Ch. 13, sec. 1.)

12
Mistakes are often the best teachers.

J. A. FROUDE, *Short Studies on Great Subjects: Education.*

13
The wrong sow by the ear.

JOHN HEYWOOD, *Proverbs.* Pt. ii, ch. 9. (1546)

He has the wrong sow by the ear.

BEN JONSON, *Every Man in His Humour,* ii, 1.

14
I refused to admit that I had made a *faux pas,* and told my critics to go to Halifax.

L. J. JENNINGS, *Chestnuts and Small Beer,* 140.

15
The man who makes no mistakes does not usually make anything.

BISHOP W. C. MAGEE, *Sermon,* Peterborough, 1868; quoted by E. J. Phelps, *Speech,* Mansion House, London, 24 Jan., 1889.

Had she not been mistaken, she would have accomplished less. (Si non errasset, fecerit illa minus.)

R. W. EMERSON, *Journal,* 1857, referring to Delia Bacon, whose *Philosophy of Shakespeare's Plays Unfolded* he had been reading.

16
How a good meaning
May be corrupted by a misconstruction!

MIDDLETON AND MASSINGER, *The Old Law.* Act i, sc. 1.

17
The shortest mistakes are always the best. (Les plus courtes erreurs sont toujours les meilleures.)

MOLIÈRE, *L'Étourdi.* Act iv, sc. 3, l. 24.

The shortest follies are the best. (Les plus courtes folies sont les meilleures.)

PIERRE CHARRON, *Traité de la Sagesse.* Bk. i, 38.

18
Mistakes remembered are not faults forgot.

R. H. NEWELL, *Columbia's Agony.* St. 9.

19
Leave no rubs nor botches in the work.

SHAKESPEARE, *Macbeth.* Act iii, sc. 1, l. 135.

20
Earth bears no balsam for mistakes;
Men crown the knave, and scourge the tool
That did his will: but thou, O Lord,
Be merciful to me, a fool.

E. R. SILL, *The Fool's Prayer.*

21
Nobody confines his mistakes to himself; people sprinkle folly among their neighbors and receive it from them in turn.

SENECA, *Epistulæ ad Lucilium.* Epis. xciv, 54.

22
The wise course is to profit from the mistakes of others. (Periculum ex aliis facto tibi quod ex usu siet.)

TERENCE, *Heauton Timorumenos,* l. 221.

Wise men learn by other men's mistakes, fools by their own.

H. G. Bohn, *Handbook of Proverbs,* p. 570.

See also under Example.

1

To make mistakes as we are on the way to knowledge is far more honourable than to escape making them through never having set out to seek knowledge.

R. C. Trench, *The Study of Words.* Lecture 7.

2

There is no mistake; there has been no mistake; and there shall be no mistake.

Duke of Wellington, *Letter to Mr. Huskisson.* Whence the slang expression, "And no mistake." (*Words on Wellington,* p. 122.)

3

The only things one never regrets are one's mistakes.

Oscar Wilde, *Picture of Dorian Gray.* Ch. 3.

MISTRESS

4

The world, as usual, wickedly inclined . . .
Whispered he had a mistress, some said *two,*
But for domestic quarrels *one* will do.

Byron, *Don Juan.* Canto i, st. 19.

5

As Juan mused on mutability,
Or on his mistress—terms synonymous.

Byron, *Don Juan.* Canto xvi, st. 20.

But on the whole they were a happy pair,
As happy as unlawful love could make them;
The gentleman was fond, the lady fair,
Their chains so slight, 'twas not worth while to break them.

Byron, *Beppo.* St. 54.

Not that he had no cares to vex,
He loved the muses and the sex;
And sometimes these so froward are,
They made him wish himself at war;
But soon his wrath being o'er, he took
Another mistress, or new book.

Byron, *Mazeppa.* St. 4.

6

A Mistress moderately fair,
And good as guardian angels are,
Only belov'd and loving me.

Abraham Cowley, *The Wish.* St. 2.

7

No, I will have mistresses.

George II, in reply to Queen Caroline, when, as she lay dying, she urged him to marry again. "Ah, good heavens," was her reply, "that doesn't prevent it." ("Non, j'aurai des maîtresses." "Ah! mon dieu! Cela n'empêche pas.")

8

A poet's Mistress is a hallowed thing.

Richard Monckton Milnes, *Tempe.*

9

Few men have wedded their sweethearts, their paramours or mistresses, but have come home by Weeping Cross, and ere long repented their bargain.

Montaigne, *Essays.* Bk. iii, ch. 5.

10

Chaste to her husband, frank to all beside,
A teeming mistress, but a barren bride.

Pope, *Moral Essays.* Epis. ii, l. 71.

11

To each of you one fair and virtuous mistress.

Shakespeare, *All's Well that Ends Well.* Act ii, sc. 3, l. 63.

Or study where to meet some mistress fine,
When mistresses from common sense are hid.

Shakespeare, *Love's Labour's Lost.* Act i, sc. 1, l. 63.

Your mistresses dare never come in rain
For fear their colours should be wash'd away.

Shakespeare, *Love's Labour's Lost.* Act iv, sc. 3, l. 270.

12

And every one his love-feat will advance
Unto his several mistress.

Shakespeare, *Love's Labour's Lost.* Act v, sc. 2, l. 123.

The bouncing Amazon, Your buskin'd mistress.

Shakespeare, *A Midsummer-Night's Dream.* Act ii, sc. 1, l. 74.

Now you are metamorphosed with a mistress.

Shakespeare, *The Two Gentlemen of Verona.* Act ii, sc. 1, l. 32.

13

How d'you like her? Puts old Velasquez in his place. A young mistress is better than an old master, eh?

H. G. Wells, *Autocracy of Mr. Parham.* Ch. 3.

14

A mistress should be like a little country retreat near the town; not to dwell in constantly, but only for a night and away.

Wycherley, *The Country Wife.* Act i.

Next to the pleasure of making a new mistress is that of being rid of an old one.

Wycherley, *The Country Wife.* Act i.

MOB, THE, see People, The

MOCKERY, see Ridicule

MODERATION

See also Content, Temperance

I—Moderation: Apothegms

15

Moderation is best. (Μέτρον ἄριστον.)

Cleobulus of Lindus, one of the seven wise men of Greece, who died 579 B.C. This phrase, his maxim, is said to have been inscribed on the wall of the temple of Apollo at Delphi. The Latin form is, "Optimus modus." (Diogenes Laertius, *Cleobulus.* Bk. i, sec. 93.)

Is not ariston metron "moderation is best"? ("Ἄριστον μέτρον an sit optimus modus?)

Cleobulus. (Ausonius, *Ludus Septem Sapientum,* l. 152.)

Observe moderation: proportion is best in all

things. (Μέτρα φυλάσσεσθαι· καιρὸς δ' ἐπὶ πᾶσιν ἄριστος.)
HESIOD, *Works and Days*, l. 694.

I, who have so much and so universally adored this ἄριστον μέτρον, "excellent moderation," of ancient times, and who have concluded the most moderate measure the most perfect, shall I pretend to an unreasonable and prodigious old age?
MONTAIGNE, *Essays*. Bk. iii, ch. 3.

Be not too zealous; moderation is best in all things. (Μηδὲν ἄγαν σπεύδειν πάντων μέσ' ἄριστα.)
THEOGNIS, *Sententiæ*. No. 335.

1
By God, Mr. Chairman, at this moment I stand astonished at my own moderation.
ROBERT CLIVE, LORD CLIVE, *Retort*, during cross-examination at Parliamentary inquiry, 1773.

1a
To find the medium asks some share of wit,
And therefore 'tis a mark fools never hit.
COWPER, *Conversation*, l. 879.

2
Little wealth, little care.
GEORGE HERBERT, *Jacula Prudentum*.

A little with quiet is the only diet.
GEORGE HERBERT, *Jacula Prudentum*.

3
There is measure in all things; certain limits, beyond and short of which right cannot be found. (Est modus in rebus, sunt certi denique fines, Quos ultra citraque nequit consistere rectum.)
HORACE, *Satires*. Bk. i, sat. 1, l. 106.

In everything, I wot, there lieth measure.
CHAUCER, *Troilus and Criseyde*. Bk. ii, l. 715. (c. 1380)

Measure is a merry mean.
JOHN RUSSELL, *Boke of Nurture*, l. 107. (c. 1450)

For measure is treasure.
FRANCIS SEGER, *School of Virtue*. (1557)

4
My glass is not large, but I drink from my glass. (Mon verre n'est pas grand, mais je bois dans mon verre.)
ALFRED DE MUSSET.

5
Moderation is the languor and sloth of the soul, as ambition is its activity and ardor. (La modération est la langueur et la paresse de l'âme, comme l'ambition en est l'activité et l'ardeur.)
LA ROCHEFOUCAULD, *Maximes*. No. 293.

6
Who wishes to travel far spares his steed. (Qui veut voyager loin ménage sa monture.)
RACINE, *Les Plaideurs*. Act i, sc. 1.

7
Things that are moderate last a long while. (Moderata durant.)
SENECA, *Troades*, l. 259.

Short is the duration of things which are immoderate. (Immodicis brevis est ætas.)
MARTIAL, *Epigrams*. Bk. vi, ep. 29, l. 7.

They are as sick that surfeit with too much as they that starve with nothing: it is no mean happiness therefore, to be seated in the mean: superfluity comes sooner by white hairs, but competency lives longer.
SHAKESPEARE, *The Merchant of Venice*. Act i, sc. 2, l. 5.

8
Be moderate, be moderate.
SHAKESPEARE, *Troilus and Cressida*. Act iv, sc. 4, l. 1.

II—Moderation: The Golden Mean

9
The golden mean is free from trips.
STEPHEN GOSSON, *Pleasant Quips*, p. 14. (1596)

Safely he jogs along the way which "Golden Mean" the sages call;
Who scales the brow of frowning Alp must face full many a slip and fall.
SIR RICHARD BURTON, *The Kasîdah*. Pt. viii, st. 12.

10
Whoso cultivates the golden mean, avoids the poverty of a hovel and the envy of a palace. (Auream quisquis mediocritatem
Diligit, tutus caret obsoleti
Sordibus tecti, caret invidenda
Sobrius aula.)
HORACE, *Odes*. Bk. ii, ode 10, l. 5.

He that holds fast the golden mean,
And lives contentedly between
The little and the great,
Feels not the wants that pinch the poor,
Nor plagues that haunt the rich man's door,
Imbittering all his state.
HORACE, *Odes*, ii, 10. (Cowper, tr.)

11
The golden rule in life is moderation in all things. (Adprime in vita esse utile, ut ne quid nimis.)
TERENCE, *Andria*, l. 61. (Act i, sc. 1.)

12
The proper mean. (Le juste milieu.)
VOLTAIRE, *Letter to Comte d'Argental*, 29 Nov., 1765; PASCAL, *Pensées*.

13
The golden mean, and quiet flow
Of truths that soften hatred, temper strife.
WORDSWORTH, *Ecclesiastical Sonnets*. Pt. iii, No. 11.

III—Moderation: Nothing in Excess

14
Nothing to excess. That is enough, or precept too will run to excess. (Nil nimium. Satis hoc, ne sit et hoc nimium.)
ANACHARSIS. (AUSONIUS [?], *Septem Sapientum Sententiæ*, l. 49.)

15
Nothing in excess. (Μηδὲν ἄγαν.)
EURIPIDES. (AUSONIUS, *Ludus Septem Sapientum*, l. 156.)

Nothing in excess. (Μηδὲν ἄγαν.)
SOLON. (DIOGENES LAERTIUS, *Solon*. Bk. i, sec. 63. Laertius also ascribes the saying to Soc-

rates, who lived two centuries later. Bk. ii, sec. 32: "Being once asked in what consisted the virtue of a young man, Socrates said, 'In doing nothing in excess.'"—Τὸ μηδὲν ἄγαν.) The more familiar Latin form is, "Ne quid nimis." With the equally famous, "Know thyself" (Γνῶθι σεαυτόν), it was inscribed on the temple of Apollo at Delphi.

1
Everything in excess is opposed to nature. (Πᾶν γάρ τὸ πολὺ πολέμιον τῇ φύσει.)

HIPPOCRATES, *Aphorisms*. Bk. ii, No. 3.

The best things carried to excess are wrong.

CHARLES CHURCHILL, *The Rosciad*, l. 1039.

2
Well observe
The rule of *Not too much*, by temperance taught.

MILTON, *Paradise Lost*. Bk. xi, l. 527.

This modest charm of not too much,
Part seen, imagined part.

WORDSWORTH, *To May*, l. 95.

3
In everything the middle course is best. All excess brings trouble to mankind. (Modus omnia nimium exhibent optimus est habitu. Nimia omnia nimium exhibent negoti hominibus ex se.)

PLAUTUS, *Pœnulus*, l. 238. (Act i, sc. 2.)

4
Between excess and famine lies a mean;
Plain, but not sordid; tho' not splendid, clean.

POPE, *Imitations of Horace: Satires*. Bk. ii, sat. 2, l. 47.

5
The too constant use even of good things is hurtful. (Bonarum rerum consuetudo pessima est.)

PUBLILIUS SYRUS, *Sententiæ*. No. 55.

He who has plenty of pepper will pepper his cabbage.

PUBLILIUS SYRUS, *Sententiæ*. No. 673.

6
It is the quality of a great soul to despise great things, and to prefer moderation to excess. (Magni animi est magna contemnere, ac mediocria malle quam nimia.)

SENECA, *Epistulæ ad Lucilium*. Epis. xxxix, 4.

7
Why then, can one desire too much of a good thing?

SHAKESPEARE, *As You Like It*. Act iv, sc. 1, l. 124.

Can we ever have too much of a good thing?

CERVANTES, *Don Quixote*. Pt. i, ch. 6.

People may have *too much* of a good *thing*.

JOHN WOLCOT, *Subjects for Painters: The Gentleman and His Wife*.

8
To gild refined gold, to paint the lily,
To throw a perfume on the violet,
To smooth the ice, or add another hue
Unto the rainbow, or with taper-light
To seek the beauteous eye of heaven to garnish,
Is wasteful and ridiculous excess.

SHAKESPEARE, *King John*. Act iv, sc. 2, l. 11.

But Shakespeare also says, 'tis very silly
"To gild refined gold, or paint the lily."

BYRON, *Don Juan*. Canto iii, st. 76.

9
Moderation is a fatal thing. Nothing succeeds like excess.

OSCAR WILDE, *A Woman of No Importance*. Act iii.

The road of excess leads to the palace of wisdom.

WILLIAM BLAKE, *Proverbs of Hell*.

There is moderation even in excess.

BENJAMIN DISRAELI, *Vivian Grey*. Bk. vi, ch. 1.

IV—Moderation: Living on Little

10
Men live better on little. (Vivitur exiguo melius.)

CLAUDIAN, *In Rufinum*. Bk. i, l. 215.

Our portion is not large, indeed;
But then how little do we need,
For Nature's calls are few!
In this the art of living lies,
To want no more than may suffice,
And make that little do.

We'll therefore relish with content,
Whate'er kind Providence has sent,
Nor aim beyond our pow'r;
For, if our stock be very small,
'Tis prudent to enjoy it all,
Nor lose the present hour.

NATHANIEL COTTON, *The Fireside*. Sts. 9, 10.

11
He who understands the limits of life knows how easy it is to procure enough to remove the pain of want and make the whole life complete and perfect. Hence he has no longer any need of things which are to be won only by labor and conflict.

EPICURUS, *Sovran Maxims*. No. 21.

12
He will always be a slave who does not know how to live upon a little. (Serviet æternum, quia parvo nesciet uti.)

HORACE, *Epistles*. Bk. i, epis. 10, l. 41.

Let's live with that small pittance which we have;
Who covets more is evermore a slave.

HERRICK, *The Covetous Still Captive*.

13
What, and how great, the virtue and the art
To live on little with a cheerful heart!
(Quæ virtus et quanta, boni, sit vivere parvo.)

HORACE, *Satires*. Bk. ii, sat. 2, l. 1. (Pope, tr.)

14
O Luxury, extravagant of resources and never satisfied with what costs little, . . . learn how little it costs to prolong life, and how little nature demands. . . . Running water and bread are enough for mankind.

LUCAN, *De Bello Civili*. Bk. iv, l. 373.

1
Thou seest how few be the things, the which if a man has at his command his life flows gently on and is divine.

MARCUS AURELIUS, *Meditations*. Bk. ii, sec. 5.

Remember this,—that very little is needed to make a happy life. (Τούτου μέμνησο ἀεί, καὶ ἔτι ἐκείνου, ὅτι ἐν ὀλιγίστοις κεῖται τὸ εὐδαιμόνως βιῶσαι.)

MARCUS AURELIUS, *Meditations*. Bk. vii, sec. 67.

2
How many things I can do without! (Πόσων ἐγὼ χρείαν οὐκ ἔχω.)

SOCRATES, on looking in the shop windows. (DIOGENES LAERTIUS, *Socrates*. Sec. 8.)

3
Man's rich with little, were his judgment true;
Nature is frugal, and her wants are few;
These few wants answer'd, brings sincere delights,
But fools create themselves new appetites.

YOUNG, *Love of Fame*. Sat. v, l. 166.

V—Moderation: Enough Is As Good As a Feast

4
Enough sufficeth for the wise. (Ἐπεὶ τὰ γ' ἀρκοῦνθ' ἱκανὰ τοῖς γε σώφροσιν.)

EURIPIDES, *Phœnissai*, l. 554.

Now that's enough! (Jam satis est.)

MARTIAL, *Epigrams*. Bk. iv, epig. 89, l. 1.

Who has enough, of no more has he need.

ROBERT HENRYSON, *Town and Country Mouse*.

Enough, with over-measure.

SHAKESPEARE, *Coriolanus*. Act iii, sc. 1, l. 140.

5
As good is enough as a great feast.

JOHN LYDGATE, *Assembly of Gods*, 59. (c. 1420)

Enough is as good as a feast.

JOHN HEYWOOD, *Proverbs*. Pt. ii, ch. 11. (1546) Also CHAPMAN, *Eastward Hoe*, iii, 2; VANBRUGH, *Relapse*, v; BICKERSTAFFE, *Love in a Village*, iii, 1, and many others.

6
"Pray take them, Sir—enough's a feast;
Eat some, and pocket up the rest."

POPE, *Imitations of Horace: Epistles*. Bk. i, epis. vii, l. 24.

7
Distribution should undo excess,
And each man have enough.

SHAKESPEARE, *King Lear*. Act iv, sc. 1, l. 73. Cited by Huey Long as his goal in his "Share the wealth" program.

8
I neither want nor yet abound,—
Enough's a feast, content is crowned.

JOSHUA SYLVESTER, *A Contented Mind*.

9
Enough is a plenty, too much is a pride.

THOMAS TUSSER, *Hundred Points of Good Husbandry: Dinner Matters*.

VI—Moderation: Its Virtues

10
Moderation, the noblest gift of Heaven. (Σωφροσύνα, δώρημα κάλλιστον Θεῶν.)

EURIPIDES, *Medea*, l. 635.

Moderation: a virtue not to be despised by the most exalted among men, and prized also by the gods.

TACITUS, *Annals*. Bk. xv, sec. 2.

11
Moderation is the silken string running through the pearl-chain of all virtues.

THOMAS FULLER, *Holy and Profane States*: Bk. iii, *Of Moderation*. Quoted by Bishop Joseph Hall in the introduction to *Christian Moderation* as an Oriental proverb.

12
True happiness springs from moderation. (Aus Mässigkeit entspringt ein reines Glück.)

GOETHE, *Die Natürliche Tochter*. Act ii, sc. 5.

13
Let him who has enough ask for nothing more. (Quod satis est cui contigit, nihil amplius optet.)

HORACE, *Epistles*. Bk. i, epis. ii, l. 46.

Give us enough but with a sparing hand.

EDMUND WALLER, *Reflections*.

You never know what is enough unless you know what is more than enough.

WILLIAM BLAKE, *Proverbs of Hell*.

14
He who desires only what is enough, is troubled neither by raging seas, nor hail-smitten vineyards, nor an unproductive farm. (Desiderantem quod satis est neque Tumultuosum sollicitat mare, . . . Non verberatæ grandine vineæ Fundusque mendax.)

HORACE, *Odes*. Bk. iii, ode 1, l. 25.

15
The moderation of fortunate people comes from the calm which good fortune gives to their tempers. (La modération des personnes heureuses vient du calme que la bonne fortune donne à leur humeur.)

LA ROCHEFOUCAULD, *Maximes*. No. 17.

Moderation is like sobriety: one would like to eat more, but one fears to make oneself ill. (La modération est comme la sobriété: on voudrait bien manger davantage, mais on craint de se faire mal.)

LA ROCHEFOUCAULD, *Maximes*. No. 507.

16
Enjoy thy possessions as if about to die, and use them sparingly, as if about to live. That man is wise who understands both these commandments, and hath applied a measure both to thrift and unthrift.

LUCIAN. (*Greek Anthology*. Bk. x, epig. 26.)

It is great riches to a man to live sparingly with an even mind. (Divitiæ grandes homini sunt, vivere parce Æquo animo.)

LUCRETIUS, *De Rerum Natura*. Bk. v, l. 1117.

17
Take this at least, this last advice, my son:

Keep a stiff rein, and move but gently on:
The coursers of themselves will run too fast,
Your art must be to moderate their haste.

OVID, *Metamorphoses*. Bk. ii, l. 147. (Addison, tr.) The story of Phaëton.

Up hill, our course is rather slow;
Down hill, how merrily we go;
But when 'tis neither up nor down,
It is a middling pace I own.

WILLIAM COMBE, *Dr. Syntax in Search of the Picturesque*. Canto xxii, l. 227.

1
In many things the middle have the best; be mine a middle station. (Πολλὰ μέσοισιν ἄριστα. Μέσος Θέλω ἐν πόλει εἶναι.)

PHOCYLIDES, *Fragment*. (ARISTOTLE, *Politics*, iv, 6, 8.)

Tenants of life's middle state,
Securely plac'd between the small and great,
Whose character, yet undebauch'd, retains
Two-thirds of all the virtue that remains.

COWPER, *Tirocinium*, l. 807.

He knows to live who keeps the middle state,
And neither leans on this side nor on that.

POPE, *Imitations of Horace: Satires*. Bk. ii, sat. 2, l. 61.

2
Give me neither poverty nor riches; feed me with food convenient for me.

Old Testament: Proverbs, xxx, 8.

3
Only moderation gives charm to life. (Nur Maas ihm Reiz.)

JEAN PAUL RICHTER, *Titan*. Zykel 145.

4
A thatched roof once covered free men; under marble and gold dwells slavery. (Culmus liberos texit, sub marmore atque auro servitus habitat.)

SENECA, *Epistulæ ad Lucilium*. Epis. xc, sec. 10.

5
In modesty of fortune there are the fewer dangers. (Ex mediocritate fortunæ, pauciora pericula sunt.)

TACITUS, *Annals*. Bk. xiv, sec. 60.

6
There is a limit to enjoyment, though the sources of wealth be boundless,
And the choicest pleasures of life lie within the ring of moderation.

M. F. TUPPER, *Proverbial Philosophy: Of Compensation*, l. 15.

VII—Moderation: Some Wishes

7
In the downhill of life when I find I'm declining,
May my lot no less fortunate be
Than a snug elbow-chair can afford for reclining,
And a cot that looks o'er the wide sea.

JOHN COLLINS, *In the Downhill of Life*.

8
Ah, yet, e'er I descend to th' grave,
May I a small House and large Garden have,
And a few Friends, and many Books, both true,
Both wise, and both delightful too.

ABRAHAM COWLEY, *The Wish*. St. 2.

This only grant me, that my means may lie
Too low for envy, for contempt too high.

ABRAHAM COWLEY, *Of Myself*.

9
Some have too much, yet still they crave;
I little have, yet seek no more:
They are but poor, though much they have,
And I am rich with little store:
They poor, I rich; they beg, I give;
They lack, I lend; they pine, I live.

SIR EDWARD DYER, *My Mind to Me a Kingdom Is*. St. 5.

10
May heaven (it's all I wish for) send
One genial room to treat a friend,
Where decent cupboard, little plate,
Display benevolence, not state.
And may my humble dwelling stand
Upon some chosen spot of land:
A pond before full to the brim,
Where cows may cool, and geese may swim;
Behind, a green like velvet neat,
Soft to the eye, and to the feet.

MATTHEW GREEN, *The Spleen*, l. 642.

11
Give me a three-legged table, a shell of clean salt, and a coat that, however coarse, will keep out the cold. (Sit mihi mensa tripes et Concha salis puri et toga, quæ defendere frigus Quamvis, crassa queat.)

HORACE, *Satires*. Bk. i, sat. 3, l. 13.

12
This is what I prayed for: a piece of land not very large, where there would be a garden, and near the house a spring of ever-flowing water, and above these a bit of woodland. More and better than this have the gods done for me. I am content.
(Hoc erat in votis: modus agri non ita magnus.
Hortus ubi et tecto vicinus jugis aquæ fons
Et paulum silvæ super his foret. Auctius atque
Di melius fecere. Bene est.)

HORACE, *Satires*. Bk. ii, sat. 6, l. 1. The opening words give expression, not to a wish, but to satisfaction as the poet looks out across his little farm, the realization of his dreams. Hence the past tense of *erat*.

Give me, ye gods, the produce of one field,
That so I neither may be rich nor poor;
And having just enough, not covet more.

DRYDEN, *Imitation of Horace*.

O grant me, Heaven, a middle state,
Neither too humble nor too great;
More than enough for nature's ends,
With something left to treat my friends.

DAVID MALLET, *Imitation of Horace*.

I've often wish'd that I had clear
For life, six hundred pounds a year;
A handsome house to lodge a friend;
A river at my garden's end;
A terrace walk, and half a rood
Of land set out to plant a wood.
SWIFT, *Imitation of Horace*. Bk. ii, sat. 6.

1 In all my wand'rings round this world of care,
In all my griefs—and God has given my share—
I still had hopes my latest hours to crown,
Amidst these humble bowers to lay me down.
GOLDSMITH, *The Deserted Village*, l. 83.

2 Ye gods! my wishes are confined
To—health of body, peace of mind,
Clean linen, and a guinea!
EDWARD LYSAGHT, *Ambition*.

3 That spot of ground pleases me in which small possession makes me happy, and where slight resources are abundant. (Illa placet tellus in qua res parva beatum Me facit et tenues luxuriantur opes.)
MARTIAL, *Epigrams*. Bk. x, ep. 96, l. 5.

If I live to grow old, as I find I go down,
Let this be my fate: in a country town,
May I have a warm house, with a stone at my gate,
And a cleanly young girl to rub my bald pate.
May I govern my passions with absolute sway,
Grow wiser and better as my strength wears away,
Without gout or stone, by a gentle decay.
WALTER POPE, *The Old Man's Wish*. (1685)

4 Mine be a cot beside the hill;
A bee-hive's hum shall soothe my ear;
A willowy brook, that turns a mill,
With many a fall, shall linger near.
SAMUEL ROGERS, *A Wish*.

5 Give me, indulgent gods! with mind serene,
And guiltless heart, to range the sylvan scene;
No splendid poverty, no smiling care,
No well-bred hate, or servile grandeur, there.
YOUNG, *Love of Fame*. Sat. i, l. 243.

MODESTY

See also Blushing, Humility

I—Modesty: Definitions

6 Modesty cannot properly be described as a virtue, for it is a feeling rather than a disposition—a kind of fear of disrepute.
ARISTOTLE, *Nicomachean Ethics*. Bk. iv, ch. 9, sec. 1.

7 Modesty is the only sure bait when you angle for praise.
LORD CHESTERFIELD, *Letters*, 8 May, 1750.

8 Modesty is that feeling by which honorable shame acquires a valuable and lasting authority.
CICERO, *De Inventione Rhetorica*. Bk. ii, 56.

9 Modesty is the citadel of beauty and of virtue. (Αἰδὼς τοῦ καλοῦ καὶ ἀρετῆς πόλις.)
DEMADES, *Peri Dodekœtias*. (MÜLLER, *Oratores Attici*. Vol. ii, p. 438.)

10 Modesty is often mistaken for secrecy, and silence for bad temper. (Plerumque modestus Occupat obscuri speciem, taciturnitus acerbi.)
HORACE, *Epistles*. Bk. i, epis. 18, l. 94.

11 Modesty, and unstained Honor, sister to Justice. (Pudor, et Justiciæ soror, Incorrupta Fides.)
HORACE, *Odes*. Bk. i, ode. 24, l. 6.

12 Modesty is to merit what shadows are to a painting; it gives it force and relief. (La modestie est au mérite ce que les ombres sont aux figures dans un tableau: elle lui donne de la force et du relief.)
LA BRUYÈRE, *Les Caractères*. Sec. 2.

13 Modesty antedates clothes and will be resumed when clothes are no more. Modesty died when clothes were born. Modesty died when false modesty was born.
MARK TWAIN. (PAINE, *Life*. Vol. iii, p. 1513.)

II—Modesty: Apothegms

14 With time diffidence dies away in man. (Ἐν χρόνῳ δ' ἀποφθίνει τὸ τάρβος ἀνθρώποισιν.)
ÆSCHYLUS, *Agamemnon*, l. 857.

Modesty does not long survive innocence.
EDMUND BURKE, *Impeachment of Warren Hastings*, 17 Feb., 1788.

15 I'm modesty personified!
W. S. GILBERT, *Ruddigore*. Act i.

I'm shy, nervous, modest, retiring, and diffident.
W. S. GILBERT, *Ruddigore*. Act i.

There's no false modesty about *you*.
W. S. GILBERT, *Ruddigore*. Act i.

16 An impudent fellow may counterfeit modesty, but I'll be hanged if a modest man can ever counterfeit impudence.
GOLDSMITH, *She Stoops to Conquer*. Act ii.

17 A truly modest fellow. (Multum demissus homo.)
HORACE, *Satires*. Bk. i, sat. 3, l. 57.

18 Modesty cannot be taught, it must be born. (Pudor doceri non potest, nasci potest.)
PUBLILIUS SYRUS, *Sententiæ*. No. 492.

Modesty, once banished, never returns. (Pudor dimissus numquam redit.)
PUBLILIUS SYRUS, *Sententiæ*. No. 498.

1
When one remains modest, not after praise but after blame, then is he really so.
JEAN PAUL RICHTER, *Hesperus*. Ch. 12.

2
Everything that is exquisite hides itself.
JOSEPH ROUX, *Meditations of a Parish Priest: Joy*. No. 50.

3
Modesty forbids what the law does not. (Quod non vetat lex, hoc vetat fieri pudor.)
SENECA, *Troades*, l. 334.

4
An act
That blurs the grace and blush of modesty.
SHAKESPEARE, *Hamlet*. Act iii, sc. 4, l. 40.

5
Not stepping o'er the bounds of modesty.
SHAKESPEARE, *Romeo and Juliet*. Act iv, sc. 2, l. 27.

III—Modesty: Its Virtues

6
Ever with the best desert goes diffidence.
ROBERT BROWNING, *A Blot in the 'Scutcheon*. Act i, sc. 2.

7
Modesty sets off one newly come to honour.
GEORGE HERBERT, *Jacula Prudentum*.

Thy modesty's a candle to thy merit.
HENRY FIELDING, *Tom Thumb the Great*. Act i, sc. 3, l. 8.

8
Modesty becomes a young man. (Decet verecundum esse adulescentem.)
PLAUTUS, *Asinaria*, l. 833. (Act v, sc. 1.)

9
I have done one braver thing
Than all the Worthies did,
And yet a braver thence doth spring,
Which is, to keep that hid.
JOHN DONNE, *The Undertaking*.

10
He full of bashfulness and truth,
Loved much, hoped little, and desired naught.
TASSO, *Jerusalem Delivered*. Bk. ii, st. 16. (Fairfax, tr.)

IV—Modesty: Its Faults

11
Modest dogs miss much meat.
JOHN RAY, *English Proverbs*.

12
Modesty in a man is a crime. Don't be modest. It is a woman's virtue.
FREDERICK WARDE, *Interview*, on his 80th birthday, 23 Feb., 1931.

13
All men have their faults; too much modesty is his.
GOLDSMITH, *The Good-Natured Man*. Act ii.

William was once a bashful youth;
His modesty was such,
That one might say (to say the truth),
He rather had too much.
WILLIAM COWPER, *Of Himself*.

14
There is a luxury in self-dispraise;
And inward self-disparagement affords
To meditative spleen a grateful feast.
WORDSWORTH, *The Excursion*. Bk. iv, l. 475.

V—Modesty in Women

15
Modesty is the beauty of women.
UNKNOWN. A Gaelic proverb.

Rare is agreement between beauty and modesty. (Rara est adeo concordia formæ Atque pudicitiæ.)
JUVENAL, *Satires*. Sat. x, l. 297. *See also under* BEAUTY.

16
Her modest looks the cottage might adorn,
Sweet as the primrose peeps beneath the thorn.
GOLDSMITH, *The Deserted Village*, l. 329.

17
Like the violet, which alone
Prospers in some happy shade,
My Castara lives unknown
To no looser eye betrayed.
WILLIAM HABINGTON, *Castara*. (1634)

18
Me of my lawful pleasure she restrain'd
And pray'd me oft forbearance; did it with
A pudency so rosy the sweet view on 't
Might well have warm'd old Saturn.
SHAKESPEARE, *Cymbeline*. Act ii, sc. 5, l. 9.

Modesty may more betray our sense
Than woman's lightness.
SHAKESPEARE, *Measure for Measure*. Act ii, sc. 2, l. 168.

19
Have you no modesty, no maiden shame,
No touch of bashfulness?
SHAKESPEARE, *A Midsummer-Night's Dream*. Act iii, sc. 2, l. 285.

20
He saw her charming, but he saw not half
The charms her downcast modesty conceal'd.
THOMSON, *The Seasons: Autumn*, l. 229.

21
There is no woman, where there's no reserve.
YOUNG, *Love of Fame*. Sat. vi, l. 45.

Let those ankles never swerve
From their exquisite reserve.
ROBERT BROWNING, *Pippa Passes: Introduction*.

22
Naked in nothing should a woman be;
But veil her very wit with modesty:
Let man discover, let her not display,
But yield her charms of mind with sweet delay.
YOUNG, *Love of Fame*. Sat. vi, l. 106.

MOMENT, see Minute

MONARCH, see King

MONEY

See also Avarice; Dollar; Gold; Marriage and Money; Riches

I—Money: Apothegms

1
Money makes the man. (Χρήματ' ἀνήρ.)
ARISTODEMUS. (ALCÆUS, *Fragments*. No. 49; DIOGENES LAERTIUS, *Thales*. Bk. i, sec. 31.)

Heed the Argive's word that cometh nearest to the very truth. "Money, money maketh man," quoth he, when reft of wealth and friends alike. (Χρήματα, χρήματ' ἀνήρ.)
PINDAR, *Isthmian Odes*. No. ii, l. 11. The Argive was Aristodemus.

2
Money makes the man.
THOMAS BECON, *Early Works*, 222. (1542)

Money maketh a man.
WILLIAM BULLEIN, *Dialogue Against the Fever Pestilence*, 102. (1564)

God makes, and apparel shapes, but it's money that finishes the man.
JOHN RAY, *English Proverbs*.

Let all the learn'd say what they can,
'Tis ready money makes the man;
Commands respect where'er we go,
And gives a grace to all we do.
WILLIAM SOMERVILLE, *Ready Money*.

3
Money is the sinews of affairs. (Τὸν πλοῦτον νεῦρα πραγμάτων.)
BION. (DIOGENES LAERTIUS, *Bion*. Bk. iv, sec. 48.)

He who first called money the sinews of affairs seems to have said this with special reference to war.
PLUTARCH, *Lives: Cleomenes*. Ch. 27, sec. 1. *See also* WAR: ITS SINEWS.

4
A fool and his money are soon parted.
GEORGE BUCHANAN, tutor to James VI of Scotland, on winning a wager from a courtier. (WALSH, *Handy-book of Literary Curiosities*, p. 380.) The proverb is of uncertain origin.

A fool and his money be soon at debate.
THOMAS TUSSER, *Five Hundred Points of Good Husbandry: Good Husbandry Lessons*.

He that gets money before he gets wit,
Will be but a short while master of it.
THOMAS FULLER, *Gnomologia*. No. 6432.

5
He that wants money wants everything.
RICHARD CUMBERLAND, *The Fashionable Lover*. Act ii, sc. 1.

A man without money is a bow without an arrow.
THOMAS FULLER, *Gnomologia*. No. 317.

The skilfullest wanting money is scorned.
JOHN RAY, *English Proverbs*, 18.

6
Be it better or be it worse,
Please you the man that bears the purse.
THOMAS DELONEY, *Thomas of Reading*.

7
Wery glad to see you, indeed, and hope our acquaintance may be a long 'un, as the gen'l'm'n said to the fi' pun' note.
DICKENS, *Pickwick Papers*. Ch. 25.

8
Money never cometh out of season.
THOMAS DRAXE, *Bibliotheca*, 82. (1633)

Money in purse will be always in fashion.
THOMAS FULLER, *Gnomologia*. No. 3435.

9
He that hath no money needeth no purse.
THOMAS DRAXE, *Bibliotheca*, 138. (1633)

No eyes in your head, nor no money in your purse?
SHAKESPEARE, *King Lear*. Act iv, sc. 6, l. 148.

10
Money maketh horses run.
JOHN FLORIO, *First Fruites*. Fo. 30. (1578)

Money makes the old mare trot and the young tit amble.
NICHOLAS BRETON, *Works*, ii, 7. (1605)

11
It is money makes the mare to trot.
JOHN WOLCOT, *Ode to Pitt*. (1790)

Will you lend me your mare to go a mile?
No, she is lame leaping o'er a stile.
But, if you will her to me spare,
You shall have money for your mare.
Oh, ho! Say you so?
Money will make the mare to go.
UNKNOWN, *Old Glees and Catches*.

12
If you would know the value of money, go and try to borrow some.
BENJAMIN FRANKLIN, *Poor Richard*, 1758.

13
They who are of the opinion that money will do everything, may very well be suspected to do everything for money.
LORD HALIFAX, *Works*, p. 242.

14
To have money is a fear, not to have it a grief.
GEORGE HERBERT, *Jacula Prudentum*.

15
Money will be slave or master. (Imperat aut servit collecta pecunia cuique.)
HORACE, *Epistles*. Bk. i, epis. 10, l. 47.

Money is a good servant but a bad master. (L'argent est un bon serviteur, mais un méchant maître.)
BACON, *Menegiana*, ii, 296. Quoting a French proverb.

16
Proud of your money you may strut,
But fortune does not change your birth.
(Licet superbus ambules pecunia,
Fortuna non mutat genus.)
HORACE, *Epodes*. No. iv, l. 5.

1
Without money and without price.
Old Testament: Isaiah, lv, 1.

2
Few listen without a desire of conviction to those who advise them to spare their money.
SAMUEL JOHNSON, *The Idler*. No. 26.

3
Loss of money is bewailed with louder lamentations than a death. (Majore tumultu Planguntur nummi quam funera.)
JUVENAL, *Satires*. Sat. xiii, l. 130.

Nothing stings more deeply than the loss of money. (Nec quicquam acrius quam pecuniæ damnum stimulat.)
LIVY, *History*. Bk. xxx, sec. 44.

He has lost his purse. (Zonam perdidit.)
HORACE, *Epistles*. Bk. ii, epis. 2, l. 40.

4
The devil of money has the better end of the staff.
SIR ROGER L'ESTRANGE, *Quevedo's Visions*, 38.

She does not know everything, but she has got hold of the right end of the stick.
BERNARD SHAW, *Saint Joan*. Sc. v.

5
The plainest print cannot be read through a gold eagle.
ABRAHAM LINCOLN, *Speech*, Springfield, Ill., 26 June, 1857.

6
A penny can do no more than it may.
JOHN LYDGATE, *The London Lyckpenny*.

For lack of money I could not speed.
JOHN LYDGATE, *The London Lyckpenny*.

7
Up and down the City Road, in and out the Eagle,
That's the way the money goes—pop goes the weasel!
W. R. MANDALE (attr.), *Pop Goes the Weasel*.

8
A little wanton money, which burned out the bottom of his purse.
SIR THOMAS MORE, *Works*, p. 195. (c. 1530)

Like an unthrift's money that burns in his purse.
SIR WILLIAM CORNWALLIS, *Essays*. Pt. ii. (1601)

My gold has burnt this twelve months in my pocket.
JAMES SHIRLEY, *Hyde Park*. Act iv, sc. 3. (1637)

9
Services for cash. (Opera pro pecunia.)
PLAUTUS, *Asinaria*, l. 172. (Act i, sc. 3.)

We purchase on Greek credit . . . cash. (Græca mercamur fide . . . dant mercem.)
PLAUTUS, *Asinaria*, l. 199. (Act i, sc. 3.) No one would trust the Greeks.

10
He writes his check. (Scribit nummos.)
PLAUTUS, *Asinaria*, l. 400. (Act ii, sc. 4.)

11
By heaven, money is a beautiful gift! (Pulchra Edepol pecunia dos est.)
PLAUTUS, *Epidicus*. Act ii, sc. 1, l. 10.

12
Lack of money is trouble without equal. (Faute d'argent, c'est douleur sans pareille.)
RABELAIS, *Works*. Bk. ii, ch. 16.

He was naturally subject to a kind of disease, which at that time they called lack of money.
RABELAIS, *Works*. Bk. ii, ch. 16.

13
No money, no Swiss. (Point d'argent, point de Suisse.)
RACINE, *Les Plaideurs*. Act i, sc. 1. Originally intended as a gibe at the venality of Swiss mercenaries, the phrase is now used to indicate that what one wants must be paid for.

14
That is but an empty purse that is full of other men's money.
JOHN RAY, *English Proverbs*.

15
The most grievous kind of destitution is to want money in the midst of wealth. (Quod genus egestatis gravissimum est, in divitiis inopes.)
SENECA, *Epistulæ ad Lucilium*. Epis. lxxiv, 4.

A beggar in the midst of wealth. (Magnas inter opes inopes.)
HORACE, *Odes*. Bk. iii, ode. 16, l. 28.

16
My lusty rustic, learn and be instructed. Cole is, in the language of the witty, money; the *ready*, the *rhino*.
SHADWELL, *The Squire of Alsatia*. Act iv. (1688)

17
As for money, enough is enough; no man can enjoy more.
SOUTHEY, *The Doctor*. Ch. 20. *See also* MODERATION: NOTHING IN EXCESS.

18
We have taught them to accept money. (Pecuniam accipere docuimus.)
TACITUS, *Germania*. Sec. 15. Of the Germans.

When it is a question of money, everybody is of the same religion.
VOLTAIRE.

19
Who in his pocket hath no money,
In his mouth he must have honey.
ROWLAND WATKINS, *Flamma Sine Fumo*.

20
Money talks. (Argent fait le jeu.)
UNKNOWN, *Baudoin de Sebourc*. Pt. xxiv, l. 443. *See also under* GOLD.

21
Why is the form of money round? Because it is to run from every man.
UNKNOWN, *Helpe to Discourse*, p. 120. (1640)

Moneys are round, and that makes them roll away.
TORRIANO, *Piazza Universale*, p. 64.

II—Money: Its Power

See also Gold: Its Power; Riches: Their Power

1
She is the Sovereign Queen of all delights;
For her the Lawyer pleads, the Soldier fights.
RICHARD BARNFIELD, *Praise of Lady Pecunia.*

2
Money is the symbol of nearly everything that is necessary for man's well-being and happiness. . . . Money means freedom, independence, liberty.
EDWARD E. BEALS, *The Law of Financial Success.*

3
Money, th' only power
That all mankind falls down before.
BUTLER, *Hudibras.* Pt. iii, canto ii, l. 1327.

Yes! ready money is Aladdin's lamp.
BYRON, *Don Juan.* Canto xii, st. 12.

4
In epochs when cash payment has become the sole nexus of man to man.
CARLYLE, *Chartism.* Ch. 2.

This bank-note world.
FITZ-GREENE HALLECK, *Alnwick Castle.*

5
The best foundation in the world is money. (El mejor cimiento en el mundo es el dinero.)
CERVANTES, *Don Quixote.* Bk. ii, ch. 20.

6
But one thing is, ye know it well enow,
Of chapmen, that their money is their plogh.
CHAUCER, *The Shipmannes Tale,* l. 287.

Money is the god of our time, and Rothschild is his prophet.
HEINE, *Wit, Wisdom and Pathos: Lutetia.*

The world's chief idol, nurse of fretting cares,
Dumb trafficker, yet understood o'er all.
WILLIAM ALEXANDER, *Doomsday: Tenth Hour.*

7
There is no fortress so strong that money cannot take it. (Nihil tam munitum, quod non expugnari pecunia possit.)
CICERO, *In Verrem.* No. 1, sec. 2.

8
As I sat at the café, I said to myself,
They may talk as they please about what they call pelf,
They may sneer as they like about eating and drinking,
But help it I cannot, I cannot help thinking
How pleasant it is to have money, heigh-ho!
How pleasant it is to have money!
ARTHUR HUGH CLOUGH, *Spectator Ab Extra.*

9
Money answereth all things.
Old Testament: Ecclesiastes, x, 19. (Pecuniæ obediunt omnia.—*Vulgate.*)

Money makes mastery.
UNKNOWN, *Liberality and Prodigality,* i, 5. (1602)

Money masters all things.
UNKNOWN, *Loyal Garland.* (1686)

10
Money is ace of trumps.
THOMAS FULLER, *Gnomologia.* No. 3438.

Money is that art which hath turned up trump.
JOHN RAY, *English Proverbs.*

11
Queen Cash gives birth and beauty. (Et genus et formam regina Pecunia donat.)
HORACE, *Epistles.* Bk. i, epis. 6, l. 37.

Sir, money, money, the most charming of all things—money, which will say more in one moment than the most eloquent lover can in years. Perhaps you will say a man is not young; I answer, he is rich; he is not genteel, handsome, witty, brave, good-humored, but he is rich, rich, rich, rich, rich,—that one word contradicts everything you can say against him.
HENRY FIELDING, *The Miser.* Act iii.

O, what a world of vile ill-favour'd faults
Looks handsome in three hundred pounds a-year.
SHAKESPEARE, *The Merry Wives of Windsor.* Act iii, sc. 4, l. 32.

12
According to the amount of money a man has in his coffers, so is he respected. (Quantum quisque sua nummorum servat in arca, Tantum habet et fidei.)
JUVENAL, *Satires.* Sat. iii, l. 143.

Money is honey, my little sonny,
And a rich man's joke is always funny.
THOMAS EDWARD BROWN, *The Doctor.*

13
Money makes the pot boil.
SIR ROGER L'ESTRANGE, *The Fables of Æsop,* p. 305. (1692)

14
The picklock that never fails. [Money]
MASSINGER, *The Unnatural Combat.* Act i, sc. 1.

15
Balzac was the first to perceive "that money was as necessary to a young man in the nineteenth century as a coat of mail was in the fifteenth."
GEORGE MOORE, *Impressions and Opinions: Balzac.*

16
Nothing but money counts nowadays: it wins honors, it wins friends; everywhere the poor man is down. (In pretio pretium nunc est: dat census honores, Census amicitias: pauper ubique jacet.)
OVID, *Fasti.* Bk. i, l. 217.

Money brings honour, friends, conquest, and realms.
MILTON, *Paradise Regained.* Bk. ii, l. 422.

17
See, I pray you, what money can do. (Videte, quæso, quid potest pecunia.)
PLAUTUS, *Stichus.* Act ii, sc. 2.

It is pretty to see what money will do.
SAMUEL PEPYS, *Diary,* 21 Mar., 1667.

1
Money is the ruling spirit of all things. (Pecunia una regimen est rerum omnium.)
PUBLILIUS SYRUS, *Sententiæ*. No. 655.

2
Money cures melancholy.
JOHN RAY, *English Proverbs.*

Money makes a man laugh.
JOHN SELDEN, *Table-Talk: Money.*

3
If money go before, all ways do lie open.
SHAKESPEARE, *The Merry Wives of Windsor.* Act ii, sc. 2, l. 175.

Money is a good soldier, sir, and will on.
SHAKESPEARE, *The Merry Wives of Windsor.* Act ii, sc. 2, l. 176.

4
Money is indeed the most important thing in the world; and all sound and successful personal and national morality should have this fact for its basis.
BERNARD SHAW, *The Irrational Knot: Preface.*

The universal regard for money is the one hopeful fact in our civilization. Money is the most important thing in the world. It represents health, strength, honour, generosity and beauty. . . . Not the least of its virtues is that it destroys base people as certainly as it fortifies and dignifies noble people.
BERNARD SHAW, *Major Barbara: Preface.*

The seven deadly sins. . . . Food, clothing, firing, rent, taxes, respectability and children. Nothing can lift those seven millstones from man's neck but money; and the spirit cannot soar until the millstones are lifted.
BERNARD SHAW, *Major Barbara.* Act iii.

5
It is money that sacks cities, and drives men forth from hearth and home; warps and seduces native innocence, and breeds a habit of dishonesty.
SOPHOCLES, *Antigone*, l. 296.

III—Money: Its Use

See also Riches: Their Use

6
Money is like muck, not good except it be spread.
FRANCIS BACON, *Essays: Of Seditions.*

7
Money was made, not to command our will,
But all our lawful pleasures to fulfil.
Shame and woe to us, if we our wealth obey;
The horse doth with the horseman run away.
ABRAHAM COWLEY, *Imitations of Horace: Epistles.* Bk. i, epis. 10, l. 75.

8
Money is trash; and he that will spend it,
Let him drink merrily, Fortune will send it.
FORD AND DEKKER, *The Sun's Darling.*

My neighbor, a jolly farmer, in the tavern barroom, thinks that the use of money is sure and speedy spending. For his part, he says, he puts his down his neck and gets the good of it.
EMERSON, *Representative Men: Montaigne.*

9
Money is like an arm or a leg—use it or lose it.
HENRY FORD, *Interview*, N. Y. *Times*, 8 Nov., 1931.

10
The use of money is all the advantage there is in having money.
BENJAMIN FRANKLIN, *Hints to Those That Would Be Rich.*

11
If thou wouldst keep money, save money;
If thou wouldst reap money, sow money.
THOMAS FULLER, *Gnomologia.* No. 2721.

12
Surely use alone
Makes money not a contemptible stone.
GEORGE HERBERT, *The Church-Porch.* St. 26.

13
Put not your trust in money, but put your money in trust.
O. W. HOLMES, *The Autocrat of the Breakfast-Table.* Ch. 2.

14
Why is fortune mine, if I may not use it? (Quo mihi fortunam, si non conceditur uti?)
HORACE, *Epistles.* Bk. i, epis. 5, l. 12.

15
Blessed is the man who has both mind and money, for he employs the latter well.
MENANDER, *Demioyplos: Fragment.*

16
You must spend money, if you wish to make money. (Necesse est facere sumptum qui quærit lucrum.)
PLAUTUS, *Asinaria*, l. 217. (Act i, sc. 3.)

17
Money begets money.
JOHN RAY, *English Proverbs.*

Money, says the proverb, makes money.
ADAM SMITH, *Wealth of Nations.* Bk. i, ch. 9.

Remember that money is of a prolific generating nature. Money can beget money, and its offspring can beget more.
BENJAMIN FRANKLIN, *Letters: To My Friend, A. B.* 1748. *See also under* DIVIDENDS.

18
Money is never spent to so much advantage as when you have been cheated out of it: for at one stroke you have purchased prudence.
SCHOPENHAUER, *Aphorisms: Wisdom of Life.*

19
Foul-cankering rust the hidden treasure frets,
But gold that's put to use more gold begets.
SHAKESPEARE, *Venus and Adonis*, l. 767.

20
Where wealth is, there lightly follows more.
GEORGE TURBERVILE, *Tragic Tales*, 22. (1587)

It is not a custom with me to keep money to look at.
GEORGE WASHINGTON, *Letter to J. P. Custis*, January, 1780.

21
In frolics dispose your pounds, shillings and pence;

For we shall be nothing a hundred years hence.
UNKNOWN. (RITSON, *English Songs*, ii, 16.)

IV—Money: Making Money

1
Making money. (Κερδαίνων.)
BIAS, when asked which occupation gives men the most pleasure. (DIOGENES LAERTIUS, *Bias*. Bk. i, sec. 87.)

There are few ways in which a man can be more innocently employed than in getting money.
SAMUEL JOHNSON, *Remark*, to Dr. Strahan. (BOSWELL, *Life*, 1775.)

2
Can anybody remember when the times were not hard, and money not scarce?
EMERSON, *Society and Solitude: Works and Days*.

3
We have heads to get money, and hearts to spend it.
FARQUHAR, *The Beaux' Stratagem*. Act i, sc. 1.

4
I am not in the least versed in the Chrematistic art.
FIELDING, *Amelia*. Bk. ix, ch. 5.

5
Money you must seek first; virtue after pelf. (Quærenda pecunia primum est; virtus post nummos!)
HORACE, *Epistles*. Bk. i, epis. 1, l. 53.

Make money, money by fair means, if you can; if not, by any means money. (Rem facias, rem, Si possis, recte, si non, quocumque modo, rem.)
HORACE, *Epistles*. Bk. i, epis. 1, l. 65.

Here Wisdom calls, "Seek Virtue first, be bold!
As gold to silver, Virtue is to gold."
There London's voice, "Get money, money still!
And then let Virtue follow if she will."
This, this the saving doctrine preach'd to all,
From low St. James's up to high St. Paul.
POPE, *Imitations of Horace: Epistles*. Bk. i, epis. 1, l. 77.

Get Place and Wealth, if possible with grace;
If not, by any means get Wealth and Place.
POPE, *Imitations of Horace: Epistles*. Bk. i, epis. 1, l. 103.

6
Money is welcome tho' it be in a dirty clout, but 'tis far more acceptable if it come in a clean handkerchief.
JAMES HOWELL, *Familiar Letters*. Bk. ii, letter 25.

7
The rule get money, still get money, boy;
No matter by what means.
BEN JONSON, *Every Man in His Humour*. Act ii, sc. 3.

8
"No matter whence the money comes, but money you must have." This is the lesson taught by skinny old nurses to little boys before they can walk; this is what every girl learns before her alphabet. ("Unde habeas quærit nemo, sed oportet habere." Hoc monstrant vetulæ pueris repentibus assæ, Hoc discunt omnes ante alpha et beta puellæ.)
JUVENAL, *Satires*. Sat. xiv, l. 207.

What is infamy so long as our money is safe? (Quid enim salvis infamia nummis?)
JUVENAL, *Satires*. Sat. i, l. 48.

9
It is easy at any moment to resign the possession of a great fortune; to acquire it is difficult and arduous. (Facile est momento quo quis velit, cedere possessione magnæ fortunæ; facere et parare eam, difficile atque arduum est.)
LIVY, *History*. Bk. xxiv, sec. 22.

10
O Lord, the sin
Done for the things there's money in.
JOHN MASEFIELD, *The Everlasting Mercy*.

11
Money tumbles into the hands of certain men as a dollar tumbles down a sewer. (Quæ sic in quosdam homines quomodo denarius in cloacam cadit.)
SENECA, *Epistulæ ad Lucilium*. Epis. 87, 17.

Fortunes . . . come tumbling into some men's laps.
BACON, *Advancement of Learning*. Bk. ii.

12
Tester I'll have in pouch, when thou shalt lack,
Base Phrygian Turk.
SHAKESPEARE, *The Merry Wives of Windsor*. Act i, sc. 3, l. 96.

Put money in thy purse.
SHAKESPEARE, *Othello*. Act i, sc. 3, l. 347.

Nothing comes amiss, so money comes withal.
SHAKESPEARE, *The Taming of the Shrew*. Act i, sc. 2, l. 82.

13
A fool may make money, but it needs a wise man to spend it.
C. H. SPURGEON, *John Ploughman*. Ch. 19.

14
But the jingling of the guinea helps the hurt that honour feels.
TENNYSON, *Locksley Hall*, l. 105.

15
It [money] has no smell. (Non olet.)
VESPASIAN, to his son Titus, when the latter blamed him for imposing a tax on urinals. (SUETONIUS, *Twelve Cæsars: Vespasian*, 23.)

The smell of gain is good, whencesoever it comes. (Lucri bonus est odor ex re Qualibet.)
JUVENAL, *Satires*. Sat. xiv, l. 204.

The savour of lucre is good, howsoever a man come by it.
THOMAS BECON, *Early Works*, 222. (1542)

So we get the chinks,
We will bear with the stinks.
SIR JOHN HARINGTON, *Metamorphosis of Ajax*, 68. (1596)

V—Money: The Love of Money

See also Avarice

1
My theme is always one, and ever was—
"Radix malorum est Cupiditas."

CHAUCER, *Pardoneres Tale: Prologue*, l. 5.

2
The love of money is the mother-city of all evils. (Τὴν φιλαργυρίαν εἶπε μητρόπολιν παντων τῶν κακῶν.)

DIOGENES. (DIOGENES LAERTIUS, *Diogenes*. Bk. vi, sec. 50.)

For the love of money is the root of all evil: which while some coveted after, they have erred from the faith, and pierced themselves through with many sorrows.

New Testament: I Timothy, vi, 10. Often incorrectly quoted, "Money is the root of all evil." The Latin is the oft-quoted, "Rad x malorum est cupiditos." Mark Twain is credited with amending this to, "Lack of monev is the root of all evil." Attributed also to Bernard Shaw.

3
The love of money and the love of learning seldom meet.

GEORGE HERBERT, *Jacula Prudentum*.

4
The love of money grows as the money itself grows. (Crescit amor nummi quantum ipsa pecunia crescit.)

JUVENAL, *Satires*. Sat. xiv, l. 139.

VI—Money: Contempt for Money

5
Thy money perish with thee.

New Testament: Acts, viii, 20.

6
I cannot afford to waste my time making money.

AGASSIZ, when offered a large sum for a course of lectures at a western college. (WHIPPLE, *Recollections of Eminent Men*.)

7
"Vile money!" True. Let's have enough
To save our thinking of such stuff.

WILLIAM ALLINGHAM, *Blackberries*.

8
Money, which is of very uncertain value, and sometimes has no value at all and even less.

CARLYLE, *Frederick the Great*. Bk. iv, ch. 3.

9
Let us despise money.

ST. JOHN CHRYSOSTOM, *The Weak Things of God*. Vol. ii, p. 59.

To despise money at the right moment is sometimes the way to make it. (Pecuniam in loco neclegere maximum interdumst lucrum.)

TERENCE, *Adelphi*, l. 216. (Act ii, sc. 2.)

10
The beggarly last doit.

COWPER, *The Task*. Bk. v, l. 321.

11
Money, thou bane of bliss and source of woe.

GEORGE HERBERT, *Avarice*.

12
What beauty is there in a piled up heap [of money]? (Quid habet pulchri constructus acervus?)

HORACE, *Satires*. Bk. i, sat. 1, l. 44.

13
Money never made any man rich, but his mind. He that can order himself to the law of nature, is not only without the sense, but the fear of poverty.

BEN JONSON, *Explorata: Amor Nummi*.

14
Money amassed with excessive care chokes many. (Plures nimia congesta pecunia cura Strangulat.)

JUVENAL, *Satires*. Sat. x, l. 12.

15
A money-mong'ring pitiable brood.

KEATS, *Addressed to Haydon*. St. 2.

16
Never do anything for money; leave gain to trades pursued for gain.

PERIANDER. (DIOGENES LAERTIUS, *Periander*. Sec. 4.)

17
Trade it may help, Society extend,
But lures the Pirate, and corrupts the friend:
It raises armies in a nation's aid,
But bribes a senate, and the land's betray'd.

POPE, *Moral Essays*. Epis. iii, l. 29.

18
Who steals my purse steals trash.

SHAKESPEARE, *Othello*. Act iii, sc. 3, l. 157.

19
The price we pay for money is paid in liberty.

R. L. STEVENSON, *Familiar Studies*, p. 138.

20
Not greedy of filthy lucre.

New Testament: I Timothy, iii, 3.

21
Whereunto is money good?
Who has it not wants hardihood,
Who has it has much trouble and care,
Who once has had it has despair.

FRIEDRICH VON LOGAU, *Sinnedichte*. (Longfellow, tr.)

22
Money—money, like everything else—is a deception and a disappointment.

H. G. WELLS, *Kipps*. Bk. ii, ch. 7.

MONK AND NUN

23
Despair makes the monk. (Desperatio facit monachum.)

ROBERT BURTON, *Anatomy of Melancholy*. Pt. iii, sec. 4, mem. 2, subs. 3. Quoted.

24
Merrily sang the monks in Ely
When Cnut, King, rowed thereby;
Row, my knights, near the land,
And hear we these monkes' song.

KING CANUTE (?), *Song of the Monks of Ely*. (c. 1030) A famous early English ballad, recorded by a monk of Ely in 1166. (SPENS, *History of the English People*.)

1
There was also a Nonne, a Prioresse,
That of her smiling was full simple and coy.
CHAUCER, *Canterbury Tales: Prologue*, l. 118.

From Eastertide to Eastertide
For ten long years her patient knees
Engraved the stones,—the fittest bride
Of Christ in all the diocese.
JOHN DAVIDSON, *A Ballad of a Nun.*

2
I like the church, I like a cowl,
I love a prophet of the soul;
And on my heart monastic aisles
Fall like sweet strains or pensive smiles;
Yet not for all his faith can see,
Would I that cowlèd churchman be.
EMERSON, *The Problem.*

3
If you become a nun, dear,
A friar I will be;
In any cell you run, dear,
Pray look behind for me.
The roses all turn pale, too;
The doves all take the veil, too;
The blind will see the show;
What! you become a nun, my dear.
I'll not believe it, no!
LEIGH HUNT, *The Nun.*

4
I envy them, those monks of old,
Their books they read, and their beads they told.
G. P. R. JAMES, *The Monks of Old.*

5
It was a friar of orders gray
Walked forth to tell his beads.
THOMAS PERCY, *The Friar of Orders Gray.* (*Reliques.* Ser. i, bk. ii, No. 18.) Arranged by Percy from fragments of old ballads.

To happy convents, bosom'd deep in vines,
Where slumber abbots purple as their wines.
POPE, *The Dunciad.* Bk. iv, l. 301.

6
I think that friars and their hoods,
Their doctrines and their maggots,
Have lighted up too many feuds,
And far too many faggots.
W. M. PRAED, *Chant of Brazen Head.* St. 8.

7
The habit does not make the monk. (L'habit ne fait point le moine.)
RABELAIS, *Works: The Author's Prologue.*

All hoods make not monks.
SHAKESPEARE, *Henry VIII.* Act iii, sc. 1, l. 23. In *Twelfth Night,* i, 5, 62, SHAKESPEARE quotes the Latin proverb, "Cucullus non facit monachum." *See also under* APPEARANCE.

8
Sacred nun . . . disciplined, ay, dieted in grace.
SHAKESPEARE, *A Lover's Complaint*, l. 260.

Love-lacking vestals and self-loving nuns.
SHAKESPEARE, *Venus and Adonis.* St. 126.

Unhappy nuns, whose common breath's a sigh.
WORDSWORTH, *Sonnet: With How Sad Steps.*

9
Ere yet, in scorn of Peter's-pence,
And number'd bead, and shrift,
Bluff Harry broke into the spence
And turn'd the cowls adrift.
TENNYSON, *The Talking Oak.* St. 12.

10
If thou wilt stand firm and grow as thou oughtest, esteem thyself as a pilgrim and stranger upon earth.
Thou must be contented for Christ's sake to be esteemed as a fool in this world, if thou desire to lead the life of a monk.
Dress and tonsure profit little; but change of heart and perfect mortification of the passions make a true monk.
THOMAS À KEMPIS, *De Imitatione Christi.* Pt. i, ch. 17.

11
O ay! the Monks, the Monks, they did the mischief!
Theirs all the grossness, all the superstition
Of a most gross and superstitious age.
UNKNOWN. (SCOTT, *The Monastery.*) Quoted as from an old play.

MONTH

12
Thirty days hath November,
April, June, and September,
February hath twenty-eight alone,
And all the rest have thirty-one.
RICHARD GRAFTON, *Abridgement of the Chronicles of England.* (1570) "A rule to know how many days every month in the year hath." Reprinted in 1577, in Harrison's *Description of England,* as an English version of these Latin hexameters:
Junius, Aprilis, Septemque, Novemque tricenos;
Unum plus reliqui, Februs tenet octo vicenos;
At si bissextus fuerit, superadditur unus.

13
Thirty days hath September,
April, June, and November,
February has twenty-eight alone,
All the rest have thirty-one;
Excepting leap year,—that's the time
When February's days are twenty-nine.
UNKNOWN. (*The Return from Parnassus.* 1606.)

Fourth, eleventh, ninth, and sixth,
Thirty days to each affix;
Every other thirty-one,
Except the second month alone.
A version common among the Friends of Chester County, Pa.

14
For hark! the last chime of the dial has ceased,
And Old Time, who his leisure to cozen,
Has finished the Months, like the flasks at a feast,
Is preparing to tap a fresh dozen.
THOMAS HOOD, *For the New Year.*

Touch'd with the dewy sadness of the time,
To think how the bright months had spent their prime.

THOMAS HOOD, *The Plea of the Midsummer Fairies*, l. 8.

1
A little month.

SHAKESPEARE, *Hamlet*. Act i, sc. 2, l. 147.

2
He hath a month's mind here to mistress Frances.

UNKNOWN, *London Prodigal*. Act i, sc. 2. (1605)

When people earnestly desire a thing, they frequently say, they have a month's mind to it.

PECK, *Desid. Curiosa*, p. 229. (1731)

MONUMENT

3
Death comes even to the monumental stones and the names inscribed thereon. (Mors etiam saxis nominibusque venit.)

AUSONIUS, *Epitaphs*. No. 32, l. 10.

No—marble and recording brass decay,
And, like the graver's mem'ry, pass away.

COWPER, *Conversation*, l. 551.

But monuments themselves memorials need.

GEORGE CRABBE, *The Borough*. Letter 2.

4
Sorry preëminence of high descent!
Above the vulgar born, to rot in state.

ROBERT BLAIR, *The Grave*, l. 154.

Proud even in death, here rot in state.

CHARLES CHURCHILL, *The Ghost*. Bk. ii, l. 726.

5
Ulysses in *Hecuba* cared not how meanly he lived, so he might find a noble tomb after death.

SIR THOMAS BROWNE, *Hydriotaphia*. Ch. 3.

6
Gold once out of the earth is no more due unto it; what was unreasonably committed to the ground, is reasonably resumed from it; let monuments and rich fabrics, not riches, adorn men's ashes.

SIR THOMAS BROWNE, *Hydriotaphia*. Ch. 3.

To extend our memories by monuments, whose death we daily pray for, and whose duration we cannot hope, without injury to our expectations in the advent of the last day, were a contradiction to our beliefs.

SIR THOMAS BROWNE, *Hydriotaphia*. Ch. 5.

7
Let not a monument give you or me hopes,
Since not a pinch of dust remains of Cheops.

BYRON, *Don Juan*. Canto i, st. 219.

So much for monuments that have forgotten
Their very record!

BYRON, *Sardanapalus*. Act v, sc. 1.

See also under OBLIVION.

8
Monuments are made for victories over strangers: domestic troubles should be covered with the veil of sadness.

JULIUS CÆSAR, refusing a monument after the battle of Pharsalia. (PLUTARCH, *Lives: Cæsar*. Ch. 56.) Charles Sumner quoted these words after the Civil War.

9
I would much rather have men ask why I have no statue than why I have one. (Μᾶλλον γὰρ βούλομαι ζητεῖσθαι, διὰ τί μου ἀνδριὰς οὐ κεῖται ἢ διὰ τί κεῖται.)

MARCUS CATO. (PLUTARCH, *Lives: Marcus Cato*. Ch. 19, sec. 4.)

10
Toils much to earn a monumental pile,
That may record the mischiefs he hath done.

COWPER, *The Task*. Bk. i, l. 276.

11
Do not, good sir, judge the dead by his monument. The stone is senseless and can cover a foul corpse as well as any other. (Μὴ λίθῳ τεκμαίρεο, ὦ λῷστε, τὸν θανόντα.)

CRINAGORAS, *Epitaph*. (*Greek Anthology*. Bk. vii, epig. 380.)

12
Yet, Corah, thou shalt from Oblivion pass;
Erect thyself thou Monumental Brass.

DRYDEN, *Absalom and Achitophel*. Pt. i, l. 632. Referring to Titus Oates.

13
The monuments of noble men are their virtues. (Γενναίων δ' ἀρεταὶ πόνων τοῖς θανοῦσιν ἄγαλμα.)

EURIPIDES, *Herakles Mainomenos*, l. 357.

14
Ye shall not pile, with servile toil,
Your monuments upon my breast,
Nor yet within the common soil
Lay down the wreck of power to rest,
Where man can boast that he has trod
On him that was "the scourge of God."

EDWARD EVERETT, *Alaric the Visigoth*. St. 3.

15
How poor remembrances are statues, tombs,
And other monuments that men erect
To princes, which remain closed rooms
Where but a few behold them.

JOHN FLORIO, *Ode*.

16
Tombs are the clothes of the dead; a grave is but a plain suit, and a rich monument is one embroidered.

THOMAS FULLER, *The Holy State: Of Tombs*.

17
There wants no marble for a tomb
Whose breast hath marble been to me.

WILLIAM HABINGTON, *To Roses in the Bosom of Castara*.

18
Not by marble graven with public records is the breath and life of goodly heroes continued after death. (Non incisa notis marmora publicis, Per quæ spiritus et vita redit bonis Post mortem ducibus.)

HORACE, *Odes*. Bk. iv, ode 8, l. 13.

19
See nations slowly wise, and meanly just,

To buried merit raise the tardy bust.
SAMUEL JOHNSON, *Vanity of Human Wishes*, l. 159.

1
He is covered by the heavens who has no sepulchral urn. (Cœlo tegitur qui non habet urnam.)
LUCAN, *De Bello Civili*. Bk. vii, l. 819.

He that unburied lies wants not his hearse,
For unto him a tomb's the Universe.
SIR THOMAS BROWNE, *Religio Medici*. Pt. i, sec. 41.

Nothing can cover his high fame but Heaven;
No pyramids set off his memories,
But the eternal substance of his greatness;
To which I leave him.
JOHN FLETCHER, *The False One*. Act ii, sc. 1.

2
Towers of silence.
ROBERT X. MURPHY. (SIR GEORGE BIRDWOOD, *Letter*, London *Times*, 8 Aug., 1905.)

3
To this man a statue of gold should be set up. (Huic decet statuam statui ex auro.)
PLAUTUS, *Bacchides*, l. 640. (Act iv, sc. 4.)

I will raise her statue in pure gold.
SHAKESPEARE, *Romeo and Juliet*. Act v, sc. 3, l. 299.

4
The erection of a monument is superfluous; our memory will endure if our lives have deserved it. (Impensa monumenti supercavua est; memoria nostri durabit, si vita meruimus.)
PLINY THE YOUNGER, *Epistles*. Bk. ix, epis. 19, sec. 3.

The marble keeps merely a cold and sad memory of a man who would else be forgotten. No man who needs a monument ever ought to have one.
HAWTHORNE, *English Note-Books:* 12 Nov., 1857, *Westminster Abbey*.

Those only deserve a monument who do not need one; that is, who have raised themselves a monument in the minds and memories of men.
WILLIAM HAZLITT, *Characteristics*. No. 388.

5
Protect his memory, and preserve his story,
Remain a lasting monument of his glory.
FRANCIS QUARLES, *Lines on Drayton's Monument*.

Like Collins, ill-starred name!
Whose lay's requital was, that tardy Fame,
Who bound no laurel round his living head,
Should hang it o'er his monument when dead.
SCOTT, *The Bridal of Triermain: Introduction*. St. 8.

6
So flits the world's uncertain span!
Nor zeal for God, nor love for man
Gives mortal monuments a date
Beyond the power of Time and Fate.
SCOTT, *Rokeby*. Canto vi, st. 1.

7
This grave shall have a living monument.
SHAKESPEARE, *Hamlet*. Act v, sc. 1, l. 320.

8
And when old time shall lead him to his end,
Goodness and he fill up one monument!
SHAKESPEARE, *Henry VIII*. Act ii, sc. 1, l. 93.

9
If charnel-houses and our graves must send
Those that we bury back, our monuments
Shall be the maws of kites.
SHAKESPEARE, *Macbeth*. Act iii, sc. 4, l. 71.

10
If a man do not erect in this age his own tomb ere he dies, he shall live no longer in monument than the bell rings and the widow weeps.
SHAKESPEARE, *Much Ado About Nothing*. Act v, sc. 2, l. 80.

There's hope a great man's memory may outlive his life half a year: but, by 'r lady, he must build churches, then; or else shall he suffer not thinking on.
SHAKESPEARE, *Hamlet*. Act iii, sc. 2, l. 142.

11
Among the knightly brasses of the graves,
And by the cold Hic Jacets of the dead!
TENNYSON, *Merlin and Vivien*, l. 750. The first two words of tombstone inscriptions were usually "Hic Jacet," Here Lies.

May no rude hand deface it,
And its forlorn *Hic jacet!*
WORDSWORTH, *Ellen Irwin, or The Braes of Kirtle*. St. 7.

12
Let it rise! Let it rise, till it meet the sun in his coming; let the earliest light of the morning gild it, and the parting day linger and play on its summit.
DANIEL WEBSTER, *Address*, on laying the corner-stone of the Bunker Hill Monument.

13
A warrior, with his shield of pride
Cleaving humbly to his side,
And hands in resignation prest,
Palm to palm, on his tranquil breast.
WORDSWORTH, *The White Doe of Rylstone*. Canto i, l. 128.

14
If you would see his monument, look around.
(Si monumentum requiris circumspice.)
CHRISTOPHER WREN, *Epitaph*, for his father, Sir Christopher Wren, inscribed on his tomb in St. Paul's cathedral, London.

Wouldst thou behold his monument? look around!
SAMUEL ROGERS, *Italy: Florence*. Referring to Massaccio.

And, talking of Epitaphs,—much I admire his,
Circumspice si Monumentum requiris;
Which an erudite Verger translated to me,
"If you ask for his monument, *Sir-come-spy-see!*"
R. H. BARHAM, *The Cynotaph*.

"Si monumentum quæris, circumspice" would be equally applicable to a physician buried in a churchyard.
HORACE SMITH, *The Tin Trumpet*.

MOON, THE

I—Moon: Apothegms

1
Thinketh, He dwelleth i' the cold o' the moon.
Thinketh He made it, with the sun to match,
But not the stars; the stars came otherwise.
ROBERT BROWNING, *Caliban upon Setebos*, l. 25.

Do I carry the moon in my pocket?
ROBERT BROWNING, *Master Hugues of Saxe-Gotha*. St. 29.

2
Doth the moon care for the barking of a dog?
ROBERT BURTON, *Anatomy of Melancholy*. Pt. ii, sec. iii, mem. 7.

The moon does not heed the barking of dogs.
JOHN RAY, *English Proverbs*, p. 208.

3
Quoth Pandarus, thou hast a full great care
Lest that the churl may fall out of the moon!
CHAUCER, *Troilus and Criseyde*. Bk. i, l. 1023.

4
And hail their queen, fair regent of the night.
ERASMUS DARWIN, *Botanic Garden*. Pt. i, canto ii, l. 90.

Now Cynthia, nam'd fair regent of the night.
JOHN GAY, *Trivia*. Bk. iii, l. 4.

The dews of summer night did fall;
The moon (sweet regent of the sky)
Silver'd the walls of Cumnor Hall,
And many an oak that grew thereby.
WILLIAM JULIUS MICKLE, *Cumnor Hall*.

5
The appearance of the face in the moon may equally well arise from interchange of parts.
EPICURUS. (DIOGENES LAERTIUS, *Epicurus*. Bk. x, sec. 95.)

6
With this pleasant, merry toy, he . . . made his friends believe the moon to be made of green cheese.
ERASMUS, *Adagia*. (Udall, tr., 1542.) This is one of the most frequently found sayings in sixteenth and seventeenth century literature.

They would make men believe that the moon is made of green cheese.
JOHN FRITH, *Antithesis*, 315. (1573)

Or think that the moon is made of a green cheese.
JOHN HEYWOOD, *Proverbs*. Bk. ii, ch. 7. (1546)

He . . . thought the moon was made of green cheese.
RABELAIS, *Works*. Bk. i, ch. 11.

He made an instrument to know
If the moon shine at full or no;
That would, as soon as e'er she shone straight,
Whether 'twere day or night demonstrate;
Tell what her d'ameter to an inch is,
And prove that she's not made of green cheese.
BUTLER, *Hudibras*. Pt. ii, canto iii, l. 261.

7
You gazed at the moon and fell in a gutter.
THOMAS FULLER, *Gnomologia*. No. 5904.

8
Fear may force a man to cast beyond the moon.
JOHN HEYWOOD, *Proverbs*. Pt. i, ch. 4. (1546)

I cast before the Moon.
JOHN LYLY, *Euphues*, p. 78. (1579)

9
We should in that but bark against the moon.
HEYWOOD AND ROWLEY, *Fortune by Land and Sea*. Act i, sc. 1.

I'd rather be a dog, and bay the moon,
Than such a Roman.
SHAKESPEARE, *Julius Cæsar*. Act iv, sc. 3, l. 27.

But thou, as blind Bayards, barkest at the moon.
THOMAS WRIGHT, *Political Poems*, ii, 53.

10
O Maker of sweet poets.
KEATS, *I Stood Tiptoe Upon a Little Hill*, l. 116. Referring to the moon.

11
Let the air strike our tune,
Whilst we show reverence to yond peeping moon.
THOMAS MIDDLETON, *The Witch*. Act v, sc. 2.

12
Another Cynthia her new journey runs,
And other planets circle other suns.
POPE, *The Dunciad*. Bk. iii, l. 243.

13
God saves the moon from the wolves.
JOHN RAY, *English Proverbs*.

To keep the moon safe from the wolves. (Garder la lune des loups.)
RABELAIS, *Works*. Bk. ii.

14
The moon is not seen where the sun shines.
JOHN RAY, *English Proverbs*.

15
That I could clamber to the frozen moon
And draw the ladder after me.
SCHOPENHAUER, *Parerga and Paralipomena*.

16
O sovereign mistress of true melancholy.
SHAKESPEARE, *Antony and Cleopatra*. Act iv, sc. 9, l. 11.

17
How now, moon-calf? How dost thine ague?
SHAKESPEARE, *The Tempest*. Act ii, sc. 2, l. 139.

18
A sweet little Venus we'll fondle between us,
When I wed my old man in the moon.
JAMES THORNTON, *My Sweetheart's the Man in the Moon*. (1892)

19
Everyone is a moon, and has a dark side which he never shows to anybody.
MARK TWAIN, *Pudd'nhead Wilson's New Calendar*.

Nay: for if that moon could love a mortal, . . .
She would turn a new side to her mortal,
Side unseen of herdsman, huntsman, steersman— . . .
Dumb to Homer, dumb to Keats—him, even!
ROBERT BROWNING, *One Word More*. Sec. 116.

See also BROWNING *under* LOVE: PROTESTATIONS.

1
Meet me by moonlight alone.
J. AUGUSTINE WADE, *Meet Me by Moonlight Alone.*

II—Moon: Description

2
Soon as the evening shades prevail,
The moon takes up the wondrous tale,
And nightly, to the listening earth,
Repeats the story of her birth.
ADDISON, *Ode.* (*Spectator.* No. 465.)

3
The moon is a silver pin-head vast,
That holds the heaven's tent-hangings fast.
W. R. ALGER, *The Use of the Moon.*

4
And from embattled clouds emerging slow,
Cynthia came riding on her silver car.
JAMES BEATTIE, *The Minstrel.* Bk. ii, l. 107.

Choose a firm cloud before it fall, and in it
Catch, ere she change, the Cynthia of this minute.
POPE, *Moral Essays.* Epis. ii, l. 19.

5
The moon, like a flower,
In heaven's high bower
With silent delight
Sits and smiles on the night.
WILLIAM BLAKE, *Night.*

6
Curving on a sky imbrued with colour,
Drifted over Fiesole by twilight;
Came she, our new crescent of a hair's-breadth.
Full she flared it, lamping Samminiato.
Rounder 'twixt the cypresses and rounder,
Perfect till the nightingales applauded.
ROBERT BROWNING, *One Word More.* Sec. 15.

7
That gentle Moon, the lesser light, the Lover's lamp, the Swain's delight,
A ruined world, a globe burnt out, a corpse upon the road of night.
SIR RICHARD BURTON, *The Kasîdah.* Pt. v, 11.

8
The moon pull'd off her veil of light,
That hides her face by day from sight
(Mysterious veil, of brightness made,
That's both her lustre and her shade),
And in the lantern of the night,
With shining horns hung out her light.
BUTLER, *Hudibras.* Pt. ii, canto i, l. 905.

9
The devil's in the moon for mischief; they
Who call'd her chaste, methinks, began too soon
Their nomenclature; there is not a day,
The longest, not the twenty-first of June,
Sees half the business in a wicked way,
On which three single hours of moonshine smile—
And then she looks so modest all the while!
BYRON, *Don Juan.* Canto i, st. 113.

10
Into the sunset's turquoise marge
The moon dips, like a pearly barge;
Enchantment sails through magic seas,
To fairyland Hesperides,
Over the hills and away.
MADISON CAWEIN, *At Sunset.*

11
Till clomb above the eastern bar
The hornèd Moon, with one bright star
Within the nether tips.
S. T. COLERIDGE, *The Ancient Mariner,* l. 209.

The moving Moon went up the sky,
And no where did abide:
Softly she was going up,
And a star or two beside.
S. T. COLERIDGE, *The Ancient Mariner,* l. 263.

12
When the hollow drum has beat to bed
And the little fifer hangs his head,
When all is mute the Moorish flute,
And nodding guards watch wearily,
Oh, then let me,
From prison free,
March out by moonlight cheerily.
GEORGE COLMAN THE YOUNGER, *Mountaineers.* Act i, sc. 2.

13
Hour after hour that passionless bright face
Climbs up the desolate blue.
DINAH MARIA MULOCK CRAIK, *Moon-Struck.*

14
How like a queen comes forth the lonely Moon
From the slow opening curtains of the clouds;
Walking in beauty to her midnight throne!
GEORGE CROLY, *Diana.*

15
The moon is distant from the sea,
And yet with amber hands
She leads him, docile as a boy,
Along appointed sands.
EMILY DICKINSON, *Poems.* Pt. iii, No. 31.

16
The man who has seen the rising moon break out of the clouds at midnight, has been present like an archangel at the creation of light and of the world.
EMERSON, *Essays, First Series: History.*

17
The moon low sailing where the waters fill
The lozenge lake, beside the banks of balm,
Gleams like a chevron on the river's arm.
BRET HARTE, *Cadet Grey.* Canto ii, st. 2.

18
A golden sickle reaping darkness down.
JAMES BARRON HOPE, *Jamestown.*

19
He who would see old Hoghton right
Must view it by the pale moonlight.
WILLIAM HAZLITT, *English Proverbs and Provincial Phrases,* p. 196.

If thou would'st view fair Melrose aright,
Go visit it by the pale moonlight.
SCOTT, *Lay of the Last Minstrel.* Canto ii, st. 1.

1
Mother of light! how fairly dost thou go
  Over those hoary crests, divinely led!
Art thou that huntress of the silver bow
  Fabled of old? Or rather dost thou tread
Those cloudy summits thence to gaze below,
Like the wild chamois from her Alpine snow,
Where hunters never climb'd—secure from dread?
  THOMAS HOOD, *Ode to the Moon*. St. 1.

2
The crimson Moon, uprising from the sea,
With large delight, foretells the harvest near.
  EDWARD HOVELL-THURLOW, *The Harvest Moon.*

3
Queen and huntress, chaste and fair,
Now the sun is laid to sleep,
Seated in thy silver chair,
State in wonted manner keep:
  Hesperus entreats thy light,
  Goddess excellently bright. . . .
  Bless us then with wishèd sight,
  Goddess excellently bright.
  BEN JONSON, *Hymn to Diana.* (*Cynthia's Revels.* Act v, sc. 3.)

4
What is there in thee, Moon! that thou should'st move
My heart so potently?
  KEATS, *Endymion*. Bk. iii, l. 142.

The moon put forth a little diamond peak,
No bigger than an unobserved star,
Or tiny point of fairy cimetar.
  KEATS, *Endymion*. Bk. iv, l. 497.

5
See yonder fire! It is the moon
Slow rising o'er the eastern hill.
It glimmers on the forest tips.
And through the dewy foliage drips
In little rivulets of light,
And makes the heart in love with night.
  LONGFELLOW, *The Golden Legend*. Pt. vi, l. 462.

6
The bent and broken moon,
Batter'd and black, as from a thousand battles,
Hangs silent on the purple walls of Heaven.
  JOAQUIN MILLER, *Ina*. Sc. 2.

7
The moon had climbed the highest hill
  Which rises o'er the source of Dee,
And from the eastern summit shed
  Her silver light on tower and tree.
  JOHN LOWE, *Mary's Dream*.

8
Unmuffle, ye faint stars; and thou fair Moon,
That wont'st to love the traveller's benison,
Stoop thy pale visage through an amber cloud,
And disinherit Chaos.
  MILTON, *Comus*, l. 331.

I walk unseen
On the dry smooth-shaven green,
To behold the wandering Moon
Riding near her highest noon,
Like one that had been led astray
Through the heav'n's wide pathless way;
And oft, as if her head she bow'd,
Stooping through a fleecy cloud.
  MILTON, *Il Penseroso*, l. 65.

9
The Moon,
Rising in clouded majesty, at length,
Apparent Queen, unveil'd her peerless light,
And o'er the dark her silver mantle threw.
  MILTON, *Paradise Lost*. Bk. iv, l. 606.

10
Like moonlight o'er a troubled sea,
Brightening the storm it cannot calm.
  THOMAS MOORE, *The Loves of the Angels*, l. 1153.

11
The moon looks On many brooks,
The brook can see no moon but this.
  THOMAS MOORE, *While Gazing on the Moon's Light*. Lines suggested by:
The moon looks upon many night flowers; the night flowers see but one moon.
  SIR WILLIAM JONES.

12
The moon was a ghostly galleon tossed upon cloudy seas.
  ALFRED NOYES, *The Highwayman*.

13
Day glimmer'd in the east, and the white Moon
Hung like a vapour in the cloudless sky.
  SAMUEL ROGERS, *Italy: The Lake of Geneva*.

14
Again thou reignest in thy golden hall,
Rejoicing in thy sway, fair queen of night!
  THOMAS ROSCOE, *To the Harvest Moon*.

15
The curled moon Was like a little feather
Fluttering far down the gulf.
  D. G. ROSSETTI, *The Blessed Damozel*. St. 10.

16
Good even, good fair moon, good even to thee;
I prithee, dear moon, now show to me
The form and the features, the speech and degree,
Of the man that true lover of mine shall be.
  SCOTT, *The Heart of Mid-Lothian*. Ch. 17.

17
The glimpses of the moon.
  SHAKESPEARE, *Hamlet*. Act i, sc. 4, l. 53.

Let us be Diana's foresters, gentlemen of the shade, minions of the moon.
  SHAKESPEARE, *I Henry IV*. Act i, sc. 2, l. 27.

18
Dull: What was a month old at Cain's birth, that's not five months old as yet?
Hol: Dictyanna, goodman Dull; Dictyanna, goodman Dull.
Dull: What is Dictyanna?

Nath: A title to Phœbe, to Luna, to the moon.
SHAKESPEARE, *Love's Labour's Lost.* Act iv, sc. 2, l. 37.

1
Upon the corner of the moon,
There hangs a vaporous drop profound.
SHAKESPEARE, *Macbeth.* Act iii, sc. 5, l. 23.

2
How sweet the moonlight sleeps upon this bank!
SHAKESPEARE, *The Merchant of Venice.* Act v, sc. 1, l. 54.

3
How slow
This old moon wanes! she lingers my desires,
Like to a step-dame or a dowager
Long withering out a young man's revenue.
SHAKESPEARE, *A Midsummer-Night's Dream.* Act i, sc. 1, l. 3.

The moon, the governess of floods.
SHAKESPEARE, *A Midsummer-Night's Dream.* Act ii, sc. 1, l. 103

The wat'ry star.
SHAKESPEARE, *Winter's Tale.* Act i, sc. 2, l. 1.

4
It is the very error of the moon;
She comes more nearer earth than she was wont,
And makes men mad.
SHAKESPEARE, *Othello.* Act v, sc. 2, l. 109.

5
Arise, fair sun, and kill the envious moon,
Who is already sick and pale with grief,
That thou her maid art far more fair than she:
Be not her maid, since she is envious.
SHAKESPEARE, *Romeo and Juliet.* Act ii, sc. 2, l. 4.

6
Romeo: Lady, by yonder blessed moon I swear,
That tips with silver all these fruit-tree tops—
Juliet: O, swear not by the moon, the inconstant moon,
That monthly changes in her circled orb,
Lest that thy love prove likewise variable.
SHAKESPEARE, *Romeo and Juliet.* Act ii, sc. 2, l. 107.

7
That orbèd maiden with white fire laden,
Whom mortals call the moon.
SHELLEY, *The Cloud,* l. 45.

Bright wanderer, fair coquette of Heaven,
To whom alone it has been given
To change and be adored forever.
SHELLEY, *Fragment: To the Moon.*

Art thou pale for weariness
Or climbing Heaven and gazing on the earth,
Wandering companionless
Among the stars that have a different birth,—
And ever changing, like a joyless eye
That finds no object worth its constancy?
SHELLEY, *Fragment: To the Moon.*

8
The young moon has fed
Her exhausted horn
With the sunset's fire.
SHELLEY, *Hellas,* l. 1031.

The moonlight's ineffectual glow:
SHELLEY, *Queen Mab.* Canto viii.

9
With how sad steps, O Moon, thou climb'st the skies!
How silently and with how wan a face!
SIR PHILIP SIDNEY, *Astrophel and Stella.* Sonnet xxxi. Quoted by Wordsworth, *Miscellaneous Sonnets.* Pt. ii, No. 23.

With what a silent and dejected pace
Dost thou, wan Moon, upon thy way advance.
HENRY KIRKE WHITE, *Angelina.*

10
I with borrow'd silver shine,
What you see is none of mine.
First I show you but a quarter,
Like the bow that guards the Tartar:
Then the half, and then the whole,
Ever dancing round the pole.
SWIFT, *On the Moon.*

11
Behold, whatever wind prevail,
Slow westering, a phantom sail—
The lonely soul of Yesterday—
Unpiloted, pursues her way.
JOHN B. TABB, *The Mid-day Moon.*

12
Moon, worn thin to the width of a quill,
In the sawn clouds flying,
How good to go, light into light, and still
Give light, dying.
SARA TEASDALE, *Moon's Ending.*

13
A maiden moon that sparkles on a sty.
TENNYSON, *The Princess.* Pt. v, l. 178.

14
Ask me no more: the moon may draw the sea.
TENNYSON, *The Princess.* Pt. vi, l. 364.

The innocent moon that nothing does but shine
Moves all the labouring surges of the world.
FRANCIS THOMPSON, *The Mirage.*

15
Pale ports o' the moon.
FRANCIS THOMPSON, *The Hound of Heaven.*

16
Lo, the moon ascending,
Up from the east the silvery round moon,
Beautiful over the house-tops, ghastly, phantom moon,
Immense and silent moon.
WALT WHITMAN, *Dirge for Two Veterans.*

17
But tenderly Above the sea
Hangs, white and calm, the hunter's moon.
J. G. WHITTIER, *The Eve of Election.* St. 1.

18
And suddenly the moon withdraws
Her sickle from the lightening skies,

And to her sombre cavern flies,
Wrapped in a veil of yellow gauze.
OSCAR WILDE, *La Fuite de la Lune.*

1
You meaner beauties of the night,
That poorly satisfy our eyes
More by your number than your light;
You common people of the skies,—
What are you when the moon shall rise?
SIR HENRY WOTTON, *On His Mistress, The Queen of Bohemia.*

2
Late, late yestreen I saw the new moon,
Wi' the auld moon in hir arm.
UNKNOWN, *Sir Patrick Spence.* St. 7. (PERCY, *Reliques.* Ser. i.)

I saw the new moon late yestreen,
Wi' the auld moon in her arm.
UNKNOWN, *Ballad.* (SCOTT, *Minstrelsy of the Scottish Border.*)

3
By the light of the moon, my friend Pierrot,
Lend me thy pen to write a word;
My candle is out, I've no more fire,
Open your door to me, for the love of God.
(Au clair de la lune, Mon ami Pierrot,
Prête moi ta plume, Pour écrire un mot;
Ma chandelle est morte, Je n'ai plus de feu,
Ouvre moi ta porte, Pour l'amour de Dieu.
UNKNOWN. French folk song, quoted by George du Maurier in *Trilby.*

MORALITY

4
Not the whiteness of years but of morals is to be praised. (Non annorum canities est laudanda, sed morum.)
AMBROSIUS, *Epistles.* Bk. i, epis. 18, sec. 7.

5
Kant, as we all know, compared the Moral Law to the starry heavens, and found them both sublime. It would, on the naturalistic hypothesis, be more appropriate to compare it to the protective blotches on the beetle's back, and to find them both ingenious.
ARTHUR J. BALFOUR, *Foundations of Belief: Naturalism and Ethics.* See 1914:8.

6
The foundations of morality are like all other foundations: if you dig too much about them the superstructure will come tumbling down.
SAMUEL BUTLER THE YOUNGER, *Note-books.*

7
A moral (like all morals) melancholy.
BYRON, *Don Juan.* Canto v, st. 63.

"Tut, tut, child!" said the Duchess. "Every thing's got a moral, if you only can find it."
LEWIS CARROLL, *Alice's Adventures in Wonderland.* Ch. 9.

Whate'er the story be, the moral's true.
DRYDEN, *University of Oxford: Prologue.*

8
Morality was held a standing jest,
And faith a necessary fraud at best.
CHARLES CHURCHILL, *Gotham.* Bk. ii, l. 597.

9
He cursed the canting moralist,
Who measures right and wrong.
JOHN DAVIDSON, *A Ballad of a Poet Born.*

To denounce moralizing out of hand is to pronounce a moral judgment.
H. L. MENCKEN, *Prejudices.* Ser. i, p. 19.

10
Let us be moral. Let us contemplate existence.
DICKENS, *Martin Chuzzlewit.* Ch. 10.

11
Morality, said Jesus, is kindness to the weak; morality, said Nietzsche, is the bravery of the strong; morality, said Plato, is the effective harmony of the whole. Probably all three doctrines must be combined to find a perfect ethic; but can we doubt which of the elements is fundamental?
WILL DURANT, *The Story of Philosophy.*

12
Men talk of "mere Morality," which is much as if one should say "Poor God, with nobody to help him."
EMERSON, *Conduct of Life: Worship.*

13
The moral system of the universe is like a document written in alternate ciphers, which change from line to line.
J. A. FROUDE, *Short Studies on Great Subjects: Calvinism.*

14
Morality, when vigorously alive, sees farther than intellect.
J. A. FROUDE, *Short Studies on Great Subjects: Divus Cæsar.*

15
It is for each man to procure himself the emotion he needs, and the morality which suits him.
RÉMY DE GOURMONT, *Decadence.*

16
We are doomed to be moral and cannot help ourselves.
JOHN HAYNES HOLMES, *Morality.*

17
Veracity is the heart of morality.
THOMAS HENRY HUXLEY, *Universities Actual and Ideal.*

18
Rhetoric takes no real account of the art in literature, and morality takes no account of the art in life.
J. W. KRUTCH, *The Modern Temper,* p. 154.

19
Morality without religion is only a kind of dead reckoning,—an endeavor to find our place on a cloudy sea.
LONGFELLOW, *Kavanagh.* Ch. 13.

20
The difference between a moral man and a man of honor is that the latter regrets a discreditable act even when it has worked.
H. L. MENCKEN, *Prejudices.* Ser. iv, p. 206.

1
I find the doctors and the sages
Have differ'd in all climes and ages,
And two in fifty scarce agree
On what is pure morality.
THOMAS MOORE, *Morality*, l. 15.

2
Never did moral thought occur
In more unlucky hour than this;
For oh! I just was leading her
To talk of love and think of bliss.
THOMAS MOORE, *The Snake*.

3
There are many religions, but there is only one morality.
RUSKIN, *Lectures on Art*. Lect. ii, sec. 37.

4
A moral fool.
SHAKESPEARE, *King Lear*. Act iv, sc. 2, l. 58.

Come, you are too severe a moraler.
SHAKESPEARE, *Othello*. Act ii, sc. 3, l. 301.

5
Absolute morality is the regulation of conduct in such a way that pain shall not be inflicted.
HERBERT SPENCER, *Essays: Prison Ethics*.

Morality knows nothing of geographical boundaries or distinctions of race.
HERBERT SPENCER, *Social Statics*. Pt. i, ch. 2.

6
If thy morals make thee dreary, depend upon it they are wrong.
R. L. STEVENSON, *A Christmas Sermon*.

7
Morals are a personal affair; in the war of righteousness every man fights for his own hand.
R. L. STEVENSON, *Lay Morals*.

8
There is no such thing as morality; it is not immoral for the tiger to eat the wolf, or the wolf the cat, or the cat the bird, and so on down; that is their business. . . . It is not immoral to create the human species—with or without ceremony; nature intended exactly these things.
MARK TWAIN. (PAINE, *Mark Twain*.)

9
Morality is simply the attitude we adopt towards people we personally dislike.
OSCAR WILDE, *An Ideal Husband*. Act ii.

Modern morality consists in accepting the standard of one's age.
OSCAR WILDE, *Picture of Dorian Gray*. Ch. 6.

10
Morality was made for man, not man for morality.
ISRAEL ZANGWILL, *Children of the Ghetto*. Bk. ii, ch. 6.

O TEMPORA! O MORES! *see under* MANNERS.

MORNING

See also Dawn, Sunrise

11
I oft had seen the dawnlight run
As red wine through the hills, and break
Through many a mist's inurning;
But, here, no earth profaned the sun;
Heaven, ocean, did alone partake
The sacrament of morning.
E. B. BROWNING, *A Sabbath Morning at Sea*.

12
Never glad, confident morning again!
ROBERT BROWNING, *The Lost Leader*.

13
The morn is up again, the dewy morn,
With breath all incense, and with cheek all bloom.
BYRON, *Childe Harold*. Canto iii, st. 98.

The breezy call of incense-breathing Morn.
THOMAS GRAY, *Elegy Written in a Country Church-yard*, l. 17.

The fresh air of incense-breathing morn.
WORDSWORTH, *Ecclesiastical Sonnets*. Pt. iii, No. 40.

14
Genial morn appears,
Like pensive Beauty smiling in her tears.
CAMPBELL, *The Pleasures of Hope*. Pt. ii, l. 95.

15
The joyous morning ran and kissed the grass
And drew his fingers through her sleeping hair.
JOHN FREEMAN, *The Wakers*.

16
All is illusion till the morning bars
Slip from the levels of the Eastern gate.
BRET HARTE, *Cadet Grey*. Canto ii, st. 13.

What lieth dark, O love, bright day will fill;
Wait for thy morning, be it good or ill.
BRET HARTE, *Cadet Grey*. Canto ii, st. 13.

17
The morn, look you, furthers a man on his road, and furthers him too in his work. (*'Ηώς τοι προφέρει μὲν ὁδοῦ, προφέρει δε καὶ ἔργου.*)
HESIOD, *Works and Days*, l. 579.

All the speed is in the morning.
ALICE HARVEY. (GABRIEL HARVEY, *Common-place Book*.)

This morning, like the spirit of a youth
That means to be of note, begins betimes.
SHAKESPEARE, *Antony and Cleopatra*. Act iv, sc. 4, l. 26.

The morning hour has gold in its mouth. (Die Morgenstunde hat Gold im Munde.)
UNKNOWN. (*Publications Modern Language Assn.*, xlii, 865.)

18
Beloved, it is morn.
A redder berry on the thorn,
A deeper yellow on the corn,
For this good day new-born.
EMILY HENRIETTA HICKEY, *Beloved, It Is Morn*. *See also under* RISING.

19
Now did the rosy-finger'd Morn arise,
And shed her sacred light along the skies.
HOMER, *Odyssey*. Bk. xiii, l. 21. (Pope, tr.)

In saffron-colored mantle from the tides
Of Ocean rose the Morning to bring light
To gods and men.
HOMER, *Iliad*. Bk. xix, l. 1. (Bryant, tr.)

1
The Morn! she is the source of sighs,
The very face to make us sad;
If but to think in other times
The same calm quiet look she had.
THOMAS HOOD, *On Melancholy*.

2
'Tis always morning somewhere in the world.
RICHARD HENGEST HORNE, *Orion*. Bk. iii, can. 2.

'Tis always morning somewhere, and above
The awakening continents, from shore to shore,
Somewhere the birds are singing evermore.
LONGFELLOW, *Birds of Killingworth*. St. 16.

3
The blessed morn has come again;
The early gray
Taps at the slumberer's window-pane,
And seems to say,
Break, break from the enchanter's chain,
Away, away!
RALPH HOYT, *Snow: A Winter Sketch*.

4
The morn was fair, the skies were clear,
No breath came o'er the sea.
CHARLES JEFFERYS, *The Rose of Allandale*.

5
Hues of the rich unfolding morn,
That, ere the glorious sun be born,
By some soft touch invisible
Around his path are taught to swell.
JOHN KEBLE, *The Christian Year: Morning*.

6
Behold how brightly breaks the morning!
Though bleak our lot, our hearts are warm.
JAMES KENNEY, *Behold How Brightly*.

7
A fine morning,
Nothing's the matter with it that I know of.
I have seen better and I have seen worse.
LONGFELLOW, *John Endicott*. Act v, sc. 2.

8
Like pearl
Dropt from the opening eyelids of the morn
Upon the bashful rose.
THOMAS MIDDLETON, *A Game of Chess*.

Under the opening eyelids of the morn.
MILTON, *Lycidas*, l. 26.

9
Ere the blabbing Eastern scout,
The nice Morn on th' Indian steep
From her cabin'd loop-hole peep.
MILTON, *Comus*, l. 138.

10
While the still morn went out with Sandals grey,
MILTON, *Lycidas*, l. 187.

Till morning fair
Came forth with pilgrim steps in amice grey.
MILTON, *Paradise Regained*. Bk. iv, l. 426.

But, look, the morn, in russet mantle clad,
Walks o'er the dew of yon high eastward hill.
SHAKESPEARE, *Hamlet*. Act i, sc. 1, l. 166.

11
Sweet is the breath of morn, her rising sweet,
With charm of earliest birds; pleasant the sun
When first on this delightful land he spreads
His orient beams, on herb, tree, fruit, and flower,
Glist'ring with dew.
MILTON, *Paradise Lost*. Bk. iv, l. 641.

12
Now morn, her rosy steps in th' eastern clime
Advancing, sow'd the earth with orient pearl.
MILTON, *Paradise Lost*. Bk. v, l. 1.

Morn,
Wak'd by the circling hours, with rosy hand
Unbarr'd the gates of light.
MILTON, *Paradise Lost*. Bk. vi, l. 2.

13
You cheat boys of their sleep, and deliver them to their masters, that their tender hands may undergo harsh strokes.
OVID, *Amores*. Bk. i, eleg. 13, l. 17. Of morning.

14
If I take the wings of the morning, and dwell in the uttermost parts of the sea.
Old Testament: Psalms, cxxxix, 9.

The Wings of the Morning.
LOUIS TRACY. Title of novel.

15
The morning like a legend long ago
Walked on the water, kindling ring on ring.
BEATRICE RAVENEL, *The Swamp*.

16
But soft! methinks I scent the morning air.
SHAKESPEARE, *Hamlet*. Act i, sc. v, l. 58.

See how the morning opes her golden gates,
And takes her farewell of the glorious sun!
SHAKESPEARE, *III Henry VI*. Act ii, sc. 1, l. 21.

The grey-eyed morn smiles on the frowning night,
Chequering the eastern clouds with streaks of light.
SHAKESPEARE, *Romeo and Juliet*. Act ii, sc. 3, l. 1.

17
Full many a glorious morning have I seen
Flatter the mountain-tops with sovereign eye.
SHAKESPEARE, *Sonnets*. No. xxxiii.

18
There comes the morning with the golden basket in her right hand bearing the wreath of beauty silently to crown the earth.
RABINDRANATH TAGORE, *Gitanjali*. No. 67.

19
Rise, happy morn, rise, holy morn,
Draw forth the cheerful day from night;
O Father, touch the east, and light
The light that shone when Hope was born.
TENNYSON, *In Memoriam*. Pt. xxx, st. 8.

1
Morn in the white wake of the morning star
Came furrowing all the orient into gold.
TENNYSON, *The Princess*. Pt. iii, l. 1.

The meek-eyed Morn appears, mother of dews.
THOMSON, *The Seasons: Summer*, l. 47.

2
Mornings are mysteries; the first world's youth,
Man's insurrection, and the future's bud,
Shroud in their births.
HENRY VAUGHAN, *Silex Scintillans: Rules and Lessons*.

MORTALITY

See also Death, the Inevitable; Oblivion

3
Learn not to esteem human things overmuch. (Γίγνωσκε τἀνθρώπεια μὴ σέβειν ἄγαν.)
ÆSCHYLUS, *Niobe*. Frag. 80.

Mortal man taketh thought only for the day, and hath no more surety than the shadow of smoke.
ÆSCHYLUS, *Fragments*. Frag. 227.

4
Who then to frail mortality shall trust
But limns on water, or but writes in dust.
FRANCIS BACON, *The World*.

5
Child of mortality, whence comest thou?
Why is thy countenance sad, and why are thine eyes red with weeping?
ANNA LETITIA BARBAULD, *Hymns in Prose*, 13.

6
The earth goeth on the earth glistering like gold;
The earth goeth to the earth sooner than it wold;
The earth builds on the earth castles and towers;
The earth says to the earth, all shall be ours.
WILLIAM BILLYNG, *Five Wounds of Christ*. (MONTGOMERY, *Christian Poets*, p. 58.) An epitaph which is cited in Ravenshaw's *Antiente Epitaphs*, p. 158. Weaver's *Funeral Monuments* (1631) states that it was used as epitaph for the Archbishop of Canterbury, in the time of Edward III.

Earth walks on Earth, glittering in gold;
Earth goes to Earth sooner than it wold;
Earth builds on Earth palaces and towers;
Earth says to Earth, Soon all shall be ours.
SCOTT, *Epitaph*. (*Notes and Queries*, 21 May, 1853.)

7
Generations pass while some trees stand, and old families last not three oaks.
SIR THOMAS BROWNE, *Hydriotaphia*. Ch. 5.

8
All bodies are subject to change; so it comes to pass that each body is mortal. (Omne corpus mutabile est; . . . ita efficitur ut omne corpus mortale sit.)
CICERO, *De Natura Deorum*. Bk. iii, ch. 12, sec. 30.

9
Sad Mortality may hide
In his ashes all her pride,
With this inscription o'er his head:
All hope of never dying here lies dead.
RICHARD CRASHAW, *On the Death of Mr. Herrys*. No. 3, l. 59.

10
To show the world that now and then
Great ministers are mortal men.
DRYDEN, *Epistles: To Sir G. Etheredge*, l. 43.

11
All things are born of earth; all things earth takes again. ("Απαντα τίκτει χθὼν, πάλιν τε λαμβάνει.)
EURIPIDES, *Antiope*. Frag. 48.

Earth all things bears and gathers in again. (Γη πάντα τίκτει καὶ πάλιν κομίζεται.)
MEANDER, *Monostikoi*. No. 89.

12
Man loses all semblance of mortality by living in the midst of immortal blessings.
EPICURUS, *Letter to Menœceus*. (DIOGENES LAERTIUS, *Epicurus*. Bk. x, sec. 135.)

13
To smell of a turf of fresh earth is wholesome for the body; no less are thoughts of mortality cordial to the soul.
THOMAS FULLER, *Holy and Profane States*. Bk. iv.

14
All flesh is grass, and all the goodliness thereof is as the flower of the field.
Old Testament: Isaiah, xl, 6.

All flesh is as grass.
New Testament: I Peter, i, 24.

Grass and hay, we are all mortal.
RICHARD BRATHWAITE, *Whimseys*, 73. (1631)

All flesh is grass, and all its glory fades
Like the fair flow'r dishevell'd in the wind.
COWPER, *The Task*. Bk. iii, l. 261.

All flesh is hay.
JOHN ERSKINE, *Gospel Sonnets: Meditations on Tobacco*.

Since all flesh is grass ere 'tis hay,
O may I in clover lie snug,
And when old Time mows me away,
Be stacked with defunct Lady Mugg!
HORACE AND JAMES SMITH, *Rejected Addresses: The Beautiful Incendiary*.

15
Mortality
Weighs heavily on me like unwilling sleep.
KEATS, *On Seeing the Elgin Marbles*.

16
All that belongs to mortals is mortal; all things pass us by, or if not, we pass them by. (Θνητὰ τὰ τῶν θνητῶν, καὶ πάντα παρέρχεται ἡμᾶς· ἢν δὲ μή, ἀλλ' ἡμεῖς αὐτὰ παρερχόμεθα.)
LUCIAN. (*Greek Anthology*. Bk. x, epig. 31.)

17
How gladly would I meet
Mortality my sentence, and be earth

Insensible, how glad would lay me down
As in my mother's lap!
MILTON, *Paradise Lost*. Bk. x, l. 775.

1
We are all mortal, and each is for himself. (Nous sommes tous mortels, et chacun est pour soi.)
MOLIÈRE, *L'École des Femmes*. Act ii, sc. 5, 4.

2
All that's bright must fade,—
The brightest still the fleetest;
All that's sweet was made
But to be lost when sweetest.
THOMAS MOORE, *All That's Bright Must Fade.*

3
Remember that thou art mortal. (Μέμνησ' ὅτι θνητὸς ὑπάρχεις.)
PHOCYLIDES, *Sententiæ*. No. 109.

Your lot is mortal; you wish for what is not mortal. (Sors tua mortalis; non est mortale quod optas.)
OVID, *Metamorphoses*. Bk. ii, l. 56.

4
Consider
The lilies of the field whose bloom is brief:—
We are as they;
Like them we fade away
As doth a leaf.
CHRISTINA ROSSETTI, *Consider*.

5
We cannot hold mortality's strong hand.
SHAKESPEARE, *King John*. Act iv, sc. 2, l. 82.

Gloucester: O, let me kiss that hand!
Lear: Let me wipe it first; it smells of mortality.
SHAKESPEARE, *King Lear*. Act iv, sc. 6, l. 134.

In them nature's copy's not eterne.
SHAKESPEARE, *Macbeth*. Act iii, sc. 2, l. 38.

6
Man's wretched state,
That flowers so fresh at morn, and fades at evening late.
SPENSER, *Faerie Queene*. Bk. iii, canto ix, st. 39.

All that in this world is great or gay
Doth as a vapour vanish and decay.
SPENSER, *The Ruines of Time*, l. 55.

7
The immortal could we cease to contemplate,
The mortal part suggests its every trait.
FRANCIS THOMPSON, *Her Portrait*. St. 7.

Why have we longings of immortal pain,
And all we long for mortal?
FRANCIS THOMPSON, *To the Setting Sun*, l. 194.

8
Old age will come; disease may come before;
Fifteen is full as mortal as threescore.
YOUNG, *Love of Fame*. Satire vi, l. 170.

All men think all men mortal but themselves.
YOUNG, *Night Thoughts*. Night i, l. 424.

MOSES

9
And he buried him in a valley in the land of Moab, over against Beth-peor: but no man knoweth of his sepulcher unto this day.
Old Testament: Deuteronomy, xxxiv, 6.

By Nebo's lonely mountain,
On this side Jordan's wave,
In a vale in the land of Moab,
There lies a lonely grave;
But no man built that sepulcher,
And no man saw it e'er,
For the angels of God upturned the sod
And laid the dead man there.
CECIL FRANCES ALEXANDER, *The Burial of Moses.*

This was the truest warrior
That ever buckled sword;
This the most gifted poet
That ever breathed a word;
And never earth's philosopher
Traced with his golden pen
On the deathless page truths half so sage
As he wrote down for men.
CECIL FRANCES ALEXANDER, *The Burial of Moses.*

10
Now the man Moses was very meek, above all the men which were upon the face of the earth.
Old Testament: Numbers, xii, 3.

Moses was a merciful, meek man, and yet with what fury did he run through the camp, and cut the throats of three-and-thirty thousand of his dear Israelites that were fallen into idolatry.
DANIEL DEFOE, *The Shortest Way with the Dissenters.*

11
Whilst you are fighting (said Panurge) I will pray God for your victory, after the example of the chivalrous Captain Moses, leader of the people of Israel. (Pendant que combaterez, je prieray Dieu pour vostre victoire, à l'exemple du chevaleureux capitaine Moses, conducteur du peuple israélicque.)
RABELAIS, *Works*. Bk. iv, ch. 37.

12
Softly his fainting head he lay
Upon his Maker's breast;
His Maker kiss'd his soul away,
And laid his flesh to rest.
ISAAC WATTS, *The Death of Moses.*

Like Moses to thyself convey,
And kiss my raptur'd soul away.
SAMUEL WESLEY, *Collection Hymn.*

Died of the kisses of the lips of God.
F. W. MYERS, *St. Paul: Of Moses.*

MOTHER AND MOTHERHOOD

I—Mother: Apothegms

13
Where there is a mother in the house, matters speed well.
AMOS BRONSON ALCOTT, *Table Talk: Nurture.*

14
Thou wilt scarce be a man before thy mother.
BEAUMONT AND FLETCHER, *Love's Cure*. Act ii, sc. 2.

But strive still to be a man before your mother.
COWPER, *Connoisseur*. Motto of No. 3.

1
The mother's heart is the child's schoolroom.
HENRY WARD BEECHER, *Life Thoughts.*

2
The sweetest sounds to mortals given
Are heard in Mother, Home, and Heaven.
WILLIAM GOLDSMITH BROWN, *Mother, Home, Heaven.*

She 's somebody's mother, boys, you know,
For all she 's aged, and poor, and slow.
MARY D. BRINE, *Somebody's Mother.* First published in *Harper's Weekly*, 2 March, 1878.

3
The many-tattered,
Little old-faced peaking sister-turned-mother.
ROBERT BROWNING, *Christmas-Eve.* Sec. 2.

4
A noble mother must have bred
So brave a son.
CAMPBELL, *Napoleon and the British Sailor.*

5
A mother is a mother still,
The holiest thing alive.
S. T. COLERIDGE, *The Three Graves.* St. 10.

6
Men are what their mothers made them.
EMERSON, *Conduct of Life: Fate.*

The future destiny of the child is always the work of the mother.
NAPOLEON BONAPARTE, *Sayings of Napoleon.*

All that I am my mother made me.
JOHN QUINCY ADAMS.

All that I am or hope to be, I owe to my angel mother.
Attributed to ABRAHAM LINCOLN.

7
Mothers' darlings make but milksop heroes.
THOMAS FULLER, *Gnomologia.* No. 3474.

A child may have too much of mother's blessing.
JOHN RAY, *English Proverbs.*

Nothing like mamma's darling for upsetting a coach.
BENJAMIN DISRAELI, *Tancred.* Bk. i, ch. 3.

Cease at length to follow thy mother. (Tandem desine matrem.)
HORACE, *Odes.* Bk. i, ode 23, l. 11.

8
Where yet was ever found a mother,
Who'd give her booby for another?
JOHN GAY, *Fables.* Pt. i, fab. 3, l. 33.

9
And Adam called his wife's name Eve; because she was the mother of all living.
Old Testament: Genesis, iii, 20.

10
What is home without a mother?
ALICE HAWTHORNE. Title of poem.

11
Put them all together, they spell "Mother,"
A word that means the world to me.
HOWARD JOHNSON, *Mother.* (1915)

12
Only a mother knows a mother's fondness.
LADY MARY WORTLEY MONTAGU, *Letter to the Countess of Bute*, 22 July, 1754.

13
He's all the mother's, from the top to toe.
SHAKESPEARE, *Richard III.* Act iii, sc. 1, l. 156.

Lord Illingworth: All women become like their mothers. That is their tragedy.
Mrs. Allonby: No man does. That is his.
OSCAR WILDE, *Woman of No Importance.* Act ii.

14
Simply having children does not make mothers.
JOHN A. SHEDD, *Salt from My Attic*, p. 38.

15
A lady who had gallantries and several children, told her husband he was like the austere man, who reaped where he did not sow.
SWIFT, *Thoughts on Various Subjects.*

16
Mother is the name for God in the lips and hearts of little children.
THACKERAY, *Vanity Fair.* Vol. ii, ch. 12.

17
Be a stepmother kindly as she will,
There's in her love some hint of winter's chill.
D'ARCY W. THOMPSON, *Sales Attici.*

A barren sow was never good to pigs.
H. G. BOHN, *Hand-Book of Proverbs*, 281.

18
God could not be everywhere and therefore he made mothers.
UNKNOWN. A Jewish proverb.

19
Does your mother know you're out?
UNKNOWN. Title of poem published in the London *Mirror*, 28 April, 1838. Afterwards a slang phrase in both England and America. (*Notes and Queries.* Ser. viii, vol. 8, p. 5.)

II—Mother: My Mother

20
Don't aim to be an earthly Saint, with eyes fixed on a star,
Just try to be the fellow that your Mother thinks you are.
WILL S. ADKIN, *Just Try to Be the Fellow.*

21
But the father's heart was broken,
And this is all he said:
"Their mother is in a casket
In the baggage coach ahead."
FRANK ARCHER, *Mother.* Later rewritten by Gussie L. Davis and renamed *In the Baggage Coach Ahead.* (1896)

22
My father urged me sair—my mother didna speak,
But she looket in my face till my heart was like to break.
LADY ANNE BARNARD, *Auld Robin Gray.*

23
My mother! when I learn'd that thou wast dead,
Say, wast thou conscious of the tears I shed?
Hover'd thy spirit o'er thy sorrowing son,
Wretch even then, life's journey just begun?

Perhaps thou gav'st me, though unseen, a kiss;
Perhaps a tear, if souls can weep in bliss—
Ah, that maternal smile! it answers—Yes.
COWPER, *On the Receipt of My Mother's Picture*, l. 21.

1
You may have tangible wealth untold;
Caskets of jewels and coffers of gold.
Richer than I you can never be—
I had a mother who read to me.
STRICKLAND GILLILAN, *The Reading Mother.*

2
Now in memory comes my mother,
As she used, in years agone,
To regard the darling dreamers
Ere she left them till the dawn.
COATES KINNEY, *Rain on the Roof.*

3
I would weave you a song, my mother, . . .
Yours the tender hand Upon my breast;
Yours the voice Sounding ever in my ears.
MADELEINE MASON-MANHEIM, *To My Mother.*

4
Me, let the tender office long engage
To rock the cradle of reposing age,
With lenient arts extend a Mother's breath,
Make languor smile, and smooth the bed of death;
Explore the thought, explain the asking eye,
And keep a while one parent from the sky!
POPE, *Epistle to Dr. Arbuthnot*, l. 408.

5 So loving to my mother
That he might not beteem the winds of heaven
Visit her face too roughly.
SHAKESPEARE, *Hamlet*. Act i, sc. 2, l. 140.

6
Mother, thou sole and only, thou not these,
Keep me in mind a little when I die,
Because I was thy first-born.
SWINBURNE, *Atalanta in Calydon: Meleager.*

7
Who ran to help me, when I fell,
And would some pretty story tell,
Or kiss the place to make it well?
My Mother.
ANN TAYLOR, *My Mother.*

8 Happy he
With such a mother! Faith in womankind
Beats with his blood, and trust in all things high
Comes easy to him, and tho' he trip and fall
He shall not blind his soul with clay.
TENNYSON, *The Princess*. Pt. vii, l. 308.

9
St. Leon raised his kindling eye,
And lifts the sparkling cup on high;
"I drink to one," he said,
"Whose image never may depart,
Deep graven on this grateful heart,
Till memory be dead." . . .
St. Leon paused, as if he would
Not breathe her name in careless mood,
Thus, lightly, to another;
Then bent his noble head, as though
To give that word the reverence due,
And gently said: "*My Mother!*"
UNKNOWN, *The Knight's Toast*. Attributed to Winthrop Mackworth Praed and to Sir Walter Scott, but not found in their works.

My mother was a lady, like yours you will allow.
EDWARD B. MARKS, *My Mother Was a Lady.* Made famous by Lottie Gilson in 1896.

III—Motherhood

10
Perhaps a better woman after all,
With chubby children hanging on my neck
To keep me low and wise.
E. B. BROWNING, *Aurora Leigh*. Bk. ii, l. 515.

11
What art can a woman be good at? Oh, vain!
What art *is* she good at, but hurting her breast
With the milk-teeth of babes, and a smile at the pain?
E. B. BROWNING, *Mother and Poet.*

The bearing and the training of a child
Is woman's wisdom.
TENNYSON, *The Princess*. Pt. v, l. 456.

12
Womanliness means only motherhood;
All love begins and ends there,—roams enough,
But, having run the circle, rests at home.
ROBERT BROWNING, *The Inn Album*. Canto vii.

13
A mother who boasts two boys was ever accounted rich.
ROBERT BROWNING, *Ivàn Ivànovitch*, l. 154.

14
Lo! at the couch where infant beauty sleeps,
Her silent watch the mournful mother keeps;
She, while the lovely babe unconscious lies,
Smiles on her slumbering child with pensive eyes.
CAMPBELL, *The Pleasures of Hope*. Pt. i, l. 225.

15
So for the mother's sake the child was dear,
And dearer was the mother for the child!
S. T. COLERIDGE, *Sonnet: To a Friend Who Asked How I Felt when the Nurse First Presented My Infant to Me.*

16
I tell you there isn't a thing under the sun that needs to be done at all, but what a man can do better than a woman, unless it's bearing children, and they do that in a poor make-shift way; it had better ha' been left to the men.
GEORGE ELIOT, *Adam Bede.*

17
Do you perhaps think that nature gave women nipples as a kind of beauty spot, not for the purpose of nourishing their children?
FAVORINUS. (AULUS GELLIUS, *Noctes Atticæ*. Bk. xii, ch. 5, sec. 7.)

1
Pooh—men!
We are done with them now,
Who had need of them then,—
I and you!
FLORENCE KIPER FRANK, *Baby*.

2
Our women have a proverb, "It is a sad burden to carry a dead man's child."
THOMAS FULLER, *Church History*. Bk. ii, sec. v. (1655)

In the first days
Of my distracting grief, I found myself
As women wish to be who love their lords.
JOHN HOME, *Douglas*. Act i, sc. 1.

3
Mine, Lord, all mine, Thy gift and loving token.
J. A. GOODCHILD, *The Firstborn*.

Beat upon mine, little heart! beat, beat!
Beat upon mine! you are mine, my sweet!
All mine from your pretty blue eyes to your feet,
My sweet!
TENNYSON, *Romney's Remorse*.

The merest grin of maternal beatitude
Is worth a world of dull virginity.
GERALD GOULD, *Monogamy*. Pt. iii, st. 4.

4
There is none,
In all this cold and hollow world, no fount
Of deep, strong, deathless love, save that within
A mother's heart.
FELICIA HEMANS, *The Siege of Valencia*.

Youth fades; love droops; the leaves of friendship fall:
A mother's secret love outlives them all.
O. W. HOLMES, *The Mother's Secret*.

If I were hanged on the highest hill,
Mother o' mine, O mother o' mine!
I know whose love would follow me still,
Mother o' mine, O mother o' mine!
RUDYARD KIPLING, *Mother o' Mine*. (*The Light That Failed: Dedication*.)

5
Beer will grow *mothery*, and ladies fair
Will grow like beer.
THOMAS HOOD, *The Stag-Eyed Lady*.

6
To bear, to nurse, to rear,
To watch and then to lose,
To see my bright ones disappear,
Drawn up like morning dews.
JEAN INGELOW, *Songs of Seven: Seven Times Six*.

7
I arose a mother in Israel.
Old Testament: Judges, v, 7.

Her children arise and call her blessed.
Old Testament: Proverbs, xxxi, 28.

8
Do you expect, forsooth, that a mother will hand down to her children principles which differ from her own? (Scilicet expectas ut tradat mater honestos Atque alios mores quam quos habet?)
JUVENAL, *Satires*. Sat. vi, l. 239.

9
How often does a gilded bed contain a woman who is lying in? (Sed jacet aurato vix ulla puerpera lecto?)
JUVENAL, *Satires*. Sat. vi, l. 594.

10
Maids must be wives and mothers, to fulfil
Th' entire and holiest end of woman's being.
FRANCES ANNE KEMBLE, *Woman's Heart*.

11
When people inquire I always just state,
"I have four nice children, and hope to have eight."
ALINE KILMER, *Ambition*.

12
I pray that our Heavenly Father may assuage the anguish of your bereavement and leave you only the cherished memory of the loved and lost, and the solemn pride that must be yours to have laid so costly a sacrifice upon the altar of freedom.
ABRAHAM LINCOLN, *Letter*, 21 Nov., 1864, to Mrs. Bixby of Boston, who lost five sons killed in battle. Said to have been drafted by John Hay, Lincoln's secretary.

13
His mother from the window look'd,
With all the longing of a mother.
JAMES LOGAN, *The Braes of Yarrow*. St. 4.

14
A woman's love
Is mighty, but a mother's heart is weak,
And by its weakness overcomes.
J. R. LOWELL, *A Legend of Brittany*. Pt. ii, st. 43.

15
A mother loves her child more than the father does, because she knows it's her own, while the father only thinks it's his.
MENANDER, *Fragments*. No. 657.

16
The bravest battle that ever was fought;
Shall I tell you where and when?
On the maps of the world you will find it not;
It was fought by the mothers of men.
JOAQUIN MILLER, *The Bravest Battle*.

17
The angels . . . singing unto one another,
Can find among their burning terms of love,
None so devotional as that of "mother."
EDGAR ALLAN POE, *To My Mother*.

18
Their mother hearts beset with fears,
Their lives bound up in tender lives.
CHRISTINA ROSSETTI, *Goblin Market*.

19
I know—yet my arms are empty,
That fondly folded seven,
And the mother heart within me
Is almost starved for heaven.
MARGARET SANGSTER, *Are the Children at Home?* *See also* DEATH AND THE CHILD.

1
The pleasing punishment that women bear.
SHAKESPEARE, *The Comedy of Errors.* Act i, sc. 1, l. 47.

My dear angel has been qualmish of late, and begins to grow remarkably round in the waist.
SMOLLETT, *Roderick Random: Conclusion.*

2
A grandam's name is little less in love,
Than is the doting title of a mother.
SHAKESPEARE, *Richard III.* Act iv, sc. 4, l. 299.

3
There will be a singing in your heart,
There will be a rapture in your eyes;
You will be a woman set apart,
You will be so wonderful and wise.
You will sleep, and when from dreams you start,
As of one that wakes in Paradise,
There will be a singing in your heart,
There will be a rapture in your eyes.
ROBERT W. SERVICE, *The Mother.*

4
And say to mothers what a holy charge
Is theirs—with what a kingly power their love
Might rule the fountains of the new-born mind.
LYDIA HUNTLY SIGOURNEY, *The Mother of Washington,* l. 33.

5
As through the drifting snow she press'd,
The babe was sleeping on her breast.
SEBA SMITH, *The Snow Storm.*

6
Oh! when a mother meets on high
The babe she lost in infancy,
Hath she not then, for pains and fears,
The day of woe, the watchful night,
For all her sorrow, all her tears,
An over-payment of delight?
SOUTHEY, *Curse of Kehama.* Canto x, st. 11.

7
Children are the anchors that hold a mother to life.
SOPHOCLES, *Phœdra.* Frag. 619.

8
The mother of the sweetest little maid,
That ever crow'd for kisses.
TENNYSON, *The Princess.* Pt. ii, l. 260.

A lusty brace
Of twins may weed her of her folly.
TENNYSON, *The Princess.* Pt. v, l. 453.

9
Is not a young mother one of the sweetest sights life shows us?
THACKERAY, *The Newcomes.* Bk. ii, ch. 13.

10
Dear little head, that lies in calm content
Within the gracious hollow that God made
In every human shoulder, where He meant
Some tired head for comfort should be laid.
CELIA THAXTER, *Song.*

11
Begin, baby boy, to recognize your mother by a smile. (Incipe, parve puer, risu cognoscere matrem.)
VERGIL, *Eclogues.* No. iv, l. 60.

12
They say that man is mighty,
He governs land and sea,
He wields a mighty scepter
O'er lesser powers that be;
But a mightier power and stronger
Man from his throne has hurled,
For the hand that rocks the cradle
Is the hand that rules the world.
WILLIAM ROSS WALLACE, *What Rules the World.* (c. 1865)

They say man rules the universe,
That subject shore and main
Kneel down and bless the empery
Of his majestic reign;
But a sovereign, gentler, mightier,
Man from his throne has hurled,
For the hand that rocks the cradle
Is the hand that rules the world.
WILLIAM STEWART ROSS, *The Hand That Rocks the Cradle.* (*Woman: Her Glory.* Vol. ii, p. 420. 1894.)

"The hand that rocks the cradle"—but today there's no such hand.
It is bad to rock the baby, they would have us understand;
So the cradle's but a relic of the former foolish days,
When mothers reared their children in unscientific ways;
When they jounced them and they bounced them, those poor dwarfs of long ago—
The Washingtons and Jeffersons and Adamses, you know.
BISHOP WILLIAM CROSWELL DOANE [?], *What Might Have Been.* A complaint that, for hygienic reasons, he was not allowed to play with his grandchild.

13
Years to a mother bring distress,
But do not make her love the less.
WORDSWORTH, *The Affliction of Margaret.*

Thou, while thy babes around thee cling,
Shalt show us how divine a thing
A woman may be made.
WORDSWORTH, *To a Young Lady.*

MOTIVE, see Purpose

MOUNTAIN

See also Hill

I—Mountain: Apothegms

14
They make of a fly an elephant, and of a molehill a mountain.
THOMAS BECON, *Catechism.* (c. 1560)

To make an elephant of a fly. ('Ελέφαντα ἐκ μυίας ποιεῖν.)
LUCIAN, *Praise of the Fly.*

She takes me for a mountain, that am but a molehill.
RICHARD BROME, *City Wit*. Act iv, sc. 1. (1653)

To make huge mountains of small mole-hills.
GABRIEL HARVEY, *Letter-Book*, p. 14. (1573)

1
They came to the Delectable Mountains.
JOHN BUNYAN, *The Pilgrim's Progress*. Pt. i.

2
Mountains interpos'd
Make enemies of nations, who had else,
Like kindred drops, been mingled into one.
COWPER, *The Task*. Bk. ii, l. 16.

There are no more Pyrenees. (Il n'y a plus de Pyrénées.)
LOUIS XIV, to his grandson, the Duke d'Anjou, on his accession to the Spanish throne. (VOLTAIRE, *Siècle de Louis XIV*. Ch. 28.) Fournier alleges that this is just another example of Voltaire inventing history, and that the phrase was really used by the Spanish Ambassador when he greeted the new king.

3
A mountain and a river are good neighbours.
GEORGE HERBERT, *Jacula Prudentum*.

4
Ye crags and peaks, I'm with you once again! . . .
O sacred forms, how proud you look!
How high you lift your heads into the sky!
How huge you are! how mighty and how free!
JAMES SHERIDAN KNOWLES, *William Tell*. Act i, sc. 2.

Mountains, ye are growing old; your ribs of granite are getting weak and rotten.
E. M. MORSE, *Mountains*.

5
A mountain was in labor, sending forth dreadful groans, and there was the highest expectation throughout the region. But it brought forth only a mouse. (Mons parturibat, gemitus immanes ciens; Eratque in terris maxima expectatio. At ille murem peperit.)
PHÆDRUS, *Fables*. Bk. iv, fab. 22, l. 1. The Latin rendering of Æsop's fable of *The Mountain in Labor*.

The mountain groaned in pangs of birth:
Great expectation filled the earth;
And lo! a mouse was born!
Metrical rendering of Phædrus, iv, 22, 1.

The mountain labors, and a ridiculous mouse is born. (Parturient montes, nascetur ridiculus mus.)
HORACE, *Ars Poetica*, l. 139.

The old fable was made good, "A mountain is in travail and then a mouse is born." (Τὸ μυθολογούμενον ὠδίνειν ὄρος, εἶτα μῦν ἀποτεκεῖν.)
PLUTARCH, *Lives: Agesilaüs*. Ch. 36, sec. 5. In Athanæus, it is Tachos himself who makes this jest upon Agesilaüs, who retorts, "Some day you will think me a lion."

6
Friends may meet,
But mountains never greet.
JOHN RAY, *English Proverbs*. An English rendering of the Greek proverb, Ὄρος ὄρει οὐ μίγνυται, "Mountain will not mingle with mountain." The French have a proverb, dating from the fifteenth century, "Entre deux montagnes vallée."

I found the proverb true that men have more privilege than mountains in meeting.
JOHN TAYLOR THE WATER-POET, *The Penniless Pilgrimage*. (1618)

Friends possibly may meet, but mountains never.
GEORGE WITHER, *Dark Lantern*, 29. (1653)

Mountains never shake hands. Their roots may touch: they may keep together some way up; but at length they part company, and rise into individual, insulated peaks. So it is with great men.
J. C. AND A. W. HARE, *Guesses at Truth*.

MOUNTAIN AND MAHOMET, *see* ADAPTABILITY.

7
Mountains are the beginning and the end of all natural scenery.
RUSKIN, *True and Beautiful: Mountains*.

8
Who digs hills because they do aspire,
Throws down one mountain to cast up a higher.
SHAKESPEARE, *Pericles*. Act i, sc. 4, l. 5.

9
As mountains are for winds,
That shake not, though they blow perpetually.
SHAKESPEARE, *Taming of the Shrew*, ii, 1, 141.

10
Longer shadows fall from lofty mountains. (Majoresque cadunt altis de montibus umbræ.)
VERGIL, *Eclogues*. No. i, l. 84.

II—Mountain: Ossa on Pelion

11
They were fain to pile Ossa on Olympus, and Pelion, with it waving forests, on Ossa, so that heaven might be scaled. (Ὄσσαν ἐπ' Οὐλύμπῳ μέμασαν θέμεν, αὐτὰρ ἐπ' Ὄσσῃ Πήλιον εἰνοσίφυλλον, ἵν' οὐρανὸς ἀμβατὸς εἴη.)
HOMER, *Odyssey*. Bk. xi, l. 315. An allusion to the myth of the Titans, who piled Mount Pelion and Mount Ossa upon Olympus in order to scale the dwelling of the gods, but were overthrown by Jupiter.

To fling Ossa upon Olympus, and to pile
Pelion with all its growth of leafy woods
On Ossa.
HOMER, *Odyssey*, xi, 315. (Bryant, tr.)

They were setting
Ossa upon Olympus, and upon
Steep Ossa heavy Pelius.
HOMER, *Odyssey*, xi, 315. (Chapman, tr.)

To the Olympian summit they essayed
To heave up Ossa, and to Ossa's crown
Branch-waving Pelion.
HOMER, *Odyssey*, xi, 315. (Cowper, tr.)

Heav'd on Olympus tottering Ossa stood;
On Ossa, Pelion nods with all his wood.
HOMER, *Odyssey*, xi, 315. (Pope, tr.)

1
To pile Pelion upon Olympus. (Pelion imposuisse Olympo.)
HORACE, *Odes*. Bk. iii, ode 4, l. 52.

2
Then the Almighty Father hurled his thunderbolts, shattering Olympus, and dashed Pelion down from underlying Ossa. (Tum pater omnipotens misso perfregit Olympum Fulmine et excussit subjectæ Pelion Ossæ.)
OVID, *Metamorphoses*. Bk. i, l. 154.

3
I would have you call to mind the strength of the ancient giants, that undertook to lay the high mountain Pelion on the top of Ossa, and set among those the shady Olympus.
RABELAIS, *Works*. Bk. iv, ch. 38.

4
Now pile your dust upon the quick and dead,
Till of this flat a mountain you have made,
To o'ertop old Pelion, on the skyish head
Of blue Olympus.
SHAKESPEARE, *Hamlet*. Act v, sc. 1, l. 274.

5
Thrice did they attempt to pile Ossa on Pelion, and over Ossa to roll leafy Olympus. (Ter sunt conati Pelio Ossam Scilicet, atque Ossæ frondosum involvere Olympum.)
VERGIL, *Georgics*. Bk. i, l. 281.

III—Mountain: Alp on Alp

6
Ah! as a pilgrim who the Alps doth pass,
Or Atlas' temples crown'd with winter's glass,
The airy Caucasus, the Apennine,
Pyrenees' clifts where sun doth never shine,
When he some heaps of hills hath overwent,
Begins to think on rest, his journey spent,
Till, mounting some tall mountain, he do find
More heights before him than he left behind.
WILLIAM DRUMMOND, *Flowers of Sion: Hymn of the Fairest Fair*, l. 149. (1623)

So pleas'd at first the tow'ring Alps we try,
Mount o'er the vales, and seem to tread the sky;
Th' eternal snows appear already past,
And the first clouds and mountains seem the last:
But those attain'd, we tremble to survey
The growing labours of the lengthen'd way;
Th' increasing prospect tires our wand'ring eyes,
Hills peep o'er hills, and Alps on Alps arise!
POPE, *Essay on Criticism*. Pt. ii, l. 25. (1711)

7
Alps on Alps in clusters swelling,
Mighty, and pure, and fit to make
The ramparts of a Godhead's dwelling!
THOMAS MOORE, *Rhymes on the Road*. Extract i, l. 26.

8
Inexperienced travellers who, finding themselves for the first time in the Alps, imagine that they can clear them with every mountain, and, when they have reached the summit, are discouraged to see higher mountains in front of them.
ROUSSEAU, *Émile*. Bk. iv. Addison used the same comparison in the *Spectator*.

9
He was like the adventurous climber on the Alps, to whom the surmounting the most dangerous precipices and ascending to the most towering peaks only shows yet dizzier heights and higher points of elevation.
SCOTT, of Napoleon, in his *Life of Napoleon*.

IV—Mountain: Description

10
Oh, thou Parnassus whom I now survey,
Not in the phrensy of a dreamer's eye,
Not in the fabled landscape of a lay,
But soaring snow-clad through thy native sky,
In the wild pomp of mountain majesty!
BYRON, *Childe Harold*. Canto i, st. 60.

11
To me
High mountains are a feeling, but the hum
Of human cities torture.
BYRON, *Childe Harold*. Canto iii, st. 72.

12
The Alps, the palaces of Nature.
BYRON, *Childe Harold*. Canto iii, st. 62.

13
Whose sunbright summit mingles with the sky.
CAMPBELL, *The Pleasures of Hope*. Pt. i, l. 4.

14
I am homesick for my mountains—
My heroic mother hills—
And the longing that is on me
No solace ever stills.
BLISS CARMAN, *The Cry of the Hill-born*.

15
Hast thou a charm to stay the morning-star
In his steep course? So long he seems to pause
On thy bald, awful head, O sovran Blanc!
S. T. COLERIDGE, *Hymn Before Sunrise in the Vale of Chamouni*, l. 1.

Thou, most awful Form!
Risest from forth thy silent sea of pines,
How silently! Around thee and above
Deep is the air and dark, substantial, black,
An ebon mass: methinks thou piercest it
As with a wedge! But when I look again
It is thine own calm home, thy crystal shrine,
Thy habitation from eternity!
O dread and silent Mount! I gazed upon thee,
Till thou, still present to the bodily sense,
Didst vanish from my thought: entranced in prayer
I worshipped the Invisible alone.
S. T. COLERIDGE, *Hymn Before Sunrise*, l. 5.

Rise, O ever rise!
Rise like a cloud of incense, from the Earth!
Thou kingly Spirit throned among the hills,
Thou dread ambassador from Earth to Heaven.
S. T. COLERIDGE, *Hymn Before Sunrise*, l. 79.

Mont Blanc is the monarch of mountains;
They crown'd him long ago,
On a throne of rocks, in a robe of clouds,
With a diadem of snow.
BYRON, *Manfred*. Act i, sc. 1, l. 62.

1
Mountains are good to look upon
But do not look too long.
They are made of granite. They will break your heart.
GRACE HAZARD CONKLING, *Mountains*.

2
The mountains lie in curves so tender
I want to lay my arm about them
As God does.
OLIVE TILFORD DARGAN, *Twilight*.

3
As some tall cliff, that lifts its awful form,
Swells from the vale, and midway leaves the storm,
Though round its breast the rolling clouds are spread,
Eternal sunshine settles on its head.
GOLDSMITH, *The Deserted Village*, l. 189.

So the loud torrent, and the whirlwind's roar,
But bind him to his native mountains more.
GOLDSMITH, *The Traveller*, l. 207.

4
On every mountain height is rest.
GOETHE, *Ein Gleiches*.

5
Mountains have a dreamy way
Of folding up a noisy day
In quiet covers, cool and gray.
LEIGH BUCKNER HANES, *Mountains in Twilight*.

God give me mountains
With hills at their knees.
LEIGH BUCKNER HANES, *Mountains*.

6
Each cloud capped mountain is a holy altar;
An organ breathes in every grove.
THOMAS HOOD, *Ode to Rae Wilson*.

7
While far below men crawl in clay and clod,
Sublimely I shall stand alone with God.
MARY SINTON LEITCH, *The Summit, Mount Everest*.

8
The rocky summits, split and rent,
Formed turret, dome, or battlement,
Or seemed fantastically set
With cupola or minaret.
SCOTT, *The Lady of the Lake*. Canto i, st. 11.

9
Rocks rich in gems, and mountains big with mines,
That on the high equator ridgy rise,
Whence many a bursting stream auriferous plays.
THOMSON, *The Seasons: Summer*, l. 646.

10
The wooded mountains. (Intonsi montes.)
VERGIL, *Eclogues*. No. v, l. 63.

MOURNING

See also Death: They Are All Gone

11
Truly lamentation is a prop of suffering. (Οἵ τοι στεναγμοὶ τῶν πόνων ἐρείσματα.)
ÆSCHYLUS, *Fragments*. Frag. 213.

12
What I do not presume to censure, I may have leave to lament.
EDMUND BURKE, *American Taxation*.

13
Ah! surely nothing dies but something mourns!
BYRON, *Don Juan*. Canto iii, st. 108.

14
Mourn, ye Graces and Loves, and all ye whom the Graces love. (Lugete, o Veneres Cupidinesque, Et quantumst hominum venustiorum.)
CATULLUS, *Odes*. No. iii, l. 1.

15
Each lonely scene shall thee restore;
For thee the tear be duly shed;
Belov'd, till life could charm no more,
And mourn'd, till Pity's self be dead.
WILLIAM COLLINS, *Dirge in Cymbeline*.

Round, round the cypress bier
Where she lies sleeping,
On every turf a tear,
Let us go weeping!
GEORGE DARLEY, *Dirge*.

16
It is better to go to the house of mourning than to go to the house of feasting.
Old Testament: Ecclesiastes, vii, 2.

17
Forever honor'd and forever mourn'd.
HOMER, *Iliad*. Bk. xxii, l. 422. (Pope, tr.)

18
We lament by the ordinance of Nature. (Naturæ imperio gemimus.)
JUVENAL, *Satires*. Sat. xv, l. 138.

Nature's law
That man was made to mourn.
BURNS, *Man Was Made to Mourn*.

Whom universal Nature did lament.
MILTON, *Lycidas*, l. 60.

19
The air is full of farewells to the dying,
And mournings for the dead.
LONGFELLOW, *Resignation*.

20
The lonely mountains o'er,
And the resounding shore,
A voice of weeping heard, and loud lament;

From haunted spring, and dale
Edg'd with poplar pale,
The parting Genius is with sighing sent,
With flower-enwoven tresses torn
The Nymphs in twilight shade of tangled thickets mourn.
MILTON, *On the Morning of Christ's Nativity*, l. 181.

1
Too innocent for coquetry, too fond for idle scorning—
O friend, I fear the lightest heart makes sometimes heaviest mourning.
CAROLINE NORTON, *Bingen on the Rhine*.

2
Then flash'd the living lightning from her eyes,
And screams of horror rend th' affrighted skies.
Not louder shrieks to pitying Heav'n are cast,
When husbands, or when lapdogs, breathe their last;
Or when rich China vessels, fall'n from high,
In glitt'ring dust and painted fragments lie!
POPE, *The Rape of the Lock*. Canto iii, l. 155.

3
Soft is the note, and sad the lay,
That mourns the lovely Rosabelle.
SCOTT, *Lay of the Last Minstrel*. Can. vi, st. 23.

4
None mourn more ostentatiously than those who are rejoicing most. (Nulli jactantius mœrent quam qui maxime lætantur.)
TACITUS, *Annals*. Bk. ii, sec. 77. *See also* GRIEF: SILENT AND VOCAL.

5
He that lacks time to mourn, lacks time to mend.
SIR HENRY TAYLOR, *Philip Van Artevelde*. Act i, sc. 5, l. 38.

How wretched is the man who never mourn'd!
YOUNG, *Night Thoughts*. Night v, l. 245.

6
I count it crime
To mourn for any overmuch.
TENNYSON, *In Memoriam*. Pt. lxxxv. *See also* DEATH: WEEP NOT THE DEAD.

7
One cry was common to them all. (Vox omnibus una.)
VERGIL, *Æneid*. Bk. v, l. 616.

8
He mourns the dead who lives as they desire.
YOUNG, *Night Thoughts*. Night ii, l. 24.

MOUSE

9
Wee sleekit, cow'rin', tim'rous beastie,
Oh, what a panic's in thy breastie!
BURNS, *To a Mouse*.

10
Don't make yourself a mouse or the cat will eat you.
CHEALES, *Proverbial Folk-lore*, 105.

11
It had need to be a wily mouse that should breed in a cat's ear.
JOHN HEYWOOD, *Proverbs*. Pt. ii, ch. 5.

It is a wily mouse
That can build his dwelling-house
Within the cattes ear.
SKELTON, *Why Come Ye Not to Court*, l. 754.

12
I gave the mouse a hole, and she is become my heir.
GEORGE HERBERT, *Jacula Prudentum*.

13
The mice were not impressed by that great house
Wherein you had your glory and your ease;
Magnificence is wasted on a mouse:
They judge all things by cheese.
RICHARD R. KIRK, *The Mice*.

14
Consider the little mouse, how sagacious an animal it is which never entrusts his life to one hole only.
PLAUTUS, *Truculentus*. Act iv, sc. 4, l. 15.

I hold a mouse's heart not worth a leek,
That hath but one hole for to sterte to.
CHAUCER, *The Wife of Bath's Prologue*, l. 572.

The mouse that always trusts to one poor hole,
Can never be a mouse of any soul.
POPE, *The Wife of Bath's Prologue*, l. 298.

The mouse that hath one hole is quickly taken.
GEORGE HERBERT, *Jacula Prudentum*.

15
When a building is about to fall down, all the mice desert it.
PLINY THE ELDER, *Historia Naturalis*. Bk. viii, sec. 103.

16
No house without mouse.
W. G. BENHAM, *Proverbs*, p. 816.

For MOUNTAIN AND MOUSE, *see* MOUNTAIN; *for* MOUSETRAP, *see* FAME: THE MOUSETRAP.

17
Not a mouse
Shall disturb this hallow'd house:
I am sent with broom before,
To sweep the dust behind the door.
SHAKESPEARE, *A Midsummer-Night's Dream*. Act v, sc. 1, l. 394.

MOUTH

See also Lips

I—Mouth: Apothegms

18
Mouth: In man, the gateway to the soul; in woman, the outlet of the heart.
AMBROSE BIERCE, *Devil's Dictionary*, p. 225.

19
These reasons made his mouth to water.
BUTLER, *Hudibras*. Pt. i, canto 3, l. 379.

20
A close mouth catches no flies.
CERVANTES, *Don Quixote*. Pt. i, ch. 11.

No flies will go down your throat if you keep your mouth shut.
C. H. SPURGEON, *John Ploughman*. Ch. 6.
See also under SILENCE.

1
He has a mouth for every matter.
THOMAS FULLER, *Gnomologia*. No. 1859.

2
One mouth doth nothing without another.
GEORGE HERBERT, *Jacula Prudentum*. *See also under* SCANDAL.

3
The hole too open under the nose
Breeds ragged shoes and tattered hose.
JAMES HOWELL, *Proverbs: Fr.-English*, 10.

He has a hole under his nose, and money runs into it.
C. H. SPURGEON, *Ploughman's Pictures*, 39.

4
A lying mouth is a stinking pit.
BEN JONSON, *Explorata: Veritas Proprium Hominis*.

5
Give him a loaf, Tom;
Quiet his mouth, that oven will be venting else.
BEN JONSON, *The Staple of News*. Act i, sc. 1. A favorite jest of the old dramatists.

6
Blind mouths! that scarce themselves know how to hold
A sheep-hook, or have learned aught else the least
That to the faithful herdman's art belongs!
MILTON, *Lycidas*, l. 119.

7
I prythee, take the cork out of my mouth that I may drink thy tidings.
SHAKESPEARE, *As You Like It*. Act iii, sc. 2, l. 213.

8
Had I as many mouths as Hydra, such an answer would stop them all.
SHAKESPEARE, *Othello*. Act ii, sc. 3, l. 308.

9
She looks as if butter wouldn't melt in her mouth.
SWIFT, *Polite Conversation*. Dial. i.

II—Mouth: Appreciations

10
Yes, like a little posy,
Your mouth so small and rosy,
A timid little posy,
Soft, drooping, rosy.
GABRIELE D'ANNUNZIO, *A Vucchella*.

11
The curves of a perfect mouth.
PAUL HAMILTON HAYNE, *Ariel*.

12
His pretty pouting mouth, witless of speech,
Lay half-way open like a rose-lipp'd shell.
THOMAS HOOD, *The Plea of the Midsummer Fairies*, l. 721.

13
It was a mouth all glowing and blest.
HEINE, *Book of Songs: New Spring*.

14
And sweet red splendid kissing mouth.
VILLON, *Complaint of the Fair Armouress*. (Swinburne, tr.)

Slave is the open mouth beneath the closed.
GEORGE MEREDITH, *The Sage Enamoured*.

15
As a pomegranate, cut in twain,
White-seeded is her crimson mouth.
OSCAR WILDE, *La Bella Donna Della Mia Mente*.

MURDER

I—Murder: Apothegms

16
The very air rests thick and heavily,
Where murder has been done.
JOANNA BAILLIE, *Orra*. Act iii, sc. 2.

17
I come fairly to kill him honestly.
BEAUMONT AND FLETCHER, *The Little French Lawyer*. Act iv, sc. 1.

18
Carcasses bleed at the sight of the murderer.
ROBERT BURTON, *Anatomy of Melancholy*. Pt. i, sec. i, mem. 2, subs. 5.

19
He could not slay a thing so fair.
BYRON, *Parisina*. St. 7.

Pity it is to slay the meanest thing.
THOMAS HOOD, *The Plea of the Midsummer Fairies*, l. 772.

20
The old fool has taken more executions in that naked country than I for the murder of my father.
CHARLES II, referring to Gov. Berkeley, of Virginia, who executed many of the adherents of Nathaniel Bacon. He was "imbittered in his last moments by the well-earned gibe." (LODGE, *English Colonies in America*.)

21
The guilt of murder is the same, whether the victim be renowned, or whether he be obscure. (Non alio facinore clari homines, alio obscuri necantur.)
CICERO, *Pro Milone*. Ch. vii, sec. 17.

22
Thou shalt not kill; but need'st not strive
Officiously to keep alive.
ARTHUR HUGH CLOUGH, *The Latest Decalogue*.

23
Murder Considered as One of the Fine Arts.
THOMAS DE QUINCEY. Title of essay.

24
Something will come of this. I hope it mayn't be human gore!
DICKENS, *Barnaby Rudge*. Ch. 4.

25
Assassination has never changed the history of the world.
BENJAMIN DISRAELI, *Speech*, House of Commons, May, 1865, on the assassination of Lincoln.

Absolutism tempered by assassination.
COUNT MÜNSTER, Hanoverian envoy at St. Petersburg, *Letter*, referring to the Russian Constitution.

1
He told how murderers walk the earth
Beneath the curse of Cain.
THOMAS HOOD, *Eugene Aram*.

When thou tillest the ground, it shall not henceforth yield unto thee her strength; a fugitive and a vagabond shalt thou be in the earth.
Old Testament: Genesis, iv, 12.

2
Even those who do not wish to kill anyone, would like the power to do it. (Qui nolunt occidere quemquam, Posse volunt.)
JUVENAL, *Satires*. Sat. x, l. 96.

3
Murder, like talent, seems occasionally to run in families.
GEORGE HENRY LEWES, *Physiology of Common Life*. Ch. 12.

4
One murder made a villain, Millions a hero.
BISHOP BEILBY PORTEUS, *Death*, l. 154.

One to destroy is murder by the law,
And gibbets keep the lifted hand in awe;
To murder thousands takes a specious name,
War's glorious art, and gives immortal fame.
YOUNG, *Love of Fame*. Sat. vii, l. 55.

5
I will kill thee a hundred and fifty ways.
SHAKESPEARE, *As You Like It*. Act v, sc. 1, 62.

That but this blow
Might be the be-all and the end-all here,
But here, upon this bank and shoal of time,
We 'ld jump the life to come.
SHAKESPEARE, *Macbeth*. Act i, sc. 7, l. 4.

I would have him nine years a-killing.
SHAKESPEARE, *Othello*. Act iv, sc. 1, l. 188.

I will kill thee, And love thee after.
SHAKESPEARE, *Othello*. Act v, sc. 2, l. 18.

Thou cutt'st my head off with a golden axe,
And smilest upon the stroke that murders me.
SHAKESPEARE, *Romeo and Juliet*. Act iii, sc. 3, l. 22.

6
No place, indeed, should murder sanctuarize.
SHAKESPEARE, *Hamlet*. Act iv, sc. 7, l. 128.

7
Do all men kill the things they do not love?
SHAKESPEARE, *The Merchant of Venice*. Act iv, sc. 1, l. 66.

Yet each man kills the thing he loves.
OSCAR WILDE, *Ballad of Reading Gaol*.

When we want to read of the deeds that are done for love, whither do we turn? To the murder column.
BERNARD SHAW, *Three Plays for Puritans: Preface*.

8
Killing no Murder.
COLONEL SILUS TITUS. Title of tract recommending the assassination of Cromwell. (*Harleian Miscellany*.)

9
Who killed Cock Robin?
"I," said the Sparrow,
"With my bow and arrow,
I killed Cock Robin."
UNKNOWN, *The Death and Burial of Cock Robin*. Probably an adaptation of John Skelton's account of the sparrow's funeral in his *Boke of Phylyp Sparowe* (c. 1504), which in turn derives from Catullus's famous elegy, "Passer mortuus est meæ puellæ."

II—Murder: Murder Will Out

10
Forby men say into his tide,
In no man's hat murder may hide.
UNKNOWN, *Cursor Mundi*, l. 1085. (c. 1290)

Murder will out, certain, it will not fail.
CHAUCER, *The Prioresses Tale*, l. 124. (c. 1386)

Murder will out, that see we day by day.
CHAUCER, *Nonne Preests Tale*, l. 232.

Yet heav'n will still have murder out at last.
MICHAEL DRAYTON, *Idea*. Sonnet iii.

11
Man cannot cover what God would reveal.
THOMAS CAMPBELL, *Lochiel's Warning*.

12
Blood, though it sleep a time, yet never dies.
The gods on murtherers fix revengeful eyes.
CHAPMAN, *The Widow's Tears*. Act v, sc. 4.

13
Murder may pass unpunish'd for a time,
But tardy justice will o'ertake the crime.
DRYDEN, *The Cock and the Fox*, l. 285.

14
Foul deeds will rise,
Though all the earth o'erwhelm them, to men's eyes.
SHAKESPEARE, *Hamlet*. Act i, sc. 2, l. 257.

For murder, though it have no tongue, will speak
With most miraculous organ.
SHAKESPEARE, *Hamlet*. Act ii, sc. 2, l. 622.

Truth will come to light; murder cannot be hid long.
SHAKESPEARE, *The Merchant of Venice*, ii, 2, 83.

III—Murder: According to Shakespeare

15
Murder most foul, as in the best it is;
But this most foul, strange and unnatural.
SHAKESPEARE, *Hamlet*. Act i, sc. 5, l. 27.

16
Thus was I, sleeping, by a brother's hand
Of life, of crown, of queen, at once dispatch'd:
Cut off even in the blossoms of my sin,
Unhousel'd, disappointed, unaneled,
No reckoning made, but sent to my account
With all my imperfections on my head.
SHAKESPEARE. *Hamlet*. Act i, sc. 5, l. 74.

He took my father grossly, full of bread;
With all his crimes broad blown, as flush as May;

And how his audit stands who knows save heaven?
SHAKESPEARE, *Hamlet*. Act iii, sc. 3, l. 80.

At gaming, swearing, or about some act
That has no relish of salvation in't;
Then trip him, that his heels may kick at heaven,
And that his soul may be as damn'd and black
As hell, whereto it goes.
SHAKESPEARE, *Hamlet*. Act iii, sc. 3, l. 91.

Oh me unhappy! I have found them lying
Close in each other's arms, and fast asleep.
But that I would not damn two precious souls,
Bought with my Saviour's blood, and send them, laden
With all their scarlet sins upon their backs,
Unto a fearful judgment, their two lives
Had met upon my rapier!
THOMAS HEYWOOD, *A Woman Killed with Kindness*. Act iv, sc. 6.

1
Confusion now hath made his masterpiece!
Most sacrilegious murder hath broke ope
The Lord's anointed temple, and stole thence
The life o' the building!
SHAKESPEARE, *Macbeth*. Act ii, sc. 3, l. 71.

Blood hath been shed ere now i' the olden time,
Ere humane statute purg'd the gentle weal;
Ay, and since too, murders have been perform'd
Too terrible for the ear.
SHAKESPEARE, *Macbeth*. Act iii, sc. 4, l. 75.

The murderers,
Steep'd in the colours of their trade, their daggers
Unmannerly breech'd with gore.
SHAKESPEARE, *Macbeth*. Act ii, sc. 3, l. 120.

2
Though in the trade of war I have slain men,
Yet do I hold it very stuff o' the conscience
To do no contrived murder: I lack iniquity
Sometimes to do me service.
SHAKESPEARE, *Othello*. Act i, sc. 2, l. 1.

Then murder's out of tune,
And sweet revenge grows harsh.
SHAKESPEARE, *Othello*. Act v, sc. 2, l. 115.

3
The great King of kings
Hath in the tables of his law commanded
That thou shalt do no murder: and wilt thou, then,
Spurn at his edict and fulfil a man's?
SHAKESPEARE, *Richard III*. Act i, sc. 4, l. 200.

Are you call'd forth from out a world of men
To slay the innocent?
SHAKESPEARE, *Richard III*. Act i, sc. 4, l. 186.

IV—Murder: Some Jingles

4
Lizzie Borden took an axe
And gave her Mother forty whacks;
When she saw what she had done,
She gave her Father forty-one.
UNKNOWN, *Lizzie Borden*. Commemorating the murder of Lizzie Borden's father and step-mother at Fall River, Mass., 4 Aug., 1892.

There's no evidence of guilt,
Lizzie Borden,
That should make your spirit wilt,
Lizzie Borden;
Many do not think that you
Chopped your father's head in two,
It's so hard a thing to do,
Lizzie Borden.
A. L. BIXBY, *To Lizzie*.

5
Up the close an' doun the stair,
But an' ben wi' Burke and Hare.
Burke's the butcher, Hare's the thief,
Knox the boy that buys the beef.
UNKNOWN, *The West Point Murders*. A series of Edinburgh crimes, committed by two degenerates named Burke and Hare for the purpose of supplying subjects for dissection to a medical college.

6
Jesse James had a wife,
She's a mourner all her life;
His children they were brave;
Oh, the dirty little coward
That shot Mr. Howard,
Has laid poor Jesse in his grave.
UNKNOWN, *Jesse James*. Old song commemorating the murder of Jesse James by Robert Ford, at St. Joseph, Mo., 3 April, 1882. James had been living under the name of Thomas Howard.

7
Two brothers in our town did dwell:
Hiram sought Heaven, but Isaac Sawtell.
UNKNOWN, *The Sawtell Murder*. A New Hampshire crime of the '90s, in which Isaac Sawtell murdered his brother Hiram.

8
The three men came in the dead of night,
In the wind and the rain and the ruts,
They held Mrs. Shann and they took the light,
And went up and stole them guts.
UNKNOWN, *The Shann Murder Case*. A Princeton undergraduate song of 1892, sung to the tune of *Don't You Hear Dem Bells*. It celebrated the arrest of a local boarding-house keeper named Shann for the murder of her husband, supposedly by poison. It was found that his intestines had been removed, and Mrs. Shann alleged that three men had driven up at midnight, one had held her, while the other two mounted to the room where her husband's body lay and eviscerated it.

9
They cut his throat from ear to ear,
His brains they battered in;
His name was Mr. William Weare,
He dwelt in Lyon's Inn.
THEODORE HOOK, *William Weare*. On the authority of John Lockhart. The lines, which refer to the murder of William Weare by John Thurtell in 1823, have also been ascribed to Lord William Lennox (see *Sporting Review*, 1839) and to William

Webb, alias "Happy Webb," a London linkman. According to Mr. E. L. Pearson, this jingle delighted Sir Walter Scott. It was at Thurtell's trial that the famous dictum was elicited that respectability consists in keeping a gig. *See under* RESPECTABILITY.

1
And ever since historian writ,
  And ever since a bard could sing,
Doth each exalt with all his wit
  The noble art of murdering.

THACKERAY, *The Chronicle of the Drum.*

MUSIC

See also Discord, Harmony, Song

I—Music: Definitions

2
Music, the greatest good that mortals know,
And all of heaven we have below.

ADDISON, *Song for St. Cecilia's Day*, l. 27.

3
There is no truer truth obtainable
By Man than comes of music.

ROBERT BROWNING, *Parleyings with Certain People: Charles Avison.*

Music tells no truths.

P. J. BAILEY, *Festus: A Village Feast.*

4
Music is well said to be the speech of angels.

CARLYLE, *Essays: The Opera.*

5
See deep enough, and you see musically; the heart of nature being everywhere music, if you can only reach it.

CARLYLE, *Heroes and Hero-Worship.* Lect. 3.

Music is in all growing things;
And underneath the silky wings
  Of smallest insects there is stirred
  A pulse of air that must be heard;
Earth's silence lives, and throbs, and sings.

GEORGE PARSONS LATHROP, *Music of Growth.*

The God of Music dwelleth out of doors.

EDITH M. THOMAS, *Music.*

There is no music in Nature, neither melody or harmony. Music is the creation of man.

H. R. HAWEIS, *Music and Morals.* Bk. i, ch. 1.

6
O Music, sphere-descended maid,
Friend of pleasure, wisdom's aid.

WILLIAM COLLINS, *The Passions*, l. 95.

7
Music is the poor man's Parnassus.

EMERSON, *Letters and Social Aims: Poetry and Imagination.*

8
Music is nothing else but wild sounds civilized into time and tune.

THOMAS FULLER, *History of the Worthies of England:* Ch. 10, *Musicians.*

9
Emotion, not thought, is the sphere of music; and emotion quite as often precedes as follows thought.

H. R. HAWEIS, *Music and Morals: Schubert.*

10
Music was a thing of the soul—a rose-lipped shell that murmured of the eternal sea—a strange bird singing the songs of another shore.

J. G. HOLLAND, *Plain Talks on Familiar Subjects: Art and Life. See also* SEA: SEA-SHELLS.

11
O sweet and healing balm of troubles. (O laborum Dulce lenimen medicumque.)

HORACE, *Odes.* Bk. i, ode 32, l. 14. Referring to music.

Music is the medicine of a troubled mind. (Musica mentis medicina mœstæ.)

WALTER HADDON, *Lucubrationes Poemata: De Musica.*

Music's the medicine of the mind.

JOHN LOGAN, *Danish Ode.*

Music's the cordial of a troubled breast,
The softest remedy that grief can find;
The gentle spell that charms our care to rest
And calms the ruffled passions of the mind.
  Music does all our joys refine,
  And gives the relish to our wine.

JOHN OLDHAM, *An Ode on St. Cecilia's Day.*

12
Music is the only one of the arts that can not be prostituted to a base use.

ELBERT HUBBARD, *A Thousand and One Epigrams*, p. 39.

Take them, you, that smile on strings, those nobler sounds than mine,
The words that never lie, or brag, or flatter, or malign.

G. K. CHESTERTON, *To M. E. W.*

13
Music remains the only art, the last sanctuary, wherein originality may reveal itself in the face of fools and not pierce their mental opacity.

JAMES HUNEKER, *Iconoclasts*, p. 142.

14
It is the only sensual pleasure without vice.

SAMUEL JOHNSON, *Apothegms.* (HAWKINS, *Johnsoniana.*)

Of all noises I think music the least disagreeable.

SAMUEL JOHNSON. (*Morning Chronicle*, 16 Aug., 1816.)

15
Yea, music is the Prophet's art
Among the gifts that God hath sent,
One of the most magnificent!

LONGFELLOW, *Christus.* Pt. iii, interlude 2.

16
Music, the mosaic of the Air.

ANDREW MARVELL, *Music's Empire.*

17
Music resembles poetry; in each
Are nameless graces which no methods teach,
And which a master-hand alone can reach.

POPE, *Essay on Criticism.* Pt. i, l. 143.

If Music and sweet Poetry agree,
As they must needs (the sister and the brother),

Then must the Love be great, 'twixt thee and
me,
Because thou lov'st the one, and I the other.
RICHARD BARNFIELD, *Sonnet: To His Friend Master R. L.*

1
The only universal tongue.
SAMUEL ROGERS, *Italy: Bergamo.*

Music is the universal language.
JOHN WILSON, *Noctes Ambrosianæ.* Ch. 27.

Music is the universal language of mankind.
LONGFELLOW, *Outre-Mer: Spanish Ballads.*

2
Music, moody food Of us that trade in love.
SHAKESPEARE, *Antony and Cleopatra,* ii, 5, 1.

3
Hell is full of musical amateurs. Music is the brandy of the damned.
BERNARD SHAW, *Man and Superman.* Act iii.

4
Music! soft charm of heav'n and earth,
Whence didst thou borrow thy auspicious
birth?
Or art thou of eternal date,
Sire to thyself, thyself as old as Fate?
EDMUND SMITH, *Ode in Praise of Music.*

5
Music is feeling, then, not sound.
WALLACE STEVENS, *Peter Quince at the Clavier.*

II—Music: Apothegms

6
The jackdaw knows nothing of music. (Nil cum fidibus graculost.)
AULUS GELLIUS, *Noctes Atticæ: Præfatio.* Sec. 19. Quoted as an old saying.

Like the ass, deaf to the lyre. (ὄνος λύρας.)
BOËTHIUS, *Philosophiæ Consolationis.* Bk. i, ch. 4. Quoting an old proverb.

Music sweeps by me as a messenger
Carrying a message that is not for me.
GEORGE ELIOT, *The Spanish Gypsy.* Bk. iii.

Because I have no ear for music, at the Concert of the Quintette Club, it looked to me as if the performers were crazy, and all the audience were making-believe crazy, in order to soothe the lunatics and keep them amused.
R. W. EMERSON, *Journals,* 1861.

I perceive you delight not in music.
SHAKESPEARE, *The Two Gentlemen of Verona.* Act iv, sc. 2, l. 66.

7
Where there's music there can't be mischief. (Donde hay Musica no puede haber cosa mala.)
CERVANTES, *Don Quixote.* Pt. ii, ch. 34.

8
And music pours on mortals
Her magnificent disdain.
EMERSON, *The Sphinx.*

9
You make as good music as a wheelbarrow.
THOMAS FULLER, *Gnomologia.* No. 5938.

10
Why should the devil have all the good tunes?
ROWLAND HILL, *Sermons.* (BROOME, *Life,* p. 93.)

I said as I sat by the edge of the sea,
A music-hall show would look bully to me;
I thought as I walked by the edge of the dunes,
Why should the Devil have all the good tunes?
FREDERICK L. ALLEN, *Familiar Quotations.* (*Atlantic Monthly,* v. 146, p. 118.)

Is it lave gaity All to the laity?
ALFRED PERCEVAL GRAVES, *Father O'Flynn.*

11
This dance of death, which sounds so musi-
cally,
Was sure intended for the *corpse de ballet.*
UNKNOWN, *On the Danse Macabre of Saint-Saëns.* (Quoted by Brander Matthews, *Recreations of an Anthologist,* p. 108, as by "an American rhymester.")

12
Musical innovation is full of danger to the State, for when modes of music change, the laws of the State always change with them.
PLATO, *The Republic.* Bk. iv, sec. 424.

13
The man who has music in his soul will be most in love with the loveliest.
PLATO, *The Republic.* Bk. iii, sec. 402.

Music and rhythm find their way into the secret places of the soul.
PLATO, *The Republic.* Bk. iii, sec. 401.

14
Music is essentially useless, as life is.
GEORGE SANTAYANA, *Little Essays,* p. 130.

What most people relish is hardly music; it is rather a drowsy reverie relieved by nervous thrills.
GEORGE SANTAYANA, *Life of Reason.* iv, 51.

15
Make battery to our ears with the loud music.
SHAKESPEARE, *Antony and Cleopatra.* Act ii, sc. 7, l. 115.

Wagner's music is better than it sounds.
BILL NYE.

16
Among all the arts, music alone can be purely religious.
MADAME DE STAËL, *Corinne.* Bk. viii, ch. 3.

As some to church repair,
Not for the doctrine, but the music there.
POPE, *Essay on Criticism.* Pt. ii, l. 142.

Light quirks of music, broken and unev'n,
Make the soul dance upon a jig to Heav'n.
POPE, *Moral Essays.* Epis. iv, l. 143.

III—Music: Music Hath Charms

17
Music hath charms to soothe a savage breast,
To soften rocks, or bend a knotted oak.
WILLIAM CONGREVE, *The Mourning Bride.* Act i, sc. 1, l. 1. (1697) Some editions read "Music has charms."

"Music hath charms to soothe the savage beast,"
And therefore proper at a sheriff's feast.
JAMES BRAMSTON, *Man of Taste.* (1729)

Rugged the breast that music cannot tame.
JOHN CODRINGTON BAMPFYLDE, *Sonnet.*

Music has charms, we all may find,
Ingratiate deeply with the mind.

When art does sound's high power advance,
To music's pipe the passions dance;
Motions unwill'd its powers have shown,
Tarantulated by a tune.
MATTHEW GREEN, *The Spleen,* l. 141. (1737)

Music has charms alone for peaceful minds.
POPE, *Sappho to Phaon,* l. 14.

1
Orpheus cou'd lead the savage race;
And trees uprooted left their place,
Sequacious of the lyre:
But bright Cecilia rais'd the wonder high'r:
When to her organ vocal breath was giv'n,
An angel heard, and straight appear'd
Mistaking earth for heav'n.
DRYDEN, *Song for St. Cecilia's Day.* St. 7.

When Orpheus strikes the trembling lyre,
The streams stand still, the stones admire;
The list'ning savages advance,
The wolf and lamb around him trip,
The bears in awkward measures leap,
And tigers mingle in the dance:
The moving woods attended as he play'd,
And Rhodophe was left without a shade.
ADDISON, *A Song for St. Cecilia's Day,* l. 33.

2
Music's force can tame the furious beast:
Can make the wolf or foaming boar restrain
His rage; the lion drop his crested mane
Attentive to the song.
MATTHEW PRIOR, *Solomon.* Bk. ii, l. 67.

3
Orpheus with his lute made trees,
And the mountain tops that freeze,
Bow themselves when he did sing:
To his music plants and flowers
Ever sprung; as sun and showers,
There had made a lasting spring.
SHAKESPEARE, *Henry VIII.* Act iii, sc. 1, l. 3.

Every thing that heard him play,
Even the billows of the sea,
Hung their heads, and then lay by.
In sweet music is such art,
Killing care and grief of heart
Fall asleep, or hearing, die.
SHAKESPEARE, *Henry VIII.* Act iii, sc. 1, l. 9.

4
Music oft hath such a charm
To make bad good, and good provoke to harm.
SHAKESPEARE, *Measure for Measure.* Act iv, sc. 1, l. 14.

5
Therefore the poet
Did feign that Orpheus drew trees, stones and floods;
Since nought so stockish, hard and full of rage,
But music for the time doth change his nature.
SHAKESPEARE, *The Merchant of Venice.* Act v, sc. 1, l. 79.

For Orpheus' lute was strung with poets' sinews,
Whose golden touch could soften steel and stones,
Make tigers tame and huge leviathans
Forsake unbounded deeps to dance on sands.
SHAKESPEARE, *The Two Gentlemen of Verona.* Act iii, sc. 2, l. 78.

IV—Music: Its Power

See also Song: Its Power

6
Music religious heats inspires,
It wakes the soul, and lifts it high,
And wings it with sublime desires,
And fits it to bespeak the Deity.
ADDISON, *A Song for St. Cecilia's Day,* l. 41.

Music exalts each joy, allays each grief.
Expels diseases, softens every pain,
Subdues the rage of poison, and the plague.
JOHN ARMSTRONG, *Art of Preserving Health.* Bk. iv, l. 512.

7
Tunes and airs, even in their own nature, have in themselves some affinity with the affections. . . . So it is no marvel if they alter the spirits. Yet generally music feedeth that disposition of the spirits which it findeth.
FRANCIS BACON, *Sylva Sylvarum.* Century ii, sec. 114.

8
Is there a heart that music cannot melt?
Alas! how is that rugged heart forlorn!
JAMES BEATTIE, *The Minstrel.* Bk. i, l. 453.

The man that hath no music in himself,
Nor is not moved with concord of sweet sounds,
Is fit for treasons, stratagems and spoils.
SHAKESPEARE, *The Merchant of Venice.* Act v, sc. 1, l. 83. Often misquoted "music in his soul." *See also* CARLYLE, *under* LAUGHTER.

9
God is its author, and not man; he laid
The key-note of all harmonies; he planned
All perfect combinations, and he made
Us so that we could hear and understand.
J. G. BRAINARD, *Music.*

10
[Music] strikes in me a deep fit of devotion, and a profound contemplation of the First Composer. There is something in it of Divinity more than the ear discovers.
SIR THOMAS BROWNE, *Religio Medici.* Pt. ii, sec. 9.

11
Who hears music, feels his solitude
Peopled at once.
ROBERT BROWNING, *Balaustion's Adventure.*

12
All the delusive seduction of martial music.
FANNY BURNEY, *Diary.* Pt. viii. (1802)

And hears thy stormy music in the drum!
CAMPBELL, *The Pleasures of Hope.* Pt. i, l. 100.

The silver, snarling trumpets 'gan to chide.
KEATS, *The Eve of St. Agnes.* St. 4.

13
When Music, Heav'nly Maid, was young,

While yet in early Greece she sung,
The Passions oft, to hear her shell,
Throng'd around her magic cell.
WILLIAM COLLINS, *The Passions*, l. 1.

1
There is in souls a sympathy with sounds,
And, as the mind is pitch'd, the ear is pleas'd
With melting airs, or martial, brisk, or grave:
Some chord in unison with what we hear
Is touch'd within us, and the heart replies.
COWPER, *The Task*. Bk. vi, l. 1.

Commemoration-mad; content to hear
(Oh wonderful effect of music's pow'r!)
Messiah's eulogy, for Handel's sake.
COWPER, *The Task*. Bk. vi, l. 635.

2
What passion cannot Music raise and quell?
DRYDEN, *Song for St. Cecilia's Day*. St. 2.

3
Now the rich stream of music winds along
Deep, majestic, smooth, and strong.
THOMAS GRAY, *The Progress of Poesy*, l. 7.

4
Music helps not the toothache.
GEORGE HERBERT, *Jacula Prudentum*.

5
Music's golden tongue
Flatter'd to tears this aged man and poor.
KEATS, *The Eve of St. Agnes*. St. 3.

6
Who carry music in their heart
Through dusky lane and wrangling mart,
Plying their daily task with busier feet,
Because their secret souls a holy strain repeat.
JOHN KEBLE, *The Christian Year: St. Matthew's Day*.

7
Such sweet compulsion doth in music lie.
MILTON, *Arcades*, l. 68.

And music, too—dear music! that can touch
Beyond all else the soul that loves it much—
Now heard far off, so far as but to seem
Like the faint, exquisite music of a dream.
THOMAS MOORE, *Lalla Rookh: The Veiled Prophet of Khorassan*.

8
And learn, my sons, the wondrous power of Noise,
To move, to raise, to ravish ev'ry heart.
POPE, *The Dunciad*. Bk. ii, l. 222.

By Music minds an equal temper know,
Nor swell too high, nor sink too low. . . .
Warriors she fires with animated sounds,
Pours balm into the bleeding lover's wounds.
POPE, *Ode on St. Cecilia's Day*, l. 22.

Music the fiercest grief can charm,
And Fate's severest rage disarm:
Music can soften pain to ease,
And make despair and madness please:
Our joys below it can improve,
And antedate the bliss above.
POPE, *Ode on St. Cecilia's Day*, l. 118.

9
I am advised to give her music o' mornings; they say it will penetrate.
SHAKESPEARE, *Cymbeline*. Act ii, sc. 3, l. 12.

Preposterous ass, that never read so far
To know the cause why music was ordain'd!
Was it not to refresh the mind of man
After his studies or his unusual pain?
SHAKESPEARE, *The Taming of the Shrew*. Act iii, sc. 1, l. 9.

10
As I went under the new telegraph-wire, I heard it vibrating like a harp high overhead. It was as the sound of a far-off glorious life, a supernal life, which came down to us, and vibrated the lattice-work of this life of ours.
H. D. THOREAU, *Journal*, 3 Sept., 1851. This entry marks Thoreau's discovery of his favorite musical instrument, to which he refers so often in subsequent pages of his journal.

11
Music hath caught a higher pace than any virtue that I know. It is the arch-reformer; it hastens the sun to its setting; it invites him to his rising; it is the sweetest reproach, a measured satire.
THOREAU, *Winter: Journal*, 8 Jan., 1842.

12
All music is what awakes from you when you are reminded by the instruments,
It is not the violins and the cornets, it is not the oboe nor the beating drums, nor the score of the baritone singer singing his sweet romanza, nor that of the men's chorus, nor that of the women's chorus.
It is nearer and farther than they.
WALT WHITMAN, *A Song for Occupations*. Pt. iv.

13
Where gripping griefs the heart would wound,
And doleful dumps the mind oppress,
There music with her silver sound,
With speed is wont to send redress.
UNKNOWN, *A Song to the Lute in Music*. (PERCY, *Reliques*.)

When griping grief the heart doth wound,
And doleful dumps the mind oppress,
Then music with her silver sound . . .
With speedy help doth lend redress.
SHAKESPEARE, *Romeo and Juliet*. Act iv, sc. 5, l. 128. An adaptation of the old song.

Sec. Mus.: I say "silver sound," because musicians sound for silver.
Peter: O, I cry you mercy. . . . It is "music with her silver sound," because musicians have no gold for sounding.
SHAKESPEARE, *Romeo and Juliet*. Act iv, sc. 5, l. 136.

14
Servant and master am I: servant of those dead, and master of those living. Through my spirit immortals speak the message that makes the world weep and laugh, and wonder

and worship. . . . For I am the instrument of God. I am Music.
UNKNOWN, *Music.* (*International Musician*, July, 1928. Recited by Walter Damrosch.)

V—Music: Its Sweetness

1
"This is the way," laughed the great god Pan
(Laughed while he sat by the river),
"The only way since gods began
To make sweet music, they could succeed."
Then, dropping his mouth to a hole in the reed,
He blew in power by the river.
E. B. BROWNING, *A Musical Instrument*. St. 5.

Sweet, sweet, sweet, O Pan!
Piercing sweet by the river!
Blinding sweet, O great god Pan!
The sun on the hill forgot to die,
And the lilies revived, and the dragon-fly
Came back to dream on the river.
E. B. BROWNING, *A Musical Instrument*. St. 6.

2
Such sweet
Soft notes as yet musician's cunning
Never gave the enraptured air.
ROBERT BROWNING, *The Pied Piper*. Pt. xii.

3
Music arose with its voluptuous swell.
BYRON, *Childe Harold*. Canto iii, st. 21.

4
The still sweet fall of music far away.
CAMPBELL, *The Pleasures of Hope*. Pt. ii, l. 112.

In hollow murmurs died away.
WILLIAM COLLINS, *The Passions*, l. 68.

The strains decay And melt away,
In a dying, dying fall.
POPE, *Ode on St. Cecilia's Day*, l. 19.

5
A solemn, strange and mingled air;
'Twas sad by fits, by starts 'twas wild.
WILLIAM COLLINS, *The Passions*, l. 27.

6
In notes by distance made more sweet.
WILLIAM COLLINS, *The Passions*, l. 60.

We are like the musician on the lake, whose melody is sweeter than he knows.
EMERSON, *Society and Solitude: Art*.

Sweetest melodies
Are those that are by distance made more sweet.
WORDSWORTH, *Personal Talk*. St. 2.

7
So just, so small, yet in so sweet a note,
It seemed the music melted in the throat.
JOHN DRYDEN, *Flower and the Leaf*, l. 199.

8
Soft as the breath of distant flutes at hours
When silent evening closes up the flowers.
JOHN GAY, *Trivia*. Bk. ii, l. 377.

9
Let me have music dying, and I seek
No more delight.
KEATS, *Endymion*. Bk. iv, l. 140.

Fading in music.
SHAKESPEARE, *The Merchant of Venice*. Act iii, sc. 2, l. 45.

10
Heard melodies are sweet, but those unheard
Are sweeter; therefore, ye soft pipes, play on;
Not to the sensual ear, but, more endear'd,
Pipe to the spirit ditties of no tone.
KEATS, *Ode on a Grecian Urn*. St. 2.

11
Who shall silence all the airs and madrigals that whisper softness in chambers?
MILTON, *Areopagitica*.

12
Can any mortal mixture of earth's mould
Breathe such divine enchanting ravishment?
MILTON, *Comus*, l. 244.

There let the pealing organ blow,
To the full voic'd quire below,
In service high, and anthems clear,
As may with sweetness, through mine ear,
Dissolve me into ecstasies,
And bring all Heav'n before mine eyes.
MILTON, *Il Penseroso*, l. 161.

And ever against eating cares,
Lap me in soft Lydian airs,
Married to immortal verse
Such as the meeting soul may pierce
In notes, with many a winding bout
Of linkèd sweetness, long drawn out.
MILTON, *L'Allegro*, l. 135.

13
Hark! the numbers soft and clear
Gently steal upon the ear.
POPE, *Ode on St. Cecilia's Day*, l. 12.

14
Here will we sit and let the sounds of music
Creep in our ears.
SHAKESPEARE, *The Merchant of Venice*. Act v, sc. 1, l. 55.

Wilt thou have music? hark! Apollo plays
And twenty caged nightingales do sing.
SHAKESPEARE, *The Taming of the Shrew: Induction*. Sc. 2, l. 37.

This music crept by me upon the waters,
Allaying both their fury and my passion
With its sweet air.
SHAKESPEARE, *The Tempest*. Act i, sc. 2, l. 391.

15
If music be the food of love, play on;
Give me excess of it, that, surfeiting,
The appetite may sicken, and so die.
That strain again! it had a dying fall:
O, it came o'er my ear like the sweet sound,
That breathes upon a bank of violets,
Stealing and giving odour!
SHAKESPEARE, *Twelfth Night*. Act i, sc. 1, l. 1.
Matthew Arnold always contended that "sound" was a misprint for "south."

If music be the food of love,
Sing on, sing on, sing on.
THOMAS D'URFEY, *Pills to Purge Melancholy:* Vol. iii, *Song*. (1661)

Is not music the food of love?
SHERIDAN, *The Rivals*. Act ii, sc. 1.

There's sure no passion in the human soul
But finds its food in music.
GEORGE LILLO, *Fatal Curiosity*. Act i, sc. 2.

1
I pant for the music which is divine;
My heart in its thirst is a dying flower;
Pour forth the sound like enchanted wine,
Loosen the notes in a silver shower;
Like a herbless plain, for the gentle rain,
I gasp, I faint, till they wake again.
SHELLEY, *Music*.

Sounds overflow the listener's brain,
So sweet, that joy is almost pain.
SHELLEY, *Prometheus Unbound*. Act ii, sc. 2.

2
If I were to begin life again, I would devote it to music. It is the only cheap and unpunished rapture upon earth.
SYDNEY SMITH, *Letter to the Countess of Carlisle*, Aug., 1844.

3
Eftsoones they heard a most melodious sound,
Of all that mote delight a dainty ear.
SPENSER, *Faerie Queene*. Bk. ii, canto xii, st. 70.

4
Music bright as the soul of light, for wings an eagle, for notes a dove.
SWINBURNE, *Bothwell*. Act ii, l. 13.

5
I shall loathe sweet tunes, where a note grown strong
Relents and recoils, and climbs and closes. . . .
I shall hate sweet music my whole life long.
SWINBURNE, *The Triumph of Time*. St. 45.

6
The music had the heat of blood,
A passion that no words can reach;
We sat together, and understood
Our own heart's speech.
ARTHUR SYMONS, *During Music*.

7
There is sweet music here that softer falls
Than petals from blown roses on the grass, . . .
Music that gentlier on the spirit lies,
Than tired eyelids upon tired eyes;
Music that brings sweet sleep down from the blissful skies.
TENNYSON, *The Lotos-Eaters: Choric Song*. St. 1.

Where light and shade repose, where music dwells
Lingering—and wandering on as loth to die;
Like thoughts whose very sweetness yieldeth proof
That they were born for immortality.
WORDSWORTH, *Ecclesiastical Sonnets*. Pt. iii, No. 43.

Soft is the music that would charm for ever.
WORDSWORTH, *Miscellaneous Sonnets*. Pt. ii, No. 9.

8
The music in my heart I bore,
Long after it was heard no more.
WORDSWORTH, *Memorials of a Tour in Scotland*. No. 9.

VI—Music: Its Sadness

9
The mellow touch of music most doth wound
The soul, when it doth rather sigh than sound.
ROBERT HERRICK, *Soft Music*.

Gentle and noble are their tempers framed,
That can be quickened with perfumes and sounds.
GEORGE CHAPMAN, *Ovid's Banquet of Sense*.

10
Fair Melody! kind Siren! I've no choice;
I must be thy sad servant evermore;
I cannot choose but kneel here and adore.
KEATS, *Endymion*. Bk. iv, l. 303.

11
Seated one day at the organ,
I was weary and ill at ease,
And my fingers wandered idly
Over the noisy keys.

I do not know what I was playing,
Or what I was dreaming then,
But I struck one chord of music
Like the sound of a great Amen.
ADELAIDE ANN PROCTER, *The Lost Chord*. As set to music, the 5th line reads, "I know not what I was playing."

As in an organ from one blast of wind
To many a row of pipes the soundboard breathes.
MILTON, *Paradise Lost*. Bk. i, l. 708.

12
I am never merry when I hear sweet music.
SHAKESPEARE, *The Merchant of Venice*. Act v, sc. 1, l. 69.

13
Inconsolable to the minuet in Ariadne.
SHERIDAN, *The Critic*. Act ii, sc. 2.

14
A lamentable tune is the sweetest music to a woeful mind.
SIR PHILIP SIDNEY, *Arcadia*. Bk. ii.

15
With a secret pain,
And smiles that seem akin to tears,
We hear the wild refrain.
WHITTIER, *At Port Royal*.

A quality
Which music sometimes has, being the Art
Which is most nigh to tears and memory.
OSCAR WILDE, *The Burden of Itys*.

VII—Music of the Spheres

16
There is music wherever there is harmony, order, or proportion; and thus far we may maintain the music of the Spheres; for those well-ordered motions and regular paces, though they give no sound to the ear, yet to

the understanding they strike a note most full of harmony.

Sir Thomas Browne, *Religio Medici*. Pt. ii, sec. 9. (1642)

1
Her voice, the music of the spheres,
So loud, it deafens mortals' ears;
As wise philosophers have thought,
And that's the cause we hear it not.

Butler, *Hudibras*. Pt. ii, canto i, l. 617.

2
There's music in the sighing of a reed;
There's music in the gushing of a rill;
There's music in all things, if men had ears:
Their earth is but an echo of the spheres.

Byron, *Don Juan*. Canto xv, st. 5.

There is beauty in the bellow of the blast,
There is grandeur in the growling of the gale.

W. S. Gilbert, *The Mikado*. Act ii.

3
And left so free mine ears,
That I might hear the music of the spheres,
And all the angels singing out of heaven.

George Chapman, *The Tears of Peace*.

4
And after shewed he him the nine spheres,
And after that the melody heard he
That cometh of those spheres thrice three,
That well is of music and melody
In this world here, and cause of harmony.

Chaucer, *The Parlement of Foules*, l. 59.

Water and Air He for the Tenor chose,
Earth made the Base, the Treble Flame arose,
To th' active Moon a quick brisk stroke he gave,
To Saturn's string a touch more soft and grave.
The motions strait, and round, and swift, and slow,
And short and long, were mixt and woven so,
Did in such artful Figures smoothly fall,
As made this decent measur'd Dance of all.
And this is Musick.

Abraham Cowley, *Davideis*. Bk. i, l. 457.

5
Let me go where'er I will
I hear a sky-born music still: . . .
'Tis not in the high stars alone,
Nor in the cup of budding flowers,
Nor in the redbreast's mellow tone,
Nor in the bow that smiles in showers
But in the mud and scum of things
There alway, alway something sings.

Emerson, *Music*.

6
When the morning stars sang together, and all the sons of God shouted for joy.

Old Testament: Job, xxxviii, 7.

7
Ring out ye crystal spheres!
Once bless our human ears,
(If ye have power to touch our senses so)
And let your silver chime
Move in melodious time;
And let the base of Heav'n's deep organ blow,
And with your ninefold harmony,
Make up full consort to th' angelic symphony.

Milton, *On the Morning of Christ's Nativity*. St. 13.

And in their motions harmony divine
So smooths her charming tones, that God's own ear
Listens delighted.

Milton, *Paradise Lost*. Bk. v, l. 625.

8
The celestial music. (La musique celeste.)

Montaigne, *Essays*. Bk. i, ch. 22.

9
"This *must* be the music," said he, "of the *spears*,
For I am curst if each note of it doesn't run through one!"

Thomas Moore, *Fudge Family in Paris*. Letter v, l. 28.

10
Sit, Jessica. Look how the floor of heaven
Is thick inlaid with patines of bright gold:
There's not the smallest orb which thou behold'st
But in his motion like an angel sings,
Still quiring to the young-eyed cherubins;
Such harmony is in immortal souls;
But whilst this muddy vesture of decay
Doth grossly close it in, we cannot hear it.

Shakespeare, *The Merchant of Venice*. Act v, sc. 1, l. 58.

11
When his veering gait
And every motion of his starry train
Seem governed by a strain
Of music, audible to him alone.

Wordsworth, *The Triad*, l. 48.

VIII—Music: The Flute

12
The flute is not an instrument which has a good moral effect; it is too exciting.

Aristotle, *Politics*. Bk. viii, ch. 6, sec. 5.

13
The soft complaining flute
In dying notes discovers
The woes of hopeless lovers,
Whose dirge is whisper'd by the warbling lute.

John Dryden, *Song for St. Cecilia's Day*.

14
A velvet flute-note fell down pleasantly
Upon the bosom of that harmony, . . .
Somewhat, half song, half odor, forth did float
As if a rose might somehow be a throat.

Sidney Lanier, *The Symphony*.

15
Govern these ventages with your fingers and thumb, give it breath with your mouth, and it will discourse most eloquent music.

Shakespeare, *Hamlet*. Act iii, sc. 2, l. 372.

You cannot play the flute by merely blowing; you must use your fingers too.

Goethe, *Sprüche in Prosa*, iii.

IX—Music: The Harp

1
His harp the sole companion of his way.
JAMES BEATTIE, *The Minstrel*. Bk. i, st. 3.

2
The lyre is welcome at the feasts of supreme Jupiter. (Dapibus supremi Grata testudo Jovis.)
HORACE, *Odes*. Bk. i, ode 32, l. 13.

3
Leave strumming at the doors of inns
To vagabonds and sharpers.
Where men seek minstrels for their sins
They shall not lack for harpers.
LAURENCE HOUSMAN, *Farewell to Town*.

4
The harp that once through Tara's halls
The soul of music shed,
Now hangs as mute on Tara's walls
As if that soul were fled.
So sleeps the pride of former days,
So glory's thrill is o'er;
And hearts, that once beat high for praise,
Now feel that pulse no more.
THOMAS MOORE, *The Harp that Once Through Tara's Halls*.

If the pulse of the patriot, soldier, or lover,
Have throbb'd at our lay, 'tis thy glory alone;
I was but as the wind, passing heedlessly over,
And all the wild sweetness I wak'd was thy own.
THOMAS MOORE, *Dear Harp of My Country*. St. 2.

'Tis believ'd that this harp which I wake now for thee
Was a siren of old who sung under the sea.
THOMAS MOORE, *Origin of the Harp*.

5
The music of the zither, the flute, and the lyre enervates the mind. (Enervant animos citharæ, lotosque, lyræque.)
OVID, *Remediorum Amoris*, l. 753.

6
He touched his harp, and nations heard, entranced,
As some vast river of unfailing source,
Rapid, exhaustless, deep, his numbers flowed,
And opened new fountains in the human heart.
POLLOK, *The Course of Time*. Bk. iv, l. 675.

7
We hanged our harps upon the willows.
Old Testament: Psalms, cxxxvii, 2.

8
Hearken, my minstrels! which of ye all
Touched his harp with that dying fall,
So sweet, so soft, so faint,
It seemed an angel's whispered call
To an expiring saint?
SCOTT, *The Bridal of Triermain*. Canto i, st. 4.

And tuned, to please a peasant's ear,
The harp a king had loved to hear.
SCOTT, *The Lay of the Last Minstrel: Introduction*, l. 25.

9
Strange! that a harp of a thousand strings
Should keep in tune so long.
ISAAC WATTS, *Hymns and Spiritual Songs*. Bk ii, No. 19.

TO HARP ON THE SAME STRING, *see under* PROVERBS.

X—Music: The Lute

10
If thou would'st have me sing and play
As once I play'd and sung,
First take this time-worn lute away,
And bring one freshly strung.
THOMAS MOORE, *If Thou Would'st Have Me Sing and Play*.

11
In a sadly pleasing strain
Let the warbling lute complain.
POPE, *Ode on St. Cecilia's Day*, l. 5.

12
Do the sounds
Which slumber in the lute, belong alone
To him who buys the chords?
SCHILLER, *Don Carlos*. Act iv, sc. 21.

13
As sweet and musical
As bright Apollo's lute, strung with his hair.
SHAKESPEARE, *Love's Labour's Lost*. Act iv, sc. 3, l. 342.

Musical as is Apollo's lute.
MILTON, *Comus*, l. 478.

14
Some dead lute-player
That in dead years had done delicious things.
SWINBURNE, *A Ballad of Life*. St. 2.

15
It is the little rift within the lute
That by and by will make the music mute
And ever widening, slowly silence all.
TENNYSON, *Merlin and Vivien*, l. 388.

XI—Music and Discord

16
So discord oft in music makes the sweeter lay.
SPENSER, *Faerie Queene*. Bk. iii, canto ii, st. 15.

Discords make the sweetest airs,
And curses are a sort of prayers.
BUTLER, *Hudibras*. Pt. iii, canto i, l. 919.

I never heard
So musical a discord, such sweet thunder.
SHAKESPEARE, *A Midsummer-Night's Dream*. Act iv, sc. 1, l. 121.

17
You had that action and counteraction which, in the natural and in the political world, from the reciprocal struggle of discordant powers draws out the harmony of the universe.
EDMUND BURKE, *Reflections on the Revolution in France*.

18
As there is music uninform'd by art.
DRYDEN, *Epistles: To Sir Robert Howard*, l. 1.

1
You think they are crusaders, sent
From some infernal clime,
To pluck the eyes of Sentiment,
And dock the tail of Rhyme,
To crack the voice of Melody,
And break the legs of Time.
O. W. HOLMES, *The Music-Grinders.*

2
Fill'd the air with barbarous dissonance.
MILTON, *Comus,* l. 550.

3
Above the pitch, out of tune, and off the hinges.
RABELAIS, *Works.* Bk. iv, ch. 19.

4
Straining harsh discords and unpleasing sharps.
SHAKESPEARE, *Romeo and Juliet.* Act iii, sc. 5, l. 28.

Melodious discord, heavenly tune harsh-sounding,
Ear's deep-sweet music, and heart's deep-sore wounding.
SHAKESPEARE, *Venus and Adonis,* l. 431.

5
How sour sweet music is,
When time is broke and no proportion kept!
So is it in the music of men's lives.
SHAKESPEARE, *Richard II.* Act v, sc. 5, l. 42.

Take but degree away, untune that string,
And, hark what discord follows!
SHAKESPEARE, *Troilus and Cressida.* Act i, sc. 3, l. 109.

And the vile squealing of the wry-neck'd fife.
SHAKESPEARE, *The Merchant of Venice.* Act ii, sc. 5, l. 30.

XII—Music: The Musician

6
But God has a few of us whom he whispers in the ear;
The rest may reason and welcome: 'tis we musicians know.
ROBERT BROWNING, *Abt Vogler.*

Therefore to whom turn I but to thee, the ineffable Name?
Builder and maker, thou, of houses not made with hands!
ROBERT BROWNING, *Abt Vogler.*

7
From this did Paganini comb the fierce
Electric sparks, or to tenuity
Pull forth the inmost wailing of the wire—
No cat-gut could swoon out so much of soul!
ROBERT BROWNING, *Red Cotton Night-cap Country.* Pt. i.

8
When a musician hath forgot his note,
He makes as though a crumb stuck in his throat.
JOHN CLARKE, *Parœmiologia,* 108. (1639)

9
Who, through long days of labor,
And nights devoid of ease,
Still heard in his soul the music
Of wonderful melodies.
LONGFELLOW, *The Day is Done.*

10
He the best of all musicians,
He the sweetest of all singers.
LONGFELLOW, *Hiawatha.* Pt. vi, l. 20.

He is dead, the sweet musician!
He has gone from us forever,
He has moved a little nearer
To the Master of all music.
LONGFELLOW, *Hiawatha.* Pt. xv, l. 56.

11
We are the music-makers,
And we are the dreamers of dreams,
Wandering by lone sea-breakers,
And sitting by desolate streams;
World-losers and world-forsakers,
Of whom the pale moon gleams:
Yet we are the movers and shakers
Of the world for ever, it seems.
ARTHUR O'SHAUGHNESSY, *The Music-Makers.*

12
The language of tones belongs equally to all mankind, and melody is the absolute language in which the musician speaks to every heart.
RICHARD WAGNER, *Beethoven.*

13
Is it not strange that sheeps' guts should hale souls out of men's bodies?
SHAKESPEARE, *Much Ado About Nothing.* Act ii, sc. 3, l. 61.

Music . . . horse-hairs and calves'-guts.
SHAKESPEARE, *Cymbeline.* Act ii, sc. 3, l. 32.

The fiddler Apollo get his sinews to make catlings on.
SHAKESPEARE, *Troilus and Cressida,* iii, 3, 303.

See to their desks Apollo's sons repair,—
Swift rides the rosin o'er the horse's hair!
In unison their various tones to tune,
Murmurs the hautboy, growls the hoarse bassoon;
In soft vibration sighs the whispering lute,
Tang goes the harpsichord, too-too the flute,
Brays the loud trumpet, squeaks the fiddle sharp,
Winds the French-horn, and twangs the tingling harp;
Till, like great Jove, the leader, figuring in,
Attunes to order the chaotic din.
HORACE AND JAMES SMITH, *Rejected Addresses: The Theatre,* l. 20.

A squeak's heard in the orchestra,
The leader draws across
The intestines of the agile cat
The tail of the noble hoss.
GEORGE T. LANIGAN, *The Amateur Orlando.* St. 8.

14
Come on and hear, come on and hear, Alexander's Ragtime Band.
IRVING BERLIN, *Alexander's Ragtime Band.* (1911)

Alexander's Ragtime Band stamped a new character on American music.
ALEXANDER WOOLLCOTT, *Irving Berlin.*

1
Hence from their resounding prison the docile winds are loosed, and repay a melody for their liberty received. (Hinc venti dociles resono se carcere solvunt, Et cantum accepta pro libertate rependunt.)
JEAN BAPTISTE DE SANTEUL, *Inscription on an Organ.*

2
There's a barrel-organ carolling across a golden street
In the city as the sun sinks low;
And the music's not immortal; but the world has made it sweet
And fulfilled it with the sunset glow.
ALFRED NOYES, *The Barrel-Organ.*

She played upon her music-box a fancy air by chance,
And straightway all her polka-dots began a lively dance.
PETER NEWELL, *Her Polka-Dots.*

3
I have a reasonable good ear in music.
Let's have the tongs and the bones.
SHAKESPEARE, *A Midsummer-Night's Dream.* Act iv, sc. 1, l. 30.

Let the music knock it.
SHAKESPEARE, *Henry VIII.* Act i, sc. 4, l. 108.

4
He was a fiddler, and consequently a rogue.
SWIFT, *Letter to Stella,* 25 July, 1711.

He could fiddle all the bugs off a sweet-potato-vine.
STEPHEN VINCENT BENÉT, *The Mountain Whip-poorwill.*

4a
Gaily the troubadour Touched his guitar.
THOMAS HAYNES BAYLY, *Welcome Me Home.*

I'll strike the light guitar.
H. S. VANDYKE, *The Light Guitar.*

5
How her fingers went when they moved by note
Through measures fine, as she marched them o'er
The yielding plank of the ivory floor.
BENJAMIN F. TAYLOR, *How the Brook Went to Mill.*

6
She ran her fingers o'er the ivory keys,
And shook a prelude from them as a bird
Shakes from its throat a song.
JAMES B. KENYON, *Twilight and Music.*

7
Five-and-thirty black slaves,
Half-a-hundred white,
All their duty but to sing
For their Queen's delight.
WILLIAM WATSON, *The Key-Board.*

Ah, the gracious tyrannies
Of her finger-tips.
WILLIAM WATSON, *The Key-Board.*

8
Her ivory hands on the ivory keys
Strayed in a fitful fantasy,
Like the silver gleam when the poplar trees
Rustle their pale leaves listlessly.
OSCAR WILDE, *In the Gold Room: A Harmony.*

10
'Tis the common disease of all your musicians, that they know no mean, to be entreated either to begin or end.
BEN JONSON, *The Poetaster.* Act ii, sc. 1.

MYSTERY

11
The lucrative business of mystery.
BURKE, *A Vindication of Natural Society.*

12
It happens, by a common vice of human nature, that we trust most to, and are most seriously frightened at, things which are strange and unknown. (Communi fit vitio naturæ, ut inusitatis atque incognitis rebus magis confidamus, vehementiusque exterreamur.)
CÆSAR, *De Bello Civili.* Bk. ii, sec. 4.

Plain truth will influence half a score of men at most in a nation, or an age, while mystery will lead millions by the nose.
HENRY ST. JOHN, *Letter,* 28 July, 1721.

13
O'er all there hung a shadow and a fear;
A sense of mystery the spirit daunted,
And said as plain as whisper in the ear,
The place is haunted.
THOMAS HOOD, *The Haunted House.*

14
Listen to voices in the upper air,
Nor lose thy simple faith in mysteries.
LONGFELLOW, *The Castle-Builder.*

15
If you go directly at the heart of a mystery, it ceases to be a mystery, and becomes only a question of drainage.
CHRISTOPHER MORLEY, *Where the Blue Begins,* p. 9.

16
There was the Door to which I found no Key;
There was the Veil through which I might not see.
OMAR KHAYYÁM, *Rubáiyát.* St. 32. (Fitzgerald, tr.)

Shall any gazer see with mortal eyes,
Or any searcher know by mortal mind?
Veil after veil will lift—but there must be
Veil upon veil behind.
EDWIN ARNOLD, *The Light of Asia.* Bk. viii.

17
Sacred mysteries. (Arcana sacra.)
TACITUS, *Germania.* Sec. 18.

18
Let not the conceit of intellect hinder thee from worshipping mystery.
M. F. TUPPER, *Proverbial Philosophy: Reading.*

N

NAIL

1
Nail is driven out by nail. (Ἥλῳ γὰρ ὁ ἧλος.)
ARISTOTLE, *Politics*. Bk. v, ch. 9, sec. 6. Quoted as a proverb.

One nail drives out another, at least!
OWEN MEREDITH, *The Portrait*.

Drive not a second nail till the first be clinched.
THOMAS FULLER, *Gnomologia*. No. 1334.

2
A nail in the wound. (Unguis in ulcere.)
CICERO, *Pro Domo Sua*. Ch. 5, sec. 12.

3
With tooth and nail.
DU BARTAS, *Devine Weekes and Workes*. Week i, day 2. (Sylvester, tr.)

4
To the nail. (Ad unguem.)
HORACE, *Satires*. Bk. i, sat. 5, l. 32; *Ars Poetica*, l. 294. In the sense of highly finished, *see under* MANNERS.

5
Speak the word, and I will help you to it upon the nail.
THOMAS NASHE, *Works*. Vol. iii, p. 59. (1596)

6
I'll never see't; for, I am sure, my nails
Are stronger than mine eyes.
SHAKESPEARE, *Antony and Cleopatra*. Act v, sc. 2, l. 223.

7
Falstaff: What, is the old king dead?
Pistol: As nail in door.
SHAKESPEARE, *II Henry IV*. Act v, sc. 3, l. 126. *See also under* DEATH.

8
Could I come near your beauty with my nails,
I 'ld set my ten commandments in your face.
SHAKESPEARE, *II Henry VI*. Act i, sc. 3, l. 144. *See also under* FINGERS.

9
Thou hittest the nail on the head.
JOHN STANBRIDGE, *Vulgaria*, B 5. (c. 1520); BEAUMONT AND FLETCHER, *Love's Cure*, ii, 1; HEYWOOD, *Proverbs*, i, 11; RABELAIS, *Works*, iii, 35.

10
Every nail driven should be as another rivet in the machine of the universe, you carrying on the work.
H. D. THOREAU, *Walden: Conclusion*.

11
A white speck upon the nails made them as sure of a gift, as if they had it already in their pockets.
UNKNOWN. (*Connoisseur*. No. 59. 1755.)

12
Cut your nails on Monday, you cut them for health;
Cut them on Tuesday, you cut them for wealth;
Cut them on Wednesday, you cut them for news;
Cut them on Thursday, a new pair of shoes;
Cut them on Friday, you cut them for sorrow;
Cut them on Saturday, a present to-morrow;
But he that on Sunday cuts his horn,
Better that he had never been born!
UNKNOWN. (HENDERSON, *Folk-Lore N. Counties*, 18.)

Hippocrates has even left directions how we should cut our nails; that is, even with the ends of the fingers, neither shorter nor longer.
H. D. THOREAU, *Walden*. Ch. 1.

NAKEDNESS, see Nudity

NAME

I—Name: Apothegms

13
I can call nothing by name if that is not his name. I call a cat a cat, and Rolet a rogue. (Je ne puis rien nommer si ce n'est pas son nom; J'appelle un chat un chat, et Rolet un fripon.)
BOILEAU, *Satires*. Sat i, l. 51.

TO CALL A SPADE A SPADE, *see under* CANDOR.

He said true things, but called them by wrong names.
ROBERT BROWNING, *Bishop Blougram's Apology*.

14
Who hath not own'd, with rapture-smitten frame,
The power of grace, the magic of a name?
CAMPBELL, *The Pleasures of Hope*. Pt. ii, l. 5.

15
"Whose name was writ in water!"
R. W. GILDER, *Keats*. *See also under* KEATS.

My name may have buoyancy enough to float upon the sea of time.
GLADSTONE, *Eton Miscellany*, Nov., 1827. Quoted.

16
And, lo! Ben Adhem's name led all the rest.
LEIGH HUNT, *Abou Ben Adhem*. *For full quotation, see* PHILANTHROPY.

17
Indeed there is a woundy luck in names, sirs,
And a main mystery, an' a man knew where
To vind it.
BEN JONSON, *Tale of a Tub*. Act iv, sc. 2.

Let us speak plain: there is more force in names
Than most men dream of; and a lie may keep
Its throne a whole age longer if it skulk
Behind the shield of some fair-seeming name.
J. R. LOWELL, *A Glance Behind the Curtain*, l. 251.

His opinion was that there was a strange kind of magic bias which good or bad names, as he called them, irresistibly impressed upon our characters and conduct. . . . How many Cæsars and Pompeys, he would say, by mere inspiration of the names, have been rendered worthy of them? And how many, he would add, are there, who might have done exceeding well in the world, had not their characters and spirits been totally depressed and Nicodemus'd into nothing?

STERNE, *Tristram Shandy*. Bk. i, ch. 19.

"Villas" now, with sounding names,
All name and door.

RICHARD LE GALLIENNE, *Love's Landmarks*.

1
There is no stone without its name. (Nullum est sine nomine saxum.)

LUCAN, *De Bello Civili*. Bk. ix, l. 973.

What is it? a learned man
Could give it a clumsy name.
Let him name it who can,
The beauty would be the same.

TENNYSON, *Maud*. Pt. ii, sec. 2, st. 2.

2
The name that dwells on every tongue,
No minstrel needs.

DON JORGE MANRIQUE, *Coplas de Manrique*. St. 54. (Longfellow, tr.)

3
My name is Legion: for we are many.

New Testament: Mark, v, 9.

A name and also an omen. (Nomen atque omen.)

PLAUTUS, *Persa*, l. 625. (Act iv, sc. 4.)

4
I have said everything when I have named the man. (Dixi omnia, cum hominem nominavi.)

PLINY THE YOUNGER, *Epistles*. Bk. iv, epis. 22.

I name no parties.

BEAUMONT AND FLETCHER, *Wit at Several Weapons*. Act ii, sc. 3.

Canst thou bring me to the party?

SHAKESPEARE, *The Tempest*. Act iii, sc. 2, l. 67.
Although it has been considered an Americanism, the older English writers frequently used "party" in the sense of "person." Shakespeare so uses it more than a score of times.

5
O name for ever sad! for ever dear!
Still breath'd in sighs, still usher'd with a tear.

POPE, *Eloisa to Abelard*, l. 31.

6
The name of the Lord is a strong tower.

Old Testament: Proverbs, xviii, 10. (Turris fortissima, nomen Domini.—*Vulgate*.)

But unto you that fear my name shall the Sun of righteousness arise with healing in his wings.

Old Testament: Malachi, iv, 2.

7
The evil wound is cured, but not the evil name.

JOHN RAY, *English Proverbs*, 18. (1670)

8
He is a fool and ever shall,
Who writes his name upon a wall.

JOHN RAY, *English Proverbs*.

Fools' names, like fools' faces,
Are often seen in public places.

UNKNOWN.

9
Thou hast a few names even in Sardis which have not defiled their garments.

New Testament: Revelation, iii, 4.

10
He who pronounces Saxe as Saxy
Would surely call an axe an axy.

J. G. SAXE, *Epigram*, when asked which was the correct pronunciation of his name.

11
I am the last of my race. My name ends with me.

SCHILLER, *Wilhelm Tell*. Act i, sc. 1, l. 100.

12
My foot is on my native heath, and my name is MacGregor.

SCOTT, *Rob Roy*. Ch. 34.

Who, noteless as the race from which he sprung,
Saved others' names, but left his own unsung.

SCOTT, *Waverley*. Ch. 13.

13
Thou hast stolen both mine office and my name.
The one ne'er got me credit, the other mickle blame.

SHAKESPEARE, *The Comedy of Errors*. Act iii, sc. 1, l. 44.

A name unmusical to the Volscians' ears,
And harsh in sound to thine.

SHAKESPEARE, *Coriolanus*. Act iv, sc. 5, l. 64.

14
O good Horatio, what a wounded name,
Things standing thus unknown, shall live behind me!

SHAKESPEARE, *Hamlet*. Act v, sc. 2, l. 355.

When we were happy we had other names.

SHAKESPEARE, *King John*. Act v, sc. 4, l. 8.

A name to be washed out with all men's tears.

SWINBURNE, *Atalanta in Calydon: Althæa*.

15
Every godfather can give a name.

SHAKESPEARE, *Love's Labour's Lost*. Act i, sc. 1, l. 93.

Giving a name, indeed, is a poetic art; all poetry, if we go to that with it, is but a giving of names.

CARLYLE, *Journal*, 18 May, 1832.

16
Who may, in the ambush of my name, strike home.

SHAKESPEARE, *Measure for Measure*. Act i, sc. 3, l. 41.

17
I cannot tell what the dickens his name is.

SHAKESPEARE, *The Merry Wives of Windsor*. Act iii, sc. 2, l. 20. (1600)

What the dickens!

THOMAS HEYWOOD, *Edward IV* Act iii, sc. 1. (1600)

18
O, Romeo, Romeo! wherefore art thou Romeo?

Deny thy father and refuse thy name:
Or if thou wilt not, be but sworn my love,
And I'll no longer be a Capulet.
SHAKESPEARE, *Romeo and Juliet*. Act ii, sc. 2, l. 33.

I cannot love my lord, and not his name.
TENNYSON, *The Marriage of Geraint*, l. 92.

1
What's in a name? that which we call a rose
By any other name would smell as sweet.
SHAKESPEARE, *Romeo and Juliet*. Act ii, sc. 2, l. 42.

That which we call a Snob, by any other name would still be snobbish.
THACKERAY, *Book of Snobs*.

2
Love hangs like light about your name
As music round the shell!
SWINBURNE, *Adieux à Marie Stuart*. Pt. iv.

3
They lent honorable names [to dishonorable things]. (Honesta nomina prætendebant.)
TACITUS, *Annals*. Bk. xiv, sec. 21.

Through superstition of a name. (Superstitione nominis.)
TACITUS, *History*. Bk. iii, sec. 58.

4
Let be my name until I make my name.
TENNYSON, *Gareth and Lynette*, l. 563.

I would rather make my name than inherit it.
THACKERAY, *The Virginians*. Ch. 26.

5
The blackest ink of Fate was sure my lot,
And, when she writ my name, she made a blot.
GEORGE VILLIERS, DUKE OF BUCKINGHAM, *The Rehearsal*. Act iii, sc. 2. (1671) Quoted by Fielding, *Amelia*. Bk. ii, ch. 9.

II—Name. Great Names

6
Some mighty man
Who beat his name on the drum of the world's ear.
BAILEY, *Festus: A Metropolis*.

7
Strong towers decay,
But a great name shall never pass away.
PARK BENJAMIN, *A Great Name*.

But he whose name is graved in the white stone
Shall last and shine when all of these are gone.
ANNE BRADSTREET, *Contemplations*.

8
Our men scarce seem in earnest now:
Distinguished names!—but 'tis, somehow,
As if they played at being names
Still more distinguished, like the games
Of children.
ROBERT BROWNING, *Waring*. Pt. i, sec. 6.

9
Round the whole world his dreaded name shall sound,
And reach to worlds, that must not yet be found.
ARBAHAM COWLEY, *Davideis*. Bk. ii, l. 834. (1656)

Nations unborn your mighty names shall sound,
And worlds applaud that must not yet be found!
POPE, *Essay on Criticism*. Pt. i, l. 193. (1711)

10
Ill did those mighty men to trust thee with their story;
That hast forgot their names who reared thee for their glory.
MICHAEL DRAYTON, *Poly-olbion*. Song iii, l. 61. Referring to Stonehenge.

11
Victorious names, who made the world obey;
Who while they liv'd, in deeds of arms excell'd,
And after death for deities were held.
DRYDEN, *The Flower and the Leaf*, l. 518.

12
Navies nor armies can exalt the state, . . .
But one great name can make a country great.
R. W. GILDER, *To James Russell Lowell*.

13
For thou art Freedom's now, and Fame's:
One of the few, the immortal names,
That were not born to die.
FITZ-GREENE HALLECK, *Marco Bozzaris*.

14
He left a name, at which the world grew pale,
To point a moral, or adorn a tale.
SAMUEL JOHNSON, *Vanity of Human Wishes*, l. 219.

15
Great names debase instead of elevating those who do not know how to sustain them. (Les grands noms abaissent au lieu d'élever ceux qui ne les savent pas soutenir.)
LA ROCHEFOUCAULD, *Maximes*. No. 94.

16
He stands the mere shadow of a mighty name. (Stat magni nominis umbra.)
LUCAN, *De Bello Civili*. Bk. i, l. 135. An adaptation of this, "Stat nominis umbra," was used by Junius as the motto prefixed to his *Letters*.

Do not concern yourself with anxiety for the shadow of a great name. (Non sit tibi curæ de magni nominis umbra.)
THOMAS À KEMPIS, *De Imitatione Christi*. Bk. iii, ch. 24, sec. 2.

17
An illustrious and ancient name. (Clarum et venerabile nomen.)
LUCAN, *De Bello Civili*. Bk. ix, l. 203.

He spreads his name throughout the whole world. (Nomen toto sparget in orbe suum.)
MARTIAL, *Epigrams*. Bk. vi, epig. 61, l. 2.

18
Those rugged names . . .
That would have made Quintilian stare and gasp.
MILTON, *Sonnets*. No. xi.

19
The dreaded name Of Demogorgon.
MILTON, *Paradise Lost*. Bk. ii, l. 965.

Must I call your master to my aid,

At whose dread name the trembling furies quake,
Hell stands abashed, and earth's foundations quake?
LUCAN, *De Bello Civili*. Bk. ii. (Rowe, tr.)

1
Wherever the bright sun of heaven shall shine,
His honour and the greatness of his name
Shall be, and make new nations.
SHAKESPEARE, *Henry VIII*. Act v, sc. 5, l. 51.

Your name is great
In mouths of wisest censure.
SHAKESPEARE, *Othello*. Act ii, sc. 3, l. 192.

2
Bright with names that men remember, loud with names that men forget.
SWINBURNE, *Eton: An Ode*.

3
To such a name for ages long,
To such a name,
Preserve a broad approach of fame,
And ever-echoing avenues of song!
TENNYSON, *Ode on the Death of the Duke of Wellington*. St. 5.

4
What a heavy burden is a name that has become too famous. (C'est un poids bien pesant qu'un nom trop tôt fameux.)
VOLTAIRE, *La Henriade*. Chant iii, l. 41.

5
Methinks their very names shine still and bright;
Apart—like glow-worms on a summer's night.
WORDSWORTH, *Ecclesiastical Sonnets*. Pt. iii, No. 5.

Yet shall thy name, conspicuous and sublime,
Stand in the spacious firmament of time,
Fixed as a star.
WORDSWORTH, *Poems Dedicated to National Independence*. Pt. ii, No. 19.

A name "fast anchored in the deep abyss of time" is like a star twinkling in the firmament, cold, silent, distant, but eternal and sublime.
WILLIAM HAZLITT, *Table Talk*.

III—Name and Fame

See also Fame

For Good Name see Reputation

6
For my name and memory, I leave it to men's charitable speeches, to foreign nations, and to the next ages.
FRANCIS BACON. From his will.

7
Bright names will hallow song.
BYRON, *Childe Harold*. Canto iii, st. 29.

8
The Glory and the Nothing of a Name.
BYRON, *Churchill's Grave*.

When I myself am nothing but a name.
ABRAHAM COWLEY, *Ode upon Occasion of a Copy of Verses of My Lord Broghill's*.

9
He left a Corsair's name to other times,
Linked with one virtue, and a thousand crimes.
BYRON, *The Corsair*. Canto iii, st. 24.

10
A poor traditionary fame
Is all that's left to grace his name.
WILLIAM COMBE, *Dr. Syntax in Search of the Picturesque*. Canto xxiv.

11
Charm'd with the foolish whistlings of a name.
ABRAHAM COWLEY, *Imitations of Vergil: Georgics*. Bk. ii, l. 486. (1647)

Ravish'd with the whistling of a name.
POPE, *Essay on Man*. Epis. iv, l. 283. (1733)

12
Some to the fascination of a name
Surrender judgment, hoodwinked.
COWPER, *The Task*. Bk. vi, l. 101.

13
Men but like visions are, time all doth claim;
He lives, who dies to win a lasting name.
WILLIAM DRUMMOND, *Sonnets*. No. xii.

14
Had swoln 'bove any Greek or Roman name.
DRYDEN, *On the Death of Lord Hastings*, l. 76. (1667)

On this foundation would I build my fame,
And emulate the Greek and Roman name.
NICHOLAS ROWE, *Jane Shore*. Act iii, sc. 1. (1714)

Above all Greek, above all Roman fame.
POPE, *Imitations of Horace: Epistles*. Bk. ii, epis. 1, l. 26. (1733)

15
There be of them, that have left a name behind them.
Apocrypha: Ecclesiasticus, xliv, 8.

16
Only a herald, who that way doth pass,
Finds his crackt name at length in the church-glass.
GEORGE HERBERT, *The Church-Porch*. St. 33.

17
I will give them an everlasting name, that shall not be cut off.
Old Testament: Isaiah, lvi, 5.

18
Then, when this body falls in funeral fire,
My name shall live, and my best part aspire.
BEN JONSON, *The Poetaster*. Act i, sc. 1.

19
To see the laurel wreath, on high suspended,
That is to crown our name when life is ended.
KEATS, *Sleep and Poetry*, l. 35.

20
The surest pledge of a deathless name
Is the silent homage of thoughts unspoken.
LONGFELLOW, *The Herons of Elmwood*.

21
Ah, with what lofty hope we came!
But we forget it, dream of fame,
And scrawl, as I do here, a name.
J. R. LOWELL, *For an Autograph*. St. 6.

1
Oh, breathe not his name! let it sleep in the shade,
Where cold and unhonour'd his relics are laid.
THOMAS MOORE, *Oh, Breathe Not His Name.*

2
And like to one he seemed whose better day
Is over to himself, though foolish fame
Shouts louder year by year his empty name.
WILLIAM MORRIS, *The Earthly Paradise: Prologue: The Wanderers*, l. 466.

A far babbled name,
The ceaseless seeker after praise and fame.
WILLIAM MORRIS, *Life and Death of Jason.* Bk. ix, l. 189.

3
Born to fail, A name without an echo
HENRY NEWBOLT, *The Non-Combatant.*

4
Perchance my name will be mingled with theirs. (Forsitan et nostrum nomen miscebitur.)
OVID, *Ars Amatoria.* Bk. iii, l. 339.

5
O! while along the stream of time thy name
Expanded flies, and gathers all its fame,
Say, shall my little bark attendant sail,
Pursue the triumph, and partake the gale?
POPE, *Essay on Man.* Epis. iv, l. 383.

6
Then shall our names,
Familiar in his mouth as household words, . . .
Be in their flowing cups freshly remember'd.
SHAKESPEARE, *Henry V.* Act iv, sc. 3, l. 51.

7
Yet leaving here a name, I trust,
That will not perish in the dust.
SOUTHEY, *My Days Among the Dead Are Passed.*

8
One day I wrote her name upon the strand,
But came the waves and washèd it away:
Again I wrote it with a second hand,
But came the tide, and made my pains his prey.
Vain man, said she, that dost in vain essay
A mortal thing so to immortalize!
For I myself shall like to this decay,
And eke my name be wipèd out likewise.
Not so (quod I) let baser things devise
To die in dust, but you shall live by fame:
My verse your virtues rare shall eternize,
And in the heavens write your glorious name.
SPENSER, *Amoretti.* Sonnet lxxv.

Alone I walked on the ocean strand,
A pearly shell was in my hand;
I stooped, and wrote upon the sand
My name, the year, the day.
As onward from the spot I passed,
One lingering look behind I cast,
A wave came rolling high and fast,
And washed my lines away.
HANNAH FLAGG GOULD, *A Name in the Sand.*

9
No sound is breathed so potent to coerce
And to conciliate, as their names who dare
For that sweet mother-land which gave them birth
Nobly to do, nobly to die.
TENNYSON, *Tiresias*, l. 116.

10
I won a noble fame;
But with a sudden frown,
The people snatched my crown,
And, in the mire, trod down
My lofty name.
THEODORE TILTON, *Sir Marmaduke's Musings.*

11
Keeps from age to age an ever-living name.
(Æternumque tenet per sæcula nomen.)
VERGIL, *Æneid.* Bk. vi, l. 235.

12
When once the trumpet of fame has sounded a poor man's name, farewell his repose for ever.
VOLTAIRE, *Letter to M. Capperonnier*, 1768.

IV—Name: Women's Names

13
Oh! no! we never mention her,
Her name is never heard;
My lips are now forbid to speak
That once familiar word.
T. H. BAYLY, *Oh! No! We Never Mention Her.*

There's a name that's never spoken,
And a mother's heart half-broken,
There is just another missing from the old home, that is all;
There is still a mem'ry living,
There's a father unforgiving,
And a picture that is turn'd toward the wall.
CHARLES GRAHAM, *The Picture That Is Turned Toward the Wall.* (1891) Suggested by a scene from the play *Blue Jeans.*

14
I have a passion for the name of "Mary,"
For once it was a magic sound to me,
And still it half calls up the realms of fairy,
Where I beheld what never was to be.
BYRON, *Don Juan.* Canto v, st. 4.

15
Sweet as the sweetest of melodies
Filling my soul with ecstasy,
Sweeter than all things to me,
The sound of my sweetheart's name.
WILL D. COBB, *The Sound of My Sweetheart's Name.* (1901)

16
I ask'd my fair one happy day,
What I should call her in my lay;
By what sweet name from Rome or Greece;
Lalage, Neaera, Chloris,
Sappho, Lesbia, or Doris,
Arethusa or Lucrece.

"Ah!" replied my gentle fair,
"Belovèd, what are names but air?
Choose thou whatever suits the line;

Call me Sappho, call me Chloris,
Call me Lalage or Doris,
Only, only call me Thine."
S. T. COLERIDGE, *Names.*

1
Brown's for Lalage, Jones for Lelia,
Robinson's bosom for Beatrice glows,
Smith is a Hamlet before Ophelia,
The glamour stays if the reason goes!
Every lover the years disclose
Is of a beautiful name made free.
One befriends, and all others are foes.
Anna's the name of names for me.
W. E. HENLEY, *Ballade of Ladies' Names.*

Ruth like a gillyflower smells and blows,
Sylvia prattles of Arcadee,
Sybil mystifies, Connie crows,
Anna's the name of names for me!
W. E. HENLEY, *Ballade of Ladies' Names.*

2
She who comes to me and pleadeth
In the lovely name of Edith.
LONGFELLOW, *Lines in a Private Album.*

3
For women's names keep murmuring like the wind
The hidden things that none for ever tells.
ERNEST RHYS, *Words.*

4
O Sophonisba! Sophonisba, O!
JAMES THOMSON, *Sophonisba.* Act iii, sc. 2. When this line was spoken, at the first performance of the play, an exasperated spectator stood up in his box and cried out, "O Jamie Thomson! Jamie Thomson, O!" and the line was altered to, "O Sophonisba! I am wholly thine!"

5
"What is thy name, fair maid?" quoth he.
"Penelophon, O King!" quoth she.
UNKNOWN, *King Cophetua and the Beggar Maid.* (PERCY, *Reliques.*) Shakespeare, quoting this old ballad in *Love's Labour's Lost* (iv, 1, 65), gives the beggar maid's name as Zenelophon.

6
Your name hangs in my heart like a bell's tongue.
ROSTAND, *Cyrano de Bergerac.* Act iii, sc. 6.

7
I do beseech you—
Chiefly, that I might set it in my prayers—
What is your name?
SHAKESPEARE, *The Tempest.* Act iii, sc. 1, l. 34.

V—Names Sweet and Ugly

8
The very names of things belov'd are dear,
And sounds will gather beauty from their sense,
As many a face thro' love's long residence
Groweth to fair instead of plain and sere.
ROBERT BRIDGES, *Growth of Love.* Sonnet 4.

9
What a name! Was it love or praise?
Speech half-asleep or song half-awake?
I must learn Spanish, one of these days,
Only for that slow sweet name's sake.
ROBERT BROWNING, *The Flower's Name.*

10
Thrice happy he whose name has been well spelt
In the despatch.
BYRON, *Don Juan.* Canto viii, st. 18.

11
Oh, Amos Cottle!—Phœbus! what a name!
BYRON, *English Bards and Scotch Reviewers,* l. 399.

A measly little gum-drop name like Percival.
HARRY LEON WILSON, *The Spenders,* p. 344.

12
Pride lives with all; strange names our rustics give
To helpless infants, that their own may live.
GEORGE CRABBE, *The Parish Register.* Pt. i.

With unpronounceable, awful names.
BRET HARTE, *The Tale of a Pony.*

13
A name?—if the party had a voice,
What mortal would be a Bugg by choice,
As a Hogg, a Grubb, or a Chubb rejoice,
Or any such nauseous blazon?
Not to mention many a vulgar name,
Which would make a doorplate blush for shame,
If doorplates were not so brazen!
HOOD, *Miss Kilmansegg: Her Christening.*

14
Have heard her sigh and soften out the name.
WALTER SAVAGE LANDOR, *Gebir.* Pt. v, l. 145.

15
And if his name be George, I'll call him Peter;
For new-made honour doth forget men's names.
SHAKESPEARE, *King John.* Act i, sc. 1, l. 186.

16
As Stephen Sly and old John Naps of Greece
And Peter Turph and Henry Pimpernell
And twenty more such names and men as these
Which never were nor no man ever saw.
SHAKESPEARE, *The Taming of the Shrew: Induction.* Sc. 2, l. 95.

17
And last of all an Admiral came,
A terrible man with a terrible name,—
A name which you all know by sight very well,
But which no one can speak, and no one can spell.
SOUTHEY, *The March to Moscow.* St. 8.

18
But Thomas, and William, and such pretty names,
Should be cleanly and harmless as doves or as lambs,
Those lovely and innocent creatures.
ISAAC WATTS, *Innocent Play.*

1
What with Gertrude, Ep and Ein,
When I hear the name of Stein,
I go creepy down the spine.
UNKNOWN. *Precious Steins.*

There's a wonderful family called Stein—
There's Gert, and there's Epp, and there's Ein;
Gert's poems are bunk,
Epp's statues are junk,
And no one can understand Ein.
UNKNOWN, *The Steins.*

VI—Name: Nicknames

2
No orator can measure in effect with him who can give good nicknames.
EMERSON, *Representative Men: Plato.*

3
A nickname is the heaviest stone that the devil can throw at a man.
HAZLITT, *Essays: On Nicknames.* Quoted.

Of all eloquence a nickname is the most concise; of all arguments the most unanswerable.
WILLIAM HAZLITT, *Essays: On Nicknames.*

4
Nicknames and whippings, when they are once laid on, no one has discovered how to take off.
W. S. LANDOR, *Imaginary Conversations: Du Paty.*

5
His intimate friends called him "Candle-ends,"
And his enemies, "Toasted-cheese."
LEWIS CARROLL, *The Hunting of the Snark.* Fit 1.

6
Known by the *sobriquet* of "The Artful Dodger."
DICKENS, *Oliver Twist.* Ch. 8.

The dodgerest of all the dodgers.
DICKENS, *Our Mutual Friend.* Bk. ii, ch. 13.

7
Called me wessel, Sammy—a wessel of wrath.
DICKENS, *Pickwick Papers.* Ch. 22.

8
I am called "Archibald the All-right"—for I am infallible.
W. S. GILBERT, *Patience.* Act i.

9
Then you can call me "Timbertoes,"—thet's wut the people likes;
Sutthin' combinin' morril truth with phrases sech ez strikes.
J. R. LOWELL, *Biglow Papers.* Ser. i, No. 8.

10
Out of his surname they have coined an epithet for a knave, and out of his Christain name a synonym for the Devil.
MACAULAY, *Essays: Niccolo Machiavelli.*

Nick Machiavel had ne'er a trick
(Tho' he gave his name to our Old Nick),
But was below the least of these,
That pass i' th' world for holiness.
BUTLER, *Hudibras.* Pt. iii, canto i, l. 1313.

11
Sunset Cox.
SAMUEL SULLIVAN COX. from a glowing description of a sunset, written by him, and printed in *Ohio State Journal,* 19 May, 1853.

12
In the parlance of the street, his first name was Jupiter; this was properly bestowed, for his word was "I command."
JAMES FORD RHODES, *History of the United States.* Referring to J. P. Morgan. "Jupiter" as a name for Morgan was originated by Thomas Hitchcock, of the New York *Sun.*

13
The bravest of the Brave. (Le brave des braves.)
MARSHAL NEY won this title at the battle of Friedland (1807). The title had previously been given to Crillon by Henry IV of France

14
Gentlemen, I give you the Bayard of India, Major James Outram of the Bombay army.
SIR CHARLES JAMES NAPIER, *Toast,* at dinner to Outram, 5 Nov., 1842.

15
O sea-green incorruptible.
CARLYLE, *French Revolution.* Pt. iii, bk. iii, ch. 1. Referring to Robespierre.

16
Some American Sobriquets:
The Old Man Eloquent: John Quincy Adams.
The American Cato: Samuel Adams.
Old Bullion: Thomas Benton.
The Plumed Knight; the Tattooed Man: James G. Blaine. (For "Plumed Knight" see 1553:10. "Tattooed Man" derived from a cartoon by Bernard Gillam in *Puck*, 16 April, 1884, captioned "Phryne Before the Chicago Tribunal," showing Blaine, clad only in a loin cloth and "magnetic pad," his body tattooed with "Mulligan letters," "Bribery," etc.)
The Tenth Muse: Anne Bradstreet.
The Sage of Wheatland: James Buchanan.
The Mill-Boy of the Slashes: Henry Clay.
The Nestor of the Press: Charles A. Dana.
The Little Giant: Stephen A. Douglas.
The Apostle of the Indians: John Eliot.
The Pathfinder: John Charles Frémont.
The Canal-Boy: James Abram Garfield.
Unconditional Surrender: U. S. Grant.
Little Ben: Benjamin Harrison.
The Cincinnatus of the West; Old Tippecanoe: William Henry Harrison.
Fighting Joe: General Joseph Hooker. Also applied to Gen. Joseph Wheeler.
Old Hickory: Andrew Jackson.
Stonewall: Thomas Jonathan Jackson.
The Sage of Monticello: Thomas Jefferson.
Light-Horse Harry: Henry Lee.
Father Abraham, Old Abe, The Rail-splitter, The Martyr President: Abraham Lincoln. In his letters to Nicolay, John Hay referred to Lincoln as "The Tycoon."

Black Eagle; Black Jack: John A. Logan. Black Jack has also been applied to General John J. Pershing.
The Swamp-Fox: Francis Marion.
Little Mac: General G. B. McClellan.
War-Horse of Democracy: Samuel Medary.
Young Hickory: James K. Polk.
Old Fuss and Feathers: Winfield Scott.
The Watch-Dog of the Treasury: Francis E. Spinner.
Old Rough and Ready: General Zachary Taylor.
The Old Roman: Allen G. Thurman.
The Sage of Greystone: Samuel J. Tilden.
The Little Magician: Martin Van Buren.
Mad Anthony: General Anthony Wayne.
The Schoolmaster of the Republic: Noah Webster.
The Quaker Poet: John G. Whittier.

NAPOLEON

I—Napoleon I

1
Crushed was Napoleon by the northern Thor,
Who knocked his army down with icy hammer.

BYRON, *Beppo*. St. 61.

And kings crept out again to feel the sun.

E. B. BROWNING, *Crowned and Buried*, St. 11.

2
The instinct of active, brave, able men, throughout the middle class everywhere, has pointed out Napoleon as the incarnate Democrat.

EMERSON, *Representative Men: Napoleon.*

Napoleon is thoroughly modern, and, at the highest point of his fortunes, has the very spirit of the newspapers.

EMERSON, *Representative Men: Napoleon.*

When you have penetrated through all the circles of power and splendor, you were not dealing with a gentleman, at last, but with an impostor and a rogue.

EMERSON, *Representative Men: Napoleon.*

3
Napoleon was a man! His life was the stride of a demigod.

GOETHE, *Conversations with Eckermann*, 1828.

You are a man!

NAPOLEON BONAPARTE, closing a conversation with Goethe at Erfurt, 2 Oct., 1808.

4
Yet spirit immortal, the tomb cannot bind thee,
But, like thine own eagle that soars to the sun,
Thou springest from bondage and leavest behind thee
A name which before thee no mortal hath won.

LYMAN HEATH, *The Grave of Bonaparte*

A little while ago I stood by the tomb of the old Napoleon, a magnificent tomb of gilt and gold, . . . and could see the only woman who ever loved him pushed aside.

R. G. INGERSOLL, *Reverie at the Tomb of Napoleon.*

I wish my ashes to repose on the banks of the Seine, in the midst of the French people I have loved so well.

NAPOLEON BONAPARTE, *Codicil to His Will*, dated 16 April, 1821.

I don't care a twopenny damn what becomes of the ashes of Napoleon Bonaparte.

DUKE OF WELLINGTON, attr. (FARMER AND HENLEY, *Slang and Its Analogues.*)

5
Napoleon healed through sword and fire the sick nation.

HEINE. (SCHERER, *History of German Literature*. Bk. ii, p. 116.)

6
Napoleon was whipped because he carried a chip on his shoulder: this is the one thing that the gods who write the laws of nations will not palliate nor excuse.

ELBERT HUBBARD, *Philistine*. Vol. xx, p. 45.

7
England took the eagle and Austria the eaglet. (L'Angleterre prit l'aigle et l'Autriche l'aiglon.)

VICTOR HUGO, applying for the first time the word l'Aiglon to Napoleon's son. Napoleon had transferred the imperial eagles of Rome to his own standard.

God was bored by him.

VICTOR HUGO. Referring to Napoleon.

8
Bonaparte's wisdom was in his thoughts, and his madness in his passions. (La sagesse de Bonaparte était dans ses pensées, et la folie dans ses passions.)

JOUBERT, *Pensées*. No. 221.

9
Even the great Napoleon could not dine twice. (Même le grand Napoléon ne pouvait pas dîner deux fois.)

ALPHONSE KARR, *Le Chemin le Plus Court.*

10
Grand, gloomy, and peculiar, he sat upon the throne a sceptred hermit, wrapped in the solitude of his own originality.

CHARLES PHILLIPS, *The Character of Napoleon.*

11
Although too much of a soldier among sovereigns, no one could claim with better right to be a sovereign among soldiers.

WALTER SCOTT, *Life of Napoleon.*

12
What! alive, and so bold, O earth?

SHELLEY, *On Hearing the News of the Death of Napoleon.*

It is no longer an event; it is only a piece of news.

TALLEYRAND, when some one exclaimed "What an event!" on learning of Napoleon's death at St. Helena. (COOPER, *Talleyrand.*)

13
Gentlemen, we have a master: this young

man does everything, can do everything, and will do everything. (Messieurs, nous avons un maître: ce jeune homme fait tout, peut tout, et veut tout.)

SIEYÈS, *Address,* to the National Assembly, speaking of Napoleon.

1
No law but his own headstrong will he knew,
No counsellor but his own wicked heart.

ROBERT SOUTHEY, *Ode, Written during the Negociations with Buonaparte.*

Pre-eminently bad among the worst.

SOUTHEY, *The Poet's Pilgrimage to Waterloo.* Pt. iv, st. 15.

2
He thought to quell the stubborn hearts of oak,
Madman!—to chain with chains, and bind with bands
That island queen who sways the floods and lands. . . .
We taught him lowlier moods.

TENNYSON, *Buonaparte.*

Though more than half the world was his,
He died without a rood his own;
And borrowed from his enemies
Six feet of ground to lie upon.

THACKERAY, *The Chronicle of the Drum.*

II—Napoleon III

3
A great unrecognized incapacity. (Une grande incapacité inconnue.)

BISMARCK, of Napoleon III. (*Letter,* 1862, while minister to France.)

Copies never succeed.

KOSSUTH, *Saying.*

4
Because we have had Napoleon the Great, must we have Napoleon the Little?

VICTOR HUGO, *Speech,* Chamber of Deputies, 17 July, 1851. (BARBOU, *Life.*)

5
We shall see Buonaparte the bastard
Kick heels with his throat in a rope.

SWINBURNE, *A Song in Time of Order, 1852.*

NATION

See also State

I—Nation: Definitions

6
The true wealth of a country lies in its men and women. If they're mean, unhappy and ill, the country is poor.

RICHARD ALDINGTON, *Colonel's Daughter,* p. 51.

And you prate of the wealth of nations, as if it were bought and sold,
The wealth of nations is men, not silk and cotton and gold.

RICHARD HOVEY, *Peace.*

7
A people is but the attempt of many
To rise to the completer life of one—
And those who live as models for the mass
Are singly of more value than they all.
Such man are you, and such a time is this,
That your sole fate concerns a nation more
Than much apparent welfare.

ROBERT BROWNING, *Luria.* Act v, l. 334.

8
I am firm in my conviction that . . . there is no calamity which a great nation can invite which equals that which follows from a supine submission to wrong and injustice, and the consequent loss of national self-respect and honor, beneath which are shielded and defended a people's safety and greatness.

GROVER CLEVELAND, *Message to Congress,* on Venezuelan question, 17 Dec., 1895. Based on draft by Richard Olney, Secretary of State. For contrasted texts see Nevins, *Grover Cleveland,* p. 640.

That nation is worthless which does not joyfully stake everything in defense of her honor.

SCHILLER, *Die Jungfrau von Orleans.* Act i, sc. 5, l. 81.

The nation's honor is dearer than the nation's comfort; yes, than the nation's life itself.

WOODROW WILSON, *Speech,* 29 Jan., 1916.

9
A nation is the unity of a people. King and parliament are the unity made visible.

S. T. COLERIDGE, *Table-Talk.*

10
Individuals may form communities, but it is institutions alone that can create a nation.

BENJAMIN DISRAELI, *Speech,* at Manchester, 1866.

Nationality is the miracle of political independence. Race is the principle of physical analogy.

BENJAMIN DISRAELI, *Speech,* House of Commons, 9 Aug., 1848.

11
A nation is a thing that lives and acts like a man, and men are the particles of which it is composed.

J. G. HOLLAND, *Plain Talks: The National Heart.*

13
Nations are the citizens of humanity, as individuals are the citizens of the nation.

MAZZINI, *Duties of Man.*

14
Nations, like men, have their infancy.

HENRY ST. JOHN, *On the Study and Use of History.*

II—Nation: Apothegms

15
And hath made of one blood all nations of men.

New Testament: Acts, xvii, 26.

All nations and kindreds and people and tongues.

New Testament: Revelation, vii, 9.

16
A treaty is the promise of a nation.

FISHER AMES, *Speech on the British Treaty,* 28 April, 1796.

1

Men, upon the whole,
Are what they can be—nations, what they would.

E. B. BROWNING, *Casa Guidi Windows*. Pt. i.

Happy are all free peoples, too strong to be dispossessed;
But blessed are those among nations who dare to be strong for the rest!

E. B. BROWNING, *A Court Lady*, l. 39.

2

Nations save, but do not revenge themselves.

GEORGES JACQUES DANTON. (TAINE, *French Revolution*.)

3

How much more are men than nations!

EMERSON, *Letters and Social Aims: Progress of Culture*.

4

Justice is as strictly due between neighbor nations as between neighbor citizens. A highwayman is as much a robber when he plunders in a gang as when single; and a nation that makes an unjust war is only a *great gang*.

BENJAMIN FRANKLIN, *Letter*, 14 March, 1785.

5

How wide the limits stand
Between a splendid and a happy land.

GOLDSMITH, *The Deserted Village*, l. 267.

A land of levity is a land of guilt.

YOUNG, *Night Thoughts: Preface*.

6

The nations are as a drop of a bucket, and are counted as the small dust of the balance.

Old Testament: Isaiah, xl, 15.

7

No nation is permitted to live in ignorance with impunity.

THOMAS JEFFERSON, *Writings*. Vol. xix, p. 407.

If a nation expects to be ignorant and free, it expects what never was and never will be.

THOMAS JEFFERSON, *Writings*. Vol. xiv, p. 382.

8

Wise nature ever, with a prudent hand,
Dispenses various gifts to ev'ry land;
To ev'ry nation frugally imparts
A genius fit for some peculiar arts.

SOAME JENYNS, *The Art of Dancing*. Canto ii, l. 55.

9

I know of no existing nation that deserves to live, and I know of very few individuals.

H. L. MENCKEN, *Prejudices*. Ser. iv, p. 208.

10

A nation's right to speak a nation's voice,
And own no power but of the nation's choice!

THOMAS MOORE, *Fudge Family in Paris*. Letter xi, l. 3.

11

Make your national conscience clean, and your national eyes will soon be clear.

RUSKIN, *Crown of Wild Olive: War*.

12

A nation strong, train'd up in arms.

SHAKESPEARE, *Titus Andronicus*. Act i, sc. 1, 30.

13

To rise by others' fall
I deem a losing gain;
All states with others' ruin built
To ruin run amain.

ROBERT SOUTHWELL, *I Envy Not Their Hap*.

A nation never falls but by suicide.

R. W. EMERSON, *Journal*, 1861.

Until nations are generous they will never be wise; true policy is generous policy; all bitterness, selfishness, etc., may gain small ends, but lose great ones.

WASHINGTON IRVING, *Letter*, March, 1823.

14

A nation's institutions and beliefs are determined by its character.

HERBERT SPENCER, *Social Statics*. Pt. ii, ch. 16, sec. 5.

15

The true greatness of nations is in those qualities which constitute the greatness of the individual.

CHARLES SUMNER, *Oration on the True Grandeur of Nations*.

16

There was never a nation great until it came to the knowledge that it had nowhere in the world to go for help.

CHARLES DUDLEY WARNER, *Studies: Comments on Canada*. Ch. 3.

17

Just pride is no mean factor in a State;
The sense of greatness keeps a nation great.

WILLIAM WATSON, *The True Patriotism*.

18

No nation is fit to sit in judgment upon any other nation.

WOODROW WILSON, *Address*, N. Y., 20 April, 1915.

III—Nation: Little Nations

19

The day of small nations has passed away; the day of empires has come.

JOSEPH CHAMBERLAIN, *Speech*. Birmingham, 13 May, 1904. *See also under* IMPERIALISM.

20

There is no such thing as a small country. The greatness of a people is no more affected by the number of its inhabitants than the greatness of an individual is measured by his height. Whoever presents a great example is great.

VICTOR HUGO, *Speech*, at Geneva, 17 Nov., 1862.

21

The nations which have put mankind and posterity most in their debt have been small states—Israel, Athens, Florence, Elizabethan England.

DEAN W. R. INGE. (MARCHANT, *Wit and Wisdom of Dean Inge*. No. 181.)

22

A little one shall become a thousand, and a small one a strong nation.

Old Testament: Isaiah, lx, 22.

She that was great among nations, and princess among provinces, how is she become tributary!
Old Testament: Lamentations, i, 1.

1
The Cry of the Little Peoples goes up to God
in vain,
For the world is given over to the cruel sons
of Cain.
RICHARD LE GALLIENNE, *The Cry of the Little Peoples.*

2
God has chosen little nations as the vessels by which He carries his choicest wines to the lips of humanity to rejoice their hearts, to exalt their vision, to strengthen their faith.
DAVID LLOYD GEORGE, *Speech*, Sept., 1914.

NATURE

See also Art and Nature; Brooks; Hills, etc.

I—Nature: Definitions

3
Nature means Necessity.
P. J. BAILEY, *Festus: Dedication.*

By fate, not option, frugal Nature gave
One scent to hyson and to wall-flower,
One sound to pine-groves and to waterfalls,
One aspect to the desert and the lake.
It was her stern necessity.
EMERSON, *Xenophanes.*

4
Whatever befalls in accordance with Nature should be accounted good. (Omnia autem, quæsecundum naturam fiunt, sunt habenda in bonis.)
CICERO, *De Senectute.* Ch. xix, sec. 71.

5
And what if all of animated nature
Be but organic harps diversely fram'd,
That tremble into thought, as o'er them
sweeps,
Plastic and vast, one intellectual breeze,
At once the soul of each, and God of all?
S. T. COLERIDGE, *The Eolian Harp*, l. 44.

6
Nature is a rag-merchant, who works up every shred and ort and end into new creations; like a good chemist whom I found, the other day, in his laboratory, converting his old shirts into pure white sugar.
EMERSON, *Conduct of Life: Considerations by the Way.*

7
Nature is what you may do. . . . Nature is the tyrannous circumstance, the thick skull, the sheathed snake, the ponderous rock-like jaw; necessitated activity, violent direction.
EMERSON, *Conduct of Life: Fate.*

Nature is no spendthrift, but takes the shortest way to her ends.
EMERSON, *Conduct of Life: Fate.*

Nature is a mutable cloud which is always and never the same.
EMERSON, *Essays, First Series: History.*

Nature, as we know her, is no saint. . . . She comes eating, drinking and sinning.
EMERSON, *Essays, Second Series: Experience.*

8
The great mother Nature will not quite tell her secret to the coach or the steamboat, but says, One to one, my dear, is my rule also, and I keep my enchantments and oracles for the religious soul coming alone, or as good as alone, in true-love.
EMERSON, *Letter to Mrs. Emerson*, 20 May, 1871.

9
Nature, in her most dazzling aspects or stupendous parts, is but the background and theatre of the tragedy of man.
JOHN MORLEY, *Critical Miscellanies: Byron.*

10
All nature is but art, unknown to thee.
POPE, *Essay on Man.* Epis. i, l. 289.
See also ART AND NATURE.

11
Meanwhile, until the world's structure is held together by philosophy, she [nature] maintains its working through hunger and through love.
SCHILLER, *Die Weltweisen.* Last stanza.

12
"Nature" is but another name for health, and the seasons are but different states of health.
H. D. THOREAU, *Journal*, 23 Aug., 1853.

Nature will bear the closest inspection. She invites us to lay our eye level with her smallest leaf, and take an insect view of its plain.
H. D. THOREAU, *Journal*, 22 Oct., 1839.

II—Nature: Apothegms

13
The never idle workshop of Nature.
MATTHEW ARNOLD, *Elegiac Poems: Epilogue.*

14
About nature consult nature herself.
FRANCIS BACON, *De Augmentis Scientiarum:* Pt. iii, *Introductio.* Stated by Bacon to be "the sole and only way in which the foundations of true and active philosophy can be established."

15
Nature is not governed except by obeying her.
FRANCIS BACON, *De Augmentis Scientiarum.* Pt. ii, bk. 1, aphor. 129.

Nature, to be commanded, must be obeyed.
FRANCIS BACON, *Novum Organum.*

16
Where man is not, nature is barren.
WILLIAM BLAKE, *Proverbs of Hell.*

17
Rich with the spoils of Nature.
SIR THOMAS BROWNE, *Religio Medici.* Pt. i, sec. 13.

18
Nature does nothing in vain. (Natura nihil agit frustra.)
SIR THOMAS BROWNE, *Religio Medici.* Pt. i, sec. 19. Quoted as "the only undisputed axiom in philosophy."

1
And muse on Nature with a poet's eye.
CAMPBELL, *The Pleasures of Hope*. Pt. ii, l. 98.

Nature indeed looks prettily in rhyme.
COWPER, *Retirement*, l. 567.

2
Nature admits no lie.
CARLYLE, *Latter-Day Pamphlets*. No. 5.

There is no pure lie, no pure malignity in nature. The entertainment of the proposition of depravity is the last profligacy and profanation. There is no skepticism, no atheism, but that.
EMERSON, *Essays, Second Series: New England Reformers*.

3
It can't be nature, for it is not sense.
CHARLES CHURCHILL, *The Farewell*, l. 200.

4
Nature abhors annihilation. (Ab interitu naturam abhorrere.)
CICERO, *De Finibus*. Bk. v, ch. 11, sec. 31.

Nature abhors a vacuum. (Natura abhorret vacuum.)
RABELAIS, *Works*. Bk. i, ch. 5. Quoted in Latin.

5
Roosevelt on the Nature-Fakirs.
EDWARD B. CLARK, *Everybody's Magazine*, June, 1907.

The modern "nature-faker" is of course an object of derision to every . . . true nature-lover.
THEODORE ROOSEVELT, *Everybody's Magazine*, Sept., 1907.

6
All Nature ministers to Hope.
HARTLEY COLERIDGE, *Sonnets*. No. 35.

In nature there is nothing melancholy.
S. T. COLERIDGE, *The Nightingale*.

No tears
Dim the sweet look that Nature wears.
LONGFELLOW, *Sunrise on the Hills*.

All Nature wears one universal grin.
FIELDING, *Tom Thumb the Great*. Act i, sc. 1.

Some touch of Nature's genial glow.
SCOTT, *The Lord of the Isles*. Canto iii, st. 14.

The saddest heart might pleasure take
To see all nature gay.
SCOTT, *Marmion*. Canto iv, st. 15.

7
Nature's self's thy Ganymede.
ABRAHAM COWLEY, *The Grasshopper*, l. 8.

8
The truth of nature lieth hid in certain deep mines and caves.
DEMOCRITUS. (BACON, *Advancement of Learning*. Bk. ii.)

9
Child of Nature, learn to unlearn.
BENJAMIN DISRAELI, *Contarini Fleming*. Pt. i, ch. 1.

10
Nature tells every secret once.
EMERSON, *Conduct of Life: Behavior*.

"Look not on Nature, for her name is fatal," said the oracle.
EMERSON, *Conduct of Life: Fate*.

11
Nature works very hard, and only hits the white once in a million throws.
EMERSON, *Conduct of Life: Considerations by the Way*.

Nature hates calculators.
EMERSON, *Essays, Second Series: Experience*.

Nature works on a method of all for each and each for all.
EMERSON, *Society and Solitude: Farming*.

12
The language of nature is the universal language.
CHRISTOPH GLUCK. (HAWEIS, *Music and Morals*. Bk. ii, sec. 85.)

13
Nature with little is content.
ROBERT HERRICK, *No Want Where There's Little*. *See also* MODERATION: LIVING ON LITTLE.

14
You may drive out Nature with a pitchfork, yet she will always hasten back. (Naturam expelles furca, tamen usque recurret.)
HORACE, *Epistles*. Bk. i, epis. 10, l. 24.

Take away the risk, set aside restraint, and Nature will spring forward, to roam at will. (Tolle periclum: Jam vaga prosiliet frenis Natura remotis.)
HORACE, *Satires*. Bk. ii, sat. 7, l. 73.

Chase Nature away, it returns at a gallop. (Chassez le naturel, il revient au galop.)
DESTOUCHES, *Glorieux*. Act iv, sc. 3.

15
To be beautiful and to be calm is the ideal of nature.
RICHARD JEFFERIES, *The Pageant of Summer*.

Deviation from Nature is deviation from happiness.
SAMUEL JOHNSON, *Rasselas*. Ch. 22.

16
All the wise world is little else, in nature,
But parasites or sub-parasites.
BEN JONSON, *Volpone*. Act iii, sc. 1.

17
To conquer Nature man broke down the gates of the Garden of Eden and came forth to meet the challenge of an unordered world.
FRANKLIN K. LANE, *Fruits of Faith*.

18
Nature does not proceed by leaps. (Natura non facit saltus.)
LINNÆUS, *Philosophia Botanica*. Sec. 77.

Nature in her operations does not proceed by leaps.
JACQUES TISSOT, *Discours Véritable de la Vie . . . du Géant Theutobocus*. (1613)

19
Nature never makes excellent things for mean, or no uses.
JOHN LOCKE, *An Essay Concerning Human Understanding*. Bk. ii, ch. 1, sec. 15.

20
All that thy seasons bring, O Nature, is fruit for me!

All things come from thee, subsist in thee, go back to thee.

MARCUS AURELIUS, *Meditations*. Bk. iv, sec. 23.

1
Beldam Nature.

MILTON, *At a Vacation Exercise in the College*, l. 48.

I have no enthusiasm for nature which the slightest chill will not instantly destroy.

GEORGE SAND.

2
And live like Nature's bastards, not her sons.

MILTON, *Comus*, l. 727.

Accuse not Nature; she hath done her part;
Do thou but thine.

MILTON, *Paradise Lost*. Bk. viii, l. 561.

Nature hath need of what she asks.

MILTON, *Paradise Regained*. Bk. ii, l. 253.

3
'Tis one and the same Nature that rolls on her course, and whoever has sufficiently considered the present state of things might certainly conclude as to both the future and the past.

MONTAIGNE, *Essays*. Bk. ii, ch. 12.

Let us a little permit Nature to take her own way; she better understands her own affairs than we.

MONTAIGNE, *Essays*. Bk. iii, ch. 13.

4
Nature forms us for ourselves, not for others; to be, not to seem.

MONTAIGNE, *Essays*. Bk. ii, ch. 37. *See also under* APPEARANCE.

5
Take Nature's path and mad Opinion's leave;
All states can reach it, and all heads conceive;
Obvious her goods, in no extreme they dwell;
There needs but thinking right and meaning well.

POPE, *Essay on Man*. Epis. iv, l. 29.

6
From Nature's chain, whatever link you strike,
Tenth, or ten thousandth, breaks the chain alike.

POPE, *Essay on Man*. Epis. i, l. 245.

7
No man finds it difficult to return to nature except the man who has deserted nature.

SENECA, *Epistulæ ad Lucilium*. Epis. 1, sec. 5.

8
Our motto, as you know, is Live according to Nature. (Nempe propositum nostrum est secundum naturam vivere.)

SENECA, *Epistulæ ad Lucilium*. Epis. v, sec. 4. Seneca is speaking of the motto of the Stoic school.

To live according to nature. (Secundum naturam vivere.)

CICERO, *De Finibus*. Bk. iv, ch. 10, sec. 26.

I sought the simple life that Nature yields.

GEORGE CRABBE, *The Village*. Bk. i.

See also LIFE: THE SIMPLE LIFE.

9
Nature hath meal and bran, contempt and grace.

SHAKESPEARE. *Cymbeline*. Act iv, sc. 2, l. 27.

10
Nature hath framed strange fellows in her time.

SHAKESPEARE, *The Merchant of Venice*. Act i, sc. 1, l. 51.

Framed in the prodigality of nature.

SHAKESPEARE, *Richard III*. Act i, sc. 2, l. 244.

For all that Nature by her mother-wit
Could frame in earth.

SPENSER, *Faerie Queene*. Bk. iv, canto x, st. 21.

11
No men sleep so soundly as they that lay their head upon Nature's lap.

JEREMY TAYLOR, *Sermons*.

12
It is the marriage of the soul with Nature that makes the intellect fruitful, and gives birth to imagination.

H. D. THOREAU, *Journal*, 21 Aug., 1851.

13
Nature is rarely allowed to enter the sacred portals of civilized society.

H. W. VAN LOON, *Multiple Man*.

14
Nature speaks in symbols and in signs.

WHITTIER, *To Charles Sumner*.

15
Few folk hae seen oftener than me Natur gettin' up i' the morning. . . . Never see ye her hair in papers.

JOHN WILSON, *Noctes Ambrosianæ*. No. 19. March, 1829.

16
Nature never did betray
The heart that loved her.

WORDSWORTH, *Lines Composed a Few Miles Above Tintern Abbey*, l. 123.

To the solid ground
Of Nature trusts the Mind that builds for aye.

WORDSWORTH, *Miscellaneous Sonnets*. Pt. i No. 34.

17
Nature's old felicities.

WORDSWORTH, *The Trosachs*.

III—Nature: Love of Nature

18
And who loves Nature more
Than he, whose painful art
Has taught and skilled his heart
To read her skill and lore?

ROBERT BRIDGES, *Spring*. Ode ii, st. 4.

19
To him who in the love of Nature holds
Communion with her visible forms, she speaks
A various language; for his gayer hours
She has a voice of gladness, and a smile
And eloquence of beauty, and she glides
Into his darker musings, with a mild
And healing sympathy, that steals away
Their sharpness, ere he is aware.

BRYANT, *Thanatopsis*, l. 1.

20
Set him before a hedgerow in a lane,

And he was happy all alone for hours.
ROBERT BUCHANAN, *Edward Crowhurst.*

1
To sit on rocks, to muse o'er flood and fell,
To slowly trace the forest's shady scene,
Where things that own not man's dominion dwell,
And mortal foot hath ne'er, or rarely been;
To climb the trackless mountain all unseen,
With the wild flock that never needs a fold;
Alone o'er steeps and foaming falls to lean;
This is not solitude; 'tis but to hold
Converse with Nature's charms, and view her stores unroll'd.
BYRON, *Childe Harold.* Canto ii, st. 25.

Dear Nature is the kindest mother still,
Though always changing, in her aspect mild;
From her bare bosom let me take my fill,
Her never-wean'd, though not her favour'd child.
BYRON, *Childe Harold.* Canto ii, st. 37.

There is a pleasure in the pathless woods,
There is a rapture on the lonely shore,
There is society where none intrudes,
By the deep Sea, and music in its roar;
I love not Man the less, but Nature more,
From these our interviews, in which I steal
From all I may be, or have been before,
To mingle with the Universe, and feel
What I can ne'er express, yet cannot all conceal.
BYRON, *Childe Harold.* Canto iv, st. 178.

2
I am a part of all you see
In Nature: part of all you feel:
I am the impact of the bee
Upon the blossom; in the tree
I am the sap—that shall reveal
The leaf, the bloom—that flows and flutes
Up from the darkness through its roots.
MADISON CAWEIN, *Penetralia.*

3
He that can draw a charm
From rocks, or woods, or weeds, or things that seem
All mute, and does it—is wise.
BRYAN WALLER PROCTER, *A Haunted Stream.*

4
Inebriate of air am I,
And debauchee of dew,
Reeling, through endless summer days,
From inns of molten blue.
EMILY DICKINSON, *Poems.* Pt. i, No. 20.

5
He who knows what sweets and virtues are in the ground, the waters, the plants, the heavens, and how to come at these enchantments, is the rich and royal man.
EMERSON, *Essays, Second Series: Nature.*

6
I do not count the hours I spend
In wandering by the sea;
The forest is my loyal friend,
Like God it useth me.
EMERSON, *Waldeinsamkeit.*

Whoso walketh in solitude,
And inhabiteth the wood,
Choosing light, wave, rock, and bird,
Before the money-loving herd,
Into that forester shall pass,
From these companions, power and grace.
EMERSON, *Woodnotes.* Pt. ii.

7
The meanest floweret of the vale,
The simplest note that swells the gale,
The common sun, the air, the skies,
To him are opening Paradise.
THOMAS GRAY, *On the Pleasure Arising from Vicissitude,* l. 49.

8
Then live who may where honied words prevail,
I with the deer, and with the nightingale!
EDWARD HOVELL-THURLOW, *When in the Woods.*

9
I have heard the mavis singing
Its love-song to the morn;
I've seen the dew-drop clinging
To the rose just newly born.
CHARLES JEFFREYS, *Mary of Argyle.*

10
Give true hearts but earth and sky,
And some flowers to bloom and die.
JOHN KEBLE, *The Christian Year: First Sunday after Epiphany.*

11
Nature, in thy largess, grant
I may be thy confidant!
F. L. KNOWLES, *To Mother Nature.*

12
I was blood-sister to the clod,
Blood-brother to the stone.
WILLIAM VAUGHN MOODY, *The Fire-Bringer*

13
For him there's a story in every breeze,
And a picture in every wave.
THOMAS MOORE, *Boat Glee.*

14
And we, with Nature's heart in tune,
Concerted harmonies.
WILLIAM MOTHERWELL, *Jeannie Morrison.*

15
O Nature, how we worship thee even against our wills! (Natura, quam te colimus inviti quoque!)
SENECA, *Hippolytus.* Act iv, l. 1116.

16
Thou, nature, art my goddess; to thy law
My services are bound.
SHAKESPEARE, *King Lear.* Act i, sc. 2, l. 1.

17
'Tis not for golden eloquence I pray,
A godlike tongue to move a stony heart—
Methinks it were full well to be apart
In solitary uplands far away,
Betwixt the blossoms of a rosy spray,
Dreaming upon the wonderful sweet face
Of Nature, in a wild and pathless place.
FREDERICK TENNYSON, *Sonnet.*

1
The sounding cataract
Haunted me like a passion: the tall rock,
The mountain, and the deep and gloomy wood,
Their colours and their forms, were then to me
An appetite; a feeling and a love,
That had no need of a remoter charm,
By thought supplied.

WORDSWORTH, *Lines Composed a Few Miles Above Tintern Abbey*, l. 76.

A lover of the meadows and the woods
And mountains; and of all that we behold
From this green earth.

WORDSWORTH, *Lines Composed a Few Miles Above Tintern Abbey*, l. 103.

2
And recognizes ever and anon
The breeze of Nature stirring in his soul.

WORDSWORTH, *The Excursion*. Bk. iv, l. 599.

As in the eye of Nature he has lived,
So in the eye of Nature let him die!

WORDSWORTH, *The Old Cumberland Beggar.*

I was yet a boy
Careless of books, yet having felt the power
Of Nature.

WORDSWORTH, *Michael*, l. 27.

As if the man had fixed his face,
In many a solitary place,
Against the wind and open sky!

WORDSWORTH, *Peter Bell*. Pt. i, st. 26.

3
He walks with nature, and her paths are peace.

YOUNG, *Night Thoughts*. Night ii, l. 188.

IV—Nature: Its Beauty

4
A painted meadow, or a purling stream.

JOSEPH ADDISON, *Letter from Italy*, l. 166.

Fountain-heads and pathless groves,
Places which pale passion loves!

BEAUMONT AND FLETCHER, *The Nice Valour: Song*. Act iii, sc. 3.

Yet nature's charms—the hills and woods—
The sweeping vales and foaming floods—
Are free alike to all.

ROBERT BURNS, *To Chloris*.

Tracing out wisdom, power, and love,
In earth or sky, in stream or grove.

JOHN KEBLE, *The Christian Year: Evening*.

Meadows trim with daisies pied,
Shallow brooks and rivers wide.

MILTON, *L'Allegro*, l. 75.

5
If Nature built by rule and square,
Than man what wiser would she be?
What wins us is her careless care,
And sweet unpunctuality.

ALFRED AUSTIN, *Nature and the Book*.

6
There are no grotesques in nature.

SIR THOMAS BROWNE, *Religio Medici*. Pt. i, sec. 19.

O Nature! a' thy shews an' forms
To feeling, pensive hearts hae charms!
Whether the summer kindly warms,
Wi' life an' light,
Or winter howls, in gusty storms,
The lang, dark night!

BURNS, *Epistle to William Simpson*. St. 14.

Nothing in Nature is unbeautiful.

TENNYSON, *The Lover's Tale*, l. 342.

7
Art, Glory, Freedom fail, but Nature still is fair.

BYRON, *Childe Harold*. Canto ii, st. 87.

8
Nature, exerting an unwearied power,
Forms, opens, and gives scent to every flower;
Spreads the fresh verdure of the field, and leads
The dancing Naiads through the dewy meads.

COWPER, *Table Talk*, l. 690.

9
Till o'er the wreck, emerging from the storm,
Immortal Nature lifts her changeful form:
Mounts from her funeral pyre on wings of flame,
And soars and shines, another and the same.

ERASMUS DARWIN, *Botanic Garden*. Pt. i, canto iv, l. 389.

10
For earth's little secret and innumerable ways,
For the carol and the colour, Lord, we bring
What things may be of thanks, and that Thou hast lent our days
Eyes to see and ears to hear and lips to sing.

JOHN DRINKWATER, *Morning Thanksgiving*.

11
When you defile the pleasant streams
And the wild bird's abiding place,
You massacre a million dreams
And cast your spittle in God's face.

JOHN DRINKWATER, *Olton Pools: To the Defilers.*

12
Ever charming, ever new,
When will the landscape tire the view?

JOHN DYER, *Grongar Hill*, l. 102.

To sit in the shade on a fine day and look upon verdure is the most perfect refreshment.

JANE AUSTEN, *Mansfield Park*. Ch. 9.

13
There is nothing so wonderful in any particular landscape as the necessity of being beautiful under which every landscape lies.

EMERSON, *Essays, Second Series: Nature*.

Miller owns this field, Locke that, and Manning the woodland beyond. But none of them owns the landscape. There is a property in the horizon which no man has but he whose eye can integrate all the parts, that is, the poet. This is the best part of these men's farms, yet to this their warranty-deeds give no title.

EMERSON, *Nature, Addresses and Lectures: Nature*.

14
How cunningly nature hides every wrinkle of

her inconceivable antiquity under roses and violets and morning dew!
EMERSON, *Letters and Social Aims: Progress of Culture.*

The rounded world is fair to see,
Nine times folded in mystery:
Though baffled seers cannot impart
The secret of its laboring heart,
Throb thine with Nature's throbbing breast,
And all is clear from east to west.
EMERSON, *Essays, Second Series: Nature.*

She paints with white and red the moors
To draw the nations out of doors.
EMERSON, *Nature.*

Nature never spares the opium or nepenthe, but wherever she mars her creatures with some deformity or defect, lays her poppies plentifully on the bruise, and the sufferer goes joyfully through life, ignorant of the ruin, and incapable of seeing it, though all the world point their finger at it every day.
EMERSON, *Representative Men: Uses of Great Men.*

1 There's gowd in the breast of the primrose pale,
An' siller in every blossom;
There's riches galore in the breeze of the vale,
And health in the wild wood's bosom.
JAMES HOGG, *There's Gowd in the Breast.*

There ev'ry bush with Nature's music rings,
There ev'ry breeze bears health upon its wings.
SAMUEL JOHNSON, *London,* l. 220.

2 Which of us is not sometimes affected, almost to despair, by the splendid vision of earth and sky?
JOHN KEBLE, *Lectures on Poetry.*

The soft south-wind, the flowers amid the grass,
The fragrant earth, the sweet sounds everywhere,
Seemed gifts too great almost for man to bear.
WILLIAM MORRIS, *Story of Rhodope.* St. 23.

3 We are what suns and winds and waters make us;
The mountains are our sponsors and the rills
Fashion and win their nurslings with their smiles.
WALTER SAVAGE LANDOR, *Hellenics.*

4 Ye marshes, how candid and simple and nothing-withholding and free
Ye publish yourselves to the sky and offer yourselves to the sea!
SIDNEY LANIER, *The Marshes of Glynn.*

Tolerant plains, that suffer the sea and the rains and the sun,
Ye spread and span like the catholic man who hath mightily won
God out of knowledge and good out of infinite pain
And sight out of blindness and purity out of a stain.
SIDNEY LANIER, *The Marshes of Glynn.*

Nature with folded hands seemed there,
Kneeling at her evening prayer!
LONGFELLOW, *Voices of the Night: Prelude.* St. 11.

5 Over our manhood bend the skies;
Against our fallen and traitor lives
The great winds utter prophecies;
With our faint hearts the mountain strives;
Its arms outstretched, the druid wood
Waits with its benedicite;
And to our age's drowsy blood
Still shouts the inspiring sea.
J. R. LOWELL, *The Vision of Sir Launfal: Prelude to Part First.*

6 Wherefore did Nature pour her bounties forth
With such a full and unwithdrawing hand,
Covering the earth with odours, fruits, and flocks,
Thronging the seas with spawn innumerable.
But all to please, and sate the curious taste?
MILTON, *Comus,* l. 710.

7 Oh, Brignall banks are wild and fair,
And Greta woods are green,
And you may gather garlands there
Would grace a summer queen.
SCOTT, *Rokeby.* Canto iii, st. 16.

8 Nature seems unspeakably grand, when, plunged in a long reverie, one hears the rippling of the waters upon a solitary strand, in the calm of a night still enkindled and luminous with the setting moon.
ETIENNE PIVART DE SENANCOUR, *Obermann.*

9 Nature's unchanging harmony.
SHELLEY, *Queen Mab.* Canto ii.

10 My banks they are furnish'd with bees,
Whose murmur invites one to sleep;
My grottoes are shaded with trees,
And my hills are white-over with sheep.
SHENSTONE, *A Pastoral Ballad:* Pt. ii, *Hope.*

11 Once, when the days were ages,
And the old Earth was young,
The high gods and the sages
From Nature's golden pages
Her open secrets wrung.
R. H. STODDARD, *Brahma's Answer.*

12 The whole wood-world is one full peal of praise.
TENNYSON, *Balin and Balan,* l. 444.

13 I care not, fortune, what you me deny:
You cannot rob me of free nature's grace;
You cannot shut the windows of the sky
Through which Aurora shows her brightening face:
You cannot bar my constant feet to trace
The woods and lawns, by living stream, at eve.
THOMSON, *Castle of Indolence.* Canto ii, st. 3.

1
O nature! all-sufficient! over all
Enrich me with the knowledge of thy works;
Snatch me to Heaven.
THOMSON, *The Seasons: Autumn*, l. 1352.

Can he forbear to join the general smile
Of Nature? can fierce passions vex his breast,
While every gale is peace, and every grove
Is melody?
THOMSON, *The Seasons: Spring*, l. 871.

2
The sun-swept spaces which the good God made.
CHARLES HANSON TOWNE, *City Children.*

3
Talk not of temples, there is one
Built without hands, to mankind given;
Its lamps are the meridian sun
And all the stars of heaven,
Its walls are the cerulean sky,
Its floor the earth so green and fair,
The dome its vast immensity
All Nature worships there!
DAVID VEDDER, *The Temple of Nature.*

Where Nature seems to sit alone,
Majestic on a craggy throne.
JOSEPH WARTON, *Ode to Fancy.*

4
I believe a leaf of grass is no less than the journey-work of the stars,
And the pismire is equally perfect, and a grain of sand, and the egg of the wren,
And the tree-toad is a chef-d'œuvre for the highest,
And the running blackberry would adorn the parlors of heaven,
And the narrowest hinge in my hand puts to scorn all machinery,
And the cow crunching with depress'd head surpasses any statue,
And a mouse is miracle enough to stagger sextillions of infidels.
WALT WHITMAN, *Song of Myself.* Sec. 31.

5
The harp at Nature's advent strung
Has never ceased to play;
The song the stars of morning sung
Has never died away.
WHITTIER, *The Worship of Nature.*

Though all the bards of earth were dead,
And all their music passed away,
What Nature wishes should be said
She'll find the rightful voice to say.
WILLIAM WINTER, *The Golden Silence.*

6
On a fair prospect some have looked,
And felt, as I have heard them say,
As if the moving time had been
A thing as steadfast as the scene
On which they gazed themselves away.
WORDSWORTH, *Peter Bell.* Pt. i, st. 16.

7
The stars of midnight shall be dear
To her; and she shall lean her ear
In many a secret place
Where rivulets dance their wayward round,
And beauty born of murmuring sound
Shall pass into her face.
WORDSWORTH, *Three Years She Grew.*

There's not a nook within this solemn pass,
But were an apt confessional.
WORDSWORTH, *The Trosachs.*

8
Such blessings Nature pours,
O'erstock'd mankind enjoy but half her stores:
In distant wilds, by human eyes unseen,
She rears her flowers, and spreads her velvet green;
Pure gurgling rills the lonely desert trace
And waste their music on the savage race.
YOUNG, *Love of Fame.* Sat. v, l. 227.

9
The little cares that fretted me,
I lost them yesterday,
Among the fields above the sea,
Among the winds at play, . . .
Among the hushing of the corn,
Where drowsy poppies nod,
Where ill thoughts die and good are born—
Out in the fields of God.
UNKNOWN, *Out in the Fields.* Published in the Boston *Sunday Globe*, 30 April, 1899, credited to *St. Paul's Magazine*, but not discovered there. Erroneously attributed to Elizabeth Barrett Browning. E. M. Tenison, in her *Life of Louise Imogen Guiney*, states that it was written by Miss Guiney "not long before her lute was broken and her pen laid aside forever." Miss Guiney went to England in 1901 and died in 1920, having previously published two collections of poems in which this one is not included. It is so obviously English—corn, for example, being used in its English sense—that it is the compiler's opinion it was written by an English author.

V—Nature: Its Cruelty

10
Nature is cruel, man is sick of blood;
Nature is stubborn, man would fain adore;
Nature is fickle, man hath need of rest;
Nature forgives no debt, and fears no grave.
MATTHEW ARNOLD, *Man and Nature.*

Nature pardons no mistakes. Her yea is yea, and her nay, nay.
EMERSON, *Nature, Addresses, and Lectures: Discipline.*

Nature's rules have no exceptions.
HERBERT SPENCER, *Social Statics: Introduction.*

11
The course of Nature seems a course of Death,
And nothingness the whole substantial thing.
P. J. BAILEY, *Festus: Water and Wood.*

12
Knowing how Nature threatens ere she springs.
ROBERT BUCHANAN. *Meg Blane.*

1
It is far from easy to determine whether she [Nature] has proved to him a kind parent or a merciless stepmother.

PLINY THE ELDER, *Historia Naturalis*. Bk. vii, sec. 1.

To man the earth seems altogether
No more a mother, but a step-dame rather.

DU BARTAS, *Devine Weekes and Workes*. Week i, day 3.

2
Nature subjects the weak to the strong. (Naturæ est enim potioribus deteriora summittere.)

SENECA, *Epistulæ ad Lucilium*. Epis. xc, sec. 4.

3
For nature is one with rapine, a harm no preacher can heal;
The Mayfly is torn by the swallow, the sparrow spear'd by the shrike,
And the whole little wood where I sit is a world of plunder and prey.

TENNYSON, *Maud*. Pt. i, sec. iv, st. 4.

4
Ah, what a warning for a thoughtless man,
Could field or grove, could any spot of earth,
Show to his eye an image of the pangs
Which it hath witnessed; render back an echo
Of the sad steps by which it hath been trod!

WORDSWORTH, *The Excursion*. Bk. vi, l. 806.

VI—Nature: Its Laws

5
Nature's great law, and law of all men's minds?—
To its own impulse every creature stirs;
Live by thy light, and earth will live by hers!

MATTHEW ARNOLD, *Religious Isolation*. St. 4.

6
I trust in Nature for the stable laws
Of beauty and utility. Spring shall plant
And Autumn garner to the end of time.

ROBERT BROWNING, *A Soul's Tragedy*. Act i.

7
For Nature in man's heart her laws doth pen.

SIR JOHN DAVIES, *Nosce Teipsum*. Sec. 26, st. 2.

8
Nature is the true law.

JOHN FLORIO, *First Fruites*, Fo. 32.

9
Against the law of nature, law of nations.

MILTON, *Samson Agonistes*, l. 889. See also LAW: VARIETIES.

10
Laws of Nature are God's thoughts thinking themselves out in the orbits and the tides.

C. H. PARKHURST, *Sermons: Pattern in Mount*.

11
Those rules of old, discover'd, not devis'd,
Are Nature still, but Nature methodized;
Nature, like Liberty, is but restrain'd
By the same laws which first herself ordain'd.

POPE, *Essay on Criticism*. Pt. i, l. 88.

VII—Nature, The Teacher

12
The study of Nature is intercourse with the Highest Mind. You should never trifle with Nature.

JEAN LOUIS AGASSIZ, *Agassiz at Penikese*.

13
Go forth under the open sky, and list
To Nature's teachings.

BRYANT, *Thanatopsis*.

Come forth into the light of things,
Let Nature be your teacher.

WORDSWORTH, *The Tables Turned*.

The house is a prison, the schoolroom's a cell;
Leave study and books for the upland and dell.

JOSEPH H. GREEN, *Morning Invitation to a Child*.

14
Never does Nature say one thing and Wisdom another. (Numquam aliud natura, aliud sapientia dicit.)

JUVENAL, *Satires*. Sat. xiv, l. 321.

Never, no never, did Nature say one thing, and Wisdom say another.

EDMUND BURKE, *Letters on a Regicide Peace*. No. 3.

Nature is always wise in every part.

EDWARD HOVELL-THURLOW, *Harvest Moon*.

15
Go, from the creatures thy instructions take:
Learn from the birds what food the thickets yield;
Learn from the beasts the physic of the field;
Thy arts of building from the bee receive;
Learn of the mole to plough, the worm to weave;
Learn of the little nautilus to sail,
Spread the thin oar, and catch the driving gale.

POPE, *Essay on Man*. Epis. iii, l. 172.

16
But any man that walks the mead,
In bud or blade or bloom, may find,
According as his humours lead,
A meaning suited to his mind.

TENNYSON, *The Day-Dream: Moral*. St. 2.

17
For I'd rather be thy child
And pupil, in the forest wild,
Than be the king of men elsewhere,
And most sovereign slave of care;
To have one moment of thy dawn,
Than share the city's year forlorn.

H. D. THOREAU, *Nature*.

18
Nature has always had more power than education. (La Nature a toujours été en eux plus forte que l'education.)

VOLTAIRE, *Life of Molière*.

Nature is more powerful than education.

BENJAMIN DISRAELI, *Contarini Fleming*. Pt. i, ch. 13.

19
"Is this," I cried,
"The end of prayer and preaching?

Then down with pulpit, down with priest,
And give us Nature's teaching!"
WHITTIER, *A Sabbath Scene.*

1
Kind Nature's charities his steps attend;
In every babbling brook he finds a friend;
While chast'ning thoughts of sweetest use, bestowed
By wisdom, moralise his pensive road.
WORDSWORTH, *Descriptive Sketches,* l. 27.

His daily teachers had been woods and rills,
The silence that is in the starry sky,
The sleep that is among the lonely hills.
WORDSWORTH, *Song at the Feast of Brougham Castle,* l. 162.

2
One impulse from a vernal wood
May teach you more of man,
Of moral evil and of good,
Than all the sages can.
WORDSWORTH, *The Tables Turned.*

3
On every thorn delightful wisdom grows;
In every rill a sweet instruction flows.
YOUNG, *Love of Fame.* Sat. i, l. 249.

Read Nature; Nature is a friend to truth;
Nature is Christian; preaches to mankind;
And bids dead matter aid us in our creed.
YOUNG, *Night Thoughts.* Night iv, l. 703.

VIII—Nature: The Book of Nature

4
After the sacred volumes of God and the Scriptures, study, in the second place, that great volume of the works and the creatures of God.
FRANCIS BACON, *Letters: To Trinity College, Cambridge.*

The volume of nature is the book of knowledge.
GOLDSMITH, *The Citizen of the World.* No. 4.

The book of Nature is the book of Fate. She turns the gigantic pages, leaf after leaf,—never re-turning one.
EMERSON, *Conduct of Life: Fate.*

Did we but pay the love we owe,
And with a child's undoubting wisdom look
On all these living pages of God's book.
J. R. LOWELL, *To the Dandelion.*

5
Believe one who knows: you will find something more in woods than in books. Trees and stones will teach you that which you can never learn from masters. (Experto crede: aliquid amplius in silvis invenies quam in libris. Ligna et lapides docebunt te quod a magistris audire non possis.)
ST. BERNARD OF CLAIRVAUX, *Epistles.* No. 106. To Master Henry Murdach, afterwards Archbishop of York.

And this our life, exempt from public haunt,
Finds tongues in trees, books in the running brooks,
Sermons in stones and good in every thing.
SHAKESPEARE, *As You Like It.* Act ii, sc. 1, l. 15.

London had been my prison; but my books
Hills and great waters, labouring men and brooks,
Ships and deep friendships and remembered days
Which even now set all my mind ablaze.
JOHN MASEFIELD, *Biography.*

6
Strange to the world, he wore a bashful look,
The fields his study, nature was his book.
ROBERT BLOOMFIELD, *The Farmer's Boy: Spring,* l. 31.

7
Out of the book of Nature's learned breast.
DU BARTAS, *Devine Weekes and Workes.* Week ii, day 4. (Sylvester, tr.)

8
See thou bring not to field or stone
The fancies found in books;
Leave authors' eyes, and fetch your own,
To brave the landscape's looks.
EMERSON, *Waldeinsamkeit.*

9
His listless length at noontide would he stretch,
And pore upon the brook that babbles by.
THOMAS GRAY, *Elegy Written in a Country Church-yard,* l. 103.

10
Nature is a volume of which God is the author.
MOSES HARVEY, *Science and Religion.*

11
What Nature has writ with her lusty wit
Is worded so wisely and kindly
That whoever has dipped in her manuscript
Must up and follow her blindly.
W. E. HENLEY, *Echoes.* No. 33.

12
Boughs are daily rifled
By the gusty thieves,
And the book of Nature
Getteth short of leaves.
THOMAS HOOD, *The Seasons.*

13
And Nature, the old nurse, took
The child upon her knee,
Saying: "Here is a story-book
Thy Father has written for thee."

"Come, wander with me," she said,
"Into regions yet untrod;
And read what is still unread
In the manuscripts of God."
LONGFELLOW, *Fiftieth Birthday of Agassiz.*

14
In nature's infinite book of secrecy
A little I can read.
SHAKESPEARE, *Antony and Cleopatra.* Act i, sc. 2, l. 9.

And meditate the Book Of Nature, ever open.
THOMSON, *The Seasons: Autumn,* l. 669.

15
O Reader! had you in your mind
Such stores as silent thought can bring,
O gentle Reader! you would find
A tale in every thing.
WORDSWORTH, *Simon Lee,* l. 65.

IX—Nature and God

1
What I call God, And fools call Nature.
ROBERT BROWNING, *The Ring and the Book: The Pope*, l. 1073.

God is seen God
In the star, in the stone, in the flesh, in the soul and the clod.
ROBERT BROWNING, *Saul*. St. 17.

2
Nature, which is the Time-vesture of God, and reveals Him to the wise, hides Him from the foolish.
CARLYLE, *Sartor Resartus*. Bk. iii, ch. 8.

[Nature], the living visible garment of God.
GOETHE, *Faust*. Pt. i, l. 50. (William P. Andrews, tr.) Quoted by CARLYLE, *Sartor Resartus*. Bk. i, ch. 8.

3
Nature, the vicar of th' almighty Lord.
CHAUCER, *The Parlement of Foules*, l. 379. Stated by Chaucer to be from Statius.

Nature, the Handmaid of God Almighty.
HOWELL, *Familiar Letters:* Bk. ii, *To Dr. T. P.*

4
At home with Nature, and at one with God!
FLORENCE EARLE COATES, *The Angelus*.

5
Nature is but a name for an effect
Whose cause is God.
COWPER, *The Task*. Bk. vi, l. 224.

His are the mountains and the valleys his,
And the resplendent rivers. His t' enjoy
With a propriety that none can feel,
But who, with filial countenance inspir'd,
Can lift to heaven an unpresumptuous eye,
And smiling say—My Father made them all!
COWPER, *The Task*. Bk. v, l. 742.

Full often too
Our wayward intellect, the more we learn
Of nature, overlooks her Author more.
COWPER, *The Task*. Bk. iii, l. 235.

6
What man has written man may read;
But God fills every root and seed
With cryptic words, too strangely set
For mortals to decipher yet.
CHARLES DALMON, *Documents*.

7
Nature is the art of God. (Deus æternus, arte sua, quæ natura est.)
DANTE, *De Monarchia*. Bk. i, l. 3.
See also ART AND NATURE.

8
And when I am stretched beneath he pines,
Where the evening star so holy shines,
I laugh at the lore and the pride of man,
At the sophist schools and the learnèd clan;
For what are they all, in their high conceit,
When man in the bush with God may meet?
EMERSON, *Good-Bye*.

Behold! the Holy Grail is found,
Found in each poppy's cup of gold;
And God walks with us as of old.
Behold! the burning bush still burns
For man, whichever way he turns;
And all God's earth is holy ground.
JOAQUIN MILLER, *Dawn at San Diego*.

9
He would adore my gifts instead of me,
And rest in Nature, not the God of Nature.
GEORGE HERBERT, *The Pulley*.

10
Nature is religious only as it manifests God.
MARK HOPKINS, *Sermon*, 30 May, 1843.

11
A voice is in the wind I do not know;
A meaning on the face of the high hills
Whose utterance I cannot comprehend.
A something is behind them: that is God.
MACDONALD, *Within and Without*. Pt. i, sc. 1.

12
Every formula which expresses a law of nature is a hymn of praise to God.
MARIA MITCHELL. Inscribed beneath her bust in Hall of Fame.

13
The perfections of Nature show that she is the image of God; her defects show that she is only his image.
PASCAL, *Pensées*. Ch. 12.

14
All are but parts of one stupendous Whole,
Whose body Nature is, and God the soul;
That changed thro' all, and yet in all the same,
Great in the earth as in th' ethereal frame,
Warms in the sun, refreshes in the breeze,
Glows in the stars, and blossoms in the trees; . . .
As full, as perfect, in a hair as heart;
As full, as perfect, in vile man that mourns,
As the rapt Seraph that adores and burns.
To him no high, no low, no great, no small;
He fills, he bounds, connects, and equals all!
POPE, *Essay on Man*. Epis. i, l. 267.

A work of skill, surpassing sense,
A labour of Omnipotence;
Though frail as dust it meet thine eye,
He form'd this gnat who built the sky.
JAMES MONTGOMERY, *The Gnat*.

Nature reads not our labels, "great" and "small";
Accepts she one and all.
JOHN VANCE CHENEY, *The Man with the Hoe: A Reply*. *See also* GREATNESS: GREAT AND SMALL.

15
Slave to no sect, who takes no private road,
But looks thro' Nature up to Nature's God.
POPE, *Essay on Man*. Epis. iv, l. 331.

It is the modest, not the presumptuous, inquirer who makes a real and safe progress in the discovery of divine truths. One follows Nature and Nature's God; that is, he follows God in his works and in his word.
LORD BOLINGBROKE, *Letter to Mr. Pope*. It was in this letter, perhaps, that Pope found the famous phrase he used in the preceding quotation.

And not from Nature up to Nature's God,
But down from Nature's God look Nature through.
ROBERT MONTGOMERY, *Luther*.

1
The heavens declare the glory of God, and the firmament sheweth his handywork.
Old Testament: Psalms, xix, 1.

2
Call it Nature, fate, fortune; all these things are names of the one and the selfsame God. (Naturam voca, fatum, fortunamque; sunt omnia unius et ejusdem Dei nomina.)
SENECA, *De Beneficiis.* Bk. iv, sec. 8.

Go thou and seek the House of Prayer!
I to the woodlands wend, and there,
In lovely Nature see the God of Love.
SOUTHEY, *Written on Sunday Morning.*

3
God, the Great Giver, can open the whole universe to our gaze in the narrow space of a single lane.
RABINDRANATH TAGORE, *Jivan-smitri.*

4
Are God and Nature then at strife,
That Nature lends such evil dreams?
So careful of the type she seems,
So careless of the single life.
TENNYSON, *In Memoriam.* Pt. lv, st. 2.

5
Nature, so far as in her lies,
Imitates God, and turns her face
To every land beneath the skies,
Counts nothing that she meets with base,
But lives and loves in every place.
TENNYSON, *On a Mourner.* St. 1.

Nature is the glass reflecting God.
YOUNG, *Night Thoughts.* Night ix, l. 1005.

6
The course of nature is the art of God.
The miracles thou call'st for, this attest;
For say, could nature nature's course control?
But, miracles apart, who sees Him not?
YOUNG, *Night Thoughts.* Night ix, l. 1266.

Take God from Nature, nothing great is left.
YOUNG, *Night Thoughts.* Night ix, l. 1591.

X—Nature: Human Nature

7
Nature is often hidden, sometimes overcome, seldom extinguished.
FRANCIS BACON, *Essays: Of Nature in Men.*

How hard it is to hide the sparks of Nature!
SHAKESPEARE, *Cymbeline.* Act iii, sc. 3, l. 79.

8
Nature stamp'd us in a heavenly mould.
CAMPBELL, *The Pleasures of Hope.* Pt. i, l. 498.

9
Never can custom conquer nature; for she is ever unconquered. (Numquam naturam mos vinceret; est enim ea semper invicta.)
CICERO, *Tusculanarum Disputationum.* Bk. v, ch. 27, sec. 78.

It is difficult indeed to change nature. (Naturam quidem mutare difficile est.)
SENECA, *De Ira.* Bk. ii, l. 20.

Nature her custom holds,
Let shame say what it will.
SHAKESPEARE, *Hamlet.* Act iv, sc. 7, l. 188.

10
Nor rural sights alone, but rural sounds,
Exhilarate the spirit, and restore
The tone of languid Nature.
COWPER, *The Task.* Bk. i, l. 182.

11
To Nature and yourself appeal,
Nor learn of others what to feel.
WILLIAM HOGARTH, *Letter to a Friend,* 1761. Quoted.

12
The faultless proprieties of nature.
MILTON, *Doctrine and Discipline of Divorce: Preface.*

13
Everything unnatural is imperfect.
NAPOLEON, *Sayings of Napoleon.*

The natural alone is permanent.
LONGFELLOW, *Kavanagh.* Ch. 13.

14
Every one follows the inclinations of his own nature. (Naturæ sequitur semina quisque suæ.)
PROPERTIUS, *Elegiæ.* Bk. iii, eleg. ix, l. 20.

All men that are ruined are ruined on the side of their natural propensities.
BURKE, *Letters on a Regicide Peace.* Letter i.

15
Nature never deceives us; it is always we who deceive ourselves. (Jamais la nature ne nous trompe; c'est toujours nous qui nous trompons.)
ROUSSEAU, *Émile.* Bk. iii.

16
One touch of nature makes the whole world kin.
SHAKESPEARE, *Troilus and Cressida.* Act iii, sc. 3, l. 175.

All argument will vanish before one touch of nature.
GEORGE COLMAN THE YOUNGER, *The Poor Gentleman.* Act v, sc. 1.

17
How sometimes nature will betray its folly,
Its tenderness, and make itself a pastime
To harder bosoms!
SHAKESPEARE, *Winter's Tale.* Act i, sc. 2, l. 151.

18
Man is not content to take nature as he finds her. He insists on making her over.
F. J. E. WOODBRIDGE, *Contrasts in Education,* p. 17.

NAVY, see SHIP

NECESSITY

19
The force of necessity is irresistible. (Τὸ τῆς ἀνάγκης ἔστ' ἀδήριτον σθένος.)
ÆSCHYLUS, *Prometheus Vinctus,* l. 105.

Necessity doth front the universe
With an invincible gesture.
ÆSCHYLUS, *Prometheus Vinctus,* l. 105. (E. B. Browning, tr.)

1
Necessity is stronger far than art. (Τέχνη δ' ἀνάγκης ἀσθενεστέρα μακρῷ.)
ÆSCHYLUS, *Prometheus Vinctus*, l. 513.

2
Every act of necessity is disagreeable. (Πᾶν γὰρ ἀναγκαῖον πρᾶγμ' ἀνιαρὸν ἔφυ.)
ARISTOTLE, *Rhetorica*. Bk. i, ch. 11, sec. 4.

3
Necessity has no law. (Legem non habet necessitas.)
ST. AUGUSTINE, *Solil. Animæ ad Deum*, c. 2, (c. 410.)

Necessity has no law. (Necessitas non habet legem.)
WILLIAM LANGLAND, *Piers Plowman*. Passus xiv, l. 45. (1377) Quoted in Latin.

For as men say, need has no law.
JOHN GOWER, *Confessio Amantis*. Bk. iv, l. 1167. (c. 1390); JOHN SKELTON, *Colyn Cloute*, l. 865. (1520) Also many later writers.

Necessity hath no law. Feigned necessities, imaginary necessities, are the greatest cozenage men can put upon the Providence of God.
OLIVER CROMWELL, *Speech*, to Parliament, 12 Sept., 1654.

4
Necessity urges desperate measures.
CERVANTES, *Don Quixote*. Pt. i, ch. 23.

5
It is necessity and not pleasure that compels him. (Necessità 'l c' induce, e non diletto.)
DANTE, *Inferno*. Canto xii, l. 87.

6
I do not see the necessity of it. (Je n'en vois pas la nécessité.)
COUNT D'ARGENSON, to the Abbé Desfontaines, who had been brought before him for publishing libels, and who excused himself by saying, "After all, I must live." (Après tout, il faut bien que je vivre.) (VOLTAIRE, *Œuvres Complètes*, xlviii, 99.) Also attributed to Count d'Argental, censor of books, by Hénault. (*Mémoires*, 4.)

The ordinary objection is of course raised: I have not the wherewithal to live. To this it may be retorted, Is there any reason why you should live?
TERTULLIAN, *De Idolatria*. Sec. 5.

7
Necessity makes an honest man a knave.
DANIEL DEFOE, *Robinson Crusoe: Serious Reflections*.

8
The necessities of things are sterner stuff than the hopes of men.
BENJAMIN DISRAELI, *Lothair*. Ch. 53.

9
Let us build altars to the Beautiful Necessity, which secures that all is made of one piece.
EMERSON, *Conduct of Life: Fate*.

We do what we must, and call it by the best names.
EMERSON, *Conduct of Life: Considerations by the Way*.

10
No man can quite exclude the element of necessity from his labor.
EMERSON, *Essays, First Series: Art*.

Necessity does everything well.
EMERSON, *Essays, Second Series: Gifts*.

11
Necessity will teach a man, however stupid he be, to be wise. (Χρεία διδάσκει, καν βραδύς τις ᾖ, σοφόν.)
EURIPIDES, *Fragments*. No. 709.

12
Not mine the saying is, but wisdom's saw:
"Stronger is naught than dread Necessity."
(Λόγος γάρ ἐστιν οὐκ ἐμός, σοφῶν δ' ἔπος,
δεινῆς ἀνάγκης οὐδὲν ἰσχύειν πλέον.)
EURIPIDES, *Helena*, l. 513. (Way, tr.)

13
Yet do I hold that mortal foolish who strives against the stress of necessity. (Τῷ δ' ἀναγκαίῳ τρόπῳ ὃς ἀντιτείνει, σκαιὸν ἡγοῦμαι βροτόν.)
EURIPIDES, *Hercules Furens*, l. 282.

Even the gods do not fight against necessity. (Ἀνάγκᾳ δ' οὐδὲ θεοὶ μάχονται.)
PITTACUS. (DIOGENES LAERTIUS, *Pittacus*. Bk. i, sec. 77.)

A wise man never refuses anything to necessity. (Necessitati sapiens nihil umquam negat.)
PUBLILIUS SYRUS, *Sententiæ*. No. 540.

Not Ares' self wars with necessity. (Πρὸς τὴν ανάγκην οὐδ' Ἄρης ἀνθίσταται.)
SOPHOCLES, *Fragments*. No. 234.

14
Necessity never made a good bargain.
BENJAMIN FRANKLIN, *Poor Richard*, 1735.

15
The three eldest children of Necessity:
God, the World and Love.
RICHARD GARNETT, *De Flagello Myrteo*.

16
Need makes the old wife trot.
HILL, *Common-place Book*, 128. (c. 1475)

Need makes the naked man run.
JOHN RAY, *English Proverbs*, 124.

Need makes the naked quean spin.
JOHN RAY, *English Proverbs*, 124.

17
Necessity, with impartial justice, allots the fates of high and low alike. (Aeque lege Necessitas Sortitur insignes et imos.)
HORACE, *Odes*. Bk. iii, ode 1, l. 14.

Dire necessity. (Dira necessitas.)
HORACE, *Odes*. Bk. iii, ode 24, l. 6.

18
Yoked in knowledge and remorse, now we come to rest,
Laughing at old villainies that Time has turned to jest;
Pardoning old necessities no pardon can efface—
That undying sin we shared in Rouen market-place.
RUDYARD KIPLING, *France*. (1913)

1
Necessity is the last and strongest weapon. (Necessitas ultimum et maximum telum est.)
LIVY, *History*. Bk. iv, sec. 28.

2
Necessity, the tyrant's plea.
MILTON, *Paradise Lost*. Bk. iv, l. 393.

Necessity is the argument of tyrants; it is the creed of slaves.
WILLIAM PITT, *Speech*, 18 Nov., 1783.

3
Necessity is a violent school-mistress. (C'est une violente maîtresse d'école que la nécessité.)
MONTAIGNE, *Essays*. Bk. i, ch. 47.

4
All idealism is falsehood in the face of necessity.
FRIEDRICH NIETZSCHE, *Ecce Homo*.

5
Yet have I found no power to vie
With thine, severe Necessity!
THOMAS LOVE PEACOCK, *Necessity*.

6
Necessity knows no shame. (Quidvis egestas imperat.)
PLAUTUS, *Asinaria*, l. 671. (Act iii, sc. 3.)

Necessity gives the law, but does not bow to it. (Necessitas dat legem non ipsa accipit.)
PUBLILIUS SYRUS, *Sententiæ*. No. 444.

7
We give necessity the praise of virtue.
QUINTILIAN, *De Institutione Oratoria*. Bk. i, ch. 8, sec. 14. (c. A. D. 90)

To make a virtue of necessity. (Faciendo de necessitate virtutem.)
MATTHEW PARIS, *Chronica Majora* (Record Ser.), i, 20. (c. 1250) This adage is common to all literatures and only a few examples need be given here.

Thus maketh virtue of necessity.
CHAUCER, *Troilus and Criseyde*. Bk. iv, l. 1586. (c. 1374)

Then is it wisdom, as it thinketh me,
To maken virtue of necessity.
CHAUCER, *The Knightes Tale*, l. 2183.

That I made virtue of necessity,
And took it well, sin that it must be.
CHAUCER, *The Squieres Tale*, l. 585.

He made a virtue of necessity. (Faisoit de necessité vertu.)
RABELAIS, *Works*. Bk. i, ch. 11; bk. v, ch. 22. (1532)

To make necessity a virtue. (Necessitatem in virtutem commutarum.)
HADRIANUS JULIUS, *Additions to the Adages of Erasmus*. (c. 1550)

To make a virtue of necessity.
SHAKESPEARE, *The Two Gentlemen of Verona*. Act iv, sc. 1, l. 62. (1594)

Teach thy necessity to reason thus:
There is no virtue like necessity.
SHAKESPEARE, *Richard II*. Act i, sc. 3, l. 279. (1595)

8
Necessity when threatening is more powerful than device of man. (Efficacior omni arte imminens necessitas.)
QUINTUS CURTIUS RUFUS, *De Rebus Gestis Alexandri Magni*. Bk. iv, sec. 3, l. 23.

9
Necessity makes even the timid brave. (Necessitas etiam timidos fortis facit.)
SALLUST, *Bellum Catilinæ*. Ch. 58, sec. 20.

Necessity makes even cowards brave.
THOMAS DAY, *Sandford and Merton*, p. 44.

Necessity and opportunity may make a coward valiant.
THOMAS FULLER, *Gnomologia*. No. 3514.

Need her courage taught.
SPENSER, *Faerie Queene*. Bk. iii, canto vii, st. 26.

10
Stern is the visage of necessity. (Ernst ist der Anblick der Nothwendigkeit.)
SCHILLER, *Wallenstein's Tod*. Act i, sc. 4, l. 45.

11
You cannot escape necessities; but you can conquer them. (Effugere non potes necessitates; potes vincere.)
SENECA, *Epistulæ ad Lucilium*. Epis. xxxi, 3

12
Whither I must, I must.
SHAKESPEARE, *I Henry IV*. Act ii, sc. 3, l. 109

13
Now sit we close about this taper here,
And call in question our necessities.
SHAKESPEARE, *Julius Cæsar*. Act iv, sc. 3, l. 164.

The deep of night is crept upon our talk,
And nature must obey necessity.
SHAKESPEARE, *Julius Cæsar*. Act iv, sc. 3, l. 226.

14
He that stands upon a slippery place
Makes nice of no vile hold to stay him up.
SHAKESPEARE, *King John*. Act iii, sc. 4, l. 137.

15
Necessity's sharp pinch!
SHAKESPEARE, *King Lear*. Act ii, sc. 4, l. 214.

O, reason not the need: our basest beggars
Are in the poorest thing superfluous:
Allow not nature more than nature needs.
SHAKESPEARE, *King Lear*. Act ii, sc. 4, l. 267.

The art of our necessities is strange,
That can make vile things precious.
SHAKESPEARE, *King Lear*. Act iii, sc. 2, l. 70.

16
If I break faith, this word shall speak for me:
I am forsworn on "mere necessity."
SHAKESPEARE, *Love's Labour's Lost*. Act i, sc. 1, l. 154.

17
Spirit of Nature! all-sufficing Power!
Necessity, thou mother of the world!
SHELLEY, *Queen Mab*. Canto vi, l. 197.

Necessity, thou tyrant conscience of the great!
SWIFT, *Ode to Dr. William Sancroft*.

18
I find no hint throughout the Universe
Of good or ill, of blessing or of curse;

I find alone Necessity Supreme.
JAMES THOMSON, *The City of Dreadful Night.* Pt. xiv.

1
Who, doomed to go in company with pain,
And fear, and bloodshed,—miserable train!—
Turns his necessity to glorious gain.
WORDSWORTH, *Character of the Happy Warrior,* l. 12.

2
Necessity the mother of invention. (Mater artium necessitas.)
UNKNOWN. A Latin proverb.

Need taught him wit.
WILLIAM HORMAN, *Vulgaria.* Fo. 52. (1519)

Necessity is the deviser of all manner of shifts.
THOMAS UNDERDOWN, *Heliodorus,* 201. (1587)

Necessity, mother of invention.
WILLIAM WYCHERLEY, *Love in a Wood.* Act iii, sc. 3. (1672) Also many later writers.

If necessity is the mother of invention, she is never more pregnant than with me.
FARQUHAR, *The Twin Rivals.* Act i, sc. 1.

Necessity—thou best of peacemakers,
As well as surest prompter of invention.
SCOTT, *Peveril of the Peak.* Ch. 26, heading.

Sheer necessity—the proper parent of an art so nearly allied to invention.
SHERIDAN, *The Critic.* Act i, sc. 2.

Want, the mistress of invention.
SUSANNAH CENTLIVRE, *The Busy-Body.* Act i, sc. 1. (1720)

NECK

3
Would that the Roman populace had but one neck. (Utinam populas Romanus unum cervicem haberet!)
CALIGULA, when incensed at the people applauding his opponents. (SUETONIUS, *Life.*) Seneca and Dion Cassius also credit the saying to Caligula, but it is ascribed to Nero by other writers.

Anger wishes all mankind had only one neck; love, that it had only one heart.
RICHTER, *Flower, Fruit and Thorn,* iv.

I love the sex, and sometimes would reverse
The tyrant's wish "that mankind only had
One neck, which he with one fell stroke might pierce":
My wish is quite as wide, but not so bad, . . .
That womankind had but one rosy mouth,
To kiss them all at once from North to South.
BYRON, *Don Juan.* Canto vi, st. 27.

4
Neck or nothing.
COLLEY CIBBER, *The Lady's Last Stake.* Act iii.

5
The stately neck is manhood's manliest part;
It takes the life-blood freshest from the heart.
With short, curled ringlets close around it spread,
How light and strong it lifts the Grecian head!
O. W. HOLMES, *A Rhymed Lesson,* l. 470.

6
They wove the lotus band to deck
And fan with pensile wreath each neck.
THOMAS MOORE, *Odes of Anacreon.* No. 69.

7
Bending down His corrigible neck.
SHAKESPEARE, *Antony and Cleopatra.* Act iv, sc. 14, l. 74.

8
I had as lief thou didst break his neck as his finger.
SHAKESPEARE, *As You Like It.* Act i, sc. 1, 153.

And break the neck
Of that proud man that did usurp his back.
SHAKESPEARE, *Richard II.* Act v, sc. 5, l. 88.

9
Falls not the axe upon the humblest neck
But first begs pardon.
SHAKESPEARE, *As You Like It.* Act iii, sc. 5, l. 5.

10
And thus I set my foot on 's neck.
SHAKESPEARE, *Cymbeline.* Act iii, sc. 3, l. 92.

NEED, see Necessity

NEEDLE

11
True as the needle to the pole.
BARTON BOOTH, *Song. See under* CONSTANCY.

12
To look for a needle in a haystack.
JOHN RAY, *English Proverbs.* From the Latin: Acum in meta fœni quærere.

He gropeth in the dark to find a needle in a bottle of hay.
ROBERT GREENE, *Works.* Vol. xi, p. 252. (1592)

To go look for a needle in a meadow.
SIR THOMAS MORE, *Works,* p. 838. (1532)

By wondrous accident perchance one may
Grope out a needle in a load of hay.
JOHN TAYLOR, *A Kicksey Winsey.* Pt. vii.

13
You might have heard a needle fall,
The hush was so profound.
H. S. LEIGH, *A Last Resource.*

14
You have touched it with a needle. (Tetigisti acu.)
PLAUTUS, *Rudens,* l. 1306. (Act v, sec. 2.) *i. e.,* "You've hit it!"

15
So delicate with her needle.
SHAKESPEARE, *Othello.* Act iv, sc. 1, l. 198.

Go ply thy needle.
SHAKESPEARE, *The Taming of the Shrew.* Act ii, sc. 1, l. 25.

16
The blooming daughter throws her needle by.
CHARLES SPRAGUE, *Curiosity.*

17
The bright little needle—the swift-flying needle,
The needle directed by beauty and art.
SAMUEL WOODWORTH, *The Needle.*

NEGRO

See also Slavery

1
The Negro, thanks to his temperament, appears to make the greatest amount of happiness out of the smallest capital.

EMERSON, *Journal.* Vol. x, p. 176.

2
Dere was an old nigga, dey call'd him Uncle Ned,
He's dead long ago, long ago.

STEPHEN COLLINS FOSTER, *Old Uncle Ned.*

3
But our captain counts the image of God—nevertheless his image—cut in ebony as if done in ivory, and in the blackest Moors he sees the representation of the King of Heaven.

THOMAS FULLER, *Holy and Profane States: The Good Sea-Captain.*

4
Can the Ethiopian change his skin, or the leopard his spots?

Old Testament: Jeremiah, xiii, 23.

A Zulu riding in a Rolls-Royce is still a Zulu.

H. W. VAN LOON, *Tolerance.*

5
All I ask for the negro is that if you do not like him, let him alone. If God gave him but little, that little let him enjoy.

ABRAHAM LINCOLN, *Speech,* Springfield, Ill., 17 July, 1858.

In the right to eat the bread . . . which his own hand earns, he [the negro] *is my equal and the equal of Judge Douglas, and the equal of every living man.*

ABRAHAM LINCOLN, *Lincoln-Douglas Debates.* First joint debate, Ottawa, Ill., 21 Aug., 1858.

6
I am endeavoring to wash an Ethiopian white. (Αἰθίοπα σμήχειν ἐπιχειρῶ.)

LUCIAN, *Adversus Indoctum.* Sec. 28.

To wash a negro white. (Æthiopem dealbare.)

UNKNOWN. A Latin proverb.

We may yet find a rose-water that will wash the negro white.

EMERSON, *Society and Solitude: Works and Days.*

Some Negroes who believe the resurrection, think that they shall rise white.

SIR THOMAS BROWNE, *Christian Morals.* Pt. ii, sec. 6.

7
Some doubt the courage of the negro. Go to Haiti and stand on those fifty thousand graves of the best soldiers France ever had, and ask them what they think of the negro's sword.

WENDELL PHILLIPS, *Toussaint L'Ouverture.*

8
Never forget that two blacks do not make a white.

BERNARD SHAW, *The Adventures of the Black Girl in Her Search for God.*

9
For more than a century before the Declaration of Independence, the negroes had been regarded as beings of an inferior order . . . so far inferior that they had no rights which a white man was bound to respect.

CHIEF-JUSTICE ROGER BROOKE TANEY, of the Supreme Court of the United States, *Decision,* in the Dred Scott case, 1857. (*Howard's Reports.* Vol. xix, p. 407.)

10
The silence, inch by inch, is there,
And the right limb for a lynch is there;
And a lean daw waits for both your eyes,
Blackbird.

RIDGELY TORRENCE, *The Bird and the Tree.*

11
The Afrikan may be Our Brother . . . But the Afrikan isn't our sister & our wife & our uncle. He isn't sevral of our brothers & all our fust wife's relashuns. He isn't our grandfather and our grate grandfather, & our Aunt in the country.

ARTEMUS WARD, *The Crisis.*

NEIGHBOR

12
A hedge between keeps friendship green.

A. B. CHEALES, *Proverbial Folk-Lore,* 93.

Love your neighbour, yet pull not down your hedge.

GEORGE HERBERT, *Jacula Prudentum.*

My apple trees will never get across
And eat the cones under his pines, I tell him.
He only says, "Good fences make good neighbors."

ROBERT FROST, *Mending Wall.*

13
You must ask your neighbour if you shall live in peace.

JOHN CLARKE, *Parœmiologia,* 203. (1639)

The most pious may not live in peace, if it does not please his wicked neighbor.

SCHILLER, *Wilhelm Tell.* Act iv, sc. 3, l. 124.

14
To God be humble, to thy friend be kind,
And with thy neighbours gladly lend and borrow;
His chance to-nicht, it may be thine to-morrow.

WILLIAM DUNBAR, *No Treasure Without Gladness.*

15
Here's talk of the Turk and the Pope, but it's my next door neighbour that does me harm.

THOMAS FULLER, *Gnomologia.* No. 2497.

What is nearest touches us most. The passions rise higher at domestic than at imperial tragedies.

SAMUEL JOHNSON, *Letter to Mrs. Thrale.*

16
Just next door 'tis cold and cheerless,
There's no carpet on the floor,
And a little heart is breaking,
In the cottage, just next door.

CHARLES K. HARRIS, *Just Next Door.* (1902)

1
All is well with him who is beloved of his neighbours.
George Herbert, *Jacula Prudentum.*

2
A bad neighbor is as great a plague as a good one is a blessing; he who enjoys a good neighbor has a precious possession.
Hesiod, *Works and Days,* l. 346.

A bad neighbor brings bad luck. (Aliquid mali esse propter vicinum malum.)
Plautus, *Mercator,* l. 772. (Act iv, sc. 4.) Quoted as a proverb.

If you're a neighbor to a neighbor who is bad, you must learn to suffer what is bad. But if you are neighbor to a neighbor who is good, more and more reciprocal good do you both teach and learn.
Menander, *Fragments,* No. 553.

3
Your own safety is at stake when your neighbor's house is in flames. (Tua res agitur, paries cum proximus ardet.)
Horace, *Epistles.* Bk. i, epis. 18, l. 84.

When a neighbor's house is on fire the flames are with difficulty kept from your own. (Proximus a tectis ignis defenditur ægre.)
Ovid, *Remediorum Amoris,* l. 625.

4
Every man's neighbour is his looking-glass.
James Howell, *Proverbs: Brit.-Eng.,* 3.

5
'Tis need that tests one's neighbor.
Henrik Ibsen, *Peer Gynt.* Act i.

6
A system in which the two great commandments were to hate your neighbour and love your neighbour's wife.
Macaulay, *Essays: Moore's Life of Byron.*

7
We are nearer neighbors to ourselves than whiteness to snow, or weight to stones.
Montaigne, *Essays.* Bk. ii, ch. 12.

8
The same reason that makes us wrangle with a neighbor causes a war between princes.
Montaigne, *Essays.* Bk. ii, ch. 12.

9
Whate'er the passion—knowledge, fame, or pelf—
Not one will change his neighbour with himself.
Pope, *Essay on Man.* Epis. ii, l. 261.

See plastic Nature working to this end,
The single atoms each to other tend,
Attract, attracted to, the next in place,
Form'd and impell'd its neighbour to embrace.
Pope, *Essay on Man.* Epis. iii, l. 9.

10
Withdraw thy foot from in thy neighbour's house; lest he be weary of thee, and so hate thee.
Old Testament: Proverbs, xxv, 17.

11
Better that man be born dumb, nay, void of reason, rather than that he employ the gifts of Providence to the destruction of his neighbor.
Quintilian, *De Institutione Oratoria.* Bk. xii, ch. 1, sec. 1.

12
There is an idea abroad among moral people that they should make their neighbours good. One person I have to make good: myself. But my duty to my neighbour is much more nearly expressed by saying that I have to make him happy—if I may.
R. L. Stevenson, *A Christmas Sermon.*

13
Love thy neighbor. ('Αγάπα τὸν πλησίον.)
Thales. (Stobæus, *Florilegium.* Pt. iii, l. 59.)

Thou shalt love thy neighbour as thyself.
Old Testament: Leviticus, xix, 18; *New Testament: Matthew,* xix, 19. It will be noted that Jesus was quoting the *Old Testament.*

Once again success has crowned
Missionary labor,
For her sweet eyes own that she
Also loves her neighbor.
G. A. Baker, *Thoughts on the Commandments.*

I love my neighbour as myself,
Myself like him too, by his leave,
Nor to his pleasure, power, or pelf
Came I to crouch, as I conceive.
John Byrom, *Careless Content.*

NELSON, HORATIO

14 She's [England] lost her Nelson now,
(A worthy man: he loved a woman well!)
Thomas Hardy, *The Dynasts,* vi, 8.

15
For he is England; Admiral,
Till the setting of her sun.
George Meredith, *Trafalgar Day.*

Admirals all, for England's sake,
Honour be yours and fame!
Henry Newbolt, *Admirals All.*

16
Keep the Nelson touch.
Henry Newbolt, *Minora Sidera.*

A PEERAGE OR WESTMINSTER ABBEY, see 2083:14.

NEW YORK CITY

17
No king, no clown, to rule this town!
William O. Bartlett, in New York *Sun,* about 1870, referring to "Boss" Tweed and Peter B. Sweeny, master-mind of the Tweed ring.

18
New York is a sucked orange.
Emerson, *Conduct of Life: Culture.*

19
Stream of the living world
Where dash the billows of strife!—
One plunge in the mighty torrent
Is a year of tamer life!
City of glorious days,
Of hope, and labor and mirth,
With room and to spare, on thy splendid bays,
For the ships of all the earth!
R. W. Gilder, *The City.*

20
In dress, habits, manners, provincialism, rou-

tine and narrowness, he acquired that charming insolence, that irritating completeness, that sophisticated crassness, that overbalanced poise that makes the Manhattan gentleman so delightfully small in his greatness.

O. HENRY, *Voice of the City: Defeat of the City.*

1
Far below and around lay the city like a ragged purple dream, the wonderful, cruel, enchanting, bewildering, fatal, great city.

O. HENRY, *Strictly Business: The Duel.*

2
Well, little old Noisyville-on-the-Subway is good enough for me.

O. HENRY, *Strictly Business: The Duel.*

If there ever was an aviary overstocked with jays it is that Yaptown-on-the-Hudson, called New York. . . . "Little old New York's good enough for us"—that's what they sing.

O. HENRY, *Gentle Grafter: A Tempered Wind.*

What else can you expect from a town that's shut off from the world by the ocean on one side and New Jersey on the other?

O. HENRY, *Gentle Grafter: A Tempered Wind.*

3
The renowned and ancient city of Gotham.

WASHINGTON IRVING, *Salmagundi.* No. xvi, Wednesday, 11 Nov., 1807, ch. 109. Chapter heading. The earliest reference to New York City as "Gotham." At the beginning of the chapter, it is referred to as "the thrice renowned and delectable city of Gotham." The proverb about the wise men of Gotham is believed to refer to Gotham, a village in Nottinghamshire, England.

4
Manhattan's a hell where culture rarely grew;
But it lets two lives do all they care to do.

ALFRED KREYMBORG, *Two Lives and Six Million.*

Harlem has a black belt where darkies dwell in a heaven where white men seek a little hell.

ALFRED KREYMBORG, *Harlem.*

New York, the hussy, was taken in sin again!

THOMAS BEER, *The Mauve Decade,* p. 141.

5
Not like the brazen giant of Greek fame,
With conquering limbs astride from land to land;
Here at our sea-washed, sunset gates shall stand
A mighty woman with a torch, whose flame
Is the imprisoned lightning, and her name
Mother of exiles.

EMMA LAZARUS, *The New Colossus.*

6
Some day this old Broadway shall climb to the skies,
As a ribbon of cloud on a soul-wind shall rise,
And we shall be lifted, rejoicing by night,
Till we join with the planets who choir their delight.
The signs in the streets and the signs in the skies
Shall make a new Zodiac, guiding the wise,
And Broadway make one with that marvelous stair
That is climbed by the rainbow-clad spirits of prayer.

VACHEL LINDSAY, *A Rhyme About an Electrical Advertising Sign.*

Give my regards to Broadway.

GEORGE M. COHAN. Title and refrain of popular song. (1904)

The Sidewalks of New York.

JAMES BLAKE AND CHARLES LAWLOR. Title and refrain of song, later made famous by Al. Smith. (1894)

7
A stillness and a sadness
Pervade the City Hall,
And speculating madness
Has left the street of Wall;
The Union Square looks really
Both desolate and dark,
And that's the case, or nearly,
From Battery to Park.

GEORGE POPE MORRIS, *Dark Days.* (c. 1860)

8
Up in the heights of the evening skies I see my City of Cities float
In sunset's golden and crimson dyes: I look and a great joy clutches my throat!
Plateau of roofs by canyons crossed: windows by thousands fire-furled—
O gazing, how the heart is lost in the Deepest City in the World.

JAMES OPPENHEIM, *New York from a Skyscraper.*

9
Who that has known thee but shall burn
In exile till he come again
To do thy bitter will, O stern
Moon of the tides of men!

JOHN REED, *Proud New York.*

10
Just where the Treasury's marble front
Looks over Wall Street's mingled nations,
Where Jews and Gentiles most are wont
To throng for trade and last quotations;
Where, hour, by hour, the rates of gold
Outrival, in the ears of people,
The quarter-chimes, serenely tolled
From Trinity's undaunted steeple.

E. C. STEDMAN, *Pan in Wall Street.*

11
City of hurried and sparkling waters! city of spires and masts!
City nested in bays! my city!

WALT WHITMAN, *Mannahatta.*

Mighty Manhattan, with spires, and
The sparkling and hurrying tides, and the ships.

WALT WHITMAN, *When Lilacs Last in the Door-Yard Bloom'd.* St. 12.

The ferries ply like shuttles in a loom.

ZOË AKINS, *This is My Hour.*

1
A little strip of an island with a row of well-fed folks up and down the middle, and a lot of hungry folks on each side.

HARRY LEON WILSON, *The Spenders*. Ch. viii.

2
We plant a tub and call it Paradise. . . . New York is the great stone desert.

ISRAEL ZANGWILL, *The Melting-Pot*. Act ii.

Vulgar of manner, overfed,
Overdressed and underbred.

BYRON R. NEWTON, *Owed to New York*. For full quotation see APPENDIX.

NEWS

For Newspapers see Press

3
A master-passion is the love of news.

GEORGE CRABBE, *The Newspaper*, l. 281.

4
When a dog bites a man that is not news, but when a man bites a dog that is news.

Usually attributed to CHARLES A. DANA, famous editor of the New York *Sun*, but the evidence favors JOHN B. BOGART, city editor of the *Sun* from 1873–1890. In a letter to the compiler, Mr. Frank M. O'Brien, the present editor of the *Sun*, says, "The late Edward P. Mitchell, Dana's right hand man for many years, told me that the author was Mr. Bogart. Mr. Mitchell was meticulous about such things, and if it had not been true I think Mr. Bogart, a most modest man, would have demurred." Stanley Walker (*City Editor*, p. 20) attributes the saying to Amos Cummings, another of Dana's editors.

Asked for a definition of news, I can give you no better answer than the one on which we were brought up in the *Sun* office. Mr. Dana used to say, "When a dog bites a man that is not news, but when a man bites a dog that is news."

RICHARD HARDING DAVIS. (HARRINGTON, *Essentials of Journalism*.)

News is as hard to hold as quicksilver, and it fades more rapidly than any morning-glory.

STANLEY WALKER, *City Editor*, p. 20.

Women, wampum and wrongdoing are always news.

STANLEY WALKER, *City Editor*, p. 44.

5
Good news may be told at any time, but ill in the morning.

GEORGE HERBERT, *Jacula Prudentum*.

Do not awake me when you have good news to communicate, with that there is no hurry. But when you bring bad news, rouse me instantly, for then there is not a moment to be lost.

NAPOLEON BONAPARTE. To his Secretary. (Quoted by Emerson, *Napoleon*.)

6
Where village statesmen talked with looks profound,
And news much older than their ale went round.

GOLDSMITH, *The Deserted Village*, l. 223.

7
News, the manna of a day.

MATTHEW GREEN, *The Spleen*, l. 169.

8
It is good news, *worthy of all acceptation*, and yet not too good to be true.

MATTHEW HENRY, *Commentaries: I Tim*. 1, 15.

9
Stay a little, and news will find you.

GEORGE HERBERT, *Jacula Prudentum*.

10
How beautiful upon the mountains are the feet of him that bringeth good tidings.

Old Testament: Isaiah, lii. 7.

As cold waters to a thirsty soul, so is good news from a far country.

Old Testament: Proverbs, xxv, 25.

11
No news is better than evil news.

JAMES I. (*Loseley MSS.*, 403. 1616.)

The best news is when we hear no news.

DONALD LUPTON, *London and Country*. No. 12. (1632)

No news is good news.

GEORGE COLMAN THE ELDER, *The Spleen*. Act i. (1776)

No news, good news. (Pas de nouvelles, bonnes nouvelles.)

MEILHAC AND HALÉVY, *La Belle Hélène*. Act ii, sc. 5.

12
Into authentical and apocryphal—
Or news of doubtful credit, as barbers' news,
And tailors' news, porters', and watermen's news . . .
Vacation news, term-news, Christmas-news.

BEN JONSON, *The Staple of News*. Act i, sc. 2.

13
Evil news fly faster still than good.

THOMAS KYD, *Spanish Tragedy*. Act i. (1594)

Ill news hath wings, and with the wind doth go:
Comfort's a cripple, and comes ever slow.

MICHAEL DRAYTON, *The Barons' Wars*. Bk. ii, st. 28. (1603)

Ill news, madam, are swallow-winged, but what's good walks on crutches.

MASSINGER, *The Picture*. Act ii, sc. 1. (1630)

It is an old saying that Ill News hath wings and Good News no legs.

MARGARET CAVENDISH, DUCHESS OF NEWCASTLE, *Sociable Companions*. Act i, sc. 1. (c. 1660)

For evil news rides post, while good news baits.

MILTON, *Samson Agonistes*, l. 1538. (1671)

Ill news is wing'd with fate, and flies apace.

DRYDEN, *Threnodia Augustalis*, l. 49. (1685)

Ill news goes quick and far.

PLUTARCH, *Of Inquisitiveness*. Quoted.

14
What, what, what,
What's the news from Swat?
Sad news, Bad news,
Comes by the cable; led
Through the Indian Ocean's bed,
Through the Persian Gulf, the Red
Sea, and the Med-

Iterranean—he's dead;
The Akhoond is dead.
GEORGE THOMAS LANIGAN, *The Akhoond of Swat*. On 22 Jan., 1878, the *London Times* published an item headed, "The Akhoond of Swat is Dead."

Who, or why, or which, or what,
Is the Akhond of Swat?
EDWARD LEAR, *The Akhond of Swat.*

1
Behold, I send my messenger before thy face.
New Testament: Mark, i, 2.

2
News, news, news, my gossiping friends,
I have wonderful news to tell.
OWEN MEREDITH, *News.*

3
My ears await your tidings. (Istuc quod adfers aures exspectant meæ.)
PLAUTUS, *Asinaria,* l. 331. (Act ii, sc. 2.)

4
Let the greatest part of the news thou hearest be the least part of what thou believest, lest the greater part of what thou believest be the least part of what is true. Where lies are easily admitted, the father of lies will not easily be excluded.
FRANCIS QUARLES, *Enchiridion*. Cent. ii, No. 50.

5
The nature of bad news infects the teller.
SHAKESPEARE, *Antony and Cleopatra.* Act i, sc. 2, l. 99.

Though it be honest, it is never good
To bring bad news: give to a gracious message
An host of tongues; but let ill tidings tell
Themselves when they be felt.
SHAKESPEARE, *Antony and Cleopatra.* Act ii, sc. 3, l. 85.

If 't be summer news,
Smile to 't before; if winterly, thou need'st
But keep that countenance still.
SHAKESPEARE, *Cymbeline.* Act iii, sc. 4, l. 12.

The first bringer of unwelcome news
Hath but a losing office, and his tongue
Sounds ever after as a sullen bell,
Remember'd tolling a departing friend.
SHAKESPEARE, *II Henry IV*. Act i, sc. 1, l. 100.

6
Ram thou thy fruitful tidings in mine ears,
That long time have been barren.
SHAKESPEARE, *Antony and Cleopatra.* Act ii, sc. 5, l. 24.

Prithee, friend,
Pour out the pack of matter to mine ear,
The good and bad together.
SHAKESPEARE, *Antony and Cleopatra.* Act ii, sc. 5, l. 53.

7
Celia: Here comes Monsieur le Beau.
Rosalind: With his mouth full of news,
Celia: Which he will put on us, as pigeons feed their young.
Rosalind: Then shall we be news-crammed.
SHAKESPEARE, *As You Like It.* Act i, sc. 2, l. 97.

Thou still hast been the father of good news.
SHAKESPEARE, *Hamlet.* Act ii, sc. 2, l. 42.

The news is not so tart.
SHAKESPEARE, *King Lear.* Act iv, sc. 2, l. 88.

8
There's villainous news abroad.
SHAKESPEARE, *I Henry IV*. Act ii, sc. 4, l. 367.

News fitting to the night
Black, fearful, comfortless and horrible.
SHAKESPEARE, *King John.* Act v, sc. 6, l. 19.

I drown'd these news in tears.
SHAKESPEARE, *III Henry VI*. Act ii, sc. 1, l. 104.

9
Pistol: Tidings do I bring, and lucky joys,
And golden times, and happy news of price.
Falstaff: I pray thee now, deliver them like a man of this world.
SHAKESPEARE, *II Henry IV*. Act v, sc. 3, l. 99.

Master, master! news, old news, and such news as you never heard of!
SHAKESPEARE, *The Taming of the Shrew.* Act iii, sc. 2, l. 30.

10
How goes it now, sir? this news which is called true is so like an old tale, that the verity of it is in strong suspicion.
SHAKESPEARE, *Winter's Tale.* Act v, sc. 2, l. 30.

11
The messenger of good news is always an object of benevolence.
SYDNEY SMITH, *Sketches of Moral Philosophy.* Lecture 22.

12
I cannot make news without straw.
WALPOLE, *Letter to the Miss Berrys,* 8 June, 1791.

13
Any news? (Μὴ τὶ καινόν.)
UNKNOWN. A Greek proverbial saying.

What's the news?
SHAKESPEARE, *Hamlet.* Act ii, sc. 2, l. 240.

What news on the Rialto?
SHAKESPEARE, *The Merchant of Venice.* Act i, sc. 3, l. 39.

NEWSPAPERS, see Press

NEWTON, SIR ISAAC

14
I do not know what I may appear to the world, but to myself I seem to have been only like a boy playing on the seashore and diverting myself in now and then finding a smoother pebble or a prettier shell than ordinary, whilst the great ocean of truth lay all undiscovered before me.
ISAAC NEWTON. (BREWSTER, *Memoirs of Newton.* Vol. ii, ch. 27.)

Collecting toys,
And trifles for choice matters, worth a sponge;
As children gath'ring pebbles on the shore.
MILTON, *Paradise Regained.* Bk. iv, l. 327.

Newton (that proverb of the mind), alas!
Declared, with all his grand discoveries recent,

That he himself felt only "like a youth
Picking up shells by the great ocean—Truth."
BYRON, *Don Juan*. Canto vii, st. 5.

1
When Newton saw an apple fall, he found . . .
A mode of proving that the earth turn'd round
In a most natural whirl, called "gravitation";
And thus is the sole mortal who could grapple,
Since Adam, with a fall or with an apple.
BYRON, *Don Juan*. Canto x, st. 1.

2
Nature and Nature's laws lay hid in Night:
God said, Let Newton be! and all was Light.
POPE, *Epitaph for Sir Isaac Newton*.

O'er Nature's laws God cast the veil of night:
Out-blaz'd a Newton's soul—and all was light.
AARON HILL, *On Sir Isaac Newton*.

3
The antechapel where the statue stood
Of Newton with his prism and silent face,
The marble index of a mind for ever
Voyaging through strange seas of thought alone.
WORDSWORTH, *The Prelude*. Bk. iii, l. 60.

NICKNAMES, see under Names

NIGHT

See also Darkness, Midnight

I—Night: Apothegms

4
Night is the sabbath of mankind,
To rest the body and the mind.
BUTLER, *Hudibras*. Pt. iii, canto 1, l. 1349.

5
The night
Shows stars and women in a better light.
BYRON, *Don Juan*. Canto ii, st. 152.

6
Night's black mantle covers all alike.
DU BARTAS, *Devine Weekes and Workes*. Week i, day 1. (c. 1580)

Night . . .
Whose pitchy mantle overveil'd the earth.
SHAKESPEARE, *I Henry VI*. Act ii, sc. 2, l. 1. (1592)

Come, civil night,
Thou sober-suited matron, all in black, . . .
With thy black mantle.
SHAKESPEARE, *Romeo and Juliet*. Act iii, sc. 2, l. 10.

Sable-vested Night, eldest of things.
MILTON, *Paradise Lost*. Bk. ii, l. 962.

7
O nights and feasts divine! (O noctes, cenæque deum!)
HORACE, *Satires*. Bk. ii, sat. 6, l. 65.

Those gay-spent, festive nights.
THOMSON, *The Seasons: Winter*, l. 1037.
See also under FEAST.

8
Watchman, what of the night?
Old Testament: Isaiah, xxi, 11.

Macbeth: What is the night?
Lady Macbeth: Almost at odds with morning, which is which.
SHAKESPEARE, *Macbeth*. Act iii, sc. 4. l. 126.

9
Night, when deep sleep falleth on men.
Old Testament: Job, iv, 13; xxxiii, 15.

The night cometh when no man can work.
New Testament: John, ix, 9.

10
Night hath a thousand eyes.
JOHN LYLY, *Maydes Metamorphosis*. Act iii, 1.

The Night has a thousand eyes,
The Day but one;
Yet the light of the bright world dies
With the dying sun.
F. W. BOURDILLON, *The Night Has a Thousand Eyes*.

11
By night comes counsel to the wise. ('Εν νυκτὶ βουλὴ τοῖς σοφοῖσι γίγνεται.)
MENANDER, *Fragments*. No. 150.

Night is the mother of counsels.
GEORGE HERBERT, *Jacula Prudentum*. The French form is "La nuit porte conseil"; the Latin, "In nocte consilium."

Night is the mother of thoughts.
JOHN FLORIO, *First Fruites*. Fo. 31. (1578)

12
What hath night to do with sleep?
MILTON, *Comus*, l. 122.

Most glorious night!
Thou wert not sent for slumber!
BYRON, *Childe Harold*. Canto iii, st. 93.

13
How sweetly did they float upon the wings
Of silence through the empty-vaulted night,
At every fall smoothing the raven down
Of darkness till it smil'd.
MILTON, *Comus*, l. 249.

Night is a stealthy, evil Raven,
Wrapt to the eyes in his black wings.
T. B. ALDRICH, *Day and Night*.

Come into the garden, Maud,
For the black bat, night, has flown.
TENNYSON, *Maud*. Pt. i, sec. 22, st. 1.

14
With him fled the shades of night.
MILTON, *Paradise Lost*. Bk. iv, l. 1015.

The shades of night were falling fast.
LONGFELLOW, *Excelsior*.

15
Let's have one other gaudy night.
SHAKESPEARE, *Antony and Cleopatra*. Act iii, sc. 13, l. 183.

Burn this night with torches.
SHAKESPEARE, *Antony and Cleopatra*. Act iv, sc. 2, l. 41.

16
Making night hideous.
SHAKESPEARE, *Hamlet*. Act i, sc. 4, l. 54.

Now the hungry lion roars,
And the wolf behowls the moon.
SHAKESPEARE, *A Midsummer-Night's Dream*. Act v, sc. 1, l. 378.

Silence, ye wolves! while Ralph to Cynthia howls,
And makes night hideous.
POPE, *The Dunciad*. Bk. iii, l. 165.

1
Dark-eyed night.
SHAKESPEARE, *King Lear*. Act ii, sc. 1, l. 121.

Come, gentle night, come, loving, black-brow'd night.
SHAKESPEARE, *Romeo and Juliet*. Act iii, sc. 2, l. 20.

Sable Night, mother of Dread and Fear,
Upon the world dim darkness doth display,
And in her vaulty prison stows the Day.
SHAKESPEARE, *The Rape of Lucrece*, l. 117.

2
'Twas night, and all the world was lulled to rest. (Omnia noctis erant placida composta quiete.)
VARRO, *Argonautica*. Frag.

3
You know not what the night will bring. (Nescis quid vesper serus ferat.)
VARRO. Title of satire. (AULUS GELLIUS, *Noctes Atticæ*, i, 22.)

4
Black night broods over the deep. (Ponto nox incubat atra.)
VERGIL, *Æneid*. Bk. i, l. 89.

5
Mine is the night, with all her stars.
EDWARD YOUNG, *Paraphrase on Job*, l. 147.

6
Wan night, the shadow-goer, came stepping in.
UNKNOWN, *Beowulf*. Pt. iii.

II—Night: Its Beauty

7
The stars are forth, the moon above the tops
Of the snow-shining mountains—Beautiful!
I linger yet with Nature, for the night
Hath been to me a more familiar face
Than that of man; and in her starry shade
Of dim and solitary loveliness
I learn'd the language of another world.
BYRON, *Manfred*. Act iii, sc. 4.

8
And soft adorings from their loves receive
Upon the honey'd middle of the night.
KEATS, *The Eve of St. Agnes*. St. 6.

9
The Night walked down the sky
With the moon in her hand.
F. L. KNOWLES, *A Memory*.

10
I heard the trailing garments of the Night
Sweep through her marble halls!
I saw her sable skirts all fringed with light
From the celestial walls!
LONGFELLOW, *Hymn to the Night*.

And Evening trails her robes of gold
Through the dim halls of Night.
SARAH H. P. WHITMAN, *Summer's Call*.

11
I felt her presence, by its spell of might,
Stoop o'er me from above;
The calm, majestic presence of the Night,
As of the one I love.
LONGFELLOW, *Hymn to the Night*.

I heard the sounds of sorrow and delight,
The manifold soft chimes,
That fill the haunted chambers of the Night,
Like some old poet's rhymes.
LONGFELLOW, *Hymn to the Night*.

O holy Night! from thee I learn to bear
What man has borne before!
Thou layest thy finger on the lips of Care,
And they complain no more.
LONGFELLOW, *Hymn to the Night*.

Peace! Peace! Orestes-like I breathe this prayer!
Descend with broad-winged flight,
The welcome, the thrice prayed-for, the most fair,
The best-beloved Night!
LONGFELLOW, *Hymn to the Night*.

12
God makes sech nights, all white an' still
Fur 'z you can look or listen,
Moonshine an' snow on field an' hill,
All silence an' all glisten.
J. R. LOWELL, *The Courtin'*.

13
Silent Night,
With this her solemn bird and this fair moon,
And these the gems of Heav'n, her starry train.
MILTON, *Paradise Lost*. Bk. iv, l. 647.

14
Bend low, O dusky Night,
And give my spirit rest,
Hold me to your deep breast,
And put old cares to flight.
Give back the lost delight
That once my soul possest,
When Love was loveliest.
LOUISE CHANDLER MOULTON, *To Night*.

15
The gods sell all things at a fair price, said an old poet. He might have added that they sell their best goods at the cheapest rate. . . . There is no entrance fee to the starlit hall of the Night.
AXEL MUNTHE, *Story of San Michele*, p. 398.

16
O Night, most beautiful and rare!
Thou giv'st the heavens their holiest hue,
And through the azure fields of air
Bring'st down the gentle dew.
THOMAS BUCHANAN READ, *Night*.

How beautiful this night! the balmiest sigh

Which vernal zephyrs breathe in evening's ear
Were discord to the speaking quietude
That wraps this moveless scene. Heaven's ebon vault,
Studded with stars unutterably bright,
Through which the moon's unclouded grandeur rolls,
Seems like a canopy which love had spread
To curtain her sleeping world.
SHELLEY, *Queen Mab*. Pt. iv, l. 1.

How beautiful is night!
A dewy freshness fills the silent air;
No mist obscures, nor cloud, nor speck, nor stain
Breaks the serene of heaven:
In full-orbed glory yonder moon divine
Rolls through the dark blue depths.
Beneath her steady ray
The desert-circle spreads
Like the round ocean, girdled with the sky.
How beautiful is night!
ROBERT SOUTHEY, *Thalaba*. Bk. i, st. 1.

1
Swiftly walk o'er the western wave,
Spirit of Night!
SHELLEY, *To Night*.

2
The star-usurping battlements of night.
GEORGE STERLING, *In Extremis*.

3
See how there the cowlèd night
Kneels on the eastern sanctuary-stair.
FRANCIS THOMPSON, *Coryambus for Autumn*.

4
Come, drink the mystic wine of Night,
Brimming with silence and the stars;
While earth, bathed in this holy light,
Is seen without its scars.
LOUIS UNTERMEYER, *The Wine of Night*.

5
Mysterious night! when our first parent knew
Thee from report divine, and heard thy name,
Did he not tremble for this lovely frame,
This glorious canopy of light and blue?
JOSEPH BLANCO WHITE, *Night and Death*.

6
Press close, bare-bosom'd night—press close, magnetic nourishing night!
Night of south winds—night of the large few stars!
Still nodding night—mad naked summer night.
WALT WHITMAN, *Song of Myself*. Sec. 21.

7
Night, sable goddess! from her ebon throne,
In rayless majesty, now stretches forth
Her leaden sceptre o'er a slumb'ring world.
Silence, how dead! and darkness, how profound!
Nor eye, nor list'ning ear, an object finds;
Creation sleeps.
YOUNG, *Night Thoughts*. Night i, l. 18.

How is night's sable mantle labour'd o'er,
How richly wrought with attributes divine!
What wisdom shines! what love! this midnight pomp,
This gorgeous arch, with golden worlds inlaid
Built with divine ambition!
YOUNG, *Night Thoughts*. Night iv, l. 385.

'Tis Nature's system of divinity,
And every student of the night inspires.
'Tis elder scripture, writ by God's own hand:
Scripture authentic! uncorrupt by man.
YOUNG, *Night Thoughts*. Night ix, l. 644.

III—Night: Its Sadness

8
A night of tears! for the gusty rain
Had ceased, but the eaves were dripping yet;
And the moon looked forth, as tho' in pain,
With her face all white and wet.
OWEN MEREDITH, *The Portrait*.

9
For now began
Night with her sullen wings to double-shade
The desert; fowls in their clay nests were couch'd,
And now wild beasts came forth, the woods to roam.
MILTON, *Paradise Regained*. Bk. i, l. 499.

10
Night is the time to weep;
To wet with unseen tears
Those graves of memory, where sleep
The joys of other years.
JAMES MONTGOMERY, *Night*.

11
Night is sadder than the hours of daylight. (Tristior nox est, quam tempora Phœbi.)
OVID, *Remediorum Amoris*, l. 585.

12
How long the night seems to one kept awake by pain. (Qu'une nuit paraît longue à la douleur qui veille!)
BERNARD JOSEPH SAURIN, *Blanche et Guiscard*. Act v, sc. 5.

The night, to him, that had no morrow.
THOMAS CAMPBELL, *O'Connor's Child*. St. 9.

There never was night that had no morn.
DINAH M. M. CRAIK, *The Golden Gate*.

This will last out a night in Russia,
When nights are longest there.
SHAKESPEARE, *Measure for Measure*. Act ii, sc. 1, l. 139.

13
The cold blast at the casement beats;
The window-panes are white;
The snow whirls through the empty streets;
It is a dreary night!
EPES SARGENT, *The Heart's Summer*.

14
Night brings our troubles to the light, rather than banishes them. (Nox exhibet molestiam, non tollit.)
SENECA, *Epistulæ ad Lucilium*. Epis. lvi, sec. 6.

1
'Tis a wild night.
SHAKESPEARE, *King Lear*. Act ii, sc. 4, l. 311.

Here's a night pities nor wise man nor fool.
SHAKESPEARE, *King Lear*. Act iii, sc. 2, l. 13.

Things that love night
Love not such nights as these.
SHAKESPEARE, *King Lear*. Act iii, sc. 2, l. 42.

'Tis a naughty night to swim in.
SHAKESPEARE, *King Lear*. Act iii, sc. 2, l. 116.

The tyranny of the open night's too rough
For nature to endure.
SHAKESPEARE, *King Lear*. Act iii, sc. 4, l. 2.

And altogether it's very bad weather,
And an unpleasant sort of a night!
R. H. BARHAM, *The Nurse's Story*.

Give not a windy night a rainy morrow.
SHAKESPEARE, *Sonnets*. No. xc.

2
O comfort-killing Night, image of hell!
Dim register and notary of shame!
Black stage for tragedies and murders fell!
Vast sin-concealing chaos! nurse of blame!
SHAKESPEARE, *The Rape of Lucrece*, l. 764.

IV—Night and Day

See also Day: Its End

3
I love night more than day—she is so lovely;
But I love night the most because she brings
My love to me in dreams which scarcely lie.
BAILEY, *Festus: Water and Wood: Midnight*.

4
God hath created nights
As well as days, to deck the varied globe.
JOHN BEAUMONT, *God Hath Created Nights*.

5
Day that I loved, day that I loved, the Night is here!
RUPERT BROOKE, *Day That I Have Loved*.

6
Most men are begotten in the night; most animals in the day.
SIR THOMAS BROWNE, *To a Friend*. Sec. 7.

7
The day is great and final. The night is for the day, but the day is not for the night.
EMERSON, *Society and Solitude: Success*.

8
Dark is a slow tide flowing between two days.
ROBERT HILLYER, *The Seventh Hill*, i, 10.

9
The day is done, and the darkness
Falls from the wings of Night,
As a feather is wafted downward
From an eagle in his flight.
LONGFELLOW, *The Day is Done*.

10
Night with her power to silence day.
GEORGE MACDONALD, *Violin Songs: My Heart*.

11
Quiet night, that brings
Rest to the labourer, is the outlaw's day,
In which he rises early to do wrong.
MASSINGER, *The Guardian*. Act ii, sc. 4.

And when night
Darkens the streets, then wander forth the sons
Of Belial, flown with insolence and wine.
MILTON, *Paradise Lost*. Bk. i, l. 500.

12
Darkness now rose,
As daylight sunk, and brought in low'ring Night,
Her shadowy offspring.
MILTON, *Paradise Regained*. Bk. iv, l. 397.

13
Day unto day uttereth speech, and night unto night sheweth knowledge.
Old Testament: Psalms, xix, 2.

14
Come day, come night, day comes at last.
CHRISTINA ROSSETTI, *Twilight*.

15
Cut short the night; use some of it for the day's business. (Circumscribatur nox, et aliquid ex illa in diem transferatur.)
SENECA, *Epistulæ ad Lucilium*. Epis. cxxii, 4.

What I take from my nights, I add to my days. (Ce que j'ôte à mes nuits, je l'ajoute à mes jours.)
JEAN ROTROU, *Venceslas*. (1647)

I must become a borrower of the night
For an hour or twain.
SHAKESPEARE, *Macbeth*. Act iii, sc. 1, l. 26.

And the best of all ways To lengthen our days
Is to steal a few hours from the night, my dear.
THOMAS MOORE, *The Young May Moon*.

But we that have but span-long life,
The thicker must lay on the pleasure;
And since time will not stay,
We'll add night to the day,
Thus, thus we'll fill the measure.
UNKNOWN, *Duet*. (c. 1795)

16
Come, seeling night,
Scarf up the tender eye of pitiful day.
SHAKESPEARE, *Macbeth*. Act iii, sc. 2, l. 46.

Night begins to muffle up the day.
GEORGE WITHER, *Mistresse of Philarete*.

17
By the clock, 'tis day,
And yet dark night strangles the travelling lamp;
Is 't night's predominance, or the day's shame,
That darkness does the face of earth entomb,
When living light should kiss it?
SHAKESPEARE, *Macbeth*. Act ii, sc. 4, l. 6.

18
Light thickens; and the crow
Makes wing to the rooky wood:
Good things of day begin to droop and drowse;
Whiles night's black agents to their preys do rouse.
SHAKESPEARE, *Macbeth*. Act iii, sc. 2, l. 50.

The night is long that never finds the day.
SHAKESPEARE, *Macbeth*. Act iv, sc. 3, l. 240.

1
This night methinks is but the daylight sick.
SHAKESPEARE, *The Merchant of Venice*. Act v, sc. 1, l. 124.

2
Wrap thy form in a mantle grey,
Star-inwrought!
Blind with thine hair the eyes of Day;
Kiss her until she be wearied out.
SHELLEY, *To Night*.

3
Day is the Child of Time,
And Day must cease to be:
But Night is without a sire
And cannot expire,
One with Eternity.
R. H. STODDARD, *Day and Night*.

4
Night is older than day by one day.
THALES. (DIOGENES LAERTIUS, *Thales*. Sec. 36.)

O majestic Night!
Nature's great ancestor! Day's elder-born!
YOUNG, *Night Thoughts*. Night ix, l. 549.

5
They wear out day and night. (Noctemque diemque fatigant.)
VERGIL, *Æneid*. Bk. viii, l. 94.

We did sleep day out of countenance, and made the night light with drinking.
SHAKESPEARE, *Antony and Cleopatra*. Act ii, sc. 2, l. 181.

6
Night holds the keys that ope the door of day.
THEODORE WATTS-DUNTON, *In a Graveyard*.

7
Day full-blown and splendid—day of the immense sun, action, ambition, laughter,
The Night follows close with millions of suns, and sleep and restoring darkness.
WALT WHITMAN, *Youth, Day, Old Age and Night*.

NIGHTINGALE

8
The nightingale, who still with sorrowing soul,
And "Itys, Itys" cry,
Bemoans a life o'erflourishing in ills.
(Ἀκόρετος βοᾶς, φεῦ, ταλαίναις φρεσὶν
Ἴτυν Ἴτυν στένουσ' ἀμφιθαλῆ κακοῖς
ἀηδὼν βίον.)
ÆSCHYLUS, *Agamemnon*, l. 1143. (Plumptre, tr.)

9
She waileth the nightingale's lament. (Θρηνεῖ δὲ γόον τὸν ἀηδόνιον.)
ÆSCHYLUS, *Fragments*. Frag. 157.

10
O sacred bird! let me at eve,
Thus wandering all alone,
Thy tender counsel oft receive,
Bear witness to thy pensive airs,
And pity Nature's common cares,
Till I forget my own.
MARK AKENSIDE, *The Nightingale*.

11
Hark! ah, the nightingale!
The tawny-throated!
Hark! from that moonlit cedar what a burst!
What triumph! hark!—what pain!
MATTHEW ARNOLD, *Philomela*.

How thick the bursts come crowding through the leaves!
Again—thou hearest?
Eternal passion! Eternal pain!
MATTHEW ARNOLD, *Philomela*.

12
Everything did banish moan
Save the Nightingale alone:
She, poor bird, as all forlorn
Lean'd her breast up-till a thorn,
And there sung the doleful'st ditty,
That to hear it was great pity.
Fie, fie fie! now would she cry;
Tereu, tereu! by and by.
RICHARD BARNFIELD, *Philomel*.

What bird so sings, yet does so wail?
O, 'tis the ravish'd nightingale—
Jug, jug, jug, jug, tereu! she cries,
And still her woes at midnight rise.
JOHN LYLY, *Spring's Welcome*.

13
A nightingale dies for shame if another bird sings better.
ROBERT BURTON, *Anatomy of Melancholy*. Pt. i, sec. ii, mem. 3, subs. 6.

14
Oh nightingale! What doth she ail?
And is she sad or jolly?
For ne'er on earth was sound of mirth
So like to melancholy.
HARTLEY COLERIDGE, *Song*.

15
'Tis the merry nightingale
That crowds, and hurries, and precipitates
With fast thick warble his delicious notes,
As he were fearful that an April night
Would be too short for him to utter forth
His love-chant, and disburthen his full soul
Of all its music!
S. T. COLERIDGE, *The Nightingale*, l. 43.

16
I wonder if it *is* a bird
That sings within the hidden tree,
Or some shy angel calling me
To follow far away?
GRACE HAZARD CONKLING, *Nightingales*.

17
Sweet bird, that sing'st away the early hours,
Of winters past or coming void of care,
Well pleased with delights which present are,
Fair seasons, budding sprays, sweet-smelling flowers.
WILLIAM DRUMMOND, *To the Nightingale*.

1
But, leaning on a thorn her dainty chest,
For fear soft sleep should steal into her breast,
Expresses in her song grief not to be expressed.
GILES FLETCHER THE YOUNGER, *Christ's Victorie and Triumph.*

Never nightingale so singeth:
Oh, she leans on thorny tree
And her poet-song she flingeth
Over pain to victory!
E. B. BROWNING, *The Lost Bower.* St. 39.

The bird forlorn
That singeth with her breast against a thorn.
THOMAS HOOD, *The Plea of the Midsummer Fairies,* l. 269.

2
The nightingale among the thick-leaved spring
That sits alone in sorrow, and doth sing
Whole nights away in mourning.
JOHN FLETCHER, *Faithful Shepherdess.* Act v.

3
Thou wast not born for death, immortal Bird!
No hungry generations tread thee down;
The voice I hear this passing night was heard
In ancient days by emperor and clown:
Perhaps the self-same song that found a path
Through the sad heart of Ruth, when, sick for home,
She stood in tears amid the alien corn;
The same that oft-times hath
Charm'd magic casements, opening on the foam
Of perilous seas, in faery lands forlorn.
KEATS, *Ode to a Nightingale.*

Adieu! adieu! thy plaintive anthem fades
Past the near meadows, over the still stream,
Up the hill-side; and now 'tis buried deep
In the next valley-glades:
Was it a vision, or a waking dream?
Fled is that music:—do I wake or sleep?
KEATS, *Ode to a Nightingale.*

Where the nightingale doth sing
Not a senseless, tranced thing,
But divine melodious truth.
KEATS, *Ode: Bards of Passion and of Mirth.*

To the red rising moon, and loud and deep
The nightingale is singing from the steep.
LONGFELLOW, *Keats.*

4
Soft as Memnon's harp at morning,
To the inward ear devout,
Touched by light, with heavenly warning
Your transporting chords ring out.
Every leaf in every nook,
Every wave in every brook,
Chanting with a solemn voice
Minds us of our better choice.
JOHN KEBLE, *The Nightingale.*

5
I had a silvery name, I had a silvery name,
I had a silvery name—do you remember
The name you cried beside the tumbling sea?
"Darling . . . darling . . . darling . . . darling . . ."
Said the Chinese nightingale.
VACHEL LINDSAY, *The Chinese Nightingale.*

6
Sweet bird that shunn'st the noise of folly,
Most musical, most melancholy!
Thee, chauntress, oft, the woods among,
I woo, to hear thy even-song.
MILTON, *Il Penseroso,* l. 61.

"Most musical, most melancholy" bird!
A melancholy bird! Oh! idle thought!
In nature there is nothing melancholy.
S. T. COLERIDGE, *The Nightingale,* l. 13.

7
All but the wakeful nightingale;
She all night long her amorous descant sung.
MILTON, *Paradise Lost.* Bk. iv, l. 602.

8
O nightingale, that on yon bloomy spray
Warblest at eve, when all the woods are still,
Thou with fresh hope the Lover's heart dost fill,
While the jolly hours lead on propitious May.
MILTON, *Sonnet: To the Nightingale.*

Thy liquid notes that close the eye of day,
First heard before the shallow cuckoo's bill,
Portend success in love.
MILTON, *Sonnet: To the Nightingale.*

That star-enchanted song falls through the air
From lawn to lawn down terraces of sound,
Darts in white arrows on the shadowed ground;
And all the night you sing.
HAROLD MONRO, *The Nightingale Near the House.*

9
There's a bower of roses by Bendemeer's stream,
And the nightingale sings round it all day long.
THOMAS MOORE, *Lalla Rookh: The Veiled Prophet.*

10
The Nightingale that in the branches sang,
Ah whence and whither flown again, who knows!
OMAR KHAYYÁM, *Rubáiyát.* St. 96. (Fitzgerald, tr.)

11
Yon nightingale, whose strain so sweetly flows,
Mourning her ravish'd young or much-loved mate,
A soothing charm o'er all the valleys throws
And skies, with notes well tuned to her sad state.
PETRARCH, *To Laura in Death.* Sonnet xliii.

1
The nightingale got no prize at the poultry show.
SIR WALTER RALEIGH THE YOUNGER, *Epigram.*

2
The sunrise wakes the lark to sing,
The moonrise wakes the nightingale.
Come, darkness, moonrise, everything
That is so silent, sweet, and pale:
Come, so ye wake the nightingale.
CHRISTINA ROSSETTI, *Bird Raptures.*

Hark! that's the nightingale,
Telling the self-same tale
Her song told when this ancient earth was young:
So echoes answered when her song was sung
In the first wooded vale.
CHRISTINA ROSSETTI, *Twilight Calm.* St. 7.

3
The angel of spring, the mellow-throated nightingale.
SAPPHO, *Fragments.* No. 39.

4
Worlds to conquer!—But Cæsar fails
To add one song To the nightingale's!
WILLIAM KEAN SEYMOUR, *Cæsar Remembers.*

5
The nightingale, if she should sing by day,
When every goose is cackling, would be thought
No better a musician than the wren.
How many things by season season'd are
To their right praise and true perfection!
SHAKESPEARE, *The Merchant of Venice.* Act v, sc. 1, l. 104.

It was the nightingale, and not the lark,
That pierced the fearful hollow of thine ear;
Nightly she sings on yond pomegranate tree.
SHAKESPEARE, *Romeo and Juliet.* Act iii, sc. 5, l. 2.

6
O Nightingale,
Cease from thy enamoured tale.
SHELLEY, *Magico Prodigioso.* Sc. 3, l. 73.

One nightingale in an interfluous wood
Satiate the hungry dark with melody.
SHELLEY, *Woodman and the Nightingale.* St. 2.

7
The nightingale as soon as April bringeth
Unto her rested sense a perfect waking,
While late bare earth, proud of new clothing, springeth,
Sings out her woes, a thorn her song-book making.
And mournfully bewailing,
Her throat in tunes expresseth
What grief her breast oppresseth.
SIR PHILIP SIDNEY, *O Philomela Fair.*

8
Where beneath the ivy shade,
In the dew-besprinkled glade,
Many a love-lorn nightingale,
Warbles sweet her plaintive tale.
SOPHOCLES, *Œdipus Coloneus,* l. 17. (Francklin, tr.)

The music of the moon
Sleeps in the plain eggs of the nightingale.
TENNYSON, *Aylmer's Field,* l. 102.

9
Lend me your song, ye Nightingales! O, pour
The mazy-running soul of melody
Into my varied verse.
THOMSON, *The Seasons: Spring,* l. 574.

The sober-suited songstress.
THOMSON, *The Seasons: Summer,* l. 746.

10
Last night the nightingale woke me,
Last night, when all was still.
It sang in the golden moonlight,
From out the woodland hill.
CHRISTIAN WINTHER, *Sehnsucht.* As translated by Théophile Marzials, for his song, *Last Night.*

11
My two passions, lilacs and nightingales, are in full bloom.
WALPOLE, *Letters: To George Montagu,* 5 May, 1761.

12
O nightingale! thou surely art
A creature of a "fiery heart":
These notes of thine—they pierce and pierce;
Tumultuous harmony and fierce!
WORDSWORTH, *O Nightingale!*

NILE, THE

13
The stream of the river Nile can water the earth, and the word of the monk Nilus can delight the mind.
GREGORY OF NAZIANZUS, *On Nilus the Great Hermit.* (*Greek Anthology.* Bk. i, epig. 100.)

14
It flows through old hushed Egypt and its sands,
Like some grave mighty thought threading a dream.
LEIGH HUNT, *Sonnet: The Nile.*

15
Son of the old moon-mountains African!
Chief of the Pyramid and Crocodile!
We call thee fruitful, and that very while
A desert fills our seeing's inward span.
KEATS, *Sonnet: To the Nile.*

O'er Egypt's land of Memory floods are level,
And they are thine, O Nile! and well thou knowest
That soul-sustaining airs and blasts of evil,
And fruits and poisons spring where'er thou flowest.
SHELLEY, *Sonnet: To the Nile.*

16
The Nile, forever new and old,
Among the living and the dead,
Its mighty, mystic stream has rolled.
LONGFELLOW, *The Golden Legend.* Pt. i.

17
It is said that dogs run when they drink in the river Nile, lest they should be seized by crocodiles.

(Canes currentes bibere in Nilo flumine,
A crocodilis ne rapiantur, traditum est.)

PHÆDRUS, *Fables*. Bk. i, fab. 25, l. 4.

Like a dog by the Nile. (Ut canis e Nilo.)

UNKNOWN. A Latin proverb, meaning restless and ill at ease.

1
E'en as the o'erflowing Nile presageth famine.

SHAKESPEARE, *Antony and Cleopatra*. Act i, sc. 2, l. 50.

The higher Nilus swells,
The more it promises: as it ebbs, the seedsman
Upon the slime and ooze scatters his grain,
And shortly comes to harvest.

SHAKESPEARE, *Antony and Cleopatra*. Act ii, sc. 7, l. 23.

2
Where's my serpent of old Nile?

SHAKESPEARE, *Antony and Cleopatra*. Act i, sc. 5, l. 25.

3
Mysterious Flood,—that through the silent sands
Hast wandered, century on century,
Watering the length of great Egyptian lands,
Which were not, but for thee.

BAYARD TAYLOR, *To the Nile*.

4
For what cause, Father Nile, or in what lands hast thou hid thy head? Because of thee thy Egypt never sues for showers, nor does the parched blade bow to Jove, the rain-giver.

TIBULLUS, *Elegies*. Bk. i, eleg. 7, l. 23.

5
It would be easier to discover the sources of the Nile. (Facilius sit Nili caput invenire.)

UNKNOWN. A Latin proverb.

NOBILITY

See also Virtue and Nobility
For Nobility of Birth, see Ancestry, Titles

6
A noble soul is like a ship at sea,
That sleeps at anchor when the ocean's calm;
But when she rages, and the wind blows high,
He cuts his way with skill and majesty.

BEAUMONT AND FLETCHER, *The Honest Man's Fortune*. Act iv, sc. 1.

7
The true standard of quality is seated in the mind; those who think nobly are noble.

ISAAC BICKERSTAFFE, *The Maid of the Mill*. Act ii, sc. 1.

The nobleman is he whose noble mind
Is filled with inborn worth, unborrowed from his kind.

DRYDEN, *Wife of Bath's Tale*, l. 384.

See also under THOUGHT.

8
Very rich he is in virtues, very noble—noble, certes;
And I shall not blush in knowing that men call him lowly born.

E. B. BROWNING, *Lady Geraldine's Courtship*. Conclusion.

9
And yet thou art the nobler of us two:
What dare I dream of, that thou canst not do?

ROBERT BROWNING, *Any Wife to Any Husband*, l. 148.

10
He is noble who has a priority among freemen, not he who has a sort of wild liberty among slaves.

EDMUND BURKE, *Letter to the King of Poland*, 1792.

11
Here all were noble, save Nobility.

BYRON, *Childe Harold*. Canto i, st. 85.

12
Unto the noble everything is good.

EURIPIDES, *Danæ: Fragment*.

I take but small account of noble birth;
For me the virtuous is the noble man;
The vicious, though his father ranked above
Great Zeus himself, I still would base-born call.

EURIPIDES, *Dictys*. Frag. 10.

13
There are epidemics of nobleness as well as epidemics of disease.

FROUDE, *Short Studies on Great Subjects: Calvinism*.

14
A noble soul alone can noble souls attract.
(Ein edler Mensch zieht edle Menschen an.)

GOETHE, *Torquato Tasso*. Act i, sc. 1, l. 59.

15
Noble blood is an accident of fortune; noble actions characterize the great. (Il sangue nobile è un accidente della fortuna; le azioni nobili caratterizzano il grande.)

GOLDONI, *Pamela*. Act i, sc. 6.

16
There is a natural aristocracy among men. The grounds of this are virtue and talents.

THOMAS JEFFERSON, *Writings*. Vol. xiii, p. 396.

17
Do you deserve to be regarded a blameless person, stalwart for the right in word and in deed? In that case I acknowledge you as a nobleman. (Sanctus haberi, Justitiæque tenax, factis dictisque mereris? Agnosco procerem.)

JUVENAL, *Satires*. Sat. viii, l. 24.

Fond man! though all the heroes of your line
Bedeck your halls, and round your galleries shine
In proud display; yet take this truth from me—
Virtue alone is true nobility! (Nobilitas sola est atque unica virtus.)

JUVENAL, *Satires*. Sat. viii, l. 20. (Gifford, tr.)

'Tis virtue, and not birth, that makes us noble;

BEAUMONT AND FLETCHER, *The Prophetess*. Act ii, sc. 3.

What tho' no grants of royal donors,

With pompous titles grace our blood;
We'll shine in more substantial honours,
And to be noble we'll be good.
UNKNOWN. *Winifreda.* (PERCY, *Reliques.*)

Howe'er it be, it seems to me,
'Tis only noble to be good.
TENNYSON, *Lady Clara Vere de Vere.* St. 7.

1
Be noble in every thought
And in every deed!
LONGFELLOW, *The Golden Legend.* Pt. ii.

Noble by birth, yet nobler by great deeds.
LONGFELLOW, *Tales of a Wayside Inn: Emma and Eginhard,* l. 82.

2
Be noble! and the nobleness that lies
In other men, sleeping, but never dead,
Will rise in majesty to meet thine own.
J. R. LOWELL, *Sonnets.* No. iv.

3
Whoso by nature 's formed for noble deeds,
E'en though his skin be dark, is nobly born.
MENANDER, *Fabulæ Incertæ.* Fragment iv, 11. Ascribed also to Epicharmus, *Fabulæ Incertæ,* cxviii, 14.

4
He is noble that hath noble conditions.
JOHN RAY, *English Proverbs.*

The more noble, the more humble.
JOHN RAY, *English Proverbs.*

5
Common natures pay with what they do, noble ones with what they are. (Gemeine Naturen Zahlen mit dem, was sie thun, edle mit dem, was sie sind.)
SCHILLER, *Unterschied der Stände.*

6
Men do not care how nobly they live, but only how long, although it is within the reach of every man to live nobly, but within no man's power to live long.
SENECA, *Epistulæ ad Lucilium.* Epis. xxii, 17.

7
His nature is too noble for the world.
SHAKESPEARE, *Coriolanus.* Act iii, sc. 1, l. 255.

Thou art the ruins of the noblest man
That ever lived in the tide of times.
SHAKESPEARE, *Julius Cæsar.* Act iii, sc. 1, l. 256.

This was the noblest Roman of them all.
SHAKESPEARE, *Julius Cæsar.* Act v, sc. 5, l. 68.

Methought thy very gait did prophesy
A royal nobleness.
SHAKESPEARE, *King Lear.* Act v, sc. 3, l. 175.

Nothing she does, or seems,
But smacks of something greater than herself,
Too noble for this place.
SHAKESPEARE, *Winter's Tale.* Act iv, sc. 4, l. 157.

8
True nobility is exempt from fear .
SHAKESPEARE, *II Henry VI.* Act iv, sc. 1, l. 129.

9
Better not to be at all Than not be noble.
TENNYSON, *The Princess.* Pt. ii, l. 79.

10
Whoe'er amid the sons
Of reason, valour, liberty, and virtue,
Displays distinguished merit, is a noble
Of Nature's own creating.
JAMES THOMSON, *Coriolanus.* Act iii, sc. 3. Hence, "Nature's nobleman."

11
There is
One great society alone on earth:
The noble Living and the noble Dead.
WORDSWORTH, *The Prelude.* Bk. xi, l. 393.

NONSENSE

12
For daring nonsense seldom fails to hit,
Like scattered shot, and pass with some for wit.
SAMUEL BUTLER, *On Modern Critics.*

For blocks are better cleft with wedges,
Than tools of sharp or subtle edges,
And dullest nonsense has been found
By some to be the most profound.
BUTLER, *Pindaric Ode.* Pt. iv, l. 82.

I suppose his nonsense suits their nonsense.
CHARLES II, referring to a foolish preacher, very popular in his parish. (WALPOLE, *Letters,* 22 Oct., 1774.)

13
Such nonsense is often heard in the schools, but one does not have to believe everything one hears. (Multa istius modi dicuntur in scholis, sed credere omnia vide ne non sit necesse.)
CICERO, *De Divinatione.* Bk. ii, ch. 13, sec. 31.

14
A doosed fine gal—well educated too—with no biggodd nonsense about her.
DICKENS, *Little Dorrit.* Bk. i, ch. 33.

15
The ropy drivel of rheumatic brains.
WILLIAM GIFFORD, *The Baviad.*

16
No one is exempt from talking nonsense; the misfortune is to do it solemnly. (Personne n'est exempt de dire des fadaises; le malheur est de les dire curieusement.)
MONTAIGNE, *Essays.* Bk. iii, ch. 1.

17
It is pleasant at times to play the madman. (Aliquando et insanire jucundum est.)
SENECA, *De Tranquillitate Animi.* Sec. 17.

18
And such a deal of skimble-skamble stuff.
SHAKESPEARE, *I Henry IV.* Act iii, sc. 1, l. 154.

19
Transcendental moonshine.
JOHN STERLING. (*Life,* p. 84.) Referring to Coleridge. Said to have been applied to Emerson by Carlyle.

20
A careless song, with a little nonsense in it now and then, does not misbecome a monarch.
WALPOLE, *Letter to Sir Horace Mann,* 1774.

A little madness in the Spring
Is wholesome even for the King.
EMILY DICKINSON, *Poems* Pt. v, No. 38.

A little nonsense now and then
Is relished by the wisest men.
UNKNOWN. Old nursery rhyme.

II—Nonsense. A Few Classic Examples

1
The conductor when he receives a fare,
Must punch in the presence of the passenjare;
A blue trip slip for an 8-cent fare,
A buff trip slip for a 6-cent fare,
A pink trip slip for a 3-cent fare,
All in the presence of the passenjare.
Punch, boys, punch, punch with care,
All in the presence of the passenjare.
ISAAC H. BROMLEY. Originally published in the New York *Tribune*, 27 Sept., 1875. Erroneously attributed to Mark Twain, because of his article, *A Literary Nightmare*, in *The Atlantic Monthly*, for February, 1876 (p. 167), in which he describes the sufferings inflicted upon him by this jingle, which, as he states, he "came across in a newspaper, a little while ago," and which he quotes inexactly. The lines were based upon an actual sign seen by Bromley in a street-car.

2
The piper he piped on the hill-top high
(*Butter and eggs and a pound of cheese*),
Till the cow said, "I die," and the goose said, "Why?"
And the dog said nothing, but searched for fleas.
C. S. CALVERLEY, *Ballad of the Period*.

3
Forever! What abysms of woe
The word reveals, what frenzy, what
Despair! For ever (printed so)
Did not . . .
Forever! 'Tis a single word!
And yet our fathers deem'd it two:
Nor am I confident they err'd;
Are you?
C. S. CALVERLEY, *Forever*.

4
If down his throat a man should choose,
In fun, to jump or slide,
He'd scrape his shoes against his teeth,
Nor dirt his own inside.
Or if his teeth were lost and gone,
And not a stump to scrape upon,
He'd see at once how very pat
His tongue lay there, by way of mat,
And he would wipe his feet on *that!*
EDMUND CANNON, *Impromptu*.

5
Aldeborontiphoscophornio!
Where left you Chrononhotonthologos?
HENRY CAREY, *Chrononhotonthologos*. Act i, sc. 1.

His cogitative faculties immersed
In cogibundity of cogitation.
HENRY CAREY, *Chrononhotonthologos*, i, 1.

To thee, and gentle Rigdom Funnidos,
Our gratulations flow in streams unbounded.
HENRY CAREY, *Chrononhotonthologos*, i, 3.

6
"Will you walk a little faster?" said a whiting to a snail,
"There's a porpoise close behind us, and he's treading on my tail!"
LEWIS CARROLL, *The Mock Turtle's Song*. (*Alice in Wonderland*. Ch. 10.)

They told me you had been to her,
And mentioned me to him:
She gave me a good character,
But said I could not swim.
LEWIS CARROLL, *Alice in Wonderland*. Ch. 12.

7
But oh, beamish nephew, beware of the day,
If your Snark be a Boojum! For then
You will softly and suddenly vanish away,
And never be met with again!
LEWIS CARROLL, *The Hunting of the Snark: The Baker's Tale*.

8
'Twas brillig, and the slithy toves
Did gyre and gimble in the wabe;
All mimsy were the borogoves,
And the mome raths outgrabe.
LEWIS CARROLL, *Jabberwocky*. (*Through the Looking-Glass*. Ch. 1.)

"And hast thou slain the Jabberwock?
Come to my arms, my beamish boy!
O frabjous day! Callooh! Callay!"
He chortled in his joy.
LEWIS CARROLL, *Jabberwocky*.

He left it dead, and with its head
He went galumphing back.
LEWIS CARROLL, *Jabberwocky*.

9
He thought he saw an Elephant,
That practised on a fife:
He looked again, and found it was
A letter from his wife.
"At length I realise," he said,
"The bitterness of Life!"
LEWIS CARROLL, *The Gardener's Song*. (*Sylvie and Bruno*.)

10
My recollectest thoughts are those
Which I remember yet;
And bearing on, as you'd suppose,
The things I don't forget.
CHARLES EDWARD CARRYL, *My Recollectest Thoughts*. (*Davy and the Goblin*.)

11
Sally Salter, she was a young teacher who taught,
And her friend, Charley Church, was a preacher who praught,
Though his enemies called him a screecher who scraught.
PHŒBE CARY, *The Lovers*.

12
So she went into the garden to cut a cabbage-leaf to make an apple-pie; and at the same time a great she-bear, coming down the street, pops its head into the shop. What! no soap? So he died, and she very imprudently married

the Barber: and there were present the Picninnies, and the Joblillies, and the Garyulies, and the grand Panjandrum himself, with the little round button at top; and they all fell to playing the game of catch-as-catch-can, till the gun powder ran out at the heels of their boots.

SAMUEL FOOTE, *An Incoherent Story*. Produced by Foote at a lecture by Charles Macklin, the latter having boasted that he could learn anything by rote on once reading it. (*Quarterly Review*, Sept., 1854). Memoirs of Foote do not mention incident. A correspondent of *Notes and Queries* (16 Nov., 1850) asserts that the author was James Quin, the actor, and, that he wrote the nonsense to test Foote's memory. Credited to Foote in Miss Edgeworth's *Harry and Lucy, Concluded* (Vol. ii, p. 155). First use of the word "panjandrum." (*The Great Panjandrum Himself*. 1885)

1
This is the Yak, so neg-li-gee;
His coiffure's like a stack of hay;
He lives so far from Any-where,
I fear the Yak neglects his hair.

OLIVER HERFORD, *The Yak*.

The rhino is a homely beast,
For human eyes he's not a feast,
But you an I will never know
Why Nature chose to make him so.
Farewell, farewell, you old rhinoceras,
I'll stare at something less prepoceros.

OGDEN NASH, *The Rhinoceras*.

2
If the man who turnips cries,
Cry not when his father dies,
'Tis a proof that he had rather
Have a turnip than his father.

SAMUEL JOHNSON, *Burlesque of Lopez de Vega*.

3
How often, oh! how often
They whispered words so soft;
How often, oh! how often,
How often, oh! how oft.

BEN KING, *How Often*. Burlesque of Longfellow's *The Bridge*.

4
On the Coast of Coromandel
Where the early pumpkins blow,
In the middle of the woods
Lived the Yonghy-Bonghy-Bò.
Two old chairs and half a candle,
One old jug without a handle,—
These were all his worldly goods.

EDWARD LEAR, *The Yonghy-Bonghy-Bò*.

5
How pleasant to know Mr. Lear!
Who has written such volumes of stuff!
Some think him ill-tempered and queer,
But a few think him pleasant enough.

EDWARD LEAR, *Lines to a Young Lady*.

6
The Owl and the Pussy-Cat went to sea
In a beautiful pea-green boat.

EDWARD LEAR, *The Owl and the Pussy-Cat*.

They dined on mince, with slices of quince,
Which they ate with a runcible spoon,
And hand in hand, on the edge of the sand,
They danced by the light of the moon.

EDWARD LEAR, *The Owl and the Pussy-Cat*.

7
The Pobble who has no toes
Had once as many as we;
When they said, "Some day you may lose them all,"
He replied, "Fish fiddle-de-dee!"
And his Aunt Jobiska made him drink
Lavender water tinged with pink,
For she said, "The World in general knows
There's nothing so good for a Pobble's toes!"

EDWARD LEAR, *The Pobble Who Has No Toes*.

8
If you lift a guinea-pig up by the tail
His eyes drop out!

F. LOCKER-LAMPSON, *A Garden Lyric*.

9
In a bowl to sea went wise men three,
On a brilliant night in June:
They carried a net, and their hearts were set
On fishing up the moon.

T. L. PEACOCK, *The Wise Men of Gotham*.

10
Flutt'ring spread thy purple Pinions,
Gentle Cupid, o'er my Heart;
I, a Slave in thy Dominions;
Nature must give Way to Art.

POPE, *Song, by a Person of Quality*.

11
A most subtle question, whether a chimera buzzing in space could devour second intentions, and was debated for ten daily sittings in the Council of Constance.

RABELAIS, *Works*. Bk. ii, ch. 7. Rabelais pretends that this nonsense was the title of a book which Pantagruel, on his visit to Paris, noticed in the library of St. Victor.

12
Bombas: So have I heard on Afric's burning shore
A hungry lion give a grievous roar,
The grievous roar echoed along the shore.
King: So have I heard on Afric's burning shore
Another lion give a grievous roar,
And the first lion thought the last a bore!

W. B. RHODES, *Bombastes Furioso*.

13
The preyful princess pierced and prick'd a pretty pleasing pricket.

SHAKESPEARE, *Love's Labour's Lost*, iv, 2, 58.

Peter Piper picked a peck of pickled peppers,
A peck of pickled peppers did Peter Piper pick;
If Peter Piper picked a peck of pickled peppers,
Where's the peck of pickled peppers that Peter Piper picked?

UNKNOWN. *Old nursery rhyme*.

14
But in a sieve I'll thither sail,

And, like a rat without a tail,
I'll do, I'll do, and I'll do.
SHAKESPEARE, *Macbeth*. Act i, sc. 3, l. 9.

They went to sea in a sieve, they did;
In a sieve they went to sea;
In spite of all their friends could say,
On a winter's morn, on a stormy day,
In a sieve they went to sea.
EDWARD LEAR, *The Jumblies*.

Far and few, far and few,
Are the lands where the Jumblies live:
Their heads are green, and their hands are blue;
And they went to sea in a sieve.
EDWARD LEAR, *The Jumblies*.

1
Said Opie Read to E. P. Roe,
"How do you like Gaboriau?"
"I like him very much indeed,"
Said E. P. Roe to Opie Read.
JULIAN STREET and JAMES MONTGOMERY FLAGG, *Read and Roe*.

2
He killed the noble Mudjokivis.
With the skin he made him mittens,
Made them with the fur side inside,
Made them with the skin side outside.
He, to get the warm side inside,
Put the inside skin side outside;
He, to get the cold side outside,
Put the warm side fur side inside.
That's why he put the fur side inside.
Why he put the skin side outside,
Why he turned them inside outside.
GEORGE A. STRONG, *The Song of Milkanwatha*.

From the Squirrel skin Marcosset
Made some mittens for our hero.
Mittens with the fur-side inside,
With the fur-side next his fingers
So's to keep the hand warm inside.
GEORGE A. STRONG, *The Song of Milkanwatha*.

When Bryan O'Lynn had no shirt to put on,
He took him a sheep skin to make him a' one.
"With the skinny side out, and the woolly side in,
'Twill be warm and convanient," said Bryan O'Lynn.
UNKNOWN, *Bryan O'Lynn*.

3
One, whom we see not, is; and one, who is not, we see;
Fiddle, we know, is diddle; and diddle, we take it, is dee.
SWINBURNE, *The Higher Pantheism in a Nutshell*.

4
There were three sailors of Bristol City
Who took a boat and went to sea.
But first with beef and captain's biscuits
And pickled pork they loaded she.

There was gorging Jack and guzzling Jimmy,
And the youngest he was little Billee.
Now when they got as far as the Equator
They'd nothing left but one split pea.
THACKERAY, *Little Billee*.

5
Mr. Finney had a turnip
And it grew behind the barn;
And it grew and it grew,
And that turnip did no harm.
UNKNOWN, *Mr. Finney's Turnip*. Has been attributed to Henry Wadsworth Longfellow, who denied its authorship in a letter to George Anderson, 11 July, 1881.

6
If all the world were paper
And all the sea were ink,
If all the trees were bread and cheese,
How should we do for drink?
UNKNOWN, *Interrogation Cantilena*. (*Wit's Recreations*. 1641)

7
Madam, I'm Adam. (Adam to Eve.)
Able was I ere I saw Elba. (Napoleon loq.)
Name no one man.
Red root put up to order.
Draw pupil's lip upward.
No, it is opposition.
No, it is opposed; art sees trade's opposition.
Examples of Palindromes—sentences which read the same forward or backward.

NOON

8
At the king's gate the subtle noon
Wove filmy yellow nets of sun.
HELEN HUNT JACKSON, *Coronation*.

9
Clearer than the noonday.
Old Testament: Job, xi, 17.

10
Morning rises into noon,
May glides onward into June!
LONGFELLOW, *Maidenhood*.

O sweet, delusive Noon,
Which the morning climbs to find,
O moment sped too soon,
And morning left behind.
HELEN HUNT JACKSON, *Noon*.

11
Another morn Ris'n on mid-noon.
MILTON, *Paradise Lost*. Bk. v, l. 310.

Another morn Risen on mid noon.
WORDSWORTH, *The Prelude*. Bk. vi, l. 197.

12
'Tis Noon;—a calm, unbroken sleep
Is on the blue waves of the deep.
GEORGE D. PRENTICE, *To an Absent Wife*.

13
With twelve great shocks of sound, the shameless noon
Was clash'd and hammer'd from a hundred towers.
TENNYSON, *Godiva*.

14
The noonday quiet holds the hill.
TENNYSON, *Œnone*.

NOSE

1
His snore is louder than his war-cry. (Μεῖζον δὲ ῥέγχοντος ἢ ἀλαλάζοντος.)
MARCUS CATO. (PLUTARCH, *Lives: Marcus Cato*. Ch. ix, sec. 5.)

There, too, full many an Aldermanic nose,
Roll'd its loud diapason after dinner.
R. H. BARHAM, *The Ghost*.

The tuneful serenade of that wakeful nightingale, his nose.
FARQUHAR, *The Beaux' Stratagem*. Act i, sc. 1.

On deck beneath the awning,
I dozing lay and yawning;
It was the grey of dawning,
Ere yet the Sun arose;
And above the funnel's roaring,
And the fitful wind's deploring,
I heard the cabin snoring
With universal nose.
THACKERAY, *The White Squall*.

There ain't no way to find out why a snorer can't hear himself snore.
MARK TWAIN, *Tom Sawyer Abroad*. Ch. 10.

2
Jolly nose! there are fools who say drink hurts the sight,
Such dullards know nothing about it;
'Tis better, with wine, to extinguish the light,
Than live always in darkness without it.
OLIVIER BASSELIN, *Vaux-de-vire*. Quoted by Ainsworth in *Jack Sheppard*. Pt. ii, ch. 5.

Nose, nose, jolly red nose,
And who gave thee this jolly red nose?
Nutmegs and Ginger, Cinnamon and Cloves,
And they gave me this jolly red nose.
THOMAS RAVENSCROFT, *Deuteromelia*, Song No 7. (1609) Quoted by Beaumont and Fletcher, *Knight of the Burning Pestle*. Act i, sc. 4.

3
My father was a freedman who wiped his nose on his sleeve.
BION. (DIOGENES LAERTIUS, *Bion*. Bk. iv, sec. 46.)

Sit down now and pray forsooth that the mucus in your nose may not run! Nay, rather wipe your nose and do not blame God!
EPICTETUS, *Discourses*. Bk. ii, ch. 16, sec. 13.

And you'd improve its shape, God wot,
And look less like a pink pug pup
If you would wipe it down, and not
Up.
EDWIN MEADE ROBINSON, *A Disagreeable Feature*.

4
Any nose May ravage with impunity a rose.
ROBERT BROWNING, *Sordello*. Bk. vi.

5
Her nose and chin they threaten ither.
BURNS, *Sic a Wife as Willie Had*.

6
He would not with a peremptory tone,
Assert the nose upon his face his own.
COWPER, *Conversation*, l. 121.

The nose of nice nobility.
COWPER, *The Task*. Bk. ii, l. 259.

7
To turn up his nose at his father's customers.
GEORGE ELIOT, *Mill on the Floss*. Bk. iii, ch. 5.

8
A fellow had cast him in the nose, that he gave so large money to such a naughty drab.
ERASMUS, *Adagia*. (Udall, tr.)

9
I can make it . . . as plain as the nose on your face.
ERASMUS, *Praise of Folly*, 25. (1516)

This is as plain as a nose in a man's face.
RABELAIS, *Works:* Bk. v, *Prologue*. (1552)

Invisible, As a nose on a man's face.
SHAKESPEARE, *The Two Gentlemen of Verona*. Act ii, sc. 1, l. 142. (1594)

As clear and as manifest as the nose in a man's face.
BURTON, *Anatomy of Melancholy*. Pt. iii, sec. iii, mem. 4, subs. 1. (1621)

10
Ah, who could have foretold that that little retroussé nose would change the laws of an empire?
(Ah, qui jamais auroit pu dire
Que ce petit nez retroussé
Changerait les lois d'un empire?)
CHARLES SIMON FAVART, *Les Trois Sultanes*. Referring to Soleiman's favorite Sultana, Roxelane. In France a retroussé nose is still referred to as a nose à la Roxelane.

Cleopatra's nose: had it been shorter, the whole aspect of the world would have been altered.
PASCAL, *Pensées*. Sec. ii, No. 162.

If Cleopatra's nose had been flat, the face of the world would have been changed.
BRANDER MATTHEWS, *Cleopatra's Nose*. A variant of Pascal's epigram.

11
He that has a great nose thinks everybody is speaking of it.
THOMAS FULLER, *Gnomologia*. No. 2129.

12
Men . . . suffer themselves to be led by the noses like brute beasts.
GOLDING, *Calvin on Deuteronomy*, cxxi. (1583)

13
I shall, to revenge former hurts, Hold their noses to grinstone.
HEYWOOD, *Proverbs*. Pt. i, ch. 5. (1546)

Hold one another's noses to the grindstone hard.
ROBERT BURTON, *Anatomy of Melancholy*. Pt. iii, sec. i, mem. 3. (1621)

Hold his nose to the grindstone, my lord.
MIDDLETON AND ROWLEY, *Spanish Gypsy*. Act iv, sc. 3. (1653)

See also under BUSINESS.

14
Another tumble! That's his precious nose!
THOMAS HOOD, *Ode to My Infant Son*.

1
Bor'd through the nose by this cheat.
JAMES HOWELL, *Forraine Travell*, p. 44.

Paying through the nose.
The origin of this phrase, meaning to pay an excessive price or at an exorbitant rate, is uncertain. It has been suggested that there is some connection with the slang word "rhino" and the Greek rhines, the nostrils. Grimm (*Deutsche Rechts Alterthümer*) states that Odin had a poll-tax in Sweden called a nose tax, because it was a penny per nose. The same legend is told of Ireland.

2
Therefore will I put my hook in thy nose . . . and will turn thee back.
Old Testament: Isaiah xxxvii, 29.

Will as tenderly be led by the nose As asses are.
SHAKESPEARE, *Othello*. Act i, sc. 3, l. 407.

3
She's an angel in a frock,
With a fascinating cock
To her nose.
F. LOCKER-LAMPSON, *My Mistress's Boots*.

And lightly was her slender nose
Tip-tilted like the petal of a flower.
TENNYSON, *Gareth and Lynette*, l. 577.

I like the saucy retroussé,
Admire the Roman, love the Greek;
But hers is none of these—it's a
Beak.
EDWIN MEADE ROBINSON, *A Disagreeable Feature*.

4
Your nose betrays what porridge you love.
THOMAS LODGE, *Rosalynde*, 91. (1590)

5
It is not given to everyone to have a nose, i. e., skill in investigating matters. (Non cuicunque datum est habere nasum.)
MARTIAL, *Epigrams*. Bk. i, ep. 42, l. 18.

Now Bill
Was a regular trump—did not like to turn nose.
R. H. BARHAM, *Patty Morgan*. Meaning to turn informer.

6
So scented the grim feature, and upturn'd
His nostril wide into the murky air.
MILTON, *Paradise Lost*. Bk. x, l. 279.

7
Give me a man with a good allowance of nose. . . . When I want any good head-work done, I always choose a man, if suitable otherwise, with a long nose.
NAPOLEON BONAPARTE. *Sayings*. (*Notes on Noses*, p. 43.)

8
To cut off one's nose to spite one's face.
PUBLILIUS SYRUS, *Sententiæ*. No. 611.

Henry IV understood well that to destroy Paris, was, as he said, to cut off his nose to spite his face.
TALLEMANT DES RÉAUX, *Historiettes*. Vol. i, ch. 1. (c. 1657)

9
It could be no other than his own man that had thrust his nose so far out of joint.
BARNABE RICH, *Apolonius and Silla*, 71. (1581)

The King is well enough pleased with her; which, I fear, will put Madam Castlemaine's nose out of joint.
PEPYS, *Diary*, 31 May, 1662.

10
Her nose, all o'er embellished with rubies, carbuncles, sapphires.
SHAKESPEARE, *The Comedy of Errors*. Act iii, sc. 2, l. 137.

11
'Twixt his finger and his thumb he held
A pouncet-box, which ever and anon
He gave his nose and took 't away again;
Who therewith angry, when it next came
there,
Took it in snuff.
SHAKESPEARE, *I Henry IV*. Act i, sc. 3, l. 37.

You abuse snuff! Perhaps it is the final cause of the human nose.
S. T. COLERIDGE, *Table Talk*, 4 Jan., 1823.

12
His nose was as sharp as a pen.
SHAKESPEARE, *Henry V*. Act ii, sc. 3, l. 17.

His lips blows at his nose, and it is like a coal of fire, sometimes plue and sometimes red.
SHAKESPEARE, *Henry V*. Act iii, sc. 6, l. 109.

13
Thou canst tell why one's nose stands i' the middle on's face? . . . Why, to keep one's eyes of either side.
SHAKESPEARE, *King Lear*. Act i, sc. 5, l. 19.

14
Take my advice and seek no further than the end of your nose. You will always know that there is something beyond that; and in that knowledge you will be hopeful and happy.
BERNARD SHAW, *The Adventures of the Black Girl in Her Search for God*.

15
Right forth on thy nose. (Recta via incede.)
JOHN STANBRIDGE, *Vulgaria*. Sig. C2. (1520)

Follow thy nose, and thou wilt be there presently.
THOMAS HEYWOOD, *Royal King*. Act i.

All that follow their noses are led by their eyes but blind men; and there's not a nose among twenty but can smell him that's stinking.
SHAKESPEARE, *King Lear*. Act ii, sc. 4, l. 68.

16
The text to turn and glose,
Like a Welshman's hose,
Or like a waxen nose.
UNKNOWN. (*Ballads from MSS.*, i, 206. 1533)

To make a nose of wax of; to wrest, manage, turn at pleasure.
COTGRAVE, *Dictionary: Tordre*. (1611)

A nose of wax, To be turned every way.
PHILIP MASSINGER, *Unnatural Combat*. Act v, sc. 2. (1639)

NOTHINGNESS

1
In the rest of Nirvana all sorrows surcease:
Only Buddha can guide to that city of Peace
Whose inhabitants have the eternal release.
ALGER, *Oriental Poetry: A Leader to Repose.*

2
People who wish to make nothing of anything advance nothing and are good for nothing. (Les gens qui ne veulent rien faire de rien n'avancent rien, et ne sont bons à rien.)
BEAUMARCHAIS, *Barbier de Séville.*

3
Nothing hath no savour.
THOMAS BECON, *Prayers*, p. 365. (1559)

Something has some savour, but nothing has no flavour.
SWIFT, *Polite Conversation.* Dial. i.

4
I have heard, indeed, that two negatives make an affirmative; but I never heard before that two nothings ever made anything.
DUKE OF BUCKINGHAM, *Speech*, House of Lords.

5
They that have nothing need fear to lose nothing.
JOHN CLARKE, *Parœmiologia*, 41.

When nothing's in, nothing can come out.
GEORGE COLMAN THE ELDER, *The Man of Business: Epilogue.*

6
As having nothing, and yet possessing all things.
New Testament: II Corinthians, vi, 10.

I've everything, though nothing; nought possess
Yet nought I ever want. (Omnia habeo neque quicquam habeo; nil quom est, nil defit tamen.)
TERENCE, *Eunuchus*, l. 243. (Act ii, sc. 2.)

6a
I hear nothings, I speak nothings, I take interest in nothing, and from nothing to nothing I travel gently down the dull way which leads to becoming nothing.
MADAME DU DEFFAND. (BRADFORD, *Portraits of Women*, p. 139.)

7
There's nothing new or true—and no matter.
EMERSON, *Representative Men: Montaigne.* Quoted as said by "my languid gentleman at Oxford."

There's nothing new, and there's nothing true, and it don't signify.
UNKNOWN. Cornish version. (*Notes and Queries.* Ser. vii, iv, 257.)

Nothing's new, and nothing's true, and nothing matters.
Attributed to LADY MORGAN, Irish novelist.

"What does anything matter!" The farce will go on.
WHISTLER, *Gentle Art of Making Enemies*, p. 31.

8
Where nothing is, nothing can come on't.
FIELDING, *Don Quixote in England.* Bk. i, ch. 3.

To whom nothing is given, of him can nothing be required.
FIELDING, *Joseph Andrews.* Bk. ii, ch. 8.

9
Nothing to do but work,
  Nothing to eat but food,
Nothing to wear but clothes
  To keep one from going nude.

Nothing to breathe but air,
  Quick as a flash 'tis gone;
Nowhere to fall but off,
  Nowhere to stand but on.
BEN KING, *The Pessimist.*

10
It is to be admitted therefore that nothing can be made out of nothing. (Nil igitur fieri de nilo posse fatendum'st.)
LUCRETIUS, *De Rerum Natura.* Bk. i, l. 206.

Nothing therefore returns to nothingness. (Haud igitur redit ad nihilum res ulla.)
LUCRETIUS, *De Rerum Natura.* Bk. i, l. 242.

Nothing proceeds from nothingness, any more than it disappears into nothingness. (Οὐδὲν γὰρ ἐκ τοῦ μηδενὸς ἔρχεται, ὥσπερ μηδεὶς τὸ οὐκ ον ἀπέρχεται.)
MARCUS AURELIUS, *Meditations.* Bk. iv, sec. 4.

Out of nothing nothing can come, and nothing can become nothing. (De nihilo nihilum, in nihilum nil posse reverti.)
PERSIUS, *Satires.* Sat. iii, l. 84.

Nothing can come from nothing. Apt and plain!
Nothing return to nothing. Good again!
PERSIUS, *Satires*, iii, 83. (Gifford, tr.)

Nothing ne hath his being of naught.
CHAUCER, *Boethius.* Bk. v, prose 1. (c. 1374)

Nothing will come of nothing.
SHAKESPEARE, *King Lear*, i, 1, 91. (1605)

Fool: Can you make no use of nothing, nuncle?
Lear: Why, no, boy; nothing can be made out of nothing.
SHAKESPEARE, *King Lear.* Act i, sc. 4, l. 143.

There is nothing falser than the old proverb which . . . is in every one's mouth. (Ex nihilo nihil fit.)
FIELDING, *Essay on Nothing.* Sec. 1. (c. 1750)

11
Nothing for nothing.
JOHN RAY, *English Proverbs.* The French form is, "Rien n'arrive pour rien."

Nothing due for nought.
THOMAS BROWN, *Works*, l. 131. (c. 1700)

Nothing is given for nothing.
OZELL, *Molière*, ii, 129. (1714)

Nothing for nothing.
MARIA EDGEWORTH, *Castle Rackrent*, p. 61. (1800)

A world where nothing is had for nothing.
A. H. CLOUGH, *Bothie of Tober-na-Vuolich.*

12
To say nothing, to do nothing, to know nothing, and to have nothing.
SHAKESPEARE, *All's Well that Ends Well*, ii, 4, 25.

I ain't never done nothin' to nobody;
I ain't never got nothin' from nobody;
And until I get somethin' from somebody, sometime,
I don't intend to do nothin' for nobody, no time
ALEX ROGERS, *Nobody*. (1905)

1
Thou art an O without a figure.
SHAKESPEARE, *King Lear*. Act i, sc. 4, l. 212.

2
Nothing is But what is not.
SHAKESPEARE, *Macbeth*. Act i, sc. 3, l. 141.

Where every something, being blent together
Turns to a wild of nothing.
SHAKESPEARE, *Merchant of Venice*, iii, 2, 183.

3
A life of nothings, nothing worth,
From that first nothing ere his birth
To that last nothing under earth.
TENNYSON, *The Two Voices*, l. 331.

4
Nothing, thou elder brother e'en to shade.
HENRY WILMOT, *Poem on Nothing*.

5
Nothing exists. (Nihil esse.)
ZENO OF ELEA. (SENECA, *Epistulæ ad Lucilium*. Epis. lxxxviii, sec. 44.)

6
From nothing I was born, and soon again I shall be nothing as at first. (Οὐδὲν ἐὼν γενόμην· πάλιν ἔσσομαι, ὡς πάρος, οὐδέν.)
UNKNOWN. (*Greek Anthology*. Bk. vii, epig. 339.)

NOVELTY

7
Always something new (or evil) out of Libya. (Ἀεὶ φέρει τι Λιβύη καινόν ἰον κακόν.)
ARISTOTLE, *H. A.*, viii, 28, 11: *Paræmiogr.*

Always something new out of Africa. (Ex Africa semper aliquid novi.)
PLINY THE ELDER, *Historia Naturalis*. Bk. viii, sec. 6. Translating the Greek proverb. Used also by Erasmus: Africa semper aliquid adfert novi.

Africa is accustomed always to produce new and monstrous things. (Afrique est coûtoumière toujours choses produire nouvelles et monstrueuses.)
RABELAIS, *Works*. Bk. v, ch. 3.

8
What is valuable is not new, and what is new is not valuable.
LORD BROUGHAM, *Essay: The Work of Thomas Young*. (*Edinburgh Review*.)

I have read their platform, . . . but I see nothing in it both new and valuable. "What is valuable is not new, and what is new is not valuable."
DANIEL WEBSTER, *Letter*, Marshfield, Mass., 1 Sept., 1848, criticising the platform of the Free Soil party. *Works*. Vol. iii. *Speech at Marshfield*, 1 Sept., 1848.

9
A rare class! (Rarum genus!)
CICERO, *De Amicitia*. Ch. 21, sec. 79. Cicero is speaking of true friends.

10
"Old things need not be therefore true,"
O brother men, nor yet the new;
Ah! still awhile the old thought retain,
And yet consider it again!
A. H. CLOUGH, *Ah! Yet Consider It Again!*

11
The thing that hath been, it is that which shall be, and that which is done is that which shall be done: and there is no new thing under the sun.
Old Testament: Ecclesiastes, i, 9.

Is there any thing whereof it may be said, See, this is new? it hath already of old time, which was before us.
Old Testament: Ecclesiastes, i, 10.

There is nothing new except what has been forgotten.
Saying attributed to MADEMOISELLE BERTIN, milliner to Marie Antoinette.

There is nothing new except that which has become antiquated.
Motto of the *Revue Rétrospective*.

12
Spick and span new.
JOHN FORD, *The Lover's Melancholy*. Act i, sc. 1; THOMAS MIDDLETON, *The Family of Love*. Act iv, sc. 3; CERVANTES, *Don Quixote*. Pt. ii, ch. 58.

13
Because thou prizest things that are
Curious and unfamiliar.
ROBERT HERRICK, *Oberon's Feast*.

14
The novelty of noon is out of date
By night.
ROBERT HILLYER, *Platitude*.

15
When I was a young man, being anxious to distinguish myself, I was perpetually starting new propositions. But I soon gave this over; for I found that generally what was new was false.
SAMUEL JOHNSON. (BOSWELL, *Life*, 1779.)

16
There's naught so easy, but when it was new
Seemed difficult of credence, and there's naught
So great, so wonderful, when first 'tis seen,
But men will later cease to marvel at it.
LUCRETIUS, *De Rerum Natura*. Bk. ii, l. 1024.

Indeed, what is there that does not appear marvellous when it comes to our knowledge for the first time?
PLINY THE ELDER, *Historia Naturalis*. Bk. vii, sec. 6.

17
Rare things please one; so greater charm belongs to early apples and to winter roses. (Rara juvant; primis sic major gratia pomis, Hibernæ pretium sic meruere rosæ.)
MARTIAL, *Epigrams*. Bk. iv, epig. 29.

Novelty is of all things the best loved. (Est quoque cunctarum novitas carissima rerum.)
OVID, *Epistulæ ex Ponto*. Bk. iii, epis. 4, l. 51.

Human nature is greedy of novelty. (Natura hominum novitatis avida.)
PLINY THE ELDER, *Historia Naturalis*. Bk. xii, sec. 5.

There are three things which the public will always clamour for, sooner or later; namely, Novelty, novelty, novelty.
THOMAS HOOD, *Announcement of Comic Annual*, 1836.

The one thing that the public dislike is novelty.
OSCAR WILDE, *Soul of Man under Socialism*.

1
I will capture your minds with sweet novelty. (Dulcique animos novitate tenebo.)
OVID, *Metamorphoses*. Bk. iv, l. 284.

2
What can happen that is beyond belief? Or what that is new? (Quid incredibile, quid novum evenit?)
SENECA, *Epistulæ ad Lucilium*. Epis. xcix, 22.

3
All, with one consent, praise new-born gawds,
Though they are made and moulded of things past,
And give to dust. that is a little gilt,
More laud than gilt o'er-dusted.
SHAKESPEARE, *Troilus and Cressida*. Act iii, sc. 3, l. 176.

NUDITY

4
Naked came we into the world, and naked shall we depart from it.
ÆSOP, *Fables*. No. 120.

And he said, Naked came I out of my mother's womb, and naked shall I return thither.
Old Testament· Job, i, 21.

Naked was I born, naked I am, I neither win nor lose.
CERVANTES, *Don Quixote*. Pt. i, ch. 25; Pt. ii, ch. 8.

See also under BIRTH.

5
The nakedness of woman is the work of God.
WILLIAM BLAKE, *Proverbs of Hell*.

6
Lives the man that can figure a naked Duke of Windlestraw addressing a naked House of Lords?
CARLYLE, *Sartor Resartus*. Bk. i, ch. 9.

7
Naked as a worm was she.
CHAUCER, *Romaunt of the Rose*. Pt. i, l. 454.

As naked and bare as a shorn sheep.
EDMUND GAYTON, *Festivous Notes on Don Quixote*, 8.

As naked as my nail.
JOHN HEYWOOD, *Play of Wether*, l. 922.

As naked as truth.
UNKNOWN, *Somers Tracts*. Vol. v, p. 491. (1647)

See also under TRUTH.

8
I'm posing for Durien the sculptor, on the next floor. I pose to him for the altogether . . . *l'ensemble*, you know—head, hands, feet—everything.
GEORGE DU MAURIER, *Trilby*, p. 18.

Nothing is so chaste as nudity. Venus herself, as she drops her garments and steps on to the model-throne, leaves behind her on the floor every weapon in her armory by which she can pierce to the grosser passions of man.
GEORGE DU MAURIER, *Trilby*, p. 99.

9
And they were both naked, the man and his wife, and were not ashamed.
Old Testament: Genesis, ii, 25.

Both naked as a needle.
WILLIAM LANGLAND, *Piers Plowman*. Passus xii, l. 162.

In naked beauty more adorned.
MILTON, *Paradise Lost*. Bk. iv, l. 713.

BEAUTY UNADORNED, *see under* BEAUTY.

10
Naked I seek the camp of those who desire nothing. (Nil cupientium Nudus castra peto.)
HORACE, *Odes*. Bk. iii, ode 16, l. 22.

11
Without clothes, but with all her insides. (Sine ornamentis, cum intestinis omnibus.)
PLAUTUS, *Pseudolus*, l. 343. (Act i, sc. 3.)

12
With presented nakedness out-face
The winds and persecutions of the sky.
SHAKESPEARE, *King Lear*. Act ii, sc. 3, l. 11.

Iago: Or to be naked with her friend in bed
An hour or more, not meaning any harm?
Othello: Naked in bed, Iago, and not mean harm!
It is hypocrisy against the devil.
SHAKESPEARE, *Othello*. Act iv, sc. 1, l. 3.

13
We shift and bedeck and bedrape us,
Thou art noble and nude and antique;
Libitina thy mother, Priapus
Thy father, a Tuscan and Greek.
We play with light loves in the portal,
And wince and relent and refrain;
Loves die, and we know thee immortal,
Our Lady of Pain.
SWINBURNE, *Dolores*. St. 7.

NUN, see Monk

O

OAK

1 The girt woak tree that's in the dell!
There's noo tree I do love so well.
WILLIAM BARNES, *The Girt Woak Tree.*

2 Heart of oak. (Corazon de encina.)
CERVANTES, *Don Quixote.* Bk. ii, ch. 70.
See also ENGLAND: HEARTS OF OAK.

3 A song to the oak, the brave old oak,
Who hath ruled in the greenwood long;
Here's health and renown to his broad green crown,
And his fifty arms so strong.
There's fear in his frown when the Sun goes down,
And the fire in the West fades out;
And he showeth his might on a wild midnight,
When the storms through his branches shout.
H. F. CHORLEY, *The Brave Old Oak.*

Then here's to the oak, the brave old oak,
Who stands in his pride alone!
And still flourish he, a hale green tree,
When a hundred years are gone!
H. F. CHORLEY, *The Brave Old Oak.*

4 The oak, when living, monarch of the wood;
The English oak, which, dead, commands the flood.
CHARLES CHURCHILL, *Gotham.* Bk. i, l. 303.

5 The talking oak To the ancient spoke.
But any tree Will talk to me.
MARY CAROLYN DAVIES, *Be Different to Trees.*

6 The monarch oak, the patriarch of the trees,
Shoots rising up, and spreads by slow degrees.
Three centuries he grows, and three he stays
Supreme in state; and in three more decays.
DRYDEN, *Palamon and Arcite.* Bk. iii, l. 1058.

7 Every oak must be an acorn.
EDWARD FITZGERALD, *Polonius,* 6. *See also under* TRIFLES.

8 Oaks may fall when reeds stand the storm.
THOMAS FULLER, *Gnomologia.* No. 3692.

9 Those green-robed senators of mighty woods,
Tall oaks, branch-charmed by the earnest stars,
Dream, and so dream all night without a stir.
KEATS, *Hyperion.* Bk. i, l. 73.

10 The tall Oak, towering to the skies,
The fury of the wind defies,
From age to age, in virtue strong,
Inured to stand, and suffer wrong.
JAMES MONTGOMERY, *The Oak.*

11 An oak whose antique root peeps out.
SHAKESPEARE, *As You Like It.* Act ii, sc. 1, l. 31.

An oak, whose boughs were moss'd with age
And high top bald with dry antiquity.
SHAKESPEARE, *As You Like It.* Act iv, sc. 3, l. 105.

12 To seel her father's eyes up close as oak.
SHAKESPEARE, *Othello.* Act iii, sc. 3, l. 210.

I am as close as oak, an absolute freemason for secrecy.
GEORGE COLMAN THE ELDER, *The Deuce Is in Him.* Act ii.

Mr. Verdant Greene had, for the first time, sported his oak.
CUTHBERT BEDE, *Verdant Greene.* Bk. i, ch. 8. To exclude visitors by closing the outer oaken door of a student's apartment.

13 There grew an ancient Tree upon the green;
A goodly Oak sometime had it been,
With arms full strong and largely displayed,
But of their leaves they were disarrayed;
The body big and mightly pight,
Thoroughly rooted, and of wond'rous height;
Whilom had been the king of the field.
SPENSER, *The Shepheardes Calender: February.*

14 It is but a simple oak
That is cut down at the first stroke.
UNKNOWN, *Paston Letters,* iii, 169. (1477)

OATH

See also Curse, Vow. For Oath in the sense of swearing, see Swearing

15 Oaths are not surety for a man, but the man for the oaths. (Οὐκ ἀνδρὸς ὅρκοι πίστις' ἀλλ' ὅρκων ἀνήρ.)
ÆSCHYLUS, *Fragments.* Frag. 222.

'Tis not the many oaths that make the truth
But the plain single vow that is vow'd true.
SHAKESPEARE, *All's Well that Ends Well.* Act iv, sc. 2, l. 21.

16 Oaths are but words, and words but wind.
BUTLER, *Hudibras.* Pt. ii, canto ii, l. 107.

For breaking of an oath and lying,
Is but a kind of self-denying,
A saint-like virtue; and from hence
Some have broke oaths by Providence.
BUTLER, *Hudibras.* Pt. ii, canto ii, l. 133.

Oaths were not purpos'd, more than law,
To keep the Good and Just in awe,

But to confine the Bad and Sinful,
Like mortal cattle in a pinfold.
BUTLER, *Hudibras*. Pt. ii, canto ii, l. 197.

He that imposes an Oath, makes it,
Not he that for convenience takes it;
Then how can any man be said
To break an oath he never made?
BUTLER, *Hudibras*. Pt. ii, canto ii, l. 377.

1
They fear not to swear anything, they spare not to promise anything. (Nil metuunt jurare, nihil promittere parcunt.)
CATULLUS, *Odes*. Ode lxiv, l. 145.

2
I will take my corporal oath on it.
CERVANTES, *Don Quixote*. Pt. i, ch. 10.

3
You may depend upon it, the more oath-taking, the more lying generally among the people.
S. T. COLERIDGE, *Table Talk*, 25 May, 1830.

4
Let him be Anathema, Maranatha.
New Testament: I Corinthians, xvi, 22. (Maranatha: The Lord cometh.)

5
Oaths terminate, as Paul observes, all strife;
Some men have surely then a peaceful life!
WILLIAM COWPER, *Conversation*, l. 55.

They fix attention, heedless of your pain,
With oaths, like rivets, forc'd into the brain;
And ev'n when sober truth prevails throughout,
They swear it, till affirmance breeds a doubt.
COWPER, *Conversation*, l. 63.

6
Oaths, used as playthings or convenient tools.
WILLIAM COWPER, *Expostulation*, l. 37.

And hast thou sworn on ev'ry slight pretence,
Till perjuries are common as bad pence,
While thousands, careless of the damning sin,
Kiss the book's outside, who ne'er look within?
COWPER, *Expostulation*, l. 384.

7
By earth, by springs, by rivers, and by streams. (Μὰ γῆν, μὰ κρήνας, μὰ ποταμούς, μὰ νάματα.)
DEMOSTHENES, his famous metrical oath. (PLUTARCH, *Lives: Demosthenes*. Sec. 9.)

8
My tongue has sworn it, but my mind is unsworn. ('Η γλῶσσ' ὀμώμοχ', ἡ δὲ φρὴν ἀνώμοτος.)
EURIPIDES, *Hippolytus*, l. 612. Quoted by Cicero (*De Officiis*. Bk. iii, ch. 29, sec. 108), who renders it into the Latin version often quoted: Juravi lingua, mentem injuratam gero.

An oath sworn with the clear understanding in one's mind that it should be performed must be kept.
CICERO, *De Officiis*. Bk. iii, ch. 29, sec. 107.

9
Would have their tale believed for their oaths,
And are like empty vessels under sail.
GEORGE HERBERT, *The Church-Porch*. St. 31.

10
An oath that is not to be made is not to be kept.
GEORGE HERBERT, *Jacula Prudentum*.

An unlawful oath is better broke than kept.
JOHN RAY, *English Proverbs*, 126.

It is great sin to swear unto a sin,
But greater sin to keep a sinful oath.
SHAKESPEARE, *II Henry VI*. Act v, sc. 1, l. 182.

An oath is of no moment, being not took
Before a true and lawful magistrate.
SHAKESPEARE, *III Henry VI*. Act i, sc. 2, l. 22.

Perhaps thou wilt object my holy oath:
To keep that oath were more impiety
Than Jephthah's, when he sacrificed his daughter.
SHAKESPEARE, *III Henry VI*. Act v, sc. 1, l. 89.

11
We mutually pledge to each other our lives, our fortunes, and our sacred honor.
THOMAS JEFFERSON, *Declaration of Independence*.

12
I take the official oath to-day with no mental reservations and with no purpose to construe the Constitution by any hypercritical rules.
LINCOLN, *First Inaugural Address*, 4 March, 1861.

You can have no oath registered in heaven to destroy the Government; while I shall have the most solemn one to "preserve, protect, and defend" it.
LINCOLN, *First Inaugural Address*, 4 March, 1861.

13
Children are to be deceived with comfits and men with oaths.
LYSANDER. (Bacon, *Advancement of Learning*, bk. ii, refers to it as "that other principle of Lysander.")

14
I know that he will rather believe me unsworn than you upon oath. (Injurato scio plus credet mihi quam jurato tibi.)
PLAUTUS, *Amphitruo*, l. 437. (Act i.)

15
You're a woman; you swear boldly. (Mulier es; audacter juras.)
PLAUTUS, *Amphitruo*, l. 836. (Act ii, sc. 2.)

16
I write a woman's oaths in water.
SOPHOCLES, *Fragments*. No. 694.

A woman's oaths are wafers, break with making.
JOHN FLETCHER, *The Chances*. Act ii, sc. 1.

17
He that sweareth to his own hurt and changeth not.
Old Testament: Psalms, xv, 4.

18
Oaths are the fossils of piety.
GEORGE SANTAYANA, *Interpretations of Poetry*, 148.

1
As false as dicers' oaths.
SHAKESPEARE, *Hamlet*. Act iii, sc. 4, l. 45.

For oaths are straws, men's faiths are wafer-cakes.
SHAKESPEARE, *Henry V*. Act ii, sc. 3, l. 52.

The strongest oaths are straw
To the fire i' the blood.
SHAKESPEARE, *The Tempest*. Act iv, sc. 1, l. 54.

2
Thou swear'st thy gods in vain.
SHAKESPEARE, *King Lear*. Act i, sc. 1, l. 162.

3
Having sworn too hard a keeping oath,
Study to break it and not break my troth.
SHAKESPEARE, *Love's Labour's Lost*. Act i, 1, 65.

What fool is not so wise
To break an oath, to win a paradise?
SHAKESPEARE, *Love's Labour's Lost*. Act iv, sc. 3, l. 72. Also *The Passionate Pilgrim*, l. 41.

4
An oath, an oath, I have an oath in heaven:
Shall I lay perjury upon my soul?
No, not for Venice.
SHAKESPEARE, *Merchant of Venice*, iv, 1, 228.

I'll take thy word for faith, not ask thine oath;
Who shuns not to break one will sure crack both.
SHAKESPEARE, *Pericles*. Act i, sc. 2, l. 120.

5
If it be ne'er so false, a true gentleman may swear it in the behalf of his friend.
SHAKESPEARE, *Winter's Tale*. Act v, sc. 2, l. 175.

7
Let my right hand forget her cunning. . . .
Let my tongue cleave to the roof of my mouth.
Old Testament: Psalms, cxxxvii, 5–6.

May my right hand forget her cunning, and my tongue cleave to the roof of my mouth, if I hesitate or waver in the support I give him [Washington].
DANIEL WEBSTER, *Supposed Speech of John Adams*.

When I cease to do that, may my tongue cleave to the roof of my mouth, and my right hand forget its cunning.
JAMES G. BLAINE, *Speech*, in U. S. Senate, 8 March, 1877, referring to his defence of Southern Unionists. (*Cong. Record*, 45th Cong., special session of Senate, p. 21.)

OBEDIENCE

I—Obedience: Apothegms

8
Obedience is the mother of success, the wife of safety. (Πειθαρχία γάρ ἐστι τῆς εὐπραξίας μήτηρ, γυνὴ σωτῆρος.)
ÆSCHYLUS, *Seven Against Thebes*, l. 224.

9
The fear of some divine and supreme powers keeps men in obedience.
BURTON, *Anatomy of Melancholy*. Pt. iii, sc. iv, mem. 1, subs. 2.

By contenting ourselves with obedience we become divine.
EMERSON, *Essays, First Series: Spiritual Laws*.

10
Obedience is the key to every door.
GEORGE MACDONALD, *Marquis of Lossie*. Ch. 53.

We must do the thing we *must*
Before the thing we *may;*
We are unfit for any trust
Till we can and do obey.
GEORGE MACDONALD, *Willie's Question*. Pt. iv.

11
All the good of which humanity is capable is comprised in obedience.
J. S. MILL, *On Liberty*. Ch. 3.

12
Even though a god, I have learnt to obey the times. (Καιρῷ δουλεύειν καὶ θεὸς ὢν ἔμαθον.)
PALLADAS, *On a Statue of Heracles*. (*Greek Anthology*. Bk. ix, epig. 441.)

13
He who takes his orders gladly, escapes the bitterest part of slavery,—doing what one does not want to do. The man who does something under orders is not unhappy; he is unhappy who does something against his will.
SENECA, *Epistulæ ad Lucilium*. Epis. lxi, sec. 3.

Let them obey our orders. (Jussisque nostris pareant.)
SENECA, *Octavia*, l. 459.

14
O calm, dishonourable, vile submission!
SHAKESPEARE, *Romeo and Juliet*, iii, 1, 76.

Obedience,
Bane of all genius, virtue, freedom, truth,
Makes slaves of men, and, of the human frame,
A mechanized automaton.
SHELLEY, *Queen Mab*. Canto iii, l. 177.

15
Give obedience where 'tis truly owed.
SHAKESPEARE, *Macbeth*. Act v, sc. 2, l. 26.

16
One so small
Who knowing nothing knows but to obey.
TENNYSON, *Guinevere*, l. 183.

17
Obedience is the courtesy due to kings.
TENNYSON, *Lancelot and Elaine*, l. 713.

Obedience is the bond of rule.
TENNYSON, *Morte d'Arthur*, l. 145.

18
What the law demands, give of your own free will. (Quod vos vis cogit, id voluntate impetret.)
TERENCE, *Adelphi*, l. 490. (Act iii, sc. 4.)

II—Obedience to God

19
I find the doing of the will of God, leaves me no time for disputing about His plans.
GEORGE MACDONALD, *Marquis of Lossie*. Ch. 72.

20
That thou art happy, owe to God;
That thou continuest such, owe to thyself,
That is, to thy obedience.
MILTON, *Paradise Lost*. Bk. v, l. 520.

1
Wouldst thou approve thy constancy, approve
First thy obedience.
MILTON, *Paradise Lost*. Bk. ix, l. 367.

2
Ascend, I follow thee, safe guide, the path
Thou lead'st me, and to the hand of heav'n submit.
MILTON, *Paradise Lost*. Bk. xi, l. 371.

I'll go where you want me to go, dear Lord,
O'er mountain or plain or sea;
I'll say what you want me to say, dear Lord,
I'll be what you want me to be.
MARY BROWN, *I'll Go Where You Want Me to Go*. The favorite hymn of William Jennings Bryan.

3
Henceforth I learn that to obey is best,
And love with fear the only God.
MILTON, *Paradise Lost*. Bk. xii, l. 561.

III—Obedience and Command

4
The man who commands efficiently must have obeyed others in the past, and the man who obeys dutifully is worthy of being some day a commander. (Qui bene imperat, paruerit aliquando necesse est, et qui modeste paret, videtur, qui aliquando imperet, dignus esse.)
CICERO, *De Legibus*. Bk. iii, ch. 2, sec. 5.

5
Obedience alone gives the right to command.
EMERSON, *Lectures and Sketches: Perpetual Forces*.

6
Who hath not served can not command.
JOHN FLORIO, *First Fruites*, Fo. 28. (1578)

7
I profess . . . so much of the Roman principle as to deem it honorable for the general of yesterday to act as a corporal today, if his services can be useful to his country.
THOMAS JEFFERSON, *Writings*. Vol. xiii, p. 186.

8
How fit he is to sway That can so well obey!
ANDREW MARVELL, *An Horatian Ode Upon Cromwell's Return from Ireland*.

9
Who best
Can suffer, best can do; best reign, who first
Well hath obeyed.
MILTON, *Paradise Regained*. Bk. iii, l. 194.

10
The worthiest and best science that may be, to wit, the knowledge how to obey, and the skill how to command.
MONTAIGNE, *Essays*. Bk. i, ch. 14.

11
There was neither command nor obedience. (Nusquam imperium, nusquam obsequium.)
PLINY THE YOUNGER, *Epistles*. Bk. viii, epis. 14.

12
Obedience is yielded more readily to one who commands gently. (Remissius imperanti melius paretur.)
SENECA, *De Clementia*. Bk. i, sec. 24.

He that most courteously commandeth, to him men most obey.
CHAUCER, *The Tale of Melibeus*. Sec. 77. (Translation of above.)

13
No one can rule except one who can be ruled. (Nemo autem regere potest, nisi qui et regni.)
SENECA, *De Ira*. Bk. iii, sec. 15.

14
Let them obey that know not how to rule.
SHAKESPEARE, *II Henry VI*. Act v, sc. 1, l. 6.

15
No man can ever end with being superior who will not begin with being inferior.
SYDNEY SMITH, *Sketches of Moral Philosophy*. Lecture 9.

16
Learn to obey before you command. (Ἄρχε πρῶτον μαθὼν ἄρχεσθαι.)
SOLON. (DIOGENES LAERTIUS, *Solon*. Bk. i, 60.)

Through obedience learn to command.
PLATO, *Leges*. Sec. 762.

17
The common saying, "He was never good master that never was scholar, nor never good captain that never was soldier."
THOMAS STARKEY, *England in the Reign of Henry VIII*. Pt. i, ch. 1.

18
No man securely commands but he who has learned to obey.
THOMAS À KEMPIS, *De Imitatione Christi*. Pt. i, ch. 20.

19
Taught to submit,
A harder lesson that than to command.
JAMES THOMSON, *Liberty*. Pt. iii, l. 156.

OBLIVION

20
The iniquity of oblivion blindly scattereth her poppy, and deals with the memory of men without distinction to merit of perpetuity. Who can but pity the founder of the pyramids? . . . Oblivion is not to be hired. The greater part must be content to be as though they had not been.
SIR THOMAS BROWNE, *Hydriotaphia*. Ch. 5, secs. 8, 9. *See also under* MONUMENT.

21
Those sacred Powers Tread on oblivion.
WILLIAM BROWNE, *Britannia's Pastorals*. Bk. ii, song 2, l. 435.

22
Without oblivion, there is no remembrance possible. When both oblivion and memory are wise, when the general soul of man is

clear, melodious, true, there may come a modern Iliad as memorial of the Past.
CARLYLE, *Cromwell's Letters and Speeches: Introduction.*

Oblivion is the dark page whereon memory writes her lightbeam characters, and makes them legible; were it all light, nothing could be read there, any more than if it were all darkness.
CARLYLE, *Essays: On History Again.*

1
And o'er the past Oblivion stretch her wing.
HOMER, *Odyssey.* Bk. xxiv, l. 557. (Pope, tr.)

1a
And if I drink oblivion of a day,
So shorten I the stature of my soul.
GEORGE MEREDITH, *Modern Love.* St. 12.

2
Far off from these, a slow and silent stream,
Lethë, the River of Oblivion, rolls
Her wat'ry labyrinth, whereof who drinks
Forthwith his former state and being forgets.
MILTON, *Paradise Lost.* Bk. ii, l. 582.

3
Cancell'd from Heav'n and sacred memory,
Nameless in dark oblivion let them dwell.
MILTON, *Paradise Lost.* Bk. vi, l. 379.

4
Where dust and damned oblivion is the tomb
Of honour'd bones.
SHAKESPEARE, *All's Well that Ends Well.* Act ii, sc. 3, l. 147.

The dust of old oblivion.
SHAKESPEARE, *Henry V.* Act ii, sc. 4, l. 87.

Razure of oblivion.
SHAKESPEARE, *Measure for Measure,* v, 1, 12.

In the swallowing gulf Of . . . dark oblivion.
SHAKESPEARE, *Richard III.* Act iii, sc. 7, l. 129.

5
And blind oblivion swallow'd cities up.
SHAKESPEARE, *Troilus and Cressida,* iii, 2, 194.

A certain Pasha, dead five thousand years,
Once from his harem fled in sudden tears,
And had this sentence on the city's gate
Deeply engraven, "Only God is great." . . .

Lost is that city's glory. Every gust
Lifts, with dead leaves, the unknown Pasha's dust,
And all is ruin, save one wrinkled gate
Whereon is written, "Only God is great."
THOMAS BAILEY ALDRICH, *A Turkish Legend.*

For, to make deserts, God, who rules mankind,
Begins with kings, and ends the work by wind.
VICTOR HUGO, *The Vanished City.*

6
What 's past and what 's to come is strew'd with husks
And formless ruin of oblivion.
SHAKESPEARE, *Troilus and Cressida,* iv, 5, 166.

7
I met a traveller from an antique land
Who said: "Two vast and trunkless legs of stone
Stand in the desert. Near them, on the sand,
Half sunk, a shattered visage lies. . . .
And on the pedestal these words appear:
'My name is Ozymandias, king of kings:
Look on my works, ye Mighty, and despair!'
Nothing beside remains. Round the decay
Of that colossal wreck, boundless and bare
The lone and level sands stretch far away."
SHELLEY, *Ozymandias of Egypt.*

Sole Lord of Lords and very King of Kings,
He sits within the desert, carved in stone;
Inscrutable, colossal, and alone,
And ancienter than memory of things. . . .
Dazed camels pause, and mute Bedouins stare.
This symbol of past power more than man's
Presages doom.
LLOYD MIFFLIN, *Sesostris.*

Where high the tombs of royal Egypt heave,
The vulture shadows with arrested wings
The indecipherable boasts of kings,
Till Arab children hear their mother's cry
And leave in mockery their toy—they leave
The skull of Pharaoh staring at the sky.
GEORGE STERLING, *Three Sonnets on Oblivion.*

8
Out of the world's way, out of the light,
Out of the ages of worldly weather,
Forgotten of all men altogether.
SWINBURNE, *The Triumph of Time.* St. 15. *See also under* FORGETFULNESS.

9
Once in Persia reigned a king
Who upon his signet ring
Graved a maxim true and wise,
Which if held before the eyes
Gave him counsel at a glance
Fit for every change and chance.
Solemn words, and these are they:
"Even this shall pass away."
THEODORE TILTON, *The King's Ring.*

And let its meaning permeate
Whatever comes, This too shall pass away.
ELLA WHEELER WILCOX, *This Too Shall Pass Away.*

10
Our name shall be forgotten in time, and no man shall have our works in remembrance, and our life shall pass away as the trace of a cloud, and shall be dispersed as a mist.
Apocrypha: Wisdom of Solomon, ii, 4.

OBSCURITY

I—Obscurity of Place

11
I give the fight up; let there be an end,
A privacy, an obscure nook for me,
I want to be forgotten even by God.
ROBERT BROWNING, *Paracelsus.* Pt. v.

For the fellow lay safe
As his mates do, the midge and the nit,
—Through minuteness, to wit.
ROBERT BROWNING, *Instans Tyrannus.*

12
As night the life-inclining stars best shows,

So lives obscure the starriest souls disclose.
George Chapman, *Hymns and Epigrams of Homer: The Translator's Epilogue*, l. 74.

1
Thy greatest praise had been to live unknown.
Charles Churchill, *The Rosciad*, l. 602.

2
Some village Hampden, that with dauntless breast
The little tyrant of his fields withstood;
Some mute, inglorious Milton here may rest,
Some Cromwell guiltless of his country's blood.
Thomas Gray, *Elegy Written in a Country Church-yard*, l. 57.

How many a rustic Milton has passed by,
Stifling the speechless longings of his heart,
In unremitting drudgery and care!
How many a vulgar Cato has compelled
His energies, no longer tameless then,
To mould a pin, or fabricate a nail!
Shelley, *Queen Mab*. Pt. v, l. 137.

There are no mute, inglorious Miltons, save in the hallucinations of poets. The one sound test of a Milton is that he function like a Milton.
H. L. Mencken, *Prejudices*. Ser. iii, p. 89.

3
There is many a rich stone laid up in the bowels of the earth, many a fair pearl laid up in the bosom of the sea, that never was seen, nor never shall be.
Joseph Hall, *Contemplations:* Bk. iv, *The Veil of Moses*. (c. 1647)

Like beauteous flowers which vainly waste their scent
Of odours in unhaunted deserts.
Edward Chamberlayne, *Pharonida*. Pt. ii, bk. 4. (1669)

Like roses, that in deserts bloom and die.
Pope, *Rape of the Lock*. Canto iv, l. 158. (1712)

And waste their music on a savage race.
Young, *Love of Fame*. Sat. v, l. 232. (1742)

Full many a gem of purest ray serene
The dark unfathom'd caves of ocean bear:
Full many a flower is born to blush unseen,
And waste its sweetness on the desert air.
Thomas Gray, *Elegy Written in a Country Church-yard*, l. 53. (1751)

"Nor waste their sweetness in the desert air."
Charles Churchill, *Gotham*. Bk. ii, l. 20. (1761) Misquoting Gray.

Unseen by all but Heaven,
Like diamond blazing in the mine.
John Keble, *The Christian Year: Third Sunday after Epiphany*. (1827)

4
Nor has he lived amiss who from birth to death has lived obscurely. (Nec vixit male, qui natus moriensque fefellit.)
Horace, *Epistles*. Bk. i, epis. 17, l. 10.

A secluded journey along the pathway of a life unnoticed. (Secretum iter et fallentis semita vitæ.)
Horace, *Epistles*. Bk. i, epis. 18, l. 103.

5
And through the palpable obscure find out
His uncouth way.
Milton, *Paradise Lost*. Bk. ii, l. 406.

6
Not to know me argues yourselves unknown.
Milton, *Paradise Lost*. Bk. iv, l. 830.

7
He has lived well who has lived obscurely. (Bene qui latuit bene vixit.)
Ovid, *Tristia*. Bk. iii, eleg. 4, l. 25.

To be Anonymous is better than to be Alexander. Cowley said it engagingly, in his little essay on *Obscurity: "Bene qui latuit, bene vixit:* he lives well that has lain well hidden."
Louise Imogen Guiney, *Patrins*.

8
May you live unenvied, and pass many pleasant years unknown to fame. (Vive sine invidia, mollesque inglorius annos Exige.)
Ovid, *Tristia*. Bk. iii, eleg. 4, l. 43.

9
How often the highest talent is wrapped in obscurity. (Ut sæpe summa ingenia in occulto latent.)
Plautus, *Captivi*, l. 165. (Act i, sc. 2.)

A long list of the illustrious obscure.
Shelley, *Adonais: Preface*.

Lives obscurely great.
Henry Newbolt, *Minora Sidera*.

10
How happy is the blameless vestal's lot!
The world forgetting, by the world forgot.
Pope, *Eloisa to Abelard*, l. 207. *See also under* Forgetfulness.

11
Thus let me live, unseen, unknown,
Thus unlamented let me die;
Steal from the world, and not a stone
Tell where I lie.
Pope, *Ode on Solitude*, l. 17.

And if for me no treasure be amass'd,
And if no future age shall hear my name,
I lurk the more secure from fortune's blast.
James Beattie, *The Minstrel*. Bk. ii, l. 131.

12
Obscurity keeps men in peace, and a cottage bestows untroubled age. (Servat placidos obscura quies Præbetque senes casa securos.)
Seneca, *Hippolytus*, l. 1126.

13
Only in the world I fill up a place, which may be better supplied when I have made it empty.
Shakespeare, *As You Like It*. Act i, sc. 2, l. 203.

14
Sweet were the days when I was all unknown.
Tennyson, *Merlin and Vivien*, l. 499.

II—Obscurity of Language

See also Style

1
Obscurity illustrated by a further obscurity.
EDMUND BURKE, *Impeachment of Warren Hastings*, 5 May, 1789.

2
If this young man expresses himself in terms too deep for *me*,
Why, what a very singularly deep young man this deep young man must be!
W. S. GILBERT, *Patience*. Act i.

3
Striving to be brief, I become obscure. (Brevis esse laboro, Obscurus fio.)
HORACE, *Ars Poetica*, l. 25.

4
You banter me by discoursing obscurely. (Ludis me obscura canendo.)
HORACE, *Satires*. Bk. ii, sat. 5, l. 58.

5
Where I am not understood, it shall be concluded that something very useful and profound is couched underneath.
SWIFT, *Tale of a Tub: Preface*.

6
Obscurity is the realm of error. (L'obscurité est le royaume de l'erreur.)
VAUVENARGUES, *Réflexions et Maximes*. No. 5.

7
Wrapping truth in obscurity. (Obscuris vera involvens.)
VERGIL, *Æneid*. Bk. vi, l. 100.

OBSERVATION

See also Research

8
Shakespeare says, we are creatures that look before and after: the more surprising that we do not look round a little, and see what is passing under our very eyes.
CARLYLE, *Sartor Resartus*. Bk. i, ch. 1.

9
The difference between landscape and landscape is small, but there is great difference in the beholders.
EMERSON, *Essays, Second Series: Nature*.

10
Seeing many things, but thou observest not; opening the ears, but he heareth not.
Old Testament: Isaiah, xlii, 20.

11
The wonders of each region view,
From frozen Lapland to Peru.
SOAME JENYNS, *Epistle to Lord Lovelace*. (c. 1747)

Let observation with extensive view,
Survey mankind from China to Peru;
Remark each anxious toil, each eager strife,
And watch the busy scenes of crowded life.
SAMUEL JOHNSON, *Vanity of Human Wishes*, l. 1. (1749)

From Paris to Peru, from Japan as far as to Rome. (De Paris au Pèrou, du Japon jusqu'à Rome.)
BOILEAU, *Satires*. Sat. viii, l. 3.

Let observation with observant view,
Observe mankind from China to Peru.
OLIVER GOLDSMITH, *Parody of Dr. Johnson*.

Let observation with extended observation observe extensively.
TENNYSON, *Parody of Dr. Johnson*. (*Memoirs of Tennyson*, by his son. Vol. ii, p. 73.)

'Tis nothing when a fancied scene's in view
To skip from Covent Garden to Peru.
STEELE, *Prologue to* AMBROSE PHILIPS's *Distressed Mother*.

12
I do love To note and to observe.
BEN JONSON, *Volpone*. Act ii, sc. 1.

13
Observation is the most enduring of the pleasures of life.
GEORGE MEREDITH, *Diana of the Crossways*. Ch. 11.

14
You all are right and all are wrong:
When next you talk of what you view,
Think others see as well as you.
REV. JAMES MERRICK, *The Chameleon*.

15
I have seen the outward appearance of the city, but I have observed the manners of men too little. (Urbis speciem vidi, hominum mores perspexi parum.)
PLAUTUS, *Persa*. Act iv, sc. 3. *See also under* MANNERS.

16
To observations which ourselves we make,
We grow more partial, for th' observer's sake.
POPE, *Moral Essays*. Epis. i, l. 11.

17
Observation, not old age, brings wisdom. (Sensus, non ætas, invenit sapientiam.)
PUBLILIUS SYRUS, *Sententiæ*. No. 638.

18
And in his brain . . . he hath strange places cramm'd
With observation.
SHAKESPEARE, *As You Like It*. Act ii, sc. 7, l. 38.

19
The observ'd of all observers.
SHAKESPEARE, *Hamlet*. Act iii, sc. 1, l. 162.

20
For he is but a bastard to the time
That doth not smack of observation.
SHAKESPEARE, *King John*. Act i, sc. 1, l. 207.

21
Armado: How hast thou purchased this experience?
Moth: By my penny of observation.
SHAKESPEARE, *Love's Labour's Lost*. Act iii, sc. 1, l. 23.

OBSTINACY

See also Opinion: Stubborn Opinion; Resolution

1
Obstinacy in a bad cause is but constancy in a good.
SIR THOMAS BROWNE, *Religio Medici*. Pt. i, 25.

'Tis known by the name of perseverance in a good cause, and of obstinacy in a bad one.
STERNE, *Tristram Shandy*. Vol. i, ch. 17.

2
For fools are stubborn in their way,
As coins are harden'd by th' allay;
And obstinacy's ne'er so stiff
As when 'tis in a wrong belief.
BUTLER, *Hudibras*. Pt. iii, canto ii, l. 481.

3
Where Obstinacy takes his sturdy stand,
To disconcert what Policy has plann'd.
COWPER, *Expostulation*, l. 298.

4
Man is a creature of a wilful head,
And hardly driven is, but eas'ly led.
SAMUEL DANIEL, *Queen's Arcadia*. Act iv, sc. 5.

5
A stiff-necked people.
Old Testament: Exodus, xxxiii, 3.

A stubborn heart shall fare evil at the last.
Apocrypha: Ecclesiasticus, iii, 26. (Cor durum habebit male in novissimo.—*Vulgate*, ii, 27.)

6
Men possessed with an idea cannot be reasoned with.
FROUDE, *Short Studies: Colonies Once More*.

7
The gods that unrelenting breast have steel'd.
And curs'd thee with a mind that cannot yield.
HOMER, *Iliad*. Bk. ix, l. 749. (Pope, tr.)

8
All this is very judicious; you may talk, sir, as you please, but I will still say what I said at first.
SAMUEL JOHNSON, *The Idler*. No. 83. [Bob Sturdy's way of closing a debate.]

9
Nor blows from pitchfork nor from ash
Can make him change his ways.
(Coups de fourches ni d'étrivères,
Ne lui font changer de manières.)
LA FONTAINE, *Fables*. Bk. ii, fab. 18.

Such fire was not by water to be drown'd,
Nor he his nature chang'd by changing ground.
(Nè spegner può, per star ne l'acqua, il fuoco;
Nè può stato mutar, per mutar loco.)
ARIOSTO, *Orlando Furioso* Canto xxviii, st. 89.

I'd rather die than change. (Mallem mori quam mutare.)
Motto of the family of Sir Walter Raleigh.

10
Obstinacy and heat of opinion are the surest proof of stupidity. Is there anything so assured, resolved, disdainful, contemplative, solemn, and serious, as an ass? (L'obstination et ardeur d'opinion est la plus seure preuve de bestise: est il rien certain, resolu, desdaigneux, contemplatif, grave, serieux, comme l'asne?)
MONTAIGNE, *Essays*. Bk. iii, ch. 8.

11
I know the stubborn temper of the man;
He may be broken, but can ne'er be bent.
(Novi ego ingenium viri
Indocile; flecti non potest, frangi potest.)
SENECA, *Thyestes*, l. 199.

'Tis best to give him way; he leads himself.
SHAKESPEARE, *King Lear*. Act ii, sc. 4, l. 301.

As headstrong as an allegory on the banks of the Nile.
SHERIDAN, *The Rivals*. Act iii, sc. 3.

12
He can never be good that is not obstinate.
THOMAS WILSON, *Maxims of Piety*, 126.

Let it be virtuous to be obstinate.
SHAKESPEARE, *Coriolanus*. Act v, sc. 3, l. 26.

OCCASION, see Opportunity

OCCUPATION

See also Business

13
Satiety of all occupation causes satiety of life. (Studiorum omnium satietas vitæ facit satietatem.)
CICERO, *De Senectute*. Ch. xx, sec. 76.

Absence of occupation is not rest.
COWPER, *Retirement*, l. 623.

There is a restlessness in inactivity; we must find occupation for kings.
W. S. LANDOR, *Imaginary Conversations: Diogenes and Plato*.

14
Oh, let us love our occupations,
Bless the squire and his relations,
Live upon our daily rations,
And always know our proper stations.
DICKENS, *The Chimes: Second Quarter*.

15
What I advise is that each contentedly practise the trade he understands. (Quam scit uterque libens censebo exerceat artem.)
HORACE, *Epistles*. Bk. i, epis. 14, l. 44.

16
"Let thine occupations be few," saith the sage, "if thou wouldst lead a tranquil life." ("Ὀλίγα πρῆσσε," φησίν, "εἰ μέλλεις εὐθυμήσειν.")
MARCUS AURELIUS, *Meditations*. Bk. iv, sec 24. Referring to Democritus (STOBÆUS, i, 100) See SENECA, *De Tranquillitate*, sec. 12.

17
Nothing is so certain as that the vices of leisure are dispersed by occupation. (Nihil tam certum est quam otii vicia negotio discuti.)
SENECA, *Epistulæ ad Lucilium*. Epis. lvi, 9

18
Farewell! Othello's occupation's gone!
SHAKESPEARE, *Othello*. Act iii, sc. 3, l. 357.

19
Thus Nero went up and down Greece and

challenged the fiddlers at their trade. Æropus, a Macedonian king, made lanterns; Harcatius, the king of Parthia, was a mole-catcher; and Biantes, the Lydian, filed needles.

JEREMY TAYLOR, *Holy Living*. Ch. i, sec. 1.

OCEAN, see Sea

OCTOBER

1
October turned my maple's leaves to gold;
The most are gone now; here and there one lingers;
Soon these will slip from out the twig's weak hold,
Like coins between a dying miser's fingers.

THOMAS BAILEY ALDRICH, *Maple Leaves*.

2
And suns grow meek, and the meek suns grow brief,
And the year smiles as it draws near its death.

BRYANT, *October: A Sonnet*.

The sweet calm sunshine of October, now
Warms the low spot; upon its grassy mould
The purple oak-leaf falls; the birchen bough
Drops its bright spoil like arrow-heads of gold.

BRYANT, *October, 1866*.

3
There is something in October sets the gypsy blood astir:
We must rise and follow her,
When from every hill of flame
She calls, and calls each vagabond by name.

BLISS CARMAN, *Vagabond Song*.

4
Hail, old October, bright and chill,
First freedman from the summer sun!
Spice high the bowl, and drink your fill!
Thank heaven, at last the summer's done!

THOMAS CONSTABLE, *Old October*.

5
There is no season when such pleasant and sunny spots may be lighted on, and produce so pleasant an effect on the feelings, as now in October.

NATHANIEL HAWTHORNE, *American Note-Books*, 7 Oct., 1841.

6
The skies they were ashen and sober;
The leaves they were crispèd and sere—
The leaves they were withering and sere;
It was night in the lonesome October
Of my most immemorial year.

EDGAR ALLAN POE, *Ulalume*.

7
October's foliage yellows with his cold.

RUSKIN, *The Months*.

8
October in New England,
And I not there to see
The glamour of the goldenrod,
The flame of the maple tree!
October in my own land . . .
I know what glory fills
The mountains of New Hampshire
And Massachusetts hills.

ODELL SHEPARD, *Home Thoughts*.

9
And close at hand, the basket stood
With nuts from brown October's wood.

WHITTIER, *Snow-Bound*.

ODOR, see Perfume

OFFENCE

10
Neither give offence to others, nor take offence from them.

ST. AMBROSE, *Letter to St. Augustine*. (TAYLOR, *Ductor Dubitantium*, i, l. 5.)

11
She hugg'd the offender and forgave the offence.

DRYDEN, *Cymon and Iphigenia*, l. 367.

How shall I lose the sin, yet keep the sense,
And love th' offender, yet detest th' offence?

POPE, *Eloisa to Abelard*, l. 191.

12
The offender never pardons.

GEORGE HERBERT, *Jacula Prudentum*.

13
What dire offence from am'rous causes springs.

POPE, *Rape of the Lock*. Canto i, l. 1.

14
No offence taken where none is meant.

W. G. BENHAM, *Proverbs*, p. 817.

If a man's armpits are unpleasant, art thou angry with him? If he has foul breath? What would be the use? The man has such a mouth, he has such armpits. Some such effluvium was bound to come from such a source.

MARCUS AURELIUS, *Meditations*. Bk. v, sec. 28.

15
A stumbling-stone and rock of offence.

New Testament: Romans, ix, 33; *I Peter*, ii, 8.

16
It is not well to see everything, to hear everything; let many causes of offence pass by us unnoticed. (Non expedit omnia videre omnia audire; multæ nos injuriæ transeant.)

SENECA, *De Ira*. Bk. iii, sec. 11.

17
O, my offence is rank, it smells to heaven.

SHAKESPEARE, *Hamlet* Act iii, sc. 3, l. 36.

The rankest compound of villainous smell that ever offended nostril.

SHAKESPEARE, *The Merry Wives of Windsor*. Act iii, sc. 5, l. 94.

If their "offence be rank," should mine be *rancour?*

THOMAS HOOD, *Ode to Rae Wilson*, l. 271.

18
In such a time as this it is not meet
That every nice offence should bear his comment.

SHAKESPEARE, *Julius Cæsar*. Act iv, sc. 3, l. 8

All's not offence that indiscretion finds
And dotage terms so.

SHAKESPEARE, *King Lear*. Act ii, sc. 4, l. 199.

The very head and front of my offending
Hath this extent, no more.

SHAKESPEARE, *Othello*. Act i, sc. 3, l. 80.

1
Time to me this truth has taught,
('Tis a treasure worth revealing)
More offend from want of thought
Than from any want of feeling.

CHARLES SWAIN, *Want of Thought*.

2
There are offences given and offences not given but taken.

IZAAK WALTON, *The Compleat Angler: Preface*.

OMEN, see Superstition

OPINION

I—Opinion: Definitions

3
Opinion is the genius, and, as it were, the foundation of all temporal happiness.

OWEN FELLTHAM, *Resolves: Of Opinion*.

4
Opinion in good men is but knowledge in the making.

MILTON, *Areopagitica*.

5
It seems to me that the nursing mother of most false opinions, both public and private, is the too high opinion which man has of himself. (Il me semble que la mère nourrice des plus faulses opinions, et publiques et particulières, c'est la trop bonne opinion que l'homme a de soy.)

MONTAIGNE, *Essays*. Bk. ii, ch. 17.

6
Truth is one forever absolute, but opinion is truth filtered through the moods, the blood, the disposition of the spectator.

WENDELL PHILLIPS, *Idols*.

7
Opinion is the mistress of fools.

W. G. BENHAM, *Proverbs*, p. 823.

8
Everything depends on opinion; ambition, luxury, greed, hark back to opinion. It is according to opinion that we suffer. (Omnia ex opinione suspensa sunt; non ambitio tantum ad illam respicit et luxuria et avaritia. Ad opinionem dolemus.)

SENECA, *Epistulæ ad Lucilium*. Epis. 78, sec. 13.

9
Opinion's but a fool, that makes us scan
The outward habit by the inward man.

SHAKESPEARE, *Pericles*. Act ii, sc. 2, l. 56.

10
All creeds and opinions are nothing but the result of chance and temperament.

J. H. SHORTHOUSE, *John Inglesant*.

11
Opinion is ultimately determined by the feelings, and not by the intellect.

HERBERT SPENCER, *Social Statics*. Pt. iii, ch. 30, sec. 8.

12
"There are no diseases, but only persons who are diseased," some doctors say, and I say that there are no opinions, but only opining persons.

MIGUEL DE UNAMUNO, *Essays and Soliloquies*, p. 156.

II—Opinion: Apothegms

13
He that complies against his will,
Is of his own opinion still,
Which he may adhere to, yet disown,
For reasons to himself best known.

BUTLER, *Hudibras*. Pt. iii, canto iii, l. 547. Often misquoted, "A man convinced against his will." *See also under* ARGUMENT.

14
A difference of opinion, though in the merest trifles, alienates little minds.

LORD CHESTERFIELD, *Letters*, 15 Jan., 1753.

The only sin which we never forgive in each other is difference of opinion.

EMERSON, *Society and Solitude: Clubs*.

It were not best that we should all think alike; it is difference of opinion that makes horse-races.

MARK TWAIN, *Pudd'nhead Wilson's Calendar*.

15
His sole opinion, whatsoe'er befall,
Centring at last in having none at all.

COWPER, *Conversation*, l. 133.

16
Opinion says hot and cold, but the reality is atoms and empty space.

DEMOCRITUS. (DIOGENES LAERTIUS, *Pyrrho*. Bk. ix, sec. 72.)

17
"I never offered an opinion till I was sixty," said the old Turk, "and then it was one which had been in our family for a century."

BENJAMIN DISRAELI, *Iskander*. Ch. 8.

18
Every opinion reacts on him who utters it.

EMERSON, *Essays, First Series: Compensation*.

19
If thou art a person that hast good authority with the company, 'twere good to look confidently, yet not scornfully, and then mildly say, "This is my opinion."

THOMAS FULLER, *Introductio ad Prudentiam*. Vol. i, p. 190.

20
Some men plant an opinion they seem to eradicate.

GEORGE HERBERT, *Jacula Prudentum*.

21
It is not often that an opinion is worth expressing, which cannot take care of itself.

O. W. HOLMES, *Medical Essays*, p. 211.

A man's opinions, look you, are generally of much more value than his arguments.

O. W. HOLMES, *The Professor at the Breakfast-Table*. Ch. 5.

22
With effervescing opinions, as with the not

yet forgotten champagne, the quickest way to let them get flat is to let them get exposed to the air.
JUSTICE O. W. HOLMES, *Opinion*, U. S. Supreme Court, 1920.

1
The average man believes a thing first, and then searches for proof to bolster his opinion.
ELBERT HUBBARD, *The Philistine*. Vol. xi, p. 36.

2
Error of opinion may be tolerated where reason is left free to combat it.
THOMAS JEFFERSON, *First Inaugural*, 4 March, 1801.

3
I never had an opinion in politics or religion which I was afraid to own.
THOMAS JEFFERSON, *Writings*. Vol. vii, p. 299.

4
How long halt ye between two opinions?
Old Testament: I Kings, xviii, 21.

5
We find scarcely any persons of good sense save those who agree with us. (Nous ne trouvons guère de gens de bon sens que ceux qui sont de notre avis.)
LA ROCHEFOUCAULD, *Maximes*. No. 347.

"My idea of an agreeable person," said Hugo Bohun, "is a person who agrees with me."
BENJAMIN DISRAELI, *Lothair*. Ch. 41.

"That was excellently observed," say I when I read a passage in another where his opinion agrees with mine. When we differ, then I pronounce him to be mistaken.
SWIFT, *Thoughts on Various Subjects*.

6
New opinions are always suspected, and usually opposed, without any other reason, but because they are not already common.
JOHN LOCKE, *An Essay Concerning Human Understanding: Dedicatory Epistle*.

7
Men are never so good or so bad as their opinions.
JAMES MACKINTOSH, *Ethical Philosophy*.

8
Remember that to change thy mind and to follow him that sets thee right, is to be none the less a free agent.
MARCUS AURELIUS, *Meditations*. Bk. viii, sec. 16.

9
Each man's opinion freely is his own
Concerning anything, or anybody.
MASSINGER, *The Fatal Dowry*. Act ii, sc. 2.

10
Size is a matter of opinion.
GEORGE MEREDITH, *Richard Feverel*. Ch. 34.

11
We can never be sure that the opinion we are endeavouring to stifle is a false opinion; and even if we were sure, stifling it would be an evil still.
JOHN STUART MILL, *On Liberty*. Ch. 2.

12
Men are tormented by their own opinions of things, and not by the things themselves.
MONTAIGNE, *Essays*. Bk. i, ch. 40. Quoted as "an ancient Greek sentence."

13
Even opinion is of force enough to make itself to be espoused at the expense of life.
MONTAIGNE, *Essays*. Bk. i, ch. 40.

14
Some praise at morning what they blame at night,
But always think the last opinion right.
POPE, *Essay on Criticism*. Pt. ii, l. 230.

15
Vain Opinion all doth sway.
THOMAS CAMPION, *Song: Whether Men*.

16
I have bought
Golden opinions from all sorts of people.
SHAKESPEARE, *Macbeth*. Act i, sc. 7, l. 33.

Fish not, with this melancholy bait,
For this fool gudgeon, this opinion.
SHAKESPEARE, *The Merchant of Venice*. Act i, sc. 1, l. 101.

17
A plague of opinion! a man may wear it on both sides, like a leather jerkin.
SHAKESPEARE, *Troilus and Cressida*. Act iii, sc. 3, l. 265.

18
Wind puffs up empty bladders; opinion, fools.
SOCRATES.

19
Following opinion, dark and blind,
That vagrant leader of the mind.
JONATHAN SWIFT, *Ode to Dr. Wm. Sancroft*.

20
You, if you were here, would think otherwise. (Tu, si hic sis, aliter sentias.)
TERENCE, *Andria*. Act ii, sc. 1, l. 10.

21
Inconsistencies of opinion, arising from changes of circumstances, are often justifiable.
DANIEL WEBSTER, *Speech*, in Senate, 25 July, 1846.

III—Opinion: So Many Men So Many Minds

22
For a thousand heads, a thousand tastes. (Quot capitum vivunt, totidem studiorum Milia.)
HORACE, *Satires*. Bk. ii, sat. 1, l. 27.

Count all the folks in the world, you'll find
A separate fancy for each separate mind.
HORACE, *Satires*, ii, 1, 27. (Conington, tr.)

23
There never were in the world two opinions alike, no more than two hairs or two grains; the most universal quality is diversity.
MONTAIGNE, *Essays*. Bk. i, ch. 37.

24
So many men, so many minds. (Quot homines tot sententiæ.)
TERENCE, *Phormio*, l. 454. (Act ii, sc. 4.)

As many heads, as many wits there been.
CHAUCER, *The Squieres Tale*, l. 195. (c. 1386)

So many men, so many wits.
RICHARD TAVERNER, *Proverbs*. Fo. 13. (1539)

So many heads so many wits.
JOHN HEYWOOD, *Proverbs*. Pt. i, ch. 3. (1546)

As the saying is, So many heads, so many wits.
QUEEN ELIZABETH, *Godly Meditation of the Christian Soul*. (1548)

IV—Opinion: Opinion Rules the World

1
Opinion governs all mankind,
Like the blind's leading of the blind.
BUTLER, *Miscellaneous Thoughts*, l. 267. (1670)

2
We are all of us more or less the slaves of opinion.
WILLIAM HAZLITT, *Political Essays: On Court Influence.*

3
Opinion can do much, and indeed she is that great lady which rules the world.
JAMES HOWELL, *Familiar Letters*. Bk. ii, No. 39.

Opinion is that high and mighty Dame
Which rules the world.
JAMES HOWELL, *Vocal Forest: Introduction.*

4
The good opinion of mankind, like the lever of Archimedes, with the given fulcrum, moves the world.
THOMAS JEFFERSON, *Writings*. Vol. xiv, p. 222.

5
Yet it is but opinion, and that must be the world's master always.
GERVASE MARKHAM, *English House-Wife*, 70. (1615)

6
In politics it is almost a triviality to say that public opinion now rules the world.
JOHN STUART MILL, *On Liberty*. Ch. 3.

7
Opinion is the queen of the world. (L'opinion est la reine du monde.)
PASCAL, *Pensées*. Sec. v, No. 311.

V—Opinion: Stubborn Opinion

8
An illogical opinion only requires rope enough to hang itself.
AUGUSTINE BIRRELL, *Obiter Dicta: The Via Media.*

9
The man who never alters his opinion is like standing water, and breeds reptiles of the mind.
WILLIAM BLAKE, *Proverbs of Hell.*

10
Stiff in opinions, always in the wrong.
DRYDEN, *Absalom and Achitophel*. Pt. i, l. 547.

11
Last of all, men vehemently in love with their own new opinions, though never so absurd, and obstinately bent to maintain them, gave those their opinions also that reverenced name of Conscience, as if they would have it seem unlawful to change or speak against them.
THOMAS HOBBES, *Leviathan*. Pt. i, ch. 7.

12
People who hold such absolute opinions
Should stay at home, in Protestant dominions,
Not travel like male Mrs. Trollopes.
THOMAS HOOD, *Ode to Rae Wilson*, l. 252.

13
Dogmatism is puppyism come to its full growth.
DOUGLAS JERROLD, *Man Made of Money*. (*Wit and Opinions of Jerrold*, p. 28.)

14
Those who never retract their opinions love themselves more than they love truth. (Ceux qui ne se rétractent jamais s'aiment plus que la vérité.)
JOUBERT, *Pensées*. No. 161.

15
The foolish and the dead alone never change their opinion.
J. R. LOWELL, *My Study Windows: Abraham Lincoln.*

16
His own opinion was his law.
SHAKESPEARE, *Henry VIII*. Act iv, sc. 2, l. 37.

17
Loyalty to petrified opinion never yet broke a chain or freed a human soul.
MARK TWAIN. Inscribed beneath his bust in Hall of Fame.

18
The deep slumber of a decided opinion.
UNKNOWN, *Thoughts for the Cloister and the Crowd*, p. 21. (Quoted by Mill, *On Liberty*.)

VI—Opinion: Other People's Opinion

19
We think as we do, mainly because other people think so.
SAMUEL BUTLER THE YOUNGER, *Note-Books*, p. 328.

20
Stay at home in your mind. Don't recite other people's opinions.
EMERSON, *Letters and Social Aims: Social Aims.*

When private men shall act with original views, the lustre will be transferred from the actions of kings to those of gentlemen.
EMERSON, *Essays, First Series: Self-Reliance.*

21
That man is best who considers everything for himself. (Οὗτος μὲν πανάριστος, ὃς αὐτὸς πάντα νοήσῃ φρασσάμενος.)
HESIOD, *Works and Days*, l. 293.

22
For the most part, we inherit our opinions. We are the heirs of habits and mental customs. Our beliefs, like the fashion of our garments, depend on where we were born.
R. G. INGERSOLL, *Why I Am an Agnostic.*

1
I very much suspect that if thinking men would have the courage to think for themselves, and to speak what they think, it would be found they do not differ in . . . opinions as much as is supposed.
THOMAS JEFFERSON, *Writings*. Vol. xiii, p. 349.

2
Opinion! which on crutches walks,
And sounds the words another talks.
DAVID LLOYD, *The Poet*, l. 55.

3
My opinion, my conviction, gains infinitely in strength and success, the moment a second mind has adopted it.
NOVALIS, *Fragment*. (Carlyle, tr.)

4
He adopts the opinion of others like a monk in the Sorbonne. (Il opine du bonnet comme un moine en Sorbonne.)
PASCAL, *Lettres Provinciales*. No. 2.

5
I have never yet given a second-hand opinion of any thing, or book, or person.
GEORGE SAINTSBURY, *Notes on a Cellar-Book*, p. x.

6
It is difficult, if not impossible, for most people to think otherwise than in the fashion of their own period.
BERNARD SHAW, *Saint Joan: Preface*.

VII—Opinion: Public Opinion

See also People: Their Fickleness

7
Public opinion is no more than this,
What people think that other people think.
ALFRED AUSTIN, *Prince Lucifer*. Act vi, sc. 2.

8
Where an opinion is general, it is usually correct.
JANE AUSTEN, *Mansfield Park*. Ch. 11.

That is true which all men say.
JOHN RAY, *English Proverbs*.

9
When the people have no other tyrant, their own public opinion becomes one.
BULWER-LYTTON, *Ernest Maltravers*. Bk. vi, ch. 5.

10
The coquetry of public opinion, which has her caprices, and must have her way.
EDMUND BURKE, *Letter to Thomas Burgh*, Dec., 1779.

11
That bloated vanity called public opinion.
EMERSON, *Miscellanies: War*.

12
Happy those who are convinced so as to be of the general opinions.
LORD HALIFAX, *Works*, p. 227.

Singularity in the right hath ruined many: happy those who are convinced of the general opinion.
BENJAMIN FRANKLIN, *Poor Richard*, 1757.

13
I traversed a dominion
Whose spokesmen spake out strong
Their purpose and opinion
Through pulpit, press, and song. . . .
I saw, in web unbroken,
Its history outwrought
Not as the loud had spoken,
But as the mute had thought.
THOMAS HARDY, *Mute Opinion*.

14
Nothing is more unjust or capricious than public opinion.
WILLIAM HAZLITT, *Characteristics*. No. 84.

Public opinion, a vulgar, impertinent, anonymous tyrant who deliberately makes life unpleasant for anyone who is not content to be the average man.
DEAN W. R. INGE, *Outspoken Essays:* Ser. i, *Our Present Discontents*.

15
The pressure of public opinion is like the pressure of the atmosphere; you can't see it—but, all the same, it is sixteen pounds to the square inch.
J. R. LOWELL, in interview with Julian Hawthorne. (BRANDER MATTHEWS, *New York Times*, 2 April, 1922.)

16
Public opinion has its natural flux and reflux.
MACAULAY, *Essays: Machiavelli*.

17
Popular opinions, on subjects not palpable to sense, are often true, but seldom or never the whole truth.
JOHN STUART MILL, *On Liberty*. Ch. 2.

18
To take by armed conquest is spasmodic and temporary, the conquest of public opinion alone is enduring.
DORA RUSSELL, *Right to Be Happy*, p. 112.

19
I know where there is more wisdom than is found in Napoleon, Voltaire, or all the ministers present and to come—in public opinion. (Je connais quelqu'un qui a plus d'esprit que Napoléon, que Voltaire, que tous les ministres présents et futurs: c'est l'opinion.)
TALLEYRAND, *Speech*, in French Senate, 1821.

OPPORTUNITY

I—Opportunity: Definitions

20
Opportunity is whoredom's bawd.
WILLIAM CAMDEN, *Remains*, p. 329. (1605)

Opportunity is the great bawd.
BENJAMIN FRANKLIN, *Poor Richard*, 1735.

Thou strong seducer, Opportunity.
DRYDEN, *II Conquest of Granada*. Act 4, sc. 3.

21
What is opportunity to the man who can't use it? An unfecundated egg, which the waves of time wash away into nonenity.
GEORGE ELIOT, *Scenes from Clerical Life: Amos Barton*.

1
Occasion is a great matter. Terence says well, "I came in time, which is the chief thing of all." Julius Cæsar understood occasion: Pompey and Hannibal did not.

LUTHER, *Table-Talk*. No. 848.

2
Opportunity is a god. (Τὸν Καιρὸν ἔφης θεόν.)

PALLADAS, quoting Menander. (*Greek Anthology*. Bk. x, epig. 52.)

3
O Opportunity, thy guilt is great!
'Tis thou that execut'st the traitor's treason:
Thou set'st the wolf where he the lamb may get;
Whoever plots the sin, thou point'st the season;
'Tis thou that spurn'st at right, at law, at reason;
And in thy shady cell, where none may spy him,
Sits Sin, to seize the souls that wander by him.

SHAKESPEARE, *The Rape of Lucrece*, l. 876.

The opportunity for doing mischief is found a hundred times a day, and of doing good once in a year. (L'occasion de faire du mal se trouve cent fois par jour, et celle de faire du bien une fois dans l'année.)

VOLTAIRE, *Zadig*.

4
Opportunity is the best captain of all endeavor. (Καιρὸς γάρ, ὅσπερ ἀνδράσιν μέγιστος ἔργου παντός ἐστ' ἐπιστάτης.)

SOPHOCLES, *Electra*, l. 75.

II—Opportunity: Apothegms

5
A man must make his opportunity, as oft as find it.

FRANCIS BACON, *Advancement of Learning: Civil Knowledge*. Sec. 3.

A wise man will make more opportunities than he finds.

BACON, *Essays: Of Ceremonies and Respects*.

6
Opportunity makes a thief.

FRANCIS BACON, *Letter to the Earl of Essex*, 1598. The earliest appearance of this axiom in English literature is in a manuscript of unknown authorship, *Hali Meidenhad* (*Early English Text Society*, 17), dating from about 1220: "Man saith that ease maketh thief."

Opportunity makes a man commit larceny.

JOHN FLORIO, *First Fruites*, Fo. 169. (1591)

7
When one door is shut, another opens. (Donde una puerta se cierra, otra se abre.)

CERVANTES, *Don Quixote*. Bk. i, ch. 21.

8
Small opportunities are often the beginning of great enterprises.

DEMOSTHENES, *In Leptinem*. Sec. 163.

9
Observe the opportunity.

Apocrypha: Ecclesiasticus, iv, 20.

10
No great man ever complains of want of opportunity.

EMERSON, *Journals*. Vol. v, p. 534.

11
Fortune once in the course of our life doth put into our hands the offer of a good turn.

SIR GEOFFREY FENTON, *Bandello*. Vol. ii, p. 148.

12
Man's extremity is God's opportunity.

JOHN FLAVEL, *A Faithful and Ancient Account of Some Late and Wonderful Sea Deliverances*. (c. 1680) Quoted by Lord Belhaven in a speech to the Scottish Parliament, 2 Nov., 1706.

13
Seek not for fresher founts afar,
Just drop your bucket where you are.

SAM WALTER FOSS, *Opportunity*.

Let down your buckets where you are.

BOOKER T. WASHINGTON, *Address*, Atlanta Exposition.

14
Keep thou from the Opportunity, and God will keep thee from the Sin.

BENJAMIN FRANKLIN, *Poor Richard*, 1744.

15
He who seizes the [right] moment is the right man. (Der den Augenblick ergreift Das ist der rechte Mann.)

GOETHE, *Faust*. Pt. i, sc. 4, l. 494.

Are you in earnest? seize this very minute.

GOETHE, *Faust: Prelude at the Theatre*, l. 303. John Anster, tr. *See* p. 2298g:3.

16
Let us snatch our opportunity from the day, my friends. (Rapiamus, amici, Occasionem de die.)

HORACE, *Epodes*. No. xiii, l. 3.

17
We sail, at sunrise, daily, "outward bound."

HELEN HUNT JACKSON, *Outward Bound*.

18
To improve the golden moment of opportunity, and catch the good that is within our reach, is the great art of life.

SAMUEL JOHNSON, *Works*. Vol. vi, p. 214.

19
The career open to talents, that was my principle.

NAPOLEON BONAPARTE. (O'MEARA, *Napoleon in Exile*.) The same principle which he expressed in another phrase, "Every French soldier carries in his knapsack the baton of a marshal of France."

To the very last, he had a kind of idea; that, namely, of *la carrière ouverte aux talents*—the tools to him that can handle them.

JOHN GIBSON LOCKHART, referring to Napoleon. (Article on Sir Walter Scott in *London and Westminster Review*, 1838.) Carlyle, in his essay on Mirabeau (1837), quotes the phrase as from "a New England book."

20
Opportunity has power everywhere; always

let your hook be hanging; where you least expect it, there will swim a fish. (Casus ubique valet; semper tibi pendeat hamus: Quo minime credas gurgite, piscis erit.)

OVID, *Ars Amatoria*. Bk. iii, l. 425.

1
Know your opportunity. (Καιρὸν γνῶθι.)

PITTACUS. (DIOGENES LAERTIUS, *Pittacus*. Bk. i, sec. 79.) Diogenes Laertius says that this apothegm belongs to Pittacus, one of the seven wise men of Greece, who died about 570 B.C. The phrase is said to have been inscribed on the temple of Apollo at Delphi.

Know your opportunity. (Γίγνωσκε καιρόν.)

PITTACUS. (AUSONIUS, *Ludus Septem Sapientum*, l. 203.)

I am come in time. (Veni in tempore.)

TERENCE, *Andria*, l. 758. Ausonius cites this as the equivalent of Pittacus' axiom.

2
Opportunity could not be more opportune. (Opportunitas non potuit opportunius.)

PLAUTUS, *Pseudolus*, l. 669. (Act ii, sc. 1.)

3
A good opportunity is seldom presented, and is easily lost. (Occasio ægre offertur, facile amittitur.)

PUBLILIUS SYRUS, *Sententiæ*. No. 487.

4
There's place and means for every man alive.

SHAKESPEARE, *All's Well that Ends Well*. Act iv, sc. 3, l. 375.

I happen, temporarily, to occupy this White House. I am a living witness that any one of your children may look to come here as my father's child has.

ABRAHAM LINCOLN, *Address*, to Ohio soldiers, 22 Aug., 1864.

5
Nor time nor place Did then adhere.

SHAKESPEARE, *Macbeth*. Act i, sc. 7, l. 51.

Never the time and the place
And the loved one all together.

ROBERT BROWNING, *Never the Time and the Place*

I've got the time, I've got the place, but it's hard to find the girl.

MACDONALD-HENRY. Title and refrain of popular song. (1910)

6
The perfect spy o' the time; The moment on 't.

SHAKESPEARE, *Macbeth*. Act iii, sc. 1, l. 131.

7
Opportunities are seldom labeled.

JOHN A. SHEDD, *Salt From My Attic*, p. 14.

8
An opportunity well taken is the only weapon of advantage.

JOHN UDALL, *To the Earl of Essex*, 15 May, 1588.

9
Turning for them who pass, the common dust
Of servile opportunity to gold.

WORDSWORTH, *Memorials of a Tour on the Continent*. No. 38.

III—Opportunity: Its Knock

10
O, once in each man's life, at least,
  Good luck knocks at his door;
And wit to seize the flitting guest
  Need never hunger more.
But while the loitering idler waits
  Good luck beside his fire,
The bold heart storms at fortune's gates,
  And conquers its desire.

L. J. BATES, *Good Luck*.

As th' pote says, Opporchunity knocks at ivry man's dure wanst. On some men's dures it hammers till it breaks down th' dure an' thin it goes in an' wakes him up if he's asleep, an' iver aftherward it wurruks f'r him as a night-watchman. On other men's dures it knocks an' runs away, an' on th' dures iv some men it knocks an' whin they come out it hits thim over th' head with an axe. But ivrywan has an opporchunity.

FINLEY PETER DUNNE, *Mr. Carnegie's Gift*.

11
Master of human destinies am I!
Fame, love, and fortune on my footsteps wait.
Cities and fields I walk; I penetrate
Deserts and seas remote, and passing by
Hovel and mart and palace, soon or late
I knock unbidden once at every gate!
If sleeping, wake—if feasting, rise before
I turn away. It is the hour of fate,
And they who follow me reach every state
Mortals desire, and conquer every foe
Save death; but those who doubt or hesitate,
Condemned to failure, penury and woe,
Seek me in vain and uselessly implore:
I answer not, and I return no more!

JOHN JAMES INGALLS, *Opportunity*. First published in *Truth*, New York, Feb., 1891.

With rustling wings, she swept from heaven and stood
Beside me where I loitered in the way.
Her brow was calm, and in her outstretched hand
She bore a gift—a virgin bud that blushed
Disparting its green sheath. . . . She spake no word,
But paused a little space and looked at me
With silent scorn; then plumed her shining wings
In sudden flight, nor ever came again.

JAMES B. KENYON, *Opportunity*.

12
They do me wrong who say I come no more
  When once I knock and fail to find you in;
For every day I stand outside your door
  And bid you wake, and rise to fight and win.

Weep not for precious chances passed away!
  Weep not for golden ages on the wane!
Each night I burn the records of the day—
  At sunrise every soul is born again!

WALTER MALONE, *Opportunity*.

The actual fact is that in this day Opportunity not only knocks at your door but is playing an anvil chorus on every man's door, and then lays for the owner around the corner with a club.

ELBERT HUBBARD. (*The Philistine*.)

IV—Opportunity: Its Forelock

1
Let nothing pass that will advantage you; hairy in front, Opportunity is bald behind. (Rem tibi quam nosces aptam dimittere noli; Fronte capillata, post est Occasio calva.)

DIONYSIUS CATO, *Disticha de Moribus*, ii, 26. In Roman mythology, *Occasio* (Occasion, or, in more idiomatic English, Opportunity) was personified as a god or goddess standing on a rotating wheel, the feet fitted with winged sandals, the head hairy in front but bald behind. Time (*Saturnus*) also had a character of Opportunity, as distinguished from Length of Years, and in this character (in Greek *Καιρός* as distinguished from *Κρόνος*) was also represented as hairy in front and bald behind.

2
Who lets slip Fortune, her shall never find;
Occasion, once passed by, is bald behind.

ABRAHAM COWLEY, *Pyramus and Thisbe*. St. 15. (1663)

Occasion . . . being bald can not easily be gotten again if she be once let slip.

WILLIAM PAINTER, *Palace of Pleasure*, i, 266. (1566)

3
Zeal and duty are not slow,
But on occasion's forelock watchful wait.

MILTON, *Paradise Regained*. Bk. iii, l. 172.

4
Opportunity has hair on her forehead, but is bald behind. If you meet her seize her, for once let slip, Jove himself cannot bring her back. (Occasio prima sui parte comosa, posteriore calva. Quam si occupasis, teneas elapsum. Non isse possit Jupiter reprehendere.)

PHÆDRUS, *Fables*. Bk. v, fab. 8.

5
"And who art thou?" "Time who subdueth all things." "Why dost thou stand on tiptoe?" "I am ever running." "Why dost thou have a pair of wings on thy feet?" "I fly with the wind." . . . "Why does thy hair hang over thy face?" "For him who meets me to take me by the forelock." "And why is the back of thy head bald?" "Because none whom I have once raced by, though he sorely wishes it, may take hold of me from behind."

POSIDIPPUS, *On a Statue of Time by Lysippus*. (*Greek Anthology*. Bk. xvi, epig. 275. *The Planudean Appendix*.) Time, here, it should be noted, is in his character of Opportunity, the word used being *Καιρός*.

"Why hast thou hair upon thy brow?"
"To seize me by, when met."
"Why is thy head then bald behind?"
"Because men wish in vain,
When I have run past on wingèd feet
To catch me e'er again."

POSIDIPPUS, *On a Statue of Time by Lysippus*. A metrical version.

6
For occasion hath all her hair on her forehead; when she is past, you may not recall her. She hath no tuft whereby you can lay hold on her, for she is bald on the hinder part of her head, and never returneth again.

RABELAIS, *Works*. Bk. i, ch. 37.

7
Let's take the instant by the forward top.

SHAKESPEARE, *All's Well that Ends Well*. Act v, sc. 3, l. 39. (1602)

We can escape even now,
So we take fleet Occasion by the hair.

SHELLEY, *The Cenci*. Act v, sc. 1, l. 36.

8
Time wears all his locks before,
Take thou hold upon his forehead;
When he flies, he turns no more,
And behind his scalp is naked.
Works adjourned have many stays,
Long demurs breed new delays.

ROBERT SOUTHWELL, *Loss in Delay*.

9
Tell her the joyous Time will not be stayed,
Unless she do him by the forelock take.

EDMUND SPENSER, *Amoretti*. Sonnet lxx. (1595)

Lose not this advantage, but take time by the fore-top.

THOMAS HEYWOOD, *The Captives*. Act iii, sc. 3. (1624)

10
The goddess occasion behind hath not one hair.

UNKNOWN, *Respublica*, iii, 6. (1553)

V—Opportunity: Now or Never

11
There is an hour in each man's life appointed
To make his happiness, if then he seize it.

BEAUMONT AND FLETCHER, *Custom of the Country*. Act ii, sc. 3, l. 85.

12
Strike, now or never!

BEAUMONT AND FLETCHER, *The Wild Goose Chase*. Act iv, sc. 1.

Strike while the iron is hot.

GEORGE FARQUHAR, *The Beaux' Stratagem*. Act iv, sc. 2. *See also under* IRON.

13
If you trap the moment before it's ripe,
The tears of repentance you'll certainly wipe;
But if once you let the ripe moment go,
You can never wipe off the tears of woe.

WILLIAM BLAKE, *Gnomic Verses*. No. 12.

14
This could but have happened once,
And we missed it, lost it forever.

ROBERT BROWNING, *Youth and Art*.

15
Now's the day and now's the hour.

BURNS, *Bannockburn*.

16
Holding occasion by the hand,
Not over nice 'twixt weed and flower,
Waiving what none can understand,
I take mine hour.

JOHN VANCE CHENEY, *This My Life*.

1
Four things come not back:
The spoken word; The sped arrow;
Time past; The neglected opportunity.
OMAR IBN, *Sayings.*

The Gods implore not,
Plead not, solicit not; they only offer
Choice and occasion, which being once passed
Return no more.
LONGFELLOW, *Masque of Pandora: Tower of Prometheus on Mount Caucasus.*

2
When fair occasion calls, 'tis fatal to delay.
LUCAN, *De Bello Civili.* Bk. i, 513. (Rowe, tr.)

3
Pluck with quick hand the fruit that quickly passes. (Quæ fugiunt, celeri carpite poma manu.)
OVID, *Ars Amatoria.* Bk. iii, l. 576.

See also LIFE AND LIVING; TIME: GATHER YE ROSEBUDS.

4
To every man there openeth
A way, and ways, and a way,
And the high soul climbs the high way,
And the low soul gropes the low;
And in between on the misty flats,
The rest drift to and fro;
But to every man there openeth
A high way and a low,
And every man decideth
The way his soul shall go.
JOHN OXENHAM, *A High Way and a Low.*

5
Oh! who art thou so fast proceeding,
Ne'er glancing back thine eyes of flame?
Mark'd but by few, through earth I'm speeding,
And Opportunity's my name.
What form is that which scowls beside thee?
Repentance is the form you see:
Learn then, the fate may yet betide thee:
She seizes them who seize not me.
THOMAS LOVE PEACOCK, *Love and Opportunity.* (*Headlong Hall.*) An imitation of Machiavelli's *Capitolo dell' Occasione.*

6
It is a maxim universally agreed upon in agriculture, that nothing must be done too late; and again, that everything must be done at its proper season; while there is a third precept which reminds us that opportunities lost can never be regained.
PLINY THE ELDER, *Historia Naturalis.* Bk. xviii, sec. 44.

7
You must be not only present in the body, but watchful in mind, if you would avail yourself of the fleeting opportunity. (Non tantum præsentis, sed vigilantis est occasionem observare properantem.)
SENECA, *Epistulæ ad Lucilium.* Epis. xxii, 3.

8
We must take the current when it serves,
Or lose our ventures.
SHAKESPEARE, *Julius Cæsar.* Act iv, sc. 3, l. 223.

Urge them while their souls
Are capable of this ambition,
Lest zeal, now melted by the windy breath
Of soft petitions, pity and remorse,
Cool and congeal again to what it was.
SHAKESPEARE, *King John.* Act ii, sc. 1, l. 475.

The time's enemies may not have this
To grace occasions.
SHAKESPEARE, *King John.* Act iv, sc. 2, l. 61.

9
Hoist up sail while gale doth last
Tide and wind stay no man's pleasure.
ROBERT SOUTHWELL, *St. Peter's Complaint.* (1595)

There is a tide in the affairs of men,
Which, taken at the flood, leads on to fortune.
SHAKESPEARE, *Julius Cæsar.* Act iv, sc. 3, l. 218. (1601)

Truly there is a tide in the affairs of men, but there is no gulf-stream setting for ever in one direction.
J. R. LOWELL, *Among My Books: New England Two Centuries Ago.*

See also TIDE; TIME: ITS FLIGHT.

VI—Opportunity: He That Will Not When He May

10
Lest, if he will not now do so while he may, afterwards, when he at last will, he may not.
UNKNOWN, *Anglo-Saxon Homily.* (c. 950) (SKEAT, *Early English Proverbs,* vi.)

11
He who will not when he may, may not when he will. (Quia qui non vult cum potest, non utique poterit cum volet.)
JOHN OF SALISBURY, *Policraticus.* Bk. viii, century 17. (c. 1150) Referred to as a proverb. St. Augustine (*Opera,* xxxviii) has it in somewhat different form: "Corrigant se, qui tales sunt, dum vivunt, ne postea velint et non possint." Which in turn harks back to *Old Testament: Isaiah,* lv, 6: "Seek ye the Lord while he may be found, call ye upon him while he is near."

He that will not when he may,
He shall not when he will.
ROBERT MANNYNG (ROBERT DE BRUNNE), *Handlyng Synne,* l. 4799. (1303)

He that will not when he may,
When he would he shall have nay.
JOHN HEYWOOD, *Proverbs.* Pt. i, ch. 3. (1546) Quoted twice by Robert Burton, *Anatomy of Melancholy,* ii, ii, 5; iii, ii, 5.

He that will not when he may,
When he desires, shall surely purchase nay.
ROBERT GREENE, *Alphonsus.* Act v, sc. 3. (1590)

12
I have known many who could not when they would, for they had not done it when they could.
RABELAIS, *Works.* Bk. iii, ch. 27.

1
Who seeks, and will not take when once 'tis offer'd,
Shall never find it more.

SHAKESPEARE, *Antony and Cleopatra*. Act ii, sc. 7, l. 89.

2
That we would do,
We should do when we would; for this "would" changes
And hath abatements and delays as many
As there are tongues, are hands, are accidents.

SHAKESPEARE, *Hamlet*. Act iv, sc. 7, l. 119.

OPPRESSION, see Tyranny

OPTIMISM

See also Pessimism

3
The one sits shivering in Fortune's smile,
Taking his joy with bated, doubtful breath.
The other, gnawed by hunger, all the while
Laughs in the face of Death.

T. B. ALDRICH, *Pessimist and Optimist*.

Two men look out through the same bars:
One sees the mud, and one the stars.

FREDERICK LANGBRIDGE [?]. This couplet is credited to Langbridge in *A Cluster of Quiet Thoughts*, published by the Religious Tract Society, but no information concerning him seems to be available. It was once credited to Clarence Hawkes, but he stated that he had merely quoted it. It has also been ascribed to Robert Louis Stevenson. There are several versions.

The optimist is blind and the pessimist bitter.

JEAN COCTEAU, *Le Rappel à l'Ordre*, p. 134.

'Twixt optimist and pessimist
The difference is droll:
The optimist sees the doughnut,
The pessimist, the hole.

MCLANDBURGH WILSON, *Optimist and Pessimist*.

Two knights contended in the list—
An optimist, a pessimist;
But each by mist was blinded so
That neither struck a single blow.

R. T. WOMBAT, *Quatrains*.

There's just as much bunk among the busters as among the boosters.

KEITH PRESTON, *Pot Shots from Pegasus*, p. 145.

4
What good I see humbly I seek to do,
And live obedient to the law, in trust
That what will come, and must come, shall come well.

EDWIN ARNOLD, *Light of Asia*. Bk. vi, l. 273.

5
The barren optimistic sophistries
Of comfortable moles.

MATTHEW ARNOLD, *To a Republican Friend*.

6
The year goes wrong, and tares grow strong,
Hope starves without a crumb;
But God's time is our harvest time,
And that is sure to come.

L. J. BATES, *Our Better Day*.

Some day Love shall claim his own
Some day Right ascend his throne,
Some day hidden Truth be known;
Some day—some sweet day.

L. J. BATES, *Some Sweet Day*.

7
Optimist: A proponent of the doctrine that black is white.

AMBROSE BIERCE, *Devil's Dictionary*, p. 239.

The Utopian is a poet who has gone astray.

DEAN W. R. INGE. (MARCHANT, *Wit and Wisdom of Dean Inge*. No. 123.)

8
My own hope is, a sun will pierce
The thickest cloud that ever stretched;
That, after Last, returns the First,
Though a wide compass round be fetched;
That what began best, can't end worst,
Nor what God blessed once, prove accurst.

ROBERT BROWNING, *Apparent Failure*.

The noble temptation to see too much in everything.

G. K. CHESTERTON, *Robert Browning*. Ch. 1.

9
One who never turned his back but marched breast forward,
Never doubted clouds would break,
Never dreamed, though right were worsted, wrong would triumph,
Held we fall to rise, are baffled to fight better,
Sleep to wake.

ROBERT BROWNING, *Asolando: Epilogue*.

No, at noon-day in the bustle of man's work-time,
Greet the unseen with a cheer!
Bid him forward, breast and back as either should be,
"Strive and thrive!" cry "Speed,—fight on, fare ever
There as here!"

ROBERT BROWNING, *Asolando: Epilogue*.

10
I find earth not grey but rosy,
Heaven not grim but fair of hue.

ROBERT BROWNING, *At the "Mermaid."*

There may be heaven; there must be hell;
Meantime, there is our earth here—well!

ROBERT BROWNING, *Time's Revenges*.

11
I see my way as birds their trackless way.
I shall arrive! what time, what circuit first,
I ask not: but unless God send his hail
Or blinding fire-balls, sleet, or stifling snow,
In some time, his good time, I shall arrive:
He guides me and the bird. In his good time!

ROBERT BROWNING, *Paracelsus*. Pt. i, l. 561.

He who, from zone to zone,
Guides through the boundless sky thy certain flight,
In the long way that I must tread alone,
Will lead my steps aright.

WILLIAM CULLEN BRYANT, *To a Waterfowl*.

Who brought me hither
Will bring me hence; no other guide I seek.
MILTON, *Paradise Regained*. Bk. i, l. 335.

1
God's in his Heaven—
All's right with the world!
ROBERT BROWNING, *Pippa Passes*. Pt. i.

We felt the universe wuz safe, an' God wuz on his throne.
SAM WALTER FOSS, *The Volunteer Organist*.

God reigneth. All is well!
O. W. HOLMES, *Hymn at the Funeral Services of Charles Sumner*.

God is, and all is well!
WHITTIER, *My Birthday*.

2
The optimist proclaims that we live in the best of all possible worlds; and the pessimist fears this is true.
BRANCH CABELL, *The Silver Stallion*, p. 112.

3
There is still sunshine on the wall.
CERVANTES, *Don Quixote*. Pt. ii, ch. 3.

God! I will not be an owl,
But sun me in the Capitol.
EMERSON, *Mithridates*.

4
I wot well clerks will say, as them leste
By arguments, that all is for the best.
CHAUCER, *The Frankeleyns Tale*, l. 158.

All is for the best in the best of possible worlds. (Tout est pour le mieux dans le meilleur des mondes possibles.)
VOLTAIRE, *Candide*. Ch. 1. This ever-recurrent phrase which Voltaire puts into the mouth of Dr. Pangloss, was a jibe at the optimist doctrines of Leibnitz.

Optimism, said Candide, is a mania for declaring when things are going badly that all is well.
VOLTAIRE, *Candide*. Ch. 19.

I hate the Pollyanna pest
Who says that All Is for the Best.
FRANKLIN P. ADAMS, *Thoughts on the Cosmos*.

5
O Light divine! we need no fuller test
That all is ordered well;
We know enough to trust that all is best
Where Love and Wisdom dwell.
C. P. CRANCH, *Oh Love Supreme*.

6
To all upon my way, Day after day,
Let me be joy, be hope. Let my life sing!
MARY CAROLYN DAVIES, *A Prayer*.

7
Whatever is is right. (Ποιότητας δὲ νόμῳ εἶναι.)
DEMOCRITUS. (DIOGENES LAERTIUS, *Democritus*. Bk. ix, sec. 45.)

8
Whatever happens at all, happens as it should. ("Ὅτι πᾶν τὸ συμβαῖνον δικαίως συμβαίνει.)
MARCUS AURELIUS, *Meditations*. Bk. iv, sec. 10.

Whatever is, is in its causes just.
DRYDEN, *Œdipus*. Act iii, sc. 1.

Whatever is, is right. Though purblind man
Sees but a part o' the chain, the nearest link:
His eyes not carrying to the equal beam,
That poises all above.
JOHN DRYDEN.

Everything that is, is reasonable. (Alles was ist, ist vernünftig.)
HEGEL, *Rechtsphilosophie: Preface*, p. 17. The full quotation is, "Was vernünftig ist, das ist wirklich: und was wirklich ist, das ist vernünftig."

And spite of Pride, in erring Reason's spite,
One truth is clear, *Whatever is, is right*.
POPE, *Essay on Man*. Epis. i, l. 293.

I know that the soul is aided
Sometimes by the heart's unrest,
And to grow means often to suffer—
But whatever is—is best.
ELLA WHEELER WILCOX, *Whatever Is, Is Best*.

9
He was fresh, and full of faith that "something would turn up."
BENJAMIN DISRAELI, *Tancred*, iii, 6. (1847)

In short, if anything turns up.
DICKENS, *David Copperfield*. Ch. xi. (1849) Mr. Micawber speaking.

10
Yet spake yon purple mountain,
Yet said yon ancient wood,
That Night or Day, that Love or Crime,
Leads all souls to the Good.
EMERSON, *The Park*.

Over the winter glaciers
I see the summer glow,
And through the wild-piled snowdrift,
The warm rosebuds below.
EMERSON, *The World-Soul*.

11
To look up and not down,
To look forward and not back,
To look out and not in,—
and
To lend a hand.
EDWARD EVERETT HALE, *Ten Times One Is Ten*. Rule of the "Harry Wadsworth Club," and afterwards adopted as motto of the Lend-a-Hand Society, founded by him in 1871.

12
Optimism is a kind of heart stimulant—the digitalis of failure.
ELBERT HUBBARD, *A Thousand and One Epigrams*, p. 80.

13
When I look in the glass I see that every line in my face means pessimism; but in spite of my face—that is my experience—I remain an optimist.
RICHARD JEFFERIES. *The Pageant of Summer*.

14
It is not raining rain to me,
It's raining daffodils;
In every dimpled drop I see
Wild flowers on distant hills.
ROBERT LOVEMAN, *April Rain*. (*Harper's Magazine*, May, 1901.)

A health unto the happy,
  A fig for him who frets!
It is not raining rain to me,
  It's raining violets.
  ROBERT LOVEMAN, *April Rain.*

1
For me Fate gave, whate'er she else denied,
A nature sloping to the southern side;
I thank her for it, though when clouds arise
Such natures double-darken gloomy skies.
  J. R. LOWELL, *An Epistle to George William Curtis: Postscript*, l. 53.

    It is good
To lengthen to the last a sunny mood.
  J. R. LOWELL, *A Legend of Brittany.* Pt. i, st. 6.

Fit for the sunshine, so, it followed him.
A happy-tempered bringer of the best
Out of the worst.
  ROBERT BROWNING, *Soul's Tragedy.* Act i, l. 64.

Since then they call him "Sunny Jim."
  MINNY MAUD HANFF (MRS. RAYMOND F AYERS), *Sunny Jim.* A series of jingles widely popular about 1902, advertising a breakfast food called Force.

2
There's a good time coming, boys!
A good time coming.
  CHARLES MACKAY, *The Good Time Coming.*

There's a gude time coming.
  SCOTT, *Rob Roy.* Ch. 32.

3
A glass is good, and a lass is good,
  And a pipe to smoke in cold weather;
The world is good, and the people are good,
  And we're all good fellows together.
  JOHN O'KEEFFE, *Sprigs of Laurel.* Act ii, sc. 1.

4
We know that all things work together for good to them that love God.
  New Testament: Romans, viii, 28.

4a
Let us gather up the sunbeams
  Lying all around our path;
Let us keep the wheat and roses,
  Casting out the thorns and chaff.
  MAY RILEY SMITH, *If We Knew* St. 6. Later set to music as a hymn, *Let Us Gather Up the Sunbeams.*

5
An optimism which is sadly and fatally at variance with actual results.
  JAN CHRISTIAAN SMUTS, *Letter*, 8 Jan., 1921.

6
Sometimes an hour of Fate's serenest weather
  Strikes through our changeful sky its coming beams;
Somewhere above us, in elusive ether,
  Waits the fulfillment of our dearest dreams.
  BAYARD TAYLOR, *Ad Amicos.*

    There may come a day
Which crowns Desire with gift, and Art with truth,
And Love with bliss, and Life with wiser youth!
  BAYARD TAYLOR, *The Picture of St. John.* Bk. iv, st. 86.

7
Then, like an old-time orator
  Impressively he rose;
"I make the most of all that comes
  And the least of all that goes."
  SARA TEASDALE, *The Philosopher.*

8
Behold, we know not anything;
  I can but trust that good shall fall,
  At last—far off—at last, to all,
And every winter change to spring.
  TENNYSON, *In Memoriam.* Pt. liv.

And all is well, tho' faith and form
  Be sunder'd in the night of fear;
  Well roars the storm to those that hear
A deeper voice across the storm.
  TENNYSON, *In Memoriam.* Pt. cxxvii, st. 1.

9
Heed not the folk who sing or say
  In sonnet sad or sermon chill,
"Alas, alack, and well-a-day!
  This round world's but a bitter pill."
  We too are sad and careful; still
    We'd rather be alive than not.
  GRAHAM R. TOMSON, *Ballade of the Optimist.*

10
What will be will be well, for what is is well.
  WALT WHITMAN, *To Think of Time.*

ORACLE

See also Prophet

11
A Delphic sword. (Δελφικὴ μάχαιρα.)
  ARISTOTLE, *Politica.* Bk. i, ch. 1, sec. 1252B. A two-edged sword, in reference to the ambiguities of the Delphic oracles.

Thou shalt go thou shalt return never in battle shalt thou perish. (Ibis redibis non morieris in bello.)
  An example of Delphic ambiguity, where the meaning depends wholly upon the punctuation, which the oracle did not supply.

12
A shallow brain behind a serious mask,
An oracle within an empty cask.
  COWPER, *Conversation*, l. 297.

13
The Oracles are dumb, No voice or hideous hum
  Runs through the arched roof in words deceiving.
Apollo from his shrine Can no more divine,
  With hollow shriek the steep of Delphos leaving.
No nightly trance, or breathed spell
Inspires the pale-ey'd Priest from the prophetic cell.
  MILTON, *On the Morning of Christ's Nativity*, l. 173.

    Or if Sion hill
Delight thee more, and Siloa's brook that flow'd
Fast by the oracle of God.
  MILTON, *Paradise Lost.* Bk. i, l. 10.

14
    I am Sir Oracle,
And, when I ope my lips, let no dog bark!
  SHAKESPEARE, *The Merchant of Venice*, i, 1, 94

There is no truth at all i' the oracle.
SHAKESPEARE, *Winter's Tale*. Act iii, sc. 2, l. 141.

When the oracle,
Thus by Apollo's great divine seal'd up,
Shall the contents discover.
SHAKESPEARE, *Winter's Tale*. Act iii, sc. 1, l. 18.

Bold as an oracle.
SHAKESPEARE, *Troilus and Cressida*. Act i, sc. 3, l. 192.

1
Thou shalt be my great Apollo. (Eris mihi magnus Apollo.)
VERGIL, *Eclogues*. No. iii, l. 104. Referring to the oracle of the temple of Apollo.

ORANGE

2
We squeeze an orange and throw away the rind.
FREDERICK THE GREAT, to La Mettraie, Sept., 1751, saying that he should want Voltaire only a year longer.

3
Is it where the flow'r of the orange blows?
FELICIA DOROTHEA HEMANS, *The Better Land*.

4
Yes, sing the song of the orange-tree,
With its leaves of velvet green;
With its luscious fruit of sunset hue,
The fairest that ever were seen.
J. K. HOYT, *The Orange-Tree*.

5
Orange bright,
Like golden lamps in a green night.
ANDREW MARVELL, *Bermudas*.

6
If I were yonder orange-tree
And thou the blossom blooming there,
I would not yield a breath of thee
To scent the most imploring air!
THOMAS MOORE, *If I Were Yonder Wave*.

7
Orange-trees
Whose fruit and blossoms in the breeze
Were wantoning together free,
Like age at play with infancy.
THOMAS MOORE, *Lalla Rookh: Paradise and the Peri*.

8
Civil as an orange, and something of that jealous complexion.
SHAKESPEARE, *Much Ado About Nothing*. Act ii, sc. 1, l. 305.

9
And every day when I've been good,
I get an orange after food.
R. L. STEVENSON, *System*.

ORATOR AND ORATORY

See also Eloquence; Speech: Speeches; Tongue

I—Orators

10
Lightnings and thunders from his mouth he hurled,
And made a chaos of the Grecian world.
("Ηστραπτ', ἐβρόντα, ξυνεκύκα τὴν Ἑλλάδα.)
ARISTOPHANES, *Acharnians*, l. 531.

11
Solon compared the people unto the sea, and orators to the winds: for that the sea would be calm and quiet, if the winds did not trouble it.
FRANCIS BACON, *Apothegms*, No. 232.

Solon wished everybody to be ready to take everybody else's part; but surely Chilo was wiser in holding that public affairs go best when the laws have much attention and the orators none.
REV. JOHN BEACON, *Letter to Earl Grey*, 1831.

12
Now your rater and debater
Is baulked by a mere spectator
Who simply stares and listens.
ROBERT BROWNING, *Pacchiarotto*. St. 7.

13
An orator is a man who says what he thinks and feels what he says.
W. J. BRYAN. (HIBBEN, *The Peerless Leader*, p. 118.)

14
For rhetoric, he could not ope
His mouth, but out there flew a trope.
BUTLER, *Hudibras*. Pt. i, canto i, l. 81.

His sober lips then did he softly part,
Whence of pure rhetoric whole streams outflow.
EDWARD FAIRFAX, *Godfrey of Bullogne*.

From whose mouth issu'd forth
Mellifluous streams that water'd all the schools
Of Academics old and new.
MILTON, *Paradise Regained*. Bk. iv, l. 276.

15
None knew, nor how, nor why, but he entwined
Himself perforce around the hearer's mind.
BYRON, *Lara*. Canto i, st. 19.

Proud of his "Hear hims," proud, too, of his vote
And lost virginity of oratory.
BYRON, *Don Juan*. Canto xiii, st. 91.

16
The Orator persuades and carries all with him, he knows not how; the Rhetorician can prove that he ought to have persuaded and carried all with him.
CARLYLE, *Essays: Characteristics*.

17
Little other than a *red-tape* talking-machine and unhappy bag of parliamentary eloquence.
CARLYLE, *Latter-Day Pamphlets*. No. 1.

Nut while the two-legged gab-machine's so plenty.
J. R. LOWELL, *Biglow Papers*. Ser. ii, No. 11.

18
Adepts in the speaking trade
Keep a cough by them ready made.
CHARLES CHURCHILL, *The Ghost*. Bk. ii, l. 545.

If a man should be out and forget his last sentence . . . then his last refuge is to begin with an Utcunque [howsoever].
SAMUEL PEPYS, *Diary*, 23 Jan., 1661.

Very good orators, when they are out, they will spit.

SHAKESPEARE, *As You Like It*. Act iv, sc. 1, l. 75.

1
He mouths a sentence as curs mouth a bone.

CHARLES CHURCHILL, *The Rosciad*, l. 322.

Nay, an thou 'lt mouth,
I'll rant as well as thou.

SHAKESPEARE, *Hamlet*. Act v, sc. 1, l. 306.

2
Let arms give place to the robe, and the laurel wreath [of the soldier] yield to the tongue [of the orator]. (Cedant arma togæ, concedat laurea linguæ.)

CICERO, *De Officiis*. Bk. i, ch. 22, sec. 77. This is the line as usually quoted, but Cicero really wrote *laudi*, not *linguæ*.

The good orator is despised, the rude soldier loved. (Spernitur orator bonus, horridus miles amatur.)

ENNIUS. (AULUS GELLIUS, *Noctes Atticæ*. Bk. xx, ch. 10, sec. 4.)

3
Loud-bawling orators are driven by their weakness to noise, as lame men to take horse.

CICERO. (PLUTARCH, *Roman Apothegms*.)

Fire in each eye, and papers in each hand,
They rave, recite, and madden round the land.

POPE, *Epistle to Dr. Arbuthnot*, l. 5.

4
You'd scarce expect one of my age
To speak in public on the stage;
And if I chance to fall below
Demosthenes or Cicero,
Don't view me with a critic's eye,
But pass my imperfections by.
Large streams from little fountains flow,
Tall oaks from little acorns grow.

DAVID EVERETT, *Lines Written for a School Declamation by a Little Boy of Seven.* (*Columbian Orator*, Boston, 1797.)

5
Men of action intervene only when the orators have finished.

ÉMILE GABORIAU, *Monsieur Lecoq*. Pt. ii, ch. 7.

6
Frequent and soft as falls the winter's snow,
Thus from his lips the copious periods flow.
(Καὶ ἔπεα νιφάδεσσιν ἐοικότα χειμερίῃσιν.)

HOMER, *Iliad*. Bk. iii, l. 222.

7
It makes a vast difference whether a god or a hero speaks. (Intererit multum, divusne loquatur an heros.)

HORACE, *Ars Poetica*, l. 114.

There is no true orator who is not a hero.

EMERSON, *Letters and Social Aims: Eloquence.*

8
Like a rough orator, that brings more truth
Than rhetoric, to make good his accusation.

PHILIP MASSINGER, *The Great Duke of Florence*. Act v, sc. 3.

9
Thence to the famous Orators repair,
Those ancient, whose resistless eloquence
Wielded at will that fierce democratie,
Shook the Arsenal, and fulmin'd over Greece,
To Macedon, and Artaxerxes' throne.

MILTON, *Paradise Regained*. Bk. iv, l. 267.

10
What orators lack in depth they make up to you in length. (Ce qui manque aux orateurs en profondeur ils vous le donnent en longuer.)

MONTESQUIEU, *Lettres*.

11
The capital of the orator is in the bank of the highest sentimentalities and the purest enthusiasms.

EDWARD G. PARKER, *The Golden Age of American Oratory*. Ch. 1.

12
I never failed to convince an audience that the best thing they could do was to go away.

T. L. PEACOCK, *Crochet Castle*. Ch. 18.

13
The remark is just—but then you have not been under the wand of the magician.

WILLIAM PITT, in 1783, referring to the eloquence of Fox.

14
An orator's virtue is to speak the truth. (Ῥήτορος δὲ τἀληθῆ λέγειν.)

PLATO, *Apologia of Socrates*, sec. 18.

15
He possesses the utmost facility and copiousness of expression, and though always extempore, his discourses have all the propriety and elegance of the most studied and elaborate compositions.

PLINY THE YOUNGER, *Epistles*. Bk. ii, epis. 3.

A man very skilled in moving to tears. (Vir movendarum lacrymarum peritissium.)

PLINY THE YOUNGER, *Epistles*. Bk. ii, epis. 11.

16
The orator is the mouth [os] of a nation.

JOSEPH ROUX, *Meditations of a Parish Priest*. Pt. ii, No. 21.

A man becomes an orator; he is born eloquent.

JOSEPH ROUX, *Meditations of a Parish Priest*. Pt. ii, No. 24.

17
Whose words all ears took captive.

SHAKESPEARE, *All's Well that Ends Well*. Act v, sc. 3, l. 17.

18
List his discourse of war, and you shall hear
A fearful battle render'd you in music:
Turn him to any cause of policy,
The Gordian knot of it he will unloose,
Familiar as his garter: that, when he speaks,
The air, a charter'd libertine, is still,
And the mute wonder lurketh in men's ears,
To steal his sweet and honey'd sentences

SHAKESPEARE, *Henry V*. Act i, sc. 1, l. 43.

19
I am no orator, as Brutus is;
But, as you know me all, a plain blunt man, . . .

For I have neither wit, nor words, nor worth,
Action, nor utterance, nor the power of speech,
To stir men's blood: I only speak right on.
SHAKESPEARE, *Julius Cæsar*. Act iii, sc. 2, l. 221.

1
So on the tip of his subduing tongue,
All kinds of arguments and question deep,
All replication prompt, and reason strong,
For his advantage still did wake and sleep:
To make the weeper laugh, the laugher weep,
He had the dialect and different skill.
SHAKESPEARE, *A Lover's Complaint*, l. 120.

Aged ears play truant at his tales
And younger hearings are quite ravished;
So sweet and voluble is his discourse.
SHAKESPEARE, *Love's Labour's Lost*. Act ii, sc. 1, l. 74.

A man in all the world's new fashion planted,
That hath a mint of phrases in his brain.
SHAKESPEARE, *Love's Labour's Lost*. Act i, sc. 1, l. 165.

2
Fear not, my lord, I'll play the orator.
SHAKESPEARE, *Richard III*. Act iii, sc. 5, l. 95.

More I could tell, but more I dare not say;
The text is old, the orator too green.
SHAKESPEARE, *Venus and Adonis*, l. 805.

3
And with a sweeping of the arm,
And a lack-lustre dead-blue eye,
Devolved his rounded periods.
TENNYSON, *A Character*.

4
Charm us, orator, till the lion look no larger than the cat.
TENNYSON, *Locksley Hall Sixty Years After*, l. 112.

II—Oratory

5
It being the nature of the mind of man, to the extreme prejudice of knowledge, to delight in the spacious liberty of generalities.
BACON, *Advancement of Learning*. Bk. ii.

Glittering and sounding generalities.
RUFUS CHOATE, *Letter*, to the Maine Whig Committee, 1856, referring to the Declaration of Independence.

See also under INDEPENDENCE DAY.

6
Most people have ears, but few have judgement; tickle those ears, and, depend upon it, you will catch their judgements, such as they are.
LORD CHESTERFIELD, *Letters*, 9 Dec., 1749.

7
Delivery is the management, with grace, of voice, countenance, and gesture. (Pronuntiatio est vocis, vultus, gestus moderatio cum venustate.)
CICERO, *Ad Herennium*. Bk. i, sec. 2.

8
Without preparation. (Ex tempore.)
CICERO, *De Oratore*. Bk. i, sec. 50.

9
The clear harangue, and cold as it is clear,
Falls soporific on the listless ear.
COWPER, *The Progress of Error*, l. 19.

The Chadband style of oratory is widely received and much admired.
DICKENS, *Bleak House*. Ch. 19.

10
Action! Action! Action!
DEMOSTHENES, when asked what three things made the perfect orator. *See under* ACT.

"Eloquence," replied the ancient orator, "is action, still action, and ever action." Action! what does that signify? Did he mean gesture? voice? attitude? bearing? delivery? movement of ideas? the vivacity of the images? . . . Yes, all this at once.
JOSEPH ROUX, *Meditations of a Parish Priest*. Pt. ii, No. 30.

I asked of my dear friend Orator Prig:
"What's the first part of oratory?" He said, "A great wig."
"And what is the second?" Then, dancing a jig
And bowing profoundly, he said, "A great wig."
"And what is the third?" Then he snored like a pig,
And puffing his cheeks out, he replied, "A great wig."
GEORGE COLMAN THE YOUNGER, *Orator Prig*.

11
Ye could waltz to it.
FINLEY PETER DUNNE, referring to Senator Beveridge's oratory.

12
Some, for fear their orations should giggle, will not let them smile.
THOMAS FULLER, *The Holy State*, p. 169.

13
He needs to acquire the art of seeming to pluck, as he goes along in the progress of his speech, as by the wayside, some flower of rhetoric.
BENJAMIN HARRISON, *Speech*, at banquet of the New England Society of Pennsylvania, 22 Dec., 1893.

14
He lays aside bombast and many-syllabled words if he wishes to touch the heart of his hearer. (Proicit ampullas et sesquipedalia verba, Si curat cor spectantis tetigisse querella.)
HORACE, *Ars Poetica*, l. 97.

15
Amplification is the vice of the modern orator. . . . Speeches measured by the hour die with the hour.
THOMAS JEFFERSON, *Writings*. Vol. xvi, p. 30.

16
Oratory is the power of beating down your adversary's arguments, and putting better in their place.
SAMUEL JOHNSON. (BOSWELL, *Life*, 1781.)

17
What is so furious and Bethlem-like as a vain sound of chosen and excellent words?
BEN JONSON, *Explorata: Lingua Sapientis*.

1
Hot air has thawed out many a cold reception.
F. M. KNOWLES, *A Cheerful Year Book.*

2
Begin low, speak slow;
Take fire, rise higher;
When most impressed
Be self-possessed;
At the end wax warm,
And sit down in a storm.
REV. JOHN LEIFCHILD, *Lines on Public Speaking.*

3
The object of oratory alone is not truth, but persuasion.
MACAULAY, *Essays: Athenian Orators.*

Poured thick and fast the burning words which tyrants quake to hear.
MACAULAY, *Virginia*, l. 92.

4
Rhetoric, or the art of speaking, is an enchantment of the soul. (Ψυχαγωγίαν οὖσαν.)
PLATO, *Phædrus.* Sec. 271.

Her chiefest business is a careful study of the affections and passions, which are, so to speak, strings and stops of the soul, requiring a very judicious fingering and striking.
PERICLES. (PLUTARCH, *Lives: Pericles.* Ch. 15, sec. 4.) After quoting Plato's phrase, given above.

There is a Truth and Beauty in Rhetoric; but it oftener serves ill turns than good ones.
WILLIAM PENN, *Fruits of Solitude.*

Rhetoric is very good or stark naught. . . . If I am not fully persuaded, I laugh at the orator.
JOHN SELDEN, *Table-Talk: Preaching.*

5
Far more effective [than books] is the spoken word. There is something in the voice, the countenance, the bearing, and the gesture of the speaker, that concur in fixing an impression upon the mind, deeper than can even vigorous writings.
PLINY THE YOUNGER, *Epistles.* Bk. ii, epis. 3.

6
It is a thing of no great difficulty to raise objections against another man's oration,—nay, it is a very easy matter; but to produce a better in its place is a work extremely troublesome.
PLUTARCH, *Of Hearing.* Sec. 6.

7
Few speeches which have produced an electrical effect on an audience can bear the colorless photography of a printed record.
LORD ROSEBERY, *Life of Pitt.* Ch. 13.

8
Nephew, what means this passionate discourse,
This peroration with such circumstance?
SHAKESPEARE, *II Henry VI.* Act i, sc. 1, l. 104.

9
With mild heat of holy oratory.
TENNYSON, *Geraint and Enid*, l. 867.

ORDER

10
Chaos often breeds life, when order breeds habit.
HENRY ADAMS, *Education of*, p. 249.

11
. . . Order means light and peace, inward liberty and free command over oneself; order is power. . . . Order is man's greatest need, and his true well-being.
AMIEL, *Journal*, 27 Jan., 1860.

12
Order is a lovely thing;
On disarray it lays its wing,
Teaching simplicity to sing.
It has a meek and lowly grace,
Quiet as a nun's face.
ANNA HEMPSTEAD ERANCH, *The Monk in the Kitchen.*

13
Good order is the foundation of all good things.
EDMUND BURKE, *Reflections on the Revolution in France.*

14
The eternal fitness of things.
SAMUEL CLARKE, *Being and Attributes of God.* (c. 1720)

The rule of right and the eternal fitness of things.
FIELDING, *Tom Jones.* Bk. iv, ch. 4. (1749)

15
Let all things be done decently and in order.
New Testament: I Corinthians, xiv, 40.

Set thine house in order.
Old Testament: Isaiah, xxxviii, 1.

16
For the world was built in order
And the atoms march in tune;
Rhyme the pipe, and Time the warder,
The sun obeys them, and the moon.
EMERSON, *Monadnock.* St. 12.

17
Confusion heard his voice, and wild uproar
Stood rul'd, stood vast infinitude confin'd;
Till at his second bidding darkness fled,
Light shone, and order from disorder sprung.
MILTON, *Paradise Lost.* Bk. iii, l. 710.

18
Order is Heav'n's first law; and, this confest,
Some are and must be greater than the rest,
More rich, more wise: but who infers from hence
That such are happier, shocks all common sense.
POPE, *Essay on Man.* Epis. iv, l. 49.

Not chaos-like together crush'd and bruis'd,
But, as the world, harmoniously confused:
Where order in variety we see,
And where, tho' all things differ, all agree.
POPE, *Windsor Forest*, l. 13.

19
The letters which I receive from Poland announce that order reigns in Warsaw. (Les

lettres que je reçois de Pologne m'annoncent que la tranquillité regne à Varsovie.)

GENERAL FRANÇOIS SEBASTIANI, in Chamber of Deputies, 16 Sept., 1831, while Minister of Foreign Affairs, announcing the fall of Poland. (DUMAS, *Mémoires*. Ser. ii, vol. iv, ch. 3.)

1
Order gave each thing view.

SHAKESPEARE, *Henry VIII*. Act i, sc. 1, l. 44.

2
The heavens themselves, the planets and this centre
Observe degree, priority, and place,
Insisture, course, proportion, season, form,
Office and custom, in all line of order.

SHAKESPEARE, *Troilus and Cressida*. Act i, sc. 3, l. 85.

3
A place for everything and everything in its place.

SAMUEL SMILES, *Thrift*, p. 66.

4
Method is good in all things. Order governs the world. The Devil is the author of confusion.

SWIFT, *Letters: To Stella*, 26 Oct., 1710.

5
Large elements in order brought,
And tracts of calm from tempest made,
And world-wide fluctuation sway'd,
In vassal tides that follow'd thought.

TENNYSON, *In Memoriam*. Pt. cxii, st. 4.

6
As order is heavenly, where quiet is had,
So error is hell, or a mischief as bad.

THOMAS TUSSER, *Points of Huswifery: Huswifery Admonitions*.

ORIGINALITY

See also Imitation, Plagiarism

7
No bird has ever uttered note
That was not in some first bird's throat;
Since Eden's freshness and man's fall
No rose has been original.

THOMAS BAILEY ALDRICH, *Originality*.

8
Not picked from the leaves of any author, but bred amongst the weeds and tares of mine own brain.

SIR THOMAS BROWNE, *Religio Medici*. Pt. i, sec. 36.

9
The merit of originality is not novelty; it is sincerity. The believing man is the original man.

CARLYLE, *Heroes and Hero-Worship*. Lect. 4.

10
What is originality? It is being one's self, and reporting accurately what we see and are.

EMERSON, *Letters and Social Aims: Quotation and Originality*.

11
Originality provokes originality.

GOETHE, *Sprüche in Prosa*.

12
A thought is often original, though you have uttered it a hundred times.

O. W. HOLMES, *The Autocrat of the Breakfast-Table*. Ch. 1.

13
Originality, I fear, is too often only undetected and frequently unconscious plagiarism.

DEAN W. R. INGE, *Wit and Wisdom: Preface*.

14
All good things which exist are the fruits of originality.

JOHN STUART MILL, *On Liberty*. Ch. 3.

Originality is the one thing which unoriginal minds cannot feel the use of.

JOHN STUART MILL, *On Liberty*. Ch. 3.

That so few now dare to be eccentric marks the chief danger of the time.

JOHN STUART MILL, *On Liberty*. Ch. 3.

15
You shall no longer take things at second or third hand, nor look through the eyes of the dead, nor feed on the spectres in books.

WALT WHITMAN, *Song of Myself*. Sec. 2.

OWL

16
To bring owls to Athens. (Γλαῦκ' εἰς Ἀθήνας.)

ARISTOPHANES, *Aves*, l. 301. The Athenian coins were stamped with an owl.

See also under PROVERBS: COALS TO NEWCASTLE.

17
The Roman senate, when within
The city walls an owl was seen,
Did cause their clergy, with lustrations . . .
The round-fac'd prodigy t' avert,
From doing town or country hurt.

BUTLER, *Hudibras*. Pt. ii, canto iii, l. 709.

18
What owl sings out of that ivy bush?

JOHN DAY, *Ile of Gulls*. Act v. (1606)

Like an owl in an ivy bush.

SWIFT, *Polite Conversation*. Dial. i.

When your hair's finely dress'd, I plainly do see,
You look like an owl in an ivy-tree.

UNKNOWN, *Poems on Costume*, 245.

19
An owl is the king of the night.

THOMAS DRAXE, *Bibliotheca*, 69. (1633)

20
Just then, with a wink and a sly normal lurch,
The owl very gravely got down from his perch, . . .
"I'm an owl; you're another. Sir Critic, good-day!"
And the barber kept on shaving.

JAMES THOMAS FIELDS, *The Owl-Critic*.

21
The owl is not accounted the wiser for living retiredly.

THOMAS FULLER, *Gnomologia*. No. 4697.

1
The owl thought her own birds fairest.
ULPIAN FULWELL, *Ars Adulandi.* (1580)

2
Can grave and formal pass for wise
When men the solemn owl despise?
JOHN GAY, *Fables: The Shepherd and the Philosopher,* l. 55. Franklin, *Poor Richard,* 1740.

3 From yonder ivy-mantled tow'r
The moping owl does to the Moon complain.
THOMAS GRAY, *Elegy Written in a Country Church-yard,* l. 9.

The wailing owl
Screams solitary to the mournful moon.
DAVID MALLET, *The Excursion.*

4
St. Agnes' Eve—Ah, bitter chill it was!
The owl, for all his feathers, was a-cold.
KEATS, *The Eve of St. Agnes,* l. 1.

5
The screech-owl, with ill-boding cry,
Portends strange things, old women say;
Stops every fool that passes by,
And frights the school-boy from his play.
LADY MARY WORTLEY MONTAGU, *The Politicians.*

6
In the hollow tree, in the old grey tower,
The spectral Owl doth dwell;
Dull, hated, despised, in the sunshine hour,
But at dusk—he's abroad and well! . . .
O, when the night falls, and roosts the fowl,
Then, then, is the reign of the Hornèd Owl!
BRYAN WALLER PROCTER, *The Owl.*

7
They say the owl was a baker's daughter.
SHAKESPEARE, *Hamlet.* Act iv, sc. 5, l. 41.

8
Then nightly sings the staring owl,
Tu-whit; Tu-who, a merry note.
SHAKESPEARE, *Love's Labour's Lost,* v, 2, 928.

The owl, . . . the fatal bellman,
Which gives the stern'st good-night.
SHAKESPEARE, *Macbeth.* Act ii, sc. 2, l. 3.

I heard the owl scream and the crickets cry.
SHAKESPEARE, *Macbeth.* Act ii, sc. 2, l. 16.

The clamorous owl that nightly hoots and wonders
At our quaint spirits.
SHAKESPEARE, *A Midsummer-Night's Dream.* Act ii, sc. 2, l. 6.

9
O you virtuous owl,
The wise Minerva's only fowl.
SIR PHILIP SIDNEY, *A Remedy for Love,* l. 77.

10
Do you think I was born in a wood to be afraid of an owl?
SWIFT, *Polite Conversation.* Dial. i.

11
When cats run home and light is come,
And dew is cold upon the ground,
And the far-off stream is dumb,
And the whirring sail goes round,
And the whirring sail goes round;
Alone and warming his five wits,
The white owl in the belfry sits.
TENNYSON, *Song: The Owl.*

When merry milkmaids click the latch,
And rarely smells the new-mown hay,
And the cock hath sung beneath the thatch
Twice or thrice his roundelay,
Twice or thrice his roundelay;
Alone and warming his five wits,
The white owl in the belfry sits.
TENNYSON, *Song: The Owl.*

12
Then lady Cynthia, mistress of the shade,
Goes, with the fashionable owls, to bed.
YOUNG, *Love of Fame.* Sat. v, l. 209.

OX

13
Thou shalt not muzzle the mouth of the ox that treadeth out the corn.
New Testament: I Corinthians, ix, 9.

14
An ox is taken by the horns, and a man by the tongue.
GEORGE HERBERT, *Jacula Prudentum.*

Take a bull by the horn and a man by his word.
JAMES HOWELL, *Proverbs,* 5.

15
It was yet but honey moon; the black ox had not trod on his nor her foot. (*i. e.* care has not come near them.)
JOHN HEYWOOD, *Proverbs.* Pt. i, ch. 7. (1546)

Now crow's foot is on her eye, and the black ox hath trod on her foot.
JOHN LYLY, *Sapho and Phao,* l. 199. (1584)

16
The old ox makes the straightest furrow.
JAMES HOWELL, *Proverbs,* 9. (1659)

Which way shall the ox go
But he needs must plough?
JAMES MAB, *Celestina,* 78.

Where shall the ox go, but he must labour?
JOHN RAY, *English Proverbs.*

17
The ox knoweth his owner, and the ass his master's crib.
Old Testament: Isaiah, i, 3.

18
And even now they crushed the sod
With stolid sense of majesty,
And stately stepped and stately trod,
As if 'twere something still to be
Kings even in captivity.
JOAQUIN MILLER, *Crossing the Plains.*

19
In time the unmanageable young oxen come to the plough; in time the horses are taught to endure the restraining bit.
(Tempore difficiles veniunt ad aratra juvenci;
Tempore lenta pati frena docentur equi.)
OVID, *Ars Amatoria.* Bk. i, l. 471.

By time the peasant's bull is made submissive to the plough. (Tempore ruricolæ patiens fit taurus aratri.)
OVID, *Tristia.* Bk. iv, eleg. 6, l. 1.

In time the savage bull sustains the yoke.
THOMAS KYD, *Spanish Tragedy.* Act ii. Quoted

by Shakespeare, *Much Ado About Nothing*. Act i, sc. 1, l. 263.

1
What have the oxen done, those faithful, guileless beasts, harmless and simple, born to a life of toil? (Quid mervere boves, animal sine fraude dolisque, Innocuum, simplex, natum tolerare labores?)

OVID, *Metamorphoses*. Bk. xv, l. 120.

And the plain ox,
That harmless, honest, guileless animal,
In what has he offended? he, whose toil,
Patient and ever ready, clothes the land
With all the pomp of harvest.

THOMSON, *The Seasons: Spring*, l. 362.

2
As an ox goeth to the slaughter.

Old Testament: Proverbs, vii, 22; *Jeremiah*, xi, 19.

3
Oxen that rattle the yoke and chain or halt in the leafy shade, what is that you express in your eyes?
It seems to me more than all the print I have read in my life.

WALT WHITMAN, *Song of Myself*.

He has the night among the gentle trees,
The dark surrounds him, and the Pleiades
Swing steady lanterns high above his head. . . .
The day is dead that gave him aching knees,
The night is his among the gentle trees.

MARTHA BANNING THOMAS, *The Ox*.

4
The cattle are grazing,
Their heads never raising;
There are forty feeding like one!

WORDSWORTH, *Written in March*.

5
The ox has spoken. (Bos locutus est.)

UNKNOWN. A Latin proverb, referring to the belief that the ox uttered omens from time to time, such as "Romans, beware!"

OYSTER

6
Nor brighter was his eye, nor moister
Than a too-long opened oyster.

ROBERT BROWNING, *The Pied Piper*. Sec. 4.

7
There are only two creatures I would envy—a horse in his wild state traversing the forests of Asia, and an oyster on some of the desert shores of Europe. The one has not a wish without enjoyment; the other has neither wish nor fear.

ROBERT BURNS. (R. W. CROMEK, *Reliques of Robert Burns*.)

8
The oyster is unseasonable and unwholesome in all months that have not the letter R in their name.

HENRY BUTTES, *Dyets Dry Dinner*. Sig N 1. (1599)

Oysters must not be eaten in those months, which in pronouncing want the letter R.

WILLIAM VAUGHAN, *Directions for Health*, p. 22. (1600)

A month without an R in it has nae richt being in the year.

JOHN WILSON, *Noctes Ambrosianæ*. No. 16.

9
But four young Oysters hurried up,
All eager for the treat:
Their coats were brushed, their faces washed,
Their shoes were clean and neat—
And this was odd, because, you know,
They hadn't any feet.

LEWIS CARROLL, *Through the Looking-Glass*. Ch. 4.

10
Ah, hapless wretch! condemn'd to dwell
For ever in my native shell;
Ordain'd to move when others please,
Not for my own content or ease;
But toss'd and buffeted about,
Now *in* the water and now *out*.
'Twere better to be born a stone,
Of ruder shape, and feeling none,
Than with a tenderness like mine,
And sensibilities so fine!

COWPER, *The Poet, the Oyster and Sensitive Plant*, l. 5.

11
Secret and self-contained, and solitary as an oyster.

DICKENS, *A Christmas Carol*. Stave 1.

12
"It's a wery remarkable circumstance, sir," said Sam, "that poverty and oysters always seem to go together."

DICKENS, *Pickwick Papers*. Ch. 22.

13
"Wery good power o' suction, Sammy," said Mr. Weller the elder. . . . "You'd ha' made an uncommon fine oyster, Sammy, if you'd been born in that station o' life."

DICKENS, *Pickwick Papers*. Ch. 23.

14
He was a bold man who first swallowed an oyster.

JAMES I OF ENGLAND. *See* WARD, *Diary*, c. 1660.

He was a bold man that first eat an oyster.

SWIFT, *Polite Conversation*. Dial ii.

15
I will not be sworn but love may transform me to an oyster; but I'll take my oath on it, till he have made an oyster of me, he shall never make me such a fool.

SHAKESPEARE, *Much Ado About Nothing*. Act ii, sc. 3, l. 25.

16
It is the sick oyster which possesses the pearl.

JOHN A. SHEDD, *Salt from My Attic*, p. 30.

17
An oyster may be crossed in love!

SHERIDAN, *The Critic*. Act iii, sc. 1.

"An oyster may be crossed in love,"—and why?
Because he mopeth idly in his shell,
And heaves a lonely subterraqueous sigh.

BYRON, *Don Juan*. Canto xiv, st. 81.

Then love was the pearl of his oyster,

And Venus rose red out of wine.
SWINBURNE, *Dolores*. St. 39.

1
There's really no end in natur to the eatin' of oisters.
JOHN WILSON, *Noctes Ambrosianæ*. No. 17. Oct., 1828.

He had often eaten oysters, but had never had enough.
W. S. GILBERT, *Bab Ballads: Etiquette*.

2
The oyster is a gentle thing
And will not come unless you sing.
UNKNOWN. (HAZLITT, *English Proverbs*, 381.)

3
Oysters are ungodly, because they are eaten without grace; uncharitable, because they leave nought but shells; and unprofitable, because they swim in wine.
UNKNOWN, *Tarltons Jests*, p. 6. (1611)

They say oysters are a cruel meat, because we eat them alive; then they are an uncharitable meat, for we leave nothing to the poor; and they are an ungodly meat, because we never say grace.
SWIFT, *Polite Conversation*. Dial. ii.

P

PAIN

See also Suffering

4
By pains men come to greater pains; . . . and by indignities to dignities.
FRANCIS BACON, *Essays: Of Great Place*.

5
World's use is cold, world's love is vain,
World's cruelty is bitter bane;
But pain is not the fruit of pain.
E. B. BROWNING, *A Vision of Poets*. St. 146.

6
Iron, left in the rain
And fog and dew,
With rust is covered.—Pain
Rusts into beauty too.
MARY CAROLYN DAVIES, *Rust*.

7
He has seen but half the universe who never has been shewn the house of Pain.
EMERSON, *Natural History of Intellect: The Tragic*.

Ah me! the Prison House of Pain!—what lessons there are bought!—
Lessons of a sublimer strain than any elsewhere taught.
FLORENCE EARLE COATES, *The House of Pain*.

8
Oh, ills of life! relentless train
Of sickness, tears, and wasting pain!
(Ὦ κακὰ θνητῶν στυγεραί τε νόσοι)
EURIPIDES, *Hippolytus*, l. 176. (Peacock, tr.)

9
So great was the extremity of his pain and anguish, that he did not only sigh but roar.
MATTHEW HENRY, *Commentaries: Job* iii, 24.

Nature knows best, and she says, *roar!*
MARIA EDGEWORTH, *Ormond*. Ch. 5. King Corny, in a paroxysm of the gout.

10
Pain is the price that God putteth upon all things.
JAMES HOWELL, *Proverbs*, p. 19.

11
Those who do not feel pain seldom think that it is felt.
SAMUEL JOHNSON, *The Rambler*. No. 48.

12
Pain is no evil, Unless it conquer us.
CHARLES KINGSLEY, *St. Maura*.

There is purpose in pain,
Otherwise it were devilish.
OWEN MEREDITH, *Lucile*. Pt. ii, canto 5, st. 8.

13
Pain is perfect misery, the worst
Of evils, and excessive, overturns
All patience.
MILTON, *Paradise Lost*. Bk. vi, l. 462.

14
Pain is no longer pain when it is past.
MARGARET JUNKIN PRESTON, *Nature's Lesson*.

"Pain is hard to bear," he cried,
"But with patience, day by day,
Even this shall pass away."
THEODORE TILTON, *All Things Shall Pass Away*.

15
It is a gain, by the loss of something, to get rid of pain. (Lucrum est dolorem posse damno exstinguere.)
PUBLILIUS SYRUS, *Sententiæ* No. 342.

16
Pain forces even the innocent to lie. (Etiam innocentes cogit mentiri dolor.)
PUBLILIUS SYRUS, *Sententiæ*. No. 171. Quoted by Francis Bacon, *Ornamenta Rationalia*. No. 8.

Torment to lie will sometimes drive
Ev'n the most innocent alive.
MONTAIGNE, *Essays*. Bk. ii, ch. 5.

Ay, but I fear you speak upon the rack,
Where men enforced do speak anything.
SHAKESPEARE, *The Merchant of Venice*. Act iii, sc. 2, l. 32.

17
No pains, no gains.
JOHN RAY, *English Proverbs*.

No pain, no palm; no thorn, no throne.
WILLIAM PENN, *No Cross, No Crown*.
See also under CROSS.

18
Pain is forgotten where gain comes.
JOHN RAY, *English Proverbs*.

When pain ends, gain ends too.
ROBERT BROWNING, *A Death in the Desert*.

1
Although today He prunes my twigs with pain,
Yet doth His blood nourish and warm my root:
Tomorrow I shall put forth buds again
And clothe myself with fruit.
CHRISTINA ROSSETTI, *From House to House.*

2
Ah, to think how thin the veil that lies
Between the pain of hell and Paradise.
GEORGE WILLIAM RUSSELL, *Janus.*

3
Remember that pain has this most excellent quality: if prolonged it cannot be severe, and if severe it cannot be prolonged.
SENECA, *Epistulæ ad Lucilium.* Epis. xciv, 7. *See also under* COMPENSATION.

4
Lord, how we lose our pains!
SHAKESPEARE, *All's Well that Ends Well,* v, 1, 24.

5
One fire burns out another's burning;
One pain is lessen'd by another's anguish.
SHAKESPEARE, *Romeo and Juliet.* Act i, sc. 2, l. 46. *See also* MISERY LOVES COMPANY.

6
I'll rack thee with old cramps,
Fill all thy bones with aches, make thee roar
That beasts shall tremble at thy din.
SHAKESPEARE, *The Tempest.* Act i, sc. 2, l. 371. Aches was originally pronounced in two syllables. John Kemble always pronounced it so.

Can by their pains and aches find
All turns and changes of the wind.
BUTLER, *Hudibras.* Pt. iii, canto 2, l. 407.

Every pain, but not heart pain;
Every ache, but not headache.
Babylonian Talmud: Shabbath, p. 11a.

7
The scourge of life, and death's extreme disgrace,
The smoke of hell,—that monster callèd Pain.
SIR PHILIP SIDNEY, *Sidera: Pain.*

8
So double was his pains so double be his praise.
SPENSER, *Faerie Queene.* Bk. i, canto 2, st. 25.

9
He loves to make parade of pain.
TENNYSON, *In Memoriam.* Pt. xxi.

10
Nothing begins, and nothing ends,
That is not paid with moan;
For we are born in other's pain,
And perish in our own.
FRANCIS THOMPSON, *Daisy.*

11
Pain with the thousand teeth.
WILLIAM WATSON, *The Dream of Man,* l. 15.

12
It changed the soul of one to sour
And passionate regret;
To one it gave unselfish power
To love and to forget.
SELDEN L. WHITCOMB, *Pain.*

13
But, soon or late, the fact grows plain
To all through sorrow's test:
The only folks who give us pain
Are those we love the best.
ELLA WHEELER WILCOX, *Cupid Wounds.*

14
When pain can't bless, heaven quits us in despair.
YOUNG, *Night Thoughts.* Night ix, l. 500.

II—Pain and Pleasure

See also Compensation

15
Pleasure must succeed to pleasure, else past pleasure turns to pain.
ROBERT BROWNING, *La Saisiaz,* l. 170.

16
Chords that vibrate sweetest pleasure,
Thrill the deepest notes of woe.
BURNS, *Sweet Sensibility.*

17
Our pains are real things, but all
Our pleasures but fantastical.
SAMUEL BUTLER, *Satire on the Weakness of Man,* l. 81.

18
Faint is the bliss, that never past thro' pain.
COLLEY CIBBER, *Love in a Riddle.* Act iii, sc. 2.

19
The more perfect the thing, the more deeply it feels pleasure, and also pain. (Quanto la cosa è più perfetta, Più senta il bene, e così la doglienza.)
DANTE, *Inferno.* Canto vi, l. 107.

20
Under pain, pleasure,—
Under pleasure, pain lies.
EMERSON, *The Sphinx.*

21
Pleasure reaches its limit in the removal of all pain.
EPICURUS, *Sovran Maxims.* No. 3.

Sweet is pleasure after pain.
DRYDEN, *Alexander's Feast,* l. 58.

We, by our suff'rings, learn to prize our bliss.
DRYDEN, *Astræa Redux,* l. 210.

For all the happiness mankind can gain
Is not in pleasure, but in rest from pain.
DRYDEN, *The Indian Emperor.* Act iv, sc. 1.

22
Pain past is pleasure.
THOMAS FULLER, *Gnomologia.* No. 3838.

Pain past is pleasure, and experience comes by it.
C. H. SPURGEON, *John Ploughman.* Ch. v.
See also MEMORY: ITS SWEETNESS.

23
If pains be a pleasure to you, profit will follow.
THOMAS FULLER, *Gnomologia.* No. 2699.

24
Men may scoff, and men may pray,
But they pay
Every pleasure with a pain.
WILLIAM ERNEST HENLEY, *Ballade of Truisms.*

25
Scorn pleasure; pleasure bought by pain is

harmful. (Sperne voluptates; nocet empta dolore voluptas.)
HORACE, *Epistles*. Bk. i, epis. 2, l. 55.

Pains are the wages of ill pleasures.
THOMAS FULLER, *Gnomologia*. No. 3839.

1
If pleasure was not followed by pain, who would forbear it?
SAMUEL JOHNSON, *The Idler*. No. 89.

2
Alas! by some degree of woe
We every bliss must gain:
The heart can ne'er a transport know,
That never feels a pain.
GEORGE LYTTELTON, *Song Written in 1753*.

Hard fate of man, on whom the heavens bestow
A drop of pleasure for a sea of woe.
SIR WILLIAM JONES, *Laura*.

3
There is a certain pleasure which is akin to pain. ("Εστιν γάρ τις ἡδονὴ λύπῃ συγγενής.)
METRODORUS. (SENECA, *Epistulæ ad Lucilium*. Epis. xcix, sec. 26.)

There is a pleasure that is born of pain.
OWEN MEREDITH, *The Wanderer:* Bk. i, *Prologue*.

Nothing gives pleasure but that which gives pain. (Rien ne chatouille qui ne pince.)
MONTAIGNE, *Essays*. Bk. iii, ch. 12.

Surrendering to pleasure means also surrendering to pain. (Si voluptati cessero, cedendum est dolori.)
SENECA, *Epistulæ ad Lucilium*. Epis. li, sec. 8.

Patrons of pleasure, posting into pain!
YOUNG, *Night Thoughts*. Night vii, l. 1198.

4
Sweet is the pleasure that springs from another's pain. (Hæc quoque ab alterius grata dolore venit.)
OVID, *Ars Amatoria*. Bk. i, l. 750. *See also* MISFORTUNE: OF OTHERS.

5
You purchase Pain with all that Joy can give,
And die of nothing but a rage to live.
POPE, *Moral Essays*. Epis. ii, l. 99.

Why, all delights are vain; but that most vain,
Which with pain purchased, doth inherit pain.
SHAKESPEARE, *Love's Labour's Lost*. Act i, sc. 1, l. 72.

6
'Tis cruel to prolong a pain, and to defer a joy.
SIR CHARLES SEDLEY, *Song: Love Still Has Something of the Sea*."

7
And painful pleasure turns to pleasing pain.
SPENSER, *Faerie Queene*. Bk. iii, canto 10, st. 60.

8
All fits of pleasure are balanced by an equal degree of pain or languor; it is like spending this year part of the next year's revenue.
SWIFT, *Thoughts on Various Subjects*.

9
With nerve and bone she weaves and multiplies
Exceeding pleasure out of extreme pain.
SWINBURNE, *Laus Veneris*.

10
Without one pleasure and without one pain.
TENNYSON, *Lucretius*, l. 268.

11
A man of pleasure is a man of pains.
YOUNG, *Night Thoughts*. Night viii, l. 793.

12
To frown at pleasure, and to smile in pain.
YOUNG, *Night Thoughts*. Night viii, l. 1054.

PAINE, THOMAS

13
In digging up your bones, Tom Paine,
Will. Cobbett has done well:
You visit him on earth again,
He'll visit you in hell.
BYRON, *Epigram*.

14
A mouse nibbling at the wing of an archangel.
ROBERT HALL, *Of Thomas Paine*. (GREGORY, *Life*.)

15
Paine was a Quaker by birth and a friend by nature. The world was his home, mankind were his friends, to do good was his religion.
ALICE HUBBARD, *An American Bible: Introduction*.

16
He was as democratic as nature, as impartial as sun and rain.
MARILLA M. RICKER, *The Philistine*. Vol. xxv, p. 104.

PAINTING

See also Art

I—Painting: Definitions

17
Painting is the intermediate somewhat between a thought and a thing.
S. T. COLERIDGE, *Table Talk*. 30 Aug., 1827.

So, if a great painter with questions you push,
"What's the first part of painting?" he'll say, "A paint-brush."
"And what is the second?" with most modest blush,
He'll smile like a cherub, and say, "A paint-brush."
"And what is the third?" he'll bow with a rush,
With a leer in his eye, he'll reply, "A paint-brush."
Perhaps this is all a painter can want:
But, look yonder—that house is the house of Rembrandt.
WILLIAM BLAKE, *On Art and Artists*. Pt. iii. *See also* DEMOSTHENES *under* ORATORS.

18
Pictures must not be too picturesque.
EMERSON, *Essays, First Series: Art*.

19
Taste appreciates pictures: connoisseurship appraises them.
J. C. AND A. W. HARE, *Guesses at Truth*.

How would any sign-post dauber know,

The worth of Titian or of Angelo?
DRYDEN, *Epistles: To Mr. Lee,* l. 51.

1
The picture that approaches sculpture nearest
Is the best picture.
LONGFELLOW, *Michael Angelo.* Pt. ii, sec. 4.

2
Painting with all its technicalities, difficulties, and peculiar ends, is nothing but a noble and expressive language, invaluable as the vehicle of thought, but by itself nothing.
RUSKIN, *True and Beautiful: Painting: Introduction.*

3
Painting is silent poetry, and poetry is painting with the gift of speech.
SIMONIDES. (PLUTARCH, *De Gloria Atheniensium,* iii, 346.

A picture is a poem without words.
CORNIFICIUS, *Auctor ad Herennium.* Bk. iv, sec. 28.

It is a pretty mocking of the life.
SHAKESPEARE, *Timon of Athens.* Act i, sc. 1, 35.

4
A picture is not wrought
By hands alone, good Padre, but by thought.
W. W. STORY, *Padre Bandelli Proses.*

I mix them with my brains, sir.
JOHN OPIE, when asked with what he mixed his colors. (SAMUEL SMILES, *Self-Help.* Ch. 5.)

The Attorney-General: The labour of two days, then, is that for which you ask two hundred guineas!
Mr. Whistler: No—I ask it for the knowledge of a lifetime.
J. MCNEILL WHISTLER, *The Gentle Art of Making Enemies,* p. 5. Under cross-examination during his suit against Ruskin.

5
Good painting is like good cooking: it can be tasted, but not explained. (La bonne peinture, c'est comme le bonne cuisine: ça se goute mais ça ne s'explique pas.
VLAMINCK, *On Painting.*

6
A life passed among pictures makes not a painter—else the policeman in the National Gallery might assert himself. As well allege that he who lives in a library must needs be a poet.
J. MCNEILL WHISTLER, *The Gentle Art of Making Enemies,* p. 26.

II—Painting: Apothegms

7
And those who paint 'em truest praise 'em most.
ADDISON, *The Campaign.* Last line. (1704)

He best can paint them who shall feel them most.
POPE, *Eloisa to Abelard.* Last line. (1717)

8
The love of gain never made a painter, but it has marred many.
WASHINGTON ALLSTON, *Lectures on Art: Aphorisms.*

9
Paint any one, and count it crime
To let a truth slip.
ROBERT BROWNING, *Fra Lippo Lippi.*

10
Paint me as I am. If you leave out the scars and wrinkles, I will not pay you a shilling.
OLIVER CROMWELL, *Remark,* to the young painter, Peter Lely, who was about to paint his portrait. This is the best known version, but what Cromwell really said was, "I desire you would use all your skill to paint my picture truly like me; but remark all these roughnesses, pimples, warts, and everything as you see me, otherwise I will never pay a farthing for it." (WALPOLE, *Anecdotes of Painting,* p. 444. *Dict. of National Biog.*)

"Paint me as I am," said Cromwell,
"Rough with age and gashed with wars;
Show my visage as you find it,
Less than truth my soul abhors."
JAMES T. FIELDS, *On a Portrait of Cromwell.*

The trouble is, the more it resembles me, the worse it looks.
EMERSON, to Daniel Chester French, who was making a bust of him. (CABOT, *A Memoir of Ralph Waldo Emerson,* p. 679.)

Hard features every bungler can command:
To draw true beauty shows a master's hand.
DRYDEN, *Epistles: To Mr. Lee, on His Alexander,* l. 53.

11
On painting and fighting look afar off.
JOHN RAY, *English Proverbs.*

12
The fellow mixes blood with his colors.
GUIDO RENI, referring to Rubens.

They dropped into the yolk of an egg the milk that flows from the leaf of a young fig-tree, with which, instead of water, gum or gumdragant, they mixed their last layer of colours.
WALPOLE, *Anecdotes of Painting.* Vol. i, ch. 2.

13
A mere copier of nature can never produce anything great.
SIR JOSHUA REYNOLDS, *Discourses on Painting.* No. 3.

There are those who think that not to copy nature is the rule for attaining perfection.
WILLIAM HAZLITT, *Table Talk: A Landscape of Poussin. See also* NATURE AND ART.

15
To sit for one's portrait is like being present at one's own creation.
ALEXANDER SMITH, *Dreamthorp: On Vagabonds.*

16
The corregiescity of Corregio.
STERNE, *Tristram Shandy.* Bk. iii, ch. 12. (1760)

The *corregioscity* of Correggio.
WILLIAM HAZLITT, *Table Talk: On the Ignorance of the Learned.* (1821)

If they could forget for a moment the correggiosity of Correggio and the learned babble of the sale-room and varnishing Auctioneer.
CARLYLE, *Frederick the Great,* iv, 3. (1860)

The Scipionism of Scipio.
EMERSON, *Essays, First Series: Self-Reliance.*

As certain as the Correggiosity of Correggio.
AUGUSTINE BIRRELL, *Obiter Dicta, Second Series: Emerson.*

How Botticellian! How Fra Angelican!
W. S. GILBERT, *Patience.* Act ii.

1
A little amateur painting in water-colour shows the innocent and quiet mind.
R. L. STEVENSON, *Virginibus Puerisque.* Pt. i.

2
He is but a landscape painter,
And a village maiden she.
TENNYSON, *The Lord of Burleigh,* l. 7.

3
Every portrait that is painted with feeling is a portrait of the artist, not of the sitter.
OSCAR WILDE, *Picture of Dorian Gray.* Ch. 1.

4
Connubial love turned Mulciber into Apelles. (Connubialis amor de Mulcibre fecit Apellem.)
UNKNOWN, *Epitaph on Quentin Matsys,* the blacksmith-painter of Antwerp.

A kiss from my mother made me a painter.
BENJAMIN WEST.

III—Painting: Praise

5
I can look for a whole day with delight upon a handsome picture, though it be but of an horse.
SIR THOMAS BROWNE, *Religio Medici.* Pt. ii, sec. 10.

6
No record of her high descent
There needs, nor memory of her name;
Enough that Raphael's colors blent
To give her features deathless fame.
WILLIAM ALLEN BUTLER, *Incognita of Raphael.*

7
Such are thy pieces, imitating life
So near, they almost conquer'd in the strife.
DRYDEN, *To Sir Godfrey Kneller,* l. 18.

A flattering painter who made it his care
To draw men as they ought to be, not as they are.
GOLDSMITH, *Retaliation,* l. 63. Of Sir Joshua Reynolds.

His pencil was striking, resistless, and grand;
His manners were gentle, complying, and bland;
Still born to improve us in every part,
His pencil our faces, his manners our heart.
OLIVER GOLDSMITH, *Retaliation,* l. 139. Of Sir Joshua Reynolds.

The canvas glow'd beyond ev'n Nature warm,
The pregnant quarry teem'd with human form.
GOLDSMITH, *The Traveller,* l. 137.

8
He displays in a painting the countenance and also the mind. (Suspendit picta vultum mentemque tabella.)
HORACE, *Epistles.* Bk. ii, epis. 1, l. 97.

By portraits I do not mean the outlines and the colouring of the human figure, but the inside of the heart and mind of man.
LORD CHESTERFIELD, *Letters,* 2 Oct., 1747.

9
No painter could give me a more living likeness. (Non potuit pictor rectius describere ejus formam.)
PLAUTUS, *Asinaria,* l. 402. (Act ii, sc. 3.)

10
Lely on animated canvas stole
The sleepy eye, that spoke the melting soul.
POPE, *Imitations of Horace: Epistles.* Bk. ii, epis. 1, l. 149.

11
This is her picture as she was:
It seems a thing to wonder on,
As though mine image in the glass
Should tarry when myself am gone.
D. G. ROSSETTI, *The Portrait.*

That's my last Duchess painted on the wall,
Looking as if she were alive. I call
That piece a wonder, now: Frà Pandolf's hands
Worked busily a day, and there she stands.
ROBERT BROWNING, *My Last Duchess.*

12
What demi-god Hath come so near creation?
SHAKESPEARE, *The Merchant of Venice.* Act iii, sc. 2, l. 116.

It tutors nature: artificial strife
Lives in these touches, livelier than life.
SHAKESPEARE, *Timon of Athens.* Act i, sc. 1, l. 37.

The painting is almost the natural man;
For since dishonour traffics with man's nature,
He is but outside: these pencill'd figures are
Even such as they give out.
SHAKESPEARE, *Timon of Athens.* Act i, sc. 1, l. 157.

Wrought he not well that painted it?
SHAKESPEARE, *Timon of Athens.* Act i, sc. 1, l. 200.

IV—Painting: Criticism

13
What has reasoning to do with the art of painting? . . . To generalize is to be an idiot.
WILLIAM BLAKE. (GILCHRIST, *Life,* i, 310.)

14
Orbaneja, the painter of Ubeda, being asked what he had painted, answered, "As it may hit;" and if he chanced to draw a cock, he wrote under it, "This is a cock."
CERVANTES, *Don Quixote.* Pt. ii, ch. 3.

15
There are only two styles of portrait painting, the serious and the smirk.
DICKENS, *Nicholas Nickleby.* Ch. 10.

16
How strongly I have felt of pictures that when you have seen one well, you must take your leave of it; you shall never see it again.
EMERSON, *Essays, Second Series: Experience.*

17
One picture in ten thousand, perhaps, ought to live in the applause of mankind, from generation to generation until the colors fade and blacken out of sight or the canvas rot entirely away.
HAWTHORNE, *The Marble Faun.* Bk. ii, ch. 12

1
Landscape painting is the obvious resource of misanthropy.
WILLIAM HAZLITT, *Criticisms on Art*, ii, 233.

Indifferent pictures, like dull people, must absolutely be moral.
WILLIAM HAZLITT, *Criticisms on Art*, i, 16.

2
Well, something must be done for May,
The time is drawing nigh—
To figure in the Catalogue,
And woo the public eye.

Something I must invent and paint;
But oh, my wit is not
Like one of those kind substantives
That answer Who and What?
THOMAS HOOD, *The Painter Puzzled*.

3
I had rather see the portrait of a dog that I know than all the allegorical paintings . . . in the world.
SAMUEL JOHNSON. (BOSWELL, *Life*, i, 364.)

4
I have seen, and heard, much of cockney impudence before now; but never expected to hear a coxcomb ask two hundred guineas for flinging a pot of paint in the public's face.
JOHN RUSKIN, in *Fors Clavigera*, 2 July, 1877, referring to Whistler's "Nocturne in Black and Gold," representing the fireworks at Cremorne. Whistler sued Ruskin for libel, asking £1000 damages, and won the verdict, with damages of a farthing. *See under* PAINTING: DEFINITIONS.

A tortoise-shell cat having a fit in a platter of tomatoes.
MARK TWAIN. His description of Turner's "The Slave Ship."

5
No picture can be good which deceives by its imitation, for the very reason that nothing can be beautiful which is not true.
RUSKIN, *Modern Painters*. Pt. i, sec. i, ch. 5, sec. 6.

6
Painters an' poets hae liberty to lie.
JOHN RAY, *Scottish Proverbs*. *See also* POETRY: POETIC LICENSE.

7
They are good furniture pictures, unworthy of praise, and undeserving of blame.
RUSKIN, *Modern Painters*. Pt. i, sec. v, ch. 5, sec. 20.

PALM

8
As the palm-tree standeth so straight and so tall,
The more the hail beats, and the more the rains fall.
SIMON DACH, *Annie of Tharaw*, l. 11. (Longfellow, tr.)

9
Through the laburnam's dropping gold
Rose the light shaft of Orient mould,
And Europe's violets, faintly sweet,
Purpled the mossbeds at its feet.
FELICIA DOROTHEA HEMANS, *The Palm-Tree*.

10
On friend and foe breathe soft and calm,
As ship with ship in battle meets;
And while the sea-gods watch the fleets,
Let him who merits, bear the palm.
(Et nobis faciles parcite et hostibus;
Concurrant paribus cum ratibus rates,
Spectant numina ponti, et
Palmam qui meruit, ferat.)
JOHN JORTIN, *Lusus Poetici: Ad Ventos*. St. 4. (W. M. F. King, tr.) "Palmam qui meruit, ferat" was the motto of Lord Nelson, and of the British Royal Naval School.

Ye gods, it doth amaze me
A man of such a feeble temper should
So get the start of the majestic world,
And bear the palm alone.
SHAKESPEARE, *Julius Cæsar*. Act i, sc. 2, l. 128.

You shall see him a palm in Athens again.
SHAKESPEARE, *Timon of Athens*. Act v, sc. 1, l. 12.

Let all be present and expect the palm, the prize of victory. (Cuncti adsint, meritæque expectent præmia palmæ.)
VERGIL, *Æneid*. Bk. v, l. 70.

11
First the high palm-trees, with branches fair,
Out of the lowly valleys did arise,
And high shoot up their heads into the skies.
SPENSER, *Virgil's Gnat*, l. 190.

12
I love the Palm,
With his leaves of beauty, his fruit of balm.
BAYARD TAYLOR, *The Arab to the Palm*.

13
Of threads of palm was the carpet spun
Whereon he kneels when the day is done,
And the foreheads of Islam are bowed as one!

To him the palm is a gift divine,
Wherein all uses of man combine,—
House, and raiment, and food, and wine!

And, in the hour of his great release,
His need of the palm shall only cease
With the shroud wherein he lieth in peace.

"Allah il Allah!" he sings his psalm,
On the Indian Sea, by the isles of balm;
"Thanks to Allah, who gives the palm!"
WHITTIER, *The Palm-Tree*.

PAN

14
And that dismal cry rose slowly
And sank slowly through the air,
Full of spirit's melancholy
And eternity's despair!
And they heard the words it said—
"Pan is dead!—Great Pan is dead—
Pan, Pan is dead."
E. B. BROWNING, *The Dead Pan*. St. 26.

By the love, He stood alone in,
His sole Godhead rose complete,
And the false gods fell down moaning
Each from off his golden seat;
All the false gods with a cry
Rendered up their deity—
Pan, Pan was dead.
E. B. BROWNING, *The Dead Pan*. St. 28.

And when, at length, "Great Pan is dead!" uprose the loud and dolorous cry,
A glamour wither'd on the ground, a splendour faded in the sky.
SIR RICHARD BURTON, *Kasîdah*. Pt. iv, st. 24.

Pan of the garden, the fold,
Pan of the bird and the beast,
Kindly, he lives as of old,
He isn't dead in the least!
PATRICK CHALMERS, *Pan Pipes*.

1
Yet half a beast is the great god Pan,
To laugh as he sits by the river.
E. B. BROWNING, *A Musical Instrument*.

2
Of Pan we sing, the best of leaders Pan,
That leads the Naiads and the Dryads forth;
And to their dances more than Hermes can,
Hear, O you groves, and hills resound his worth.
BEN JONSON, *Pan's Anniversary Hymn*.

Pan himself,
The simple shepherd's awe-inspiring god!
WORDSWORTH, *The Excursion*. Bk. iv, l. 886.

3
Great Pan is dead. (Πὰν ὁ μέγας τέθνηκε.)
PLUTARCH, *De Defectu Oraculorum*. Sec. xvii. Plutarch is relating the legend that at the hour of the Saviour's agony, a cry of "Great Pan is dead!" swept across the waves in the hearing of certain mariners, and the oracles were silent.

A ship laden with passengers drove with the tide near the Isles of Paxi, when a loud voice was heard calling unto one Thanus. The voice then said aloud to him, "When you are arrived at Palados, take care to make it known that the great god Pan is dead."
PLUTARCH, *Isis and Osiris*.

Suddenly there came gasping towards them a pale Jew dripping with blood, a crown of thorns on his head, bearing a great cross of wood on his shoulder, and he cast the cross on the high table of the gods, so that the golden goblets trembled and fell, and the gods grew dumb and pale, and ever paler, till they melted in utter mist.
HEINE, *Reisebilder: City of Lucca*. Ch. 6.

PANSY

4
Of all the bonny buds that blow
In bright or cloudy weather,
Of all the flowers that come and go
The whole twelve months together,
This little purple pansy brings
Thoughts of the sweetest, saddest things.
MARY E. BRADLEY, *Heartsease*.

5
Pansies for ladies all—(I wis
That none who wear such brooches miss
A jewel in the mirror).
E. B. BROWNING, *A Flower in a Letter*.

6
Cornelia: I pray, what flowers are these?
Gazetta: The pansy this.
Cornelia: Oh, that's for lovers' thoughts.
GEORGE CHAPMAN, *All Fools*. Act ii, sc. 1, l. 248.

Pray, love, remember: and there is pansies, that's for thoughts.
SHAKESPEARE, *Hamlet*. Act iv, sc. 5, l. 176.

7
The delicate thought, that cannot find expression,
For ruder speech too fair,
That, like thy petals, trembles in possession,
And scatters on the air.
BRET HARTE, *The Mountain Heart's-Ease*.

8
Heart's ease! one could look for half a day
Upon this flower, and shape in fancy out
Full twenty different tales of love and sorrow,
That gave this gentle name.
MARY HOWITT, *Heart's Ease*.

9
There is a flower I wish to wear,
But not until first worn by you. . . .
Heart's ease . . . of all earth's flowers most rare;
Bring it; and bring enough for two.
WALTER SAVAGE LANDOR, *Heart's-Ease*.

10
The pansy freak'd with jet.
MILTON, *Lycidas*, l. 144.

I send thee pansies while the year is young,
Yellow as sunshine, purple as the night;
Flowers of remembrance, ever fondly sung
By all the chiefest of the Sons of Light;
And if in recollection lives regret
For wasted days and dreams that were not true,
I tell thee that the "pansy freak'd with jet"
Is still the heart's ease that the poets knew.
Take the sweetness of a gift unsought,
And for the pansies send me back a thought.
SARAH DOUDNEY, *Pansies*.

11
The beauteous pansies rise
In purple, gold, and blue,
With tints of rainbow hue
Mocking the sunset skies.
THOMAS J. OUSELEY, *Angel of the Flowers*.

12
Heart's ease or pansy, pleasure or thought,
Which would the picture give us of these?
Surely the heart that conceived it sought
Heart's ease.
SWINBURNE, *A Flower Piece by Fantin*.

PARADISE

See also Heaven

1
In the nine heavens are eight Paradises;
Where is the ninth one? In the human breast.
Only the blessed dwell in th' Paradises,
But blessedness dwells in the human breast.
WILLIAM R. ALGER, *Poetry of the Orient: The Ninth Paradise.*

2
For he that lives retired in mind and spirit
Is still in Paradise.
BEAUMONT AND FLETCHER, *The Nice Valour.* Act v, sc. 2.

3
Too much of words or yet too few! What to thy Godhead easier than
One little glimpse of Paradise to ope the eyes and ears of man?
SIR RICHARD BURTON, *The Kasîdah.* Pt. ii, st. 12.

4
For he on honey-dew hath fed,
And drunk the milk of Paradise.
S. T. COLERIDGE, *Kubla Khan,* l. 53.

On the tongue of such an one they shed a honeyed dew, and from his lips drop gentle words.
HESIOD, *Theogony,* l. 83.

5
Not in mine eyes alone is Paradise.
DANTE, *Paradise.* Canto xviii, l. 21.

6
Nor count compartments of the floors,
But mount to paradise
By the stairway of surprise.
EMERSON, *Merlin.*

7
Unto you is paradise opened.
Apocrypha: II Esdras, viii, 52.

8
O Paradise! O Paradise!
Who doth not crave for rest?
Who would not seek the happy land
Where they that love are blest?
FREDERICK WILLIAM FABER, *Paradise.*

9
He that will enter into Paradise must come with the right key.
THOMAS FULLER, *Gnomologia.* No. 2347.

Thou hast the keys of Paradise, O just, subtle, and mighty opium!
THOMAS DE QUINCEY, *Confessions of an English Opium-Eater.* Pt. ii.

10
The fruit of the tree of knowledge always drives man from some paradise or other.
DEAN W. R. INGE. (MARCHANT, *Wit and Wisdom of Dean Inge.* No. 198.)

11
Paradise is (as from the Learn'd I gather)
A quire of blest Souls circling in the Father.
ROBERT HERRICK, *Paradise.*

12
Dry your eyes—O dry your eyes,
For I was taught in Paradise
To ease my breast of melodies.
KEATS, *Faery Song.*

13
Verily for the pious is a blissful abode
Gardens and vineyards
Damsels with swelling breasts of suitable age
And a brimming cup.
MAHOMET, *Sara,* 78.

14
Must I thus leave thee, Paradise? thus leave
Thee, native soil, these happy walks and shades,
Fit haunt of Gods?
MILTON, *Paradise Lost.* Bk. xi, l. 269.

15
The Paradise of Fools, to few unknown.
MILTON, *Paradise Lost.* Bk. iii, l. 496. *See also* FOOL: FOOL'S PARADISE.

16
If God hath made this world so fair,
Where sin and death abound,
How beautiful, beyond compare,
Will paradise be found!
JAMES MONTGOMERY, *The Earth is Full of God's Goodness.*

17
One morn a Peri at the gate
Of Eden stood disconsolate.
MOORE, *Lalla Rookh: Paradise and the Peri.*

18
Nor did they think that they might long draw breath
In such an earthly Paradise as this.
WILLIAM MORRIS, *Life and Death of Jason.* Bk. vi, l. 508.

The young men well nigh wept, and e'en the wise
Thought they had reached the gate of Paradise.
WILLIAM MORRIS, *Life and Death of Jason.* Bk. xiii, l. 51.

For, oh! if there be an Elysium on earth,
It is this, it is this.
THOMAS MOORE, *Lalla Rookh: The Light of the Haram.*

19
With dreamful eyes
My spirit lies
Under the walls of Paradise.
THOMAS BUCHANAN READ, *Drifting.*

Around this lovely valley rise
The purple hills of Paradise.
J. T. TROWBRIDGE, *Midsummer.*

20
The loves that meet in Paradise shall cast out fear,
And Paradise hath room for you and me and all.
CHRISTINA ROSSETTI, *Saints and Angels.*

21
There must have been a charming climate in Paradise. The temperature was perfect; and connubial bliss, I allot, was real jam up.
SAM SLICK, *Human Nature,* p. 273.

1
Shiftless and shy, gentle and kind and frail,
Poor wanderer, bewildered into vice,
You are freed at last from seas you could not sail,
A wreck upon the shores of Paradise.
J. C. SQUIRE, *An Epitaph.*

2
And paint the gates of Hell with Paradise.
TENNYSON, *The Princess.* Pt. iv, l. 113.

3
There is no expeditious road
To pack and label men for God,
And save them by the barrel-load.
Some may perchance, with strange surprise,
Have blundered into Paradise.
FRANCIS THOMPSON, *A Judgement in Heaven: Epilogue.* St. 2.

PARDON, see Forgiveness

PARENTS

See also Children and Parents; Father, Mother

4
Reverence for parents—this standeth written third among the statutes of Justice, to whom supreme honor is due. (Τὸ γὰρ τεκόντων σέβας τρίτον τόδ' ἐν θεσμίοις Δίκας γέγραπται μεγιστοτίμου.)
ÆSCHYLUS, *Suppliants,* l. 707. Referring to the three great laws ascribed to Triptolemus by Plutarch: to honor parents, to worship the gods with the fruit of the earth, and to hurt no living creature.

Honour thy father and thy mother: that thy days may be long upon the land which the Lord thy God giveth thee.
Old Testament: Exodus, xx, 12. The fifth Commandment.

Honor the gods, reverence parents. (Θεοὺς τίμα, γονέας αἰδοῦ.)
SOLON. (DIOGENES LAERTIUS, *Solon.* Bk. i, sec. 60.)

To love our parents is the first law of nature. (Diligere parentes prima naturæ lex est.)
VALERIUS MAXIMUS, *De Factis Dictisque.* Bk. v, ch. 4, sec. 7.

5
Lovers grow cold, men learn to hate their wives,
And only parents' love can last our lives.
ROBERT BROWNING, *Pippa Passes.*

6
The childless cherubs well might envy thee
The pleasures of a parent.
BYRON, *Cain.* Act iii, sc. 1, l. 171.

7
Conduct thyself towards thy parents as thou wouldst wish thy children to conduct themselves towards thee.
ISOCRATES, *Ad Demonicum,* iv. 14.

8
In general those parents have the most reverence who deserve it; for he that lives well cannot be despised.
SAMUEL JOHNSON, *Rasselas.* Ch. 26.

The notion that parents are entitled to respect simply because they are parents is preposterous. The stream of obligation runs strongly the other way. A child owes its parents no gratitude whatever for bringing him into the world (as Swift sardonically said, while they were thinking of something else).
JOHN MACY, *About Women,* p. 116.

9
The virtue of parents is a great dowry. (Dos est magna parentium Virtus.)
HORACE, *Odes.* Bk. iii, ode 24, l. 21.

10
Whence do you derive the power and privilege of a parent, when you, though an old man, do worse things than your child?
JUVENAL, *Satires.* Sat. xiv, l. 56.

Few parents act in such a manner as much to enforce their maxims by the credit of their lives.
SAMUEL JOHNSON, *Works,* xi, 72.

If parents want honest children they should be honest themselves.
R. G. INGERSOLL, *How to Reform Mankind.*

11
One moment makes a father, but a mother
Is made by endless moments, load on load.
JOHN G. NEIHARDT, *Eight Hundred Rubles.*

12
My son, hear the instruction of thy father, and forsake not the law of thy mother.
Old Testament: Proverbs, i, 8.

Hearken unto thy father that begat thee, and despise not thy mother when she is old.
Old Testament: Proverbs, xxiii, 22.

The eye that mocketh at his father, and despiseth to obey his mother, the ravens of the valley shall pick it out, and the young eagles shall eat it.
Old Testament: Proverbs, xxx, 17.

What heavy guilt upon him lies!
How cursed is his name!
The ravens shall pick out his eyes,
And eagles eat the same.
ISAAC WATTS, *Obedience.*

13
Everything is dear to its parent. (Τῷ τεκόντι πᾶν φίλον.)
SOPHOCLES, *Œdipus Coloneus,* l. 1108.

No fathers or mothers think their children ugly.
CERVANTES, *Don Quixote.*

So both the Raven and the Ape think their own young the fairest.
SIR THOMAS MORE, *Utopia.*

The parent who could see his boy as he really is, would shake his head and say; "Willie is no good: I'll sell him."
STEPHEN B. LEACOCK, *The Lot of the Schoolmaster.*

PARIS

14
Good Americans, when they die, go to Paris.
THOMAS GOLD APPLETON. Perpetuated by

Oliver Wendell Holmes, in the *Autocrat of the Breakfast-Table*, ch. 6, as a saying of one of the "Seven Wise Men of Boston."

Mrs. Allonby: They say, Lady Hunstanton, that when good Americans die they go to Paris.
Lady Hunstanton: Indeed? And when bad Americans die, where do they go to?
Lord Illingworth: Oh, they go to America.
OSCAR WILDE, *A Woman of No Importance*. Act i.

1
Fair, fantastic Paris.
E. B. BROWNING, *Aurora Leigh*. Bk. vi, l. 81.

2
At Paris it was, at the Opera there;—
And she looked like a queen in a book that night,
With the wreath of pearl in her raven hair,
And the brooch on her breast, so bright.
BULWER-LYTTON, *Aux Italiens*.

3
Paris is the place in the world where, if you please, you may best unite the *utile* and the *dulce*.
LORD CHESTERFIELD, *Letters*, 30 April, 1750.

4
Paris is terribly derisive of all absurd pretensions but its own.
EMERSON, *Uncollected Lectures: Table-Talk*.

5
Beautiful carriages from Champs Elysees
Filled with fair maidens on cushions easy.
GEORGINA FARRER. Quoted by Edith Sitwell, *Collected Poems*, as "the worst poetry ever written."

6
Paris is well worth a Mass. (Paris vaut bien une Messe.)
HENRY IV, referring to his conversion to Catholicism in order to gain Paris and the crown of France. Fournier doubts if Henry was so undiplomatic as to have said this.

7
Paris is nothing but an immense hospitality.
VICTOR HUGO, *Appeal to German Army to Spare Paris*, 1870.

The café of Europe.
ABBÉ GALIANI, *Epigram*.

What's Paris but a circus, fair,
To tempt this west world's open purse
With tawdry trinkets, toys bizarre?
Ah, would that she were nothing worse!
JOAQUIN MILLER, *A Song of Creation*. Sec. 24.

8
Every fresh day's research into the city brings increasing disappointment. . . . Everything is planed, smoothed, and set to an oppressive regularity . . . in short, Paris is the plainest city in Europe.
RICHARD JEFFERIES, *The Plainest City in Europe*.

9
All Paris goes to see it. (Tout Paris va voir.)
MOLIÈRE, *L'Impromptu de Versailles*. Sc. 5, l. 75.

10
Secrets travel fast in Paris.
NAPOLEON I, *Sayings of Napoleon*.

11
Paris is the middle-aged woman's paradise.
PINERO, *The Princess and the Butterfly*. Act i.

I think every wife has a right to insist upon seeing Paris.
SYDNEY SMITH, *Letters: To Countess Grey*, 11 Sept., 1835.

12
You who have ever been to Paris, know;
And you who have not been to Paris—go!
JOHN RUSKIN, *A Tour Through France*. St. 12.

13
A street there is in Paris famous,
For which no rhyme our language yields,
Rue Neuve des Petits Champs its name is—
The New Street of the Little Fields.
THACKERAY, *The Ballad of Bouillabaisse*.

14
Prince, give praise to our French ladies
For the sweet sound their speaking carries;
'Twixt Rome and Cadiz many a maid is,
But no good girl's lip out of Paris.
FRANÇOIS VILLON, *Ballade des Femmes de Paris*. (Swinburne, tr.)

Good talkers are only found in Paris.
FRANÇOIS VILLON, *Ballade des Femmes de Paris*.

PARK

15
Public money is scarcely ever so well employed as in securing bits of waste ground and keeping them as open spaces.
ARTHUR HELPS, *Friends in Council*. Bk. i, ch. 10.

16
The proud park takes away the dwellings from the poor. (Abstulerat miseris tecta superbus ager.)
MARTIAL, *De Spectaculis*, ii, 8.

What had been the delights of the lord are now the delights of the people. (Deliciæ populi, quæ fuerant domini.)
MARTIAL, *De Spectaculis*, ii, 12. Of land given to public use.

17
The lungs of London.
WILLIAM WINDHAM, *Debate*, House of Commons. 30 June, 1808.

If the Parks be "the lungs of London," we wonder what Greenwich Fair is—a periodical breaking out, we suppose—a sort of spring rash.
DICKENS, *Sketches by Boz: Greenwich Fair*.

PARTING

See also Farewell; Meeting and Parting

18
Some weep because they part,
And languish broken-hearted.
And others—O my heart!—
Because they never parted.
THOMAS BAILEY ALDRICH, *The Difference*.

Good-night! I have to say good-night
To such a host of peerless things!

Good-night unto the slender hand
All queenly with its weight of rings;
Good-night to fond uplifted eyes,
Good-night to chestnut braids of hair,
Good-night unto the perfect mouth,
And all the sweetness nestled there—
The snowy hand detains me; then
I have to say, Good-night again.

THOMAS BAILEY ALDRICH, *Palabras Carinosas.*

Good-night! good-night! as we so oft have said
Beneath this roof at midnight, in the days
That are no more, and shall no more return.
Thou hast but taken thy lamp and gone to bed;
I stay a little longer, as one stays
To cover up the embers that still burn.

LONGFELLOW, *Three Friends of Mine.* Pt. iv.

1
Now in the summit of love's topmost peak
Kiss and we part; no farther can we go.

ALFRED AUSTIN, *Sonnet: Love's Wisdom.*

To meet, to know, to love—and then to part,
Is the sad tale of many a human heart.

S. T. COLERIDGE, *Couplet Written in a Volume of Poems.*

Since there's no help, come, let us kiss and part;
Nay, I have done, you get no more of me;
And I am glad, yea, glad with all my heart,
That thus so cleanly I myself can free.
Shake hands for ever, cancel all our vows,
And when we meet at any time again,
Be it not seen in either of our brows
That we one jot of former love retain.
Now at the last gasp of Love's latest breath,
When, his pulse failing, Passion speechless lies,
When Faith is kneeling by his bed of death,
And Innocence is closing up his eyes:
Now, if thou wouldst, when all have given him over,
From death to life thou might'st him yet recover.

MICHAEL DRAYTON, *Idea.* Sonnet lxi.

And must we part?
Well—if we must, we must—and in that case
The less said the better.

SHERIDAN, *The Critic.* Act ii, sc. 2.

2
Heart to heart
And lips to lips! Yet once more, ere we part,
Clasp me and make me thine, as mine thou art!

ROBERT BROWNING, *In a Gondola.*

3
We meet to part; yet asks my sprite, Part we to meet? Ah! is it so?

SIR RICHARD BURTON, *The Kasîdah.* Pt. i, st. 12.

4
When we two parted In silence and tears,
Half broken-hearted To sever for years.

BYRON, *When We Two Parted.*

Such partings break the heart they fondly hope to heal.

BYRON, *Childe Harold.* Canto i, st. 10.

5
Good-bye, Dolly, I must leave you,
Though it breaks my heart to go;
Something tells me I am needed
At the front to fight the foe.

WILL D. COBB, *Good-Bye, Dolly Gray.* (1900)

6
Kathleen Mavourneen, the grey dawn is breaking,
The horn of the hunter is heard on the hill;
The lark from her light wing the bright dew is shaking—
Kathleen Mavourneen! what, slumbering still?
Oh, hast thou forgotten how soon we must sever?
Oh, hast thou forgotten this day we must part?
It may be for years, and it may be for ever!
Oh, why art thou silent, thou voice of my heart?

LOUISA MACARTNEY CRAWFORD, *Kathleen Mavourneen.* "Kathleen Mavourneen" was "Big Tim" Sullivan's pseudonym for a promissory note, the reference being to the line, "It may be for years, and it may be for ever."

7
Parting is all we know of heaven,
And all we need of hell.

EMILY DICKINSON, *Poems.* Pt. i, No. 96.

8
One kind kiss before we part,
Drop a tear and bid adieu:
Though we sever, my fond heart
Till we meet shall pant for you.

ROBERT DODSLEY, *The Parting Kiss.*

9
Only in the agony of parting do we look into the depths of love.

GEORGE ELIOT, *Felix Holt.* Ch. 44.

In every parting there is an image of death.

GEORGE ELIOT, *Scenes of Clerical Life: Amos Barton.* Ch. 10. A variation of the French proverb, "To part is to die a little." (Partir c'est mourir un peu.)

10
Excuse me, then! you know my heart;
But dearest friends, alas! must part.

JOHN GAY, *Fables.* Pt. i, fab. 51.

But fate ordains that dearest friends must part.

YOUNG, *Love of Fame.* Sat. ii, l. 232.

11
"Adieu," she cried, and waved her lily hand.

JOHN GAY, *Sweet William's Farewell.*

So sweetly she bade me adieu,
I thought that she bade me return.

WILLIAM SHENSTONE, *A Pastoral Ballad.* Pt. i.

I now bid you a welcome adoo.

ARTEMUS WARD, *The Shakers.*

12
The day goes by like a shadow o'er the heart,
With sorrow where all was delight:
The time has come when the darkies have to part,
Then my old Kentucky Home, good-night!

STEPHEN COLLINS FOSTER, *My Old Kentucky Home.*

1
The day is gone, and all its sweets are gone!
Sweet voice, sweet lips, soft hand, and softer breast.
KEATS, *Sonnet: The Day is Gone.*

2
Say "au revoir" but not "good-bye,"
Though past is dead, Love cannot die.
HARRY KENNEDY, *Say "Au Revoir" but Not "Good-bye."* (1893) Sung at the author's grave a few years later by Helen Mora, the great female baritone, whom it had made famous.

3
Thou art gone from my gaze like a beautiful dream.
GEORGE LINLEY, *Thou Art Gone.*

4
They who go
Feel not the pain of parting; it is they
Who stay behind that suffer.
LONGFELLOW, *Michael Angelo:* Pt. i, *Prologue.*

The one who goes is happier
Than those he leaves behind.
EDWARD POLLOCK, *The Parting Hour.*

5
The shore he was never to see again. (Litora numquam Ad visus reditura suos.)
LUCAN, *De Bello Civili.* Bk. iii, l. 5.

Now a' is done that men can do,
And a' is done in vain;
My love and native land, farewell,
For I maun cross the main,
BURNS, *The Farewell.*

And soon, too soon, we part with pain,
To sail o'er silent seas again.
THOMAS MOORE, *The Meeting of the Ships.*

6
Honey Boy, I hate to see you leaving;
Honey Boy, you know my heart is grieving.
JACK NORWORTH, *Honey Boy.* (1907)

7
If we must part forever,
Give me but one kind word to think upon,
And please myself withal, whilst my heart's breaking.
THOMAS OTWAY, *The Orphan.* Act v, sc. 2.

8
Some jealousy of someone's heir,
Some hopes of dying broken-hearted,
A miniature, a lock of hair,
The usual vows—and then we parted.
W. M. PRAED, *The Belle of the Ball.* St. 12.

9
In vain you tell your parting lover
You wish fair winds may waft him over.
Alas! what winds can happy prove,
That bear me far from what I love?
MATTHEW PRIOR, *A Song.*

10
He that parts us shall bring a brand from heaven,
And fire us hence like foxes.
SHAKESPEARE, *King Lear.* Act v, sc. 3, l. 22.

11
'Tis almost morning; I would have thee gone:
And yet no further than a wanton's bird;
Who lets it hop a little from her hand,
Like a poor prisoner in his twisted gyves,
And with a silk thread plucks it back again,
So loving-jealous of his liberty.
SHAKESPEARE, *Romeo and Juliet.* Act ii, sc. 2, l. 177.

Good night, good night! parting is such sweet sorrow,
That I shall say good night till it be morrow.
SHAKESPEARE, *Romeo and Juliet.* Act ii, sc. 2, l. 185.

Eyes, look your last!
Arms, take your last embrace!
SHAKESPEARE, *Romeo and Juliet.* Act v, sc. 3, l. 112.

12
I remember the way we parted,
The day and the way we met;
You hoped we were both broken-hearted,
And knew we should both forget.
SWINBURNE, *An Interlude.*

We twain shall not remeasure
The ways that left us twain;
Nor crush the lees of pleasure
From sanguine grapes of pain.
A. C. SWINBURNE, *Rococo.*

13
She went her unremembering way,
She went and left in me
The pang of all the partings gone,
And partings yet to be.
FRANCIS THOMPSON, *Daisy.* St. 12.

14
Shall I bid her go? what and if I do?
Shall I bid her go and spare not?
Oh no, no, no! I dare not.
UNKNOWN, *Corydon's Farewell to Phillis.* (PERCY, *Reliques.* Bk. ii, No. 10.)

Sir Toby: Shall I bid him go?
Clown: What an if you do?
Sir Toby: Shall I bid him go and spare not?
Clown: O no, no, no, no, you dare not.
SHAKESPEARE, *Twelfth Night.* Act ii, sc. 3, l. 118.

PARTY, see Politics

PASSION

See also Anger; Love and Lust

15
We also are men of like passions with you.
New Testament: Acts, xiv, 15.

Shepherds and ministers are both men; their nature and passions are the same, the modes of them only different.
LORD CHESTERFIELD, *Letters,* 10 May, 1748.

16
Only I discern
Infinite passion, and the pain
Of finite hearts that yearn.
ROBERT BROWNING, *Two in the Campagna.*

17
Femininely meaneth furiously,
Because all passions in excess are female.
BYRON, *Sardanapalus.* Act iii, sc. 1.

1
What is young passion but a gusty breeze
Ruffling the surface of a shallow flood?
HARTLEY COLERIDGE, *Sonnets*. No. 31.

The passionate young hours
When sorrow sang, and joy, for rapture, wept.
ROSALIE M. JONAS, *Temptation*.

2
Nor can a man of passions judge aright,
Except his mind be from all passions free.
SIR JOHN DAVIES, *Nosce Teipsum:* Sec. 4, st. 18.

3
We are ne'er like angels till our passion dies.
THOMAS DEKKER, *II The Honest Whore*. Act i, sc. 2.

4
Man is only truly great when he acts from the passions.
BENJAMIN DISRAELI, *Coningsby*. Bk. iv, ch. 13.

5
His passion cast a mist before his sense,
And either made, or magnified the offence.
DRYDEN, *Palamon and Arcite*. Bk. ii, l. 334.

Where passion rules, how weak does reason prove!
DRYDEN, *The Rival Ladies*. Act ii, sc. 1.

6
Sad as a wasted passion.
GEORGE ELIOT, *Spanish Gypsy*. Bk. i.

7
Passion, though a bad regulator, is a powerful spring.
EMERSON, *Conduct of Life: Considerations by the Way*.

8
Passion overcometh sober thought;
And this is cause of direst ills to men.
(*Θυμὸς δε κρείσσων τῶν ἐμῶν βουλευμάτων, ὅσπερ μεγίστων αἴτιος κακῶν βροτοῖς.*)
EURIPIDES, *Medea*, l. 1079.

9
The fit's upon me now!
Come quickly, gentle lady;
The fit's upon me now.
JOHN FLETCHER, *Wit Without Money*. Act v, sc. 4.

10
When passion entereth at the fore-gate, wisdom goeth out of the postern.
THOMAS FULLER, *Gnomologia*. No. 5564.

11
Though thou canst not pull thy passions out by the roots, yet it's in thy power to hold them down, for a time at least.
FULLER, *Introductio ad Prudentiam*, ii, 29.

12
And ev'n the proudest goddess, now and then,
Would lodge a night among the sons of men;
To vulgar deities descends the fashion,
Each, like her betters. had her earthly passion.
JOHN GAY, *Trivia*. Bk. ii, l. 111.

13
Great passions are incurable diseases: the very remedies make them worse.
GOETHE, *Conversations with Eckermann*.

14
Let never man be bold enough to say,
Thus, and no farther shall my passion stray:
The first crime, past, compels us into more,
And guilt grows *fate*, that was but *choice*, before.
AARON HILL, *Athelwold*. Act v.

15
Speed passion's ebb as you greet its flow—
To have, to hold, and in time let go!
LAURENCE HOPE, *The Teak Forest*.

16
Bee to the blossom, moth to the flame;
Each to his passion; what's in a name?
HELEN HUNT JACKSON, *Vanity of Vanities*.

17
Passion plucks no berries from the myrtle and ivy.
SAMUEL JOHNSON, *Works*, ii, 148.

18
The passions are the only orators which always persuade. (Les passions sont les seuls orateurs qui persuadent toujours.)
LA ROCHEFOUCAULD, *Maximes*. No. 8.

If we resist our passions, it is more because of their weakness than because of our strength. (Si nous résistons à nos passions, c'est plus par leur faiblesse que par notre force.)
LA ROCHEFOUCAULD, *Maximes*. No. 122.

19
The passions are merely different kinds of self-love. (Les passions ne sont que les divers goûts de l'amour-propre.)
LA ROCHEFOUCAULD, *Maximes Posthumes*. No. 531.

All the passions are nothing but different degrees of heat and cold of the blood. (Toutes les passions ne sont autre chose que les divers degrés de la chaleur et de la froideur du sang.)
LA ROCHEFOUCAULD, *Maximes Supprimées*. No. 564.

20
It is curious that we should be more anxious to conceal our best passions than our worst.
WALTER SAVAGE LANDOR, *Letter to Southey*, 1811.

21
It is with our passions, as it is with fire and water, they are good servants but bad masters.
SIR ROGER L'ESTRANGE, *Æsop*, 38.

22
Take heed lest passion sway
Thy judgement to do aught, which else free will
Would not admit.
MILTON, *Paradise Lost*. Bk. viii, l. 635.

May I govern my passions with absolute sway,
And grow wiser and better as my strength wears away.
WALTER POPE, *The Old Man's Wish*.

23
All passions that suffer themselves to be relished and digested are but moderate.
MONTAIGNE, *Essays*. Bk. i, ch. 2.

1 Passion is power,
And, kindly tempered, saves. All things declare
Struggle hath deeper peace than sleep can bring.
WILLIAM VAUGHN MOODY, *The Masque of Judgment*. Act iii, sc. 2.

2
It is a difficult thing for man to resist the natural necessity of mortal passions.
PLUTARCH, *Whom God is Slow to Punish.*

3
All subsists by elemental strife;
And passions are the elements of life.
POPE, *Essay on Man*. Epis. i, l. 169.

As fruits ungrateful to the planter's care,
On savage stocks inserted, learn to bear,
The surest Virtues thus from Passions shoot,
Wild Nature's vigour working at the root.
POPE, *Essay on Man*. Epis. ii, l. 181.

4
On life's vast ocean diversely we sail,
Reason the card, but Passion is the gale.
POPE, *Essay on Man*. Epis. ii, l. 107.

What Reason weaves, by Passion is undone.
POPE, *Essay on Man*. Epis. ii, l. 42.

Where passion leads or prudence points the way.
ROBERT LOWTH, *The Choice of Hercules.*

5
Search then the Ruling Passion: there alone,
The wild are constant, and the cunning known;
The fool consistent, and the false sincere;
Priests, princes, women, no dissemblers here.
POPE, *Moral Essays*. Epis. i, l. 174.

The ruling Passion, be it what it will,
The ruling Passion conquers Reason still.
POPE, *Moral Essays*. Epis. iii, l. 153.

And you, brave Cobham! to the latest breath,
Shall feel your Ruling Passion strong in death.
POPE, *Moral Essays*. Epis. i, l. 262.

If you can engage people's pride, love, pity, ambition, (or whatever is their prevailing passion) on your side, you need not fear what their reason can do against you.
LORD CHESTERFIELD, *Letters,* 8 Feb., 1746.

6
On diff'rent senses diff'rent objects strike;
Hence diff'rent passions more or less inflame,
As strong or weak the organs of the frame;
And hence one Master-passion in the breast,
Like Aaron's serpent, swallows up the rest.
POPE, *Essay on Man*. Epis. ii, l. 128.

In the human breast
Two master-passions cannot co-exist.
THOMAS CAMPBELL, *Theodric,* l. 488.

One passion doth expel another still.
GEORGE CHAPMAN, *Monsieur D'Olive*. Act v, 1.

7
It is a harder lot to be a slave to one's passions than to tyrants.
PYTHAGORAS. (STOBÆUS, *Florilegium*. Pt. vi, l. 47.)

8
Passions are likened best to floods and streams:
The shallow murmur, but the deep are dumb.
SIR WALTER RALEIGH, *The Silent Lover*. (Altissima quæque flumina minimo sono labuntur.—Quintus Curtius Rufus.) For attribution to Raleigh, see CAYLEY, *Life of Raleigh*, i, 3. *See also* 2126:5.

9
Her passions are made of nothing but the finest part of pure love.
SHAKESPEARE, *Antony and Cleopatra*. Act i, sc. 2, l. 151.

10 Give me that man
That is not passion's slave, and I will wear him
In my heart's core, ay, in my heart of heart.
SHAKESPEARE, *Hamlet*. Act iii, sc. 2, l. 76.

11
What to ourselves in passion we propose,
The passion ending, doth the purpose lose.
SHAKESPEARE, *Hamlet*. Act iii, sc. 2, l. 204.

I never heard a passion so confused,
So strange, outrageous, and so variable.
SHAKESPEARE, *The Merchant of Venice*. Act ii, sc. 8, l. 12.

12
You are eaten up with passion.
SHAKESPEARE, *Othello*. Act iii, sc. 3, l. 391.

O well-painted passion!
SHAKESPEARE, *Othello*. Act iv, sc. 1, l. 268.

13
A man in passion rides a horse that runs away with him.
C. H. SPURGEON, *Ploughman's Pictures,* 143.

In wayward passions lost and vain pursuits.
THOMSON, *The Seasons: Summer,* l. 1801.

14
True quietness of heart is won by resisting our passions, not by obeying them.
THOMAS À KEMPIS, *De Imitatione Christi*. Pt. iii, ch. 25.

15
Don't be in a passion, Tam, for passion is the most unbecoming thing in the Warld.
VANBRUGH, *The Relapse*. Act iii, sc. 1.

16
Does his own fatal passion become to each man his God? (Sua cuique deus fit dira cupido?)
VERGIL, *Æneid*. Bk. ix, l. 185.

17
All the passions are extinguished with old age. (Toutes les passions s'éteignant avec l'age.)
VOLTAIRE, *Stances ou Quatrains*. After Pibrac.
See also AGE: ITS COMPENSATIONS.

18
The seas are quiet when the winds give o'er;
So calm are we when passions are no more.
EDMUND WALLER, *On the Last Verses in the Book.*

The sea's my mind, which calm would be
Were it from winds (my passions) free;
But out, alas! no sea I find
Is troubled like a lover's mind.
Within it rocks and shallows be:
Despair and fond credulity.
SIR JOHN SUCKLING, *Love's World.*

1
Passion and prejudice govern the world; only under the name of reason.

JOHN WESLEY, *Letter to Joseph Benson*, 5 Oct., 1770.

2
She parried Time's malicious dart,
And kept the years at bay,
Till passion entered in her heart
And aged her in a day!

ELLA WHEELER WILCOX, *The Destroyer.*

PAST

See also Antiquity, Memory, Time, Yesterday

I—Past: Apothegms

3
Oh! leave the past to bury its own dead.

WILFRID SCAWEN BLUNT, *To One Who Would Make a Confession.*

Let the dead Past bury its dead!

LONGFELLOW, *A Psalm of Life.*

Why should we grope among the dry bones of the past, or put the living generation into masquerade out of its faded wardrobe?

EMERSON, *Essays, Second Series: Lecture.*

4
Let all things passed pass.

JOHN HEYWOOD, *Proverbs*. Pt. ii, ch. 9. (1546)

Let bygans be bygans.

FRANCIS NETHERSOLE, *Parables*, 5.

By-gones be by-gones, and fair play for time to come.

SAMUEL PALMER, *Moral Essay on Proverbs.*

5
What is past, even the fool knows. (Ῥεχθὲν δέ τε νήπιος ἔγνω.)

HOMER, *Iliad*. Bk. xvii, l. 32.

6
A eulogist of bygone days. (Laudator temporis acti.)

HORACE, *Ars Poetica*, l. 173.

The "good old times"—all times, when old, are good.

BYRON, *The Age of Bronze*, l. 1.

Say not thou, What is the cause that the former days were better than these? for thou dost not inquire wisely concerning this.

Old Testament: Ecclesiastes, vii, 10.

See also under ANTIQUITY.

7
We live in time, and the past must always be the most momentous part of it.

LIONEL JOHNSON, *Post Liminium*, 211.

8
Safe in the hallowed quiets of the past.

J. R. LOWELL, *The Cathedral*, l. 235.

9
Our past has gone into history.

MCKINLEY, *Speech*, at Memphis, 30 April, 1901.

The past at least is secure.

DANIEL WEBSTER, *Speech*, on Foote's Resolution, Senate, 26 Jan., 1830.

10
The Past is a bucket of ashes.

CARL SANDBURG, *Prairie.*

11
Those who cannot remember the past are condemned to repeat it.

GEORGE SANTAYANA, *Life of Reason*, p. 284.

12
Nothing is certain except the past. (Nihil nisi quod preteriit certum est.)

SENECA, *De Consolatione ad Marciam*. Sec. 22.

13
The dark backward and abysm of time.

SHAKESPEARE, *The Tempest*. Act i, sc. 2, l. 50.

What's past is prologue.

SHAKESPEARE, *The Tempest*. Act ii, sc. 1, l. 253.

14
The past, like an inspired rhapsodist, fills the theatre of everlasting generations with her harmony.

SHELLEY. (BIRRELL, *Obiter Dicta: Second Series: The Muse of History.*)

15
The eternal landscape of the past.

TENNYSON, *In Memoriam*. Pt. xlvi.

Thro' all the faultful Past.

TENNYSON, *The Princess*. Pt. vii, l. 232.

II—Past: The Irrevocable Past

16
This only is denied even to God: the power to undo the past. (Μόνου γὰρ αὐτοῦ καὶ θεὸς στερίσκεται, ἀγένητα ποιεῖν ἅσσ' ἂν ᾖ πεπραγμένα.)

AGATHON. (ARISTOTLE, *Nicomachean Ethics*. Bk. vi, ch. 2, sec. 6.)

Even Time, the father of all, cannot undo the past, whether right or wrong. (Τῶν δὲ πεπραγμένων ἐν δίκα τε καὶ παρὰ δίκαν, ἀποίητον οὐδ' ἂν χρόνος ὁ πάντων πατὴρ δύναιτο θέμεν ἔργων τέλος.)

PINDAR, *Olympian Odes*. Ode ii, l. 16.

Virtue's achievement, Folly's crime,
Whate'er of guilt or good the past has known,
Not e'en the Sire of all things, mighty Time,
Hath power to change, or make the deed undone.

PINDAR, *Olympian Odes*. Ode ii, l. 16.

17
Odin . . . of all powers the mightiest far art thou,
Lord over men on Earth, and Gods in Heaven;
Yet even from thee thyself hath been withheld
One thing: to undo what thou thyself hast rul'd.

MATTHEW ARNOLD, *Balder Dead: Funeral*, l. 254.

18
Thou unrelenting past.

BRYANT, *To the Past.*

19
Yet will the Father not render vain whatever now is past, nor will he alter and undo what once the fleeting hour has brought. (Non tamen irritum, Quodcumque retro est, efficiet, neque Diffinget infec.umque reddet, Quod fugiens semel hora vexit.)

HORACE, *Odes*. Bk. iii, ode 29, l. 45.

Not heaven itself upon the past has power.

DRYDEN, *Imitation of Horace*, iii, 29, 71.

1
Nor deem the irrevocable Past
As wholly wasted, wholly vain,
If, rising on its wrecks, at last
To something nobler we attain.
LONGFELLOW, *The Ladder of St. Augustine.*

2
But past who can recall, or done undo?
Not God Omnipotent.
MILTON, *Paradise Lost.* Bk. ix, l. 926.

3
Neither can the wave that has passed be called back; nor can the hour which has gone by return. (Nec quæ præteriit, iterum revocabitur unda, Nec quæ præteriit, hora redire potest.)
OVID, *Ars Amatoria.* Bk. iii, l. 63.

4
O that Jupiter would give back to me the years that are past! (O mihi præteritos referat si Juppiter annos.)
VERGIL, *Æneid.* Bk. viii, l. 560.

Nothing can bring back the hour
Of splendour in the grass, of glory in the flower.
WORDSWORTH, *Intimations of Immortality,* l. 181.

III—Past: Its Memory

5
Ah, the Past, the pearl-gift thrown
To hogs, time's opportunity we made
So light of, only recognized when flown!
ROBERT BROWNING, *Jocoseria: Jochanan Hakkadosh.*

The past is in its grave,
Though its ghost haunts us.
ROBERT BROWNING, *Pauline.*

But how carve way i' the life that lies before,
If bent on groaning ever for the past?
ROBERT BROWNING, *Balaustion's Adventure.*
See also under REMORSE.

No past is dead for us, but only sleeping, Love.
HELEN HUNT JACKSON, *At Last.*

7
This is the place. Stand still, my steed,
Let me review the scene,
And summon from the shadowy Past
The forms that once have been.
LONGFELLOW, *A Gleam of Sunshine.*

7a
Ah, me! what a world this was to live in two or three centuries ago, when it was getting itself discovered! . . . Then man was courting Nature, now he has married her. Every mystery is dissipated. The planet is familiar as the trodden pathway running between towns.
ALEXANDER SMITH, *Dreamthorp: On Vagabonds.*

8
Dead and gone, the days we had together,
Shadow-stricken all the lights that shone
Round them, flown as flies the blown-foam's feather,
Dead and gone.
SWINBURNE, *Past Days.*

9
But the tender grace of a day that is dead
Will never come back to me.
TENNYSON, *Break, Break, Break.*

So sad, so strange, the days that are no more.
TENNYSON, *The Princess.* Pt. iv, l. 35.

O Death in Life, the days that are no more.
TENNYSON, *The Princess:* Pt. iv, l. 40.

10
Old, unhappy, far-off things,
And battles long ago.
WORDSWORTH, *The Solitary Reaper.*

11
'Tis greatly wise to talk with our past hours,
And ask them what report they bore to heaven.
YOUNG, *Night Thoughts.* Night ii, l. 376.

IV—Past and Present

12
A sensible man judges of present by past events. (Ἔννους τὰ καινὰ τοῖς πάλαι τεκμαίρεται.)
SOPHOCLES, *Œdipus Tyrannus,* l. 916.

We read the past by the light of the present, and the forms vary as the shadows fall, or as the point of vision alters.
J. A. FROUDE. *Short Studies on Great Subjects: Society in Italy. See also under* EXPERIENCE.

13
The Present is the living sum-total of the whole Past.
CARLYLE, *Essays: Characteristics.*

The present contains nothing more than the past, and what is found in the effect was already in the cause.
HENRI BERGSON, *Creative Evolution.* Ch. 1.

14
Underneath the surface of Today,
Lies Yesterday, and what we call the Past,
The only thing which never can decay.
EUGENE LEE-HAMILTON, *Roman Baths.*

Things bygone are the only things that last:
The present is mere grass, quick-mown away;
The Past is stone, and stands forever fast.
EUGENE LEE-HAMILTON, *Roman Baths.*

15
The dogmas of the quiet past are inadequate to the stormy present.
ABRAHAM LINCOLN, *Second Annual Message to Congress,* 1862.

16
Consult the dead upon things that were,
But the living only on things that are.
LONGFELLOW, *The Golden Legend.* Pt. i.

17
O there are Voices of the Past,
Links of a broken chain,
Wings that can bear me back to Times
Which cannot come again;
Yet God forbid that I should lose
The echoes that remain!
ADELAIDE ANN PROCTER, *Voices of the Past.*

18
Why is it that the meed of changeless fame
Is grudged the present, granted to the past?
JAMES EDWIN ROGERS, *To George Waring.*

1
Past and to come, seems best; things present, worst.
SHAKESPEARE, *II Henry IV*. Act i, sc. 3, l. 108.

2
Thou who stealest fire
From the fountains of the past,
To glorify the present.
TENNYSON, *Ode to Memory*.

3
He praises all thing that is gone;
Of present thing he praises none.
UNKNOWN, *Cursor Mundi*, l. 3577. (c. 1375)

He praised the present and abused the past,
Reversing the good custom of old days.
BYRON, *Don Juan*. Canto iii, st. 79.

See also under AGE, THE.

V—Past and Future

4
Making all futures fruits of all the pasts.
EDWIN ARNOLD, *Light of Asia*. Bk. v, l. 432.

What is past is past. There is a future left to all men, who have the virtue to repent and the energy to atone.
BULWER-LYTTON, *Lady of Lyons*. Act iv, sc. 1.

5
You can never plan the future by the past.
EDMUND BURKE, *Letter to a Member of the National Assembly*.

The best prophet of the future is the past.
BYRON, *Letter*, 28 Jan., 1821.

6
I watch the wheels of Nature's mazy plan,
And learn the future by the past of man.
CAMPBELL, *Pleasures of Hope*. Pt. i, l. 319.

Study the past, if you would divine the future.
CONFUCIUS, *Analects*.

The best way to suppose what may come is to remember what is past.
LORD HALIFAX, *Works*, p. 249.

I know of no way of judging the future but by the past.
PATRICK HENRY, *Speech*, in Virginia Convention, March, 1775.

7
Indemnity for the past and security for the future.
CHARLES JAMES FOX, *Letter to Hon. T. Maitland*. (RUSSELL, *Memorials of Fox*, iii, 345.)

8
The Past is like a funeral gone by,
The Future comes like an unwelcome guest.
EDMUND GOSSE, *Sonnet: May-Day*.

9
She knew the future, for the past she knew.
JOHN LANGHORNE, *The Country Justice*, l. 214.

10
Look not mournfully into the Past. It comes not back again. Wisely improve the Present. It is thine. Go forth to meet the shadowy Future, without fear, and with a manly heart.
LONGFELLOW, *Hyperion*: Bk. i, *Motto*.

11
For hope shall brighten days to come,
And memory gild the past!
THOMAS MOORE, *Song*.

12
The future is only the past again, entered through another gate.
PINERO, *The Second Mrs. Tanqueray*. Act iv.

13
We will not anticipate the past; so mind, young people,—our retrospection will be all to the future.
SHERIDAN, *The Rivals*. Act iv, sc. 2.

14
Man hath a weary pilgrimage
As through the world he wends,
On every stage, from youth to age,
Still discontent attends;
With heaviness he casts his eye
Upon the road before,
And still remembers with a sigh
The days that are no more.
ROBERT SOUTHEY, *Remembrance*.

15
The past unsighed for, and the future sure.
WORDSWORTH, *Laodamia*, l. 100.

PATIENCE

See also Endurance, Waiting

I—Patience: Apothegms

16
Patience and shuffle the cards. (Paciencia y barajar.)
CERVANTES, *Don Quixote*. Pt. ii, ch. 23.

17
How far then, Catiline, will you abuse our patience? (Quosque tandem abutere, Catilina, patientia nostra?)
CICERO, *In Catilinam*. No. i, ch. 1, sec. 1.

18
Though God take the sun out of heaven, yet we must have patience.
GEORGE HERBERT, *Jacula Prudentum*.

19
Let patience grow in your garden.
JOHN HEYWOOD, *Proverbs*. Pt. i, ch. 11. (1546)

Patience is a flower that grows not in every garden.
HOWELL, *Familiar Letters*. Bk. i, No. 58.

20
Ye have heard of the patience of Job.
New Testament: James, v, 11. *See also* JOB.

21
In your patience possess ye your souls.
New Testament: Luke, xxi, 19.

And see all sights from pole to pole,
And glance, and nod, and bustle by;
And never once possess our soul
Before we die.
MATTHEW ARNOLD, *A Southern Night*. St. 18.

22
Have patience and endure. (Perfer et obdura.)
OVID, *Amores*. Bk. iii, eleg. 11, l. 7.

23
Patience provoked often turns to fury. (Furor fit læsa sæpius patientia.)
PUBLILIUS SYRUS, *Sententiæ*. No. 289.

Beware the fury of a patient man.
DRYDEN, *Absalom and Achitophel*. Pt. i, l. 1005.

I do oppose My patience to his fury.
SHAKESPEARE, *The Merchant of Venice*. Act iv, sc. 1, l. 10.

1
There is nothing so bitter, that a patient mind can not find some solace for it. (Nihil tam acerbum est in quo non æquus animus solatium inveniat.)
SENECA, *De Animi Tranquillitate*. Sec. 10.

2
You tread upon my patience.
SHAKESPEARE, *I Henry IV*. Act i, sc. 3, l. 4.

3
Though patience be a tired mare, yet she will plod.
SHAKESPEARE, *Henry V*. Act ii, sc. 1, l. 26.

4
I will with patience hear.
SHAKESPEARE, *Julius Cæsar*. Act i, sc. 2, l. 169.

I will be the pattern of all patience.
SHAKESPEARE, *King Lear*. Act iii, sc. 2, l. 36.

God grant us patience!
SHAKESPEARE, *Love's Labour's Lost*. Act i, sc. 1, l. 197.

5
That which in mean men we intitle patience
Is pale cold cowardice in noble breasts.
SHAKESPEARE, *Richard II*. Act i, sc. 2, l. 33.

6
There is between my will and all offences
A guard of patience.
SHAKESPEARE, *Troilus and Cressida*. Act v, sc. 2, l. 53.

I will not be myself, nor have cognition
Of what I feel: I am all patience.
SHAKESPEARE, *Troilus and Cressida*. Act v, sc. 2, l. 63.

7
She pined in thought,
And with a green and yellow melancholy,
She sat like patience on a monument,
Smiling at grief.
SHAKESPEARE, *Twelfth Night*. Act ii, sc. 4, l. 115.

Like Patience gazing on kings' graves, and smiling
Extremity out of act.
SHAKESPEARE, *Pericles*. Act v, sc. 1, l. 139.

Dame Patience sitting there I found,
With face pale, upon a hill of sand.
CHAUCER, *Parlement of Foules*, l. 242.

That Patience-on-a-Monument kind of look.
HENLEY AND STEVENSON, *Beau Austin*. Act i, sc. 2.

8
Strike, but hear. (Πάταξον μέν, ἄκουσον δέ.)
THEMISTOCLES, to Eurybiades, when the latter, during an argument, raised his staff to strike him. (PLUTARCH, *Lives: Themistocles*. Ch. 11, sec. 3.) The Latin form is: Verbera, sed audi.

That ancient and patient request, "Verbera, sed audi."
BACON, *Advancement of Learning*. Bk. ii.

9
All men commend patience, although few be willing to practise it.
THOMAS À KEMPIS, *De Imitatione Christi*. Pt. iii, ch. 12.

'Tis all men's office to speak patience
To those that wring under the load of sorrow,
But no man's virtue nor sufficiency
To be so moral when he shall endure
The like himself.
SHAKESPEARE, *Much Ado About Nothing*. Act v, sc. 1, l. 27.

See also MISFORTUNE OF OTHERS.

10
At the least bear patiently, if thou canst not joyfully.
THOMAS À KEMPIS, *De Imitatione Christi*. Pt. iii, ch. 57.

II—Patience: Sovereign Remedy

11
Patience is a plaister for all sores.
CERVANTES, *Don Quixote*. Pt. ii, ch. 1. (D'Urfey, tr.) (1694)

Be plastered with patience.
WILLIAM LANGLAND, *Piers Plowman*. Passus xx, l. 89. (c. 1393)

Patience is sorrow's salve.
CHURCHILL, *Prophecy of Famine*, l. 363.

12
Patience is the best medicine that is for a sick man.
JOHN FLORIO, *First Fruites*. Fo. 44. (1578)

Patience, which is the leech of all offence.
JOHN GOWER, *Confessio Amantis*. Bk. iii, l. 614.

13
Patience perforce is medicine for a mad dog.
JAMES HOWELL, *Proverbs*, 11.

Patience perforce is a remedy for a mad dog.
RABELAIS, *Works*. Bk. v, ch. 1.

14
Patience, sov'reign o'er transmuted ill.
SAMUEL JOHNSON, *The Vanity of Human Wishes*, l. 360.

15
Patience is the best remedy for every trouble. (Animus æquos optimum est ærumnæ condimentum.)
PLAUTUS, *Rudens*, l. 402. (Act ii, sc. 3.)

Patience is a remedy for every disease.
THOMAS WILSON, *Arte of Rhetorique*, 206. (1560)

16
Every misfortune is subdued by patience. (Superanda omnis fortuna ferendo est.)
VERGIL, *Æneid*. Bk. v, l. 710.

III—Patience: Its Virtues

17
I worked with patience, which means almost power.
E. B. BROWNING, *Aurora Leigh*. Bk. iii, l. 204.

18
Our patience will achieve more than our force.
EDMUND BURKE, *Reflections on the Revolution in France*.

1
Patience is a high virtue, certàin,
For it vanquisheth, as this clerk seyn,
Things that regour should never attain.
CHAUCER, *The Frankeleyns Tale*, l. 773.

Sufferance is a sovereign virtue.
LANGLAND, *Piers Plowman*. Passus xi, l. 370.

Patience, which alike to the Pagan and the Christian world, to the Oriental and the Occidental mind, is the greatest virtue of man.
GEORGE EDWARD WOODBERRY, *Virgil*.

2
His patient soul endures what Heav'n ordains,
But neither feels nor fears ideal pains.
GEORGE CRABBE, *The Borough*. Letter 17.

3
A patient man's a pattern for a king.
THOMAS DEKKER, *II The Honest Whore*. Fin.

4
The worst speak something good; if all want sense,
God takes a text, and preacheth patience.
GEORGE HERBERT, *The Church-Porch*. St. 72.

"Work and wait," is what God says to us in Creation and in Providence.
J. G. HOLLAND, *Gold-Foil: Patience*.

5
What cannot be removed, becomes lighter through patience. (Levius fit patientia Quicquid corrigere est nefas.)
HORACE, *Odes*. Bk. i, ode 24, l. 19.

6
Patience is the strongest of strong drinks, for it kills the giant Despair.
DOUGLAS JERROLD, *Jerrold's Wit: Patience*.

7
Patience—in patience there is safety.
LABOULAYE, *Abdallah*. Ch. 20.

8
The patient overcome. (Pacientes vincunt.)
LANGLAND, *Piers Plowman*. Passus xiv, l. 138.

Patient men win the day.
JOHN CLARKE, *Parœmiologia*, 242.

He that has patience may compass anything.
RABELAIS, *Works*. Bk. iv, ch. 48.

9
By patience and time we sever
What strength and rage could never.
(Patience et longueur de temps
Font plus que force ni que rage.)
LA FONTAINE, *Fables*. Bk. ii, fab. 11.

10
Rule by patience, Laughing Water!
LONGFELLOW, *Hiawatha*. Pt. x.

11
Endurance is the crowning quality,
And patience all the passion of great hearts.
J. R. LOWELL, *Columbus*, l. 241.

Endurance is nobler than strength, and patience than beauty.
RUSKIN, *The Two Paths*. Lecture iv, sec. 3.

12
Some find the fruit like Hercules—
For such the moon and sun may stop;
Yet never doubt that Sisyphus
Achieved at last the mountain top.
SCUDDER MIDDLETON, *The Journey*.

13
Arm th' obdured breast
With stubborn patience as with triple steel.
MILTON, *Paradise Lost*. Bk. ii, l. 568.

14
Patience, which is a great part of justice. (Patientia, quæ pars magna justitiæ est.)
PLINY THE YOUNGER, *Epistles*.

15
Patience is bitter, but its fruit is sweet. (La patience est amère, mais son fruit est doux.)
ROUSSEAU, *Émile*.

16
Whosoever hath not patience, neither doth he possess philosophy.
SADI, *Gulistan*. Ch. 3, tale 1.

17
How poor are they that have not patience!
SHAKESPEARE, *Othello*. Act ii, sc. 3, l. 376.

Patience, thou young and rose-lipp'd cherubin.
SHAKESPEARE, *Othello*. Act iv, sc. 2, l. 63.

18
But patience perforce; he must abide
What future and his fate on him will lay.
SPENSER, *Faery Queene*. Bk. iii, canto 10, st. 3.

Since you will buckle fortune on my back,
To bear her burthen, whether I will or no,
I must have patience to endure the load.
SHAKESPEARE, *Richard III*. Act iii, sc. 7, l. 228.

19
Patience is the art of hoping. (La patience est l'art d'espérer.)
VAUVENARGUES, *Réflexions*. No. 251.

20
One to whom
Long patience hath such mild composure given,
That patience now doth seem a thing of which
He hath no need.
WORDSWORTH, *Animal Tranquillity and Decay*.

IV—Patience: Its Faults

21
Patience is a flatterer, sir—and an ass, sir.
APHRA BEHN, *Feigned Courtezans*. Act iii, sc. 1.

22
He preacheth patience that never knew pain.
H. G. BOHN, *Hand-Book of Proverbs*, 381.

23
There is however a limit at which forbearance ceases to be a virtue.
EDMUND BURKE, *Observations on a Late Publication on the Present State of the Nation*.

But there are times when patience proves at fault.
ROBERT BROWNING, *Paracelsus*. Pt. iii.

There was a time when Patience ceased to be a virtue. It was long ago.
CHARLOTTE PERKINS GILMAN, *The Forerunner*.

24
Patience with poverty is all a poor man's remedy.
JOHN CLARKE. *Parœmiologia*, 15.

Patience, virtue of the poor.
RICHARD FLECKNOE, *Diarium*, 6.

Patience, the beggar's virtue.
PHILIP MASSINGER, *A New Way to Pay Old Debts*. Act v, sc. 1.

1
Patience is the virtue of an ass,
That trots beneath his burden, and is quiet.
GEORGE GRANVILLE, *Heroic Love*. Act i.

Patience is sottish, and impatience does
Become a dog that's mad.
SHAKESPEARE, *Antony and Cleopatra*, iv, 15, 79.

PATRICK, SAINT

See also Ireland

2
Oh! St. Patrick was a gentleman
Who came of decent people;
He built a church in Dublin town,
And on it put a steeple.
HENRY BENNETT, *Saint Patrick*.

So, success attend St. Patrick's fist,
For he's a saint so clever;
Oh! he gave the snakes and toads a twist,
And bothered them forever!
HENRY BENNETT, *Saint Patrick*.

Oh, thou tormenting Irish lay!
I've got thee buzzing in my brain,
And cannot turn thee out again.
ELIZA COOK, *St. Patrick's Day*.

3
On the eighth day of March it was, some people say,
That Saint Pathrick at midnight he first saw the day,
While others declare 'twas the ninth he was born . . .
Till Father Mulcahy, who showed them their sins,
Said, "No one could have two birthdays, but a twins."
Says he, "Boys, don't be fightin' for eight or for nine,
Don't be always dividin', but sometimes combine;
Combine eight and nine, and seventeen is the mark,
So let that be his birthday." "Amen!" says the clerk.
SAMUEL LOVER, *The Birth of St. Patrick*.

PATRIOTISM

See also America, England, Father of His Country, Flag

I—Patriotism: Definitions

4
Patriotism is a lively sense of collective responsibility. Nationalism is a silly cock crowing on its own dunghill.
RICHARD ALDINGTON, *Colonel's Daughter*, p. 49.

5
Patriotism has its roots deep in the instincts and the affections. Love of country is the expansion of filial love.
D. D. FIELD, *Speeches: A Memorial Address*.

There is no limit to the noble aspirations which the words "my country" may evoke.
DEAN W. R. INGE. (MARCHANT, *Wit and Wisdom of Dean Inge*. No. 154.)

6
Patriotism is the last refuge of a scoundrel.
SAMUEL JOHNSON, (BOSWELL, *Life*, 1775.)

7
Patriotism is a kind of religion; it is the egg from which wars are hatched.
GUY DE MAUPASSANT, *My Uncle Sosthenes*.

8
Patriotism is often an arbitrary veneration of real estate above principles.
G. J. NATHAN, *Testament of a Critic*, p. 16.

9
True patriotism is of no party.
SMOLLETT, *The Adventures of Sir Launcelot Greaves*. Ch. 9. *See also* POLITICS AND PARTY.

10
There are no points of the compass on the chart of true patriotism.
ROBERT C. WINTHROP, *Letter to Boston Commercial Club*. 12 June, 1879.

Patriotism knows neither latitude nor longitude. It is not climatic.
E. A. STORRS, *Political Oratory*. Ch. 2.

II—Patriotism: Apothegms

10a
The Beautiful, the Sacred—
Which, in all climes, men that have hearts adore
By the great title of their mother country!
BULWER-LYTTON, *Richelieu*. Act iv, sc. 2.

11
To make us love our country, our country ought to be lovely.
EDMUND BURKE, *Reflections on the Revolution in France*.

He loves his country best who strives to make it best.
R. G. INGERSOLL, *Decoration Day Oration, 1882*.

Best they honour thee
Who honour in thee only what is best.
WILLIAM WATSON, *The True Patriotism*.

12
He who loves not his country, can love nothing.
BYRON, *The Two Foscari*. Act iii, sc. 1.

He, with liberal and enlargèd mind,
Who loves his country, cannot hate mankind.
CHARLES CHURCHILL, *The Farewell*, l. 300.

13
I am French, I am Chauvin. (J'suis Français, j'suis Chauvin.)
THÉODORE AND HIPPOLYTE COGNIARD, *La Cocarde Tricolore*. Produced in Paris, 19 March, 1831. In the play, Chauvin is a young recruit, who is always singing couplets with the above refrain. Said to have been drawn from Nicholas Chauvin, sergeant in Napoleon's army, and extravagant patriot.

Since your marriage you have entered into chauvinism.
BAYARD AND DUMANOIR, *Aides-de-Camp*. (1842)

1
How can a man be said to have a country when he has no right to a square inch of soil?

HENRY GEORGE, *Social Problems*. Ch. 2.

2
Nothing is more shameful than ignorance of one's Fatherland. (Nihil magis pudendum quam ignarum esse suæ Patriæ.)

GABRIEL HARVEY, *Note,* written in Humphrey Lloyd's *Breviary of Britain.*

3
We don't want to fight,
But, by Jingo, if we do,
We've got the ships, we've got the men,
We've got the money too.

G. W. HUNT, *We Don't Want to Fight*. An English music hall song of 1878, when the country was on the verge of intervening in the Russo-Turkish war on behalf of the Turks. The Russophobes became known as Jingoes, and the term came to be applied generally to super-patriots, itching to go to war on the slightest provocation.

By the living Jingo.

GOLDSMITH, *The Vicar of Wakefield*. Ch. 10.

4
Indeed, I tremble for my country when I reflect that God is just.

THOMAS JEFFERSON, *Notes on Virginia: Manners.*

5
That man is little to be envied, whose patriotism would not gain force upon the plain of Marathon, or whose piety would not grow warmer among the ruins of Iona.

SAMUEL JOHNSON, *A Journey to the Western Islands: Inch Kenneth.*

6
Why should patriotism and pessimism be identical? Hope is the mainspring of patriotism.

DAVID LLOYD GEORGE, *Speech,* House of Commons, Oct., 1919.

7
And thus we see on either hand
We name our blessings whence they've sprung;
We call our country Father Land,
We call our language Mother Tongue.

SAMUEL LOVER, *Father Land and Mother Tongue.*

8
We find them cracking up the country they belong to.

JAMES PAYN, *By Proxy*. Ch. 1.

9
I am already married to my country.

WILLIAM PITT, THE YOUNGER, when Horace Walpole tried to arrange a marriage between him and Mademoiselle Necker, afterwards Madame de Staël, in 1783. (CROKER, *Memoirs*, ii, 340.)

He married public virtue in his early days, but seemed forever afterwards to be quarreling with his wife.

ROBERT HALL, of Bishop Watson. (GREGORY, *Life.*)

10
Man was not born for himself alone, but for his country.

PLATO, *Epistles:* No. ix, *To Archytas*. Quoted by Cicero (*De Finibus*, ii, 14, 45): Non sibi se soli natum meminerit sed patriæ.

11
Who dare to love their country, and be poor.

POPE, *On His Grotto at Twickenham.*

12
Don't spread patriotism too thin.

THEODORE ROOSEVELT. (*Metropolitan Magazine,* July, 1918.)

13
It is glorious to serve one's country by deeds; even to serve her by words is a thing not to be despised. (Pulchrum est bene facere rei publicæ, etiam bene dicere haud absurdum est.)

SALLUST, *Catiline*. Sec. 3.

14
For country, children, hearth, and home. (Pro patria, pro liberis, pro aris atque focis.)

SALLUST, *Catiline*. Sec. 59.

Strike—till the last armed foe expires;
Strike—for your altars and your fires;
Strike—for the green graves of your sires;
God—and your native land!

FITZ-GREENE HALLECK, *Marco Bozzaris.*

15
A fatherland focuses a people.

ISRAEL ZANGWILL, *Children of the Ghetto.* Bk. ii, ch. 15.

III—Patriotism: My Country

16
The die was now cast; I had passed the Rubicon. Swim or sink, live or die, survive or perish with my country was my unalterable determination.

JOHN ADAMS, *Works*. Vol. iv, p. 8. In a conversation with Jonathan Sewell, in 1774. Quoted by Webster in his *Supposed Speech of John Adams.*

Live or die, sink or swim.

GEORGE PEELE, *Edward I*. (c. 1586)

17
To that loved land, where'er he goes,
His tenderest thoughts are cast;
And dearer still, through absence, grows
The memory of the past.

JAMES DRUMMOND BURNS, *The Exile.*

18
Because all earth, except his native land,
To him is one wide prison, and each breath
Of foreign air he draws seems a slow poison,
Consuming but not killing.

BYRON, *The Two Foscari*. Act i, sc. 1.

The more I saw of foreign countries, the more I loved my own. (Plus je vis l'étranger, plus j'aimais ma patrie.)

LAURENT DE BELLOY, *Siège de Calais.*

The more I see of other countries the more I love my own.

MADAME DE STAËL, *Corinne.*

1
O Heaven! he cried, my bleeding country save!

CAMPBELL, *The Pleasures of Hope*. Pt. i, l. 359.

2
Dear are our parents, dear are our children, neighbors, companions; but all the affections of all men are bound up in one native land. (Cari sunt parentes, cari liberi, propinqui, familiares; sed omnes omnium caritates patria una complexa est.)

CICERO, *De Officiis*. Bk. i, ch. 17, sec. 57.

Our country is the common parent of all. (Patria est communis omnium parens.)

CICERO, *In Catilinam*. No. i, sec. 7.

Dear, sweet and pleasing to us all is the soil of our native land. (Solum patriæ omnibus est carum, dulce, atque jucundum.)

CICERO, *In Catilinam*. No. iv, sec. 8.

3
But more, my country's love demands the lays;
My country's be the profit; mine the praise.

JOHN GAY, *Trivia*. Bk. i, l. 21.

4
They love their land because it is their own,
And scorn to give aught other reason why.

FITZ-GREENE HALLECK, *Connecticut*.

5
He serves me most, who serves his country best.

HOMER, *Iliad*. Bk. x, l. 201. (Pope, tr.)

Our country's welfare is our first concern,
And who promotes that best, best proves his duty.

WILLIAM HAVARD, *Regulus*. Act iii, sc. 3.

6
God gave all men all earth to love,
But since our hearts are small,
Ordained for each one spot should prove
Belovèd over all.

RUDYARD KIPLING, *Sussex*.

7
Opposed to these, a hovering band
Contended for their father-land;
Peasants, whose new-found strength had broke
From manly necks th' ignoble yoke,
And beat their fetters into swords,
On equal terms to fight their lords.

MONTGOMERY, *The Patriot's Pass-Word*.

Marshall'd once more, at freedom's call
They came to conquer or to fall.

MONTGOMERY, *The Patriot's Pass-Word*.

8
What bosom beats not in his country's cause?

POPE, *Prologue to Addison's Cato*, l. 24.

9
Duty's claim and country's call
Shall be conscience for us all!

J. L. RENTOUL, *Australia's Battle Hymn*.

10
Breathes there the man, with soul so dead,
Who never to himself hath said,
This is my own, my native land?
Whose heart hath ne'er within him burn'd
As home his footsteps he hath turn'd
From wandering on a foreign strand?

SCOTT, *Lay of the Last Minstrel*. Canto vi, st. 1.

Land of my sires! What mortal hand
Can e'er untie the filial band
That knits me to thy rugged strand!

SCOTT, *Lay of the Last Minstrel*. Canto vi, st. 2.

Where's the coward that would not dare
To fight for such a land?

SCOTT, *Marmion*. Canto iv, st. 30.

11
I do love
My country's good with a respect more tender,
More holy and profound, than mine own life.

SHAKESPEARE, *Coriolanus*. Act iii, sc. 3, l. 112.

12
This day is call'd the feast of Crispian:
He that outlives this day, and comes safe home,
Will stand a tip-toe when this day is named,
And rouse him at the name of Crispian.

SHAKESPEARE, *Henry V*. Act iv, sc. 3, l. 40.

13
One drop of blood drawn from thy country's bosom,
Should grieve thee more than streams of foreign gore.

SHAKESPEARE, *I Henry VI*. Act iii, sc. 3, l. 54.

Who is here so vile that will not love his country?

SHAKESPEARE, *Julius Cæsar*. Act iii, sc. 2, l. 35.

14
I vow to thee, my country—all earthly things above—
Entire and whole and perfect, the service of my love.

CECIL SPRING-RICE, *I Vow to Thee, My Country*. See APPENDIX for full quotation.

15
The arm that drives its unbought blows
With all a patriot's scorn,
Might brain a tyrant with a rose,
Or stab him with a thorn.

HENRY TIMROD, *A Cry to Arms*.

16
Our country is that spot to which our heart is bound. (La patrie est aux lieux où l'âme est enchainée.)

VOLTAIRE, *Le Fanatisme*, i, 2.

17
I would not change my native land
For rich Peru with all her gold.

ISAAC WATTS, *Praise for Birth*.

18
Let our object be, our country, our whole country, and nothing but our country.

DANIEL WEBSTER, *Address, at the laying of the corner-stone of the Bunker Hill Monument*, 17 June, 1825.

19
The land we from our fathers had in trust,
And to our children will transmit, or die:
This is our maxim, this our piety.

WORDSWORTH, *Poems Dedicated to National Independence*. Pt. ii, No. 11.

Our land is the dearer for our sacrifices. The blood of our martyrs sanctifies and enriches it. Their spirit passes into thousands of hearts. How costly is the progress of the race. It is only by the giving of life that we can have life.
REV. E. J. YOUNG, *Lesson of the Hour*. (*Monthly Religious Mag*., May, 1865.)

IV—Patriotism and Death

See also Soldier: How Sleep the Brave

1
What pity is it
That we can die but once to serve our country!
ADDISON, *Cato*. Act iv, sc. 4.

I only regret that I have but one life to lose for my country.
NATHAN HALE, *Last Words*, 22 Sept., 1776. (STEWART, *Life of Nathan Hale*. Ch. 7.)

2
For body-killing tyrants cannot kill
The public soul—the hereditary will
That, downward as from sire to son it goes,
By shifting bosoms more intensely glows:
Its heirloom is the heart, and slaughtered men
Fight fiercer in their orphans o'er again.
THOMAS CAMPBELL, *Lines on Poland*, l. 146.

3
Glory to them that die in this great cause!
THOMAS CAMPBELL, *Stanzas to the Memory of the Spanish Patriots*, l. 37.

The patriot's blood's the seed of Freedom's tree.
CAMPBELL, *To the Spanish Patriots*, l. 13.

There is a victory in dying well
For Freedom,—and ye have not died in vain.
CAMPBELL, *To the Spanish Patriots*, l. 3.

4
Happy the death of him who pays the debt of nature for his country's sake. (O fortunata mors, quæ naturæ debita pro patria est potissimum reddita!)
CICERO, *Philippicæ*. No. iv, ch. 12, sec. 31.

Can a few days of life equal the happiness of dying for one's country?
NAPOLEON BONAPARTE, *Sayings of Napoleon*.

5
No one would ever have exposed himself to death for his country without the hope of immortality. (Nemo unquam sine magna spe immortalitatis se pro patria offeret ad mortem.)
CICERO, *Tusculanarum Disputationum*. Bk. i, ch. 15, sec. 33.

6
And they who for their country die
Shall fill an honored grave,
For glory lights the soldier's tomb,
And beauty weeps the brave.
J. R. DRAKE, *To the Defenders of New Orleans*.

7
I gave my life for freedom—This I know;
For those who bade me fight had told me so.
W. N. EWER, *Five Souls*.

8
A glorious death is his
Who for his country falls.
(Οὐ οἱ ἀεικὲς ἀμυνομένῳ περὶ πάτρης τεθνάμεν.)
HOMER, *Iliad*. Bk. xv, l. 496. (Derby, tr.)

And for our country 'tis a bliss to die.
HOMER, *Iliad*. Bk. xv, l. 583. (Pope, tr.)

9
It is sweet and glorious to die for one's country. (Dulce et decorum est pro patria mori.)
HORACE, *Odes*. Bk. iii, ode 2, l. 13.

Who would not die for his dear country's cause!
HORACE, *Odes*. Bk. iii, ode 2, l. 13. (Fielding, tr., *Tom Jones*. Bk. xii, ch. 3.)

"Tempt not death!" cried his friends; but he bade them good-bye,
Saying, "Oh! it is sweet for our country to die!"
EPES SARGENT, *The Death of Warren*.

10
Not afraid to die for cherished friends or fatherland. (Non ille pro caris amicis Aut patria timidus perire.)
HORACE, *Odes*. Bk. iv, ode 9, l. 51.

11
And how can man die better
Than facing fearful odds,
For the ashes of his fathers
And the temples of his gods?
MACAULAY, *Horatius*. St. 27.

12
'Twere sweet to sink in death for Truth and Freedom!
Yes, who would hesitate, for who could bear
The living degradation we may know
If we do dread death for a sacred cause?
TERENCE MCSWINEY, *Lines* written when a boy. (*Nation*, 3 Nov., 1920.) McSwiney was Lord Mayor of Cork in 1920, was arrested by the British for treason in August of that year and died after a long hunger strike.

13
Far dearer, the grave or the prison,
Illumed by one patriot name,
Than the trophies of all who have risen
On Liberty's ruins to fame.
THOMAS MOORE, *Forget Not the Field*.

14
A man who is good enough to shed his blood for his country is good enough to be given a square deal afterwards.
THEODORE ROOSEVELT, *Life of Benton*.

15
Had I a dozen sons, each in my love alike and none less dear than thine and my good Marcius, I had rather had eleven die nobly for their country than one voluptuously surfeit out of action.
SHAKESPEARE, *Coriolanus*. Act i, sc. 3, l. 24.

16
If it be the pleasure of heaven that my country shall require the poor offering of my life, the victim shall be ready at the appointed hour of sacrifice, come when that hour may.
DANIEL WEBSTER, *Supposed Speech of John Adams*.

17
They went where duty seemed to call,
They scarcely asked the reason why;
They only knew they could but die,

And death was not the worst of all!
J. G. WHITTIER, *Lexington.*

1
There is one certain means by which I can be sure never to see my country's ruin: I will die in the last ditch.
WILLIAM III, PRINCE OF ORANGE. (HUME, *History of England.* Ch. 65.)

2
And shall Trelawney die, and shall Trelawney die?
Then thirty thousand Cornish boys will know the reason why.
UNKNOWN. Old ballad popular throughout Cornwall, referring to the imprisonment of the seven Bishops by James II, in 1688, Trelawney being Bishop of Bristol. (MACAULAY, *History of England.* Ch. 8.)

And have they fixed the where, and when?
And shall Trelawney die?
Here's thirty thousand Cornish men
Will know the reason why!
ROBERT STEPHEN HAWKER, *Song of the Western Men.* Mr. Hawker wrote this song in 1825, taking the refrain from the old ballad referred to above. Davies Gilbert, President of the Royal Society, reprinted it as an old one, and Sir Walter Scott was deceived into thinking it "the solitary people's song of the seventeenth century."

V—Patriotism: Its Faults

3
Patriotism is not enough. I must have no hatred or bitterness towards anyone.
EDITH CAVELL, *Conversation with the Rev. Mr. Gahan,* 11 Oct., 1915, the night before her execution at Brussels by the Germans.

Such is the patriot's boast, where'er we roam,
His first, best country, ever is at home.
And yet, perhaps, if countries we compare,
And estimate the blessings which they share,
Though patriots flatter, still shall wisdom find
An equal portion dealt to all mankind.
GOLDSMITH, *The Traveller,* l. 73.
See also COSMOPOLITANISM.

4
Never was patriot yet, but was a fool.
DRYDEN, *Absalom and Achitophel.* Pt. i, l. 968.

A patriot is a fool in ev'ry age.
POPE, *Epilogue to the Satires.* Dial. i, l. 41.

5
When a nation is filled with strife then do patriots flourish.
LAO-TSZE, *The Simple Way.* No. 18.

6
You'll never have a quiet world till you knock the patriotism out of the human race.
BERNARD SHAW, *O'Flaherty V. C.*

7
It would therefore seem obvious that patriotism as a feeling is a bad and harmful feeling, and as a doctrine is a stupid doctrine. For it is clear that if each people and each State considers itself the best of peoples and States, they all dwell in a gross and harmful delusion.
TOLSTOY, *Patriotism and Government.*

8
A great and lasting war can never be supported on this principle [patriotism] alone. It must be aided by a prospect of interest, or some reward.
WASHINGTON, *Letter to John Banister,* Valley Forge, 21 April, 1778.

9
Patriotism has become a mere national self assertion, a sentimentality of flag-cheering with no constructive duties.
H. G. WELLS, *The Future in America.*

VI—Patriotism: Patriots

10
From distant climes, o'er wide-spread seas we come,
Though not with much éclat or beat of drum;
True patriots all; for be it understood
We left our country for our country's good.
GEORGE BARRINGTON (?), *Prologue for the Opening of the Playhouse at Sydney, New South Wales,* 16 Jan., 1796. Barrington, whose real name was Waldron, was transported to Botany Bay in 1790 for theft, and he and his fellow convicts acted in a production of Edward Young's tragedy, *The Revenge,* for which Barrington is said to have written the prologue. His authorship of the lines has been questioned. R. S. Lambert, in *The Prince of Pickpockets,* ch. 8, asserts that they were written by Henry Carter, "a gentleman of considerable literary attainments," who died in 1806.

And bold and hard adventures t' undertake,
Leaving his country for his country's sake.
HENRY FITZGEFFREY, *Life and Death of Sir Francis Drake.* St. 213. (1600)

'Twas for the good of my country that I should be abroad. Anything for the good of one's country—I'm a Roman for that.
GEORGE FARQUHAR, *The Beaux' Stratagem.* Act iii, sc. 2, l. 89. (1706)

11
These gentry are invariably saying all they can in dispraise of their native land; and it is my opinion, grounded upon experience, that an individual who is capable of such baseness would not hesitate at the perpetration of any villainy, for next to the love of God, the love of country is the best preventive of crime.
GEORGE BORROW, *The Bible in Spain.* Ch. 4.

12
For what were all these country patriots born?
To hunt, and vote, and raise the price of corn?
BYRON, *The Age of Bronze.* St. 14.

13
A steady patriot of the world alone,
The friend of every country—but his own.
GEORGE CANNING, *The New Morality.*

14
Patriots are grown too shrewd to be sincere,

And we too wise to trust them.
COWPER, *The Task*. Bk. v, l. 495.

For when was public virtue to be found
When private was not? Can he love the whole
Who loves no part? He be a nation's friend
Who is, in truth, the friend of no man there?
COWPER, *The Task*. Bk. v, l. 502.

1
Patriots have toil'd, and in their country's cause
Bled nobly; and their deeds, as they deserve,
Receive proud recompense.
COWPER, *The Task*. Bk. v, l. 704.

2
Patriots in peace, assert the people's right;
With noble stubbornness resisting might.
DRYDEN, *Epistles: To John Driden of Chesterton*, l. 184.

Then, seiz'd with fear, yet still affecting fame,
Usurped a patriot's all-atoning name.
DRYDEN, *Absalom and Achitophel*. Pt. i, l. 178.

3
The flaming patriot, who so lately scorched us in the meridian, sinks temperately to the west, and is hardly felt as he descends.
JUNIUS, *Letters*. Letter 54, 15 Aug., 1771.

4
Brave men and worthy patriots, dear to God, and famous to all ages.
MILTON, *Tractate of Education*.

5
Who stabs at this my heart, stabs at a kingdom;
These veins are rivers, and these arteries
Are very roads, this body is your country.
STEPHEN PHILLIPS, *Herod*. Act ii.

6
I never was a good son or a good brother or a good patriot in the sense of thinking that my mother and my sister and my native country were better than other people's, because I happened to belong to them.
BERNARD SHAW, *The Irrational Knot*. Ch. 6.

7
None loves his king and country better,
Yet none was ever less their debtor.
SWIFT, *A Pastoral Dialogue*.

8
The ever lustrous name of patriot
To no man be denied because he saw
Wherein his country's wholeness lay the flaw,
Where, on her whiteness, the unseemly blot.
WILLIAM WATSON, *Sonnet*.

9
If I ever love another country, damn ME!
UNKNOWN. Retort of discouraged Confederate private to General Polk. (THOMPSON, *Presidents I've Known*, p. 186.)

PATRONAGE

See also Politics: Office-Holding

10
"O dear Mother Outline! of wisdom most sage,
What's the first part of painting?" She said. "Patronage."
"And what is the second, to please and engage?"
She frowned like a fury, and said: "Patronage."
"And what is the third?" She put off old age,
And smil'd like a siren, and said: "Patronage."
WILLIAM BLAKE, *On Art and Artists*. Pt. iv.

11
The mud of English patronage
Grows round his feet, and keeps him down.
ROBERT BUCHANAN, *Edward Crowhurst*.

12
But now for a Patron, whose name and whose glory
At once may illustrate and honour my story.
BURNS, *To the Hon. C. J. Fox*.

13
And thou shalt prove how salt a savor hath
The bread of others, and how hard the path
To climb and to descend the stranger's stairs!
DANTE, *Paradiso*. Canto xvii, l. 58.

14
Is not a Patron, my Lord, one who looks with unconcern on a man struggling for life in the water, and, when he has reached ground, encumbers him with help?
SAMUEL JOHNSON, *Letter to the Earl of Chesterfield*, 7 Feb., 1755. (BOSWELL, *Life*, 1775.) Johnson's explanation to Boswell of the letter was: "Sir, after making great professions, he had, for many years, taken no notice of me; but when my *Dictionary* was coming out, he fell a scribbling in *The World* about it. Upon which, I wrote him a letter expressed in civil terms, but such as might shew him that I did not mind what he said or wrote, and that I had done with him."

Patron: Commonly a wretch who supports with insolence, and is paid with flattery.
SAMUEL JOHNSON, *Dictionary of the English Language*.

15
Mæcenas, sprung from royal stock, my bulwark and my glory dearly cherished. (Mæcenas atavis edite regibus, O et præsidium et dulce decus meum.)
HORACE, *Odes*. Bk. i, ode 1, l. 1.

Let there be Mæcenases, Flaccus, and there will not be wanting Vergils. (Sint Mæcenates non derunt, Flacce, Marones.)
MARTIAL, *Epigrams*. Bk. viii, ep. 56.

16
We should seek support from merit, not from patrons; he has sufficient patrons who does rightly. (Virtute ambire oportet, non favitoribus; Sat habet favitorum semper, qui recte facit.)
PLAUTUS, *Amphitruo: Prologue*, l. 78.

It matters not a featherweight whether patron or client is the better man. (Pluma haud interest, patronus an cliens probior siet.)
PLAUTUS, *Mostellaria*, l. 408. (Act ii, sc. 1.)

1
No man's talents, however brilliant, can raise him from obscurity, unless they find scope, opportunity, and also a patron to commend them. (Neque enim cuiquam tam clarum statim ingenium, ut possit emergere, nisi illi materia, occasio, fautor etiam commendatorque contingat.)

PLINY THE YOUNGER, *Epistles*. Bk. vi, epis. 23.

2
My soul's earth's god, and body's fostering patron.

SHAKESPEARE, *Love's Labour's Lost*. Act i, sc. 1, l. 222.

3
Getting Patronage is the whole art of life. A man cannot have a career without it.

BERNARD SHAW, *Captain Brassbound's Conversion*. Act iii.

4
Refuse to endure the haughty insolence [of patrons]. (Mitte superba pati fastidia.)

UNKNOWN. An adaptation of Vergil's "superba pati fastidia." (*Eclogues*, ii, 15.)

PAYMENT

5
Alas! how deeply painful is all payment! . . .
They hate a murderer much less than a claimant. . . .
Kill a man's family, and he may brook it—
But keep your hands out of his breeches' pocket.

BYRON, *Don Juan*. Canto x, st. 79.

While punctual beaux reward the grateful notes,
And pay for poems—when they pay for coats.

BYRON, *English Bards and Scotch Reviewers*, l. 797.

6
What you will have, quoth God, pay for it and take it.

EMERSON, *Essays, First Series: Compensation*. Quoted as a proverb.

7
He that payeth aforehand hath never his work well done.

JOHN FLORIO, *Second Frutes*, Fo. 39.

Pay beforehand and your work will be behindhand.

JOHN RAY, *English Proverbs*.

Pay-before-hand's never well served.

SCOTT, *The Bride of Lammermoor*. Ch. 3.

8
Glad that he . . . had paid her his debt in her own coin.

ROBERT GREENE, *Works*. Vol. vii, p. 133. (1589)

I would pay him in his own coin.

APHRA BEHN, *Lucky Chance*. Act i, sc. 2.

She pays him in his own coin.

SWIFT, *Polite Conversation*. Dial. iii.

I am accustomed to pay men back in their own coin. (Ich bin gewohnt in der Münze wiederzuzahlen in der man mich bezahlt.)

BISMARCK, *Speech*, to the Ultramontanes, 1870

9
A good prayer is master of another man's purse.

GEORGE HERBERT, *Jacula Prudentum*.

10
If I can't pay, why I can owe.

JOHN HEYWOOD, *Be Merry, Friends*.

11
Light is the dance, and doubly sweet the lays,
When, for the dear delight, another pays.

HOMER, *Odyssey*. Bk. i, l. 205. (Pope, tr.)

He thought I was to pay the piper.

CONGREVE, *Love for Love*. Act ii, sc. 5.

I am not at all in the humor to pay the fiddlers for others to dance. (Je ne suis point d'humeur à payer les violons pour faire danser les autres.)

MOLIÈRE, *La Comtesse d'Escarbagnas*. Sc. 8.

Always those that dance must pay the music.

JOHN TAYLOR THE WATER-POET, *Taylor's Feast*, p. 98. (1638)

He who pays the piper can call the tune.

JOHN RAY, *English Proverbs*.

12
He loveth well to be at good fare, but he will pay no shot.

WILLIAM HORMAN, *Vulgaria*. Fo. 165. (1519)

I will pay for my shot.

JOHN BOURCHIER, LORD BERNERS, *Huon of Burdeux*, 704. (c. 1534)

Have paid scot and lot there any time this eighteen years.

BEN JONSON, *Every Man in His Humour*. Act iii, sc. 3.

Every man must pay his scot.

EMERSON, *Conduct of Life: Wealth*.

13
He that pays last payeth but once.

JAMES HOWELL, *Proverbs*, 4. (1659)

He that pays last never pays twice.

THOMAS FULLER, *Gnomologia*. No. 2246.

14
The time for payment comes, early or late,
No earthly debtor but accounts to Fate.

JOHN MASEFIELD, *The Widow in the Bye Street*.

15
Till thou hast paid the uttermost farthing.

New Testament: Matthew, v, 26; *Luke* xii, 59.

Pay me that thou owest.

New Testament: Matthew, xviii, 28.

16
Pay and pray too.

DANIEL ROGERS, *Matrimonial Honour*, 53.

He that cannot pay, let him pray.

THOMAS FULLER, *Gnomologia*. No. 6362.

To pray and pay too is the devil.

DANIEL DEFOE, *Everybody's Business*.

17
Base is the slave that pays.

SHAKESPEARE, *Henry V*. Act ii, sc. 1, l. 100.

18
He is well paid that is well satisfied.

SHAKESPEARE, *The Merchant of Venice*. Act iv, sc. 1, l. 415.

1
Now nothing but pay, pay,
With, laugh and lay down,
Borough, city, and town.
SKELTON, *Why Come Ye Not to Court*, l. 926.

Pass the hat for your credit's sake, and pay, pay, pay!
KIPLING, *The Absent-Minded Beggar.*

2
Pay what you owe, and what you're worth you'll know.
C. H. SPURGEON, *John Ploughman.* Ch. 12.

He [Sir Pitt Crawley] had an almost invincible repugnance to paying anybody, and could only be brought by force to discharge his debts.
THACKERAY, *Vanity Fair.* Bk. i, ch. 9.

Tho' I owe much, I hope long trust is given,
And truly mean to pay all bills in Heaven.
UNKNOWN. *Epitaph,* Barnwell Churchyard.

3
Who quick be to borrow, and slow be to pay,
Their credit is naught, go they never so gay.
THOMAS TUSSER, *Five Hundred Points of Good Husbandry: January's Abstract.*

4
You could not well expect to go in without paying, but you may pay without going in.
ARTEMUS WARD, *Notice at Door of the Tent.*

5
Who cannot pay with money, must pay with his body. (Luat in corpore, qui non habet in aere.)
UNKNOWN. A law maxim.

PEACE

See also War and Peace

I—Peace: Definitions

6
Peace is liberty in tranquillity.
CICERO, *Philippicæ.* No. ii, sec. 44.

7
Those Christians best deserve the name
Who studiously make peace their aim;
Peace, both the duty and the prize
Of him that creeps and him that flies.
COWPER, *The Nightingale and Glow-Worm.*

8
The first and fundamental law of Nature, which is, *to seek peace and follow it.*
THOMAS HOBBES, *Leviathan.* Pt. i, ch. 14.

9
Peace is the nurse of Ceres; Ceres is the foster-child of Peace. (Pax Cererem nutrit; pacis alumna Ceres.)
OVID, *Fasti.* Bk. i, l. 704.

Peace,
Dear nurse of arts, plenties and joyful births.
SHAKESPEARE, *Henry V.* Act v, sc. 2, l. 34.

10
People are always expecting to get peace in heaven: but you know whatever peace they get there will be ready-made. Whatever making of peace *they* can be blest for, must be on the earth here.
RUSKIN, *The Eagle's Nest.* Lecture ix.

You may either win your peace or buy it: win it, by resistance to evil; buy it, by compromise with evil.
JOHN RUSKIN, *The Two Paths.* Lecture v.

11
A peace is of the nature of a conquest;
For then both parties nobly are subdued,
And neither party loser.
SHAKESPEARE, *II Henry IV.* Act iv, sc. 2, l. 89.

12
Peace is the healing and elevating influence of the world.
WOODROW WILSON, *Address,* Philadelphia, 10 May, 1915.

II—Peace: Apothegms

13
To plunder, to slaughter, to steal, these things they misname empire; and where they make a desert, they call it peace. (Atqui ubi solitudinem faciunt, pacem appellant.)
CALGACUS, addressing the Britons at the battle of the Grampians, referring to the Romans. (TACITUS, *Agricola.* Sec. 30.)

Yet there we follow but the bent assign'd
By fatal Nature to man's warring kind:
Mark! where his carnage and his conquests cease!
He makes a solitude, and calls it—peace!
BYRON, *The Bride of Abydos.* Canto ii, l. 428.

14
Go in peace. ("Ερπε χαίρων.)
CALLIMACHUS, *Epitaph for a Priestess.* (*Greek Anthology.* Bk. vii, epig. 728.)

Go in peace. (Vade in pace.)
Vulgate: Exodus, iv, 18.

15
Thank God for peace! Thank God for peace, when the great gray ships come in!
GUY WETMORE CARRYL, *When the Great Gray Ships Come In.*

16
Nor is heaven always at peace. (Nec sidera pacem Semper habent.)
CLAUDIAN, *De Bello Gothico,* l. 62.

Where there is peace, God is.
GEORGE HERBERT, *Jacula Prudentum.* No. 729.

17
Peace rules the day, where reason rules the mind.
WILLIAM COLLINS, *Hassan,* l. 68.

18
Though peace be made, yet it is interest that keeps peace.
OLIVER CROMWELL, *Speech,* in Parliament, 4 Sept., 1654. He refers to it as "a maxim not to be despised"

If we will have Peace without a worm in it, lay we the foundations of Justice and Righteousness.
OLIVER CROMWELL, *Speech,* 23 Jan., 1656. (*Letters and Speeches,* iv, 13.)

19
The god of Victory is said to be one-handed, but Peace gives victory to both sides.
EMERSON, *Journal,* 1867.

1
Let us have peace!

U. S. GRANT, *Letter Accepting the Nomination to the Presidency*, 29 May, 1868.

2
How beautiful upon the mountains are the feet of him that bringeth good tidings, that publisheth peace.

Old Testament: Isaiah, lii, 7.

3
Peace, peace; when there is no peace.

Old Testament: Jeremiah, vi, 14; viii, 11.

4
Peace courts his hand, but spreads her charms in vain;
"Think nothing gain'd," he cries, "till nought remain."

SAMUEL JOHNSON, *The Vanity of Human Wishes*, l. 199.

5
The days of peace and slumberous calm are fled.

KEATS, *Hyperion*. Bk. ii, l. 335.

6
Peace at any price. (Paix à tout prix.)

LAMARTINE. (ARTHUR HUGH CLOUGH, *Letters and Remains*, p. 105.)

The Ministry of peace at any price. (Le Ministère de la Paix à tout prix.)

ARMAND CARREL, referring to the Périer ministry. (*National*, 13 March, 1831.)

We love peace, as we abhor pusillanimity; but not peace at any price. There is a peace more destructive of the manhood of living man than war is destructive of his material body. Chains are worse than bayonets.

DOUGLAS JERROLD, *Specimens of Jerrold's Wit: Peace.*

Though not a "peace-at-any-price" man, I am not ashamed to say that I am a peace-at-almost-any-price man.

SIR JOHN LUBBOCK, *The Use of Life*. Ch. 11. Lord Palmerston sneered at John Bright as a "peace-at-any-price man."

Professional pacifists, the peace-at-any-price, non-resistance, universal arbitration people, are seeking to Chinafy this country.

THEODORE ROOSEVELT, *Speech*, San Francisco.

If I must choose between peace and righteousness, I choose righteousness.

THEODORE ROOSEVELT, *Unwise Peace Treaties.*

There is a price which is too great to pay for peace, and that price can be put in one word. One cannot pay the price of self-respect.

WOODROW WILSON, *Speech*, Des Moines, 1 Feb., 1916.

7
Glory to God in the highest, and on earth peace, good will toward men.

New Testament: Luke, ii, 14.

Peace be to this house.

New Testament: Luke, x, 5. (Pax huic domui. —*Vulgate.*)

Peace be within thy walls, and prosperity within thy palaces.

Old Testament: Psalms, cxxii, 7.

That peace which made thy prosperous reign to shine,
That peace thou leavest to thy imperial line,
That peace, oh, happy shade, be ever thine.

DRYDEN, *Threnodia Augustalis*. St. 9.

8
Blessed are the peace-makers.

New Testament: Matthew, v, 9. (Beati pacifici.—*Vulgate.*)

Your "if" is the only peace-maker; much virtue in "if."

SHAKESPEARE, *As You Like It*. Act v, sc. 4, l. 107.

I hate your *ifs*.

STERNE, *Tristram Shandy*. Bk. i, ch. 12.

9
Agree with thine adversary quickly, whiles thou art in the way with him.

New Testament: Matthew, v, 25.

If it be possible, as much as lieth in you, live peaceably with all men.

New Testament: Romans, xii, 18.

10
Fair peace is becoming to men; fierce anger belongs to beasts. (Candida pax homines, trux decet ira feras.)

OVID, *Ars Amatoria*. Bk. iii, l. 502.

11
An equal doom clipp'd Time's blest wings of peace.

PETRARCH, *To Laura in Death*. Sonnet xlviii.

12
Her ways are ways of pleasantness, and all her paths are peace.

Old Testament: Proverbs, iii, 17.

13
Still in thy right hand carry gentle peace,
To silence envious tongues.

SHAKESPEARE, *Henry VIII*. Act iii, sc. 2, l. 445.

Enrich the time to come with smooth-faced peace,
With smiling plenty and fair prosperous days!

SHAKESPEARE, *Richard III*. Act v, sc. 5, l. 33.

14
No more shall . . . Peace
Pipe on her pastoral hillock a languid note,
And watch her harvest ripen.

TENNYSON, *Maud*. Pt. ii, sec. 6, st. 2.

15
Peace is always beautiful.

WALT WHITMAN, *The Sleepers*.

16
Who gives a nation peace, gives tranquillity to all.

HORACE WALPOLE, *Letter to Sir Horace Mann*, 3 Oct., 1762.

17
It must be a peace without victory.

WOODROW WILSON, *Address*, to U. S. Senate, 22 Jan., 1917.

Open covenants of peace openly arrived at. . . . Absolute freedom of navigation upon the seas outside territorial waters alike in peace and in war. . . . The removal, so far as possible, of all economic barriers and the establishment of an equality of trade conditions among all nations. . . . Adequate guarantees given and taken that national armaments will be reduced to the lowest point consistent with domestic safety.

WOODROW WILSON, *Address*, to Congress, 8 Jan., 1918. First four of *Fourteen Points*.

III—Peace with Honor

1
Lord Salisbury and myself have brought you back peace—but a peace, I hope, with honour.

BENJAMIN DISRAELI, *Speech*, after Berlin Congress, 16 July, 1878.

2
With peace and honour I am willing to spare anything so as to keep all ends together.

SAMUEL PEPYS, *Diary*, 25 May, 1663.

3
If peace cannot be maintained with honour, it is no longer peace.

LORD JOHN RUSSELL, *Speech*, at Greenock, Sept., 1853.

4
That it shall hold companionship in peace
With honour, as in war.

SHAKESPEARE, *Coriolanus*. Act iii, sc. 2, l. 49.

We have made peace
With no less honour to the Antiates
Than shame to the Romans.

SHAKESPEARE, *Coriolanus*. Act v, sc. 6, l. 79.

5
Not thus doth Peace return!
A blessed visitant she comes;
Honour in his right hand
Doth lead her like a bride.

ROBERT SOUTHEY, *Carmina Aulica*. Sec. 5.

6
Peace with honor.

THEOBALD, COUNT OF CHAMPAGNE, *Letter to Louis the Great*. c. 1125. (WALTER MAP, *De Nugis Curialium*, p. 220); SIR KENELM DIGBY, *Letter to Lord Bristol*, 27 May, 1625.

He had rather spend £10,000 on Embassies to keep or procure peace with dishonour, than £10,000 on an army that would have forced peace with honour.

SIR ANTHONY WELDON, *The Court and Character of King James*, p. 185. (1650)

IV—Peace: World Peace

7
To make peace in Europe possible, the last representative of the pre-war generation must die and take his pre-war mentality into the grave with him.

EDUARD BENEŠ, *Interview*, Dec., 1929.

8
As I read this to-day what a change! The world convulsed by war as never before. Men slaying each other like wild beasts.

ANDREW CARNEGIE, *Autobiography*. The abrupt close of the manuscript.

9
War will never yield but to the principles of universal justice and love, and these have no sure root but in the religion of Jesus Christ.

WILLIAM ELLERY CHANNING, *Lecture on War*

Peace cannot be kept by force. It can only be achieved by understanding.

ALBERT EINSTEIN, *Notes on Pacifism*.

10
An end to these bloated armaments.

BENJAMIN DISRAELI, *Speech*, advocating disarmament, 1862. *See also under* PREPAREDNESS.

11
Instead of by battles and Œcumenical Councils, the rival portions of humanity will one day dispute each other's excellence in the manufacture of little cakes.

FOURIER. (EMERSON, *Lectures and Biographical Sketches: The Man of Letters*.)

12
The only foes that threaten America are the enemies at home, and these are ignorance, superstition and incompetence.

ELBERT HUBBARD, *The Philistine*. Vol. xx, p. 36.

13
The closeness of their [the nations'] intercourse will assuredly render war as absurd and impossible by-and-by, as it would be for Manchester to fight with Birmingham, or Holborn Hill with the Strand.

LEIGH HUNT, *Poems: Preface*.

14
They shall beat their swords into ploughshares, and their spears into pruning-hooks: nation shall not lift up sword against nation, neither shall they learn war any more.

Old Testament: Isaiah, ii, 4; *Joel*, iii, 10; *Micah*, iv, 3.

The wolf also shall dwell with the lamb, and the leopard shall lie down with the kid.

Old Testament: Isaiah, xi, 6.

15
An association of men who will not quarrel with one another is a thing which never yet existed, from the greatest confederacy of nations down to a town-meeting or a vestry.

THOMAS JEFFERSON, *Letter to John Taylor*, 1798.

You have not been mistaken in supposing my views and feeling to be in favor of the abolition of war. . . . I hope it is practicable, by improving the mind and morals of society, to lessen the disposition to war; but of its abolition I despair.

THOMAS JEFFERSON, *Writings*. Vol. xviii, p. 298.

16
An angel with a trumpet said,
"Forevermore, forevermore,
The reign of violence is o'er!"

LONGFELLOW, *The Occultation of Orion*. St. 6.

Were half the power that fills the world with terror,
Were half the wealth bestowed on camps and courts,
Given to redeem the human mind from error,

There were no need of arsenals and forts.
H. W. LONGFELLOW, *The Arsenal at Springfield.*

Peace! and no longer from its brazen portals
The blast of War's great organ shakes the skies!
But beautiful as songs of the immortals,
The holy melodies of love arise.
LONGFELLOW, *The Arsenal at Springfield.*

1
Buried was the bloody hatchet;
Buried was the dreadful war-club;
Buried were all warlike weapons,
And the war-cry was forgotten.
Then was peace among the nations.
LONGFELLOW, *Hiawatha.* Pt. xiii, l. 7.

2
War in men's eyes shall be
A monster of iniquity
In the good time coming.
Nations shall not quarrel then,
To prove which is the stronger;
Nor slaughter men for glory's sake;—
Wait a little longer.
CHARLES MACKAY, *The Good Time Coming.*

3
No war, or battle's sound
Was heard the world around;
The idle spear and shield were high up hung.
MILTON, *Hymn on the Morning of Christ's Nativity,* l. 53.

4
To discover a system for the avoidance of war is a vital need of our civilization; but no such system has a chance while men are so unhappy that mutual extermination seems to them less dreadful than continued endurance of the light of day.
BERTRAND RUSSELL, *The Conquest of Happiness,* p. 15.

5
For lo! the days are hastening on,
By prophet-bards foretold,
When with the ever-circling years,
Comes round the age of gold;
When Peace shall over all the earth
Its ancient splendors fling
And the whole world send back the song
Which now the angels sing.
EDMUND HAMILTON SEARS, *The Angels' Song.* *See also under* CHRISTMAS.

6
The time of universal peace is near:
Prove this a prosperous day, the three-nook'd world
Shall bear the olive freely.
SHAKESPEARE, *Antony and Cleopatra.* Act iv, sc. 6, l. 4.

7
Let the bugles sound the *Truce of God* to the whole world forever.
CHARLES SUMNER, *Oration: The True Grandeur of Nations.*

8
The battlefield as a place of settlement of disputes is gradually yielding to arbitral courts of justice.
WILLIAM HOWARD TAFT, *Dawn of World Peace.* (*U. S. Bureau of Education Bulletin.* No. 8.)

9
Ah! when shall all men's good
Be each man's rule, and universal Peace
Lie like a shaft of light across the land,
And like a lane of beams athwart the sea?
TENNYSON, *The Golden Year,* l. 47.

Till the war-drum throbb'd no longer, and the battle-flags were furl'd
In the Parliament of man, the Federation of the world.
ALFRED TENNYSON, *Locksley Hall,* l. 127.

10
Who can fancy warless men?
Warless? war will die out late then. Will it ever? late or soon?
Can it, till this outworn earth be dead as yon dead world the moon?
TENNYSON, *Locksley Hall Sixty Years After,* l. 173.

11
The League of Nations is a declaration of love without the promise of marriage.
ADMIRAL VON TIRPITZ. (*So Say the Wise,* p. 167.)

'Tis startin' a polis foorce to prevint war. . . . How'll they be ar-rmed? What a foolish question. They'll be ar-rmed with love, if coorse.
FINLEY PETER DUNNE, *On Making a Will.* Referring to W. J. Bryan's speech on League of Nations, 1920.

12
Beautiful that war and all its deeds of carnage, must in time be utterly lost;
That the hands of the sisters Death and Night incessantly softly wash again and ever again, this soiled world.
WALT WHITMAN, *Drum-Taps: Reconciliation.*

13
When Earth, as if on evil dreams,
Looks back upon her wars,
And the white light of Christ outstreams
From the red disk of Mars,

His fame who led the stormy van
Of battle well may cease;
But never that which crowns the man
Whose victory was Peace.
WHITTIER, *William Francis Bartlett.*

14
God for His service needeth not proud work of human skill;
They please Him best who labour most in peace to do His will.
WORDSWORTH, *The Poet's Dream,* l. 65.

15
The High Contracting Parties solemnly declare in the names of their respective peoples that they condemn recourse to war for the solution of international controversies, and renounce it as an instrument of national

policy in their relations with one another. The High Contracting Parties agree that the settlement or solution of all disputes or conflicts of whatever nature or of whatever origin they may be, which may arise among them, shall never be sought except by pacific means.

Articles I and II of the Pact of Paris.

V—Peace: Its Faults

1
And Peace it self is War in Masquerade.

DRYDEN, *Absalom and Achitophel*. Pt. i, l. 752; pt. ii, l. 269.

2
My argument is that War makes rattling good history; but Peace is poor reading.

THOMAS HARDY, *The Dynasts*. Act ii, sc. 5.

3
It is mutual cowardice that keeps us in peace. Were one-half of mankind brave, and one-half cowards, the brave would be always beating the cowards. Were all brave, they would lead a very uneasy life; all would be continually fighting: but being all cowards, we go on very well.

SAMUEL JOHNSON. (BOSWELL, *Life*, 28 April, 1778.)

4
Now we suffer the ills of a long peace; luxury, more cruel than warfare, has overshadowed us. (Nunc patimur longæ pacis mala; sævior armis Luxuria incubuit.)

JUVENAL, *Satires*. Sat. vi, l. 292.

The cankers of a calm world and a long peace.

SHAKESPEARE, *I Henry IV*. Act iv, sc. 2, l. 33.

5
The inglorious arts of peace.

ANDREW MARVELL, *An Horatian Ode Upon Cromwell's Return from Ireland*.

6
Nor is this peace, the nurse of drones and cowards,
Our health, but a disease.

MASSINGER, *The Maid of Honour*. Act i, sc. 1.

7
The brazen throat of war had ceased to roar:
All now was turn'd to jollity and game,
To luxury and riot, feast and dance.

MILTON, *Paradise Lost*. Bk. xi, l. 709.

Peace to corrupt no less than war to waste.

MILTON, *Paradise Lost*. Bk. xi, l. 780.

8
No more to watch at night's eternal shore,
With England's chivalry at dawn to ride;
No more defeat, faith, victory,—O! no more
A cause on earth for which we might have died.

HENRY NEWBOLT, *Peace*.

9
For peace do not hope; to be just you must break it.

JOHN BOYLE O'REILLY, *Rules of the Road*.

10
War its thousands slays, Peace its ten thousands.

BEILBY PORTEUS, *Death*, l. 178.

11
Plenty and peace breeds cowards: hardness ever
Of hardiness is mother.

SHAKESPEARE, *Cymbeline*. Act iii, sc. 6, l. 21.

12
In this weak piping time of peace.

SHAKESPEARE, *Richard III*. Act i, sc. 1, l. 24.

13
Beware of the man who does not return your blow.

BERNARD SHAW, *Maxims for Revolutionists*.

There are pacifists in pleasure as well as pacifists in war. The latter are called cowards. The former are called leading moral citizens.

G. J. NATHAN, *The World in Falseface*.

14
Even war is better than a miserable peace. (Miseram pacem vel bello bene mutari.)

TACITUS, *Annals*. Bk. iii, sec. 44.

Down with a patched-up peace, sow seeds of wicked war! (Disice compositam pacem, sere crimina belli.)

VERGIL, *Æneid*. Bk. vii, l. 339.

15
Why do they prate of the blessings of peace? we have made them a curse,
Pickpockets, each hand lusting for all that is not its own;
And lust of gain, in the spirit of Cain, is it better or worse
Than the heart of the citizen hissing in war on his own hearthstone?

TENNYSON, *Maud*. Pt. i, sec. 1, st. 6.

When a Mammonite mother kills her babe for a burial-fee,
And Timour-Mammon grins on a pile of children's bones,
Is it peace or war? better, war! loud war by land and by sea,
War with a thousand battles, and shaking a hundred thrones!

TENNYSON, *Maud*. Pt. i, sec. 1, st. 12.

16
Verily I do think
War is as hateful almost, and well-nigh
As ghastly, as this terrible Peace, whereby
We halt forever on the crater's brink,
And feed the wind with phrases.

WILLIAM WATSON, *Ver Tenebrosum*. It was a President of the French Senate who spoke of "The pernicious poison of a premature peace."

VI—Peace of Mind

See also Tranquillity

17
Peace, peace is what I seek, and public calm:
Endless extinction of unhappy hates.

MATTHEW ARNOLD, *Merope*, l. 101.

18
Thou hast touched me and I have been trans-

lated into thy peace. (Tetigisti me et exarsi in pacem tuam.)
ST. AUGUSTINE, *Confessions*. Bk. x, ch. 27.

That peace which the world cannot give.
Book of Common Prayer: Evening Prayer.

Nothing can bring you peace but yourself.
EMERSON, *Essays: Of Self-Reliance.*

1
After dreams of horror, comes again
The welcome morning with its rays of peace.
BRYANT, *Mutation*, l. 5.

2
The Pilgrim they laid in a large upper chamber, whose window opened toward the sunrising; the name of the chamber was Peace, where he slept till break of day, and then he awoke and sang.
JOHN BUNYAN, *The Pilgrim's Progress*. Pt. i.

3
In his will is our peace. (In la sua voluntade è nostra pace.)
DANTE, *Paradiso*. Bk. iii, l. 85.

4
Peace be to you.
Old Testament: Genesis, xliii, 23, etc. (Pax vobiscum.—*Vulgate*.)

The peace of God which passeth all understanding.
New Testament: Philippians, iv, 7.

5
When a man finds no peace within himself it is useless to seek it elsewhere. (Quand on ne trouve pas son repos en soi-même, il est inutile de le chercher ailleurs.)
LA ROCHEFOUCAULD, *Maximes Supprimées*, 571.

6
I shall not hold my little peace; for me
There is no peace but one.
ALICE MEYNELL, *The Poet to the Birds.*

7
I knew by the smoke, that so gracefully curl'd
Above the green elms, that a cottage was near,
And I said, "If there's peace to be found in the world,
A heart that was humble might hope for it here!"
THOMAS MOORE, *Ballad Stanzas*. Said to refer to the old Redfield farm at Batavia, N. Y., where the poet passed a night in 1804.

8
Joy is like restless day; but peace divine
Like quiet night;
Lead me, O Lord, till perfect day shall shine
Through Peace to Light.
ADELAIDE ANN PROCTER, *Per Pacem ad Lucem.*

9
But sometimes, through the Soul of Man,
Slow moving o'er his pain,
The moonlight of a perfect peace
Floods heart and brain.
WILLIAM SHARP, *The White Peace.*

11
We should have much peace if we would not busy ourselves with the sayings and doings of others.
THOMAS À KEMPIS, *De Imitatione Christi*. Pt. i, ch. 11.

Thy peace shall be in much patience.
THOMAS À KEMPIS, *De Imitatione Christi*. Pt. iii, ch. 25.

12
To be glad of life because it gives you the chance to love and to work and to play and to look up at the stars, to be satisfied with your possessions but not contented with yourself until you have made the best of them, to despise nothing in the world except falsehood and meanness and to fear nothing except cowardice, to be governed by your admirations rather than by your disgusts, to covet nothing that is your neighbor's except his kindness of heart and gentleness of manners, to think seldom of your enemies, often of your friends, and every day of Christ, and to spend as much time as you can, with body and with spirit, in God's out-of-doors, these are little guide-posts on the footpath to peace.
HENRY VAN DYKE, *The Footpath to Peace.*

13
Peace begins just where ambition ends.
YOUNG, *Night Thoughts*. Night v, l. 940.

PEACH

14
And the soft gold-down on her silken chin
Is like the under side of a ripe peach.
ROBERT BUCHANAN, *Polypheme's Passion.*

15
A little peach in the orchard grew,—
A little peach of emerald hue;
Warmed by the sun and wet by the dew,
It grew.

One day, passing that orchard through,
That little peach dawned on the view
Of Johnny Jones and his sister Sue—
Them two. . . .

Hard trials for them two,
Johnny Jones and his sister Sue,
And the peach of emerald hue,
That grew:

Listen to my tale of woe!

John took a bite and Sue took a chew,
And then the trouble began to brew,—
Trouble the doctor could n't subdue.
Too true!

Under the turf where the daisies grew
They planted John and his sister Sue,
And their little souls to the angels flew,—
Boo hoo!
EUGENE FIELD, *The Little Peach.*

16
The peach will have wine, and the fig water.
JOHN GRANGE, *Golden Aphroditis*. (1577)

17
An apple is an excellent thing—until you have tried a peach!
GEORGE DU MAURIER, *Trilby*, p. 256.

18
Give me women as soft, and as delicate, and

as velvet as my peaches! . . . with peaches and women, it's only the side next the sun that's tempting.

OUIDA, *Strathmore*.

1
As touching peaches in general, the very name in Latin, whereby they are called Persica, doth evidently show that they were brought out of Persia first.

PLINY, *Historia Naturalis*. Bk. xv, sec. 13.

2
Pill [peel] a fig for your friend, and a peach for your enemy.

JOHN RAY, *English Proverbs*. From the Italian, "Al amico cura gli il fico, al inimico il persico."

3
The ripest peach is highest on the tree.

JAMES WHITCOMB RILEY, *The Ripest Peach*.

4
Oh, Persica, Persica, pale and fair,
With a ripe blush on your cheek,
How pretty—how very pretty you are,
Until you begin to speak!
As for a heart and soul, my dear,
You have not enough to sin;
Outside so fair, like a peach you are,
With a stone for a heart within.

W. W. STORY, *Persica*.

PEACOCK

5
Like an imperial peacock stalk abroad
(That royal bird, whose tail's a diadem).

BYRON, *Don Juan*. Canto vii, st. 74.

6
And stately peacocks with their splendid eyes.

THOMAS HOOD, *Plea of the Midsummer Fairies*.

Like a peacock whose eyes are inclin'd to his tail.

THOMAS HOOD, *A Parthian Glance*.

7
To Paradise, the Arabs say,
Satan could never find the way
Until the peacock led him in.

CHARLES GODFREY LELAND, *The Peacock*.

8
And like a peacock sweep along his tail.

SHAKESPEARE, *I Henry VI*. Act iii, sc. 3, l. 6.

Why, he stalks up and down like a peacock,—a stride and a stand.

SHAKESPEARE, *Troilus and Cressida*. Act iii, sc. 3, l. 251.

9
Proud as peacocks.

SHERLOCKE, *Hatcher of Heresies*. (1565)

The pride of the peacock is the glory of God.

WILLIAM BLAKE, *Proverbs of Hell*.

"Fly pride," says the peacock.

SHAKESPEARE, *The Comedy of Errors*. Act iv, sc. 3, l. 81.

And there they placed a peacock in his pride.

TENNYSON, *Gareth and Lynette*, l. 829.

10
She is a peacock in everything but beauty.

OSCAR WILDE, *Picture of Dorian Gray*. Ch. 1.

PEARL

11
If that a pearl may in a toad's head dwell,
And may be found too in an oyster shell.

JOHN BUNYAN, *The Pilgrim's Progress: The Author's Apology for His Book*, l. 89.

Has a pearl less whiteness
Because of its birth?

THOMAS MOORE, *Desmond's Song*.

12
They [the Russians] came to the court balls dropping pearls and vermin.

MACAULAY, *History of England*. Ch. 23.

13
Give not that which is holy unto the dogs, neither cast ye your pearls before swine, lest they trample them under their feet, and turn again and rend you.

New Testament: Matthew, vii, 6.

Men should not put pearles white
To-fore rude swine.

JOHN LYDGATE, *Minor Poems*, p. 188.

Introducing a fine woman to you is casting pearls before swine.

BERNARD SHAW, *How He Lied to Her Husband*.

And the precious pearls ye strowen to hogs.

UNKNOWN. (WRIGHT, *Political Poems*, ii, 110. 1401)

See also under SWINE.

14
When he had found one pearl of great price.

New Testament: Matthew, xiii, 46.

15
This treasure of an oyster.

SHAKESPEARE, *Antony and Cleopatra*. Act i, sc. 5, l. 44.

16
One whose hand
Like the base Indian, threw a pearl away
Richer than all his tribe.

SHAKESPEARE, *Othello*. Act v, sc. 2, l. 346.

PEDANTRY

17
Pedantry consists in the use of words unsuitable to the time, place, and company.

S. T. COLERIDGE, *Biographia Literaria*. Ch. 10.

18
He who is in some measure a pedant, though he may be wise, cannot be a very happy man.

WILLIAM HAZLITT, *Round Table*. Vol. ii, p. 28.

19
A profound man, who has become hollow.

VICTOR HUGO, *Ninety-Three*. Pt. ii, bk. iii, ch. 1. He was speaking of Sieyès, and echoing Talleyrand's epigram, also of Sieyès: Profond, hem! vous voulez dire, peut-être, creux: Perhaps you mean hollow. Jean d'Alembert has already said of French philosophers: They believe themselves profound, while they are merely hollow.

20
Pedantry is the dotage of knowledge.

HOLBROOK JACKSON, *Anatomy of Bibliomania*, p. 150.

1
An artist may visit a museum, but only a pedant can live there.
GEORGE SANTAYANA, *Life of Reason*, iv, 129.

2
Bold in thy applause,
The Bard shall scorn pedantic laws.
SCOTT, *Marmion:* Canto v, *Introduction.*

3
The vacant skull of a pedant generally furnishes out a throne and a temple for vanity.
WILLIAM SHENSTONE, *Books and Writers.*

4
Figures pedantical.
SHAKESPEARE, *Love's Labour's Lost*, v, 2, 408.

How fiery and forward our pedant is!
SHAKESPEARE, *Taming of the Shrew*, iii, 1, 48.

5
A reasoning, self-sufficing thing,
An intellectual All-in-all.
WORDSWORTH, *A Poet's Epitaph*. St. 8.

PELICAN

6
What, wouldst thou have me turn pelican, and feed thee out of my own vitals?
CONGREVE, *Love for Love*. Act ii, sc. 1.

7
By them there sat the loving pelican,
Whose young ones, poison'd by the serpent's sting,
With her own blood to life again doth bring.
MICHAEL DRAYTON, *Noah's Flood.*

8
Like the kind, life-retiring pelican,
Repast them with my blood.
SHAKESPEARE, *Hamlet*. Act iv, sc. 5, l. 146.

That blood already, like the pelican,
Hast thou tapp'd out and drunkenly caroused.
SHAKESPEARE, *Richard II*. Act ii, sc. 1, l. 126.

9
A wonderful bird is the pelican!
His bill will hold more than his belican.
He can take in his beak
Food enough for a week
But I'm darned if I see how the helican.
DIXON L. MERRITT, *The Pelican*. One of Woodrow Wilson's favorite limericks.

PEN

See also Press, Writing

9a
He dipped his pen into the tears of the human race, and with celestial clearness wrote down what he conceived to be eternal truths.
JOHN P. ALTGELD, *In Memoriam, Henry George.*

10
Art thou a pen, whose task shall be
To drown in ink What writers think?
Oh, wisely write, That pages white
Be not the worse for ink and thee!
ETHEL LYNN BEERS, *The Gold Nugget.*

11
Whose noble praise
Deserves a quill pluckt from an angel's wing.
DOROTHY BERRY, *Sonnet*. (Preface to Diana Primrose's *Chain of Pearls*, 1699.)

The pen wherewith thou dost so heavenly sing
Made of a quill from an angel's wing.
HENRY CONSTABLE, *Sonnet*. (Note to Todd's *Milton*. Vol. v, p. 454.)

For what made that in glory shine so long
But poets' Pens, pluckt from Archangels' wings?
JOHN DAVIES, *Bien Venu.*

The sacred Dove a quill did lend
From her high-soaring wing.
FRANCIS NETHERSOLE, *Preface to Giles Fletcher's Christ's Victory.*

The feather, whence the pen
Was shaped that traced the lives of these good men,
Dropped from an Angel's wing.
WORDSWORTH, *Ecclesiastical Sonnets:* Pt. iii, No. 5, *Walton's Book of Lives.*

12
I had rather stand in the shock of a basilisk, than in the fury of a merciless pen.
SIR THOMAS BROWNE, *Religio Medici*. Pt. ii, sec. 4.

13
Oh! nature's noblest gift, my grey goose-quill!
Slave of my thoughts, obedient to my will,
Torn from thy parent-bird to form a pen,
That mighty instrument of little men!
BYRON, *English Bards and Scotch Reviewers*, l. 7.

14
Break, my boy, your pens, and forsake the useless muses. (Frange, puer, calamos, et inanes desere Musas.)
CALPURNIUS, *Eclogues*. No. iv, l. 23.

15
The pen is the tongue of the mind. (La pluma es lengua del alma.)
CERVANTES, *Don Quixote*. Bk. v, ch. 16.

16
Pen and ink is wit's plough.
JOHN CLARKE, *Parœmiologia*, 35. (1639)

How strange that men,
Who guide the plough, should fail to guide the pen.
GEORGE CRABBE, *The Parish Register:* Pt. ii.

17
I dip my pen in the blackest ink, because I am not afraid of falling into my inkpot.
EMERSON, *Conduct of Life: Worship.*

18
Goose, bee and calf govern the world. (Anser, apis, vitulus, populos et regna gubernant.)
JAMES HOWELL, *Familiar Letters*. Bk. ii, letter 2. Quoted. Meaning pen, wax and parchment.

19
The pen became a clarion.
LONGFELLOW, *Monte Cassino*. St. 13.

20
One that excels the quirks of blazoning pens.
SHAKESPEARE, *Othello*. Act ii, sc. 1, l. 63.

21
Let there be gall enough in thy ink, though thou write with a goose-pen, no matter.
SHAKESPEARE, *Twelfth Night*. Act iii, sc. 2, l. 52.

No gall has ever poisoned my pen. (Aucun fiel n'a jamais empoisonné ma plume.)
CRÉBILLON, *Discours de Réception.*

1
Ask my pen,—it governs me,—I govern not it.
STERNE, *Tristram Shandy.* Bk. vi, ch. 6.

2
There's no wound deeper than a pen can give,
It makes men living dead, and dead men live.
JOHN TAYLOR, *A Kicksey-Winsey.* Pt. vii.

II—Pen and Sword

3
Beneath the rule of men entirely great,
The pen is mightier than the sword.
BULWER-LYTTON, *Richelieu.* Act ii, sc. 2.

4
From this it appears how much more cruel the pen may be than the sword. (Hinc quam sic calamus sævior ense, patet.)
ROBERT BURTON, *Anatomy of Melancholy.* Pt. i, sec. ii, mem. 4, subs. 4.

5
A sword less hurt does, than a pen.
WILLIAM KING, *The Eagle and Robin,* l. 82.

6
So much had the pen, under the king, the advantage over the sword. (Tant la plume a eu sous le roi d'avantage sur l'épée.)
SAINT-SIMON, *Mémoires.* Vol. iii, p. 517. (1702)

7
Thou canst hurt no man's fame with thy ill word;
Thy pen is full as harmless as thy sword.
SIR CARR SCROPE, *On the Earl of Rochester.*

8
Many wearing rapiers are afraid of goose-quills.
SHAKESPEARE, *Hamlet.* Act ii, sc. 2, l. 359.

9
Pens are most dangerous tools, more sharp by odds
Than swords, and cut more keen than whips or rods.
JOHN TAYLOR, *News from Hell, Hull, and Halifax: Three Satirical Lashes,* l. 1.

10
Cæsar had perished from the world of men,
Had not his sword been rescued by his pen.
HENRY VAUGHAN, *On Sir Thomas Bodley's Library.*

PENITENCE, see Remorse, Repentance

PEOPLE, THE

I—People: Apothegms

11
To worship the people is to be worshipped.
FRANCIS BACON, *De Augmentis Scientiarum:* Pt. i, bk. 6, ch. 30, *Popularitas.*

12
All the rabble of the ship, hag, tag, and rag.
JOHN BALE, *Vocacyon.* (*Harl. Miscel.*, vi, 459. 1553)

For all were there, tag and ragge, cut and long-tail.
SAMUEL HARSNETT, *Declaration of Egregious Popish Impostures,* 50. (1603)

Tag and rag, cut and long tail, everyone that can eat an egg.
JOHN CLARKE, *Paræmiologia,* 236. (1639)

That rabble rout, tag rag and bobtail.
UNKNOWN, *Just Defence of John Bastwick,* 16. (1645)

The tag-rag people.
SHAKESPEARE, *Julius Cæsar.* Act i, sc. 2, l. 263.

13
The public is poor.
EDMUND BURKE, *Speech,* House of Commons, 11 Feb., 1780. Often quoted, "The state is always poor."

14
Man has set man against man, Washed against Unwashed.
CARLYLE, *The French Revolution.* Pt. ii, bk. 2, ch. 4.

The great unwashed.
This phrase has been attributed to Henry Peter Brougham and to Edmund Burke. Sir Walter Scott is said to have applied it to the laboring class.

We begin to understand what is meant by the lowest classes, the great unwashed.
SYDNEY WATSON, *Wops the Waif.* Ch. 3.

15
The safety of the people shall be the highest law. (Salus populi suprema lex esto.)
CICERO, *De Legibus.* Bk. iii, ch. 3, sec. 8.

The safety of the State is the highest law. (Salus populi suprema lex.)
JUSTINIAN, *Twelve Tables.*

The noblest motive is the public good.
RICHARD STEELE, *The Spectator.* No. 200.

That grounded maxim,
So rife and celebrated in the mouths
Of wisest men, that to the public good
Private respects must yield.
MILTON, *Samson Agonistes,* l. 865.

There is not any thing in the world more abused than this sentence, *Salus populi suprema lex esto.*
JOHN SELDEN, *Table-Talk: People.*

16
The dregs of the people. (Fæx populi.)
CICERO, *Epistulæ ad Quintum Fratrem.* Bk. ii, epis. 9, sec. 5.

17
Public wrongs are but popular rights in embryo.
CHARLES JOHN DARLING, *Scintillæ Juris.*

18
Those three most intractable beasts, the owl, the serpent, and the people. (Γλαυκὶ καὶ δράκοντι καὶ δήμῳ.)
DEMOSTHENES, referring to the Athenians. (PLUTARCH, *Lives: Demosthenes.* Sec. 26.)

19
I was told that the Privileged and the People formed Two Nations.
BENJAMIN DISRAELI, *Sybil.* Bk. iv, ch. 8.

1
If by the people you understand the multitude, the *hoi polloi,* 'tis no matter what they think; they are sometimes in the right, sometimes in the wrong; their judgment is a mere lottery.
DRYDEN, *Essay on Dramatic Poetry.*

The many; the multitude. (Οἱ πολλοί.)
UNKNOWN. A proverbial Greek phrase.

2
He who serves the public is a poor animal. (Wer dem Publicum dient, ist ein armes Thier.)
GOETHE, *Sprüche in Reimen,* iii.

3
I shall on all subjects have a policy to recommend, but none to enforce against the will of the people.
U. S. GRANT, *First Inaugural Address,* 4 March, 1869.

4
Knowing as "the man in the street" (as we call him at Newmarket) always does, the greatest secrets of kings, and being the confidant of their most hidden thoughts.
CHARLES FULKE GREVILLE, *Memoirs,* 22 March, 1830.

The man in the street does not know a star in the sky.
EMERSON, *Conduct of Life: Worship.*

5
When the people contend for their liberty, they seldom get anything by their victory but new masters.
LORD HALIFAX, *Works,* p. 483.

6
The people cannot see, but they can feel.
JAMES HARRINGTON, *Oceana,* p. 483.

They who have put out the people's eyes, reproach them of their blindness.
JOHN MILTON, *Works.* Vol. i, p. 192.

7
To scorn the envious rabble. (Malignum Spernere vulgus.)
HORACE, *Odes.* Bk. ii, ode 16, l. 39.

I hate the vulgar herd and hold it far. (Odi profanum vulgus et arceo.)
HORACE, *Odes.* Bk. iii, ode 1, l. 1.

Hence ye profane; I hate you all;
Both the great vulgar, and the small.
HORACE, *Odes,* iii, 1. (Cowley, tr.)

Hence, far hence, ye vulgar herd! (Procul O procul este profani.)
VERGIL, *Æneid.* Bk. vi, l. 258.

I hate the vulgar popular cattle.
ROBERT BUCHANAN, *Fine Weather on the Digentia.*

8
To despise the popular talk. (Populi contemnere voces.)
HORACE, *Satires.* Bk. i, sat. 1, l. 65. *See also under* RUMOR.

9
Then Jack, and Tom, and Will, and Dick shall meet and censure me and my council.
JAMES I. (FULLER, *Church History.* Bk x, sec. 1. 1604.)

I neither care what Tom, or Jack, or Dick said.
JOHN TAYLOR THE WATER-POET, *Sir Gregory Nonsense,* 16. (1622)

Though Dick, Tom, and Jack
Will serve you and your pack.
ALEXANDER BROME, *The Royalist's Answer.* (1660)

Tom, Dick, and Harry were not to censure them and their convert.
JOHN ADAMS, *Works.* Vol. x, p. 351. (c. 1800)

10
No doubt but ye are the people, and wisdom shall die with you.
Old Testament: Job, xii, 2.

11
The venal herd. (Venale pecus.)
JUVENAL, *Satires.* Sat. viii, l. 62.

A venal pack. (Grex venalium.)
SUETONIUS, *De Viris Illustribus: De Clar. Rhet.* Sec. 1.

12
The Lord prefers common-looking people. That is the reason He makes so many of them.
ABRAHAM LINCOLN. (JAMES MORGAN, *Our Presidents,* vi; C. T. WETTSTEIN, *Was Abraham Lincoln an Infidel,* p. 84.)

It rather occurs to me that it's the commonplace people who *do* things.
STEPHEN LEACOCK, *The Soul Call.*

13
All go free when multitudes offend. (Quidquid multis peccatur inultum est.)
LUCAN, *De Bello Civili.* Bk. v, l. 260.

14
The public, with its mob yearning to be instructed, edified and pulled by the nose, demands certainties; . . . but there are no certainties.
H. L. MENCKEN, *Prejudices,* 1st ser., p. 46.

15
All ranks and classes,
Down to that new Estate, "the masses."
THOMAS MOORE, *The Fudges in England.* Letter iv, l. 101. Gladstone is said to have used the phrase, "The classes and the masses."

16
Common sense, in so far as it exists, is all for the bourgeoisie. Nonsense is the privilege of the aristocracy. The worries of the world are for the common people.
GEORGE JEAN NATHAN, *Autobiography of an Attitude.*

17
Forbear to lay on the multitude the reproach of a few. (Parcite paucarum diffundere crimen in omnes.)
OVID, *Ars Amatoria.* Bk. iii, l. 9.

1
Let the people think they govern and they will be governed.
WILLIAM PENN, *Some Fruits of Solitude*, l. 67.

2
It is a sin for a plebeian to grumble in public. (Palam mutire plebeio piaculum est.)
PHÆDRUS, *Fables*. Bk. iii, 34.

3
Have I inadvertently said some evil thing? (*Οὐ δή πού τι κακὸν λέγων ἐμαυτὸν λέληθα.*)
PHOCION, when one of his sentences in a public debate was universally applauded. (PLUTARCH, *Lives: Phocion*. Ch. 10, sec. 3.)

What provokes you to risibility, sir? Have I said anything that you understand? Then I ask pardon of the rest of the company.
SAMUEL JOHNSON, *Remark*. (RICHARD CUMBERLAND, *Recollections*.)

4
It is an ancient axiom of statecraft that you can always give the public anything but you can never take away what you once have given, without enormous trouble.
W. B. PITKIN, *Twilight of the American Mind*, p. 222.

5
It is too easy to go over to the majority. (Facile transitur ad plures.)
SENECA, *Epistulæ ad Lucilium*. Epis. vii, sec. 6.

We go with the crowd. (Populo nos damus.)
SENECA, *Epistulæ ad Lucilium*. Epis. xcix, 17.

"It is always best on these occasions to do what the mob do."—"But suppose there are two mobs?" suggested Mr. Snodgrass.—"Shout with the largest," replied Mr. Pickwick.
DICKENS, *Pickwick Papers*. Ch. 13.

6
The mob tramples on the coward. (Calcat jacentem vulgus.)
SENECA, *Octavia*, l. 455.

7
Art thou officer?
Or art thou base, common and popular?
SHAKESPEARE, *Henry V*. Act iv, sc. 1, l. 37.

8
The views of the mob are neither bad nor good. (Neque mala, vel bona, quæ vulgus putet.)
TACITUS, *Annals*. Bk. vi, sec. 22.

Sometimes the common people see correctly; sometimes they err. (Interdum vulgus rectum videt, est ubi peccat.)
HORACE, *Epistles*. Bk. ii, epis. 1, l. 63.

9
A cowardly rabble, bold only in tongue. (Vulgus ignavum et nihil ultra verba ausurum.)
TACITUS, *History*. Bk. iii, sec. 58.

10
The public be damned.
WILLIAM H. VANDERBILT, *Retort*, to Clarence Dresser, a reporter for the Chicago *Tribune*, in 1883, when asked whether the public had been consulted about the proposed discontinuance of a fast mail train to Chicago over the New York Central Railroad. Vanderbilt had explained that the train didn't pay. "Are you working for the public or for your stockholders?" the reporter asked. "The public be damned! I'm working for my stockholders," was Vanderbilt's reply. Henry Clews is the authority for this version of the incident. (See letters in N. Y. *Times*, 25 Aug., 1918; N. Y. *Herald*, 1 Oct., 1918; 28 Oct., 1918.) *See* 2298i:6.

11
The base rabble are enraged; now brands and stones fly. (Sævitque animus ignobile volgus, Iamque faces et saxa volant.)
VERGIL, *Æneid*. Bk. i, l. 149.

12
Our Lords on high,
Who call the underworld of man
An assish, mulish, packhorse clan.
JOHN WOLCOT, *Liberty's Last Squeak*.

13
The poor taxpaying people. (Misera contribuens plebs.)
UNKNOWN, *Law*, adopted by the Hungarian Diet, 1751. Art. 37.

II—People: Vox Populi, Vox Dei

14
A people's voice is a mighty power. (*Φήμη γε μέντοι δημόθρους μέγα σθένει.*)
ÆSCHYLUS, *Agamemnon*, l. 938.

15
The voice of the people is the voice of God. (Vox populi, vox dei.)
ALCUIN, *Epistle to Charlemagne*. c. 800. (*Admonitio ad Carolum Magnum: Works*. Epis. 127.) The context is: "We would not listen to those who were wont to say the voice of the people is the voice of God, for the voice of the mob is near akin to madness." (Nec audiendi sunt qui solent dicere vox populi, vox dei; cum tumultus vulgi semper insaniæ proxima est.) Walter Reynolds, Archbishop of Canterbury, took "Vox Populi, Vox Dei" as the text of his sermon when Edward III ascended the throne, 1 Feb., 1327. Referred to as a proverb as early as 920 by William of Malmesbury (*De Gestis Pont*, fo. 114.)

16
The voice of the people is in some ways divine. (*Θεός νύ τίς ἐστι καὶ αὐτή.*)
HESIOD, *Works and Days*, l. 764. (c. 735 B. C.)

The voice of the people has about it something divine. (Vox populi habet aliquid divinum.)
FRANCIS BACON, *De Augmentis Scientiarum*. Pt. i, bk. 6, ch. 9.

Do not wonder if the common people speak more truly than those of higher rank; for they speak with more safety.
FRANCIS BACON, *De Augmentis Scientiarum*. Pt. i, bk. 6, ch. 9.

17
People's voice is God's voice, men say.
THOMAS HOCCLEVE, *De Regimine Principum*. 104. (1412)

1
Surely the voice of the public, when it calls so loudly, and only for mercy, ought to be heard

SAMUEL JOHNSON, *Letter to Boswell*, 1777.

2
The People's voice is odd;
It is, and it is not, the voice of God.

POPE, *Imitations of Horace: Epistles*, ii, 1, 89.

3
Sacred is the speech of the people. (Sacra populi lingua est.)

SENECA, *Rhetor. Controv.*, i, l. 10. So quoted by Büchmann (*Geflügelte Worte*), but the correct reading is now generally held to be, "Sacra populi digna est."

4
Scripture calling the voice of the people the voice of God. (Scriptoria dicente vox populi, vox Dei.)

POPE SYLVESTER II, *Epistles*. Possibly a misreading of *Isaiah*, lxvi, 6: "A voice from the temple, a voice of God."

5
It is the folly of too many to mistake the echo of a London coffee-house for the voice of the kingdom.

SWIFT, *The Conduct of the Allies*.

III—People: Their Virtues

6
The conscience of a people is their power.

DRYDEN, *The Duke of Guise*. Act i, sc. 1.

7
March without the people, and you march into night: their instincts are a finger-pointing of Providence, always turned toward real benefit.

EMERSON, *Conduct of Life: Power*. Quoted as having been said by "a French deputy from the tribune."

When I see how much each virtuous and gifted person, whom all men consider, lives affectionately with scores of excellent people who are not known far from home, and perhaps with great reason reckons these people his superiors in virtue and in the symmetry and force of their qualities,—I see what cubic values America has, and in these a better certificate of civilization than great cities or enormous wealth.

EMERSON, *Society and Solitude: Civilization*.

8
About things on which the public thinks long, it commonly attains to think right.

SAMUEL JOHNSON, *Works*. Vol. iii, p. 90.

9
For as we come and as we go (and deadly-soon go we!)
The people, Lord, Thy people, are good enough for me!

RUDYARD KIPLING, *A Pilgrim's Way*.

And, Amorite or Eremite, or General Averagee,
The people, Lord, Thy people, are good enough for me!

RUDYARD KIPLING, *A Pilgrim's Way*.

10
Why should there not be a patient confidence in the ultimate justice of the people? Is there any better or equal hope in the world?

ABRAHAM LINCOLN, *First Inaugural Address*, 4 March, 1861.

11
The common crowd is wiser because it is just as wise as it need be. (Plus sapit vulgus quia tantum, quantum opus est, sapit.)

LACTANTIUS, *Divinarum Institutionum*. Bk. iii, sec. 5.

12
The people docile to the yoke. (Ad juga cur faciles populi.)

LUCAN, *De Bello Civili*. Bk. ii, l. 314.

13
For the crowd, the incredible has sometimes more power and is more credible than truth.

MENANDER, *Fragments*. No. 622.

14
Great lords have pleasures, the people have joy. (Les grands seigneurs ont des plaisirs, le peuple a de la joie.)

MONTESQUIEU.

15
The supremacy of the people tends to liberty. (Populi imperium juxta libertatem.)

TACITUS, *Annals*. Bk. vi, sec. 42.

15a
Folks are better than angels.

EDWARD THOMPSON TAYLOR, minister of the Seamen's Bethel, in North Square, Boston, Mass., when his friends tried to comfort him, as he lay dying in 1871, by assuring him that he would soon be among the angels.

16
The mind of the people is like mud,
From which arise strange and beautiful things.

W. J. TURNER, *Talking with Soldiers*.

IV—People: Their Faults

17
Nothing moderate is pleasing to the crowd.

BACON, *De Augmentis Scientiarum*. Pt. i, bk. 6.

It is not given to the world to be moderate.

GOETHE, *Conversations with Eckermann*.

18
The Public is an old woman. Let her maunder and mumble.

THOMAS CARLYLE, *Journal*, 1835.

19
The public! why, the public's nothing better than a great baby.

THOMAS CHALMERS, *Letter*.

The public is just a great baby.

JOHN RUSKIN, *Sesame and Lilies*. Sec. i, 40. Paraphrasing Chalmers.

20
The public! How many fools does it take to make a public? (Le public! Combien faut-il de sots pour faire un public?)

SEBASTIEN CHAMFORT, *Maximes*.

Why then, I say, the Public is a fool.

POPE, *Imitations of Horace: Epistles*, ii, 1, 94.

21
The herd of mankind can hardly be said to think; their notions are almost all adoptive;

and, in general, I believe it is better that it should be so, as such common prejudices contribute more to order and quiet than their own separate reasonings would do, uncultivated and unimproved as they are.

LORD CHESTERFIELD, *Letters,* 7 Feb., 1749.

1
The rabble values few things according to truth, but many according to rumor. (Vulgus ex veritate pauca, ex opinione multa æstimat.)

CICERO, *Pro Roscio Comœdo.* Sec. 10.

2
If it has to choose who is to be crucified, the crowd will always save Barabbas.

JEAN COCTEAU, *Le Rappel à l'Ordre,* p. 31.

3
Nor is the people's judgment always true:
The most may err as grossly as the few.

DRYDEN, *Absalom and Achitophel.* Pt. i, l. 781.

Yet be not blindly guided by the throng;
The multitude is always in the wrong.

WENTWORTH DILLON, *Essay on Translated Verse,* l. 183.

The public is a bad guesser.

THOMAS DE QUINCEY, *Essays: Protestantism.*

4
So void of pity is th' ignoble crowd,
When others' ruin may increase their store!

DRYDEN, *Annus Mirabilis.* St. 250.

5
Leave this hypocritical prating about the masses. Masses are rude, lame, unmade, pernicious in their demands and influence, and need not to be flattered, but to be schooled. . . . The mass are animal, in pupilage, and near chimpanzee. But the units, whereof the mass is composed, are neuters, every one of which may be grown to a queen-bee.

EMERSON, *Conduct of Life: Considerations by the Way.*

The people are to be taken in very small doses. If solitude is proud, so is society vulgar.

EMERSON, *Essays: Society and Solitude.*

6
The public have neither shame nor gratitude.

WILLIAM HAZLITT, *Characteristics.* No. 85.

There is not a more mean, stupid, dastardly, pitiful, selfish, spiteful, envious, ungrateful animal than the Public. It is the greatest of cowards, for it is afraid of itself.

HAZLITT, *Table Talk: On Living to One's-Self.*

The public pays with ingratitude.

JOHN RAY, *English Proverbs.*

Ingratitude is monstrous, and for the multitude to be ingrateful, were to make a monster of the multitude.

SHAKESPEARE, *Coriolanus.* Act ii, sc. 3, l. 9.

7
Reason stands aghast at the sight of an "unprincipled, immoral, incorrigible" public; and the word of God abounds in such threats and denunciations, as must strike terror into the heart of every believer.

RICHARD HURD, *Sermon.* (Vol. iv, 1.)

There was not that variety of beasts in the ark, as is of beastly natures in the multitude.

BEN JONSON, *Explorata: Vulgi Mores.*

8
And what the people but a herd confus'd,
A miscellaneous rabble, who extol
Things vulgar?

MILTON, *Paradise Regained.* Bk. iii, l. 49.

9
Let a man proclaim a new principle. Public sentiment will surely be on the other side.

THOMAS B. REED. (W. A. ROBINSON, *Life.*)

10
Who that is pleased by virtue can please the mob? It takes trickery to win the mob's approval. (Quis enim placere populo potest, cui placet virtus? Malis artibus popularis favor quæritur.)

SENECA, *Epistulæ ad Lucilium.* Epis. xxix, 11.

'Faith there have been many great men that have flattered the people, who ne'er loved them.

SHAKESPEARE, *Coriolanus.* Act ii, sc. 2, l. 8.

I will not choose what many men desire,
Because I will not jump with common spirits,
And rank me with the barbarous multitudes.

SHAKESPEARE, *The Merchant of Venice.* Act ii, sc. 9, l. 31.

V—People: Their Fickleness

See also Opinion: Public Opinion

11
But when the Crier cried, "O Yes!" the people cried, "O No!"

R. H. BARHAM, *Aunt Fanny.*

12
O stormy people, unsad and ever untrue,
And undiscreet, and changing as a vane,
Delighting ever in rumble that is new,
For like the moon ay waxe ye and wane!

CHAUCER, *The Clerkes Tale,* l. 939. Unsad: i. e., unstable. Rumble: i. e., rumor.

13
No man who depends upon the caprice of the ignorant rabble can be accounted great. (Qui ex errore imperitæ multitudinis pendet, hic in magnis viris non est habendus.)

CICERO, *De Officiis.* Bk. i, ch. 19, sec. 65.

14
Nothing is more uncertain than a dependence upon public bodies. They are moved like the wind, but rather more uncertain.

ABRAHAM CLARK, *Letter to James Caldwell,* 7 March, 1777.

15
The fickle mob ever changes along with the prince. (Mobile mutantur semper cum principe vulgus.)

CLAUDIAN, *Panegyricus de Quarto Consulatu Honorii Augusti,* l. 302.

16
I have never wished to cater to the crowd; for what I know they do not approve, and what they approve I do not know. (Numquam volui populo placere. Nam quæ ego

scio, non probat populus; quæ probat populus, ego nescio.)
EPICURUS, *Fragments*. Frag. 187.

I do not hunt for the votes of the inconstant multitude. (Non ego ventosæ plebis suffragia venor.)
HORACE, *Epistles*. Bk. i, epis. 19, l. 37.

1
It is a good part of sagacity to have known the foolish desires of the crowd and their unreasonable notions. (Bona prudentiæ pars est nosse stultas vulgi cupiditates, et absurdas opiniones.)
ERASMUS, *De Utilitate Colloquiorum: Preface*.

2
The mob of fickle citizens. (Mobilium turba Quiritium.)
HORACE, *Odes*. Bk. i, ode 1, l. 7.

3
The Roman mob follows after Fortune, as it always did, and hates those who have been condemned. (Turba Remi sequitur Fortunam, ut semper, et odit Damnatos.)
JUVENAL, *Satires*. Sat. x, l. 74.

4
Nothing is so uncertain or so worthless as the judgments of the mob. (Nil tam incertum nec tam inæstimabile est quam animi multitudinis.)
LIVY, *History*. Bk. xxxi, sec. 34

5
Our slippery people,
Whose love is never link'd to the deserver
Till his deserts are past.
SHAKESPEARE, *Antony and Cleopatra*. Act i, sc. 2, l. 192.

6
He that depends
Upon your favours, swims with fins of lead,
And hews down oaks with rushes.
SHAKESPEARE, *Coriolanus*. Act i, sc. 1, l. 183.

An habitation giddy and unsure
Hath he that buildeth on the vulgar heart.
SHAKESPEARE, *II Henry IV*. Act i, sc. 3, l. 89.

7
Was ever feather so lightly blown to and fro as this multitude?
SHAKESPEARE, *II Henry VI*. Act iv, sc. 8, l. 57.

Look, as I blow this feather from my face,
And as the air blows it to me again,
Obeying with my wind when I do blow,
And yielding to another when it blows,
Commanded always by the greater gust;
Such is the lightness of you common men.
SHAKESPEARE, *III Henry VI*. Act iii, sc. 1, l. 84.

8
The wavering mob is torn by opposite opinions. (Scinditur incertum studia in contraria volgus.)
VERGIL, *Æneid*. Bk. ii, l. 39.

VI—People: Their Tyranny

9
The tyranny of a multitude is a multiplied tyranny.
EDMUND BURKE, *Letter to Thomas Mercer*, 26 Feb., 1790.

The people are the masters.
EDMUND BURKE, *Speech*, House of Commons, 11 Feb., 1780.

10
I think I hear a little bird, who sings
The people by and by will be the stronger.
BYRON, *Don Juan*. Canto viii, st. 50.

The people will come to their own at last,—
God is not mocked forever.
JOHN HAY, *The Sphynx of the Tuileries*.

11
The people's right remains; let those who dare
Dispute their power, when they the judges are.
DRYDEN, *Character of a Good Parson*, l. 121.

12
That worst of tyrants, an usurping crowd.
HOMER, *Iliad*. Bk. ii, l. 242. (Pope, tr.)

Oppress'd by multitudes, the best may fall.
HOMER, *Iliad*. Bk. xi, l. 587. (Pope, tr.)

13
True worth . . . neither takes up nor lays aside the ax at the fickle mob's behest. (Virtus . . . Nec sumit aut ponit secures Arbitrio popularis auræ.)
HORACE, *Odes*. Bk. iii, ode 2, l. 17.

14
The people arose as one man.
Old Testament: Judges, xx, 8.

15
There is no tyranny so despotic as that of public opinion among a free people.
DONN PIATT, *Memories of the Men who Saved the Union: Lincoln*.

16
What, shall the mob dictate my policy? (Πόλις γὰρ ἡμῖν ἁμὲ χρὴ τάσσειν ἐρεῖ.)
SOPHOCLES, *Antigone*, l. 734.

What are the rank tongues
Of this vile herd, grown insolent with feeding,
That I should prize their noisy praise, or dread
Their noisome clamour?
BYRON, *Sardanapalus*. Act i, sc. 2.

17
Our supreme governors, the mob.
HORACE WALPOLE, *Letters: To Sir Horace Mann*, 7 Sept., 1743.

VII—People: The Many-Headed Multitude

18
That great enemy of reason, virtue, and religion, the Multitude, that numerous piece of monstrosity . . . more prodigious than Hydra.
SIR THOMAS BROWNE, *Religio Medici*. Pt. ii, sec. 1.

19
This many-headed monster, Multitude.
SAMUEL DANIEL, *History of the Civil War*. Bk. ii, st. 13.

The many-headed monster, The giddy multitude.
MASSINGER, *Unnatural Combat*. Act iii, sc. 2.

20
The mob has many heads but no brains.
THOMAS FULLER, *Gnomologia*. No. 4653.

A Mob's a Monster; Heads enough, but no Brains.
BENJAMIN FRANKLIN, *Poor Richard*, 1747.

1 Thou art a many-headed beast. (Belua multorum es capitum.)
HORACE, *Epistles*. Bk. i, epis. 1, l. 76.

The many-headed monster of the pit.
POPE, *Imitations of Horace: Epistles*. Bk. ii, epis. 1, l. 305.

The multitude of the gross people, being a beast of many heads.
ERASMUS, *Adagia*. No. 122.

O weak trust of the many-headed multitude.
SIR PHILIP SIDNEY, *Arcadia*, p. 226.

That beast of many heads, the staggering multitude.
JOHN WEBSTER, *The Malcontent*. Act iii, sc. 3.

2 The blunt monster with uncounted heads,
The still-discordant wavering multitude.
SHAKESPEARE, *II Henry IV: Induction*, l. 18.

He himself stuck not to call us the many-headed multitude.
SHAKESPEARE, *Coriolanus*. Act ii, sc. 3, l. 17.

3 Trust not the populace; the crowd is many-minded.
PHOCYLIDES, *Gnomai*. No. 89. (Attr.)

4 Well, if a King's a lion, at the least
The people are a many-headed beast.
POPE, *Imitations of Horace: Epistles*. Bk. i, epis. 1, l. 120.

5 Who o'er the herd would wish to reign,
Fantastic, fickle, fierce, and vain?
Vain as the leaf upon the stream,
And fickle as a changeful dream;
Fantastic as a woman's mood,
And fierce as Frenzy's fevered blood.
Thou many-headed monster-thing,
O who would wish to be thy king?
SCOTT, *The Lady of the Lake*. Canto v, st. 30.

6 The beast With many heads butts me away.
SHAKESPEARE, *Coriolanus*. Act iv, sc. 1, l. 1.

VIII—People: The Mob's Insanity

7 Every numerous assembly is *mob*, let the individuals who compose it be what they will.
LORD CHESTERFIELD, *Letters*, 18 March, 1751.

8 A mob is a society of bodies voluntarily bereaving themselves of reason. . . . A mob is man voluntarily descending to the nature of the beast.
EMERSON, *Essays, First Series: Compensation*.

9 The angry buzz of a multitude is one of the bloodiest noises in the world.
LORD HALIFAX, *Works*, p. 219.

10 Vanquishing the clamor of the mob. (Popularis Vincentem strepitus.)
HORACE, *Ars Poetica*, l. 81.

11 All we have a right to say is that individuals are occasionally guided by reason, crowds never.
DEAN W. R. INGE. (MARCHANT, *Wit and Wisdom of Dean Inge*. No. 229.)

12 Men who are rogues by retail, are extremely honest in the gross; they love morality. (Les hommes, fripons en détail, sont en gros de très honnêtes gens; ils aiment la moralité.)
MONTESQUIEU, *Spirit of the Laws*. Bk. xxv, ch. 2.

The Mob destroys spiritual values by accepting them; it destroys great men by adopting their principles.
FRANK K. NOTCH, *King Mob*, p. 63.

13 The mass never comes up to the standard of its best member, but on the contrary degrades itself to a level with the lowest.
H. D. THOREAU, *Journal*, 14 March, 1838.

PERFECTION

See also Faults: Faultlessness

14 They are perfect—how else? they shall never change:
We are faulty—why not? we have time in store.
ROBERT BROWNING, *Old Pictures in Florence*. St. 16.

What's come to perfection perishes.
Things learned on earth we shall practise in heaven;
Works done least rapidly Art most cherishes.
ROBERT BROWNING, *Old Pictures in Florence*. St. 17.

15 All his perfections were so rare,
The wit of man could not declare
Which single virtue, or which grace
Above the rest had any place.
SAMUEL BUTLER, *Hudibras's Elegy*, l. 41.

16 Oh! she was perfect past all parallel—
Of any modern female saint's comparison.
BYRON, *Don Juan*. Canto i, st. 17.

Her goodness doth disdain comparison,
And, but herself, admits no parallel.
MASSINGER, *The Duke of Milan*. Act iv, sc. 3.

None but itself can be its parallel.
LEWIS THEOBALD, *The Double Falsehood*. Act iii, sc. 1. This is persistently misquoted, "None but himself."

What noble presence in himself! (Quantum instar in ipso!)
VERGIL, *Æneid*. Bk. vi, l. 865.

She can be imitated by none, nor paralleled by any but by herself.
UNKNOWN, *Inscription Under the Portrait of*

Colonel Strangeways. (DODD, *Epigrammatists,* p. 533.)

1
By different methods different men excel,
But where is he who can do all things well?
CHARLES CHURCHILL, *Epistle to William Hogarth,* l. 573.

Or if, once in a thousand years,
A perfect character appears.
CHARLES CHURCHILL, *The Ghost.* Bk. iii, l. 207.

2
Everything splendid is rare, and nothing is harder to find than perfection. (Quidem omnia præclara, rara, nec quicquam difficilius quam reperire quod sit omni ex parte in suo genere perfectum.)
CICERO, *De Amicitia.* Ch. 21, sec. 79

3
So slow
The growth of what is excellent; so hard
T' attain perfection in this nether world.
COWPER, *The Task.* Bk. i, l. 83.

4
The world globes itself in a drop of dew. The microscope cannot find the animalcule which is less perfect for being little.
EMERSON, *Essays, First Series: Compensation.*

5
The desire of perfection is the worst disease that ever afflicted the human mind.
FONTANES, *Address to Napoleon, in behalf of the French Senate,* 1804.

6
The very pink of perfection.
GOLDSMITH, *She Stoops to Conquer.* Act i, sc. 1.

The Pink of Perfection.
T. H. BAYLY, *Loves of the Butterflies.*

7
Be ye therefore perfect, even as your Father which is in heaven is perfect.
New Testament: Matthew, v, 48.

8
Trifles make perfection, and perfection is no trifle.
MICHELANGELO. (C. C. COLTON, *Lacon.*)

9
God made thee perfect, not immutable.
MILTON, *Paradise Lost.* Bk. v, l. 524.

When I approach
Her loveliness, so absolute she seems, . . .
That what she wills to do or say,
Seems wisest, virtuousest, discreetest, best.
MILTON, *Paradise Lost.* Bk. viii, l. 546.

10
'Tis true, perfection none must hope to find
In all the world, much less in womankind.
POPE, *January and May,* l. 190.

11
Was never eye did see that face,
Was never ear did hear that tongue,
Was never mind did mind his grace,
That ever thought the travel long;
But eyes and ears and ev'ry thought
Were with his sweet perfections caught.
MATTHEW ROYDON, *An Elegie, or Friend's Passion for His Astrophill.* (1593) Referring to Sir Philip Sidney.

12
Do you seek Alcides' equal? None is, except himself. (Quæris Alcides parem? Nemo est nisi ipse.)
SENECA, *Hercules Furens,* l. 84.

He was equal only to himself.
SIR WILLIAM TEMPLE, referring to Cæsar. (GRANGER, *Biographical History.*)

13
The demi-Atlas of this earth, the arm
And burgonet of men.
SHAKESPEARE, *Antony and Cleopatra.* Act i, sc. 5, l. 23. Referring to Antony.

She did make defect perfection.
SHAKESPEARE, *Antony and Cleopatra.* Act ii, sc. 2, l. 236.

14
Whose dear perfection hearts that scorn'd to serve
Humbly call'd mistress.
SHAKESPEARE, *All's Well that Ends Well.* Act v, sc. 3, l. 18.

15
Thou art the nonpareil.
SHAKESPEARE, *Macbeth.* Act iii, sc. 4, l. 20.

I had else been perfect,
Whole as the marble, founded as the rock,
As broad and general as the casing air.
SHAKESPEARE, *Macbeth.* Act iii, sc. 4, l. 21.

16
How many things by season season'd are
To their right praise and true perfection!
SHAKESPEARE, *The Merchant of Venice.* Act v, sc. 1, l. 107.

It is the witness still of excellency
To put a strange face on his own perfection.
SHAKESPEARE, *Much Ado About Nothing.* Act ii, sc. 3, l. 48.

17
No perfection is so absolute,
That some impurity doth not pollute.
SHAKESPEARE, *The Rape of Lucrece.* St. 122.

Every thing that grows
Holds in perfection but a little moment.
SHAKESPEARE, *Sonnets.* No. xv.

But you, O you,
So perfect and so peerless, are created
Of every creature's best!
SHAKESPEARE, *The Tempest.* Act iii, sc. 1, l. 46.

18
If, one by one, you wedded all the world,
Or from the all that are took something good,
To make a perfect woman, she you kill'd
Would be unparallel'd.
SHAKESPEARE, *Winter's Tale.* Act v, sc. 1, l. 13.

Women will love her, that she is a woman
More worth than any man; men, that she is
The rarest of all women.
SHAKESPEARE, *Winter's Tale.* Act v, sc. 1, l. 110.

1
Our erected wit maketh us know what perfection is, and yet our infected will keepeth us from reaching unto it.

SIR PHILIP SIDNEY, *The Defense of Poesie.*

2
A man cannot have an idea of perfection in another, which he was never sensible of in himself.

STEELE, *The Tatler.* No. 227.

3
No perfect thing is too small for eternal recollection.

ARTHUR SYMONDS, *Introduction to Coleridge's "Biographia Literaria."*

4
I thought I could not breathe in that fine air,
That pure severity of perfect light.

TENNYSON, *Guinevere,* l. 640.

5
To keep in sight Perfection, and adore
The vision, is the artist's best delight;
His bitterest pang, that he can ne'er do more
Than keep her long'd-for loveliness in sight.

WILLIAM WATSON, *Epigrams.*

6
In this broad earth of ours,
Amid the measureless grossness and the slag,
Enclosed and safe within its central heart,
Nestles the seed Perfection.

WALT WHITMAN, *Song of the Universal.* Pt. i. Inscribed beneath his bust in Hall of Fame.

7
Let other bards of angels sing,
Bright suns without a spot;
But thou art no such perfect thing:
Rejoice that thou art not!

WORDSWORTH, *To ——.*

8
Counsels of perfection.

UNKNOWN. A theological term of great antiquity applied to works of supererogation.

II—Perfection: The Broken Mould

9
There never was such beauty in another man.
Nature made him, and then broke the mould.
(Non è un si bello in tante altre persone,
Natura il fece, e poi roppe la stampa.)

ARIOSTO, *Orlando Furioso.* Canto x, st. 84.

One can say without exaggeration that nature, after she had made him, broke the mould. (L'on peut dire sans hyperbole, que la nature, que la après l'avoir fait en cassa la moule.)

ANGELO CONSTANTINI, *La Vie de Scaramouche.*

The mould is lost wherein was made
This a *per se* of all.

ALEXANDER MONTGOMERIE, *The Cherrie and the Slae.* (1597)

10 Nature's richest, sweetest store,
She made an Hoyland, and can make no more.

THOMAS CHATTERTON, *To Miss Hoyland.*

12
No autumn, nor no age ever approach
This heavenly piece, which nature having wrought
She lost her needle, and did then despair
Ever to work so lively and so fair.

MASSINGER AND FIELD, *The Fatal Dowry.*

For Nature had but little clay
Like that of which she moulded him.

T. L. PEACOCK, *Headlong Hall.* Ch. 5.

The gods—a kindness I with thanks must pay—
Have form'd me of a coarser kind of clay.

CHARLES CHURCHILL, *The Rosciad,* l. 1065.

13
Crack nature's moulds, all germens spill at once
That make ingrateful man!

SHAKESPEARE, *King Lear.* Act iii, sc. 2, l. 9.

14
I think Nature hath lost the mould
Where she her shape did take;
Or else I doubt if Nature could
So fair a creature make.

UNKNOWN, *A Praise of his Lady.* (*Tottel's Miscellany,* 1557.)

15
The idea that Nature lost the perfect mould has been a favourite one with all song-writers and poets, and is found in the literature of all European nations.

UNKNOWN, *Book of English Songs,* p. 28.

PERFUME

16
Gentle and noble are their tempers framed,
That can be quickened with perfumes and sounds.

GEORGE CHAPMAN, *Ovid's Banquet of Sense.*

17
Does it not betray itself by its odor? (Non olet?)

CICERO, *Orator.* Sec. 45.

18
I cannot talk with civet in the room,
A fine puss-gentleman that's all perfume;
The sight's enough—no need to smell a beau.

COWPER, *Conversation,* l. 283.

And all your courtly civet-cats can vent,
Perfume to you, to me is excrement.

POPE, *Epilogue to the Satires.* Dial. ii, l. 183.

But O! too common ill, I brought with me
That, which betray'd me to mine enemy,
A loud perfume, which at my entrance cried
E'en at thy father's nose; so were we spied. . . .
Had it been some bad smell he would have thought
That his own feet, or breath, that smell had wrought.

JOHN DONNE, *Elegy iv; The Perfume.*

19
The sweetest essences are always confined in the smallest glasses.

JOHN DRYDEN, *Essays.* Vol. ii, p. 178.

20
Look not for musk in a dog-kennel.

H. G. BOHN, *Hand-Book of Proverbs,* p. 445.

1
I curl up my nose for a savory smell. (Nasum nidore supinor.)
HORACE, *Satires*. Bk. ii, sat. 7, l. 38.

2
There is nothing like an odour to stir memories.
WILLIAM MCFEE, *The Market*. *See also under* VIOLET.

3
He thought her penny scent a sweeter thing
Than precious ointment out of alabaster.
MASEFIELD, *The Widow in the Bye Street*.

4
A stream of rich distill'd perfumes.
MILTON, *Comus*, l. 556.

5
Sabean odours from the spicy shore
Of Arabie the blest.
MILTON, *Paradise Lost*. Bk. iv, l. 162.

This casket India's glowing gems unlocks,
And all Arabia breathes from yonder box.
POPE, *The Rape of the Lock*. Canto i, l. 133.

All the perfumes of Arabia will not sweeten this little hand.
SHAKESPEARE, *Macbeth*. Act v, sc. 1, l. 57.

6
An amber scent of odorous perfume
Her harbinger.
MILTON, *Samson Agonistes*, l. 720.

7
The smell of an onion from the mouth of the lovely is sweeter than that of a rose in the hand of the ugly.
SADI, *Rose Garden: Hatefulness of Old Husbands*.

8
He who frequents the perfumer's shop and lingers even for a short time, will carry with him the scent of the place. (Qui in unguentaria taberna resederunt et paullo diutius commorati sunt, odorem secum loci ferunt.)
SENECA, *Epistulæ ad Lucilium*. Epis. cviii, 4.

9
So perfumed that The winds were love-sick.
SHAKESPEARE, *Antony and Cleopatra*, ii, 2, 198.

A strange invisible perfume hits the sense.
SHAKESPEARE, *Antony and Cleopatra*, ii, 2, 217.

10
The perfumed tincture of the roses.
SHAKESPEARE, *Sonnets*. No. liv.

Perfume for a lady's chamber.
SHAKESPEARE, *Winter's Tale*. Act iv, sc. 4, l. 225.

11
Let me have them very well perfumed:
For she is sweeter than perfume itself
To whom they go to.
SHAKESPEARE, *Taming of the Shrew*, i, 2, 152.

11a
My very heart faints and my whole soul grieves
At the moist rich smell of the rotting leaves.
TENNYSON, *Song*.

II—Perfume: No Scent the Best Scent

12
Pickles are one thing, balsam another; away with scents! Neither to smell rank nor to smell sweet pleases me. (Salgama non noc sunt, quod balsama: cedite odores. Nec male olere mihi, nec bene olere placet.)
AUSONIUS, *Epigrams*. No. 84.

13
Still to be neat, still to be drest,
As you were going to a feast;
Still to be powder'd, still perfumed:
Lady, it is to be presumed,
Though art's hid causes are not found,
All is not sweet, all is not sound.
BEN JONSON, *Epicœne: Song*. Act i.

14
He does not smell well who always has a nice scent upon him. (Non bene olet, qui bene semper olet.)
MARTIAL, *Epigrams*. Bk. ii, epig. 12, l. 4.

'Tis doubt, my Postumus, he that doth smell
So sweetly always, smells not very well.
MARTIAL, *Epigrams*, ii, 12. (Fletcher, tr.)

15
I prefer rather than to smell well not to smell of anything at all. (Malo, quam bene olere, nil olere.)
MARTIAL, *Epigrams*. Bk. vi, epig. 55.

You laugh at us that we of nothing savour;
Rather smell so than sweeter (by your favour).
MARTIAL, *Epigrams*, vi, 55. (Florio, tr.)

16
He who smells good always does not smell good. (Non bene olet qui bene semper olet.)
PETRONIUS, *Fragments*. No. 24.

17
A woman smells well when she smells of nothing. (Mulier recte olet ubi nihil olet.)
PLAUTUS, *Mostellaria*, l. 273. (Act i, sc. 3.)

Then smells a woman purely well,
When she of nothing else doth smell.
MONTAIGNE, *Essays*. Bk. i, ch. 55.

As women do smell well, which smell of nothing.
FRANCIS MERES, *Palladis*, 32. (1598)

18
The best scent for the person is no scent at all. (Optimus odor in corpore est nullus.)
SENECA, *Epistulæ ad Lucilium*. Epis. cviii, 16.

19
They that smell least, smell best.
UNKNOWN, *New Help to Discourse*, p. 245. (1669)

PERIL, see Danger

PERSEVERANCE

See also Resolution; Trifles; Water and Rock

20
With a wink of his eye, His friend made reply
In his jocular manner, sly, caustic, and dry,
"Still the same boy, Bassanio—never say 'die'!"
R. H. BARHAM, *The Merchant of Venice*.

1
Even the woodpecker owes his success to the fact that he uses his head and keeps pecking away until he finishes the job he starts.
COLEMAN COX, *Perseverance.*

So! And did it yell
Till it became all voice?
Cicada-shell!
BASHŌ, *Persistence.* (Henderson, tr.)

2
A pretty good firm is "Watch & Waite,"
And another is "Attit, Early & Layte;"
And still another is "Doo & Dairet;"
But the best is probably "Grinn & Barrett."
WALTER G. DOTY, *The Best Firm.*

3
They did not strike twelve the first time.
EMERSON, *English Traits.* Ch. 19.

4
Step after step the ladder is ascended.
GEORGE HERBERT, *Jacula Prudentum.*

Let thy mind still be bent, still plotting, where,
And when, and how thy business may be done.
Slackness breeds worms; but the sure traveller,
Though he alight sometimes, still goeth on.
GEORGE HERBERT, *The Church-Porch.* St. 57.

5
I will spit in my hands, and take better hold.
JOHN HEYWOOD, *Proverbs,* Pt. ii, ch. 4. (1546)

Hold on with a bulldog grip, and chew and choke as much as possible.
ABRAHAM LINCOLN, *Telegram to General Grant,* at siege of Petersburgh, 17 August, 1864.

Stick to your aim; the mongrel's hold will slip,
But only crowbars loose the bulldog's grip;
Small as he looks, the jaw that never yields
Drags down the bellowing monarch of the fields.
O. W. HOLMES, *A Rhymed Lesson,* l. 286.

6
Men who had had their fortunes to build,
And—much to their credit—had richly filled
Their purses by *pursy-verance.*
THOMAS HOOD, *Miss Kilmansegg: Marriage.*

7
God is with those who persevere.
Koran. Ch. 8.

Slow and steady wins the race.
DAVID LLOYD, *Fables: The Hare and Tortoise.*

8
Flinch not, neither give up nor despair, if thou dost not invariably succeed in acting from right principles.
MARCUS AURELIUS, *Meditations.* Bk. v, sec. 9.

9
"Brave admiral, say but one good word:
What shall we do when hope is gone?"
The words leapt like a leaping sword:
"Sail on! sail on! sail on! and on!"
JOAQUIN MILLER, *Columbus.*

10
And the saying grew, as sayings will grow
From hard endeavor and bangs and bumps:
"He got in a mighty hard row of stumps;
But he tried, and died trying to hoe his row."
JOAQUIN MILLER, *A Hard Row of Stumps.*

11
For a just man falleth seven times and riseth up again.
Old Testament: Proverbs, xxiv, 16.

'Tis a lesson you should heed:
Try, try, try again.
If at first you don't succeed,
Try, try, try again.
WILLIAM E. HICKSON, *Try and Try Again.*

12
When men are arrived at the goal, they should not turn back.
PLUTARCH, *Of the Training of Children.*

13
Persevere and never fear.
W. G. BENHAM, *Proverbs,* p. 825.

14
There is nothing which persevering effort and unceasing and diligent care cannot overcome. (Nihil est quod non expugnet pertinax opera, et intenta ac diligens cura.)
SENECA, *Epistulæ ad Lucilium.* Epis. 1, sec. 6.
See also under DIFFICULTY.

15
Perseverance is more efficacious than violence; and many things which cannot be overcome when they stand together, yield themselves up when taken little by little.
SERTORIUS. (PLUTARCH, *Lives: Sertorius.* Ch. 16, sec. 4.)

16
Perseverence, dear my lord,
Keeps honour bright: to have done is to hang
Quite out of fashion, like a rusty mail
In monumental mockery.
SHAKESPEARE, *Troilus and Cressida.* Act iii, sc. 3, l. 150.

17
Neither to change, nor falter, nor repent;
This, like thy glory, Titan, is to be
Good, great, and joyous, beautiful and free;
This is alone Life, Joy, Empire and Victory.
SHELLEY, *Prometheus.* Act iv, l. 575.

18
Nothing is achieved before it be thoroughly attempted.
SIR PHILIP SIDNEY, *Arcadia.* Bk. ii.

19
By perseverance the snail reached the ark.
C. H. SPURGEON, *Salt-Cellars.*

20
'Tain't no use to sit and whine
'Cause the fish ain't on your line;
Bait your hook an' keep on tryin',
Keep a-goin'!
FRANK L. STANTON, *Keep A-goin'.*

21
It's dogged as does it. It ain't thinking about it.
ANTHONY TROLLOPE, *Last Chronicle of Barset.* Vol. i, ch. 61.

1
Persevere, and preserve yourself for better days. (Durate, et vosmet rebus servate secundis.)
VERGIL, *Æneid*. Bk. i, l. 207.

Persevere: it is thy part. Perhaps on the unhappy happier days shall wait. (Perge: decet. Forsan miseros meliora sequentur.)
VERGIL, *Æneid*. Bk. xii, l. 153.

Endure and persist; this pain will turn to your good by and by. (Prefer et obdura; dolor hic tibi proderit olim.)
OVID, *Amores*. Bk. iii, eleg. 11, l. 7.

2
It is not necessary to hope in order to undertake, or to succeed in order to persevere.
WILLIAM THE SILENT, *Apothegms*.

PERSONALITY

See also Character, Individuality

3
So intrinsical is every man unto himself, that some doubt may be made, whether any would exchange his being, or substantially become another man.
SIR THOMAS BROWNE, *To a Friend:* Sec. 23.

4
Sancho Panza by name is my own self, if I was not changed in the cradle.
CERVANTES, *Don Quixote*. Pt. ii, ch. 30.

5
Each the known track of sage philosophy
Deserts, and has a byway of his own:
So much the restless eagerness to shine,
And love of singularity, prevail.
DANTE, *Paradiso*. Canto xxix, l. 89. (Cary, tr.)

6
I am the owner of the sphere,
Of the seven stars and the solar year,
Of Cæsar's hand, and Plato's brain,
Of Lord Christ's heart, and Shakespeare's strain.
EMERSON, *Essays, First Series: History: Motto*.

7
As I am, so I see.
EMERSON, *Essays, Second Series: Experience*.

8
Singularity may be good sense at home, but it must not go much abroad.
LORD HALIFAX, *Works*, p. 254.

9
There are three Johns: 1, the real John; known only to his Maker; 2, John's ideal John, never the real one, and often very unlike him; 3, Thomas's ideal John, never the real John, nor John's John, but often very unlike either.
O. W. HOLMES, *The Autocrat of the Breakfast-Table*. Ch. 3.

Every man has three characters: that which he exhibits, that which he has, and that which he thinks he has.
ALPHONSE KARR.

10
Such a man in truth am I. (Nimirum hic ego sum.)
HORACE, *Epistles*. Bk. i, epis. 15, l. 42.

Such am I and you; but what I am you cannot be; what you are anyone may be. (Hoc ego, tuque sumus: sed quod sum, non potes esse: Tu quod es, e populo quilibet esse potest.)
MARTIAL, *Epigrams*. Bk. v, epig. 13.

Such you and I: like me you cannot be;
Fortune may make a cobbler like to thee.
MARTIAL, *Epigrams*, v, 13. (Hay, tr.)

11
I am four monkeys.
One hangs from a limb,
tail-wise,
chattering at the earth;
another is cramming his belly with cocoanut;
the third is up in the top branches,
quizzing the sky;
and the fourth—
he's chasing another monkey.
How many monkeys are you?
ALFRED KREYMBORG, *The Tree*.

12
And now each man bestride his hobby, and dust away his bells to what tune he pleases.
CHARLES LAMB, *Essays of Elia: All Fool's Day*.

13
I am bigger than anything that can happen to me. All these things, sorrow, misfortune and suffering, are outside my door. I am in the house and I have a key.
CHARLES F. LUMMIS.

14
The secret of the universe, as by slow degrees it reveals itself to us, turns out to be personality.
J. C. POWYS, *The Complex Vision*, p. 194.

15
Absent he is a character understood, but present he is a force respected.
GEORGE SANTAYANA, *Interpretations of Poetry and Religion*, p. 273.

16
Personality is to a man what perfume is to a flower.
CHARLES M. SCHWAB, *Ten Commandments of Success*.

17
As accidental as my life may be, or as that random humour is, which governs it, I know nothing, after all, so real or substantial as myself.
LORD SHAFTESBURY, *Characteristics*. Vol. ii, p. 353.

18
Who is it that can tell me who I am?
SHAKESPEARE, *King Lear*. Act i, sc. 4, l. 250.

No, I am that I am.
SHAKESPEARE, *Sonnets*. No. cxxi.

19
But this main-miracle that thou art thou,

With power on thine own act and on the world.
TENNYSON, *De Profundis*. Last lines.

1
For an impenetrable shield, stand inside yourself.
H. D. THOREAU, *Journal*, 27 June, 1840.

1a
Momentous to himself as I to me
Hath each man been that ever woman bore.
WILLIAM WATSON, *Epigrams*. No. 22.

2
Nothing endures but personal qualities.
WALT WHITMAN, *Song of the Broad-Axe*. Sec. 4.

What is commonest, cheapest, nearest, easiest, is Me.
WALT WHITMAN, *Song of Myself*, Sec. xiv.

PERSUASION

See also Argument

3
He spake, and straight
Upon his lips Persuasion sate.
(Πρὸς δέ γ' αὐτοῦ τῷ τάχει
Πειθώ τις ἐπεκάθητο τοῖσι χείλεσιν.)
EUPOLIS, *Dæmoi*. Frag. 94.

4
Charming women can true converts make.
We love the precepts for the teacher's sake.
FARQUHAR, *The Constant Couple*. Act v, sc. 3.

5
The persuasion of the fortunate sways the doubtful.
GEORGE HERBERT, *Jacula Prudentum*.

6
He, from whose lips divine persuasion flows.
HOMER, *Iliad*. Bk. vii, l. 143. (Pope, tr.)

Persuasive speech, and more persuasive sighs,
Silence that spoke, and eloquence of eyes.
HOMER, *Iliad*. Bk. xiv, l. 251. (Pope, tr.)

Enchanting tongues Persuasive.
MILTON, *Paradise Regained*. Bk. ii, l. 158.

Persuasion hung upon his lips.
STERNE, *Tristram Shandy*. Bk. i, ch. 19.

7
Yet hold it more humane, more heav'nly, first.
By winning words to conquer willing hearts,
And make persuasion do the work of fear.
MILTON, *Paradise Regained*. Bk. i, l. 221.

8
Sulla proceeded by persuasion, not by force of arms.
PLUTARCH, *Lives: Lysander and Sulla*. Ch. 2.

9
Graced as thou art with all the power of words,
So known, so honour'd, at the House of Lords.
POPE, *Imitations of Horace: Epistles*. Bk. i, epis. 6, l. 48.

Persuasion tips his tongue whene'er he talks,
And he has chambers in King's Bench walks.
COLLEY CIBBER, *Parody on Pope's Lines*.

10
By long forbearing is a prince persuaded.
Old Testament: Proverbs, xxv, 15.

11
He did entreat me, past all saying nay.
SHAKESPEARE, *The Merchant of Venice*. Act iii, sc. 2, l. 232.

PERVERSITY

12
Men take more pains to lose themselves than would be requisite to keep them in the right road.
KENELM HENRY DIGBY, *The Broad Stone of Honour: Godefridus*.

13
Perverseness makes one squint-eyed.
GEORGE HERBERT, *Jacula Prudentum*.

14
All things can corrupt perverted minds. (Omnia perversas possunt corrumpere mentes.)
OVID, *Tristia*. Bk ii, l. 301.

There is nothing, Antipho, which cannot be perverted in the telling. (Nihil est, Antipho, Quin male narrando possit depravarier.)
TERENCE, *Phormio*, l. 696. (Act iv, sc. 4.)

15
'Zounds, sir, you are one of those that will not serve God if the devil bid you.
SHAKESPEARE, *Othello*. Act i, sc. 1, l. 109.

16
They won't when you would, and will when you won't. (Nolunt ubi velis, ubi nolis cupiunt ultro.)
TERENCE, *Eunuchus*, l. 813. (Act iv, sc. 7.)
See also under OPPORTUNITY.

PESSIMISM

See also Melancholy, Optimism

17
Just because there's fallen
A snowflake on his forehead
He must go and fancy
'Tis winter all the year.
THOMAS BAILEY ALDRICH, *A Snowflake*.

18
Nothing is in general more gloomy and monotonous than declamations on the hollowness and transitoriness of human life and grandeur.
MATTHEW ARNOLD, *Essays in Criticism*, p. 434.

19
Pessimism, when you get used to it, is just as agreeable as optimism.
ARNOLD BENNETT, *Things that Have Interested Me: The Slump in Pessimism*.

20
Pessimism, a thing unfit for a white man; a thing like opium, that may often be a poison and sometimes a medicine, but never a food for us, who are driven by an inner command not only to think but to live, not only to live but to grow, and not only to grow but to build.
G. K. CHESTERTON, *The Victorian Age in Literature*, p. 195.

21
That man, I trow, is doubly curst,

Who of the best doth make the worst;
And he I'm sure is doubly blest,
Who of the worst can make the best:
To sit and sorrow and complain,
Is adding folly to our pain.

WILLIAM COMBE, *Dr. Syntax in Search of the Picturesque*. Canto xxvi, l. 135.

1
The self-styled decadent insists on lying down in the belief that he is hopelessly paralyzed.

HAVELOCK ELLIS, *The Soul of Spain*, p. 410.

2
I know those miserable fellows, and I hate them, who see a black star always riding through the light and colored clouds in the sky overhead.

EMERSON, *Conduct of Life: Considerations by the Way*.

Come let us sit and watch the sky,
And fancy clouds, where no clouds be.

THOMAS HOOD, *Ode to Melancholy*, l. 17.

3
There are people who have an appetite for grief, pleasure is not strong enough and they crave pain, mithridatic stomachs which must be fed on poisoned bread, natures so doomed that no prosperity can sooth their ragged and dishevelled desolation.

EMERSON, *Natural History of Intellect: The Tragic*.

4
Oh, don't the days seem lank and long,
When all goes right and nothing goes wrong?
And isn't your life extremely flat
With nothing whatever to grumble at?

W. S. GILBERT, *Princess Ida*. Act iii.

5
A pessimist is one who has been intimately acquainted with an optimist.

ELBERT HUBBARD, *A Thousand and One Epigrams*, p. 121.

6
A bilious philosopher's opinion of the world can only be accepted with a pinch of salt, of Epsom salt by preference.

ALDOUS HUXLEY, *Proper Studies*, p. 320.

7
Polydore: Let us embrace, and from this very moment
Vow an eternal misery together.
Monimia: And wilt thou be a very faithful wretch,
Never grow fond of cheerful peace again?
Wilt thou with me study to be unhappy,
And find out ways t' increase affliction?

THOMAS OTWAY, *The Orphan*. Act iv, sc. 2. Found in original printed edition but sometimes omitted in later versions.

8
My pessimism goes to the point of suspecting the sincerity of the pessimists.

JEAN ROSTAND, *Journal d'un Caractère*.

9
Do you know what a pessimist is? A man who thinks everybody as nasty as himself, and hates them for it.

BERNARD SHAW, *An Unsocial Socialist*. Ch. 5.

10
Nothing is right and nothing is just;
We sow in ashes and reap in dust.

MARY MONTGOMERY SINGLETON, *A Reverie*.

11
Welcome, kindred glooms, Congenial horrors, hail!

THOMSON, *The Seasons: Winter*, l. 5.

12
Fond World, adieu; come, Death, and close my eyes;
More Geese than Swans now live; more Fools than Wise.

UNKNOWN, *Fond World Adieu*.

PETER

13
Saint Peter sat by the celestial gate:
His keys were rusty, and the lock was dull.

BYRON, *Vision of Judgment*. St. 1.

Till Peter's keys some christened Jove adorn.

POPE, *The Dunciad*. Bk. iii, l. 109.

14
There is a difference between Peter and Peter. (Algo va de Pedro á Pedro.)

CERVANTES, *Don Quixote*. Pt. i, ch. 47.

15
As one who crucified Paul that Peter might go free. (Tanquam si quis crucifigeret Paulum ut redimeret Petrum.)

HERBERT OF BOSHAM, *Life of St. Thomas of Canterbury*, p. 287. (c. 1175)

16
Give not Saint Peter so much, to leave Saint Paul nothing.

GEORGE HERBERT, *Jacula Prudentum*.

17
Who praiseth St. Peter does not blame St. Paul.

GEORGE HERBERT, *Jacula Prudentum*.

Praise Peter, but don't find fault with Paul.

W. G. BENHAM, *Proverbs*, p. 827.

18
Peter in, and Paul out.

JOHN RAY, *Proverbs: Scottish*.

19
How should God approve that you rob Peter, and give this robbery to Paul, in the name of Christ?

JOHN WYCLIFFE, *Works*. Vol. iii, p. 174. (1383)

20
To rob Peter, and give it Paul, it were not alms but great sin.

UNKNOWN, *Jacob's Well*, 138. (c. 1440)

The lands of Westminster so dilapidated by Bishop Thirlby . . . the rest laid out for reparation to the church of St. Paul; pared almost to the quick in these days of rapine. From hence first came that significant byword (as is said by some) of robbing Peter to pay Paul.

PETER HEYLYN, *History of the Reformation*,

121. (1661) There is, of course, no basis for this theory.

By robbing Peter he paid Paul, he kept the moon from the wolves, and was ready to catch larks if ever the heavens should fall.
RABELAIS, *Works*. Bk. i, ch. 11.

1
Full twenty times was Peter feared,
For once that Peter was respected.
WORDSWORTH, *Peter Bell*. Pt. i, st. 3.

2
Peter deny'd His Lord and cry'd.
UNKNOWN, *The New England Primer*. (1777)

PHILANTHROPY

See also Brotherhood, Charity, Gifts, Help

I—Philanthropy: Apothegms

3
Gifts and alms are the expressions, not the essence, of this virtue.
ADDISON, *The Guardian*. No. 166.

4
All human Weal and Woe learn thou to make thine own.
JAMES BEATTIE, *The Minstrel*. Bk. i, st. 29.

And, from the prayer of Want, and plaint of Woe,
O never, never turn away thine ear!
Forlorn, in this bleak wilderness below,
Ah! what were man, should Heaven refuse to hear!
JAMES BEATTIE, *The Minstrel*. Bk. i, st. 29.

5
Mankind will not be reasoned out of the feelings of humanity.
BLACKSTONE, *Commentaries*. Bk. i, sec. 5.

6
Man's work is to labour and leaven—
As best he may—earth here with heaven.
ROBERT BROWNING, *Of Pacchiarotto*.

7
He scorn'd his own, who felt another's woe.
CAMPBELL, *Gertrude of Wyoming*. Pt. i, st. 24.

More skill'd to raise the wretched than to rise.
GOLDSMITH, *The Deserted Village*, l. 148.

We rise by raising others—and he who stoops above the fallen, stands erect.
R. G. INGERSOLL, *Tribute to Roscoe Conkling*.

8
Wipe the nose of your neighbor's son, and take him into your house.
CERVANTES, *Don Quixote*. Pt. ii, ch. 5.

9
Shall he who soars, inspired by loftier views,
Life's little cares and little pains refuse?
Shall he not rather feel a double share
Of mortal woe, when doubly arm'd to bear?
GEORGE CRABBE, *The Library*, l. 648.

10
It is easy to live for others; everybody does.
EMERSON, *Journals*. Vol. vii, p. 46.

11
We owe to man higher succors than food and fire. We owe to man man.
EMERSON, *Society and Solitude: Domestic Life*.

12
My Lady Bountiful.
FARQUHAR, *The Beaux' Stratagem*. Act i, sc. 1.

13
Respect us, human, and relieve us, poor.
HOMER, *Odyssey*. Bk. ix, l. 318. (Pope, tr.)

It never was our guise
To slight the poor, or aught humane despise.
HOMER, *Odyssey*. Bk. xiv, l. 65. (Pope, tr.)

14
I was a father to the poor.
Old Testament: Job, xxix, 16.

Blessed is he that considereth the poor.
Old Testament: Psalms, xli, 1.

I am the friend of the unfriended poor.
SHELLEY, *To Cambria*.

The poor must be wisely visited and liberally cared for, so that mendicity shall not be tempted into mendacity, nor want exasperated into crime.
ROBERT C. WINTHROP, *Yorktown Oration*, 1881.

15
I was a stranger, and ye took me in.
New Testament: Matthew, xxv, 35.

16
Benevolence is the distinguishing characteristic of man. As embodied in man's conduct, it is called the path of duty.
MENCIUS, *Works*. Bk. vii, pt. ii, ch. 16.

17
What is done for another is done for oneself. (Quod jessu alterius solvitur pro eo est quasi ipsi solutum esset.)
PAULUS, *Digest*. Bk. i, l. 17. Afterwards rendered by Boniface VIII: "Qui facit per alium facit per se." (*Maxim. Sexti. Corp. Jur.*, v, 12.)

18
For this relief, much thanks: 'tis bitter cold,
And I am sick at heart.
SHAKESPEARE, *Hamlet*. Act i, sc. i, l. 8.

19
To a man of honour (said I) the unfortunate need no introduction.
SMOLLETT, *Adventures of Ferdinand Count Fathom*. Ch. 62.

20
Feel for others—in your pocket.
C. H. SPURGEON, *Salt-Cellars*.

21
I am a man, and nothing in man's lot can be indifferent to me. (Homo sum; humani nil a me alienum puto.)
TERENCE, *Heauton Timoroumenos*, l. 77. St. Augustine states that this line was received with great applause by the audience.

I am a man as well as a Roman, and nothing human is foreign to me.
EMERSON, *Uncollected Lectures: Table-Talk*. An adaptation of Terence.

Nothing human foreign was to him.
JAMES THOMSON, *To the Memory of Lord Talbot*, l. 282.

22
Only those live who do good.
TOLSTOY, *My Confession*. Ch. 3.

1
To think without confusion, clearly,
To love his fellow-men sincerely.
HENRY VAN DYKE, *Four Things.*

2
Never to blend our pleasure or our pride
With sorrow of the meanest thing that feels.
WORDSWORTH, *Hart-leap Well.* Pt. ii, l. 179.

II—Philanthropy: Do It Now

3
Often have I heard it said, What good thing you do, do not defer it. (Semper audivi dici, Quod bene potes facere noli differe.)
ALBERTANO OF BRESCIA, *Liber Consolationis et Consilii.* (1246)

4
"There is an old proverb," quoth she [Dame Prudence], "sayeth: that 'the goodness that thou mayst do this day, do it, and abide not nor delay it not till tomorrow.'"
CHAUCER, *The Tale of Melibeus.* Sec. 71. (c. 1373)

5
However, while I crawl upon this planet I think myself obliged to do what good I can in my narrow domestic sphere, to all my fellow-creatures, and to wish them all the good I cannot do.
LORD CHESTERFIELD, *Letter to the Bishop of Waterford,* 22 Jan., 1780.

6
I expect to pass through this world but once. Any good therefore that I can do, or any kindness that I can show to any fellow creature, let me do it now. Let me not defer or neglect it, for I shall not pass this way again.
Attributed to STEPHEN GRELLET, an American Quaker of French birth (1773-1855), but not found in his writings. This quotation shares with the "mouse-trap" quotation the honor of being the best known and the most mysterious as to authorship. It has been credited to Emerson; to Edward Courtenay, Earl of Devon, owing to a slight resemblance to his epitaph (see under Gifts: Giving and Receiving); to John Wesley, William Penn, Thomas Carlyle, and many others. It is probable that Grellet was the author. The sentiment is, of course, a very old one.

The old Quaker was right: I expect to pass through life but once. If there is any kindness, or any good thing I can do to my fellow beings, let me do it now. I shall pass this way but once.
WILLIAM C. GANNETT, *Blessed be Drudgery.*

7
Having lately had a loud call from God to arise and go hence, I am convinced that if I attempt anything of this kind at all I must not delay any longer.
JOHN WESLEY, *Explanatory Notes upon the New Testament: Preface.* (1754)

III—Philanthropy: Its Virtues

8
Now there was at Joppa a certain disciple named Tabitha, which by interpretation is called Dorcas: this woman was full of good works and almsdeeds which she did.
New Testament: Acts, ix, 36.

9
A little common sense, goodwill, and a tiny dose of unselfishness could make this goodly earth into an earthly paradise.
RICHARD ALDINGTON, *Colonel's Daughter,* 51.

10
We praise those who love their fellow-men. ("Οθεν τοὺς φιλανθρώπους ἐπαινοῦμεν.)
ARISTOTLE, *Nicomachean Ethics.* Bk. viii, ch. 1, sec. 3.

11
There are, while human miseries abound,
A thousand ways to waste superfluous wealth,
Without one fool or flatterer at your board,
Without one hour of sickness or disgust.
ARMSTRONG, *Art of Preserving Health.* Bk. ii, l. 195.

12
What does Man see or feel or apprehend
Here, there, and everywhere, but faults to mend,
Omissions to supply,—one wide disease
Of things that are, which Man at once would ease,
Had will but power and knowledge?
ROBERT BROWNING, *Francis Furini.* Sec. 9.

13
He who bestows his goods upon the poor,
Shall have as much again, and ten times more.
JOHN BUNYAN, *The Pilgrim's Progress.* Pt. ii.

14
To rest the weary and to soothe the sad,
Doth lesson happier men, and shames at least the bad.
BYRON, *Childe Harold.* Canto ii, st. 68.

The drying up a single tear has more
Of honest fame, than shedding seas of gore.
BYRON, *Don Juan.* Canto viii, st. 3.

15
In nothing do men more nearly approach the gods than in doing good to their fellow-men. (Homines ad deos nulla re propius accedunt quam salutem hominibus dando.)
CICERO, *Pro Ligario.* Ch. 12, sec. 38.

16
Youth, beauty, graceful action seldom fail:
But common interest always will prevail;
And pity never ceases to be shown
To him who makes the people's wrongs his own.
DRYDEN, *Absalom and Achitophel.* Pt. i, l. 723.

17
There is no beautifier of complexion, or form, or behavior, like the wish to scatter joy and not pain around us.
EMERSON, *Conduct of Life: Behavior.*

18
Who kindly sets a wanderer on his way
Does e'en as if he lit another's lamp by his:

No less shines his, when he his friend's hath lit.
(Homo, qui erranti comiter monstrat viam,
Quasi lumen de suo lumine accendat, facit.
Nihilo minus ipsi lucet, cum illi accenderit.)
ENNIUS. (CICERO, *De Officiis*. Bk. i, ch. 16, sec. 51.)

1
W'en you see a man in woe,
Walk right up and say "hullo."
Say "hullo" and "how d'ye do,"
"How's the world a-usin' you?" . . .

W'en you travel through the strange
Country t'other side the range,
Then the souls you've cheered will know
Who you be, an' say "hullo."
SAM WALTER FOSS, *Hullo*.

2
The most acceptable service of God is doing good to man.
BENJAMIN FRANKLIN, *Autobiography*. Ch. 1.

He's true to God who's true to man; wherever wrong is done,
To the humblest and the weakest, 'neath the all-beholding sun.
J. R. LOWELL, *On the Capture of Fugitive Slaves near Washington*. St. 7.

3
Let us not be weary in well-doing: for in due season we shall reap, if we faint not.
New Testament: Galatians, vi, 9.

Be not weary in well-doing.
New Testament: II Thessalonians, iii, 13.

4
The hands that help are holier than the lips that pray.
R. G. INGERSOLL, *The Children of the Stage*.

5
Walk life's dark ways, ye seem to say,
With love's divine foreknowing
That where man sees but withered leaves,
God sees sweet flowers growing.
ALBERT LAIGHTON, *Under the Leaves*.

6
'Tis a kingly action, believe me, to assist the fallen. (Regia, crede mihi, res est succurrere lapsis.)
OVID, *Epistulæ ex Ponto*. Bk. ii, epis. 9, l. 11.

To pity distress is but human; to relieve it is Godlike.
HORACE MANN, *Lectures on Education*. Lect. 6.

'Tis not enough to help the feeble up,
But to support him after.
SHAKESPEARE, *Timon of Athens*. Act i, sc. 1, l. 107.

7
It is a pleasure appropriate to man, for him to save a fellow-man, and gratitude is acquired in no better way. (Conveniens homini est hominem servare voluptas, Et melius nulla quæritur arte favor.)
OVID, *Epistulæ ex Ponto*. Bk. ii, epis. ix, l. 39.

8
He that loves but half of Earth
Loves but half enough for me.
ARTHUR QUILLER-COUCH, *The Comrade*.

9
Neither can any man live happily who has regard to himself alone, and converteth all things to his own profit; thou must live for thy neighbor if thou wouldst live for thyself.
SENECA, *Epistulæ ad Lucilium*. Epis. 48, sec. 3.

IV—Philanthropy: Its Faults

10
The most melancholy of human reflections, perhaps, is that, on the whole, it is a question whether the benevolence of mankind does most harm or good.
WALTER BAGEHOT, *Physics and Politics*, p. 188.

No people do so much harm as those who go about doing good.
MANDELL CREIGHTON. (CREIGHTON, *Life*.)

11
I tell thee, thou foolish philanthropist, that I grudge the dollar, the dime, the cent I give to such men as do not belong to me and to whom I do not belong.
EMERSON, *Essays, First Series: Self-Reliance*.

12
Take egotism out, and you would castrate the benefactors.
EMERSON, *Journals*. Vol. ix, p. 519.

13
Benevolent people are very apt to be one-sided and fussy, and not of the sweetest temper if others will not be good and happy in their way.
SIR ARTHUR HELPS, *Friends in Council*. Bk. i, ch. 6.

14
To be the friend of the human race is not at all in my line. (L'ami du genre humain n'est point du tout mon fait.)
MOLIÈRE, *Le Misanthrope*. Act i, sc. 1, l. 64.

15
You find people ready enough to do the Samaritan, without the oil and twopence.
SYDNEY SMITH. (LADY HOLLAND, *Memoir of Smith*, i, 261.) The reference is to *Luke*, x, 34, 35.

16
Nine parts of self-interest gilt over with one part of philanthropy.
HERBERT SPENCER, *Social Statics*. Pt. iii, ch. 28, sec. 3. *See also under* CHARITY.

17
As for doing good, that is one of the professions that are full.
HENRY DAVID THOREAU, *Walden: Economy*.

18
Philanthropy seems to me to have become simply the refuge of people who wish to annoy their fellow-creatures.
OSCAR WILDE, *An Ideal Husband*. Act i.

V—Philanthropists

19
He has put to hazard his ease, his security,

his interest, his power, even his darling popularity, for the benefit of a people whom he has never seen.
EDMUND BURKE, *Speech,* on Mr. Fox's East-India Bill. House of Commons, 1 Dec., 1783.

1
The friend of man, to vice alone a foe.
BURNS, *Epitaph on His Father.*

Friend to the friendless, to the sick man health,
With generous joy he viewed his modest wealth.
S. T. COLERIDGE, *Lines Written at the King's Arms, Ross.*

He treads unemulous of fame or wealth,
Profuse of toil, and prodigal of health.
ERASMUS DARWIN, *Philanthropy of Mr. Howard.*

2
I love my country better than my family, but I love human nature better than my country.
FÉNELON, *Télémaque.*

3
Their chat on various subjects ran,
But most what each had done for man.
JOHN GAY, *Fables.* Pt. ii, fab. 13.

4
A kind and gentle heart he had,
To comfort friends and foes;
The naked every day he clad,
When he put on his clothes.
GOLDSMITH, *Elegy on the Death of a Mad Dog.*

5
Large was his bounty, and his soul sincere,
Heav'n did a recompense as largely send:
He gave to Mis'ry all he had, a tear,
He gain'd from Heav'n ('twas all he wish'd) a friend.

No farther seek his merits to disclose,
Or draw his frailties from their dread abode,
(There they alike in trembling hope repose,)
The bosom of his Father and his God.
THOMAS GRAY, *Elegy Written in a Country Church-yard: The Epitaph.*

Scatter plenty o'er a smiling land.
GRAY, *Elegy Written in a Country Churchyard,* l. 63.

6
You hear that boy laughing?—You think he's all fun;
But the angels laugh, too, at the good he has done;
The children laugh loud as they troop at his call,
And the poor man that knows him laughs loudest of all!
O. W. HOLMES, *The Boys.*

7
He held his seat; a friend to human race.
HOMER, *Iliad.* Bk. vi, l. 18. (Pope, tr.)

8
A man rich in substance, and beloved of all men; for he dwelt in a house by the high-road and was wont to give entertainment to all. ('Αφνειὸς βιότοιο, φίλος δ' ἦν ἀνθρώποισι· πάντας γὰρ φιλέεσκεν ὁδῷ ἔπι οἰκία ναίων.)
HOMER, *Iliad.* Bk. vi, l. 14.

Depart from the highway and transplant thyself in some enclosed ground, for it is hard for a tree which stands by the wayside to keep her fruit till it be prime.
ST. JOHN CHRYSOSTOM.

There are hermit souls that live withdrawn
In the peace of their self-content;
There are souls like stars that dwell apart,
In a fellowless firmament;
There are pioneer souls that blaze their paths
Where highways never ran,—
But let me live by the side of the road,
And be a friend to man.
SAM WALTER FOSS, *The House by the Side of the Road.*

Ah me, why did they build my house by the road to the market town?
RABINDRANATH TAGORE, *The Gardener.* No. 4.

9
In ev'ry sorrowing soul I pour'd delight,
And Poverty stood smiling in my sight.
HOMER, *Odyssey.* Bk. xvii, l. 505. (Pope, tr.)

10
Abou Ben Adhem (may his tribe increase!)
Awoke one night from a deep dream of peace,
And saw, within the moonlight in his room,
Making it rich, and like a lily in bloom,
An angel writing in a book of gold:—
Exceeding peace had made Ben Adhem bold,
And to the presence in the room he said,
"What writest thou?"—The Vision rais'd its head,
And, with a look made all of sweet accord,
Answer'd, "The names of those who love the Lord."
"And is mine one?" said Abou. "Nay, not so,"
Replied the angel. Abou spoke more low,
But cheerly still; and said, "I pray thee, then,
Write me as one that loves his fellow men."

The angel wrote, and vanish'd. The next night
It came again with a great wakening light,
And show'd the names whom love of God had blest,
And lo! Ben Adhem's name led all the rest.
LEIGH HUNT, *Abou Ben Adhem.*

11
He is one of those wise philanthropists who in a time of famine would vote for nothing but a supply of toothpicks.
DOUGLAS JERROLD, *Douglas Jerrold's Wit.*

The milk of human kindness ran
In rich abundance in his breast,
It left thin grease stains on the tan
Of his asbestos vest.
PAUL TANAQUIL, *Philanthropist.*

1
I was eyes to the blind, and feet was I to the lame.
Old Testament: Job, xxix, 15.

2
Officious, innocent, sincere,
Of every friendless name the friend.
SAMUEL JOHNSON, *On the Death of Dr. Robert Levet.*

In Misery's darkest cavern known,
His useful care was ever nigh,
Where hopeless Anguish pour'd his groan,
And lonely Want retir'd to die.
SAMUEL JOHNSON, *On the Death of Dr. Robert Levet.*

3
He believed that he was born, not for himself, but for the whole world. (Nec sibi sed toti genitum se credere mundo.)
LUCAN, *De Bello Civili.* Bk. ii, l. 383.

4
And chiefly for the weaker by the wall,
You bore that lamp of sane benevolence.
GEORGE MEREDITH, *To a Friend Lost.*

5
For his bounty
There was no winter in 't; an autumn 'twas
That grew the more by reaping.
SHAKESPEARE, *Antony and Cleopatra*, v, 2, 87.

6
He saw the goodness, not the taint,
In many a poor, do-nothing creature,
And gave to sinner and to saint,
But kept his faith in human nature.
E. C. STEDMAN, *Horace Greeley.*

7
Myself not ignorant of adversity, I have learned to befriend the unhappy. (Non ignara mali miseris succurrere disco.)
VERGIL, *Æneid.* Bk. i, l. 630.

8
His love was like the liberal air,—
Embracing all, to cheer and bless;
And every grief that mortals share
Found pity in his tenderness.
WILLIAM WINTER, *I. H. Bromley.*

9
For thou wert still the poor man's stay,
The poor man's heart, the poor man's hand;
And all the oppressed, who wanted strength,
Had thine at their command.
WORDSWORTH, *Rob Roy's Grave*, l. 109.

PHILISTIA

10
The people who believe most that our greatness and welfare are proved by our being very rich, and who most give their lives and thoughts to becoming rich, are just the very people whom we call the Philistines.
MATTHEW ARNOLD, *Culture and Anarchy.* (1869)

11
Taking that terrible modern weapon, the pen, in his hand, he passed the remainder of his life [from 1830] in one fierce battle. What was that battle? the reader will ask. It was a life and death battle with Philistinism.
MATTHEW ARNOLD, *Essays in Criticism: Heine.* (1865)

It was in this essay that Arnold introduced into England from Germany the term "philistine." This word was his chief contribution to the process of disintegrating Victorianism.
HUGH KINGSMILL, *Matthew Arnold*, p. 256.

12
Philistine must have originally meant, in the mind of those who invented the nickname, a strong, dogged, unenlightened opponent of the children of the light.
MATTHEW ARNOLD, *Essays in Criticism: Heine.*

Arnold defines a Philistine as a "strong, dogged, unenlightened opponent of the chosen people," a definition which, when one reflects what the chosen people were like, raises a doubt about the justice of using Philistine as a synonym for an enemy of art and culture.
HUGH KINGSMILL, *Matthew Arnold*, p. 257.

Philistine, as a term applied to the ill-behaved and ignorant, or to persons of low and materialistic ideas, is said to have originated from a sermon preached from this text at Jena in 1693 at the funeral of a student killed in a "town and gown" quarrel. Ever afterwards the students at German universities called the townsmen "Philisters." Matthew Arnold probably heard it there.

Philistine—a term of contempt applied by prigs to the rest of their species.
LESLIE STEPHEN.

13
Of all the places on the map,
Some queer and others queerer,
Arcadia is dear to me,
Philistia is dearer.

They never puzzle me with Greek,
Nor drive me mad with Ibsen;
Yet over forms as fair as Eve's
They wear the gowns of Gibson.
BLISS CARMAN, *In Philistia.*

14
The Philistines be upon thee, Samson.
Old Testament: Judges, xvi, 9.

The Philistines have invaded the land.
Old Testament: I Samuel, xxiii, 27.

15
Philistia, triumph thou because of me.
Old Testament: Psalms, lx, 8. A plain in southeastern Palestine, the land of commonplace.

16
Tell it not in Gath, publish it not in the streets of Askalon, lest the daughters of the Philistines rejoice.
Old Testament: II Samuel, i, 20.

Bid Fame be dumb, and tremble to proclaim
In heathen Gath, or Ascalon, our shame,
Lest proud Philistia, lest our haughty foe,
With impious scorn insult our solemn woe.
W. C. SOMERVILLE, *The Lamentation of David.*

PHILOSOPHY

I—Philosophy: Definitions

1
Unintelligible answers to insoluble problems.
HENRY ADAMS, defining philosophy. (Quoted by BERT LESTON TAYLOR, *The So-Called Human Race*, p. 154.)

2
All good and moral philosophy, as was said, is but a handmaid to religion.
BACON, *Advancement of Learning*. Bk. ii.

A little philosophy inclineth man's mind to atheism; but depth in philosophy bringeth men's minds about to religion.
BACON, *Essays: Atheism.*

A little skill in antiquity inclines a man to Popery; but depth in that study brings him about again to our religion.
THOMAS FULLER, *The Holy State: The True Church Antiquary.*

3
Metaphysics is the finding of bad reasons for what we believe on instinct.
F. H. BRADLEY, *Appearance and Reality*. Ch. 14.

Metaphysics I detested. The science appeared to me an elaborate, diabolical invention for mystifying what was clear, and confounding what was intelligible.
W. E. AYTOUN, *Norman Sinclair.*

4
Philosophy is common-sense in a dress suit.
OLIVER S. BRASTON, *Philosophy.*

5
Before Philosophy can teach by Experience, the Philosophy has to be in readiness, the Experience must be gathered and intelligibly recorded.
CARLYLE, *Essays: On History.*

6
Philosophy, the mother of all the arts. (Philosophia vero, omnium mater artium.)
CICERO, *Tusculanarum Disputationum*. Bk. i, ch. 26, sec. 64.

That great mother of the sciences.
FRANCIS BACON, *De Augmentis Scientiarum*. Pt. ii, bk. 1, aphor. 80. Referring to natural philosophy.

7
The true medicine of the mind is philosophy. (Est profecto animi medicina, philosophia.)
CICERO, *Tusculanarum Disputationum*. Bk. iii, ch. 3, sec. 6.

I look to philosophy to provide an antidote to sorrow.
CICERO, *Academicarum Quæstionum*. Bk. i, ch. 3, sec. 11.

Adversity's sweet milk, philosophy.
SHAKESPEARE, *Romeo and Juliet*, iii, 3, 55.

8
The science of sciences. (Scientia scientiarum.)
S. T. COLERIDGE, *Biographia Literaria*. Ch. 12. Referring to philosophy.

9
Philosophy—the thoughts of men about human thinking, reasoning and imagining, and the real values in human existence.
CHARLES W. ELIOT, *Inscription*, Public Library, Warren, Pa.

10
Philosophy is the account which the mind gives to itself of the constitution of the world.
EMERSON, *Representative Men: Plato.*

11
The beginning of philosophy . . . is a consciousness of a man's own weakness and impotence with reference to the things of real importance in life.
EPICTETUS, *Discourses*. Bk. ii, ch. 11, sec. 1.

Behold the beginning of philosophy!—a recognition of the conflict between the opinions of men.
EPICTETUS, *Discourses*. Bk. ii, ch. 11, sec. 13.

12
What is the first business of one who practises philosophy? To part with self-conceit. For it is impossible for any one to begin to learn what he thinks he already knows.
EPICTETUS, *Discourses*. Bk. ii, ch. 17, sec. 1.

What is philosophy? Does it not mean preparation to face the things which may come upon us?
EPICTETUS, *Discourses*. Bk. iii, ch. 10, sec. 5.

13
Philosophy goes no further than probabilities, and every assertion keeps a doubt in reserve.
J. A. FROUDE, *Short Studies on Great Subjects: Calvinism.*

14
A modest confession of ignorance is the ripest and last attainment of philosophy.
R. D. HITCHCOCK, *Eternal Atonement: Secret Things of God.*

15
Philosophy is doubt. (Philosopher c'est doubter.)
MONTAIGNE, *Essays*. Bk. ii, ch. 3.

The first step towards philosophy is incredulity.
DENIS DIDEROT, *Remark*, during his last conversation.

16
Philosophy is the highest music. (Φιλοσοφίας μὲν οὔσης μεγίστης μουσικῆς.)
PLATO, *Phædo*. Sec. 61.

17
Philosophy is nothing but Discretion.
JOHN SELDEN, *Table-Talk: Philosophy.*

18
Philosophy calls for plain living, but not for penance. (Frugalitatem exigit philosophia, non pœnam.)
SENECA, *Epistulæ ad Lucilium*. Epis. v, sec. 5.

Philosophy does the going, and wisdom is the goal. (Illa venit, ad hanc venitur.)
SENECA, *Epistulæ ad Lucilium*. Epis. 89, sec. 7.

19
The philosopher is Nature's pilot. And there

you have our difference: to be in hell is to drift: to be in heaven is to steer.

BERNARD SHAW, *Man and Superman*. Act iii.

1

To be a philosopher is not merely to have subtle thoughts, nor even to found a school, but so to love wisdom as to live according to its dictates, a life of simplicity, independence, magnanimity, and trust.

H. D. THOREAU, *Walden*. Ch. 1.

How can a man be a philosopher and not maintain his vital heat by better methods than other men?

H. D. THOREAU, *Walden*. Ch. 1.

II—Philosophy: Apothegms

2

Those that study particular sciences and neglect philosophy are like Penelope's wooers, who made love to the waiting-women.

ARISTIPPUS. (BACON, *Apothegms*. No. 189.)

3

A deep occult philosopher.

BUTLER, *Hudibras*. Pt. i, canto i, l. 537.

4

I *won't* philosophise, and *will* be read.

BYRON, *Don Juan*. Canto x, st. 28.

5

But all be that he was a philosopher,
Yet had he but little gold in coffer.

CHAUCER, *Canterbury Tales: Prologue*, l. 297.

6

The Arabians say that Abul Khain, the mystic, and Abu Ali Seena, the philosopher, conferred together; and, on parting, the philosopher said, "All that he sees I know"; and the mystic said, "All that he knows I see."

EMERSON, *Representative Men: Swedenborg*.

7

To a philosopher no circumstance, however trifling, is too minute.

GOLDSMITH, *The Citizen of the World*. No. 30.

8

A countryman, one of nature's philosophers, with rough mother-wit. (Rusticus, abnormis sapiens, crassaque Minerva.)

HORACE, *Satires*. Bk. ii, sat. 2, l. 3.

Hast any philosophy in thee, shepherd?

SHAKESPEARE, *As You Like It*. Act iii, sc. 2, l. 22.

9

Be a philosopher; but, amidst all your philosophy, be still a man.

DAVID HUME, *Essays*. No. 39.

10

The philosophic climate of our time inevitably forces its own clothing on us.

WILLIAM JAMES, *Varieties of Religious Experience*, p. 432.

11

All men are Philosophers, to their inches.

BEN JONSON, *The Magnetic Lady*. Act i, sc. 1.

It is neither possible nor necessary for all men, nor for many, to be philosophers.

S. T. COLERIDGE, *Biographia Literaria*. Ch. 12.

12

There are philosophies which are unendurable not because men are cowards, but because they are men.

LUDWIG LEWISOHN, *Modern Drama*, p. 222.

13

[They] fetch their precepts from the Cynic tub.

MILTON, *Comus*, l. 708. The tub from which Diogenes lectured.

14

That stone, . . .
Philosophers in vain so long have sought.

MILTON, *Paradise Lost*. Bk. iii, l. 600.

15

Philosophy drips gently from his tongue
Who hath three meals a day in guarantee.

CHRISTOPHER MORLEY, *So This Is Arden*.

16

The whole life of the philosopher is a preparation for death. (Τὸ μελέτημα αὐτὸ ἐστι τῶν φιλοσόφων, λύσις καὶ χωρισμὸς ψυχῆς ἀπὸ σώματος.)

PLATO, *Phædo*. Sec. 67D. Cicero, (*Tusculanarum Disputationum*. Bk. i, ch. 30, sec. 74) gives it: Tota philosophorum vita commentatio mortis est.

17

I am safe, he is now philosophizing. (Salvus sum, jam philosophatur.)

PLAUTUS, *Pseudolus*, l. 974. (Act iv, sc. 2.)

18

There are more things in heaven and earth, Horatio,
Than are dreamt of in your philosophy.

SHAKESPEARE, *Hamlet*. Act i, sc. 5, l. 166.

Of your philosophy you make no use,
If you give place to accidental evils.

SHAKESPEARE, *Julius Cæsar*. Act iv, sc. 3, l. 145.

19

Clearness marks the sincerity of philosophers. (La clarté est la bonne foi des philosophes.)

VAUVENARGUES, *Pensées Diverses*. No. 365.

20

Books bear him up awhile, and make him try
To swim with bladders of philosophy.

JOHN WILMOT, EARL OF ROCHESTER, *A Satire Against Mankind*, l. 20.

21

In years that bring the philosophic mind.

WORDSWORTH, *Ode on the Intimations of Immortality*. St. 10.

The bosom-weight, your stubborn gift,
That no philosophy can lift.

WORDSWORTH, *Presentiments*, l. 25.

III—Philosophy: Its Virtues

22

The calm lights of mild philosophy.

ADDISON, *Cato*. Act i, sc. 1, l. 14.

23

What I have gained from philosophy is the ability to feel at ease in any society.

ARISTIPPUS. (DIOGENES LAERTIUS, *Aristippus* Bk. ii, sec. 68.)

I have gained this by philosophy: that I do without being ordered what others do only from fear of the law.

ARISTOTLE. (DIOGENES LAERTIUS, *Aristotle.* Bk. v, sec. 20.)

I have gained at least this from philosophy: to be prepared for every fortune.

DIOGENES. (DIOGENES LAERTIUS, *Diogenes.* Sec. 63.)

1
Natural philosophy, next to the word of God, is the surest medicine for superstition.

FRANCIS BACON, *De Augmentis Scientiarum.* Pt. ii, bk. 1, aphor. 89.

2
To take things as they be—
That's my philosophy.
No use to holler, mope, or cuss—
If they was changed they might be wuss.

JOHN KENDRICK BANGS, *A Philosopher.*

To take what passes in good part
And keep the hiccups from the heart.

JOHN BYROM, *Careless Content.*

3
Sublime Philosophy!
Thou art the Patriarch's ladder, reaching heaven,
And bright with beck'ning angels.

BULWER-LYTTON, *Richelieu.* Act iii, sc. 1, l. 4.

4
Philosophy can never be praised as much as she deserves, since she enables every man who obeys her precepts to pass every season of his life free from worry. (Numquam igitur laudari satis digne philosophia poterit, cui qui pareat omne tempus ætatis sine molestia possit degere.)

CICERO, *De Senectute.* Ch. i, sec. 2.

Divine philosophy! by whose pure light
We first distinguish, then pursue the right.

JUVENAL, *Satires.* Sat. xiii, l. 254. (Gifford, tr.)

O philosophy, life's guide! O searcher-out of virtue and expeller of vice! What would we and every age of men have been without thee?

CICERO, *Tusculanarum Disputationum.* Bk. v, ch. 2, sec. 5.

5
Philosophy! the great and only heir
Of all the human knowledge which has been
Unforfeited by man's rebellious sin.

ABRAHAM COWLEY, *To the Royal Society.*

6
If you would enjoy real freedom, you must be the slave of philosophy. (Philosophiæ servias oportet, ut tibi contingat vera libertas.)

EPICURUS, *Fragments.* No. 199. (SENECA, *Epistulæ ad Lucilium.* Epis. viii, sec. 7.)

7
But above all 'tis pleasantest to get
The top of high philosophy, and sit
On the calm, peaceful, flourishing head of it.

LUCRETIUS, *De Rerum Natura.* Bk. ii, l. 6. (Creech, tr.)

8
How charming is divine Philosophy!
Not harsh, and crabbed as dull fools suppose,
But musical as is Apollo's lute,
And a perpetual feast of nectar'd sweets,
Where no crude surfeit reigns.

MILTON, *Comus,* l. 476.

9
The first thing which philosophy attempts to give is fellow-feeling with all men. (Hoc primum philosophia promittit, sensum communem.)

SENECA, *Epistulæ ad Lucilium.* Epis. v, sec. 4.

If there is any good in philosophy, it is this—that it never looks into pedigrees. (Si quid est aliud in philosophia boni, hoc est, quod stemma non inspicit.

SENECA, *Epistulæ ad Lucilium.* Epis. xliv, sec. 1.

10
Without philosophy the mind is sickly, and the body, too, though it may be very powerful, is strong only as that of a madman is strong.

SENECA, *Epistulæ ad Lucilium.* Epis. xv, sec. 2.

Life is the gift of the immortal gods, but living well is the gift of philosophy. (Deorum immortalium munus sit quod vivimus, philosophiæ quod bene vivimus.)

SENECA, *Epistulæ ad Lucilium.* Epis. xc, sec. 1.

11
To suck the sweets of sweet philosophy.

SHAKESPEARE, *The Taming of the Shrew.* Act i, sc. 1, l. 28.

IV—Philosophy: Its Faults

12
As for the philosophers, they make imaginary laws for imaginary commonwealths; and their discourses are as the stars, which give little light, because they are so high.

FRANCIS BACON, *Advancement of Learning: Civil Knowledge.*

13
Beside, he was a shrewd philosopher,
And had read ev'ry text and gloss over;
Whate'er the crabbed'st author hath,
He understood b' implicit faith.

BUTLER, *Hudibras.* Pt. i, canto i, l. 127.

There was an ancient sage philosopher,
That had read Alexander Ross over,
And swore the world, as he could prove,
Was made of fighting and of love.

BUTLER, *Hudibras.* Pt. i, canto ii, l. 1.

14
No statement is too absurd for some philosophers to make. (Nihil tam absurde dici potest quod non dicatur ab aliquo philosophorum.)

CICERO, *De Divinatione.* Bk. ii, ch. 58, sec. 119.

15
I hate the philosopher who is not wise for himself. (Μισῶ σοφιστὴν, ὅστις οὐχ αὑτῷ σοφός.)

EURIPIDES, *Fragments.* Frag. 72.

Many talk like philosophers and live like fools.

H. G. BOHN, *Hand-Book of Proverbs.*

See also under WISDOM.

1
Philosophers dwell in the moon.
JOHN FORD, *Lover's Melancholy*. Act iii, sc. 3

A pindaric book-keeper, an arithmetician in the clouds.
EDMUND BURKE, *Impeachment of Warren Hastings*, 5 May, 1789.

2
This same philosophy is a good horse in the stable, but an arrant jade on a journey.
GOLDSMITH, *The Good-Natured Man*. Act i.

3
Do not all charms fly
At the mere touch of cold philosophy?
KEATS, *Lamia*. Pt. ii, l. 229.

Philosophy will clip an Angel's wings,
Conquer all mysteries by rule and line,
Empty the haunted air, the gnomèd mine—
Unweave a rainbow.
KEATS, *Lamia*. Pt. ii, l. 234.

4
Undoubtedly the study of the more abstruse regions of philosophy . . . always seems to have included an element not very much removed from a sort of insanity.
JOHN KEBLE, *Lectures on Poetry*. No. 34.

5
Philosophy triumphs easily over past and future evils, but present evils triumph over it. (La philosophie triomphe aisément des maux passés et des maux à venir, mais les maux présents triomphent d'elle.)
LA ROCHEFOUCAULD, *Maximes*. No. 22.

For there was never yet philosopher
That could endure the toothache patiently.
SHAKESPEARE, *Much Ado About Nothing*. Act v, sc. 1, l. 35.

6
There is no record in human history of a happy philosopher.
H. L. MENCKEN, *Prejudices*.

7
O foolishness of men! that lend their ears
To those budge doctors of the Stoic fur.
MILTON, *Comus*, l. 706.

Vain wisdom all, and false philosophy.
MILTON, *Paradise Lost*. Bk. ii, l. 565.

8
In earthy mire philosophy may slip.
SCOTT, *The Poacher*.

9
Emanating from high-browed philosophers. (Quæ ingenti supercilio philosophi jactant.)
SENECA, *Epistulæ ad Lucilium*. Epis. xciv, 9.

"HIGH-BROW," *see under* EDUCATION.

10
Philosophy! the lumber of the schools,
The roguery of alchemy: and we the bubbled fools
Spend all our present stock in hopes of golden rules.
SWIFT, *Ode to Sir W. Temple*. Pt. ii.

11
Hold thou the good; define it well;
For fear divine Philosophy
Should push beyond her mark, and be
Procuress to the Lords of Hell.
TENNYSON, *In Memoriam*. Pt. liii.

12
Say, Not so, and you will outcircle the philosophers.
H. D. THOREAU, *Journal*, 26 June, 1840.

13
Why should not grave Philosophy be styled,
Herself, a dreamer of a kindred stock,
A dreamer yet more spiritless and dull?
WORDSWORTH, *The Excursion*. Bk. iii, l. 338.

14
To ridicule philosophy is truly philosophical. (Se moquer de la philosophie, c'est vraiment philosopher.)
PASCAL, *Pensées*. Pt. vii, No. 35.

PHYSICIAN, see Doctor

PIETY

15
One's piety is best displayed in his pursuits.
A. B. ALCOTT, *Table Talk: Creeds*.

16
The weaker sex, to piety more prone.
WILLIAM ALEXANDER, EARL OF STIRLING, *Doomsday: The Fifth Hour*. St. 55.

Piety is sweet to infant minds.
WORDSWORTH, *The Excursion*. Bk. iv, l. 799.

17
One day lived after the perfect rule of piety, is to be preferred before sinning immortality.
SIR THOMAS BROWNE, *To a Friend*. Sec. 29.

18
Religious persecution may shield itself under the guise of a mistaken and overzealous piety.
EDMUND BURKE, *Impeachment of Warren Hastings*, 17 Feb., 1788.

19
There's nothing so absurd or vain,
Or barbarous, or inhumane,
But if it lay the least pretence
To piety and godliness,
Or tender-hearted conscience,
And zeal for gospel-truths profess,
Does sacred instantly commence.
SAMUEL BUTLER, *On a Hypocritical Nonconformist*. St. 1.

20
Piety and holiness of life will win the favor of the gods. (Deos placetos pietas efficiet et sanctitas.)
CICERO, *De Officiis*. Bk. ii, ch. 3, sec. 11.

Piety is the foundation of all virtues. (Pietas fundamentum est omnium virtutum.)
CICERO, *Pro Cnæo Plancio*. Sec. 12.

21
No solemn, sanctimonious face I pull,
Nor think I'm pious when I'm only bilious.
THOMAS HOOD, *Ode to Rae Wilson*, l. 43.

"Rogue that I am," he whispers to himself,
"I lie—I cheat—do anything for pelf,
But who on earth can say I am not pious?"
THOMAS HOOD, *Ode to Rae Wilson*, l. 186.

1
No piety delays the wrinkles. (Nec pietas moram Rugis.)
HORACE, *Odes*. Bk. ii, ode 14, l. 1.

2
Piety is the tinfoil of pretense.
ELBERT HUBBARD, *A Thousand and One Epigrams*, p. 91.

2a
True piety is this: to look on all things with a master eye, and mind at peace.
LUCRETIUS, *De Rerum Natura*. Bk. v, l. 1202.

3
There is no piety but amongst the poor.
THOMAS RANDOLPH, *On the Content He Enjoys in the Muses*.

4
Glistening semblances of piety.
SHAKESPEARE, *Henry V*. Act ii, sc. 2, l. 117.

Thou villain, thou art full of piety.
SHAKESPEARE, *Much Ado About Nothing*, iv, 2, 81.

O cruel, irreligious piety!
SHAKESPEARE, *Titus Andronicus*, i, 1, 130.

5
From Piety, whose soul sincere
Fears God and knows no other fear.
WILLIAM SMYTH, *Ode for the Installation of the Duke of Gloucester as Chancellor of Cambridge*.

6
Volumes might be written upon the impiety of the pious.
HERBERT SPENCER, *First Principles*. Ch. 5, sec. 31.

PILGRIM FATHERS

See also Puritans

7
Wild was the day; the wintry sea
Moaned sadly on New England's strand,
When first the thoughtful and the free,
Our fathers, trod the desert land.
BRYANT, *The Twenty-Second of December*.

8
They fell upon an ungenial climate . . . that called out the best energies of the men, and of the women too, to get a mere subsistence out of the soil. In their efforts to do that, they cultivated industry and frugality at the same time—which is the real foundation of the greatness of the Pilgrims.
ULYSSES S GRANT, *Speech*, New England Society Dinner, 22 Dec., 1880.

9
What sought they thus afar?
Bright jewels of the mine?
The wealth of seas, the spoils of war?
—They sought a faith's pure shrine!
FELICIA DOROTHEA HEMANS, *The Landing of the Pilgrim Fathers*.

Ay call it holy ground,
The soil where first they trod!
They have left unstained what there they found—
Freedom to worship God!
FELICIA DOROTHEA HEMANS, *The Landing of the Pilgrim Fathers*.

10
O Exile of the wrath of kings!
O Pilgrim Ark of Liberty!
The refuge of divinest things,
Their record must abide in thee!
JULIA WARD HOWE, *Our Country*.

11
Down to the Plymouth Rock, that had been to their feet as a doorstep
Into a world unknown,—the corner-stone of a nation!
LONGFELLOW, *The Courtship of Miles Standish*. Pt. v, st. 2.

12
Our Pilgrim stock wuz pithed with hardihood.
J. R. LOWELL, *Biglow Papers*. Ser. ii, No. 6.

They talk about their Pilgrim blood,
Their birthright high and holy!
A mountain-stream that ends in mud
Methinks is melancholy.
J. R. LOWELL, *Interview with Miles Standish*.

13
Answer—thou refuge of the freeman's need—
Thou for whose destinies no kings looked out,
Nor sages to resolve some mighty doubt—
Thou simple Mayflower of the salt-sea mead!
RICHARD MONCKTON MILNES, *Columbus and the Mayflower*.

14
Give it only the fulcrum of Plymouth Rock, an idea will upheave the continent.
WENDELL PHILLIPS, *Speech*, New York, 21 Jan., 1863.

Neither do I acknowledge the right of Plymouth to the whole rock. No, the rock underlies all America: it only crops out here.
WENDELL PHILLIPS, *Speech*, dinner of the Pilgrim Society at Plymouth, 21 Dec., 1855.

15
The Pilgrim spirit has not fled:
It walks in noon's broad light;
And it watches the bed of the glorious dead,
With the holy stars by night.
JOHN PIERPONT, *The Pilgrim Fathers*.

16
The Pilgrims rose, at this, God's word,
And sailed the wintry seas:
With their own flesh nor blood conferred,
Nor thought of wealth or ease.

They left the towers of Leyden town,
They left the Zuyder Zee;
And where they cast their anchor down,
Rose Freedom's realm to be.
JEREMIAH EAMES RANKIN, *The Word of God to Leyden Came*.

PINE

17
Desert-loving pine, whose emerald scalp
Nods to the storm.
BYRON, *Prophecy of Dante*. Canto ii, l. 63.

18
Risest from forth thy silent sea of pines.
S. T. COLERIDGE, *Hymn before Sunrise in the Vale of Chamouni*.

1
'Twas on the inner bark, stripped from the
pine,
Our father pencilled this epistle rare.
THOMAS D'URFEY, *What-Cheer*. Canto ii.

2
As sunbeams stream through liberal space
And nothing jostle or displace,
So waved the pine-tree through my thought
And fanned the dreams it never brought.
EMERSON, *Woodnotes*. Pt. ii.

Who liveth by the rugged pine
Foundeth a heroic line;
Who liveth in the palace hall
Waneth fast and spendeth all.
EMERSON, *Woodnotes*. Pt. ii.

3
The pine wishes herself a shrub when the axe is at her root.
THOMAS FULLER, *Gnomologia*. No. 4705.

4
Like two cathedral towers these stately pines
Uplift their fretted summits tipped with
cones;
The arch beneath them is not built with
stones,
Not Art but Nature traced these lovely lines,
And carved this graceful arabesque of vines;
No organ but the wind here sighs and moans,
No sepulchre conceals a martyr's bones,
No marble bishop on his tomb reclines.
Enter! the pavement, carpeted with leaves,
Gives back a softened echo to thy tread!
Listen! the choir is singing; all the birds,
In leafy galleries beneath the eaves,
Are singing! listen, ere the sound be fled,
And learn there may be worship without
words.
LONGFELLOW, *My Cathedral*.

Yes, the pine is the mother of legends; what food
For their grim roots is left when the thousand-
yeared wood,
The dim-aisled cathedral, whose tall arches
spring
Light, sinewy, graceful.
J. R. LOWELL, *The Growth of the Legend*.

Under the yaller pines I house,
When sunshine makes 'em all sweet-scented,
An' hear among their furry boughs
The baskin' west-wind purr contented.
J. R. LOWELL, *Biglow Papers*. Ser. ii, No. 10.

5
The archèd walks of twilight groves,
And shadows brown that Sylvan loves,
Of pine.
MILTON, *Il Penseroso*, l. 133.

6
Thus yields the cedar to the axe's edge,
Whose arms gave shelter to the princely eagle,
Under whose shade the ramping lion slept,
Whose top-branch overpeer'd Jove's spread-
ing tree,
And kept low shrubs from winter's powerful
wind.
SHAKESPEARE, *III Henry VI*. Act v, sc. 2, l. 11.

Ay me! the bark peel'd from the lofty pine,
His leaves will wither and his sap decay.
SHAKESPEARE, *The Rape of Lucrece*, l. 1167.

7
And wind, that grand old harper, smote
His thunder-harp of pines.
ALEXANDER SMITH, *A Life Drama*.

8
Here also grew the rougher rinded pine,
The great Argoan ship's brave ornament,
Whom golden fleece did make an heavenly
sign;
Which coveting, with his high top's extent,
To make the mountains touch the stars divine,
Decks all the forest with embellishment.
EDMUND SPENSER, *Virgils Gnat*, l. 209.

The sailing pine.
SPENSER, *The Faerie Queene*. Bk. i, canto i, st. 8.

9
Ancient Pines,
Ye bear no record of the years of man.
Spring is your sole historian.
BAYARD TAYLOR, *The Pine Forest of Monterey*.

PIONEER

10
Pioneering does not pay.
ANDREW CARNEGIE. (HENDRICK, *Life*.)

11
There are pioneer souls that blaze their paths
Where highways never ran.
SAM WALTER FOSS, *The House by the Side of the Road*.

12
O willing hearts turned quick to clay,
Glad lovers holding death in scorn,
Out of the lives ye cast away
The coming race is born.
LAURENCE HOUSMAN, *The Settlers*.

13
There, till the vision he foresaw,
Splendid and whole arise,
And unimagined Empires draw
To council 'neath his skies,
The immense and brooding Spirit still
Shall quicken and control.
Living he was the land, and dead,
His soul shall be her soul.
RUDYARD KIPLING, *C. J. Rhodes*. Read at his burial, 10 April, 1902.

The gull shall whistle in his wake, the blind wave
break in fire.
He shall fulfil God's utmost will, unknowing His
desire.
And he shall see old planets change and alien
stars arise,
And give the gale his seaworn sail in shadow of
new skies.
Strong lust of gear shall drive him forth and
hunger arm his hand,

To win his food from the desert rude, his pittance from the sand.
RUDYARD KIPLING, *The Voortrekker*.

1
Shall I tell you who he is, this key figure in the arch of our enterprise? That slender, dauntless, plodding, modest figure is the American pioneer. . . . His is this one glory —he found the way.
FRANKLIN K. LANE, *The American Pioneer*.

2
His echoing axe the settler swung
Amid the sea-like solitude,
And, rushing, thundering, down were flung
The Titans of the wood. . . .
Humble the lot, yet his the race,
When Liberty sent forth her cry,
Who thronged in conflict's deadliest place,
To fight—to bleed—to die!
ALFRED B. STREET, *The Settler*.

3
Their fame shrinks not to names and dates
On votive stone, the prey of time;—
Behold where monumental States
Immortalize their lives sublime.
W. H. VENABLE, *The Founders of Ohio*.

4
Conquering, holding, daring, venturing as we go the unknown ways,
Pioneers! O pioneers!
WALT WHITMAN, *Pioneers! O Pioneers*.

O Pioneers!
WILLA CATHER. Title of novel.

5
The paths to the house I seek to make,
But leave to those to come the house itself.
WALT WHITMAN, *Thou Mother with Thy Equal Brood*.

PITY

See also Love and Pity

6
Pity makes the world
Soft to the weak and noble for the strong.
EDWIN ARNOLD, *Light of Asia*. Bk. v, l. 416.

Pity and need Make all flesh kin.
EDWIN ARNOLD, *The Light of Asia*. Bk. vi, l. 73.

7
Pity is the deadliest feeling that can be offered to a woman.
VICKI BAUM, *And Life Goes On*, p. 201.

8
Compassion will cure more sins than condemnation.
BEECHER, *Proverbs from Plymouth Pulpit*.

9
There are some people who are only at their best when they are to be pitied.
ARNOLD BENNETT, *Cupid and Commonsense*. Act iv.

10
Compassion breathes along the savage mind.
BYRON, *Don Juan*. Canto viii, st. 106.

11
A soul that pity touched, but never shook.
CAMPBELL, *Gertrude of Wyoming*. Pt. i, st. 23.

12
O'er friendless grief Compassion shall awake,
And smile on innocence, for Mercy's sake!
CAMPBELL, *Pleasures of Hope*. Pt. ii, l. 455.

13
Humblest of heart, highest of reverence,
Benign flower, crown of virtues all.
CHAUCER, *The Compleynte Unto Pity*, l. 57.

For pity runneth soon in gentle heart.
CHAUCER, *The Knightes Tale*, l. 903. Apparently Chaucer's favorite line, for he repeated it in *The Marchantes Tale*, l. 742; *The Squieres Tale*, l. 471; and *The Legend of Good Women*, l. 503.

14
A heart to pity and a hand to bless.
CHURCHILL, *The Prophecy of Famine*, l. 178.

15
Here pity most doth show herself alive,
When she is dead.
(Qui vive la pietà quando è ben morta.)
DANTE, *Inferno*. Canto xx, l. 28. (Cary, tr.)

16
But they that han't pity, why I pities they.
CHARLES DIBDIN, *True Courage*.

Taught by the power that pities me,
I learn to pity them.
GOLDSMITH, *A Ballad*, l. 23. (*The Vicar of Wakefield*. Ch. 8.)

17
More helpful than all wisdom is one draught of simple human pity that will not forsake us.
GEORGE ELIOT, *Mill on the Floss*. Bk. vii, ch. 1.

18
Careless their merits or their faults to scan,
His pity gave ere charity began.
GOLDSMITH, *The Deserted Village*, l. 161.

19
Ah! were she pitiful as she is fair,
Or but as mild as she is seeming so!
ROBERT GREENE, *The Praise of Fawnia*.

20
He that pities another remembers himself.
GEORGE HERBERT, *Jacula Prudentum*.

21
Shutteth up his bowels of compassion.
New Testament: I John, iii, 17.

The wretched have no compassion.
SAMUEL JOHNSON, *Letters*. Vol. ii, p. 215.

22
It is of the Lord's mercies that we are not consumed, because his compassions fail not.
Old Testament: Lamentations, iii, 22.

23
No anger find in thee, but pity and ruth.
MILTON, *Sonnets: To a Virtuous Lady*.

24
I have no longing for things great and fair,
Beauty and strength and grace of word or deed;
For all sweet things my soul has ceased to care;
Infinite pity—that is all its need.
J. B. B. NICHOLS, *During Music*.

1
I warn you beforehand so to have pity on others that others may not have to take pity on you. (Præmonstro tibi Ut ita te aliorum miserescat, ne tui alios misereat.)
PLAUTUS, *Trinummus*. Act ii, sc. 2, l. 61.

2
She knows as well as anyone
That Pity, having played, soon tires.
E. A. ROBINSON, *The Poor Relation.*

3
'Tis true: 'tis pity; And pity 'tis 'tis true.
SHAKESPEARE, *Hamlet*. Act ii, sc. 2, l. 97.

'Twas strange, 'twas passing strange.
'Twas pitiful, 'twas wondrous pitiful.
SHAKESPEARE, *Othello*. Act i, sc. 3, l. 160.

But yet the pity of it, Iago! O Iago, the pity of it, Iago!
SHAKESPEARE, *Othello*. Act iv, sc. 1, l. 206.

4
My pity hath been balm to heal their wounds
SHAKESPEARE, *III Henry VI*. Act iv, sc. 8, l. 41.

5
And pluck commiseration of his state
From brassy bosoms and rough hearts of
flint.
SHAKESPEARE, *The Merchant of Venice*. Act iv, sc. 1, l. 30.

6
Soft pity enters at an iron gate.
SHAKESPEARE, *The Rape of Lucrece*, l. 595.

No beast so fierce but knows some touch of pity.
SHAKESPEARE, *Richard III*. Act i, sc. 2, l. 71.

My friend, I spy some pity in thy looks.
SHAKESPEARE, *Richard III*. Act i, sc. 4, l. 270.

Tear-falling pity dwells not in this eye.
SHAKESPEARE, *Richard III*. Act iv, sc. 2, l. 66.

7
If I die, no soul shall pity me:
Nay, wherefore should they, since that I
myself
Find in myself no pity to myself.
SHAKESPEARE, *Richard III*. Act v, sc. 3, l. 201.

Is there no pity sitting in the clouds,
That sees into the bottom of my grief?
SHAKESPEARE, *Romeo and Juliet*. Act iii, sc. 5, l. 198.

8
Men must learn now with pity to dispense;
For policy sits above conscience.
SHAKESPEARE, *Timon of Athens*. Act iii, sc. 2, l. 93.

Pity is the virtue of the law,
And none but tyrants use it cruelly.
SHAKESPEARE, *Timon of Athens*. Act iii, sc. 5, 8.

9
Nothing but the Infinite pity is sufficient for the infinite pathos of human life.
J. H. SHORTHOUSE, *John Inglesant*. Vol. i, ch. 6.

10
Wide and sweet and glorious as compassion.
SWINBURNE, *Dunwich*. Pt. i, st. 8.

11
So left alone, the passions of her mind,
As winds from all the compass shift and
blow,
Made war upon each other for an hour,
Till pity won.
TENNYSON, *Godiva*, l. 32.

12
O brother man! fold to thy heart thy brother.
Where pity dwells, the peace of God is there.
J. G. WHITTIER, *Worship*. St. 13.

PLACE

13
It is not the places that grace men, but men the places.
AGESILAÜS, *Remark*, as he accepted an inferior seat. (PLUTARCH, *Laconic Apothegms*.)

No post the man Ennobles;—man the post!
BULWER-LYTTON, *King Arthur*. Bk. xii.

The place does not make the man, nor the sceptre the king. Greatness is from within.
ROBERT G. INGERSOLL, *Voltaire*.

Where Macgregor sits, there is the head of the table.
UNKNOWN. Referring to Rob Roy Macgregor. Quoted by Emerson, *The American Scholar*, as "Macdonald."

14
Nothing is more annoying than a low man raised to a high position. (Asperius nihil est humili cum surgit in altum.)
CLAUDIAN, *In Eutropium*. Bk. i, l. 181.

15
The prerogative of place.
FRIEDRICH DEDEKIND, *Grobianus*. Bk. i, ch. 4.

16
He who thinks his place below him will certainly be below his place.
LORD HALIFAX, *Works*, p. 182.

17
When baseness is exalted, do not bate
The place its Honour, for the person's sake.
The shrine is that which thou dost venerate;
And not the beast, that bears it on his back.
GEORGE HERBERT, *The Church-Porch*. St. 45.

18
All things have their place, knew we how to place them.
GEORGE HERBERT, *Jacula Prudentum*.

A place for everything, and everything in its place.
EMERSON, *Journal*, 2 Aug., 1857. Quoted.

19
Each man has his own place. (Est lucus uni Cuique suus.)
HORACE, *Satires*. Bk. i, sat. 9, l. 50.

20
Let each keep to the place properly allotted to it. (Singula quæque locum teneant sortita decentem.)
HORACE, *Ars Poetica*, l. 92.

Accept the place the divine providence has found for you.
EMERSON, *Essays, First Series: Self-Reliance.*

Sit in your place, and none can make you rise.
GEORGE HERBERT, *Jacula Prudentum*. No. 368.

1
God attributes to place
No sanctity, if none be thither brought
By men who there frequent.
MILTON, *Paradise Lost*. Bk. xi, l. 832.

2
There is no greater immorality than to occupy a place you cannot fill.
NAPOLEON I, to his brother Joseph, King of Spain. (BERCOVICI, in *Liberty*, 6 Dec., 1930.)

3
The place is dignified by the doer's deed.
SHAKESPEARE, *All's Well that Ends Well*. Act ii, sc. 3, l. 132.

There 's place and means for every man alive.
SHAKESPEARE, *All's Well that Ends Well*. Act iv, sc. 3, l. 375.

4
Towering in her pride of place.
SHAKESPEARE, *Macbeth*. Act ii, sc. 4, l. 12.

5
O place, O form,
How often dost thou with thy case, thy habit,
Wrench awe from fools!
SHAKESPEARE, *Measure for Measure*. Act ii, sc. 4, l. 12.

O place and greatness! millions of false eyes
Are stuck upon thee.
SHAKESPEARE, *Measure for Measure*, iv, 1, 60

6
It is a maxim, that those to whom everybody allows the second place have an undoubted title to the first.
SWIFT, *Tale of a Tub: Dedication*.

PLAGIARISM

See also Imitation, Quotation

I—Plagiarism: Condemnation

7
They lard their lean books with the fat of others' works.
ROBERT BURTON, *Anatomy of Melancholy: Democritus to the Reader*.

8
Who, to patch up his fame—or fill his purse—
Still pilfers wretched plans, and makes them worse;
Like gypsies, lest the stolen brat be known,
Defacing first, then claiming for his own.
CHARLES CHURCHILL, *The Apology*, l. 232.

Steal!—to be sure they may; and egad, serve your best thoughts as gypsies do stolen children, disfigure them to make 'em pass for their own.
SHERIDAN, *The Critic*. Act i, sc. 1.

[Witches] steal young children out of their cradles, *ministerio dæmonum*, and put deformed in their rooms, which we call changelings.
ROBERT BURTON, *Anatomy of Melancholy*. Pt. i, sec. ii, mem. 1, subs. 3.

9
To copy beauties, forfeits all pretence
To fame—to copy faults, is want of sense.
CHARLES CHURCHILL, *The Rosciad*, l. 457.

10
Because they commonly make use of treasure found in books, as of other treasure belonging to the dead and hidden underground; for they dispose of both with great secrecy, defacing the shape and image of the one as much as of the other.
SIR WILLIAM D'AVENANT, *Gondibert: Preface*.

The Plagianism of orators is the art, or an ingenious and easy mode, which some adroitly employ, to change, or disguise, all sorts of speeches of their own composition, or that of other authors, for their pleasure, or their utility; in such a manner that it becomes impossible even for the author himself to recognise his own work, his own genius, and his own style, so skilfully shall the whole be disguised.
SIEUR DE RICHE-SOURCE, *The Mask of Orators*. (Quoted by ISAAC D'ISRAELI, *Curiosities of Literature: Professors of Plagiarism*, who says that Riche-Source invented "plagianism" to describe a peculiarly artful kind of literary theft.)

11
They steal my thunder!
JOHN DENNIS.

Our author, for the advantage of this play [*Appius and Virginia*], had invented a new species of thunder, . . . the very sort that at present is used in the theatre. The tragedy itself was coldly received, notwithstanding such assistance, and was acted but a short time. Some nights after, Mr. Dennis, being in the pit at the representation of *Macbeth*, heard his own thunder made use of; upon which he rose in a violent passion, and exclaimed, with an oath, that it was his thunder. "See how the rascals use me!" said he. "They will not let my play run, and yet they steal my thunder!"
Biographia Britannica. Vol. v, p. 103.

12
He that readeth good writers and picks out their flowers for his own nose, is like a fool.
STEPHEN GOSSON, *The School of Abuse: Loiterers*. (1579)

13
Nothing is stolen: my Muse, though mean,
Draws from the spring she finds within.
MATTHEW GREEN, *The Spleen*, l. 13.

14
My books need no title or judge to prove them; your page stares you in the face and says, "You are a thief!" (Indice non opus est nostris nec judice libris; Stat contra dicitque tibi tua pagina "Fur es.")
MARTIAL, *Epigrams*. Bk. i, epig. 53.

Why, simpleton, do you mix your verses with mine? What have you to do, foolish man, with writings that convict you of theft? Why do you attempt to associate foxes with lions, and make owls pass for eagles? Though you had one of Ladas's legs, you would not be able, blockhead, to run with the other leg of wood.
MARTIAL, *Epigrams*. Bk. x, ep. 100.

15
Every generation has the privilege of stand-

ing on the shoulders of the generation that went before; but it has no right to pick the pockets of the first-comer.
BRANDER MATTHEWS, *Recreations of an Anthologist*, p. 20.

1
For such kind of borrowing as this, if it be not bettered by the borrower, among good authors is accounted plagiary.
MILTON, *Iconoclasts*. Ch. 23.

2
I recover my property wherever I find it. (Je reprends mon bien où je le trouve.)
MOLIÈRE, taking possession of and using several times in his *Les Fourberies de Scapin*, the famous phrase, "What the devil was he doing in that galley?" (Que diable allait-il faire dans cette galère?), which he claimed Cyrano de Bergerac had stolen from him and used in his *Pédant Joué* (Act ii, sc. 4). Emerson (*Letters and Social Aims*) attributed the *mot* to Marmontel.

3
He liked those literary cooks
Who skim the cream of others' books;
And ruin half an author's graces
By plucking *bon-mots* from their places.
HANNAH MORE, *Florio, the Bas-Bleu*.

4
It brings praise to me that you and those like you, copy my words into your books. (Mihi parta laus est, quod tu, quod similes tui, Vestras in chartas verba transfertis mea.)
PHÆDRUS, *Fables:* Bk. v, *Prologue*, l. 17.

5
In comparing various authors with one another, I have discovered that some of the gravest and latest writers have transcribed, word for word, from former works, without making acknowledgment.
PLINY THE ELDER, *Historia Naturalis:* Bk. i, *Dedication*. Sec. 22.

6
Next o'er his books his eyes began to roll,
In pleasing memory of all he stole;
How here he sipp'd, how there he plunder'd snug,
And suck'd all o'er like an industrious bug.
POPE, *The Dunciad*. Bk. i, l. 127.

Little would be left you, I'm afraid,
If all your debts to Greece and Rome were paid.
POPE, *Prologue, Designed for Mr. D'Urfey's Last Play*, l. 13.

7
Most writers steal a good thing when they can,
And when 'tis safely got 'tis worth the winning.
The worst of 't is we now and then detect 'em,
Before they ever dream that we suspect 'em.
BRYAN WALLER PROCTER, *Diego de Montillo*.

8
Libertas et natale solum:
Fine words! I wonder where you stole 'em.
SWIFT, *Verses Occasioned by Whitshed's Motto on His Coach*, 1724. Whitshed was the Chief-Justice who twice prosecuted the "Drapier." The motto is mentioned repeatedly in the *Drapier Letters*.

9
I wrote these lines, another wears the bays:
Thus you for others build your nests, O birds:
Thus you for others bear your fleece, O sheep:
Thus you for others honey make, O bees:
Thus you for others drag the plough, O kine!
(Hos ego versiculos feci, tulit alter honores:
Sic vos non vobis nidificatis aves:
Sic vos non vobis vellera fertis oves:
Sic vos non vobis mellificatis apes:
Sic vos non vobis fertis arata boves.)
VERGIL, *Epigram*. (CAIUS TIBERIUS DONATUS, *Life of Vergil*, p. 17. Brummer's edn. in Latin.) The story is that a versifier named Bathyllus had stolen a distich of Vergil's in honor of Augustus, and, in the presence of the Emperor, Vergil wrote beneath the distich four lines beginning, "Sic vos non vobis," and challenged Bathyllus to complete them. He was unable to do so, and Vergil did it as above.

The seed ye sow, another reaps;
The wealth ye find, another keeps;
The robe ye weave, another wears;
The arms ye forge, another bears.
SHELLEY, *Song to the Men of England*.

10
Read my little fable:
He that runs may read.
Most can raise the flowers now,
For all have got the seed.
TENNYSON, *The Flower*.

Though I am young, I scorn to flit
On the wings of borrowed wit.
GEORGE WITHER, *The Shepherd's Hunting*.

11
Who borrow much, then fairly make it known,
And damn it with improvements of their own.
YOUNG, *Love of Fame*. Sat. iii, l. 23.

II—Plagiarism: Excuse

12
We can say nothing but what has been said. . . . Our poets steal from Homer. . . . Our storydressers do as much; he that comes last is commonly best.
ROBERT BURTON, *Anatomy of Melancholy: Democritus to the Reader*.

When 'Omer smote 'is bloomin' lyre,
He'd 'eard men sing by land an' sea;
An' what he thought 'e might require,
'E went an' took—the same as me!
RUDYARD KIPLING, *Barrack-Room Ballads: Introduction*.

Thus the artless songs I sing
Do not deal with anything
New or never said before.
RUDYARD KIPLING, *A General Summary*.

That's of no consequence; all that can be said is,

that two people happened to hit on the same thought—and Shakespeare made use of it first, that's all.

SHERIDAN, *The Critic*. Act iii, sc. 1.

1
Then why should those who pick and choose
The best of all the best compose,
And join it by Mosaic art,
In graceful order, part to part,
To make the whole in beauty suit,
Not merit as complete repute
As those who with less art and pains
Can do it with their native brains?

SAMUEL BUTLER, *Satire upon Plagiaries*, l. 109.

2
It is as difficult to appropriate the thoughts of others as it is to invent.

EMERSON, *Letters and Social Aims: Quotation and Originality*.

3
It has come to be practically a sort of rule in literature, that a man, having once shown himself capable of original writing, is entitled thenceforth to steal from the writings of others at discretion. Thought is the property of him who can entertain it, and of him who can adequately place it.

EMERSON, *Representative Men: Shakespeare*.

Every man is a borrower and a mimic, life is theatrical and literature a quotation.

EMERSON, *Society and Solitude: Success*.

Take the whole range of imaginative literature, and we are all wholesale borrowers. In every matter that relates to invention, to use, or beauty or form, we are borrowers.

WENDELL PHILLIPS, *Lecture: The Lost Arts*.

4
You have a memory that would convict any author of plagiarism in any court of literature in the world.

JOHN HAWKESWORTH. *Remark*, to Dr. Johnson. (KEARSLEY, *Johnsoniana*. No. 600.)

5
Though old the thought and oft exprest,
'Tis his at last who says it best.

J. R. LOWELL, *For an Autograph*. St. 1.

6
The bees pillage the flowers here and there but they make honey of them which is all their own; it is no longer thyme or marjolaine: so the pieces borrowed from others he will transform and mix up into a work all his own.

MONTAIGNE, *Essays*. Bk. i, ch. 25.

Amongst so many borrowed things, I am glad if I can steal one, disguising and altering it for some new service.

MONTAIGNE, *Essays*. Bk. iii, ch. 12.

7
Poesy, drawing within its circle all that is glorious and inspiring, gave itself but little concern as to where its flowers originally grew.

KARL OTTFRIED MÜLLER. (EMERSON, *Quotation and Originality*.)

8
Whatever is well said by another, is mine. (Quicquid bene dictum est ab ullo, meum est.)

SENECA, *Epistulæ ad Lucilium*. Epis. xvi, 7.

9
Not a translation—only taken from the French.

SHERIDAN, *The Critic*. Act i, sc. 1.

10
I have thus played the sedulous ape to Hazlitt, to Lamb, to Wordsworth, to Sir Thomas Browne, to Defoe, to Hawthorne, to Montaigne, to Baudelaire and to Obermann.

R. L. STEVENSON, *Memories and Portraits*. Ch. 4.

11
Nothing is said nowadays that has not been said before. (Nullumst jam dictum quod non sit dictum prius.)

TERENCE, *Eunuchus: Prologue*, l. 41.

Perish those who said our good things before us. (Pereant qui ante nos nostra dixerent.)

ÆLIUS DONATUS. (ST. JEROME, *Commentaries: Ecclesiastes*. Ch. 1.) Referring to the phrase of Terence.

Their writings are thefts which they have made from us in advance. (Leurs écrits sont des vols qu'ils nous ont faits d'avance.)

ALEXIS PIRON, *Epigram*.

12
All the makers of dictionaries, all compilers who do nothing else than repeat backwards and forwards the opinions, the errors, the impostures, and the truths already printed, we may term plagiarists; but honest plagiarists, who arrogate not the merit of invention.

VOLTAIRE, *A Philosophical Dictionary: Plagiarism*.

Call them if you please bookmakers, not authors; range them rather among second-hand dealers than plagiarists.

VOLTAIRE, *A Philosophical Dictionary: Plagiarism*.

PLATITUDE

13
I am *not* fond of uttering platitudes
In stained-glass attitudes.

W. S. GILBERT, *Patience*. Act 1.

14
Thou say'st an undisputed thing
In such a solemn way.

O. W. HOLMES, *To an Insect*.

15
The moral commonplaces.

SIR PHILIP SIDNEY, *Apology for Poetry*. Pt. ii, sec. 1.

16
Hail to Martin Farquhar Tupper!
Who, when he bestrides the crupper
Of Pegasus, gets the upper
Hand of poets more renowned; . . .
Suited to all times and latitudes,

By the everlasting platitudes.
RICHARD HENRY STODDARD, *Proverbial Philosophy.*

1
In modern life nothing produces such an effect as a good platitude. It makes the whole world kin.
OSCAR WILDE, *An Ideal Husband.* Act i.

PLATO

2
And as when Plato did in the cradle thrive,
Bees to his lips brought honey from their hive.
WILLIAM BROWNE, *Britannia's Pastorals.* Pt. ii.

3
Oh, Plato! Plato! you have paved the way,
With your confounded fantasies, to more
Immoral conduct by the fancied sway
Your system feigns o'er the controlless core
Of human hearts, than all the long array
Of poets and romancers.
BYRON, *Don Juan.* Canto i, st. 116.

An attachment *à la* Plato for a bashful young potato, or a not-too-French French bean.
W. S. GILBERT, *Patience.* Act i.

4
From a wedding-banquet he has passed to that city which he had founded for himself and planted in the sky.
DIOGENES LAERTIUS, *Epitaph on Plato.* (Bk. iii, sec. 45.) Plato is said to have died at a wedding-banquet.

5
Out of Plato come all things that are still written and debated among men of thought. Great havoc makes he among our originalities. . . . Plato is philosophy and philosophy Plato,—at once the glory and the shame of mankind, since neither Saxon nor Roman have availed to add any idea to his categories.
EMERSON, *Representative Men: Plato.*

Plato has no external biography. If he had lover, wife, or children, we hear nothing of them. He ground them all into paint.
EMERSON, *Representative Men: Plato.*

6
See there the olive grove of Academe,
Plato's retirement, where the Attic bird
Trills her thick-warbl'd notes the summer long.
MILTON, *Paradise Regained.* Bk. iv, l. 244.

7
Come hither, O fire-god, Plato has need of thee. ("Ηφαιστε, πρόμολ' ὧδε· Πλάτων νύ τι σεῖο χατίζει.)
PLATO, consigning to the flames, after listening to Socrates, the manuscript of a tragedy he had written in competition for a prize.

8
Philosophy did not find Plato already a nobleman, it made him one. (Platonem non accepit nobilem philosophia, sed fecit.)
SENECA, *Epistulæ ad Lucilium.* Epis. xliv, 3.

9
He, if anyone, had the highest meed of praise for wisdom, and was too great for envy.
UNKNOWN, *Epitaph on Plato.* (*Greek Anthology*, vii, 60.)

Ariston's son, whom every good man honors, because he discerned the divine life.
UNKNOWN, *Epitaph on Plato.* (*Greek Anthology*, vii, 61.)

PLAYS, see Stage

PLEASURE

See also Delight; Happiness; Joy; Pain and Pleasure

I—Pleasure: Definitions

10
The great pleasure in life is doing what people say you cannot do.
WALTER BAGEHOT, *Literary Studies.* Vol. i, p. 171.

11
Pleasure may perfect us as truly as prayer.
W. E. CHANNING, *Note-Book: Joy.*

12
Nor do I call pleasures idleness, or time lost, provided they are the pleasures of a rational being.
LORD CHESTERFIELD, *Letters,* 30 Oct., 1747.

Distinguish carefully between the pleasures of a man of fashion, and the vices of a scoundrel; pursue the former, and abhor the latter, like a man of sense.
LORD CHESTERFIELD, *Letters,* 25 Jan., 1750.

Pleasure must not, nay, cannot, be the business of a man of sense and character; but it may be, and is, his relief, his reward.
LORD CHESTERFIELD, *Letters,* 8 May, 1750.

13
The pleasure of life is according to the man that lives it, and not according to the work or place.
EMERSON, *Conduct of Life: Fate.*

14
Wherefore we call pleasure the alpha and omega of a blessed life. Pleasure is our first and kindred good. (Ταύτην γὰρ ἀγαθὸν πρωτον καὶ συγγενικὸν ἔγνωμεν.)
EPICURUS, *Letter to Menœceus.* (DIOGENES LAERTIUS, *Epicurus.* Bk. x, sec. 128.)

When we say, then, that pleasure is the end and aim of life, we do not mean the pleasures of the prodigal or the pleasures of sensuality. . . . By pleasure we mean the absence of pain in the body and of trouble in the soul.
EPICURUS, *Letter to Menœceus.* (DIOGENES LAERTIUS, *Epicurus.* Bk. x, sec. 131.)

Some sages have defin'd
Pleasure the sov'reign bliss of humankind.
POPE, *January and May,* l. 440.

It is impossible to live pleasantly without living wisely and well and justly; and it is impossible to live wisely and well and justly without living pleasantly.
EPICURUS, *Sovran Maxims.* No. 5.

1
The *sine qua non* of pleasure is virtue, for it is the one thing without which pleasure cannot be

EPICURUS (DIOGENES LAERTIUS, *Epicurus*. Bk. x, sec. 138.)

Pleasure the servant, Virtue looking on.

BEN JONSON, *Pleasure Reconciled to Virtue*.

Pleasure is nought but virtue's gayer name.

YOUNG, *Night Thoughts*. Night viii, l. 573.

2
I know not how to conceive the good, apart from the pleasures of taste, sexual pleasures, the pleasures of sound, and the pleasures of beautiful form.

EPICURUS. (DIOGENES LAERTIUS, *Epicurus*. Bk x, sec. 6.)

The main Maxim of Epicurus's Philosophy was to trust to his Senses and follow his nose.

RICHARD BENTLEY, *Boyle Lectures*, ii, 79.

For he was Epicurus owen son.

CHAUCER, *Canterbury Tales: Prologue*, l. 336.

3
There are only three pleasures in life pure and lasting, and all are derived from inanimate things—books, pictures, and the face of nature.

HAZLITT, *Criticisms on Art*. Vol. i, p. 40.

4
Pleasure is far sweeter as a recreation, than a business.

R. D. HITCHCOCK, *Eternal Atonement*, viii.

5
Pleasure, or wrong or rightly understood,
Our greatest evil or our greatest good.

POPE, *An Essay on Man* Epis. ii, l. 91.

Pleasure, we both agree, is man's chief good;
Our only contest, what deserves the name.

YOUNG, *Night Thoughts*. Night viii, l. 1027.

6
Learn thou, whate'er the motive they may call,
That Pleasure is the aim, and Self the spring of all.

ROBERT SOUTHEY, *The Poet's Pilgrimage to Waterloo*. Pt. ii, canto i, st. 22.

II—Pleasure: Apothegms

7
Perils commonly ask to be paid in pleasures.

FRANCIS BACON, *Essays: Of Love*.

8
Pleasure's devious way.

BURNS, *The Vision*.

9
Oh Pleasure! you're indeed a pleasant thing.
Although one must be damned for you, no doubt.

BYRON, *Don Juan*. Canto i, st. 119.

10
I'm going to "go it" a bit before *I* settle down. I *have* gone it a *bit* already, and I'm going to "go it" a bit *more*.

HENRY J. BYRON, *Our Boys*. Act i.

11
Leave business to idlers, and wisdom to fools: they have need of 'em: wit, be my faculty, and pleasure my occupation.

CONGREVE, *The Old Batchelor*. Act i, sc. 1.

The rule of my life is to make business a pleasure, and pleasure my business.

AARON BURR, *Letter to Pichon*.

12
When Sissy got into the school here . . . her father was as pleased as Punch.

DICKENS, *Hard Times*. Bk. i, ch. 6.

I was (as the poet says) as pleased as Punch.

THOMAS MOORE, *Letter to Lady Donegal*.

13
It is the part of the wise man to resist pleasures, but of a foolish one to be a slave to them.

EPICTETUS, *Fragments*. No. 111.

14
Follow pleasure, and then will pleasure flee;
Flee pleasure, and pleasure will follow thee.

HEYWOOD, *Proverbs*. Pt. i, ch. 10.

Thus pleasure oft eludes our grasp,
Just when we think to grip her;
And hunting after Happiness
We only hunt a slipper.

THOMAS HOOD, *The Epping Hunt: Moral*.

Pleasure is very seldom found where it is sought.

SAMUEL JOHNSON, *The Idler*. No. 58.

In life there is nothing more unexpected and surprising than the arrivals and departures of pleasure. If we find it in one place to-day, it is vain to seek it there to-morrow. You can not lay a trap for it.

ALEXANDER SMITH, *City Poem: A Boy's Dream*.

Pleasure-seekers never find theirs.

ELBERT HUBBARD, *Epigrams*.

See also under WOOING.

15
The public pleasures of far the greater part of mankind are counterfeit.

SAMUEL JOHNSON, *The Idler*. No. 18.

16
I fly from pleasure, because pleasure has ceased to please.

SAMUEL JOHNSON, *Rasselas*. Ch. 3.

17
It is rarity that gives zest to pleasure. (Voluptas commendat rarior usus.)

JUVENAL, *Satires*. Sat. xi, l. 208.

Pleasure deferred is keenest; in cold we enjoy the sun, in sunshine, shade. (Sustentata venus gratissima; frigora soles, Sole juvant umbræ.)

OVID, *Remediorum Amoris*, l. 405.

Who will in time present from pleasure refrain,
Shall in time to come the more pleasure obtain.

JOHN HEYWOOD, *Proverbs*. Pt. i, ch. 11.

18
He that loves pleasure, must for pleasure fall

CHRISTOPHER MARLOWE, *Faustus*. Act v, sc. 4.

19
They need their pious exercises less

Than schooling in the Pleasures.
GEORGE MEREDITH, *A Certain People.*

1
Pleasure safely enjoyed is the less valued. (Quæ venit ex tuto, minus est accepta voluptas.)
OVID, *Ars Amatoria.* Bk. iii, l. 603.
For FORBIDDEN PLEASURE *see* PROHIBITION.

2
Pleasures are ever in our hands or eyes,
And when in act they cease, in prospect rise.
POPE, *Essay on Man.* Epis. ii, l. 123.

3
Pleasures the sex, as children birds, pursue,
Still out of reach, yet never out of view.
POPE, *Moral Essays.* Epis. ii, l. 231.

All human race, from China to Peru,
Pleasure, howe'er disguis'd by art, pursue.
THOMAS WARTON, *Universal Love of Pleasure.* *See also under* OBSERVATION.

4
I consider the world as made for me, not me for the world. It is my maxim therefore to enjoy it while I can, and let futurity shift for itself.
SMOLLETT, *Roderick Random.* Ch. 45. *See also* LIFE AND LIVING.

5
The human mind always runs downhill from toil to pleasure. (Hominum ab labore proclive ad libidinem.)
TERENCE, *Andria,* l. 78. (Act i, sc. 1.)

6
You have an immense pleasure to come.
JAMES TOWNLEY, *High Life Below Stairs.* Act ii, sc. 1. Referring to the reading of Shakespeare.

Why, then, your ladyship has one pleasure to come.
SWIFT, *Polite Conversation.* Dial. i. Referring to reading a play called *Love in a Hollow Tree.*

7
His own special pleasure attracts each one. (Trahit sua quemque voluptas.)
VERGIL, *Eclogues.* No. ii, l. 65.

8
Simple pleasures . . . are the last refuge of the complex.
OSCAR WILDE, *Aphorisms.* No. 35.

9
No civilized man ever regrets a pleasure.
OSCAR WILDE, *Picture of Dorian Gray.* Ch. 6.

10
Gay pleasure! proud ambition is her slave.
YOUNG, *Night Thoughts.* Night viii, l. 527.

III—Pleasure: Its Delight

11
Then top and maintop crowd the sail,
Heave Care owre side!
And large, before Enjoyment's gale,
Let's tak' the tide.
BURNS, *Epistle to James Smith.* St. 11.

12
Mingle your cares with pleasure now and then. (Interpone tuis interdum gaudia curis.)
DIONYSIUS CATO, *Disticha de Moribus.* Bk. iii, No. 7. *See also under* NONSENSE.

13
Whenever you are sincerely pleased, you are nourished.
EMERSON, *Conduct of Life: Considerations by the Way.*

14
By happy alchemy of mind
They turn to pleasure all they find.
MATTHEW GREEN, *The Spleen,* l. 610.

15
A day in such serene enjoyment spent
Is worth an age of splendid discontent.
JAMES MONTGOMERY, *Greenland.*

16
God made all pleasures innocent.
CAROLINE NORTON, *Lady of La Garaye.* Pt. i.

17
Pleasure in moderation relaxes and tempers the spirit. (Modica voluptas laxat animos et temperat.)
SENECA, *De Ira.* Bk. ii, sec. 20.

18
There's not a minute of our lives should stretch
Without some pleasure.
SHAKESPEARE, *Antony and Cleopatra.* Act i, sc. 1, l. 46.

Pleasure and action make the hours seem short.
SHAKESPEARE, *Othello.* Act ii, sc. 3, l. 385.

19
Man could direct his ways by plain reason, and support his life by tasteless food; but God has given us wit, and flavour, and brightness, and laughter, and perfumers, to enliven the days of man's pilgrimage, and to "charm his pained steps over the burning marle."
SYDNEY SMITH, *Dangers and Advantages of Wit.*

'Tis sweet to be awaken'd by the lark,
Or lull'd by falling waters; sweet the hum
Of bees, the voice of girls, the song of birds,
The lisp of children, and their earliest words.
BYRON, *Don Juan.* Canto i, st. 123.

20
I built my soul a lordly pleasure-house,
Wherein at ease for aye to dwell.
I said, "O Soul, make merry and carouse,
Dear soul, for all is well."
TENNYSON, *The Palace of Art.* St. 1.

21
Compassed round by pleasure.
WORDSWORTH, *The Excursion.* Bk. iii, l. 380.

That sweet taste of pleasure unpursued.
WORDSWORTH, *The Old Cumberland Beggar.*

22
Pleasure's the mistress of ethereal powers;
For her contend the rival gods above;
Pleasure's the mistress of the world below; . . .
What is the pulse of this so busy world?
The love of pleasure: that, thro' ev'ry vein,

Throws motion, warmth, and shuts out death
from life.
YOUNG, *Night Thoughts*. Night viii, l. 533.

The love of pleasure is man's eldest-born,
Born in his cradle, living to his tomb;
Wisdom, her younger sister, tho' more grave,
Was meant to minister, and not to mar,
Imperial pleasure, queen of human hearts.
YOUNG, *Night Thoughts*. Night viii, l. 595.

IV—Pleasure: Its Sting

1
No more deadly curse has been given by nature to man than carnal pleasure. From it come treason and overthrow of states. There is no criminal purpose and no evil deed which the lust for pleasure will not drive men to undertake. Since nature—or some god, perhaps—has given to man nothing more excellent than his intellect, therefore this divine gift has no deadlier foe than pleasure; for where lust holds despotic sway self-control has no place, and in pleasure's realm there is not a single spot where virtue can put her foot.
ARCHYTAS OF TARENTUM. (CICERO, *De Senectute*. Ch. xii, sec. 39.)

There is nothing so hateful and so pernicious as pleasure, since, if indulged in too much and too long, it turns the light of the soul into utter darkness. (Quocirca nihil esse tam detestabile tamque pestiferum quam voluptatem, si quidem ea, cum major esset longior, omne animi lumen exstingueret.)
ARCHYTAS OF TARENTUM. (CICERO, *De Senectute*. Ch. xii, sec. 41.)

Carnal pleasure hinders deliberation, is at war with reason, blindfolds the eyes of the mind, so to speak, and has no fellowship with virtue. (Impedit consilium voluptas, rationi inimica est, mentis ut ita dicam præstringit oculos, nec habet ullum cum virtute commercium.
CICERO, *De Senectute*. Ch. xii, sec. 42.

2
Punish not thyself with pleasure; glut not thy sense with palative delights.
SIR THOMAS BROWNE, *Christian Morals*. Pt. ii, sec. 1.

3
Pleasure (whene'er she sings, at least)'s a
siren,
That lures, to flay alive, the young beginner.
BYRON, *Don Juan*. Canto iii, st. 36.

Though sages may pour out their wisdom's
treasure,
There is no sterner moralist than Pleasure.
BYRON, *Don Juan*. Canto iii, st. 65.

4
Pleasure is the rock which most young people split upon: they launch out with crowded sails in quest of it, but without a compass to direct their course, or reason sufficient to steer the vessel.
LORD CHESTERFIELD, *Letters*, 27 March, 1747.

Every virtue, they say, has its kindred vice; every pleasure, I am sure, has its neighbouring disgrace.
LORD CHESTERFIELD, *Letters*, 5 Feb., 1750.

5
In everything satiety closely follows the greatest pleasures. (Omnibus in rebus voluptatibus maximis fastidium finitimum est.)
CICERO, *De Oratore*. Bk. iii, sec. 25.

But not even pleasure to excess is good:
What most elates then sinks the soul as low.
THOMSON, *Castle of Indolence*. Canto i, st. 63.

6
And pleasure brings as surely in her train
Remorse, and Sorrow, and vindictive Pain.
COWPER, *The Progress of Error*, l. 43.

Pleasure admitted in undue degree
Enslaves the will, nor leaves the judgment free.
COWPER, *The Progress of Error*, l. 269.

Pleasure is labour too, and tires as much.
COWPER, *Hope*, l. 20.

Pleasure, . . .
That reeling goddess with the zoneless waist
And wand'ring eyes, still leaning on the arm
Of Novelty, her fickle frail support.
COWPER, *The Task*. Bk. iii, l. 51.

7
No pleasure is in itself evil, but the things which produce certain pleasures entail annoyance many times greater than the pleasures themselves.
EPICURUS, *Sovran Maxims*. No. 8.

8
Fly that present joy,
Which in time will breed annoy.
JOHN FLORIO, *Second Frutes*, 99. (1591)

Fell all present pleasure that gives the future pain.
WODROEPHE, *Spared Hours*, 277. (1623)

Fly the pleasure that bites tomorrow.
GEORGE HERBERT, *Jacula Prudentum*.

9
In war, hunting, and love,
Men for one pleasure a thousand griefs prove.
GEORGE HERBERT, *Jacula Prudentum*.

A life of pleasure is therefore the most unpleasing life in the world.
GOLDSMITH, *The Citizen of the World*. No. 44.

10
From the midst of the fountains of pleasures there rises something of bitterness which torments us amid the very flowers. (Medio de fonte leporum Surgit amari aliquit quod in ipsis floribus angat.)
LUCRETIUS, *De Rerum Natura*. Bk. iv, l. 1133.

11
There is no pleasure unalloyed. (Usque adeo nulla est sincera voluptas.)
OVID, *Metamorphoses*. Bk. vii, l. 453.

The sweetest rose hath his prickle.
JOHN LYLY, *Euphues*, p. 33. (1579)
See also ROSE AND THORN.

12
The bait of sin. (Κακοῦ δέλεαρ.)
PLATO, *Timæus*. Sec. 69 D.

Plato happily calls pleasure "the bait of sin," evidently because men are caught therewith like fish. (Divine Plato "escam malorum" appellat voluptatem quod es videlicet homines capiantur ut pisces.)

CICERO, *De Senectute*. Ch. xiii, sec. 44.

Pleasure is the greatest incentive to evil.

PLATO. (PLUTARCH, *Lives: Life of Cato the Censor*).

Pleasure is an inciter to vileness. (Voluptas est illecebra turpitudinis.)

CICERO, *De Legibus*. Bk. i, ch. 11, sec. 31.

Pleasure's a sin, and sometimes sin's a pleasure.

BYRON, *Don Juan*. Canto i, st. 133.

1
Never pleasure without repentance.

JOHN RAY, *English Proverbs*.

Short pleasure, long lament.

JOHN RAY, *English Proverbs*. The French form is, "De court plaisir, long repentir."

After drought commyth rayne,
After pleasure commyth payne.

UNKNOWN. (*Reliq. Antiquæ*, 323.)

2
All the instances of pleasure have a sting in the tail.

JEREMY TAYLOR, *Holy Living*. Ch. ii, sec. 1.

To think o' the sting that's in the tail of pleasure!

WILLIAM CONGREVE, *Old Batchelor: Epilogue*.

Pleasure, such as leaves no sting behind!

SAMUEL ROGERS, *Human Life*, l. 482.

3
Too oft is transient pleasure the source of endless woe. (Zu oft ist kurze Lust die Quelle langer Schmerzen!)

WIELAND, *Oberon*. Pt. ii, l. 52.

4
Sure as night follows day,
Death treads in pleasure's footsteps round the world,
When pleasure treads the paths which reason shuns.

YOUNG, *Night Thoughts*. Night v, l. 863.

V—Pleasure: Its Transitoriness

5
The race of delight is short, and pleasures have mutable faces.

SIR THOMAS BROWNE, *Christian Morals*. Pt. ii, sec. 1.

6
But pleasures are like poppies spread:
You seize the flow'r, its bloom is shed;
Or like the snow falls in the river,
A moment white—then melts for ever.

BURNS, *Tam o' Shanter*, l. 59.

7
Where is delight? and what are pleasures now?—
Moths that a garment fret.

MARY E. COLERIDGE, *Mandragora*.

8
'Tis a sight to engage me, if anything can,
To muse on the perishing pleasures of man;
Though his life be a dream, his enjoyments, I see,
Have a being less durable even than he.

WILLIAM COWPER, *The Poplar-Field*.

Some pleasures live a month and some a year,
But short the date of all we gather here.

COWPER, *Retirement*, l. 459.

9
The shortest pleasures are the sweetest.

FARQUHAR, *The Twin Rivals*. Act iii, sc. 3.

10
Play the man.
Look not on pleasures as they come, but go.

GEORGE HERBERT, *The Church-Porch*. St. 72.

11
The roses of pleasure seldom last long enough to adorn the brow of him who plucks them; for they are the only roses which do not retain their sweetness after they have lost their beauty.

HANNAH MORE, *Essays: On Dissipation*.

12
This is a brief and not a true pleasure. (Brevis est hæc, et non vera voluptas.)

OVID, *Heroides*. Epis. xix, l. 65.

13
Pleasures are transient, honors are immortal.

PERIANDER. (DIOGENES LAERTIUS, *Periander*. Sec. 4.)

14
Spangling the wave with lights as vain
As pleasures in this vale of pain,
That dazzle as they fade.

SCOTT, *The Lord of the Isles*. Canto i, st. 23.

15
Pleasure is frail like a dewdrop, while it laughs it dies.

RABINDRANATH TAGORE, *The Gardener*. No. 27.

16
Pleasure comes, but not to stay;
Even this shall pass away.

THEODORE TILTON, *All Things Shall Pass Away*.

17
Pleasure that most enchants us
Seems the soonest done;
What is life with all it grants us,
But a hunting run?

G. J. WHYTE-MELVILLE, *A Lay of the Ranston Bloodhounds*.

VI—Pleasure: The Art of Pleasing

18
He more had pleased us had he pleased us less.

ADDISON, *English Poets*. Referring to Cowley.

19
I would rather please one good man than many bad. (Bono probari malo quam multis malis.)

PITTACUS. (AUSONIUS [?], *Septem Sapientum Sententiæ*, l. 9.)

20
He pleases every one but can not please him-

self. (Il plaît à tout le monde et ne saurait se plaire.)
BOILEAU, *Satires*, ii. Referring to Molière.

1 Most arts require long study and application; but the most useful of all, that of pleasing, only the desire.
LORD CHESTERFIELD, *Letters*, 8 May, 1750.

He makes people pleased with him by first making them pleased with themselves.
LORD CHESTERFIELD, *Letters*, 18 Jan., 1750.

Pleasure is necessarily reciprocal; no one feels, who does not at the same time give it. To be pleased one must please.
LORD CHESTERFIELD, *Letters*, 9 July, 1750.

The art of pleasing is to seem pleased.
WILLIAM HAZLITT, *Round Table: On Manner*

For we that live to please must please to live.
SAMUEL JOHNSON, *Prologue on the Opening of the Drury Lane Theatre*.

Men seldom give pleasure where they are not pleased themselves.
SAMUEL JOHNSON, *The Rambler*. No. 74.

They who are pleased themselves must always please.
THOMSON, *Castle of Indolence*. Canto i, st. 15.

2 Too much desire to please pleasure divorces.
GEORGE CHAPMAN, *Ovid's Banquet of Sense*.

The greatest mistake is the trying to be more agreeable than you can be.
WALTER BAGEHOT, *Biographical Studies*, p. 294.

3 If you mean to profit, learn to please.
CHARLES CHURCHILL, *Gotham*. Bk. ii, l. 88.

4 Who pleases one against his will.
CONGREVE, *The Way of the World: Epilogue*.

5 Thus always teasing others, always teas'd,
His only pleasure is—to be displeas'd.
COWPER, *Conversation*, l. 345.

6 Whate'er he did was done with so much ease,
In him alone, 'twas natural to please.
DRYDEN, *Absalom and Achitophel*. Pt. i, l. 27.

Whoever would be pleased and please,
Must do what others do with ease.
ROBERT NUGENT, *Epistle to a Lady*.

7 He must rise early, yea, not at all go to bed, who will have every one's good word.
THOMAS FULLER, *Holy War*. Bk. iv, ch. 14. (1639)

He had need rise betimes that would please everybody.
JOHN RAY, *English Proverbs*, 132. (1670) The French form is, "Qui veut plaire à tout le monde doit se lever de bonne heure."

He that all men will please shall never find ease.
JOHN CLARKE, *Parœmiologia*, 282. (1639)

He that would please all and himself too,
Undertakes what he cannot do.
JAMES HOWELL, *Proverbs*, 5. (1670)

Who seeks to please all men each way,
And not himself offend,
He may begin his work to-day,
But God knows where he'll end.
SAMUEL ROWLANDS, *Epigrams*.

8 He is very foolish who aims at pleasing all the world and his father. (Est bien fou du cerveau qui prétend contenter tout le monde et son pere.)
LA FONTAINE, *Fables*. Bk. iii, fab. 1.

9 He pleased you by not studying to please.
GEORGE LYTTELTON, *Progress of Love*. Pt. iii.

10 The man who gives pleasure is as charitable as he who relieves suffering.
GEORGE MOORE, *Impressions and Opinions: Dramatists and Their Literature*.

11 By whatever gifts you can please, please. (Quacumque potes dote placere, place.)
OVID, *Ars Amatoria*. Bk. i, l. 596.

You alone please me. (Tu mihi sola places.)
OVID, *Ars Amatoria*. Bk. i, l. 42.

12 Do not care how many, but whom, you please. (Non quam multis placeas, sed qualibus stude.)
PUBLILIUS SYRUS, *Sententiæ*.

Satisfy a few; to please many is bad. (Mach' es Wenigen recht; vielen gefallen ist schlimm.)
SCHILLER, *Votivtafeln*.

13 I do not exist to please you. (Non tibi spiro.)
SIR PHILIP SIDNEY, *Arcadia*. Motto on title-page.

Be you pig or god, I am marjoram, and do not breathe for you. (Sis sus, sis divus, sum caltha, et non tibi spiro.)
COLERIDGE, *Aids to Reflection*. Vol. i, p. 13.

14 In great affairs, it is difficult to please all. (Ἐν μεγάλοις πασιν ἁδεῖν χαλεπόν.)
SOLON. (PLUTARCH, *Lives: Solon*. Sec. 25.)

15 For not even Jove can please all, whether he rains or does not rain. (Οὐδὲ γὰρ ὁ Ζεὺς Οὔθ' ὕων οὔτ' ἀνεχων πάντεσσ' ἁνδάνει.)
THEOGNIS, *Elegies*. No. 26.

VII—Pleasure: The Man of Pleasure

16 A man of pleasure, in the vulgar acceptation of that phrase, means only a beastly drunkard, an abandoned whoremaster, and a profligate swearer and curser.
LORD CHESTERFIELD, *Letters*, 27 March, 1747.

The true pleasures of a gentleman are those of the table, but within the bound of moderation; good company, that is to say, people of merit; moderate play, which amuses, without any interested views; and sprightly gallant conversations with women of fashion and sense.
LORD CHESTERFIELD, *Letters*, 24 Feb., 1747.

No man takes pleasures truly who does not earn them by previous business; and few people do business well who do nothing else.
CHESTERFIELD, *Letters,* 7 Aug., 1749.

I know a great many men, who call themselves men of pleasure, but who, in truth, have none.
LORD CHESTERFIELD, *Letters,* 5 Feb., 1750.

1
No blinder bigot, I maintain it still,
Than he who must have pleasure, come what will.
COWPER, *Hope,* l. 594.

2
Who cannot live on twenty pound a year,
Cannot on forty: he's a man of pleasure,
A kind of thing that's for itself too dear.
GEORGE HERBERT, *The Church-Porch.* St. 30.

3
A life of pleasure requires an aristocratic setting to make it interesting.
GEORGE SANTAYANA, *Life of Reason.* Vol. ii, 135.

4
A man devoted to pleasure. (Homo voluptati obsequens.)
TERENCE, *Hecyra,* l. 459. (Act iii, sc. 5.)

PLOT, see Conspiracy

POE, EDGAR ALLAN

5
Ah, much he suffered in his day:
He knelt with Virtue, kissed with Sin—
Wild Passion's child, and Sorrow's twin,
A meteor that had lost its way!

He walked with goblins, ghouls, and things
Unsightly,—terrors and despairs;
And ever in the starry airs
A dismal raven flapped its wings!
THOMAS BAILEY ALDRICH, *A Poet's Grave.*

I've an idea that if Poe had been an exemplary, conventional, tax-oppressed citizen, like Longfellow, his few poems, as striking as they are, would not have made so great a stir.
ALDRICH, *Letter to Stedman,* 15 Nov., 1900.

6
Proud, mad, but not defiant,
He touched at heaven and hell.
Fate found a rare soul pliant
And rung her changes well.
Alternately his lyre,
Stranded with strings of fire,
Led earth's most happy choir,
Or flashed with Israfel.
J. H. BONER, *Poe's Cottage at Fordham.*

7
You mean the jingle-man!
RALPH WALDO EMERSON, referring to Edgar Allan Poe. (HOWELLS, *Literary Friends and Acquaintances,* p. 63.)

8
There comes Poe, with his raven, like Barnaby Rudge,
Three fifths of him genius and two fifths sheer fudge.
J. R. LOWELL, *A Fable for Critics,* l. 1297.

9
O raven death that shrouds your luminous head!
Not you, but your biographers are dead.
JOHN MACY, *Couplets in Criticism: Poe.*

10
The sad great gifts the austere Muses bring
In their stern hands to make their poets of
Were laid on him that he might wildly sing
Of Beauty, Death and Love.
EDWIN MARKHAM, *Our Israfel.*

Weird wraiths companioned him, but none the less,
Amid the forms of ghoul and ghost and gnome,
Figures were wont to roam
Of light and loveliness.
CLINTON SCOLLARD, *At the Grave of Poe.*

He walked with shadows, and yet who shall say
We are not all as shadows, we who fare
Toward one dim bourn along life's fateful way,
Sharing the griefs and joys once his to share.
CLINTON SCOLLARD, *At the Grave of Poe.*

11
If Poe from Pike The Raven stole,
As his accusers say,
Then to embody Adam's soul,
God plagiarized the clay.
JOHN B. TABB, *Plagiarism.*

12
A certain tyrant, to disgrace
The more a rebel's resting place,
Compelled the people every one
To hurl, in passing there, a stone,
Which done, behold, the pile became
A monument to keep the name.
And thus it is with Edgar Poe;
Each passing critic has his throw,
Nor sees, defeating his intent,
How lofty grows the monument.
JOHN B. TABB, *Poe's Critics.*

POETRY

See also Song, Writing

I—Poetry: Definitions

13
Poetry is simply the most beautiful, impressive, and widely effective mode of saying things, and hence its importance.
MATTHEW ARNOLD, *Essays in Criticism: Heine.*

The eternal objects of poetry, among all nations, and at all times, are actions; human actions; possessing an inherent interest in themselves, and which are to be communicated in an interesting manner by the art of the poet.
MATTHEW ARNOLD, *Sohrab and Rustum: Preface.*

14
Poetry is devil's wine. (Poesis est vinum dæmonum.)
ST. AUGUSTINE, *Contra Academicos.* Sec. 1.

Did not one of the fathers in great indignation call poesy, vinum dæmonum?
BACON, *Advancement of Learning.* Bk. ii.

1
It [poetry] was ever thought to have some participation of divineness, because it doth raise and erect the mind.
BACON, *Advancement of Learning*. Bk. ii.

Poetry is itself a thing of God;
He made His prophets poets; and the more
We feel of poesie do we become
Like God in love and power.
P. J. BAILEY, *Festus: Proëm*, l. 5.

God Himself is the best Poet,
And the Real is His song.
E. B. BROWNING, *The Dead Pan*. St. 36.

Poetry, the language of the gods.
SAMUEL ROGERS, *Italy*.

2
Poetry, not finding the actual world exactly conformed to its idea of good and fair, seeks to accommodate the shows of things to the desires of the mind, and to create an ideal world better than the world of experience.
FRANCIS BACON, paraphrasing Aristotle. (EMERSON, *Natural History of Intellect: Milton*.)

3
Poetry should be vital—either stirring our blood by its divine movements, or snatching our breath by its divine perfection. To do both is supreme glory, to do either is enduring fame.
AUGUSTINE BIRRELL, *Obiter Dicta:* Ser. i, *Browning's Poetry*.

4
Poetry and religion are a product of the smaller intestines.
DR. CABANIS. (CARLYLE, *Signs of the Times*.)

5
There is no heroic poem in the world but is at bottom a biography, the life of a man; also it may be said, there is no life of a man, faithfully recorded, but is a heroic poem of its sort, rhymed or unrhymed.
CARLYLE, *Essays: Memoirs of Scott*.

The finest poetry was first experience.
EMERSON, *Representative Men: Shakespeare*.

6
Poetry which has been defined as the harmonious unison of man with nature.
CARLYLE, *Essays: Early German Literature*.

Poetry, therefore, we will call *musical Thought*. The Poet is he who *thinks* in that manner.
CARLYLE, *Heroes and Hero-Worship: The Hero as Poet*.

Giving a name, indeed, is a poetic art; all poetry, if we go to that with it, is but a giving of names.
CARLYLE, *Journal*, 18 May, 1832.

7
Poetry, the eldest sister of all art, and parent of most.
WILLIAM CONGREVE, *The Way of the World: Dedication*.

Poetry, the queen of arts.
THOMAS SPRAT, *Ode upon the Poems of Abraham Cowley*.

Poetry is an art, and chief of the fine arts: the easiest to dabble in, the hardest in which to reach true excellence.
E. C. STEDMAN, *Victorian Poets*. Ch. 5.

8
Poems come like boats
With sails for wings;
Crossing the sky swiftly
They slip under tall bridges
Of cloud.
HILDA CONKLING, *Poems*.

9
Good poetry could not have been otherwise written than it is. The first time you hear it, it sounds rather as if copied out of some invisible tablet in the Eternal mind, than as if arbitrarily composed by the poet. The feeling of all great poets has accorded with this. They found the verse, not made it. The muse brought it to them.
EMERSON, *Essays, First Series: Art*.

10
It does not need that a poem should be long. Every word was once a poem.
EMERSON, *Essays, Second Series: The Poet*.

Every poem should be made up of lines that are poems.
EMERSON, *Journals*. Vol. vii. p. 523.

Finally, most of us [imagist poets] believe that concentration is the very essence of poetry.
AMY LOWELL, *Imagist Poetry*.

11
Only that is poetry which cleanses and mans me.
EMERSON, *Letters and Social Aims: Inspiration*.

Poetry is faith. To the poet the world is virgin soil; all is practicable; the men are ready for virtue; it is always time to do right. . . The test of the poet is the power to take the passing day and hold it up to a divine reason. . . . Poetry is the consolation of mortal men.
EMERSON, *Letters and Social Aims: Poetry and Imagination*.

Poetry is the only verity—the expression of a sound mind speaking after the ideal, not after the apparent.
EMERSON, *Letters and Social Aims: Poetry and Imagination*.

Poetry must be as new as foam and as old as the rock.
EMERSON, *Journals*.

12
Words are rather the drowsy part of poetry; imagination the life of it.
OWEN FELLTHAM, *Resolves: Poets and Poetry*.

13
Poems, the hop-grounds of the brain.
MATTHEW GREEN, *The Spleen*, l. 506.

14
Poetry is to philosophy what the Sabbath is to the rest of the week.
J. C. AND A. W. HARE, *Guesses at Truth*.

Science sees signs; Poetry the thing signified.
J. C. AND A. W. HARE, *Guesses at Truth*.

1
I am the reality of things that seem;
The great transmuter, melting loss to gain.
ELLA HEATH, *Poetry.*

2
It is not enough for poems to have beauty; they must have charm, and lead the hearer's soul where they will. (Non satis est pulchra esse poemata; dulcia sunto Et quocumque volent animum auditoris agunto.)
HORACE, *Ars Poetica*, l. 99.

A poem is like a picture: one strikes your fancy more, the nearer you stand; another, the farther away. . . . This pleased but once; that, though ten times called for, will always please (Ut pictura poesis: erit quæ, si propius stes, Te capiat magis, et quædam, si longius abstes. . . . Hæc placuit semel, hæc deciens repetita placebit.)
HORACE, *Ars Poetica*, l. 361.

3
The question is whether a noble song is produced by nature or by art. I neither believe in mere labor being of avail without a rich vein of talent, nor in natural cleverness which is not educated. (Natura fieret laudabile carmen an arte, Quæsitum est: ego nec studium sine divite vena, Nec rude quid prosit video ingenium.)
HORACE, *Ars Poetica*, l. 408.

'Tis not sufficient to combine
Well-chosen words in a well-ordered line.
(Non satis est puris versum perscribere verbis.)
HORACE, *Satires*. Bk. i, sat. 4, l. 54.

4
Poetry is the bill and coo of sex.
ELBERT HUBBARD, *Epigrams.*

5
The essence of poetry is invention; such invention as, by producing something unexpected, surprises and delights.
SAMUEL JOHNSON, *English Poets: Waller.*

6
All good verses are like impromptus made at leisure. (Tous les vers excellents sont comme des impromptus faits à loisir.)
JOUBERT, *Pensées*. No. 291.

7
A drainless shower
Of light is Poesy: 'tis the supreme of power;
'Tis might half slumb'ring on its own right arm.
KEATS, *Sleep and Poetry*, l. 237.

Poetry should surprise by a fine excess, and not by singularity.
KEATS, *Letter to John Taylor*, 27 Feb., 1818

8
Poetry, native and true poetry, is nothing else than each poet's innermost feeling issuing in rhythmic language.
JOHN KEBLE, *Lectures on Poetry*. No. 22.

The true poem is the poet's mind.
EMERSON, *Essays, First Series: Of History.*

9
The essence of all poetry is to be found, not in high-wrought subtlety of thought, nor in pointed cleverness of phrase, but in the depths of the heart and the most sacred feelings of the men who write.
JOHN KEBLE, *Lectures on Poetry*. No. 28.

Let us therefore deem the glorious art of Poetry a kind of medicine divinely bestowed upon man.
JOHN KEBLE, *Lectures on Poetry: Dedication.*

10
A poem should not mean But be.
ARCHIBALD MACLEISH, *Ars Poetica.*

11
Poetry is a comforting piece of fiction set to more or less lascivious music.
H. L. MENCKEN, *Prejudices*. Ser. iii, p. 150.

12
The pearl Is a disease of the oyster.
A poem Is a disease of the spirit
Caused by the irritation
Of a granule of Truth
Fallen into that soft gray bivalve
We call the mind.
CHRISTOPHER MORLEY, *Bivalves.*

13
I would define, in brief, the Poetry of words as the Rhythmical Creation of Beauty. Its sole arbiter is Taste.
EDGAR ALLAN POE, *The Poetic Principle.*

Poetry is a criticism of life in terms of beauty.
MRS. GEORGE PIERCE. (*Forum*, Aug., 1928.)

14
Poetry is a language that tells us, through a more or less emotional reaction, something that cannot be said.
E. A. ROBINSON, *Newspaper Interview.*

15
I should define poetry as the exquisite expression of exquisite impressions.
JOSEPH ROUX, *Meditations of a Parish Priest*. Pt. i, No. 3.

Poetry is truth in its Sunday clothes.
JOSEPH ROUX, *Meditations of a Parish Priest*. Pt. i, No. 76.

16
Poetry is the journal of a sea animal living on land, wanting to fly in the air. Poetry is a search for syllables to shoot at the barriers of the unknown and the unknowable. Poetry is a phantom script telling how rainbows are made and why they go away.
CARL SANDBURG, *Poetry Considered*. (*Atlantic Monthly*, March, 1923.)

Poetry is the achievement of the synthesis of hyacinths and biscuits.
CARL SANDBURG, *Poetry Considered*. (*Atlantic Monthly*, March, 1923.) *See also* HYACINTH.

17
Poetry is the record of the best and happiest moments of the happiest and best minds.
SHELLEY, *A Defense of Poetry.*

A poem is the very image of life expressed in its eternal truth.
SHELLEY, *A Defense of Poetry.*

1
Poetry is the companion of camps.
SIR PHILIP SIDNEY, *Apologie for Poetrie*. Pt. ii.
2
Poetry is the natural language of all worship.
MADAME DE STAËL, *Germany*. Pt. ii, ch. 10.
3
Poetry implies the whole truth, philosophy expresses a particle of it.
H. D. THOREAU, *Journal*, 26 June, 1852.

Poetry is nothing but healthy speech.
H. D. THOREAU, *Journal*, 4 Sept., 1841.
4
Whatever may have been the case in years gone by, the true use for the imaginative faculty of modern times is to give ultimate vivification to facts, to science, and to common lives, endowing them with the glows and glories and final illustriousness which belong to every real thing, and to real things only. Without that ultimate vivification—which the poet or other artist alone can give—reality would seem incomplete, and science, democracy, and life itself, finally in vain.
WALT WHITMAN, *A Backward Glance O'er Travel'd Roads*.

The messages of great poems to each man and woman are, Come to us on equal terms, only then can you understand us. We are no better than you, what we inclose you inclose, what we enjoy you may enjoy.
WALT WHITMAN, *Leaves of Grass: Preface*.
5
Poetry is the spontaneous overflow of powerful feelings: it takes its origin from emotion recollected in tranquillity.
WORDSWORTH, *Lyrical Ballads: Preface*.

II—Poetry: Apothegms

6
I would be the Lyric ever on the lip,
Rather than the Epic memory lets slip.
THOMAS BAILEY ALDRICH, *Lyrics and Epics*.

In Nature's open book
An epic is the sea,
A lyric is the brook:—
Lyrics for me!
FRANK DEMPSTER SHERMAN, *Lyrics*.
7
Poetry fettered fetters the human race.
WILLIAM BLAKE, *Marriage of Heaven and Hell*.
8
Poetry is the worst mask in the world behind which folly and stupidity could attempt to hide their features.
BRYANT, *Lectures on Poetry: The Nature of Poetry*.
9
Why then we should drop into poetry.
DICKENS, *Our Mutual Friend*. Bk. i, ch. 5.

Poetry's unnat'ral; no man ever talked poetry 'cept a beadle on boxin' day, or Warren's blackin' or Rowland's oil, or some o' them low fellows.
DICKENS, *Pickwick Papers*. Ch. 33.
10
There are great arts now, but no poetry celebrates them.
EMERSON, *Journals*, 1864.
11
Amateurs and women have but the feeblest ideas of poetry.
GOETHE, *Conversations with Eckermann*.
12
A verse may find him who a sermon flies,
And turn delight into a sacrifice.
GEORGE HERBERT, *The Church-Porch*. St. 1.
13
As civilization advances, poetry almost necessarily declines.
MACAULAY, *Essays: Mitford's History of Greece*.
14
A prize poem is like a prize sheep. . . . In general, prize sheep are good for nothing but to make tallow candles, and prize poems are good for nothing but to light them.
MACAULAY, *On the Royal Society of Literature*. Par. 8.
15
Those who have souls meet their fellows there.
GEORGE MEREDITH, *Diana of the Crossways*, ch. 1.
16
Fit to give weight to smoke. (Dare pondus idonea fumo.)
PERSIUS, *Satires*. Sat. v, l. 20. Referring to a page of poetry.
17
The profoundest gift of the spirit of poetry is the gift of peace.
J. C. POWYS, *The Meaning of Culture*, p. 57.
18
The elegancy, facility, and golden cadence of poesy.
SHAKESPEARE, *Love's Labour's Lost*. Act iv, sc. 2, l. 126.

Much is the force of heaven-bred poesy.
SHAKESPEARE, *The Two Gentlemen of Verona*. Act iii, sc. 2, l. 71.
19
You cannot hear the planet-like music of poetry.
SIR PHILIP SIDNEY, *Apologie for Poetrie*. Pt. ii. *See also* MUSIC OF THE SPHERES.
20
I would rather have written that poem, gentlemen, than take Quebec to-morrow.
MAJOR-GENERAL JAMES WOLFE, the night before he was killed on the Plains of Abraham (13 Sept., 1759), referring to Gray's *Elegy Written in a Country Church-yard*. (HUME, *History of England*, ch. 30.)
21
Verses are children of the lyre;
They should be sung, not read.
(Les vers sont enfants de la lyre;
Il faut les chanter, non les lire.)
UNKNOWN, *Les Vers*.

III—Poetry: Rhyme and Reason

1
Still may syllabes jar with time,
Still may reason war with rhyme,
Resting never!

Ben Jonson, *A Fit of Rhyme Against Rhyme.*

Here is rhyme, not empty of reason.

Ben Jonson, *Volpone: Prologue.*

2
Yea, marry, now it is somewhat, for now it is rhyme, whereas before it was neither rhyme nor reason.

Sir Thomas More, to a friend who had versified an indifferent book. (Francis Bacon, *Apothegms.* No. 287.)

3
Rosalind: But are you so much in love as your rhymes speak?
Orlando: Neither rhyme nor reason can express how much.

Shakespeare, *As You Like It.* Act iii, sc. 2, l. 418. Also *Comedy of Errors,* ii, 2; *Merry Wives of Windsor,* v, 5. Used frequently thereafter by other writers.

4
Rhyme yet out of reason.

John Skelton, *Against Garnesche.* No. iii, l. 128. (c. 1520)

5
I was promised on a time
To have reason for my rhyme;
From that time unto this season,
I received not rhyme nor reason.

Edmund Spenser, *Lines on His Promised Pension.* An apocryphal story relates that in 1590 Queen Elizabeth ordered Lord Burghley, the Lord Treasurer, to pay Spenser a hundred pounds, and when he objected to the amount, she said, "Then give him what is reason." Whereupon Burghley let the matter rest altogether, until the poet, by a rhymed appeal to his sovereign, secured the hundred pounds. It is certain that, in February, 1591, he did secure a pension of fifty pounds.

IV—Poetry: Its Power and Beauty

6
Gold, glory, greed! I loved you not for long;
Wine, women, war! seductive, but not strong;
One passion lasts—the deathless lust of Song.

Edmund Vance Cooke, *From the Book of Extenuations: David.*

7
And the shamed listeners knew the spell
That still enchants the years,
When the world's commonplaces fell
In music on their ears.

John Davidson, *A Ballad of a Poet Born.*

8
To ransom one lost moment with a rhyme,
Or, if fate cries and grudging gods demur,
To clutch Life's hair, and thrust one naked phrase
Like a lean knife between the ribs of Time.

Alfred Bruce Douglas, *The City of the Soul.*

9
Olympian bards who sung
Divine ideas below,
Which always find us young,
And always keep us so.

Ralph Waldo Emerson, *The Poet.*

Blake, Homer, Job, and you,
Have made old wine-skins new.
Your energies have wrought
Stout continents of thought.

Marianne Moore, *That Harp You Play So Well.*

10
God sent his Singers upon earth
With songs of sadness and of mirth,
That they might touch the hearts of men,
And bring them back to heaven again.

Longfellow, *The Singers.*

11
Never did Poesy appear
So full of heaven to me, as when
I saw how it would pierce through pride and fear
To the lives of coarsest men.

Lowell, *Incident in a Railroad Car.* St. 18.

Gently touching with the charm of poetry.
(Musæo contigens cuncta lepore.)

Lucretius, *De Rerum Natura.* Bk. iv, sec. 9.

12
We hold that the most wonderful and splendid proof of genius is a great poem produced in a civilized age.

Macaulay, *Essays: On Milton.*

13
Let the crowd delight in worthless things; for me may golden-haired Apollo minister full cups from the Castalian spring.
(Vilia miretur vulgus; mihi flavus Apollo
Pocula Castalia plena ministret aqua.)

Ovid, *Amores.* Bk. i, eleg. 15, l. 35. This couplet was used as the motto on the title page of Shakespeare's *Venus and Adonis.*

Great poets need no gentle reader; they hold him captive, however unwilling or hard to please.
(Non opus est magnis placido tectore poetis;
Quamlibet invitum difficilemque tenent.)

Ovid, *Epistulæ ex Ponto.* Bk. iii, epis. 4, l. 9.

Thanks, Muse, to thee; for thou dost lend me comfort, thou dost come as rest, as balm, to my sorrow. Thou art guide and comrade both.
(Gratia, Musa, tibi: nam tu solacia præbes
Tu curæ requies, tu medicina venis.
Tu dux et comes est.)

Ovid, *Tristia.* Bk. iv, eleg. 10, l. 117.

14
Drive my dead thoughts over the universe,
Like withered leaves, to quicken a new birth;
And, by the incarnation of this verse,
Scatter, as from an unextinguished hearth
Ashes and sparks, my words among mankind!
Be through my lips to unawakened Earth
The trumpet of a prophecy!

Shelley, *Ode to the West Wind.* Sec. 5.

1
A poem round and perfect as a star.
ALEXANDER SMITH, *A Life Drama*. Sc. 2.

2
Yea, is not even Apollo, with hair and harp-string of gold,
A bitter God to follow, a beautiful God to behold?
SWINBURNE, *Hymn to Proserpine*, l. 7.

3
Your lay, heavenly bard, is to me even as sleep on the grass to the weary, as in summer heat the slaking of thirst in a dancing rill of sweet water.
(Tale tuum carmen nobis, divine poeta,
Quale sopor fessis in gramine, quale per æstum
Dulcis aquæ saliente sitim restinguere rivo.)
VERGIL, *Eclogues*. No. v, l. 45.

V—Poetry and Immortality

4
No slightest golden rhyme he wrote
That held not something men must quote;
Thus by design or chance did he
Drop anchors to posterity.
T. B. ALDRICH, *A Hint from Herrick*.

Only write a dozen lines, and rest on your oars forever.
EMERSON, *Journals*. Vol. vii, p. 539.

I would rather risk for future fame upon one lyric than upon ten volumes.
OLIVER WENDELL HOLMES.

One simile that solitary shines
In the dry Desert of a thousand lines,
Or lengthen'd thought, that gleams thro' many a page,
Has sanctified whole poems for an age.
POPE, *Imitations of Horace: Epistles*. Bk. ii, epis. i, l. 111.

5
Sappho survives, because we sing her songs;
And Æschylus, because we read his plays!
ROBERT BROWNING, *Cleon*.

6
Poets alone are sure of immortality; they are the truest diviners of nature.
BULWER-LYTTON, *Caxtoniana*. Essay 27.

7
Like him I strive in hope my rhymes
May keep my name a little while,—
O child, who knows how many times
We two have made the angels smile!
WILLIAM CANTON, *A New Poet*.

8
Poets by Death are conquer'd but the wit
Of poets triumphs over it.
ABRAHAM COWLEY, *The Praise of Poetry*. Ode i, l. 13.

9
Even the gods must go;
Only the lofty Rhyme
Not countless years o'erthrow,—
Not long array of time.
AUSTIN DOBSON, *Ars Victrix*.

10
His instant thought the poet spoke,
And filled the age his fame;
An inch of ground the lightning strook
But lit the sky with flame.
EMERSON, *The Poet*.

11
Let no one honor me with tears, nor bury me with lamentation. Why? Because I fly from lip to lip, living in the mouths of men.
(Nemo me lacrymis decoret nec funera fletu
Faxit. Cur? volito vivus per ora virum.)
ENNIUS. Part of his epitaph. (CICERO, *Tusculanarum Disputationum*. Bk. i, ch. 15, sec. 34.)

I have reared a monument more enduring than bronze and loftier than the royal pyramids, one that no wasting rain, no unavailing north wind can destroy; no, not even the unending years nor the flight of time itself. I shall not wholly die. The greater part of me shall escape oblivion. (Exegi monumentum ære perennius Regalique situ pyramidum altius; Quod non imber edax, non Aquilo impotens Possit diruere aut innumerabilis Annorum series et fuga temporum. Non omnis moriar, multaque pars mei Vitabit Libitinam.)
HORACE, *Odes*. Bk. iii, ode 30, l. 1.

I've reared a monument alone
More durable than brass or stone;
Whose cloudy summit is more hid
Than regal height of pyramid.
HORACE, *Odes*, iii, 30, 1. (Coles, tr.)

Now have I finished a work which neither the wrath of Jove, nor fire, nor steel, nor all-consuming time can destroy. Welcome the day which can destroy only my body in ending my uncertain life. In my better part I shall be raised to immortality above the lofty stars, and my name shall never die.
OVID, *Metamorphoses*. Bk. xv, l. 871.

Not marble, nor the gilded monuments
Of princes, shall outlive this powerful rhyme.
SHAKESPEARE, *Sonnets*. No. lv.

12
Homer's harp is broken and Horace's lyre is unstrung, and the voices of the great singers are hushed; but their songs—their songs are immortal. O friend! what moots it to them or to us who gave this epic or that lyric to immortality? The singer belongs to a year, his song to all time.
EUGENE FIELD, *Love Affairs of a Bibliomaniac*, p. 99.

What difference does it make who spoke the words? They were uttered for the world. (Quid interest quis dixerit? Omnibus dixit.)
SENECA, *Epistulæ ad Lucilium*. Epis. xiv, 18.

Only to Beauty Time belongs;
Men may perish, But not their songs.
LOUIS GINSBERG, *Only to Beauty*.

13
Singing and rejoicing,
As aye since time began,
The dying earth's last poet
Shall be the earth's last man.
ANASTASIUS GRÜN, *The Last Poet*.

1
Thou shalt not all die; for while Love's fire shines
Upon his altar, men shall read thy lines.
ROBERT HERRICK, *Upon Himself.*

2
In his own verse the poet still we find,
In his own page his memory lives enshrined,
As in their amber sweets the smothered bees,—
As the fair cedar, fallen before the breeze,
Lies self-embalmed amidst the mouldering trees.
O. W. HOLMES, *Bryant's Seventieth Birthday.*

3
Where go the poet's lines?—
Answer, ye evening tapers!
Ye auburn locks, ye golden curls,
Speak from your folded papers!
O. W. HOLMES, *The Poet's Lot.*

4
Still breathes the love, still glows the ardor imparted to the lyre by the Æolian girl. (Spirat adhuc amor, Vivuntque commissi calores Æoliæ fidibus puellæ.)
HORACE, *Odes.* Bk. iv, ode 9, l. 10. Referring to Sappho.

The poet remains, dismember him as you will. (Invenias etiam disjecta membra poetæ.)
HORACE, *Satires.* Bk. i, sat. 4, l. 62.

5
Little snatch of ancient song,
What has made thee live so long?
Flying on thy wings of rhyme
Lightly down the depths of time.
W. E. H. LECKY, *On an Old Song.*

All things perish, and the strongest
Often do not last the longest;
The stately ship is seen no more,
The fragile skiff attains the shore;
And while the great and wise decay,
And all their trophies pass away,
Some sudden thought, some careless rhyme,
Still floats above the wrecks of Time.
W. E. H. LECKY, *On an Old Song.*

The bards sublime,
Whose distant footsteps echo
Through the corridors of Time.
LONGFELLOW, *The Day Is Done.*

6
Doth it not thrill thee, Poet,
Dead and dust though thou art,
To feel how I press thy singing
Close to my heart?
RICHARD LE GALLIENNE, *The Passionate Reader to His Poet.*

Like the river, swift and clear,
Flows his song through many a heart.
LONGFELLOW, *Oliver Basselin* St. 11.

7
O ye dead Poets, who are living still
Immortal in your verse, though life be fled,
And ye, O living Poets, who are dead
Though ye are living, if neglect can kill,
Tell me if in the darkest hours of ill,
With drops of anguish falling fast and red
From the sharp crown of thorns upon your head,
Ye were not glad your errand to fulfil?
LONGFELLOW, *The Poets.*

8
The Poet is the only potentate;
His sceptre reaches o'er remotest zones;
His thought remembered and his golden tones
Shall, in the ears of nations uncreate,
Roll on for ages and reverberate
When Kings are dust beside forgotten thrones.
LLOYD MIFFLIN, *The Sovereigns.*

9
Lap me in soft Lydian airs,
Married to immortal verse.
MILTON, *L'Allegro,* l. 136.

Wisdom married to immortal verse.
WORDSWORTH, *The Excursion.* Bk. vii, l. 536.

10
Remember me a little then, I pray,
The idle singer of an empty day.
WILLIAM MORRIS, *Earthly Paradise: Apology.*

11
Gowns will be rent to rags and gems and gold broken to fragments, but the fame which song brings lasts for ever. (Scindentur vester, gemmæ frangentur et aurum; Carmina quam tribuent, fama perennis erit.)
OVID, *Amores.* Bk. i, eleg. 10, l. 61.

Yea, though hard rocks and though the tooth of the enduring ploughshare perish with passing time, song is untouched by death. (Ergo, cum silices, cum dens patientis aratri Depereant ævo, carmina morte carent.)
OVID, *Amores.* Bk. i, eleg. 15, l. 31.

The poet's work endures. (Durat opus vatum.)
OVID, *Amores.* Bk. iii, eleg. 9, l. 29.

12
'Twas he that ranged the words at random flung,
Pierced the fair pearls and them together strung.
PILPAY, *Anvar-i Suhaili.* (Eastwick, tr.)

Go boldly forth, my simple lay,
Whose accents flow with artless ease,
Like orient pearls at random strung.
HAFIZ, *Song.* (Sir William Jones, tr.)

These pearls of thought in Persian gulfs were bred,
Each softly lucent as a rounded moon;
The diver Omar plucked them from their bed,
FitzGerald strung them on an English thread.
J. R. LOWELL, *In a Copy of Omar Khayyám.*

Jewels five-words-long
That on the stretch'd forefinger of all Time
Sparkle for ever.
TENNYSON, *The Princess.* Pt. ii, l. 355.

It came to him in rainbow dreams,
Blent with the wisdom of the sages,
Of spirit and of passion born;
In words as lucent as the morn
He prisoned it, and now it gleams
A jewel shining through the ages.
L. M. MONTGOMERY, *The Poet's Thought.*

1
Call it not vain:—they do not err
Who say that when the poet dies
Mute Nature mourns her worshipper,
And celebrates his obsequies.
SCOTT, *Lay of the Last Minstrel.* Canto v, st. 1.

2
I would rather be remembered by a song than by a victory.
ALEXANDER SMITH, *Dreamthorp: Men of Letters.*

There is no mere earthly immortality that I envy so much as the poet's. If your name is to live at all, it is so much better to have it live in people's hearts than only in their brains!
O. W. HOLMES, *The Poet at the Breakfast-Table.* Ch. 4.

3
How best to build the imperishable lay.
ROBERT SOUTHEY, *Carmen Nuptiale: Proem.*

He knew
Himself to sing, and build the lofty rhyme.
MILTON, *Lycidas,* l. 10.

4
To have the deep Poetic heart
Is more than all poetic fame.
TENNYSON, *The New Timon.*

5
Empires dissolve and peoples disappear:
Song passes not away.
Captains and conquerors leave a little dust,
And kings a dubious legend of their reign;
The swords of Cæsars, they are less than rust:
The poet doth remain.
WILLIAM WATSON, *Lacrimæ Musarum.*

VI—Poetry and Fame

6
How many, most famous while they lived, are utterly forgotten for want of writers! (Quam multos clarissimos suis temporibus viros scriptorum inops deleuit oblivio!)
BOETHIUS, *Philosophiæ Consolationis.* Bk. ii, prosa 7.

7
Verse, like the laurel, its immortal meed,
Should be the guerdon of a noble deed.
COWPER, *Charity,* l. 292.

Ofttimes with unseemly verse poets debase noble deeds. (Fere scriptores carmine fœdo Splendida facta linunt.)
HORACE, *Epistles.* Bk. ii, epis. 1, l. 236.

8
Their name, their years, spelt by th' unletter'd Muse.
GRAY, *Elegy in a Country Church-yard.* St. 20.

9
'Tis the Muse forbids the hero worthy of renown to perish; she enthrones him in the heavens. (Dignum laude virum Musa vetat mori: Cælo Musa beata.)
HORACE, *Odes.* Bk. iv, ode 8, l. 28.

Song forbids victorious deeds to die.
SCHILLER, *The Artists.*

10
Many heroes lived before Agamemnon; but all are overwhelmed in unending night, unwept, unknown, because they lacked a sacred bard.
(Vixere fortes ante Agamemnona
Multi; sed omnes inlacrimabiles
Urgentur ignotique longa
Nocte, carent quia vate sacro.)
HORACE, *Odes.* Bk. iv, ode 9, st. 7.

Before Atrides men were brave:
But ah! oblivion dark and long
Has locked them in a tearless grave,
For lack of consecrating song.
HORACE, *Odes,* iv, 9. (Conington, tr.)

Many valiant chiefs of old
Greatly lived and died before
Agamemnon, Grecian bold,
Waged the ten years' famous war.
But their names, unsung, unwept,
Unrecorded, lost and gone,
Long in endless night have slept,
And shall now no more be known.
HORACE, *Odes,* iv, 9. (Swift, tr.)

Brave men were living before Agamemnon
And since, exceeding valorous and sage,
A good deal like him too, but quite the same none;
But then they shone not on the poet's page.
BYRON, *Don Juan.* Canto i, st. 5.

Vain was the Chief's, the Sage's pride!
They had no Poet, and they died.
In vain they schemed, in vain they bled!
They had no Poet, and are dead.
POPE, *Imitations of Horace: Odes.* Bk. iv, ode 9, l. 13.

They built with bronze and gold and brawn,
The inner Vision still denied;
Their conquests . . . Ask oblivion! . . .
"They had no poet, and they died."
DON MARQUIS, *They Had No Poet.*

11
Past ruined Ilion Helen lives,
Alcestis rises from the shades;
Verse calls them forth; 'tis verse that gives
Immortal youth to mortal maids.

Soon shall Oblivion's deepening veil
Hide all the peopled hills you see,
The gay, the proud, while lovers hail
These many summers you and me.
W. S. LANDOR, *Past Ruined Ilion.*

12
How mighty, how sacred is the poet's task! He snatches all things from destruction and gives immortality to mortal men.
(O Sacer et magnus vatum labor! omnia fato
Eripis et populis donas mortalibus ævum.)
LUCAN, *De Bello Civili.* Bk. ix, l. 980.

13
Song makes great deeds immortal, cheats the tomb,
And hands down fame to ages yet to come.

(Carmine fit vivax virtus: expersque sepulcri,
Notitiam seræ posteritatis habet.)
OVID, *Epistulæ ex Ponto*. Bk. iv, epis. 8, l. 47.

1
I'll make thee glorious by my pen
And famous by my sword.
MARQUIS OF MONTROSE, *My Dear and Only Love.*

I'll make thee famous by my pen
And glorious by my sword.
SCOTT, *Legend of Montrose*. Ch. 15. An incorrect quotation of Montrose's lines.

2
'Tis meet for the great to be hymned in fairest song, for every noble deed dieth if suppressed in silence. (Πρέπει δ' ἐσλοῖσιν ὑμνεῖσθαι . . . καλλίσταις ἀοιδαῖς· . . . θνᾴσκει δὲ σιγαθὲν καλὸν ἔργον.)
PINDAR, *Alexandro Amynta*. Frag. 85.

3
Ascendant Phœbus watch'd that hour with care,
Averted half your parents' simple prayer,
And gave you beauty, but denied the pelf
That buys your sex a tyrant o'er itself. . . .
Kept dross for Duchesses, the world shall know it,
To you gave Sense, Good-humour, and a Poet.
POPE, *Moral Essays*. Epis. ii, l. 285.

4
When falls the soldier brave,
Dead at the feet of wrong,
The poet sings and guards his grave
With sentinels of song.
ABRAM J. RYAN, *Sentinel Songs*.

5
Your monument shall be my gentle verse,
Which eyes not yet created shall o'er-read,
And tongues to be your being shall rehearse
When all the breathers of this world are dead;
You still shall live—such virtue hath my pen—
Where breath most breathes, even in the mouths of men.
SHAKESPEARE, *Sonnets*. No. lxxxi.

6
Thy lord shall never die, the whiles this verse
Shall live, and surely it shall live for ever:
For ever it shall live, and shall rehearse
His worthy praise, and virtues dying never,
Though death his soul do from his body sever:
And thou thyself herein shalt also live:
Such grace the heavens do to my verses give.
SPENSER, *The Ruines of Time*, l. 253.

How many great ones may remembered be
Which in their days most famously did flourish,
Of whom no word we hear nor sign we see
But as things wiped out with a sponge do perish
Because they living cared not to cherish
No gentle wits, thro' pride or covetize,
Which might their name forever memorize.
SPENSER, *The Ruines of Time*, l. 358.

How strange a paradox is true,
That men who lived and died without a name,
Are the chief heroes in the sacred lists of fame.
SWIFT, *Ode to the Athenian Society*.

7
Illustrious acts high raptures do infuse,
And every conqueror creates a muse.
EDMUND WALLER, *Panegyric on Cromwell.*

Yet what he sung in his immortal strain,
Though unsuccessful, was not sung in vain; . . .
Like Phœbus thus, acquiring unsought praise,
He catched at love and filled his arm with bays.
EDMUND WALLER, *The Story of Phœbus and Daphne Applied.*

8
A great deal, my dear liege, depends
On having clever bards for friends.
What had Achilles been without his Homer?
A tailor, woollen-draper, or a comber!
JOHN WOLCOT, *A Moral Reflection: To George III.*

Small thought was his, in after-time
E'er to be hitched into a rhyme.
SCOTT, *Marmion:* Canto vi, *Introduction.*

9
Shall poesy, like law, turn wrong to right,
And dedications wash an Æthiop white?
YOUNG, *Love of Fame*. Sat. i, l. 27.

VII—Poetry and Love

10
There's many a would-be poet at this hour
Rhymes of a love that he hath never wooed,
And o'er his lamplit desk in solitude
Deems that he sitteth in the Muses' bower.
ROBERT BRIDGES, *The Growth of Love*. St. 11.

Young men, ay and maids,
Too often sow their wild oats in tame verse.
E. B. BROWNING, *Aurora Leigh*. Bk. i, l. 948.

11
Verse and nothing else have I to give you.
Other heights in other lives, God willing:
All the gifts from all the heights, your own, Love!
ROBERT BROWNING, *One Word More*. Sec. 12.

12
Love thou, and if thy love be deep as mine,
Thou wilt not laugh at poets.
BULWER-LYTTON, *Richelieu*. Act i, sc. 1, l. 177.

13
When amatory poets sing their loves
In liquid lines mellifluously bland,
And pair their rhymes as Venus yokes her doves.
BYRON, *Don Juan*. Canto v, st. 1.

Ovid's a rake, as half his verses show him,
Anacreon's morals are a still worse sample,
Catullus scarcely has a decent poem,
I don't think Sappho's Ode a good example,
Although Longinus tells us there is no hymn
Where the sublime soars forth on wings more ample;
But Virgil's songs are pure, except that horrid one
Beginning with "Formosum Pastor Corydon."
BYRON, *Don Juan*. Canto i, st. 42.

1
A Poet without Love were a physical and metaphysical impossibility.
CARLYLE, *Essays: Burns.*

A poet not in love is out at sea;
He must have a lay-figure.
P. J. BAILEY, *Festus: Home.*

Test of the poet is knowledge of love,
For Eros is older than Saturn or Jove.
EMERSON, *Quatrains: Casella.*

2
Oh love will make a dog howl in rhyme.
FLETCHER, *Queen of Corinth.* Act iv, sc. 1.

3
Poetry has not often been worse employed than in dignifying the amorous fury of a raving girl.
SAMUEL JOHNSON, *Works.* Vol. iv, p. 15.

4
Touchstone: Truly, I would the gods had made thee poetical.
Audrey: I do not know what "poetical" is: is it honest in deed and word? is it a true thing?
Touchstone: No, truly; for the truest poetry is the most feigning; and lovers are given to poetry.
SHAKESPEARE, *As You Like It.* Act iii, sc. 3, l. 15.

Never durst poet touch a pen to write
Until his ink were temper'd with Love's sighs.
SHAKESPEARE, *Love's Labour's Lost.* Act iv, sc. 3, l. 346.

5
But since he died, and poets better prove,
Theirs for their style I'll read, his for his love.
SHAKESPEARE, *Sonnets.* No. xxxii.

6
Song, made in lieu of many ornaments
With which my love should duly have been deck'd.
EDMUND SPENSER, *Epithalamion,* l. 427.

7
Had his fingers been able to toy with her hair
Would they then have written the verses fair?
JAMES THOMSON, *Art.* St. 3.

8
If Thought and Love desert us, from that day
Let us break off all commerce with the Muse.
WORDSWORTH, *Poems Suggested During a Tour.* No. 48.

VIII—Poetry and Poverty

9
A man should live in a garret aloof,
And have few friends, and go poorly clad,
With an old hat stopping the chink in the roof,
To keep the Goddess constant and glad.
THOMAS BAILEY ALDRICH, *The Flight of the Goddess.*

For who sings commonly so merry a note
As he that cannot chop or change a groat?
RICHARD BARNFIELD, *The Shepherd's Content.* St. 29.

10
Poets evermore are scant of gold.
E. B. BROWNING, *Aurora Leigh.* Bk. v, l. 1199.

11
Poverty is the Muse's patrimony.
ROBERT BURTON, *Anatomy of Melancholy.* Pt. i, sec. 2, mem. 3, subs. 15.

12
It is not poetry that makes men poor,
For few do write that were not so before,
And those that have writ best, had they been rich,
Had ne'er been clapp'd with a poetic itch.
SAMUEL BUTLER, *Miscellaneous Thoughts,* l. 440.

13
Let such forego the poet's sacred name,
Who rack their brains for lucre, not for fame.
BYRON, *English Bards and Scotch Reviewers,* l. 177.

No Muse is proof against a golden shower.
SAMUEL GARTH, *Claremont,* l. 14.

14
The man who weds the sacred Muse
Disdains all mercenary views.
CHARLES CHURCHILL, *The Ghost.* Bk. iii, l. 919.

15
Feel you the barren flattery of a rhyme?
Can poets soothe you, when you pine for bread,
By winding myrtle round your ruin'd shed?
GEORGE CRABBE, *The Village.* Bk. i.

16
If I'd as much money as I could tell,
I never would cry my songs to sell.
ADELAIDE CRAPSEY, *Vendor's Song.*

17
The poet is never the poorer for his song.
EMERSON, *Society and Solitude: Works and Days.*

18
A Cure for Poetry:—Seven wealthy towns contend for Homer dead,
Through which the living Homer begged his bread.
BENJAMIN FRANKLIN, *Poor Richard,* 1739. Quoting Thomas Seward. See 911:5.

My father discouraged me [from becoming a poet] by ridiculing my performances, and telling me verse-makers were generally beggars.
BENJAMIN FRANKLIN, *Autobiography.* Ch. 1.

19
And thou, sweet Poetry, thou loveliest maid,
Still first to fly where sensual joys invade; . . .
Thou source of all my bliss and all my woe,
That found'st me poor at first, and keep'st me so.
GOLDSMITH, *The Deserted Village,* l. 407.

Could a man live by it, it were not unpleasant employment to be a poet.
GOLDSMITH, *Letter to H. Goldsmith,* Feb., 1759.

20
Poets, Being poor,
Must use words with economy.
WILLIAM GRIFFITH, *Laconic.*

1
Poets, henceforth for pensions need not care,
Who call you beggars, you may call them liars,
Verses are grown such merchantable ware,
That now for Sonnets, sellers are, and buyers.
SIR JOHN HARINGTON, *A Comfort for Poor Poets.* 1633. (*Epigrams.* Bk. i, epig. 41.)

In rhyme, fine tinkling rhyme and flowing verse,
With now and then some sense; and he was paid for it,
Regarded and rewarded; which few poets are nowadays.
BEN JONSON, *Masque of the Fortunate Isles.* Alluding to Henry Scogan, tutor to the sons of Henry IV.

2
Barefaced poverty drove me to writing verses. (Paupertas impulit audax Ut versus facerem.)
HORACE, *Epistles.* Bk. ii, epis. 2, l. 51.

Indignation leads to the making of poetry. (Facit indignatio versum.)
JUVENAL, *Satires.* Sat. i, l. 79.

And poets by their sufferings grow,—
As if there were no more to do,
To make a poet excellent,
But only want and discontent.
SAMUEL BUTLER, *Miscellaneous Thoughts.* l. 437.

Most wretched men
Are cradled into poetry by wrong;
They learn in suffering what they teach in song.
SHELLEY, *Julian and Maddalo,* l. 544.

3
Dreaming on nought but idle poetry,
That fruitless and unprofitable art,
Good unto none; but least to the professors.
BEN JONSON, *Every Man in His Humour.* Act i, sc. 1.

4
You who compose sublime poetry in a cramped attic, that you may come forth worthy of an ivy wreath and an ugly statue. Beyond this, you have no hope of anything.
JUVENAL, *Satires.* Sat. vii, l. 27.

Let such as have not got a passport from nature be content with happiness, and leave to the poet the unrivalled possession of his misery, his garret, and his fame.
GOLDSMITH, *The Poet.* (*Critical Review,* 1759.)

5
Poverty! thou source of human art,
Thou great inspirer of the poet's song!
EDWARD MOORE, *Hymn to Poverty.*

Necessity may be the mother of lucrative invention, but it is the death of poetical.
WILLIAM SHENSTONE, *Writing and Books,* 63.

6
I am the poet of the poor. (Pauperibus vates ego sum.)
OVID, *Ars Amatoria.* Bk. ii, l. 165.

7
Poets were once the care of chieftains and of kings. (Cura ducum fuerant olim regumque poetæ.)
OVID, *Ars Amatoria.* Bk. iii, l. 405.

In a foolish world
The poet would be king.
WILLIAM GRIFFITH, *Demos.*

8
The bard whom pilfer'd pastorals renown,
Who turns a Persian tale for half-a-crown,
Just writes to make his barrenness appear,
And strains from hard-bound brains eight lines a year.
POPE, *Epistle to Dr. Arbuthnot,* l. 179.

9
For ne'er
Was flattery lost on Poet's ear;
A simple race! they waste their toil
For the vain tribute of a smile.
SCOTT, *Lay of the Last Minstrel.* Can. iv, st. 35.

Friendship, esteem, and fair regard,
And praise, the poet's best reward!
SCOTT, *Rokeby.* Canto i, st. 27.

10
Princess, inscribe beneath my name,
"He never begged, he never sighed,
He took his medicine as it came";
For this the poets lived—and died.
J. C. SQUIRE, *Ballade of the Poetic Life.*

11
And mighty Poets in their misery dead.
WORDSWORTH, *Resolution and Independence.* St. 17.

I thought of Chatterton, the marvellous Boy,
The sleepless Soul that perished in his pride;
Of Him who walked in glory and in joy
Following his plough, along the mountain-side:
By our own spirits are we deified:
We Poets in our youth begin in gladness;
But thereof come in the end despondency and madness.
WORDSWORTH, *Resolution and Independence.*

Poetry has never brought in enough to buy shoe-strings.
WILLIAM WORDSWORTH, *Remark.*

12
On earth what hath the poet? An alien breath.
THEODORE WATTS-DUNTON, *In a Graveyard.*

IX—Poetry: Its Technique

See also Sonnet; Writing: Careful Writing

13
Great thoughts in crude, unshapely verse set forth
Lose half their preciousness and ever must.
Unless the diamond with its own rich dust
Be cut and polished, it seems little worth.
THOMAS BAILEY ALDRICH, *On Reading.* Probably referring to Whitman.

14
I think it will be found that the grand style arises in poetry when a noble nature, poetically gifted, treats with simplicity or with severity a serious subject.
MATTHEW ARNOLD, *Controversy with Professor Newman on the Right Method of Translating Homer.*

1
Time was, ere yet in these degenerate days
Ignoble themes obtain'd ignoble praise,
When sense and wit with poesy allied,
No fabled graces, flourish'd side by side;
From the same fount their inspiration drew,
And, rear'd by taste, bloom'd fairer as they grew.

BYRON, *English Bards and Scotch Reviewers*, l. 103.

Yet Truth sometimes will lend her noblest fires,
And decorate the verse herself inspires:
This fact, in Virtue's name, let Crabbe attest,—
Though Nature's sternest painter, yet the best.

BYRON, *English Bards, Scotch Reviewers*, 855.

2
Let the verse the subject fit,
Little subject, little wit.
Namby Pamby is your guide.

HENRY CAREY, *Namby-Pamby*. (*Poems on Several Occasions*, p. 55. 1729) A satire on Ambrose Philips, of whose first name "Namby-Pamby" was intended as a diminutive.

And Namby-Pamby he preferr'd for wit.

POPE, *The Dunciad*. Bk. iii, l. 322. (1729) Also referring to Philips; changed in later editions to "Lo! Ambrose Philips is preferr'd for wit."

His namby-pamby madrigals of love.

WILLIAM GIFFORD, *The Baviad*. (1794) For Macaulay's note see APPENDIX.

3
Who often, but without success, have pray'd
For apt Alliteration's artful aid.

CHARLES CHURCHILL, *Prophecy of Famine*, l. 85.

Begot by butchers, but by bishops bred,
How high his Honour holds his haughty head.

UNKNOWN, *On Cardinal Wolsey*.

An Austrian army awfully arrayed,
Boldly by battery besieged Belgrade.

A. A. WATTS, *The Siege of Belgrade*. Alliterative poems in Latin are quite common, famous examples being those by Hamconius and Hucbald in C, and Placentius in P.

4
A poet does not work by square or line.

COWPER, *Conversation*, l. 789.

5
It is not metres, but a metre-making argument that makes a poem.

EMERSON, *Essays, Second Series: The Poet*.

Matches are made in heaven, and for every thought its proper melody and rhyme exists, though the odds are immense against our finding it, and only genius can rightly say the banns.

EMERSON, *Social Aims: Poetry and Imagination*.

6
A comic theme cannot be expressed in tragic verse. (Versibus exponi tragicis res comica non volt.)

HORACE, *Ars Poetica*, l. 89.

7
Poets one and all cannot brook the toil and tedium of the file. (Non offenderet unum Quemque poetarum limæ labor et mora.)

HORACE, *Ars Poetica*, l. 291.

O Poet, then, forbear
The loosely-sandalled verse,
Choose rather thou to wear
The buskin—strait and terse.
Leave to the tyro's hand
The limp and shapeless style;
See that thy form demand
The labour of the file.

AUSTIN DOBSON, *Ars Victrix*. A paraphrase of *L'Art*, by Théophile Gautier.

8
Return to the forge the badly-turned verses. (Male tornatos incudi reddere versus.)

HORACE, *Ars Poetica*, l. 441.

Put your parchment in the closet and keep it back until the ninth year. (Nonumque prematur in annum, Membranis intus positis.)

HORACE, *Ars Poetica*, l. 388.

I sit with sad civility, I read
With honest anguish and an aching head,
And drop at last, but in unwilling ears,
This saving counsel, "Keep your piece nine years."
"Nine years!" cries he, who, high in Drury Lane,
Lull'd by soft zephyrs thro' the broken pane,
Rhymes ere he wakes, and prints before Term ends,
Obliged by hunger and request of friends.

POPE, *Epistle to Dr. Arbuthnot*, l. 37.

9
Wheresoe'er I turn my view,
All is strange, yet nothing new:
Endless labour all along,
Endless labour to be wrong:
Phrase that Time has flung away,
Uncouth words in disarray,
Trick'd in antique ruff and bonnet,
Ode, and elegy, and sonnet.

SAMUEL JOHNSON, *Lines in Imitation of a Well-Known Author*. (BOSWELL, *Life*, 18 Sept., 1777. Croker's note.) A parody of Thomas Warton.

10
They write a verse as smooth, as soft as cream;
In which there is no torrent, nor scarce stream.

BEN JONSON, *Explorata: Ingeniorum*. Not. 5.

Soft creeping words on words the sense compose,
At ev'ry line they stretch, they yawn, they doze.

POPE, *The Dunciad*. Bk. ii. l. 389.

Smooth verse, inspired by no unlettered Muse.

WORDSWORTH, *The Excursion*. Bk. v, l. 262.

11
There are nine and sixty ways of constructing tribal lays,
And — every — single — one — of — them — is — right!

KIPLING, *In the Neolithic Age*.

12
gods i am pent in a cockroach
i with the soul of a dante
am mate and companion of fleas
i with the gift of a homer
must smile when a mouse calls me pal
tumble bugs are my familiars
this is the punishment meted
because i have written vers libre

DON MARQUIS, *the wail of archy*.

Writing free verse is like playing tennis with the net down.
ROBERT FROST, *Address,* at Milton Academy, Milton, Mass., 17 May, 1935.

Among our literary scenes,
Saddest this sight to me.
The graves of little magazines
That died to make verse free.
KEITH PRESTON, *The Liberators.*

1
I always make the first verse well, but I have trouble in making the others. (Je fais toujours bien le premier vers; mais j'ai peine à faire les autres.)
MOLIÈRE, *Les Précieuses Ridicules.* Sc. 11.

Nothing so difficult as a beginning
In poesy, unless perhaps the end.
BYRON, *Don Juan.* Canto iv, st. 1.

2
Confined to common life thy numbers flow,
And neither soar too high nor sink too low;
There strength and ease in graceful union meet,
Though polished, subtle, and though poignant, sweet;
Yet powerful to abash the front of crime
And crimson error's cheek with sportive rhyme.
(Verba togæ sequeris junctura callidus acri,
Ore teres modico, pallentis radere mores
Doctus et ingenuo culpam defigere ludo.)
PERSIUS, *Satires.* Sat. v, l. 14. (Gifford, tr.)

3
'Tis more to guide than spur the Muse's steed,
Restrain his fury than provoke his speed:
The winged courser, like a gen'rous horse,
Shows most true metal when you check his course.
POPE, *Essay on Criticism.* Pt. i, l. 84.

Some drily plain, without invention's aid,
Write dull receipts how poems may be made.
POPE, *Essay on Criticism.* Pt. i, l. 114.

The Muse whose early voice you taught to sing,
Prescribed her heights, and pruned her tender wing.
POPE, *Essay on Criticism.* Pt. iii, l. 176. Referring to Walsh, Pope's early patron.

4
Poets, like painters, thus unskill'd to trace
The naked nature and the living grace,
With gold and jewels cover every part,
And hide with ornaments their want of Art.
POPE, *Essay on Criticism.* Pt. ii, l. 93.

Poets heap virtues, painters gems, at will,
And show their zeal, and hide their want of skill.
POPE, *Moral Essays.* Epis. ii, l. 185.

5
His noble negligences teach
What others' toils despair to reach.
PRIOR, *Alma.* Canto ii, l. 7.

6
Hark at the lips of this pink whorl of shell
And you shall hear the ocean's surge and roar;
So in the quatrain's measure, written well,
A thousand lines shall all be sung in four!
FRANK DEMPSTER SHERMAN, *A Quatrain.* *See also* SEA: SEA-SHELLS.

7
Must intimate the whole, and say the smallest part.
WILLIAM WETMORE STORY, *The Unexpressed.*

8
Re-write the thrice re-written. Strive to say
Some older nothing in some newer way.
J. ST. LOE STRACHEY, *The Poetaster.*

9
Then, rising with Aurora's light,
The Muse invok'd, sit down to write;
Blot out, correct, insert, refine,
Enlarge, diminish, interline.
SWIFT, *On Poetry.*

Poets lose half the praise they should have got,
Could it be known what they discreetly blot.
EDMUND WALLER, *Upon the Earl of Roscommon's Translation of Horace,* l. 41.

For his chaste Muse employed her heaven-taught lyre
None but the noblest passions to inspire,
Not one immoral, one corrupted thought,
One line, which dying he could wish to blot.
GEORGE LYTTELTON, *Prologue to Thomson's Coriolanus.*

10
For I will for no man's pleasure
Change a syllable or measure;
Pedants shall not tie my strains
To our antique poets' veins;
Being born as free as these,
I will sing as I shall please.
GEORGE WITHER, *The Shepherd's Hunting.*

X—Poetry: Rhyme

11
Rhyme the rudder is of verses,
With which, like ships, they steer their courses.
BUTLER, *Hudibras.* Pt. i, canto i, l. 463.

12
Rhyme is the rock on which thou art to wreck.
DRYDEN, *Absalom and Achitophel.* Pt. ii, l. 486.

Till barbarous nations, and more barbarous times,
Debased the majesty of verse to rhymes.
DRYDEN, *To the Earl of Roscommon,* l. 11.

And rhyme began t' enervate Poetry.
DRYDEN, *To Sir Godfrey Kneller,* l. 50.

13
And like the canter of the rhymes,
That had a hoofbeat in their sound.
LONGFELLOW, *The Wayside Inn: Interlude before The Mother's Ghost.*

14
The troublesome and modern bondage of Rhyming.
MILTON, *Paradise Lost: Preface.*

Rhyme being no necessary Adjunct or true Ornament of Poem or good Verse, in longer Works especially, but the Invention of a barbarous Age, to set off wretched matter and lame Meter.
MILTON, *Paradise Lost: Preface.*

15
So I told them in rhyme,
For of rhymes I had store.
ROBERT SOUTHEY, *The Cataract of Lodore.*

Thick calf, fat foot, and slim knee,
Mounted on roof and chimney.

HORACE AND JAMES SMITH, *Rejected Addresses.* This couplet was introduced "by way of bravado, in answer to one who alleged that the English language contained no rhyme to chimney."

XI—Poetry: Metre

1
And the rolling anapæstic
Curled like vapour over shrines!

E. B. BROWNING, *Wine of Cyprus.* St. 10.

2
The fatal facility of the octosyllabic verse.

BYRON, *The Corsair: Preface.*

3
Trochee trips from long to short;
From long to long in solemn sort
Slow Spondee stalks; strong foot! yet ill able
Ever to come up with dactyl trisyllable.
Iambics march from short to long;—
With a leap and a bound the swift Anapæsts throng;
One syllable long, with one short at each side,
Amphibrachys hastes with a stately stride;—
First and last being long, middle short, Amphimacer
Strikes his thundering hoofs like a proud high-bred Racer.

S. T. COLERIDGE, *Metrical Feet.*

4
In the hexameter rises the fountain's silvery column:
In the pentameter aye falling in melody back.

S. T. COLERIDGE, *The Ovidian Elegiac Metre.*

Strongly it bears us along in swelling and limitless billows;
Nothing before and nothing behind but the sky and the ocean.

S. T. COLERIDGE, *The Homeric Hexameter.*

So the Hexameter, rising and singing, with cadence sonorous,
Falls; and in refluent rhythm back the Pentameter flows.

LONGFELLOW, *Elegiac Verse.*

5
A long syllable following a short is called an Iambus. (Syllaba longa brevi subjecta vocatur Iambus.)

HORACE, *Ars Poetica,* l. 251.

The bitter but wholesome iambic.

SIR PHILIP SIDNEY, *Apologie for Poetrie.* Pt. ii.

6
These equal syllables alone require,
Tho' oft the ear the open vowels tire,
While expletives their feeble aid do join,
And ten low words oft creep in one dull line.

POPE, *Essay on Criticism.* Pt. ii, l. 144.

XII—Poetry: Poetic Licence

7
Poets and painters, as all artists know,
May shoot a little with a lengthened bow. . . .
But make not monsters spring from gentle dams—
Birds breed not vipers, tigers nurse not lambs.

BYRON, *Hints from Horace,* l. 15.

8
The freer utterances of the poet's licence. (Poetarum licentiæ liberiora.)

CICERO, *De Oratore.* Bk. iii, ch. 38, sec. 153.

9
A man may be an admirable poet without being an exact chronologer.

DRYDEN, *Æneid: Dedication.*

Some force whole regions, in despite
O' geography, to change their site;
Make former times shake hands with latter,
And that which was before come after.
But those that write in rhyme still make
The one verse for the other's sake;
For one for sense, and one for rhyme,
I think 's sufficient at one time.

BUTLER, *Hudibras.* Pt. ii, canto i, l. 23.

10
According to that old verse . . . Astronomers, painters and poets may lie by authority.

SIR JOHN HARINGTON, *Apologie of Poetry.* Par. 3. (1591)

Besides, we Poets lie by good authority.

SIR JOHN HARINGTON, *Epigrams.* Bk. ii, No. 184.

Poets and painters by authoritie
As well as travelers we say may lie.

ROBERT HEATH, *Epigrams,* 35.

11
Painters and poets have always had an equal licence to dare anything. (Pictoribus atque poetis Quidlibet audendi semper fuit æqua potestas.)

HORACE, *Ars Poetica,* l. 9.

This the just right of poets ever was,
And will be still, to coin what words they please.

JOHN OLDHAM, *Horace's Art of Poetry Imitated.*

12
Measureless pours forth the creative licence of poets, nor trammels its utterance with history's truth. (Exit in immensum fecunda licentia vatum, Obligat historica nec sua verba fide.)

OVID, *Amores.* Bk. iii, eleg. 12, l. 41.

Good-bye to the fictions of the poets. (Valeant mendacia vatum.)

OVID, *Fasti.* Bk. vi, l. 253.

13
Using, as his habit is, a poet's licence. (Usus Poetæ, ut moris est, licentia.)

PHÆDRUS, *Fables.* Bk. iv, fab. 25, l. 8.

14
Fiction is the privilege of poets. (Tamen poetis mentiri licet.)

PLINY THE YOUNGER, *Epistles.* Bk. vi, epis. 21.

Odds life! must one swear to the truth of a song?

MATTHEW PRIOR, *A Better Answer*

In poetry there is always fallacy, and sometimes fiction.
SCOTT, *The Bride of Lammermoor*. Ch. 21.

1
And thought a lie in verse or prose the same;
That not in fancy's maze he wander'd long,
But stoop'd to truth, and moraliz'd his song.
POPE, *Epistle to Dr. Arbuthnot*, l. 339.

Fierce wars and faithful loves shall moralize my song.
SPENSER, *Faerie Queene: Introduction*. St. 1.

2
Poetic licence. (Licentia poetica.)
SENECA, *Naturales Quæstiones*, xliv, 1.

3
Unjustly poets we asperse:
Truth shines the brighter clad in verse,
And all the fictions they pursue
Do but insinuate what is true.
SWIFT, *To Stella*.

XIII—Poetry and Verse

4
I little read those poets who have made
A noble art a pessimistic trade,
And trained their Pegasus to draw a hearse
Through endless avenues of drooping verse.
THOMAS BAILEY ALDRICH, *Pessimistic Poets*.

What though, like a lady's waist,
All his lines are overlaced?
UNKNOWN, *To Thomas Bailey Aldrich*. (*Daily Tatler*, November, 1896.)

5
Our witty Boston Autocrat, Oliver Wendell Holmes, once playfully declared that Mr. Smith and Mrs. Brown were the two most popular poets in the United States. He had in mind the Reverend Samuel F. Smith, to whom we are indebted for "My Country, 'Tis of Thee," and Mrs. Phoebe Hinsdale Brown, who wrote the famous hymn which begins, "I love to steal away awhile from every slumbering care."
C. A. BROWNE, *The Story of Our National Ballads*.

6
One fine day,
Says Mister Mucklewraith to me. says he,
"So! you've a poet in your house," and smiled.
"A poet? God forbid," I cried; and then
It all came out: how Andrew slyly sent
Verse to the paper; how they printed it
In Poet's Corner.
ROBERT BUCHANAN, *Poet Andrew*, l. 161.

7
A quaint farrago of absurd conceits,
Out-babying Wordsworth and out-glittering Keats.
BULWER-LYTTON, *The New Timon*. Pt. i.

8
I too can hunt a poetaster down.
BYRON, *English Bards and Scotch Reviewers*, l. 1064.

9
Swans sing before they die—'twere no bad thing
Did certain persons die before they sing.
S. T. COLERIDGE, *Epigram*.

Sir, I admit your general rule,
That every poet is a fool,
But you yourself may serve to show it,
That every fool is not a poet.
S. T. COLERIDGE, *Epigram*.

Your poem must eternal be,
Dear Sir! it cannot fail!
For 'tis incomprehensible,
And without head or tail.
S. T. COLERIDGE, *To the Author of the Ancient Mariner*.

10
Made poetry a mere mechanic art.
COWPER, *Table Talk*, l. 654.

11
Doeg, though without knowing how or why,
Made still a blund'ring kind of melody;
Spurr'd boldly on, and dash'd through thick and thin,
Through sense and nonsense, never out nor in;
Free from all meaning, whether good or bad,
And in one word, heroically mad.
DRYDEN, *Absalom and Achitophel*. Pt. ii, l. 412. "Doeg": Elkanah Settle.

O gracious God! How far have we
Profan'd thy Heav'nly gift of Poesy!
Made prostitute and profligate the Muse,
Debas'd to each obscene and impious use,
Whose Harmony was first ordain'd Above,
For Tongues of Angels and for Hymns of Love!
DRYDEN, *To the Pious Memory of Mrs. Anne Killigrew*. St. 4.

12
Oh, hapless land of mine! whose country-presses
Labour with poets and with poetesses;
Where Helicon is quaffed like beer at table,
And Pegasus is "hitched" in every stable.
A. J. H. DUGANNE, *Parnassus in Pillory*.

Their scallop-shells so many bring
The fabled founts of song to try,
They've drained, for aught I know, the spring
Of Aganippe dry.
WHITTIER, *My Namesake*. St. 3.

13
Thy trivial harp will never please
Or fill my craving ear;
Its chords should ring as blows the breeze,
Free, peremptory, clear. . . .
The kingly bard
Must smite the chords rudely and hard,
As with hammer or with mace.
EMERSON, *Merlin*.

14
Modern poets mix too much water with their ink. (Neuere Poeten thun viel Wasser in die Tinte.)
GOETHE, *Sprüche in Prosa*, iii. Quoting Sterne.

15
Verses void of thought, sonorous trifles. (Versus inopes rerum nugæque canoræ.)
HORACE, *Ars Poetica*, l. 322.

His verses run with a halting foot. (Incomposito pede currere versus.)
HORACE, *Satires*. Bk. i, sat. 10, l. 9.

The line, too, labours, and the words move slow
POPE, *Essay on Criticism*. Pt. ii, l. 171.

This is the very false gallop of verses.
SHAKESPEARE, *As You Like It*. Act iii, sc. 2, l. 119.

1
Great noble wits, be good unto yourselves,
And make a difference 'twixt poetic elves
And poets: all that dabble in the ink
And defile quills are not those few can think.
BEN JONSON, *The Staple of News: Prologue*.

2
They sway'd about upon a rocking-horse.
And thought it Pegasus.
JOHN KEATS, *Sleep and Poetry*, l. 186.

3
Some ladies now make pretty songs,
And some make pretty nurses:
Some men are good for righting wrongs,
And some for writing verses.
F. LOCKER-LAMPSON, *The Jester's Plea*.

4
The zeal of fools offends at any time,
But most of all the zeal of fools in rhyme.
POPE, *Imitations of Horace: Epistles*. Bk. ii, epis. 1, l. 406.

5
And that would set my teeth nothing on edge
Nothing so much as mincing poetry:
'Tis like the forced gait of a shuffling nag.
SHAKESPEARE, *I Henry IV*. Act iii, sc. 1, l. 133.

6
A flawless cup: how delicate and fine
The flowing curve of every jewelled line!
Look, turn it up or down, 'tis perfect still,—
But holds no drop of life's heart-warming wine.
HENRY VAN DYKE, *The Empty Quatrain*.

7
There have been many most excellent poets that never versified, and now swarm many versifiers that need never answer to the name of poets.
SIR PHILIP SIDNEY, *Apologie for Poetrie*. Pt. ii.

One may be a poet without versing, and a versifier without poetry.
SIR PHILIP SIDNEY, *Apologie for Poetrie*. Pt. ii.

8
Men endowed with highest gifts,
The vision and the faculty divine;
Yet wanting the accomplishment of verse.
WORDSWORTH *The Excursion*. Bk. i, l. 78.

XIV—Poetry and Prose

9
Who all in raptures their own works rehearse.
And drawl out measur'd prose, which they call verse.
CHARLES CHURCHILL, *Independence*, l. 295.

And with poetic trappings grace thy prose.
COWPER, *The Task*. Bk. v, l. 679.

10
For all those pretty knacks you compose,
Alas, what are they but poems in prose?
SIR JOHN DENHAM, *To the Five Members of the Hon. House of Commons*, l. 41.

11
I wish our clever young poets would remember my homely definitions of prose and poetry; that is, prose,—words in their best order; poetry,—the best words in their best order.
S. T. COLERIDGE, *Table Talk*, 12 July, 1827.

Poetry has done enough when it charms, but prose must also convince.
H. L. MENCKEN, *Prejudices*. Ser. iii, p. 166.

12
A kind of hobbling prose,
That limped along, and tinkled in the close.
DRYDEN, *To the Earl of Roscommon*, l. 13.

13
Our poetry in the eighteenth century was prose; our prose in the seventeenth, poetry.
J. C. AND A. W. HARE, *Guesses at Truth*.

14
Truth is enough for prose:
Calmly it goes
To tell just what it knows.

For verse, skill will suffice—
Delicate, nice
Casting of verbal dice.

Poetry, men attain
By subtler pain
More flagrant in the brain—

An honesty unfeigned,
A heart unchained,
A madness well restrained.
CHRISTOPHER MORLEY, *At the Mermaid Cafeteria*.

15
And he whose fustian 's so sublimely bad,
It is not poetry, but prose run mad.
POPE, *Epistle to Dr. Arbuthnot*, l. 187.

Who says in verse what others say in prose.
POPE, *Imitations of Horace: Epistles*. Bk. ii, epis. i, l. 202.

16
One merit of poetry few persons will deny: it says more and in fewer words than prose.
VOLTAIRE, *A Philosophical Dictionary: Poets*.

17
There is in Poesy a decent pride,
Which well becomes her when she speaks to Prose,
Her younger sister.
YOUNG, *Night Thoughts*. Night v, l. 64.

XV—Poetry Old and New

18
And Marlowe, Webster, Fletcher, Ben,
Whose fire-hearts sowed our furrows when
The world was worthy of such men.
E. B. BROWNING, *A Vision of Poets*, l. 400.

God's prophets of the Beautiful,
These Poets were.
E. B. BROWNING, *A Vision of Poets*, l. 292.

1
You speak As one who fed on poetry.
BULWER-LYTTON, *Richelieu*. Act i, sc. 1.

2
Oh, the bards of olden days, blessed bards in song-craft skilled,
Happy henchmen of the Muses, when the field was yet untilled.
CHŒRILUS. (ARISTOTLE, *Rhetoric*. Bk. iii, ch. 14, sec. 4. Sandys, tr.)

3
In every cell and every blooming bower
The sweetness of old lays is hovering still.
HARTLEY COLERIDGE, *Whither Is Gone the Wisdom and the Power?*

I love the old melodious lays
Which softly melt the ages through,
The songs of Spenser's golden days,
Arcadian Sidney's silver phrase,
Sprinkling our noon of time with freshest morning dew.
WHITTIER, *Proem*.

4
Subtract from many modern poets all that may be found in Shakespeare, and trash will remain.
C. C. COLTON, *Lacon*. No. 568.

5
My Muse is rightly of the English strain,
That cannot long one fashion entertain.
MICHAEL DRAYTON, *Idea*.

6
You admire, Vacerra, only the poets of old and praise only those who are dead. Pardon me, Vacerra, if I think death too great a price to pay for your praise.
MARTIAL, *Epigrams*. Bk. viii, ep. 49.

7
It stands on record, that in Richard's times
A man was hang'd for very honest rhymes.
POPE, *Imitations of Horace: Satires*. Bk. ii, sat. 1. l. 145. Referring, perhaps, to John Ball, reputed author of "When Adam dolve and Eve span, Who was then the gentleman?", hanged during the reign of Richard II. *See* ANCESTRY.

8
Poets that lasting marble seek
Must come in Latin or in Greek.
EDMUND WALLER, *Of English Verse*.

9
Old-fashioned poetry, but choicely good.
WALTON, *The Compleat Angler*. Pt. i, ch. 4.

It was written in the homespun verse of that time and people.
BENJAMIN FRANKLIN, *Autobiography*. Ch. 1.

10
Come Muse migrate from Greece and Ionia,
Cross out please those immensely overpaid accounts, . . .
Placard "Removed" and "To Let" on the rocks of your snowy Parnassus, . . .
For know a better, fresher, busier sphere,
a wide, untried domain awaits, demands you.
WALT WHITMAN, *Song of the Exposition*. Sec. 2.

POETS

I—Poets: Definitions

11
Poets are all who love, who feel great truths,
And tell them.
P. J. BAILEY, *Festus: Another and a Better World*.

Many are poets who have never penn'd
Their inspiration, and perchance the best: . . .
Many are poets but without the name,
For what is poesy but to create
From overfeeling good or ill; and aim
At an external life beyond our fate?
BYRON, *The Prophecy of Dante*. Canto iv, l. 1.

12 For poets (bear the word),
Half-poets even, are still whole democrats.
E. B. BROWNING, *Aurora Leigh*. Bk. iv, l. 314.

13
All great poets have been men of great knowledge.
BRYANT, *Lectures on Poetry: Relation of Poetry to Time and Place*.

No man was ever yet a great poet without being at the same time a profound philosopher.
S. T. COLERIDGE, *Biographia Literaria*. Ch. 15.

14
He that works and *does* some Poem, not he that merely *says* one, is worthy of the name of Poet.
CARLYLE, *Cromwell's Letters and Speeches: Introduction*.

How does the poet speak to men with power, but by being still more a man than they.
CARLYLE, *Essays: Burns*.

It is a man's sincerity and depth of vision that makes him a poet.
CARLYLE, *Heroes and Hero-Worship*. Lect. iii.

15
Most joyful let the Poet be;
It is through him that all men see.
WILLIAM ELLERY CHANNING, *The Poet of the Old and New Times*.

16
Party-Poets are like wasps, who dart
Death to themselves, but to their foes but smart.
GEORGE CRABBE, *The Newspaper*, l. 11.

17
A poet is the painter of the soul.
ISAAC D'ISRAELI, *Literary Character*. Ch. 20.

The poet must be alike polished by an intercourse with the world as with the studies of taste; one to whom labour is negligence, refinement a science, and art a nature.
ISAAC D'ISRAELI, *Literary Character of Men of Genius: Vers de Société*.

18
Poets should be law-givers; that is, the boldest lyric inspiration should not chide and insult, but should announce and lead the civil code, and the day's work.
EMERSON, *Essays, First Series: Of Prudence*.

The sign and credentials of the poet are that he announces that which no man has foretold.
EMERSON, *Essays, Second Series: The Poet*.

1
What are our poets, take them as they fall,
Good, bad, rich, poor, much read, not read at all?
Them and their works in the same class you'll find—
They are the mere wastepaper of mankind.
BENJAMIN FRANKLIN, *Paper.*

2
The poet is the truest historian.
JAMES ANTHONY FROUDE, *Homer.*

We call those poets who are first to mark
Through earth's dull mist the coming of the dawn,—
Who see in twilight's gloom the first pale spark,
While others only note that day is gone.
O. W. HOLMES, *Memorial Verses: Shakespeare.*

Poets, the first instructors of mankind.
HORACE, *Ars Poetica,* l. 449. (Dillon, tr.)

The true poet is all-knowing! he is an actual world in miniature.
NOVALIS, *Fragment.* (Carlyle, tr.)

3
A poet is that which by the Greeks is called κατ' ἐξοχὴν, ὁ Ποιητής, a maker, or a feigner: . . . from the word ποιεῖν, which signifies to make, or feign. Hence he is called a poet.
BEN JONSON, *Explorata: Poeta.*

4
If men will impartially, and not asquint, look toward the offices and function of a poet, they will easily conclude to themselves the impossibility of any man's being the good poet without first being a good man.
BEN JONSON, *Volpone: Dedication.*

A poet's soul must contain the perfect shape of all things good, wise and just. His body must be spotless and without blemish, his life pure, his thoughts high, his studies intense.
AUGUSTINE BIRRELL, *Obiter Dicta: Second Series: Milton.*

5
They shall be accounted poet kings
Who simply tell the most heart-easing things.
JOHN KEATS, *Sleep and Poetry,* l. 267.

6
Nothing is more certain than that great poets are no sudden prodigies but slow results.
J. R. LOWELL, *My Study Windows: Chaucer.*

7
He who would not be frustrate of his hope to write well hereafter in laudable things ought himself to be a true poem.
MILTON, *Apology for Smectymnuus.*

He who would write heroic poems should make his whole life a heroic poem.
CARLYLE, *Essays: Schiller.*

8
A poet is a nightingale who sits in darkness and sings to cheer its own solitude with sweet sounds.
SHELLEY, *A Defence of Poetry.*

Poets are the hierophants of an unapprehended inspiration; the mirrors of the gigantic shadows which futurity casts upon the present.
SHELLEY, *A Defence of Poetry.*

9
The tadpole poet will never grow into anything bigger than a frog; not though in that stage of development he should puff and blow himself till he bursts with windy adulation at the heels of the laureled ox.
SWINBURNE, *Under the Microscope.*

II—Poets: Apothegms

10
An eager meagre servant of the Muses. (Μουσάων θεράπων ὀτρηρός.)
ARISTOPHANES, *The Birds,* l. 909.

11
They all are off their native heath—
Shake, Mulleary and Go-ethe.
H. C. BUNNER, *Shake, Mulleary and Go-ethe.*

12
When people say, "I've told you *fifty* times,"
They mean to scold, and very often do;
When poets say, "I've written *fifty* rhymes,"
They make you dread that they'll recite them too.
BYRON, *Don Juan.* Canto i, st. 108.

13
Spare the poet for his subject's sake.
COWPER, *Charity,* l. 636.

They best can judge a poet's worth,
Who oft themselves have known
The pangs of a poetic birth
By labours of their own.
COWPER, *To Dr. Darwin.* St. 2.

Poets! not in Arabia alone
You get beheaded when your skill is gone.
THOMAS BAILEY ALDRICH, *The World's Way.*

14
Idleness, that is the curse of other men, is the nurse of poets.
D'ARCY CRESSWELL, *The Poet's Progress.*

15
All men are poets at heart.
EMERSON, *Nature, Addresses, and Lectures: Literary Ethics.*

Every man will be a poet if he can; otherwise a philosopher or man of science. This proves the superiority of the poet.
H. D. THOREAU, *Journal,* 11 April, 1852.

16
The experience of each new age requires a new confession, and the world seems always waiting for its poet.
EMERSON, *Essays, Second Series: the Poet.*

17
The poet's business is not to save the soul of man but to make it worth saving.
JAMES ELROY FLECKER. (UNTERMEYER, *Modern British Poetry,* p. 533.)

18
Those who err follow the poets.
The Koran. Ch. 26. The Oriental belief is that poets are prompted by devils with such scraps of angels' converse as they can hear by stealth.

1
Next to being a great poet, is the power of understanding one.

LONGFELLOW, *Hyperion*. Bk. ii, ch. 3.

2
He is upbraidingly called a Poet, as if it were a most contemptible nickname.

BEN JONSON, *Explorata: Jam Literæ Sordent.*

Slight not the songsmith.

WILLIAM WATSON, *England My Mother*. Pt. i.

3
He does not write whose verses no one reads. (Non scribit, cujus carmina nemo legit.)

MARTIAL, *Epigrams*. Bk. iii, ep. 9, l. 2.

Enthusiast, go, unstring the lyre;
In vain thou sing'st if none admire,
How sweet soe'er the strain.

WILLIAM WHITEHEAD, *The Enthusiast.*

4
God's most candid critics are those of his children whom he has made poets.

SIR WALTER RALEIGH THE YOUNGER, *Oxford Poetry, 1914: Preface.*

5
The poet who does not revere his art, and believe in its sovereignty, is not born to wear the purple.

E. C. STEDMAN, *Poets of America*. Ch. 9.

6
For pointed satire I would Buckhurst choose,
The best good man with the worst-natured muse.

JOHN WILMOT, EARL OF ROCHESTER, An allusion to Horace, *Satires*. Bk. i, sat. 10, l. 64.

Thou best humour'd man with the worst humour'd muse.

GOLDSMITH, *Retaliation; Postscript*, last line. Quoted. Referring to Caleb Whitefoord.

But you're *our* partic'lar author, you're our patriot and our friend,
You're the poet of the cuss-word an' the swear.

EDGAR WALLACE, *Tommy to his Laureate*. Referring to Rudyard Kipling.

III—Poets: Born, Not Made

7
Sure there are poets which did never dream
Upon Parnassus, nor did taste the stream
Of Helicon; we therefore may suppose
Those made not poets, but the poets those.

SIR JOHN DENHAM, *Cooper's Hill.*

8
Each year new consuls and proconsuls are made; but not every year is a king or a poet born. (Consules fiunt quotannis et novi proconsules: Solus aut rex aut poeta non quotannis nascitur.)

FLORUS, *De Qualitate Vitæ*. Fragment 8. Hence the proverb, "Poeta nascitur, non fit," the poet is born, not made.

And, therefore, is an old proverb, Orator fit, poeta nascitur.

SIR PHILIP SIDNEY, *Apologie for Poetrie.* (1595)

9
A good poet's made as well as born.

BEN JONSON, *To the Memory of Shakespeare.*

10
The god makes not the poet; but
The thesis, vice-versa put,
Should Hebrew-wise be understood:
And means, the poet makes the god.

MATTHEW PRIOR, *Epistle to Fleetwood Shepherd.* No. i, l. 62.

11
No man is so born a poet but that he needs to be regenerated into a poetic artist.

JOHN STERLING, *Essays and Tales: Thoughts and Images.*

IV—Poets: Their Madness

12
All poets are mad.

ROBERT BURTON, *Anatomy of Melancholy. Democritus to the Reader.*

13
For that fine madness still he did retain,
Which rightly should possess a poet's brain.

DRAYTON, *To Henry Reynolds: Of Poets and Poesy*, l. 109.

The man is mad, or else he's writing verses. (Aut insanit homo aut versus facit.)

HORACE, *Satires*. Bk. ii, sat. 7, l. 117. The line is spoken by Davus, Horace's slave, referring to his master's eccentric habits.

14
Perhaps no person can be a poet, or even enjoy poetry, without a certain unsoundness of mind.

MACAULAY, *Essays: Milton.*

15
Prince of sweet songs made out of tears and fire.
A harlot was thy nurse, a God thy sire;
Shame soiled thy song, and song assoiled thy shame.
But from thy feet now death has washed the mire,
Love reads out first, at head of all our choir,
Villon, our sad bad glad mad brother's name.

SWINBURNE, *Ballad of François Villon: Envoi.*

Mad verse, sad verse, glad verse and bad verse.

JOHN TAYLOR THE WATER-POET. Title of book. (1644)

How sad and mad and bad it was,
But then, how it was sweet!

ROBERT BROWNING, *Confessions.*

V—Poets: Their Inspiration

16
Shuddering they drew her garments off—and found
A robe of sackcloth next the smooth, white skin.
Such, poets, is your bride, the Muse! young, gay,
Radiant, adorn'd outside; a hidden ground
Of thought and of austerity within.

MATTHEW ARNOLD, *Austerity of Poetry.*

1
The world but feels the present's spell,
The poet feels the past as well;
Whatever men have done, might do,
Whatever thought, might think it too.
MATTHEW ARNOLD, *Bacchanalia*. Pt. ii, l. 65.

Not deep the Poet sees, but wide.
MATTHEW ARNOLD, *Resignation*, l. 212.

Poets, who bear buckets to the well
Of ampler draught.
E. B. BROWNING, *Aurora Leigh*. Bk. vi, l. 135.

2
For as nightingales do upon glow-worms feed,
So poets live upon the living light.
P. J. BAILEY, *Festus: Home*.

3
I cast my nets in many streams
To catch the silver fish of dreams.
KARLE WILSON BAKER, *Poet Songs*.

4
The "vision and the faculty divine"
Come not by dreaming; he whose eye is clear
To read the present, reads the future sign,
The truest seer.
HENRY MONTAGU BUTLER, *The Seer*. See 1529:8.

5
Homer's words are as costly and admirable to Homer as Agamemnon's victories are to Agamemnon.
EMERSON, *Essays, Second Series: The Poet*.

6
Like a Chimborazo under the line, running up from a torrid base through all the climates of the globe.
EMERSON, *Essays, Second Series: The Poet*.

With a poet, as with a mountain, the altitude is reckoned by the highest point.
R. U. JOHNSON, *Poems of Fifty Years: Preface*.

7
Do not judge the poet's life to be sad because of his plaintive verses and confessions of despair. Because he was able to cast off his sorrows into these writings, therefore went he onward free and serene to new experiences.
EMERSON, *Journals*. Vol. v, p. 520.

Slow comes the verse that real woe inspires:
Grief unaffected suits but ill with art,
Or flowing numbers with a bleeding heart.
THOMAS TICKELL, *To the Earl of Warwick, on the Death of Mr. Addison*, l. 6.

8
'Tis one of the mysteries of our condition that the poet seems sometimes to have a mere talent,—a chamber in his brain into which an angel flies with divine messages, but the man, apart from this privilege, commonplace. . . . Poets are not to be seen.
EMERSON, *Journals*. Vol. x, p. 360.

9
Turnpike is one thing and blue sky another. Let the poet, of all men, stop with his inspiration. The inexorable rule in the muse's court, *either inspiration or silence*, compels the bard to report only his supreme moments.
EMERSON, *Letters and Social Aims: Poetry and Imagination*.

10
If bright the sun, he tarries,
All day his song is heard;
And when he goes he carries
No more baggage than a bird.
EMERSON, *The Poet*.

Ever the Poet *from* the land
Steers his bark and trims his sail;
Right out to sea his courses stand,
New worlds to find in pinnace frail.
EMERSON, *Quatrains: Poet*.

Tell men what they knew before,
Paint the prospect from their door,
Give to barrows, trays, and pans
Grace and glimmer of romance.
EMERSON, *Quatrain*.

11
Whatever can happen to man has happened so often that little remains for fancy or invention. We have all been born; we have most of us been married; and so many have died before us, that our deaths can supply but few materials for a poet.
SAMUEL JOHNSON, *Works*, ii, 408. (Hawkins, ed.)

Knowledge of the subject is to the poet what durable materials are to the architect.
SAMUEL JOHNSON, *Works*, ii, 408.

To tell of disappointment and misery, to thicken the darkness of futurity, and perplex the labyrinth of uncertainty, has always been a delicious employment of the poets.
SAMUEL JOHNSON, *Works*, iv, 110.

12
A stewed poet? he doth sit like an unbraced drum, with one of his heads beaten out; for that you must note, a poet hath two heads as a drum has: one for making, the other repeating!
BEN JONSON, *The Staple of News: Induction*.

13
Bards of Passion and of Mirth,
Ye have left your souls on earth!
Ye have souls in heaven too,
Double-lived in regions new.
JOHN KEATS, *Ode*. Written on the blank page before Beaumont and Fletcher's *The Fair Maid of the Inn*, and thus addressed to these bards in particular.

14
As fire is kindled by fire, so is a poet's mind kindled by contact with a brother poet.
JOHN KEBLE, *Lectures on Poetry*. No. 16.

15
Content, with meagre scrip and pilgrim staff,
Singing he journeys through the changeful years;
At whiles, he stays to laugh with those that laugh;
Anon, his way lies through the Vale of Tears.
JAMES B. KENYON, *The Singing Pilgrim*.

He flings a Romany ballad
Out through his prison bars
And, deaf, he sings of nightingales
Or, blind, he sings of stars.

MARY SINTON LEITCH, *The Poet.*

1
Nine-tenths of the best poetry of the world has been written by poets less than thirty years old; a great deal more than half of it has been written by poets under twenty-five.

H. L. MENCKEN, *Prejudices.* Ser. iii, p. 147.

2
Read from some humbler poet,
Whose songs gushed from his heart,
As showers from the clouds of summer,
Or tears from the eyelids start;

Who, through long days of labor,
And nights devoid of ease,
Still heard in his soul the music
Of wonderful melodies.

LONGFELLOW, *The Day Is Done.*

3
Poets have forgotten that the first lesson of literature, no less than of life, is the learning how to burn your own smoke; that the way to be original is to be healthy; . . . and that to make the common marvellous . . . is the test of genius.

J. R. LOWELL, *My Study Windows: Chaucer.*

4
A poet, soaring in the high region of his fancies, with his garland and singing robes about him.

MILTON, *Church Government.* Bk. ii, Intro.

5
Through moving waters of his mind
He daily drags thought's seine along,
Hoping within its mesh to find
A song!

J. R. MORELAND, *The Poet.*

6
Dreamer of dreams, born out of my due time,
Why should I strive to set the crooked straight?
Let it suffice me that my murmuring rhyme
Beats with light wing against the ivory gate,
Telling a tale not too importunate
To those who in the sleepy region stay,
Lulled by the singer of an empty day.

WILLIAM MORRIS, *Earthly Paradise: Apology.*

7
Whether verses are good for aught, I doubt; they have always been my bane. . . . Would that the Muses had looked away when I began to write, and Phœbus refused to aid me when my attempt was new. (An prosint, dubium, nocuerunt carmina semper; . . . Aversis utinam tetigissem carmina Musis, Phœbus et inceptum destituisset opus!)

OVID, *Amores.* Bk. iii, eleg. 12, l. 13.

8
There is a god within us; we are in touch with heaven: from celestial places comes our inspiration. (Est deus in nobis, et sunt commercia cæli: Sedibus ætheriis spiritus ille venit.)

OVID, *Ars Amatoria.* Bk. iii, l. 549.

There is a god within us. It is when he stirs that our bosom warms; it is his impulse that sows the seeds of inspiration. (Est deus in nobis; agitante calescimus illo: Impetus hic sacræ semina mentis habet.)

OVID, *Fasti.* Bk. vi, l. 5.

9
To build from matter is sublimely great,
But gods and poets only can create.

WILLIAM PITT, *To the Unknown Author of the Battle of the Sexes.*

10
All good poets, epic as well as lyric, compose their beautiful poems not as works of art, but because they are inspired and possessed.

PLATO, *Ion.* Sec. 533.

Poets utter great and wise things which they do not themselves understand.

PLATO, *The Republic.* Bk. ii, sec. 5.

11
If I could dwell Where Israfel
Hath dwelt, and he where I,—
He might not sing so wildly well
A mortal melody,
While a bolder note than his might swell
From my lyre within the sky.

EDGAR ALLAN POE, *Israfel.*

12
While pensive Poets painful vigils keep,
Sleepless themselves to give their readers sleep.

POPE, *The Dunciad.* Bk. i, l. 93.

13
Curst be the verse, how well soe'er it flow,
That tends to make one worthy man my foe,
Give Virtue scandal, Innocence a fear,
Or from the soft-eyed virgin steal a tear!

POPE, *Epistle to Dr. Arbuthnot,* l. 283.

14
Where stray ye, Muses! in what lawn or grove, . . .
In those fair fields where sacred Isis glides,
Or else where Cam his winding vales divides?

POPE, *Pastorals: Summer,* l. 23.

Rise, honest Muse! and sing the Man of Ross.

POPE, *Moral Essays.* Epis. iii, l. 250. The Man of Ross was John Kyrle, of Herefordshire.

15
Verse comes from Heav'n, like inward light;
Mere human pains can ne'er come by't;
The god, not we, the poem makes;
We only tell folks what he speaks.

PRIOR, *Epistle to Fleetwood Shepherd,* l. 41.

16
Sweet the exultance of song, but the strain that precedes it is sweeter,
And never was poem yet writ, but the meaning outmastered the metre.

RICHARD REALF, *Indirection.*

No song's pinions ever can
Quite out-soar the heart of man!

RICHARD ROWLEY, *To a Poet.*

1
The degree in which a poet's imagination dominates reality is, in the end, the exact measure of his importance and dignity.

GEORGE SANTAYANA, *The Life of Reason*. Vol. iv, p. 114.

2
O for a Muse of fire, that would ascend
The brightest heaven of invention.

SHAKESPEARE, *Henry V: Prologue*, l. 1.

3
The poet's eye, in a fine frenzy rolling,
Doth glance from heaven to earth, from earth to heaven;
And as imagination bodies forth
The forms of things unknown, the poet's pen
Turns them to shapes, and gives to airy nothing
A local habitation and a name.

SHAKESPEARE, *A Midsummer-Night's Dream*. Act v, sc. 1, l. 12.

4
Thus, great with child to speak, and helpless in my throes,
Biting my truant pen, beating myself for spite:
"Fool!" said my Muse to me, "look in thy heart, and write."

SIR PHILIP SIDNEY, *Astrophel and Stella*. Sonnet i. See 2251:10.

For voices pursue him by day,
And haunt him by night,
And he listens, and needs must obey,
When the Angel says, "Write!"

LONGFELLOW, *The Poet and His Songs*.

Would you have your songs endure?
Build on the human heart!

ROBERT BROWNING, *Sordello*. Bk. ii.

"Give me a theme," the little poet cried,
"And I will do my part,"
" 'Tis not a theme you need," the world replied;
"You need a heart."

R. W. GILDER, *Wanted, a Theme*.

5
The poet in a golden clime was born,
With golden stars above;
Dower'd with the hate of hate, the scorn of scorn,
The love of love.

TENNYSON, *The Poet*.

6
Vex not thou the poet's mind
With thy shallow wit;
Vex not thou the poet's mind,
For thou canst not fathom it.
Clear and bright it should be ever,
Flowing like a crystal river,
Bright as light, and clear as wind.

TENNYSON, *The Poet's Mind*.

7
The Poet gathers fruit from every tree,
Yea, grapes from thorns and figs from thistles he.
Plucked by his hand, the basest weed that grows
Towers to a lily, reddens to a rose.

WILLIAM WATSON, *Four Epigrams*.

The statue—Buonarroti said—doth wait,
Thralled in the block for me to liberate.
The poem—saith the poet—wanders free
Till I betray it to captivity.

WILLIAM WATSON, *Four Epigrams*.

VI—Poets: Their Virtues

8
Happy who in his verse can gently steer
From grave to light, from pleasant to severe.
(Heureux qui, dans ses vers, sait d'une voix légère
Passer de grave au doux, du plaisant au sévère.)

BOILEAU, *L'Art Poétique*. Canto i, l. 75. (Dryden, tr.)

Form'd by thy converse, happily to steer
From grave to gay, from lively to severe.

POPE, *Essay on Man*. Epis. iv, l. 379.

9
O brave poets, keep back nothing,
Nor mix falsehood with the whole!
Look up Godward; speak the truth in
Worthy song from earnest soul:
Hold, in high poetic duty,
Truest Truth the fairest Beauty!

E. B. BROWNING, *The Dead Pan*. St. 39.

10
I reckon, when I count at all,
First Poets—then the Sun—
Then Summer—then the Heaven of God—
And then the list is done.
But looking back—the first so seems
To comprehend the whole—
The others look a needless show,
So I write Poets—All.

EMILY DICKINSON, *Poems*. Pt. vi, No. 9.

11
True poets are the guardians of the state.

WENTWORTH DILLON, *Essay on Translated Verse*, l. 356.

12
There was never poet who had not the heart in the right place.

EMERSON, *Society and Solitude: Success*.

13
By many hands the work of God is done,
Swart toil, pale thought, flushed dream, he spurneth none:
Yea! and the weaver of a little rhyme
Is seen his worker in his own full time.

RICHARD LE GALLIENNE, *English Poems: Inscription*, p. 105.

14
All that is best in the great poets of all countries is not what is national in them, but what is universal.

LONGFELLOW, *Kavanagh*. Ch. 20.

15
The clear, sweet singer with the crown of snow

Not whiter than the thoughts that housed
below!
J. R. LOWELL, *Epistle to George William Curtis: Postscript*, l. 43.

1
"But how divine is utterance!" she said. "As we to the brutes, poets are to us."
GEORGE MEREDITH, *Diana of the Crossways*. Ch. 16.

2
Bravo, O poet! (Euge, poeta!)
PERSIUS, *Satires*. Sat. i, l. 75.

The flower of poets. (Flos poetarum.)
PLAUTUS, *Casina: Prologue*, l. 18.

He could songes make and well indite.
CHAUCER, *Canterbury Tales: Prologue*, l. 95.

3
Let me for once presume t' instruct the times,
To know the Poet from the man of rhymes:
'Tis he who gives my breast a thousand pains.
Can make me feel each passion that he feigns,
Enrage, compose, with more than magic art,
With pity and with terror tear my heart,
And snatch me o'er the earth, or thro' the air,
To Thebes, to Athens, when he will, and
where.
POPE, *Imitations of Horace: Epistles*. Bk. ii, epis. i, l. 340.

The varying verse, the full resounding line,
The long majestic march, and energy divine.
POPE, *Imitations of Horace: Epistles*. Bk. ii, epis. i, l. 268. Referring to Dryden.

4
I learnt life from the poets.
MADAME DE STAËL, *Corinne*. Bk. xviii, ch. 5.

5
He is a poet strong and true
Who loves wild thyme and honey-dew;
And like a brown bee works and sings
With morning freshness on his wings,
And a golden burden on his thighs,—
The pollen-dust of centuries!
MAURICE THOMPSON, *Wild Honey*.

6
Blessings be with them—and eternal praise,
Who gave us nobler loves, and nobler
cares,—
The Poets, who on earth have made us heirs
Of truth and pure delight by heavenly lays!
WORDSWORTH, *Personal Talk*. Sonnet iv.

7
His virtues formed the magic of his song.
UNKNOWN, *Inscription*, on the tomb of William Cowper, l. 10. (See HAYLEY, *Life of Cowper*. Vol. iv, p. 189.)

VII—Poets: Their Shortcomings

8
I agree with one of your reputable critics that a taste for drawing-rooms has spoiled more poets than ever did a taste for gutters.
THOMAS BEER, *The Mauve Decade*, p. 235.

9
"Poets needs must be
Or men or women—more's the pity"—"Ah,
But men, and still less women, happily,
Scarce need be poets."
E. B. BROWNING, *Aurora Leigh*. Bk. ii, l. 90.

10
I do distrust the poet who discerns
No character or glory in his times.
E. B. BROWNING, *Aurora Leigh*. Bk. v, l. 189.

Your poet who sings how Greeks
That never were, in Troy which never was,
Did this or the other impossible great thing.
ROBERT BROWNING, *Mr. Sludge "The Medium."*

11
Yet half a beast is the great god Pan,
To laugh as he sits by the river,
Making a poet out of a man:
The true gods sigh for the cost and the pain—
For the reed that grows nevermore again
As a reed with the reeds in the river.
E. B. BROWNING, *A Musical Instrument*.

12
I have never yet known a poet who did not think himself the best. (Adhuc neminem cognovi poetam, qui sibi non optimus videretur.)
CICERO, *Tusculanarum Disputationum*. Bk. v, ch. 22, sec. 63.

13
The worst tragedy for a poet is to be admired
through being misunderstood.
JEAN COCTEAU, *Le Rappel à l'Ordre*, p. 10.

14
Poor slaves in metre, dull and addle-pated,
Who rhyme below ev'n David's Psalms trans-
lated.
DRYDEN, *Absalom and Achitophel*. Pt. ii, l. 402.

Poets, like disputants, when reasons fail,
Have one sure refuge left, and that's to rail.
DRYDEN, *All for Love: Epilogue*, l. 1.

15
Poets have often nothing poetical about them except their verses.
EMERSON, *Conduct of Life: Behavior*.

Poets are prosy in their common talk,
As the fast trotters, for the most part, walk.
O. W. HOLMES, *The Banker's Secret*.

16
Our poets are men of talents who sing, and not the children of music.
EMERSON, *Essays, Second Series: The Poet*.

17
Of course poets have morals and manners of their own, and custom is no argument with them.
THOMAS HARDY, *Hand of Ethelberta*. Ch. 2.

18
Beggar is jealous of beggar and poet of poet.
(Καὶ πτωχὸς πτωχῷ φθονέει καὶ ἀοιδὸς ἀοιδῷ.)
HESIOD, *Works and Days*, l. 26.

Envy's a sharper spur than pay:
No author ever spar'd a brother;
Wits are gamecocks to one another.
JOHN GAY, *Fables: The Elephant and the Bookseller*, l. 74.

Poets are sultans, if they had their will;
For every author would his brother kill.
ROGER B. ORRERY, *Prologues*.

Every poet in his kind
Is bit by him that comes behind.
SWIFT, *On Poetry: A Rhapsody*, l. 341.

1
That poets should be mediocre, neither men, nor gods, nor booksellers ever permitted. (Mediocribus esse poetis Non homines, non di, non concessere columnæ.)
HORACE, *Ars Poetica*, l. 372.

Third-rate poets no one knows, and but few know those who are good. (Mediocres poetas nemo novit; bonos pauci.)
TACITUS, *Dialogues de Oratoribus*. Sec. 10.

Let's strive to be the best; the Gods, we know it,
Pillars and men, hate an indifferent Poet.
ROBERT HERRICK, *Parcel-gilt Poetry*.

For there's no second-rate in poetry.
JOHN OLDHAM, *An Ode on St. Cecilia's Day*.

2
Men of sense fear to come in contact with a raging poet. (Vesanum tetigisse timent fugientque poetam Qui sapiunt.)
HORACE, *Ars Poetica*, l. 455.

All these fear verses and detest poets. (Omnes hi metuunt versus, odere poetas.)
HORACE, *Satires*. Bk. i, sat. 4, l. 33.

I hate all Boets and Bainters.
GEORGE I OF ENGLAND. (CAMPBELL, *Life of Lord Mansfield*, ch. 30, note.)

But was there ever such stuff as the great part of Shakespeare? Is it not sad stuff? But one must not say so.
GEORGE III OF ENGLAND, *Remark*, to Miss Burney.

3
Doctors undertake a doctor's work; carpenters handle carpenter's tools: but, skilled or unskilled, we scribble poetry, all alike.
HORACE, *Epistles*. Bk. ii, epis. 1, l. 116.

4
The irritable tribe of poets. (Genus irritabile vatum.)
HORACE, *Epistles*. Bk. ii, epis. 2, l. 102.

We poets are, in every age and nation,
A most absurd, wrong-headed generation.
SOAME JENYNS, *Imitation of Horace*. Bk. ii, epis. 1.

We poets are (upon a poet's word)
Of all mankind, the creatures most absurd.
POPE, *Imitations of Horace: Epistles*. Bk. ii, epis. 1, l. 358.

A poetical tempest arises. (Poetica surgit Tempestas.)
JUVENAL, *Satires*. Sat. xii, l. 24.

5
It costs less to keep a lion than a poet; the poet's belly is more capacious. (Constat leviori belua sumptu Nimirum et capiunt plus intestina poetæ.)
JUVENAL, *Satires*. Sat. vii, l. 77.

6
The passionate heart of the poet is whirl'd
into folly and vice.
TENNYSON, *Maud*. Pt. i, sec. 4.

7
Dear Madam, take it from me, no Man . . . is more dreadful than a Poet.
WILLIAM WYCHERLEY, *Love in a Wood*. (1672)

I am as barren and hidebound as one of your scribbling poets.
WYCHERLEY, *Love in a Wood*. Act i, sc. 2.

VIII—The Poet and His Song

See also Song and Singer

8
Dropped feathers from the wings of God
My little songs and snatches are.
KARLE WILSON BAKER, *Poet Songs*.

9
And I made a rural pen,
And I stained the water clear,
And I wrote my happy songs
Every child may joy to hear.
WILLIAM BLAKE, *Reeds of Innocence*.

10
Content, as random fancies might inspire,
If his weak harp at times or lonely lyre
He struck with desultory hand, and drew
Some softened tones, to Nature not untrue.
W. L. BOWLES, *Sonnet*.

11
O my uncared-for songs, what are ye worth,
That in my secret book, with so much care,
I write you, this one here and this one there,
Marking the time and order of your birth?
ROBERT BRIDGES, *The Growth of Love*. St. 51.

12
Many tender souls
Have strung their losses on a rhyming thread,
As children cowslips.
E. B. BROWNING, *Aurora Leigh*. Bk. i, l. 946.

13
Piping a vagrant ditty free from Care.
ROBERT BUCHANAN, *Pastoral Pictures*.

14
Some rhyme a neebor's name to lash;
Some rhyme (vain thought!) for needfu' cash;
Some rhyme to court the country clash,
An' raise a din;
For me, an aim I never fash—
I rhyme for fun.
BURNS, *Epistle to James Smith*. St. 5.

I am nae poet, in a sense,
But just a rhymer like by chance,
An' hae to learning nae pretence;
Yet, what the matter?
Whene'er my Muse does on me glance,
I jingle at her.
BURNS, *Epistle to John Lapraik*. St. 9.

15
There is a pleasure in poetic pains
Which only poets know
COWPER, *The Task*. Bk. ii, l. 285. Quoted by Wordsworth, *Miscellaneous Sonnets*. Sonnet xix, l. 1.

16
Yea, though he sang not, he was unto song

A light, a benediction.
JOHN DRINKWATER, *The Dead Critic.*

1
Good people all, of every sort,
Give ear unto my song;
And if you find it wondrous short,
It cannot hold you long.
OLIVER GOLDSMITH, *Elegy on the Death of a Mad Dog.*

2
To write a verse or two, is all the praise
That I can raise.
GEORGE HERBERT, *Praise.*

I sing of brooks, of blossoms, birds, and bowers,
Of April, May, of June, and July flowers;
I sing of May-poles, hock-carts, wassails, wakes,
Of bridegrooms, brides, and of their bridal-cakes.
I write of Youth, of Love, and have access
By these, to sing of cleanly wantonness.
I sing of dews, of rains, and, piece by piece,
Of balm, of oil, of spice, and ambergris.
I sing of times trans-shifting; and I write
How roses first came red, and lilies white.
ROBERT HERRICK, *The Argument of His Book.*

3
I sometimes sit beneath a tree
And read my own sweet songs.
O. W. HOLMES, *The Last Reader.*

I know not why, but even to me
My songs seem sweet when read to thee.
HENRY TIMROD, *A Trifle.*

4
For dear to Gods and man is sacred song.
Self-taught I sing; by Heav'n, and Heav'n alone,
The genuine seeds of poesy are sown.
HOMER, *Odyssey.* Bk. xxii, l. 382. (Pope, tr.)

5
A humble bard, I fashion laborious songs.
(Operosa parvus Carmina fingo.)
HORACE, *Odes.* Bk. iv, ode 2, l. 31.

But if you rank me among lyric bards,
With my exalted head I touch the stars.
(Quodsi me lyricis vatibus inseris,
Sublimi feriam sidera vertice.)
HORACE, *Odes.* Bk. i, ode 1, l. 35.

6
My poesy was, "The deeper, the sweeter."
BEN JONSON, *Every Man in His Humour.* Act ii, sc. 4.

7
But since the world with writing is possest,
I'll versify in spite; and do my best
To make as much waste-paper as the rest.
JUVENAL, *Satires.* Sat. i, l. 23. (Dryden, tr.)

8
Could I but speak it and show it,
This pleasure more sharp than pain,
That baffles and lures me so,
The world should once more have a poet,
Such as it had
In the ages glad,
Long ago!
J. R. LOWELL, *In the Twilight.*

9
Lo! he am I whose light verse yields to none;
Reader, thy love, not awe, methinks I've won
Let greater men strike loftier notes: I earn
Enough if my small themes oft to thy hands return.
(Ille ego sum nulli nugarum laude secundus
Quem non miraris sed puto, lector, amas.
Majores majora sonent: mihi parva locuto
Sufficit in vestras sæpe redire manus.)
MARTIAL, *Epigrams.* Bk. ix, epig. 1.

10
Better be a cornfed bard, writing lyrics by the yard, with an appetite so gay it won't balk at prairie hay, than to have a mighty pile, and forget the way to smile!
WALT MASON, *Plutocrat and Poet.*

11
More safe I sing with mortal voice, unchang'd
To hoarse or mute, though fall'n on evil days,
On evil days though fall'n, and evil tongues.
MILTON, *Paradise Lost.* Bk. vii, l. 24.

12
My unpremeditated verse.
MILTON, *Paradise Lost.* Bk. ix, l. 24.

And as in Beauty's bower he pensive sate,
Pour'd forth this unpremeditated lay,
To charms as fair as those that soothed his happier day.
BYRON, *Childe Harold.* Canto i, st. 84.

The unpremeditated lay.
SCOTT, *The Lay of the Last Minstrel: Introduction,* l. 18.

A bard here dwelt, more fat than bard beseems
Who, void of envy, guile, and lust of gain,
On virtue still, and nature's pleasing themes,
Poured forth his unpremeditated strain.
JAMES THOMSON, *The Castle of Indolence.* Canto i, st. 68. Thomson himself is meant by "a bard here dwelt," and in a footnote he says: "The following lines of this stanza were writ by a friend of the author." The friend is supposed to have been Lord Lyttelton.

13
As yet a child, nor yet a fool to fame,
I lisp'd in numbers, for the numbers came.
POPE, *Epistle to Dr. Arbuthnot,* l. 127.

In numbers warmly pure and sweetly strong.
WILLIAM COLLINS, *Ode to Simplicity,* l. 3.

By magic numbers and persuasive sound.
CONGREVE, *The Mourning Bride.* Act i, sc. 1.

To add to golden numbers golden numbers.
THOMAS DEKKER, *Patient Grissell.* Act i, sc. 1.

14
For I was taught in Paradise
To ease my breast of melodies.
KEATS, *Faery Song.*

15
And song is as foam that the sea-winds fret,
Though the thought at its heart should be deep as the sea.
SWINBURNE, *Poems and Ballads. Second Series: Dedication.*

16
Ring out, ring out my mournful rhymes,
But ring the fuller minstrel in!
TENNYSON, *In Memoriam.* Pt. cvi, st. 5.

1
I do but sing because I must,
And pipe but as the linnets sing.
Tennyson, *In Memoriam*. Pt. xxi, st. 6.

I sing but as the linnet sings.
Goethe, *Wilhelm Meister:* Bk. ii, ch. 11, *The Harper's Song*. (Carlyle, tr.)

Soft as a bubble sung
Out of a linnet's lung.
Ralph Hodgson, *Eve*.

I was singing as a bird mourns. (Je chantais comme l'oiseau gémit.)
Lamartine, *Le Poète Mourant*.

2
The Doric reed once more
Well-pleased, I tune.
Thomson, *The Seasons: Autumn*, l. 3.

3
I, too, have songs; me also the shepherds call a poet, but I trust them not. For as yet, methinks, I sing nothing worthy of a Varius or a Cinna, but gabble as a goose among melodious swans. (Sed argutos inter strepere anser olores.)
Vergil, *Eclogues*. No. ix, l. 33.

When to my haughty spirit I rehearse
My verse,
Faulty enough it seems; yet sometimes when
I measure it by that of other men,
Why, then—
I see how easily it might be worse.
J. T. Trowbridge, *An Odious Comparison*.

4
Wake, Betsy, wake, my sweet galoot!
Rise up, fair lady, while I touch my lute!
Artemus Ward, *Among the Fenians*.

5
I sound my barbaric yawp over the roofs of the world.
Walt Whitman, *Song of Myself*. Sec. 52.

6
If I had peace to sit and sing,
Then I could make a lovely thing;
But I am stung with goads and whips,
So I build songs like iron ships.
Let it be something for my song,
If it is sometimes swift and strong.
Anna Wickham, *The Singer*.

7
Surely there was a time I might have trod
The sunlit heights, and from life's dissonance
Struck one clear chord to reach the ears of
God.
Oscar Wilde, *Helas!* Lines prefixed to his poems, Paris edition, 1903.

8
I have seized life by the poetic side.
Franz Woepcke. (Emerson, *Journals*, 1868.)

9
The moving accident is not my trade;
To freeze the blood I have no ready arts:
'Tis my delight, alone in summer shade,
To pipe a simple song for thinking hearts.
Wordsworth, *Hart-leap Well*. Pt. ii, st. 1.

He murmurs near the running brooks
A music sweeter than their own.
Wordsworth, *A Poet's Epitaph*, l. 39.

The harvest of a quiet eye
That broods and sleeps on his own heart.
Wordsworth, *A Poet's Epitaph*, l. 51.

POISON

10
When the Fates will, two poisons work for good. (Cum fata volunt, bina venena juvant.)
Ausonius, *Epigrams*. No. iii, l. 12.

Venom destroys venom.
Langland, *Piers Plowman*. Passus xxi, l. 156.

11
The gnat that sings his summer's song
Poison gets from Slander's tongue.
The poison of the snake and newt
Is the sweat of Envy's foot.
The poison of the honey-bee
Is the artist's jealousy. . . .
The strongest poison ever known
Came from Cæsar's laurel crown.
William Blake, *Auguries of Innocence*, l. 45.

12
The poisons are our principal medicines, which kill the disease, and save the life.
Emerson, *Conduct of Life: Considerations by the Way*.

13
Tobacco, coffee, alcohol, hashish, prussic acid, strychnine, are weak dilutions: the surest poison is time.
Emerson, *Society and Solitude: Old Age*.

14
The coward's weapon, poison.
Phineas Fletcher, *Sicelides*. Act v, sc. 3.

15
One drop of poison infecteth the whole tun of wine.
John Lyly, *Euphues*, p. 39.

A little poison embitters much sweetness.
Unknown, *Old English Homilies*. Ser. i, p. 23. (c. 1175)

16
What to some is food, to others may be sharp poison. (Quod aliis cibus est, aliis fuat acre venenum.)
Lucretius, *De Rerum Natura*. Bk. iv, l. 638.

What's one man's poison, signior,
Is another's meat or drink.
Beaumont and Fletcher, *Love's Cure*. Act iii, sc. 2.

And one man's meat, another's poison is.
John Taylor the Water-Poet, *Works*, p. 254.

Wan Lo has made an amazing discovery.
"I have found," he cries,
"That what is one man's poison
Is another man's poison."
Henry Harrison, *Wan Lo Tanka*.

17
A little poison now and then: that causeth pleasant dreams; and much poison at last for an easy death.
Nietzsche, *Thus Spake Zarathustra*. Sec. 5.

1
Wicked poisons lurk in sweet honey. (Inpia sub dulci melle venena latent.)
Ovid, *Amores*. Bk. i, eleg. 8, l. 104.
See also Sweetness: Sweet and Bitter.

2
I know too well the poison and the sting
Of things too sweet.
Adelaide Ann Procter, *Per Pacem ad Lucem.*

3
Poison is drunk from cups of gold. (Venenum in auro bibitur.)
Seneca, *Thyestes*, l. 453.

Poison is poison though it comes in a golden cup.
Thomas Adams, *Works*, p. 705. (1630)

4
I bought an unction of a mountebank,
So mortal that, but dip a knife in it,
Where it draws blood no cataplasm so rare,
Collected from all simples that have virtue
Under the moon, can save the thing from death
That is but scratch'd withal.
Shakespeare, *Hamlet*. Act iv, sc. 7, l. 142.

Then, venom, to thy work.
Shakespeare, *Hamlet*. Act v, sc. 2, l. 333.

5
In poison there is physic.
Shakespeare, *II Henry IV*. Act i, sc. 1, l. 137.

Sweet, sweet, sweet poison for the age's tooth.
Shakespeare, *King John*. Act i, sc. 1, l. 213.

6
They love not poison that do poison need.
Shakespeare, *Richard II*. Act v, sc. 6, l. 38.

7
Let me have
A dram of poison, such soon-speeding gear
As will disperse itself through all the veins
That the life-weary taker may fall dead
And that the trunk may be discharg'd of breath
As violently as hasty powder fir'd
Doth hurry from the fatal cannon's womb.
Shakespeare, *Romeo and Juliet*. Act v, sc. 1, l. 59.

8
Oh! you do bear a poison in your mind
That would not let you rest in Paradise.
Charles Jeremiah Wells, *Joseph and His Brethren*. Act iii, sc. 1.

9
He kissed her cold corpse a thousand times o'er,
And called her his jewel though she was no more;
And he drank all the pison like a lovyer so brave,
And Villikins and Dinah lie buried in one grave.
Unknown, *Villikins and Dinah*. George Augustus Sala (*Autobiography*) states that this ballad is older than the age of Elizabeth; modern version interpolated by Henry Mayhew in his *Wandering Minstrel*.

POLAND

10
Hope of the half-defeated; house of gold,
Shrine of the sword and tower of ivory.
Hilaire Belloc.

Mr. Belloc has put the Polish ideal into lines dedicated to a great Polish shrine.
Chesterton, *Generally Speaking*, p. 53.

11
She, like the eagle, will renew her age,
And fresh historic plumes of Fame put on,—
Another Athens after Marathon,
Where eloquence shall fulmine, arts refine.
Thomas Campbell, *Lines on Poland*, l. 30.

12
He smote the sledded Polacks on the ice.
Shakespeare, *Hamlet*. Act i, sc. 1, l. 63.

13
The heart of Poland hath not ceased
To quiver, tho' her sacred blood doth drown
The fields, and out of every smouldering town
Cries to Thee.
Tennyson, *Poland*, l. 3.

POLICE

14
Ah, take one consideration with another—
A policeman's lot is not a happy one.
W. S. Gilbert, *The Pirates of Penzance*. Act ii.

15
A fiend, a fury, pitiless and rough;
A wolf, nay, worse, a fellow all in buff;
A back-friend, a shoulder-clapper, one that countermands
The passages of alleys, creeks and narrow lands;
A hound that runs counter and yet draws dry-foot well;
One that before the judgement carries poor souls to hell.
Shakespeare, *The Comedy of Errors*. Act iv, sc. 2, l. 35.

16
Thou art pinch'd for't now.
Shakespeare, *The Tempest*. Act v, sc. 1, l. 74.

17
Policemen are soldiers who act alone; soldiers are policemen who act in unison.
Herbert Spencer, *Social Statics*. Pt. iii, ch. 21, sec. 8.

18
A lidless watcher of the public weal.
Tennyson, *The Princess*. Pt. iv, l. 306.

19
You'll be copped, then.
Thomas Terrell, *Lady Delmar*. Act i.

There were cries of "Coppers, coppers!" in the yard.
Thomas Terrell, *Lady Delmar*. Act i.

POLICY, see Cunning

POLITENESS, see Courtesy, Manners

POLITICS

See also Statesman; Vote and Voting

I—Politics: Definitions

1
Man is a political animal. (Πολιτικὸν ὁ ἄνθρωπος.)

Aristotle, *Politics*. Bk. i, ch. 1, sec. 10. The complete quotation is: "And why man is a political animal in a greater measure than any bee or any gregarious animal, is clear. For nature does nothing without purpose, and man alone of the animals possesses speech."

Learn'd or unlearn'd, we all are politicians.

Soame Jenyns, *Imitations of Horace*. Bk. ii, epis. 1.

2
There is no gambling like politics.

Benjamin Disraeli, *Endymion*. Ch. 82.

There is nothing in which the power of circumstances is more evident than in politics.

Benjamin Disraeli, *Life of Bentinck*.

3
A good deal of our politics is physiological.

Emerson, *Conduct of Life: Fate*.

4
Politics, like religion, hold up torches of martyrdom to the reformers of error.

Thomas Jefferson, *Writings*. Vol xiii, p. 69.

There is a holy mistaken zeal in politics as well as religion. By persuading others we convince ourselves.

Junius, *Letters*. No. 35, 19 Dec., 1769.

5
Those who would treat politics and morality apart will never understand the one or the other.

John Morley, *Rousseau*, p. 380. (1876) He adds, "In politics the choice is constantly between two evils."

6 Politics is the science of exigencies.

Theodore Parker, *Ten Sermons: Of Truth*.

Politics is the science of how who gets what, when and why.

Sidney Hillman, *Political Primer*. (1944) La Follette called politics "economics in action."

7
It is the first business of men, the school to mediocrity, to the covetously ambitious a sty, to the dullard his amphitheatre, arms of Titans to the desperately enterprising, Olympus to the genius.

George Meredith, *Diana of the Crossways*. Ch. i. Of Politics.

8
There is no more perfect endowment in man than political virtue.

Plutarch, *Lives: Aristides and Marcus Cato*. Ch. 3.

9
I tell you Folks, all Politics is Apple Sauce.

Will Rogers, *The Illiterate Digest*, p. 30.

10
Those two amusements for all fools of eminence, Politics or Poetry.

Richard Steele, *The Spectator*. No. 43.

Politics and theology are the only two really great subjects.

Harriet Grote. Quoted by W. E. Gladstone, *Letter to Lord Rosebery*. 16 Sept., 1880. (Morley, *Life of Gladstone*. Bk. viii, ch. 1.)

11
Politics is perhaps the only profession for which no preparation is thought necessary.

R. L. Stevenson, *Yoshida-Torajiro*.

We trust a man with making constitutions on less proof of competence than we should demand before we gave him our shoe to patch.

J. R. Lowell, *On a Certain Condescension in Foreigners*.

12
Politics . . . are but the cigar-smoke of a man.

H. D. Thoreau, *Walking*.

13
Politics I conceive to be nothing more than the science of the ordered progress of society along the lines of greatest usefulness and convenience to itself.

Woodrow Wilson, *Address*, Pan-American Scientific Congress, Washington, D.C., 6 Jan., 1916.

II—Politics: Apothegms

14
Politics make strange bedfellows:

Charles Dudley Warner, *My Summer in a Garden*. Ch. 15. (1871) Frequently quoted, for example, by J. S. Bassett, *Life of Andrew Jackson*, p. 351. (1911)

16
Magnanimity in politics is not seldom the truest wisdom; and a great empire and little minds go ill together.

Edmund Burke, *Conciliation with America*.

17
Vain hope, to make people happy by politics!

Carlylé. (Froude, *Thomas Carlyle, First Forty Years: Journal*, 10 Oct., 1831.)

18
In politics, what begins in fear usually ends in folly.

S. T. Coleridge, *Table Talk*, 5 Oct., 1830.

19
The practice of politics in the East may be defined by one word—dissimulation.

Benjamin Disraeli, *Contarini Fleming*. Pt. v, ch. 10.

20
In politics experiments mean revolutions.

Benjamin Disraeli, *Popanilla*. Ch. 4. Note, dated 1828.

Finality is not the language of politics.

Benjamin Disraeli, *Speech*, 28 Feb., 1859.

21
As I sat opposite the Treasury Bench, the Ministers reminded me of those marine landscapes not unusual on the coasts of South America. You behold a range of exhausted volcanoes.

Benjamin Disraeli, *Speech*. Manchester, 3 April, 1872.

1
No politics disturb their mind.
OLIVER GOLDSMITH, *The Logicians Refuted,* l. 24.

Politics we bar, They are not our bent.
W. S. GILBERT, *Princess Ida.* Act i.

2
It is the good of public life that it supplies agreeable topics and general conversation.
SAMUEL JOHNSON, *Letters.* Vol. i, p. 343.

3
Agitate, agitate, agitate.
LORD MELBOURNE. (TORRENS, *Life of Lord Melbourne.* Vol. i, p. 320.) *See also under* ACTION.

4
The immemorial political-economic principle that it never will get well if you pick it.
H. L. MENCKEN, *What is Going on in the World.* (*American Mercury,* Nov., 1933, p. 257.)

5
In political discussion heat is in inverse proportion to knowledge.
J. G. C. MINCHIN, *The Growth of Freedom in the Balkan Peninsula.*

When quacks with pills political would dope us
When politics absorbs the livelong day,
I like to think about the star Canopus,
So far, so far away! . . .

For after one has had about a week of
The arguments of friends as well as foes,
A star that has no parallax to speak of
Conduces to repose.
BERT LESTON TAYLOR, *Canopus.*

6
The quicksands of politics.
BASIL MONTAGUE, *Essays: Bacon's Works.*

7
There is no Canaan in politics.
WENDELL PHILLIPS, *Speech: Public Opinion,* 28 Jan., 1852.

8
Civilization dwarfs political machinery.
WENDELL PHILLIPS, *Speech,* on the election of Lincoln, 7 Nov., 1860.

9
'Tis not juggling that is to be blamed, but much juggling, for the world cannot be governed without it.
JOHN SELDEN, *Table-Talk: Juggling.*

10
Political changes should never be made save after overcoming great resistance.
SPENCER, *Principles of Ethics.* Sec. 468.

III—Politics: Their Corruption

11
The age of virtuous politics is past.
COWPER, *The Task.* Bk. v, l. 493.

12
I am sufficiently behind the scenes to know the worth of political life. I am quite an infidel about it, and shall never be converted.
DICKENS, *David Copperfield.* Ch. 43.

13
What a vicious practice is this of our politicians at Washington pairing off! as if one man who votes wrong, going away, could excuse you, who mean to vote right, for going away; or as if your presence did not tell in more ways than in your vote. Suppose the three hundred heroes at Thermopylæ had paired off with three hundred Persians: would it have been all the same to Greece, and to history?
EMERSON, *Conduct of Life: Considerations by the Way.*

14
Politics is a deleterious profession, like some poisonous handicrafts.
EMERSON, *Conduct of Life: Power.*

In politics and in trade, bruisers and pirates are of better promise than talkers and clerks.
EMERSON, *Essays, Second Series: Manners.*

There is a certain satisfaction in coming down to the lowest ground of politics, for we get rid of cant and hypocrisy.
EMERSON, *Representative Men: Napoleon.*

15
They politics like ours profess,
The greater prey upon the less.
MATTHEW GREEN, *The Grotto,* l. 69.

16
State-business is a cruel trade; good-nature is a bungler in it.
LORD HALIFAX, *Works,* p. 217.

17
You can't adopt politics as a profession and remain honest.
LOUIS MCHENRY HOWE, *Address,* to Columbia University School of Journalism, 17 Jan., 1933.

No man, I fear, can effect great benefits for his country without some sacrifice of the minor virtues.
SYDNEY SMITH. (LADY HOLLAND, *Memoir.*)

Scrupulous people are not suited to great affairs.
TURGOT.

18
O ye who lead, Take heed!
Blindness we may forgive, but baseness we will smite.
WILLIAM VAUGHN MOODY, *An Ode in Time of Hesitation.*

19
With what grace could I face the men who were driven out of the Republican party by the crooked work at the convention of 1912, and ask them to support for President the head devil [Elihu Root] of the whole thing? How could I face them and say, "The emergency is so great that I must ask you to forget the burglary of 1912, and put this unconvicted felon in the White House?"
THEODORE ROOSEVELT. (THOMPSON: *Presidents I've Known,* p. 204.)

20
In public life, instead of modesty, incorruptibility, and honesty, shamelessness, bribery, and rapacity hold sway. (Ad rem publicam

. . . pro pudore, pro abstentia, pro virtute, audacia, largito, avarita vigebant.)

SALLUST, *Catiline*. Sec. 3.

1
In politics I am sure it is even a Machiavelian holy maxim, "That some men should be ruined for the good of others."

SWIFT, *Essay on English Bubbles*.

The public path of life Is dirty.

YOUNG, *Night Thoughts*. Night viii, l. 373.

IV—Politics: Their Reformation

2
To convince a poor voter by the common argument of promised reforms is merely to corrupt him with hope.

CHARLES JOHN DARLING, *Scintillæ Juris*.

3
When shall the softer, saner politics,
Whereof we dream, have play in each proud land?

THOMAS HARDY, *Departure*, l. 11.

4
The purification of politics is an iridescent dream. Government is force. . . . The Decalogue and the Golden Rule have no place in a political campaign. . . . The commander who lost the battle through the activity of his moral nature would be the derision and jest of history.

JOHN J. INGALLS, *Article*, New York *World*, 1890.

5
Most schemes of political improvement are very laughable things.

SAMUEL JOHNSON. (BOSWELL, *Life*, ii, 102.)

6
As it was in the beginning,
Is to-day official sinning,
And shall be for evermore.

RUDYARD KIPLING, *A General Summary*.

V—Politics: Measures Not Men

7
Measures, not men.

LORD CHESTERFIELD, *Letter*, 6 March, 1742; EARL OF SHELBURNE, *Letter*, 11 July, 1765.

Measures, not men, have always been my mark.

GOLDSMITH, *The Good-Natured Man*. Act ii, sc. 1. (1768)

8
It is necessary that I should qualify the doctrine of its being not men, but measures, that I am determined to support. In a monarchy it is the duty of parliament to look at the men as well as at the measures.

LORD BROUGHAM, *Speech*, House of Commons. Nov., 1830.

9
Of this stamp is the cant of "Not men but measures"; a sort of charm by which many people get loose from every honourable engagement.

EDMUND BURKE, *Thoughts on the Cause of the Present Discontents*. (1770)

10
Away with the cant of "Measures, not men!" —the idle supposition that it is the harness and not the horses that draw the chariot along. No Sir, if the comparison must be made, if the distinction must be taken, men are everything, measures comparatively nothing.

GEORGE CANNING, *Speech*, against the Addington Ministry, 1801.

11
It used to be an applauded political maxim, "Measures, not men." I venture to denounce the soundness of this maxim, and to propose "Men, not measures." . . . Better a hundred times an honest administration of an erroneous policy than a corrupt administration of a good one.

E. J. PHELPS, *Address*, at dinner N. Y. Chamber of Commerce, 19 Nov., 1889.

VI—Politics: Parties

12
All political parties die at last of swallowing their own lies.

JOHN ARBUTHNOT. (RICHARD GARNETT, *Life of Emerson*, p. 165.)

13
When great questions end, little parties begin.

WALTER BAGEHOT, *English Constitution*, p. 261.

14
Party divisions, whether on the whole operating for good or evil, are things inseparable from free government.

EDMUND BURKE, *Observations on a Publication, "The Present State of the Nation."*

15
Being of no party,
I shall offend all parties:—never mind!
My words, at least, are more sincere and hearty
Than if I sought to sail before the wind.

BYRON, *Don Juan*. Canto ix, st. 26.

16
In these days, more emphatically than ever, "to live, signifies to unite with a party or to make one."

CARLYLE, *Signs of the Times*.

17
Party honesty is party expediency.

GROVER CLEVELAND, *Interview, New York Commercial Advertiser*. 19 Sept., 1889.

They have proved themselves offensive partisans and unscrupulous manipulators of local party management.

GROVER CLEVELAND, *Letter to George William Curtis*, 25 Dec., 1884.

18
To sacrifice one's honour to one's party is so unselfish an act that our most generous statesmen have not hesitated to do it.

CHARLES JOHN DARLING, *Scintillæ Juris*.

I always voted at my party's call,
And never thought of thinking for myself at all!
I thought so little, they rewarded me

By making me the ruler of the Queen's navee!
W. S. GILBERT, *Pinafore*. Act i.

1
Party is organized opinion.
BENJAMIN DISRAELI, *Speech*, Oxford, 25 Nov., 1864.

2
I believe that without party Parliamentary Government is impossible.
BENJAMIN DISRAELI, *Speech*, Manchester, 3 April, 1872.

All free governments are party governments.
JAMES A. GARFIELD, *Remarks*, on the death of Oliver H. P. Morton, House of Representatives, 18 Jan., 1878.

3
Still violent, whatever cause he took,
But most against the party he forsook;
For renegadoes, who ne'er turn by halves,
Are bound in conscience to be double knaves.
DRYDEN, *Absalom and Achitophel*. Pt. ii, l. 364.

4
At home the hateful names of parties cease,
And factious souls are wearied into peace.
DRYDEN, *Astræa Redux*, l. 312.

5
The vice of our leading parties in this country is that they do not plant themselves on the deep and necessary grounds to which they are respectively entitled, but lash themselves to fury in the carrying of some local and momentary measure, nowise useful to the commonwealth. Of the two great parties which at this hour almost share the nation between them, I should say that one has the best cause, and the other contains the best men.
EMERSON, *Essays, Second Series: Politics*.

In our political parties, compute the power of badges and emblems. See the great ball which they roll from Baltimore to Bunker Hill! Witness the cider-barrel, the log-cabin, the hickory-stick, the palmetto.
EMERSON, *Essays, Second Series: The Poet*.

6
Who, born for the universe, narrow'd his mind,
And to party gave up what was meant for mankind.
OLIVER GOLDSMITH, *Retaliation*, l. 31.

7
The best party is but a kind of conspiracy against the rest of the nation. . . . Ignorance maketh men go into a party, and shame keepeth them from going out of it.
LORD HALIFAX, *Works*, p. 225.

8
He serves his party best who serves the country best.
RUTHERFORD B. HAYES, *Inaugural Address*, 5 March, 1877.

He serves me most who serves his country best.
HOMER, *Iliad*. Bk. x, l. 201. (Pope, tr.)

9
If I could not go to heaven but with a party, I would not go there at all.
THOMAS JEFFERSON, *Letter to Francis Hopkinson*, 1789.

10
Faction, Disappointment's restless child.
SOAME JENYNS, *On the Late Attempt on His Majesty's Life*.

And clamorous Faction, gagged and bound,
Gasping its life out on the ground.
RICHARD REALF, *Apocalypse*.

11
Our differences are policies, our agreements principles.
WILLIAM MCKINLEY, *Speech*, at Des Moines, 1901.

12
A party of order or stability and a party of progress or reform are both necessary elements of a healthy state of political life.
JOHN STUART MILL, *On Liberty*. Ch. 2.

13
Any party which takes credit for the rain must not be surprised if its opponents blame it for the drought.
DWIGHT W. MORROW, *Campaign Speech*, Oct., 1930.

14
Party-spirit, which at best is but the madness of many, for the gain of a few.
POPE, *Letter to Blount*, 27 Aug., 1714.

Party is the madness of the many for the gain of a few.
POPE, *Thoughts on Various Subjects*. Sometimes mistakenly ascribed to Swift.

15
A good party is better than the best man that ever lived.
THOMAS B. REED. (W. A. ROBINSON, *Life*.)

16
The first advice I have to give the party is that it should clean its slate.
LORD ROSEBERY, *Speech*, Chesterfield, 16 Dec., 1901.

17
You tell me I am a party man. I hope I shall always be so.
SYDNEY SMITH, *Peter Plymley Letters*. No. 1.

18
He shall be disfranchised who, in time of faction, takes neither side.
SOLON, *Tables of the Law*. (PLUTARCH, *Lives: Solon*. Sec. 20.)

19
When I first came into Parliament, Mr. Tierney, a great Whig authority, used always to say that the duty of an Opposition was very simple—it was to oppose everything and propose nothing.
LORD STANLEY, *Debate*, 4 June, 1841.

The Duty of an Opposition is to oppose.
LORD RANDOLPH CHURCHILL, quoting George Tierney.

VII—Politics: Liberal and Conservative

1
He belonged to the third party, the quiddists or quids, being the tertium quid, . . . which had no name, but was really an anti-Madison movement.

HENRY ADAMS, *John Randolph*, p. 182.

2
You want a seat? Then boldly sate your itch;
Be very radical, and very rich.

ALFRED AUSTIN, *The Golden Age.*

3
The Right Honourable gentleman [Sir Robert Peel] caught the Whigs bathing and walked away with their clothes.

BENJAMIN DISRAELI, *Speech,* House of Commons, 28 Feb., 1845.

4
A conservative government is an organized hypocrisy.

BENJAMIN DISRAELI, *Speech,* House of Commons, 17 March, 1845. *See* CONSERVATISM.

5
It [Liberalism] is the introduction into the practical business of life of the highest kind—namely, politics—of philosophical ideas instead of political principle.

BENJAMIN DISRAELI, *Speech,* House of Commons, 5 June, 1848.

The liberal deviseth liberal things; and by liberal things shall he stand.

Old Testament: Isaiah, xxxii, 8.

6
What is a communist? One who has yearnings
For equal division of unequal earnings.

EBENEZER ELLIOT, *Epigram.*

Parlor bolshevism.

THEODORE ROOSEVELT, *Metropolitan Magazine,* June, 1918.

7
The Democratic party is the party of the Poor marshalled against the Rich. . . . But they are always officered by a few self-seeking deserters from the Rich or Whig party.

EMERSON, *Journals,* 1857.

The Democratic party is like a mule—without pride of ancestry or hope of posterity.

EMORY STORRS, *Speech,* during campaign of 1888. Also attributed to William C. Linton, Ignatius Donnelly and Judge Gay Gordon.

The Democratic party is like a man riding backward in a railroad car; it never sees anything until it has got past it.

THOMAS B. REED. (ROBINSON, *Life.*)

The penguin flies backwards because he doesn't care to see where he's going, but wants to see where he's been.

FRED ALLEN, *The Backward View.*

Yes, I am a Democrat still, very still.

DAVID B. HILL. When asked, on his return from the Democratic convention of 1896 if he was still a Democrat.

8
Deprived of all they had [by Cromwell], they took to a wild life of robbery, and were called Tories, from the Irish word meaning a plunderer.

W. S. GREGG, *Irish History,* p. 62.

A gentleman had a red Ribband in his hat . . . he said it signified that he was a Tory. What's that? said she. He answered, An Irish rebel . . . I hear that . . . instead of Cavalier and Roundhead, they are now called Torys and Wiggs.

OLIVER HEYWOOD, *Diaries,* 24 Oct., 1681.

9
Where you see a Whig you see a rascal. . . . The first Whig was the devil.

SAMUEL JOHNSON, *Miscellanies.* Vol. ii, p. 393; and BOSWELL, *Life,* 1778.

Whig: The name of a faction.

SAMUEL JOHNSON, *Dictionary of the English Language.*

10
A wise Tory and a wise Whig, I believe, will agree. Their principles are the same, though their modes of thinking are different.

SAMUEL JOHNSON, *Of Tory and Whig.* Written statement given to Boswell, 1783.

11
There is always some basic principle that will ultimately get the Republican party together. If my observations are worth anything, that basic principle is the cohesive power of public plunder.

A. J. MCLAURIN, *Speech,* U. S. Senate, May, 1906.

Stalwart Republicans.

JAMES G. BLAINE. Coined in 1877 to describe the group in Congress who fought to sustain the privileges of Republicans in the South.

The Republicans have their splits right after election and Democrats have theirs just before an election.

WILL ROGERS, *Syndicate Article,* 29 Dec., 1930.

12
Socialism is simply the degenerate capitalism of bankrupt capitalists. Its one genuine object is to get more money for its professors.

H. L. MENCKEN, *Prejudices.* Ser. iii, p. 109.

13
I have never given way to that puritanical feeling of the Whigs against dining with Tories.

Tory and Whig in turn shall be my host;
I taste no politics in boiled and roast.

SYDNEY SMITH, *Letter to John Murray,* 1834.

14
He thinks like a Tory and talks like a Radical, and that's so important now-a-days.

OSCAR WILDE, *Lady Windermere's Fan* Act ii.

15
Toryism is an innate principle o' human nature—Whiggism but an evil habit.

JOHN WILSON, *Noctes Ambrosianæ,* No. 4.

16
By "radical" I understand one who goes too

far; by "conservative" one who does not go far enough; by "reactionary" one who won't go at all. I suppose I must be a "progressive," which I take to be one who insists on recognizing new facts, adjusting policies to facts and circumstances as they arise.

WOODROW WILSON, *Speech*, N. Y., 29 Jan., 1911.

By a progressive I do not mean a man who is ready to move, but a man who knows where he is going when he moves.

WOODROW WILSON, *Speech*, St. Paul, Minn., 9 Sept., 1919.

1
A man of hope and forward-looking mind.

WORDSWORTH, *The Excursion*. Bk. vii, l. 276.

For "right" and "left" as applied to conservatives and liberals, see APPENDIX.

VIII—Politics: Expediency

2
I am invariably of the politics of people at whose table I sit, or beneath whose roof I sleep.

GEORGE BORROW, *The Bible in Spain*. Ch. 16.

And so God save the regent, church, and King!
Which means that I like all and every thing.

BYRON, *Beppo*. St. 48.

3
In politics if thou wouldst mix,
And mean thy fortunes be,
Bear this in mind: Be deaf and blind,
Let great folks hear and see.

ROBERT BURNS, *At the Globe Tavern*. No. 4.

4
Principle is ever my motto, not expediency.

BENJAMIN DISRAELI, *Sybil*. Bk. ii, ch. 2.

5
He [Sir Condy] . . . was very ill-used by the Government about a place that was promised him and never given, after his supporting them against his conscience very honourably, and being greatly abused for it, which hurt him greatly, he having the name of a great patriot in the country before.

MARIA EDGEWORTH, *Castle Rackrent: Continuation of Memoirs*.

6
The greatest superstition now entertained by public men is that hypocrisy is the royal road to success.

R. G. INGERSOLL, *Speech*, Thirteen Club Dinner, 13 Dec., 1886.

7
A marciful Providunce fashioned us holler,
O' purpose thet we might our princerples swaller.

J. R. LOWELL, *Biglow Papers*. Ser. i, No. 4.

It ain't by princerples nor men
My preudunt course is steadied:
I scent wich pays the best, an' then
Go into it baldheaded.

J. R. LOWELL, *Biglow Papers*: Ser. i, No. 6.

Ez to my princerples, I glory
In hevin' nothin' o' the sort;
I aint a Whig, I aint a Tory,
I'm jest a canderdate, in short.

J. R. LOWELL, *Biglow Papers*. Ser. i, No. 7.

Now warn't thet a system wuth pains in presarvin',
Where the people found jints an' their frien's done the carvin'?

J. R. LOWELL, *Biglow Papers*. Ser. ii, No. 5.

8
I keep my principle, that of living and dying the vicar of Bray.

REV. SYMON SYMONDS. Bray is a village in Berkshire, England, and tradition asserts that Symon Symonds, the vicar there, preserved his incumbency for half a century by being twice Protestant and twice Catholic under Henry VIII, Edward VI, Mary, and Elizabeth. (FULLER, *Worthies of Berkshire*.)

In good King Charles's golden days,
When loyalty no harm meant,
A zealous high-churchman was I,
And so I got preferment. . . .
And this is law that I'll maintain
Until my dying day, sir,
That whatsoever king shall reign,
Still I'll be Vicar of Bray, sir.

UNKNOWN, *The Vicar of Bray*. (c. 1700) Sometimes ascribed to a Colonel Fuller, an officer in the army of George I.

He held it safer to be of the religion of the King or Queen that was in being, for he knew that he came raw into the world, and accounted it no point of wisdom to be broiled out of it.

JOHN TAYLOR THE WATER-POET, *The Old, Old, Very Old Man*. (1635)

Whatever I can say or do,
I'm sure not much avails;
I shall still Vicar be of Bray,
Whichever side prevails.

SAMUEL BUTLER, *Tale of the Cobbler and the Vicar of Bray*.

I dare be bold, you're one of those
Have took the covenant,
With cavaliers are cavaliers
And with the saints, a saint.

SAMUEL BUTLER, *Tale of the Cobbler and the Vicar of Bray*.

I loved no King since Forty One
When Prelacy went down,
A Cloak and Band I then put on,
And preached against the Crown.

SAMUEL BUTLER, *The Turn-Coat*.

I never doubted of the prudent versatility of your Vicar of Bray.

LORD CHESTERFIELD, *Letters*, 15 Nov., 1756.

9
From whatever direction the wind is, the sail is shifted accordingly. (Utquomque est ventus, quasi navi in mari.)

PLAUTUS, *Pœnulus*, l. 754.

Not a weathercock on the top of the edifice, exalted for my levity and versatility, and of no use but to indicate the shiftings of every fashionable gale.

EDMUND BURKE, *Speech*, at Bristol, 1780.

1
My pollertics, like my religion, bein of a exceedin accommodatin character.
ARTEMUS WARD, *The Crisis.*

IX—Politics: The Politician

2
It is as hard and severe a thing to be a true politician as to be truly moral.
BACON, *Advancement of Learning.* Bk. ii.

3
Surely, as there are mountebanks for the natural body, so there are mountebanks for the political body: men who undertake great cures; and perhaps have been lucky in two or three experiments, but want the grounds of science, and therefore cannot hold out.
BACON, *Essays: Of Boldness.*

4
There are three classes of politicians—those who under pressure of an existing evil seek for change; . . . those who, with conscious and definite aim, plant the great Hereafter in the Now; . . . and thirdly, those who with clear eye discern the dependence of the Hereafter upon the Now, and because they shrink from the Hereafter, refuse to take the step which renders it inevitably certain.
GEORGE BRIMLEY, *Essays: Wordsworth's Poems.*

5
I was not swaddled and rocked and dawdled into a legislator.
EDMUND BURKE, *Letter to a Noble Lord.*

6
An honest politician is one who, when he is bought, will stay bought.
SIMON CAMERON, Republican Boss of Pennsylvania, about 1860. Quoted by Thomas B. Reed. (ROBINSON, *Life.*)

7
Pelting each other for the public good.
COWPER, *Charity,* l. 623.

8
It is wonderful how little mischief we can do with all our trouble.
MANDELL CREIGHTON. (CREIGHTON, *Life.*)

9
Demagogues are the mob's lacqueys. (Τοὺς δημαγωγοὺς ὄχλου διακόνους.)
DIOGENES. (DIOGENES LAERTIUS, *Diogenes.* Bk. vi, sec. 24.) *See also under* PEOPLE.

In every age the vilest specimens of human nature are to be found among demagogues.
MACAULAY, *History of England.* Ch. 5.

10
One who is a master of jibes and flouts and jeers.
BENJAMIN DISRAELI, *Speech,* House of Commons, 1874, referring to the Marquis of Salisbury.

11
For politicians neither love nor hate.
DRYDEN, *Absalom and Achitophel.* Pt. i, l. 223.

Politicians neither love nor hate. Interest, not sentiment, directs them.
LORD CHESTERFIELD, *Letters,* 23 Dec., 1748.

12
To the people they're ollers ez slick ez molasses,
An' butter their bread on both sides with The Masses.
J. R. LOWELL, *Biglow Papers.* Ser. i, No. 4.

We're the original friends o' the nation,
All the rest air a paltry an' base fabrication.
J. R. LOWELL, *Biglow Papers.* Ser. ii, No. 5.

13
Skilled to pull wires, he baffles Nature's hope,
Who sure intended him to stretch a rope.
J. R. LOWELL, *The Boss.* Probably referring to Boss Tweed, of New York.

Whitewashed, he quits the politicians' strife
At ease in mind, with pockets filled for life.
J. R. LOWELL, *Tempora Mutantur.*

But John P. Robinson, he
Sez they did n't know everythin' down in Judee.
J. R. LOWELL, *Biglow Papers.* Ser. i, No. 3.

14
Once there were two brothers. One ran away to sea, the other was elected Vice-President, and nothing was ever heard of either of them again.
THOMAS R. MARSHALL, *Recollections.*

15
To scholars who become politicians the comic role is usually assigned; they have to be the good conscience of a state policy.
NIETZSCHE, *Human, All-Too-Human.* Bk. ii, p. 468.

We cannot safely leave politics to politicians, or political economy to college professors.
HENRY GEORGE, *Social Problems,* p. 9.

16
They [politicians] are the semi-failures in business and the professions, men of mediocre mentality, dubious morals, and magnificent commonplaceness.
W. B. PITKIN, *The Twilight of the American Mind,* p. 81.

17
The conduct of a wise politician is ever suited to the present posture of affairs. Often by foregoing a part he saves the whole, and by yielding in a small matter secures a greater.
PLUTARCH, *Lives: Publicola and Solon.*

18
Old politicians chew on wisdom past,
And totter on in bus'ness to the last.
POPE, *Moral Essays.* Epis. i, l. 228.

Coffee, which makes the politician wise,
And see thro' all things with his half-shut eyes.
POPE, *The Rape of the Lock.* Canto iii, l. 117.

19
There lies beneath this mossy stone
A politician who
Touched a live issue without gloves,
And never did come to.
KEITH PRESTON, *Epitaph.*

1
Perhaps been poorly rich, and meanly great,
The slave of pomp, a cipher in the state.
RICHARD SAVAGE, *The Bastard*, l. 39.

2
It might be the pate of a politician, . . . one that would circumvent God.
SHAKESPEARE, *Hamlet*. Act v, sc. 1, l. 86.

This vile politician.
SHAKESPEARE, *I Henry IV*. Act i, sc. 3, l. 241.

3
Get thee glass eyes;
And, like a scurvy politician, seem
To see the things thou dost not.
SHAKESPEARE, *King Lear*. Act iv, sc. 6, l. 174.

4
Or that eternal want of pence,
Which vexes public men.
TENNYSON, *Will Waterproof's Lyrical Monologue*, l. 43.

5
I'm not a politician and my other habits air good.
ARTEMUS WARD, *Fourth of July Oration.*

You won't be able to find such another pack of poppycock gabblers as the present Congress.
ARTEMUS WARD, *Travels: Things in New York.*

6
Lord of the golden tongue and smiting eyes;
Great out of season and untimely wise:
A man whose virtue, genius, grandeur, worth,
Wrought deadlier ill than ages can undo.
WILLIAM WATSON, *The Political Luminary.*

The earth's high places who attain to fill
By most indomitably sitting still, . . .
Find in the golden mean their proper bliss,
And doing nothing, never do amiss;
But lapt in men's good graces live, and die
By all regretted, nobody knows why.
WILLIAM WATSON, *Sketch of a Political Character.*

7
Things get very lonely in Washington sometimes. The real voice of the great people of America sometimes sounds faint and distant in that strange city. You hear politics until you wish that both parties were smothered in their own gas.
WOODROW WILSON, *Speech,* St. Louis, Mo., 5 Sept., 1919.

It is easy enough to see why a man goes to the poor house or the penitentiary. Its becawz he can't help it. But why he should woluntarily go and live in Washinton, is intirely beyond my comprehension.
ARTEMUS WARD, *Interview with the Prince Napoleon.*

At Washington, where an insignificant individual may trespass on a nation's time.
EMERSON, *Uncollected Lectures: Social Aims.*

X—Politics: Office-Holding

8
No man who ever held the office of President would congratulate a friend on obtaining it. He will make one man ungrateful, and a hundred men his enemies, for every office he can bestow.
JOHN ADAMS, referring to the election of his son, John Quincy Adams, to the Presidency. (QUINCY, *Figures of the Past*, p. 74.)

Every time I bestow a vacant office I make a hundred discontented persons and one ingrate. (Toutes les fois que je donne une place vacante, je fais cent mécontents et un ingrat.)
LOUIS XIV. (VOLTAIRE, *Siècle de Louis XIV*.)

9
In order to distribute the offices according to merit it is necessary for the citizens to know each other's personal characters. . . . Haphazard decision is unjust, and this must obviously prevail in a numerous community.
ARISTOTLE, *Politica*. Bk. vii, ch. 4, sec. 7.

But we'll hae ane frae 'mang oursels,
A man we ken, and a' that.
BURNS, *Heron Election Ballad.*

10
Examine the Honours List and you will know exactly how a government feels in its inside. When the Honours List is full of rascals, millionaires, and er—chumps,—you may be quite sure that the Government is dangerously ill.
ARNOLD BENNETT, *The Title*. Act i.

Literature is always a good card to play for Honours. It makes people think that Cabinet ministers are educated.
ARNOLD BENNETT, *The Title*. Act iii.

11
Office will show the man. ('Αρχὰ ἄνδρα δείξει.)
BIAS. (ARISTOTLE, *Nicomachean Ethics*. Bk. v, ch. 1, sec. 16.)

Office shows the man. ('Αρχὴ ἄνδρα δείκνυσιν.)
PITTACUS. (DIOGENES LAERTIUS, *Pittacus*. Bk. i, sec. 77.)

12
Can you let me know what positions you have at your disposal with which to reward deserving Democrats?
WILLIAM JENNINGS BRYAN, *Letter to Walter W. Vick,* Receiver General, 20 Aug., 1913.

I am glad to have the public know that I appreciate the services of those who work in politics and feel an interest in seeing them rewarded.
WILLIAM JENNINGS BRYAN, *Interview,* N. Y. *Times,* 16 Jan., 1915.

The folks down south like you, but they are tired of going into the post office and having their mail handed to them by a Republican.
O. O STEALEY, *Letter to W. J. Bryan.* (THOMPSON, *Presidents I've Known*, p. 51.)

13
In their nomination to office they will not appoint to the exercise of authority as to a pitiful job, but as to a holy function.
EDMUND BURKE, *Reflections on the Revolution in France.*

An upright minister asks, *what* recommends a man; a corrupt minister, *who*.
C. C. COLTON, *Lacon: Reflections*. No. 9.

1
The only difference, after all their rout,
Is that the one is *in*, the other *out*.
CHARLES CHURCHILL, *The Conference*, l. 165.

The grand contention's plainly to be seen,
To get some men put out, and some put in.
DEFOE, *The True-Born Englishman: Intro.*

2
A most wretched custom is our electioneering and scrambling for office. (Misserima omnimo est ambitio honorumque contentio.)
CICERO, *De Officiis*. Bk. i, ch. 25, sec. 87.

This office-seeking is a disease. It is even catching.
GROVER CLEVELAND, *Interview*, in 1885. (NEVINS, *Grover Cleveland*, p. 235.)

3
From plots and treasons Heav'n preserve my years,
But save me most from my petitioners!
DRYDEN, *Absalom and Achitophel*. Pt. i, l. 985.

4
Take from the United States the appointment of postmasters and let the towns elect them, and you deprive the Federal Government of half a million defenders.
EMERSON, *Journals*, 1860.

I have heard in highest places the shameless doctrine avowed by men grown old in public office that the true way by which power should be gained in the Republic is to bribe the people with the offices created for their service.
GEORGE F. HOAR, *Speech*, at impeachment trial of Secretary W. W. Belknap, in 1876. (HOAR, *Autobiography of Seventy Years*, i, 307.)

What are we here for, except the offices?
WEBSTER FLANAGAN, leader of the Republican party in Texas, at the national Republican convention, in 1880. (*Dict. Amer. Biog.*, vi, 453. See also *The Nation*, 10 June, 1880.)

5
But the President has paid dear for his White House. It has commonly cost him all his peace and the best of his manly attributes.
EMERSON, *Essays, First Series: Compensation*.

Even in the White House one must keep house with oneself.
SILAS BENT, *Justice O. W. Holmes*, p. 254.

6
Of the various executive duties, no one excited more anxious concern than that of placing the interests of our fellow citizens in the hands of honest men, with understanding sufficient for their stations. No duty is at the same time more difficult to fulfil.
THOMAS JEFFERSON, *Letter to Elias Shipman*, 12 July, 1801.

No duty the Executive has to perform is so trying as to put the right man in the right place.
THOMAS JEFFERSON. As quoted by J. B. McMaster, *History of the People of the United States*. Vol. ii, p. 586.

I have always believed that success would be the inevitable result if the two services, the army and the navy, had fair play, and if we sent the right man to fill the right place.
SIR AUSTEN HENRY LAYARD, *Speech*, in Parliament, 15 Jan., 1855.

7
Whenever a man has cast a longing eye on offices, a rottenness begins in his conduct.
THOMAS JEFFERSON, *Letter to T. Coxe*, 1799.

8
Few die and none resign.
THOMAS JEFFERSON, *Letter to a Committee of Merchants of New Haven*, 12 July, 1801. The exact words were, "If a due participation of office is a matter of right, how are vacancies to be obtained? Those by death are few: by resignation, none."

9
Wherefore the Little Tin Gods harried their little tin souls,
Seeing he came not from Chatham, jingled no spurs at his heels,
Knowing that, nevertheless, was he first on the Government rolls
For the billet of "Railway Instructor to Little Tin Gods on Wheels."
RUDYARD KIPLING, *Public Waste*. The phrase "Little tin gods on wheels" has been attributed to Robert Grant.

10
It is easier to appear worthy of a position one does not hold, than of the office which one fills. (Il est plus facile de paraître digne des emplois qu'on n'a pas que de ceux que l'on exerce.)
LA ROCHEFOUCAULD, *Maximes*. No. 164.

11
Office a fund for ballot-brokers made
To pay the drudges of their gainful trade;
Our cities taught what conquered cities feel
By ædiles chosen that they might safely steal.
LOWELL, *Epistle to George William Curtis*.

Mere pegs to hang an office on.
LOWELL, *An Interview with Miles Standish*. St. 13.

Constitoounts air hendy to help a man in,
But arterwards don't weigh the heft of a pin.
LOWELL, *The Biglow Papers*. Ser. i, No. 4.

12
To place and power all public spirit tends,
In place and power all public spirit ends;
Like hardy plants, that love the air and sky,
When *out*, 'twill thrive—but taken *in*, 'twill die!
THOMAS MOORE, *Corruption*, l. 149.

13
There's not a particle of doubt
We've turned a bunch of rascals out,
And put a nice clean aggregation
In very serious temptation.
KEITH PRESTON, *Post-election Misgivings*.

14
My business, Sir, you'll quickly guess,

Is to desire some little place:
And fair pretensions I have for't,
Much need, and very small desert.

MATTHEW PRIOR, *Epistle to Fleetwood Shepherd*. No. 2.

1
But long I will not be Jack out of office.

SHAKESPEARE, *I Henry VI*. Act i, sc. 1, l. 175.

Some folks are Jacks-in-office, fond of power.

JOHN WOLCOT, *The Louisiad*. Canto iv. (1800)

See also under JACK.

2
O, that estates, degrees, and offices
Were not derived corruptly, and that clear
honour
Were purchased by the merit of the wearer!

SHAKESPEARE, *The Merchant of Venice*. Act ii, sc. 9, l. 41.

3
Every man who takes office in Washington either grows or swells, and when I give a man an office, I watch him carefully to see whether he is swelling or growing.

WOODROW WILSON, *Address*, Washington, 15 May, 1916.

XI—Politics: Public Office a Public Trust

4
For the administration of the government, like the office of a trustee, must be conducted for the benefit of those entrusted to one's care, not of those to whom it is entrusted.

CICERO, *De Officiis*. Bk. i, ch. 25, sec. 85.

5
All political power is a trust.

CHARLES JAMES FOX, *Speech*, 1788.

6
To execute laws is a royal office; to execute orders is not to be a king. However, a political executive magistracy, though merely such, is a great trust.

EDMUND BURKE, *Reflections on the Revolution in France*. (1790)

All persons possessing any portion of power ought to be strongly and awfully impressed with an idea that they act in trust, and that they are to account for their conduct in that trust to the one great Master, Author, and Founder of society.

EDMUND BURKE, *Reflections on the Revolution in France*.

7
All power is a trust; that we are accountable for its exercise; that from the people and for the people all springs, and all must exist.

BENJAMIN DISRAELI, *Vivian Grey*. Bk. vi, ch. 7. (1826)

The English doctrine that all power is a trust for the public good.

MACAULAY, *Essays: Horace Walpole*. (1833)

8
It is not fit the public trusts should be lodged in the hands of any till they are first proved and found fit for the business they are to be entrusted with.

MATTHEW HENRY, *Commentaries: Timothy*, iii. (1708)

9
No religious test shall ever be required as a qualification to any office or public trust under the United States.

Constitution of the United States. Art. vi, sec. 3. (1787)

10
When a man assumes a public trust, he should consider himself as public property.

THOMAS JEFFERSON. In a conversation with Baron Humboldt. (RAYNER, *Life of Jefferson*, p. 356.)

11
Government is a trust, and the officers of the government are trustees; and both the trust and the trustees are created for the benefit of the people.

HENRY CLAY, *Speech*, at Lexington, Ky., 16 May, 1829.

12
The very essence of a free government consists in considering offices as public trusts, bestowed for the good of the country, and not for the benefit of an individual or a party.

JOHN C. CALHOUN, *Speech*, 13 Feb., 1835.

13
An' in convartin' public trusts
To very privit uses.

J. R LOWELL, *The Biglow Papers*. Ser. i, No. 6. (1848)

14
The phrase, "public office is a public trust," has of late become common property.

CHARLES SUMNER, *Speech*, U. S. Senate, 31 May, 1872.

The public offices are a public trust.

W. W. CRAPO, *Speech*, Republican State Convention, Mass., 1881.

Public office is a public trust, the authority and opportunities of which must be used as absolutely as the public moneys for the public benefit.

DORMAN B. EATON, *The "Spoils" System and Civil-Service Reform*. Ch. iii.

15
Public officials are the trustees of the people.

GROVER CLEVELAND, *Letter Accepting Nomination for Mayor of Buffalo*, 1881.

Public officers are the servants and agents of the people to execute laws which the people have made.

GROVER CLEVELAND, *Letter Accepting Nomination for Governor of New York*, 7 Oct., 1882.

But what man is fit to hold office? Only he who regards political office as a public trust.

A. S. HEWITT, *Address*, at opening Brooklyn bridge, 24 May, 1883.

16
Public office is a public trust.

WILLIAM C. HUDSON, a newspaper man whc

was asked to write a campaign document summarizing the achievements of Grover Cleveland, at the opening of his first Presidential campaign, in June, 1884, and who produced this slogan from various utterances by Cleveland. Sometimes attributed to Dan Lamont, Cleveland's campaign manager.

1
Your every voter, as surely as your chief magistrate, under the same high sanction, though in a different sphere, exercises a public trust.

GROVER CLEVELAND, *Inaugural*, 4 Mar., 1885.

XII—Politics: Familiar Phrases *

See also America: Famous Phrases

2
This day the caucus club meets . . . in the garret of Tom Dawes, the adjutant of the Boston regiment.

JOHN ADAMS, *Diary*, ii, 164, Feb., 1753. The first known instance of the printed use of "caucus," whose origin is uncertain.

3
No expedient ever devised could equal it [a debased currency] in efficiency for fertilizing the rich man's field with the sweat of the poor man's brow.

JOHN QUINCY ADAMS. (J. T. ADAMS, *America's Tragedy*.)

With Mr. Slingsby, of the Tower, who did inform me mightily in several things—among others, that the heightening or lowering of money is only a cheat, and do good to some particular men, which, if I can but remember how, I am now by him fully convinced of.

SAMUEL PEPYS, *Diary*, 2 Oct., 1666.

4
I placed it where it would do the most good.

OAKES AMES, *Letter to Henry S. McComb*, referring to Crédit Mobilier stock distributed to members of Congress in 1872.

5
Winfield Scott Hancock is a good man weighing 250 pounds.

WILLIAM O. BARTLETT, *Editorial*, New York *Sun*, 19 Oct., 1880. Hancock was described in the same editorial as "pure, patriotic and good, a fit man to be President."

6
This new page opened in the book of our public expenditures, and this new departure taken, which leads into the bottomless gulf of civil pensions and family gratuities.

THOMAS HART BENTON, *Speech*, U. S. Senate, April, 1841, against a grant to the widow of President William Henry Harrison. Harrison had died on April 4, exactly a month after assuming office.

7
The contempt of that large-minded gentleman is so wilting; his haughty disdain, his grandiloquent swell, his majestic, supereminent, overpowering turkey-gobbler strut has been so crushing to myself and all the members of this House, that I know it was an act of the greatest temerity for me to venture upon a controversy with him. . . . Hyperion to a satyr, Thersites to Hercules, mud to marble, dunghill to diamond, a singed cat to a Bengal tiger, a whining puppy to a roaring lion.

JAMES G. BLAINE, *Speech*, House of Representatives, 30 April, 1886, referring to Roscoe Conkling, who never forgave him. (*Congressional Globe*, 1st session, 39th Cong., p. 2299.)

Becurled and perfumed grandee gazed at by the gallery-gapers.

H. J. ECKENRODE, referring to Roscoe Conkling. (MUZZEY, *James G. Blaine*, p. 144.)

8
The right honourable gentleman [Robert Lowe, Viscount Sherbrooke] is the first of the new party who has retired into his political cave of Adullam and he has called about him everyone that was in distress and everyone that was discontented.

JOHN BRIGHT, *Speech on the Reform Bill*, March, 1866, referring to Mr. Horsman and other liberals.

David therefore departed thence, and escaped to the cave Adullam; and when his brethren and all his father's house heard it, they went down thither to him.

Old Testament: I Samuel, xxii, 1.

9
John A. Logan is the Head Centre, the Hub, the King Pin, the Main Spring, Mogul, and Mugwump of the final plot.

ISAAC HILL BROMLEY, *Impeach Logan*. Editorial in N. Y. *Tribune*, 16 Feb., 1877.

Mugwump D. O. Bradley.

Headline N. Y. *Sun*, 23 March, 1884. Applied by the *Sun*, 15 June, 1884, to the "independents" of the Blaine-Cleveland campaign.

A mugwump is a person educated beyond his intellect.

HORACE PORTER, *Speech*, during Cleveland-Blaine campaign, 1884. The *Nation* defined a mugwump as "a man who, for some reason or other, is unable to vote his regular party ticket." An Algonquin Indian word, meaning "Big Chief," used in Eliot's translation of the Bible, 1661. Said to have been first used in its political sense by the Indianapolis *Sentinel* in 1872. Thomas B. Reed called them "long-tailed birds of Paradise."

Very few . . . take an active part in politics, however interested they may be in public affairs.

BRYCE, *American Commonwealth*, ii, iii, 379.

A mugwump is one of those boys who always has his mug on one side of the political fence and his wump on the other.

ALBERT J. ENGEL, *Speech*, House of Representatives, 23 April, 1936. Credited also to Harold Willis Dodds, President of Princeton University

10
I shall not help crucify mankind upon a cross of gold. I shall not aid in pressing down

* For additional phrases see APPENDIX.

upon the bleeding brow of labor this crown of thorns.

WILLIAM JENNINGS BRYAN, *Speech*, House of Representatives, 22 Dec., 1894.

You shall not press down upon the brow of labor this crown of thorns; you shall not crucify mankind upon a cross of gold.

WILLIAM JENNINGS BRYAN, *Speech*, before National Democratic Convention, Chicago, 10 July, 1896. Concluding sentence.

1

The enemy's country.

WILLIAM JENNINGS BRYAN. Phrase used by him in the 1896 campaign to describe the East, specifically New York.

I never said, "Great is Tammany and Croker is its prophet." Bryan did.

CHAMP CLARK, *Memories*.

In a consistent, albeit futile gesture, therefore, he [Bryan] resolved to invade "The enemy's country" and formally accept his nomination at Madison Square Garden—"the champion of Lazarus at the gates of Dives."

PAXTON HIBBEN, *The Peerless Leader*, p. 197. The first quoted phrase was Bryan's, the second was coined by Edward C. Little.

Ours is no sapling, chance-sown by the fountain,
Blooming at Beltane, in winter to fade.

SCOTT, *The Lady of the Lake:* Canto ii, st. 19. Quoted by Senator Vest in nominating Richard Parks Bland for the Presidency at Chicago, in 1896, referring to Bryan.

2

We are Republicans, and we don't propose to leave our party and identify ourselves with the party whose antecedents have been rum, Romanism, and rebellion.

REV. SAMUEL DICKINSON BURCHARD, *Speech of Congratulation*, to James G. Blaine, at Fifth Avenue Hotel, New York City, 29 Oct., 1884, as spokesman for a party of clergymen gathered to assure him of their support in his presidential campaign. There is good reason to believe that the phrase "rum, Romanism, and rebellion," which Blaine failed to repudiate promptly, lost him the Presidency. Cleveland carried New York by a plurality of 1047, and the state's electoral vote decided the election. Burchard was a Presbyterian clergyman, whom Edward P. Mitchell in the New York *Sun* described as "a Silurian or early Paleozoic bigot."

The combined power of rebellion, Catholicism and whiskey.

JAMES A. GARFIELD, *Letter*, 1876, when he thought Tilden elected, explaining how it had happened. (CALDWELL, *James A. Garfield*, p. 251.)

3

One of those damn literary fellers.

SIMON CAMERON, *Speech*, U. S. Senate, 7 March, 1876, referring to Richard Henry Dana, whose nomination as Minister to Great Britain had just been sent to the Senate by President Grant. Cameron was Senator from Pennsylvania, and succeeded in defeating the nomination. (C. F. ADAMS, *Life of R. H. Dana*, ii, 376.)

What could you expect from a man who had snubbed seventy Senators!

SIMON CAMERON, in 1870, referring to Judge Ebenezer Rockwood Hoar, whose nomination to the Supreme Court by President Grant the Senate had rejected. Judge Hoar had antagonized the Senate, while Attorney-General by refusing to treat appointments to judgeships as Senate patronage. (*Proceedings Mass. Hist. Society*, 2d series, ix, 304; *Dict. Amer. Biog.*, ix, 86.)

4

He has peculiar powers as an assailant, and almost always, even when attacked, gets himself into that attitude by making war upon his accuser; and he has, withal, an instinct for the jugular and the carotid artery, as unerring as that of any carnivorous animal.

RUFUS CHOATE, referring to John Quincy Adams. (SAMUEL GILMAN BROWN, *Memoir of Rufus Choate*, p. 417. A note states that this is "from the memorandum of Hon. Charles A. Peabody." Quoted in ALEXANDER, *Four Famous New Yorkers*, p. 17.)

5

I would rather be right than president.

HENRY CLAY. To Preston, of Kentucky, when told that his advocacy of the Missouri compromise measures of 1850 would injure his chances for the Presidency.

The gentleman need not worry. He will never be either.

THOMAS B. REED. Retorting to Congressman Springer, when he quoted Clay's statement (W. A. ROBINSON, *Life*.)

Bargain and Corruption.

The cry that "barred the door of the Presidency to Henry Clay." (*Dictionary of American Biography*, ii, 324.)

6

It is a condition which confronts us, not a theory.

GROVER CLEVELAND, *Annual Message*, 1887. Referring to the tariff.

7

Let it alone; let it pass. (Laissez faire; laissez passer.)

JEAN BAPTISTE COLBERT, finance minister of Louis XIV of France. (*See* speech by Lord John Russell, *London Times*, 2 April, 1840.) Attributed also to Gournay, Minister of Commerce, 1751. Quoted by Adam Smith, *Wealth of Nations*.

8

A halcyon and vociferous occasion.

ROSCOE CONKLING, *Speech*.

9

I do not choose to run for President in 1928.

CALVIN COOLIDGE. Statement to press in 1927.

"I do not choose" means in the Yankee language "I am determined not to."

C. W. THOMPSON, *Presidents I've Known*, p. 345.

In my opinion, it was never meant to bring about the results it did. . . . The President hoped to be the nominee, expected to be the nominee, and was disappointed and distressed when he was not chosen by the convention.

IRWIN HOOD ("IKE") HOOVER, *Forty-Two Years in the White House*, p. 177.

I should like to be known as a former president who tries to mind his own business.

CALVIN COOLIDGE. (*Cosmopolitan Magazine*, May, 1930.)

He looks as if he had been weaned on a pickle.

ALICE ROOSEVELT LONGWORTH, characterizing Mr. Coolidge, by quoting her physician. (*Crowded Hours*, p. 337.)

1

The convention will be deadlocked, and after the other candidates have gone their limit, some twelve or fifteen men, worn out and bleary-eyed for lack of sleep, will sit down, about two o'clock in the morning, around a table in a smoke-filled room in some hotel, and decide the nomination. When that time comes, Harding will be selected.

HARRY M. DAUGHERTY, campaign manager for Warren G. Harding, predicting with uncanny accuracy the method of Harding's nomination for the Presidency by the Republican National Convention at Chicago, 12 June, 1920. The "smoke-filled room" was Colonel George Harvey's room at the Blackstone Hotel. The convention was deadlocked between General Leonard Wood and Governor Frank O. Lowden, and about two o'clock on the morning of Saturday, 12 June, a small group of the "party elders" got together and selected Harding as a compromise candidate. (*See* the New York *Times*, 13 June, 1920; MARK SULLIVAN, *Our Times*, vol. vi, p. 37.)

We drew to a pair of deuces and filled.

WARREN G. HARDING, commenting on his nomination, just after it had been made, to a group of reporters who had rushed to him, demanding a statement. The phrase is familiar to every poker player. To "fill" means to succeed in getting a "full house," a hand consisting of a pair and three of a kind.

2

"Hargrave," said his Lordship, "if you want any information upon points of practical politics."

BENJAMIN DISRAELI, *Vivian Grey*. Ch. 14. (1826) The first known appearance in print of the phrase, "practical politics."

Out of the range of practical politics.

GLADSTONE. Referring to the abolition of the Established Church in Ireland, April, 1867. (O'CONNOR, *The Parnell Movement*, p. 216.)

It would be interesting to imagine the first President of the United States confronted with some one who had ventured to approach him upon the basis of what is now commonly called "practical politics."

HENRY CODMAN POTTER, *Address*, Washington Centennial service, 30 April, 1889.

3

The first favourite was never heard of, the second favourite was never seen after the distance post, all the ten-to-oners were in the rear, and a dark horse which had never been thought of, and which the careless St. James had never even observed in the list, rushed past the grand stand in sweeping triumph.

BENJAMIN DISRAELI, *The Young Duke*. Bk. i, ch. 5. (1831)

Who is the dark horse he has in his stable?

THACKERAY, *Adventures of Philip*.

4

We went across, but they won't come across.

A. VICTOR (VIC) DONAHEY, U. S. Senator from Ohio, explaining his vote against American adherence to the World Court, 30 Jan., 1935, referring to American participation in the World War and the refusal of the Allies to pay their debts to the United States. To "come across" is American vernacular for paying up.

5

I could travel from Boston to Chicago by the light of my own effigies.

STEPHEN A. DOUGLAS, in 1854, after the passage of the Kansas-Nebraska bill, which he had supported. (RHODES, *History of the United States*, Vol. i, p. 496.)

6

Water flowed like wine.

WILLIAM M. EVARTS, describing a dinner at the White House in 1877, during the administration of Rutherford B. Hayes, whose wife was a Prohibitionist.

7

I am a biger man than old Grant.

LAFAYETTE FITZHUGH, of Texas, *Letter*, written to a constituent in 1875. Fitzhugh, who had been sergeant-at-arms of the Confederate Senate, had managed to secure an appointment as file clerk of the document room of the House of Representatives, when the Democrats recovered control of the House and its patronage in 1875. (See New York *Sun*, 8 Oct., 1916.) The saying has been attributed also to Webster Flanagan and to Tom Ochiltree.

8

I will leave the leader of the opposition, for the present, floundering and foundering in the Straits of Malacca.

GLADSTONE, *Speech*, at Greenwich, Jan., 1874. Referring to Disraeli's accusation that the Liberal government had neglected British interests in the Straits of Malacca.

The country has, I think, made up its mind to close this career of plundering and blundering.

DISRAELI, *Letter to Lord Grey de Wilton*, Oct., 1873.

Support a compatriot against a native, however the former may blunder or plunder.

R. F. BURTON, *Explorations of the Highroads of Brazil*. Vol. i, p. 11. (c. 1869)

The foreign policy of the noble earl . . . may be summed up in two truly expressive words: "meddle" and "muddle."

LORD DERBY, *Speech*, House of Lords, Feb., 1864, referring to Earl Russell.

1
What's the use of wasting dynamite when insect-powder will do?

SENATOR CARTER GLASS, in an unpublished speech, Democratic caucus, 1913.

2
Here comes another of the Spell-binders!

WILLIAM CASSIUS GOODLOE. Referring to the Republican stump-speakers in campaign of 1888, who were publicised as holding their audiences spell-bound.

3
I have the courage of my opinions, but I have not the temerity to give a political blank cheque to Lord Salisbury.

SIR WILLIAM EDWARD GOSCHEN, *Speech*, in Parliament, 19 Feb., 1884.

4
Who will burden himself with your liturgical parterre when the burning questions [brennende Fragen] of the day invite to very different toils?

HAGENBACH, *Grundlinien der Liturgik und Homiletik*. (1803)

The burning question of the day.

BENJAMIN DISRAELI, *Speech*, House of Commons, March, 1873.

5
We'll stand pat!

MARK HANNA. When asked by a reporter to state the issue of the 1900 campaign to reelect McKinley. Hence the sobriquet, "standpatters." (See STODDARD, *As I Knew Them*, p. 259.) "Stand pat" is a poker term, meaning that the player is satisfied with the cards dealt to him, and desires no new ones.

I felt as if I were before this speech tarred with the brush of being a thick-and-thinnite.

A. J. BALFOUR, *Speech*, 9 Jan., 1900. The British for standpatter.

6
One thing, if no more, I have gained by my custom-house experience—to know a politician. It is a knowledge which no previous thought, or power of sympathy, could have taught me, because the animal, or the machine rather, is not in nature.

HAWTHORNE, *Note Books*, 15 March, 1840. Said to be the origin of "machine politics."

Such is the operation of the machine, as now established, that . . . scarcely an individual is certain of his political existence.

DUKE OF WELLINGTON, *Letter to Thomas Raikes*, 12 Sept., 1845. (*Raikes-Wellington Correspondence*, p. 384.)

They call the system—I do not coin the phrase, I adopt it because it carries its own meaning—the system they call "invisible government."

ELIHU ROOT. Referring to boss rule, specifically to Thomas C. Platt, of New York.

7
If the Man Higher Up is ever found, take my assurance for it, he will be a large, pale man with blue wristlets showing under his cuffs, and he will be sitting to have his shoes polished within sound of a bowling alley, and there will be somewhere about him turquoises.

O. HENRY, *Man About Town*.

8
We in America today are nearer to the final triumph over poverty than ever before in the history of any land. The poorhouse is vanishing from among us. We have not yet reached the goal, but given a chance to go forward with the policies of the last eight years, and we shall soon, with the help of God, be within sight of the day when poverty shall be banished from this nation.

HERBERT HOOVER, *Speech*, 11 Aug., 1928, accepting the Republican nomination for President.

Ours is a land . . . filled with millions of happy homes, blessed with comfort and opportunity. . . . In no nation are the fruits of accomplishment more secure. . . . I have no fears for the future of our country. It is bright with hope.

HERBERT HOOVER, *Inaugural*, 4 March, 1929.

They are playing politics at the expense of human misery.

HERBERT HOOVER, *Statement to the Press*, 9 Dec., 1930. Referring to members of Congress who had introduced bills for unemployment relief.

9
Like an armed warrior, like a plumed knight, James G. Blaine marched down the halls of the American Congress and threw his shining lance full and fair against the brazen forehead of every traitor to his country and every maligner of his fair reputation.

ROBERT G. INGERSOLL, *Speech*, nominating Blaine for President, at the National Republican Convention, Cincinnati, 15 June, 1876. (*Proceedings of the Convention*, p. 73–75.)

Let us believe that in the silence of the receding world, he heard the great waves breaking on a farther shore, and felt already upon his wasted brow the breath of the Eternal Morning.

R. G. INGERSOLL, *Eulogy of James G. Blaine*.

Mulligan letters.

Letters supposed to show corruption on the part of James G. Blaine in various railroad and land deals in 1869. Used with deadly effect during his campaign against Cleveland, they "probably barred the door of the Presidency to him forever." (*Dict. Amer. Biog.*, ii, 324.)

1
No sooner does he hear any of his brothers mention reform or retrenchment, than up he jumps.

WASHINGTON IRVING, *The Sketch Book: John Bull.* (1820)

I am for peace, for retrenchment, and for reform,—thirty years ago the great watchwords of the great Liberal Party.

JOHN BRIGHT, *Speech,* Birmingham, 28 April, 1859. The phrase dates from 1830, when it was probably said by William IV to Earl Grey in an interview, 17 Nov., 1830, and is in *H. B.'s Cartoons,* No. 93, 26 Nov., 1830. (*See* MOLESWORTH, *History of the Reform Bill of 1832,* p. 98. Also WARREN, *Ten Thousand a Year,* 1839, where it is inscribed on the banner of Tittlebat Titmouse.)

2
John Marshall has made his decision: now let him enforce it!

PRESIDENT ANDREW JACKSON, referring to the Supreme Court decision in Worcester vs. Georgia, 3 March, 1832, which upheld the right of the Cherokee Indians to remain in possession of their land, from which the state was trying to eject them. (GREELEY, *The American Conflict,* vol. i, p. 106.)

3
We are swinging round the circle.

ANDREW JOHNSON, *Speech,* on the Presidential Reconstruction tour, August, 1866.

4
It was not free silver that frightened the plutocratic leaders. What they feared then, what they fear now, is free men.

TOM JOHNSON, *My Story,* p. 109.

5
Allow me to introduce to you my particular friend, Mr. George O. Evans. . . . He understands Addition, Division, and Silence.

WILLIAM H. KEMBLE, while State Treasurer of Pennsylvania, in a letter to Titian J. Coffey, recommending a political protégé, March, 1867. Published in the New York *Sun,* 20 June, 1872, the phrase soon became famous.

Multiplication, Division and Silence.

MATTHEW STANLEY QUAY, political boss of Pennsylvania, when asked the qualification for a ring or trust. (Every schoolboy knows that "Addition, Division and Silence" was not spoken by Bill Tweed, but written by Matt Quay.—BRANDER MATTHEWS, New York *Times Book Review,* 1 Jan., 1922.)

6
The brains trust.

JAMES M. KIERAN, of the New York *Times,* in a conversation with Franklin D. Roosevelt, at Hyde Park, N.Y., in August, 1932, referring to the group of Columbia University professors with whom Mr. Roosevelt was consulting concerning his campaign speeches. The phrase was promptly seized upon by the newspapers, and soon modified to "brain trust."

When the first American general staff was appointed from among the army's bright young men and fair-haired boys, some of the old Indian fighters and plains soldiers grumbled, and one of them said, "It's a damned brain trust."

Parenthetically, this was the same old Commissary General Weston who once wise-cracked on General Greely's fitness to be entrusted with the command of many men. Greely had won his rank in the Signal Corps, where the duties are largely technical. He achieved glory in his historic Arctic expedition with a small squad—not all of whom came back. Weston's comment was:—"He never commanded more than ten soldiers—and he ate three of them."

Weston's crack about the Brain Trust lived. One day at Krum Elbow, in the summer of 1932, some bright news-hawk saw a group of young "intellectuals" hanging about Hyde Park and recalled Weston's old wise-crack—"Moley and the brain trust." It stuck.

HUGH S. JOHNSON, *Syndicated Article,* 12 July, 1935. The General Greely referred to was Major General Adolphus Washington Greely, who headed a disastrous government Arctic expedition in 1881. Hyde Park is the country residence of Franklin D. Roosevelt, in Dutchess County, New York. "Moley" is Raymond Moley, a college professor who, in 1932 and for some time thereafter, was one of Mr. Roosevelt's most trusted advisers.

7
If the policy of the government upon vital questions affecting the whole people is to be irrevocably fixed by decisions of the Supreme Court, . . . the people will have ceased to be their own rulers, having to that extent practically resigned their government into the hands of that eminent tribunal.

ABRAHAM LINCOLN, *First Inaugural Address,* 4 March, 1861. (*Forum,* Aug., 1935, p. 66.)

8
I do not allow myself to suppose that either the convention or the League have concluded to decide that I am either the greatest or best man in America, but rather they have concluded it is not best to swap horses while crossing the river, and have further concluded that I am not so poor a horse that they might not make a botch of it in trying to swap.

ABRAHAM LINCOLN, *Address,* to a delegation of the National Union League, which had called to congratulate him on his renomination as the Republican presidential candidate, 9 June, 1864. (RHODES, *Hist. of the U. S.,* iv, 470; NICOLAY AND HAY, *Complete Works of Abraham Lincoln,* ii, 532.)

I have not permitted myself, gentlemen, to conclude that I am the best man in the country, but I am reminded in this connection of an old Dutch farmer who remarked that it was not best to swap horses while crossing a stream.

ABRAHAM LINCOLN. Version of above speech by W. O. Stoddard. (RAYMOND, *Life and Public Services of Abraham Lincoln,* p. 500.)

1
Boon-doggle.

ROBERT H. LINK, Eagle Scout, of Rochester, N Y., claims to have coined the word in 1926. and to have applied it, in 1929, to the plaited leather neck-strap on his son's Boy Scout uniform. (See *Literary Digest*, 1 June, 1935, p 3.) The *English Dialect Dictionary*, however. states that it is of Scottish origin, and means a marble obtained as a gift. It came to public attention in the spring of 1935 during an investigation in New York City of the relief activities conducted by the F. D. Roosevelt administration there. It was discovered that there were classes in boon-doggling, that is the plaiting of leather neck-straps, and the public at once hilariously adopted the word to describe any occupation which was a waste of time and money, especially if connected with New Deal activities.

Boon-doggles are like old-type lanyards. They are made of plaited leather. Scouts have been making them for years as uniform ornaments all over the world.

UNKNOWN, *Boon-doggles*. (*Scouting*, March, 1930)

If we can boon-doggle our way out of the depression, that word is going to be enshrined in the hearts of the American people for years to come.

FRANKLIN D. ROOSEVELT, *Speech*, Newark, N. J., 18 Jan., 1936.

2
The cordial understanding. (L'entente cordiale.)

LOUIS PHILIPPE, *Speech*, from the throne, January, 1843, referring to the friendly relations existing between France and England, during Guizot's administration of foreign affairs. QUEEN VICTORIA, *Letter to Lord John Russell*, 7 Sept., 1848.

The cordial understanding which exists between the governments of France and Great Britain (La cordiale entente qui existe entre le gouvernement français et celui de la Grande-Bretagne.)

UNKNOWN, *Article*, in *Le Charivari*, Paris, 6 Jan., 1844, reviewing a speech by Guizot.

The people of two nations [French and English] must be brought into mutual dependence by the supply of each other's wants. There is no other way of counteracting the antagonism of language and race. It is God's own method of producing an *entente cordiale*.

RICHARD COBDEN, *Letter to M. Michel Chevalier*, Sept., 1859.

3
A kin' o' hangin' roun' an' settin' on the fence,
Till Prov'dunce pinted how to jump.

J. R. LOWELL, *The Biglow Papers*. Ser. ii, No. 3. (1862)

4
There are some things so elastic that even the heavy roller of democracy cannot flatten them altogether down.

J. R. LOWELL, *On a Certain Condescension in Foreigners*.

The steam-roller was first heard of in American politics in June, 1908, when it was applied by Oswald F. Schuette, of the Chicago *Inter-Ocean*, to the methods employed by the Roosevelt-Taft majority in the Republican National Committee in over-riding the protests against seating Taft delegates from Alabama and Arkansas.

H. L. MENCKEN, *American Language*, p. 372.

5
What piece of work have you now in hand?
None in hand, if it like your Majesty, but I am devising a platform in my head.

JOHN LYLY, *Alexander and Campaspe*. Act v, sc. 4. (1584)

The wisdom of a lawmaker consisteth not only in a platform of justice, but in the application thereof.

BACON, *Advancement of Learning*, ii, 355. (1623)

Because the things did not work forth your platform.

OLIVER CROMWELL, *Letters*. Vol. iii, p. 89. (1655)

He can soon quit the way wherein he was, and become religious, after the manner of this novel platform.

PATRICK, *Parable of the Pilgrim*, p. 206. (1687)

The Whigs, whether on the Lexington platform or some other non-committal platform, will be and must be at once known as the party that opposed their country in her just and generous war.

UNKNOWN, *Resolutions of the Democratic National Convention*, 30 May, 1844. So far as known, the first recorded use of platform in this sense in America. (See the New York *Herald*, 6 May, 1848.)

6
Frauds of which a lame duck on the stock exchange would be ashamed.

MACAULAY, *Mirabeau*. (*Miscellany*, ii, 95.) In England a lame duck is a defaulter on the Exchange, in America a defeated Congressman, but lame-duck Congresses were abolished in 1934.

I'll have no lame duck's daughter in my family.

THACKERAY, *Vanity Fair*. Ch. 13.

President Lincoln selected Hale [John Parker Hale, appointed minister to Spain] out of general kindness and good will to the lame ducks.

E. L. PIERCE, *Memoir and Letters of Charles Sumner*. Vol. iv, p. 255.

NOTE: This section of familiar political phrases is continued in the APPENDIX.

XIII—Politics: Campaign Slogans

7
Tippecanoe and Tyler too.

Republican campaign slogan, 1840. "Tippecanoe" was William Henry Harrison, who had won an indecisive victory over the Indians in 1811, at the spot where Tippecanoe Creek empties into the Wabash. Attributed to Orson E. Woodbury.

1
Fifty-four forty, or fight!

WILLIAM ALLEN, *Speech*, U. S. Senate, 1844. Adopted as the slogan of the war party, in the presidential election of James K. Polk, 1844. "During the same session war with England regarding the Oregon question seemed imminent. . . . The Democratic convention of 1844 had demanded the reoccupation of the whole of Oregon up to 54° 40′, with or without war with England. Stephen A. Douglas was one of the small band of congressmen who shouted for 'fifty-four forty' to the bitter end. It was therefore humiliating to find the new President willing to compromise with Great Britain on the forty-ninth parallel."—*Dic. Am. Biog.*, v, 398.

2
We stand for free soil.

LEONARD BACON. Motto for the *Independent*, which he helped to found and edited in 1848.

3
Young America!

Slogan of an important group of the Democratic party during campaign of 1852.

The position and duties of Young America.

EDWIN DE LEON (Charleston, 1845), first formulation of Young America idea, in commencement address at South Carolina College, in 1845. The idea was that if there was to be a Young America, the younger generation must seize political power and participate directly in the affairs of the world. (M. E. CURTI, *American Historical Review*, xxxii, 34.)

4
Free soil, free men, free speech, Fré-mont.

Republican slogan in campaign of 1856.

Oh! we'll give 'em Jessie
When we rally round the polls.

Song used by FRÉMONT's supporters in the Presidential campaign of 1856.

5
Peace at any price; peace and union.

Rallying cry Fillmore Campaign, 1856.

6
Repudiate the repudiators.

WILLIAM PITT FESSENDEN, *Speech*, presidential campaign of 1868. The phrase became one of the slogans of the campaign.

7
Turn the rascals out!

CHARLES A. DANA, used first in the New York *Sun*, and afterwards as the slogan of Greeley's campaign against Grant in 1872.

8
Hurrah for Maria,
Hurrah for the kid,
I voted for Grover
And am damn glad I did.

Campaign song, Blaine-Cleveland campaign, 1884, the reference being to Maria Halpin, of Buffalo, N. Y., the mother of Cleveland's reputed illegitimate child. Cleveland always doubted its paternity. (For full story, see NEVINS, *Grover Cleveland*, pp. 163–167.)

Ma! ma! where's my Pa?
Up in the White House, darling,
Making the laws, working the cause,
Up in the White House, dear.

H. R. MONROE, *Ma! Ma! Where's My Pa?* (1884) Referring to the Maria Halpin scandal. Adopted by the Democrats as a campaign jingle in the form: "Ma! Ma! where's my pa? Gone to the White House, ha, ha, ha!"

Tell the truth.

GROVER CLEVELAND, when asked by his campaign managers what they should do about the scandal. (*Harper's Weekly*, 16 Aug., 1884.)

9
Blaine, Blaine, Blaine,
The continental liar from the State of Maine,
Burn this letter!

Campaign jingle used by Democrats during Blaine-Cleveland campaign, referring to an incriminating letter written by Blaine to a business associate named Warren G. Fisher, which he had endorsed on the back, "Burn this letter." (NEVINS, *Grover Cleveland*, p. 161.)

I do not engage in criminal practise.

GEORGE WILLIAM CURTIS, when asked why he did not speak for Blaine during the Blaine-Cleveland campaign of 1884. (NEVINS, *Grover Cleveland*, p. 178.) MUZZEY (*Life of Blaine*, p. 307) attributes the phrase to Roscoe Conkling.

10
We'll hang Jay Gould to a sour apple tree.

Sung by campaign crowd in New York during Blaine-Cleveland campaign of 1884. (NEVINS, *Grover Cleveland*, p. 186.)

11
He's all right!

Prohibition campaign slogan, 1884, referring to John P. St. John, candidate for President. He had been a Republican party leader, and the Republicans started the cry, "What's the matter with St. John?" The reply was, "Oh, he's all right!" Intended to be ironic, it was promptly adopted by the Prohibitionists. Isaac Goldberg (*Tin Pan Alley*, p. 64) asserts that Tony Pastor originated the phrase in New York City in 1884, when Abram S. Hewitt was running for Mayor. Pastor wrote a song with the refrain, "What's the matter with Hewitt?" To which the orchestra, and as many of the audience as agreed, would bellow back, "He's all right!" Used also in the Harrison campaign in 1888.

12
Yes, grandfather's hat fits Ben—fits Ben;
He wears it with dignified grace, Oh yes!
So rally again and we'll put Uncle Ben
Right back in his grandfather's place.

UNKNOWN, *Campaign Song*, 1888. "Ben" was Benjamin Harrison, Republican candidate for President, whose grandfather was General William Henry Harrison.

Grandpa's Pants Won't Fit Benny.

Democratic slogan in campaign of 1888.

13
If the American people want me for this high office, I shall be only too willing to

serve them. . . . Since studying this subject I am convinced that the office of President is not such a very difficult one to fill.

ADMIRAL GEORGE DEWEY, announcing his candidacy, 4 April, 1900.

1
Grover, Grover, Four years more of Grover;
In we'll go, Out they'll go,
Then we'll be in clover.

Democratic campaign song in 1892. Sung to the air of the berceuse in *Wang:*

Baby, baby, Bless the darling baby;
Down she goes, Up she goes,
Ninety times high as the moon.

J. CHEEVER GOODWIN, *Wang*. Act i.

Wanamaker runs the Sunday School,
Morton runs the bar,
Baby McKee runs the White House,
And by God, here we are!

UNKNOWN. Democratic campaign slogan, 1892, referring to Postmaster-General John Wanamaker, superintendent of a Philadelphia Sunday School; Vice-President Levi P. Morton, who owned the Shoreham hotel, in Washington; and "Baby" McKee, Harrison's small grandson.

The prophet and the ballot-box—both stuffed.

THOMAS B. REED, suggested as a slogan for the Democratic party in 1892.

2
Liliuokalani,
Give us your little brown hannie.

Popular jingle, referring to the Hawaiian annexation question, Feb., 1893. Liliuokalani was Queen of the Hawaiian Islands.

3
Elect McKinley, the Advance Agent of Prosperity!

Republican campaign slogan, 1896.

4
The full dinner pail.

Republican campaign slogan, 1900, alleged to have been coined by the editor of *Judge*.

5
Ev'ry time I come to town,
The boys keep kickin' my dawg aroun';
Makes no dif'rence if he is a houn',
They gotta quit kickin' my dawg aroun'.

WEBB M. OUNGST, *They Gotta Quit Kickin' My Dawg Aroun'*. Published in 1912, and the slogan of the campaign for Champ Clark in that year.

6
The New Freedom.

WOODROW WILSON. Used as the slogan of his first campaign. Grover Cleveland said of it: "Sounds fine—I wonder what it means."

7
You have laid upon me this double obligation: "We are relying upon you, Mr. President, to keep us out of war, but we are relying upon you, Mr. President, to keep the honor of the nation unstained."

WOODROW WILSON, *Speech*, at Cleveland, 29 Jan., 1916.

I am the friend of peace and mean to preserve it for America so long as I am able. . . . War can come only by the wilful acts and aggressions of others.

WOODROW WILSON, *Address* to Congress, 26 Feb., 1917.

He kept us out of war!

MARTIN H. GLYNN, *Keynote Speech*, National Democratic Convention, St. Louis, June 15, 1916. Referring to Woodrow Wilson. The phrase became the Democratic slogan of the campaign.

8
The fathers who gave us this government were not graduated from soap-boxes

JOSEPH S. SCOTT, *Speech*, nominating Herbert Hoover, Chicago, 15 June, 1932.

POPE, THE, see under Rome

POPE, ALEXANDER

9
Heroes and Kings! your distance keep;
In peace let one poor Poet sleep,
Who never flatter'd folks like you:
Let Horace blush, and Virgil too.

POPE, *For One Who Would Not Be Buried in Westminster Abbey*.

Under this Marble, or under this Sill,
Or under this Turf, or ev'n what they will, . . .
Lies one who ne'er car'd, and still cares not, a pin
What they said, or may say, of the mortal within;
But who, living and dying, serene, still and free,
Trusts in God that as well as he was he shall be.

POPE, *Another on the Same*.

10
Yes I am proud; I must be proud to see
Men, not afraid of God, afraid of me.

POPE, *Epilogue to the Satires*. Dial. ii, l. 208.

The great honour of that boast is such,
That hornets and mad dogs may boast as much.

T. K. HERVEY, *The Difference between Verbal and Practical Virtue*.

11
One whom it was easy to hate, but still easier to quote.

BIRRELL, *Obiter Dicta: Second Series: Pope*.

12
Where sense with sound, and ease with weight combine,
In the pure silver of Pope's ringing line.

BULWER-LYTTON, *The New Timon*.

13
O Pope, had I thy satire's darts
To gie the rascals their deserts,
I'd rip their rotten, hollow hearts
An' tell aloud
Their jugglin', hocus-pocus arts
To cheat the crowd!

BURNS, *To the Rev. John M'Math*. St. 7.

14
Pope came off clean with Homer; but, they say,
Broome went before, and kindly swept the way.

JOHN HENLEY, *On Pope's Translation of Homer*. William Broome was employed by Pope to translate Homer from the original.

15
No poet? Calculated commonplace?

Ten razor blades in one neat couplet case!
JOHN MACY, *Couplets in Criticism: Pope.*

POPPY

1
The Poppy hath a charm for pain and woe.
MARY A. BARR, *White Poppies.*

The poppy opes her scarlet purse of dreams.
SHARMEL IRIS, *Early Nightfall.*

2
Full-blown poppies, overcharged with rain
Decline the head, and drooping kiss the plain.
HOMER, *Iliad.* Bk. viii, l. 371. (Pope, tr.)

3
Central depth of purple,
Leaves more bright than rose,
Who shall tell what brightest thought
Out of darkness grows?
LEIGH HUNT, *Poppies.*

4
Through the dancing poppies stole
A breeze, most softly lulling to my soul.
KEATS, *Endymion.* Bk. i, l. 566.

On one side is a field of drooping oats,
Through which the poppies show their scarlet coats,
So pert and useless, that they bring to mind
The scarlet coats that pester human-kind.
KEATS, *Epistle to My Brother George,* l. 127.

5
Every castle of the air
Sleeps in the fine black grains, and there
Are seeds for every romance, or light
Whiff of a dream for a summer night.
AMY LOWELL, *Sword Blades and Poppy Seed.*

Visions for those too tired to sleep,
These seeds cast a film over eyes which weep.
AMY LOWELL, *Sword Blades and Poppy Seed.*

6
In Flanders fields the poppies blow
Between the crosses, row on row.
JOHN MCCRAE, *In Flanders Fields.*

And would it not be proud romance
Falling in some obscure advance,
To rise, a poppy field of France?
WILLIAM ALEXANDER PERCY, *Poppy Fields.*

7
Find me next a Poppy posy,
Type of his harangues so dozy.
MOORE, *Wreaths for the Ministers.*

8
Let but my scarlet head appear
And I am held in scorn;
Yet juice of subtile virtue lies
Within my cup of curious dyes.
CHRISTINA ROSSETTI, *"Consider the Lilies of the Field."*

9
O simple flower, you speak the tongue
That tear-drops answer; North and South,
The lips of lovers as they clung,
Spake your sweet language, mouth to mouth.
JOEL ELIAS SPINGARN, *Italian Poppies.*

10
Summer set lip to earth's bosom bare,
And left the flushed print in a poppy there.
FRANCIS THOMPSON, *The Poppy.*

POPULARITY

See also Applause; People, The

11
An ordinary song or ballad that is the delight of the common people cannot fail to please all such readers as are not unqualified for the entertainment by their affectation or ignorance. . . . For it is impossible that anything should be universally tasted and approved by the multitude, though they are only the rabble of the nation, which hath not in it some peculiar aptness to please and gratify the mind of man.
ADDISON, *The Spectator,* No. 70.

12
Such kings of shreds have wooed and won her,
Such crafty knaves her laurel owned,
It has become almost an honor
Not to be crowned.
THOMAS BAILEY ALDRICH, *Popularity.*

13
And Hobbs, Nobbs, Stokes and Nokes combine
To paint the future from the past,
Put blue into their line.

Hobbs hints blue,—straight he turtle eats:
Nobbs prints blue,—claret crowns his cup:
Nokes outdares Stokes in azure feats,—
Both gorge. Who fished the murex up?
What porridge had John Keats?
ROBERT BROWNING, *Popularity.*

14
Their [the public's] favour in an author's cap's a feather,
And no great mischief's done by their caprice.
BYRON, *Don Juan.* Canto i, st. 199.

15
The tumultuous love of the populace must be seized and enjoyed in its first transports; there is no hoarding of it to use upon occasions; it will not keep.
LORD CHESTERFIELD, *Account of the Dutch Republic.* Footnote.

16
The popular breeze. (Aura popularis.)
CICERO, *De Haruspicum Responsis.* Ch. 20, 43.

17
The people's chosen flower, Persuasion's marrow. (Flos delibatus populi, Suadæque medulla.)
QUINTUS ENNIUS, *De Cetego.*

18
When one has a good table, one is always in the right. (Quand on a bonne table on a toujours raison.)
COLLIN D'HARLEVILLE, *M. de Crac.* Sc. 4.

1
Popularity is a crime from the moment it is sought; it is only a virtue when men have it whether they will or no.
LORD HALIFAX, *Works*, p. 232.

2
Popularity disarms envy in well-disposed minds. Those are ever the most ready to do justice to others, who feel that the world has done them justice.
WILLIAM HAZLITT, *Characteristics*. No. 12.

3
Popularity is glory in copper pieces. (La popularité c'est la gloire en gros sous.)
VICTOR HUGO.

4
To some men popularity is always suspicious. Enjoying none themselves, they are prone to suspect the validity of those attainments which command it.
GEORGE HENRY LEWES, *Spanish Drama*. Ch. 3.

5
Honour, glory, and popular praise,
Rocks whereon greatest men have oftest wreck'd.
MILTON, *Paradise Regained*. Bk. ii, l. 227.

6
Safer with multitudes to stray,
Than tread alone a fairer way:
To mingle with the erring throng,
Than boldly speak ten millions wrong.
ROBERT NUGENT, *Epistle to a Lady*.

7
The popularity of a bad man is as treacherous as himself. (Gratia malorum tam infida est quam ipsi.)
PLINY THE YOUNGER, *Epistles*. Bk. i, epis. 5.

8
When Fortune favors us, Popularity bears her company.
PUBLILIUS SYRUS, *Sententiæ*. No. 275.

9
I know what pathway leads to popularity. (Sciam, quæ via ad istum favorem ferat.)
SENECA, *Epistulæ ad Lucilium*. Epis. xxix, 12.

10
All tongues speak of him, and the bleared sights
Are spectacled to see him.
SHAKESPEARE, *Coriolanus*. Act ii, sc. 1, l. 221.

I have seen the dumb men throng to see him and
The blind to hear him speak: matrons flung gloves,
Ladies and maids their scarfs and handkerchers,
Upon him as he pass'd, the nobles bended,
As to Jove's statue, and the commons made
A shower and thunder with their caps and shouts.
SHAKESPEARE, *Coriolanus*. Act ii, sc. 1, l. 278.

The ladies call him sweet;
The stairs, as he treads on them, kiss his feet.
SHAKESPEARE, *Love's Labour's Lost*. Act v, sc. 2, l. 329.

Some shout him, and some hang upon his car,
To gaze in 's eyes, and bless him. Maidens wave
Their 'kerchiefs, and old women weep for joy;
While others, not so satisfied, unhorse
The gilded equipage, and, turning loose
His steeds, usurp a place they well deserve.
COWPER, *The Task*. Bk. vi, l. 698.

11
Enfeoff'd himself to popularity.
SHAKESPEARE, *I Henry IV*. Act iii, sc. 2, l. 69.

12
That empty and ugly thing called popularity.
R. L. STEVENSON, *A Letter to a Young Gentleman*.

13
These heroes—erst extolling—
A fickle public drops;
Folks chase a ball that's rolling,
And kick it when it stops.
UNKNOWN, *Popularity*. (*Life*, April, 1900.) Apropos of Dewey and Hobson.

14
God will not love thee less, because men love thee more.
MARTIN FARQUHAR TUPPER, *Proverbial Philosophy: Of Self-Acquaintance*.

POSITION, see Place

POSSESSION

15
I die,—but first I have possess'd,
And come what may, I *have been* blest.
BYRON, *The Giaour*, l. 1114.

16
So various is the human mind;
Such are the frailties of mankind!
What at a distance charmed our eyes,
Upon attainment, droops, and dies.
JOHN CUNNINGHAM, *Hymen*.

The thing possessed is not the thing it seems.
SAMUEL DANIEL, *The History of the Civil War*. Bk. ii, st. 104.

All things that are,
Are with more spirit chased than enjoy'd.
SHAKESPEARE, *The Merchant of Venice*. Act ii, sc. 6, l. 12.

17
Possession means to sit astride of the world,
Instead of having it astride of you.
CHARLES KINGSLEY, *The Saint's Tragedy*. Act i, sc. 2.

18
Aspiration sees only one side of every question; possession, many.
LOWELL, *Among My Books: New England Two Centuries Ago*.

19
Bliss in possession will not last.
JAMES MONTGOMERY, *The Little Cloud*, l. 177.

20
What is not ours charms more than our own. (Capiunt animos plus aliena suis.)
OVID, *Ars Amatoria*. Bk. i, l. 348. *See also under* DISCONTENT.

1
An object in possession never retains the same charms it had in pursuit. (Nihil enim æque gratum est adeptis, quam concupiscentibus.)
PLINY THE YOUNGER, *Epistles*. Bk. ii, epis. 15.

When I behold what pleasure is Pursuit,
What life, what glorious eagerness it is,
Then mark how full Possession falls from this,
How fairer seems the blossom than the fruit,—
I am perplext, and often stricken mute,
Wondering which attained the higher bliss,
The winged insect, or the chrysalis
It thrust aside with unreluctant foot.
T. B. ALDRICH, *Pursuit and Possession*.

See also under WOOING.

2
What our contempt doth often hurl from us,
We wish it ours again.
SHAKESPEARE, *Antony and Cleopatra*. Act i, sc. 2, l. 127.

For it so falls out
That what we have we prize not to the worth
Whiles we enjoy it, but being lack'd and lost,
Why, then we rack the value; then we find
The virtue that possession would not show us
Whiles it was ours.
SHAKESPEARE, *Much Ado About Nothing*. Act iv, sc. 1, l. 219.

Not to understand a treasure's worth
Till time has stol'n away the slighted good,
Is cause of half the poverty we feel,
And makes the world the wilderness it is.
COWPER, *The Task*. Bk. vi, l. 50.

3
She is mine own,
And I as rich in having such a jewel
As twenty seas, if all their sand were pearl,
The water nectar, and the rocks pure gold.
SHAKESPEARE, *The Two Gentlemen of Verona*. Act ii, sc. 4, l. 168.

4
No one worth possessing
Can be quite possessed.
SARA TEASDALE, *Advice to a Girl*.

5
The want of a thing is perplexing enough, but the possession of it is intolerable.
SIR JOHN VANBRUGH, *The Confederacy*. Act i, sc. 3.

POSSESSION NINE POINTS OF THE LAW, *see under* LAW: APOTHEGMS.

POSSESSIONS

See also Property, Riches, Wealth

I—Definitions and Apothegms

6
I carry all my possessions with me. (Omnia mea porto mecum.)
BIAS. (CICERO, *Paradoxa*, i, 2.)

All my goods are with me. (Omnia bona mea mecum sunt.)
STILPO. (SENECA, *Epistulæ ad Lucilium*. Epis. ix.)

For what one has in black and white,
One can carry home in comfort.
(Denn was man schwarz auf weiss besitzt
Kann man getrost nach Hause tragen.)
GOETHE, *Faust*. Act i, sc. 4, l. 42.

7
As much as thou hast, so much art thou worth.
CERVANTES, *Don Quixote*. Pt. ii, ch. 20.

What a man has, so much he is sure of.
CERVANTES, *Don Quixote*. Pt. ii, ch. 43.

We are Goddes stewardes all, nought of our owne we bare.
THOMAS CHATTERTON, *Excelente Balade of Charitie*.

8
As having nothing, and yet possessing all things.
New Testament: II Corinthians, vi, 10.

Lord of himself, though not of lands;
And having nothing, yet hath all.
SIR HENRY WOTTON, *The Character of a Happy Life*.

9
The feeling of satiety, almost inseparable from large possessions, is a surer cause of misery than ungratified desires.
BENJAMIN DISRAELI, *Lothair*. Ch. 25.

10
Much will have more.
EMERSON, *Society and Solitude: Works and Days*.

11
This, and this alone, I contend for—that he who makes should have; that he who saves should enjoy.
HENRY GEORGE, *Social Problems*. Ch. 9.

12
Would ye both eat your cake and have your cake?
JOHN HEYWOOD, *Proverbs*. Pt. i, ch. 9. (1546)
GEORGE HERBERT, *The Size*.

I can't, I trow,
Both eat my cake and have it too.
ROBERT HEATH, *Occasional Poems*, 19 .

13
Let me possess what I now have, or even less, that I may enjoy my remaining days—if the gods grant any to remain. (Sit mihi quod nunc est, etiam minus, ut mihi vivam Quod superest ævi, si quid superesse volunt di.)
HORACE, *Epistles*. Bk. i, epis. 18, l. 107.

See also under CONTENT.

15
Is it not lawful for me to do what I will with mine own?
New Testament: Matthew, xx, 15.

16
All the possessions of mortals are mortal. (Mortale est omne mortalium bonum.)
METRODORUS, *Fragments*. Frag. 35.

You can never consider that as your own which can be changed. (Nil proprium ducas quod mutari potest.)
PUBLILIUS SYRUS, *Sententiæ*. No. 416.

1
What is mine is dear to me, as his own is dear to every man. (Meus mihi, suos cuique est carus.)
PLAUTUS, *Captivi*, l. 400. (Act ii, sc. 2.)

An ill-favoured thing, sir, but mine own.
SHAKESPEARE, *As You Like It*. Act v, sc. 4, l. 61.

2
What is thine own hold as thine own. (Quod tuum est, teneas tuum.)
PLAUTUS, *Cistellaria*, l. 768. (Act iv, sc. 2.)

Get what you can, and keep what you get. (Lucri quidquid est, id domum trahere oportet.)
PLAUTUS, *Mostellaria*, l. 801. (Act iii, sc. 2.)

That's a dismal word, the very worst of words, "had," when one has nothing. (Miserum istac verbum et pessimum est, habuisse, et nihil habere.)
PLAUTUS, *Rudens*, l. 1321. (Act v, sc. 2.)

3
What is thine is mine, and all mine is thine. (Quod tuomst meumst, omne meum est autem tuom.)
PLAUTUS, *Trinummus*. Act ii, sc. 2.

What's mine is yours and what is yours is mine.
SHAKESPEARE, *Measure for Measure*, v, 1, 543.

He who says, What is mine is yours and what is yours is yours, is a saint. He who says, What is yours is mine and what is mine is mine, is a wicked man.
Babylonian Talmud: Aboth, v, 13.

4
It is better to have a little than nothing.
PUBLILIUS SYRUS, *Sententiæ*. No. 484.

To know how to do without is to possess. (C'est posséder les biens que savoir s'en passer.)
REGNARD, *Joueur*, iv, 13.

See also under MODERATION.

5
What difference does it make how much you have? What you do not have amounts to much more. (Quid enim refert quantum habeas? Multo illud plus est quos non habes.)
SENECA. (AULUS GELLIUS, *Noctes Atticæ*. Bk. xii, ch. 2, sec. 13.)

No man can swim ashore and carry his baggage with him. (Nemo cum sarcinis enatat.)
SENECA, *Epistulæ ad Lucilium*. Epis. xxii, 12.

6
To have may be taken from us, to have had, never. (Habere crepitur, habuisse numquam.)
SENECA, *Epistulæ ad Lucilium*. Epis. xcviii, 11.

7
Let's choose executors and talk of wills:
And yet not so, for what can we bequeath
Save our deposed bodies to the ground? . . .
Nothing can we call our own but death
And that small model of the barren earth
Which serves as paste and cover to our bones.
SHAKESPEARE, *Richard II*. Act iii, sc. 2, l. 148.

8
They well deserve to have
That know the strong'st and surest way to get.
SHAKESPEARE, *Richard II*. Act iii, sc. 3, l. 200.

The good old rule
Sufficeth them, the simple plan,
That they should take who have the power,
And they should keep who can.
WORDSWORTH, *Rob Roy's Grave*. St. 9.

9
Saw from his windows nothing save his own.
TENNYSON, *Aylmer's Field*, l. 21.

I am amused to see from my window here how busily man has divided and staked off his domain. God must smile at his puny fences running hither and thither everywhere over the land.
H. D. THOREAU, *Journal*, 20 Feb., 1842.

It [land] gives one position, and prevents one from keeping it up.
OSCAR WILDE, *The Importance of Being Earnest*. Act i.

10
I'm the only thing in my house I can call my own. (Ego meorum solus sum meus.)
TERENCE, *Phormio*, l. 587. (Act iv, sc. 1.)

10a
Papa's having and mama's having is not like having one's self. (Fu yu mu yu wu ju tzŭ yu.)
UNKNOWN. A Chinese proverb.

II—Possessions: To Him Who Hath

11
Unto every one that hath shall be given, and he shall have abundance; but from him that hath not shall be taken away even that which he hath.
New Testament: Matthew, xxv, 29; *Mark*, iv, 25.

To him that hath, we are told,
Shall be given. Yes, by the Cross!
To the rich man fate sends gold,
To the poor man loss on loss.
THOMAS BAILEY ALDRICH, *From The Spanish*.

12
If you are poor now, Æmilius, you will always be poor. Wealth is given today to none save the rich. (Semper pauper eris, si pauper es, Æmiliane. Dantur opes nullis nunc nisi divitibus.)
MARTIAL, *Epigrams*. Bk. v, epig. 81.

All strive to give to the rich man.
THOMAS FULLER, *Gnomologia*. No 544.

We give to the rich and take from the poor.
GEORGE HERBERT, *Jacula Prudentum*.

13
Everything goes to him who wants nothing.
JOHN RAY, *English Proverbs*. The French form is: "Tout va à qui n'a pas besoin."

By right or wrong,
Lands and goods go to the strong,
Property will brutely draw
Still to the proprietor;
Silver to silver creep and wind,
And kind to kind.
EMERSON, *The Celestial Love*.

14
"Poor deer," quoth he, "thou makest a testament

As worldlings do, giving thy sum of more
To that which had too much."

SHAKESPEARE, *As You Like It*. Act ii, sc. 1, l. 47.

1
How unfair it is that those who have less are always adding to the possessions of those who have more. (Quam inique comparatumst, ei qui minus habent Ut semper aliquid addant ditioribus.)

TERENCE, *Phormio*, l. 41. (Act i, sc. 1.)

For now a few have all, and all have nought.

SPENSER, *Mother Hubberds Tale*.

POST, see Letter

POST, see Letter

POSTERITY

2
The care of posterity is most in them that have no posterity.

BACON, *Essays: Of Parents and Children*.

3
Not to the Past, but to the Future, looks true nobility, and finds its blazon in posterity.

BULWER-LYTTON, *The Lady of Lyons*. Act. ii, sc. 1.

People will not look forward to posterity, who never look backward to their ancestors.

EDMUND BURKE, *Reflections on the Revolution in France*.

4
Be careful of this—it is my carte de visite to posterity.

CHAMPOLLION. On his death-bed, as he gave the printer the revised proofs of his Egyptian Grammar.

I look upon *Leaves of Grass* . . . as my definitive carte de visite to the coming generations of the New World.

WALT WHITMAN, *A Backward Glance o'er Travel'd Roads*.

5
He thinks posterity a packhorse, always ready to be loaded.

BENJAMIN DISRAELI, *Speech*, 3 June, 1862.

Posterity is a most limited assembly. Those gentlemen who reach posterity are not much more numerous than the planets.

BENJAMIN DISRAELI, *Speech*. 3 June, 1862.

6
The love of posterity is the consequence of the necessity of death. If a man were sure of living forever here, he would not care about his offspring.

HAWTHORNE, *American Note Books*. *See also under* SON.

7
Posterity, thinned by the crimes of its ancestors. (Vitio parentum Rara juventus.)

HORACE, *Odes*. Bk. i, ode 2, l. 23.

Posterity pays for the sins of their fathers. (Culpam majorum posteri luunt.)

QUINTUS CURTIUS RUFUS, *De Rebus Gestis Alexandri Magni*. Bk. vii, sec. 5.

Herself the solitary scion left
Of a time-honour'd race.

BYRON, *The Dream*. St. 2.

8
Believe it, posterity! (Credite, posteri.)

HORACE, *Odes*. Bk. ii, ode 19, l. 2.

He lives to posterity. (Vivit ad posteros.)

SENECA, *Epistulæ ad Lucilium*. Epis. xciii, 5.

9
Our descendants will be still far unhappier than we are. Would I not be a criminal if, notwithstanding this view, I should provide for progeny, i. e., for unfortunates?

ALEXANDER VON HUMBOLDT. Conversation with Arago in 1812.

10
The ancients said *our ancestors*, we say *posterity*. (Les anciens disaient *nos ancêtres*, nous disons *la postérité*.)

JOUBERT, *Pensées*. No. 228.

11
Posterity, that high court of appeal which is never tired of eulogising its own justice and discernment.

MACAULAY, *Essays: Machiavelli*.

Like Sir Condy Rackrent in the tale, she survived her own wake, and overheard the judgment of posterity.

MACAULAY, *Essays: Madame d'Arblay*. Referring to Miss Edgeworth's novel, *Castle Rackrent*.

12
Leaving no posterity:
'Twas not their infirmity,
It was married chastity.

SHAKESPEARE, *Phœnix and the Turtle*, l. 59.

13
All his successors, gone before him, have done 't; and all his ancestors that come after him, may.

SHAKESPEARE, *Merry Wives of Windsor*, i, 1, 14.

14
What is thy body but a swallowing grave,
Seeming to bury that posterity
Which by the rights of time thou needs must have,
If thou destroy them not in dark obscurity?

SHAKESPEARE, *Venus and Adonis*, l. 757.

15
We are always doing, says he, something for Posterity, but I would fain see Posterity do something for us.

ADDISON, *The Spectator*. No. 583. (1712)

The man was laughed at as a blunderer who said in a public business: "We do much for posterity; I would fain see them do something for us."

MRS. ELIZABETH MONTAGU, *Letters*, 1 Jan., 1742.

As to posterity, I may ask (with somebody whom I have forgot) what has it ever done to oblige me?

THOMAS GRAY, *Letter to Dr. Warton*, 8 March, 1758.

As though there were a tie,
And obligation to posterity!
We get them, bear them, breed and nurse.
What has posterity done for us,

That we. lest they their rights should lose,
Should trust our necks to gripe of noose?
JOHN TRUMBULL, *McFingal*. Canto ii, l. 121. (1775)

Why should we put ourselves out of the way to do anything for posterity? What has posterity done for us?
SIR BOYLE ROCHE, *Speech,* in Irish Parliament, 1780. (FLAKINER, *Studies in Irish History.*)

Few can be induced to labor exclusively for posterity. Posterity has done nothing for us.
ABRAHAM LINCOLN, *Speech,* 22 Feb., 1842.

1
Think of your ancestors and your posterity. (Majores vestros et posteros cogitate.)
TACITUS, *Agricola.* Sec. 32.

Think of your forefathers! Think of your posterity!
JOHN QUINCY ADAMS, *Speech,* Plymouth, Mass., 22 Dec., 1802.

See also under ANCESTRY.

2
Posterity gives to every man his proper praise. (Suum cuique decus posteritas rependit.)
TACITUS, *Annals.* Bk. iv, sec. 35.

Posterity pays every man his honour.
BEN JONSON, *Fall of Sejanus.* Act iii, sc. 1.

3
Our children's children, and those who shall be descended from them. (Nati natorum, et qui nascentur ab illis.)
VERGIL, *Æneid.* Bk. iii, l. 98.

CONTEMPORANEOUS POSTERITY, *see under* FOREIGNERS.

POT

4
Said the pot to the kettle, "Get away, blackface!" (Dijó la sarten á la caldera, quitate allá ojinegra.)
CERVANTES, *Don Quixote.* Pt. ii, ch. 67.

Do not let the kettle call the pot black-arse!
APHRA BEHN, *Feigned Courtesan.* Act v, sc. 4.

Dares thus the kettle to rebuke our sin!
Dares thus the kettle say the pot is black!
FIELDING, *Covent Garden Tragedy.* Act ii, sc. 5.

The raven said to the rook, "Stand away, blackcoat."
THOMAS FULLER, *Gnomologia.* No. 4729.

Thou art a bitter bird, said the raven to the starling.
JOHN RAY, *English Proverbs,* 195.

The raven chides blackness.
SHAKESPEARE, *Troilus and Cressida,* ii, 3, 221.

The poker scoffs at the shovel. (Le fourgon se mocque de la pelle.)
MONTAIGNE, *Essays.* Bk. iii, ch. 5.

5
We'll find out rich husband to make you the pot boil.
SIR WILLIAM D'AVENANT, *Play-House to be Let.* Act v. (c. 1663)

Glory is excellent, but will not make the national pot boil.
CARLYLE, *Frederick the Great,* xvi, 2; vi, 151

She teaches you economy, which makes the pot to boil.
CHRISTOPHER SMART, *Ballads.* No. 13.

I think this piece will help to boil thy pot.
JOHN WOLCOT, *The Bard Complimenteth Mr. West.* (c. 1790) Probably the origin of the term "pot-boiler."

6
How agree the kettle and earthen pot together?
APOCRYPHA: *Ecclesiasticus,* xiii, 2.

The earthen pot must keep clear of the brass kettle.
H. G. BOHN, *Handbook of Proverbs,* p 503.

7
A pot that belongs to many is ill stirred and worse boiled.
THOMAS FULLER, *Gnomologia.* No. 360.

See also under COOK.

8
What's the use of watching? A watched pot never boils.
MRS. GASKELL, *Mary Barton.* Ch. 31.

9
Neither pot broken nor water spilt.
JOHN HEYWOOD, *Proverbs.* Pt. i, ch. ii. In other words, "No harm done."

10
The weaker goeth to the pot, as all days see.
JOHN HEYWOOD, *Proverbs.* Pt. ii, ch. 5.

11
The pot boils badly. (Olla male fervet.)
PETRONIUS, *Satyricon.* Sec. 38. Meaning that things do not go favorably.

When the pot boils over, it cooleth itself.
THOMAS FULLER, *Gnomologia.* No. 5602.

12
One pot sets another boiling.
W. G. BENHAM, *Proverbs,* p. 822.

13
Little pot is soon hot.
JOHN RAY, *English Proverbs.*

Now, were not I a little pot and soon hot, my very lips might freeze to my teeth.
SHAKESPEARE, *The Taming of the Shrew.* Act iv, sc. 1, l. 6.

POTTER AND POTTERY

See also Man and the Potter

14
Thy moist clay is pliant to command,
Unwrought, and easy to the potter's hand:
Now take the mould; now bend thy mind to feel
The first sharp motions of the forming wheel.
DRYDEN, *Third Satire of Persius.* l. 38.

15
Dear Tom, this brown jug that now foams with mild ale,—
In which I will drink to sweet Nan of the vale,—
Was once Toby Fillpot, a thirsty old soul

As e'er drank a bottle, or fathomed a bowl;
In bousing about 'twas his praise to excel,
And among jolly topers he bore off the bell.
FRANCIS FAWKES, *The Brown Jug.*

1
The potter is at enmity with the potter. (Καὶ κεραμεὺς κεραμεῖ κοτέει.)
HESIOD, *Works and Days*, l. 25.

2
There's a joy without canker or cark,
There's a pleasure eternally new,
'Tis to gloat on the glaze and the mark
Of china that's ancient and blue;
Unchipp'd, all the centuries through
It has pass'd, since the chime of it rang,
And they fashion'd it, figures and hue,
In the reign of the Emperor Hwang.
ANDREW LANG, *Ballade of Blue China.*

I am content to be a bric-a-bracker and a Ceramiker.
MARK TWAIN, *A Tramp Abroad.* Ch. 20.

3
Every potter praises his own pot.
H. G. BOHN, *Hand-Book of Proverbs.*

4
No handycraft can with our art compare,
For pots are made of what we potters are.
UNKNOWN. Motto of 18th century potters, often used on glazed ware. Another version was used by Longfellow in an introduction to *Kéramos*, and is sometimes mistakingly ascribed to him.

Turn, turn, my wheel! Turn round and round
Without a pause, without a sound:
So spins the flying world away!
This clay, well mixed with marl and sand,
Follows the motion of my hand;
For some must follow, and some command,
Though all are made of clay!
LONGFELLOW, *Kéramos*, l. 1.

POVERTY

See also Misery; Poetry and Poverty; Want

I—Poverty: Definitions

5
Poverty does not mean the possession of little, but the non-possession of much. (Paupertas enim est non quæ pauca possidet, sed quæ multa non possidet.)
ANTIPATER, *Fragments.* No. 54. (SENECA, *Epistulæ ad Lucilium.* Epis. lxxxvii, sec. 39.)

It is not the man who has too little, but the man who craves more, that is poor. (Non qui parum habet, sed qui plus cupit, pauper est.)
SENECA, *Epistulæ ad Lucilium.* Epis. ii, sec. 6.

He is not poor that hath little, but he that desireth much.
GEORGE HERBERT, *Jacula Prudentum.*

6
Poverty is the discoverer of all the arts. (Paupertas . . omnium artium repertrix.)
APOLLONIUS DYSCOLUS, *De Magia.* Sec. 18.

Poverty . . . instructress in all the arts. (Paupertas . . . omnes artes perdocet.)
PLAUTUS, *Stichus.* Act ii, sc. 1.

Poverty is the mother of all the arts and trades.
TORRIANO, *Piazza Universale*, 214.
See also under NECESSITY.

7
Poverty is the muses' patrimony.
ROBERT BURTON, *Anatomy of Melancholy.* Pt. i, sec. ii, mem. 3, subs. 15.

Poverty! thou source of human art,
Thou great inspirer of the poet's song!
EDWARD MOORE, *Hymn to Poverty.*
See also POETRY AND POVERTY.

8
Poverty is the mother of crime. (Mater crimunum necessitas tollitur.)
CASSIODORUS, *Variæ.* Bk. ix, sec. 13.

Poverty, the mother of manhood. (Fecunda virorum paupertas.)
LUCAN, *De Bello Civili.* Bk. i, l. 165.

Poverty, the mother of temperance. (Πενία μητέρα σωφροσύνας.)
PALLADAS. (*Greek Anthology.* Bk. x, epig. 61.)

Mother of Miseries.
SOUTHEY, *Vision of the Maid of Orleans.* Bk. iii.

Poverty, mother of health. (Paupertas sanitatis mater.)
VINCENT OF BEAUVAIS, *Speculum Historiale.* Bk. x, ch. 71.

9
Poverty, the reward of honest fools.
COLLEY CIBBER, *Richard III.* (Altered), ii, 2.

10
Poverty consists in feeling poor.
EMERSON, *Society and Solitude: Domestic Life.*

There is no ill on earth which mortals fly
With so much dread as abject poverty. . . .
And yet thou art no formidable foe,
Except to little souls, who think thee so!
STEPHEN DUCK, *Poverty.*

11
Contented poverty is an honorable estate. (Honesta res est læta paupertas.)
EPICURUS, *Fragments.* No. 475.

12
Poverty is no vice, but an inconvenience.
JOHN FLORIO, *Second Frutes.* Fo. 105.

He found it inconvenient to be poor.
COWPER, *Charity*, l. 189.

Poverty is no disgrace to a man, but it is confoundedly inconvenient.
SYDNEY SMITH. (LADY HOLLAND, *Memoir.* Vol. i.)

13
Poverty is not a shame, but the being ashamed of it is.
THOMAS FULLER, *Gnomologia.* No. 3908.

Poverty is no sin.
GEORGE HERBERT, *Jacula Prudentum.*

'Tis true that poverty is not a sin,
But all the same 'tis best to keep it in.
(La pauvreté n'est pas un péché,
Mieux vaut cependant la cacher.)
UNKNOWN. A French proverb.

1
He is not poor who has enough for his needs. (Pauper enim non est, cui rerum suppetit usus.)
HORACE, *Epistles*. Bk. i, epis. 12, l. 4.

I do not regard a man as poor, if the little which remains is enough for him. (Non puto pauperem, cui quantulumcumque superest, sat est.)
SENECA, *Epistulæ ad Lucilium*. Epis. i, sec. 5.
See also under MODERATION.

2
To have nothing is not poverty. (Non est paupertas habere nihil.)
MARTIAL, *Epigrams*. Bk. xi, ep. 32.

3
Poverty is a hateful blessing. (Paupertas est odibile bonum.)
VINCENT OF BEAUVAIS, *Speculum Historiale*. Bk. x, ch. 71.

II—Poverty: Apothegms

4
There is no man so poor but what he can afford to keep one dog. And I have seen them so poor that they could afford to keep three.
JOSH BILLINGS, *On Poverty*.

5
Poverty makes strange bedfellows.
BULWER-LYTTON, *The Caxtons*. Pt. iv, ch. 4.

6
Over the hill to the poor-house I'm trudgin' my weary way.
WILL CARLETON, *Over the Hill to the Poor-house*.

Rattle his bones over the stones,
He's only a pauper whom nobody owns.
THOMAS NOEL, *The Pauper's Drive*.

7
Of all God's creatures, man Alone is poor.
JANE WELSH CARLYLE, *To a Swallow Building Under Our Eaves*.

8
Living from hand to mouth.
DU BARTAS, *Devine Weekes and Workes*. Week ii, day 1. (Sylvester, tr.)

9
As poor as Job.
JOHN GOWER, *Confessio Amantis*. Bk. v, l. 2505. (1390) *See also under* JOB.

As poor as church mice.
JOHN OZELL, *Molière*, iv, 38.

10
The poor man alone,
When he hears the poor moan,
From a morsel a morsel will give.
THOMAS HOLCROFT, *Gaffer Gray*.

Few, save the poor, feel for the poor.
LETITIA ELIZABETH LANDON, *The Poor*.

11
What mean ye that ye beat my people to pieces, and grind the faces of the poor?
Old Testament: Isaiah, iii, 15.

12
Here we all live in pretentious poverty. (Hic vivimus ambitiosa Paupertate omnes.)
JUVENAL, *Satires*. Sat. iii, l. 182.

13
Women that bake and brew, butchers and cooks,
They are the people that harm the poor.
WILLIAM LANGLAND, *Piers Plowman*. Part iv.

14
The wretch, at summing up his misspent days,
Found nothing left, but poverty and praise.
JOHN OLDHAM, *A Satire: Spenser Dissuading the Author*, l. 182.

15
It is natural for a poor man to count his flock. (Pauperis est numerare pecus.)
OVID, *Metamorphoses*. Bk. xiii, l. 824.

16
So shall thy poverty come as one that travelleth, and thy want as an armed man.
Old Testament: Proverbs, vi, 11. The revised version is, "So shall thy poverty come as a robber."

17
He that hath pity upon the poor lendeth unto the Lord.
Old Testament: Proverbs, xix, 17.

18
No one lives so poor as he is born. (Nemo tam pauper vivit quam natus est.)
SENECA, *Quare Bonis Viris*.

19
My friends are poor but honest.
SHAKESPEARE, *All's Well that Ends Well*. Act i, sc. 3, l. 201.

An honest exceeding poor man.
SHAKESPEARE, *The Merchant of Venice*. Act ii, sc. 2, l. 54.

20
Steep'd me in poverty to the very lips.
SHAKESPEARE, *Othello*. Act iv, sc. 2, l. 50.

Steeped to the lips in misery.
LONGFELLOW, *Goblet of Life*. St. 11.

21
O world, how apt the poor are to be proud!
SHAKESPEARE, *Twelfth Night*. Act iii, sc. 1, 138.

The devil wipes his tail with the poor man's pride.
JOHN RAY, *English Proverbs*, 21.
See also PRIDE: APOTHEGMS.

22
Those who minister to poverty and disease are accomplices in the two worst of all crimes.
BERNARD SHAW, *Maxims for Revolutionists*.

23
Yes, we will do almost anything for the poor man, anything but get off his back.
TOLSTOY. (HUNTINGDON, *Philanthropy and Morality*.)

24
How punctually God's poor arise to serve
Mammon and Greed!
CHARLES HANSON TOWNE, *Manhattan*.

25
As for the virtuous poor, one can pity them,

of course, but one cannot possibly admire them.

OSCAR WILDE, *The Soul of a Man under Socialism.*

III—Poverty: Its Prevalence

1
Come away! Poverty's catching.

APHRA BEHN, *II The Rover.* Act i, sc. 1.

2
Well, let the world change on,—still must endure
While earth is earth, one changeless race, the poor!

BULWER-LYTTON, *The New Timon.* Pt. i, st. 1.

3
Three million paupers . . . these are but items in the sad ledger of despair.

CARLYLE, *Latter-Day Pamphlets.* No. 1.

4
For one poor Man there are an hundred indigent.

BENJAMIN FRANKLIN, *Poor Richard,* 1746.

5
For ye have the poor always with you.

New Testament: Matthew, xxvi, 11; *Mark,* xiv, 7; *John,* xii, 8.

6
Where are those troops of Poor, that throng'd of yore
The good old Landlord's hospitable door?

POPE, *Satires of Dr. Donne.* Satire ii, l. 113.

7
No society can surely be flourishing and happy, of which the far greater part of the members are poor and miserable.

ADAM SMITH, *Wealth of Nations.* Bk. i, ch. 8.

8
The awful phantom of the hungry poor.

HARRIET PRESCOTT SPOFFORD, *A Winter's Night.*

9
Whene'er I take my walks abroad,
How many poor I see.

ISAAC WATTS, *Praise for Mercies Spiritual and Temporal.*

Whene'er I walk the public ways,
How many poor that lack ablution
Do probe my heart with pensive gaze,
And beg a trivial contribution!

OWEN SEAMAN, *The Bitter Cry of the Great Unpaid.*

Whene'er I walk this beauteous earth
How many poor I see,
But as I never speaks to them,
They never speaks to me.

UNKNOWN, *Travesty of Seaman's Bitter Cry of the Great Unpaid.*

IV—Poverty: Its Compensations

10
Christ himself was poor. . . . And as he was himself, so he informed his apostles and disciples, they were all poor, prophets poor, apostles poor.

ROBERT BURTON, *Anatomy of Melancholy.* Pt. ii, sec. ii, mem. 3, subs. 1.

The greatest man in history was the poorest.

EMERSON, *Society and Solitude: Domestic Life.*

11
Thank God for poverty
That makes and keeps us free,
And lets us go our unobtrusive way,
Glad of the sun and rain,
Upright, serene, humane,
Contented with the fortune of a day.

BLISS CARMAN, *The Word at Saint Kavin's.*

They who have nothing have little to fear,
Nothing to lose or to gain.

MADISON CAWEIN, *The Bellman.*

12
Now let my bed be hard
No care take I;
I'll make my joy like this
Small Butterfly;
Whose happy heart has power
To make a stone a flower.

WILLIAM H. DAVIES, *The Example.*

13
Remember to bear patiently the burden of poverty. (Paupertatis onus patienter ferre memento.)

DIONYSIUS CATO, *Disticha de Moribus.* Bk. i, No. 21.

14
"Ignorance," says Ajax, "is a painless evil"; so, I should think, is dirt, considering the merry faces that go along with it.

GEORGE ELIOT, *Mr. Gilfil's Love Story.*

15
O happy unown'd youths! your limbs can bear
The scorching dog-star and the winter's air,
While the rich infant, nurs'd with care and pain,
Thirsts with each heat and coughs with every rain!

JOHN GAY, *Trivia.* Bk. ii, l. 145.

16
Let not Ambition mock their useful toil,
Their homely joys, and destiny obscure;
Nor Grandeur hear with a disdainful smile
The short and simple annals of the poor.

THOMAS GRAY, *Elegy Written in a Country Church-yard,* l. 29.

17
Happier he, the peasant, far,
From the pangs of passion free,
That breathes the keen yet wholesome air
Of ragged penury.

THOMAS GRAY, *On the Pleasure Arising from Vicissitude.* This stanza is said to have been added to Gray's poem by his biographer, the Rev. William Mason.

Poverty has no means to feed its passion, yet it is not worth while to wish to be poor because of that. (Non habet, unde suum paupertas pascat amorem: Non tamen hoc tanti est, pauper ut esse velis.)

OVID, *Remediorum Amoris,* l. 749.

1

Poverty, when it is voluntary, is never despicable, but takes an heroical aspect.
  WILLIAM HAZLITT, *Table Talk*. Pt. i, ser. 2.

2

The loss of wealth is loss of dirt,
As sages in all times assert;
The happy man's without a shirt.
  JOHN HEYWOOD, *Be Merry, Friends*.

I hold him rich, al had he not a shirt.
  CHAUCER, *Wife of Bath's Tale*, l. 330.

3

Who can sing so merry a note
As he that cannot change a groat?
  JOHN HEYWOOD, *Proverbs*. Pt. i, ch. 12. (1546)

Rich men never whistle, poor men always do; bird-songs are in the hearts of the people.
  STEPHEN B. ELKINS, *Speech*, 1906.

4

Wrapped in my virtue, I woo honest Poverty, undowered though she be. (Virtute me involvo probamque Pauperiem sine dote quæro.)
  HORACE, *Odes*. Bk. iii, ode, 29, l. 55.

Content with poverty, my soul I arm;
And virtue, though in rags, will keep me warm.
  HORACE, *Odes*, iii, 29, 55. (Dryden, tr.)

5

Yes! in the poor man's garden grow,
  Far more than herbs and flowers,
Kind thoughts, contentment, peace of mind,
  And joy for weary hours.
  MARY HOWITT, *The Poor Man's Garden*.

Cultivate poverty like a garden herb, sage.
  H. D. THOREAU, *Walden: Conclusion*.

6

The penniless traveler may sing before thieves. (Cantabit vacuus coram latrone viator.)
  JUVENAL, *Satires*. Sat. x, l. 22.

The traveller, freighted with a little wealth,
Sets forth at night, and makes his way by
    stealth; . . .
While, void of care, the beggar trips along,
And, in the spoiler's presence, trolls his song.
  JUVENAL, *Satires*, x. (Gifford, tr.)

If you are empty-handed, the highwayman passes you by; even along an infested road, the poor travel in peace. (Nudum latro transmittit; etiam in obsessa via pauperi pax est.)
  SENECA, *Epistulæ ad Lucilium*. Epis. xiv, 10.

A poor man, that beareth no riches on him by the way, may boldly sing before thieves.
  CHAUCER, *Boethius*. Bk. ii, prose 5.

The poor man before the thief doth sing.
  JOHN LYDGATE, *Fall of Princes*. Bk. iii, l. 582.

7

How safe and easy the poor man's life and his humble dwelling! (O vitæ tuta facultas Pauperis angustique lares!)
  LUCAN, *De Bello Civili*. Bk. v, l. 527.

There is nothing perfectly secure but poverty.
  LONGFELLOW, *Final Memorials: Letter*, 13 Nov., 1872.

8

Blessed be ye poor: for yours is the kingdom of God.
  New Testament: Luke, vi, 20.

9

The gods protect the poor. (Ἀεὶ νομίζονθ' οἱ πένητες τῶν θεῶν.)
  MENANDER, *The Lady of Leucas: Fragment*.

Religion always sides with poverty.
  GEORGE HERBERT, *The Church Militant*.

10

Fortune takes least from him to whom she has given least. (Minimum eripit Fortuna, cui minimum dedit.)
  PUBLILIUS SYRUS, *Sententiæ*. No. 386.

11

It is not poverty that we praise, it is the man whom poverty cannot humble or bend. (Laudatur enim non paupertas, sed ille, quem paupertas non summittit nec incurvat.)
  SENECA, *Epistulæ ad Lucilium*. Epis. 82, 11.

12

The couch of turf, softer than Tyrian purple, often soothes to fearless slumber. (Cæspes Tyrio millior ostro solet inpavidos ducere somnos.)
  SENECA, *Hercules Œtæus*, l. 644.

Less wildly does Fortune rage among humble folks, and more lightly does God smite the more lightly blessed. (Minor in parvis Fortuna furit Leviusque ferit leviora deus.)
  SENECA, *Hippolytus*, l. 1124.

13

The town's poor seem to me often to live the most independent lives of any.
  H. D. THOREAU, *Walden: Conclusion*.

14

        By breathing in content
The keen, the wholesome, air of poverty,
And drinking from the well of homely life.
  WORDSWORTH, *The Excursion*. Bk. i, l. 306.

15

No man should commend poverty but he who is poor. (Nemo paupertatem commendaret nisi pauper.)
  ST. BERNARD, *Sermons*.

He must have a great deal of godliness who can find any satisfaction in being poor.
  CERVANTES, *Don Quixote*. Pt. ii, ch. 44.

'Tis mighty easy, o'er a glass of wine,
On vain refinements vainly to refine,
To laugh at poverty in plenty's reign,
To boast of apathy when out of pain.
  CHARLES CHURCHILL, *The Farewell*, l. 47.

V—Poverty: Its Penalties

16

All the days of the poor are evil.
  Babylonian Talmud: Kethuboth, p. 110b.

If you've ever really been poor, you remain poor at heart all your life.
  ARNOLD BENNETT. (MAUGHAM, *Introduction to "The Old Wives' Tale."*)

17

The rude inelegance of poverty.
  R. BLOOMFIELD, *Farmer's Boy: Autumn*, l. 82.

1
Poverty makes some humble, but more malignant.
BULWER-LYTTON, *Eugene Aram*. Bk. i, ch. 7.

2
Squeamishness was never yet bred in an empty pocket.
J. B. CABELL, *The Cream of the Jest*, p. 86.

3
If thou be poor, thy brother hateth thee,
And all thy friends flee fro thee, alas!
CHAUCER, *Man of Law's Prologue*, l. 22.

The poor make no new friends.
LADY DUFFERIN, *Lament of the Irish Emigrant*.

4
What can a poor man do but love and pray?
HARTLEY COLERIDGE, *Sonnets*. No. 30.

5
The cottage is sure to suffer for every error of the court, the cabinet, or the camp.
C. C. COLTON, *Lacon: Reflections*. No. 5.

6
The poor, inur'd to drudgery and distress,
Act without aim, think little, and feel less,
And no where, but in feign'd Arcadian scenes,
Taste happiness, or know what pleasure means.
WILLIAM COWPER, *Hope*, l. 7.

A wise man poor
Is like a sacred book that's never read,—
To himself he lives, and to all else seems dead.
This age thinks better of a gilded fool
Than of a threadbare saint in wisdom's school.
THOMAS DEKKER, *Old Fortunatus*. Act i, sc. 1.

7
I live on broken wittles—and I sleep on the coals.
DICKENS, *David Copperfield*. Ch. 5.

An' what poor cot-folk pit their painch in,
I own it's past my comprehension.
ROBERT BURNS, *The Twa Dogs*. St. 9.

8
The life of the poor is the curse of the heart.
Apocrypha: Ecclesiasticus, xxxviii, 19.

Poverty demoralizes.
EMERSON, *Conduct of Life: Wealth*.

9
So helpless is poverty. (Ἀπορία τὸ δυστυχεῖν.)
EURIPIDES, *Ion*, l. 971.

10
There's no scandal like rags, nor any crime so shameful as poverty.
FARQUHAR, *The Beaux' Stratagem*. Act i, sc. 1.

Needy knife-grinder! whither are ye going?
Rough is the road, your wheel is out of order;
Bleak blows the blast—your hat has got a hole in it.
So have your breeches.
GEORGE CANNING, *The Friend of Humanity and the Knife-Grinder*.

It's a little awt at elbows.
CIBBER, *The Provok'd Husband*. Act iv, sc. 1.

11
There is no virtue that poverty destroyeth not.
JOHN FLORIO, *First Fruites*. Fo. 32.

12
Light purse, heavy heart.
BENJAMIN FRANKLIN, *Poor Richard*, 1733.

No wonder that his soul was sad,
When not one penny piece he had.
CHRISTINA ROSSETTI, *Johnny*.

13
Chill penury repress'd their noble rage,
And froze the genial current of the soul.
GRAY, *Elegy Written in a Country Churchyard*. St. 13.

14
Poverty parteth fellowship.
JOHN HEYWOOD, *Proverbs*. Pt. i, ch. 12. (1546)

Kind was she, and my friends were free,
But poverty parts good company.
JOANNA BAILLIE, *Poverty Parts Good Company*.

15
The shame and ostracism of poverty. (Paupertatis pudor et fuga.)
HORACE, *Epistles*. Bk. i, epis. 18, l. 24.

May squalid poverty be far from my home. (Pauperies immunda domus procul absit.)
HORACE, *Epistles*. Bk. ii, epis. 2, l. 199.

Cruel poverty. (Sæva paupertas.)
HORACE, *Odes*. Bk. i, ode 12, l. 43.

16
The man who has lost his purse will go wherever you wish. (Ibit eo, quo vis, qui zonam perdidit.)
HORACE, *Epistles*. Bk. ii, epis. 2, l. 40.

Poverty, that base reproach, bids us do or suffer anything. (Magnum pauperies opprobrium jubet Quidvis et facere et pati.)
HORACE, *Odes*. Bk. iii, ode 24, l. 42.

There are many things which ragged men dare not say. (Plurima sunt quæ Non audent homines pertusa dicere læna.)
JUVENAL, *Satires*. Sat. v, l. 130.

To be poor and independent is very nearly an impossibility.
WILLIAM COBBETT, *Advice to Young Men: To a Young Man*.

My poverty, but not my will, consents.
SHAKESPEARE, *Romeo and Juliet*. Act v, sc. 1, l. 75.

The poor man is never free; he serves in every country. (Le pauvre n'est point libre; il sert en tout pays.)
VOLTAIRE, *Les Guèbres*. Act iii, sc. 1.

17
All crimes are safe but hated poverty.
This, only this, the rigid law pursues.
SAMUEL JOHNSON, *London*, l. 159.

A man guilty of poverty easily believes himself suspected.
SAMUEL JOHNSON, *The Rambler*. No. 26.

18
Poverty is a great enemy to human happiness; it certainly destroys liberty, and it makes some virtues impracticable, and others extremely difficult.
SAMUEL JOHNSON. (BOSWELL, *Life*, iv, 157.)

1
Nothing in poverty so ill is borne,
As its exposing men to grinning scorn.
JUVENAL, *Satires*. Sat. iii, l. 152. (Oldham, tr.)

O Poverty, thy thousand ills combined
Sink not so deep into the generous mind,
As the contempt and laughter of mankind.
(Nil habet infelix paupertas durius in se,
Quam quod ridiculos homines facit.)
JUVENAL, *Satires*. Sat. iii, l. 152. (Gifford, tr.)

Everywhere the poor man is despised. (Pauper ubique jacet.)
OVID, *Fasti*. Bk. i, l. 218.

Poverty causes me to be ridiculed. (Paupertas fecit ut ridiculus forem.)
PLAUTUS, *Stichus*. Act i, sc. 3, l. 20.

2
They do not easily rise whose abilities are repressed by poverty at home. (Haud facile emergunt quorum virtutibus Res angusta domi.)
JUVENAL, *Satires*. Sat. iii, l. 164.

To be poor, and to seem poor, is a certain method never to rise.
GOLDSMITH, *On Concealing Our Wants*.

To *be* poor and *seem* poor is the very devil.
SIR ARTHUR HELPS, *Friends in Council*, ii, 7.

This mournful truth is ev'rywhere confess'd,
Slow rises worth, by poverty depress'd.
SAMUEL JOHNSON, *London*, l. 176.

3
It is the world's one crime its babes grow dull,
Its poor are ox-like, limp and leaden-eyed.
Not that they starve, but starve so dreamlessly, . . .
Not that they die, but that they die like sheep.
VACHEL LINDSAY, *The Leaden-Eyed*.

4
A blind man is a poor man, and blind a poor man is;
For the former seeth no man, and the latter no man sees.
FRIEDRICH VON LOGAU, *Sinngedichte*. (Longfellow, tr.)

5
Nothing is more luckless than a poor man. (Πένητος οὐδέν ἐστι δυστυχέστερον.)
MENANDER, *Fragments*. No. 597.

Fortune, that arrant whore,
Ne'er turns the key of the poor.
SHAKESPEARE, *King Lear*. Act ii, sc. 4, l. 52.

6
The poor man must labor while life lasts, for idleness cannot support even the frugal life.
MENANDER, *Fragments*. No. 634.

A poor man, though he speak the truth, is not believed. (Πένης λέγων τἀληθὲς οὐ πιστεύεται.)
MENANDER, *Fragments*. No. 856.

7
Poverty may be an unescapable misfortune, but that no more makes it honorable than a cocked eye is made honorable by the same cause.
H. L. MENCKEN, *Prejudices*. Ser. iii, p. 17.

8
But to the world no bugbear is so great
As want of figure and a small estate.
To either India see the merchant fly,
Scared at the spectre of pale Poverty!
See him with pains of body, pangs of soul,
Burn thro' the Tropics, freeze beneath the Pole!
POPE, *Imitations of Horace: Epistles*, i, 1, 67.

The prevalent fear of poverty among the educated classes is the worst moral disease from which our civilization suffers.
WILLIAM JAMES, *Varieties of Religious Experience*, p. 370.

9
In a change of rule among the citizens, the poor change nothing except the name of their master. (In principatu commutando civium, Nil præter domini nomen mutant pauperes.)
PHÆDRUS, *Fables*. Bk. i, fab. 15.

10
The poor live miserably in every way. (Omnibus modis qui pauperes sunt homines miseri vivont.)
PLAUTUS, *Rudens*, l. 290. (Act ii, sc. 1.)

His drink, the running stream; his cup, the bare
Of his palm closed; his bed, the hard, cold ground.
THOMAS SACKVILLE, *Mirrour for Magistrates: Misery*.

Worse housed than your hacks and your pointers,
Worse fed than your hogs and your sheep.
CHARLES KINGSLEY, *The Bad Squire*.

11
The destruction of the poor is their poverty.
Old Testament: Proverbs, x, 15.

12
Poverty is the only load which is the heavier the more loved ones there are to assist in supporting it.
RICHTER, *Flower, Fruit, Thorn Pieces*. Ch. 10.

13
Money is very slow to come where there is poverty.
SENECA, *Epistulæ ad Lucilium*. Epis. ci, sec. 2.

14
They brought one Pinch, a hungry lean-faced villain,
A mere anatomy, a mountebank,
A threadbare juggler, and a fortune-teller,
A needy, hollow-eyed, sharp-looking wretch;
A living-dead man.
SHAKESPEARE, *The Comedy of Errors*, v, 1, 238.

Houseless poverty.
SHAKESPEARE, *King Lear*. Act iii, sc. 4, l. 26.

His rawbone cheeks, through penury and pine,
Were shrunk into his jaws, as he did never dine
SPENSER, *Faerie Queene*. Bk. i, canto 9, st. 35

15
'Tis infamous, I grant it, to be poor.
SMOLLETT, *Advice*, l. 2.

Hark ye, Clinker, you are a most notorious offender. You stand convicted of sickness, hunger, wretchedness, and want.
SMOLLETT, *Humphrey Clinker*.

1
Poverty is to me a wretched crushing load. (Paupertas mihi onus visumst et miserum et grave.)

TERENCE, *Phormio*, l. 94. (Act i, sc. 1.)

VI—Poverty and Riches

2
The rich feast, the poor fast;
The dogs dine, the poor pine.

THOMAS ADAMS, *Works*, p. 39. (1630)

3
Poverty is an anomaly to rich people. It is very difficult to make out why people who want dinner do not ring the bell.

BAGEHOT, *Literary Studies*. Vol. ii, p. 160.

At length I recollected the thoughtless saying of a great princess, who, on being informed that the country people had no bread, replied, "Then let them eat cake." (Enfin je me rappelai le pis-aller d'une grande princesse à qui l'on disait que les paysans n'avaient pas de pain, et qui répondit: "Qu'ils mangent de la brioche.")

JEAN-JACQUES ROUSSEAU, *Confessions*. Bk. vi, ninth paragraph from end. Usually attributed to Marie Antoinette, after her arrival in France in 1770, but the sixth book of the *Confessions* was written two or three years before that date. It is difficult to translate "brioche," which is not exactly cake, but a bun or fancy bread something like Scotch scones.

Marie Antoinette made only one mistake. She should have said, "Let them eat hokum."

WESTBROOK PEGLER, *Fair Enough*, 5 Dec., 1934.

She had an idea from the very sound
That people with naught were naughty.

HOOD, *Miss Kilmansegg: Her Education*.

4
God only, who made us rich, can make us poor.

E. B. BROWNING, *Sonnets from Portuguese*, 24.

5
There are only two families in the world, the Haves and the Have Nots.

CERVANTES, *Don Quixote*. Pt. ii, ch. 20.

That these two parties still divide the world—
Of those that want, and those that have: and still
The same old sore breaks out from age to age,
With much the same result.

TENNYSON, *Walking to the Mail*, l. 69.

6
A poor man who does not flatter, and a rich man who is not proud, are passable characters; but they are not equal to the poor who are cheerful, and the rich who yet love the rules of propriety.

CONFUCIUS, *Analects*. Bk. i, ch. 15.

7
The rich grow poor, the poor become purse-
proud.

COWPER, *Hope*, l. 18.

8
Wealth is crime enough to him that's poor.

SIR JOHN DENHAM, *Cooper's Hill*, l. 122.

9
Poverty brought into conformity with the law of nature is great wealth. (Magnæ divitiæ sunt lege naturæ composita paupertas.)

EPICURUS, *Fragments*. No. 477. (SENECA, *Epistulæ ad Lucilium*. Epis. iv, sec. 10.)

10
The pleasures of the rich are bought with the tears of the poor.

THOMAS FULLER, *Gnomologia*. No. 4707.

I don't 'old with Wealth. What *is* Wealth? Labour robbed out of the poor.

H. G. WELLS, *Kipps*. Bk. ii, ch. 4.

11
Ye friends to truth, ye statesmen, who survey
The rich man's joys increase, the poor's de-
cay,
'Tis yours to judge, how wide the limits
stand
Between a splendid and a happy land.

GOLDSMITH, *The Deserted Village*, l. 265.

The nakedness of the indigent world may be clothed from the trimmings of the vain.

GOLDSMITH, *The Vicar of Wakefield*. Ch. 4.

12
Poverty breeds wealth; and wealth in its turn breeds poverty. The earth, to form the mould, is taken out of the ditch; and whatever may be the height of the one will be the depth of the other.

J. C. AND A. W. HARE, *Guesses at Truth*.

13
The greatest luxury of riches is, that they enable you to escape so much good advice. The rich are always advising the poor, but the poor seldom venture to return the compliment.

SIR ARTHUR HELPS, *Brevia*.

14
God could have made all rich, or all men
poor;
But why He did not, let me tell wherefore:
Had all been rich, where then had Patience
been?
Had all been poor, who had His Bounty seen?

ROBERT HERRICK, *Riches and Poverty*.

15
Two of a thousand things are disallow'd,
A lying rich man, and a poor man proud.

ROBERT HERRICK, *Two Things Odious*.

16
My soul . . . will not own a notion so unholy,
As thinking that the rich by easy trips
May go to heav'n, whereas the poor and lowly
Must work their passage, as they do in ships.

THOMAS HOOD, *Ode to Rae Wilson*, l. 129.

17
Stitch! stitch! stitch!
In poverty, hunger, and dirt,
And still with a voice of dolorous pitch,
Would that its tone could reach the Rich,
She sang this "Song of the Shirt!"

THOMAS HOOD, *The Song of the Shirt*. St. 11.

18
A beggar in the midst of plenty. (Magnas inter opes inops.)

HORACE, *Odes*. Bk. iii, ode 16, l. 28.

Plenty has made me poor. (Inopem me copia fecit.)
Ovid, *Metamorphoses*. Bk. iii, l. 466.

With much we surfeit, plenty makes us poor.
Drayton, *Legend of Matilda the Fair.*

And plenty makes us poor.
Dryden, *The Medal*, l. 126.

Whose wealth was want, whose plenty made him poor.
Spenser, *Faerie Queene*. Bk. i, canto iv, st. 29.

For he that needs five thousand pound to live,
Is full as poor as he that needs but five.
George Herbert, *The Church-Porch*. St. 18.

1
If you are poor, distinguish yourself by your virtues; if rich, by your good deeds.
Joubert, *Pensées*. No. 74.

2
Rich men direct you to their furniture, poor ones divert you from it.
Lamb, *Last Essays of Elia: Captain Jackson.*

3
Neither locks had they to their doors nor bars to their windows;
But their dwellings were open as day and the hearts of the owners;
There the richest was poor and the poorest lived in abundance.
Longfellow, *Evangeline*. Pt. i, sec. 1, l. 36.

4
The Little Sister of the Poor . . .
The Poor, and their concerns, she has
Monopolized, because of which
It falls to me to labor as
A Little Brother of the Rich.
E. S. Martin, *A Little Brother of the Rich.*

Those whom we strive to benefit
Dear to our hearts soon grow to be;
I love my Rich, and I admit
That they are very good to me.
Succor the poor, my sisters,—I
While heaven shall still vouchsafe me health
Will strive to share and mollify
The trials of abounding wealth.
E. S. Martin, *A Little Brother of the Rich.*

5
Painless poverty is better than embittered wealth. (Πενίαν τ' ἄλυπον μᾶλλον ἢ πλοῦτον πικρόν.)
Menander, *Fragments*. No. 588.

6
For ever must the rich man hate the poor.
William Morris, *The Earthly Paradise: Bellerophon at Argos*, l. 515.

7
It is better to endure straightened Fortune than the arrogance of the wealthy.
Palladas. (*Greek Anthology*. Bk. x, epig. 93.)

8
When the trumpets sound, the savage's knife stands drawn at the rich man's throat; the poor man's rags are the amulet of safety. (Cum sonuere tubæ, jugulo stat divite ferrum Barbaricum: tenuis præbia pannus habet.)
Petronius, *Fragments*. No. 80.

Poverty is safe; riches are exposed to danger. (Tuta est hominum tenuitas; Magnæ periclo sunt opes obnoxiæ.)
Phædrus, *Fables*. Bk. ii, fab. 7, l. 13.

9
The poor, wishing to imitate the powerful, perish. (Inops, potentem dum vult imitari, perit.)
Phædrus, *Fables*. Bk. i, fab. 24, l. 1.

10
I trust no rich man who is officiously kind to a poor man. (Nemini credo, qui large blandus est dives pauperi.)
Plautus, *Aulularia*, l. 196. (Act ii, sc. 2.)

11
Oh impudence of wealth! with all thy store
How darest thou let one worthy man be poor?
Pope, *Imitations of Horace: Satires*. Bk. ii, sat. 2, l. 117.

12
But Satan now is wiser than of yore,
And tempts by making rich, not making poor.
Pope, *Moral Essays*. Epis. iii, l. 351.

13
Who am I to condemn you, O Dives,
I who am as much embittered
With poverty
As you with useless riches?
Ezra Pound, *To Dives.*

14
Bear wealth; poverty will bear itself.
John Ray, *English Proverbs.*

15
The pride of the rich makes the labours of the poor.
W. Gurney Benham, *Quotations, Proverbs, and Household Words*, p. 849. Sometimes stated the other way, "The labours of the poor make the pride of the rich."

16
Riches come better after poverty than poverty after riches.
John Ray, *English Proverbs.*

It is still her use
To let the wretched man outlive his wealth,
To view with hollow eye and wrinkled brow
An age of poverty.
Shakespeare, *The Merchant of Venice*. Act iv, sc. 1, l. 268.

17
But she was rich, and he was poor,
And so it might not be.
John Godfrey Saxe, *The Way of the World.*

18
He who has made a fair compact with poverty is rich. (Cui cum paupertas bene convenit, dives est.)
Seneca, *Epistulæ ad Lucilium*. Epis. iv, 11.

A man is sheltered just as well by a thatch as by a roof of gold. (Bene hominem culmo quam auro tegi.)
Seneca, *Epistulæ ad Lucilium*. Epis. viii, 5.

That which makes poverty a burden, makes riches also a burden. It matters little whether you lay a sick man on a wooden or a golden bed, for whithersoever he be moved he will carry his malady with him.

SENECA, *Epistulæ ad Lucilium*. Epis. xvii, sec. 12.

1
No, madam, 'tis not so well that I am poor, though many of the rich are damned.

SHAKESPEARE, *All's Well that Ends Well*. Act. i, sc. 3, l. 17.

2
If thou art rich, thou'rt poor;
For, like an ass whose back with ingots bows,
Thou bear'st thy heavy riches but a journey,
And death unloads thee.

SHAKESPEARE, *Measure for Measure*. Act iii, sc. 1, l. 25.

3
When rich villains have need of poor ones
Poor ones may make what price they will.

SHAKESPEARE, *Much Ado About Nothing*. Act iii, sc. 3, l. 121.

4
Poor and content is rich and rich enough,
But riches fineless is as poor as winter
To him that ever fears he shall be poor.

SHAKESPEARE, *Othello* Act iii, sc. 3, l. 172.

The world affords no law to make thee rich;
Then be not poor, but break it.

SHAKESPEARE, *Romeo and Juliet*. Act v, sc. 1, l. 73.

5
For often evil men are rich, and good men poor;
But we will not exchange with them
Our virtue for their wealth, since one abides alway,
While riches change their owners every day.

SOLON, *Fragments*. Frag. 15. (PLUTARCH, *Lives: Solon*. Sec. 3.)

6
Many who appear to be struggling with adverse fortune are happy: and many, that wallow in wealth, are most wretched. (Multos qui conflictari adversis videantur, beatos; ac plerosque, quanquam magnas per opes, miserrimos.)

TACITUS, *Annals*. Bk. vi, sec. 22.

God help the rich; the poor can sleep with their windows shut.

BERT LESTON TAYLOR, *The So-Called Human Race*, p. 9.

7
Happy must be the State
Whose ruler heedeth more
The murmurs of the poor
Than flatteries of the great.

WHITTIER, *King Solomon and the Ants*.

8
I know how to be rich and still enjoy all the little comforts of poverty.

HARRY LEON WILSON, *The Spenders*, p. 24.

POWER

9
I am more and more convinced that man is a dangerous creature; and that power, whether vested in many or a few, is ever grasping, and like the grave, cries "Give, give!"

ABIGAIL ADAMS, *Letter to Her Husband*, 27 Nov., 1775.

10
Give me a lever long enough, and a fulcrum strong enough, and single-handed I can move the world.

ARCHIMEDES OF SYRACUSE. (PAPPUS ALEXANDER, *Collectio*, viii, 10; PLINY, *Historia Naturalis*, vii, 37.) Sometimes quoted: "Give me where to stand and I will move the world," or "Give me a base and I will move the world."

If there were another world, and I could go to it, I could move this.

ARCHIMEDES. (PLUTARCH, *Lives: Marcellus*. Ch. 14, sec. 7.)

Don't talk to me of your Archimedes' lever. . . . Give me the right word and the right accent and I will move the world.

JOSEPH CONRAD, *A Personal Record: Preface*.

11
The seeds of godlike power are in us still:
Gods are we, Bards, Saints, Heroes, if we will.

MATTHEW ARNOLD, *Written in Emerson's Essays*.

12
It is the solecism of power, to think to command the end, and yet not to endure the mean.

FRANCIS BACON, *Essays: Of Empire*.

It is a strange desire, to seek power, and to lose liberty; or to seek power over others, and to lose power over a man's self.

FRANCIS BACON, *Essays: Of Great Place*.

13
He hath no power that hath not power to use.

P. J. BAILEY, *Festus: A Visit*.

14
Energy is Eternal Delight.

WILLIAM BLAKE, *Proverbs of Hell*.

15
Then wakes the power which in the age of iron
Burst forth to curb the great and raise the low.

BULWER-LYTTON, *Richelieu*. Act iv, sc. 2.

16
The greater the power the more dangerous the abuse.

EDMUND BURKE, *Speech*, House of Commons, 7 Feb., 1771.

Power gradually extirpates from the mind every humane and gentle virtue.

BURKE, *A Vindication of Natural Society*.

17 Dim with the mist of years, grey flits the shade of power.

BYRON, *Childe Harold*. Canto ii, st. 2.

1
Power is so far from being desirable in itself, that it sometimes ought to be refused, and sometimes to be resigned.
CICERO, *De Officiis*. Bk. i, ch. 20, sec. 68.

Next to the assumption of power was the responsibility of relinquishing it.
BENJAMIN DISRAELI, *Speech*, House of Commons, 27 May, 1841.

2
By his own prowess. (Suo Marte.)
CICERO, *Philippicæ*. No. ii, ch. 37, sec. 95.

3
To know the pains of power, we must go to those who have it; to know its pleasures, we must go to those who are seeking it: the pains of power are real, its pleasures imaginary.
C. C. COLTON, *Lacon*. Vol. i, No. 427.

You shall have joy, or you shall have power, said God; you shall not have both.
EMERSON, *Journals*. Vol. vi, p. 282.

What is grandeur, what is power?
Heavier toil, superior pain.
THOMAS GRAY, *Ode for Music*, l. 57.

I have never been able to conceive how any rational being could propose happiness to himself from the exercise of power over others.
THOMAS JEFFERSON, *Writings*. Vol. xiii, p. 18.

Power, like a desolating pestilence,
Pollutes whate'er it touches.
SHELLEY, *Queen Mab*. Canto iii, l. 176.

4
Whoever can do as he pleases, commands when he entreats. (Qui peut ce qui lui plaît, commande alors qu'il prie.)
CORNEILLE, *Sertorius*. Act iv, sc. 2.

5
Increase of power begets increase of wealth.
COWPER, *The Task*. Bk. iv, l. 580.

6
The depositary of power is always unpopular.
BENJAMIN DISRAELI, *Coningsby*. Bk. iv, ch. 13.

My opinion is that power should always be distrusted, in whatever hands it is placed.
SIR WILLIAM JONES, *Letter to Lord Althorpe*, 5 Oct., 1782.

7
All empire is no more than power in trust.
DRYDEN, *Absalom and Achitophel*. Pt. i, l. 411.
See also POLITICS, sec. 11.

8
For what can Pow'r give more than food
and drink,
To live at ease, and not be bound to think?
DRYDEN, *The Medal*, l. 235.

9
There is always room for a man of force, and he makes room for many.
EMERSON, *Conduct of Life: Power*.

10
It was Watt who told King George III that he dealt in an article of which kings were said to be fond—Power.
EMERSON, *Letters and Social Aims: Inspiration*.

11
From high to higher forces
The scale of power uprears,
The heroes on their horses,
The gods upon their spheres.
EMERSON, *Life*.

12
The love of power may be as dominant in the heart of a peasant as of a prince.
J. T. HEADLEY, *Miscellanies: Alison's History of Europe*.

13
Power . . . is the measure of manhood.
J. G. HOLLAND, *Plain Talks: Self-Help*.

14
Power weakens the wicked.
JAMES HOWELL, *Proverbs*, p. 6. (1659)

Unlimited power is apt to corrupt the minds of those who possess it.
WILLIAM PITT, EARL OF CHATHAM, *Speech*, House of Lords, 9 Jan., 1770.

Power tends to corrupt and absolute power corrupts absolutely.
LORD ACTON, *Essays on Freedom and Power*, p. 365. (Beacon Press, 1948.) *See* 2298y:12.

15
Power flows to the man who knows how.
ELBERT HUBBARD, *The Philistine*, Vol. xi, p. 50.

17
To be out of place is not necessarily to be out of power.
SAMUEL JOHNSON, *Debates*. (*Works*, xi, 111.)
See also POLITICS: OFFICE-HOLDING.

18
For when was power beneficent in vain?
SAMUEL JOHNSON, *Irene*.

'Tis god-like to have power, but not to kill.
BEAUMONT AND FLETCHER, *The Chances*. Act ii, sc. 2. *See also under* GIANT.

19
There is nothing which power cannot believe of itself, when it is praised as equal to the gods. (Nihil est quod credere de se Non possit, quum laudatur dis æqua potestas.)
JUVENAL, *Satires*. Sat. iv, l. 70.

O what is it proud slime will not believe
Of his own worth, to hear it equal praised
Thus with the gods?
BEN JONSON, *Sejanus*. Act i, sc. 2.

20
From the summit of power men no longer turn their eyes upward, but begin to look about them.
J. R. LOWELL, *Among My Books: New England*.

21
Little he loved, but power the most of all;
And that he seemed to scorn, as one who
knew

By what foul paths men choose to crawl thereto.
J. R. LOWELL, *A Legend of Brittany*. St. 17.

1
His rod revers'd,
And backward mutters of dissevering power.
MILTON, *Comus*, l. 816.

2
Power admits no equal, and dismisses friendship for flattery.
EDWARD MOORE, *The Foundling*. Act i.

3
A partnership with the powerful is never safe. (Nunquam est fidelis cum potente societas.)
PHÆDRUS, *Fables*. Bk. i, fab. 5, l. 1.

4
Whether with Reason or with Instinct blest,
Know, all enjoy that power which suits them best.
POPE, *Essay on Man*. Epis. iii, l. 79.

5
So mightiest powers by deepest calms are fed,
And sleep, how oft, in things that gentlest be!
BRYAN WALLER PROCTER, *The Sea in Calm*, l. 13.

6
The highest power may be lost by misrule. (Male imperando summum imperium amittitur.)
PUBLILIUS SYRUS, *Sententiæ*. No. 373.

7
The powers that be are ordained of God.
New Testament: Romans, xiii, 1.

8
Power is always passing to the best man from the hands of his inferior. (Imperium semper ad optumum quemque a minus bono transfertur.)
SALLUST, *Catiline*. Sec. 2.

Power is always gradually stealing away from the many to the few, because the few are more vigilant and consistent.
SAMUEL JOHNSON, *The Adventurer*, No. 45.

Power is ever stealing from the many to the few.
WENDELL PHILLIPS, *Address: Public Opinion*, Boston, 28 Jan., 1852.

9
Power is easily retained by the qualities by which it was first won. (Imperium facile eis artibus retinetur quibus initio partum est.)
SALLUST, *Catiline*. Sec. 2.

Power is more certainly retained by wary measures than by daring counsels. (Potentium cautis quam acribus consiliis tutius haberi.)
TACITUS, *Annals*. Bk. xi, sec. 29.

10
Power on an ancient consecrated throne,
Strong in possession, founded in old custom;
Power by a thousand tough and stringy roots
Fixed to the people's pious nursery-faith.
SCHILLER, *Wallenstein*. Act iv, sc. 4. (Coleridge, tr.)

11
The Monarch drank, that happy hour,
The sweetest, holiest draught of Power.
SCOTT, *The Lady of the Lake*. Canto vi, st. 28.

Power laid his rod of rule aside,
And Ceremony doffed his pride.
SCOTT, *Marmion:* Canto vi, *Introduction*, l. 40.

12
'Tis not seasonable to call a man traitor that has an army at his heels.
JOHN SELDEN, *Table-Talk: Traitor*.

It is ill arguing with the master of thirty legions.
FAVORINUS. Yielding to the Emperor Hadrian in an argument. (PLUTARCH, *Apothegms*.)

13
He who is too powerful seeks power beyond his power. (Quod non potest vult posse qui nimium potest.)
SENECA, *Hippolytus*, l. 215.

14
No pent-up Utica contracts your powers,
But the whole boundless continent is yours.
JONATHAN MITCHELL SEWALL, *Prologue to Addison's "Cato."* Written for a performance of the play at the Bow Street Theatre, Portsmouth, N. H. Sewall is drawing a parallel between the events of the American Revolution and those of the play, in which (Act i, sc. 1) occur the words, "But what can Cato do . . . Pent up in Utica?" Park Benjamin adopted the couplet as the motto of his paper, *The New World*.

15
The awful shadow of some unseen Power
Floats, tho' unseen, amongst us.
SHELLEY, *Hymn to Intellectual Beauty*, l. 1.

16
Each would the sweets of sov'reign Rule devour,
While Discord waits upon divided power.
STATIUS, *Thebais*. Bk. i, l. 182. (Pope, tr.)

17
Lust of power is the most flagrant of all the passions. (Cupido dominandi cunctis affectibus flagrantior est.)
TACITUS, *Annals*. Bk. xv, sec. 53.

Power acquired by guilt was never used for a good purpose. (Imperium flagitio acquisitum nemo unquam bonis artibus exercuit.)
TACITUS, *History*. Bk. i, sec. 30.

Everything slave-like for the sake of power. (Omnia serviliter pro dominatione.)
TACITUS, *History*. Bk. i, sec. 36.

18
In the struggle for power there is no middle course between the highest elevation and destruction. (Imperium cupientibus nihil medium inter summa et præcipitia.)
TACITUS, *History*. Bk. ii, sec. 74.

19
If you would be powerful, pretend to be powerful.
HORNE TOOKE. (EMERSON, *Conduct of Life: Considerations by the Way*.)

PRAISE

See also Applause, Compliment, Flattery

I—Praise: Definitions

1
Praise undeserv'd is satire in disguise.
BROADHURST [?], *To the Celebrated Beauties of the British Court.* (BELL, *Fugitive Poetry.* Vol. iii, p. 118.)

When one good line did once my wonder raise
In Br——st's works, I stood resolv'd to praise,
And had, but that the modest author cries,
"Praise undeserv'd is satire in disguise."
UNKNOWN, *On a Certain Line of Mr. Br——.* (*The Garland,* London, 1721.) This epigram, which was signed B., is the only clue to the author of this famous line. It is assumed that the name was Broadhurst.

Praise undeserv'd is scandal in disguise.
POPE, *Imitations of Horace: Epistles.* Bk. ii, epis. 1, l. 413. (1733) Pope encloses the line in quotation marks.

Why, praise is satire in these sinful days.
PAUL WHITEHEAD, *Manners.*

Praise is rebuke to the man whose conscience alloweth it not.
M. F. TUPPER, *Proverbial Philosophy: Of Commendation.*

2
Praise is but the shadow of virtue.
SAMUEL BUTLER, *Remains.* Vol. ii, p. 118.

3
Praises of the unworthy are felt by ardent minds as robberies of the deserving.
S. T. COLERIDGE, *Biographia Literaria.* Ch. 3.

4
It is as great a spite to be praised in the wrong place, and by a wrong person, as can be done to a noble nature.
BEN JONSON, *Explorata: Non Vulgi Sunt.*

Praise that stings like shame.
SWINBURNE, *In Sepulcretis.* St. 1.

5
Be silent, Praise,
Blind guide with siren voice, and blinding all
That hear thy call.
JOHN KEBLE, *The Christian Year: Wednesday before Easter.*

6
All praise is foreign, but of true desert;
Plays round the head, and comes not to the heart.
WILLIAM MASON, *Musæus.*

7
Among the smaller duties of life I hardly know any one more important than that of not praising where praise is not due.
SYDNEY SMITH, *Sketches of Moral Philosophy.* Lecture 9.

8
The art of praising began the art of pleasing. (L'art de louer commença l'art de plaire.)
VOLTAIRE, *La Pucelle.* Chant xx.

9
I now perceived
That we are praised, only as men in us
Do recognise some image of themselves,
An abject counterpart of what they are,
Or the empty thing that they would wish to be.
WORDSWORTH, *The Borderers.* Act iv, l. 1822.

II—Praise: Apothegms

10
Praise is deeper than the lips.
ROBERT BROWNING, *Hervé Riel.* St. 9.

11
He wants worth who dares not praise a foe.
DRYDEN, *Conquest of Granada.* Act ii, sc. 1.

12
Praise without profit puts little into the pot.
THOMAS FULLER, *Gnomologia.* No. 3922.

Praise makes good men better and bad men worse.
THOMAS FULLER, *Gnomologia.* No. 3918.

13
Good people all, with one accord,
Lament for Madam Blaize,
Who never wanted a good word—
From those who spoke her praise.
GOLDSMITH, *An Elegy on Mrs. Mary Blaize.*

14
Out of the mouth of babes and sucklings thou hast perfected praise.
New Testament: Matthew, xxi, 16; *Psalms,* viii, 2.

15
And touch'd their golden harps, and hymning prais'd
God and his works.
MILTON, *Paradise Lost.* Bk. vii, l. 258.

16
I am deaf with praises, and all dazed with flowers.
STEPHEN PHILLIPS, *Herod.* Act i.

17
Poetic Justice, with her lifted scale,
Where, in nice balance, truth with gold she weighs,
And solid pudding against empty praise.
POPE, *The Dunciad.* Bk. i, l. 52.

18
Be thou the first true merit to befriend;
His praise is lost who stays till all commend.
POPE, *Essay on Criticism.* Pt. ii, l. 274.

19
Forbear to mention what thou canst not praise.
MATTHEW PRIOR, *Carmen Seculare,* l. 106.

20
Unless new praise arises even the old is lost. (Laus nova nisi oritur etiam vetus amittitur.)
PUBLILIUS SYRUS, *Sententiæ.* No. 326.

Old praise dies unless you feed it.
GEORGE HERBERT, *Jacula Prudentum.* No. 695.

21
Praise a fool and you water his folly.
W. G. BENHAM, *Proverbs,* p. 826.

1
I will praise any man that will praise me.
SHAKESPEARE, *Antony and Cleopatra*, ii, 6, 91.

You were ever good at sudden commendations.
SHAKESPEARE, *Henry VIII*. Act v, sc. 3, l. 122.

In thy condign praise.
SHAKESPEARE, *Love's Labour's Lost*, i, 2, 26.

2
Old John of Gaunt, time-honoured Lancaster.
SHAKESPEARE, *Richard II*. Act i, sc. 1, l. 1.

3
Praise is the best diet for us, after all.
SYDNEY SMITH. (LADY HOLLAND, *Memoir*. Vol. i.)

3a
A part of man's praise may be told in his presence; the whole in his absence.
Babylonian Talmud: Erubin, p. 63a.

4
Their silence is sufficient praise. (Tacent, satis laudant.)
TERENCE, *Eunuchus*, l. 476. (Act iii, sc. 2.)

III—Praise: Love of Praise

See also Flattery: Love of Flattery

5
We are all imbued with the love of praise. (Trahimur omnes laudis studio.)
CICERO, *Pro Archia Poeta*. Ch. 11, sec. 26.

6
The praise of a fool is incense to the wisest of us.
BENJAMIN DISRAELI, *Vivian Grey*. Bk. vii, ch. 2.

7
What cannot praise effect in mighty minds,
When flattery soothes, and when ambition blinds?
DRYDEN, *Absalom and Achitophel*. Pt. i, l. 303.

8
We thirst for approbation, yet cannot forgive the approver.
EMERSON, *Essays, First Series: Circles*.

9
Spite of all modesty, a man must own a pleasure in the hearing of his praise.
FARQUHAR, *The Twin Rivals*. Act iii, sc. 2.

The modesty of praise wears gradually away.
SAMUEL JOHNSON, *Lives of the Poets: Halifax*.

Modesty is the only sure bait when you angle for praise.
LORD CHESTERFIELD, *Letters*, 17 May, 1750.

10
What woman can resist the force of praise?
JOHN GAY, *Trivia*. Bk. i, l. 260.

Beauty's elixer vitæ, praise.
COVENTRY PATMORE, *The Angel in the House*: Bk. ii, *Prologue*.

Delightful praise!—like summer rose,
That brighter in the dew-drop glows,
The bashful maiden's cheek appear'd.
SCOTT, *The Lady of the Lake*. Canto ii, st. 24.

When all the world conspires to praise her,
The woman's deaf and does not hear.
POPE, *On a Certain Lady at Court*.

The sweeter sound of woman's praise.
MACAULAY, *Lines Written on the Night of 30th of July, 1847*.

11
Of praise a mere glutton, he swallow'd what came,
And the puff of a dunce, he mistook it for fame;
Till his relish grown callous, almost to displease,
Who pepper'd the highest was surest to please.
GOLDSMITH, *Retaliation*, l. 109. Referring to David Garrick.

12
Do you swell with the love of praise? (Laudis amore tumes?)
HORACE, *Epistles*. Bk. i, epis. 1, l. 36

So light and so small a thing it is which casts down or restores a mind greedy of praise. (Sic leve, sic parvum est, animum quod laudis avarum Subruit ac reficit.)
HORACE, *Epistles*. Bk. ii, epis. 1, l. 179.

13
For they loved the praise of men more than the praise of God.
New Testament: John, xii, 43.

14
He that departs with his own honesty
For vulgar praise, doth it too dearly buy.
BEN JONSON, *Epigrams*. No. 2.

15
Usually we praise only to be praised. (On ne loue d'ordinaire que pour être loué.)
LA ROCHEFOUCAULD, *Maximes*. No. 146.

The refusal of praise is a wish to be praised twice. (Le refus des louanges est un désir d'être loué deux fois.)
LA ROCHEFOUCAULD, *Maximes*. No. 149.

16
We are apt to love praise, but not to deserve it. But if we would deserve it, we must love virtue more than that.
WILLIAM PENN, *Fruits of Solitude*.

17
To what base ends, and by what abject ways,
Are mortals urged thro' sacred lust of praise!
POPE, *Essay on Criticism*. Pt. ii, l. 320.

Itch of vulgar praise.
POPE, *Moral Essays*. Epis. i, l. 60.

Whose Ruling Passion was the lust of praise.
POPE, *Moral Essays*. Epis. i, l. 181.

His passion still, to covet gen'ral praise,
His life, to forfeit it a thousand ways.
POPE, *Moral Essays*. Epis. i, l. 196.

18
The greatest efforts of the race have always been traceable to the love of praise, as its greatest catastrophes to the love of pleasure.
JOHN RUSKIN, *Sesame and Lilies*. Sec. i, 3.

19
Praises, of whose taste the wise are fond
SHAKESPEARE, *Richard II*. Act ii, sc. 1, l. 18.

1
Cram 's with praise, and make 's
As fat as tame things: one good deed, dying tongueless,
Slaughters a thousand waiting upon that.
Our praises are our wages.
SHAKESPEARE, *Winter's Tale*. Act i, sc. 2, l. 91.

Farewell, Bristolia's dingy piles of brick,
Lovers of mammon, worshippers of trick!
Ye spurned the boy who gave you antique lays,
And paid for learning with your empty praise.
THOMAS CHATTERTON, *Last Verses*.

2
He who loves praise loves temptation.
THOMAS WILSON, *Maxims of Piety*, p. 114.

3
The most pleasing of all sounds, that of your own praise. ("Ἥδιστον ἄκουσμα ἔπαινος.")
XENOPHON, *Heiro*. Ch. 1, sec. 14.

4
The love of praise, howe'er concealed by art,
Reigns, more or less, and glows, in ev'ry heart:
The proud, to gain it, toils on toils endure;
The modest shun it, but to make it sure.
YOUNG, *Love of Fame*. Sat. i, l. 51.

As love of pleasure into pain betrays,
So most grow infamous through love of praise.
YOUNG, *To the Right Hon. Mr. Dodington*.

IV—Praise of the Living

5
Every one that has been long dead has a due proportion of praise allotted him, in which, whilst he lived, his friends were too profuse and his enemies too sparing.
ADDISON, *The Spectator*. No. 101.

To hear the world applaud the hollow ghost
Which blamed the living man.
MATTHEW ARNOLD, *Growing Old*.

6
Him who ne'er listen'd to the voice of praise,
The silence of neglect can ne'er appall.
JAMES BEATTIE, *The Minstrel*. Bk. i, st. 2.

And hearts that once beat high for praise
Now feel that pulse no more.
THOMAS MOORE, *The Harp That Once Thro' Tara's Halls*.

Praise cannot wound his generous spirit now.
SAMUEL ROGERS, *Voyage of Columbus*. Canto i.

They have their passing paragraphs of praise,
And are forgotten.
ROBERT SOUTHEY, *The Victory*, l. 9.

7
The pathway of the living we can beautify and grace;
We can line it deep with roses and make earth a happier place.
But we've done all mortals can do, when our prayers are softly said
For the souls of those who travel o'er the pathway of the dead.
EDGAR GUEST, *The Pathway of the Living*.

8
Don't strew me with roses after I'm dead.
When Death claims the light of my brow,
No flowers of life will cheer me: instead
You may give me my roses now!
THOMAS F. HEALEY, *Give Me My Roses Now*.

A rose to the living is more
Than sumptuous wreaths to the dead.
NIXON WATERMAN, *A Rose to the Living*.

9
Then wherefore waste the rose's bloom
Upon the cold, insensate tomb?
Can flowery breeze, or odour's breath,
Affect the still, cold sense of death?
Oh no; I ask no balm to steep
With fragrant tears my bed of sleep:
But now, while every pulse is glowing,
Now let me breathe the balsam flowing.
THOMAS MOORE, *Odes of Anacreon*. Ode xxxii.

10
And so I charge ye, by the thorny crown,
And by the cross on which the Saviour bled,
And by your own soul's hope of fair renown,
Let something good be said.
JAMES WHITCOMB RILEY, *Let Something Good Be Said*.

11
Oh, friends! I pray to-night,
Keep not your roses for my dead, cold brow:
The way is lonely, let me feel them now.
ARABELLA EUGENIA SMITH, *If I Should Die To-night*. Erroneously attributed to Robert C. V. Myers, Alice Cary and Abram J. Ryan. Claimed without foundation by Irvine Dungan. (See STEVENSON, *Famous Single Poems*.)

If I should die to-night,
And you should come in deepest grief and woe,
And say, "Here's that ten dollars that I owe,"
I might arise in my large white cravat
And say, "What's that?" . . .
But I'd drop dead again!
BEN KING, *If I Should Die To-night*.

12
Closed eyes can't see the white roses;
Cold hands can't hold them, you know!
Breath that is stilled can not gather
The odors that sweet from them blow.
Death, with a peace beyond dreaming
Its children of earth doth endow;
Life is the time we can help them—
So give them the flowers now!
UNKNOWN, *Give Them the Flowers Now*.

Bring me all your flowers to-day—
Whether pink, or white, or red;
I'd rather have one blossom now
Than a truckload when I'm dead.
UNKNOWN, *Kindness During Life*.

13
Do not keep the alabaster boxes of your love and tenderness sealed up until your friends are dead. . . . Fill their lives with sweetness. . . . Postmortem kindness does

not cheer the burdened spirit. Flowers on the coffin cast no fragrance backward over the weary way.

UNKNOWN, *The Alabaster Boxes,* attributed to Warren P. Lovett, George W. Childs, Ben Selling, and others.

V—Praise of Gods and Men

1
The praise of so mean a creature was degrading to me. (Quæ quidem conlaudatio hominis turpissimi mihi ipsi erat pæne turpis.)

CICERO, *In Pisonem.* Ch. 29, sec. 72.

Of whom to be disprais'd were no small praise.

MILTON, *Paradise Regained.* Bk. iii, l. 56.

2
Nothing so soon the drooping spirits can raise
As praises from the men whom all men praise.

ABRAHAM COWLEY, *Ode upon Occasion of a Copy of Verses of My Lord Broghill's.*

Approbation from Sir Hubert Stanley is praise indeed.

THOMAS MORTON, *A Cure for the Heartache.* Act v, sc. 2. Usually quoted "Praise from Sir Hubert."

3
Be not extravagantly high in expression of thy commendations of men thou likest: It may make the hearers' stomach rise.

THOMAS FULLER, *Introductio ad Prudentiam.* Vol. i, p. 51.

Long open panegyric drags at best,
And praise is only praise when well address'd.

JOHN GAY, *Epistles.* Epis. i, l. 29.

4
Praising all alike is praising none.

JOHN GAY, *Epistles.* Epis. i, l. 114.

He who praises everybody praises nobody.

SAMUEL JOHNSON. (BOSWELL, *Life.* Vol. iii, p. 225, note.)

5
I would both sing thy praise and praise thy singing.

HUGH HOLLAND, *To Giles Farnaby.*

6
Sweet is the scene where genial friendship plays
The pleasing game of interchanging praise.

O. W. HOLMES, *An After Dinner Poem.*

7
Praise me not too much,
Nor blame me, for thou speakest to the Greeks
Who know me.

HOMER, *Iliad.* Bk. x, l. 289. (Bryant, tr.)

Praise none too much, for all are fickle.

GEORGE HERBERT, *Jacula Prudentum.*

8
I like you, Tom! and in these lays
Give honest worth its honest praise.

THOMAS HOOD, *Stanzas to Tom Woodgate.*

9
A continual feast of commendation is only to be attained by merit or by wealth.

SAMUEL JOHNSON, *The Rambler.* No. 193.

10
I should have praised you more had you praised me less. (Je vous louerais davantage si vous m'aviez loué moins.)

LOUIS XIV, *Remark,* to Bossuet.

11
Praise from you delights me, father, you a man deserving praise. (Lætus sum laudari me abs te, pater, a laudato viro.)

NÆVIUS. (CICERO, *Tusculanarum Disputationum.* Bk. iv, ch. 31, sec. 67.)

I am pleased to be praised by a man whom every one praises. (Lætus sum laudari a laudato viro.)

CICERO, *Epistolæ ad Familiares.* Bk. v, epis. 12.

It is not the least praise to have pleased distinguished men. (Principibus placuisse viris non ultima laus est.)

HORACE, *Epistles.* Bk. i, epis. 17, l. 35.

A word or nod from a good man is worth more than a thousand arguments from others.

PLUTARCH, *Lives: Phocion.* Ch. 5, sec. 4.

12
Praise, the fine diet which we're apt to love,
If given to excess, does hurtful prove.

JOHN OLDHAM, *A Letter from the Country to a Friend in Town.*

Praise is like ambergris: a little whiff of it, and by snatches, is very agreeable; but when a man holds a whole lump of it to your nose, it is a stink, and strikes you down.

POPE, *Thoughts on Various Subjects.*

13
And make her chronicle as rich with praise
As is the ooze and bottom of the sea
With sunken wreck and sumless treasuries.

SHAKESPEARE, *Henry V.* Act i, sc. 2, l. 163.

14
To you! to you! all song of praise is due;
Only in you my song begins and endeth.

SIR PHILIP SIDNEY, *Astrophel and Stella: First Song.*

And round thee with the breeze of song
To stir a little dust of praise.

TENNYSON, *In Memoriam.* Pt. lxxv.

15
On him and on his high endeavour
The light of praise shall shine for ever.

WORDSWORTH, *The White Doe of Rylstone.* Canto v, l. 1214.

VI—Praise and Blame

16
For if it be but half-denied,
'Tis half as good as justified.

BUTLER, *Hudibras.* Pt. iii, canto ii, l. 803.

17
Teasing with blame, excruciating with praise.

BYRON, *Beppo.* St. 74.

18
I praise loudly, I blame softly.

CATHERINE II OF RUSSIA, *Maxims.*

1
Thus neither the praise nor the blame is our own.
COWPER, *Letter to Mr. Newton.*

2
This misery those dreary souls sustain
Who passed their lives without or praise or
blame. (Questo misero modo
Tengon l'anime triste di coloro,
Che visser senza infamia e senza lodo.)
DANTE, *Inferno.* Canto iii, l. 34.

Now God bless all true workers, let us pray:
The night-time cometh when we all must rest:
Strive we, and do, lest by-and-by we sit
In that blind life to which all other fate
Is cause for envy; with the naked souls
Who never lived, knowing nor praise nor blame,
But kept themselves in mean neutrality,
Hateful alike to God and to His foes.
EMILY HENRIETTA HICKEY, *Michael Villiers, Idealist.*

3
It is more shameful to be praised faintly and coldly than to be censured violently and severely. For the man who reviles is regarded as unjust and hostile, but one who praises faintly is regarded as a friend, who would like to praise but can find nothing to commend.
FAVORINUS. (AULUS GELLIUS, *Noctes Atticæ.* Bk. xix, ch. 3, sec. 1.)

When needs he must, yet faintly then he praises;
Somewhat the deed, much more the means he
raises:
So marreth what he makes, and praising most,
dispraises.
PHINEAS FLETCHER, *The Purple Island.* Canto vii, st. 67.

Damn with faint praise, assent with civil leer,
And, without sneering, teach the rest to sneer.
POPE, *Epistle to Dr. Arbuthnot,* l. 201.

Well, well, is a word of malice.
JOHN RAY, *English Proverbs.*

With faint praises one another damn.
WYCHERLEY, *The Plain-Dealer: Prologue,* l. 6.

4
He that praiseth publicly will slander privately.
THOMAS FULLER, *Gnomologia.* No. 2250.

5
Praise from a friend, or censure from a foe,
Are lost on hearers that our merits know.
HOMER, *Iliad.* Bk. x, l. 293. (Pope, tr.)

6
Cold Approbation gave the lingering bays,
For those who durst not censure, scarce could
praise.
SAMUEL JOHNSON, *Prologue at the Opening of the Drury Lane Theatre,* l. 13.

7
Few are wise enough to prefer useful reproof to treacherous praise. (Peu de gens sont assez sages pour préférer le blâme qui leur est utile à la louange qui les trahit.)
LA ROCHEFOUCAULD, *Maximes.* No. 147.

There are reproaches which praise and praises which reproach. (Il y a des reproches qui louent et des louanges qui médisent.)
LA ROCHEFOUCAULD, *Maximes.* No. 148.

We blame or praise most things merely because it is the fashion. (On loue et on blâme la plupart des choses parce que c'est la mode de les louer ou de les blâmer.)
LA ROCHEFOUCAULD, *Maximes Posthumes.* No. 533.

8
Be sparing in praising and more so in blaming. (Parum lauda, vitupera parcius.)
WILLIAM LANGLAND, *Piers Plowman.* Quoted.

9
A man's accusations of himself are always believed, his praises never.
MONTAIGNE, *Essays.* Bk. iii, ch. 8.

10
Fear not the anger of the wise to raise;
Those best can bear reproof who merit praise.
POPE, *Essay on Criticism.* Pt. iii, l. 23.

11
Such is the mode of these censorious days,
The art is lost of knowing how to praise.
JOHN SHEFFIELD, *On Mr. Hobbes,* l. 1.

VII—Praise: Self-Praise

See also Boasting

12
Praise yourself daringly, something always sticks. (Audacter te vendita, semper aliquid hæret.)
FRANCIS BACON, *Apothegms. See also under* SLANDER.

13
He who discommendeth others obliquely commendeth himself.
SIR THOMAS BROWNE, *Christian Morals.* Pt. i, sec. 34.

14
Self-praise and self-depreciation are alike absurd. (Τὸ ἐπαινεῖν αὐτὸν ὥσπερ τὸ λοιδορεῖν ἄτοπον εἶναι.)
MARCUS CATO. (PLUTARCH, *Aristides and Cato.* Ch. 5, sec. 2.)

15
Self-praise debaseth.
CERVANTES, *Don Quixote.* Pt. i, ch. 16.

He that praiseth himself spattereth himself.
GEORGE HERBERT, *Jacula Prudentum.*

16
On their own merits modest men are dumb.
GEORGE COLMAN THE YOUNGER, *The Heir at Law: Epilogue.*

17
He whose own worth doth speak, need not speak his own worth.
THOMAS FULLER, *The Holy State,* p. 147.

Neither praise nor dispraise thyself, thy actions serve the turn.
GEORGE HERBERT, *Jacula Prudentum.*

1
All censure of a man's self is oblique praise. . . . It has all the invidiousness of self-praise, and all the reproach of falsehood.
SAMUEL JOHNSON. (BOSWELL, *Life*, 1778.)

One prefers to speak evil of himself rather than not speak of himself at all. (On aime mieux dire du mal de soi-même que de n'en point parler.)
LA ROCHEFOUCAULD, *Maximes*. No. 138.

2
You are pretty,—we know it; and young,—it is true; and rich,—who can deny it? But when you praise yourself extravagantly, Fabulla, you appear neither rich, nor pretty, nor young.
MARTIAL, *Epigrams*. Bk. i, ep. 64.

3
What would have been a great source of honor if another had related it, becomes nothing when the doer relates it himself. (Quod magnificum referente alio fuisset, ipso, qui gesserat, recensente vanescit.)
PLINY THE YOUNGER, *Epistles*. Bk. i, epis. 8.

4
Some, valuing those of their own side or mind,
Still make themselves the measure of mankind:
Fondly we think we honour merit then,
When we but praise ourselves in other men.
POPE, *Essay on Criticism*. Pt. ii, l. 252.

5
He who praises himself will soon find some-one to deride him. (Qui se ipsum laudat, cito derisorem invenit.)
PUBLILIUS SYRUS, *Sententiæ*. No. 588.

6
A man commends himself in praising that which he loves. (Quod quisque amat laudando commendat sibi.)
PUBLILIUS SYRUS, *Sententiæ*. No. 599.

7
Every man praises his own wares.
JOHN RAY, *English Proverbs*.

8
Say nothing good of yourself, you will be distrusted; say nothing bad of yourself, you will be taken at your word.
JOSEPH ROUX, *Meditations of a Parish Priest: Joy*. No. 22.

9
This comes too near the praising of myself.
SHAKESPEARE, *Merchant of Venice*, iii, 4, 22.

10
The trumpet of his own virtues.
SHAKESPEARE, *Much Ado About Nothing*. Act v, sc. 2, l. 87. (1598)

Or I should not blush so often as I do, by blowing the trumpet of my own praise.
THOMAS KNIGHT, *Turnpike Gate*. Act i, sc. 1. (1799)

If you wish in this world to advance
Your merits you're bound to enhance;
You must stir it and stump it,
And blow your own trumpet.
Or, trust me, you haven't a chance.
W. S. GILBERT, *Ruddigore*. Act i.

The fellow is blowing his own strumpet.
W. S. GILBERT, of a theatrical manager who was puffing an actress who was also his mistress. (PEARSON, *Gilbert and Sullivan*, Pt. iii.)

11
Oscar Wilde: When you and I are together, we never talk about anything except ourselves.
Whistler: No, no, Oscar, you forget—when you and I are together, we never talk about anything except me.
WHISTLER, *The Gentle Art of Making Enemies*, p. 66.

12
Hast thou that ancient, true-said saw forgot,
That a man's praise, in his own mouth, doth stink?
UNKNOWN, *Times Whistle*. Pt. iii, l. 1089. (c. 1614)

PRAYER

I—Prayer: Definitions

13
Prayer is the spirit speaking truth to Truth.
P. J. BAILEY, *Festus: Elsewhere*.

Truth is what prays in man, and a man is continually at prayer when he lives according to truth.
SWEDENBORG, *Apocalypse Explained*, p. 493.

14
This is that incense of the heart,
Whose fragrance smells to Heaven.
NATHANIEL COTTON, *The Fireside*. St. 11.

15
Prayer is the little implement
Through which men reach
Where presence is denied them.
EMILY DICKINSON, *Poems*. Pt. i, No. 80.

16
Ejaculations are short prayers darted up to God on emergent occasions.
THOMAS FULLER, *Good Thoughts in Bad Times*. Sec. v.

17
Prayer should be the key of the day and the lock of the night.
THOMAS FULLER, *Gnomologia*. No. 3927.

18
Prayers and Praises are those spotless two
Lambs, by the Law, which God requires as due.
ROBERT HERRICK, *God's Part*.

The imperfect offices of prayer and praise.
WORDSWORTH, *The Excursion*. Bk. i, l. 216.

19
A single grateful thought towards heaven is the most complete prayer.
LESSING, *Minna von Barnhelm*. Act ii, sc. 7.

20
Prayer is a strong wall and fortress of the church; it is a goodly Christian's weapon.
LUTHER, *Table Talk: Of Prayer*.

21
Prayer is the soul's sincere desire,
Uttered or unexpressed,
The motion of a hidden fire
That trembles in the breast.

Prayer is the burden of a sigh,
The falling of a tear,
The upward glancing of an eye
When none but God is near.
JAMES MONTGOMERY, *What Is Prayer?*

Prayers, the sweet ambassadors to God,
The heralds to prepare a better life.
FRANCIS ROUS, *Thule.*

1
There is a bridge, whereof the span
Is rooted in the heart of man,
And reaches, without pile or rod,
Unto the Great White Throne of God.

Its traffic is in human sighs,
Fervently wafted to the skies;
'Tis the one pathway from Despair,
And it is called the Bridge of Prayer.
GILBERT THOMAS, *The Unseen Bridge.*

2
Prayer is The world in tune,
A spirit-voice, And vocal joys,
Whose echo is heaven's bliss.
HENRY VAUGHAN, *The Morning Watch.*

3
Prayer, man's rational prerogative.
WORDSWORTH, *Ecclesiastical Sonnets.* Pt. ii, No. 23.

II—Prayer: Apothegms

4
Prayers plough not! Praises reap not!
WILLIAM BLAKE, *Proverbs of Hell.*

5
No man ever prayed heartily without learning something.
EMERSON, *Miscellanies: Nature.*

6
And fools, who came to scoff, remain'd to pray.
GOLDSMITH, *The Deserted Village,* l. 180.

7
Who goes to bed, and doth not pray,
Maketh two nights to every day!
GEORGE HERBERT, *Charms and Knots.*

He who ceases to pray ceases to prosper.
W. G. BENHAM, *Proverbs,* p. 783.

He that forgets to pray
Bids not himself good-morrow nor good-day.
THOMAS RANDOLPH, *Necessary Observations.* Precept 1.

8
Prayers and provender hinder no journey.
GEORGE HERBERT, *Jacula Prudentum.* No. 273.

9
Men ought always to pray, and not to faint.
New Testament: Luke, xviii, 1.

Watch and pray.
New Testament: Matthew, xxvi, 41; *Mark,* xiii, 33; xiv, 38; *Luke,* xxii, 40, 46. (Vigilate et orate.—*Vulgate.*)

Pray without ceasing.
New Testament: I Thessalonians, v, 17.

Pray for us.
New Testament: II Thessalonians, iii, 1. (Orate pro nobis.—*Vulgate.*)

Watch to-night, pray to-morrow.
SHAKESPEARE, *I Henry IV.* Act ii, sc. 4, l. 305.

10
To pray well is the better half of study.
MARTIN LUTHER, *Table Talk: Of Prayer.*

11
God warms his hands at man's heart when he prays.
MASEFIELD, *Widow in the Bye Street.* Pt. vi.

12
Do you wish to find out the really sublime?
Repeat the Lord's Prayer.
NAPOLEON I, *Sayings of Napoleon.*

13
I was immersed in prayer. (In prece totus eram.)
OVID, *Fasti.* Bk. xi, l. 251.

14
In times of tribulation, suspense, affliction, we ought indeed, in seeking deliverance, to try *everything*—even prayer.
A. W. PINERO, *The Freaks.* Act ii.

15
The monkey's paternoster. (Patenostre du singe.)
RABELAIS, *Works.* Bk. i, ch. 11. A proverbial expression for meaningless muttering.

16
Pray devoutly, but hammer stoutly.
W. G. BENHAM, *Proverbs,* p. 827. *See also* GOD: GOD HELPS THEM THAT HELP THEMSELVES.

17
He has mickle prayer but little devotion.
JOHN RAY, *Proverbs: Scottish.*

18
Fear drives the wretched to prayer. (In vota miseros ultimus cogit timor.)
SENECA, *Agamemnon,* l. 510.

19
Nothing costs so much as what is bought by prayers. (Nulla res carius constat quam quæ precibus empta est.)
SENECA, *De Beneficiis.* Bk. ii, sec. 1. *See* FAVORS.

20
Nay, that's past praying for.
SHAKESPEARE, *I Henry IV.* Act ii, sc. 4, l. 211.

"Amen" Stuck in my throat.
SHAKESPEARE, *Macbeth.* Act ii, sc. 2, l. 31.

I could not say "Amen,"
When they did say "God bless us!"
SHAKESPEARE, *Macbeth.* Act ii, sc. 2, l. 30.

Let me say "amen" betimes, lest the devil cross my prayer.
SHAKESPEARE, *Merchant of Venice,* iii, 1, 22.

21
Battering the gates of heaven with storms of prayer.
TENNYSON, *St. Simeon Stylites,* l. 7.

Making their lives a prayer.
WHITTIER, *To A. K. on Receiving a Basket of Sea Mosses.*

III—Prayer: Its Power

1
Just my vengeance complete,
The man sprang to his feet,
Stood erect, caught at God's skirts, and prayed!
—So, *I* was afraid!

ROBERT BROWNING, *Instans Tyrannus.*

2
And Satan trembles when he sees
The weakest saint upon his knees.

COWPER, *Exhortation to Prayer.*

3
The prayer of faith shall save the sick.

New Testament: James, v, 15.

The highest prayer is not one of faith merely; it is demonstration. Such prayer heals sickness, and must destroy sin and death.

MARY BAKER EDDY, *Science and Health,* p. 16.

4
He who fashions sacred images of gold or marble does not make them gods; he makes them such who prays to them. (Qui fingit sacros auro vel marmore vultus, Non facit ille deos: qui rogat, ille facit.)

MARTIAL, *Epigrams.* Bk. viii, ep. 24, l. 5.

Who is this before whose presence idols tumble to the sod?
While he cries out—"Allah Akbar! and there is no god but God!"

WILLIAM R. WALLACE, *El Amin: The Faithful.*

4a
Whosoever shall say unto this mountain, Be thou removed and be thou cast into the sea; and shall not doubt in his heart, but shall believe that those things which he saith shall come to pass; he shall have whatsoever he saith. Therefore I say unto you, What things soever ye desire, when ye pray, believe that ye receive them, and ye shall receive them.

New Testament: Mark, xi, 23, 24.

All things, whatsoever ye shall ask in prayer, believing, ye shall receive.

New Testament: Matthew, xxi, 22.

5
They who have steeped their souls in prayer
Can every anguish calmly bear.

RICHARD MONCKTON MILNES, *Sayings of Rabia.*

6
But that from us aught should ascend to Heav'n
So prevalent as to concern the mind
Of God high-bless'd, or to incline His will,
Hard to belief may seem; yet this will Prayer.

MILTON, *Paradise Lost.* Bk. xi, l. 143.

7
Prayer moves the arm which moves the world,
And brings salvation down.

JAMES MONTGOMERY, *Prayer.*

Prayer moves the Hand which moves the world.

JOHN AIKMAN WALLACE, *There Is an Eye That Never Sleeps,* l. 19.

8
Prayers travel more strongly when said in unison. (Conjunctas fortius ire preces.)

PETRONIUS, *Fragments.* No. 92.

Though private prayer be a brave design,
Yet public hath more promises, more love.

GEORGE HERBERT, *The Church-Porch.* St. 67.

To pray together, in whatever tongue or ritual, is the most tender brotherhood of hope and sympathy that men can contract in this life.

MADAME DE STAËL, *Corinne.* Bk. x, ch. 5.

Their ill-tasted home-brewed prayer
To the State's mellow forms prefer.

MATTHEW GREEN, *The Spleen,* l. 336.

Where a few villagers on bended knees
Find solace which a busy world disdains.

WORDSWORTH, *Ecclesiastical Sonnets.* Pt. iii, 17.

9
From every place below the skies
The grateful song, the fervent prayer,—
The incense of the heart,—may rise
To heaven, and find acceptance there.

JOHN PIERPONT, *Every Place a Temple.*

10
More things are wrought by prayer
Than this world dreams of.

TENNYSON, *Morte d'Arthur,* l. 247.

11
Lord, what a change within us one short hour
Spent in Thy presence will avail to make!
What heavy burdens from our bosoms take!
What parchèd grounds refresh as with a shower!

RICHARD CHENEVIX TRENCH, *Prayer.*

Time spent on the knees in prayer will do more to remedy heart strain and nerve worry than anything else.

GEORGE DAVID STEWART, *Lecture,* to his students at New York University.

12
Glory be unto her whose word
Sends her dear lord to bitter fight;
Although he conquer by his sword,
She to the praise has equal right;
He with the sword in battle, she at home with prayer,
Both win the victory, and both the glory share.

HARTMAN VON AUE. (WALSH, *Golden Treasury of Medieval Literature,* p. 112.)

13
Prayer ardent opens Heaven.

YOUNG, *Night Thoughts.* Night viii, l. 721.

14
In ev'ry storm that either frowns, or falls,
What an asylum has the soul in prayer!

YOUNG, *Night Thoughts.* Night ix, l. 1350.

The sure relief of prayer.

WORDSWORTH, *Miscellaneous Sonnets.* Pt. ii, 15.

15
Doubt not but God who sits on high,
Thy secret prayers can hear;
When a dead wall thus cunningly
Conveys soft whispers to the ear.

UNKNOWN, *Stanza Inscribed in the Whispering Gallery of Gloucester Cathedral.*

IV—Prayer: The Good Prayer

16
Know that thou art freed from all desires when thou hast reached such a point that thou prayest to God for nothing except what thou

canst pray for openly. (Tunc scito esse te omnibus cupiditatibus solutum, cum eo perveneris, ut nihil deum roges, nisi quod rogare possis palam.)

ATHENODORUS, *Fragment: De Superstitione.* (SENECA, *Epistulæ ad Lucilium.* Epis. x, 5.)

Prayers all men may hear. (Aperto vivere voto.)

PERSIUS, *Satires.* Sat. ii, l. 7.

Live among men as if God beheld you; speak with God as if men were listening. (Sic vive cum hominibus, tamquam deus videat; sic loquere cum deo, tamquam homines audiant.)

SENECA, *Epistulæ ad Lucilium.* Epis. x, sec. 5.

One way they look, another way they steer,
Pray to the gods, but would have mortals hear.

YOUNG, *Love of Fame.* Sat. i, l. 73.

1
Whoso will pray, he must fast and be clean,
And fat his soul, and make his body lean.

CHAUCER, *The Somnours Tale,* l. 171.

2
He prayeth well who loveth well
Both man and bird and beast.
He prayeth best who loveth best
All things both great and small;
For the dear God who loveth us,
He made and loveth all.

S. T. COLERIDGE, *The Ancient Mariner.* Pt. vii.

3
The prayer of the farmer kneeling in his field to weed it, the prayer of the rower kneeling with the stroke of his oar, are true prayers heard throughout nature.

EMERSON, *Essays, First Series: Self-Reliance.*

4
To pray . . . is to desire; but it is to desire what God would have us desire. He who desires not from the bottom of his heart, offers a deceitful prayer.

FÉNELON, *Advice Concerning Prayer.*

5
So a good prayer, though often used, is still fresh and fair in the ears and eyes of Heaven.

THOMAS FULLER, *Good Thoughts.* Sec. xii.

6
Thou canst not pray to God without praying to Love, but mayest pray to Love without praying to God.

RICHARD GARNETT, *De Flagello Myrteo,* xiii.

7
In prayer the lips ne'er act the winning part
Without the sweet concurrence of the heart.

ROBERT HERRICK, *The Heart.*

And, when I pray, my heart is in my prayer.

LONGFELLOW, *Giles Corey.* Act ii, sc. 3.

My prayers
Are not words duly hallow'd, nor my wishes
More worth than empty vanities; yet prayers
and wishes
Are all I can return.

SHAKESPEARE, *Henry VIII.* Act ii, sc. 3, l. 67.

8
A man can pray unbidden from a hassock,
And, passing by the customary cassock,
Kneel down remote upon the simple sod.
And sue in forma pauperis to God.

THOMAS HOOD, *Ode to Rae Wilson,* l. 206.

9
Thus she stood amid the stooks,
Praising God with sweetest looks.

THOMAS HOOD, *Ruth.*

10
You should pray for a sound mind in a sound body; for a stout heart that has no fear of death. (Orandum est ut sit mens sana in corpore sano; Fortem posce animum mortis terrore carentem.)

JUVENAL, *Satires.* Sat. x, l. 356.

Pray for a sound mind and for good health, first of soul and then of body. . . . Call boldly upon God; you will not be asking him for that which belongs to another.

SENECA, *Epistulæ ad Lucilium.* Epis. x, sec. 4.

Let our unceasing, earnest prayer
Be, too, for light,—for strength to bear
Our portion of the weight of care,
That crushes into dumb despair
One half the human race.

LONGFELLOW, *The Goblet of Life.* St. 10.

O, do not pray for easy lives. Pray to be stronger men. Do not pray for tasks equal to your powers. Pray for powers equal to your tasks.

PHILLIPS BROOKS, *Going Up to Jerusalem.* (In *Visions and Tasks,* p. 330.)

11
Full on this casement shone the wintry moon,
And threw warm gules on Madeline's fair breast,
As down she knelt for heaven's grace and boon;
Rose-bloom fell on her hands, together prest,
And on her silver cross soft amethyst,
And on her hair a glory, like a saint:
She seemed a splendid angel, newly drest,
Save wings, for heaven.

KEATS, *The Eve of St. Agnes.* St. 25.

12
In all thou dost first let thy Prayers ascend,
And to the Gods thy Labours first commend,
From them implore Success, and hope a prosperous End.

PYTHAGORAS, *Golden Verses,* l. 49. (DACIER, *Life of Pythagoras.*)

13
It may never be mine,
The loaf or the kiss or the kingdom
Because of beseeching;
But I know that my hand
Is an arm's length nearer the sky
For reaching.

EDWIN QUARLES, *Petition.*

14
A short prayer enters heaven; a long drink empties the can (Brevis oratio penetrat cælum; longa potatio evacuat scyphos.)

RABELAIS, *Works* Bk. i, ch. 41.

A short prayer winneth heaven.

UNKNOWN, *Good Wyfe Wold a Pylgremage,* l. 167. (c. 1460)

1
Prayers are heard in heaven very much in proportion to our faith. Little faith will get very great mercies, but great faith still greater.

CHARLES HADDEN SPURGEON, *Gleanings Among the Sheaves: Believing Prayer.*

I am groping for the keys
Of the heavenly harmonies.

WHITTIER, *Andrew Rykman's Prayer.*

V—Prayer: The Useless Prayer

2
"Oh, God, if I were sure I were to die to-night I would repent at once." It is the commonest prayer in all languages.

J. M. BARRIE, *Sentimental Tommy*, p. 98.

3
The prayers of Abel linked to deeds of Cain.

BYRON, *The Island.* Canto ii, st. 4.

4
Two went to pray? O, rather say,
One went to brag, the other to pray;
One stands up close and treads on high,
Where the other dares not lend his eye;
One nearer to God's altar trod,
The other to the altar's God.

RICHARD CRASHAW, *Two Went Up to the Temple to Pray.*

Prayer that craves a particular commodity, anything less than all good, is vicious. . . . Prayer as a means to a private end is meanness and theft.

EMERSON, *Essays, First Series: Self-Reliance.*

5
He who prays without confidence cannot hope that his prayers will be granted.

FÉNELON, *Maximes: On Prayer.*

6
God He rejects all Prayers that are slight,
And want their poise: words ought to have their weight.

ROBERT HERRICK, *Prayers Must Have Poise.*

7
Fool! why do you in vain beseech with childish prayers things which no day ever did bring, will bring, or could bring? (Stulte, quid hæc frustra votis puerilibus optas, Quæ non ulla tibi, fertque, feretque dies?)

OVID, *Tristia.* Bk. iii, eleg. 8, l. 11.

Do not waste time in praying. (Ne tempora perde precando.)

OVID, *Metamorphoses.* Bk. xi, l. 286.

8
He pray'd by quantity,
And with his repetitions, long and loud,
All knees were weary.

POLLOK, *The Course of Time.* Pt. viii, l. 628.

9
Do not pray for yourself: you do not know what will help you.

PYTHAGORAS. (LAERTIUS, *Pythagoras.* Sec. 9.)

10
Don't ask for what you'll wish you hadn't got. (Postea noli rogare, quod inpetrare nolueris.)

SENECA, *Epistulæ ad Lucilium.* Epis. xcv, 1.

We often want one thing and pray for another, not telling the truth even to the gods. (Sæpe aliud volumus, aliud optamus et verum ne dis quidem dicimus.)

SENECA, *Epistulæ ad Lucilium.* Epis. xcv, 2.

What we seek we shall find; what we flee from flees from us; as Goethe said, "What we wish for in youth, comes in heaps on us in old age," too often cursed with the granting of our prayer: and hence the high caution, that, since we are sure of having what we wish, we beware to ask only for high things.

EMERSON, *Conduct of Life: Fate.*

11
My words fly up, my thoughts remain below:
Words without thoughts never to heaven go.

SHAKESPEARE, *Hamlet.* Act iii, sc. 3, l. 97.

When I would pray and think, I think and pray
To several subjects; Heaven hath my empty words.

SHAKESPEARE, *Measure for Measure,* ii, 4, 1.

12
Common people do not pray; they only beg.

BERNARD SHAW, *Misalliance,* p. 57.

13
Complaint is the largest tribute heaven receives, and the sincerest part of our devotion.

SWIFT, *Thoughts on Various Subjects.*

14
Nor are any prayers, unless righteous, heard by the gods. (Neque a Diis nisi justas supplicium preces audiri.)

TACITUS, *Annals.* Bk. iii, sec. 36.

15
" 'Twas then belike," Honorious cried,
"When you the public fast defied,
Refused to heav'n to raise a prayer,
Because you'd no connections there."

JOHN TRUMBULL, *McFingal.* Canto i, l. 541.

16
Cease to think that the decrees of the gods can be turned aside by prayers. (Desine fata deum flecti sperare precando.)

VERGIL, *Æneid.* Bk. vi, l. 376.

17
Though smooth be the heartless prayer, no ear in heaven will mind it;
And the finest phrase falls dead, if there is no feeling behind it.

ELLA WHEELER WILCOX, *Art and Heart.*

18
"What is good for a bootless bene?"
With these dark words begins my Tale;
And their meaning is, whence can comfort spring
When Prayer is of no avail?

WORDSWORTH, *The Force of Prayer.* St. 1.

VI—Prayer: Answered Prayer

19
Long tarries destiny, but comes to those who pray. (Τὸ μόρσιμον μένει πάλαι, εὐχομένοις δ' ἂν ἔλθοι.)

ÆSCHYLUS, *Chœphoræ,* l. 464. (Plumptre, tr.)

20
God answers sharp and sudden on some prayers,

And thrusts the thing we have prayed for in
our face,
A gauntlet with a gift in 't.
E. B. BROWNING, *Aurora Leigh*. Bk. ii, l. 952.

1
She knows omnipotence has heard her prayer
And cries, "It shall be done—sometime, somewhere."
OPHELIA G. BROWNING, *Unanswered*.

2
They never sought in vain that sought the Lord aright!
BURNS, *The Cotter's Saturday Night*. St. 6.

A generous prayer is never presented in vain.
R. L. STEVENSON, *The Merry Men*.

3
But this she knows, in joys and woes,
That saints will aid if men will call;
For the blue sky bends over all!
S. T. COLERIDGE, *Christabel:* Pt. i, *Conclusion*.

4
Our vows are heard betimes! and Heaven takes care
To grant, before we can conclude the pray'r:
Preventing angels met it half the way,
And sent us back to praise, who came to pray.
DRYDEN, *Britannia Rediviva*, l. 1.

5
Grant folly's prayers that hinder folly's wish,
And serve the ends of wisdom.
GEORGE ELIOT, *The Spanish Gypsy*. Bk. iv.

6
God, who's in Heav'n, will hear from thence,
If not to th' sound, yet to the sense.
ROBERT HERRICK, *God Hears Us*.

7
Who hearkens to the gods, the gods give ear.
HOMER, *Iliad*. Bk. i, l. 280. (Bryant, tr.)

A god when angry is moved by the voice of prayer. (Flectitur iratus voce rogante deus.)
OVID, *Ars Amatoria*. Bk. i, l. 442.

8
So spake he in prayer, and Zeus, the counsellor, heard him, and a part the Father granted him, and a part denied.
HOMER, *Iliad*. Bk. xvi, l. 249.

Ae half the prayer wi' Phœbus grace did find
And t'other half he whistled down the wind.
(Audiit et voti Phœbus succedere partem
Mente dedit, partem volucris dispersit in auras.)
VERGIL, *Æneid*. Bk. xi, l. 794. (Scott, tr., *Waverley*. Ch. 43.)

9
Your Father knoweth what things ye have need of, before ye ask Him.
New Testament: Matthew, vi, 8.

Leave it to the gods to decide what is best for us and most suitable to our circumstances. (Permittes ipsis expendere numinibus quid Conveniat nobis rebusque sit utile nostris.)
JUVENAL, *Satires*. Sat. x, l. 347.

10
Ask, and it shall be given you; seek, and ye shall find; knock, and it shall be opened unto you.
New Testament: Matthew, vii, 7.

Every one that asketh receiveth; and he that seeketh findeth.
New Testament: Matthew, vii, 8.

11
Who rises from Prayer a better man, his prayer is answered.
GEORGE MEREDITH, *The Ordeal of Richard Feverel*. Ch. 12.

12
My debts are large, my failures great, my shame secret and heavy; yet when I come to ask for my good, I quake in fear lest my prayer be granted.
RABINDRANATH TAGORE, *Gitanjali*. No. 28.

13
I have never made but one prayer to God, a very short one: "O Lord, make my enemies ridiculous." And God granted it.
VOLTAIRE, *Letter to M. Damiliville*, 16 May, 1767.

14
When the gods wish to punish us they answer our prayers.
OSCAR WILDE, *An Ideal Husband*. Act ii.

Prayer must never be answered: if it is, it ceases to be prayer and becomes a correspondence.
OSCAR WILDE, *Remark*, to Laurence Housman.

VII—Prayer: Unanswered Prayer

15
Of course I prayed—
And did God care?
He cared as much
As on the air
A bird had stamped her foot
And cried "Give me!"
EMILY DICKINSON, *Poems*. Pt. v, No. 38.

16
Is there never a chink in the world above
Where they listen for words from below?
JEAN INGELOW, *Supper at the Mill: The Mother's Song*.

17
If by prayer
Incessant I could hope to change the will
Of him who all things can, I would not cease
To weary him with my assiduous cries:
But prayer against his absolute decree
No more avails than breath against the wind,
Blown stifling back on him that breathes it forth:
Therefore to his great bidding I submit.
MILTON, *Paradise Lost*. Bk. xi, l. 307.

18
O sad estate
Of human wretchedness; so weak is man,
So ignorant and blind, that did not God
Sometimes withhold in mercy what we ask,
We should be ruined at our own request.
HANNAH MORE, *Moses in the Bulrushes*. Pt. i.

19
We, ignorant of ourselves,
Beg often our own harms, which the wise powers

Deny us for our good; so find we profit
By losing of our prayers.
SHAKESPEARE, *Antony and Cleopatra*. Act ii, sc. 1, l. 5.

Who finds not Providence all good and wise,
Alike in what it gives, and what denies?
POPE, *Essay on Man*. Epis. i, l. 205.

Good when he gives, supremely good,
Nor less when he denies,
E'en crosses from his sovereign hand
Are blessings in disguise.
JAMES HERVEY, *Hymn*.

See also under BLESSING.

VIII—Prayer: Praying

1
A child may say amen
To a bishop's prayer, and feel the way it goes.
E. B. BROWNING, *Aurora Leigh*. Bk. ii, l. 337.

2
Ave Maria! 'tis the hour of prayer!
BYRON, *Don Juan*. Canto iii, st. 103.

'Twas the hour when rites unholy
Called each Paynim voice to prayer.
THOMAS CAMPBELL, *The Turkish Lady*.

3
Father of Light! great God of Heaven!
Hear'st thou the accents of despair?
Can guilt like man's be e'er forgiven?
Can vice atone for crimes by prayer?
BYRON, *The Prayer of Nature*. St. 1.

4
O sweeter than the marriage-feast,
'Tis sweeter far to me,
To walk together to the kirk
With a goodly company:

To walk together to the kirk,
And all together pray,
While each to his great Father bends,
Old men, and babes, and loving friends
And youths and maidens gay.
S. T. COLERIDGE, *The Ancient Mariner*. Pt. vii.

5
White Captain of my soul, lead on;
I follow thee, come dark or dawn.
Only vouchsafe three things I crave:
Where terror stalks, help me be brave!
Where righteous ones can scarce endure
The siren call, help me be pure!
Where vows grow dim, and men dare do
What once they scorned, help me be true!
ROBERT FREEMAN, *Prayer*.

6
O Lord of Courage grave,
O Master of this night of Spring!
Make firm in me a heart too brave
To ask Thee anything.
JOHN GALSWORTHY, *The Prayer*.

7
Lord, dismiss us with thy blessing,
Hope, and comfort from above;
Let us each, thy peace possessing,
Triumph in redeeming love.
ROBERT HAWKER, *Benediction*.

8
Brightest and best of the sons of the morning,
Dawn on our darkness, and lend us thine aid.
REGINALD HEBER, *Epiphany*.

9
Father, I scarcely dare to pray,
So clear I see, now it is done,
How I have wasted half my day,
And left my work but just begun.
HELEN HUNT JACKSON, *A Last Prayer*.

10
Abide with me from morn till eve,
For without Thee I cannot live:
Abide with me when night is nigh,
For without Thee I dare not die.
JOHN KEBLE, *The Christian Year: Evening*.

And help us, this and every day,
To live more nearly as we pray.
JOHN KEBLE, *The Christian Year: Morning*.

11
I kneel not now to pray that thou
Make white one single sin,—
I only kneel to thank thee, Lord,
For what I have not been.
HARRY KEMP, *A Prayer*.

12
I ask and wish not to appear
More beauteous, rich or gay:
Lord, make me wiser every year,
And better every day.
CHARLES LAMB, *A Birthday Thought*.

13
O Lord my God, I have trusted in thee;
O Jesu my dearest one, now set me free.
In prison's oppression, in sorrow's obsession,
I weary for thee.
With sighing and crying bowed down as dying,
I adore thee, I implore thee, set me free!
(O Domine Deus! speravi in te;
O care mi Jesu! nunc libera me.
In dura catena, in misera poëna,
Disidero te.
Languendo, jemendo, et genuflectendo,
Adoro, imploro, ut liberes me!)
MARY, QUEEN OF SCOTS. Written in her Book of Devotion before her execution. (Swinburne, tr., *Mary Stewart*. Act v, sc. 1.)

14
When the last sea is sailed and the last shal low charted,
When the last field is reaped and the last harvest stored,
When the last fire is out and the last guest departed,
Grant the last prayer that I shall pray, Be good to me, O Lord!
JOHN MASEFIELD, *D'Avalos' Prayer*.

15
Lord, help me live from day to day
In such a self-forgetful way,
That even when I kneel to pray,
My prayer shall be for—*others*.
CHARLES D. MEIGS, *Others*.

1
Let not that happen which I wish, but that which is right. (Μή μοι γένοιθ' ἃ βούλομ' ἀλλ' ἃ συμφέρει.)
MENANDER, *Fragment.*

Not what we wish, but what we want,
Oh! let thy grace supply,
The good unask'd, in mercy grant;
The ill, though ask'd, deny.
JAMES MERRICK, *Hymn.*

2
As down in the sunless retreats of the Ocean,
Sweet flowers are springing no mortal can see,
So, deep in my soul the still prayer of devotion
Unheard by the world, rises silent to Thee.
MOORE, *As Down in the Sunless Retreats.*

2a
Socrates: O beloved Pan and all ye other gods of this place, grant to me that I be made beautiful in my soul within, and that all external possessions be in harmony with my inner man. May I consider the wise man rich; and may I have such wealth as only the self-restrained man can endure.—Do we need anything more, Phædrus? For me that prayer is enough. Phædrus: Let me also share in this prayer; for friends have all things in common. (Κοινὰ γὰρ τὰ τῶν φίλων.)
PLATO, *Phædrus.* Conclusion. *See under* FRIEND.

I prayed the prayer of Plato old:
God make thee beautiful within,
And let thine eyes the good behold
In everything save sin!
J. G. WHITTIER, *My Namesake.* St. 43.

3
Without ceasing I make mention of you always in my prayers.
New Testament: Romans, i, 9.

Farewell! if ever fondest prayer
For other's weal avail'd on high,
Mine will not all be lost in air,
But waft thy name beyond the sky.
BYRON, *Farewell! If Ever Fondest Prayer.*

I would not exchange the prayer of the deceased [Mrs. Sheppard] in my behalf for the united glory of Homer, Cæsar, and Napoleon, could such be accumulated upon a living head.
BYRON, *Letter to Mr. Sheppard.* (MOORE, *Life of Byron.*)

Pray, sweet, for me, that I may be
Faithful to God and thee.
EMILY HENRIETTA HICKEY, *Beloved, It Is Morn.*

Nymph, in thy orisons
Be all my sins remember'd.
SHAKESPEARE, *Hamlet.* Act iii, sc. 1, l. 89.

4
Now that the sun is gleaming bright,
Implore we, bending low,
That He, the Uncreated Light,
May guide us as we go.
ADAM DE ST. VICTOR, *Guide Us, Lord.* A paraphrase of an old Latin hymn, sung at the death-bed of William the Conqueror.

5
Bow, stubborn knees; and, heart with strings of steel,
Be soft as sinews of the new-born babe.
SHAKESPEARE, *Hamlet.* Act iii, sc. 3, l. 70.

Make of your prayers one sweet sacrifice,
And lift my soul to heaven.
SHAKESPEARE, *Henry VIII.* Act ii, sc. 1, l. 77.

Now I am past all comforts here, but prayers.
SHAKESPEARE, *Henry VIII.* Act iv, sc. 2, l. 123.

6
His worst fault is, that he is given to prayer; he is something peevish that way; but nobody but has his fault.
SHAKESPEARE, *Merry Wives of Windsor,* i, 4, 13.

7
She prayed, that never prayed before.
SHAKESPEARE, *Taming of the Shrew,* iv, 1, 81.

8
Four things which are not in thy treasury,
I lay before thee, Lord, with this petition:—
My nothingness, my wants,
My sins, and my contrition.
ROBERT SOUTHEY, *Occasional Pieces.* No. 19.

9
Holy Father, in thy mercy,
Hear our anxious prayer.
Keep our loved ones, now far absent,
'Neath Thy care.
ISABELLA S. STEPHENSON, *Hymn.*

10
The day returns and brings us the petty round of irritating concerns and duties. Help us to play the man, help us to perform them with laughter and kind faces; let cheerfulness abound with industry. Give us to go blithely on our business all this day, bring us to our resting beds weary and content and undishonored, and grant us in the end the gift of sleep.
ROBERT LOUIS STEVENSON, *Prayer.*

11
For what are men better than sheep or goats
That nourish a blind life within the brain,
If, knowing God, they lift not hands of prayer
Both for themselves and those who call them friend?
TENNYSON, *Morte d'Arthur,* l. 301.

12
While Thee I seek, protecting Power,
Be my vain wishes stilled;
And may this consecrated hour
With better hopes be filled.
HELEN MARIA WILLIAMS, *Trust in Providence.*

13
If she, with those soft eyes in tears,
Day after day in her first years,
Must kneel and pray for grace from Thee,
What far, far deeper need have we!
How hardly, if she win not heaven,
Will *our* wild errors be forgiven!
NATHANIEL PARKER WILLIS, *"Chamber Scene."*

Ah! a seraph may pray for a sinner,
But a sinner must pray for himself.
CHARLES MONROE DICKINSON, *The Children*

Her cushion's threadbare with her constant prayer.
YOUNG, *Love of Fame.* Satire vi, l. 78.

14
I pray the prayer the Easterners do:

May the peace of Allah abide with you.
(Salaam Aleikum.)
UNKNOWN, *Peace Be With You.*

PREACHER AND PREACHING

I—Preacher: Definitions

1
For the preacher's merit or demerit,
It were to be wished the flaws were fewer
In the earthen vessel, holding treasure
Which lies as safe in a golden ewer;
But the main thing is, does it hold good measure?
Heaven soon sets right all other matters!
ROBERT BROWNING, *Christmas-Eve.* Pt. xxii.

I praise the heart, and pity the head of him,
And refer myself to Thee, instead of him.
ROBERT BROWNING, *Christmas-Eve.* Pt. xxii.

2
For his religion, it was fit
To match his learning and his wit:
'Twas Presbyterian true blue;
For he was of that stubborn crew
Of errant saints, whom all men grant
To be the true Church Militant;
Such as do build their faith upon
The holy text of pike and gun;
Decide all controversies by
Infallible artillery;
And prove their doctrine orthodox,
By Apostolic blows and knocks.
BUTLER, *Hudibras.* Pt. i, canto 1, l. 189.

3
My profession is to keep secrets.
CERVANTES, *Don Quixote.* Pt. ii, ch. 1. It is a priest speaking.

4
Priests are extremely like other men, and neither the better or worse for wearing a gown or a surplice.
LORD CHESTERFIELD, *Letters,* 10 May, 1748.

Vows can't change nature; priests are only men.
ROBERT BROWNING, *The Ring and the Book.* Pt. i, l. 1057.

All pastors are alike
To wand'ring sheep, resolv'd to follow none.
COWPER, *The Task.* Bk. vi, l. 890.

5
For we preach not ourselves, but Christ Jesus the Lord: . . . But we have this treasure in earthen vessels, that the excellency of the power may be of God, and not of us.
New Testament: II Corinthians, iv, 5, 7.

Judge not the preacher; for he is thy Judge:
If thou mislike him, thou conceiv'st him not.
God calleth preaching folly. Do not grudge
To pick our treasures from an earthen pot.
The worst speak something good: if all want sense,
God takes a text, and preacheth patience.
GEORGE HERBERT, *The Church-Porch.* St. 72.

6
He that negotiates between God and man,
As God's ambassador, the grand concerns
Of judgment and of mercy, should beware
Of lightness in his speech.
COWPER, *The Task.* Bk. ii, l. 463.

7
Alas for the unhappy man that is called to stand in the pulpit, and *not* give the bread of life.
EMERSON, *Address to the Senior Class in Divinity College, Cambridge,* 15 July, 1838.

8
The Clergy in this sense, of Divine Institution, that God hath made mankind so weak that it must be deceived.
LORD HALIFAX, *Works,* p. 221.

9
Even ministers of good things are like torches, a light to others, waste and destruction to themselves.
RICHARD HOOKER. Quoted as "that admirable saying," by Gladstone, in 1880. (MORLEY, *Life of Gladstone.* Bk. viii, ch. 1.)

10
What bishops like best in their clergy is a dropping-down-deadness of manner.
SYDNEY SMITH, *First Letter to Archdeacon Singleton.*

They admire the Vicar of Bray, whose principle was to be Vicar of Bray, whether the church was Protestant or Popish.
C. H. SPURGEON, *John Ploughman.* Ch. 18.
See also POLITICS: EXPEDIENCY.

11
A genius in a reverend gown
Must ever keep its owner down;
'Tis an unnatural conjunction,
And spoils the credit of the function.
SWIFT, *To Dr. Delany.*

Now hear an allusion:—A mitre, you know,
Is divided above, but united below.
If this you consider, our emblem is right;
The bishops divide, but the clergy unite.
SWIFT, *On the Irish Bishops.*

12
I never saw, heard, nor read that the clergy were beloved in any nation where Christianity was the religion of the country. Nothing can render them popular but some degree of persecution.
SWIFT, *Thoughts on Religion.*

II—Preacher: Apothegms

13
The parson knows enough who knows a Duke.
COWPER, *Tirocinium,* l. 403.

14
Keeping our hearts warm and our heads cool, we clergy need do nothing emphatically.
DICKENS, *Mystery of Edwin Drood.* Ch. 16.

15
Taylor, the Shakespeare of divines.
His words are music in my ear,
I see his cowlèd portrait dear;
And yet, for all his faith could see,

I would not the good bishop be.
EMERSON, *The Problem.*

1
A Mr. Wilkinson, a clergyman.
EDWARD FITZGERALD, telling Tennyson of the man to whom his sister was engaged. Tennyson seized upon the fact that the words made a line of blank verse, and aptly illustrated Wordsworth's weakest manner. (See BENSON, *Life of Fitzgerald*, p. 62.)

2
To a philosophic eye the vices of the clergy are far less dangerous than their virtues.
GIBBON, *Decline and Fall.* Ch. 49.

3
It is by the Vicar's skirts that the
Devil climbs into the Belfry.
LONGFELLOW, *Spanish Student.* Act i, sc. 2.

4
Touch not mine anointed, and do my prophets no harm.
Old Testament: I Chronicles, xvi, 22; *Psalms*, cv, 15. The text upon which "Benefit of Clergy" (Beneficium clericorum aut clergicorum) was grounded. In England, the privilege was at first restricted to ecclesiastical places and persons, but in 1274 was extended to all persons who could read, and in 1691 to women. Such a person could not be put to death, but was branded on the hand. It was abolished in 1827. In America, the Congress passed an act in 1790 prohibiting benefit of clergy in any case of conviction of a capital crime.

Without Benefit of Clergy.
RUDYARD KIPLING. Title of short story. Kipling used the phrase in the sense of unmarried.

When want of learning kept the laymen low,
And none but priests were authoriz'd to know;
When what small knowledge was, in them did dwell;
And he a god, who could but read or spell.
JOHN DRYDEN, *Religio Laici*, l. 372.

5
A Curate—there is something which excites compassion in the very name of a Curate!
SYDNEY SMITH, *Persecuting Bishops.*

Ah me! I was a pale young curate then.
W. S. GILBERT, *The Sorcerer.* Act i.

The mildest curate going.
W. S. GILBERT, *The Rival Curates.*

The curate—he was fatter than his cure!
TENNYSON, *Edwin Morris*, l. 15.

III—Preachers: Their Virtues

6
I met a preacher there I knew, and said:
"Ill and o'erwork'd, how fare you in this scene?"
"Bravely!" said he; "for I of late have been
Much cheer'd with thoughts of Christ, the living bread."
MATTHEW ARNOLD. *East London.*

7
I venerate the man whose heart is warm,
Whose hands are pure, whose doctrine and whose life,
Coincident, exhibit lucid proof
That he is honest in the sacred cause.
COWPER, *The Task.* Bk. ii, l. 372.

Would I describe a preacher, . . .
I would express him simple, grave, sincere;
In doctrine uncorrupt; in language plain,
And plain in manner; decent, solemn, chaste,
And natural in gesture; much impress'd
Himself, as conscious of his awful charge,
And anxious mainly that the flock he feeds
May feel it too; affectionate in look,
And tender in address, as well becomes
A messenger of grace to guilty men.
COWPER, *The Task.* Bk. ii, l. 394.

8
There, where a few torn shrubs the place disclose,
The village preacher's modest mansion rose.
A man he was to all the country dear,
And passing rich with forty pounds a year;
Remote from towns he ran his godly race,
Nor e'er had chang'd, nor wished to change, his place.
GOLDSMITH, *The Deserted Village*, l. 139.

But in his duty prompt at every call,
He watch'd and wept, he pray'd and felt, for all.
GOLDSMITH, *The Deserted Village*, l. 165.

At church, with meek and unaffected grace,
His looks adorn'd the venerable place;
Truth from his lips prevail'd with double sway,
And fools, who came to scoff, remain'd to pray.
GOLDSMITH, *The Deserted Village*, l. 177.

E'en children follow'd with endearing wile,
And pluck'd his gown, to share the good man's smile. . . .
To them his heart, his love, his griefs were given,
But all his serious thoughts had rest in Heaven.
As some tall cliff, that lifts its awful form,
Swells from the vale, and midway leaves the storm,
Though round its breast the rolling clouds are spread,
Eternal sunshine settles on its head.
GOLDSMITH, *The Deserted Village*, l. 183.

9
As pleasant songs, at morning sung,
The words that dropped from his sweet tongue
Strengthened our hearts; or, heard at night,
Made all our slumbers soft and light.
LONGFELLOW, *The Golden Legend.* Pt. i.

Skilful alike with tongue and pen,
He preached to all men everywhere
The Gospel of the Golden Rule,
The New Commandment given to men,
Thinking the deed, and not the creed,
Would help us in our utmost need.
LONGFELLOW, *Tales of a Wayside Inn: Prelude*, l. 217.

1
He of their wicked ways
Shall them admonish, and before them set
The paths of righteousness.
MILTON, *Paradise Lost*. Bk. xi, l. 808.

2
It comes now into my mind to observe that I am sensible that I have been a little too free to make mirth with the minister of our ship, he being a very sober and upright man.
SAMUEL PEPYS, *Diary*, 11 April, 1660.

A minister, but still a man.
POPE, *Epistle to James Craggs*.

3
And truths divine came mended from that tongue.
POPE, *Eloisa to Abelard*, l. 66.

4
He was a shrewd and sound divine,
Of loud Dissent the mortal terror;
And when, by dint of page and line,
He 'stablished Truth, or started Error,
The Baptist found him far too deep,
The Deist sighed with saving sorrow,
And the lean Levite went to sleep,
And dreamed of eating pork to-morrow.
WINTHROP MACKWORTH PRAED, *The Vicar*.

His sermon never said or showed
That Earth is foul, that Heaven is gracious,
Without refreshment on the road
From Jerome, or from Athanasius;
And sure a righteous zeal inspired,
The hand and head that penned and planned them,
For all who understood, admired—
And some who did not understand them.
WINTHROP MACKWORTH PRAED, *The Vicar*.

5
I have taught you, my dear flock, for above thirty years how to live; and I will show you in a very short time how to die.
GEORGE SANDYS, *Anglorum Speculum*, p. 903.

He taught them how to live and how to die.
WILLIAM SOMERVILLE, *In Memory of the Rev. Mr. Moore*, l. 21.

See also under LIFE AND DEATH.

6
Thou art no Sabbath-drawler of old saws,
Distill'd from some worm-canker'd homily.
TENNYSON, *To J. M. K.*

7
God's true priest is always free;
Free, the needed truth to speak,
Right the wronged, and raise the weak.
WHITTIER, *The Curse of the Charter-Breakers*.

IV—Preachers: Their Faults

8
Vile avarice and pride, from Heaven accurst,
In all are ill, but in a church-man worst.
WILLIAM ALEXANDER, *Doomsday: The Seventh Hour*. St. 86.

And of all plagues with which mankind are curst,
Ecclesiastic tyranny's the worst.
DANIEL DEFOE, *The True-Born Englishman*. Pt. ii, l. 299.

Inquisitorious and tyrannical duncery [of prelaty].
MILTON, *Reason of Church Government:* Bk. ii, *Introduction*.

9
First, the preacher speaks through his nose:
Second, his gesture is too emphatic:
Thirdly, to waive what's pedagogic,
The subject-matter itself lacks logic:
Fourthly, the English is ungrammatic.
ROBERT BROWNING, *Christmas-Eve*. Pt. xxii.

The pig-of-lead-like pressure
Of the preaching man's immense stupidity.
ROBERT BROWNING, *Christmas-Eve*. Pt. iii.

10
Hear how he clears the points o' Faith
Wi' rattlin' an' thumpin'!
Now meekly calm, now wild in wrath,
He's stampin', an' he's jumpin'!
BURNS, *The Holy Fair*. St. 13.

11
Cleric before and Lay behind;
A lawless linsey-woolsey brother,
Half of one order, half another.
BUTLER, *Hudibras*. Pt. i, canto iii, l. 1226.

12
The things that mount the rostrum with a skip,
And then skip down again; pronounce a text;
Cry hem: and, reading what they never wrote,
Just fifteen minutes, huddle up their work,
And with a well-bred whisper close the scene!
COWPER, *The Task*. Bk. ii, l. 409.

13
There is not in the universe a more ridiculous nor a more contemptible animal than a proud clergyman.
FIELDING, *Amelia*. Bk. x, ch. 10.

That pride to pampered priesthood dear.
BYRON, *Childe Harold*. Canto ii, st. 44.

Cleric pride,
Whose reddening cheek no contradiction bears.
JAMES THOMSON, *Liberty*. Pt. iv, l. 62.

14
A country clergyman with a one story intellect and a one-horse vocabulary.
O. W. HOLMES, *The Autocrat of the Breakfast-Table*. Ch. ii.

15
Not one of those self-constituted saints,
Quacks—not physicians—in the cure of souls.
THOMAS HOOD, *Ode to Rae Wilson*, l. 14.

16
Preaching the people for profit of the belly,
And glosing the Gospel as them good liked.
LANGLAND, *Piers Plowman*. Passus i, l. 57.

Many chaplains are chaste, but charity is wanting;
There are none harder nor hungrier than men of holy church.
LANGLAND, *Piers Plowman*. Passus ii, l. 187.

For with the Princes of Pride the Preachers dwelleth.
LANGLAND, *Piers Plowman's Creed*, l. 705.

1
We dislike the man who tries
To give us title clear
To any mansion in the skies
An' grab our title here.
DOUGLAS MALLOCH, *Behind a Spire.*

2
So clomb this first grand thief into God's fold;
So since into his church lewd hirelings climb.
Thence up he flew, and on the Tree of Life,
The middle Tree and highest there that grew,
Sat like a cormorant.
MILTON, *Paradise Lost.* Bk. iv, l. 192.

3
Clericalism, that is the enemy! (Le cléricalisme, voilà l'ennemi!)
ALPHONSE PEYRAT, *Speech*, 1859.

4
Dulness is sacred in a sound divine.
POPE, *The Dunciad.* Bk. ii, l. 352.

A little, round, fat, oily man of God.
THOMSON, *Castle of Indolence.* Canto i, st. 69.

V—Preachers: Priests

5
Once have a priest for an enemy, good-bye
To peace.
SARAH FLOWER ADAMS, *Vivia Perpetua.* Act iii, sc. 2.

6
The Jackdaw sat on the Cardinal's chair!
Bishop and abbot and prior were there;
Many a monk, and many a friar,
Many a knight, and many a squire,
With a great many more of lesser degree,—
In sooth a goodly company;
And they served the Lord Primate on bended knee.
Never, I ween, Was a prouder seen,
Read of in books, or dreamt of in dreams,
Than the Cardinal Lord Archbishop of Rheims!
R. H. BARHAM, *The Jackdaw of Rheims.*

7
In brief, I don't stick To declare Father Dick—
So they call'd him, "for short"—was a "Regular Brick,"
A metaphor taken—I have not the page aright—
Out of an ethical work by the Stagyrite.
R. H. BARHAM, *The Brothers of Birchington.* The reference is to Aristotle, *Nicomachean Ethics*, sec. i, where he defines a happy man as a faultless cube.

Och! Father O'Flynn, you've the wonderful way wid you,
All ould sinners are wishful to pray wid you,
All the young childer are wild for to play wid you,
You've such a way wid you, Father avick!
Still, for all you've so gentle a soul,
Gad, you've your flock in the grandest control,
Checking the crazy ones,
Coaxin' onaisy ones,
Liftin' the lazy ones on wid the stick.
ALFRED PERCEVAL GRAVES, *Father O'Flynn.*

Once the Bishop looked grave at your jest,
Till this remark sent him off with the rest:
"Is it lave gaity
All to the laity?
Cannot the clargy be Irishmen too?"
ALFRED PERCEVAL GRAVES, *Father O'Flynn.*

8
They said this mystery never shall cease:
The priest promotes war, and the soldier peace.
WILLIAM BLAKE, *Gnomic Verses.* No. 3.

9
As the caterpillar chooses the fairest leaves to lay her eggs on, so the priest lays his curse on the fairest joys.
WILLIAM BLAKE, *Proverbs of Hell.*

10
Mothers, wives, and maids,
These be the tools wherewith priests manage fools.
ROBERT BROWNING, *The Ring and the Book.* Bk. iv, l. 503.

11
Those vegetables of the Catholic creed
Are apt exceedingly to run to seed.
BYRON, *Don Juan.* Canto xiv, st. 81. Referring to monks.

And, from long residence upon your living, are become a kind of holy vegetable.
SYDNEY SMITH, *Peter Plymley's Letters.* No. 1.

12
Oh, laugh or mourn with me, the rueful jest,
A cassock'd huntsman, and a fiddling priest!
COWPER, *The Progress of Error*, l. 110.

A priest,
A piece of mere church-furniture at best.
COWPER, *Tirocinium*, l. 424.

The priest he merry is, and blithe
Three-quarters of a year,
But oh! it cuts him like a scythe
When tithing time draws near.
COWPER, *Yearly Distress.* St. 2.

13
In pious times, ere priestcraft did begin,
Before polygamy was made a sin.
DRYDEN, *Absalom and Achitophel.* Pt. i, l. 1.

14
But the black earthly spirit of the priest wounded my life.
GEORGE FOX, *Account of His Mission.*

15
Bad priests bring the devil into the church.
THOMAS FULLER, *Gnomologia.* No. 835.

16
But now I see well the old proverb is true:
That parish priest forgetteth that ever he was clerk!
JOHN HEYWOOD, *Tyb*, 86. (1533)

The proverb old is come to pass,
The priest when he begins the mass
Forgets that ever clerk he was.
RICHARD JOHNSON, *The Crown Garland of Golden Roses*, 48. (1612)

There goes the parson, oh! illustrious spark.
And there, scarce less illustrious, goes the clerk!
COWPER, *On Observing Some Names of Little Note.*

1
A wealthy priest, but rich without a fault.
HOMER, *Iliad*. Bk. v, l. 16. (Pope, tr.)

Say, ye priests, what does gold do in the sacred place? (Dicite, pontifices, in sacro quid facit aurum?)
PERSIUS, *Satires*. Sat. ii, l. 69.

2
In every country and in every age, the priest has been hostile to liberty He is always in alliance with the despot, abetting his abuses in return for protection to his own.
THOMAS JEFFERSON, *Writings*. Vol. xiv, p. 119.

3
The priest is always with the herd and against the individual.
HUGH KINGSMILL, *Matthew Arnold*, p. 192.

4
New Presbyter is but Old Priest writ large.
MILTON, *On the New Forcers of Conscience.*

5
But first among the Priests dissension springs,
Men who attend the altar, and should most
Endeavour peace.
MILTON, *Paradise Lost*. Bk. xii, l. 353.

When knaves fall out, honest men get their goods; when priests dispute, we come at the truth.
BENJAMIN FRANKLIN, *Poor Richard*, 1742.

6
Ridden you need not fear to be,
By prophet or by priest,
Since Balaam's dead.—and none but he
Would choose you for his beast.
REV. JOHN SAMUEL B MONSELL, *On a Public Man Proclaiming That He Would Not Be "Priest Ridden."*

7
Patience and perséverance
Made a Bishop of His Reverence.
Attributed to Head-master MULLAN, of the National school at Waterside, Londonderry, Ireland.

8
What baron or squire or knight of the shire
Lives half so well as a holy friar?
JOHN O'KEEFFE, *The Friar of Orders Grey.*

9
At length Erasmus, that great injur'd name,
(The glory of the priesthood and the shame!)
Stemm'd the wild torrent of a barb'rous age,
And drove those holy Vandals off the stage.
POPE, *Essay on Criticism*. Pt. iii, l. 134.

10
I have seen nobody since I saw you, but persons in orders. My only varieties are vicars, rectors, curates, and every now and then (by way of turbot) an archdeacon.
SYDNEY SMITH, *Letter to Miss Berry*, 28 Jan., 1843.

Embryos and idiots, eremites and friars,
White, black, and grey, with all their trumpery.
MILTON, *Paradise Lost*. Bk. iii, l. 474.

11
So the priests hated him, and he
Repaid their hate with cheerful glee.
SHELLEY, *Rosalind and Helen*, l. 689.

12
Perhaps thou wert a Priest,—if so, my struggles
Are vain, for priestcraft never owns its juggles.
HORACE SMITH, *Address to a Mummy*. St. 4.

13
The snowy-banded dilettante,
Delicate-handed priest.
TENNYSON, *Maud*. Pt. i, sec. 8.

14
What village parson would not like to be pope?
VOLTAIRE, *Letters on the English*. No. 5.

No priestling, small though he may be,
But wishes some day Pope to be.
HEINRICH HEINE, *Confessions.*

15
A priest, ye cry, a priest!—lame shepherds they,
How shall they gather in the straggling flock?
Dumb dogs that bark not—how shall they compel
The loitering vagrants to the Master's fold?
Fitter to bask before the blazing fire,
And snuff the mess neat-handed Phillis dresses,
Than on the snow-wreath battle with the wolf.
UNKNOWN, *The Reformation*. (SCOTT, *The Monastery*.)

VI—Preaching

16
I preached as never sure to preach again,
And as a dying man to dying men.
RICHARD BAXTER, *Love Breathing Thanks and Praise.*

Let us, even to the wearing of our tongues to the stumps, preach and pray.
JOHN BRADFORD, *Sermon on Repentance.*

I shook the sermon out of my mind.
JOHN BUNYAN, *Grace Abounding.*

17
Well stored with pious frauds, and like most discourses of the sort, much better calculated for the private advantage of the preacher than the edification of the hearers.
EDMUND BURKE, *Observations on a Publication, "The Present State of the Nation."*

18
I'll grunt a real Gospel-groan.
BURNS, *Epistle to James Tait.*

19
And pulpit, drum ecclesiastic,
Was beat with fist instead of a stick.
BUTLER, *Hudibras*. Pt. i, canto 1, l. 11.

By thy language cabalistic,
By thy cymbal, drum, and his stick.
UNKNOWN, *The Debauchée*. Sometimes attributed to Thomas Stanley.

1
The foolishness of preaching.
New Testament: I Corinthians, i, 21.

2
How oft, when Paul has serv'd us with a text,
Has Epictetus, Plato, Tully, preach'd!
COWPER, *The Task*. Bk. ii, l. 539.

He bangs and bethwacks them,—their backs he salutes
With the whole tree of knowledge torn up by the roots;
His sermons with satire are plenteously verjuiced,
And he talks in one breath of Confutzee, Cass, Zerduscht.
J. R. LOWELL, *A Fable for Critics*, l. 707.

His hearers can't tell you on Sunday beforehand,
If in that day's discourse they'll be Bibled or Koraned.
J. R. LOWELL, *A Fable for Critics*, l. 786. Of Theodore Parker.

One may as well preach a respectable mythology as anything else.
MRS. HUMPHRY WARD, *Robert Elsmere*, i, 5.

3
His weekly drawl, Though short, too long.
COWPER, *Hope*, l. 199.

I preach for ever; but I preach in vain.
GEORGE CRABBE, *The Parish Register*. Pt. ii.

The parson exceeds not an hour in preaching, because all ages have thought that a competency.
GEORGE HERBERT, *Priest to the Temple*. Ch. 7.

Talks much, and says just nothing for an hour.
Truth and the text he labours to display,
Till both are quite interpreted away.
CHRISTOPHER PITT, *On the Art of Preaching*.

With patient inattention hear him prate.
GEORGE MEREDITH, *Bellerophon*. St. 4.

4
Go forth and preach impostures to the world,
But give them truth to build on.
DANTE, *Vision of Paradise*. Canto xxix, l. 116.

5
God preaches,—a noted clergyman,—
And the sermon is never long;
So instead of getting to heaven at last,
I'm going all along!
EMILY DICKINSON, *Poems*. Pt. ii, No. 57.

6
More vacant pulpits would more converts make.
DRYDEN, *The Hind and Panther*. Pt. iii, l. 182.

7
One may prefer fresh eggs, though laid by a fowl of the meanest understanding, but why fresh sermons?
GEORGE ELIOT, *Theophrastus Such: Looking Backward*.

8
I like the silent church before the service begins, better than any preaching.
EMERSON, *Essays, First Series: Self-Reliance*.

9
Great sermons lead the people to praise the preacher. Good preaching leads the people to praise the Saviour.
CHARLES G. FINNEY, *Autobiography*, p. 72.

10
None preaches better than the ant, and she says nothing.
BENJAMIN FRANKLIN, *Poor Richard*, 1736.

The lilies say: Behold how we
Preach without words of purity.
CHRISTINA ROSSETTI, *Consider the Lilies*.

11
They shall gnaw a file, and flee unto the mountains of Hepsidam whar the lion roareth and the Wang Doodle mourneth for its first born—ah!
UNKNOWN, *A Burlesque Sermon*. A travesty on the Hardshell Baptist sermons preached by itinerant preachers on the Mississippi about 1850. Ascribed to various writers, among them Andrew Harper and William P. Brannan. (See S. P. AVERY, *The Harp of a Thousand Strings*, so named from a similar burlesque sometimes attributed to Joshua S. Morris. Also *Choice Selections*, No. 9; *Humorous Hits*.)

12
Resort to sermons, but to prayers most:
Praying's the end of preaching.
GEORGE HERBERT, *The Church-Porch*. St. 69.

13
Calling all sermons contrabands,
In that great Temple that's not made with hands.
THOMAS HOOD, *Ode to Rae Wilson*, l. 369.

14
Sir, a woman preaching is like a dog's walking on his hind legs. It is not done well: but you are surprised to find it done at all.
SAMUEL JOHNSON. (BOSWELL, *Life*, 1763.)

15
The top of the hill he will ne'er come nigh reaching
Till he learns the distinction 'twixt singing and preaching.
J. R. LOWELL, *A Fable for Critics*, l. 1584. Referring to himself.

I shall never be a poet till I get out of the pulpit, and New England was all meeting-house when I was growing up.
J. R. LOWELL, *Letter to Norton*, 28 Aug., 1865.

16
Go ye into all the world, and preach the gospel to every creature.
New Testament: Mark, xvi, 15.

17
Only the sinner has a right to preach.
CHRISTOPHER MORLEY, *Tolerance*, p. 863.

18
A lazy, poor sermon.
SAMUEL PEPYS, *Diary*, 1660.

A good, honest, and painful sermon.
SAMUEL PEPYS, *Diary*, 17 March, 1661.

A very good and seraphic kind of a sermon too good for an ordinary congregation.

SAMUEL PEPYS, *Diary*, 24 May, 1668. Of a sermon by "Jervas Fullword."

1
The gracious Dew of Pulpit Eloquence,
And all the well-whip'd cream of courtly Sense.

POPE, *Epilogue to the Satires*. Dial. i, l. 69.

2
Parson's coming up the hill,
Meaning mighty well:
Thinks he's preached the doubters down.
And old men never tell.

JOHN CROWE RANSOM, *Under the Locusts*.

3
To preach long, loud, and Damnation, is the way to be cried up. We love a man that Damns us, and we run after him again to save us.

JOHN SELDEN, *Table-Talk: Damnation*.

"Parson," said I, "you pitch the pipe too low."

TENNYSON, *Edwin Morris*, l. 52.

4
The excellency of this text is that it will suit any sermon; and of this sermon, that it will suit any text.

STERNE, *Tristram Shandy*. Bk. vi, ch. 11.

"Dear sinners all," the fool began, "man's life is but a jest,
A dream, a shadow, bubble, air, a vapour at the best.
In a thousand pounds of law I find not a single ounce of love,
A blind man killed the parson's cow in shooting at the dove;
The fool that eats till he is sick must fast till he is well,
The wooer who can flatter most will bear away the belle." . . .
And then again the women screamed, and every staghound bayed;
And why? because the motley fool so wise a sermon made.

GEORGE W. THORNBURY, *The Jester's Sermon*.

He bowed his head, and bent his knee
Upon the monarch's silken stool;
His pleading voice arose: "O Lord,
Be merciful to me, a fool!"

EDWARD ROWLAND SILL, *The Fool's Prayer*.

5
A fool is he that comes to preach or prate,
When men with swords their right and wrong debate.
(Chi contra i colpi, o la dovuta offesa,
Mentr' arde la tenzon, misura e pesa?)

TASSO, *Jerusalem Delivered*. Bk. v, st. 57.

6
Preach not because you have to say something, but because you have something to say.

RICHARD WHATELY, *Apothegms*.

7
The deep soul-moving sense
Of religious eloquence.

WORDSWORTH, *Poems Dedicated to National Independence*. Pt. ii, No. 45.

VII—Preaching and Practice

See also Consistency; Example and Precept; Word and Deed

8
Of right and wrong he taught
Truths as refined as ever Athens heard;
And (strange to tell) he practis'd what he preach'd.

JOHN ARMSTRONG, *The Art of Preserving Health*. Bk. iv, l. 301.

9
A preacher should live perfectly and do as he teaches truly.

JOHN AWDELAY, *Poems*, p. 31. (c. 1426)

10
He preaches well who lives well. (Bien Predica quien bien vive.)

CERVANTES, *Don Quixote*. Pt. ii, ch. 20.

He preaches well that lives well.

THOMAS FULLER, *Gnomologia*. No. 2006.

The best of all the preachers are the men who live their creeds.

EDGAR A. GUEST, *Sermons We See*.

For if a priest be foul, on whom we trust,
No wonder is a lewd man to rust; . . .
Well ought a priest example for to give,
By his cleanness, how that his sheep should live.

CHAUCER, *The Canterbury Tales*. Prol. l. 501.

11
The proud he tam'd, the penitent he cheer'd:
Nor to rebuke the rich offender fear'd.
His preaching much, but more his practice wrought—
(A living sermon of the truths he taught—)
For this by rules severe his life he squar'd,
That all might see the doctrine which they heard.

DRYDEN, *Character of a Good Parson*, l. 75.

12
A good example is the best sermon.

THOMAS FULLER, *Gnomologia*. No. 146.
FRÁNKLIN, *Poor Richard*, 1747.

Examples draw when precept fails,
And sermons are less read than tales.

PRIOR, *The Turtle and the Sparrow*, l. 192.

The sermon edifies, the example destroys. (Le sermon edifie, l'exemple detruit.)

ABBÉ DE VILLIERS, *L'Art de Prêcher*.

13
And, as a bird each fond endearment tries,
To tempt its new-fledg'd offspring to the skies,
He tried each art, reprov'd each dull delay,
Allur'd to brighter worlds, and led the way.

GOLDSMITH, *The Deserted Village*, l. 167.

Just men, by whom impartial laws were given,
And saints who taught and led the way to Heaven.

THOMAS TICKELL, *To the Earl of Warwick, on the Death of Mr. Addison*, l. 41.

14
Till that learned men live as they teach.

LANGLAND, *Piers Plowman*, v, 118. (c. 1393)

15
Practice yourself what you preach. (Facias ipse quod faciamus suades.)

PLAUTUS, *Asinaria*, l. 644. (Act iii, sc. 3.)

We must practise what we preach.
SIR ROGER L'ESTRANGE, *Seneca's Morals*. Ch. ii. (c. 1680)

Practise what you preach.
YOUNG, *Love of Fame*. Sat. iii, l. 48.

1
An ounce of practice is worth a pound of preaching.
JOHN RAY, *English Proverbs*.

An ounce of mother-wit is worth a pound of clergy.
ANDREW MARVELL, *Growth of Popery*. Quoted as "the homely Scotch proverb." SYDNEY SMITH, *A Persecuting Bishop*. Quoted.

2
Preachers say, Do as I say, not as I do.
JOHN SELDEN, *Table-Talk: Preaching*.
See also WORD AND DEED.

3
Do not, as some ungracious pastors do,
Show me the steep and thorny way to heaven;
Whiles, like a puff'd and reckless libertine,
Himself the primrose path of dalliance treads,
And recks not his own rede.
SHAKESPEARE, *Hamlet*. Act i, sc. 3, l. 47.

If to do were as easy as to know what were good to do, chapels had been churches and poor men's cottages princes' palaces. It is a good divine that follows his own instructions: I can easier teach twenty what were good to be done, than be one of the twenty to follow mine own teaching.
SHAKESPEARE, *The Merchant of Venice*. Act i, sc. 2, l. 13.

4
In truth, sublime words make not a man holy and just: but a virtuous life maketh him dear to God.
THOMAS À KEMPIS, *De Imitatione Christi*. Ch. 1.

PRECEDENT

See also Example; Law: Precedent

5
Set it down to thyself, as well to create good precedents, as to follow them.
FRANCIS BACON, *Essays: Of Great Place*.

6
To follow foolish precedents, and wink
With both our eyes, is easier than to think.
COWPER, *Tirocinium*, l. 255.

7
For men are prone to go it blind
Along the calf-paths of the mind,
And work away from sun to sun
To do what other men have done. . . .
But how the wise old wood-gods laugh,
Who saw the first primeval calf. . . .
For thus such reverence is lent
To well-established precedent.
SAM WALTER FOSS, *The Calf-Path*.

8
The acts of to-day become the precedents of to-morrow.
FARRER HERSCHELL, *Speech*, 23 May, 1878.

What yesterday was fact to-day is doctrine.
JUNIUS, *Letters: Dedication*.

9
The tradition of the elders.
New Testament: Matthew, xv, 2; *Mark*, vii, 3

Tradition, thou art for suckling children,
Thou art the enlivening milk for babes,
But no meat for men is in thee.
STEPHEN CRANE, *Tradition*.

Tradition wears a snowy beard, romance is always young.
WHITTIER, *Mary Garvin*.

10
Who lasts a century can have no flaw;
I hold that Wit a classic, good in law.
POPE, *Imitations of Horace: Epistles*. Bk. ii, epis. 1, l. 55.

11
I'll show thee a precedent.
SHAKESPEARE, *I Henry IV*. Act ii, sc. 4, l. 37.

12
But, ah, who ever shunn'd by precedent
The destined ill she must herself assay?
SHAKESPEARE, *A Lover's Complaint*, l. 155.

13
Is not Precedent indeed a King of men?
SWINBURNE, *A Word from the Psalmist*.

14
All things which are now regarded as of great antiquity were once new, and what we to-day maintain by precedents will hereafter become a precedent. (Omnis quæ nunc vetustissima creduntur, nova fuere, . . . et quod hodie exemplis tuemur, inter exempla erit.)
TACITUS, *Annals*. Bk. xi, sec. 24.

15
The more ancient the abuse the more sacred it is.
VOLTAIRE, *Les Guèbres*. Act i, sc. 1.

PRECEPT, see Example and Precept

PREJUDICE

16
A prejudice is a vagrant opinion without visible means of support.
AMBROSE BIERCE, *The Devil's Dictionary*.

17
But his eddication to his ruination had not been over nice,
And his stupid skull was choking full of vulgar prejudice.
ROBERT BUCHANAN, *Phil Blood's Leap*.

18
Prejudice renders a man's virtue his habit, and not a series of unconnected acts. Through just prejudice, his duty becomes a part of his nature.
EDMUND BURKE, *Reflections on the Revolution in France*.

19
What extravagancy is not man capable of entertaining, when once his shackled reason is led in triumph by fancy and prejudice!
LORD CHESTERFIELD, *Letters*, 27 Sept., 1748.

Our prejudices are our mistresses; reason is at best our wife, very often heard indeed, but seldom minded.
LORD CHESTERFIELD, *Letters*, 13 April, 1752.

Prejudice is never easy unless it can pass itself off for reason.
WILLIAM HAZLITT, *Sketches and Essays: On Prejudice*.

1
As in politics so in literary action a man wins friends for himself mostly by the passion of his prejudices and by the consistent narrowness of his outlook.
JOSEPH CONRAD, *A Personal Record: Preface*.

2
A system-grinder hates the truth.
EMERSON, *Journals*. Vol. iii, p. 523.

3
Drive out prejudices by the door, they will come back by the window. (Chassez les préjugés par la porte, ils rentreront par la fenêtre.)
FREDERICK THE GREAT, *Letter to Voltaire*, 19 March, 1771.

4
Prejudices are the props of civilization.
ANDRÉ GIDE, *The Counterfeiters*. Pt. i, ch. 2.

5
How many a useless stone we find
Swallowed in that capacious blind
Faith-swollen gullet, our ancestral mind.
CHARLOTTE PERKINS GILMAN, *Forerunner*.

6
I can promise to be upright but not to be unprejudiced.
GOETHE, *Sprüche in Prosa*, iii.

Fortunately for serious minds, a bias recognized is a bias sterilized.
A. EUSTACE HAYDON, *Quest of the Ages*, p. 202.

7
Prejudice is the child of ignorance.
WILLIAM HAZLITT, *Sketches and Essays: On Prejudice*.

8
Without the aid of prejudice and custom, I should not be able to find my way across the room.
WILLIAM HAZLITT, *Sketches and Essays: On Prejudice*.

I am, in plainer words, a bundle of prejudices—made up of likings and dislikings.
CHARLES LAMB, *Essays of Elia: Imperfect Sympathies*.

9
It is the test of reason and refinement to be able to subsist without bugbears.
WILLIAM HAZLITT, *Emancipation of the Jews*.

10
To be prejudiced is always to be weak.
SAMUEL JOHNSON, *Taxation No Tyranny*.

Remember, when the judgment's weak the prejudice is strong.
KANE O'HARA, *Midas*. Act i, sc. 4.

11
One may no more live in the world without picking up the moral prejudices of the world than one will be able to go to hell without perspiring.
H. L. MENCKEN, *Prejudices*. Ser. ii, p. 174.

12
Put no trust in any thought that is not born in the open to the accompaniment of free bodily motion. All prejudices take their origin in the intestines. A sedentary life is the real sin against the Holy Ghost.
FRIEDRICH NIETZSCHE, *Ecce Homo*.

13
There is nothing stronger than human prejudice.
WENDELL PHILLIPS, *Speech*, 28 Jan., 1852.

14
If ever from an English heart,
O here let prejudice depart!
SCOTT, *Marmion:* Canto i, *Introduction*.

15
I will buy with you, sell with you, talk with you, walk with you, and so following; but I will not eat with you, drink with you, nor pray with you.
SHAKESPEARE, *The Merchant of Venice*. Act i, sc. 3, l. 36.

16
We all decry prejudice, yet are all prejudiced.
HERBERT SPENCER, *Social Statics*. Pt. ii, ch. 17, sec. 2.

17
It is never too late to give up our prejudices.
H. D. THOREAU, *Walden*. Ch. 1.

18
Prejudices, friend, are the kings of the vulgar herd. (Les préjugés, ami, sont les rois du vulgaire.)
VOLTAIRE, *Le Fanatisme*, ii, 4.

PREPAREDNESS

19
The commonwealth of Venice in their armoury have this inscription: "Happy is that city which in time of peace thinks of war."
ROBERT BURTON, *Anatomy of Melancholy*. Pt. ii, sec. 2, mem. 6.

20
Forewarned, forearmed; to be prepared is half the victory.
CERVANTES, *Don Quixote*. Pt. ii, ch. 17.

Unforeseen, they say, is unprepared.
DRYDEN, *Palamon and Arcite*. Bk. ii, l. 74.

Forewarned, forearmed.
BENJAMIN FRANKLIN, *Poor Richard*, 1736.

21
They who are best prepared for war have it most in their power to live in peace. (*"Οτι τοῖς κάλλιστα πολεμεῖν παρεσκευασμενοις, τούτοις μάλιστα ἔξεστιν εἰρήνην ἄγειν.*)
DIO CHRYSOSTOM, *First Discourse on Kingship*. Sec. 27.

To be prepared for war is one of the most effectual means of preserving peace.
GEORGE WASHINGTON, *Address*, to Congress,

8 Jan., 1790. Theodore Roosevelt misquoted Washington's words in an address at the University of Pennsylvania: "To be prepared for war is the most effective means to promote peace."

1
A man-of-war is the best ambassador.
OLIVER CROMWELL. (CARLYLE, *Life.*)

2
The time is coming, it will soon be come
When those who dare not fight
For God or for the right,
Shall fight for peace.
AUBREY THOMAS DE VERE, *Liberalism.*

3
The lawyers have always . . . some reserve of sovereignty, tantamount to the Rob Roy rule that might makes right. America should affirm and establish that in no instance should the guns go in advance of the perfect right.
EMERSON, *Journals,* 1866.

We have all grown up in the sight of frigates and navy yards, of armed forts and islands, of arsenals and militia. . . . One is scared to find at what a cost the peace of the globe is kept.
EMERSON, *Miscellanies: War.*

The Saviour came. With trembling lips
He counted Europe's battleships.
"Yet millions lack their daily bread.
So much for Calvary!" He said.
NORMAN GALE, *The Second Coming.*

4
'Tis safest making peace with sword in hand.
FARQUHAR, *Love and a Bottle.* Act v, sc. 3.

5
A disarmed peace is weak.
GEORGE HERBERT, *Jacula Prudentum.* No. 624.

6
The first blow is as much as two.
GEORGE HERBERT, *Jacula Prudentum.* No. 907. (1640)

The first blow is half the battle.
GOLDSMITH, *She Stoops to Conquer.* Act ii, sc. 1.

Which spills the foremost foeman's life,
That party conquers in the strife.
SCOTT, *The Lady of the Lake.* Canto iv, st. 6.

"Thrice is he armed that hath his quarrel just"—
And four times he who gets his fist in fust.
ARTEMUS WARD, *Shakespeare Up-to-Date. See also under* JUSTICE: ITS POWER.

7
Set thine house in order.
Old Testament: Isaiah, xxxviii, 1. (Dispone domui tuæ.—*Vulgate.*) Often misquoted, "Put your house in order."

8
To aim at such a navy as the greater European nations possess would be a foolish and wicked waste of the energies of our countrymen. It would be to pull on our own heads that load of military expense which makes the European laborer go supperless to bed.
THOMAS JEFFERSON, *Writings.* Vol. vii, p. 241.

The good sense of the people will always be found to be the best army.
THOMAS JEFFERSON, *Writings.* Vol. vi, p. 55.

No nation ever had an army large enough to guarantee it against attack in time of peace or insure it victory in time of war.
CALVIN COOLIDGE, *Address,* 6 Oct., 1925.

9
Ef you want peace, the thing you've gut to du
Is jes' to show you're up to fightin', tu.
J. R. LOWELL, *Biglow Papers.* Ser. ii, No. 2.

God, give us Peace! not such as lulls to sleep,
But sword on thigh and brow with purpose knit!
And let our Ship of State to harbor sweep,
Her ports all up, her battle-lanterns lit,
And her leashed thunders gathering for their leap.
J. R. LOWELL, *The Washers of the Shroud.*

10
Let your loins be girded about, and your lights burning.
New Testament: Luke, xii, 35.

Then Christian began to gird up his loins, and to address himself to his journey.
BUNYAN, *The Pilgrim's Progress.* Pt. i.

11
There is no record in history of a nation that ever gained anything valuable by being unable to defend itself.
H. L. MENCKEN, *Prejudices.* Ser. v, p. 33.

12
He who is not prepared to-day, will be less so to-morrow. (Qui non est hodie, cras minus aptus erit.)
OVID, *Remediorum Amoris,* l. 94.

13
We should provide in peace what we need in war. (Prospicere in pace oportet quod bellum juvet.)
PUBLILIUS SYRUS, *Sententiæ.* No. 709.

14
One sword keeps another in the sheath.
GEORGE HERBERT, *Jacula Prudentum.* No 725.

Who carries a sword, carries peace. (Qui porte épée, porte paix.)
UNKNOWN. A French Proverb. A variant is, "Baton porte paix," A cudgel brings peace.

15
There is a homely adage which runs: "Speak softly and carry a big stick; you will go far."
THEODORE ROOSEVELT, *Address,* Minnesota State Fair, 2 Sept., 1901. Elsewhere he referred to this saying as "a West African proverb." H. F. Pringle (*Theodore Roosevelt,* p. 214) says Roosevelt quoted the proverb to Henry L. Sprague, 22 Jan., 1900. No one knows where he picked it up, but it may be an English rendering of the saying attributed to Henri IV of France, "Le bâton qui porte paix," The stick which brings peace.

Broomstick preparedness.
THEODORE ROOSEVELT, *The Great Adventure.*

16
It is most meet we arm us 'gainst the foe;
For peace itself should not so dull a kingdom, . . .

But that defences, musters, preparations,
Should be maintain'd, assembled and collected,
As were a war in expectation.
SHAKESPEARE, *Henry V*. Act ii, sc. 4, l. 15.

1
Peace the offspring is of Power.
BAYARD TAYLOR, *A Thousand Years.*

2
Who desires peace, let him prepare for war. (Qui desiderat pacem, præparet bellum.)
VEGETIUS, *De Rei Militari:* Bk. iii, *Prologue.*

Like as a wise man in time of peace prepares for war. (In pace ut sapiens aptarit idonea bello.)
HORACE, *Satires*. Bk. ii, sat. 2, l. 111.

Peace prepares for war. (Pax paritur bello.)
CORNELIUS NEPOS, *Epaminondas*, v. Statius (*Thebais*, vii, 554) has it: "Sævis pax quæritur annis."

And who stands safest? tell me, is it he
That spreads and swells in puff'd prosperity,
Or bless'd with little, whose preventing care
In peace provides fit arms against a war?
POPE, *Imitations of Horace: Satires.* Bk. ii, sat. 2, l. 125.

PRESENT, THE

See also Life; Past and Present; Time; Today

I—Present: Definitions

3
Let's ev'n compound, and for the present live,
'Tis all the ready money Fate can give.
ABRAHAM COWLEY, *To Dr. Scarborough.*
See also LIFE AND LIVING.

4
The present is an indivisible point which cuts in two the length of an infinite line.
DIDEROT. (MORLEY, *Diderot and the Encyclopaedists.* Vol. ii, p. 283.)

5
This passing moment is an edifice
Which the Omnipotent cannot rebuild.
EMERSON, *Life.*

6
The present is a powerful deity. (Die Gegenwart ist eine mächtige Göttin.)
GOETHE, *Torquato Tasso*. Act iv, sc. 4.

7
The present is the necessary product of all the past, the necessary cause of all the future.
R. G. INGERSOLL, *What Is Religion?*

8
Learn that the present hour alone is man's.
SAMUEL JOHNSON, *Irene*. Act iii, sc. 2, l. 33.

9
No time like the present.
MARY DE LA R. MANLEY, *The Lost Lover.* Act iv, sc. 1. (1696) SCOTT, *The Fair Maid of Perth.* Ch. 2. (1828)

10
The present is our own; but while we speak
We cease from its possession, and resign
The stage we tread on to another race
As vain, and gay, and mortal as ourselves.
THOMAS LOVE PEACOCK, *Time*, l. 9.

The present changes so quickly that we are not aware of our life at the moment of living it.
GEORGE MOORE, *Ave*, p. 8.
See also TIME: ITS FLIGHT.

11
The present alone can make no man wretched. (Nemo tantum præsentibus miser est.)
SENECA, *Epistulæ ad Lucilium.* Epis. v, sec. 9.

The present is never a happy state to any being.
SAMUEL JOHNSON. (BOSWELL, *Life*, 1775.)

12
The Present, the Present is all thou hast
For thy sure possessing;
Like the patriarch's angel hold it fast
Till it gives its blessing.
J. G. WHITTIER, *My Soul and I.* St. 34.

II—Present: The Everlasting Now

13
Dear Land to which Desire for ever flees;
Time doth no present to our grasp allow;
Say in the fix'd Eternal shall we seize
At last the fleeting Now?
BULWER-LYTTON, *The First Violets.*

The Now, that indivisible point which studs the length of infinite line
Whose ends are nowhere, is thine all, the puny all thou callest thine.
SIR RICHARD BURTON, *The Kasidah.* Pt. ix, st. 34.

14
Nothing is there to come, and nothing past,
But an eternal now does always last.
ABRAHAM COWLEY, *Davideis.* Bk. i, l. 360. (1656). Cowley points out, in a note to these lines, that St. Thomas Aquinas called eternity "Nunc stans," a standing Now. Their paraphrase in Hugh Boyd's translation from Petrarch, made about 1820, and given below, should be noted.

The time will come when every change shall cease,
This quick revolving wheel shall rest in peace:
No summer then shall glow, nor winter freeze;
Nothing shall be to come, and nothing past,
But an eternal now shall ever last.
PETRARCH, *The Triumph of Eternity*, l. 119. (Boyd, tr.)

One of our poets—which is it?—speaks of an *everlasting now.* If such a condition of existence were offered to us in this world, and it were put to the vote whether we should accept the offer and fix all things immutably as they are, who are they whose votes would be given in the affirmative?
ROBERT SOUTHEY, *The Doctor.* Ch. 25.
See also under ETERNITY.

15
An everlasting Now reigns in nature, which hangs the same roses on our bushes which charmed the Roman and the Chaldean in their hanging gardens.
EMERSON, *Society and Solitude: Works and Days.*

1
We're curus critters: Now ain't jes' the minute
Thet ever fits us easy while we're in it;
Long ez 'twus futur', 'twould be perfect bliss—
Soon ez it's past, *thet* time's wuth ten o' this;
An' yit there ain't a man thet need be told
Thet Now's the only bird lays eggs o' gold.
J. R. LOWELL, *Biglow Papers*. Ser. ii, No. 6.

2
"Now" is the watchword of the wise.
C. H. SPURGEON, *Salt-Cellars*.

3
Out of the moment Now
Rises the god To-Be,
The light upon his brow
Is from eternity.
J. H. WHEELOCK, *To the Modern Man*.

4
In what alone is ours, the living Now.
WORDSWORTH, *Memorials of a Tour in Italy*. No. 10.

III—Present and Future
See also Today and Tomorrow

5
The present interests me more than the past and the future more than the present.
BENJAMIN DISRAELI, *Lothair*. Ch. 24.

6
Present joys are more to flesh and blood
Than a dull prospect of a distant good.
DRYDEN, *The Hind and Panther*. Pt. iii, l. 364.

7
Those who live to the future must always appear selfish to those who live to the present.
EMERSON, *Essays, Second Series: Character*.

8
In the moment of our talking envious time has ebbed away.
Seize the present; trust to-morrow e'en as little as you may.
(Dum loquimur, fugerit invida
Ætas: carpe diem, quam minimum credula postero.)
HORACE, *Odes*. Bk. i, ode 11. (Conington, tr.)

Trust no Future, howe'er pleasant!
Let the dead Past bury its dead!
Act,—act in the living Present!
Heart within, and God o'erhead!
LONGFELLOW, *A Psalm of Life*.

9
Let the soul be joyful in the present, disdaining anxiety for the future, and tempering bitter things with a serene smile. (Lætus in præsens animus quod ultra est Oderit curare at amara lento Temperet risu.)
HORACE, *Odes*. Bk. ii, ode 16, l. 25.

10
The future is purchased by the present.
SAMUEL JOHNSON, *The Rambler*. No. 178.

The present is big with the future. (Le présent est gros d'avenir.)
LEIBNITZ.

11
The future works out great men's purposes;
The present is enough for common souls,
Who never looking forward, are indeed
Mere clay, wherein the footprints of their age
Are petrified forever.
J. R. LOWELL, *A Glance Behind the Curtain*. St. 6.

12
Ah, take the Cash, and let the Credit go,
Nor heed the rumble of a distant Drum!
OMAR KHAYYÁM, *Rubáiyát*. (Fitzgerald, tr.)

13
If people take no care for the future, they will soon have to sorrow for the present.
W. G. BENHAM, *Proverbs*, p. 789. Chinese.

14
And the future is dark, and the present is spread
Like a pillow of thorns for thy slumberless head.
SHELLEY, *Prometheus Unbound*. Act i, l. 562.

15
Oh, the dulness and hardness of the human heart, which thinketh only of present things and provideth not more for things to come. (O hebetudo et duritia cordis humani, quod solum præsentia mediatur, et futura non magis prævidet!)
THOMAS À KEMPIS, *De Imitatione Christi*. Bk. i, ch. 23, sec. 3.

16
Such is; what is to be?
The pulp so bitter, how shall taste the rind?
FRANCIS THOMPSON, *The Hound of Heaven*.

PRESS, THE
I—Press: Apothegms

17
Harmony seldom makes a headline.
SILAS BENT, *Strange Bedfellows*, p. 179.

18
"Twelve Spadissins" were seen, by the yellow eye of Journalism, "arriving recently out of Switzerland."
CARLYLE, *The French Revolution*. Pt. ii, bk. 3, ch. 3.

This "Present" book, indeed, is blue, but the hue of its thought is yellow.
H. D. THOREAU, *Familiar Letters*.

It is time for scientists, alienists, and psychological investigators to make a careful study of the Yellow literary atmosphere.
CHARLES DUDLEY WARNER, *The Yellows in Literature*. (*Harper's Magazine*, xc, 481.)

"Yellow journalism" traces its origin to these comics of the Hearst and Pulitzer newspapers, a phrase credited to Ervin Wardman, who, before he died in January, 1923, was publisher of Munsey's *Herald*.
JOHN K. WINKLER, *W. R. Hearst*, p. 110.

For forty years he has carried out, rather literally, the dictum of Mr. Dooley that the mission of a modern newspaper is to "comfort the afflicted and afflict the comfortable."

JOHN K. WINKLER, *W. R. Hearst*, p. 12.

1
Did Charity prevail, the press would prove
A vehicle of virtue, truth, and love.

COWPER, *Charity*, l. 624.

2
This folio of four pages, happy work!
Which not ev'n critics criticise.

COWPER, *The Task*. Bk. iv, l. 50.

3
Old, old man, it is the wisdom of the age.

STEPHEN CRANE, *The Black Riders*. No. xi.

4
To give me information is thy office. (Σὸν τὸ μηνύειν ἐμοί.)

EURIPIDES, *Suppliants*, l. 98.

5
The newspapers of either side,
These joys of every Englishman.

ANDREW LANG, *The New Millennium*.

6
Three hostile newspapers are more to be feared than a thousand bayonets.

NAPOLEON I, *Sayings of Napoleon*.

7
The dull duty of an editor.

POPE, *Preface to the Works of Shakespeare*.

8
News value.

JULIAN RALPH. Phrase coined in 1892, in a talk at Columbia, to Brander Matthews's class in English. (THOMAS BEER, *The Mauve Decade*.)

9
It is always the unreadable that occurs.

OSCAR WILDE, *The Decay of Lying*.

II—Press: The Fourth Estate

10
The gallery in which the reporters sit has become a fourth estate of the realm.

MACAULAY, *Essays: Hallam's Constitutional History*. Tenth paragraph from end. (Published in the *Edinburgh Review*, Sept., 1828.)

Burke said there were Three Estates in Parliament; but, in the Reporters' Gallery yonder, there sat a *Fourth Estate* more important far than they all.

CARLYLE, *Heroes and Hero-Worship: The Hero as Man of Letters*. 1839. The statement is not found in Burke's published works, and it is probable that Carlyle inadvertently attributed the phrase to Burke instead of to Macaulay.

11
A Fourth Estate, of Able Editors, springs up.

CARLYLE, *The French Revolution*. Pt. i, bk. 6, ch. 5. (1837)

12
One of them was dressed like a Monk in his frock, draggled-tail'd and booted: the other like a Falconer with a lure and a long-tailed hawk on his fist: the third like a Solicitor, with a large bag: . . . the fourth look'd like one of your Vine Barbers. . . . Pantagruel enquir'd of one of their Coxwain's Crew who those persons were? He answer'd that they were the Four Estates of the Island.

RABELAIS, *Works*. Bk. iv, ch. 48. (1532)

13
You have been a long time talking of the three estates; there is a fourth which, if not well looked to, will turn us all out of doors—the army.

LORD FALKLAND, *Speech*, in Parliament, 1638. The "three estates of the realm" are the Lords Spiritual, the Lords Temporal, and the Commons.

None of our political writers . . . take notice of any more than three estates, namely, Kings, Lords and Commons . . passing by in silence that very large and powerful body which form the fourth estate in the community . . . the Mob.

FIELDING, *Covent Garden Journal*, 13 June, 1752. See also MONTAIGNE, *Essays*. Bk. i, ch. 22.

14
Mr. Fox's Board of Commissioners. which Mr. Pultenay and Mr. Pitt clamoured against as a Fourth Estate, was to be responsible to Parliament. Mr. Pitt's Fourth Estate, of the Queen and her Council, is to have no responsibility.

UNKNOWN, *Article, Gazetteer and New Daily Advertiser*, 30 Jan., 1789.

III—Press: Its Liberty

15
What have the Germans gained by their boasted freedom of the press except the liberty to abuse each other?

GOETHE, *Table-Talk*. (1809)

16
The press restrained! nefandous thought!
In vain our sires have nobly fought:
While free from force the press remains,
Virtue and Freedom cheer our plains.

MATTHEW GREEN, *The Spleen*, l. 394.

17
No government ought to be without censors; and where the press is free none ever will.

THOMAS JEFFERSON, *Writings*. Vol. viii, p. 406.

When the press is free and every man able to read, all is safe.

THOMAS JEFFERSON, *Writings*. Vol. xiv, p. 382.

18
The liberty of the press is the *palladium* of all the civil, political, and religious rights of an Englishman.

JUNIUS, *Letters: Dedication*.

19
Here shall the Press the People's right maintain,
Unawed by influence and unbribed by gain;
Here patriot Truth her glorious precepts draw,

Pledged to Religion, Liberty, and Law.

JOSEPH STORY, *Motto of the Salem Register.* Adopted 1802. (STORY, *Life of Joseph Story.* Vol. i, ch. vi.)

IV—Press: Its Power

1
Great is Journalism. Is not every able Editor a Ruler of the World, being a persuader of it?

CARLYLE, *The French Revolution.* Pt. ii, bk. i, ch. 4.

The true Church of England, at this moment, lies in the Editors of its newspapers. These preach to the people daily, weekly.

CARLYLE, *Signs of the Times.*

2
The penny-papers of New York do more to govern this country than the White House at Washington.

WENDELL PHILLIPS, *Address: The Press.*

We live under a government of men and morning newspapers.

WENDELL PHILLIPS, *Address: The Press.*

3
Thay sed the press was the Arkymedian Leaver which moved the wurld.

ARTEMUS WARD, *Artemus Ward, His Book: The Press. See also under* POWER.

4
In America the President reigns for four years, and Journalism governs for ever and ever.

OSCAR WILDE, *The Soul of a Man Under Socialism.*

V—Press: Its Virtues

5
They consume a considerable quantity of our paper manufacture, employ our artisans in printing, and find business for great numbers of indigent persons.

ADDISON, *The Spectator.* No. 367.

I would . . . earnestly advise them for their good to order this paper to be punctually served up, and to be looked upon as a part of the tea equipage.

ADDISON, *The Spectator.* No. 10.

6
Newspapers are the schoolmasters of the common people. That endless book, the newspaper, is our national glory.

HENRY WARD BEECHER, *Proverbs from Plymouth Pulpit: The Press.*

7
Only a newspaper! Quick read, quick lost,
Who sums the treasure that it carries hence?
Torn, trampled underfoot, who counts thy cost,
Star-eyed intelligence?

MARY CLEMMER, *The Journalist.*

8
I believe it has been said that one copy of the [London] *Times* contains more useful information than the whole of the historical works of Thucydides.

RICHARD COBDEN, *Speech,* Manchester, 27 Dec., 1850. (MORLEY, *Life of Cobden.* Vol. ii, p. 429, note.)

9
He comes, the herald of a noisy world,
With spatter'd boots, strapp'd waist, and frozen locks;
News from all nations lumb'ring at his back.

COWPER, *The Task.* Bk. iv, l. 5.

10
The newspaper, which does its best to make every square acre of land and sea give an account of itself at your breakfast-table.

EMERSON, *Society and Solitude: Works and Days.*

Behold the whole huge earth sent to me hebdomadally in a brown-paper wrapper!

J. R. LOWELL, *Biglow Papers.* Ser. i, No. 6.

11
Then hail to the Press! chosen guardian of freedom!
Strong sword-arm of justice! bright sunbeam of truth!

HORACE GREELEY, *The Press.*

12
Were it left to me to decide whether we should have a government without newspapers, or newspapers without a government, I should not hesitate a moment to prefer the latter.

THOMAS JEFFERSON, *Writings.* Vol. vi, p. 55.

13
Trade hardly deems the busy day begun
Till his keen eye along the sheet has run;
The blooming daughter throws her needle by,
And reads her schoolmate's marriage with a sigh;
While the grave mother puts her glasses on,
And gives a tear to some old crony gone.
The preacher, too, his Sunday theme lays down
To know what last new folly fills the town;
Lively or sad, life's meanest, mightiest things,
The fate of fighting cocks, or fighting kings.

CHARLES SPRAGUE, *Curiosity.*

VI—Press: Its Faults

14
Can it be maintained that a person of any education can learn anything worth knowing from a penny paper? It may be said that people may learn what is said in Parliament. Well, will that contribute to their education?

ROBERT CECIL, *Speech,* House of Commons, 1861.

15
How shall I speak thee, or thy pow'r address,
Thou god of our idolatry, the Press?
By thee, religion, liberty, and laws
Exert their influence and advance their cause;
By thee, worse plagues than Pharaoh's land befell,

Diffus'd, make earth the vestibule of hell;
Thou fountain, at which drink the good and wise;
Thou ever bubbling spring of endless lies;
Like Eden's dread probationary tree,
Knowledge of good and evil is from thee.

COWPER, *The Progress of Error*, l. 460.

1
The more of these instructors a man reads, the less he will infallibly understand.

GEORGE CRABBE, *The Newspaper: To the Reader*.

One editor will sometimes convey his abuse with more decency, and colour his falsehood with more appearance of probability than another.

CRABBE, *The Newspaper: To the Reader*.

These things have their use; and are, besides, vehicles of much amusement: but this does not outweigh the evil they do to society, and the irreparable injury they bring upon the character of individuals.

CRABBE, *The Newspaper: To the Reader*.

2
I sing of News, and all those vapid sheets
The rattling hawker vends through gaping streets;
Whate'er their name, whate'er the time they fly,
Damp from the press, to charm the reader's eye:
For, soon as morning dawns with roseate hue,
The Herald of the morn arises too;
Post after Post succeeds, and, all day long,
Gazettes and Ledgers swarm, a noisy throng.
When evening comes, she comes with all her train
Of Ledgers, Chronicles, and Posts again,
Like bats, appearing when the sun goes down,
From holes obscure and corners of the town.

GEORGE CRABBE, *The Newspaper*.

3
What is the newspaper but a sponge or invention for oblivion?

EMERSON, *Natural History of Intellect: Memory*.

They have ceased to publish the "Newgate Calendar" and the "Pirate's Own Book" since the family newspapers . . . have quite superseded them in the freshness as well as the horror of their records of crime.

EMERSON, *Society and Solitude: Works and Days*.

4
Caused by a dearth of scandal should the vapours
Distress our fair ones—let them read the papers.

DAVID GARRICK, *Prologue to Sheridan's "School for Scandal."*

5
A reply to a newspaper attack resembles very much the attempt of Hercules to crop the Hydra, without the slightest chance of his ultimate success.

THEODORE HOOK, *Gilbert Gurney*. Vol. ii, ch. 1.

6
The man who never looks into a newspaper is better informed than he who reads them, inasmuch as he who knows nothing is nearer the truth than he whose mind is filled with falsehoods and errors.

THOMAS JEFFERSON, *Writings*. Vol. xi, p. 224.

Perhaps an editor might . . . divide his paper into four chapters, heading the first, Truths; 2d, Probabilities; 3d, Possibilities; 4, Lies.

THOMAS JEFFERSON, *Writings*. Vol. xi, l. 224.

7
Newspapers always excite curiosity. No one ever lays one down without a feeling of disappointment.

CHARLES LAMB, *Last Essays of Elia: Detached Thoughts on Books and Reading*.

8
The press is like the air, a chartered libertine.

WILLIAM PITT, *Letter to Lord Grenville*, 1757.

The newspapers! Sir, they are the most villainous—licentious—abominable—infernal—not that I ever read them—no—I make it a rule never to look into a newspaper.

SHERIDAN, *The Critic*. Act i, sc. 1.

9
Blessed are they who never read a newspaper, for they shall see Nature, and, through her, God.

THOREAU, *Essays and Other Writings*, p. 254.

10
I have been reading the morning paper. I do it every morning—well knowing that I shall find in it the usual depravities and basenesses and hypocrisies and cruelties that make up civilization, and cause me to put in the rest of the day pleading for the damnation of the human race.

MARK TWAIN, *Letter to W. D. Howells*, 1899.

11
In old days men had the rack. Now they have the press.

OSCAR WILDE, *The Soul of Man Under Socialism*.

VII—Press: The Press-Men

12
Nor ever once ashamed, so we be named
Press-men; Slaves of the Lamp; Servants of Light.

SIR EDWIN ARNOLD, *The Tenth Muse*. St. 18.

13
Journalists say a thing that they know isn't true, in the hope that if they keep on saying it long enough it *will* be true.

ARNOLD BENNETT, *The Title*.

14
If there's a hole in a' your coats,
I rede you tent it:
A chield's amang you takin' notes,

And faith he'll prent it.
ROBERT BURNS, *On the Late Captain Grose's Peregrinations Thro' Scotland.* St. 1.

When found make a note of.
DICKENS, *Dombey and Son.* Bk. i, ch. 15. Adopted as the motto of *Notes and Queries.*

Note this before my notes.
There's not a note of mine that's worth the noting.
SHAKESPEARE, *Much Ado About Nothing.* Act ii, sc. 3, l. 56.

1
A would-be satirist, a hired buffoon,
A monthly scribbler of some low lampoon,
Condemn'd to drudge, the meanest of the mean,
And furbish falsehoods for a magazine.
BYRON, *English Bards and Scotch Reviewers,* l. 975.

Newspaper wits, and sonneteers,
Gentlemen bards, and rhyming peers.
CHARLES CHURCHILL, *The Ghost.* Bk. ii, l. 513.

2
To serve thy generation, this thy fate:
"Written in water," swiftly fades thy name;
But he who loves his kind does, first and late,
A work too great for fame.
MARY CLEMMER, *The Journalist.*

3
As for the press, I am myself a "gentleman of the press," and I have no other escutcheon.
BENJAMIN DISRAELI, *Speech,* House of Commons, 18 Feb., 1853.

4
With much communication will he tempt thee, and smiling upon thee will get out thy secrets.
Apocrypha: Ecclesiasticus, xiii, 11.

5
Ask how to live? Write, write, write anything;
The world's a fine believing world, write news!
JOHN FLETCHER, *Wit Without Money.* Act ii.

6
I am a printer, and a printer of news; and I do hearken after them, wherever they be at any rates; I'll give anything for a good copy now, be it true or false, so it be news.
BEN JONSON, *News from the New World.*

7
He wrote for certain papers which, as everybody knows,
Is worse than serving in a shop or scaring off the crows.
RUDYARD KIPLING, *Delilah.*

8
The highest reach of a news-writer is an empty Reasoning on Policy, and vain Conjectures on the public Management.
LA BRUYÈRE, *Les Caractères.* Ch. 1.

The News-writer lies down at Night in great Tranquillity, upon a piece of News which corrupts before Morning, and which he is obliged to throw away as soon as he awakes.
LA BRUYÈRE, *Les Caractères.* Ch. 1.

9
Every newspaper editor owes tribute to the devil. (Tout faiseur de journaux doit tribut au Malin.)
LA FONTAINE, *Letter to Simon de Troyes,* 1686.

10
I have always thought that I would like to be a newspaper man myself, because I love the classics and I love good literature.
JOHN P. O'BRIEN, *Speech,* to a company of journalists, while mayor of New York, 1933.

11
But I'll report it.
SHAKESPEARE, *Coriolanus.* Act i, sc. 9, l. 2.

He will print them, without a doubt, for he cares not what he puts into the press.
SHAKESPEARE, *The Merry Wives of Windsor.* Act ii, sc. 1, l. 79.

12
Ah, ye knights of the pen! May honour be your shield, and truth tip your lances! Be gentle to all gentle people. Be modest to women. Be tender to children. And as for the Ogre Humbug, out sword, and have at him.
THACKERAY, *Roundabout Papers: Ogres.*

13
The thorn in the cushion of the editorial chair.
THACKERAY, *Roundabout Papers: The Thorn in the Cushion.*

14
An Ambassador is a man of virtue sent to lie abroad for his country; a news-writer is a man without virtue who lies at home for himself.
SIR HENRY WOTTON, when twitted on his famous definition of an Ambassador by a newspaperman. (*Reliquæ Wottonianæ.*)
See also under DIPLOMACY.

PRETENCE, see HYPOCRISY

PRICE

See also Worth

I—Price: Apothegms

15
Buy not what you want, but what you need; what you do not need is dear at a farthing. (Emas non quod opus est, sed quod necesse est; quod non opus est, asse carum est.)
CATO, *Reliquæ.* (JORDAN, p. 79.) Quoted by Seneca, *Epistulæ ad Lucilium.* Epis. xciv, sec. 27.

Never, from a mistaken economy, buy a thing you do not want because it is cheap; or, from a silly pride, because it is dear.
LORD CHESTERFIELD, *Letters,* 10 Jan., 1749.

Never buy what you do not want because it is cheap; it will be dear to you.
THOMAS JEFFERSON, *Writings.* Vol. xvi, p. 111.

16
What costs little is valued less.
CERVANTES, *Don Quixote.* Pt. i, ch. 34.

What we obtain too cheaply we esteem too

lightly; it is dearness only which gives everything its value.
THOMAS PAINE, *The Crisis: Introduction.*

1
You cannot make a cheap palace.
EMERSON, *Journals,* 1857.

Magnificence cannot be cheap, for what is cheap cannot be magnificent.
SAMUEL JOHNSON, *Works.* Vol. v, p. 458.

2
Earth gets its price for what Earth gives us;
The beggar is taxed for a corner to die in,
The priest hath his fee who comes and shrives us,
We bargain for the graves we lie in;
At the devil's booth are all things sold,
Each ounce of dross costs its ounce of gold.
J. R. LOWELL, *Vision of Sir Launfal:* Pt. i, *Prelude.*

3
Things of greatest profit are set forth with least price.
JOHN LYLY, *Euphues.*

4
The things are most dear to us which have cost us most. (Les choses nous sont plus chères, qui nous ont plus cousté.)
MONTAIGNE, *Essays.* Bk. ii, ch. 8.

5
No mortal thing can bear so high a price,
But that with mortal thing it may be bought.
SIR WALTER RALEIGH, *Love the Only Price of Love.*

6
The highest price a man can pay for a thing is to ask for it.
W. G. BENHAM, *Proverbs,* p. 846.

7
There is hardly anything in the world that some man cannot make a little worse and sell a little cheaper, and the people who consider price only are this man's lawful prey.
Attributed to JOHN RUSKIN, but not found in his works.

All works of taste must bear a price in proportion to the skill, taste, time, and expense and risk attending their invention and manufacture. Those things called dear are, when justly estimated, the cheapest: they are attended with much less profit to the artist than those which everybody calls cheap. Beautiful forms and compositions are not made by chance, nor can they ever, in any material, be made at small expense. A competition for cheapness and not excellence of workmanship is the most frequent and certain cause of the rapid decay and entire destruction of arts and manufactures.
JOSIAH WEDGWOOD, *Dearness and Cheapness.*

Not how cheap, but how good.
WILLIAM MORRIS.

8
Her price is fall'n.
SHAKESPEARE, *King Lear.* Act i, sc. 1, l. 200.

I know my price.
SHAKESPEARE, *Othello.* Act i, sc. 1, l. 10.

II—Price: "All Men Have Their Price"

9
'Tis pleasant purchasing our fellow creatures;
And all are to be sold, if you consider
Their passions, and are dext'rous; some by features
Are brought up, others by a warlike leader,
Some by a place—as tend their years or natures;
But most by ready cash—but all have prices,
From crowns to kicks, according to their vices.
BYRON, *Don Juan.* Canto v, st. 27.

10
Still as of old men by themselves are priced—
For thirty pieces Judas sold himself, not Christ.
HESTER H. CHOLMONDELEY. Quoted by her sister, Mary Cholmondeley, as heading to Chapter 11, *Diana Tempest.* Quoted by Robert Hugh Benson at end of chapter, *Herod,* in *Christ in the Church.*

11
All those men have their price.
SIR ROBERT WALPOLE. (WILLIAM COXE, *Memoirs of Sir Robert Walpole.* Vol. iv, p. 369.) The context is as follows: "Flowery oratory he [Walpole] despised. He ascribed to the interested views of themselves or their relatives the declarations of pretended patriots, of whom he said, 'All those men have their price.'"

Every man has his price.
Attributed to SIR ROBERT WALPOLE, but probably a misquotation. A. F. Robbins, in the *Gentleman's Magazine* (No. iv, p. 589), asserts that Walpole used this phrase in a speech either in November or December, 1734. Horace Walpole denies this, and claims that it was falsely attributed to Sir Robert by his enemies. (*Letter,* 26 Aug., 1785.)

I know the price of every man in this house except three.
Attributed to SIR ROBERT WALPOLE. (*Notes and Queries,* 11 May, 1907, p. 367.) Latham's *Famous Sayings and Their Authors* asserts that Walpole made this remark to Lord John Leveson-Gower, and that it was from this that the misquotation, "Every man has his price" arose.

12
It is an old maxim that every man has his price.
SIR WILLIAM WYNDHAM. (*The Bee,* vol. viii, p. 97. 1733.)

Every man is to be had one way or another, and every woman almost any way.
LORD CHESTERFIELD, *Letters,* 5 June, 1750.

Every man has his price, and every woman her figure.
UNKNOWN. A modern variant.

PRIDE

See also Self-Respect, Vanity

I—Pride: Definitions

1
'Tis pride, rank pride, and haughtiness of soul;
I think the Romans call it Stoicism.
ADDISON, *Cato*. Act i, sc. 4.

2
Pampered vanity is a better thing, perhaps, than starved pride.
JOANNA BAILLIE, *The Election*. Act ii, sc. 2.

3
A proud man is always hard to be pleased, because he hath too great expectations from others.
RICHARD BAXTER, *Christian Ethics*.

4
No barbarousness beside
Is half so barbarous as pride.
SAMUEL BUTLER, *Satire Upon the Weakness and Misery of Man*, l. 64.

5
Pride, Envy, Avarice—these are the sparks
Have set on fire the hearts of all men.
(Superba, invidia ed avarizia sono
Le tre faville ch' hanno i cuori accesi.)
DANTE, *Inferno*. Canto vi, l. 74.

6
There is no pride on earth like the pride of intellect and science.
R. D. HITCHCOCK, *Eternal Atonement: Secret Things of God*.

A pride there is of rank—a pride of birth,
A pride of learning, and a pride of purse,
A London pride—in short, there be on earth
A host of prides, some better and some worse;
But of all prides, since Lucifer's attaint,
The proudest swells a self-elected saint.
THOMAS HOOD, *Ode to Rae Wilson*, l. 314.

7
Pride and conceit were the original sin of man.
LE SAGE, *Gil Blas*. Bk. vii, ch. 3.

8
Pride is the spring of malice and desire of revenge, and of rash anger and contention.
ARCHBISHOP LEIGHTON, *Works*. Vol. iv, p. 147.

9
Pride grows greater in prosperity, nor is it easy to bear good fortune with undisturbed mind. (Luxuriant animi rebus plerumque secundis, Nec facile est æqua commoda mente pati.)
OVID, *Ars Amatoria*. Bk. ii, l. 438.

Pride grows, forsooth, by the reflection in the mirror. (Scilicet a speculi sumuntur imagine fastus.)
OVID, *Amores*. Bk. ii, eleg. 17, l. 9.
See also under BEAUTY.

10
Ask for what end the heav'nly bodies shine,
Earth for whose use,—Pride answers, "'Tis for mine:
For me kind Nature wakes her genial power,
Suckles each herb, and spreads out ev'ry flower; . . .
Seas roll to waft me, suns to light me rise;
My footstool earth, my canopy the skies."
POPE, *Essay on Man*. Epis. i, l. 131.

All the parts of the universe I have an interest in: the earth serves me to walk upon; the sun to light me; the stars have their influence upon me.
MONTAIGNE, *Essays*. Bk. ii, ch. 12.

11
Some glory in their birth, some in their skill,
Some in their wealth, some in their bodies' force,
Some in their garments, though new-fangled ill;
Some in their hawks and hounds, some in their horse;
And every humour hath his adjunct pleasure,
Wherein it finds a joy above the rest.
SHAKESPEARE, *Sonnets*. No. xci.

12
Pride Howe'er disguised in its own majesty,
Is littleness.
WORDSWORTH, *Lines Left Upon a Seat in a Yew-tree*, l. 50.

13
This passion with a pimple have I seen
Retard a cause, and give a judge the spleen.
YOUNG, *Love of Fame*. Sat. i, l. 109.

14
Pride, that impartial passion, reigns through all,
Attends our glory, nor deserts our fall.
YOUNG, *Love of Fame*. Sat. i, l. 203.

Pride, like an eagle, builds among the stars;
But Pleasure, lark-like, nests upon the ground.
YOUNG, *Night Thoughts*. Night v, l. 19.

Pride, like hooded hawks, in darkness soars,
From blindness bold, and tow'ring to the skies.
YOUNG, *Night Thoughts*. Night vi, l. 324.

II—Pride: Apothegms

15
They be high in the instep and standeth in their own conceit.
ANDREW BOORDE, *Introduction to Knowledge*. Ch. 26. (1542)

He is so high in the instep and so strait laced.
JOHN HEYWOOD, *Proverbs*. Pt. i, ch. 11.

She's high in the instep (*i.e.* proud and haughty).
BAKER, *Northants Glossary*.

16
Proud as a peacock.
HENRY BRADSHAW, *St. Werburga*, 69. (1513)
See also under PEACOCK.

Proud as Lucifer.
UNKNOWN. (WRIGHT, *Political Poems*, i, 315. c. 1394); BAILEY, *Festus: A Country Town*.

17
Proud with the proud, yet courteously proud.
BYRON, *Don Juan*. Canto xv, st. 15.

18
The proud will sooner lose than ask their way.
CHARLES CHURCHILL, *The Farewell*. l. 330.

1
And the Devil did grin, for his darling sin
Is pride that apes humility.
S. T. COLERIDGE, *The Devil's Thoughts.*

He pass'd a cottage with a double coach-house,
A cottage of gentility;
And he owned with a grin That his favourite sin
Is pride that apes humility.
ROBERT SOUTHEY, *The Devil's Walk.* St. 8. Coleridge's poem, of seventeen stanzas, was published in 1799; in 1827, Southey rewrote it and expanded it to fifty-seven stanzas.

They are proud in humility; proud in that they are not proud.
ROBERT BURTON, *Anatomy of Melancholy.* Pt. ii, sec. ii, mem. 3, subs. 14.

One may be humble out of pride.
MONTAIGNE, *Essays.* Bk. ii, ch. 17.

How much pride you expose to view, Diogenes, in seeming not to be proud.
PLATO. (DIOGENES LAERTIUS, *Diogenes.* Sec. 26.)

2
Lo, here one may see that there is none worse
Than is a proud heart and a beggar's purse.
ROBERT COPLAND, *The Hye Wey to the Spyttel Hous,* l. 977. (c. 1532)

Pride and poverty are ill met, yet often seen together.
THOMAS FULLER, *Gnomologia.* No. 3933.

Pride may lurk under a thread-bare cloak.
THOMAS FULLER, *Gnomologia.* No. 3947.

A man may be poor in purse, yet proud in spirit.
JOHN MASON, *McGuffey's Third Reader,* p. 110.

See also POVERTY: APOTHEGMS.

3
The proud are always most provoked by pride.
COWPER, *Conversation,* l. 160.

4
Pride that dines on vanity sups on contempt.
H. G. BOHN, *Hand-Book of Proverbs,* p. 476.

Pride breakfasted with Plenty, dined with Poverty, supped with Infamy.
BENJAMIN FRANKLIN, *Poor Richard,* 1757.

5
Pride had rather go out of the way than go behind.
THOMAS FULLER, *Gnomologia.* No. 3937.

6
Pride in prosperity turns to misery in adversity.
THOMAS FULLER, *Gnomologia.* No. 3940. *See also under* PROSPERITY.

7
Pride never feels pain.
FULLER, *Pisgah Sight.* Bk. iv, ch. 6, sec. 7.

Pride feels no cold.
JOHN RAY, *English Proverbs.*

All that the proud can feel of pain.
BYRON, *Prometheus,* l. 8.

8
Pride is as loud a beggar as want, and a great deal more saucy.
LORD HALIFAX, *Works,* p. 181.

9
Pride costs us more than hunger, thirst, and cold.
WILLIAM HONE, *Year-book,* 1612; THOMAS JEFFERSON, *Writings,* xvi, 111.

Pride brings want, want makes rogues, rogues come to be hanged, and the devil's alone the gainer.
SIR JOHN VANBRUGH, *Æsop.* Act iv, sc. 2.

Overdone pride makes naked side.
UNKNOWN, *How the Good Wife,* l. 95.

10
Now gaudy pride corrupts the lavish age.
JOHN GAY, *Trivia.* Bk. i, l. 114.

11
Oh, why should the spirit of mortal be proud?
Like a swift-flitting meteor, a fast-flying cloud,
A flash of the lightning, a break of the wave,
He passeth from life to his rest in the grave.
WILLIAM KNOX, *Oh, Why Should the Spirit of Mortal Be Proud?* The favorite hymn of Abraham Lincoln.

12
If we had no pride ourselves, we would not lament that of others. (Si nous n'avions point d'orgueil, nous ne nous plaindrions pas de celui des autres.)
LA ROCHEFOUCAULD, *Maximes.* No. 34.

13
Pride that licks the dust.
POPE, *Epistle to Dr. Arbuthnot,* l. 333.

14
He smarteth most who hides his smart,
And sues for no compassion.
SIR WALTER RALEIGH, *The Silent Lover.*

15
The passions grafted on wounded pride are the most inveterate; they are green and vigorous in old age.
GEORGE SANTAYANA, *Little Essays,* p. 22.

16
An avenging god pursues the proud. (Sequitur superbos ultor a tergo deus.)
SENECA, *Hercules Furens,* l. 385.

17
Prouder than rustling in unpaid-for silk.
SHAKESPEARE, *Cymbeline.* Act iii, sc. 3, l. 24.

18
Pride went before, ambition follows him.
SHAKESPEARE, *II Henry VI.* Act i, sc. 1, l. 180.

For he will never follow any thing
That other men begin.
SHAKESPEARE, *Julius Cæsar.* Act ii, sc. 1, l. 151.

19
Two curs shall tame each other; pride alone
Must tarre the mastiffs on.
SHAKESPEARE, *Troilus and Cressida.* Act i, sc. 3, l. 391.

20
I do hate a proud man, as I hate the engendering of toads.
SHAKESPEARE, *Troilus and Cressida.* Act ii, sc. 3, l. 170.

1
Pride hath no other glass
To show itself but pride.
SHAKESPEARE, *Troilus and Cressida*. Act iii, sc. 3, l. 47.

2
Too coy to flatter, and too proud to serve,
Thine be the joyless dignity to starve.
SMOLLETT, *Advice*, l. 236.

3
You've done yourselves proud.
MARK TWAIN, *Innocents at Home*. Ch. 5.

4
Did pride to pride oppose, and scorn to scorn.
EDMUND WALLER, *To a Friend*.

I have not paid the world
The evil and the insolent courtesy
Of offering it my baseness for a gift.
WILLIAM WATSON, *Apologia*.

5
He that fancies he is perfect, may lose that by pride which he attained by grace.
BISHOP THOMAS WILSON, *Maxims of Piety*, p. 108.

6
Our pride misleads, our timid likings kill.
WORDSWORTH, *Memorials of a Tour on the Continent*: Pt. ii, *Desultory Stanzas*.

7
It's pride that puts this country down;
Man, take thine old cloak about thee.
UNKNOWN, *Take Thine Old Cloak About Thee*. (PERCY, *Reliques*. Ser. i, bk. ii, No. 7.)

'Tis pride that pulls the country down.
SHAKESPEARE, *Othello*. Act ii, sc. 3, l. 98. Quoting the old ballad.

III—Pride Goeth Before a Fall

8
The pride of them at last should have a fall.
ALEXANDER BARCLAY, *Shyp of Folys*, ii, 161. (1509)

Inord'nate pride will have a fall.
JOHN SKELTON, *Against Garnesche*. No. iv, l. 158. (c. 1520)

Pride must have a fall, and break the neck
Of that proud man that did usurp his back.
SHAKESPEARE, *Richard II*. Act v, sc. 5, l. 88. (1595)

Pride shall have a fall, and it always was and will be so.
DICKENS, *Dombey and Son*. Ch. 59. (1848)

9
Pride goeth forth on horseback grand and gay,
But cometh back on foot, and begs its way.
LONGFELLOW, *The Bell of Atri*. St. 6.

10
Pride goeth before destruction, and a haughty spirit before a fall.
Old Testament: Proverbs, xvi, 18.

11
My pride fell with my fortunes.
SHAKESPEARE, *As You Like It*. Act i, sc. 2, l. 264.

My high-blown pride At length broke under me.
SHAKESPEARE, *Henry VIII*. Act iii, sc. 2, l. 361.

12
The lowly hart doth win the love of all,
But pride at last is sure of shameful fall.
GEORGE TURBERVILLE, *To Piero: of Pride*.

IV—Pride and Shame

13
Shame is Pride's cloak.
WILLIAM BLAKE, *Proverbs of Hell*.

14
Pride goes before, shame follows after.
UNKNOWN, *Jacob's Well*, 70. (c. 1440)

Pride goeth before, but shame do it ensue.
ALEXANDER BARCLAY, *Shyp of Folys*, ii, 164. (1509)

Pride goeth before, and shame cometh behind.
UNKNOWN, *Treatise of a Gallant*. (c. 1510)

15
Let pride go afore, shame will follow after.
GEORGE CHAPMAN, *Eastward Hoe*. Act iv, sc. 1.

16
When pride rides, shame lacqueys.
THOMAS FULLER, *Gnomologia*. No. 5567.

17
Pride will have a fall; for pride goeth before and shame cometh after.
JOHN HEYWOOD, *Proverbs*. Pt. i, ch. 10. (1546)

18
When pride is in the saddle, mischief and shame are on the crupper.
LOUIS XI OF FRANCE. (*Countryman's New Commonwealth*, 26. (1647)

19
When pride cometh, then cometh shame.
Old Testament: Proverbs, xi, 2.

V—Pride: Its Virtues

20
He who would climb and soar aloft
Must needs keep ever at his side
The tonic of a wholesome pride.
ARTHUR HUGH CLOUGH, *The Higher Courage*.

21
Though pride is not a virtue, it is the parent of many virtues.
CHURTON COLLINS, *Aphorisms*.

22
There is a paradox in pride: it makes some men ridiculous, but prevents others from becoming so.
C. C. COLTON, *Lacon*.

23
Pride is handsome, economical; pride eradicates so many vices, letting none subsist but itself, that it seems as if it were a great gain to exchange vanity for pride. . . . Only one drawback: proud people are intolerably selfish, and the vain are gentle and giving.
EMERSON, *Essays: Conduct of Life*.

24
The truly proud man knows neither superiors nor inferiors. The first he does not admit of: the last he does not concern himself about.
WILLIAM HAZLITT, *Characteristics*. No. 112.

The vile are only vain, the great are proud.
BYRON, *Marino Faliero*. Act ii, sc. 1.

1
Proud bearing is appropriate to proud fortunes. (Secundas fortunas decent superbiæ.)
PLAUTUS, *Stichus*. Act ii, sc. 2.

Be exceeding proud. Stand upon your gentility, and scorn every man. Speak nothing humbly.
BEN JONSON, *Every Man in His Humour*. Act iii, sc. 4.

2
Why, who cries out in pride,
That can therein tax any private party?
Doth it not flow as hugely as the sea?
SHAKESPEARE, *As You Like It*. Act ii, sc. 7, l. 70.

But, sure, he's proud, and yet his pride becomes him.
SHAKESPEARE, *As You Like It*. Act iii, sc. 5, l 114.

3
Was never in this world aught worthy tried,
Without some spark of such self-pleasing pride.
SPENSER, *Amoretti*. Sonnet v.

VI—Pride: Its Faults

4
Pride hated stands, and doth unpitied fall.
WILLIAM ALEXANDER, *Doomsday: The Fourth Hour*. St. 85.

Thus unlamented pass the proud away,
The gaze of fools, and pageant of a day!
POPE, *Elegy to the Memory of an Unfortunate Lady*, l. 43.

5
Of all the lunacies earth can boast,
The one that must please the devil the most
Is pride reduced to the whimsical terms
Of causing the slugs to despise the worms.
ROBERT BROUGH, *The Tent-Maker's Story*.

Curs'd pride, that creeps securely in,
And swells a haughty worm.
ISAAC WATTS, *Sincere Praise*.

6
The sad rhyme of the men who proudly clung
To their first fault, and withered in their pride.
ROBERT BROWNING, *Paracelsus*. Pt. iv.

7
But his heart was swollen, and turned aside,
By deep, interminable pride.
BYRON, *The Siege of Corinth*. St. 21.

8
There be, whose loveless wisdom never failed
In self-adoring pride securely mailed.
CAMPBELL, *The Pleasures of Hope*. Pt. ii, l. 9.

9
How blind is Pride! what Eagles we are still
In matters that belong to other men!
What Beetles in our own!
GEORGE CHAPMAN, *All Fooles*. Act iv, sc. 1.

See also under FAULTS.

10
My thoughtless youth was wing'd with vain desires;
My manhood, long misled by wandering fires,
Follow'd false lights; and, when their glimpse was gone,
My pride struck out new sparkles of her own.
Such was I, such by nature still I am;
Be thine the glory, and be mine the shame.
DRYDEN, *The Hind and the Panther*. Pt. i, l. 72.

I was not ever thus, nor pray'd that Thou
Shouldst lead me on;
I loved to choose and see my path, but now
Lead Thou me on!
I loved the garish day, and, spite of fears,
Pride ruled my will: remember not past years.
JOHN HENRY NEWMAN, *The Pillar of the Cloud*.

Alas, I have loved pride and praise, like others worse or worthier.
M. F. TUPPER, *Proverbial Philosophy: Second Series: The End*.

11
Pride is the sworn enemy to content.
THOMAS FULLER, *Gnomologia*. No. 3944.

Pride and grace dwell never in one place.
THOMAS FULLER, *Gnomologia*. No. 6273.

But was ever Pride contented,
Or would Folly ere be taught?
W. S. LANDOR, *An Arab to His Mistress*.

12
How insolent is upstart pride!
JOHN GAY, *Fables*. Pt. i, fab. 24.

13
Pride is the cause of allë woe.
JOHN GOWER, *Confessio Amantis*. Bk. i, l. 3006.

14
Hating that solemn vice of greatness, pride.
BEN JONSON, *On Lady Bedford*.

15
There are such as fain would be the worst
Amongst all men, since best they cannot be,
So strong is that wild lie that men call pride.
WILLIAM MORRIS, *The Earthly Paradise: The Hill of Venus*. Sts. 184, 185.

16
Of all the causes which conspire to blind
Man's erring judgment, and misguide the mind,
What the weak head with strongest bias rules,
Is Pride, the never failing vice of fools.
POPE, *Essay on Criticism*. Pt. ii, l. 1.

Whatever Nature has in worth denied,
She gives in large recruits of needful Pride;
For as in bodies, thus in souls, we find,
What wants in blood and spirits, swell'd with wind:
Pride, where Wit fails, steps in to our defence,
And fills up all the mighty void of Sense.
POPE, *Essay on Criticism*. Pt. ii, l. 5.

17
In pride, in reas'ning pride, our error lies;
All quit their sphere, and rush into the skies!
Pride still is aiming at the bless'd abodes,
Men would be Angels, Angels would be Gods.
POPE, *Essay on Man*. Epis. i, l. 123.

Pride (of all others the most dangerous fault)

Proceeds from want of sense, or want of thought.
The men who labour and digest things most,
Will be much apter to despond than boast.

WENTWORTH DILLON, *Essay on Translated Verse*, l. 161.

1
Save me alike from foolish Pride
Or impious Discontent.

POPE, *Universal Prayer*, l. 33.

2
In general, pride is at the bottom of all great mistakes.

RUSKIN, *True and Beautiful: Conception of God.*

3
He that is proud eats up himself: pride is his own glass, his own trumpet, his own chronicle; and whatever praises itself but in the deed, devours the deed in the praise.

SHAKESPEARE, *Troilus and Cressida.* Act ii, sc. 3, l. 164.

He is so plaguy proud that the death-tokens of it
Cry "No recovery."

SHAKESPEARE, *Troilus and Cressida.* Act ii, sc. 3, l. 187.

4
For often a man's own angry pride
Is cap and bells for a fool.

TENNYSON, *Maud.* Pt. i, sec. 6, st. 7.

PRIEST

See Preacher: Priest

PRIMROSE

5
Ring-ting! I wish I were a Primrose,
A bright yellow Primrose, blowing in the Spring!

WILLIAM ALLINGHAM, *Wishing.*

Primrose, first-born child of Ver,
Merry springtime's harbinger.

BEAUMONT AND FLETCHER, *The Two Noble Kinsmen.* Act i, sc. 1.

The sweet Infanta of the year.

ROBERT HERRICK, *The Primrose.*

6
The primrose banks how fair!

BURNS, *My Chloris, Mark How Green.*

7
"I could have brought you some primroses, but I do not like to mix violets with anything." "They say primroses make a capital salad," said Lord St. Jerome.

BENJAMIN DISRAELI, *Lothair.* Ch. 13.

8
First came the primrose,
On the bank high,
Like a maiden looking forth
From the window of a tower.

SYDNEY DOBELL, *A Chanted Calendar.*

9
Why do ye weep, sweet Babes? can tears
Speak grief in you
Who were but born
Just as the modest morn
Teem'd her refreshing dew?

ROBERT HERRICK, *To Primroses Fill'd With Morning Dew.*

10
A tuft of evening primroses,
O'er which the mind may hover till it dozes.

KEATS, *I Stood Tiptoe*, l. 107.

11
Bountiful Primroses,
With outspread heart that needs the rough leaves' care.

GEORGE MACDONALD, *Wild Flowers.*

12
Bring the rathe primrose that forsaken dies.

MILTON, *Lycidas*, l. 142.

13
In this low vale, the promise of the year,
Serene, thou openest to the nipping gale,
Unnoticed and alone, thy tender elegance.

HENRY KIRKE WHITE, *To an Early Primrose.*

14
Primroses, the Spring may love them;
Summer knows but little of them.

WORDSWORTH, *Foresight.*

15
A primrose by a river's brim
A yellow primrose was to him,
And it was nothing more.

WORDSWORTH, *Peter Bell.* Pt. i, st. 12.

16
The Primrose for a veil had spread
The largest of her upright leaves;
And thus, for purposes benign,
A simple flower deceives.

WORDSWORTH, *A Wren's Nest*, l. 57.

PRINCE

See also King, Royalty

17
Princes are like to heavenly bodies, which cause good or evil times, and which have much veneration, but no rest.

FRANCIS BACON, *Essays: Of Empire.*

Kings are like stars: they rise and set, they have
The worship of the world, but no repose.

SHELLEY, *Hellas*, l. 195.

18
The prince who
Neglects or violates his trust is more
A brigand than a robber-chief.

BYRON, *The Two Foscari.* Act ii, sc. 1.

19
The Prince exists for the sake of the State, not the State for the sake of the Prince.

ERASMUS, *Adagia.*

Princely offspring of Braganza,
Erin greets thee with a stanza.

BYRON, *To the Infanta.*

A prince is the first servant and first magistrate of the state.

FREDERICK THE GREAT, the motto of his political testament, written in French with his own hand. (*Memoirs of Brandebourg.*)

The freedom princes owe their people is the freedom of law, of which you are only the minister and first depositary.

JEAN BAPTISTE MASSILLON, in a sermon to Louis XV.

The king will show that he belongs to the republic, not the republic to him.

SENECA, *De Clementia*. Bk. i, sec. 19.

See also under KING.

1
Who made thee a prince and a judge over us?

Old Testament: Exodus, ii, 14.

2
Trouble not your head with the tyranny of princes for you may catch cold therein from the wind of complication.

JAMES ELROY FLECKER, *Hassan*.

The Wind of Complication.

SUSAN ERTZ. Title of book of short stories.

3
Experience has shewn that between the prisons and the graves of princes, the distance is very small.

SIR MICHAEL FOSTER, *Foster's Crown Cas.*, 1762. (*Discourse I*, c. 1. s. 3.)

4
A yeoman upon his legs is higher than a prince upon his knees.

THOMAS FULLER, *Gnomologia*. No. 488.

5
Princes and lords may flourish, or may fade;
A breath can make them, as a breath has made.

GOLDSMITH, *The Deserted Village*, l. 53.

6
Of a new prince, new bondage.

GEORGE HERBERT, *Jacula Prudentum*.

When the prince fiddles, the subjects must dance. (Was die Fürsten geigen, mussen die Unterthanen tanzen.)

UNKNOWN. A German proverb.

7
Madame, bear in mind
That princes govern all things—save the wind.

VICTOR HUGO, *The Infanta's Rose*.

8
A prince without letters is a Pilot without eyes. All his government is groping.

BEN JONSON, *Explorata: Illiteratus Princeps*.

Learning in a prince is like a dangerous knife in the hands of a madman.

DANIEL TUVILL, *Vade Mecum*, 16. (1638)

9
The devotion which one gives to princes is an inferior self-love. (La dévotion qu'on donne aux princes est un second amour-propre.)

LA ROCHEFOUCAULD, *Maximes Posthumes*. No. 518.

10
The punishment of bad princes is to be thought worse than they are. (Le châtiment des mauvais princes est d'être crus pires qu'ils ne sont.)

JOUBERT, *Pensées*. No. 195.

11
A Prince's greatest virtue is to know his own. (Principis est virtus maxima nosce suos.)

MARTIAL, *Epigrams*. Bk. viii, epig. 15.

12
Go now and cultivate princes. (I, cole nunc reges.)

MARTIAL, *Epigrams*. Bk. x, epig. 96.

13
For princes never more make known their wisdom,
Than when they cherish goodness where they find it.

MASSINGER, *Great Duke of Florence*. Act i, sc. 1.

14
If the prince of a State love benevolence, he will have no opponent in all the empire.

MENCIUS, *Works*. Bk. iv, pt. i, ch. 7.

15
The secret counsels of princes are a troublesome burden to such as have only to execute them. (C'est une importune garde, du secret des princes, à qui n'en à que faire.)

MONTAIGNE, *Essays*. Bk. iii, ch. 1.

But still remember, that a prince's secrets
Are balm concealed; but poison if discovered.

MASSINGER, *The Duke of Milan*. Act i, sc. 3.

16
Put not your trust in princes.

Old Testament: Psalms, cxlvi, 3.

17
The fortune of princes changes with their character. (Fortuna simul cum moribus immutatur.)

SALLUST, *Catiline*. Sec. 2.

18
The sword protects the prince. Still better, loyalty. (Ferrum tuetur principem. Melius fides.)

SENECA, *Octavia*, l. 457.

19
The shepherd's homely curds,
His cold thin drink out of his leathern bottle,
His wonted sleep under a fresh tree's shade,
All which secure and sweetly he enjoys,
Is far beyond a prince's delicates,
His viands sparkling in a golden cup,
His body couched in a curious bed,
When care, mistrust, and treason waits on him.

SHAKESPEARE, *III Henry VI*. Act ii, sc. 5, l. 47.

20
The hearts of princes kiss obedience,
So much they love it: but to stubborn spirits
They swell, and grow as terrible as storms.

SHAKESPEARE, *Henry VIII*. Act iii, sc. 1, l. 162.

O how wretched
Is that poor man that hangs on princes' favours!
There is, betwixt that smile we would aspire to,
That sweet aspect of princes, and their ruin,
More pangs and fears than wars or women have.

SHAKESPEARE, *Henry VIII*. Act iii, sc. 2, l. 366.

21
Yet in bestowing, madam,

He was most princely.
SHAKESPEARE, *Henry VIII*. Act iv, sc. 2, l. 56.

1
Princes are the glass, the school, the book,
Where subjects' eyes do learn, do read, do look.
SHAKESPEARE, *The Rape of Lucrece*. St. 88.

Like prince, like people. (Qualis rex, talis grex.)
UNKNOWN. A Latin proverb.

2
A begging prince what beggar pities not?
SHAKESPEARE, *Richard III*. Act i, sc. 4, l. 270.

3
Remember who you are,
A prince, born for the good of other men;
Whose god-like office is to draw the sword
Against oppression, and set free mankind.
THOMAS SOUTHERNE, *Oroonoko*. Act iii, sc. 3.

4
Princes are mortal, the commonwealth is eternal. (Principes mortales, rempublican æternam.)
TACITUS, *Annals*. Bk. iii, sec. 6.

5
The princes among us are those who forget themselves and serve mankind.
WOODROW WILSON, *Speech*, Washington, 31 March, 1916.

Princes of courtesy, merciful, proud and strong.
HENRY NEWBOLT, *Craven*.

6
The prince that is feared of many must of necessity fear many.
UNKNOWN, *Politeuphuia*, 79. (1669)

See also FEAR: FEARED AND FEARING.

PRINCIPLE

7
Every principle contains in itself the germs of a prophecy.
S. T. COLERIDGE, *Biographia Literaria*. Ch. 10.

8
When independence of principle consists in having no principle on which to depend.
C. C. COLTON, *Lacon: Preface*.

9
Principles do not mainly influence even the principled; we talk on principle, but we act on interest.
W. S. LANDOR, *Imaginary Conversations: Banos and Alpuente*.

I *don't* believe in princerple,
But, oh, I *du* in interest!
J. R. LOWELL, *Biglow Papers*. Ser. i, No. 6.

10
Ez to my princerples, I glory
In hevin' nothin' o' the sort.
J. R. LOWELL, *Biglow Papers*. Ser. i, No. 7.

11
Flinch not, neither give up nor despair, if the achieving of every act in accordance with right principle is not always continuous with thee.
MARCUS AURELIUS, *Meditations*. Bk. v, sec. 9.

12
Their feet through faithless leather meet the dirt;
And oftener chang'd their principles than shirt.
YOUNG, *Epistle to Mr. Pope*. No. i, l. 277.

PRINTING

See also Press

13
The art preservative of arts. (Ars artium omnium conservatrix.)
Inscription, on façade of the house at Haarlem, Holland, formerly occupied by Laurent Koster, one of the reputed inventors of printing. The inscription ran: "Memoræ Sacrum Typographia Ars Artium Omnium Conservatrix Hic Primum Inventa Circa Annum MCCCCXL." It is first mentioned about 1628.

14
The printing-press is either the greatest blessing or the greatest curse of modern times, one sometimes forgets which.
J. M. BARRIE, *Sentimental Tommy*, p. 58.

Th' printin'-press isn't wondherful. What's wondherful is that annybody shud want it to go on doin' what it does.
FINLEY PETER DUNNE, *On the Midway*.

15
Ready-writing which we call Printing.
CARLYLE, *On Heroes and Hero-Worship: The Hero as Man of Letters*.

He who first shortened the labour of Copyists by device of *Movable Types* was disbanding hired Armies and cashiering most Kings and Senates, and creating a whole new Democratic world: he had invented the Art of printing.
CARLYLE, *Sartor Resartus*. Bk. i, ch. 5.

16
For when news is printed,
It leaves, sir, to be news; while 'tis but written,
Tho' it be ne'er so false, it runs news still. . . .
See divers men's opinions! unto some
The very printing of 'em makes them news;
That have not the heart to believe anything
But what they see in print.
BEN JONSON, *The Staple of News*. Act i, sc. 1.

The thing is written. It is true. (Cela est escrit. Il est vray.)
RABELAIS, *Works*.

I love a ballad in print o' life, for then we are sure they are true.
SHAKESPEARE, *Winter's Tale*. Act iv, sc. 4, l. 264.

If it is in print, it must be true.
W. G. BENHAM, *Proverbs*, p. 788.

If you see it in the Sun it's so.
CHARLES A. DANA, *Motto of the New York Sun*.

17
Though an angel should write, still 'tis *devils* must print.
THOMAS MOORE, *The Fudge Family in England*. Letter 3.

1
'Sdeath, I'll print it, And shame the fools.
POPE, *Epistle to Dr. Arbuthnot*, l. 61.

2
All this I speak in print, for in print I found it.
SHAKESPEARE, *The Two Gentlemen of Verona*. Act ii, sc. 1, l. 175.

3
And whereas, before, our forefathers had no other books but the score and the tally, thou hast caused printing to be used, and, contrary to the king, his crown and dignity, thou hast built a paper-mill.
SHAKESPEARE, *II Henry VI*. Act iv, sc. 7, l. 39.

4
The jour printer with gray head and gaunt jaws works at his case,
He turns his quid of tobacco while his eyes blurr with the manuscript.
WALT WHITMAN, *Song of Myself*. Sec. 15.

PRISON

5
Prisons are built with stones of Law, brothels with bricks of Religion.
WILLIAM BLAKE, *Proverbs of Hell*.

6
In durance vile here must I wake and weep,
And all my frowsy couch in sorrow steep.
BURNS, *Epistle from Esopus to Maria*, l. 57.

In durance vile.
WILLIAM KENDRICK, *Falstaff's Wedding*. Act i, sc. 2; EDMUND BURKE, *Thoughts on the Present Discontents*. (1770) The Oxford Dictionary states that this phrase has been traced back to 1513.

What boots it him from death to be unbound,
To be captived in endless durance?
SPENSER, *Faerie Queene*. Bk. iii, canto v, st. 42.

7
As he went through Cold-Bath Fields he saw
A solitary cell;
And the Devil was pleased, for it gave him a hint
For improving his prisons in Hell.
S. T. COLERIDGE, *The Devil's Thoughts*. St. 8.

Sometimes they shut you up in jail—
Dark, and a filthy cell;
I hope the fellows built them jails
Find 'em down in hell.
EDWIN FORD PIPER, *Bindlestiff*.

8
Away with him to the deepest dungeon beneath the castle moat.
DICKENS, *Nicholas Nickleby*. Ch. 29.

9
Golden fetters. (Χρυσαὶ πέδαι.)
DIOGENES. (ERASMUS, *Chiliades Adajiorum*, "*Amor*.")

A fool I do him firmly hold,
That loves his fetters, though they were of gold.
SPENSER, *Faerie Queene*. Bk. iii, canto ix, st. 8.

No man loveth his fetters, be they made of gold.
JOHN HEYWOOD, *Proverbs*. Bk. i, ch. viii.

Then, when I am thy captive, talk of chains.
MILTON, *Paradise Lost*. Bk. iv, l. 970.

10
Stone walls do not a prison make,
Nor iron bars a cage;
Minds innocent and quiet take
That for an hermitage;
If I have freedom in my love,
And in my soul am free,
Angels alone, that soar above,
Enjoy such liberty.
RICHARD LOVELACE, *To Althea from Prison*. (1642)

That which the world miscalls a jail,
A private closet is to me. . . .
Locks, bars, and solitude together met,
Make me no prisoner, but an anchoret.
LORD ARTHUR CAPEL, *Written in Confinement*. (1649) Also attributed to Sir Roger L'Estrange. (*Notes and Queries*, 10 April, 1909, p. 288.)

Double grills with great nails, triple doors, heavy bolts, to wicked souls you represent hell; but to the innocent you are only wood, stones, iron.
(Doubles grilles à gros cloux,
Triples portes, forts verroux,
Aux âmes vraiment méchantes
Vous représentez l'enfer:
Mais aux âmes innocentes
Vous n'êtes que de bois, des pierres, du fer.)
PELLISSON-FONTANIER, *Written on the Wall of His Cell in the Bastille*.

11
Nor stony tower, nor walls of beaten brass,
Nor airless dungeon, nor strong links of iron,
Can be retentive to the strength of spirit.
SHAKESPEARE, *Julius Cæsar*. Act i, sc. 7, l. 93.

Might I but through my prison once a day
Behold this maid: all corners else o' the earth
Let liberty make use of; space enough
Have I in such a prison.
SHAKESPEARE, *The Tempest*. Act i, sc. 2, l. 490.

12
Come, let's away to prison:
We two alone will sing like birds i' the cage.
SHAKESPEARE, *King Lear*. Act v, sc. 3, l. 8.

We'll wear out
In a wall'd prison, packs and sects of great ones
That ebb and flow by the moon.
SHAKESPEARE, *King Lear*. Act v, sc. 3, l. 17.

Our cage
We make a quire, as doth the prison'd bird,
And sing our bondage freely.
SHAKESPEARE, *Cymbeline*. Act iii, sc. 3, l. 42.

13
Whilst we have prisons it matters little which of us occupies the cells.
BERNARD SHAW, *Maxims for Revolutionists*.

The most anxious man in a prison is the governor.
BERNARD SHAW, *Maxims for Revolutionists*.

14
Even savage animals, if you keep them confined, forget their natural courage. (Etiam

fera animalia, si clausa teneas, virtutis obliviscuntur.)

TACITUS, *History*. Bk. iv, sec. 64.

1
I know not whether Laws be right,
Or whether Laws be wrong;
All that we know who lie in gaol
Is that the wall is strong;
And that each day is like a year,
A year whose days are long.

OSCAR WILDE, *The Ballad of Reading Gaol*. Pt. v, st. 1.

This too I know—and wise it were
If each could know the same—
That every prison that men build
Is built with bricks of shame,
And bound with bars, lest Christ should see
How men their brothers maim.

OSCAR WILDE, *The Ballad of Reading Gaol*. Pt. v, st. 3.

The vilest deeds like poison weeds
Bloom well in prison-air:
It is only what is good in Man
That wastes and withers there:
Pale Anguish keeps the heavy gate
And the Warder is Despair.

OSCAR WILDE, *The Ballad of Reading Gaol*. Pt. v, st. 5.

But though lean Hunger and green Thirst
Like asp with adder fight,
We have little care of prison fare,
For what chills and kills outright
Is that every stone one lifts by day
Becomes one's heart by night.

OSCAR WILDE, *The Ballad of Reading Gaol*. Pt. v, st. 9.

PRIZE, see Reward

PROCRASTINATION

See also Delay

2
Often have I heard it said, What good thing you can do, do not defer it. (Semper audivi dici, Quod bene potes facere noli differre.)

ALBERTANO OF BRESCIA, *Liber Consolationis et Consilii*. (1246)

3
By and by never comes. (Modo, et modo, non habebant modum.)

ST. AUGUSTINE, *Confessions*. Bk. viii, ch. 5, sec. 12.

By and by is easily said.

SHAKESPEARE, *Hamlet*. Act iii, sc. 2, l. 403.

4
It is an undoubted truth, that the less one has to do, the less time one finds to do it in. One yawns, one procrastinates, one can do it when one will, and therefore one seldom does it at all.

LORD CHESTERFIELD, *Letters*, 30 Sept., 1757.

5
No idleness, no laziness, no procrastination; never put off till to-morrow what you can do to-day.

LORD CHESTERFIELD, *Letters*, 26 Dec., 1749.

Chesterfield adds that this was the rule of "the famous and unfortunate Pensionary De Witt." The axiom is repeated in the letter of 5 Feb., 1750.

Never leave that till to-morrow which you can do to-day.

BENJAMIN FRANKLIN, *Poor Richard*.

There is a maxim, "Never put off till to-morrow what you can do to-day." It is a maxim for sluggards. A better reading of it is, "Never do to-day what you can as well do to-morrow," because something may occur to make you regret your premature action.

AARON BURR. (PARTON, *Life of Aaron Burr*, p. 150.)

6
Whatsoever thou mayest do to-night defer not till to-morrow.

MILES COVERDALE, *The Christian State of Matrimony*, i, 3. (1541)

7
Procrastination brings loss, delay danger. (Dilatio damnum habet, mora periculum.)

ERASMUS, *Colloquia: Adolescens*.

Nothing so perilous as procrastination.

LYLY, *Euphues*, p. 65. (1579)

8
One of these days is none of these days.

H. C. BOHN, *Handbook of Proverbs*, p. 471; BENHAM, *Proverbs*, p. 822.

9
The procrastinating man is ever struggling with ruin. (Αἰεὶ δ' ἀμβολιεργὸς ἀνὴρ ἄτῃσι παλαίει.)

HESIOD, *Works and Days*, l. 413.

10
He who defers this work from day to day,
Does on a river's bank expecting stay,
Till the whole stream, which stopped him, should be gone,
That runs, and as it runs, for ever will run on.
(Qui recte vivendi prorogat horam,
Rusticus exspectat dum defluat amnis; at ille
Labitur et labetur in omne volubilis ævum.)

HORACE, *Epistles*. Bk. i, epis. 2, l. 41. (Cowley, tr.)

11
procrastination is the
art of keeping
up with yesterday

DON MARQUIS, *certain maxims of archy*.

12
Two anons and a by-and-by is an hour-and-a-half.

JOHN RAY, *English Proverbs*.

13
While we are postponing life speeds by. (Dum differtur, vita transcurrit.)

SENECA, *Epistulæ ad Lucilium*. Epis. i, sec. 3.

14
The patient dies while the physician sleeps;
The orphan pines while the oppressor feeds;
Justice is feasting while the widow weeps;
Advice is sporting while infection breeds.

SHAKESPEARE, *The Rape of Lucrece*, l. 904.

1
Procrastination is the thief of time:
Year after year it steals, till all are fled,
And to the mercies of a moment leaves
The vast concerns of an eternal scene.
YOUNG, *Night Thoughts*. Night i, l. 392.

Punctuality is the thief of time.
OSCAR WILDE, *Picture of Dorian Gray*. Ch. 3.

PRODIGALITY

I—Prodigality: Apothegms

2
When thrift is in the town, he is in the field.
FRANCIS BACON, *Promus*. No. 675.

3
Why, do nothing, be like a gentleman, be idle, . . . make ducks and drakes with shillings.
GEORGE CHAPMAN, *Eastward Hoe*, i, 1. (1605)

Played at duck and drake with gold, like pebbles.
JAMES SHIRLEY, *Cupid and Death*. (1653)

What figured slates are best to make
On watery surface duck and drake.
BUTLER, *Hudibras*. Pt. ii, canto 3, l. 301. (1664)

A stone thrown into the water, and making circles ere it sink, it is called a duck and a drake and a half-penny cake.
UNKNOWN, *Nomenclator*, 299. (1585)
See also under CIRCLES.

4
Let friends of prodigals say what they will,
Spendthrifts at home, abroad are spendthrifts still.
CHARLES CHURCHILL, *The Candidate*, l. 519.

5
Profusion apes the noble part
Of liberality of heart,
And dullness of discretion.
COWPER, *Friendship*. St. 1.

6
Squandering wealth was his peculiar art;
Nothing went unrewarded but desert.
Beggar'd by fools, whom still he found too late;
He had his jest, and they had his estate.
DRYDEN, *Absalom and Achitophel*. Pt. i, l. 559.

The premature expenditure of money is the function of the foolish.
WILLIAM GARRETT, *The Man in the Mirror*.

7
The prodigal robs his heir, the miser himself.
THOMAS FULLER, *Gnomologia*. No. 4722.

'Tis strange the Miser should his cares employ
To gain those riches he can ne'er enjoy;
Is it less strange the Prodigal should waste
His wealth to purchase what he ne'er can taste?
POPE, *Moral Essays*. Epistle iv, l. 1.

8
A princely mind will undo a private family.
LORD HALIFAX, *Works*, p. 27.

9
Free livers on a small scale; who are prodigal within the compass of a guinea.
WASHINGTON IRVING, *The Stout Gentleman*.

10
On parchment wings his acres take their flight.
SOAME JENYNS, *The Modern Fine Gentleman*.

11
See! The difference 'twixt the covetous and the prodigal!
The covetous man never has money, and
The prodigal will have none shortly!
BEN JONSON, *The Staple of News*. Act i, sc. 1.

12
We commonly say of a prodigal man that he is no man's foe but his own.
BISHOP JOHN KING, *Lecture on Jonah*. (1594)
See also under ENEMY.

13
I can get no remedy against this consumption of the purse: borrowing only lingers and lingers it out, but the disease is incurable.
SHAKESPEARE, *II Henry IV*. Act i, sc. 2, l. 263.

14
When they will not give a doit to relieve a lame beggar, they will lay out ten to see a dead Indian.
SHAKESPEARE, *The Tempest*. Act ii, sc. 2, l. 20.

The beggarly last doit.
COWPER, *The Task*. Bk. v, l. 316.

15
You must consider that a prodigal course
Is like the sun's; but not, like his, recoverable.
SHAKESPEARE, *Timon of Athens*. Act iii, sc. 4, l. 12.

16
A spending hand that alway poureth out,
Hath need to have a bringer-in as fast.
SIR THOMAS WYATT, *How to Use the Court and Himself Therein*, l. 1.

17
This lady glories in profuse expense,
And thinks distraction is magnificence.
YOUNG, *Love of Fame*. Satire vi, l. 55.

II—Prodigality: The Prodigal Son

18
The younger son gathered all together, and took his journey into a far country, and there wasted his substance with riotous living.
New Testament: Luke, xv, 13.

And bring hither the fatted calf, and kill it.
New Testament: Luke, xv, 23.

When prodigals return great things are done.
A. A. DOWTY, *The Siliad*. (BEETON, *Christmas Annual*. 1873.)

A returning prodigal is not to be exchanged for gold. (Lang tzŭ 'hui 'tou chin pu 'huan.)
UNKNOWN. A Chinese proverb.

19
Shall I keep your hogs and eat husks with them? What prodigal portion have I spent, that I should come to such penury?
SHAKESPEARE, *As You Like It*. Act i, sc. 1, l. 40.

20
He that goes in the calf's skin that was killed for the Prodigal.
SHAKESPEARE, *Comedy of Errors*, iv, 3, 17.

Prodigals lately come from swine-keeping.
SHAKESPEARE, *I Henry IV*. Act iv, sc. 2, l. 38.

21
How like the prodigal doth she return

With over-weather'd ribs!

SHAKESPEARE, *The Merchant of Venice*. Act ii, sc. 6, l. 17.

1
I have received my proportion, like the prodigious son.

SHAKESPEARE, *The Two Gentlemen of Verona*. Act ii, sc. 3, l. 3.

PROFESSOR, see Teacher

PROGRESS

2
Progress, man's distinctive mark alone,
Not God's, and not the beast's;
God is, they are,
Man partly is, and wholly hopes to be.

ROBERT BROWNING, *A Death in the Desert*.

Progress is
The law of life, man is not man as yet.

ROBERT BROWNING, *Paracelsus*. Pt. v.

3
A race that binds
Its body in chains and calls them Liberty,
And calls each fresh link Progress.

ROBERT BUCHANAN, *Political Mystics: Titan and Avatar*.

What we call "Progress" is the exchange of one nuisance for another nuisance.

HAVELOCK ELLIS, *Impressions and Comments*. Ser. i, p. 16.

4
Now, by St. Paul, the work goes bravely on.

COLLEY CIBBER, *Richard III* (altered). Act iii, sc. 1.

5
It is the darling delusion of mankind that the world is progressive in religion, toleration, freedom, as it is progressive in machinery.

MONCURE D. CONWAY, *Dogma and Science*.

6
So long as all the increased wealth which modern progress brings, goes but to build up great fortunes, to increase luxury, and make sharper the contest between the House of Have and the House of Want, progress is not real and cannot be permanent.

HENRY GEORGE, *Progress and Poverty: Introductory*.

Social progress makes the well-being of all more and more the business of each; it binds all closer and closer together in bonds from which none can escape.

HENRY GEORGE, *Social Problems*.

7
All that is human must retrograde if it does not advance.

EDWARD GIBBON, *Decline and Fall of the Roman Empire*. Ch. 71.

He who moves not forward goes backward!
A capital saying!

GOETHE, *Herman and Dorothea*. Canto iii, 66.

Applaud us when we run, console us when we fall, cheer us when we recover, but let us pass on—for God's sake, let us pass on.

EDMUND BURKE [?].

8
Slackness breeds worms; but the sure traveller,
Though he alight sometimes, still goeth on.

GEORGE HERBERT, *The Church-Porch*. St. 57.

9
Cost is the father and compensation is the mother of progress.

J. G. HOLLAND, *Plain Talks: Cost and Compensation*.

We rise by things that are under our feet;
By what we have mastered of good and gain;
By the pride deposed and the passion slain,
And the vanquished ills that we hourly meet.

J. G. HOLLAND, *Gradation*.

10
All progress begins with a crime.

ELBERT HUBBARD, *A Thousand and One Epigrams*, p. 109.

11
There is no greater disloyalty to the great pioneers of human progress than to refuse to budge an inch from where they stood.

DEAN W. R. INGE. (MARCHANT, *Wit and Wisdom of Dean Inge*. No. 176.)

12
Harsh and brutal systems slowly give place to gentler ones. The stars in their courses have all along fought against Sisera and his kind. The way of the transgressor has proved to be not only difficult but impossible. The universe is against it.

RUFUS M. JONES. (NEWTON, *My Idea of God*, p. 57.)

13
From lower to the higher next,
Not to the top, is Nature's text;
And embryo Good, to reach full stature,
Absorbs the Evil in its nature.

J. R. LOWELL, *Festina Lente: Moral*.

14
New times demand new measures and new men;
The world advances, and in time outgrows
The laws that in our fathers' day were best;
And, doubtless, after us, some purer scheme
Will be shaped out by wiser men than we.

J. R. LOWELL, *A Glance Behind the Curtain*.

New occasions teach new duties, time makes ancient good uncouth;
They must upward still and onward, who would keep abreast of truth.

J. R. LOWELL, *The Present Crisis*.

15
A single breaker may recede; but the tide is evidently coming in.

MACAULAY, *Essays: Southey's Colloquies*.

16
We're driven back for our next fray
A newer strength to borrow,
And where the vanguard camps to-day,
The rear shall rest to-morrow.

GERALD MASSEY, *Song: 'Tis Weary Watching*.

Not enjoyment, and not sorrow,
Is our destined end or way;

But to act, that each to-morrow
Find us farther than to-day.
LONGFELLOW, *A Psalm of Life.*

1
That in our proper motion we ascend
Up to our native seat: descent and fall
To us is adverse.
MILTON, *Paradise Lost.* Bk. ii, l. 75.

2
I forge ahead, nor can the opposing rush,
That sways all else, my onward progress check,
But bears me on against a whirling world.
(Nitor in adversum, nec me, qui cætera, vincit
Impetus, et rapido contrarius evehor orbi.)
OVID, *Metamorphoses.* Bk. ii, l. 72. (King, tr.)

3
Every step of progress the world has made has been from scaffold to scaffold and from stake to stake.
WENDELL PHILLIPS, *Speech for Woman's Rights,* 15 Oct., 1851.

Life means progress, and progress means suffering.
H. W. VAN LOON, *Tolerance,* p. 89.

4
For my own part I am persuaded that everything advances by an unchangeable law through the eternal constitution and association of latent causes, which have been long before predestinated.
QUINTUS CURTIUS RUFUS, *De Rebus Gestis Alexandri Magni.* Bk. v, ch. 11, sec. 10.

5
There is a period of life when we go back as we advance. (Il est un terme de la vie au-delà duquel en rétrograde en avançant.)
ROUSSEAU, *Émile.* Ch. 2.

6
The greater part of progress is the desire to progress. (Magna pars est profectus velle proficere.)
SENECA, *Epistulæ ad Lucilium.* Epis. lxxi, 36.

7
Progress, therefore, is not an accident, but a necessity. . . . It is a part of nature.
HERBERT SPENCER, *Social Statics.* Pt. i, ch. 2.

8
Men, my brothers, men the workers, ever reaping something new:
That which they have done but earnest of the things that they shall do.
TENNYSON, *Locksley Hall,* l. 117.

9
Onward the chariot of the Untarrying moves;
Nor day divulges him nor night conceals;
Thou hear'st the echo of unreturning hooves
And thunder of irrevocable wheels.
WILLIAM WATSON, *Epigrams.* No. xvii.

10
And step by step, since time began,
I see the steady gain of man.
WHITTIER, *The Chapel of the Hermits.*

I have seen that Man moves over with each new generation into a bigger body, more awful, more reverent and more free than he has had before.
GERALD STANLEY LEE, *Crowds.* Pt. ii, ch. 3.

11
Progress is the realization of Utopias.
OSCAR WILDE, *The Soul of Man under Socialism.*

PROHIBITION

See also Temperance

I—Prohibition: Its Effect

12
Forbid us thing, that thing desyren we.
CHAUCER, *Wife of Bath's Prologue,* l. 519.

Forbidden wares sell twice as dear.
SIR JOHN DENHAM, *Natura Naturata,* l. 16.

Forbidden fruit a flavor has
That lawful orchards mocks;
How luscious lies the pea within
The pod that Duty locks!
EMILY DICKINSON, *Poems.* Pt. i, No. 87.

13
Vicious actions are not hurtful because they are forbidden, but forbidden because they are hurtful.
BENJAMIN FRANKLIN, *Autobiography.* Ch. 1.

14
If God had laid all common, certainly
Man would have been th' incloser; but since now
God hath impal'd us, on the contrary
Man breaks the fence, and every ground will plough.
GEORGE HERBERT, *The Church-Porch.* St. 4.

15
"Much sweeter," she saith, "more acceptable
Is drink, when it is stolen privily,
Than when it is taken in form avowable."
JOHN LYDGATE, *The Remedy of Love.*

Venison stolen is aye the sweeter,
The ferther the narrower fet the better!
JOHN LYDGATE, *The Remedy of Love.*

16
So glister'd the dire Snake, and into fraud
Led Eve, our credulous Mother, to the Tree
Of Prohibition, root of all our woe.
MILTON, *Paradise Lost.* Bk. ix, l. 643.

17
What is lawful has no charm; what is unlawful pricks one more keenly on. (Quod licet, ingratum est; quod non licet acrius urit.)
OVID, *Amores.* Bk. ii, eleg. 19, l. 3.

We are always striving for things forbidden, and desiring those denied us. (Nitimur in vetitum semper cupimusque negata.)
OVID, *Amores.* Bk. iii, eleg. iv, l. 17.

Whatever is guarded we desire the more; the very care invites the thief; few love what they may have. (Quidquid servatur cupimus magis, ipsaque furem Cura vocat; pauci, quod sinit alter, amant.)
OVID, *Amores.* Bk. iii, eleg. 4, l. 25.

So great is man's hunger for forbidden food! (Fames homini vetitorum tanta ciborum est!)
OVID, *Metamorphoses*. Bk. xv, l. 138.

Only forbidden pleasures are loved immoderately; when lawful, they do not excite desire. (Diliguntur immodice sola quæ non licent; . . . non nutrit ardorem concupiscendi, ubi frui licet.)
QUINTILIAN, *Declamationes*, xiv, 18.

Things forbidden have a secret charm. (Prævalent illicita.)
TACITUS, *Annals*. Bk. xiii, sec. 1.

1
As stolen love is pleasant to a man, so is it also to a woman. (Utque viro furtiva venus, sic gratta puellæ.)
OVID, *Ars Amatoria*. Bk. i, l. 275.

How glowing guilt exalts the keen delight!
POPE, *Eloisa to Abelard*, l. 230.

2
Stolen waters are sweet, and bread eaten in secret is pleasant.
Old Testament: Proverbs, ix, 17.

Pleasure stolen being sweetest.
MASSINGER, *City Madam*. Act ii, sc. 1. (1632)

Stolen meat is sweetest.
HEAD AND KIRKMAN, *English Rogue: Preface*. (1671)

Stolen sweets are best.
COLLEY CIBBER, *Rival Fools*. Act i. (1709)

Stolen glances, sweeter for the theft.
BYRON, *Don Juan*. Canto i, st. 74. (1818)

Stolen sweets are always sweeter:
Stolen kisses much completer;
Stolen looks are nice in chapels:
Stolen, stolen be your apples.
THOMAS RANDOLPH, *Song of Fairies*.

3
The pleasure of all things, amongst the ignorant, increases with the very danger which should repel. (Omnium enim rerum voluptas, apud imperitos, ipso quo fugare debet periculo, crescit.)
SENECA, *De Beneficiis*. Bk. vii, sec. 9.

4
He found out a new thing—namely, that to promise not to do a thing is the surest way in the world to make a body want to go and do that very thing.
MARK TWAIN, *The Adventures of Tom Sawyer*. Ch. 22.

II—Prohibition: The Eighteenth Amendment

5
See Social-life and Glee sit down
All joyous and unthinking,
Till, quite transmugrify'd, they're grown
Debauchery and Drinking.
ROBERT BURNS, *An Address to the Unco Guid*.

6
In all matters having to do with the personal habits and customs of large numbers of our people, we must be certain that the established processes of legal change are followed.
WOODROW WILSON, *Veto Message*, on the Volstead Act, 27 Oct., 1919.

7
It is here at last—dry America's first birthday. At one minute past twelve to-morrow morning a new nation will be born. . . . To-night John Barleycorn makes his last will and testament. Now for an era of clear thinking and clean living.
UNKNOWN, *Anti-Saloon League Manifesto*, 15 Jan., 1920.

Good-bye, John. You were God's worst enemy. You were Hell's best friend. I hate you with a perfect hatred.
BILLY SUNDAY, *Funeral Oration*, over John Barleycorn, Norfolk, Va., 16 Jan., 1920.

But the cheerful Spring came kindly on,
And show'rs began to fall:
John Barleycorn got up again,
And sore surpris'd them all.
ROBERT BURNS, *John Barleycorn*. St. 3.

Of old, all invitations ended
With the well-known *R.S.V.P.*,
But now our laws have been amended
The hostess writes *B.Y.O.B.*
CHRISTOPHER MORLEY, *Thoughts on Being Invited to Dinner*. "B.Y.O.B.," it should perhaps be explained, means "Bring your own booze."

8
There are conditions relating to its [prohibition's] enforcement which savor of a nationwide scandal. It is the most demoralizing factor in our public life.
WARREN G. HARDING, *Message to Congress*, 8 Dec., 1922.

9
Vice, crime, immorality, disease, insanity, corruption, and a general disregard for law, directly traceable to the unenforceability of the Volstead Act, are increasing with alarming rapidity.
CONGRESSMAN GEORGE J. SCHNEIDER, of Wisconsin. (*Congressional Record*, 69th Congress, 1st session, p. 629.)

Industry, commerce, art, literature, music, learning, entertainment, and benevolence all find their finest expression in this saloonless land.
Anti-Saloon League Statement, N. Y. *Times*, 26 Nov., 1925.

10
One out of the twelve disciples went wrong.
JOHN W. HARRELD, Senator from Oklahoma, minimizing the fact that 875 agents of the government's prohibition enforcement service, one-twelfth of the entire force, had been dismissed for corruption. (*Congressional Record*, 69th Congress, 1st session, p. 80.)

11
Our country has deliberately undertaken a great social and economic experiment, noble in motive and far-reaching in purpose.
HERBERT HOOVER, *Letter to Senator William E. Borah*, 28 Feb., 1928. Repeated by Hoover

in address at Stanford University accepting the Republican nomination for President.

1
The Commission, by a large majority, does not favor the repeal of the Eighteenth Amendment. I am in accord with this view.

HERBERT HOOVER, *Letter of Transmissal,* accompanying Wickersham Report, Jan., 1931.

We expect legislation to conform to public opinion, not public opinion to yield to legislation.

Report of Wickersham Commission, 20 Jan., 1931.

The whole subject is one of great difficulty.

GEORGE W. WICKERSHAM, *Interview,* after submission of his report on prohibition.

Prohibition has made nothing but trouble.

ALPHONSE CAPONE, *Newspaper interview.*

2
All I kin git out o' the Wickersham position on prohibition is that the distinguished jurist seems to feel that if we'd let 'em have it the problem o' keepin' 'em from gittin' it would be greatly simplified.

KIN HUBBARD, *Abe Martin's Broadcast,* p. 125.

3
The prohibition law, written for weaklings and derelicts, has divided the nation, like Gaul, into three parts—wets, drys, and hypocrites.

MRS. CHARLES H. SABIN, *Address,* 9 Feb., 1931.

4
You cannot write on the banner of the Democratic party the skull and crossbones of an outlaw trade.

JOSEPH T. ROBINSON, U. S. Senator from Arkansas, replying to Raskob's state control of liquor plan, before the Democratic National Committee, 5 March, 1931.

5
In the meantime alcohol produces a delightful social atmosphere that nothing else can produce.

ARNOLD BENNETT, *Things That Have Interested Me: For and Against Prohibition.*

6
A young prohibition worker had his office in the Burr Block [Lincoln, Neb., 1890] with Bryan and Charley Dawes. He had been baptized William Eugene, but he came to be known to fame as "Pussyfoot" Johnson.

PAXTON HIBBEN, *The Peerless Leader,* p. 125.

7
The law of Maine will hardly take effect while the law of fermentation stands unrepealed on the pages of heaven's statute book. The strictest Sabbath edict never could keep the Puritan ale from working on Sunday.

O. W. HOLMES, *Address,* before the New England Society in New York, December, 1865, referring to the passage of the Maine prohibition law.

A law made to be habitually and openly violated is a frightful demoralizer of society. A law notoriously despised by many that appear as its public advocates, which takes many a vote from the same hand that an hour later is lifted trembling to the voter's lips with the draught that quiets at once his nerves and his conscience.

O. W. HOLMES, *Address,* before the New England Society in New York, December, 1885, referring to the Maine prohibition law.

8
It is mighty difficult to get drunk on 2.75 per cent beer.

HERBERT HOOVER, *Statement to the Press,* while Food Administrator, 5 June, 1918.

9
As for prohibition, it is going to be recorded as one of the results of the European War, foreseen by nobody.

STEPHEN LEACOCK, *The Woman Question.*

10
Whether or not the world would be vastly benefited by a total banishment from it of all intoxicating drinks seems not now an open question. Three-fourths of mankind confess the affirmative with their tongues, and I believe all the rest acknowledge it in their hearts.

ABRAHAM LINCOLN, *Address,* before the Washington Society of Springfield, Ill., 22 Feb., 1842.

Prohibition will work great injury to the cause of temperance. It is a species of intemperance within itself, for it goes beyond the bounds of reason, in that it attempts to control a man's appetite by legislation and makes a crime out of things that are not crimes.

Statement attributed to ABRAHAM LINCOLN, in handbill circulated in 1887, during a campaign to close saloons. In *Wet Slanders of Abraham Lincoln,* by Albert Porter, the author says that a copy of this handbill was sent to Lincoln's biographers, Nicolay and Hay, and they declared that they were unable to discover the statement in any of his papers or speeches. *Every Evening,* 12 Feb., 1926, states that there are affidavits extant to the effect that Col. John B. Goodwin, of Atlanta, Ga., admitted he had fabricated the statement.

11
Brown home-brew served for wine.

MARGARET J. PRESTON, *The First Thanksgiving Day.*

12
There is as much chance of repealing the Eighteenth Amendment as there is for a humming-bird to fly to the planet Mars with the Washington Monument tied to its tail.

MORRIS SHEPPARD, Senator from Texas, *Newspaper Interview,* 24 Sept., 1930.

13
We drained the flask we dared not keep
And laughed and talked ourselves to sleep.

J. C. SQUIRE, *Approaching New York.*

14
In the whole course of history, there's been no government that could alter the laws of nature. When by mere legislation man can

stop fruit from fermenting of its own accord after it falls to the ground, he can talk about a law of prohibition. The very word destroys its meaning. You can't prohibit nature.

E. TEMPLE THURSTON, *Mr. Bottleby Does Something.*

1
It was the Eighteenth Amendment that for the first time in our history challenged the integrity of the compact between the States and struck at the heart of our Federal system —the principles of local self-government.

OSCAR W. UNDERWOOD, *Drifting Sands of Party Politics*, p. 365.

2
Temperance is moderation in the things that are good and total abstinence from the things that are bad.

FRANCES E. WILLARD. "The accepted definition when the W.C.T.U. was organized as a total abstinence society in 1874, and handed down through its records."—MRS. ELLA A. BOOLE, *Letter to Compiler*, 10 June, 1932.

3
There is as much whisky consumed in Iowa now as before . . . "for medicinal purposes only," and on the boot-leg plan.

Editorial: Omaha Herald, 1889.

The bootlegger is a grim spectre to the anti-prohibitionist. He is a man who wears boots in whose tops are concealed a flask or two of liquor.

Editorial: Voice, N. Y., 17 July, 1890.

PROMISE

I—Promise: Apothegms

4
Promise is most given when the least is said.

GEORGE CHAPMAN, *Hero and Leander*, l. 234.

5
Promise is debt.

CHAUCER, *Man of Law's Tale: Prologue.*

6
There was never promise made, but it was broken or kept.

QUEEN ELIZABETH. (JOHN DEE, *Diary*, p. 37.)

7
A man apt to promise is apt to forget.

THOMAS FULLER, *Gnomologia*, No. 271.

He promises like a merchantman and pays like a man-of-war.

THOMAS FULLER, *Gnomologia*. No. 2007.

8
You never bade me hope, 'tis true;
  I asked you not to swear:
But I looked in those eyes of blue,
  And read a promise there.

GERALD GRIFFIN, *You Never Bade Me Hope.*

9
Promise is a promise, dough you make it in de dark er de moon.

JOEL CHANDLER HARRIS, *Nights with Uncle Remus*, Ch. 39.

10
Some persons make promises for the pleasure of breaking them.

WILLIAM HAZLITT, *Characteristics*, p. 145.

11
Many promises impair confidence. (Multa fidem promissa levant.)

HORACE, *Epistles*. Bk. ii, epis. 2, l. 10.

12
Ah! what a fine promise La Châtre has! (Ah! le bon billet qu'a La Châtre!)

NINON DE L'ENCLOS, when taking another lover, after promising the Marquis de La Châtre to be faithful to him in his absence. "It became," says Sainte-Beuve, "a proverb upon empty assurances."

13
A promise to men in grief is lightly broken.

JOHN MASEFIELD, *The Wild Swan.*

14
Be sure to promise: what harm is there in promises? In promises anyone can be rich. (Promittas facito: quid enim promittere lædit? Pollicitis dives quilibet esse potest.)

OVID, *Ars Amatoria*. Bk. i, l. 443. The way to win a woman.

Promise, promise; want for no promising.

GEORGE CHAPMAN, *Monsieur d'Olive*. Act iii, sc. 1.

Promise, large promise, is the soul of an advertisement.

SAMUEL JOHNSON, *The Idler*. No. 40.

15
To promise seas and mountains. (Maria montisque polliceri.)

SALLUST, *Catiline*. Ch. xxiii, sec. 3.

Promising mountains of gold. (Montis auri pollicens.)

TERENCE, *Phormio*, l. 68.

16
Promises and pie-crust are made to be broken.

SWIFT, *Polite Conversation*. Dial. i.

Fair promises avail but little,
Like too rich pie-crust, they're so brittle.

EDWARD WARD, *Hudibras Redivivus*. Pt. v, canto vii, l. 9.

II—Promise and Performance

17
If we've promised them aught, let us keep our
  promise!

ROBERT BROWNING, *The Pied Piper*. Pt. xv.

18
Great promise, small performance.

JOHN HEYWOOD, *Epigrams*. Cent. v, No. 10.

Those who are quick to promise are generally slow to perform.

C. H. SPURGEON, *Ploughman's Pictures*, 18.

19
Half the promises people say were never kept were never made.

E. W. HOWE, *Howe's Monthly.*

20
We promise according to our hopes, and perform according to our fears. (Nous promettons selon nos espérances, et nous tenons selon nos craintes.)

LA ROCHEFOUCAULD, *Maximes*. No. 38.

21
Fair words fat few; great promises without

performance, delight for the time, but irk ever after.

JOHN LYLY, *Euphues and His England*, p. 476.

1 Giants in
Their promises, but, those obtained, weak pigmies
In their performance.

MASSINGER, *Great Duke of Florence*. Act ii, sc. 3.

2
Begin to supplement your promises with deeds. (Incipe pollicitis addere facta tuis.)

OVID, *Amores*. Bk. ii, eleg. 16, l. 48.

His presents are falling short of his promises. (Quia non suppetunt dictis data.)

PLAUTUS, *Asinaria*, l. 56. (Act i, sc. 1.)

3
Thy promises are like Adonis' gardens
That one day bloom'd and fruitful were the next.

SHAKESPEARE, *I Henry VI*. Act i, sc. 6, l. 6.

He was ever precise in promise-keeping.

SHAKESPEARE, *Measure for Measure*, i, 2, 76.

And though he promise to his loss,
He makes his promise good.

TATE AND BRADY, *Psalm XV*.

4
His promises were, as he then was, mighty;
But his performance, as he is now, nothing.

SHAKESPEARE, *Henry VIII*. Act. iv, sc. 2, l. 41.

Promising is the very air o' the time; it opens the eyes of expectation: performance is ever the duller for his act; and, but in the plainer and simpler kind of people, the deed of saying is quite out of use.

SHAKESPEARE, *Timon of Athens*. Act v, sc. 1, l. 24.

He will spend his mouth, and promise, like Brabbler the hound; but when he performs, astronomers foretell it.

SHAKESPEARE, *Troilus and Cressida*, v, 1, 97.

5
And be these juggling fiends no more believ'd,
That palter with us in a double sense:
That keep the word of promise to our ear,
And break it to our hope.

SHAKESPEARE, *Macbeth*. Act v, sc. 8, l. 19.

6
They promise mountains, and perform molehills.

C. H. SPURGEON, *Ploughman's Pictures*, 18.

6a
The righteous promise little and perform much; the wicked promise much and perform not even a little.

Babylonian Talmud: Baba Metsia, p. 87a.

PROOF

7
What is now proved was once only imagin'd.

WILLIAM BLAKE, *Proverbs of Hell*.

8
The proof of the pudding is the eating.

CERVANTES, *Don Quixote*. Pt. ii, ch. 24.

9
Compassed about with so great a cloud of witnesses.

New Testament: Hebrews, xii, 1.

10
We must never assume that which is incapable of proof.

G. H. LEWES, *Physiology of Common Life*. Ch. 13.

11
You cannot demonstrate an emotion or prove an aspiration.

JOHN MORLEY, *Rousseau*, p. 402.

12
The event proves the act. (Exitus acta probat.)

OVID, *Heroides*. Eleg. ii, l. 85. Adopted as a motto by George Washington.

13
For when one's proofs are aptly chosen,
Four are as valid as four dozen.

MATTHEW PRIOR, *Alma*. Canto i, l. 514.

14
He who furnishes a voucher for his statements argues himself unknown. (Qui notorem dat, ignotus est.)

SENECA, *Epistulæ ad Lucilium*. Epis. 39, sec. 2.

15
Who finds the heifer dead and bleeding fresh
And sees fast by a butcher with an axe,
But will suspect 'twas he that made the slaughter?

SHAKESPEARE, *II Henry VI*. Act iii, sc. 2, l. 188.

Sir, he made a chimney in my father's house, and the bricks are alive at this day to testify it; therefore deny it not.

SHAKESPEARE, *II Henry VI*. Act iv, sc. 2, l. 156.

16 To vouch this, is no proof,
Without more wider and more overt test
Than these thin habits and poor likelihoods
Of modern seeming do prefer against him.

SHAKESPEARE, *Othello*. Act i, sc. 3, l. 106.

Be sure of it; give me the ocular proof.

SHAKESPEARE, *Othello*. Act iii, sc. 3, l. 360.

See also under EYE.

Where are the evidence that do accuse me?

SHAKESPEARE, *Richard III*. Act i, sc. 4, l. 188.

17
For nothing worthy proving can be proven,
Nor yet disproven.

TENNYSON, *The Ancient Sage*, l. 66.

18
Prove all things; hold fast that which is good.

New Testament: I Thessalonians, v, 21.

19
Some circumstantial evidence is very strong, as when you find a trout in the milk.

H. D. THOREAU, *Journal*, 11 Nov., 1850.

PROPERTY

See also Possessions

20
That man does not possess his estate; his estate possesses him.

BION, of a niggardly rich man. (DIOGENES LAERTIUS, *Bion*. Bk. iv, sec. 50.)

If a man owns land, the land owns him.

EMERSON, *Conduct of Life: Wealth*.

My cow milks me.

EMERSON, *Journals*. Vol. v, p. 406.

1
The power of perpetuating our property in our families is one of the most valuable and interesting circumstances belonging to it, and that which tends the most to the perpetuation of society itself.

EDMUND BURKE, *Reflections on the Revolution in France.*

2
Property has its duties as well as its rights.

THOMAS DRUMMOND, *Letter to the Landlords of Tipperary,* 22 May, 1838. "The letter was jointly composed by Wolfe, Drummond and Chief Baron Pigot, and none of them was afterwards able to say who suggested the celebrated phrase."—MCLENNAN, *Memoir of Thomas Drummond,* p. 338. It is usually credited to Drummond, and is engraved on the pedestal of his statue in the City Hall, Dublin. Disraeli appropriated the phrase without credit in his novel, *Sybil,* bk. ii, ch. 11.

We mustn't forget that property has duties even if other people forget that it has rights.

HENRY ARTHUR JONES, *The Triumph of the Philistines.* Act i.

3
Some people talk of morality, and some of religion, but give me a little snug property.

MARIA EDGEWORTH, *The Absentee.* Ch. 2.

4
Whence you obtain your property no one inquires, but it is necessary that you have it. (Unde habeas quærit nemo; sed oportet habere.)

ENNIUS. (JUVENAL, *Satires.* Sat. xiv, l. 206.)

How you get it, that is the question; whether by right or by wrong. (Quo modo habeas, id refert, jurene anne injuria.)

PLAUTUS, *Rudens,* l. 1069. (Act iv, sc. 4.)

I don't care how, as long as I get it. (Mea nil re fert, dum potiar modo.)

TERENCE, *Eunuchus,* l. 320. (Act ii, sc. 3.)

See also MONEY: MAKING MONEY.

5
What we call real estate—the solid ground to build a house on—is the broad foundation on which nearly all the guilt of this world rests.

HAWTHORNE, *The House of the Seven Gables: The Flight of the Two Owls.*

6
Endeavor vigorously to increase your property. (Rem strenuus auge.)

HORACE, *Epistles.* Bk. i, ep. 7, l. 71.

Rich in lands, rich in money put out to usury. (Dives agris, dives positis in fœnore nummis.)

HORACE, *Ars Poetica,* l. 421; *Satires,* i, 2, 13.

7
The personal right to acquire property, which is a natural right, gives to property, when acquired, a right to protection, as a social right.

JAMES MADISON, *Writings.* Vol. iv, p. 51.

8
Worth now lies in what a man is worth: property gives honors, property brings friendships; everywhere the poor man is trodden down. (In pretio pretium nunc est; dat census honores, Census amicitias; pauper ubique jacet.)

OVID, *Fasti.* Bk. i, l. 217.

9
Property is theft. (La propriété, c'est le vol.)

P. J. PROUDHON, *Principle of Right.* Ch. 1.

Exclusive property is a theft against nature. (La propriété exclusive est un vol dans la nature.)

JEAN PIERRE BRISSOT.

Property, says Prudhon, is theft. That is the only perfect truism that has been uttered on the subject.

BERNARD SHAW, *Maxims for Revolutionists.*

10
Whether we force the man's property from him by pinching his stomach, or pinching his fingers, makes some difference anatomically; morally, none whatsoever.

RUSKIN, *The Two Paths.* Lect. v, sec. 3.

11
Property assures what toil acquires.

RICHARD SAVAGE, *Of Public Spirit,* l. 39.

12
My son! the road the human being travels, . . .
Curves round the cornfield and the hill of vines,
Honouring the holy bounds of property!

SCHILLER, *Die Piccolomini.* Act i, sc. 4. (Coleridge, tr.)

13
Lord of thy presence and no land beside.

SHAKESPEARE, *King John.* Act i, sc. 1, l. 137.

14
Dosn't thou 'ear my 'erse's legs, as they canters awaäy?
Proputty, proputty, proputty—that's what I 'ears them saäy.

TENNYSON, *Northern Farmer, New Style.* St. 1.

15
Give a man the secure possession of a bleak rock, and he will turn it into a garden; give him a nine years' lease of a garden, and he will convert it into a desert. . . . The magic of property turns sand into gold.

ARTHUR YOUNG, *Travels in France,* 30 July, and 7 Nov., 1787.

PROPHECY AND PROPHETS

I—Prophecy

16
The passion of prying into futurity makes a striking part of the history of human nature.

ROBERT BURNS, *Hallowe'en: Introduction.*

17
Of all the horrid, hideous notes of woe,
Sadder than owl-songs or the midnight blast,
Is that portentous phrase, "I told you so,"
Utter'd by friends, those prophets of the past.

BYRON, *Don Juan.* Canto xiv, st. 50.

18
Ancestral voices prophesying war.

S. T. COLERIDGE, *Kubla Khan.*

19
We know in part, and we prophesy in part.

New Testament: I Corinthians, xiii, 9.

1
Sweet is the harp of prophecy; too sweet
Not to be wrong'd by a mere mortal touch.
COWPER, *The Task*. Bk. vi, l. 747.

Mean you to prophesy, or but to preach?
COWPER, *Table Talk*, l. 479.

2
Divinations, and soothsayings, and dreams are vain.
Apocrypha: Ecclesiasticus, xxxiv, 5.

All prophecies make sad reading when their term has elapsed.
JOSEPH W. KRUTCH, *The Modern Temper*, p. 59.

The prophesying business is like writing fugues; it is fatal to everyone save the man of absolute genius.
H. L. MENCKEN, *Prejudices*. Ser. i, p. 31.

3
Thy voice sounds like a prophet's word;
And in its hollow tones are heard
The thanks of millions yet to be.
FITZ-GREENE HALLECK, *Marco Bozzaris*.

4
Whatever I state either will come to pass or will not; truly the great Apollo has given me the art of divination. (Quidquid dicam, aut erit aut non: Divinare etenim magnus mihi donat Apollo.)
HORACE, *Satires*. Bk. ii, sat. 5, l. 59.

5
Your sons and your daughters shall prophesy, your old men shall dream dreams, your young men shall see visions.
Old Testament: Joel, ii, 28.

Your sons and your daughters shall prophesy, and your young men shall see visions, and your old men shall dream dreams.
New Testament: Acts, ii, 17.

6
I will eat exceedingly, and prophesy.
BEN JONSON, *Bartholomew Fair*. Act i.

7
Can ye not discern the signs of the times?
New Testament: Matthew, xvi, 3.

8
O, my prophetic soul! My uncle!
SHAKESPEARE, *Hamlet*. Act i, sc. 5, l. 40.

9
There is a history in all men's lives,
Figuring the nature of the times deceased;
The which observed, a man may prophesy.
SHAKESPEARE, *II Henry IV*. Act iii, sc. 1, l. 80.

Over thy wounds now do I prophesy.
SHAKESPEARE, *Julius Cæsar*. Act iii, sc. 1, l. 259.

10
If you can look into the seeds of time,
And say which grain will grow and which will
not,
Speak then to me, who neither beg nor fear
Your favours nor your hate.
SHAKESPEARE, *Macbeth*. Act i, sc. 3, l. 58.

11
I prophesied that, though I never told anybody.
HORACE AND JAMES SMITH, *Rejected Addresses*. No. 5, *Hampshire Farmer's Address*.

PROPHECY AND PROPHETS

12
I am about to die, and that is the hour in which men are gifted with prophetic power.
SOCRATES. (PLATO, *Apology*. Sec. 30.)

'Tis the sunset of life gives me mystical lore.
THOMAS CAMPBELL, *Lochiel's Warning*, l. 55.

Some long experienced souls in the world, before their dislodging, arrive to the height of prophetic spirits.
ERASMUS, *The Praise of Folly*.

Till old experience do attain
To something like prophetic strain.
MILTON, *Il Penseroso*, l. 173.

II—Prophecy: The Prophet

See also Oracle

13
When the prophet beats the ass,
The angel intercedes.
E. B. BROWNING, *Aurora Leigh*. Bk. viii, l. 795.

14
The prophet's mantle, ere his flight began,
Dropt on the world—a sacred gift to man.
CAMPBELL, *The Pleasures of Hope*. Pt. i, l. 43.

15
It is surprising that an augur can see an augur without smiling. (Mirabile videtur quod non redeat haruspex cum haruspicum viderit.)
CICERO, *De Natura Deorum*. Bk. i, ch. 26, 71.

16
In yonder grave a Druid lies.
COLLINS, *Ode on the Death of Mr. Thomson*.

17
Each prophet comes presently to identify himself with his thought, and to esteem his hat and shoes sacred.
EMERSON, *Essays, Second Series: Nature*.

18
He is the best diviner who conjectures well. (Μάντις δ' ἄριστος ὅστις εἰκάζει καλῶς.)
EURIPIDES, *Fragments*.

I shall always consider the best guesser the best prophet. (Bene qui conjiciet, vatem hunc perhibebo optimum.)
CICERO, *De Divinatione*. Bk. ii, sec. 5.

The best qualification of a prophet is to have a good memory.
LORD HALIFAX, *Works*, p. 249.

19
Prophet of evil! never hadst thou yet
A cheerful word for me. To mark the signs
Of coming mischief is thy great delight,
Good dost thou ne'er foretell nor bring to
pass.
HOMER, *Iliad*. Bk. i, l. 138. (Bryant, tr.)

And better skill'd in dark events to come.
HOMER, *Odyssey*. Bk. v, l. 219. (Pope, tr.)

20
God has granted to every people a prophet in its own tongue.
The Koran. (EMERSON, *Representative Men: Napoleon*.)

God, when he makes the prophet, does not unmake the man.
JOHN LOCKE. (EMERSON, *Representative Men: Swedenborg*.)

1
Thine was the prophet's vision, thine
The exultation, the divine
Insanity of noble minds,
That never falters nor abates,
But labors and endures and waits,
Till all that it foresees it finds,
Or what it cannot find creates!
LONGFELLOW, *Kéramos.*

2
It takes a mind like Dannel's, fact, ez big ez all ou' doors
To find out thet it looks like rain arter it fairly pours.
J. R. LOWELL, *The Biglow Papers.* Ser. i, No. 9, l. 97.

3
Beware of false prophets, which come to you in sheep's clothing, but inwardly they are ravening wolves.
New Testament: Matthew, vii, 15.

Take heed of a prophetess.
GEORGE HERBERT, *Jacula Prudentum.*

4
A prophet is not without honour, save in his own country, and in his own house.
New Testament: Matthew, xiii, 57; *Mark,* vi, 4; *Luke,* iv, 24; *John,* iv, 44.

No man has been a prophet, not only in his own house, but in his own country, saith the experience of histories.
MONTAIGNE, *Essays.* Bk. iii, ch. 2.

5
What should I be but a prophet and a liar,
Whose mother was a leprechaun, whose father was a friar?
Teethed on a crucifix and cradled under water,
What should I be but the fiend's god-daughter?
EDNA ST. VINCENT MILLAY, *The Singing-Woman from the Wood's Edge.*

6
No nightly trance, or breathed spell
Inspires the pale-ey'd Priest from the prophetic cell.
MILTON, *Hymn on the Morning of Christ's Nativity,* l. 179.

7
That Prophet ill sustains his holy call,
Who finds not heav'ns to suit the tastes of all.
THOMAS MOORE, *Lalla Rookh: The Veiled Prophet,* l. 558.

8
No prophecy of the scripture is of any private interpretation.
New Testament: II Peter, i, 20.

9
I ought to let my hair grow and set up for a fortune-teller. (Capillum promittam optimumst occipiamque hariolari.)
PLAUTUS, *Rudens,* l. 376. (Act ii, sc. 3.)

10
"Prophet!" said I, "thing of evil—prophet still, if bird or devil!"
EDGAR ALLAN POE, *The Raven.* St. 16.

11
With the fond maids in palmistry he deals;
They tell the secret first which he reveals.
MATTHEW PRIOR, *Henry and Emma,* l. 134.

12
Is Saul also among the prophets?
Old Testament: I Samuel, x, 11.

13
"In the name of the Prophet—figs!"
HORACE AND JAMES SMITH, *Rejected Addresses: Johnson's Ghost.*

14
How long have you been a sectary astronomical?
SHAKESPEARE, *King Lear.* Act i, sc. 2, l. 166.

15
Prophets are all a money-getting tribe. (Τὸ μαντικὸν γὰρ πᾶν φιλάργυρον γένος.)
SOPHOCLES, *Antigone,* l. 1055.

16
He'd rather choose that I should die
Than his prediction prove a lie.
SWIFT, *On the Death of Dr. Swift,* l. 131.

17
Alas for the ignorant minds of the Seers! (Heu vatum ignaræ mentes!)
VERGIL, *Æneid.* Bk. iv, l. 65.

18
He too was a king, and the augur best beloved of king Turnus; yet he could not by augury avert his doom. (Rex idem et regi Turno gratissimus augur; Sed non augurio potuit depellere pestem.)
VERGIL, *Æneid.* Bk. ix, l. 327.

19
Prognostics do not always prove prophecies, at least the wisest prophets make sure of the event first.
HORACE WALPOLE, *Letter to Thomas Walpole,* 9 Feb., 1785.

My gran'ther's rule was safer 'n 'tis to crow:
Don't never prophesy—onless ye know.
J. R. LOWELL, *Mason and Slidell.*

20
Your fathers, where are they? And the prophets, do they live forever?
Old Testament: Zechariah, i, 5.

PROSPERITY

I—Prosperity: Its Dangers

21
Prosperity is a feeble reed. (C'est un faible roseau que la prospérité.)
DANIEL D'ANCHÈRES, *Tyr et Sidon.*

22
In prosperity, when the stream of life flows according to our wishes, let us diligently avoid all arrogance, haughtiness and pride. (In rebus prosperis et ad voluntatem nostram flu-

entibus superbiam magnopere, fastidium arrogantiamque fugiamus.)

CICERO, *De Officiis*. Bk. i, ch. 26, sec. 90.

In prosperity one should resolve nothing arrogantly or vindictively against anyone. (In secundis rebus nihil in quemquam superbe ac violenter consulere decet.)

LIVY, *History*. Bk. xlv, sec. 8.

1
And you shall find the greatest enemy
A man can have is his prosperity.

SAMUEL DANIEL, *Philotas: Dedication*, l. 13.

2
Everything in the world may be endured, except only a succession of prosperous days. (Alles in der Welt lässt sich ertragen,
Nur nicht eine Reihe von schönen Tagen.)

GOETHE, *Sprüche in Reimen*, iii.

3
Prosperity lets go the bridle.

H. G. BOHN, *Hand-Book of Proverbs*, p. 476.

Prosperity destroys fools, and endangers the wise.

H. G. BOHN, *Hand-Book of Proverbs*, p. 476.

4
As you bear your prosperity, Celsus, so shall we bear with you. (Ut tu fortunam, sic nos te, Celse, feremus.)

HORACE, *Epistles*. Bk. i, epis. 8, l. 17.

5
The prosperous man is never sure that he is loved for himself. (Felix se nescit amari.)

LUCAN, *De Bello Civili*. Bk. vii, l. 727.

Prosperity makes few friends. (La prospérité fait peu d'amis.)

VAUVENARGUES, *Réflexions*. No. 17.

6
Pride waxes in prosperity, nor is it easy to bear good fortune with equal mind. (Luxuriant animi rebus plerumque secundis, Nec facile est æqua commoda mente pati.)

OVID, *Ars Amatoria*. Bk. ii, l. 437.

Prosperity can change man's nature; and seldom is any one cautious enough to resist the effects of good fortune. (Res secundæ valent commutare naturam, et raro quisquam erga bona sua satis cautus est.)

QUINTUS CURTIUS RUFUS, *De Rebus Gestis Alexandri Magni*. Bk. x, ch. 1, sec. 40.

7
How much does great prosperity overspread the mind with darkness. (Quantum caliginis mentibus nostris objicit magna felicitas!)

SENECA, *De Brevitate Vitæ*. Sec. 13.

When God has once begun to oppress the prosperous, he bears down hard. To such an end do mighty fortunes come. (Semel profeto premere felices deus Cum cœpit, urget. Hos habent magna exitus.)

SENECA, *Hercules Œtæus*, l. 713.

8
Seeing upon how slippery a place
Fortune for mortals and misfortune stand,
The man who lives at ease should ever look
For rocks ahead, and when he prospers most
Watch lest he suffer shipwreck unawares.

SOPHOCLES, *Philoctetes*, l. 502.

9
We are corrupted by prosperity. (Felicitate corrumpimur.)

TACITUS, *History*. Bk. i, sec. 15.

10
Let me see no other conflict but with prosperity. If my path run on before me level and smooth, it is all a mirage; in reality it is steep and arduous as a chamois pass.

H. D. THOREAU, *Journal*, 25 June, 1840.

11
Prosperity doth bewitch men, seeming clear;
As seas do laugh, show white, when rocks are near.

JOHN WEBSTER, *The White Devil*. Act v, sc. 6.

II—Prosperity and Adversity

12
If Fortune favors, no need for toil.
If Fortune aids not, so much the less toil.
(Si fortuna juvat, nihil laboris:
Si non adjuvat, hoc minus laboris.)

AUSONIUS [?], *Septem Sapientum Sententiæ: No. 4, Periander*.

If Fortune favors, do not rejoice;
If Fortune thunders, do not despond.
(Si fortuna juvat, caveto tolli:
Si fortune tunat caveto mergi.)

AUSONIUS [?], *Septem Sapientum Sententiæ*. Another rendering.

13
Prosperity is the blessing of the Old Testament; adversity is the blessing of the New, which carrieth the greater benediction.

FRANCIS BACON, *Essays: Of Adversity*.

Prosperity is not without many fears and distastes; and adversity is not without comforts and hopes.

FRANCIS BACON, *Essays: Of Adversity*.

14
He who swells in prosperity, will shrink in adversity.

H. G. BOHN, *Hand-Book of Proverbs*, 401.

It is a sign of weakness not to bear prosperity as well as adversity with moderation. (Ut adversus res, sic secundas immoderate ferre levitatis est.)

CICERO, *De Officiis*. Bk. i, ch. 26, sec. 90.

15
Reverse cannot befall that fine Prosperity
Whose sources are interior.
As soon Adversity
A diamond overtake.

EMILY DICKINSON, *Poems*. Pt. v, No. 8.

16
In the day of prosperity be joyful, but in the day of adversity consider.

Old Testament: Ecclesiastes, vii, 14.

In prosperity, caution; in adversity, patience.

JOHN RAY, *English Proverbs*.

Take your part as it cometh, of rough and eke of smooth.

UNKNOWN, *Beryn*, 37. (c. 1400)

1
Adversity is easier borne than prosperity forgot.

THOMAS FULLER, *Gnomologia*. No. 763.

2
Prosperity is a great teacher; adversity is a greater.

WILLIAM HAZLITT, *Sketches and Essays: On the Conversation of Lords.*

3
Hopeful in adversity, fearful in prosperity, is the heart that is prepared for weal or woe. (Sperat infestis, metuit secundis, Alteram sortem bene preparatum Pectus.)

HORACE, *Odes*. Bk. ii, ode 10, l. 13.

If hindrances obstruct thy way,
Thy magnanimity display.
And let thy strength be seen:
But O, if Fortune fill thy sail
With more than a propitious gale,
Take half thy canvas in.

HORACE, *Odes*, ii, 10. (Cowper, tr.)

4
Adversity is wont to reveal genius, prosperity to hide it. (Ingenium res adversæ nudare solent, celare secundæ.)

HORACE, *Satires*. Bk. ii, sat. 8, l. 73.

See also POETRY AND POVERTY.

5
Remember that there is nothing stable in human affairs; therefore avoid undue elation in prosperity, or undue depression in adversity.

ISOCRATES, *Ad Demonicum*, iv, 42.

6
We need greater virtues to sustain good than evil fortune. (Il faut de plus grandes vertus pour soutenir la bonne fortune que la mauvaise.)

LA ROCHEFOUCAULD, *Maximes*. No. 25.

See also under FORTUNE.

7
In prosperity he is brave, in doubtful fortune a runaway. (Re secunda fortis est, dubia fugax.)

PHÆDRUS, *Fables*. Bk. v, fab. 2, l. 13.

8
Prosperity proves the fortunate, adversity the great. (Secunda felices, adversa magnos probent.)

PLINY THE YOUNGER, *Panegyric*. Sec. 31.

9
Prosperity makes friends, adversity tries them.

PUBLILIUS SYRUS, *Sententiæ*. No. 872.

See also FRIENDS AND ADVERSITY.

10
We become wiser in the midst of adversity; it is prosperity that takes away righteousness. (Melius in malis sapimus; secunda rectum auferunt.)

SENECA, *Epistulæ ad Lucilium*. Epis. 94, sec. 74.

Affliction teacheth a wicked person some time to pray: Prosperity never.

BEN JONSON, *Explorata: Afflictio Pia Magistra.*

11
The good things which belong to prosperity are to be wished; but the good things that belong to adversity are to be admired. (Bona rerum secundarum, optabilia; adversarum, mirabilia.)

SENECA. (BACON, *Essays: Of Adversity.*)

Happy is he who knows how to bear the estate of either slave or king, and who can match his countenance with either lot. For he who bears his ills with even soul has robbed misfortune of its power.

(Felix quisque novit famulum
Regemque pati vultusque suos
Variare potest. Rapuit vires
pondusque malis casus animo
Qui tulit æquo.)

SENECA, *Hercules Œtæus*, l. 228.

12
Welcome the sour cup of prosperity! Affliction may one day smile again; and until then, sit thee down, sorrow!

SHAKESPEARE, *Love's Labour's Lost*. Act i, sc. 1, l. 316.

13
All men, when prosperity is at its height, ought then chiefly to consider in what way they will endure disaster. (Omnis, quom secundæ res sunt maxumæ, tum maxume Meditari secum oportet quo pacto advorsam ærum nam ferant.)

TERENCE, *Phormio*, l. 241. (Act ii, sc. 1.)

14
To me, Cyrus, it appears more difficult to find a man that bears prosperity well, than one that bears adversity well; for prosperity creates presumption in most men, but adversity brings sobriety to all.

XENOPHON, *Cyropædia*. Bk. viii, ch. 4, sec. 14

Adversity is sometimes hard upon a man; but for one man who can stand prosperity, there are a hundred that will stand adversity.

CARLYLE, *Heroes and Hero-Worship: The Hero as Man of Letters.*

I'll say this fer adversity—people seem to be able to stand it, an' that's more'n I kin say fer prosperity.

KIN HUBBARD, *Abe Martin's Broadcast*, p. 79.

15
Affliction is the good man's shining scene:
Prosperity conceals his brightest ray;
As night to stars, woe lustre gives to man.

YOUNG, *Night Thoughts*. Night ix, l. 406.

III—Prosperity: Public

16
Prosperity is only an instrument to be used, not a deity to be worshipped.

CALVIN COOLIDGE, *Speech*, 11 June, 1928.

17
Prosperity cannot be restored by raids upon the public treasury.

HERBERT HOOVER, *Statement to the Press*, 9 Dec., 1930.

18
Agriculture, manufactures, commerce and

navigation, the four pillars of our prosperity, are the most thriving when left most free to individual enterprise.
THOMAS JEFFERSON, *Writings*. Vol. iii, p. 337.

1
Surer to prosper than prosperity
Could have assured us.
MILTON, *Paradise Lost*. Bk. ii, l. 39.

2
Plenty is the child of peace.
WILLIAM PRYNNE, *Histrio-Mastix*. Act i, sc. 1.

3
If the period of prosperity could be expressed in a single word, that word would be confidence; and if the period of adversity, as we call it, could be expressed in a single word, that word would be distrust.
THOMAS B. REED. (W. A. ROBINSON, *Life*.)

4
There shall be in England seven halfpenny loaves sold for a penny: the three-hooped pot shall have ten hoops; and I will make it a felony to drink small beer.
SHAKESPEARE, *II Henry VI*. Act iv, sc. 2, l. 71.

5
Prosperity's the very bond of love.
SHAKESPEARE, *Winter's Tale*. Act iv, sc. 4, l. 583.

6
We were living in a fairyland of exorbitance, called "prosperity." Poverty is much better.
UNKNOWN. (*The New Yorker*, 7 Feb., 1931.)

7
O how portentous is prosperity!
How, comet-like, it threatens, while it shines!
YOUNG, *Night Thoughts*. Night v, l. 915.

PROSTITUTE, see Whore

PROTECTION, see Tariff

PROVERBS AND FAMILIAR SAYINGS

I—Proverbs: Definitions

8
Certainly apothegms are of excellent use. They are "mucrones verborum," pointed speeches. Cicero prettily called them "salinas," salt pits, that you may extract salt out of and sprinkle it where you will. They serve to be interlaced in continued speech. They serve to be recited upon occasion of themselves. They serve, if you take out the kernel of them and make them your own.
FRANCIS BACON, *Apothegms: Introduction*.

This delivering of knowledge in distinct and disjointed aphorisms doth leave the wit of man more free to turn and toss, and to make use of that which is so delivered to more several purposes and applications.
FRANCIS BACON, *Maxims of the Law: Preface*.

There is some degree of licentiousness and error in forming axioms.
FRANCIS BACON, *Novum Organum: Summary of the Second Part*. Aphorism 17.

9
The genius, wit, and spirit of a nation are discovered in its proverbs.
FRANCIS BACON, *Essays:*

The proverbs of a nation furnish the index to its spirit, and the results of its civilization.
J. G. HOLLAND, *Gold-Foil: An Exordial Essay*.

Maxims are the condensed good sense of nations.
SIR JAMES MACKINTOSH. (Quoted on the title page of Broom's *Legal Maxims*.)

10
There is a certain list of vices committed in all ages, and declaimed against by all authors, which will last as long as human nature; or digested into commonplaces may serve for any theme, and never be out of date until Doomsday.
SIR THOMAS BROWNE, *Pseudodoxia Epidemica*.

11
I do not say a proverb is amiss when aptly and seasonably applied; but to be forever discharging them, right or wrong, hit or miss, renders conversation insipid and vulgar.
CERVANTES, *Don Quixote*. Pt. ii, ch. 43.

This formal fool, your man, speaks naught but proverbs,
And speak men what they can to him he'll answer
With some rhyme, rotten sentence, or old saying,
Such spokes as ye ancient of ye parish use.
HENRY PORTER, *Two Angry Women of Abington*. Sc. 3. (1599)

Sigh'd forth proverbs,
That hunger broke stone walls, that dogs must eat,
That meat was made for mouths, that the gods sent not
Corn for the rich man only.
SHAKESPEARE, *Coriolanus*. Act i, sc. 1, l. 209.

12
There is no proverb which is not true. (No hay refran que no sea verdadero.)
CERVANTES, *Don Quixote*.

13
A proverb is a short sentence based on long experience.
CERVANTES, *Don Quixote*.

Proverbs are the daughters of daily experience. (Spreekworden zijn dochters der dagelijksche ondervinding.)
UNKNOWN. A Dutch proverb.

14
Most maxim-mongers have preferred the prettiness to the justness of a thought, and the turn to the truth.
LORD CHESTERFIELD, *Letters*, 15 Jan., 1753.

Proverbs are art—cheap art. As a general rule they are not true; unless indeed they happen to be mere platitudes.
JOSEPH CONRAD, *Gaspar Ruiz*. Ch. 5.

In all pointed sentences, some degree of accuracy must be sacrificed to conciseness.
SAMUEL JOHNSON, *Works*. Vol. x, p. 286.

1
Proverbial expressions and trite sayings are the flowers of the rhetoric of a vulgar man. . . . A man of fashion never has recourse to proverbs and vulgar aphorisms.

LORD CHESTERFIELD, *Letters*, 27 Sept., 1749.

Never utter the truism, but live it among men.

EMERSON, *Journals*. Vol. iii, p. 455.

To repeat what has been said a thousand times is commonplace.

WILLIAM HAZLITT, *Works*. Vol. i, p. 381.

2
Mean narrow maxims which enslave mankind,
Ne'er from its bias warp thy settled mind.

CHURCHILL, *The Prophecy of Famine*, l. 163.

The mind of man, when its daily maxims are put before it, revolts from anything so stupid, so mean, so poor.

WALTER BAGEHOT, *Literary Studies*. Vol. ii, p. 266.

3
A man of maxims only is like a Cyclops with one eye, and that eye placed in the back of his head.

S. T. COLERIDGE, *Table Talk*, 24 June, 1827.

4
Proverbs are easily made in cold blood.

DICKENS, *Barnaby Rudge*. Ch. 14.

5
Thou shalt become an astonishment, a proverb, and a byword, among all nations.

Old Testament: Deuteronomy, xxviii, 37.

Constant popping off of proverbs will make thee a byword thyself.

THOMAS FULLER, *Intro. ad Prudentiam*, i, 196.

6
Syllogisms do breed or rather are all the variety of man's life. They are the steps by which we walk in all our businesses.

SIR KENELM DIGBY, *Man's Soul*, p. 29.

7
The wise make proverbs and fools repeat them.

ISAAC D'ISRAELI, *Curiosities of Literature*. Ser. ii, vol. i, p. 449.

8
Despise not the discourse of the wise, but acquaint thyself with their proverbs; for of them thou shalt learn instruction.

Apocrypha: Ecclesiasticus, viii, 8.

9
He gave good heed, and sought out, and set in order many proverbs.

Old Testament: Ecclesiastes, xii, 9.

These proverbs, which contained the wisdom of many ages and nations, I assembled and formed into a connected discourse prefixed to the Almanack of 1757, as the harangue of a wise old man to the people attending an auction.

BENJAMIN FRANKLIN, *Autobiography*. Ch. 1. Franklin's memory seems to have been wrong in this, for his reference is undoubtedly to the preface to *Poor Richard* for 1758.

10
Proverbs, like the sacred books of each nation, are the sanctuary of the intuitions.

EMERSON, *Essays, First Series: Compensation*.

11
A proverb is much matter decocted into few words.

THOMAS FULLER, *Worthies of England*. Ch. 2.

Well short in words and well lang in wit.

FRÈRE LORENZ, *Le Somme des Vices et des Vertus*. (1279) Referring to the Lord's Prayer.

12
Don't you go believing in sayings, Picotee; they are all made by men, for their own advantage.

THOMAS HARDY, *Hand of Ethelberta*. Ch. 20.

13
Stories and sayings they will well remember.

GEORGE HERBERT, *Priest to the Temple*. Ch. 7.

14
There are words and maxims whereby you may soothe the pain and cast much of the malady aside. (Sunt verba et voces, quibus hunc lenire dolorem Possis et magnam morbi deponere partem.)

HORACE, *Epistles*. Bk. i, epis. 1, l. 34. Referring to avarice.

15
The People's Voice the voice of God we call;
And what are proverbs but the People's Voice?

JAMES HOWELL, *Before a Great Volume of Proverbs*.

16
Pointed axioms and acute replies fly loose about the world, and are assigned successively to those whom it may be the fashion to celebrate.

SAMUEL JOHNSON, *Lives of the Poets: Waller*.

17
A maxim is the exact and noble expression of an important and unquestionable truth. (Une maxime est l'expression exacte et noble d'une vérité importante et incontestable.)

JOUBERT, *Pensées*. No. 137.

18
A proverb is no proverb to you till life has illustrated it.

KEATS, *Letters*, p. 305.

19
As I pass through my incarnations in every age and race,
I make my proper prostrations to the Gods of the Market Place.
Peering through reverent fingers, I watch them flourish and fall,
And Gods of the Copybook Headings, I notice, outlast them all.

RUDYARD KIPLING, *The Gods of the Copybook Headings*.

We were living in trees when they met us. They showed us each in turn
That Water would certainly wet us, as Fire would certainly burn:

But we found them lacking in Uplift, Vision and
Breadth of Mind,
So we left them to teach the Gorillas while we
followed the March of Mankind. . . .
As it will be in the future, it was at the birth
of Man—
There are only four things certain since Social
Progress began:—
That the Dog returns to his Vomit and the Sow
returns to her mire,
And the burnt Fool's bandaged finger goes wabbling back to the fire.

RUDYARD KIPLING, *The Gods of the Copybook Headings.*

1
Nothing is so useless as a general maxim.

MACAULAY, *Essays: Machiavelli.*

2
Proverbs are the wisdom of the streets.

W. G. BENHAM, *Proverbs*, p. 828.

Copper coinage of wisdom is the way of proverbs.

GEORGE MEREDITH, *Sandra Belloni.* Ch. 40.

3
A maker of maxims is synonymous with a pessimist. (*Maximist, pessimist.*)

JOSEPH ROUX, *Meditations of a Parish Priest: Prelude.*

4
A proverb is one man's wit and all men's wisdom.

LORD JOHN RUSSELL. (MACKINTOSH, *Memoirs.* Vol. ii, p. 473.) Usually quoted, "The wisdom of many, the wit of one."

5
Almost every wise saying has an opposite one, no less wise, to balance it.

GEORGE SANTAYANA, *Little Essays*, p. 237.

7
The proverb is something musty.

SHAKESPEARE, *Hamlet.* Act iii, sc. 2, l. 359.

For I am proverb'd with a grandsire phrase.

SHAKESPEARE, *Romeo and Juliet.* Act i, sc. 4, l. 37.

A most remarkably long-headed, flowing-bearded, and patriarchal proverb.

DICKENS, *Martin Chuzzlewit.* Ch. 13.

9
Patch grief with proverbs.

SHAKESPEARE, *Much Ado About Nothing.* Act v, sc. 1, l. 17.

10
I can tell thee where that saying was born.

SHAKESPEARE, *Twelfth Night.* Act i, sc. 5, l. 9.

An old saying, that was a man when King Pepin of France was a little boy.

SHAKESPEARE, *Love's Labour's Lost*, iv, 1, 121.

11
A short saying oft contains much wisdom.

SOPHOCLES, *Aletes.* Frag. 99.

Much of the wisdom of the world is not wisdom.

EMERSON, *Works.* Vol. i, p. 155.

12
There is a strong feeling in favor of cowardly and prudential proverbs. . . . Most of our pocket wisdom is conceived for the use of mediocre people, to discourage them from ambitious attempts, and generally console them in their mediocrity.

R. L. STEVENSON, *Crabbed Age and Youth.*

14
With a little hoard of maxims preaching
down a daughter's heart.

TENNYSON, *Locksley Hall*, l. 94.

Maxims of the mud.

TENNYSON, *Merlin and Vivien*, l. 49.

15
It is more trouble to make a maxim than it is to do right.

MARK TWAIN, *Pudd'nhead Wilson's New Calendar.*

16
The maxims of men reveal their characters. (Les maximes des hommes décèlent leur cœur.)

VAUVENARGUES, *Réflexions.* No. 107.

II—Proverbs and Familiar Sayings *

The proverbs and sayings which follow are grouped alphabetically according to the key word. Only those are included here which do not fall naturally under other subject headings. "The great refusal" (il gran rifiuto), for example, will be found under Refusal.

17
I will tell you in verse the cities, names, and
sayings of the seven sages:
Cleobulus of Lindus said, "Moderation is
best." (Μέτρον ἄριστον.)
Chilon in hollow Lacedæmon said, "Know
thyself." (Γνῶθι σεατόν.)
Periander, who dwelt in Corinth, said, "Master anger." (Χόλου κρατέειν.)
Pittacus, who was from Mytilene, said,
"Nothing in excess." (Οὐδὲν ἄγαν.)
And Solon, in holy Athens, "Look at the end
of life." (Τέρμα δ' ὁρᾶν βιότοιο.)
Bias of Priene declared that "Most men are
bad." (Τοὺς πλέονας κακίους.)
And Thales of Miletus said, "Shun suretyship." (Ἐγγύην φεύγειν.)

UNKNOWN. (*Greek Anthology.* Bk. ix, epig. 366.)

* Only a few of the best known and most important proverbs have been included in this book. Any one interested in pursuing the subject further should consult the source-books. One of the most important of these is the collection of Latin proverbs (*Sententiæ*), including many translations from the Greek, made by Publilius Syrus, about 40 B.C. Erasmus also made a noteworthy collection (*Adagia*), translated into English by Richard Taverner in 1539. The principal early English collections are: John Heywood, *Proverbs* (1546); John Florio, *First Fruites* (1578), and *Second Frutes* (1591); George Herbert, *Jacula Prudentum* (1640); James Howell, *Proverbs* (1659); John Ray, *English Proverbs* (1670); Thomas Fuller, *Gnomologia* (1732). There are, of course, many modern collections.

1
"You I love, and you alone."
"And so in love says every one."
"Virtue alone is an estate."
"But money's virtue, gold is fate."
"I scorn your gold, and yet I love."
"I'm poor; let's see how kind you'll prove."
"Let love alone be our debate."
"She loves enough that does not hate."

Daniel Defoe, *Moll Flanders*, p. 103. Moll and one of her lovers are capping proverbs.

2
As Love and I late harbour'd in one inn,
With proverbs thus each other entertain:
"In love there is no lack," thus I begin;
"Fair words make fools," replieth he again;
"Who spares to speak doth spare to speed," quoth I;
"As well," saith he, "too forward as too slow";
"Fortune assists the boldest," I reply;
"A hasty man," quoth he, "ne'er wanted woe";
"Labour is light where love," quoth I, "doth pay";
Saith he, "Light burden's heavy, if far borne";
Quoth I, "The main lost, cast the by away";
"Y'have spun a fair thread," he replies in scorn.
And having thus awhile each other thwarted
Fools as we met, so fools again we parted.

Michael Drayton, *Proverbs.*

A

3
A. E. I. O. U.

Frederick III, Emperor of the Holy Roman Empire (1415–1493), had these vowels stamped upon coins and medals and inscribed upon public buildings. They were originally used at the coronation of his predecessor, Albert II, signifying, "Albertus Electus Imperator Optamus Vivat." After Frederick's coronation, the motto was changed to "Archidux Electus Imperator Optime Vivat." Still later to "Austria est imperare orbi universo" (German, "Alles Erdreich ist Oesterreich unterthan"), Austria is to rule the whole universe.

4
"He must be a first-rater," said Sam. "A 1," replied Mr. Roker.

Dickens, *Pickwick Papers*. Ch. 41.

He was six foot o' man, A 1,
Clear grit an' human natur'.

J. R. Lowell, *The Courtin'*.

5
I am Alpha and Omega, the beginning and the ending, saith the Lord.

New Testament: Revelation, i, 8. Alpha is the first and Omega the last letter of the Greek alphabet.

I am Alpha and Omega, the beginning and the end, the first and the last.

New Testament: Revelation, xii, 13.

I am not the first, and shall not be the last.

John Ray, *English Proverbs.* From the Latin proverb, "Primus non sum nec imus."

Undoubtedly you have not been the first, and you will not be, as I suppose, the last.
(Vous n'avez pas été sans doute la première,
Et vous ne serez pas, que je crois, la dernière.)

Molière, *Dépit Amoureux.* Act ii, sc. 9, l. 57.

6
Apache; les Apaches.

Stoddard Dewey. Dewey suggested this name, in 1890, to a French reporter seeking a phrase to describe the La Chapelle gang of desperadoes who were terrorizing Paris.

7
To hold by the apron strings.

John Ray, *English Proverbs.* (1678)

B

8
Between you and me and the bed-post, young master has quarrelled with old master.

Bulwer-Lytton, *Eugene Aram.* Bk. iv, ch. 1.

Between you and me and the general post.

Dickens, *Nicholas Nickleby.* Ch. 10.

9
You whirled them to the back of beyont.

Scott, *The Antiquary.*

10
We saw a knot of others, about a baker's dozen.

Rabelais, *Works.* Bk. v, ch. 22. A baker's dozen is thirteen for twelve. At one time a heavy penalty was inflicted on bakers for short weight, and consequently they added a surplus number of loaves, called the inbread, to avoid all risk of incurring the fine. The thirteenth was the "vantage loaf."

The pleasant institution of napa—the petty gratuity added by the dealer to anything bought—grew the pleasanter, drawn out into Gallicized lagnappe.

G. W. Cable, *Creoles of Louisiana.* Ch. 16. More usually spelled lagniappe, and in current use in the South, especially Louisiana.

11
That bates Bannagher!

William Carleton, *Traits and Stories of the Irish Peasantry: Three Tasks.* (1830)

That bangs Banagher!

William Black, *White Heather.* Ch. 40. (1885)

This beats Bannagher.

W. B. Yeats, *Fairy Tales of the Irish Peasantry*, p. 196.

Banagher is a village in King's Co., on the Shannon. When anything very unusual or unexpected occurs, the people say, "Well, that bangs Banagher!"

P. W. Joyce, *English As We Speak It.*

12
All my eye and Betty Martin.

Carr, *Craven Dialect*, i, 128. A retort to anyone trying to humbug.

Who was Betty Martin, and wherefore should she be so often mentioned in connection with my precious eye or yours?
SOUTHEY, *The Doctor*. Ch. 125.

Only your eye and Miss Elizabeth Martin.
PLANCHÉ, *Extravaganzas*, iv, 158.

1
Big-endians and Little-endians.
JONATHAN SWIFT, *Gulliver, Voyage to Lilliput*. The controversy was as to whether a boiled egg should be broken at the big or little end Big-endians signified the Catholics and Little-endians the Protestants.

2
The Blue Ribbon of the Turf.
BENJAMIN DISRAELI, referring to the Derby. (*Life of Lord George Bentinck*.)

3
Talking of boots. (À propos de bottes.)
REGNARD, *Le Distrait*. A French proverb, applied to sayings or doings which are without motive or relevance. Said to have arisen in the time of Francis I, when a man who had been decided against (debouté) in a lawsuit, told the king that he had been "debotté" (debooted).

4
Now Dragon could kill a wolf in a brace of shakes.
CHARLES READE, *The Cloister and the Hearth*. Ch. 93.

5
The green new broom sweepeth clean.
HEYWOOD, *Proverbs*. Pt. ii, ch. 1. (1546)

Ah, well I wot that a new broom sweepeth clean.
JOHN LYLY, *Euphues*, p. 89. (1579)

6
His palfrey was as brown as a berry.
CHAUCER, *Canterbury Tales: Prologue*, l. 207. (c. 1386)

Thy nose is as brown as a berry.
JOHN TATHAM, *Love Crowns the End*. (1640)

7
For Warwick was a bug that fear'd us all.
SHAKESPEARE, *III Henry VI*. Act v, sc. 2, l. 2.

8
A Big Butter-and-Egg Man.
TEXAS GUINAN, introducing from the floor of her night club in New York a generous stranger who, one night in 1924, paid all the cover charges and distributed $50 bills to the entertainers, and who refused to reveal his name, remarking only that he was in the dairy produce business. The phrase became popular as a designation for a reckless spender or a financial "angel," and was used by George Kaufman as the title for a comedy produced in 1925.

C

9
Your cake is dough, and all your fat in the fire.
THOMAS BECON, *Prayers*, 277. (1559)

My cake is dough.
SHAKESPEARE, *The Taming of the Shrew*. Act v, sc. 1, l. 145. (1594)

10
Set the cart before the horse.
JOHN HEYWOOD, *Proverbs*. Pt. ii, ch. 7. (1546)

Others set carts before the horses.
RABELAIS, *Works*. Bk. v, ch. 22.

To make the plough go before the horse.
JAMES I, *Letter to the Lord Keeper*, July, 1617.

It is folly to put the plough in front of the oxen. (Folie est mettre la charrue devant les bœufs.)
RABELAIS, *Works*. Bk. ii, ch. 11.

11
But catch who that catch might.
JOHN GOWER, *Confessio Amantis*. Bk. vii, l. 4422. (c. 1390)

They catch that catch may, keep and hold fast.
JOHN SKELTON, *Magnyfycence*, l. 1773. (1520)

There's catch as catch can, hit or miss, luck is all.
KANE O'HARA, *Midas*. Act ii, sc. 8. (1761)

12
Carthage should be destroyed. (Delenda est Carthago.)
MARCUS CATO, who ended every speech in the Roman Senate with the words, "Ceterum censeo Carthaginem esse delendam." (PLUTARCH, *Lives: Marcus Cato*. Ch. 27, sec. 1. The Greek is: Καρχηδόνα μὴ εἶναι.)

13
If I can give that Cerberus a sop, I shall be at rest for one day.
WILLIAM CONGREVE, *Love for Love*. Act i, sc. 1. Cerberus, in Roman mythology, is the three-headed dog which guards the entrance to the infernal regions. Whenever a person died, a cake was placed in his hand, to be used as a sop to Cerberus, so that the dead might pass without molestation.

To Cerberus they give a sop
His triple barking mouth to stop.
SWIFT, *On Poetry*, l. 213.

These realms huge Cerberus makes ring with his triple-throated baying, his monstrous bulk crouching in the cavern opposite. To him, seeing the snakes now bristling on his neck, the seer flung a morsel drowsy with honey and drugged meal. . . . The warder buried in sleep, Æneas wins the entrance, and swiftly leaves the bank of that stream whence none return. (Melle soporatam et medicatis frugibus offam Obicit.)
VERGIL, *Æneid*. Bk. vi, l. 417.

14
'Tis as cheap sitting as standing.
SWIFT, *Polite Conversation*. Dial. i.

15
I believe he would make three bits of a cherry. (Je croy qu'il feroit d'une cerise trois morceaux.)
RABELAIS, *Works*. Bk. v, ch. 28.

The old rule of never to make two bites of a cherry.
WILLIAM MAGINN, *O'Doherty's Maxims*, 69. (1824)

Two Bites of a Cherry.
T. B. ALDRICH, Title of story.

1
Clear as a bell.
JOHN RAY. *English Proverbs*, 203. (1670)

Clear as crystal.
UNKNOWN, *Cursor Mundi*, l. 376. (c. 1290)

As clear as the day.
MILES COVERDALE, *Christian State of Matrimony*. Sig. D 8. (1541)

Clearer than the noonday.
Old Testament: Job, xi, 17.

Is it not clearer than the sun at noon-day?
GABRIEL HARVEY, *Letter-Book*, 66. (1579)

As clear as a whistle.
JOHN BYROM, *Epistle to Lloyd*. (1773)

2
Seeing the coast clear, . . . he sate him down.
THOMAS LODGE, *Rosalynde*. (1590)

Herod is now sent home The coast is clear for the return of that holy family
JOSEPH HALL, *Contemplations*, i, 6 (1612)

The coast was clear.
MICHAEL DRAYTON, *Nymphidia*. (1627)

3
Confusion worse confounded.
MILTON, *Paradise Lost*. Bk. ii, l. 996.

Confusion unconfus'd.
YOUNG, *Night Thoughts*. Night ix, l. 1117.

4
I seem to be the person marked for displeasure, and was almost literally sent to Coventry.
DAVID GARRICK, *Correspondence*. Vol ii, p. 237. The phrase is said to have originated during the Civil War in England, when doubtful officers were sent to the garrison at Coventry.

This again sent me to Coventry for the rest of the dinner.
MADAME D'ARBLAY, *Diary*. Vol. ii, p. 427.

Send them into everlasting Coventry.
EMERSON, *Essays, Second Series: Manners*.

5
Who covers thee discovers thee.
CERVANTES, *Don Quixote*. Pt. ii, ch. 5.

6
I warrant you lay abed till the cows came home.
SWIFT, *Polite Conversation*. Dial. 2. (1738)

You may rezoloot till the cows come home.
JOHN HAY, *Banty Jim*.

7
As fruitful a place as any the crow flies over.
BUNYAN, *The Pilgrim's Progress*. Pt. ii.

8
What with her merry sporting, and good nourishing, I began to gather up my crumbs.
JOHN LYLY, *Euphues*, p. 302. (1580) Meaning to be convalescent.

I am recovering and picking up my crums apace.
HOWELL, *Letters*. Bk. i, sec. 2, let. 1.

9
Young maids were as cold as cucumbers.
BEAUMONT AND FLETCHER, *Cupid's Revenge*. Act i, sc. 1. (1615)

Cool as a cucumber could see
The rest of womankind.
JOHN GAY, *Poems*, ii, 278. (1720)

I rose as cool as a cucumber.
SIR WALTER SCOTT, *Journal*, 7 July, 1829.

10
Curfew shall not ring to-night!
ROSE HARTWICK THORPE, *Curfew Must Not Ring To-night*.

11
Cut and come again.
GEORGE CRABBE, *Tales of the Hall*. Pt. vii, l. 27.

D

12
I do not know the lady, but damn her at a venture.
CHARLES LAMB, to an insufferable fellow-guest at a dinner, who was inquiring persistently as to Lamb's acquaintance with persons of note: "Do you know So-and-So? Do you know Thus-and-Thus? Do you know Miss ——?" "No, madam, I do not," Lamb replied, "but damn her at a venture." (*See* LUCAS, *Charles Lamb*. Vol. i, p. 440.)

13
Then all the children of Israel went out, and the congregation was gathered together as one man from Dan even unto Beersheba.
Old Testament: Judges, xx, 1.

14
After us the deluge. (Après nous le déluge.)
MADAME DE POMPADOUR, to Louis XV, after the French defeat at Rossbach, 5 Nov., 1757. The attribution is by J. B. D. Després, in an essay on Madame de Pompadour, in *Mémoires de Madame de Hausset*, p. xix. Sainte-Beuve and La Tour also attribute the saying to her, but LAROUSSE, *Fleurs Historiques*, attributes it to the King. It was original with neither, for it is an old French proverb cited in many collections, and usually applied to spendthrifts.

15
Where's Brummel? Dish'd. Where's Long Pole Wellesley? Diddled.
BYRON, *Don Juan*. Canto xi, st. 77.

16
And whosoever shall not receive you, nor hear you, when ye depart thence, shake off the dust under your feet, for a testimony against them.
New Testament: Mark, vi, 11.

And whosoever shall not receive you, nor hear your words, when ye depart out of that house or city, shake off the dust of your feet.
New Testament: Matthew, x, 14.

E

17
I find a greater fault in myself in suffering another to cut the earth from under my feet.
GEOFFREY FENTON, *Bandello*, ii, 10. (1567)

The grass had been cut from under his feet.
GEORGE PETTIE, *Petite Pallace*, i, 121. (1576)

Thus will you cut the ground from 'neath his feet.
W. S. GILBERT, *Rosencrantz and Guildenstern*.

18
Eclipse first, the rest nowhere.
DENNIS O'KELLY, owner of Eclipse, at Epsom, 3 May, 1769. (*Annals of Sporting*, ii, 271.)

1
Beware how you give any edged tool
Unto a young child and unto a fool.
WILLIAM WAGER, *Longer Thou Livest.* (1568)

It is not good jesting with edged tools.
STEPHEN GOSSON, *School of Abuse,* 57. (1579)

2
It will cost nothing but a little elbow-grease.
UNKNOWN, *New Dict. Canting Crew.* (1690)

Elbow grease gives the best polish.
ROBERT FORBY, *Vocab. East Anglia,* 431.

3
"Now we are even," quoth Steven, when he gave his wife six blows to one.
SWIFT, *Letter to Stella,* 20 Jan., 1711.

F

4
It is a far cry to Lochow.
SCOTT, *Rob Roy.* Ch. 29, note. Lochow and the adjacent districts formed the original seat of the Campbells.

5
You may go farther and fare worse. (Nota mala res optumast.)
PLAUTUS, *Trinummus,* l. 63.

You might have gone further and fared worse.
JOHN HEYWOOD, *Proverbs.* Pt. ii, ch. 4 (1546)

I may go farther and fare worse.
JAMES SHIRLEY, *Love in a Maze.* Act ii, sc. 2.

6
He findeth that surely bindeth.
JOHN BALE, *Kynge Johan,* l. 1897. (c. 1540)

Then catch and hold while I may, fast bind, fast find
JOHN HEYWOOD, *Proverbs.* Pt. i, ch. 3. (1546)

Fast bind, fast find;
A proverb never stale in thrifty mind.
SHAKESPEARE, *The Merchant of Venice.* Act ii, sc. 5, l. 54. (1596)

7
The fat is in the fire.
JOHN HEYWOOD, *Proverbs.* Pt. i, ch. 3. (1546)

All the fat's in the fire.
SMOLLETT, *The Reprisal.* Act i, sc. 8.

8
First come, first served.
HENRY BRINKELOW, *Complaint of Roderick Mors.* Ch. 17. (c. 1540); BEN JONSON, *Bartholomew Fair.* Act ii, sc. 5. (1614)

Whoso that first to mill cometh, first grinds.
CHAUCER, *Wife of Bath's Tale: Prologue,* l. 389 (c. 1386)

9
This is . . . as fit as a fiddle.
WILLIAM HAUGHTON, *English-Men for My Money.* Act iv, sc. 1. (1616)

Looking fit and taut as a fiddle.
R. L. STEVENSON, *Treasure Island.* Ch. 30.

10
His nose as flat as a cake beaten to his face.
ERASMUS, *Adagia.* (Udall, tr. 1542)

Beat all your feathers as flat as pancakes.
THOMAS MIDDLETON, *The Roaring Girl.* Act ii, sc. 1. (1611)

He has crushed his nose . . . as flat as a pancake.
STERNE, *Tristram Shandy.* Bk. iii, ch. 27. (1758)

11
Flat as a flounder.
JOHN FLETCHER, *Women Pleased.* Act ii, sc. 4. (c. 1625)

He laid him squat as a flounder.
RABELAIS, *Works.* Bk. i, ch. 27.

12
This is a pretty flimflam.
BEAUMONT AND FLETCHER, *The Little French Lawyer.* Act iii, sc. 3. (1620)

They with a courtly trick or a flim-flam,
Do nod at me, whilst I the noddy am.
JEREMY TAYLOR, *Works.* (1630)

13
I'll have a fling.
JOHN FLETCHER, *Rule a Wife and Have a Wife.* Act iii, sc. 5. (1624)

14
Fresh and flourishing as the flowers in May.
LEWIS WAGER, *Mary Magdalene* B. 1. (1566)

As fresh as flowers in May.
THOMAS HEYWOOD, *The Fair Maid of the West.* Pt. ii, act i. (1631)

With sweetness fresh as any rose.
JOHN LYDGATE, *Troy Book.* Bk. v, l. 2897. (1420)

That was right fair and fresh as morning rose.
SPENSER, *The Faerie Queene.* Bk. ii, canto ix, st. 36. (1590)

As fresh as a daisy.
EATON STANNARD BARRETT, *Heroine,* iii, 155. (1815)

As fresh as any daisy.
DICKENS, *Cricket on the Hearth.* Chirp 2.

You are looking as fresh as paint.
F. E. SMEDLEY, *Frank Fairlegh.* Ch. 41. (1850)

15
In his own grease I made him fry.
CHAUCER, *Wife of Bath's Prologue,* l. 487. (c. 1386)

Thus is he fried in his own grease.
JOHN LYDGATE, *Temple of Glass,* 14. (c. 1400)

Fat enough to be stewed in their own liquor.
THOMAS FULLER, *Holy and Profane States,* p. 396. (1642)

I stew all night in my own grease.
NATHANIEL COTTON, *Virgil Travestie,* p. 35. (1791)

Let them stew in their own juice.
BISMARCK, to Mr. Malet at Meaux, referring to the French (LABOUCHERE, *Diary of a Besieged Resident.*)

To live on their own juices. (Suo sibi suco vivont.)
PLAUTUS, *Captivi,* l. 81.

16
Out of the frying-pan into the fire. (Pervenimus igitur de calcaria in carbonarium.)
TERTULLIAN, *De Carne Christi.* Ch. 6.

But as the flounder doth,
Leap out of the frying pan into the fire.
JOHN HEYWOOD, *Proverbs.* Pt. ii, ch. 5. (1546)

Leap they like a flounder out of a frying-pan into the fire.
Sir Thomas More, *Works*, p. 179. (1557)

But I was saved, as is the flounder, when
He leapeth from the dish into the fire.
Sir John Harington, *Orlando Furioso*. Bk. xiii, st. 28. (1591)

As Æsop's fishes, they leap from the frying-pan into the fire itself.
Robert Burton, *Anatomy of Melancholy*. Pt. i, sec. 4, mem. 1. (1621)

As the saying is, the people who would avoid the slavery of freemen, which is smoke and appearance, has fallen under the tyranny of slaves, which is fire.
Plato, *The Republic*. Sec. 569.

1
To leap out of the hall into the kitchen, or out of Christ's blessing into the warm sun.
John Palsgrave, *Acolastus*. Sig. H3. (1540) The proverb refers to the haste of the congregation to leave the church after the benediction has been pronounced.

Good king, thou must approve the common saw,
That out of heaven's benediction comest
To the warm sun!
Shakespeare, *King Lear*. Act ii, sc. 2, l. 166.

Out of God's blessing into the warm sun.
Cervantes, *Don Quixote*. Pt. i, bk. 3, ch. 4. Motteux takes the saying to mean "Out of the frying pan into the fire," which is an error. "From better to worse" would be nearer its meaning.

2
I'll make the fur
Fly 'bout the ears of the old cur.
Butler, *Hudibras*. Pt. i, canto iii, l. 278.

G

3
Higher than Gilderoy's kite.
Said to be an allusion to the high gallows on which a notorious robber, Patrick McGregor, alias Gilderoy, was hanged at Edinburgh, July, 1638, from which his body looked like a kite.

They hung him high aboon the rest,
He was sae trim a boy;
There died the youth whom I loved best,
My handsome Gilderoy.
Unknown, *Gilderoy*. (Percy, *Reliques*. Ser. i, bk. iii, No. 12.) The greater the crime the higher the gallows was at one time a practical legal axiom.

4
Add to golden numbers golden numbers.
Thomas Dekker, *Patient Grissell*. Act i, sc. 1.

5
Gone, glimmering.
Byron, *Childe Harold*. Canto ii, st. 2.

6
By all that's good and glorious.
Byron, *Sardanapalus*. Act i, sc. 2.

7
But for the grace of God there goes John Bradford.
John Bradford, on seeing some criminals on the way to execution, c. 1553. A traditional ascription. (See *Dictionary of National Biography*, vol. vi, p. 159.) The saying has been incorrectly attributed to John Bunyan and to John Wesley.

8
But for this whoreson cutting of throats, it goes a little against the grain.
Dryden, *Amboyna*. Act i, sc. 1. (1673)

Hither, though much against the grain,
The Dean has carried Lady Jane.
Swift, *Works*. Vol. 14, p. 250. (c. 1730)

Which again, naturally, rubs against the grain of Mr. Bazzard.
Dickens, *Edwin Drood*. Ch. 20.

9
I will go against the hair in all things, so I may please thee in any thing.
John Lyly, *Euphues*, p. 394. (1580)

He is . . . merry against the hair.
Shakespeare, *Troilus and Cressida*. Act i, sc. 2, l. 26. (1609)

10
The more he thought on't, the madder he grew,
Until he vowed by the great horn spoon,
Unless they did the thing that was right,
He'd give them a licking, and that pretty soon.
Unknown, *French Claim*. (McCarty, *National Song Book*, i, 222. 1842.)

Sez Mr. Foote,
"I should like to shoot
The holl gang, by the gret horn spoon!" sez he.
J. R. Lowell, *The Debate in the Sennit*.

H

11
He waxed hail fellow with him.
William Horman, *Vulgaria*, 148. (1519)

They would be hail fellow well-met with him.
Thomas Becon, *Catechism*, 561. (c. 1550)

Hail fellow well met, all dirty and wet;
Find out, if you can, who's master, who's man.
Swift, *My Lady's Lamentation*.

If he be not fellow with the best king, thou shalt find the best king of good fellows.
Shakespeare, *Henry V*. Act v, sc. 2, l. 261.

12
The half is more than the whole. (Τὸ ἥμισυ τοῦ παντὸς πλεῖον εἶναι.)
Pittacus. (Diogenes Laertius, *Pittacus*. Bk. i, sec. 75.)

Fools! they know not how much the half exceeds the whole. (Νήπιοι, οὐδὲ ἴσασιν ὅσῳ πλέον ἥμισυ παντὸς.)
Hesiod, *Works and Days*, l. 40.

That's just, if the half shall judge the whole.
John Heywood, *Proverbs*. Pt. i, ch 13. (1546)

13
He is handsome that handsome does.
John Gay, *Wife of Bath*, iii, 1. (1713)

Handsome is that handsome does.
Goldsmith, *Vicar of Wakefield*. Ch. 1. (1766)

Goodly is he that goodly doeth.
ANTHONY MUNDAY, *Sundry Examples*, 78. (1580)

He is proper that proper doth.
THOMAS DEKKER, *Shoemaker's Holiday*. Act ii, sc. 3. (1600)

1
"I say, old boy, where do you hang out?" Mr. Pickwick replied that he was at present suspended at the George and Vulture.
DICKENS, *The Pickwick Papers*. Ch. 30.

2
A harper is laughed at who plays always on the same string. (Citharœdus Ridetur, chorda qui semper oberrat eadem.)
HORACE, *Ars Poetica*, l. 355.

He should harp no more upon that string.
SIR THOMAS MORE, *Works*, p. 49. (1557)

Harp not on that string, madam; that is past.
SHAKESPEARE, *Richard III*. Act iv, sc. 4, l. 364. (1592)

Not good it is to harp on the frayed string.
WILLIAM MORRIS, *The Earthly Paradise: Bellerophon at Argos*, l. 479.

"Harp and carp, Thomas!" she said,
"Harp and carp along wi' me."
UNKNOWN, *Thomas the Rhymer*.

3
John Jones may be described as one of the has beens.
WILLIAM HONE, *Every-Day Book*, ii, 820. (1826)

4
Over head and heels. (Per caputque pedesque.)
CATULLUS, *Carmina*. Ode xvii, l. 9.

Over head and ears in love.
SWIFT, *Polite Conversation*. Dial. 1.

5
From the crown of his head to the sole of his foot.
SHAKESPEARE, *Much Ado About Nothing*. Act iii, sc. 2, l. 9; PLINY, *Historia Naturalis*, vii, 17; BEAUMONT AND FLETCHER, *Honest Man's Fortune*, ii, 2; THOMAS MIDDLETON, *A Mad World, My Masters*, i, 3; etc.

From her little finger-tips to the topmost hair of her head. (Usque ab unguiculo ad capillum summum.)
PLAUTUS, *Epidicus*, l. 623. (Act v, sc. 1.)

6
And he smote them hip and thigh with a great slaughter.
Old Testament: Judges, xv, 8.

7
Honey, you shall be well desired in Cyprus.
SHAKESPEARE, *Othello*. Act ii, sc. 1, l. 207.

8
By hook or crook.
JOHN WYCLIFFE, *Controversial Tracts*. (c. 1380); HEYWOOD, *Proverbs*, i, 11, and many others. On certain manors tenants were authorized to take as much wood as they could gather by hook or crook, that is, as much of the underwood as could be cut with a hook (billhook), and as much of the loose timber as could be collected by means of a crook.

Nor will suffer this book
By hook ne by crook Printed for to be.
JOHN SKELTON, *Colyn Cloute*, l. 1239. (1523)

In hope her to attain by hook or crook.
SPENSER, *The Faerie Queene*. Bk. iii, canto i, st. 17. (1596)

Which he by hook or crook has gather'd
And by his own inventions father'd.
BUTLER, *Hudibras*. Pt. iii, canto i, l. 109.

9
How not to do it.
DICKENS, *Little Dorrit*. Bk. i, ch. 10.

10
For 'tis all one a hundred years hence.
UNKNOWN, *Bagford Ballads*, ii, 722. (1675); A. W. PINERO, *Benefit of the Doubt*. Act ii.

A hundred years from now, dear heart,
We shall not care at all.
It will not matter then a whit,
The honey or the gall.
JOHN BENNETT, *In a Rose Garden*.

I

11
An inch in a miss is as good as an ell.
WILLIAM CAMDEN, *Remains*. (1614)

An inch in missing is as bad as an ell.
THOMAS FULLER, *Gnomologia*. (1732)

He was very near being a poet—but a miss is as good as a mile, and he always fell short of the mark.
SCOTT, *Journal*, 3 Dec., 1825.

A narrow shave, but a miss is as good as a mile.
BERNARD SHAW, *Arms and the Man*. Act i.

12
Give an inch and you'll take an ell.
JOHN HEYWOOD, *Proverbs*. Pt. ii, ch. 9. (1546)

Give a knave an inch, he'll take an ell.
JOHN TAYLOR THE WATER-POET, *Works*, 168. (1630)

J

13
Ye may fly up to the roost with Jackson's hens.
UNKNOWN, *Misogonus*, iv, 2. (1577) To become bankrupt.

14
Let them all go to Jericho,
And ne'er be seen again.
MERCURIUS AULICUS. (1648) (*Athenæum*, 14 Nov., 1874.)

15
The frolicsome company had begun to practise the ancient and now forgotten pastime of high jinks.
SCOTT, *Guy Mannering*. Ch. 36. High jinks was a game of forfeits, in which one was chosen by lot to perform some ridiculous task.

Captain Jinks.
CLYDE FITCH, title of play produced 1901, derived from an old song, "Captain Jinks, of the Horse Marines."

L

1
"Lambe them, lads! lambe them!" a cant phrase derived from the fate of Dr Lambe, an astrologer and quack, of the time of Charles I, who was knocked on the head by the rabble.
SCOTT, *Peveril of the Peak*. Ch. 42.

2
Who in a row like Tom could lead the van,
Booze in the ken, or at the spellken hustle?
Who queer a flat? Who (spite of Bow-street's ban)
On the high toby-spice so flash the muzzle?
Who on a lark, with black-eyed Sal (his blowing),
So prime, so swell, so nutty, and so knowing?
BYRON, *Don Juan*. Canto xi, st. 19.

3
It's a long run that never turns.
JOHN RAY, *English Proverbs*, 117. (1768)
It's a long lane that has no turning.
RICHARDSON, *Clarissa Harlowe*, iv, 237.

4
As large as life.
MARIA EDGEWORTH, *Lame Jervas*. Ch. 2. (1799)
As large as life and quite as natural.
CUTHBERT BEDE, *Verdant Green*. Ch. 6. (1853)
As large as life, and twice as natural.
LEWIS CARROLL, *Through the Looking-Glass*. Ch. 7. (1871)

5
The last, but not the least.
JOHN LYLY, *Euphues*, p. 343. (1580)
Though last, not least.
SPENSER, *Colin Clout*, l. 444. (1595)
Although the last, not least.
SHAKESPEARE, *King Lear*, i, 1, 85. (1605)

6
Give me back my legions! (Legiones redde!)
EMPEROR AUGUSTUS, to the dead Quintillius Varus, after his defeat by Arminius. (SUETONIUS, *Twelve Cæsars: Augustus, 23.*)

7
The life of Riley.
The origin of this phrase has not been found. It perhaps originated from the song, "Is that Mr. Riley?" popular in the 90's. See APPENDIX.
My name is Kelly, but I'm living the life of Riley just the same.
HARRY PEASE and ED. G. NELSON, title and refrain of song. (1919)

8
Doctor Livingstone, I presume?
HENRY M. STANLEY. Stanley's greeting when he found David Livingstone in the heart of the African jungle, 10 Nov., 1871. For further account see APPENDIX.

M

9
Nor stare in a man's face, as if he had spied a mare's nest.
CASA, *Galateo*, iii, 1576. (Peterson, tr.)
What mare's nest hast thou found?
BEAUMONT AND FLETCHER, *Bonduca*, v, 2 (1614)
He has found a mare's nest and laughs at the eggs.
D'URFEY, *Tales Tragic and Comical*, 216. (1704)

10
Tell that to the marines—the sailors won't believe it.
SCOTT, *Redgauntlet* Ch. 13. Quoted as an old saying. TROLLOPE, *The Small House at Allington*.
Right—that will do for the marines.
BYRON, *The Island* Canto ii, st. 21.
Henceforth, whenever we cast doubt upon a tale that lacketh likelihood, we will tell it to the marines. If they believe it, it is safe to say it is true.
W. P DRURY, English novelist, in the preface to his *The Tadpole of an Archangel, The Petrified Eye, and Other Stories* (1904), relates how Charles II said this to Samuel Pepys, after hearing a tall story about some flying fish. *See also* APPENDIX, p 2283·4.
'E isn't one o' the reg'lar Line, nor 'e isn't one of the crew.
'E's a kind of a giddy harumfrodite—soldier an' sailor too!
RUDYARD KIPLING, *Soldier an' Sailor Too*.
The marines have landed, and the situation is well in hand.
RICHARD HARDING DAVIS, *Cable*, from Panama, 1885.

11
In the very midst of the matter (In medias res.)
HORACE, *Ars Poetica*, l. 148 Horace is describing how Homer, in the Odyssey, begins "in medias res."

12
I'm from Missouri; you've got to show me.
WILLARD D. VANDIVER, *Speech*, while Representative from Missouri, at a naval banquet in Philadelphia. (1899) "Colonel Vandiver, at least, was the means by which the expression gained nation-wide currency."—*Literary Digest*, 28 Jan., 1922.

13 Please, sir, I want some more. . . .
Oliver Twist has asked for more.
DICKENS, *Oliver Twist*. Ch. 2.

14
Much of a muchness.
VANBRUGH AND CIBBER, *The Provok'd Husband*. Act i, sc. 1. (1727)
They are all pretty much of a muchness.
CHARLES READE, *It Is Never Too Late to Mend*. Ch. 18.

15
Let us return to the sheep· i. e., to the subject. (Revenons à nos moutons.)
PIERRE BLANCHET, *La Farce de Maistre Pierre Patelin*, l. 1291 (c. 1460) Used also by Brueys in his *L'Avocat Patelin*, taken from Blanchet's play. In the play, a cloth-dealer prosecutes his shepherd for stealing some of his sheep, and employs the advocate Patelin, but perceives, as he is in the midst of his evidence, that the advocate is wearing a suit made of stolen cloth. He is so troubled by this that his mind keeps wandering from the stolen sheep to the stolen cloth, while the judge tries to keep him to his story by adjuring him, "*Revenons à nos moutons.*" As *mouton* is French for both sheep and mutton, British waggery (or ignorance) has transformed the phrase into, "Let us stick to our muttons."

Let us get back to our sheep. (Retournons à nos moutons.)
RABELAIS, *Works*. Bk. iii, ch. 34.

1a
Sick o' th' mulligrubs with eating chopt hay.
JOHN RAY, *English Proverbs*, 77 (1678) SWIFT, *Polite Conversation*. Dial. i. (1738)

N

1
Some say it's naughty, but it's really very nice.
UNKNOWN. English music-hall song, 1875.

It's naughty but it's nice.
UNKNOWN. (*Tattle*, 19 July, 1896, p. 2.)

She knew how to be "so naughty and so nice" in the way that society in London likes and never punishes.
OUIDA, *Moths*. Ch. 15.

2
Neck or nothing; come down or I'll fetch you down.
SWIFT, *Polite Conversation*. Dial. 1.

3
And now is the time come to feather my nest.
UNKNOWN. *Respublica* Act i, sc. 1. (1553)

How well I feathered my nest.
RABELAIS, *Works*. Bk. ii, ch. 17.

4
It was nuts to him to tell the guests.
HEAD AND KIRKMAN, *English Rogue*, iii, 102. (1674) "Nuts," in the sense of something pleasurable, was used by Fletcher, Marvell, Cotton, and many others.

For oh, 'twas nuts to the Father of lies.
THOMAS MOORE, *A Case of Libel*.

P

5
For now thou art in thy Pee and Kue.
THOMAS DEKKER, *Satiro-matrix*. (1602)

Bring in a quart of Maligo right true:
And look, you rogue, that it be Pee and Kew.
SAMUEL ROWLANDS, *Knave of Hearts*, l. 20. (1612)

You must mind your P's and Q's.
HANNAH COWLEY, *Who's the Dupe?* Act i, sc. 2. (1779) The expression is said to derive from the old custom of hanging up a slate in a tavern with P. and Q. marked on it, for pints and quarts, under which were written the names of the customers, and checks for the number of P's and Q's.

And I full five-and-twenty year
Have always been school-master here;
And almost all you know and see
Have learned their P's and Q's from me.
WILLIAM COMBE, *Dr. Syntax's Tour in Search of Consolation*.

6
The passive resistance of the Tolbooth-gate.
SCOTT, *The Heart of Midlothian*. Ch. 6 (1818)

7
Well then, o'er shoes, o'er boots. And in for a penny, in for a pound.
EDWARD RAVENSCROFT, *The Canterbury Guests*. Act v, sc. 1. (1695)

In for a mill, in for a million.
EMERSON, *Essays, Second Series: Experience*.

8
Nobody seem'd one penny the worse!
R. H. BARHAM, *The Jackdaw of Rheims*. St. 8.

9
Pigs is Pigs.
ELLIS PARKER BUTLER. Title of story dealing with guinea pigs.

Railway Porter (to old lady travelling with a menagerie of pets): "Station Master say, Mum, as cats is 'dogs', and rabbits is 'dogs', and so's parrots; but this ere 'tortis' is a insect, so there ain't no charge for it."
CHARLES KEENE, in *Punch*, 6 March, 1869.

10
As plain as a pike-staff.
SHERLOCKE, *Hatcher of Heresies*. (1565)

11
We cannot. (Non possumus.)
POPE CLEMENT VII, to Henry VIII, who demanded a divorce from Catherine of Aragon. It has since been the formula of such refusals.

12
Practice makes perfect. (Μελέτη τὸ πᾶν.)
PERIANDER, his motto. (DIOGENES LAERTIUS, *Periander*. Sec. 6.)

13
Every one heard that I'd written the book and got it in the press. After that, I might have been a gold-fish in a glass bowl for all the privacy I got.
H. H. MUNRO (SAKI), *The Innocence of Reginald*. (1904) Irvin Cobb used the phrase "No more privacy than a gold-fish" in describing his sojourn in a hospital, and is often credited with its invention.

14
Such as he is, he's my prize-packet.
A. W. PINERO, *Preserving Mr. Panmure*. Act ii.

Q

15
Whatever I tell you is on the Q. T.
UNKNOWN, *Talkative Man from Poplar*. Broadside ballad, 1870.

16
Simon Peter said unto him, Lord, whither goest thou?
New Testament: John, xiii, 36. (Quo vadis, Domine?—*Vulgate*.)

Thomas saith unto him, Lord, we know not whither thou goest; and how can we know the way?
New Testament: John, xiv, 5.

Quo Vadis?
HENRYK SIENKIEWICZ. Title of novel.

R

17
Modified rapture.
W. S. GILBERT, *The Mikado*. Act i.

18
Scratch the Russian, you will find the Tartar. (Grattez le russe, vous trouverez le tartare.)
NAPOLEON BONAPARTE, *Remark*, at St. Helena. *See* HUGO, *Le Rhin: Conclusion*, vii.

19
To recant. (Palinodiam canere.)
MACROBIUS, *Satires*. Sat. vii, l. 5.

2
To knit a rope of sand.
BACON, *Promus*. No. 778.

O woman, woman, thy vows are ropes of sand.
CORYE, *Generous Enemies*, ii, 1.

I leave to my said children a great chest full of broken promises and cracked oaths; likewise a vast cargo of ropes made with sand.
UNKNOWN. (*Somers Tracts*, xiii, 144.)

For he a rope of sand could twist
As tough as learned Sorbonist,
And weave fine cobwebs, fit for skull
That's empty when the moon is full.
BUTLER, *Hudibras*. Pt. i, canto i, l. 157.

3
Till we be rotten can we not be ripe.
CHAUCER, *Reves Tale: Prologue*, l. 21. (c. 1386)

Soon ripe soon rotten. (Cito maturum cito putridum.)
JOHN HEYWOOD, *Proverbs*, i, 10. (1546)

4
To have a Rowland for an Oliver.
EDWARD HALL, *Chronicles*, p. 266. (1548) A blow for a blow; tit for tat. Roland and Oliver were two of Charlemagne's Paladins, who fought for five days on an island in the Rhine, without either gaining the advantage.

She will always have a Rowland for your Oliver.
JAMES HOWELL, *Familiar Letters*. Vol. ii, p. 665.

England all Rowlands and Olivers bred.
SHAKESPEARE, *I Henry VI*. Act i, sc. 2, l. 30.

S

4a
As the saying is.
GEORGE FARQUHAR, *The Beaux' Stratagem*. (1707) Repeated frequently throughout the play.

5
And Aaron shall lay both his hands upon the head of the live goat, and confess over him all the iniquities of the children of Israel, . . . putting them upon the head of the goat, and shall send him away by the hand of a fit man into the wilderness.
Old Testament: Leviticus, xvi, 21. The word "Scapegoat" was employed in 1530 by Tindale as a translation of the Hebrew "Azazel." (*Vulgate:* caper emissarius.)

6
Thought I to myself, we shall never come off scot-free.
RABELAIS, *Works*. Bk. v, ch. 15.

7
Up to the scratch.
WILLIAM HAZLITT, *The Fight*.

8
In season, out of season.
New Testament: II Timothy, iv, 2.

9
The second blow makes the fray; the second word makes the bargain.
FRANCIS BACON, *Colours of Good and Evil*.

10
And the Gileadites took the passages of Jordan before the Ephraimites: and it was so, that when those Ephraimites which were escaped said, Let me go over, that the men of Gilead said unto him, Art thou an Ephraimite? If he said, Nay; then said they unto him, say now Shibboleth: and he said Sibboleth: for he could not frame to pronounce it right. Then they took him, and slew him at the passages of Jordan.
Old Testament: Judges, xii, 5, 6.

11
It needs more skill than I can tell
To play the second fiddle well.
C. H. SPURGEON, *Salt-Cellars*.

12
The real Simon Pure.
SUSANNAH CENTLIVRE, *A Bold Stroke for a Wife*. Act v, sc. 1. (1710)

13
All in sunder it burst in six or in seven.
UNKNOWN, *Avowyne of Arthur*, 65. (c. 1340)

Set the world on six and seven.
CHAUCER, *Troilus*. Bk. iv, l. 622. (c. 1374)

There is a proverb, omnem jacere aliam, to cast at dice, by which is signified, to set all on six and seven.
ERASMUS, *Adagia*. (Udall, tr.) "Probably a fanciful alteration of *to set on cinque and sice*, these being the two highest numbers." —*Oxford Dictionary*.

And every thing is left at six and seven.
SHAKESPEARE, *Richard II*, ii, 2, 122. (1595)

Fair moon, to thee I sing,
Bright regent of the heavens;
Say, why is everything
Either at sixes or at sevens?
W. S. GILBERT, *H. M. S. Pinafore*. Act ii.

14
Slide, Kelly, slide!
J. W. KELLY. Title of popular song written in 1889, and referring to the prowess of Michael Kelly (1857–1894), of the Chicago and Boston baseball teams, as a base runner.

14a
Zooks, he 's up to snuff!
JOHN POOLE, *Hamlet Travestie*. Act ii, sc. 1. (1811)

15
I here lay *incog.* for at least three seconds; snug was the word.
RICHARD STEELE, *The Lover*, 11 March, 1714.

Away, away! take all your scaffolds down,
For snug 's the word: My dear! we 'll live in town.
POPE, *Imitations of Horace: Epistles*. Bk. i, epis. 1, l. 146. (1738)

Here Skugg lies snug As a bug in a rug.
BENJAMIN FRANKLIN, *Letter to Miss Georgiana Shipley*, 26 Sept., 1772.

16
A giddy son of a gun.
SWIFT, *The Battle of the Books*. (1697)

17
You're complaining to a stepmother. (Apud novercam querere.)
PLAUTUS, *Pseudolus*, l. 314. (Act i, sc. 3.)

18
He 'as had a stinger.
JOHN FLETCHER, *Wit Without Money*. Act iv, sc. 1. (1639)

'Tis a stinger.
THOMAS MIDDLETON, *More Dissemblers Besides Women*. Act iii, sc. 2. (1657)

1
The more thou stir it the worse it will be.
CERVANTES, *Don Quixote*. Bk. iii, ch. 8.

1a
"Must you stay? Can't you go?"
Legend to cartoon in *Punch*, 18 Jan., 1905, representing the French Governor of Madagascar speaking to the Russian Admiral Rodjestvensky, who had made a prolonged stay at Madagascar, while on his way to meet the Japanese fleet.

2
Turn every stone. (Πάντα κινῆσαι πέτρον.)
EURIPIDES, *Heracleidæ*, l. 1002. An echo of the response given by the Delphian oracle to Polycrates, when he asked what would be the best method of finding a treasure buried by Mardonius, one of Xerxes' generals, on the field of Platæa. The oracle replied, Πάντα λίθον κίνει, "Turn every stone." (LEUTSCH AND SCHNEIDEWIN, *Corpus Paræmiographorum Græcorum*, i, 146.)

He will refuse no labour nor leave no stone unturned, to pick up a penny.
GILBERT WALKER, *Dice-Play*. (c. 1550)

3
Seldom mosseth the marblestone that men oft treadeth.
LANGLAND, *Piers Plowman*. Pas. x, l. 10. (1362)

The rolling stone never gathereth moss.
JOHN HEYWOOD, *Proverbs*. Pt. i, ch. 11. (1546)

The stone that is rolling can gather no moss;
Who often removeth is sure of a loss.
THOMAS TUSSER, *Five Hundred Points of Good Husbandry: Husbandry Lessons*. (1557)

4
Within a stone's throw of it.
CERVANTES, *Don Quixote*. Pt. i, ch. 9.

5
With a favoring stream. (Secundo amni.)
LIVY, *History*. Bk. xliv, sec. 31.

6
To strive against the stream. (Dirigere bracchia contra torrentum.)
JUVENAL, *Satires*. Sat. iv, l. 89.

In vain it is to strive against the stream.
ROBERT GREENE, *Alphonsus*, i, 1. (c. 1590)

7
Mr. Longman, who had struck me of a heap.
RICHARDSON, *Pamela*, ii, 119. (1740)

Struck me all of a heap.
SHERIDAN, *The Duenna*. Act ii, sc. 2.

8
Matters will go swimmingly.
CERVANTES, *Don Quixote*. Pt. ii, ch. 36.

T

9
Let him take it or leave it. (Aut agat aut desistat.)
SUETONIUS, *Tiberius*. Ch. xxiv, sec. 2.

Take it or leave it.
THOMAS KILLIGREW, *Thomaso*. Act. i, sc. 4, (1664)

10
Ha—what a devil have I caught—a Tartar?
APHRA BEHN, *Feign'd Courtezans*. Act iv, sc. 2. (c. 1680)

I'm sure catching a husband is catching a Tartar.
COLLEY CIBBER, *Lady's Last Stake*. Act ii, 1.

A poor good-natur'd mean-spirited creetur, as went out fishing for a wife one day, and caught a Tartar.
DICKENS, *Barnaby Rudge*. Ch. 80.

11
"You're an amiably-disposed young man, I don't think," resumed Mr. Weller.
DICKENS, *Pickwick Papers*. Ch. 38.

12
Through thick and through thin.
CHAUCER, *The Reves Tale*, l. 148. (c. 1386)

Through thick and thin, both over Hill and Plain.
DU BARTAS, *Devine Weekes and Workes*. Week ii, day 4. (Sylvester, tr. 1590.)

Through thick and thin, both over bank and bush.
SPENSER, *The Faerie Queene*. Bk. iii, canto i, st. 17. (1596)

I must follow him through thick and thin.
CERVANTES, *Don Quixote*. Pt. ii, ch. 33.

Spurred boldly on, and dashed through thick and thin.
DRYDEN, *Absalom and Achitophel*. Pt. ii, l. 414.

Through perils of both wind and limb,
Through thick and thin she follow'd him.
BUTLER, *Hudibras*. Pt. i, canto 2, l. 370.

And all agog
To dash through thick and thin.
COWPER, *John Gilpin*. St. 10.

13
Not to be handled with a pair of tongs.
JOHN CLARKE, *Paræmiologia*, 34. (1639)

Without a pair of tongs no man will touch her.
UNKNOWN, *Wit Restor'd*, 159. (1658)

I will not touch her with a pair of tongs.
THOMAS FULLER, *Gnomologia*. No. 2649.

14
Touch me not.
New Testament: John, xx, 17. (Noli me tangere.—*Vulgate*.)

15
To touch to the quick. (Χρῷ τοῦτο μὴ χαίρειν τινά.)
SOPHOCLES, *Ajax*, l. 786.

16
One good turn asketh another.
JOHN HEYWOOD, *Proverbs*. Pt. i, ch. 11. (1546)

One good turn deserves another.
BEAUMONT AND FLETCHER, *The Little French Lawyer*. Act iii, sc. 2. (1647)

U

17
I had her in my power—up a tree, as the Americans say.
THACKERAY, *Major Gahagan*. Ch. 5.

18
Perceptively intense and consummately utter. They are indeed jolly utter.
W. S. GILBERT, *Patience*. Act ii.

Oh, so all-but!
W. S. GILBERT, *Patience*. Act ii.

W

19
The thing passed off like water from a duck's back.
MAGINN, *O'Doherty's Maxims*, 128. (1824)

1
The longest way round is the shortest way home.
H. G. BOHN, *Foreign Proverbs: Italian.*

The farthest way about is the nearest way home
ROBERTSON, *Phraseology Generalis*, 1300.

The furthest way about, t' o'ercome,
In the end does prove the nearest home.
BUTLER, *Hudibras.* Pt. ii, canto i, l. 227.

The road to resolution lies by doubt:
The next way home's the farthest way about.
QUARLES, *Emblems.* Bk. iv, emb. 2. (1635)

2
Something given that way.
BEAUMONT AND FLETCHER, *The Lovers' Progress.* Act i, sc. 1.

3
Let well alone, as the saying is. (Actum. aiunt, ne agas.)
TERENCE, *Phormio*, l. 419. (Act ii, sc. 3.)

It is well, it works well, let well alone.
PEACOCK, *Misfortunes of Elphin.* Ch. 2. (1829)

Let well alone, lad, and ill too at times.
KINGSLEY, *Water Babies.* Ch. 1. (1863)

4
What price Salvation?
BERNARD SHAW, *Major Barbara.* Act ii.

What Price Glory?
MAXWELL ANDERSON AND LAURENCE STALLINGS. Title of play, produced 3 Sept., 1924.

5
A proper place for men to sow their wild oats—where they will not spring up. (Istic oportet observi mores malos, Si in obserendo possint interfieri.)
PLAUTUS, *Trinummus.* Act iv, sc. 4, l. 128.

He has not yet sown all his wild oats.
UNKNOWN, *Misogonus*, ii, 3. (1577)

Youth ne'er aspires to virtues perfect grown
Till his wild oats be sown.
THOMAS NASHE, *Works*, vi, 152. (1600)

5a
I'll clip his wings.
CHRISTOPHER MARLOWE, *The Massacre at Paris.* Act iii, sc. 2. (1590)

To clip the wings
Of their high-flying arbitrary Kings.
DRYDEN, *Virgil's Georgics.* Bk. iv, l. 161.

6
Many a one goes for wool and comes back shorn.
CERVANTES, *Don Quixote.* Pt. i, ch. 7.

7
Much cry and little wool.
JOHN FORTESCUE, *De Laudibus Legium Angliæ.* Ch. 10. (c. 1475)

Great cry and little wool.
STEPHEN GOSSON, *School of Abuse*, 28. (1579)

Thou wilt at best but suck a bull,
Or shear swine, all cry and no wool.
BUTLER, *Hudibras.* Pt. i, canto i. l. 851. (1663)

8
Let the worst come to the worst.
CERVANTES, *Don Quixote.* Pt. i, ch. 5.

If the worst comes to the worst.
UNKNOWN. *Discovery of Knights of the Poste.* Sig. C3. (1597) In frequent use thereafter.

III—Familiar Sayings: Shakespearean

9
Thus must I from the smoke into the smother.
SHAKESPEARE, *As You Like It.* Act i, sc. 2, l. 299.

10
Thou art in a parlous state.
SHAKESPEARE, *As You Like It.* Act iii, sc. 2, l. 45.

11
Not with bag and baggage, yet with scrip and scrippage.
SHAKESPEARE, *As You Like It.* Act iii, sc. 2, l. 170. (1599) In use as early as 1550 (HULOET. *Abcedarium Anglico-Latinum*); credited to Froissart by Lord Berners. (Vol. i, ch. 320.)

12
Can one desire too much of a good thing?
SHAKESPEARE, *As You Like It.* Act iv, sc. 1, l. 123.

13
"So so" is good, very good, very excellent good; and yet it is not; it is but so so.
SHAKESPEARE, *As You Like It.* Act v, sc. 1, l. 29

Breathe twice and cry "so, so."
SHAKESPEARE, *The Tempest.* Act iv, sc. 1, l. 45

14
We are for you.
SHAKESPEARE, *As You Like It.* Act v, sc. 3, l. 10

15
I holp to frame thee.
SHAKESPEARE, *Coriolanus.* Act v, sc. 3, l. 63.

The maid will I frame.
SHAKESPEARE, *Measure for Measure*, iii, 1, 266.

16
That it should come to this!
SHAKESPEARE, *Hamlet.* Act i, sc. 2, l. 137.

17
I know a hawk from a handsaw.
SHAKESPEARE, *Hamlet* Act ii, sc. 2, l. 397 Handsaw is probably a corruption of hernshaw, a heron: I know a hawk from a heron —the bird of prey from the prey itself.

18
What's Hecuba to him, or he to Hecuba?
SHAKESPEARE, *Hamlet.* Act. ii, sc. 2, l. 585.

19
The observed of all observers.
SHAKESPEARE, *Hamlet.* Act iii, sc. 1, l. 162.

20
Tear a passion to tatters . . . to split the ears of the groundlings.
SHAKESPEARE, *Hamlet.* Act iii, sc. 2, l. 11.

21
It out-herods Herod.
SHAKESPEARE, *Hamlet.* Act iii, sc. 2, l. 16.

22
To hold, as 'twere, the mirror up to nature.
SHAKESPEARE, *Hamlet.* Act iii, sc. 2, l. 24.

23
Make the judicious grieve.
SHAKESPEARE, *Hamlet.* Act iii, sc. 2, l. 29.

1
Not to speak it profanely.
SHAKESPEARE, *Hamlet*. Act iii, sc. 2, l. 34.

2
Here's metal more attractive.
SHAKESPEARE, *Hamlet*. Act iii, sc. 2, l. 116.

3
Let the galled jade wince, our withers are unwrung.
SHAKESPEARE, *Hamlet*. Act iii, sc. 2, l. 253.

4
Now might I do it pat.
SHAKESPEARE, *Hamlet*. Act iii, sc. 3, l. 73.

5
How absolute the knave is! we must speak by the card, or equivocation will undo us.
SHAKESPEARE, *Hamlet*. Act v, sc. 1, l. 148.

6
We'll put the matter to the present push.
SHAKESPEARE, *Hamlet*. Act v, sc. 1, l. 318.

7
The phrase would be more german to the matter, if we could carry cannon by our sides.
SHAKESPEARE, *Hamlet*. Act v, sc. 2, l. 165.

8
A hit, a very palpable hit.
SHAKESPEARE, *Hamlet*. Act v, sc. 2, l. 292.

9
God save the mark!
SHAKESPEARE, *I Henry IV*. Act i, sc. 3, l. 56.

10
If he fall in, good night!
SHAKESPEARE, *I Henry IV*. Act i, sc. 3, l. 194.

This wicked world was once my dear delight;
Now all my conquests, all my charms, good night!
POPE, *The Wife of Bath: Prologue*, l. 225.

11
Nay, I will; that's flat.
SHAKESPEARE, *I Henry IV*. Act i, sc. 3, l. 218.

I'll not march through Coventry with them, that's flat.
SHAKESPEARE, *I Henry IV*. Act iv, sc. 2, l. 42.

That's flat.
SHAKESPEARE, *Love's Labour's Lost*. Act iii, sc. 1, l. 102.

12
I know a trick worth two of that.
SHAKESPEARE, *I Henry IV*. Act ii, sc. 1, l. 41.

13
Not an inch further.
SHAKESPEARE, *I Henry IV*. Act ii, sc. 3, l. 117.

14
Show it a fair pair of heels.
SHAKESPEARE, *I Henry IV*. Act ii, sc. 4, l. 53.

15
I sent him Bootless home.
SHAKESPEARE, *I Henry IV*. Act iii, sc. 1, l. 66.

16
Let me tell the world.
SHAKESPEARE, *I Henry IV*. Act v, sc. 2, l. 66.

17
Away, you scullion! you rampallion! you fustilarian!
SHAKESPEARE, *II Henry IV*. Act ii, sc. 1, l. 65.

18
I'll tickle your catastrophe.
SHAKESPEARE, *II Henry IV*. Act ii, sc. 1, l. 66.

19
With all appliances and means to boot.
SHAKESPEARE, *II Henry IV*. Act iii, sc. 1, l. 29.

20
Most forcible Feeble.
SHAKESPEARE, *II Henry IV*. Act iii, sc. 2, l. 179.

21
Under which king, Besonian? speak, or die.
SHAKESPEARE, *II Henry IV*. Act v, sc. 3, l. 117.
Recruits sent from Spain to Rome were called *besogni*, because they were in need of everything, from the Italian *bisogno*, need.

Great men oft die by vile bezonians.
SHAKESPEARE, *II Henry VI*. Act iv, sc. 1, l. 134.

Base and pilfering besognios and marauders.
SCOTT, *The Monastery*. Ch. 16.

22
To this gear the sooner the better.
SHAKESPEARE, *II Henry VI*. Act i, sc. 4, l. 17.

23
A fig for Peter!
SHAKESPEARE, *II Henry VI*. Act ii, sc. 3, l. 67.

Figo for thy friendship!
SHAKESPEARE, *Henry V*. Act iii, sc. 6, l. 60.

24
We will fall for it?
SHAKESPEARE, *Julius Cæsar*. Act ii, sc. 1, l. 128.

25
Thou shalt see me at Philippi.
SHAKESPEARE, *Julius Cæsar*. Act iv, sc. 3, l. 284. This is the warning addressed to Brutus by the ghost of Cæsar. The story is told by Plutarch (*Lives: Cæsar*. Ch. 69), where the phantom says, "I am thy evil genius, Brutus, and thou shalt see me at Philippi." (Ὁ *σός, ὦ Βροῦτε, δαίμων κακός· ὄψει δέ με περὶ Φιλίππους.*)

26
Bell, book, and candle shall not drive me back.
SHAKESPEARE, *King John*. Act iii, sc. 3, l. 12.

27
May's new-fangled mirth.
SHAKESPEARE, *Love's Labour's Lost*. Act i, sc. 1, l. 106.

More new-fangled than an ape.
SHAKESPEARE, *As You Like It*. Act iv, sc. 1, l. 152.

Some [glory] in their garments, though new-fangled ill.
SHAKESPEARE, *Sonnets*. No. xci.

28
The rational hind Costard.
SHAKESPEARE, *Love's Labour's Lost*. Act i, sc. 2, l. 123.

29
Bon, bon, fort bon! Priscian a little scratched, 'twill serve.
SHAKESPEARE, *Love's Labour's Lost*. Act v, sc. 1, l. 31.

1
Master, let me take you a button-hole lower.
SHAKESPEARE, *Love's Labour's Lost.* Act v, sc. 2, l. 706. (1592)

I'll bring him a button-hole lower.
JAMES SHIRLEY, *Triumph of Peace.* (1634)

We . . . took your grandees down a peg.
SAMUEL BUTLER, *Hudibras.* Bk. ii, canto 2, l. 522. (1664)

To take a peg lower.
JOHN RAY, *English Proverbs,* p. 189. (1670)

I must take her down a peg or so.
MRS. FRANCES SHERIDAN, *The Dupe.* Act iv, sc. 4. (1760)

2
Coigne of vantage.
SHAKESPEARE, *Macbeth.* Act i, sc. 6, l. 7.

3
At one fell swoop.
SHAKESPEARE, *Macbeth.* Act iv, sc. 3, l. 219.

4
Say that I said so.
SHAKESPEARE, *Measure for Measure,* iii, 2, 195.

5
I will presently to Saint Luke's: there, at the moated grange, resides this dejected Mariana.
SHAKESPEARE, *Measure for Measure,* iii, 1, 276.

Mariana in the moated grange.
TENNYSON, *Motto: Mariana.*

6
My business in this state
Made me a looker on here in Vienna.
SHAKESPEARE, *Measure for Measure,* v, 1, 318.

7
What 's mine is yours and what is yours is mine.
SHAKESPEARE, *Measure for Measure,* v, 1, 543.

8
Nay, but I bar to-night: you shall not gauge me
By what we do to-night.
SHAKESPEARE, *Merchant of Venice,* ii, 2, 208.

9
From the four corners of the earth they come.
SHAKESPEARE, *Merchant of Venice,* ii, 7, 39.

From the four corners of the world do haste.
DU BARTAS, *Devine Weekes and Workes.* Week i, day 2. (Sylvester, tr.)

10
It will go hard with poor Antonio.
SHAKESPEARE, *Merchant of Venice,* iii, 2, 293.

11
Now, infidel, I have you on the hip.
SHAKESPEARE, *Merchant of Venice,* iv, 1, 334.

12
You Banbury cheese!
SHAKESPEARE, *The Merry Wives of Windsor.* Act i, sc. 1, l. 130. Bardolph is speaking to Slender, and has in mind the proverb, "As thin as Banbury cheese."

13
We burn daylight.
SHAKESPEARE, *The Merry Wives of Windsor.* Act ii, sc. 1, l. 54.

14
Shall we wag?
SHAKESPEARE, *The Merry Wives of Windsor* Act ii, sc. 1, l. 238.

Let us wag, then.
SHAKESPEARE, *The Merry Wives of Windsor.* Act ii, sc. 3, l. 101.

15
This is the short and the long of it.
SHAKESPEARE, *The Merry Wives of Windsor.* Act ii, sc. 2, l. 60. (1600)

This is the short and the long, and the sum of all.
THOMAS NASHE, *Death of Martin Mar-Prelate.* (1589)

16
O, understand my drift.
SHAKESPEARE, *The Merry Wives of Windsor.* Act ii, sc. 2, l. 251.

17
I will smite his noddles.
SHAKESPEARE, *The Merry Wives of Windsor.* Act iii, sc. 1, l. 128.

18
I can not tell what the dickens his name is.
SHAKESPEARE, *The Merry Wives of Windsor.* Act iii, sc. 2, l. 19.

19
A man of my kidney.
SHAKESPEARE, *The Merry Wives of Windsor.* Act iii, sc. 5, l. 117.

20
God speed, fair Helena! whither away?
SHAKESPEARE, *A Midsummer-Night's Dream.* Act i, sc. 1, l. 180.

21
Masters, spread yourselves.
SHAKESPEARE, *A Midsummer-Night's Dream.* Act i, sc. 2, l. 19.

22
O spite! O hell! I see you all are bent
To set against me for your merriment.
SHAKESPEARE, *A Midsummer-Night's Dream.* Act iii, sc. 2, l. 145.

You all did see that on the Lupercal
I thrice presented him a kingly crown,
Which he did thrice refuse.
SHAKESPEARE, *Julius Cæsar.* Act iii, sc. 2, l. 100

"You all" is the Southern plural for you.
UNKNOWN. *Nashville Banner,* 24 July, 1921.

23
I'll go with thee, cheek by jole.
SHAKESPEARE, *A Midsummer-Night's Dream.* Act iii, sc. 2, l. 338.

24
Thy honesty and love doth mince this matter.
SHAKESPEARE, *Othello.* Act ii, sc. 3, l. 247.

Mince the matter.
CERVANTES, *Don Quixote: Author's Preface.*

25
But they must blab.
SHAKESPEARE, *Othello.* Act iv, sc. 1, l. 29.

26
'Tis neither here nor there.
SHAKESPEARE, *Othello.* Act iv, sc. 3, l. 59.

27
It makes us, or it mars us.
SHAKESPEARE, *Othello.* Act v, sc. 1, l. 4.

1
Shall I seem crest-fall'n in my father's sight?
SHAKESPEARE, *Richard II*. Act i, sc. 1, l. 188.

2
A knot you are of damned blood-suckers.
SHAKESPEARE, *Richard III*. Act iii, sc. 3, l. 6.

3
Welcome, my lord: I dance attendance here.
SHAKESPEARE, *Richard III*. Act iii, sc. 7, l. 56.

4
I am not in the vein.
SHAKESPEARE, *Richard III*. Act iv, sc. 2, l. 122.

5
Tetchy and wayward.
SHAKESPEARE, *Richard III*. Act iv, sc. 4, l. 168.

6
I think there be six Richmonds in the field.
Five have I slain to-day instead of him.
SHAKESPEARE, *Richard III*. Act v, sc. 4, l. 11. Hence: "Another Richmond in the field."

7
Nay, if thy wits run the wild-goose chase, I have done.
SHAKESPEARE, *Romeo and Juliet*. Act ii, sc. 4, l. 75. (See Persius, iii, 61: An passim sequeris corvos testaque lutoque.)

Why do you lead me a wild-goose chase?
CERVANTES, *Don Quixote*. Pt. i, ch. 6.

8
I'll not budge an inch.
SHAKESPEARE, *The Taming of the Shrew: Induction*. Sc. 1, l. 13.

9
Sir, give him head: I know he'll prove a jade.
SHAKESPEARE, *The Taming of the Shrew*. Act i, sc. 2, l. 249.

10
That's but a cavil.
SHAKESPEARE, *The Taming of the Shrew*. Act ii, sc. 1, l. 392.

11
Fie, doff this habit, shame to your estate,
An eye-sore to our solemn festival.
SHAKESPEARE, *The Taming of the Shrew*. Act iii, sc. 2, l. 102.

12
Nay, I have ta'en you napping, gentle love.
SHAKESPEARE, *The Taming of the Shrew*. Act iv, sc. 2, l. 46.

13
From the still-vex'd Bermoothes.
SHAKESPEARE, *The Tempest*. Act i, sc. 2, l. 229.

14
We know what belongs to frippery.
SHAKESPEARE, *The Tempest*. Act iv, sc. 1, l. 226.

15
How camest thou in this pickle?
SHAKESPEARE, *The Tempest*. Act v, sc. 1, l. 281.

Stew'd in brine, Smarting in lingering pickle.
SHAKESPEARE, *Antony and Cleopatra*. Act ii, sc. 5, l. 66.

16
Say, wall-eyed slave.
SHAKESPEARE, *Titus Andronicus*. Act v, sc. 1, l. 44.

17
Our firebrand brother, Paris. burns us all.
SHAKESPEARE, *Troilus and Cressida*. Act ii, sc. 2, l. 110.

18
I have them at my fingers' ends.
SHAKESPEARE, *Twelfth Night*. Act i, sc. 3, l. 83.

19
Faith, I can cut a caper.
SHAKESPEARE, *Twelfth Night*. Act i, sc. 3, l. 129.

20
'Tis in grain, sir, 'twill endure wind and weather.
SHAKESPEARE, *Twelfth Night*. Act i, sc. 5, l. 256.

21
Westward-ho!
SHAKESPEARE, *Twelfth Night*. Act iii, sc. 1, l. 146. Used by Charles Kingsley as title of novel.

22
Hob, nob, is his word: give 't or take 't.
SHAKESPEARE, *Twelfth Night*. Act iii, sc. 4, l. 262.

23
Anon, sir, I'll be with you again.
SHAKESPEARE, *Twelfth Night*. Act iv, sc. 3, l. 131.

24
What is 't that you took up so gingerly?
SHAKESPEARE, *The Two Gentlemen of Verona*. Act i, sc. 2, l. 70.

25
And if it please you, so: if not, why, so.
SHAKESPEARE, *The Two Gentlemen of Verona*. Act ii, sc. 1, l. 137.

IV—Familiar Sayings: Americanisms

See also under America

26
How old is Ann?
UNKNOWN. In the New York *Press*, October 16, 1903, appeared the following problem: "Mary is 24 years old. She is twice as old as Ann was when she was as old as Ann is now. How old is Ann now?"

27
His name was George F. Babbitt, and . . . he was nimble in the calling of selling houses for more than people could afford to pay.
SINCLAIR LEWIS, *Babbitt*, p. 2. (1922)

28
Who hit [or struck] Billy Patterson?
It has been impossible to verify any of the stories which purport to explain this expression. One story is to the effect that in a row at the corner of Baltimore and Charles Streets, Baltimore, a man named Billy Patterson was struck by somebody and went around inquiring "Who hit me?" till it became a joke. Another is that a student at a medical college died from fright during a hazing some eighty years ago, after being struck a mock blow, and at the inquest the great question was "Who struck Billy Patterson?" until it developed that no one had really struck him. Still another version places the locale at Lancaster, Pa.

1
It's "bold," it's "clever" and it's "cute,"
And so is this my blurb.

GELETT BURGESS, *Burgess Unabridged*, p. 7. Blurb: an inspired testimonial; a sound like a publisher.

2
Are you a bromide?

GELETT BURGESS. Title of essay. (*Smart Set*, April, 1906.)

Bromides and Sulphites.

GELETT BURGESS. Two words coined in 1907, the first to indicate the majority of mankind, who all think and talk alike, the latter the select minority who "eliminate the obvious from their conversation."

3
Nothing doing. That's just "baloney." Everybody knows I can't lay bricks.

ALFRED E. SMITH, at the laying of the cornerstone of the New York State Office Building, when asked to permit a motion picture showing him actually laying the brick. His secretary states that "it is impossible to say exactly when the Governor first used the expression 'baloney.'"

I am for gold dollars against baloney dollars.

ALFRED E. SMITH, *Editorial, New Outlook*, Dec., 1933, referring to the devaluation experiments of Roosevelt administration.

No matter how thin you slice it, it's still baloney.

ALFRED E. SMITH, *Speech*, 1936.

4
Bonehead.

CHARLES DRYDEN, reviving an old word, in newspaper article describing the famous play in which Fred Merkle, first baseman of the New York Giants, failed to touch second base in the deciding game of the 1908 championship series, at Polo Grounds, New York City, 23 Sept. The error lost the game for the Giants, and a riot followed. (See SULLIVAN, *Our Times*. Vol. iii, p. 541.)

5
The practice for which W. E. Woodward, in a novel [*Bunk*] published in 1923, invented the word "debunking."

F. L. ALLEN, *Only Yesterday*, p. 236.

Bunk is mental junk.

GEORGE W. LYON and O. F. PAGE. A definition submitted simultaneously by these two men, strangers to each other, in a contest sponsored by *The Forum*, Sept., 1927, p. 449.

6
I acknowledge the corn.

CHARLES A. WICKLIFFE, of Kentucky, in debate in House of Representatives in 1828. (DE VERE, *Americanisms*.)

7
Gibson has drawn the true American girl. He is the American Du Maurier. . . . As soon as the world saw Gibson's ideal it bowed down in adoration, saying: "Lo, at last the typical American girl." . . . The girls themselves held her as their portrait and strove to live up to the likeness. Thus did nature follow in the footsteps of art and thus did the Gibson girl become legion.

UNKNOWN. *Editorial. New York World*, 1896.

8
What things we see when we don't have a gun!

UNKNOWN. Troy (N. Y.) *Times*, 26 Dec., 1883.

10
They say that the lady from Philadelphia, who is staying in town, is very wise. Suppose I go and ask her what is best to be done?

LUCRETIA P. HALE, *Peterkin Papers*. Ch. 1.

11
Another phrase, which often glides in music from the lip,
Is one of fine significance and beauty, "Let her rip!"

PARK BENJAMIN, *Hard Times*.

12
Mollycoddles instead of vigorous men.

THEODORE ROOSEVELT, *Speech*, Cambridge, Mass., 23 Feb., 1907.

The large mollycoddle vote—the people who are soft physically and morally.

THEODORE ROOSEVELT, *Autobiography*. Ch. 7. When asked to define mollycoddle, Roosevelt quoted Herodotus (*History*. Bk. ii, sec. 35); who, describing the habits of the Egyptians, writes: Οὐρεουσι αἱ μὲν γυναῖκες ὀρθαί, οἱ δὲ ἄνδρες κατήμενοι.

Hold him up to scorn as a mollycoddle and a milksop.

THACKERAY, *English Humorists: Fielding*.

13
Don't throw a monkey-wrench into the machinery!

PHILANDER JOHNSON, *Shooting Stars*. (See *Everybody's Magazine*, May, 1920.)

14
Nifty! (short for *magnificat*).

BRET HARTE, *The Tale of a Pony*.

15
Andrew Jackson, Esq., proved a bill of sale from Hugh McGary to Gasper Mansker, for a negro man, which was O. K.

Archives of Sumner County, Tenn., 6 Oct., 1790. This has long been held to be the first recorded use of O.K., but James Parton suggested in 1859 (*Life of Andrew Jackson*, vol. i, p. 136) that O.K. was a misreading of O.R., Order Recorded, and recent investigation has proved this to be the case. Woodrow Wilson preferred to believe that it derived from a Choctaw word, "Okeh," meaning "It is so," and wrote it in that form on papers which had his approval. But the actual origin of the term is quite uncertain.

The People is Oll Korrect.

Wording of a banner displayed at a Harrison and Tyler meeting at Urbana, Ohio, 15 Sept., 1840 (See Columbus, Ohio, *Dispatch*, 3 Sept., 1933.)

16
It depends upon whose ox is gored.

Fable 8, in NOAH WEBSTER'S *American Spelling Book*, is called *The Partial Judge*, in which an ox is gored by a bull. The expression is said to have originated from this.

1
Stuffed shirt.

Attributed to FAY TEMPLETON, who chucked it at a plunger named John Gates, about 1899, meaning a tremendous nobody.

2
Why is this thus? What is the reason of this thusness?

ARTEMUS WARD, *Moses, the Sassy.*

3
But the following year struck her smiling career
With a dull and a sickening thud!

GUY WETMORE CARRYL, *Red Riding Hood.*

4
The Total Depravity of Inanimate Things.

KATHERINE KENT WALKER. Title of essay, *Atlantic Monthly*, Sept., 1864.

5
We are bound toward the scuppers,
And the time has come to act,
Or we'll both be on our uppers
For a fact!

GUY WETMORE CARRYL, *How a Cat Was Annoyed and a Poet Was Booted.*

6
As you are not prepared, as the Americans say, *to go the whole hog*, we will part good friends.

FREDERICK MARRYAT, *Japhet.* Ch. 54. (1836) *Notes and Queries* (27 Sept., 1851) says the phrase is of Irish origin, where a shilling is called a "hog," so that "To go the whole hog" means to spend a whole shilling. An editorial writer on the *Democratic Press*, of Philadelphia, claims to have used it in the summer of 1827. See the *Arkansas Advocate*, 21 Aug., 1835.

7
Gone where the woodbine twineth.

JAMES FISK. At Congressional investigation of Black Friday, (Sept., 1869), referring to the money he had lost in the attempt to corner gold. When asked what the phrase meant, he is said to have answered, "Up the spout."

PROVIDENCE

See also Destiny; Fate; War and Providence

I—Providence: Definitions and Apothegms

7a
The ways of Heav'n are dark and intricate,
Puzzled in mazes, and perplex'd with errors;
Our understanding traces them in vain,
Lost and bewilder'd in the fruitless search;
Nor sees with how much art the windings run,
Nor where the regular confusion ends.

ADDISON, *Cato.* Act i, sc. 1.

8
Providence labors with quaint instruments, dilapidating Troy by means of a wooden rocking-horse, and loosing sin into the universe through a half-eaten apple.

JAMES BRANCH CABELL, *Cream of the Jest*, p. 87.

9
He does not, like Bolingbroke, patronise Providence.

CARLYLE, *Essays: Voltaire.*

10
Providence has been called the baptismal name of Chance, but a devout person would say that Chance is a nickname of Providence. (Quelqu'un disait que la Providence était le nom de baptême du Hasard, quelque dévot dira que le Hasard est un sobriquet de la Providence.)

CHAMFORT, *Maximes et Pensées.* Pt. i.

11
Providence has a wild, rough, incalculable road to its end, and it is of no use to try to whitewash its huge, mixed instrumentalities, or to dress up that terrific benefactor in a clean shirt and white neckcloth of a student in divinity.

EMERSON, *Conduct of Life: Fate.*

A pistareen-Providence, which, whenever the good man wants a dinner, makes that somebody shall knock at his door, and leave a half-dollar.

EMERSON, *Conduct of Life: Fate.*

12
What is the operation we call Providence? There lies the unspoken thing, present, omnipresent. Every time we converse we translate it into speech.

EMERSON, *Essays, Second Series: New England Reformers.*

13
Providence has many different aspects. (Πολλαὶ μορφαὶ τῶν δαιμονίων.)

EURIPIDES, *Alcestis*, l. 1159.

But they that are above
Have ends in everything.

BEAUMONT AND FLETCHER, *The Maid's Tragedy.* Act v, sc. 4.

14
Why doth IT so and so, and ever so,
This viewless, voiceless Turner of the Wheel?

THOMAS HARDY, *The Dynasts: Fore Scene: Spirit of the Pities.*

15
The ways of the Gods are full of Providence. (Τὰ τῶν θεῶν προνοίας μεστά.)

MARCUS AURELIUS, *Meditations.* Bk. ii, sec. 3.

16
The lap of providence.

HUMPHREY PRIDEAUX, *Directions to Churchwardens*, p. 105.

17
Providence provides for the provident.

W. G. BENHAM, *Proverbs*, p. 828.

18
Call it Nature, Fate, Fortune; all these are names of the one and selfsame God. (Naturam voca, fatum, fortunamque; sunt omnia unius et ejusdem Dei nomina.)

SENECA, *De Beneficiis.* Bk. iv, sec. 8.

19
Heaven is above all yet; there sits a judge
That no king can corrupt.

SHAKESPEARE, *Henry VIII* Act iii, sc. 1, l. 100.

For every event is a judgment of God. (Denn aller Ausgang ist ein Gottesurtheil.)
SCHILLER, *Wallenstein's Tod*. Act i, sc. 7, l. 32.

He hears the judgment of the King of kings.
TENNYSON, *Geraint and Enid*, l. 801.

1
There are many scapegoats for our sins, but the most popular is providence.
MARK TWAIN, *More Tramps Abroad*.

II—Providence: Its Power

2
When a storm bloweth, sent of the gods, we needs must endure it, toiling without complaint. (Θεόθεν δὲ πνέοντ' οὖρον ἀνάγκη τλῆναι καμάτοις ἀνοδύρτοις.)
ÆSCHYLUS [?], *Fragments*. Frag. 246.

3
Heaven's all-subduing will
With good, the progeny of ill,
Attempereth every state below.
MARK AKENSIDE, *Ode on the Winter Solstice*.

4
The rich man in his castle,
The poor man at his gate,
God made them, high or lowly,
And ordered their estate.
CECIL FRANCES ALEXANDER, *All Things Bright*.

5
Providence cares for every hungry mouth.
ROBERT BROWNING, *Ferishtah's Fancies: The Eagle*.

If heaven send no supplies,
The fairest blossom of the garden dies.
WILLIAM BROWNE, *Visions*. Ch. 5.

6
'Tis Providence alone secures
In every change, both mine and yours.
COWPER, *A Fable: Moral*.

7
O thou, whose certain eye foresees
The fix'd events of fate's remote decrees.
HOMER, *Odyssey*. Bk. iv, l. 627. (Pope, tr.)

8
He maketh his sun to rise on the evil and on the good, and sendeth rain on the just and on the unjust.
New Testament: Matthew, v, 45.

9
The Ball no question makes of Ayes and Noes,
But Here or There as strikes the Player goes;
And He that toss'd you down into the Field,
He knows about it all—HE knows—HE knows!
OMAR KHAYYÁM, *Rubáiyát*, 70. (Fitzgerald, tr.)

The Moving Finger writes; and, having writ,
Moves on: nor all your Piety nor Wit
Shall lure it back to cancel half a Line
Nor all your Tears wash out a Word of it
OMAR KHAYYÁM, *Rubáiyát*, 71. (Fitzgerald, tr.)

10
Divine power plays with human affairs. (Ludit in humanis divina potentia rebus.)
OVID, *Epistulæ ex Ponto*. Bk. iv, epis. 3, l. 49.

11
Go, wiser thou! and in thy scale of sense
Weigh thy opinion against Providence;
Call imperfection what thou fanciest such;
Say, here he gives too little, there too much;
Destroy all creatures for thy sport or gust,
Yet cry, if man's unhappy, God's unjust.
POPE, *Essay on Man*. Epis. i, l. 113.

12
He putteth down one and setteth up another.
Old Testament: Psalms, lxxv, 7.

13
It is not so with Him that all things knows
As 'tis with us that square our guess by shows;
But most it is presumption in us when
The help of heaven we count the act of men.
SHAKESPEARE, *All's Well that Ends Well*. Act ii, sc. 1, l. 152.

14
There's a divinity that shapes our ends,
Rough-hew them how we will.
SHAKESPEARE, *Hamlet*. Act v, sc. 2, l. 10.

O God, thy arm was here;
And not to us, but to thy arm alone,
Ascribe we all!
SHAKESPEARE, *Henry V*. Act iv, sc. 8, l. 111.

But He, that hath the steerage of my course,
Direct my sail!
SHAKESPEARE, *Romeo and Juliet*. Act i, sc. 4, l. 112.

15
Arming myself with patience
To stay the providence of some high powers
That govern us below.
SHAKESPEARE, *Julius Cæsar*. Act v, sc. 1, l. 106.

16
A greater power than we can contradict
Hath thwarted our intents.
SHAKESPEARE, *Romeo and Juliet*. Act v, sc. 3, l. 153.

17
Every drunken skipper trusts to Providence. But one of the ways of Providence with drunken skippers is to run them on the rocks.
BERNARD SHAW, *Heartbreak House*. Act iii.

18
He maketh kings to sit in soverainty;
He maketh subjects to their power obey;
He pulleth down, he setteth up on high;
He gives to this, from that he takes away;
For all we have is his: what he list do he may.
SPENSER, *Faerie Queene*. Bk. v, canto ii, st. 41.

19
The mighty power of the gods ordains it. (Cælestum vis magna jubet.)
VERGIL, *Æneid*. Bk. vii, l. 432.

Events of all sorts creep or fly exactly as God pleases.
COWPER, *Letter to Lady Hesketh*, 11 June, 1792.

See also GOD: MAN PROPOSES BUT GOD DISPOSES.

III—Providence: Its Beneficence

1
Confide ye aye in Providence,
For Providence is kind:
An' bear ye a' life's changes
Wi' a calm an' tranquil mind.
Tho' pressed and hemmed on every side,
Ha'e faith, an' ye'll win through;
For ilka blade o' grass
Keeps its ain drap o' dew.
JAMES BALLANTINE, *Its Ain Drap o' Dew.*

"Oh! pilot, 'tis a fearful night,
There's danger on the deep!
I'll come and pace the deck with thee,
I do not dare to sleep."
"Go down!" the sailor cried, "go down!
This is no place for thee;
Fear not, but trust in Providence,
Wherever thou mayst be."
THOMAS HAYNES BAYLY, *The Pilot.*

2
Judge not the Lord by feeble sense,
But trust Him for His grace;
Behind a frowning Providence
He hides a smiling face.
COWPER, *Light Shining Out of Darkness.*

3
We sometimes had those little rubs which Providence sends to enhance the value of its favours.
GOLDSMITH, *The Vicar of Wakefield.* Ch. 1.

4
We ought to feel deep cheerfulness, as I may say, that a happy Providence kept it from being any worse.
HARDY, *Far from the Madding Crowd.* Ch. 8.

5
Behind the dim unknown,
Standeth God within the shadow, keeping watch above his own.
J. R. LOWELL, *The Present Crisis.* St. 8.

6
The lot assigned to every man is suited to him, and suits him to itself.
MARCUS AURELIUS, *Meditations.* Bk. iii, sec. 4.

God gives to ev'ry man
The virtue, temper, understanding, taste,
That lifts him into life, and lets him fall
Just in the niche he was ordain'd to fill.
COWPER, *The Task.* Bk. iv, l. 789.

7
Are not two sparrows sold for a farthing? and one of them shall not fall on the ground without your Father.
New Testament: Matthew, xi, 29.

He that doth the ravens feed,
Yea, providently caters for the sparrow,
Be comfort to my age!
SHAKESPEARE, *As You Like It.* Act ii, sc. 3, l. 43.

There's a special providence in the fall of a sparrow. If it be now, 't is not to come; if it be not to come, it will be now; if it be not now, yet it will come: the readiness is all.
SHAKESPEARE, *Hamlet.* Act v, sc. 2, l. 230.

8
Eye me, blest Providence, and square my trial
To my proportion'd strength.
MILTON, *Comus,* l. 329.

9
The sun shall not smite thee by day, nor the moon by night.
Old Testament: Psalms, cxxi, 6.

10
Come wealth or want, come good or ill,
Let young and old accept their part,
And bow before the Awful Will,
And bear it with an honest heart.
THACKERAY, *The End of the Play.*

11
So, darkness in the pathway of Man's life
Is but the shadow of God's providence,
By the great Sun of Wisdom cast thereon;
And what is dark below is light in Heaven.
WHITTIER, *Tauler,* l. 79.

12
While Thee I seek, protecting Power,
Be my vain wishes stilled;
And may this consecrated hour
With better hopes be filled.
HELEN MARIA WILLIAMS, *Trust in Providence.*

13
We rather think, with grateful mind sedate,
How Providence educeth, from the spring
Of lawless will, unlooked-for streams of good,
Which neither force shall check nor time abate.
WORDSWORTH, *Miscellaneous Sonnets.* Pt. iii, No. 4. Of Henry VIII.

PRUDENCE

See also Discretion

I—Prudence: Definitions

14
By prudence, which the Greeks call φρόνησις, we understand the practical knowledge of things to be sought, and of things to be avoided. (Prudentiam enim, quam Græci φρόνησιν dicunt, aliam quandam intellegimus, quæ est rerum expetendarum fugiendarumque scientia.)
CICERO, *De Officiis.* Bk. i, ch. 43, sec. 153.

I prefer silent prudence to loquacious folly. (Malo indisertam prudentiam, quam loquacem stultitiam.)
CICERO, *De Oratore.* Bk. iii, sec. 35.

15
Prudence is God taking thought for oxen.
EMERSON, *Essays, First Series: Prudence.*

16
The greatest good is prudence; a more precious thing even than philosophy; from it spring all the other virtues.
EPICURUS, *Letter to Menœceus.* (DIOGENES LAERTIUS, *Epicurus.* Bk. x, sec. 132.)

17
That man is prudent who neither hopes nor fears anything from the uncertain events of the future.
ANATOLE FRANCE, *The Procurator of Judea.*

1
Wise venturing is the most commendable part of human prudence.
LORD HALIFAX, *Works*, p. 245.

2
One has no protecting power save prudence. (Nullum numen habes si sit prudentia.)
JUVENAL, *Satires*. Sat. x, l. 365; sat. xiv, l. 315.

No divinity is absent if Prudence is present. (Nullum numen abest si sit Prudentia.)
JUVENAL, *Satires*. Sat. x, l. 365. Adapted.

II—Prudence: Apothegms

3
Prudence is of no service unless it be prompt.
FRANCIS BACON, *De Augmentis Scientiarum:* Pt. i, bk. 6. *Promptitudo*.

4
Hearken with your ears that ye may know prudence.
Apocrypha: Baruch, iii, 9. (Douay.)

5
Early and provident fear is the mother of safety.
EDMUND BURKE, *Speech*, on the Unitarian petition, 11 May, 1792. *See under* FEAR.

For those that fly may fight again,
Which he can never do that's slain.
BUTLER, *Hudibras*. Pt. iii, canto 3, l. 243. *See under* DISCRETION *for other quotations.*

6
Achilles, though invulnerable, never went to battle but completely armed.
LORD CHESTERFIELD, *Letters*, 15 Jan., 1753.

7
Precaution is better than cure. (Præstat cautela quam medela.)
COKE, *Institutes*.

Prevention is the daughter of intelligence.
SIR WALTER RALEIGH, *Letter to Sir Robert Cecil*, 10 May, 1593.

8
The cautious seldom err.
CONFUCIUS, *Analects*. Bk. iv, ch. 23.

9
Chance fights ever on the side of the prudent. (Πᾶσιν γὰρ εὐφρονοῦσι συμμαχεῖ τύχη.)
EURIPIDES, *Peirithous*. Frag.

10
One virtue he had in perfection, which was prudence—often the only one that is left us at seventy-two.
GOLDSMITH, *The Vicar of Wakefield*. Ch. 2.

11
Every one stretcheth his legs according to his coverlet.
GEORGE HERBERT, *Jacula Prudentum* (1640)

He who does not stretch himself according to the coverlet finds his feet uncovered. (Wer sich nicht nach der Decke streckt, dem bleiben die Füsse unbedeckt.)
GOETHE, *Sprüche in Reimen*, iii.

I shall cut my coat after my cloth.
JOHN HEYWOOD, *Proverbs*. Pt. i, ch. 8. (1546)
See also under ADAPTABILITY.

12
Prudence is always in season. (La prudence est toujours de saison.)
MOLIÈRE, *Dépit Amoureux*. Act v, sc. 8, l. 8.

13
Prudence is the first thing to desert the wretched. (Miseros prudentia prima relinquit.)
OVID, *Epistulæ ex Ponto*. Bk. iv, epis. 12, l. 47.

14
The prudent man looketh well to his going.
Old Testament: Proverbs, xiv, 15.

15
As he is slow he is sure.
STEELE, *The Spectator*. No. 140. *See also under* CERTAINTY.

16
I won't quarrel with my bread and butter.
SWIFT, *Polite Conversation*. Dial. 1.

17
It becomes a wise man to try negotiation before arms. (Omnia prius experiri verbis quam armis sapientem decet.)
TERENCE, *Eunuchus*. Act v, sc. 1, l. 19.

III—Prudence: Look Before You Leap

18
Look ere thou leap, whose literal sense is, Do nothing suddenly or without advisement.
WILLIAM TYNDALE, *The Obedience of a Christian Man*, 304. (1528)

Look ere you leap.
JOHN HEYWOOD, *Proverbs*. Pt. i, ch. 2. (1546)

19
Look ere you leap, see ere you go,
It may be for thy profit so.
THOMAS TUSSER, *Five Hundred Points of Good Husbandry*. Ch. 56. (1573)

20
He that looketh not before he leapeth
May chance to stumble before he sleepeth.
WILLIAM PAINTER, *Palace of Pleasure*, iii, 53. (1567)

21
Thou shouldst have looked before thou hadst leapt.
BEN JONSON, *Eastward Hoe*. Act v, sc. 1. (1605)

22
Let every man look before he leaps.
CERVANTES, *Don Quixote*. Pt. ii, ch. 14. (1615)

23
'Tis good to look before thou leap.
MARTIN PARKER, *An Excellent New Medley*. (*Roxburghe Ballads*. 1643.)

24
Try therefore before you trust; look before you leap
JOHN TRAPP, *Commentaries: I Peter*. (1660)
Trapp traces the saying back to St. Bernard.

25
Look before you ere you leap,
For as you sow, ye are like to reap.
BUTLER, *Hudibras*. Pt. ii, canto 2, l. 501. (1664)

26
I love to look before I leap.
STEELE, *Tender Husband*. Act iii, sc. 2. (1705)

1
Look twice before you leap.
CHARLOTTE BRONTË, *Shirley*. Ch. 9. (1849)

2
Always wise men go back for to leap the further.
UNKNOWN, *Melusine*. Ch. 20. (14th century French romance.)

One must draw back to leap the better. (Il faut reculer pour mieux sauter.)
MONTAIGNE, *Essays*. Bk. i, ch. 38.

IV—Prudence: Make Haste Slowly

3
Make haste slowly. (Σπεῦδε βραδέως.)
CÆSAR AUGUSTUS. (AULUS GELLIUS, *Noctes Atticæ*. Bk. x, ch. 11, sec. 5.) Aulus Gellius says that the Emperor used these two Greek words in conversation and in his letters, "by which he recommended that to accomplish a result we should use at once the promptness of energy and the delay of carefulness." Suetonius (*Lives of the Cæsars: The Deified Augustus*, xxv, 4) attributes to him the familiar Latin form, "Festina lente." Franklin used it in *Poor Richard*, April, 1744. The German form is, "Eile mit Weile."

Hasten slowly. (Hâtez-vous lentement.)
BOILEAU, *L'Art Poétique*. Canto i, l. 171.

5
Festination may prove precipitation; deliberating delay may be wise cunctation.
SIR THOMAS BROWNE, *Christian Morals*. Pt. i, sec. 33. Paraphrasing Cæsar Augustus.

6
He hasteth well that wisely can abide.
CHAUCER, *The Tale of Melibeus*. Sec. 13. Quoted as a proverb, and used also in *Troilus and Criseyde*, bk. i, l. 956.

V—Prudence: Two Strings to the Bow

7
I will well that every man be amorous and love, but that he have two strings on his bow.
WILLIAM CAXTON, *Jason*, 57. (c. 1477)

'Tis true no lover has that pow'r
T' enforce a desperate amour,
As he that has two strings t' his bow,
And burns for love and money too.
BUTLER, *Hudibras*. Pt. iii, canto 1, l. 1.

8
I hope you will remember that who seeketh two strings to one bow, he may shoot strong but never straight.
QUEEN ELIZABETH, *Letter to James VI*. (*Letters*. No. 10. 1585)

Yes, I had two strings to my bow; both golden ones, egad! and both cracked.
FIELDING, *Love in Several Masques*. Act v, sc. 13.

10
You have many strings to your bow.
JOHN HEYWOOD, *Proverbs*. Pt. i, ch. 11. (1546)

11
Have more strings to thy bow than one; it is safe riding at two anchors.
JOHN LYLY, *Euphues*, p. 116. (1579)

12
In the stormy night it is well that anchors twain be let down from the swift ship.
PINDAR, *Olympian Odes*. Ode vi, l. 100.

A ship is safer when two cables hold it, and an anxious mother, if she rear twins, has less to dread. (Nam melius duo defendunt retinacula navim, Tutius et geminos anxia mater alit.)
PROPERTIUS, *Elegies*. Bk. ii, eleg. 22, l. 41.

Good riding at two anchors, men have told,
For if one fail, the tother may hold.
JOHN HEYWOOD, *Proverbs*. Pt. ii, ch. 9. (1546)

13
I think it better to have two strings to my bow. (Commodius esse opinor duplici spe utier.)
TERENCE, *Phormio*, l. 603. (Act iv, sc. 2.)

I will well that every man be amorous and love but that he have two strings on his bow.
WILLIAM CAXTON, *Jason*, 57. (c. 1477)

It is always good for one to have two strings to his bow.
JOHN FLORIO, *First Fruites*. Fo. 6. (1578)

So that every man lawfully ordained must bring a bow which hath two strings, a title of present right and another to provide for future possibility or chance.
RICHARD HOOKER, *Laws of Ecclesiastical Polity*. Bk. v, ch. 80. (1597)

A wise man's bow goes with a two-fold string.
JOHN DAY, *Ile of Gulls*. Act ii, sc. 2. (1606)

Archers ever
Have two strings to a bow; and shall great Cupid
(Archer of archers both in men and women),
Be worse provided than a common archer?
GEORGE CHAPMAN, *Bussy d'Ambois*. Act ii, sc. 1. (1607)

'Tis good in every case, you know,
To have two strings unto our bow.
CHARLES CHURCHILL, *The Ghost*. Bk. iv, l. 1282. (1761)

VI—Prudence: Admonitions

14
He that cannot see well, let him go softly.
FRANCIS BACON, *Baconiana*, p. 65.

Where the road bends abruptly take short steps.
ERNEST BRAMAH, *Kai Lung's Golden Hours*.

Do not adjust your sandals while passing through a melon field; nor yet arrange your hat beneath an orange tree.
ERNEST BRAMAH, *Kai Lung's Golden Hours*.

15
It is always good
When a man has two irons in the fire.
BEAUMONT AND FLETCHER, *The Faithful Friends*. Act i, sc. 2.

16
It is a common saying that it is best first to catch the stag, and afterwards, when he has been caught, to skin him. (Vulgariter dicitur, quod primum oportet cervum capere, et postea, cum captus fuerit, illum excoriare.)
HENRY DE BRACTON, *De Legibus et Consuetudinibus Angliæ*. Bk. iv, pt. i, ch. 2, sec. 4. (c. 1240) *See also under* FOLLY.

17
It is the part of a wise man to keep himself

to-day for to-morrow, and not to venture all his eggs in one basket.
CERVANTES, *Don Quixote*. Bk. iii, ch. 9.

1
Let us not throw the rope after the bucket. (No arrojemos la soga tras el caldero.)
CERVANTES, *Don Quixote*. Pt. ii, ch. 9.

2
They had best not stir the rice, though it sticks to the pot.
CERVANTES, *Don Quixote*. Pt. ii, ch. 37.

3
Never put thy thumbs between two back teeth.
CERVANTES, *Don Quixote*. Pt. ii, ch. 43.

Between the tree and your finger never put the bark. (Entre l'arbre et le doigt il ne faut point mettre l'écorce.)
MOLIÈRE, *Le Médicin Malgré Lui*. Act i, sc. 2. Referred to as a saying of Cicero.

4
The branch is better that bowen will to wind
Than that that breaks.
CHAUCER, *Troilus and Criseyde*. Bk. i, l. 257. (c. 1374)

Rather to bow than break is profitable;
Humility is a thing commendable.
UNKNOWN, *Moral Proverbs of Christian*. (1390)

Better is to bow than break.
JOHN HEYWOOD, *Proverbs*. Pt. i, ch. 9. (1546)

I bend and do not break. (Je plie et ne romps pas.)
LA FONTAINE, *Fables*. Bk. i, fab. 22.

5
If thou meet a red man and a bearded woman, greet them three mile off.
JOHN FLORIO, *First Fruites*. Fo. 30. (1578)

The red is wise, the brown trusty,
The pale envious, and the black lusty. . . .
To a red man read thy rede,
With a brown man break thy bread,
At a pale man draw thy knife,
From a black man keep thy wife.
ROBERT TOFTE, *Blazon of Jealousy*, 21. (1615)

He is false by nature that has a black head and a red beard.
THOMAS FULLER, *Gnomologia*. No. 1915.

6
Wonder at hills, keep on the plain;
Praise the sea, on shore remain.
JOHN FLORIO, *Second Frutes*. Fo. 99. (1591)

Praise the mountains, but love the plains.
JOHN WODROEPE, *Spared Hours*, 277. (1623)

Praise a hill, but keep below;
Praise the sea, but keep on land.
GEORGE HERBERT, *Jacula Prudentum*. (1640)

Commend the sea, but keep thyself ashore.
JAMES HOWELL, *Familiar Letters*, ii, 666. (1659)

7
Whose house is of glass must not throw stones at another.
GEORGE HERBERT, *Jacula Prudentum*. (1640)

Nobody should throw stones whose house is made of glass.
CHARLES SHADWELL, *The Sham Prince*. Act i, sc. 2. (1720)

Don't throw stones at your neighbors, if your own windows are glass.
BENJAMIN FRANKLIN, *Poor Richard*, 1736.

One who has a head of glass should never engage in throwing stones.
JOHN GROSE, *Olio*, 281. (1793)

People who live in glass houses have no right to throw stones.
BERNARD SHAW, *Widowers' Houses*. Act ii. (1892)

8
He that goes barefoot must not plant thorns.
GEORGE HERBERT, *Jacula Prudentum*. (1640)

He that scatters thorns, let him not go barefoot.
BENJAMIN FRANKLIN, *Poor Richard*, 1736.

9
Put your trust in God, my boys, and keep your powder dry.
OLIVER CROMWELL, as they were about to cross a stream to attack the enemy. (HAYES, *Ballads of Ireland*. Vol. i, p. 191.)

10
Open not thine heart to every man.
Apocrypha: Ecclesiasticus, viii, 19.

11
To women's fore parts do not aspire,
From a mule's hinder part retire,
And shun all parts of monk or friar.
JOHN FLORIO, *Second Frutes*. Fo. 99. (1591)

Take heed of an ox before, an ass behind, and a monk on all sides.
JOHN RAY, *English Proverbs*. (1670) Cited as from the Spanish.

Beware of a mule's hind foot, a dog's tooth, and a woman's tongue.
C. H. SPURGEON, *Ploughman's Pictures*, 118.

The Boldest Farmer heeds the Cautious Rule
To stand Behind the Bull, Before the Mule.
ARTHUR GUITERMAN, *A Poet's Proverbs*, p. 106.

12
He [Mather] was a man who never missed any occasion of giving instruction; and upon this he said to me, "You are young and have the world before you; stoop as you go through it, and you will miss many hard thumps."
BENJAMIN FRANKLIN, *Letter to Dr. Mather*.

13
Speak with contempt of none, from slave to king;
The meanest bee hath, and will use, a sting.
BENJAMIN FRANKLIN, *Poor Richard*, 1743.

14
A stitch in time may save nine.
THOMAS FULLER, *Gnomologia*. No. 6291. (1732)

15
I desire not the lowest; I am incapable of

the highest; I keep quiet. (Imum nolo; summum nequeo; quiesco.)

BISHOP JOSEPH HALL, *Motto*, on his vicarage, Hawsted, Suffolk, England. (c. 1601)

Tar-baby ain't sayin' nuthin', en brer Fox, he lay low.

JOEL CHANDLER HARRIS, *Legends of the Old Plantation*. Ch. xii.

1
Grasp not at much, for fear thou losest all.

GEORGE HERBERT, *The Size*.

2
It is good to have a hatch before the door.

JOHN HEYWOOD, *Proverbs*. Pt. i, ch. 11.

3
Take things always by their smooth handle.

THOMAS JEFFERSON, *Writings*. Vol. xvi, p. 111.

4
The first years of man must make provision for the last.

SAMUEL JOHNSON, *Rasselas*. Ch. 17.

5
Better to go on foot than ride and fall.

THOMAS MIDDLETON, *Micro-Cynicon*. Sat. v.

6
If you have any care for me, take care of yourself! (Si tibi cura mei, sit tibi cura tui!)

OVID, *Heroides*. Epis. xiii, l. 166.

7
Be modest in good fortune, prudent in misfortune. (Εὐτυχῶν μὲν μέτριος ἴσθι, ἀτυχῶν δὲ φρόνιμος.)

PERIANDER. (STOBÆUS, *Florilegium*. Pt. iii, l. 79.)

In time of stress show thyself brave and valiant!
Yet wisely reef thy sails when swollen by too fair
a breeze.
(Rebus angustis animosus atque
Fortis appare: sapienter idem
Contrahes vento nimium secundo
Turgida vela.)

HORACE, *Odes*. Bk. ii, ode 10, l. 21.

But O! if Fortune fill thy sail
With more than a propitious gale,
Take half thy canvas in.

HORACE, *Odes*, ii, 10. (Cowper, tr.)

Set thy sails warily,
Tempests will come;
Steer thy course steadily;
Christian, steer home!

CAROLINE ANNE SOUTHEY, *Mariner's Hymn*.

8
Be prudent, and if you hear, . . . some insult or some threat, . . . have the appearance of not hearing it.

GEORGE SAND, *Handsome Lawrence*. Ch. 2.

9
Wake not a sleeping wolf. To wake a wolf is as bad as to smell a fox.

SHAKESPEARE, *II Henry IV*. Act i, sc. 2, l. 173.
See also under WOLF.

10
Watch thou and wake when others be asleep.

SHAKESPEARE, *II Henry VI*. Act i, sc. 1, l. 249.

11
My ventures are not in one bottom trusted,
Nor to one place.

SHAKESPEARE, *The Merchant of Venice*. Act i, sc. 1, l. 42. (1596)

Venture not all in one bottom.

JOHN CLARKE, *Parœmiologia*, 95. (1639)

12
What need the bridge much broader than the flood?

SHAKESPEARE, *Much Ado About Nothing*, i, 1, 318.

13
Use another's foot to kick a dog. (Pieh jên chiao 'ti 'chüan.)

UNKNOWN. A Chinese proverb.

In buying needles examine the eyes. (Mai chên 'kan 'kung.)

UNKNOWN. A Chinese proverb.

14
Hug the shore, and let the oar-blade graze the rocks on the left; let others keep to the deep! (Litus ama et læva stringat sine palmula cautes; Altum alii teneant.)

VERGIL, *Æneid*. Bk. v, l. 163.

Great Estates may venture more,
But little Boats must keep near Shore.

BENJAMIN FRANKLIN, *Poor Richard*, 1751.

VII—Prudence: Its Virtues

15
Know, one false step is ne'er retriev'd,
And be with caution bold.

THOMAS GRAY, *On the Death of a Favourite Cat*, l. 38.

16
Man never heeds enough from hour to hour what he should shun. (Quid quisque vitet, numquam homini satis Cautum est in horas.)

HORACE, *Odes*. Bk. ii, ode 13, l. 13.

17
A prudence undeceiving, undeceived,
That nor too little, nor too much believed,
That scorned unjust Suspicion's coward fear,
And, without weakness, knew to be sincere.

GEORGE LYTTELTON, *Monody to the Memory of Lady Lyttelton*.

18
The man within the coach that sits,
And to another's skill submits,
Is safer much (whate'er arrives),
And warmer too, than he that drives.

MATTHEW PRIOR, *Alma*. Canto iii, l. 137.

19
He is free from danger who, even when he is safe, is on his guard. (Caret periculo, qui etiam cum est tutus cavet.)

PUBLILIUS SYRUS, *Sententiæ*. No. 127.

It is the part of a fool to give counsel to others, but himself not to be on his guard. (Sibi non cavere, et aliis consilium dare, Stultum esse.)

PHÆDRUS, *Fables*. Bk. i, fab. 9, l. 1.

20
Who fears all snares falls into none. (Qui omnes insidias timet, in nullas incidit.)

PUBLILIUS SYRUS, *Sententiæ*. No. 585.

1
You will conquer more surely by prudence than by passion. (Consilio melius vincas quam iracundia.)
PUBLILIUS SYRUS, *Sententiæ*. No. 107.

We accomplish more by prudence than by force. (Plura consilio quam vi perficimus.)
TACITUS, *Annals*. Bk. ii, sec. 26.

2
An ounce of prudence is worth a pound of gold.
SMOLLETT, *Roderick Random*. Ch. 15.

Whatever satisfies souls is true;
Prudence entirely satisfies the craving and glut of souls.
WALT WHITMAN, *Song of Prudence*, l. 40.

3
Who never wins can rarely lose,
Who never climbs as rarely falls.
WHITTIER, *To James T. Fields*. St. 13.

4
It is better to walk than to run; it is better to stand than to walk; it is better to sit than to stand: it is better to lie than to sit.
UNKNOWN. A Hindu proverb.

VIII—Prudence: Its Faults

5
Prudence is a rich, ugly old maid, courted by Incapacity.
WILLIAM BLAKE, *Proverbs of Hell*.

6
The prudent man may direct a state; but it is the enthusiast who regenerates it, or ruins.
BULWER-LYTTON, *Rienzi*. Bk. i, ch. 8.

7
Observe the prudent; they in silence sit,
Display no learning, and affect no wit;
They hazard nothing, nothing they assume,
But know the useful art of *acting dumb*.
GEORGE CRABBE, *Tales: The Patron*, l. 315.

Too eager caution shows some danger's near,
The bully's bluster proves the coward's fear.
GEORGE CRABBE, *The Parish Register*. Pt. i, l. 353.

8
Carefulness bringeth age before the time.
Apocrypha: Ecclesiasticus, xxx, 24.

9
The world is filled with the proverbs and acts and winkings of a base prudence; . . . a prudence which adores the Rule of Three, which never subscribes, which never gives, which seldom lends, and asks but one question of any project,—Will it bake bread?
EMERSON, *Essays, First Series: Prudence*.

10
Prudence keeps life safe, but does not often make it happy.
SAMUEL JOHNSON, *The Idler*. No. 57.

11
He could pledge himself to eternity, but shrank from being bound to eleven o'clock on the morrow morning.
GEORGE MEREDITH, *Sandra Belloni*. Ch. 20.

12
Refusing to accept as great a share
Of hazard as of honour.
MILTON, *Paradise Lost*. Bk. ii, l. 452.

13
He that is overcautious will accomplish little. (Wer gar zu viel bedenkt, wird wenig leisten.)
SCHILLER, *Wilhelm Tell*. Act iii, sc. 1, l. 72.
See also under TIMIDITY.

14
It is by the goodness of God that in our country we have those three unspeakably precious things: freedom of speech, freedom of conscience, and the prudence never to practice either.
MARK TWAIN, *Pudd'nhead Wilson's Calendar*.

IX—Prudence and Forethought

15
Advisement is good before the need.
CHAUCER, *Troilus and Criseyde*. Bk. ii, l. 343.

Let this proverb a lore unto you be,
"Too late y-were, quod Beauty, when it past."
CHAUCER, *Troilus and Criseyde*. Bk. ii, l. 398.

16
That should be considered long which can be decided but once. (Deliberandum est diu, quod statuendum semel.)
PUBLILIUS SYRUS, *Sententiæ*. No. 153.

When any great design thou dost intend,
Think on the means, the manner, and the end.
SIR JOHN DENHAM, *Of Prudence*.

17
Looking before and after.
SHAKESPEARE, *Hamlet*. Act iv, sc. 4, l. 37.

Shakespeare says, we are creatures that look before and after, the more surprising that we do not look round a little and see what is passing under our very eyes.
CARLYLE, *Sartor Resartus*. Bk. i, ch. 1.

18
Ay, and you had any eye behind you, you might see more detraction at your heels than fortunes before you.
SHAKESPEARE, *Twelfth Night*. Act ii, sc. 5, l. 148.

19
I have anticipated all things, and traversed them in thought. (Omnia præcepi atque animo mecum ante peregi.)
VERGIL, *Æneid*. Bk. vi, l. 105.

PRUDERY

See also Reformers

20
You have only, when before your glass, to keep pronouncing to yourself nimini-pimini; the lips cannot help taking their plie.
JOHN BURGOYNE, *The Heiress*. Act iii, sc. 2.

Father is rather vulgar, my dear. The word Papa, besides, gives a very pretty form to the lips. Papa, potatoes, poultry, prunes, and prism are all very good words for the lips; especially prunes and prism. You will find it serviceable, in the formation of a demeanour, if you sometimes say to yourself in company—on entering a room, for instance—Papa, potatoes, poultry, prunes and prism, prunes and prism.
DICKENS, *Little Dorrit*. Bk. ii, ch. 5.

1
At this every lady drew up her mouth as if going to pronounce the letter P.
GOLDSMITH, *Letter to R. Bryanton*, Sept., 1758.

2
Disdainful prudes, who ceaseless ply
The superb muscle of the eye.
MATTHEW GREEN, *The Spleen*, l. 119.

3
Prudery pretends to have only those passions that it cannot feel.
R. G. INGERSOLL, *Art and Morality*.

4
In England, the garden of Beauty is kept
By a dragon of prudery placed within call.
MOORE, *We May Roam Through This World*.

5
Hence, far hence, ye prudes! (Procul hinc, procul este, severæ!)
OVID, *Amores*. Bk. ii, eleg. 1, l. 3.

6
What is Prudery? 'Tis a beldam,
Seen with Wit and Beauty seldom. . . .
'Tis a virgin hard of feature,
Old, and void of all good-nature;
Lean and fretful; would seem wise,
Yet plays the fool before she dies.
POPE, *Answer to Mrs. Howe*.

Every thing nat'ral, and easy, and true, is ca'd coorse.
JOHN WILSON, *Noctes Ambrosianæ*. Ch. 26.

7
Comstockery is the world's standing joke at the expense of the United States. It confirms the deep-seated conviction of the Old World that America is a provincial place, a second-rate town civilization, after all.
BERNARD SHAW, *Interview*, N. Y. *Times*, 26 Sept., 1905, commenting upon the action of the New York Public Library in relegating his *Man and Superman* to the reserved shelves, an action which he thought Anthony Comstock had inspired. It was Comstock who had complained to the police of Shaw's play, *Mrs. Warren's Profession*, in 1904, and caused it to be closed.

Our art is all a mockery Of Bokery-Comstockery.
ARTHUR GUITERMAN, *A Wail*. (N. Y. *Times*, 11 Dec., 1906.) "Bokery" refers to Edward Bok, then editor of *The Ladies' Home Journal*. Comstock was the New York head of the Society for the Suppression of Vice.

8
Will Honeycomb calls these over-offended ladies the outrageously virtuous.
RICHARD STEELE, *Spectator*. No. 266.

PUBLIC, THE, see People, The

PUBLICITY

9
The great art in writing advertisements is the finding out a proper method to catch the reader's eye; without which a good thing may pass over unobserved, or be lost among commissions of bankrupt.
ADDISON, *The Tatler*. No. 224.

Advertisements are of great use to the vulgar. First of all, as they are instruments of ambition. A man that is by no means big enough for the Gazette, may easily creep into the advertisements; by which means we often see an apothecary in the same paper of news with a plenipotentiary, or a running footman with an ambassador.
ADDISON, *The Tatler*. No. 224.

10
As gaslight is found to be the best nocturnal police, so the universe protects itself by pitiless publicity.
EMERSON, *Conduct of Life: Worship*. The phrase, "Pitiless publicity," was popularized by Woodrow Wilson. *See* 2282:2.

11
In every field of human endeavor, he that is first must perpetually live in the white light of publicity.
THEODORE F. MACMANUS, *The Penalty of Leadership*. (*Sat. Eve. Post*, 2 Jan., 1915.)

12
Great is advertisement with little men.
OWEN SEAMAN, *Ode to Spring in the Metropolis*.

PUN

I—Puns: Their Faults and Virtues

13
The seeds of punning are in the minds of all men, and though they may be subdued by reason, reflection, and good sense, they will be very apt to shoot up in the greatest genius.
ADDISON, *The Spectator*. No. 61.

A turn for punning, call it Attic salt.
BYRON, *English Bards and Scotch Reviewers*, l. 68.

14
But still a pun I do detest,
'Tis such a paltry, humbug jest;
They who've least wit can make them best.
WILLIAM COMBE, *Dr. Syntax in Search of the Picturesque*. Canto xxvi.

15
A man who could make so vile a pun would not scruple to pick a pocket.
JOHN DENNIS. (*Gentleman's Magazine*. Vol. li, p. 324.)

The critic [Dennis] immediately started up and left the room, swearing that any man who could make such an execrable pun would pick his pocket.
UNKNOWN, *Article* in *The Public Advertiser*, London, 12 Jan., 1779.

And however our Dennises take offence,
A double meaning shows double sense;
And if proverbs tell truth, A double tooth
Is Wisdom's adopted dwelling.
THOMAS HOOD, *Miss Kilmansegg: Her Honeymoon*, l. 1881.

16
Rare compound of oddity, frolic, and fun!
Who relish'd a joke, and rejoic'd in a pun.
GOLDSMITH, *Retaliation*, l. 149.

1
People that make puns are like wanton boys that put coppers on the railroad tracks.

O. W. Holmes, *The Autocrat of the Breakfast-Table*. Ch. 1.

2
My little dears, who learn to read,
Pray early learn to shun
That very foolish thing indeed
The people call a pun.

Theodore Edward Hook, *Cautionary Verses to Youth of Both Sexes*.

3
A pun is a noble thing *per se*. O never bring it in as an accessory! . . . it fills the mind; it is as perfect as a sonnet; better.

Charles Lamb, *Letter to S. T. Coleridge*.

4
It often happens a bad pun
Goes farther than a better one.

W. S. Landor, *Last Fruit Off an Old Tree*. No. 92.

5
How every fool can play upon the word!

Shakespeare, *The Merchant of Venice*. Act iii, sc. 5, l. 48.

6
I have mentioned puns. They are, I believe, what I have denominated them—the wit of words. They are exactly the same to words which wit is to ideas, and consist in the sudden discovery of relations in language.

Sydney Smith, *Sketches of Moral Philosophy*. Lecture 10.

Puns are in very bad repute. . . . The wit of words is so miserably inferior to the wit of ideas that it is very deservedly driven out of good company.

Sydney Smith, *Sketches of Moral Philosophy*.

7
I am thankful that my name is obnoxious to no pun.

William Shenstone, *Egotisms*.

Pun-provoking thyme.

Shenstone, *The Schoolmistress*. St. 11.

II—Puns: A Few Examples

8
Mr. Hay was rather hazy and Mr. Wu was rather woozy.

Alvey A. Adee. Referring to conference between John Hay and Wu Ting-fang during the Boxer uprising.

9
The Window has Four Little Panes;
But One have I—
The Window Panes are in its Sash;
I Wonder Why!

Gelett Burgess, *Panes*.

10
In all quarters of Paris, and to every store,
While McFlimsey in vain stormed, scolded, and swore,
They footed the streets, and he footed the bills.

William Allen Butler, *Nothing to Wear*.

11
There are months which nature grows more merry in—
March has its hares, and May must have its heroine.

Byron, *Don Juan*. Canto i, st. 102.

12
How funny it'll seem to come out among the people who walk with their heads downwards. The antipathies, I think.

Lewis Carroll, *Alice's Adventures in Wonderland*, p. 5.

13
Whoever weds the young lawyer at C.
Will surely have prospects most cheering,
For what must his person and intellect be,
When even his name is "N. Deering"?

Lydia Maria Child, *On Nathaniel Deering Moving to Canaan*.

14
So stooping down, as needs he must
Who cannot sit upright,
He grasped the mane with both his hands,
And eke with all his might.

William Cowper, *John Gilpin*.

15
Burgoyne, alas, unknowing future fates,
Could force his way through woods, but not through Gates.

David Edwards, *On Burgoyne's Surrender*. General Gates was the commander of the American army.

The very day that General Lee,
Flower of Southern chivalry,
Baffled and beaten, backward reeled
From a stubborn Meade and a barren field.

Bret Harte, *John Burns of Gettysburg*. General Meade was in command of the Union forces.

16
We found on his nails, which were taper,
What is frequent in tapers,—that's wax.

Bret Harte, *Plain Language From Truthful James*.

17
My sense of sight is very keen,
My sense of hearing weak.
One time I saw a mountain pass,
But could not hear its peak.

Oliver Herford, *My Sense of Sight*.

18
Ben Battle was a soldier bold,
And used to war's alarms;
But a cannon-ball took off his legs,
So he laid down his arms.

Thomas Hood, *Faithless Nelly Gray*.

For here I leave my second leg,
And the Forty-second Foot!

Thomas Hood, *Faithless Nelly Gray*.

19
His death, which happen'd in his berth,
At forty-odd befell;
They went and told the sexton, and
The sexton toll'd the bell.

Thomas Hood, *Faithless Sally Brown*.

1
Upon your cheek I may not speak,
Nor on your lip be warm,
I must be wise about your eyes,
And formal with your form.
THOMAS HOOD, *I'm Not a Single Man.*

2
Heaven never heard his cry, nor did
The ocean heed his *caul.*
THOMAS HOOD, *The Sea Spell.*

3
The famous Gate of Billing
That does not lead to cooing.
THOMAS HOOD, *The Turtles.*

4
Phœbus, sitting one day in a laurel-tree's shade,
Was reminded of Daphne, of whom it was made,
For the god being one day too warm in his wooing,
She took to the tree to escape his pursuing;
Be the cause what it might, from his offers she shrunk,
And, Ginevra-like, shut herself up in a trunk.
J. R. LOWELL, *A Fable for Critics,* l. 1.

5
In Ethics—'tis you that can check,
In a minute, their doubts and their quarrels;
Oh! show but that mole on your neck,
And 'twill soon put an end to their morals.
THOMAS MOORE, *To Fanny.*

6
When Dido found Æneas would not come,
She mourned in silence, and was Di-do-dumb.
RICHARD PORSON, *Facetiæ Cantabrigienses.* Porson had boasted that he could rhyme on any subject, and being asked to rhyme upon the three Latin gerunds, which, in the old Eton Latin grammar, are called *-di, -do, -dum,* produced the couplet given above.

7
We wanted Li Wing But we winged Willie Wong,
A sad but excusable Slip of the tong.
KEITH PRESTON, *Lapsus Linguæ.*

8
When the Rudyards cease from Kipling
And the Haggards Ride no more.
J. K. STEPHEN, *Lapsus Calami.*

PUNISHMENT

See also Retribution

I—Punishment: Apothegms

9
All punishment is mischief. All punishment in itself is evil.
JEREMY BENTHAM, *Principles of Morals and Legislation.* Ch. 15, sec. 1.

10
The world does not grow better by force or by the policeman's club.
WILLIAM J GAYNOR, *Letters and Speeches,* p. 314.

11
My punishment is greater than I can bear.
Old Testament: Genesis, iv, 13.

12
It is grievous to be caught. (Deprendi miserum est.)
HORACE, *Satires.* Bk. i, sat. 2, l. 134.

13
The power of punishment is to silence, not to confute.
SAMUEL JOHNSON, *Works.* Vol. ix, p. 499.

14
The object of punishment is, prevention from evil; it never can be made impulsive to good.
HORACE MANN, *Lectures and Reports on Education.* Lecture 7.

Men are not hanged for stealing horses, but that horses may not be stolen.
LORD HALIFAX, *Works,* 229.

The best of us being unfit to die, what an inexpressible absurdity to put the worst to death!
HAWTHORNE, *Journals,* 13 Oct., 1851.

II—Punishment: Just and Unjust

15
When by just vengeance guilty mortals perish,
The gods behold the punishment with pleasure,
And lay th' uplifted thunderbolt aside.
ADDISON, *Cato.* Act iii, sc. 4.

See they suffer death,
But in their deaths remember they are men;
Strain not the laws to make their tortures grievous.
ADDISON, *Cato.* Act iii, sc. 5.

16
Severity breedeth fear, but roughness breedeth hate. Even reproofs from authority ought to be grave, and not taunting.
FRANCIS BACON, *Essays: Of Great Place.*

17
Let the punishment be equal with the offence. (Noxiæ poena par esto.)
CICERO, *De Legibus.* Bk. iii, ch. 20.

Care should be taken that the punishment does not exceed the guilt. (Cavendum est ne major poena quam culpa sit.)
CICERO, *De Officiis.* Bk. i, ch. 25, sec. 89.

Let us have a system which assigns just penalties to offenses, lest you flay with the terrible scourge what calls only for the strap. (Adsit Regula, peccatis quæ poenas inroget æquas, Ne scutica dignum horribili sectere flagello.)
HORACE, *Satires.* Bk. i, sat. 3, l. 117.

The punishment, methinks, exceeds the offense.
CHARLES I, a soldier having invoked a blessing on him after having been struck by an officer. (HUME, *History of England.* Ch. 22.)

My object all sublime
I shall achieve in time—
To let the punishment fit the crime—
The punishment fit the crime.
W. S. GILBERT, *The Mikado.* Act ii.

18
Anger is to be very specially avoided in

inflicting punishment. (Prohibenda autem maxime est ira in puniendo.)

CICERO, *De Officiis*. Bk i, ch 25, sec. 89.

It is to be desired that those who are at the head of the commonwealth be like the laws, which are moved to punish, not by anger, but by justice.

CICERO, *De Officiis*. Bk. i, ch. 25, sec. 89.

But he is the peer of the gods whom reason, not anger, animates, and who, weighing the guilt, can with deliberation balance the punishment. (Dis proximus ille, Quem ratio, non ira movet, qui facta rependens Consilio punire potest.)

CLAUDIAN, *Panigyricus Dictus Manlio Theodoro Consuli*, l. 227.

He, who has committed a fault, is to be corrected both by advice and by force, kindly and harshly, and to be made better for himself as well as for another, not without chastisement, but without passion.

SENECA, *De Ira*. Bk. i, sec. 14.

1
Tell them the men that placed him here
Are friends unto the times;
But at a loss to find his guilt,
They can't commit his crimes.

DEFOE, *Hymn to the Pillory*. Conclusion.

2
In all cases where two have joined to commit an offence, punish one of the two lightly.

GEORGE MEREDITH, *Richard Feverel*. Ch. 27.

3
Let the ruler be slow to punish, swift to reward. (Sed piger ad poenas princeps, ad præmia velox.)

OVID, *Epistulæ ex Ponto*. Bk. i, epis. 2, l. 123.

4
Let those who have deserved their punishment, bear it patiently. (Æquo animo poenam, qui meruere, ferunt.)

OVID, *Amores*. Bk. ii, eleg. 7, l. 12.

Every one should bear patiently the results of his own conduct. (Sua quisque exempla debet æquo animo pati.)

PHÆDRUS, Bk. i, fab. 26, l. 12.

5
It is a smaller thing to suffer punishment than to have deserved it. . . . The punishment can be removed, the fault will remain forever. (Estque pati poenam, quam meruisse, minus. . . . Poena potest demi, culpa perennis erit.)

OVID, *Epistulæ ex Ponto*. Bk. i, epis. 1, l. 62.

Patiently must we bear whatever suffering is our desert; the punishment which comes without deserving, comes as a matter for bewailing. (Leniter, ex merito quidquid patiare, ferendum est; Quæ venit indigno poena, dolenda venit.)

OVID, *Heroides*. Eleg. v, l. 7.

6 But if the first Eve
Hard doom did receive,
When only one apple had she,
What a punishment new
Shall be found out for you,
Who tasting have robb'd the whole tree?

POPE, *To Lady Mary Wortley Montagu*.

7
The time that precedes punishment is the severest part of it. (Quod antecedit tempus, maxima venturi supplicii pars est.)

SENECA, *De Beneficiis*. Bk. ii, sec. 5.

8
Bid that welcome
Which comes to punish us, and we punish it
Seeming to bear it lightly.

SHAKESPEARE, *Antony and Cleopatra*, iv, 14, 36.

Let death come now! 'tis right to die!
Right to be punished!

ROBERT BROWNING, *Pippa Passes*.

9
There needeth not the hell that bigots frame
To punish those who err: Earth in itself
Contains at once the evil and the cure;
And all-sufficing Nature can chastise
Those who transgress her law,—she only knows
How justly to proportion to the fault
The punishment it merits.

SHELLEY, *Queen Mab*. Canto iii, l. 79.

10
That's the penalty we have to pay for our acts of foolishness,—someone else always suffers for them.

ALFRED SUTRO, *The Perfect Lover*. Act ii.

11
Every great example of punishment has in it some injustice, but the suffering individual is compensated by the public good. (Habet aliquid ex iniquo omne magnum exemplum, quod contra singulos, utilitate publica rependitus.)

TACITUS, *Annals*. Bk. xiv, sec. 44.

III—Punishment: Its Certainty

See also Justice: Its Certainty; Retribution: Its Certainty

12
The sword of heaven is not in haste to smite,
Nor yet doth linger.

DANTE, *Paradiso*. Canto xxii, l. 16. (Cary, tr.)

13
There is no den in the wide world to hide a rogue. Commit a crime, and the earth is made of glass. . . . The laws and substances of nature become penalties to the thief.

EMERSON, *Essays, First Series: Compensation*.

Crime and punishment grow out of one stem. Punishment is a fruit that unsuspected ripens within the flower of the pleasure which concealed it.

EMERSON, *Essays, First Series: Compensation*.

That is the bitterest of all,—to wear the yoke of our own wrong-doing.

GEORGE ELIOT, *Daniel Deronda*. Bk. v, ch. 36.

14
Punishment is lame, but it comes.

GEORGE HERBERT, *Jacula Prudentum*.

15
Punishment follows close on guilt. (Culpam poena premit comes.)

HORACE, *Odes*. Bk iv, ode 5, l. 24.

1
By his own verdict no guilty man was ever acquitted. (Se judice, nemo nocens absolvitur.)

JUVENAL, *Satires*. Sat. xiii, l. 2. *See also under* CRIME.

2
But that two-handed engine at the door
Stands ready to smite once, and smite no more.

MILTON, *Lycidas*, l. 130.

3
One day brings the punishment which many days demand (Unus dies poenam affert quam multi irrogant.)

PUBLILIUS SYRUS, *Sententiæ*. No. 692.

4
Good luck frees many men from punishment, but no man from fear (Multos fortuna liberat poena, metu neminem.)

SENECA, *Epistulæ ad Lucilium*. Epis. xcvii, 15.

5
Crime can never go unpunished, since the punishment of crime lies in the crime itself. (Nec ullum scelus . . inpunitum est, quoniam sceleris in scelere supplicium est.)

SENECA, *Epistulæ ad Lucilium* Epis. xcvii, 14.

The greatest chastisement that a man may receive who hath outraged another, is to have done the outrage; and there is no man who is so rudely punished as he that is subject to the whip of his own repentance.

SENECA, *De Ira*. Bk. iii, sec. 26.

Disgrace does not consist in the punishment, but in the crime. (Non nella pena, Nell' delitto è la infamia.)

ALFIERI, *Antigone*. Act i, sc. 3.

For crime is all the shame of punishment.

DANIEL DEFOE, *Hymn to the Pillory*.

See also under SHAME.

6
There is no greater punishment for vice than that it is dissatisfied with itself and its deeds. (Nec ulla major poena nequitiæ est quam quod sibi ac suis displicet.)

SENECA, *Epistulæ ad Lucilium*. Epis. xlii, sec. 2.

7
Even if at first we hide the perjury, yet in the end comes Punishment on noiseless feet. (Si quis primo perjuria celat, Sera tamen tacitis Poena venit pedibus.)

TIBULLUS, *Odes*. Bk. i, ode 9, l. 3.

8
Each of us suffers his own Spirit. (Quisquis suos patimur Manes.)

VERGIL, *Æneid*. Bk. vi, l. 743.

9
The soul itself its awful witness is.
Say not in evil doing, "No one sees."

J. G. WHITTIER, *The Inward Judge*.

IV—Punishment: Its Forms

10
Some have been beaten till they know
What wood a cudgel's of by th' blow:
Some kick'd until they can feel whether
A shoe be Spanish or neat's leather.

BUTLER, *Hudibras*. Pt. ii, canto 1, l. 221.

11
Forty stripes save one.

New Testament: II Corinthians, xi, 24.

A rod is for the back of him that is void of understanding.

Old Testament: Proverbs, x, 13.

A whip for the horse, a bridle for the ass, and a rod for the fool's back.

Old Testament: Proverbs, xxvi, 3.

Judgments are prepared for scorners, and stripes for the back of fools.

Old Testament: Proverbs, xix, 29.

11a
She sifted the meal, she gimme the huss;
She baked the bread, she gimme the crus';
She biled the meat, she gimme the bone;
She gimme a kick, and sent me home!

DAVID CROCKETT, of an aunt who had treated him shabbily when he was a boy. (*Century Magazine*, April, 1894, p. 851.)

12
'Tis I that call, remember Milo's end,
Wedged in that timber which he strove to rend.

WENTWORTH DILLON, *Essay on Translated Verse*.

13
It's very hard to lose your cash,
But harder to be shot.

O. W. HOLMES, *The Music Grinders*.

14
The greatest punishment is to be despised by your neighbors, the world, and members of your family.

E. W. HOWE, *Howe's Monthly*.

15
Just prophet, let the damn'd one dwell
Full in the sight of Paradise,
Beholding heaven and feeling hell.

THOMAS MOORE, *Lalla Rookh: The Fire Worshippers*, l. 1028.

16
Say-all-you-know shall go with clouted head,
Say-nought-at-all is beaten.

WILLIAM MORRIS, *The Earthly Paradise: The Lovers of Gudrun*, l. 121.

17
My father hath chastised you with whips, but I will chastise you with scorpions.

Old Testament: I Kings, xii, 11; *II Chronicles*, x, 14.

20
Thou shalt be whipp'd with wire, and stew'd in brine,
Smarting in lingering pickle.

SHAKESPEARE, *Antony and Cleopatra*. Act ii, sc. 5, l. 65.

For him at least I have a rod in pickle.

KANE O'HARA, *Midas*. Act ii, sc. 1.

Something lingering, with boiling oil in it, I fancy. Something of that sort. I think boiling oil occurs in it, but I'm not sure, I know it's something humorous, but lingering, with either boiling oil or melted lead.

W. S. GILBERT, *The Mikado*. Act ii.

1
Off with his guilty head!

SHAKESPEARE, *III Henry VI*. Act v, sc. 5, l. 3.

Off with his head—so much for Buckingham!

CIBBER, *Richard III* (altered). Act iv, sc. 3.

Your great goodness, out of holy pity,
Absolved him with an axe.

SHAKESPEARE, *Henry VIII*. Act iii, sc. 2, l. 263.

2
Pinch the maids as blue as bilberry.

SHAKESPEARE, *The Merry Wives of Windsor*. Act v, sc. 5, l. 49.

Some of us will smart for it.

SHAKESPEARE, *Much Ado About Nothing*. Act v, sc. 1, l. 109.

3
You will have words for your punishment, but for me there will be blows. (Tibi erunt parata verba, huic homini verbera.)

TERENCE, *Heauton Timorumenos*, l. 356. (Act ii, sc. 3.)

4
Poor Floyd Ireson, for his hard heart,
Tarred and feathered and carried in a cart
By the women of Marblehead!

WHITTIER, *Skipper Ireson's Ride*.

PURITANS

See also Pilgrim Fathers

5
Round-heads and wooden-shoes are standing-jokes.

ADDISON, *The Drummer: Prologue*.

6
The Puritan has been made a popular scape-goat, and the word has become a catch-basin for undeserved reproaches.

SILAS BENT, *Justice O. W. Holmes*, p. 54.

7
It never frightened a Puritan when you bade him stand still and listen to the speech of God. His closet and his church were full of the reverberations of the awful, gracious, beautiful voice for which he listened.

PHILLIPS BROOKS, *Sermons: The Seriousness of Life*.

He made little, too little of sacraments and priests, because God was so intensely real to him. What should he do with lenses who stood thus full in the torrent of the sunshine.

PHILLIPS BROOKS, *Sermons: The Seriousness of Life*.

8
A sect, whose chief devotion lies
In odd perverse antipathies;
In falling out with that or this,
And finding somewhat still amiss;
More peevish, cross, and splenetic,
Than dog distract, or monkey sick:
That with more care keep holy-day
The wrong, than others the right way;
Compound for sins they are inclin'd to,
By damning those they have no mind to:
Still so perverse and opposite,
As if they worshipp'd God for spite.

BUTLER, *Hudibras*. Pt. i, canto i, l. 207.

9
A puritan is a person who pours righteous indignation into the wrong things.

G. K. CHESTERTON, *Interview*, N. Y. *Times*, 21 Nov., 1930.

10
There was a State without kings or nobles; there was a church without a bishop; there was a people governed by grave magistrates which it had elected, and equal laws which it had framed.

RUFUS CHOATE, *Speech*, before the New England Society, 22 Dec., 1843.

It [Calvinism] established a religion without a prelate, a government without a king.

GEORGE BANCROFT, *History of the United States*. Vol iii, ch. 6.

Oh, we are weary pilgrims; to this wilderness we bring
A Church without a bishop, a State without a King.

UNKNOWN, *The Puritan's Mistake*.

11
'Twas founded be th' Puritans to give thanks f'r bein' presarved fr'm the Indyans, an' we keep it to give thanks we are presarved fr'm th' Puritans.

FINLEY PETER DUNNE, *Thanksgiving*.

12
The Puritan through Life's sweet garden goes
To pluck the thorn and cast away the rose,
And hopes to please by this peculiar whim,
The God who fashioned it and gave it him.

KENNETH HARE, *The Puritan*.

13
My Fathers and Brethren, this is never to be forgotten that New England is originally a plantation of religion, not a plantation of trade.

JOHN HIGGINSON, *Election Sermon*, 27 May, 1663.

14
He had stiff knees, the Puritan,
That were not good at bending.

J. R. LOWELL, *An Interview with Miles Standish* St. 12.

15
Puritanism, believing itself quick with the seed of religious liberty, laid, without knowing it, the egg of democracy.

J. R. LOWELL, *Among My Books: New England Two Centuries Ago*.

Puritanism meant something when Captain Hodgson, riding out to battle through the morning mist, turns over the command of his troop to a lieutenant, and stays to hear the prayer of a cornet, there was "so much of God in it."

J. R. LOWELL, *Among My Books: New England Two Centuries Ago*.

1
The Puritan hated bear-baiting, not because it gave pain to the bear, but because it gave pleasure to the spectators.

MACAULAY, *History of England.* Vol. i, ch. 2.

Even bear-baiting was esteemed heathenish and unchristian: the sport of it, not the inhumanity, gave offence.

HUME, *History of England.* Vol. i, ch. 62.

2
As Puritans they prominently wax,
And none more kindly gives and takes hard knocks.
Strong psalmic chanting, like to nasal cocks,
They join to thunderings of their hearty thwacks.
But naughtiness, with hoggery, not lacks.

GEORGE MEREDITH, *A Certain People.*

3
What the Puritans gave the world was not thought, but action.

WENDELL PHILLIPS, *Speech,* 21 Dec., 1855.

The Puritan did not stop to think; he recognized God in his soul, and acted.

WENDELL PHILLIPS, *Speech.* 18 Dec., 1859.

4
The Puritan was not a man of speculation. He originated nothing. His principles are to be found broadcast in the centuries behind him. His speculations were all old. . . . The distinction between his case and that of others was simply that he practised what he believed.

WENDELL PHILLIPS, *The Puritan Principle.*

5
Old times were changed, old manners gone;
A stranger filled the Stuarts' throne;
The bigots of the iron time
Had called his harmless art a crime.

SCOTT, *The Lay of the Last Minstrel: Introduction.*

6
Maria: Marry, sir, sometimes he is a kind of puritan.
Sir Andrew: O, if I thought that, I 'ld beat him like a dog!
Maria: What, for being a puritan?

SHAKESPEARE, *Twelfth Night.* Act ii, sc. 3, l. 151.

But one puritan amongst them, and he sings psalms to hornpipes.

SHAKESPEARE, *Winter's Tale.* Act iv, sc. 3, l. 46.

7
Strait-laced, but all-too-full in bud
For puritanic stays.

TENNYSON, *The Talking Oak,* l. 59.

PURITY

See also Chastity

8
Of the nature of the sun, which passeth through pollutions, and itself remains as pure as before.

BACON, *Advancement of Learning.* Bk. ii.

Yes—for a spirit, pure as hers,
Is always pure, even while it errs;
As sunshine, broken in the rill,
Though turned astray, is sunshine still.

THOMAS MOORE, *Lalla Rookh: The Fire-Worshippers.*

9
The pure soul
Shall mount on native wings, disdaining little sport,
And cut a path into the heaven of glory,
Leaving a track of light for men to wonder at.

WILLIAM BLAKE, *King Edward the Third.*

10
There's a woman like a dew-drop, she's so purer than the purest.

ROBERT BROWNING, *A Blot in the 'Scutcheon.* Act i, sc. 3.

As pure as a pearl,
And as perfect: a noble and innocent girl.

OWEN MEREDITH, *Lucile.* Pt. ii, canto vi, st. 16.

11
Brief, brave, and glorious was his young career. . . . He had kept
The whiteness of his soul, and thus men o'er him wept.

BYRON, *Childe Harold.* Canto iii, st. 57.

The purity of his life was the brightness of his glory.

SIR JAMES MACKINTOSH, of Henry Grattan.

12
The purest soul that e'er was sent
Into a clayey tenement.

THOMAS CAREW, *Epitaph on the Lady Mary Villiers.*

There fled the purest soul that ever dwelt
In mortal clay.

TOBIAS SMOLLETT, *The Regicide.* Act v, sc. 8.

A purer soul and one more like yourselves.
Ne'er entered at the golden gates of bliss.

D. G. ROSSETTI, *Lady Jane Grey.* Act i, sc. 1.

13
The blossoms opening to the day,
The dews of heaven refined,
Could nought of purity display
To emulate his mind.

GOLDSMITH, *A Ballad.* (*Vicar of Wakefield.* Ch. 8.)

14
Purity is the feminine, Truth the masculine, of Honour.

J. C. AND A. W. HARE, *Guesses at Truth.* Pt. i.

Purity of mind and conduct is the first glory of a woman.

MADAME DE STAËL, *Germany.* Pt. iii, ch. 19.

15
To doubt her pureness were to want a heart.

TENNYSON, *Lancelot and Elaine,* l. 1366.

16
Blessed are the pure in heart: for they shall see God.

New Testament: Matthew, v, 8.

Blest are the pure in heart,
For they shall see our God.

JOHN KEBLE, *The Christian Year: The Purification.*

Still to the lowly soul
He doth Himself impart,
And for His cradle and His throne
Chooseth the pure in heart.
JOHN KEBLE, *The Christian Year: The Purification.*

For in heaven there's a lodge, and St. Peter keeps the door,
And none can enter in but those that are pure.
UNKNOWN, *The Masonic Hymn.* Stated by J. H. Dixon (*Ancient Poems*, Percy Society, 1846) to be "a very ancient production."

1
Like the stain'd web that whitens in the sun,
Grow pure by being purely shone upon.
THOMAS MOORE, *Lalla Rookh: The Veiled Prophet of Khorassan.*

2
Unto the pure all things are pure.
New Testament: Titus, i, 15.

With the pure thou wilt show thyself pure.
Old Testament: II Samuel, xxii, 27; *Psalms*, xviii, 26.

The better a man is, the less ready is he to suspect dishonesty in others. (Ut quisque est vir optimus, ita difficillime esse alios improbos suspicatur.)
CICERO, *Epistolæ ad Quintum Fratrem.* Bk. i, epis. 1, sec. 4.

3
The stream is always purer at its source. (Les choses valent toujours mieux dans leur source.)
PASCAL, *Lettres Provinciales*, iv.

What will the stream become in its long course,
Since 'tis so dark and turbid at the source?
(Qual diverra quel fiume
Nel lungo suo cammino,
Se al fonte ancor vicino
È torbido così?)
METASTASIO, *Morte d'Abele*, i.

4
My good blade carves the casques of men,
My tough lance thrusteth sure,
My strength is as the strength of ten,
Because my heart is pure.
TENNYSON, *Sir Galahad*, l. 1.

5
Whose life was like the violet sweet,
As climbing jasmine pure.
WORDSWORTH, *Elegiac Stanzas.*

PURPOSE

See also Intention

6
I live for those who love me, for those who know me true;
For the heaven that smiles above me, and awaits my spirit too;
For the cause that lacks assistance, for the wrong that needs resistance,
For the future in the distance, and the good that I can do.
G. LINNÆUS BANKS. *My Aim.*

7
Never ascribe to an opponent motives meaner than your own.
J. M. BARRIE, *Rectorial Address.* St. Andrew's, 3 May, 1922.

8
The aim, if reached or not, makes great the life;
Try to be Shakespeare, leave the rest to fate!
ROBERT BROWNING, *Bishop Blougram's Apology.*

Greatly begin! Though thou have time
But for a line, be that sublime—
Not failure, but low aim is crime.
J. R. LOWELL, *For an Autograph.*

9
Better have failed in the high aim, as I,
Than vulgarly in the low aim succeed,—
As, God be thanked! I do not.
ROBERT BROWNING, *The Inn Album.* Pt. iv, l. 450.

One great aim like a guiding star, above.
ROBERT BROWNING, *Colombe's Birthday.* Pt. ii, l. 215.

Who aimeth at the sky,
Shoots higher much than he that means a tree.
GEORGE HERBERT, *The Church-Porch.* St. 56.

See also under ASPIRATION.

10
That low man seeks a little thing to do,
Sees it and does it:
This high man, with a great thing to pursue,
Dies ere he knows it.
This low man goes on adding one to one,
His hundred's soon hit:
This high man, aiming at a million,
Misses an unit.
ROBERT BROWNING, *A Grammarian's Funeral*, l. 113.

Lofty designs must close in like effects.
ROBERT BROWNING, *A Grammarian's Funeral*, l. 146.

11
The soul o' the purpose, ere 'tis shaped as act,
Takes flesh i' the world, and clothes itself a king,
But when the act comes, stands for what 'tis worth.
ROBERT BROWNING, *Luria.* Act iii.

12
A man without a purpose is soon down at zero. Better to have a bad purpose than no purpose at all.
THOMAS CARLYLE, *Remark*, to Churton Collins.

What makes life dreary is the want of motive.
GEORGE ELIOT, *Daniel Deronda.* Bk. viii, ch. 65.

Purpose is what gives life a meaning.
C. H. PARKHURST, *Sermons: Pattern in the Mount.*

13
Each natural agent works but to this end,—
To render that it works on like itself.
CHAPMAN, *Bussy d'Ambois.* Act iii, sc. 1.

1
But nathelees his purpose held he still,
As lordes do, when they will have their will.
CHAUCER, *The Clerkes Tale*, l. 524.

2
It was a favourite remark of the late Mr. Whitbread's that no man does anything from a single motive.
S. T. COLERIDGE, *Biographia Literaria*. Ch. 11.

3
The one prudence in life is concentration; the one evil is dissipation: and it makes no difference whether our dissipations are coarse or fine. . . . Everything is good which takes away one plaything and delusion more, and drives us home to add one stroke of faithful work.
EMERSON, *Conduct of Life: Power*.

4
We aim above the mark to hit the mark. Every act hath some falsehood or exaggeration in it.
EMERSON, *Essays, Second Series: Nature*.

Cock'd—fired—and miss'd his man—but gain'd his aim.
BYRON, *The Waltz*, l. 22.

5
Slight not what's near, through aiming at what's far. (Μή νυν τά πόρρω ταγγύθεν μεθεὶς σκόπει.)
EURIPIDES, *Rhesus*, l. 482.

"Do the thing that is next," saith the proverb,
And a nobler shall yet succeed:
'Tis the motive exalts the action;
'Tis the doing, and not the deed.
MARGARET JUNKIN PRESTON, *The First Proclamation of Miles Standish*.

6
A good archer is not known by his arrows but his aim.
THOMAS FULLER, *Gnomologia*. No. 135.

Nor will the arrow always strike the mark at which it was aimed. (Nec semper feriet quodcumque minabitur arcus.)
HORACE, *Ars Poetica*, l. 350.

7
When thou dost purpose aught (within thy power),
Be sure to do it, though it be but small.
GEORGE HERBERT, *The Church-Porch*. St. 20.

Who sweeps a room, as for thy laws,
Makes that and th' action fine.
GEORGE HERBERT, *The Elixir*, l. 19.

8
Childhood may do without a grand purpose, but manhood cannot.
J. G. HOLLAND, *Plain Talks: Work and Play*.

9
Neither the rage of his fellow citizens commanding what is base, nor the angry look of threatening tyrant, can shake the upright and determined man from his firm purpose. (Justum et tenacem propositi virum, Non civium ardor prava jubentium, Non vultus instantis tyranni Mente quatit solida.)
HORACE, *Odes*. Bk. iii, ode 3, l. 1.

10
However brilliant an action may be, it should not be accounted great when it is not the result of a great purpose. (Quelque éclatante que soit une action, elle ne doit pas passer pour grande lorsqu'elle n'est pas l'effet d'un grand dessein.)
LA ROCHEFOUCAULD, *Maximes*. No. 160.

11
The Almighty has his own purposes.
ABRAHAM LINCOLN, *Second Inaugural Address*, 4 March, 1865.

Men are not flattered by being shown that there has been a difference of purpose between the Almighty and them.
ABRAHAM LINCOLN, *Letter to Thurlow Weed*, 14 March, 1865.

12
Purpose clean as light from every taint.
J. R. LOWELL, *Under the Old Elm*.

13
But in what shape they choose,
Dilated or condens'd, bright or obscure,
Can execute their aery purposes.
MILTON, *Paradise Lost*. Bk. i, l. 428.

14
Speak thy purpose out;
I love not mystery or doubt.
SCOTT, *Rokeby*. Canto iii, st. 11.

15
He who would arrive at the appointed end must follow a single road and not wander through many ways. (Qui, quo destinavit, pervenire vult, unam sequatur viam, non per multas vagetur.)
SENECA, *Epistulæ ad Lucilium*. Epis. xlv, 1.

Stick to your brewery, and you will be the great brewer of London. Be brewer, and banker, and merchant, and manufacturer, and you will soon be in the Gazette.
NATHAN ROTHSCHILD, to Sir Thomas Buxton in his youth. (EMERSON, *Conduct of Life: Power*.)

16
When a man does not know what harbor he is making for, no wind is the right wind. (Ignoranti, quem portum petat, nullus suus ventus est.)
SENECA, *Epistulæ ad Lucilium*. Epis. lxxi, 3.

No wind makes for him that hath no intended port to sail unto.
MONTAIGNE, *Essays*. Bk. ii, ch. 1.

He gains no wind that has no port in view,
But drifteth vainly with a listless crew;
The favoring breeze for him with firm-held helm—
No storm or breakers can him overwhelm!
DON SEITZ, *In Praise of War: To Woodrow Wilson*.

17
May I never

To this good purpose, that so fairly shows,
Dream of impediment.
SHAKESPEARE, *Antony and Cleopatra*. Act ii, sc. 2, l. 146.

1
Purpose is but the slave to memory,
Of violent birth, but poor validity.
SHAKESPEARE, *Hamlet*. Act iii, sc. 2, l. 198.

2
Purposes mistook Fall'n on the inventors' heads.
SHAKESPEARE, *Hamlet*. Act v, sc. 2, l. 395.

Men may construe things after their fashion,
Clean from the purpose of the things themselves.
SHAKESPEARE, *Julius Cæsar*. Act i, sc. 3, l. 34.

3
We shall express our darker purpose.
SHAKESPEARE, *King Lear*. Act i, sc. 1, l. 36.

No compunctious visitings of nature
Shake my fell purpose.
SHAKESPEARE, *Macbeth*. Act i, sc. 5, l. 46.

The time and my intents are savage-wild,
More fierce and more inexorable far
Than empty tigers or the roaring sea.
SHAKESPEARE, *Romeo and Juliet*. Act v, sc. 3, l. 37.

My purpose is, indeed, a horse of that colour.
SHAKESPEARE, *Twelfth Night*. Act ii, sc. 3, l 181.

4
Infirm of purpose!
SHAKESPEARE, *Macbeth*. Act ii, sc. 2, l. 52.

The flighty purpose never is o'ertook,
Unless the deed go with it.
SHAKESPEARE, *Macbeth*. Act iv, sc. 1, l. 146.

5
Pursue worthy aims. (Τὰ σπουδαῖα μελέτα.)
SOLON. (DIOGENES LAERTIUS, *Solon*. Bk. i, sec. 60.)

6
Yet I doubt not thro' the ages one increasing purpose runs,
And the thoughts of men are widen'd with the process of the suns.
TENNYSON, *Locksley Hall*, l. 137.

7
Full of great aims and bent on bold emprise.
JAMES THOMSON, *The Castle of Indolence*. Canto ii, st. 14.

8
A noble aim,
Faithfully kept, is as a noble deed;
In whose pure sight all virtue doth succeed.
WORDSWORTH, *Poems dedicated to National Independence and Liberty*. Pt. ii, No. 19.

The man who consecrates his hours
By vigorous effort and an honest aim,
At once he draws the sting of life and death.
YOUNG, *Night Thoughts*. Night ii, l. 185.

PYRAMID, see Egypt

Q

QUACK

See also Prophet

9
A quack's words are heard, but no one trusts himself to him when he is sick. (Tamquam pharmacopolam. Nam ejus verba audiuntur, verum se ei nemo committat, si æger est.)
CATO. (AULUS GELLIUS, *Noctes Atticæ*, i, 15.)

10
Out, you impostors!
Quack salving, cheating mountebanks! your skill
Is to make sound men sick, and sick men kill.
MASSINGER, *The Virgin-Martyr*. Act iv, sc. 1.

Quacks—not physicians.
THOMAS MOORE, *Ode to Rae Wilson*. Quack is an abbreviation of Quacksalver, and dates from 1638.

Running after Quacks and Mountebanks for medicines and remedies.
DANIEL DEFOE.

See also under DOCTOR; MEDICINE.

11
Quackery gives birth to nothing; gives death to all things.
CARLYLE, *Heroes and Hero-Worship*. Lecture 1.

12
Void of all honour, avaricious, rash,
The daring tribe compound their boasted trash—
Tincture of syrup, lotion, drop, or pill;
All tempt the sick to trust the lying bill.
GEORGE CRABBE, *The Borough*. Letter vii, l. 75.

From powerful causes spring th' empiric's gains,
Man's love of life, his weakness, and his pains;
These first induce him the vile trash to try,
Then lend his name, that other men may buy.
GEORGE CRABBE, *The Borough*. Letter vii, l. 124.

QUARRELING

See also Discord

I—Quarreling: Definitions and Apothegms

13
When civil dudgeon first grew high,
And men fell out, they knew not why;
When hard words, jealousies and fears,
Set folks together by the ears,
And made them fight, like mad or drunk,
For dame Religion as for punk; . . .
Then did Sir Knight abandon dwelling,
And out he rode a colonelling.
SAMUEL BUTLER, *Hudibras*. Pt. i, canto 1, l. 1.

14
In all private quarrels the duller nature is triumphant by reason of its dullness.
GEORGE ELIOT, *Felix Holt*. Ch. 9.

15
When we quarrel, how we wish we had been blameless!
EMERSON, *Journals*. Vol. ix, p. 497.

1
"I did not mean to abuse the cloth; I only said your conclusion was a non sequitur." "You're another," cries the sergeant, "an' you come to that, no more a sequitur than yourself."
FIELDING, *Tom Jones*. Bk ix, ch. 6.

"Sir," said Mr. Tupman, "you're a fellow." "Sir," said Mr. Pickwick, "you're another."
DICKENS, *Pickwick Papers*. Ch. 15.

2
Let there be no strife, I pray thee, between me and thee.
Old Testament: Genesis, xiii, 8.

3
A man of strife and a man of contention.
Old Testament: Jeremiah, xv, 10.

4
Quarrels do not last long if the wrong is only on one side. (Les querelles ne dureraient pas longtemps si le tort n'était que d'un côté.)
LA ROCHEFOUCAULD, *Maximes*. No. 496.

Weakness on both sides is, as we know, the motto of all quarrels.
VOLTAIRE, *Philosophical Dictionary*.

5
Quarrelsome dogs get dirty coats.
SAMUEL LOVER, *Handy Andy*. Ch. 46.

Like dogs that snarl about a bone,
And play together when they've none.
BUTLER, *Hudibras*. Pt. iii, canto 1, l. 27.

6
Prone to bitter quarrelling. (Amaris litibus aptus.)
MARTIAL, *Epigrams*. Bk. xii, ep. 69, l. 3.

7
Be dumb, Thou spirit of contradiction!
PHILIP MASSINGER, *The Picture*. Act i, sc. 2.

8
Above all, avoid quarrels caused by wine. (Jurgia præcipue vino stimulata caveto.)
OVID, *Ars Amatoria*. Bk. i, l. 591.

9
We never meet together but we be at daggers drawing.
JOHN PALSGRAVE, *Acolastus*. Fo. 1. (1540)

From spiteful words they fell to daggers drawing.
SIR JOHN HARINGTON, *Epigrams*. Bk. i, 91. (1618)

Have always been at daggers-drawing,
And one another clapper-clawing.
BUTLER, *Hudibras*. Pt. ii, canto 2, l. 79. (1664)

We should be at daggers drawn.
MRS. HENRY WOOD, *Life's Secret*. Pt. i, ch. 2.

10
You will stir up the hornets. (Irritabis crabrones.)
PLAUTUS, *Amphitruo*, l. 707. (Act ii, sc. 2.)

Stir up the hornets. (Irriter les freslons.)
RABELAIS, *Works*. Bk. ii.

11
Agreement is made more precious by disagreement. (Discordia fit carior concordia.)
PUBLILIUS SYRUS, *Sententiæ*. No. 151. *See also* LOVE: LOVERS' QUARRELS.

12
As cross as two sticks.
SCOTT, *Journal*, 2 Nov., 1831.

She scolded her maid and was as cross as two sticks.
THACKERAY, *The Newcomes*. Ch. 33.

13
And each upon his rival glared,
With foot advanced, and blade half bared.
SCOTT, *The Lady of the Lake*. Canto ii, st. 34.

Quarrelers do not live long.
SCOTT, *St. Ronan's Well*. Ch. 8.

14
If you'll patch a quarrel.
SHAKESPEARE, *Antony and Cleopatra*, ii, 2, 52.

15
O sir, we quarrel in print, by the book; as you have books for good manners: I will name you the degrees. The first, the Retort Courteous; the second, the Quip Modest; the third, the Reply Churlish; the fourth, the Reproof Valiant; the fifth, the Countercheck Quarrelsome; the sixth, the Lie with Circumstance; the seventh, the Lie Direct. All these you may avoid but the Lie Direct; and you may avoid that too, with an If. . . . Your If is the only peace-maker; much virtue in If.
SHAKESPEARE, *As You Like It*. Act v, sc. 4, l. 94.

16
As quarrelous as the weasel.
SHAKESPEARE, *Cymbeline*. Act iii, sc. 4, l. 162.

Carp and quarrel.
SHAKESPEARE, *King Lear*. Act i, sc. 4, l. 222.

He is a devil in private brawls: souls and bodies hath he divorced three. . . . Hob, nob, is his word; give 't or take 't.
SHAKESPEARE, *Twelfth Night*. Act iii, sc. 4, l. 259.

17
Beware
Of entrance to a quarrel; but being in,
Bear 't that the opposed may beware of thee.
SHAKESPEARE, *Hamlet*. Act i, sc. 3, l. 65.

18
No quarrel, but a slight contention.
SHAKESPEARE, *III Henry VI*. Act i, sc. 2, l. 6.

19
In a false quarrel there is no true valour.
SHAKESPEARE, *Much Ado About Nothing*. Act v, sc. 1, l. 120.

20
The quarrel is a very pretty quarrel as it stands; we should only spoil it by trying to explain it.
SHERIDAN, *The Rivals*. Act iv, sc. 3.

21
For souls in growth, great quarrels are great emancipations.
LOGAN PEARSALL SMITH, *Afterthoughts*.

22
It takes two to make a quarrel. ('Εμοὶ γαρ οὐ πρόσεστι ταῦτα.)
SOCRATES. (DIOGENES LAERTIUS, *Socrates*. Bk. ii, sec. 36.)

A quarrel is quickly settled when deserted by one party: there is no battle unless there be two. (Cadit statim simultas, ab altera parte deserta; nisi pariter, non pugnant.)

SENECA, *De Ira*. Bk. ii, sec. 34.

1
Some strand of our own misdoing is involved in every quarrel.

R. L. STEVENSON, *Prince Otto*.

2
There is no such test of a man's superiority of character as in the well-conducting of an unavoidable quarrel.

SIR HENRY TAYLOR, *The Statesman*, p. 101.

3
Na. na. abide. we have a crow to pull.

UNKNOWN, *Towneley Plays*, xviii. (c. 1410)

I've a crow to pluck wi' ye.

JOHN WILSON, *The Projectors*. Act v. (1665)

4
Lord Chatham. with his sword undrawn,
Is waiting for Sir Richard Strachan;
Sir Richard, longing to be at 'em,
Is waiting for the Earl of Chatham.

UNKNOWN, *Epigram*. (*Morning Chronicle*, London. 1809.) See under Chatham, *Dict. Nat. Biog.*, for another version. The reference is to the recriminations following the failure of the expedition against Walcheren in 1809. Admiral Strachan referred to Pitt as "the late Earl of Chatham," because of his dilatoriness.

II—Quarreling: Its Folly

5
Those who in quarrels interpose,
Must often wipe a bloody nose.

JOHN GAY, *Fables*. Pt. i, No. 34; FRANKLIN, *Poor Richard*, 1740.

So when two dogs are fighting in the streets,
When a third dog one of the two dogs meets:
With angry teeth he bites him to the bone,
And this dog smarts for what that dog has done.

FIELDING, *Tom Thumb the Great*. Act i, sc. 5, l. 55.

Thus when a barber and collier fight,
The barber beats the luckless collier—white;
The dusty collier heaves his ponderous sack,
And, big with vengeance, beats the barber—black.
In comes the brick-dust man, with grime o'erspread,
And beats the collier and the barber—red;
Black, red, and white, in various clouds are toss'd,
And in the dust they raise the combatants are lost.

CHRISTOPHER SMART, *Soliloquy of the Princess Periwinkle* in *A Trip to Cambridge*.

We must have bloody noses and cracked crowns.

SHAKESPEARE, *I Henry IV*. Act ii, sc. 3, l. 96.

6
Dissensions, like small streams, are first begun,
Scarce seen they rise, but gather as they run:
So lines that from their parallel decline,
More they proceed the more they still disjoin.

GARTH, *The Dispensary*. Canto viii, l. 184.

7
But curb thou the high spirit in thy breast,
For gentle ways are best, and keep aloof
From sharp contentions.

HOMER, *Iliad*. Bk. ix, l. 317. (Bryant, tr.)

This is no time nor fitting place to mar
The mirthful meeting with a wordy war.

BYRON, *Lara*. Canto i, st. 23.

8
He wrangles about goat's wool, and donning his armor, fights for trifles. (Rixatur de lana sæpe caprina. Propugnat nugis armatus.)

HORACE, *Epistles*. Bk. i, epis. 18, l. 15. The question of whether the hair of goats could be called *lana*, or wool, was proverbial for a matter of no importance.

Thou! why, thou wilt quarrel with a man that hath a hair more, or a hair less, in his beard than thou hast: thou wilt quarrel with a man for cracking nuts, having no other reason but because thou hast hazel eyes: what eye but such an eye would spy out such a quarrel? Thy head is as full of quarrels as an egg is full of meat.

SHAKESPEARE, *Romeo and Juliet*. Act iii, sc. 1, l. 18.

9
And bitter waxed the fray;
Brother with brother spake no word
When they met in the way.

JEAN INGELOW, *Strife and Peace*.

10
And of their vain contest appear'd no end.

JOHN MILTON, *Paradise Lost*. Bk. ix, l. 1189.

11
But from sharp words and wits men pluck no fruit,
And gathering thorns they shake the tree at root.

SWINBURNE, *Atalanta in Calydon: Chorus*.

12
And musing on the little lives of men,
And how they mar this little by their feuds.

TENNYSON, *Sea Dreams*, l. 48.

QUEEN

13
Your queens Are generally prosperous in reigning.

BYRON, *Don Juan*. Canto x, st. 47.

14
I know that I have but the body of a weak and feeble woman; but I have the heart of a King, and of a King of England, too.

QUEEN ELIZABETH, to the troops assembled at Tilbury, in 1588, to oppose the Spanish Armada. (HUME, *History of England*.)

15
A queen devoid of beauty is not queen;
She needs the royalty of beauty's mien.

VICTOR HUGO, *Eviradnus*, v.

16
Our queen,

The imperial jointress to this warlike state.
SHAKESPEARE, *Hamlet*. Act i, sc. 2, l. 8.

The fairest queen that ever king received.
SHAKESPEARE, *II Henry VI*. Act i, sc. 1, l. 16.

She had all the royal makings of a queen;
As holy oil, Edward Confessor's crown,
The rod, and bird of peace, and all such emblems
Laid nobly on her.
SHAKESPEARE, *Henry VIII*. Act iv, sc. 1, l. 87.

1
I would not be a queen For all the world.
SHAKESPEARE, *Henry VIII*. Act ii, sc. 3, l. 24.

2
A partial world will listen to my lays,
While Anna reigns, and sets a female name
Unrival'd in the glorious lists of fame.
YOUNG, *The Force of Religion*. Bk. i, l. 6.

3
With the selfsame sunlight shining upon her,
Shining down on her ringlets' sheen,
She is standing somewhere—she I shall honor,
She that I wait for, my queen, my queen!
UNKNOWN, *My Queen*.

QUESTION

4
To beg the question. (ἀρχῃ αἰτεῖν.)
ARISTOTLE, *Organon: Prior Analytics*. Bk. ii, ch. 16. (c. 340 B.C.) A logical fallacy, assuming a proposition which involves the conclusion. The Latin is "Petitio principii," to beg the chief point.

5
What song the Sirens sang, or what name Achilles assumed when he hid himself among the women, though puzzling questions, are not beyond all conjecture.
SIR THOMAS BROWNE, *Hydriotaphia*. Ch. v, sec. 4.

6
Mony e'en spiers the gat then ken right weel.
SUSANNAH CENTLIVRE, *Woman Keeps a Secret*. Act iii.

What sent the messengers to hell
Was asking what they knew full well.
SCOTT, *Waverley*. Ch. 24.

7
Time has made this question without question.
SIR EDWARD COKE, *Institutes*. No. iii, sec. 302.

8 The $64 question.
Quiz show, *Take It or Leave It,* born April 21, 1940, contributed "the $64 question" to the American language. Contestants are called upon to answer seven questions for progressive payoffs, from $1 to $64, and the $64 or last question became a household phrase for a question almost impossible to answer. —*News-Week*, 18 Sept., 1950, p. 36.

9 Nothing questioneth, nothing learneth.
THOMAS FULLER, *Gnomologia*. No. 2241.

Courage to ask questions; courage to expose our ignorance.
EMERSON, *Social Aims*.

10
Ask me no questions, and I'll tell you no fibs.
GOLDSMITH, *She Stoops to Conquer*. Act iii.

11
Avoid a questioner, for such a man is also a tattler. (Percontatorem fugito; nam garrulus idem est.)
HORACE, *Epistles*. Bk. i, epis. 18, l. 69.

Questioning is not a mode of conversation among gentlemen.
SAMUEL JOHNSON. (BOSWELL, *Life*, 1776.)

12
I keep six honest serving-men
(They taught me all I knew):
Their names are What and Why and When
And How and Where and Who.
RUDYARD KIPLING, *The Serving-Men*.

13
Hard questions must have hard answers. (Τὰς ἀποκρίσεις ἀπόρους εἶναι.)
PLUTARCH, *Lives: Alexander*. Ch. 64, sec. 4.

Hard are those questions;—answer harder still.
YOUNG, *Night Thoughts*. Night ix, l. 1532.

That's a blazing strange answer.
DICKENS, *A Tale of Two Cities*. Bk. i, ch. 2.

But answer came there none.
SCOTT, *Bridal of Triermain*. Canto iii, st. 10.

I pause for a reply.
SHAKESPEARE, *Julius Cæsar*. Act iii, sc. 2, l. 36.

14
It is not every question that deserves an answer.
PUBLILIUS SYRUS, *Sententiæ*. No. 581.

15
When anyone explains himself guardedly, nothing is more uncivil than to put a new question.
JEAN PAUL RICHTER, *Hesperus*. Ch. 3.

16
A question not to be asked.
SHAKESPEARE, *I Henry IV*. Act ii, sc. 4, l. 451.

How needless was it then to ask the question!
SHAKESPEARE, *Love's Labour's Lost*. Act ii, sc. 1, l. 117.

That is not the question.
SHAKESPEARE, *The Merry Wives of Windsor*. Act i, sc. 1, l. 227.

17
Questions are never indiscreet. Answers sometimes are.
OSCAR WILDE, *An Ideal Husband*. Act i.

18
The greatest men
May ask a foolish question, now and then.
JOHN WOLCOT, *The Apple Dumpling and the King*.

QUIET

See also Peace: Peace of Mind; Rest

19
An inability to stay quiet, . . . is one of the most conspicuous failings of mankind.
WALTER BAGEHOT, *Physics and Politics*, p. 186.

1
Quiet to quick bosoms is a hell.
BYRON, *Childe Harold*. Canto iii, st. 42.

2
Spared and blessed by Time, Looking tranquillity.
BYRON, *Childe Harold*. Canto iv, st. 146.

How reverend is the face of this tall pile, . . .
Looking tranquillity.
CONGREVE, *The Mourning Bride*. Act ii, sc. 1.

How reverend is the view of these hush'd heads,
Looking tranquillity!
CHARLES LAMB, *Essays of Elia: A Quaker Meeting*.

But common quiet is mankind's concern.
DRYDEN, *Religio Laici*, l. 450.

3
Be restful. ('Ηρεμία χρῆσθαι.)
CHILON. (DIOGENES LAERTIUS, *Chilon*. Sec. 70.)

4
Tranquillity! thou better name
Than all the family of Fame!
S. T. COLERIDGE, *Ode to Tranquillity*.

5
It is better to die of hunger, but in a state of freedom from grief and fear, than to live in plenty, but troubled in mind.
EPICTETUS [?], *Encheiridion*. Sec. 12.

6
To husband out life's taper at the close,
And keep the flames from wasting by repose.
GOLDSMITH, *The Deserted Village*, l. 87.

7
A little with quiet Is the only diet.
GEORGE HERBERT, *Jacula Prudentum*.

8
Anything for a quiet life.
THOMAS HEYWOOD, *Captives*. Act iii, sc. 3.
See also LIFE: THE SIMPLE LIFE.

9
Quietness is best.
HOLLAND, *Cheshire Glossary*, p. 453.

10
In quietness and confidence shall be your strength.
Old Testament: Isaiah, xxx, 15.

12
He is as quiet as a lamb.
WILLIAM LANGLAND, *Piers Plowman*. Passus vi, l. 43. (1362)

Still as a lamb.
JOHN LYDGATE, *Fall of Princes*. Bk. i, l. 6934. (1440)

I will sit as quiet as a lamb.
SHAKESPEARE, *King John*. Act iv, sc. 1, l. 80. (1596)

Was wont to be as still as mouse.
RICHARD FLECKNOE, *Diarium*, 9. (1656)

As quiet as a mouse in his hole.
SCOTT, *Redgauntlet*. Ch. 16. (1824)

Quiet as a street at night.
RUPERT BROOKE, *Retrospect*.

The holy time is quiet as a nun.
WORDSWORTH, *It is a Beauteous Evening*.

13
But I live
For ever in a deep deliberate bliss,
A spirit sliding through tranquillity.
STEPHEN PHILLIPS, *Marpessa*.

14
Better is a dry morsel, and quietness therewith, than a house full of sacrifices with strife.
Old Testament: Proverbs, xvii, 1.

15
Sometimes quiet is an unquiet thing. (Interdum quies inquieta est.)
SENECA, *Epistulæ ad Lucilium*. Epis. lvi, sec. 8.

The violent desire for quiet grew into a tumult. (Affectatio quietis in tumultum evaluit.)
TACITUS, *History*. Bk. i, sec. 80.

16
Passionless bride, divine Tranquillity.
TENNYSON, *Lucretius*, l. 265.

17
Study to be quiet.
New Testament: I Thessalonians, iv, 11.

Dwell with yourself; "study to be quiet." (Tecum habita.)
PERSIUS, *Satires*. Sat. iv, l. 52.

18
The best of men have ever loved repose:
They hate to mingle in the filthy fray;
Where the soul sours, and gradual rancour grows,
Imbitter'd more from peevish day to day.
THOMSON, *Castle of Indolence*. Canto i, st. 17.

19
Tranquillity comprehends every wish I have left, and I think I should not even ask what news there is.
HORACE WALPOLE, *Letter to Sir Horace Mann*, 22 Feb., 1771.

20
That blessed mood,
In which the burden of the mystery,
In which the heavy and the weary weight
Of all this unintelligible world,
Is lightened.
WORDSWORTH, *Lines Composed a Few Miles Above Tintern Abbey*, l. 37.

QUIXOTE, see Cervantes

QUOTATION

See also Plagiarism

21
One must be a wise reader to quote wisely and well.
A. B. ALCOTT, *Table Talk: Quotation*.

22
There is not less wit nor invention in applying rightly a thought one finds in a book, than in being the first author of that thought. Cardinal du Perron has been heard to say that the happy application of a verse of Virgil has deserved a talent.
PIERRE BAYLE, *Dictionnaire*. Vol. ii, p. 1077.

The art of quotation requires more delicacy in the practice than those conceive who can see nothing more in a quotation than an extract.
ISAAC D'ISRAELI, *Curiosities of Literature: Quotation.*

1
'Twas counted learning once, and wit,
To void but what some author writ,
And when men understood by rote,
By as implicit sense to quote.
SAMUEL BUTLER, *Satire upon Plagiaries*, l. 99.

All which he understood by rote,
And, as occasion serv'd, would quote.
BUTLER, *Hudibras*. Pt. i, canto 1, l. 135.

Perverts the Prophets, and purloins the Psalms.
BYRON, *English Bards and Scotch Reviewers*, l. 326.

2
The wisdom of the wise, and the experience of ages, may be preserved by quotations.
ISAAC D'ISRAELI, *Curiosities of Literature: Quotation.*

The greater part of our writers, . . . have become so original, that no one cares to imitate them: and those who never quote in return are seldom quoted.
D'ISRAELI, *Curiosities of Literature: Quotation.*

One may quote till one compiles.
D'ISRAELI, *Curiosities of Literature: Quotation.*

3
The adventitious beauty of poetry may be felt in the greater delight which a verse gives in happy quotation than in the poem.
EMERSON, *Essays, First Series: Art.*

4
By necessity, by proclivity, and by delight, we all quote. We quote not only books and proverbs, but arts, sciences, religion, customs, and laws; nay, we quote temples and houses, tables and chairs by imitation.
EMERSON, *Letters and Social Aims: Quotation and Originality.*

Every book is a quotation; and every house is a quotation out of all forests and mines and stone quarries.
EMERSON, *Representative Men: Plato.*

Quotation confesses inferiority.
EMERSON, *Letters and Social Aims: Quotation and Originality.*

5
Next to the originator of a good sentence is the first quoter of it.
EMERSON, *Letters and Social Aims: Quotation and Originality.*

6
We are as much informed of a writer's genius by what he selects as by what he originates. . . . A passage from one of the poets, well recited, borrows new interest from the rendering. As the journals say, "The italics are ours."
EMERSON, *Letters and Social Aims: Quotation and Originality.*

A great man quotes bravely, and will not draw on his invention when his memory serves him with a word as good.
EMERSON, *Quotation and Originality.*

In his immense quotation and allusion we quickly cease to discriminate between what he quotes and what he invents. 'Tis all Plutarch by right of eminent domain, and all property vests in the emperor.
EMERSON, *Representative Men: Plutarch.*

7
Nothing gives an author so much pleasure as to find his works respectfully quoted by other learned authors.
BENJAMIN FRANKLIN, *Pennsylvania Almanach.*

To be occasionally quoted is all the fame I care for.
ALEXANDER SMITH, *Dreamthorp: Men of Letters.*

8
Classical quotation is the parole of literary men all over the world.
SAMUEL JOHNSON. (BOSWELL, *Life*, 1781.)

9
Every Quotation contributes something to the stability or enlargement of the language.
SAMUEL JOHNSON, *Preface to Dictionary.*

One advantage there certainly is in quotation, that if the authors cited be good, there is at least so much worth reading in the book of him who quotes them.
SAMUEL JOHNSON. (BOSWELL, *Life.*)

10
A good saying often runs the risk of being thrown away when quoted as the speaker's own. (C'est souvent hasarder un bon mot et vouloir le perdre que de le donner pour sien.)
LA BRUYÈRE, *Les Caractères: De la Société et la Conversation.*

11
Pardon a quotation: I hate it.
WALTER SAVAGE LANDOR, *Imaginary Conversations: Southey and Porson.*

12
He that has but ever so little examined the citations of writers cannot doubt how little credit the quotations deserve, where the originals are wanting; and, consequently, how much less quotations of quotations can be relied on.
JOHN LOCKE, *Essay Concerning Human Understanding*. Bk. iv, ch. 16, sec. 11.

Nor suffers Horace more in wrong translations
By wits, than critics in as wrong quotations.
POPE, *Essay on Criticism*. Pt. iii, l. 104.

The little honesty existing among authors is to be seen in the outrageous way in which they misquote from the writings of others.
SCHOPENHAUER, *On Authorship.*

A forward critic often dupes us
With sham quotations *peri hupsos*,
And if we have not read Longinus,
Will magisterially outshine us.
Then, lest with Greek he over-run ye,
Procure the book for love or money,

Translated from Boileau's translation,
And quote quotation on quotation.
SWIFT, *On Poetry*.

1
I quote others only in order the better to express myself.
MONTAIGNE, *Essays*. Bk. i, ch. 25.

2
I have made here merely a nosegay of other people's flowers, and have provided nothing of my own except the thread which holds them together. (J'ay seylement faict icy un amas des fleurs estrangieres, n'y ayant fourny du mien que le filet à les lier.)
MONTAIGNE, *Essays*. Bk. iii, ch. 12.

I am but a gatherer and disposer of other men's stuff.
SIR HENRY WOTTON, *Elements of Architecture: Preface*.

A book which hath been culled from the flowers of all books.
GEORGE ELIOT, *The Spanish Gypsy*. Bk. ii.

3
He ranged his tropes, and preached up patience,
Backed his opinion with quotations.
PRIOR, *Paulo Purganti and His Wife*, l. 143.

4
Always verify your quotations.
DR. MARTIN JOSEPH ROUTH, President of Magdalen College, *Advice*, given to Dean John William Burgon, then fellow of Oriel College. (BURGON, *Memoir of Dr. Routh*.) The word "quotations" was changed to "references" in later editions of the book, and is usually so quoted.

5
A fine quotation is a diamond on the finger of a man of wit, and a pebble in the hand of a fool.
JOSEPH ROUX, *Meditations of a Parish Priest*. Pt. i, sec. 74.

6
Some for renown, on scraps of learning dote,
And think they grow immortal as they quote.
To patch-work learn'd quotations are allied:
Both strive to make our poverty our pride.
YOUNG, *Love of Fame*. Satire i, l. 89.

Proud of his learning (just enough to quote).
BYRON, *Don Juan*. Canto xiii, st. 91.

With just enough of learning to misquote.
BYRON, *English Bards and Scotch Reviewers*, l. 66.

R

RAGE, see Anger

RAILROAD

7
The progress of invention is really a threat. Whenever I see a railroad I look for a republic.
EMERSON, *Journals*, 1866.

8
These railroads—could but the whistle be made musical, and the rumble and the jar got rid of—are positively the greatest blessing that the ages have wrought out for us. They give us wings; they annihilate the toil and dust of pilgrimage; they spiritualize travel!
HAWTHORNE, *House of Seven Gables*. Ch. 17.

9
Your railroad, when you come to understand it, is only a device for making the world smaller.
RUSKIN, *Modern Painters*. Pt. iv, ch. 17, sec. 35.

Going by railroad I do not consider as travelling at all; it is merely being "sent" to a place, and very little different from becoming a parcel.
JOHN RUSKIN, *Modern Painters*. Bk. iii, pt. 4, ch. 17, sec. 24.

10
If railroads are not built, how shall we get to heaven in season? But if we stay at home and mind our business. who will want railroads? We do not ride on the railroad; it rides upon us.
H. D. THOREAU, *Walden*. Ch. 2.

11
Commuter—one who spends his life
In riding to and from his wife;
A man who shaves and takes a train,
And then rides back to shave again.
E. B. WHITE, *The Commuter*.

RAIN

I—Rain: Apothegms

12
After the rain cometh the fair weather.
ÆSOP, *Fables*. Bk. ii, fab. 8. (Caxton, tr. 1484)

After the showers at length would come a sun.
CHRISTOPHER MIDDLETON, *Famous Historie of Chinon*, 26. (1597)

13
A foot deep of rain Will kill hay and grain,
But three feet of snow Will make them come mo'.
BLACKMORE, *Lorna Doone*. Ch. 50. Quoted as an old saying.

14
It shall rain dogs and polecats.
RICHARD BROME, *City Wit*. Act iv, sc. 1. (1653)

He was sure it would rain cats and dogs.
SWIFT, *Polite Conversation*. Dial. ii.

It cannot rain but it pours.
SWIFT, *Prose Miscellanies: Title*.

It never rains but it pours.
THOMAS GRAY, *Letter to Dr. Wharton*, 2 Feb., 1771; MALKIN, tr., *Gil Blas*, i, 9 (1809); CHARLES KINGSLEY, *Yeast*. Ch. 6 (1848).

1
Though it rain daggers with their points downward.
ROBERT BURTON, *Anatomy of Melancholy*. Pt. iii, sec. ii, mem. 3.

2
When the heaven is shut up, and there is no rain.
Old Testament: II Chronicles, vi, 26.

3
A sunshiny shower Won't last half an hour.
MICHAEL DENHAM, *Proverbs*, 8.

When God wills, no wind but brings rain.
GEORGE HERBERT, *Jacula Prudentum*. No. 328. The proverb appears in many languages.

The hollow winds begin to blow,
The clouds look black, the glass is low.
EDWARD JENNER, *Signs of Rain*.

4
Extraordinary rains pretty generally fall after great battles.
PLUTARCH, *Lives: Caius Marius*.

5
When it rains, it rains on all alike.
W. G. BENHAM, *Proverbs*, p. 870. Hindoo.

He sendeth rain on the just and on the unjust.
New Testament: Matthew, v, 45.

6
For the rain it raineth every day.
SHAKESPEARE, *Twelfth Night*. Act v, sc. 1, l. 401; *King Lear*. Act iii, sc. 2, l. 77.

7
A coming shower your shooting corns presage.
SWIFT, *Description of a City Shower*.

8
The useful trouble of the rain.
TENNYSON, *Geraint and Enid*, l. 770.

9
Jove, the rain-giver. (Jupiter pluvius.)
TIBULLUS, *Elegies*. Bk. i, eleg. 7, l. 26.

He shall come down like rain upon the mown grass.
Old Testament: Psalms, lxxii, 6.

10
Close the stream now, lads; the meadows have drunk enough! (Claudite jam rivos, pueri; sat prata biberunt.)
VERGIL, *Eclogues*. No. iii, l. 111.

11
St. Swithin's day, if thou dost rain,
For forty days it will remain.
UNKNOWN, old adage concerning St. Swithin's day, July 15. The French have a similar rhyme about St. Médard's day, June 8.

Now if on Swithin's feast the welkin lours,
And every penthouse streams with hasty showers.
Twice twenty days shall clouds their fleeces drain
And wash the pavements with incessant rain.
JOHN GAY, *Trivia*. Bk. i, l. 182.

O here, "St. Swithin's, the 15 day, variable weather, for the most part rain," good! "for the most part rain." Why, it should rain forty days after, now, more or less."
BEN JONSON, *Every Man Out of His Humour*. Act i, sc. 1.

St. Swithin is christening the apples.
HONE, *Every Day Book*. Vol. i, p. 960.

II—Rain: Description

12
We knew it would rain, for the poplars showed
The white of their leaves, the amber grain
Shrunk in the wind,—and the lightning now
Is tangled in tremulous skeins of rain.
T. B. ALDRICH, *Before the Rain*.

13
A little rain will fill
The lily's cup which hardly moists the field.
EDWIN ARNOLD, *Light of Asia*. Bk. vi, l. 215.

14
The August cloud . . . suddenly
Melts into streams of rain.
BRYANT, *Sella*, l. 433.

15
Soon dries the rain-drop on the April leaf!
BULWER-LYTTON, *New Timon*. Pt. iii, sec. 3.

16
The raindrops' showery dance and rhythmic beat,
With tinkling of innumerable feet.
ABRAHAM COLES, *The Microcosm Hearing*.

17
The thirsty earth soaks up the rain,
And drinks, and gapes for drink again;
The plants suck in the earth, and are
With constant drinking fresh and fair.
ANACREON, *Odes*. No. 21. (Cowley, tr.)

18
Welcome falls the imprisoning rain—dear hermitage of nature.
EMERSON, *Nature, Addresses and Lectures: Literary Ethics*.

19
Fall on me like a silent dew,
Or like those maiden showers,
Which, by the peep of day, do strew
A baptism o'er the flowers.
ROBERT HERRICK, *To Music, to Becalm His Fever*.

Like morning dew that in a pleasant shower
Drops pearls into the bosom of a flower.
THOMAS RANDOLPH, *The Jealous Lovers*.

20
How it pours, pours, pours,
In a never-ending sheet!
How it drives beneath the doors!
How it soaks the passer's feet!
How it rattles on the shutter!
How it rumples up the lawn!
How 'twill sigh, and moan, and mutter,
From darkness until dawn.
ROSSITER JOHNSON, *Rhyme of the Rain*.

21
And a thousand recollections
Weave their air-threads into woof,
As I listen to the patter
Of the rain upon the roof.
COATES KINNEY, *Rain on the Roof*.

1
The day is cold, and dark, and dreary;
It rains, and the wind is never weary;
The vine still clings to the mouldering wall,
But at every gust the dead leaves fall,
And the day is dark and dreary.
LONGFELLOW, *The Rainy Day.*

2
The ceaseless rain is falling fast,
And yonder gilded vane,
Immovable for three days past,
Points to the misty main.
LONGFELLOW, *Travels by the Fireside.* St. 1.

3
The gentleness of rain was in the wind.
SHELLEY, *Fragment: Rain-Wind.*

The good-will of the rain that loves all leaves.
MARKHAM, *Lincoln, The Man of the People.*

RAINBOW

4
And, lo! in the dark east, expanded high,
The rainbow brightens to the setting Sun!
JAMES BEATTIE, *The Minstrel.* Bk. i, st. 30.

5 'Tis sweet to view on high
The rainbow, based on ocean, span the sky.
BYRON, *Don Juan.* Canto i, st. 122.

6
Triumphal arch, that fill'st the sky
When storms prepare to part,
I ask not proud Philosophy
To teach me what thou art.
THOMAS CAMPBELL, *To the Rainbow.* St. 1.

Still seem, as to my childhood's sight,
A midway station given
For happy spirits to alight
Betwixt the earth and heaven.
THOMAS CAMPBELL, *To the Rainbow.* St. 2.

The rainbow never tells me
That gust and storm are by;
Yet she is more convincing
Than philosophy.
EMILY DICKINSON, *Further Poems.* No. 48.

Some day Jane shall Have, she Hopes,
Rainbows for her Skipping Ropes.
DOROTHY ALDIS, *Skipping Ropes.*

7
The sun athwart the cloud thought it no sin
To use my land to put his rainbows in.
EMERSON, *Nature.*

8
Over her hung a canopy of state,
Not of rich tissue, nor of spangled gold,
But of a substance, though not animate,
Yet of a heavenly and spiritual mould,
That only eyes of spirits might behold.
GILES FLETCHER, *The Rainbow,* l. 33.

9
I do set my bow in the cloud, and it shall be for a token of a covenant between me and the earth.
Old Testament: Genesis, ix, 13.

God's glowing covenant.
HOSEA BALLOU, *MS. Sermons.*

Bright pledge of peace and sunshine! the sure tie
Of thy Lord's hand, the object of His eye!
When I behold thee, though my light be dim,
Distinct, and low, I can in thine see Him
Who looks upon thee from His glorious throne,
And minds the covenant between all and One.
HENRY VAUGHAN, *The Rainbow.*

10
God loves an idle rainbow
No less than labouring seas.
RALPH HODGSON, *Poems,* p. 59.

11
What skilful limner e'er would choose
To paint the rainbow's varying hues,
Unless to mortal it were given
To dip his brush in dyes of heaven?
SCOTT, *Marmion.* Canto vi, st. 5.

12
Mild arch of promise! on the evening sky
Thou shinest fair with many a lovely ray,
Each in the other melting.
SOUTHEY, *The Evening Rainbow.*

13 Whatso looks lovelily
Is but the rainbow on life's weeping rain.
FRANCIS THOMPSON, *Ode on the Setting Sun,* l. 192.

14
Hung on the shower that fronts the golden West,
The rainbow bursts like magic on mine eyes!
In hues of ancient promise there imprest;
Frail in its date, eternal in its guise.
CHARLES TENNYSON TURNER, *The Rainbow.*

15
My heart leaps up when I behold
A rainbow in the sky.
WORDSWORTH, *My Heart Leaps Up.*

Rain, rain, and sun! a rainbow in the sky!
TENNYSON, *The Coming of Arthur,* l. 401.

16
The rainbow comes and goes,
And lovely is the rose.
WORDSWORTH, *Intimations of Immortality.* Pt. ii.

17
Where the rainbow rests is a crock of gold.
UNKNOWN. (See *Notes and Queries.* Ser. i, vol. 2, p. 512.)

18
The rainbow in the morning
Is the shepherd's warning
To carry his coat on his back.
The rainbow at night
Is the shepherd's delight,
For then no coat will he lack.
UNKNOWN. (INWARDS, *Weather Lore,* p. 112.)

A rainbow in the morning
Is the Shepherd's warning;
But a rainbow at night
Is the Shepherd's delight.
UNKNOWN. (HONE, *Every Day Book,* i, 670.)

If in the morning the rainbow appear, it signifyeth moisture; if in the evening it spend itself, fair weather ensueth.
LEONARD DIGGES, *Prognostication.* (1555)

RAKE

1
He was a rake among scholars and a scholar among rakes.

MACAULAY, *Essays: Aiken's Life of Addison.*

2
Women who like, and will have for a hero, a rake! how soon are you not to learn that you have taken bankrupts to your bosoms, and that the putrescent gold that attracted you is the slime of the Lake of Sin!

GEORGE MEREDITH, *Richard Feverel.* Ch. 15.

3
Every woman is at heart a rake.

POPE, *Moral Essays.* Epis. ii, l. 216. See 1255:3

Few men can be men of pleasure, every man may be a rake.

LORD CHESTERFIELD, *Letters,* 25 Jan., 1750.

4
A reformed rake makes the best husband.

W. G. BENHAM, *Proverbs,* p. 727. "Rake," an abbreviation of "rake-hell," dates from 1663.

RANK, see Ancestry

RASCAL, see Knave

RAT

5
It is the wisdom of rats, that will be sure to leave a house somewhat before it fall.

BACON, *Essays: Of Wisdom for a Man's Self.*

It is a great house still, . . . but it is a ruin none the less, and the rats fly from it.

DICKENS, *Dombey and Son.* Ch. 59.

A rotten carcass of a boat, . . . the very rats
Instinctively have quit it.

SHAKESPEARE, *The Tempest.* Act i, sc. 2, l. 5.

6
Anything like the sound of a rat
Makes my heart go pit-a-pat!

ROBERT BROWNING, *The Pied Piper.*

7
Yf they smell a ratt,
They grisely chide and chatt.

JOHN SKELTON, *The Image of Hypocrisy.* (c. 1520) *Works,* i, 51. (1843)

I smell a rat.

THOMAS MIDDLETON, *Blurt, Master-Constable.* Act iv, sc. 1. (1602)

Now you talk of a cat, Cicely, I smell a rat.

THOMAS HEYWOOD, *A Woman Killed with Kindness.* Act iv, sc. 4. (1603)

Do you not smell a rat?

BEN JONSON, *A Tale of a Tub.* Act iv, sc. 3. (1633)

Quoth Hudibras, I smell a rat;
Ralpho, thou dost prevaricate.

SAMUEL BUTLER, *Hudibras.* Pt. i, canto i, l. 821. (1663) Frequently thereafter.

8
The rat is the concisest tenant.
He pays no rent.— . . .
Hate cannot harm
A foe so reticent.

EMILY DICKINSON, *Poems.* Pt. ii, No. 35.

9
Too late repents the rat when caught by the cat.

JOHN FLORIO, *Second Frutes,* 165.

10
Die here in a rage, like a poisoned rat in a hole.

SWIFT, *Letter to Bolingbroke,* 21 March, 1729.

RAVEN

11
The raven said to the rook, "Stand away, black coat!"

THOMAS FULLER, *Gnomologia.* No. 4729.

Thou art a bitter bird, said the raven to the starling.

JOHN RAY, *English Proverbs,* 195.

See also under POT.

12
He pardons ravens but storms at doves. (Dat veniam corvis, vexat censura columbas.)

JUVENAL, *Satires.* Sat. ii, l. 63.

Who will not change a raven for a dove?

SHAKESPEARE, *A Midsummer-Night's Dream.* Act ii, sc. 2, l. 114.

13
Rarer even than a white raven. (Corvo quoque rarior albo.)

JUVENAL, *Satires.* Sat. vii, l. 202.

14
Beware of the Raven at Zurich,
'Tis a bird of omen ill;
A noisy and an unclean bird,
With a very, very long bill.

H. W. LONGFELLOW, *Journal,* 11 Aug., 1836. The entry is as follows: "Prepared to leave Zurich. At the Hotel du Corbeau they brought us a most exorbitant bill, whereupon I made the following beautiful lines." The quatrain is repeated, with minor variations, in *Hyperion.* Bk. iii, ch. 3.

15
He [Grenville] was the raven of the House of Commons, always croaking defeat in the midst of triumphs.

MACAULAY, *Essays: The Earl of Chatham.*

16
The Raven's house is built with reeds,—
Sing woe, and alas is me!
And the Raven's couch is spread with weeds,
High on the hollow tree;
And the Raven himself, telling his beads
In penance for his past misdeeds,
Upon the top I see.

THOMAS D'ARCY MCGEE, *The Penitent Raven.*

17
The raven once in snowy plumes was drest,
White as the whitest dove's unsullied breast,
Fair as the guardian of the Capitol,
Soft as the swan; a large and lovely fowl,
His tongue, his prating tongue has changed him quite
To sooty blackness from the purest white.

OVID, *Metamorphoses.* Bk. ii, l. 569. (Addison, tr.)

1
It wasn't for nothing—that raven croaking on my left hand just now. (Non temere est quod corvos cantat nunc ab læva manu.)
PLAUTUS, *Aulularia*, l. 624. (Act iv, sc. 3.)

That raven on yon left-hand oak
(Curse on his ill-betiding croak)
Bodes me no good.
JOHN GAY, *Fables: The Farmer's Wife and the Raven*, l. 27. *See also* SUPERSTITION: OMENS.

2
Ghastly, grim, and ancient Raven, wandering from the nightly shore,—
Tell me what thy lordly name is on the night's Plutonian shore?
Quoth the Raven, "Nevermore!"
EDGAR ALLAN POE, *The Raven*. St. 8.

Take thy beak from out my heart, and take thy form from off my door!
Quoth the Raven, "Nevermore!"
EDGAR ALLAN POE, *The Raven*. St. 17.

And the Raven, never flitting, still is sitting, still is sitting
On the pallid bust of Pallas just above my chamber door;
And his eyes have all the seeming of a demon's that is dreaming,
And the lamplight o'er him streaming throws his shadow on the floor;
And my soul from out that shadow that lies floating on the floor,
Shall be lifted—nevermore!
EDGAR ALLAN POE, *The Raven*. St. 18.

Raven from the dim dominions
On the Night's Plutonian shore,
Oft I hear thy dusky pinions
Wave and flutter round my door—
See the shadow of thy pinions
Float along the moonlit floor.
SARAH HELEN POWER WHITMAN, *The Raven*.

3
Bring up a raven and it will peck out your eyes.
W. G. BENHAM, *Proverbs*, 745. Spanish.

4
The croaking raven doth bellow for revenge.
SHAKESPEARE, *Hamlet*. Act iii, sc. 2, l. 264.

5
O, it comes o'er my memory,
As doth the raven o'er the infected house,
Boding to all.
SHAKESPEARE, *Othello*. Act iv, sc. 1, l. 20.

6
Did ever raven sing so like a lark,
That gives sweet tidings of the sun's uprise?
SHAKESPEARE, *Titus Andronicus*. Act iii, sc. 1, l. 158.

READING

See also Books, Libraries

I—Reading: How to Read

7
Read not to contradict and confute; nor to believe and take for granted; nor to find talk and discourse; but to weigh and consider. Some books are to be tasted, others to be swallowed, and some few to be chewed and digested: that is, some books are to be read only in parts, others to be read, but not curiously, and some few to be read wholly, and with diligence and attention.
FRANCIS BACON, *Essays: Of Studies*.

Some books are only cursorily to be tasted of.
FULLER, *Holy and Profane State: Of Books*.

8
All rests with those who read. A work or thought
Is what each makes it to himself.
P. J. BAILEY, *Festus: Proem*, l. 326.

9
Reading is not a duty, and has consequently no business to be made disagreeable.
AUGUSTINE BIRRELL, *Obiter Dicta: Second Series: The Office of Literature*.

Books soon are painful to my failing sight,
And oftener read from duty than delight.
GEORGE CRABBE, *Tales: Widow's Tale*, l. 127.

10
Read, mark, learn, and inwardly digest.
Book of Common Prayer: Collect for the Second Sunday in Advent.

11
It is impossible to read properly without using all one's engine-power. If we are not tired after reading, common-sense is not in us.
ARNOLD BENNETT, *Things that Have Interested Me: Translating Literature into Life*.

12
We get no good
By being ungenerous, even to a book,
And calculating profits,—so much help
By so much reading. It is rather when
We gloriously forget ourselves and plunge
Soul-forward, headlong, into a book's profound,
Impassioned for its beauty and salt of truth—
'Tis then we get the right good from a book.
E. B. BROWNING, *Aurora Leigh*. Bk. i, l. 702.

13
If that thou wilt not read, let it alone;
Some love the meat, some love to pick the bone.
JOHN BUNYAN, *The Pilgrim's Progress: The Author's Apology for His Book*.

14
What we should read is not the words, but the man whom we feel to be behind the words.
SAMUEL BUTLER THE YOUNGER, *Note-Books*, p. 94.

15
We have not *read* an author till we have seen his object, whatever it may be, as *he* saw it.
CARLYLE, *Essays: Goethe's Helena*.

Reading is seeing by proxy.
HERBERT SPENCER, *Study of Sociology*. Ch. 15.

1
It's with blood that letters enter. (La Letra con sangre entra.)
CERVANTES, *Don Quixote*. Pt. ii, ch. 36.

2
There is a great deal of difference between the eager man who wants to read a book, and the tired man who wants a book to read.
G. K. CHESTERTON, *Charles Dickens*, p. 99.

3
It is poor traveling that is only to arrive, and it is poor reading that is only to find out how the book ends.
ARTHUR COLTON, *The Reader*, Feb., 1909.

4
Some read to think,—these are rare; some to write,—these are common; and some to talk,—and these form the great majority.
C. C. COLTON, *Lacon*.

5
In its leaves that day We read no more. (Quel giorno più non vi leggemmo avante.)
DANTE, *Inferno*. Canto v, l. 138. (Cary, tr.)

When the last reader reads no more.
O. W. HOLMES, *The Last Reader*.

6
There is an art of reading, as well as an art of thinking, and an art of writing.
ISAAC D'ISRAELI, *Literary Character*. Ch. 11.

The art of reading is to skip judiciously.
P. G. HAMERTON, *Intellectual Life*. Pt. iv, let. 4.

7
One must be a great inventor to read well.
EMERSON, *Nature, Addresses, and Lectures: The American Scholar*.

'Tis the good reader that makes the good book.
EMERSON, *Society and Solitude: Success*.

If I do not read, nobody will.
EMERSON, *Journals*. Vol. iii, p. 460.

We read often with as much talent as we write.
EMERSON, *Journals*. Vol. x, p. 67.

8
All good and true book-lovers practise the pleasing and improving avocation of reading in bed.
EUGENE FIELD, *Love Affairs of a Bibliomaniac*, p. 31.

9
The use of books for pleasure is the most satisfactory recreation; without having acquired the power of reading for pleasure, none of us can be independent.
VISCOUNT GREY, *Fallodon Papers: Recreation*.

10
A man ought to read just as inclination leads him; for what he reads as a task will do him little good.
SAMUEL JOHNSON. (BOSWELL, *Life*, 1763.)

11
What is twice read is commonly better remembered than what is transcribed.
SAMUEL JOHNSON, *The Idler*. No. 74.

12
There be some men are born only to suck out the poison of books.
SAMUEL JOHNSON. (BOSWELL, *Life*.)

13
It may be well to wait a century for a reader, as God has waited six thousand years for an observer.
JOHN KEPLER. (BREWSTER, *Martyrs of Science*, p. 197.)

If the Almighty God waited six thousand years for one to see what he had made, I may surely wait two hundred for one to understand what I have written.
CARLYLE, *Miscellanies: Voltaire*. Of Kepler.

14
As you read it out it begins to grow your own. (Dum recitas, incipit esse tuus.)
MARTIAL, *Epigrams*. Bk. i, epig. 39.

15
And better had they ne'er been born
Who read to doubt, or read to scorn.
SCOTT, *The Monastery*. Ch. 12.

Waverley drove through the sea of books, like a vessel without a pilot or a rudder.
SCOTT, *Waverley*. Ch. 3.

16
Of all the artificial relations formed between mankind, the most capricious and variable is that of author and reader.
LORD SHAFTESBURY, *Characteristics*, iii, 227.

17
Sometimes I read a book with pleasure, and detest the author.
SWIFT, *Thoughts on Various Subjects*.

18
If thou wilt receive profit, read with humility, simplicity and faith; and seek not at any time the fame of being learned.
THOMAS À KEMPIS, *De Imitatione Christi*. Pt. i. ch. 5.

19
To read well, that is, to read true books in a true spirit, is a noble exercise.
H. D. THOREAU, *Walden: Reading*.

Books must be read as deliberately and reservedly as they were written.
H. D. THOREAU, *Walden: Reading*.

The works of the great poets have never yet been read by mankind, for only great poets can read them. . . . Most men have learned to read to serve a paltry convenience, . . . but of reading as a noble intellectual exercise they know little or nothing.
H. D. THOREAU, *Walden: Reading*.

20
Learn to read slow: all other graces
Will follow in their proper places.
WILLIAM WALKER, *The Art of Reading*.

II—Reading: What to Read

21
It is not wide reading but useful reading that tends to excellence.
ARISTIPPUS. (DIOGENES LAERTIUS, *Aristippus*. Bk. ii, sec. 71.)

22
Preserve proportion in your reading. Keep your view of men and things extensive.
THOMAS ARNOLD, *Address to His Scholars*.

1
In science, read by preference the newest works; in literature, the oldest. The classics are always modern.
Bulwer-Lytton, *Caxtoniana: Hints on Mental Culture.*

For what are the classics but the noblest recorded thoughts of man? They are the only oracles which are not decayed.
H. D. Thoreau, *Walden: Reading.*

2
Let blockheads read what blockheads wrote.
Lord Chesterfield, *Letters,* 1 Nov., 1750.

3
The mind, relaxing into needful sport,
Should turn to writers of an abler sort,
Whose wit well manag'd, and whose classic style,
Give truth a lustre, and make wisdom smile.
Cowper, *Retirement,* l. 715.

4
The three practical rules, then, which I have to offer, are,—1. Never read any book that is not a year old. 2. Never read any but famed books. 3. Never read any but what you like.
Emerson, *Society and Solitude: Books.*

I wish only to read that book it would have been a disaster to omit.
Emerson, *Uncollected Lectures: Books; Journals,* ix, 429.

Every book is worth reading which sets the reader in a working mood.
Emerson, *Uncollected Lectures: Resources.*

5
Turn over with nightly and daily labor. (Nocturna versate manu, versate diurna.)
Horace, *Ars Poetica,* l. 269. Of reading the Greek authors.

6
One should not read to swallow all, but rather see what one has use for.
Henrik Ibsen, *Peer Gynt.* Act iv.

7
Was there ever anything written by mere man that was wished longer by its readers, excepting *Don Quixote, Robinson Crusoe,* and the *Pilgrim's Progress*?
Samuel Johnson, *Remark.* (Piozzi, *Johnsoniana.*)

8
Read this of which life can say: " 'Tis my own." (Hoc lege, quod possit dicere vita "Meum est.")
Martial, *Epigrams.* Bk. x, epig. 4, l. 8.

9
Read much, but not many books. (Multum legendum esse, non multa.)
Pliny the Younger, *Epistles.* Bk. vii, epis. 9; Benjamin Franklin, *Poor Richard,* 1738.

From one that reads but one book . . . the Lord deliver us.
Howell, *Proverbs: Ital.-Eng.,* 7. (1659)

10
No man can read with profit that which he cannot learn to read with pleasure.
Noah Porter, *Books and Reading.* Ch. 1

11
Life being short and the quiet hours of it few, we ought to waste none of them in reading valueless books.
John Ruskin, *Sesame and Lilies: Preface.*

Life is too short for reading inferior books.
James Bryce, *Address,* Rutgers College, 10 Nov., 1911.

If time is precious, no book that will not improve by repeated readings deserves to be read at all.
Carlyle, *Essays: Goethe's Helena.*

12
You must linger among a limited number of master-thinkers, and digest their works, if you would derive ideas which shall win firm hold in your mind.
Seneca, *Epistulæ ad Lucilium.* Epis. ii, sec. 2.

It is not the reading of many books which is necessary to make a man wise or good, but the well-reading of a few, could he be sure to have the best.
Richard Baxter, *Christian Directory.* Pt. ii, ch. 16.

A few books thoroughly digested, rather than hundreds but gargled in the mouth.
Francis Osborne, *Advice to a Son.*

13
You complain that in your part of the world there is a scant supply of books. But it is quality, rather than quantity, that matters; a limited list of reading benefits; a varied assortment serves only for delight.
Seneca, *Epistulæ ad Lucilium.* Epis. xlv, sec. 1.

14
Digressions, incontestably, are the sunshine;—they are the life, the soul of reading!
Sterne, *Tristram Shandy.* Bk. i, ch. 22.

15
Nothing is worth reading that does not require an alert mind.
Charles Dudley Warner, *Backlog Studies.* No. 1.

III—Reading: Its Benefits

16
Reading is to the mind, what exercise is to the body. As by the one, health is preserved, strengthened, and invigorated; by the other, virtue, which is the health of the mind, is kept alive, cherished, and confirmed.
Addison, *The Tatler.* No. 147.

17
Reading maketh a full man; conference a ready man; and writing an exact man.
Francis Bacon, *Essays: Of Studies.*

Reading makes a full man—meditation a profound man—discourse a clear man.
Benjamin Franklin, *Poor Richard,* 1738.

1
Histories make men wise; poets, witty; the mathematics, subtile; natural philosophy, deep; morals, grave; logic and rhetoric, able to contend.

FRANCIS BACON, *Essays: Of Studies.*

Books have always a secret influence on the understanding; we cannot at pleasure obliterate ideas: he that reads books of science, though without any fixed desire of improvement, will grow more knowing; he that entertains himself with moral or religious treatises, will imperceptibly advance in goodness; the ideas which are often offered to the mind, will at last find a lucky moment when it is disposed to receive them.

SAMUEL JOHNSON, *The Adventurer.* No. 137.

2
Of all the human relaxations which are free from guilt, none so dignified as reading.

EGERTON BRYDGES, *The Ruminator.* No. 24.

3
Who is he . . . that will not be much lightened in his mind by reading of some enticing story, true or feigned?

ROBERT BURTON, *Anatomy of Melancholy: Democritus to the Reader.*

4
Let us assume that entertainment is the sole end of reading; even so, I think you would hold that no mental employment is so broadening to the sympathies or so enlightening to the understanding. Other pursuits belong not to all times, all ages, all conditions; but this gives stimulus to our youth and diversion to our old age; this adds a charm to success, and offers a haven of consolation to failure. Through the night-watches, on all our journeyings, and in our hours of ease, it is our unfailing companion.

CICERO, *Pro Archia Poeta.* Ch. vii, sec. 16.

5
Ah! happy he who thus, in magic themes
O'er worlds bewitch'd, in early rapture dreams,
Where wild Enchantment waves her potent wand,
And Fancy's beauties fill her fairy land.

GEORGE CRABBE, *The Library,* l. 563.

6
The delight of opening a new pursuit, or a new course of reading, imparts the vivacity and novelty of youth even to old age.

ISAAC D'ISRAELI, *Literary Character of Men of Genius.* Ch. 22.

7
Our high respect for a well-read man is praise enough of literature.

EMERSON, *Letters and Social Aims: Quotation and Originality.*

If we encountered a man of rare intellect, we should ask him what books he read.

EMERSON, *Letters and Social Aims: Quotation and Originality.*

It is a tie between men to have read the same book

EMERSON, *Journals,* 1864.

8
My early and invincible love of reading, . . . I would not exchange for the treasures of India.

EDWARD GIBBON, *Memoirs.*

9
He that loves reading, has everything within his reach. He has but to desire, and he may possess himself of every species of wisdom to judge and power to perform.

WILLIAM GODWIN, *Enquirer: Early Taste for Reading.*

10
In a polite age, almost every person becomes a reader, and receives more instruction from the Press than the Pulpit.

GOLDSMITH, *Citizen of the World.* Letter 75.

The first time I read an excellent book, it is to me just as if I had gained a new friend: when I read over a book I have perused before, it resembles the meeting with an old one.

GOLDSMITH, *Citizen of the World.* Letter 83.

11
Every reader who holds a book in his hand is free of the inmost minds of men past and present; . . . he needs no introduction to the greatest.

FREDERIC HARRISON, *The Choice of Books,* p. 7.

12
Read anything five hours a day, and you will soon be learned.

SAMUEL JOHNSON. (BOSWELL, *Life.*)

13
I love to lose myself in other men's minds. When I am not walking, I am reading; I cannot sit and think. Books think for me.

CHARLES LAMB, *Last Essays of Elia: Detached Thoughts on Books and Reading.*

14
Have you ever rightly considered what the mere ability to read means? That it is the key which admits us to the whole world of thought and fancy and imagination? to the company of saint and sage, of the wisest and the wittiest at their wisest and wittiest moment? That it enables us to see with the keenest eyes, hear with the finest ears, and listen to the sweetest voices of all time?

J. R. LOWELL, *Democracy and Other Addresses: Books and Libraries.*

15
I was so allured to read that no recreation came to me better welcome.

MILTON, *An Apology for Smectymnuus.*

16
He that I am reading seems always to have the most force.

MONTAIGNE, *Essays.* Bk. ii, ch. 12.

17
To love to read is to exchange hours of ennui for hours of delight.

MONTESQUIEU, *Pensées.*

1
Reading nourishes the mind, and refreshes it when it is wearied with study, though not without study. (Alit lectio ingenium et studio fatigatum, non sine studio tamen, reficit.)
SENECA, *Epistulæ ad Lucilium*. Epis. lxxiv, 1.

2
He reads much;
He is a great observer and he looks
Quite through the deeds of men.
SHAKESPEARE, *Julius Cæsar*. Act i, sc. 2, l. 201.

Exceedingly well read.
SHAKESPEARE, *I Henry IV*. Act iii, sc. 1, l. 166.

One who, to all the heights of learning bred,
Read books and men, and practised what he read.
GEORGE STEPNEY, *To the Earl of Carlisle*.

3
He hath never fed of the dainties that are bred in a book; he hath not eat paper, as it were; he hath not drunk ink: his intellect is not replenished; he is only an animal, only sensible in the duller parts.
SHAKESPEARE, *Love's Labour's Lost*. Act iv, sc. 2, l. 25.

4
People say that life is the thing, but I prefer reading.
LOGAN PEARSALL SMITH, *Afterthoughts*.

5
Give a man a pipe he can smoke,
Give a man a book he can read:
And his home is bright with a calm delight,
Though the room be poor indeed.
JAMES THOMSON, *Gifts*.

6
The habit of reading is the only enjoyment in which there is no alloy; it lasts when all other pleasures fade.
ANTHONY TROLLOPE, *Speech*, 7 Dec., 1868.

IV—Reading: Its Dangers

7
But so many books thou readest,
But so many schemes thou breedest,
But so many wishes feedest,
That thy poor head almost turns.
MATTHEW ARNOLD, *The Second Best*.

8
Affects all books of past and modern ages,
But reads no further than their title-pages.
SAMUEL BUTLER, *Satires: Human Learning*.

Kiss the book's outside, who ne'er look within.
COWPER, *Expostulation*, l. 389.

9
And let a scholar all Earth's volumes carry,
He will be but a walking dictionary.
GEORGE CHAPMAN, *Tears of Peace*, l. 270.

10
With various readings stored his empty skull,
Learn'd without sense, and venerably dull.
CHARLES CHURCHILL, *The Rosciad*, l. 591.

11
A man may as well expect to grow stronger by always eating as wiser by always reading. . . . 'Tis thought and digestion which makes books serviceable, and gives health and vigour to the mind.
JEREMY COLLIER, *Essays: Of the Entertainment of Books*.

12
Guanoed her mind by reading French novels.
BENJAMIN DISRAELI, *Tancred*. Bk. ii, ch. 9.

13
Those book-learnèd fools who miss the world.
JOHN DRINKWATER, *From Generation to Generation*.

14
You will see me any morning in the park
Reading the comics and the sporting page.
Particularly I remark
An English countess goes upon the stage,
A Greek was murdered at a Polish dance,
Another bank defaulter has confessed.
I keep my countenance.
T. S. ELIOT, *Portrait of a Lady*.

15
He might be a very clever man by nature for aught I know, but he laid so many books upon his head that his brains could not move.
ROBERT HALL. (GREGORY, *Life of Hall*.) Referring to Kippis.

16
Reading is sometimes an ingenious device for avoiding thought.
HELPS, *Friends in Council*. Bk. ii, ch. 1.

17
If I had spent as much time in reading as other men of learning, I should have been as ignorant as they.
THOMAS HOBBES. (D'ISRAELI, *Curiosities of Literature*. Vol. ii, p. 179.)

18
He has left off reading altogether, to the great improvement of his originality.
CHARLES LAMB, *Last Essays of Elia: Detached Thoughts on Books and Reading*.

19
Reading furnishes the mind only with materials of knowledge; it is thinking makes what we read ours.
JOHN LOCKE, *Conduct of Understanding:* Sec. 20, *Reading*.

Reading without thinking may indeed make a rich common-place, but 'twill never make a clear head.
JOHN NORRIS, *Of the Advantages of Thinking*.

20
Night after night,
He sat and bleared his eyes with books.
LONGFELLOW, *The Golden Legend*. Pt. i.

21
For reading new books is like eating new bread,
One can bear it at first, but by gradual steps he
Is brought to death's door of a mental dyspepsy.
J. R. LOWELL, *A Fable for Critics*, l. 104.

1
A reading-machine, always wound up and going,
He mastered whatever was not worth the knowing.
J. R. LOWELL, *A Fable for Critics*, l. 164.

In books a prodigal, they say,
A living cyclopedia.
COTTON MATHER, *Epitaph on Anne Bradstreet*.

2
His classical reading is great: he can quote
Horace, Juvenal, Ovid and Martial by rote.
He has read Metaphysics, . . . Spinoza and Kant
And Theology too: I have heard him descant
Upon Basil and Jerome. Antiquities, art,
He is fond of. He knows the old masters by heart.
OWEN MEREDITH, *Lucile*. Canto ii, pt. 4.

3
Who reads
Incessantly, and to his reading brings not
A spirit and judgment equal or superior, . . .
Uncertain and unsettl'd still remains,
Deep vers'd in books and shallow in himself.
MILTON, *Paradise Regained*. Bk. iv, l. 322.

4
For men that read much and work little are as bells, the which do sound to call others, and they themselves never enter into the church.
THOMAS NORTH, *Diall of Princes*, 138. (1557)

5
More true knowledge comes by meditation than by reading; for much reading is an oppression of the mind, and extinguishes the natural candle, which is the reason of so many senseless scholars in the world.
WILLIAM PENN, *Advice to His Children*.

6
The bookful blockhead, ignorantly read,
With loads of learned lumber in his head,
With his own tongue still edifies his ears,
And always list'ning to himself appears.
POPE, *Essay on Criticism*. Pt. iii, l. 53.

7
In reading of many books is distraction. (Distringit librorum multitudo.)
SENECA, *Epistulæ ad Lucilium*. Epis. ii, sec. 3.

8
To pass from hearing literature to reading it is to take a great and dangerous step.
R. L. STEVENSON, *Random Memories*.

9
Who readeth much, and never meditates,
Is like the greedy eater of much food,
Who so surcloys his stomach with his cates,
That commonly they do him little good.
JOSHUA SYLVESTER, *Tetraticha*.

10
Verily, when the day of judgment comes, we shall not be asked what we have read, but what we have done.
THOMAS À KEMPIS, *De Imitatione Christi*. Pt. i, ch. 3.

V—Reading and Running

11
But truths on which depends our main concern,
That 'tis our shame and mis'ry not to learn,
Shine by the side of ev'ry path we tread
With such a lustre, he that runs may read.
COWPER, *Tirocinium*, l. 77.

12
And reads, though running, all these needful motions.
DU BARTAS, *Devine Weekes and Workes*. Week i, day 1. (Sylvester, tr.)

13
Write the vision, and make it plain upon tables, that he may run that readeth it.
Old Testament: Habakkuk, ii, 2. Frequently misquoted, "that he who runs may read."

Read my little fable:
He that runs may read.
TENNYSON, *The Flower*. St. 5.

REASON

See also Faith and Reason; Instinct and Reason

I—Reason: Definitions

14
Every man's reason is every man's oracle.
LORD BOLINGBROKE, *Of the True Use of Retirement and Study*. Letter ii.

Every man's own reason is his best Œdipus.
SIR THOMAS BROWNE, *Religio Medici*. Pt. i, sec. 6.

Your own reason is the only oracle given you by heaven, and you are answerable for, not the rightness, but the uprightness of the decision.
THOMAS JEFFERSON, *Writings*. Vol. x, p. 178.

Reason is my augury, and my interpretation of the future; by it I have practised divination, and obtained knowledge. (Augurium ratio est, et conjectura futuri: Hac divinavi notitiamque tuli.)
OVID, *Tristia*. Bk. i, eleg. 9, l. 51.

15
Wherefore I assert:—if Reason's only function were to heighten our pleasure, that were vindication enough.
ROBERT BRIDGES, *Testament of Beauty*. Bk. i, l. 202.

16
Reason is Life's sole arbiter, the magic Labyrinth's single clue.
SIR RICHARD BURTON, *Kasîdah*. Pt. vii, st. 22.

17
Reason to rule and mercy to forgive;
The first is law, the last prerogative.
DRYDEN, *Hind and the Panther*. Pt. i, l. 261.

Subdue
By force, who reason for their law refuse,
Right reason for their law.
MILTON, *Paradise Lost*. Bk. vi, l. 40.

See also under LAW.

18
Reason is not measured by size or height, but

by principle. (Λόγου γὰρ μέγεθος οὐ μήκει οὐδ' ὕψει κρίνεται, ἀλλὰ δόγμασιν.)

EPICTETUS, *Discourses*. Ch. 12, sec. 26.

1 To a rational being, to act according to nature and according to reason is the same thing. (Τῷ λογικῷ ζῴῳ ἡ αὐτὴ πρᾶξις κατὰ φύσιν ἐστὶ καὶ κατὰ λόγον.)

MARCUS AURELIUS, *Meditations*. Bk. vii, 11.

2 Unto the good their reason ever is a god. (Θεός ἐστι τοῖς χρηστοῖς ἀεὶ ὁ νοῦς γάρ, ὡς ἔοικεν.)

MENANDER, *Adelphoi*. Frag. 11.

3 Say first, of God above or Man below
What can we reason but from what we know?

POPE, *Essay on Man*. Epis. i, l. 17.

4 The soul of man is divided into three parts, intelligence, reason, and passion. Intelligence and passion are possessed by other animals, but reason by man alone. . . . Reason is immortal, all else is mortal.

PYTHAGORAS. (DIOGENES LAERTIUS, *Pythagoras*. Bk. viii, sec. 30.)

5 Reason is nothing else but a portion of the divine spirit set in a human body. (Ratio autem nihil aliud est quam in corpus humanum pars divini spiritus mersa.)

SENECA, *Epistulæ ad Lucilium*. Epis. lxvi, 12.

6 Reason, the choicest gift bestowed by heaven. (Φρένας, πάντων ὅσ' ἐστὶ κτημάτων ὑπέρτατον.)

SOPHOCLES, *Antigone*, l. 683.

7 And what is reason? Be she thus defin'd:
Reason is upright stature in the soul.

YOUNG, *Night Thoughts*. Night vii, l. 1440.

II—Reason: Apothegms

8 It must be so,—Plato, thou reason'st well!

ADDISON, *Cato*. Act v, sc. 1, l. 1.

9 Sweet reasonableness.

MATTHEW ARNOLD, *St. Paul and Protestantism: Preface*. A phrase used by Arnold many times.

10 It is not necessary to believe things in order to reason about them. (Il n'est pas nécessaire de tenir les choses pour en raisonner.)

BEAUMARCHAIS, *Le Barbier de Séville*. Act v, sc. 4.

11 He who will not reason, is a bigot; he who cannot is a fool; and he who dares not, is a slave.

SIR WILLIAM DRUMMOND, *Academical Question: Preface*.

12 Let us first of all follow reason, it is the surest guide. It warns us itself of its feebleness and informs us of its own limitations.

ANATOLE FRANCE, *Credo of a Sceptic*, p. 79.

13 O Reason! when will thy long minority expire?

HAZLITT, *Literary Remains*. Vol. ii, p. 453.

14 Hearken to reason, or she will be heard.

GEORGE HERBERT, *Jacula Prudentum*.

Reason governs the wise man and cudgels the fool.

H. G. BOHN, *Hand-Book of Proverbs*, 479.

If you will not hear Reason, she will surely rap your knuckles.

BENJAMIN FRANKLIN, *Poor Richard*, 1758.

15 Setting themselves against reason, as often as reason is against them.

THOMAS HOBBES, *Tripos: Epistle Dedicatory*.

16 We have not enough strength to follow reason absolutely. (Nous n'avons pas assez de force pour suivre toute notre raison.)

LA ROCHEFOUCAULD, *Maximes*. No. 42.

We have not enough reason to use all our strength. (Nous n'avons pas assez de raison pour employer toute notre force.)

MADAME DE GRIGNAN, reversing La Rochefoucauld, to illustrate how the reverse of his maximes was often as true as the original. (MADAME DE SÉVIGNÉ, *Lettres*, vi, 527.)

17 To be rational is so glorious a thing, that two-legged creatures generally content themselves with the title.

JOHN LOCKE, *Letter to Antony Collins, Esq.*

18 Always take the short cut; and that is the rational one. Therefore say and do everything according to soundest reason.

MARCUS AURELIUS, *Meditations*. Bk. iv, sec. 51. *See also* SENSE: COMMON SENSE.

19 To be pointedly rational is a greater difficulty for me than a fine delirium.

GEORGE MEREDITH, *Diana of the Crossways*. Ch. 1.

20 Indu'd With sanctity of reason.

MILTON, *Paradise Lost*. Bk. vii, l. 507.

21 Every extreme doth perfect reason flee,
And wishes wisdom with sobriety.
(La parfaite raison fuit toute extrémité,
Et veut que l'on soit sage avec sobriété.)

MOLIÈRE, *Le Misanthrope*. Act i, sc. 1, l. 151.

22 What is now reason was formerly impulse. (Quod nunc ratio est, impetus ante fuit.)

OVID, *Remediorum Amoris*, l. 10. *See also* INSTINCT AND REASON.

23 We must be fortified . . . by reason against all adversities.

PLUTARCH, *Lives: Solon*. Sec. 7.

24 The feast of reason and the flow of soul.

POPE, *Imitations of Horace: Satires*. Bk. ii, sat. 1, l. 128.

1
Some folks dey would 'a' beat him:
Now, dat would only heat him;
I know jes' how to treat him:
You mus' *reason* wid a mule.
IRWIN RUSSELL, *Nebuchadnezzar.*

2
Nothing is to be done without reason. (Nihil sine ratione faciendum est.)
SENECA, *De Beneficiis.* Bk. iv, sec. 10.

3
And reason pandars will.
SHAKESPEARE, *Hamlet.* Act iii, sc. 4, l. 88.

O, strange excuse,
When reason is the bawd to lust's abuse!
SHAKESPEARE, *Venus and Adonis,* l. 791.

4
But since the affairs of men rest still incertain,
Let 's reason with the worst that may befall.
SHAKESPEARE, *Julius Cæsar.* Act v, sc. 1, l. 96.

5
Be led by reason. (Νοῦν ἡγεμόνα ποιοῦ.)
SOLON. (DIOGENES LAERTIUS, *Solon.* Bk. i, sec. 60.)

6
The man who listens to Reason is lost: Reason enslaves all whose minds are not strong enough to master her.
BERNARD SHAW, *Maxims for Revolutionists.*

The reasonable man adapts himself to the world: the unreasonable one persists in trying to adapt the world to himself. Therefore all progress depends on the unreasonable man.
BERNARD SHAW, *Maxims for Revolutionists.*

7
Impassion'd logic, which outran
The hearer in its fiery course.
TENNYSON, *In Memoriam.* Pt. cix, st. 2.

8
In human affairs there is always, somehow, a slight majority on the side of reason.
HENRY VAN DYKE, attr. But Dr. van Dyke writes, "I don't think this is mine; it sounds more like Emerson."

9
I can stand brute force, but brute reason is quite unbearable. There is something unfair about its use. It is hitting below the intellect.
OSCAR WILDE, *Picture of Dorian Gray.* Ch. 3.

10
Abstrusest matter, reasonings of the mind
Turned inward.
WORDSWORTH, *The Excursion.* Bk. i, l. 65.

III—Reason: Its Power

11
Reason is the mistress and queen of all things. (Domina omnium et regina ratio.)
CICERO, *Tusculanarum Disputationum.* Bk. ii, ch. 21.

And this I know, for kinde wit me taught,
That reason shall reign and realms govern.
LANGLAND, *Piers Plowman.* Passus iv, l. 440.

12
Within the brain's most secret cells
A certain Lord Chief Justice dwells,
Of sovereign power, whom, one and all,
With common voice, we Reason call.
CHARLES CHURCHILL, *The Ghost.* Bk. iv, l. 125.

13
Reason and speech, which bring men together and unite them in a sort of natural society. Nor in anything are we further removed from the nature of wild beasts. (Ratio et oratio quæ . . . conciliat inter se homines, conjungitque naturali quadam societate; neque ulla re longius absumus a natura ferarum.)
CICERO, *De Officiis.* Bk. i, ch. 16, sec. 50.

A man without reason is a beast in season.
JOHN RAY, *English Proverbs.*

A man that doth not use his reason is a tame beast; a man that abuses it is a wild one.
LORD HALIFAX, *Works,* p. 254.

A beast, that wants discourse of reason.
SHAKESPEARE, *Hamlet.* Act i, sc. 2, l. 150.

14
Reason, which is, as it were, the light and lamp of life. (Ratio . . . quasi quædam lux, lumenque vitæ.)
CICERO, *Academicarum Quæstionum.* Bk. i, ch. 5, sec. 8.

We walk evermore
To higher paths by brightening Reason's lamp.
GEORGE ELIOT, *The Spanish Gypsy.* Bk. ii.

15
O Youth, alas, why wilt thou not incline
And unto rulèd reason bowe thee,
Since Reason is the very straight line
That leadeth folk into felicity?
THOMAS HOCCLEVE, *La Male Regle.* (1425)

16
We may take Fancy for a companion, but must follow Reason as our guide.
SAMUEL JOHNSON, *Letter to Boswell,* 1774.

If but a beam of sober Reason play,
Lo, Fancy's fairy frost-work melts away!
ROGERS, *Pleasures of Memory.* Pt. ii, l. 427.

While Reason drew the plan, the Heart inform'd
The moral page, and Fancy lent it grace.
JAMES THOMSON, *Liberty.* Pt. iv, l. 262.

17
Nothing can be lasting when reason does not rule. (Nihil potest esse diuturnum cui non subest ratio.)
QUINTUS CURTIUS RUFUS, *De Rebus Gestis Alexandri Magni,* iv, 14, 19.

18
If you wish to subject all things to yourself, subject yourself to reason. (Si vis omnia tibi subicere, te subice rationi.)
SENECA, *Epistulæ ad Lucilium.* Epis. 37, sec. 4.

19
The will of man is by his reason sway'd.
SHAKESPEARE, *A Midsummer-Night's Dream.* Act ii, sc. 2, l. 115.

20
All the tools with which mankind works upon its fate are dull, but the sharpest among them is the reason.
CARL VAN DOREN, *Many Minds,* p. 209.

IV—Reason: Its Weakness

1
Between craft and credulity, the voice of reason is stifled.

EDMUND BURKE, *Letter to the Sheriffs of Bristol.*

2
Reason, which ought always to direct mankind, seldom does; but passions and weaknesses commonly usurp its seat, and rule in its stead.

LORD CHESTERFIELD, *Letters,* 15 Feb., 1754.

Address yourself generally to the senses, to the heart, and to the weaknesses of mankind, but very rarely to their reason.

LORD CHESTERFIELD, *Letters,* 6 Feb., 1752.

3
Few have reason, most have eyes.

CHARLES CHURCHILL, *The Ghost.* Bk. iv, l. 186.

4
Error lives
Ere reason can be born. Reason, the power
To guess at right and wrong, the twinkling lamp
Of wand'ring life, that winks and wakes by turns,
Fooling the follower between shade and shining.

CONGREVE, *The Mourning Bride.* Act iii, sc. 1.

Dim as the borrow'd beams of moon and stars
To lonely, weary, wand'ring travellers,
Is Reason to the soul: and as on high
Those rolling fires discover but the sky,
Not light us here; so Reason's glimmering ray
Was lent, not to assure our doubtful way,
But guide us upward to a better day.
And as those nightly tapers disappear,
When day's bright lord ascends our hemisphere;
So pale grows Reason at Religion's sight;
So dies, and so dissolves in supernatural light.

DRYDEN, *Religio Laici,* l. 1.

Reason, thou vain impertinence,
Deluding hypocrite, begone! . . .
At best thou'rt but a glimmering light,
Which serves not to direct our way;
But, like the moon, confounds our sight,
And only shows it is not day.

UNKNOWN, *Reason.* (*Miscellany Poems and Translations by Oxford Hands.* 1685.)

5
All is but jest, all dust, all not worth two peason:
For why in man's matters is neither rhyme nor reason.
(Omnia sunt rusus, sunt pulvis, et omnia nil sunt:
Res hominum cunctæ, nam ratione carent)

DEMOCRITUS, *Idylls.* (PUTTENHAM, *Arte of English Poesie,* p. 125.) *See also* POETRY: RHYME AND REASON.

Reason, Justice and Equity never had weight enough on the face of the earth to govern the councils of men.

THOMAS A. EDISON. (*Golden Book,* April, 1931.)

If ever there was a bigger lie, my dear Daddy, than any other, it is that man is a reasonable creature.

H. G. WELLS, *Mr. Britling Sees It Through.* Bk. ii, ch. 4, sec. 18.

6
Ah, when to the heart of man
Seemed it ever less than a treason
To go with the drift of things,
To yield with a grace to reason
And bow and accept the end
Of a love, or a season?

ROBERT FROST, *Reluctance.*

7
Reason exercises merely the function of preserving order, is, so to say, the police in the region of art. In life it is mostly a cold arithmetician summing up our follies.

HEINE, *Wit, Wisdom, and Pathos: Art Notes.*

8
To think that two and two are four
And neither five nor three
The heart of man has long been sore
And long 'tis like to be.

A. E. HOUSMAN, *Last Poems,* p. 69.

9
On human actions reason tho' you can,
It may be Reason, but it is not Man.

POPE, *Moral Essays.* Epis. i, l. 25.

What Reason weaves, by Passion is undone.

POPE, *An Essay on Man.* Epis. ii, l. 42.

10
Who reasons wisely is not therefore wise;
His pride in reas'ning, not in acting, lies.

POPE, *Moral Essays.* Epis. i, l. 117.

11
Reason perhaps teaches certain bourgeois virtues, but it does not make either heroes or saints.

MIGUEL DE UNAMUNO, *Tragic Sense of Life,* p. 293.

12
Reason, an ignis fatuus of the mind.

JOHN WILMOT, *A Satire Against Mankind,* l. 11. An imitation of Boileau.

V—Reason: Reasons

See also Motive, Purpose

13
Reasons are not like garments, the worse for wearing.

EARL OF ESSEX, *Letter to Lord Willoughby.* (See *Notes and Queries.* Ser. x, vol. 2, p. 23.)

14
I will it, I so order, let my will stand for a reason. (Hoc volo, sic jubeo, sit pro ratione voluntas.)

JUVENAL, *Satires.* Sat. vi, l. 223. *See also* WOMAN: A WOMAN'S REASON.

15
The heart has reasons of which reason has no knowledge. (Le cœur a ses raisons, que la raison ne connaît point.)

PASCAL, *Pensées.* No. 277.

1
'Zounds, an I were at the strappado, or all the racks in the world, I would not tell you on compulsion. Give you a reason on compulsion! if reasons were as plentiful as blackberries, I would give no man a reason upon compulsion, I.

SHAKESPEARE, *I Henry IV*. Act ii, sc. 4, l. 262.

2
Good reasons must, of force, give place to better.

SHAKESPEARE, *Julius Cæsar*. Act iv, sc. 3, l. 203.

My reasons are both good and weighty.

SHAKESPEARE, *The Taming of the Shrew*. Act i, sc. 1, l. 252.

Strong reasons make strong actions.

SHAKESPEARE, *King John*. Act iii, sc. 4, l. 182.

3
His reasons are as two grains of wheat hid in two bushels of chaff: you shall seek all day ere you find them, and when you have them, they are not worth the search.

SHAKESPEARE, *The Merchant of Venice*. Act i, sc. 1, l. 115.

VI—Reason: Why and Wherefore

4
Whatever Sceptic could inquire for,
For every why he had a wherefore.

BUTLER, *Hudibras*. Pt. i, canto i, l. 131.

5
Never mind the why and wherefore.

W. S. GILBERT, *H. M. S. Pinafore*. Act ii, sc. 1.

6
Why and Wherefore set out one day,
To hunt for a wild Negation.
They agreed to meet at a cool retreat
On the Point of Interrogation.

OLIVER HERFORD, *Metaphysics*.

7
Without why or wherefore. (Nec quid nec quare.)

PETRONIUS, *Satyricon*. Sec. 37.

8
The "why" is plain as way to parish church.

SHAKESPEARE, *As You Like It*. Act ii, sc. 7, l. 52.

9
Ant. S.: Shall I tell you why?
Dro. S.: Ay, sir, and wherefore; for they say every why hath a wherefore.

SHAKESPEARE, *The Comedy of Errors*. Act ii, sc. 2, l. 43.

There is occasions and causes why and wherefore in all things.

SHAKESPEARE, *Henry V*. Act v, sc. 1, l. 3.

10
It fits thee not to ask the reason why.

SHAKESPEARE, *Pericles*. Act i, sc. 1, l. 157.

VII—Reason: To Make the Worse Appear the Better Reason

11
To make the worse appear the better reason. (Τὸν ἥττω δὲ λόγον κρείττω ποιεῖν.)

ARISTOTLE, *Rhetorica*. Bk. ii, ch. 24, sec. 11.

12
Aristophanes turns Socrates into ridicule for making the worse appear the better reason. (Τὸν ἥττω λόγον κρείττω ποιοῦντα.)

DIOGENES LAERTIUS, *Socrates*. Bk. ii, sec. 19.

For comic writers charge Socrates with making the worse appear the better reason. (Nam et Socrati objiciunt comici, docere eum quomodo pejorem causam meliorem faciat.)

QUINTILIAN, *De Institutione Oratoria*. Bk. ii, ch. 17, sec. 1.

13
His tongue
Dropt manna, and could make the worse appear
The better reason.

MILTON, *Paradise Lost*. Bk. ii, l. 112.

14
He makes black white, and white he turns to black. (Candida de nigris, et de candentibus atra.)

OVID, *Metamorphoses*. Bk. xi, l. 314.

And finds with keen, discriminating sight,
Black's not so black—nor white so very white.

GEORGE CANNING, *The New Morality*.

See also RIGHT AND WRONG.

15
There is a demand these days for men who can make wrong appear right. (Eis nunc præmiumst, qui recta prava faciunt.)

TERENCE, *Phormio*, l. 771. (Act v, sc. 2.)

REBELLION

See also Revolution

16
The devil was the first o' th' name
From whom the race of rebels came.

BUTLER, *Miscellaneous Thoughts*, l. 169.

The worst of rebels never arm
To do their king or country harm,
But draw their swords to do them good,
As doctors cure by letting blood.

BUTLER, *Miscellaneous Thoughts*, l. 181.

17
Men seldom, or rather never for a length of time and deliberately, rebel against anything that does not deserve rebelling against.

CARLYLE, *Essays: Goethe's Works*.

18
A little rebellion now and then is a good thing, and as necessary in the political world as storms in the physical.

THOMAS JEFFERSON, *On Shays' Rebellion*. (*Writings*. Vol. vi, p. 64.)

19
No doubt but it is safe to dwell
Where ordered duties are;
No doubt the cherubs earn their wage
Who wind each ticking star;
No doubt the system is quite right!—
Sane, ordered, regular;
But how the rebel fires the soul
Who dares the strong gods' ire.

DON MARQUIS, *The Rebel*.

1
It doesn't take a majority to make a rebellion; it takes only a few determined leaders and a sound cause.
H. L. MENCKEN, *Prejudices*. Ser. v, p. 141.

2
Rebellion! foul, dishonouring word,
Whose wrongful blight so oft has stain'd
The holiest cause that tongue or sword
Of mortal ever lost or gain'd.
How many a spirit, born to bless,
Hath sunk beneath that with'ring name,
Whom but a day's, an hour's success,
Had wafted to eternal fame!
THOMAS MOORE, *Lalla Rookh: The Fire Worshippers: Prologue*. Pt. ii, l. 91.

3
Rebels in Cork are patriots at Madrid.
THOMAS MOORE, *The Sceptic*, l. 58.

4
But in the gross and scope of my opinion,
This bodes some strange eruption to our state.
SHAKESPEARE, *Hamlet*. Act i, sc. 1, l. 68.

5
Rebellion in this land shall lose his sway,
Meeting the check of such another day.
SHAKESPEARE, *I Henry IV*. Act v, sc. 5, l. 41.

Quenching the flame of bold rebellion
Even with the rebels' blood.
SHAKESPEARE, *II Henry IV: Induction*, l. 26.

Rebellion, flat rebellion!
SHAKESPEARE, *King John*. Act iii, sc. 1, l. 298.

Unthread the rude eye of rebellion.
SHAKESPEARE, *King John*. Act v, sc. 4, l. 11.

6
The remedy for the tumult was another tumult. (Remedium tumultus fuit alius tumultus.)
TACITUS, *History*. Bk. ii, sec. 68.

7
The most seditious is the most cowardly. (Seditiosissimus quisque ignavus.)
TACITUS, *History*. Bk. iv, sec. 34.

8
Rebellion to tyrants is obedience to God.
UNKNOWN. From an inscription on the cannon near which the ashes of President John Bradshaw were buried, on the top of a high hill near Martha Bay, in Jamaica.—STILES, *History of the Three Judges of King Charles I*. Bradshaw was Lord President of the parliamentary commission which tried Charles I, and pronounced sentence. He was buried in Westminster Abbey, but his body was dug up in 1660, hanged and reburied at Tyburn. Attributed also to Benjamin Franklin. (RANDOLPH, *Life of Jefferson*. Vol. iii, p. 585.)

RECREATION

See also Exercise

9
Mingle your cares with pleasure now and then. (Interpone tuis interdum gaudia curis.)
DIONYSIUS CATO, *Disticha de Moribus*. Bk. iii, No. 7.

10
At times Apollo wakes with the lyre his slumbering song, and does not always stretch the bow. (Quondam cithara tacentem Suscitat musam neque semper arcum Tendit Apollo.)
HORACE, *Odes*. Bk. ii, ode 10, l. 18.

The bow, if never unbent, will lose its power. (Arcus, si numquam cesses tendere, mollis erit.)
OVID, *Heroides*. Epis. iv, l. 91.

11
The bow that's always bent will quickly break;
But if unstrung will serve you at your need.
So let the mind some relaxation take
To come back to its task with fresher heed.
PHÆDRUS, *Fables*. Bk. iii, fable 14. (King, tr.)

Straining breaks the bow, and relaxation relieves the mind. (Arcum intensio frangit, animum remisso.)
PUBLILIUS SYRUS, *Sententiæ*. No. 388.

12
Sweet recreation barr'd, what doth ensue
But moody and dull melancholy,
Kinsman to grim and comfortless despair,
And at her heels a huge infectious troop
Of pale distemperatures, and foes to life?
SHAKESPEARE, *The Comedy of Errors*, v, 1, 78.

13
These should be hours for necessities,
Not for delights; times to repair our nature
With comforting repose, and not for us
To waste these times.
SHAKESPEARE, *Henry VIII*. Act v, sc. 1, l. 3.

To walk abroad, and recreate yourselves.
SHAKESPEARE, *Julius Cæsar*. Act iii, sc. 2, l. 256.

REDEMPTION, see Salvation

REFLECTION

See also Thought: Second Thought

14
The next time you go out to a smoking party, young feller, fill your pipe with that 'ere reflection.
DICKENS, *Pickwick Papers*. Ch. 16. (1836)

Put that in your pipe . . . and smoke it.
R. H. BARHAM, *The Lay of St. Odille*. St. 14. (1840) See 2018:12.

Let the *Tribune* put all this in its pipe and smoke it.
UNKNOWN, *Editorial*, Richmond, Va., *Enquirer*, 7 Feb., 1860.

15
Remembrance and reflection how allied!
POPE, *Essay on Man*. Epis. i, l. 225.

16
In vain sedate reflections we would make,
When half our knowledge we must snatch, not take.
POPE, *Moral Essays*. Epis. i, l. 39.

The learn'd reflect on what before they knew.
POPE, *Essay on Criticism*. Pt. iii, l. 181.

17
Till then, my noble friend, chew upon this.
SHAKESPEARE, *Julius Cæsar*. Act i, sc. 2, l. 171.

1
A soul without reflection, like a pile
Without inhabitant, to ruin runs.
YOUNG, *Night Thoughts*. Night v, l. 596.

REFORM AND REFORMERS

I—Reform

2
To innovate is not to reform.
EDMUND BURKE, *A Letter to a Noble Lord.*

3
The oyster-women lock'd their fish up,
And trudged away to cry, No Bishop.
BUTLER, *Hudibras*. Pt. i, canto 2, l. 537.

4
All reform except a moral one will prove unavailing.
CARLYLE, *Essays: Corn Law Rhymes.*

5
Every reform, however necessary, will by weak minds be carried to an excess which will itself need reforming.
S. T. COLERIDGE, *Biographia Literaria*. Ch. 1.

6
All zeal for a reform, that gives offence
To peace and charity, is mere pretence.
COWPER, *Charity*, l. 533.

7
'Tis such a light as putrefaction breeds
In fly-blown flesh whereon the maggot feeds,
Shines in the dark, but, usher'd into day,
The stench remains, the lustre dies away.
COWPER, *Conversation*, l. 675. Of bigots and reformers.

8
Reforms are less to be dreaded than revolutions, for they cause less reaction.
CHARLES JOHN DARLING, *Scintillæ Juris.*

9
Every project in the history of reform, no matter how violent and surprising, is good when it is the dictate of a man's genius and constitution, but very dull and suspicious when adopted from another.
EMERSON, *Essays, Second Series: New England Reformers.*

10
Every reform is only a mask under cover of which a more terrible reform, which dares not yet name itself, advances.
EMERSON, *Journals*. Vol. vii, p. 205.

The history of persecution is a history of endeavors to cheat nature, to make water run up hill, to twist a rope of sand.
EMERSON, *Essays, First Series: Compensation.*

11
Reform is affirmative, conservatism negative; conservatism goes for comfort, reform for truth. . . . Conservatism makes no poetry, breathes no prayer, has no invention; it is all memory. Reform has no gratitude, no prudence, no husbandry.
EMERSON, *Nature, Addresses, and Lectures: The Conservative.*

Reform kicks with hoofs; it runs to egotism and bloated self-conceit.
EMERSON, *Nature, Addresses, and Lectures: The Conservative.*

12
Reform must come from within, not from without. You cannot legislate for virtue.
CARDINAL GIBBONS, *Address*, at Baltimore, 13 Sept., 1909.

Any essential reform must, like charity, begin at home.
JOHN MACY, *About Women*, p. 126.

13
Reforming schemes are none of mine;
To mend the world's a vast design:
Like theirs, who tug in little boat,
To pull to them the ship afloat.
MATTHEW GREEN, *The Spleen*, l. 357.

14
No True Reform has ever come to pass
Unchallenged by a Lion and an Ass.
ARTHUR GUITERMAN, *A Poet's Proverbs*, p. 9.

15
It is essential to the triumph of reform that it should never succeed.
WILLIAM HAZLITT, *Aphorisms on Man*. No. 16.

16
When we reflect how difficult it is to move or deflect the great machine of society, how impossible to advance the notions of a whole people suddenly to ideal right, we see the wisdom of Solon's remark, that no more good must be attempted than the nation can bear.
THOMAS JEFFERSON, *Writings*. Vol. x, p. 255.

17
Ah Love! could thou and I with Fate conspire
To grasp this sorry Scheme of Things entire,
Would not we shatter it to bits—and then
Remould it nearer to the Heart's Desire!
OMAR KHAYYÁM, *Rubáiyát*. St. 99. (Fitzgerald, tr.)

18
The race could save one-half its wasted labor
Would each reform himself and spare his neighbor.
FRANK PUTNAM, *Reform*. *See also under* NEIGHBOR.

II—Reformers

See also Fanaticism, Prudery

19
So long as there are earnest believers in the world, they will always wish to punish opinions, even if their judgment tells them it is unwise, and their conscience that it is wrong.
BAGEHOT, *Literary Studies*. Vol. ii, p. 423.

Nothing is more unpleasant than a virtuous per son with a mean mind.
BAGEHOT, *Literary Studies*. Vol. ii, p. 373.

20
And the voice of man shall call,
"He is fallen like us all,
Though the weapon of the Lord was in his hand:"

And thine epitaph shall be—
"He was wretched ev'n as we;"
And thy tomb shall be unhonoured in the land.
ROBERT BUCHANAN, *Modern Warrior*. St. 7.

1
It is a general error to suppose the loudest complainers for the public to be the most anxious for its welfare.
EDMUND BURKE, *Observations on a Publication, "The Present State of the Nation."*

2
In hope to merit Heaven by making earth
a Hell.
BYRON, *Childe Harold*. Canto i, st. 20.

And hated all for love of Jesus Christ.
CHRISTINA ROSSETTI, *A Portrait*.

3
No fidget and no reformer, just
A calm observer of ought and must,
BLISS CARMAN, *The Joys of the Road*.

4
Suspect, in general, those who remarkably affect any one virtue. . . . I say suspect them, for they are commonly impostors; but do not be sure that they are always so; for I have sometimes known saints really religious, blusterers really brave, reformers of manners really honest, and prudes really chaste.
LORD CHESTERFIELD, *Letters*, 19 Dec., 1749.

5
He wooed the daunted odalisques,
He kissed each downcast nude;
He whispered that an angel's robe
Is mostly attitude.
NATHALIA CRANE, *The First Reformer*.

He cursed the canting moralist,
Who measures right and wrong.
JOHN DAVIDSON, *A Ballad of a Poet Born*.

6
For both were bigots—fateful souls that
plague the gentle world.
JOHN DAVIDSON, *A Woman and Her Son*.

A bigot is a person who, under an atheist king, would be an atheist. (Un dévot est celui qui, sous un Roi athée, serait athée.)
LA BRUYÈRE, *Les Caractères*. Pt. iv, No. 39.

A bigot delights in public ridicule, for he begins to think he is a martyr.
SYDNEY SMITH, *Peter Plymley Letters*. No. 1.

7
When we see a special reformer, we feel like asking him, What right have you, sir, to your one virtue?
EMERSON, *Essays, Second Series: New England Reformers*.

The Reformer believes that there is no evil coming from Change which a deeper thought cannot correct.
EMERSON, *Journals*, 1864.

8
No man's person I hate, though his conduct
I blame;
I can censure a vice, without stabbing a name.
To amend—not reproach—is the bent of my
mind;
A reproof is half lost when ill nature is joined.
Where merit appears, though in rags, I re-
spect it,
And plead virtue's cause, should the whole
world reject it.
BENJAMIN FRANKLIN, *Poor Richard*, 1734.

9
Moderate reformers always hate those who go beyond them.
J. A. FROUDE, *Life and Letters of Erasmus*. Lecture 20.

10
Those who are fond of setting things to rights, have no great objection to seeing them wrong.
WILLIAM HAZLITT, *Characteristics*, p. 148.

11
The hammer and the anvil are the two hemispheres of every true reformer's character.
J. G. HOLLAND, *Gold-Foil: Anvils and Hammers*.

The moral bully, though he never swears,
Nor kicks intruders down his entry stairs,
Though meekness plants his backward-sloping
hat,
And non-resistance ties his white cravat,
Though his black broadcloth glories to be seen
In the same plight with Shylock's gabardine,
Hugs the same passion to his narrow breast
That heaves the cuirass on the trooper's chest,
Hears the same hell-hounds yelling in his rear
That chase from port the maddened buccaneer,
Feels the same comfort while his acrid words
Turn the sweet milk of kindness into curds . . .
As the scarred ruffian of the pirate's deck,
When his long swivel rakes the staggering wreck!
O. W. HOLMES, *The Moral Bully*.

12
Most reformers wore rubber boots and stood on glass when God sent a current of Commonsense through the Universe.
ELBERT HUBBARD, *Epigrams*.

13
The selfish wish to govern is often mistaken for a holy zeal in the cause of humanity.
ELBERT HUBBARD, *The Philistine*. Vol. v, p. 194.

Nine parts of self-interest gilt over with one part of philanthropy.
HERBERT SPENCER, *Social Statics*. Pt. iii, ch. 28.

14
The Fabian is the man who does what he can, and thanks heaven that things are not worse.
ELBERT HUBBARD, *Philistine*. Vol. xvii, p. 4.

We must do what we can, improve every opportunity, and like Quintus Fabius, who was never defeated, reform the government, not overthrow it. . . . We must take the present social order and build upon it.
WILLIAM MORRIS. Defining the policy of the Fabian Society.

15
A single zealot may become persecutor, and better men be his victims.
THOMAS JEFFERSON, *Notes on Virginia*.

1
A concern with the perfectibility of mankind is always a symptom of thwarted or perverted development.
HUGH KINGSMILL, *Matthew Arnold*, p. 151.

2
Pray you use your freedom,
And. so far as you please, allow me mine,
To hear you only; not to be compelled
To take your moral potions.
MASSINGER, *The Duke of Milan*. Act iv, sc. 3.

3
That man is thought a dangerous knave,
Or zealot plotting crime,
Who for advancement of his kind
Is wiser than his time.
RICHARD MONCKTON MILNES, *The Men of Old*.

4
All reformers are bachelors.
GEORGE MOORE, *Bending of the Bough*. Act i.

5
For virtue's self may too much zeal be had;
The worst of madmen is a saint run mad.
POPE, *Imitations of Horace: Epistles*. Bk. i, epis. 6, l. 26.

6
Every reform movement has a lunatic fringe.
THEODORE ROOSEVELT. Speaking of the Progressive Party, in 1913.

Men who form the lunatic fringe in all reform movements.
THEODORE ROOSEVELT, *Autobiography*. Ch. 7.

7
Swift-footed to uphold the right
And to uproot the wrong.
CHRISTINA ROSSETTI, *Noble Sisters*.

8
The people who are regarded as moral luminaries are those who forego ordinary pleasures themselves and find compensation in interfering with the pleasures of others.
BERTRAND RUSSELL, *Sceptical Essays*, p. 109.

Both claim the legal right to the pursuit of other people's happiness.
ELBERT HUBBARD, *Philistine*. Vol. xxv, p. 52.

9
That man is a weakling and degenerate who struggles and maligns the order of the universe and would rather reform the gods than reform himself. (Ille pusillus et degener, qui obluctatur et de ordine mundi male existimat et emendare mavult deos quam se.)
SENECA, *Epistulæ ad Lucilium*. Epis. cvii, 12.

10
We are told by Moralists with the plainest faces that immorality will spoil our looks.
LOGAN PEARSALL SMITH, *Afterthoughts*.

11
God did not make man a hound-dog to scent out evil.
JOHN TIMOTHY STONE, *Everyday Religion*.

Moralists on the scent of evil will perpetrate any villainy in the name of God.
GEORGE WILLIAM RUSSELL.

12
Long-winded schismatics shall rule the roast,
And Father Christmas mourn his revels lost.
SWIFT, *The Swan Tripe Club in Dublin*.

13
One of the never solved enigmas of life is the number of people that bear a commission from no one, who, as a rule, are least informed on the principles of government, but who insist on exercising the power of government to make their neighbors live the lives they desire to prescribe for them.
OSCAR W. UNDERWOOD, *Drifting Sands of Party Politics*, p. 365.

14
Young man, behold the fate of a reformer.
VOLTAIRE. To a young humanitarian, pointing to a crucifix.

For him who fain would teach the world
The world holds hate in fee—
For Socrates, the hemlock cup;
For Christ, Gethsemane.
DON MARQUIS, *The Wages*.

Socrates drinking the hemlock,
And Jesus on the rood.
W. H. CARRUTH, *Each in His Own Tongue*.

15
A reformer is a guy who rides through a sewer in a glass-bottomed boat.
JAMES J. WALKER. Newspaper interview.

REFORMATION

16
And ye were as a firebrand plucked out of the burning.
Old Testament: Amos, iv, 11.

A new heart also will I give you, and a new spirit will I put within you.
Old Testament: Ezekiel, xxxvi, 26.

17
Make me over in the morning from the rag-bag of the world.
BLISS CARMAN, *Spring Song*.

18
But 'tis the talent of our English nation,
Still to be plotting some new reformation.
DRYDEN, *Sophonisba: Prologue*, l. 9.

19
When doctrines meet with general approbation,
It is not heresy, but reformation.
DAVID GARRICK, *Epigram*.

20
As soon as men have understanding enough to find a fault, they have enough to see the danger of mending it.
LORD HALIFAX, *Works*, p. 244.

21
When they saw the Englishmen at the weakest, they turned the leaf and sang another song.
EDWARD HALL, *Chronicle*, 180. (1548)

Except such men think themselves wiser than Cicero for teaching of eloquence, they must be content to turn a new leaf.
ROGER ASCHAM, *Scholemaster*, 155. (1570)

I . . . resolved to turn over a new leaf, and live honestly.
LE SAGE, *Gil Blas*. Bk. v, ch. 1. (Smollett, tr.)

1
He bought a Bible of the new translation,
And in his life he show'd great reformation;
He walkèd mannerly and talkèd meekly;
He heard three lectures and two sermons weekly;
He vow'd to shun all companies unruly,
And in his speech he used no oath but "truly."
SIR JOHN HARINGTON, *Of a Precise Tailor*.

Some scruple rose, but thus he eas'd his thought:
"I'll now give sixpence where I gave a groat;
Where once I went to church, I'll now go twice—
And am so clear too of all other vice."
POPE, *Moral Essays*. Epis. iii, l. 365.

2
To make a crooked stick straight, we bend it the contrary way.
MONTAIGNE, *Essays*. Bk. iii, ch. 10.

3
Some positive persisting fops we know,
Who, if once wrong, will needs be always so;
But you with pleasure own your errors past,
And make each day a critique on the last.
POPE, *Essay on Criticism*. Pt. iii, l. 9.

4
It is never too late to tread the path to honesty. (Sera numquam est ad bonos mores via.)
SENECA, *Agamemnon*, l. 242.

Vice to forsake is better late than never.
LYDGATE, *Assembly of Gods*. St. 172. (1420)

Better to amend late than never.
UNKNOWN. *Petition to the Mayor of London*, 1433.

Amends may never come too late.
THOMAS LODGE AND ROBERT GREENE, *A Looking-Glass for London*. (c. 1590)

It is never over-late to mend.
JAMES HOWELL, *Familiar Letters*. Bk. iv, No. 38.

It Is Never Too Late to Mend.
CHARLES READE. Title of novel. (1856)

Though deep in mire, wring not your hands and weep;
I lend my arm to all who say "I can!"
No shame-faced outcast ever sank so deep
But yet might rise and be again a man!
WALTER MALONE, *Opportunity*.

5
My desolation does begin to make
A better life.
SHAKESPEARE, *Antony and Cleopatra*. Act v, sc. 2, l. 1.

6
Yet herein will I imitate the sun;
Who doth permit the base contagious clouds
To smother up his beauty from the world,
That, when he please again to be himself,
Being wanted, he may be more wonder'd at,
By breaking through the foul and ugly mists.
SHAKESPEARE, *I Henry IV*. Act i, sc. 2, l. 220.

So, when this loose behaviour I throw off, . . .
My reformation, glittering o'er my fault,
Shall show more goodly, and attract more eyes
Than that which hath no foil to set it off.
SHAKESPEARE, *I Henry IV*. Act i, sc. 2, l. 231.

7
I'll purge, and leave sack, and live cleanly, as a nobleman should do.
SHAKESPEARE, *I Henry IV*. Act v, sc. 4, l. 168.

When wilt thou leave fighting o' days and foining o' nights, and begin to patch up thine old body for heaven?
SHAKESPEARE, *II Henry IV*. Act ii, sc. 4, l. 250.

8
Never came reformation in a flood.
SHAKESPEARE, *Henry V*. Act i, sc. 1, l. 33.

Mend when thou canst; be better at thy leisure.
SHAKESPEARE, *King Lear*. Act ii, sc. 4, l. 231.

9
Every generation needs regeneration.
C. H. SPURGEON, *Salt-Cellars*.

10
And ah for a man to arise in me,
That the man I am may cease to be!
TENNYSON, *Maud*, l. 396.

Presume not that I am the thing I was.
SHAKESPEARE, *II Henry IV*. Act v, sc. 5, l. 60.

11
Hops, Reformation, Bays, and Beer
Came into England all in one year.
UNKNOWN, *Old Rhyme*.

Turkeys, Carpes, Hops, Picarel and Beer
Came into England, all in one year.
UNKNOWN, *Old Rhyme*. (EDMUND HOWES, *Annals or Chronicles*, 1631.) The time of the innovations was about 1518.

REFUSAL

12
Do not strike him dead with a denial,
But hold him up in life, and cheer his soul
With the faint glimmering of a doubtful hope.
ADDISON, *Cato*. Act iii, sc. 2.

13
He could refuse more gracefully than other people could grant.
LORD CHESTERFIELD, *Letters*, 18 Nov., 1748. Of the Duke of Marlborough.

Whom she refuses she treats still
With so much sweet behaviour,
That her refusal, through her skill,
Looks almost like a favour.
WILLIAM CONGREVE. (As quoted in the House of Commons by Mr. F. E. Smith, later Lord Birkenhead, referring to Mr. Asquith.)

Who refuses courteously grants half your suit. (Pars benefici est, quod petitur si belle neges.)
PUBLILIUS SYRUS, *Sententiæ*. No. 469.

14
The great refusal. (Il gran rifiuto.)
DANTE, *Inferno*. Canto iii, l. 60. Supposed to refer to the resignation of Pope Celestine V, in 1294.

Il gran rifiuto—Henry James's desertion of America.
W. S. MAUGHAM, *Cakes and Ale*, p. 152.

1
He who refuses nothing will soon have nothing to refuse. (Quisquis nil negat, fellat.)
MARTIAL, *Epigrams*. Bk. xii, ep. 79.

2
One made the observation of the people of Asia that they were all slaves to one man, merely because they could not pronounce that syllable No.
PLUTARCH, *Morals: Of Bashfulness*.

Nay has the same number of letters as aye. (Tantas Letras tiene un no como un si.)
CERVANTES, *Don Quixote*. Pt. i, ch. 22.

3
It is kindness to refuse immediately what you intend to deny. (Pars beneficii est, quod petitur, si cito neges.)
PUBLILIUS SYRUS, *Sententiæ*. No. 470.

He is less disappointed who is promptly refused. (Minus decipitur cui negatur celeriter.)
PUBLILIUS SYRUS, *Sententiæ*. No. 366.

4
A reason for refusing is never wanting to an avaricious man. (Negandi causa avaro numquam deficit.)
PUBLILIUS SYRUS, *Sententiæ*. No. 423.

5
Who grants a doubtful hope to sufferers, refuses. (Dubiam salutem qui dat adflictis negat.)
SENECA, *Œdipus*, l. 213.

6
Not Hebrew, Arabic, Syriac, Coptic, nor even the Chinese language, seems half so difficult to me as the language of refusal.
WILLIAM SHENSTONE, *Egotisms*.

REGRET

See also Remorse, Repentance

7
A series of congratulatory regrets.
BENJAMIN DISRAELI, *Speech*, 30 July, 1878.

8
The beginning of compunction is the beginning of a new life.
GEORGE ELIOT, *Felix Holt*. Ch. 13.

9
Nor cast one longing, ling'ring look behind.
THOMAS GRAY, *Elegy Written in a Country Church-yard*. St. 22.

10
Thou wilt lament
Hereafter, when the evil shall be done
And shall admit no cure.
HOMER, *Iliad*. Bk. ix, l. 308. (Bryant, tr.)

11
O lost days of delight, that are wasted in doubting and waiting!
O lost hours and days in which we might have been happy!
LONGFELLOW, *Tales of a Wayside Inn*: Pt. iii, *The Theologian's Tale*.

12
But years shall see the cypress spread,
Immutable as my regret.
T. L. PEACOCK, *Beneath the Cypress Shade*.

13
The mind longs for what it has missed. (Animus quod perdidit optat.)
PETRONIUS ARBITER, *Satyricon*.

14
Familiar as an old mistake,
And futile as regret.
E. A. ROBINSON, *Bewick Finzer*.

15
For who, alas, has lived,
Nor in the watches of the night recalled
Words he has wished unsaid and deeds undone?
SAMUEL ROGERS, *Reflections*, l. 52.

16
Look in my face: my name is Might-have-been;
I am also called No-more. Too-late, Farewell.
D. G. ROSSETTI, *A Superscription*. (*Sonnets*. No. 97.)

These poor Might-Have-Beens,
These fatuous ineffectual yesterdays.
W. E. HENLEY, *Rhymes and Rhythms*. No. 13.

Ashes of roses these, and yet—
They are the things which I regret.
JOHN D. SWAIN, *Ballade of François Villon, As He Was About to Die*. (*Critic*, vol. 42, p. 73.)

17
There's nothing in the world to me
So dear as my regret.
LORD DE TABLEY, *The Churchyard on the Sands*.

18
O last regret, regret can die!
TENNYSON, *In Memoriam*. Pt. lxxviii, st. 5.

19
Deep as first love, and wild with all regret.
TENNYSON, *The Princess*. Pt. iv, l. 39.

20
I desire rather to feel compunction than to know its definition.
THOMAS À KEMPIS, *De Imitatione Christi*. Pt. i, ch. 1.

21
Make the most of your regrets. . . . To regret deeply is to live afresh.
H. D. THOREAU, *Journal*, 13 Nov., 1839.

22
For of all sad words of tongue or pen,
The saddest are these: "It might have been!"
WHITTIER, *Maud Muller*, l. 105.

If, of all sad words of tongue or pen,
The saddest are, "It might have been,"
More sad are these we daily see,
"It is, but it hadn't ought to be."
BRET HARTE, *Mrs. Judge Jenkins*.

I plowed "Perhaps," I planted "If" therein,
And sadly harvested "It Might Have Been."
ARTHUR GUITERMAN, *A Poet's Proverbs*, p. 65.

We might have been—these are but common words,
And yet they make the sum of life's bewailing.
LETITIA ELIZABETH LANDON, *Three Extracts from the Diary of a Week*.

And of all glad words of prose or rhyme,
The gladdest are, "Act while there yet is time."
FRANKLIN P. ADAMS, *Maud Muller Mutatur.*

The *Moral* is that gardeners pine,
Whene'er no pods adorn the vine.
Of all sad words experience gleans,
The saddest are: "It *might* have beans."
(I did not make this up myself:
'Twas in a book upon my shelf.
It's witty, but I don't deny
It's rather Whittier than I.)
GUY WETMORE CARRYL, *How Jack Found that Beans May go Back on a Chap.*

1
When love in the faint heart trembles,
And the eyes with tears are wet,
O, tell me what resembles
Thee, young Regret?
GEORGE EDWARD WOODBERRY, *Agathon.*

2
But now it is too late to speak of had-I-wist!
UNKNOWN, *Beryn,* l. 2348. (c. 1400) A common expression of regret in the writings of the period.

Beware of Had I wist!
JOHN SKELTON, *Magnificence,* l. 213. (1529) Sometimes attributed to Queen Elizabeth.

Had I wist cometh too late.
GABRIEL HARVEY, *Commonplace Book.* (1600)

RELIGION

See also Christianity; Creeds; Superstition and Religion; Theology

I—Religion: Definitions

3
The efficacy of religion lies precisely in what is not rational, philosophic, nor eternal; its efficacy lies in the unforeseen, the miraculous, the extraordinary. Thus religion attracts more devotion according as it demands more faith—that is to say, as it becomes more incredible to the profane mind. The philosopher aspires to explain away all mysteries, to dissolve them into light. Mystery on the other hand is demanded and pursued by the religious instinct; mystery constitutes the essence of worship.
AMIEL, *Journal,* 5 June, 1870.

Methinks there be not impossibilities enough in Religion for an active faith.
SIR THOMAS BROWNE, *Religio Medici.* Pt. i, 9.

Religion without mystery ceases to be religion.
BISHOP WILLIAM THOMAS MANNING, *Sermon,* 2 Feb., 1930.

4
Religion—that voice of the deepest human experience.
MATTHEW ARNOLD, *Culture and Anarchy: Sweetness and Light.*

5
The true religion is built upon the rock; the rest are tossed upon the waves of time.
BACON, *Essays: Of Vicissitude of Things*

A religion that is jealous of the variety of learning, discourse, opinions, and sects, as misdoubting it may shake the foundations, or that cherisheth devotion upon simplicity and ignorance, as ascribing ordinary effects to the immediate working of God, is adverse to knowledge.
FRANCIS BACON, *Of the Interpretation of Nature.* Ch. 25.

6
Religion—a daughter of Hope and Fear, explaining to Ignorance the nature of the Unknowable.
AMBROSE BIERCE, *The Devil's Dictionary.*

Impiety—your irreverence toward my deity.
AMBROSE BIERCE, *The Devil's Dictionary.*

7
The body of all true religion consists, to be sure, in obedience to the will of the Sovereign of the world, in a confidence in His declarations, and in imitation of His perfections.
EDMUND BURKE, *Reflections on the Revolution in France.*

8
My altars are the mountains and the ocean,
Earth, air, stars,—all that springs from the great Whole,
Who hath produced and will receive the soul.
BYRON, *Don Juan.* Canto iii, st. 104.

Each cloud-capped mountain is a holy altar;
An organ breathes in every grove;
And the full heart's a Psalter,
Rich in deep hymns of gratitude and love.
THOMAS HOOD, *Ode to Rae Wilson,* l. 385.

9
It is well said, in every sense, that a man's religion is the chief fact with regard to him. . . . By religion I do not mean here the church-creed which he professes. . . . This is not what I call religion, . . . but the thing a man does practically believe; the thing a man does practically lay to heart, and know for certain, concerning his vital relations to this mysterious Universe, and his duty and destiny there, . . . that is his religion.
CARLYLE, *Heroes and Hero-Worship: The Hero as Divinity.*

A man's "religion" consists not of the many things he is in doubt of and tries to believe, but of the few he is assured of, and has no need of effort for believing.
CARLYLE, *Latter-Day Pamphlets.* No. 8.

10
Religion is the sense of ultimate reality, of whatever meaning a man finds in his own existence or the existence of anything else.
G. K. CHESTERTON, *Come to Think of It.*

11
Religion is life, philosophy is thought; religion looks up, friendship looks in. We need both thought and life, and we need that the two shall be in harmony.
JAMES FREEMAN CLARKE, *Ten Great Religions,* Pt. i, ch. 7, sec. 9

1
Religion, harsh, intolerant, austere,
Parent of manners like herself severe.
COWPER, *Table Talk*, l. 612.

2
Sacred relig'on! Mother of Form and Fear!
SAMUEL DANIEL, *Musophilus*. St. 47.

3
Religion must always be a crab fruit; it cannot be grafted and keep its wild beauty.
EMERSON, *Conduct of Life: Worship*.

What is called religion effeminates and demoralizes.
EMERSON, *Conduct of Life: Worship*.

4
God builds his temple in the heart on the ruins of churches and religions.
EMERSON, *Conduct of Life: Worship*.

5
All the religion we have is the ethics of one or another holy person.
EMERSON, *Journals*, June, 1865.

The religions of the world are the ejaculations of a few imaginative men.
EMERSON, *Journals*.

All the popular religions in the world are made apprehensible by an array of legendary personages.
BERNARD SHAW, *Saint Joan: Preface*.

6
There are at bottom but two possible religions—that which rises in the moral nature of man, and which takes shape in moral commandments, and that which grows out of the observation of the material energies which operate in the external universe.
J. A. FROUDE, *Short Studies: Calvinism*.

Everywhere the human soul stands between a hemisphere of light and another of darkness; on the confines of two everlasting hostile empires, Necessity and Freewill.
CARLYLE, *Essays: Goethe's Works*.

7
The religion which allies itself with injustice to preach down the natural aspirations of the masses is worse than atheism.
HENRY GEORGE, *The Land Question*, p. 96.

8
The inquiry into a dream is another dream.
LORD HALIFAX, *Works*, p. 249.

Religion is the mother of dreams. Over the gray world, ruined by deluge and death, it has sought ever, and found, the arching rainbow of hope.
A. E. HAYDON, *The Quest of the Ages*, p. 205.

9
Religion is a stalking-horse to shoot other fowl.
GEORGE HERBERT, *Jacula Prudentum*.

10
Religion is not a dogma, nor an emotion, but a service.
R. D. HITCHCOCK, *Eternal Atonement*.

11
Pure religion and undefiled before God and the Father is this, To visit the fatherless and widows in their affliction, and to keep himself unspotted from the world.
New Testament: James, i, 27.

All religion relates to life, and the life of religion is to do good.
SWEDENBORG, *Doctrine of Life*, p. 1.

12
To one man religion is his literature and his science; to another, his delight and his duty.
JOUBERT, *Pensées*. No. 26.

The religion of one age is ever the poetry of the next.
EMERSON, *Uncollected Lectures: Character*.

Religion is the elder sister of Philosophy.
W. S. LANDOR, *Imaginary Conversations: David Hume and John Home*.

13
A man's religion is the truth he lives habitually, subconsciously and consciously.
BENJAMIN C. LEEMING, *Imagination*.

14
Possibly if a true estimate were made of the morality and religions of the world, we should find that the far greater part of mankind received even those opinions and ceremonies they would die for, rather from the fashions of their countries and the constant practice of those about them than from any conviction of their reasons.
JOHN LOCKE, *On Education*. Sec. 146.

14a
Religion is the sigh of the oppressed creature, the feelings of a heartless world, just as it is the spirit of unspiritual conditions. It is the opium of the people.
KARL MARX, *Introduction to a Critique of the Hegelian Philosophy of Right*. (*Deutsch-Franz-Ösische Jahrbücher*, 1844; RÜHLE, *Karl Marx*, p. 57.)

15
The friend of him who has no friend—Religion.
JAMES MONTGOMERY, *The Pillow*, l. 152.

16
Religion is an attempt, a noble attempt, to suggest in human terms more-than-human realities.
CHRISTOPHER MORLEY, *Religio Journalistici*, 35.

17
Religion is the dominion of the soul. It is the hope of life, the anchor of safety, the deliverance of the soul.
NAPOLEON I. (O'MEARA, *Napoleon in Exile*.)

18
My own mind is my own church.
THOMAS PAINE, *The Age of Reason*. Ch. 1.

19
Humanity and Immortality consist neither in reason, nor in love; not in the body, nor in the animation of the heart of it, nor in the thoughts and stirrings of the brain of it;—but in the dedication of them all to Him who will raise them up at the last day.
RUSKIN, *Stones of Venice*. Vol. i, ch. 2.

20
Religion is not a hearsay, a presumption, a

supposition; is not a customary pretension and profession; is not an affectation of any mode; is not a piety of particular fancy, consisting of some pathetic devotions, vehement expressions, bodily severities, affected anomalies, and aversion from the innocent usages of others; but consisteth in a profound humility, and a universal charity.

BENJAMIN WHICHCOTE, *Sermons*.

True religion doth clear the mind from all impotent and unsatiable desires, which do abuse and toss a man's soul, and make it restless and unquiet. It sets a man free from eager and impetuous loves, from vain and disappointing hopes, from lawless and exorbitant appetites, from frothy and empty joys, from dismal, presaging fears, and anxious, self-devouring cares.

BENJAMIN WHICHCOTE, *Sermons*.

1
Each is not for its own sake,
I say the whole earth and all the stars in the sky are for religion's sake.
I say no man has ever yet been half devout enough,
None has ever yet adored or worship'd half enough,
None has begun to think how divine he himself is, and how certain the future is.
I say that the real and permanent grandeur of these States must be their religion.

WALT WHITMAN, *Starting from Paumanok*. Sec. 7.

II—Religion: Apothegms

2
Nothing is so fatal to religion as indifference, which is at least, half infidelity.

EDMUND BURKE, *Letter to William Smith*. 29 Jan., 1795.

3
Man is by his constitution a religious animal.

EDMUND BURKE, *Reflections on the Revolution in France*.

Man has been rather defined as a religious than a rational creature.

JAMES HARRINGTON, *Oceana*, p. 484. (1656)

Every man, either to his terror or consolation, has some sense of religion.

JAMES HARRINGTON, *Oceana*, p. 484.

4
Politics and the pulpit are terms that have little agreement. No sound ought to be heard in the church but the healing voice of Christian charity. . . . Surely the church is a place where one day's truce ought to be allowed to the dissensions and animosities of mankind.

EDMUND BURKE, *Reflections on the Revolution in France*.

When policy puts on religious cloak.

WILLIAM ALEXANDER, *Doomsday: The Second Hour*. St. 22.

When Kings interfere in matters of religion, they enslave instead of protecting it.

FÉNELON, *Advice*, to the Pretender, Son of James II of England.

5
They make it a principle of their religion outwardly to conform to any religion.

BURKE, *Speech*, on the bill for the relief of Protestant dissenters, House of Commons, 1773.

He left his old religion for an estate, and has not had time to get a new one, but stands like a dead wall between church and synagogue, or like the blank leaves between the Old and New Testament.

SHERIDAN, *The Duenna*. Act i, sc. 3.

See also POLITICS: EXPEDIENCY.

6
The writers against religion, whilst they oppose every system, are wisely careful never to set up any of their own.

BURKE, *Vindication of Natural Society: Preface*.

7
His religion at best is an anxious wish—like that of Rabelais, a great Perhaps.

CARLYLE, *Essays: Burns*.

The grand perhaps.

ROBERT BROWNING, *Bishop Bloughram's Apology*. *See* RABELAIS *under* DEATH: LAST WORDS.

8
God is for men and religion for women.

JOSEPH CONRAD, *Nostromo*.

9
Religion does not censure or exclude
Unnumber'd pleasures, harmlessly pursu'd.

COWPER, *Retirement*, l. 783.

We do ourselves wrong, and too meanly estimate the holiness above us, when we deem that any act or enjoyment good in itself, is not good to do religiously.

HAWTHORNE, *The Marble Faun*. Bk. ii, ch. 7

Religion without joy,—it is no religion.

THEODORE PARKER, *Of Conscious Religion*.

Let us start a new religion with one commandment, "Enjoy thyself."

ISRAEL ZANGWILL, *Children of the Ghetto*. Bk. ii, ch. 6.

10
Religion should be the rule of life, not a casual incident of it.

BENJAMIN DISRAELI, *Lothair*. Ch. 17.

11
Begin where we will, we are pretty sure in a short space to be mumbling our ten commandments.

EMERSON, *Essays, First Series: Prudence*.

12
The religions we call false were once true.

EMERSON, *Lectures and Biographical Sketches: Character*.

Time consecrates;
And what is grey with age becomes religion.

SCHILLER, *Die Piccolomini*. Act iv, sc. 4. (Coleridge, tr.)

13
We measure all religions by their civilizing power.

EMERSON, *Uncollected Lectures: Natural Religion*.

A complete nation does not import its religion.

EMERSON, *Uncollected Lectures: Character*.

1
Religion is the best armour in the world, but the worst cloak.

THOMAS FULLER, *Gnomologia*. No. 4011.

2
Fools make the text, and men of wit the commentaries. (Les sots font le texte, et les hommes d'esprit les commentaires.)

ABBÉ FERDINANDO GALIANI, *Of Politics*.

They have the texts in their favor, but I'm sorry for the texts.

ROYER-COLLARD, disapproval of the doctrine of grace by the fathers of Port-Royal.

So much the worse for the texts.

VOLTAIRE.

3
Man, without religion, is the creature of circumstances.

J. C. AND A. W. HARE, *Guesses at Truth*. Bk. i.

Educate men without religion and you make them but clever devils.

DUKE OF WELLINGTON, *Remark*.

4
Some persons, instead of making religion for their God, are content to make a god of their religion.

SIR ARTHUR HELPS, *Brevia*.

5
Religion stands on tiptoe in our land,
Ready to pass to the American strand.

GEORGE HERBERT, *The Church Militant*, l. 235.

6
Religion can bear no jesting.

GEORGE HERBERT, *Jacula Prudentum*.

Religion, credit and the eye are not to be touched.

GEORGE HERBERT, *Jacula Prudentum*.

7
Religion's in the heart, not in the knee.

DOUGLAS JERROLD, *The Devil's Ducat*.

8
To be of no church is dangerous. Religion, of which the rewards are distant, and which is animated only by Faith and Hope, will glide by degrees out of the mind, unless it be invigorated and reimpressed by external ordinances, by stated calls to worship, and the salutary influence of example.

SAMUEL JOHNSON, *Lives of the Poets: Milton*.

9
Whoso fighteth for the religion of God, whether he be slain or be victorious, we will give him a great reward.

The Koran. Ch. 4.

10
All religions die of one disease, that of being found out.

JOHN MORLEY.

11
It is right to be religious, but one should shun religiosity. (Religentem esse oportet; religiosus ne fuas.)

NIGIDIUS FIGULUS, *Commentariorum Grammaticorum*. Bk. xi. Quoted as from an early poet. Aulus Gellius (*Noctes Atticæ*, iv, 9, 1) points out that the ending "osus" always implies an excessive amount of the quality in question.

12
To be furious in religion is to be irreligiously religious.

WILLIAM PENN, *Fruits of Solitude*.

13
The truth of religion is in its ritual and the truth of dogma is in its poetry.

J. C. POWYS, *The Complex Vision*, p. 232.

I realized that ritual will always mean throwing away something; *Destroying* our corn or wine upon the altar of our gods.

G. K. CHESTERTON, *Tremendous Trifles: Secret of a Train*.

14
All false religion is in conflict with nature. (Toute fausse religion combat la nature.)

ROUSSEAU, *Julie*. Pt. iv, letter 10.

The luxury of false religion is to be unhappy.

SYDNEY SMITH, *Letter to Francis Horner*, 25 Nov., 1816.

15
I believe all that I can understand of religion, and I respect the rest without rejecting it. (Je crois de la religion tout ce que j'en puis comprendre, et respecte le reste sans le rejeter.)

ROUSSEAU, *Julie*. Pt. 5, Letter 3.

Religion has nothing more to fear than not being sufficiently understood.

STANISLAUS, KING OF POLAND, *Maxims*. No. 36.

16
In religion, as in friendship, they who profess most are the least sincere.

SHERIDAN, *The Duenna*. Act iii, sc. 3.

17
A religious life is a struggle and not a hymn.

MADAME DE STAËL, *Corinne*. Bk. x, ch. 5.

18
The poor creatures . . . seated themselves on the "anxious benches."

FRANCES M. TROLLOPE, *Domestic Manners of the Americans*. Ch. 8. (1832)

In front of the pulpit there was a space railed off and strewn with straw, which I was told was the anxious seat, and on which sat those who were touched by their consciences.

FREDERICK MARRYAT, *Diary in America*, 1839.

Folks got up . . . and worked their way . . . to the mourners' bench, with the tears running down their faces.

MARK TWAIN. (*Century Magazine*, Feb., 1885.)

19
Religion hath no landmarks.

M. F. TUPPER, *Of Estimating Character*.

20
I would rather think of my religion as a gamble than to think of it as an insurance premium.

STEPHEN S. WISE, *Religion*.

21
The crooked end obedient spirits draws,

The pointed, those rebels who spurn at Christian laws.
(Curva trahit mites, pars pungit acuta rebelles.)

UNKNOWN, *On a Crosier*. (BROUGHTON, *Dictionary of Religions*.) A crosier at Toulouse is said to bear the motto: "Curva trahit, quos virga regit, pars ultima pungit." A crosier is curved at the top and pointed at the bottom.

III—Religion: Its Virtues

1
Religion tends to speak the language of the heart, which is the language of friends, lovers, children, and parents.

E. S. AMES. (NEWTON, *My Idea of God*, p. 246.)

2
The spiritual virtue of a sacrament is like light: although it passes among the impure, it is not polluted. (Spiritalis enim virtus sacramenti ita est ut lux: etsi per immundos transeat, non inquinatur.)

ST. AUGUSTINE, *Johannis Evang*. Ch. 1, sec. 15.

3
Religion converts despair, which destroys, into resignation, which submits.

COUNTESS OF BLESSINGTON, *Commonplace Book*.

4
Religion, if in heav'nly truths attir'd,
Needs only to be seen to be admir'd.

COWPER, *Expostulation*, l. 492.

5
There is no age which religion does not become. (Nullam ætatem non decet religio.)

ERASMUS, *Colloquia: Pietas Puerilis*.

6
Religion always sides with poverty.

GEORGE HERBERT, *The Church Militant*, l. 252.

7
With sweet kind natures, as in honey'd cells,
Religion lives, and feels herself at home.

THOMAS HOOD, *Ode to Rae Wilson*, l. 308.

8
The enduring value of religion is in its challenge to aspiration and hope in the mind of man.

ERNEST M. HOPKINS. (DURANT, *On the Meaning of Life*, p. 75.)

9
The highest flights of charity, devotion, trust, patience, bravery, to which the wings of human nature have spread themselves have been flown for religious ideals.

WILLIAM JAMES, *Varieties of Religious Experience*, p. 259.

9a
Nobody can deny but religion is a comfort to the distressed, a cordial to the sick, and sometimes a restraint on the wicked; therefore, whoever would laugh or argue it out of the world, without giving some equivalent for it, ought to be treated as a common enemy.

MARY WORTLEY MONTAGU, *Letter to the Countess of Bute*, 1752, referring to Swift.

10
Religion's all. Descending from the skies
To wretched man, the goddess in her left
Holds out this world, and, in her right, the next.

YOUNG, *Night Thoughts*. Night iv, l. 550.

IV—Religion: Its Faults

11
Religion brought forth riches, and the daughter devoured the mother. (Religio peperit divitias et filia devoravit matrem.)

ST. BERNARD, *Saying*. (REUSNER, *Ænigmatographia*. Pt. i, p. 361. 1602.)

12
No priestcraft can longer make man content with misery here in the hope of compensation hereafter.

G. STANLEY HALL, *Senescence*, p. 483.

13
Formal religion was organized for slaves: it offered them consolation which earth did not provide.

ELBERT HUBBARD, *Philistine*. Vol. xxv, p. 89.

14
Religion has reduced Spain to a guitar, Italy to a hand-organ, and Ireland to exile.

ROBERT G. INGERSOLL, *Gov. Rollin's Fast Day Proclamation*.

15
What excellent fools Religion makes of men!

BEN JONSON, *Sejanus*. Act v.

Fanatic fools, that in those twilight times,
With wild religion cloaked the worst of crimes!

JOHN LANGHORNE, *The Country Justice*. Pt. iii, l. 122.

16
It is, I think, an error to believe that there is any need of religion to make life seem worth living.

SINCLAIR LEWIS. (DURANT, *On the Meaning of Life*, p. 37.)

17
Long time men lay oppress'd with slavish fear;
Religion's tyranny did domineer. . . .
At length a mighty one of Greece began
T' assert the natural liberty of man,
By senseless terrors and vain fancies led
To slavery. Straight the conquer'd phantoms fled.

LUCRETIUS, *De Rerum Natura*. Bk. i, l. 63. (Creech, tr.) The reference is to Epicurus.

Too often in time past religion has brought forth criminal and shameful actions. (Sæpius olim Religio peperit scelerosa atque impia facta.)

LUCRETIUS, *De Rerum Natura*. Bk. i, l. 84.

How many evils has religion caused! (Tantum religio potuit suadere malorum!)

LUCRETIUS, *De Rerum Natura*. Bk. i, l. 102.

18
Religion
Hides many mischiefs from suspicion.

MARLOWE, *The Jew of Malta*. Act i, sc. 2.

19
I fear this iron yoke of outward conformity hath left a slavish print upon our necks.

MILTON, *Prose Works*. Vol. ii, p. 97.

1
Men never do evil so completely and cheerfully as when they do it from religious conviction.
PASCAL, *Pensées*. Sec. xiv, No. 895.

2
Religion, which true policy befriends,
Designed by God to serve man's noblest ends,
Is by that old deceiver's subtle play
Made the chief party in its own decay,
And meets the eagle's destiny, whose breast
Felt the same shaft which his own feathers
 drest.
KATHERINE PHILIPS, *On Controversies in Religion*.

3
 In religion
What damned error, but some sober brow
Will bless it, and approve it with a text?
SHAKESPEARE, *The Merchant of Venice*. Act iii, sc. 2, l. 77

4
Your northern religions, harsh and bitter as your skies.
SHORTHOUSE, *John Inglesant*. Vol. ii, ch. 6.

5
But mark me well; Religion is my name;
An angel once, but now a fury grown,
Too often talked of, but too little known.
SWIFT, *The Swan Tripe Club in Dublin*.

V—Religion: Its Unity

See also Creeds

6
Children of men! the unseen Power, whose
 eye
 For ever doth accompany mankind,
Hath look'd on no religion scornfully
 That men did ever find.
MATTHEW ARNOLD, *Progress*. St. 10.

7
One religion is as true as another.
ROBERT BURTON, *Anatomy of Melancholy*. Pt. iii, sec. iv, mem. 2, subs. 1.

8
I would no more quarrel with a man because of his religion than I would because of his art.
MARY BAKER EDDY, *Miscellany*, p. 270.

9
I do not find that the age or country makes the least difference; no, nor the language the actors spoke, nor the religion which they professed, whether Arab in the desert, or Frenchman in the Academy. I see that sensible men and conscientious men all over the world were of one religion,—the religion of well-doing and daring.
EMERSON, *Lectures and Biographical Sketches: The Preacher*.

10
I confidently expect that in the future even more than in the past, faith in an order, which is the basis of science, will not be dissevered from faith in an Ordainer, which is the basis of religion.
ASA GRAY. Inscribed beneath his bust in the Hall of Fame.

11
All religions must be tolerated, . . . for in this country every man must get to heaven his own way.
FREDERICK THE GREAT, *Note*, on margin of report concerning Roman Catholic schools, 22 June, 1740. (CARLYLE, *Frederick the Great*.)

Perhaps those simple souls might teach
 Lessons as high as we could set them,
And if they're striving heaven to reach
 Their own strange road,—by all means let
 them!
R. O. CREWE-MILNES, *Easter in Florence*.

12
Those who obey their conscience are of my religion, and I am of the religion of all those who are brave and good.
HENRY IV OF FRANCE, *Letter to Manaud de Batz*.

13
We cannot make a religion for others, and we ought not to let others make a religion for us. Our own religion is what life has taught us.
DEAN W. R. INGE. (MARCHANT, *Wit and Wisdom of Dean Inge*. No. 1.)

14
I must ever believe that religion substantially good which produces an honest life, and we have been authorized by one whom you and I equally respect, to judge of the tree by its fruit.
THOMAS JEFFERSON, *Writings*. Vol. xiv, p. 197.

I never told my own religion, nor scrutinized that of another. I never attempted to make a convert, nor wished to change another's creed. I have ever judged of others' religion by their lives . . . for it is from our lives and not from our words, that our religion must be read.
THOMAS JEFFERSON, *Writings*. Vol. xv, p 60

On the whole we must repeat the often repeated saying, that it is unworthy a religious man to view an irreligious one either with alarm or aversion; or with any other feeling than regret, and hope, and brotherly commiseration.
CARLYLE, *Essays: Voltaire*.

15
Sir, I think all Christians, whether Papists or Protestants, agree to the essential articles, and that their differences are trivial, and rather political than religious.
SAMUEL JOHNSON. (BOSWELL, *Life*, 1763.)

16
The Earl of Shaftesbury said at last . . . "Men of sense are really but of one religion." Upon which says the lady of a sudden, "Pray, my lord, what religion is that which men of sense agree in?" "Madam," says the Earl, "men of sense never tell."
ARTHUR ONSLOW, Speaker of the House of Commons, *Footnote* to Bishop Gilbert Bur-

net's notice of the Earl of Shaftesbury, *History of His Own Times,* Vol. i, bk. 1, sec. 96. Froude tells a similar anecdote of Samuel Rogers (*Short Studies on Great Subjects: A Plea for the Free Discussion of Theological Difficulties*), but this was probably a confusion of memory on Froude's part. The saying has also been attributed to Benjamin Franklin, who probably repeated it upon some occasion.

Old Lord Shaftesbury, conferring with Major Wildman about the many sects of religion, "All wise men are of the same religion." Whereupon a lady in the room . . . demanded what that religion was, To whom Lord Shaftesbury straight replied, "Madam, wise men never tell."

JOHN TOLAND, *Clidophorus.*

"As for that," said Waldenshare, "sensible men are all of the same religion." "Pray, what is that?" inquired the Prince. "Sensible men never tell."

BENJAMIN DISRAELI, *Endymion.* Ch. 81. Borrowed from Lord Shaftesbury.

1
Every religion is good that teaches man to be good.

THOMAS PAINE, *Rights of Man.* Pt. ii, ch. v.

2
The humble, meek, merciful, just, pious and devout souls are everywhere of one religion and when death has taken off the mask, they will know one another, though the diverse liveries they wore here make them strangers.

WILLIAM PENN, *Some Fruits of Solitude.*

3
There is nothing wanting to make all rational and disinterested people in the world of one religion, but that they should walk together every day.

POPE, *Thoughts on Various Subjects.*

4
Religion is like the fashion. One man wears his doublet slashed, another laced, another plain; but every man has a doublet. So every man has his religion. We differ about trimming.

JOHN SELDEN *Table-Talk: Religion.*

5
There is only one religion, though there are a hundred versions of it.

BERNARD SHAW, *Plays Pleasant and Unpleasant:* Vol. ii, *Preface.*

6
It was his opinion that no honest man would swerve from the principles in which he was bred, whether Turkish, Protestant or Roman.

SMOLLETT, *Roderick Random.* Ch. 42.

7
There is no very important difference between a New Englander's religion and a Roman's. We both worship in the shadow of our sins: they erect the temples for us. Jehovah has no superiority to Jupiter.

H. D. THOREAU, *Journal,* 5 June. 1853.

8
We are all of the same religion without knowing it.

VOLTAIRE, *Sermon by "Josias Rossette."*

9
He dared not mock the Dervish whirl
The Brahmin's rite, the Lama's spell;
God knew the heart; Devotion's pearl
Might sanctify the shell.

WHITTIER, *My Namesake.*

10
They who differ pole-wide serve
Perchance the common Master,
And other sheep He hath than they
Who graze one narrow pasture!

WHITTIER, *A Spiritual Manifestation.*

VI—Religion: Its Dissensions

See also Christianity: Its Faults; Church: Its Faults

11
The greatest vicissitude of things amongst men is the vicissitude of sects and religions.

FRANCIS BACON, *Essays: of Vicissitude of Things.*

12
When Popes damn Popes, and councils damn them all,
And Popes damn councils, what must Christians do?

RICHARD BAXTER, *Hypocrisy.*

13
Kings, that made laws, first broke them; and the Gods,
By teaching us religion first, first set the world at odds.

APHRA BEHN, *The Golden Age.* St. 4.

14
Can such bitterness enter into the heart of the devout? (Tant de fiel entre-t-il dans l'âme des dévots?)

BOILEAU, *Le Lutrin,* i, 12.

15
The religion of one seems madness unto another.

SIR THOMAS BROWNE, *Hydriotaphia.* Ch. 2.

16
Dissent, not satisfied with toleration, is not conscience, but ambition.

EDMUND BURKE, *Speech,* on the Acts of Uniformity, House of Commons, Feb., 1772.

All Protestantism, even the most cold and passive, is a sort of dissent. But the religion most prevalent in our northern colonies is a refinement on the principle of resistance; it is the dissidence of dissent, and the Protestantism of the Protestant religion.

EDMUND BURKE, *Conciliation with America.*

17
Old religious factions are volcanoes burnt out.

EDMUND BURKE, *Speech,* on the petition of the Unitarians, House of Commons, 11 May, 1792.

18
Synods are mystical Bear-gardens,

Where Elders, Deputies, Church-wardens,
And other Members of the Court,
Manage the Babylonish sport.

BUTLER, *Hudibras*. Pt. i, canto 3, l. 1095.

Religion spawn'd a various rout
Of petulant capricious sects,
The maggots of corrupted texts,
That first run all religion down,
And after every swarm its own.

BUTLER, *Hudibras*. Pt. iii, canto 2, l. 8.

As if Religion were intended
For nothing else but to be mended.

BUTLER, *Hudibras*. Pt. i, canto 1, l. 205.

1
A convert's but a fly that turns about,
After his head's cut off, to find it out.

BUTLER, *Miscellaneous Thoughts*, l. 775.

2
No truly great man, from Jesus Christ down, ever founded a sect.

THOMAS CARLYLE, *Journal*.

Do not call yourself Lutherans, call yourself Christians. Has Luther been crucified for the world?

MARTIN LUTHER.

3
Life and the Universe show spontaneity;
Down with ridiculous notions of Deity!
Churches and creeds are lost in the mists;
Truth must be sought with the Positivists.

MORTIMER COLLINS, *The Positivists*.

4
Men will wrangle for religion; write for it; fight for it; die for it; anything but—*live* for it.

C. C. COLTON, *Lacon: Reflections*. No. 25.

Bigotry murders Religion, to frighten fools with her ghost.

C. C. COLTON, *Lacon: Reflections*. No. 101.

5
Religion should extinguish strife,
And make a calm of human life;
But friends that chance to differ
On points which God has left at large,
How fiercely will they meet and charge,
No combatants are stiffer!

COWPER, *Friendship*, l. 133.

6
Against her foes Religion well defends
Her sacred truths, but often fears her friends. . . .
But most she fears the controversial pen,
The holy strife of disputatious men.

GEORGE CRABBE, *The Library*, l. 248.

7
O how far removed
Predestination! is thy foot from such
As see not the First Cause entire.

DANTE, *Paradiso*. Canto xx, l. 122.

8
I do not prescribe fire and faggot, but, as Scipio said of Carthage, Delenda est Carthago.

DANIEL DEFOE, *The Shortest Way with the Dissenters*.

9
I knew a witty physician who . . . used to affirm that if there was disease in the liver, the man became a Calvinist, and if that organ was sound, he became a Unitarian.

EMERSON, *Essays, Second Series: Experience*.

I would not do for a Methodist preacher, for I am a poor horseman. I would not suit the Baptists, for I dislike water. I would fail as an Episcopalian, for I am no ladies' man.

JOHN HAY, *Letter*. (THAYER, *Life and Letters of John Hay*, i, 59.)

I have noticed all my life that many people think they have religion when they are troubled with dyspepsia.

INGERSOLL, *Liberty of Man, Woman and Child*.

A spleeny Lutheran.

SHAKESPEARE, *Henry VIII*. Act iii, sc. 2, l. 99.

10
Sects are stoves, but fire keeps its old properties through them all.

EMERSON, *Journals*, 1861.

Religion is the relation of the soul to God, and therefore the progress of sectarianism marks the decline of religion. Religion is as effectually destroyed by bigotry as by indifference.

EMERSON, *Journals*.

11
'Tis a strange thing, Sam, that among us people can't agree the whole week because they go different ways upon Sundays.

FARQUHAR, *Letter from Leyden*, 15 Oct., 1700.

12
The ecclesiastical writers, who, in the heat of religious faction, are apt to despise the profane virtues of sincerity and moderation.

EDWARD GIBBON, *Decline and Fall of the Roman Empire*. Ch. 26.

13
All sects seem to me to be right in what they assert, and wrong in what they deny.

GOETHE, *Conversations with Eckermann*.

14
Most men's anger against religion is as if two men should quarrel for a lady they neither of them care for.

LORD HALIFAX, *Works*, p. 221.

15
The Temple is a good, a holy place,
But quacking only gives it an ill savour;
While saintly mountebanks the porch disgrace,
And bring religion's self into disfavour.

THOMAS HOOD, *Ode to Rae Wilson*, l. 175.

16
It is becoming impossible for those who mix at all with their fellow-men to believe that the grace of God is distributed denominationally.

DEAN W. R. INGE. (MARCHANT, *Wit and Wisdom of Dean Inge*. No. 201.)

17
Every sect is a moral check on its neighbour. Competition is as wholesome in religion as in commerce.

W. S. LANDOR, *Imaginary Conversations: Martin and Jack*.

1
Beware of him the days that he takes Communion. (Gardez-vous bien de lui les jours qu'il communie.)

Du Lorens, *Satires*. Bk. i.

2
Persecution produced its natural effect on them. It found them a sect; it made them a faction.

Macaulay, *History of England*. Ch. 1.

Persecution is a bad and indirect way to plant religion.

Sir Thomas Browne, *Religio Medici*. Pt. i, sec. 25.

But he turned up his nose at their mumming and shamming,
And cared (shall I say?) not a d—— for their damming;
So they first read him out of their church, and next minute
Turned round and declared he had never been in it.

J. R. Lowell, *A Fable for Critics*, l. 759.

3
There is no disagreement greater than one which proceeds from religion. (Nulla discordia major quam quæ a religione fit.)

Montanus, *In Micah*.

Difference of religion breeds more quarrels than difference of politics.

Wendell Phillips, *Speech*, 7 Nov., 1860.

4
So shall they build me altars in their zeal,
Where knaves shall minister, and fools shall kneel:
Where Faith may mutter o'er her mystic spell,
Written in blood—and Bigotry may swell
The sail he spreads for Heav'n with blasts from hell!

Thomas Moore, *Lalla Rookh: The Veiled Prophet of Khorassan*. Pt. iii, l. 584.

5
We have a Calvinistic creed, a Popish liturgy, and an Arminian clergy.

William Pitt, Earl of Chatham. (Prior, *Life of Burke*. Ch. 10. 1790.)

6
Upright Quakers please both man and God.

Pope, *The Dunciad*. Bk. iv, l. 208.

The sedate, sober, silent, serious, sad-coloured sect.

Thomas Hood, *The Doves and the Crows*.

Her parents held the Quaker rule,
Which doth the human feeling cool.

Charles Lamb, *Hester*.

7
Religion, blushing, veils her sacred fires,
And unawares Morality expires.

Pope, *The Dunciad*. Bk. iv, l. 649.

8
I think while zealots fast and frown,
And fight for two or seven,
That there are fifty roads to town,
And rather more to Heaven.

W. M. Praed, *The Chant of the Brazen Head*. St. 8.

9
I always thought
It was both impious and unnatural
That such immanity and bloody strife
Should reign among professors of one faith.

Shakespeare, *I Henry VI*. Act v, sc. 1, l. 11.

Religious love put out Religion's eye.

Shakespeare, *A Lover's Complaint*, l. 250.

10
We have just enough religion to make us hate, but not enough to make us love, one another.

Swift, *Thoughts on Various Subjects*. No. 1.

11
What religion is he of? Why, he is an Anythingarian.

Swift, *Polite Conversation*. Dial. 1.

12
The race of men, while sheep in credulity, are wolves for conformity.

Carl Van Doren, *Why I Am an Unbeliever*.

13
The Methodists love your big sinners, as proper subjects to work upon.

Horace Walpole, *Letter to Sir Horace Mann*, 3 May, 1749.

14
Place before your eyes two precepts, and only two. One is Preach the Gospel; and the other is, Put down enthusiasm. . . . The Church of England in a nutshell.

Mrs. Humphry Ward, *Robert Elsmere*. Bk. ii, ch. 16. Referring to the valedictory of Archbishop Sutton, on the consecration of Bishop Reginald Heber to the See of Calcutta.

The merit claimed for the Anglican Church is, that if you let it alone, it will let you alone.

Emerson, *Journals*. Vol. viii, p. 368.

15
To damn for falling short
Of what they could not do,
For not believing the report
Of that which was not true.

Charles Wesley, *Epigram on Calvinism*.

We are God's chosen few;
All others will be damned;
There is no place in Heaven for you,
We can't have Heaven crammed.

Credited to Jonathan Swift by F. J. Gilman, *Evolution of the English Hymn*, but not found in Swift's works. Directed at the Calvinists. Quoted in Lord Fisher's *Memoirs*.

You can and you can't,—You shall and you shan't—You will and you won't—You'll be damned if you do—And you'll be damned if you don't.

Lorenzo Dow, *Reflections on the Love of God*. Defining Calvinism.

Die and be damned.

Thomas Mortimer. Referring to the Calvinistic doctrine of eternal punishment.

16
There is nothing more unnatural to religion than contentions about it.

Benjamin Whichcote, *Sermons*.

REMEDY, see Medicine

REMEMBRANCE, see Memory

REMORSE

See also Conscience: Guilty; Guilt; Repentance

1
A man's first care should be to avoid the reproaches of his own heart.
ADDISON, *Sir Roger de Coverley Papers: Sir Roger on the Bench.*

2
Nor ear can hear nor tongue can tell
The tortures of that inward hell!
BYRON, *The Giaour.* l. 748.

There is no future pang
Can deal that justice on the self condemn'd
He deals on his own soul.
BYRON, *Manfred.* Act iii, sc. 1.

Thy nights are banished from the realms of sleep!—
Yes! they may flatter thee, but thou shalt feel
A hollow agony which will not heal,
For thou art pillowed on a curse too deep.
BYRON, *Lines on Hearing Lady Byron Was Ill.*

3
Remorse is as the heart in which it grows;
If that be gentle, it drops balmy dews
Of true repentance; but if proud and gloomy,
It is the poison tree, that pierced to the inmost,
Weeps only tears of poison.
S. T. COLERIDGE, *Remorse.* Act i, sc. 1.

The Past lives o'er again
In its effects, and to the guilty spirit
The ever-frowning Present is its image.
S. T. COLERIDGE, *Remorse.* Act i, sc. 2.
See also PAST AND PRESENT.

4
Reproach cuts deeper than the keenest sword,
And cleaves my heart.
CONGREVE, *The Mourning Bride.* Act iv, sc. 1.

5
Remorse, the fatal egg by Pleasure laid.
COWPER, *The Progress of Error,* l. 239.

6
Remorse begets reform.
COWPER, *The Task.* Bk. v, l. 618.

Remorse does but add to the evil which bred it, when it promotes not penitence, but despair.
ARTHUR HELPS, *Friends in Council.* Bk. i, ch. 3.

7
Better to stand ten thousand sneers than one abiding pang, such as time could not abolish, of bitter self-reproach.
THOMAS DE QUINCEY, *Confessions of an English Opium-Eater.* Pt. i.

8
Remorse is memory awake.
EMILY DICKINSON, *Poems.* Pt. i, No. 69.

9
The hearts of good men admit of atonement. (Ἀκεσταί τοι φρένες ἐσθῶν.)
HOMER, *Iliad.* Bk. xiii, l. 115.

10
There's Morbid, all bile, and verjuice, and nerves,
Where other people would make preserves,
He turns his fruits into pickles:
Jealous, envious, and fretful by day,
At night, to his own sharp fancies a prey,
He lies like a hedgehog rolled up the wrong way,
Tormenting himself with his prickles.
THOMAS HOOD, *Mrs. Kilmansegg: Her Dream.*

11
Man, wretched man, whene'er he stoops to sin,
Feels, with the act, a strong remorse within
JUVENAL, *Satires.* Sat. xiii, l. 1 (Gifford, tr.)

Trust me, no tortures which the poets feign,
Can match the fierce, the unutterable pain,
He feels, who night and day, devoid of rest,
Carries his own accuser in his breast.
JUVENAL, *Satires.* Sat. xiii, l. 217. (Gifford, tr.)

A torture kept for those who know,
Know every thing, and—worst of all—
Know and love Virtue while they fall!
THOMAS MOORE, *Loves of the Angels: Second Angel's Story,* l. 1144.

12
When the scourge
Inexorably, and the torturing hour
Calls us to penance.
MILTON, *Paradise Lost.* Bk. ii, l. 90.

Whose iron scourge and torturing hour
The Bad affright, afflict the best!
THOMAS GRAY, *Hymn to Adversity,* l. 3.

To ease the anguish of a torturing hour.
SHAKESPEARE, *A Midsummer-Night's Dream.* Act v, sc. 1, l. 37

And braved the tyrant in his torturing hour
CAMPBELL, *Pleasures of Hope.* Pt. i, l 548.

13
Take thy beak from out my heart and take thy form from off my door!
Quoth the Raven, "Nevermore!"
EDGAR ALLAN POE, *The Raven.*

14
Remorse goes to sleep during a prosperous period and wakes up in adversity (Le remords s'endort durant un destin prospère et s'aigrit dans l'adversité.)
ROUSSEAU, *Confessions.* Bk. i, ch. 2. *See also* PROSPERITY AND ADVERSITY.

15
High minds, of native pride and force,
Most deeply feel thy pangs, Remorse!
Fear for their scourge mean villains have,
Thou art the torturer of the brave!
SCOTT, *Marmion.* Canto iii, l 200

'Tis when the wound is stiffening with the cold,
The warrior first feels pain—'tis when the heat
And fiery fever of the soul is past,
The sinner feels remorse.
SCOTT, *The Monastery.* Ch. 23. Quoted as from "an old play."

1
When thou shalt be disedged by her
That now thou tirest on, how thy memory
Will then be pang'd by me.
SHAKESPEARE, *Cymbeline*. Act iii, sc. 4, l. 96.

2
Leave her to heaven
And to those thorns that in her bosom lodge,
To prick and sting her.
SHAKESPEARE, *Hamlet*. Act i, sc. 5, l. 86.

3
I could accuse me of such things that it were better my mother had not borne me.
SHAKESPEARE, *Hamlet*. Act iii, sc. 1, l. 125.

4
The image of a wicked heinous fault
Lives in his eye: that close aspect of his
Does show the mood of a much troubled breast.
SHAKESPEARE, *King John*. Act iv, sc. 2, l. 71.

5
Make thick my blood;
Stop up the access and passage to remorse,
That no compunctious visitings of nature
Shake my fell purpose.
SHAKESPEARE, *Macbeth*. Act i, sc. 5, l. 44.

Thou sure and firm-set earth,
Hear not my steps, which way they walk, for fear
Thy very stones prate of my whereabout.
SHAKESPEARE, *Macbeth*. Act ii, sc. 1, l. 56.

6
Better be with the dead . . .
Than on the torture of the mind to lie
In restless ecstasy.
SHAKESPEARE, *Macbeth*. Act iii, sc. 2, l. 19.

O, full of scorpions is my mind.
SHAKESPEARE, *Macbeth*. Act iii, sc. 2, l. 36.

Infected minds
To their deaf pillows will discharge their secrets.
SHAKESPEARE, *Macbeth*. Act v, sc. 1, l. 80.

7
Abandon all remorse;
On horror's head horrors accumulate.
SHAKESPEARE, *Othello*. Act iii, sc. 3, l. 369.

Farewell, remorse: all good to me is lost;
Evil, be thou my good.
MILTON, *Paradise Lost*. Bk. iv, l. 109.

8
O that the vain remorse which must chastise
Crimes done, had but as loud a voice to warn,
As its keen sting is mortal to avenge!
SHELLEY, *The Cenci*. Act v, sc. 1, l. 2.

9
Oh! you do bear a poison in your mind
That would not let you rest in Paradise.
C. J. WELLS, *Joseph and His Brethren*. Act iii, sc. 1.

10
Men who can hear the Decalogue, and feel
No self-reproach.
WORDSWORTH, *Old Cumberland Beggar*, l. 136.

RENOWN, see Fame

REPENTANCE

See also Conscience: Guilty; Guilt; Remorse

11
Repent one day before your death.
Babylonian Talmud: Shabbath, p. 153a.

"Would a man 'scape the rod?"
Rabbi Ben Karshook saith,
"See that he turn to God
The day before his death."
"Ay, could a man inquire
When that will come!" I say.
The Rabbi's eye shoots fire—
"Then let him turn to-day!"
ROBERT BROWNING, *Ben Karshook's Wisdom*.

I ne'er repented anything yet in my life,
And scorn to begin now.
BEAUMONT AND FLETCHER, *Queen of Corinth*. Act iv, sc. 1.

And he who seeks repentance for the Past
Should woo the Angel Virtue in the future!
BULWER-LYTTON, *The Lady of Lyons*. Act v, sc. 2. Concluding lines.

12
To sigh, yet not recede; to grieve, yet not repent!
GEORGE CRABBE, *Tales of the Hall*. Bk. iii, last line.

Without any snivelling signs of contrition or repentance.
GEORGE LYTTELTON, *Dialogues of the Dead*.

13
His soul smelt pleasant as rain-wet clover.
"I have sinned and repented and that's all over.
In his dealings with heathen, the Lord is hard,
But the humble soul is his spikenard."
STEPHEN VINCENT BENÉT, *King David*.

14
In all my life, I have never repented but of three things: that I trusted a woman with a secret, that I went by sea when I might have gone by land, and that I passed a day in idleness.
MARCUS CATO. (PLUTARCH, *Lives: Marcus Cato*. Ch. 9, sec. 6; RABELAIS, *Works*, iv, 24.)

15
Ye sorrowed to repentance.
New Testament: II Corinthians, vii, 9.

16
No power can the impenitent absolve. (Ch' assolver non si può, chi non si pente.)
DANTE, *Inferno*. Canto xxvii, l. 118.

The true physician does not preach repentance, he offers absolution.
H. L. MENCKEN, *Prejudices*. Ser. iii, p. 269.

17
I decline to buy repentance at the cost of ten thousand drachmas. (Οὐκ ὠνοῦμαι μυρίων δραχμῶν μεταμέλειαν.)
DEMOSTHENES, refusing to pay the famous courtesan, Lais, the fee she demanded. (AULUS GELLIUS, *Noctes Atticæ*. Bk. i, ch. 8, sec. 6.)

18
Repentance is the virtue of weak minds.
DRYDEN, *The Indian Emperor*. Act iii, sc. 1.

The spirit burning but unbent,
May writhe—rebel—the weak alone repent.
BYRON, *The Corsair*. Canto ii, st. 10.

What 'twas weak to do,
'Tis weaker to lament, once being done.
SHELLEY, *The Cenci*. Act v, sc. 3, l. 111.

Never to repent and never to reproach others, these are the first steps to wisdom.
DENIS DIDEROT, *Pensées*.

1
Repentance is but want of power to sin.
DRYDEN, *Palamon and Arcite*. Bk. iii, l. 813.

2
He that repents of his own act, either is, or was a fool by his own confession.
THOMAS FULLER, *Gnomologia*. No. 2264.

3
Restore to God His due in tithe and time;
A tithe purloin'd cankers the whole estate.
GEORGE HERBERT, *The Church-Porch*. St. 65.

Repentance is good, but innocence better.
UNKNOWN.

4
To stand publicly in the Stool of Repentance, acknowledging their former transgressions.
EDWARD HYDE, EARL OF CLARENDON, *Narrative of the Rebellion*. Pt. xiii, sec. 48. (1674) A stool of repentance, also called "cutty-stool," was formerly placed in Scottish churches for offenders, especially against chastity.

5
A noble mind disdains not to repent.
HOMER, *Iliad*. Bk. xv, l. 227. (Pope, tr.)

6
A death-bed repentance seldom reaches to restitution.
JUNIUS, *Letters: Dedication*.

He well repents that will not sin, yet can;
But Death-bed sorrow rarely shews the man.
NATHANIEL LEE, *Princess of Cleve*. Act iv, sc. 3.

7
It is too late to repent of fighting, once you have buckled on the helmet. (Galeatum sero duelli Pænitet.)
JUVENAL, *Satires*. Sat. i, l. 169.

8
Our repentance is not so much sorrow for the ill we have done, as fear of the ill that may happen to us in consequence. (Notre repentir n'est pas tant un regret du mal que nous avons fait, qu'une crainte de celui qui nous en peut arriver.)
LA ROCHEFOUCAULD, *Maximes*. No. 180.

9
Joy shall be in heaven over one sinner that repenteth, more than over ninety and nine just persons, which need no repentance.
New Testament: Luke, xv, 7.

When prodigals return great things are done.
A. A. DOWTY, *The Siliad*. (BEETON, *Christmas Annual*, 1873.)

See also PRODIGALITY: THE PRODIGAL SON.

10
To do it no more is the truest repentance.
MARTIN LUTHER, *Of Repentance*.

Repentance for past crimes is just and easy;
But Sin-no-more's a task too hard for mortals.
SIR JOHN VANBRUGH, *The Relapse*. Act v, sc. 4.

11
Come, fill the Cup, and in the fire of Spring
Your Winter-garment of Repentance fling:
The Bird of Time has but a little way
To flutter—and the Bird is on the Wing.
OMAR KHAYYÁM, *Rubáiyát*, 7. (Fitzgerald, tr.)

12
Sweet tastes have sour closes;
And he repents on thorns that sleeps in beds of roses.
FRANCIS QUARLES, *Emblems*. Bk. i, No. 7.

Amid the roses, fierce repentance rears
Her snaky crest: a quick-returning pang
Shoots through the conscious heart.
THOMSON, *The Seasons: Spring*, l. 999.

13
It is never too late to repent.
JOHN RAY, *English Proverbs*.

He comes never late who comes repentant.
JUAN DE HOROZCO, *Manasses, Rey de India*, iii.

And while the lamp holds out to burn,
The vilest sinner may return.
ISAAC WATTS, *Hymns*. Bk. i, Hymn 88.

14
Repentance always comes behind.
CLEMENT ROBINSON, *Handful of Pleasant Delights*, p. 38. (1584)

Harm done, too late followeth repentance.
JOHN LYDGATE, *Fall of Princes*. Bk. iii, l. 915. (c. 1440)

When all is gone, repentance comes too late.
THOMAS FULLER, *Gnomologia*. No. 5545.

15
The dream is short, repentance long. (Der Wahn ist kurtz, die Reu ist lang.)
SCHILLER, *Lied von der Glocke*.

16
But with the morning cool repentance came.
SCOTT, *Rob Roy*. Ch. 12.

But with the morning cool reflection came.
SCOTT, *Chronicles of the Canongate*. Ch. 4.

17
He who repents his sins is well-nigh innocent. (Quem pænitet peccasse pæne est innocens.)
SENECA, *Agamemnon*, l. 243.

Who after his transgression doth repent,
Is half, or altogether, innocent.
HERRICK, *Penitence*.

18
Try what repentance can; what can it not?
Yet what can it when one can not repent?
SHAKESPEARE, *Hamlet*. Act iii, sc. 3, l. 65.

Well, I'll repent, and that suddenly, while I am in some liking; I shall be out of heart shortly, and then I shall have no strength to repent.
SHAKESPEARE, *I Henry IV*. Act iii, sc. 3, l. 5.

Well, if my wind were but long enough to say my prayers, I would repent.
SHAKESPEARE, *The Merry Wives of Windsor*. Act iv, sc. 5, l. 105.

19
Forgive me, Valentine: if hearty sorrow

Be a sufficient ransom for offence,
I tender 't here; I do as truly suffer,
As e'er I did commit.

SHAKESPEARE, *The Two Gentlemen of Verona*. Act v, sc. 4, l. 74.

1
The world will not believe a man repents;
And this wise world of ours is mainly right.

TENNYSON, *Geraint and Enid*, l. 899.

2
We all go astray, but the least imprudent
Is he who the earliest comes to repent.
(Chacun s'égare, et le moins imprudent
Est celui-là qui plus tôt se repent.)

VOLTAIRE, *Nanine*. Act ii, sc. 10.

To err is human; but contrition felt for the crime distinguishes the virtuous from the wicked. (D'uomo è il fallir, ma dal malvagio il buono Scerne il dolor del fallo.)

ALFIERI, *Rosmunda*. Act iii, sc. 1.

3
Repentance must be something more than mere remorse for sins: it comprehends a change of nature befitting heaven.

LEW WALLACE, *Ben Hur*. Bk. vi, ch. 2.

4
There's no repentance in the grave.

ISAAC WATTS, *Solemn Thoughts*.

REPUBLIC, see Democracy

REPUTATION

I—Reputation: Definitions

5
Where reputation is, almost every thing becometh; but where it is not, it must be supplied by punctilios and compliments.

FRANCIS BACON, *Advancement of Learning: Civil Knowledge*. Sec. 3.

6
To disregard what the world thinks of us is not only arrogant but utterly shameless. (Neglegere quid de se quisque sentiat, non solum arrogantis est, sed etiam omnino dissoluti.)

CICERO, *De Officiis*. Bk. i, ch. 28, sec. 99.

The contempt of good reputation is called impudence.

THOMAS HOBBES, *Leviathan*. Pt. i, ch. 6.

7
Reputation is the life of the mind, as breath is the life of the body.

GRACIAN, *Complete Gentleman*, 96. (Saldkeld, tr.)

8
The invisible thing called a Good Name is made up of the breath of numbers that speak well of you.

LORD HALIFAX, *Works*, p. 37.

9
The great difficulty is first to win a reputation; the next to keep it while you live; and the next to preserve it after you die.

B. R. HAYDON, *Table Talk*.

10
Your reputation will never correspond with the amount of your labor. (Reponsura tuo numquam est par fama labori.)

HORACE, *Satires*. Bk. ii, sat. 8, l. 65.

How many people live on the reputation of the reputation they might have made!

O. W. HOLMES, *The Autocrat of the Breakfast-Table*. Ch. 3.

11
The blaze of a reputation cannot be blown out, but it often dies in the socket.

SAMUEL JOHNSON, *Letter to Mrs. Thrale*, 1 May, 1780.

12
A great reputation is a great noise: the more there is made, the farther off it is heard.

NAPOLEON, *Sayings*. (EMERSON, *Representative Men: Napoleon*.)

13
Reputation demands words, but renown can be content with men's judgments. (Fama vocem utique desiderat, claritas potest etiam citra vocem contingere contenta judicio.)

SENECA, *Epistulæ ad Lucilium*. Epis. cii, sec. 17.

14
It sometimes happens that a person, when not known, shines by a good reputation, who, when he is present, is disagreeable to them that see him.

THOMAS À KEMPIS, *De Imitatione Christi*. Pt. i, ch. 8.

Men . . . have their reputation by distance.

BEN JONSON, *Explorata: Decipimur Specie*.

15
One man lies in his words and gets a bad reputation; another in his manners, and enjoys a good one.

H. D. THOREAU, *Journal*, 25 June, 1852.

II—Reputation: Apothegms

16
'Tis better never to be named than to be ill spoken of.

SUSANNAH CENTLIVRE, *The Basset Table*. Act i.

17
And reputation bleeds in ev'ry word.

CHARLES CHURCHILL, *The Apology*, l. 48.

At every word a reputation dies.

POPE, *Rape of the Lock*. Canto iii, l. 16.

I see my reputation is at stake;
My fame is shrewdly gored.

SHAKESPEARE, *Troilus and Cressida*. Act iii, sc. 3, l. 227.

Convey a libel in a frown,
And wink a reputation down.

SWIFT, *Journal of a Modern Lady*.

18
All reputations each age revises. Very few immutable men has history to show

EMERSON, *Journals*. Vol. v, p. 312.

The reputations of the nineteenth century will one day be quoted to prove its barbarism.

EMERSON, *Representative Men: Uses of Great Men*.

1
A man has a reputation, and is no longer free, but must respect it.
EMERSON, *Society and Solitude: Works and Days.*

2
Many a man's reputation would not know his character if they met on the street.
ELBERT HUBBARD, *The Philistine.* Vol. iv, p. 82.

3
Reputations, like beavers and cloaks, shall last some people twice the time of others.
DOUGLAS JERROLD, *Specimens of Jerrold's Wit: Reputations.*

4
No man, however great, is known to everybody and no man, however solitary, is known to nobody.
GEORGE MOORE, *Impressions: A Great Poet.*

5
The worst of me is known, and I can say that I am better than my reputation. (Das Aergste weiss die Welt von mir, und ich Kann sagen, ich bin besser als mein Ruf.)
SCHILLER, *Marie Stuart.* Act iii, sc. 4, l. 208.

6
Read not my blemishes in the world's report.
SHAKESPEARE, *Antony and Cleopatra.* Act ii, sc. 3, l. 5.

7
There was worlds of reputation in it, but no money.
MARK TWAIN, *A Yankee at the Court of King Arthur.* Ch. 9.

8
The only way to compel men to speak good of us is to do it.
VOLTAIRE, *History of Charles XII: Preliminary Discourse.*

9
Associate yourself with men of good quality if you esteem your own reputation; for 'tis better to be alone than in bad company.
GEORGE WASHINGTON, *Rules of Civility.* No. 56. *See also under* COMPANION.

III—Reputation: Its Value

10
A good name is better than precious ointment.
Old Testament: Ecclesiastes, vii, 1.

A good name is rather to be chosen than great riches.
Old Testament: Proverbs, xxii, 1.

A good name is a second life, and the groundwork of eternal existence.
BHASCARA ACHARYA, *Lilawati.* (LONGFELLOW, *Kavanagh.* Ch. 4.)

Good renomme is better than richesse.
ANTHONY WOODVILLE, *Dictes,* 64. (1477)

Good name is worth gold.
UNKNOWN, *How the Good Wife,* l. 75. (1460)

For wise men and old seyn good name is worth gold.
UNKNOWN, *Plasidas,* 166. (1597)

11
A good name is better than great riches. (Mas vale el buen Nombre que muchas riquezas.)
CERVANTES, *Don Quixote.* Pt. ii, ch. 15. (1615)

A good reputation is a fair estate.
THOMAS FULLER, *Gnomologia.* No. 172. (1732)

A good reputation is more valuable than money. (Bona opinio hominum tutior pecunia est.)
PUBLILIUS SYRUS, *Sententiæ.* No. 108.

12
A good name endureth for ever.
Apocrypha: Ecclesiasticus, xli, 13.

A good report
Makes men live long, although their life be short.
ROWLAND WATKYNS, *Flamma Sine Fumo: A Good Report.*

13
It is reasonable to rejoice, as the day declines, to find that it has been spent with the approbation of mankind.
SAMUEL JOHNSON, *Letters.* Vol. ii, p. 369.

14
My good name is nevertheless unstained; and so far I have lived without reproach. (Fama tamen clara est, et adhuc sine crimine vixi.)
OVID, *Heroides.* Epis. xvii, l. 17.

My good name, which was as white as a tulip.
WYCHERLEY, *Love in a Wood.* Act iv, sc. 1.

15
It's a fine thing to have a finger pointed at one! (At pulchrum est digito monstrari.)
PERSIUS, *Satires.* Sat. i, l. 28.

16
If I can only keep my good name, I shall be rich enough. (Ego si bonam famam mihi servasso, sat ero dives.)
PLAUTUS, *Mostellaria,* l. 228. (Act i, sc. 3.)

17
An honourable reputation is a second patrimony. (Honestus rumor alterum est patrimonium.)
PUBLILIUS SYRUS, *Sententiæ.* No. 246.

To an upright man a good reputation is the greatest inheritance. (Probo bona fama maxima est hereditas.)
PUBLILIUS SYRUS, *Sententiæ.* No. 537.

He dying bequeathed to his son a good name,
Which unsullied descended to me.
JOHN O'KEEFFE, *The Farmer.* Act i.

18
A good name keeps its lustre in the dark.
JOHN RAY, *English Proverbs,* 18.

If one's name be up, he may lie in bed.
JOHN RAY, *English Proverbs.*

19
I would to God, thou and I knew where a commodity of good names were to be bought.
SHAKESPEARE, *I Henry IV.* Act i, sc. 2, l. 93.

20
Good name in man and woman, dear my lord,
Is the immediate jewel of their souls:
Who steals my purse steals trash; 'tis something, nothing;

'Twas mine, 'tis his, and has been slave to thousands;
But he that filches from me my good name
Robs me of that which not enriches him,
And makes me poor indeed.

SHAKESPEARE, *Othello*. Act iii, sc. 3, l. 155.

Who steals a bugle-horn, a ring, a steed,
Or such like worthless thing, has some discretion;
'Tis petty larceny: not such his deed
Who robs us of our fame, our best possession.

BERNI, *Orlando Innamorata*. Canto lv.

Reputation is a jewel.

VANBRUGH, *The Provoked Wife*. Act i, sc. 2.

1

The purest treasure mortal times afford
Is spotless reputation: that away,
Men are but gilded loam or painted clay.

SHAKESPEARE, *Richard II*. Act i, sc. 1, l. 177.

'T is better to be vile than vile esteem'd,
When not to be receives reproach of being,
And the just pleasure lost which is so deem'd
Not by our feeling, but by others' seeing.

SHAKESPEARE, *Sonnets*. No. cxxi.

IV—Reputation: Its Worthlessness

2

The solar system has no anxiety about its reputation.

EMERSON, *Conduct of Life: Worship*.

3

O reputation, reputation! how many a worthless man hast thus set up on high! (*Ὦ δόξα δόξα, μυρίοισι δὴ βροτῶν οὐδὲν γεγῶσι βίοτον ὤγκωσας μέγαν.*)

EURIPIDES, *Andromache*, l. 319.

4

I consider him of small account who esteems himself just as the popular breath may chance to raise him. (Ich halte nichts von dem, der von sich denkt Wie ihn das Volk vielleicht erheben möchte.)

GOETHE, *Iphigenia auf Tauris*. Act ii, sc. 1.

Reputation is but a synonym of popularity: dependent on suffrage, to be increased or diminished at the will of the voters.

MRS. ANNA JAMESON, *Memoirs and Essays: Washington Allston*.

5

Most people judge men only by their vogue or by their fortune. (La plupart des gens ne jugent des hommes que par la vogue qu'ils ont, ou par leur fortune.)

LA ROCHEFOUCAULD, *Maximes*. No. 212.

6

Woe unto you, when all men shall speak well of you!

New Testament: Luke, vi, 26.

7

Those who have been most celebrated have not always been the most illustrious. (Illustrium alia clariora esse, alia majora.)

PLINY THE YOUNGER, *Epistles*. Bk. iii, epis. 16.

8

Seeking the bubble reputation
Even in the cannon's mouth.

SHAKESPEARE, *As You Like It*. Act ii, sc. 7, l. 152.

Reputation is a bubble which a man bursts when he tries to blow it for himself.

EMMA CARLETON. (*The Philistine*, xi, 82.)

9

Cassio: Reputation! reputation! reputation! O, I have lost my reputation! I have lost the immortal part of myself, and what remains is bestial. . . .
Iago: Reputation is an idle and most false imposition; oft got without merit, and lost without deserving.

SHAKESPEARE, *Othello*. Act ii, sc. 3, l. 262.

10

To be mis-spoken and mis-seen of men,
Which is not for high-seated hearts to fear.

SWINBURNE, *Bothwell*. Act i, sc. 1.

V—Reputation in Women

11

Nothing is so delicate as the reputation of a woman; it is at once the most beautiful and most brittle of all human things.

FANNY BURNEY, *Evelina*. Letter 39.

12

The reputation of a woman may also be compared to a mirror of crystal, shining and bright, but liable to be sullied by every breath that comes near it.

CERVANTES, *Don Quixote*. Pt. i, bk. iv, ch. 33.

13

Flavia, most tender of her own good name,
Is rather careless of her sister's fame.

COWPER, *Charity*, l. 453.

14

Must I live 'twixt spite and fear,
Every day grow handsomer,
And lose my reputation?

JOHN GAY, *The Lady's Lamentation*.

15

For a strolling damsel bears a doubtful reputation. (Denn ein wanderndes Mädchen ist immer von schwankendem Rufe.)

GOETHE, *Hermann und Dorothea*, vii, 93.

16

Her name, that was as fresh
As Dian's visage, is now begrimed and black.

SHAKESPEARE, *Othello*. Act iii, sc. 3, l. 386.

VI—Reputation: Its Loss

17

Who can see worse days than he that yet living doth follow at the funeral of his own reputation?

FRANCIS BACON, *Essays: On Death*. Sec. 11. (The authenticity of this essay is doubted.)

18

It is a maxim with me that no man was ever written out of reputation but by himself.

RICHARD BENTLEY. (MONK, *Life of Bentley*. Vol. i, ch. 6.)

No book was ever written down by any but itself.
EMERSON, *Essays, First Series: Spiritual Laws.*

1
Take away my good name and take away my life.
THOMAS FULLER, *Gnomologia.* No. 4306.

2
How many worthy men have we seen survive their own reputation!
MONTAIGNE, *Essays.* Bk. ii, ch. 16.

3
I have offended reputation,
A most unnoble swerving.
SHAKESPEARE, *Antony and Cleopatra.* Act iii, sc. 11, l. 49.

4
Thy death-bed is no lesser than thy land
Wherein thou liest in reputation sick.
SHAKESPEARE, *Richard II.* Act ii, sc. 1, l. 95.

5
The breath
Of accusation kills an innocent name,
And leaves for lame acquittal the poor life,
Which is a mask without it.
SHELLEY, *The Cenci.* Act iv, sc. 4, l. 137.

6
Bankrupt in fortune and reputation.
SHERIDAN, *School for Scandal.* Act i, sc. 1.

VII—Reputation: Its Recovery

7
A wounded reputation is seldom cured.
H. G. BOHN, *Hand-Book of Proverbs,* p. 304.

8
Reputation crackt is a Venice-glass broke.
THOMAS FULLER, *Gnomologia.* No. 4021.

Glass, China, and Reputation, are easily crack'd and never well mended.
BENJAMIN FRANKLIN, *Poor Richard,* 1750.

9
A lost good name is ne'er retriev'd.
JOHN GAY, *Fables: The Fox at the Point of Death,* l. 46.

10
An ill wound is cured, not an ill name.
GEORGE HERBERT, *Jacula Prudentum.*

11
Who swerves from innocence, who makes divorce
Of that serene companion—a good name,
Recovers not his loss; but walks with shame,
With doubt, with fear, and haply with remorse.
WORDSWORTH, *The River Duddon.* Sonnet xxx.

RESEARCH

12
Those hateful persons called Original Researchers.
J. M. BARRIE, *My Lady Nicotine.* Ch. 14.

13
As is your sort of mind,
So is your of sort of search: you'll find
What you desire.
ROBERT BROWNING, *Easter-Day.* Pt. vii, l. 3.

14
We are as much gainers by finding a new property in the old earth as by acquiring a new planet.
EMERSON, *Representative Men: Uses of Great Men.*

15
Nothing can be more miserable than the man who goes through the whole round of things, and pries into the things beneath the earth. (Τὰ νέρθεν γᾶς ἐρευνῶντος.)
MARCUS AURELIUS, *Meditations.* Bk. ii, sec. 13.

Nothing has such power to broaden the mind as the ability to investigate systematically and truly all that comes under thy observation in life.
MARCUS AURELIUS, *Meditations.* Bk. iii, sec. 2.

16
Seek, and ye shall find; knock, and it shall be opened unto you.
New Testament: Matthew, vii, 7.

He that seeketh findeth.
JOHN HEYWOOD, *Proverbs,* i, 10.

Seek till you find and you'll not lose your labour.
JOHN RAY, *English Proverbs,* 200.

17
Like following life thro' creatures you dissect,
You lose it in the moment you detect.
POPE, *Moral Essays.* Epis. i, l. 29.

18
Far must thy researches go
Wouldst thou learn the world to know;
Thou must tempt the dark abyss
Wouldst thou prove what *Being* is;
Naught but firmness gains the prize,
Naught but fullness makes us wise,
Buried deep truth ever lies.
SCHILLER, *Proverbs of Confucius.* (Bowring, tr.)

19
Nothing is so difficult but that it may be found out by seeking. (Nil tam difficile est quin quærendo investigari possiet.)
TERENCE, *Heauton Timorumenos,* l. 675. (Act iv, sc. 2.)

Attempt the end, and never stand to doubt;
Nothing's so hard but search will find it out.
ROBERT HERRICK, *Seek and Find.*

See also under DIFFICULTY.

RESEMBLANCE, see Likeness

RESIGNATION

See also Patience

20
Do not kick against the pricks. (Πρὸς κέντρα μὴ λακτιζε.)
ÆSCHYLUS, *Agamemnon,* l. 1624.

It is folly to kick against the pricks. (Advorsum stimulum calces.)
TERENCE, *Phormio,* l. 78. (Act i, sc. 2.)

It is hard for thee to kick against the pricks.
New Testament: Acts, ix, 5; xxvi, 14.

If you strike the goads with your fists, your hands suffer most. (Si stimulos pugnis cædis manibus plus dolet.)

PLAUTUS, *Truculentus*. Act iv, sc. 2, l. 54.

1 Take no sorrow of the thing lost which may not be recovered.

ÆSOP, *Fables*, ii, 270. (Caxton, tr.)

It's no use crying over spilt milk.

W. S. GILBERT, *Foggarty's Fairy*. Act i.

2 Thy will be done, though in my own undoing.

SIR THOMAS BROWNE, *Religio Medici*. Pt. ii, sec. 15, conclusion.

Then let us cheerfu' acquiesce,
Nor make our scanty pleasures less,
By pining at our state.

BURNS, *Epistle to Davie*.

3 Resignation open-eyed, conscious, and informed by love, is the only one of our feelings for which it is impossible to become a sham.

JOSEPH CONRAD, *A Personal Record: Preface*.

4 To be resign'd when ills betide,
Patient when favours are denied,
And pleased with favours given;—
Dear Chloe, this is wisdom's part,
This is that incense of the heart
Whose fragrance smells to heaven.

NATHANIEL COTTON, *The Fireside*. St. 11.

5 It's over, and can't be helped, and that's one consolation, as they always say in Turkey.

DICKENS, *Pickwick Papers*. Ch. 23.

6 Dare to look up to God and say, "Use me henceforward as Thou wilt; I am of one mind with Thee; I am Thine; I ask exemption from nothing that pleases Thee; lead me where Thou wilt; clothe me in any dress Thou choosest."

EPICTETUS, *Discourses*. Bk. ii, ch. 16, sec. 42.

What is the law of God? To guard what is his own, not to lay claim to what is not his own, but to make use of what is given him, and not to yearn for what has not been given.

EPICTETUS, *Discourses*. Bk. ii, ch. 16, sec. 28.

Give what thou canst, without thee we are poor;
And with thee rich, take what thou wilt away.

COWPER, *The Task*. Bk. v, l. 905.

7 Let him give up his place like a guest well filled. (Cedat uti conviva satur.)

HORACE, *Satires*. Bk. i, sat. 1, l. 119.

Sinks to the grave in unperceiv'd decay,
While Resignation gently slopes the way.

GOLDSMITH, *The Deserted Village*, l. 110. (1770) In later editions, Goldsmith changed "sinks" to "bends."

An age that melts with unperceiv'd decay,
And glides in modest innocence away.

SAMUEL JOHNSON, *Vanity of Human Wishes*, l. 292. (1749)

And varied life steal unperceiv'd away.

SAMUEL JOHNSON, *Irene*. Act ii, sc. 7.

8 Father, if thou be willing, remove this cup from me: nevertheless, not my will, but thine, be done.

New Testament: Luke, xxii, 42.

It seem'd so hard at first, mother, to leave the blessed sun,
And now it seems as hard to stay, and yet His will be done!

TENNYSON, *The May Queen: Conclusion*.

9 To will what God doth will, that is the only science
That gives us any rest.

MALHERBE, *Consolation*. St. 7. (Longfellow, tr.)

That's best
Which God sends. 'Twas His will: it is mine.

OWEN MEREDITH, *Lucile*. Pt. ii, canto 6, st. 29.

Not as we wanted it,
But as God granted it.

SIR ARTHUR QUILLER-COUCH, *To Bearers*.

10 What doctrine call ye this, *Che sera, sera:*
What will be, shall be?

CHRISTOPHER MARLOWE, *Dr. Faustus*. Act i, l. 75. *See also under* FATE.

11 If God be appeased, I can not be wretched. (Placato possum non miser esse deo.)

OVID, *Tristia*. Bk. i, eleg. 3, l. 40.

12 That tender compromise called resignation is only an eloquent name for the dying down, the wearing thin, of the vital impulse in us.

J. C. POWYS, *The Meaning of Culture*, p. 17.

13 Let that please man which has pleased God. (Placeat homini quidquid deo placuit.)

SENECA, *Epistulæ ad Lucilium*. Epis. lxxiv, 20.

One help in misfortune is to endure and submit to necessity. (Unum est levamentum malorum pati et necessitatibus suis obsequi.)

SENECA, *De Ira*. Bk. iii, sec. 16.

14 I am tied to the stake, and I must stand the course.

SHAKESPEARE, *King Lear*. Act iii, sc. 7, l. 53.

Thus ready for the way of life or death,
I wait the sharpest blow.

SHAKESPEARE, *Pericles*. Act i, sc. 1, l. 54.

15 When some great sorrow, like a mighty river,
Flows through your life with peace-destroying power
And dearest things are swept from sight forever,
Say to your heart each trying hour:
"This, too, will pass away."

LANTA WILSON SMITH [?], *This, Too, Will Pass Away*.

16 God's plans, like lilies, pure and white, unfold;

We must not tear the close-shut leaves apart—
Time will reveal the chalices of gold.
MARY LOUISE RILEY SMITH, *Sometime.*

1
Come wealth or want, come good or ill,
Let young and old accept their part,
And bow before the Awful Will,
And bear it with an honest heart.
THACKERAY, *The End of the Play.*

2
To kiss the rod.
UNKNOWN, *Roman de Renart.* (c. 1200. William Caxton, tr. 1481)

And presently all humble kiss the rod.
SHAKESPEARE, *The Two Gentlemen of Verona.* Act i, sc. 2, l. 59.

RESOLUTION

See also Obstinacy, Perseverance, Purpose

3
I will neither yield to the song of the siren nor the voice of the hyena, the tears of the crocodile nor the howling o' the Wolf.
GEORGE CHAPMAN, *Eastward Hoe.* Act v, sc. 1.

His way once chose, he forward thrust outright,
Nor stepped aside for dangers or delight.
ABRAHAM COWLEY, *Davideis.* Bk. iv, l. 361.

4
The soldier, armed with resolution.
CIBBER, *Richard III* (altered). Act ii, sc. 1.

5 Be as a tower, that, firmly set,
Shakes not its top for any blast that blows.
DANTE, *Purgatorio.* Canto v, l. 14. (Cary, tr.)

6
I am in earnest—I will not equivocate—I will not excuse—I will not retreat a single inch AND I WILL BE HEARD.
WILLIAM LLOYD GARRISON, *Salutatory of the Liberator.* Vol. i, No. 1, 1 Jan., 1831.

7
There is no such thing in man's nature as a settled and full resolve either for good or evil, except at the very moment of execution.
HAWTHORNE, *Twice-Told Tales: Fancy's Show Box.*

8
Hast thou attempted greatness?
Then go on;
Back-turning slackens resolution.
ROBERT HERRICK, *Regression Spoils Resolution.*

9
Be firm! One constant element in luck
Is genuine solid old Teutonic pluck.
O. W. HOLMES, *A Rhymed Lesson,* l. 282.

10
Resolve, and thou art free.
LONGFELLOW, *The Masque of Pandora.* Pt. vi.

Let us, then, be up and doing,
With a heart for any fate;
Still achieving, still pursuing,
Learn to labor and to wait.
LONGFELLOW, *A Psalm of Life.*

11
In life's small things be resolute and great
To keep thy muscle trained: know'st thou when Fate
Thy measure takes, or when she'll say to thee,
"I find thee worthy; do this deed for me"?
J. R. LOWELL, *Sayings.* No. 1.

12
All things are what you make them. (Omnes res perinde sunt ut agas.)
PLAUTUS, *Pseudolus,* l. 578. (Act ii, sc. 1.)

13
The road to resolution lies by doubt.
FRANCIS QUARLES, *Emblems.* Bk. iv, No. 2.

14
Now truce, farewell, and ruth, begone!
SCOTT, *The Lady of the Lake.* Canto v, st. 14.

15
Never tell your resolution beforehand.
JOHN SELDEN, *Table-Talk: Wisdom.*

16
And thus the native hue of resolution
Is sicklied o'er with the pale cast of thought.
SHAKESPEARE, *Hamlet.* Act iii, sc. 1, l. 84.

How terrible is constant resolution.
SHAKESPEARE, *Henry V.* Act ii, sc. 4, l. 35.

How high a pitch his resolution soars!
SHAKESPEARE, *Richard II.* Act i, sc. 1, l. 109.

18
Hearts resolved and hands prepared.
SMOLLETT, *Ode to Leven Water.*

19
'Tis fix'd, th' irrevocable doom of Jove;
No force can bend me, no persuasion move.
STATIUS, *Thebais.* Bk. i, l. 413. (Pope, tr.)

His mind remains unshaken. (Mens immota manet.)
VERGIL, *Æneid.* Bk. iv, l. 449.

RESPECTABILITY

20
How much of priceless life were spent
With men that every virtue decks,
And women models of their sex.
ROBERT BROWNING, *Respectability.*

21
"The Discobolus is out here because he is vulgar—
He has neither vest nor pants with which to cover his limbs;
I, sir, am a person of the most respectable connections—
My brother-in-law is haberdasher to Mr. Spurgeon."
O God! O Montreal!
SAMUEL BUTLER, *A Psalm of Montreal.* Written after visiting the Montreal Museum of Natural History, and finding the Discobolus stuck away in a corner because, as the custodian said, he was rather vulgar.

In the bosom of her respectable family resided Camilla.
FANNY BURNEY, *Camilla.* Bk. i, ch. 1.

22
Least is he marked that doth as most men do.
MICHAEL DRAYTON, *The Owl.*

23
Men are respectable only as they respect.
EMERSON, *Lectures and Sketches: Sovereignty of Ethics.*

Is there no respect of place, persons, nor time in you?

SHAKESPEARE, *Twelfth Night*. Act ii, sc. 3, l. 99.

I had so great a respect for the memory of Henry IV, that had a victim I was pursuing taken refuge under his statue on the Pont Neuf, I would have spared his life.

CARTOUCHE, the famous French brigand. (SPENCER, *Social Statics*. Pt. iv, ch. 30, sec. 6.)

1

"*Bourgeois,*" I observed, "is an epithet which the riff-raff apply to what is respectable, and the aristocracy to what is decent."

ANTHONY HOPE, *The Dolly Dialogues*. No. 17.

2

Respectability is the dickey on the bosom of civilization.

ELBERT HUBBARD, *A Thousand and One Epigrams*.

The only man to me who is not respectable is the man who consumes more than he produces.

ELBERT HUBBARD, *Philistine*. Vol. xx, p. 36.

3

To be respectable implies a multitude of little observances, from the strict keeping of Sunday, down to the careful tying of a cravat.

VICTOR HUGO, *Toilers of the Sea*. Pt. i, bk. 3, ch. 12.

4

Respectable means rich, and decent means poor. I should die if I heard my family called decent.

THOMAS LOVE PEACOCK, *Crochet Castle*. Ch. 3.

5

Men have to do some awfully mean things to keep up their respectability.

BERNARD SHAW, *Fanny's First Play*. Act iii.

We are ashamed of everything that is real about us. . . . The more things a man is ashamed of the more respectable he is.

BERNARD SHAW, *Man and Superman*. Act i.

6

'Tis the misfortune of worthy people that they are cowards. (Un des plus grands malheurs des honnêtes gens c'est qu'ils sont des lâches.)

VOLTAIRE. (EMERSON, *Conduct of Life: Fate*.)

7

Q. What sort of a person was Mr. Weare?
A. He was always a respectable person.
Q. What do you mean by respectable?
A. He kept a gig.

UNKNOWN, *Evidence* at the trial of John Thurtell for the murder of William Weare, in 1823. *See* MURDER: SOME JINGLES.

Thus does society naturally divide itself into four classes: Noblemen, Gentlemen, Gigmen, and Men.

CARLYLE, *Essays: Boswell*. Note.

REST

See also Idleness; Leisure; Night and Rest; Quiet; Sleep

8

Rest is not idleness, and to lie sometimes on the grass under the trees on a summer's day, listening to the murmur of the water, or watching the clouds float across the blue sky, is by no means a waste of time.

LORD AVEBURY, *Ease of Life*. Ch. 4.

9

The end and the reward of toil is rest.

JAMES BEATTIE, *The Minstrel*. Bk. ii, l. 136.

10

Quietly rested under the drums and tramplings of three conquests.

SIR THOMAS BROWNE, *Hydriotaphia*. Ch. 5.

Never weather-beaten sail more willing bent to shore;
Never tired pilgrim's limbs affected slumber more.

THOMAS CAMPION, *Never Weather-beaten Sail*.

11

Rest is for the dead.

THOMAS CARLYLE. (FROUDE, *The First Forty Years*. Vol. ii, ch. 5.)

LAST REST, *see under* DEATH.

12

Ah, what is more blessed than to put care aside, when the mind lays down its burden, and spent with distant travel, we come home again and rest on the couch we longed for? This, this alone, is worth all such toils. (O quid solutis est beatius curis, Cum mens onus reponit, as peregrino Labore fessi venimus larem ad nostrum Desideratoque acquiescimus lecto? Hoc est, quod unumst pro laboribus tantis.)

CATULLUS, *Odes*. Ode xxxi, l. 7.

13

Absence of occupation is not rest;
A mind quite vacant is a mind distress'd.

COWPER, *Retirement*, l. 623.

14

Rest is not quitting The busy career,
Rest is the fitting Of self to one's sphere.

'Tis the brook's motion, Clear without strife,
Fleeing to ocean After its life.

'Tis loving and serving The Highest and Best!
'Tis onwards! unswerving, And that is true rest.

JOHN SULLIVAN DWIGHT, *Rest*. Sts. 4, 5, 7. Partly a paraphrase of Goethe.

15

Rest comes at length, though life be long and dreary;
The day must dawn, and darksome night be passed.

F. W. FABER, *Hark, Hark, My Soul!*

Time comes with the morning
And rest with the night.

LONGFELLOW, *Curfew*.

16

Amidst these restless thoughts this rest I find,

For those that rest not here, there's rest behind.

THOMAS GATAKER, *B. D.*

1
For too much rest itself becomes a pain.

HOMER, *Odyssey*. Bk. xv, l. 429. (Pope, tr.)

This hardest penal toil, reluctant rest.

WILLIAM WATSON, *To a Friend.*

2
Think not of rest; though dreams be sweet,
Start up, and ply your heavenward feet.

JOHN KEBLE, *The Christian Year: Second Sunday in Advent.*

We wish him health; he sighs for rest,
And Heaven accepts the prayer.

JOHN KEBLE, *The Christian Year: Restoration of the Royal Family.*

3
When Earth's last picture is painted and the tubes are twisted and dried,
When the oldest colours have faded, and the youngest critic has died,
We shall rest, and, faith, we shall need it—lie down for an æon or two,
Till the Master of All Good Workmen shall put us to work anew.

RUDYARD KIPLING, *When Earth's Last Picture Is Painted.*

Master, I've filled my contract, wrought in Thy many lands;
Not by my sins wilt Thou judge me, but by the work of my hands.
Master, I've done Thy bidding, and the light is low in the west,
And the long, long shift is over . . . Master, I've earned it—Rest.

ROBERT W. SERVICE, *Song of the Wage Slave.*

4
Come unto me, all ye that labour and are heavy laden, and I will give you rest.

New Testament: Matthew, xi, 28.

5
Rest is sweet after strife.

OWEN MEREDITH, *Lucile*. Pt. i, canto 6, st. 25.

Rest springs from strife, and dissonant chords beget
Divinest harmonies.

LEWIS MORRIS, *Love's Suicide.*

6
Night is the time for rest;
How sweet, when labours close,
To gather round an aching breast
The curtain of repose.

JAMES MONTGOMERY, *Night.*

7
Take rest; a field that has rested gives a bountiful crop. (Da requiem; requietus ager bene credita reddit.)

OVID, *Ars Amatoria*. Bk. ii, l. 351.

It is well to lie fallow for a while.

MARTIN F. TUPPER, *Of Good in Things Evil.*

8
What is without periods of rest will not endure. (Quod caret alterna requie, durabile non est.)

OVID, *Heroides*. Epis. iv, l. 89.

9
Beyond the last horizon's rim,
Beyond adventure's farthest quest,
Somewhere they rise, serene and dim,
The happy, happy Hills of Rest.

ALBERT BIGELOW PAINE, *The Hills of Rest.*

10
Rest a while and run a mile.

PALSGRAVE, *L'Éclaircissement de la Langue Française*, p. 436.

Rest and success are fellows.

W. G. BENHAM, *Proverbs*, p. 829.

11
Rest, rest, perturbed spirit!

SHAKESPEARE, *Hamlet*. Act i, sc. 5, l. 183.

12
An old man, broken with the storms of state,
Is come to lay his weary bones among ye;
Give him a little earth for charity!

SHAKESPEARE, *Henry VIII*. Act iv, sc. 2, l. 21.

The cardinal, partly from the fatigues of his journey, partly from the agitation of his anxious mind, was seized with a disorder that turned into a dysentery; and he was able with some difficulty to reach Leicester Abbey. When the abbot and the monks advanced to receive him with much respect, and reverence, he told them that he had come to lay his bones among them; then he immediately took to his bed, whence he never rose more.

HUME, *History of England*. Ch. 30.

13
Sleep after toil, port after stormy seas,
Ease after war, death after life, does greatly please.

SPENSER, *The Faerie Queene*. Bk. i, canto ix, st. 40.

14
And rest, that strengthens into virtuous deeds,
Is one with prayer.

BAYARD TAYLOR, *Temptation of Hassan Ben Khaled*. St. 4.

15
That is a sure place of rest from labor. (Requies ea certa laborum.)

VERGIL, *Æneid*. Bk. iii, l. 393.

God has given us this repose. (Deus nobis hæc otia fecit.)

VERGIL, *Eclogues*. No. 1, l. 6.

16
Rest, free from care, and a life without knowledge of deceit. (Secura quies, et nescia fallere vita.)

VERGIL, *Georgics*. Bk. ii, l. 467.

17
"Rest and be Thankful."

WORDSWORTH. Title of sonnet, quoted from an inscription on a stone seat at the head of Glencroe, in the Scottish highlands.

RESULTS, see Consequences

RESURRECTION, see Judgment Day

RETRIBUTION

See also Consequences, Punishment, Revenge

I—Retribution: Its Law

1
Eye for eye, tooth for tooth, hand for hand, foot for foot.

Old Testament: Deuteronomy, xix, 21.

Breach for breach, eye for eye, tooth for tooth: as he hath caused a blemish in a man, so shall it be done to him again.

Old Testament: Leviticus, xxiv, 20.

If a man destroy the eye of another man, they shall destroy his eye.

HAMMURABI, *King of Babylon, Code*. Sec. 196. (c. 2100 B.C.)

Ye have heard that it hath been said, An eye for an eye, and a tooth for a tooth: But I say unto you, That ye resist not evil: but whosoever shall smite thee on thy right cheek, turn to him the other also.

New Testament: Matthew, v, 38, 39.

2
Whoso sheddeth man's blood, by man shall his blood be shed.

Old Testament: Genesis, ix, 6.

It will have blood; they say, blood will have blood.

SHAKESPEARE, *Macbeth*. Act iii, sc. 5, l. 122.

Blood will have blood, revenge beget revenge,
Evil must come of evil.

SOUTHEY, *Madoc in Wales*. Pt. vii, l. 45.

3
My road shall be the road I made;
All that I gave shall be repaid.

JOHN MASEFIELD, *A Creed*.

4
And with what measure ye mete, it shall be measured to you again.

New Testament: Matthew, vii, 2.

II—Retribution: The Mills of the Gods

5
God's mill grinds slow but sure. (Ὀψὲ θεῶν ἀλέουσι μύλοι, ἀλέουσι δὲ λεπτά.)

Proverbiæ Cod. Coisl. No. 396. (GAISFORD, *Parœmiologia Græca*, 164.)

6
God's mill grinds slow, but sure.

GEORGE HERBERT, *Jacula Prudentum*.

God's mills grind slow,
But they grind woe.

WILLIAM R. ALGER, *Poetry of the Orient: Delayed Retribution*.

7
Though the mills of God grind slowly, yet they grind exceeding small;
Though with patience he stands waiting, with exactness grinds he all.

FRIEDRICH VON LOGAU, *Sinngedichte*. (Longfellow, tr. *Poetic Aphorisms: Retribution*.)

8
The mill of God grinds late, but grinds to powder.

R. C. TRENCH, *Proverbs*, 140.

Kabira wept when he beheld the millstone roll;
Of that which passes 'twixt the stones, nought goes forth whole.

UNKNOWN, *The Bag-o-Behar*. (Eastwick, tr.)

III—Retribution: Its Certainty

See also Justice: Its Certainty; Punishment: Its Certainty

9
There never yet was human power
Which could evade, if unforgiven,
The patient search and vigil long
Of him who treasures up a wrong.

BYRON, *Mazeppa*. Sec. 10.

10
His Martinmas comes to every pig.

CERVANTES, *Don Quixote*. Pt. ii, ch. 62. In Spain, pigs are usually killed on St. Martin's Day.

11
Whatever any one desires from another, the same returns upon himself.

EMERSON, *Uncollected Lectures: Natural Religion*.

12
The ways of the gods are slow, but mighty at last to fulfil. (Χρόνια μὲν τὰ τῶν θεῶν πως, εἰς τέλος δ' οὐκ ἀσθενῆ.)

EURIPIDES, *Ion*, l. 1615. (*Oracula Sibyllina*, viii, 14.)

Vengeance comes not slowly either upon you or any other wicked man, but steals silently and imperceptibly, placing its foot on the bad.

EURIPIDES, *Fragment*.

God does not pay at the end of every week, but He pays.

ANNE OF AUSTRIA. To Cardinal Mazarin.

Jupiter is slow looking into his note-book, but he always looks.

ZENOBIUS, *Sententiæ*. Cent. iv, No. 11.

13
So comes a reck'ning when the banquet's o'er,
The dreadful reck'ning, and men smile no more.

JOHN GAY, *The What D'ye Call It*. Act ii, sc. 9.

14
Rarely does Retribution, albeit of halting gait, fail to overtake the guilty, though he gain the start. (Raro antecedentem scelestum Deseruit pede Poena claudo.)

HORACE, *Odes*. Bk. iii, ode 2, l. 31.

And though the villain 'scape awhile he feels
Slow vengeance, like a bloodhound at his heels.

HORACE, *Odes*, iii, 2, 31. (Swift, tr.)

15
The wrath of the gods may be great, but it assuredly is slow. (Ut sit magna, tamen certe lenta ira deorum est.)

JUVENAL, *Satires*. Sat. xiii, l. 100.

16
And will not Jupiter call upon himself, think you? Do you imagine that he has condoned everything because, when it thunders, the sacred fire rends in twain an oak tree rather than you and your house?

PERSIUS, *Satires*. Sat. ii, l. 23.

All who bring to court false cases supported by false witnesses, all who before the magistrate deny on oath their honest debts, them we note and take their names to Jove. Day by day He knows who they be that do seek evil here on earth. When the wicked here expect to win their suits by perjury, or press false claims before the judge, the case adjudged is adjudged again by Him. And the fine He fines them far exceeds their gains in courts of law.

PLAUTUS, *Rudens: Prologue*, l. 13.

Ah, wretch! even though one may at first conceal his perjuries, yet retribution creeps on, though late, with noiseless step. (Ah, miser! et si quis primo perjuria celat, Sera tamen tacitis Poena venit pedibus.)

TIBULLUS, *Odes*. Bk. i, ode 9, l. 3.

The divine wrath is slow indeed in vengeance but it makes up for its tardiness by the severity of the punishment. (Lento quidem gradu ad vindictam divina procedit ira, sed tarditatem supplicii gravitate compensat.)

VALERIUS MAXIMUS, *Annals*. Bk. i, ch. 1, sec. 3.

And though circuitous and obscure
The feet of Nemesis, how sure!

WILLIAM WATSON, *Europe at the Play*.

1
It is advantageous that the gods should be believed to attend to the affairs of man; and the punishment for evil deeds, though sometimes late, is never fruitless.

PLINY THE ELDER, *Historia Naturalis*. Bk. ii, ch. 5, sec. 10.

2
The speech that suggested itself was said to be that which the phantom of Cleonice dinned into the ears of the tyrant who murdered her—"Tu cole justitiam; teque atque alios manet ultor."

SCOTT, *Count Robert of Paris*. Ch. 24. Reply of Agelastes to one of the men of Alexius Comnenus, Emperor of Greece. (Do thou cultivate justice: for thee and for others there remains an avenger.—OVID, *Metamorphoses*.)

3
After your fling
Watch for the sting.

UNKNOWN. (BRIDGE, *Cheshire Proverbs*, 7.)

IV—Retribution: As Ye Sow, So Shall Ye Reap

4
As you sow y' are like to reap.

BUTLER, *Hudibras*. Pt. ii, canto 2, l. 504.

5
All the children of men, as they sow in sorsow, so afterwards they reap, they bring forth for death.

CYNEWULF, *Christ*, l. 84. (8th century.)

6
He that sows iniquity shall reap sorrow.

THOMAS FULLER, *Gnomologia*. No. 2306.

7
Whatsoever a man soweth, that shall he also reap.

New Testament: Galatians, vi, 7.

8
They have sown the wind, and they shall reap the whirlwind.

Old Testament: Hosea, viii, 7.

Sowing the wind to reap the whirlwind.

SCOTT, *Black Dwarf*. Ch. 18.

9
As he brews, so shall he drink.

BEN JONSON, *Every Man in His Humour*. Act ii, sc. 1.

And who so wicked ale breweth,
Full oft he must the worse drink.

JOHN GOWER, *Confessio Amantis*. Pt. iii.

Let her brew as she has baked.

PEPYS, *Diary*, 15 Aug., 1664.

As they bake they shall brew,
Old Nick and his crew.

DAVID GARRICK, *May-Day*. Sc. 2.

"As they bake, so they will brew," philosophized Mr. Challis.

DE MORGAN, *It Never Can Happen Again*. Ch. 5.

10
He that plants thorns must never expect to gather roses.

PILPAY, *Fables: The Ignorant Physician*.

11
As you have sown, so also shall you reap. (Ut sementem feceris, ita et metes.)

PINARIUS RUFUS. (CICERO, *De Oratore*. Bk. ii, sec. 65.)

Such as ye have sown must ye needs reap.

JOHN LYDGATE, *Assembly of Gods*, 37. (c. 1420)

12
Sow'd cockle reap'd no corn.

SHAKESPEARE, *Love's Labour's Lost*. Act iv, sc. 3, l. 383.

13
Men must reap the things they sow,
Force from force must ever flow.

SHELLEY, *Lines Written Among the Euganean Hills*, l. 231.

14
The Fates are just; they give us but our own;
Nemesis ripens what our hands have sown.

WHITTIER, *To a Southern Statesman*. Addressed to John C. Calhoun in 1846.

V—Retribution: Hoist With His Own Petard

15
Let the smith who made them wear
The shackles which he did prepare.
(Compedes, quas ipse fecit, ipsus ut gestet faber.)

AUSONIUS, *De Bissula: Præfatio*, l. 6.

16
The thorns which I have reap'd are of the tree
I planted; they have torn me, and I bleed.
I should have known what fruit would spring from such a seed.

BYRON, *Childe Harold*. Canto iv, st. 10.

1 'Twas thine own genius gave the final blow,
And help'd to plant the wound that laid thee low:
So the struck eagle, stretch'd upon the plain,
No more through rolling clouds to soar again,
View'd his own feather on the fatal dart,
And wing'd the shaft that quiver'd in his heart.

BYRON, *English Bards and Scotch Reviewers*, l. 839. Referring to the death of Henry Kirke White. *See also under* EAGLE.

2 Remember Milo's end,
Wedged in that timber which he strove to rend.

DILLON, *Essay on Translated Verse*, l. 87.

3 Once in an age the biter should be bit.

THOMAS D'URFEY, *Richmond Heiress: Epilogue*.

I think she merits equal praise
That has the wit to bite the biter.

WARD, *Nuptial Dialogues*. Pt. ii, l. 179.

The greatest sharp some day will find another sharper wit;
It always makes the Devil laugh to see a biter bit.

C. G. LELAND, *El Capitan-General*.

4 He that diggeth a pit shall fall into it.

Old Testament: Ecclesiastes, x, 8.

Whoso diggeth a pit shall fall therein; and he that rolleth a stone, it will return upon him.

Old Testament: Proverbs, xxvi, 27.

He made a pit and digged it, and is fallen into the ditch which he made.

Old Testament: Psalms, vii, 15.

The heathen are sunk into the pit that they made: in the net which they hid is their own foot taken.

Old Testament: Psalms, ix, 15.

Our enemies have beat us to the pit.

SHAKESPEARE, *Julius Cæsar*. Act v, sc. 5, l. 23.

5 Nemesis is that recoil of Nature, not to be guarded against, which ever surprises the most wary transgressor.

EMERSON, *Journals*, 1864.

Nothing which we don't invite.

EMERSON, *Uncollected Lectures: Natural Religion*.

6 The camel set out to get him horns, and was shorn of his ears. (Camelus desiderans cornua etiam aures predidit.)

ERASMUS, *Adagia*. A free translation of a Greek proverb from Apostolius, ix, 8, 43.

Many go out for wool, and come home shorn.

CERVANTES, *Don Quixote*. Pt. ii, ch. 37.

If such as came for wool, sir, went home shorn,
Where is the wrong I did them?

ROBERT BROWNING, *Mr. Sludge "The Medium."*

7 'Twas he
Gave heat unto the injury, which returned
Like a petard ill lighted, into the bosom
Of him gave fire to it.

JOHN FLETCHER, *Fair Maid of the Inn*. Act ii.

8 Evil planned harms the plotter most. (Ἡ δὲ κακὴ βουλὴ τῷ βουλεύσαντι κακίστη.)

HESIOD, *Works and Days*, l. 266.

9 To be left alone
And face to face with my own crime, had been
Just retribution.

LONGFELLOW, *The Masque of Pandora*. Pt. viii.

10 Let them fall into the snare which they have laid. (In laqueos quos posuere, cadant.)

OVID, *Ars Amatoria*. Bk. i, l. 646.

There is no juster law than that the contrivers of death should perish by their own contrivances. (Neque enim lex æquior ulla est, Quam necis artifices arte perire sus.)

OVID, *Ars Amatoria*. Bk. i, l. 655.

11 Would that I had not; but my fate drew me on to be clever to my own hurt. (Non equidem vellem; sed me mea fata trahebant; Inque meas poenas ingeniosus eram.)

OVID, *Tristia*. Bk. ii, l. 341.

12 Those who plot the destruction of others often fall themselves. (Sæpe intereunt aliis meditantes necem.)

PHÆDRUS, *Fables: Appendix*. Fab. vi, l. 11.

13 We are paid in our own coin. (Dedi malum, et accepi.)

PLINY THE YOUNGER, *Epistles*. Bk. iii, epis. 9.

14 Misdeeds often return to their author. (Sæpe in magistrum scelera redierunt sua.)

SENECA, *Thyestes*, l. 311.

15 For 'tis the sport to have the enginer
Hoist with his own petar.

SHAKESPEARE, *Hamlet*. Act iii, sc. 4, l. 206. A petard was an iron canister filled with gunpowder, used for blowing up gates and barricades in time of war. There was always danger that the engineer who fired the petard would be blown up by it.

16 Why, as a woodcock to mine own springe, Osric;
I am justly kill'd with mine own treachery.

SHAKESPEARE, *Hamlet*. Act v, sc. 2, l. 317.

In seeking tales and informations
Against this man, whose honesty the devil
And his disciples only envy at,
Ye blew the fire that burns ye.

SHAKESPEARE, *Henry VIII*. Act v, sc. 3, l. 110.

17 We but teach
Bloody instructions, which, being taught, return
To plague the inventor: this even-handed justice
Commends the ingredients of our poison'd chalice
To our own lips.

SHAKESPEARE, *Macbeth*. Act i, sc. 7, l. 8.

She hath eaten up all her beef, and she is herself in the tub.
SHAKESPEARE, *Measure for Measure*, iii, 2, 58.

1
Those who inflict must suffer, for they see
The work of their own hearts, and this must be
Our chastisement or recompense.
SHELLEY, *Julian and Maddalo*, l. 482.

2
With his own sword I cut his throat. (Suo sibi gladio hunc jugulo.)
TERENCE, *Adelphi*, l. 958. (Act v, sc. 8.)

He that first made the gin should handsell it.
JOHN TATHAM, *The Scots Figgaries*. Act ii. (1652)

He that invented the Maiden first hanselled it.
JOHN KELLY, *Scottish Proverbs*, 140. Referring to the Regent Morton, inventor of "the maiden," a sort of guillotine, of which he was the first victim.

3
You have mixed the mess, and you must eat it up. (Tute hoc intristi; tibi omnest exedendum.)
TERENCE, *Phormio*, l. 318. (Act ii, sc. 2.)

The wine is poured, it must be drunk. (Le vin est versé, il faut le boire.)
ARMAND JOSEPH DE CHAROST. To Louis XIV, at the siege of Douai, in 1667, as the king attempted to retire from the firing line. (TRENCH, *Proverbs and Their Lessons*, ii, 43.)

4
But as some muskets so contrive it
As oft to miss the mark they drive at,
And though well aimed at duck or plover
Bear wide, and kick their owners over.
JOHN TRUMBULL, *McFingal*. Canto i, l. 95.

5
Beat by hot hail, and wet with bloody rain,
The myriad-handed pioneer may pour,
And the wild West with the roused North combine
To heave the engineer of evil with his mine.
WHITTIER, *To a Southern Statesman*.

6
Every man's judgment returns to his own door.
UNKNOWN, *Proverbs of Alfred*. A 84. (c. 1275)

REVELRY, see Feast and Festival

REVENGE

See also Punishment; Retribution; Woman: A Woman's Vengeance

I—Revenge: Definitions

7
Revenge is a kind of wild justice; which the more man's nature runs to, the more ought law to weed it out.
BACON, *Essays: Of Revenge*.

8
Vengeance is not cured by another vengeance, nor a wrong by another wrong; but each increaseth and aggreggeth the other.
CHAUCER, *Melibeus*. Sec. 31, l. 2475.

9
The noblest vengeance is to forgive.
H. G. BOHN, *Hand-Book of Proverbs*, p. 512.

To forget a wrong is the best revenge.
JOHN RAY, *English Proverbs*, 92.

'Tis more noble to forgive, and more manly to despise, than to revenge an Injury.
BENJAMIN FRANKLIN, *Poor Richard*, 1752.

Forgiveness and a smile is the best revenge.
SAMUEL PALMER, *Essays on Proverbs*, 81.

To revenge is no valour, but to bear.
SHAKESPEARE, *Timon of Athens*. Act iii, 5, 39

Living well is the best revenge.
GEORGE HERBERT, *Jacula Prudentum*. No. 520.

11
Vengeance is mine; I will repay, saith the Lord. Therefore if thine enemy hunger, feed him; if he thirst, give him drink: for in so doing thou shalt heap coals of fire on his head.
New Testament: Romans, xii, 19, 20. The last phrase is quoted from *Proverbs*, xxv, 22.

Vengeance is a morsel for God. (Vendetta, boccon di Dio.)
UNKNOWN. An Italian proverb. (See TRENCH, *Proverbs and Their Lessons*, iii, 55.)

Vengeance to God alone belongs;
But, when I think on all my wrongs,
My blood is liquid flame!
SCOTT, *Marmion*. Canto vi, st. 7.

12
Call it not
Revenge! thus sanctified and thus sublimed,
'Tis duty, 'tis devotion.
ROBERT SOUTHEY, *Roderick*. Pt. iii, l. 397.

There are things
Which make revenge a virtue by reflection,
And not an impulse of mere anger.
BYRON, *Marino Faliero*. Act iv, sc. 2.

Souls made of fire, and children of the sun,
With whom revenge is virtue.
YOUNG, *The Revenge*. Act v, sc. 2.

II—Revenge: Apothegms

13
Revenge in person's certainly no virtue,
But then 'tis not *my* fault if *others* hurt you.
BYRON, *Don Juan*. Canto i, st. 30.

14
He meditates revenge who least complains.
DRYDEN, *Absalom and Achitophel*. Pt. i, l. 446.

15
Revenge is profitable, gratitude is expensive.
EDWARD GIBBON, *Decline and Fall of the Roman Empire*. Ch. 11.

16
Have ye him on the hip.
JOHN HEYWOOD, *Proverbs*. Pt ii, ch. 5. (1546)

In fine he doth apply one special drift
Which was to get the pagan on the hip.
SIR JOHN HARINGTON, *Orlando Furioso*. Bk. xlvi, l. 117. (1591)

If I can catch him once upon the hip,
I will feed fat the ancient grudge I bear him.
SHAKESPEARE, *The Merchant of Venice*. Act i, sc. 3, l. 47. (1596)

Now, infidel, I have you on the hip.
SHAKESPEARE, *The Merchant of Venice*. Act iv, sc. 1, l. 334.

I'll have our Michael Cassio on the hip.
SHAKESPEARE, *Othello*. Act ii, sc. 1, l. 314. (1604)

1
T' avenge a private, not a public wrong.
HOMER, *Iliad*. Bk. i, l. 208. (Pope, tr.)

2
Behold, on wrong Swift vengeance waits.
HOMER, *Odyssey*. Bk. viii, l. 367. (Pope, tr.)

Long trains of ill may pass unheeded, dumb,
But vengeance is behind, and justice is to come.
THOMAS CAMPBELL, *Stanzas to the Memory of the Spanish Patriots*, l. 44.

A growing dread of vengeance at his heels.
COWPER, *Truth*, l. 258.

Vengeance, though it comes with leaden feet, strikes with iron hands.
RICHARDSON, *Clarissa Harlowe*, iv, 120.

See also RETRIBUTION: ITS CERTAINTY.

3
Now Vengeance has a brood of eggs,
But Patience must be hen.
GEORGE MEREDITH, *Archduchess Anne*. St. 12.

4
Which, if not victory, is yet revenge.
MILTON, *Paradise Lost*. Bk. ii, l. 105.

5
A brave revenge Ne'er comes too late.
THOMAS OTWAY, *Venice Preserved*. Act iii, sc. 2.

6
Vengeance lies open to patient craft. (Vindicta docili quia patet sollertiæ.)
PHÆDRUS, *Fables*. Bk. i, fab. 28, l. 2.

My vengeance is easy. (Facilis vindicta est mihi.)
PHÆDRUS, *Fables*. Bk. i, fab. 29, l. 10.

7
Tit for tat. (Par pari respondet.)
PLAUTUS, *Truculentus*. Act ii, l. 47; JOHN HEYWOOD, *Proverbs*. Pt. ii, ch. 4.

To give a Rowland for an Oliver.
EDWARD HALL, *Chronicles*, 266. (1548)

See also under PROVERBS.

8
Revenge is an inhuman word. (Inhumanum verbum est ultio.)
SENECA, *De Ira*. Bk. ii, sec. 31.

Revenge is a confession of pain. (Ultio doloris confessio.)
SENECA, *De Ira*. Bk. iii, sec. 5.

9
Let's make us medicines of our great revenge,
To cure this deadly grief.
SHAKESPEARE, *Macbeth*. Act iv, sc. 3, l. 214.

10
Can vengeance be pursued further than death?
SHAKESPEARE, *Romeo and Juliet*. Act v, sc. 3, l. 55.

Vile is the vengeance on the ashes cold,
And envy base, to bark at sleeping fame.
SPENSER, *Faerie Queene*. Bk. ii, canto 8, st. 13.

11
Thus the whirligig of time brings in his revenges.
SHAKESPEARE, *Twelfth Night*. Act v, sc. 1, l. 385.

The wheel is come full circle.
SHAKESPEARE, *King Lear*. Act v, sc. 3, l. 174.

12
The Christless code
That must have life for a blow.
TENNYSON, *Maud*. Pt. ii, sec. 1, st. 1.

See also RETRIBUTION: ITS LAW.

13
Arise from my ashes, unknown avenger! (Exoriare, aliquis nostris ex ossibus ultor.)
VERGIL, *Æneid*. Bk. iv, l. 625. The dying imprecation of Dido upon the false Æneas. Said to have been written on the wall of his dungeon by Philip Strozzi, before killing himself, when imprisoned by Cosmo I, Grand Duke of Tuscany.

III—Revenge: Its Sweetness

14
I love a dire revenge:
Give me the man that will all others kill,
And last himself.
BEAUMONT AND FLETCHER, *The Little French Lawyer*. Act iv, sc. 1.

15
Too many there be to whom a dead enemy smells well, and who find musk and amber in revenge.
SIR THOMAS BROWNE, *Christian Morals*. Pt. iii, sec. 12. *See also under* ENEMY.

16
Revenge is a luscious fruit which you must leave to ripen.
ÉMILE GABORIAU, *File 113*. Ch. 10.

17
'Tis sweet to love; but when with scorn we meet,
Revenge supplies the loss with joys as great.
GEORGE GRANVILLE, *British Enchanters*. Act v, sc. 1.

18
It [revenge] is sweeter far than flowing honey. (*Ὅς τε πολὺ γλυκίων μέλιτος καταλειβομένοιο.*)
HOMER, *Iliad*. Bk. xviii, l. 109.

"Vengeance is good, sweeter than life itself." Yes; so say the ignorant. (At vindicta bonum vita jucundius ipsa. Nempe hoc indocti.)
JUVENAL, *Satires*. Sat. xiii, l. 180.

19
Though sweet are our friendships, our hopes, our affections,
Revenge on a tyrant is sweetest of all.
THOMAS MOORE, *Avenging and Bright*.

20
Vengeance is sweet.
WILLIAM PAINTER, *Palace of Pleasure*, ii, 35. (1566)

O revenge, how sweet thou art!
BEN JONSON, *The Silent Woman*. Act iv, sc. 5. (1609)

It is a devilish phrase in the mouth of men,
That revenge is sweet.
UNKNOWN, *Whole Duty of Man: Sunday*, 16. (1658)

1
To be revenged on an enemy is to obtain a second life. (Inimicum ulcisci vitam accipere est alteram.)
PUBLILIUS SYRUS, *Sententiæ*. No. 270.

IV—Revenge: Its Folly

2
A man that studieth revenge keeps his own wounds green, which otherwise would heal and do well.
BACON, *Essays: Of Revenge.*

3
No animal revenge,
No brute-like punishment of bad by worse.
ROBERT BROWNING, *Luria*. Act iv.

4
An act by which we make one friend and one enemy is a losing game; because revenge is a much stronger principle than gratitude.
C. C. COLTON, *Lacon*. Vol. i, No. 98.

5
Revenge proves its own executioner.
JOHN FORD, *The Broken Heart*. Act v, sc. 2.

6
There's small revenge in words, but words may be greatly revenged.
BENJAMIN FRANKLIN, *Poor Richard*, 1735.

7
He that will venge every wrath,
The longer he liveth the less he hath.
HILLS, *Commonplace-Book*, p. 140. (c. 1495)

Had I revenged been of every harm,
My coat had never kept me half so warm.
GEORGE GASCOIGNE, *Posies*, p. 147. (1575)

If I had revenged all wrong,
I had not worn my skirts so long.
JOHN RAY, *English Proverbs*, p. 136.

8
Revenge, that thirsty dropsy of our souls,
Which makes us covet that which hurts us most,
Is not alone sweet, but partakes of tartness.
MASSINGER, *A Very Woman*. Act iv, sc. 2.

9
Revenge, at first though sweet,
Bitter ere long back on itself recoils.
MILTON, *Paradise Lost*. Bk. ix, l. 171.

10
It is foolish to wish to be avenged on your neighbor by setting his house on fire. (Stultum est vicinum velle ulcisci incendio.)
PUBLILIUS SYRUS, *Sententiæ*. No. 659.

11
Murder's out of tune,
And sweet revenge grows harsh.
SHAKESPEARE, *Othello*. Act v, sc. 2, l. 115.

12
It costs more to revenge injuries than to bear them.
BISHOP THOMAS WILSON, *Maxims*. No. 303.

V—Revenge: Threats of Revenge

13
Revenge is now the cud that I do chew.
BEAUMONT AND FLETCHER, *Queen of Corinth*. Act iv, sc. 1.

14
I am accustomed to pay men back in their own coin. (Ich bin gewohnt in der Münze wiederzuzahlen in der man mich bezahlt.)
BISMARCK, *Speech*, to the Ultramontanes, 1870.
See also under PAYMENT.

15
Vengeance, deep-brooding o'er the slain,
Had locked the source of softer woe,
And burning pride and high disdain
Forbade the rising tear to flow.
SCOTT, *The Lay of the Last Minstrel*. Canto i, st. 9.

16
By this leek, I will most horribly revenge.
SHAKESPEARE, *Henry V*. Act v, sc. 1, l. 49.

I will have such revenges on you both
That all the world shall——I will do such things,
What they are, yet I know not; but they shall be
The terrors of the earth.
SHAKESPEARE, *King Lear*. Act ii, sc. 4, l. 282.

17
If a Jew wrong a Christian, what is his humility? Revenge. If a Christian wrong a Jew, what should his sufferance be by Christian example? Why, revenge. The villany you teach me, I will execute, and it shall go hard but I will better the instruction.
SHAKESPEARE, *The Merchant of Venice*. Act iii, sc. 1, l. 71.

If it will feed nothing else, it will feed my revenge.
SHAKESPEARE, *The Merchant of Venice*. Act iii, sc. 1, l. 56.

18
O, that the slave had forty thousand lives!
One is too poor, too weak for my revenge
SHAKESPEARE, *Othello*. Act iii, sc. 3, l. 442.

Had all his hairs been lives, my great revenge
Had stomach for them all.
SHAKESPEARE, *Othello*. Act v, sc. 2, l. 74.

19
Like to the Pontic sea,
Whose icy current and compulsive course
Ne'er feels retiring ebb, but keeps due on
To the Propontic and the Hellespont,
Even so my bloody thoughts, with violent pace,
Shall ne'er look back, ne'er ebb to humble love,
Till that a capable and wide revenge
Swallow them up.
SHAKESPEARE, *Othello*. Act iii, sc. 3, l. 453.

Vengeance is in my heart, death in my hand,
Blood and revenge are hammering in my head.
SHAKESPEARE, *Titus Andronicus*. Act ii, sc. 3, l. 38.

20
Material for future hatred, which he stores up in his heart, to bring it out augmented in bitterness. (Odia in longum jaciens, quæ reconderet, auctaque promeret.)
TACITUS, *Annals*. Bk. i, sec. 69.

REVOLUTION

See also Rebellion

1
Revolutions are not about trifles, but spring from trifles.

ARISTOTLE, *Politica*. Bk. v, ch. 3, sec. 1.

2
The surest way to prevent seditions, if the times do bear it, is to take away the matter of them.

FRANCIS BACON, *Essays: Of Seditions and Troubles.*

3
A reform is a correction of abuses; a revolution is a transfer of power.

EDWARD BULWER-LYTTON, *Speech,* House of Commons, on the Reform Bill of 1866.

4
Forgive me. Some women bear children in strength,
And bite back the cry of their pain in self-scorn;
But the birth-pangs of nations will wring us at length
Into wail such as this—and we sit on forlorn
When the man-child is born.

E. B. BROWNING, *Mother and Poet.*

5
Every revolution contains in it something of evil.

EDMUND BURKE, *An Appeal from the New to the Old Whigs.*

6
The first step to empire is revolution, by which power is conferred.

EDMUND BURKE, *Impeachment of Warren Hastings,* 16 Feb., 1788.

7
Do you suppose, then, that revolutions are made with rose-water? (Voulez-vous, donc, qu'on vous fasse des révolutions à l'eau-rose?)

SEBASTIEN CHAMFORT, *Retort,* to Marmontel, who deplored the excesses of the French Revolution. (MARMONTEL, *Mémoires d'un Père*. Bk. xiv.)

Revolutions are not made with rose-water.

BULWER-LYTTON, *The Parisians*. Bk. v, ch. 7.

8
An oppressed people are authorized, whenever they can, to rise and break their fetters.

HENRY CLAY, *Speech,* House of Representatives, 24 March, 1818.

If by the mere force of numbers a majority should deprive a minority of any clearly written constitutional right, it might, in a moral point of view, justify revolution—certainly would if such a right were a vital one.

LINCOLN, *First Inaugural Address,* 4 March, 1861.

9
Longing not so much to change things as to overturn them. (Non tam commutandarum, quam evertendarum rerum cupidos.)

CICERO, *De Officiis*. Bk. ii, ch. 1, sec. 3.

10
I have ever been of opinion that revolutions are not to be evaded.

BENJAMIN DISRAELI, *Coningsby*. Bk. iv, ch. 11.

11
Every revolution was first a thought in one man's mind.

EMERSON, *Essays, First Series: History.*

Every man carries a revolution in his waist-coat pocket.

R. W. EMERSON. Referring to the inhabitants of Boston.

12
The worst of revolutions is a restoration. . . . The people of England, in my opinion, committed a worse offense by the unconstitutional restoration of Charles II than even by the death of Charles I.

CHARLES JAMES FOX, *Speech,* House of Commons, 10 Dec., 1795.

13
I am the signet which marks the page where the revolution has been stopped; but when I die it will turn the page and resume its course. (Je suis le signet qui marque la page où la révolution s'est arrêtée; mais quand je serai mort, elle tournera le feuillet et reprendra sa marche.)

NAPOLEON BONAPARTE, *Remark,* to Count Molé.

14
Revolutions are not made: they come. A revolution is as natural a growth as an oak. It comes out of the past. Its foundations are laid far back.

WENDELL PHILLIPS, *Speech,* at Boston, to the Anti-Slavery Society, 28 Jan., 1852.

Insurrection of thought always precedes insurrection of arms.

WENDELL PHILLIPS, *Speech,* 1 Nov., 1859.

15
Sire, it is not a revolt,—it is a revolution. (Mon sire, ce n'est pas une révolte,—c'est une révolution.)

DUC DE ROCHEFOUCAULD-LIANCOURT, to Louis XVI, King of France, on the evening of 14 July, 1789, after the fall of the Bastille. He had hastened to Versailles to apprise the king of the event, and the King had exclaimed, "Mais, c'est une révolte!" (CARLYLE, *French Revolution*. Pt. i, bk. 5, ch. 7.)

16
I know and all the world knows, that revolutions never go backwards.

WILLIAM HENRY SEWARD, *Speech: The Irrepressible Conflict,* Oct., 1858.

Revolutions never go backward.

WENDELL PHILLIPS, *Speech: Progress,* 17 Feb., 1861.

17
Revolutions have never lightened the burden

of tyranny: they have only shifted it to another shoulder.
BERNARD SHAW, *Revolutionist's Handbook: Preface.*

The effect of every revolt is merely to make the bonds galling.
H. L. MENCKEN, *Prejudices.* Ser. ii, p. 245.

We all think that Mr. Roosevelt is only the Kerensky of this revolution.
WILLIAM ALBERT WIRT, quoting, so he claimed, an unnamed "brain-truster" before the Interstate Commerce Committee of the House of Representatives, 23 March, 1934.

1
Repression is the seed of revolution.
DANIEL WEBSTER, *Speech,* 1845.

REWARD

I—Reward: Definitions and Apothegms

2
Let a man contend to the uttermost
For his life's set prize, be it what it will!
ROBERT BROWNING, *The Statue and the Bust.*

3
'Tis an old lesson; Time approves it true,
And those who know it best, deplore it most;
When all is won that all desire to woo,
The paltry prize is hardly worth the cost.
BYRON, *Childe Harold.* Canto ii, st. 35.

The prize is not without dust. (Palma non sine pulvere.)
UNKNOWN. A Latin proverb.
See also under PALM.

4
The "wages" of every noble work do yet lie in Heaven or else nowhere.
CARLYLE, *Past and Present.* Bk. iii, ch. 12.

For blessings ever wait on virtuous deeds;
And though a late, a sure reward succeeds.
WILLIAM CONGREVE, *The Mourning Bride.* Act v. Concluding lines.

5
The reward of one duty is the power to fulfil another.
GEORGE ELIOT, *Daniel Deronda.* Bk. vi, ch. 46.

7
'Tis toil's reward, that sweetens industry,
As love inspires with strength the enraptur'd thrush.
EBENEZER ELLIOT, *Corn Law Rhymes.* No. 7.

6
The labourer is worthy of his reward.
New Testament: I Timothy, v, 18. *See also under* LABOR.

8
What is vulgar, and the essence of all vulgarity, but the avarice of reward? 'Tis the difference of artisan and artist, of talent and genius, of sinner and saint. The man whose eyes are nailed, not on the nature of his act, but on the wages, whether it be money, or office, or fame, is almost equally low.
EMERSON, *Conduct of Life: Worship.*

9
Service without reward is punishment.
GEORGE HERBERT, *Jacula Prudentum.*

10
Those sweet rewards, which decorate the brave,
'Tis folly to decline.
SAMUEL JOHNSON, *Lines Added to an Ode by Sir William Jones.*

11
Give, I pray, a reward worthy of my genius. (Da, precor, ingenio præmia digna meo.)
OVID, *Tristia.* Bk. iii, eleg. 11, l. 50.

12
The reward of a thing rightly done is to have done it. (Recte facti fecisse merces est.)
SENECA, *Epistulæ ad Lucilium.* Epis. 81, sec. 20.

The reward of a thing well done is to have done it.
EMERSON, *Essays: New England Reformers.*

The reward of well-doing is the doing, and the fruit of our duty is our duty.
MONTAIGNE, *Essays.* Bk. ii, ch. 16.

The reward for a good deed is to have done it.
ELBERT HUBBARD, *The Philistine,* xx, 139.

[He] rewards His deeds with doing them.
SHAKESPEARE, *Coriolanus.* Act ii, sc. 2, l. 131.

A generous action is its own reward.
WILLIAM WALSH, *Upon Quitting His Mistress.*
See also VIRTUE: ITS REWARDS.

13
Who would run, that's moderately wise,
A certain danger for a doubtful prize?
JOHN POMFRET, *Love Triumphant,* l. 85.

14
Is there no bright reversion in the sky
For those who greatly think, or bravely die?
POPE, *Elegy to an Unfortunate Lady,* l. 9.

15
Of old those met rewards who could excel,
And such were prais'd who but endeavour'd well;
Tho' triumphs were to gen'rals only due,
Crowns were reserv'd to grace the soldiers too.
POPE, *Essay on Criticism.* Pt. ii, l. 310.

Rewards, that either would to Virtue bring
No joy, or be destructive of the thing:
How oft by these at sixty are undone
The virtues of a saint at twenty-one!
POPE, *Essay on Man.* Epis. iv, l. 181.

16
Desert and reward, I can assure her, seldom keep company.
RICHARDSON, *Clarissa Harlowe,* iv, 120.

17
In that day's feats, . . .
He prov'd best man i' the field, and for his meed
Was brow-bound with the oak.
SHAKESPEARE, *Coriolanus.* Act ii, sc. 2, l. 99.

18
I never knew yet but rebuke and check was the reward of valour.
SHAKESPEARE, *II Henry IV.* Act iv, sc. 3, l. 35.

1
There is tears for his love; joy for his fortune; honour for his valour; and death for his ambition.

SHAKESPEARE, *Julius Cæsar*. Act iii, sc. 2, l. 30.

Learning to the Studious; Riches to the Careful; Power to the Bold; Heaven to the Virtuous.

BENJAMIN FRANKLIN, *Poor Richard*, 1754.

2
Preferment goes by letter and affection.

SHAKESPEARE, *Othello*. Act i, sc. 1, l. 36.

3
I give thee thanks in part of thy deserts,
And will with deeds requite thy gentleness.

SHAKESPEARE, *Titus Andronicus*. Act i, sc. 1, l. 236.

4
Through long-lived pressure of obscure distress,
Still to be strenuous for the bright reward.

WORDSWORTH, *Sonnet: To B. R. Haydon.*

5
A leather medal his reward should be,
A leather medal and an LL.D.

UNKNOWN, *Harvardina*, iii, 147.

II—Reward: The Goal, Not the Prize

6
Be it jewel or toy,
Not the prize gives the joy,
But the striving to win the prize.

BULWER-LYTTON, *The Boatman.*

7
Perhaps the reward of the spirit who tries
Is not the goal but the exercise.

EDMUND VANCE COOKE, *Prayer.*

8
The virtue lies
In the struggle, not the prize.

R. M. MILNES, *The World to the Soul.*

9
The deed is everything, the glory naught. (Die That ist alles, nichts der Ruhm.)

GOETHE, *Faust*. Pt. ii, act iv, sc. 1. (Bayard Taylor, tr.)

10
Not in rewards, but in the strength to strive,
The blessing lies.

J. T. TROWBRIDGE, *Twoscore and Ten.*

11
And set his heart upon the goal,
Not on the prize.

WILLIAM WATSON, *In Laleham Churchyard.* St. 11. A tribute to Matthew Arnold, published in the *Spectator*, 30 Aug., 1890.

RHETORIC, see Grammar

RHINE, THE

See also Germany

12
You shall never have it,
The free German Rhine.
(Sie sollen ihn nicht haben
Den freien, deutschen Rhein.)

BECKER, *Der Rhein*. Alfred de Musset wrote a *riposte, Nous l'avons eu, Votre Rhin Allemand* (We have had it, your German Rhine), which appeared in the *Athenæum*, 13 Aug., 1870.

13
Majestic Rhine, . . .
A blending of all beauties,—streams and dells,
Fruit, foliage, crag, wood, corn-field, mountain, vine,
And chiefless castles breathing stern farewells.

BYRON, *Childe Harold*. Canto iii, st. 46.

The castled crag of Drachenfels
Frowns o'er the wide and winding Rhine,
Whose breast of waters broadly swells
Between the banks which bear the vine;
And hills all rich with blossom'd trees,
And fields which promise corn and wine,
And scatter'd cities crowning these,
Whose far white walls along them shine.

BYRON, *Childe Harold*. Canto iii, st. 55, (1).

14
The lordly, lovely Rhine.

THOMAS CAMPBELL, *The Child and Hind*, l. 23.

15
On the Rhine, on the Rhine, there grow our vines. (Am Rhein, am Rhein, da wachsen uns're Reben.)

MATTHIAS CLAUDIUS, *Rheinweinlied.*

16
In Köhln, a town of monks and bones,
And pavements fang'd with murderous stones
And rags and hags, and hideous wenches;
I counted two and seventy stenches,
All well defined, and several stinks!
Ye Nymphs that reign o'er sewers and sinks,
The river Rhine, it is well known,
Doth wash your city of Cologne;
But tell me, Nymphs, what power divine
Shall henceforth wash the river Rhine?

COLERIDGE, *Cologne.*

17
The Rhine! the Rhine! a blessing on the Rhine!

LONGFELLOW, *Hyperion*. Bk. i, ch. 2.

Beneath me flows the Rhine, and, like the stream of Time, it flows amid the ruins of the Past.

LONGFELLOW, *Hyperion*. Bk. i, ch. 3.

18
The Rhine, the Rhine, the German Rhine!
Who guards today my stream divine?
(Zum Rhein, zum Rhein, zum deutschen Rhein!
Wer will des Stromes Hüter sein?)

MAX SCHNECKENBURGER, *Die Wacht am Rhein.*

RICHES

See also Gold; Mammon; Money; Possessions; Poverty and Riches

I—Riches: Definitions

19
I cannot call riches better than the baggage of virtue. The Roman word is better, *Impedimenta*. For as the baggage is to an army, so is riches to virtue. It cannot be spared, nor left behind, but it hindreth the march; yea, and

the care of it, sometimes, loseth or disturbeth the victory.

FRANCIS BACON, *Essays: Of Riches.*

For what are riches, empire, pow'r,
But larger means to gratify the will?

WILLIAM CONGREVE, *The Mourning Bride.* Act ii, sc. 9.

1
Surplus wealth is a sacred trust which its possessor is bound to administer in his lifetime for the good of the community.

ANDREW CARNEGIE, *The Gospel of Wealth.*

2
Communism is a hateful thing. . . . But the communism of combined wealth and capital . . . is not less dangerous than the communism of oppressed poverty and toil.

GROVER CLEVELAND, *Annual Message,* 1888.

3
Wealth is an application of mind to nature; and the art of getting rich consists not in industry, much less in saving, but in a better order, a timeliness, in being at the right spot.

EMERSON, *Conduct of Life: Wealth.*

It is the perpetual tendency of wealth to draw on the spiritual class, not in this coarse way, but in plausible and covert ways.

EMERSON, *Lectures and Biographical Sketches: The Man of Letters.*

4
The ideal social state is not that in which each gets an equal amount of wealth, but in which each gets in proportion to his contribution to the general stock.

HENRY GEORGE, *Social Problems.* Ch. 6.

5
It cannot be repeated too often that the safety of great wealth with us lies in obedience to the new version of the Old World axiom—*Richesse oblige.*

HOLMES, *A Mortal Antipathy: Introduction.*

6
Know from the bounteous heavens all riches flow;
And what man gives, the gods by man bestow.

HOMER, *Odyssey.* Bk. xviii, l. 26. (Broome, tr.)

7
It is great riches to a man to live sparingly with an even mind. (Divitiæ grandes homini sunt, vivere parce Æquo animo.)

LUCRETIUS, *De Rerum Natura.* Bk. v, l. 1117.
See also under MODERATION.

8
Riches, the incentives to evil, are dug out of the earth. (Effodiuntur opes, irritamenta malorum.)

OVID, *Metamorphoses.* Bk. i, l. 140.

9
Usefulness is value in the hands of the valiant. Wealth is the possession of the valuable by the valiant.

RUSKIN, *Ad Valorem.*

10
The people of this country are not jealous of fortunes, however great, which have been built up by the honest development of great enterprises, which have been actually earned by business energy and sagacity: they are jealous only of speculative wealth, of the wealth which has been piled up by no effort at all, but only by shrewd wits playing on the credulity of others. . . . This is "predatory wealth," and is found in stock markets.

WOODROW WILSON, *Address,* N. Y., 13 April, 1908.

It is almost as difficult to reconcile the principles of republican society with the existence of billionaires as of dukes.

THOMAS WENTWORTH HIGGINSON.

II—Riches: Apothegms

11
No man's fortune can be an end worthy of his being.

BACON, *Advancement of Learning.* Bk. ii.

12
The man who dies rich dies disgraced.

ANDREW CARNEGIE, *The Gospel of Wealth.*

The amassing of wealth is one of the worst species of idolatry, no idol more debasing.

ANDREW CARNEGIE, *Memorandum,* made in 1868, and found among his papers after his death.

Malefactors of great wealth.

THEODORE ROOSEVELT, *Speech,* Provincetown, Mass., 20 Aug., 1907.

13
As rich as Crœsus. (Superare Crassum divitiis.)

CICERO, *Epistulæ ad Atticum.* Bk. i, epis. 4, fin.

14
An Embarrassment of Riches. (Embarras de Richesse.)

D'ALLAINVAL, Title of comedy, 1726. Often quoted, "Embarass des richesses." Played at the Haymarket, London, in a translation by John Ozell, 9 Oct., 1738.

15
A rich man is an honest man, no thanks to him, for he would be a double knave to cheat mankind when he had no need of it.

DANIEL DEFOE, *Serious Reflections.*

16
Riches are gotten with pain, kept with care, and lost with grief.

THOMAS FULLER, *Gnomologia.* No. 4043.

17
The house laughs with silver. (Ridet argento domus.)

HORACE, *Odes.* Bk. iv, ode 11, l. 6.

Knowledge makes one laugh, but wealth makes one dance.

GEORGE HERBERT, *Jacula Prudentum.* No. 950.

18
If every man who wears a laced coat (that he can pay for) was extirpated, who would miss them?

SAMUEL JOHNSON, *Miscellanies.* Vol. i, p. 253.

19
I come to see what riches thou bearest in thy breeches.

BEN JONSON, *The Staple of News.* Act i, sc. 1.

1
Excess of wealth is cause of covetousness.

MARLOWE, *The Jew of Malta*. Act i, sc. 2.

See also under AVARICE.

2
I am rich beyond the dreams of avarice.

EDWARD MOORE, *The Gamester*. Act ii, sc. 2. (1753)

We are not here to sell a parcel of boilers and vats, but the potentiality of growing rich beyond the dreams of avarice.

SAMUEL JOHNSON, *Remark*, at the sale of Thrale's brewery. He was one of the executors of the estate, and at the sale, as Boswell says, was "bustling about like an excise-man." (BOSWELL, *Life*, 1781)

3
And all your fortune lies beneath your hat.

JOHN OLDHAM, *Lines to a Friend About to Leave the University*.

4
He heapeth up riches, and knoweth not who shall gather them.

Old Testament: Psalms, xxxix, 6.

5
No man was ever as rich as all men ought to be.

W. G. BENHAM, *Proverbs*, p. 816.

6
A golden bit does not make a better horse. (Non faciunt meliorem equum aurei freni.)

SENECA, *Epistulæ ad Lucilium*. Epis. xli, 6.

7
We must spurn riches, the diploma of slavery. (Spernendæ opes: auctoramenta sunt servitutum.)

SENECA, *Epistulæ ad Lucilium*. Epis. civ, 34.

Dare, my guest, to despise riches. (Aude, hospes, contemnere opes.)

VERGIL, *Æneid*. Bk. viii, l. 364.

8
Rich men without convictions are more dangerous in modern society than poor women without chastity.

BERNARD SHAW, *Plays, Pleasant and Unpleasant: Preface*.

9
He that is proud of riches is a fool. For if he be exalted above his neighbours because he hath more gold, how much inferior is he to a gold mine!

JEREMY TAYLOR, *Holy Living: Of Humility*.

10
Superfluous wealth can buy superfluities only. Money is not required to buy one necessary of the soul.

H. D. THOREAU, *Walden: Conclusion*.

11
A rich person ought to have a strong stomach.

WALT WHITMAN, *Collect*, p. 324.

III—Riches: Their Acquisition

12
He may love riches that wanteth them, as much as he that hath them.

RICHARD BAXTER, *Christian Ethics*.

13
The Gospel of Wealth advocates leaving free the operation of laws of accumulation.

ANDREW CARNEGIE, *The Gospel of Wealth: Advantages of Poverty*.

14
If the search for riches is sure to be successful, though I should become a groom with whip in hand to get them, I will do so. As the search may not be successful, I will follow after that which I love.

CONFUCIUS, *Analects*. Bk. vii, ch. 11. (EMERSON, *Letters and Social Aims: Social Aims*.)

15
There are only three ways by which any individual can get wealth—by work, by gift, or by theft. And, clearly, the reason why the workers get so little is that the beggars and thieves get so much.

HENRY GEORGE, *Social Problems*, p. 84.

16
Base wealth preferring to eternal praise.

HOMER, *Iliad*. Bk. xxiii, l. 368. (Pope, tr.)

The ungovernable passion for wealth. (Opum furiosa cupido.)

OVID, *Fasti*. Bk. i, l. 211.

17
He who wants riches, wants them at once. (Dives qui fieri vult, et cito vult fieri.)

JUVENAL, *Satires*. Sat. xiv, l. 176.

18
No just man ever became rich all at once. (Οὐθεὶς ἐπλούτησε ταχέως δίκαιος ὤν.)

MENANDER, *The Toady*, l. 42.

No good man ever became suddenly rich. (Repente dives nemo factus est bonus.)

PUBLILIUS SYRUS, *Sententiæ*. No. 643. Loeb.

19
If at great things thou would'st arrive,
Get riches first, get wealth, and treasure heap.

MILTON, *Paradise Regained*. Bk. ii, l. 426.

See also MONEY: MAKING MONEY.

20
The man who gets rich quickly must economize quickly, or he'll go hungry quickly. (Qui homo mature quæsivit pecuniam, Nisi eam mature parsit, mature esurit.)

PLAUTUS, *Curculio*, l. 380. (Act iii, sc. 1.)

21
He that maketh haste to be rich shall not be innocent.

Old Testament: Proverbs, xxviii, 20.

22
The shortest way to riches is by contempt of riches. (Brevissima ad divitias per contemptum divitiarum via est.)

SENECA, *Epistulæ ad Lucilium*. Epis. lxii, 3.

23
Knowing how to make money and also how to keep it; either one of these gifts might make a rich man.

SENECA, *Epistulæ ad Lucilium*. Epis. ci, 3.

IV—Riches: Their Use

See also Money: Its Use

1
Riches are for spending.
Francis Bacon, *Essays: Of Expense.*

2
Be not penny-wise; riches have wings, and sometimes they fly away of themselves, sometimes they must be set flying to bring in more.
Francis Bacon, *Essays: Of Riches.*

Penny wise and pound foolish.
William Camden, *Remains*, p. 330. (1605); Robert Burton, *Anatomy of Melancholy: Democritus to the Reader*, p. 35. (1621)

Riches have wings, and grandeur is a dream.
Cowper, *The Task*. Bk. iii, l. 263.

Riches, like insects, when conceal'd they lie,
Wait but for wings, and in their season fly.
Pope, *Moral Essays*. Epis. iii, l. 169.

Riches certainly make themselves wings; they fly away as an eagle toward heaven.
Old Testament: Proverbs, xxiii, 5.

"What is wealth?" the king would say,
"Even this shall pass away."
Theodore Tilton, *All Things Shall Pass Away.*

3
A man that keeps riches and enjoys them not is like an ass that carries gold and eats thistles.
Thomas Fuller, *Gnomologia*. No. 312.

These riches are possess'd, but not enjoy'd!
Homer, *Odyssey*. Bk. iv, l. 118. (Pope, tr.)

4
He is not fit for riches who is afraid to use them.
Thomas Fuller, *Gnomologia*. No. 1934.

Riches abuse them that know not how to use them.
Thomas Fuller, *Gnomologia*. No. 4040.

5
What good to you is a vast weight of silver and gold, if in terror you stealthily bury it in a hole in the ground? (Quid juvat immensum te argenti pondus et auri Furtim defossa timidum deponere terra?)
Horace, *Satires*. Bk. i, sat. 1, l. 41.

6
Wealth is not his who has it, but his who enjoys it.
James Howell, *Proverbs, Ital.-Eng.*, 12; Franklin, *Poor Richard*, 1736.

7
It is better to live rich than to die rich.
Samuel Johnson. (Boswell, *Life*, 1773.)

Life is short. The sooner that a man begins to enjoy his wealth the better.
Samuel Johnson. (Boswell, *Life*, 1773.)

8
The shade of the rich man will carry nothing to his abode in the other world. (Nil feret ad manes divitis umbra suos.)
Ovid, *Tristia*. Bk. v, eleg. 14, l. 12.

You are wealthy. And what is the end of it? When you depart, do you trail your riches after you as you are being pulled to your tomb? You gather wealth by spending time, but you cannot pile up a heavier measure of life.
Palladas. (*Greek Anthology*. Bk. x, epig. 60.)

If your riches are yours, why don't you take them with you to t'other world?
Benjamin Franklin, *Poor Richard*, 1751.

They'll make no pocket in my shroud.
Joaquin Miller, *The Dead Millionaire.*

9 They who know all the wealth they have,
are poor;
He's only rich that cannot tell his store.
Sir John Suckling, *Against Fruition.*

Not he that knows the wealth he has is poor,
But he that dares not touch, nor use, his store.
Edmund Waller, *Answer to Suckling's Verses.*

10
Riches get their value from the mind of their possessor; they are blessings to those who know how to use them. curses to those who do not. (Atque hæc perinde sunt ut illius animust qui ea possidet; Qui uti scit ei bona; illi qui non utitur recte mala.)
Terence, *Heauton Timorumenos*, l. 195.

V—Riches: Master and Servant

11
Wealth is a good servant, a very bad mistress.
Francis Bacon, *De Augmentis Scientiarum*. Pt. i, bk. 6, *Divitiæ*.

12
If we command our wealth, we shall be rich and free; if our wealth commands us, we are poor indeed.
Edmund Burke, *Letters on a Regicide Peace.*

13
[The rich] are indeed rather possessed by their money than possessors.
Robert Burton, *Anatomy of Melancholy*. Pt. i, sec. ii, mem. 3, subs. 12.

14
Riches serve wise men, but command a fool: for a covetous man serveth his riches, and not they him.
Pierre Charron. (Quoted by William Penn, *No Cross, No Crown*, xiii. 1669) Fuller, *Gnomologia*, 4047.

15
Riches either serve or govern the possessor. (Imperat aut servit collecta pecunia cuique.)
Horace, *Epistles*. Bk. i, epis. 10, l. 47.

VI—Riches: Their Power

See also Money: Its Power

16
As wealth is power, so all power will infallibly draw wealth to itself by some means or other.
Edmund Burke, *Speech*, House of Commons, 11 Feb., 1780.

It is the interest of the commercial world that wealth should be found everywhere.
Edmund Burke, *Letter to Samuel Span.*

1
Wealth had done wonders—taste not much.
BYRON, *Don Juan*. Canto v, st. 94.

2
Aristocracy of Feudal Parchment has passed away with a mighty rushing; and now, by a natural course, we arrive at Aristocracy of the Moneybag.
CARLYLE, *The French Revolution*. Vol. iii, bk. vii, ch. 7, par. 1.

3
Men desire riches for the enjoyment of pleasure. (Expetuntur divitiæ ad . . . perfruendas voluptates.)
CICERO, *De Officiis*. Bk. i, ch. 8, sec. 25.

For what are riches, empire, power,
But larger means to gratify the will?
WILLIAM CONGREVE, *The Mourning Bride*. Act ii, sc. 2.

4
Morals today are corrupted by our worship of riches. (Corrupti mores depravatique sunt admiratione divitarium.)
CICERO, *De Officiis*. Bk. ii, ch. 20, sec. 71.

5
Riches rule the roast.
THOMAS FULLER, *Gnomologia*. No. 4046.

6
All things, divine and human—virtue, fame, honor—are slaves to the beauty of riches. (Omnis enim res, virtus, fama, decus, divina humanaque pulchris Divitiis parent.)
HORACE, *Satires*. Bk. ii, sat. 3, l. 94.

Both rank and valour, without wealth, are more worthless than seaweed. (Et genus et virtus, nisi cum re, vilior alga est.)
HORACE, *Satires*. Bk. ii, sat. 5, l. 8.

Wealth excuses folly. (Stultitiam patiuntur opes.)
HORACE, *Epistles*. Bk i, epis. 18, l. 29.

7
Among us most sacred of all is the majesty of wealth. (Inter nos sanctissima divitiarum Majestas.)
JUVENAL, *Satires*. Sat i, l. 113.

8
Wealth may be an excellent thing, for it means power, it means leisure, it means liberty.
J. R. LOWELL, *Speech*, Harvard Anniversary.

But wealth is a great means of refinement; and it is a security for gentleness, since it removes disturbing anxieties.
IK MARVEL, *Reveries of a Bachelor: Over His Cigar*.

9
Riches cover a multitude of woes. (Πλοῦτος δὲ πολλῶν ἐπικαλυμμ' ἐστὶν κακῶν.)
MENANDER, *The Boetian Girl: Fragment*.

10
The most valuable of all human possessions, next to a superior and disdainful air, is the reputation of being well to do.
H. L. MENCKEN, *Prejudices*. Ser. iii, p. 310.

11
And Wealth, more bright with Virtue joined,
Brings golden Opportunity.
PINDAR, *Olympian Odes*. Ode ii, l. 96. (Abraham Moore, tr.)

12
The sense to value riches, with the art
T' enjoy them, and the virtue to impart; . . .
Join with economy magnificence;
With splendour charity, with plenty health.
POPE, *Moral Essays* Epis. iii, l. 219.

13
O the divinity of being rich!
THOMAS RANDOLPH, *Hey for Honesty*. Act ii, sc. 8.

14
Wealth makes wit waver.
SCOTT, *St. Ronan's Well*. Ch. 15.

15
A competence is vital to content.
YOUNG, *Night Thoughts*. Night vi, l. 506.

VII—Riches: Rich Men Have No Faults

16
Riches are able to solder up abundance of flaws.
CERVANTES, *Don Quixote*. Pt. i, ch. 3.

Rich men have no faults.
THOMAS FULLER, *Gnomologia*. No. 4036.

Rich men's spots are covered with money.
THOMAS FULLER, *Gnomologia*. No. 4039.

17
The foolish sayings of the rich pass for wise saws in society. (Las necedades del rico por sentencias pasan en el mundo.)
CERVANTES, *Don Quixote*. Pt. ii, ch. 43.

The jests of the rich are ever successful.
GOLDSMITH, *The Vicar of Wakefield*. Ch. 7.

Get wealth—wealth makes the dullard's jest
Seem witty when true wit falls flat.
T. B. ALDRICH, *Nourmadee*. Conclusion.

18
And he was competent whose purse was so.
COWPER, *The Task*. Bk. ii, l. 742.

19
Now I have got an ewe and a lamb, everyone cries, Welcome, Peter.
THOMAS FULLER, *Gnomologia*. No. 3690.

Now I have a sheep and a cow, everybody bids me good-morrow.
BENJAMIN FRANKLIN, *Poor Richard*, 1736.

As long as I am rich reputed,
With solemn voice I am saluted;
But wealth away once worn,
Not one will say good morn.
UNKNOWN. (*Reliq. Antiquæ*, p. 207. c. 1525)

20
He who has made his "pile" will be famous, brave and just. (Quas qui construxerit ille Clarus erit, fortis, justus.)
HORACE, *Satires*. Bk. ii, sat. 3, l. 96.

21
First as to his fortune, for the last question that will be asked will be as to his morals.

(Protenus ad censum, de moribus ultima fiet Quæstio)

JUVENAL, *Satires*. Sat. iv, l. 140.

We all ask whether he is wealthy; none whether he is good. (An dives omnes quærimus; nemo an bonus.)

SENECA, *Epistulæ ad Lucilium*. Quoting Euripides.

1
So he be rich, even a barbarian pleases. (Dummodo sit dives, barbarus ipse placet.)

OVID, *Ars Amatoria*. Bk. ii, l. 276.

2
A man of wealth is dubb'd a man of worth.

POPE, *Imitations of Horace: Epistles*, i, 1, 81.

3
The learned pate Ducks to the golden fool.

SHAKESPEARE, *Timon of Athens*. Act iv, sc. 3, l. 18.

4
The wealthiest man among us is the best.

WORDSWORTH, *Poems Dedicated to National Independence*. Pt. i, No. 13.

4a
To gain wealth is easy; to keep it hard. ('Chuang yeh yung i shou yeh nan.)

UNKNOWN. A Chinese proverb.

VIII—Riches: True Riches

5
I have mental joys and mental health,
Mental friends and mental wealth,
I've a wife that I love and that loves me;
I've all but riches bodily.

WILLIAM BLAKE, *Mammon*.

6
Lay not up for yourselves treasure upon earth; where the rust and moth doth corrupt.

Book of Common Prayer: The Communion.

7
Not to be avaricious is money; not to be fond of buying is a revenue; but to be content with our own is the greatest and most certain wealth of all. (Non esse cupidum, pecunia est; non esse emacem, vectigal est; contentum vero suis rebus esse, maximæ sunt, certissimæque divitiæ.)

CICERO, *Paradoxa*, vi, 3.

8
Without a rich heart, wealth is an ugly beggar.

EMERSON, *Essays, Second Series: Manners*.

9
If you wish to make Pythocles rich, do not add to his store of money, but subtract from his desires.

EPICURUS, *Fragments*. No. 135.

One is not rich by what one owns, but more by what one is able to do without with dignity

IMMANUEL KANT. *See also under* MODERATION.

10
How much richer are you than millions of people who are in want of nothing!

FIELDING, *Amelia*. Bk. iii, ch. 11.

11
A little house well-fill'd, a little land well-till'd, and a little wife well-will'd, are great riches.

JOHN RAY, *English Proverbs;* FRANKLIN, *Poor Richard*, 1735.

12
And passing rich with forty pounds a year.

GOLDSMITH, *The Deserted Village*, l. 142.

13
The way to make thy son rich is to fill
His mind with rest, before his trunk with riches:
For wealth without contentment climbs a hill
To feel those tempests which fly over ditches.

GEORGE HERBERT, *The Church-Porch*. St. 19.

14
Not oaks alone are trees, nor roses flowers;
Much humble wealth makes rich this world of ours.

LEIGH HUNT, *On Reading Pomfret's "Choice."*

15
He is rich enough who does not want bread. (Satis dives qui pane non indiget.)

ST. JEROME, *Epistles*. Ep. 125.

He is rich enough that needeth neither to flatter nor to borrow.

THOMAS FULLER, *Gnomologia*. No. 1942.

16
Wealth in the home; comfortable circumstances. (Res ampla domi.)

JUVENAL, *Satires*. Sat. xii, l. 10.

17
He is rich, not that hath much, but that coveteth least.

JOHN NORTHBROOKE, *Dicing, etc.*, 48. (c. 1577)

18
What riches have you that you deem me poor,
Or what large comfort that you call me sad?
Tell me what makes you so exceeding glad:
Is your earth happy or your heaven sure?

GEORGE SANTAYANA, *What Riches Have You?*

19
Do you ask what is the proper limit to wealth? It is, first, to have what is necessary; and, second, to have what is enough. (Primus habere quod necesse est, proximus quod sat est.)

SENECA, *Epistulæ ad Lucilium*. Epis. ii, sec. 6.

20
A man is rich in proportion to the number of things which he can afford to let alone.

H. D. THOREAU, *Walden: Where I Lived, and What I Lived For.*

IX—Riches and Happiness

21
He frivols through the livelong day,
He knows not Poverty, her pinch.
His lot seems light, his heart seems gay;
He has a cinch.

FRANKLIN P. ADAMS, *The Rich Man*.

A mind releas'd
From anxious thoughts how wealth may be increas'd.

WILLIAM COWPER, *Retirement*, l. 139.

22
Since all the riches of this world
May be gifts from the devil and earthly kings,
I should suspect that I worshipped the devil

If I thanked my God for worldly things.
WILLIAM BLAKE, *Riches.*

1
But I have learned a thing or two; I know as
sure as fate,
When we lock up our lives for wealth, the
gold key comes too late.
WILL CARLETON, *The Ancient Miner's Story.*

2
Beware of ambition for wealth; for there is nothing so characteristic of narrowness and littleness of soul as the love of riches; and there is nothing more honorable and noble than indifference to money.
CICERO, *De Officiis.* Bk. i, ch. 20, sec. 68.

3
Nature's wealth has its bounds and is easy to procure; but the wealth of vain fancies recedes to infinity.
EPICURUS, *Sovran Maxims.* No. 15.

Riches increase to a monstrous extent; yet there is always something wanting to our still imperfect fortune. (Improbæ Crescunt divitiæ; tamen Curtæ nescio quid semper abest rei.)
HORACE, *Odes.* Bk. iii, ode 24, l. 62.

4
Great wealth and content seldom live together.
THOMAS FULLER, *Gnomologia.* No. 1771.

For one rich man that is content, there are a hundred that are not.
H. G. BOHN, *Handbook of Proverbs,* p. 357.

5
Who hath not heard the rich complain
Of surfeits, and corporeal pain?
He barr'd from every use of wealth,
Envies the ploughman's strength and health.
GAY, *Fables: The Cookmaid, Turnspit, and Ox.*

Dame Nature gave him comeliness and health,
And Fortune (for a passport) gave him wealth.
WALTER HARTE, *Eulogius,* l. 411.

6
Alas! the joys that fortune brings
Are trifling, and decay;
And those who prize the paltry things,
More trifling still than they.
GOLDSMITH, *A Ballad.* (*Vicar of Wakefield,* 8.)

7
He that hides treasure
Imagines every one thinks of that place.
MIDDLETON AND MASSINGER, *The Old Law.* Act iv, sc. 2.

8
It is a common proverb, Divesque miserque, a rich man, and a miserable.
THOMAS NASHE, *Works.* Vol. vi, p. 99.

9
What riches give us let us then inquire:
Meat, fire, and clothes. What more? Meat,
clothes and fire.
POPE, *Moral Essays.* Epis. iii, l. 79.

There is a limit to enjoyment, though the sources of wealth be boundless.
M. F. TUPPER, *Proverbial Philosophy: Of Compensation.*

10
If riches increase, set not your heart upon them.
Old Testament: Psalms, lxii, 10.

If riches increase, let thy mind hold pace with them; and think it not enough to be Liberal but Munificent.
SIR THOMAS BROWNE, *Christian Morals.* Pt. i, sec. 5.

11
He enjoys riches most who needs them least. (Is maxime divitiis fruitur, qui minime divitiis indiget.)
SENECA, *Epistulæ ad Lucilium.* Epis. xiv, 17.

12
Wealth lightens not the hearts and cares of men. (Non optibus mentes hominum curæque levantur.)
TIBULLUS, *Elegies.* Bk. iii, eleg. 3, l. 21.

13
Can wealth give happiness? look round and
see
What gay distress! what splendid misery!
Whatever fortune lavishly can pour,
The mind annihilates, and calls for more!
YOUNG, *Love of Fame.* Sat. v, l. 393.

X—Riches: An Evil

14
Those that have wealth must be watchful and
wary,
Power, alas! naught but misery brings!
T. H. BAYLY, *I'd Be a Butterfly.*

15
Machiavel says virtue and riches seldom settle on one man.
ROBERT BURTON, *Anatomy of Melancholy.* Pt. ii, sec. ii, mem. 2, subs. 1.

Our Lord commonly giveth Riches to such gross asses, to whom he affordeth nothing else that is good.
MARTIN LUTHER, *Colloquies,* p. 90.

It was very prettily said that we may learn the little value of fortune by the persons on whom Heaven is pleased to bestow it.
RICHARD STEELE, *The Tatler.* No. 203.

If Heaven had looked upon riches to be a valuable thing, it would not have given them to such a scoundrel.
SWIFT, *Letter to Miss Vanhomrigh,* 12 Aug., 1720.

16
Great wealth always supports the party in power, no matter how corrupt it may be. It never exerts itself for reform, for it instinctively fears change.
HENRY GEORGE, *Social Problems,* p. 85.

17
Ill fares the land, to hastening ills a prey,
Where wealth accumulates, and men decay.
GOLDSMITH, *The Deserted Village,* l. 51.

18
Riches oft bring harm and ever fear.
JOHN HEYWOOD, *Proverbs.* Pt. i, ch. 12.

1
As money grows, care and greed for greater riches follow after. (Crescentem sequitur cura pecuniam Majorumque fames.)
HORACE, *Odes*. Bk. iii, ode 16, l. 17.

2
Wealth first, the ready pander of all sin,
Brought foreign manners, foreign vices in.
JUVENAL, *Satires*. Sat. vi, l. 440. (Gifford, tr.)

3
Common sense among men of fortune is rare. (Rarus enim ferme sensus communis in illa Fortuna.)
JUVENAL, *Satires*. Sat. viii, l. 73.

4
Great wealth implies great loss.
LAO-TSZE, *The Simple Way*. No. 44.

5
The rich man's son inherits cares;
The bank may break, the factory burn,
A breath may burst his bubble shares,
And soft white hands could hardly earn
A living that would serve his turn.
J. R. LOWELL, *The Heritage*.

6
It is easier for a camel to go through the eye of a needle, than for a rich man to enter into the kingdom of God.
New Testament: Matthew, xix, 24.

It is as hard to come as for a camel
To thread the postern of a small needle's eye.
SHAKESPEARE, *Richard II*. Act v, sc. 5, l. 16.

How hardly shall they that have riches enter into the kingdom of God!
New Testament: Luke, xviii, 24; *Mark*, x, 24.

Remember that sore saying spoken once
By Him that was the truth, "How hard it is
For the rich man to enter into heaven!"
Let all rich men remember that hard word.
TENNYSON, *Queen Mary*. Act iv, sc. 3, l. 134.

7
The greater your fortune, the greater your cares. (Plus est sollicitus magis beatus.)
PERIANDER. (AUSONIUS [?], *Septem Sapientum Sententiæ*, l. 23.)

He who multiplies Riches multiplies Cares.
BENJAMIN FRANKLIN, *Poor Richard*, 1744.

As the carle riches, he wretches.
JOHN RAY, *Proverbs: Scottish*.

8
Riches are a cause of evil, not because, of themselves, they do any evil, but because they goad men on to evil. (Divitias esse causam malorum, non quia ipsæ faciunt aliquid, sed quia facturos inritant.)
POSIDONIUS. (SENECA, *Epistulæ ad Lucilium*. Epis. lxxxvii, sec. 31.)

9
A great fortune is a great slavery. (Magna servitus est magna fortuna.)
SENECA, *Ad Polybium de Consolatione*. Sec. 26.

Gilded ceilings disturb men's rest, and purple robes cause watchful nights. Oh, if the hearts of rich men were laid bare, what fears would be seen therein!
SENECA, *Hercules Œtæus*, l. 646.

10
It is the wretchedness of being rich that you have to live with rich people.
LOGAN PEARSALL SMITH, *Afterthoughts*.

11
Wealth breeds satiety, satiety outrage.
SOLON. (DIOGENES LAERTIUS, *Solon*. Sec. 15.)

12
The rich man's wealth is most enemy unto his health.
GEORGE WHETSTONE, *The English Myrror*, 14. (1586)

RIDDLE

13
If ye had not ploughed with my heifer, ye had not found out my riddle.
Old Testament: Judges, xiv, 18.

Riddle me, riddle me ree.
UNKNOWN. Old saying, meaning read my riddle correctly.

It may well be doubted whether human ingenuity can construct an enigma of the kind which human ingenuity may not, by proper application resolve.
EDGAR ALLAN POE, *The Gold Bug*.

14
What animal goes on four legs in the morning, two at noon, and three in the evening?
The riddle of the Sphinx. The Sphinx, in Greek legend, was a monster with the head and breasts of a woman, the body of a dog, the tail of a serpent, the paws of a lion, and a human voice. It frequented the neighborhood of Thebes, propounded riddles and devoured the people who could not solve them. The Thebans had been told by an oracle that the Sphinx would destroy herself if her riddle was solved, so the king promised his crown and his sister Jocasta to whoever should answer it. This was done by Œdipus, who observed that a man walked on all fours when a child, erect in the noon of life, and supported by a stick in old age. The Sphinx, on hearing the answer, dashed her head against a rock.

The Sphinx must solve her own riddle.
EMERSON, *Essays, First Series: History*.

As that Theban monster that propos'd her riddle,
And him, who solv'd it nor devour'd.
MILTON.

I am plain Davus, not Œdipus [the solver of riddles.] (Davus sum, non Œdipus.)
TERENCE, *Andria*, l. 194. (Act i, sc. 2.)

15
All that we caught, we left behind, and carried away all that we did not catch. ("Ὅσσ' ἕλομεν λιπόμεσθ', ὅσα δ' οὐχ ἕλομεν φερομεσθα.)
The riddle, as recorded by PLUTARCH, and in *The Contest of Homer and Hesiod*, which caused the death of Homer, through vexation at his inability to solve it. It was propounded by some boys whom Homer met

as they were returning from fishing, when he asked them if they had caught anything. They referred to fleas or lice, not to fish.

Beware of the riddle of the young boys. (Ἀλλὰ νέων παίδων αἴνιγμα φύλαξαι.)

UNKNOWN. Oracle given to Homer. (*Greek Anthology*. Bk. xiv, No. 65.)

In Ios the boys, weaving a riddle at the bidding of the Muses, vexed to death Homer, the singer of heroes.

ALCÆUS OF MESSENE, *On Homer*. (*Greek Anthology*. Bk. vii, No. 1.)

Hereupon Homer remembered the oracle and, perceiving that the end of his life had come, composed his own epitaph. And while he was retiring from that place, he slipped in a clayey place and fell upon his side, and died, it is said, the third day after.

ALCIDAMUS, *The Contest of Homer and Hesiod*. Sec. 326.

1
There was a man bespake a thing,
Which when the owner home did bring,
He that made it did refuse it:
And he that brought it would not use it,
And he that hath it doth not know
Whether he hath it yea or no.

SIR JOHN DAVIES, *Riddle Upon a Coffin*.

2
Much upon this riddle runs the wisdom of the world.

SHAKESPEARE, *Measure for Measure*. Act iii, sc. 2, l. 242.

3
You have not the Book of Riddles about you, have you?

SHAKESPEARE, *The Merry Wives of Windsor*. Act i, sc. 1, l. 209.

4
A handless man had a letter to write,
And he who read it had lost his sight;
The dumb repeated it word for word,
And deaf was the man who listened and heard.

WILLIAM WHEWELL, *A Riddle*.

A handless man a letter did write,
A dumb dictated it word for word;
The person who read it had lost his sight,
And deaf was he who listened and heard.

GEORGE BORROW, *The Bible in Spain*. A more accurate translation of an old Spanish riddle than that of Whewell.

5
'Twas whispered in heaven, 'twas muttered in hell.

HORACE SMITH, *A Riddle on the Letter H*.

'Twas in heaven pronounced, and 'twas muttered in hell,
And echo caught faintly the sound as it fell;
On the confines of earth 'twas permitted to rest,
And the depth of the ocean its presence confessed . . .
Yet in shade let it rest, like a delicate flower,
Ah, breathe on it softly,—it dies in an hour.

CATHARINE FANSHAWE, *A Riddle on the Letter H*. Often wrongly credited to Lord Byron.

RIDER AND RIDING, see Horsemanship

RIDICULE

See also Laughter and Scorn; Satire; Sneer

I—Ridicule: Definitions and Apothegms

6
I defy the wisest man in the world to turn a truly good action into ridicule.

FIELDING, *Joseph Andrews*. Bk. iii, ch. 6.

7
Jeerers must be content to taste of their own broth.

H. G. BOHN, *Hand-Book of Proverbs*, p. 436.

He who laughs and is himself ridiculous, bears a double share of ridicule.

LORD SHAFTESBURY, *Characteristics*. Pt. i, 83.

8
We grow tired of everything but turning others into ridicule, and congratulating ourselves on their defects.

HAZLITT, *The Plain Speaker*. Vol. i, p. 318.

9
Thus to turn serious matters to sport. (Ita vertere seria ludo.)

HORACE, *Ars Poetica*, l. 226.

10
A man more quickly learns and more easily recalls what he derides than what he approves and esteems. (Discit enim citius meminitque libentius illud Quod quis deridet, quam quod probat et veneratur.)

HORACE, *Epistles*. Bk. ii, epis. 1, l. 262.

The little crow moves our ridicule, stripped of its stolen colors. (Movet cornicula risum, Furtivis nudata coloribus.)

HORACE, *Epistles*. Bk. i, epis. 3, l. 19.

11
On the day of resurrection, those who have indulged in ridicule will be called to the door of Paradise, and have it shut in their faces. They will be called to another door, and again, on reaching it, will see it closed against them; and so on ad infinitum.

The Koran.

12
Mockery is often poverty of wit. (La moquerie est souvent l'indigence d'esprit.)

LA BRUYÈRE, *Les Caracteres*. Ch. 5.

13
You are scoffing and use your turned-up nose too freely. (Rides et nimis uncis Naribus indulges.)

PERSIUS, *Satires*. Sat. i, l. 40.

14
Sacred to ridicule his whole life long,
And the sad burden of some merry song.

POPE, *Imitations of Horace: Satires*. Bk. ii, sat. 1, l. 79.

15
Ridicule . . . often checks what is absurd, and fully as often smothers that which is noble.

SCOTT, *Quentin Durward*. Ch. 24.

1
Shall quips and sentences and these paper bullets of the brain awe a man from the career of his humour?

SHAKESPEARE, *Much Ado About Nothing*. Act ii, sc. 3, l. 249.

2
Scoffing cometh not of wisdom.

SIR PHILIP SIDNEY, *Apologie for Poetrie:* Pt. ii, *Objections Stated.*

3
The spirit, Sir, is one of mockery.

R. L. STEVENSON, *The Suicide Club.*

4
Mockery is the fume of little hearts.

TENNYSON, *Guinevere*, l. 628.

II—Ridicule: The Test of Truth

5
Jane borrow'd maxims from a doubting school,
And took for truth the test of ridicule;
Lucy saw no such virtue in a jest,
Truth was with her of ridicule the test.

GEORGE CRABBE, *Tales of the Hall*. Bk. viii, l. 126. (1819)

7
Truth, 'tis supposed, may bear all lights; and one of those principal lights or natural mediums by which things are to be viewed in order to a thorough recognition is ridicule itself.

ANTHONY ASHLEY COOPER, LORD SHAFTESBURY, *Essay on the Freedom of Wit and Humour*. Pt. i, sec. 1. (1709)

How comes it to pass, then, that we appear such cowards in reasoning, and are so afraid to stand the test of ridicule?

LORD SHAFTESBURY, *A Letter Concerning Enthusiasm.* (1708)

We have oftener than once endeavoured to attach some meaning to that aphorism, vulgarly imputed to Shaftesbury, which however we can find nowhere in his works, that "ridicule is the test of truth."

CARLYLE, *Essays: Voltaire.*

It is commonly said, and more particularly by Lord Shaftesbury, that ridicule is the best test of truth.

LORD CHESTERFIELD, *Letters*, 6 Feb., 1752.

RIDICULOUSNESS

8
They that are serious in ridiculous things will be ridiculous in serious affairs.

CATO THE ELDER. (PLUTARCH, *Roman Apothegms.*)

9
I distrust those sentiments that are too far removed from nature, and whose sublimity is blended with ridicule; which two are as near one another as extreme wisdom and folly.

DESLANDES, *Réflexions sur les Grands Hommes qui Sont Morts en Plaisantant.*

10
There is nothing one sees oftener than the ridiculous and magnificent, such close neighbors that they touch. (L'on ne saurait mieux faire voir que le magnifique et le ridicule sont si voisins qu'ils se touchent.)

FONTENELLE, *Dialogues des Morts.* (1683)

11
The ridiculous usually touches the sublime. (En général, le ridicule touche au sublime.)

MARMONTEL, *Œuvres Completes.* Vol. v, p. 188.

12
From the sublime to the ridiculous is but a step. (Du sublime au ridicule il n'y a qu'un pas.)

NAPOLEON BONAPARTE, to the Abbé du Pradt, on his return from Russia, referring to the retreat from Moscow. (DU PRADT, *Histoire de l'Ambassade dans la Grande Duché de Varsovie*, p. 215.) The saying has been attributed also to Talleyrand.

There is but one step from triumph to ruin.

NAPOLEON BONAPARTE. (LOCKHART, *Life.*)

13
The sublime and the ridiculous are so close that they touch.

EDWARD LORD OXFORD, *Commonplace-Book.*

14
The sublime and the ridiculous are often so nearly related that it is difficult to class them separately. One step above the sublime makes the ridiculous, and one step above the ridiculous makes the sublime again.

THOMAS PAINE, *The Age of Reason.* Pt. ii.

RIGHT

For Might and Right, see Might

I—Right: Apothegms

15
Rather stand up, assured with conscious pride,
Alone, than err with millions on thy side.

CHARLES CHURCHILL, *Night*, l. 381. *See also under* ERROR.

16
But 'twas a maxim he had often tried,
That right was right, and there he would abide.

GEORGE CRABBE, *Tales of the Hall.* Tale xv, l. 365.

For right is right, since God is God,
And right the day must win;
To doubt would be disloyalty,
To falter would be sin.

F. W. FABER, *The Right Must Win.* St. 18.

Because right is right, to follow right
Were wisdom in the scorn of consequence.

TENNYSON, *Œnone*, l. 147.

17
Be sure you are right, then go ahead.

DAVID CROCKETT, *Motto*, during War of 1812.

18
Right as a trivet.

DICKENS, *Pickwick Papers.* Ch. 16. (1837); BARHAM, *Auto-da-fé.* (1847)

And she as right as my leg,

Shall give him leave to touze her.
THOMAS D'URFEY, *Quixote*. Pt. iii, act iii, sc. 2. (1696)

Right as a line.
JOHN HEYWOOD, *Proverbs*. Pt. i, ch. 11. (1546)

Right as a ram's horn.
LYDGATE, *Minor Poems*, p. 171. (c. 1430)

Right as rain.
WILLIAM RAYMOND, *Love and Quiet Life*, p. 108. (1894)

Right as my glove.
SCOTT, *Antiquary*. Ch. 30. (1816)

1
The axioms of geometry translate the laws of ethics.
EMERSON, *Uncollected Lectures: Natural Religion.*

2
Can any man have a higher notion of the rule of right and the eternal fitness of things?
FIELDING, *Tom Jones*. Bk. iv, ch. 4.

3
Unto it boldly let us stand,
God will give right the upper hand.
HUMPHREY GIFFORD, *For Soldiers.*

4
I am right, And you are right,
And all is right as right can be.
W. S. GILBERT, *The Mikado*. Act i.

5
Too fond of the right to pursue the expedient.
GOLDSMITH, *Retaliation*, l. 40.

6
If mankind had wished for what is right, they might have had it long ago.
WILLIAM HAZLITT, *Plain Speaker*, i, 325.

7
Not always right in all men's eyes,
But faithful to the light within.
OLIVER WENDELL HOLMES, *A Birthday Tribute.*

8
I care and pray for what is true and right, and to this I am wholly given. (Quid verum atque decens curo et rogo, et omnis in hoc sum.)
HORACE, *Epistles*. Bk. i, epis. 1, l. 11.

9
For the ultimate notion of right is that which tends to the universal good; and when one's acting in a certain manner has this tendency he has a right thus to act.
FRANCIS HUTCHESON, *A System of Moral Philosophy*. Bk. ii, ch. 3. *See also* HAPPINESS: THE GREATEST HAPPINESS OF THE GREATEST NUMBER.

10
If some great Power would agree to make me always think what is true and do what is right, on condition of being turned into a sort of clock and wound up every morning before I got out of bed, I should instantly close with the offer.
T. H. HUXLEY, *Materialism and Idealism.*

11
My principle is to do whatever is right, and leave consequences to him who has the disposal of them.
THOMAS JEFFERSON, *Writings*. Vol. xiii, p. 387.

Do what thou oughtst, and come what come can.
GEORGE HERBERT, *Jacula Prudentum*. No. 813.

He will hew to the line of right, let the chips fly where they may.
ROSCOE CONKLING, *Speech*, at Republican National Convention, Chicago, 1880, referring to General Grant.

12
With malice toward none; with charity for all; with firmness in the right, as God gives us to see the right.
ABRAHAM LINCOLN, *Second Inaugural Address*, 4 March, 1865.

They say that if you do this you will be standing with the Abolitionists. I say stand with anybody that stands right. Stand with him while he is right and part with him when he goes wrong.
ABRAHAM LINCOLN, *Speech*, Peoria, Ill., 16 Oct., 1854. The following, attributed to Lincoln, but not found, is probably based upon the above speech: "I am not bound to win, but I am bound to be true. I am not bound to succeed, but I am bound to live up to what light I have. I must stand with anybody that stands right; stand with him while he stands right, and part company with him when he goes wrong."

13
They are slaves who dare not be
In the right with two or three.
J. R. LOWELL, *Stanzas on Freedom.*

14
No one can have a true idea of right until he does it; any genuine reverence for it until he has done it often and with cost; any peace ineffable in it, till he does it always and with alacrity.
JAMES MARTINEAU, *Endeavours after Christian Life*. Ch. 15.

15
Right is better than law. (Τὸ καλῶς ἔχον που κρεῖττόν ἐστι καὶ νόμου.)
MENANDER, *The Carthaginian: Fragment.*

16
The victories of Right are born of strife.
SIR LEWIS MORRIS, *The Ode of Evil.*

17
And spite of pride, in erring reason's spite,
One truth is clear, Whatever is, is right.
POPE, *Essay on Man*. Epis. i, l. 293. *See also under* OPTIMISM.

18
Rightness expresses of actions, what *straightness* does of lines; and there can no more be two kinds of right action than there can be two kinds of straight line.
HERBERT SPENCER, *Social Statics*. Ch. 32, sec. 4.

19
None of us has a patent on being right.
MILLARD E. TYDINGS, *Speech*, U. S. Senate.

20
However the battle is ended,

Though proudly the victor comes,
With flaunting flags and neighing nags
And echoing roll of drums;
Still truth proclaims this motto
In letters of living light:
No question is ever settled
Until it is settled right.

ELLA WHEELER WILCOX, *Settle the Question Right*. "No question is ever settled until it is settled right," has been attributed to Abraham Lincoln.

Men are never so likely to settle a question rightly as when they discuss it freely.

MACAULAY, *Essays: Southey's Colloquies.*

1
The right is more precious than peace.

WOODROW WILSON, *War Message to Congress*, 2 April, 1917.

II—Right and Wrong

2
One may go wrong in many different ways, but right only in one, which is why it is easy to fail and difficult to succeed—easy to miss the target and difficult to hit it.

ARISTOTLE, *Nicomachean Ethics*. Bk. ii, sec. 14.

Better, though difficult, the right way to go,
Than wrong, tho' easy, where the end is woe.

BUNYAN, *The Pilgrim's Progress*. Pt. i.

All other ways are wrong, all other guides are false. . . . There is but one road that leads to Corinth.

WALTER PATER, *Marius the Epicurean*. Ch. 24.

3
I trust in God—the right shall be the right
And other than the wrong, while he endures.

ROBERT BROWNING, *A Soul's Tragedy*. Act i.

In the great right of an excessive wrong.

ROBERT BROWNING, *The Ring and the Book: The Other Half-Rome*, l. 1055.

4
But, dash my buttons, though you put it strong,
It's my opinion you're more right than wrong.

ROBERT BUCHANAN, *The Last of the Hangmen.*

5
Indiscriminate mashing up of right and wrong into a patent treacle.

CARLYLE, *Latter-Day Pamphlets*. No. 2.

6
I prefer to do right and get no thanks, rather than to do wrong and get no punishment.

MARCUS CATO. (PLUTARCH, *Lives: Marcus Cato*. Ch. 8, sec. 9.)

7
Though syllogisms hang not on my tongue,
I am not surely always in the wrong!
'Tis hard if all is false that I advance—
A fool must now and then be right, by chance.

COWPER, *Conversation*, l. 93.

8
Good and bad are but names very readily transferable to that or this; the only right is what is after my constitution; the only wrong what is against it.

EMERSON, *Essays, First Series: Self-Reliance.*

9
To be engaged in opposing wrong affords, under the conditions of our mental constitution, but a slender guarantee for being right.

GLADSTONE, *Time and Place of Homer: Introduction.*

11
We are not satisfied to be right, unless we can prove others to be wrong.

WILLIAM HAZLITT, *Note-Books*, p. 236.

12
Right and wrong exist in the nature of things. Things are not right because they are commanded, nor wrong because they are prohibited.

R. G. INGERSOLL, *The Ghosts.*

13
It is not that you do wrong by design, but that you should never do right by mistake.

JUNIUS, *Letters: To the Duke of Grafton*. Letter xii, 30 May, 1769.

14
When everyone is wrong, everyone is right. (Quand tout le monde a tort, tout le monde a raison.)

LA CHAUSSÉE, *La Gouvernante*. Act i, sc. 3.

15
Wrong ever builds on quicksands, but the Right
To the firm center lays its moveless base.

JAMES RUSSELL LOWELL, *Prometheus*, l. 116.

16
For aye Valerius loathed the wrong,
And aye upheld the right.

MACAULAY, *Battle of Lake Regillus*. St. 18.

17
He that would sing, but hath no song,
Must speak the right, denounce the wrong.

GEORGE MACDONALD, *How Shall He Sing?*

18
In wise deport, spake much of right and wrong,
Of justice, of religion, truth, and peace,
And judgement from above.

MILTON, *Paradise Lost*. Bk. xi, l. 662.

19
The passionate love of Right, the burning hate of Wrong.

LEWIS MORRIS, *The Diamond Jubilee.*

The love of the Right, tho' cast down, the hate of victorious Ill,
All are sparks from the central fire of a boundless will.

LEWIS MORRIS, *A New Orphic Hymn.*

20
I see the right, and I approve it too,
Condemn the wrong, and yet the wrong pursue.
(Video meliora proboque, deteriora sequor.)

OVID, *Metamorphoses*. Bk. vii, l. 20. (Garth, tr.)

1
Two blacks make no white.

H. G. BOHN, *Proverbs*, p. 548. To which is usually added, "Two wrongs do not make a right."

To prove by reason, in reason's despite,
That right is wrong, and wrong is right,
And white is black, and black is white.

ROBERT SOUTHEY, *All for Love*. Pt. ix, st. 29.

2
To do and dare, and die at need,
But while life lasts, to fight—
For right or wrong a simple creed,
But simplest for the right.

JAMES JEFFREY ROCHE, *Gettysburg*.

3
Swift-footed to uphold the right
And to uproot the wrong.

CHRISTINA ROSSETTI, *Noble Sisters*.

4
Right now is wrong, and wrong that was is right,
As all things else in time are changed quite.

SPENSER, *The Faerie Queene:* Bk. v, *Prologue*. St. 4. *See also* REASON: TO MAKE THE WORSE APPEAR THE BETTER REASON.

5
It often falls, in course of common life,
That right long time is overborne of wrong.

SPENSER, *Faerie Queene*. Bk. v, canto xi, st. 1.

6
A man finds he has been wrong at every preceding stage of his career, only to deduce the astonishing conclusion that he is at last entirely right.

R. L. STEVENSON, *Crabbed Age and Youth*.

7
Wrong and right
Are twain forever: nor, though night kiss day,
Shall right kiss wrong and die not.

SWINBURNE, *Marino Faliero*. Act iv, sc. 2.

7a
The greatest right in the world is the right to be wrong.

HARRY WEINBERGER, *The First Casualties in War*. (New York *Evening Post*, 10 Apr., 1917.)

III—Rights

8
They made and recorded a sort of institution and digest of anarchy, called the Rights of Man.

EDMUND BURKE, *Speech*. (*Works*, iii, 221.)

The sacred rights of man are not to be rummaged from among old parchments or musty records. They are written as with a sunbeam in the whole volume of human nature by the hand of divinity itself and can never be erased by mortal power.

ALEXANDER HAMILTON. *See also under* INDEPENDENCE DAY.

9
What people have always sought is equality of rights before the law. For rights that were not open to all alike would be no rights. (Jus enim semper est quæsitium æquabile; neque enim aliter esset jus.)

CICERO, *De Officiis*. Bk. ii, ch. 12, sec. 42.

10
Public wrongs are but popular rights in embryo.

SIR CHARLES DARLING, *Scintillæ Juris*.

11
Wherever there is a human being, I see God-given rights inherent in that being, whatever may be the sex or complexion.

WILLIAM LLOYD GARRISON. (*Life*. Vol. iii, 390.)

12
Every man has by the law of nature a right to such a waste portion of the earth as is necessary for his subsistence.

SIR THOMAS MORE, *Utopia*. Bk. ii.

The equal right of all men to the use of land is as clear as their equal right to breathe the air—it is a right proclaimed by the fact of their existence. For we cannot suppose that some men have a right to be in this world, and others no right.

HENRY GEORGE, *Progress and Poverty*. Bk. vii, ch. 1.

13
What rights are his that dare not strike for them?

TENNYSON, *The Last Tournament*, l. 525.

RIGHTEOUSNESS

14
What is all righteousness that men devise?
What—but a sordid bargain for the skies?

WILLIAM COWPER, *Truth*, l. 75.

15
Be not righteous over much, neither make thyself over wise.

Old Testament: Ecclesiastes, vii, 16.

My son, these maxims make a rule,
And lump them aye thegither:
The Rigid Righteous is a fool,
The Rigid Wise anither.

BURNS, *Address to the Unco Guid: Motto*. A paraphrase of Ecclesiastes, vii, 16.

16
He was righteous in his own eyes.

Old Testament: Job, xxxii, 1.

17
Righteousness exalteth a nation.

Old Testament: Proverbs, xiv, 34.

18
I have been young and now am old; yet have I not seen the righteous forsaken, nor his seed begging bread.

Old Testament: Psalms, xxxvii, 25.

The righteous shall flourish like the palm tree: he shall grow like a cedar of Lebanon.

Old Testament: Psalms, xcii, 12. (Justus ut palma florebit.—*Vulgate*.)

RISING

See also Bed, Sleep

I—Rising Early: Its Virtues

19
The early bird catches the worm.

WILLIAM CAMDEN, *Remains*, p. 333. (1605)

And it is the early bird, as the saying goes, that gets the rations.

R. L. STEVENSON, *Treasure Island*. Ch. 30.

The early bird gets the late one's breakfast.
CHAMBERLAIN, *West Worcester Words*, 39.

The early tire gits the roofin' tack.
KIN HUBBARD, *Abe Martin's Broadcast*, p. 118.

1
At grammar-school I learned a verse, that is this: *Sanat, sanctificat et ditat surgere mane.* That is to say, Early rising maketh a man holy in body, holier in soul, and richer in goods.
ANTHONY FITZHERBERT, *Husbandry*, 101. (1523)

Rise you early in the morning, for it hath properties three:
Holiness, health, and happy wealth, as my father taught me.
HUGH RHODES, *Boke of Nurture*, 72. (1577)

Early to bed and early to rise,
Make a man healthy and wealthy and wise.
JOHN RAY, *English Proverbs*, 38. (1670)

2
Who riseth late must trot all the day.
BENJAMIN FRANKLIN, *The Way to Wealth.*

3
He that will thrive must rise at five;
He that hath thriven may lie till seven;
He that will never thriven may lie till eleven.
GABRIEL HARVEY, *Marginalia*, 102. (c. 1590)

Cock crows in the morning to tell us to rise,
And he who lies late will never be wise;
For early to bed and early to rise
Is the way to be healthy and wealthy and wise.
UNKNOWN. *Old Nursery Rhyme.*

4
He that riseth first is first dressed.
GEORGE HERBERT, *Jacula Prudentum.*

5
He that hath the name to be an early riser may sleep till noon.
JAMES HOWELL, *Proverbs*, 11. (1659)

6
Go to bed with the lamb and rise with the lark.
JOHN LYLY, *Euphues and His England*, p. 229.

To rise with the lark and go to bed with the lamb.
NICHOLAS BRETON, *Court and Country.*

Rise with the lark, and with the lark to bed.
JAMES HURDIS, *The Village Curate.*

7
Awake, the morning shines, and the fresh field
Calls us; we lose the prime, to mark how spring
Our tended plants, how blows the citron grove,
What drops the myrrh, and what the balmy reed,
How nature paints her colours, how the bee
Sits on the bloom, extracting liquid sweet.
MILTON, *Paradise Lost*. Bk. v, l. 20.

8
An early stirrer, by the rood!
SHAKESPEARE, *II Henry IV*. Act iii, sc. 2, l. 3.

I am glad I was up so late; for that's the reason I was up so early.
SHAKESPEARE, *Cymbeline*. Act ii, sc. 3, l. 37.

Not to be abed after midnight is to be up betimes.
SHAKESPEARE, *Twelfth Night*. Act ii, sc. 3, l. 1.

9
Yet never sleep the sun up. Prayer shou'd
Dawn with the day. There are set, awful hours
'Twixt heaven and us. The manna was not good
After sun-rising; far day sullies flowers.
Rise to prevent the sun; sleep doth sin glut,
And heaven's gate opens when the world's is shut
HENRY VAUGHAN, *Silex Scintillans: Rules and Lessons*. St. 2.

II—Rising Early: Its Drawbacks

10
Oh! how I hate to get up in the morning,
Oh! how I'd love to remain in bed;
For the hardest blow of all
Is to hear the bugler call,
"You've got to get up, you've got to get up,
You've got to get up this morning!"
IRVING BERLIN, *Oh! How I Hate to Get Up in the Morning*. Written at Camp Upton, 1917.

O it's nice to get up in the mornin' when the sun begins to shine,
At four or five or six o'clock in the good old summer time;
When the snow is snowin' and it's murky overhead,
O it's nice to get up in the mornin', but it's nicer to lie in bed.
HARRY LAUDER, *It's Nice to Get Up in the Morning*. (1913)

11
Heaven's help is better than early rising.
CERVANTES, *Don Quixote*. Pt. ii, ch. 34.

12
Prone on my back I greet arriving day,
A day no different than the one just o'er;
When I will be, to practically say,
Considerable like I have been before.
Why then get up? Why wash, why eat, why pray?
—Oh, leave me lay!
ELEANOR PRESCOTT HAMMOND, *Oh, Leave Me Lay*. Published anonymously in the *Contributors' Column* of the *Atlantic Monthly* for August, 1922, as "by a well-known scholar."

13
They were early up, and never the nearer.
JOHN HEYWOOD, *Proverbs*. Pt. i, ch. 2. (1546)

Wherein the poet's fortune is, I fear,
Still to be early up, but ne'er the near.
BEN JONSON, *Tale of a Tub: Epilogue.* (1633)

14
Let Taylor preach, upon a morning breezy,
How well to rise while night and larks are flying—
For my part, getting up seems not so easy
By half as *lying*.
THOMAS HOOD, *Morning Meditations.*

Wherefore should master rise before the hens
Have laid the eggs?
THOMAS HOOD, *Morning Meditations.*

A man that's fond precociously of *stirring*,
Must be a *spoon!*
THOMAS HOOD, *Morning Meditations.*

1
Yonder see the morning blink:
The sun is up, and up must I,
To wash and dress and eat and drink
And look at things and talk and think
And work, and God knows why.
A. E. HOUSMAN, *Last Poems*. No. 11.

2
Many a good man has caught his death of cold getting up in the middle of the night to go home.
LUKE MCLUKE, *Epigram*.

3
He that blesseth his friend with a loud voice, rising early in the morning, it shall be counted a curse to him.
Old Testament: Proverbs, xxvii, 14.

4
Yes; bless the man who first invented sleep, . . .
But blast the man with curses loud and deep, . . .
Who first invented, and went round advertising,
That artificial cut-off—Early Rising.
JOHN GODFREY SAXE, *Early Rising*.

III—Rising: Exhortations

5
Up rose the sun, and up rose Emelye.
CHAUCER, *The Knightes Tale*, l. 1415.

6
Waste not these hours so fresh and gay;
Leave thy soft couch and haste away.
JOANNA BAILLIE, *Wake, Lady*.

7
Arise! come down! and, heart to heart,
Love, let me clasp in thee all these—
The sunbeam, of which thou art part,
And all the rapture of the breeze!—
Arise! come down! loved that thou art!
MADISON CAWEIN, *Morning Serenade*.

8
Awake thee, my lady love, wake thee and rise!
The sun through the bower peeps into thine eyes!
GEORGE DARLEY, *Sylvia: Serenade*.

9
Awake, awake, the morn will never rise,
Till she can dress her beauty at your eyes.
WILLIAM D'AVENANT, *Morning*.

10
All want day till thy beauty rise;
For the grey morn breaks from thine eyes.
NATHANIEL FIELD, *Matin Song*.

11
O swan of slenderness, Dove of tenderness,
Jewel of joys, arise!
ALFRED PERCEVAL GRAVES, *The Little Red Lark*.

12
Pack, clouds, away, and welcome, day,
With night we banish sorrow.
Sweet air, blow soft; mount, lark, aloft
To give my Love good-morrow!
THOMAS HEYWOOD, *Matin Song*.

13
And winking Mary-buds begin
To ope their golden eyes:
With everything that pretty bin,
My lady sweet, arise.
SHAKESPEARE, *Cymbeline*. Act ii, sc. 3, l. 26.

14
A birdie with a yellow bill
Hopped upon the window sill,
Cocked his shining eye and said:
"Ain't you 'shamed, you sleepy-head?"
R. L. STEVENSON, *Time to Rise*.

RIVALRY

15
Heaven cannot brook two suns, nor earth two masters.
ALEXANDER THE GREAT, to Darius. (PLUTARCH, *Apothegms*.)

We could not stall together
In the whole world.
SHAKESPEARE, *Antony and Cleopatra*, v, 1, 39.

Two stars keep not their motion in one sphere;
Nor can one England brook a double reign.
SHAKESPEARE, *I Henry IV*. Act v, sc. 4, l. 65.

There was a Brutus once that would have brook'd
The eternal devil to keep his state in Rome
As easily as a king.
SHAKESPEARE, *Julius Cæsar*. Act i, sc. 2, l. 159.

For monarchs ill can rivals brook,
Even in a word, or smile, or look.
SCOTT, *Marmion*. Canto v, st. 13.

16
Rival and imitator of my studies. (Æmulo atque imitatore studiorum.)
CICERO, *Pro Marcello*. Ch. i, sec. 2.

17
Sternhold himself he out-Sternholded.
JOHN GAY, *Verses to be Placed Under the Picture of Sir Richard Blackmore*.

18
No man keeps such a jealous lookout as a rival.
J. C. AND W. A. HARE, *Guesses at Truth*.

19
Rivalry is good for mortals. (Ἀγαθὴ δ' Ἔρις ἥδε βροτοῖσιν.)
HESIOD, *Works and Days*, l. 24.

20
Without rivals thou lovest alone thyself and thine. (Sine rivali teque et tua solus amares.)
HORACE, *Ars Poetica*, l. 444.

A man who loved himself without having any rivals. (Un homme qui s'aimait sans avoir de rivaux.)
LA FONTAINE, *Rochefoucauld*.

21
Whoever strives, O Julius, to rival Pindar, relies on wings fastened with wax by Dædalean craft, and is doomed to give his name to some crystal sea.
(Pindarum quisquis studet æmulari,
Jule, ceratis ope Dædalea
Nititur pinnis vitreo daturus
Nomina ponto.)
HORACE, *Odes*. Bk. iv, ode 2, l. 1. Horace is alluding to the story of Icarus, who fell into the sea, afterwards called Icarian.

1
Assured of worthiness we do not dread
Competitors; we rather give them hail
And greeting in the lists where we may fail: . . .
So that I draw the breath of finer air,
Station is nought, nor footways laurel-strewn,
Nor rivals tightly belted for the race.
Goodspeed to them! My place is here or there;
My pride is that among them I have place:
And thus I keep this instrument in tune.

GEORGE MEREDITH, *Internal Harmony.*

1a
Endure a rival with patience. (Rivalem patienter habe.)

OVID, *Ars Amatoria.* Bk. ii, l. 539.

2
In arms and science 'tis the same;
Our rival's hurts create our fame.

MATTHEW PRIOR, *Alma.* Canto i, l. 196.

3
Nothing is ever done beautifully which is done in rivalship, nor nobly which is done in pride.

JOHN RUSKIN, *Ethics of the Dust.*

4
And each upon his rival glared,
With foot advanced, and blade half bared.

SCOTT, *The Lady of the Lake.* Canto ii, st. 34.

The obligation of our blood forbids
A gory emulation 'twixt us twain.

SHAKESPEARE, *Troilus and Cressida,* iv, 5, 122.

5
"Rivals" in the primary sense of the word, are those who dwell on the banks of the same river. . . . There is no such fruitful source of contention as a water-right.

RICHARD CHENEVIX TRENCH, *The Study of Words.* Lecture 7.

RIVER

I—Rivers: Apothegms

6
A river is the cosiest of friends. You must love it and live with it before you can know it.

G. W. CURTIS, *Lotus-Eating: Hudson and Rhine.*

7
A thousand years hence, the river will run as it did.

THOMAS FULLER, *Gnomologia.* No. 436.

8
Two ways the rivers
Leap down to different seas, and as they roll
Grow deep and still, and their majestic presence
Becomes a benefaction to the towns
They visit.

LONGFELLOW, *The Golden Legend.* Pt. v.

9
Men travel far to see a city, but few seem curious about a river. Every river has, nevertheless, its individuality, its great silent interest. Every river has, moreover, its influence over the people who pass their lives within sight of its waters.

H. S. MERRIMAN. *The Sowers.* Ch. 2.

10
He that had never seen a river imagined the first he met to be the sea.

MONTAIGNE, *Essays.* Bk. i, ch. 26.

11
Rivers are roads that move and carry us whither we wish to go. (Les rivières sont des chemins qui marchant et qui portent où l'on veut aller.)

PASCAL, *Pensées.* No. 17.

12
He who knows not the way to the sea, should seek a river for companion. (Viam qui nescit, qua deveniat ad mare, Eum oportet amnem quærere comitem sibi.)

PLAUTUS, *Pœnulus,* l. 627. (Act iii, sc. 3.)

Follow the river and you will get to sea.

JOHN RAY, *English Proverbs.*

13
The deepest rivers flow with the smallest noise. (Altissima quæque flumina minimo sono labuntur.)

QUINTUS CURTIUS RUFUS, *De Rebus Gestis Alexandri Magni. See also* WATER: STILL WATERS.

14
Rain added to a river that is rank
Perforce will force it overflow its bank.

SHAKESPEARE, *Venus and Adonis,* l. 71.

15
The river glideth at his own sweet will.

WORDSWORTH, *Sonnet: Composed upon Westminster Bridge.*

II—Rivers: Their Source

16
Ye rivers, backwards run! (Redite sursum flumina!)

AUSONIUS, *Epistles.* Frag. 35.

17
Upward to their fountains the sacred rivers run. (Ἀνω ποταμῶν ἱερῶν χωρουσι παγαί.)

EURIPIDES, *Medea,* l. 410. Meaning that things are upside down.

18
The soul aspiring pants its source to mount,
As streams meander level with their fount.

ROBERT MONTGOMERY, *The Omnipresence of the Deity.* Pt. i.

We take this on the whole to be the worst similitude in the world. In the first place, no stream meanders or can possibly meander level with the fount. In the next place, if streams did meander level with their founts, no two motions can be less like each other than that of meandering level and that of mounting upwards.

MACAULAY, *Review of Montgomery's Poems.* (*Edinburgh Review,* April, 1830.) Montgomery evidently thought Macaulay's criticism well founded, for these lines were omitted from subsequent editions of the poem

19
Your mountains shall bend
And your streams ascend,
Ere Margaret be our foeman's bride!

SCOTT, *Lay of the Last Minstrel.* Canto i, st. 18.

1
Of nothing comes nothing: springs rise not above
Their source in the far-hidden heart of the mountains:
Whence then have descended the Wisdom and Love
That in man leap to light in intelligent fountains?
J. T. TROWBRIDGE, *The Missing Leaf*. St. 11.

III—Rivers: Description

2
And see the rivers how they run
Through wood and mead, in shade and sun,
Sometimes swift, sometimes slow,
Wave succeeding wave, they go
A various journey to the deep.
Like human life to endless sleep.
JOHN DYER, *Grongar Hill*, l. 93.

See the rivers, how they run,
Changeless toward a changeless sea.
CHARLES KINGSLEY, *The Saint's Tragedy*. Act ii, sc. 2.

3
Like streams that keep a summer mind
Snow-hid in Jenooary.
J. R. LOWELL, *The Courtin'*.

4
By shallow rivers, to whose falls
Melodious birds sing madrigals.
CHRISTOPHER MARLOWE, *The Passionate Shepherd to His Love*. Included in *The Passionate Pilgrim*, 1599; quoted by Shakespeare, *The Merry Wives of Windsor*. Act iii, sc. 1, l. 17. 1600.

5
There is a river in Macedon; and there is also moreover a river at Monmouth; . . . and there is salmons in both.
SHAKESPEARE, *Henry V*. Act iv, sc. 7, l. 28.

6
The current that with gentle murmur glides,
Thou know'st, being stopp'd, impatiently doth rage;
But when his fair course is not hindered,
He makes sweet music with the enamell'd stones,
Giving a gentle kiss to every sedge
He overtaketh in his pilgrimage.
SHAKESPEARE, *The Two Gentlemen of Verona*. Act ii, sc. 7, l. 25.

7
I chatter, chatter, as I flow
To join the brimming river,
For men may come and men may go,
But I go on for ever.
TENNYSON, *The Brook*, l. 47.

8
No check, no stay, this streamlet fears:
How merrily it goes.
'Twill murmur on a thousand years
And flow as now it flows.
WORDSWORTH, *The Fountain*. St. 6.

A sea-green river, proud to lave,
With current swift and undefiled,
The towers of old Lucerne.
WORDSWORTH, *Memorials of a Tour on the Continent*. No. 32.

IV—Rivers: Individual Rivers

See also Nile, Rhine, Thames

9
Flow gently, sweet Afton, among thy green braes!
Flow gently, I'll sing thee a song in thy praise.
BURNS, *Flow Gently, Sweet Afton*.

10
In Xanadu did Kubla Khan
A stately pleasure-dome decree;
Where Alph, the sacred river, ran
Through caverns measureless to man
Down to a sunless sea.
S. T. COLERIDGE, *Kubla Khan*.

11
Ayr, gurgling, kiss'd his pebbled shore,
O'erhung with wild woods thickening green;
The fragrant birch and hawthorn hoar
Twin'd amorous round the raptur'd scene.
BURNS, *Thou Lingering Star*. St. 3.

Farewell, the bonnie banks of Ayr.
BURNS, *The Banks of Ayr*.

12
Yet I will look upon thy face again,
My own romantic Bronx, and it will be
A face more pleasant than the face of men.
Thy waves are old companions. I shall see
A well-remembered form in each old tree
And hear a voice long loved in thy wild minstrelsy.
JOSEPH RODMAN DRAKE, *The Bronx*.

13
In those fair fields where sacred Isis glides,
Or else where Cam his winding vales divides.
POPE, *Pastorals: Summer*, l. 25.

14
Out of the hills of Habersham,
Down the valleys of Hall,
I hurry amain to reach the plain;
Run the rapid and leap the fall,
Split at the rock, and together again
Accept my bed, or narrow or wide,
And flee from folly on every side
With a lover's pain to attain the plain,
Far from the hills of Habersham,
Far from the valleys of Hall.
SIDNEY LANIER, *The Song of the Chattahoochee*.

15
How sweet to move at summer's eve
By Clyde's meandering stream,
When Sol in joy is seen to leave
The earth with crimson beam.
ANDREW PARK, *The Banks of Clyde*.

16
From the heart of the mighty mountains strong-souled for my fate I came,

My far-drawn track to a nameless sea through a land without a name; . . .
I stayed not, I could not linger; patient, resistless, alone,
I hewed the trail of my destiny deep in the hindering stone.
SHARLOT M. HALL, *Song of the Colorado.*

1
Then I saw the Congo, creeping through the black,
Cutting through the jungle with a golden track.
VACHEL LINDSAY, *The Congo.*

2
Flow on, lovely Dee, flow on, thou sweet river,
Thy banks' purest stream shall be dear to me ever.
JOHN TAIT, *The Banks of the Dee.*

O Mary, go and call the cattle home, . . .
Across the sands o' Dee.
CHARLES KINGSLEY, *The Sands o' Dee.*

3
Ye banks and braes o' bonny Doon,
How can ye bloom sae fresh and fair!
BURNS, *The Banks o' Doon.*

4
On Linden, when the sun was low,
All bloodless lay the untrodden snow,
And dark as winter was the flow
Of Iser, rolling rapidly.
THOMAS CAMPBELL, *Hohenlinden.*

5
Thou soft-flowing Keedron, by thy silver stream
Our Saviour at midnight, when Cynthia's pale beam
Shone bright on the waters, would oftentimes stray,
And lose in thy murmurs the toils of the day.
MARIA DE FLEURY, *Thou Soft-Flowing Keedron.*

6
On this I ponder
Where'er I wander,
And thus grow fonder,
Sweet Cork, of thee,—
With thy bells of Shandon,
That sound so grand on
The pleasant waters
Of the river Lee.
FRANCIS SYLVESTER MAHONY (FATHER PROUT), *The Bells of Shandon.*

7
On Leven's banks, while free to rove,
And tune the rural pipe to love,
I envied not the happiest swain
That ever trod the Arcadian plain.
Pure stream! in whose transparent wave
My youthful limbs I wont to lave;
No torrents stain thy limpid source,
No rocks impede thy dimpling course,
That sweetly warbles o'er its bed.
With white, round, polish'd pebbles spread.
TOBIAS SMOLLETT, *Ode to Leven Water.*

8
Slowly it moves, and in a mystic silence,
It draws me wondering,
Out through its shadowy portals to the ocean
Where sails are blossoming.
MARY SINTON LEITCH, *The River.* The Lynnhaven.

9
Ol' man river, dat ol' man river,
He must know sumpin', but don't say nothin',
He just keeps rollin', he keeps on rollin' along.
OSCAR HAMMERSTEIN 2d, *Ol' Man River.* (1927) Referring to the Mississippi.

Rasselas was the fourth son of the mighty emperor in whose dominions the Father of Waters begins his course.
SAMUEL JOHNSON, *Rasselas.* Dr. Johnson refers to the Nile. The Mississippi has also been called the Father of Waters. Its name is from the Algonquin for Great Water.

10
Or lose thyself in the continuous woods
Where rolls the Oregon, and hears no sound,
Save his own dashings.
W. C. BRYANT, *Thanatopsis.*

11
And Potomac flowed calmly, scarce heaving her breast,
With her low-lying billows all bright in the west,
For a charm as from God lulled the waters to rest
Of the fair-rolling river.
PAUL HAMILTON HAYNE, *Beyond the Potomac.*

12
By the blue rushing of the arrowy Rhone.
BYRON, *Childe Harold.* Canto iii, st. 71.

13
Alone by the Schuylkill a wanderer rov'd,
And bright were its flowery banks to his eye;
But far, very far, were the friends that he lov'd,
And he gaz'd on its flowery banks with a sigh.
THOMAS MOORE, *Lines Written on Leaving Philadelphia.*

14
On the gentle Severn's sedgy bank.
SHAKESPEARE, *I Henry IV.* Act i, sc. 3, l. 98.

Swift Severn's flood;
Who then, affrighted with their bloody looks,
Ran fearfully among the trembling reeds.
SHAKESPEARE, *I Henry IV.* Act i, sc. 3, l. 103.

15
Way down upon de Swanee ribber,
Far, far away,
Dere's wha my heart is turning ebber,
Dere's wha de old folks stay.
STEPHEN COLLINS FOSTER, *Old Folks at Home.*

16
Those graceful groves that shade the plain,
Where Tiber rolls majestic to the main,

And flattens, as he runs, the fair campagne.
OVID, *Metamorphoses*. Bk. xiv, l. 8. (Garth, tr.) *See also under* ROME.

1
Says Tweed to Till—
"What gars ye rin sae still?"
Says Till to Tweed—
"Though ye rin with speed
And I rin slaw,
For ae man that ye droon
I droon twa."
UNKNOWN, *Two Rivers*.

2
From Stirling Castle we had seen
The mazy Forth unravelled;
Had trod the banks of Clyde and Tay,
And with the Tweed had travelled;
And when we came to Clovenford,
Then said my *"winsome Marrow,"*
"Whate'er betide, we'll turn aside,
And see the Braes of Yarrow."
WORDSWORTH, *Yarrow Unvisited*. St. 1.

3
O lovely river of Yvette!
O darling river! like a bride,
Some dimpled, bashful, fair Lisette,
Thou goest to wed the Orge's tide. . . .

O lovely river of Yvette!
O darling stream! on balanced wings
The wood-birds sang the chansonette
That here a wandering poet sings.
LONGFELLOW, *To the River Yvette*.

ROAD

See also Wanderlust

4
On the beaten road there is tolerable travelling; but it is sore work, and many have to perish, fashioning a path through the impassable!
CARLYLE, *On Heroes and Hero-Worship: The Hero as Man of Letters*.

I will find a way or make one. (Viam inveniam aut faciam.)
HANNIBAL. Referring to the passage of the Alps.

It was a noble Roman
In Rome's imperial day,
Who heard a coward croaker
Before the battle say:
"They're safe in such a fortress;
There is no way to shake it."—
"On, on!" exclaimed the hero,
"I'll find a way, or make it!"
UNKNOWN, *On Fort Sumter*.

5
Before the Roman came to Rye or out to Severn strode,
The rolling English drunkard made the rolling English road.
A reeling road, a rolling road, that rambles round the shire,
And after him the parson ran, the sexton and the squire.
A merry road, a mazy road, and such as we did tread
That night we went to Birmingham by way of Beachy Head.
G. K. CHESTERTON, *The Rolling English Road*.

6
This road is not passable,
Not even jackassable.
JESSE DOUGLAS, *Epigram*. Referring to an Indiana road in 1839.

7
The rule of the road is a paradox quite,
Both in riding and driving along;
If you keep to the left, you are sure to be right,
If you keep to the right you are wrong;
But in walking the streets 'tis a different case,
To the right it is right you should bear;
Whereas to the left should be left enough space
For those whom you chance to meet there.
HENRY ERSKINE, *The Rule of the Road*. (*Notes and Queries*, 27 Aug., 1910.)

8
Any road leads to the end of the world.
EDWARD FITZGERALD, *Polonius*, 86.

9
Great roads the Romans built that men might meet,
And walls to keep strong men apart, secure.
Now centuries are gone, and in defeat
The walls are fallen, but the roads endure.
ETHELYN MILLER HARTWICH, *What Shall Endure?*

10
Keep the common road and thou'rt safe.
THOMAS FULLER, *Gnomologia*. No. 3118.

11
A long, forlorn, uncomfortable way!
HOMER, *Iliad*. Bk. vi, l. 248. (Pope, tr.)

12
What was now but a path has become a high road. (Et modo quæ fuerat semita, facta via est.)
MARTIAL, *Epigrams*. Bk. vii, ep. 6.

13
A broad and ample road, whose dust is gold,
And pavement stars.
MILTON, *Paradise Lost*. Bk. vii, l. 577.

14
The road was a ribbon of moonlight over the purple moor.
ALFRED NOYES, *The Highwayman*.

15
The way to rest is pain;
The road to resolution lies by doubt;
The next way home's the farthest way about.
FRANCIS QUARLES, *Emblems*. Bk i., No. 2. *See also* WAY *under* PROVERBS.

16
What is the use of running when you are on the wrong road?
W. G. BENHAM, *Proverbs*, p. 868.

1
I like a road that leads away to prospects bright and fair,
A road that is an ordered road, like a nun's evening prayer;
But best of all I love a road that leads to God knows where.

CHARLES HANSON TOWNE, *The Best Road of All.*

2
Here is the place where the road divides into two parts. (Hic locus est partes ubi se via findit in ambas.)

VERGIL, *Æneid.* Bk. vi, l. 540.

3
Had you seen this road before it was made,
You would lift up your hands and bless General Wade.

UNKNOWN, *The Highland Road.* The reference is to General George Wade, who, in 1726–29, employed 500 soldiers in roadmaking in the Highlands. (*See* J. P. ANDREW, *Anecdotes.*)

ROBBER, see Thief

ROBIN

4
Robin, Robin Redbreast,
O Robin dear!
And a crumb of bread for Robin,
His little heart to cheer.

WILLIAM ALLINGHAM, *Robin Redbreast.*

5
A robin redbreast in a cage
Puts all heaven in a rage.

WILLIAM BLAKE, *Auguries of Innocence.*

6
The robin is the one
That speechless from her nest
Submits that home and certainty
And sanctity are best.

EMILY DICKINSON, *Poems.* Pt. ii, No. 6.

7
Sweet Robin, I have heard them say
That thou wert there upon the day
The Christ was crowned in cruel scorn,
And bore away one bleeding thorn;
And so the blush upon thy breast,
In shameful sorrow, was impressed;
And thence thy genial sympathy
With our redeemed humanity.

GEORGE WASHINGTON DOANE, *Robin Redbreast.*

Bearing His cross, while Christ passed forth forlorn,
His God-like forehead by the mock crown torn,
A little bird took from that crown one thorn.
To soothe the dear Redeemer's throbbing head:
That bird did what she could; His blood, 'tis said,
Down dropping, dyed her tender bosom red.

HOSKYNS-ABRAHALL, *The Redbreast: A Brêton Legend.*

On fair Britannia's isle, bright bird,
A legend strange is told of thee,—
'Tis said thy blithesome song was hushed
While Christ toiled up Mount Calvary, . . .
'Twas then, dear bird, the legend says,
That thou, from out His crown, didst tear
The thorns, to lighten the distress,
And ease the pain that He must bear,
While pendant from thy tiny beak
The gory points thy bosom pressed,
And crimsoned with thy Saviour's blood
The sober brownness of thy breast.

DELLE W. NORTON, *To the Robin Redbreast.*

8
The household bird, with the red stomacher.

JOHN DONNE, *Epithalamion on The Lady Elizabeth and Count Palatine,* l. 8.

9
You have learned . . . to relish a love-song, like a robin-redbreast.

SHAKESPEARE, *The Two Gentlemen of Verona.* Act ii, sc. 1, l. 19.

10
The Redbreast, sacred to the household gods.

THOMSON, *The Seasons: Winter,* l. 246.

11
Call for the robin-redbreast and the wren,
Since o'er shady groves they hover,
And with leaves and flowers do cover
The friendless bodies of unburied men.

JOHN WEBSTER, *The White Devil.* Act v, sc. 4.

12
Art thou the bird whom Man loves best,
The pious bird with the scarlet breast,
Our little English Robin;
The bird that comes about our doors
When Autumn-winds are sobbing?
Art thou the Peter of Norway Boors?
Their Thomas in Finland,
And Russia far inland?
The bird that, by some name or other
All men who know thee call their brother?

WORDSWORTH, *The Redbreast Chasing the Butterfly,* l. 1.

ROGUE, see Knave

ROMANCE

13
All's cold and grey without it [romance].
They that have had it have slipped in and out of heaven.

J. M. BARRIE, *What Every Woman Knows.* Act ii.

14
Parent of golden dreams, Romance!
Auspicious queen of childish joys,
Who lead'st along, in airy dance,
Thy votive train of girls and boys.

BYRON, *To Romance.*

15
Romance, like a ghost, eludes touching. It is always where you were, not where you are.

G. W. CURTIS, *Lotus-Eating: Saratoga.*

16
Every form of human life is romantic.

T. W. HIGGINSON, *A Plea for Culture.*

1
"Farewell, Romance!" the Cave-men said:
"With bone well carved he went away.
Flint arms the ignoble arrowhead,
And jasper tips the spear to-day.
Changed are the Gods of Hunt and Dance,
And He with these. Farewell, Romance!" . . .
Confound Romance! . . . And all unseen
Romance brought up the nine-fifteen.

RUDYARD KIPLING, *The King.*

2
He loved the twilight that surrounds
The borderland of old romance.

LONGFELLOW, *Tales of a Wayside Inn: Prelude.*

3
The young who avoid that region [romance] escape the title of fool at the cost of a celestial crown.

GEORGE MEREDITH, *Diana of the Crossways.* Ch. 1.

4
Apes and ivory, skulls and roses, in junks of old Hong-Kong,
Gliding over a sea of dreams to a haunted shore of song.

ALFRED NOYES, *Apes and Ivory.*

4a
Romance is a love affair in other than domestic surroundings.

SIR WALTER RALEIGH THE YOUNGER, *Essays.* (Quoted by BERT LESTON TAYLOR, *The So-Called Human Race,* p. 295.)

5
To romance we owe the spirit of adventure, the code of honour, both masculine and feminine.

GEORGE SANTAYANA, *The Genteel Tradition at Bay.*

6
Tradition wears a snowy beard. Romance is always young.

WHITTIER, *Mary Garvin,* l. 16.

7
Romance should never begin with sentiment. It should begin with science and end with a settlement.

OSCAR WILDE, *An Ideal Husband.* Act iii.

The worst of having a romance of any kind is that it leaves one so unromantic.

OSCAR WILDE, *The Picture of Dorian Gray.* Ch. 1.

8
When one is in love, one always begins by deceiving oneself, and one always ends by deceiving others. That is what the world calls a romance.

OSCAR WILDE, *The Picture of Dorian Gray* Ch. 4.

In love, one first deceives oneself and then others—and that is what is called romance.

JOHN L. BALDERSTON, *Berkeley Square.* p. 63

9
Lady of the Mere,
Sole-sitting by the shores of old romance.

WORDSWORTH, *Poems on the Naming of Places.* No. 4, l. 37.

ROME

I—Rome: Apothegms

10
A thousand roads lead men forever to Rome.

ALAIN DE LILLE, *Liber Parábolarum,* l. 591. (1175)

Right as diverse paths lead diverse folk the right way to Rome.

CHAUCER, *A Treatise on the Astrolabe,* l. 44. (c. 1380)

All roads lead to Rome, but our antagonists
Think we are able to choose different paths.
(Tous chemins vont à Rome; ainsi nos concurrents
Crurent pouvoir choisir des sentiers différents.)

LA FONTAINE, *Fables.* Bk. xii, fab. 27.

11
All roads take to Rome.

CHARLES READE, *Cloister and the Hearth.* Ch. 24.

12
I found Rome brick and left it marble. (Urbem marmoream se relinquere, quam latericiam accepisset.)

CÆSAR AUGUSTUS. (SUETONIUS, *De Vita Cæsarum: Divus Augustus.* Bk. ii, ch. 28, sec. 3.) This saying is given another meaning by Dion Cassius (lvi, 589), who applies it to Cæsar's consolidation of the government, in the following form: "That Rome, which I found built of mud, I shall leave you firm as a rock." Strictly speaking, "latericiam" means "of sun-dried brick." *(See under* LAW *for Lord Brougham's fine use of the saying.)*

13
To Rome for everything. (Á Roma por todo.)

CERVANTES, *Don Quixote.* Pt. ii, ch. 52.

Every one soon or late comes round by Rome.

ROBERT BROWNING, *Ring and Book.* Bk. v, l. 296.

14
I am a Roman citizen. (Civis Romanus sum.)

CICERO, *In Verrem.* No. vi, sec. 57. Describing the case of Publius Gavius, beaten with rods in the forum of Messina, "while in the meantime no groan was heard, no cry amid all this pain and between the sound of the blows, except the words, 'I am a Roman citizen.'"

As the Roman in days of old held himself free from indignity when he could say *Civis Romanus sum,* so also a British subject shall feel confident that the watchful eye and strong arm of England will protect him against injustice and wrong.

LORD PALMERSTON, *Speech,* House of Commons, 25 June, 1850.

I would have the English republic respected as ever the Roman commonwealth was.

OLIVER CROMWELL. (CARLYLE, *Life.*)

By the terror of the Roman name. (Terrore nominis Romani.)

TACITUS, *Annals.* Bk. iv, sec. 24.

15
Butchered to make a Roman holiday.

BYRON, *Childe Harold.* Canto iv, st. 141.

16
O happy Fate for the Roman State
Was the date of my great Consulate!

(O fortunatam natam me consule Romam.)
CICERO. (JUVENAL, *Satires*. Sat. x, l. 122.) A line ridiculed for egoism and cacophony.

1
What can I do at Rome? I do not know how to lie. (Quid Romæ faciam? mentiri nescio.)
JUVENAL, *Satires*. Sat. iii, l. 41.

I cannot abide, O citizens, a Rome of Greeks. (Non possum ferre, Quirites, Græcam urbem.)
JUVENAL, *Satires*. Sat. iii, l. 60.

2
All things at Rome have their price. (Omnia Romæ Cum pretio.)
JUVENAL, *Satires*. Sat. iii, l. 183.

All things are saleable at Rome. (Omnia venalia Romæ.)
SALLUST, *Jugurtha*, ch. 8, sec. 1.
See also PRICE: ALL MEN HAVE THEIR PRICE.

3
It appears to me that nothing romantic or poetical can coexist with what is Roman.
The Romans were a blunt, flat people.
W. S. LANDOR, *Letter to Southey*, 30 Nov., 1809.

4
It is the nature of a Roman to do and suffer bravely. (Et facere et pati fortiter Romanum est.)
LIVY, *History*. Bk. ii, sec. 12.

6
Rome was not built in a day. (Neque protinus uno est Condita Roma die.)
PIETRO ANGELO MANZOLLI (Palingenius, pseud.), *Zodiacus Vitæ*. Bk. xii, l. 460.

Rome ne fut pas faite toute en un jour.
UNKNOWN, *Li Proverbe au Vilain*, 43. (c. 1190)

Rome was not built in a day.
CERVANTES, *Don Quixote*. Pt. ii, ch. 71; BEAUMONT AND FLETCHER, *Little French Lawyer*. Act i, sc. 3, etc.

7
Let's do it after the high Roman fashion.
SHAKESPEARE, *Antony and Cleopatra*. Act iv, sc. 15, l. 87.

I am more an antique Roman than a Dane.
SHAKESPEARE, *Hamlet*. Act v, sc. 2, l. 352.

8
Not that I loved Cæsar less, but that I loved
Rome more.
SHAKESPEARE, *Julius Cæsar*. Act iii, sc. 2, l. 23.

I had rather be a dog, and bay the moon,
Than such a Roman.
SHAKESPEARE, *Julius Cæsar*. Act iv, sc. 3, l. 27.

9
This was the noblest Roman of them all.
SHAKESPEARE, *Julius Cæsar*. Act v, sc. 5, l. 68.

Thou sleepest, Brutus, and yet Rome is in chains. (Tu dors, Brutus, et Rome est dans les fers.)
VOLTAIRE, *La Mort de César*. Act ii, sc. 2.

10
Thou art a Roman; be not barbarous.
SHAKESPEARE, *Titus Andronicus*. Act i, sc. 1, 378.

11
The last of the Romans. (Romanorum ultimus.)
TACITUS, *Annals*. Bk. iv, sec. 34. Referring to Caius Cassius.

The last of all the Romans, fare thee well!
SHAKESPEARE, *Julius Cæsar*. Act v, sc. 3, l. 99.

12
Not yet had Romulus traced the walls of the Eternal City. (Romulus æternæ nondum formaverat urbis Mœnia.)
TIBULLUS, *Elegies*. Bk. ii, eleg. 5, l. 23.

You cheer my heart, who build as if Rome would be eternal.
AUGUSTUS CÆSAR to Piso. (PLUTARCH, *Apothegms*.)

13
The walls of lofty Rome. (Altæ mœnia Romæ.)
VERGIL, *Æneid*. Bk. i, l. 7.

14
So great a labor was it to found the Roman race. (Tantæ molis erat Romanam condere gentem.)
VERGIL, *Æneid*. Bk. i, l. 33.

15
Neither holy, nor Roman, nor Empire.
VOLTAIRE, *Essay on the Morals of the Holy Empire of the Hapsburgs*.

16
Rare are the buttons of a Roman's breeches,
In antiquarian eyes surpassing riches.
JOHN WOLCOT, *Peter's Prophecy*.

17
The Roman Senate and People. (Senatus Populusque Romanus.)
The motto of Rome, denoted on Roman banners, coins, etc., by the letters, S. P. Q. R. Rabelais (*Works*, bk. iii, ch. 32) explains them as meaning, "Si Peu Que Rien," So little as to be nothing.

II—Rome: In Rome Do as the Romans Do

18
When I am here [at Milan] I do not fast on Saturday; when I am at Rome, I fast on a Saturday. (Quando hic sum, non jejuno Sabbato; quando Romæ sum, jejuno Sabbato.)
ST. AMBROSE, *Advice to St. Augustine*.

When you are in Rome, live in the Roman style; when you are elsewhere, live as they live there. (Cum fueris Romæ, Romano vivito more; cum fueris alibi, vivito sicut ibi.)
ST. AMBROSE. As quoted by Jeremy Taylor, *Ductor Dubitantium*. Bk. i, ch. 1, sec. 5.

19
My mother, having joined me at Milan, found that the church there did not fast on Saturdays as at Rome, and was at a loss what to do. I consulted St. Ambrose, of holy memory, who replied, "When I am at Rome, I fast on a Saturday; when I am at Milan, I do not. Follow the custom of the church where you are."
ST. AUGUSTINE, *Epistle to Januarius*. (Epis. ii,

sec. 18.) Also *Epistle to Casualanus.* (Epis. xxxvi, sec. 32.)

1
When they are at Rome, they do there as they see done.

ROBERT BURTON, *Anatomy of Melancholy.* Pt. iii, sec. iv, mem. 2, subs. 1.

When thou art at Rome, do as thou shalt see. (Cuando á Roma fueres, Haz como vieres.)

CERVANTES, *Don Quixote.* Pt. ii, ch. 54.

2
Isocrates adviseth Demonicus, when he came to a strange city, to worship by all means the gods of the place.

ROBERT BURTON, *Anatomy of Melancholy.* Pt. iii, sec. iv, mem. 1, subs. 5.

Good-breeding, as it is called, . . . is different in almost every country, and merely local; and every man of sense imitates and conforms to that local good-breeding of the place he is at.

LORD CHESTERFIELD, *Letters,* 2 Oct., 1747.

When you are abroad, live in the manner of the place. (Cum fueris alibi, vivito more loci.)

Quoted by Don Diego, as warrant for following Henry VIII.'s religion while in England.

Aristo Punico ingenio inter pœnas usus.

LIVY, *History.* Bk. xxxiv, sec. 61.

3
That is to say, if your religion's Roman,
And you at Rome would do as Romans do,
According to the proverb,—although no man,
If foreign, is obliged to fast; and you,
If Protestant, or sickly, or a woman,
Would rather dine in sin on a ragout—
Dine, and be d—d! I don't mean to be coarse,
But that's the penalty, to say no worse.

BYRON, *Beppo.* St. 9.

4
When thou art at Rome, do after the dome;
When thou art elsewhere, do as they do there.

HILL, *Commonplace Book,* 130. (c. 1490)

5
Ye may not sit in Rome and strive with the Pope.

DAVID FERGUSON, *Scottish Proverbs,* p. 112.

6
"When in Rome do as the Romans do" is the surest road to success.

BERNARD SHAW, *Radio Address,* 11 July, 1932.

III—Rome: Her Greatness

7
First among cities, the home of gods, is golden Rome. (Prima urbes inter, divum domus, aurea Roma.)

AUSONIUS, *Ordo Urbium Nobilium,* l. 1.

That queen of nations, absolutely great.

WILLIAM ALEXANDER, *Doomsday: The Sixth Hour.* St. 77.

8
A city greater than any upon earth, whose amplitude no eye can measure, whose beauty no imagination can picture, who raises a golden head amid the neighboring stars and with her seven hills imitates the seven regions of heaven, mother of arms and of law, who extends her sway over all the earth and was the earliest cradle of justice, this is the city which, sprung from humble beginnings, has stretched to either pole, and from one small place extended its power so that upon it the sun never sets. (In geminos axes parváque a sede profecta Dispersit cum sole manus.)

CLAUDIAN, *De Consulatu Stilichonis.* Bk. iii, l. 130. *See also under* ENGLAND, SPAIN.

She alone among nations has received into her bosom those whom she has conquered, and has cherished all humanity as her sons, and not as her slaves.

CLAUDIAN, *De Consulatu Stilichonis.* Bk. iii, l. 150.

9
But I will sing above all monuments,
Seven Roman hills, the world's seven wonderments.

JOACHIM DU BELLAY, *Ruins of Rome.* St. 2. (Spenser, tr.)

Rome only might to Rome comparèd be,
And only Rome could make great Rome to tremble.

JOACHIM DU BELLAY, *Ruins of Rome.* St. 6. (Spenser, tr.)

10
Cease to admire the smoke, wealth, and noise of prosperous Rome. (Omitte mirari beatæ Fumum et opes strepitumque Romæ.)

HORACE, *Odes.* Bk. iii, ode 29, l. 11.

11
In tears I tossed my coin from Trevi's edge.
A coin unsordid as a bond of love—
And, with the instinct of the homing dove,
I gave to Rome my rendezvous and pledge.
And when imperious Death
Has quenched my flame of breath,
Oh, let me join the faithful shades that throng that fount above.

ROBERT UNDERWOOD JOHNSON, *Italian Rhapsody.*

12
The grandeur that was Rome.

EDGAR ALLAN POE, *To Helen.*

13
On this foundation would I build my fame,
And emulate the Greek and Roman name.

NICHOLAS ROWE, *Jane Shore.* Act iii, sc. 1.

14
Imperial diadem of Rome.

SHAKESPEARE, *Titus Andronicus.* Act i, sc. 1, 6.

Hail, Rome, victorious in thy mourning weeds!

SHAKESPEARE, *Titus Andronicus.* Act i, sc. 1, 70.

15
'Twas glory once to be a Roman;
She makes it glory, now, to be a man.

BAYARD TAYLOR, *The National Ode.*

16
The Romans, lords of the world. (Romanos, rerum dominos.)

VERGIL, *Æneid.* Bk. i, l. 282.

Remember. O Roman, these shall be thy arts; to rule the nations with thy sway, to crown Peace with Law, to spare the humble and to tame the proud. (Tu regnere imperio populos, Romane, memento (Hae tibi erunt artes) pacique imponere morem, Parcere subjectis et debellare superbos.)

VERGIL, *Æneid*. Bk. vi, l. 851.

1
The city, Melibœus, which they call Rome, I, fool that I am, imagined to be like this town of ours. (Urbem quam dicunt Romam, Melibœe, putavi Stultus ego, huic nostræ similem.)

VERGIL, *Eclogues*. No. i, l. 20.

This city has reared her head as high among all other cities as cypresses oft do among the bending osiers. (Verum hæs tantum alias inter caput extulit urbes, Quantum lenta solent inter viburna cupressi.)

VERGIL, *Eclogues*. No. i, l. 24.

IV—Rome: Her Ruin

2
Oh Rome! my country! city of the soul!
The orphans of the heart must turn to thee,
Lone mother of dead empires!

BYRON, *Childe Harold*. Canto iv, st. 78.

The Niobe of nations! there she stands,
Childless and crownless, in her voiceless woe;
An empty urn within her wither'd hands,
Whose holy dust was scatter'd long ago.

BYRON, *Childe Harold*. Canto iv, st. 79.

"While stands the Coliseum, Rome shall stand;
When falls the Coliseum, Rome shall fall;
And when Rome falls—the world."
From our own land
Thus spake the pilgrims o'er this mighty wall
In Saxon times.

BYRON, *Childe Harold*. Canto iv, st. 145.

3
I've stood upon Achilles' tomb,
And heard Troy doubted; time will doubt of Rome.

BYRON, *Don Juan*. Canto iv, st. 101.

4
What was built by the toil of countless leaders, knit together through so many years by Roman hands, one coward traitor instantly overthrew. (Quod mille ducum peperere labores, Quod tantis Romana manus contexuit annis, Proditor unus iners angusto tempore vertit.)

CLAUDIAN, *In Rufinum*. Bk. ii, l. 51.

5
All the incongruous things of past incompatible ages
Seem to be treasured up here to make fools of present and future.

CLOUGH, *Amours de Voyage*. Canto i, sec. 1.

6
Now conquering Rome doth conquered Rome inter,
And she the vanquished is, and vanquisher.
To show us where she stood there rests alone
Tiber; and that too hastens to be gone.
Learn, hence what fortune can. Towns glide away;
And rivers, which are still in motion, stay.

JOACHIM DU BELLAY, *Ruins of Rome*. St. 3. (William Browne, tr.)

Rome now of Rome is th' only funeral,
And only Rome of Rome hath victory;
Nor aught save Tiber hast'ning to his fall
Remains of all: O world's inconstancy.
That which is firm doth flit and fall away,
And that is flitting doth abide and stay.

JOACHIM DU BELLAY, *Ruins of Rome*. St. 3. (Edmund Spenser, tr.)

7
The barbarians who broke up the Roman empire did not arrive a day too soon.

EMERSON, *Conduct of Life: Considerations by the Way*.

8
A city for sale, and doomed to speedy destruction, if it finds a purchaser. (Urbem venalem et mature perituram, si emptorem invenerit!)

JUGURTHA, looking back at Rome, as he left it. (SALLUST, *Jugurtha*. Ch. 35, sec. 10.)

9
Though Cato lived, though Tully spoke,
Though Brutus dealt the godlike stroke,
Yet perished fated Rome.

ROBERT NUGENT, *Epistle to a Lady*.

10
The man who first ruined the Roman people was he who first gave them treats and gratuities.

PLUTARCH, *Lives: Coriolanus*. Ch. 14, sec. 3. Quoted as a wise remark.

11
See the wild waste of all-devouring years;
How Rome her own sad sepulchre appears!
With nodding arches, broken temples spread,
The very tombs now vanish'd like their dead!
Imperial wonders rais'd on nations spoil'd,
Where mix'd with slaves the groaning martyrs toil'd.

POPE, *Epistle to Mr. Addison*, l. 1.

12
By her own wealth is haughty Rome brought low. (Frangitur ipsa suis Roma superba bonis.)

PROPERTIUS, *Elegies*. Bk. iii, eleg. 13, l. 60.

13
Go thou to Rome,—at once the Paradise,
The grave, the city, and the wilderness.

SHELLEY, *Adonais*. St. 49.

14
O weakness of the Great! O folly of the Wise!
Where now the haughty Empire that was spread
With such fond hope? Her very speech is dead.

WORDSWORTH, *Memorials of a Tour in Italy* No. 28, l. 64.

V—Rome: The Church of Rome

1
Rome has spoken; the case is concluded. (Roma locuta est; causa finita est.)

St. Augustine, *Sermons.* No. cxxxi, sec. 10. The context is: "The case is finished; would that heresy might sometime come to an end as well!" (Causa finita est; utinam aliquando error finiatur!)

2
Outside of the Catholic church everything may be had except salvation. (Extra Ecclesiam Catholicam totum potest præter salutem.)

St. Augustine, *Works.* Vol. ix, p. 122. The context is: "You may have Orders and Sacraments, you may sing Alleluia and answer Amen, you may hold the Gospel and have and preach the faith in the name of the Father, the Son, and the Holy Ghost; but nowhere except in the Catholic Church can salvation be found."

Outside the Church there is no salvation. (Extra Ecclesiam nulla salus.)

St. Cyprian, *Epistles.* No. iv, sec. 4; No. lxii, sec. 18.

3
It is the Mass that matters.

Augustine Birrell, *What, Then, Did Happen at the Reformation?* (*Nineteenth Century,* April, 1896.)

4
Though Rome's gross yoke
Drops off, no more to be endured,
Her teaching is not so obscured
By errors and perversities
That no truth shines athwart the lies.

Robert Browning, *Christmas-Eve.* Sec. 11.

The raree-show of Peter's successor.

Robert Browning, *Christmas-Eve.* Sec. 22.

Good, strong, thick, stupefying incense-smoke.

Robert Browning, *The Bishop Orders His Tomb at Saint Praxed's.*

5
Being a man I may come to be Pope.

Cervantes, *Don Quixote.* Pt. ii, ch 47.

6
St. Peter is very well at Rome. (Bien se está San Pedro á Roma.)

Cervantes, *Don Quixote.* Pt. ii, ch. 41, 53, 59.

7
The church of Rome,
Mixing two governments that ill assort,
Hath missed her footing, fallen into the mire,
And there herself and burden much defiled.

Dante, *Purgatorio.* Canto xvi, l. 129. (Cary, tr.)

8
Defoe says there were a hundred thousand stout country-fellows in his time ready to fight to the death against popery, without knowing whether popery was a man or a horse.

William Hazlitt, *Sketches: On Prejudice.*

No popery!

Cry of the mob at the doors of the House of Commons, 2 June, 1780. (Hume, *History of England.* Ch. 21.)

No popery, no slavery!

Motto woven in ribbons worn in 1681 when a new parliament was summoned at Oxford. (Hume, *History of England.* Ch. 25.)

9
The Papacy is no other than the ghost of the deceased Roman Empire, sitting crowned upon the grave thereof.

Thomas Hobbes, *Leviathan.* Pt. iii, ch. 42.

10
Religion went to Rome, subduing those,
Who, that they might subdue, made all their foes.

George Herbert, *The Church Militant,* l. 61.

11
Why leave a serious, moral, pious home,
Scotland, renown'd for sanctity of old,
Far distant Catholics to rate and scold
For—doing as the Romans do at Rome?

Thomas Hood, *Ode to Rae Wilson,* l. 243.

12
Well has the name of Pontifex been given
Unto the Church's head, as the chief builder
And architect of the invisible bridge
That leads from earth to heaven.

Longfellow, *The Golden Legend.* Pt. v.

13
The Catholic Church . . . was great and respected before the Saxon had set foot on Britain. . . . And she may still exist in undiminished vigour when some traveller from New Zealand shall, in the midst of a vast solitude, take his stand on a broken arch of London Bridge to sketch the ruins of St. Paul's.

Macaulay, *Essays: Ranke's History of the Popes.* Often referred to as Macaulay's New Zealander. First published in the *Edinburgh Review,* Oct., 1840. See also under Greece the quotation from his essay on *Mitford's Greece.*

There is not, and there never was on this earth, a work of human policy so well deserving of examination as the Roman Catholic Church. . . . No other institution is left standing which carries the mind back to the times when the smoke of sacrifice rose from the Pantheon, and when camelopards and tigers abounded in the Flavian Amphitheatre.

Macaulay, *Essays: Ranke's History of the Popes.*

The proudest royal houses are but of yesterday, when compared with the line of the Supreme Pontiffs. That line we trace back in an unbroken series from the pope who crowned Napoleon in the nineteenth century to the pope who crowned Pepin in the eighth; and far beyond the time of Pepin the august dynasty extends, till it is lost in the twilight of fable.

Macaulay, *Essays: Ranke's History of the Popes.*

1
Till Peter's keys some christen'd Jove adorn,
And Pan to Moses lends his Pagan horn.

POPE, *The Dunciad*. Bk. iii, l. 109.

2
The Order of Jesuits is a sword whose handle is at Rome and whose point is every where. (L'institut des Jesuites est une épée dont la poignée est à Rome et la pointe partout.)

ABBÉ RAYNAL, *Letter to Mlle. Volland.* (DUPIN, *Procès de Tendance.*)

The Society of Jesus is a sword, the blade of which is in France, and the handle in Rome.

D'AUBIGNE, *Anti-Coton,* attributing the saying to a Pole.

A sword, the hilt of which is at Rome, and the point everywhere.

ANDRÉ M. J. DUPIN, in a legal argument in 1825.

Sow a Jesuit, reap a revolter.

JEROME BONAPARTE, in the French Assembly, in 1877.

The Jesuits of the Revolution.

CHARLES FRANÇOIS DUMOURIEZ, speaking of the Girondists. (*Mémoirs,* iii, 314.) Carlyle thought it too hard a name. (*French Revolution,* ii, v, 2.)

3
Hitherto I have sought the key of heaven bent over: now I have found it.

SIXTUS V, who simulated decrepitude before his election as Pope, and threw away his crutches afterward. (TALLEMANT, *Historiettes,* x, 74.)

"Why, Father, is the net removed?" "Son, it hath caught the fish."

ROBERT BROWNING, *The Pope and the Net.*

4
Once I journeyed far from home
To the gate of holy Rome;
There the Pope, for my offence,
Bade me straight, in penance, thence
Wandering onward, to attain
The wondrous land that hight Cokaigne.

ROBERT WACE, *The Land of Cokaigne.*

5
All Babylon lies low; Luther destroyed the roof, Calvin the walls, but Socinus the foundations. (Tota jacet Babylon; destruxit lecta Lutherus, Calvinus muros, sed fundamenta Socinus.)

UNKNOWN, *Epigram.*

6
Where the Pope is, Rome is. (Dove è il Papa, ivi è Roma.)

UNKNOWN. An Italian proverb.

ROOSEVELT, THEODORE

I—Roosevelt: Apothegms

7
You called me a megalomaniac—
I called you a Serpent's Tooth.

FRANKLIN P. ADAMS, *T. R. to W. H. T.* (Theodore Roosevelt to William H. Taft.)

At three o'clock Thursday afternoon, Theodore Roosevelt will walk on the waters of Lake Michigan.

UNKNOWN. Text of poster distributed by an unknown humorist in Chicago, 17 June, 1912, on the eve of the Republican convention which nominated Taft.

8
If I was him I'd call the book "Alone in Cubia."

FINLEY PETER DUNNE, referring to Roosevelt's *The Rough Riders,* a history of his campaign in Cuba during the Spanish-American war. "Rough Riders" was the popular name of the regiment, composed largely of cowboys, which Roosevelt had raised, and of which he was second in command, under Colonel Leonard Wood.

9
Now look, that damned cowboy is President of the United States.

MARK HANNA, referring to Roosevelt, in conversation with H. H. Kohlsaat on McKinley funeral train from Buffalo, 16 Sept., 1901.

10
The Constitution rides behind
And the Big Stick rides before,
(Which is the rule of precedent
In the reign of Theodore).

WALLACE IRWIN, *The Ballad of Grizzly Gulch.*

11
Theodore! with all thy faults—

WILLIAM M. LAFFAN, *Editorial,* in New York *Sun,* 11 August, 1904, indicating that the *Sun,* which had fought Roosevelt for years, would support him in his campaign for the presidency against Alton B. Parker.

12
He has subjugated Wall street.

JOSEPH PULITZER's summation in the New York *World,* of Roosevelt's achievement as a "trust-buster."

13
Theodore, if there is one thing more than another for which I admire you, it is your original discovery of the ten commandments.

THOMAS B. REED. (W. A. ROBINSON, *Life.*)

14
He keeps a gentleman's cellar.

PHILIP J. ROOSEVELT, when testifying in Theodore Roosevelt's libel suit against George H. Newett, editor of *Iron Ore,* at Marquette, Mich., in 1913. Newett had stated in his paper that Roosevelt was a person who "gets drunk frequently." Roosevelt won the suit.

15
Our hero is a man of peace,
Preparedness he implores;
His sword within its scabbard sleeps,
But mercy, how it snores!

MCLANDBURGH WILSON, *A Man of Peace.*

16
Teddy-bear.

In November 1902, Roosevelt, on a hunting trip near Smedes, Miss., refused to shoot a small bear which had been brought into camp for him to kill. The incident was cartooned by Berryman, and the vogue of the Teddy bear started. The first model for the Teddy bear is said to have been made by Fräulein Gretel Steiff, in Geingen, Swabia, in 1904. (*New Yorker*, 28 Feb., 1931, p. 11.)

II—Roosevelt: Eulogies

1
He entered all the portals of the world,
A vibrant, thrilled, exhaustless, restless soul,
Riding at last the very stars—
Asleep.
ROBERT H. DAVIS, *Roosevelt*.

2
And, cow-boys or dough-boys,
We'll follow his drum, boys,
Who never said, "Go, boys!"
But always said. "Come. boys!"
ARTHUR GUITERMAN, *Our Colonel*.

4
Concerning brave Captains
Our age hath made known
For all men to honour,
One standeth alone,
Of whom, o'er both oceans
Both peoples may say:
"Our realm is diminished
With Great-Heart away."
RUDYARD KIPLING, *Great-Heart*.

The Interpreter then called for a man-servant of his, one Great-heart, and bid him take sword, and helmet, and shield.
JOHN BUNYAN, *The Pilgrim's Progress*. Pt. ii.

5
Friend of the humblest man, peer of the highest,
Knight of the lance that was never at rest—
O there are tears for him,
O there are cheers for him—
Liberty's champion. Cid of the West!
EDNA DEAN PROCTOR, *Cid of the West*.

6
Pilot and Prophet! as the years increase
The sorrow of your passing will not cease.
We love to think of you still moving on
From sun to blazing sun.
CHARLES HANSON TOWNE, *Pilot and Prophet*.

7
A smack of Lord Cromer, Jeff Davis a touch of him;
A little of Lincoln, but not very much of him;
Kitchener, Bismarck, and Germany's Will,
Jupiter, Chamberlain, Buffalo Bill.
UNKNOWN, *Roosevelt!* An English estimate, 1901.

7a
A tower is fallen, a star is set. Alas! alas for Celin!
UNKNOWN, *Lamentation for the Death of Celin*. (LOCKHART, tr., *Spanish Ballads*, p. 118.) Senator Henry Cabot Lodge began his eulogy of Theodore Roosevelt with these words.

ROSE

I—Rose: Apothegms

8
It was roses, roses all the way.
ROBERT BROWNING, *The Patriot*.

9 Oh, no man knows
Through what wild centuries
Roves back the rose.
WALTER DE LA MARE, *All That's Past*.

10
You with your roses, rosy is your charm; but what do you sell, yourself or the roses, or both? (Ἡτὰ ῥόδα, ῥοδόεσσαν ἔχεις χάριν.)
DIONYSIUS THE SOPHIST. (*Greek Anthology*. Bk. v, epig. 81.)

Poor Peggy hawks nosegays from street to street
Till—think of that who find life so sweet!—
She hates the smell of roses.
THOMAS HOOD, *Miss Kilmansegg: Her Birth*.

11
The said questions were asked with licence, and that it should remain under the rose. (Sub rosa.)
SIR ROBERT DYMOKE, *Letter to Stephen Vaughan*, 1546. (*State Papers, Henry VIII*, ii, 200.) The phrase, "sub rosa," meaning secretly, is of unknown origin. With the ancients the rose was emblematic of secrecy, and when a host hung a rose above his tables, his guests understood that all words spoken under it were to remain secret. Later, roses were carved as decorations on the ceilings of council chambers and confessionals, with the same significance.

The rose is the flower of Venus; and Love, in order that her sweet dishonesties might be hidden, dedicated this gift of his mother to Harpocrates, the god of silence. Hence the host hangs the rose over his friendly tables, that his guests may know that beneath it what is said will be regarded as secret.
(Est rosa flos veneris; quo dulcia furta laterent,
Harpocrati matris dona dicavit amor.
Inde rosam mensis hospes suspendit amicis,
Convivæ ut sub ea dicta tacenda sciant.)
UNKNOWN, *Rosa Flos Veneris*.

We all love a pretty girl—under the rose.
ISAAC BICKERSTAFFE, *Love in a Village*, ii, 2.

Under the rose, since here are none but friends,
(To own the truth) we have some private ends.
SWIFT, *Epilogue to a Benefit Play for the Distressed Weavers*.

12
It never will rain roses: when we want
To have more roses we must plant more trees.
GEORGE ELIOT, *The Spanish Gypsy*. Bk. iii.

13
Then in that Parly, all those powers
Voted the Rose the Queen of flowers.
ROBERT HERRICK, *The Parliament of Roses*.

14
What would the rose with all her pride be worth,
Were there no sun to call her brightness forth?
THOMAS MOORE, *Love Alone*. St. 2.

1
Rose of the Desert! thus should woman be
Shining uncourted, lone and safe, like thee.
THOMAS MOORE, *Rose of the Desert.*

Rose of the Garden! such is woman's lot—
Worshipp'd while blooming—when she fades, forgot.
THOMAS MOORE, *Rose of the Desert.*

2
As rich and purposeless as is the rose:
Thy simple doom is to be beautiful.
STEPHEN PHILLIPS, *Marpessa,* l. 51.

3
I shall never be friends again with roses.
SWINBURNE, *The Triumph of Time.* St. 45.

4
And is there any moral shut
Within the bosom of the rose?
TENNYSON, *The Day-Dream: Moral.*

6
Far off, most secret, and inviolate Rose,
Enfold me in my hour of hours.
WILLIAM BUTLER YEATS, *The Secret Rose.*

Red Rose, proud Rose, sad Rose of all my days!
Come near me, while I sing the ancient ways.
W. B. YEATS, *To the Rose upon the Rood of Time.*

Rose of all Roses, Rose of all the World!
W. B. YEATS, *The Rose of Battle.*

Rose is a rose is a rose is a rose.
GERTRUDE STEIN, *Geography and Plays: Sacred Emily.* (1922)

Speaking of the device of rose is a rose is a rose is a rose, it was I who found it in one of Gertrude Stein's manuscripts and insisted upon putting it as a device on the letter paper, on the table linen and anywhere that she would permit that I would put it.
GERTRUDE STEIN, *The Autobiography of Alice B. Toklas,* p. 169.

II—Rose: Its Beauty

7
The rose that all are praising,
Is not the rose for me;
Too many eyes are gazing
Upon the faultless tree.
But there's a rose in yonder glen
That scorns the gaze of other men;
For me its beauty saving,—
Oh! that's the rose for me.
T. H. BAYLY, *The Rose that All are Praising.*

8
"For if I wait," said she,
"Till time for roses be,
For the moss-rose and the musk-rose,
Maiden-blush and royal-dusk rose,
What glory then for me
In such a company?—
Roses plenty, roses plenty,
And one nightingale for twenty!"
E. B. BROWNING, *A Lay of the Early Rose.*

9
Yon rose-buds in the morning dew,
How pure amang the leaves sae green!
BURNS, *To Chloris.*

While rose-buds scarcely show'd their hue,
But coyly linger'd on the thorn.
MONTGOMERY, *The Adventures of a Star.*

10
He came and took me by the hand
Up to a red rose tree,
He kept His meaning to Himself,
But gave a rose to me.

I did not pray Him to lay bare
The mystery to me;
Enough the rose was Heaven to smell,
And His own face to see.
RALPH HODGSON, *The Mystery.*

11
It was not in the winter
Our loving lot was cast:
It was the time of roses,
We plucked them as we passed.
THOMAS HOOD, *Ballad.*

12
The roses that in yonder hedge appear
Outdo our garden buds which bloom within;
But since the hand may pluck them every day,
Unmarked they bud, bloom, drop, and drift away.
JEAN INGELOW, *The Four Bridges.* St. 61.

13
A Rose is sweeter in the bud than full blown.
JOHN LYLY, *Euphues and His England,* p. 314.

The rose is fairest when 't is budding new,
And hope is brightest when it dawns from fears;
The rose is sweetest washed with morning dew,
And love is loveliest when embalmed in tears.
SCOTT, *The Lady of the Lake.* Canto iv, st. 1.

The budding rose above the rose full blown.
WORDSWORTH, *The Prelude.* Bk. xi, l. 121.

Blinded alike from sunshine and from rain,
As though a rose should shut, and be a bud again.
JOHN KEATS, *The Eve of St. Agnes.* St. 27.

14
A root in the right soil,
Sun, rain, and a man's toil;
That, as a wise man knows,
Is all there is to a rose.
ORGILL MACKENZIE, *Whitegates.*

15
Sweet as the rose that died last year is the rose that is born to-day.
COSMO MONKHOUSE, *A Dead March.*

16
Rose, thou art the sweetest flower
That ever drank the amber shower;
Rose, thou art the fondest child
Of dimpled Spring, the wood-nymph wild.
THOMAS MOORE, *Odes of Anacreon.* Ode xliv.

O rose! the sweetest blossom,
Of spring the fairest flower;
O rose! the joy of heaven.
JAMES GATES PERCIVAL, *Anacreontic.*

Sometimes, when on the Alpine rose,
  The golden sunset leaves its ray,
So like a gem the flow'ret glows,
  We thither bend our headlong way;
And though we find no treasure there,
We bless the rose that shines so fair.
  THOMAS MOORE, *The Crystal-Hunters.*

1
And the rose, like a nymph to the bath addrest,
Which unveiled the depth of her glowing
    breast,
Till, fold after fold, to the fainting air,
The soul of her beauty and love lay bare.
  SHELLEY, *The Sensitive Plant.* Pt. i, l. 29.

2
Roses all that's fair adorn;
Rosy-fingered is the morn;
Rosy-armed the nymphs are seen;
Rosy-skinned is Beauty's queen.
  CHARLES WESLEY, *Anacreontic.*

3
You violets that first appear,
  By your pure purple mantles known,
Like the proud virgins of the year,
  As if the spring were all your own,
  What are you when the rose is blown?
  SIR HENRY WOTTON, *To His Mistress, Elizabeth of Bohemia.*

III—Rose and Thorn

4
Thus to the Rose, the Thistle:
  Why art thou not of thistle-breed?
Of use thou'dst, then, be truly,
  For asses might upon thee feed.
  F. M. BODENSTEDT, *The Rose and Thistle.* (Frederick Ricord, tr.)

5
But ne'er the rose without the thorn.
  ROBERT HERRICK, *The Rose.*

There is no rose . . . in garden, but there is some thorn.
  JOHN LYDGATE, *Bochas.* Prol., 9. (1430)

No rose without a thorn.
  JOHN RAY, *English Proverbs.*

The sweetest rose hath his prickle.
  JOHN LYLY, *Euphues*, p. 33. (1579)

I took her for a rose, but she breedeth a burr.
  JOHN HEYWOOD, *Proverbs.* Pt. i, ch. 10.

6
But the rose leaves herself upon the briar,
For winds to kiss and grateful bees to feed.
  KEATS, *On Fame*, l. 9.

7
Flowers of all hue, and without thorn the rose.
  MILTON, *Paradise Lost.* Bk. iv, l. 256.

8
When the rose perishes, the hard thorn is left behind. (Riget amissa spina relicta rosa.)
  OVID, *Ars Amatoria.* Bk. ii, l. 116.

9
The prickly thorn often bears soft roses. (Sæpe creat molles aspera spina rosas.)
  OVID, *Epistulæ ex Ponto.* Bk. ii, epis. 2, l. 34.

Often is the nettle nearest to the rose. (Urticæ proxima sæpe rosa est.)
  OVID, *Remediorum Amoris*, l. 46.

10
There is no gathering the rose without being pricked by the thorns.
  PILPAY, *Fables: The Two Travellers.*

He that plants thorns must never expect to gather roses.
  PILPAY, *Fables: The Ignorant Physician.*
See also under RETRIBUTION.

11
Better be stung by a nettle than pricked by a rose.
  H. G. BOHN, *Handbook of Proverbs*, p. 327.

12
The rose does not bloom without thorns; would that the thorns did not outlive the rose.
  JEAN PAUL RICHTER, *Titan.* Zykel 105.

13
The rose saith in the dewy morn,
  I am most fair;
Yet all my loveliness is born
Upon a thorn.
  CHRISTINA ROSSETTI, *Consider the Lilies of the Field.*

14
The rose and thorn, the treasure and dragon, joy and sorrow, all mingle into one.
  SADI, *Gulistan:* Ch. vii, Apologue 19.

15
From off this brier pluck a white rose with
    me.
  SHAKESPEARE, *I Henry VI.* Act ii, sc. 4, l. 30.

But, alack, my hand is sworn
Ne'er to pluck thee from thy thorn.
  SHAKESPEARE, *Love's Labour's Lost*, iv, 3, 111.

16
I am the one rich thing that morn
  Leaves for the ardent noon to win;
Grasp me not, I have a thorn,
  But bend and take my being in.
  HARRIET PRESCOTT SPOFFORD, *The Rose.*

17
This world that we're a-livin' in
  Is mighty hard to beat;
You git a thorn with every rose,
  But *ain't* the roses *sweet!*
  FRANK L. STANTON, *This World.*

18
The thorns he spares when the rose is taken;
  The rocks are left when he wastes the plain;
The wind that wanders, the weeds wind-
    shaken,
      These remain.
  SWINBURNE, *A Forsaken Garden.* St. 3.

19
The best rose-bush, after all, is not that which has the fewest thorns but that which bears the finest roses.
  HENRY VAN DYKE, *Fisherman's Luck.* Ch. viii.

IV—Rose: Its Frailty

20
As long as is one day, so long is the rose's life;

Her brief youth and age go hand in hand.
(Quam longa una dies, ætas tam longa rosarum:
Cum pubescenti juncta senecta brevis.)
AUSONIUS, *De Rosis Nascentibus*, l. 43.

1
The bloom of a rose passes quickly away,
And the pride of a Butterfly dies in a day.
JOHN CUNNINGHAM, *The Rose and the Butterfly.*

2
All June I bound the rose in sheaves,
Now, rose by rose, I strip the leaves.
ROBERT BROWNING, *One Way of Love.*

3
Loveliest of lovely things are they
On earth that soonest pass away.
The rose that lives its little hour
Is prized beyond the sculptured flower.
BRYANT, *A Scene on the Banks of the Hudson.*

4
Great is the rose
Infected by the tomb,
Yet burgeoning
Indifferent to death.

Great is the rose
That challenges the crypt,
And quotes millenniums
Against the grave.
NATHALIA CRANE, *Song from Tadmor.*

5
The fairest and the sweetest rose
In time must fade and beauty lose.
JOHN FLORIO, *Second Frutes*, 105.

6
Because the rose must fade,
Shall I not love the rose?
RICHARD WATSON GILDER, *Song.*

7
It is written on the rose
In its glory's full array:
Read what those buds disclose—
"Passing away."
FELICIA DOROTHEA HEMANS, *Passing Away.*

Sweet rose, whose hue, angry and brave,
Bids the rash gazer wipe his eye,
Thy root is ever in its grave,
And thou must die.
GEORGE HERBERT, *Virtue.*

She bloomed on earth, where the loveliest things
Have the saddest dower;
And Rose, she lived as the roses live,
For the space of an hour.
(Mais elle était du monde, où les plus belles choses
Ont le pire destin;
Et Rose, elle e vécu ce que vivent les roses,
L'espace d'un matin.)
FRANÇOIS DE MALHERBE, *Rose.* In a letter of condolence to M. du Perrier on the loss of his daughter, Rose.

8
Roses are beauty, but I never see
Those blood drops from the burning heart of June
Glowing like thought upon the living tree,
Without a pity that they die so soon,
Die into petals, like those roses old,
Those women, who were summer in men's hearts
Before the smile upon the Sphinx was cold.
JOHN MASEFIELD, *Sonnets.* No. 18.

9
'Tis the last rose of summer,
Left blooming alone;
All her lovely companions
Are faded and gone;
No flower of her kindred,
No rose-bud is nigh,
To reflect back her blushes,
Or give sigh for sigh.
THOMAS MOORE, *The Last Rose of Summer.*

10
Each Morn a thousand Roses brings, you say;
Yes, but where leaves the Rose of Yesterday?
OMAR KHAYYÁM, *Rubáiyát.* St. 9. (Fitzgerald, tr.)

The roses of seven hundred years
Have flamed and passed away
Since Omar steeped in golden tears
The Rose of Yesterday.
ADAM LINDSAY GORDON, *The Rose of Yesterday.*

11
When I have pluck'd the rose,
I cannot give it vital growth again,
It needs must wither: I'll smell it on the tree.
SHAKESPEARE, *Othello.* Act v, sc. 2, l. 13.

12
Sweet rose, fair flower, untimely pluck'd, soon vaded,
Pluck'd in the bud, and vaded in the spring!
SHAKESPEARE [?], *Passionate Pilgrim*, l. 131.

13
De rose is sweet, but de rose can't stay,
But I'm mighty glad when it blooms my way;
De night fall dark but de Lawd send day,
An' de good Lawd know my name.
FRANK L. STANTON, *De Good Lawd Know My Name.*

14
The year of the rose is brief;
From the first blade blown to the sheaf,
From the thin green leaf to the gold,
It has time to be sweet and grow old,
To triumph and leave not a leaf.
SWINBURNE, *The Year of the Rose.*

15
The fairest things have fleetest end:
Their scent survives their close,
But the rose's scent is bitterness
To him that loved the rose!
FRANCIS THOMPSON, *Daisy.* St. 10.

V—Rose: Its Perfume

1
I'll pu' the budding rose, when Phœbus peeps in view,
For it's like a baumy kiss o' her sweet bonie mou.

BURNS, *The Posie.*

2
I am not the rose, but I have lived with the rose. (Je ne suis pas la rose, mais j'ai vécu avec elle.)

H. B. CONSTANT. (HAYWARD, *Letters of Mrs. Piozzi: Introduction.*) In his *Gulistan,* Sadi represents a lump of clay still perfumed by the petals fallen from the rose-trees.

Yet, O thou beautiful Rose!
Queen rose, so fair and sweet,
What were lover or crown to thee
Without the Clay at thy feet?

JULIA C. R. DORR, *The Clay to the Rose.*

3
The jar will long keep the fragrance of what it was steeped in when new. (Quo semel est imbuta recens, servabit odorem Testa diu.)

HORACE, *Epistles.* Bk. i, epis. 2, l. 69.

You may break, you may shatter the vase, if you will,
But the scent of the roses will hang round it still.

THOMAS MOORE, *Farewell!—But Whenever You Welcome the Hour.*

You may break, you may shatter Watkins if you will, but the scent of the Roederer will hang round him still.

THOMAS BAILEY ALDRICH, *Marjorie Daw.*

4
And the rose herself has got
Perfume which on earth is not.

KEATS, *Bards of Passion and of Mirth,* l. 15.

5
And sweeten'd every musk-rose of the dale.

MILTON, *Comus,* l. 496.

6
The rose distils a healing balm
The beating pulse of pain to calm.

THOMAS MOORE, *Odes of Anacreon.* Ode lv.

There was never a daughter of Eve but once, ere the tale of her years be done,
Shall know the scent of the Eden Rose, but once beneath the sun;
Though the years may bring her joy or pain, fame, sorrow or sacrifice,
The hour that brought her the scent of the Rose, she lived it in Paradise.

SUSAN K. PHILLIPS, *The Eden-Rose.* (Published anonymously in St. Louis *Globe Democrat,* 13 July, 1878. Quoted by Kipling in *Mrs. Hauksbee Sits Out.*)

7
Fell on the upturn'd face of these roses
That gave out, in return for the love-light,
Their odorous souls in an ecstatic death.

EDGAR ALLAN POE, *To Helen,* l. 11.

8
Die of a rose in aromatic pain.

POPE, *Essay on Man,* epis. i, l. 200.

9
The rose looks fair, but fairer we it deem
For that sweet odour which doth in it live.

SHAKESPEARE, *Sonnets.* No. liv.

How fair is the Rose! what a beautiful flower!
The glory of April and May!
But the leaves are beginning to fade in an hour,
And they wither and die in a day.

Yet the Rose has one powerful virtue to boast,
Above all the flowers of the field:
When its leaves are all dead, and fine colours are lost,
Still how sweet a perfume it will yield!

ISAAC WATTS, *The Rose.*

VI—Rose: Red and White

10
Red as rose of Harpocrate.

E. B. BROWNING, *Isobel's Child,* l. 32.

A white rosebud for a guerdon.

E. B. BROWNING, *The Romance of the Swan's Nest.* St. 12.

11
Ah, ah, Cytherea! Adonis is dead.
She wept tear after tear with the blood which was shed,
And both turned into flowers for the earth's garden-close,
Her tears, to the windflower; his blood, to the rose.

E. B. BROWNING, *A Lament for Adonis.* St. 6.

12
Red as a rose is she.

S. T. COLERIDGE, *The Ancient Mariner.* Pt. i, st. 9. Used by Rhoda Broughton as title for a novel.

13
In Heaven's happy bowers
There blossom two flowers,
One with fiery glow
And one as white as snow;
While lo! before them stands,
With pale and trembling hands,
A spirit who must choose
One, and one refuse.

R. W. GILDER, *The White and Red Rose.*

14
Roses at first were white,
Till they co'd not agree
Whether my Sappho's breast,
Or they more white sho'd be.

But being vanquisht quite,
A blush their cheeks bespread:
Since which (believe the rest)
The Roses first came red.

ROBERT HERRICK, *How Roses Came Red.*

15
Rose of the desert, thou art to me
An emblem of stainless purity,—
Of those who, keeping their garments white,
Walk on through life with steps aright.

DAVID M. MOIR, *The White Rose.*

1
Then will I raise aloft the milk-white rose,
With whose sweet smell the air shall be perfumed.
SHAKESPEARE, *II Henry VI.* Act i, sc. 1, l. 254.

Hoary-headed frosts
Fall in the fresh lap of the crimson rose.
SHAKESPEARE, *A Midsummer-Night's Dream.* Act ii, sc. 1, l. 107.

The red rose on triumphant brier.
SHAKESPEARE, *A Midsummer-Night's Dream.* Act iii, sc. 1, l. 96.

2
Rosebuds, yellow and red,
Done in a prim, straight row,
Just on the edge of the thread,
Neither above nor below;
Each one shaded the same—
With all the art that she knew—
Making her cross-stitched name,
Ann Elizabeth Drew.
UNKNOWN, *The Sampler.*

VII—Rose and Love

3
She wore a wreath of roses,
The night that first we met.
T. H. BAYLY, *She Wore a Wreath of Roses.*

He wore, I think, a chasuble, the day when first we met.
BRET HARTE, *The Ritualist.*

4
O Rose, who dares to name thee?
No longer roseate now, nor soft, nor sweet,
But pale and hard and dry as stubble wheat,—
Kept seven years in a drawer, thy titles shame thee.
E. B. BROWNING, *A Dead Rose.*

It was nothing but a rose I gave her,—
Nothing but a rose
Any wind might rob of half its savor,
Any wind that blows. . . .

Withered, faded, pressed between these pages,
Crumpled, fold on fold,—
Once it lay upon her breast, and ages
Cannot make it old!
HARRIET PRESCOTT SPOFFORD, *A Sigh.*

5
You smell a rose through a fence:
If two should smell it, what matter?
E. B. BROWNING, *Lord Walter's Wife,* l. 9.

6
The morning was beautiful, mild and serene,
All nature had waked from repose;
Maternal affection came silently in
And placed in my bosom a rose.
MARY ANN BUTLER, *Whitsuntide Rose.* (WHITE, *Life of Mrs. Ann Seton,* p. 477.)

7
When love came first to Earth, the Spring
Spread rose-beds to receive him.
THOMAS CAMPBELL, *When Love Came First.*

And I will make thee beds of roses,
And a thousand fragrant posies.
CHRISTOPHER MARLOWE, *The Passionate Shepherd to his Love.* St. 3. (1599)

There will we make our peds of roses,
And a thousand fragrant posies.
SHAKESPEARE, *The Merry Wives of Windsor.* Act iii, sc. 1, l. 19. (1600)

8
Or risen from play at your pale raiment's hem
God, grown adventurous from all time's repose,
Of your tall body climbed the ivory Tower
And kissed upon your mouth the mystic Rose.
G. K. CHESTERTON, *A Little Litany.*

Till the roses' lips grew pale with her sighs.
ROSE TERRY COOKE, *Rêve du Midi.*

9
A rose I marked, and might have plucked; but she
Blushed as she bent, imploring me to spare her,
Nor spoil her beauty by such rivalry.
AUBREY DE VERE, *Flowers I Would Bring.*

10
She's just like a rose with a broken stem,
That is plucked and then cast aside;
The garden of love has no place for them,
When their fragrance and perfume have died.
For you can't take the stain from a woman's name,
Nor a flaw from the purest gem,
She chooses her path and must bear the blame—
She's a rose with a broken stem.
CARROLL FLEMING, *A Rose with a Broken Stem.* (1901)

11
If you were a white rose Columbine,
And I were a Harlequin,
I'd leap and sway on my spangled hips,
And blow you a kiss with my finger tips,
And woo a smile to your petal lips
With every glittering spin.
CROSBIE GARSTIN, *A Fantasy.*

12
Oh, raise your deep-fringed lids that close
To wrap you in some sweet dream's thrall;
I am the spectre of the rose
You wore but last night at the ball.
THÉOPHILE GAUTIER, *The Spectre of the Rose*

13
I sent my love two roses,—one
As white as driven snow,
And one a blushing royal red,
A flaming Jacqueminot. . . .

My heart sank when I met her: sure
I had been overbold,
For on her breast my pale rose lay
In virgin whiteness cold.

Yet with low words she greeted me,
With smiles divinely tender;
Upon her cheek the red rose dawned,—
The white rose meant surrender.
JOHN HAY, *The White Flag.*

Should this fair rose offend thy sight,
Placed in thy bosom bare,
'Twill blush to find itself less white,
And turn Lancastrian there.
JAMES SOMERVILLE, *The White Rose.*

1
The sweetest flower that blows,
I give you as we part
For you it is a rose
For me it is my heart.
FREDERICK PETERSON, *At Parting.*

2
I saw the rose-grove blushing in pride,
I gathered the blushing rose—and sigh'd—
I come from the rose-grove, mother,
I come from the grove of roses.
GIL VICENTE, *I Come from the Rose-grove, Mother.* (John Bowring, tr.)

3
Go, lovely rose—
Tell her that wastes her time and me,
That now she knows,
When I resemble her to thee,
How sweet and fair she seems to be.
EDMUND WALLER, *Go, Lovely Rose.*

Yet, though thou fade,
From thy dead leaves let fragrance rise;
And teach the maid
That goodness Time's rude hand defies,
That virtue lives when beauty dies.
HENRY KIRKE WHITE, *Additional Stanza to Waller's "Go, Lovely Rose."*

ROYALTY, see King

RUDENESS, see Manners: Bad Manners

RUIN

I—Ruin: Apothegms

4
A ruin—yet what ruin! from its mass
Walls, palaces, half-cities, have been rear'd.
BYRON, *Childe Harold.* Canto iv, st. 143. Referring to the Coliseum at Rome.

Tully was not so eloquent as thou,
Thou nameless column with the buried base!
BYRON, *Childe Harold.* Canto iv, st. 110.

5
There is a temple in ruin stands,
Fashion'd by long-forgotten hands;
Two or three columns, and many a stone,
Marble and granite, with grass o'ergrown!
Out upon time! it will leave no more
Of the things to come than the things before!
BYRON, *The Siege of Corinth.* St. 18.

While in the progress of their long decay,
Thrones sink to dust, and nations pass away.
EARL OF CARLISLE, *On the Ruins of Pæstum.*
See also under OBLIVION

Crumpling a pyramid, humbling a rose,
The dust has its reasons wherever it goes.
NATHALIA CRANE, *The Dust.*

6
Men moralise among ruins.
BENJAMIN DISRAELI, *Tancred.* Bk. v, ch. 5.

There's a fascination frantic
In a ruin that's romantic.
W. S. GILBERT, *The Mikado.* Act ii.

7
So many great nobles, things, administrations,
So many high chieftains, so many brave nations,
So many proud princes, and power so splendid,
In a moment, a twinkling, all utterly ended.
JACOPONE, *De Contemptu Mundi.* (Coles, tr., *Old Gems in New Settings,* p. 75.)

One minute gives invention to destroy;
What to rebuild, will a whole age employ.
CONGREVE, *The Double-Dealer.* Act i, sc. 3.

8
With ruin upon ruin, rout on rout.
MILTON, *Paradise Lost.* Bk. ii, l. 996.

Havoc, and spoil, and ruin are my gain.
MILTON, *Paradise Lost.* Bk. ii, l. 1009.

9
Prostrate the beauteous ruin lies; and all
That shared its shelter, perish in its fall.
WILLIAM PITT THE YOUNGER. (*Poetry of the Anti-Jacobin.* No. 36.)

10
Remains of rude magnificence.
SCOTT, *Marmion.* Canto iv, st. 11.

A fairer sight perchance than when it frown'd in power.
ROBERT SOUTHEY, *The Poet's Pilgrimage to Waterloo.* Pt. i, canto 4, st. 30.

11
To build up cities an age is needed, but an hour destroys them. A forest is long in growing, but in a moment is reduced to ashes. (Urbes constituit ætas: hora dissolvit: momento fit cinis: diu sylva.)
SENECA, *Naturales Questiones.* Bk. iii, sec. 27.

12
We two will sink on the wild waves of ruin,
Even as a vulture and a snake outspent
Drop twisted in inextricable fight,
Into a shoreless sea.
SHELLEY, *Prometheus Unbound.* Act iii, sc. 1.

13
Red ruin, and the breaking up of laws.
TENNYSON, *Guinevere,* l. 423.

14
It gathers ruin as it rolls along.
JAMES THOMSON, *Britannia,* l. 215.

15
Lovely in death the beauteous ruin lay;
And if in death still lovely, lovelier there;
Far lovelier! pity swells the tide of love.
YOUNG, *Night Thoughts.* Night iii, l. 104.

16
Final ruin fiercely drives
Her ploughshare o'er creation!
YOUNG, *Night Thoughts.* Night ix, l. 167

Stern ruin's ploughshare drives elate
Full on thy bloom.

BURNS, *To a Mountain Daisy*.

II—Ruin: Babylon and London

1
Babylon is fallen, is fallen.

Old Testament: Isaiah. xxi, 9.

Babylon the great is fallen, is fallen.

New Testament: Revelation, xviii, 2.

Babylon,
Learned and wise, hath perished utterly,
Nor leaves her speech one word to aid the sigh
That would lament her.

WORDSWORTH, *Ecclesiastical Sonnets*. Pt. i, No. 25.

It [Tyre] shall be a place for the spreading of nets in the midst of the sea.

Old Testament: Ezekiel, xxvi, 5.

2
And when 'midst fallen London they survey
The stone where Alexander's ashes lay,
Shall own with humble pride the lesson just
By Time's slow finger written in the dust.

ANNA LETITIA BARBAULD, *Eighteen Hundred and Eleven*. (1811) The original of Macaulay's New Zealander.

She may still exist in undiminished vigour, when some traveller from New Zealand shall, in the midst of a vast solitude, take his stand on a broken arch of London Bridge to sketch the ruins of St. Paul's.

MACAULAY, *Essays: Ranke's History of the Popes*. (*Edinburgh Review*, Oct., 1840.) Referring to the Roman Catholic Church. *See also* ROME: THE CHURCH OF ROME.

3
What cities, as great as this, have . . . promised themselves immortality! Posterity can hardly trace the situation of some. The sorrowful traveller wanders over the awful ruins of others. . . . Here stood their citadel, but now grown over with weeds; there their senate-house, but now the haunt of every noxious reptile; temples and theatres stood here, now only an undistinguished heap of ruins.

GOLDSMITH, *The Bee*: No. iv, *A City Night-Piece*. (27 Oct., 1759.)

When London shall be a habitation of bitterns, when St. Paul and Westminster Abbey shall stand shapeless and namelesss ruins in the midst of an unpeopled marsh, when the piers of Waterloo Bridge shall become the nuclei of islets of reeds and osiers, and cast the jagged shadows of their broken arches on the solitary stream, some Transatlantic commentator will be weighing in the scales of some new and now unimagined system of criticism the respective merits of the Bells and the Fudges and their historians.

SHELLEY, *Peter Bell the Third: Dedication*. (1819)

At last, some curious traveller from Lima will visit England, and give a description of the ruins of St. Paul's, like the editions of Balbec and Palmyra.

HORACE WALPOLE, *Letter to Horace Mann*. 24 Nov., 1774.

When I have been indulging this thought I have, in imagination, seen the Britons of some future century, walking by the banks of the Thames, then overgrown with weeds and almost impassable with rubbish. The father points to his son where stood St. Paul's, the Monument, the Bank, the Mansion House, and other places of the first distinction.

UNKNOWN, *Humorous Thoughts on the Removal of the Seat of Empire and Commerce*. (*London Magazine*, 1745.)

4
Who knows but that hereafter some traveller like myself will sit down upon the banks of the Seine, the Thames, or the Zuyder Zee, where now, in the tumult of enjoyment, the heart and the eyes are too slow to take in the multitude of sensations,—who knows but that he will sit down solitary amid silent ruins, and weep a people inurned, and their greatness changed into an empty name?

CONSTANTIN CHASSEBŒUF, COMTE DE VOLNEY, *Ruines*. Ch. 2. (1791)

5
Where now is Britain? . . .
Even as the savage sits upon the stone
That marks where stood her capitols, and hears
The bittern booming in the weeds, he shrinks
From the dismaying solitude.

HENRY KIRKE WHITE, *Time*. (1803)

6
The state of England and the once prosperous city of London, [described] in a letter from an American Traveller, dated from the ruinous portico of St. Paul's, in the year 2199, to a friend settled in Boston, the metropolis of the Western Empire.

Subtitle of *Poems by a Young Nobleman Lately Deceased* [the second Lord Lyttelton] published at London in 1780.

III—Ruin: Personal

7
All men that are ruined, are ruined on the side of their natural propensities.

BURKE, *On a Regicide Peace*.

So fond are mortal men
Fall'n into wrath divine,
As their own ruin on themselves to invite.

MILTON, *Samson Agonistes*, l. 1682.

8
He's undone, horse and man.

JOHN CLARKE, *Parœmiologia*, 86. (1639)

9
The road to ruin is always in good repair; the travellers pay the expense of it.

W. G. BENHAM, *Proverbs*, p. 850.

10
Ruin seize thee, ruthless king!

THOMAS GRAY, *The Bard*. Pt. i, st. i, l. 1.

1
Going to ruin is silent work.
W. G. BENHAM, *Proverbs*, p. 767.

2
Rejoicing that he has made his way by ruin. (Gaudensque viam fecisse ruina.)
LUCAN, *De Bello Civili*. Bk. i, l. 150. Referring to Julius Cæsar.

3
Thou art the ruins of the noblest man
That ever lived in the tide of times.
SHAKESPEARE, *Julius Cæsar*. Act iii, sc. 1, l. 256.

4
It's all up, all over, you're done for. (Actumst, ilicet, peristi.)
TERENCE, *Eunuchus*, l. 54. (Act i, sc. 1.)

Truly, sir, when a man is ruined, 'tis but the duty of a Christian to tell him of it.
FARQUHAR, *The Twin Rivals*. Act i, sc. 1.

RULE

5
No rule is so general, which admits not some exception.
ROBERT BURTON, *Anatomy of Melancholy*. Pt. i, sec. ii, mem. 2, subs. 3. (1621)

There is no rule without an exception.
CERVANTES, *Don Quixote*. Pt. ii, ch. 18.

The exception proves the rule.
JOHN WILSON, *The Cheats: To the Reader*. (1664)

Exceptions only prove the rule.
BYRON, *Letters and Journals*. Vol. i, p. 204.

6
For nothing goes for sense or light,
That will not with old rules jump right.
BUTLER, *Hudibras*. Pt. i, canto 3, l. 135.

7
I don't see the use in drawin' hard and fast rules. You only have to break 'em.
JOHN GALSWORTHY, *Eldest Son*. Act i, sc. 2.

8
Rules and models destroy genius and art.
WILLIAM HAZLITT, *On Taste*.

8a
What he doth, he doth by rule of thumb, and not by art.
SIR WILLIAM HOPE. *The Fencing-Master*, 157. (1692)

No rule so good as rule of thumb, if it hit.
JOHN KELLY, *Scottish Proverbs*, 256. (1791)

9
Obtruding false rules pranked in reason's garb.
MILTON, *Comus*, l. 759.

10
Rules and precepts are of no value without natural capacity. (Nihil præcepta arque artes valere nisi adjuvante natura.)
QUINTILIAN, *De Institutione Oratoria: Præfatio*. Sec. 26.

11
I have not kept my square; but that to come
Shall all be done by the rule.
SHAKESPEARE, *Antony and Cleopatra*. Act ii, sc. 3, l. 6.

RULER

12
Who made thee a ruler and a judge over us?
New Testament: Acts, vii, 27.

13
He who is to be a good ruler must have first been ruled, as the saying is. (Τόν τε γὰρ μέλλοντα καλῶς ἄρχειν ἀρχθῆναι φασι δεῖν πρῶτον.)
ARISTOTLE, *Politics*. Bk. vii, ch. 13, sec. 4. *See also* OBEDIENCE AND COMMAND.

14
'Tis a very fine thing to be father-in-law
To a very magnificent three-tailed bashaw.
GEORGE COLMAN THE YOUNGER, *Blue Beard*. Act iii, sc. 4.

A Pooh-Bah paid for his services!
W. S. GILBERT, *The Mikado*. Act i.

15
Resolv'd to ruin or to rule the state.
DRYDEN, *Absalom and Achitophel*. Pt. i, l. 174.

16
Lord of human kind.
DRYDEN, *The Spanish Friar*. Act ii, sc. 1.

Pride in their port, defiance in their eye,
I see the lords of humankind pass by.
GOLDSMITH, *The Traveller*, l. 327.

The Lords of creation men we call.
EMILY ANNE SHULDHAM, *Lords of Creation*.

The demi-Atlas of this earth.
SHAKESPEARE, *Antony and Cleopatra*, i, 5, 23.

17
To manage men one ought to have a sharp mind in a velvet sheath.
GEORGE ELIOT, *Romola*. Bk. i, ch. 39.

Iron hand in a velvet glove.
Attributed to CHARLES V; used also by Napoleon. (CARLYLE, *Latter-Day Pamphlets*, 11.)

Gentle of speech, but absolute of rule.
LONGFELLOW, *Emma and Eginhard*, l. 20.

18
His fair large front and eye sublime declar'd
Absolute rule.
MILTON, *Paradise Lost*. Bk iv, l. 300.

19
Let the ruler be slow in punishing, swift in rewarding. (Piger ad poenas princeps, ad præmia velox.)
OVID, *Epistulæ ex Ponto*. Bk. i, epis. 2, l. 121.

20
He shall rule them with a rod of iron.
New Testament: Revelation, ii, 27; xii, 5; xix, 15.

21
Unjust rule never endures perpetually. (Iniqua numquam regna perpetuo manent.)
SENECA, *Medea*, l. 196.

22
He who fears odium over much, does not know how to rule. (Odia qui nimium timet, Regnare nescit.)
SENECA, *Œdipus*, l. 703.

23
Each would the sweets of sov'reign rule devour,
While discord waits upon divided power.
STATIUS, *Thebais*. Bk. i, l. 182. (Pope, tr.)

1
Which shall to all our nights and days to come
Give solely sovereign sway and masterdom.
SHAKESPEARE, *Macbeth*. Act i, sc. 5, l. 70.

2
The desire to rule is more vehement than all the passions. (Cupido dominandi cunctis affectibus flagrantior est.)
TACITUS, *Annals*. Bk. xv, sec. 53.

3
He that only rules by terror
Doeth grievous wrong.
Deep as hell I count his error.
Let him hear my song.
TENNYSON, *The Captain*, l. 1.

4
We shall exult, if they who rule the land
Be men who hold its many blessings dear,
Wise, upright, valiant; not a servile band
Who are to judge of danger which they fear,
And honour which they do not understand.
WORDSWORTH, *Poems Dedicated to National Independence*. Pt. i, No. 27.

5
Whatsoever ye brag or boast,
My master yet shall rule the roast.
UNKNOWN, *Carpenter's Tools*. (c. 1400) (HALLIWELL, *Nugæ Poeticæ*, 17.)

He ruleth all the roast
With bragging and with boast.
JOHN SKELTON, *Why Come Ye Not to Court?* l. 200. (c. 1520) Of Cardinal Wolsey.

Nay, if riches might rule the roast,
Behold what cause I have to boast!
JOHN HEYWOOD, *Four Plays*. (c. 1540) (HAZLITT, *Old Plays*, i, 361.)

She doth rule the roast, she wears the keys.
WILLIAM BULLEIN, *Dialogue Against the Fever Pestilence*. (1564)

Suffolk, the new-made duke that rules the roast.
SHAKESPEARE, *II Henry VI*. Act i, sc. 1, l. 109. (1590)

I never strove to rule the roast,
She ne'er refused to pledge my toast.
MATTHEW PRIOR, *Turtle and Sparrow*. (1719)

RUMOR

See also Scandal

6
Avoid the talk of men. For talk is mischievous, light, and easily raised, but hard to bear and difficult to escape. Talk never wholly dies away when voiced by many people.
HESIOD, *Works and Days*, l. 760.

7
I believe there is nothing amongst mankind swifter than rumor. (Nullam rem citiorem apud homines esse, quam famam, reor.)
PLAUTUS, *Fragment*. From a lost play.

Enemies carry a report in form different from the original. (Nam inimici famam non ita ut nata est ferunt.)
PLAUTUS, *Persa*, l. 351. (Act iii, sc. 1.)

8
The flying rumours gather'd as they roll'd,
Scarce any tale was sooner heard than told;
And all who told it added something new,
And all who heard it made enlargements too.
POPE, *The Temple of Fame*, l. 468.

What some invent the rest enlarge.
SWIFT, *Journal of a Modern Lady*.

9
In calamity any rumor is believed. (Ad calamitatem quilibet rumor valet.)
PUBLILIUS SYRUS, *Sententiæ*. No. 17.

Idle rumors were also added to reasonable apprehensions. (Vana quoque ad veros accessit fama timores.)
LUCAN, *De Bello Civili*. Bk. i, l. 469.

Rumour doth double, like the voice and echo,
The numbers of the fear'd.
SHAKESPEARE, *II Henry IV*. Act iii, sc. 1, l. 97.

10
Rumour is a great traveller.
W. G. BENHAM, *Proverbs*, p. 830.

11
I cannot tell how the truth may be;
I tell the tale as 'twas said to me.
SCOTT, *The Lay of the Last Minstrel*. Canto ii, st. 22.

I tell the tale as 'twas told to me.
BRET HARTE, *A Newport Romance*, l. 2. A popular misquotation of Scott's line.

12
I from the orient to the drooping west,
Making the wind my post-horse, still unfold
The acts commenced on this ball of earth:
Upon my tongues continual slanders ride,
The which in every language I pronounce,
Stuffing the ears of men with false reports.
SHAKESPEARE, *II Henry IV: Induction*, l. 3.

Rumour is a pipe
Blown by surmises, jealousies, conjectures.
SHAKESPEARE, *II Henry IV: Induction*, l. 15.

We hold rumour
From what we fear, yet know not what we fear,
But float upon a wild and violent sea
Each way and move.
SHAKESPEARE, *Macbeth*. Act iv, sc. 2, l. 19.

13
Rumor does not always err; it sometimes even elects a man. (Haud semper erret fama; aliquando et elegit.)
TACITUS, *Agricola*. Sec. 9.

14
To scatter dark rumors amongst the crowd. (Spargere voces In volgum ambiguas.)
VERGIL, *Æneid*. Bk. ii, l. 98.

Rumor, of all evils the most swift. Speed lends her strength, and she gains vigor as she goes; small at first through fear, soon she mounts to heaven, and walks the ground with head hidden in the clouds. (Fama, malum qua non aliud velocius ullum, Obilitate viget virisque adquirit eundo; Parva metu primo, mox sese attollit in

auras Ingrediturque solo et caput inter nubila condit.)
VERGIL, *Æneid*. Bk. iv, l. 174.

The rumor forthwith flies abroad throughout the little town. (Fama volat parvam subito volgata per urbem.)
VERGIL, *Æneid*. Bk. viii, l. 554.

A hundred tongues, a hundred mouths, a voice of iron. (Linguæ centum sint, oraque centum Ferrea vox.)
VERGIL, *Georgics*. Bk. ii, l. 44.

RUST

1
It is better to wear out than to rust out.
RICHARD CUMBERLAND, BISHOP OF PETERBOROUGH, when a friend told him that he would wear himself out by his incessant labors. (BOSWELL, *Tour to the Hebrides*, p. 18, note; HORNE, *Sermon on the Duty of Contending for the Truth*) The saying was attributed to George Whitefield, the famous Methodist preacher, by Southey. (*Life of Wesley*. Vol. ii, l. 170.)

If I rest, I rust. (Rast' ich. so rost' ich.)
MARTIN LUTHER, *Maxims*.

2
There is rust upon locks and hinges,
And mould and blight on the walls,
And silence faints in the chambers,
And darkness waits in the halls.
LOUISE C. MOULTON, *The House of Death*.

3
I were better to be eaten to death with a rust than to be scoured to nothing with perpetual motion.
SHAKESPEARE, *II Henry IV*. Act i, sc. 2, l. 245.

4
How dull it is to pause, to make an end,
To rust unburnish'd, not to shine in use.
TENNYSON, *Ulysses*, l. 22.

The brightest blades grow dim with rust.
O. W. HOLMES, *Chanson without Music*.

S

SABBATH

I—Sabbath: Its Observance

5
Sunday clears away the rust of the whole week.
ADDISON, *The Spectator*. No. 112.

6
I sing the sabbath of eternal rest.
WILLIAM ALEXANDER, *Doomsday: The First Hour*. St. 1.

7
There are many people who think that Sunday is a sponge to wipe out all the sins of the week.
HENRY WARD BEECHER, *Life Thoughts*.

8
Of all the days that 's in the week
I dearly love but one day—
And that 's the day that comes betwixt
A Saturday and Monday;
For then I'm drest all in my best
To walk abroad with Sally;
She is the darling of my heart,
And she lives in our alley.
HENRY CAREY, *Sally in Our Alley*.

9
'Tis sweet to him, who all the week
Through city-crowds must push his way,
To stroll alone through fields and woods,
And hallow thus the Sabbath-day.
S. T. COLERIDGE, *Home-Sick*. St. 1.

10
How still the morning of the hallow'd day!
Mute is the voice of rural labour, hush'd
The ploughboy's whistle, and the milkmaid's song.
JAMES GRAHAME, *The Sabbath*.

Hail Sabbath! thee I hail, the poor man's day.
JAMES GRAHAME, *The Sabbath*.

Yes, child of suffering, thou may'st well be sure
He who ordained the Sabbath loves the poor!
O. W. HOLMES, *Urania*, l. 325.

11
Gently on tiptoe Sunday creeps,
Cheerfully from the stars he peeps,
Mortals all are asleep below,
None in the village hears him go;
Even chanticleer keeps very still,
For Sunday whispered, 'twas his will.
JOHN PETER HEBEL, *Sunday Morning*.

12
Sundays observe: think when the bells do chime
'Tis angels' music.
GEORGE HERBERT, *The Church-Porch*. St. 65.

A Sabbath well spent brings a week of content,
And health for the toils of the morrow;
But a Sabbath profan'd,
Whatso'er may be gain'd,
Is a certain forerunner of sorrow.
SIR MATTHEW HALE, *Golden Maxim*. Said to be "a poetical rendering of a passage in a letter to his children."

13
O day most calm, most bright,
The fruit of this, the next world's bud, . . .
The week were dark, but for thy light:
Thy torch doth show the way.
GEORGE HERBERT, *Sunday*, l. 1.

The other days and thou
Make up one man; whose face thou art,
Knocking at heaven with thy brow:
The worky-days are the back-part;
The burden of the week lies there.
GEORGE HERBERT, *Sunday*, l. 8.

On Sunday heaven's gate stands ope;
Blessings are plentiful and rife,
More plentiful than hope.
GEORGE HERBERT, *Sunday*, l. 29.

Thou art a day of mirth,
And, where the week-days trail upon the ground,
Thy flight is higher.
GEORGE HERBERT, *Sunday*, l. 57.

Day of all the week the best,
Emblem of eternal rest.
JOHN NEWTON, *Saturday Evening*. (1774)

1
Day of the Lord, as all our days should be!
LONGFELLOW, *John Endicott*. Act ii, sc. 2.

Take the Sunday with you through the week,
And sweeten with it all the other days.
LONGFELLOW, *Michael Angelo*. Pt. i, st. 5.

2
So sang they, and the empyrean rung
With Hallelujahs: Thus was Sabbath kept.
MILTON, *Paradise Lost*. Bk. vii, l. 633.

3
See Christians, Jews, one heavy sabbath keep,
And all the western world believe and sleep!
POPE, *The Dunciad*. Bk. iii, l. 99.

No place is sacred, not the church is free,
Ev'n Sunday shines no Sabbath-day to me.
POPE, *Epistle to Dr. Arbuthnot*, l. 11.

4
Now once a week, upon the Sabbath day,
It is enough to do our small devotion,
And then to follow any merrie motion.
SPENSER, *Mother Hubberds Tale*, l. 456.

5
The Sabbaths of Eternity,
One Sabbath deep and wide.
TENNYSON, *St. Agnes' Eve*. St. 3.

II—Sabbath: The Blue Sabbath

6
We have it on good authority that it is lawful to pull an ass out of the pit on the Sabbath day. Well, there never was a bigger ass, nor a deeper pit.
HENRY WARD BEECHER, to his attorneys, who came to consult him one Sunday, during the Tilton-Beecher trial, in the fall of 1874. (*Dict. of Amer. Biog.*, ii, 134.)

Golf may be played on Sunday, not being a game within view of the law, but being a form of moral effort.
STEPHEN BUTLER LEACOCK, *Why I Refuse to Play Golf*.

7
To Banbury came I, O profane one!
Where I saw a Puritane one
Hanging of his cat on Monday,
For killing of a mouse on Sunday.
RICHARD BRATHWAITE, *Barnabee's Journal*. (1638) "Banbury Saint" was slang for an over-strained Puritan.

8
Reforming saints! too delicately nice!
By whose decrees, our sinful souls to save,
No Sunday tankards foam, no barbers shave;
And beer undrawn, and beards unmown, display
Your holy reverence for the sabbath-day.
BYRON, *English Bards and Scotch Reviewers*, l. 633.

Sunday shaven, Sunday shorn,
Better hadst thou ne'er been born!
UNKNOWN. (HENDERSON, *Folk Lore*, 18.)

9
The Sabbath, as now recognized and enforced, is one of the main pillars of Priestcraft and Superstition, and the stronghold of a merely ceremonial Religion.
WILLIAM LLOYD GARRISON. (*Life*. Vol. iii, p. 224.)

10
Who backs his rigid Sabbath, so to speak,
Against the wicked remnant of the week.
THOMAS HOOD, *Ode to Rae Wilson*, l. 183.

The Saints!—the aping Fanatics that talk
All cant and rant, and rhapsodies high-flown—
That bid you baulk A Sunday walk,
And shun God's work as you should shun your own.
THOMAS HOOD, *Ode to Rae Wilson*, l. 357.

Now really, this appears the common case,
Of putting too much Sabbath into Sunday—
But what is your opinion, Mrs. Grundy?
THOMAS HOOD, *An Open Question*.

For MRS. GRUNDY *see* SOCIETY: CONVENTION.

11
And he said unto them, The sabbath was made for man, and not man for the sabbath.
New Testament: Mark, ii, 27.

12
For, bless the gude mon, gin he had his ain way,
He 'd na let a cat on the Sabbath say "mew;"
Nae birdie maun whistle, nae lambie maun play,
An' Phœbus himsel' could na travel that day,
As he 'd find a new Joshua in Andie Agnew.
THOMAS MOORE, *Sunday Ethics*. St. 3.

SACRIFICE, see Self-Sacrifice

SADNESS, see Grief, Melancholy, Sorrow

SAFETY

13
He who goes the lowest builds the safest.
P. J. BAILEY, *Festus: Home*.

Often, to our comfort, shall we find
The sharded beetle in a safer hold
Than is the full-wing'd eagle.
SHAKESPEARE, *Cymbeline*. Act iii, sc. 3, l. 19.

14
Safe shall be my going,
Secretly armed against all death's endeavour;
Safe though all safety's lost; safe where men fall;

And if these poor limbs die, safest of all.
RUPERT BROOKE, *1914: Safety.*

1
Oh! are they safe? we ask not of success.
BYRON, *The Corsair.* Canto i, st. 5.

2
Who can hope to be safe? who sufficiently cautious?
Guard himself as he may, every moment's an ambush.
(Quid quisque vitet, nunquam homini satis
Cautum est in horas.)
HORACE, *Odes.* Bk. ii, ode 13, l. 13. (Lytton, tr.)

3
The strongest tower has not the highest wall.
Think well of this, when you sit safe at home.
WILLIAM MORRIS, *The Earthly Paradise: The Story of Cupid and Psyche,* l. 896.

4
Let others seek what is safe. Utter misery is safe; for the fear of any worse event is taken away. (Tuta petant alii: fortuna miserrima tuta est, Nam timor eventus deterioris abest.)
OVID, *Epistulæ ex Ponto.* Bk. ii, eleg. 2, l. 31.

5
Safety lies in the middle course. (Medio tutissimus ibis.)
OVID, *Metamorphoses.* Bk. ii, l. 137. *See also under* MODERATION.

6
If still you be disposed to rhyme,
Go try your hand a second time.
Again you fail: yet Safe's the word;
Take courage, and attempt a third.
JONATHAN SWIFT, *On Poetry.* (1733)

Safe is the word.
JOHN KELLY, *Scottish Proverbs,* 291. (1721)

7
He is safe from danger who is on guard even when safe. (Caret periculo qui etiam tutus cavet.)
PUBLILIUS SYRUS, *Sententiæ.* No. 127.

He that's secure is not safe.
BENJAMIN FRANKLIN, *Poor Richard,* 1748.

The way to be safe is never to be secure.
THOMAS FULLER, *Gnomologia.* No. 4820.

Be wary, then; best safety lies in fear.
SHAKESPEARE, *Hamlet.* Act i, sc. 3, l. 43.

Security Is mortals' chiefest enemy.
SHAKESPEARE, *Macbeth.* Act iii, sc. 5, l. 32.

8
Better ride safe in the dark, says the proverb, than in daylight with a cut-throat at your elbow.
SCOTT, *Kenilworth.* Ch. viii.

9
Out of this nettle, danger, we pluck this flower, safety.
SHAKESPEARE, *I Henry IV.* Act ii, sc. 3, l. 11.

10
I would give all my fame for a pot of ale and safety.
SHAKESPEARE, *Henry V.* Act iii, sc. 2, l. 13.

11
What is safe is distasteful; in rashness there is hope. (Ingrata quæ tuta; ex temeritate spes.)
TACITUS, *History.* Bk. iii, sec. 26.

There is always safety in valor.
EMERSON, *English Traits: The Times.*

In ourselves,
In our own honest hearts and chainless hands,
Will be our safeguard.
THOMAS NOON TALFOURD, *Ion.*

12
The only safety for the conquered is to expect no safety. (Una salus victis nullam sperare salutem.)
VERGIL, *Æneid.* Bk. ii, l. 354.

13
It is man's perdition to be safe when he ought to die for the truth.
RICHARD VINES, *Sermon,* preached at St. Margaret's, Westminster, before the House of Commons, 30 Nov., 1642.

Though love repine, and reason chafe,
There came a voice without reply,—
"'Tis man's perdition to be safe,
When for the truth he ought to die."
EMERSON, *Quatrains: Sacrifice.*

A ship in harbor is safe, but that is not what ships are built for.
JOHN A. SHEDD, *Salt from My Attic,* p. 20.

SAILOR, see under Sea

SAINT

14
Saint: a dead sinner revised and edited.
AMBROSE BIERCE, *The Devil's Dictionary.*

15
There are many (questionless) canonised on earth, that shall never be Saints in Heaven.
SIR THOMAS BROWNE, *Religio Medici.* Pt. i, sec. 34.

All are not saints that go to church.
UNKNOWN, *Poor Robin Almanac,* 1687.

16
The soberest saints are more stiff-neckèd
Than th' hottest-headed of the wicked.
BUTLER, *Miscellaneous Thoughts,* l. 306.

The rigid saint, by whom no mercy's shown
To saints whose lives are better than his own.
CHARLES CHURCHILL, *Epistle to Hogarth,* l. 25.

17
Sacred on earth; designed a saint above!
SAMUEL DANIEL, *Sonnets to Delia.* No. vi.

Saints, to do us good, Must be in heaven.
ROBERT BROWNING, *The Ring and the Book.* Pt. vi, l. 176.

18
Every saint, as every man, comes one day to be superfluous.
EMERSON, *Journals,* 1864.

A saint is a sceptic once in every twenty-four hours.
EMERSON, *Journals*, 1864.

1
I don't like your way of conditioning and contracting with the saints. Do this and I'll do that! Here's one for t'other. Save me and I'll give you a taper or go on a pilgrimage.
ERASMUS, *The Shipwreck*.

2
The saint who works no miracles has few pilgrims.
W. G. BENHAM, *Proverbs*, p. 850.

3
To every saint his own candle.
THOMAS FULLER, *Gnomologia*.

Like saint, like offering.
JOHN RAY, *English Proverbs*.

4
The tears of Saints more sweet by far
Than all the songs of sinners are.
ROBERT HERRICK, *Tears*.

5
Those Saints, which God loves best,
The Devil tempts not least.
ROBERT HERRICK, *Temptation*.

6
The greatest saint may be a sinner that never got down to "hard pan."
O. W. HOLMES, *The Guardian Angel*. Ch. 30.

7
A black-leg saint, a spiritual hedger.
THOMAS HOOD, *Ode to Rae Wilson*, l. 180.

8
The way of this world is to praise dead saints and persecute living ones.
NATHANIEL HOWE, *Sermon*.

9
Look in, and see Christ's chosen saint
In triumph wear his Christ-like chain;
No fear lest he should swerve or faint;
"His life is Christ, his death is gain."
JOHN KEBLE, *The Christian Year: Saint Luke*.

10
Would you enjoy soft nights and solid dinners?
Faith, gallants, board with saints and bed with sinners.
POPE, *Epilogue to Mr. Rowe's Jane Shore*, l. 23.

11
A saint in crape is twice a saint in lawn.
POPE, *Moral Essays*. Epis. i, l. 136.

12
Precious in the sight of the Lord is the death of his saints.
Old Testament: Psalms, cxvi, 15.

13
A young Saint an old Devil, (mark this, an old saying, and as true a one, as a young Whore an old Saint.)
RABELAIS, *Works*. Bk. iv, ch. 64. *See also* AGE AND YOUTH.

It is easier to make a saint out of a libertine than out of a prig.
GEORGE SANTAYANA, *Little Essays*, p. 253.

14
A saint may be defined as a person of heroic virtue whose private judgment is privileged.
BERNARD SHAW, *Saint Joan: Preface*.

15
Thou hast damnable iteration and art indeed able to corrupt a saint.
SHAKESPEARE, *I Henry IV*. Act i, sc. 2, l. 101.

Such an injury would vex a very saint.
SHAKESPEARE, *The Taming of the Shrew*. Act iii, sc. 2, l. 28.

'Twould a saint provoke.
POPE, *Moral Essays*. Epis. i, l. 246.

16
I hold you as a thing ensky'd and sainted.
SHAKESPEARE, *Measure for Measure*. Act i, sc. 4, l. 34.

17
O cunning enemy, that, to catch a saint,
With saints dost bait thy hook!
SHAKESPEARE, *Measure for Measure*. Act ii, sc. 2, l. 180.

18
The only difference between the saint and the sinner is that every saint has a past and every sinner has a future.
OSCAR WILDE, *A Woman of No Importance*. Act iii.

19
The saint's day over, good bye to the saint. (La fête passée, adieu le saint.)
UNKNOWN. A French proverb. *See also* DEVIL: SICK AND WELL.

SALT

20
Salt of truth.
E. B. BROWNING, *Aurora Leigh*. Bk. i, l. 708.

21
I could sit at rich men's tables,—though the courtesies that raised me,
Still suggested clear between us the pale spectrum of the salt.
E. B. BROWNING, *Lady Geraldine's Courtship*. St. 9.

22
Men must eat many a peck of salt together before the claims of friendship are fulfilled. (Multos modios salis simul edendos esse, ut amicitia munus expletum sit.)
CICERO, *De Amicitia*. Ch. xix, sec. 67. Referred to as a well-known adage.

It is a true saying that a man must eat a peck of salt with his friend before he knows him.
CERVANTES, *Don Quixote*. Pt. i, ch. 1.

23
Trust no one until you have eaten much salt with him. (Nemini fidas, nisi cum quo prius multos medios salis absumpseris.)
CICERO, *De Amicitia*. Pt. xix, sec. 67.

Before you make a friend, eat a bushel of salt with him.
GEORGE HERBERT, *Jacula Prudentum*. No. 620.

24
Salt seasons all things.
JOHN FLORIO, *Second Frutes*, 53.

Of all smells, bread; of all tastes, salt.
GEORGE HERBERT, *Jacula Prudentum*. No. 166.

1 His [Lot's] wife looked back from behind him, and she became a pillar of salt.
Old Testament: Genesis, xix, 26.

This would make a man a man of salt.
SHAKESPEARE, *King Lear*. Act iv, sc. 6, l. 199.

2 Help me to salt, help me to sorrow.
JOHN GLYDE, JR., *Norfolk Garland*, 44.

3 It is a foolish bird that stayeth the laying of salt on her tail.
JOHN LYLY, *Euphues and His England*, p. 327. (1580)

As boys catch sparrows by flinging salt upon their tails.
SWIFT, *Tale of a Tub* Sec. 8.

4 Salt is good: but if the salt have lost his saltness, wherewith will ye season it? Have salt in yourselves.
New Testament: Mark, ix, 50.

Ye are the salt of the earth: but if the salt have lost his savour, wherewith shall it be salted?
New Testament: Matthew, v, 13.

5 It is a covenant of salt for ever before the Lord unto thee and to thy seed with thee.
Old Testament: Numbers, xviii, 19.

I have eaten your bread and salt,
I have drunk your water and wine.
RUDYARD KIPLING, *Departmental Ditties: Dedication*.

6 Not worth his salt. (Non valet lotium suum.)
PETRONIUS, *Satyricon*. Sec. 57.

7 Attic salt. (Sal Atticum.)
PLINY, *Historia Naturalis*. Bk. xxxi, ch. 7, sec. 41. A term for refined wit.

A turn for punning, call it Attic salt.
BYRON, *English Bards and Scotch Reviewers*, l. 68.

8 A grain of salt being added. (Addito salis grano.)
PLINY, *Historia Naturalis*. Bk. xxiii, sec. 8 He is telling the story of Pompey, who, when he took the palace of Mithridates, discovered the antidote against poison, "to be taken fasting, a grain of salt being added." Hence "cum grano salis," with a grain of salt.

9 Spilt salt is never all gathered.
W. G. BENHAM, *Proverbs*, p. 837.

The salt is spilt.
JOHN GAY, *Fables*. Pt. i, fab. 37. An omen of bad luck.

10 Salt rheum.
SHAKESPEARE, *The Comedy of Errors*. Act iii, sc. 2, l. 131.

Salt tears.
SHAKESPEARE, *A Midsummer-Night's Dream* Act ii. sc. 2, l. 92

Salt scorn.
SHAKESPEARE, *Troilus and Cressida*. Act i, sc 3, l. 371.

11 Make use of thy salt hours
SHAKESPEARE, *Hamlet*. Act iii, sc. 2, l. 166.

The salt in them is hot.
SHAKESPEARE, *King John*. Act v, sc. 7, l. 45.

Salt imagination. [*i e.*, salacious]
SHAKESPEARE, *Measure for Measure*. Act v, sc. 1, l. 406.

Salt Cleopatra.
SHAKESPEARE, *Antony and Cleopatra*. Act ii, sc. 1, l. 21.

12 We have some salt of our youth in us.
SHAKESPEARE, *The Merry Wives of Windsor*. Act ii, sc. 3, l. 50.

As salt as wolves in pride.
SHAKESPEARE, *Othello*. Act iii, sc. 3, l. 404.

SALVATION

13 What must I do to be saved?
New Testament: Acts, xvi, 30.

Despair of being saved, "except thou be born again."
This kind of despair is one of the first steps to heaven.
RICHARD BAXTER, *Saint's Rest*. Ch. 6.

For *my* salvation must its doom receive,
Not from what *others*, but what *I* believe.
DRYDEN, *Religio Laici*, l. 303.

No one can be redeemed by another. No God and no saint is able to shield a man from the consequences of his evil doings. Every one of us must become his own redeemer
SUBHADRA BHIKSHU, *A Buddhist Catechism*.

Salvation is from God only. (Solo Deus salus.)
UNKNOWN. A Latin motto.

14 The elect are those who will; the non-elect are those who won't.
HENRY WARD BEECHER, *Life Thoughts*.

15 The fearless man is his own salvation.
ROBERT BRIDGES, *The First Seven Divisions*. 5 Dec., 1917.

16 Behold, now is the accepted time; behold, now is the day of salvation.
New Testament: II Corinthians, vi, 2.

17 Souls are not saved in bundles.
EMERSON, *Conduct of Life: Worship*.

18 The knowledge of sin is the beginning of salvation (Initium est salutis notitia peccati.)
EPICURUS, *Fragments*. Frag. 522. (SENECA, *Epistulæ ad Lucilium*. Epis xxviii sec. 9.)

19 I know that my redeemer liveth.
Old Testament: Job, xix, 25.

1
I am the door [bâb]: by me if any man enter in, he shall be saved.
New Testament: John, x, 9. Bâbism was founded by Mirza Ali Mohammed, who told the people that he was the bâb or door through which all must pass to enter Paradise.

2
Say, Heav'nly Powers, where shall we find such love,
Which of ye will be mortal to redeem
Man's mortal crime, and just th' unjust to save?
MILTON, *Paradise Lost*. Bk. iii, l. 213.

And now without redemption all mankind
Must have been lost, adjudg'd to Death and Hell
By doom severe.
MILTON, *Paradise Lost*. Bk. iii, l. 222.

3
The will to be saved means a great deal. (Hoc multum est, velle servari.)
SENECA, *Epistulæ ad Lucilium*. Epis. iii, sec. 3.

A man may be damned for despairing to be saved.
JEREMY TAYLOR, *Holy Living*, p. 259.

4
It were pity but they should suffer salvation, body and soul.
SHAKESPEARE, *Much Ado About Nothing*. Act iii, sc. 3, l. 3.

5
And for a helmet, the hope of salvation.
New Testament: I Thessalonians, v, 8. (Galea spes salutis.—*Vulgate*.)

6
Salvation by the cross. (In cruce salus.)
THOMAS À KEMPIS, *De Imitatione Christi*. Bk. ii, ch. 2.

With crosses, relics, crucifixes,
Beads, pictures, rosaries, and pixes,—
The tools of working our salvation
By mere mechanic operation.
BUTLER, *Hudibras*. Pt. iii, canto 1, l. 1495.

7
There is no expeditious road
To pack and label men for God,
And save them by the barrel-load.
FRANCIS THOMPSON, *A Judgement in Heaven: Epilogue*.

SATAN, see Devil

SATIRE

See also Laughter and Scorn; Ridicule

8
He that hath a satirical vein, as he maketh others afraid of his wit, so he had need be afraid of others' memory.
FRANCIS BACON, *Essays: Of Discourse*.

When there's more Malice shown than Matter,
On the Writer falls the Satyr.
BENJAMIN FRANKLIN, *Poor Richard*, 1747.

9
Level at beauty and at wit,
The fairest mark is easiest hit.
BUTLER, *Hudibras*. Pt. ii, canto 1, l. 663.

10
I'll publish, right or wrong:
Fools are my theme, let Satire be my song.
BYRON, *English Bards and Scotch Reviewers*, l. 5.

Strange! that a Man who has wit enough to write a Satire should have folly enough to publish it.
BENJAMIN FRANKLIN, *Poor Richard*, 1742.

11
And that sarcastic levity of tongue,
The stinging of a heart the world hath stung.
BYRON, *Lara*. Canto i, st. 5.

12
Sarcasm I now see to be, in general, the language of the devil.
CARLYLE, *Sartor Resartus*. Bk. ii, ch. 4.

13
When satire flies abroad on falsehood's wing,
Short is her life, and impotent her sting;
But when to truth allied, the wound she gives
Sinks deep, and to remotest ages lives.
CHARLES CHURCHILL, *The Author*, l. 217.

Why should we fear; and what? the laws?
They all are arm'd in virtue's cause;
And aiming at the self-same end,
Satire is always virtue's friend.
CHURCHILL, *The Ghost*. Bk. iii, l. 943.

14
Satire is a lonely and introspective occupation, for nobody can describe a fool to the life without much patient self-inspection.
FRANK MOORE COLBY, *Simple Simon*.

15
Crack the satiric thong.
COWPER, *The Task*. Bk. iii, l. 26.

And I must twist my little gift of words
Into a scourge of rough and knotted cords
Unmusical, that whistle as they swing
To leave on shameless backs their purple sting.
J. R. LOWELL, *Epistle to George William Curtis*.

16
Unless a love of virtue light the flame,
Satire is, more than those he brands, to blame;
He hides behind a magisterial air
His own offences, and strips others bare.
COWPER, *Charity*, l. 491.

When scandal has new minted an old lie,
Or tax'd invention for a fresh supply,
'Tis call'd a satire.
COWPER, *Charity*, l. 513.

17
Satire has always shone among the rest,
And is the boldest way, if not the best,
To tell men freely of their foulest faults;
To laugh at their vain deeds and vainer thoughts.
DRYDEN, *Essay Upon Satire*, l. 11.

1
The arrows of sarcasm are barbed with contempt. . . . It is the sneer of the satire, the ridicule, that galls and wounds.

WASHINGTON GLADDEN, *Things Old and New: Taming the Tongue.*

2
It is difficult *not* to write satire. (Difficile est satiram non scribere.)

JUVENAL, *Satires.* Sat. i, l. 29.

3
Men are satirical from vanity more often than from malice. (On est d'ordinaire plus médisant par vanité que par malice.)

LA ROCHEFOUCAULD, *Maximes.* No. 483.

4
Satire should, like a polished razor keen,
Wound with a touch that's scarcely felt or seen.
Thine is an oyster knife, that hacks and hews;
The rage, but not the talent, to abuse.

MARY WORTLEY MONTAGU, *To the Imitator of the First Satire of Horace.* [Pope.]

5
I wear my Pen as others do their Sword.
To each affronting sot I meet, the word
Is *Satisfaction:* straight to thrusts I go,
And pointed satire runs him through and through.

JOHN OLDHAM, *Satire upon a Printer,* l. 35.

6
I have never put anyone on the rack by a biting poem, nor does my verse denounce any man's crimes. (Non ego mordaci distrinxi carmine quemquam; Nec meus ullius crimina versus habet.)

OVID, *Tristia.* Bk. ii, l. 563.

Who, for the poor renown of being smart,
Would leave a sting within a brother's heart?

EDWARD YOUNG, *Love of Fame.* Sat. ii, l. 113.

7
Satire or sense, alas! can Sporus feel?
Who breaks a butterfly upon a wheel?

POPE, *Epistle to Dr. Arbuthnot,* l. 307. ["Sporus," Lord John Hervey.]

For who would be satirical
Upon a thing so very small?

SWIFT, *Dr. Delany's Villa.*

8
There are to whom my satire seems too bold;
Scarce to wise Peter complaisant enough,
And something said of Chartres much too rough.

POPE, *Imitations of Horace: Satires.* Bk. ii, sat. 1, l. 2.

Satire 's my weapon, but I 'm too discreet
To run amuck, and tilt at all I meet.

POPE, *Imitations of Horace: Satires.* Bk. ii, sat. 1, l. 69.

9
The flash of that satiric rage,
Which, bursting on the early stage,
Branded the vices of the age,
And broke the keys of Rome.

SCOTT, *Marmion.* Canto iv, st. 7.

10
That is some satire, keen and critical.

SHAKESPEARE, *A Midsummer-Night's Dream.* Act v, sc. 1, l. 54.

11
I'll tell thee what, prince; a college of wit-crackers cannot flout me out of my humour. Dost thou think I care for a satire or an epigram?

SHAKESPEARE, *Much Ado About Nothing.* Act v, sc. 4, l. 101.

12
Let there be gall enough in thy ink, though thou write with a goose-pen, no matter.

SHAKESPEARE, *Twelfth Night.* Act iii, sc. 2, l. 52.

13
Satire is a sort of glass wherein beholders do generally discover everybody's face but their own, which is the chief reason for that kind reception it meets with in the world.

SWIFT, *The Battle of the Books: Preface.*

Each line shall stab, shall blast, like daggers and like fire.

SWIFT, *Ode: Dr. William Sancreff.*

14
Satire lies about literary men while they live and eulogy lies about them when they die. (La satire ment sur les gens de lettres pendant leur vie, et l'éloge ment après leur mort.)

VOLTAIRE, *Lettre à Bordes,* 10 Jan., 1769.

15
N. B.—This is rote Sarcastikul.

ARTEMUS WARD, *A Visit to Brigham Young.*

SAVAGERY

16
They led their wild desires to woods and caves,
And thought that all but savages were slaves.

DRYDEN, *Absalom and Achitophel.* Pt. i, l. 55.

17
Ere the base laws of servitude began,
When wild in woods the noble savage ran.

DRYDEN, *Conquest of Granada.* Act i, sc. 1.

When in a barbarous age, with blood defiled,
The human savage roam'd the gloomy wild.

FALCONER, *The Shipwreck.* Canto iii, l. 1.

18
Savages, who have only what is necessary, converse in figures.

EMERSON, *Nature, Studies and Addresses: Language.*

Dirty savages, extemporizing from hand to mouth.

EMERSON, *Uncollected Lectures: Public and Private Education.*

19
A rude and savage man of Ind.

SHAKESPEARE, *Love's Labour's Lost.* Act iv, sc. 3, l. 222.

1
This is the bloodiest shame, the wildest savagery.
SHAKESPEARE, *King John*. Act iv, sc. 3, l. 48.

2
Savageness begets savageness.
HERBERT SPENCER, *Education*. Ch. 3.

3
I will take some savage woman, she shall rear my dusky race.
Iron-jointed, supple-sinew'd, they shall dive, and they shall run,
Catch the wild goat by the hair, and hurl their lances in the sun;
Whistle back the parrot's call, and leap the rainbows of the brooks,
Not with blinded eyesight poring over miserable books.
TENNYSON, *Locksley Hall*, l. 168.

SAVING, see Thrift

SCANDAL

See also Calumny, Rumor, Slander

I—Scandal: Definitions

4
In things that a man would not be seen in himself, it is a point of cunning to borrow the name of the world; as to say, "The world says." or "There is a speech abroad."
FRANCIS BACON, *Essays: Of Cunning*.

Everybody says it, and what everybody says must be true.
J. FENIMORE COOPER, *Miles Wallingford*. Ch. 30. For "Gossip column" see 2298i:4.

5
That abominable tittle-tattle,
Which is the cud eschew'd by human cattle.
BYRON, *Don Juan*. Canto xii, st. 43.

6
Gossip is a sort of smoke that comes from the dirty tobacco-pipes of those who diffuse it; it proves nothing but the bad taste of the smoker.
GEORGE ELIOT, *Daniel Deronda*. Bk. ii, ch. 13.

7
Gossip is vice enjoyed vicariously.
ELBERT HUBBARD, *Philistine*. Vol. xix, p. 104.

8
The opposite of gossip about men and affairs is often the truth. (Le contraire des bruits qui courent des affaires ou des personnes est souvent la vérité.)
LA BRUYÈRE, *Les Caractères*. Pt. xii.

9
Gossips are people who have only one relative in common, but that relative the highest possible; namely God.
CHRISTOPHER MORLEY, *Religio Journalistici*, 13.

10
Gossip is charming! History is merely gossip. But scandal is gossip made tedious by morality.
OSCAR WILDE, *Lady Windermere's Fan*. Act iii.

II—Scandal: Apothegms

11
That which passes out of one mouth passes into a hundred ears.
ERNEST BRAMAH, *Kai Lung's Golden Hours*.

12
Dead scandals form good subjects for dissection.
BYRON, *Don Juan*. Canto i, st. 31.

And dye conjecture with a darker hue.
BYRON, *Lara*. Canto ii, st. 6.

13
In the case of scandal, as in that of robbery, the receiver is always thought as bad as the thief.
LORD CHESTERFIELD, *Letters*, 19 Oct., 1748.

Seem always ignorant of all matters of private scandal and defamation, though you should hear them a thousand times; for the parties affected always look upon the receiver to be almost as bad as the thief.
LORD CHESTERFIELD, *Letters*, 15 Jan., 1753.

14
The words she spoke of Mrs. Harris, lambs could not forgive . . . nor worms forget.
DICKENS, *Martin Chuzzlewit*. Ch. 40.

15
The more you are talked about, the less powerful you are.
BENJAMIN DISRAELI, *Endymion*. Ch. 36.

16
For a bird of the air shall carry the voice.
Old Testament: Ecclesiastes, x, 20. *See under* BIRD: APOTHEGMS.

17
A gossip speaks ill of all and all of her.
THOMAS FULLER, *Gnomologia*. No. 186.

18
Scandal will rub out like dirt when it is dry.
THOMAS FULLER, *Gnomologia*. No. 4076.

Knowing, what all experience serves to show,
No mud can soil us but the mud we throw.
J. R. LOWELL, *Epistle to George William Curtis*.

19
Common fame is mostly to blame.
THOMAS FULLER, *Gnomologia*. No. 6120.

Common fame is seldom to blame.
JOHN RAY, *English Proverbs*.

"Common fame is seldom to blame," is the baser proverb.
R. C. TRENCH, *Proverbs*, 13.

20
I shall make a song of the Queen of Crete
Who had nine panthers at her feet,
Who wore bright brooches in her hair—
And her private life was her own affair.
JOHN GRIMES, *The Queen of Crete*.

21
Gossips are frogs—they drink and talk.
GEORGE HERBERT, *Jacula Prudentum*. No. 271.

22
It's merry when gossips meet.
BEN JONSON, *The Staple of News: Induction*.

1
It is at home, not in public, one washes one's dirty linen. (C'est en famille, ce n'est pas en publique. qu'on lave son linge sale.)

NAPOLEON BONAPARTE, *Speech*, to the French Legislative Assembly, on his return from Elba in 1815.

The king has sent me some of his dirty linen to wash; I will wash yours another time.

VOLTAIRE, *Reply to General Manstein*, referring to Frederick the Great.

2
The chameleon, who is said to feed upon nothing but air, has of all animals the nimblest tongue.

SWIFT, *Thoughts on Various Subjects.*

3
You do not know it but you are the talk of all the town. (Fabula, nec sentis, tota jactaris in urba.)

OVID, *Amores*. Bk. iii, eleg. 1, l. 21.

He shall mourn, and shall be marked out for the gossip of the whole town. (Flebit et insignis tota cantabitur urbe.)

HORACE, *Satires*. Bk. ii, sat. 1, l. 46.

We in the world's wide mouth
Live scandalized and foully spoken of.

SHAKESPEARE, *I Henry IV*. Act i, sc. 3, l. 153.

4
Tell it not in Gath, publish it not in the streets of Askelon.

Old Testament: II Samuel, i, 20.

5
For greatest scandal waits on greatest state.

SHAKESPEARE, *The Rape of Lucrece*, l. 1006.

Never yet
Was noble man but made ignoble talk.

TENNYSON, *Lancelot and Elaine*, l. 1080.

No scandal about Queen Elizabeth, I hope?

SHERIDAN, *The Critic*. Act ii, sc. 1.

6
Well, for my part, I believe there never was a scandalous tale without some foundation.

SHERIDAN, *The School for Scandal*. Act ii, sc. 2.

The basis of every scandal is an absolutely immoral certainty.

OSCAR WILDE, *A Woman of No Importance*. Act i.

How awful to reflect that what people say of us is true.

LOGAN PEARSALL SMITH, *Afterthoughts.*

7
Swift flies each tale of laughter, shame or folly,
Caught by Paul Pry, and carried home to Polly.

CHARLES SPRAGUE, *Curiosity*, l. 329.

8
There is nothing that can't be made worse by telling. (Nil est Quin male narrando possit depravarier.)

TERENCE, *Phormio*, l. 696. (Act iv, sc. 4.)

9
There is only one thing in the world worse than being talked about, and that is not being talked about.

OSCAR WILDE, *Picture of Dorian Gray*. Ch. 1.

10
They say. What do they say? Let them say. (Λέγουσιν ἃ θέλουσιν. Λεγέτωσαν. Οὐ μέλει μοι.)

UNKNOWN. Greek inscription on rings found at Pompeii. Used by Bernard Shaw as a motto over his fireplace, as taken from "an ancient Frenchman."

They say. Quhat say they? Let thame say.

Charm inscribed over doors of houses in Scotland during the sixteenth century; also the motto of the Scottish Earls Marischal, given by them to Marischal College.

"They say" is half a lie.

PALMER, *Moral Essays on Proverbs*, p. 261.

Have you heard of the terrible family They,
And the dreadful venomous things They say?
Why, half the gossip under the sun,
If you trace it back, you will find begun
In that wretched House of They.

ELLA WHEELER WILCOX, *"They Say."*

III—Scandal: Its Baseness

11
To converse with Scandal is to play at Losing Loadum; you must lose a good name to him, before you can win it for yourself.

WILLIAM CONGREVE, *Love for Love*. Act i, sc. 2. In "Losing Loadum" the game is to *lose* tricks.

12
Whoever keeps an open ear
For tattlers will be sure to hear
The trumpet of contention;
Aspersion is the babbler's trade,
To listen is to lend him aid,
And rush into dissension.

COWPER, *Friendship*, l. 97.

13
In a contempt for the gabble of today's opinions the secret of the world is to be learned.

EMERSON, *Nature, Studies and Addresses: Literary Ethics.*

14
And there's a lust in man no charm can tame
Of loudly publishing his neighbor's shame;
On eagles' wings immortal scandals fly,
While virtuous actions are but born and die.

JUVENAL, *Satires*. Sat. ix, l. 102. (Stephen Harvey, tr.)

Assail'd by scandal and the tongue of strife,
His only answer was, a blameless life;
And he that forg'd, and he that threw, the dart,
Had each a brother's int'rest in his heart!

COWPER, *Hope*, l. 576.

15
All the wickedness I know of any in our convent
I cough up in our cloisters and all the world hears it.

LANGLAND, *Piers Plowman: Seven Sins.*

1
The rolling fictions grow in strength and size,
Each author adding to the former lies.
OVID, *Metamorphoses*, xii, 56. (Swift, tr.)

A cruel story runs on wheels, and every hand oils the wheels as they run.
OUIDA, *Wisdom, Wit and Pathos: Moths.*

2
To babble and to talk is most tolerable and not to be endured.
SHAKESPEARE, *Much Ado About Nothing*. Act iii, sc. 3, l. 36.

3
Ye think the rustic cackle of your bourg
The murmur of the world!
TENNYSON, *Geraint and Enid*, l. 276.

Below me, there, is the village, and looks how quiet and small!
And yet bubbles o'er like a city, with gossip, scandal, and spite.
TENNYSON, *Maud*, l. 108.

IV—Scandal Mongers

4
I doubt if he bathed before he dressed.
A brasier?—the pagan, he burned perfumes!
You see it is proved what the neighbours guessed:
His wife and himself had separate rooms.
ROBERT BROWNING, *House.*

5
The mair they talk I'm kend the better;
E'en let them clash!
BURNS, *The Poet's Welcome to His Love-Begotten Daughter*. St. 2.

6
Now, the best way to do is to do as you please,
For your mind, if you have one, will then be at ease.
Of course you will meet with all sorts of abuse,
But don't try to stop it, it is of no use,
For people will talk.
SAMUEL DODGE, *People Will Talk.*

7
Do not be so impatient to set the town right concerning the unfounded pretensions and the false reputation of certain men of standing. They are laboring harder to set the town right concerning themselves, and will certainly succeed.
EMERSON, *Essays, Second Series: New England Reformers.*

The commanding eye of his neighborhood, which held him to decorum. . . . But . . . the censors of action are as numerous and as near in Paris, as in Littleton or Portland; the gossip is as prompt and vengeful.
EMERSON, *Conduct of Life: Worship.*

8
Pleasant as it is to hear
Scandal tickling in our ear
Ev'n of our own mothers;
In the chit chat of the day,
To us is pay'd, when we're away,
What we lent to others.
JOHN GAY, *The Lady's Lamentation.*

9
And though you duck them ne'er so long,
Not one salt drop e'er wets their tongue;
'Tis hence they scandal have at will,
And that this member ne'er lies still.
JOHN GAY, *The Mad Dog*. Last lines.

10
Fierce to invent some sort of scandal against anyone. (Quælibet in quemvis opprobria fingere sævus.)
HORACE, *Epistles*. Bk. i, epis. 15, l. 30.

Talk of unusual swell of waist
In maid of honour loosely laced.
MATTHEW GREEN, *The Spleen*, l. 188.

11
He's gone, and who knows how he may report
Thy words by adding fuel to the flame?
MILTON, *Samson Agonistes*, l. 1350.

12
The mind conscious of innocence despises false reports: but we are a set always ready to believe a scandal. (Conscia mens recti famæ mendacia risit, Sed nos in vitium credula turba sumus.)
OVID, *Fasti*. Bk. iv, l. 311.

13
To John I owed great obligation;
But John unhappily thought fit
To publish it to all the nation;
Sure John and I are more than quit.
MATTHEW PRIOR, *An Epigram.*

14
How hard soe'er it be to bridle wit,
Yet memory oft no less requires the bit.
How many hurried by its force away,
Forever in the land of gossips stray.
BENJAMIN STILLINGFLEET, *Essay on Conversation.*

15
Tattlers also, and busybodies, speaking things which they ought not.
New Testament: I Timothy, v, 13.

Some mumble-news, some trencher-knight, some Dick.
SHAKESPEARE, *Love's Labour's Lost*. Act v, sc. 2, l. 464.

16
The serpent's tongue.
SHAKESPEARE, *A Midsummer-Night's Dream.* Act v, sc. 1, l. 440.

She is not old, she is not young,
The Woman with the Serpent's Tongue.
The haggard cheek, the hungering eye,
The poisoned words that wildly fly,
The famished face, the fevered hand—
Who slights the worthiest in the land,
Sneers at the just, contemns the brave,

And blackens goodness in its grave.
WILLIAM WATSON, *The Woman with the Serpent's Tongue.*

To think that such as she can mar
Names that among the noblest are!
That hands like hers can touch the springs
That move who knows what men and things!
That on *her* will *their* fates have hung!
The Woman with the Serpent's Tongue.
WILLIAM WATSON, *The Woman with the Serpent's Tongue.* Richard Le Gallienne wrote a réplique to this poem, "The poet with the coward's heart."

Skill'd by a touch to deepen scandal's tints
With all the kind mendacity of hints,
While mingling truth with falsehood—sneers with smiles—
A thread of candour with a web of wiles;
A plain blunt show of briefly-spoken seeming,
To hide her bloodless heart's soul-harden'd scheming;
A lip of lies; a face form'd to conceal;
And, without feeling, mock at all who feel;
With a vile mask the Gorgon would disown,—
A cheek of parchment, and an eye of stone.
BYRON, *A Sketch from Private Life,* l. 55.

Her mouth is a honey-blossom,
No doubt, as the poet sings;
But within her lips, the petals,
Lurks a cruel bee that stings.
WILLIAM DEAN HOWELLS, *The Sarcastic Fair.*

1
He rams his quill with scandal, and with scoff,
But 'tis so very foul, it won't go off.
YOUNG, *Epistles to Pope.* Epis. i, l. 199.

V—Scandal and Women

2
Nut while the two-legged gab-machine's so plenty.
J. R. LOWELL, *Biglow Papers,* Ser. ii, No. 11.

3
From loveless youth to unrespected age,
No passion gratified except her rage:
So much the Fury still outran the Wit,
The pleasure miss'd her, and the scandal hit.
Who breaks with her provokes revenge from Hell,
But he's a bolder man who dares be well.
POPE, *Moral Essays.* Epis. ii, l. 125.

4
Her tea she sweetens, as she sips, with scandal.
SAMUEL ROGERS, *Written to be Spoken by Mrs. Siddons.*

Love and scandal are the best sweeteners of tea.
FIELDING, *Love in Several Masques.* Act iv, sc. 2.

Scandal's the sweetener of a *female* feast.
YOUNG, *Love of Fame.* Sat. vi, l. 353.

5
Nor do they trust their tongues alone,
But speak a language of their own;
Can read a nod, a shrug, a look,
Far better than a printed book;
Convey a libel in a frown,
And wink a reputation down;
Or, by the tossing of a fan,
Describe the lady and the man.
SWIFT, *Journal of a Modern Lady,* l. 188.

Ladies, your most obedient.—Mercy on me! here is the whole set! a character dead at every word, I suppose.
SHERIDAN, *The School for Scandal.* Act ii, sc. 2.
See also under REPUTATION.

SCHOLAR

See also Learning, Study

6
The rich physician, honour'd lawyer ride,
Whilst the poor scholar foots it by their side.
(Dat Galenus opes, dat Justinianus honores,
Sed genus et species cogitur ire pedes.)
ROBERT BURTON, *Anatomy of Melancholy.* Pt. i, sec. ii, mem. 3, subs. 15. A footnote refers to Buchanan, eleg. lib.

And to this day is every scholar poor;
Gross gold from them runs headlong to the boor.
ROBERT BURTON, *Anatomy of Melancholy.* Pt. i, sec. ii, mem. 3, subs. 15.

Mark what ills the scholar's life assail,
Toil, envy, want, the patron, and the jail.
SAMUEL JOHNSON, *The Vanity of Human Wishes,* l. 157.

7
The scholar who cherishes the love of comfort, is not fit to be deemed a scholar.
CONFUCIUS, *Analects.* Bk. xiv, ch. 3.

8
I offer perpetual congratulation to the scholar; he has drawn the white lot in life.
EMERSON, *Lectures and Biographical Sketches: The Man of Letters.*

I cannot forgive a scholar his homeless despondency.
EMERSON, *Lectures and Biographical Sketches: The Man of Letters.*

9
Every man is a scholar potentially, and does not need any one good so much as this of right thought.
EMERSON, *Lectures and Biographical Sketches: The Man of Letters.*

Shall I tell you the secret of the true scholar? It is this: Every man I meet is my master in some point, and in that I learn of him.
EMERSON, *Letters and Social Aims: Greatness.*

10
The office of the scholar is to cheer, to raise, and to guide men by showing them facts amidst appearances.
EMERSON, *Nature, Addresses, and Lectures: The American Scholar.*

The scholar is the student of the world; and of what worth the world is, and with what emphasis it accosts the soul of man, such is the worth, such the call of the scholar.
EMERSON, *Nature, Addresses, and Lectures: Literary Ethics.*

1
He [the scholar] must be a solitary, laborious, modest, and charitable soul. He must embrace solitude as a bride. . . . That he may become acquainted with his thoughts.
EMERSON, *Nature, Addresses, and Lectures: Literary Ethics.*

To talk in public, to think in solitude, to read and to hear, to inquire and to answer inquiries, is the business of a scholar.
SAMUEL JOHNSON, *Rasselas.* Ch. 8.

Where should the scholar live? In solitude, or in society? in the green stillness of the country, where he can hear the heart of Nature beat, or in the dark, gray town, where he can hear and feel the throbbing heart of man?
LONGFELLOW, *Hyperion.* Bk. i, ch. 8.

2
Hell is paved with the skulls of great scholars.
GILES FIRMIN, *The Real Christian. See also* HELL: ITS PAVEMENT.

3
The world's great men have not commonly been great scholars, nor its great scholars great men.
O. W. HOLMES, *The Autocrat of the Breakfast-Table.* Ch. 6.

4
The classic scholar is he whose blood is most nuptial to the webbed bottle. . . . Port hymns to his conservatism.
GEORGE MEREDITH, *The Egoist.* Ch. 19.

5
The ink of the scholar is more sacred than the blood of the martyr.
MOHAMMED, *Tribute to Reason.*

6
A mere scholar, a mere ass.
ROBERT BURTON, *The Anatomy of Melancholy.* Pt. i, sec. ii, memb. 3, subsec. 15.

A mere scholar is a mere—you know the old proverb.
SUSANNAH CENTLIVRE, *Stolen Heiress.* Act i.

A scholar at court is an ass among apes.
JOHN CLARKE, *Parœmiologia,* 145.

This scholar, rake, Christian, dupe, gamester, and poet.
DAVID GARRICK, *Jupiter and Mercury.*

He was a rake among scholars, and a scholar among rakes.
MACAULAY, *Essays: Aikin's Life of Addison.* Referring to Sir Richard Steele.

7
He is yet a scholar, than which kind of man there is nothing so simple, so sincere, none better.
PLINY, of Isæus, the Greek sophist. (BURTON, *Anatomy of Melancholy,* i, ii, 3, 15.)

8
Love seldom haunts the breast where learning lies,
And Venus sets ere Mercury can rise.
Those play the scholars who can't play the men,
And use that weapon which they have, their pen.
POPE, *The Wife of Bath: Prologue,* l. 369.

9
He was a scholar, and a ripe and good one;
Exceeding wise, fair-spoken and persuading:
Lofty and sour to them that loved him not,
But to those men that sought him sweet as summer.
SHAKESPEARE, *Henry VIII.* Act iv, sc. 2, l. 51.

A scholar and a soldier.
SHAKESPEARE, *The Merchant of Venice.* Act i, sc. 2, l. 124.

Gentleman and scholar.
BURNS, *The Twa Dogs. See also under* GENTLEMAN.

SCHOOL, see Education

SCIENCE

I—Science: Definitions

10
Science is the labour and handicraft of the mind; poetry can only be considered its recreation.
FRANCIS BACON, *Description of the Intellectual Globe.* Ch. 1.

Science is for those who learn; poetry, for those who know.
JOSEPH ROUX, *Meditations of a Parish Priest.* Pt. i, No. 71.

11
What we might call, by way of eminence, the *dismal science.*
THOMAS CARLYLE, *The Nigger Question.* Referring to political economy and "social science."

The science of sciences. (Scientia scientiarum.)
S. T. COLERIDGE, *Biographia Literaria.* Ch. 12. Referring to philosophy. *See also under* PHILOSOPHY.

The science of fools with long memories.
PLANCHÉ, *Preliminary Observations: Pursuivant of Arms.* Speaking of Heraldry.

12
What art was to the ancient world, science is to the modern.
BENJAMIN DISRAELI, *Coningsby.* Bk. iv, ch. 1.

Science and art belong to the whole world, and the barriers of nationality vanish before them.
GOETHE, *Remark,* to a German historian, 1813

13
Science distinguishes a man of honour from one of those athletic brutes whom undeservedly we call heroes.
DRYDEN, *Fables: Preface. See also under* GAME.

14
Men love to wonder, and that is the seed of our science.
EMERSON, *Society and Solitude: Works and Days.*

15
Geometry, which is the only science that it

hath pleased God hitherto to bestow on mankind.

THOMAS HOBBES, *Leviathan*. Pt. i, ch. 4.

And Lucy, dear child, mind your arithmetic. . . . What would life be without arithmetic, but a scene of horrors?

SYDNEY SMITH, *Letters: To Miss* ——, 22 July, 1835.

1
Science is the topography of ignorance.

O. W. HOLMES, *Medical Essays*, p. 211.

Equipped with his five senses, man explores the universe around him and calls the adventure Science.

EDWIN POWELL HUBBLE, *Science*.

Human science is uncertain guess.

MATTHEW PRIOR, *Solomon*. Bk. i, l. 740.

True science teaches, above all, to doubt and to be ignorant.

MIGUEL DE UNAMUNO, *The Tragic Sense of Life*, p. 93.

2
A series of judgments, revised without ceasing, goes to make up the incontestable progress of science.

DUCLAUX, *Pasteur*, p. 111.

3
Science is nothing but perception.

PLATO, *Theætetus*. Sec. 182.

4
Economics, the science of managing one's own household. (Οἰκονομικὴν, administrandæ familiaris rei scientiam.)

SENECA, *Epistulæ ad Lucilium*. Epis. 89, sec. 10.

5
Science is the great antidote to the poison of enthusiasm and superstition.

ADAM SMITH, *The Wealth of Nations*. Bk. v, pt. 3, sec. 3.

6
Technocracy.

WILLIAM H. SMYTH. Used first by him in *Industrial Management*, March, 1919.

Scientific reorganization of national energy and resources, coördinating industrial democracy to effect the will of the people.

WILLIAM H. SMYTH, definition of technocracy. (*Concerning Irascible Strong*, 1926.)

Scientific management.

FREDERICK W. TAYLOR. Evolved as name for the "Taylor system" about 1910. (SULLIVAN, *Our Times*. Vol. iv, p. 77.)

7
Science is organized knowledge.

HERBERT SPENCER, *Education*. Ch. 2.

8
Science when well digested is nothing but good sense and reason.

STANISLAUS, King of Poland, *Maxims*. No. 43.

Science is a first-rate piece of furniture for a man's upper-chamber, if he has common-sense on the ground floor.

O. W. HOLMES, *The Poet at the Breakfast-Table*. Ch. 5.

Science is madness if good sense does not cure it. (Ciencia es locura Si buen senso no la cura.)

UNKNOWN. A Spanish proverb.

9
Science is a cemetery of dead ideas.

MIGUEL DE UNAMUNO, *The Tragic Sense of Life*, p. 90.

10
To define it rudely but not inaptly, engineering is the art of doing that well with one dollar which any bungler can do with two after a fashion.

ARTHUR M. WELLINGTON, *The Economic Theory of Railway Location: Introduction*.

II—Science: Apothegms

11
While bright-eyed Science watches round.

THOMAS GRAY, *Ode for Music*, l. 11.

Like truths of Science waiting to be caught.

TENNYSON, *The Golden Year*, l. 17.

12
Every science has been an outcast.

R. G. INGERSOLL, *The Liberty of Man, Woman and Child*.

13
Science is . . . like virtue, its own exceeding great reward.

CHARLES KINGSLEY, *Health and Education: Science*.

14
One Science only will one genius fit,
So vast is Art, so narrow human wit.

POPE, *Essay on Criticism*. Pt. i, l. 60.

15
[We] do not learn for want of time
The sciences which should become our country.

SHAKESPEARE, *Henry V*. Act v, sc. 2, l. 58.

16
Only when genius is married to science, can the highest results be produced.

HERBERT SPENCER, *Education*. Ch. 1.

17
Science moves, but slowly, slowly, creeping on from point to point.

ALFRED TENNYSON, *Locksley Hall*, l. 134.

Mystics always hope that science will some day overtake them.

BOOTH TARKINGTON, *Looking Forward*, p. 112.

III—Science: Its Shortcomings

18
'Twas thus by the glare of false science betray'd,
That leads, to bewilder; and dazzles, to blind.

JAMES BEATTIE, *The Hermit*. St. 5.

19
The atoms of Democritus,
And Newton's particles of light
Are sands upon the Red Sea shore,
Where Israel's tents do shine so bright.

WILLIAM BLAKE, *Mock On, Voltaire, Rousseau*.

1
Knowledge is not happiness, and science
But an exchange of ignorance for that
Which is another kind of ignorance.
BYRON, *Manfred.* Act ii, sc. 4.

2
O star-eyed Science, hast thou wandered
there,
To waft us home the message of despair?
CAMPBELL, *Pleasures of Hope.* Pt. ii, l. 325.

When Science from Creation's face
Enchantment's veil withdraws,
What lovely visions yield their place
To cold material laws!
THOMAS CAMPBELL, *To the Rainbow.*

3
Why does this magnificent applied science which saves work and makes life easier bring us so little happiness? The simple answer runs: Because we have not yet learned to make sensible use of it.
ALBERT EINSTEIN, *Address,* California Institute of Technology, Feb., 1931.

4
'Tis a short sight to limit our faith in laws to those of gravity, of chemistry, of botany, and so forth.
EMERSON, *Conduct of Life: Worship.*

5
O Timothy, keep that which is committed to thy trust, avoiding profane and vain babblings, and oppositions of science falsely so called.
New Testament: I Timothy, vi, 20.

The humble knowledge of thyself is a surer way to God than the deepest search after science.
THOMAS À KEMPIS, *De Imitatione Christi.* Pt. i, ch. 3.

6
Science robs men of wisdom and usually converts them into phantom beings loaded up with facts.
MIGUEL DE UNAMUNO, *Essays and Soliloquies,* p. 55.

7
But beyond the bright searchlights of science,
Out of sight of the windows of sense,
Old riddles still bid us defiance,
Old questions of Why and of Whence.
W. C. D. WHETHAM, *Recent Development of Physical Science,* p. 10.

8
The higher we soar on the wings of science, the worse our feet seem to get entangled in the wires.
UNKNOWN. (*The New Yorker,* 7 Feb., 1931.)

IV—Science: The Scientist

9
He would pore by the hour o'er a weed or a
flower,
Or the slugs that come crawling out after a
shower.
R. H. BARHAM, *The Knight and the Lady.*

10
Oh! what a noble heart was here undone,
When Science' self destroyed her favourite
son.
BYRON, *English Bards and Scotch Reviewers,* l. 835. Referring to Henry Kirke White, who died as a result of over-study.

11
A man, always studying one subject, will view the general affairs of the world through the coloured prism of his own atmosphere.
BENJAMIN DISRAELI, *Speech,* House of Commons, 15 Feb., 1849.

12
Go thou to thy learned task,
I stay with the flowers of spring:
Do thou of the ages ask
What me the hours will bring.
EMERSON, *Quatrains: Botanist.*

And all their botany is Latin names.
EMERSON, *Blight,* l. 22.

I pull a flower from the woods,—
A monster with a glass
Computes the stamens in a breath,
And has her in a class.
EMILY DICKINSON, *Poems.* Pt. ii, No. 20.

Physician art thou?—one, all eyes,
Philosopher!—a fingering slave,
One that would peep and botanize
Upon his mother's grave?
WORDSWORTH, *A Poet's Epitaph,* l. 17.

13
Put by the Telescope!
Better without it man may see,
Stretch'd awful in the hush'd midnight,
The ghost of his eternity.
COVENTRY PATMORE, *The Unknown Eros.*

14
Go, wondrous creature! mount where Science
guides;
Go, measure earth, weigh air, and state the
tides;
Instruct the planets in what orbs to run,
Correct old Time, and regulate the sun. . . .
Go, teach Eternal Wisdom how to rule—
Then drop into thyself, and be a fool!
POPE, *Essay on Man.* Epis. ii, l. 19.

Of science and logic he chatters,
As fine and as fast as he can;
Though I am no judge of such matters,
I'm sure he's a talented man.
W. M. PRAED, *The Talented Man.*

15
Small have continual plodders ever won
Save base authority from others' books.
These earthly godfathers of heaven's lights
That give a name to every fixed star
Have no more profit of their shining nights
Than those that walk and wot not what
they are.
Too much to know is to know nought but
fame:

And every godfather can give a name.
SHAKESPEARE, *Love's Labour's Lost*. Act i, sc. 1, l. 86.

Human pride
Is skilful to invent most serious names
To hide its ignorance.
SHELLEY, *Queen Mab*. Pt. vii, l. 24.

1
He thrids the labyrinth of the mind,
He reads the secret of the star,
He seems so near and yet so far,
He looks so cold: she thinks him kind.
TENNYSON, *In Memoriam*. Pt. xcvii, st. 6.

SCORN

See also Contempt, Ridicule, Sneer

2
Not scorn'd in heav'n, though little notic'd here.
COWPER, *On the Receipt of My Mother's Picture*, l. 73.

3
He that rejoiceth to scorn folk in vain,
When he were lothest shall scorned be again.
JOHN LYDGATE, *Fall of Princes*. Bk. iii, l. 601. (c. 1440)

4
Methought a scornful and malignant curl
Show'd on the lips of that malicious churl.
THOMAS HOOD, *Plea of the Midsummer Fairies*, l. 220. *See also* LAUGHTER AND SCORN.

5
He hears
On all sides, from innumerable tongues,
A dismal universal hiss, the sound
Of public scorn.
MILTON, *Paradise Lost*. Bk. x, l. 506.

6
Nor sitteth in the seat of the scornful.
Old Testament: Psalms, i, 1.

7
When one is marching toward the goal of honor, one should scorn scorn itself. (Ad honesta vadenti contemnendus est ipse contemptus.)
SENECA, *Epistulæ ad Lucilium*. Epis. lxxvi, 4.

8
Panurge suddenly lifted up in the air his right hand and put the thumb thereof into the nostril of the same side, holding his four fingers straight out.
RABELAIS, *Works*. Bk. ii, ch. 19. The gesture known as the "Spanish fan."

The Sacristan he said no word to indicate a doubt,
But he put his thumb unto his nose, and he spread his fingers out.
R. H. BARHAM, *Nell Cook*.

9
What, my dear Lady Disdain!
SHAKESPEARE, *Much Ado About Nothing*. Act i, sc. 1, l. 119.

Disdain and scorn ride sparkling in her eyes.
SHAKESPEARE, *Much Ado About Nothing*. Act iii, sc. 1, l. 51.

I have learned thy arts, and now
Can disdain as much as thou!
THOMAS CAREW, *Disdain Returned*.

10
Scorn at first makes after-love the more.
SHAKESPEARE, *The Two Gentlemen of Verona*. Act iii, sc. 1, l. 95.

11
A fixed figure for the time of scorn
To point his slow unmoving finger at!
SHAKESPEARE, *Othello*. Act iv, sc. 2, l. 54. "Time of scorn" a misprint, perhaps, for "hand of scorn."

So let him stand through ages yet unborn,
Fix'd statue on the pedestal of scorn!
BYRON, *The Curse of Minerva*, l. 206.

12
O, what a deal of scorn looks beautiful
In the contempt and anger of his lip!
SHAKESPEARE, *Twelfth Night*. Act iii, sc. 1, l. 157.

13
Scorn tempering wrath, yet anger sharpening scorn.
SOUTHEY, *Madoc in Wales*. Pt. xv, l. 102.

14
Scorn'd, to be scorn'd by one that I scorn,
Is that a matter to make me fret?
TENNYSON, *Maud*, l. 444.

15
Scornful dogs will eat dirty puddings.
SWIFT, *Polite Conversation*. Dial. 1.

SCOTLAND AND THE SCOTS

I—Scotland: Apothegms

16
God's will be done. It came with a lass and will go with a lass.
JAMES V OF SCOTLAND, on his death-bed, when informed of the birth of a daughter. The Scottish crown was brought into the Stuart family through Margery Bruce, daughter of Robert Bruce, who married Walter Stuart. The daughter born to James V was Mary Queen of Scots, whose son James removed to England and called himself James I of England and VI of Scotland.

17
Peebles Body (to townsman supposed to be in London): E-eh Mac! you're sune hume again.
Mac: E-eh, it's just a ruinous place that! Mun, a had na' been there abune two hoours when Bang went saxpence.
BIRKET FOSTER. A joke published in *Punch*, 5 Dec., 1868, with a drawing by Charles Keene. The story had been communicated to Keene by Foster, who had it from Sir John Gilbert.

18
The Campbells are comin'.
ROBERT T. S. LOWELL, *The Relief of Lucknow*.

The warpipes are pealing, "The Campbells are coming."

They are charging and cheering. O dinna ye hear it?
ALEXANDER MACLAGAN, *Jennie's Dream.*

But the Gordons know what the Gordons dare,
When they hear the pipers playing.
HENRY NEWBOLT, *The Gay Gordons.*

These are Clan-Alpine's warriors true;
And, Saxon,—I am Roderick Dhu!
SCOTT, *The Lady of the Lake.* Canto v, st. 9.

The plaided warriors of the North.
SCOTT, *The Lady of the Lake.* Canto vi, st. 19.

1
Mutton old and claret good were Caledonia's forte,
Before the Southron taxed her drink and poisoned her with port.
CHARLES NEAVES, *Beef and Potatoes.*

Firm and erect the Caledonian stood;
Sound was his mutton, and his claret good;
"Let him drink port!" the English statesman cried:
He drank the poison, and his spirit died.
UNKNOWN. (DODD, *Epigrammatists.*)

2
Stands Scotland where it did?
SHAKESPEARE, *Macbeth.* Act iv, sc. 3, l. 164.

3
I look upon Switzerland as an inferior sort of Scotland.
SYDNEY SMITH, *Letter to Lord Holland,* 1815.

4
'Twould better heat a man
Than two Bath faggots or Scotch warming-pan.
SAMUEL WESLEY, *Maggots,* 36. "Scotch warming-pan" derives from the story of the traveller who asked to have his bed warmed, and the maid-servant immediately undressed and lay down in it.

Expecting all the welcome of a lover.
(A "Highland welcome" all the wide world over).
BYRON, *Don Juan.* Canto vi, st. 13.

5
There grows a bonnie brier bush in our kailyard.
UNKNOWN. Line from a Scottish Jacobite song used by Ian Maclaren as a motto for his story, *Beside the Bonnie Brier Bush,* 1894. Hence, "kailyard school." A kailyard is a cabbage garden or kitchen garden attached to a small cottage.

II—Scotland: Praise

6
Give me but one hour of Scotland,—
Let me see it ere I die!
W. E. AYTOUN, *Charles Edward at Versailles,* l. 211.

It was a' for our rightfu' king
We left fair Scotland's strand.
BURNS, *It Was A' for Our Rightfu' King.*

It's guid to be merry and wise,
It's guid to be honest and true,
It's guid to support Caledonia's cause
And bide by the buff and the blue.
BURNS, *Here's a Health to Them that's Awa.*

7
O Scotia! my dear, my native soil!
For whom my warmest wish to Heaven is sent!
Long may thy hardy sons of rustic toil
Be blest with health, and peace, and sweet content!
BURNS, *The Cotter's Saturday Night,* l. 172.

8
Scotland, thy mountains, thy valleys and fountains
Are famous in story—the birth-place of song.
ALEXANDER CRAWFORD, *Scotland.*

9
From the lone shieling of the misty island
Mountains divide us, and the waste of seas,
Yet still the blood is strong, the heart is Highland,
And we in dreams behold the Hebrides.
JOHN GALT, *Canadian Boat Song.* (*Blackwood's Magazine,* Sept., 1829; *Noctes Ambrosianæ.* No. 46.) The poem is introduced into the *Noctes Ambrosianæ* by Christopher North (John Wilson), as "from a friend of mine now in upper Canada," where Galt had been serving as secretary to a land-purchase company. It has been attributed both to Wilson and to John G. Lockhart, and also to Hugh Montgomerie, twelfth Earl of Eglinton. "Shieling" is Scotch for a small hut or dwelling.

Then Scotland's right and Scotland's might,
And Scotland's hills for me;
We'll drink a cup to Scotland yet,
Wi' a' the honours three.
HENRY SCOTT RIDDELL, *Scotland Yet.*

10
O Caledonia, stern and wild,
Meet nurse for a poetic child!
Land of brown heath and shaggy wood,
Land of the mountain and the flood,
Land of my sires! what mortal hand
Can e'er untie the filial band,
That knits me to thy rugged strand!
SCOTT, *Lay of the Last Minstrel.* Canto vi, st. 2.

Where's the coward that would not dare
To fight for such a land!
SCOTT, *Marmion.* Canto iv, st. 30.

Still from the sire the son shall hear
Of the stern strife and carnage drear
Of Flodden's fatal field,
When shivered was fair Scotland's spear
And broken was her shield!
SCOTT, *Marmion.* Canto vi, st. 34.

Stand to your arms, then, and march in good order;
England shall many a day
Tell of the bloody fray,
When the Blue Bonnets came over the Border.
SCOTT, *Border Song.* (*The Monastery.* Ch. 25.)

11
There is not such a word

Spoke of in Scotland as this term of fear.
SHAKESPEARE, *I Henry IV*. Act iv, sc. 1, l. 84

1
Mourn, hapless Caledonia, mourn
Thy banished peace, thy laurels torn!
SMOLLETT, *The Tears of Scotland.*

What foreign arms could never quell
By civil rage and rancour fell.
SMOLLETT, *The Tears of Scotland.*

2
My heart's in the Highlands, my heart is not here;
My heart's in the Highlands a-chasing the deer.
UNKNOWN, *The Strong Walls of Derry*. Robert Burns used these lines from this old song for his own song, *My Heart's in the Highlands*.

III—Scotland: Some Gibes

3
Caledonia's ours.
And well I know within that bastard land
Hath Wisdom's goddess never held command;
A barren soil, where Nature's germs, confined
To stern sterility, can stint the mind;
Whose thistle well betrays the niggard earth,
Emblem of all to whom the land gives birth;
Each genial influence nurtured to resist;
A land of meanness, sophistry, and mist.
BYRON, *The Curse of Minerva*, l. 130.

4
Treacherous Scotland, to no int'rest true.
DRYDEN, *On the Death of Cromwell.* St. 17.

That garret of the earth—that knuckle-end of England—that land of Calvin, oat-cakes, and sulphur.
SYDNEY SMITH. (LADY HOLLAND, *Memoir*. Ch. 2.)

5
In my youth, a Highland gentleman measured his importance by the number of men his domain could support. After some time the question was, to know how many great cattle it would feed. Today we are come to count the number of sheep. I suppose posterity will ask how many rats and mice it can feed.
EMERSON, *Lectures and Biographical Sketches: The Man of Letters*. Quoting "a Scotch mountaineer."

6
If the Scotch knew enough to go in when it rained, they would never get any outdoor exercise.
SIMEON FORD, *My Trip to Scotland.*

7
Oats,—a grain which is generally given to horses, but in Scotland supports the people.
SAMUEL JOHNSON, *Dictionary of the English Language*.

Joh. Mayor, in the first book of his *History of Scotland*, contends much for the wholesomeness of oaten bread: it was objected to him, then living at Paris in France, that his countrymen fed on oats, and base grain. . . . And yet Wecker out of Galen calls it horse-meat, and fitter for juments than men to feed on.
ROBERT BURTON, *Anatomy of Melancholy* Pt i, sec. 2, mem. 2, subs. 1.

The halesome parritch, chief o' Scotia's food
BURNS, *The Cotter's Saturday Night*, l. 92.

8
We cultivate literature on a little oatmeal. (Tenui musam meditamur avena.)
SYDNEY SMITH. (LADY HOLLAND, *Memoir*. Vol. i.)

The motto I proposed for the [Edinburgh] *Review* was, "Tenui musam meditamur avena"; but this was too near the truth to be admitted; so we took our present grave motto from Publius Syrus, of whom none of us, I am sure, had read a single line.
SYDNEY SMITH (LADY HOLLAND, *Memoir* Vol i.)

The judge is condemned when a guilty person is acquitted. (Judex damnatur cum nocens absolvitur.)
PUBLILIUS SYRUS, *Sententiæ*. No. 288. Adopted as the motto of the *Edinburgh Review*.

Oatmeal marks not only the child's breakfast, it is the favourite food of the Edinburgh reviewers. Thus do extremes meet.
E. V. LUCAS, *Domesticities*, p. 24.

9
One Scottish mile, now and then, may well stand for a mile and a half or two English.
JOHN TAYLOR THE WATER-POET, *The Penniless Pilgrimage: Continuation in Prose.* (1618)

IV—Scotland: The Scots

10
Nowhere beats the heart so kindly
As beneath the tartan plaid!
W. E. AYTOUN, *Charles Edward at Versailles*, l. 219.

As Dr. Johnson never said, is there any Scotsman without charm?
J. M. BARRIE, *Address*, Edinburgh University.

11
There are few more impressive sights in the world than a Scotsman on the make.
J. M. BARRIE, *What Every Woman Knows* Act ii.

A young Scotsman of your ability, let loose upon the world with three hundred pounds, what could he not do? It's almost appalling to think of; especially if he went among the English.
J. M. BARRIE, *What Every Woman Knows*. Act i.

12
I've sometimes thought that the difference between the Scotch and the English is that the Scotch are hard in all other respects but soft with women, and the English are hard with women and soft in all other respects.
J. M. BARRIE, *What Every Woman Knows*. Act ii.

The ardent disposition of the Scotch. (Perfervidum ingenium Scotorum.)
A proverb of unknown origin.

1
You've forgotten the grandest moral attribute of a Scotsman, Maggie, that he'll do nothing which might damage his career.
J. M. BARRIE, *What Every Woman Knows*. Act ii.

2
Trust yow no Skott.
ANDREW BOORD, *Letter to Thomas Cromwell*, 1 April, 1536.

3
But bring a Scotsman frae his hill,
Clap in his cheek a Highland gill,
Say, such is royal George's will,
And there's the foe!
He has nae thought but how to kill
Twa at a b'ow.
ROBERT BURNS, *The Author's Earnest Cry and Prayer: Postscript*. St. 29.

Scots, wha hae wi' Wallace bled,
Scots, wham Bruce has aften led,
Welcome to your gory bed,
Or to victorie!
BURNS, *Scots, Wha Hae*.

The Scot will not fight till he see his own blood.
SCOTT, *Fortunes of Nigel*. Ch. 1.

4
The Scots are steadfast—not their clime.
CAMPBELL, *The Pilgrim of Glencoe*, l. 14.

5
Only a few industrious Scots perhaps, who indeed are dispersed over the face of the whole earth. But as for them, there are no greater friends to Englishmen and England, when they are out on't, in the world, than they are. And for my own part, I would a hundred thousand of them were there [Virginia] for we are all one countrymen now, ye know, and we should find ten times more comfort of them there than we do here.
GEORGE CHAPMAN, *Eastward Hoe*. Act iii, sc. 2. James I was offended at this reflection on his countrymen and compelled its deletion, threatening the authors, Chapman, Jonson, and Marston, with imprisonment.

6
The Scots are poor, cries surly English pride;
True is the charge, nor by themselves denied.
Are they not then in strictest reason clear,
Who wisely come to mend their fortunes here?
CHURCHILL, *The Prophecy of Famine*, l. 195.

7
Your proper child of Caledonia believes in his rickety bones that he is the salt of the earth . . . He is the one species of human animal that is taken by all the world to be fifty per cent cleverer and pluckier and honester than the facts warrant. He is the daw with a peacock's tail of his own painting. He is the ass who has been at pains to cultivate the convincing roar of a lion.
T. W. H. CROSLAND, *The Unspeakable Scot*.

8
A Scottishman and a Newcastle grindstone travel all the world over.
THOMAS FULLER, *Worthies of England*. Vol. ii, p. 543. (1662)

In every corner of the world you will find a Scot, a rat, and a Newcastle grindstone.
JOHN GIBSON LOCKHART, *Life of Scott*. Vol. v, p. 99. Quoted as an old saying.

You come of a race of men the very wind of whose name has swept the ultimate seas.
J. M. BARRIE, *Rectorial Address*, University of St. Andrew's, 3 May, 1922.

9
We will not lose a Scot.
THOMAS FULLER, *Worthies of England*. Vol. ii, p. 542. Meaning nothing of importance.

10
The Scotch are a nation of gentlemen.
GEORGE IV, *Saying*, according to Sir Walter Scott. (See *Noctes Ambrosianæ*, Nov., 1830.)

11
Much may be made of a Scotchman if he be caught young.
SAMUEL JOHNSON. (BOSWELL, *Life*, 1772.)

12
The noblest prospects which a Scotchman ever sees is the highroad that leads him to England.
SAMUEL JOHNSON, to Mr. Ogilvie, when the latter remarked that "Scotland had a great many noble wild prospects." (BOSWELL, *Life*, 1763.)

In all my travels I never met with any one Scotchman but what was a man of sense. I believe everybody of that country that has any, leaves it as fast as they can.
FRANCIS LOCKIER, *Scotchmen*.

13
I have been trying all my life to like Scotchmen, and am obliged to desist from the experiment in despair.
CHARLES LAMB, *Essays of Elia: Imperfect Sympathies*.

14
Bitin' and scratchin' is Scotch folks' wooing.
JOHN RAY, *Proverbs: Scottish*.

15
It's ill taking the breeks off a Hielandman.
SCOTT, *Rob Roy*. Ch. 27.

16
It requires a surgical operation to get a joke well into a Scotch understanding. Their only idea of wit . . . is laughing immoderately at stated intervals.
SYDNEY SMITH. (LADY HOLLAND, *Memoir* Ch. 2.)

The whole [Scotch] nation hitherto has been void of wit and humour, and even incapable of relishing it.
WALPOLE, *Letter to Sir Horace Mann*, 1778.

1
The Scotch have no way of redeeming the credit of their understandings, but by avowing that they have been consummate villains. Stavano bene; per star meglio, stanno qui.
HORACE WALPOLE, *Letter to the Rev. William Mason*, 28 Aug., 1778.

SCOTT, SIR WALTER

2
The Ariosto of the North.
BYRON, *Childe Harold*. Canto iv, st. 40.

3
It can be said of him, when he departed he took a Man's life with him. No sounder piece of British manhood was put together in that eighteenth century of Time.
CARLYLE, *Essays: Lockhart's Life of Scott*.

4
On Waterloo's ensanguined plain
Lie tens of thousands of the slain;
But none by sabre or by shot
Fell half so flat as Walter Scott.
THOMAS, LORD ERSKINE, *Epigram*, on Scott's *Field of Waterloo*.

4a
His morality is not in purple patches, ostentatiously obtrusive, but woven in through the very texture of the stuff.
MARIA EDGEWORTH, *Helen*. Vol. i, ch. 12. (1834) Referring to Sir Walter Scott. See also APPENDIX, p. 2296.

SCRATCHING

5
Mules may ease each other's itch. (Mutuum muli scalpant.)
AUSONIUS, *Technopægnion*. Pt. iv, l. 12.

6
Itch . . . also is pleasing.
FRANCIS BACON, *Natural History*, vii, 694.

Scratching is one of the pleasantest gratifications of nature, especially with the hand. (Si est la gratterie des gratifications de nature les plus douces, et autant à main.)
MONTAIGNE, *Essays*. Bk. iii, ch. 13.

7
Itch and ease can no man please.
FRANCIS BACON, *Promus*. No. 486.

8
I claw oft where it does not itch.
ALEXANDER BARCLAY, *Eglogs*. No. 30. (c. 1510)

Thou makest me claw where it itcheth not.
JOHN HEYWOOD, *Proverbs*. Pt. ii, ch. 8.

'Twould make one scratch where 't does not itch,
To see fools live poor to die rich.
THOMAS SHADWELL, *Woman Captain*. Act i.

9
And he, whom in itching no scratching will forbear,
He must bear the smarting that shall follow there.
THOMAS FULLER, *Gnomologia*. No. 2449.

Itch is more intolerable than smart.
THOMAS FULLER, *Gnomologia*. No. 3114.

10
You'll scratch a beggar before you die.
THOMAS FULLER, *Gnomologia*. No. 6035.

She'll never scratch a grey head.
SWIFT, *Polite Conversation*. Dial. 3.

11
'Tis better than riches to scratch when it itches.
UNKNOWN. An English proverb.

12
Scratch my head, Peaseblossom.
SHAKESPEARE, *A Midsummer-Night's Dream*. Act iv, sc. 1, l. 7.

13
She loved not the savour of tar nor of pitch,
Yet a tailor might scratch her where'er she did itch.
SHAKESPEARE, *The Tempest*. Act ii, sc. 2, l. 55.

I would thou didst itch from head to foot and I had the scratching of thee.
SHAKESPEARE, *Troilus and Cressida*, ii, 1, 30.

14
God bless the Duke of Argyle.
UNKNOWN. A humorous phrase supposed to be addressed to Scotchmen when they scratch themselves. The story goes that the Duke of Argyle erected posts on his estates for his cattle to rub themselves against, and his herdsmen, as they rubbed their own backs against the posts, uttered this blessing.

SCRIPTURE, see Bible

SCULPTURE

See also ART

15
Appeal, fair stone,
From God's pure heights of beauty against man's wrong!
. . . and strike and shame the strong,
By thunders of white silence.
E. B. BROWNING, *Hiram Powers' "Greek Slave."*

Too fair to worship, too divine to love.
HENRY HART MILMAN, *The Belvidere Apollo*.

So stands the statue that enchants the world.
THOMSON, *The Seasons: Summer*, l. 1347. Referring to the Venus de Medici.

16
I've seen much finer women, ripe and real,
Than all the nonsense of their stone ideal.
BYRON, *Don Juan*. Canto ii, st. 118.

17
A sculptor wields
The chisel, and the stricken marble grows
To beauty.
BRYANT, *The Flood of Years*, l. 42.

Carved with figures strange and sweet,
All made out of the carver's brain.
S. T. COLERIDGE, *Christobel*. Pt. i, l. 179.

18
The statue is then beautiful when it begins to be incomprehensible.
EMERSON, *Essays, First Series: Compensation*.

19
Sculpture is more divine, and more like Nature,

That fashions all her works in high relief,
And that is sculpture. This vast ball, the Earth,
Was moulded out of clay, and baked in fire;
Men, women, and all animals that breathe
Are statues and not paintings.
LONGFELLOW, *Michael Angelo*. Pt. iii, sec. 5.

Sculpture is more than painting. It is greater
To raise the dead to life than to create
Phantoms that seem to live.
LONGFELLOW, *Michael Angelo*. Pt. iii, sec. 5.

1
With chiselled touch
The stone unhewn and cold
Becomes a living mould.
The more the marble wastes,
The more the statue grows.
MICHELANGELO, *Sonnet*. (Mrs. Roscoe, tr.)

2
Nought but images,
Lifelike but lifeless, wonderful but dead.
WILLIAM MORRIS, *Life and Death of Jason*. Bk. viii, l. 258.

3
The drab washwoman dazed and breathless, ray-chiseled in the golden stream,
Is a magic statue standing deathless—her tub and soap-suds touched with Dream.
JAMES OPPENHEIM, *Saturday Night*.

4
Not Nature, but Art, made the Bacchant frenzied, mixing madness with the stone.
PAULUS SILENTIARIUS, *On a Bacchant in Byzantium*. (*Greek Anthology*. Bk. xvi, epig. 57.)

5
Either Zeus came to earth to show his form to thee,
Phidias, or thou to heaven hast gone the god to see.
PHILIPPUS, *On the Statue of Zeus at Olympia*. (*Greek Anthology*. Bk. xvi, epig. 81.)

Not from a vain or shallow thought
His awful Jove young Phidias brought.
EMERSON, *The Problem*.

6
He is not a man but a statue. (Ἀπ' ἀνδρός, ἀλλ' ἀπ' ἀνδριάντος.)
PHRYNE, of Xenocrates, when he repulsed her advances. (DIOGENES LAERTIUS, *Xenocrates*. Bk. iv, ch. 2, sec. 7.)

7
The Paphian Queen to Cnidos made repair
Across the tide to see her image there:
Then looking up and round the prospect wide,
When did Praxiteles see me thus? she cried.
PLATO, *On the Cnidian Aphrodite of Praxiteles*. (*Greek Anthology*. Bk. xvi, epig. 160.)

8
A Mercury is not made out of any block of wood. (Ex quovis ligno non fit Mercurius.)
PYTHAGORAS. (APULEIUS, *Metamorphoses*.)

9
The sculptor does not work for the anatomist, but for the common observer of life and nature.
RUSKIN, *True and Beautiful: Sculpture*.

10
From a living being the gods made me a stone, but Praxiteles from a stone made me alive again.
UNKNOWN, *On a Statue of Niobe*. (*Greek Anthology*. Bk. xvi, epig. 129.)

Then marble, soften'd into life, grew warm.
POPE, *Imitations of Horace: Epistles*. Bk. ii, epis. 1, l. 147.

And the cold marble leapt to life a god.
H. H. MILMAN, *The Belvedere Apollo*.
See also GOLDSMITH, *under* PAINTING.

SEA, THE

See also Ship

I—Sea: Apothegms

11
Every sea is sea. (Πᾶσα θάλασσα θάλασσα.)
ANTIPATER. (*Greek Anthology*. Bk. vii, epig. 639.)

12
That great fishpond, the sea.
THOMAS DEKKER, *I The Honest Whore*. Act i, sc. 2. (c. 1635)

Nay, I'll send printed scrolls beyond
To neighbours o'er the Herring Pond.
THOMAS D'URFEY, *Pills to Purge Melancholy:* Pt. ii, *The Fable of the Lady, the Lurcher, and the Marrow-Puddings*. (1661)

Easier rents and taxes will tempt many of your countrymen to cross the herring-pond.
UNKNOWN, *England's Path to Wealth*. (1722)

He'll plague you now he's come over the herring-pond.
SCOTT, *Guy Mannering*. Ch. 34.

The herring-pond is wide.
ROBERT BROWNING, *Mr. Sludge "The Medium."* Third line from end.

And bid the broad Atlantic roll
A ferry of the free.
EMERSON, *Ode*, Concord, 4 July, 1857.

13
The sea doth wash away all human ills. (Θάλασσα κλύζει πάντα τανθρώπων κακά.)
EURIPIDES, *Iphigenia in Tauris*, l. 1193. Quoted by Plato when cured of an illness in Egypt by the use of sea-water. (DIOGENES LAERTIUS, *Plato*. Sec. 6.)

14
All the rivers run into the sea; yet the sea is not full.
Old Testament: Ecclesiastes, i, 7.

All earth's full rivers can not fill
The sea that drinking thirsteth still.
CHRISTINA ROSSETTI, *By the Sea*.

15
Old Indefatigable
Time's right-hand man, the sea.
W. E. HENLEY, *To J. A. C.*

1
The loud-resounding sea. (Πολυφλοισβοιο θαλάσσης.)
Homer, *Iliad*. Bk. ix, l. 182.

Far-spooming Ocean.
Keats, *Endymion*. Bk. iii, l. 70.

The always wind-obeying deep.
Shakespeare, *The Comedy of Errors*. Act i, sc. 1, l. 64.

2
The old man of the sea. (Γέρων ἅλιος.)
Homer, *Odyssey*. Bk. iv, l. 349.

3
A lull like the lull of the treacherous sea.
Thomas Hood, *Miss Kilmansegg: Her Will*.

4
The burden of the desert of the sea.
Old Testament: Isaiah, xxi, 1.

5
Hitherto shalt thou come, but no further: and here shall thy proud waves be stayed.
Old Testament: Job, xxxviii, 11.

6
Past are three summers since she first beheld
The ocean; all around the child await
Some exclamation of amazement here.
She coldly said, her long-lasht eyes abased,
Is this the mighty ocean? is this all?
W. S. Landor, *Gebir*. Bk. v.

These lines were especially singled out for admiration by Shelley, Humphrey Davy, Scott, and many remarkable men.
John Forster, *Life of Landor*. Vol. i, p. 95.

7
The dim, dark sea, so like unto Death,
That divides and yet unites mankind!
Longfellow, *The Building of the Ship*, l. 166.

8
The rising world of waters dark and deep.
Milton, *Paradise Lost*. Bk. iii, l. 11.

9
Distinct as the billows, yet one as the sea.
James Montgomery, *The Ocean*. St. 6.

10
For still it savoured of the bitter sea.
William Morris, *Life and Death of Jason*. Bk. xii, l. 109.

11
Deep calleth unto deep.
Old Testament: Psalms, xlii, 7.

Under every deep a lower deep opens.
Emerson, *Essays, First Series: Circles*.

12
I love the sea: she is my fellow-creature.
Francis Quarles, *Emblems*. Bk. v, No. 6.

13
And the sea gave up the dead which were in it.
New Testament: Revelation, xx, 13.

We shall part no more in the wind and the rain,
Where thy last farewell was said;
But perhaps I shall meet thee and know thee again
When the sea gives up her dead.
Jean Ingelow, *Supper at the Mill: Mother Sings*.

14
And I saw a new heaven and a new earth: for the first heaven and the first earth were passed away; and there was no more sea.
New Testament: Revelation, xxi, 1.

15
The sea hath no king but God alone.
D. G. Rossetti, *The White Ship*.

16
Inestimable stones, unvalued jewels,
All scattered in the bottom of the sea.
Shakespeare, *Richard III*. Act i, sc. 4, l. 27.

Rich and various gems inlay
The unadorned bosom of the Deep.
Milton, *Comus*, l. 22.

In chambers deep, Where waters sleep,
What unknown treasures pave the floor!
Edward Young, *Ocean*. St. 24.

See also under Obscurity.

17
Salt flood.
Shakespeare, *Romeo and Juliet*. Act iii, sc. 5, l. 135.

Neptune's salt wash.
Shakespeare, *Hamlet*. Act iii, sc. 2, l. 166.

Salt wave.
Shakespeare, *Love's Labour's Lost*. Act v, sc. 1, l. 61.

The great naked sea shouldering a load of salt.
Carl Sandburg, *Adelaide Crapsey*.

18
Unpath'd waters.
Shakespeare, *Winter's Tale*. Act iv, sc. 4, 577.

The Sea
That shuts still as it opes, and leaves no tracts
Nor prints of precedent for poor men's facts.
George Chapman, *Bussy d'Ambois*. Act i, sc. 1.

19
The slimy caverns of the populous deep.
Shelley, *Alastor*, l. 307.

20
The heavy blue chain of the sea didst thou, O just man, endure.
Taliessin. To an exile on an island. (Emerson, *Poetry and Imagination*.)

21
A few swimming in the vast deep. (Rari nantes in gurgite vasto.)
Vergil, *Æneid*. Bk. i, l. 118.

For all, that here on earth we dreadful hold,
Be but as bugs to fearen babes withal,
Comparèd to the creatures in the seas entrall.
Spenser, *Faerie Queene*. Bk. ii, canto xii, st. 25.

22
On all sides nothing but sky and sea. (Cælum undique, et unidque pontus.)
Vergil, *Æneid*. Bk. iii, l. 193.

Like the round ocean, girdled with the sky.
Robert Southey, *Thalaba*. Bk. i, l. 9.

The world of waters wild.
James Thomson, *Britannia*, l. 27.

23
Sea, that breakest for ever, that breakest and never art broken.
William Watson, *Hymn to the Sea*. Pt. ii.

1
Have sight of Proteus rising from the sea,
Or hear old Triton blow his wreathèd horn.
WORDSWORTH, *The World Is Too Much with Us.*

From thy dead lips a clearer note is born
Than ever Triton blew from wreathèd horn.
O. W. HOLMES, *The Chambered Nautilus.*

II—Sea: Description

2
The multitudinous laughter of the sea. (Ποντίων τε κυμάτων ἀνήριθμον γέλασμα.)
ÆSCHYLUS, *Prometheus Bound,* l. 89. (De Quincey, tr.)

Ye waves
That o'er the interminable ocean wreathe
Your crispèd smiles.
ÆSCHYLUS, *Prometheus Bound,* l. 89.

The many-twinkling smile of ocean.
JOHN KEBLE, *The Christian Year: Second Sunday after Trinity.*

3
Old ocean's gray and melancholy waste.
BRYANT, *Thanatopsis,* l. 44.

The wavy waste.
THOMAS HOOD, *Ode to Rae Wilson,* l. 7.

4
Roll on, thou deep and dark-blue Ocean, roll!
Ten thousand fleets sweep over thee in vain;
Man marks the earth with ruin, his control
Stops with the shore; upon the watery plain
The wrecks are all thy deed, nor doth remain
A shadow of man's ravage.
BYRON, *Childe Harold.* Canto iv, st. 179.

Dark-heaving;—boundless, endless, and sublime—
The image of Eternity—the throne
Of the Invisible; even from out thy slime
The monsters of the deep are made; each zone
Obeys thee; thou goest forth, dread, fathomless, alone.
BYRON, *Childe Harold.* Canto iv, st. 183.

5
Unchangeable save to thy wild waves' play;
Time writes no wrinkle on thine azure brow;
Such as creation's dawn beheld, thou rollest now.
BYRON, *Childe Harold.* Canto iv, st. 182.

And Thou, vast Ocean! on whose awful face
Time's iron feet can print no ruin trace.
ROBERT MONTGOMERY, *The Omnipresence of the Deity.* Pt. i, st. 20.

The sea appears today just as it did on the first day of creation. (La mer reparait telle qu'elle fut au premier jour de la création.)
MADAME DE STAËL, *Corinne.* Bk. i, ch. 4.

6
And I have loved thee, Ocean! and my joy
Of youthful sports was on thy breast to be
Borne, like thy bubbles, onward. From a boy
I wanton'd with thy breakers, . . .
And trusted to thy billows far and near,
And laid my hand upon thy mane—as I do here.
BYRON, *Childe Harold.* Canto iv, st. 184.

I'll bid him welcome, clap his mane,
And hug his breakers to my breast.
GEORGE GRAY, *The Storm.*

He laid his hand upon "the Ocean's mane,"
And played familiar with his hoary locks.
POLLOK, *The Course of Time.* Bk. iv, l. 689.

7
Behold the Sea,
The opaline, the plentiful and strong,
Yet beautiful as is the rose in June,
Fresh as the trickling rainbow of July;
Sea full of food, the nourisher of kinds,
Purger of earth, and medicine of men;
Creating a sweet climate by my breath,
Washing out harms and griefs from memory,
And, in my mathematic ebb and flow,
Giving a hint of that which changes not.
EMERSON, *Sea-Shore.*

8
The sea, unmated creature, tired and lone,
Makes on its desolate sands eternal moan.
F. W. FABER, *The Sorrowful World.*

It keeps eternal whisperings around
Desolate shores.
KEATS, *Sonnet: On the Sea.*

The hollow murmur of the ocean-tide.
JAMES BEATTIE, *The Minstrel.* Bk. i, l. 340.

9
Sweet is the bitter sea, and the clear green in which the gaze seeks the soul, looking through the glass into itself. The sea thinks for me as I listen and ponder; the sea thinks, and every boom of the wave repeats my prayer.
RICHARD JEFFERIES, *The Story of My Heart.*

10
Who hath desired the Sea? Her excellent loneliness rather
Than forecourts of kings, and her outermost pits than the streets where men gather?
RUDYARD KIPLING, *The Sea and the Hills.*

11
My soul is full of longing
For the secret of the sea,
And the heart of the great ocean
Sends a thrilling pulse through me.
LONGFELLOW, *The Secret of the Sea.*

"Wouldst thou,"—so the helmsman answered,
"Learn the secret of the sea?
Only those who brave its dangers
Comprehend its mystery!"
LONGFELLOW, *The Secret of the Sea.*

What are the wild waves saying,
Sister, the whole day long,
That ever amid our playing,
I hear but their low, lone song?
JOSEPH EDWARDS CARPENTER, *What Are the Wild Waves Saying?*

The sea, Floy, what is it that it keeps on saying?
DICKENS, *Dombey and Son.* Ch. 8.

1
And like the wings of sea-birds
Flash the white caps of the sea.
LONGFELLOW, *Twilight*.

2
She knows all sighs and she knows all sinning,
And they whisper out in her breaking wave:
She has known it all since the far beginning,
Since the grief of that first grave.
She shakes the heart with her stars and thunder
And her soft low word when the winds are late;
For the Sea is Woman, the Sea is Wonder—
Her other name is Fate!
EDWIN MARKHAM, *Virgilia*.

3
But, visiting sea, your love doth press
And reach in further than you know,
And fills all these; and when you go
There's loneliness in loneliness.
ALICE MEYNELL, *Song*.

4
Before their eyes in sudden view appear
The secrets of the hoary deep, a dark
Illimitable Ocean, without bound,
Without dimension, where length, breadth, and height,
And time and place are lost; where eldest Night
And Chaos, ancestors of Nature, hold
Eternal anarchy, amidst the noise
Of endless wars, and by confusion stand.
For hot, cold, moist, and dry, four champions fierce,
Strive here for mast'ry.
MILTON, *Paradise Lost*. Bk. ii, l. 890.

5
The sea! the sea! the open sea!
The blue, the fresh, the ever free!
Without a mark, without a bound,
It runneth the earth's wide regions round;
It plays with the clouds; it mocks the skies;
Or like a cradled creature lies.
BRYAN WALLER PROCTER, *The Sea*.

6
The old, old sea, as one in tears,
Comes murmuring with foamy lips,
And knocking at the vacant piers,
Calls for its long lost multitude of ships.
THOMAS BUCHANAN READ, *Come, Gentle Trembler*. Wrongly quoted in Mark Twain's *Life on the Mississippi*. Ch. 22.

7
The whole ocean flamed as one wound.
KING REGNER LODBROK. (EMERSON, *Poetry and Imagination*.)

8
By winds the sea is lashed to storm, but if it be
Unvexed, it is of all things most amenable.
SOLON, *Fragments*. Frag. 9.

9
For every wave with dimpled face
That leap'd upon the air,
Had caught a star in its embrace
And held it trembling there.
AMELIA C. WELBY, *Twilight at Sea*. St. 4.

10
To me the sea is a continual miracle,
The fishes that swim—the rocks—the motion of the waves—the ships with men in them,
What stranger miracles are there?
WALT WHITMAN, *Miracles*.

Thou sea that pickest and cullest the race in time, and unitest nations,
Suckled by thee, old husky nurse, embodying thee,
Indomitable, untamed as thee.
WALT WHITMAN, *Song for All Seas, All Ships*.

The glad indomitable sea.
BLISS CARMAN, *A Sea Child*.

Majestic main,
A secret world of wonders in thyself.
THOMSON, *A Hymn on the Seasons*, l. 52.

III—Sea: In Calm

11
The tender azure of the unruffled deep.
BYRON, *Childe Harold*. Canto i, st. 19.

12
It is easy to spread the sails to propitious winds. (Facile est ventis dare vela secundis.)
MANILIUS, *Astronomica*. Sec. 3.

When the sea is calm the careless sailor takes his ease. (Cum mare compositum est, secura navita cessat.)
OVID, *Ars Amatoria*. Bk. iii, l. 259.

Any one can hold the helm when the sea is calm.
PUBLILIUS SYRUS, *Sententiæ*. No. 358.

In a calm sea every man is a pilot.
JOHN RAY, *English Proverbs*.

When winds are steady and skies are clear,
Every hand the ship would steer;
But soon as ever the wild winds blow,
Every hand would go below.
D'ARCY WENTWORTH THOMPSON, *Sales Attici*.

13
The sea being smooth,
How many shallow bauble boats dare sail
Upon her patient breast.
SHAKESPEARE, *Troilus and Cressida*. Act i, sc. 3, l. 34.

14
There is no dashing of billows when the sea is calm. (In tranquillo non tumultuatur.)
SENECA, *Epistulæ ad Lucilium*. Epis. 98, sec. 7.

15
There the sea I found
Calmed as a cradled child in dreamless slumber bound.
SHELLEY, *The Revolt of Islam*. Canto i, st. 15.

IV—Sea: In Storm

16
O pilot! 'tis a fearful night,
There's danger on the deep.
THOMAS HAYNES BAYLY, *The Pilot*.

A daring pilot in extremity;
Pleas'd with the danger, when the waves went high
He sought the storms.
DRYDEN, *Absalom and Achitophel.* Pt. i, l. 159.

1

How Bishop Aidan foretold to certain seamen a storm that would happen, and gave them some holy oil to lay it.
VENERABLE BEDE, *Ecclesiastical History.* Vol. iii, ch. 15, *Heading.*

Remember to throw into the sea the oil which I give to you, when straightway the winds will abate, and a calm and smiling sea will accompany you throughout your voyage.
VENERABLE BEDE, *Ecclesiastical History.* Bk. iii, ch. 15. Hence the expression, "To throw oil on troubled waters."

All seas are made calm and still with oil; and therefore the divers under the water do spirt and sprinkle it abroad with their mouths because it dulceth and allayeth the unpleasant nature thereof, and carrieth a light with it.
PLINY, *Historia Naturalis.* Bk. ii, ch. 103.

Why does pouring oil on the sea make it clear and calm? Is it because the winds, slipping the smooth oil, have no force, nor cause any waves?
PLUTARCH, *Morals: Natural Questions.* Sec. 12.

2

The sea heaves up, hangs loaded o'er the land,
Breaks there and buries its tumultuous strength.
ROBERT BROWNING, *Luria.* Act i.

3

Come hither, hither, my little page!
Why dost thou weep and wail?
Or dost thou dread the billows' rage,
Or tremble at the gale?
But dash the tear-drop from thine eye;
Our ship is swift and strong,
Our fleetest falcon scarce can fly
More merrily along.
BYRON, *Childe Harold.* Canto i, st. 13. *Song.*

Come hither! come hither! my little daughtèr,
And do not tremble so;
For I can weather the roughest gale
That ever wind did blow.
LONGFELLOW, *The Wreck of the Hesperus.*

4

The hell of waters! where they howl and hiss,
And boil in endless torture.
BYRON, *Childe Harold.* Canto iv, st. 69.

In Biscay's sleepless bay.
BYRON, *Childe Harold.* Canto i, st. 14.

5

Thou glorious mirror, where the Almighty's form
Glasses itself in tempests.
BYRON, *Childe Harold.* Canto iv, st. 183.

6

'T was when the seas were roaring
With hollow blasts of wind;
A damsel lay deploring,
All on a rock reclin'd.
JOHN GAY, *The What d'ye Call It.* Act ii, sc. 8.

7

The breaking waves dash'd high
On a stern and rock-bound coast,
And the woods, against a stormy sky,
Their giant branches toss'd.
FELICIA DOROTHEA HEMANS, *The Landing of the Pilgrim Fathers in New England.*

8

He goes a great voyage that goes to the bottom of the sea.
H. G. BOHN, *Hand-Book of Proverbs,* p. 371.
See also SHIPWRECK.

9

Bursts as a wave that from the clouds impends,
And swell'd with tempests on the ship descends;
White are the decks with foam; the winds aloud
Howl o'er the masts, and sing thro' ev'ry shroud:
Pale, trembling, tired, the sailors freeze with fears;
And instant death on ev'ry wave appears.
HOMER, *Iliad.* Bk. xv, l. 752. (Pope, tr.)

The wild sea roars and lashes the granite cliffs below,
And round the misty islets the loud tempests blow.
MARY HOWITT, *The Sea-Fowler.*

10

He maketh the deep to boil like a pot.
Old Testament: Job, xli, 31.

11

Let him who knows not how to pray go to sea.
JOHN RAY, *English Proverbs.*

He that will learn to pray, let him go to Sea.
GEORGE HERBERT, *Jacula Prudentum.* No. 84.

12

And all day long the stone
Felt how the wind was blown;
And all night long the rock
Stood the sea's shock;
While, from the window, I
Looked out, and wondered why,
Why at such length
Such force should fight such strength.
JOHN MASEFIELD, *Watching by a Sick-bed.*

13

Look when the clouds are blowing
And all the winds are free:
In fury of their going
They fall upon the sea.
But though the blast is frantic,
And though the tempest raves,
The deep immense Atlantic
Is still beneath the waves.
F. W. H. MYERS, *Wind, Moon and Tides.*

When winds are raging o'er the upper ocean
And billows wild contend with angry roar,
'Tis said, far down beneath the wild commotion
That peaceful stillness reigneth evermore.
HARRIET BEECHER STOWE. *Hymn.*

1
Wherever I look, there is naught but sea and air—sea swollen with billows, air athreat with clouds; and between them are the hum and roar of the cruel winds. (Quocumque aspicio, nihil est, nisi pontus et aër, Fluctibus hic tumidus, nubinus ille minax. Inter utrumque fremunt inmani murmure venti.)
OVID, *Tristia*. Bk. i, eleg. 2, l. 23.

The storm is master; man, like a ball,
Is toss'd 'twixt wind and billow.
(Der Sturm ist Meister; Wind und Welle spielen
Ball mit dem Menschen.)
SCHILLER, *Wilhelm Tell*. Act iv, sc. 1, l. 59

We are carried up to the heaven by the circling wave, and immediately the wave subsiding, we descend to the lowest depths. (Tollimur in cælum curvato gurgite, et idem Subducta ad Manis imos descendimus unda.)
VERGIL, *Æneid*. Bk. iii, l. 564.

Ocean into tempest wrought
To waft a feather or to drown a fly.
YOUNG, *Night Thoughts*. Night i, l. 153.

2
As far as I could ken thy chalky cliffs,
When from thy shore the tempest beat us back,
I stood upon the hatches in the storm.
SHAKESPEARE, *II Henry VI*. Act iii, sc. 2, l. 101

3
Blow wind, swell billow, and swim bark!
The storm is up, and all is on the hazard.
SHAKESPEARE, *Julius Cæsar*. Act v, sc. 1, l. 67.

4
Cease, rude Boreas, blustering railer!
List, ye landsmen all, to me:
Messmates, hear a brother sailor
Sing the dangers of the sea.
GEORGE A. STEVENS, *The Storm*.

5
Yet winds to seas
Are reconcil'd at length, and sea to shore.
MILTON, *Samson Agonistes*, l. 961.

V—Sea: Sailing

6
Once more upon the waters! yet once more!
And the waves bound beneath me as a steed
That knows his rider.
BYRON, *Childe Harold*. Canto iii, st. 2.

This quiet sail is as a noiseless wing
To waft me from distraction.
BYRON, *Childe Harold*. Canto iii, st. 85.

7
O'er the glad waters of the dark-blue sea,
Our thoughts as boundless, and our souls as free,
Far as the breeze can bear, the billows foam,
Survey our empire, and behold our home!
BYRON, *The Corsair*. Canto i, st. 1.

8
Give me a spirit that on this life's rough sea
Loves t' have his sails fill'd with a lusty wind.
Even till his sail-yards tremble, his masts crack,
And his rapt ship run on her side so low
That she drinks water, and her keel plows air.
GEORGE CHAPMAN, *Byron's Conspiracy*. Act iii, sc. 1.

9
The ship was cheered, the harbour cleared,
Merrily did we drop
Below the kirk, below the hill,
Below the lighthouse top.
S. T. COLERIDGE, *Ancient Mariner*. Pt. i, st. 6.

We were the first that ever burst
Into that silent sea.
S. T. COLERIDGE, *Ancient Mariner*. Pt ii, st. 5.

10
But oars alone can ne'er prevail
To reach the distant coast;
The breath of heav'n must swell the sail,
Or all the toil is lost.
COWPER, *Human Frailty*. St. 6.

And all the way, to guide their chime,
With falling oars they kept the time.
ANDREW MARVELL, *Bermudas*.

Faintly as tolls the evening chime,
Our voices keep tune and our oars keep time.
THOMAS MOORE, *A Canadian Boat-Song*.

11
A wet sheet and a flowing sea,—
A wind that follows fast,
And fills the white and rustling sail,
And bends the gallant mast,—
And bends the gallant mast, my boys,
While, like the eagle free,
Away the good ship flies, and leaves
Old England on the lee.
ALLAN CUNNINGHAM, *A Wet Sheet and a Flowing Sea*.

12
Well, then—our course is chosen, spread the sail,
Heave oft the lead, and mark the soundings well;
Look to the helm, good master; many a shoal
Marks this stern coast, and rocks, where sits the Siren,
Who, like ambition, lures men to their ruin
WILLIAM FALCONER, *The Shipwreck*. Quoted by Scott, *Kenilworth*. Ch. 17.

13
Thus, thus I steer my bark, and sail
On even keel with gentle gale.
MATTHEW GREEN, *The Spleen*, l. 814.

Though pleased to see the dolphins play,
I mind my compass and my way.
MATTHEW GREEN, *The Spleen*, l. 826.

For me, my craft is sailing on,
Through mists to-day, clear seas anon.
Whate'er the final harbor be,
'Tis good to sail upon the sea!
JOHN KENDRICK BANGS, *The Voyage*.

14
Come o'er the moonlit sea,

The waves are brightly glowing.
CHARLES JEFFERYS, *The Moonlit Sea.*

1
Some love to roam o'er the dark sea's foam,
Where the shrill winds whistle free.
CHARLES MACKAY, *Some Love to Roam.*

2
"Ahoy! and O-ho! and it's who's for the ferry?"
(The briar's in bud and the sun going down)
"And I'll row ye so quick and I'll row ye so steady,
And 't is but a penny to Twickenham Town."
THÉOPHILE MARZIALS, *Twickenham Ferry.*

3
Well pleas'd they slack their course, and many a league
Cheer'd with the grateful smell old Ocean smiles.
MILTON, *Paradise Lost.* Bk. iv, l. 164.

4
Thus far we run before the wind.
ARTHUR MURPHY, *The Apprentice.* Act i, sc. 1, l. 344.

But the principal failing occurred in the sailing,
And the Bellman, perplexed and distressed,
Said he *had* hoped, at least, when the wind blew due East,
That the ship would *not* travel due West!
LEWIS CARROLL, *The Hunting of the Snark.*

5
Simple and strong and desolate and daring,
Leaps to the great embraces of the sea.
FREDERIC W. H. MYERS, *St. Paul.*

6
We have ploughed the vast ocean in a fragile bark. (Nos fragili ligno vastum sulcavimus æquor.)
OVID, *Epistulæ ex Ponto.* Bk. i, epis. 4, l. 35.

7
I'm on the sea! I'm on the sea!
I am where I would ever be,
With the blue above and the blue below,
And silence wheresoe'er I go.
BRYAN WALLER PROCTER, *The Sea.*

8
A life on the ocean wave,
A home on the rolling deep,
Where the scattered waters rave,
And the winds their revels keep!
EPES SARGENT, *A Life on the Ocean Wave.*

9
Upon the gale she stooped her side,
And bounded o'er the swelling tide,
As she were dancing home;
The merry seamen laughed to see
Their gallant ship so lustily
Furrow the green sea-foam.
SCOTT, *Marmion.* Canto ii, st. 1.

10
Behold the threaden sails,
Borne with the invisible and creeping wind,
Draw the huge bottoms through the furrow'd sea,
Breasting the lofty surge.
SHAKESPEARE, *Henry V.* Act iii, *Prologue*, l. 10.

Sail like my pinnace to these golden shores.
SHAKESPEARE, *The Merry Wives of Windsor.* Act i, sc. 3, l. 89.

11
Gentle airs
Curl'd the blue deep, and bright the summer sun
Play'd o'er the summer ocean, when our barks
Began their way. And they were gallant barks
As ever through the raging billows rode;
And many a tempest's buffeting they bore.
Their sails all swelling with the eastern breeze,
Their tighten'd cordage clattering to the mast,
Steady they rode the main.
SOUTHEY, *Madoc in Wales.* Pt. iv, l. 5.

Day after day, with one auspicious wind,
Right to the setting sun we held our course. . . .
Day after day, day after day the same,—
A weary waste of waters!
SOUTHEY, *Madoc in Wales.* Pt. iv, l. 16.

And still at morning where we were at night,
And where we were at morn, at nightfall still,
The centre of that drear circumference,
Progressive, yet no change!
SOUTHEY, *Madoc in Wales.* Pt. iv, l. 83.

12
I will go back to the great sweet mother,
Mother and lover of men, the sea.
I will go down to her, I and none other,
Close with her, kiss her and mix her with me.
SWINBURNE, *The Triumph of Time.* St. 33. *See also* WANDERLUST.

13
Rocked in the cradle of the deep
I lay me down in peace to sleep;
Secure I rest upon the wave,
For Thou, O Lord! hast power to save.
EMMA HART WILLARD, *Rocked in the Cradle of the Deep.* Written at sea, 14 July, 1831.

VI—Sea: Sailors

14
Great seamen . . . in tall ships ribbed with brass,
To put a girdle round about the world.
GEORGE CHAPMAN, *Bussy d'Ambois.* Act i, sc. 1. A proverbial expression for a voyage around the world.

I'll put a girdle round about the earth in forty minutes.
SHAKESPEARE, *A Midsummer-Night's Dream.* Act ii, sc. 1, l. 175.

He hath put a girdle 'bout the world,
And sounded all her quicksands.
JOHN WEBSTER, *Duchess of Malfi.* Act iii, sc. 2.

Round the world and home again,
That's the sailor's way.
WILLIAM ALLINGHAM, *Homeward Bound.*

Wherever waves can roll, and winds can blow.
CHARLES CHURCHILL, *The Farewell.*

1
While the hollow oak our palace is,
Our heritage the sea.
ALLAN CUNNINGHAM, *A Wet Sheet and a Flowing Sea.*

2
For they say there's a Providence sits up aloft,
To keep watch for the life of poor Jack!
CHARLES DIBDIN, *Poor Jack.*

There's a sweet little cherub that sits up aloft,
To keep watch for the life of poor Jack.
CHARLES DIBDIN, *Poor Jack.*

For if bold tars are Fortune's sport,
Still are they Fortune's care.
CHARLES DIBDIN, *The Blind Sailor.*

3
Mayhap you have heard that as dear as their lives
All true-hearted tars love their ships and their wives.
CHARLES DIBDIN, *The Nancy.*

In every mess I find a friend,
In every port a wife.
CHARLES DIBDIN, *Jack in His Element.*

They 'll tell thee sailors, when away,
In every port a mistress find.
JOHN GAY, *Sweet William's Farewell.*

A seafaring man may have a sweetheart in every port; but he should steer clear of a wife as he would avoid a quicksand.
SMOLLETT, *The Adventures of Sir Launcelot Greaves.* Ch. 21.

4
Here, a sheer hulk, lies poor Tom Bowling,
The darling of our crew;
No more he'll hear the tempest howling,
For death has broached him to.
His form was of the manliest beauty,
His heart was kind and soft;
Faithful, below, he did his duty;
But now he's gone aloft.
CHARLES DIBDIN, *Tom Bowling.*

5
Skill'd in the globe and sphere, he gravely stands,
And, with his compass, measures seas and lands.
DRYDEN, *Sixth Satire of Juvenal,* l. 760.

6
The wonder is always new that any sane man can be a sailor.
EMERSON, *English Traits,* p. 36.

7
Your seamen are like your element, always tempestuous.
FARQUHAR, *Sir Harry Wildair.* Act i, sc. 1.

A rude and boisterous captain of the sea.
JOHN HOME, *Douglas.* Act iv, sc. 1.

The skipper stormed and tore his hair,
Hauled on his boots and roared at Marden—
"Nantucket 's sunk and here we are
Right over old Marm Hackett's garden!"
JAMES T. FIELDS, *The Nantucket Skipper.*

8
Now landsmen all, whoever you may be,
If you want to rise to the top of the tree,
If your soul isn't fettered to an office stool,
Be careful to be guided by this golden rule—
Stick close to your desks and never go to sea,
And you all may be Rulers of the Queen's Navee!
W. S. GILBERT, *H. M. S. Pinafore.* Act i.

9
Sailors should never be shy.
W. S. GILBERT, *H. M. S. Pinafore.* Act i.

Sailors are but worldly men, and little prone to lead serious and thoughtful lives.
W. S. GILBERT, *Ruddigore.* Act i.

10 Oak and brass of triple fold
Encompassed sure that heart, which first made bold
To the raging sea to trust a fragile bark.
(Illi robur et æs triplex
Circa pectus erat, qui fragilem truci
Commissit pelago ratem Primus.)
HORACE, *Odes.* Bk. i, ode 3, l. 9. (Conington, tr.)

11
The hungry sea is fatal to sailors. (Exitio est avidum mare nautis.)
HORACE, *Odes.* Bk. i, ode 28, l. 18.

Trust to a plank, draw precarious breath,
At most seven inches from the jaws of death.
(Confisus ligno, digitis a morte remotus
Quattuor aut septem, si sit latissima, tædæ.)
JUVENAL, *Satires.* Sat. xii, l. 58.

Avoid business with the sea, and put thy mind to the ox-drawn plough, if it is any joy to thee to see the end of a long life. On land there is length of days, but on the sea it is difficult to find a man with gray hair.
PHALÆCUS, *Epigram.* (*Greek Anthology.* Bk. vii, No. 650.)

Ships are but boards, sailors but men: there be land-rats and water-rats, land-thieves and water-thieves, I mean pirates, and then there is the peril of waters, winds and rocks.
SHAKESPEARE, *The Merchant of Venice,* i, 3, 22.

12
Of all the husbands on the earth,
The sailor has the finest berth,
For in 'is cabin he can sit
And sail and sail—and let 'er knit.
WALLACE IRWIN, *A Grain of Salt.*

A baby was sleeping, Its mother was weeping,
For her husband was far on the wild-raging sea.
SAMUEL LOVER, *The Angel's Whisper.*

13
No man will be a sailor who has contrivance enough to get himself into a jail; for being in a ship is being in jail with the chance of being drowned. . . . A man in a jail has more room, better food, and commonly better company.
SAMUEL JOHNSON, (BOSWELL, *Life,* 1759.)

What is a ship but a prison?
ROBERT BURTON, *Anatomy of Melancholy*. Pt. ii, sec. iii, mem. 4.

1
Roll down—roll down to Rio—
Roll really down to Rio!
Oh, I'd love to roll to Rio
Some day before I'm old!
KIPLING, *Just-So Stories: Armadilloes.*

2
There were gentlemen and there were seamen in the navy of Charles the Second. But the seamen were not gentlemen; and the gentlemen were not seamen.
MACAULAY, *History of England*. Vol. i, ch. 3.

3
A white color is a disgrace in a sailor: he should be swarthy from the sea-water and the rays of the sun. (Candidus in nauta turpis color: æquoris unda Debet et a radiis sideris esse niger.)
OVID, *Ars Amatoria*. Bk. i, l. 723.

4
Seek, sailor, the safe harbors. (Tutos, pete, navita, portus.)
OVID, *Fasti*. Bk. iv, l. 625.

A Passage perillus makyth a Port pleasant.
UNKNOWN, *Motto*, inscribed on a harbor wall on the Lake of Como.

Did you voyage all unspoken, small and lonely?
Or with fame, the happy fortune of the few?
So you win the Golden Harbour, in the old way;
There's the old sea welcome waiting there for you.
RONALD A. HOPWOOD, *The Old Way*. (London *Times*, 16 Sept., 1916.)

They saw the cables loosened, they saw the gangways cleared,
They heard the women weeping, they heard the men that cheered;
Far off, far off, the tumult faded and died away,
And all alone the sea-wind came singing up the Bay.
HENRY NEWBOLT, *The Sailing of the Long Ships*.

5
The seaman sets his sails to suit the wind. (Utcumque in alto ventust, exim velum vortitur.)
PLAUTUS, *Epidicus*, l. 49. (Act i, sc. 1.)

6
There is no pleasure sailors have greater than sighting from the deep the distant land. (Voluptas nullast navitis . . . quam quom ex alto procul terram conspiciunt.)
PLAUTUS, *Menæchmi*, l. 226. (Act ii, sc. 1.)

Pass we the joys and sorrows sailors find,
Coop'd in their winged sea-girt citadel,
The foul, the fair, the contrary, the kind,
As breezes rise and fall and billows swell,
Till on some jocund morn—lo, land! and all is well.
BYRON, *Childe Harold*. Canto ii, st. 28.

7
They that go down to the sea in ships, that do business in great waters; these see the works of the Lord, and his wonders in the deep.
Old Testament: Psalms, cvii, 23, 24.

8
Like a drunken sailor on a mast;
Ready, with every nod, to tumble down
Into the fatal bowels of the deep.
SHAKESPEARE, *Richard III*. Act iii, sc. 4, l. 101.

9
I make good the old saying, we sailors get money like horses, and spend it like asses.
SMOLLETT, *Peregrine Pickle*. Ch. 2.

Strike up the band, here comes a sailor,
Cash in his hand, just off a whaler;
Stand in a row, don't let him go;
Jack's a cinch, but every inch a sailor.
ANDREW B. STERLING, *Strike Up the Band*. (1900)

10
There were three sailors of Bristol city
Who took a boat and went to sea.
But first with beef and captain's biscuits
And pickled pork they loaded she.

There was gorging Jack and guzzling Jimmy,
And the youngest he was little Billee.
Now when they got as far as the Equator
They'd nothing left but one split pea.
THACKERAY, *Little Billee*.

Oh, I am a cook and a captain bold
And the mate of the *Nancy* brig,
And a bo'sun tight and a midshipmite
And the crew of the captain's gig.
W. S. GILBERT, *The Yarn of the Nancy Bell.*

11
Why, Jack's the king of all,
For they all love Jack.
FREDERICK E. WEATHERLY, *They All Love Jack. See also under* JACK.

12
Six days shalt thou labor and do all thou art able,
And on the seventh—holystone the decks and scrape the cable.
UNKNOWN, *The Philadelphia Catechism*. (DANA, *Two Years Before the Mast*. Ch. 3.)

VII—Sea and Land

13
Whenever you can make your journey by land, do not make it by sea. (Quando terra iter facere possis, ne mari facias.)
APOSTOLIUS. *Adagia* Cent. ii, sec. 54. One of the three things in his life which Cato Major repented was having made a journey by sea when he could have gone by land. (PLUTARCH, *Lives: Marcus Cato*. Ch. 9, 6.)

There are many advantages in sea-voyaging, but security is not one of them.
SADI. (EMERSON, *English Traits: The Voyage*.)

14
They are ill discoverers that think there is no land, when they can see nothing but sea.
BACON, *Advancement of Learning*. Bk. ii.

15
An everywhere of silver,
With ropes of sand

To keep it from effacing
The track called land.
EMILY DICKINSON, *Poems*. Pt. ii, No. 22.

1
A strong nor'wester's blowing, Bill;
Hark! don't ye hear it roar, now?
Lord help 'em, how I pities them
Unhappy folks on shore now!
CHARLES DIBDIN, *The Sailor's Consolation*. This poem is sometimes attributed to William Pitt, the song-writer.

My eyes! what tiles and chimney-pots
About their heads are flying!
CHARLES DIBDIN, *The Sailor's Consolation*.

The shore has perils unknown to the deep.
GEORGE ILES, *Jottings*.

2
Women and cowards on the land may lie,
The sea's a tomb that's proper for the brave.
DRYDEN, *Annus Mirabilis*. St. 101.

3
Where the broad ocean leans against the land.
GOLDSMITH, *The Traveller*, l. 284.

4
Praise the sea, but keep on land.
GEORGE HERBERT, *Jacula Prudentum*. No. 485.

Being on sea, sail: being on land, settle.
GEORGE HERBERT, *Jacula Prudentum*. No. 414.

5
What though the sea be calm? Trust to the shore:
Ships have been drown'd, where late they danc'd before.
HERRICK, *Safety on the Shore*.

6
Love the sea? I dote upon it—from the beach.
DOUGLAS JERROLD, *Specimens of Jerrold's Wit: Love of the Sea*.

7
When men come to like a sea life they are not fit to live on land.
SAMUEL JOHNSON. (BOSWELL, *Life*, 1776.)

They scorn the strand who sail upon the sea.
H. D. THOREAU, *The Fisher's Boy*.

8
The land is dearer for the sea,
The ocean for the shore.
LUCY LARCOM, *On the Beach*. St. 11.

9
He who loves the ocean
And the ways of ships
May taste beside a mountain pool
Brine on his lips.
MARY SINTON LEITCH, *He Who Loves the Ocean*.

10
It is a pleasure for to sit at ease
Upon the land, and safely for to see
How other folks are tossèd on the seas
That with the blustering winds turmoilèd be.
LUCRETIUS. (AMYOT, *Introduction to Plutarch*. North, tr. 1579.)

11
With whisper of her mellowing grain,
With treble of brook and bud and tree,
Earth joys for ever to sustain
The bass eternal of the sea.
RODEN NOEL, *Beatrice*.

12
What have you to do with the sea? You should have been content with land. (Quid tibi cum pelago? Terra contenta fuisses.)
OVID, *Amores*. Bk. iii, eleg. 8, l. 49.

13
By sea and by land. (Per mare, per terras.)
OVID, *Heroides*. Epis. vii, p. 88; epis. xiv, l. 101.

14
Ye gentlemen of England
That live at home at ease,
Ah! little do you think upon
The dangers of the seas.
MARTIN PARKER, *Ye Gentlemen of England*.

Ye who dwell at home,
Ye do not know the terrors of the main!
SOUTHEY, *Madoc in Wales*. Pt. iv, l. 178.

15
I am the tomb of a shipwrecked man, and that opposite is the tomb of a husbandman. So death lies in wait alike on sea and land.
PLATO. (*Greek Anthology*. Bk. vii, epig. 265.)

And Christians love in the turf to lie,
Not in watery graves to be;
Nay, the very fishes will sooner die
On the land than in the sea.
THOMAS HOOD, *The Mermaid of Margate*, l. 65.

16
I never was on the dull, tame shore,
But I loved the great sea more and more.
BRYAN WALLER PROCTER, *The Sea*.

17
Now would I give a thousand furlongs of sea for an acre of barren ground.
SHAKESPEARE, *The Tempest*. Act i, sc. 1, l. 70.

18
Hug the shore, let others keep to the deep. (Litus ama, . . . altum alii teneant.)
VERGIL, *Æneid*. Bk. v, l. 163.

19
Of Christian souls more have been wrecked on shore
Than ever were lost at sea.
CHARLES H. WEBB, *With a Nantucket Shell*.

VIII—Sea: Seasickness

20
He felt that chilling heaviness of heart,
Or rather stomach, which, alas! attends,
Beyond the best apothecary's art,
The loss of love, the treachery of friends. . . .
No doubt he would have been much more pathetic,
But the sea acted as a strong emetic.
BYRON, *Don Juan*. Canto ii, st. 21.

The best of remedies is a beef-steak
Against sea-sickness: try it, sir, before

You sneer, and I assure you this is true,
For I have found it answer—so may you.
BYRON, *Don Juan*. Canto ii, st. 13.

There 's not a sea the passenger e'er pukes in
Turns up more dangerous breakers than the
Euxine.
BYRON, *Don Juan*. Canto v, st. 5.

1
The bounding pinnace play'd a game
Of dreary pitch and toss;
A game that, on the good dry land,
Is apt to bring a loss!
THOMAS HOOD, *The Sea-Spell*, l. 21.

2
What of the poor man? . . . He hires a boat and gets just as sick as the rich man who sails in his yacht. (Quid pauper? . . . Conducto navigio æque Nauseat ac locuples quem ducit priva triremis.)
HORACE, *Epistles*. Bk. i, epis. 1, l. 91.

3
You may be sure that the reason Ulysses was shipwrecked on every possible occasion was not because of the anger of the sea-god; he was simply subject to sea-sickness. (Nausiator erat.)
SENECA, *Epistulæ ad Lucilium*. Epis. liii, sec. 4.

4
We all like to see people sea-sick when we are not ourselves.
MARK TWAIN, *The Innocents Abroad*. Ch. 3.

IX—Sea: Sea-Shells

5
I wiped away the weeds and foam,
I fetched my sea-born treasures home;
But the poor, unsightly, noisome things
Had left their beauty on the shore,
With the sun and the sand and the wild uproar.
EMERSON, *Each and All*.

6
But I have sinuous shells of pearly hue; . . .
Shake one, and it awakens; then apply
Its polisht lips to your attentive ear,
And it remembers its august abodes,
And murmurs as the ocean murmurs there.
W. S. LANDOR, *Gebir*. Bk. i, l. 159.

In the upper room I lay, and heard far off
The unsleeping murmur like a shell.
R. L. STEVENSON, *To S. C.*

7
The hollow sea-shell, which for years hath
stood
On dusty shelves, when held against the ear
Proclaims its stormy parent, and we hear
The faint, far murmur of the breaking flood.
We hear the sea. The Sea? It is the blood
In our own veins, impetuous and near.
EUGENE LEE-HAMILTON, *Sea-shell Murmurs*.

8
The soul of music slumbers in the shell,
Till waked and kindled by the master's spell;
And feeling hearts—touch them but rightly
—pour
A thousand melodies unheard before!
SAMUEL ROGERS, *Human Life*, l. 361.

9
Gather a shell from the strown beach
And listen at its lips: they sigh
The same desire and mystery,
The echo of the whole sea's speech.
D. G. ROSSETTI, *The Sea-Limits*.

From within were heard
Murmurings, whereby the monitor expressed
Mysterious union with its native sea.
WORDSWORTH, *The Excursion*. Bk. iv, l. 1138.

10
I send thee a shell from the ocean-beach;
But listen thou well, for my shell hath speech.
Hold to thine ear And plain thou'lt hear
Tales of ships.
CHARLES H. WEBB, *With a Nantucket Shell*.

11
It is perhaps a more fortunate destiny to have a taste for collecting shells than to be born a millionaire.
R. L. STEVENSON, *Lay Morals*.

X—Sea: Freedom of the Sea

12
Thus much is certain: that he that commands the sea is at great liberty, and may take as much and as little of the war as he will.
BACON, *Essays: Of Kingdoms and Estates*.

13
To all nations their empire will be dreadful, because their ships will sail wherever billows roll or winds can waft them.
SIR JOHN DALRYMPLE, *Memoirs of Great Britain and Ireland*. Vol. iii, p. 152.

14
The most advanced nations are always those who navigate the most.
EMERSON, *Society and Solitude: Civilization*.

15
That the persons of our citizens shall be safe in freely traversing the ocean, that the transportation of our own produce, in our own vessels, to the markets of our own choice, and the return to us of the articles we want for our own use, shall be unmolested, I hold to be fundamental, and the gauntlet that must be forever hurled at him who questions it.
THOMAS JEFFERSON, *Writings*. Vol. xiv, p. 301.

16
The trident of Neptune is the sceptre of the world. (Le trident de Neptune est le sceptre du monde.)
ANTOINE LEMIÈRRE, *Commerce*.

17
I deliver to you a fleet that is mistress of the seas. (Θαλασσοκρατοῦν τὸ ναυτικὸν παραδίδωσιν.)
LYSANDER, when handing over the command of the fleet to Callicratidas, 406 B.C. (PLUTARCH, *Lives: Lysander*. Ch. 6, sec. 2.)

1
The sea indeed is assuredly common to all. (Mare quidem commune certo 'st omnibus.)
PLAUTUS, *Rudens*, l. 975. (Act iv, sc. 3.)

And seas but join the regions they divide.
POPE, *Windsor Forest*, l. 400.

The seas are but a highway between the doorways of the nations.
FRANKLIN K. LANE, *The American Pioneer.*

2
He who commands the sea has command of everything. (Qui mari teneat, eum necesse rerum potiri.)
THEMISTOCLES. (CICERO, *Epistolæ ad Atticum*, x, 8.)

3
Guarded with ships, and all our sea our own.
EDMUND WALLER, *To My Lord of Falkland.*

SEASONS, THE

See also Spring, Summer, Autumn, Winter

4
The tendinous part of the mind, so to speak, is more developed in winter; the fleshy, in summer. I should say winter had given the bone and sinew to literature, summer the tissues and the blood.
JOHN BURROUGHS, *The Snow-Walkers.*

5
Therefore all seasons shall be sweet to thee,
Whether the summer clothe the general earth
With greenness, or the redbreast sit and sing
Betwixt the tufts of snow on the bare branch
Of mossy apple-tree.
S. T. COLERIDGE, *Frost at Midnight*, l. 65.

6
Four seasons fill the measure of the year.
KEATS, *The Human Seasons.*

Perceiv'st thou not the process of the year,
How the four seasons in four forms appear,
Resembling human life in ev'ry shape they wear?
Spring first, like infancy, shoots out her head,
With milky juice requiring to be fed: . . .
Proceeding onward whence the year began,
The Summer grows adult, and ripens into man. . . .
Autumn succeeds, a sober, tepid age,
Not froze with fear, nor boiling into rage; . . .
Last, Winter creeps along with tardy pace.
Sour is his front, and furrow'd is his face.
OVID, *Metamorphoses*, xv, 296. (Dryden, tr.)

Sing a song of Spring-time, the world is going round,
Blown by the south wind, listen to its sound. . . .
Sing a song of Summer, the world is nearly still,
The mill-pond has gone to sleep, and so has the mill. . . .
Sing a song of Autumn, the world is going back;
They glean in the corn-field, and stamp on the stack. . . .
Sing a song of Winter, the world stops dead;
Under snowy coverlid flowers lie abed.
COSMO MONKHOUSE, *A Song of the Seasons.*

Then, how merry are the times!
The Spring times! the Summer times! . . .
Now, how solemn are the times!
The Winter times! the Night times! . . .
Sing then, hopeful are all times!
Winter, Spring, Summer times!
BRYAN W. PROCTER, *A Song for the Seasons.*

These, as they change, Almighty Father, these
Are but the varied God. The rolling year
Is full of Thee. Forth in the pleasing Spring
Thy beauty walks, thy tenderness and love. . . .
Then comes thy glory in the Summer-months,
With light and heat refulgent. Then thy sun
Shoots full perfection through the swelling year. . . .
Thy bounty shines in Autumn unconfined,
And spreads a common feast for all that lives.
In Winter awful thou! with clouds and storms
Around thee thrown, tempest o'er tempest rolled,
Majestic darkness! On the whirlwind's wing
Riding sublime.
JAMES THOMSON, *A Hymn on the Seasons*, l. 1.

Spring, the low prelude of a lordlier song;
Summer, a music without hint of death:
Autumn, a cadence, lingeringly long:
Winter, a pause;—the Minstrel-Year takes breath.
WILLIAM WATSON, *The Year's Minstrelsy.*

7
Our seasons have no fixed returns,
Without our will they come and go;
At noon our sudden summer burns,
Ere sunset all is snow.
J. R. LOWELL, *To* ——. St. 2.

8
Autumn to winter, winter into spring,
Spring into summer, summer into fall,—
So rolls the changing year, and so we change;
Motion so swift, we know not that we move.
DINAH MARIA MULOCK CRAIK, *Immutable.*

9
Autumn brings fruit; summer is fair with harvest; spring gives flowers; winter is relieved by fire. (Poma dat autumnus; formosa est messibus æstas; Ver præbet flores; igne levatur hiemps.)
OVID, *Remediorum Amoris*, l. 187.

10
Each changing season doth its poison bring,
Rheums chill the winter, agues blast the spring.
MATTHEW PRIOR, *Ode to the Memory of Colonel Villiers*, l. 49.

11
Winter brings cold weather, and we must shiver. Summer returns with its heat, and we must sweat. (Hiems frigora adducit: algendum est. Ætas calores refert: æstuandum est.)
SENECA, *Epistulæ ad Lucilium*. Epis. cvii, 7.

12
January grey is here,
Like a sexton by her grave;
February bears the bier,
March with grief doth howl and rave,
And April weeps—but, O ye Hours!
Follow with May's fairest flowers.
SHELLEY, *Dirge for the Year*. St. 4.

1
January snowy; February flowy; March blowy.
April show'ry; May flow'ry; June bow'ry.
July moppy; August croppy; September poppy.
October breezy; November wheezy; December freezy.

RICHARD BRINSLEY SHERIDAN, *The Calendar.*

Spring: slippy, drippy, nippy.
Summer: showery, flowery, bowery.
Autumn: hoppy, croppy, poppy.
Winter: wheezy, sneezy, breezy.

UNKNOWN, *The Seasons.* (*Athenæum,* 22 Feb., 1862.)

2
Sing a song of seasons!
Something bright in all!
Flowers in the summer,
Fires in the fall.

R. L. STEVENSON, *Autumn Fires.*

3
Ah! welaway! Seasons flower and fade.

TENNYSON, *Song.* St. 1.

4
Barnaby bright, Barnaby bright,
The longest day and the shortest night;
Lucy light, Lucy light,
The shortest day and the longest night.

UNKNOWN, *Old Rhyme.* Referring to St. Barnabas' Day, the summer solstice; and St. Lucy's Day, the winter solstice.

SECRET

I—Secret: Apothegms

5
For this thing was not done in a corner.

New Testament: Acts, xxvi, 26.

As witnesses that the things were not done in a corner.

GENERAL THOMAS HARRISON, *Defence at His Trial.* (*Trial of Twenty Regicides, 1660,* p. 39.)

6
Two things only a man cannot hide: that he is drunk, and that he is in love.

ANTIPHANES OF MACEDONIA, *Fragment.* (MEINEKE, *Frag. Comicorum Græcorum,* iii, 3.)

7
There is no secrecy comparable to celerity.

FRANCIS BACON, *Essays: Of Delays.*

8
When we desire to confine our words, we commonly say they are spoken under the rose.

SIR THOMAS BROWNE, *Vulgar Errors: Of Speaking Under the Rose. See also* ROSE: APOTHEGMS.

9
The open secret. (El secreto á voces.)

CALDERON. Title of play.

10
I shall be as secret as the grave.

CERVANTES, *Don Quixote.* Pt. ii, ch. 62.

11
Our story a secret! Lord help you—tell 'em Queen Anne's dead.

GEORGE COLMAN THE YOUNGER, *The Heir-at-Law.* Act i, sc. 1.

12
He only is secret who never was trusted.

CONGREVE, *Love for Love.* Act iii, sc. 3.

13
The secret things belong unto the Lord our God.

Old Testament: Deuteronomy, xxix, 29.

14
The secrets of life are not shown except to sympathy and likeness.

EMERSON, *Representative Men: Montaigne.*

15
There are secrets in all families.

FARQUHAR, *The Beaux' Stratagem.* Act iii, sc. 3.

Some of the roofs are plum-color,
Some of the roofs are gray,
Some of the roofs are silverstone,
And some are made of clay;
But under every gabled close
There's a secret hid away.

ESTHER LILIAN DUFF, *Not Three, But One.*

There is a skeleton in every house.

UNKNOWN, *Italian Tales of Humor, Gallantry and Romance.*

They have a skeleton in their closets, as well as their neighbours.

THACKERAY, *The Newcomes.* Ch. 55.

It is in truth a most contagious game:
HIDING THE SKELETON shall be its name.

GEORGE MEREDITH, *Modern Love.* St. 17.

Every man—even the most cynical—has one enthusiasm—he is earnest about some one thing. If there is a skeleton—there is also an *idol* in the cupboard!

JOHN OLIVER HOBBES, *The Ambassador.* Act ii.

16
Those house them best who house for secrecy.

THOMAS HARDY, *Heiress and Architect.* St. 6.

17
He that tells a secret is another's servant.

GEORGE HERBERT, *Jacula Prudentum.*

Thy secret is thy prisoner; if thou let it go thou art a prisoner to it.

JOHN RAY, *Adagia Hebraica,* 408. (1678)

A secret is your slave if you keep it, your master if you lose it.

UNKNOWN. An Arabian proverb.

18
Three may keep counsel if two be away.

JOHN HEYWOOD, *Proverbs.* Pt. ii, ch. 5. (1546)

Two may keep counsel if one be away.

JOHN LYLY, *Euphues,* p. 67. (1579)

Two may keep counsel when the third 's away.

SHAKESPEARE, *Titus Andronicus,* iv, 2, 144. (1593)

Two may keep counsel, putting one away.

SHAKESPEARE, *Romeo and Juliet,* ii, 4, 209. (1595)

Three may keep a secret if two of them are dead.

BENJAMIN FRANKLIN, *Poor Richard,* 1735.

A secret between two is a secret of God; a secret among three is everybody's secret. (Secret de deux, secret de Dieu; Secret de trois, secret de tous.)

UNKNOWN. A French proverb.

1
Secret path marks secret foe.
SCOTT, *The Lady of the Lake.* Canto v, st. 8.

2
Leave in concealment what has long been concealed. (Latere semper patere, quod latuit diu.)
SENECA, *Œdipus*, l. 826.

Men conceal the past scenes of their lives. (Vitæ poscænia celant.)
LUCRETIUS, *De Rerum Natura.* Bk. iv, l. 1182.

3
Seal up your lips, and give no words but
mum:
The business asketh silent secrecy.
SHAKESPEARE, *II Henry VI.* Act i, sc. 2, l. 89.

Persuade me not; I will make a Star-chamber matter of it.
SHAKESPEARE, *The Merry Wives of Windsor.* Act i, sc. 1, l. 1.

I pray you, turn the key and keep our counsel.
SHAKESPEARE, *Othello.* Act iv, sc. 2, l. 94.

Wherefore are these things hid?
SHAKESPEARE, *Twelfth Night.* Act i, sc. 3, l. 133.

4
Secrecy is the seal of speech, and occasion the seal of secrecy.
SOLON. (DIOGENES LAERTIUS, *Solon.* Sec. 14.)

5
A secret is a weapon and a friend. Man is God's secret, Power is man's secret, Sex is woman's secret.
JAMES STEPHENS, *The Crock of Gold.*

II—Secrets: Their Betrayal

6
Little secrets are commonly told again, but great ones are generally kept.
LORD CHESTERFIELD, *Letters*, 13 Sept., 1748.

If a fool knows a secret, he tells it because he is a fool; if a knave knows one, he tells it wherever it is his interest to tell it. But women and young men are very apt to tell what secrets they know from the vanity of having been trusted.
LORD CHESTERFIELD, *Letters, Sentences, and Maxims.*

The vanity of being known to be entrusted with a secret is generally one of the chief motives to disclose it.
SAMUEL JOHNSON, *The Rambler*, No. 13.

7
None are so fond of secrets as those who do not mean to keep them; such persons covet secrets as a spendthrift covets money, for the purpose of circulation.
C. C. COLTON, *Lacon.* No. 40.

8
Never inquire into another man's secret; but conceal that which is intrusted to you, though pressed both by wine and anger to reveal it. (Arcanum neque tu scrutaberis illius umquam, Commissumque teges et vino tortus et ira.)
HORACE, *Epistles.* Bk. i, epis. 18, l. 37.

9
They wish to know the family secrets, and to be feared accordingly. (Scire volunt secreta domus, atque inde timeri.)
JUVENAL, *Satires.* Sat. iii, l. 113.

10
We confide our secret through friendship, but it escapes through love. (L'on confie son secret dans l'amitié, mais il échappe dans l'amour.)
LA BRUYÈRE, *Les Caractères.* Pt. iv.

11
When a secret is revealed, it is the fault of the man who confided it. (Toute révélation d'un secret est la faute de celui qui l'a confié.)
LA BRUYÈRE, *Les Caractères.* Pt. v.

How can we expect another to guard our secret if we have not been able to guard it ourselves? (Comment prétendons-nous qu'un autre garde notre secret, si nous n'avons pas pu le garder nous-mêmes?)
LA ROCHEFOUCAULD, *Maximes Supprimées.* No. 584.

I have play'd the fool, the gross fool, to believe
The bosom of a friend will hold a secret
Mine own could not contain.
MASSINGER, *The Unnatural Combat.* Act v, sc. 2, l. 1.

12
Nothing is secret, that shall not be made manifest.
New Testament: Luke, viii, 17.

And that which you have spoken in the ear in closets shall be proclaimed upon the housetops.
New Testament: Luke, xii, 3.

13
Mind, it's all *entre nous*,
But you know, love, I never keep secrets
from you.
THOMAS MOORE, *The Fudge Family in Paris.* Letter i, l. 67.

14
Sooner will men hold fire in their mouths than keep a secret. (Nam citius flammas mortales ore tenebunt quam secreta tegant.)
PETRONIUS, *Fragments.* No. 86.

15
Some secret truths, from learned pride conceal'd,
To maids alone and children are reveal'd.
POPE, *The Rape of the Lock.* Canto i, l. 37.

16
You are in a pitiable condition when you have to conceal what you wish to tell. (Miserum est tacere cogi, quod cupias loqui.)
PUBLILIUS SYRUS, *Sententiæ.* No. 348.

17
He who gives up the smallest part of a secret has the rest no longer in his power.
JEAN PAUL RICHTER, *Titan.* Zykel 123.

18
If you wish another to keep your secret, first

keep it yourself. (Alium silere quod voles, primus sile.)

SENECA, *Hippolytus*, l. 876.

You can take better care of your secret than another can.

EMERSON, *Journals*, 1863.

1
If you have hitherto conceal'd this sight
Let it be tenable in your silence still;
And whatsoever else shall hap to-night,
Give it an understanding, but no tongue.

SHAKESPEARE, *Hamlet*. Act 1, sc. 2, l. 247.

2
If you wish to preserve your secret, wrap it up in frankness.

ALEXANDER SMITH, *Dreamthorp: On the Writing of Essays*.

3
Shy and unready men are great betrayers of secrets; for there are few wants more urgent for the moment than the want of something to say.

SIR HENRY TAYLOR, *The Statesman*, p. 131.

4
I am full of leaks, and I let secrets out hither and yon (Plenus rimarum sum, hac atque illac perfluo.)

TERENCE, *Eunuchus*, l. 105. (Act i, sc. 2.)

These are weighty secrets, and we must whisper them.

SARAH CHAUNCEY WOOLSEY, *Secrets*.

III—Secrets and Women

5
The parties in both cases Enjoining secrecy,—
Inviolable compact To notoriety.

EMILY DICKINSON, *Poems*. Pt. ii, No. 32.

6
Thus through a woman was the secret known;
Tell us, and in effect you tell the town.

DRYDEN, *The Wife of Bath, Her Tale*, l. 201.

Oil and water—woman and a secret—
Are hostile properties.

BULWER-LYTTON, *Richelieu*. Act i, sc. 1.

7
A man can keep another person's secret better than his own: a woman, on the contrary, keeps her secret though she blabs all others

LA BRUYÈRE, *Les Caractères*. Pt. v.

8
Nothing is so oppressive as a secret: women find it difficult to keep one long; and I know a goodly number of men who are women in this regard
(Rien ne pèse tant qu'un secret:
Le porter loin est difficile aux dames;
Et je sais même sur ce fait
Bon nombre d'hommes que sont femmes.)

LA FONTAINE, *Fables* Bk. viii, fab. 6.

9
A free-tongued woman,
And very excellent at telling secrets.

MIDDLETON AND MASSINGER, *The Old Law*. Act iv, sc. 2.

10
Thou wilt not utter what thou dost not know,
And so far will I trust thee, gentle Kate.

SHAKESPEARE, *I Henry IV*. Act ii, sc. 3, l. 114.

11
Is there whom you detest, and seek his life?
Trust no soul with the secret—but his wife.

YOUNG, *Love of Fame*. Sat. vi, l. 389.

SECTS, see Religion: Dissensions

SELF-CONFIDENCE

12
You carry Cæsar and Cæsar's fortune. (Cæsarem vehis Cæsarisque fortunam. Or, Cæsarem portas et fortunam ejus.)

JULIUS CÆSAR, to the pilot, Amyclas, when their boat was imperilled by a storm. (SUETONIUS, *Lives of the Cæsars: Julius*. Sec. 58. Also PLUTARCH, *Lives: Cæsar*. Sec. 38.)

You are uneasy; you never sailed with *me* before, I see.

ANDREW JACKSON, to an elderly man who showed signs of fear while sailing with Jackson down Chesapeake Bay in an old steamboat. (PARTON, *Life of Jackson*. Vol iii, p. 493.)

13
Most happy he who is entirely self-reliant, and who centres all his requirements in himself alone. (Beatissimus, qui est totus aptus ex sese, quisque in se uno sua ponit omnia.)

CICERO, *Paradoxa*, ii.

By his own prowess (Suo Marte.)

CICERO, *Philippicæ*. No. ii, ch. 37, sec. 95.

14
Nor fate, nor chance, nor any star commands
Success and failure—naught but your own
hands.

SAMUEL VALENTINE COLE, *Works and Days*.

15
Self-trust is the essence of heroism.

EMERSON, *Essays, First Series: Heroism*.

Trust thyself: every heart vibrates to that iron string.

EMERSON, *Essays, First Series: Self-Reliance*.

16
Self-confidence is the first requisite to great undertakings.

SAMUEL JOHNSON, *Works*. Vol. iv, p. 6.

Self-trust is the first secret of success.

EMERSON, *Society and Solitude: Success*.

Those who believe that they are exclusively in the right are generally those who achieve something.

ALDOUS HUXLEY, *Proper Studies*, p. 243.

17
The confidence which we have in ourselves engenders the greatest part of that we have in others (La confiance que l'on a en soi fait naître le plus grande partie de celle que l'on a aux autres.)

LA ROCHEFOUCAULD, *Maximes Supprimées*, 624.

18
When the trumpet sounds the signal of danger, man hastens to join his comrades, no matter what the cause that calls them to arms. He rushes into the thickest of the fight,

and amid the uproar of battle regains confidence in himself and in his powers.
LAMARTINE, *Méditations Poétiques.*

1
The promises of this world are for the most part vain phantoms, and to confide in one's self, and become something of worth and value, is the best and safest course.
MICHELANGELO. (EMERSON, *Society and Solitude: Success.*)

2
All my hope for all my help is myself.
MONTAIGNE, *Essays.* Bk. iii, ch. 9. *See also* GOD: GOD HELPS THEM THAT HELP THEMSELVES.

3
On he moves,
Careless of blame while his own heart approves.
SAMUEL ROGERS, *Human Life,* l. 577.

4
Then where is truth, if there be no self-trust?
SHAKESPEARE, *The Rape of Lucrece,* l. 158.

5
For he that of himself is most secure,
Shall find his state most fickle and unsure.
SPENSER, *Visions of the World's Vanitie.* St. 12.

It is easy—terribly easy—to shake a man's faith in himself. To take advantage of that to break a man's spirit is devil's work.
BERNARD SHAW, *Candida.*

6
In ourselves,
In our own honest hearts and chainless hands,
Will be our safeguard.
THOMAS NOON TALFOURD, *Ion.* Act v.

7
He lean'd not on his fathers, but himself.
TENNYSON, *Aylmer's Field,* l. 56.

8
Let every man's hope be in himself. (Spes sibi quisque.)
VERGIL, *Æneid.* Bk. xi, l. 309.

There is no dependence that can be sure but a dependence upon one's self.
JOHN GAY, *Letter to Swift,* 9 Nov., 1729.

SELF-CONTROL

9
I count him braver who overcomes his desires than him who conquers his enemies; for the hardest victory is the victory over self.
ARISTOTLE. (STOBÆUS, *Florilegium,* p. 223.)

No man is such a conqueror as the man who has defeated himself.
HENRY WARD BEECHER, *Proverbs from Plymouth Pulpit.*

When the fight begins within himself
A man's worth something.
ROBERT BROWNING, *Bishop Blougram's Apology.*

10
Prudent, cautious self-control
Is wisdom's root.
BURNS, *A Bard's Epitaph.*

11
The enemy is within the gates; it is with our own luxury, our own folly, our own criminality that we have to contend.
CICERO, *In Catilinam.* No. ii, ch. 5, sec. 11.

12
Coolness and absence of heat and haste indicate fine qualities.
EMERSON, *Essays, Second Series: Manners.*

13
Thrice noble is the man who of himself is king.
PHINEAS FLETCHER, *Apollyonists.* Canto iii, 10.

14
Few are fit to be entrusted with themselves.
THOMAS FULLER, *Gnomologia.* No. 1523.

15
Thou shalt rule a broader realm by subduing a greedy heart than shouldst thou join Libya to distant Gades. (Latius regnes avidum domando Spiritum, quam si Libyam remotis Gadibus jungas.)
HORACE, *Odes.* Bk. ii, ode 2, l. 9.

16
Nothing gives one person so much advantage over another as to remain always cool and unruffled under all circumstances.
THOMAS JEFFERSON, *Writings.* Vol. xix, p. 241.

17
Than self-restraint there is nothing better.
LAO-TSZE, *The Simple Way.* No. 5.

18
He is strong who conquers others; he who conquers himself is mighty.
LAO-TSZE, *The Simple Way.* No. 33.

He conquers twice who conquers himself in victory. (Bis vincit qui se vincit in victoria.)
PUBLILIUS SYRUS, *Sententiæ.* No. 74.

19
But I will write of him who fights
And vanquishes his sins,
Who struggles on through weary years
Against himself and wins.
CAROLINE LE ROW, *True Heroism.*

20
It is by presence of mind in untried emergencies that the native metal of a man is tested.
LOWELL, *My Study Windows: Lincoln.*

Such power there is in clear-eyed self-restraint.
J. R. LOWELL, *Under the Old Elm.*

21
Vanquish your feelings and your wrath, you who conquer other things. (Vince animos, iramque tuam, qui cetera vincis.)
OVID, *Heroides.* Eleg. iii, l. 85.

There is a victory and defeat—the first and best of victories, the lowest and worst of defeats—which each man gains or sustains at the hands not of another, but of himself.
PLATO, *Laws.* Pt. i, sec. 3. (Jowett, tr.)

22
I am myself my own commander. (Egomet sum mihi imperator.)
PLAUTUS, *Mercator,* l. 853. (Act v, sc. 2.)

And mistress of herself, tho' china fall.
POPE, *Moral Essays*. Epis. ii, l. 268.

1
He that is slow to anger is better than the mighty; and he that ruleth his spirit than he that taketh a city.
Old Testament: Proverbs, xvi, 32.

2
How shall I be able to rule over others, that have not full power and command of myself?
RABELAIS, *Works*. Bk. i, ch. 52.

In vain he seeketh others to suppress,
Who hath not learn'd himself first to subdue.
SPENSER, *Faerie Queene*. Bk. vi, canto 1, st. 41.

3
Power belongs to the self-possessed. (L'empire est au phlégmatique.)
ANTOINE SAINT-JUST, to Robespierre, when the latter gave way to passion at a meeting oi the Committee of Public Safety.

"Keep cool, and you command everybody," said Saint-Just; and the wily old Talleyrand would still say, *Surtout, messieurs, pas de zêle*,—"Above all, gentlemen, no heat."
EMERSON, *Letters and Social Aims: Social Aims.*

4
Rule lust, temper tongue, and bridle the belly.
JOHN RAY, *English Proverbs*, p. 20.

5
To know one's self is the true; to strive with one's self is the good; to conquer one's self is the beautiful.
JOSEPH ROUX, *Meditations of a Parish Priest*. Pt. x, No. 60.

6
The use of self-control is like the use of brakes on a train. It is useful when you find yourself going in the wrong direction, but merely harmful when the direction is right.
BERTRAND RUSSELL, *Marriage and Morals*, p. 311.

7
He is most powerful who has power over himself. (Potentissimum esse qui se habet in potestate.)
SENECA, *Epistulæ ad Lucilium*. Epis. xc, sec. 34.

To master one's self is the greatest mastery. (Imperare sibi maximum imperium est.)
SENECA, *Epistulæ ad Lucilium*. Epis. cxiii, 31.

8
Keep yourself within yourself.
SHAKESPEARE, *Antony and Cleopatra*. Act ii, sc. 3, l. 75.

I pray you, school yourself.
SHAKESPEARE, *Macbeth*. Act iv, sc. 2, l. 15.

Hast thou command? by him that gave it thee,
From a pure heart command thy rebel will.
SHAKESPEARE, *The Rape of Lucrece*, l. 624.

9
Brave conquerors,—for so you are,
That war against your own affections
And the huge army of the world's desires.
SHAKESPEARE, *Love's Labour's Lost*. Act i, sc. 1, l. 8.

10
Man who man would be,
Must rule the empire of himself; in it
Must be supreme, establishing his throne
On vanquished will, quelling the anarchy
Of hopes and fears, being himself alone.
SHELLEY, *Sonnet: Political Greatness.*

11
Self-reverence, self-knowledge, self-control,
These three alone lead life to sovereign power.
TENNYSON, *Œnone*, l. 142.

12
Who has a harder fight than he who is striving to overcome himself? (Quis habet fortius certamen quam qui nititur vincere seipsum?)
À KEMPIS, *De Imitatione Christi*. Pt. i, ch. 3.

13
Lord of himself, though not of lands.
HENRY WOTTON, *Character of a Happy Life.*

Lord of himself—that heritage of woe!
BYRON, *Lara*. Canto i, st. 2.

SELF-DECEIT, see Deceit

SELF-DEFENCE

14
Self-defence is a virtue,
Sole bulwark of all right.
BYRON, *Sardanapalus*. Act ii, sc. 1.

15
Self-defence is Nature's eldest law.
DRYDEN, *Absalom and Achitophel*. Pt. i, l. 458.

16
The sum of the right of Nature, which is, "by all means we can to defend ourselves."
THOMAS HOBBES, *Leviathan*. Pt. i, ch. 14.

17
Fear God and take your own part.
THEODORE ROOSEVELT, *Heading*, ch. 1, book of same name.

I learnt to read and sew, to fear God, and to take my own part.
GEORGE BORROW, *Lavengro*. Ch. 86. (1851) Isopel Berners is speaking.

See also under PREPAREDNESS.

SELF-DENIAL

18
The more a man denies himself, so much the more will he receive from the gods. (Quanto quisque sibi plura negaverit, Ad dis plura feret.)
HORACE, *Odes*. Bk. iii, ode 16, l. 21.

19
In order that you may please you ought to be forgetful of self. (Ut placeas, debes immemor esse tui.)
OVID, *Amores*. Bk. i, eleg. 14, l. 38.

20
Self-denial is not a virtue: it is only the effect of prudence on rascality.
BERNARD SHAW, *Maxims for Revolutionists.*

21
Never preferring himself to others; thus very readily you may find praise without envy, and friends to your taste. (Nunquam præponens se aliis; ita facillime Sine invidia invenias laudem, et amicos pares.)
TERENCE. *Andria*. Act i, sc. 1, l. 38.

1
Self-denial is the shining sore on the leprous body of Christianity.
OSCAR WILDE. (HARRIS, *Oscar Wilde*, p. 340.)

SELF-KNOWLEDGE

2
Once read thy own breast right,
And thou hast done with fears!
Man gets no other light,
Search he a thousand years.
MATTHEW ARNOLD, *Empedocles on Etna*, l. 142.

3
Condemn no poor man, mock no simple man, which proud fools . . . love to do; but find fault with yourself and with none other.
ROGER ASCHAM, *Advice to Lord Warwick's Servant.*

4
Weigh not thyself in the scales of thy own opinion, but let the judgement of the judicious be the standard of thy merit.
SIR THOMAS BROWNE, *Christian Morals*. Pt. ii, sec. 8.

5
Lord deliver me from myself.
SIR THOMAS BROWNE, *Religio Medici*. Pt. ii, sec. 10.

6
And I,—what I seem to my friend, you see:
What I soon shall seem to his love, you guess:
What I seem to myself, do you ask of me?
No hero, I confess.
ROBERT BROWNING, *A Light Woman.*

7
O wad some Pow'r the giftie gie us
To see oursels as ithers see us!
It wad frae monie a blunder free us.
An' foolish notion:
What airs in dress an' gait wad lea'e us,
An' ev'n devotion!
ROBERT BURNS, *To a Louse.*

'Tis one of human nature's laws
To see ourselves without our flaws.
R. T. WOMBAT, *Quatrains.*

8
As men of inward light are wont
To turn their optics in upon 't
BUTLER, *Hudibras*. Pt. iii, canto 1, l. 481.

9
As light increases we see ourselves to be worse than we thought.
FÉNELON, *Spiritual Letters to Women*. No. 8.

It is in general more profitable to reckon up our defects than to boast of our attainments.
CARLYLE, *Essays: Signs of the Times.*

10
I have to live with myself, and so
I want to be fit for myself to know;
I want to be able as days go by,
Always to look myself straight in the eye.
I don't want to stand with the setting sun
And hate myself for the things I've done.
EDGAR A. GUEST, *Myself.*

Just stand aside and watch yourself go by,
Think of yourself as "he" instead of "I."
STRICKLAND GILLILAN, *Watch Yourself Go By.*

Confront yourself and look you in the eye—
Just stand aside and watch yourself go by.
STRICKLAND GILLILAN, *Watch Yourself Go By.*

11
The first step to self-knowledge is self-distrust. Nor can we attain to any kind of knowledge, except by a like process.
J. C. AND A. W. HARE, *Guesses at Truth*, p. 454.

12
Only by knowledge of that which is not Thyself, shall thyself be learned.
OWEN MEREDITH, *Know Thyself.*

13
I know myself better than any doctor can. (Sed sum quam medico notior ipse mihi.)
OVID, *Epistulæ ex Ponto*. Bk. i, epis. 3, l. 92.

Not if I know myself at all.
CHARLES LAMB, *Essays of Elia: The Old and New Schoolmaster.*

14
Man is so made that by continually telling him he is a fool he believes it, and by continually telling it to himself he makes himself believe it. For man holds an inward talk with himself alone, which it behoves him to regulate well.
PASCAL, *Pensées*. No. 536.

As I walk'd by myself, I talk'd to myself,
And myself replied to me;
And the questions myself then put to myself,
With their answers, I give to thee.
BERNARD BARTON, *Colloquy With Myself.* (1826)

15
Live within thyself, and thou wilt discover how small a stock is there. (Tecum habita: noris quam sit tibi curta supellex.)
PERSIUS, *Satires*. Sat. iv, l. 52.

16
All our knowledge is, ourselves to know.
POPE, *Essay on Man*. Epis. iv, l. 398.

Know then thyself, presume not God to scan;
The proper study of mankind is Man.
POPE, *Essay on Man*. Epis ii, l. 1.

See also MAN: THE STUDY OF MAN.

17
Allow not sleep to draw near to your languorous eyelids
Until you have reckoned up each several deed of the daytime:
"Where went I wrong? Did what? And what to be done was left undone?"
Starting from this point, review, then, your acts, and thereafter remember:
Censure yourself for the acts that are base, but rejoice in the goodly.
PYTHAGORAS (?), *Golden Verses*. (EPICTETUS, *Discourses*. Bk. iii, ch. 10, sec. 2.)

Sum up at night what thou hast done by day;
And in the morning what thou hast to do.
Dress and undress thy soul; mark the decay

And growth of it; if, with thy watch, that too
Be down, then wind up both; since we shall be
Most surely judg'd, make thy accounts agree.

GEORGE HERBERT, *The Church-Porch*. St. 76.

Let not soft slumber close your eyes,
Before you've recollected thrice
The train of action through the day!
Where have my feet chose out their way?
What have I learnt, where'er I've been,
From all I've heard, from all I've seen?
What have I more that's worth the knowing?
What have I done that's worth the doing?
What have I sought that I should shun?
What duty have I left undone,
Or into what new follies run?
These self-inquiries are the road
That lead to virtue and to God.

ISAAC WATTS, *Self Examination*.

'Tis greatly wise to talk with our past hours,
And ask them what report they bore to heaven;
And how they might have borne more welcome news.

YOUNG, *Night Thoughts*. Night ii, l. 376.

1
Nothing requires a rarer intellectual heroism than willingness to see one's equation written out.

GEORGE SANTAYANA, *Little Essays*, p. 37.

To understand oneself is the classic form of consolation; to elude oneself is the romantic.

GEORGE SANTAYANA, *Words of Doctrine*, p. 200.

2
If you wish to know yourself observe how others act. If you wish to understand others look into your own heart.

SCHILLER, *Votive Tablets: Xenien*.

3
Whenever I wish to enjoy the quips of a clown, I am not compelled to hunt far; I can laugh at myself.

SENECA, *Epistulæ ad Lucilium*. Epis. 50, sec. 2.

4
What you think of yourself is much more important than what others think of you. (Multo autem ad rem magis pertinet, qualis tibi videaris quam qualis aliis.)

SENECA, *Epistulæ ad Lucilium*. Epis. xxix, 11.

One self-approving hour whole years outweighs
Of stupid starers, and of loud huzzas;
And more true joy Marcellus exiled feels,
Than Cæsar with a senate at his heels.

POPE, *Essay on Man*. Epis. iv, l. 255.

For these attacks do not contribute to make us frail but rather show us to be what we are.

THOMAS À KEMPIS, *De Imitatione Christi*. Bk. i, ch. 16.

5
On him does death weigh heavily, who, known to others all too well, dies to himself unknown. (Illi mors gravis incubat Qui, notus nimis omnibus, Ignotus moritur sibi.)

SENECA, *Thyestes*, l. 401.

He knoweth the universe, and himself he knoweth not. (Il connaît l'univers, et ne se connaît pas.)

LA FONTAINE, *Fables*. Bk. viii, fab. 26.

Every one is least known to himself, and it is very difficult for a man to know himself (Minime sibi quisque notus est, et difficillime de se quisque sentit.)

CICERO, *De Oratore*. Bk. iii, sec. 9.

I know all save myself alone.

FRANÇOIS VILLON, *Autre Ballade: Refrain*

He dies known by all, and yet unknown to himself. (Il muert connu de tous et ne se connaît pas.)

UNKNOWN, *Addition à la Vie de Vauquelain des Yvetaux*, p. 12.

6
Go to your bosom;
Knock there, and ask your heart what it doth know
That's like my brother's fault.

SHAKESPEARE, *Measure for Measure*. Act ii, sc. 2, l. 136.

7
Not on the outer world
For inward joy depend;
Enjoy the luxury of thought,
Make thine own self friend;
Not with the restless throng,
In search of solace roam,
But with an independent zeal
Be intimate at home.

LYDIA HUNTLY SIGOURNEY, *Know Thyself*.

8
Great God, I ask thee for no meaner pelf
Than that I may not disappoint myself.

H. D. THOREAU, *My Prayer*.

9
We can secure the people's approval, if we do right and try hard; but our own is worth a hundred of it, and no way has been found out of securing that.

MARK TWAIN, *Pudd'nhead Wilson's New Calendar*.

10
The kingdom of heaven is within you: and whosoever knoweth himself shall find it.

UNKNOWN, *New Sayings of Jesus*. (Greek papyrus discovered in 1903.)

II—Self-Knowledge: Know Thyself

11
Make it thy business to know thyself, which is the most difficult lesson in the world.

CERVANTES, *Don Quixote*. Pt. ii, ch. 42.

The knowledge of thyself will preserve thee from vanity.

CERVANTES, *Don Quixote*. Pt. ii, ch. 43.

12
Full wise is he that can himselven know.

CHAUCER, *The Monkes Tale*, l. 1449.

Men who know themselves are no longer fools; they stand on the threshold of the Door of Wisdom.

HAVELOCK ELLIS, *Impressions and Comments*. Ser. iii, p. 66.

13
Do your deed, and know yourself. (Fay ton faict, et te cognoy.)

MONTAIGNE, *Essays*. Bk. i, ch. 3.

1
Know thyself. (Γνῶθι σαυτόν.)

THALES. (DIOGENES LAERTIUS, *Thales*. Sec. 40.) Diogenes Laertius asserts that this belongs to Thales, one of the seven wise men of Greece, although Antisthenes, in his *Successions of Philosophers,* attributes it to Phemonoë, and others to Chilon and to Solon. It was the first of the three maxims inscribed on the Temple of Apollo at Delphi. The others were "Nothing too much" (Μηδὲν ἄγαν), and "Give surety, and trouble is at hand" (Ἐγγύα, πάρα δ' ἄτη).

I commend my "know thyself," which is still preserved on a column at Delphi. (Commendo nostrum γνῶθι σεαυτόν, nosce te, Quod in columna jam tenetur Delphica.)

CHILON. (AUSONIUS, *Ludus Septem Sapientum,* l. 138.)

That irksome toil produces most excellent fruit—to distinguish what you can endure and what you cannot; by night and day to examine what you are doing, what you have done, down to the smallest atom. All virtues—self-respect, honor, fortitude—lie in this.

AUSONIUS, *Ludus Septem Sapientum,* l. 140.

The ancients gave us the injunction, "Know thyself." (Διὰ τοῦτο παρήγγελλον οἱ παλαιοὶ τὸ Γνῶθι σαυτόν.)

EPICTETUS, *Discourses*. Bk. i, ch. 18, sec. 18.

2
Know thyself. (Nosce te.)

CICERO, *Tusculanarum Disputationum*. Bk. i, ch. 22, sec. 52. The commonly used form of the proverb. The full quotation is: Cum igitur: *Nosce te,* dicit, hoc dicit: *Nosce animum tuum,* "When then Apollo says, 'Know thyself,' he says, 'Know thy soul.'" (BURTON, *Anatomy of Melancholy,* ii, 3, 8.)

From heaven descended the precept, "Know thyself." (E cælo descendit γνῶθι σεαυτόν.)

JUVENAL, *Satires*. No. xi, l. 27. It should be noted that σαυτόν is a contraction of σεαυτόν, and that sometimes one is used and sometimes the other. Originally the word was separated, as in Homer, who always writes, σ' αὐτόν.

3
The saying, "Know thyself," is silly. It were more practical to say, "Know other folks." (Γνῶθι τοὺς ἄλλους.)

MENANDER, *Thrasyleon: Fragment.*

If the "Know thyself" (Γνῶθι σαυτὸν) of the oracle were an easy thing for every man, it would not be held to be a divine injunction.

PLUTARCH, *Lives: Demosthenes*. Ch. 3. sec. 2.

Γνῶθι σεαυτὸν!—and is this the prime
And heaven-sprung adage of the olden time! . . .
Vain sister of the worm,—life, death, soul, clod—
Ignore thyself, and strive to know thy God!

S. T. COLERIDGE, *Self-Knowledge.*

Well said the wisdom of earth, O mortal, know thyself;
But better the wisdom of heaven, O man, learn thou thy God.

M. F. TUPPER, *Of Self-Acquaintance.*

SELF-LOVE

See also Selfishness, Vanity

4
It is the nature of extreme self-lovers, as they will set an house on fire, and it were but to roast their eggs.

BACON, *Essays: Of Wisdom for a Man's Self.*

5
There 's lang-tochered Nancy maist fetters his fancy,—
But the laddie's dear sel' he lo'es dearest of a'.

BURNS, *There 's a Youth in This City.*

6
The "Golden calf of self-love."

CARLYLE, *Essays: Burns.*

7
Every living creature loves itself. (Omne animal se ipsum diligere.)

CICERO, *De Finibus*. Bk. v, ch. 10. sec. 27.

All men love themselves. (Sese omnes amant.)

PLAUTUS, *Captivi*. Act iii, sc. 1.

8
A lover of himself, without any rival. (Se ipse amans sine rivali.)

CICERO, *Epistolæ ad Quintum Fratrem,* iii, 8.

Love yourself and your own affairs without any rival. (Sine rivali te et tua solus amares.)

HORACE, *Ars Poetica,* l. 444.

He that falls in love with himself, will have no rivals.

BENJAMIN FRANKLIN, *Poor Richard,* 1739.

9
Self-love is a principle of action; but among no class of human beings has nature so profusely distributed this principle of life and action as through the whole sensitive family of genius.

ISAAC D'ISRAELI, *Literary Character of Men of Genius*. Ch. 15.

10
Self-love is often rather arrogant than blind; it does not hide our faults from ourselves, but persuades us that they escape the notice of others.

SAMUEL JOHNSON, *The Rambler*. No. 155.

Self-love is a busy prompter.

SAMUEL JOHNSON, *Works*. Vol. vii, p. 323.

11
Self-love is the greatest of all flatterers. (L'amour-propre est le plus grand de tous les flatteurs.)

LA ROCHEFOUCAULD, *Maximes*. No. 2.

Behold the fine appointment he makes with me! That man never did love anyone but himself! (Voyez le beau rendezvous qu'il me donne! Cet homme là n'a jamais aimé que lui-même.)

MADAME DE MAINTENON, when Louis XIV, in dying, said, Nous nous renverrons bientôt. "We shall meet again soon."

12
View yourselves
In the deceiving mirror of self-love.

MASSINGER, *Parliament of Love*. Act i, sc. 5.

1
Through very love of self himself he slew.
GEORGE MEREDITH, *The Egoist: Prelude.*

2
Oft times nothing profits more
Than self-esteem, grounded on just and right.
MILTON, *Paradise Lost*. Bk. viii, l. 571.

3
Two principles in Human Nature reign,
Self-love to urge, and Reason to restrain; . . .
Self-love, the spring of motion, acts the soul;
Reason's comparing balance rules the whole. . . .
Most strength the moving principle requires;
Active its task, it prompts, impels, inspires:
Sedate and quiet the comparing lies,
Form'd but to check, delib'rate, and advise.
Self-love still stronger, as its objects nigh;
Reason's at distance, and in prospect lie.
POPE, *Essay on Man*. Epis. ii, l. 59.

Self-love but serves the virtuous mind to wake,
As the small pebble stirs the peaceful lake;
The centre mov'd, a circle straight succeeds,
Another still, and still another spreads;
Friends, parent, neighbour, first it will embrace;
His country next; and next all human race.
POPE, *Essay on Man*. Epis. iv, l. 363.

Reason, Passion, answer one great aim;
True Self-love and Social are the same.
POPE, *Essay on Man*. Epis. iv, l. 396.

4
Be always displeased at what thou art, if thou desire to attain to what thou art not; for where thou hast pleased thyself, there thou abidest.
FRANCIS QUARLES, *Emblems*. Bk. iv, No. 3.

5
Self-love is a mote in every man's eye.
JOHN RAY, *English Proverbs*, p. 130. (1678) FULLER, *Gnomologia*. No. 4093. (1732) A variant is, "Self-love makes the eyes blind."

6
Self-love makes more libertines than love. (L'amour-propre fait plus de libertins que l'amour.)
ROUSSEAU, *Émile*. Bk. iv.

7
Self-love, which is the most inhibited sin in the canon.
SHAKESPEARE, *All's Well that Ends Well*, i, 1, 158.

Self-love, my liege, is not so vile a sin
As self-neglecting.
SHAKESPEARE, *Henry V*. Act ii, sc. 4, l. 74.

She cannot love,
Nor take no shape nor project of affection,
She is so self-endeared.
SHAKESPEARE, *Much Ado About Nothing*, ii, 1, 54.

8
I have looked upon the world for four times seven years; and since I could distinguish betwixt a benefit and an injury, I never found man that knew how to love himself.
SHAKESPEARE, *Othello*. Act i, sc. 3, l. 312.

9
Self-love and love of the world constitute hell.
SWEDENBORG, *Apocalypse Explained*. Par. 1144.

10
I am myself my own nearest of kin; I am dearest to myself. (Proximus sum egomet mihi.)
TERENCE, *Andria*, l. 635. (Act iv, sc. 1.)

I to myself am dearer than a friend.
SHAKESPEARE, *Two Gentlemen of Verona*, ii, 6, 23.

Sin of self-love possesseth all mine eye
And all my soul and all my every part.
SHAKESPEARE, *Sonnets*. No. lxii.

11
Every man is sorry for himself. (Nostri nosmet pænitet.)
TERENCE, *Phormio*, l. 172. (Act i, sc. 3.)

12
Offended self-love never forgives. (L'amour-propre offensé ne pardonne jamais.)
JEAN DE VIZÉ, *Les Aveux Difficiles*. Act vii.

13
Self-love never dies. (L'amour-propre ne meurt jamais.)
VOLTAIRE, *Stances ou Quatrains*. After Pibrac.

Self-love is the instrument of our preservation; it resembles the provision for the perpetuity of mankind:—it is necessary, it is dear to us, it gives us pleasure, and we must conceal it.
VOLTAIRE, *Philosophical Dictionary: Self-Love.*

14
Would you hurt a man keenest, strike at his self-love.
LEW WALLACE, *Ben Hur*. Bk. vi, ch. 2.

15
To love oneself is the beginning of a life-long romance.
OSCAR WILDE, *An Ideal Husband*. Act iii.

16
Rule No. Six: Don't take yourself so damn seriously.
UNKNOWN. Originated in the Allied Maritime Transport Council in 1917, according to Mr. Dwight Morrow. (See Raleigh, N. C., *News and Observer*, 25 May, 1933.)

SELF-PRAISE, see Praise

SELF-PRESERVATION

17
Self-preservation is the first law of nature.
SAMUEL BUTLER, *Remains*, ii, 27. (c. 1675); SMOLLETT, *Peregrine Pickle*. Ch. 57. (1751)

18
Nature has endowed every species of living creature with the instinct of self-preservation. (Generi animantium omni est a natura tributum.)
CICERO, *De Officiis*. Bk. i, ch. 4, sec. 11.

19
An animal's first impulse is self-preservation. (Τὴν δὲ πρώτην ὁρμήν φασι τὸ ζῷον ἴσχειν ἐπὶ τὸ τηρεῖν ἑαυτό.)
DIOGENES LAERTIUS, *Zeno*. Bk. vii, sec. 85. Explaining a Stoic doctrine.

1
Self preservation is of natural law.
JOHN DONNE, *Biathanatos*. Sig. AA (c. 1610)

Self-preservation is the first of laws.
DRYDEN, *Spanish Friar*. Act iv, sc. 2. (1681)

Self-preservation, nature's first great law.
ANDREW MARVELL, *Hodge's Vision*. (1675)

Self-preservation should exert itself, 'tis then indeed the first principle of nature.
CHARLES SHADWELL, *Irish Hospitality*. Act v, sc. 1. (1720)

1a
The good but pine; the order of the day
Is—prey on others, or become a prey.
HOWARD FISH, *The Wrongs of Man* (1819)

SELF-RESPECT

See also Pride

2
The reverence of a man's self is, next religion, the chiefest bridle of all vices.
FRANCIS BACON, *New Atlantis*.

Self-respect—that corner-stone of all virtue.
SIR JOHN HERSCHEL, *Address*, 20 Jan., 1833.

3
I desire so to conduct the affairs of this administration that if at the end, when I come to lay down the reins of power, I have lost every other friend on earth, I shall at least have one friend left, and that friend shall be down inside of me.
ABRAHAM LINCOLN, *Reply to Missouri Committee of Seventy*, 1864.

4
He that respects himself is safe from others,
He wears a coat of mail that none can pierce.
LONGFELLOW, *Michael Angelo*. Pt. ii, sec. 3.

5
Never esteem anything as of advantage to thee that shall make thee break thy word or lose thy self-respect (*Μή τιμήσῃς ποτὲ ὡς συμφέρον σεαυτοῦ, ὃ ἀναγκάσει σε ποτὲ τὴν πίστιν παραβῆναι, τὴν αἰδῶ ἐγκαταλιπεῖν*)
MARCUS AURELIUS, *Meditations* Bk iii; sec. 7

6
It is necessary to the happiness of man that he be mentally faithful to himself.
THOMAS PAINE, *The Age of Reason* Ch i.

7
Respect gods before demi-gods, heroes before men, and first among men your parents; but respect yourself most of all.
PYTHAGORAS, *Golden Maxims*. (DIOGENES LAERTIUS, *Pythagoras*. Bk. viii, sec. 23.)

8
Self-respect is the noblest garment with which a man may clothe himself, the most elevating feeling with which the mind can be inspired.
SAMUEL SMILES, *Self Help*. Ch. 10.

9
Revere thyself, and yet thyself despise.
YOUNG, *Night Thoughts*. Night vi, l. 128.

SELF-SACRIFICE

10
Inwardness, mildness, and self-renouncement do make for man's happiness
MATTHEW ARNOLD, *Literature and Dogma*. Ch 3.

11
He never errs who sacrifices self.
BULWER-LYTTON, *The New Timon*. Pt. iv, sec. 3.

Self sacrifice which denies common sense is not a virtue. It's a spiritual dissipation.
MARGARET DELAND.

12
Self-sacrifice is the real miracle out of which all the reported miracles grew.
EMERSON, *Society and Solitude: Courage*.

13
Sacrifice is the first element of religion, and resolves itself in theological language into the love of God
J A FROUDE, *Short Studies: Sea Studies*.

In common things, the law of sacrifice takes the form of positive duty
J. A. FROUDE, *Short Studies: Sea Studies*.

As soon as sacrifice becomes a duty and necessity to the man, I see no limit to the horizon which opens before me
ERNEST RENAN.

15
Was anything real ever gained without sacrifice of some kind?
ARTHUR HELPS, *Friends in Council*. Bk. ii, 1.

16
Present your bodies a living sacrifice, holy, acceptable unto God.
New Testament: Romans, xii, 1.

17
Harsh towards herself, towards others full of
ruth
CHRISTINA ROSSETTI, *A Portrait*.

18
Upon such sacrifices, my Cordelia,
The gods themselves throw incense.
SHAKESPEARE, *King Lear*. Act v, sc. 3, l. 20.

19
Self-sacrifice enables us to sacrifice other people without blushing.
BERNARD SHAW, *Maxims for Revolutionists*.

20
A flower when offered in the bud
Is no vain sacrifice.
ISAAC WATTS, *Early Religion*.

21
The awful beauty of self-sacrifice.
WHITTIER, *Amy Wentworth*, l. 16.

22
Give unto me, made lowly wise,
The spirit of self-sacrifice.
WORDSWORTH, *Ode to Duty* St. 8.

High sacrifice, and labour without pause
Even to the death:—else wherefore should the eye
Of man converse with immortality?
WORDSWORTH, *Poems Dedicated to National Independence*. Pt. ii, No. 14.

SELFISHNESS

See also Self-Love

I—Selfishness: Apothegms

1
Man seeks his own good at the whole world's cost.
ROBERT BROWNING, *Luria*. Act i.

2
At the king's court, my brother,
Each man for himself, there is none other.
CHAUCER, *The Knightes Tale*, l. 323. (c. 1386)

Where every man is for himself,
And no man for all.
ROBERT CROWLEY, *Works*, p. 11. (1550)

Every one for his home, every one for himself. (Chacun chez soi, chacun pour soi.)
ANDRÉ DUPIN, *Procès de Tendance*.

Every man for himself and God for us all.
JOHN HEYWOOD, *Proverbs*. Pt. ii, ch. 9. (1546)

Every man for himself, his own ends, the devil for all.
BURTON, *Anatomy of Melancholy*. Pt. iii, sec. 1.

3
By whatever name we call
The ruling tyrant, Self is all in all.
CHARLES CHURCHILL, *The Conference*, l. 177.

4
The least pain in our little finger gives us more concern and uneasiness, than the destruction of millions of our fellow-beings.
WILLIAM HAZLITT, *Works*. Vol. x, p. 324.

5
In high places regard for others is rarely to be found. (Rarus enim ferme sensus communis in illa Fortuna.)
JUVENAL, *Satires*. Sat. viii, l. 73.

6
Not a deed would he do, nor a word would he utter,
Till he'd weighed its relations to plain bread and butter.
J. R. LOWELL, *A Fable for Critics*, l. 186.

But somehow, when the dogs hed gut asleep,
Their love o' mutton beat their love o' sheep.
J. R. LOWELL, *Biglow Papers*. Ser. ii, No. 11.

7
We always took care of number one.
FREDERICK MARRYAT, *Frank Mildmay*. Ch. 19.

8
There are two levers for moving men—interest and fear.
NAPOLEON BONAPARTE, *Sayings of Napoleon*.

John Adams . . . said . . . Reason, Justice and Equity never had weight enough on the face of the earth to govern the councils of men. It is interest alone which does it.
THOMAS JEFFERSON, *Writings*. Vol. i, p. 49.

For the world is ruled by interest alone. (Denn nur vom Nutzen wird die Welt regiert.)
SCHILLER, *Wallenstein's Tod*. Act i, sc. 6, l. 37.

9
Everyone was eloquent in behalf of his own cause. (Proque sua causa quisque disertus erat.)
OVID, *Fasti*. Bk. iv, l. 112.

10
As for the largest-hearted of us, what is the word we write most often in our cheque-books?—"Self."
EDEN PHILLPOTTS, *A Shadow Passes*.

11
Because I do not wish to perish alone, I desire you to perish with me. (Quia perire solus nolo, te cupio perire mecum.)
PLAUTUS, *Epidicus*, l. 77. (Act i, sc. 1.)

12
My tunic is nearer to me than my mantle. (Tunica propior pallio est.)
PLAUTUS, *Trinummus*. Act v, sc. 2, l. 30.

The shirt is nearer than the coat.
THOMAS FULLER, *Gnomologia*. No. 4745.

Close sits my shirt, but closer my skin.
JOHN RAY, *English Proverbs*.

Near is my petticoat, but nearer is my smock.
JOHN RAY, *English Proverbs*.

13
No one is second to himself. (Nemo sibi secundus.)
RABELAIS, *Letter*, 15 Feb., 1536. Quoted as a proverb.

14
Self do, self have.
JOHN RAY, *English Proverbs*.

15
What need we any spur but our own cause,
To prick us to redress.
SHAKESPEARE, *Julius Cæsar*. Act ii, sc. 1, l. 123.

16
Self the spring of all.
SOUTHEY, *The Poet's Pilgrimage to Waterloo*. Pt. ii, canto 1, st. 22.

17
Everyone sets his own good before his neighbor's. (Omnis sibi malle melius esse quam alteri.)
TERENCE, *Andria*, l. 427. (Act ii, sc. 5.) Quoted as a proverb.

II—Selfishness: Its Faults

18
Like a hog, or dog in the manger, he doth only keep it because it shall do nobody else good, hurting himself and others.
ROBERT BURTON, *Anatomy of Melancholy*. Pt. i, sec. 2, mem. 3, subs. 12.

19
You mayn't be changed to a bird though you live
As selfishly as you can;
But you will be changed to a smaller thing—
A mean and selfish man.
PHŒBE CARY, *A Legend of the Northland*.

20
Selfishness is the greatest curse of the human race.
W. E. GLADSTONE, *Speech*, Hawarden, 28 May, 1890.

1
Virtues lose themselves in self-interest, as streams lose themselves in the sea. (Les vertus se perdent dans l'intérêt, comme les fleuves se perdent dans la mer.)

LA ROCHEFOUCAULD, *Maximes*. No. 171.

2
He that lives not somewhat to others, liveth little to himself.

MONTAIGNE, *Essays*. Bk. iii, ch. 10.

No man is born unto himself alone;
Who lives unto himself, he lives to none.

FRANCIS QUARLES, *Esther*. Sec i, med. 1.

3
Self is the medium through which Judgment's ray
Can seldom pass without being turn'd astray.

THOMAS MOORE, *The Sceptic*, l. 41.

4
High though his titles, proud his name,
Boundless his wealth as wish can claim,—
Despite those titles, power, and pelf,
The wretch, concentred all in self,
Living, shall forfeit fair renown,
And, doubly dying, shall go down
To the vile dust from whence he sprung,
Unwept, unhonoured, and unsung.

SCOTT, *Lay of the Last Minstrel*. Canto vi, st. 1.

Then dropt into the grave, unpitied and unknown!

JAMES BEATTIE, *The Minstrel*. Bk. i, l. 9.

Without a grave, unknell'd, uncoffin'd, and unknown.

BYRON, *Childe Harold*. Canto iv, st. 179.

Unwept, unhonor'd, uninterr'd he lies!

HOMER, *Iliad*. Bk. xxii, l. 484. (Pope, tr.)

Unwept, unnoted, and for ever dead!

HOMER, *Odyssey*. Bk. v, l. 402. (Pope, tr.)

Unrespited, unpitied, unrepriev'd,
Ages of hopeless end.

MILTON, *Paradise Lost*. Bk. ii, l. 185.

Thy fate unpitied, and thy rites unpaid.

POPE, *Elegy to the Memory of an Unfortunate Lady*, l. 48.

Unwept, unshrouded, and unsepulchred.

ROBERT SOUTHEY, *A Tale of Paraguay*. Canto i, st. 11.

5
That which serves and seeks for gain,
And follows but for form,
Will pack when it begins to rain,
And leave thee in the storm.

SHAKESPEARE, *King Lear*. Act ii, sc. 4, l. 79.

6
Suicidal Selfishness, that blights
The fairest feelings of the opening heart.

SHELLEY, *Queen Mab*. Pt. v, l. 16.

Undisguising Selfishness, that sets
On each its price, the stamp-mark of her reign.
Even love is sold; the solace of all woe
Is turned to deadliest agony.

SHELLEY, *Queen Mab*. Pt. v, l. 187.

7
Himself unto himself he sold:
Upon himself himself did feed;
Quiet, dispassionate and cold.

TENNYSON, *A Character*, l. 26.

8
The selfish heart deserves the pains it feels.

YOUNG, *Night Thoughts*. Night i, l. 300.

Nothing in nature, much less conscious being,
Was e'er created solely for itself.

YOUNG, *Night Thoughts*. Night ix, l. 704.

III—Selfishness: Its Virtues

9
Keep all you have and try for all you can.

BULWER-LYTTON, *King Arthur*. Bk. ii, l. 70.

10
I have heard said, eke times twice twelve,
"He is a fool that will forget himselve."

CHAUCER, *Troilus and Criseyde*. Bk. v, l. 97.

All sensible people are selfish.

EMERSON, *Conduct of Life: Considerations by the Way*.

Where all are selfish, the sage is no better than the fool, and only rather more dangerous.

J. A. FROUDE, *Short Studies on Great Subjects: Party Politics*.

11
It is reasonable that everyone should measure himself by his own standard and measurement. (Metiri se quemque suo modulo ac pede verum est.)

HORACE, *Epistles*. Bk. i, epis. 7, l. 98.

12
Be, as so many are now, rich for yourself, poor for your friends. (Esto, ut nunc multi, dives tibi, pauper amicis.)

JUVENAL, *Satires*. Sat. v, l. 113.

The same people who can deny others everything are famous for refusing themselves nothing.

LEIGH HUNT, *Table Talk: Catherine II*. Note.

Or monarch's hands that let not bounty fall
Where want cries some, but where excess begs all.

SHAKESPEARE, *A Lover's Complaint*, l. 41.

13
Selfishness, Love's cousin.

KEATS, *Isabella*. St. 31.

Twin-sister of Religion, Selfishness!

SHELLEY, *Queen Mab*. Pt. v, l. 22.

14
I have yet to find a man worth his salt in any direction who did not think of himself first and foremost. . . . The man who thinks of others before he thinks of himself may become a Grand Master of the Elks, a Socialist of parts, or the star guest of honor at public banquets, but he will never become a great or successful artist, statesman, or even clergyman.

G. J. NATHAN, *Testament of a Critic*, p. 6.

15
This is the plain truth: every one ought to keep a sharp eye for the main chance. (Vera dico: ad suom quemque hominem quæstum esse æquomst callidum.)

PLAUTUS, *Asinaria*, l. 186. (Act i, sc. 3.) *See also under* CHANCE.

1
The primary and sole foundation of virtue or of the proper conduct of life is to seek our own profit.
SPINOZA, *Ethics*. Pt. iv, prop. 20 (1674)

2
Selfishness is calm, a force of nature: you might say the trees were selfish.
R. L. STEVENSON, *Ethical Studies*, p. 83.

SENSE, SENSES

I—Sense: Good Sense

See also Sound and Sense

3
Common sense (which, in truth, is very uncommon) is the best sense I know of.
LORD CHESTERFIELD, *Letters*, 27 Sept., 1748.

4
Who would die a martyr to sense in a country where the religion is folly?
CONGREVE, *Love for Love*. Act i, sc. 2.

5
Through Sense and Non-sense, never out nor in.
DRYDEN, *Absalom and Achitophel*. Pt. ii, l. 415.

Preferring sense, from chin that's bare,
To nonsense throned in whiskered hair.
MATTHEW GREEN, *The Spleen*, l. 760.

6
Common Sense, which, one would say, means the shortest line between two points.
EMERSON, *Journals*, March, 1866.

7
Be sober, and to doubt prepense,
These are the sinews of good sense.
SIR WILLIAM HAMILTON, *Notes on Reid*. (EPICHARMUS, *Fragments*. No. 255.)

8
Where Sense is wanting, everything is wanting.
LORD HALIFAX, *Works*, p. 248.

9
Between good sense and good taste there is the difference between cause and effect. (Entre le bon sens et le bon goût il y a la différence de la cause à son effet.)
LA BRUYÈRE, *Les Caractères*. Pt. 12.

If poverty is the mother of crimes, want of sense is the father.
LA BRUYÈRE, *Les Caractères*. Pt. 2.

10
Sword of Common Sense! Our surest gift.
GEORGE MEREDITH, *To the Comic Spirit*, l. 1.

11
A bit of sound sense is what makes men; the rest is all rubbish. (Corcillum est quod homines, facit, cetera quisquilia omnia.)
PETRONIUS, *Satyricon*. Sec. 75.

12
Good Sense, which only is the gift of Heav'n,
And tho' no science, fairly worth the sev'n.
POPE, *Moral Essays*. Epis. iv, l. 43.

And splendour borrows all her rays from sense.
POPE, *Moral Essays*. Epis. iv, l. 180.

Fool! 'tis in vain from wit to wit to roam:
Know, Sense, like Charity, "begins at home."
POPE, *Umbra*, l. 15.

13
God send you mair sense and me mair siller.
JOHN RAY, *Proverbs: Scottish*.

14
At Christmas I no more desire a rose
Than wish a snow in May's new-fangled mirth;
But like of each thing that in season grows.
SHAKESPEARE, *Love's Labour's Lost*. Act i, sc. 1, l. 105.

15
Common sense is not so common. (Le sens commun n'est pas si commun.)
VOLTAIRE, *Philosophical Dictionary: Self-Love*.

16
Plain sense but rarely leads us far astray.
YOUNG, *Night Thoughts*. Night vi, l. 278.

Sense is our helmet, wit is but the plume;
The plume exposes, 'tis our helmet saves.
Sense is the diamond, weighty, solid, sound;
When cut by wit, it casts a brighter beam;
Yet, wit apart, it is a diamond still.
YOUNG, *Night Thoughts*. Night viii, l. 1259.

II—Senses, The

See also Ear, Eye, etc.

17
Huzzaed out of my seven senses.
ADDISON, *The Spectator*. No. 616.

I am almost frightened out of my seven senses.
CERVANTES, *Don Quixote*. Pt. i, ch. 9.

18
They received the use of the five operations of the Lord and in the sixth place he imparted them understanding, and in the seventh speech, an interpreter of the cogitations thereof.
Apocrypha: Ecclesiasticus, xvii, 5.

19
Moral qualities rule the world, but at short distances the senses are despotic.
EMERSON, *Essays, Second Series: Manners*.

20
Whate'er in her Horizon doth appear,
She is one Orb of Sense, all Eye, all aery Ear.
HENRY MORE, *Antidote Against Atheism*.

21
All spread their charms, but charm not all alike;
On diff'rent senses diff'rent objects strike.
POPE, *Essay on Man*. Epis. ii, l. 127.

22
What thin partitions Sense from Thought divide!
POPE, *Essay on Man*. Epis. i, l. 226. (1733)

Thin partitions do divide
The bounds where good and ill reside;
That nought is perfect here below,
But *bliss* still bordering upon woe.
UNKNOWN. Published in the *Weekly Magazine*, Edinburgh, vol. xxii, p. 50 (1770), and attributed to Robert Burns.

The frontiers between sense and spirit are the devil's hunting-grounds.

COVENTRY PATMORE, *Memoirs*. Vol. ii, p. 70.

1
The wanton stings and motions of the sense.

SHAKESPEARE, *Measure for Measure*. Act i, sc. 4, l. 59.

2
Those obstinate questionings
Of sense and outward things,
Fallings from us, vanishings;
Blank misgivings of a Creature
Moving about in worlds not realized.

WORDSWORTH, *Intimations of Immortality*, l. 145.

3
A languid, leaden iteration reigns,
And ever must, o'er those, whose joys are joys
Of sight, smell, taste.

YOUNG, *Night Thoughts*. Night iii, l. 373.

SENTIMENT, see Feeling

SENTIMENTALISM

4
The barrenest of all mortals is the sentimentalist.

CARLYLE, *Characteristics*.

Is not Sentimentalism twin-sister to Cant, if not one and the same with it?

CARLYLE, *French Revolution*. Pt. i, bk. 2, ch. 7.

5
Society is infested by persons who, seeing that the sentiments please, counterfeit the expression of them. These we call sentimentalists,—talkers who mistake the description for the thing, saying for having.

EMERSON, *Letters and Social Aims: Social Aims*.

6
Sentimentalists are they who seek to enjoy without incurring the Immense Debtorship for a thing done.

GEORGE MEREDITH, *Richard Feverel*. Ch. 24.

The sentimental people fiddle harmonics on the string of sensualism.

GEORGE MEREDITH, *Diana of the Crossways*. Ch. 1. The word "sentimental" is said to have been used for the first time in a letter written in 1740 by Laurence Sterne.

7
Sentimentality is the error of supposing that quarter can be given or taken in moral conflicts.

BERNARD SHAW, *Maxims for Revolutionists*.

8
I sit with my toes in a brook,
And if any one axes forwhy?
I hits them a rap with my crook,
For 'tis sentiment does it, says I.

HORACE WALPOLE, *Epigram*. (CUNNINGHAM, *Life of Walpole*.)

SEPARATION

See also Absence, Parting

9
A God, a God their severance rul'd;
And bade betwixt their shores to be
The unplumb'd, salt, estranging sea.

MATTHEW ARNOLD, *To Marguerite. See also under* SOLITUDE.

They stood aloof, the scars remaining,
Like cliffs which had been rent asunder;
A dreary sea now flows between.

S. T. COLERIDGE, *Christabel*. Pt. ii, l. 421.

Atom from atom yawns as far
As moon from earth, or star from star.

R. W. EMERSON, *Nature*.

10
Dear heart! take it sadly home to thee,—there is no co-operation . . . The dearest friends are separated by impassable gulfs.

EMERSON, *Essays: Society and Solitude*.

11
They grew in beauty side by side,
They filled one home with glee:
Their graves are severed far and wide
By mount and stream and sea.

FELICIA HEMANS, *The Graves of a Household*.

12
You to the left and I to the right,
For the ways of men must sever—
And it may be for a day and a night,
And it well may be forever.
But whether we meet or whether we part,
(For our ways are past our knowing)
A pledge from the heart to its fellow heart,
On the ways we all are going!
Here's luck!
For we know not where we are going.

RICHARD HOVEY, *At the Crossroads*.

13
One only hope my heart can cheer,—
The hope to meet again.

GEORGE LINLEY, *Song*.

14
Who shall separate us from the love of Christ?

New Testament: Romans, viii, 35.

Who shall separate? (Quis separabit?)

Motto of Order of St. Patrick.

15
Life and these lips have long been separated.

SHAKESPEARE, *Romeo and Juliet*. Act iv, sc. 5, l. 27.

16
I'm sitting on the stile, Mary,
Where we sat side by side.

HELEN SELINA SHERIDAN, *Lament of the Irish Emigrant*.

SERENITY

See also Quiet

17
Smiling always with a never fading serenity of countenance, and flourishing in an immortal youth.

ISAAC BARROW, *Duty of Thanksgiving*.

18
Live on! No touch of time shall cause
One wrinkle on thy smooth, unruffled brow!

ROBERT BUCHANAN, *Balder the Beautiful*. Pt. iii, 2.

1
Serene I fold my hands and wait,
Nor care for wind or tide nor sea;
I rave no more 'gainst time or fate,
For lo! my own shall come to me.
JOHN BURROUGHS, *Waiting*.

2
After a storm comes a calm.
MATTHEW HENRY, *Commentaries: Acts*, ix.

There is no joy but calm.
TENNYSON, *The Lotos Eaters: Choric Song*.

If after every tempest come such calms,
May the winds blow till they have waken'd death!
SHAKESPEARE, *Othello*. Act ii, sc. 1, l. 187.

3
Calmness is great advantage: he that lets
Another chafe, may warm him at his fire.
GEORGE HERBERT, *The Church-Porch*. St. 53.

Keep cool: it will be all one a hundred years hence.
EMERSON, *Representative Men: Montaigne*.
See also ANGER: ITS CONTROL.

4
Remember to preserve an even mind in adverse circumstances, and likewise in prosperity a mind free from over-weening joy. (Æquam memento rebus in arduis
Servare mentem, non secus in bonis
Ab insolenti temperatam
Lætitia.)
HORACE, *Odes*. Bk. ii, ode 3, l. 1. *See also* PROSPERITY AND ADVERSITY.

5
The serenity of the wise is merely the art of imprisoning their agitation in the heart. (La constance des sages n'est que l'art de renfermer leur agitation dans le cœur.)
LA ROCHEFOUCAULD, *Maximes*. No. 20.

6
The star of the unconquered will,
He rises in my breast,
Serene, and resolute, and still,
And calm, and self possessed.
LONGFELLOW, *The Light of Stars*. St. 7.

7
There is in stillness oft a magic power
To calm the breast when struggling passions lower;
Touched by its influence, in the soul arise
Diviner feelings, kindred with the skies.
JOHN HENRY NEWMAN, *Solitude*.

Serene yet strong, majestic yet sedate,
Swift without violence, without terror great.
MATTHEW PRIOR, *Carmen Seculare*, l. 282.

8
If human things went ill or well;
If changing empires rose or fell;
The morning passed, the evening came,
And found this couple still the same.
MATTHEW PRIOR, *An Epitaph*.

9
It is the nature of a great mind to be calm and undisturbed. (Magni animi est proprium, placidum esse tranquillumque.)
SENECA, *De Clementia*. Bk. i, sec. 5.

10
Serene amidst the savage waves. (Sævis tranquillus in undis.)
WILLIAM OF ORANGE, *Motto*.

11
Serene will be our days and bright,
And happy will our nature be,
When love is an unerring light,
And joy its own security.
WILLIAM WORDSWORTH, *Ode to Duty*, l. 17.

SERPENT

I—Serpent: Definitions and Apothegms

12
Think'st thou there are no serpents in the world
But those that slide along the grassy sod,
And sting the luckless foot that presses them?
There are who in the path of social life
Do bask their spotted skins in Fortune's sun,
And sting the soul.
JOANNA BAILLIE, *De Montfort*. Act i, sc. 2.

Vipers, that creep where man disdains to climb,
And, having wound their loathsome track to the top
Of this huge, mouldering monument of Rome,
Hang hissing at the nobler man below.
GEORGE CROLY, *Catiline's Reply to the Charges of Cicero*.

13
Man spurns the worm, but pauses ere he wake
The slumbering venom of the folded snake:
The first may turn—but not avenge the blow;
The last expires—but leaves no living foe.
BYRON, *The Corsair*. Canto i, st. 11.

14
Now the serpent was more subtle than any beast of the field.
Old Testament: Genesis, iii, 1.

Some flow'rets of Eden ye still inherit,
But the trail of the Serpent is over them all!
THOMAS MOORE, *Lalla Rookh: Paradise and the Peri*, l. 206.

15
Johnson said that he could repeat a complete chapter of "The Natural History of Iceland" from the Danish of Horrebow, the whole of which was exactly thus: "There are no snakes to be met with throughout the whole island."
BOSWELL, *Life of Samuel Johnson*, 1778. This is Chapter 72. But Chapter 42 is still shorter: "There are no owls of any kind in the whole island."

17
Put a snake in your bosom, and it will sting when it is warm.
JOHN KELLY, *Scottish Proverbs*, 61 (1721)

Every desire is a viper in the bosom, who, when he was chill, was harmless, but when warmth gave him strength, exerted it in poison.
SAMUEL JOHNSON. (BOSWELL, *Life*, 8 Dec., 1763.)

There was a snake that dwelt in Skye,
Over the misty sea, oh;
He lived upon nothing but gooseberry-pie,
For breakfast, dinner, and tea, oh!

HENRY JOHNSTONE, *The Fastidious Serpent.*

1 When you see a snake, never mind where he came from.

W. G. BENHAM, *Proverbs*, p. 872.

2 Where's my serpent of old Nile?

SHAKESPEARE, *Antony and Cleopatra*, i, 5, 25.

Your serpent of Egypt is bred now of your mud by the operation of your sun: so is your crocodile.

SHAKESPEARE, *Antony and Cleopatra*, ii, 7, 29.

Hast thou the pretty worm of Nilus there,
That kills and pains not?

SHAKESPEARE, *Antony and Cleopatra*, v, 2, 243.

3 It is the bright day that brings forth the adder;
And that craves wary walking.

SHAKESPEARE, *Julius Cæsar*. Act ii, sc. 1, l. 14.

4 We have scotch'd the snake, not kill'd it:
She'll close and be herself, whilst our poor malice
Remains in danger of her former tooth.

SHAKESPEARE, *Macbeth*. Act iii, sc. 2, l. 13.

What, wouldst thou have a serpent sting thee twice?

SHAKESPEARE. *The Merchant of Venice*, iv, 1, 69.

5 There the snake throws her enamell'd skin.

SHAKESPEARE, *A Midsummer-Night's Dream*. Act ii, sc. 1, l. 255.

6 Who sees the lurking serpent steps aside.

SHAKESPEARE, *The Rape of Lucrece*, l. 361.

7 Away from here, lads; a chill snake lurks in the grass. (Frigidus, o pueri, fugite hinc, latet anguis in herba.)

VERGIL, *Eclogues*. No. ii, l. 93.

Beware from her that in thy bosom sleepeth;
Ware fro the serpent that so slyly creepeth
Under the grass, and stingeth subtilly.

CHAUCER, *The Somnours Tale*, l. 1993. (c. 1386)

There's a snake in the grass. (Anguis sub viridi herba.)

FRANCIS BACON, *Essays: Of a King*.

But the serpent lurked under the grass, and under sugared speech was hid pestiferous poison.

EDWARD HALL, *Chronicles*, 236. (1548)

Take heed of the snake in the grass, or the padd in the straw.

GABRIEL HARVEY, *Works*. Vol. ii, p. 294. (1593)

There is a snake in the bush.

ANDREW YARRONTON, *England's Improvement*, p. 101.

Serpents lie where flowers grow.

UNKNOWN, *The Spanish Lady's Love*.

8 If the snake could hear and the slow-worm could see,
Neither man nor beast should e'er go free.

UNKNOWN, *Old Rhyme*. (*N. and Q.*, ii, i, 401.)

If I could hear as well as see,
No man in life could master me.

UNKNOWN. (PARISH, *Sussex Dictionary*, 14.) It is a country superstition that the marks on the adder's belly form these words.

II—Serpent: The Viper and the Cappadocian

9 An evil viper once bit a Cappadocian, but it died itself, having tasted the venomous blood. (Καππαδόκην ποτ' ἔχιδνα κακὴ δάκεν· ἀλλὰ καὶ αὐτὴ κάτθανε, γευσαμένη αἵματος ἰοβόλου.)

DEMODOCUS OF LEROS. (*Greek Anthology*. Bk. xi, epig. 237.) The Latin form is: "Vipera Cappadocem nocitura momordit; at illa gustato periit sanguine Cappadocis."

Yesterday near Charenton, a snake bit Jean Fréron. What do you think happened? It was the serpent that died.
(Hier auprès de Charenton,
Un serpent mordit Jean Fréron.
Que croyez-vous qu'il arriva?
Ce fut le serpent qui creva.)

VOLTAIRE, *Imitation of Demodocus*. (*Œuvres Complètes*, iii, 1002.) Attributed also to Piron. There are various other French versions of this epigram. (*See Notes and Queries*, 30 March, 1907.)

10 While Fell was reposing himself in the hay,
A reptile concealed bit his leg as he lay;
But, all venom himself, of the wound he made light,
And got well, while the scorpion died of the bite.

LESSING, *Paraphrase of Demodocus*.

The dog, to gain his private ends,
Went mad, and bit the man. . . .
The man recovered of the bite,
The dog it was that died.

GOLDSMITH, *Elegy on the Death of a Mad Dog*.

11 A serpent, which is touched with human saliva, perishes, and even commits suicide by biting itself.

LUCRETIUS, *De Rerum Natura*. Bk. iv, l. 640.

All men carry about them that which is poison to serpents: for if it be true that is reported, they will no better abide the touching with man's spittle than scalding water cast upon them: but if it happen to light within their chawes or mouth, especially if it come from a man that is fasting, it is present death.

PLINY, *Historia Naturalis*. Bk. vii, ch. 2. (Holland, tr.)

SERVANT

I—Servant: Apothegms

12 His lordship may compel us to be equal upstairs but there will never be equality in the servants' hall.

J. M. BARRIE, *The Admirable Crichton*. Act i.

1
Maidservants, I hear people complaining, are getting instructed in the "ologies."
CARLYLE, *Inaugural Address at Edinburgh.*

2
Do not rashly give credence to a wife complaining of servants. (Nil temere uxori de servis crede querenti.)
DIONYSIUS CATO (?), *Disticha de Moribus.* Bk. i, No. 8.

3
In all the necessaries of life there is not a greater plague than servants.
COLLEY CIBBER, *She Would and She Would Not.* Act i, sc. 1.

4
He should be faithful, ugly, and fierce. (Ut sit fidelis, ut sit deformis, ut sit ferox.)
ERASMUS, *Convivium Poeticum.* Giving the three qualifications of a good servant.

The face of a pig, the ears of an ass, the feet of a stag, a padlock on his mouth, and a sword at his side.
CHRISTOPHER JOHNSON, *The Trusty Servant.* (c. 1560)

Never in the way and never out of the way.
CHARLES II, referring to Sidney Godolphin; a phrase afterwards used to describe a good valet. (MACAULAY, *History of England.* Vol. i, p. 265.)

Servants should put on patience when they put on a livery.
THOMAS FULLER, *Gnomologia.* No. 4101.

5
A servant and a cock should be kept but a year.
THOMAS FULLER, *Gnomologia.* No. 389.

6
If you pay not a servant his wages, he will pay himself.
THOMAS FULLER, *Gnomologia.* No. 2778.

He can give little to his servant that licks his knife.
GEORGE HERBERT, *Jacula Prudentum.*

7
No surly porter stands in guilty state
To spurn imploring famine from the gate.
GOLDSMITH, *The Deserted Village,* l. 105.

A pampered menial drove me from the door,
To seek a shelter in an humbler shed.
THOMAS MOSS, *The Beggar's Petition.* "Pampered menial" is Oliver Goldsmith's. Moss submitted his poem to Goldsmith before it was published, and the latter substituted "pampered menial" for the original's more commonplace "liveried servant."

A great man's overfed great man, what the Scotch call Flunkey.
CARLYLE, *Essays: Samuel Johnson.*

8
A servant that is diligent, honest and good
Must sing at his work like a bird in the wood.
ROBERT GREENE, *Works.* Vol. vii, p. 311. (1590)

9
Empty chambers make foolish maids.
GEORGE HERBERT, *Jacula Prudentum.*

10
Disgust turns the stomach, should the servant touch the cup with his greasy hands. (Magna movet stomacho fastidia, seu puer unctis Tractavit calicem manibus.)
HORACE, *Satires.* Bk. ii, sat. 4, l. 78.

11
Every great house is full of saucy servants. (Maxima quæque domus servis est plena superbis.)
JUVENAL, *Satires.* Sat. v, l. 66.

It is not becoming for a servant to be arrogant. (Non decet superbum esse hominem servum.)
PLAUTUS, *Asinaria,* l. 470. (Act ii, sc. 4.)

Great men's servants think themselves great.
W. G. BENHAM, *Proverbs,* p. 770.

Who wishes to be ill-served, let him keep plenty of servants. (Chi vuol esser mal servito, tenga assai famiglia.)
UNKNOWN. An Italian proverb.

12
The tongue of a bad servant is his worst part. (Lingua mali pars pessima servi.)
JUVENAL, *Satires.* Sat. ix, l. 120.

A servant had better know too much than say too much. That's wisdom on his part. (Plus scire satiust quam loqui servom hominem. Ea sapientia est.)
PLAUTUS, *Epidicus,* l. 60. (Act i, sc. 1.)

Pitchers have ears, and I have many servants.
SHAKESPEARE, *The Taming of the Shrew.* Act iv, sc. 4, l. 52. *See also under* EARS.

13
Is thy servant a dog, that he should do this great thing?
Old Testament: II Kings, viii, 13. Quoted by Sydney Smith when advised to have his portrait painted by Landseer.

14
We are unprofitable servants: we have done that which was our duty to do.
New Testament: Luke, xvii, 10.

15
A faithful and good servant is a real godsend, but truly 'tis a rare bird in the land.
LUTHER, *Table Talk.* Sec. clvi. Paraphrasing Juvenal, vi, 165. *See under* SWAN.

16
He that is greatest among you shall be your servant.
New Testament: Matthew, xxiii, 11.

17
Well done, thou good and faithful servant: thou hast been faithful over a few things, I will make thee ruler over many things.
New Testament: Matthew, xxv, 21.

O good old man, how well in thee appears
The constant service of the antique world,
When service sweat for duty, not for meed!
Thou art not for the fashion of these times,
Where none will sweat but for promotion.
SHAKESPEARE, *As You Like It.* Act ii, sc. 3, l. 56.

18
Nor let too pretty a maid-servant wait upon

you. (Nec nimium vobis formosa ancilla ministret.)

Ovid, *Ars Amatoria*. Bk. iii, l. 665.

Let thy maidservant be faithful, strong and homely.

Benjamin Franklin, *Poor Richard*, 1736.

1
So many servants, so many enemies. (Totidem hostes esse quot servos.)

Seneca, *Epistulæ ad Lucilium*. Epis. xlvii, sec. 5. Quoted as a proverb.

2
Every good servant does not all commands:
No bond but to do just ones.

Shakespeare, *Cymbeline*. Act v, sc. 1, l. 6.

3
You gentlemen's gentlemen are so hasty.

Sheridan, *The Rivals*. Act ii, sc. 2. Referring to a valet.

4
When you have done a fault be always pert and insolent, and behave yourself as if you were the injured person.

Swift, *Directions to Servants*.

5
The sooty yoke of kitchen-vassalage.

Tennyson, *Gareth and Lynette*, l. 469.

6
A baker's wife may bite of a bun,
A brewer's wife may drink of a tun,
A fish-monger's wife may feed of a cunger,
But a servingman's wife may starve for hunger.

Unknown, *Servingman's Comfort*. (*Inedited Tracts*, 166. 1598)

II—Servant and Master

7
If you would have good servants, see that you be good masters.

Richard Baxter, *Works*. Vol. iv, p. 290.

8
The truest report comes from a man's servants. (Verior fama e domesticis emanat.)

Cicero, *De Petitione Consulatus*. Sec. 6 Adapted. Quoted in this form by Francis Bacon.

The highest panegyric . . . that private virtue can receive is the praise of servants.

Samuel Johnson, *The Rambler*. No. 68.

Few men have been admired by their servants. (Peu d'hommes ont esté admiré par leurs domestiques.)

Montaigne, *Essays*. Bk. iii, ch. 2.

See also Hero and Valet.

9
Masters, give unto your servants that which is just and equal.

New Testament: Colossians, iv, 1.

Servants, be obedient to them that are your masters . . . not with eyeservice, as menpleasers; but as the servants of Christ.

New Testament: Ephesians, vi, 5.

10
From kings to cobblers 't is the same;
Bad servants wound their masters' fame.

John Gay, *Fables*. Pt. ii, fab. 6.

11
As with the servant, so with his master; as with the maid, so with her mistress.

Old Testament: Isaiah, xxiv, 2.

Like master, like man, *see under* Master.

12
A devoted old servant cancels the name of master.

Axel Munthe, *Story of San Michele*, p. 490.

13
A master is usually what his servants choose to make him. If they're good, he is good; if they are bad, it makes him bad. (Ut servi volunt esse erum, ita solet, Boni sunt, bonust; improbi sunt, malus fit.)

Plautus, *Mostellaria*, l. 872. (Act iv, sc. 1.)

14
Take care that you do not let your servant excel you in doing right. (Cave sis te superare servom siris faciundo bene.)

Plautus, *Bacchides*, l. 402. (Act iii, sc. 2.)

15
'Tis the master shames me, not the servitude. (Domini pudet, Non servitutis.)

Seneca, *Troades*, l. 989.

16
Servants talk about their master behind his back when they may not talk in his presence. (Isti domino loquantur, quibus coram domino loqui non licet.)

Seneca, *Epistulæ ad Lucilium*. Epis. xlvii, 4.

17
Servants must their masters' minds fulfil.

Shakespeare, *The Comedy of Errors*. Act iv, sc. 1, l. 113.

18
The stone that is rolling can gather no moss;
For master and servant oft changing is loss.

Thomas Tusser, *Five Hundred Points of Good Husbandry: Housewifely Admonitions*.

SERVICE

I—Service: Definitions

19
We are his,
To serve him nobly in the common cause,
True to the death, but not to be his slaves.

Cowper, *The Task*. Bk. v, l. 343. Referring to the King.

20
Command was service; humblest service done
By willing and discerning souls was glory.

George Eliot, *Agatha*.

21
When I have attempted to join myself to others by services, it proved an intellectual trick,—no more. They eat your service like apples, and leave you out. But love them, and they feel you, and delight in you all the time.

Emerson, *Essays, Second Series: Of Gifts*.

Serve and thou shalt be served. If you love and serve men, you cannot, by any hiding or stratagem, escape the remuneration.
EMERSON, *Lectures and Biographical Studies: The Sovereignty of Ethics.*

1
Who seeks for aid
Must show how service sought can be repaid.
OWEN MEREDITH, *Siege of Constantinople.*

2
They also serve who only stand and wait.
MILTON, *Sonnet: On His Blindness.*

3
If I have done the public any service, it is due to patient thought.
ISAAC NEWTON, *Remark to Dr. Bentley.*

4
For what hard heart would not all service do
To help a fair, a chaste, a woman too?
FRANCIS ROUS, *Thule.*

5
Service is no heritage.
SHAKESPEARE, *All's Well that Ends Well.* Act i, sc. 3, l. 26.

Service is no inheritance.
SWIFT, *Directions to Servants: General Rules.*

6
It did me yeoman's service.
SHAKESPEARE, *Hamlet.* Act v, sc. 2, l. 36.

7
Alas and alas! you may take it how you will, but the services of no single individual are indispensable. Atlas was just a gentleman with a protracted nightmare!
R. L. STEVENSON, *An Apology for Idlers.*

8
Enough, if something from our hands have power
To live, and act, and serve the future hour.
WORDSWORTH, *After-Thought.*

9
Small service is true service while it lasts:
Of humblest Friends, bright Creature! scorn not one:
The Daisy, by the shadow that it casts,
Protects the lingering dew-drop from the Sun.
WORDSWORTH, *To a Child.*

II—Service to God

10
All service is the same with God,
With God, whose puppets, best and worst,
Are we: there is no last nor first.
ROBERT BROWNING, *Pippa Passes.* Pt. iv.

Our voluntary service He requires,
Not our necessitated.
MILTON, *Paradise Lost.* Bk. v, l. 529.

They serve God well, Who serve his creatures.
CAROLINE NORTON, *The Lady of La Garaye: Conclusion,* l. 9.

11
God curse Moawiyah. If I had served God as well as I have served him, He would never have damned me to all eternity.
SWAMWRA, to the Governor of Basra, when deposed by the Caliph in 675. (See OCKLEY, *History of Saracens.* Hegira 54, A. D. 673.)

Had I but written as many odes in praise of Muhammad and Ali as I have composed for King Mahmud, they would have showered a hundred blessings on me.
ABUL KASIM FIRDUSI, *The Shahnemeh.* (c. 1000)

12
Had I but served God as diligently as I have served my king, he would not have given me over in my grey hairs. But this is the just reward that I must receive for my indulgent pains and study, not regarding my service to God, but only to my prince.
CARDINAL WOLSEY, to Sir William Kingston, Constable of the Tower, at Leicester Abbey, 5 Nov., 1530. Wolsey, accused of high treason, was being conducted to London, but was overtaken by illness on the road, stopped at Leicester, and died there. (HUME, *History of England.* Ch. 30.)

Had I but served my God with half the zeal
I served my king, he would not in mine age
Have left me naked to mine enemies.
SHAKESPEARE, *Henry VIII.* Act iii, sc. 2, l. 455. (1612)

13
Had I served God as well in every part
As I did serve my king and master still,
My scope had not this season been so short,
Nor would have had the power to do me ill.
THOMAS CHURCHYARD, *Death of Morton.* (1593)

SERVILITY

See also Slave

14
Always mistrust a subordinate who never finds fault with his superior.
CHURTON COLLINS, *Aphorisms.*

15
Servitude that hugs her chain.
THOMAS GRAY, *Ode for Music,* l. 6.

16
They kiss the hand by which they are oppressed. (Illam osculantur, qua sunt oppressi, manum.)
PHÆDRUS, *Fables.* Bk. v, fab. 1, l. 5.

Many kiss the hand they wish cut off.
GEORGE HERBERT, *Jacula Prudentum.*

17
Learn to lick betimes; you know not whose tail you may go by.
JOHN RAY, *English Proverbs,* 117. (1670)

Wit that can creep, and pride that licks the dust.
POPE, *Epistle to Dr. Arbuthnot,* l. 333.

For aye thy foot-licker.
SHAKESPEARE, *The Tempest.* Act iv, sc. 1, l. 219.

18
More vile Than is a slave in base servility.
SHAKESPEARE, *I Henry VI.* Act v, sc. 3, l. 113.

Dogs, easily won to fawn on any man.
SHAKESPEARE, *Richard II.* Act iii, sc. 2, l. 130.

1
Away with slavish weeds and servile thoughts.
SHAKESPEARE, *Titus Andronicus*. Act ii, sc. 1, 18.

Supple knees
Feed arrogance and are the proud man's fees.
SHAKESPEARE, *Troilus and Cressida*. Act iii, sc. 3, l. 48.

2
Full little knowest thou that hast not tried,
What hell it is, in suing long to bide:
To lose good days, that might be better spent;
To waste long nights in pensive discontent;
To speed today, to be put back tomorrow;
To feed on hope, to pine with fear and sorrow; . . .
To fret thy soul with crosses and with cares;
To eat thy heart through comfortless despairs;
To fawn, to crouch, to wait, to ride, to run,
To spend, to give, to want, to be undone.
SPENSER, *Mother Hubberds Tale*, l. 895.

SEXES

See also Man and Woman

3
Sex to the last.
DRYDEN, *Cymon and Iphigenia*, l. 368.

4
Virtue attired in woman see, . . .
And forget the He and She.
JOHN DONNE, *The Undertaking*.

5
Breathes there a man with hide so tough
Who says two sexes aren't enough?
SAMUEL HOFFENSTEIN, *The Sexes*.

6
A woman never forgets her sex. She would rather talk with a man than an angel, any day.
O. W. HOLMES, *The Poet at the Breakfast-Table*. Ch. 4.

7
Freud and his three slaves, Inhibition, Complex and Libido.
SOPHIE KERR, *The Age of Innocence*. (*Sat. Eve. Post*, 9 April, 1932.)

8
This world consists of men, women, and Hervey's.
LADY MARY WORTLEY MONTAGU, *Letters*. Vol. i, p. 67. The reference is to John Hervey, whom Pope attacked in *The Dunciad* as "Lord Fanny." The saying has been wrongly attributed to Charles Pigott. (*Jockey Club*. Pt. ii, p. 4.)

As the French say, there are three sexes,—men, women, and clergymen.
SYDNEY SMITH. (LADY HOLLAND, *Memoir*. Vol. i, p. 262.)

The jibe of European scholars that there are three sexes in America—men, women, and professors.
JOEL E. SPINGARN.

This country is inhabited by saints, sinners, and Beechers.
DR. LEONARD BACON.

9
As the man beholds the woman,
As the woman sees the man,
Curiously they note each other,
As each other only can.
Never can the man divest her
Of that wondrous charm of sex;
Ever must she, dreaming of him,
That same mystic charm annex.
BRYAN WALLER PROCTER, *The Sexes*.

He was close on to six feet tall, of military bearing, and of such extraordinary vitality that young ladies asserted they could feel him ten feet away.
C. HARTLEY GRATTAN, *Bitter Bierce*, p. 39. Referring to Ambrose Bierce.

'Tisn't beauty, so to speak, nor good talk necessarily. It's just It. Some women'll stay in a man's memory if they once walked down a street.
RUDYARD KIPLING, *Mrs. Bathurst*. (1904)

10
The son of the female is the shadow of the male.
SHAKESPEARE, *II Henry IV*. Act iii, sc. 2, l. 141.

11
The nonsense of the old women (of both sexes).
STERNE, *Tristram Shandy*. Vol. v, ch. 16.

In company with several other old ladies of both sexes.
DICKENS, *Little Dorrit*. Pt. i, ch. 17.

12
The little rift between the sexes is astonishingly widened by simply teaching one set of catchwords to the girls and another to the boys.
ROBERT LOUIS STEVENSON, *Virginibus Puerisque*. Pt. i.

13
I lose my respect for the man who can make the mystery of sex the subject of a coarse jest, yet, when you speak earnestly and seriously on the subject, is silent.
H. D. THOREAU, *Journal*, 12 April, 1852.

14
In the argot of the sub-deb, "U.S.A." has long ago lost its patriotic meaning. It now stands for "Universal Sex Appeal."
MARY DAY WINN, *Adam's Rib*, p. 17. *See also under* LOVE AND LUST.

Sex is the tabasco sauce which an adolescent national palate sprinkles on every course in the menu.
MARY DAY WINN, *Adam's Rib*, p. 8.

15
Sometimes, through pride, the sexes change their airs;
My lord has vapours, and my lady swears.
YOUNG, *Love of Fame*. Pt. iii, l. 136.

Some sexes change their sexes now
and make a mere man wonder how.
ALFRED KREYMBORG, *Outmoded*.

SHADOW

1
If you measure your shadow, you will find it no greater than before.
ARCHIDAMUS III, KING OF SPARTA, to Philip of Macedon, who sent him a haughty letter after his victory at Chæronea. (PLUTARCH, *Apothegms.*) The French say, "Un petit homme projette parfois une grande ombre" (A little man sometimes casts a great shadow).

2
Man, shackled to his shadow, cannot move
Without the base companionship of self.
ALFRED AUSTIN, *Fortunatus the Pessimist*. Act i, sc. 4.

Always there is a black spot in our sunshine—it is the shadow of ourselves.
CARLYLE, *Sartor Resartus*. Bk. 2, ch. 9.

Vain truly is the hope of your swiftest Runner to escape "from his own Shadow!"
CARLYLE, *Sartor Resartus*. Bk. ii, ch. 6.

His shadow for his sole attendant.
LA FONTAINE, *Fables: The Use of Knowledge*. Bk. ii, fab. 18.

3
Catch not at the shadow and lose the substance.
H. G. BOHN, *Hand-Book of Proverbs*, p. 335. Founded on the fable of the dog and his reflection in the water.

4
Think not thy own shadow longer than that of others, nor delight to take the altitude of thyself.
SIR THOMAS BROWNE, *Christian Morals*, i, 14.

5
The worthy gentleman [Mr. Coombe] . . . has feelingly told us, what shadows we are, and what shadows we pursue.
EDMUND BURKE, *Speech*, Bristol, Sept., 1780.

We know not substance; 'mid the shades shadows ourselves we live and die.
SIR RICHARD BURTON, *Kasîdah*. Pt. vi, st. 5.

6
Strange to relate, but wonderfully true,
That even shadows have their shadows too!
CHARLES CHURCHILL, *The Rosciad*, l. 411.

The picture of a shadow is a positive thing.
LOCKE, *Essay Concerning Human Understanding*. Bk. ii, ch. 8, sec. 5.

7
Our days on the earth are as a shadow.
Old Testament: I Chronicles, xxix, 15.

Passeth as doth a shadow upon the wall.
CHAUCER, *The Shipmannes Tale*, l. 9.

Come like shadows, so depart!
SHAKESPEARE, *Macbeth*. Act iv, sc. 1, l. 111.

8
Oh for a lodge in some vast wilderness,
Some boundless contiguity of shade.
COWPER, *The Task*. Bk. ii, l. 1.

The unpierc'd shade.
MILTON, *Paradise Lost*. Bk. iv, l. 245.

Or ruminate in the contiguous shade.
THOMSON, *The Seasons: Winter*, l. 86.

Chequer'd shadow.
SHAKESPEARE, *Titus Andronicus*. Act ii, sc. 3, 15.

9
Shadows are not enough.
ELLEN GLASGOW, *The Sheltered Life*, p. 36.

10
A hunter of shadows, himself a shade. (Τοὺς αὐτὸς κατέπεφνεν ἐν οἰοπόλοισιν ὄρεσσι.)
HOMER, *Odyssey*. Bk. xi, l. 574. Referring to Orion.

We all laugh at pursuing a shadow, though the lives of the multitude are devoted to the chase.
WILLIAM WORDSWORTH. *See also under* GHOST.

11
On yon bare knoll the pointed cedar shadows
Drowse on the crisp, gray moss.
J. R. LOWELL, *An Indian Summer Reverie*.

12
Follow a shadow, it still flies you;
Seem to fly it, it will pursue.
BEN JONSON, *Song: That Women Are But Men's Shadows*. *See also under* WOOING.

13
Shall the shadow go forward ten degrees, or go back ten degrees? And Hezekiah answered, It is a light thing for the shadow to go down ten degrees: nay, but let the shadow return backward ten degrees.
Old Testament: II Kings, xx, 9, 10.

Like Hezekiah's, backward runs
The shadow of my days.
TENNYSON, *Will Waterproof's Lyrical Monologue*. St. 5. The original version, altered in 1853 ed. to: "Against its fountain upward runs The current of my days."

14
To fight with a shadow (whether one's own or another's) passeth for the proverbial expression of a vain and useless act.
THOMAS FULLER, *History of Cambridge University*, 592. (1659)

Alas! must it ever be so?
Do we stand in our own light, wherever we go,
And fight our own shadows forever?
OWEN MEREDITH, *Lucile*. Pt. ii, canto 2, st. 5.

15
Syene, and where the shadow both way falls,
Meroë, Nilotic isle.
MILTON, *Paradise Regained*. Bk. iv, l. 70.

16
Every light has its shadow.
H. G. BOHN, *Handbook of Proverbs*, p. 349.

Thus shadow owes its birth to light.
JOHN GAY, *Fables: The Persian, the Sun, and the Cloud*, l. 10.

17
Some there be that shadows kiss;
Such have but a shadow's bliss.
SHAKESPEARE, *The Merchant of Venice*, ii, 9, 66.

The best in this kind are but shadows.
SHAKESPEARE, *A Midsummer-Night's Dream*. Act v, sc. 1, l. 213.

18
Shadows to-night
Have struck more terror to the soul of Richard

Than can the substance of ten thousand
  soldiers.
  SHAKESPEARE, *Richard III*. Act v, sc. 3, l. 216.

1 The awful shadow of some unseen Power
Floats, though unseen, amongst us.
  SHELLEY, *Hymn to Intellectual Beauty*, l. 1.

2 For this I see, that we, all we that live,
Are but vain shadows, unsubstantial dreams.
(Εἴδωλ' ὅσοιπερ ζῶμεν ἢ κούφην σκιάν.)
  SOPHOCLES, *Ajax*, l. 126. (Plumptre, tr.)

Behold! human beings living in a sort of underground den . . . they see only their own shadows, or the shadows of one another, which the fire throws on the opposite wall of the cave.
  PLATO, *The Republic*. Bk. vii, sec. 514.

We are but dust and shadow. (Pulvis et umbra sumus.)
  HORACE, *Odes*. Bk. iv, ode 7, l. 16.

3 The Shadow cloak'd from head to foot,
Who keeps the keys of all the creeds.
  TENNYSON, *In Memoriam*. Pt. xxiii, sts. 1, 2.

4 The longer shadows fall from the lofty mountains. (Majoresque cadunt altis de montibus umbræ.)
  VERGIL, *Eclogues*. No. i, l. 84.

5 The setting sun doubles the lengthening shadows. (Sol crescentis decedens duplicat umbræ.)
  VERGIL, *Eclogues*. No. iii, l. 67.

When the sun sets, shadows, that showed at
  noon
But small, appear most long and terrible.
  NATHANIEL LEE, *Œdipus*.

And now his shadow reach'd her as she run,
His shadow lengthen'd by the setting sun.
  POPE, *Windsor Forest*, l. 193.

But why lament the common lot
  That all must share so soon;
Since shadows lengthen with the day,
  That scarce exist at noon?
  MRS. ALARIC A. WATTS, *Requiem of Youth*.

6 That shadow my likeness that goes to and fro
  seeking a livelihood, chattering, chaffering,
How often I find myself standing and looking
  at it where it flits,
How often I question and doubt whether that
  is really me.
  WALT WHITMAN, *That Shadow My Likeness*.

7 Again the shadow moveth o'er
The dial-plate of time!
  J. G. WHITTIER, *The New Year*, l. 3.

SHAKESPEARE

8 This was Shakespeare's form;
Who walked in every path of human life,
Felt every passion, and to all mankind
Doth now, will ever, that experience yield
Which his own genius only could acquire.
  MARK AKENSIDE, *For a Statue of Shakespeare*.

9 Bonnet in hand, obsequious and discreet,
The butcher that served Shakespeare with his
  meat
Doubtless esteemed him little, as a man
Who knew not how the market prices ran.
  THOMAS BAILEY ALDRICH, *Points of View*.

10 Others abide our question. Thou art free.
We ask and ask; Thou smilest and art still,
Out-topping knowledge.
  MATTHEW ARNOLD, *Shakespeare*.

11 Live ever you, at least in Fame live ever:
Well may the body die, but Fame dies never.
  RICHARD BARNFIELD, *A Remembrance of Some English Poets*.

12 Renowned Spenser, lie a thought more nigh
To learned Chaucer, and rare Beaumont lie
A little nearer Spenser, to make room
For Shakespeare in your threefold, fourfold
  tomb.
  WILLIAM BASSE, *On Shakespeare*. (1616)

13 There, Shakespeare, on whose forehead climb
The crowns o' the world: O eyes sublime
With tears and laughters for all time!
  E. B. BROWNING, *A Vision of Poets*, l. 298.

14 As I declare our Poet, him
Whose insight makes all others dim.
A thousand poets pried at life
And only one amid the strife
Rose to be Shakespeare.
  ROBERT BROWNING, *Christmas-Eve*. Sec. 16.

Shakespeare!—to such names sounding, what
  succeeds
Fitly as silence?
  ROBERT BROWNING, *The Names*.

15 Shake was a dramatist of note;
He lived by writing things to quote.
  H. C. BUNNER, *Shake, Mulleary and Go-ethe*.

16 How often in the summer-tide,
His graver business set aside,
Has stripling Will, the thoughtful-eyed,
  As to the pipe of Pan,
Stepped blithesomely with lover's pride
  Across the fields to Anne.
  RICHARD BURTON, *Across the Fields to Anne*.

But were it to my fancy given
To rate her charms, I'd call them heaven;
For though a mortal made of clay,
Angels must love Anne Hathaway;
She hath a way so to control,
To rapture the imprisoned soul,
And sweetest heaven on earth display,

That to be heaven Anne hath a way;
She hath a way,
Anne Hathaway,—
To be heaven's self Anne hath a way.

CHARLES DIBDIN, *A Love Dittie*. In his novel *Hannah Hewitt*. (1795) Anne Hathaway was the maiden name of Shakespeare's wife. These verses have often been attributed to Shakespeare, and a biting irony read into them.

1

And rival all but Shakespeare's name below.

CAMPBELL, *Pleasures of Hope*. Pt. i, l. 472.

2

If I say that Shakespeare is the greatest of intellects, I have said all concerning him. But there is more in Shakespeare's intellect than we have yet seen. It is what I call an unconscious intellect; there is more virtue in it than he himself is aware of.

CARLYLE, *Essays: Characteristics of Shakespeare.*

3

Happy in tragic and in comic powers,
Have we not Shakspeare?—is not Jonson ours?
For them, your natural judges, Britons, vote;
They'll judge like Britons, who like Britons wrote.

CHARLES CHURCHILL, *The Rosciad*, l. 223.

Things of the noblest kind his genius drew,
And look'd through Nature at a single view:
A loose he gave to his unbounded soul,
And taught new lands to rise, new seas to roll;
Call'd into being scenes unknown before,
And passing Nature's bounds, was something more.

CHARLES CHURCHILL, *The Rosciad*, l. 264.

4

Our *myriad-minded* Shakespeare—*ἀνὴρ μυριόνους*, a phrase which I have borrowed from a Greek monk, who applies it to a Patriarch of Constantinople. It seems to belong to Shakespeare, *de jure singulari, et ex privilegio naturæ.*

S. T. COLERIDGE, *Biographia Literaria*. Ch. 15.

Shakespeare is of no age.

S. T. COLERIDGE, *Table Talk*.

5

His want of erudition was a most happy and productive ignorance; it forced him back upon his own resources, which were exhaustless.

C. C. COLTON, *Lacon*. Vol. i, No. 198.

6

The making of Shakespeare's mind was like the making of the world.

WILLIAM JOHNSON CORY. (M. E. COLERIDGE, *Gathered Leaves*, p. 323.)

7

Shakespeare, thou hadst as smooth a comic vein,
Fitting the sock, and in thy natural brain,
As strong conception, and as clear a rage,
As any one that traffick'd with the stage.

MICHAEL DRAYTON, *Elegy to Henry Reynolds*. (1627)

8

Shakespear, who (taught by none) did first impart
To Fletcher wit, to labouring Jonson art;
He, Monarch-like, gave those his subjects law,
And is that Nature which they paint and draw.

DRYDEN, *Prologue to His Version of The Tempest*, l. 5.

But Shakespear's magic could not copied be;
Within that circle none durst walk but he.

DRYDEN, *Prologue to His Version of The Tempest*, l. 19.

Heav'n, that but once was prodigal before,
To Shakespear gave as much; she could not give him more.

DRYDEN, *To Mr. Congreve*, l. 62.

9

When Shakspeare is charged with debts to his authors, Landor replies: "Yet he was more original than his originals. He breathed upon dead bodies and brought them into life."

EMERSON, *Letters and Social Aims: Quotation and Originality.*

The passages of Shakspeare that we most prize were never quoted until within this century.

EMERSON, *Letters and Social Aims: Quotation and Originality.*

10

It is difficult not to be intemperate in speaking of Shakspeare. . . . If the world were on trial, it is the perfect success of this one man that might justify such expenditure of geology, chemistry, fauna, and flora, as the world was. And, I suppose, if Intellect perceives and converses "in climes beyond the solar road," they probably call this planet, not Earth, but Shakspeare.

EMERSON, *Journals*, 1864.

Shakspeare's fault that the world appears so empty. He has educated you with his painted world, and this real one seems a huckster's shop.

EMERSON, *Journals*, 1864.

11

Nor sequent centuries could hit
Orbit and sum of Shakspeare's wit.

EMERSON, *Solution*, l. 39.

I see all human wits
Are measured by a few;
Unmeasured still my Shakspeare sits,
Lone as the blessed Jew.

EMERSON, *Quatrains: Shakspeare.*

What point of morals, of manners, of economy, of philosophy, of religion, of taste, of the conduct of life, has he not settled? What mystery has he not signified his knowledge of? What office, or function, or district of man's work, has he not remembered? What king has he not taught state, as Talma taught Napoleon? What maiden has not found him finer than her delicacy? What lover has he not outloved? What sage has he not outseen? What gentleman has he not instructed in the rudeness of his behavior?

EMERSON, *Representative Men: Shakspeare.*

Shakspeare's principal merit may be conveyed in saying that he of all men best understands the English language, and can say what he will.

EMERSON, *Representative Men: Uses of Great Men.*

1

I saw Hamlet Prince of Denmark played; but now the old plays began to disgust this refined age.

JOHN EVELYN, *Diary*, 26 Oct., 1661.

The play-bill which is said to have announced the tragedy of Hamlet, the character of the Prince of Denmark being left out.

SCOTT, *The Talisman: Introduction.*

2

Nature's darling.

THOMAS GRAY, *Progress of Poesy.* Pt. iii, l. 84.

I know the signs of an immortal man—
Nature's chief darling, and illustrious mate.

THOMAS HOOD, *The Plea of the Midsummer Fairies*, l. 941.

3

If we wish to know the force of human genius we should read Shakspeare. If we wish to see the insignificance of human learning we may study his commentators.

WILLIAM HAZLITT, *Table Talk: On the Ignorance of the Learned.*

4

Mellifluous *Shakespeare*, whose enchanting Quill
Commandeth Mirth or Passion, was but *Will*.

THOMAS HEYWOOD, *Hierarchie of the Blessed Angels.* (1635)

5

Shakespeare was an intellectual ocean, whose waves touched all the shores of thought, . . . towards which all rivers ran, and from which now the isles and continents of thought receive their dew and rain.

ROBERT G. INGERSOLL, *Shakespeare.*

Shakespeare has done more for woman than all the other dramatists of the world.

ROBERT G. INGERSOLL, *Shakespeare.*

6

The stream of Time, which is continually washing the dissoluble fabrics of other poets, passes without injury by the adamant of Shakespeare.

SAMUEL JOHNSON, *Preface to the Works of Shakespeare.*

When Learning's triumph o'er her barbarous foes
First rear'd the stage, immortal Shakespeare rose;
Each change of many-colour'd life he drew,
Exhausted worlds, and then imagin'd new:
Existence saw him spurn her bounded reign,
And panting Time toil'd after him in vain.
His powerful strokes presiding Truth impress'd,
And unresisted Passion storm'd the breast.

SAMUEL JOHNSON, *Prologue at the Opening of Drury Lane Theatre*, l. 1.

Corneille is to Shakespeare as a clipped hedge to a forest.

SAMUEL JOHNSON, *The Rambler.* No. 160.

7

This Figure, that thou here seest put,
It was for gentle Shakespeare cut;
Wherein the Graver had a strife
With Nature, to out-doo the life:
O, could he but have drawne his wit
As well in brasse, as hė hath hit
His face; the Print would then surpasse
All, that was ever writ in brasse.
But, since he cannot, Reader, looke
Not on his Picture, but his Booke.

BEN JONSON, *To the Reader.* These verses were printed facing the portrait of Shakespeare prefixed as a frontispiece to the first folio edition of his works, 1623.

8

Soul of the Age!
The applause! delight! the wonder of our stage!
My Shakespeare, rise; I will not lodge thee by
Chaucer, or Spenser, or bid Beaumont lie
A little further, to make thee a room:
Thou art a monument, without a tomb,
And art alive still, while thy book doth live
And we have wits to read, and praise to give.

BEN JONSON, *To the Memory of My Beloved Master, William Shakespeare, and What He Hath Left Us*, l. 17. Printed on the fifth preliminary leaf to the first folio, 1623.

And though thou hadst small Latin, and less Greek,
From thence to honour thee, I would not seek
For names.

BEN JONSON, *To the Memory of Shakespeare*, l. 31.

Triumph, my Britain, thou hast one to show,
To whom all scenes of Europe homage owe.
He was not of an age, but for all time!

BEN JONSON, *To the Memory of Shakespeare*, l. 41.

Nature herself was proud of his designs,
And joy'd to wear the dressing of his lines!
Which were so richly spun, and woven so fit,
As, since, she will vouchsafe no other wit.

BEN JONSON, *To the Memory of Shakespeare*, l. 47.

Yet must I not give Nature all: thy Art,
My gentle Shakespeare, must enjoy a part.
For though the poet's matter Nature be,
His art doth give the fashion.

BEN JONSON, *To the Memory of Shakespeare*, l. 55.

For a good poet's made, as well as born,
And such wert thou. Look how the father's face
Lives in his issue; even so, the race
Of Shakespeare's mind and manners brightly shines
In his well-turnėd and true filėd lines:
In each of which he seems to shake a lance,
As brandish'd at the eyes of ignorance.

BEN JONSON, *To the Memory of Shakespeare*, l. 64.

Sweet Swan of Avon! what a sight it were

To see thee in our waters yet appear.
BEN JONSON, *To the Memory of Shakespeare*, l. 71.

Shakespeare, at length thy pious fellows give
The world thy works: thy works, by which outlive
Thy tomb, thy name must: when that stone is rent.
And Time dissolves thy Stratford monument,
Here we alive shall view thee still. This book,
When brass and marble fade, shall make thee look
Fresh to all ages.
LEONARD DIGGES, *To the Memorie of the Deceased Authour Maister, W. Shakespeare.* Eighth preliminary leaf to first folio, 1623.

His days are done, that made the dainty plays,
Which made the Globe of heav'n and earth to ring.
HUGH HOLLAND, *Upon the Lines and Life of the Famous Scenicke Poet, Master William Shakespeare.* Sixth preliminary leaf to the first folio, 1623.

We wonder'd (Shakespeare) that thou went'st so soon
From the World's-Stage, to the Grave's-Tyring-room.
We thought thee dead, but this thy printed worth,
Tells thy spectators, that thou went'st but forth
To enter with applause. An actor's art,
Can die, and live, to act a second part.
JAMES MABBE [?], *To the Memorie of W. Shake-speare. Eighth preliminary leaf to the first folio,* 1623.

1
I remember, the players have often mentioned it as an honour to Shakespeare, that in his writing (whatsoever he penn'd) he never blotted out a line. My answer hath been, would he had blotted a thousand.
BEN JONSON, *Explorata: De Shakespeare Nostrat.*

2
Shakespeare is not our poet, but the world's,—
Therefore on him no speech!
W. S. LANDOR, *To Robert Browning.*

3
The great poet who foreruns the ages,
Anticipating all that shall be said!
LONGFELLOW, *Sonnet on Mrs. Kemble's Readings from Shakespeare.*

Now you who rhyme, and I who rhyme,
Have not we sworn it, many a time,
That we no more our verse would scrawl,
For Shakespeare he had said it all!
R. W. GILDER, *The Modern Rhymer.*

4
Then to the well-trod stage anon,
If Jonson's learned sock be on,
Or sweetest Shakespear, fancy's child,
Warble his native wood-notes wild.
MILTON, *L'Allegro*, l. 131.

What needs my Shakespear for his honour'd bones,
The labour of an age in piled stones,
Or that his hallow'd reliques should be hid
Under a star-ypointing pyramid?
Dear son of memory, great heir of Fame,
What need'st thou such weak witness of thy name?
Thou in our wonder and astonishment
Hast built thyself a live-long monument, . . .
And so sepulchr'd in such pomp dost lie,
That kings for such a tomb would wish to die.
MILTON, *On Shakespear.* (1630)

5
And one wild Shakespeare, following Nature's lights,
Is worth whole planets, fill'd with Stagyrites.
THOMAS MOORE, *The Sceptic*, l. 121.

6
I know of no more heartrending reading than Shakespeare. How a man must have suffered to be so much in need of playing the clown.
FRIEDRICH NIETZSCHE, *Ecce Homo.*

7
Shakespeare (whom you and every playhouse bill
Style the divine! the matchless! what you will),
For gain, not glory, wing'd his roving flight,
And grew immortal in his own despite.
POPE, *Imitations of Horace: Epistles.* Bk. ii, epis. 1, l. 69.

Or damn all Shakespeare, like th' affected fool
At court, who hates whate'er he read at school.
POPE, *Imitations of Horace: Epistles.* Bk. ii, epis. 1, l. 105.

8
He seems to have known the world by intuition, to have looked through nature at one glance.
POPE, *Preface to the Works of Shakespeare.*

9
Hour after hour he loved to pore
On Shakespeare's rich and varied lore.
SCOTT, *Rokeby.* Canto i, st. 24.

10
With the single exception of Homer, there is no eminent writer, not even Sir Walter Scott, whom I despise so entirely as I despise Shakespeare when I measure my mind against his. . . . It would positively be a relief to me to dig him up and throw stones at him.
BERNARD SHAW, *Dramatic Opinions and Essays.* Vol. v, p. 2.

11
And he the man, whom Nature self had made
To mock her self, and Truth to imitate,
With kindly counter under Mimic shade,
Our pleasant Willy, ah! is dead of late:
With whom all joy and jolly merriment
Is also deaded, and in dolour drent.
SIR PHILIP SIDNEY, *Tears of the Muses.*

12
Realms yet unborn, in accents now unknown,
Thy song shall learn, and bless it for their own.
CHARLES SPRAGUE, *Shakespeare Ode.*

1
No man ever spake as he that bade our England be but true,
Keep but faith with England fast and firm, and none should bid her rue;
None may speak as he: but all may know the sign that Shakespeare knew.

A. C. SWINBURNE, *England: An Ode.* Pt. ii, st. 7.

2
The two Great Unknowns, the two Illustrious Conjecturabilities! They are the best known unknown persons that have ever drawn breath upon the planet.

MARK TWAIN, *Shakespeare Dead?* Ch. 3. Referring to the Devil and Shakespeare.

3
To the preëxistent Shakespeare wisdom was offered, but he declined it, and took only genius.

JONES VERY. (EMERSON, *Journals,* 1865.)

4
Shakespeare is a savage with sparks of genius which shine in a dreadful darkness of night. (Shakespeare est un sauvage avec des etincelles de génie qui brillent dans une nuit horrible.)

VOLTAIRE, *Irène: Preliminary Letter.*

When I gained a fuller acquaintance with the speech, I perceived that the English were right. . . . They saw, as I did, the gross faults of their favorite author, but they felt better than I his beauties, all the more remarkable because they are lightning flashes which have sent forth their gleams in profoundest night.

VOLTAIRE. (Quoted by Thomas Lounsbury in his *Shakespeare and Voltaire: First Impressions of Shakespeare.*)

5
He was a great playwright, a great humorist, the sweetest laugher in the world.

H. G. WELLS. From a symposium in the *Strand Magazine* on the six greatest men in history.

6
They were built out of music.

OSCAR WILDE, *The Critic as Artist.* Pt. i. Referring to Shakespeare's plays.

7
There is not anything of human trial
That ever love deplored or sorrow knew,
No glad fulfilment and no sad denial,
Beyond the pictured truth that Shakespeare drew.

WILLIAM WINTER, *Ashes.*

8
The sightless Milton, with his hair
Around his placid temples curled;
And Shakespeare at his side,—a freight
If clay could think and mind were weight,
For him who bore the world!

WORDSWORTH, *The Italian Itinerant.* Pt. i, st. 1.

9
Few of the university pen plays well, they smell too much of that writer Ovid, and talk too much of Proserpina and Jupiter. Why, here's our fellow Shakespeare puts them all down.

UNKNOWN, *Return from Parnassus.* Act iv, sc. 3. Printed in 1606, and acted before that date by the students of St. John's College, Cambridge.

10
Good frend for Jesvs sake forbeare,
To digg the dust encloased heare.
Blese be ye man yt spares thes stones.
And curst be he yt moves my bones.

UNKNOWN, *Epitaph,* on Shakespeare's tombstone in Stratford Church. Said to have been chosen by him, but not from his pen. The lines are rudely engraved in capital letters on the stone slab which covers his body, the last line an evident imitation of the damnation clause so frequent in Roman sepulchral inscriptions.

11
Stay Passenger, why goest thou by so fast?
Read if thou canst, whom envious Death hath plast,
With in this monument Shakspeare: with whome,
Quick nature dide: whose name doth deck ys Tombe,
Far more then cost: sieh all, yt He hath writt,
Leaves living art, but page, to serve his witt.

UNKNOWN, *Epitaph,* on the monument in Stratford Church, erected before 1623.

SHAME

See also Pride and Shame

12
Why shameful, if the spectators do not think so? (Τί δ' αἰσχρόν, ἢν μὴ τοῖς θεωμένοις δοκῇ.)

ARISTOPHANES, *The Frogs,* l. 1475.

Shame is as it is taken.

JOHN HEYWOOD, *Proverbs.* Pt. i, ch. 9.

See also THOUGHT: ITS POWER.

13
Shame is an ornament to the young, a disgrace to the old, since an old man ought not to do anything of which he need be ashamed. The virtuous man does not feel shame, if shame is the feeling caused by base actions, since the virtuous man does not do base actions. Shame is a mark of a base man, and springs from a character capable of doing a shameful act.

ARISTOTLE, *Nicomachean Ethics* Bk. iv, ch. 9, sec. 3.

The eyes are the abode of shame. (Τὸ ἐν ὀφθαλμοῖς εἶναι αἰδῶ.)

ARISTOTLE, *Rhetoric.* Bk. ii, ch. 6, sec. 18. Referred to as a proverb.

14
It is a shame not to be shameless. (Pudet non esse impudentem.)

ST. AUGUSTINE, *Confessions.* Bk. ii, ch. 9, last line.

For while he holds that nothing is so damned

And shameful, as to be ashamed.
SAMUEL BUTLER, *On a Hypocritical Nonconformist*. St. 5.

None but the shamefaced lose. (Il n'y a que les honteux qui perdent.)
UNKNOWN. A French proverb.

1
Whilst shame keeps its watch, virtue is not wholly extinguished in the heart.
EDMUND BURKE, *Reflections on the Revolution in France*.

2
It is the crime which makes the shame, and not the scaffold. (C'est le crime qui fait la honte, et non pas l'échafaud.)
CORNEILLE, *Comte d'Essex*. Act iv, sc. 3. Quoted by Charlotte Corday in a letter to her father after her murder of Marat.

The shame is in the crime, not in the punishment.
VOLTAIRE, *Artemire*. Act iv.

See also CRIME; PUNISHMENT: ITS CERTAINTY.

3
Less shame a greater fault would palliate. (Maggior difetto men vergogna lava.)
DANTE, *Inferno*. Canto xxx, l. 142.

4
Love taught him shame; and shame, with love at strife,
Soon taught the sweet civilities of life.
DRYDEN, *Cymon and Iphigenia*, l. 133.

5
There is a shame which is glory and grace.
Apocrypha: Ecclesiasticus, iv, 21.

Of all sweet passions Shame the loveliest.
LORD ALFRED DOUGLAS, *In Praise of Shame*.

6
On shameful things shame everywhere attends. (Κἀκεῖ τά γ' αἰσχρὰ κανθάδ' αἰσχύνην ἔχει.)
EURIPIDES, *Andromache*, l. 244.

7
He that has no shame has no conscience.
THOMAS FULLER, *Gnomologia*. No 2148.

Where there is no shame there is no honour.
W. G. BENHAM, *Proverbs*, p. 873.

Where there is no shame, the kingdom is insecure. (Ubi non est pudor, . . . Instabile regnum est.)
SENECA, *Thyestes*, l. 215.

Man is a beast when shame stands off from him.
SWINBURNE, *Phædra: Hippolytus*.

8
Shame to them that think shame.
SIR JOHN HARINGTON, *Metamorphosis of Ajax*, 104. *See also under* EVIL: HONI SOIT.

9
If yet not lost to all the sense of shame.
HOMER, *Iliad*. Bk. vi, l. 350. (Pope, tr.)

I count him lost who is lost to shame. (Nam ego illum perisse dico quoi quidem periit pudor.)
PLAUTUS, *Bacchides*, l. 485. (Act iii, sc. 3.)

10
It is the false shame of fools which tries to cover unhealed sores. (Stultorum incurata malus pudor ulcera celat.)
HORACE, *Epistles*. Bk. i, epis. 16, l. 24.

11
Shame arises from the fear of men, conscience from the fear of God.
SAMUEL JOHNSON. (REYNOLDS, *Recollections of Johnson*.)

12
There smites nothing so sharp, nor smelleth so sour, As shame.
WILLIAM LANGLAND, *Piers Plowman*. Pt. xi.

13
The worst kind of shame is being ashamed of frugality or poverty. (Pessimus quidem pudor vel est parsimoniæ vel frugalitatis.)
LIVY, *History*. Bk. xxxiv, sec. 4.

14
Where shame is, there is fear.
MILTON, *Church Government*. Ch. 3.

Here shame dissuades him, there his fear prevails,
And each by turns his aching heart assails.
OVID, *Metamorphoses*. Bk. iii, 73. (Addison, tr.)

15
What shame forbade me speak, Love bade me write. (Dicere quæ puduit, scribere jussit amor.)
OVID, *Heroides*. Epis. iv, l. 10.

16
It is easier to bear shame than annoyance. (Nimio id quod pudet facilius fertur quam illud quod piget.)
PLAUTUS, *Pseudolus*, l. 281. (Act i, sc. 3.)

17
No penance can absolve our guilty fame;
Nor tears, that wash out sin, can wash out shame.
MATTHEW PRIOR, *Henry and Emma*, l. 312.

18
There is hope of salvation where shame reproaches a man. (Spes est salutis ubi hominem objurgat pudor.)
PUBLILIUS SYRUS, *Sententiæ*. No. 633.

Where there is yet shame, there may in time be virtue.
SAMUEL JOHNSON, *Works*. Vol. x, p. 319.

19
Shame, when once 'tis gone, knows no return. (Et qui redire cum perit nescit pudor.)
SENECA, *Agamemnon*, l. 113.

Past shame once, and past all amendment.
JOHN REDFORD, *Wit and Science*, 840. (c. 1530)

Past shame, past grace.
JOHN RAY, *Changes of World*, 214. (1692)

Shame leaves us by degrees.
SAMUEL DANIEL, *Complaint of Rosamond*. St. 64.

20
Shame hath a bastard fame, well managed;
Ill deeds are doubled with an evil word.
SHAKESPEARE, *The Comedy of Errors*, iii, 2, 19.

O shame! where is thy blush? Rebellious hell,
If thou canst mutine in a matron's bones,
To flaming youth let virtue be as wax,
And melt in her own fire: proclaim no shame
When the compulsive ardour gives the charge,
Since frost itself as actively doth burn,
And reason panders will.
SHAKESPEARE, *Hamlet*. Act iii, sc. 4, l. 82.

All is confounded, all!
Reproach and everlasting shame
Sits mocking in our plumes.
SHAKESPEARE, *Henry V.* Act iv, sc. 5, l. 3.

1
Makest thou this shame thy pastime?
SHAKESPEARE, *King Lear.* Act ii, sc. 4, l. 5.

Must I hold a candle to my shames?
SHAKESPEARE, *The Merchant of Venice.* Act ii, sc. 6, l. 41.

2 He was not born to shame:
Upon his brow shame is ashamed to sit.
SHAKESPEARE, *Romeo and Juliet.* Act iii, sc. 2, l. 91.

Shame and dishonour sit
By his grave ever;
Blessing shall hallow it,—
Never, O never!
SCOTT, *Marmion.* Canto iii, st. 11.

3
We live in an atmosphere of shame. We are ashamed of everything that is real about us; ashamed of ourselves, of our relatives, of our incomes, of our accents, of our opinions, of our experience, just as we are ashamed of our naked skins.
BERNARD SHAW, *Man and Superman.* Act i.

4
In shame there is no comfort, but to be beyond all bounds of shame.
SIR PHILIP SIDNEY, *Arcadia.* Bk. ii.

5
The most curious offspring of shame is shyness.
SYDNEY SMITH, *Lecture on the Evil Affections.*

As sheepish as a fox captured by a fowl. (Honteux comme un renard qu'une poule aurait pris.)
LA FONTAINE, *Fables.* Bk. i, fab. 18.

6
Shame is shame, whether thou think'st or not.
STOBÆUS, *Florilegium.* Pt. v, l. 82.

7
He is without sense of shame or glory, as some men are without the sense of smelling.
SWIFT, *Character of Lord Wharton.*

8
I never wonder to see men wicked, but I often wonder not to see them ashamed.
SWIFT, *Thoughts on Various Subjects.*

9
They say sin touches not a man so near
As shame a woman; yet he too should be
Part of the penance, being more deep than she
Set in the sin.
SWINBURNE, *Tristram of Lyonesse: The Sailing of the Swallow,* l. 360.

Shame, that stings sharpest of the worms in hell.
SWINBURNE, *Marino Faliero.* Act ii, sc. 1.

10
Shame is the eldest daughter of uncleanness.
JEREMY TAYLOR, *Holy Living.* Ch. ii, sec. 3.

11
Deep in his heart boils overwhelming shame. (Æstuat ingens Imo in corde pudor.)
VERGIL, *Æneid.* Bk. x, l. 870.

12
I have known all evils; virtue can surmount them, but what generous heart can endure shame? (J'ai connu tous les maux, la vertu les surmonte; Mais quel cœur généreux peut supporter la honte?)
VOLTAIRE, *Zulime.* Act i, sc. 5.

13
Shame followed shame—and woe supplanted woe—
Is this the only change that time can show?
WORDSWORTH, *Poems Dedicated to National Independence.* Pt. i, No. 28.

SHAMROCK, see Ireland

SHEEP AND SHEPHERD

I—Sheep: Apothegms

14
Till now I thought the proverb did but jest
Which said a black sheep is a biting beast.
THOMAS BASTARD, *Chrestoleros.* Bk. iv, ep. 20. (1598)

The black sheep is a perilous beast.
UNKNOWN, *Six Ballads.* No. 4. (c. 1550)

Even now, now, very now, an old black ram
Is tupping your white ewe.
SHAKESPEARE, *Othello.* Act i, sc. 1, l. 88.

15
Every sheep with its fellow. (Cada oveja con su pareja.)
CERVANTES, *Don Quixote. See also* BIRDS OF A FEATHER.

16
As soon goeth the young lambskin to the market as the old ewe's.
JOHN HEYWOOD, *Proverbs.* Pt. ii, ch. 4.

As soon comes the lamb's skin to market as the auld tup's.
SCOTT, *Bride of Lammermoor.* Ch. 4.

17
The scab of one sheep, or the mange of one pig, destroys an entire herd. (Grex totus in agris Unius scabie cadit.)
JUVENAL, *Satires.* Sat. ii, l. 79.

One scabbed sheep infecteth all the fold.
HILLS, *Common-place Book,* p. 129. (c. 1530)

One sickly sheep infects the flock,
And poisons all the rest.
ISAAC WATTS, *Against Evil Company.*

I am a tainted wether of the flock,
Meetest for death
SHAKESPEARE, *The Merchant of Venice.* Act iv, sc. 1, l. 114.

18
Other sheep I have, which are not of this fold: them also I must bring, and they shall hear my voice; and there shall be one fold and one shepherd.
New Testament: John, x, 16.

There were ninety-and-nine that safely lay
In the shelter of the fold;
But one was out in the hills away,
Far off from the gates of gold,—

Away in the mountains wild and bare,
Away from the tender Shepherd's care.
ELIZABETH CLEPHANE, *The Lost Sheep.*

De massa ob de sheepfol',
Dat guards de sheepfol' bin,
Look out in de gloomerin' meadows,
Wha'r de long night rain begin—
So he call to de hirelin' shepa'd,
"Is my sheep, is dey all come in?—
My sheep, is dey all come in?"
SARAH P. MCLEAN GREENE, *De Sheepfol'.*

1
As sheep that have not a shepherd.
Old Testament: I Kings, xxii, 17.

2
And before him shall be gathered all nations: and he shall separate them one from another, as a shepherd divideth his sheep from the goats.
New Testament: Matthew, xxv, 32.

3
The mountain sheep are sweeter,
But the valley sheep are fatter;
We therefore deemed it meeter
To carry off the latter.
T. L. PEACOCK, *War Song of Dinas Vawr.* (*Misfortunes of Elphin.* Ch. 11.)

4
It is the nature of sheep always to follow the first, wheresoever it goes; which makes Aristotle, lib. 9, *de Hist. Animal.* mark them for the most silly and foolish animals in the world.
RABELAIS, *Works.* Bk. iv, ch. 8.

One sheep follows another.
JOHN RAY, *English Proverbs.*

One sheep will leap the ditch when another goes first.
SCOTT, *Old Mortality.* Ch. 36.

Sheep follow sheep.
The Talmud. Sec. 62.

5
As good be hanged for a sheep as a lamb.
JOHN RAY, *English Proverbs. See also under* HANGING.

6
Then will he look as fierce as a Cotswold lion.
NICHOLAS UDALL, *Ralph Roister Doister.* Act iv, sc. 6 (1566). *See also under* LION.

7
Little Bo-peep has lost her sheep,
And can't tell where to find them;
Leave them alone, and they'll come home,
Wagging their tails behind them.
UNKNOWN, *Bo-peep.*

II—Sheep and Wolf

8
It is hard to have wolf full and wether whole.
CHAUCER, *Troilus and Criseyde.* Bk. iv, l. 1373.

9
The death of the wolf is the health of the sheep.
JOHN FLORIO, *First Fruites.* Fo. 31.

10
The dust raised by the sheep does not choke the wolf.
THOMAS FULLER, *Gnomologia.* No. 4491.

11
He that will be made a sheep shall find wolves enough.
GABRIEL HARVEY, *Works.* Vol. ii, p. 38. Quoted as a proverb.

He that makes himself a sheep shall be eat by the wolf.
GEORGE HERBERT, *Jacula Prudentum.*

Make yourselves sheep and the wolves will eat you.
BENJAMIN FRANKLIN, *Poor Richard.* Quoted as an Italian proverb.

He that makes himself a sheep will find that the wolves are not all dead.
C. H. SPURGEON, *John Ploughman.* Ch. 4.

12
He that will needs be a sheep, cannot greatly grudge to be bitten with a fox.
BRIAN MELBANCKE, *Philotinus.* Sig. Bb4. (1583)

He that will make himself a sheep, it is no matter though the wolves do eat him.
BARNABE RICH, *Irish Hubbub,* 4. (1619)

13
It is a foolish sheep that makes the wolf his confessor.
JOHN RAY, *English Proverbs,* 23.

14
You have entrusted the sheep to the wolf. (Lupo ovem commisisti.)
TERENCE, *Eunuchus,* l. 832. (Act v, sc. 1.)

III—Shepherd

15
Sooth 't were a pleasant life to lead,
With nothing in the world to do
But just to blow a shepherd's reed,
The silent season thro',
And just to drive a flock to feed,—
Sheep—quiet, fond and few!
LAMAN BLANCHARD, *Dolce far Niente.* St. 1.

16
In summer's heat, and winter's cold,
He fed his flock, and penn'd the fold.
JOHN GAY, *Fables: Introduction.*

17
For kings have often fears when they do sup,
Where shepherds dread no poison in their cup.
ROBERT GREENE, *The Shepherd's Wife's Song.*

The shepherd's homely curds,
His cold thin drink out of his leather bottle,
His wonted sleep under a fresh tree's shade,
All which secure and sweetly he enjoys,
Is far beyond a prince's delicates,
His viands sparkling in a golden cup,
His body couched in a curious bed,
When care, mistrust, and treason waits on him.
SHAKESPEARE, *III Henry VI.* Act ii, sc. 5, l. 47.

18
My name is Norval; on the Grampian hills
My father feeds his flocks; a frugal swain,

Whose constant cares were to increase his store.
And keep his only son, myself, at home.
JOHN HOME, *Douglas.* Act ii, sc. 1.

1
And every shepherd tells his tale
Under the hawthorn in the dale.
MILTON, *L'Allegro*, l. 67. "Tells his tale": i. e., counts his sheep.

2
Sleepest or wakest thou, jolly shepherd?
Thy sheep be in the corn;
And for one blast of thy minikin mouth,
Thy sheep shall take no harm.
SHAKESPEARE, *King Lear.* Act iii, sc. 6, l. 42.

3
My flocks feed not,
My ewes breed not,
My rams speed not,
All is amiss.
SHAKESPEARE [?], *The Passionate Pilgrim*, l. 245.

SHELLEY, PERCY BYSSHE

4
In his poetry, as well as in his life, Shelley was indeed "a beautiful and *ineffectual* angel, beating in the void his luminous wings in vain."
ARNOLD, *Literature and Dogma: Shelley.*

5
Ah, did you once see Shelley plain,
And did he stop and speak to you,
And did you speak to him again?
How strange it seems and new!
ROBERT BROWNING, *Memorabilia.*

6
For they who shrank from his mad human ache
Call him high Shelley now and praise his wake.
ALFRED KREYMBORG, *A Man Whom Men Deplore.*

7
Knight-errant of the Never-ending Quest,
And Minstrel of the Unfulfilled Desire;
For ever tuning thy frail earthly lyre
To some unearthly music.
HENRY VAN DYKE, *Shelley.*

8
Shelley, lyric lord of England's lordliest singers, here first heard
Ring from lips of poets crowned and dead the Promethean word
Whence his soul took fire, and power to outsoar the sunward-soaring bird.
A. C. SWINBURNE, *Eton: An Ode.*

9
'Tis no mean fortune to have heard
A singer who, if errors blurred
His sight, had yet a spirit stirred
By vast desire,
And ardour fledging the swift word
With plumes of fire.
WILLIAM WATSON, *Shelley's Centenary.*

All the rapturous heart of things
Throbs through his own.
WILLIAM WATSON, *Shelley's Centenary.*

10
Shelley, the hectic, flamelike rose of verse,
All colour, and all odour, and all bloom,
Steeped in the moonlight, glutted with the sun,
But somewhat lacking root in homely earth.
WILLIAM WATSON, *To Edward Dowden*, l. 46.

SHERIDAN, RICHARD BRINSLEY

11
Good at a fight, but better at a play;
Godlike in giving, but the devil to pay.
BYRON, *On a Cast of Sheridan's Hand.*

12
The flash of Wit, the bright Intelligence,
The beam of Song, the blaze of Eloquence,
Set with their Sun, but still have left behind
The enduring produce of immortal Mind;
Fruits of a genial morn, and glorious noon,
A deathless part of him who died too soon.
BYRON, *On the Death of Sheridan*, l. 27.

The matchless dialogue, the deathless wit,
Which knew not what it was to intermit;
The glowing portraits, fresh from life, that bring
Home to our hearts the truth from which they spring;
These wondrous beings of his Fancy, wrought
To fulness by the fiat of his thought. . . .
Long shall we seek his likeness—long in vain,
And turn to all of him which may remain,
Sighing that Nature form'd but one such man,
And broke the die—in moulding Sheridan.
BYRON. *On the Death of Sheridan*, l. 49.

See also under PERFECTION.

13
Whose mind was an essence, compounded with art
From the finest and best of all other men's pow'rs:—
Who rul'd, like a wizard, the world of the heart,
And could call up its sunshine, or bring down its show'rs:—
Whose humour, as gay as the fire-fly's light,
Play'd round every subject, and shone as it play'd;—
Whose wit, in the combat, as gentle as bright,
Ne'er carried a heart-stain away on its blade.
THOMAS MOORE, *On the Death of Sheridan*, l. 37.

SHIP

See also Sea

I—Ship: Apothegms

14
He holds him with his skinny hand,
"There was a ship," quoth he.
S. T. COLERIDGE, *The Ancient Mariner.* Pt. i.

14a
Everything was 'ship-shape and Bristol fashion.'
R. H. DANA, *Two Years Before the Mast.* Ch 22. (1840)

15
Yet never ship upon the sea
Bears blessed merchandise for me.
JOHN DRINKWATER, *Vigil.*

If all the ships I have at sea
Should come a-sailing home to me,
Ah, well! the harbor would not hold
So many ships as there would be
If all my ships came home from sea.
ELLA WHEELER WILCOX, *My Ships.*

1
The true ship is the ship builder.
EMERSON, *Essays, First Series: Of History.*

2
A great ship asks deep waters.
GEORGE HERBERT, *Jacula Prudentum.*

3
To be in the same boat. (Ταῦτ' ἐμοὶ ζυγὸν τρίβεις.)
HERODAS, *Sententiæ*, vi, 12.

Therefore the sinner and the saint
Are often in the selfsame boat.
EDWARD WARD, *Nuptial Dialogues.* Pt. ii, l. 360.

4
Women are jealous of ships. They always suspect the sea. They know they're three of a kind when it comes to a man.
EUGENE O'NEILL, *Mourning Becomes Electra.* Act i.

Ships, young ships,
I do not wonder men see you as women—
You in the white length of your loveliness
Reclining on the sea!
SALLY BRUCE KINSOLVING, *Ships.*

5
Who wishes to give himself an abundance of trouble, let him equip these two things, a ship and a woman. No two things involve more bother, for neither is ever sufficiently adorned.
PLAUTUS, *Pœnulus,* l. 210. (Act i, sc. 2.)

A ship is ever in need of repairing.
JOHN TAYLOR, *A Navy of Landships.*

6
Let our barks across the pathless flood
Hold different courses.
SCOTT, *Kenilworth.* Ch. 29.

7
It would have been as though he were in a boat of stone with masts of steel, sails of lead, ropes of iron, the devil at the helm, the wrath of God for a breeze, and hell for his destination.
EMORY A. STORRS, *Speech,* Chicago, 1866, referring to President Johnson, who had threatened to use troops to compel Congress to adjourn.

8
Your ships are the wooden walls.
THEMISTOCLES, interpreting an oracle received by the Athenians. (HERODOTUS, *History.* Bk. vii, sec. 143.)

The wooden wall alone shall remain unconquered. (*τεῖχος ξύλινον.*)
The second reply of the Pythian oracle to the Athenians, 480 B.C. (HERODOTUS, *History.* Bk. vii, sec. 141.)

The credit of the Realm, by defending the same with Wooden Walls, as Themistocles called the Ships of Athens.
LINSCHOTEN. *London: Preface.*

There's not a ship that sails the ocean,
But every climate, every soil,
Must bring its tribute, great or small,
And help to build the wooden wall!
LONGFELLOW, *Building of the Ship,* l. 66.

See also ENGLAND: BRITANNIA RULES THE WAVES

9
The ships rest upon the beach. (Stant littore puppes.)
VERGIL, *Æneid.* Bk. vi, l. 901.

10
One ship drives east and another drives west
With the self-same winds that blow,
'Tis the set of the sails and not the gales
Which tells us the way to go.
ELLA WHEELER WILCOX, *Winds of Fate.*

II—Ship: Description

11
But the ships, they carries me long, long ways,
An' draws far places near.
J. J. BELL, *On the Quay.*

12
Gray sail against the sky,
Gray butterfly!
Have you a dream for going,
Or are you only the blind wind's blowing?
DANA BURNET, *A Sail at Twilight.*

13
She walks the waters like a thing of life,
And seems to dare the elements to strife.
BYRON, *The Corsair.* Canto i, st. 3.

She bears her down majestically near,
Speed on her prow, and terror in her tier.
BYRON, *The Corsair.* Canto iii, st. 15.

14
And ships were drifting with the dead
To shores where all was dumb!
THOMAS CAMPBELL, *The Last Man,* l. 19.

Ships that sailed for sunny isles,
But never came to shore.
THOMAS KIBBLE HERVEY, *The Devil's Progress.*

A capital ship for an ocean trip
Was "The Walloping Window-blind";
No gale that blew dismayed her crew
Or troubled the captain's mind.
CHARLES EDWARD CARRYL, *The Walloping Window-blind.* (From *Davy and the Goblin,* p. 89.)

15
Till next day, There she lay,
In the Bay of Biscay, O!
ANDREW CHERRY, *The Bay of Biscay, O!*

16
As ships, becalmed at eve, that lay
With canvas drooping, side by side,
Two towers of sail at dawn of day
Are scarce long leagues apart descried.
ARTHUR HUGH CLOUGH, *Qua Cursum Ventus.*

17
All in the Downs the fleet was moor'd.
JOHN GAY, *Sweet William's Farewell.*

18
For she *is* such a smart little craft,
Such a neat little, sweet little craft—
Such a bright little, Tight little,

Slight little, Light little,
Trim little, slim little craft!
W. S. GILBERT, *Ruddigore*. Act ii.

1
This is the ship of pearl, which, poets feign,
Sails the unshadowed main,—
The venturous bark that flings
On the sweet summer wind its purpled wings.
O. W. HOLMES, *The Chambered Nautilus*.

2
Scarce one tall frigate walks the sea
Or skirts the safer shores
Of all that bore to victory
Our stout old Commodores.
O. W. HOLMES, *At a Dinner to Farragut*.

Ships,
Fraught with the ministers and instruments
Of cruel war.
SHAKESPEARE, *Troilus and Cressida: Prologue*.

This new Katterfelto, his show to complete,
Means his boats should all sink as they pass by our fleet;
Then as under the ocean their course they steer right on,
They can pepper their foes from the bed of old Triton.
HENRY KIRKE WHITE, *The Wonderful Juggler*. (1803) An anticipation of the submarine.

3
There be triple ways to take, of the eagle or the snake,
Or the way of a man with a maid;
But the sweetest way to me is a ship's upon the sea,
In the heel of the North-East Trade.
RUDYARD KIPLING, *The Long Trail*.

The Liner she's a lady, an' she never looks nor 'eeds—
The Man-o'-War's 'er 'usband, an' 'e gives 'er all she needs;
But, oh, the little cargo-boats, that sail the wet seas roun',
They're just the same as you an' me a-plyin' up an' down!
RUDYARD KIPLING, *The Liner She's a Lady*.

Lord, Thou hast made this world below the shadow of a dream,
An', taught by time, I tak' it so—exceptin' always Steam.
From coupler-flange to spindle-guide I see Thy Hand, O God—
Predestination in the stride o' yon connectin'-rod.
KIPLING, *M'Andrew's Hymn*, l. 1.

4
Build me straight, O worthy Master!
Stanch and strong, a goodly vessel
That shall laugh at all disaster,
And with wave and whirlwind wrestle!
LONGFELLOW, *The Building of the Ship*, l. 1.

She starts,—she moves,—she seems to feel
The thrill of life along her keel!
LONGFELLOW, *The Building of the Ship*, l. 349.

5
And the wind plays on those great sonorous harps, the shrouds and masts of ships.
LONGFELLOW, *Hyperion*. Bk. i, ch. 7.

6
Long since, when all the docks were filled
With that sea beauty man has ceased to build.
JOHN MASEFIELD, *Ships*.

7
The barge she sat in, like a burnish'd throne,
Burn'd on the water: the poop was beaten gold;
Purple the sails, and so perfumed that
The winds were love-sick with them; the oars were silver,
Which to the tune of flutes kept stroke, and made
The water which they beat to follow faster,
As amorous of their strokes.
SHAKESPEARE, *Antony and Cleopatra*. Act ii, sc. 2, l. 196.

8
She comes majestic with her swelling sails,
The gallant Ship; along her watery way,
Homeward she drives before the favouring gales;
Now flirting at their length the streamers play,
And now they ripple with the ruffling breeze.
SOUTHEY, *Sonnets*. No. xix.

Thou bring'st the sailor to his wife,
And travell'd men from foreign lands,
And letters unto trembling hands:
And, thy dark freight, a vanish'd life.
TENNYSON, *In Memoriam*. Pt. x.

9
And the stately ships go on
To their haven under the hill.
TENNYSON, *Break, Break, Break*. St. 3.

10
Ships dim-discovered dropping from the clouds.
THOMSON, *The Seasons: Summer*, l. 946.

11
Whoever you are, motion and reflection are especially for you,
The divine ship sails the divine sea for you.
WALT WHITMAN, *Song of the Rolling Earth*.

12
Speed on the ship! But let her bear
No merchandise of sin,
No groaning cargo of despair
Her roomy hold within;
No Lethean drug for Eastern lands,
Nor poison-draught for ours;
But honest fruits of toiling hands
And Nature's sun and showers.
WHITTIER, *The Ship-Builders*.

SHIPWRECK

13
What matter in what wreck we reached the shore,

So we both reached it?

WILFRID SCAWEN BLUNT, *To One Who Would Make a Confession.*

1

He perhaps reads of a shipwreck on the coast of Bohemia.

EDMUND BURKE, *On the Sublime and Beautiful:* Pt. i, *Introduction.*

2

Then rose from sea to sky the wild farewell!
Then shriek'd the timid, and stood still the brave;
Then some leap'd overboard with dreadful yell,
As eager to anticipate their grave;
And the sea yawn'd around her like a hell,
And down she suck'd with her the whirling wave.

BYRON, *Don Juan.* Canto ii, st. 52.

He sinks into thy depths with bubbling groan.

BYRON, *Childe Harold.* Canto iv, st. 179.

A solitary shriek—the bubbling cry
Of some strong swimmer in his agony.

BYRON, *Don Juan.* Canto ii, st. 53.

But hark! what shriek of death comes in the gale,
And in the distant ray what glimmering sail
Bends to the storm?—Now sinks the note of fear!
Ah! wretched mariners!—no more shall day
Unclose his cheering eye to light ye on your way!

ANN RADCLIFFE, *Mysteries of Udolpho: Shipwreck.*

3

Let us think of them that sleep,
Full many a fathom deep,
By thy wild and stormy steep,
Elsinore!

THOMAS CAMPBELL, *Battle of the Baltic.*

4

He who will not be ruled by the rudder, must be ruled by the rock.

ISAAC D'ISRAELI, *Curiosities of Literature.* Vol. ii, p. 454.

5

And for a winding sheet a wave,
I had, and all the ocean for my grave.

DRYDEN, *The Conquest of Granada.* Pt. ii, act ii, sc. 1. (1670)

A lady that was drowned at sea and had a wave for her winding sheet.

GEORGE VILLIERS, *The Rehearsal.* (1671)

6

The ship hangs hovering on the verge of death,
Hell yawns, rocks rise, and breakers roar beneath! . . .
In vain the cords and axes were prepared,
For every wave now smites the quivering yard;
High o'er the ship they throw a dreadful shade,
Then on her burst in terrible cascade. . . .
Again she plunges! hark! a second shock
Bilges the splitting vessel on the rock—
Down on the vale of death, with dismal cries,
The fated victims shuddering cast their eyes. . . .
Ah Heaven!—behold her crashing ribs divide!
She loosens, parts, and spreads in ruin o'er the tide.

WILLIAM FALCONER, *The Shipwreck.* Canto iii, l. 610.

"We are lost!" the captain shouted,
As he staggered down the stairs.

JAMES THOMAS FIELDS, *Ballad of the Tempest.*

7

He who has suffered shipwreck, fears to sail
Upon the seas, though with a gentle gale.

ROBERT HERRICK, *Shipwreck.*

8

When Crew and Captain understand each other to the core,
It takes a gale and more than a gale to put their ship ashore.

RUDYARD KIPLING, *"Together."*

9

And fast through the midnight dark and drear,
Through the whistling sleet and snow,
Like a sheeted ghost, the vessel swept
Tow'rds the reef of Norman's Woe.

LONGFELLOW, *The Wreck of the Hesperus.*

10

Each man makes his own shipwreck. (Naufragium sibi quisque facit.)

LUCAN, *De Bello Civili.* Bk. i, l. 503. Said of sailors leaping from a wreck into the sea.

They make glorious shipwreck who are lost in seeking worlds.

LESSING. (Quoted by Emerson, *Journals*, 1867.)

11

Down, down beneath the deep,
That oft in triumph bore him,
He sleeps a sound and peaceful sleep,
With the salt waves dashing o'er him.

HENRY FRANCIS LYTE, *The Sailor's Grave.*

Sleep on, sleep on, thou mighty dead!
A glorious tomb they've found thee;
The broad blue sky above thee spread,
The boundless ocean round thee.

HENRY FRANCIS LYTE, *The Sailor's Grave.*

Kings have no such couch as thine,
As the green that folds thy grave.

TENNYSON, *A Dirge.* St. 6.

12

It was that fatal and perfidious bark,
Built in th' eclipse, and rigg'd with curses dark,
That sunk so low that sacred head of thine.

MILTON, *Lycidas,* l. 100.

13

Like ships that have gone down at sea,
When heaven was all tranquillity!

THOMAS MOORE, *Lalla Rookh: The Light of the Harem,* l. 189.

14

I have seen a man drowned in the sea who laughed at shipwreck, and I said, "Never was the wave more just." (Vidi ego naufragium qui risit in æquora mergi, Et "numquam" dixi "justior unda fuit.")

OVID, *Tristia*. Bk. v, eleg. 8, l. 11.

1

He wrongly accuses Neptune, who makes shipwreck a second time. (Improbe Neptunum accusat, qui iterum naufragium facit.)

PUBLILIUS SYRUS, *Sententiæ*. No. 264.

2

To make shipwreck in port. (Naufragium in portu facere.)

QUINTILIAN, *De Institutione Oratoria*. Bk. xii, sec. 23. Quoted as a proverb.

3

No dust have I to cover me,
My grave no man may show;
My tomb is this unending sea,
And I lie far below.
My fate, O stranger, was to drown;
And where it was the ship went down
Is what the sea-birds know.

E. A. ROBINSON, *Inscription by the Sea*. (From the *Greek Anthology*.)

A sailor buried on this shore
Bids you set sail.
For many a gallant bark, when I was lost,
Weathered the gale.

EVELYN BARING, LORD CROMER, *From the Greek Anthology*.

4

Though his bark cannot be lost,
Yet it shall be tempest-tost.

SHAKESPEARE, *Macbeth*. Act i, sc. 3, l. 24.

5

'Tis double death to drown in ken of shore.

SHAKESPEARE, *The Rape of Lucrece*, l. 1114.

Lord, Lord! methought, what pain it was to drown!
What dreadful noise of waters in mine ears!
What ugly sights of death within mine eyes!
Methought I saw a thousand fearful wrecks;
Ten thousand men that fishes gnaw'd upon;
Wedges of gold, great anchors, heaps of pearl,
Inestimable stones, unvalued jewels,
All scatter'd in the bottom of the sea:
Some lay in dead men's skulls; and, in those holes
Where eyes did once inhabit, there were crept,
As 't were in scorn of eyes, reflecting gems.

SHAKESPEARE, *Richard III*. Act i, sc. 4, l. 21.

The wills above be done! but I would fain die a dry death.

SHAKESPEARE, *The Tempest*. Act i, sc. 1, l. 67.

6

My son i' the ooze is bedded; and
I'll seek him deeper than e'er plummet sounded
And with him there lie mudded.

SHAKESPEARE, *The Tempest*. Act iii, sc. 3, l. 100.

Deeper than did ever plummet sound.

SHAKESPEARE, *The Tempest*. Act v, sc. 1, l. 56.

7

Here and there they are seen swimming in the vast flood. (Apparent rari nantes in gurgite vasto.)

VERGIL, *Æneid*. Bk. i, l. 118.

8

Or, shipwrecked, kindles on the coast
False fires, that others may be lost.

WORDSWORTH, *To the Lady Fleming*, l. 69.

9

I made a prosperous voyage when I suffered shipwreck.

ZENO, referring to the fact that he was shipwrecked on a voyage from Phœnicia to Peiræus, and so came to Athens, where he studied philosophy under Crates. (DIOGENES LAERTIUS, *Zeno*. Bk. vii, sec. 4.)

10

A common shipwreck is a consolation to all. (Commune naufragium omnibus est consolatio.)

UNKNOWN. A Latin proverb. *See also* MISERY LOVES COMPANY.

SHOE

11

"Who are you?" said the stocking to the shoe.
Said the shoe to the stocking,
"How terribly shocking,
For such as you to say to a shoe,
Who are you?"

ANGE FAGNANO, *Strife*.

12

Or, if thee list not wait for dead men's shoon.

BISHOP JOSEPH HALL, *Satires*. Bk. ii, sat. 5. (1597)

He that looks after dead-men's shoes, may chance to go barefoot.

JAMES MABBE, *Celestina*, 24. (1631)

13

Now for good luck, cast an old shoe after me.

JOHN HEYWOOD, *Proverbs*. Pt. i, ch. 9. (1546) *See also* 1226:17, under LUCK.

14

Let not the shoe be too large for the foot.

LUCIAN, *Pro Imaginibus*. Sec. 10.

Let firm, well hammer'd soles protect thy feet
Thro' freezing snows, and rains, and soaking sleet.
Should the big last extend the shoe too wide,
Each stone will wrench the unwary step aside;
The sudden turn may stretch the swelling vein,
The cracking joint unhinge, or ankle sprain;
And when too short the modish shoes are worn,
You 'll judge the seasons by your shooting corn.

JOHN GAY, *Trivia*. Bk. i, l. 33.

I was not made of common calf,
Nor ever meant for country loon;
If with an axe I seem cut out,
The workman was no cobbling clown;
A good jack boot with double sole he made,
To roam the woods, or through the rivers wade.

GIUSEPPE GIUSTI, *The Chronicle of the Boot*.

15

My galligaskins, that have long withstood
The winter's fury, and encroaching frosts,
By time subdued (what will not time subdue!),
A horrid chasm disclosed.

JOHN PHILIPS, *The Splendid Shilling*, l. 121.

16

We ought not to treat living creatures like

shoes or pots and pans, which, when worn with use, we throw away.
PLUTARCH, *Lives: Marcus Cato*. Ch. 5, sec. 5.

1
No one of you can tell me where my shoe pinches.
PLUTARCH, *Lives: Æmilius Paulus*. Ch. 5, sec. 2. Relating the story of a Roman, who made this response to friends who demanded why he had divorced his wife without apparent cause.

Each knows where the shoe pinches him. (Cada uno sabe donde la aprieta el Zapato.)
CERVANTES, *Don Quixote*. Pt. i, ch. 32.

But I wot best where wringeth me my shoe.
CHAUCER, *The Marchantes Tale*, l. 309.

Those who wear the shoe know best where it pinches.
C. H. SPURGEON, *John Ploughman*. Ch. 16.

Others may guess where the shoe wrings, besides him that wears it.
JOHN LYLY, *Euphues*, p. 413.

2
You cannot put the same shoe on every foot.
PUBLILIUS SYRUS, *Sententiæ*. No. 596.

All shoes fit not all feet.
THOMAS D'URFEY, *Quixote*. Act v, sc. 2.

All feet tread not in one shoe.
GEORGE HERBERT, *Jacula Prudentum*. No. 493.

For still when all is said the rule stands fast
That each man's shoe be made on his own last.
(Metiri se quemque suo modulo ac pede verum est.)
HORACE, *Epistles*. Bk. i, epis. 7, l. 98. (Conington, tr.)

To each foot its own shoe. (A chaque pied son soulier.)
MONTAIGNE, *Essays*. Bk. iii, ch. 13.

3
'Tis the same to him who wears a shoe, as if the whole earth were covered with leather.
EMERSON, *Conduct of Life: Wealth*. Quoted as a Persian proverb.

4
Hark! the boy calls thee to his destin'd stand,
And the shoe shines beneath his oily hand.
JOHN GAY, *Trivia*. Bk. ii, l. 101.

5
One said he wondered that leather was not dearer than any other thing. Being demanded a reason: because, saith he, it is more stood upon than any other thing in the world.
WILLIAM HAZLITT, *Shakespeare Jest Books: Conceits, Flashes and Whimzies*. No. 86.

6
The shoe will hold with the sole.
JOHN HEYWOOD, *Proverbs* Pt. ii, ch. 5. (1546.)

Who should hold with the shoe but the sole?
UNKNOWN *Peddler's Prophecy*, l. 730. (1595)

7
Oh, where did hunter win
So delicate a skin
For her feet?
You lucky little kid,
You perished, so you did,
For my sweet.
F LOCKER-LAMPSON, *To My Mistress's Boots*.

8
And put
My clouted brogues from off my feet.
SHAKESPEARE, *Cymbeline*. Act iv, sc. 2, l. 213.

9
Tip at the toe, live to see woe;
Wear at the side, live to be a bride;
Wear at the ball, live to spend all;
Wear at the heel, live to save a deal.
UNKNOWN, *The Wear of Shoes*. Old rhyme.

SHOEMAKER

10
I do not think that shoemaker a good workman who makes a great shoe for a little foot.
AGESILAUS THE GREAT, to one commending an orator for his skill in amplifying petty matters. (PLUTARCH, *Laconic Apothegms*.)

11
Let not the cobbler go above his last. (Ne sutor supra crepidam.)
APELLES. He was in the habit of hanging his pictures where they could be seen by the passers-by, and listening to their comments. One day a shoemaker criticised the shoes in a certain picture, and found next day that they had been repainted. Proud of his success as a critic, he began to find fault with the thigh of the figure, when Apelles called out from behind the canvas, "Shoemaker, don't go above your last!" (Sutor, ne supra crepidam judicaret. PLINY THE ELDER, *Historia Naturalis*. Bk. xxxv, ch. 10, sec. 36.) Lucian tells the same story of Phidias.

Let not the cobbler go beyond his last. (Ne sutor ultra crepidam.)
ERASMUS, quoting the proverb in the form generally used And the usual rendering is, of course, "Cobbler, stick to your last."

Remember, cobbler, to keep to your leather. (Memento, in pellicula, cerdo, tenere tua.)
MARTIAL, *Epigrams* Bk. iii, p. 16, l. 6.

Do you not perceive that you are speaking beyond your hammer? (Non sentis, inquit, te ultra malleum loqui?)
ATHENÆUS, to a blacksmith criticising music.

The title of Ultracrepidarian critics has been given to those persons who find fault with small and insignificant details.
WILLIAM HAZLITT, *Table Talk* Essay xxii.

12
'Tis a maxim with me, that an hale cobbler is a better man than a sick king
ISAAC BICKERSTAFFE, *Love in a Village* Act i, sc. 5.

13
Him that makes shoes goes barefoot himself.
ROBERT BURTON, *Anatomy of Melancholy: Democritus to the Reader*

When we see a man with bad shoes, we say it is no wonder, if he is a shoemaker. (Quand

nous voyons un homme mal chaussé, nous disons que ce n'est pas merveille, s'il est chaussetier.)
MONTAIGNE, *Essays*. Bk. i, ch. 24.

Who is worse shod than the shoemaker's wife?
JOHN HEYWOOD, *Proverbs*. Pt. i, ch. 11.

1
Ye tuneful cobblers! still your notes prolong,
Compose at once a slipper and a song;
So shall the fair your handiwork peruse,
Your sonnets sure shall please—perhaps your shoes.
BYRON, *English Bards and Scotch Reviewers*, l. 791.

2
A man cannot make a pair of shoes *rightly* unless he do it in a devout manner.
THOMAS CARLYLE, *Letter to Erskine*, 22 Oct., 1842.

3
A shoemaker's son is a prince born.
THOMAS DELONEY, *The Gentle Craft*. Ch. 9.

4
The shoemaker makes a good shoe because he makes nothing else.
EMERSON, *Letters and Social Aims: Greatness*.

5
Mock not the cobbler for his black thumbs.
THOMAS FULLER, *The Holy and the Profane State: Of Jesting*.

6
Oh, her heart's adrift with one
On an endless voyage gone!
Night and morning
Hannah's at the window binding shoes.
LUCY LARCOM, *Hannah Binding Shoes*.

7
I am but, as you would say, a cobbler. . . . Truly, sir, all that I live by is with the awl. . . . I am indeed, sir, a surgeon to old shoes; when they are in great danger I recover them. As proper men as ever trod upon neat's leather have gone upon my handiwork.
SHAKESPEARE, *Julius Cæsar*. Act i, sc. 1, l. 9.

Hans Grovendraad, an honest clown,
By cobbling in his native town,
Had earned a living ever.
His work was strong and clean and fine,
And none who served at Crispin's shrine
Was at his trade more clever.
JAN VAN RYSWICK, *Hans Grovendraad*. (F. W. Ricord, tr.)

8
When boots and shoes are torn up to the lefts,
Cobblers must thrust their awls up to the hefts.
NATHANIEL WARD, *The Simple Cobbler of Aggawam in America*. Title page.

9
Marry, because you have drank with the King,
And the King hath so graciously pledg'd you,
You shall no more be call'd shoemakers,
But you and yours, to the world's end,
Shall be call'd the Trade of the Gentle Craft.
ROBERT GREENE (?), *George-a-Greene*, sig. F 4b. (a. 1592) The king referred to was Edward IV, who, in one of his disguises, is said to have drunk with a party of shoemakers and pledged them. The term, "gentle craft," probably arose from the legend that St. Crispin, after he left Rome for Soissons to preach Christianity, supported himself by shoemaking.

I'll . . . fall to my old trade of the gentle craft the cobbler.
ROBERT WILSON, *Cobbler's Prophecy*, l. 1677. (1594)

Brave shoemakers, all gentlemen of the gentle craft.
THOMAS DEKKER, *The Shoemaker's Holiday*. Act iii, sc. 1. (1600)

When young of Crispin's gentle craft by trade.
EDWARD WARD, *History of the Grand Rebellion*. Pt. iii, l. 464.

SIGH

10
The sighing of a contrite heart.
Book of Common Prayer: Litany.

11
Had sighed to many, though he loved but one.
BYRON, *Childe Harold*. Canto i, st. 5.

12
And sighed, and wept, and said no more.
CHAUCER, *Chaucer's Dream*, l. 931. Usually attributed to Chaucer, but probably spurious. The line is borrowed from Alan de Lisle (or de Insulis), *De Planctu Naturæ*.

Sigh'd and look'd, and sigh'd again.
DRYDEN, *Alexander's Feast*, l. 120.

Sighed and looked unutterable things.
THOMSON, *The Seasons: Summer*, l. 1188.

13
Not such sorrowful sighs as men make
For woe, or else when that folk be sick,
But easy sighs, such as been to like.
CHAUCER, *Troilus and Criseyde*. Bk. iii, l. 1361.

And easy sighs, such as folk draw in love.
HENRY HOWARD, *Prisoner in Windsor*.

14
Drew a long, long sigh, and wept a last adieu!
COWPER, *On the Receipt of My Mother's Picture*, l. 30.

15
To sigh, yet not recede; to grieve, yet not repent.
GEORGE CRABBE, *Tales of the Hall*. Bk. iii.

To sigh, yet feel no pain.
THOMAS MOORE, *The Blue Stocking*. Song ii.

16
When he is here, I sigh with pleasure—
When he is gone, I sigh with grief.
W. S. GILBERT, *The Sorcerer*. Act i.

17
The sigh that rends thy constant heart
Shall break thy Edwin's too.
GOLDSMITH, *A Ballad: The Hermit*. (*Vicar of Wakefield*. Ch. 8.)

18
Implores the passing tribute of a sigh.
THOMAS GRAY, *Elegy Written in a Country Church-yard*, l. 80.

1
My soul has rest, sweet sigh! alone in thee.
PETRARCH, *To Laura in Death*. Sonnet liv.

Oh, if you knew the pensive pleasure
That fills my bosom when I sigh,
You would not rob me of a treasure
Monarchs are too poor to buy.
SAMUEL ROGERS, *To* ——. St. 2.

Sighs
Which perfect Joy, perplex'd for utterance,
Stole from her sister Sorrow.
TENNYSON, *The Gardener's Daughter*, l. 249.

2
Speed the soft intercourse from soul to soul,
And waft a sigh from Indus to the Pole.
POPE, *Eloisa to Abelard*, l. 57.

3
Words may be false and full of art;
Sighs are the natural language of the heart.
THOMAS SHADWELL, *Psyche*. Act iii.

4
He raised a sigh so piteous and profound,
That it did seem to shatter all his bulk
And end his being.
SHAKESPEARE, *Hamlet*. Act ii, sc. 1, l. 94.

5
A plague of sighing and grief! it blows a man up like a bladder.
SHAKESPEARE, *I Henry IV*. Act ii, sc. 4, l. 364.

6
Hushed be that sigh, be dry that tear,
Nor let us lose our Heaven here.
SHERIDAN, *Dry Be That Tear*.

7
Never sigh, but send.
SWIFT, *Polite Conversation*. Dial. 1.

SIGHT

See also Eyes

8
By heaven! it is a splendid sight to see.
BYRON, *Childe Harold*. Canto i, st. 40.

It was a thing to see, not hear.
BYRON, *Parisina*. St. 14.

A sight to dream of, not to tell!
S. T. COLERIDGE, *Christabel*. Pt. i, l. 253.

A sight to delight in.
SOUTHEY, *The Cataract of Lodore*, l. 68.

A sight to make an old man young.
TENNYSON, *The Gardener's Daughter*, l. 140.

9
How inferior for *seeing* with, is your brightest train of fireworks to the humblest farthing candle!
CARLYLE, *Essays: Diderot*.

10
What you see, yet cannot see over, is as good as infinite.
CARLYLE, *Sartor Resartus*. Bk. ii, ch. 1.

11
You can see farther into a millstone than he.
CERVANTES, *Don Quixote*. Pt. ii, ch. 28.

I can see as far into the mill-stone as the best of you.
DRYDEN, *Amphitryon*. Act v. (1690)

She had seen far in a millstone.
JOHN HEYWOOD, *Proverbs*. Pt. i, ch. 10. (1546)

12
The sense of sight is the keenest of all our senses. (Acerrimum ex omnibus nostris sensibus esse sensum videndi.)
CICERO, *De Oratore*. Bk. ii, l. 87.

The sight of a man hath the force of a lion.
GEORGE HERBERT, *Jacula Prudentum*. No. 613.

13
We see through a glass, darkly.
New Testament: I Corinthians, xiii, 12.

14
One man does not see everything. (Εἷς δ' ἀνὴρ οὐ πάνθ' ὁρᾷ.)
EURIPIDES, *Phœnissæ*, l. 745.

I see much, but I say little, and do less.
JOHN HEYWOOD, *Proverbs*. Pt. i, ch. 11.

15
What went ye out into the wilderness to see? A reed shaken with the wind? But what went ye out for to see? A man clothed in soft raiment?
New Testament: Matthew, xi, 7; *Luke*, vii, 24.

16
Then purg'd with euphrasy and rue
The visual nerve, for he had much to see.
MILTON, *Paradise Lost*. Bk. xi, l. 414.

18
They come to see, they come to be seen. (Spectatum veniunt, veniunt spectentur ut ipsæ.)
OVID, *Ars Amatoria*. Bk. i, l. 99.

She who is eager to see is eager also to be seen.
CERVANTES, *Don Quixote*, Pt. ii, ch. 49.

And for to see, and eke for to be seen.
CHAUCER, *Wife of Bath's Prologue*, l. 552.

Come chiefly but to see, and to be seen.
SIR JOHN HARINGTON, *Of Going to Bathe*. (*Epigrams*. Bk. i, epig. 58.)

We are persons of quality, I assure you, and women of fashion, and come to see and to be seen.
BEN JONSON, *The Staple of News: Induction*.

As many more Crowd round the door,
To see them going to see it.
THOMAS HOOD, *Miss Kilmansegg: Her Fancy Ball*.

19
Seeing is believing. (Pluris est oculatus testis unus, quam auriti decem.)
PLAUTUS, *Truculentus*. Act ii, sc. 6; FARQUHAR, *The Recruiting Officer*. Act iv, sc. 3. (1706)

20
The longer we live the more strange sights we see.
JOHN RAY, *Proverbs: Scottish*.

21
The greatest thing a human soul ever does in this world is to see something. Hundreds of people can talk for one who thinks, but thou-

sands can think for one who can see. To see clearly is poetry, prophecy and religion all in one.

RUSKIN, *Modern Painters*. Vol. iii, pt. iv, ch. 16.

There is only one way of seeing things rightly, and that is, seeing the whole of them.

JOHN RUSKIN, *The Two Paths*. Lecture 2.

1 O, woe is me,
To have seen what I have seen, see what I see!

SHAKESPEARE, *Hamlet*. Act iii, sc. 1, l. 168.

2 My business in this state
Made me a looker on here in Vienna.

SHAKESPEARE, *Measure for Measure*, v, 1, 318.

3
Better see rightly on a pound a week than squint on a million.

BERNARD SHAW, *Plays, Pleasant and Unpleasant: Preface.*

4
The Spanish fleet thou canst not see—because—
It is not yet in sight!

SHERIDAN, *The Critic*. Act ii, sc. 2. OUT OF SIGHT OUT OF MIND, *see under* ABSENCE.

For any man with half an eye
What stands before him may espy;
But optics sharp it needs I ween,
To see what is not to be seen.

JOHN TRUMBULL, *McFingal*. Canto i, l. 67.

5
The sight of you is good for sore eyes.

SWIFT, *Polite Conversation*. Dial. i.

A sight for sair een.

JOHN WILSON, *Noctes Ambrosianæ*, 3 Oct., 1825.

6
Seeing I saw not, hearing not I heard;
Tho', if I saw not, yet they told me all
So often that I speak as having seen.

TENNYSON, *The Princess*. Pt. vi, l. 3.

7
We see things not as they are, but as we are.

H. M. TOMLINSON, *Out of Soundings*, p. 149.

7a
All of which, most piteous, I saw, and much of which I was. (Quæque ipse miserrima vidi, et quorum pars magna fui.)

VERGIL, *Æneid*. Bk. ii, l. 5.

SILENCE

I—Silence: Definitions

8
Silence is gain to many of mankind. (Πολλοῖς γάρ ἐστι κέρδος ἡ σιγὴ βροτῶν.)

ÆSCHYLUS, *Prometheus*. Frag. 103.

Silence is a healing for all ailments.

Babylonian Talmud: Megillah, p. 18a.

9
Silence is the virtue of fools, so he rightly said to the silent man: "If you are wise, you are a fool; if you are a fool, you are wise."

BACON, *De Augmentis Scientiarum: Loquacitas.*

Silence is the wit of fools. (Le silence est l'esprit des sots.)

LA BRUYÈRE, *Les Caractères: Conversation.*

10
Silence is the eternal duty of man.

CARLYLE, *Inaugural Address at Edinburgh.*

Silence, the great Empire of Silence: higher than all stars; deeper than the Kingdom of Death! It alone is great; all else is small.

CARLYLE, *Heroes and Hero-Worship*. Lect. vi.

Silence is the element in which great things fashion themselves together.

CARLYLE, *Sartor Resartus*. Bk. iii, ch. 3.

11
The uttered part of a man's life, let us always repeat, bears to the unuttered, unconscious part a small unknown proportion.

CARLYLE, *Essays: Memoirs of the Life of Scott.*

Of every noble work the silent part is best
Of all expression that which cannot be expressed.

W. W. STORY, *The Unexpressed.*

12
Silence is the mother of Truth.

BENJAMIN DISRAELI, *Tancred*. Bk. iv, ch. 4.

13
The ancient sentence said, Let us be silent for so are the gods. Silence is a solvent that destroys personality, and gives us leave to be great and universal.

EMERSON, *Essays, First Series: Intellect.*

14
Silence is true wisdom's best reply.

EURIPIDES, *Fragments*. Frag. 947.

Silence is man's chief learning. ('Η μεγάλη παίδευσις ἐν ἀνθρώποισι σιωπή.)

PALLADAS. (*Greek Anthology*. Bk. x, epig. 46.)

Aurispa nothing writes though learn'd, for he
By a wise silence seems more learn'd to be.

JANUS PANNONIUS, *On Aurispa.*

15
Stillborn silence! thou that art
Flood-gate of the deeper heart!

RICHARD FLECKNOE, *Silence.*

16
Silence is one great art of conversation. He is not a fool who knows when to hold his tongue.

WILLIAM HAZLITT, *Characteristics*. No. 59.

Silence and modesty are very valuable qualities in the art of conversation. (Le silence et la modestie sont qualités très commodes à la conversation.)

MONTAIGNE, *Essays*. Bk. i, ch. 25.

That silence is one of the great arts of conversation is allowed by Cicero himself, who says, there is not only an art, but even an eloquence in it.

HANNAH MORE, *Essays on Various Subjects: Thoughts on Conversation.*

17
Silence is strength. (Qui silet, est firmus.)

OVID, *Remediorum Amoris*, l. 697.

Love silence, even in the mind; for thoughts are to that as words are to the body, troublesome: much speaking, as much thinking, spends. True silence is the rest of the mind; and it is to the spirit what sleep is to the body, nourishment and refreshment.

WILLIAM PENN, *Advice to His Children.*

1
Silence is the soul of war.
MATTHEW PRIOR, *Ode in Imitation of Horace.*

2
Silence is the perfectest herald of joy: I were but little happy. if I could say how much.
SHAKESPEARE, *Much Ado About Nothing.* Act ii, sc. 1, l. 317.

3
Silence is the gratitude of true affection.
SHERIDAN, *Pizarro.* Act ii, sc. 1.

II—Silence: Apothegms

4
Deep vengeance is the daughter of deep silence. (Alta vendetta D'alto silenzio è figlia.)
ALFIERI, *La Congiura de' Pazzi.* Act i, sc. 1.

Silent people are dangerous. (Les gens sans bruit sont dangereux.)
LA FONTAINE, *Fables.* Bk. vii, fab. 23.

O have a care of natures that are mute!
GEORGE MEREDITH, *Modern Love.* St. 35.

Silent anguish is the more dangerous. (La douleur qui se tait n'en est que plus funeste.)
RACINE, *Andromaque.* Act iii, sc. 3.
See also GRIEF: SILENT AND VOCAL.

5
The silence of the people is a lesson for kings. (Le silence du peuple est la leçon des rois.)
BEAUVAIS, *Funeral Oration for Louis XV.*

6
I kept silence, yea even from good words; but it was pain and grief to me.
Book of Common Prayer: Psalter: Psalms, xxxix, 3.

7
Lo, I am silent and curb my mouth. (Ἰδοὺ σιωπῶ κἀπιλάζυμαι στόμα.)
EURIPIDES, *Andromache,* l. 250.

Keep shut the doors of thy mouth even from the wife of thy bosom.
The Talmud.
See also under MOUTH.

8
Silence is fine jewel for a woman, but it's little worn.
THOMAS FULLER, *Gnomologia.* No. 4166.

9
Silence is become his mother-tongue.
GOLDSMITH, *The Good-Natured Man.* Act ii.

10
The most silent people are generally those who think most highly of themselves.
WILLIAM HAZLITT, *Characteristics.* No. 91.

11
If the crow could feed in silence, he would have more meat and much less quarreling and envy. (Sed tacitus pasci si posset corvus, haberet Plus dapis et rixæ multo minus invidiæque.)
HORACE, *Epistles.* Bk. i, epis. 17, l. 50.

12
Not much talk—a great, sweet silence.
HENRY JAMES, *A Bundle of Letters.* Letter 4.

13
She shall be as mute as a fish.
JOHN MELTON, *Astrologaster,* 38. (1620)

"Dumb as a drum with a hole in it, sir," replied Sam.
DICKENS, *Pickwick Papers.* Ch. 25.

14
Eternal silence be their doom.
MILTON, *Paradise Lost.* Bk. vi, l. 385.

15
Mum is counsel.
JOHN PALSGRAVE, *Acolastus.* Sig. B2. (1540)

I will say nought but mum, and mum is counsel.
JOHN HEYWOOD, *Proverbs.* Pt. ii, ch. 5. (1546)

Mum's the word.
GEORGE COLMAN THE YOUNGER, *Battle of Hexham.* Act ii, sc. 1. (c. 1789)

But mum's the word; least said is soonest mended.
THOMAS COGAN, *John Buncle, Junior,* i, 237.

Little said is soon amended.
WRIGHT, *Songs: Philip and Mary.* (c. 1555)

And I oft have heard defended,—
Little said is soonest mended.
GEORGE WITHER, *The Shepherd's Hunting.*

16
Hesiod might as well have kept his breath to cool his pottage.
PERIANDER. (PLUTARCH, *Morals: The Banquet of the Seven Wise Men.*)

Spare your breath to cool your porridge.
CERVANTES, *Don Quixote.* Pt. ii, ch. v.; RABELAIS, *Works.* Bk. v, ch. 28.

I'll keep my breath to cool my porridge.
THOMAS DELONEY, *Gentle Craft.* Pt. ii, ch. 3. (c. 1598) In frequent use thereafter.

But if I get among the glum
I hold my tongue to tell the troth,
And keep my breath to cool my broth.
JOHN BYROM, *Careless Content.*

17
Bekker is silent in seven languages. (Bekker schweigt in sieben Sprachen.)
SCHLEIERMACHER. (ZELTER, *Letter to Goethe,* 15 Mar., 1830.)

18
To silence another, first be silent yourself. (Alium silere quod voles, primus sile.)
SENECA, *Hippolytus,* l. 876.

19
Silence is taught by life's many misfortunes. (Tacere multis discitur vitæ malis.)
SENECA, *Thyestes,* l. 319.

20
The rest is silence.
SHAKESPEARE, *Hamlet.* Act v, sc. 2, l. 369.

21
Silence is only commendable
In a neat's tongue dried and a maid not vendible.
SHAKESPEARE, *The Merchant of Venice.* Act i, sc. 1, l. 111.

1
Out of this silence yet I pick'd a welcome.
SHAKESPEARE, *A Midsummer-Night's Dream.* Act v, sc. 1, l. 100.

2
They froze me into silence.
SHAKESPEARE, *Timon of Athens.* Act ii, sc. 2, l. 222.

3
Is it a party in a parlour?
Cramm'd just as they on earth were cramm'd—
Some sipping punch, some sipping tea,
But, as you by their faces see,
All silent and all damn'd!
WORDSWORTH, *Peter Bell,* l. 516, in original edition, 1819; omitted from later editions.

III—Silence Gives Consent

4
I keep silence because I approve the plan. (Νῦν δ' ἡσυχίαν ἄγειν . . . ἀλλὰ τὴν γνώμην ἐπαινῶν.)
ARISTIDES. (PLUTARCH, *Lives: Aristides,* 8, 6.)

5
Silence gives consent. (Qui tacet, consentire videtur.)
Canon Law: Decretals. Bk. v, ch. 12, sec. 43. The favorite maxim of Pope Boniface VIII.

Silence, madam, consents.
JOHN LYLY, *Endymion.* Act v, sc. 3. (1591)

Silence gives consent.
GOLDSMITH, *The Good-Natured Man.* Act ii. (1768) In common use thereafter.

6
His silence answers yes. (Φησὶν σιωπῶν.)
EURIPIDES, *Orestes,* l. 1592.

Thy very silence is confession. (Αὐτὸ δὲ τὸ σιγᾶν ὁμολογοῦντός ἐστί σου.)
EURIPIDES, *Iphigenia at Aulis,* l. 1142.

7
She half consents who silently denies.
OVID, *Helen to Paris.* (Dryden, tr.)

He that is still seemeth as he granteth.
THOMAS USK, *Testament of Love.* (c. 1387)

Whoso holdeth him still doth assent.
UNKNOWN, *Partonope,* 467. (c. 1490)

8
But that you shall not say I yield being silent,
I would not speak.
SHAKESPEARE, *Cymbeline.* Act ii, sc. 3, l. 99.

8a
One manner of consent is, when a man is still and telleth not.
JOHN WYCLIFFE, *Selected Works,* iii, 349. (c. 1380)

This proverb was said full long ago: 'Who so holdeth him still doth assent.'
UNKNOWN, *Partonope,* 467. (c. 1490)

IV—Silence: Its Virtues

9
Silence may do good, and can do little harm.
RICHARD BRATHWAITE, *English Gentleman,* 51. (1630)

Silence seldom hurts.
THOMAS FULLER, *Gnomologia.* No. 4170.

10
It is harmful to no one to have been silent. (Nulli tacuisse nocet.)
DIONYSIUS CATO, *Disticha de Moribus,* i, 12.

11
If you will still live at ease,
Hear and see, and hold your peace.
JOHN FLORIO, *Second Frutes,* Fo. 101. (1591)

Hear, see, and be silent, if you wish to live in peace. (Audi, vide, tace, si vis vivere in pace.)
UNKNOWN, *Gesta Romanorum: Folliculus.*

12
There is likewise a reward for faithful silence. (Est et fideli tuta silentio Merces.)
HORACE, *Odes.* Bk. iii, ode 2, l. 25.

13
Silence is as full of potential wisdom and wit as the unhewn marble of great sculpture.
ALDOUS HUXLEY, *Point Counter Point,* p. 10.

14
Silence is the safest role for the man who distrusts himself. (Le silence est le parti le plus sûr de celui qui se défie de soi-même.)
LA ROCHEFOUCAULD, *Maximes.* No. 79.

15
In silence God brings all to pass. ("Απαντα σιγῶν ὁ θεὸς ἐξεργάζεται.)
MENANDER, *Fragments.* No. 818.

16
All things, save silence only, bring repentance. (Μόνη σιωπὴ μεταμέλειαν οὐ θέρει.)
MENANDER, *Fragments.* No. 1105.

Be silent and safe—silence never betrays you.
J. B. O'REILLY, *Rules of the Road.* St. 2.

17
Let a fool hold his tongue and he will pass for a sage. (Taciturnitas stulto homini pro sapientia est.)
PUBLILIUS SYRUS, *Sententiæ.* No. 914.

Even a fool, when he holdeth his peace, is counted wise.
Old Testament: Proverbs, xvii, 28.

18
Wise men say nothing in dangerous times.
JOHN SELDEN, *Table-Talk: Wisdom.*

V—Silence: Its Eloquence

19
Silence never shows itself to so great an advantage, as when it is made the reply to calumny and defamation.
ADDISON, *The Tatler.* No. 133.

The best apology against false accusers is silence and sufferance, and honest deeds set against dishonest words.
MILTON, *Apology for Smectymnuus: Intro.*

And *I* too talk, and lose the touch
I talk of. Surely, after all,
The noblest answer unto such
Is kindly silence when they brawl.
TENNYSON, *The After Thought.* (*Punch,* 7 March, 1846.) Altered in the published poems to: "Is perfect stillness when they brawl."

20
Silence is more eloquent than words.
CARLYLE, *Heroes and Hero-Worship.* Lect. ii.

There are moments when silence, prolong'd and unbroken,
More expressive may be than all words ever spoken.

OWEN MEREDITH, *Lucile*. Pt. ii, canto 1, st. 20.

Well-timed silence hath more eloquence than speech.

M. F. TUPPER, *Proverbial Philosophy: Of Discretion.*

1

The silent organ loudest chants
The master's requiem.

EMERSON, *Dirge*. Last lines.

2

There is the silent criticism of silence, worth all the rest.

HELPS, *Friends in Council*. Bk. ii, ch. 2.

3

Silence that spoke, and eloquence of eyes.

HOMER, *Iliad*. Bk. xiv, l. 252. (Pope, tr.)

When they hold their tongues they cry out (*i.e.* their silence is eloquent). (Cum tacent clamant.)

CICERO, *In Catilinam*. No. i, sec. 8.

Even silence may be eloquent in love.

CONGREVE, *The Old Batchelor*. Act ii, sc. 2.

Silence in love bewrays more woe
Than words, though ne'er so witty:
A beggar that is dumb, you know,
May challenge double pity.

SIR WALTER RALEIGH, *The Silent Lover*. St. 9.

4

There is an eloquent silence: it serves sometimes to approve, sometimes to condemn; there is a mocking silence; there is a respectful silence.

LA ROCHEFOUCAULD, *Réflexions Diverses:* Pt. iv, *De la Conversation.*

5

Why, know you not soul speaks to soul?
I say the use of words shall pass—
Words are but fragments of the glass,
But silence is the perfect whole.

JOAQUIN MILLER, *Why, Know You Not?*

Grant me the power of saying things
Too simple and too sweet for words.

COVENTRY PATMORE, *The Angel in the House*. Bk. i, canto i, prelude 1.

6

I'll speak to thee in silence.

SHAKESPEARE, *Cymbeline*. Act v, sc. 4, l. 29.

See also under FACE.

7

The silence often of pure innocence
Persuades when speaking fails.

SHAKESPEARE, *Winter's Tale*. Act ii, sc. 2, l. 41.

8

Come then, expressive Silence, muse His praise.

THOMSON, *A Hymn on the Seasons*, l. 118.

VI—Silence and Speech

9

Both silent, when there is need, and speaking in season. (Σιγῶν θ' ὅπου δεῖ καὶ λέγων τὰ καίρια.)

ÆSCHYLUS, *Prometheus*, Frag. 118.

It is a great thing to know the season for speech and the season for silence. (Magna res est vocis et silentii tempora nosse.)

SENECA, *De Moribus*. Sec. 74.

There is a time of speaking and a time of being still.

WILLIAM CAXTON, *Charles the Grete*, 56. (1485)

Let him now speak, or else hereafter for ever hold his peace.

Book of Common Prayer: Solemnization of Matrimony.

Now speak, Or be for ever silent.

MASSINGER, *The Duke of Milan*. Act iv, sc. 3.

10

"Dost thou now at length think me a philosopher?" To which he bitingly replied, "I would have thought thee one if thou hadst held thy peace." (Intellexeram si tacuisses.)

BOËTHIUS, *Philosophiæ Consolationis*. Bk. ii, prosa 7. Hence the phrase, "Si tacuisses, philosophus mansisses," If you had been silent, you would have remained a philosopher.

Better to remain silent and be thought a fool than to speak out and remove all doubt.

ABRAHAM LINCOLN. (*Golden Book*, Nov., 1931.)

An ignorant man is wisest if he remains silent, hiding his speech like a disgraceful disease.

PALLADAS. (*Greek Anthology*.) Bk. x, epig. 98.

Do you wish people to think well of you? Don't speak. (Voulez-vous qu'on croie du bien de vous? n'en dites pas.)

PASCAL, *Pensées*. Appendix to ch. 29, No. 15.

If thou wouldst be known a wise man, let thy words show thee so; if thou doubt thy words, let thy silence feign thee so. It is not a greater point of wisdom to discover knowledge than to hide ignorance.

FRANCIS QUARLES, *Enchiridion*. Cent. iii, No. 57.

O my Antonio, I do know of these,
That therefore only are reputed wise,
For saying nothing.

SHAKESPEARE, *The Merchant of Venice*, i, 1, 95.

11

An event has happened, upon which it is difficult to speak, and impossible to be silent.

EDMUND BURKE, *Impeachment of Warren Hastings*, 5 May, 1789.

12

Under all speech that is good for anything there lies a silence that is better. Silence is deep as Eternity; Speech is shallow as Time.

CARLYLE, *Essays: Memoirs of the Life of Scott.*

Speech is great, but silence is greater.

CARLYLE, *Characteristics of Shakespeare.*

As the Swiss inscription says: *Sprechen ist silbern, Schweigen ist golden*—Speech is silvern, Silence is golden; or, as I might rather express it, Speech is of Time, Silence is of Eternity.

CARLYLE, *Sartor Resartus*. Bk. iii, ch. 3.

Silence sweeter is than speech.

DINAH M. M. CRAIK, *Magnus and Morna*. Sc. 3.

Speech is better than silence; silence is better than speech.
EMERSON, *Essays, Second Series: Nominalist and Realist.*

Silence more musical than any song.
CHRISTINA ROSSETTI, *Sonnet: Rest.*

The dark is at the end of every day,
And silence is the end of every song.
E. A. ROBINSON, *Woman and the Wife.*

1
When you have nothing to say, say nothing.
C. C. COLTON, *Lacon: Reflections.* No. 183.

2
Let thy speech be better than silence, or be silent.
DIONYSIUS THE ELDER, *Fragments* Frag 6.

Be silent or let thy words be worth more than silence.
PYTHAGORAS. (STOBÆUS, *Florilegium* Pt.34,l 7.)

3
There are some silent people who are more interesting than the best talkers.
BENJAMIN DISRAELI, *Endymion.* Ch. 35.

4
Speech is often barren, but silence also does not necessarily brood over a full nest.
GEORGE ELIOT, *Felix Holt.* Ch. 16.

5
Not able to speak, but unable to hold his tongue. (Οὐ λέγειν δεινός, ἀλλὰ σιγᾶν ἀδύνατος.)
EPICHARMUS, *Fragments.* No. 272.

Though he could not speak, he could not be silent. (Qui cum loqui non posset, tacere non potuit.)
AULUS GELLIUS, *Noctes Atticæ.* Bk. i, ch. 15, sec. 16. Paraphrasing Epicharmus.

It is a sad thing when men have neither wit to speak well nor judgment to hold their tongues.
LA BRUYÈRE, *Les Caractères: Des Hommes.*

He must have leave to speak that cannot hold his tongue.
JOHN RAY, *English Proverbs.*
See also TONGUE: HOLDING THE TONGUE.

6
It is safer to keep silence than to speak. (Ἀσφαλέστερον γὰρ τοῦ λέγειν τὸ σιγᾶν.)
EPICTETUS [?], *Enchiridion.* Frag. 29.

7
Of the best society it used to be said: their speech instructs the mind, and their silence the feelings.
GOETHE, *Sprüche in Prosa.*

8
He that speaks sows, and he that holds his peace gathers.
GEORGE HERBERT, *Jacula Prudentum.*

He that speaks doth sow, he that holds his peace doth reap.
JOHN RAY, *English Proverbs,* 24.

9
Let every man be swift to hear, slow to speak, slow to wrath.
New Testament: James, i, 19.

10
You hesitate to stab me with a word,
And know not Silence is the sharper sword.
R. U. JOHNSON, *To One Who Has Forgotten.*

11
What shall I say to you? What can I say
Better than silence is?
LONGFELLOW, *Morituri Salutamus,* l. 128.

12
Silence is a very small virtue, but to speak what should not be uttered is a heinous crime. (Exigua est virtus præstare silentia rebus: At contra gravis est culpa tacenda loqui.)
OVID, *Ars Amatoria.* Bk. ii, l. 603.

13
Silence at the proper season is wisdom and better than any speech.
PLUTARCH. *Morals: On Education.*

Silence is wisdom, when speaking is folly.
THOMAS FULLER, *Gnomologia.* No. 4169.

14
Be silent always when you doubt your sense,
And speak, tho' sure, with seeming diffidence.
POPE, *Essay on Criticism.* Pt. iii, l. 7.

15
A man of virtue, judgment, and prudence speaks not until there is silence.
SADI, *The Gulistan.* Ch. 4, No. 7.

16
Be check'd for silence,
But never tax'd for speech.
SHAKESPEARE, *All's Well that Ends Well.* Act i, sc. 1, l. 76.

17
Anon, as patient as the female dove,
When that her golden couplets are disclosed,
His silence will sit drooping.
SHAKESPEARE, *Hamlet.* Act v, sc. 1, l. 309.

18
Silence after grievous things is good, . . .
For words divide and rend;
But silence is most noble till the end.
SWINBURNE, *Atalanta in Calydon: Chorus.*

Peace and be wise; no gods love idle speech.
SWINBURNE, *Atalanta in Calydon: Meleager.*

19
I have been breaking silence these twenty-three years and have hardly made a rent in it. Silence has no end; speech is but the beginning of it.
H. D. THOREAU, *Journal,* 9 Feb., 1841.

20
Fear oftentimes restraineth words,
But makes not thought to cease;
And he speaks best who hath the skill
When for to hold his peace.
THOMAS VAUX, *Of a Contented Mind.*

For many have been harmed by speech,—
Through thinking, few, or none.
THOMAS VAUX, *Of a Contented Mind.*

21
All were with one accord silent, and deeply attentive held their peace. (Conticuere omnes, intentique ora tenebant.)
VERGIL, *Æneid.* Bk. ii, l. 1.

Why do you compel me to break my deep silence? (Quid me alta silentia cogis Rumpere?)
VERGIL, *Æneid*. Bk. x, l. 63.

1 The sweet voice into silence went,
A silence which was almost pain.
WHITTIER, *The Grave by the Lake*. St. 45.

2 He knew the precise psychological moment when to say nothing.
OSCAR WILDE, *Picture of Dorian Gray*. Ch. 2.

3 I have often repented speaking, but never of holding my tongue. (Dixisse me aliquando pœnituit, tacuisse nunquam.)
XENOCRATES. (VALERIUS MAXIMUS, *Annals*. Bk. vii, ch. 2, sec. 7.) Plutarch attributes the saying to Simonides.

I have often regretted having spoken, never having kept silent. (Sæpius locutum, nunquam me tacuisse Pœnitet.)
PUBLILIUS SYRUS, *Sententiæ*. No. 1070.

We often repent of what we have said, but never, never, of that which we have not.
THOMAS JEFFERSON, *Writings*. Vol. xiv, p. 117.

We seldom repent talking too little, but very often talking too much.
LA BRUYÈRE, *Les Caractères: Des Hommes*.

4 A wise old owl sat on an oak,
The more he saw the less he spoke;
The less he spoke the more he heard;
Why aren't we like that wise old bird?
EDWARD HERSEY RICHARDS, *A Wise Old Owl*. Quoted by John D. Rockefeller, Sr., and used by Calvin Coolidge as motto over the fireplace of his home at Northampton, Mass.

VII—Silence: Stillness

5 Three things are ever silent—Thought, Destiny, and the Grave.
BULWER-LYTTON, *Harold*. Bk. x, ch. 2.

There be
Three silent things:
The falling snow . . . the hour
Before the dawn . . . the mouth of one
Just dead.
ADELAIDE CRAPSEY, *Triad*.

Three Silences there are: the first of speech,
The second of desire, the third of thought.
LONGFELLOW, *The Three Silences of Molinos*.

Silence! Oh well are Death and Sleep and Thou
Three brethren named.
SHELLEY, *Fragment: To Silence*.

There are haunters of the silence, ghosts that hold the heart and brain.
MADISON CAWEIN, *Haunters of the Silence*.

And they three passed over the white sands, between the rocks, silent as the shadows.
S. T. COLERIDGE, *The Wanderings of Cain*.

6 All Heaven and Earth are still, though not in sleep,
But breathless, as we grow when feeling most.
BYRON, *Childe Harold*. Canto iii, st. 89.

There was silence deep as death;
And the boldest held his breath.
THOMAS CAMPBELL, *Battle of the Baltic*. St. 2.

7 The splendor of Silence,—of snow-jeweled hills and of ice.
INGRAM CROCKETT, *Orion*.

8 O golden Silence, bid our souls be still,
And on the foolish fretting of our care
Lay thy soft touch of healing unaware!
JULIA CAROLINE RIPLEY DORR, *Silence*.

Remember what peace there may be in silence.
MAX EHRMANN, *Desiderata*.

9 An horrid stillness first invades the ear,
And in that silence we the tempest fear.
DRYDEN, *Astræa Redux*, l. 7.

10 And silence, like a poultice, comes
To heal the blows of sound.
O. W. HOLMES, *The Music-Grinders*. St. 10.

11 There is a silence where hath been no sound,
There is a silence where no sound may be,
In the cold grave—under the deep deep sea,
Or in wide desert where no life is found.
THOMAS HOOD, *Sonnet: Silence*.

12 Noiseless as fear in a wide wilderness.
JOHN KEATS, *The Eve of St. Agnes*. St. 28.

13 Thou foster-child of Silence and slow Time.
JOHN KEATS, *Ode on a Grecian Urn*, l. 2.

14 Hoeder, the blind old god
Whose feet are shod with silence.
LONGFELLOW, *Tegnér's Drapa*. St. 6.

15 I have known the silence of the stars and of the sea,
And the silence of the city when it pauses,
And the silence of a man and a maid, . . .
And the silence for which music alone finds the word.
EDGAR LEE MASTERS, *Silence*.

16 Silence sleeping on a waste of ocean.
PERCY SOMERS PAYNE, *Rest*.

17 Ha! no more moving? Still as the grave.
SHAKESPEARE, *Othello*. Act v, sc. 2, l. 93.

I will be silent as the grave.
HENRY BROOKE, *Marriage Contract*. Act i, sc. 2.

18 It takes a man to make a room silent.
H. D. THOREAU, *Journal*, 9 Feb., 1839.

19 Our noisy years seem moments in the being
Of the eternal Silence.
WORDSWORTH, *Intimations of Immortality*. 158.

The silence that is in the starry sky.
WORDSWORTH, *Song at the Feast of Brougham Castle*, l. 163.

SIMPLICITY

See also Life: The Simple Life

1
What is true, simple and sincere is most congenial to man's nature. (Quod verum, simplex, sincerumque sit, id esse naturæ hominis aptissimum.)
CICERO, *De Officiis*. Bk. i, ch. 4, sec. 13.

2
Elegant as simplicity, and warm as ecstasy.
COWPER, *Table Talk*, l. 588.

3
Hail! divine lady Simplicity, child of glorious Temperance, beloved by good men. All who practise righteousness venerate thy virtue.
CRATES, *Hymn to Simplicity*. (*Greek Anthology*. Bk. x, epig. 104.)

4
Nothing is more simple than greatness; indeed, to be simple is to be great.
EMERSON, *Nature, Addresses, and Lectures: Literary Ethics*.

The greatest truths are the simplest: and so are the greatest men.
J. C. AND A. W. HARE, *Guesses at Truth*.

And, as the greatest only are,
In his simplicity sublime.
TENNYSON, *Ode on the Death of the Duke of Wellington*, l. 33.

5
Generally nature hangs out a sign of simplicity in the face of a fool.
THOMAS FULLER, *The Holy and Profane States: Of Natural Fools*. Maxim 1.

How blessed are we that are not simple men!
SHAKESPEARE, *Winter's Tale*. Act iv, sc. 4, l. 771.

7
Oh! what a power has white simplicity!
KEATS, *Written on the Blank Space at the End of Chaucer's Tale of "The Flower and the Leaf."*

8
Cultivate simplicity, Coleridge.
CHARLES LAMB, to S. T. Coleridge. *See also* GRACE: THE GRACES.

9
Perfect simplicity is unconsciously audacious.
GEORGE MEREDITH, *The Ordeal of Richard Feverel*. Ch. 1.

10
Simplicity of character is no hindrance to subtlety of intellect.
JOHN MORLEY, *Life of Gladstone*. Vol. i, 194.

11
Simplicity, most rare in our age. (Ævo rarissima nostro, Simplicitas.)
OVID, *Ars Amatoria*. Bk. i, l. 241.

12
In Wit a man; Simplicity a child.
POPE, *Epitaph on Mr. Gay*, l. 2.

13
For never anything can be amiss
When simpleness and duty tender it.
SHAKESPEARE, *A Midsummer-Night's Dream*. Act v, sc. 1, l. 82.

Tongue-tied simplicity
In least speak most, to my capacity.
SHAKESPEARE, *A Midsummer-Night's Dream*. Act v, sc. 1, l. 104.

14
Simplicity and liberality, qualities which beyond a certain limit lead to ruin.
TACITUS, *Annals*. Bk. iii, sec. 1.

15
Blissful are the simple, for they shall have much peace.
THOMAS À KEMPIS, *De Imitatione Christi*. Pt. i, ch. 11.

Blessed simplicity. (Beata simplicitas.)
THOMAS À KEMPIS, *De Imitatione Christi*. Pt. iv, ch. 18.

O holy simplicity. (O sancta simplicitas!)
JOHN HUSS, *Last Words*, at the stake, 1415.

16
Simplicity, simplicity, simplicity! I say, let your affairs be as two or three, and not a hundred or a thousand. . . . Simplify, simplify.
H. D. THOREAU, *Walden*. Ch. 2.

In gloomy tones we need not cry:
"How many things there are to buy!"
Here is a thought for you and me:
"The best things in life are free." . . .
The more we look, the more we see
How many precious things are free.
The heart will find more than the eye
Of things we do not need to buy.
JOHN MARTIN, *These Things Are Free*.

17
Simplicity is a state of mind.
CHARLES WAGNER, *The Simple Life*. Ch. 2.

A man is simple when his chief care is the wish to be what he ought to be, that is honestly and naturally human.
CHARLES WAGNER, *The Simple Life*. Ch. 2.

18
Often ornateness goes with greatness;
Oftener felicity comes of simplicity.
WILLIAM WATSON, *Art Maxims*.

19
The art of art, the glory of expression and the sunshine of the light of letters, is simplicity.
WALT WHITMAN, *Leaves of Grass: Preface*.

SIN

See also Crime, Evil, Guilt, Offence, Vice, Wickedness

I—Sin: Definitions

20
This miry slough is such a place as cannot be mended; it is the descent whither the scum and filth that attends conviction for sin doth continually run, and therefore it is called the Slough of Despond.
JOHN BUNYAN, *Pilgrim's Progress*. Pt. i.

21
It is lawful for no one to sin. (Peccare nemini licet.)
CICERO, *Tusculanarum Disputationum*. Bk. v ch. 19, sec. 55.

1
That which we call sin in others is experiment for us.
EMERSON, *Essays, Second Series: Experience.*

Naught that delights is sin.
BEN JONSON, *Explorata.*

2
There is often a sin of omission as well as of commission. (Ἀδικεῖ πολλάκις ὁ μὴ ποιῶν τι, οὐ μόνον ὁ ποιῶν τι.)
MARCUS AURELIUS, *Meditations.* Bk. ix, sec. 5.

3
Nor custom, nor example, nor vast numbers
Of such as do offend, make less the sin.
MASSINGER, *The Picture.* Act iv, sc. 2, l. 1.

4
All that defiles comes from within. (Πᾶν τὸ λυμαινόμενόν ἐστιν ἔνδοθεν.)
MENANDER, *Fragments.* No. 540.

Our outward act is prompted from within,
And from the sinner's mind proceeds the sin.
MATTHEW PRIOR, *Henry and Emma,* l. 481.

Sin is a state of mind, not an outward act.
WILLIAM SEWELL, *Passing Thoughts on Religion: Wilful Sin.*

5
One who is free to sin, sins less; the very power weakens the seeds of sin. (Cui peccare licet, peccat minus; ipsa potestas Semina nequitiæ languidiora facit.)
OVID, *Amores.* Bk. iii, eleg. 4, l. 9.

Who's free to sin, sins less: the very power
Robs evildoing of its choicest flower.
OVID, *Amores,* iii, 4, 9. (King, tr.)

See also under PROHIBITION.

6
My sin is the black spot which my bad act makes, seen against the disk of the Sun of Righteousness.
C. H. PARKHURST, *Sermons: Pattern in the Mount.*

7
Sins in the regenerate are only the breaking forth of leaves in the trunk that is felled.
COVENTRY PATMORE. (CHAMPNEYS, *Memoirs.* Vol. ii, p. 75.)

8
It seems that sin is geographical. From this conclusion it is only a small step to the further conclusion that the notion of "sin" is illusory.
BERTRAND RUSSELL, *Sceptical Essays,* p. 16.

9
More men abstain from forbidden actions because they are ashamed of sinning, than because their inclinations are good. (Plures enim pudore peccandi quam bona voluntate prohibitis abstinent.)
SENECA, *Epistulæ ad Lucilium.* Epis. 83, 20.

It makes a great difference whether a person is unwilling to sin, or does not know how. (Multum interest utrum peccare aliquis nolit an nesciat.)
SENECA, *Epistulæ ad Lucilium.* Epis. 90, 46.

10
He does not sin who sins without intent. (Haut est nocens quicumque non sponte est nocens.)
SENECA, *Hercules Œtaeus,* l. 886.

Our compell'd sins
Stand more for number than for accompt.
SHAKESPEARE, *Measure for Measure.* Act ii, sc. 4, l. 57.

11
To say of shame—what is it?
Of virtue—we can miss it;
Of sin—we can but kiss it,
And it's no longer sin.
SWINBURNE, *Before Dawn.* St. 5.

II—Sin: Apothegms

12
Lay not this sin to their charge.
New Testament: Acts, vii, 60.

13
An original something, fair maid, you would win me
To write—but how shall I begin?
For I fear I have nothing original in me—
Excepting Original Sin.
THOMAS CAMPBELL, *To a Young Lady Who Asked Me to Write Something Original for Her Album.*

14
Here some are thinkin' on their sins,
An' some upo' their claes.
BURNS, *The Holy Fair,* l. 82.

16
Sin brought death, and death will disappear with the disappearance of sin.
MARY BAKER EDDY, *Science and Health,* p. 426.

17
Little sins make room for great, and one brings in all.
THOMAS EDWARDS, *Gangrene of Heresy.*

'Twas but one little drop of sin
We saw this morning enter in,
And lo! at eventide the world is drown'd.
JOHN KEBLE, *The Christian Year: Sexagesima.*

18
Every man carries the bundle of his sins
Upon his own back.
JOHN FLETCHER, *Rule a Wife and Have a Wife.* Act iv.

Each man shall bear his own sin without doubt.
WILLIAM MORRIS, *Life and Death of Jason.* Bk. xvii, l. 122.

19
Sin is not hurtful because it is forbidden, but it is forbidden because it is hurtful. Nor is a duty beneficial because it is commanded, but it is commanded because it is beneficial.
BENJAMIN FRANKLIN, *Poor Richard,* 1739.

20
Sin writes histories, goodness is silent. (Das Uebel macht eine Geschichte und das Gute keine.)
GOETHE. (RIEMER, *Mittheilungen über Goethe,* ii, 9.) *See also under* HISTORY.

1
The new shame of old sins.
JOHN GOWER, *Confessio Amantis.* Bk. vii.

Commit The oldest sins the newest kind of ways?
SHAKESPEARE, *II Henry IV.* Act iv, sc. 5, l. 126.

Sin, every day, takes out a new patent for some new invention.
E. P. WHIPPLE, *Essays: Romance of Rascality.*

The sins they sinned in Eden, boys,
Are bad enough for me.
CHRISTOPHER MORLEY, *A Glee Upon Cider.*

2
I do confess that I abhor and shrink
From schemes, with a religious willy-nilly,
That frown upon Saint Giles's sins, but blink
The peccadilloes of all Piccadilly.
THOMAS HOOD, *Ode to Rae Wilson,* l. 121.

3
Through sin do men reach the light.
ELBERT HUBBARD, *Epigrams.*

4
Woe unto them that draw iniquity with cords of vanity, and sin as it were with a cart rope!
Old Testament: Isaiah, v, 18.

5
Harm watch, harm catch.
BEN JONSON, *Bartholomew Fair.* Act v, sc. 3.

6
Custom in sin gives sin a lovely dye;
Blackness in Moors is no deformity.
MIDDLETON AND DEKKER, *The Honest Whore.* Pt. ii, act ii, sc. 1. *See also under* VICE.

7
Fixed as a habit or some darling sin.
JOHN OLDHAM, *A Letter from the Country.*

One little weakness, we are apt to fancy, all men must be allowed, and we even claim a certain indulgence for that apparent necessity of nature which we call our besetting *sin.*
HENRY DRUMMOND, *Natural Law in the Spiritual World,* p. 185.

8
See Sin in state, majestically drunk,
Proud as a peeress, prouder as a punk.
POPE, *Moral Essays.* Epis. ii, l. 69.

9
Fools make a mock at sin.
Old Testament: Proverbs, xiv, 9.

10
A sinful heart makes feeble hand.
SCOTT, *Marmion.* Canto vi, st. 31.

11
If we desire to judge all things justly, we must first persuade ourselves that none of us is without sin.
SENECA, *De Ira.* Bk. ii, sec. 28.

He that is without sin among you, let him cast the first stone.
New Testament: John, viii, 7.

12
We are all sinful. Therefore whatever we blame in another we shall find in our own bosoms. (Omnes mali sumus. Quidquid itaque in alio reprehenditur, id unusquisque in suo sinu inveniet.)
SENECA, *De Ira.* Bk. iii, sec. 26.
See also JUDGMENT: THE MOTE AND THE BEAM.

13
He who does not forbid sin when he can, encourages it. (Qui non vetat peccare cum possit, jubet.)
SENECA, *Troades,* l. 291.

14
I am a man More sinn'd against than sinning.
SHAKESPEARE, *King Lear.* Act iii, sc. 2, l. 59.

15
Some sins do bear their privilege on earth.
SHAKESPEARE, *King John.* Act i, sc. 1, l. 261.

16
Thy sin's not accidental, but a trade.
SHAKESPEARE, *Measure for Measure,* iii, 1, 149.

17
Few love to hear the sins they love to act.
SHAKESPEARE, *Pericles.* Act i, sc. 1, l. 92.

18
Though some of you with Pilate wash your hands
Showing an outward pity; yet you Pilates
Have here deliver'd me to my sour cross,
And water cannot wash away your sin.
SHAKESPEARE, *Richard II.* Act iv, sc. 1, l. 239.

19
Sin is too dull to see beyond himself.
TENNYSON, *Queen Mary.* Act v, sc. 2.

20
It would be better to eschew sin than to flee death. (Melius esset peccata cavere quam mortem fugere.)
THOMAS À KEMPIS, *De Imitatione Christi.* Bk. i, ch. 23, sec. 5.

21
We cannot well do without our sins; they are the highway of our virtue.
H. D. THOREAU, *Journal,* 22 March, 1842.

22
When one has broken the tenth commandment, the others are not of much account.
MARK TWAIN, *Pudd'nhead Wilson's Calendar.*

22a
Lecherie . . . is one of the seven deadly sins.
UNKNOWN, *Ayenbite,* 9. (1340)

Now it is bihovely thing to tell which been the deadly sins. . . Of the root of these seven sins then is Pride, the general root of all harms; for of this root springeth certain branches, as Ire, Envy, Accidie or Sloth, Avarice or Coveitise, Gluttony, and Lechery.
CHAUCER, *Canterbury Tales: The Persones Tale.* Sec. 23. (c. 1386) See also 1335:4.

III—Sin: The Eleventh Commandment

23
Verily the sin lieth in the scandal.
APHRA BEHN, *The Roundheads.* Act iii, sc. 2.

Scandal is the greatest part of the offence.
DRYDEN, *Limberham.* Act i, sc. 1.

'Tis the talk and not the intrigue that's the crime.
GRANVILLE, *The She Gallants.* Act iii, sc. 1.

24
The sin
Is in itself excusable; to be taken
Is a crime.
JOHN FLETCHER, *Lover's Progress.* Act iv, sc. 1.

1
The sin is not in the sinning, but in the being found out.

W. G. BENHAM, *Proverbs*, p. 851.

2
Guard yourself from being found out, so that you may sin freely. (D'être pincé te garderas, Afin de fauter librement.)

PRINCE DE JOINVILLE, *Memoirs*, adding that this "Eleventh Commandment, according to the late Lord Clarendon, sums up all the rest."

After all, the eleventh commandment [thou shalt not be found out] is the only one that is vitally important to keep in these days.

BERTHA H. BUXTON, *Jenny of the Prince's*, iii, 314. (1879)

3
The sin is merely in the noise which one makes;
It is only the scandal which makes the offence.
(Le mal n'est jamais que dans l'éclat qu'on fait;
Le scandale du monde est ce qui fait l'offense.)

MOLIÈRE, *Le Tartuffe*. Act iv, sc. 5, l. 118.

4
Their best conscience
Is not to leave 't undone, but keep 't unknown.

SHAKESPEARE, *Othello*. Act iii, sc. 3, l. 203.

5
The girl who can her fault deny
Will always at the end be winner;
'Tis she who does for pardon cry
That's held the sinner.

F. A. WRIGHT, *The Complaisant Swain*.

IV—Sin: Repentance and Forgiveness

See also Forgiveness

6
To abstain from sin when a man cannot sin is to be forsaken by sin, not to forsake it.

ST. AUGUSTINE, *Sermons: De Pœnitentibus*. (Jeremy Taylor, tr., *Works*, vii, 206.)

Therefore I rede you this counsel take,
Forsaketh sin, ere sin you forsake.

CHAUCER, *The Phisiciens Tale*, l. 285.

Unto each man comes a day when his favorite sins all forsake him,
And he complacently thinks he has forsaken his sins.

JOHN HAY, *Distichs*.

7
The proper process of unsinning sin
Is to begin well doing.

ROBERT BROWNING, *The Ring and the Book*. Pt. iv, l. 285.

8
Who sins and mends commends himself to God.

CERVANTES, *Don Quixote*. Pt. ii, ch. 28.

Take away the motive, and the sin is taken away. (Quitada la causa, se quita el pecado.)

CERVANTES, *Don Quixote*. Pt. ii, ch. 67.

9
For to sin, indeed, is human: but to persevere in sin is not human but altogether satanic. (Peccare, quidem, humanum est; at in peccatis perseverare, id non humanum est, sed omnino satanicum.)

ST. CHRYSOSTOM, *Adhortatio at Theodorum Lapsum*, i, 14.

To do sin is mannish, but certes to persevere long in sin is the work of the devil.

CHAUCER, *The Tale of Melibeus*. Sec. 29. Quoted as a proverb.

He that falls into sin is a man; that grieves at it, is a saint; that boasteth of it, is a devil.

THOMAS FULLER, *The Holy and the Profane State: Of Self-Praising*.

God pardons those who do through frailty sin,
But never those that persevere therein.

ROBERT HERRICK, *Pardon*.

Man-like is it to fall into sin,
Fiend-like is it to dwell therein,
Christ-like is it for sin to grieve,
God-like is it all sin to leave.

FRIEDRICH VON LOGAU, *Sinngedichte: Sin*. (Longfellow, tr., *Poetic Aphorisms*.)

10
When once the sin has fully acted been,
Then is the horror of the trespass seen.

ROBERT HERRICK, *Sin Seen*.

11
Owning her weakness,
Her evil behaviour,
And leaving with meekness,
Her sins to her Saviour!

THOMAS HOOD, *The Bridge of Sighs*.

12
Palliation of a sin is the hunted creature's refuge and final temptation. Our battle is ever between spirit and flesh. Spirit must brand the flesh, that it may live.

GEORGE MEREDITH, *Diana of the Crossways*. Ch. 1.

13
But unless I had sinned, what had there been for you to pardon? (Sed nisi peccassem, quid tu concedere posses?)

OVID, *Tristia*. Bk. ii, l. 32.

14
A sin confessed is half forgiven.

JOHN RAY, *English Proverbs*. The French form is: Péché avoué est à moitié pardonné.

The blackest sin is clear'd with absolution.

SHAKESPEARE, *The Rape of Lucrece*. St. 51.

15
When thy lovely sin has been
Wasted in a long despair,
World-forgetting, it may look
Upon thee with an angel air.

GEORGE WILLIAM RUSSELL, *Ancestry*.

16
Why does no one confess his sins? Because he is still in their grasp. Only he who has awoke from sleep can tell his dreams. (Quare vitia sua nemo confitetur? Quia etiam nunc in illis est; somnium narrare vigilantis est.)

SENECA, *Epistulæ ad Lucilium*. Epis. liii, 8.

1
The sin
That neither God nor man can well forgive.
TENNYSON, *Sea Dreams*, l. 62.

2
But he who never sins can little boast
Compared to him who goes and sins no more!
The "sinful Mary" walks more white in heaven
Than some who never "sinn'd and were forgiven!"
N. P. WILLIS, *The Lady Jane*. Canto ii, st. 44.

3
But the sin forgiven by Christ in Heaven
By man is cursed alway!
N. P. WILLIS, *Unseen Spirits*.

4
Young Timothy Learnt sin to fly.
UNKNOWN, *The New England Primer*. (1777)

V—Sin: Its Punishment

See also Punishment

5
One leak will sink a ship; and one sin will destroy a sinner.
JOHN BUNYAN, *The Pilgrim's Progress*. Pt. ii.

6
I waive the quantum o' the sin,
The hazard of concealing:
But, och! it hardens a' within,
And petrifies the feeling!
BURNS, *Epistle to a Young Friend*.

7
And out of his own bowels spins
A rack and torture for his sins.
SAMUEL BUTLER, *Satire Upon the Weakness and Misery of Man*, l. 173.

8
The righteous sometimes pay for the sinners. (Pagan á las veces justos por pecadores.)
CERVANTES, *Don Quixote*. Pt. i, ch. 7.

9
For a fresh sin a fresh penance. (Á Pecado nuevo, penitencia nueva.)
CERVANTES, *Don Quixote*. Pt. i, ch. 30.

10
Sin let loose speaks punishment at hand.
COWPER, *Expostulation*, l. 160.

11
The way of sinners is made plain with stones, but at the end thereof is the pit of hell.
Apocrypha: Ecclesiasticus, xxi, 10.

Sin makes its own hell, and goodness its own heaven.
MARY BAKER EDDY, *Science and Health*, p. 196.

Sinners, you are making a bee-line from time to eternity.
LORENZO DOW, *Sermons*. Vol. i, p. 215.

12
The gods visit the sins of the fathers upon the children.
EURIPIDES, *Fragments*. No. 970.

I the Lord thy God am a jealous God, visiting the iniquity of the fathers upon the children unto the third and fourth generation of them that hate me.
Old Testament: Exodus, xx, 5.

They enslave their children's children who make compromise with sin.
J. R. LOWELL, *The Present Crisis*. St. 9.

This is thy eld'st son's son,
Infortunate in nothing but in thee:
Thy sins are visited in this poor child;
The canon of the law is laid on him,
Being but the second generation
Removed from thy sin-conceiving womb.
SHAKESPEARE, *King John*. Act ii, sc. 1, l. 177.

The son pays the father's debts. (Fu 'chien chai tzŭ 'huan 'chien.)
UNKNOWN. A Chinese proverb.

13
Hell gives us art to reach the depth of sin;
But leaves us wretched fools, when we are in.
JOHN FLETCHER [?], *Queen of Corinth*, iv, 3.

14
Three fatal Sisters wait upon each sin:
First, Fear and Shame without, then Guilt within.
ROBERT HERRICK, *Three Fatal Sisters*.

15
Men are punished by their sins, not for them.
ELBERT HUBBARD, *The Philistine*. Vol. xi, p. 7.

16
The mere wish to sin entails the penalty, for he who meditates a crime within his breast has all the guilt of the deed. (Patitur poenas peccandi sola voluntas. Nam scelus intra se tacitum qui cogitat ullum, Facti crimen habet.)
JUVENAL, *Satires*. Sat. xiii, l. 208.

17
The sin ye do by two and two ye must pay for one by one!
RUDYARD KIPLING, *Tomlinson*, l. 62.

It takes two bodies to make one seduction.
GUY WETMORE CARRYL. (BEER, *Mauve Decade*, p. 197.

Every sin is the result of a collaboration.
STEPHEN CRANE.

18
The sins committed by many pass unpunished. (Quidquid multis peccatur inultum est.)
LUCAN, *De Bello Civili*. Bk. v, l. 260.

If Jupiter hurled his thunderbolts as often as men sinned, he would soon be out of thunderbolts. (Si, quotiens peccant homines, sua fulmina mittat Juppiter, exiguo tempore inermis erit.)
OVID, *Tristia*. Bk. ii, l. 33.

19
Anger and just rebuke, and judgement giv'n,
That brought into this world a world of woe,
Sin and her shadow Death, and Misery
Death's harbinger.
MILTON, *Paradise Lost*. Bk. ix, l. 10.

20
Be sure your sin will find you out.
Old Testament: Numbers, xxxii, 23.

21
Indulgent gods, grant me this one sin in safety, that is enough. Let a second offense bear its

punishment. (Di faciles, peccasse semel concedite tuto, Et satis est; poenam culpa secunda ferat!)

Ovid, *Amores*. Bk. ii, eleg. 14, l. 43.

'Tis not unjust that for *one* sin beauty should pay no forfeit. (Æquum est impune licere numina formosis lædere vestra semel.)

Tibullus, *Odes*. Bk. i, ode 9, l. 5.

1
The way of transgressors is hard.

Old Testament: Proverbs, xiii, 15.

2
The wages of sin is death.

New Testament: Romans, vi, 23.

3
Sin can be well-guarded, but free from anxiety it cannot be. (Tuta scelera esse possunt; secura esse non possunt.)

Seneca, *Epistulæ ad Lucilium*. Epis. xcvii, 13.

Some have sinned with safety, but none with peace of soul. (Scelus aliqua tutum, nulla securum tulit.)

Seneca, *Hippolytus*, l. 164.

Man may securely sin, but safely never.

Ben Jonson, *The Forest*. Epode 11.

4
The chief and greatest punishment for sin is the fact of having sinned. (Prima et maxima peccantium est poena pecasse.)

Seneca, *Epistulæ ad Lucilium*. Epis. xcvii, 14.
See also Punishment: Its Certainty.

5
Then is sin struck down like an ox, and iniquity's throat cut like a calf.

Shakespeare, *II Henry VI*. Act iv, sc. 2, l. 29.

6
Our sins, like to our shadows,
When our day is in its glory, scarce appear:
Towards our evening how great and monstrous
They are!

Sir John Suckling, *Aglaura*.

6a
There is no death without sin.

Babylonian Talmud: Shabbath, fo. 55a.

Sin kills the sinner and will continue to kill him as long as he sins.

Mary Baker Eddy, *Science and Health*, p. 203.

7
Have no hope of concealment when thou art planning sin. God knows of it, and lets no sin be hidden. (Nec tibi celandi spes sit peccare paranti; Scit deus, occultos qui vetat esse dolos.)

Tibullus, *Odes*. Bk. i, ode 9, l. 22.

8
But they that sin are enemies to their own life.

Apocrypha: Tobit, xii, 10.

And worst of enemies, their Sins were arm'd
Against them.

Robert Southey, *Roderick*. Pt. i, l. 53.

VI—Sin: Sinners

9
Sin we have explain'd away;
Unluckily, the sinners stay.

William Allingham, *Blackberries*.

10
There is no sinner like a young saint.

Aphra Behn, *The Rover*. Pt. i, act i, sc. 2.
See also under Age and Youth.

11
Thy sins and hairs may no man equal call,
For, as thy sins increase, thy hairs do fall.

John Donne, *A Licentious Person*.

The longer thread of life we spin,
The more occasion still to sin.

Robert Herrick, *Long Life*.

12
The greater the sinner's name, the more signal the guilt of sin. (Omne animi vitium tanto conspectuis in se Crimen habet.)

Juvenal, *Satires*. Sat. viii, l. 140.

13
Be a sinner, and sin mightily, but more mightily believe and rejoice in Christ. (Esto pecator et pecca fortiter, sed fortius fide et gaude in Christo.)

Martin Luther, *Letter to Melanchthon* (*Epistolæ Lutheri*. Vol. i, p. 345.)

14
God be merciful to me a sinner.

New Testament: Luke, xviii, 13. (Deus propitius esto mihi peccatori.—*Vulgate*.)

16
A large part of mankind is angry not with the sins, but with the sinners. (Magna pars hominum est quæ non peccatis irascitur, sed peccantibus.)

Seneca, *De Ira*. Bk. ii, sec. 28.

17
From scalp to sole one slough and crust of sin,
Unfit for earth, unfit for heaven, scarce meet
For troops of devils, mad with blasphemy.

Tennyson, *St. Simeon Stylites*, l. 2.

18
'Tis easier work if we begin
To fear the Lord betimes;
While sinners, that grow old in sin,
Are hardened in their crimes.

Isaac Watts, *Advantages of Early Religion*.

SINCERITY

See also Candor

19
His resolve is not to seem the bravest, but to be. (Οὐ γαρ δοκεῖν ἄριστος, ἀλλ' εἶναι θέλει.)

Æschylus, *Seven Against Thebes*, l. 592. The Latin version of this maxim is "Esse quam videre," to be rather than to seem.

He preferred to be, rather than to seem, virtuous. (Esse quam videri bonus malebat.)

Sallust, *Catilina*. Sec. 54.

Be what thou seemest! live thy creed!

Horatius Bonar, *He Liveth Long Who Liveth Well*.

Man should be ever better than he seems.

Aubrey de Vere, *A Song of Faith*.

20
Resolve to be thyself: and know, that he

Who finds himself, loses his misery.
MATTHEW ARNOLD, *Self-Dependence*, l. 31.

1
It matters not what men assume to be
Or good, or bad, they are but what they are.
P. J. BAILEY, *Festus: Water and Wood.*

2
Private sincerity is a public welfare.
C. H. BARTOL, *Radical Problems: Individualism.*

3
Thou must be true thyself,
If thou the truth wouldst teach.
HORATIUS BONAR, *Be True.*

Don't be "consistent," but be simply *true.*
O. W. HOLMES, *The Professor at the Breakfast-Table.* Ch. 2.

4
All must be earnest in a world like ours.
HORATIUS BONAR, *Our One Life.*

Be earnest, earnest, earnest; mad, if thou wilt:
Do what thou dost as if the stake were heaven,
And that thy last deed ere the judgment-day.
KINGSLEY, *The Saint's Tragedy.* Act ii, sc. 7.

5
Loss of sincerity is loss of vital power.
C. N. BOVEE, *Summaries of Thought: Sincerity.*

6
The sincere alone can recognise sincerity.
CARLYLE, *Heroes and Hero-Worship: The Hero as King.*

7
Everything you reprove in another, you must carefully avoid in yourself. (Omnia quæ vindicaris in altero, tibi ipsi vehementer fugienda sunt.)
CICERO, *In Verrem.* No. ii, sec. 3.

8
I may not hope from outward forms to win
The passion and the life, whose fountains are within.
COLERIDGE, *Dejection*, l. 45.

9
Sincerity is the luxury allowed, like diadems and authority, only to the highest rank. . . . Every man alone is sincere.
EMERSON, *Essays, First Series: Friendship.*

Never was a sincere word utterly lost.
EMERSON, *Essays, First Series: Spiritual Laws.*

Profound sincerity is the only basis of talent as of character.
EMERSON, *Essays: Natural History of Intellect.*

Every sincere man is right.
EMERSON, *Essays: Natural History of Intellect.*

The honest man must keep faith with himself; his sheet anchor is sincerity.
EMERSON, *Uncollected Lectures: Table Talk.*

10
Wrought in sad sincerity.
EMERSON, *The Problem.*

11
At last be true; no gesture now let spring
But from supreme sincerity of art;
Let him who plays the monarch be a king,
Who plays the rogue, be perfect in his part.
JOHN ERSKINE, *At the Front.*

12
Of all the evil spirits abroad at this hour in the world, insincerity is the most dangerous.
FROUDE, *Short Studies on Great Subjects: Education.*

13
He is one that will not plead that cause wherein his tongue must be confuted by his conscience.
THOMAS FULLER, *The Holy and the Profane State: The Good Advocate.* Bk. ii, ch. 1.

14
A silent address is the genuine eloquence of sincerity.
GOLDSMITH, *The Good-Natured Man.* Act ii.

15
The only conclusive evidence of a man's sincerity is that he gave *himself* for a principle.
J. R. LOWELL, *Among My Books: Rousseau.*

Sincerity is impossible, unless it pervade the whole being, and the pretence of it saps the very foundation of character.
J. R. LOWELL, *Essays: Pope.*

16
Be content to seem what you really are. (Ut tandem videaris unus esse.)
MARTIAL, *Epigrams.* Bk. x, epig. 83.

I'm what I seem; not any dyer gave,
But nature dyed this color that I have.
(Non est lana mihi mendax nec mutor aheno.
Sic placeant Tyriæ: me mea tinxit ovis.)
MARTIAL, *Epigrams.* Bk. xiv, epig. 133.

17
There is no greater delight than to be conscious of sincerity on self-examination.
MENCIUS, *Works.* Bk. vii, ch. 4.

18
Then grow as God hath planted, grow
A lordly oak or daisy low,
As He hath set His garden; be
Just what thou art, or grass or tree.
JOAQUIN MILLER, *With Love to You and Yours.* Pt. ii, sec. 8.

If you can't be a pine on the top of the hill,
Be a scrub in the valley—but be
The best little scrub by the side of the rill;
Be a bush if you can't be a tree.
DOUGLAS MALLOCH, *Be the Best of Whatever You Are.*

19
I want to see you shoot the way you shout.
THEODORE ROOSEVELT, *Speech,* Madison Square Garden, N. Y., Oct., 1917.

20
My way must be straight out. True with the tongue,
False with the heart—I may not, cannot be.
SCHILLER, *Die Piccolomini.* Act iii, sc. 3. (Coleridge, tr.)

21
Let us say what we feel, and feel what we say; let speech harmonize with life. (Quod sentimus loquamur, quod loquimur sentiamus; concordet sermo cum vita.)
SENECA, *Epistulæ ad Lucilium.* Epis. lxxv, 4.

1
Nor are these empty-hearted whose low sound
Reverbs no hollowness.
SHAKESPEARE, *King Lear*. Act i, sc. 1, l. 155.

I do profess to be no less than I seem; to serve him truly that will put me in trust; to love him that is honest; to converse with him that is wise, and says little; to fear judgement; to fight when I cannot choose; and to eat no fish.
SHAKESPEARE, *King Lear*. Act i, sc. 4, l. 14.

Men should be what they seem;
Or those that be not, would they might seem none.
SHAKESPEARE, *Othello*. Act iii, sc. 3, l. 126.

Bashful sincerity and comely love.
SHAKESPEARE, *Much Ado About Nothing*. Act iv, sc. 1, l. 55.

2
It is dangerous to be sincere unless you are also stupid.
BERNARD SHAW, *Maxims for Revolutionists*.

A little sincerity is a dangerous thing, and a great deal of it is absolutely fatal.
OSCAR WILDE, *The Critic as Artist*. Pt. ii.

3
That my weak hand may equal my firm faith,
And my life practise more than my tongue saith.
HENRY DAVID THOREAU, *My Prayer*.

4
Men, that would blush at being thought sincere.
YOUNG, *Night Thoughts*. Night viii, l. 285.

SISTER

5
My sister! my sweet sister! if a name
Dearer and purer were, it should be thine.
BYRON, *Epistle to Augusta*, l. 1.

6
Gone are those three, those sisters rare
With wonder-lips and eyes ashine.
One was wise, and one was fair,
And one was mine.
ARTHUR DAVISON FICKE, *The Three Sisters*.

7
Being used but sisterly salutes to feel,
Insipid things—like sandwiches of veal.
THOMAS HOOD, *Bianca's Dream*, l. 263. *See also under* KISS.

8
What did the Colonel's Lady think?
Nobody never knew.
Somebody asked the Sergeant's Wife,
An' she told 'em true!
When you get to a man in the case,
They're like as a row of pins—
For the Colonel's Lady an' Judy O'Grady
Are sisters under their skins!
RUDYARD KIPLING, *The Ladies*.

E'en a woman, and commanded
By such poor passion as the maid that milks.
SHAKESPEARE, *Antony and Cleopatra*. Act iv, sc. 15, l. 72.

9
For there is no friend like a sister,
In calm or stormy weather,
To cheer one on the tedious way,
To fetch one if one goes astray,
To lift one if one totters down,
To strengthen whilst one stands.
CHRISTINA ROSSETTI, *Goblin Market*. Conclusion.

10
O, never say hereafter
But I am truest speaker: you call'd me brother
When I was but your sister.
SHAKESPEARE, *Cymbeline*. Act v, sc. 5, l. 375.

A ministering angel shall my sister be.
SHAKESPEARE, *Hamlet*. Act v, sc. 1, l. 264.

11
The weird sisters.
SHAKESPEARE, *Macbeth* Act iv, sc. 1, l. 32.

Two sisters from the same old home
Now meet no more in life;
For one the smiles of fortune fair,
For one its frown and strife.
Their paths are parted far and wide,
Since they were young and gay,
And so the simple story runs,
Of life from day to day.
CHARLES A. WILSON, *Two Sisters from the Same Old Home, or, Life from Day to Day*. (1899)

SKEPTICISM, see Doubt

SKILL

12
'Tis God gives skill,
But not without men's hands: He could not make
Antonio Stradivari's violins Without Antonio.
GEORGE ELIOT, *Stradivarius*, l. 151.

13
Skill to do comes of doing.
EMERSON, *Society and Solitude: Old Age*.

14
Skill is stronger than strength.
W. G. BENHAM, *Proverbs*, p. 834. The French form is, "L'adresse surmonte la force."

15
Skill and confidence are an unconquered army.
GEORGE HERBERT, *Jacula Prudentum*. No. 622.

16
This sort of thing takes a deal of training.
W. S. GILBERT, *Ruddigore*.

17
All things require skill but an appetite.
GEORGE HERBERT, *Jacula Prudentum*.

18
And skill's a joy to any man.
JOHN MASEFIELD, *Everlasting Mercy*, l. 600.

19
To show our simple skill,
That is the true beginning of our end.
SHAKESPEARE, *A Midsummer-Night's Dream*. Act v, sc. 1, l. 110.

20
Like an arrow shot
From a well-experienced archer hits the mark
His eye doth level at.
SHAKESPEARE, *Pericles*. Act i, sc. 1, l. 163.

21
Masterful skill. (Arte magistra.)
VERGIL, *Æneid*. Bk. viii, l. 442; bk. xii, l. 427.

SKIN

1
You are come off now with a whole skin.
CERVANTES, *Don Quixote*. Pt. i, ch. 5.

It is good sleeping in a whole skin.
JOHN RAY, *English Proverbs*.

Your skins are whole.
SHAKESPEARE, *The Merry Wives of Windsor*. Act iii, sc. 1, l. 111.

2
A fair skin often covers a crooked mind.
W. G. BENHAM, *Proverbs*, p. 720.

3
Can the Ethiopian change his skin, or the leopard his spots?
Old Testament: Jeremiah, xiii, 23. *See also under* CHANGE.

4
Skin for skin, yea, all that a man hath will he give for his life.
Old Testament: Job, ii, 4.

5
My skin hangs about me like an old lady's loose gown.
SHAKESPEARE, *I Henry IV*. Act iii, sc. 3, l. 3.

6
His silver skin laced with his golden blood.
SHAKESPEARE, *Macbeth*. Act ii, sc. 3, l. 118.

I'll not shed her blood;
Nor scar that whiter skin of her than snow,
And smooth as monumental alabaster.
SHAKESPEARE, *Othello*. Act v, sc. 2, l. 3.

SKULL

See also Head

7
Remove yon skull from out the scatter'd heaps:
Is that a temple where a God may dwell?
Why ev'n the worm at last disdains her shatter'd cell!
Look on its broken arch, its ruin'd wall,
Its chambers desolate, and portals foul:
Yes, this was once Ambition's airy hall,
The dome of Thought, the palace of the Soul.
BYRON, *Childe Harold*. Canto ii, st. 5, 6.

8
That skull had a tongue in it, and could sing once. . . . And now my Lady Worm's; chapless, and knocked about the mazzard with a sexton's spade.
SHAKESPEARE, *Hamlet*. Act v, sc. 1, l. 83.

9
Behold this ruin! 'Twas a skull
Once of ethereal spirit full!
This narrow cell was Life's retreat;
This place was Thought's mysterious seat!
What beauteous pictures fill'd that spot,
What dreams of pleasure, long forgot!
Nor Love, nor Joy, nor Hope, nor Fear,
Has left one trace, one record here.
ANNA JANE VARDILL, *Lines to a Skull*. (Published in *European Magazine*, Nov., 1816, with signature V.) Claimed by J. D. Gordman, Robert Philip, and others.

SKY

10
Oh "darkly, deeply, beautifully blue!"
As some one somewhere sings about the sky.
BYRON, *Don Juan*. Canto iv, st. 110.

Blue, darkly, deeply, beautifully blue,
In all its rich variety of shades,
Suffused with glowing gold.
SOUTHEY, *Madoc in Wales*. Pt. i, canto v, l. 102. Referring to dolphins, not to the sky, as Byron supposed.

11
And they were canopied by the blue sky,
So cloudless, clear, and purely beautiful
That God alone was to be seen in heaven.
BYRON, *The Dream*. St. 4.

Naught is seen in the vault on high
But the moon, and the stars, and the cloudless sky.
JOSEPH RODMAN DRAKE, *Culprit Fay*. St. 1.

The very clouds have wept and died
And only God is in the sky.
JOAQUIN MILLER, *The Ship in the Desert*.

12
Just take a trifling handful, O philosopher!
Of magic matter: give it a slight toss over
The ambient ether—and I don't see why
You shouldn't make a sky.
MORTIMER COLLINS, *Sky-Making: To Professor Tyndall*.

13
The mountain at a given distance
In amber lies;
Approached, the amber flits a little,—
And that's the skies!
EMILY DICKINSON, *Poems*. Pt. i, No. 45.

14
Under the cold sky. (Sub Jove frigido.)
HORACE, *Odes*. Bk. i, ode 1, l. 25.

15
The sky
is that beautiful old parchment
in which the sun and the moon
keep their diary.
ALFRED KREYMBORG, *Old Manuscript*.

16
And that inverted Bowl they call the Sky,
Whereunder crawling coop'd we live and die,
Lift not your hands to *It* for help—for it
As impotently moves as you or I.
OMAR KHAYYÁM, *Rubáiyát*. St. 72. (Fitzgerald, tr.)

17
Phaëton, if he were alive, would shun the sky. (Vitaret cœlum Phaëton, si viverat.)
OVID, *Tristia*. Bk. i, eleg. 1, l. 79.

18
The heavens declare the glory of God, and the firmament sheweth his handywork.
Old Testament: Psalms, xix, 1.

19
The wrathful skies

Gallow the very wanderers of the dark,
And make them keep their caves.
SHAKESPEARE, *King Lear*. Act iii, sc. 2, l. 43.

1
What if the sky fell? (Quid si nunc cælum ruat?)
TERENCE, *Heauton Timorumenos*, l. 719. (Act iv, sc. 3.) Quoted as a proverb.

If the sky fall, we shall catch larks. (Si les nues tomboyent esperoyt prendre les alouettes.)
RABELAIS, *Works*. Bk. i, ch. 11.

If the sky falls, the pots will be broken. (Si el cielo se cae, quebrarse han las ollas.)
The Spanish form of the proverb.

2
Sometimes gentle, sometimes capricious, sometimes awful, never the same for two moments together; almost human in its passions, almost spiritual in its tenderness, almost Divine in its infinity.
RUSKIN, *The True and Beautiful: The Sky*.

3
Look you, this brave o'erhanging firmament, this majestical roof fretted with golden fire, why, it appears no other thing to me than a foul and pestilent congregation of vapours.
SHAKESPEARE, *Hamlet*. Act ii, sc. 2, l. 312.

4
Heaven's face doth glow.
SHAKESPEARE, *Hamlet*. Act iii, sc. 4, l. 48.

Heaven's ebon vault,
Studded with stars unutterably bright,
Through which the moon's unclouded grandeur rolls,
Seems like a canopy which Love had spread
To curtain her sleeping world.
SHELLEY, *Queen Mab*. Pt. iv, l. 4.

5
The Lord descended from above
And bow'd the heavens high;
And underneath his feet he cast
The darkness of the sky.
THOMAS STERNHOLD, *A Metrical Version of Psalm civ*. St. 1.

6
Never yet
Had heavèn appear'd so blue, nor earth so green.
TENNYSON, *The Holy Grail*, l. 364.

Of evening tinct,
The purple-streaming amethyst is thine.
THOMSON, *The Seasons: Summer*, l. 150.

Green calm below, blue quietness above.
WHITTIER, *The Pennsylvania Pilgrim*. St. 113.

7
Before the pageant of the skies
Nightly his spirit bowed.
L. FRANK TOOKER, *He Bringeth Them unto Their Desired Haven*.

8
It becomes wearisome constantly to watch the arch of heaven. (Tædet cæli convexa tueri.)
VERGIL, *Æneid*. Bk. iv, l. 451.

9
Over all the sky—the sky! far, far out of reach, studded, breaking out, the eternal stars.
WALT WHITMAN, *Bivouac on a Mountain Side*.

10
I never saw a man who looked
With such a wistful eye
Upon that little tent of blue
Which prisoners call the sky,
And at every drifting cloud that went
With sails of silver by.
OSCAR WILDE, *Ballad of Reading Gaol*. Pt. i, st. 3.

11
The soft blue sky did never melt
Into his heart; he never felt
The witchery of the soft blue sky!
WORDSWORTH, *Peter Bell*. Pt. i, st. 15.

SKYLARK, see Lark

SLANDER

See also Calumny, Rumor, Scandal

I—Slander: Definitions

12
Slander, dog's eloquence. (Canina eloquentia.)
APPIUS CLAUDIUS. (QUINTILIAN, *De Institutione Oratoria*. Bk. xii, ch. 9, sec. 9.)

Squint-eyed Slander plies th' unhallow'd tongue.
JAMES BEATTIE, *The Judgment of Paris*. St. 109.

13
Slander is a shipwreck by a dry tempest.
GEORGE HERBERT, *Jacula Prudentum*.

14
Slander is a most serious evil; it implies two who do wrong, and one who is doubly wronged.
ARTABANUS. (HERODOTUS, *History*. Bk. vii, 10.)

Slander slays three persons: the speaker, the spoken to, and the spoken of.
Babylonian Talmud: Arachin, p. 15b.

A Slander counts by Threes its victims, who
Are Speaker, Spoken Of, and Spoken To.
ARTHUR GUITERMAN, *A Poet's Proverbs*, p. 39.

An evil-speaker differs from an evil-doer only in opportunity. (Maledicus a malefico non distat nisi occasione.
QUINTILIAN, *De Institutione Oratoria*. Bk. xii, ch. 9, sec. 9.

Tale-bearers are just as bad as the tale-makers.
SHERIDAN, *The School for Scandal*. Act i, sc. 1.

The partaker is as bad as the thief.
SWIFT, of William III's motto, "Recipit non rapuit."

15
Slander, that worst of poisons, ever finds
An easy entrance to ignoble minds.
JOHN HERVEY, *Paraphrase of Juvenal*.

16
Defamation is becoming a necessity of life; insomuch that a dish of tea in the morning or evening cannot be digested without this stimulant.
THOMAS JEFFERSON, *Writings*. Vol. xi, p. 224.

1
If slander be a snake, it is a winged one—it flies as well as creeps.
Douglas Jerrold, *Specimens of Jerrold's Wit: Slander.*

2
We commonly slander through vanity more often than through malice. (On est d'ordinaire plus médisant par vanité que par malice.)
La Rochefoucauld, *Maximes.* No. 483.

3
Slander, the foulest whelp of Sin.
Pollok, *The Course of Time.* Bk. viii, l. 726.

Slander, meanest spawn of hell—
And women's slander is the worst.
Tennyson, *The Letters.* St. 5.

4
What is slander? A verdict of "guilty" pronounced in the absence of the accused, with closed doors, without defence or appeal, by an interested and prejudiced judge.
Joseph Roux, *Meditations of a Parish Priest: Mind.* No. 67.

Believe not each accusing tongue,
As most weak mortals do;
But still believe that story wrong
Which ought not to be true.
Richard Brinsley Sheridan, *Sheridaniana.*

There are two sides to a story,
Hear them both before you blame;
For a woman's crowning glory
Is a fair, unblemished name!
Heaven holds no gift that's grander,
So beware of idle slander;
There are two sides to a story—
Right and wrong!
Will A. Heelan and J. Fred Helf, *There Are Two Sides to a Story.* (1900) Popularized by Florence Brooks. See 99:3.

5
'Tis slander,
Whose edge is sharper than the sword, whose tongue
Outvenoms all the worms of Nile, whose breath
Rides on the posting winds and doth belie
All corners of the world: kings, queens, and states,
Maids, matrons, nay, the secrets of the grave
This viperous slander enters.
Shakespeare, *Cymbeline.* Act iii, sc. 4, l. 35.

Whose whisper o'er the world's diameter,
As level as the cannon to his blank,
Transports his poison'd shot.
Shakespeare, *Hamlet.* Act iv, sc. 1, l. 41.

Slander's mark was ever yet the fair;
The ornament of beauty is suspect,
A crow that flies in heaven's sweetest air.
So thou be good, slander doth but approve
Thy worth the greater.
Shakespeare, *Sonnets.* No. lxx.

6
Soft-buzzing slander—silky moths, that eat
An honest name.
James Thomson, *Liberty.* Pt. iv, l. 619.

7
Slander, the immortal daughter of self-love and idleness. (La Médisance est la fille immortelle De l'Amour-propre et de l'Oisivité.)
Voltaire, *La Calomnie.*

II—Slander: Apothegms

8
Slander flings stones at itself.
Thomas Fuller, *Gnomologia.* No. 4183. (1732)

Who by aspersions throw a stone
At th' head of others, hit their own.
George Herbert, *Charms and Knots.*

If I tell a malicious lie, in order to affect any man's fortune or character, I may indeed injure him for some time; but I shall be sure to be the greatest sufferer myself at last.
Lord Chesterfield, *Letters,* 21 Sept., 1747.
See also under Retribution.

9
It is said that self-praise stinks in the nostrils. For the kind of smell that arises from the unjust abuse of others, people have no nose at all.
Goethe, *Sprüche in Prosa.*

10
It may be a slander, but it is no lie.
John Heywood, *Proverbs.* Pt. ii, ch. 7. (1546)

That is no slander, sir, which is a truth.
Shakespeare, *Romeo and Juliet.* Act iv, sc. 1, l. 33.

11
A generous heart repairs a slanderous tongue.
Homer, *Odyssey.* Bk. viii, l. 432. (Pope, tr.)

12
The tooth of slander. (Dente Theonino.)
Horace, *Epistles.* Bk. i, epis. 18, l. 82. A proverbial expression for calumny, of unknown origin. Theon is supposed to have been a satirical poet.

13
Brand him who will with base report,—
He shall be free from mine.
Scott, *Bridal of Triermain.* Canto ii, st. 18.

To speak no slander, no, nor listen to it.
Tennyson, *Guinevere,* l. 468.

14
Thee nor carketh care nor slander.
Tennyson, *A Dirge.* St. 2.

III—Slander: Its Baseness

15
The man that dares traduce, because he can
With safety to himself, is not a man.
Cowper, *Expostulation,* l. 432.

16
If you mean wild beasts, the slanderer's; if tame ones, the flatterer's.
Diogenes, when asked which beast's bite was the most dangerous. (Seneca, *Epistles.*)

The most dangerous of wild beasts is a slanderer; of tame ones a flatterer.
H. G. Bohn, *Hand-Book of Proverbs,* p. 511.

17
Each man swore to do his best

To damn and perjure all the rest.
BUTLER, *Hudibras.* Pt. i, canto ii, l. 631.

1
Leaving behind them horrible dispraise. (Di sè lasciando orribili dispregi!)
DANTE, *Inferno.* Canto viii, l. 51. (Cary, tr.)

2
I hate the man who builds his name
On ruins of another's fame.
JOHN GAY, *Fables.* Fab. xlv, l. 1.

3
The world delights to tarnish shining names,
And to trample the sublime in the dust.
(Es liebt die Welt, das Strahlende zu schwärzen
Und das Erhabne in den Staub zu ziehn.)
SCHILLER, *Die Jungfrau von Orleans.*

Since we cannot attain to it, let us avenge ourselves by abusing it. (Puisque nous ne la pouvons aveindre, vengeons nous à en mesdire.)
MONTAIGNE, *Essays.* Bk. iii, ch. 7. Referring to greatness.

4
Innuendo, into which one must read more meaning than was intended to meet the ear. (Suspiciosæ, in quibus plus intellegendum esset quam audiendum.)
SENECA, *Epistulæ ad Lucilium.* Epis. cxiv, 1.

5
Foul whisperings are abroad.
SHAKESPEARE, *Macbeth.* Act v, sc. 1, l. 79.

One that is as slanderous as Satan.
SHAKESPEARE, *The Merry Wives of Windsor.* Act v, sc. 5, l. 163.

A slave whose gall coins slanders like a mint.
SHAKESPEARE, *Troilus and Cressida.* Act i, sc. 3, l. 193.

6
That foul bird of rapine whose whole prey
Is man's good name.
TENNYSON, *Merlin and Vivien,* l. 726.

Defaming and defacing, till she left
Not even Lancelot brave nor Galahad clean.
TENNYSON, *Merlin and Vivien,* l. 802.

IV—Slander: Its Power

7
Quick-circulating slanders mirth afford;
And reputation bleeds in every word.
CHARLES CHURCHILL, *The Apology,* l. 47. *See also under* REPUTATION.

8
Cut Men's throats with whisperings.
BEN JONSON, *Sejanus.* Act i, sc. 1.

9
Truth shall retire Bestuck with sland'rous darts.
MILTON, *Paradise Lost.* Bk. xii, l. 535.

10
Destroy his fib, or sophistry—in vain!
The creature's at his dirty work again.
POPE, *Epistle to Dr. Arbuthnot,* l. 91.

11
He that repeateth a matter separateth very friends.
Old Testament: Proverbs, xvii, 9.

I'll devise some honest slanders
To stain my cousin with: one doth not know
How much an ill word may empoison liking.
SHAKESPEARE, *Much Ado About Nothing.* Act iii, sc. 1, l. 84.

Alas! they had been friends in youth;
But whispering tongues can poison truth.
S. T. COLERIDGE, *Christabel.* Pt. ii, l. 408.

12
For slander lives upon succession,
For ever housed where it gets possession.
SHAKESPEARE, *The Comedy of Errors.* Act iii, sc. 1, l. 105.

13
What king so strong,
Can tie the gall up in the slanderous tongue?
SHAKESPEARE, *Measure for Measure.* Act iii, sc. 2, l. 198.

Done to death by slanderous tongues.
SHAKESPEARE, *Much Ado About Nothing.* Act v, sc. 3, l. 3.

14
Slander'd to death by villains,
That dare as well answer a man indeed
As I dare take a serpent by the tongue.
SHAKESPEARE, *Much Ado About Nothing.* Act v, sc. 1, l. 88.

15
I will be hang'd, if some eternal villain,
Some busy and insinuating rogue,
Some cogging, cozening slave, to get some office,
Have not devis'd this slander.
SHAKESPEARE, *Othello.* Act iv, sc. 2, l. 130.

I am disgrac'd, impeach'd and baffled here,
Pierced to the soul with slander's venom'd spear.
SHAKESPEARE, *Richard II.* Act i, sc. 1, l. 170.

Slander,
Whose sting is sharper than the sword's.
SHAKESPEARE, *Winter's Tale.* Act ii, sc. 3, l. 85.

16
The breath
Of accusation kills an innocent name,
And leaves for lame acquittal the poor life,
Which is a mask without it.
SHELLEY, *The Cenci.* Act iv, sc. 4, l. 137.

17
Detraction and spite are received with eager ears. (Obtrectatio et livor pronis auribus accipiuntur.)
TACITUS, *History.* Bk. i, sec. 1.

This ill-wresting world is grown so bad,
Mad slanderers by mad ears believed be.
SHAKESPEARE, *Sonnets.* No. cxl.

18
The tiny-trumpeting gnat can break our dream
When sweetest; and the vermin voices here
May buzz so loud—we scorn them, but they sting.
TENNYSON, *Lancelot and Elaine,* l. 137.

19
Slander that is raised is ill to fell.
UNKNOWN, *How the Good Wife,* l. 25. (c 1460)

V—Slander: Contempt for Slander

1
One may even scourge me, so it be in my absence.

ARISTOTLE, when told that some one had slandered him. (DIOGENES LAERTIUS, *Aristotle,* sec. 18.)

Better he speak where we are both known, than where we are both unknown.

PHILIP OF MACEDON, when advised to banish a man who had spoken ill of him. (FRANCIS BACON, *Apothegms.* No. 103.)

If I am
Traduced by ignorant tongues, which neither know
My faculties nor person, yet will be
The chronicles of my doing, let me say,
'Tis but the fate of place, and the rough brake
That virtue must go through.

SHAKESPEARE, *Henry VIII.* Act i, sc. 2, l. 71.

2
The man that despiseth slander deserveth it.

LORD HALIFAX, *Works,* p. 255.

3
That they speak [evil of me] is not the point; that they do not speak it justly, that is the point. (Quin dicant non est: merito ut ne dicant, id est.)

PLAUTUS, *Trinummus.* Act i, sc. 2.

4
Spiteful songs, if despised, are soon forgotten; but if you show displeasure, they seem to be admitted as true. (Carmina . . . spreta exolescunt; si irascare, agnita videntur.)

TACITUS, *Annals.* Bk. iv, sec. 34.

Where it concerns himself,
Who's angry at a slander, makes it true.

BEN JONSON, *Catiline.* Act iii, sc. 1.

VI—Slander: Admonitions

5
Carry no tales, be no common teller of news, be not inquisitive of other men's talk, for those that are desirous to hear what they need not, commonly be ready to babble what they should not.

ROGER ASCHAM, *Advice to Lord Warwick's Servant.*

6
Though the quickness of thine ear were able to reach the noise of the moon, which some think it maketh in its rapid revolution; though the number of thy ears should equal Argus his eyes; yet stop them all with the wise man's wax, and be deaf unto the suggestions of talebearers, calumniators, pickthank or malevolent delators, who, while quiet men sleep, sowing the tares of discord and division, distract the tranquillity of charity and all friendly society.

SIR THOMAS BROWNE, *Christian Morals.* Pt. i, sec. 20.

7
Avoid gossip lest you come to be regarded as its originator; for silence harms no one, but speech is harmful. (Rumorem fuge, ne incipias novus auctor haberi; Nam nulli tacuisse nocet nocet esse locutum.)

DIONYSIUS CATO, *Disticha de Moribus.* Bk. i, No. 12.

8
Don't be a Prittle-prattle, nor Prate-apace, nor be a minding anything but what is said to you.

ERASMUS, *The Schoolmaster's Admonitions.*

9
Ever have an eye as to what and to whom you speak concerning any man. (Quid de quoque viro, et cui dicas, sæpe videto.)

HORACE, *Epistles.* Bk. i, epis. 18, l. 68.

10
Speak no ill of a friend, nor even of an enemy. (Φίλον μὴ λέγειν κακῶς, ἀλλὰ μηδὲ ἐχθρόν.)

PITTACUS. (DIOGENES LAERTIUS, *Pittacus.* Bk. i, sec. 78.)

Hear no ill of a friend, nor speak any of an enemy.

BENJAMIN FRANKLIN, *Poor Richard,* 1739.

11
Slander-mongers and those who listen to slander, if I had my way, would all be strung up, the talkers by the tongue, the listeners by the ears. (Homines qui gestant quique auscultant crimina, Si meo arbitratu liceat, omnes pendeant, Gestores linguis, auditores auribus.)

PLAUTUS, *Pseudolus,* l. 427. (Act i, sc. 5.)

12
I ne'er with Wits or Witlings pass'd my days
To spread about the itch of verse and praise;
Nor like a puppy daggled thro' the town
To fetch and carry sing-song up and down.

POPE, *Epistle to Dr. Arbuthnot,* l. 223.

13
Publish not men's secret faults, for by disgracing them you make yourself of no repute.

SADI, *Gulistan: Rules for Conduct.* No. 39.

Thy friend has a friend, and thy friend's friend has a friend, so be discreet.

The Talmud.

14
Refrain your tongue from backbiting, for . . . the mouth that belieth slayeth the soul.

Apocrypha: Wisdom of Solomon, i, 11.

Rebuke backbiters, and encourage them not by hearkening to their tales.

SAMUEL BAGSTER, *Christian Politics.*

15
If for a tranquil mind you seek,
These things observe with care:
Of whom you speak, to whom you speak,
And how, and when, and where.

UNKNOWN, *A Rule of Conduct.* Quoted by Edwin Booth.

SLAVERY

I—Slavery: Definitions and Apothegms

16
So free we seem, so fettered fast we are!

ROBERT BROWNING, *Andrea del Sarto.*

Born slaves, bred slaves,
Branded in the blood and bone slaves.
ROBERT BROWNING, *A Soul's Tragedy*. Act i.

So we are slaves,
The greatest as the meanest.
BYRON, *The Two Foscari*. Act ii, sc. 1.

Nations of slaves, with tyranny debas'd,
(Their Maker's image more than half defac'd).
ADDISON, *The Campaign*, l. 81.

1
Slavery they can have anywhere. It is a weed that grows in every soil.
EDMUND BURKE, *Speech on Conciliation with America*.

2
As the slave departs, the man returns.
CAMPBELL, *The Pleasures of Hope*. Pt. i, l. 348.

Was man ordained the slave of man to toil,
Yoked with the brutes, and fettered to the soil?
CAMPBELL, *The Pleasures of Hope*. Pt. i, l. 495.

3
He that is one man's slave, is free from none.
CHAPMAN, *The Gentleman Usher*. Act i, sc. 1.

4
Excessive liberty leads both nations and individuals into excessive slavery. (Nimia libertas et populis et privatis in nimiam servitutem cadit.)
CICERO, *De Republica*. Bk. i, sec. 44.

5
I own I am shock'd at the purchase of slaves,
And fear those who buy them and sell them are knaves;
What I hear of their hardships, their tortures, and groans,
Is almost enough to draw pity from stones.
COWPER, *Pity for Poor Africans*, l. 1. (1788)

He blam'd and protested, but join'd in the plan;
He shar'd in the plunder, but pitied the man.
COWPER, *Pity for Poor Africans*, l. 43.

6
Base in kind, and born to be a slave.
COWPER, *Table Talk*, l. 28.

7
I would not have a slave to till my ground,
To carry me, to fan me while I sleep,
And tremble when I wake, for all the wealth
That sinews bought and sold have ever earn'd.
COWPER, *The Task*. Bk. ii, l. 29.

8
Under the whip of the driver, the slave shall feel his equality with saints and heroes.
EMERSON, *Conduct of Life: Worship*.

Slavery it is that makes slavery; freedom, freedom. The slavery of women happened when the men were slaves of kings.
EMERSON, *Miscellanies: Women*.

9
Freedom and slavery! the one is the name of virtue, and the other of vice, and both are acts of the will.
EPICTETUS, *Fragments*. No. 8.

10
Slaves bought with a price do not put up with unjust treatment from their masters; will you, Roman citizens born to power, endure slavery with patience?
GAIUS MEMMIUS. (SALLUST, *Jugurtha*. Ch. xxxi, sec. 11.)

11
Corrupted freemen are the worst of slaves.
DAVID GARRICK, *The Gamesters: Prologue*.

12
Nothing in the world is lawless except a slave.
J. C. AND A. W. HARE, *Guesses at Truth*.

13
He loves his bonds, who, when the first are broke,
Submits his neck unto a second yoke.
ROBERT HERRICK, *Hesperides*. No. 42.

14
Whatever day
Makes man a slave, takes half his worth away.
HOMER, *Odyssey*. Bk. xvii, l. 392. (Pope, tr.)

15
Men! whose boast it is that ye
Come of fathers brave and free,
If there breathe on earth a slave,
Are ye truly free and brave?
J. R. LOWELL, *Stanzas on Freedom*.

They are slaves who fear to speak
For the fallen and the weak; . . .
They are slaves who dare not be
In the right with two or three.
J. R. LOWELL, *Stanzas on Freedom*.

16
It is useless, believe me, to be the slave of a slave, even though he be a friend: let him be free who shall wish to be my master.
(Non bene, crede mihi, servo servitur amico:
Sit liber, dominus qui volet esse meus.)
MARTIAL, *Epigrams*. Bk. ii, epig. 32, l. 7.

17
Better the devil's than a woman's slave.
MASSINGER, *Parliament of Love*. Act ii, sc. 2.

18
Retain a free man's mind though slave, and slave thou shalt not be. ('Ελευθέρως δούλευε· δοῦλος οὐκ ἔσει.)
MENANDER [?], *Fragments*. Frag. 857.

Man's mind and not his master makes him slave.
R. U. JOHNSON, *To the Spirit of Byron*.

They set the slave free, striking off his chains. . .
Then he was as much of a slave as ever. . . .
His slavery was not in his chains,
But in himself . . .
They can only set free men free . . .
And there is no need of that:
Free men set themselves free.
JAMES OPPENHEIM, *The Slave*.

The blow that liberates the slave
But sets the master free.
JAMES JEFFREY ROCHE, *Gettysburg*.

See also under MASTER.

19
He gave us only over beast, fish, fowl,
Dominion absolute; that right we hold
By His donation; but man over men
He made not lord, such title to himself

Reserving, human left from human free.
MILTON, *Paradise Lost*. Bk. xii, l. 67.

1
And ne'er shall the sons of Columbia be slaves,
While the earth bears a plant, or the sea rolls its waves.
ROBERT TREAT PAINE, *Adams and Liberty*. (1798)

2
Slave before slave, and master before master. (Δοῦλος πρὸ δούλου, δεσπότης πρὸ δεσπότου.)
PHILEMON, *Fragment*. (ARISTOTLE, *Politics*. Bk. i, ch. 2, sec. 22.)

3
None can be free who is a slave to, and ruled by, his passions.
PYTHAGORAS, (STOBÆUS, *Florilegium*. Pt. xviii, l. 23.)

Show me a man who is not a slave. One is a slave to lust, another to greed, another to ambition, and all men are slaves to fear. I will name you an ex-consul who is slave to an old hag, a millionaire who is slave to a serving-maid; I will show you youths of the noblest birth in serfdom to pantomime players! No servitude is more disgraceful than that which is self-imposed. (Nulla servitus turpior est quam voluntaria.)
SENECA, *Epistulæ ad Lucilium*. Epis. 47, sec. 17.

4
Slavery enchains a few; more enchain themselves to slavery. (Paucos servitus, plures servitutem tenent.)
SENECA, *Epistulæ ad Lucilium*. Epis. 22. 11.

The most onerous slavery is to be a slave to oneself.
SENECA, *Naturales Questiones:* Bk. iii, *Præfatio*. Sec. 17.

So every bondman in his own hand bears
The power to cancel his captivity.
SHAKESPEARE, *Julius Cæsar*. Act i, sc. 3, l. 101.

5
The foulest death is preferable to the fairest slavery. (Præferendam esse spurcissimam mortem servitute mundissimæ.)
SENECA, *Epistulæ ad Lucilium*. Epis. 70, 21.

It is far better to be a mortal freeman than an immortal slave.
R. G. INGERSOLL, *Voltaire*.

6
As many have been killed by the wrath of slaves as by that of kings. (Non pauciores servorum ira cecidisse quam regnum.)
SENECA, *Epistulæ ad Lucilium*. Epis. iv, sec. 8.

7
O, what a rogue and peasant slave am I!
SHAKESPEARE, *Hamlet*. Act ii, sc. 2, l. 576.

A base slave,
A hilding for a livery, a squire's cloth,
A pantler, not so eminent.
SHAKESPEARE, *Cymbeline*. Act ii, sc. 3, l. 127.

8
You have among you many a purchased slave,
Which, like your asses and your dogs and mules,
You use in abject and in slavish parts,
Because you bought them.
SHAKESPEARE, *The Merchant of Venice*. Act iv, sc. 1, l. 90.

The distinguishing sign of slavery is to have a price, and to be bought for it.
RUSKIN, *Crown of Wild Olive: War*.

9
Disguise thyself as thou wilt, still, Slavery! said I,—still thou art a bitter draught!
LAURENCE STERNE, *Sentimental Journey: The Passport: The Hotel at Paris*.

10
The thrall in person may be free in soul.
TENNYSON, *Gareth and Lynette*, l. 162.

11
O men, made for slavery! (O homines, ad servitutem paratos!)
TIBERIUS. (TACITUS, *Annals*. Bk. iii, sec. 65.)

12
Slavery is as ancient as war, and war as human nature.
VOLTAIRE, *Philosophical Dictionary: Slaves*.

II—Slavery in England

13
The meanest Briton scorns the highest slave.
ADDISON, *The Campaign*, l. 300.

14
It could not, in the opinion of His Majesty's Government, be classified as slavery in the extreme acceptance of the word without some risk of terminological inexactitude.
WINSTON CHURCHILL, *Speech*, House of Commons, 22 Feb., 1906. Referring to Chinese labor in South Africa.

15
Slaves cannot breathe in England; if their lungs
Receive our air, that moment they are free;
They touch our country, and their shackles fall.
COWPER, *The Task*. Bk. ii, l. 40.

I speak in the spirit of the British law, which makes liberty commensurate with and inseparable from British soil; which proclaims even to the stranger and sojourner, the moment he sets his foot upon British earth, that the ground on which he treads is holy and consecrated by the genius of universal emancipation.
JOHN PHILPOT CURRAN, *British Law*.

16
A soil whose air is deemed too pure for slaves to breathe in.
FRANCIS HARGRAVE, *Argument in Somersett Habeas Corpus Case*, 14 May, 1772. James Somersett was a negro slave from Jamaica who accompanied his master to England, and claimed his freedom. The decision upheld the argument of Hargrave, Somersett's counsel, that slaves could not exist in England.

Every man who comes to England is entitled to the protection of the English law, whatever oppression he may heretofore have suffered, and whatever may be the colour of his skin, whether it is black, or whether it is white. (Quamvis ille niger, quamvis tu candidus.)

WILLIAM MURRAY, EARL OF MANSFIELD, *Decision,* in Somersett Habeas Corpus Case, May, 1772. (*State Trials.* Vol. xx, p. 1.)

Lord Mansfield first established the grand doctrine that the air of England is too pure to be breathed by a slave.

LORD JOHN CAMPBELL, *Lives of the Lord Chancellors.* Vol. ii, p. 418.

Foreign slaves as soon as they come within the limits of France are free. (Servi peregrini, ut primum Galliæ fines penetraverunt, eodem momento liberi sunt.)

BODINUS, a French jurist of the 17th century. (*Works.* Bk. i, ch. 4.)

1
Am I not a man and brother?

JOSIAH WEDGWOOD, *Motto,* on medallion designed by Wedgwood, 1787, representing a negro in chains, with one knee on the ground and both hands raised to heaven. Adopted as the seal of the Anti-Slavery Society of London.

2
O true yoke-fellow of Time,
Duty's intrepid liegeman, see, the palm
Is won, and by all Nations shall be worn!
The blood-stained Writing is for ever torn;
And thou henceforth wilt have a good man's calm,
A great man's happiness; thy zeal shall find
Repose at length, firm friend of human kind!

WORDSWORTH, *Poems Dedicated to National Independence.* Pt. ii, No. 3. To Thomas Clarkson, on the passing of the bill for abolition of the slave trade, March, 1807.

A Briton, even in love, should be
A subject, not a slave!

WORDSWORTH, *Poems Founded on the Affections.* No. 10, l. 19.

III—Slavery in America

3
If those laws of the southern states by virtue of which slavery exists there and is what it is, are not wrong, nothing is wrong.

LEONARD BACON, *Slavery Discussed: Preface.* (1846)

If slavery is not wrong, nothing is wrong.

LINCOLN, *Letter to A. G. Hodges,* 4 April, 1864.

4
God has put into every white man's hand a whip to flog the black.

CARLYLE, *Letter to Emerson,* 1848.

5
There shall be neither slavery nor involuntary servitude in the said territory.

NATHAN DANE, *Article,* added to the Ordinance for the Government of the Northwest Territory, 1787. (*Indiana Hist. Soc. Pub.* No. 1, p. 69.)

No more slave States and no more slave territory.

SALMON P. CHASE, *Platform Resolutions,* adopted by the Free-Soil National Convention, 9 Aug., 1848.

6
I do not see how a barbarous community and a civilized community can constitute a state. I think we must get rid of slavery or we must get rid of freedom.

EMERSON, *The Assault upon Mr. Sumner's Speech,* 26 May, 1856.

"A house divided against itself cannot stand." I believe this government cannot endure permanently half-slave and half-free. I do not expect the Union to be dissolved—I do not expect the house to fall—but I do expect it will cease to be divided. It will become all one thing, or all the other. Either the opponents of slavery will arrest the further spread of it, and place it where the public mind shall rest in the belief that it is in the course of ultimate extinction; or its advocates will push it forward, till it shall become alike lawful in all the States, old as well as new—North as well as South.

ABRAHAM LINCOLN, *Speech,* at the Republican state convention, Springfield, Ill., 17 June, 1858.

Where Slavery is, there Liberty cannot be; and where Liberty is, there Slavery cannot be.

CHARLES SUMNER, *Slavery and the Rebellion.* Speech before the N. Y. Young Men's Republican Union, 5 Nov., 1864.

Either be wholly slaves, or wholly free.

DRYDEN, *The Hind and the Panther.* Pt. ii, l. 285.

7
Resolved: That the compact which exists between the North and the South is a covenant with death and an agreement with hell, involving both parties in atrocious criminality, and should be immediately annulled.

WILLIAM LLOYD GARRISON, *Resolution,* adopted by the Massachusetts Anti-Slavery Society, 27 Jan., 1843.

8
In all social systems there must be a class to do the mean duties. . . . It constitutes the very mudsills of society. . . . Fortunately for the South, she found a race adapted to that purpose. . . . We use them for that purpose and call them slaves.

JAMES H. HAMMOND, *Speech,* U. S. Senate, March, 1858.

9
Whitee—as well as blackee—man-cipation.

THOMAS HOOD, *The Monkey Martyr.*

11
I intend no modification of my oft-expressed wish that all men everywhere could be free.

ABRAHAM LINCOLN, *Letter to Horace Greeley,* 22 Aug., 1862. (RAYMOND, *History of Lincoln's Administration.*)

In giving freedom to the slave we assure freedom

to the free,—honorable alike in what we give and what we preserve.

Abraham Lincoln, *Second Annual Message to Congress,* 1 Dec., 1862.

It is my last card, and I will play it and may win the trick.

Abraham Lincoln, referring to the Emancipation Proclamation. (Robert C. Winthrop, *Diary,* Sharon Springs, N. Y., 31 July, 1863.) Judge Edwards Pierrepont described to Winthrop a visit paid by him to the President on the Sunday preceding the issuing of the Proclamation, during the course of which he alleged that Lincoln made the remark as quoted.

Whenever I hear anyone arguing for slavery, I feel a strong impulse to see it tried on him personally.

Lincoln, *Address,* 17 March, 1865.

1 Out from the land of bondage 'tis decreed our
slaves shall go,
And signs to us are offered as erst to Pharaoh;
If we are blind, their exodus, like Israel's of
yore,
Through a Red Sea is doomed to be, whose
surges are of gore.

J. R. Lowell, *On the Capture of Certain Fugitive Slaves Near Washington.* (1850)

But libbaty's a kind o' thing
Thet don't agree with niggers.

J. R. Lowell, *The Biglow Papers.* Ser. i, No. 6.

2 Slavery is in flagrant violation of the institutions of America—direct government—over all the people, by all the people, for all the people.

Theodore Parker, *Sermon,* Music Hall, Boston, 4 July, 1858. *See also under* Democracy.

3 No slave is here:—our unchained feet
Walk freely as the waves that beat
Our coast.

James Gates Percival, *New England.*

4 An irrepressible struggle between opposing and enduring forces.

W. H. Seward, *Speech,* at Rochester, N. Y., 25 Oct., 1858, referring to slavery.

5 This is a world of compensations, and he who would *be* no slave must consent to *have* no slave. Those who deny freedom to others deserve it not for themselves, and, under a just God, they cannot long retain it.

Charles Sumner, *Letter,* 6 April, 1859, declining to attend festival in honor of anniversary of Jefferson's birthday. Has been wrongly attributed to Abraham Lincoln, who probably quoted it.

By the Law of Slavery, man, created in the image of God, is divested of the human character, and declared to be a mere chattel.

Charles Sumner, *The Anti-Slavery Enterprise.* Address at New York, 9 May, 1859.

6 We preach Democracy in vain while Tory and Conservative can point to the other side of the Atlantic and say: "There are nineteen millions of the human race free absolutely, governing themselves—the government of all, by all, for all; but instead of being a consistent republic, it is one widespread confederacy of free men for the enslavement of a nation of another complexion."

George Thompson, *Speech,* House of Commons, 1851.

7 Under a government which imprisons any unjustly, the true place for a just man is also a prison, . . . the only house in a slave State in which a free man can abide with honor.

H. D. Thoreau, *The Duty of Civil Disobedience.*

8 Mister Ward, don't yur blud bile at the thawt that three million and a half of your culled brethren air a clanking their chains in the South?—Sez I, not a bile! Let 'em clank!

Artemus Ward, *His Book: Oberlin.*

9 I never mean, unless some particular circumstances should compel me to do it, to possess another slave by purchase, it being among my first wishes to see some plan adopted by which slavery in this country may be abolished by law.

George Washington, *Letter to John Francis Mercer,* 9 Sept., 1786. *Writings,* xxix, 5.

10 That execrable sum of all villainies commonly called the slave-trade.

John Wesley, *Journal,* 12 Feb., 1772.

Perjury only filches your neighbor's rights. Man-stealing takes rights and neighbor too.

Wendell Phillips, *Progress.* Address delivered at Boston, 17 Feb., 1861.

11 Our fellow-countrymen in chains!
Slaves, in a land of light and law!
Slaves, crouching on the very plains
Where rolled the storm of Freedom's
war! . . .
What! mothers from their children riven!
What! God's own image bought and sold!
Americans to market driven,
And bartered as the brute for gold!

Whittier, *Expostulation,* l. 1. (1842)

SLEEP

See also Bed; Night and Rest

I—Sleep: Apothegms

12 What probing deep
Has ever solved the mystery of sleep?

T. B. Aldrich, *Human Ignorance.*

The mystery Of folded sleep.

Tennyson, *A Dream of Fair Women,* l. 262.

1
We sleep, but the loom of life never stops and the pattern which was weaving when the sun went down is weaving when it comes up tomorrow.

HENRY WARD BEECHER, *Life Thoughts*, p. 12.

2
Strange state of being! (for 'tis still to be)
Senseless to feel, and with seal'd eyes to see.

BYRON, *Don Juan*. Canto iv, st. 30.

For sleep is awful.

BYRON, *Don Juan*. Canto ii, st. 143.

Into dreadful slumber lull'd.

TENNYSON, *Eleänore*, l. 30.

3
Our life is two-fold: Sleep hath its own world,
A boundary between the things misnamed
Death and existence: Sleep hath its own world,
And a wide realm of wild reality.

BYRON, *The Dream*, l. 1.

4
While we are asleep, we are all equal.

CERVANTES, *Don Quixote*. Pt. ii, ch. 43.

5
I shall sleep like a top.

SIR WILLIAM D'AVENANT, *The Rivals*. Act iii. (1668)

Juan slept like a top, or like the dead.

BYRON, *Don Juan*. Canto ii, st. 134.

5a
Or snorted we in the Seven Sleepers' den?

JOHN DONNE, *The Good-Morrow*. (1633)

The Seven Sleepers of Ephesus, who had been slumbering two hundred years in a cavern of Mount Celion.

S. BARING-GOULD, *Curious Myths of the Middle Ages*, p. 101. (1869)

6
He is so wary that he sleeps like a hare, with his eyes open.

THOMAS FULLER, *Gnomologia*. No. 1947.

Which sleepeth (as they say) her eyes being open.

GUAZZO, *Civile Conversation*. (PETTIE, tr. 1581)

7
You counsel me to take counsel of my pillow.

GABRIEL HARVEY, *Letter-Book*, p. 21. (1573)

8
Perhaps no man shall ever know whether it is better to wear nightcaps or not.

SAMUEL JOHNSON. (BOSWELL, *Life*.)

9
Sleep such as makes the darkness brief.
(Somnus qui faciat breves tenebras.)

MARTIAL, *Epigrams*. Bk. x, epig. 47, l. 11.

10
Now may our heiress fair on both ears sleep.
('Επ' ἀμφότερα νῦν ἠπίκληρος ἡ καλὴ μέλλει καθευδήσειν.)

MENANDER, *Plocium*. Frag. 402.

You can sleep on both ears: i. e., in security. (In aurem utramvis otiose ut dormias.)

TERENCE, *Heauton Timorumenos*. l. 342.

Then truly live I like one that sleepeth on both his ears.

JOHN PALSGRAVE, *Acolastus*. C 4. (1540)

Supine amidst our flowing store,
We slept securely, and we dreamt of more.

DRYDEN, *Threnodia Augustalis*, l. 14.

11
O, we're a' noddin', nid, nid, noddin';
O, we're a' noddin' at our house at hame.

CAROLINA NAIRNE, *We're a' Noddin'*.

12
No one when asleep is good for anything.

PLATO. (DIOGENES LAERTIUS, *Plato*. Sec. 39.)

13
He sleeps well who knows not that he sleeps ill. (Bene dormit, qui non sentit quod male dormiat.)

PUBLILIUS SYRUS, *Sententiæ*. No. 77. FRANCIS BACON, *Ornamenta Rationalia*. No. 5.

What blessed ignorance equals this,
To sleep—and not to know it?

THOMAS HOOD, *Miss Kilmansegg: Her Dream*.

14
I never sleep comfortably except when I am at sermon or when I pray to God. (Je ne dors jamais bien à mon aise sinon quand je suis au sermon, ou quand je prie Dieu.)

RABELAIS, *Works*. Bk. i, ch. 41.

15
Sleep, riches, and health, to be truly enjoyed, must be interrupted.

RICHTER, *Flower, Fruit, and Thorn*. Ch. 8.

16
We did sleep day out of countenance.

SHAKESPEARE, *Antony and Cleopatra*, ii, 2, 181.

He sleeps by day More than the wild-cat.

SHAKESPEARE, *The Merchant of Venice*, ii, 5, 47.

17
I would 'twere bed-time, Hal, and all well.

SHAKESPEARE, *I Henry IV*. Act v, sc. 1, l. 125.

Winding up days with toil and nights with sleep.

SHAKESPEARE, *Henry V*. Act iv, sc. 1, l. 296.

18
I have an exposition of sleep come upon me.

SHAKESPEARE, *A Midsummer-Night's Dream*. Act iv, sc. 1, l. 42.

I let fall the windows of mine eyes.

SHAKESPEARE, *Richard III*. Act iv, sc. 3, l. 116.

19
Whatever moves, or toils, or grieves, hath its appointed sleep.

SHELLEY, *Stanzas*. April, 1814.

20
I sleep, but my heart waketh.

Old Testament: Song of Solomon, v, 2.

21
I am going to the land of Nod.

SWIFT, *Polite Conversation*. Dial. iii. (1738)

22
Who can wrestle against Sleep?—Yet is that giant very gentleness.

MARTIN FARQUHAR TUPPER, *Of Beauty*.

A little more sleep and a little more slumber.

ISAAC WATTS, *The Sluggard*.

II—Sleep: Care-Charmer Sleep

24
What means this heaviness that hangs upon me?

This lethargy that creeps through all my
senses?
Nature, oppress'd and harrass'd out with care,
Sinks down to rest.
ADDISON, *Cato*. Act v, sc. 1.

1
Sweet are the slumbers of the virtuous man.
ADDISON, *Cato*. Act v, sc. 4.

2
Heaven trims our lamps while we sleep.
A. B. ALCOTT, *Table Talk: Sleep*.

Sleep is a sort of innocence and purification. Blessed be He who gave it to the poor sons of men as the sure and faithful companion of life, our daily healer and consoler.
AMIEL, *Journal*, 20 March, 1853.

3
Silken rest Tie all thy cares up!
BEAUMONT AND FLETCHER, *Four Plays in One:* Sc. 4, *Triumph of Love*.

4
Blessings on him that first invented sleep! It covers a man, thoughts and all, like a cloak; it is meat for the hungry, drink for the thirsty, heat for the cold, and cold for the hot. It is the current coin that purchases cheaply all the pleasures of the world, and the balance that sets even king and shepherd, fool and sage.
CERVANTES, *Don Quixote*. Pt. ii, ch. 68. Quoted by Sterne, *Tristram Shandy*, iv, 15.

"God bless the man who first invented sleep!"
So Sancho Panza said and so say I;
And bless him, also, that he didn't keep
His great discovery to himself, nor try
To make it,—as the lucky fellow might—
A close monopoly by patent-right.
J. G. SAXE, *Early Rising*.

5
So long as I am asleep I have neither fear nor hope, trouble nor glory.
CERVANTES, *Don Quixote*. Pt. ii, ch. 68.

Sleep is the best cure for waking troubles.
CERVANTES, *Don Quixote*. Pt. ii, ch. 70.

6
O sleep! it is a gentle thing,
Beloved from pole to pole!
To Mary Queen the praise be given!
She sent the gentle sleep from Heaven
That slid into my soul.
S. T. COLERIDGE, *The Ancient Mariner*. Pt. v.

7
Her gentle limbs did she undress,
And lay down in her loveliness.
S. T. COLERIDGE, *Christabel*. Pt. i, l. 237.

For she belike hath drunken deep
Of all the blessedness of sleep!
S. T. COLERIDGE, *Christabel*. Pt. ii, l. 375.

8
I met at eve the Prince of Sleep,
His was a still and lovely face,
He wandered through a valley steep.
Lovely in a lonely place.
WALTER DE LA MARE, *I Met at Eve*.

9
Sleep, Silence' child, sweet father of soft
rest,
Prince, whose approach peace to all mortals
brings,
Indifferent host to shepherds and to kings,
Sole comforter of minds with grief op-
prest.
WILLIAM DRUMMOND, *Sonnets*. No. 9.

10
Come, Sleep, and with thy sweet deceiving
Lock me in delight awhile.
JOHN FLETCHER, *The Woman-Hater*.

11
O sleep! in pity thou art made
A double boon to such as we;
Beneath closed lids and folds of deepest
shade,
We think we see.
NATHANIEL FROTHINGHAM, *The Sight of the Blind*.

12
Oh, lightly, lightly tread!
A holy thing is sleep,
On the worn spirit shed,
And eyes that wake to weep.
FELICIA DOROTHEA HEMANS, *The Sleeper*.

13
Dream, who loves dreams! forget all grief;
Find in sleep's nothingness relief.
LIONEL JOHNSON, *Oxford Nights*.

14
O magic sleep! O comfortable bird,
That broodest o'er the troubled sea of the
mind
Till it is hush'd and smooth! O unconfin'd
Restraint! imprison'd liberty! great key
To golden palaces, strange minstrelsy,
Fountains grotesque, new trees, bespangled
caves,
Echoing grottoes, full of tumbling waves
And moonlight; aye, to all the mazy world
Of silvery enchantment!—who, upfurl'd
Beneath thy drowsy wing a triple hour,
But renovates and lives?
KEATS, *Endymion*. Bk. i, l. 453.

O soft embalmer of the still midnight,
Shutting, with careful fingers and benign,
Our gloom-pleas'd eyes, embower'd from the
light,
Enshaded in forgetfulness divine:
O soothest Sleep!
KEATS, *To Sleep*.

15
Bed is the boon for me!
It's well to bake and sweep,
But hear the word of old Lizette:
It's better than all to sleep.
AGNES LEE, *Old Lizette on Sleep*.

16
Cool Sleep, thy reeds, in solemn ranks,
That murmur peace to me by midnight's
streams,
At dawn I pluck, and dayward pipe my flock
of dreams.
PERCY MACKAYE, *To Sleep*.

1
By the Gate of Sleep we enter the Enchanted Valleys.
WILLIAM SHARP, *The Enchanted Valleys.*

2
Enfold me in thy mystical embrace,
Thou sovereign gift of God, most sweet, most blest,
O happy Sleep!
ADA LOUISE MARTIN, *Sleep.*

3
The dovecote doors of sleep.
ALICE MEYNELL, *At Night.*

The dewy-feather'd sleep.
MILTON, *Il Penseroso*, l. 146.

The timely dew of sleep.
MILTON, *Paradise Lost*. Bk. iv, l. 614.

4
Sleep, dear Sleep, sweet harlot of the senses,
Delilah of the spirit, you unnerve
The strong man's knees, depose his laughing brain,
And make him a mere mass of steady breathing.
CHRISTOPHER MORLEY, *Sleep.*

5
Blessed are the sleepy, for they shall soon drop off.
NIETZSCHE, *Thus Spake Zarathustra: Of the Chairs of Virtue.*

6
Take me upon thy breast,
O river of rest.
Draw me down to thy side,
Slow-moving tide.
GRACE FALLOW NORTON, *O Sleep.*

7
O Sleep, thou rest of all things, Sleep, gentlest of the gods, peace of the soul, who puttest care to flight. (Somne, quies rerum, placidissime, Somne, deorum, Pax animi, quem cura fugit.)
OVID, *Metamorphoses*. Bk. xi, l. 623.

8
He that sleeps feels not the tooth-ache.
SHAKESPEARE, *Cymbeline*. Act v, sc. 4, l. 177.

9
Methought I heard a voice cry, "Sleep no more!
Macbeth does murder sleep," the innocent sleep,
Sleep that knits up the ravell'd sleave of care,
The death of each day's life, sore labour's bath,
Balm of hurt minds, great nature's second course,
Chief nourisher in life's feast.
SHAKESPEARE, *Macbeth*. Act ii, sc. 2, l. 35.

The season of all natures, sleep.
SHAKESPEARE, *Macbeth*. Act iii, sc. 4, l. 141.

Sleep, that sometimes shuts up sorrow's eye,
Steal me awhile from mine own company.
SHAKESPEARE, *A Midsummer-Night's Dream*. Act iii, sc. 2, l. 435.

10
Sleep, the fresh dew of languid love, the rain
Whose drops quench kisses till they burn again.
SHELLEY, *Epipsychidion*, l. 558.

11
Come, Sleep! O Sleep, the certain knot of peace,
The baiting-place of wit, the balm of woe,
The poor man's wealth, the prisoner's release,
Th' indifferent judge between the high and low!
SIR PHILIP SIDNEY, *Astrophel and Stella*. Sonnet 39.

12
Gentle sleep!
Scatter thy drowsiest poppies from above;
And in new dreams not soon to vanish, bless
My senses with the sight of her I love.
HORACE SMITH, *Poppies and Sleep.*

13
Sleep's the only medicine that gives ease. ('Αλλ' ἐὰν χρεὼν ἔκηλον εὕδειν.)
SOPHOCLES, *Philoctetes*, l. 768.

Sleep is better than medicine.
JOHN RAY, *English Proverbs.*

14
Thou hast been call'd, O Sleep! the friend of Woe,
But 'tis the happy who have call'd thee so.
SOUTHEY, *The Curse of Kehama*. Pt. xv, st. 12.

15
I am tired of tears and laughter,
And men that laugh and weep
Of what may come hereafter
For men that sow to reap:
I am weary of days and hours,
Blown buds of barren flowers,
Desires and dreams and powers,
And everything but sleep.
SWINBURNE, *The Garden of Proserpine*. St. 2.

Thou art more than the day or the morrow, the seasons that laugh or that weep;
For these give joy and sorrow; but thou, Proserpina, sleep.
Sweet is the treading of wine, and sweet the feet of the dove;
But a goodlier gift is thine than foam of the grapes or love.
SWINBURNE, *Hymn to Proserpine*, l. 3.

16
The end is come of pleasant places,
The end of tender words and faces,
The end of all, the poppied sleep.
SWINBURNE, *Ilicet*. St. 1.

All gifts but one the jealous God may keep
From our soul's longing, one he cannot—sleep.
This, though he grudge all other grace to prayer,
This grace his closed hand cannot choose but spare.
This, though his ear be sealed to all that live,
Be it lightly given or lothly, God must give.
SWINBURNE, *Tristram of Lyonesse: Prelude*, l. 205.

1
To sleep! to sleep! The long bright day is done,
And darkness rises from the fallen sun.
To sleep! to sleep!
Whate'er thy joys, they vanish with the day;
Whate'er thy griefs, in sleep they fade away.
To sleep! to sleep!
Sleep, mournful heart, and let the past be past!
Sleep, happy soul! all life will sleep at last.
To sleep! to sleep!

TENNYSON, *The Foresters*. Act i, sc. 3, *Song*.

2
To tired limbs and over-busy thoughts,
Inviting sleep and soft forgetfulness.

WORDSWORTH, *The Excursion*. Bk. iv, l. 1323.

3
Tir'd Nature's sweet restorer, balmy sleep!
He, like the world, his ready visit pays
Where fortune smiles; the wretched he forsakes;
Swift on his downy pinion flies from woe,
And lights on lids unsullied with a tear.

YOUNG, *Night Thoughts*. Night i, l. 1.

III—Sleep: Wishes

4
Still believe that ever round you
Spirits float who watch and wait;
Nor forget the twain who found you
Sleeping nigh the Golden Gate.

BESANT AND RICE, *The Case of Mr. Lucraft and Other Tales*, p. 92.

5
Visit her, gentle Sleep! with wings of healing,
And may this storm be but a mountain-birth,
May all the stars hang bright above her dwelling,
Silent as though they watched the sleeping Earth!

S. T. COLERIDGE, *Dejection*, l. 128.

6
Softly, O midnight hours!
Move softly o'er the bowers
Where lies in happy sleep a girl so fair:
For ye have power, men say,
Our hearts in sleep to sway
And cage cold fancies in a moonlight snare.

AUBREY DE VERE, *Softly, O Midnight Hours*.

7
Sleep sweet within this quiet room,
O thou! who'er thou art,
And let no mournful yesterday
Disturb thy quiet heart. . . .
Forget thyself and all the world,
Put out each feverish light.
The stars are watching overhead.
Sleep sweet! Good night! Good night!

ELLEN HUNTINGTON GATES, *Sweet Sleep*. Originally written by Mrs. Gates as a motto for a silken quilt made by a friend, the first line reading, "Sleep sweet beneath this silken quilt."

8
Breathe thy balm upon the lonely,
Gentle Sleep!
As the twilight breezes bless
With sweet scents the wilderness,
Ah, let warm white dove-wings only
Round them sweep!

LUCY LARCOM, *Sleep Song*.

9
Dreams of the summer night!
Tell her, her lover keeps
Watch! while in slumbers light
She sleeps! My lady sleeps!

LONGFELLOW, *Spanish Student*. Act i, sc. 3.

10
To all, to each, a fair good-night,
And pleasing dreams, and slumbers light!

WALTER SCOTT, *Marmion: L'Envoy*.

Good night, good night! As sweet repose and rest
Come to thy heart, as that within my breast!

SHAKESPEARE, *Romeo and Juliet*. Act ii, sc. 2, l. 123.

11
On your eyelids crown the god of sleep,
Charming your blood with pleasing heaviness:
Making such difference 'twixt wake and sleep,
As is the difference betwixt day and night,
The hour before the heavenly-harness'd team
Begins his golden progress in the east.

SHAKESPEARE, *I Henry IV*. Act iii, sc. 1, l. 217.

Enjoy the honey-heavy dew of slumber.

SHAKESPEARE, *Julius Cæsar*. Act ii, sc. 1, l. 230.

Sleep dwell upon thine eyes, peace in thy breast!
Would I were sleep and peace, so sweet to rest!

SHAKESPEARE, *Romeo and Juliet*. Act ii, sc. 2, l. 187.

Sleep rock thy brain.

SHAKESPEARE, *Hamlet*. Act iii, sc. 2, l. 237.

12
Good night, good sleep, good rest from sorrow,
To these that shall not have good morrow;
The gods be gentle to all these.

SWINBURNE, *Ilicet*. St. 8.

13
Slumbers sweet thy mercy send us,
Holy dreams and hopes attend us,
This livelong night.

RICHARD WHATELY, *Evening Hymn*.

IV—Sleep: Prayers and Lullabies

14
Sleep an' let me to my wark—
A' thae claes to airn—
Jenny wi' the airn teeth,
Come an' tak' the bairn!

ALEXANDER ANDERSON, *Jenny Wi' the Airn Teeth*.

15
When the sheep are in the fauld, and a' the kye at hame,
And all the weary world to sleep are gane.

LADY ANNE BARNARD, *Auld Robin Gray*.

1
Sleep, sleep, beauty bright,
Dreaming in the joys of night;
Sleep, sleep; in thy sleep
Little sorrows sit and weep.
William Blake, *Cradle Song.*

2
Fly away, Kentucky Babe, fly away to rest,
Lay yo' kinky, woolly head on yo' mammy's breast,—
Close yo' eyes in sleep.
Richard Henry Buck, *Kentucky Babe.* (1896)

Go to sleep, my little piccaninny, . . .
Mammy's little Alabama coon.
Hattie Starr, *Little Alabama Coon.* (1893) Sung by Frankie Raymond in *Aladdin, Jr.*

3
Golden slumbers kiss your eyes,
Smiles awake you when you rise.
Sleep, pretty wantons, do not cry,
And I will sing a lullaby.
Rock them, rock them, lullaby.
Thomas Dekker, *Patient Grissil: Lullaby.*

4
If thou wilt close thy drowsy eyes,
My mulberry one, my golden son,
The rose shall sing thee lullabies,
My pretty cosset lambkin!
Eugene Field, *Armenian Lullaby.*

5
Wynken, Blynken, and Nod one night
Sailed off in a wooden shoe—
Sailed on a river of crystal light
Into a sea of dew.
Eugene Field, *Wynken, Blynken, and Nod.*

6
I lay me down to sleep with little care
Whether my waking find me here or there.
Mary Woolsey Howland, *Rest.*

7
Like infant's slumbers, pure and light.
John Keble, *The Christian Year: Evening.*

Thou driftest gently down the tides of sleep.
Longfellow, *To a Child,* l. 115.

8
Sleep, baby, sleep!
Thy father's watching the sheep,
Thy mother's shaking the dreamland tree,
And down drops a little dream for thee.
Sleep, baby, sleep!
Elizabeth Prentiss, *Cradle Song.*

9
I will both lay me down in peace, and sleep: for thou, Lord, only makest me dwell in safety.
Old Testament: Psalms, iv, 8.

10
O, hush thee, my babie, thy sire was a knight,
Thy mother a lady both lovely and bright;
The woods and the glens, from the towers which we see,
They all are belonging, dear babie, to thee.
Scott, *Lullaby of an Infant Chief.*

11
Hush, my dear, lie still and slumber!
Holy angels guard thy bed!
Heavenly blessings without number
Gently falling on thy head.
Isaac Watts, *A Cradle Hymn.*

12
Now I lay me down to sleep,
I pray the Lord my soul to keep;
If I should die before I wake,
I pray the Lord my soul to take.
Unknown, *Prayer at Lying Down.* (*New England Primer,* 1737.) A few editions give the reading, "I pray, Thee, Lord."

Now I lay me down to sleep,
I pray Thee, Lord, my soul to keep;
When in the morning light I wake,
Lead Thou my feet, that I may take
The path of love for Thy dear sake.
Unknown, *Now I Lay Me: Revised.*

I lay me down in peace and sleep,
For thou, dear Lord, my soul will keep.
And as I rest, this prayer I make:
To do thy will when I awake.
Grenville Kleiser, *Evening Prayer.*

N.R.A. me down to sleep,
I pray the Lord my codes I'll keep;
If I should bust before I wake,
A.F.O.L. my plant will take.
Unknown, *Now I Lay Me: New Deal Version.* For the benefit of future generations, it may be worth explaining that in the summer of 1933, a government agency known as the National Recovery Administration, which was declared unconstitutional by the U. S. Supreme Court in 1935, endeavored to regulate American industry by a series of codes, establishing wages and working hours; and the American Federation of Labor sought to organize the country's workers in order to enforce them. The whole movement, of which the N.R.A. was only a part, was known as the "New Deal."

13
Hush-a-bye, baby, on the tree-top,
When the wind blows, the cradle will rock;
When the bough breaks, the cradle will fall,
And down will come baby, cradle, and all.
Unknown. *Old Nursery Rhyme. The Book Lover* (Feb., 1904) says it was the first poem produced on American soil, by a youth who came over in the Mayflower. It has also been attributed to Charles Blake.

V—Sleep of Little and Great

14
Art thou poor, yet hast thou golden slumbers?
O sweet content!
Thomas Dekker, *Patient Grissil: Song.*

15
The sleep of a labouring man is sweet.
Old Testament: Ecclesiastes, v, 12.

Sleep is sweet to the labouring man.
John Bunyan, *The Pilgrim's Progress: The Author's Apology.*

Weariness
Can snore upon the flint, when resty sloth
Finds the down pillow hard.
Shakespeare, *Cymbeline.* Act iii, sc. 6, l. 33.

1 Soft sleep does not disdain the humble cottage of the peasant, nor the shady bank, nor the valley by zephyrs fanned. (Somnus agrestium Lenis vivorum non humilis domos Fastidit umbrosamque ripam, Non Zephyris agitata Tempe.)

HORACE, *Odes*. Bk. iii, ode 1, l. 21.

2 The lowliest cot will give thee peaceful sleep,
While Gaius tosses on his bed of down.

MARTIAL, *Epigrams*. Bk. ix, epig. 92, l. 3.

Why rather, sleep, liest thou in smoky cribs,
Upon uneasy pallets stretching thee, . . .
Than in the perfum'd chambers of the great,
Under the canopies of costly state,
And lull'd with sound of sweetest melody?
O thou dull god, why liest thou with the vile
In loathsome beds, and leavest the kingly couch
A watch-case or a common 'larum-bell?

SHAKESPEARE, *II Henry IV*. Act iii, sc. 1, l. 9.

Canst thou, O partial sleep, give thy repose
To the wet sea-boy in an hour so rude,
And in the calmest and most stillest night,
With all appliances and means to boot,
Deny it to a king? Then happy low, lie down!
Uneasy lies the head that wears a crown.

SHAKESPEARE, *II Henry IV*. Act iii, sc. 1, l. 26.

Yet not so sound and half so deeply sweet
As he whose brow with homely biggen bound
Snores out the watch of night.

SHAKESPEARE, *II Henry IV*. Act iv, sc. 5, l. 26.

VI—Sleep and Health

3 It is recorded of Methusalem, who, being the longest liver, may be supposed to have best preserved his health, that he slept always in the open air; for, when he had lived five hundred years, an angel said to him, "Arise, Methusalem, and build thee an house, for thou shalt live yet five hundred years longer." But Methusalem answered and said, "If I am to live but five hundred years longer, it is not worth while to build me an house; I will sleep in the air, as I have been used to do."

BENJAMIN FRANKLIN, *Letter to Miss* ——, on the art of procuring pleasant dreams. The story is one of Franklin's pleasant inventions.

4 One hour's sleep before midnight is worth three afterwards.

GEORGE HERBERT, *Jacula Prudentum*. (1640)

5 It does not become a man of counsel to sleep the whole night through. (Οὐ χρὴ παννύχιον εὕδειν βουληφόρον ἄνδρα.)

HOMER, *Iliad*. Bk. ii, l. 24.

6 I never take a nap after dinner but when I have had a bad night, and then the nap takes me.

SAMUEL JOHNSON. (BOSWELL, *Life*, 1775.)

7 For his sleep
Was aery light, from pure digestion bred.

MILTON, *Paradise Lost*. Bk. v, l. 3.

8 Sleep after luncheon is not good. (Non bonust somnus de prandio.)

PLAUTUS, *Mostellaria*, l. 697. (Act iii, sc. 2.)

For much sleep is not medicinal in middle of the day.

JOHN RUSSELL, *Boke of Nature*, l. 952.

Let your midday sleep be short or none at all. (Sit brevis aut nullus tibi somnus meridianus.)

UNKNOWN, *Maxim, School of Salerno*.

9 Five hours sleep a traveller, seven a scholar, eight a merchant, and eleven every knave.

TORRIANO, *Piazza Universale*, 114. (1666)

Six hours for a man, seven for a woman, and eight for a fool. The precept seems to be based on the Latin lines: Sex horis dormire sat est juvenique senique, Septem vix pigro, nulli concedimius octo.

Collectio Salernitana, v, 7. (*Notes and Queries*, xi, v, 52.)

10 When it is time to turn over, it is time to turn out. (Or exactly, "When one begins to turn in bed, it is time to get up.")

DUKE OF WELLINGTON, *Maxims and Table-Talk*.

VII—Sleep: Brother of Death

See also Death: The Last Sleep

11 Since the brother of death daily haunts us with dying mementoes.

SIR THOMAS BROWNE, *Hydriotaphia*. Ch. v, sec. 9.

And Sleep, Death's brother, yet a friend to life,
Gave wearied Nature a restorative.

SAMUEL BUTLER, *Repartees Between Cat and Puss*.

12 Care-charmer Sleep, son of the sable Night,
Brother to Death, in silent darkness born;
Relieve my languish, and restore the light.

SAMUEL DANIEL, *Sonnets to Delia*. No. xlvi.

Care-charming Sleep, thou easer of all woes,
Brother to Death . . . thou son of Night.

JOHN FLETCHER, *Valentinian*. Act v, sc. 2.

13 One brother anticipates another—Sleep before Death.

DIOGENES, when roused from slumber a little before his death. (PLUTARCH, *Apothegms: Diogenes*.)

14 Sleep, the brother of Death. (Ὕπνον, κασίγνητον Θανάτοιο.)

HESIOD, *Theogony*, l. 756.

There she met Sleep, the brother of Death. (Ἔνθ' Ὕπνῳ ξύμβλητο, κασιγνήτῳ Θανάτοιο.)

HOMER, *Iliad*. Bk. xiv, l. 231.

Then Sleep and Death, two twins of winged race,
Of matchless swiftness, but of silent pace.
HOMER, *Iliad*. Bk. xvi, l. 831. (Pope, tr.)

Death's own brother, Sleep. (Consanguineus Leti Sopor.)
VERGIL, *Æneid*. Bk. vi, l. 278.

1 Heavy Sleep, the Cousin of Death.
THOMAS SACKVILLE, *Sleep*.

2 How wonderful is Death,
Death and his brother Sleep!
One, pale as yonder waning moon
With lips of lurid blue;
The other, rosy as the morn
When throned on ocean's wave
It blushes o'er the world:
Yet both so passing wonderful!
SHELLEY, *Queen Mab*, l. 1. *Queen Mab* was written in 1813. Two years later, Shelley wrote another poem, *The Dæmon of the World*, which began with the same lines.

3 When in the down I sink my head,
Sleep, Death's twin-brother, times my breath.
TENNYSON, *In Memoriam*. Pt. lxvii.

Sleep, kinsman thou to death and trance
And madness, thou hast forged at last
A night-long present of the past.
TENNYSON, *In Memoriam*. Pt. lxxi.

VIII—Sleep: Death's Counterfeit

4 Sleep is like death, and after sleep
The world seems new begun;
White thoughts stand luminous and firm,
Like statues in the sun;
Refreshed from supersensuous founts,
The soul to clearer vision mounts.
WILLIAM ALLINGHAM, *Sleep*.

5 Death without dying—living, but not Life.
SIR EDWIN ARNOLD, *The Light of the World*. Bk. iv, l. 164.

6 We term sleep a death . . . by which we may be literally said to die daily; in fine, so like death, I dare not trust it without my prayers.
SIR THOMAS BROWNE, *Religio Medici*. Pt. ii, sec. 12.

Sleep is a death: O make me try,
By sleeping, what it is to die;
And as gently lay my head
On my grave, as now my bed.
SIR THOMAS BROWNE, *Religio Medici*. Pt. ii, sec. 12.

7 Sleep falls like snowflakes, and it seems
'Tis always drifting into dreams;
But Death falls like the snow at sea,
And drifts into Eternity.
FRANCIS CARLIN, *Sleep*.

8 Sleep, I have heard say, has only one fault, that it is like death; for between a sleeping man and a dead man there is very little difference.
CERVANTES, *Don Quixote*. Pt. ii, ch. 68.

9 Sleep's but a short death; death's but a longer sleep.
PHINEAS FLETCHER, *Apollyonists*. Canto i, st. 6.

10 There will be sleeping enough in the grave.
BENJAMIN FRANKLIN, *Poor Richard*, 1758. A parody of a popular saying, "Thou shalt sorrow enough in hell," derived from a tale in the *Gesta Romanorum*.

11 O fool, what else is sleep but the image of chill death? (Stulte, quid est somnus, gelidæ nisi mortis imago?)
OVID, *Amores*. Bk. ii, eleg. ix, l. 41.

12 Lived she?—in sooth 't were hard to tell,
Sleep counterfeited Death so well.
W. M. PRAED, *The Bridal of Belmont*, l. 238.

13 O sleep, thou ape of death, lie dull upon her!
And be her sense but as a monument.
SHAKESPEARE, *Cymbeline*. Act ii, sc. 2, l. 31.

14 Shake off this downy sleep, death's counterfeit,
And look on death itself!
SHAKESPEARE, *Macbeth*. Act ii, sc. 3, l. 81.

O'er their brows death-counterfeiting sleep
With leaden legs and batty wings doth creep.
SHAKESPEARE, *A Midsummer-Night's Dream*. Act iii, sc. 2, l. 364.

Thy eyes' windows fall,
Like death, when he shuts up the day of life;
Each part, deprived of supple government,
Shall, stiff and stark and cold, appear like death.
SHAKESPEARE, *Romeo and Juliet*. Act iv, sc. 1, l. 100.

15 Sleep, death's ally.
ROBERT SOUTHWELL, *St. Peter's Complaint*.

16 For next to Death is Sleep to be compared:
Therefore his house is unto his annext.
SPENSER, *Faerie Queene*. Bk. ii, canto vii, st. 25.

17 Deep rest and sweet, most like indeed to death's own quietness. (Dulcis et alta quies, placidæque simillima morti.)
VERGIL, *Æneid*. Bk. vi, l. 522.

18 Come, gentle sleep! attend thy votary's prayer,
And, though death's image, to my couch repair;
How sweet, though lifeless, yet with life to lie,
And, without dying, O how sweet to die!
THOMAS WARTON, *Latin Epigram on Sleep*. (John Wolcot, tr.)

19 Each night we die,
Each morn are born anew: each day, a life!
YOUNG, *Night Thoughts*. Night ii, l. 286.

IX—Sleep: Insomnia

1 Slumber everywhere! . . .
But I in chilling twilight stand and wait
At the portcullis of thy castle gate,
Longing to see the charmèd door of dreams
Turn on its noiseless hinges, delicate Sleep!
THOMAS BAILEY ALDRICH, *Invocation to Sleep.*

2
Come to me now! O, come! benignest sleep!
And fold me up, as evening doth a flower,
From my vain self, and vain things which have power
Upon my soul to make me smile or weep.
And when thou comest, oh, like Death be deep.
PATRICK PROCTOR ALEXANDER, *Sleep.*

3
Sleep I can get nane For thinking on my dearie.
BURNS, *Simmer's a Pleasant Time.*

4
In vain from side to side he throws
His form, in courtship of repose.
BYRON, *The Siege of Corinth.* St. 13.

My slumbers, if I slumber, are not sleep,
But a continuance of enduring thought.
BYRON, *Manfred.* Act i, sc. 1.

Sleep, Which will not be commanded.
BYRON, *Marino Faliero.* Act iv, sc. 1.

5
And I with sobs did pray—
O let me be awake, my God!
Or let me sleep alway.
S. T. COLERIDGE, *The Ancient Mariner.* Pt. vi.

6
Sister Simplicitie!
Sing, sing a song to me,—
Sing me to sleep!
Some legend low and long,
Slow as the summer song
Of the dull Deep.
SIDNEY DOBELL, *A Sleep Song.*

7
Those only can sleep who do not care to sleep.
EMERSON, *Society and Solitude: Works and Days.*

Still last to come where thou art wanted most.
WORDSWORTH, *To Sleep.*

8
Insomnia never comes to a man who has to get up at exactly six o'clock. Insomnia troubles only those who can sleep any time.
ELBERT HUBBARD, *Philistine.* Vol. xxv, p. 78.

9
But sleep stole on me unawares,
Even on me at last;
Though drop by drop the minutes faint,
Like hours at midnight passed.
HARRIET ELEANOR KING, *The First of June.*

10
Over the edge of the purple down,
Where the single lamplight gleams,
Know ye the road to the Merciful Town
That is hard by the Sea of Dreams—
Where the poor lay their wrongs away,
And the sick may forget to weep?
But we—pity us! Oh, pity us!
We wakeful; ah, pity us!—
We must go back with Policeman Day—
Back from the City of Sleep!
RUDYARD KIPLING, *The City of Sleep.* St. 1.

For I am weary, and am overwrought
With too much toil, with too much care distraught,
And with the iron crown of anguish crowned.
Lay thy soft hand upon my brow and cheek,
O peaceful Sleep!
LONGFELLOW, *Sleep.*

11
I have forgotten how to sigh—
Remembered how to sleep.
DOROTHY PARKER, *The Danger of Writing Defiant Verse.*

12
I will not give sleep to mine eyes, or slumber to mine eyelids.
Old Testament: Psalms, cxxxii, 4; *Proverbs,* vi, 4.

13
Sleep came at length, but with a train
Of feelings true and fancies vain,
Mingling, in wild disorder cast,
The expected future with the past.
SCOTT, *Rokeby.* Canto i, st. 2.

14
I have not slept one wink.
SHAKESPEARE, *Cymbeline.* Act iii, sc. 4, l. 103.

And for my soul I cannot sleep a wink.
POPE, *Imitations of Horace: Satires,* ii, 1, 12.

15
I'll wake mine eye-balls blind first.
SHAKESPEARE, *Cymbeline.* Act iii, sc. 4, l. 104.

16 O sleep, O gentle sleep,
Nature's soft nurse, how have I frighted thee,
That thou no more wilt weigh my eyelids down
And steep my senses in forgetfulness?
SHAKESPEARE, *II Henry IV.* Act iii, sc. 1, l. 5.

Who, with a body fill'd and vacant mind,
Gets him to rest, cramm'd with distressful bread.
SHAKESPEARE, *Henry V.* Act iv, sc. 1, l. 286.

17
At their chamber-door I'll beat the drum
Till it cry sleep to death.
SHAKESPEARE, *King Lear.* Act ii, sc. 4, l. 119.

18
Our foster-nurse of nature is repose,
The which he lacks; that to provoke in him,
Are many simples operative, whose power
Will close the eye of anguish.
SHAKESPEARE, *King Lear.* Act iv, sc. 4, l. 12.

19
Sleep shall neither night nor day
Hang upon his pent-house lid.
SHAKESPEARE, *Macbeth.* Act i, sc. 3, l. 19.

Not poppy, nor mandragora,
Nor all the drowsy syrups of the world
Shall ever medicine thee to that sweet sleep
Which thou ow'dst yesterday.
SHAKESPEARE, *Othello.* Act iii, sc. 3, l. 330.

Give me to drink mandragora.
SHAKESPEARE, *Antony and Cleopatra,* i, 5, 4.

1
O, I have pass'd a miserable night,
So full of ugly sights, of ghastly dreams,
That, as I am a Christian faithful man,
I would not spend another such a night,
Though 'twere to buy a world of happy days.
SHAKESPEARE, *Richard III*. Act i, sc. 4, l. 2.

All the wild trash of sleep, without the rest.
YOUNG, *Night Thoughts*. Night viii, l. 70.

2
And Sleep shall obey me,
And visit thee never,
And the Curse shall be on thee
For ever and ever.
SOUTHEY, *The Curse of Kehama*. Pt. ii, st. 14.

3
Sleep vanishes before the house of care. (Somnus sollicitas deficit ante domus.)
TIBULLUS, *Elegies*. Bk. iii, eleg. 4, l. 20. *See also under* CARE.

4
A flock of sheep that leisurely pass by,
One after one; the sound of rain, and bees
Murmuring; the fall of rivers, winds and seas,
Smooth fields, white sheets of water, and pure sky;
I have thought of all by turns and yet do lie
Sleepless! . . .
Come, blessed barrier between day and day,
Dear mother of fresh thoughts and joyous health!
WORDSWORTH, *To Sleep*.

If, my dear, you seek to slumber,
Count of stars an endless number;
If you still continue wakeful,
Count the drops that make a lakeful;
Then, if vigilance yet above you
Hover, count the times I love you;
And if slumber still repel you,
Count the times I did not tell you.
FRANKLIN P. ADAMS, *Lullaby*.

5
The wakey nights.
SIR THOMAS WYATT, *Complaint upon Love*.

SLEEVELESS

6
To make . . . a sleeveless errand.
JOHN HEYWOOD, *Proverbs*. Pt. i, ch. 7. (1546)

A sleeveless errand.
SHAKESPEARE, *Troilus and Cressida*. Act v, sc. 4, l. 9. (1601)

To whose house I went upon a sleeveless errand.
UNKNOWN, *Jacke of Dover*, 4. (1604)

7
Having, under a Sleeveless Pretence, been deny'd a Combat.
WILLIAM HONE, *Every-Day Book*, ii, 782. (1726)

Neither feign for thyself any sleeveless excuse.
JOHN LYLY, *Euphues*, p. 114. (1579)

8
He . . . had no honourable mode of avoiding the sleeveless quarrel fixed on him.
SCOTT, *Familiar Letters*, ii, 111. (1821)

9
And measureth his goodness, not by sleeveless words.
THOMAS USK, *Testament of Love*. (c. 1387)

Sleeveless talk.
UNKNOWN, *Jacob's Well*, 181. (c. 1440)

10
Now this was the guise in which the messengers journeyed: one sleeve was on the cap of each of them in front, as a sign that they were messengers, in order that through what hostile land soever they might pass, no harm might be done them.
UNKNOWN, *Mabinogion: The Dream of Mayen Wledig*. (Lady Guest, tr.)

Without the sleeve they might never be able to perform their errand.
WARWICK BOND, *Note*, to his edition of Lyly's Works, iii, 503.

SLOTH, see Idleness, Indolence

SMILE

I—Smile: Apothegms

11
There is a smile of Love,
And there is a smile of Deceit,
And there is a smile of smiles
In which these two smiles meet.
WILLIAM BLAKE, *Smile and Frown*.

12
Her bright smile haunts me still.
JOSEPH EDWARDS CARPENTER. Title of popular song of 1880's.

13
What I saw was equal ecstasy:
One universal smile it seemed of all things.
(Ciò ch' io vedeva, mi sembiava un riso
Dell' universo.)
DANTE, *Paradiso*. Canto xxvii, l. 5.

All Nature wears one universal grin.
FIELDING, *Tom Thumb the Great*. Act i, sc. 1.

14
In came Mrs. Fezziwig, one vast substantial smile.
DICKENS, *A Christmas Carol*. Stave 2.

15
His smile is sweetened by his gravity.
GEORGE ELIOT, *Spanish Gypsy*. Bk. i.

His wise, rare smile is sweet with certainties.
W. E. HENLEY, *In Hospital: The Chief*.

16
He smiled a kind of sickly smile and curled up on the floor,
And the subsequent proceedings interested him no more.
BRET HARTE, *The Society Upon the Stanislaus*.

17
In his heart he smiled a sardonic smile. (Μείδησε δὲ θυμῷ σαρδάνιον μάλα τοῖον.)
HOMER, *Odyssey*. Bk. xx, l. 301.

Your laugh is of the sardonic kind.
CAIUS GRACCHUS, when his adversaries laughed at his defeat by unfair means when applying

for a third tribuneship. (PLUTARCH, *Lives: Caius Gracchus*, ch. 12, sec. 5.) The sardonic smile was supposed to be an involuntary distention of the muscles of the mouth occasioned by a bitter plant, *Sardonia herba*, which came from Sardinia. Hence, γέγως σαρδόνιος, bitter or sardonic smile or laughter, laughter that is forced or mocking.

1
Make two grins grow where there was only a grouch before.
ELBERT HUBBARD, *Pig-Pen Pete*.

2
Nods, and becks, and wreathèd smiles.
MILTON, *L'Allegro*, l. 28.

A smile that glow'd
Celestial rosy red, love's proper hue.
MILTON, *Paradise Lost*. Bk. viii, l. 618.

3
Smiles from reason flow
To brute deny'd, and are of love the food.
MILTON, *Paradise Lost*. Bk. ix, l. 239.

4
Smiling, as some fly had tickled slumber.
SHAKESPEARE, *Cymbeline*. Act iv, sc. 2, l. 210.

5
An thou canst not smile as the wind sits, thou 'lt catch cold shortly.
SHAKESPEARE, *King Lear*. Act i, sc. 4, l. 112.

6
The heaving of my lungs provokes me to ridiculous smiling.
SHAKESPEARE, *Love's Labour's Lost*. iii, 1, 78.

7
A smile recures the wounding of a frown.
SHAKESPEARE, *Venus and Adonis*, l. 465.

8
To hear him speak, and sweetly smile,
You were in Paradise the while.
SIR PHILIP SIDNEY, *A Friend's Passion for His Astrophel*.

9
The smile that won't come off.
JOSEPH W. STANDISH. Title and refrain of popular song. (1903) Said to have originated with Carolyn Wells, as the winning slogan in a contest, c. 1900.

10
And, as when
A stone is flung into some sleeping tarn,
The circle widens till it lip the marge,
Spread the slow smile thro' all her company.
TENNYSON, *Pelleas and Ettarre*, l. 88.

The slow wise smile.
TENNYSON, *The Miller's Daughter*, l. 5.

11
Wrinkles should merely indicate where smiles have been.
MARK TWAIN, *Pudd'nhead Wilson's New Calendar*.

12
Yet, if successful, thou wilt be adored—
Lo, like a Cheshire cat our Court will grin!
JOHN WOLCOT, *Works*. Vol. ii, p. 424.

13
When you call me that, *smile!*
OWEN WISTER, *The Virginian*, p. 28. *See* 2298j:1.

II—Smile: Women's Smiles

14
Her smile is as the litten West,
Nigh-while the sun is gone.
THOMAS ASHE, *Old Jane*.

Her very frowns are fairer far
Than smiles of other maidens are.
HARTLEY COLERIDGE, *Song: She Is Not Fair*.

15
They smile so when one's right, and when one's wrong
They smile still more.
BYRON, *Don Juan*. Canto ii, st. 164.

16
Give me your smile, the lovelight in your eyes,
Life could not hold a fairer paradise.
LEONARD COOKE, *The Sunshine of Your Smile*. Popular song of 1915.

17
But O, her artless smile's mair sweet
Than hinny or than marmalete.
JAMES HOGG, *My Love She's But a Lassie Yet*.

18
The odor is the rose;
The smile, the woman.
ROBERT UNDERWOOD JOHNSON, *Her Smile*.

19
Smooth flow the waves, the zephyrs gently play,
Belinda smil'd, and all the world was gay.
POPE, *The Rape of the Lock*. Canto ii, l. 51.

When bold Sir Plume had drawn Clarissa down,
Chloe stepp'd in, and kill'd him with a frown;
She smiled to see the doughty hero slain,
But, at her smile, the beau revived again.
POPE, *The Rape of the Lock*. Canto v, l. 67.

20
Blest as the immortal gods is he,
The youth who fondly sits by thee,
And hears and sees thee all the while
Softly speak and sweetly smile.
SAPPHO, *To ——*.

(Ille mi par esse deo videtur,
Ille, si fas est, superare divos,
Qui, sedans adversus, identidem te
Spectat et audit Dulce ridentem.)
CATULLUS, *Odes*. No. li, l. 1.

Softly speak and sweetly smile.
ADDISON, *Spectator*. Vol. iii, No. 229. (Tr. from Boileau.)

21
Heaven hath no mouth, and yet is said to smile
After your style:
No more hath earth, yet that smiles too,
Just as you do.
AURELIAN TOWNSEND, *To the Lady May*. (c. 1635)

22
I feel in every smile a chain.
JOHN WOLCOT, *Pindariana*.

23
And she hath smiles to earth unknown;
Smiles, that with motion of their own

Do spread, and sink, and rise.
WORDSWORTH, *Louisa*. St. 2.

III—Smile: Deceitful Smiles

1
Oh sir, she smiled, no doubt,
Whene'er I passed her; but who passed without
Much the same smile?
ROBERT BROWNING, *My Last Duchess*.

2
Smile with an intent to do mischief, or cozen him whom he salutes.
ROBERT BURTON, *Anatomy of Melancholy: Democritus to the Reader*.

3
But own'd, that smile, if oft observed and near,
Waned in its mirth, and wither'd to a sneer.
BYRON, *Lara*. Canto i, st. 17.

4
From thy own smile I snatch'd the snake.
BYRON, *Manfred*. Act i, sc. 1.

There is a snake in thy smile, my dear,
And bitter poison within thy tear.
SHELLEY, *The Cenci: Song*. Act v, sc. 4.

5
The smiler with the knife under the cloak.
CHAUCER, *The Knightes Tale*, l. 1141.

He surest strikes that smiling gives the blow.
SUSANNAH CENTLIVRE, *The Beau's Duel: Epilogue*.

6
But he smiled, as he sat by the table,
With the smile that was childlike and bland.
BRET HARTE, *Plain Language from Truthful James*.

But his smile it was pensive and childlike.
BRET HARTE, *Plain Language from Truthful James*.

7
Eternal smiles his emptiness betray,
As shallow streams run dimpling all the way.
POPE, *Epistle to Dr. Arbuthnot*, l. 315. *See also under* WATER.

Egnatius, because he has white teeth, is everlastingly smiling. If people come to the prisoner's bench, when the counsel for the defence is making everyone cry, he smiles: if they are mourning at the funeral of a dear son, when the bereaved mother is weeping for her only boy, he smiles: whatever it is, wherever he is, whatever he is doing, he smiles. It is a disease he has. (Quicquid est, ubicumquest, quodcumque agit, renidet. Hunc habet morbum.)
CATULLUS, *Odes*. Ode 29, l. 1.

8
One may smile, and smile, and be a villain.
SHAKESPEARE, *Hamlet*. Act i, sc. 5, l. 108.

Why I can smile and murder while I smile.
SHAKESPEARE, *III Henry VI*. Act iii, sc. 2, l. 182.

There's daggers in men's smiles.
SHAKESPEARE, *Macbeth*. Act ii, sc. 3, l. 146.

9
Seldom he smiles, and smiles in such a sort
As if he mock'd himself and scorn'd his spirit,
That could be moved to smile at any thing.
SHAKESPEARE, *Julius Cæsar*. Act i, sc. 2, l. 205.

Of such vinegar aspect
That they'll not show their teeth by way of smile,
Though Nestor swear the jest be laughable.
SHAKESPEARE, *The Merchant of Venice*. Act i, sc. 1, l. 54.

10
With silent smiles of slow disparagement.
TENNYSON, *Guinevere*, l. 14.

11
And Milo's lurking marble smile.
WILLIAM WATSON, *Termonde*.

IV—Smile and Tear

See also Laughter and Tears

12
Smiles form the channel of a future tear.
BYRON, *Childe Harold*. Canto ii, st. 97.

And if she met him, though she smiled no more,
She looked a sadness sweeter than her smile.
BYRON, *Don Juan*. Canto i, st. 72.

Of all tales 'tis the saddest—and more sad,
Because it makes us smile.
BYRON, *Don Juan*. Canto xiii, st. 9.

13
The social smile, the sympathetic tear.
THOMAS GRAY, *The Alliance of Education and Government*, l. 37.

14
Why comes not death to those who mourn?—
He never smiled again!
FELICIA HEMANS, *He Never Smiled Again*.

'Tis hard to smile when one would weep,
To speak when one would silent be;
To wake when one would wish to sleep,
And wake to agony.
ANNE HUNTER, *The Lot of Thousands*.

15
A smile is ever the most bright and beautiful with a tear upon it. What is the dawn without the dew? The tear is rendered by the smile precious above the smile itself.
W. S. LANDOR, *Imaginary Conversations: Dante and Gemma Donati*.

16
All kin' o' smily round the lips,
An' teary round the lashes.
J. R. LOWELL, *The Courtin'*.

17
As Jupiter
On Juno smiles, when he impregns the clouds
That shed May flowers.
MILTON, *Paradise Lost*. Bk. iv, l. 499.

18
Behold who ever wept, and in his tears
Was happier far than others in their smiles.
PETRARCH, *The Triumph of Eternity*, l. 95.

19
With a smile on her lips and a tear in her eye.
SCOTT, *Lochinvar*. (*Marmion*. Canto v, st. 12.)

Reproof on her lip, but a smile in her eye.
SAMUEL LOVER, *Rory O'More*.

1
Nobly he yokes
A smiling with a sigh, as if the sigh
Was that it was, for not being such a smile;
The smile mocking the sigh.
SHAKESPEARE, *Cymbeline.* Act iv, sc. 2, l. 51.

Triumphs for nothing and lamenting toys
Is jollity for apes and grief for boys.
SHAKESPEARE, *Cymbeline.* Act iv, sc. 2, l. 193.

2
You have seen
Sunshine and rain at once: her smiles and tears
Were like a better way: those happy smilets,
That play'd on her ripe lip, seem'd not to know
What guests were in her eyes: which parted thence,
As pearls from diamonds dropp'd.
SHAKESPEARE, *King Lear.* Act iv, sc. 3, l. 19.

Venus smiles not in a house of tears.
SHAKESPEARE, *Romeo and Juliet.* Act iv, sc. 1, l. 8.

3
'Tis easy enough to be pleasant,
When life flows along like a song;
But the man worth while is the one who will smile
When everything goes dead wrong;
For the test of the heart is trouble,
And it always comes with the years,
But the smile that is worth the praise of earth
Is the smile that comes through tears.
ELLA WHEELER WILCOX, *Worth While.*

It's easy to fight when everything's right
And you're mad with the thrill and the glory;
It's easy to cheer when victory's near,
And wallow in fields that are gory.
It's a different song when everything's wrong,
When you're feeling infernally mortal;
When it's ten against one, and hope there is none,
Buck up, little soldier, and chortle!
ROBERT W. SERVICE, *Carry On.*

SMITH

4
The first artificer of death; the shrewd
Contriver who first sweated at the forge,
And forc'd the blunt and yet unbloodied steel
To a keen edge, and made it bright for war. . . .
And the first smith was the first murd'rer's son.
COWPER, *The Task.* Bk. v, l. 213.

And he sang: "Hurra for my handiwork!"
And the red sparks lit the air;
Not alone for the blade was the bright steel made;
And he fashioned the first ploughshare.
CHARLES MACKAY, *Tubal Cain.* St. 4.

And fitfully you still may see the grim smiths ranking round,
All clad in leathern panoply, their broad hands only bare;
Some rest upon their sledges here, some work the windlass there.
SAMUEL FERGUSON, *The Forging of the Anchor.*

5
The smith hath always a spark in his throat.
THOMAS FULLER, *Gnomologia.* No. 4754.
Meaning he is always thirsty.

He is not a blacksmith, but he has a spark in his throat.
C. H. SPURGEON, *Plowman's Pictures,* 39.

6
I heard that Smug the smith, for ale and spice
Sold all his tools, and yet he kept his vice.
SIR JOHN HARINGTON, *Of a Drunken Smith.* (*Epigrams.* Bk. iv, epig. 301.)

7
The smith and his penny both are black.
GEORGE HERBERT, *Jacula Prudentum.*

8
As great Pythagoras of yore,
Standing beside the blacksmith's door,
And hearing the hammers, as they smote
The anvils with a different note,
Stole from the varying tones, that hung
Vibrant on every iron tongue,
The secret of the sounding wire,
And formed the seven-chorded lyre.
LONGFELLOW, *To a Child,* l. 175.

And the smith his iron measures hammered to the anvil's chime;
Thanking God, whose boundless wisdom makes the flowers of poesy bloom
In the forge's dust and cinders, in the tissues of the loom.
LONGFELLOW, *Nuremberg,* l. 34.

9
Under a spreading chestnut-tree
The village smithy stands;
The smith, a mighty man is he,
With large and sinewy hands;
And the muscles of his brawny arms
Are strong as iron bands.
LONGFELLOW, *The Village Blacksmith,* l. 1.
The tree was really a horse-chestnut.

Week in, week out, from morn till night,
You can hear his bellows blow;
You can hear him swing his heavy sledge,
With measured beat and slow,
Like a sexton ringing the village bell,
When the evening sun is low.
LONGFELLOW, *The Village Blacksmith,* l. 13.

10
In other part stood one who at the forge
Labouring, two massy clods of iron and brass
Had melted.
MILTON, *Paradise Lost.* Bk. xi, l. 560.

11
From whence came Smith, albe he knight or squire,
But from the smith that forgeth at the fire?
RICHARD ROWLANDS, *Restitution of Decayed Intelligence,* p. 310. (c. 1600)

Fate tried to conceal him by naming him Smith.
O. W. HOLMES, *The Boys.* Of Samuel Francis Smith, author of *America.*

Here lies what had nor birth, nor shape, nor fame;
No gentleman! no man! no-thing! no name! . . .
More, shrunk to Smith—and Smith's no name at all.

POPE, *Epitaph on James More-Smythe.*

The Smiths never had any arms, and have invariably sealed their letters with their thumbs.

SYDNEY SMITH. (LADY HOLLAND, *Memoir*. Vol. i, p. 244.)

1
I saw a smith stand with his hammer, thus,
The whilst his iron did on the anvil cool,
With open mouth swallowing a tailor's news.

SHAKESPEARE, *King John*. Act iv, sc. 2, l. 193.

2
The painful smith, with force of fervent heat,
The hardest iron soon doth mollify,
That with his heavy sledge he can it beat,
And fashion it to what he it list apply.

SPENSER, *Amoretti*. Sonnet xxxii.

SMOKING, see Tobacco

SNAIL

3
Whereso'er he roam,—
Knock when you will,—he's sure to be at home.

VINCENT BOURNE, *The Snail*. (Charles Lamb, tr.)

The snail, which everywhere doth roam,
Carrying his own house still, still is at home.

JOHN DONNE, *To Sir Henry Wotton.*

I can tell you why a snail has a house . . .
To put his head in

SHAKESPEARE. *King Lear*. Act i, sc. 5, l. 30.

4
He was a sort of snail which crawled over a man in his sleep and left its slime.

JOHN SINGLETON COPLEY. Referring to an artist named Carter. (DUNLAP, *History of the Arts of Design in the U.S.*, i, 129.)

5
An inadvertent step may crush the snail
That crawls at ev'ning in the public path;
But he that has humanity, forewarn'd,
Will tread aside, and let the reptile live.

COWPER, *The Task*. Bk. vi, l. 564.

6
Like snails I see the people go
Along the pavement, row on row;
And each one on his shoulder bears
His coiling shell of petty cares—
The spiral of his own affairs.

ELEANOR HAMMOND, *From a Street Corner.*

7
Wise emblem of our politic world,
Sage snail, within thine own self curled,
Instruct me softly to make haste,
Whilst these my feet go slowly fast.

RICHARD LOVELACE, *The Snail.*

8
The slow snail climbeth the tower at last, though the swift swallow mount it sooner.

JOHN LYLY, *Euphues*, p. 419.

9
You have beaten the snail in slowness. (Vicistis cochleam tarditudine.)

PLAUTUS, *Pœnulus*, l. 532. (Act iii, sc. 1.)

There he comes, in a snail's trot.

GEORGE COLMAN THE YOUNGER, *John Bull*. Act iii, sc. 1. (1803)

He is easy-paced, this snail.

JOHN DONNE, *To Sir Henry Wotton.*

I will thitherward hie me in haste like a snail.

JOHN HEYWOOD, *Proverbs*. Pt. i, ch. 9. (1546)

10
The snail, whose tender horns being hit,
Shrinks backward in his shelly cave with pain,
And there, all smother'd up, in shade doth sit,
Long after fearing to creep forth again.

SHAKESPEARE, *Venus and Adonis*, l. 1033.

11
"The snail," says the Hindoo, "sees nothing but his own shell, and thinks it the grandest palace in the universe."

SYDNEY SMITH, *Peter Plymley Letters*. No. 10.

SNAKE, see Serpent

SNEER

See also Ridicule, Scorn

12
There was a laughing devil in his sneer.

BYRON, *The Corsair* Canto i, st. 9.

And shaped his weapon with an edge severe,
Sapping a solemn creed with solemn sneer.

BYRON, *Childe Harold*. Canto iii, st. 107.

13
Better to stand ten thousand sneers than one abiding pang, such as time could not abolish, of bitter self-reproach.

THOMAS DE QUINCEY, *Confessions of an English Opium Eater*. Pt. i.

14
I can't help it, I was born sneering.

W. S. GILBERT, *The Mikado*. Act i.

15
Ill-suited to the sharp sneers of these men. (Minus aptus acutis Naribus horum hominum.)

HORACE, *Satires*. Bk. i, sat. 3, l. 29.

16
Sir spokesman, sneers are weakness veiling rage

GEORGE MEREDITH, *A Ballad of Fair Ladies in Revolt*. St. 42.

17
Who can refute a sneer?

WILLIAM PALEY, *Moral Philosophy*. Vol. ii, bk. v, ch. 9.

18
"You laugh," he says, "and indulge too much in curved nostrils." ("Rides," ait, "et nimis uncis Naribus indulges.")

PERSIUS, *Satires*. Sat. i, l. 40.

19
Damn with faint praise, assent with civil leer,
And without sneering, teach the rest to sneer.

POPE, *Epistle to Dr. Arbuthnot*, l. 201.

1
I fancy that it is just as hard to do your duty when men are sneering at you as when they are shooting at you.
WOODROW WILSON, *Speech*, Brooklyn Navy Yard, 11 May, 1914.

SNEEZING

2
He's a friend at a sneeze; the most you can get of him is a God bless you.
THOMAS FULLER, *Gnomologia*. No. 2436.

Will you demand of me, whence this custom ariseth, to bless and say God help to those that sneeze? We produce three sorts of wind: that issuing from below is too undecent; that from the mouth implieth some reproach of gourmandise; the third is sneezing: and because it cometh from the head, and is without imputation, we thus kindly entertain it. Smile not at this subtlety; it is (as some say) Aristotle's.
MONTAIGNE, *Essays*. Bk. iii, ch. 6.

3
He hath sneezed thrice; turn him out of the hospital.
JAMES HOWELL, *Proverbs*, p. 2.

4
(Hang it, I shall sneeze till spring!)
Snuff is a delicious thing.
LEIGH HUNT, *Sneezing*.

5
Just where the breath of life his nostrils drew,
A charge of snuff the wily virgin threw;
The gnomes direct, to every atom just,
The pungent grains of titillating dust.
Sudden, with starting tears each eye o'erflows,
And the high dome re-echoes to his nose.
POPE, *The Rape of the Lock*. Canto v, l. 81.

6
Sneeze on a Sunday morning fasting,
You'll enjoy your true love to everlasting.
UNKNOWN. (DYER, *English Folk-Lore*, p. 239.)

Sneeze on a Monday, you sneeze for danger;
Sneeze on a Tuesday, you kiss a stranger;
Sneeze on a Wednesday, you sneeze for a letter;
Sneeze on a Thursday, for something better;
Sneeze on a Friday, you sneeze for sorrow;
Sneeze on a Saturday, your sweetheart tomorrow;
Sneeze on a Sunday, your safety seek,
The Devil will have you the whole of the week.
UNKNOWN. (HARLAND, *Lancs. Folk-Lore*, p. 68.)

SNOB

7
Don't be proud and turn up your nose
At poorer people in plainer clothes;
But learn, for the sake of your soul's repose,
That all proud flesh, where'er it grows,
Is liable to irritation.
S. S. COX, *Because You Flourish in Worldly Affairs*.

8
I attach but little value to rank or wealth, but the line must be drawn somewhere. A man in that station may be brave and worthy, but at every step he would commit solecisms that society would never pardon.
W. S. GILBERT, *H. M. S. Pinafore*. Act i.

9
Snobbery is but a point in time. Let us have patience with our inferiors. They are ourselves of yesterday.
ISAAC GOLDBERG, *Tin Pan Alley*.

10
We are all snobs of the Infinite, parvenus of the Eternal.
JAMES HUNEKER, *Iconoclasts*, p. 16.

11
Ain't a snob a fellow as wants to be taken for better bred, or richer, or cleverer, or more influential than he really is?
CHARLES LEVER, *One of Them*. Ch. 39.

12
Heaven grant him now some noble nook,
For, rest his soul! he'd rather be
Genteelly damn'd beside a Duke,
Than sav'd in vulgar company.
THOMAS MOORE, *Epitaph on a Tuft-Hunter*.

13
Now she is dead she greets Christ with a nod.—
(He was a carpenter)—*but she knows God*.
VIRGINIA MCCORMICK, *The Snob*.

14
Say what strange motive, Goddess! could compel
A well-bred Lord t' assault a gentle Belle?
O say what stranger cause, yet unexplor'd,
Could make a gentle Belle reject a Lord?
POPE, *The Rape of the Lock*. Canto i, l. 7.

15
Perpetual nosing after snobbery at least suggests the snob.
R. L. STEVENSON, *Some Gentlemen in Fiction*.

16
Rough to common men,
But honeying at the whisper of a lord.
TENNYSON, *The Princess: Prologue*, l. 114.

17
He who meanly admires a mean thing is a Snob—perhaps that is a safe definition of the character.
THACKERAY, *Book of Snobs*. Ch. 2.

It is impossible, in our condition of Society, not to be sometimes a Snob.
THACKERAY, *Book of Snobs*. Ch. 3.

The state of society, viz. Toadyism, organized; base Man-and-Mammon worship, instituted by command of law;—snobbishness, in a word, perpetuated.
THACKERAY, *Book of Snobs*. Ch. 3.

That which we call a snob, by any other name would still be snobbish.
THACKERAY, *Book of Snobs*. Ch. 18.

No one succeeds better than Mr. Thackeray in cutting his coat according to his cloth. Here he flattered the aristocracy; but when he crossed the Atlantic, George Washington became the idol of his worship.

EDMUND YATES. (*Town Talk*, 12 June, 1858.)

1
A tuft-hunter is a snob, a parasite is a snob. the man who allows the manhood within him to be awed by a coronet is a snob. The man who worships mere wealth is a snob.

ANTHONY TROLLOPE, *Life of Thackeray*, p. 56.

SNOW

I—Snow: Apothegms

2
Ye, farewell all the snow of ferne year!

CHAUCER, *Troilus and Criseyde*, l. 1176.

Where are the snows of yesteryear? (Où sont les neiges d'antan?)

FRANÇOIS VILLON, *Ballade des Dames du Temps Jadis*. (Rossetti, tr.)

One burden answers, ever and aye,
"Nay, but where is the last year's snow?"

VILLON, *Ballade des Dames du Temps Jadis*. (Lang, tr.)

But where are the snows of last year? That was the greatest concern of Villon, the Parisian poet. (Mais où sont les neiges d'antan? C'estoit le plus grand soucy qu'eust Villon, le poète parisien.)

RABELAIS, *Works*. Bk. ii, ch. 14.

Where's the snow
That fell the year that's fled—where's the snow?

SAMUEL LOVER, *The Snow*.

3
You came as seasonably as snow in summer.

THOMAS FULLER, *Gnomologia*. No. 5869.

As profitable as snow in harvest.

UNKNOWN, *Pedlar's Prophecy*, l. 237. (1595)

4
Whether you boil snow or pound it, you can have but water of it.

GEORGE HERBERT, *Jacula Prudentum*. No. 176.

5
Snow is white and lieth in the dike,
And every man lets it lie;
Pepper is black, and hath a good smack,
And every man doth it buy.

HILL, *Commonplace-Book*, p. 128. (c. 1495)

For thou wilt lie upon the wings of night
Whiter than new snow on a raven's back.

SHAKESPEARE, *Romeo and Juliet*. Act iii, sc. 2, l. 18.

6
"The gates are mine to open,
As the gates are mine to close,
And I abide in my Mother's house,"
Said our Lady of the Snows.

RUDYARD KIPLING, *Our Lady of the Snows*. Referring to Canada. In Italian, "Sancta Maria ad Nives"; in French, "Notre Dame des Neiges"; many Catholic churches so-called after the famous legend.

7
The pity of the snow, that hides all scars.

EDWIN MARKHAM, *Lincoln, The Man of the People*.

8
They are pulling geese in Scotland, so here it snows.

SAMUEL PEGGE THE ELDER, *Derbicisms*, p. 138. (1791)

The old lady up in the sky is picking her geese pretty hard to-day.

DICKENS, *The Holly Tree*. Branch 1.

9
A little snow, tumbled about,
Anon becomes a mountain.

SHAKESPEARE, *King John*. Act iii, sc. 4, l. 176.

10
Right, as snow in harvest.

SHAKESPEARE, *Richard III*. Act i, sc. 4, l. 248.

II—Snow: Description

11
Lo, what wonders the day hath brought,
Born of the soft and slumbrous snow!

ELIZABETH AKERS ALLEN, *Snow*.

12
And out of the frozen mist the snow
In wavering flakes begins to glow;
Flake after flake
They sink in the dark and silent lake.

BRYANT, *The Snow-Shower*.

Through the sharp air a flaky torrent flies,
Mocks the slow sight, and hides the gloomy skies;
The fleecy clouds their chilly bosoms bare,
And shed their substance on the floating air.

GEORGE CRABBE, *Inebriety*, l. 17.

13
Whenever a snowflake leaves the sky,
It turns and turns to say "Good-by!
Good-by, dear clouds, so cool and gray!"
Then lightly travels on its way.

MARY MAPES DODGE, *Snowflakes*.

But when a snowflake, brave and meek,
Lights on a rosy maiden's cheek,
It starts—"How warm and soft the day!"
"'Tis summer!" and it melts away.

MARY MAPES DODGE, *Snowflakes*.

14
Announced by all the trumpets of the sky,
Arrives the snow, and, driving o'er the fields,
Seems nowhere to alight: the whited air
Hides hills and woods, the river, and the heaven,
And veils the farm-house at the garden's end.
The sled and traveller stopped, the courier's feet
Delayed, all friends shut out, the housemates sit
Around the radiant fireplace, enclosed
In a tumultuous privacy of storm.

EMERSON, *The Snow-Storm*, l. 1.

Come, see the north wind's masonry.
Out of an unseen quarry evermore
Furnished with tile, the fierce artificer
Curves his white bastions with projected roof
Round every windward stake, or tree, or door.

EMERSON, *The Snow-Storm*, l. 10.

The frolic architecture of the snow.
EMERSON, *The Snow-Storm*, l. 28.

1
Out of the bosom of the Air,
Out of the cloud-folds of her garments shaken,
Over the woodlands brown and bare,
Over the harvest-fields forsaken,
Silent, and soft, and slow
Descends the snow.
LONGFELLOW, *Snow-Flakes*.

2
What heart could have thought you?—
Past our devisal (A filigree petal!)
Fashioned so purely, Fragilely, surely.
FRANCIS THOMPSON, *To a Snow-Flake*.

Through the hushed air the whitening shower descends,
At first thin-wavering; till at last the flakes
Fall broad and wide and fast, dimming the day
With a continual flow. The cherished fields
Put on their winter-robe of purest white.
'Tis brightness all; save where the new snow melts
Along the mazy current.
JAMES THOMSON, *The Seasons: Winter*, l. 229.

3
Oh! the snow, the beautiful snow,
Filling the sky and the earth below; . . .
Beautiful snow, from the heavens above,
Pure as an angel and fickle as love!
JOHN WHITAKER WATSON, *Beautiful Snow*. Fraudulently claimed by no less than seven people. (See STEVENSON, *Famous Single Poems*, p. 178.)

4
Like an army defeated
The snow hath retreated.
WILLIAM WORDSWORTH, *Written in March*.

5
I saw fair Chloris walk alone,
Whilst feather'd rain came swiftly down,
As Jove descended from his tower
To court her in a silver shower
The wanton snow flew on her breast
Like little birds unto their nest,
But, overcome with whiteness there,
For grief it thaw'd into a tear;
Thence falling on her garment's hem,
To deck her, froze into a gem.
WILLIAM STRODE, *On Chloris Walking in the Snow*.

SOCIETY

I—Society: Definitions

6
Man seeketh in society comfort, use, and protection.
BACON, *Advancement of Learning*. Bk. ii.

Man was formed for society.
WILLIAM BLACKSTONE, *Of the Nature of Laws in General*.

[Man] is a social animal. (Sociale animal est.)
SENECA, *De Beneficiis*. Bk. vii, sec. 1.

7
The bond of human society is reason and speech. (In universi generis humani sociatate . . . vinculum est ratio et oratio.)
CICERO, *De Officiis*. Bk. i, ch. 16, sec. 50.

8
Fine society is only a self-protection against the vulgarities of the street and the tavern. . . . 'Tis an exclusion and a precinct. . . . It is an unprincipled decorum; an affair of clean linen and coaches, of gloves, cards, and elegance in trifles.
EMERSON, *Conduct of Life: Considerations by the Way*.

Society is a masked ball, where every one hides his real character, and reveals it by hiding.
EMERSON, *Conduct of Life: Worship*.

Society is a joint stock company, in which the members agree, for the better securing of his bread to each shareholder, to surrender the liberty and culture of the eater.
EMERSON, *Essays, First Series: Self-Reliance*.

Society is frivolous, and shreds its day into scraps, its conversation into ceremonies and escapes.
EMERSON, *Essays, Second Series: Character*.

Society is a hospital of incurables.
EMERSON, *New England Reformers*.

9
Society never advances.
EMERSON, *Essays, First Series: Self-Reliance*.

No society can ever be so large as one man.
EMERSON, *New England Reformers*.

10
Here is the use of society: it is so easy with the great to be great.
EMERSON, *Essays: Society and Solitude*.

When a man meets his fitting mate society begins.
EMERSON, *Uncollected Lectures: Social Aims*.

It is rendering mutual service to men of virtue and understanding to make them acquainted with one another.
THOMAS JEFFERSON, *Writings*. Vol. vi, p. 424.

11
The spirit of truth and the spirit of freedom —they are the pillars of society.
HENRIK IBSEN, *Pillars of Society*. Act iv.

12
Society is the union of men and not the men themselves. (La Société est l'union des hommes, et non pas les hommes.)
MONTESQUIEU, *L'Esprit des Lois*. Bk. x, sec. 3.

13
The difference between what is commonly called ordinary company and good company is only hearing the same things said in a little room or in a large salon.
POPE, *Thoughts on Various Subjects*.

14
The problem of building a human society is always the difficulty of establishing a relation between individual and communal happiness.
DORA RUSSELL, *The Right to Be Happy*, p. 255.

1
Society is like the air, necessary to breathe, but insufficient to live on.
GEORGE SANTAYANA, *Little Essays*.

2
Society, saith the text, is the happiness of life.
SHAKESPEARE, *Love's Labour's Lost*, iv, 2, 167.

3
Society exists for the benefit of its members; not the members for the benefit of society.
SPENCER, *Principles of Ethics*. Sec. 222.

4
A society cannot be founded only on the pursuit of pleasure and power; a society can only be founded on the respect for liberty and justice.
TAINE, *Hist. English Literature*. Bk. ii, ch. 11.

5
What men call social virtue, good fellowship, is commonly but the virtue of pigs in a litter, which lie close together to keep each other warm.
H. D. THOREAU, *Journal*, 23 Oct., 1852.

6
Society therefore is as ancient as the world.
VOLTAIRE, *Philosophical Dictionary: Policy*.

7
There is
One great society alone on earth:
The noble Living and the noble Dead.
WORDSWORTH, *The Prelude*. Bk. xi, l. 393.

II—Society: Apothegms

8
Brothers, I am sorry I have got no Morrison's Pill for curing the maladies of Society.
CARLYLE, *Past and Present*. Bk. i, ch. 4.

9
I want you to see Peel, Stanley, Graham, Sheil, Russell, Macaulay, Old Joe, and so on. They are all upper-crust here.
THOMAS C. HALIBURTON, *Sam Slick in England*. Ch. 24. (1843)

Those families, you know, are our upper crust, not upper ten thousand.
J. FENIMORE COOPER, *Ways of the Hour*. Ch. 6. (1850)

At present there is no distinction among the upper ten thousand of the city.
N. P. WILLIS. *Necessity for a Promenade Drive*. (1860)

Warren . . . is a novus homo, and only a Conservative on that account; it being the quickest method to gain admission among the Upper Ten.
JAMES PAYN, *By Proxy*. Ch. 36. (1878)

A rout which . . . embraces a tithe of the Upper Ten Thousand, is conventionally described . . . by the epithets 'small' and 'early.'
G. O. TREVELYAN, *Interludes*, p. 286. (1905)

There are only about four hundred people in New York Society.
WARD MCALLISTER. A boast at the Union Club, after he had cut down the list of guests for the ball given by Mrs. William Astor, 1 Feb., 1892. The phrase was caught up by the newspapers, and passed into the idiom of the language. (*Dict. of Amer. Biog.*)

10
The Brahmin caste of New England. This is the harmless, inoffensive, untitled aristocracy referred to.
OLIVER WENDELL HOLMES, *Elsie Venner*. Ch. 1.

11
Mrs. Montagu has dropt me. Now, Sir, there are people whom one should like very well to drop, but would not wish to be dropt by.
SAMUEL JOHNSON. (BOSWELL, *Life*, iv, 73.)

12
He might have proved a useful adjunct, if not an ornament, to society.
CHARLES LAMB, *Eliana: Captain Starkey*.

13
But the fact is, a man may do very well with a very little knowledge and scarce be found out, in mixed company.
CHARLES LAMB, *Essays of Elia: The Old and the New Schoolmaster*.

14
A town that boasts inhabitants like me
Can have no lack of good society!
LONGFELLOW, *The Birds of Killingworth*.

15
The Don Quixote of one generation may live to hear himself called the savior of society by the next.
J. R. LOWELL, *Essays: Don Quixote*.

16
What quality are they of?
SHAKESPEARE, *Measure for Measure*, ii, 1, 59.

17
A few yards in London cement, or dissolve friendship.
SYDNEY SMITH. (EMERSON, *Considerations by the Way*.)

18
Ah, you flavour everything; you are the vanille of society.
SYDNEY SMITH. (LADY HOLLAND, *Memoir*. Vol. i, p. 262.)

19
The genteel comedy of the polite world.
SMOLLETT, *The Adventures of Ferdinand Count Fathom*. Ch. 1.

20
Pray, madam, who were the company? Why, there was all the world and his wife.
SWIFT, *Polite Conversation*. Dial. iii. (1738)

He welcomes at once all the world and his wife.
CHRISTOPHER ANSTEY, *New Bath Guide*, p. 140. (1767)

21
Society waits unform'd, and is for a while between things ended and things begun.
WALT WHITMAN, *Thoughts: Of These Years*.

22
She tried to found a salon, but only succeeded in opening a restaurant.
OSCAR WILDE, *Picture of Dorian Gray*. Ch. 1.

23
Gerald: I suppose Society is wonderfully delightful?

Lord Illingworth: To be in it is merely a bore. But to be out of it is simply a tragedy.
OSCAR WILDE, *A Woman of No Importance.* Act iii.

The wise man sometimes flees from society from fear of being bored. (Le sage quelquefois évite le monde, de peur d'être ennuyé.)
LA BRUYÈRE, *Les Caractères.* Pt. v.

1
Society became my glittering bride.
WORDSWORTH, *The Excursion.* Bk. iii, l. 735.

III—Society: Its Virtues

2
The social hours, swift-wing'd, unnotic'd fleet.
BURNS, *The Cotter's Saturday Night,* l. 39.

3
Society, friendship, and love
Divinely bestow'd upon man.
COWPER, *Verses: Alexander Selkirk,* l. 17.

4
Why should your fellowship a trouble be,
Since man's chief pleasure is society?
SIR JOHN DAVIES, *Orchestra.* St. 32.

5
The thoughts of the best minds always become the last opinion of Society.
EMERSON, *Correspondence of Carlyle and Emerson,* i, 29.

6
Of all the cordials known to us, the best, safest, and most exhilarating, with the least harm, is society.
EMERSON, *Society and Solitude: Clubs.*

7
Without society, and a society to our taste, men are never contented.
THOMAS JEFFERSON, *Writings.* Vol. vi, p. 15.

8
It is an extreme evil to depart from the company of the living before you die.
SENECA, *De Tranquillitate Animi.* Sec. 1.

For it is most true that a natural and secret hatred and aversation towards society in any man, hath somewhat of the savage beast.
FRANCIS BACON, *Essays: Of Friendship.*

9
A little society is needful to show a man his failings.
R. L. STEVENSON, *Ethical Studies,* p. 82.

10
Company keeps our rind from growing too coarse and rough.
HORACE WALPOLE, *Letter to George Montagu,* 22 Sept., 1765.

IV—Society: Its Faults

11
Dante standing, studying his angel,—
In there broke the folk of his Inferno.
Says he—"Certain people of importance"
(Such he gave his daily dreadful line to)
"Entered and would seize, forsooth, the poet."
Says the poet—"Then I stopped my painting."
ROBERT BROWNING, *One Word More.* Sec. 5.

12
Society is now one polish'd horde,
Form'd of two mighty tribes, the Bores and Bored.
BYRON, *Don Juan.* Canto xiii, st. 95.

13
The visit paid, with ecstasy we come,
As from a seven years transportation, home.
COWPER, *Conversation,* l. 399.

The painful ceremony of receiving and returning visits.
SMOLLETT, *Peregrine Pickle.* Ch. 5.

14
Oh to the club, the scene of savage joys,
The school of coarse good-fellowship and noise.
COWPER, *Conversation,* l. 421.

Club: An assembly of good fellows, meeting under certain conditions.
SAMUEL JOHNSON, *Dictionary.*

15
On the approach of Spring, I withdraw without reluctance from the noisy and extensive scene of crowds without company and dissipation without pleasure.
EDWARD GIBBON, *Memoirs.* Vol. i, p. 116.

16
Ermined and minked and Persian-lambed,
Be-puffed (be-painted, too, alas!)
Be-decked, be-diamonded—be-damned!
The Women of the Better Class.
OLIVER HERFORD, *The Women of the Better Class.*

17
For one of the pleasures of having a rout
Is the pleasure of having it over.
THOMAS HOOD, *Miss Kilmansegg: Her Dream.* St. 3.

18
I live in the crowds of jollity, not so much to enjoy company as to shun myself.
SAMUEL JOHNSON, *Rasselas.* Ch. 16.

19
Society is no comfort To one not sociable.
SHAKESPEARE, *Cymbeline.* Act iv, sc. 2, l. 12.

20
No society can surely be flourishing and happy, of which the far greater part of the members are poor and miserable.
ADAM SMITH, *Wealth of Nations.* Bk. i, ch. 8.

21
Other people are quite dreadful. The only possible society is oneself.
OSCAR WILDE, *An Ideal Husband.* Act iii.

22
High society is for those who have stopped working and no longer have anything important to do.
WOODROW WILSON, *Address,* Washington, 24 Feb., 1915.

23
The dreary intercourse of daily life.
WORDSWORTH, *Lines Composed a Few Miles Above Tintern Abbey,* l. 131.

V—Society and Convention

1
"I am afraid." replied Elinor, "that the pleasantness of an employment does not always evince its propriety."

JANE AUSTEN, *Sense and Sensibility*. Ch. 13.

2
Conventionality is not morality. Self-righteousness is not religion. To attack the first is not to assail the last. To pluck the mask from the face of the Pharisee, is not to lift an impious hand to the Crown of Thorns.

CHARLOTTE BRONTË, *Jane Eyre: Preface.*

3
It's wiser being good than bad;
It's safer being meek than fierce:
It's fitter being sane than mad.

ROBERT BROWNING, *Apparent Failure.*

4
For a "mixt company" implies, that, save
Yourself and friends, and half a hundred more,
Whom you may bow to without looking grave,
The rest are but a vulgar set.

BYRON, *Beppo*. St. 59.

5
In general, the more completely cased with formulas a man may be, the safer, happier is it for him.

CARLYLE, *Past and Present*. Bk. ii, ch. 17.

6
the Cambridge ladies who live in furnished souls
are unbeautiful and have comfortable minds . . .
they believe in Christ and Longfellow, both dead.

E. E. CUMMINGS, *Sonnets: Realities.*

7
My business in the social system is to be agreeable; I take it that everybody's business in the social system is to be agreeable.

DICKENS, *Bleak House*. Ch. 18.

8
Society everywhere is in conspiracy against the manhood of every one of its members. . . . The virtue in most request is conformity. Self-reliance is its aversion. It loves not realities and creators, but names and customs.

EMERSON, *Essays, First Series: Self-Reliance.*

Society will pardon much to genius and special gifts, but, being in its nature a convention, it loves what is conventional, or what belongs to coming together.

EMERSON, *Essays, Second Series: Manners.*

Comme il faut, is the Frenchman's description of good society.

EMERSON, *Essays, Second Series: Manners.*

9
The snow is lying very deep,
My house is sheltered from the blast.
I hear each muffled step outside,
I hear each voice go past.

But I'll not venture in the drift
Out of this bright security,
Till enough footsteps come and go
To make a path for me.

AGNES LEE, *Convention.*

10
Where it is a duty to worship the sun it is pretty sure to be a crime to examine the laws of heat.

JOHN MORLEY, *Miscellanies: Voltaire.*

11
What will Mrs. Grundy say?

THOMAS MORTON, *Speed the Plough*. (1798)

Mrs. Grundy, in the play, is a neighbor and obsession of Dame Ashfield, who constantly refers to her, wondering what she will think or say. Mrs. Grundy never appears. It was this play which, on 8 Feb., 1798, at Covent Garden, introduced Mrs. Grundy into English literature.

Aleways ding-dinging Dame Grundy into my ears— What will Mrs. Grundy zay? er, What will Mrs. Grundy think?

THOMAS MORTON, *Speed the Plough*. Act i, sc. 1.

The world's an ugly world. Offend
Good people, how they wrangle!
Their manners that they never mend,—
The characters they mangle!
They eat, and drink, and scheme, and plod,—
They go to church on Sunday;
And many are afraid of God—
And more of Mrs. Grundy.

F. LOCKER-LAMPSON, *The Jester's Plea.*

There be four things that keep us all from having our own way,—
Money, Fortune, Mrs. Grundy, and Policeman A.

D'ARCY THOMPSON, *Sales Attici.*

12
Custom and convention govern human action.
(Νόμῳ δὲ καὶ ἔθει πάντα τοὺς ἀνθρώπους πράττειν.)

PYRRHO. (DIOGENES LAERTIUS, *Pyrrho*. Bk. ix, sec. 61.)

Society has only one law, and that is custom.

P. G. HAMERTON, *Intellectual Life*. Pt. vi, let. 1.

13
Conventional people are roused to fury by departure from convention, largely because they regard such departure as a criticism of themselves.

BERTRAND RUSSELL, *The Conquest of Happiness*, p. 131.

14
Keep decorum.

SHAKESPEARE, *Antony and Cleopatra*, i, 2, 77.

Let them cant about decorum
Who have characters to lose.

BURNS, *The Jolly Beggars.*

15
Men like conventions because men made them.

BERNARD SHAW, *Misalliance*, p. 64.

16
To say what you think will certainly damage you in society; but a free tongue is worth more than a thousand invitations.

LOGAN PEARSALL SMITH, *Afterthoughts.*

VI—Society and Solitude

1
Solitude is very sad,
Too much company twice as bad.
WILLIAM ALLINGHAM, *Blackberries.*

Society than solitude is worse,
And man to man is still the greatest curse.
ANNA LETITIA BARBAULD, *Ovid to His Wife.*

2
If from society we learn to live,
'Tis solitude should teach us how to die.
BYRON, *Childe Harold.* Canto iv, st. 33.

3
There is a society in the deepest solitude.
ISAAC D'ISRAELI, *Literary Character of Men of Genius.* Ch. 10.

4
Solitude is impracticable, and society fatal.
EMERSON, *Essays: Society and Solitude.*

The solitary worshipper knows the essence of the thought: the scholar in society sees only its fair face.
EMERSON, *Journals,* 1864.

5
Solitude is as needful to the imagination as society is wholesome for the character.
J. R. LOWELL, *Among My Books: Dryden.*

6
Solitude is often the best society.
W. G. BENHAM, *Proverbs,* p. 835.

For solitude sometimes is best society,
And short retirement urges sweet return.
MILTON, *Paradise Lost.* Bk. ix, l. 249.

7
I love tranquil solitude,
And such society
As is quiet, wise, and good.
SHELLEY, *Song: Rarely, Rarely Comest Thou.*

SOLDIER

See also War

I—Soldier: Apothegms

8
It were better to be a soldier's widow than a coward's wife.
T. B. ALDRICH, *Mercedes.* Act ii, sc. 2.

9
One can be a soldier without dying, and a lover without sighing.
EDWIN ARNOLD, *Adzuma.* Act ii, sc. 5.

10
To take a soldier without ambition is to pull off his spurs.
FRANCIS BACON, *Essays: Of Ambition.*

Ambition, The soldier's virtue.
SHAKESPEARE, *Antony and Cleopatra.* Act iii, sc. 1, l. 22.

11
Man is a military animal,
Glories in gunpowder, and loves parade.
P. J. BAILEY, *Festus: A Metropolis.*

12
Soldiers in peace are like chimneys in summer.
WILLIAM CECIL, LORD BURGHLEY, *Ten Precepts.*

13
She was so accustomed to fast riding with our cavalry . . . she does not know how to treat a doughboy.
MRS. GEORGE A. CUSTER, *Letter,* March, 1867.
In the Civil War, infantrymen were called doughboys from their large brass buttons. In the World War, it was applied to all branches of the service.

14
A serjeant is a soldier with a halbert, and a drummer is a soldier with a drum.
JUSTICE DENISON, *Judgment,* Lloyd v. Wooddall. (I Black, 30.)

15
Eh-oh, my little brother,
They rigged you up in state,
In a khaki coat and gun to tote,
But you never could learn to hate.
MARTIN FEINSTEIN, *In Memoriam.*

16
Cowards in scarlet pass for men of war.
GEORGE GRANVILLE, *She Gallants.* Act v, sc. 1.

Uniforms were often masks [to hide cowards] . . . When my journal appears, many statues must come down.
DUKE OF WELLINGTON, *Sayings.*

All are not soldiers that go to the wars. (No son soldados todos los que van á la guerra.)
UNKNOWN. A Spanish proverb.

17
Every man thinks meanly of himself for not having been a soldier.
SAMUEL JOHNSON. (BOSWELL, *Life,* 1778.)

18
It ain't the guns or armament, or the money they can pay,
It's the close coöperation that makes them win the day;
It ain't the individual, nor the army as a whole,
But the everlastin' teamwork of every bloomin' soul.
J. MASON KNOX [?], *Coöperation.* These lines have been attributed to other writers. They were claimed for Mr. Knox in a letter from his wife to the New York *Times,* 1 Aug., 1920.

19
Courage, in soldiers, is a dangerous profession they follow to earn their living. (La valeur est, dans les simples soldats, un métier périlleux qu'ils ont pris pour gagner leur vie.)
LA ROCHEFOUCAULD, *Maximes.* No. 214.

20
In arms the Austrian phalanx stood,
A living wall, a human wood.
JAMES MONTGOMERY, *The Patriot's Pass-Word,* l. 1.

An Austrian army, awfully arrayed,
Boldly by battery besieged Belgrade;
Cossack commanders cannonading come,
Dealing destruction's devastating doom.
ALARIC ALEXANDER WATTS, *The Siege of Belgrade.* A study in alliteration. First appeared in the Winchester, Eng., *Trifler,* 7 May, 1817. Attributed to Isaac J. Reeve,

and the Rev. Benjamin Poulter, but definitely claimed for Watts, by his son. (*Life of Alaric Alexander Watts.* Vol. i, p. 118.)

1
I love a brave soldier who has undergone the baptism of fire.

NAPOLEON BONAPARTE. (O'MEARA, *Napoleon in Exile,* 2 Aug., 1817.)

Louis has just received his baptism of fire.

NAPOLEON III, *Letter to the Empress Eugénie,* 10 Aug., 1870, after the battle of Saarbrück, referring to their son.

I heard the bullets whistle; and believe me, there is something charming in the sound.

GEORGE WASHINGTON, *Letter to his Mother,* after his encounter with the French at Great Meadows, 3 May, 1754.

That shall be my music in the future!

CHARLES XII OF SWEDEN, on hearing for the first time the whistling of bullets in battle, at Copenhagen.

2
The worse the man, the better the soldier.

NAPOLEON BONAPARTE, *Sayings of Napoleon.*

3
They know no country, own no lord,
Their home the camp, their law the sword.

SILVIO PELLICO, *Enfernio de Messina.* Act v, sc. 2.

4
He also made other laws himself, one of which provides that those who are maimed in war shall be maintained at the public charge.

PLUTARCH, *Lives: Solon.* Sec. 31. Referring to Peisistratus.

5
But off with your hat and three times three
for Columbia's true-blue sons:
The men below who batter the foe—the men
behind the guns!

JOHN JEROME ROONEY, *The Men Behind the Guns.*

6
[The Russians] dashed on towards that thin red line tipped with steel.

W. H. RUSSELL, *Letter from the Crimea, London Times,* 25 Oct., 1854. Also in his *British Expedition in the Crimea,* p. 187. (See *Notes and Queries,* Ser. 8, vol. vii, p. 191, for letter from Russell claiming credit for authorship of "the thin red line.")

The spruce beauty of the slender red line. . . . Soon the men of the column began to see that, though the line was slender, it was very rigid and exact.

ALEXANDER WILLIAM KINGLAKE, *Invasion of the Crimea.* Vol. iii, pp. 248, 455. (1868)

See also KIPLING, *under* SOLDIERS, sec. 5.

7
Ah, what delight to be a soldier! (Ah, quel plaisir d'être soldat!)

EUGÈNE SCRIBE, *Dame Blanche.*

8
The chief bond of the soldier is his oath of allegiance and his love for the flag. (Primum militiæ vinculum est religio et signorum amor.)

SENECA, *Epistulæ ad Lucilium.* Epis. xcv, 35

9
When a soldier was the theme, my name
Was not far off.

SHAKESPEARE, *Cymbeline.* Act iii, sc. 3, l. 59.

10
Food for powder, food for powder; they'll fill a pit as well as better: tush, man, mortal men, mortal men.

SHAKESPEARE, *I Henry IV.* Act iv, sc. 2, l. 71.

Far and near and low and louder
On the roads of earth go by,
Dear to friends and food for powder,
Soldiers marching, all to die.

A. E. HOUSMAN, *A Shropshire Lad.* No. 35.

Food for Acheron. (Acheruntis pabulum.)

PLAUTUS, *Casina,* l. 157. (Act ii, sc. 1.)

11
Give them great meals of beef and iron and steel, they will eat like wolves and fight like devils.

SHAKESPEARE, *Henry V.* Act iii, sc. 7, l. 161.

No soldier can fight unless he is properly fed on beef and beer.

DUKE OF MARLBOROUGH, *Sayings.*

An army, like a serpent, travels on its belly.

FREDERICK THE GREAT, *Epigram.*

The soup makes the soldier. (La soupe fait le soldat.)

UNKNOWN. A French proverb.

12
I said, an elder soldier, not a better:
Did I say "better"?

SHAKESPEARE, *Julius Cæsar.* Act iv, sc. 3, l. 56.

13
Fie, my lord, fie! a soldier, and afeard?

SHAKESPEARE, *Macbeth.* Act v, sc. 1, l. 41.

Mere prattle, without practice,
Is all his soldiership.

SHAKESPEARE, *Othello.* Act i, sc. 1, l. 26.

14
It is just as fitting for a soldier to be ignorant of some things, as that he should know others. (Tam nescire quædam milites, quam scire oportet.)

TACITUS, *History.* Bk. i, sec. 83.

15
A military gent I see—and while his face I
scan,
I think you'll all agree with me—He came
from Hindostan.

THACKERAY, *The Newcomes.* Bk. i, ch. 1.

16
Ten good soldiers, wisely led,
Will beat a hundred without a head.

D'ARCY THOMPSON, *Paraphrase of Euripides.*

17
It is not a fair deal to take a man from a farm or a factory, clap a tin hat on his head, and then shoot him if his nerve fails.

ERNEST THURTLE, *Speech,* House of Commons, on bill to abolish death penalty for desertion.

1
All soldiers run away, madam.
DUKE OF WELLINGTON, when asked whether British soldiers ever ran away.

2
Of boasting more than of a bomb afraid,
A soldier should be modest as a maid.
YOUNG, *Love of Fame*. Sat. iv, l. 251.

3
On becoming soldiers we have not ceased to be citizens.
UNKNOWN, *Humble Representation*, addressed to Parliament by Cromwell's soldiers, 1647.

When we assumed the soldier, we did not lay aside the citizen.
GEORGE WASHINGTON, *Address*, to the provincial Congress of New York, 26 June, 1775. The quotation is inscribed on the memorial amphitheatre in Arlington Cemetery.

4
Here rests in honored glory an American soldier known but to God.
Inscription, on the tomb of the Unknown Soldier in Arlington National Cemetery.

II—Soldiers: Their Virtues

5
Glory is the sodger's prize;
The sodger's wealth is honour.
BURNS, *The Sodger's Return*, l. 59.

6
The army is a school in which the miser becomes generous, and the generous prodigal; miserly soldiers are like monsters, very rarely seen.
CERVANTES, *Don Quixote*. Pt. i, ch. 39.

7
Dear God, I raised my boy to be a soldier;
I tried to make him strong of will and true.
FLORENCE EARLE COATES, *A Soldier*. An answer to a popular song of the early World War period, *I Did Not Raise My Boy to Be a Soldier*, written by Albert Bryan and published in 1914. In 1917, Bryan climbed aboard the patriotic band-wagon by writing *It's Time for Ev'ry Boy to Be a Soldier;* in 1916, J. Will Callahan produced, *I'm Going to Raise My Boy to Be a Soldier*, and in 1917, Happy Mack turned out *I Didn't Raise My Boy to be a Slacker*. All were fleetingly popular.

The man who has not raised himself to be a soldier, and the woman who has not raised her boy to be a soldier for the right, neither one of them is entitled to citizenship in the Republic.
THEODORE ROOSEVELT, *Speech*, to the Soldiers at Camp Upton, 1917.

8
He stands erect; his slouch becomes a walk;
He steps right onward, martial in his air,
His form and movement.
COWPER, *The Task*. Bk. iv, l. 639.

9
That little bronze button,
Still keep it in view,
And honor the wearers,
Once brave boys in blue.
ADAM CRAIG, *The Little Bronze Button*. (1899)

Ye living soldiers of the mighty war,
Once more from roaring cannon and the drums,
And bugles blown at morn, the summons comes;
Forget the halting limb, each wound and scar:
Once more your Captain calls to you;
Come to his last review!
R. W. GILDER, *The Burial of Grant*.

10
Last night, among his fellow-roughs
He jested, quaffed, and swore;
A drunken private of the Buffs,
Who never looked before.
To-day, beneath the foeman's frown,
He stands in Elgin's place,
Ambassador from Britain's crown,
And type of all her race.
FRANCIS H. DOYLE, *The Private of the Buffs*.

So let his name through Europe ring!
A man of mean estate,
Who died as firm as Sparta's king,
Because his soul was great.
FRANCIS H. DOYLE, *The Private of the Buffs*.

From softness only softness comes;
Urged by a bitterer shout within,
Men of the trumpets and the drums
Seek, with appropriate discipline,
That Glory past the pit or wall
Which contradicts and stops the breath,
And with immortalizing gall
Builds the most stubborn things on death.
OLIVER GOGARTY, *Marcus Curtius*.

11
The broken soldier, kindly bade to stay,
Sat by his fire, and talk'd the night away,
Wept o'er his wounds, or, tales of sorrow done,
Shoulder'd his crutch, and show'd how fields were won.
GOLDSMITH, *The Deserted Village*, l. 155.

12
If soldier,
Chase brave employments with a naked sword
Throughout the world. Fool not, for all may have
If they dare try, a glorious life, or grave.
GEORGE HERBERT, *The Church-Porch*. St. 15.

13
The man-at-arms is the only man.
IBSEN, *Lady Inger*. Act i. Quoted as a proverb.

14
So 'ere's *to* you, Fuzzy-Wuzzy, at your 'ome in the Soudan;
You're a pore benighted 'eathen but a first-class fightin' man.
RUDYARD KIPLING, *"Fuzzy-Wuzzy."*

Ah there, Piet!—picked up be'ind the drive!
The wonder wasn't 'ow 'e fought, but 'ow 'e kep' alive,
With nothin' in 'is belly, on 'is back, or to 'is feet—
I've known a lot o' men behave a dam' sight worse than Piet.
RUDYARD KIPLING, *Piet*.

15
The soldier should be fear-inspiring; not decked with gold and silver, but relying on

his courage and his steel. . . . Valor is the soldier's adornment.
LIVY, *History*. Bk. ix, sec. 40.

1
They carved at the meal With gloves of steel,
And they drank the red wine through the helmet barred.
SCOTT, *Lay of the Last Minstrel*. Canto i, st. 4.

A soldier's but a man; A life's but a span;
Why, then, let a soldier drink.
SHAKESPEARE, *Othello*. Act ii, sc. 3, l. 73.

2
A soldier,
Full of strange oaths and bearded like the pard,
Jealous in honour, sudden and quick in quarrel,
Seeking the bubble reputation
Even in the cannon's mouth.
SHAKESPEARE, *As You Like It*. Act ii, sc. 7, l. 149.

Arm'd at point exactly, cap-a-pe.
SHAKESPEARE, *Hamlet*. Act i, sc. 2, l. 200.

All furnished, all in arms,
All plumed like estridges that with the wind
Baited like eagles having lately bathed;
Glittering in golden coats, like images;
As full of spirit as the month of May,
And gorgeous as the sun at midsummer.
SHAKESPEARE, *I Henry IV*. Act iv, sc. 1, l. 97.

3
I am a soldier and unapt to weep
Or to exclaim on fortune's fickleness.
SHAKESPEARE, *I Henry VI*. Act v, sc. 3, l. 133.

They are soldiers,
Witty, courteous, liberal, full of spirit.
SHAKESPEARE, *III Henry VI*. Act i, sc. 2, l. 42.

He is a soldier fit to stand by Cæsar.
SHAKESPEARE, *Othello*. Act ii, sc. 3, l. 126.

'Tis the soldiers' life
To have their balmy slumbers waked with strife.
SHAKESPEARE, *Othello*. Act ii, sc. 3, l. 257.

5
Let it be your pride, therefore, to show all men everywhere not only what good soldiers you are, but also what good men you are. . . . Let us set for ourselves a standard so high that it will be a glory to live up to it, and then let us live up to it and add a new laurel to the crown of America.
WOODROW WILSON, *Address*, to the soldiers of the National Army, 1917.

6
When captains courageous, whom death could not daunt,
Did march to the siege of the city of Gaunt,
They mustered their soldiers by two and by three,
And the foremost in battle was Mary Ambree.
UNKNOWN, *Mary Ambree*. (PERCY, *Reliques*.)

Captains Courageous.
RUDYARD KIPLING. Title of boy's story.

III—Soldiers: Their Faults

7
The Soldier, arm'd with Sword & Gun,
Palsied strikes the Summer's Sun. . . .
Nought can deform the Human Race
Like to the Armour's iron brace.
WILLIAM BLAKE, *Auguries of Innocence*.

8
For he was of that noble trade
That demi-gods and heroes made,
Slaughter, and knocking on the head,
The trade to which they all were bred.
BUTLER, *Hudibras*. Pt. i, canto 2, l. 321.

9
Mouths without hands; maintain'd at vast expense,
In peace a charge, in war a weak defence.
DRYDEN, *Cymon and Iphigenia*, l. 401.

10
The soldiers of America have killed more Americans, twenty times over, than they have foreign foes.
ELBERT HUBBARD, *The Philistine*. Vol. xx, p. 38.

11
No faith and no honor is found in men who follow camps. (Nulla fides pietasque viris qui castra sequuntur.)
LUCAN, *De Bello Civili*. Bk. x, l. 407.

12
The braggart warrior. (Miles gloriosus.)
PLAUTUS. Title of comedy.

Each year his mighty armies marched forth in gallant show,
Their enemies were targets, their bullets they were tow.
BÉRANGER, *Le Roi d'Yvetot*. (Thackeray, tr.)

13
Telling me . . . it was great pity, so it was,
This villanous saltpetre should be digg'd
Out of the bowels of the harmless earth,
Which many a good tall fellow had destroy'd
So cowardly; and but for these vile guns,
He would himself have been a soldier.
SHAKESPEARE, *I Henry IV*. Act i, sc. 3, l. 57

If I be not ashamed of my soldiers, I am a soused gurnet.
SHAKESPEARE, *I Henry IV*. Act iv, sc. 2, l. 12.

14
A soldier is an anachronism of which we must get rid.
BERNARD SHAW, *The Devil's Disciple*. Act iii.

I never expect a soldier to think.
BERNARD SHAW, *The Devil's Disciple*. Act iii.

15
True, quoth my Uncle Toby, thou didst very right, Trim, as a soldier—but certainly very wrong as a man.
STERNE, *Tristram Shandy*. Bk. vi, ch. 8.

A soldier, cried my Uncle Toby, interrupting the corporal, is no more exempt from saying a foolish thing, Trim, than a man of letters— But not so often, an' please your honour, replied the corporal.
STERNE, *Tristram Shandy*. Bk. viii, ch. 19.

1
Many believe that subtlety is wanting in military genius. (Credunt plerique militaribus ingeniis subtilitatem deesse.)
TACITUS, *Agricola*. Sec. 9.

IV—Soldiers and the Fair Sex

2
The young hussar,
The whisker'd votary of waltz and war.
BYRON, *The Waltz*, l. 15.

3
We know, Mr. Weller—we, who are men of the world—that a good uniform must work its way with the women, sooner or later.
DICKENS, *Pickwick Papers*. Ch. 37.

4
Such is the country maiden's fright,
When first a red-coat is in sight,
Behind the door she hides her face;
Next time at distance eyes the lace.
JOHN GAY, *Fables: The Tame Stag*.

Gold lace has a charm for the fair.
W. S. GILBERT, *Patience*. Act i.

The love that loves a scarlet coat,
Should be more uniform!
THOMAS HOOD, *Faithless Nelly Gray*.

5
The sex is ever to a soldier kind.
HOMER, *Odyssey*. Bk. xiv, l. 246. (Pope, tr.)

He's an absent-minded beggar, and his weaknesses are great—
But we and Paul must take him as we find him—
He is out on active service, wiping something off a slate—
And he's left a lot of little things behind him!
RUDYARD KIPLING, *The Absent-Minded Beggar*.

There are girls he walked with casual. They'll be sorry now he's gone,
For an absent-minded beggar they will find him,
But it ain't the time for sermons with the winter coming on.
We must help the girl that Tommy's left behind him!
RUDYARD KIPLING, *The Absent-Minded Beggar*.

6
But we are soldiers;
And may that soldier a mere recreant prove,
That means not, hath not, or is not in love!
SHAKESPEARE, *Troilus and Cressida*. Act i, sc. 3, l. 286.

7
When the military man approaches, the world locks up its spoons and packs off its womankind.
BERNARD SHAW, *Man and Superman*.

8
What female heart can withstand a red-coat? I think this should be a part of female education. As you have the rocking-horse to accustom them to ride, I would have military dolls in the nursery, to harden their hearts against officers and red-coats.
SYDNEY SMITH. (LADY HOLLAND, *Memoir*. Vol. i, p. 313.)

9
Malbrouck is off to the wars; . . .
I don't know when he'll return.
(Malbrouck s'en va-t-en guerre;
Mironton, mironton, mirontaine,
Malbrouck s'en va-t-en guerre,
Ne sait quand reviendra.)
UNKNOWN, *Malbrouck*. A famous old French song, sometimes attributed to Madame de Sévigné, and supposed to refer to the unsuccessful expedition against St. Malo made by Charles, Third Duke of Marlborough, in 1758. Found in many collections; popularized by Marie Antoinette about 1780; introduced by Beaumarchais into *Le Mariage de Figaro*, and by George Du Maurier into *Trilby*. Sung to the air of "We won't go home till morning."

O. send Lewis Gordon hame
And the lad I mauna name,
Though his back be at the wa'
Here's to him that's far awa'.
WILLIAM GEDDES [?], *Lewis Gordon*.

The unreturning brave.
BYRON, *Childe Harold*. Canto iii, st. 27.

V—Soldiers and Public Ingratitude

10
For a soldier I listed, to grow great in fame,
And be shot at for sixpence a day.
CHARLES DIBDIN, *Charity*.

How happy's the soldier who lives on his pay,
And spends half-a-crown out of sixpence a day!
JOHN O'KEEFFE, *The Poor Soldier*.

Ninepunce a day fer killin' folks comes kind o' low fer murder.
J. R. LOWELL, *The Biglow Papers*. Ser. i, No. 2.

11
For it's Tommy this, an' Tommy that, an' "Chuck 'im out, the brute!"
But it's "Saviour of 'is country" when the guns begin to shoot.
RUDYARD KIPLING, *Tommy*.

Then it's Tommy this, an' Tommy that, an' "Tommy, 'ow's yer soul?"
But it's "Thin red line of 'eroes" when the drums begin to roll.
RUDYARD KIPLING, *Tommy*.

We aren't no thin red 'eroes, nor we aren't no blackguards too,
But single men in barricks, most remarkable like you;
An' if sometimes our conduck isn't all your fancy paints,
Why, single men in barricks don't grow into plaster saints.
RUDYARD KIPLING, *Tommy*.

The world's wicked.
We are men, not saints, sweet lady.
MASSINGER, *Unnatural Combat*. Act i, sc. 1.

Tommy Atkins, as a sobriquet of the British soldier, comes from the imaginary name "Thomas Atkins," employed in 1815 in connection with *The Soldier's Account Book*, called into use by the War Office. "Thomas Atkins" appeared in the sample forms accompanying the official circular letter, 31 August, 1815.

1
The painful warrior famoused for fight,
After a thousand victories once foil'd,
Is from the book of honour razed quite,
And all the rest forgot for which he toil'd.
SHAKESPEARE, *Sonnets*. No. xxv.

Our God and soldier we alike adore,
When at the brink of ruin, not before;
After deliverance, both alike requited,
Our God forgotten, and our soldiers slighted.
FRANCIS QUARLES, *Epigram*. *See also* DEVIL: SICK AND WELL.

And when they're worn,
Hacked, hewn with constant service, thrown aside,
To rust in peace, and rot in hospitals.
THOMAS SOUTHERNE, *The Loyal Brother*.

2
Some for hard masters, broken under arms,
In battle lopt away, with half their limbs,
Beg bitter bread thro' realms their valour saved.
YOUNG, *Night Thoughts*. Night i, l. 250.

VI—Soldiers: Officers

3
The honorable thing, that which makes the real general, is to have clean hands. (Καλὸν δὲ καὶ στρατηγικὸν ἀληθῶς ἡ περὶ τὰς χεῖρας ἐγκράτεια.)
ARISTIDES, to Themistocles. (PLUTARCH, *Lives: Aristides*. Ch. 24, sec. 4.)

The greatest general is he who makes the fewest mistakes.
NAPOLEON BONAPARTE, *Sayings of Napoleon*.

I made all my generals out of mud.
NAPOLEON BONAPARTE, *Sayings of Napoleon*.

It is the part of a good general to talk of success, not of failure. (Ἐπεὶ στρατηλάτου χεηστοῦ τὰ κρείσσω μηδὲ τἀνδεᾶ λέγειν.)
SOPHOCLES, *Œdipus Coloneus*, l. 1429.

The proper qualities of a general are judgment and deliberation. (Ratio et consilium propriæ ducis artes.)
TACITUS, *History*. Bk. iii, sec. 20.

To know when to retreat and to dare to do it.
DUKE OF WELLINGTON, when asked what was the best test of greatness in a general. (FRASER, *Words on Wellington*, p. 35.)

4
We can make majors and officers every year, but not scholars.
ROBERT BURTON, *Anatomy of Melancholy*. Pt. i, sec. ii, mem. 3, subs. 15.

I am sorry it was not a general—I could make more of them.
ABRAHAM LINCOLN, *Remark*, when he heard of the death of a private.

If he is mad, I wish he would bite my other generals.
GEORGE II, *Retort*, to one who complained that Gen. James Wolfe was a madman.

Get me the brand, and I'll send a barrel to my other generals.
ABRAHAM LINCOLN, *Retort*, when told that General Grant was drinking too much whiskey.

5
Turenne's small change. (La monnaie de M. Turenne.)
MADAME DE CORNUEL, referring to the eight generals appointed to take Turenne's place. (*Nouvelle Biographie Universelle*.)

6
Captains are casual things.
JOHN FLETCHER, *Rule a Wife and Have a Wife*. Act iii.

An army all of captains, used to pray
And stiff in fight, but serious drill's despair,
Skilled to debate their orders, not obey.
J. R. LOWELL, *Under the Old Elm*. Referring to the Continental army.

That in the captain's but a choleric word,
Which in the soldier is flat blasphemy.
SHAKESPEARE, *Measure for Measure*. Act ii, sc. 2, l. 130.

The courageous captain of complements.
SHAKESPEARE, *Romeo and Juliet*. Act ii, 4, 19.

See now comes the captain all daubed with gold lace.
SWIFT, *The Grand Question Debated*.

6a
Hail, ye indomitable heroes, hail!
Despite of all your generals, ye prevail.
WALTER SAVAGE LANDOR, *The Crimean Heroes*.

Grant lies asleep in his great white tomb, where the Hudson tides run deep;
And Sheridan and Sherman lie on marble beds asleep; . . .
But what of the men those heroes led: of Smith and Robinson?
REGINALD WRIGHT KAUFFMAN, *Heroes of Yesterday*.

7
I have heard, in such a way as to believe it, of your recently saying that both the army and the government needed a dictator. . . . Only those generals who gain successes can set up dictators. What I ask of you now is military success, and I will risk the dictatorship.
ABRAHAM LINCOLN, *Letter to Major-General Joseph Hooker*, appointing him commander of the Army of the Potomac, 26 Jan., 1863.

8
I personally wish Jacob Freese, of New Jersey, to be appointed colonel of a colored regiment, and this regardless of whether he can tell the exact shade of Julius Cæsar's hair.
ABRAHAM LINCOLN *Letter to Secretary of War Stanton*.

9
"Companions," said he [Saturninus], "you have lost a good captain, to make of him a bad general."
MONTAIGNE, *Essays*. Bk. iii, ch. 9.

1
Yet, trained in camps, he knew the art
To win the soldier's hardy heart.
They love a captain to obey,
Boisterous as March, yet fresh as May;
With open hand and brow as free,
Lover of wine and minstrelsy;
Ever the first to scale a tower,
As venturous in a lady's bower:—
Such buxom chief shall lead his host
From India's fires to Zembla's frost.

SCOTT, *Marmion*. Canto iii, st. 4.

2
It is a bad soldier who grumbles when following his commander. (Malus miles est qui imperatorem gemens sequitur.)

SENECA, *Epistulæ ad Lucilium*. Epis. cvii, sec. 10.

3
If you have a station in the file,
Not i' the worst rank of manhood, say 't.

SHAKESPEARE, *Macbeth*. Act iii, sc. 1, l. 102.

4
'Tis the curse of service,
Preferment goes by letter and affection,
Not by the old gradation, where each second
Stood heir to the first.

SHAKESPEARE, *Othello*. Act i, sc. 1, l. 35.

Worked himself, step by step, through each preferment,
From the ranks upwards. And verily, it gives
A precedent of hope, a spur of action
To the whole corps, if once in their remembrance
An old, deserving soldier makes his way.

SCHILLER, *Wallenstein*. Pt. i, act i, sc. 1. (Coleridge, tr.)

5
Cassio, I love thee;
But never more be officer of mine.

SHAKESPEARE, *Othello*. Act ii, sc. 3, l. 248.

5a
A thousand soldiers are easily got, but a single general is hard to find. ('Chien ping i tê i chiang nan 'chiu.)

UNKNOWN. A Chinese proverb.

VII—Soldiers: How Sleep the Brave

6
Lay him low, lay him low,
In the clover or the snow!
What cares he? he cannot know:
Lay him low!

GEORGE HENRY BOKER, *Dirge for a Soldier*.

He rush'd into the field, and, foremost fighting, fell.

BYRON, *Childe Harold*. Canto iii, st. 23.

He slept an iron sleep,—
Slain fighting for his country.

HOMER, *Iliad*. Bk. xi, l. 285. (Bryant, tr.)

7
In the field of proud honour—our swords in our hands,
Our King and our Country to save—
While victory shines on life's last ebbing sands,
O! who would not die with the brave!

BURNS, *Song of Death*, l. 16.

Oh who would not sleep with the brave?

A. E. HOUSMAN, *Lancer*, l. 2.

8
I see before me the Gladiator lie:
He leans upon his hand—his manly brow
Consents to death, but conquers agony.

BYRON, *Childe Harold*. Canto iv, st. 140.

9
How sleep the brave, who sink to rest,
By all their country's wishes blest!
When Spring, with dewy fingers cold,
Returns to deck their hallow'd mold,
She there shall dress a sweeter sod
Than Fancy's feet have ever trod.

By fairy hands their knell is rung,
By forms unseen their dirge is sung;
There Honour comes, a pilgrim grey,
To bless the turf that wraps their clay,
And Freedom shall a-while repair,
To dwell a weeping hermit there!

WILLIAM COLLINS, *Ode Written in 1746*.

The snow shall be their winding-sheet,
And every turf beneath their feet
Shall be a soldier's sepulchre.

THOMAS CAMPBELL, *Hohenlinden*. St. 8.

10
Toll for the brave—
The brave! that are no more:
All sunk beneath the wave,
Fast by their native shore.

COWPER, *On the Loss of the Royal George*.

Far in foreign fields from Dunkirk to Belgrad.
Lie the soldiers and chiefs of the Irish Brigade.

THOMAS DAVIS, *Battle Eve of the Brigade*.

11
We meet neath the sounding rafter,
And the walls around are bare;
As they shout back our peals of laughter,
It seems that the dead are there.
Ho! stand to your glasses steady!
'T is all we have left to prize.
A cup to the dead already,—
Hurrah for the next that dies!

BARTHOLOMEW DOWLING, *The Revel*.

And hands that wist not though they dug a grave,
Undid the hasps of gold, and drank, and gave,
And he drank after, a deep glad kingly draught:
And all their life changed in them, for they quaffed
Death; if it be death so to drink, and fare
As men who change and are what these twain were.

SWINBURNE, *Tristram of Lyonesse: The Sailing of the Swallow*, l. 789.

13
It is a sign of a soldier to believe that there is nothing left of man after death, except a corpse. (Militare est credere nihil hominis superesse post mortem, nisi cadaver.)

ERASMUS, *Hippeus Anippos*.

Old soldiers never die, they just fade away.

GENERAL DOUGLAS MACARTHUR, *Address*, before a joint meeting of U.S. Congress, April 19, 1951, quoting an old army ballad. *See* 2298h:4.

1
Under the sod and the dew,
  Waiting the Judgment Day;
Love and tears for the Blue,
  Tears and love for the Gray.
  FRANCIS MILES FINCH, *The Blue and the Gray.*

Each for his land, in a fair fight,
  Encountered, strove, and died,
And the kindly earth that knows no spite
  Covers them side by side.
  RUDYARD KIPLING, *The American Rebellion: After.*

Sleep sweetly in your humble graves,
Sleep, martyrs of a fallen cause.
  HENRY TIMROD, *Ode.*

2
He that stepped forward to follow the flag,
To ride with a saber or march with a Krag,
You'll find now, with thousands, shipped home in a bag,
  Just a little brass tag.
  EDGAR A. GUEST, *A Little Brass Tag.*

3
Let those who have no homes at all,
Go battle for a long one.
  THOMAS HOOD, *The Volunteer*, l. 69.

4
In a wood they call the Rouge Bouquet,
There is a new-made grave today,
Built by never a spade nor pick,
Yet covered with earth ten metres thick.
There lie many fighting men,
  Dead in their youthful prime.
Never to laugh nor love again
  Nor taste the Summertime.
  JOYCE KILMER, *Rouge Bouquet.*

If any question why we died,
Tell them, because our fathers lied.
  RUDYARD KIPLING, *Epitaphs of the War: Common Form.*

5
We have met on a great battlefield of that war. We have come to dedicate a portion of that field as a final resting-place for those who here gave their lives that that nation might live. It is altogether fitting and proper that we should do this. But in a larger sense, we cannot dedicate, we cannot consecrate, we cannot hallow this ground. The brave men, living and dead, who struggled here, have consecrated it far above our poor power to add or detract. The world will little note, nor long remember, what we say here, but it can never forget what they did here.
  ABRAHAM LINCOLN, *Gettysburg Address*, 19 Nov., 1863.

These heroes are dead. They died for liberty—they died for us. They are at rest. They sleep in the land they made free, under the flag they rendered stainless, under the solemn pines, the sad hemlocks, the tearful willows, the embracing vines. They sleep beneath the shadows of the clouds, careless alike of sunshine or storm, each in the windowless palace of rest. Earth may run red with other wars—they are at peace. In the midst of battles, in the roar of conflict, they found the serenity of death.
  R. G. INGERSOLL, *Memorial Day Vision.*

6
Nicanor lay dead in his harness.
  Apocrypha: II Maccabees, xv, 28.

7
Take up our quarrel with the foe:
To you from failing hands we throw
  The torch; be yours to hold it high.
  If ye break faith with us who die
We shall not sleep, though poppies grow
    In Flanders fields.
  JOHN MCCRAE, *In Flanders Fields.* First published in *Punch*, London, 8 Dec., 1915.

Your flaming torch aloft we bear,
With burning heart an oath we swear
To keep the faith, to fight it through,
To crush the foe or sleep with you
  In Flanders fields.
  C. B. GALBREATH, *Answer to In Flanders Fields.*

8
When soldiers brave death, they drive him into the ranks of the enemy.
  NAPOLEON, *Address to His Soldiers*, two days after the battle of Jena.

9
"And where do we go now?" brave Bingham said,
And Bethell, with his feet among the dead
Feeling the slant plate sink, the waters thrust,
Answered him cheerily, "Why, to heaven I trust."
  ROBERT NICHOLS, *The Souls of the Righteous.*

O loved, living, dying, heroic soldier,
All, all, my joy, my grief, my love, are thine!
  ROBERT NICHOLS, *Fulfilment.*

10
A soldier of the Legion lay dying in Algiers,
There was lack of woman's nursing, there was dearth of woman's tears; . . .
And he said, "I never more shall see my own, my native land;
Take a message, and a token, to some distant friends of mine,
For I was born at Bingen,—at Bingen on the Rhine."
  CAROLINE NORTON, *Bingen on the Rhine.*

11
The muffled drum's sad roll has beat
  The soldier's last tattoo;
No more on Life's parade shall meet
  The brave and fallen few.
On Fame's eternal camping-ground
  Their silent tents are spread,
And Glory guards, with solemn round,
  The bivouac of the dead.
  THEODORE O'HARA, *The Bivouac of the Dead.*

Nor shall your story be forgot,
  While Fame her record keeps,
Or Honor points the hallowed spot
  Where Valor proudly sleeps.
  THEODORE O'HARA, *The Bivouac of the Dead*

1
The sunshine streaming upon Salmon's height
Is not so sweet and white
As the most heretofore sin-spotted Soul
That darts to its delight
Straight from the absolution of a faithful fight.

COVENTRY PATMORE, *Peace.*

2
Soldiers are citizens of death's grey land.

SIEGFRIED SASSOON, *Dreamers.*

3
Soldier, rest! thy warfare o'er,
Dream of fighting fields no more;
Sleep the sleep that knows not breaking,
Morn of toil, nor night of waking.

SCOTT, *The Lady of the Lake.* Canto i, st. 31.

Death had he seen by sudden blow,
By wasting plague, by tortures slow,
By mine or breach, by steel or ball,
Knew all his shapes and scorned them all.

SCOTT, *Rokeby.* Canto i, st. 8.

Fell as he was in act and mind,
He left no bolder heart behind:
Then, give him, for a soldier meet,
A soldier's cloak for winding sheet.

SCOTT, *Rokeby.* Canto vi, st. 33.

4
O, wither'd is the garland of the war,
The soldier's pole is fallen.

SHAKESPEARE, *Antony and Cleopatra.* Act iv, sc. 15, l. 64.

Cut is the branch that might have grown full straight,
And burnèd is Apollo's laurel bough,
That sometime grew within this learnèd man.

MARLOWE, *Doctor Faustus.* Final chorus.

5
Died with their swords in hand.

SHAKESPEARE, *Cymbeline.* Act i, sc. 1, l. 36.

O, farewell, honest soldier.

SHAKESPEARE, *Hamlet.* Act i, sc. 1, l. 16.

God's soldier be he!
Had I as many sons as I have hairs,
I would not wish them to a fairer death,
And so, his knell is knoll'd.

SHAKESPEARE, *Macbeth.* Act v, sc. 8, l. 47.

6
Sleep, soldiers! still in honored rest
Your truth and valor wearing:
The bravest are the tenderest,—
The loving are the daring.

BAYARD TAYLOR, *The Song of the Camp.*

7
Home they brought her warrior dead.

TENNYSON, *The Princess.* Pt. v, l. 532.

8
Where are the boys of the old Brigade,
Who fought with us side by side?

F. E. WEATHERLY, *The Old Brigade.*

Not in the Abbey proudly laid
Find they a place or part;
The gallant boys of the old Brigade,
They sleep in Old England's heart.

F. E. WEATHERLY, *The Old Brigade.*

9
Not a drum was heard, not a funeral note,
As his corse to the rampart we hurried;
Not a soldier discharged his farewell shot
O'er the grave where our hero we buried.

CHARLES WOLFE, *The Burial of Sir John Moore After Corunna.* In 1908, R. C. Newick published a pamphlet at Bristol, England, contending that this poem was written by a private soldier named Joseph Wolfe, a member of the squad which dug Moore's grave, but the ascription to Charles Wolfe is undoubtedly correct.

No useless coffin enclosed his breast,
Not in sheet or in shroud we wound him;
But he lay like a warrior taking his rest
With his martial cloak around him.

Few and short were the prayers we said,
And we spoke not a word of sorrow;
But we steadfastly gazed on the face that was dead,
And we bitterly thought of the morrow. . . .

Slowly and sadly we laid him down,
From the field of his fame fresh and gory;
We carved not a line, and we raised not a stone,
But we left him alone with his glory.

WOLFE, *The Burial of Sir John Moore.*

10
Dead on the field of honor. (Mort au champ d'honneur.)

Response to the roll-call for Théophile Malo, La Tour d'Auvergne, in his company after his death in action at Oberhausen, 27 June, 1800, according to an order of Napoleon, still in force.

SOLITUDE

See also Society and Solitude

I—Solitude: Definitions and Apothegms

11
It had been hard for him that spake it to have put more truth and untruth together, in few words, than in that speech: "Whosoever is delighted in solitude is either a wild beast, or a god."

FRANCIS BACON, *Essays: Of Friendship.*

12
To fly from need not be to hate mankind.

BYRON, *Childe Harold.* Canto iii, st. 59.

13
The secret of solitude is that there is no solitude.

JOSEPH COOK, *Boston Monday Lectures: Conscience.*

14
There is one means of procuring solitude which to me, and I apprehend to all men, is effectual, and that is to go to the window and look at the stars.

EMERSON, *Journals.* Vol. iii, p. 263.

Inspiration makes solitude anywhere.

EMERSON, *Nature, Addresses, and Lectures: Literary Ethics.*

15
When you have closed your doors, and dark-

ened your room, remember never to say that you are alone, for you are not alone; God is within, and your genius is within,—and what need have they of light to see what you are doing?

EPICTETUS, *Discourses*. Bk. i, ch. 14.

A solitude is the audience-chamber of God.

W. S. LANDOR, *Imaginary Conversations: Lord Brooke and Sir Philip Sidney*.

1
"And nobody with me at sea but myself."

GOLDSMITH, *The Haunch of Venison*, l. 60. Quoted from a letter of Henry Frederick, Duke of Cumberland, to Lady Grosvenor, a correspondence which, in 1770, gave great delight to scandal-mongers.

All by my own-alone self.

JOEL CHANDLER HARRIS, *Nights with Uncle Remus*. Ch. 36.

2
Woe unto him that is never alone, and cannot bear to be alone.

P. G. HAMERTON, *The Intellectual Life*. Pt. ix, letter 6.

3
The strongest man in the world is he who stands most alone.

HENRIK IBSEN, *An Enemy of the People*. Act v.

The more powerful and original a mind, the more it will incline towards the religion of solitude.

ALDOUS HUXLEY, *Proper Studies*, p. 218.

4
Now the New Year reviving old Desires,
The thoughtful Soul to Solitude retires.

OMAR KHAYYÁM, *Rubáiyát*. St. 4. (Fitzgerald, tr.)

5
You must show him . . . by leaving him severely alone.

CHARLES STEWART PARNELL, *Speech at Ennis*, 19 Sept., 1880.

7
Solitude vivifies; isolation kills.

JOSEPH ROUX, *Meditations of a Parish Priest*. Pt. v, No. 60.

8
Time is not here, nor days, nor months, nor years,
An everlasting NOW of solitude!

SOUTHEY, *Thalaba*. Bk. i, sec. 28. *See also* PRESENT: THE EVERLASTING NOW.

9
I never found the companion that was so companionable as solitude.

THOREAU, *Walden: Solitude*.

10
O! lost to virtue, lost to manly thought,
Lost to the noble sallies of the soul!
Who think it solitude, to be alone.

YOUNG, *Night Thoughts*. Night iii, l. 6.

II—Solitude: Its Virtues

11
Converse with men makes sharp the glittering wit,
But God to man doth speak in solitude.

JOHN STUART BLACKIE, *Highland Solitude*.

'Tis solitude should teach us how to die
It hath no flatterers; vanity can give
No hollow aid; alone—man with his God must strive.

BYRON, *Childe Harold*. Canto iv, st. 33.

12
O Solitude, the soul's best friend,
That man acquainted with himself dost make.

CHARLES COTTON, *The Retirement*.

13
Solitude is the nurse of enthusiasm, and enthusiasm is the true parent of genius. In all ages solitude has been called for—has been flown to.

ISAAC D'ISRAELI, *Literary Character of Men of Genius*. Ch. 10.

So vain is the belief
That the sequestered path has fewest flowers.

THOMAS DOUBLEDAY, *The Poet's Solitude*.

14
Go cherish your soul; expel companions; set your habits to a life of solitude; then will the faculties rise fair and full within.

EMERSON, *Nature, Addresses, and Lectures: Literary Ethics*.

I am sure of this, that by going much alone a man will get more of a noble courage in thought and word than from all the wisdom that is in books.

EMERSON, *Journals*, 1833.

What a saving grace is in poverty and solitude, that the obscure youth learns the practice instead of the literature of his Virtues!

EMERSON, *Journals*, 1864.

15
Living in solitude till the fulness of time, I still kept the dew of my youth and the freshness of my heart.

HAWTHORNE: Inscribed beneath his bust in Hall of Fame.

16
By all means use sometimes to be alone.
Salute thyself: see what thy soul doth wear. . . .
Who cannot rest till he good fellows find,
He breaks up house, turns out of doors his mind.

GEORGE HERBERT, *The Church-Porch*. St. 25.

17
Two paradises 'twere in one,
To live in Paradise alone.

ANDREW MARVELL, *The Garden*.

18
Wisdom's self
Oft seeks to sweet retired Solitude,
Where with her best nurse Contemplation
She plumes her feathers, and lets grow her wings,
That in the various bustle of resort
Were all too ruffl'd, and sometimes impair'd.

MILTON, *Comus*, l. 375.

Solitude is the best nurse of wisdom.

LAURENCE STERNE, *Letters*. No. 82.

Impulses of deeper birth
Have come to him in solitude.
WORDSWORTH, *A Poet's Epitaph*, l. 47.

1
O blessed solitude! O sole blessedness. (O beata solitudo! O sola beatitudo.)
CORNELIUS MUYS, *Solitudo*. (1566)

I praise the Frenchman, his remark was shrewd—
"How sweet, how passing sweet is solitude!"
But grant me still a friend in my retreat,
Whom I may whisper—Solitude is sweet.
COWPER, *Retirement*, l. 739. The quotation has been attributed to LA BRUYÈRE.

2
Hail, mildly pleasing Solitude,
Companion of the wise and good;
But from whose holy piercing eye
The herd of fools and villains fly.
Oh! how I love with thee to walk,
And listen to thy whispered talk,
Which innocence and truth imparts,
And melts the most obdurate hearts.
JAMES THOMSON, *Hymn on Solitude*, l. 1.

I will arise and go now, and go to Innisfree,
And a small cabin build there, of clay and wattles made:
Nine bean-rows will I have there, a hive for the honey-bee,
And live alone in the bee-loud glade.
W. B. YEATS, *The Lake Isle of Innisfree.*

3
O sacred solitude! divine retreat!
Choice of the prudent! envy of the great,
By thy pure stream, or in thy waving shade,
We court fair wisdom, that celestial maid.
YOUNG, *Love of Fame*. Satire v, l. 254.

III—Solitude: Its Faults

4
Solitude affects some people like wine; they must not take too much of it, for it flies to the head.
MARY COLERIDGE, *Gathered Leaves*, p. 223.

5
Oh, solitude! where are the charms
That sages have seen in thy face?
Better dwell in the midst of alarms,
Than reign in this horrible place.
COWPER, *Verses Supposed to be Written by Alexander Selkirk.*

6
Woe to him that is alone when he falleth; for he hath not another to help him up.
Old Testament: Ecclesiastes, iv, 10. (Væ soli.—*Vulgate.*)

The wise saith, "Woe him that is alone,
For, and he fall, he hath no help to rise."
CHAUCER, *Troilus and Criseyde*. Bk. i, l. 694.

Woe be to him that lust to be alone,
For if he falle, helpe hath he none.
THOMAS HOCCLEVE, *De Regimine Principum.*

7
Solitude is dangerous to reason, without being favourable to virtue. . . . Remember that the solitary mortal is certainly luxurious, probably superstitious, and possibly mad.
SAMUEL JOHNSON, *Miscellanies*. Vol. i, p. 219.

Solitude is pasturage for suspicion.
GEORGE MEREDITH, *Sandra Belloni*. Ch. 28.

8
In solitude
What happiness, who can enjoy alone,
Or all enjoying, what contentment find?
MILTON, *Paradise Lost*. Bk. viii, l. 364.

9
Overbearing austerity is always the companion of solitude. (Τὴν ἐρημίᾳ σύνοικον αὐθάδειαν μὴ ὑπομείναντας.)
PLATO, *Epistle to Dion*. (PLUTARCH, *Lives: Alcibiades and Coriolanus*. Ch. 2, sec. 2.)

Solitude would ripen a plentiful crop of despots.
EMERSON, *Essays, Second Series: Nominalist and Realist.*

10
Solitude prompts us to all kinds of evil. (Omnia nobis mala solitudo persuadet.)
SENECA, *Epistulæ ad Lucilium*. Epis. xxv, 6.

There are some solitary wretches who seem to have left the rest of mankind only as Eve left Adam, to meet the devil in private.
POPE, *Thoughts on Various Subjects.*

IV—Solitude and the Crowd

11
Little do men perceive what solitude is, and how far it extendeth. For a crowd is not company, and faces are but a gallery of pictures, and talk but a tinkling cymbal, where there is no love.
SIR FRANCIS BACON, *Essays: Of Friendship.*

But 'midst the crowd, the hum, the shock of men,
To hear, to see, to feel, and to possess,
And roam along, the world's tired denizen,
With none who bless us, none whom we can bless, . . .
This is to be alone; this, this is solitude!
BYRON, *Childe Harold*. Canto ii, st. 26.

Among them, but not of them.
BYRON, *Childe Harold*. Canto iii, st. 113.

How lonely we are in the world! . . . You and I are but a pair of infinite isolations, with some fellow-islands a little more or less near to us.
THACKERAY, *Pendennis*. Ch. 16.

12
The time when, most of all, you should withdraw into yourself is when you are forced to be in a crowd.
EPICURUS, *Fragments*. No. 209.

13
Far from the sweet society of men.
HOMER, *Odyssey*. Bk. xxi, l. 394. (Pope, tr.)

Far from the madding crowd's ignoble strife,
Their sober wishes never learn'd to stray;
Along the cool sequester'd vale of life
They kept the noiseless tenor of their way.
THOMAS GRAY, *Elegy Written in a Country Church-yard*. St. 19.

Far from the clank of crowds.
WALT WHITMAN, *Starting from Paumanok*. Sec. 1.

1
Man dwells apart, though not alone,
He walks among his peers unread;
The best of thoughts which he hath known
For lack of listeners are not said.
JEAN INGELOW, *Afternoon at a Parsonage: Afterthought.*

2
Oh that I had in the wilderness a lodging place of wayfaring men; that I might leave my people, and go from them! for they be all adulterers, an assembly of treacherous men.
Old Testament: Jeremiah, ix, 2. (Quis dabit me in solitudine diversorium viatorum.—*Vulgate.*)

Oh for a lodge in some vast wilderness,
Some boundless contiguity of shade,
Where rumour of oppression and deceit,
Of unsuccessful or successful war,
Might never reach me more.
COWPER, *The Task.* Bk. ii, l. 1.

O Solitude! if I must with thee dwell,
Let it not be among the jumbled heap
Of murky buildings: climb with me the steep,—
Nature's observatory; . . . let me thy vigils keep
'Mongst boughs pavilion'd, where the deer's swift leap
Startles the wild bee from the foxglove bell.
KEATS, *Sonnet: O Solitude.*

3
We need not bid, for cloistered cell,
Our neighbour and our work farewell.
JOHN KEBLE, *The Christian Year: Morning.*

The city does not take away, neither does the country give, solitude; solitude is within us.
JOSEPH ROUX, *Meditations of a Parish Priest: The Country.* No. 48.

4
Avoid the reeking herd,
Shun the polluted flock,
Live like that stoic bird
The eagle of the rock.
ELINOR WYLIE, *The Eagle and the Mole.*

5
I should have then this only fear:
Lest men, when they my pleasures see,
Should hither throng to live like me,
And so make a city here.
ABRAHAM COWLEY, *The Wish.*

V—Solitude and Loneliness

6
Yes: in the sea of life enisl'd,
With echoing straits between us thrown,
Dotting the shoreless watery wild,
We mortal millions live alone.
MATTHEW ARNOLD, *To Marguerite.*

7
Indeed, though in a wilderness, a man is never alone, not only because he is with himself and his own thoughts, but because he is with the Devil, who ever consorts with our solitude. . . . There is no such thing as solitude, nor anything that can be said to be alone and by itself, but God.
SIR THOMAS BROWNE, *Religio Medici.* Pt. ii, sec. 11.

8
When is man strong until he feels alone?
ROBERT BROWNING, *Colombe's Birthday.* Act iii.

He travels the fastest who travels alone.
RUDYARD KIPLING, *The Winners.*

See also under MARRIAGE AND CELIBACY.

9
Alone!—that worn-out word,
So idly spoken, and so coldly heard;
Yet all that poets sing, and grief hath known,
Of hope laid waste, knells in that word—
ALONE!
BULWER-LYTTON, *The New Timon.* Pt. ii.

I am as one who is left alone at a banquet, the lights dead and the flowers faded.
BULWER-LYTTON, *Last Days of Pompeii.* Ch. 5.

I feel like one who treads alone
Some banquet-hall deserted,
Whose lights are fled, whose garlands dead,
And all but he departed!
THOMAS MOORE, *Oft, in the Stilly Night.*

10
Then forth uprose that lone wayfaring man.
CAMPBELL, *Gertrude of Wyoming.* Pt. i, st. 27.

All perished!—I alone am left on earth!
To whom nor relative nor blood remains,
No!—not a kindred drop that runs in human veins!
CAMPBELL, *Gertrude of Wyoming.* Pt. iii, st. 17.

11
Alone, alone, all, all alone,
Alone on a wide wide sea!
S. T. COLERIDGE, *The Ancient Mariner.* Pt. iv.

So lonely 'twas, that God himself
Scarce seemèd there to be.
S. T. COLERIDGE, *The Ancient Mariner.* Pt. vii.

12
I am a lone lorn creetur and everythink goes contrairy with me.
DICKENS, *David Copperfield.* Ch. 3.

13
Thrice happy he, who by some shady grove,
Far from the clamorous world, doth live his own;
Though solitary, who is not alone,
But doth converse with that eternal love.
WILLIAM DRUMMOND, *Urania.*

In solitude, where we are *least* alone.
BYRON, *Childe Harold.* Canto iii, st. 90.

14
Everything begins from loneliness.
JOHN ERSKINE, *Adam and Eve.* Ch. 1.

One aged man—one man—can't fill a house.
ROBERT FROST, *An Old Man's Winter Night.*

15
He will not take me where he goes,
He's deaf to me and blind.
Always, I am left at home,
Sitting in my mind.
AMANDA BENJAMIN HALL, *The Wanderer.*

1
Why should we faint and fear to live alone,
Since all alone, so Heaven has will'd, we die,
Nor e'en the tenderest heart, and next our own,
Knows half the reasons why we smile and sigh?
JOHN KEBLE, *The Christian Year: 24th Sunday after Trinity.*

I shall die alone. (Je mourrai seul.)
PASCAL, *Pensées.*

My life must linger on alone.
BYRON, *Parisina.* St. 12.

I have trodden the winepress alone.
Old Testament: Isaiah, lxiii, 3.

We enter the world alone, we leave it alone.
FROUDE, *Short Studies on Great Subjects: Sea Studies. See also under* BIRTH.

I must plough my lonely furrow alone.
LORD ROSEBERY, *Letter,* 19 July, 1901.

2
You will be sad if you are alone. (Tristis eris si solus eris.)
OVID, *Remediorum Amoris,* l. 583.

3
I am never less alone than when alone. (Minus solum, cum quam solus esset.)
SCIPIO AFRICANUS. (CICERO, *De Officiis.* Bk. iii, ch. 1, sec. 1.)

A good man is never less alone than when alone, as Themistocles said.
THOMAS LODGE, *The Divel Conjured.* (1596)

I was never less alone than when by myself.
EDWARD GIBBON, *Memoirs.* Vol. i, p. 117.

Never less alone than when alone.
SAMUEL ROGERS, *Human Life,* l. 759.

A wise man is never less alone than when he is alone.
SWIFT, *Essays: The Faculties of the Mind.*

4
They are never alone that are accompanied with noble thoughts.
SIR PHILIP SIDNEY, *Arcadia.* Bk. i. (1598)

He is never alone that is accompanied with noble thoughts.
JOHN FLETCHER, *Love's Cure.* Act iii, sc. 3. (1647)

Through the wide world he only is alone
Who lives not for another. Come what will,
The generous man has his companion still.
SAMUEL ROGERS, *Human Life,* l. 702.

5
Why should I feel lonely? is not our planet in the Milky Way?
H. D. THOREAU, *Walden: Solitude.*

SON

See also Fathers and Sons

6
Who is there that has not suffered the extremity of woe, weeping for a son? (Καὶ τίς ὃς οὐκ ἔτλη κακὸν ἔσχατον υἱέα κλαύσας.)
APOLLONIDES, *Epigram.* (*Greek Anthology.* Bk. vii, No. 389.)

I knew my son was mortal. (Ἤιδειν θνητὸν γεγεννηκώς.)
XENOPHON, when his son was killed in battle. (DIOGENES LAERTIUS, *Xenophon.* Sec. 8.)

He was not all a father's heart could wish;
But oh, he was my son!—my only son.
JOANNA BAILLIE, *Orra.* Act iii, sc. 2.

O lord! my boy, my Arthur, my fair son!
My life, my joy, my food, my all the world!
My widow-comfort, and my sorrow's cure!
SHAKESPEARE, *King John.* Act iii, sc. 4, l. 103.

The boy was the very staff of my age, my very prop.
SHAKESPEARE, *The Merchant of Venice.* Act ii, sc. 2, l. 70.

7
That unfeather'd two-legged thing, a son.
DRYDEN, *Absalom and Achitophel.* Pt. i, l. 170.

8
Gods! How the son degenerates from the sire!
HOMER, *Iliad.* Bk. iv, l. 451. (Pope, tr.)

Few sons attain the praise
Of their great sires, and most their sires' disgrace.
HOMER, *Odyssey.* Bk. ii, l. 315. (Pope, tr.)

He follows his father with unequal steps. (Sequiturque patrem non passibus æquis.)
VERGIL, *Æneid.* Bk. ii, l. 724.

Ah me! how seldom see we sons succeed
Their fathers' praise!
JOSEPH HALL, *Satires.* Bk. iv, No. 3.

9
He only half dies who leaves an image of himself in his sons. (Muore per metà chi lascia un' immagine di se stesso nei figli.)
GOLDONI, *Pamela.* Act ii, sc. 2.

The survivorship of a worthy man in his son is a pleasure scarce inferior to the hopes of the continuance of his own life.
RICHARD STEELE, *The Spectator,* 10 Oct., 1711.

Your work was waste? Maybe your share
Lay in the hour you laughed and kissed;
Who knows but that your son shall wear
The laurels that his father missed?
LAURENCE HOPE, *The Masters.*

10
His father, the sculptor, fashioned him for a pocket-Hercules.
EDWARD LAW, LORD ELLENBOROUGH, of Michael Angelo Taylor, very short of stature but very well-knit. (CAMPBELL, *Life.*)

11
That thou art my son, I have partly thy mother's word, partly my own opinion, but chiefly a villainous trick of thine eye and a foolish hanging of thy nether lip, that doth warrant me.
SHAKESPEARE, *I Henry IV.* Act ii, sc. 4, l. 443.

12
A son who is the theme of honour's tongue;
Amongst a grove, the very straightest plant.
SHAKESPEARE, *I Henry IV.* Act i, sc. 1, l. 81.

Kent: Is not this your son, my lord?
Gloucester: His breeding, sir, hath been at my

charge: I have so often blushed to acknowledge him, that now I am brazed to it.
Kent: I cannot conceive you.
Gloucester: Sir, this young fellow's mother could: whereupon she grew round-wombed, and had, indeed, sir, a son for her cradle ere she had a husband for her bed.
SHAKESPEARE, *King Lear.* Act i, sc. 1, l. 7.

1
A wayward son, spiteful and wrathful.
SHAKESPEARE, *Macbeth.* Act iii, sc. 5, l. 11.

Good wombs have borne bad sons.
SHAKESPEARE, *The Tempest.* Act i, sc. 2, l. 120.

SONG

See also Ballad, Poetry

I—Song: Apothegms

2
Everything ends in songs. (Tout finit par des chansons.)
BEAUMARCHAIS, *Le Mariage de Figaro.* Last line.

3
Sing a song of sixpence.
BEAUMONT AND FLETCHER, *Bonduca.* Act v, 2.

Sing a song of sixpence, a pocket full of rye,
Four-and-twenty blackbirds baked in a pie.
UNKNOWN, *Old Nursery Rhyme.*

4
It is the best of all trades to make songs, and the second best to sing them.
HILAIRE BELLOC, *On Song.*

5
But how the subject-theme may gang,
Let time and chance determine;
Perhaps it may turn out a sang,
Perhaps turn out a sermon.
ROBERT BURNS, *Epistle to a Young Friend.*

I think, whatever mortals crave,
With impotent endeavour,
A wreath—a rank—a throne—a grave—
The world goes round forever;
I think that life is not too long,
And therefore I determine,
That many people read a song,
Who will not read a sermon.
W. M. PRAED, *Chant of the Brazen Head.* St. 1.

What will a child learn sooner than a song?
POPE, *Imitations of Horace: Epistles.* Bk. ii, epis. 1, l. 205.

6
Unlike my subject now . . . shall be my song;
It shall be witty and it shan't be long.
LORD CHESTERFIELD, *Impromptu,* on Sir Thomas Robinson, of Rokeby, who was both tall and stupid. (MAHON, *Chesterfield's Letters: Preface.*)

On Tuesday, July 18, I found tall Sir Thomas Robinson sitting with Johnson.
BOSWELL, *Life of Johnson,* 18 July, 1763.

7
And heav'n had wanted one immortal song.
DRYDEN, *Absalom and Achitophel.* Pt. i, l. 197.

8
I see you have a singing face—a heavy, dull, sonata face.
FARQUHAR, *The Inconstant.* Act ii, sc. 1.

Come, sing now, sing; for I know you sing well;
I see you have a singing face.
JOHN FLETCHER, *Wild Goose Chase.* Act ii, 2.

You know you haven't got a singing face.
W. B. RHODES, *Bombastes Furioso.*

9
What is the voice of song, when the world lacks the ear of taste?
HAWTHORNE, *The Snow Image: Canterbury Pilgrims.*

10
And now am I their song, yea, I am their byword.
Old Testament: Job, xxx, 9.

11
As a singer you're a great dancer.
AMY LESLIE, to George Primrose. (MARKS, *They All Sang,* p. 67.)

12
Sphere-born harmonious sisters, Voice and Verse.
MILTON, *At a Solemn Music,* l. 2.

13
I care not who writes the laws of a country so long as I may listen to its songs.
G. J. NATHAN, *The World in Falseface: Foreword. See also under* BALLAD.

14
The song that we hear with our ears is only the song that is sung in our hearts.
OUIDA, *Wisdom, Wit, and Pathos: Ariadne.*

It sank deep into his heart, like the melody of a song sounding from out of childhood's days.
JEAN PAUL RICHTER, *Hesperus.* Ch. 12.

15
Song is untouched by death. (Carmina morte carent.)
OVID, *Amores.* Bk. i, eleg. 15, l. 32. *See also* POETRY AND IMMORTALITY.

16
Give in return for old wine, a new song. (Redde cantionem, veteri pro vino, novam.)
PLAUTUS, *Stichus.* Act v, sc. 6, l. 8.

I know a man . . . sold a goodly manor for a song.
SHAKESPEARE, *All's Well that Ends Well.* Act iii, sc. 2, l. 10.

I bought it for a song.
JOHN CROWNE, *Regulus.* Act ii, sc. 1. (1694)

Hence comes the common saying, and commoner practice, of parting with money for a song.
SWIFT, *Tale of a Tub.* Sec. 9. (1704)

All this for a song!
WILLIAM CECIL, LORD BURGHLEY, Lord High Treasurer, when commanded by Queen Elizabeth to give Edmund Spenser a hundred pounds.

17
A beau and witling perish'd in the throng,
One died in metaphor, and one in song.
POPE, *The Rape of the Lock.* Canto v, l. 59.

1
A very excellent good-conceited thing; after, a wonderful sweet air, with admirable rich words to it.
SHAKESPEARE, *Cymbeline*. Act ii, sc. 3, l. 18.

2
Come, sing me a bawdy song; make me merry.
SHAKESPEARE, *I Henry IV*. Act iii, sc. 3, l. 16.

When Satan makes impure verses, Allah sends a divine tune to cleanse them.
BERNARD SHAW, *The Adventures of the Black Girl in Her Search for God*.

3
Warble, child; make passionate my sense of hearing.
SHAKESPEARE, *Love's Labour's Lost*, iii, 1, 1.

The sly whoresons
Have got a speeding trick to lay down ladies;
A French song and a fiddle has no fellow.
SHAKESPEARE, *Henry VIII*. Act i, sc. 3, l. 39.

To each word a warbling note.
SHAKESPEARE, *A Midsummer-Night's Dream*. Act v, sc. 1, l. 405.

He hath songs for man or woman, of all sizes.
SHAKESPEARE, *Winter's Tale*. Act iv, sc. 4, l. 191.

4
Cicala to cicala is dear, and ant to ant, and hawk to hawk, but to me the muse and song.
THEOCRITUS, *Idylls*. No. 9, st. 2. (Lang, tr.)

Your song, divine poet, is to me even as sleep is to the weary. (Tale tuum carmen nobis, divine poeta, Quale sopor fessis.)
VERGIL, *Eclogues*. No. v, l. 45.

II—Song: Singing and Working

5
The mouth which is busy with song is not busy with the grapes. (Bouche qui mord à la chanson ne mord pas à la grappe.)
EDMOND ABOUT, *Les Mariages de Paris*. Quoted as a proverb.

6
'Tis a sure sign work goes on merrily, when folks sing at it.
ISAAC BICKERSTAFFE, *The Maid of the Mill*. Act i, sc. 1.

7
Gloomy cares will be lightened by song. (Minuentur atræ Carmine curæ.)
HORACE, *Odes*. Bk. iv, ode 11, l. 35.

He who sings scares away his woes. (Quien Canta Sus males espanta.)
CERVANTES, *Don Quixote*. Pt. i, ch. 22.

8
They sing, they will pay. (Ils chantent, ils payeront.)
CARDINAL MAZARIN, when he heard the Parisian populace singing, after the imposition of some new taxes. Originally a patois: "S'ils cantent la chansonette, ils pageront."

Slavedrivers know well enough that when the slave is singing a hymn to liberty he is consoling himself for his slavery and not thinking about breaking his chain.
MIGUEL DE UNAMUNO, *Essays and Soliloquies*, p. 94.

9
Men, even when alone, lighten their labors by song, however rude. (Etiam singulorum fatigatio quamlibet se rudi modulatione solatur.)
QUINTILIAN, *De Institutione Oratoria*. Bk. i, ch. 10, sec. 16.

10
Knitting and withal singing, and it seemed that her voice comforted her hands to work.
SIR PHILIP SIDNEY, *Arcadia*. Bk. i.

She makes her hand hard with labour, and her heart soft with pity: and when winter evenings fall early (sitting at her merry wheel), she sings a defiance to the giddy wheel of fortune . . . and fears no manner of ill because she means none.
SIR THOMAS OVERBURY, *A Fair and Happy Milk-maid*.

Verse sweetens toil, however rude the sound;
She feels no biting pang the while she sings,
Nor as she turns the giddy wheel around,
Revolves the sad vicissitudes of things.
RICHARD GIFFORD, *Contemplation*. (1753) Samuel Johnson, who was fond of tinkering with other men's poetry, changed the second line of this stanza to "All at her work the village maiden sings."

The sad vicissitude of things.
LAURENCE STERNE, *Sermon: The Character of Shimel*. (1767)

III—Song: Any Words Good Enough

11
Nothing is capable of being well set to music that is not nonsense.
ADDISON, *The Spectator*. No. 18.

To varnish nonsense with the charms of sound.
CHARLES CHURCHILL, *The Apology*, l. 219.

This particularly rapid, unintelligible patter,
Isn't generally heard, and if it is it doesn't matter!
W. S. GILBERT, *Ruddigore*. Act ii.

12
For music any words are good enough.
ARISTOPHANES, *The Birds*. (Planché, tr.)

13
That which is not worth saying is sung. (Ce qui ne vaut pas la peine d'être dit, on le chante.)
BEAUMARCHAIS, *Barbier de Séville*. Act i, sc. 1.

Let a man try the very uttermost to *speak* what he means, before singing is had recourse to.
THOMAS CARLYLE, *Journal*, 17 Nov., 1843, referring to poetry.

14
Why "words for music" are almost invariably trash now, though the words of Elizabethan songs are better than any music, is a gloomy and difficult question.
W. S. LANDOR, *Essays: T. H. Bayly*.

1
As for the words, there will be no difference between the words that are and are not set to music; both will conform to the same laws.
PLATO, *The Republic*. Bk. iii, sec. 398.

2
Soft words, with nothing in them, make a song.
EDMUND WALLER, *To Mr. Creech*.

IV—Song: Its Power

See also Music: Its Power

3
Her fingers witched the chords they passed along,
And her lips seemed to kiss the soul in song.
THOMAS CAMPBELL, *Theodric*. l. 30.

How oft, from yonder window o'er the lake,
Her song of wild Helvetian swell and shake
Has made the rudest fisher bend his ear
And rest enchanted on his oar to hear!
THOMAS CAMPBELL, *Theodric*, l. 42.

4
At ev'ry close she made, th' attending throng
Replied, and bore the burden of the song:
So just, so small, yet in so sweet a note,
It seem'd the music melted in the throat.
DRYDEN, *The Flower and the Leaf*, l. 197.

5
'Tis not in the high stars alone,
Nor in the cups of budding flowers,
Nor in the redbreast's mellow tone,
Nor in the bow that smiles in showers,
But in the mud and scum of things
There alway, alway something sings.
EMERSON, *The Poet*. Frag. 14.

The leaguèd might of trivial things
Wars with the soul that dreams and sings.
DON MARQUIS, *The Singer*.

6
When I but hear her sing, I fare
Like one that raisèd, holds his ear
To some bright star in the supremest Round;
Through which, besides the light that's seen,
There may be heard, from Heaven within,
The rests of Anthems, that the Angels sound.
OWEN FELLTHAM, *Lusoria*. No. xxxiv. This is the poem beginning, "When, dearest, I but think of thee," usually attributed to Sir John Suckling, but Felltham claimed it, and modern criticism is disposed to support the claim.

Where thro' the long-drawn aisle and fretted vault
The pealing anthem swells the note of praise.
THOMAS GRAY, *Elegy Written in a Country Church-yard*, l. 39.

Compared with these, Italian trills are tame;
The tickled ears no heartfelt raptures raise.
BURNS, *The Cotter's Saturday Night*. l. 115.

The fineness which a hymn or psalm affords
Is when the soul unto the lines accords.
GEORGE HERBERT, *A True Hymn*.

7
Song wins grace with the gods above, and with the gods below. (Carmine di superi placantur, carmine Manes.)
HORACE, *Epistles*. Bk. ii, epis. 1, l. 138.

8
The song on its mighty pinions,
Took every living soul, and lifted it gently to heaven.
LONGFELLOW, *Children of the Lord's Supper*, l. 44.

For doth not Song
To the whole world belong?
Is it not given wherever tears can fall,
Wherever hearts can melt or blushes glow,
Or mirth or sadness mingle as they flow,
A heritage to all?
ISA CRAIG KNOX, *On the Centenary of Burns*

9
Listen to that song and learn it!
Half my kingdom would I give,
As I live,
If by such songs you would earn it!
LONGFELLOW, *The Saga of King Olaf*. Pt. v.

Such songs have power to quiet
The restless pulse of care,
And come like the benediction
That follows after prayer.
LONGFELLOW, *The Day Is Done*. St. 9.

10
Or bid the soul of Orpheus sing
Such notes as, warbled to the string,
Drew iron tears down Pluto's cheek.
MILTON, *Il Penseroso*, l. 105.

But would you sing, and rival Orpheus' strain.
The wond'ring forests soon should dance again;
The moving mountains hear the powerful call.
And headlong streams hang list'ning in their fall!
POPE, *Pastorals: Summer*, l. 81.

None knew whether
The voice or lute was most divine,
So wondrously they went together.
THOMAS MOORE, *Lalla Rookh: Prologue*. No. 2.

11
A persuasive thing is song; let girls learn to sing. (Res est blanda canor; discant cantare puellæ.)
OVID, *Ars Amatoria*. Bk. iii, l. 315.

The rude sea grew civil at her song,
And certain stars shot madly from their spheres
To hear the sea-maid's music.
SHAKESPEARE, *A Midsummer-Night's Dream*. Act ii, sc. 1, l. 152.

An admirable musician: O! she will sing the savageness out of a bear.
SHAKESPEARE, *Othello*. Act iv, sc. 1, l. 198.

12
The song that nerves a nation's heart
Is in itself a deed.
TENNYSON, *The Charge of the Heavy Brigade: Epilogue*.

1
To kindle war by song. (Martem accendere cantu.)
VERGIL, *Æneid*. Bk. vi, l. 165.

2
Nothing but songs is wanting here. (Nihil hic nisi carmina desunt.)
VERGIL, *Eclogues*. No. viii, l. 67.

V—Song: The Old Songs

See also Ballads

3
I cannot sing the old songs
I sang long years ago,
For heart and voice would fail me,
And foolish tears would flow;
For bygone hours come o'er my heart
With each familiar strain;
I cannot sing the old songs,
Or dream those dreams again.
CHARLOTTE ALINGTON BARNARD, *I Cannot Sing the Old Songs*. Mrs. Barnard wrote under the pseudonym of Claribel. (c. 1860)

I cannot sing the old songs
Though well I know the tune,
Familiar as a cradle-song
With sleep-compelling croon;
Yet though I'm filled with music,
As choirs of summer birds,
"I cannot sing the old songs"—
I do not know the words.
ROBERT J. BURDETTE, *Songs Without Words*.

I can not sing the old songs now!
It is not that I deem them low,
'Tis that I can't remember how
They go.
CHARLES STUART CALVERLEY, *Changed*.

4
Sing me the songs I delighted to hear,
Long, long ago, long ago.
T. H. BAYLY, *The Long Ago*.

Old songs, the precious music of the heart!
WORDSWORTH, *Poems Dedicated to National Independence*. Pt. ii, No. 12.

5
He play'd an ancient ditty, long since mute,
In Provence call'd "La belle dame sans mercy."
KEATS, *The Eve of St. Agnes*. St. 33. "La Belle Dame, sans Merci" is a poem by Alain Chartier, sometimes attributed to Jean Marot. Keats also wrote a poem with that title. See 2187:16.

6
O Carril, raise again thy voice! let me hear the song of Selma, which was sung in my halls of joy, when Fingal, king of shields, was there, and glowed at the deeds of his fathers.
OSSIAN, *Fingal*. Bk. iii, st. 1.

7
To sing a song that old was sung.
SHAKESPEARE, *Pericles:* Act i, *Prelude*, l. 1.

And stretched metre of an antique song.
SHAKESPEARE, *Sonnets*. No. xvii.

Songs consecrate to truth and liberty.
SHELLEY, *To Wordsworth*, l. 12.

8
In the years fled, Lips that are dead
Sang me that song.
MRS. R. A. M. STEVENSON, *Song*.

9 Those high songs of thine
That stung the sense like wine,
Or fell more soft than dew or snow by night.
SWINBURNE, *To Victor Hugo*. St. 6.

10
A love-song I had somewhere read,
An echo from a measured strain,
Beat time to nothing in my head
From some odd corner of the brain.
It haunted me, the morning long,
With weary sameness in the rhymes,
The phantom of a silent song,
That went and came a thousand times.
TENNYSON, *The Miller's Daughter*. St. 9.

11
You sing the same old song. (Cantilenam eandem canis.)
TERENCE, *Phormio*, l. 495. (Act iii, sc. 2.)

Bring the good old bugle, boys! we'll sing another song—
Sing it with a spirit that will start the world along—
Sing it as we used to sing it, fifty thousand strong,
While we were marching through Georgia.
HENRY CLAY WORK, *Marching Through Georgia*.

VI—Song and Singer

See also Poet and His Song

12
Of all the friends I used to love,
My harp remains alone;
Its faithful voice seems still to be
An echo of my own.
My tears, when I bend over it,
Will fall upon its string;
Yet those who hear me little think
I'm saddest when I sing.
T. H. BAYLY, *I'm Saddest When I Sing*.

For now to sorrow must I tune my song,
And set my harp to notes of saddest woe.
MILTON, *The Passion*, l. 8.

Our sweetest songs are those which tell of saddest thought.
SHELLEY, *To a Skylark*. St. 18.

I can't sing. As a singist I am not a success. I am saddest when I sing. So are those who hear me. They are sadder even than I am.
ARTEMUS WARD, *Lecture*.

At what I sing there's some may smile,
While some, perhaps, will sigh.
THOMAS MOORE, *Nets and Cages*, l. 11.

13
And ever as he went some merry lay he sung.
JAMES BEATTIE, *The Minstrel*. Bk. i, l. 27.

14 Let the singing singers
With vocal voices, most vociferous,
In sweet vociferation out-vociferize
Even sound itself.
HENRY CAREY, *Chrononhotonthologos*. Act i, sc. 1.

1
He could songes make, and well endite.
CHAUCER, *Canterbury Tales: Prologue,* l. 95.

He knew
Himself to sing, and build the lofty rhyme.
MILTON, *Lycidas,* l. 10.

2
On the beryl-rimmed rebecs of Ruby
Brought fresh from the hyaline streams,
She played on the banks of the Yuba
Such songs as she heard in her dreams.
THOMAS HOLLEY CHIVERS, *Lily Adair.*

Y'ought to hyeah dat gal a-warblin'
Robins, la'ks an' all dem things
Heish de mouffs an' hides dey faces
When Malindy sings.
PAUL LAURENCE DUNBAR, *When Malindy Sings.*

3
A wandering minstrel I—
A thing of shreds and patches,
Of ballads, songs, and snatches,
And dreamy lullaby
W. S. GILBERT, *The Mikado.* Act i.

Sing, minstrel, sing us now a tender song
Of meeting and parting, with the moon in it.
STEPHEN PHILLIPS, *Ulysses.* Act i, sc. 1.

4
A few can touch the magic string,
And noisy Fame is proud to win them:—
Alas for those that never sing,
But die with all their music in them!
O. W. HOLMES, *The Voiceless.* St. 1.

Songs may be mute; for songs may exist unsung, but voices exist only while they sound.
W. S. LANDOR, *Imaginary Conversations: Abbé Delille and Landor.*

5
Because the road was steep and long
And through a dark and lonely land,
God set upon my lips a song
And put a lantern in my hand.
JOYCE KILMER, *Love's Lantern.*

6
In the ink of our sweat we will find it yet,
The song that is fit for men!
FREDERIC LAWRENCE KNOWLES, *The Song.*

8
He touch'd the tender stops of various quills,
With eager thought warbling his Doric lay.
MILTON, *Lycidas,* l. 188.

9
Sweetest the strain when in the song
The singer has been lost.
ELIZABETH STUART PHELPS, *The Poet and the Poem.*

10
In Heaven a spirit doth dwell
Whose heart-strings are a lute;
None sing so wildly well
As the angel Israfel.
EDGAR ALLAN POE, *Israfel.*

And the angel Israfel, who has the sweetest voice of all God's creatures.
GEORGE SALE, *Preliminary Discourse to the Koran,* iv, 71. Often wrongly attributed to the *Koran.* Thomas Moore has the correct attribution in *Lalla Rookh,* pt. viii, l. 419, footnote; but Poe attributes it to the *Koran,* although he got it either from Sale, whose work he had reviewed, or from Moore. He interpolated the phrase, "whose heart-strings are a lute," which appears neither in the *Koran,* nor Sale, nor Moore, and which is undoubtedly his own. Thomas Holley Chivers, a Georgia physician and versifier, appropriated it, together with many other of Poe's phrases, and then alleged that Poe had stolen them from him. (See WOODBERRY, *Life of Poe,* i, 180.)

11
The sweet psalmist of Israel.
Old Testament: II Samuel, xxiii, 1.

12
Scenes sung by him who sings no more!
His bright and brief career is o'er,
And mute his tuneful strains.
SCOTT, *The Lord of the Isles.* Canto iv, st. 11.

For him, no minstrel raptures swell.
SCOTT, *The Lay of the Last Minstrel.* Canto vi, l. 8.

Why then a final note prolong,
Or lengthen out a closing song?
SCOTT, *Marmion: L'Envoi.*

He ceased. But still their trembling ears retained
The deep vibrations of his witching song.
JAMES THOMSON, *The Castle of Indolence.* Canto i, st. 20.

13
Sing, siren, for thyself.
SHAKESPEARE, *The Comedy of Errors.* Act iii, sc. 2, l. 47.

The Siren waits thee, singing song for song.
W. S. LANDOR, *To Robert Browning.*

14
Sing again, with your dear voice revealing
A tone
Of some world far from ours,
Where music and moonlight and feeling
Are one.
SHELLEY, *To Jane.*

15
And round thee with the breeze of song
To stir a little dust of praise.
TENNYSON, *In Memoriam.* Pt. lxxv.

Short swallow-flights of song, that dip
Their wings in tears, and skim away.
TENNYSON, *In Memoriam.* Pt. xlviii.

16
Swift, swift, and bring with you
Song's Indian summer!
FRANCIS THOMPSON, *A Carrier Song.* St. 2.

17
I do not sing unbidden. (Non injussa cano.)
VERGIL, *Eclogues.* No. vi, l. 9.

18
Enough of mournful melodies, my lute!
Be henceforth joyous, or be henceforth mute.
Song's breath is wasted when it does but fan
The smouldering infelicity of man.
WILLIAM WATSON, *Epigrams*

VII—Song: Discords

1
The tenor's voice is spoilt by affectation,
And for the bass, the beast can only bellow;
In fact, he had no singing education,
An ignorant, noteless, timeless, tuneless fellow.
BYRON, *Don Juan*. Canto iv, st. 87.

Heard at conventicle, where worthy men,
Misled by custom, strain celestial themes
Through the prest nostril.
COWPER, *The Task*. Bk. ii, l. 437.

2
And when that choir got up to sing,
I couldn't catch a word;
They sung the most doggonedest thing
A body ever heard!
WILL CARLETON, *The New Church Organ*.

Then they began to sing
That extremely lovely thing,
"Scherzando! ma non troppo, ppp."
W. S. GILBERT, *The Story of Prince Agib*.

3
Sir Joseph: Can you sing?
Ralph: I can hum a little, your honour.
W. S. GILBERT, *H. M. S. Pinafore*. Act i.

Only a rash man ever asks me to hum.
W. S. GILBERT, when Sullivan asked him to hum a tune.

4
There is this vice in all singers, that if asked to sing among their friends they are never so inclined, but unasked they never leave off. (Omnibus hoc vitium est cantoribus, inter amicos Ut numquam inducant animum cantare rogati, Injussi numquam desistant.)
HORACE, *Satires*. Bk. i, sat. 3, l. 1.

5
He praised unblushingly her notes, for he was false as they.
RUDYARD KIPLING, *Army Headquarters*.

6
Man was never meant to sing:
And all his mimic organs e'er expressed
Was but an imitative howl at best.
JOHN LANGHORNE, *The Country Justice*, ii, 223.

Their lean and flashy songs
Grate on their scrannel pipes of wretched straw.
MILTON, *Lycidas*, l. 123.

7
I count it but time lost to hear such a foolish song.
SHAKESPEARE, *As You Like It*. Act v, sc. 3, l. 41.

Nay, now you are too flat
And mar the concord with too harsh a descant.
SHAKESPEARE, *Two Gentlemen of Verona*, i, 2, 94.

VIII—Song and Love

8
It's the song of a merryman, moping mum,
Whose soul was sad, and whose glance was glum,
Who sipped no sup, and who craved no crumb
As he sighed for the love of a ladye.
W. S. GILBERT, *Yoemen of the Guard*. Act i.

9
And when, beside me in the dale,
He carolled lays of love,
His breath lent fragrance to the gale
And music to the grove.
GOLDSMITH, *A Ballad*. (*Vicar of Wakefield*. Ch. 8.)

The swain responsive to the milkmaid sung.
GOLDSMITH, *The Deserted Village*, l. 117.

10
So she poured out the liquid music of her voice to quench the thirst of his spirit.
HAWTHORNE, *Mosses from an Old Manse: The Birthmark*.

She sang the tears into his eyes,
The heart out of his breast.
CHRISTINA ROSSETTI, *Maiden-Song*.

11
Bow down. my song, before her presence high.
MORTON LUCE, *Thysia*. Sonnet iii.

12
But I can only offer you, my sweet,
The songs I made on many a night of stars.
Yet have I worshipped honor, loving you.
THEODORE MAYNARD, *If I Had Ridden Horses*.

As a skylark to the sky,
Up into thy breast I fly;
As a sea-shell of the sea
Ever shall I sing of thee.
GEORGE MEREDITH, *Lines*.

13
My heart is dead, my veins are cold:
I may not, must not, sing of love.
SCOTT, *Lay of the Last Minstrel*. Canto ii, 30.

14
Every night he comes
With music of all sorts and songs composed
To her unworthiness: it nothing steads us
To chide him from our eaves; for he persists
As if his life lay on 't.
SHAKESPEARE, *All's Well that Ends Well*. Act iii, sc. 7, l. 39.

Thou hast by moonlight at her window sung
With feigning voice verses of feigning love.
SHAKESPEARE, *A Midsummer-Night's Dream*. Act i, sc. 1, l. 30.

15
Song like a rose should be;
Each rhyme a petal sweet;
For fragrance, melody,
That when her lips repeat
The words, her heart may know
What secret makes them so.
Love, only Love!
FRANK DEMPSTER SHERMAN, *Song*.

16
Singing is sweet, but be sure of this,
Lips only sing when they cannot kiss.
JAMES THOMSON (B. V.), *Sunday Up the River*.

And what's a careless kiss or so
To one remembered song?
THEODOSIA GARRISON, *The Kerry Lads*.

IX—Some Familiar Refrains and Choruses *

1
Tin Pan Alley.

MONROE H. ROSENFELD. Said to be the title of an article on the music business published by Rosenfeld in a New York newspaper about 1892. (See GOLDBERG, *Tin Pan Alley*, p. 173.) Also claimed by Robert H. Duiree, who died at Carmel, Cal., 5 Oct., 1935. Just before his death, Duiree issued a statement to the press alleging that he had coined the phrase many years ago as a name for West Twenty-Eighth Street, then the home of many music publishing houses, while walking through the street with Epes W Sargent, dramatic critic for the New York *Morning Telegraph*, who used it in his paper next day. No date was given.

2
Mister Jefferson Lord, play that barber shop chord,
That soothing harmony, it makes an awful, awful hit with me.
Play that strain, just to please me, again, . . .
Oh, Lord, play that barber shop chord!

WILLIAM TRACEY, *Play that Barber Shop Chord*. (c. 1910) Music by Lewis Muir.

That strain again! It had a dying fall.

SHAKESPEARE, *Twelfth Night*. Act i, sc. 1, l. 4.

The willing harmonizer inevitably asks sooner or later, "What has quartet singing to do with a barber shop? . . Whatever the historical association may be, anyone familiar with quartet singing knows "barber shop swipes" by ear. Those harmonies, generally moving in opposite directions while the melody stands still, are recognized by the musical treatises. But they are called by very different names, such as tonic, dominant and subdominant, of which the first alone has a truly tonsorial fragrance.

SIGMUND SPAETH, *Barber Shop Ballads: Preface*.

3
I wonder who's kissing her now,
Wonder who's teaching her now,
Wonder who's looking into her eyes,
Breathing sighs, telling lies.

FRANK R. ADAMS and WILL M. HOUGH, *I Wonder Who's Kissing Her Now*. (1909) Music by J. E. Howard. First sung in a musical comedy, *The Prince of To-night*.

4
Take back the heart thou gavest,
What is my anguish to thee?
Take back the freedom thou cravest,
Leaving the fetters to me.

CHARLOTTE ALINGTON BARNARD (CLARIBEL), *Take Back the Heart*. (1860)

5
I'll be loving you, always. . . .

* This section is continued in the Appendix, and many other refrains and choruses will be found scattered throughout the book under appropriate headings. *She Was Bred in Old Kentucky*, for example, will be found under Kentucky, *Carry Me Back to Old Virginny* under *Virginia*, and so on. To find the refrain desired, consult the INDEX AND CONCORDANCE for its keyword.

Not for just an hour,
Not for just a day,
Not for just a year, but always.

IRVING BERLIN, *Always*. (1925)

Everybody's doin' it now.

IRVING BERLIN. Title and refrain. (1911)

Remember we found a lonely spot,
And after I learned to care a lot,
You promised that you'd forget me not,
But you forgot to remember.

IRVING BERLIN, *Remember*. (1925)

What'll I do when you are far away
And I am blue, what'll I do, what'll I do?

IRVING BERLIN, *What'll I Do*. (1923)

6
East side, West side,
All around the town,
The tots sing "Ring-a-Rosie,
London Bridge is falling down";
Boys and girls together,
Me and Mamie Rourke,
Tripped the light fantastic
On the sidewalks of New York.

JAMES W. BLAKE, *The Sidewalks of New York*. (1894) Music by Charles B. Lawlor. Used as a campaign song for Alfred E. Smith in the presidential campaign of 1928.

7
In de ebening by the moonlight, you could hear us darkies singing,
In de ebening by the moonlight, you could hear de banjo ringing;
How de old folks would enjoy it, they would sit all night and listen,
As we sang in the ebening by de moonlight.

JAMES A. BLAND, *In the Evening by the Moonlight*. (1880) Bland was a Virginia negro, and proclaimed himself to be "the best Ethiopian song-writer in the world," perhaps not an overstatement. The unforgettable *Carry Me Back to Old Virginny* was also his. See under VIRGINIA.

8
Bunch up your conversation, that's what I demand,
And don't forget you're talkin' to a Lady.

HENRY M. BLOSSOM, JR., *Don't Forget You're Talking to a Lady*. (1902) Music by George A. Spink.

9
Get in your place and take a back seat,
Go way back and sit down.

ELMER BOWMAN, *Go Way Back and Sit Down*. (1901) Music by Al. Johns.

10
If you want to win her hand,
Let the maiden understand
That she's not the only pebble on the beach.

HENRY BRAISTEAD, *You're Not the Only Pebble on the Beach* (1896) Sung by the "Little Magnet," Lottie Gilson, for years.

11
When you ain't got no money, well you needn't come 'round.

CLARENCE S. BREWSTER. Title and refrain of

song set to music by A. B. Sloane in 1898. One of May Irwin's hits.

1
Oh, you beautiful doll!
SEYMOUR BROWN. Title and refrain. (1911)

2
Just for the sake of Society,
  Baby is sad and 'lone,
Just for a thing called Propriety,
  Mother's heart's turning to stone.

ALFRED BRYAN, *Just for the Sake of Society.* (1904) Music by Kerry Mills. The terrible situation was that the heartless mother had gone to a ball, leaving her baby alone, and it fell into the fire and was burned to death.

Smother me with kisses, hon, and kill me with love,
Wrap yourself around me like a serpent 'round a dove.

ALFRED BRYAN, *Smother Me with Kisses.* (1914) Music by Harry Carroll. Introduced by Lillian Lorraine at the New York Winter Garden.

Sometime, someday, somewhere,
'Mid other scenes more fair,
Your eyes of blue my face will view,
And its sad look of care:
Because my heart was true,
To soothe my dark despair,
With glances sweet my gaze you'll meet,
Sometime, someday, somewhere.

ALFRED BRYAN, *Sometime, Someday, Somewhere.* (1903) Music by Al. Johns. See 1216:6

Who paid the rent for Mrs. Rip Van Winkle
When Rip Van Winkle went away?

ALFRED BRYAN, *Who Paid the Rent for Mrs. Rip Van Winkle?* Featured by Sam Bernard in *The Belle of Bond Street,* 1914.

3
The Rhine may be fine, but a cold stein for mine,
  Down where the Wurzburger flows.

VINCENT P. BRYAN, *Down Where the Wurzburger Flows.* (1902) Music by Harry Von Tilzer. Sung by the incomparable Nora Bayes, just entering vaudeville, who became known as "the Wurzburger Girl." When she carried the song to London, the *London Times* asked "why she did not sing about the Thames" instead of some "western American stream."

Come, come, come, and make eyes with me,
  Under the Anheuser Bush.

ANDREW B. STERLING, *Under the Anheuser Bush.* (1903) Music by Harry Von Tilzer. Also popularized by Nora Bayes.

4
Tammany, Tammany,
Big Chief sits in his tepee,
Cheering braves to victory.
Tammany, Tammany,
Swamp 'em, swamp 'em, get the "wampum,"
  Tammany.

VINCENT BRYAN, *Tammany.* (1905) Music by Gus Edwards. First sung at the annual smoker of the National Democratic Club of New York City in the fall of 1905. Afterwards introduced by Jefferson De Angelis in *Fantana* at the Lyric Theatre, New York City. Official song of Tammany Hall.

5
There are smiles that make us happy,
  There are smiles that make us blue,
There are smiles that steal away the teardrops
  As the sunbeams steal away the dew.
There are smiles that have a tender meaning,
  That the eyes of love alone may see,
But the smiles that fill my life with sunshine
  Are the smiles that you give to me.

J. WILL CALLAHAN, *Smiles.* (c. 1917) Music by Lee S. Roberts.

6
'Member dat rainy eve dat I drove you out,
  Wid nothing but a fine tooth comb?
I knows I'se to blame; well, ain't dat a shame?
  Bill Bailey, won't you please come home?

HUGHIE CANNON, *Bill Bailey, Won't You Please Come Home?* (1902) Introduced by John Queen in a farce comedy called *Town Topics,* at Newburgh, N. Y., it quickly produced a whole crop of songs dealing with the troubles of the Bailey family; among them:

I wonder why Bill Bailey don't come home?
FRANK FOGERTY. Title and refrain. (1902)

I ain't got time to stay, I'll do no work this day,
'Cause I'm happy since Bill Bailey came back home.

BILLY JOHNSON, *Since Bill Bailey Came Back Home.* (1902) Music by Seymour Furth.

7
You can't keep a good man down.
M. F. CAREY. Title and refrain. (1900)

8
'Tis years since last we met,
  And we may not meet again;
I have struggled to forget,
  But the struggle was in vain;
For her voice lives on the breeze,
  And her spirit comes at will;
In the midnight on the seas,
  Her bright smile haunts me still.

J. E. CARPENTER, *Her Bright Smile Haunts Me Still.* (1883) Music by W. T. Wrightson.

9
So won't you grant me all my wishes,
Won't you sprinkle me with kisses,
If you want my love to grow?

EARL CARROLL, *Sprinkle Me With Kisses.* (1915) Music by Ernest R. Ball. Sung by Evelyn Nesbit.

10
Then drill, ye Tarriers, drill,
Drill, ye Tarriers, drill,
Oh, it's work all day without sugar in your tay
When ye work beyant on the railway,
And drill, ye Tarriers, drill.

THOMAS F. CASEY, *Drill, Ye Tarriers, Drill.* (1888) "Tarriers" was the name given unskilled Irish laborers in New York, engaged in drilling out rock in making excavations for new buildings. The song was introduced to the town in Hoyt's *A Brass Monkey*, which opened at the Bijou Theatre, 15 Oct., 1888, and instantly became popular.

1
Oh, Mandy Lee, I love you, 'deed I do, my Mandy Lee,
Your eyes they shine like diamonds, love, to me.
THURLAND CHATTAWAY, *Mandy Lee.* (1899)

2
I'm sorry, dear, so sorry, dear,
I'm sorry I made you cry!
Won't you forget? won't you forgive?
Don't let us say good-bye!
One little word, one little smile,
One little kiss won't you try?
It breaks my heart to hear you sigh,
I'm sorry I made you cry!
N. J. CLESI, *I'm Sorry I Made You Cry.* (1918)

3
Too proud to beg, too honest to steal,
I know what it is to be wanting a meal;
My tatters and rags I try to conceal,
I'm one of the Shabby Genteel.
HARRY CLIFTON, *Shabby Genteel.* (c. 1870)

4
I can't tell why I love you, but I do.
WILL D. COBB. Title and refrain. (1900)

I don't want money—don't you think that's funny?
Come closer, honey, I'll tell you true;
I don't want jewelry, fine clothes or foolery
When I grows up, I wants just you.
WILL D. COBB, *I Don't Want Money.* (1901) Music by Gus Edwards.

NOTE: For continuation of this section, see APPENDIX.

SONNET

5
Rafael made a century of sonnets.
ROBERT BROWNING, *One Word More.* Sec. 2.

6
What is a sonnet? 'Tis the pearly shell
That murmurs of the far-off murmuring sea;
A precious jewel carved most curiously;
It is a little picture painted well.
RICHARD WATSON GILDER, *The Sonnet.*

7
There Sackville's sonnets sweetly sauced
And featly fined be.
JASPER HEYWOOD, *Metrical Preface to the Thyestes of Seneca.*

8
For, of all compositions, he thought that the sonnet
Best repaid all the toil you expended upon it.
J. R. LOWELL, *A Fable for Critics,* l. 368.

9
The sonnet is a trunk, and you must pack
With care, to ship frail baggage far away;
The octet is the trunk; sestet, the tray;

10
Tight, but not overloaded, is the knack.
CHRISTOPHER MORLEY, *Thoughts While Packing a Trunk.*

A sonnet is a moment's monument,—
Memorial from the Soul's eternity
To one dead deathless hour.
D. G. ROSSETTI, *The Sonnet.*

11
A torturer of phrases into sonnets.
SCOTT, *Auchindrane.* Pt. iii, ch. 1.

12
I had rather than forty shillings I had my Book of Songs and Sonnets here.
SHAKESPEARE, *The Merry Wives of Windsor.* Act i, sc. 1, l. 205.

13
Will you then write me a sonnet in praise of my beauty?
SHAKESPEARE, *Much Ado About Nothing.* Act v, sc. 2, l. 4.

Deep-brain'd sonnets.
SHAKESPEARE, *A Lover's Complaint,* l. 209.

A halting sonnet of his own pure brain.
SHAKESPEARE, *Much Ado About Nothing.* Act v, sc. 4, l. 87.

14
The Sonnet is a world, where feelings caught
In webs of phantasy, combine and fuse
Their kindred elements 'neath mystic dews
Shed from the ether round man's dwelling wrought.
JOHN ADDINGTON SYMONDS, *The Sonnet.*

Spare thou no pains; carve thought's pure diamond
With fourteen facets, scattering fire and light.
JOHN ADDINGTON SYMONDS, *The Sonnet.*

Our Sonnet's world hath two fixed hemispheres:
This, where the sun with fierce strength masculine
Pours his keen rays and bids the noonday shine;
That, where the moon and the stars, concordant powers,
Shed milder rays, and daylight disappears
In low melodious music of still hours.
JOHN ADDINGTON SYMONDS, *The Sonnet.*

15
A sonnet is a wave of melody:
From heaving waters of the impassioned soul
A billow of tidal music one and whole
Flows, in the "octave"; then, returning free,
Its ebbing surges in the "sestet" roll
Back to the deeps of Life's tumultuous sea.
THEODORE WATTS-DUNTON, *The Sonnet's Voice.*

16
Scorn not the Sonnet; Critic, you have frowned,
Mindless of its just honours; with this key
Shakespeare unlocked his heart; the melody
Of this small lute gave ease to Petrarch's wound; . . . and, when a damp
Fell round the path of Milton, in his hand
The Thing became a trumpet; whence he blew

Soul-animating strains—alas, too few!
WILLIAM WORDSWORTH, *Scorn Not the Sonnet.*

"With this same key
Shakespeare unlocked his heart," once more!
Did Shakespeare? If so, the less Shakespeare he!
ROBERT BROWNING, *House.* St. 10.

Shall I sonnet-sing you about myself?
Do I live in a house you would like to see?
Is it scant of gear, has it store of pelf?
"Unlock my heart with a sonnet key?"
No: thanking the public, I must decline.
ROBERT BROWNING, *House.* St. 1.

"Scorn not the sonnet," though its strength be sapped,
Nor say malignant its inventor blundered;
The corpse that here in fourteen lines is wrapped
Had otherwise been covered with a hundred.
RUSSELL H. LOINES, *On a Magazine Sonnet.*

SORROW

See also Grief; Joy and Sorrow; Melancholy; Woe

I—Sorrow: Definitions

1
Sorrow is knowledge.
BYRON, *Manfred.* Act i, sc. 1.

'Tis held that sorrow makes us wise.
TENNYSON, *In Memoriam.* Pt. cviii.

2
For Sorrow's a woman a man may take
And know, till his heart and body break.
SAMUEL HOFFENSTEIN, *Sorrow That Cries.*

3
There is no wisdom in useless and hopeless sorrow, but there is something in it so like virtue, that he who is wholly without it cannot be loved.
SAMUEL JOHNSON, *Letter to Mrs. Thrale,* 1781.

4
Sorrow is a kind of rust of the soul, which every new idea contributes in its passage to scour away.
SAMUEL JOHNSON, *The Rambler.* No. 47.

5
Sorrow, the great idealizer.
J. R. LOWELL, *Among My Books: Spenser.*

6
Our size of sorrow,
Proportion'd to our cause, must be as great
As that which makes it.
SHAKESPEARE, *Antony and Cleopatra.* Act iv, sc. 15, l. 4.

Sorrow breaks seasons and reposing hours,
Makes the night morning, and the noon-tide night.
SHAKESPEARE, *Richard III.* Act i, sc. 4, l. 76.

7
Sorrow is held the eldest child of sin.
JOHN WEBSTER, *Duchess of Malfi.* Act v, sc. 5.

Sorrow is good for nothing but sin.
THOMAS FULLER, *Gnomologia.* No. 4232.

8
Where there is sorrow, there is holy ground.
OSCAR WILDE, *De Profundis.*

II—Sorrow: Apothegms

9
Nothing comes to us too soon but sorrow.
P. J. BAILEY, *Festus: Home*

10
The busy bee has no time for sorrow.
WILLIAM BLAKE *Proverbs of Hell.*

Sorrow preys upon Its solitude. . . .
The busy have no time for tears.
BYRON, *The Two Foscari.* Act iv, sc. 1.

11
All sorrows are less with bread. (Los duelos con Pan son menos.)
CERVANTES, *Don Quixote.* Pt. ii, ch. 13.

Fat sorrow is better than lean sorrow.
THOMAS FULLER, *Gnomologia.* No. 1507.

A lean sorrow is hardest to bear.
SARA ORNE JEWETT, *Life of Nancy,* p. 278.

There are few sorrows, however poignant, in which a good income is of no avail.
LOGAN PEARSALL SMITH, *Afterthoughts.*

12
If you wish to live a life free from sorrow, think of what is going to happen as if it had already happened.
EPICTETUS, *Fragments.* No. 158.

Why should we
Anticipate our sorrows? 'Tis like those
That die for fear of death.
SIR JOHN DENHAM, *The Sophy.*

To grieve for evils is often wrong; but it is much more wrong to grieve without them.
SAMUEL JOHNSON, *Letters.* Vol. ii, p. 23.
See also TROUBLE: NEVER TROUBLE TROUBLE.

13
Sorrow comes unsent for.
THOMAS FULLER, *Gnomologia.* No. 4230.

Sorrows are visitors that come without invitation.
C. H. SPURGEON, *John Ploughman.* Ch. 5.

14
When sorrow is asleep wake it not.
THOMAS FULLER, *Gnomologia.* No. 5569.

When sorrow sleepeth, wake it not,
But let it slumber on.
MARY A. STODART, *Song.*

Without the door let sorrow lie.
GEORGE WITHER, *Christmas.*

15
Sinks my sad soul with sorrow to the grave.
HOMER, *Iliad.* Bk. xxii, l. 543. (Pope, tr.)

Bring down my gray hairs with sorrow to the grave.
Old Testament: Genesis, xlii, 38.

Smit with exceeding sorrow unto Death.
TENNYSON, *The Lover's Tale,* l. 590.

16
The world will never be long without some good reason to hate the unhappy.
SAMUEL JOHNSON, *The Adventurer.* No. 99.

17
We often console ourselves for being unhappy by a certain pleasure in appearing so. (On se console souvent d'être malheureux

par un certain plaisir qu'on trouve à le paraître.)

La Rochefoucauld, *Maximes Supprimées.* No. 573.

1
Humanity is fortunate, because no man is unhappy except by his own fault. (Bono loco res humanæ sunt, quod nemo nisi vitio suo miser est.)

Seneca, *Epistulæ ad Lucilium.* Epis. lxx, 15.

2
I cannot sing: I'll weep, and word it with thee;
For notes of sorrow out of tune are worse
Than priests and fanes that lie.

Shakespeare, *Cymbeline.* Act iv, sc. 2, l. 240.

3
More in sorrow than in anger.

Shakespeare, *Hamlet.* Act i, sc. 2, l. 232.

4
Hysterica passio, down, thy climbing sorrow.

Shakespeare, *King Lear.* Act ii, sc. 4, l. 58.

All's cheerless, dark, and deadly.

Shakespeare, *King Lear.* Act v, sc. 3, l. 290.

Affliction may one day smile again; and till then, sit thee down, sorrow!

Shakespeare, *Love's Labour's Lost.* Act i, sc. 1, l. 316.

5
To show an unfelt sorrow is an office
Which the false man does easy.

Shakespeare, *Macbeth.* Act ii, sc. 3, l. 142.

See also Grief: Silent and Vocal.

6
Past sorrows, let us moderately lament them;
For those to come, seek wisely to prevent them.

John Webster, *Duchess of Malfi.* Act iii, sc. 2.

III—Sorrow: A Blessing

7
The path of sorrow, and that path alone,
Leads to the land where sorrow is unknown;
No trav'ller ever reach'd that blest abode
Who found not thorns and briars in his road.

Cowper, *An Epistle to a Protestant Lady in France,* l. 9.

8
Who ne'er his bread in sorrow ate,
Who ne'er the mournful midnight hours
Weeping upon his bed has sate,
He knows you not, ye Heavenly Powers.
(Wer nie sein Brod mit Thränen ass,
Wer nie die kummervollen Nächte
Auf seinem Bette weinend sass,
Der kennt euch nicht, ihr himmlischen Mächte.)

Goethe, *Wilhelm Meister.* Bk. ii, ch. 13. (Longfellow, tr., used as the motto for *Hyperion.* Bk. i.)

9
I walked a mile with Sorrow
And ne'er a word said she;
But, oh, the things I learned from her
When Sorrow walked with me.

Robert B. Hamilton, *Along the Road.*

10
How beautiful, if sorrow had not made
Sorrow more beautiful than Beauty's self.

Keats, *Hyperion.* Bk. i, l. 35.

Come then, Sorrow! Sweetest Sorrow!
Like an own babe I nurse thee on my breast:
I thought to leave thee, And deceive thee,
But now of all the world I love thee best.

Keats, *Endymion.* Bk. iv, l. 279.

11
A grace within his soul hath reigned
Which nothing else can bring;
Thank God for all that I have gained
By that high sorrowing.

Richard Monckton Milnes, *Sorrow.*

Do not cheat thy heart and tell her
"Grief will pass away,
Hope for fairer times in future,
And forget to-day."
Tell her, if you will, that sorrow
Need not come in vain;
Tell her that the lesson taught her
Far outweighs the pain.

Adelaide Ann Procter, *Friend Sorrow.*

12
This sorrow's heavenly;
It strikes where it doth love.

Shakespeare, *Othello.* Act v, sc. 2, l. 21.

13
All pains are nothing in respect of this,
All sorrows short that gain eternal bliss.

Edmund Spenser, *Amoretti.* Sonnet lxiii.

14
Lives there whom pain hath evermore pass'd by
And sorrow shunned with an averted eye?
Him do thou pity, him above the rest,
Him of all hopeless mortals most unbless'd.

William Watson, *Epigrams.*

15
A soul, by force of sorrows high,
Uplifted to the purest sky
Of undisturbed humanity!

Wordsworth, *The White Doe of Rylstone.* Canto ii, l. 585.

IV—Sorrow: Its Relief

16
Sing away sorrow, cast away care.

Cervantes, *Don Quixote.* Pt. i, ch. 8.

17
For 'tis some ease our sorrows to reveal
If they to whom we shall impart our woes,
Seem but to feel a part of what we feel,
And meet us with a sigh, but at the close.

Samuel Daniel, *The Tragedy of Cleopatra* Act iv, sc. 1.

Some ease it is hid sorrows to declare.

Francis Davison, *A Complaint.*

So sorrow is cheered by being poured
From one vessel into another.

Thomas Hood, *Miss Kilmansegg: Her Misery.*

'Tis something to lighten with words a fated sor-

row. (Est aliquid, fatale malum per verba levare.)
OVID, *Tristia*. Bk. v, eleg. 1, l. 59.

See also GRIEF: VOCAL AND SILENT.

1
Remove sorrow from thee: for sorrow hath killed many, and there is no profit therein.
Apocrypha: Ecclesiasticus, xxx, 23.

Chase Anguish, and doubt, and fear, and sorrow, and pain,
From mortal or immortal minds.
MILTON, *Paradise Lost*. Bk. i, l. 557.

2
And sorrow and sighing shall flee away.
Old Testament: Isaiah, xxxv, 10.

Sorrow is never long without a dawn of ease.
SAMUEL JOHNSON, *Works*. Vol. xi, p. 99.

3
Earth has no sorrow that Heaven cannot heal.
THOMAS MOORE, *Come, Ye Disconsolate*.

The longest sorrow finds at last relief.
WILLAM ROWLEY, *New Wonder*. Act iv. sc. 1.

4
The wounds of the unhappy endure through the night. (In noctis spatium miserorum vulnera durant.)
PETRONIUS, *Fragments*. No. 121.

5
Wherever sorrow is, relief would be.
SHAKESPEARE, *As You Like It*. Act iii, sc. 5, 86.

6
For gnarling sorrow hath less power to bite
The man that mocks at it and sets it light.
SHAKESPEARE, *Richard II*. Act i, sc. 3, l. 292.

Fell sorrow's tooth doth never rankle more
Than when it bites, but lanceth not the sore.
SHAKESPEARE, *Richard II*. Act i, sc. 3, l. 302.

In wooing sorrow let's be brief,
Since, wedding it, there is such length in grief.
SHAKESPEARE, *Richard II*. Act v, sc. 1, l. 93.

7
If sorrow can admit society,
Tell o'er your woes again by viewing mine.
SHAKESPEARE, *Richard III*. Act iv, sc. 4, l. 38.

8
Sorrow concealed, like an oven stopp'd,
Doth burn the heart to cinders where it is.
SHAKESPEARE, *Titus Andronicus*. Act ii, sc. 4, 36.

9
To weep with them that weep doth ease some deal;
But sorrow flouted at is double death.
SHAKESPEARE, *Titus Adronicus*. Act iii, sc. 1, 245.

10
Stay but to-morrow, and your present sorrow will be weary, and will lie down to rest.
JEREMY TAYLOR, *Sermons*. Vol. i, p. 327.

V—Sorrow: The Common Lot

11
Why waste a word, or let a tear escape,
While other sorrows wait you in the world?
ROBERT BROWNING, *Balaustion's Adventure*.

12
How selfish Sorrow ponders on the past,
And clings to thoughts now better far removed!
BYRON, *Childe Harold*. Canto ii, st. 96.

13
But sorrow return'd with the dawning of morn,
And the voice in my dreaming ear melted away.
THOMAS CAMPBELL, *The Soldier's Dream*.

14
Men die, but sorrow never dies;
The crowding years divide in vain,
And the wide world is knit with ties
Of common brotherhood in pain.
SUSAN COOLIDGE, *The Cradle Tomb in Westminster Abbey*.

But when I came to Heartbreak Hill,
Silver touched the sea;
I knew that many and many a soul
Was climbing close to me;
I knew I walked that weary way
In a great company.
HELEN GRAY CONE, *Heartbreak Road*.

15
When I was young, I said to Sorrow,
"Come, and I will play with thee!"
He is near me now all day,
And at night returns to say,
"I will come again to-morrow—
I will come and stay with thee."
AUBREY DE VERE, *Song: When I Was Young*.

16
Heavy the sorrow that bows the head
When love is alive and hope is dead!
W. S. GILBERT, *H. M. S. Pinafore*. Act i.

17
To each his suff'rings; all are men,
Condemn'd alike to groan,—
The tender for another's pain,
Th' unfeeling for his own.
Yet ah! why should they know their fate?
Since sorrow never comes too late.
THOMAS GRAY, *On a Distant Prospect of Eton College*, l. 91.

18
Sorrows our portion are: ere hence we go,
Crosses we must have; or, hereafter, woe.
ROBERT HERRICK, *Sorrows*.

19
When sparrows build and the leaves break forth
My old sorrow wakes and cries.
JEAN INGELOW, *Supper at the Mill: Mother's Song*.

20
O, sorrow! Why dost borrow
Heart's lightness from the merriment of May?
KEATS, *Endymion*. Bk. iv, l. 164.

To Sorrow I bade good morrow,
And thought to leave her far away behind;
But cheerly, cheerly, She loves me dearly;
She is so constant to me, and so kind.
KEATS, *Endymion*. Bk. iv, l. 173.

1
I have a silent sorrow here,
A grief I'll ne'er impart.
KOTZEBUE, *The Stranger.* Act iv, sc. 1.

2
Is it nothing to you, all ye that pass by? behold. and see if there be any sorrow like unto my sorrow.
Old Testament: Lamentations, i, 12.

Much then I learned and much can show
Of human guilt and human woe,
Yet ne'er have in my wanderings known
A wretch whose sorrows matched my own!
SCOTT, *Rokeby.* Canto iv, st. 23.

3
Believe me, every man has his secret sorrows, which the world knows not; and oftentimes we call a man cold when he is only sad.
LONGFELLOW, *Hyperion.* Bk. iii, ch. 4.

Into each life some rain must fall,
Some days must be dark and dreary.
LONGFELLOW, *The Rainy Day.*

Nor indolence, nor pleasure, nor the fret
Of restless passions that would not be stilled,
But sorrow, and a care that almost killed,
Kept me from what I may accomplish yet.
LONGFELLOW, *Mezzo Cammin.*

4
Our days and nights
Have sorrows woven with delights.
MALHERBE, *To Cardinal Richelieu.* (Longfellow, tr.) *See also* JOY AND SORROW.

5
And Sorrow tracketh wrong,
As echo follows song.
HARRIET MARTINEAU, *Hymn: On, on, for ever. See also under* RETRIBUTION.

6
A weary lot is thine, fair maid,
A weary lot is thine!
To pull the thorn thy brow to braid,
And press the rue for wine!
SCOTT, *Rokeby.* Canto iii, st. 28.

7
There is no day without sorrow. (Nulla dies mærore caret.)
SENECA, *Troades,* l. 77.

Each new morn
New widows howl, new orphans cry, new sorrows
Strike heaven on the face.
SHAKESPEARE, *Macbeth.* Act iv, sc. 3, l. 4.

8
When sorrows come, they come not single spies,
But in battalions!
SHAKESPEARE, *Hamlet.* Act iv, sc. v, l. 78. *See also under* MISFORTUNE, 1322:5.

9
O, if thou teach me to believe this sorrow,
Teach thou this sorrow how to make me die.
SHAKESPEARE, *King John.* Act iii, sc. 1, l. 29.

I will instruct my sorrows to be proud;
For grief is proud and makes his owner stoop.
SHAKESPEARE, *King John.* Act iii, sc. 1, l. 68.

Here I and sorrows sit;
Here is my throne, bid kings come bow to it.
SHAKESPEARE, *King John.* Act iii, sc. 1, l. 73.

10
But now will canker sorrow eat my bud,
And chase the native beauty from his cheek.
SHAKESPEARE, *King John.* Act iii, sc. 4, l. 82.

Hath sorrow struck
So many blows upon this face of mine,
And made no deeper wounds?
SHAKESPEARE, *Richard II.* Act iv, sc. 1, l. 277.

11
Storming her world with sorrow's wind and rain.
SHAKESPEARE, *A Lover's Complaint.* l. 7.

Ah, do not, when my heart hath 'scaped this sorrow,
Come in the rearward of a conquer'd woe;
Give not a windy night a rainy morrow,
To linger out a purposed overthrow.
SHAKESPEARE, *Sonnets.* No. xc.

12
I have, as when the sun doth light a storm,
Buried this sigh in wrinkle of a smile:
But sorrow, that is couch'd in seeming gladness,
Is like that mirth fate turns to sudden sadness.
SHAKESPEARE, *Troilus and Cressida.* Act i, sc. 1, l. 37.

13
Sorrow so royally in you appears,
That I will deeply put the fashion on.
SHAKESPEARE, *II Henry IV.* Act v, sc. 2, l. 51.

14
It stirs
Too much of suffocating sorrow!
SHELLEY, *Rosalind and Helen,* l. 66.

15
O Sorrow, wilt thou rule my blood,
Be sometimes lovely like a bride,
And put thy harsher moods aside,
If thou wilt have me wise and good?
TENNYSON, *In Memoriam.* Pt. lix, st. 2.

Your sorrow, only sorrow's shade,
Keeps real sorrow far away.
TENNYSON, *Margaret.* St. 4.

16
Some natural sorrow, loss, or pain,
That has been, and may be again.
WORDSWORTH, *The Solitary Reaper,* l. 23.

SOUL

See also Immortality and the Soul

I—Soul: Definitions

17
Soul is the Man.
THOMAS CAMPION, *Are You What Your Fair Looks Express?*

18
The soul of man is larger than the sky,
Deeper than ocean, or the abysmal dark
Of the unfathom'd centre.
HARTLEY COLERIDGE, *To Shakespeare.*

19
A soul,—a spark of the never-dying flame

that separates man from all the other beings of earth.

J. FENIMORE COOPER, *Afloat and Ashore*. Ch. 12.

1
Our souls sit close and silently within,
And their own web from their own entrails spin;
And when eyes meet far off, our sense is such,
That, spider-like, we feel the tenderest touch.

DRYDEN, *Marriage-à-la-Mode*. Act ii, sc. 1.

2
The Supreme Critic on the errors of the past and the present, and the only prophet of that which must be, is that great nature in which we rest as the earth lies in the soft arms of the atmosphere; that Unity, that Over-Soul, within which every man's particular being is contained and made one with all other.

EMERSON, *Essays, First Series: The Over-Soul*.

The one thing in the world, of value, is the active soul.

EMERSON, *Nature, Addresses, and Lectures: The American Scholar*.

3
Whether or not the philosophers care to admit that we have a soul, it seems obvious that we are equipped with something or other which generates dreams and ideals, and which sets up values.

JOHN ERSKINE. (DURANT, *On the Meaning of Life*, p. 39.)

4
By the word soul, or psyche, I mean that inner consciousness which aspires. By prayer I do not mean a request preferred to a deity; I mean . . . intense aspiration.

RICHARD JEFFERIES, *The Story of My Heart*.

5
The soul's a sort of sentimental wife,
That prays and whimpers of the higher life.

RICHARD LE GALLIENNE, *The Decadent to His Soul*.

6
For every soul is a circus,
And every mind is a tent,
And every heart is a sawdust ring
Where the circling race is spent.

VACHEL LINDSAY, *Every Soul is a Circus*.

7
Hands of invisible spirits touch the strings
Of that mysterious instrument, the soul,
And play the prelude of our fate. We hear
The voice prophetic, and are not alone.

LONGFELLOW, *The Spanish Student*. Act i, sc. 3, l. 111.

8
Men do not know what the nature of the soul is, whether it is engendered with us or whether it is infused into us at our birth; whether it perishes with us, dissolved by death, or whether it haunts the gloomy shades and bottomless pits of Orcus, or whether, by divine influence, it infuses itself into other animals.
(Ignoratur enim, quæ sit natura animæ;
Nata sit, an contra nascentibus insinuetur;
Et simul intereat nobiscum, morte diremta,
An tenebras Orci visat, vastasque lacunas:
An pecudes alias divinitus insinuet se.)

LUCRETIUS, *De Rerum Natura*. Bk. i, l. 113.

So the soul cannot exist separate from the body, and the man himself, whose body seems as it were the urn of the soul.

LUCRETIUS, *De Rerum Natura*. Bk. iii, l. 553.

My mind is incapable of conceiving such a thing as a soul. I may be in error, and man may have a soul; but I simply do not believe it.

THOMAS A. EDISON, *Do We Live Again?*

Nobody knows how the idea of a soul or the supernatural started It probably had its origin in the natural laziness of mankind.

JOHN B. WATSON, *Behaviorism*, p. 3.

9
A soul is a troublesome possession, and when man developed it he lost the Garden of Eden.

SOMERSET MAUGHAM, *Red*.

10
The soul on earth is an immortal guest,
Compelled to starve at an unreal feast.

HANNAH MORE, *Reflections of King Hezekiah*, l. 125.

11
There is a divinity within our breast. (Deus est in pectore nostro.)

OVID, *Epistulæ ex Ponto*. Bk. iii, epis. 4, l. 93.

12
Of all things which a man has, next to the gods, his soul is the most divine and most truly his own.

PLATO, *Laws*. Bk. iv, sec. 252.

13
The soul has in itself a capacity for affection, and loves just as naturally as it perceives, understands, and remembers.

PLUTARCH, *Lives: Solon*. Sec. 7.

14
Do you ask where the Supreme Good dwells? In the soul. And unless the soul be pure and holy, there is no room in it for God. (Quis sit summi boni locus quæris? Animus. Hic nisi purus ac sanctus est, deum non capit.)

SENECA, *Epistulæ ad Lucilium*. Epis. 87, 21.

The soul is more powerful than any sort of fortune; . . . of its own power it can produce a happy life, or a wretched one. (Valentior enim omni fortuna animus est.)

SENECA, *Epistulæ ad Lucilium*. Epis. 98, 2.

The soul is our king. (Rex noster est animus.)

SENECA, *Epistulæ ad Lucilium*. Epis. 114, 24.

The soul has this proof of its divinity: that divine things delight it. (Animus hoc habet argumentum divinitatis suæ, quod illum divina delectant.)

SENECA, *Naturales Questiones*. Bk. i, *Præfatio*.

15
Mine eternal jewel.

SHAKESPEARE, *Macbeth*. Act iii, sc. 1, l. 68.

1

My soul is an enchanted Boat,
Which, like a sleeping swan, doth float
Upon the silver waves of thy sweet singing;
And thine doth like an Angel sit
Beside the helm conducting it,
Whilst all the winds with melody are ringing.

SHELLEY, *Prometheus Unbound*. Act ii, sc. 5, l. 72.

2

The human soul is a silent harp in God's quire, whose strings need only to be swept by the divine breath to chime in with the harmonies of creation.

H. D. THOREAU, *Journal*, 10 Aug., 1838.

The soul has that measureless pride which revolts
from every lesson but its own.

WALT WHITMAN, *Song of Prudence*, l. 43.

3

What then do you call your soul? What idea have you of it? You cannot of yourselves, without revelation, admit the existence within you of anything but a power unknown to you of feeling and thinking.

VOLTAIRE, *A Philosophical Dictionary: Soul.*

4

But who would force the Soul tilts with a straw
Against a Champion cased in adamant.

WORDSWORTH, *Ecclesiastical Sonnets*. Pt. iii, 7.

For the Gods approve
The depth, and not the tumult, of the soul.

WORDSWORTH, *Laodamia*, l. 75. Emerson (*Uncollected Lectures: Natural Religion*) attributes this to Socrates. See 913:19.

5

Amazing pomp! redouble this amaze;
Ten thousand add; add twice ten thousand more;
Then weigh the whole; one soul outweighs them all.

YOUNG, *Night Thoughts*. Night vii, l. 995.

6

And I have written three books on the soul,
Proving absurd all written hitherto,
And putting us to ignorance again.

ROBERT BROWNING, *Cleon*, l. 57.

II—Soul: Apothegms

7

My soul still flies above me for the quarry it shall find.

WILLIAM ROSE BENÉT, *The Falconer of God.*

8

The soul's Rialto hath its merchandise;
I barter curl for curl upon that mart.

E. B. BROWNING, *Sonnets from the Portuguese*. No. xix

And he that makes his soul his surety,
I think, does give the best security.

BUTLER, *Hudibras*. Pt. iii, canto i, l. 203.

When by habit a man cometh to have a bargaining soul, its wings are cut so that it can never soar.

LORD HALIFAX, *Works*, p. 253.

Most people sell their souls and live with a good conscience on the proceeds.

LOGAN PEARSALL SMITH, *Afterthoughts.*

9

This soul, to whom Luther and Mahomet were
Prisons of flesh.

JOHN DONNE, *Progress of the Soul*. No. i, st. 7.

10

The soul is lost by mimicking soul.

EMERSON, *Uncollected Lectures: Table Talk.*

11

The soul is not where it lives, but where it loves.

H. G. BOHN, *Hand-Book of Proverbs*, p. 515.

The proverb is, 'Homo non est ubi animat, sed amat.'

THOMAS FULLER, *Worthies of England*, iii, 310.

12

Spontaneously to God should tend the soul,
Like the magnetic needle to the Pole.

THOMAS HOOD, *Ode to Rae Wilson*, l. 115.
See also under CONSTANCY.

13

Why do you hasten to remove anything which hurts your eye, while if something affects your soul, you postpone the cure until next year?

HORACE, *Epistles*. Bk. i, epis. 2, l. 38.

14

Soul, thou hast much goods laid up for many years; take thine ease, eat, drink, and be merry.

New Testament: Luke, xii, 19; *Ecclesiastes*, viii, 15. *See also under* EATING.

15

For what is a man profited, if he shall gain the whole world, and lose his own soul? or what shall a man give in exchange for his soul?

New Testament: Matthew, xvi, 26.

16

Ah, what a dusty answer gets the soul
When hot for certainties in this our life!

GEORGE MEREDITH, *Modern Love*, St. 50.

Dusty Answer.

ROSAMOND LEHMAN. Title of novel.

17

Lack of wealth is easily repaired; but poverty of soul is irreparable. (La pauvreté des biens est aysee à guerir; la pauvreté de l'âme, impossible.)

MONTAIGNE, *Essays*. Bk. iii, ch. 10.

18

I will hew great windows for my soul.

ANGELA MORGAN, *Room.*

I wish thar was winders to my Sole, sed I, so that you could see some of my feelins.

ARTEMUS WARD, *The Showman's Courtship.*

19

Above the vulgar flight of common souls.

ARTHUR MURPHY, *Zenobia*. Act v, sc. 1, l. 154.

20

O souls, bent down to earth, and void of heavenly things. (O curvæ in terris animæ et cælestium inanes.

PERSIUS, *Satires*. Sat. ii, l. 61.

21

Stript to the naked soul.

POPE, *Lines to Mrs. Grace Butler*. (*Sussex Garland*. No. 9.) Attr. also to Charles Yorke.

1
My soul is continually in my hand.
Old Testament: Psalms, cxix, 109. (Anima mea in manibus meis semper.—*Vulgate.*)

2
Would you damn your precious soul?
RABELAIS, *Pantagruel.* Bk. v, ch. 54.

Well, God's above all; and there be souls must be saved, and there be souls must not be saved.
SHAKESPEARE, *Othello.* Act ii, sc. 3, l. 105.

Thinkest thou I 'll endanger my soul gratis?
SHAKESPEARE, *The Merry Wives of Windsor.* Act ii, sc. 2, l. 16.

3
Poor men have no souls.
JOHN RAY, *English Proverbs.*

4
My soul to-day Is far away
Sailing the Vesuvian Bay.
THOMAS BUCHANAN READ, *Drifting.*

6
Now my soul hath elbow-room.
SHAKESPEARE, *King John.* Act v, sc. 7, l. 28.

7
No seed shall perish which the soul hath sown.
JOHN ADDINGTON SYMONDS, *Sonnet: A Belief.*

8
Star to star vibrates light; may soul to soul
Strike thro' a finer element of her own?
TENNYSON, *Aylmer's Field,* l. 578.

9
Be careless in your dress if you must, but keep a tidy soul.
MARK TWAIN, *Pudd'nhead Wilson's Calendar.*

10
I played with fire, did counsel spurn, . . .
But never thought that fire would burn,
Or that a soul could ache.
HENRY VAUGHAN, *Garland.* (1655)

My soul is all an aching void.
CHARLES WESLEY, *Hymn.*

No craving void left aching in the breast.
POPE, *Eloisa to Abelard,* l. 94.

III—Souls: Good and Bad

11
Calm Soul of all things! make it mine
To feel, amid the city's jar,
That there abides a place of thine,
Man did not make, and can not mar!
MATTHEW ARNOLD, *Lines Written in Kensington Gardens,* l. 37.

12
A soul as white as Heaven.
BEAUMONT AND FLETCHER, *The Maid's Tragedy.* Act iv, sc. 1.

The man who in this world can keep the whiteness of his soul, is not likely to lose it in any other.
ALEXANDER SMITH, *Dreamthorp.* Ch. 1.

13
God help all poor souls lost in the dark.
ROBERT BROWNING, *Heretic's Tragedy.* St. 10.

'T is an awkward thing to play with souls,
And matter enough to save one's own.
ROBERT BROWNING, *A Light Woman.*

14
I trust in my own soul, that can perceive
The outward and the inward, Nature's good
And God's.
ROBERT BROWNING, *A Soul's Tragedy.* Act i.

15
Of what avail to have a soul derived from above, and to lift the head on high, if, after the manner of beasts, men go astray? (Quid mentem traxisse polo, quid profuit altum Erexisse caput, pecudum si more pererrant?)
CLAUDIAN, *De Raptu Proserpinæ.* Bk. iii, l. 41.

16
Two souls, alas! reside within my breast,
And each withdraws from and repels its brother.
GOETHE, *Faust.* Pt. i, sc. 2. (Taylor, tr.)

I feel two natures struggling within me.
GEORGE GRAY BARNARD. Title of group of statuary.

The lark soars up in the air,
The toad sits tight in his hole;
And I would I were certain which of the pair
Were the truer type of my soul!
F. ANSTEY, *Stanza Written in Depression Near Dulwich.*

In me there meet a combination of antithetical elements which are at eternal war with one another.
W. S. GILBERT, *H. M. S. Pinafore.* Act i.

17
Awake, my Soul, and with the Sun,
Thy daily stage of Duty run;
Shake off dull Sloth, and early rise,
To pay thy Morning Sacrifice.
BISHOP THOMAS KEN, *Morning Hymn.* (1695)

Build thee more stately mansions, O my soul,
As the swift seasons roll!
Leave thy low-vaulted past!
Let each new temple, nobler than the last,
Shut thee from heaven with a dome more vast,
Till thou at length art free,
Leaving thine outgrown shell by life's unresting sea!
O. W. HOLMES, *The Chambered Nautilus.*

18
I count that soul exceeding small
That lives alone by book and creed,—
A soul that has not learned to read.
JOAQUIN MILLER, *The Larger College.*

Ah! there be souls none understand;
Like clouds, they cannot touch the land.
Unanchored ships, they blow and blow,
Sail to and fro, and then go down
In unknown seas that none shall know,
Without one ripple of renown.

Call these not fools; the test of worth
Is not the hold you have of earth.
Ay, there are gentlest souls sea-blown
That know not any harbor known.
Now it may be the reason is,
They touch on fairer shores than this.
JOAQUIN MILLER, *The Ship in the Desert,* xxii.

19
There was a little Man, and he had a little Soul;

And he said, "Little Soul, let us try, try, try!"
THOMAS MOORE, *Little Man and Little Soul.*

1
The soul's calm sunshine and the heartfelt joy.
POPE, *Essay on Man.* Epis. iv, l. 168.

2
The soul alone renders us noble. (Animus facit nobilem.)
SENECA, *Epistulæ ad Lucilium.* Epis. xliv, 5.

3
Thou turn'st mine eyes into my very soul;
And there I see such black and grained spots
As will not leave their tinct.
SHAKESPEARE, *Hamlet.* Act iii, sc. 4, l. 89.

4
The soul of man is like the rolling world,
One half in day, the other dipt in night;
The one has music and the flying cloud,
The other, silence and the wakeful stars.
ALEXANDER SMITH, *Horton.*

My soul is a dark ploughed field
In the cold rain;
My soul is a broken field
Ploughed by pain.
SARA TEASDALE, *The Broken Field.*

5
A sinful soul possess'd of many gifts,
A spacious garden full of flowering weeds.
TENNYSON, *To ——.*

What profits now to understand
The merits of a spotless shirt—
A dapper boot—a little hand—
If half the little soul is dirt.
TENNYSON, *The New Timon and the Poets.* (Published in *Punch,* 28 Feb., 1846, in answer to attack made by Bulwer-Lytton in *The New Timon* when Tennyson received a pension.)

6
"Two things," the wise man said, "fill me with awe:
The starry heavens and the moral law."
Nay, add another wonder to thy roll.—
The living marvel of the human soul!
HENRY VAN DYKE, *Stars and the Soul.* A reference to Kant. See 1914:8.

7
And keeps that palace of the soul serene.
EDMUND WALLER, *Of Tea,* l. 9.

The palace of the soul.
BYRON, *Childe Harold.* Canto ii, st. 6. *See also under* SKULL.

8
A charge to keep I have,
A God to glorify:
A never-dying soul to save,
And fit it for the sky.
CHARLES WESLEY, *Christian Fidelity.*

IV—Soul and Body

9 To man, propose this test—
Thy body at its best,
How far can it project thy soul on its lone way?
ROBERT BROWNING, *Rabbi Ben Ezra.* St. 8.

10
Whoe'er thou art, O reader, know
That Death has murdered Johnny!
And here his body lies fu' low—
For saul he ne'er had ony.
ROBERT BURNS, *On Wee Johnny.* John Wilson, the printer of Burns's poems, at Kilmarnock.

11
A fiery soul, which working out its way,
Fretted the pigmy body to decay,
And o'er informed the tenement of clay.
DRYDEN, *Absalom and Achitophel.* Pt. i, l. 156.

He was one of a lean body and visage, as if his eager soul, biting for anger at the clog of his body, desired to fret a passage through it.
THOMAS FULLER, *Life of the Duke of Alva.*

For the sword outwears its sheath,
And the soul wears out the breast.
BYRON, *So We'll Go No More a Roving.*

12
Though a sound body cannot restore an unsound mind, yet a good soul can, by its virtue, render the body the best possible.
EMERSON, *Representative Men: Plato. See also* MIND AND BODY.

13
It is much more necessary to cure the soul than the body, for death is better than a bad life. (Ψυχὴν σώματος ἀναγκαιότερον ἰᾶσθαι· τοῦ γὰρ κακῶς ζῆν τὸ τεθνάναι κρεῖσσον.)
EPICTETUS [?], *Encheiridion.* Frag. 32.

14
The soul needs few things, the body many.
GEORGE HERBERT, *Jacula Prudentum.*

The body is sooner dressed than the soul.
GEORGE HERBERT, *Jacula Prudentum.*

15
The body, laden with yesterday's vices, drags down the soul as well, and fastens to the earth a fragment of the divine spirit. (Corpus onustum Hesternis vitiis animum quoque prægravat una Atque adfigit humo divinæ particulam auræ.)
HORACE, *Satires.* Bk. ii, sat. 2, l. 77.

16
The limbs will quiver and move after the soul is gone.
SAMUEL JOHNSON. (NORTHCOTE, *Johnsoniana,* p. 487.)

17
There is nothing the body suffers that the soul may not profit by.
GEORGE MEREDITH, *Diana of the Crossways.* Ch. 1.

18
The soul is nothing apart from the senses.
PROTAGORAS. (DIOGENES LAERTIUS, *Protagoras.* Bk. ix, sec. 51.)

The body is the socket of the soul.
JOHN RAY, *English Proverbs.*

The perfect body is itself the soul.
GEORGE SANTAYANA, *Before a Statue of Achilles.*

19
It is the soul, and not the strong-box, which

should be filled. (Animum impleri debere, non arcam.

SENECA, *Epistulæ ad Lucilium*. Epis. xcii, sec. 32.

1
So every spirit, as it is more pure,
And hath in it the more of heavenly light,
So it the fairer body doth procure
To habit in, and it more fairly dight,
With cheerful grace and amiable sight.
For, of the soul, the body form doth take,
For soul is form, and doth the body make.

EDMUND SPENSER, *Hymn in Honour of Beauty*, l. 127.

For what is form, or what is face,
But the soul's index, or its case?

NATHANIEL COTTON, *Pleasure*.

2
How should I gauge what beauty is her dole,
Who cannot see her countenance for her soul,
As birds see not the casement for the sky?
And as 'tis check they prove its presence by,
I know not of her body till I find
My flight debarred the heaven of her mind.

FRANCIS THOMPSON, *Her Portrait*.

3
Our life is but the Soul made known by its fruits, the body. The whole duty of man may be expressed in one line: Make to yourself a perfect body.

H. D. THOREAU, *Journal*, 21 June, 1840.

V—Soul: The Unconquered Soul

4
No coward soul is mine,
No trembler in the world's storm-troubled sphere:
I see Heaven's glories shine,
And faith shines equal, arming me from fear.

EMILY BRONTË, *Last Verses*.

5
My feet are heavy now but on I go,
My head erect beneath the tragic years.

JOHN DAVIDSON, *I Felt the World A-spinning on Its Nave*.

6
The soul selects her own society,
Then shuts the door;
On her divine majority
Obtrude no more.

EMILY DICKINSON, *Poems*. Pt. i, No. 13.

8
Let fortune empty her whole quiver on me.
I have a soul that, like an ample shield,
Can take in all, and verge enough for more.

DRYDEN, *Don Sebastian*. Act i. sc. 1.

Give ample room, and verge enough.

THOMAS GRAY, *The Bard*, l. 51.

9
Out of the night that covers me,
Black as the pit from pole to pole,
I thank whatever gods may be
For my unconquerable soul.

W. E. HENLEY, *Invictus*.

Out of the light that dazzles me,
Bright as the sun from pole to pole,
I thank the God I know to be
For Christ, the Conqueror of my soul.

DOROTHEA DAY, *Victus*.

Dame Nature doubtless has designed
A man the monarch of his mind.

JOHN BYROM, *Careless Content*.

10
It matters not how strait the gate,
How charged with punishments the scroll,
I am the master of my fate:
I am the captain of my soul.

W. E. HENLEY, *Invictus*.

I am the captain of my soul;
I rule it with stern joy;
And yet I think I had more fun
When I was cabin boy.

KEITH PRESTON, *An Awful Responsibility*.

Arise, O Soul, and gird thee up anew,
Though the black camel Death kneel at thy gate;
No beggar thou that thou for alms shouldst sue:
Be the proud captain still of thine own fate.

JAMES B. KENYON, *The Black Camel*.

Mistress of mine own self and mine own soul.

TENNYSON, *The Foresters*. Act iv, sc. 1.

See also under SELF-CONTROL.

11
God gave thy soul brave wings; put not those feathers
Into a bed, to sleep out all ill weathers.

GEORGE HERBERT, *The Church-Porch*. St. 14.

12
Only a sweet and virtuous soul,
Like seasoned timber, never gives,
But though the whole world turn to coal.
Then chiefly lives.

GEORGE HERBERT, *Virtue*.

13
A frame of adamant, a soul of fire,
No dangers fright him, and no labours tire.

SAMUEL JOHNSON, *The Vanity of Human Wishes*, l. 191.

14
Give thanks, O heart, for the high souls
That point us to the deathless goals. . . .
The company of souls supreme
The conscripts of the Mighty Dream. . . .
Brave souls that took the perilous trail
And felt the vision could not fail.

EDWIN MARKHAM, *Conscripts of the Dream*.

15
Lord of myself, accountable to none.
But to my conscience, and my God alone.

JOHN OLDHAM, *Satire Addressed to a Friend*.

16
Make thee a soul that will abide; only that endures to the end. (Iam molire animum, qui duret; . . . Solus ad extremos permanet ille rogos.)

OVID, *Ars Amatoria*. Bk. ii, l. 119.

1
'Tis my soul
That I thus hold erect as if with stays,
And decked with daring deeds instead of ribbons.
EDMOND ROSTAND, *Cyrano de Bergerac*. Act i, sc. 4.

2
I love a soul not all of wood,
Predestined to be good,
But true to the backbone
Unto itself alone
And false to none;
Born to its own affairs,
Its own joys and own cares;
By which the work that God begun
Is finished, and not undone.
H. D. THOREAU, *Conscience*.

3
They have mighty souls beating in narrow breasts. (Ingentes animos angusto in corpore versant.)
VERGIL, *Georgics*. Bk. iv, l. 83.

Little bodies have great souls.
JOHN RAY, *English Proverbs*.

What a mighty soul in a narrow bosom. (Welch' höher Geist in einer engen Brust.)
GOETHE, *Torquato Tasso*. Act ii, sc. 3, l. 199.

4
What do you suppose will satisfy the soul, except to walk free and own no superior?
WALT WHITMAN, *Laws for Creations*.

Ever the undiscouraged, resolute, struggling soul of man; . . .
Ever the soul dissatisfied, curious, unconvinced at last;
Struggling to-day the same—battling the same.
WALT WHITMAN, *Life*.

O my brave soul! O farther farther sail!
O daring joy, but safe! are they not all the seas of God?
O farther, farther, farther sail!
WALT WHITMAN, *Passage to India*. Sec. 9.

5
And the most difficult of tasks to keep
Heights which the soul is competent to gain.
WORDSWORTH, *The Excursion*. Bk. iv, l. 138.

VI—Soul: Its Last Journey

6
To-day the journey is ended,
I have worked out the mandates of fate;
Naked, alone, undefended,
I knock at the Uttermost Gate.
Behind is life and its longing,
Its trial, its trouble, its sorrow,
Beyond is the Infinite Morning
Of a day without a to-morrow.
WENONAH STEVENS ABBOTT, *A Soul's Soliloquy*.

7
There's a quiet harbor somewhere
For the poor a-weary soul
H. H. BROWNELL, *The Burial of the Dane*.

8
A happy soul, that all the way
To heaven hath a summer day. . . .
And, when life's sweet fable ends,
Soul and body part like friends:—
No quarrels, murmurs, no delay;
A kiss, a sigh, and so away.
RICHARD CRASHAW, *In Praise of Lessius's Rules of Health*, l. 33.

9
Gentle little soul, hastening away, my body's guest and comrade, whither goest thou now, pale, fearful, pensive, not jesting, as of old?
(Animula, vagula, blandula
Hospes comesque corporis,
Quæ nunc abibis in loca,
Pallidula, rigida, nudula,
Nec, ut soles, dabis joca?)
HADRIAN, *Morientis, Ad Animam Suam* (ÆLIUS SPARTIANUS, *Life of the Emperor Hadrian*.)

Ah! gentle, fleeting, wav'ring sprite,
Friend and associate of this clay!
To what unknown region borne,
Wilt thou now wing thy distant flight?
No more with wonted humour gay,
But pallid, cheerless, and forlorn.
HADRIAN, *Ad Animam Suam*. (Byron, tr.)

Vital spark of heav'nly flame,
Quit, oh quit, this mortal frame!
Trembling, hoping, ling'ring, flying,
Oh, the pain, the bliss of dying! . . .
Hark! they whisper; angels say,
Sister Spirit, come away!
POPE, *The Dying Christian to His Soul*. (*The Spectator*, 15 Nov., 1711.)

Poor little pretty, fluttering thing,
Must we no longer live together?
And dost thou prune thy trembling wing,
To take thy flight thou know'st not whither?
Thy humorous vein, thy pleasing folly
Lies all neglected, all forgot:
And pensive, wavering, melancholy,
Thou dread'st and hop'st thou know'st not what.
HADRIAN, *Ad Animam Suam*. (Prior, tr.)

Ma petite âme, ma mignonne,
Tu t'en vas donc, ma fille, et Dieu sçache où tu vas:
Tu pars seulette, nuë, et tremblotante, helas!
Que deviendra ton humeur folichonne!
Que deviendront tant de jolis ébats!
HADRIAN, *Ad Animam Suam*. (Fontanelle, tr.) Prior quotes Fontanelle's version before his own.

10
Ah, the souls of those that die
Are but sunbeams lifted higher.
LONGFELLOW, *The Golden Legend*. Pt. iv: *The Cloisters*, l. 19.

The dust's for crawling, heaven's for flying,
Wherefore, O Soul, whose wings are grown,
Soar upward to the sun!
EDGAR LEE MASTERS, *The Spoon River Anthology: Julian Scott*.

11
Return unto thy rest, my soul,

From all the wanderings of thy thought,
From sickness unto death made whole,
Safe through a thousand perils brought.
JAMES MONTGOMERY, *Rest for the Soul.*

1
I reflected, how soon in the cup of Desire
The pearl of the soul may be melted away;
How quickly, alas, the pure sparkle of fire
We inherit from heav'n, may be quench'd in the clay.
THOMAS MOORE, *Stanzas.*

2
My soul, the seas are rough, and thou a stranger
In these false coasts; O keep aloof; there's danger;
Cast forth thy plummet; see, a rock appears;
Thy ship wants sea-room; make it with thy tears.
FRANCIS QUARLES, *Emblems.* Bk. iii, No. 11.

3
Go, Soul, the Body's guest,
Upon a thankless arrant:
Fear not to touch the best,
The truth shall be thy warrant:
Go, since I needs must die,
And give the World the lie.
SIR WALTER RALEIGH, *The Lie.* Probably written by Raleigh during his imprisonment, 1592. Found in a manuscript of 1593. Has also been attributed to Sir John Davies, Joshua Sylvester, Lord Pembroke and Richard Edwards.

Tell zeal, it lacks devotion;
Tell love, it is but lust;
Tell time, it is but motion;
Tell flesh, it is but dust!
And wish them not reply,
For thou must give the lie.
SIR WALTER RALEIGH, *The Lie.*

Yet stab at thee that will,
No stab the soul can kill!
SIR WALTER RALEIGH, *The Lie.*

4
And the souls mounting up to God
Went by her like thin flames.
D. G. ROSSETTI, *The Blessed Damozel.*

5
Her soul from earth to Heaven lies,
Like the ladder of the vision,
Wheron go To and fro,
In ascension and demission,
Star-flecked feet of Paradise.
FRANCIS THOMPSON, *Scala Jacobi Portaque Eburnea.*

VII—Soul: Transmigration

6
Animals share with us the privilege of having a soul.
PYTHAGORAS. (DIOGENES LAERTIUS, *Pythagoras.* Bk. viii, sec. 13.)

The soul, bound now in this creature, now in that, goes on a round ordained of necessity.
PYTHAGORAS. (DIOGENES LAERTIUS, *Pythagoras.* Bk. viii, sec. 14.)

I was Euphorbus at the siege of Troy.
PYTHAGORAS.

When I was a shepherd on the plains of Assyria.
THOREAU.

7
Our souls are deathless, and ever, when they have left their former seat, do they live in new abodes and dwell in the bodies that have received them. (Morte carent animæ semperque priore relicta Sede novis domibus vivunt habitantque receptæ.)
OVID, *Metamorphoses.* Bk. xv, l. 158.

8
The soul is immortal, and is clothed successively in many bodies.
PLATO. (DIOGENES LAERTIUS, *Plato.* Sec. 40.)

I hold that when a person dies
His soul returns again to earth;
Arrayed in some new flesh-disguise
Another mother gives him birth.
With sturdier limbs and brighter brain
The old soul takes the roads again.
JOHN MASEFIELD, *A Creed.*

9
Thou almost makest me waver in my faith
To hold opinion with Pythagoras,
That souls of animals infuse themselves
Into the trunks of men.
SHAKESPEARE, *The Merchant of Venice.* Act iv, sc. 1, l. 130.

Clown: What is the opinion of Pythagoras concerning wildfowl?
Malvolio: That the soul of our grandam might haply inhabit a bird.
SHAKESPEARE, *Twelfth Night.* Act iv, sc. 2, l. 54.

SOUND

I—Sound: Definitions

10
A thousand trills and quivering sounds
In airy circles o'er us fly,
Till, wafted by a gentle breeze,
They faint and languish by degrees,
And at a distance die.
ADDISON, *Ode for St. Cecilia's Day.* St. 6.

11
No sound is dissonant which tells of Life.
S. T. COLERIDGE, *This Lime-Tree Bower My Prison,* l. 76.

12
There is in souls a sympathy with sounds.
COWPER, *The Task.* Bk. vi, l. 1.

13
Own, by neglecting sorrow's wound,
The consanguinity of sound.
MATTHEW GREEN, *The Spleen,* l. 152.

14
There is no sound but shall find some lovers, as the bitterest confections are grateful to some palates.
BEN JONSON, *Explorata: Consuetudo.*

1
A sound so fine there's nothing lives
'Twixt it and silence.

JAMES SHERIDAN KNOWLES, *Virginius*. Act v, 2.

2
Not many sounds in life, and I include all urban and rural sounds, exceed in interest a *knock at the door*.

LAMB, *Essays of Elia: Valentine's Day*.

3
Sonorous metal blowing martial sounds.

MILTON, *Paradise Lost*. Bk. i, l. 540.

4
And empty heads console with empty sound.

POPE, *The Dunciad*. Bk. iv, l. 542.

5
Momentary as a sound.

SHAKESPEARE, *A Midsummer-Night's Dream*. Act i, sc. 1, l. 143.

Idle sounds resembling parasites.

SHAKESPEARE, *Venus and Adonis*, l. 848.

Low, sweet, faint sounds, like the farewell of ghosts.

SHELLEY, *Prometheus Unbound*. Act ii, sc. 1, 158.

6 Sweet is every sound,
Sweeter thy voice, but every sound is sweet;
Myriads of rivulets hurrying thro' the lawn,
The moan of doves in immemorial elms,
And murmuring of innumerable bees.

TENNYSON, *The Princess*. Pt. vii, l. 203.

And beauty born of murmuring sound.

WORDSWORTH, *Three Years She Grew*.

7
Sugar is not so sweet to the palate as sound to the healthy ear.

H. D. THOREAU, *Journal*. (EMERSON, *Thoreau*.)

II—Sound and Sense

8
If the speaker's words sound discordant with his fortunes, the Romans in box and pit alike, will raise a loud guffaw. (Si dicentis erunt fortunis absona dicta, Romani tollent equites peditesque cachinnum.)

HORACE, *Ars Poetica*, l. 112.

To all proportioned terms he must dispense
And make the sound a picture of the sense.

CHRISTOPHER PITT, *Imitation of Horace, Ars Poetica*, l. 112.

The sound must seem an echo to the sense.

POPE, *Essay on Criticism*. Pt. ii, l. 15.

Take care of the sense and the sounds will take care of themselves.

LEWIS CARROLL, *Alice in Wonderland*. Ch. 9.

9
It has more sound than value. (Plus sonat quam valet.)

SENECA, *Epistulæ ad Lucilium*. Epis. xl, sec. 5.

10
Sound is more than sense.

LOGAN PEARSALL SMITH, *Afterthoughts*.

11
Mr. Hannaford's utterances have no meaning; he's satisfied if they sound clever.

ALFRED SUTRO, *The Walls of Jericho*. Act i.

SPAIN AND THE SPANIARDS

11a
The Spaniard is a bad servant but a worse master.

THOMAS ADAMS, *Sermons*. Vol. i, p. 116. (1629)

12
Poor Isabella's dead, whose abdication
Set all tongues wagging in the Spanish nation.
For that performance 'twere unfair to scold her:
She wisely left a throne too hot to hold her.
To History she'll be no royal riddle—
Merely a plain parched pea that jumped the griddle.

AMBROSE BIERCE, *Devil's Dictionary*, p. 11.

13
A whale stranded upon the coast of Europe.

EDMUND BURKE, *Speech, House of Commons*. Referring to Spain. The original sentence was, "A whale stranded upon the sea shore of Europe."

14
Oh, Christ! it is a goodly sight to see
What Heaven hath done for this delicious land!

BYRON, *Childe Harold*. Canto i, st. 15.

Oh, lovely Spain! renown'd romantic land!

BYRON, *Childe Harold*. Canto i, st. 35.

15
A nation swoln with ignorance and pride,
Who lick yet loathe the hand that waves the sword.

BYRON, *Childe Harold*. Canto i, st. 16.

The land of war and crimes.

BYRON, *Childe Harold*. Canto ii, st. 16.

16
Her soil has felt the foot-prints, and her clime
Been winnowed by the wings of Liberty.

THOMAS CAMPBELL, *Stanzas to the Memory of the Spanish Patriots*, l. 30.

17
All evil comes from Spain; all good from the north.

SIR THOMAS CHALONER, *Letter from Florence*, 1597. "A common proverb in every man's mouth." (*Notes and Queries*, 10th Ser., Vol. ii, p. 23.)

18
Well here's to the Maine, and I'm sorry for Spain,
Said Kelly and Burke and Shea.

J. I. C. CLARKE, *The Fighting Race*.

19
Perhaps they may count me a beggar here,
With never a roof for the wind and the rain,
But there is the sea with its wave-lashed pier,
And over the sea lies Spain.

C. W. COLEMAN, *Over the Sea Lies Spain*.

20
Singed the Spanish king's beard.

SIR FRANCIS DRAKE. (KNIGHT, *Pictorial History of England*, iii, 215.)

He has singed the beard of the King of Spain.
H. W. LONGFELLOW, *A Dutch Picture.*

1
Illustrious monarch of Iberia's soil.
PHILIP FRENEAU, *Columbus to Ferdinand.*

2
Proud daughter of that monarch, upon whom,
Though elsewhere it grow dark, sun never sets.
(Altera figlia Di quel monarcha a cui
Nè anco, quando annotta, il Sol tramonta.)
GUARINI, *Pastor Fido.* (1585) Referring to Catherine of Austria. Philip II of Spain is supposed to have said, "The sun never sets upon my empire."

The sun never sets upon my dominions.
ALEXANDER THE GREAT. (WILLIAMS, *Life.* Ch. 13.) This was a boast repeated by many writers: for Rome by Claudian (*De Consulatu Stilichonis,* iii, 139); Ovid (*Fasti,* ii, 136); Tibullus (*Elegiæ,* ii, 5, 58); Vergil (*Æneid,* vi, 795); for Portugal by Camoens (*Lusiad,* i, 8); for Philip II by James Howell (*Familiar Letters*).

It may be said of the Hollanders as of the Spaniards, that the sun never sets upon their dominions.
THOMAS GAGE, *New Survey of the West Indies: Epistle Dedicatory.* (1648)
See also under ENGLAND.

3
The king of Spain is a great potentate, who stands with one foot in the east and the other in the west; and the sun never sets that it does not shine on some of his dominions.
BALTHASAR SCHUPPIUS, *Abgenötigte Ehrenrettung.* (1660)

4
The richest man in Christendom I'm called;
On my dominions never sets the sun.
(Ich heisse
Der reichste Mann in der getauften Welt;
Die Sonne geht in meinem Staat nicht unter.)
SCHILLER, *Don Carlos.* Act i, sc. 6, l. 60.

The sun never sets on the immense empire of Charles V.
SCOTT, *Life of Napoleon.* Ch. 59.

5
Why should the brave Spanish soldiers brag? The sun never sets in the Spanish dominions, but ever shineth on one part or other we have conquered for our king.
CAPTAIN JOHN SMITH, *Advertisements for the Unexperienced, etc.* (*Mass. Hist. Soc. Coll.,* Ser. iii, vol. 3, l. 49.)

SPARROW

6
Sparrow, my lady's pet, with whom she often plays. (Passer, deliciæ meæ puellæ, Quicum ludere.)
CATULLUS, *Odes.* No. ii, l. 1.

Mourn, ye Loves and Graces, My lady's sparrow is dead, her pet, whom she loved more than her very eyes. (Lugete, O Veneres Cupidinesque, . . . Passer mortuus est meæ puellæ, Quem plus illa oculis suis amabat.)
CATULLUS, *Odes.* No. iii, l. 1.

Tell me not of joy: there's none
Now my little sparrow's gone;
He, just as you, Would toy and woo.
WILLIAM CARTWRIGHT, *Lesbia's Sparrow.*

7
I thought the sparrow's note from heaven,
Singing at dawn on the alder bough;
I brought him home, in his nest, at even;
He sings the song, but it cheers not now,
For I did not bring home the river and sky;—
He sang to my ear,—they sang to my eye.
EMERSON, *Each and All,* l. 13.

8
He's cheerful in weather so bitterly cold
It freezes your bones to the marrow;
I'll admit he's a beggar, a gangster, a bum,
But I take off my hat to the sparrow.
MINNA IRVING, *The Sparrow.*

9
The sparrows chirped as if they still were proud
Their race in Holy Writ should mentioned be.
LONGFELLOW, *The Birds of Killingworth.* St. 2.
See under PROVIDENCE.

SPEECH

See also Conversation, Freedom of Speech, Oratory, Silence and Speech, Talk, Tongue

I—Speech: Definitions

10
Speech is the image of life. (Γόγον εἴδολον τοῦ βίου.)
DEMOCRITUS, *Idylls.* (BRATHWAIT, *English Gentleman,* 51. 1641)

A man's character is revealed by his speech. ('Ανδρὸς χαρακτὴρ ἐκ λόγου γνωριζεται.)
MENANDER, *The Flute Girl: Fragment.*

Man's speech is like his life. (Οἷος ὁ βίος, τοιοῦτος καὶ ὁ λογος.)
SOCRATES. (CICERO, *Tusculanarum Disputationum,* v, 47.)

A man cannot speak but he judges himself.
EMERSON, *Essays, First Series: Compensation.*

Language most shews a man: Speak, that I may see thee.
BEN JONSON, *Explorata: Oratio Imago Animi.*
See also LANGUAGE: SINCERITY.

11
Usage, in whose hands lies the judgment, the right and the rule of speech. (Usus, Quem penes arbitrium est et jus et norma loquendi.)
HORACE, *Ars Poetica,* l. 71.

12
Speech is the only benefit man hath to express his excellency of mind above other creatures. It is the Instrument of Society. . . . In all speech, words and sense are as the body and the soul.
BEN JONSON, *Explorata: De Orationis Dignitate.*

1
Speech is the mirror of the soul; as the man, so is his speech. (Sermo animi est imago; qualis vir, talis et oratio est.)
PUBLILIUS SYRUS, *Sententiæ*. No. 1073.

Speech is the picture of the mind.
JOHN RAY, *English Proverbs*.

Speech is the index and mirror of the soul.
T. W. ROBERTSON, *Nightingale*. Pt. i.

2
God, all-powerful Creator of nature and Architect of the world, has impressed man with no character so proper to distinguish him from other animals, as by the faculty of speech.
QUINTILIAN, *De Institutione Oratoria*. Bk. ii, ch. 17, sec. 2.

3
Speech is the mirror of action. (Λόγον εἴδωλον εἶναι τῶν ἔργων.)
SOLON. (DIOGENES LAERTIUS, *Solon*. Bk. i, sec. 58.)

4
All speech, written or spoken, is a dead language, until it finds a willing and prepared hearer.
R. L. STEVENSON, *Lay Morals*.

5
The speech of men is like embroidered tapestries, since, like them, it must be extended in order to display its patterns, but when it is rolled up it conceals and distorts them.
THEMISTOCLES, to Artaxerxes. (PLUTARCH, *Lives: Themistocles*. Ch. 29, sec. 3.)

His speeches are like cyprus trees; they are tall and comely, but bear no fruit.
PHOCION. (PLUTARCH, *Lives: Phocion*.)

6
All speech is a hazard; oftener than not it is the most hazardous kind of deed.
MIGUEL DE UNAMUNO, *The Life of Don Quixote*. *See also* WORD AND DEED.

7
Speech, thought's canal! speech, thought's criterion, too!
Thought in the mine, may come forth gold or dross;
When coin'd in words, we know its real worth.
YOUNG. *Night Thoughts*. Night ii, l. 469.

II—Speech: Apothegms

8
Though I say it that should not.
JOHN LYLY, *Mother Bombie*. Act v, sc. 3. (1594)

I say it—that should not say it.
BEN JONSON, *Every Man Out of His Humour*. Act ii, sc. 1. (1599)

To say the truth, though I say 't that should not say 't.
BEAUMONT AND FLETCHER, *Wit at Several Weapons*. Act ii, sc. 2. (1609)

9
What I *have* said, Charles Middlewick, 's my ultipomatum.
HENRY J. BYRON, *Our Boys*. Act ii.

10
That's nothing to what I could say if I chose.
LEWIS CARROLL, *Alice's Adventures in Wonderland*. Ch. 9.

"Then you should say what you mean," the March Hare went on.
"I do," Alice hastily replied; "at least—at least I mean what I say—that's the same thing, you know."
"Not the same thing a bit!" said the Hatter.
CARROLL, *Alice's Adventures in Wonderland*, 7.

11
He himself said it. (Ipse dixit.)
CICERO, *De Natura Deorum*. Bk. i, ch. 5, sec. 10. Referring to the Pythagoreans.

Pythagoras, to whom was applied the phrase, "The Master said" (Αὐτὸς ἔφα), which passed into a proverb of ordinary life.
DIOGENES LAERTIUS, *Pythagoras*. Bk. viii, 46.

12
I speak this by permission, and not of commandment.
New Testament: I Corinthians, vii, 6.

13
The bearings of this observation lays in the application on it.
DICKENS, *Dombey and Son*. Ch. 23.

14
We never speak as we pass by.
FRANK EGERTON. Refrain of song. (1883)

15
I can't say fairer than that, can I?
W. S. GILBERT, *Ruddigore*. Act i.

16
I will speak something notable, new, and hitherto unsaid by any other mouth. (Dicam insigne, recens, adhuc Indictum ore alio.)
HORACE, *Odes*. Bk. iii, ode 25, l. 7.

Now I'll say something to remember.
ROBERT BROWNING, *A Soul's Tragedy*. Act i.

17
Out of the abundance of the heart the mouth speaketh.
New Testament: Matthew, xii, 34. (Ex abundantia cordis os loquitur.—*Vulgate*.)

18
For more than forty years I have been speaking prose without knowing it. (Il y a plus de quarante ans que je dis de la prose sans que j'en susse rien.)
MOLIÈRE, *Le Bourgeois Gentilhomme*, ii, 4, 179.

He speaks to a dead man: i. e., he wastes words. (Verba faciet mortuo.)
PLAUTUS, *Pœnulus*, l. 840. (Act iv, sc. 2.)

The words are spoken to a dead man. (Verba fiunt mortuo.)
TERENCE, *Phormio*, l. 1015. (Act v, sc. 8.)

19
He never speaks but his mouth opens.
JOHN RAY, *English Proverbs*, 193.

20
I do not much dislike the matter, but
The manner of his speech.
SHAKESPEARE, *Antony and Cleopatra*, ii, 2, 113

21
Say, and speak thick.
SHAKESPEARE, *Cymbeline*. Act iii, sc. 2, l. 58.

What should we speak of
When we are old as you? when we shall hear
The rain and wind beat dark December, how,
In this our pinching cave, shall we discourse
The freezing hours away?
SHAKESPEARE, *Cymbeline*. Act iii, sc. 3, l. 35.

1
I will speak daggers to her, but use none.
SHAKESPEARE, *Hamlet*. Act iii, sc. 2, l. 414.

Nor shall it be your excuse, that, murderer as you are, you have spoken daggers, but used none.
SHELLEY, *Adonais: Preface*.

She speaks poniards, and every word stabs.
SHAKESPEARE, *Much Ado About Nothing*. Act ii, sc. 1, l. 255.

2
Runs not this speech like iron through your blood?
SHAKESPEARE, *Much Ado About Nothing*. Act v, sc. 1, l. 252.

He speaks plain cannon fire, and smoke and bounce.
SHAKESPEARE, *King John*. Act ii, sc. 1, l. 462.

3
Mend your speech a little,
Lest it may mar your fortunes.
SHAKESPEARE, *King Lear*. Act i, sc. 1, l. 95.

Thou but offend'st thy lungs to speak so loud.
SHAKESPEARE, *The Merchant of Venice*. Act iv, sc. 1, l. 140.

4
She has brown hair, and speaks small like a woman.
SHAKESPEARE, *The Merry Wives of Windsor*. Act i, sc. 1, l. 48.

You may speak as small as you will.
SHAKESPEARE, *A Midsummer-Night's Dream*. Act i, sc. 2, l. 52.

I'll speak in a monstrous little voice.
SHAKESPEARE, *A Midsummer-Night's Dream*. Act i, sc. 2, l. 54.

5
There was speech in their dumbness, language in their very gesture.
SHAKESPEARE, *Winter's Tale*. Act v, sc. 2. l. 14.

6
I am not surprised, for I have heard him speak very disrespectfully of the Equator.
SYDNEY SMITH, to Sir John Leslie, when the latter complained to him that Francis Jeffrey had attacked in the *Edinburgh Review*, an article of his dealing with the North Pole, and when he complained, had retorted, "Oh, damn the North Pole!" (GREVILLE, *Memoirs*, 1833; LADY HOLLAND, *Memoir*. Ch. 2.)

Insultin' the sun and quarrellin' wi' the equator.
JOHN WILSON, *Noctes Ambrosianæ*. No. 24. May, 1830.

7
God giveth speech to all, song to the few.
WALTER CHALMERS SMITH, *Olrig Grange*. Bk. i, *Editorial*, l. 15.

8
He said enough. Enough said.
GERTRUDE STEIN, *Enough Said*. The poem consists of these words, five times repeated.

9
The first duty of man is to speak; that is his chief business in this world.
R. L. STEVENSON, *Talk and Talkers*.

Who hath given man speech? or who hath set therein
A thorn for peril and a snare for sin?
SWINBURNE, *Atalanta in Calydon: Chorus*.

God's great gift of speech abused
Makes thy memory confused.
TENNYSON, *A Dirge*. St. 7.

III—Speech: Speaking Well

10
The speaking in perpetual hyperbole is comely in nothing but in love.
FRANCIS BACON, *Essays: Of Love*.

11
Every man, who can speak at all, can speak elegantly and correctly if he pleases, by attending to the best authors and orators; and. indeed, I would advise those who do not speak elegantly, not to speak at all; for I am sure they will get more by their silence than by their speech.
LORD CHESTERFIELD, *Letters*, 26 Dec., 1749.

The manner of speaking is full as important as the matter, as more people have ears to be tickled, than understandings to judge.
LORD CHESTERFIELD, *Letters*, 9 July, 1750.

12
Let your speech be always with grace, seasoned with salt.
New Testament: Colossians, iv, 6.

13
Though I be rude in speech.
New Testament: II Corinthians, xi, 6.

Rude am I in my speech,
And little bless'd with the soft phrase of peace.
SHAKESPEARE, *Othello*. Act i, sc. 3, l. 81.

14
The music that can deepest reach,
And cure all ill, is cordial speech.
EMERSON, *Conduct of Life: Considerations by the Way*.

15
In chatter excellent, but unable quite to speak. (Λαλεῖν ἄριστος, ἀδυνατώτατος λέγειν.)
EUPOLIS, *Fragments*. No. 95.

He speaks one word nonsense and two that have nothing in them.
THOMAS FULLER, *Gnomologia*, No. 2025.

16
Speak clearly, if you speak at all;
Carve every word before you let it fall.
O. W. HOLMES, *A Rhymed Lesson*, l. 408.

[Learning] knit her brows and stamped her angry foot
To hear a Teacher call a rōōt a rŏŏt.
O. W. HOLMES, *A Rhymed Lesson*, l. 406.

1
The flowering moments of the mind
Drop half their petals in our speech.
O. W. HOLMES, *To My Readers*. St. 11.

2
His speech flowed from his tongue sweeter than honey. (Τοῦ καὶ ἀπὸ γλώσσης μέλιτος γλυκίων ῥέεν αὐδή.)
HOMER, *Iliad*. Bk. i, l. 245.

The poetry of speech.
BYRON, *Childe Harold*. Canto iv, st. 58.

The sweet music of speech.
COWPER, *Verses: Alexander Selkirk*.

3
The greatest things gain by being said simply; they are spoiled by emphasis. But one must say little things nobly, because they are propped up by expression, tone and manner.
LA BRUYÈRE, *Les Caractères*. Pt. ii, No. 82.

To speak and to offend, with some people, are but one and the same thing.
LA BRUYÈRE, *Les Caractères: Du Cœur*.

4
One speaks little when vanity does not make one speak. (On parle peu quand la vanité ne fait pas parler.)
LA ROCHEFOUCAULD, *Maximes*. No. 137.

It is never more difficult to speak well than when one is ashamed to be silent. (Il n'est jamais plus difficile de bien parler que quand on a honte de se taire.)
LA ROCHEFOUCAULD, *Maximes Posthumes*. No. 556.

5
He will no more speak fast, than he will run, for fear his tongue should go before his wit.
SIR ROGER L'ESTRANGE, *Of Seneca's Epistles*.

6
When we make ourselves understood, we always speak well, and all your fine diction serves no purpose. (Quand on se fait entendre, on parle toujours bien, Et tous vos beaux dictons ne servent pas de rien.)
MOLIÈRE, *Les Femmes Savantes*. Act ii, sc. 6.

7
Nor have I readiness in speaking. (Nec mihi dicere promptum.)
OVID, *Metamorphoses*. Bk. xiii, l. 10.

8
Grant me the power of saying things
Too simple and too sweet for words.
COVENTRY PATMORE, *The Angel in the House:* Bk. i, sec. 1, *Prelude*.

9
You are skilled in knowing what to say and what not to say. (Dicenda tacendave calles.)
PERSIUS, *Satires*. Sat. iv, l. 5.

10
Speak after the manner of men.
New Testament: Romans, vi, 19.

11
His ready speech flowed fair and free,
In phrase of gentlest courtesy;
Yet seemed that tone and gesture bland
Less used to sue than to command.
SCOTT, *The Lady of the Lake*. Canto i, st. 21.

12
An angry man speaks in an angry way, an excitable man in a flurried way, and an effeminate man in a style that is soft and unresisting. (Iracundi hominis iracunda oratio est, commoti nimis incitata, delicati tenera et fluxa.)
SENECA, *Epistulæ ad Lucilium*. Epis. cxiv, 20.

The sailor speaks of winds, the ploughman of oxen;
The soldier tells his wounds, the shepherd his sheep.
(Navita de ventis, de tauris narrat arator;
Enumerat miles vulnera, pastor oves.)
PROPERTIUS, *Elegies*. Bk. ii, eleg. 1, l. 43

13
To speak much is one thing, to speak to the point is another. (Χωρὶς τό τ' εἰπεῖν πολλὰ καὶ τὰ καίρια.)
SOPHOCLES, *Œdipus Coloneus*, l. 808.

14
His speech is a burning fire.
SWINBURNE, *Atalanta in Calydon: Chorus*.

15
He knew the most effective time for speaking. (Qui novit mollissima fandi tempora.)
VERGIL, *Æneid*. Bk. iv, l. 293.

I had a thing to say,
But I will fit it with some better time.
SHAKESPEARE, *King John*. Act iii, sc. 3, l. 25.

It may be right; but you are i' the wrong
To speak before your time.
SHAKESPEARE, *Measure for Measure*. Act v, sc. 1, l. 85.

16
Choice word and measured phrase, above the reach
Of ordinary men; a stately speech;
Such as grave Livers do in Scotland use.
WORDSWORTH, *Resolution and Independence*. St. 14.

IV—Speech: Loquacity

See also Talk: Loquacity; Words: Verbosity

17
Uncurbed, unfettered, uncontrolled of speech,
Unperiphrastic, bombastiloquent.
('Απεριλάλητον, καμποφακελορρήμονα.)
ARISTOPHANES, *The Frogs*, l. 837. Referring to Æschylus.

18
The habit of common and continuous speech is a symptom of mental deficiency.
BAGEHOT, *Literary Studies*. Vol. i, p. 47.

19
His speech was a fine sample, on the whole,
Of rhetoric, which the learn'd call *"rigmarole"*
BYRON, *Don Juan*. Canto i, st. 174.

In that manner vulgarly, but significantly, called rigmarole.
SAMUEL JOHNSON. (BOSWELL, *Life*, i, 191, note.)

1
Had that calm look which seemed to all assent,
And that complacent speech which nothing meant.
GEORGE CRABBE, *Parish Register*. Pt. i, l. 744.

2
Of the reinless lips that will own no master, . . .
One is the end of them, even disaster.
EURIPIDES, *Bacchanals*, l. 386.

3
He that speaks lavishly shall hear as knavishly.
THOMAS FULLER, *Gnomologia*. No. 6367.

4
I feel as stupid, from all you've said
As if a mill-wheel whirled in my head.
(Mir wird von alledem so dumm,
Als ging 'mir ein Mühlrad im Kopf herum.)
GOETHE, *Faust:* Act i, *Schulerscene*.

5
Stop not, unthinking, every friend you meet
To spin your wordy fabric in the street;
While you are emptying your colloquial pack,
The fiend *Lumbago* jumps upon his back.
O. W. HOLMES, *A Rhymed Lesson*, l. 336.

6
He has a rage for saying something when there's nothing to be said.
SAMUEL JOHNSON, *Remark*, to Dr. Burney, referring to Warburton. (BOSWELL, *Life*, 1758.)

7
But as they hedn't no gret things to say,
An' sed 'em often, I come right away.
J. R. LOWELL, *The Biglow Papers*. Ser. ii, *Mason and Slidell*.

8
They think that they shall be heard for their much speaking.
New Testament: Matthew, vi, 7.

9
With patient inattention hear him prate.
GEORGE MEREDITH, *Bellerophon*. St. 4.

10
And 'tis remarkable that they
Talk most who have the least to say.
MATTHEW PRIOR, *Alma*. Canto ii, l. 345.

In general those who nothing have to say
Contrive to spend the longest time in doing it;
They turn and vary it in every way,
Hashing it, stewing it, mincing it, *ragouting* it.
J. R. LOWELL, *An Oriental Apologue*. St. 15.

11
What cracker is this same that deafs our ears
With this abundance of superfluous breath?
SHAKESPEARE, *King John*. Act ii, sc. 1, l. 147.

12
Why have I blabbed?
SHAKESPEARE, *Troilus and Cressida*. Act iii, sc. 2, l. 132.

13
She sits tormenting every guest,
Nor gives her tongue one moment's rest,
In phrases batter'd, stale, and trite,
Which modern ladies call polite.
SWIFT, *The Journal of a Modern Lady*.

V—Speech: With Discretion

See also Silence and Speech

14
The wise man, before he speaks, will consider well what he speaks, to whom he speaks, and where and when. (Sapiens, ut loquatur, multa prius considerat, quid dicat, aut cui dicat, quo in loco, et tempora.)
ST. AMBROSE, *De Officiis Ministrorum*. Bk. i, ch. 10, sec. 35.

Si sapiens fore vis, sex serva quæ tibi mando:
Quid dicas, et ubi, de quo, cui, quomodo, quando.
UNKNOWN, *Six Things to be Observed*. (*Notes and Queries*, 23 Dec., 1911, p. 516.)

If that thou wilt speak aright,
Six things thou must observe then:
What thou speakest, and of what wight,
Where, to whom, why, and when.
UNKNOWN, *Whatever Thou Say, Advise Thee Well*. (MS. Trinity College, Cambridge, c. 1530.)

If you your lips would keep from slips
Five things observe with care;
To whom you speak, of whom you speak,
And how, and when, and where.
W. E. NORRIS, *Thirlby Hall*, i, 315. Quoted.

If you your ears would keep from jeers,
These things keep meekly hid:
Myself and me, or my and mine,
Or how I do or did.
W. E. NORRIS, *Thirlby Hall*, i, 315. Quoted.

15
Discretion of speech is more than eloquence.
FRANCIS BACON, *Essays: Of Discourse*.

And let him be sure to leave other men their turns to speak.
FRANCIS BACON, *Essays: Of Discourse*.

There is no man but speaketh more honestly than he can do or think.
BACON, *Advancement of Learning*. Bk. ii.

16
You, having a large and fruitful mind, should not so much labour what to speak as to find what to leave unspoken. Rich soils are often to be weeded.
FRANCIS BACON, *Letter to Coke*, expostulating with him on his verbosity.

17
Speak not at all, in any wise, till you have somewhat to speak; care not for the reward of your speaking, but simply and with undivided mind for the truth of your speaking.
CARLYLE, *Essays: Biography*.

There is endless merit in a man's knowing when to have done.
CARLYLE, *Essays: Francia*.

18
A wise man, then, sets hatch before the door,
And, whilst he may, doth square his speech with heed.
THOMAS DELONEY, *Strange Histories*, l. 70.

Think all you speak; but speak not all you think:
Thoughts are your own; your words are so no more.
Where Wisdom steers, wind cannot make you sink:
Lips never err, when she does keep the door.
HENRY DELAUNE, *Epigram.*
See also THOUGHT AND SPEECH.

1
Blessed is the man who having nothing to say, abstains from giving us wordy evidence of the fact.
GEORGE ELIOT, *Theophrastus Such.* Ch. iv.

2
He that speaks without care shall remember with sorrow.
THOMAS FULLER, *Gnomologia.* No. 2311.

Speaking without thinking is shooting without aiming.
W. G. BENHAM, *Proverbs,* p. 837.

3
Think well of what you say and to whom you say it. (Quid de quoque viro et cui dicas, sæpe videto.)
HORACE, *Epistles.* Bk. i, epis. 18, l. 68.

Think twice before you speak and then say it to yourself.
ELBERT HUBBARD, *The Philistine.* Cover, No. 4.

4
No, never say nothin' without you're compelled tu,
An' then don't say nothin' thet you can be held tu.
J. R. LOWELL, *Biglow Papers.* Ser. ii, No. 5.

5
It is better to guard speech than to guard wealth. (Κρείσσων γαρ μύθων ἢ κτεάνων φυλακή.)
LUCIAN. (*Greek Anthology.* Bk. x, epig. 42.)

6
The man is wise who speaketh few things. (Vir sapit qui pauca loquitur.)
WILLIAM LILLY, *Grammatices Rudimentis,* p. 42. (a. 1522) Quoted by SHAKESPEARE, *Love's Labour's Lost,* iv, 2, 82.

7
But ye, keep ye on earth
Your lips from over-speech,
Loud words and longing are so little worth,
And the end is hard to reach.
SWINBURNE, *Atalanta in Calydon: Chorus.*

VI—Speech: To Conceal Thought

For Candid Speech, see Candor

8
He who does not make his words rather serve to conceal than discover the sense of his heart, deserves to have it pulled out like a traitor's, and strewn publicly to the rabble.
SAMUEL BUTLER, *Remains,* ii, 25. (1759)

The true use of speech is not so much to express our wants as to conceal them.
GOLDSMITH, *The Bee.* No. 3. An echo of Butler, whose *Remains* he had just reviewed.

9
The heart seldom feels what the mouth expresses. (Le cœur sent rarement ce que la bouche exprime.)
JEAN CAMPISTRON, *Pompeia,* xi, 5.

10
Speech is . . . the art of . . . stifling and suspending thought.
CARLYLE, *Sartor Resartus.* Bk. iii, ch. 3.

11
Speech both conceals and reveals the thoughts of men. (Sermo hominum mores et celat et indicat idem.)
DIONYSIUS CATO, *Disticha de Moribus.* Bk. i, No. 26.

12
The carl spake one thing, but he thought another.
CHAUCER, *The Freres Tale,* l. 270.

13
The brow, the eyes, the countenance very often deceive us; but most often of all the speech. (Frons, oculi, vultus, persæpe mentiuntur; oratio vero sæpissime.)
CICERO, *Epistolæ ad Quintum Fratrem.* Bk. i, ch. 1, sec. 5.

14
These authors do not avail themselves of the invention of letters for the purpose of conveying, but of concealing their ideas.
LORD HOLLAND, *Life of Lope de Vega.*

15
Speech was made to open man to man, and not to hide him; to promote commerce, and not betray it.
DAVID LLOYD, *State Worthies.* Vol. i, p. 503. (1665)

Speech has been given to man to express his thought. (La parole a été donnée à l'homme pour exprimer sa pensée.)
MOLIÈRE, *La Mariage Forcé.* Sc. 4, l. 186.

16
The smooth speeches of the wicked are full of treachery. (Habent insidias hominis blanditiæ mali.)
PHÆDRUS, *Fables.* Bk. i, fab. 19, l. 1.

17
In their declamations and speeches they made use of words to veil and muffle their design.
PLUTARCH, *On Hearing.* Sec. 5. Referring to the Sophists.

The great sophism of all sophisms being equivocation or ambiguity of words and phrase.
BACON, *Advancement of Learning.* Bk. ii.

With reconciling words and courteous mien
Turning into sweet milk the sophist's spleen.
KEATS, *Lamia.* Pt. ii, l. 171.

Dark-brow'd sophist, come not anear;
All the place is holy ground.
TENNYSON, *The Poet's Mind.* St. 2.

18
It is easy for men to say one thing and think another.
PUBLILIUS SYRUS, *Sententiæ.* No. 322.

19
He that speaks me fair and loves me not, I'll speak him fair and trust him not.
JOHN RAY, *English Proverbs,* 24.

Speak fair and think what you will.
JOHN RAY, *English Proverbs,* 144.

1
A knavish speech sleeps in a foolish ear.
SHAKESPEARE, *Hamlet.* Act iv, sc. 2, l. 25.

2
It oft falls out,
To have what we would have, we speak not what we mean.
SHAKESPEARE, *Measure for Measure.* Act ii, sc. 4, l. 117.

3
Speech was given to the ordinary sort of men whereby to communicate their mind, but to wise men whereby to conceal it.
ROBERT SOUTH, *Sermon,* preached in Westminster Abbey, 30 April, 1676.

4
Speech was given to man to disguise his thoughts. (La parole a été donnée à l'homme pour déguiser sa pensée.)
TALLEYRAND. (BARÈRE, *Talleyrand,* vi. HAREL, *Le Nain Jaune.*) Harel afterwards alleged that the *mot* was really his own, and that he had put it into Talleyrand's mouth.

When Harel wished to put a joke or witticism into circulation, he was in the habit of connecting it with some celebrated name, on the chance of reclaiming it if it took. Thus he assigned to Talleyrand, in the *Nain Jaune,* the phrase, "Speech was given to man to disguise his thoughts."
FOURNIER, *L'Esprit dans l'Histoire.*

5
Men use thought only to justify their wrongdoing, and employ speech only to conceal their thoughts. (Ils ne se servent de la pensée que pour autoriser leurs injustices, et emploient les paroles que pour déguiser leurs pensées.)
VOLTAIRE, *Dialogues:* No. xiv, *Le Chapon et la Poularde.* (1766)

We must distinguish between speaking to deceive and being silent to be reserved. (Il faut distinguer entre parler pour tromper et se taire pour être impénétrable.)
VOLTAIRE, *Essai sur les Mœurs.* Sec. 163.

6
Where nature's end of language is declined,
And men talk only to conceal the mind.
YOUNG, *Love of Fame.* Sat. ii, l. 207.

VII—Speech: Speeches

See also Oratory

7
There is no inspiration in evil and . . . no man ever made a great speech on a mean subject.
EUGENE V. DEBS, *Efficient Expression.*

8
I will sit down now, but the time will come when you will hear me.
BENJAMIN DISRAELI, *Maiden Speech,* House of Commons, 1837.

9
The speeches of one that is desperate, which are as wind.
Old Testament: Job, vi, 26.

10
Strong men delight in forceful speech. Soldiers relish a speaker delivering himself a little unreservedly.
JOHN KEBLE, *Lectures on Poetry.* No. 25.

11
Ha, my friend, get me out of danger; you can deliver your speech afterwards. (Hé, mon ami, tire-moi de danger; Tu feras après ta harangue.)
LA FONTAINE, *Fables.* Bk. i, No. 19.

Knowin' the ears long speeches suit air mostly made to match.
J. R. LOWELL, *Biglow Papers.* Ser ii, No. 3.

12
I shall make you an impromptu at my leisure. (Je vous ferai un impromptu à loisir.)
MOLIÈRE, *Les Précieuses Ridicules.* Act i, sc. 11, l. 124.

Ward has no heart, they say, but I deny it;
He has a heart, and gets his speeches by it.
SAMUEL ROGERS, *Impromptu Epitaph upon Lord Dudley,* alluding to the story that Dudley carefully practised the speeches which he pretended were extempore.

13
Forgotten—like a maiden speech,
Which all men praise, but none remember.
WINTHROP MACKWORTH PRAED, *To a Lady.*

14
What is the short meaning of this long harangue? (Was ist der langen Rede kurzer Sinn?)
SCHILLER, *Piccolomini.* Act i, sc. 2, l. 160.

15
Even the most timid man can deliver a bold speech. (Est enim oratio etiam timidissimis audax.)
SENECA, *Epistulæ ad Lucilium.* Epis. xxvi, sec. 6.

16
I would be loath to cast away my speech, for besides that it is excellently well penned, I have taken great pains to con it.
SHAKESPEARE, *Twelfth Night.* Act i, sc. 5, l. 184.

17
On the day of the dinner of the Oystermongers' Company, what a noble speech I thought of in the cab!
THACKERAY, *Roundabout Papers: On Two Papers I Intended to Write.*

SPELL, see Charm

SPENSER, EDMUND

18
Old Spenser next, warm'd with poetic rage,
In ancient tales amus'd a barb'rous age.
ADDISON, *The Greatest English Poets,* l. 17.

The palfrey pace and the glittering grace,
Of Spenser's magical song.
ROBERT BUCHANAN, *Cloudland.*

1
Like Spenser ever in thy Faery Queene,
Whose like (for deep conceit) was never seen:
Crown'd mayst thou be unto thy more renown
(As King of Poets) with a Laurel Crown.
RICHARD BARNFIELD, *Remembrance of Some English Poets.*

Spenser to me, whose deep conceit is such
As, passing all conceit, needs no defence.
RICHARD BARNFIELD, *To His Friend, Master R. I.* This couplet is also in *The Passionate Pilgrim.* St. 8.

2
Discouraged, scorn'd, his writings vilified,
Poorly—poor man—he liv'd; poorly—poor man—he died.
PHINEAS FLETCHER, *The Purple Island.* Canto iv, st. 19.

3
The nobility of the Spencers has been illustrated and enriched by the trophies of Marlborough, but I exhort them to consider the Faerie Queene as the most precious jewel of their coronet.
EDWARD GIBBON, *Memoirs,* p. 3.

4
A silver trumpet Spenser blows,
And, as its martial notes to silence flee,
From a virgin chorus flows
A hymn in praise of spotless Chastity.
'Tis still! Wild warblings from the Æolian lyre
Enchantment softly breathe, and tremblingly expire.
KEATS, *Ode to Apollo.* St. 6.

5
The English Virgil.
JOHN KEBLE, *Lectures on Poetry.* No. 5.

6
Here nigh to Chaucer, Spenser, stands thy hearse,
Still nearer standst thou to him in thy verse.
Whilst thou didst live, lived English poetry;
Now thou art dead, it fears that it shall die.
UNKNOWN, *Epitaph on Spenser.* (CAMDEN, *Reges Reginæ Nobiles.* 1606.)

SPIDER

7
There webs were spread of more than common size,
And half-starved spiders prey'd on half-starved flies.
CHARLES CHURCHILL, *The Prophecy of Famine,* l. 327.

8
Much like a subtle spider, which doth sit
In middle of her web, which spreadeth wide:
If aught do touch the utmost thread of it,
She feels it instantly on every side.
SIR JOHN DAVIES, *The Immortality of the Soul:* Sec. 18, *Feeling.*

Or almost like a spider, who, confin'd
In her web's centre, shakt with every wind,
Moves in an instant if the buzzing fly
Stirs but a string of her lawn canopy.
DU BARTAS, *Devine Weekes and Workes.* Week i, day 6. (Sylvester, tr.)

9
A spider sewed at night
Without a light
Upon an arc of white. . . .
His strategy
Was physiognomy.
EMILY DICKINSON, *Poems.* Pt. ii, No. 27.

The spider as an artist
Has never been employed. . . .
Neglected son of genius,
I take thee by the hand.
EMILY DICKINSON, *Poems.* Pt. ii, No. 95.

9a
The spider lost her distaff, and is ever since forced to draw her thread through her tail.
THOMAS FULLER, *Gnomologia.* No. 4766.

10
"Will you walk into my parlour?" said a Spider to a Fly;
" 'Tis the prettiest little parlour that ever you did spy."
MARY HOWITT, *The Spider and the Fly.*

11
The spider's touch, how exquisitely fine,
Feels at each thread, and lives along the line.
POPE, *Essay on Man.* Epis. i, l. 217.

SPIRIT

See also Soul

12
For then
The bowstring of my spirit was not slack.
CAMPBELL, *Gertrude of Wyoming.* Pt. iii, st. 14.

13
I envy no mortal, though ever so great,
Nor scorn I a wretch for his lowly estate;
But what I abhor and esteem as a curse
Is poorness of Spirit, not poorness of Purse.
HENRY CAREY, *General Reply to the Libelling Gentry.*

14
It is the spiritual always which determines the material.
CARLYLE, *On Heroes and Hero-Worship.* Lect. v.

15
Not of the letter, but of the spirit: for the letter killeth, but the spirit giveth life.
New Testament: II Corinthians, iii, 6.

It is the Spirit that quickeneth.
New Testament: John, vi, 63.

16
Then shall the dust return to the earth as it was: and the spirit shall return unto God who gave it.
Old Testament: Ecclesiastes, xii, 7.

17
Every spirit makes its house, but afterwards the house confines the spirit.
EMERSON, *Conduct of Life: Fate.*

1
The spirits of just men made perfect.
New Testament: Hebrews, xii, 23.

2
More brightly must my spirit shine
Since grace of beauty is not mine.
JANIE SCREVEN HEYWARD, *The Spirit's Grace.*

3
Into thy hands I commend my spirit.
New Testament: Luke, xxiii, 46. (In manus tuas commendo spiritum meum.—*Vulgate.*)

4
The spirit indeed is willing, but the flesh is weak.
New Testament: Matthew, xxvi, 41.

The spirit truly is ready, but the flesh is weak.
New Testament: Mark, xiv, 38. (Spiritus quidem promptus est, caro autem infirma.—*Vulgate.*)

5
A spirit superior to every weapon. (Teloque animus præstantior omni.)
OVID, *Metamorphoses*. Bk. iii, l. 54.

Of my own spirit let me be
In sole though feeble mastery.
SARA TEASDALE, *Mastery.*

See also SOUL: THE UNCONQUERED SOUL.

6
The ornament of a meek and quiet spirit, which is in the sight of God of great price.
New Testament: I Peter, iii, 4.

7
A wounded spirit who can bear?
Old Testament: Proverbs, xviii, 14.

8
The choice and master spirits of this age.
SHAKESPEARE, *Julius Cæsar*. Act iii, sc. 1, 163.

9
Spirits are not finely touch'd
But to fine issues.
SHAKESPEARE, *Measure for Measure*. Act i, sc. 1, l. 36.

10
It is a dangerous grieving of the spirit, when, instead of drawing ourselves to the spirit, we will labour to draw the Spirit to us.
RICHARD SIBBES, *The Fountain Sealed.*

The life of any one can by no means be changed after death; an evil life can in no wise be converted into a good life, or an infernal into an angelic life: because every spirit, from head to foot, is of the character of his love, and therefore, of his life; and to convert this life into its opposite, would be to destroy the spirit utterly.
SWEDENBORG, *Heaven and Hell*, p. 527.

SPIRITS

See also Ghosts

11
Why, a spirit is such a little, little thing, that I have heard a man, who was a great scholar, say that he'll dance ye a hornpipe upon the point of a needle.
ADDISON, *The Drummer*. Act i, sc. 1.

Some who are far from atheists, may make themselves merry with that conceit of thousands of spirits dancing at once upon a needle's point.
RALPH CUDWORTH, *True Intellectual System of the Universe*. Vol. iii, p. 497.

How many angels can dance on the point of a very fine needle without jostling each other?
ISAAC D'ISRAELI, *Curiosities of Literature: Quodlibets*. Paraphrasing an idea in St. Thomas Aquinas, *Summa.*

12
Somewhere—in desolate wind-swept space—
In Twilight-land—in No-man's-land—
Two hurrying Shapes met face to face,
And bade each other stand.

"And who are you?" cried one a-gape,
Shuddering in the gloaming light.
"I know not," said the second Shape,
"I only died last night!"
THOMAS BAILEY ALDRICH, *Identity.*

13
We are spirits clad in veils;
Man by man was never seen;
All our deep communing fails
To remove the shadowy screen.
CHRISTOPHER PEARSE CRANCH, *Gnosis.*

14
We spirits have just natures
We had for all the world, when human creatures;
And, therefore, I, that was an actress here,
Play all my tricks in hell, a goblin there.
DRYDEN, *Tyrannick Love: Epilogue.*

15
Aërial spirits, by great Jove design'd
To be on earth the guardians of mankind:
Invisible to mortal eyes they go,
And mark our actions, good or bad, below:
The immortal spies with watchful care preside,
And thrice ten thousand round their charges glide:
They can reward with glory or with gold,
A power they by Divine permission hold.
HESIOD, *Works and Days*, l. 164.

Millions of spiritual creatures walk the earth
Unseen, both when we wake, and when we sleep.
MILTON, *Paradise Lost*. Bk. iv, l. 677.

Know, then, unnumber'd Spirits round thee fly,
The light militia of the lower sky.
POPE, *Rape of the Lock*. Canto i, l. 41.

See also ANGEL: GUARDIAN ANGEL.

16
The spirit-world around this world of sense
Floats like an atmosphere, and everywhere
Wafts through these earthly mists and vapors dense
A vital breath of more ethereal air.
LONGFELLOW, *Haunted Houses*. St. 6.

So from the world of spirits there descends
A bridge of light, connecting it with this,
O'er whose unsteady floor, that sways and bends,
Wander our thoughts above the dark abyss.
LONGFELLOW, *Haunted Houses*. St. 10.

1
Spirits when they please
Can either sex assume, or both; so soft
And uncompounded is their essence pure,
Not tied or manacl'd with joint or limb,
Nor founded on the brittle strength of bones,
Like cumbrous flesh; but in what shape they choose,
Dilated or condens'd, bright or obscure,
Can execute their aerie purposes,
And works of love or enmity fulfil.
MILTON, *Paradise Lost*. Bk. i, l. 423.

Spirits that live throughout
Vital in every part, not as frail man
In entrails, heart or head, liver or reins,
Cannot but by annihilating die;
Nor in their liquid texture mortal wound
Receive, no more than can the fluid air:
All heart they live, all head, all eye, all ear,
All intellect, all sense, and as they please,
They limb themselves, and colour, shape or size
Assume, as likes them best, condense or rare.
MILTON, *Paradise Lost*. Bk. vi, l. 344.

2
Raise no more spirits than you can conjure down.
JOHN RAY, *English Proverbs*.

3
Whether in sea or fire, in earth or air,
The extravagant and erring spirit hies
To his confine.
SHAKESPEARE, *Hamlet*. Act i, sc. 1, l. 153.

4
Glendower: I can call spirits from the vasty deep.
Hotspur: Why, so can I, or so can any man;
But will they come when you do call for them?
SHAKESPEARE, *I Henry IV*. Act iii, sc. 1, l. 53.

5
Black spirits and white, red spirits and grey,
Mingle, mingle, mingle, while you mingle may.
SHAKESPEARE, *Macbeth*. Act iv, sc. 1, l. 43. (1606) THOMAS MIDDLETON, *The Witch*. Act v, sc. 2. (c. 1615) Probably a snatch of a traditional song.

6
My little spirit, see,
Sits in a foggy cloud, and stays for me.
SHAKESPEARE, *Macbeth*. Act iii, sc. 5, l. 34.

7
I will be correspondent to command,
And do my spiriting gently.
SHAKESPEARE, *The Tempest*. Act i, sc. 2, l. 297.

8
A pard-like spirit, beautiful and swift.
SHELLEY, *Adonais*. St. xxxii.

9
Take, O boatman, thrice thy fee,—
Take, I give it willingly;
For, invisible to thee,
Spirits twain have crossed with me.
UHLAND, *The Passage*. (Sarah Austin, tr.)

SPORT, see Game, Hunting

SPRING

See also April

10
Tantarrara! the joyous Book of Spring
Lies open, writ in blossoms.
WILLIAM ALLINGHAM, *Daffodil*.

But when shall spring visit the mouldering urn?
O when shall it dawn on the night of the grave?
JAMES BEATTIE, *The Hermit*. St. 4.

11
Spring beckons! All things to the call respond,
The trees are leaving and cashiers abscond.
AMBROSE BIERCE, *Devil's Dictionary*, p. 15.

12
O thou with dewy locks, who lookest down
Thro' the clear windows of the morning, turn
Thine angel eyes upon our western isle,
Which in full choir hails thy approach, O Spring!
WILLIAM BLAKE, *To Spring*, l. 1.

Beneath the crisp and wintry carpet hid
A million buds but stay their blossoming;
And trustful birds have built their nests amid
The shuddering boughs, and only wait to sing
Till one soft shower from the south shall bid,
And hither tempt the pilgrim steps of Spring.
ROBERT BRIDGES, *The Growth of Love*. Sonnet vi.

13
The year 's at the spring
And day 's at the morn;
Morning 's at seven;
The hill-side 's dew-pearled;
The lark 's on the wing;
The snail 's on the thorn;
God 's in his heaven—
All 's right with the world!
ROBERT BROWNING, *Pippa Passes: Morning*.

14
Now spring returns: but not to me returns
The vernal joy my better years have known;
Dim in my breast life's dying taper burns,
And all the joys of life with health are flown.
MICHAEL BRUCE, *Elegy Written in Spring*.

15
In days when daisies deck the ground,
And blackbirds whistle clear,
With honest joy our hearts will bound
To see the coming year.
BURNS, *Epistle to Davie*.

Now Nature hangs her mantle green
On every blooming tree,
And spreads her sheets o' daisies white
Out-owre the grassy lea.
BURNS, *Lament of Mary Queen of Scots*.

Again rejoicing Nature sees
Her robe assume its vernal hues,
Her leafy locks wave in the breeze,
All freshly steep'd in morning dews.
BURNS, *And Maun I Still on Menie Doat?*

1
Spring comes laughing down the valley
All in white, from the snow
Where the winter's armies rally
Loth to go. . . .
Every tree is loud with birds.
Bourgeon, heart,—do thy part!
Raise a slender stalk of words
From a root unseen.
AMELIA JOSEPHINE BURR, *New Life.*

2
She comes with gusts of laughter,—
The music as of rills;
With tenderness and sweetness,
The wisdom of the hills.
BLISS CARMAN, *Over the Wintry Threshold.*

3
The season pricketh every gentle heart,
And maketh him out of his sleep to start.
CHAUCER, *The Knightes Tale,* l. 1045.

For surely in the blind deep-buried roots
Of all men's souls to-day
A secret quiver shoots.
RICHARD HOVEY, *Spring.*

4
I have not yet lived long
Enough to be so young
As the old innocence
Of the eternal Spring.
RICHARD CHURCH, *In April.*

5
'Tis a month before the month of May,
And the Spring comes slowly up this way.
S. T. COLERIDGE, *Christabel.* Pt. i, l. 21.

6
Spring, Spring, beautiful Spring.
ELIZA COOK, *Spring.*

7
"Spring goes," you say; "suns set."
So be it! Why be glum?
Enough, the spring has come.
JAMES COUSINS, *A Starling's Spring Rondel.*

The days are before us for weeping and sorrow . . .
To-day it is spring!
SAROJINI NAIDU, *Ecstasy.*

Yet ah, that Spring should vanish with the Rose!
OMAR KHAYYÁM, *Rubáiyát.* St. 96. (Fitzgerald, tr.)

Spring flies, and with it all the train it leads:
And flowers, in fading, leave us but their seeds.
SCHILLER, *Farewell to the Reader.*

Sweet Spring, full of sweet days and roses,
A box where sweets compacted lie;
My music shows ye have your closes,
And all must die.
GEORGE HERBERT, *Virtue.* St. 3.

Spring counts no seed and gleans no treasure. . . . Summer kisses her tired eyes, and takes her crown and sceptre.
EDEN PHILLPOTTS, *The Girl and the Faun.*

8
Spring hangs her infant blossoms on the trees,
Rock'd in the cradle of the western breeze.
COWPER, *Tirocinium,* l. 43.

9
If there comes a little thaw,
Still the air is chill and raw,
Here and there a patch of snow,
Dirtier than the ground below,
Dribbles down a marshy flood;
Ankle-deep you stick in mud
In the meadows while you sing,
"This is Spring."
C. P. CRANCH, *A Spring Growl.*

10
The spring's behaviour here is spent
To make the world magnificent.
JOHN DRINKWATER, *May Garden.*

11
And still the nearer to the Spring we go,
More limpid, more unsoil'd, the waters flow.
DRYDEN, *Religio Laici,* l. 340.

12
Daughter of Heaven and Earth, coy Spring,
With sudden passion languishing,
Teaching barren moors to smile,
Painting pictures mile on mile,
Holds a cup of cowslip-wreaths,
Whence a smokeless incense breathes.
EMERSON, *May-Day,* l. 1.

When the trellised grapes their flowers unmask,
And the new-born tendrils twine,
The old wine darkling in the cask
Feels the bloom on the living vine,
And bursts the hoops at hint of spring.
EMERSON, *May-Day,* l. 77.

13
Now the lusty spring is seen;
Golden yellow, gaudy blue,
Daintily invite the view.
JOHN FLETCHER, *Valentinian: Love's Emblems.*

14
Eternal Spring, with smiling Verdure here
Warms the mild Air, and crowns the youthful Year.
GARTH, *The Dispensary.* Canto iv, l. 298.

15
Lo! where the rosy bosom'd Hours,
Fair Venus' train appear,
Disclose the long-expecting flowers,
And wake the purple year!
THOMAS GRAY, *Ode on the Spring,* l. 1.

And the glad earth, caressed by murmuring showers,
Wakes like a bride, to deck herself with flowers!
HENRY SYLVESTER CORNWELL, *May.*

When Spring unlocks the flowers to paint the laughing soil.
REGINALD HEBER, *Hymn for Seventh Sunday after Trinity.*

The Spring 's already at the gate
With looks my care beguiling;
The country round appeareth straight
A flower-garden smiling.
HEINE, *Book of Songs: New Spring.*

I come, I come! ye have called me long.
I come o'er the mountains with light and song!
Ye may trace my step o'er the wakening earth,
By the winds which tell of the violet's birth,
By the primrose-stars, in the shadowy grass,
By the green leaves opening as I pass.
FELICIA HEMANS, *The Voice of Spring.*

1
Spring in the world!
And all things are made new!
RICHARD HOVEY, *Spring.*

2
The sweet season, that bud and bloom forth brings,
With green hath clad the hill, and eke the vale.
HENRY HOWARD, *Description of Spring.*

3
In the tassel-time of Spring.
R. U. JOHNSON, *Before the Blossom.*

4
I wonder if the tides of spring
Will always bring me back again
Mute rapture at the simple thing
Of lilacs blooming in the rain.
THOMAS S. JONES, JR., *Beyond.*

Alas, for us no second spring,
Like mallows in the garden-bed.
ANDREW LANG, *Triolets after Moschus.*

5
The lovely town was white with apple-blooms,
And the great elms o'erhead
Dark shadows wove on their aerial looms,
Shot through with golden thread.
LONGFELLOW, *Hawthorne.* St. 2.

6
Came the Spring with all its splendor,
All its birds and all its blossoms,
All its flowers, and leaves, and grasses.
LONGFELLOW, *Hiawatha.* Pt. xxi, l. 109.

Then came the lovely spring with a rush of blossoms and music,
Flooding the earth with flowers, and the air with melodies vernal.
LONGFELLOW, *Tales of a Wayside Inn:* Pt. iii, *The Theologian's Tale.*

7
Every clod feels a stir of might,
An instinct within it that reaches and towers,
And, groping blindly above it for light,
Climbs to a soul in grass and flowers.
J. R. LOWELL, *The Vision of Sir Launfal: Prelude.*

The holy spirit of the Spring
Is working silently.
GEORGE MACDONALD, *Songs of Spring Days.* Pt. ii.

8
This wind is called Zephyrus, whose mild
And fruitful birth gets the young Spring with child,
Filling her womb with such delicious heat,
As breeds the blooming rose and violet.
SHACKERLEY MARMION, *Cupid and Psyche.*

9
Wag the world how it will,
Leaves must be green in spring.
HERMAN MELVILLE, *Malvern Hill.*

10
O Spring! I know thee. Seek for sweet surprise
In the young children's eyes.
But I have learnt the years, and know the yet
Leaf-folded violet.
ALICE MEYNELL, *In Early Spring.*

11
Spring rides no horses down the hill,
But come on foot, a goose-girl still.
And all the loveliest things there be
Come simply so, it seems to me.
EDNA ST. VINCENT MILLAY, *The Goose-Girl.*

12
In those vernal seasons of the year, when the air is calm and pleasant, it were an injury and sullenness against Nature not to go out and see her riches, and partake in her rejoicing with heaven and earth.
MILTON, *Tractate of Education.*

13
The Spring returns!
Triumphant through the wider-archèd cope
She comes, she comes, unto her tyranny,
And at her coronation are set ope
The prisons of the mind, and man is free!
CHARLES LEONARD MOORE, *The Spring Returns.*

14
Sound, jocund strains; on pipe and viol sound,
Young voices sing;
Wreathe every door with snow-white voices round,
For lo! 't is Spring!
Winter has passed with its sad funeral train,
And Love revives again.
LEWIS MORRIS, *Life-Music.*

15
Spring, the sweet Spring, is the pleasant year's king.
THOMAS NASHE, *Spring.*

16
Gentle Spring! in sunshine clad,
Well dost thou thy power display!
For Winter maketh the light heart sad,
And thou, thou makest the sad heart gay.
CHARLES D'ORLÉANS, *Spring.* (Longfellow, tr.)

17
It was then perpetual spring. (Ver erat æternum.)
OVID, *Metamorphoses.* Bk. i, l. 107.

Here is eternal spring. (Hic ver assiduum.)
VERGIL, *Georgics.* Bk. ii, l. 149.

18
There is no time like Spring,
When life's alive in every thing.
CHRISTINA ROSSETTI, *Spring.*

19
Never yet was a springtime,
Late though lingered the snow,
That the sap stirred not at the whisper

Of the southwind, sweet and low;
Never yet was a springtime
When the buds forgot to blow.
MARGARET ELIZABETH SANGSTER, *Awakening.*

1
I sing the first green leaf upon the bough,
The tiny kindling flame of emerald fire,
The stir amid the roots of reeds, and how
The sap will flush the briar.
CLINTON SCOLLARD, *Song in March.*

2
The vernal sun new life bestows
Even on the meanest flower that blows.
SCOTT, *Marmion:* Canto i, *Introduction,* l. 63.

3
When daffodils begin to peer,
With heigh! the doxy over the dale,
Why, then comes in the sweet o' the year;
For the red blood reigns in the winter's pale.
SHAKESPEARE, *Winter's Tale.* Act iv, sc. 3, l. 1.

4
For, lo, the winter is past, the rain is over and gone; the flowers appear on the earth; the time of the singing of birds is come, and the voice of the turtle is heard in our land.
Old Testament: Song of Solomon, ii, 11, 12.

5
Fresh Spring, the herald of love's mighty king,
In whose coat-armour richly are display'd
All sorts of flowers the which on earth do spring
In goodly colours gloriously array'd.
EDMUND SPENSER, *Amoretti.* Sonnet lxx.

So forth issued the Seasons of the year:
First, lusty Spring, all dight in leaves of flowers
That freshly budded and new blooms did bear
(In which a thousand birds had built their bowers,
That sweetly sung, to call forth paramours).
SPENSER, *Faerie Queene.* Bk. vii, canto vii, st. 28.

6
When the hounds of spring are on winter's traces,
The mother of months in meadow or plain
Fills the shadows and windy places
With lisp of leaves and ripple of rain.
SWINBURNE, *Atalanta in Calydon: Chorus.*

7
Once more the Heavenly Power
Makes all things new,
And domes the red-plough'd hills
With loving blue;
The blackbirds have their wills,
The throstles too.
TENNYSON, *Early Spring.* St. 1.

8
Dip down upon the northern shore,
O sweet new-year delaying long;
Thou doest expectant Nature wrong;
Delaying long, delay no more.
TENNYSON, *In Memoriam.* Pt. lxxxiii.

Now fades the last long streak of snow,
Now burgeons every maze of quick
About the flowering squares, and thick
By ashen roots the violets blow.
TENNYSON, *In Memoriam.* Pt. cxv.

And even into my inmost ring
A pleasure I discern'd,
Like those blind motions of the spring,
That show the year is turn'd.
TENNYSON, *The Talking Oak,* l. 173.

The boyhood of the year.
TENNYSON, *Sir Launcelot and Queen Guinevere.* St. 3.

9
Come, gentle Spring, ethereal mildness, come;
And from the bosom of yon dropping cloud,
While music wakes around, veiled in a shower
Of shadowing roses, on our plains descend.
THOMSON, *The Seasons: Spring,* l. 1.

Fair-handed Spring unbosoms every grace—
Throws out the snow-drop and the crocus first.
THOMSON, *The Seasons: Spring,* l. 529.

10
Spring, with that nameless pathos in the air
Which dwells in all things fair,
Spring, with her golden suns and silver rain,
Is with us once again.
HENRY TIMROD, *Spring.*

The good-wife oped the window wide,
The good-man spanned his plough;
'Tis time to run, 'tis time to ride,
For Spring is with us now.
CHARLES GODFREY LELAND, *Spring.*

11
Now the woods are in leaf, now the year is in its greatest beauty. (Nunc frondent sylvæ, nunc formosissmus annus.)
VERGIL, *Eclogues.* No. iii, l. 57.

In spring heat returns to the bones. (Vere calor redit ossibus.)
VERGIL, *Georgics.* Bk. iii, l. 272.

12
We have not a leaf, yet, large enough to make an apron for a Miss Eve of two years old.
HORACE WALPOLE, *Letter to George Montagu,* 6 May, 1770.

13
Again the blackbirds sing; the streams
Wake, laughing, from their winter dreams,
And tremble in the April showers
The tassels of the maple flowers.
J. G. WHITTIER, *The Singer.* St. 20.

II—Spring and Love

14
When things were as fine as could possibly be
I thought 'twas the spring; but alas it was she.
JOHN BYROM, *A Pastoral.*

15
One of love's April fools.
CONGREVE, *The Old Batchelor.* Act i, sc. 1.

16
Men are the devil—they all bring woe.
In winter it's easy to say just "No"

Men are the devil, that's one sure thing,
But what are you going to do in spring?
MARY CAROLYN DAVIES, *Men Are the Devil.*

A trap's a very useful thing:
Nature in our path sets Spring.
It is a trap to catch us two,
It is planned for me and you.
MARY CAROLYN DAVIES, *Traps.*

1
All the veneration of Spring connects itself with love. . . . Even the frog and his mate have a new and gayer coat for this benign occasion.
EMERSON, *Journals.* Vol. ix, p. 178.

2
Spring! and the buds against the sky;
Heart, forget that you saw
The little brown bird that fluttered by—
The bird with the wisp of straw.
CAROLINE GILTINAN, *Spring.*

3
In spring time, the only pretty ring time,
When birds do sing, hey ding a ding, ding:
Sweet lovers love the spring.
SHAKESPEARE, *As You Like It.* Act v, sc. 3, l. 20

4
Love, whose month is ever May.
SHAKESPEARE, *Love's Labour's Lost.* Act iv, sc. 3, l. 102.

Of temper amorous as the first of May.
TENNYSON, *The Princess.* Pt. i, l. 2.

He has a hard heart who does not love in May. (Moult a dur cuer qui en Mai n'aime.)
UNKNOWN, *Roman de la Rose.*

5
It is the season now to go
About the country high and low,
Among the lilacs hand in hand,
And two by two in fairy land.
R. L. STEVENSON, *Underwoods.* No. 4.

Now the hedged meads renew
Rustic odour, smiling hue,
And the clean air shines and twinkles as the world goes wheeling through;
And my heart springs up anew,
Bright and confident and true,
And my old love comes to meet me in the dawning and the dew.
R. L. STEVENSON, *My Old Love.*

6
In the spring a livelier iris changes on the burnish'd dove;
In the spring a young man's fancy lightly turns to thoughts of love.
TENNYSON, *Locksley Hall,* l. 19.

7
When Spring is old, and dewy winds
Blow from the south, with odors sweet,
I see my love, in shadowy groves,
Speed down dark aisles on shining feet.
MAURICE THOMPSON, *Atalanta's Race.*

8
Love knows no winter; no, no! It is, and remains the sign of spring.
(Die Liebe wintert nicht;
Nein, nein! Ist und bleibt Frühlings-Schein.)
LUDWIG TIECK, *Herbstlied.*

9
This is the time when bit by bit
The days begin to lengthen sweet
And every minute gained is joy—
And love stirs in the heart of a boy.
KATHERINE TYNAN, *Turn o' the Year.*

10
The flowers that bloom in the spring, Tra la,
Have nothing to do with the case.
W. S. GILBERT, *The Mikado.* Act ii.

STAGE

See also Acting; Life: A Play; World: A Stage

I—Stage: Apothegms

11
No play would I have rather seen. (Nullos his mallem ludos spectasse.)
HORACE, *Satires.* Bk. ii, sat. 8, l. 79. Referring to a banquet which a friend was describing.

As good as a play!
CHARLES II, while listening to the debate in Parliament on Lord Ross's Divorce Bill. (MACAULAY, *Essays: The Life of Sir William Temple.*)

12
Drama—what literature does at night.
GEORGE JEAN NATHAN, *Testament of a Critic.*

Great drama is the reflection of a great doubt in the heart and mind of a great, sad, gay man.
GEORGE JEAN NATHAN, *Materia Critica.*

13
The stage was unadorned. (Scena sine arte fuit.)
OVID, *Ars Amatoria.* Bk. i, l. 106.

14
The play, I remember, pleased not the million; 'twas caviare to the general.
SHAKESPEARE, *Hamlet.* Act ii, sc. 2, l. 457.

15
The play's the thing.
SHAKESPEARE, *Hamlet.* Act ii, sc. 2, l. 633.

16
A hit, a very palpable hit.
SHAKESPEARE, *Hamlet.* Act v, sc. 2, l. 292.

17
When my cue comes, call me, and I will answer.
SHAKESPEARE, *A Midsummer-Night's Dream.* Act iv, sc. 1, l. 204.

18
Where they do agree on the stage, their unanimity is wonderful!
SHERIDAN, *The Critic.* Act ii, sc. 2.

19
To have degenerated into theatrical arts. (Ad theatrales artes degeneravisse.)
TACITUS, *Annals.* Bk. xiv, sec. 21.

20
Come, children, let us shut up the box and the puppets, for our play is played out.
THACKERAY, *Vanity Fair.* Conclusion.

II—Stage: Its Influence

1
Plays make mankind no better, and no worse.
BYRON, *Hints from Horace*, l. 370.

2
A moral expression at the close of a lewd play is much like a pious expression in the mouth of a dying man. . . . The doctor comes too late for the disease and the antidote is much too weak for the poison.
JEREMY COLLIER, *The Immorality of the English Stage.*

3
To me it seems as if when God conceived the world, that was Poetry; He formed it, and that was Sculpture; He colored it, and that was Painting; He peopled it with living beings, and that was the grand, divine, eternal Drama.
CHARLOTTE CUSHMAN. (STEBBINS, *Charlotte Cushman.*)

4
Keen satire is the business of the stage.
GEORGE FARQUHAR, *The Beaux' Stratagem: Prologue*, l. 2.

5
There is nothing but heathenism to be learned from plays.
FIELDING, *Joseph Andrews.* Bk. iii, ch. 11.

6
Life's moving pictures, well-wrought plays,
To others' grief attention raise:
Here, while the tragic fictions glow,
We borrow joy by pitying woe;
There gaily comic scenes delight,
And hold true mirrors to our sight.
MATTHEW GREEN, *The Spleen*, l. 131.

7
Behind the curtain's mystic fold
The glowing future lies unrolled.
BRET HARTE, *Address: Opening of the California Theatre, San Francisco*, 19 Jan., 1870.

8
In all ages the drama, through its portrayal of the acting and suffering spirit of man, has been more closely allied than any other art to his deeper thoughts concerning his nature and his destiny.
LUDWIG LEWISOHN, *The Modern Drama*, p. 1.

9
It hath evermore been the notorious badge of prostituted strumpets and the lewdest Harlots, to ramble abroad to Plays, to Playhouses; whither no honest, chaste or sober Girls or Women, but only branded Whores and infamous Adulteresses, did usually resort in ancient times.
WILLIAM PRYNNE, *Histrio-Mastix.*

That popular Stage-plays are sinful, heathenish, lewd, ungodly Spectacles, and most pernicious Corruptions; condemned in all ages, as intolerable Mischiefs to Churches, to Republics, to the manners, minds and souls of men.
WILLIAM PRYNNE, *Histrio-Mastix.*

10
I have heard
That guilty creatures sitting at a play
Have by the very cunning of the scene
Been struck so to the soul that presently
They have proclaim'd their malefactions.
SHAKESPEARE, *Hamlet.* Act ii, sc. 2, l. 617.

A woman that hath made away her husband,
And sitting to behold a tragedy,
At Lynn, a town in Norfolk,
Acted by players travelling that way,—
Wherein a woman that had murder'd hers
Was ever haunted by her husband's ghost;
The passion written by a feeling hand,
And acted by a good tragedian,—
She was so moved with the sight thereof
As she cried out, "The play was made by her,"
And openly confess'd her husband's murder.
UNKNOWN, *A Warning for Fair Women.* (An Elizabethan drama sometimes ascribed to Shakespeare.)

III—Stage: Plays Good and Bad

11
The growing drama has outgrown such toys
Of simulated stature, face, and speech:
It also peradventure may outgrow
The simulation of the painted scene, . . .
And take for a worthier stage the soul itself,
Its shifting fancies and celestial lights,
With all its grand orchestral silences
To keep the pauses of its rhythmic sounds.
E. B. BROWNING, *Aurora Leigh.* Bk. v, l. 335.

12
We have the challenge of the mighty line—
God grant us grace to give the countersign.
JOHN DRINKWATER, *Lines for the Opening of Birmingham Repertory Theatre.*

13
There is a mode in plays as well as clothes.
DRYDEN, *Rival Ladies: Prologue.*

14
Prologues precede the piece in mournful verse,
As undertakers walk before the hearse.
DAVID GARRICK, *The Apprentice: Prologue.*

Prologues, like compliments, are loss of time;
'Tis penning bows and making legs in rhyme.
GARRICK, *Prologue to Crisp's Virginia.*

If it be true that good wine needs no bush, 'tis true that a good play needs no epilogue.
SHAKESPEARE, *As You Like It: Epilogue*, l. 3.

14a
The observance or violation of the three unities of time, place, and action.
HAZLITT, *Table Talk.* Essay 22.

The unities, sir [said Mr. Curdle], are a completeness—a kind of a universal dovetailedness with regard to place and time—a sort of a general oneness. . . . I take those to be the dramatic unities, so far as I have been enabled to bestow attention upon them.
DICKENS, *Nicholas Nickleby.* Ch. 24.

15
If you fashion a fresh character, have it kept

to the end as it was in the beginning, consistent with itself. (Personam formare novam, servetur ad imum, qualis ad incepto processerit, et sibi constet.)

HORACE, *Ars Poetica*, l. 126. Of play-writing.

Nor let Medea slaughter her children in the sight of the audience. (Nec pueros coram populo Medea trucidet.)

HORACE, *Ars Poetica*, l. 185.

1
The last act crowns the play.

FRANCIS QUARLES, *Respice Finem*. (*Emblems*. Bk. i, No. 15.) See 1125:5.

The first Act's doubtful, but we say
It is the last commends the Play.

ROBERT HERRICK, *The Plaudite*.

Act first, this Earth, a stage so gloom'd with woe
You all but sicken at the shifting scenes.
And yet be patient. Our Playwright may show
In some fifth act what this wild Drama means.

TENNYSON, *The Play*.

ALL THE WORLD'S A STAGE, *see under* WORLD.

2
Theseus: Is there no play
To ease the anguish of a torturing hour? . . .
Philostrate: A play there is, my lord, some ten words long,
Which is as brief as I have known a play;
But by ten words, my lord, it is too long,
Which makes it tedious; for in all the play
There is not one word apt, one player fitted.

SHAKESPEARE, *A Midsummer-Night's Dream*. Act v, sc. 1, l. 61.

3
Through all the drama—whether damn'd or not—
Love gilds the scene, and women guide the plot.

R. B. SHERIDAN, *The Rivals: Epilogue*, l. 5.

4
Lo, where the Stage, the poor, degraded Stage,
Holds its warped mirror to a gaping age!

CHARLES SPRAGUE, *Curiosity*, l. 127.

5
What are the plays of to-day? There're either so chock-full of intellect that they send you to sleep,—or they reek of sentiment till you yearn for the smell of a cabbage.

ALFRED SUTRO, *The Man in the Stalls*.

IV—Stage: Comedy and Tragedy

6
A perfect Tragedy is the noblest production of human nature.

ADDISON, *The Spectator*. No. 39.

7
Your true right tragedy is enacted on the stage of a man's soul, and with the man's reason as lone auditor.

BRANCH CABELL, *Cream of the Jest*, p. 236.

8
A talent for comedy equal to that of the Greeks. (Comica ut æquato virtus polleret honore Cum Græcis.)

GAIUS CÆSAR, referring to Terence. (SUETONIUS, *Lives: Terence*. Sec. 5.)

9
And Tragedy should blush as much to stoop
To the low mimic follies of a farce,
As a grave matron would to dance with girls.

HORACE, *Ars Poetica*, l. 272. (Dillon, tr.)

10
You know the rites to jocund Flora dear,
The festive quips and licence of the rout;
Why on the scene, stern Cato, enter here?
Did you then enter only to go out?
(Nosses jocosæ dulce cum sacrum Floræ
Festosque lusus et licentiam volgi,
Cur in theatrum, Cato severe, venisti?
An ideo tantum veneras, ut exires?)

MARTIAL, *Epigrams:* Bk. i, *Introduction*. The reference is to a story told by Valerius Maximus (ii, x, 8) to the effect that at the Floralia in 55 B. C., Cato left the theatre on finding that his presence checked the licence of the actors.

11
The theatre is no place for painful speculation; it is a place for diverting representation.

H. L. MENCKEN, *Prejudices*. Ser. i, p. 201.

12
Attic tragedies of stateliest and most regal argument.

MILTON, *Tractate of Education*.

13
A long, exact, and serious comedy;
In ev'ry scene some moral let it teach,
And, if it can, at once both please and preach.

POPE, *Epistle to Miss Blount*, l. 22.

What dear delight to Britons farce affords!
Ever the taste of mobs, but now of lords.

POPE, *Imitations of Horace: Epistles*. Bk. ii, epis. 1, l. 310.

A comedy is often only a farce—by a deceased dramatist.

ARTHUR WING PINERO.

14
As in comedies, where all the characters find out everything. (Ut in comœdiis Omnia omnes ubi resciscunt.)

TERENCE, *Hecyra*, l. 866. (Act v, sc. 4.)

Pat he comes like the catastrophe of the old comedy.

SHAKESPEARE, *King Lear*. Act i, sc. 1, l. 147.

V—Stage: The Audience

15
"Do you come to the play without knowing what it is?" "O, yes, Sir, yes, very frequently. I have no time to read play-bills. One merely comes to meet one's friends, and show that one's alive."

FANNY BURNEY, *Evelina*. Letter 20.

16
Some very foolish influence rules the pit,
Not always kind to sense, or just to wit.

DRYDEN, *Epistles: To Mr. Southerne*, l. 3.

There still remains, to mortify a wit,
The many-headed monster of the pit.

POPE, *Imitations of Horace: Epistles*. Bk. ii, epis. 1, l. 304.

1
Like hungry guests, a sitting audience looks:
Plays are like suppers: poets are the cooks.
The founder's you: the table is this place:
The carvers we: the prologue is the grace.
Each act, a course; each scene, a different dish.
FARQUHAR, *The Inconstant: Prologue*, l. 1.

When first upon the stage a play appears
'Tis not the multitude a poet fears,
Who, from example, praise or damn by rote,
And give their censure as some members vote.
But if in the expecting box or pit
The wretch discerns one true, substantial wit,
Tow'rds him his doubtful sight he'll still direct,
Whose very looks can all his faults detect.
ANNE FINCH, COUNTESS OF WINCHILSEA, *Aristomenes: Prologue*, l. 1.

2
The stage but echoes back the public voice;
The drama's laws, the drama's patrons give,
For we that live to please, must please to live.
SAMUEL JOHNSON, *Prologue at the Opening of the Drury Lane Theatre*, l. 52.

3
Would you were come to hear, not see a play. . . .
The maker . . . he'd have you wise,
Much rather by your ears than by your eyes.
BEN JONSON, *The Staple of News: Prologue.*

4
I don't think the audience noticed it.
GEORGE KELLY, *The Torch-Bearers.* Act ii.

5
Fit audience find, though few.
MILTON, *Paradise Lost.* Bk. vii, l. 31.

6
'Tis ten to one this play can never please
All that are here: some come to take their ease,
And sleep an act or two; . . . others to hear the city
Abused extremely, and to cry "That's witty!"
SHAKESPEARE, *Henry VIII: Epilogue*, l. 1.

7
In other things the knowing artist may
Judge better than the people; but a play,
(Made for delight, and for no other use)
If you approve it not, has no excuse.
EDMUND WALLER, *The Maid's Tragedy: Prologue*, l. 35.

STARS

I—Stars: Definitions

8
What are ye orbs?
The words of God? the Scriptures of the skies?
P. J. BAILEY, *Festus: Everywhere.*

9
The pale populace of Heaven.
ROBERT BROWNING, *Balaustion's Adventure*, l. 205.

10
Ah! the lamps numberless,
The mystical jewels of God,
The luminous, wonderful,
Beautiful lights of the Veil!
ROBERT BUCHANAN, *Book of Orm: First Song.*

11
Flowers of the sky! ye, too, to age must yield,
Frail as your silken sisters of the field!
ERASMUS DARWIN, *Economy of Vegetation.* Canto iv.

Silently one by one, in the infinite meadows of heaven,
Blossomed the lovely stars, the forget-me-nots of the angels.
LONGFELLOW, *Evangeline.* Pt. i, sec. 3.

Stars are the Daisies that begem
The blue fields of the sky,
Beheld by all and everywhere,
Bright prototypes on high.
DAVID MACBETH MOIR, *The Daisy.* St. 5.

Wide are the meadows of night
And daisies are shining there,
Tossing their lovely dews,
Lustrous and fair;
And through these sweet fields go,
Wanderers amid the stars—
Venus, Mercury, Uranus, Neptune,
Saturn, Jupiter, Mars.
WALTER DE LA MARE, *The Wanderers.*

12
The stars are golden fruit upon a tree
All out of reach.
GEORGE ELIOT, *The Spanish Gypsy.* Bk. ii.

13
Let there be lights in the firmament of the heaven to divide the day from the night.
Old Testament: Genesis, i, 14.

14
The stars, bright sentinels of the skies.
WILLIAM HABINGTON, *Dialogue between Night and Araphil*, l. 3. (c. 1630)

The stars, heav'n sentry, wink and seem to die.
NATHANIEL LEE, *Theodosius.* (c. 1680)

And the sentinel stars set their watch in the sky.
THOMAS CAMPBELL, *The Soldier's Dream.* (1805)

The quenchless stars, so eloquently bright,
Untroubled sentries of the shadow'y night.
ROBERT MONTGOMERY, *Omnipresence of the Deity.* (1828)

15
The stars
That nature hung in Heav'n, and fill'd their lamps
With everlasting oil, to give due light
To the misled and lonely traveller.
MILTON, *Comus*, l. 197.

And made the stars,
And set them in the firmament of Heav'n
T' illuminate the earth, and rule the day
In their vicissitude, and rule the night.
MILTON, *Paradise Lost.* Bk. vii, l. 348.

Who rounded in his palm these spacious orbs. . .
Numerous as glittering gems of morning dew,
Or sparks from populous cities in a blaze,

And set the bosom of old night on fire?
YOUNG, *Night Thoughts*. Night ix, l. 1275.

1
There's husbandry in heaven;
Their candles are all out.
SHAKESPEARE, *Macbeth*. Act ii, sc. 1, l. 4.

These blessed candles of the night.
SHAKESPEARE, *The Merchant of Venice*. Act v, sc. 1, l. 220.

The burning tapers of the sky.
SHAKESPEARE, *Titus Andronicus*. Act iv, sc. 2, l. 89.

2
The stars are mansions built by Nature's hand,
And, haply, there the spirits of the blest
Dwell, clothed in radiance, their immortal vest.
WORDSWORTH, *Sonnets*. Pt. ii, Sonnet 25.

Brightest seraph, tell
In which of all these shining orbs hath man
His fixed seat, or fixed seat hath none,
But all these shining orbs his choice to dwell.
MILTON, *Paradise Lost*. Bk. iii, l. 667.

3
'Tis Nature's system of divinity,
And every student of the night inspires.
'Tis elder scripture, writ by God's own hand:
Scripture authentic! uncorrupt by man.
YOUNG, *Night Thoughts*. Night ix, l. 642.

II—Stars: Apothegms

4
There be more stars, God wot, than a pair.
CHAUCER, *Parlement of Foules*, l. 595.

Two stars keep not their motion in one sphere.
SHAKESPEARE, *I Henry IV*. Act v, sc. 4, l. 65.

5
Hast thou a charm to stay the morning-star?
S. T. COLERIDGE, *Hymn Before Sun-rise in the Vale of Chamouni*, l. 1.

6
And yet more light
Shines out the Julian star,
As moon outglows each lesser light.
(Micat inter omnes
Iulium sidus, velut inter ignes
Luna minores.)
HORACE, *Odes*. Bk. i, ode 12, l. 47.

Led by the light of the Mæonian star.
POPE, *Essay on Criticism*. Pt. iii, l. 89.

7
And all the spangled host keep watch in squadrons bright.
MILTON, *On the Morning of Christ's Nativity*, l. 21.

The planets in their stations list'ning stood.
MILTON, *Paradise Lost*. Bk. vii, l. 563.

8
The starry cope Of Heav'n.
MILTON, *Paradise Lost*. Bk. iv, l. 992.

Heaven's ebon vault
Studded with stars unutterably bright.
SHELLEY, *Queen Mab*. Pt. iv, l. 4.

9
There is no easy road from the earth to the stars. (Non est ad astra mollis e terris via.)
SENECA, *Hercules Furens*, l. 437.

Through hardship to the stars. (Per aspera ad astra.)
A proverbial phrase probably derived from Seneca. Motto of the State of Kansas.

Thus is accomplished the journey to the stars. (Sic itur ad astra.)
VERGIL, *Æneid*. Bk. ix, l. 641.

10
He that strives to touch the stars,
Oft stumbles at a straw.
SPENSER, *Shepheardes Calender, July*, l. 99.

11
Nothing is fixed, that mortals see or know,
Unless perhaps some stars be so.
SWIFT, *Ode: Dr. Wm. Sancroft*.

Bright Star! would I were steadfast as thou art!
JOHN KEATS, *Last Sonnet*.

12
Twinkle, twinkle, little star!
How I wonder what you are,
Up above the world so high,
Like a diamond in the sky!
ANN TAYLOR, *The Star*.

13
Too low they build, who build beneath the stars.
YOUNG, *Night Thoughts*. Night viii, l. 215.

Hitch your wagon to a star.
EMERSON, *Society and Solitude: Civilization*. *For full quotation, see under* ASPIRATION.

14
Though my soul may set in darkness, it will rise in perfect light;
I have loved the stars too fondly to be fearful of the night.
UNKNOWN, *An Old Astronomer to His Pupil*. (Galileo) Originally published in *Morning Sky Map*. Oct., 1920.

We have loved the stars too fondly to be fearful of the night.
Inscription on slab covering the ashes of John and Phœbe Brashear, in the crypt of the observatory at Allegheny, Pa., where they labored together for many years.

III—Stars: Their Beauty

15
The Spacious Firmament on high,
With all the blue Ethereal sky,
And spangled Heav'ns, a shining Frame,
Their great Original proclaim.
ADDISON, *Ode*. (*The Spectator*. No. 465. 23 Aug., 1712. Suggested by the 19th *Psalm*. See 1834:18.)

In Reason's ear they all rejoice,
And utter forth a glorious voice;
For ever singing as they shine,
"The Hand that made us is divine."
ADDISON, *Ode*.

16
And you, ye stars,

Who slowly begin to marshal,
As of old, in the fields of heaven,
Your distant, melancholy lines!
MATTHEW ARNOLD, *Empedocles on Etna*, l. 276.

1
The stars,
Which stand as thick as dewdrops on the fields
Of heaven.
P. J. BAILEY, *Festus: Heaven.*

2
Behind the western bars
The shrouded day retreats,
And unperceived the stars
Steal to their sovran seats.
ROBERT BRIDGES, *The Clouds Have Left the Sky.*

3
Sky—what a scowl of cloud
Till, near and far,
Ray on ray split the shroud:
Splendid, a star!
ROBERT BROWNING, *Two Poets of Croisic*, l. 5.

4
The sad and solemn Night
Hath yet her multitude of cheerful fires;
The glorious host of light.
BRYANT, *Hymn to the North Star*, l. 1.

The number is certainly the cause. The apparent disorder augments the grandeur, for the appearance of care is highly contrary to our idea of magnificence. Besides, the stars lie in such apparent confusion, as makes it impossible on ordinary occasions to reckon them. This gives them the advantage of a sort of infinity.
EDMUND BURKE, *On the Sublime and the Beautiful: Magnificence.*

5
Every sphere
That gems the starry girdle of the year.
CAMPBELL, *Pleasures of Hope*. Pt. ii, l. 193.

6
There is one glory of the sun, and another glory of the moon, and another glory of the stars; for one star differeth from another star in glory.
New Testament: I Corinthians, xv, 41.

The stars that have most glory, have no rest.
SAMUEL DANIEL, *History of the Civil War.* Bk. viii, st. 104.

7
Teach me your mood, O patient stars!
Who climb each night the ancient sky,
Leaving on space no shade, no scars,
No trace of age, no fear to die.
RALPH WALDO EMERSON, *The Poet.*

8
Two things fill the mind with ever new and increasing wonder and awe—the starry heavens above me and the moral law within me.
IMMANUEL KANT, *Critique of Pure Reason: Conclusion.* See also 1345:5.

No sight that the human eyes can look upon is more provocative of awe than is the night sky scattered thick with stars.
LLEWELYN POWYS, *Impassioned Clay*, p. 6.

9
But when eve's silent footfall steals
Along the eastern sky,
And one by one to earth reveals
Those purer fires on high.
JOHN KEBLE, *The Christian Year: Fourth Sunday after Trinity.*

God be thanked for the Milky Way that runs across the sky.
That's the path that my feet would tread whenever I have to die.
Some folks call it a Silver Sword, and some a Pearly Crown.
But the only thing I think it is, is Main Street, Heaventown.
JOYCE KILMER, *Main Street.*

The stars come forth to listen
To the music of the sea.
LONGFELLOW, *The Golden Legend*. Pt. v, *The Inn at Genoa*, l. 55.

Then stars arise, and the night is holy.
LONGFELLOW, *Hyperion*. Bk. i, ch. 1.

10
And also there's a little star
So white a virgin's it must be:—
Perhaps the lamp my love in heaven
Hangs out to light the way for me.
THÉOPHILE MARZIALS, *Song.*

11
But soon, the prospect clearing,
By cloudless starlight on he treads,
And thinks no lamp so cheering
As that light which Heaven sheds.
THOMAS MOORE, *I'd Mourn the Hopes.*

12
The skies are painted with unnumber'd sparks,
They are all fire and every one doth shine,
But there 's but one in all doth hold his place.
SHAKESPEARE, *Julius Cæsar*. Act iii, sc. 1, l. 63.

Look how the floor of heaven
Is thick inlaid with patines of bright gold.
SHAKESPEARE, *The Merchant of Venice*. Act v, sc. 1, l. 58.

13
Each separate star
Seems nothing but a myriad scattered stars
Break up the Night, and make it beautiful.
BAYARD TAYLOR, *Lars*. Bk. iii, conclusion.

14
When the stars pitch the golden tents
Of their high encampment on the plains of night.
FRANCIS THOMPSON, *To a Child Heard Repeating Her Mother's Verses.*

With battlements that on their restless fronts
Bore stars.
WORDSWORTH, *The Excursion*. Bk. ii, l. 844.

15
The twilight hours, like birds flew by,
As lightly and as free;
Ten thousand stars were in the sky,
Ten thousand on the sea.

For every wave with dimpled face
That leap'd upon the air,
Had caught a star in its embrace
And held it trembling there.
AMELIA C. WELBY, *Twilight at Sea*. St. 4.

I was thinking the day most splendid till I saw what the not-day exhibited;
I was thinking this globe enough till there sprang out so noiseless around me myriads of other globes.
WALT WHITMAN, *Night on the Prairies.*

1
Though wise men come not, nor angels sing,
Still the stars shine for comforting.
MARGARET WIDDEMER, *Stars.*

IV—Stars: Their Influence

2
Is there not
A tongue in every star that talks with man,
And wooes him to be wise?
ANNA LETITIA BARBAULD, *A Summer Evening's Meditation,* l. 48.

3
No star ever rose
And set, without influence somewhere.
OWEN MEREDITH, *Lucile*. Pt. ii, canto vi, sec. 40.

4
This hairy meteor did announce
The fall of sceptres and of crowns.
BUTLER, *Hudibras*. Pt. i, canto i, l. 247.

As shaking terrors from his blazing hair,
A sanguine comet gleams through dusky air.
TASSO, *Jerusalem Delivered,* l. 581. (Hoole, tr.)

The stars shall be rent into threds of light,
And scatter'd like the beards of comets.
JEREMY TAYLOR, *Christ's Advent to Judgement.*

5
Cry out upon the stars for doing
Ill offices, to cross their wooing.
BUTLER, *Hudibras*. Pt. iii, canto i, l. 17.

6
Ye stars! which are the poetry of Heaven!
If in your bright leaves we would read the fate
Of men and empires,—'tis to be forgiven,
That in our aspirations to be great,
Our destinies o'erleap their mortal state,
And claim a kindred with you; for ye are
A beauty and a mystery, and create
In us such love and reverence from afar,
That fortune, fame, power, life, have named themselves a star.
BYRON, *Childe Harold*. Canto iii, st. 88.

So may we read, and little find them cold:
Not frosty lamps illumining dead space,
Not distant aliens, not senseless Powers.
The fire is in them whereof we are born;
The music of their motion may be ours.
GEORGE MEREDITH, *Meditation under Stars,* 5.

7
The stars rule men but God rules the stars.
(Astra regunt homines, sed regit astra Deus.)
CELLARIUS, *Harmonica Macrocosmica: Preface.* (1661)

8
Canst thou bind the sweet influences of Pleiades, or loose the bands of Orion?
Old Testament: Job, xxxviii, 31.

Canst thou guide Arcturus with his sons?
Old Testament: Job, xxxviii, 32.

9
The stars in their courses fought against Sisera.
Old Testament: Judges, v, 20.

10
Thus some, who have the stars survey'd,
Are ignorantly led
To think those glorious lamps were made
To light Tom Fool to bed.
NICHOLAS ROWE, *On a Fine Woman Who Had a Dull Husband.*

This is the excellent foppery of the world, that, when we are sick in fortune,—often the surfeit of our own behaviour,—we make guilty of our disasters the sun, the moon, and the stars: as if we were villains by necessity; fools by heavenly compulsion; knaves, thieves, and treachers, by spherical predominance; drunkards, liars, and adulterers by an enforced obedience of planetary influence; and all that we are evil in, by a divine thrusting on: an admirable evasion whoremaster of man, to lay his goatish disposition to the charge of a star!
SHAKESPEARE, *King Lear*. Act i, sc. 2, l. 128.

11
When Princes meet, astrologers may mark it
An ominous conjunction, full of boding,
Like that of Mars with Saturn.
SCOTT, *Quentin Durward*. Ch. 31. Quoted as from "An old play."

12
Eat, speak, and move, under the influence of the most received star; and though the devil lead the measure, such are to be followed.
SHAKESPEARE, *All's Well that Ends Well.* Act ii, sc. 1, l. 56.

The stars above us govern our conditions.
SHAKESPEARE, *King Lear*. Act iv, sc. 3, l. 35.

A breath thou art,
Servile to all the skyey influences.
SHAKESPEARE, *Measure for Measure.* Act iii, sc. 1, l. 9.

There's some ill planet reigns:
I must be patient till the heavens look
With an aspect more favourable.
SHAKESPEARE, *Winter's Tale*. Act ii, sc. 1, l. 105.

12a
A man gazing at the stars is proverbially at the mercy of the puddles on the road.
ALEXANDER SMITH, *Dreamthorp: Men of Letters.*

13
But who can count the stars of heaven?
Who sing their influence on this lower world?
THOMSON, *The Seasons: Winter,* l. 528.

V—Stars: Morning and Evening

14
Star that bringest home the bee,

And sett'st the weary labourer free!
THOMAS CAMPBELL, *Song to the Evening Star.*

1
The morning stars sang together, and all the sons of God shouted for joy.
Old Testament: Job, xxxviii, 7.

2
There is no light in earth or heaven
But the cold light of stars;
And the first watch of night is given
To the red planet Mars.
LONGFELLOW, *The Light of Stars.* St. 2.

3
The star that bids the shepherd fold,
Now the top of Heav'n doth hold.
MILTON, *Comus,* l. 93.

Oft till the star that rose, at ev'ning bright,
Toward Heav'n's descent had slop'd his westering wheel.
MILTON, *Lycidas,* l. 30.

So sinks the day-star in the ocean bed
MILTON, *Lycidas,* l. 168.

Th' evening star, Love's harbinger.
MILTON, *Paradise Lost.* Bk. xi, l. 584.

Fairest of stars, last in the train of night,
If better thou belong not to the dawn,
Sure pledge of day.
MILTON, *Paradise Lost.* Bk. v, l. 166.

4
Hither, as to their fountain, other stars
Repairing, in their golden urns draw light,
And hence the morning planet gilds his horns.
MILTON, *Paradise Lost.* Bk. vii, l. 364.

5
And the daystar arise in your hearts.
New Testament: II Peter, i, 19.

6
Hesperus bringing together
All that the morning star scattered.
SAPPHO, *Fragments.* No. 14. (Carman, tr.)

7
Look, the unfolding star calls up the shepherd.
SHAKESPEARE, *Measure for Measure.* Act iv, sc. 2, l. 219.

8
That full star that ushers in the even.
SHAKESPEARE, *Sonnets.* No. cxxxii.

9
Many a night from yonder ivied casement, ere I went to rest,
Did I look on great Orion sloping slowly to the west.
TENNYSON, *Locksley Hall,* l. 7.

Many a night I saw the Pleiads, rising thro' the mellow shade,
Glitter like a swarm of fireflies tangled in a silver braid.
TENNYSON, *Locksley Hall,* l. 9.

VI—Stars: "My Star"

10
What matter to me if their star is a world?
Mine has opened its soul to me; therefore I love it.
ROBERT BROWNING, *My Star.*

My star, God's glow-worm!
ROBERT BROWNING, *Popularity.*

11
I await my star. (J'attends mon astre.)
CARLO ALBERTO, *King of Sardinia.* Adopted as the motto of his house, the House of Savoy. When Victor Emmanuel opened the first parliament in Rome, Nov., 1871, the common people peered all day into an unclouded sky searching for the Star of Savoy.

12
"If thou," he answered, "follow but thy star,
Thou canst not miss at last a glorious haven."
(Ed egli a me: "Se tu segui tua stella,
Non puoi fallire al glorioso porto."
DANTE, *Inferno.* Canto xv, l. 55. (Cary, tr.)

Courage, brother! do not stumble,
Though thy path be dark as night;
There's a star to guide the humble,
Trust in God and do the Right.
NORMAN MACLEOD, *Trust in God.*

13
A man must stoop sometimes to his star, but he must never lie down to it.
LORD HALIFAX, *Works,* p. 238.

14
My good stars, that were my former guides,
Have empty left their orbs, and shot their fires
Into the abysm of hell.
SHAKESPEARE, *Antony and Cleopatra.* Act iii, sc. 13, l. 145.

15
What different lots our stars accord!
This babe to be hail'd and woo'd as a Lord!
And that to be shunned like a leper!
One, to the world's wine, honey, and corn,
Another, like Colchester native, born
To its vinegar, only, and pepper.
THOMAS HOOD, *Miss Kilmansegg: Her Birth,* l. 93.

16
Our Jovial star reign'd at his birth.
SHAKESPEARE, *Cymbeline.* Act v, sc. 4, l. 105.

I find my zenith doth depend upon
A most auspicious star, whose influence
If now I court not but omit, my fortunes
Will ever after droop.
SHAKESPEARE, *The Tempest.* Act i, sc. 2, l. 181.

17
Grapples with his evil star.
TENNYSON, *In Memoriam.* Sec. lxiv.

VII—Stars and Love

18
Surely the stars are images of love.
P. J. BAILEY, *Festus: Garden and Bower by the Sea.*

19
When stars are in the quiet skies,
Then most I pine for thee;
Bend on me then thy tender eyes,
As stars look on the sea.
BULWER-LYTTON, *When Stars Are in the Quiet Skies.*

1
The stars of the night
Will lend thee their light,
Like tapers clear without number.
ROBERT HERRICK, *The Night-Piece to Julia.*

2
When sunset flows into golden glows,
And the breath of the night is new,
Love finds afar eve's eager star—
That is my thought of you.
ROBERT UNDERWOOD JOHNSON, *Star Song.*

3
Stars of the summer night!
Far in yon azure deeps
Hide, hide your golden light!
She sleeps! My lady sleeps!
LONGFELLOW, *The Spanish Student: Serenade.* Act i, sc. 3.

4
When twilight dews are falling soft
Upon the rosy sea, love,
I watch the star, whose beam so oft
Has lighted me to thee, love.
THOMAS MOORE, *When Twilight Dews.*

5
Thou lookest on the stars, my Star? Would I were heaven, to look on thee with many eyes! ('Αστέρας εἰσαθρεῖς ἀστὴρ ἐμός. εἴθε γενοίμην Οὐρανός, ὡς πολλοῖς ὄμμασιν εἰς σὲ βλέπω.)
PLATO. (*Greek Anthology.* Bk. vii, epig. 669.)

Or soar aloft to be the Spangled Skies
And gaze upon her with a thousand eyes!
S. T. COLERIDGE, *Lines: On an Autumnal Evening,* l. 69.

O that my spirit were yon heaven of night,
Which gazes on thee with its thousand eyes.
SHELLEY, *The Revolt of Islam.* Canto ix, st. 36.

6
Her blue eyes sought the west afar,
For lovers love the western star.
SCOTT, *The Lay of the Last Minstrel.* Canto iii, st. 24.

VIII—Stars and Science

7
The starry Galileo, with his woes.
BYRON, *Childe Harold.* Canto iv, st. 54.

8
Oh never star
Was lost here but it rose afar.
ROBERT BROWNING, *Waring.* Pt. ii.

No star is ever lost we once have seen,
We always may be what we might have been.
ADELAIDE ANN PROCTER, *A Legend of Provence.*

And like a fiery planet mount and burn.
N. P. WILLIS, *Parrhasius.*

9
Like the lost pleiad seen no more below.
BYRON, *Beppo.* St. 14.

Why, who shall talk of thrones, of sceptres riven?
Bowed be our hearts to think of what *we* are,
When from its height afar
A world sinks thus—and yon majestic heaven
Shines not the less for that one vanished star!
FELICIA DOROTHEA HEMANS, *The Lost Pleiad.* The line from Byron quoted above is used as a motto for this poem.

All for Love, or the Lost Pleiad.
STIRLING COYNE. Title of play, produced in London, 16 Jan., 1838.

10
A wise man,
Watching the stars pass across the sky,
Remarked:
In the upper air the fireflies move more slowly.
AMY LOWELL, *Meditation.*

11
Around the ancient track marched, rank on rank,
The army of unalterable law.
GEORGE MEREDITH, *Lucifer in Starlight.*

The stars of heaven are free because
In amplitude of liberty
Their joy is to obey the laws.
WILLIAM WATSON, *The Things That Are More Excellent.* St. 4.

13
At night astronomers agree.
MATTHEW PRIOR, *Phillis's Age.* St. 3.

Devotion! Daughter of astronomy!
An undevout astronomer is mad.
YOUNG, *Night Thoughts.* Night ix, l. 770.

14
These earthly godfathers of heaven's lights
That give a name to every fixed star
Have no more profit of their shining nights
Than those that walk and know not what they are.
SHAKESPEARE, *Love's Labour's Lost.* Act i, sc. 1, l. 88.

STATE

See also Government, Nation

15
Not stones, nor timber, nor the art of building constitute a state; but wherever men are who know how to defend themselves, there is a city and a fortress.
ALCÆUS, *Ode.* Fragment. (ARISTIDES, *Orations.* Vol. ii.) Only a single line remains of the ode, of which Aristides gives this summary: Fighting men are the city's walls.

What constitutes a State?
Not high-crown'd battlement or labour'd mound,
Thick wall or moated gate;
Not cities proud with spires and turrets crown'd; . . .
No:—men, high-minded men, . . .
Men who their duties know,
But know their rights, and, knowing, dare maintain . . .
These constitute a State.
SIR WILLIAM JONES, *An Ode in Imitation of Alcæus. See also under* CITY.

The noble spirit of the metropolis is the life-blood of the state, collected at the heart.
JUNIUS, *Letters.* No. 37, 19 Mar., 1770.

1
States, as great engines, move slowly.
BACON, *Advancement of Learning*. Bk. ii.

2
A thousand years scarce serve to form a state;
An hour may lay it in the dust.
BYRON, *Childe Harold*. Canto ii, st. 84.

3
Ah me! what mighty perils wait
The man who meddles with a State.
CHARLES CHURCHILL, *The Duellist*. Bk. iii, st. 1.

4
Better one suffer, than a nation grieve.
DRYDEN, *Absalom and Achitophel*. Pt. i, l. 416.

But what's one woman's fortune more or less
Beside the schemes of kings!
THOMAS HARDY, *The Dynasts*. Part ii, vi, 3.

It was only one life. What is one life in the affairs of a state?
BENITO MUSSOLINI. (GENERAL SMEDLEY E. BUTLER, *Address*, before the Contemporary Club, Phila., 19 Jan., 1931.) The Navy Department ordered General Butler court-martialed for making this speech, in which he accused Mussolini of not stopping when his automobile ran down a child, but the order was afterwards countermanded. Mussolini denied that such an incident had ever occurred.

I heard a shriek, . . . a shapeless little form lying in the road back of us. "Look, Your Excellency!" I cried. "Never look back, my friend, always look forward," he [Mussolini] answered without turning, and we roared ahead.
CORNELIUS VANDERBILT, JR., *Farewell to Fifth Avenue*, p. 163.

5
To educate the wise man, the State exists; and with the appearance of the wise man, the State expires.
EMERSON, *Essays, Second Series: Politics*.

6
The men are ripe of Saxon kind
To build an equal state—
To take the statute from the mind,
And make of duty fate.
RALPH WALDO EMERSON, *Ode*.

7
A State is never greater than when all its superfluous hands are employed in the service of the public.
DAVID HUME, *Essays: Of Commerce*.

8
The incredible cunning of the monstrous plan
Whereby the spider State has set its web for Man.
R. U. JOHNSON, *The Crowned Republic*.

9
States, like men, have their growth, their manhood, their decrepitude, their decay.
W. S. LANDOR, *Imaginary Conversations: Pollio and Calvus*.

All empires die of indigestion.
NAPOLEON BONAPARTE, *Sayings of Napoleon*.

9a
While the state exists there is no freedom; when there is freedom there will be no state.
LENIN, *The State and Revolution*, p. 79. (International Publishers.)

10
Here pulling down, and there erecting new.
Founding a firm state by proportions true.
ANDREW MARVELL, *The First Anniversary*.

States are not made, nor patched; they grow,
Grow slow through centuries of pain,
And grow correctly in the main.
MASEFIELD, *The Everlasting Mercy*. St. 60.

11
The worth of a State in the long run is the worth of the individuals composing it.
JOHN STUART MILL, *On Liberty*. Ch. 5.

12
The state is the association of men, and not men themselves; the citizen may perish, and the man remain.
MONTESQUIEU, *Spirit of the Laws*. Bk. x, ch. 3.

13
The State and the family are for ever at war.
GEORGE MOORE, *The Bending of the Bough*. Act i.

14
State, but a golden prison, to live in,
And torture free-born minds.
SIR WALTER RALEIGH, *A Farewell to the Vanities of the World*.

15
Something is rotten in the state of Denmark.
SHAKESPEARE, *Hamlet*. Act i, sc. 4, l. 90.

16
Cares of state.
SHAKESPEARE, *King Lear*. Act i, sc. 1, l. 51.

17
The state has nothing whatever to do with theological errors which do not violate the common rules of morality.
SYDNEY SMITH, *Peter Plymley Letters*. No. 1.

18
For as, of all the ways of life, but one—
The path of duty—leads to happiness;
So in their duty States must find at length
Their welfare, and their safety, and their strength.
ROBERT SOUTHEY, *Carmen Nuptiale*. St. 65.

19
Chiefs are mortal, the commonwealth is eternal. (Principes mortales, rempublicam æternam.)
TACITUS, *Annals*. Bk. iii, sec. 6.

Individuals pass like shadows; but the commonwealth is fixed and eternal.
EDMUND BURKE, *Speech*, House of Commons, 11 Feb., 1780.

STATESMAN

See also Government, Politics

20
A constitutional statesman is in general a

man of common opinions and uncommon abilities.

WALTER BAGEHOT, *Biographical Studies*, p. 2.

1

It is strange so great a statesman should
Be so sublime a poet.

BULWER-LYTTON, *Richelieu*. Act i, sc. 2.

2

A disposition to preserve, and an ability to improve, taken together, would be my standard of a statesman.

EDMUND BURKE, *Reflections on the Revolution in France*.

The three ends which a statesman ought to propose to himself in the government of a nation, are—1. Security to possessors; 2. Facility to acquirers; and 3. Hope to all.

S. T. COLERIDGE, *Table Talk*, 25 June, 1831.

3

Who's in or out, who moves this grand machine,
Nor stirs my curiosity nor spleen:
Secrets of state no more I wish to know
Than secret movements of a puppet-show:
Let but the puppets move, I've my desire,
Unseen the hand which guides the master-wire.

CHARLES CHURCHILL, *Night*, l. 257.

4

Most statesmen have long noses, which is very lucky because most of them cannot see further than the length of them.

Attributed to PAUL CLAUDEL in the *Golden Book*, July, 1930, but disclaimed by him in a letter to the compiler.

5

The disencumber'd Atlas of the state.

COWPER, *Retirement*, l. 394.

6

Statesmen are always sick of one disease,
And a good pension gives them present ease:
That's the specific makes them all content
With any king and any government.

DANIEL DEFOE, *The True-Born Englishman: Introduction*.

7

The world is wearied of statesmen whom democracy has degraded into politicians.

BENJAMIN DISRAELI, *Lothair*. Ch. 17.

A statesman makes the occasion, but the occasion makes the politician.

G. S. HILLARD, *Life and Services of Daniel Webster*.

A statesman is a successful politician who is dead.

THOMAS B. REED. (LODGE, *The Democracy of the Constitution*, p. 191.) Senator Henry Cabot Lodge, in a magazine article, told the story of the editor who thereupon telegraphed Reed, "Why don't you die and become a statesman?" To which Reed wired back, "No; fame is the last infirmity of a noble mind."

8

His life has been one great Appropriation Clause. He is a burglar of others' intellects. . . . There is no statesman who has committed political petty larceny on so great a scale.

BENJAMIN DISRAELI, *Speech*, 15 May. 1846, referring to Sir Robert Peel.

9

Art thou a statesman,
And canst not be a hypocrite? Impossible!
Do not distrust thy virtues.

DRYDEN, *Don Sebastian*. Act ii, sc. 1.

10

It is the duty of a minister to stand like a wall of adamant between the people and the sovereign.

GLADSTONE, *Speech*, at Garston, 14 Nov., 1868.

11

There is one statesman of the present day of whom I always say that he would have escaped making the blunders that he has made if he had only ridden more in omnibuses.

SIR ARTHUR HELPS, *Friends in Council*. Ser. ii, ch. 17.

12

D'ye think that statesmen's kindnesses proceed
From any principles but their own need?

SIR ROBERT HOWARD, *The Vestal Virgin*.

A ginooine statesman should be on his guard,
Ef he *must hev* beliefs, not to b'lieve 'em tu hard.

J. R. LOWELL, *Biglow Papers*. Ser. ii, No. 5.

13

In them is plainest taught, and easiest learnt,
What makes a Nation happy, and keeps it so,
What ruins Kingdoms, and lays Cities flat.

MILTON, *Paradise Regained*. Bk. iv, l. 361. Referring to the great statesmen of England.

14

The minds of some of our statesmen, like the pupil of the human eye, contract themselves the more, the stronger light is shed upon them.

THOMAS MOORE, *Corruption and Intolerance: Preface*.

15

You can always get the truth from an American statesman after he has turned seventy, or given up all hope of the Presidency.

WENDELL PHILLIPS, *Speech*, 7 Nov., 1860.

16

Statesmen are not only liable to give an account of what they say or do in public, but there is a busy inquiry made into their very meals, beds, marriages, and every other sportive or serious action.

PLUTARCH, *Political Precepts*.

17

Who would not praise Patricio's high desert,
His hand unstain'd, his uncorrupted heart,
His comprehensive head? all int'rests weigh'd,
All Europe saved, yet Britain not betray'd!

POPE, *Moral Essays*. Epis. i, l. 81.

1
The foul corruption-gendered swarm of state.
ROBERT SOUTHEY, *Joan of Arc*. Bk. iv, l. 94.

2
The mode of flattery which, being at once safe and efficacious, is the best adapted to the purposes of a statesman, is the flattery of listening.
SIR HENRY TAYLOR, *The Statesman*, 238.

3
And statesmen at her council met
Who knew the seasons when to take
Occasion by the hand, and make
The bounds of freedom wider yet.
TENNYSON, *To the Queen*.

O Statesmen, guard us, guard the eye, the soul
Of Europe, keep our noble England whole.
TENNYSON, *Ode on the Death of the Duke of Wellington*. St. 7.

A lidless watcher of the public weal.
TENNYSON, *The Princess*. Pt. iv, l. 306.

4
In statesmanship
To strike too soon is oft to miss the blow.
TENNYSON, *Queen Mary*. Act iii, sc. 6.

5
In statesmanship get the formalities right, never mind about the moralities.
MARK TWAIN, *Pudd'nhead Wilson's New Calendar*.

6
Why don't you show us a statesman who can rise up to the Emergency, and cave in the Emergency's head?
ARTEMUS WARD, *Things in New York*.

STATUE, see Monument

STEALING, see Thief

STEAM

7
Soon shall thy arm, unconquer'd steam! afar
Drag the slow barge, or drive the rapid car;
Or on wide-waving wings expanded bear
The flying chariot through the field of air.
ERASMUS DARWIN, *The Botanic Garden*. Pt. i, canto i, l. 289. (1792)

8
Strong-shouldered steam.
EMERSON, *Conduct of Life: Wealth*.

Steam, the enemy of space and time, with its enormous strength and delicate applicability, which is made in hospitals to bring a bowl of gruel to a sick man's bed, and can twist beams of iron like candy-braids. . . . Steam is an apt scholar and a strong-shouldered fellow.
EMERSON, *Society and Solitude: Works and Days*.

9
Fulton knocked at the door of Napoleon with steam, and was rejected; and Napoleon lived long enough to know that he had excluded a greater power than his own.
HORATIO GREENOUGH, *Remark*, to Emerson. (EMERSON, *Success*.)

10
Steam, that great civilizer.
FREEMAN HUNT, *American Merchants: Introduction*.

11
Steam is a tyrant.
JOHN WILSON, *Noctes Ambrosianæ*. No. 36, Nov., 1834.

STOMACH, see Belly

STORM

See also Sea in Storm, Shipwreck

12
And, pleas'd the Almighty's orders to perform,
Rides in the whirlwind and directs the storm.
ADDISON, *The Campaign*, l. 291.

And proud his mistress' orders to perform,
Rides in the whirlwind, and directs the storm.
POPE, *The Dunciad*. Bk. iii, l. 263. The last line borrowed from Addison.

Ride the air In whirlwind.
MILTON, *Paradise Lost*. Bk. ii, l. 540.

13
The tempest's howl, it soothes my soul,
My griefs it seems to join;
The leafless trees my fancy please,
Their fate resembles mine!
BURNS, *Winter: A Dirge*.

14
Without was Nature's elemental din.
THOMAS CAMPBELL, *Theodric*, l. 474.

15
He used to raise a storm in a wine-ladle. (Excitabat fluctus in simpulo.)
CICERO, *De Legibus*. Bk. iii, ch. 16, sec. 36. Quoted as a proverb. Erasmus, *Adagia* ii, ii, 73.

I have seen a greater storm in a boiling saucepan.
DORION, ridiculing the description of a tempest in the *Nauplius* of Timotheus. (ATHENÆUS, *Deipnosophistæ*, viii, 19.)

A storm in a cream bowl.
DUKE OF ORMOND, *Letter to the Earl of Arlington*, 28 Dec., 1678.

It is a tempest in a glass of water. (C'est une tempête dans un verre d'eau.)
GRAND DUKE PAUL OF RUSSIA, referring to an insurrection in Geneva.

A Storm in a Teacup.
BERNARD BAYLE. Title of comedietta performed at London, 20 March, 1854.

16
Any port in a storm, they say.
JAMES COBB, *First Floor*. Act ii, sc. 2.

"Any port in a storm" was the principle on which I was prepared to act.
R. L. STEVENSON, *St. Ives*. Ch. 25.

17
Every storm hath his calm.
ROBERT GREENE, *Works*. Vol. viii, p. 101. (1590)

After a storm comes a calm.
SIR WILLIAM D'AVENANT, *Cruel Brother*. Act i.

After a storm comes a calm.
MATTHEW HENRY, *Commentaries: Acts ix.*
See also under QUIET.

1
Storms make oaks take deeper root.
GEORGE HERBERT, *Jacula Prudentum.*

2
The beating of her restless heart
Still sounding through the storm.
O. W. HOLMES, *The Steamboat*, l. 27.

The pulses of her iron heart
Go beating through the storm.
EMERSON, *Society and Solitude: Civilization.* Misquoting and improving on Holmes.

3
As the days grow longer, the storms grow stronger.
J. O. HALLIWELL, *Nature Songs.*

4
A little gale will soon disperse that cloud . . .
For every cloud engenders not a storm.
SHAKESPEARE, *III Henry VI*. Act v, sc. 3, l. 10.

5
I have seen tempests, when the scolding winds
Have rived the knotty oaks, and I have seen
The ambitious ocean swell and rage and foam,
To be exalted with the threatening clouds:
But never till to-night, never till now,
Did I go through a tempest dropping fire.
SHAKESPEARE, *Julius Cæsar*. Act i, sc. 3, l. 5.

Blow, winds, and crack your cheeks! rage! blow!
You cataracts and hurricanes, spout
Till you have drench'd our steeples!
SHAKESPEARE, *King Lear*. Act iii, sc. 2, l. 1.

Since I was man,
Such sheets of fire, such bursts of horrid thunder,
Such groans of roaring wind and rain, I never
Remember to have heard.
SHAKESPEARE, *King Lear*. Act iii, sc. 2, l. 45.

Alack, the night comes on, and the bleak winds
Do sorely ruffle.
SHAKESPEARE, *King Lear*. Act ii, sc. 4, l. 303.

6
When clouds appear, wise men put on their cloaks;
When great leaves fall, the winter is at hand;
When the sun sets, who doth not look for night?
Untimely storms make men expect a dearth.
SHAKESPEARE, *Richard III*. Act ii, sc. 3, l. 32.

STORY, see Tale

STRAW

7
And Pharaoh commanded . . . Ye shall no more give the people straw to make brick, as heretofore: let them go and gather straw for themselves.
Old Testament: Exodus, v, 7.

8
The last straw breaks the camel's back.
JOHN RAY, *English Proverbs.*

The last straw breaks the laden camel's back.
DICKENS, *Dombey and Son*. Ch. 2.

'Tis the last feather that breaks the horse's back.
THOMAS FULLER, *Gnomologia*. No. 5120.

It is not the last drop that empties the water-clock, but all that has previously flowed out. (Quemadmodum clepsydram non extremum stillicidium exhaurit, sed quicquid ante defluxit.)
SENECA, *Epistulæ ad Lucilium*. Epis. xxiv, 20.

9
We catch hold of hopes . . . as drowning men do upon thorns, or straws.
L'ESTRANGE, *Seneca's Epistles*, xviii. (c. 1680)

The dear implacable, like a drowning man, catches at a straw to save herself!
RICHARDSON, *Clarissa Harlowe*, vi, 5.

10
The suburb of their straw-built citadel.
MILTON, *Paradise Lost*. Bk. i, l. 773.

11
Take a straw and throw it up into the air,—you shall see by that which way the wind is.
JOHN SELDEN, *Table-Talk: Libels.*

Such straws of speech show how blows the wind.
CHARLES READE, *Cloister and Hearth*. Ch. 56.

12
I did not care one straw. (Ego non flocci pendere.)
TERENCE, *Eunuchus*, l. 411. (Act iii, sc. 1.)

STRAWBERRY

13
Doubtless God could have made a better berry, but doubtless God never did.
DR. WILLIAM BUTLER, referring to the strawberry. (Thomas Fuller, *Worthies of England: Suffolk*, calls Butler the "Æsculapius of our age." Quoted in Walton's *Compleat Angler*, 2nd edition, pt. i, ch. 5.) See 672:6.

One of the chiefest doctors of England was wont to say that God could have made, but God never did make, a better berry.
ROGER WILLIAMS, *Key Into the Language of America*, p. 98. (1643)

14
Strawberries lose their flavor in garden beds.
EMERSON, *Essays, First Series: Prudence.*

15
The strawberry grows underneath the nettle
And wholesome berries thrive and ripen best
Neighbour'd by fruit of baser quality.
SHAKESPEARE, *Henry V*. Act i, sc. 1, l. 60.

Roses and violets are ever the sweeter and more odoriferous that grow near unto garlic and onions.
MONTAIGNE, *Essays*. Bk. iii, ch. 9.

STRENGTH

16
Strengthen me by sympathizing with my strength not my weakness.
AMOS BRONSON ALCOTT, *Table-Talk: Sympathy.*

17
Such strength as a man has he should use. (Quod est, eo decet uti.)
CICERO, *De Senectute*. Ch. 9, sec. 27.

1
My strength is made perfect in weakness.
New Testament: II Corinthians, xii, 9.

2
As thy days, so shall thy strength be.
Old Testament: Deuteronomy, xxxiii, 25.

3
We acquire the strength we have overcome.
EMERSON, *Conduct of Life: Considerations by the Way*.

It is as easy for the strong man to be strong, as it is for the weak to be weak.
EMERSON, *Essays, First Series: Self-Reliance*.

4
Success to the strongest, who are always, at last, the wisest and best.
EMERSON, *Uncollected Lectures: Public and Private Education*.

Not two strong men th' enormous weight could raise,
Such men as live in these degen'rate days.
HOMER, *Iliad*. Bk. v, l. 371; bk. xii, l. 539. (Pope, tr.)

5
It is not strength, but art, obtains the prize,
And to be swift is less than to be wise.
HOMER, *Iliad*. Bk. xxiii, l. 383. (Pope, tr.)

Brute strength bereft of reason falls by its own weight. (Vis consili expers mole ruit sua.)
HORACE, *Odes*. Bk. iii, ode 4, l. 65.

'Tis slight, not strength, that gives the greatest lift.
MIDDLETON, *Michaelmas Term*. Act iv, sc. 1.

What is strength without a double share
Of wisdom? vast, unwieldy, burdensome,
Proudly secure, yet liable to fall
By weakest subtleties, not made to rule,
But to subserve where wisdom bears command.
MILTON, *Samson Agonistes*, l. 53.

6
Their strength is to sit still.
Old Testament: Isaiah, xxx, 7.

7
They that wait upon the Lord shall renew their strength.
Old Testament: Isaiah, xl, 31.

8
Only be thou strong and very courageous.
Old Testament: Joshua, i, 7.

9
But noble souls, through dust and heat,
Rise from disaster and defeat
The stronger.
LONGFELLOW, *The Sifting of Peter*. St. 7.

10
And weaponless himself,
Made arms ridiculous.
MILTON, *Samson Agonistes*, l. 130.

Like Teneriff or Atlas, unremov'd.
MILTON, *Paradise Lost*. Bk. iv, l. 987.

11
The stronger always succeeds. (Plus potest qui plus valet.)
PLAUTUS, *Truculentus*. Act iv, sc. 3, l. 30.
See also MIGHT and RIGHT.

12
They go from strength to strength.
Old Testament: Psalms, lxxxiv, 7.

13
Be strong, and quit yourselves like men.
Old Testament: I Samuel, iv, 9.

14
His limbs were cast in manly mould,
For hardy sports or contest bold.
SCOTT, *The Lady of the Lake*. Canto i, st. 21.

15
Profaned the God-given strength, and marred the lofty line.
SCOTT, *Marmion*: Canto i, *Introduction*, l. 283.

When you want to lose what strength you have.
PYTHAGORAS, when asked when a man should consort with a woman. (DIOGENES LAERTIUS, *Pythagoras*. Sec. 10.)

16
He who has great strength should use it lightly. (Minimum decet libere cui multum licet.)
SENECA, *Troades*, l. 336.

O, it is excellent
To have a giant's strength; but it is tyrannous
To use it like a giant.
SHAKESPEARE, *Measure for Measure*. Act ii, sc. 2, l. 107.

17
The strength Of twenty men.
SHAKESPEARE, *Romeo and Juliet*. Act v, sc. 1, l. 78.

18
Nero, which in the Sabine tongue means strong and valiant. (Nero, quo significatur lingua Sabina fortis ac strenuus.)
SUETONIUS, *Tiberius*. Sec. 2.

He is a second Hercules. (Ἄλλος οὗτος Ἡρακλῆς.)
THEMISTOCLES. (PLUTARCH, *Lives: Theseus*. Ch. 29, sec. 3.) Plutarch says that Themistocles originated this phrase.

19
Let our strength be the law of justice: for that which is feeble is found to be nothing worth.
Apocrypha: Wisdom of Solomon, ii, 11.

STRIFE, see Discord, Quarreling

STUDY

See also Scholar

I—Study: Apothegms

20
Boys should study those things which will be useful to them when they are grown up.
ARISTIPPUS. (DIOGENES LAERTIUS, *Aristippus*. Bk. ii, sec. 80.)

21
Crafty men contemn studies; simple men admire them; and wise men use them.
FRANCIS BACON, *Essays: Of Studies*.

22
I would live to study, and not study to live.
FRANCIS BACON, *Letter to King James I*. (*Letters and Speeches*, p. 321.)

1
When night hath set her silver lamp on high,
Then is the time for study.
P. J. BAILEY, *Festus: A Village Feast.*

2
Concentrate though your coat-tails be on fire.
J. M. BARRIE, *Tommy and Grizel,* p. 22.

3
There is no satiety in study. (Non est ulla studiorum satietas.)
ERASMUS, *Colloquia: Scholastic Studies.*

4
Whence is thy learning? hath thy toil
O'er books consum'd the midnight oil?
JOHN GAY, *Fables: Introduction,* l. 15.

Walkers, at leisure, Learning's flowers may spoil,
Nor watch the wasting of the midnight oil.
JOHN GAY, *Trivia.* Bk. ii, l. 557.

I trimm'd my lamp, consum'd the midnight oil.
WILLIAM SHENSTONE, *Elegies.* No. xi, st. 7. (1758)

My temples throb, my pulses boil,
I'm sick of Song, and Ode, and Ballad—
So, Thyrsis, take the Midnight Oil,
And pour it on a lobster salad.
THOMAS HOOD, *To Minerva.*

5
Who learns by Finding Out has sevenfold
The Skill of him who learned by Being Told.
ARTHUR GUITERMAN, *A Poet's Proverbs,* p. 73.

6
It seems to me (said she) that you are in some brown study.
JOHN LYLY, *Euphues,* p. 80. (1579)

A brown study.
SWIFT, *Polite Conversation.* Dial. 1.

7
As turning the logs will make a dull fire burn, so changes of studies a dull brain.
LONGFELLOW, *Drift-Wood: Table Talk.*

8
See there the olive grove of Academe,
Plato's retirement, where the Attic bird
Trills her thick-warbl'd notes the summer long.
MILTON, *Paradise Regained.* Bk. iv, l. 244.

9
I am slow of study.
SHAKESPEARE, *A Midsummer-Night's Dream.* Act i, sc. 2, l. 69.

II—Study: The Smell of the Lamp

10
Thy words smell of the apron.
ANTIGONUS I, to Aristodemus, supposed to be a cook's son, when the latter advised him to moderate his gifts and expenses. (PLUTARCH, *Apothegms.*)

11
Knowledge . . . will smell of the lamp.
C. C. COLTON, *Lacon: Preface.* (1820)

12
This little volume of mine smelleth of the oil and candle.
JOHN GRANGE, *Golden Aphroditis.* N 1. (1577)

A well-labour'd sermon that smelt of the candle.
SIR JOHN HARINGTON. (*Nugæ Antiquæ.* Vol. ii, p. 190.) 1608.

Your last letter, . . . I found it smelt of the lamp.
JAMES HOWELL, *Familiar Letters.* Bk. ii, No. 21.

13
A work not smelling of the lamp.
BEN JONSON, *The Staple of News: Prologue.*

14
They smell of the lamp. (Ἐλλυχνίων ὄζειν.)
PYTHEAS, referring to the orations of Demosthenes, and alluding to the underground cave which the philosopher used as a study, and which was lighted only by a lamp. Demosthenes retorted, "Yes, but your lamp and mine, my friend, do not witness the same labors." (PLUTARCH, *Lives: Demosthenes:* Sec. 8.) In his *Life of Timoleon,* Plutarch applies the expression to over-finished paintings, as well as to labored writing. The Latin proverb is, "Lucernam olet."

The saying of Pytheas is common and much spoken of, that the orations of Demosthenes smelled all of the candle, for that the same did in the night season write and record such things as he had to say to the people in the day time.
ERASMUS, *Adagia.* (Udall, tr., 379.) 1542.

15
A man who thinks much of his words as he writes them will generally leave behind him work that smells of oil.
ANTHONY TROLLOPE, *Autobiography.* Ch. 10.

III—Study: Its Virtues

16
Studies serve for delight, for ornament, and for ability.
FRANCIS BACON, *Essays: Of Studies.*

Histories make men wise; poets, witty; the mathematics, subtile; natural philosophy, deep; moral, grave; logic and rhetoric, able to contend.
FRANCIS BACON, *Essays: Of Studies.*

The faithful study of the liberal arts humanizes character. (Ingenuas dedicisse fideliter artes Emollit mores.)
OVID, *Epistulæ ex Ponto.* Bk. ii, epis. 9, l. 47.

17
Hiving wisdom with each studious year.
BYRON, *Childe Harold.* Canto iii, st. 107.

18
We spent them not in toys, in lusts, or wine,
But search of deep philosophy,
Wit, eloquence, and poetry;
Arts which I lov'd, for they, my friend, were thine.
ABRAHAM COWLEY, *On the Death of Mr. William Harvey.*

19
Beholding the bright countenance of truth in the quiet and still air of delightful studies.
MILTON, *Reason of Church Government: Introduction.* Bk. ii.

1
Common studies, pursued in the same spirit, in all civilized countries, form, beyond the restrictions of diverse and often hostile nationalities, a great country which no war profanes, no conqueror menaces.

GASTON PARIS, *Address*, Collège de France, 1870.

2
For sure no minutes bring us more content,
Than those in pleasing, useful studies spent.

JOHN POMFRET, *The Choice*, l. 31.

3
What is the end of study? let me know.
Why, that to know, which else we should not know.
Things hid and barr'd, you mean, from common sense?
Ay, that is study's god-like recompense.

SHAKESPEARE, *Love's Labour's Lost*. Act i, sc. 1, l. 55.

Balk logic with acquaintance that you have,
And practise rhetoric in your common talk;
Music and poesy use to quicken you;
The mathematics and the metaphysics
Fall to them as you find your stomach serves you;
No profit grows where is no pleasure ta'en;
In brief, sir, study what you most affect.

SHAKESPEARE, *The Taming of the Shrew*. Act i, sc. 1, l. 34.

4
One of the best methods of rendering study agreeable is to live with able men, and to suffer all those pangs of inferiority which the want of knowledge always inflicts.

SYDNEY SMITH, *On the Conduct of the Understanding*. Lecture 2.

5
With unwearied fingers drawing out
The lines of life, from living knowledge hid.

SPENSER, *Faerie Queene*. Bk. iv, canto ii, st. 48.

IV—Study: Its Faults

6
To spend too much time in studies is sloth.

FRANCIS BACON, *Essays: Of Studies*.

7
Who studies ancient laws and rites,
Tongues, arts and arms, and history,
Must drudge, like Selden, days and nights,
And in the endless labour die.

RICHARD BENTLEY, *Who Strives to Mount Parnassus' Hill*.

8
Much study had made him very lean,
And pale, and leaden-eyed.

HOOD, *The Dream of Eugene Aram*, l. 29.

9
We learn our lessons not for life, but for the lecture-room. (Non vitæ sed scholæ decimus.)

SENECA, *Epistulæ ad Lucilium*. Epis. cvi, 12.

The studious class are their own victims; they are thin and pale, their feet are cold, their heads are hot, the night is without sleep, the day a fear of interruption,—pallor, squalor, hunger, and egotism.

EMERSON, *Representative Men: Montaigne*.

10
Study is like the heaven's glorious sun
That will not be deep-search'd with saucy looks:
Small have continual plodders ever won
Save base authority from others' books.

SHAKESPEARE, *Love's Labour's Lost*, i, 1, 84.

So study evermore is overshot:
While it doth study to have what it would
It doth forget to do the thing it should,
And when it hath the thing it hunteth most,
'Tis won as towns with fire, so won, so lost.

SHAKESPEARE, *Love's Labour's Lost*, i, 1, 143.

STUPIDITY

See also Fools

11
We are growing serious, and, let me tell you, that's the very next step to being dull.

ADDISON, *The Drummer*. Act iv, sc. 6.

I find we are growing serious, and then we are in great danger of being dull.

CONGREVE, *The Old Batchelor*. Act ii, sc. 2.

12
O Dulness! portion of the truly blest!
Calm shelter'd haven of eternal rest!
Thy sons ne'er madden in the fierce extremes
Of Fortune's polar frost, or torrid beams.

BURNS, *Epistle to Robert Graham*, l. 56.

13
Learn'd, without sense, and venerably dull.

CHARLES CHURCHILL, *The Rosciad*, l. 592.

Fill a dull man to the brim with knowledge and he will not become less dull.

ARTHUR BALFOUR, *Essays and Addresses*, p. 10.

14
Prudent Dulness marked him for a mayor.

CHARLES CHURCHILL, *The Rosciad*, l. 596.

15
Your blunderer is as sturdy as a rock.

COWPER, *The Progress of Error*, l. 539.

16
Shadwell alone of all my sons is he
Who stands confirm'd in full stupidity.
The rest to some faint meaning make pretence,
But Shadwell never deviates into sense.

DRYDEN, *Mac Flecknoe*, l. 17.

17
Nature delights in punishing stupid people.

EMERSON, *Journals*. Vol. v, p. 238.

18
I don't know what a moron is,
And I don't give a damn.
I'm thankful that I am not one—
My God! Perhaps I am.

HENRY PRATT FAIRCHILD, *The Great Economic Paradox*. (*Harper's Magazine*, May, 1932)

See the happy moron,
He doesn't give a damn.

I wish I were a moron;
My God, perhaps I am!

UNKNOWN, *The Moron*. (Quoted in the *Journal of Heredity* by its editor, Robert Cook, who states that he "lifted" the stanza from some British publication.) Often attributed to Dorothy Parker, who writes the compiler, "I never saw it before." See also 2296:9.

1
Allow me to offer my congratulations on the admirable skill you have shown in missing the mark. Not to have hit once in so many trials, argues the most splendid talents for missing.

EMPEROR GALERIUS, to a soldier who had missed the mark many times in succession. (Quoted by DE QUINCEY, *Works*, xiv, 161.)

2
The fault rests with the gods, who have made her so stupid. (La faute en est aux dieux, qui la firent si bête.)

JEAN DE GRESSET, *Méchant*. Act ii, sc. 7.

3
Dull as an alderman at church, or a fat lapdog after dinner.

THOMAS HOLCROFT, *Duplicity*. Act i, sc. 1.

He must be dull as a Dutch commentator.

SOAME JENYNS, *Imitation of Horace*, ii, 1.

4
You would swear that he was born in the foggy air of Bœotia. (Bœotum in crasso jurares ære natum.)

HORACE, *Epistles*. Bk. i, l. 244. Bœotia was proverbial for the stupidity of its inhabitants, as the city of Kampen is in Holland.

5
An Athenian blockhead is the worst of all blockheads.

SAMUEL JOHNSON. (BOSWELL, *Life*, 1729.)

6
Why, Sir, Sherry is dull, naturally dull; but it must have taken him a great deal of pains to become what we now see him. Such an excess of stupidity, Sir, is not in Nature.

SAMUEL JOHNSON, referring to Sheridan. (BOSWELL, *Life*, 1763.)

He is not only dull himself, but the cause of dulness in others.

SAMUEL JOHNSON. (BOSWELL, *Life*, 1784.)

I'm the saftest o' the fam'ly!
I'm the simple Johnnie Raw!

HARRY LAUDER AND BOB BEATON, *The Saftest o' the Fam'ly*. (1904)

7
It is the dull man who is always sure, and the sure man who is always dull.

H. L. MENCKEN, *Prejudices*. Ser. ii, p. 101.

8
Obstinacy and heat of opinion are the surest proof of stupidity. Is there anything so assured, resolved, disdainful, contemplative, solemn, and serious, as the ass?

MONTAIGNE, *Essays*. Bk. iii, ch. 8.

9
Dulness! whose good old cause I yet defend,
With whom my Muse began, with whom shall end.

POPE, *The Dunciad*. Bk. i, l. 165.

10
And gentle Dulness ever loves a joke.

POPE, *The Dunciad*. Bk. ii, l. 34.

Too dull for laughter, for reply too mad.

POPE, *Epigram*.

11
Much was believ'd, but little understood,
And to be dull was construed to be good.

POPE, *Essay on Criticism*. Pt. iii, l. 130.

12
Against stupidity the very gods
Themselves contend in vain.

SCHILLER, *The Maid of Orleans*. Act iii, sc. 6.

13
You have been a boggler ever.

SHAKESPEARE, *Antony and Cleopatra*, iii, 13, 110.

And duller shouldst thou be than the fat weed
That roots itself in ease on Lethe wharf.

SHAKESPEARE, *Hamlet*. Act i, sc. 5, l. 32.

A dull and muddy-mettled rascal.

SHAKESPEARE, *Hamlet*. Act ii, sc. 2, l. 594.

14
Peter was dull—he was at first
Dull,—Oh, so dull—so very dull!
Whether he talked, wrote, or rehearsed—
Still with his dulness was he cursed—
Dull—beyond all conception—dull.

SHELLEY, *Peter Bell the Third*. Pt. vii, st. 11.

15
It is to be noted that when any part of this paper appears dull, there is a design in it.

RICHARD STEELE, *The Tatler*. No. 38.

A late facetious writer who told the public that whenever he was dull they might be assured there was a design in it.

FIELDING, *Tom Jones*. Bk. v, ch. 1.

16
Blest fertile Dulness! mothering surmise, rumor, report, as stagnant water, flies, whose happy votaries, stung by every hatch, divinely itch, and more divinely scratch!

SYLVIA TOWNSEND WARNER, *Opus 7*.

17
There is no sin but stupidity.

OSCAR WILDE, *The Critic as Artist*. Pt. ii.

A thick head can do as much damage as a hard heart.

HAROLD WILLIS DODDS.

18
I have a great admiration for stupidity.

OSCAR WILDE, *An Ideal Husband*. Act ii.

Whenever a man does a thoroughly stupid thing, it is always from the noblest motives.

OSCAR WILDE, *Picture of Dorian Gray*. Ch. 6.

STYLE

See also Words: Use; Writing: Manner

I—Style: Definitions

19
The style is the man himself. (Le style est l'homme même.)

BUFFON, *Discourse*, at reception into French Academy, 1753.

The style is the man; and some will add that, thus unsupported, it does not amount to much of a man. It is a sort of fighting and profane parody of the Old Testament.
G. K. CHESTERTON, *The Victorian Age in Literature*, p. 185. Referring to Swinburne.

1
It is most true, *stylus virum arguit*,—our style bewrays us.
ROBERT BURTON, *Anatomy of Melancholy: Democritus to the Reader.*

A chaste and lucid style is indicative of the same personal traits in the author.
HOSEA BALLOU, *Sermons.*

2
And, after all, it is style alone by which posterity will judge of a great work, for an author can have nothing truly his own but his style.
ISAAC D'ISRAELI, *Literary Miscellanies: Style.*

3
A man's style is his mind's voice.
EMERSON, *Journals.* Vol. x, p. 457.

The style of an author should be the image of his mind, but the choice and command of language is the fruit of exercise.
EDWARD GIBBON, *Miscellaneous Works.* Vol. i, p. 145.

4
Form is the Golden Vase wherein Thought, that fleeting essense, is preserved to Posterity.
ANATOLE FRANCE. (COURNOS, *Modern Plutarch*, p. 29.)

5
What is called style in writing or speaking is formed very early in life, while the imagination is warm and impressions are permanent.
THOMAS JEFFERSON, *Writings.* Vol. v, p. 185.

Style! style! why, all writers will tell you that it is the very thing which can least of all be changed. A man's style is nearly as much a part of him as his physiognomy, his figure, the throbbing of his pulse,—in short, as any part of his being is at least subjected to the action of the will.
FÉNELON, *Dialogues sur l'Eloquence.*

6
Master alike in speech and song
Of fame's great antiseptic—Style,
You with the classic few belong
Who tempered wisdom with a smile.
J. R. LOWELL, *To Oliver Wendell Holmes on His Seventy-fifth Birthday.* St. 15.

7
Wit belongs to the man, style to the author.
MAUPERTUIS, *Letter to Frederick the Great*, 19 Nov., 1745.

8
For style beyond the genius never dares. (Che stilo oltra l'ingegno non si stende.)
PETRARCH, *Morte di Laura.* Sonnet 68.

9
Expression is the dress of thought, and still
Appears more decent as more suitable.
POPE, *Essay on Criticism.* Pt. ii, l. 118. (1712)

Style is the dress of thoughts.
LORD CHESTERFIELD, *Letters.* 24 Nov., 1749.

Dress covers the mortal body and adorns it, but style is the vehicle of the spirit.
SYDNEY SMITH, *Letter to Miss Harcourt*, 1842.

Style is what gives value and currency to thought.
AMIEL, *Journal: Introduction.*

10
Style, after all, rather than thought, is the immortal thing in literature.
ALEXANDER SMITH, *Dreamthorp: On the Writing of Essays.*

II—Style: Good Style

11
Sound words, I know, Timothy is to use,
And old wives' fables he is to refuse;
But yet grave Paul him nowhere did forbid
The use of parables; in which lay hid
That gold, those pearls, and precious stones that were
Worth digging for, and that with greatest care.
JOHN BUNYAN, *The Pilgrim's Progress: The Author's Apology for His Book.*

May I not write in such a style as this?
In such a method, too, and yet not miss
My end—thy good?
JOHN BUNYAN, *The Pilgrim's Progress: The Author's Apology for His Book.*

12
Nor can one word be chang'd but for a worse.
HOMER, *Odyssey.* Bk. viii, l. 192. (Pope, tr.)

A strict and succinct style is that, where you can take away nothing without loss, and that loss to be manifest.
BEN JONSON, *Explorata: Consuetudo.*

13
Clear arrangement. (Lucidus ordo.)
HORACE, *Ars Poetica*, l. 41.

14
With a nice taste and care in weaving words together, you will express yourself most happily, if a skillful setting makes a familiar word new. (In verbis etiam tenuis cautusque serendis Dixeris egregie, notum si callida verbum Reddiderit junctura novum.)
HORACE, *Ars Poetica*, l. 46.

It has ever been, and ever will be, permitted to issue words stamped with the mint-mark of the day. (Licuit semperque licebit Signatum præsente nota producere nomen.)
HORACE, *Ars Poetica*, l. 58.

A man coins not a new word without some peril and less fruit; for if it happen to be received, the praise is but moderate; if refused, the scorn is assured.
BEN JONSON, *Explorata: De Orationis Dignitate.*

15
Well-rounded phrase. (Ore rotundo.)
HORACE, *Ars Poetica.* l. 323. The words are applied to style, not utterance, although commonly quoted as referring to the latter.

Your language is that of the toga, skilled in clever phrasing, rounded but not full-mouthed. (Verba togæ sequeris junctura callidus acri, Ore teres modico.)

PERSIUS, *Satires*. Sat. v, l. 14. That is, the language of the cultivated class.

1
The chief virtue of a style is perspicuity, and nothing so vicious in it as to need an interpreter. Words borrowed of antiquity do lend a kind of majesty to style, and are not without their delight sometimes. For they have the authority of years, and out of their intermission do win themselves a kind of grace-like newness. But the eldest of the present, and newest of the past language, is the best.

BEN JONSON, *Explorata: Consuetudo*.

2
Before employing a fine word, find a place for it. (Avant d'employer un beau mot, faites-lui une place.)

JOUBERT, *Pensées*. No. 302.

3
I think that too many stops stop the way, and that every sixth or seventh is uncalled for.

W. S. LANDOR, *Letter to John Forster*, 1854. Of punctuation.

4
A careful felicity of style. (Curiosa felicitas.)

PETRONIUS, *Satyricon*. Sec. 118.

5
When an old phrase fits the occasion, it's well used. (Scitumst, per tempus si obviamst, verbum vetus.)

PLAUTUS, *Pœnulus*, l. 135. (Act i, sc. 1.)

6
Style has no fixed laws; it is changed by the usage of the people, never the same for any length of time. (Oratio certam regulam non habet; consuetudo illam civitatis, quæ numquam in eodem diu stetit, versat.)

SENECA, *Epistulæ ad Lucilium*. Epis. cxiv, 13.

7
The word is well culled, chose, sweet and apt, I do assure you, sir, I do assure.

SHAKESPEARE, *Love's Labour's Lost*, v, 1, 98.

Proper words in proper places.

SWIFT, *Definition of a Good Style*.

As to the Adjective: when in doubt, strike it out.

MARK TWAIN, *Pudd'nhead Wilson's Calendar*.

8
Clearness ornaments profound thoughts. (La clarté orne les pensées profondes.)

VAUVENARGUES, *Réflexions et Maximes*. No. 4.

When things are small the terms should still be so,
For low words please us when the theme is low.

VIDA, *De Arte Poetica*. (Pitt, tr.)

Abstruse and mystic thoughts you must express
With painful care, but seeming easiness;
For truth shines brightest thro' the plainest dress.

WENTWORTH DILLON, *Essay on Translated Verse*, l. 216.

Clarity, the greatest of legislative and judicial virtues, like the sunshine, revealing and curative.

CHARLES E. HUGHES, *Address*, Feb., 1931.

9
All styles are good except the tiresome kind. (Tous les genres sont bons, hors le genre ennuyeux.)

VOLTAIRE, *L'Enfant Prodigue: Preface*.

10
That graceful manner of thinking in Virgil seems to me to be more than style, if I do not refine too much: and I admire, I confess, Mr. Addison's phrase, that Virgil "tossed about his dung with an air of majesty."

WALPOLE, *Letter to Pinkerton*, 26 June, 1785.

III—Style: Bad Style

11
That's not good language that all understand not.

GEORGE HERBERT, *Jacula Prudentum*.

That must be fine, for I understand nothing of it. (Oui, ça est si beau, que je n'y entends goutte.)

MOLIÈRE, *Le Médecin Malgré Lui*. Act ii, sc. 4.

12
We say it is a fleshy style, when there is much periphrasis and circuit of words; and when, with more than enough, it grows fat and corpulent; *arvina orationis*, full of suet and tallow.

BEN JONSON, *Explorata: Carnosa*.

The fleshly gentlemen [Swinburne, Baudelaire and Rossetti] have bound themselves by solemn league and covenant to extol fleshliness as the distinct and supreme end of poetic and pictorial art.

ROBERT BUCHANAN, *Fleshly School of Poetry*.

13
The gloomy companions of a disturbed imagination; the melancholy madness of poetry, without the inspiration.

JUNIUS, *Letters*. No. 7, 3 March, 1769.

14
It frequently happens that where the second line is sublime, the third, in which he meant to rise still higher, is perfect bombast.

LONGINUS, *On the Sublime*. Sec. 3. Referring to Lucan's style.

That passage is what I call the sublime dashed to pieces by cutting too close with the fiery four-in-hand round the corner of nonsense.

S. T. COLERIDGE, *Table Talk*. 20 Jan., 1834.

15
Ornate rhetoric taught out of the rule of Plato.

MILTON, *Tractate of Education*.

Taffeta phrases, silken terms precise,
Three-piled hyperboles, spruce affectation,
Figures pedantical; these summer-flies
Have blown me full of maggot ostentation.

SHAKESPEARE, *Love's Labour's Lost*, v, 2, 407.

Flowers of rhetoric, in sermons and serious discourses, are like the blue and red flowers in corn, pleasing to them who come only for amusement, but prejudicial to him who would reap the profit.

SWIFT, *Thoughts on Various Subjects*.

The flowery style is not unsuitable to public speeches or addresses, which amount only to compliment. The lighter beauties are in their place when there is nothing more solid to say; but the flowery style ought to be banished from a pleading, a sermon, or a didactic work.

VOLTAIRE, *Philosophical Dictionary: Style.*

1
Some by old words to fame have made pretence,
Ancients in phrase, mere moderns in their sense;
Such labour'd nothings, in so strange a style,
Amaze the unlearn'd, and make the learned smile.

POPE, *Essay on Criticism.* Pt. ii, l. 124.

In a style, to be sure, of remarkable fullness,
But which nobody reads on account of its dullness.

J. G. SAXE, *Pyramus and Thisbe.*

2
It is no less degenerate to use no words except those which are striking, high-sounding, and poetical, avoiding what is familiar and usual. (Quam nolle nisi splendidis uti ac sonantibus et poeticis, necessaria atque in usu posita vitare.)

SENECA, *Epistulæ ad Lucilium.* Epis. cxiv, 14.

It begins to hunt for novelties in speech, summoning and displaying obsolete and old fashioned words, or coining and misshaping unknown words.

SENECA, *Epistulæ ad Lucilium.* Epis. cxiv, 10.

With others it is not so much an arrangement of words, as it is a setting to music, so wheedling and soft is their gliding style.

SENECA, *Epistulæ ad Lucilium.* Epis. cxiv, 16.

3
Base is the style and matter mean withall.

SPENSER, *Mother Hubberds Tale,* l. 44.

4
His style is chaos illumined by flashes of lightning. As a writer, he has mastered everything except language.

OSCAR WILDE, *The Decay of Lying.* Referring to George Meredith.

SUCCESS

I—Success: Definitions

5
Have little care that Life is brief,
And less that Art is long.
Success is in the silences
Though Fame is in the song.

BLISS CARMAN, *Songs from Vagabondia: Envoy.*

6
In all things, success depends upon previous preparation, and without such preparation there is sure to be failure.

CONFUCIUS, *Analects.* (EMERSON, *Uncollected Lectures: Public and Private Education.*)

7
Success is the child of Audacity.

BENJAMIN DISRAELI, *Iskander.* Ch. 4.

8
The secret of success is constancy to purpose.

BENJAMIN DISRAELI, *Speech,* 24 June, 1870.

9
The things you must scramble and elbow for are not worth having; not one of them. They are the swill of life, my son; leave them to swine.

E. S. MARTIN, *A Father to His Freshman Son.*

10
There is only one success—to be able to spend your life in your own way.

CHRISTOPHER MORLEY, *Where the Blue Begins,* p. 85.

He has achieved success who has lived well, laughed often, and loved much.

MRS. A. J. STANLEY, *What Constitutes Success.*

11
Only he is successful in his business who makes that pursuit which affords him the highest pleasure sustain him.

H. D. THOREAU, *Journal,* 10 Jan., 1851.

12
Success, a sort of suicide, Is ruin'd by success.

YOUNG, *Resignation.* Pt. ii, l. 299.

13
Success shall be in thy courses tall,
Success in thyself, which is best of all,
Success in thy hand, success in thy foot,
In struggle with man, in battle with brute.

SVEND VONVED. Ancient Norse ballad.

II—Success: Apothegms

14
'Tis not in mortals to command success,
But we'll do more, Sempronius; we'll deserve it.

ADDISON, *Cato.* Act i, sc. 2.

But though the place I never gain,
Herein lies comfort for my pain:
I will be worthy of it.

ELLA WHEELER WILCOX, *I Will be Worthy of It.*

15
Success in men's eyes is God and more than God. (Τὸ δ' εὐτυχεῖν, τόδ' ἐν βροτοῖς θεός τε καὶ θεοῦ πλέον.)

ÆSCHYLUS, *Chœphoroi,* l. 59.

16
I have found it! I have found it! (Eureka! Eureka!)

ARCHIMEDES. (VITRUVIUS, *De Architectura,* ix, 215.)

When the idea flashed across his mind, the philosopher sprang out of the bath, exclaiming, "Heureka! heureka!" and without waiting to dress himself, ran home to try the experiment.

VITRUVIUS, of Archimedes, who discovered a method of testing the purity of Hiero's crown, while in the bath.

17
Success is full of promise till men get it; and then it is a last-year's nest from which the birds have flown.

HENRY WARD BEECHER, *Life Thoughts.*

1
Success makes a fool seem wise.
H. G. BOHN, *Hand-Book of Proverbs*, p. 492.

The only infallible criterion of wisdom to vulgar judgments—success.
EDMUND BURKE, *Letter to a Member of the National Assembly*, 1791.

But, Lord! to see what success do, whether with or without reason, and making a man seem wise.
SAMUEL PEPYS, *Diary*. 15 Aug., 1666.

2
God will estimate Success one day.
BROWNING, *Prince Hohenstiel-Schwangau*, 1219.

3
The true touchstone of desert—success.
BYRON, *Marino Faliero*. Act i, sc. 2.

4
One never rises so high as when one does not know where one is going.
OLIVER CROMWELL, *Remark*, to M. Bellièvre. (CARDINAL DE RETZ, *Memoirs*.)

5
Nothing succeeds like success. (Rien ne réussit comme le succès.)
DUMAS, *Ange Pitou*. Bk. i, p. 72. (1854) Quoting a French proverb of unknown origin.

Gentlemen, this is no humbug.
DR. JOHN C. WARREN, of Boston, after operating for the first time on a patient under the influence of ether administered by Dr. William T. G. Morton, at the Massachusetts General Hospital, 16 Oct., 1846. F. P. A. states that he added, "Nothing succeeds like success."

6
One thing is forever good;
That one thing is Success.
EMERSON, *Destiny*, l. 45.

7
Self-trust is the first secret of success.
EMERSON, *Society and Solitude: Success*.

8
Show that you know this only: never to fail to get what you desire; never to fall into what you would avoid.
EPICTETUS, *Discourses*. Bk. ii, ch. 1, sec. 37.

9
Success is never blamed.
THOMAS FULLER, *Gnomologia*. No. 4273.

Everything is subservient to success, even grammar. (Tout obéit au succès, même la grammaire.)
VICTOR HUGO, *Les Misérables*.

10
The success of any great moral enterprise does not depend upon numbers.
WILLIAM LLOYD GARRISON, *Life*. Vol. iii, p. 473.

Experience has always shown, and reason also, that affairs which depend on many seldom succeed.
GUICCIARDINI, *Storia d'Italia*.

11
Like the British Constitution, she owes her success in practice to her inconsistencies in principle.
THOMAS HARDY, *Hand of Ethelberta*. Ch. 9.

12
Every man who can be a first-rate something—as every man can be who is a man at all—has no right to be a fifth-rate something; for a fifth-rate something is no better than a first-rate nothing.
J. G. HOLLAND, *Plain Talks: Self-Help*.

13
'Tis man's to fight, but Heaven's to give success.
HOMER, *Iliad*. Bk. vi, l. 427. (Pope, tr.) *See also under* GOD: APOTHEGMS.

14
In the full tide of successful experiment.
THOMAS JEFFERSON, *First Inaugural*, 4 March, 1801.

15
Success serves men as a pedestal. It makes them seem greater, when not measured by reflection. (Le succès sert aux hommes de piédestal; il les fait paraître plus grands, si la réflexion ne les mesure.)
JOUBERT, *Pensées*. No. 148.

16
If Fortune wishes to make a man estimable, she gives him virtue; if she wishes to make him esteemed, she gives him success. (Si la fortune veut rendre un homme estimable, elle lui donne des vertus; si elle veut le rendre estimé, elle lui donne des succès.)
JOUBERT, *Pensées*. No. 149.

17
Return'd Successful beyond hope.
MILTON, *Paradise Lost*. Bk. x, l. 462.

He said he'd bring home the bacon, and the honey boy has gone and done it.
"TINY" JOHNSON, mother of Jack Johnson, when the latter defeated Jeffries at Reno, 4 July, 1910. Attributed also to Bob Armstrong, negro trainer of pugilists. (N. Y. *Sun*, 20 July, 1933.)

18
Either attempt it not, or succeed. (Aut non temptaris, aut perfice.)
OVID, *Ars Amatoria*. Bk. i, l. 389. Altered by Thomas Sackville, Earl of Dorset, for his motto, to, "Aut nunquam tentes, aut perfice."

19
Nothing is so impudent as Success—unless it be those she favours.
J. R. PLANCHÉ, *Success*. (Burletta, 1825.)

20
Promotion cometh neither from the east, nor from the west, nor from the south.
Old Testament: Psalms, lxxv, 6.

21
Homo novus. (A new man.)
SALLUST, *Catilina*. Ch. 23, sec. 6. Meaning one who has just risen to success.

22
His head was turned by too great success. (Motum illi felicitate nimia caput.)
SENECA, *Epistulæ ad Lucilium*. Epis. cxiv, 8.

23
Take care to get what you like or you will be forced to like what you get.
BERNARD SHAW, *Maxims for Revolutionists*. *See also under* PRAYER.

1
A great devotee of the Gospel of Getting On.
SHAW, *Mrs. Warren's Profession.* Act. iv.

2
Life lives only in success.
BAYARD TAYLOR, *Amran's Wooing.* St. 5.

3
To attain . . . the Unattainable.
TENNYSON, *Timbuctoo,* l. 196.

4
We never know, believe me, when we have succeeded best.
UNAMUNO, *Essays and Soliloquies,* p. 144.

5
Triumphing at last. (Tandem triumphans.)
UNKNOWN, *Motto,* inscribed on the standard of the Young Pretender, Charles Edward Stuart, on his landing in Scotland, 1745.

III—Success: How It Is Won

6
Those things which are not practicable are not desirable. There is nothing in the world really beneficial that does not lie within the reach of an informed understanding and a well-directed pursuit.
EDMUND BURKE, *Speech on the Plan for Economical Reform,* 11 Feb., 1780.

7
Presence of mind and courage in distress
Are more than armies to procure success.
DRYDEN, *Aureng-Zebe.* Act ii.

8
The race is not to the swift, nor the battle to the strong, neither yet bread to the wise, nor yet riches to men of understanding, nor yet favour to men of skill; but time and chance happeneth to them all.
Old Testament: Ecclesiastes, ix, 11.

Not to the swift, the race:
Not to the strong, the fight:
Not to the righteous, perfect grace:
Not to the wise, the light.

But often faltering feet
Come surest to the goal;
And they who walk in darkness meet
The sunrise of the soul.
HENRY VAN DYKE, *Reliance.*

The race by vigour, not by vaunts, is won.
POPE, *The Dunciad.* Bk. ii, l. 59.

9
Born for success he seemed,
With grace to win, with heart to hold,
With shining gifts that took all eyes.
EMERSON, *In Memoriam,* l. 60.

10
Be studious in your profession, and you will be learned. Be industrious and frugal, and you will be rich. Be sober and temperate, and you will be healthy. Be in general virtuous, and you will be happy. At least, you will, by such conduct, stand the best chance for such consequences.
BENJAMIN FRANKLIN, *Letter to John Alleyn.*

If you want to know whether you are destined to be a success or a failure in life, you can easily find out. The test is simple and it is infallible. Are you able to save money? If not, drop out. You will lose.
JAMES J. HILL.

11
If you can dream—and not make dreams your master;
If you can think—and not make thoughts your aim;
If you can meet with Triumph and Disaster
And treat those two impostors just the same; . . .
If you can fill the unforgiving minute
With sixty seconds' worth of distance run,
Yours is the Earth and everything that's in it,
And—which is more—you'll be a Man, my son!
RUDYARD KIPLING, *If—.* Said to have been written with George Washington in mind.

12 There are only two ways of getting on in the world: by one's own industry, or by the stupidity of others. (Il n'y a au monde que deux manières de s'élever, ou par sa propre industrie, ou par l'imbécillité des autres.)
LA BRUYÈRE, *Les Caractères: Biens de Fortune.*

13
The talent of success is nothing more than doing what you can do well; and doing well whatever you do, without a thought of fame.
LONGFELLOW, *Hyperion.* Bk. i, ch. 8.

To know how to wait is the great secret of success.
DE MAISTRE.

14
The man who seeks one thing in life, and but one,
May hope to achieve it before life be done;
But he who seeks all things, wherever he goes,
Only reaps from the hopes which around him he sows
A harvest of barren regrets.
OWEN MEREDITH, *Lucile.* Pt. i, canto ii, sec. 4.

15
I have always observed that to succeed in the world one should seem a fool, but be wise. (J'ai toujours vu que, pour réussir dans le monde, il fallait avoir l'air fou et être sage.)
MONTESQUIEU, *Pensées Diverses.*

16
The success of most things depends upon knowing how long it will take to succeed. (Le succès de la plupart des choses dépend de voir combien il faut de temps pour réussir.)
MONTESQUIEU, *Pensées Diverses.*

17
If you wish to reach the highest, begin at the lowest. (Si vis ad summum progredi ab infimo ordire.)
PUBLILIUS SYRUS, *Sententiæ.* No. 647.

1
Have more than thou showest,
Speak less than thou knowest,
Lend less than thou owest,
Ride more than thou goest,
Learn more than thou trowest,
Set less than thou throwest;
Leave thy drink and thy whore,
And keep in-a-door,
And thou shalt have more
Than two tens to a score.

SHAKESPEARE, *King Lear*. Act i, sc. 4, l. 131.

2
Success, remember, is the reward of toil. (Ὅρα, πόνου τοι χωρὶς οὐδὲν εὐτυχεῖ.)

SOPHOCLES, *Electra*, l. 945.

3
If you would win success, go with the crowd,
Nor like a fool against the current strive.

W. W. STORY, *A Primitive Christian in Rome*.

4
All succeeds with people who are sweet and cheerful. (Tout réussit aux gens qui sont doux et joyeux.)

VOLTAIRE, *Le Dépositaire*.

5
Success begins with a fellow's will—
It's all in the state of mind.

WALTER D. WINTLE, *Thinking*.

He started to sing as he tackled the thing
That couldn't be done, and he did it.

EDGAR A. GUEST, *It Couldn't be Done*.

5a
If the plow cannot reach it, the harrow can. (Li pu chao pa yeh chao.)

UNKNOWN. A Chinese proverb.

A hundred shots and a hundred hits. (Pai fo pai chung.)

UNKNOWN. A Chinese proverb.

IV—Success: Its Penalties

See also Greatness: Its Penalties

6
Yet the success of plans and the advantage to be derived from them do not at all times agree, seeing the gods claim to themselves the right to decide as to the final result.

AMMIANUS MARCELLINUS, *Annales*. Bk. xxv, 3.

Success, the mark no mortal wit,
Or surest hand, can always hit:
For whatsoe'er we perpetrate,
We do but row, we're steer'd by Fate,
Which in success oft disinherits,
For spurious causes, noblest merits.

BUTLER, *Hudibras*. Pt. i, canto i, l. 879.

7
Hast thou not learn'd, what thou art often told,
A truth still sacred, and believ'd of old,
That no success attends on spears and swords
Unblest, and that the battle is the Lord's?

COWPER, *Expostulation*, l. 350.

8 The odium of success is hard enough to bear, without the added ignominy of popular applause.

R. B. CUNNINGHAME-GRAHAM, *Success*.

9
The moral flabbiness born of the exclusive worship of the bitch-goddess Success.

WILLIAM JAMES, *Letter to H. G. Wells*, 11 Sept., 1906.

Success—"the bitch-goddess, Success," in William James's phrase—demands strange sacrifices from those who worship her.

ALDOUS HUXLEY, *Proper Studies*, p. 318.

10
The incomputable perils of success.

J. R. LOWELL, *Under the Old Elm*.

11
Mighty things haste to destruction—such is the limit ordained by heaven to success. (In se magna ruunt: lætis hunc numina rebus Crescendi pœuere modum.)

LUCAN, *De Bello Civili*. Bk. i, l. 81.

12
When the shore is won at last,
Who will count the billows past?

JOHN KEBLE, *The Christian Year: St. John the Evangelist's Day*.

13
Success has brought many to destruction. (Successus ad perniciem multos devocat.)

PHÆDRUS, *Fables*. Bk. iii, fab. 5, l. 1.

Success has ruined many a man.

BENJAMIN FRANKLIN, *Poor Richard*, 1752.

V—Success and Failure

See also Failure; Victory and Defeat

14
'Twixt failure and success the point's so fine
Men sometimes know not when they touch the line.
Just when the pearl was waiting one more plunge,
How many a struggler has thrown up the sponge! . . .
Then take this honey from the bitterest cup:
"There is no failure save in giving up!"

HENRY AUSTIN, *Perseverance Conquers All*.

15
If this be then success, 'tis dismaller
Than any failure.

E. B. BROWNING, *Aurora Leigh*. Bk. v, l. 433.

16
For thence,—a paradox
Which comforts while it mocks,—
Shall life succeed in that it seems to fail:
What I aspired to be,
And was not, comforts me:
A brute I might have been, but would not sink i' the scale.

ROBERT BROWNING, *Rabbi Ben Ezra*. St. 7.

17
Well, if I don't succeed, I *have* succeeded,
And that's enough.

BYRON, *Don Juan*. Canto xii, st. 17.

The secret of success in life is known only to those who have not succeeded.

CHURTON COLLINS, *Aphorisms*. No. 40.

Success is counted sweetest
By those who ne'er succeed.
EMILY DICKINSON, *Poems*. Pt. i, No. 1.

1
Failure is often that early morning hour of darkness which precedes the dawning of the day of success.
LEIGH MITCHELL HODGES, *Success*.

2
Not in the clamor of the crowded street,
Not in the shouts and plaudits of the throng,
But in ourselves, are triumph and defeat.
LONGFELLOW, *The Poets*.

3
How far high failure overleaps the bounds of
low success.
LEWIS MORRIS, *The Epic of Hades: Marsyas*, l. 211.

4
To stand upon the ramparts and die for our principles is heroic, but to sally forth to battle and win for our principles is something more than heroic.
FRANKLIN D. ROOSEVELT, *Speech*, nominating Alfred E. Smith for the presidency, Houston, Tex., June, 1928.

5
We learn wisdom from failure much more than from success. We often discover what *will* do, by finding out what will not do; and probably he who never made a mistake never made a discovery.
SAMUEL SMILES, *Self-Help*. Ch. 11.

6
What though success will not attend on all,
Who bravely dares must sometimes risk a fall.
SMOLLETT, *Advice*, l. 207. *See also under* FALL.

7
Our business in this world is not to succeed, but to continue to fail, in good spirits.
R. L. STEVENSON, *Ethical Studies*, p. 84.

7a
I cannot give you the formula for success, but I can give you the formula for failure—which is: Try to please everybody.
HERBERT BAYARD SWOPE, *Address*, at dinner given in his honor by Interfaith in Action, 20 December, 1950.

8
This proverb flashes thro' his head,
"The many fail, the one succeeds."
TENNYSON, *The Day-Dream*, l. 115.

Some shall reap that never sow
And some shall toil and not attain.
MADISON CAWEIN, *Success*.

SUFFERING

9
Courage! Suffering when it climbs highest, lasts not long. (Θάρσει· πόνου γὰρ τἄκρον οὐκ ἔχει χρόνον.)
ÆSCHYLUS, *Fragments*. Frag. 190.

11
Tragedy is in the eye of the observer, and not in the heart of the sufferer.
EMERSON, *Natural Hist. of Intellect: Tragic*.

12
To each his suff'rings: all are men,
Condemn'd alike to groan;
The tender for another's pain,
Th' unfeeling for his own.
THOMAS GRAY, *Ode on a Distant Prospect of Eton College*, l. 91.

13
For he who much has suffer'd, much will know.
HOMER, *Odyssey*. Bk. xv, l. 436. (Pope, tr.)

14
If you suffer, thank God!—it is a sure sign that you are alive.
ELBERT HUBBARD, *Epigrams*.

15
Present sufferings seem far greater to men than those they merely dread. (Graviora quæ patiantur videntur jam hominibus quam quæ metuant.)
LIVY, *History*. Bk. iii, sec. 39.

16
Know how sublime a thing it is
To suffer and be strong.
LONGFELLOW, *The Light of Stars*, l. 36.

17
My being hath been but a living death,
With a continued torture.
PHILIP MASSINGER, *The Guardian*. Act ii, sc. 4.

18
Our torments also may in length of time
Become our elements.
MILTON, *Paradise Lost*. Bk. ii, l. 274.

19
Civilized mankind has of will ceased to torture, but in our process of being civilized we have won, I suspect, intensified capacity to suffer.
S. WEIR MITCHELL, *Characteristics*. Ch. 1.

Is it so, O Christ in heaven, that the highest suffer most,
That the strongest wander farthest, and more hopelessly are lost,
That the mark of rank in nature is capacity for pain,
That the anguish of the singer makes the sweetness of the strain?
SARAH WILLIAMS, *Is It So, O Christ in Heaven?*

20
Racks, gibbets, halters were their arguments.
JOHN OLDHAM, *Satires Upon the Jesuits*: No. 1, *Gernet's Ghost*.

21
For I reckon that the sufferings of this present time are not worthy to be compared with the glory which shall be revealed in us.
New Testament: Romans, viii, 18.

22
The shirt of Nessus is upon me.
SHAKESPEARE, *Antony and Cleopatra*. Act iv, sc. 12, l. 43.

23
Poor Tom 's a-cold.
SHAKESPEARE, *King Lear*. Act iii, sc. 4, l. 151.

Ho! why dost thou shiver and shake, Gaffer Grey?

And why does thy nose look so blue?
THOMAS HOLCROFT, *Gaffer Grey*.

1
Thy old groans ring yet in my ancient ears.
SHAKESPEARE, *Romeo and Juliet*. Act ii, sc. 3, 74.

2
O, I have suffer'd
With those that I saw suffer.
SHAKESPEARE, *The Tempest*. Act i, sc. 2, l. 5.

He could *afford* to suffer
With those whom he saw suffer.
WORDSWORTH, *The Excursion*. Bk. i, l. 370.

3
For there are . . . sufferings which have no tongue.
SHELLEY, *The Cenci*. Act iii, sc. 1.

4
Yet tears to human suffering are due;
And mortal hopes defeated and o'erthrown
Are mourned by man, and not by man alone.
WORDSWORTH, *Laodamia*, l. 164.

SUFFRAGE, see Votes and Voting

SUICIDE

I—Suicide: Apothegms

5
The common damned shun their society.
ROBERT BLAIR, *The Grave*, l. 415. Referring to suicides in Hell.

While foulest fiends shun thy society.
NATHANIEL LEE, *Rival Queens*. Act v, sc. 1, l. 86.

They dread to meet thee, poor unfortunate!
Whose crime it was, on Life's unfinished road,
To feel the stepdame buffetings of fate.
THOMAS CAMPBELL, *Lines on the Grave of a Suicide*.

6
Not to be content with life is the unsatisfactory state of those who destroy themselves.
SIR THOMAS BROWNE, *To a Friend*. Sec. 26.

7
Nine men in ten are suicides.
BENJAMIN FRANKLIN, *Poor Richard*, 1749.

8
And there he hung till he was dead
As any nail in town,—
For though distress had cut him up,
It could not cut him down!
THOMAS HOOD, *Faithless Nelly Gray*.

9
It does not hurt, my Pætus. (Pæte, non dolet.)
ARRIA, wife of Pætus, as she held out the knife to him after she had stabbed herself. He had been ordered to commit suicide because of cowardice. (PLINY THE YOUNGER, *Epistles*. Bk. iii, epis. 16.)

When chaste Arria was offering to her Pætus that sword which with her own hand she had drawn from out her breast: "If thou believest me," she said, "the wound I have inflicted has no smart; but the wound thou shalt inflict—this, for me, Pætus, has the smart."
MARTIAL, *Epigrams*. Bk. i, epig. 13.

10
There is left us Ourselves to end ourselves.
SHAKESPEARE, *Antony and Cleopatra*, iv, 14, 21.

Is it sin
To rush into the secret house of death,
Ere death dare come to us?
SHAKESPEARE, *Antony and Cleopatra*, iv, 15, 80.

This mortal house I'll ruin.
SHAKESPEARE, *Antony and Cleopatra*, v, 2, 51.

11
Against self-slaughter
There is a prohibition so divine
That cravens my weak hand.
SHAKESPEARE, *Cymbeline*. Act iii, sc. 4, l. 78.

Or that the Everlasting had not fix'd
His canon 'gainst self-slaughter.
SHAKESPEARE, *Hamlet*. Act i, sc. 2, l. 131.

12
By self and violent hands Took off her life.
SHAKESPEARE, *Macbeth*. Act v, sc. 8, l. 70.

With blade, with bloody blameful blade,
He bravely broach'd his boiling bloody breast.
SHAKESPEARE, *A Midsummer-Night's Dream*. Act v, sc. 1, l. 147.

13
I will incontinently drown myself.
SHAKESPEARE, *Othello*. Act i, sc. 3, l. 306.

The more pity that great folk should have countenance in this world to drown or hang themselves, more than their even Christian.
SHAKESPEARE, *Hamlet*. Act v, sc. 1, l. 29.

And now I'm here, from this here pier, it is my fixed intent
To jump as Mister Levi did from off the monument.
R. H. BARHAM, *Aunt Fanny*.

Ah, yes! the sea is still and deep,
All things within its bosom sleep!
A single step, and all is o'er;
A plunge, a bubble, and no more.
LONGFELLOW, *The Golden Legend*: Pt. v, *The Inn at Genoa*.

If you like not hanging, drown yourself! take some course
For your reputation.
PHILIP MASSINGER, *A New Way to Pay Old Debts*. Act ii, sc. 1.

13a
In church your grandsire cut his throat;
To do the job too long he tarried:
He should have had my hearty vote
To cut his throat before he married.
JONATHAN SWIFT, *On an Upright Judge*.

14
There is no refuge from confession but suicide; and suicide is confession.
DANIEL WEBSTER, *Argument on the Murder of Captain Wilde*, 6 April, 1830.

II—Suicide: Its Folly

15
Suicide is the worst form of murder, because it leaves no opportunity for repentance.
CHURTON COLLINS, *Aphorisms*.

16
When Fannius from his foe did fly,
Himself with his own hands he slew;
Who e'er a greater madman knew,
Life to destroy for fear to die?

(Hostem cum fugeret, se Fannius ipse peremit.
Hoc, rogo, non furor est, ne moriare, mori?)
MARTIAL, *Epigrams*. Bk. ii, epig. 80.

It is folly to die through fear of dying. The executioner is upon you; wait for him. (Stultitia est timore mortis mori. Venit qui occidat. Expecta.)
SENECA, *Epistulæ ad Lucilium*. Epis. lxx, sec. 8.

Who doubting tyranny, and fainting under
Fortune's false lottery, desperately run
To death, for dread of death; that soul's most stout,
That, bearing all mischance, dares last it out.
BEAUMONT AND FLETCHER, *The Honest Man's Fortune*. Act iv, sc. 1.

Why should we
Anticipate our sorrows? 'Tis like those
That die for fear of death.
SIR JOHN DENHAM, *The Sophy*.

The beasts had committed suicide to save themselves from slaughter.
JOHN BRIGHT, *Speech,* at Birmingham, 1867. Referring to the Conservatives.

III—Suicide: Its Wisdom

1
We are in the power of no calamity while death is in our own.
SIR THOMAS BROWNE, *Religio Medici*. Pt. i, 44.

The sweetest gift nature has bequeathed us . . . is that she has left us the key of the fields.
MONTAIGNE, *Essays*. Bk. ii, ch. 3.

Happy men that have the power to die.
TENNYSON, *Tithonus*, l. 70.

But now that refuge of despair is shut,
For other lives have twined themselves with mine.
JOHN DAVIDSON, *Lammas*.

2
What, does he who is at liberty to leave the banquet when he will, and play the game no longer, keep on annoying himself by staying?
EPICTETUS, *Discourses*. Bk. ii, ch. 16, sec. 37.

3
If suicide be supposed a crime, it is only cowardice can impel us to it. If it be no crime, both prudence and courage should engage us to rid ourselves at once of existence when it becomes a burden. It is the only way that we can then be useful to society, by setting an example which, if imitated, would preserve every one his chance for happiness in life, and would effectually free him from all danger or misery.
DAVID HUME, *Essays: Suicide*.

4
Just as I shall select my ship when I am about to go on a voyage, or my house when I propose to take a residence, so I shall choose my death when I am about to depart from life.
SENECA, *Epistulæ ad Lucilium*. Epis. lxx, 11.

5
Tranquillity can be purchased at the cost of a pin-prick. (Puncto securitas constat.)
SENECA, *Epistulæ ad Lucilium*. Epis. lxx, 16.

6
He is truly great who has not only given himself the order to die, but has found the means. (Ille vir magnus est, qui mortem sibi non tantum imperavit, sed invenit.)
SENECA, *Epistulæ ad Lucilium*. Epis. lxx, 25.

7
That self hand,
Which writ his honour in the acts it did,
Hath, with the courage which the heart did lend it,
Splitted the heart.
SHAKESPEARE, *Antony and Cleopatra*. Act v, sc. 1, l. 21.

Bravest at the last,
She levell'd at our purposes, and, being royal,
Took her own way.
SHAKESPEARE, *Antony and Cleopatra*. Act v, sc. 2, l. 338.

She drank Prussic acid without any water,
And died like a Duke-and-a-Duchess's daughter!
R. H. BARHAM, *The Tragedy*.

8
You good gods, give me
The penitent instrument to pick the bolt,
Then, free for ever!
SHAKESPEARE, *Cymbeline*. Act v, sc. 4, l. 9.

9
To be, or not to be: that is the question:
Whether 'tis nobler in the mind to suffer
The slings and arrows of outrageous fortune,
Or to take arms against a sea of troubles,
And by opposing end them?
SHAKESPEARE, *Hamlet*. Act iii, sc. 1, l. 56.

For who would bear the whips and scorns of time,
The oppressor's wrong, the proud man's contumely,
The pangs of despised love, the law's delay,
The insolence of office, and the spurns
That patient merit of the unworthy takes,
When he himself might his quietus make
With a bare bodkin?
SHAKESPEARE, *Hamlet*. Act iii, sc. 1, l. 70.

10
But life, being weary of these worldly bars,
Never lacks power to dismiss itself.
SHAKESPEARE, *Julius Cæsar*. Act i, sc. 3, l. 96.

He that cuts off twenty years of life
Cuts off so many years of fearing death.
SHAKESPEARE, *Julius Cæsar*. Act iii, sc. 1, l. 101.

11
Let it not be call'd impiety,
If in this blemish'd fort I make some hole
Through which I may convey this troubled soul.
SHAKESPEARE, *The Rape of Lucrece*. St. 168.

12
Why should I, beastlike as I find myself,
Not manlike end myself?—our privilege—

What beast has heart to do it?
TENNYSON, *Lucretius*, l. 231.

Again the voice spake unto me:
"Thou art so steep'd in misery,
Surely 't were better not to be."
TENNYSON, *The Two Voices*, l. 46.

1
Though the Garden of thy Life be wholly waste, the sweet flowers withered, the fruit-trees barren, over its wall hang ever the rich dark clusters of the Vine of Death, within easy reach of thy hand, which may pluck of them when it will.
JAMES THOMSON, *The City of Dreadful Night*. Pt. i, note.

IV—Suicide: Its Cowardice

2
Self-murder! name it not; our island's shame;
That makes her the reproach of neighb'ring states.
ROBERT BLAIR, *The Grave*, l. 403.

Our time is fixed, and all our days are number'd;
How long, how short, we know not:—this we know,
Duty requires we calmly wait the summons,
Nor dare to stir till Heaven shall give permission.
ROBERT BLAIR, *The Grave*, l. 417.

3
The divinity who rules within us forbids us to quit this world without his command. (Vetat dominans ille in nobis deus, injussu hinc nos suo demigrare.)
CICERO, *Tusculanarum Disputationum*. Bk. i, ch. 30, sec. 74.

Death may be call'd in vain, and cannot come,
Tyrants can tie him up from your relief:
Nor has a Christian privilege to die. . . .
Brutus and Cato might discharge their souls,
And give them furlo's for another world:
But we like sentries are oblig'd to stand
In starless nights, and wait th' appointed hour.
DRYDEN, *Don Sebastian*. Act ii, sc. 1.

The thought is Cicero's, but how it is intensified by the "starless nights"! Dryden, I suspect, got it from his favorite, Montaigne.
J. R. LOWELL, *My Study Windows: Dryden*.

4
Fool! I mean not
That poor-souled piece of heroism, self-slaughter;
Oh no! the miserablest day we live
There's many a better thing to do than die!
GEORGE DARLEY, *Ethelstan*.

5
Self-destruction is the effect of cowardice in the highest extreme.
DANIEL DEFOE, *An Essay Upon Projects: Of Projectors*.

He is as cowardly
That longer fears to live, as he that fears to die.
PHINEAS FLETCHER, *The Purple Island*. Canto x, st. 8.

6
Who quits a world where strong temptations try,
And, since 'tis hard to combat, learns to fly!
OLIVER GOLDSMITH, *The Deserted Village*, l. 101.

7
When all the blandishments of life are gone,
The coward sneaks to death, the brave live on.
(Rebus in angustis facile est contemnere vitam:
Fortiter ille facit qui miseresse potest.)
MARTIAL, *Epigrams*. Bk. xi, 56. (Sewell, tr.)

8
Yet we should not,
Howe'er besieged, deliver up our fort
Of life, till it be forced.
MASSINGER, *The Guardian*. Act ii, sc. 4.

This life's a fort committed to my trust,
Which I must not yield up till it be forced:
Nor will I. He's not valiant that dares die,
But he that boldly bears calamity.
MASSINGER, *The Maid of Honour*. Act iv, sc. 3.

9
It is the rôle of cowardice, not of courage, to crouch in a hole, under a massive tomb, to avoid the blows of fortune. (C'est le rôle de la couardise, non de la vertu, de s'aller tapir dans un creux, sous un tombe massive, pour éviter les coups de la fortune.)
MONTAIGNE, *Essays*. Bk. ii, ch. 3.

10
To wish for death is a coward's part. (Timidi est optare necem.)
OVID, *Metamorphoses*. Bk. iv, l. 115.

11
We men are in a kind of prison and must not set ourselves free or run away. (*Ὡς ἔν τινι φρουρᾷ ἐσμεν οἱ ἄνθρωποι καὶ οὐ δεῖ δὴ ἑαυτὸν ἐκ ταύτης λύειν οὐδ' ἀποδιδράσκειν.*)
PLATO, *Phædo*. Sec. 62.

Nor at all can tell
Whether I mean this day to end myself,
Or lend an ear to Plato where he says,
That men like soldiers may not quit the post
Allotted by the Gods.
TENNYSON, *Lucretius*, l. 145.

12
You ever-gentle gods, take my breath from me;
Let not my worser spirit tempt me again
To die before you please!
SHAKESPEARE, *King Lear*. Act iv, sc. 6, l. 221.

13
Less base the fear of death than fear of life.
YOUNG, *Night Thoughts*. Night v, l. 441.

SUMMER

I—Summer: Apothegms

14
Summer has set in with his usual severity.
S. T. COLERIDGE, *Letter to Charles Lamb*, May, 1826.

If that the *summer* is not too severe.
BYRON, *The Vision of Judgment*. St. 55. A note to this passage says, "An allusion to Horace Walpole's expression in a letter," but Charles Lamb, in a letter to Bernard Barton (16 May, 1826), states that a letter received by him from Coleridge began with this phrase.

Summer, as my friend Coleridge waggishly writes, has set in with its usual severity.
LAMB, *Letter to V. Novello*, 9 May, 1826.

1
Summer is gone on swallow's wings.
THOMAS HOOD, *The Departure of Summer*.

2
There is something of summer in the hum of insects.
W. S. LANDOR, *Letter to Southey*, 1810.

Do what we can, summer will have its flies.
EMERSON, *Essays, First Series: Prudence*.

3
Expect Saint Martin's summer, halcyon days.
SHAKESPEARE, *I Henry VI*. Act i, sc. 2, l. 131.

The middle summer's spring.
SHAKESPEARE, *A Midsummer-Night's Dream*. Act ii, sc. 1, l. 82.

The Indian Summer, the dead Summer's soul.
MARY CLEMMER, *Presence*, l. 62.

3a
The present time of the year has been named the 'silly season.'
UNKNOWN, *Article*, London *Punch*, 9 Sept., 1871. Referring to August and September, when newspapers, for lack of real news, fill their columns with trivialities.

II—Summer: Its Beauty

4
Bring back the singing; and the scent
Of meadowlands at dewy prime;—
Oh, bring again my heart's content,
Thou Spirit of the Summertime!
WILLIAM ALLINGHAM, *Song*.

5
Now simmer blinks on flowery braes,
And o'er the crystal streamlet plays.
BURNS, *The Birks of Aberfeldy*.

6
I question not if thrushes sing,
If roses load the air;
Beyond my heart I need not reach
When all is summer there.
JOHN VANCE CHENEY, *Love's World*.

7
Here is the ghost Of a summer that lived for us,
Here is a promise Of summers to be.
W. E. HENLEY, *Rhymes and Rhythms*. No. 8.

8
All labourers draw hame at even,
And can to others say,
"Thanks to the gracious God of heaven,
Whilk sent this summer day."
ALEXANDER HUME, *Evening*. St. 2.

O summer day beside the joyous sea!
O summer day so wonderful and white,
So full of gladness and so full of pain!
Forever and forever shalt thou be
To some the gravestone of a dead delight,
To some the landmark of a new domain.
LONGFELLOW, *A Summer Day by the Sea*.

9
Where'er you walk cool gales shall fan the glade;
Trees, where you sit, shall crowd into a shade;
Where'er you tread, the blushing flowers shall rise,
And all things flourish where you turn your eyes.
POPE, *Pastorals: Summer*, l. 73.

10
Rough winds do shake the darling buds of May,
And summer's lease hath all too short a date.
SHAKESPEARE, *Sonnets*. No. xviii.

11
In the good old summer time,
In the good old summer time,
Strolling thro' the shady lanes,
With your baby mine;
You hold her hand and she holds yours,
And that's a very good sign
That she's your tootsey-wootsey
In the good old summer time.
REN SHIELDS, *In the Good Old Summer Time*. (1902) Music by George Evans. Sung by Blanche Ring in *The Defender*.

12
Then came the jolly Summer, being dight
In a thin silken cassock, coloured green,
That was unlinèd all, to be more light.
SPENSER, *Faerie Queene*. Bk. vii, canto vii, st. 29.

13
Pale in her fading bowers the Summer stands,
Like a new Niobe with claspèd hands,
Silent above the flowers, her children lost,
Slain by the arrows of the early Frost.
RICHARD HENRY STODDARD, *Ode*.

14
Pride of summer passing by
With lordly laughter in her eye.
SWINBURNE, *The Tale of Balen*. Pt. ii, st. 1.

Strong summer, dumb with rapture, bound
With golden calm the woodlands round.
SWINBURNE, *The Tale of Balen*. Pt. vii, st. 14.

15
The Summer looks out from her brazen tower,
Through the flashing bars of July.
FRANCIS THOMPSON, *A Corymbus for Autumn*.

16
From brightening fields of ether fair-disclosed,
Child of the sun, refulgent Summer comes.
THOMSON, *The Seasons: Summer*, l. 1.

17
O, softly on yon banks of haze,
Her rosy face the Summer lays!
J. T. TROWBRIDGE, *Midsummer*.

18
Sumer is icumen in,
Lhude sing cuccu!
UNKNOWN, *Cuckoo Song*. The oldest song in the English language, written, probably in

1226, by a monk at Reading Abbey, somewhat questionably identified as John of Fornsete. Original in the Harleian MS., No. 978. The music to which it was sung still survives.

III—Summer: Its Heat

1
O thou who passest thro' our valleys in
Thy strength, curb thy fierce steeds, allay the heat
That flames from their large nostrils! Thou, O Summer,
Oft pitched'st here thy golden tent, and oft
Beneath our oaks hast slept, while we beheld
With joy thy ruddy limbs and flourishing hair.

WILLIAM BLAKE, *To Summer*.

2
O for a lodge in a garden of cucumbers!
O for an iceberg or two at control!
O for a vale that at midday the dew cumbers!
O for a pleasure trip up to the pole!

ROSSITER JOHNSON, *Ninety-Nine in the Shade*.

As a lodge in a garden of cucumbers.

Old Testament: Isaiah, i, 8.

3
But see, the shepherds shun the noonday heat,
The lowing herds to murmuring brooks retreat,
To closer shades the panting flocks remove:
Ye Gods! and is there no relief for love?

POPE, *Pastorals: Summer*, l. 85.

4
Summer's parching heat.

SHAKESPEARE, *II Henry VI*. Act i, sc. 1, l. 81.

5
Heat, ma'am! It was so dreadful here that I found there was nothing left for it but to take off my flesh and sit in my bones.

SYDNEY SMITH. (LADY HOLLAND, *Memoir*. Ch. 9.)

6
The dogged dog-days had begun to bite.

JOHN TAYLOR, *A Very Merry-Wherry-Ferry Voyage*, l. 6.

7
All-conquering heat, oh, intermit thy wrath!
And on my throbbing temples potent thus
Beam not so fierce! Incessant still you flow,
And still another fervent flood succeeds,
Pour'd on the head profuse. In vain I sigh,
And restless turn, and look around for night:
Night is far off; and hotter hours approach.

THOMSON, *The Seasons: Summer*, l. 451.

SUN

I—Sun: Apothegms

8
Fabricius finds certain spots and clouds in the sun.

ROBERT BURTON, *Anatomy of Melancholy*. Pt. ii, sec. ii, mem. 3.

The sun is not all spots.

AUGUSTINE BIRRELL, *Obiter Dicta, Second Series: John Milton*.

9
Make hay while the sun shines.

CERVANTES, *Don Quixote*. Pt. i, ch. 11.

10
As thick as motes in the sun-beam.

CHAUCER, *Wife of Bath's Tale*, l. 12.

As thick and numberless
As the gay motes that people the sunbeams.

MILTON, *Il Penseroso*, l. 7.

11
The sun shines on both sides of the hedge.

DENHAM, *Proverbs*, 49.

The vernal sun new life bestows
Even on the meanest flower that blows.

SCOTT, *Marmion:* Canto i, *Introduction*, l. 63.

The selfsame sun that shines upon his court
Hides not his visage from our cottage but
Looks on alike.

SHAKESPEARE, *Winter's Tale*. Act iv, sc. 4, l. 454.

12
Stand a little out of my sun. (*Μικρόν ἀπὸ τοῦ ἡλίου μετάστηθι*.)

DIOGENES to Alexander, when the latter asked if there was anything he could do for him. (PLUTARCH, *Lives: Alexander*. Ch. 14, sec. 2.)

13
The sun, too, visits cesspools and is not defiled. (*Ἥλιος εἰς τοὺς αποπάτους, ἀλλ' οὐ μιαίνεται*.)

DIOGENES. (DIOGENES LAERTIUS, *Diogenes*. Bk. vi, sec. 63.)

The sun, which passeth through pollutions and itself remains as pure as before.

FRANCIS BACON, *Advancement of Learning*. Bk. ii. (1623)

The sun his fairness never he tines,
Though he on the muck heap shines.

ROBERT MANNYNG (or ROBERT DE BRUNNE), *Handlyng Synne*, l. 2299. (1303)

The sun shineth upon the dunghill and is not corrupted.

JOHN LYLY, *Euphues*, p. 43. (1579)

As sunshine, broken in the rill,
Though turn'd aside, is sunshine still!

THOMAS MOORE, *Lalla Rookh: The Fire-Worshippers*.

The sun reflecting upon the mud of strands and shores is unpolluted in his beam.

JEREMY TAYLOR, *Holy Living*. Ch. i, sec. 3. (1650)

14
Out of the solar walk and Heaven's highway.

DRYDEN, *Threnodia Augustalis*, l. 353.

In climes beyond the solar road.

THOMAS GRAY, *The Progress of Poesy*, l. 54.

15
Let not the sun look down and say, Inglorious here he lies.

BENJAMIN FRANKLIN, *Poor Richard*, 1758.

16
In every country the sun rises in the morning.

GEORGE HERBERT, *Jacula Prudentum*.

Sad soul, take comfort, nor forget
That sunrise never failed us yet.

CELIA THAXTER, *The Sunrise Never Failed Us Yet*.

1
The sun, too, will blind you if you persist in gazing at it. (Sol etiam cæcat, contra si tendere pergas.)
LUCRETIUS, *De Rerum Natura*. Bk. iv, l. 326.

But who can gaze upon the sun in heaven?
TENNYSON, *Lancelot and Elaine*, l. 123.

2
Suppose the chariot of the sun were given you: what would you do? (Finge datos currus: quid ages?)
OVID, *Metamorphoses*. Bk. ii, l. 74. Apollo's question to Phaëton.

Why, so this gallant will command the sun.
SHAKESPEARE, *The Taming of the Shrew*. Act iv, sc. 3, l. 198.

3
The sun is a faithful artist, but his choice of emphasis is often too ironical to be intelligible to human faculty.
SIR WALTER RALEIGH THE YOUNGER, *Oxford Poetry 1914: Preface*.

4
He that walks in the sun, though he walk not for that purpose, must needs become sunburned. (Qui in solem venit, licet non in hoc venerit, colorabitur.)
SENECA, *Epistulæ ad Lucilium*. Epis. cxiii, 4.

To be still hot summer's tanlings.
SHAKESPEARE, *Cymbeline*. Act iv, sc. 4, l. 29. (1610)

He that walketh in the sun shall be tanned.
DAVID TUVILL, *Vade Mecum*, p. 56. (1638)

5
I 'gin to be aweary of the sun.
SHAKESPEARE, *Macbeth*. Act v, sc. 5, l. 49.

6
Written as with a sunbeam.
TERTULLIAN, *De Resurrectione Carnis*. Ch. 47.

Such words fall too often on our cold and careless ears with the triteness of long familiarity; but to Octavia . . . they seemed to be written in sunbeams.
F. W. FARRAR, *Darkness and Dawn*. Ch. 46.

The great duties of life are written with a sunbeam.
JOHN JORTIN, *Sermons*. (1751)

7
Who would dare say the sun is false? (Solem quis dicere falsum Audeat?)
VERGIL, *Georgics*. Bk. i, l. 463.

8
Whose dwelling is the light of setting suns.
WORDSWORTH, *Lines Composed a Few Miles Above Tintern Abbey*, l. 97. A line described by Tennyson as "almost the grandest in the English language."

9
A sunbeam took human shape when he was born.
ISRAEL ZANGWILL, *The Melting-Pot*. Act i.

II—Sun: Its Praise

10
The sun, centre and sire of light,
The keystone of the world-built arch of heaven.
P. J. BAILEY, *Festus: Heaven*.

See the sun!
God's crest upon His azure shield, the Heavens.
P. J. BAILEY, *Festus: A Mountain*.

See the gold sunshine, patching,
And streaming and streaking across
The grey-green oaks; and catching,
By its long brown beard, the moss.
P. J. BAILEY, *Festus: Earth's Surface*.

11
And if the sun would ever shine, there would I dwell.
ANNE BRADSTREET, *Contemplations*.

12
Pleasantly, between the pelting showers, the sunshine gushes down.
BRYANT, *The Cloud on the Way*, l. 18.

13
The God of life and poesy and light,—
The Sun.
BYRON, *Childe Harold*. Canto iv, st. 161.

And representative of the Unknown—
Who chose thee for His shadow!
BYRON, *Manfred*. Act iii, sc. 2.

14
The glorious lamp of Heav'n, the radiant sun,
Is Nature's eye.
DRYDEN, *The Fable of Acis*, l. 165. (OVID, *Metamorphoses*. Bk. xiii.)

Thou sun, of this great world both eye and soul.
MILTON, *Paradise Lost*. Bk. v, l. 171.

Lamp of the world, light of this universe.
JOSHUA SYLVESTER, *The Chariot of the Sun*.

15
High in his chariot glow'd the lamp of day.
FALCONER, *The Shipwreck*. Canto i, pt. 3, l. 3.

16
The great luminary
Aloof the vulgar constellations thick,
That from his lordly eye keep distance due,
Dispenses light from far.
MILTON, *Paradise Lost*. Bk. iii, l. 576.

17
O thou that with surpassing glory crown'd,
Look'st from thy sole dominion like the God
Of this new world; at whose sight all the stars
Hide their diminish'd heads!
MILTON, *Paradise Lost*. Bk. iv, l. 32.

Ye little stars, hide your diminish'd rays.
POPE, *Moral Essays*. Epis. iii, l. 282.

18
Blest power of sunshine!—genial Day,
What balm, what life is in thy ray!
To feel thee is such real bliss,
That had the world no joy but this,
To sit in sunshine calm and sweet,—
It were a world too exquisite
For man to leave it for the gloom,
The deep, cold shadow, of the tomb.
THOMAS MOORE, *Lalla Rookh: The Fire-Worshippers, Third Day*, l. 342.

1
The glorious sun,
Stays in his course and plays the alchemist,
Turning with splendour of his precious eye
The meagre cloddy earth to glittering gold.
SHAKESPEARE, *King John*. Act iii, sc. 1, l. 77.

Gilding pale streams with heavenly alchemy.
SHAKESPEARE, *Sonnets*. No. xxxiii.

2
That orbed continent the fire
That severs day from night.
SHAKESPEARE, *Twelfth Night*. Act v, sc. 1, l. 278.

3
In the warm shadow of her loveliness,
He kissed her with his beams.
SHELLEY, *The Witch of Atlas*. St. 2.

4
Fairest of all the lights above,
Thou sun, whose beams adorn the spheres,
And with unwearied swiftness move,
To form the circles of our years.
ISAAC WATTS, *Sun, Moon and Stars, Praise Ye the Lord*.

5
Give me the splendid silent sun with all his beams full-dazzling!
WALT WHITMAN, *Give Me the Splendid Silent Sun*.

6
The sunshine seemed to bless,
The air was a caress.
WHITTIER, *The Maids of Attitash*. St. 24.

7
The sun's gold would not seem pure gold
Unless the sun were in the sky:
To take him thence and chain him near
Would make his beauty disappear.
WILLIAM WINTER, *Love's Queen*.

III—Sun: Rising and Setting

8
Men rather honour the sun rising than the sun going down.
GEORGE CHAPMAN, *Alphonsus*. Act i, sc. 1.

Most men worship the rising sun.
THOMAS FULLER, *Gnomologia*. No. 3470.

Welcome, young Sunrise, since Voltaire is about to set!
FREDERICK THE GREAT, to Baculard d'Arnaud. Frederick wrote, "Voltaire est à son couchant, Vous êtes à votre aurore." The rendering is Carlyle's.

9
Let others hail the rising sun;
I bow to that whose course is run.
DAVID GARRICK, *On the Death of Mr. Pelham*.

10
More worship the rising than the setting sun. (*Τὸν ἥλιον ἀνατέλλοντα πλείονες ἢ δυόμενον προσκυνοῦσιν*.)
POMPEY, to Sulla. (PLUTARCH, *Lives: Pompey*. Ch. 14, sec. 3.)

You forsake the setting to court the rising sun.
TIBERIUS, to Macro, when the latter seemed favoring Caligula. (TACITUS, *Annals*. Bk. vi, sec. 46.)

11
Men shut their doors against a setting sun.
SHAKESPEARE, *Timon of Athens*. Act i, sc. 2, l. 150.

12
The Sun came up upon the left,
Out of the sea came he!
And he shone bright, and on the right
Went down into the sea.
S. T. COLERIDGE, *The Ancient Mariner*. Pt. i.

The Sun now rose upon the right:
Out of the sea came he,
Still hid in mist, and on the left
Went down into the sea.
S. T. COLERIDGE, *The Ancient Mariner*. Pt. ii.

So sinks the day-star in the ocean bed,
And yet anon repairs his drooping head,
And tricks his beams, and with new spangled ore
Flames in the forehead of the morning sky.
MILTON, *Lycidas*, l. 168.

13
When the sun shines let foolish gnats make sport,
But creep in crannies when he hides his beams.
SHAKESPEARE, *The Comedy of Errors*. Act ii, sc. 2, l. 30.

IV—Sun: Sunrise

See also Dawn, Morning

14
And led by silence more majestical
Than clash of conquering arms, He comes! He Comes!
And strikes out flame from the adoring hills.
ALICE BROWN, *Sunrise on Mansfield Mountain*.

15
The sun is bright on heaven's brow,
The world's fresh blood runs fleet;
Time is as young as ever now,
Nature as fresh and sweet.
JOHN DAVIDSON, *A Ballad of Euthanasia*.

16
And all the small fowls singing on the spray
Welcome the lord of light, the lamp of day.
GAVIN DOUGLAS, *Morning in May*.

17
I saw myself the lambent easy light
Gild the brown horror, and dispel the night.
DRYDEN, *Hind and Panther*. Pt. ii, l. 658.

18
Now from the smooth deep ocean-stream the sun
Began to climb the heavens, and with new rays
Smote the surrounding fields.
HOMER, *Iliad*. Bk. vii, l. 525. (Bryant, tr.)

19
Father of rosy day,
No more thy clouds of incense rise;
But waking flow'rs,
At morning hours,

Give out their sweets to meet thee in the skies.
THOMAS HOOD, *Hymn to the Sun*. St. 4.

1
Night's son was driving
His golden-haired horses up;
Over the eastern firths
High flashed their manes.
KINGSLEY, *The Longbeards' Saga*, l. 122.

2
Thou shalt sleep in thy clouds, careless of the voice of the morning.
MACPHERSON, *Ossian: Address to the Sun.*

3
The east is blossoming! Yea, a rose,
Vast as the heavens, soft as a kiss,
Sweet as the presence of woman is,
Rises and reaches, and widens and grows
Large and luminous up from the sea,
And out of the sea, as a blossoming tree,
Richer and richer, so higher and higher,
Deeper and deeper it takes its hue;
Brighter and brighter it reaches through
The space of heaven and the place of stars,
Till all is as rich as a rose can be,
And my rose-leaves fall into billows of fire.
JOAQUIN MILLER, *Sunrise in Venice.*

4
Right against the Eastern gate,
Where the great Sun begins his state.
MILTON, *L'Allegro*, l. 59.

5
Whether the sun, predominant in Heav'n,
Rise on the earth, or earth rise on the sun, . . .
Solicit not thy thoughts with matters hid,
Leave them to God above, him serve and fear.
MILTON, *Paradise Lost*. Bk. viii, l. 160.

"But," quoth his neighbour, "when the sun
From East to West his course has run,
How comes it that he shows his face
Next morning in his former place?"
"Ho! there's a pretty question, truly!"
Replied our wight, with an unruly
Burst of laughter and delight,
So much his triumph seemed to please him.
"Why, blockhead! he goes back at night,
And that's the reason no one sees him!"
HORACE SMITH, *The Astronomical Alderman.*

6
And see—the Sun himself!—on wings
Of glory up the East he springs.
Angel of Light! who from the time
Those heavens began their march sublime,
Hath first of all the starry choir
Trod in his Maker's steps of fire!
THOMAS MOORE, *Lalla Rookh: The Fire-Worshippers, Second Day*, l. 25.

7
Wake! for the Sun, who scatter'd into flight
The Stars before him from the Field of Night,
Drives Night along with them from Heav'n, and strikes
The Sultan's Turret with a Shaft of Light.
OMAR KHAYYÁM, *Rubáiyát*. St. 1. (Fitzgerald, tr.)

8
The morning sun has now smiled upon the roofs. (Matutinus sol tectis arrisit.)
PETRONIUS, *Fragments*. No. 5.

9
Day, peeping from the east, makes the sun turn from black to red, like a boiled lobster.
RABELAIS, *Works*. Bk. v, ch. 7.

The sun had long since, in the lap
Of Thetis, taken out his nap,
And, like a lobster boil'd, the morn
From black to red began to turn.
BUTLER, *Hudibras*. Pt. ii, canto 2, l. 29.

10
Hark, hark! the lark at heaven's gate sings,
And Phœbus 'gins arise.
SHAKESPEARE, *Cymbeline*. Act ii, sc. 3, l. 21.

11
The hour before the heavenly-harness'd team
Begins his golden progress in the east.
SHAKESPEARE, *I Henry IV*. Act iii, sc. 1, l. 221.

An hour before the worshipp'd sun
Peer'd forth the golden window of the east.
SHAKESPEARE, *Romeo and Juliet*. Act i, sc. 1, l. 125.

12
For night's swift dragons cut the clouds full fast,
And yonder shines Aurora's harbinger:
At whose approach, ghosts, wandering here and there,
Troop home to churchyards.
SHAKESPEARE, *A Midsummer-Night's Dream*. Act iii, sc. 2, l. 379.

He fires the proud tops of the eastern pines
And darts his light through every guilty hole.
SHAKESPEARE, *Richard II*. Act iii, sc. 2, l. 42.

As when the golden sun salutes the morn,
And, having gilt the ocean with his beams,
Gallops the zodiac in his glistering coach,
And overlooks the highest-peering hills.
SHAKESPEARE, *Titus Andronicus*. Act ii, sc. 1, l. 5.

13
At last, the golden oriental gate
Of greatest heaven 'gan to open fair,
And Phœbus, fresh as bridegroom to his mate,
Came dancing forth, shaking his dewy hair.
SPENSER, *Faerie Queene*. Bk. i, canto v, st. 2.

14
And yonder fly his scattered golden arrows,
And smite the hills with day.
BAYARD TAYLOR, *The Poet's Journal: Third Evening: Morning.*

But yonder comes the powerful King of Day,
Rejoicing in the east.
THOMSON, *The Seasons: Summer*, l. 81.

15
See how there The cowlèd Night
Kneels on the Eastern sanctuary-stair.
FRANCIS THOMPSON, *A Corymbus for Autumn.*

16
It is true, I never assisted the sun materially

in his rising; but, doubt not, it was of the last importance only to be present at it.
HENRY DAVID THOREAU, *Walden*. Ch. 1.

1
The rising sun complies with our weak sight,
First gilds the clouds, then shows his globe of light
At such a distance from our eyes, as though
He knew what harm his hasty beams would do.
EDMUND WALLER, *To the King, Upon His Majesty's Happy Return*, l. 1.

V—Sun: Sunset

See also Evening, Twilight

2
Come watch with me the azure turn to rose
In yonder West: the changing pageantry,
The fading alps and archipelagoes,
And spectral cities of the sunset-sea.
T. B. ALDRICH, *Miracles*.

3
The sun had gone down fiery red;
And if, that evening, he laid his head
In Thetis's lap beneath the seas,
He must have scalded the goddess's knees.
R. H. BARHAM, *The Witches' Frolic*.

As far as Phœbus first doth rise,
Until in Thetis' lap he lies.
SIR ARTHUR GORGES, *Ode*.

4
The sun descending in the west,
The evening star does shine;
The birds are silent in their nest,
And I must seek for mine.
WILLIAM BLAKE, *Night*.

5
The sacred lamp of day
Now dipt in western clouds his parting ray.
WILLIAM FALCONER, *The Shipwreck*. Canto ii, l. 27.

6
For the Elysians the sun seems always to have just set.
BENJAMIN DISRAELI, *The Infernal Marriage*. Pt. iv, ch. 2.

7
Behold him setting in his western skies,
The shadows lengthening as the vapours rise.
DRYDEN, *Absalom and Achitophel*. Pt. i, l. 268.

8
Oft did I wonder why the setting sun
Should look upon us with a blushing face:
Is't not for shame of what he hath seen done,
Whilst in our hemisphere he ran his race?
LYMAN HEATH, *On the Setting Sun*.

9
A late lark twitters from the quiet skies;
And from the west,
Where the sun, his day's work ended,
Lingers as in content,
There falls on the old, grey city
An influence luminous and serene,
A shining peace.
W. E. HENLEY, *Margaritæ Sorori*. St. 1.

The smoke ascends
In a rosy-and-golden haze. The spires
Shine, and are changed. In the valley
Shadows rise. The lark sings on. The sun,
Closing his benediction,
Sinks, and the darkening air
Thrills with a sense of the triumphing night—
Night with her train of stars
And her great gift of sleep.
W. E. HENLEY, *Margaritæ Sorori*. St. 2.

10
Now deep in ocean sunk the lamp of light,
And drew behind the cloudy veil of night.
HOMER, *Iliad*. Bk. viii, l. 605. (Pope, tr.)

11
The sun is a-wait at the ponderous gate of the West.
SIDNEY LANIER, *The Marshes of Glynn*.

12
Down sank the great red sun, and in golden, glimmering vapors
Veiled the light of his face, like the Prophet descending from Sinai.
LONGFELLOW, *Evangeline*. Pt. i, sec. 4.

After a day of cloud and wind and rain
Sometimes the setting sun breaks out again,
And, touching all the darksome woods with light,
Smiles on the fields, until they laugh and sing,
Then like a ruby from the horizon's ring,
Drops down into the night.
LONGFELLOW, *Hanging of the Crane*. Pt. vii.

13
The sun is set; and in his latest beams
Yon little cloud of ashen gray and gold,
Slowly upon the amber air unrolled,
The falling mantle of the Prophet seems.
LONGFELLOW, *A Summer Day by the Sea*.

14
The west is broken into bars
Of orange, gold, and gray;
Gone is the sun, come are the stars,
And night infolds the day.
GEORGE MACDONALD, *Songs of Summer Nights*.

15
And the gilded car of day,
His glowing axle doth allay
In the steep Atlantic stream.
MILTON, *Comus*, l. 95.

16
The skies yet blushing with departing light.
When fallen dews with spangles deck'd the glade,
And the low sun had lengthen'd ev'ry shade.
POPE, *Pastorals: Autumn*, l. 98.

17
Long on the wave reflected lustres play.
SAMUEL ROGERS, *Pleasures of Memory*. Pt. i, l. 94.

18
God is at the anvil, beating out the sun;
Where the molten metal spills,
At His forge among the hills
He has hammered out the glory of a day that's done.
LEW SARETT, *God Is at the Anvil*.

1
No pale gradations quench his ray,
No twilight dews his wrath allay;
With disk like battle-target red
He rushes to his burning bed,
Dyes the wide wave with bloody light,
Then sinks at once—and all is night.
SCOTT, *Rokeby*. Canto vi, st. 21.

2
The lonely sunsets flare forlorn
Down valleys dreadly desolate;
The lonely mountains soar in scorn
As still as death, as stern as fate.
ROBERT W. SERVICE, *Land That God Forgot*.

3
The west yet glimmers with some streaks of day.
SHAKESPEARE, *Macbeth*. Act iii, sc. 3, l. 5.

4
The setting sun, and music at the close,
At the last taste of sweets, is sweetest last.
SHAKESPEARE, *Richard II*. Act ii, sc. 1, l. 12.

5
When the sun sets, who doth not look for night?
SHAKESPEARE, *Richard III*. Act ii, sc. 3, l. 34.

6
The weary sun hath made a golden set,
And, by the bright track of his fiery car,
Gives signal of a goodly day to-morrow.
SHAKESPEARE, *Richard III*. Act v, sc. 3, l. 19.

7
The beams of sunset hung their rainbow hues
High 'mid the shifting domes of sheeted spray
That canopied his path o'er the waste deep.
SHELLEY, *Alastor*, l. 334.

When, as a token at parting, munificent Day, for remembrance,
Gives, unto men that forget, Ophirs of fabulous ore.
WILLIAM WATSON, *Hymn to the Sea*. Pt. iii, l. 15.

Touched by a light that hath no name,
A glory never sung,
Aloft on sky and mountain wall
Are God's great pictures hung.
WHITTIER, *Sunset on the Bearcamp*. St. 3.

8
There sinks the nebulous star we call the sun.
TENNYSON, *The Princess*. Pt. iv, l. 1.

9
Nobody of any real culture ever talks nowadays about the beauty of a sunset. Sunsets are quite old-fashioned. They belong to the time when Turner was the last note in art.
OSCAR WILDE, *The Decay of Lying*.

VI—Sun and Moon

10
That hour of the day when, face to face, the rising moon beholds the setting sun.
LONGFELLOW, *Hyperion*. Bk. ii, ch. 10.

11
Courses even with the sun
Doth her mighty brother run.
BEN JONSON, *The Gipsies Metamorphosed*.

12
And God made two great lights, great for their use
To man, the greater to have rule by day
The less by night altern.
MILTON, *Paradise Lost*. Bk. vii, l. 346.

13
The sun to me is dark
And silent as the moon,
When she deserts the night
Hid in her vacant interlunar cave.
MILTON, *Samson Agonistes*, l. 86.

14
And teach me how
To name the bigger light, and how the less,
That burn by day and night.
SHAKESPEARE, *The Tempest*. Act i, sc. 2, l. 334.

15
L'Abbé de Ville proposed a toast.
His master, as the rising Sun;
Reisbach then gave the Empress Queen,
As the bright Moon, and much praise won.
The earl of Stair, whose turn came next,
Gave for his toast his own King Will,
As Joshua, the son of Nun,
Who made both Sun and Moon stand still.
UNKNOWN. (*Anecdote Library*, 1822.) The Empress Queen was Maria Theresa. The same anecdote is related of other men, notably of Benjamin Franklin, who, at a banquet in England, after toasts to Great Britain as the sun which gives light to the whole earth, and to France as the moon whose magic rays move the earth's tides, is said to have toasted Washington "the Joshua of America, who commanded the sun and moon to stand still —and they obeyed."

SUNDAY, see Sabbath

SUN-DIAL

I—Sun-Dial: Its Mission

16
Think: the shadow on the dial
For the nature most undone,
Marks the passing of the trial,
Proves the presence of the sun.
E. B. BROWNING, *The Fourfold Aspect*, l. 107.

17
The dial tells the golden-lighted hours
In gardens fair with roses.
DOROTHY COOPER JOHNSON, *Country Gardens*.

18
The old dial . . . stood as the garden god of Christian gardens. . . . It spoke of moderate labours, of pleasures not protracted after sunset, of temperance, and good hours. . . . The shepherd "carved it out quaintly in the sun"; and, turning philosopher by the very occupation, provided it with mottoes more touching than tombstones.
CHARLES LAMB, *Essays of Elia: The Old Benchers of the Inner Temple*.

Thou breathing dial! since thy day began
The present hour was ever mark'd with shade.
W. S. LANDOR, *The Sun-Dial*.

1
Carve out the dials quaintly, point by point,
Thereby to see the minutes how they run.
How many make the hour full complete;
How many hours bring about the day.
SHAKESPEARE, *III Henry VI*. Act ii, sc. 5, l. 24.

2
A sun-dial which keeps very good time.
MARK TWAIN, *Autobiography*. Vol. ii, p. 222.

II—Sun-Dial Mottoes

2a
I am a Shade: a Shadowe too arte thou:
I marke the Time: saye, Gossip, dost thou so?
AUSTIN DOBSON, *The Sundial*.

3
Once at a potent leader's voice I stayed;
Once I went back when a good monarch prayed;
Mortals, howe'er we grieve, howe'er deplore,
The flying shadow will return no more.
WILLIAM HAMILTON, *Sun-dial Motto*. (CHALMERS, *Poets of Scotland*, xv, 620.)

4
Plant the seed of time so deep—
Time that shall outgrow all flowers—
That you shall forget to weep,
Beholding such a host of hours.
ROBERT HUNT, *Legend for a Sun-dial*.

5
A lumine motus. (I am moved by the light.)
MAETERLINCK, *Measure of the Hours· Motto*.

6
I mark my hours by shadow;
Mayest thou mark thine by sunshine.
C. B. HILTON-TURVEY, *The Sundial*, (*The Van Haavens*.)

7
Time can never take
What Time did not give;
When your shadows have all passed,
I shall live.
HENRY VAN DYKE, *The Dial*.

8
Hours fly, Flowers die.
New days, New ways,
Pass by. Love stays.
HENRY VAN DYKE, *For Katrina's Sun-Dial*.

9
Time is
Too Slow for those who Wait,
Too Swift for those who Fear,
Too Long for those who Grieve,
Too Short for those who Rejoice,
But for those who Love
Time is not.
HENRY VAN DYKE, *For Katrina's Sun-Dial*.

10
With warning hand I mark Time's rapid flight
From life's glad morning to its solemn night;
Yet, through the dear God's love, I also show
There's Light above me by the Shade below.
WHITTIER, *Inscription on a Sun-dial for Dr. Henry I. Bowditch*.

11
He knows but from its shade the present hour.
WORDSWORTH, *An Evening Walk*, l. 42.

12
Horas non numero nisi serenas. (I count only the hours that are bright.)
UNKNOWN. Ancient sun-dial inscription.

Horas non numero nisi serenas is the motto of a sun-dial near Venice. There is a softness and harmony in the words and in the thought unparalleled. Of all conceits it is surely the most classical. "I count only the hours that are serene."
WILLIAM HAZLITT, *On a Sun-Dial*.

There stands in the garden of old St. Mark
A sun-dial quaint and gray.
It takes no heed of the hours which in dark
Pass o'er it day by day.
It has stood for ages amid the flowers
In that land of sky and song.
"I number none but the cloudless hours,"
Its motto the live day long.
WILLIAM C. DOANE, *Of a Sun-Dial in Venice*.

Let others tell of storms and showers,
I'll only mark your sunny hours.
UNKNOWN. A variation of the foregoing.

13
The Natural Clock-work by the mighty ONE
Wound up at first, and ever since have gone.
Inscription on sun-dial on south porch of Seaham church, Durham, England.

14
Our life's a flying shadow, God the pole,
The index pointing to Him is our soul;
Death the horizon, when our sun is set,
Which will through Christ a resurrection get.
Inscription on sun-dial, Glasgow cathedral.

15
Give God thy heart, thy service, and thy gold;
The day wears on, and time is waxing old.
Inscription on sun-dial in the cloister garden of cathedral at Gloucester, England.

16
Hours are Time's shafts, and one comes winged with death.
Inscription on the clock at Keir House.

17
Amende to-day and slack not,
Deythe cometh and warneth not,
Tyme passeth and speketh not.
Inscription on ancient sun-dial at Moccas Hall, near Hereford, England.

18
Vivite, ait, fugie. (Live ye, he says, I flee.)
Motto on sun-dial of Bishop Francis Atterbury, at Rochester, England.

19
As the long hours do pass away,
So doth the life of man decay.
Inscription on sun-dial in garden of Royal Hotel, Sevenoaks, Kent, England.

SUNFLOWER

20
Ah sunflower, weary of time,
Who countest the steps of the Sun,
Seeking after that sweet golden clime
Where the traveller's journey is done.
WILLIAM BLAKE, *The Sunflower*.

1
The seal a sun-flower; "Elle vous suit partout,"
The motto, cut upon a white cornelian.

BYRON, *Don Juan*. Canto i, st. 198. Elle vous suit partout: She follows you everywhere.

As the sunflower turns on her god when he sets,
The same look which she turn'd when he rose.

THOMAS MOORE, *Believe Me, if All Those Endearing Young Charms.*

In the course of the evening, you find chance for certain
Soft speeches to Anne, in the shade of the curtain:
You tell her your heart can be likened to *one* flower,
"And that, O most charming of women, 's the sunflower,
Which turns"—here a clear nasal voice, to your terror,
From outside the curtain, says, "That's all an error"

J. R. LOWELL, *A Fable for Critics*, l. 266.

2
Light-enchanted Sunflower, thou
Who gazest ever true and tender
On the sun's revolving splendour!

CALDERON, *Magico Prodigioso*. Sc. 3, l. 66. (Shelley, tr.)

Restless Sunflower, cease to move.

CALDERON, *Magico Prodigioso*. Sc. 3, l. 76. (Shelley, tr.)

3
The Sunflow'r, thinking 'twas for him foul shame
To nap by daylight, strove t' excuse the blame;
It was not sleep that made him nod, he said,
But too great weight and largeness of his head.

ABRAHAM COWLEY, *The Poppy*, l. 102.

4
With zealous steps he climbs the upland lawn,
And bows in homage to the rising dawn;
Imbibes with eagle eye the golden ray,
And watches, as it moves, the orb of day.

ERASMUS DARWIN, *Loves of the Plants*. Canto i, l. 225.

5
Eagle of flowers! I see thee stand,
And on the sun's noon-glory gaze;
With eye like his, thy lids expand,
And fringe their disk with golden rays:
Though fix'd on earth, in darkness rooted there,
Light is thine element, thy dwelling air,
Thy prospect heaven.

JAMES MONTGOMERY, *The Sun-flower.*

Heavily hangs the broad sunflower
Over its grave in the earth so chilly.

TENNYSON, *Song*.

6
But one, the lofty follower of the sun,
Sad when he sets, shuts up her yellow leaves,
Drooping all night; and, when he warm returns,
Points her enamour'd bosom to his ray.

THOMSON, *The Seasons: Summer*, l. 216.

SUPERSTITION

I—Superstition: Definitions

7
Superstition is the reproach of the Deity.

FRANCIS BACON, *Essays: Of Superstition.*

The master of superstition is the people; and in all superstition, wise men follow fools.

FRANCIS BACON, *Essays: Of Superstition.*

There is a superstition in avoiding superstition.

FRANCIS BACON, *Essays: Of Superstition.*

8
Superstition, that poisons and destroys all peace of mind. (Superstitio, qua qui est imbutus quietus esse numquam potest.)

CICERO, *De Finibus*. Bk. i, ch. 18, sec. 60.

9
A superstition is a premature explanation that overstays its time.

GEORGE ILES, *Jottings.*

10
The greatest burden in the world is superstition, not only of ceremonies in the church, but of imaginary and scarecrow sins at home.

MILTON, *Doctrine and Discipline of Divorce.*

11
It was necessary to succumb to superstitions, which are, more than ourselves, the kings of nations. (Il fallut succomber aux superstitions, qui sont, bien plus que nous, les rois des nations.)

VOLTAIRE, *Eryphile*. Act iii, sc. 2.

II—Superstition: Its Folly

12
I perceive that in all things ye are too superstitious.

New Testament: Acts, xvii, 22.

All superstition from thy breast repel.

JOHN GAY, *Trivia*. Bk. i, l. 175.

Better be dumb than superstitious.

BEN JONSON, *Elegy on My Muse*, l. 73.

13
Sickness and sorrows come and go, but a superstitious soul hath no rest.

ROBERT BURTON, *Anatomy of Melancholy*. Pt. iii, sec. iv, mem. 1, subs. 3.

14
Superstition, which is widespread among the nations, has taken advantage of human weakness to cast its spell over the mind of almost every man. (Superstitio, fusa per gentis, oppressit omnium fere animos atque hominum imbecillitatem occupavit.)

CICERO, *De Divinatione*. Bk. ii, ch. 72, sec. 148.

15
All people have their blind side—their superstitions.

CHARLES LAMB, *Essays of Elia: Mrs. Battle's Opinions on Whist.*

For not to rank nor sex confined
Is this vain ague of the mind.

SCOTT, *Rokeby*. Canto ii, st. 11.

16
Look, how the world's poor people are amazed

At apparitions, signs and prodigies!
SHAKESPEARE, *Venus and Adonis*, l. 925.

No natural exhalation in the sky,
No scope of nature, no distemper'd day,
No common wind, no customed event,
But they will pluck away his natural cause
And call them meteors, prodigies and signs,
Abortives, presages and tongues of heaven.
SHAKESPEARE, *King John*. Act iii, sc. 4, l. 153.

Ghost, kelpie, wraith,
And all the trumpery of vulgar faith.
CAMPBELL, *The Pilgrim of Glencoe*, l. 188.

He put this engine [a watch] to our ears, which made an incessant noise like that of a water-mill: and we conjecture it is either some unknown animal or the god that he worships, but we are more inclined to the latter opinion.
SWIFT, *Gulliver's Travels: Voyage to Lilliput*.

1
A pupil in the many-chambered school
Where superstition weaves her airy dreams.
WORDSWORTH, *The Excursion*. Bk. iv, l. 609.

III—Superstition and Religion

2
A great fear . . . is the parent of superstition; but a discreet and well-guided fear produced religion.
JEREMY TAYLOR, *Holy Living*, p. 317.

I can hardly think there was ever any scared into Heaven.
SIR THOMAS BROWNE, *Religio Medici*. Pt. i, sec. 59.

3
Superstition is the religion of feeble minds.
EDMUND BURKE, *Reflections on the Revolution in France*.

Superstition is the only religion of which base souls are capable. (La superstition est la seule religion dont soient capables les âmes basses.)
JOUBERT, *Pensées*. No. 27.

4
Foul Superstition! howsoe'er disguised,
Idol, saint, virgin, prophet, crescent, cross,
For whatsoever symbol thou art prized,
Thou sacerdotal gain, but general loss!
Who from true worship's gold can separate thy dross?
BYRON, *Childe Harold*. Canto ii, st. 44.

For superstition will survive,
Purer religion to perplex.
APHRA BEHN, *On Desire*.

5
Superstition consists in a senseless fear of the gods, religion in the pious worship of them. (Superstitio, in qua inest inanis timor Deorum; religio, quæ deorum pio cultu continetur.)
CICERO, *De Natura Deorum*. Bk. i, sec. 42.

The destruction of superstition does not mean the destruction of religion. (Superstitio tollenda religio tollitur.)
CICERO, *De Divinatione*. Bk. ii, ch. 72, sec. 148.

6
O! Superstition is the giant shadow
Which the solicitude of weak mortality,
Its back towards Religion's rising sun,
Casts on the thin mist of th' uncertain future.
S. T. COLERIDGE, *Fragments*. No. 42.

7
Superstition is godless religion, devout impiety.
JOSEPH HALL, *Of the Superstitious*.

8
A foolish superstition introduces the influences of the gods even in the smallest matters. (Minimis etiam rebus prava religio inserit deos.)
LIVY, *History*. Bk. xxvii, sec. 23.

9
Superstition is related to this life, religion to the next; superstition is allied to fatality, religion to virtue; it is by the vivacity of earthly desires that we become superstitious; it is, on the contrary, by the sacrifice of these desires that we become religious.
MADAME DE STAËL. (ABEL STEVENS, *Life of Madame de Staël*. Ch. 34.)

10
Crush the infamous thing! (Écrasez l'infâme!)
VOLTAIRE, *Letter to d'Alembert*, 23 June, 1760. "By *infâme*," he wrote, "you will understand that I mean superstition: as for religion, I love and respect it as you do." Voltaire adopted this phrase as his motto.

IV—Superstition: Omens
See also Luck

11
And on a Friday fell all this mischance.
CHAUCER, *The Nonne Preestes Tale*, l. 521.

12
Matrons, who toss the cup, and see
The grounds of fate in grounds of tea.
CHARLES CHURCHILL, *The Ghost*. Bk. i, l. 117.

13
Certain signs precede certain events. (Certis rebus certa signa præcurrerent.)
CICERO, *De Divinatione*. Bk. i, ch. 52, sec. 118.

Coming events cast their shadows before.
CAMPBELL, *Lochiel's Warning*, l. 56.

Often do the spirits
Of great events stride on before the events,
And in to-day already walks to-morrow.
SCHILLER, *Wallenstein's Tod*. Act v, sc. 1. (Coleridge, tr.)

Against ill chances men are ever merry;
But heaviness foreruns the good event.
SHAKESPEARE, *II Henry IV*. Act iv, sc. 2, l. 81.

And in such indexes, although small pricks
To their subsequent volumes, there is seen
The baby figure of the giant mass
Of things to come at large.
SHAKESPEARE, *Troilus and Cressida*. Act i, sc. 3, l. 343.

14
Nay I have had some omens: I got out of bed

backwards too this morning, without premeditation; pretty good that too; but then I stumbled coming down stairs, and met a weasel; bad omens those: some bad, some good, our lives are chequer'd.

CONGREVE, *Love for Love*. Act ii, sc. 2.

Alas! you know the cause too well;
The salt is spilt, to me it fell;
Then to contribute to my loss,
My knife and fork were laid across:
On Friday, too! the day I dread!
Would I were safe at home in bed!
Last night (I vow to Heav'n 'tis true)
Bounce from the fire a coffin flew.
Next post some fatal news shall tell:
God send my Cornish friends be well!

JOHN GAY, *Fables: The Farmer's Wife and the Raven.*

1
Send a bird of omen; . . . let him appear upon my right hand.

HOMER, *Iliad*. Bk. xxiv, l. 310.

How happily rose I on my right side to-day.

PALSGRAVE, *Acolastus*. M 3. (1540)

2
The menacing gods filled earth, sky, and sea with portents. (Prodigiis terras implerunt, æthera, pontum.)

LUCAN, *De Bello Civili*. Bk. i, l. 525.

3
It is a bad sign; a Roman would have turned back.

NAPOLEON BONAPARTE, when his horse stumbled and threw him as he was about to cross the Nieman on his invasion of Russia, 24 June, 1812. (LOCKHART, *Life*.) Malesherbes had said it before him.

4
There is something in omens. (Omina sunt aliquid.)

OVID, *Amores*. Bk. i, eleg. 12, l. 3.

5
You shall be rewarded for that omen, Sir Omener! (Ob istuc omen, ominator, capies quod te condecet.)

PLAUTUS, *Amphitruo*, l. 722. (Act ii, sc. 2.)

6
It's a bad sign when a man in a sweat shivers. (Pro monstro extemplo est, quando qui sudat tremit.)

PLAUTUS, *Asinaria*, l. 289. (Act ii, sc. 2.)

7
This day black omens threat the brightest fair,
That e'er deserv'd a watchful spirit's care.

POPE, *The Rape of the Lock*. Canto ii, l. 101.

8
Midnight hags,
By force of potent spells, of bloody characters,
And conjurations horrible to hear,
Call fiends and spectres from the yawning deep,
And set the ministers of hell at work.

NICHOLAS ROWE, *Jane Shore*. Act iv, sc. 1, l. 240.

9
Release, ye gods, release the mind from such omens. (Solvite tantis animum monstris, Solvite Superi!)

SENECA, *Hercules Furens*, l. 1063.

10
Some devils ask but the parings of one's nail,
A rush, a hair, a drop of blood, a pin,
A nut, a cherry-stone;
But she, more covetous, would have a chain.
Master, be wise; an if you give it her,
The devil will shake her chain and fright us with it.

SHAKESPEARE, *The Comedy of Errors*. Act iv, sc. 3, l. 72.

11
In what particular thought to work I know not:
But in the gross and scope of my opinion,
This bodes some strange eruption to our state.

SHAKESPEARE, *Hamlet*. Act i, sc. 1, l. 67.

12
The graves stood tenantless, and the sheeted dead
Did squeak and gibber in the Roman streets:
As stars with trains of fire and dews of blood,
Disasters in the sun.

SHAKESPEARE, *Hamlet*. Act i, sc. 1, l. 113.

Fierce fiery warriors fought upon the clouds,
In ranks and squadrons and right form of war,
Which drizzled blood upon the Capitol.

SHAKESPEARE, *Julius Cæsar*. Act ii, sc. 2, l. 19.

And ghosts did shriek and squeal about the streets.
O Cæsar! these things are beyond all use,
And I do fear them.

SHAKESPEARE, *Julius Cæsar*. Act ii, sc. 2, l. 24.

13
At my nativity
The front of heaven was full of fiery shapes,
Of burning cressets; and at my birth
The frame and huge foundation of the earth
Shaked like a coward.

SHAKESPEARE, *I Henry IV*. Act iii, sc. 1, l. 13.

The owl shriek'd at my birth, an evil sign;
The night-crow cried, aboding luckless time.
Dogs howled.

SHAKESPEARE, *III Henry VI*. Act v, sc. 6, l. 47.

14
These late eclipses in the sun and moon portend no good to us: though the wisdom of nature can reason it thus and thus, yet nature finds itself scourged by the sequent effects: love cools, friendship falls off, brothers divide: in cities, mutinies; in countries, discord; in palaces, treason; and the bond cracked 'twixt son and father.

SHAKESPEARE, *King Lear*. Act i, sc. 2, l. 112.

The night had been unruly: where we lay,
Our chimneys were blown down; and, as they say,
Lamentings heard i' the air; strange screams of death,
And prophesying with accents terrible

Of dire combustion and confused events
New hatch'd to the woeful time: the obscure bird
Clamour'd the livelong night: some say, the earth
Was feverous and did shake.
SHAKESPEARE, *Macbeth*. Act ii, sc. 3, l. 59.

Stones have been known to move and trees to speak.
SHAKESPEARE, *Macbeth*. Act iii, sc. 4, l. 123.

The bay-trees in our country are all wither'd
And meteors fright the fixed stars of heaven;
The pale-faced moon looks bloody on the earth
And lean-look'd prophets whisper fearful change;
Rich men look sad and ruffians dance and leap,
The one in fear to lose what they enjoy,
The other to enjoy by rage and war:
These signs forerun the death or fall of kings.
SHAKESPEARE, *Richard II*. Act ii, sc. 4, l. 8.

1
By the pricking of my thumbs,
Something wicked this way comes.
SHAKESPEARE, *Macbeth*. Act iv, sc. 1, l. 44.

2
Then it was not for nothing that my nose fell a-bleeding on Black-Monday.
SHAKESPEARE, *The Merchant of Venice*. Act ii, sc. 5, l. 24.

If a man's nose bleeds one drop at the left nostril it is a sign of good luck, and *vice versa*.
SIR JOHN MELTON, *Astrologaster*. (1620)

3
It is the part of men to fear and tremble,
When the most mighty gods by tokens send
Such dreadful heralds to astonish us.
SHAKESPEARE, *Julius Cæsar*. Act i, sc. 3, l. 54.

SURETY

4
Act as surety, and ruin is at hand. ('Εγγύα, πάρα δ' ἄτα.)
CHILON. (DIOGENES LAERTIUS, *Chilon*. Bk. i, sec. 73.) Diogenes Laertius states that this was Chilon's apothegm, but it has also been ascribed to Thales of Miletus. It was one of the three maxims inscribed upon the temple of Apollo at Delphi. *See under* MODERATION.

Act as surety, and ruin stands near you. (Εη ἐγγύα, πάρα δ' ἄτα, græce dicimus: Latinum est, Sponde, noxa set præsto tibi.)
THALES. (AUSONIUS, *Ludus Septem Sapientum*, l. 180.)

I could give a thousand instances to prove that those who give bond or bail appear at the bar of regret. (Per mille possem currere exempla, ut probem Prædes vadesque pænitudinis reos.)
AUSONIUS, *Ludus Septem Sapientum*, l. 182.

Having consented to be one of three sureties, I was caught. So did the inscription at Delphi hold good for once, that suretyship is woe.
CRATINUS THE YOUNGER, *Fragment*.

Be surety for another and harm is at hand.
RICHARD TAVERNER, *Proverbs*, 20. (1539)

5
A person who can't pay gets another person who can't pay to guarantee that he can pay. Like a person with two wooden legs getting another person with two wooden legs to guarantee that he has got two natural legs. It don't make either of them able to do a walking match.
DICKENS, *Little Dorrit*. Pt. i, ch. 23.

6
My son, if thou be surety for thy friend, if thou hast stricken thy hand with a stranger,
Thou art snared with the words of thy mouth.
Old Testament: Proverbs, vi, 1–2.

My son, if I, Hafiz, thy father, take hold of thy knees in my pain,
Demanding thy name on stamped paper, one day or one hour—refrain.
Are the links of thy fetters so light that thou cravest another man's chain?
RUDYARD KIPLING, *Certain Maxims of Hafiz*. No. 19.

7
He that is surety for a stranger shall smart for it: and he that hateth suretiship is sure.
Old Testament: Proverbs, xi, 15.

He who is surety is never sure.
C. H. SPURGEON, *John Ploughman*. Ch. 4.

8
One of the greatest in the Christian world
Shall be my surety.
SHAKESPEARE, *All's Well that Ends Well*. Act iv, sc. 4, l. 3.

Procure your sureties for your days of answer.
SHAKESPEARE, *Richard II*. Act iv, sc. 1, l. 159.

Have pity; I'll be his surety.
SHAKESPEARE, *The Tempest*. Act i, sc. 2, l. 475.

9
But yet I 'll make assurance double sure,
And take a bond of fate.
SHAKESPEARE, *Macbeth*. Act iv, sc. 1, l. 83.

He is one who may
Make our assurance doubly sure.
BYRON, *Marino Faliero*. Act ii, sc. 2, 1. 156.

SUSPICION

See also Distrust; Trust: Its Folly

10
Superabundance of suspicion is a kind of political madness.
FRANCIS BACON, *De Augmentis Scientiarum: Suspicio*.

Suspicion absolves faith.
FRANCIS BACON, *De Augmentis Scientiarum: Suspicio*.

11
Suspicions amongst thoughts are like bats amongst birds, they ever fly by twilight.
FRANCIS BACON, *Essays: Of Suspicion*.

There is nothing makes a man suspect much, more than to know little.
FRANCIS BACON, *Essays: Of Suspicion*.

Suspicions that the mind, of itself, gathers, are but buzzes; but suspicions that are artificially nourished and put into men's heads by the tales and whisperings of others, have stings.
FRANCIS BACON, *Essays: Of Suspicion*.

1
And, when his first suspicions dimly stole,
Rebuked them back like phantoms from his
soul.
THOMAS CAMPBELL, *Theodric*, l. 232.

2
There is one safeguard known generally to the wise, which is an advantage and security to all, but especially to democracies as against despots—suspicion.
DEMOSTHENES, *Philippics*. No. ii, sec. 24.

It was a maxim with Foxey—our revered father, gentlemen—"Always suspect everybody."
DICKENS, *The Old Curiosity Shop*. Ch. 66.

3
Always suspect that which seems probable, and begin by believing what appears incredible.
ÉMILE GABORIAU, *Monsieur Lecoq*. Ch. 8. The maxim which Lecoq followed.

4
Suspicion is rather a virtue than a fault, as long as it doth like a dog that *watcheth*, and doth not *bite*.
LORD HALIFAX, *Works*, p. 247.

5
He that hath suspicion is rarely at fault.
W. G. BENHAM, *Proverbs*, p. 778.

Your suspicion is not without wit and judgement.
SHAKESPEARE, *Othello*. Act iv, sc. 2, l. 215.

6
He that will live of all cares dispossessed
Must shun the bad, ay, and suspect the best.
ROBERT HERRICK, *Suspicion Makes Secure*.

7
The hawk suspects the snare, and the pike the covered hook. (Accipiterque Suspectos laqueos, et opertum miluus hamum.)
HORACE, *Epistles*. Bk. i, epis. 16, l. 50.

8
Suspicion is no less an enemy to virtue than to happiness.
SAMUEL JOHNSON, *The Rambler*. No. 79.

Suspicion is very often a useless pain.
SAMUEL JOHNSON. (BOSWELL, *Life*. iii, 135.)

9
Suspicion follows close on mistrust. (Argwohnen folgt auf Misstrauen.)
LESSING, *Nathan der Weise*. Act v, sc. 8.

10
Banish squint suspicion.
MILTON, *Comus*, l. 413.

11
And oft though wisdom wake, suspicion sleeps
At wisdom's gate, and to simplicity
Resigns her charge, while goodness thinks no
ill
Where no ill seems.
MILTON, *Paradise Lost*. Bk. iii, l. 686.

12
Suspicion is the badge of base-born minds,
And calculation never understands.
VIRGINIA MOORE, *Tragic Conclusions*.

13
Suspicion's but at best a coward's virtue.
THOMAS OTWAY, *Venice Preserved*. Act iii. sc. 1.

Suspicion is the companion of mean souls.
THOMAS PAINE, *Common Sense*. Ch. iii.

14
All seems infected that th' infected spy,
As all looks yellow to the jaundic'd eye.
POPE, *Essay on Criticism*. Pt. ii, l. 358.

15
The losing side is full of suspicion. (Ad tristem partem strenua est suspicio.)
PUBLILIUS SYRUS, *Sententiæ*. No. 7.

16
All is not well; I doubt some foul play.
SHAKESPEARE, *Hamlet*. Act i, sc. 2, l. 255.

17
Suspicion all our lives shall be stuck full of eyes.
SHAKESPEARE, *I Henry IV*. Act v, sc. 2, l. 8.

See what a ready tongue suspicion hath!
SHAKESPEARE, *II Henry IV*. Act i, sc. 1, l. 84.

Hath not the world one man but he will wear his cap with suspicion?
SHAKESPEARE, *Much Ado About Nothing*. Act i, sc. 1, l. 200.

18
Bid suspicion double-lock the door.
SHAKESPEARE, *Venus and Adonis*, l. 448.

19
If I shall be condemn'd
Upon surmises, all proofs sleeping else
But what your jealousies awake, I tell you,
'Tis rigour and not law.
SHAKESPEARE, *Winter's Tale*. Act iii, sc. 2, l. 112.

20
All persons, as they grow less prosperous, grow more suspicious. (Omnes, quibus res sunt minus secundæ magis sunt, nescio quomodo, Suspiciosi.)
TERENCE, *Adelphi*, l. 605. (Act iv, sc. 3.)

SWALLOW

I—Swallow: One Swallow Does Not Make Summer

21
One swallow does not make spring, nor does one fine day. (*Μία γὰρ χελιδὼν ἔαρ οὐ ποιεῖ, οὐδε μία ἡμέρα.*)
ARISTOTLE, *Nicomachean Ethics*. Bk. i, ch. 7, sec. 16.

One swallow does not make summer. (Una Golondrina sola no hace verano.)
CERVANTES, *Don Quixote*. Pt. i, ch. 13.

One swallow maketh not summer.
JOHN HEYWOOD, *Proverbs*. Bk. ii, ch. 5. (1546)

22
One foul wind no more makes a winter, than one swallow makes a summer.
DICKENS, *Martin Chuzzlewit*. Ch. 43.

23
One swallow proveth not that summer is near.
JOHN NORTHBROOKE, *Treatise against Dancing* (1577)

1
It's surely summer, for there's a swallow:
Come one swallow, his mate will follow,
The bird race quicken and wheel and thicken.
CHRISTINA ROSSETTI, *A Bird Song*. St. 2.

2
The swallow follows not summer more willing than we your lordship.
SHAKESPEARE, *Timon of Athens*. Act iii, sc. 6, l. 31.

3
It is not one swallow that bringeth in summer.
RICHARD TAVERNER, *Proverbs*, 25. (1539)

Nay soft (said the widow) one swallow makes not a summer, nor one meeting a marriage.
THOMAS DELONEY, *Jacke of Newberie*. Ch. 1. (c. 1597)

II—Swallow: Description

4
In truth, I rather take it thou hast got
By instinct wise much sense about thy lot,
And hast small care
Whether an Eden or a desert be
Thy home, so thou remain'st alive, and free
To skim the air.
JANE WELSH CARLYLE, *To a Swallow Building under Our Eaves*.

5
Down comes rain drop, bubble follows;
On the house-top one by one
Flock the synagogue of swallows,
Met to vote that autumn's gone.
THÉOPHILE GAUTIER, *Life, a Bubble*.

6
But, as old Swedish legends say,
Of all the birds upon that day,
The swallow felt the deepest grief,
And longed to give her Lord relief,
And chirped when any near would come.
"Hugswala swala swal honom!"
Meaning, as they who tell it deem,
Oh, cool, oh. cool and comfort Him!
CHARLES GODFREY LELAND, *The Swallow*.

7
The swallow is come! The swallow is come!
O, fair are the seasons, and light
Are the days that she brings with her dusky wings,
And her bosom snowy white!
LONGFELLOW, *Hyperion*. Bk. ii, ch. 1.

8
The swallow is not ensnared by men because of its gentle nature. (At caret insidiis hominum, quia mitis, hirundo.)
OVID, *Ars Amatoria*. Bk. ii, l. 149.

9
Come, summer visitant, attach
To my reed roof your nest of clay,
And let my ear your music catch,
Low twittering underneath the thatch
At the grey dawn of day.
CHARLOTTE SMITH, *The First Swallow*.

10
Swallow, my sister, O sister swallow,
How can thine heart be full of the spring?
A thousand summers are over and dead.
What hast thou found in the spring to follow?
What hast thou found in thy heart to sing?
What wilt thou do when the summer is shed?
SWINBURNE, *Itylus*. St. 1.

For where thou fliest I shall not follow,
Till life forget and death remember,
Till thou remember and I forget.
SWINBURNE, *Itylus*. St. 5.

11
Nature's licensed vagabond, the swallow.
TENNYSON, *Queen Mary*. Act v, sc. 1, l. 12.

12
The swallow sweeps
The slimy pool, to build his hanging house.
THOMSON, *The Seasons: Spring*, l. 654.

SWAN

See also Goose

13
A swan swam in a silver lake,
And gracefully swam the swan.
MRS. E. L. AVELINE, *The Vain Swan*.

On thy fairy bosom, silver lake,
The wild swan spreads his snowy sail,
And round his breast the ripples break
As down he bears before the gale.
JAMES GATES PERCIVAL, *To Seneca Lake*.

14
And swans seem whiter if swart crows be by.
DUBARTAS, *Devine Weekes and Workes*. Week i, day 1. (Sylvester, tr.)

Such as ne'er saw swans
May think crows beautiful.
MASSINGER, *Great Duke of Florence*. Act iii.

15
There 's double beauty whenever a swan
Swims on a lake, with her double thereon.
THOMAS HOOD, *Miss Kilmansegg: Her Honeymoon*, l. 1852.

The swan on still St. Mary's Lake
Float double, swan and shadow!
WORDSWORTH, *Yarrow Unvisited*, l. 43.

16
As rare a bird upon the earth as a black swan.
(Rara avis in terris nigroque simillima cycno.)
JUVENAL, *Satires*. Sat. vi, l. 165.

17
The swan, with arched neck
Between her white wings mantling proudly, rows
Her state with oary feet.
MILTON, *Paradise Lost*. Bk. vii, l. 438.

Like some full-breasted swan
That, fluting a wild carol ere her death,
Ruffles her pure cold plume, and takes the flood
With swarthy webs.
TENNYSON, *The Passing of Arthur*, l. 434.

18
I have seen a swan
With bootless labour swim against the tide,
And spend her strength with over-matching waves.
SHAKESPEARE, *III Henry VI*. Act i, sc. 4, l. 19.

All the water in the ocean
Can never turn the swan's black legs to white,
Although she lave them hourly in the flood.
SHAKESPEARE, *Titus Andronicus*, iv, 2, 101.

2 The stately-sailing swan
Gives out his snowy plumage to the gale,
And, arching proud his neck, with oary feet
Bears forward fierce, and guards his osier-isle,
Protective of his young.
THOMSON, *The Seasons: Spring*, l. 778.

II—Swans: Their Death-Song

3
The jealous swan, against his death that singeth.
CHAUCER, *Parlement of Foules*, l. 342. (c. 1370)

The yellow swan famous and agreeable,
Against his death melodiously singing.
JOHN LYDGATE, *Minor Poems*, p. 157. (c. 1430)

Thus, like a dying swan, to a sad tune, I sing my own dirge.
MASSINGER, *Emperor of the East*, v, 3. (1631)

Thus on Mæander's flowery margin lies
Th' expiring swan, and as he sings he dies.
POPE, *The Rape of the Lock*. Canto v, l. 65.

4
Not without cause is the swan dedicated to Apollo, because, foreseeing his happiness in death, he dies with a song of rapture.
CICERO, *Tusculanarum Disputationum*. Bk. i, ch. 30, sec. 73.

The swan murmurs sweet strains with failing tongue, itself the minstrel of its own death. (Dulcia defecta modulatur carmina lingua Cantator, cygnus, funeris ipse sui.)
MARTIAL, *Epigrams*. Bk. xiii, epig. 77.

A Latin proverb, *Cygnea cantio*, which among the common people is termed a lightning before death.
THOMAS COGAN, *Haven of Health*, 135. (1584)
See 397:13.

The cock swan is an emblem or representation of an affectionate and true husband to his wife above all other fowls; for the cock swan holdeth himself to one female only, and for this cause nature hath conferred on him a gift before all others; that is, to die so joyfully, that he sings sweetly when he dies; upon which the poet saith:
Dulcia defecta modulatur carmina lingua,
Cantator, cygnus, funeris ipse sui, etc.
SIR EDWARD COKE, *Decision*, the Case of Swans, 1600. (4 *Rep.* 85.)

5
Death darkens his eyes, and unplumes his wings,
Yet the sweetest song is the last he sings:
Live so, my Love, that when death shall come,
Swan-like and sweet it may waft thee home.
GEORGE WASHINGTON DOANE, *The Swan*.

6
The immortal swan that did her life deplore.
GILES FLETCHER, *Temptation and Victory of Christ*.

7
The dying swan, when years her temples pierce,
In music-strains breathes out her life and verse,
And, chanting her own dirge, tides on her wat'ry hearse.
PHINEAS FLETCHER, *Purple Island*. Canto i.

8
'Tis strange that death should sing.
I am the cygnet to this pale faint swan,
Who chants a doleful hymn to his own death,
And from the organ-pipe of frailty sings
His soul and body to their lasting rest.
SHAKESPEARE, *King John*. Act v, sc. 7, l. 20.

9
He makes a swan-like end, Fading in music.
SHAKESPEARE, *Merchant of Venice*, iii, 2, 44.

I will play the swan, and die in music.
SHAKESPEARE, *Othello*. Act v, sc. 2, l. 247.

There, swan-like, let me sing and die.
BYRON, *Don Juan*. Canto iii, st. 86.

10
And now this pale swan in her watery nest
Begins the sad dirge of her certain ending.
SHAKESPEARE, *The Rape of Lucrece*, l. 1161.

11
Will you not admit that I have as much of the spirit of prophecy in me as the swans? For they, when they perceive approaching death, sing more merrily than ever, rejoicing in the thought that they are going to the god they serve.
SOCRATES. (PLATO, *Phædo*. Sec. 84, fin.)

12
The wild swan's death-hymn took the soul
Of that waste place with joy
Hidden in sorrow. At first to the ear
The warble was low, and full and clear.
TENNYSON, *The Dying Swan*. St. 3.

SWEARING

See also Cursing. For Swearing, in the sense of taking an oath, see Oath, Vow

I—Swearing: Apothegms

13
'Tis strange—the Hebrew noun which means "I am,"
The English always use to govern d—n.
BYRON, *Don Juan*. Canto i, st. 14.

Ethelberta breathed a sort of exclamation, not right out, but stealthily, like a parson's damn.
THOMAS HARDY, *Hand of Ethelberta*. Ch. 26.

Seeing would certainly have led to D—ing.
THOMAS HOOD, *Legend of Navarre*.

Jack was embarrass'd—never hero more,
And as he knew not what to say, he swore.
BYRON, *The Island*. Canto iii, st. 5.

14
He that sweareth deep, sweareth like a lord.
SIR THOMAS ELYOT, *The Governour*, i, 26. (1531)

He swore like a trooper.
D. M. MOIR, *Mansie Wauch*. Ch. 14. (1824)

If you swear till you are black in the face, I shan't believe you.
FANNY BURNEY, *Evelina*, ii, 23. (1778)

I'd swear, till I was black in the face, he was innocent.
THACKERAY, *Pendennis*. Ch. 55. (1859)

1
I'm Gormed—and I can't say no fairer than that!
DICKENS, *David Copperfield*. Ch. 63.

2
Most bitter Billingsgate rhetoric.
EDMUND GAYTON, *Festivous Notes on Don Quixote*, p. 60. (1654)

Such Billingsgate language as should not come out of the mouth of any man.
ROGER NORTH, *Lives of the Norths*, i, 288 Muirhead (*Blue Guide to London*, p. 398) states that Billingsgate, as a synonym for coarse language, is an unjust aspersion on fish-porters.

Rather too close an imitation of that language which is used in the apostolic occupation of trafficking in fish.
SYDNEY SMITH, *Letters to Archdeacon Singleton*. No. 3.

3 Bad language or abuse
I never, never use,
Whatever the emergency;
Though "Bother it" I may
Occasionally say,
I never never use a big, big D.
W. S. GILBERT, *H. M. S. Pinafore*. Act i.

One word alone is all that strikes the ear,
One short, pathetic, simple word, . . .
"Oh, dear!"
ROBERT BLOOMFIELD, *The Farmer's Boy: Autumn*, l. 157.

4
It's most enough to make a deacon swear.
J. R. LOWELL, *The Biglow Papers*. Ser ii, No. 2.

5
When I swear after mine own fashion, it is only by God; the directest of all oaths.
MONTAIGNE, *Essays*. Bk. iii, ch. 5.

6
He speaks Bear-garden.
JOHN RAY, *English Proverbs*, 66. (1678)

This is brave Bear-garden language.
JEREMY COLLIER, *Short View of the Immorality and Profaneness of the English Stage*, p. 232. (1698)

He's as great a master of ill language as ever was bred at a Bear-garden.
EDWARD WARD, *London Terræfilius*. No. iii, p. 29. (1707)

7
He'll swear dagger out of sheath; he'll swear the devil out of hell.
JOHN RAY, *English Proverbs*, p. 271.

When he's excited he uses language that would make your hair curl.
W. S. GILBERT, *Ruddigore*. Act i.

Full of strange oaths.
SHAKESPEARE, *As You Like It*. Act ii, sc. 7, l. 150.

Foam'd at the mouth, and swore.
SHAKESPEARE, *Cymbeline*. Act v, sc. 5, l. 276.

8
Swear me, Kate, like a lady as thou art,
A good mouth-filling oath, and leave "in sooth,"
And such protest of pepper-gingerbread,
To velvet-guards and Sunday-citizens.
SHAKESPEARE, *I Henry IV*. Act iii, sc. 1, l. 258.

9
Swearing till my very roof was dry.
SHAKESPEARE, *The Merchant of Venice*, iii, 2, 206.

10
You taught me language; and my profit on 't
Is, I know how to curse.
SHAKESPEARE, *The Tempest*. Act i, sc. 2, l. 363.

11
"Our armies swore terribly in Flanders," cried my Uncle Toby, "but nothing to this."
STERNE, *Tristram Shandy*. Bk. iii, ch. 11.

12
A footman may swear, but he cannot swear like a lord. He can swear as often, but can he swear with equal delicacy, propriety and judgment?
SWIFT, *Polite Conversation: Introduction*.

II—Swearing: Its Virtues

13
Some fresh new oath that is not stale, but will rin round in the mouth.
ROGER ASCHAM, *The Scholemaster*.

14
Take not God's name in vain; select
A time when it will have effect.
AMBROSE BIERCE, *The Devil's Dictionary: The Decalogue Revised*.

15
Damn braces. Bless relaxes.
WILLIAM BLAKE, *Proverbs of Hell*.

16
I confess to some pleasure from the stinging rhetoric or a rattling oath.
EMERSON, *Journals*, 1840.

17
Page . . . take my hat . . . and go down into the courtyard and swear for me for just a short half-hour. I will swear for you when you wish it. (Paige . . . tiens ici mon bonnet . . . et va en la basse court jurer une petite demie heure pour moy. Je jureray pour toy quand tu vouldras.)
RABELAIS, *Works*. Bk. iii, ch. 36.

18
A whoreson jackanapes must take me up for swearing; as if I borrowed mine oaths of him and might not spend them at my pleasure. . . . When a gentleman is disposed to swear, it is not for any standers-by to curtail his oaths, ha?
SHAKESPEARE, *Cymbeline*. Act ii, sc. 1, l. 4.

It comes to pass oft that a terrible oath, with a swaggering accent sharply twanged off, gives manhood more approbation than ever proof itself would have earned him.
SHAKESPEARE, *Twelfth Night*. Act iii, sc. 4, l. 196.

19
In certain trying circumstances, urgent circumstances, desperate circumstances, profanity furnishes a relief denied even to prayer.
MARK TWAIN, *Pudd'nhead Wilson's Calendar*.

III—Swearing: Its Faults

1
The more you are averse to base actions, the more you should keep yourself from licence in language. (Quantum a rerum turpitudine abes, tantum te a verborum libertate sejungas.)
CICERO, *Pro Cœlio*. Pt. iii, sec. 8.

2
But mutters coward curses as he goes.
JOHN GAY, *Trivia*. Bk. ii, l. 64.

3
Take not His name, who made thy mouth, in vain;
It gets thee nothing, and hath no excuse.
GEORGE HERBERT, *The Church-Porch*. St. 10.

Lust and wine plead a pleasure, avarice gain;
But the cheap swearer through his open sluice
Lets his soul run for nought, as little fearing.
Were I an Epicure, I could bate swearing.
GEORGE HERBERT, *The Church-Porch*. St. 10.

When thou dost tell another's jest, therein
Omit the oaths, which true wit cannot need.
GEORGE HERBERT, *The Church-Porch*. St. 11.

4
Who spits against heaven, it falls in his face.
GEORGE HERBERT, *Jacula Prudentum*.

5
Things past recovery
Are hardly cur'd with exclamations.
MARLOWE, *The Jew of Malta*. Act i, l. 470.

6
And each blasphemer quite escape the rod,
Because the insult 's not on man but God?
POPE, *Epilogue to Satires*. Dialogue ii, l. 195.

7
To swear at all, except when absolutely necessary, is unbecoming to a man of sense. (In totum jurare, nisi ubi necesse est, gravi viro parum convenit.)
QUINTILIAN, *De Institutione Oratoria*. Bk. ix, ch. 2, sec. 98.

8
Why, what an ass am I! This is most brave,
That I, the son of a dear father murder'd,
Prompted to my revenge by heaven and hell,
Must, like a whore, unpack my heart with words,
And fall a-cursing, like a very drab,
A scullion!
SHAKESPEARE, *Hamlet*. Act ii, sc. 2, l. 611.

SWEETNESS

I—Sweetness: Apothegms

9
Mind cannot follow it, nor words express
Her infinite sweetness.
DANTE, *Paradiso*. Canto xiv, l. 75. (Cary, tr.)

10
No sweet without some sweat.
THOMAS FULLER, *Gnomologia*. No. 3632.

No sweat, no sweet.
SAMUEL SMILES, *Self-Help*. Ch. 10.

11
And spicèd dainties, every one,
From silken Samarcand to cedar'd Lebanon.
KEATS, *The Eve of St. Agnes*. St. 30.

11a
Short and sweet if I were judge, a piece surely worthy praise.
THOMAS LODGE, *A Defence of Play*. (1580)

Both short and sweet some say is best.
THOMAS MIDDLETON, *The Spanish Gipsy*, iv, 3. (1623)

Better short and sweet than long and lax.
JOHN KELLY, *Scottish Proverbs*. (1721)

12
A wilderness of sweets.
MILTON, *Paradise Lost*. Bk. v, l. 294.

13
You are sweeter than sweet honey. (Melle dulci dulcior tu es.)
PLAUTUS, *Asinaria*, l. 614. (Act iii, sc. 3.)

Sweeter also than honey and the honeycomb.
Old Testament: Psalms, xix, 10.

Sweet as dew Shut in a lily's golden core.
MARGARET JUNKIN PRESTON, *Agnes*.

The sweetest thing that ever grew
Beside a human door!
WORDSWORTH, *Lucy Gray*. St. 2.

14
Sweets to the sweet: farewell!
SHAKESPEARE, *Hamlet*. Act v, sc. 1, l. 266.

The sweetest garland to the sweetest maid.
THOMAS TICKELL, *To a Lady with a Present of Flowers*, l. 4.

15
They surfeited with honey and began
To loathe the taste of sweetness, whereof a little
More than a little is by much too much.
SHAKESPEARE, *I Henry IV*. Act iii, sc. 2, l. 71.

To pile up honey upon sugar, and sugar upon honey, to an interminable tedious sweetness.
LAMB, *Essays of Elia: A Chapter on Ears*.

16
So sweet was ne'er so fatal.
SHAKESPEARE, *Othello*. Act v, sc. 2, l. 20.

17
Ah that such sweet things should be fleet,
Such fleet things sweet!
SWINBURNE, *Félise*. St. 22.

18
Sweet as love,
Or the remembrance of a generous deed.
WORDSWORTH, *The Prelude*. Bk. vi, l. 682.

II—Sweetness: Sweet and Sour

19
The bitter goes before the sweet. Yea, and for as much as it doth, it makes the sweet the sweeter.
JOHN BUNYAN, *The Pilgrim's Progress*. Pt. ii.

The little sweet doth kill much bitterness.
KEATS, *Isabella*. St. 13.

20
No tasting earth's true food for men,
Its sweet in sad, its sad in sweet.
ROBERT BROWNING, *Dîs Aliter Visum*. St. 25.

21
The bud may have a bitter taste,
But sweet will be the flower.
COWPER, *Light Shining Out of Darkness*.

1 Much I muse,
How bitter can spring up. when sweet is sown.
(Come uscir può di dolce seme amaro.)

DANTE, *Paradiso*. Canto viii, l. 93. (Cary, tr.)

2
He deserves not sweet that will not taste of sour.

THOMAS FULLER, *Gnomologia*. No. 1834.

He hath not deserved this sweet before he hath tasted some sour.

HENRY GOLDINGHAM, *Garden Plot*, p. 60. (c. 1575)

Take the sweet with the sour.

JOHN HEYWOOD, *Proverbs*. Pt. ii, ch. 4. (1546)

He that desireth the sweet to assay,
He must taste bitter, this is no nay.

UNKNOWN, *Dialogues of Creatures*. No. 21. (c. 1535)

3
Sweet meat must have sour sauce.

BEN JONSON, *The Poetaster*. Act iii, sc. 1.

4
What is to some sad and bitter, may seem to others particularly sweet. (Aliis quod triste et amarum est, Hoc tamen esse aliis possit prædulce videri.)

LUCRETIUS, *De Rerum Natura*. Bk. iv, l. 638.

5
Life to have its sweets must have its sours.
Love isn't always two souls picking flowers.

JOHN MASEFIELD, *The Widow in the Bye Street*. Pt. iv, st. 25.

6
Ah, what a mixture of sweet and bitter you serve me now! (Dulce amarumque una nunc misces mihi.)

PLAUTUS, *Pseudolus*, l. 63. (Act i, sc. 1.)

7
Flee what is sweet if it can turn to bitterness. (Dulce etiam fugias, fieri quod amarum potest.)

PUBLILIUS SYRUS, *Sententiæ*. No. 167.

8
Touch you the sourest points with sweetest terms.

SHAKESPEARE, *Antony and Cleopatra*. Act ii, sc. 2, l. 24.

Speak sweetly, man, although thy looks be sour.

SHAKESPEARE, *Richard II*. Act iii, sc. 2, l. 193.

9
The bitter past, more welcome is the sweet.

SHAKESPEARE, *All's Well that Ends Well*. Act v, sc. 3, l. 334.

10
The sweets we wish for turn to loathed sours
Even in the moment that we call them ours.

SHAKESPEARE, *The Rape of Lucrece*, l. 867.

11
Things sweet to taste prove in digestion sour.

SHAKESPEARE, *Richard II*, i, 3, 236. (1595)

What is sweet in the mouth is bitter in the stomach.

UNKNOWN, *Politeuphuia*, 172. (1669)

Good in the mouth and bad in the maw.

THOMAS FULLER, *Gnomologia*. No. 5511.

It is sweet in the mouth but bitter in the belly.

CHARLES KINGSLEY, *Westward Ho*. Ch. 11.

12
Sweet is the rose, but grows upon a briar;
Sweet is the juniper, but sharp his bough;
Sweet is the eglantine, but pricketh near;
Sweet is the firbloom, but his branches rough;
Sweet is the cypress, but his rind is tough;
Sweet is the nut. but bitter is his pill;
Sweet is the broom-flower, but yet sour enough;
And sweet is moly, but his root is ill.
So every sweet with sour is tempered still.

SPENSER, *Amoretti*. Sonnet xxvi.

Every excess causes a defect; every defect an excess. Every sweet hath its sour; every evil its good. . . . For every grain of wit there is a grain of folly. For everything you have missed, you have gained something else; and for every thing you gain, you lose something.

EMERSON, *Essays, First Series: Compensation*.

Every white will have its black
And every sweet its sour.

UNKNOWN, *Sir Cauline*. Pt. ii, l. 1. (c. 1450); (PERCY, *Reliques*. Ser. i, No. 4.)

See also under COMPENSATION.

13 One loving hour
For many years of sorrow can dispense:
A dram of sweet is worth a pound of sour.

SPENSER, *Faerie Queene*. Bk. i, canto 3, st. 30.

SWIMMING

14
It is one method to practise swimming with bladders, and another to practise dancing with heavy shoes.

BACON, *Advancement of Learning*. Bk. ii.

But swam, 'till Fortune threw a rope,
Buoyant on bladders filled with hope.

MATTHEW GREEN, *The Spleen*, l. 51.

My whole life, since I was left to myself to swim, as they say, without bladders.

JAMES HOWELL, *Pre-eminence of Parliament*, 17.

Little wanton boys that swim on bladders.

SHAKESPEARE, *Henry VIII*. Act iii, sc. 2, l. 359.

15 Not to swim
I' th' lead o' th' current, were almost to sink.

BEAUMONT AND FLETCHER, *Two Noble Kinsmen*. Act i, sc. 2.

16
He could, perhaps, have pass'd the Hellespont,
As once (a feat on which ourselves we prided)
Leander. Mr. Ekenhead. and I did.

BYRON, *Don Juan*. Canto ii, st. 105.

I read it in the story-book, that, for to kiss his dear,
Leander swam the Hellespont,—and I will swim this here.

O. W. HOLMES, *The Ballad of the Oysterman*.

17
They told me you had been to her,
And mentioned me to him:
She gave me a good character,
But said I could not swim.

LEWIS CARROLL, *Alice in Wonderland*. Ch. 13.

1
Good swimmers at length are drowned.
GEORGE HERBERT, *Jacula Prudentum.*

2
He may lightly swim that is held up by the chin.
HILL, *Commonplace-Book*, p. 129. (c. 1490)

It is easy to swim when the head is held up.
JOHN RAY, *Proverbs: Scottish.*

3
You will swim without cork; i. e., you will get on without help. (Nabis sine cortice.)
HORACE, *Satires*. Bk. i, sat. 4, l. 120.

3a
Oh! the old swimmin'-hole! whare the crick so still and deep
Looked like a baby-river that was laying half asleep.
J. W. RILEY, *The Old Swimmin'-hole.*

4
Or sink or swim.
SHAKESPEARE, *I Henry IV*. Act i, sc. 3, l. 194.

Ye reck not whether I float or sink.
CHAUCER, *The Compleynte of Pite*, l. 110. (c. 1368) Repeated in *The Knight's Tale*, l. 1539.

They care not whether they sink or swim.
THOMAS STARKEY, *England*, i, 3, 85. (1538)

5
An unpractised swimmer plunging still,
With too much labour drowns for want of skill.
SHAKESPEARE, *The Rape of Lucrece*, l. 1098.

I saw him beat the surges under him,
And ride upon their backs; . . . his bold head
'Bove the contentious waves he kept, and oar'd
Himself with his good arms in lusty stroke.
SHAKESPEARE, *The Tempest*. Act ii, sc. 1, l. 114.

6
I can swim like a duck.
SHAKESPEARE, *The Tempest*. Act ii, sc. 2, l. 133.

I can swim like a fish.
JOHN FLETCHER, *The Sea-Voyage*, i, 1. (1622)

7
A purer passion, a lordlier leisure,
A peace more happy than lives on land,
Fulfils with pulse of diviner pleasure
The dreaming head and the steering hand.
I lean my cheek to the cold grey pillow,
The deep soft swell of the full broad billow,
And close mine eyes for delight past measure,
And wish the wheel of the world would stand.
SWINBURNE, *A Swimmer's Dream*. Pt. v, st. 2.

SWINE

8
Root, hog, or die. This is the refrain of each of the nine verses of the Bull-Whacker's Epic.
J. H. BEADLE, *Life in Utah*, p. 227.

8a
A man cannot make a cheverill purse of a sow's ear.
COTGRAVE, *French-English Dictionary: Pigeon*. (1611) Quoting a proverb already old.

You will never make a satin purse of a sow's ear.
JAMES HOWELL, *English Proverbs*. (1659)

You can't make a silk purse out of a sow's ear.
SWIFT, *Polite Conversation*. Dial ii. (1738)
RICHARDSON, *Clarissa Harlowe*, iv, 119. (1748)

9
Thus says the prophet of the Turk:
Good mussulman, abstain from pork;
There is a part in ev'ry swine
No friend or follower of mine
May taste, whate'er his inclination,
On pain of excommunication. . . .
But for one piece they thought it hard
From the whole hog to be debarr'd. . . .
With sophistry their sauce they sweeten,
Till quite from tail to snout 'tis eaten.
COWPER, *Love of the World Reproved*, l. 1.

10
Though he love not to buy the pig in the poke.
JOHN HEYWOOD, *Proverbs*. Pt. i, ch. 9. (1546)

In doing of aught let your wit bear a stroke
For buying or selling of pig in a poke.
THOMAS TUSSER, *Five Hundred Points of Good Husbandry: September*. (1557)

He is a fool that will buy a pig in a poke.
ROBERT GREENE, *Works*. Vol. ii, p. 121.

11
You have a wrong sow by the ear.
BUTLER, *Hudibras*. Pt. ii, 3, 580. See 1324:13.

12
He keeps a parlour boarder of a pig.
THOMAS HOOD, *The Irish Schoolmaster*, l. 39.

14
The pig, if I am not mistaken,
Supplies us sausage, ham, and bacon.
Let others say his heart is big—
I call it stupid of the pig.
OGDEN NASH, *The Pig.*

15
How instinct varies in the grovelling swine.
POPE, *Essay on Man*. Epis. i, l. 221.

16
The hog that ploughs not, nor obeys thy call,
Lives on the labours of this lord of all.
POPE, *Essay on Man*. Epis. iii, l. 41.

17
'Tis old, but true, Still swine eats all the draff.
SHAKESPEARE, *Merry Wives of Windsor*, iv, 2, 109.

18
Pearl enough for a swine.
SHAKESPEARE, *Love's Labour's Lost*. Act iv, sc. 2, l. 91. *See also under* PEARL.

19
Weke, weke! so cries a pig prepared to the spit.
SHAKESPEARE, *Titus Andronicus*. Act iv, sc. 2, 146.

SWORD

See also Pen and Sword

20
What rights the brave? The sword!
What frees the slave? The sword!
What cleaves in twain the despot's chain,
And makes his gyves and dungeons vain?
The sword!
MICHAEL J. BARRY, *The Sword.*

He knew me and named me
The War-Thing, the Comrade,
Father of honour, And giver of kingship,
The fame-smith, the song-master,
Bringer of women.
W. E. HENLEY, *The Song of the Sword*, 43.

1
Take away the sword;
States can be saved without it.
BULWER-LYTTON, *Richelieu.* Act iii, sc. 1.

The sword, indeed, is never out of fashion,—
The Devil has care of *that.*
BULWER-LYTTON, *Richelieu.* Act i, sc. 1.

2
The trenchant blade Toledo trusty,
For want of fighting was grown rusty,
And ate into itself for lack
Of somebody to hew and hack.
BUTLER, *Hudibras.* Pt. i, canto 1, l. 359.

I give him three years and a day to match my Toledo,
And then we'll fight like dragons.
MASSINGER, *The Maid of Honour.* Act ii, sc. 2.

3
Arras they pricked and curtains with their swords,
And wounded several shutters and some boards.
BYRON, *Don Juan.* Canto i, st. 143.

4
For the sword outwears its sheath,
And the soul wears out the breast.
BYRON, *So We'll Go No More a Roving.*

5
Who has tied that little fellow to his sword?
CICERO, seeing his little son-in-law, Dolabella, with a long sword at his side. (FORSYTH, *Life.*)

Seeing Lentulus, his son-in-law, a man of very small stature, walking up, with a long sword at his side, he called out, "Who has tied my son-in-law to that sword?"
ERASMUS, *Adagia.*

Grac'd with a sword, and worthier of a fan.
COWPER, *The Task.* Bk. i, l. 771.

6
Great is the licence of the sword. (Magna gladiorum est licentia.)
CICERO, *Epistulæ ad Atticum.* Bk. iv, epis. 9.

7
Better die with the sword than by the sword.
SAMUEL DANIEL, *History of Civil War,* vii, 26.

8
A leaden sword in an ivory scabbard. (In eburna vagina plumbeus gladius.)
DIOGENES, of a fop. (LAERTIUS, *Diogenes.*)

Good sword has often been in poor scabbard.
W. G. BENHAM, *Proverbs,* p. 768.

8a
None could do such feats with Scanderbeg's sword as himself.
WILLIAM GURNALL, *The Christian in Complete Armour,* ii, 239. (1658) "Scanderbeg" was George Castriota, an Albanian patriot (1403–68).

Scanderbeg's sword must have Scanderbeg's arm.
THOMAS FULLER, *Gnomologia.* No. 4077. (1732)

9
Impatient straight to flesh his virgin sword.
HOMER, *Odyssey.* Bk. xx, l. 381. (Pope, tr.)

Full bravely hast thou flesh'd Thy maiden sword.
SHAKESPEARE, *I Henry IV.* Act v, sc. 4, l. 133.

10
Civilly by the sword.
BEN JONSON, *Every Man in His Humour,* iv, 5.

11
The fierce tigress of India lives in peace with her fellow; bears live in harmony with bears. But man thinks nothing of beating out the deadly sword on the accursed anvil. (Indica tigris agit rabida cum tigride pacem Perpetuam, sævis inter se convenit ursis. Ast homini ferrum letale induce nefanda Produxisse parum est.)
JUVENAL, *Satires.* Sat. xv, l. 163.

Who was the first to produce the fear-inspiring sword? How cruel and truly steel-hearted was he! (Quis fuit, horrendos primus qui protulit enses? Quam ferus et vere ferreus ille fuit!)
TIBULLUS, *Odes.* Bk. i, eleg. 10, l. 1.

See also under SMITH.

12
The cross has been carried forward on the hilt of the sword.
E. M. MACDONALD, *The Truth Seeker.*

13
Cowards and faint-hearted runaways
Look for orations when the foe is near:
Our swords shall play the orators for us.
MARLOWE, *Tamburlaine the Great.* Pt. i, l. 326.

Our right is in our swords.
BRENNUS, KING OF THE GAULS, to the Roman Ambassador, 390 B. C.

14
Some undone widow sits upon mine arm,
And takes away the use of 't; and my sword,
Glued to my scabbard, with wrong'd orphans' tears,
Will not be drawn.
MASSINGER, *New Way to Pay Old Debts,* v, 1.

15
Then said Jesus unto him, Put up again thy sword into his place: for all they that take the sword shall perish with the sword.
New Testament: Matthew, xxvi, 52.

He that strikes with the sword shall be beaten with the scabbard.
JOHN HEYWOOD, *Proverbs.* Pt. ii, ch. 7. (1546)

16
Violence, . . . oppression and sword law.
MILTON, *Paradise Lost.* Bk. xi, l. 671.

17
Young fire-eyed disputants, who deem their swords,
On points of faith, more eloquent than words.
MOORE, *Lalla Rookh: The Veiled Prophet,* l. 18.

18
There are but two powers in the world, the sword and the mind. In the long run the sword is always beaten by the mind.
NAPOLEON I, *Sayings of Napoleon.*

19
Snatch away the sword from one who is beside herself. (Eripite isti gladium, quæ suist impos animi.)
PLAUTUS, *Casina,* l. 629. (Act iii, sc. 5.)

Never put a sword in a madman's hand.
JAMES KELLY, *Scottish Proverbs,* p. 264.

No skill in swordsmanship, however just,
Can be secure against a madman's thrust.
COWPER, *Charity*, l. 509.

1
Don't stir the fire with a sword. (Πῦρ μαχαίρᾳ μὴ σκαλεύειν.)
PYTHAGORAS. (DIOGENES LAERTIUS, *Pythagoras*. Sec. 17.)

To your folly add bloodshed, and stir the fire with the sword. (Adde cruorem Stultitiæ, atque ignem gladio scrutare.)
HORACE, *Satires*. Bk. ii, sat. 3, l. 275.

2
It is now as in the olden days when the sword ruled all things. (Es ist hier wie in den alten Zeiten Wo die kninge noch alles that bedeuten.)
SCHILLER, *Wallenstein's Lager*. Sc. vi, l. 140.

3
This is his sword;
I robb'd his wound of it; behold it stain'd
With his most noble blood.
SHAKESPEARE, *Antony and Cleopatra*. Act v, sc. 1, l. 24.

I that with my sword quarter'd the world.
SHAKESPEARE, *Antony and Cleopatra*. Act iv, sc. 14, l. 57.

Your own good blade must win the rest.
SCOTT, *The Lady of the Lake*. Canto v, st. 7.

4
So we measured swords and parted.
SHAKESPEARE, *As You Like It*. Act v, sc. 4, l. 91.

And sheathed their swords for lack of argument.
SHAKESPEARE, *Henry V*. Act iii, sc. 1, l. 21.

5
Come, and get thee a sword, though made of lath.
SHAKESPEARE, *II Henry VI*. Act iv, sc. 2, l. 1.

6
Men Are as the time is: to be tender-minded
Does not become a sword.
SHAKESPEARE, *King Lear*. Act v, sc. 3, l. 30.

7
O goodly usage of those antique times,
In which the sword was servant unto right!
SPENSER, *The Faerie Queene*. Bk. iii, canto i, st. 13.

8
Let the sword decide. (Decernere ferro.)
VERGIL, *Æneid*. Bk. xii, l. 282.

The arbitrament of swords.
SHAKESPEARE, *Cymbeline*. Act i, sc. 4, l. 53.

9
Terrible he rode alone,
With his yemen sword for aid;
Ornament it carried none
But the notches on the blade.
UNKNOWN, *The Death Feud*. St. 14. (Translation of an Arab war song, signed J. S. M., *Tait's Edinburgh Magazine*, July, 1850.)

SYMPATHY

10
A brother's suff'rings claim a brother's pity.
ADDISON, *Cato*. Act i, sc. 1.

When your own tooth aches, then you know how to sympathise with one having the tooth-ache. ('Chih 'têng fang chih 'chih 'têng jên.)
UNKNOWN. A Chinese proverb.

Needs there groan a world in anguish just to teach us sympathy?
ROBERT BROWNING, *La Saisiaz*, l. 312.

13
Not only hear, but patronize, befriend them,
And where ye justly can commend, commend them;
And aiblins, when they winna stand the test,
Wink hard, and say: "The folks hae done their best!"
BURNS, *Scots Prologue for Mrs. Sutherland's Benefit-Night*, l. 37.

14
I would help others out of a fellow-feeling.
ROBERT BURTON, *Anatomy of Melancholy: Democritus to the Reader*.

A fellow feeling makes one wondrous kind.
DAVID GARRICK, *Epilogue on Quitting the Theatre*, June, 1776.

A fellow-feeling makes us wondrous kind.
BYRON, *English Bards and Scotch Reviewers*, l. 258. Misquoting Garrick.

15
How often do the clinging hands, though weak,
Clasp round strong hearts that otherwise would break.
M. ELIZABETH CROUSE, *Strength of Weakness*.

16
Jobling, there *are* chords in the human mind.
DICKENS, *Bleak House*. Ch. 20.

17
Nature has cast me in so soft a mould,
That but to hear a story feigned for pleasure,
Of some sad lover's death, moistens my eyes,
And robs me of my manhood.
DRYDEN, *All for Love*. Act iv, sc. 1.

18
Our souls sit close and silently within,
And their own web from their own entrails spin;
And when eyes meet far off, our sense is such,
That, spider like, we feel the tenderest touch.
DRYDEN, *Marriage-à-la-Mode*. Act ii, sc. 1.

Striking the electric chain wherewith we are darkly bound.
BYRON, *Childe Harold*. Canto iv, st. 23.

19
Harmony of aim, not identity of conclusion, is the secret of the sympathetic life.
EMERSON, *Essays, First Series: Friendship*.

20
We sink as easily as we rise, through sympathy
EMERSON, *Essays: Society and Solitude*.

21
The secrets of life are not shown except to sympathy and likeness.
EMERSON, *Representative Men: Montaigne*.

1
The man who melts
With social sympathy, though not allied,
Is of more worth than a thousand kinsmen.
EURIPIDES, *Orestes*, l. 846. *See also under* PHILANTHROPY.

2
Sympathy without relief is like mustard without beef.
R. L. GALES, *Vanished Country Folk*, p. 204.

3
The poem hangs on the berry bush
When comes the poet's eye;
The street begins to masquerade
When Shakespeare passes by.
The Christ sees white in Judas' heart
And loves His traitor well;
The God, to angel His new heaven,
Explores His lowest hell.
W. C. GANNETT, *We See as We Are*.

4
Our sympathy is cold to the relation of distant misery.
EDWARD GIBBON, *Decline and Fall of the Roman Empire*. Ch. 49.

5
He watch'd and wept, he pray'd and felt, for all.
GOLDSMITH, *The Deserted Village*, l. 166.

6
The craving for sympathy is the common boundary-line between joy and sorrow.
J. C. AND A. W. HARE, *Guesses at Truth*.

7
Accept these grateful tears! for thee they flow,
For thee, that ever felt another's woe!
HOMER, *Iliad*. Bk. xix, l. 319. (Pope, tr.)

Yet, taught by time, my heart has learned to glow
For others' good, and melt at others' woe.
HOMER, *Odyssey*. Bk. xviii, l. 269. (Pope, tr.) William Broome translated Book xviii for Pope, but Pope supplied the polish.
See also under WOE.

8
Sensibility of mind is indeed the parent of every virtue, but it is the parent of much misery, too.
THOMAS JEFFERSON, *Writings*. Vol. xix, p. 46.

9
People in distress never think that you feel enough.
SAMUEL JOHNSON. (BOSWELL, *Life*, ii, 469.)

10
E'en from good words thyself refrain,
And tremblingly admit
There is no anodyne for pain
Except the shock of it.
So, when thine own dark hour shall fall,
Unchallenged canst thou say:
"I never worried *you* at all,
For God's sake go away!"
RUDYARD KIPLING, *The Comforters*. St. 8.

11
No one is so accursed by fate,
No one so utterly desolate,
But some heart, though unknown,
Responds unto his own.
LONGFELLOW, *Endymion*. St. 8.

Somewhere or other there must surely be
The face not seen, the voice not heard,
The heart that not yet—never yet—ah me!
Made answer to my word.
CHRISTINA ROSSETTI, *Somewhere or Other*.

12
My heart, which by a secret harmony
Still moves with thine, join'd in connection sweet.
MILTON, *Paradise Lost*. Bk. x, l. 358.

13
A man should keep his heart-strings tightly drawn. (Misericordia se abstinere hominem oportet.)
PLAUTUS, *Mostellaria*, l. 802. (Act iii, sc. 2.)

Never elated while one man's oppress'd;
Never dejected while another's bless'd.
POPE, *Essay on Man*. Epis. iv, l. 323.

14
There is much satisfaction in work well done; praise is sweet; but there can be no happiness equal to the joy of finding a heart that understands.
VICTOR ROBINSON, *William Godwin*. (*The Truth Seeker*, 6 Jan., 1906.)

15
Rejoice with them that do rejoice, and weep with them that weep.
New Testament: Romans, xii, 15.

16
Bring thy soul and interchange with mine.
SCHILLER, *Votive Tablets: Value and Worth*.

17
Let our finger ache, and it induces
Our other healthful members even to that sense.
SHAKESPEARE, *Othello*. Act iii, sc. 4, l. 146.
See also under HEAD.

18
A heart at leisure from itself,
To soothe and sympathise.
ANNA LETITIA WARING, *Father, I Know that All My Life*.

19
And nothing, not God, is greater to one than one's self is,
And whoever walks a furlong without sympathy walks to his own funeral drest in his shroud.
WALT WHITMAN. *Song of Myself*. Sec. 48.

20
The homely sympathy that heeds
The common life our nature breeds;
A wisdom fitted to the needs
Of hearts at leisure.
WORDSWORTH, *To the Daisy*, l. 53.

T

TAILOR

See also Dress

I—Tailor: Apothegms

1
Great is the Tailor, but not the greatest.
CARLYLE, *Essays: Goethe's Works.*

2
Sartor resartus. (The patched-up tailor.)
THOMAS CARLYLE, Title of book, 1833.

3
The tailor that makes not a knot loseth a stitch.
THOMAS FULLER, *Gnomologia.* No. 4786.

4
A tailor, though a man of upright dealing,—
True but for lying,—honest but for stealing.
SIR JOHN HARINGTON, *Of a Precise Tailor.*

5
Be sure your tailor is a man of sense;
But add a little care, a decent pride,
And always err upon the sober side.
O. W. HOLMES, *A Rhymed Lesson,* l. 425.

6
Tailor, thou art a vermin,
Worse than the same thou prosecut'st and prick'st
In subtle seam.
BEN JONSON, *The Staple of News.* Act i, sc. 1.

I cannot abide a talking tailor.
BEN JONSON, *The Staple of News.* Act i, sc. 1.

7
There is knavery in all trades, but most in tailors.
ROGER L'ESTRANGE, *Æsop,* 161.

Truth among clothiers has less harbor than a louse upon a threadbare cloth.
WILLIAM SPELMAN, *Dialogue,* p. 116. (1580)

8
Let every tailor keep to his goose.
W. G. BENHAM, *Proverbs,* p. 800.

9
Lie ten nights awake, carving the fashion of a new doublet.
SHAKESPEARE, *Much Ado About Nothing.* Act ii, sc. 3, l. 18.

II—Tailor: The Tailor Makes the Man

10
God makes and the tailor shapes.
JOHN BULWER, *Anthropomet.,* 256. (1650)

God makes and apparel shapes, but 'tis money that finishes a man.
THOMAS FULLER, *Gnomologia.* No. 1680.

A man made by God and not by a tailor.
ANDREW JACKSON, referring to Sam Houston. (MCELROY, *Grover Cleveland,* ii, 258.)

11
For though the tailor makes the man, the cook yet makes the dishes.
JOHN FLETCHER, *The Bloody Brother.* Act iii, sc. 2. (1616)

Believe it, sir,
That clothes do much upon the wit, as weather
Does on the brain; and thence, sir, comes your proverb,
The tailor makes the man.
BEN JONSON, *The Staple of News.* Act i, sc. 1. (1625)

What a fine man Hath your tailor made you!
MASSINGER, *City Madam.* Act i, sc. 2. (1658)

12
By a new creation of my tailor's
I've shook off old mortality.
JOHN FORD, *Fancies Chaste and Noble.* Act i, sc. 3.

13
Thy tailor! . . . that poor shred
Can bring more to the making up of a man,
Than can be hoped from thee; thou art his creature;
And did he not, each morning, new create thee,
Thou'dst stink and be forgotten.
MASSINGER, *The Fatal Dowry.* Act iii, sc. 1.

14
Get me some French tailor
To new-create you.
MASSINGER, *The Renegade.* Act iii, sc. 1.

Yes, if they would thank their maker,
And seek no further; but they have new creators,
God tailor and god mercer.
MASSINGER, *A Very Woman.* Act iii, sc. 1, l. 161.

15
Thy tailor, rascal, . . . made those clothes,
Which, as it seems, make thee.
SHAKESPEARE, *Cymbeline.* Act iv, sc. 2, l. 81.

16
Cornwall: Thou art a strange fellow: a tailor make a man?
Kent: Ay, a tailor, sir; a stone-cutter or a painter could not have made him so ill, though he had been but two hours at the trade.
SHAKESPEARE, *King Lear.* Act ii, sc. 2, l. 61.

III—Tailor: Nine Tailors Make a Man

17
They say three tailors go to the making up of a man.
DEKKER AND WEBSTER, *Northward Hoe.* Act ii. (1607)

Two tailors go to a man.
UNKNOWN, *Tarlton's Jests,* p. 20. (1611)

Some foolish knave at first began the slander that three tailors are one man.
JOHN TAYLOR THE WATER-POET, *Works,* p. 73. (1630)

18
Like to nine tailors, who, if rightly spell'd
Into one man are monosyllabel'd.
JOHN CLEVELAND, *Poems,* p. 23. (1639)

Just like the manhood of nine tailors.
BUTLER, *Hudibras*. Pt. i, canto 2, l. 22. (1663)

Nine tailors make but one man.
JOHN RAY, *English Proverbs*. (1670)

1
Does it not stand on record that the English Queen Elizabeth, receiving a deputation of eighteen tailors, addressed them with a "Good morning, gentlemen both!"
CARLYLE, *Sartor Resartus*. Bk. iii, ch. 11.

Thou wretched Fraction, wilt thou be the ninth part even of a tailor?
CARLYLE, *Francia*.

2
It takes nine tailors to make a man. (Il faut neuf tailleurs pour faire un homme.)
UNKNOWN. A Breton proverb, quoted by Comte de la Villemarque.

TALE

I—Tale: Apothegms

3
Tell me the tales that to me were so dear,
Long, long ago,—long, long ago.
THOMAS HAYNES BAYLY, *Long, Long Ago*.

The story always old, and always new.
ROBERT BROWNING, *The Ring and the Book*. Pt. ii, l. 214.

A tale of the times gone by. (Ein Mährchen aus alten Zeiten.)
HEINE, *Die Lorelei*.

Unwritten, half-forgotten tales of old.
WILLIAM MORRIS, *Life and Death of Jason*. Bk. xi, l. 464.

'Tis an old tale, and often told.
SCOTT, *Marmion*. Canto ii, st. 27.

But now the mystic tale that pleas'd of yore
Can charm an understanding age no more.
ADDISON, *An Account of the Greatest English Poets*, l. 23.

4
I wrote tales beside,
Carved many an article on cherry-stones
To suit light readers.
E. B. BROWNING, *Aurora Leigh*. Bk. iii, l. 317.

5
Who will, may hear Sordello's story told.
Who would has heard Sordello's story told.
ROBERT BROWNING, *Sordello*. First and last lines. It was Tennyson who remarked that he had been able to understand only two lines of *Sordello*, the first and the last, and both of them were lies.

6
When we meet next we'll have a tale to tell.
BYRON, *Don Juan*. Canto v, st. 84.

Story! God bless you! I have none to tell, Sir.
GEORGE CANNING, *The Friend of Humanity and the Knife Grinder*.

7
Let every fellow tell his tale about.
CHAUCER, *The Knightes Tale*, l. 32.

Sey forth thy tale, and tarry not the time.
CHAUCER, *The Reeves Prologue*, l. 51.

8
For though myself be a full vicious man,
A moral tale yet I you telle can.
CHAUCER, *The Pardoneres Prologue*, l. 131.

Listen, every one
That listen may, unto a tale
That's merrier than the nightingale.
LONGFELLOW, *Tales of a Wayside Inn*: Pt. iii, *The Sicilian's Tale*.

9
This tale's a fragment from the life of dreams.
S. T. COLERIDGE, *Phantom or Fact?*

10
Believe not every tale.
Apocrypha: Ecclesiasticus, xix, 15.

This story will never go down.
HENRY FIELDING, *Tumble-Down Dick*. Air 1.

11
The tale runs as it pleases the teller.
THOMAS FULLER, *Gnomologia*. No. 4783.

12
Lest men suspect your tale untrue,
Keep probability in view.
JOHN GAY, *Fables: The Painter Who Pleased Nobody*, l. 1.

13
A good tale ill told is a bad one.
JOHN RAY, *English Proverbs*, p. 135.

No tale so good but may be spoiled in the telling.
W. G. BENHAM, *Proverbs*, p. 817.

Mar a curious tale in telling it.
SHAKESPEARE, *King Lear*. Act i, sc. 4, l. 35.

A tale never loses in the telling.
C. H. SPURGEON, *John Ploughman*. Ch. 6.

14
Soft as some song divine, thy story flows.
HOMER, *Odyssey*. Bk. xi, l. 458. (Pope, tr.)

15
Why do you laugh? Change but the name and the tale is told of you. (Quid rides? Mutato nomine de te Fabula narratur.)
HORACE, *Satires*. Bk. i, sat. 1, l. 69.

How strive you? *De te fabula!*
ROBERT BROWNING, *The Statue and the Bust*, last line.

16
I am always at a loss to know how much to believe of my own stories.
WASHINGTON IRVING, *Tales of a Traveller: Preface*.

17
A story without a head (or beginning). (Ἀκέφαλος μῦθος.)
PLATO, *Phædrus*. Sec. 264.

18
And thereby hangs a tale.
SHAKESPEARE, *As You Like It*, ii, 7, 28; iv, l. 60; *Merry Wives of Windsor*, i, 4, 159; *Othello*, iii, 1, 8; *Taming of Shrew*, iv, 1, 60.

19
Mark now, how a plain tale shall put you down.
SHAKESPEARE, *I Henry IV*. Act ii, sc. 4, l. 281.

I will a round unvarnish'd tale deliver.
SHAKESPEARE, *Othello*. Act i, sc. 3, l. 90.

1
And when thou comest thy tale to tell,
Smooth not thy tongue with filed talk.
SHAKESPEARE [?], *Passionate Pilgrim*, l. 305.

An honest tale speeds best being plainly told.
SHAKESPEARE, *Richard III*. Act iv, sc. 4, l. 358.

A whispering tale in a fair lady's ear,
Such as would please.
SHAKESPEARE, *Romeo and Juliet*. Act i, sc. 5, l. 25.

2
He cometh unto you with a tale which holdeth children from play, and old men from the chimney corner.
SIR PHILIP SIDNEY, *The Defense of Poesy*. Pt. ii.

Such wondrous tales as childhood loves to hear.
SOUTHEY, *Joan of Arc*. Bk. i, l. 227.

3
What cometh once in may never out, for fear of telling tales out of school.
WILLIAM TYNDALE, *Practice of Prelates*, 249. (1530)

Beware of the porter's lodge for carrying tales out of school.
JOHN FORD, *Fancies*. Act i, sc. 2. (1638)

Fie, miss! fie! tell tales out of school?
THOMAS SHADWELL, *The True Widow*. Act iv, sc. 1. (1679)

4
The first law of story-telling. . . . "Every man is bound to leave a story better than he found it."
MRS. HUMPHRY WARD, *Robert Elsmere*. Bk. i, ch. 3.

II—Tale: Cock-and-Bull Stories

5
A schoolboy's tale, the wonder of an hour!
BYRON, *Childe Harold*. Canto ii, st. 2.

6
If we take it for a Canterbury tale, why do we not refute it?
THOMAS CRANMER, *Sermon on Rebellion*. (c. 1545)

We might as well spend that time in reading of profane histories, of Canterbury tales, or fit of Robin Hood.
HUGH LATIMER, *Seven Sermons*, 49. (1549)

That foolish young girl held us all in a Canterbury story; I thought she would never have done with it.
DANIEL DEFOE, *Roxana*. (1724)

7
What a tale of a cock and a bull he told my father.
JOHN DAY, *Law Trickes*. Act iv, sc. 2. (1608)

Thou talk'st of cocks and bulls.
BEAUMONT AND FLETCHER, *Chances*. Act ii, sc. 4. (1625)

Things which some call a cock and a bull, and others the product of a lively imagination.
THOMAS BROWN, *Works*. Vol. ii, p. 94. (1702)

And then tell a familiar tale of a cock and a bull, and a whore and a bottle.
CONGREVE, *Way of the World*. Act iii, sc. 15.

8
Old wives' foolish tales of Robin Hood.
ERASMUS, *Adagia*. (Udall, tr., 1542)

This is a tale of Robinhood, which to believe, might show my wits but weak.
SIR JOHN HARINGTON, *Orlando Furioso*, xlv, 105. (1591)

From idle tales of Robin Hood, the blessed Lord of Heaven deliver me.
NICHOLAS BRETON, *Works*, i, 8. (1600)

9
He tells old wives' tales appropriate to the case. (Garrit aniles Ex re fabellas.)
HORACE, *Satires*. Bk. ii, sat. 6, l. 77.

A fool he is for his most felicity
Is to believe the tales of an old wife.
ALEXANDER BARCLAY, *Ship of Fools*, i, 72. (1509)

Thinking every old wives' tale to be a truth.
JOHN LYLY, *Euphues*, p. 347.

The Old Wives Tale.
GEORGE PEELE. Title of play (c. 1585); ARNOLD BENNETT. Title of Novel.

10
This is a fair tale of a tub told us of his election.
SIR THOMAS MORE, *Confutation of Tyndale's Answers*. (1532)

Ye say they follow your law,
And vary not a shaw,
Which is a tale of a tub.
JOHN BALE, *Three Laws*. Pt. ii. (1538)

Having entertained the fellow with a tale of a tub.
DANIEL DEFOE, *Memoirs of a Cavalier*, p. 97.

Tale of a Tub.
BEN JONSON. Title of play; JONATHAN SWIFT. Title of satire.

Do not believe what I tell you here any more than if it were some tale of a tub.
RABELAIS, *Works*. Bk. iv, ch. 38.

Note: A tale of a tub is a cock-and-bull story, a rigmarole, usually told with intent to deceive; a tale of Robin Hood is a fiction, usually told as such; a Canterbury tale is a traditional story designed to amuse, and sometimes long-winded; an old wives' tale is any marvellous, legendary story.

III—Tale: Twice-Told Tales

11
'Tis hard to venture where our betters fail,
Or lend fresh interest to a twice-told tale.
BYRON, *Hints from Horace*, l. 183.

12
A tale twice told is cabbage twice sold.
THOMAS FULLER, *Gnomologia*. No. 429.

It ought to be a good tale that is twice told.
THOMAS FULLER, *Gnomologia*. No. 3041.

13
It is an irksome thing to tell again a plain-told tale. (Ἐχθρὸν δέ μοί ἐστιν αὖτις ἀριζήλως εἰρημένα μυθολογεύειν.)
HOMER, *Odyssey*. Bk. xii, last line.

And what so tedious as a twice told tale?
HOMER, *Odyssey*. Bk. xii, last line. (Pope, tr.)

1
Often would he tell the same tale in other words. (Ille referre aliter sæpe solebat idem.)
OVID, *Ars Amatoria*. Bk. ii, l. 128.

2
A good tale is none the worse for being twice told.
SCOTT, *Old Mortality*. Ch. 7.

3
Life is as tedious as a twice-told tale.
SHAKESPEARE, *King John*. Act iii, sc. 4, l. 108.

IV—Tale: Long-Winded Tales

See also Brevity

4
Various and strange was the long-winded tale.
JAMES BEATTIE, *The Minstrel*. Bk. i, l. 388.

5
Three stories high, long, dull, and old
As great lords' stories often are.
GEORGE COLMAN THE YOUNGER, *The Maid of the Moor*.

6
A story, in which native humour reigns,
Is often useful, always entertains:
A graver fact, enlisted on your side,
May furnish illustration, well applied;
But sedentary weavers of long tales
Give me the fidgets, and my patience fails.
COWPER, *Conversation*, l. 203.

A tale should be judicious, clear, succinct;
The language plain, and incidents well link'd;
Tell not as new what every body knows;
And, new or old, still hasten to a close.
COWPER, *Conversation*, l. 235.

7
It is a foolish thing to make a long prologue, and to be short in the story itself.
Apocrypha: II Maccabees, ii, 32.

This is a long preamble of a tale.
CHAUCER, *Wife of Bath's Prologue*, l. 831.

"Skoal! to the Northland! skoal!"
—Thus the tale ended.
LONGFELLOW, *The Skeleton in Armor*.

8
O, Sir! the story will make your heart bleed, . . . but it is too long to be told now.
STERNE, *Tristram Shandy*. Bk. ii, ch. 17.

But that's another story.
RUDYARD KIPLING, *Soldiers Three: Mulvaney*.

V—Tale: Sad Tales

9
All the piteous tales that tears
Have water'd since the world was born.
THOMAS HOOD, *Ode to Melancholy*, l. 11.

10
The tale is worth the hearing; and may move
Compassion, perhaps deserve your love
And approbation.
MASSINGER, *Believe as You List: Prologue*.

11
I will tell ye now
What never yet was heard in tale or song,
From old or modern bard, in hall or bower.
MILTON, *Comus*, l. 43.

12
Masters, I have to tell a tale of woe,
A tale of folly and of wasted life,
Hope against hope, the bitter dregs of strife,
Ending, where all things end, in death at last.
WILLIAM MORRIS, *The Earthly Paradise: Prologue*. St. 6.

13
I could a tale unfold whose lightest word
Would harrow up thy soul.
SHAKESPEARE, *Hamlet*. Act i, sc. 5, l. 15.

I had as lief you would tell me of a mess of porridge.
SHAKESPEARE, *Merry Wives of Windsor*, iii, 1, 64.

A sad tale's best for winter: I have one
Of sprites and goblins.
SHAKESPEARE, *Winter's Tale*. Act ii, sc. 1, l. 25.

14
Come listen to my mournful tale,
Ye tender hearts and lovers dear;
Nor will you scorn to heave a sigh,
Nor need you blush to shed a tear.
WILLIAM SHENSTONE, *Jemmy Dawson*.

For seldom shall she hear a tale
So sad, so tender, yet so true.
WILLIAM SHENSTONE, *Jemmy Dawson*.

Listen to my tale of woe.
EUGENE FIELD. See 1475:15.

15
A lamentation and an ancient tale of wrong,
Like a tale of little meaning tho' the words are strong.
TENNYSON, *The Lotos-eaters*, l. 118.

16
I shudder as I tell it. (Horresco referens.)
VERGIL, *Æneid*. Bk. ii, l. 204.

TALENT

See also Genius and Talent

17
To do easily what is difficult for others is the mark of talent.
AMIEL, *Journal*, 17 Dec., 1856.

Talent is habitual facility of execution.
EMERSON, *Essays: Natural History of Intellect*.

18
Her talents were of the more silent class.
BYRON, *Don Juan*. Canto vi, st. 49.

19
Few boys are born with talents that excel,
But all are capable of living well.
COWPER, *Tirocinium*, l. 509.

20
The difference between talents and character is adroitness to keep the old and trodden round, and power and courage to make a new road to new and better goals.
EMERSON, *Essays, First Series: Circles*.

Profound sincerity is the only basis of talent, as of character.
EMERSON, *Essays: Natural History of Intellect*.

Talent is developed in retirement; character is formed in the rush of the world. (Es bildet ein Talent sich in der Stille, Sich ein Charakter in dem Strom der Welt.)

GOETHE, *Tasso*. Act i, sc. 2.

1
Each man has his own vocation. The talent is the call.

EMERSON, *Essays, First Series: Spiritual Laws*.

Each man has an aptitude born with him.

EMERSON, *Society and Solitude: Success*.

Every man has his gift, and the tools go to him that can use them.

CHARLES KINGSLEY, *Saint's Tragedy*. Act ii, sc. 6.

2
Talents differ; all is well and wisely put;
If I cannot carry forests on my back,
Neither can you crack a nut.

EMERSON, *Fable*.

3
And sure th' Eternal Master found
His single talent well employ'd.

SAMUEL JOHNSON, *On the Death of Mr. Robert Levet*. St. 7.

That one talent which is death to hide.

MILTON, *Sonnet: On His Blindness*.

And I was afraid, and went and hid thy talent in the earth.

New Testament: Matthew, xxv, 25.

4
Let us not overstrain our talents, lest we do nothing gracefully. (Ne forçons point notre talent; Nous ne ferions rien avec grâce.)

LA FONTAINE, *Fables*. Bk. iv, fab. 5.

5
Let the path be open to talent.

NAPOLEON BONAPARTE, *Sayings of Napoleon*.

6
Hidden talent counts for nothing. (Occultæ musicæ nullum esse respectum.)

NERO, quoting a Greek proverb, when arranging to make his début as a singer. (SUETONIUS, *Lives: Nero*. Ch. 20, sec. 2.) Suetonius records that the début was made at Naples. The theatre was shaken by an earthquake shock while Nero was singing, but he finished the number. The theatre collapsed just after the audience dispersed.

Hide not your talents, they for use were made.
What's a Sun-dial in the Shade?

BENJAMIN FRANKLIN, *Poor Richard*, 1750.

The Fairies were invited to be present at the birth of my son, and each one conferred a talent on him—he possesses them all. Unfortunately we had forgotten to invite an old fairy, who, arriving after all the others, exclaimed, "He shall have all the talents, except that to make good use of them."

DUCHESSE D'ORLEANS, referring to the Duc d'Orleans, Regent of France during the minority of Louis XV. (IRVING, *The Great Mississippi Bubble*.)

7
Often the greatest talents lie unseen. (Sæpe summa ingenia in occulto latent.)

PLAUTUS, *Captivi*, l. 165. (Act i, sc. 2.)

8
Nathaniel: A rare talent!
Dull: If a talent be a claw, look how he claws him with a talent.

SHAKESPEARE, *Love's Labour's Lost*, iv, 2, 64.

9
Talents angel-bright,
If wanting worth, are shining instruments
In false ambition's hand, to finish faults
Illustrious, and give infamy renown.

YOUNG, *Night Thoughts*. Night vi, l. 273.

TALK

See also Conversation, Speech

I—Talk: Definitions

10
A great thing is a great book, but greater than all is the talk of a great man.

BENJAMIN DISRAELI, *Coningsby*. Bk. iii, ch. 1.

11
The most fluent talkers or most plausible reasoners are not always the justest thinkers.

WILLIAM HAZLITT, *Essays: On Prejudice*.

12
Talking is like playing on the harp; there is as much in laying the hands on the strings to stop their vibration as in twanging them to bring out their music.

HOLMES, *Autocrat of Breakfast-Table*. Ch. 1.

13
The man who talks to unburthen his mind is the man to delight you.

SAMUEL JOHNSON. (BOSWELL, *Life*, iii, 247.)

14
A good talker, even more than a good orator, implies a good audience.

LESLIE STEPHEN, *Life of Samuel Johnson*. Ch. 3.

15
All natural talk is a festival of ostentation; and by the laws of the game each accepts and fans the vanity of the other.

R. L. STEVENSON, *Memories and Portraits: Talk and Talkers*.

II—Talk: Apothegms

16
Two great talkers will not travel far together.

GEORGE BORROW, *Lavengro*. Ch. 35. Cited as a Spanish proverb.

17
"The time has come," the Walrus said,
"To talk of many things:
Of shoes—and ships—and sealing-wax—
Of cabbages—and kings—
And why the sea is boiling hot—
And whether pigs have wings."

CARROLL, *Through the Looking-Glass*. Ch. 4.

18
When I can't talk sense, I talk metaphor.

JOHN PHILPOT CURRAN. (MOORE, *Life of Sheridan*, ii, 29, note.)

19
True he can talk, and yet he is no speaker. (*Λαλεῖν ἄριστος, ἀδυνατώτατος λέγειν.*)

EUPOLIS, *Demes*. (PLUTARCH, *Lives: Alcibiades*, xiii, 2.) Of Alcibiades.

Talkative rather than eloquent. (Loquax magis quam facundus.)
SALLUST, *History*. Bk. iv, sec. 43.

1
Time will explain it all. He is a talker, and needs no questioning before he speaks.
EURIPIDES, *Æolus*. Fragment 38.

2
People may come to do anything almost, by talking of it.
SAMUEL JOHNSON. (BOSWELL, *Life*, v, 286.)

4
You talk just like a book. (Vous parlez tout comme un livre.)
MOLIÈRE, *Don Juan*. Act i, sc. 2, l. 100.

5
Strange the difference of men's talk!
SAMUEL PEPYS, *Diary*, 1660.

6
A hotch-potch of talk. (Sartago loquendi.)
PERSIUS, *Satires*. Sat. i, l. 80.

You are talking cobble-stones. (Lapides loqueris.)
PLAUTUS, *Aulularia*, l. 152. (Act ii, sc. 1.)

This is idle talk. (Verba multa facimus.)
PLAUTUS, *Pseudolus*, l. 638. (Act ii, sc. 1.)

7
The talk of the lips tendeth only to penury.
Old Testament: Proverbs, xiv, 23.

8
I'll talk a word with this same learned Theban.
SHAKESPEARE, *King Lear*. Act iii, sc. 4, l. 162.

9
And all talk died, as in the grove all song
Beneath the shadow of some bird of prey.
TENNYSON, *Pelleas and Ettarre*, l. 594.

III—Talk: Table-Talk

10
In dinner talk it is perhaps allowable to fling any faggot rather than let the fire go out.
J. M. BARRIE, *Tommy and Grizel*, p. 34.

11
A civil guest
Will no more talk all, than eat all the feast.
GEORGE HERBERT, *The Church-Porch*. St. 51.

12
A table-talker rich in sense,
And witty without wit's pretence.
COTTON MATHER, *Epitaph on Anne Bradstreet*.

13
And not to serve for table-talk.
MONTAIGNE, *Essays*. Bk. ii, ch. 3.

Let it serve for table-talk.
SHAKESPEARE, *The Merchant of Venice*. Act iii, sc. 5, l. 93.

14
In after dinner talk,
Across the walnuts and the wine.
TENNYSON, *The Miller's Daughter*. St. 4.

IV—Talk: Admonitions

15
Talk often, but never long: in that case, if you do not please, at least you are sure not to tire your hearers.
LORD CHESTERFIELD, *Letters*, 19 Oct., 1748.

16
Men of your kidney talk little; they glory in taciturnity, and cut their hair shorter than their eyebrows. (Rarus sermo illis et magna libido tacendi Atque supercilio brevior coma.)
JUVENAL, *Satires*. Sat. ii, l. 14.

17
We know well enough that we should not talk of our wives, but we seem not to know that we should talk still less of ourselves. (On sait assez qu'il ne faut guère parler de sa femme, mais on ne sait pas assez qu'on devrait encore moins parler de soi.)
LA ROCHEFOUCAULD, *Maximes*. No. 364.

18
Let your talk be such as is worthy of belief, and your words such as are commonly used. (Sit tibi credibilis sermo, consuetaque verba.)
OVID, *Ars Amatoria*. Bk. i, l. 467.

19
Talk to every woman as if you loved her, and to every man as if he bored you.
OSCAR WILDE, *A Woman of No Importance*. Act iii.

V—Talk: Familiar Talk

20
The charm and playfulness of his talk. (Lepos et festivitas orationis.)
CICERO, *De Oratore*. Bk. ii, sec. 56.

21
They would talk of nothing but high life, and high-lived company; with other fashionable topics, such as pictures, taste, Shakespeare, and the musical glasses.
GOLDSMITH, *The Vicar of Wakefield*. Ch. 9.

22
No season now for calm, familiar talk.
HOMER, *Iliad*. Bk. xxii, l. 169. (Pope, tr.)

23
And the talk slid north, and the talk slid south,
With the sliding puffs from the hookah-mouth.
Four things greater than all things are,—
Women and Horses and Power and War.
KIPLING, *Ballad of the King's Jest*.

24
To beguile with talk the slow-moving hours. (Tarde tempora narrando fallat.)
OVID, *Tristia*. Bk. iii, eleg. 3, l. 11.

We were wont to spend long hours in talking, the day not sufficing for our discourse. (Solebamus consumere longa loquendo Tempora, sermonem deficiente die.)
OVID, *Tristia*. Bk. v, eleg. 13, l. 28.

25
His talk was like a stream which runs
With rapid change from rocks to roses:

It slipped from politics to puns:
  It passed from Mahomet to Moses:
Beginning with the laws which keep
  The planets in their radiant courses,
And ending with some precept deep
  For dressing eels or shoeing horses.

WINTHROP MACKWORTH PRAED, *The Vicar.*

1
Come, let's now talk with deliberation, fair and softly, as lawyers go to heaven.

RABELAIS, *Works.* Bk. v, ch. 28.

2
Let's talk of graves, of worms, and epitaphs; . . .
Let's choose executors and talk of wills.

SHAKESPEARE, *Richard II.* Act iii, sc. 2, l. 145.

3
I am not one who oft or much delight
To season my fireside with personal talk.

WORDSWORTH, *Personal Talk.* No. 1.

VI—Talk: Loquacity

See also Speech: Loquacity; Words: Verbosity

4
The talk of empty-headed, vain and tiresome babblers . . . has justly been thought to come from the lips and not from the heart. The tongue ought not to be unrestrained and rambling, but guided by cords connected with the inmost breast.

AULUS GELLIUS, *Noctes Atticæ.* Bk. i, ch. 15, sec. 1.

5
It would talk; Lord, how it talked!

BEAUMONT AND FLETCHER, *The Scornful Lady.* Act iv, sc. 1.

Then he will talk—good gods, how he will talk!

NATHANIEL LEE, *Alexander the Great.* Act i, sc. 1.

How you do talk!

SHAKESPEARE, *Henry VIII.* Act ii, sc. 3, l. 44.

Poor prattler, how thou talk'st!

SHAKESPEARE, *Macbeth.* Act iv, sc. 2, l. 64.

6
Folded his two hands and let them talk,
Watching the flies that buzzed! and yet no fool.

ROBERT BROWNING, *An Epistle,* l. 123.

7
So much they talked, so very little said.

CHARLES CHURCHILL, *The Rosciad,* l. 550.

8
He who talks much says many foolish things. (Qui parle beaucoup dit beaucoup de sottises.)

CORNEILLE, *Le Menteur: Sequel.* Act iii, sc. 1.

Much talk, much foolishness.

The Talmud.

9
But far more numerous was the herd of such,
Who think too little, and who talk too much.

DRYDEN, *Absalom and Achitophel.* Pt. i, l. 533.

Those that merely talk and never think.

BEN JONSON, *An Epistle, Answering One that Asked to be Sealed of the Tribe of Ben,* l. 9.

They never taste who always drink;
They always talk who never think.

MATTHEW PRIOR, *Upon a Passage in the Scaligeriana.* The French say, "Moins on pense, plus on parle" (The less people think, the more they talk).

10
Though I'm anything but clever,
I could talk like that for ever.

W. S. GILBERT, *H. M. S. Pinafore.* Act ii.

11
He who talks much cannot always talk well. (Chi parla troppo non può parlar sempre bene.)

GOLDONI, *Pamela.* Act i, sc. 6.

12
And there's our well-dressed gentleman, who sits,
By right divine, no doubt, among the wits,
Who airs his tailor's patterns when he walks,
The man that often speaks, but never talks.

O. W. HOLMES, *The Banker's Secret,* l. 63.

13
Whom the disease of talking still once possesseth, he can never hold his peace. Nay, rather than he will not discourse, he will hire men to hear him.

BEN JONSON, *Explorata: Optanda: Thersites Homeri.*

14
Oft has it been my lot to mark
A proud, conceited, talking spark.

JAMES MERRICK, *The Chameleon.*

15
You interrupt him with your talking. (Sermone huic obsonas.)

PLAUTUS, *Pseudolus.* Act i, sc. 2, l. 74.

16
Talkativeness has another plague attached to it, even curiosity; for praters wish to hear much that they may have much to say.

PLUTARCH, *Morals: Of Talkativeness.*

17
Talk thy tongue weary: speak.

SHAKESPEARE, *Cymbeline.* Act iii, sc. 4, l. 115.

18
If I chance to talk a little wild, forgive me;
I had it from my father.

SHAKESPEARE, *Henry VIII.* Act i, sc. 4, l. 26.

19
                The red wine first must rise
In their fair cheeks, my lord; then we shall have 'em
Talk us to silence.

SHAKESPEARE, *Henry VIII.* Act i, sc. 4, l. 43.

20
For the watch to babble and to talk is most tolerable and not to be endured.

SHAKESPEARE, *Much Ado About Nothing.* Act iii, sc. 3, l. 37.

With vollies of eternal babble.

BUTLER, *Hudibras.* Pt. iii, canto 2, l. 453.

They only babble who practise not reflection.

SHERIDAN, *Pizarro.* Act i, sc. 1.

21
A gentleman, nurse, that loves to hear him-

self talk, and will speak more in a minute than he will stand to in a month.

SHAKESPEARE, *Romeo and Juliet*. Act ii, sc. 4, l. 155.

1
In my youth people talked about Ruskin; now they talk about drains.

MRS. HUMPHRY WARD, *Robert Elsmere*. Bk. ii, ch. 12.

TARIFF, THE

2
Protection and patriotism are reciprocal. This is the road that all great nations have trod.

J. C. CALHOUN, *Speech*, House of Representatives, 12 Dec., 1811.

3
It is a condition that confronts us—not a theory.

GROVER CLEVELAND, *Annual Message*, 1887, referring to the tariff.

There's one more President for us in Protection.

JAMES G. BLAINE, *Letter*, Dec., 1887, after Cleveland's tariff message.

4
Free trade is not a principle, it is an expedient.

BENJAMIN DISRAELI, *Speech on Import Duties*, 25 April, 1843.

Protection is not a principle, but an expedient.

DISRAELI, *Speech*, 17 March, 1845.

5
Free-trade, they [parties] concede, is very well as a principle, but it is never quite time for its adoption.

EMERSON, *Letters and Social Aims: Poetry and Imagination*.

6
What more incongruous than the administering of custom-house oaths and the searching of trunks and hand-bags under the shadow of "Liberty Enlightening the World"?

HENRY GEORGE, *Protection or Free Trade*. Ch. 9.

7
The tariff question is a local question.

WINFIELD SCOTT HANCOCK, *Interview*, Paterson, N. J., *Daily Guardian*, 8 Oct., 1880, during his campaign for the Presidency, a remark widely ridiculed and which helped to lose him the election.

8
Our interest will be to throw open the doors of commerce, and to knock off all its shackles, giving perfect freedom to all persons for the vent of whatever they may choose to bring into our ports, and asking the same in theirs.

THOMAS JEFFERSON, *Writings*. Vol. ii, p. 240.

We should encourage home manufactures to the extent of our own consumption of everything of which we raise the raw material.

THOMAS JEFFERSON, *Writings*. Vol. xii, p. 236.

I do not mean to say that it may not be for the general interest to foster for awhile certain infant manufactures, until they are strong enough to stand against foreign rivals, but when evident that they will never be so, it is against right to make the other branches of industry support them.

THOMAS JEFFERSON, *Writings*. Vol. xv, p. 432.

9
It accorded well with two favorite ideas of mine, of leaving commerce free, and never keeping an unnecessary soldier.

THOMAS JEFFERSON, *Writings*. Vol. xvii, p. 330.

10
I have come to a resolution myself, as I hope every good citizen will, never again to purchase any article of foreign manufacture which can be had of American make, be the difference of price what it may.

THOMAS JEFFERSON, *Writings*. Vol. xix, p. 223.

11
Free trade, one of the greatest blessings which a government can confer on a people, is in almost every country unpopular.

MACAULAY, *Essays: Mitford's History of Greece*.

12
The tariff is the Gulf Stream of politics. It flows through both parties, and each is trying to catch the other in bathing and steal his clothes.

PATRICK FRANCIS MURPHY, *Speech*, at Manhattan Club.

13
This talk bout the Revenoo is of the bosh, boshy.

ARTEMUS WARD, *Things in New York*.

TASTE

14
Every one carries his own inch-rule of taste, and amuses himself by applying it, triumphantly, wherever he travels.

HENRY ADAMS, *Education of*, p. 182.

15
Want of taste plays the chief part among men and plethora of words. (Ἀμουσία τὸ πλέον μέρος ἐν βροτοῖσι, λόγων τε πλῆθος.)

CLEOBULUS. (DIOGENES LAERTIUS, *Cleobulus*. Bk. i, sec. 91.)

16
Other virtues are in request in the field and workyard, but a certain degree of taste is not to be spared in those we sit with.

EMERSON, *Essays, Second Series: Manners*.

Those who are esteemed umpires of taste are often persons who have acquired some knowledge of admired pictures or sculptures, and have an inclination for whatever is elegant; but if you inquire whether they are beautiful souls, and whether their own acts are like fair pictures, you learn that they are selfish and sensual.

EMERSON, *Essays, Second Series: The Poet*.

17
Men lose their tempers in defending their taste.

EMERSON, *Journals*. Vol. ii, p. 147.

1
Love of beauty is Taste. . . . The creation of beauty is Art.
EMERSON, *Nature, Addresses: Beauty.*

2
You can't get high æsthetic tastes like trousers, ready made.
W. S. GILBERT, *Patience.* Act ii.

3
Shocking to Taste, and to Fine Arts a treason.
THOMAS HOOD, *Ode to Rae Wilson,* l. 285.

4
A fine judgment in discerning art. (Judicium subtile videndis artibus.)
HORACE, *Epistles.* Bk. ii, epis. 1, l. 242.

A judge of matters of taste. (Elegantiæ arbiter.)
TACITUS, *Annals.* Bk. xvi, sec. 18. Usually quoted: Arbiter elegantiarum.

5
Men have not all the same tastes and likes. . . . Their tastes vary, and they call for widely different things. (Non omnes eadem mirantur amantque. . . . Poscentes vario multum diversa palato.)
HORACE, *Epistles.* Bk. ii, epis. 2, l. 58.

There are as many thousands of tastes as there are living men. (Quot capitum vivunt, totidem studiorum Milia.)
HORACE, *Satires.* Bk. ii, sat. 1, l. 27.

Such and so various are the tastes of men.
AKENSIDE, *Pleasures of Imagination,* iii, 567.

Now who shall arbitrate?
Ten men love what I hate,
Shun what I follow, slight what I receive.
ROBERT BROWNING, *Rabbi Ben Ezra.* St. 22.

In different courses different tempers run;
He hates the moon, I sicken at the sun.
Wound up at twelve at noon, his clock goes right;
Mine better goes, wound up at twelve at night.
CHARLES CHURCHILL, *Night,* l. 81.

6
The wild vicissitudes of taste.
SAMUEL JOHNSON, *Prologue on the Opening of the Drury Lane Theatre,* l. 48.

7
Taste is the literary conscience of the soul. (Le goût est la conscience littéraire de l'âme.)
JOUBERT, *Pensées.* No. 366.

8
I wish you all sorts of prosperity, with a little more taste.
LE SAGE, *Gil Blas.* Bk. vii, ch. 4.

9
Well, for those who like that sort of thing I should think that is just about the sort of thing they would like.
ABRAHAM LINCOLN, *Remark,* to Robert Dale Owen, the spiritualist, who had insisted on reading to him a long manuscript on spiritism, and then asked his opinion of it. (GROSS, *Lincoln's Own Stories,* p. 96.)

10
Taste here were sacrilege.
WILLIAM MASON, *English Garden.* Bk. ii, l. 20.

11
Every man to his taste. (Chacun à son goût.)
MONTAIGNE, *Essays.* Bk. i, ch. 16. Quoting an old French proverb.

Every one as they like, as the woman said when she kissed her cow.
PETER MOTTEUX, tr., *Rabelais.* Bk. v, ch. 29.

12
No one thing pleases all: one man gathers thorns and another roses. (Non omnibus unum est quod placet: hic spinas colligit, ille rosas.)
PETRONIUS, *Fragments.* No. 74.

13
Talk what you will of taste, my friend, you'll find
Two of a face as soon as of a mind.
POPE, *Imitations of Horace: Epistles,* ii, 2, 268.

One likes the pheasant's wing, and one the leg;
The vulgar boil, the learned roast an egg.
POPE, *Imitations of Horace: Epistles,* ii, 2, 84.

But different taste in different men prevails,
And one is fired by heads, and one by tails.
POPE, *A Sermon Against Adultery,* l. 35.

14
I have always suspected public taste to be a mongrel product, out of affectation by dogmatism.
R. L. STEVENSON, *Virginibus Puerisque.* Pt. i.

15
There can be no disputing about tastes. (De gustibus non est disputandum.)
JEREMY TAYLOR, *Reflections upon Ridicule,* p. 122. Quoting a widely used Latin proverb.

TAXES

16
Neither will it be that a people over-laid with taxes should ever become valiant. . . . No people over-charged with tribute is fit for empire.
FRANCIS BACON, *Essays: Of the True Greatness of Kingdoms.*

17
To tax and to please, no more than to love and to be wise, is not given to men.
EDMUND BURKE, *On American Taxation.*

We ought not to be quite so ready with our taxes, until we can secure the desired representation.
EDMUND BURKE, *State of the Nation.* (*Works,* ii, 138.) 1769.

Taxation without representation is tyranny.
JAMES OTIS, *Argument on the Illegality of the Writs of Assistance,* Feb., 1761. See APPENDIX, p. 2296.

The corruption of democracies proceeds directly from the fact that one class imposes the taxes and another class pays them. The constitutional principle, 'No taxation without representation,' is utterly set at nought.
DEAN W. R. INGE, *Outspoken Essays,* i, 11.

18
[Lord Suffolk] at last paid his tribute to the common treasury to which we all must be taxed.
EDMUND BURKE, *Speech,* House of Commons, 11 Feb., 1780.

1
What is't to us if taxes rise or fall?
Thanks to our fortune, we pay none at all.
CHARLES CHURCHILL, *Night*, l. 264.

No statesman e'er will find it worth his pains
To tax our labours, and excise our brains.
CHARLES CHURCHILL, *Night*, l. 271.

2
Revenues, the sinews of the state. (Vectigalia, nervos rei publicæ.)
CICERO, *Pro Lege Manilia*. Ch. 7, 17. *See* WAR.

3
In sooth, the sorrow of such days
Is not to be express'd,
When he that takes and he that pays
Are both alike distress'd.
COWPER, *The Yearly Distress*. St. 5.

4
Of all debts men are least willing to pay the taxes. What a satire is this on government! Everywhere they think they get their money's worth, except for these. Hence the less government we have the better—the fewer laws and the less confided power.
EMERSON, *Essays, Second Series: Politics*.

5
Was it Bonaparte who said that he found vices very good patriots?—"he got five millions from the love of brandy, and he should be glad to know which of the virtues would pay him as much." Tobacco and opium have broad backs, and will cheerfully carry the load of armies.
EMERSON, *Society and Solitude: Civilization*.

6
But in this world, nothing is certain but death and taxes. (Mais dans ce monde, il n'y a rien d'assure que la mort et les impôts.)
BENJAMIN FRANKLIN, *Letter to Leroy*, 1789.

"It was as true," said Mr. Barkis, . . . "as taxes is. And nothing's truer than them."
DICKENS, *David Copperfield*. Ch. 21.

7
Taxation must not lead men into temptation, by requiring trivial oaths, by making it profitable to lie, to swear falsely, to bribe or to take bribes. . . . Taxation must not take from individuals what rightfully belongs to individuals.
HENRY GEORGE, *The Condition of Labor*, p. 11.

8
No one should be permitted to hold natural opportunities without a fair return to all for any special privilege thus accorded to him, and that value which the growth and improvement of a community attaches to land should be taken for the use of the community. . . . We are in favor of raising all public revenues by a single tax upon land values.
HENRY GEORGE, *The Single Tax Theory*.

9
All taxes must, at last, fall upon agriculture.
GIBBON, *Decline and Fall of the Roman Empire*. Ch. 8.

10
Robin: On Tuesday I made a false income tax return. *All:* Ha! ha! *1st Ghost:* That's nothing. *2nd Ghost:* Nothing at all. *3rd Ghost:* Everybody does that. *4th Ghost:* It's expected of you.
W. S. GILBERT, *Ruddigore*. Act ii.

11
Unnecessary taxation is unjust taxation.
ABRAM S. HEWITT. Democratic platform, 1884.

12
The purse of the people is the real seat of sensibility. Let it be drawn upon largely, and they will then listen to truths which could not excite them through any other organ.
THOMAS JEFFERSON, *Writings*. Vol. x, p. 59.

The marvel of all history is the patience with which men and women submit to burdens unnecessarily laid upon them by their governments.
WILLIAM H. BORAH, *Speech*, U. S. Senate.

13
Excise: A hateful tax levied upon commodities.
SAMUEL JOHNSON, *Dictionary*.

14
Taxes milks dry, but, neighbor, you'll allow
Thet havin' things onsettled kills the cow.
LOWELL, *Biglow Papers: Mason and Slidell*.

Taxes are paid in the sweat of every man that labors.
F. D. ROOSEVELT, *Speech*, at Pittsburgh, Pa., 19 October, 1932. During first campaign.

15
O that there might in England be
A duty on Hypocrisy,
A tax on humbug, an excise
On solemn plausibilities.
HENRY LUTTRELL, *An Aspiration*.

16
That the power of taxing it [the bank] by the States may be exercised so as to destroy it, is too obvious to be denied. . . . That the power to tax involves the power to destroy [is] not to be denied.
CHIEF JUSTICE JOHN MARSHALL, *Decision*, McCulloch v. Maryland. 1819. (*Wheat.*, iv, 427, 431.) Usually quoted, "The power to tax is the power to destroy." Marshall was echoing Daniel Webster, who, during his argument in the case (p. 327), stated, "An unlimited power to tax involves, necessarily, the power to destroy."

The power to tax is not the power to destroy while this court sits.
JUSTICE O. W. HOLMES, *Dissenting Opinion*, Panhandle Oil Co. v. Knox. 1928. (227 U.S., 218, 223.)

17
"I would," says Fox, "a tax devise
That shall not fall on me."
"Then tax receipts," Lord North replies,
"For those you never see."
RICHARD BRINSLEY SHERIDAN, *Epigram*.

18
We can inform Jonathan what are the inevitable consequences of being too fond of glory:—Taxes upon every article which enters the

mouth, or covers the back, or is placed on the foot . . . taxes on everything on earth, and in the waters under the earth.

SYDNEY SMITH, *Essays: Review of Seybert's Statistical Annals of the United States.*

The schoolboy whips his taxed top, the beardless youth manages his taxed horse with a taxed bridle, on a taxed road; and the dying Englishman, pouring his medicine, which has paid seven per cent., flings himself back on his chintz bed, which has paid twenty-two per cent., and expires in the arms of an apothecary, who has paid a license of a hundred pounds for the privilege of putting him to death.

SYDNEY SMITH, *Essays: Review of Seybert's Annals.*

1
Men who prefer any load of infamy, however great, to any pressure of taxation, however light.

SYDNEY SMITH, *Letters on American Debts.*

2
It is the part of a good shepherd to shear his flock, not flay it. (Boni pastoris esse tondere pecus, non deglubere.)

TIBERIUS CÆSAR, to certain governors who recommended burdensome taxes. (SUETONIUS, *Lives: Tiberius.* Ch. xxxii, sec. 2.)

What am I now to take out of all this scarcity? (Quid ego ex hac inopia nunc capiam?)

TERENCE, *Phormio,* l. 167. (Act i, sc. 3.)

TEA

3
The would-be wits and can't-be gentlemen,
I leave them to their daily "tea is ready,"
Smug coterie, and literary lady.

BYRON, *Beppo.* St. 76.

4
Tea! thou soft, thou sober, sage, and venerable liquid, . . . thou female tongue-running, smile-smoothing, heart-opening, wink-tippling cordial, to whose glorious insipidity I owe the happiest moment of my life, let me fall prostrate.

COLLEY CIBBER, *The Lady's Last Stake.* Act i, sc. 1.

5
Free yourselves from the slavery of tea and coffee and other slopkettle.

WILLIAM COBBETT, *Advice to Young Men.* Ch. 1.

Oh some are fond of Spanish wine and some are fond of French,
And some 'll swallow tay and stuff fit only for a wench.

JOHN MASEFIELD, *Captain Stratton's Fancy.*

6
Retired to tea and scandal, according to their ancient custom.

WILLIAM CONGREVE, *The Double-Dealer.* Act i, sc. 1.

Love and scandal are the best sweeteners of tea.

FIELDING, *Love in Several Masques.* Act iv, sc. 2.

7
Now stir the fire, and close the shutters fast,
Let fall the curtains, wheel the sofa round,
And, while the bubbling and loud hissing urn
Throws up a steamy column, and the cups,
That cheer but not inebriate, wait on each,
So let us welcome peaceful ev'ning in.

COWPER, *The Task.* Bk. iv, l. 36. (1785)

[Tar water] is of a nature so mild and benign and proportioned to the human constitution as to warm without heating, to cheer but not inebriate.

BISHOP GEORGE BERKELEY, *Siris.* Sec. 217. (1744) Quoted by SCOTT, *St. Ronan's Well: Heading,* ch. 7.

8
Polly put the kettle on, we'll all have tea.

DICKENS, *Barnaby Rudge.* Ch. 17.

9
Tea, though ridiculed by those who are naturally coarse in their nervous sensibilities, . . . will always be the favourite beverage of the intellectual.

THOMAS DE QUINCEY, *Confessions of an English Opium-Eater.*

10
There is a great deal of poetry and fine sentiment in a chest of tea.

EMERSON, *Letters and Social Aims: Inspiration; Representative Men: Montaigne.*

11
We had a kettle: we let it leak:
Our not repairing it made it worse.
We haven't had any tea for a week. . . .
The bottom is out of the Universe!

RUDYARD KIPLING, *Natural Theology.*

12
Soft yielding minds to water glide away,
And sip, with Nymphs, their elemental tea.

POPE, *Rape of the Lock.* Canto i, l. 61.

Here, thou, great Anna! whom three realms obey,
Dost sometimes counsel take—and sometimes tea.

POPE, *Rape of the Lock.* Canto iii, l. 7. It should be remembered that in Pope's day, tea was pronounced tay.

13
Thank God for tea! What would the world do without tea? how did it exist? I am glad I was not born before tea.

SYDNEY SMITH. (LADY HOLLAND, *Memoir.* Vol. i, p. 383.)

14
Venus her myrtle, Phœbus has his bays;
Tea both excels, which she vouchsafes to praise. . . .
The Muse's friend, tea does our fancy aid,
Repress those vapours which the head invade,
And keeps that palace of the soul serene.

EDMUND WALLER, *Of Tea.*

15
For her own breakfast she'll project a scheme,
Nor take her tea without a stratagem.

YOUNG, *Love of Fame.* Sat. vi, l. 190.

TEACHING

See also Education

I—Teaching: Definitions and Apothegms

1
To know how to suggest is the great art of teaching.

AMIEL, *Journal,* 16 Nov., 1864.

I do not teach, I only tell. (Je n'enseigne point, je raconte.)

MONTAIGNE, *Essays.* Bk. iii, ch. 2.

2
'Tis the taught already that profits by teaching.

ROBERT BROWNING, *Christmas-Eve.* Pt. iv.

3
He is wise who can instruct us and assist us in the business of daily virtuous living.

CARLYLE, *Essays: Schiller.*

4
The master loseth his time to learn
When the disciple will not hear.

CHAUCER, *Romaunt of the Rose,* l. 2149.

5
What greater or better gift can we offer the republic than to teach and instruct our youth? (Quod enim munus reipublicæ afferre majus meliusve possumus, quam si docemus atque erudimus juventutem?)

CICERO, *De Divinatione.* Bk. ii, ch. 2, sec. 4.

6
Not only is there an art in knowing a thing, but also a certain art in teaching it. (Nam non solum scire aliquid artis est, sed quædam ars etiam docendi.)

CICERO, *De Legibus.* Bk. ii, ch. 19, sec. 47.

7
It is always safe to learn, even from our enemies—seldom safe to venture to instruct, even our friends.

C. C. COLTON, *Lacon.* Pt. i, No. 284.

8
Examinations are formidable, even to the best prepared, for the greatest fool may ask more than the wisest man can answer.

C. C. COLTON, *Lacon.* Pt. i, No. 322.

9
Seek to delight, that they may mend mankind.
And, while they captivate, inform the mind.

COWPER, *Hope,* l. 758.

10
The schools became a scene
Of solemn farce, where Ignorance in stilts,
His cap well lin'd with logic not his own,
With parrot tongue perform'd the scholar's part,
Proceeding soon a graduated dunce.

COWPER, *The Task.* Bk. ii, l. 735.

11
It is the supreme art of the teacher to awaken joy in creative expression and knowledge.

ALBERT EINSTEIN, *Motto,* for the astronomy building of Junior College, at Pasadena, Calif.

12
There is no teaching until the pupil is brought into the same state or principle in which you are; a transfusion takes place; he is you and you are he; then is a teaching, and by no unfriendly chance or bad company can he ever quite lose the benefit.

EMERSON, *Essays, First Series: Spiritual Laws.*

13
It is a luxury to learn; but the luxury of learning is not to be compared with the luxury of teaching.

R. D. HITCHCOCK, *Eternal Atonement: Receiving and Giving.*

14
While the colt has a tender neck and is able to learn, the trainer teaches him to go as his rider directs. (Fingit equum tenera docilem cervice magister Ire viam qua monstret eques.)

HORACE, *Epistles.* Bk. i, epis. 2, l. 64.

15
Instruction enlarges the powers of the mind. (Doctrina sed vim promovet insitam.)

HORACE, *Odes.* Bk. iv, ode 4, l. 33.

16
If you love instruction, you will be well instructed. (Ἐὰν ᾖς φιλομαθής, ἔσει πολυμαθής.)

ISOCRATES, *Ad Dæmonicum.* Sec. 18. Roger Ascham (*The Schoolmaster*) states that this motto was inscribed in golden letters above the door of Isocrates' school.

17
Very few men are wise by their own counsel; or learned by their own teaching. For he that was only taught by himself, had a fool to his master.

BEN JONSON, *Explorata: Consilia.*

18
The guidance of our mind is of more importance than its progress. (La direction de notre esprit est plus importante que son progrès.)

JOUBERT, *Pensées.* No. 266.

19
Those having torches will pass them on to others. (Λαμπάδια ἔχοντες διαδώσουσιν ἀλλήλοις.)

PLATO, *The Republic.* Sec. 328.

Who kindly sets a wanderer on his way
Does e'en as if he lit another's lamp by his:
No less shines his, when he his friend's hath lit.
(Homo, qui erranti comiter monstrat viam,
Quasi lumen de suo lumine accendat, facit.
Nihilo minus ipsi lucet, cum illi accenderit.)

ENNIUS. (CICERO, *De Officiis.* Bk. i, ch. 16, sec. 51.)

Ministers of good things are like torches, a light to others, waste and destruction to themselves.

RICHARD HOOKER Quoted by Gladstone, 1880. (MORLEY, *Life of Gladstone.* Bk. viii, ch. 1.)

20
Men must be taught as if you taught them not,
And things unknown proposed as things forgot.

POPE, *Essay on Criticism.* Pt. iii, l. 15.

1
The teaching makes the difficulty. (Difficultatem facit doctrina.)
QUINTILIAN, *De Institutione Oratoria*. Bk. x, ch. 3.

2
Men learn while they teach. (Homines, dum docent, discunt.)
SENECA, *Epistulæ ad Lucilium*. Epis. vii, sec. 9.

And gladly would he learn, and gladly teach.
CHAUCER, *Canterbury Tales: Prologue*, l. 310.

Men learn when they teach.
HUGH RHODES, *Boke of Nurture*.

3
Is it this nonsense we teach with sour and pale faces? (Hoc est, quod tristes docemus et pallidi?)
SENECA, *Epistulæ ad Lucilium*. Epis. 48, sec. 7.

4
Highly fed and lowly taught.
SHAKESPEARE, *All's Well that Ends Well*. Act ii, sc. 2, l. 3.

Better fed than taught.
JOHN TAYLOR THE WATER-POET, *Jack-a-Lent*.

5
To teach a teacher ill beseemeth me.
SHAKESPEARE, *Love's Labour's Lost*. Act ii, sc. 1, l. 108.

6
Delightful task! to rear the tender thought,
To teach the young idea how to shoot.
THOMSON, *The Seasons: Spring*, l. 1152.

II—Teaching: The Teacher

7
Brought up in this city at the feet of Gamaliel.
New Testament: Acts, xxii, 3.

8
A schoolmaster should have an atmosphere of awe, and walk wonderingly, as if he was amazed at being himself.
WALTER BAGEHOT, *Literary Studies*. Vol. i, p. 52.

9
The hawk-nosed, high-cheek-boned Professor. . . .
The sallow, virgin-minded, studious
Martyr to mild enthusiasm.
ROBERT BROWNING, *Christmas-Eve*. Pt. xiv.

10
Here lie Willie Michie's banes:
O Satan, when ye tak him,
Gie him the schulin o' your weans,
For clever deils he'll mak them!
ROBERT BURNS, *For Mr. William Michie*.

11
Look out, gentlemen, the schoolmaster is abroad!
LORD BROUGHAM, *Address*, London Mechanics' Institute, 1825, referring to the secretary, John Reynolds, a schoolmaster.

Let the soldier be abroad if he will, he can do nothing in this age. There is another personage,—a personage less imposing in the eyes of some, perhaps insignificant. The schoolmaster is abroad, and I trust to him, armed with his primer, against the soldier, in full military array.
LORD BROUGHAM, *Speech*, 29 Jan., 1828.

The victory of the Prussians over the Austrians was a victory of the Prussian over the Austrian schoolmaster.
PRIVY COUNCILLOR PESCHEL. (*Ausland*. No. 19, 17 July, 1866.)

The Prussian schoolmaster won the battle of Sadowa. (Der preussiche Schulmeister hat die Schlacht bei Sadowa gewonnen.)
VON MOLTKE, *Speech*, Reichstag, 16 Feb., 1874.

12
'Tis pleasing to be school'd in a strange tongue
By female lips and eyes—that is, I mean,
When both the teacher and the taught are young.
BYRON, *Don Juan*. Canto ii, st. 164.

13
Respectable Professors of the Dismal Science.
CARLYLE, *Latter-Day Pamphlets*. No. 1. Used with reference to political economy.

14
A teacher should be sparing of his smile.
COWPER, *Charity*, l. 490.

15
We loved the doctrine for the teacher's sake.
DANIEL DEFOE, *Character of the Late Dr. Annesley*. *See also* HOLMES *under* CREED.

16
Consider that I laboured not for myself only, but for all them that seek learning.
Apocrypha: Ecclesiasticus, xxxiii, 17.

17
He teaches who gives and he learns who receives.
EMERSON, *Essays, First Series: Spiritual Laws*.

The man who can make hard things easy is the educator.
EMERSON, *Journals*, 1861.

The Spirit only can teach. Not any sensual, not any liar, not any slave can teach.
EMERSON, *Nature, Addresses and Lectures: An Address Delivered before the Senior Class in Divinity College, Cambridge, 15 July, 1838*.

18
A mere professor, spite of all his cant, is
Not a whit better than a Mantis,—
An insect, of what clime I can't determine,
That lifts its paws most parson-like, and thence,
By simple savages—thro' sheer pretence—
Is reckon'd quite a saint amongst the vermin.
THOMAS HOOD, *Ode to Rae Wilson*, l. 87.

19
Now owls are not really wise—they only look that way. The owl is a sort of college professor.
ELBERT HUBBARD, *Epigrams*.

20
Our American professors like their literature clear, cold, pure, and very dead.
SINCLAIR LEWIS, *Address*, Swedish Academy, 12 Dec., 1930.

1
The average schoolmaster is and always must be essentially an ass, for how can one imagine an intelligent man engaging in so puerile an avocation?
H. L. MENCKEN, *Prejudices*. Ser. iii, p. 244.

2
Beside yon straggling fence that skirts the way,
With blossom'd furze unprofitably gay,
There, in his noisy mansion, skill'd to rule,
The village master taught his little school;
A man severe he was, and stern to view;
I knew him well, and every truant knew;
Well had the boding tremblers learn'd to trace
The day's disasters in his morning face;
Full well they laugh'd, with counterfeited glee,
At all his jokes, for many a joke had he;
Full well the busy whisper, circling round,
Convey'd the dismal tidings when he frown'd;
Yet he was kind; or if severe in aught,
The love he bore to learning was in fault.
GOLDSMITH, *The Deserted Village*, l. 193.

3
The vanity of teaching often tempteth a man to forget he is a blockhead.
LORD HALIFAX, *Works*, p. 240.

4
The times were hard when Rip to manhood grew;
They always will be when there's work to do.
He tried at farming,—found it rather slow,—
And then at teaching—what he didn't know.
O. W. HOLMES, *Rip Van Winkle, M. D.*, l. 7.

5
For him the Teacher's chair became a throne.
LONGFELLOW, *Parker Cleaveland*.

6
Teacher, spare your simple flock. . . . Let the dismal rods, sceptres of pedagogues, have a rest. (Ludi magister, parce simplici turbæ; . . . ferulæque tristes, sceptra pædagogorum, cessant.)
MARTIAL, *Epigrams*. Bk. x, epig. 62.

The twig is so easily bended
I have banished the rule and the rod:
I have taught them the goodness of knowledge,
They have taught me the goodness of God:
My heart is the dungeon of darkness,
Where I shut them for breaking a rule;
My frown is sufficient correction;
My love is the law of the school.
CHARLES M. DICKINSON, *The Children*.

7
Let such teach others who themselves excel,
And censure freely who have written well.
POPE, *Essay on Criticism*. Pt. i, l. 15.

8
Woe upon ye
And all such false professors.
SHAKESPEARE, *Henry VIII*. Act iii, sc. 1, l. 114.

9
When I am forgotten, . . . say, I taught thee.
SHAKESPEARE, *Henry VIII*. Act iii, sc. 2, l. 432.

10
Schoolmasters will I keep within my house,
Fit to instruct her youth.
SHAKESPEARE, *The Taming of the Shrew*. Act i, sc. 1, l. 94.

I do present you with a man of mine,
Cunning in music and the mathematics.
SHAKESPEARE, *The Taming of the Shrew*. Act ii, sc. 1, l. 55.

11
I am not a teacher: only a fellow-traveller of whom you asked the way. I pointed ahead—ahead of myself as well as of you.
BERNARD SHAW, *Getting Married*.

12
He who can, does. He who cannot, teaches.
BERNARD SHAW, *Maxims for Revolutionists*.

13
Seven pupils in the class
Of Professor Callias,
Listen silent while he drawls,—
Three are benches, four are walls.
HENRY VAN DYKE, *The Professor*.

14
Everybody who is incapable of learning has taken to teaching.
OSCAR WILDE, *The Decay of Lying*.

15
He is either dead or teaching school. (Ἢ τεθνηκεν ἢ διδάσκει γράμματα.)
ZENOBIUS. Quoted by Erasmus, *Adagia:* "Aut mortuus est aut docet litteras."

16
The same persons telling to the same people the same things about the same things. (Οἱ αὐτοὶ περὶ τῶν αὐτῶν τοῖς αὐτοῖς τὰ αὐτά.)
UNKNOWN. A Greek proverb. Quoted by Isaac le Grange, apropos of teachers.

TEARS

See also Laughter and Tears; Smile and Tear

I—Tears: Definitions

17
Every tear from every eye
Becomes a babe in eternity.
WILLIAM BLAKE, *Auguries of Innocence*.

18
Tears are the noble language of the eye.
ROBERT HERRICK, *Hesperides*. No. 150.

Tears, though th' are here below the sinner's brine,
Above they are the Angels' spiced wine.
ROBERT HERRICK, *Upon Tears*.

Our present tears here, not our present laughter,
Are but the handsells of our joys hereafter.
ROBERT HERRICK, *Tears*.

19
A winy vapour melting in a tear.
HOMER, *Odyssey*. Bk. xix, l. 143. (Pope, tr.)

1
Sweet tears! the awful language, eloquent
Of infinite affection, far too big for words.
POLLOK, *The Course of Time*. Bk. v, l. 633.

2
Sweet drop of pure and pearly light,
In thee the rays of Virtue shine;
More calmly clear, more mildly bright,
Than any gem that gilds the mine.
SAMUEL ROGERS, *On a Tear*.

3
Eye-offending brine.
SHAKESPEARE, *Twelfth Night*. Act i, sc. 1, l. 30.

4
Of all the languages of earth in which the human kind confer
The Master Speaker is the Tear: it is the Great Interpreter.
FREDERIC RIDGELY TORRENCE, *The House of a Hundred Lights*.

5
Tears are the silent language of grief.
VOLTAIRE, *A Philosophical Dictionary: Tears*.

6
Hast thou ever weigh'd a sigh,
Or studied the philosophy of tears?
YOUNG, *Night Thoughts*. Night v, l. 516.

II—Tears: Apothegms

7
The welling fountains of my tears are utterly dried up. (Κλαυμάτων ἐπίσσυτοι πηγαὶ κατεσβήκασιν.)
ÆSCHYLUS, *Agamemnon*, l. 887.

Oh that my head were waters, and mine eyes a fountain of tears.
Old Testament: Jeremiah, ix, 1.

If you go over desert and mountain,
Far into the country of Sorrow, . . .
You shall certainly come to the fountain
At length,—to the Fountain of Tears.
ARTHUR O'SHAUGHNESSY, *The Fountain of Tears*.

Silver key of the fountain of tears.
SHELLEY, *Fragment: To Music*.

8
Why mournest thou, Rachel, shedding bitter tears? Because I see my children slain I shed tears.
AGATHIAS SCHOLASTICUS, *On Rachel*. (*Greek Anthology*. Bk. i, epig. 43.)

Rachel weeping for her children.
New Testament: Matthew, ii, 18.

Raining the tears of lamentation.
SHAKESPEARE, *Love's Labour's Lost*, v, 2, 819.

9
Nothing dries sooner than a tear. (Nihil lacrima citius arescit.)
APOLLONIUS. (CICERO, *De Inventione Rhetorica*. Bk. i, sec. 56; *Ad Herrenium*. Bk. ii, sec. 31.) FRANKLIN, *Poor Richard*, 1757.

Nothing dries sooner than a woman's tears.
THOMAS FULLER, *Gnomologia*. No. 3661.

Never a tear bedims the eye
That time and patience will not dry.
BRET HARTE, *The Lost Galleon*, l. 33.

The tear down childhood's cheek that flows
Is like the dew-drop on the rose;
When next the summer breeze comes by
And waves the bush, the flower is dry.
SCOTT, *Rokeby*. Canto iv, st. 11.

10
It is not possible that a child of these tears should be lost. (Fieri non potest, ut filius istarum lachrimarum pereat.)
ST. AUGUSTINE, *Confessions*. Ch. xii. The answer of the Bishop to St. Augustine's mother, when she wept for her son's heresies.

11
It is the wisdom of crocodiles, that shed tears when they would devour.
BACON, *Essays: Of Wisdom for a Man's Self*.

To these crocodile tears they will add sobs, fiery sighs, and sorrowful countenance.
ROBERT BURTON, *Anatomy of Melancholy*. Pt. iii, sec. ii, mem. 2, subs. 4.

The crocodile shrowdeth greatest treason under most pitiful tears.
JOHN LYLY, *Euphues*, p. 75. (1579)

Lepidus: What manner o' thing is your crocodile? . . . 'Tis a strange serpent.
Antony: 'Tis so. And the tears of it are wet.
SHAKESPEARE, *Antony and Cleopatra*, ii, 7, 46.

The mournful crocodile
With sorrow snares relenting passengers.
SHAKESPEARE, *II Henry VI*. Act iii, sc. 1, l. 226.

Crocodiles wept tears for thee.
ALFRED TENNYSON, *A Dirge*. St. 4.

12
Tell Alyttes, from me, to make his diet of onions.
BIAS, advising an enemy to weep. (DIOGENES LAERTIUS, *Bias*. Bk. i, sec. 84.)

Onions can make even heirs and widows weep.
BENJAMIN FRANKLIN, *Poor Richard*, 1734.

The tears live in an onion that should water this sorrow.
SHAKESPEARE, *Antony and Cleopatra*, i, 2, 177.

And if the boy have not a woman's gift
To rain a shower of commanded tears,
An onion will do well for such a shift,
Which in a napkin being close convey'd
Shall in despite enforce a watery eye.
SHAKESPEARE, *The Taming of the Shrew: Induction*. Sc. i, l. 124.

13
The busy have no time for tears.
BYRON, *The Two Foscari*. Act iv, sc. 1.

Weep if thou wilt, but weep not all too long;
Or weep and work, for work will lead to song.
GEORGE MACDONALD, *Within and Without*. Pt. iv, *Introductory Sonnet*, l. 6.

14
Why wakest thou the sleeping tear? (Τί δάκρυον εὗδον ἐγείρεις.)
CALLIMACHUS, *Fragmenta Incertæ*. No. 103.

15
It will grieve me so to the heart, that I shall cry my eyes out.
CERVANTES, *Don Quixote*. Pt. i, ch. 11.

1
He loves thee well that makes thee weep.
CERVANTES, *Don Quixote*. Pt. i, ch. 20.

2
What argufies snivelling and piping your eye?
CHARLES DIBDIN, *Poor Jack*.

Blest if I don't think he's got a main in his head, as is always turned on.
DICKENS, *Pickwick Papers*. Ch. 16.

3
Waste not fresh tears over old griefs.
EURIPIDES, *Alexander*. Frag. 44.

4
You weep, and you are the master! (Vous pleurez, et vous êtes le maître!)
MARIE MANCHINI, to Louis XIV (c. 1658), when he permitted her uncle, Cardinal Mazarin, to send her away from Paris. See MADAME DE MOTTEVILLE, *Mémoires*.

You are emperor, my lord, and you weep! (Vous êtes empereur, seigneur, et vous pleurez!)
5 RACINE, *Bérénice*. Act iv, sc. 5. (1670)

In tears I was born, and after tears I die, finding the whole of life a place of many tears. (*Δακρυχέων γενόμην, καὶ δακρύσας ἀποθνήσκω· δάκυσι δ' ἐν πολλοῖς τὸν βίον εὗρον ὅλον.*)
PALLADAS. (*Greek Anthology*. Bk. x, epig. 84.)

Art thou a child of tears,
Cradled in care and woe?
JOHN KEBLE, *The Christian Year: Circumcision*.

6
Tears are for the conquered there, and for the conqueror, Death. (Κλαίει ὁ νικηθεὶς, ὁ δὲ νικήσας ἀπόλωλεν.)
PLUTARCH, *Lives: Demosthenes*. Sec. 21. Quoted as an oracular saying.

7
There's no seeing one's way through tears.
W. G. BENHAM, *Proverbs*, p. 856.

8
God shall wipe away all tears from their eyes.
New Testament: Revelation, vii, 17; xxi, 4.

9
In youth, one has tears without grief: in age griefs without tears.
JOSEPH ROUX, *Meditations of a Parish Priest*. Pt. v, No. 55.

10
If you have tears, prepare to shed them now.
SHAKESPEARE, *Julius Cæsar*. Act iii, sc. 2, l. 173.

How now, foolish rheum!
SHAKESPEARE, *King John*. Act iv, sc. 1, l. 33.

Our tears are not yet brew'd.
SHAKESPEARE, *Macbeth*. Act ii, sc. 3, l. 129.

11
How much better it is to weep at joy than to joy at weeping!
SHAKESPEARE, *Much Ado About Nothing*. Act i, sc. 1, l. 29.

12
To drown the eyes in tears. (Οὐκέτι πηγὰς δύναμαι δακρύων.)
SOPHOCLES, *Antigone*, l. 803.

13
Hence those tears. (Hinc illæ lacrimæ.)
TERENCE, *Andria*, l. 126. (Act i, sc. 1.) Quoted by Horace, *Epistles*. Bk. i, epis. 19, l. 41. The phrase became proverbial in Latin literature, and was used even when there were no actual tears shed.

Hence rage and tears. (Inde iræ et lacrimæ.)
JUVENAL, *Satires*. Sat. i, l. 168.

Hinc illæ lachrymæ. Thence flows the cause of the main grievance.
BEN JONSON, *Magnetic Lady*. Act i, sc. 1.

Why these weeps?
ARTEMUS WARD, *Artemus Ward's Lecture*.

14
You cannot cleanse your heart with tears.
RICHARD CHENEVIX TRENCH, *The Story of Justin Martyr*, l. 132.

15
The chiefest sanctity of a temple is that it is a place to which men go to weep in common.
MIGUEL DE UNAMUNO, *The Tragic Sense of Life*, p. 17.

16
There are tears for misfortune. (Sunt lacrimæ rerum.)
VERGIL, *Æneid*. Bk. i, l. 462.

Yet tears to human suffering are due.
WORDSWORTH, *Laodamia*, l. 164.

III—Tears: A Blessing

17
Thus after a season of tears a sober and softened joy may return to us.
AMIEL, *Journal*, 21 Sept., 1868.

18
So it clears,
And so we rain our skies blue.
E. B. BROWNING, *Aurora Leigh*. Bk. vii, l. 227.

Thank God, bless God, all ye who suffer not
More grief than ye can weep for; . . . those tears will run
Soon in long rivers down the lifted face,
And leave the vision clear for stars and sun.
E. B. BROWNING, *Tears*.

19
The soul would have no rainbow
Had the eyes no tears.
JOHN VANCE CHENEY, *Tears*.

20
Weeping is the ease of woe.
RICHARD CRASHAW, *St. Mary Magdalene*, l. 56.

21
"It opens the lungs, washes the countenance, exercises the eyes, and softens down the temper," said Mr. Bumble. "So cry away."
DICKENS, *Oliver Twist*. Ch. 37.

22
The tear forgot as soon as shed,
The sunshine of the breast.
THOMAS GRAY, *Ode on a Distant Prospect of Eton College*, l. 43.

23
Made a man's eyes friends with delicious tears.
LEIGH HUNT, *Jaffàr*.

Tears are blessings, let them flow.
HARRY HUNTER, *Song.*

2
When nature gave tears to man, she proclaimed him tender-hearted; and tenderness is the best quality in man. (Mollissima corda Humano generi dare se natura fatetur, Quæ lacrimas dedit; hæc nostri pars optima sensus.)
JUVENAL, *Satires.* Sat. xv, l. 131.

Dear Lord, though I be changed to senseless clay,
And serve the potter as he turns his wheel,
I thank Thee for the gracious gift of tears!
T. B. ALDRICH, *Two Moods.* Pt. ii.

The gift of tears is (as has been said) the best gift of God to suffering man.
JOHN KEBLE, *Lectures on Poetry.* No. 16.

3
It is only to the happy that tears are a luxury.
THOMAS MOORE, *Lalla Rookh: Prologue No. 2.*

4
Truly it is allowed us to weep; by weeping we disperse our wrath; and tears course over the bosom like a flowing stream. (Flere licet certe; flendo defundimus iram, Perque sinum lacrimæ fluminis instar eunt.)
OVID, *Heroides.* Epis. viii, l. 61.

There is a certain joy in weeping, for by tears grief is sated and relieved. (Est quædam flere voluptas; Expletur lacrimis egeriturque dolor.)
OVID, *Tristia.* Bk. iv, eleg. 3, l. 37.

5
Tears soothe suffering eyes.
JEAN PAUL RICHTER, *Flower, Fruit, and Thorn Pieces.* Bk. iv, ch. 23.

6
Tears fall, no matter how we try to check them, and by being shed they ease the soul. (Excidunt etiam retinentibus lacrimæ et animum profusæ levant.)
SENECA, *Epistulæ ad Lucilium.* Epis. xcix, 16.

7
The liquid drops of tears that you have shed
Shall come again, transform'd to orient pearl,
Advantaging their loan with interest
Of ten times double gain of happiness.
SHAKESPEARE, *Richard III.* Act iv, sc. 4, l. 321.

IV—Tears: Weeping

8
The flower which the wind has shaken
Is soon filled again with rain;
So does my heart fill slowly with tears,
O Foam-driver, Wind-of-the-vineyards,
Until you return.
RICHARD ALDINGTON, *Images.* No. 6.

9
Frequent tears have run
The colours from my life, and left so dead
And pale a stuff, it were not fitly done
To give the same as pillow to thy head.
E. B. BROWNING, *Sonnets From the Portuguese.* No. 8.

10
"I weep for you," the Walrus said:
"I deeply sympathize."
With sobs and tears he sorted out
Those of the largest size,
Holding his pocket-handkerchief
Before his streaming eyes.
LEWIS CARROLL, *Through the Looking-Glass.* Ch. 4.

11
It's such a little thing to weep,
So short a thing to sigh;
And yet by trades the size of these
We men and women die!
EMILY DICKINSON, *Poems.* Pt. i, No. 91.

12
What precious drops are those
Which silently each other's track pursue,
Bright as young diamonds in their infant dew?
DRYDEN, *II Conquest of Granada.* Act iii, sc. 1.

Not a sigh nor a tear my pain discloses,
But they fall silently, as dew on roses.
DRYDEN, *Secret Love.* Act iv, sc. 2.

13
But nothing could a charm impart
To soothe the stranger's woe;
For grief was heavy at his heart,
And tears began to flow.
GOLDSMITH, *A Ballad.* (*Vicar of Wakefield.* Ch. 8.)

14
And weep the more because I weep in vain.
THOMAS GRAY, *Sonnet: On the Death of Richard West.*

15
Weep not, my wanton, smile upon my knee,
When thou art old there's grief enough for thee.
ROBERT GREENE, *Menaphon: Song.*

16
Such pretty flowers, like to orphans young,
To speak by tears, before ye have a tongue.
ROBERT HERRICK, *To Primroses Filled With Morning Dew.*

17
My tears must stop, for every drop
Hinders needle and thread.
THOMAS HOOD, *The Song of the Shirt.*

Oh! would I were dead now,
Or up in my bed now,
To cover my head now
And have a good cry.
THOMAS HOOD, *A Table of Errata.*

18
Shed no tear! O shed no tear!
The flower will bloom another year.
Weep no more! O weep no more!
Young buds sleep in the root's white core.
JOHN KEATS, *Faery Songs.* No. 1, l. 1.

19
E'en like the passage of an angel's tear
That falls through the clear ether silently.
KEATS, *Sonnet: To One Who Has Been Long in City Pent.*

1
Give me thy tears: I ask not for thy kiss,
Or for thy smile—but only for thy tears.
RICHARD LE GALLIENNE, *From a Lover's Note-book.*

Give other friends your lighted face,
The laughter of the years;
I come to crave a greater grace—
Bring me your tears.
EDWIN MARKHAM, *Your Tears.*

I do not beg the flower, the fruit,
Your summer wears;
Some winter hour when joy is mute,
Give me your tears.
JOHN RICHARD MORELAND, *Petition.*

2
A flood of thoughts came o'er me
That filled my eyes with tears.
LONGFELLOW, *The Bridge.* St. 6.

3
But only human eyes can weep.
ANDREW MARVELL, *Eyes and Tears,* l. 48.

4
The setting is all of rubies red,
And pearls which a Peri might have kept.
For each ruby there my heart hath bled:
For each pearl my eyes have wept.
OWEN MEREDITH, *The Portrait.*

5
Weep not, nor pity thine own life too much.
WILLIAM MORRIS, *Life and Death of Jason.* Bk. xiii, l. 315.

6
Some reckon their age by years,
Some measure their life by art;
But some tell their days by the flow of their tears,
And their lives by the moans of their heart.
ABRAM J. RYAN, *The Rosary of My Tears.*

7
The big round tears
Coursed one another down his innocent nose.
SHAKESPEARE, *As You Like It.* Act ii, sc. 1, 38.

The big round tears run down his dappled face.
THOMSON, *The Seasons: Autumn,* l. 454.

8
No longer will I be fool,
To put the finger in the eye and weep.
SHAKESPEARE, *The Comedy of Errors.* Act ii, sc. 2, l. 205.

9
Draw them to Tiber banks, and weep your tears
Into the channel, till the lowest stream
Do kiss the most exalted shores of all.
SHAKESPEARE, *Julius Cæsar.* Act i, sc. 1, l. 63.

Why, man, if the river were dry, I am able to fill it with my tears.
SHAKESPEARE, *The Two Gentlemen of Verona.* Act ii, sc. 3, l. 58.

She by the river sat, and sitting there,
She wept, and made it deeper by a tear.
ROBERT HERRICK, *Upon Julia, Weeping.*

10
Tears, idle tears, I know not what they mean,
Tears from the depth of some divine despair
Rise in the heart, and gather to the eyes,
In looking on the happy autumn-fields,
And thinking of the days that are no more.
TENNYSON, *The Princess.* Pt. iv, l. 21. *See also under* MEMORY.

11
She bid me take life easy, as the grass grows on the weirs;
But I was young and foolish, and now am full of tears.
W. B. YEATS, *Down By the Sally Gardens.*

V—Tears of Sympathy

See also Philanthropy

12
What gem hath dropp'd and sparkles o'er his chain?
The tear most sacred, shed for other's pain,
That starts at once—bright—pure—from pity's mine,
Already polish'd by the hand divine!
BYRON, *The Corsair.* Canto ii, st. 15.

13
There is a tear for all that die,
A mourner o'er the humblest grave.
BYRON, *On the Death of Sir Peter Parker, Bart.*

14
No radiant pearl, which crested Fortune wears,
No gem that twinkling hangs from Beauty's ears,
Not the bright stars which Night's blue arch adorn,
Nor rising suns that gild the vernal morn,
Shine with such lustre as the tear that flows
Down Virtue's manly cheek for others' woes,
ERASMUS DARWIN, *The Botanic Garden.* Pt. ii, canto 3, l. 459.

15
Ope the sacred source of sympathetic tears.
THOMAS GRAY, *Progress of Poesy,* l. 94.

16
The tribute of a tear is all I crave.
HOMER, *Odyssey.* Bk. ii, l. 89. (Pope, tr.)

None are so desolate but something dear,
Dearer than self, possesses or possess'd
A thought, and claims the homage of a tear.
BYRON, *Childe Harold.* Canto ii, st. 24.

17
If you would have me weep, you must first feel grief yourself. (Si vis me flere, dolendum est Primum ipsi tibi.)
HORACE, *Ars Poetica,* l. 102. *See also under* FEELING.

18
He must not float upon his watery bier
Unwept, and welter to the parching wind,
Without the meed of some melodious tear
MILTON, *Lycidas,* l. 12.

19
The glorious Angel, who was keeping
The gates of Light, beheld her weeping;
And, as he nearer drew and listen'd

To her sad song, a tear-drop glisten'd
Within his eyelids, like the spray
From Eden's fountain, when it lies
On the blue flow'r, which—Bramins say—
Blooms nowhere but in Paradise.
THOMAS MOORE, *Lalla Rookh: Paradise and the Peri*, l. 28.

A tear so limpid and so meek
It would not stain an angel's cheek.
SCOTT, *The Lady of the Lake*. Canto ii, st. 22.

1
And wiped our eyes
Of drops that sacred pity hath engender'd.
SHAKESPEARE, *As You Like It*. Act ii, sc. 7, l. 122.

Those that can pity, here
May, if they think it well, let fall a tear.
SHAKESPEARE, *Henry VIII: Prologue*, l. 5.

2
Those eyes of thine from mine have drawn salt tears,
Shamed their aspect with store of childish drops.
SHAKESPEARE, *Richard III*. Act i, sc. 2, l. 154.

And wet his grave with my repentant tears.
SHAKESPEARE, *Richard III*. Act i, sc. 2, l. 216.

My tears that fall Prove holy water on thee.
SHAKESPEARE, *Cymbeline*. Act v, sc. 5, l. 268.

3
Then can I drown an eye, unused to flow,
For precious friends hid in death's dateless night,
And weep afresh love's long since cancell'd woe,
And moan the expense of many a vanish'd sight.
SHAKESPEARE, *Sonnets*. No. xxx.

I so lively acted with my tears
That my poor mistress, moved therewithal,
Wept bitterly.
SHAKESPEARE, *The Two Gentlemen of Verona*. Act iv, sc. 4, l. 174.

4
Who in telling such things can refrain from tears? (Quis talia fando . . . Temperet a lacrimis?)
VERGIL, *Æneid*. Bk. ii, l. 6.

5
Our funeral tears, from diff'rent causes, rise.
YOUNG, *Night Thoughts*. Night v, l. 522.

VI—Tears of Men

6
Talk not of grief till thou hast seen the tears of warlike men!
FELICIA HEMANS, *Bernardo del Carpio*, l. 26.

A child will weep a bramble's smart,
A maid to see her sparrow part,
A stripling for a woman's heart;
But woe awaits a country when
She sees the tears of bearded men.
SCOTT, *Marmion*. Canto v, st. 16.

7
Thrice he assay'd, and thrice, in spite of scorn,
Tears, such as angels weep, burst forth.
MILTON, *Paradise Lost*. Bk. i, l. 619.

8
Look, they weep;
And I, an ass, am onion-eyed; for shame,
Transform us not to women.
SHAKESPEARE, *Antony and Cleopatra*. Act iv, sc. 2, l. 34.

9
Too much of water hast thou, poor Ophelia,
And therefore I forbid my tears: but yet
It is our trick; nature her custom holds,
Let shame say what it will.
SHAKESPEARE, *Hamlet*. Act iv, sc. 7, l. 186.

10
All my mother came into mine eyes
And gave me up to tears.
SHAKESPEARE, *Henry V*. Act iv, sc. 6, l. 31.

See, see what showers arise,
Blown with the windy tempest of my heart.
SHAKESPEARE, *III Henry VI*. Act ii, sc. 5, l. 85.

What I should say
My tears gainsay; for every word I speak,
Ye see, I drink the water of mine eyes.
SHAKESPEARE, *III Henry VI*. Act v, sc. 4, l. 73.

11
Cromwell, I did not think to shed a tear
In all my miseries; but thou hast forced me,
Out of thy honest truth, to play the woman.
SHAKESPEARE, *Henry VIII*. Act iii, sc. 2, l. 428.

O, I could play the woman with mine eyes.
SHAKESPEARE, *Macbeth*. Act iv, sc. 3, l. 230.

12
These foolish drops do something drown my manly spirit.
SHAKESPEARE, *The Merchant of Venice*. Act ii, sc. 3, l. 13.

13
Did he break into tears? . . . There are no faces truer than those that are so washed.
SHAKESPEARE, *Much Ado About Nothing*. Act i, sc. 1, l. 24.

One whose subdued eyes,
Albeit unused to the melting mood,
Drop tears as fast as the Arabian trees
Their medicinal gum.
SHAKESPEARE, *Othello*. Act v, sc. 2, l. 348.

14
Scorn the proud man that is asham'd to weep.
YOUNG, *Night Thoughts*. Night iii, l. 108.

VII—Tears of Women

15
A lady's tears are silent orators.
BEAUMONT AND FLETCHER, *Love's Cure*. Act iii, sc. 3.

With the persuasive language of a tear.
CHARLES CHURCHILL, *The Times*, l. 308.

Tears are sometimes as weighty as words. (Interdum lacrimæ pondera vocis habent.)
OVID, *Epistulæ ex Ponto*. Bk. iii, epis. 1, l. 158.

16
So bright the tear in Beauty's eye,

Love half regrets to kiss it dry.
BYRON, *The Bride of Abydos*. Canto i, st. 8.

For Beauty's tears are lovelier than her smile.
CAMPBELL, *The Pleasures of Hope*. Pt. i, l. 180.

There shall he love, when genial morn appears,
Like pensive Beauty smiling in her tears.
CAMPBELL, *The Pleasures of Hope*. Pt. ii, l. 95.

Yet ah, how lovely in her tears!
SAMUEL ROGERS, *Jacqueline*. Pt. i, l. 10.

1
Oh! too convincing—dangerously dear—
In woman's eye the unanswerable tear!
That weapon of her weakness she can wield,
To save, subdue—at once her spear and shield.
BYRON, *The Corsair*. Canto ii, st. 15.

What lost a world, and bade a hero fly?
The timid tear in Cleopatra's eye.
BYRON, *The Corsair*. Canto ii, st. 15.

2
And the tear that is wip'd with a little address,
May be follow'd perhaps by a smile.
COWPER, *The Rose*, l. 19. *See also* SMILE AND TEAR.

3
Then Niobe dissolves into a tear.
JOHN GAY, *Trivia*. Bk. i, l. 168.

Like Niobe, all tears.
SHAKESPEARE, *Hamlet*. Act i, sc. 2, l. 149.

4
She would have made a splendid wife, for crying only made her eyes more bright and tender.
O. HENRY, *Options*.

5
Women laugh when they can and weep when they will.
GEORGE HERBERT, *Jacula Prudentum*.

6
She has an abundant supply of tears always ready, awaiting her command to flow. (Uberibus semper lacrimis semperque paratis In statione sua atque expectantibus illam, Quo jubeat manaere modo.)
JUVENAL, *Satires*. Sat. vi, l. 273.

She makes a shower of rain as well as Jove.
SHAKESPEARE, *Antony and Cleopatra*. Act i, sc. 2, l. 156.

7
She's somewhere in the sunlight strong,
Her tears are in the falling rain.
RICHARD LE GALLIENNE, *Song*.

8
By ready tears a woman can always gain a respite for her soul's suffering.
MENANDER, *Fragments*. No. 599.

9
Why do you spoil those tender eyes with tears? (Quid teneros lacrimis corrumpis ocellos?)
OVID, *Ars Amatoria*. Bk. i, l. 129.

10
Tears too are useful; with tears you can melt iron. (Et lacrimæ prosunt: lacrimis admanata movebis.)
OVID, *Ars Amatoria*. Bk. i, l. 659.

Let your eyes learn to drop tears at command. (Quin etiam discant oculi lacrimare coacti.)
OVID, *Amores*. Bk. i, eleg. 8, l. 83.

11
Do not be moved by women's tears; they have taught their eyes to weep. (Neve puellarum lacrimis moveare, caveto; Ut flerent, oculos erudiere suos.)
OVID, *Remediorum Amoris*, l. 689.

For women, when they list, can cry.
POPE, *January and May*, l. 786.

12
When the big lip and wat'ry eye
Tell me the rising storm is nigh.
PRIOR, *The Lady's Looking-Glass*, l. 33.

13
Many indeed shed tears for show, and as soon as an onlooker is gone they have dry eyes. (Plerique enim lacrymas fundunt, ut ostendant; et toties siccos oculos habent, quoties spectator defuit.)
SENECA, *De Tranquillitate Animi*. Sec. 15.

14
Tears, . . . the best brine a maiden can season her praise in.
SHAKESPEARE, *All's Well that Ends Well*. Act i, sc. 1, l. 55.

15
I will weep for nothing, like Diana in the fountain, and I will do that when you are disposed to be merry.
SHAKESPEARE, *As You Like It*. Act iv, sc. 1, l. 156.

16
At a few drops of women's rheum, which are
As cheap as lies.
SHAKESPEARE, *Coriolanus*. Act v, sc. 6, l. 46.

17
Ere yet the salt of most unrighteous tears
Had left the flushing in her galled eyes.
SHAKESPEARE, *Hamlet*. Act i, sc. 2, l. 154.

Then fresh tears
Stood on her cheeks, as doth the honey-dew
Upon a gather'd lily almost wither'd.
SHAKESPEARE, *Titus Andronicus*. Act iii, sc. 1, l. 111.

18
O father, what a hell of witchcraft lies
In the small orb of one particular tear!
SHAKESPEARE, *A Lover's Complaint*, l. 288.

Women's weapons, water-drops.
SHAKESPEARE, *King Lear*. Act ii, sc. 4, l. 280.

19
And he, a marble to her tears, is washed with them, but relents not.
SHAKESPEARE, *Measure for Measure*. Act iii, sc. 1, l. 239.

20
If that the earth could teem with woman's tears,
Each drop she falls would prove a crocodile
SHAKESPEARE, *Othello*. Act iv, sc. 1, l. 256.

1
I loved thee for the tear thou couldst not hide.
TENNYSON, *The Bridesmaid*.

Why wilt thou ever scare me with thy tears?
TENNYSON, *Tithonus*, l. 46.

2
One small pretended tear, which, with grievous rubbing of the eyes, she could scarcely squeeze out by force. (Una falsa lacrimula, Quam oculos terendo misere vix vi expresserit.)
TERENCE, *Eunuchus*, l. 67. (Act i, sc. 1.)

3
Grief is the unhappy charter of our sex:
The gods who gave us readier tears to shed,
Gave us more cause to shed them.
WILLIAM WHITEHEAD, *Creusa*.

4
Crying is the refuge of plain women, but the ruin of pretty ones.
OSCAR WILDE, *Lady Windermere's Fan*. Act i.

5
It is as great pity to see a woman weep as a goose to go barefoot.
UNKNOWN, *A Hundred Merry Tales*, x, 20. (1526)

VIII—Tears: Tearlessness

6
A stoic of the woods—a man without a tear.
THOMAS CAMPBELL, *Gertrude of Wyoming*. Pt. i, st. 23.

Mute and magnificent, without a tear.
DRYDEN, *Threnodia Augustalis*, l. 52.

7
He bids me dry the last—the first—
The only tears that ever burst
From Outalissi's soul.
THOMAS CAMPBELL, *Gertrude of Wyoming*. Pt. iii, st. 39.

8
I wept not, so of stone grew I within. (Io non piangeva, si dentro impietrai.)
DANTE, *Inferno*. Canto xxxiii, l. 49.

9
"Oh, weep with me, Daphne," he sighed, "for you know it's
A terrible thing to be pestered with poets!"
But, alas, she is dumb, and the proverb holds good,
She never will cry till she's out of the wood!
J. R. LOWELL, *A Fable for Critics*, l. 73.

10
Tell me, you wingèd winds,
That round my pathway roar,
Know ye not some spot
Where mortals weep no more?
CHARLES MACKAY, *Tell Me Ye Winds*.

11
Nothing is here for tears, nothing to wail
Or knock the breast.
MILTON, *Samson Agonistes*, l. 1721

I cannot weep; for all my body's moisture
Scarce serves to quench my furnace-burning heart.
SHAKESPEARE, *III Henry VI*. Act ii, sc. 1, l. 79.

No, I'll not weep:
I have full cause of weeping; but this heart
Shall break into a hundred thousand flaws
Or ere I 'll weep.
SHAKESPEARE, *King Lear*. Act ii, sc. 4, l. 286.

12
Hush'd be that sigh, be dry that tear,
Nor let us lose our Heaven here.
Dry be that tear!
R. B. SHERIDAN, *Dry be That Tear*.

13
Weep no more, lady, weep no more,
Thy sorrow is in vain,
For violets pluckt, the sweetest showers
Will ne'er make grow again.
UNKNOWN, *The Friar of Orders Gray*. (PERCY, *Reliques*. Ser. i, bk. 2, No. 18.)

Oh! sing unto my roundelay;
Oh! drop the briny tear with me;
Dance no more at holiday;
Like a running river be.
THOMAS CHATTERTON, *Ælla: Minstrel's Song*.

Weep no more, nor sigh, nor groan,
Sorrow calls no time that's gone:
Violets pluck'd the sweetest rain
Makes not fresh nor grow again.
JOHN FLETCHER, *Queen of Corinth*. Act iv, sc. 1. Perhaps a spurious addition to the play.

Weep no more, my lady, oh! weep no more today!
STEPHEN COLLINS FOSTER, *My Old Kentucky Home*.

TEMPERAMENT

14
Perhaps he confuses temperament, character and individuality? . . . Individuality is a matter of psychology; temperament, a matter of sensation or æsthetics; character alone is a matter of morals.
AMIEL, *Journal*, 30 Aug., 1869. Referring to Schopenhauer.

15
So well she acted all and every part
By turns—with that vivacious versatility,
Which many people take for want of heart.
They err—'tis merely what is call'd mobility,
A thing of temperament and not of art,
Though seeming so, from its supposed facility;
And false—though true; for surely they're sincerest
Who're strongly acted on by what is nearest.
BYRON, *Don Juan*. Canto xvi, st. 97.

16
The nerves, they are the man.
CABANIS. (EMERSON, *Montaigne*.)

17
Betsy, like all good women, had a temper of her own.
WILL CARLETON, *Betsy and I Are Out*.

Of all bad things by which mankind are cursed,
Their own bad tempers surely are the worst.
RICHARD CUMBERLAND, *Menander.*

A lady of what is commonly called an uncertain temper—a phrase which being interpreted signifies a temper tolerably certain to make everybody more or less uncomfortable.
DICKENS, *Barnaby Rudge.* Ch. 7.

Good temper is an estate for life.
WILLIAM HAZLITT, *Plain Speaker: On Personal Character.*

1 Our temperatures differ in capacity of heat, or, we boil at different degrees.
EMERSON, *Society and Solitude: Eloquence.*

2 It is often temperament which makes men brave and women chaste. (Le tempérament font souvent la valeur des hommes et la vertu des femmes.)
LA ROCHEFOUCAULD, *Maximes.* No. 220.

3 There was no resisting the vortex of his temperament.
CHARLES LAMB, *Last Essays of Elia: Captain Jackson.*

4 Sensitive, swift to resent, but as swift in atoning for error.
LONGFELLOW, *The Courtship of Miles Standish:* Pt. ix, *The Wedding Day.* St. 3.

5 Though I am not splenitive and rash,
Yet have I something in me dangerous.
SHAKESPEARE, *Hamlet.* Act v, sc. 1, l. 284.

6 You know the fiery quality of the duke.
SHAKESPEARE, *King Lear.* Act ii, sc. 4, l. 93.

He's full of alteration and self-reproving.
SHAKESPEARE, *King Lear.* Act v, sc. 1, l. 3.

7 Who can be wise, amazed, temperate and furious,
Loyal and neutral, in a moment?
SHAKESPEARE, *Macbeth.* Act ii, sc. 3, l. 114.

8 Were not I a little pot and soon hot, my very lips might freeze to my teeth.
SHAKESPEARE, *The Taming of the Shrew.* Act iv, sc. 1, l. 5.

9 These flashes on the surface are not he.
He has a solid base of temperament.
TENNYSON, *The Princess.* Pt. iv, l. 234.

10 Suit your manner to the man. (Ut homo'st, ita morem geras.)
TERENCE, *Adelphi,* l. 431.

TEMPERANCE

See also Moderation

11 Health, longevity, beauty, are other names for personal purity; and temperance is the regimen for all.
A. B. ALCOTT, *Table Talk: Habits.*

12 Temperance is a bridle of gold.
ROBERT BURTON, *Anatomy of Melancholy.* Pt. ii, sec. ii, mem. 1, subs. 2.

13 Let us become more cheerful and we will become a more temperate people. . . . Men cannot be driven into temperance.
WILLIAM ELLERY CHANNING, *Works,* p. 112.

14 Temperance is the firm and moderate dominion of reason over passion and other unrighteous impulses of the mind. (Temperantia est rationis in libidinem atque in alios non rectos impetus animi firma et moderata dominatio.)
CICERO, *De Inventione Rhetorica.* Bk. ii, ch. 54, sec. 164.

Temperance consists in foregoing bodily pleasures. (Temperantia autem constat ex prætermittendis voluptatibus corporis.)
CICERO, *De Natura Deorum.* Bk. iii, ch. 15, 38.

15 Temp'rate in every place—abroad, at home,
Thence will applause, and hence will profit come;
And health from either he in time prepares
For sickness, age, and their attendant cares.
CRABBE, *The Borough.* Letter xvii, l. 198.

16 Eat not to dullness; drink not to elevation.
BENJAMIN FRANKLIN, *Autobiography.* Ch. 1. Temperance, the first of thirteen virtues which Franklin tried to practise. The others were silence, order, resolution, frugality, industry, sincerity, justice, moderation, cleanliness, tranquillity, chastity, humility.

17 If we give more to the flesh than we ought, we nourish an enemy; if we give not to her necessity what we ought, we destroy a citizen.
ST. GREGORY, *Homilies.* No. 3.

18 Drink not the third glass, which thou canst not tame,
When once it is within thee; but before
Mayst rule it, as thou list: and pour the shame,
Which it would pour on thee, upon the floor.
It is most just to throw that on the ground,
Which would throw me there, if I keep the round.
GEORGE HERBERT, *The Church-Porch.* St. 5.

19 If all the world
Should in a pet of temperance feed on pulse,
Drink the clear stream, and nothing wear but freize,
Th' all-giver would be unthank'd, would be unprais'd, . . .
And we should serve him as a grudging master, . . .

And live like Nature's bastards, not her sons.
MILTON, *Comus*, l. 720.

1
Impostor do not charge most innocent Nature,
As if she would her children should be riotous
With her abundance; she, good cateress,
Means her provision only to the good
That live according to her sober laws,
And holy dictate of spare Temperance.
MILTON, *Comus*, l. 762.

2
Temperance controls our desires; some it hates and routs, others it regulates and restores to a healthy measure. Temperance knows that the best measure of the appetites is not what you want to take, but what you ought to take.
SENECA, *Epistulæ ad Lucilium*. Epis. 88, sec. 29.

3
Though you can guess what temperance should be,
You know not what it is.
SHAKESPEARE, *Antony and Cleopatra*. Act iii, sc. 13, l. 121.

Make less thy body hence, and more thy grace;
Leave gormandizing.
SHAKESPEARE, *II Henry IV* Act v, sc. 5, l. 56.

Ask God for temperance; that's the appliance only
Which your disease requires.
SHAKESPEARE, *Henry VIII*. Act i, sc. 1, l. 124.

4
I prefer temperance hotels—although they sell worse liquor than any other kind of hotels.
ARTEMUS WARD, *Temperance*.

5
Temperance is the nurse of chastity.
WILLIAM WYCHERLEY, *Love in a Wood*. Act iii, sc. 3.

TEMPTATION

6
It is good to be without vices, but it is not good to be without temptations.
WALTER BAGEHOT, *Biographical Studies*, p. 237.

7
If thou wilt go seek for a thief, no wonder if thou be robbed. . . . If thou wilt go seek fire to put in the thatch, no wonder if thy house be burned. . . . If thou canst not keep at a distance nor forbear the presence of the bait, thou art not like to forbear the sin.
RICHARD BAXTER, *Works*. Vol. iii, p. 447.

8
Why comes temptation but for man to meet
And master and make crouch beneath his foot,
And so be pedestaled in triumph?
ROBERT BROWNING, *The Ring and the Book: The Pope*, l. 1185.

9
What 's done we partly may compute,
But know not what 's resisted.
BURNS, *Address to the Unco Guid*, l. 63.

10
So you tell yourself you are pretty fine clay
To have tricked temptation and turned it away,
But wait, my friend, for a different day;
Wait till you want to want to!
EDMUND VANCE COOKE, *Desire*.

11
The subtlest tempter has the smoothest style;
Sirens sing sweetest when they would betray.
MICHAEL DRAYTON, *Legend of Matilda the Fair*.

12
As the Sandwich Islander believes that the strength and valor of the enemy he kills passes into himself, so we gain the strength of the temptation we resist.
EMERSON, *Essays, First Series: Compensation*.

13
How much, preventing God, how much I owe
To the defences thou hast round me set;
Example, custom, fear, occasion slow,—
These scornèd bondmen were my parapet.
I dare not peep over this parapet
To gauge with glance the roaring gulf below,
The depths of sin to which I had descended,
Had not these me against myself defended.
RALPH WALDO EMERSON, *Grace*.

We love to overlook the boundaries which we do not wish to pass.
SAMUEL JOHNSON, *The Rambler*. No. 114.

14
'Tis easy to resist where none invade.
SIR JOHN HARINGTON, *Orlando Furioso*. Bk. xliii, st. 25.

It is easy to keep a castle that was never assaulted.
THOMAS FULLER, *Gnomologia*. No. 2924.

15
For we're only poor weak mortals, after all,
Sons of apple-eating Adam, prone to fall.
OTTO A. HARBACH, *Madam Sherry*. Act iii.

16
Beware of the beginnings of vice. Do not delude yourself with the belief that it can be argued against in the presence of the exciting cause. Nothing but *actual flight* can save you.
BENJAMIN ROBERT HAYDON, *Table Talk*. *See also under* BEGINNING.

17
Many a dangerous temptation comes to us in fine gay colours, that are but skin-deep.
MATTHEW HENRY, *Commentaries, Genesis*, iii.

18
No man is tempted so, but may o'ercome,
If that he has a will to masterdom.
ROBERT HERRICK, *Temptations*.

Temptations hurt not, though they have access:
Satan o'ercomes none, but by willingness.
ROBERT HERRICK, *Temptations*.

The devil tempts us not—'tis we tempt him,

Reckoning his skill with opportunity.
GEORGE ELIOT, *Felix Holt*. Ch. 47.

1
There are temptations that require all of one's strength to yield to.
ELBERT HUBBARD, *The Philistine*, xx, 86.

Do you really think that it is weakness that yields to temptation? I tell you that there are terrible temptations which it requires strength, strength and courage, to yield to.
OSCAR WILDE, *An Ideal Husband*. Act ii.

2
Blessed is the man that endureth temptation: for when he is tried, he shall receive the crown of life.
New Testament: James, i, 12.

3
Honest bread is very well—it's the butter that makes the temptation.
DOUGLAS JERROLD, *The Catspaw*.

4
Let us not lose heart in temptation.
ST. JOHN CHRYSOSTOM, *The Word of Praise*.

5
When the clergyman's daughter drinks nothing but water,
She's certain to finish on gin!

If the aunt of the vicar has never touched liquor,
Look out when she finds the champagne!
RUDYARD KIPLING, *Sons of the Suburbs*. These are two of the choruses from this unpublished poem of five eight-line stanzas, never included in Kipling's collected works.

6
Her smile, her voice, her face, were all temptation,
All subtle flies to trouble man the trout.
JOHN MASEFIELD, *The Widow in the Bye Street*. Pt. i, st. 16.

7
You may be lustrous as a star, with all the virtues in you canned, but if you fool around with tar you'll blacken up to beat the band.
WALT MASON, *At the Theatre*.

8
Lead us not into temptation, but deliver us from evil.
New Testament: Matthew, vi, 13; *Luke*, xi, 4.

From all blindness of heart; from pride, vainglory, and hypocrisy; from envy, hatred, and malice, and all uncharitableness.
Book of Common Prayer: Litany.

9
Watch and pray, that ye enter not into temptation.
New Testament: Matthew, xxvi, 41; *Mark*, xiii, 33; xiv, 38; *Luke*, xxii, 40, 46.

10
So gloz'd the Tempter.
MILTON, *Paradise Lost*. Bk. ix, l. 549.

Squat like a toad, close at the ear of Eve.
MILTON, *Paradise Lost*. Bk. iv, l. 800.

11
May God defend me from myself. (Defienda me Dios de my.)
MONTAIGNE, *Essays*. Bk. iii, ch. 13. Quoted as a maxim.

12
If you have overcome your inclination and not been overcome by it, you have reason to rejoice. (Tu si animum vicisti potius quam animus te est quod gaudeas.)
PLAUTUS, *Trinummus*, l. 310. Act ii, sc. 2, l. 24.

13
The devil was piqued such saintship to behold,
And long'd to tempt him like good Job of old;
But Satan now is wiser than of yore.
And tempts by making rich, not making poor.
POPE, *Moral Essays*. Epis. iii, l. 349.

The tempter saw his time; the work he plied;
Stocks and subscriptions poured on ev'ry side,
Till all the demon makes his full descent
In one abundant shower of cent per cent,
Sinks deep within him, and possesses whole,
Then dubs Director, and secures his soul.
POPE, *Moral Essays*. Epis. iii, l. 369.

Bell, book, and candle shall not drive me back,
When gold and silver becks me to come on.
SHAKESPEARE, *King John*. Act iii, sc. 3, l. 12.

14
My son, if sinners entice thee, consent thou not.
Old Testament: Proverbs, i, 10.

15
That no man put a stumbling-block or an occasion to fall in his brother's way
New Testament: Romans, xiv, 13.

16
How oft the sight of means to do ill deeds
Make deeds ill done!
SHAKESPEARE, *King John*. Act iv, sc. 2, l. 219.
See also under OPPORTUNITY.

17
Devils soonest tempt, resembling spirits of light.
SHAKESPEARE, *Love's Labour's Lost*. Act iv, sc. 3, l. 257.

18
I am that way going to temptation,
Where prayers cross.
SHAKESPEARE, *Measure for Measure*. Act ii, sc. 2, l. 158.

19
The tempter or the tempted, who sins most?
SHAKESPEARE, *Measure for Measure*. Act ii, sc. 2, l. 163.

I was one of the tempted, and not one of the strong.
ARTHUR WING PINERO, *The Profligate*. Act iii.

20
Most dangerous
Is that temptation that doth goad us on
To sin in loving virtue.
SHAKESPEARE, *Measure for Measure*. Act ii, sc. 2, l. 181.

1
The fiend is at mine elbow and tempts me.
Shakespeare, *The Merchant of Venice*. Act ii, sc. 2, l. 2. *See also under* Devil.

Well, my conscience says, "Launcelot, budge not." "Budge," says the fiend: "budge not," says my conscience. "Conscience," say I, "you counsel well." "Fiend," say I, "you counsel well."
Shakespeare, *The Merchant of Venice*. Act ii, sc. 2, l. 19.

2
I never tempted her with word too large;
But, as a brother to his sister, show'd
Bashful sincerity and comely love.
Shakespeare, *Much Ado About Nothing*. Act iv, sc. 1, l. 53.

3
Tempt not a desperate man.
Shakespeare, *Romeo and Juliet*. Act v, sc. 3, l. 59.

Sometimes we are devils to ourselves,
When we will tempt the frailty of our powers,
Presuming on their changeful potency.
Shakespeare, *Troilus and Cressida*. Act iv, sc. 4, l. 97.

4
Never resist temptation: prove all things: hold fast that which is good.
Bernard Shaw, *Maxims for Revolutionists.*

5
Many men have too much will power. It's won't power they lack.
John A. Shedd, *Salt from My Attic*, p. 16.

6
Let a man be but as earnest in praying against a temptation as the tempter is in pressing it, and he needs not proceed by a surer measure.
Bishop Robert South, *Sermons*. Vol. vi, sermon 10.

7
Ay me! how many perils do enfold
The righteous man, to make him daily fall,
Were not that Heavenly Grace doth him uphold
And steadfast Truth acquit him out of all!
Spenser, *Faerie Queene*. Bk. i, canto viii, st. 1.

8
For how many years did Mr. Pepys continue to make and break his little vows? And yet I have not heard that he was discouraged in the end.
R. L. Stevenson, *Virginibus Puerisque*. Pt. ii.

9
Hold the hand that is helpless and whisper,
"They only the victory win
Who have fought the good fight and have vanquished the demon that tempts us within."
William Wetmore Story, *He and She*.

10
Fire tries iron, and temptation tries a just man.
Thomas à Kempis, *De Imitatione Christi*. Bk. i, ch. 13.

11
There are several good protections against temptation, but the surest is cowardice.
Mark Twain, *Pudd'nhead Wilson's New Calendar*.

It is easier to stay out than get out.
Mark Twain, *Pudd'nhead Wilson's New Calendar*.

12
"Propinquity does it"—as Mrs. Thornburgh is always reminding us.
Mrs. Humphry Ward, *Robert Elsmere*. Bk. i, ch. 1.

13
Could'st thou boast, O child of weakness!
O'er the sons of wrong and strife,
Were there strong temptations planted
In thy path of life?
Whittier, *What the Voice Said*. St. 8.

14
I can resist everything except temptation.
Oscar Wilde, *Lady Windermere's Fan*. Act i.

The only way to get rid of a temptation is to yield to it.
Oscar Wilde, *Picture of Dorian Gray*. Ch. 2.

TENNYSON, ALFRED

15
Of borrowed notes, the mock-bird's modish tune,
The jingling medley of purloined conceits,
Out-babying Wordsworth and out-glittering Keats;
Where all the airs of patchwork pastoral chime
To drown the ears in Tennysonian rhyme!
Bulwer-Lytton, *The New Timon*. Pt. i, sec. 6.

You talk of tinsel! why, we see
The old mark of rouge upon your cheeks.
You prate of Nature! you are he
That spilt his life among the cliques.
Tennyson, *The New Timon and the Poets*. Tennyson's rejoinder to Bulwer-Lytton's attack. Published in *Punch*, 28 Feb., 1846. *See also* Souls: Good and Bad.

Ah God! the petty fools of rhyme
That shriek and sweat in pigmy wars
Before the stony face of Time,
And look'd at by the silent stars;
Who hate each other for a song,
And do their little best to bite
And pinch their brethren in the throng,
And scratch the very dead for spite.
Tennyson, *Literary Squabbles*. Originally printed in *Punch*, 7 March, 1846, entitled *After-thought*. Referring to the attack by Bulwer-Lytton.

16
He [Tennyson] has a great deal to say; but he had much more power of expression than was wanted for anything he had to say. He could not think up to the height of his own towering style.
G. K. Chesterton, *The Victorian Age in Literature*, p. 165.

1
Brother of the greatest poets, true to nature, true to art;
Lover of Immortal Love, uplifter of the human heart;
Who shall cheer us with high music, who shall sing, if thou depart?
HENRY VAN DYKE, *Tennyson.*

2
Death's little rift hath rent the faultless lute:
The singer of undying songs is dead.
WILLIAM WATSON, *Lacrimæ Musarum.*

3
Now finalè to the shore,
Now land and life finalè and farewell,
Now Voyager depart, . . .
Embrace thy friends, leave all in order,
To port and hawser's tie no more returning,
Depart upon thy endless cruise old Sailor.
WALT WHITMAN, *Now Finalè to the Shore.*

TERROR, see Fear

THAMES, THE

4
And the thronged river toiling to the main.
HARTLEY COLERIDGE, *The Thames.*

5
O, could I flow like thee! and make thy stream
My great example, as it is my theme;
Tho' deep yet clear, tho' gentle yet not dull;
Strong without rage, without o'erflowing full.
SIR JOHN DENHAM, *Cooper's Hill,* l. 189.

Serene yet strong, majestic yet sedate,
Swift without violence, without terror great.
MATTHEW PRIOR, *Carmen Seculare,* l. 282. Imitating Denham.

6
Say, Father Thames, for thou hast seen
Full many a sprightly race
Disporting on thy margent green,
The paths of pleasure trace.
THOMAS GRAY, *On a Distant Prospect of Eton College,* l. 21.

7
The great street paved with water, filled with shipping,
And all the world's flags flying and seagulls dipping.
JOHN MASEFIELD, *Biography,* l. 53.

8
Flow proudly, Thames! the emblem bright
And witness of succeeding years!
Flow on, in freedom's sacred light,
Nor stained with blood, nor swelled with tears.
Sweet is thy course, and clear, and still.
THOMAS LOVE PEACOCK, *The Genius of the Thames,* Pt. ii, st. 13.

9
That mysterious forest below London Bridge.
JOHN RUSKIN, *Modern Painters.* Bk. i, pt. ix, ch. 9, sec. 7.

10
Slow let us trace the matchless vale of Thames:
Fair-winding up to where the Muses haunt
In Twit'nam's bowers.
THOMSON, *The Seasons: Summer,* l. 1425.

11
He had to restrain himself from . . . accosting some passer-by with the question, "Say! But is this little wet ditch here the Historical River Thames?"
H. G. WELLS, *Mr. Britling Sees It Through.* Bk. i, ch. 1.

12
The river glideth at his own sweet will:
Dear God! the very houses seem asleep;
And all that mighty heart is lying still!
WORDSWORTH, *Sonnet: Composed upon Westminster Bridge.*

THANKSGIVING DAY

13
Come, ye thankful people, come,
Raise the song of Harvest-home!
HENRY ALFORD, *Thanksgiving Day.*

Heap high the board with plenteous cheer, and gather to the feast,
And toast the sturdy Pilgrim band whose courage never ceased.
Give praise to that All-Gracious One by whom their steps were led,
And thanks unto the harvest's Lord who sends our "daily bread."
ALICE WILLIAMS BROTHERTON, *The First Thanksgiving Day.*

14
Thanksgiving-day, I fear,
If one the solemn truth must touch,
Is celebrated, not so much
To thank the Lord for blessings o'er,
As for the sake of getting more!
WILL CARLETON, *Captain Young's Thanksgiving.*

15
Over the river and through the wood,
Now grandmother's cap I spy!
Hurrah for the fun!
Is the pudding done?
Hurrah for the pumpkin pie!
LYDIA MARIA CHILD, *Thanksgiving Day.*

16
So once in every year we throng
Upon a day apart,
To praise the Lord with feast and song
In thankfulness of heart.
ARTHUR GUITERMAN, *The First Thanksgiving.*

17
And taught by thee the Church prolongs
Her hymns of high thanksgiving still.
KEBLE, *The Christian Year: St. Luke the Evangelist.* St. 18.

18
Our rural ancestors, with little blest,
Patient of labour when the end was rest,

Indulged the day that housed their annual grain,
With feasts, and off'rings, and a thankful strain.

POPE, *Imitations of Horace: Epistles*. Bk. ii, epis. 1, l. 241.

1
Gather the gifts of Earth with equal hand;
Henceforth ye too may share the birthright soil,
The corn, the wine, and all the harvest-home.

E. C. STEDMAN, *The Feast of Harvest*.

2
And let these altars, wreathed with flowers
And piled with fruits, awake again
Thanksgivings for the golden hours,
The early and the latter rain!

WHITTIER, *For an Autumn Festival*. St. 12.

Ah! on Thanksgiving day, when from East and from West,
From North and South, come the pilgrim and guest,
When the gray-haired New Englander sees round his board
The old broken links of affection restored,
When the care-wearied man seeks his mother once more,
And the worn matron smiles where the girl smiled before.
What moistens the lip and what brightens the eye?
What calls back the past, like the rich Pumpkin pie?

WHITTIER, *The Pumpkin*. St. 3.

THEATRE, see Stage

THEOLOGY

See also Doctrine

3
Sacred and inspired divinity, the sabaoth and port of all men's labours and peregrinations.

BACON, *Advancement of Learning*. Bk. ii.

4
He could raise scruples dark and nice,
And after solve 'em in a trice;
As if Divinity had catched
The itch, on purpose to be scratched.

BUTLER, *Hudibras*. Pt. i, canto i, l. 163.

I have only a small flickering light to guide me in the darkness of a thick forest. Up comes a theologian and blows it out.

DIDEROT.

5
And after hearing what our Church can say,
If still our reason runs another way,
That private reason 'tis more just to curb,
Than by disputes the public peace disturb.
For points obscure are of small use to learn,
But common quiet is mankind's concern.

DRYDEN, *Religio Laici*, l. 445.

6
The broad ethics of Jesus were quickly narrowed to village theologies.

EMERSON, *Conduct of Life: Fate*.

7
The cure for false theology is mother-wit.

EMERSON, *Conduct of Life: Worship*.

8
Men are better than their theology. Their daily life gives it the lie.

EMERSON, *Essays, First Series: Compensation*.

9
Theology is Anthropology. (Die Theologie ist die Anthropologie.)

FEUERBACH, *Wesen des Christenthums*.

10
Theology is an attempt to explain a subject by men who do not understand it. The intent is not to tell the truth but to satisfy the questioner.

ELBERT HUBBARD, *Philistine*. Vol. xx, p. 81.

11
Get theology out of education. Nothing should be taught in school that somebody does not know. . . . Let us put theology out of religion. Theology has always sent the worst to heaven, the best to hell.

R. G. INGERSOLL, *Myth and Miracle*.

It is an old habit with theologians to beat the living with the bones of the dead.

R. G. INGERSOLL, *Reply to Archbishop Farrar*.

Any stigma will do to beat a dogma.

PHILIP GUEDALLA.

12
Theology hath vexed me ten score times;
The more I muse thereon the mistier it seemeth,
And the deeper I divine, the darker me thinketh it.

WILLIAM LANGLAND, *Piers Plowman*. Passus xii, l. 129.

13
Blessed is the man that hath not walked in the way of Sacramentarians, nor sat in the seat of the Zwinglians, nor followed the Council of the Zurichers.

MARTIN LUTHER, *Parody of First Psalm*.

14
Women are hardly fit to treat on matters of theology. (Les femmes ne sont guères propres à traicter les matières de la theologie.)

MONTAIGNE, *Essays*. Bk. i, ch. 56.

15
My theology, briefly, Is that the Universe
Was Dictated But not Signed.

CHRISTOPHER MORLEY, *Safe and Sane*.

16
Matter of the breviary, elementary theology. (Matière de breviare.)

RABELAIS, *Works*. Bk. ii.

17
So oft in theologic wars,
The disputants, I ween,
Rail on in utter ignorance
Of what each other mean,
And prate about an Elephant
Not one of them has seen!

J. G. SAXE, *The Blind Men and the Elephant*.

1
The Board of Longitude objected to his theology.

SAMUEL SMILES, *Invention and Industry*. Ch. 3. Referring to Dr. Priestley's rejection as astronomer to Captain Cook's expedition.

2
He breathed into theology a humane spirit.

UNKNOWN. Inscription on pedestal of statue of W. E. Channing in the Public Garden, Boston.

THIEVING

3
To rob even a corpse. (Τὸ κἂν ἀπὸ νεκροῦ φέρειν.)

ARISTOTLE, *Rhetoric*. Bk. ii, ch. 6, sec. 5. Quoted as a proverb.

4
Every rascal is not a thief, but every thief is a rascal. (Οὐ γὰρ πᾶς πονηρὸς κλέπτες, ἀλλ' ὁ κλέπτης πᾶς πονηρός.)

ARISTOTLE, *Rhetoric*. Bk. ii, ch. 24, sec. 5.

All are not thieves that dogs bark at.

JOHN RAY, *English Proverbs*, p. 26.

5
Opportunity makes a thief.

FRANCIS BACON, *Letter to the Earl of Essex*.

If the thief has no opportunity, he thinks himself honorable.

The Talmud. See also under OPPORTUNITY.

6
To keep my hands from picking and stealing, and my tongue from evil speaking, lying, and slandering.

Book of Common Prayer: Catechism.

7
'Twas a thief said the last kind word to Christ:
Christ took the kindness and forgave the theft.

BROWNING, *Ring and the Book*. Bk. vi, l. 869.

8
But for your petty, picking, downright thievery,
We scorn it as we do board-wages.

BYRON, *Werner*. Act ii, sc. 1.

9
A thief myself, I know the tracks of a thief. (Φωρὸς δ' ἴχνια φὼρ ἔμαθον.)

CALLIMACHUS, *Epigrams*. No. 44.

10
In a very plain sense the proverb says, Call one a thief and he will steal.

CARLYLE, *Sartor Resartus*. Bk. ii, ch. 1.

11
Thieves are never rogues among themselves.

CERVANTES, *Don Quixote*. Pt. ii, ch. 60.

Even thieves have a code of laws to observe and obey. (Quin etiam leges latronum esse dicuntur, quibus pareant, quas observent.)

CICERO, *De Officiis*. Bk. ii, ch. 11, sec. 40.

What thieves make a point of honour of; I mean that of being honest to one another.

DEFOE, *Colonel Jack*. Ch. 1.

There is honour among thieves.

SCOTT, *Redgauntlet*. Ch. 10.

A plague upon it when thieves cannot be true one to another!

SHAKESPEARE, *I Henry IV*. Act ii, sc. 2, l. 29.

12
A thief of venison . . .
Can keep a forest best of any man.

CHAUCER, *The Phisiciens Tale*, l. 83.

Always set a thief to catch a thief: the greatest deer-stealers make the best park-keepers.

THOMAS FULLER, *Church History of Britain*. Pt. iv, sec. 3. (1655)

Set a thief to catch a thief.

ROBERT HOWARD, *The Committee*. Act i. (1665)

Knavery is the best defense against a knave.

ZENO. (PLUTARCH, *Apothegms*.)

13
How great his theft who robs himself!

NATHANIEL COTTON, *Pleasure*.

In labor as in life there can be no cheating. The thief steals from himself.

EMERSON, *Essays, First Series: Compensation.*

14
And he that stole has learn'd to steal no more.

COWPER, *Hope*, l. 523.

He that is once a thief is ever more in danger.

LANGLAND, *Piers Plowman*. Passus xv, l. 146.

15
When false thieves fall out true men come to their own.

JOHN DAY, *Blind Beggar*. Act iv, sc. 1. (1600)

When knaves fall out, honest men come by their own.

SAMUEL PALMER, *Essays on Proverbs*, p. 327.

16
One thief knoweth another.

THOMAS DRAXE, *Bibliotheca Scholas. Instruct.*

A thief knows a thief, as a wolf knows a wolf.

THOMAS FULLER, *Gnomologia*. No. 430.

16a
When a felon 's not engaged in his employment,
Or maturing his felonious little plans,
His capacity for innocent enjoyment
Is just as great as any honest man's.

W. S. GILBERT, *The Pirates of Penzance*. Act ii.

17
When it thunders the thief becomes honest.

GEORGE HERBERT, *Jacula Prudentum. See also under* DEVIL.

18
The Friar preached against stealing, and had a goose in his sleeve.

GEORGE HERBERT, *Jacula Prudentum. See also under* JUDGE.

19
Change be no robbery.

JOHN HEYWOOD, *Proverbs*. Pt. ii, ch. 4. (1546)

Exchange is no robbery.

C. H. SPURGEON, *Salt-cellars*.

20
Robbers spring up by night to cut a man's throat. (Ut jugulent hominem, surgunt de nocte latrones.)

HORACE, *Epistles*. Bk. i, epis. 2, l. 32.

21
If from my thousand pecks you steal but one,
My loss is small, but you're by sin undone.
(Nam de mille fabæ modiis cum surripis unum,

Damnum est, non facinus, mihi pacto lenius isto.)

HORACE, *Epistles*. Bk. i, epis. 16, l. 55.

Easy it is
Of a cut loaf to steal a shive, we know.

SHAKESPEARE, *Titus Andronicus*. Act ii, sc. 1, 86.

1
Now Barabbas was a robber.

New Testament: John, xviii, 40.

Now Barabbas was a publisher.

THOMAS CAMPBELL. "It was Thomas Campbell who wrote 'Now Barabbas was a publisher,' whether in a Bible or otherwise is not authentically recorded, and forwarded it to a friend; but Mr. Murray was not the publisher to whom it referred, nor was Lord Byron, as has been so frequently stated, the author of the joke."—SAMUEL SMILES, *Memoirs and Correspondence of John Murray*. Vol. i, p. 336. See also WHYTE, *Memoir of William Heinemann*, p. 44.

2
No one shall be a thief with me as his helper. (Me nemo ministro Fur erit.)

JUVENAL, *Satires*. Sat. iii, l. 46.

3
What a liberal confounding of those pedantic distinctions of *meum* and *tuum!*

LAMB, *Essays of Elia: The Two Races of Men*.

4
All men love to appropriate to themselves the belongings of others; it is a universal desire; only the manner of doing it differs. (Tous les hommes aiment à s'approprier le bien d'autrui; c'est un sentiment général; la manière seule de le faire en est différente.)

LE SAGE, *Gil Blas*. Bk. i, ch. 5.

5
In vain we call old notions fudge,
And bend our conscience to our dealing;
The Ten Commandments will not budge,
And stealing *will* continue stealing.

JAMES RUSSELL LOWELL, *International Copyright*. Adopted as motto by the American Copyright League. Written 20 Nov., 1885.

6
And fell among thieves.

New Testament: Luke, x, 30.

7
My house shall be called the house of prayer; but ye have made it a den of thieves.

New Testament: Matthew, xxi, 13; *Mark*, xi, 17; *Luke*, xix, 46.

8
If the goodman of the house had known in what watch the thief would come, he would have watched.

New Testament: Matthew, xxiv, 43.

9
Both are thieves, the receiver as well as the stealer. (Ἀμφότεροι κλῶπες, καὶ ὁ δεξάμενος, καὶ ὁ κλέψας.)

PHOCLIDES, *Sententiæ*. (STOBÆUS, *Florilegium*.)

The receiver's as bad as the thief.

JOHN RAY, *English Proverbs*.

10
Great thieves hang little ones.

W. G. BENHAM, *Proverbs*, p. 770.

Thieves at home must hang; but he that puts
Into his overgorg'd and bloated purse
The wealth of Indian provinces, escapes.

COWPER, *The Task*. Bk. i, l. 736.

We hang little thieves and take off our hats to great ones. (Kleine Diebe hängt man, vor grossen zieht man den Hut ab.)

UNKNOWN. A German proverb.

11
Hang a thief when he's young and he'll no steal when he's auld.

ANDREW HENDERSON, *Scottish Proverbs*.

12
A sacrilegious thief.

SHAKESPEARE, *Cymbeline*. Act v, sc. 5, l. 220.

A cutpurse of the empire.

SHAKESPEARE, *Hamlet*. Act iii, sc. 4, l. 99.

13
Rob me the exchequer.

SHAKESPEARE, *I Henry IV*. Act iii, sc. 3, l. 205.

14
Pirates may make cheap pennyworths of their pillage
And purchase friends and give to courtesans,
Still reveling like lords till all be gone;
While as the silly owner of the goods
Weeps over them and wrings his hapless hands.

SHAKESPEARE, *II Henry VI*. Act i, sc. 1, l. 222.

It is when pirates count their booty that they become mere thieves.

BOLITHO, *Twelve Against the Gods: Intro.*, p. 8.

They inwardly resolved that so long as they remained in the business their piracies should not again be sullied with the crime of stealing.

MARK TWAIN, *Tom Sawyer*. Ch. 13.

15
Every true man's apparel fits your thief.

SHAKESPEARE, *Measure for Measure*, iv, 2, 46.

16
"Convey," the wise it call. "Steal!" foh! a fico for the phrase!

SHAKESPEARE, *Merry Wives of Windsor*, i, 3, 32.

O, good! convey? conveyors are you all,
That rise thus nimbly by a true king's fall.

SHAKESPEARE, *Richard II*. Act iv, sc. 1, l. 317.

17
The most peaceable way for you, if you do take a thief, is to let him show himself what he is and steal out of your company.

SHAKESPEARE, *Much Ado About Nothing*, iii, 3, 61.

18
Flat burglary as ever was committed.

SHAKESPEARE, *Much Ado About Nothing*, iv, 2, 52.

19
The robb'd that smiles steals something from the thief.

SHAKESPEARE, *Othello*. Act i, sc. 3, l. 208.

He that is robb'd, not wanting what is stol'n,
Let him not know 't, and he 's not robb'd at all.

SHAKESPEARE, *Othello*. Act iii, sc. 3, l. 342.

What loss feels he that wots not what he loses?
WILLIAM BROOME, *Merry Beggars*. Act i, sc. 1.

1 I'll example you with thievery:
The sun 's a thief, and with his great attraction
Robs the vast sea: the moon 's an arrant thief,
And her pale fire she snatches from the sun:
The sea 's a thief, whose liquid surge resolves
The moon into salt tears: the earth 's a thief,
That feeds and breeds by a composture stolen
From general excrement: each thing 's a thief.
SHAKESPEARE, *Timon of Athens*, iv, 3, 438.

2 O, theft most base,
That we have stol'n what we do fear to keep!
SHAKESPEARE, *Troilus and Cressida*, ii, 2, 92.

3
Save a thief from the gallows and he will cut your throat.
WILLIAM CAMDEN, *Remains*, 311. (1614) Quoted by SMOLLET, *Humphrey Clinker*.

Save a thief from the gallows and he will help to hang you.
ARTHUR GOLDING, *Calvin on Deuteronomy*. (1583) There are several other variations.

This is true, by all hallows,
Deliver a thief from the gallows,
And he shall wait thee to rob or slay.
UNKNOWN, *Sir Beves of Hamtoun*, l. 969. (14th century.)

Anoint a scoundrel and he will wound you; wound him and he will anoint you.
RABELAIS, *Works*. Bk. i, ch. 32.

4
Pickpockets, each hand lusting for all that is not its own.
TENNYSON, *Maud*. Pt. i, sec. 1, st. 6.

5
Why should I deprive my neighbour
Of his goods against his will?
Hands were made for honest labour,
Not to plunder or to steal.
ISAAC WATTS, *The Thief*.

6
He that prigs what isn't his'n,
When he's cotched 'll go to prison.
"HOPPY" WEBB. (On the authority of Lord William Lennox.)

THIRST

7
The panting thirst that scorches in the breath
Of those that die the soldier's fiery death.
BYRON, *Lara*. Canto ii, st. 16.

8
The fountains themselves are athirst. (Fontes ipsi sitiunt.)
CICERO, *Epistolæ ad Quintum Fratrem*. Bk. iii, ch. 1, sec. 4.

9
Hunger is bitter, but the worst
Of human pangs, the most accursed
Of Want's fell scorpions, is Thirst.
ELIZA COOK, *Melaia*.

10
Go not to the pot for every thirst.
GEORGE HERBERT, *Jacula Prudentum*. The French say, "Qui est maître de sa soif est maître de sa santé" (He who is master of his thirst is master of his health).

11
And pines with thirst amidst a sea of waves.
HOMER, *The Odyssey*. Bk. xi, l. 722. (Pope, tr.)

There, with water everywhere, dry thirst burns the throat. (Illic interaquas urit sitis arida fauces.)
PETRONIUS, *Fragments*. No. 87.

Water, water, every where,
And all the boards did shrink;
Water, water, every where,
Nor any drop to drink.
S. T. COLERIDGE, *The Ancient Mariner*. Pt. ii, st. 9. Often incorrectly quoted, "And not a drop to drink."

12
Tantalus, thirsty wretch, catches at the streams that fly from his lips. (Tantalus a labris sitiens fugientia captat Flumina.)
HORACE, *Satires*. Bk. i, sat. 1, l. 69.

He [Tantalus] seeks water in the midst of water. (Quærit aquas in aquis.)
OVID, *Amores*. Bk. ii, eleg. 2, l. 43.

No water is obtainable to thee, Tantalus. (Tibi Tantale, nullæ Deprenduntur aquæ.)
OVID, *Metamorphoses*. Bk. iv, l. 458.

13
I drank at every vine.
The last was like the first.
I came upon no wine
So wonderful as thirst.
EDNA ST. VINCENT MILLAY, *Feast*.

14
Whenever I see thee thirst, cup in hand, I apply it to my lips more for thy sake than for drinking.
PHILOSTRATUS, *Letters*. No. 24.

The thirst that from the soul doth rise,
Doth ask a drink divine;
But might I of Jove's nectar sup,
I would not change for thine.
BEN JONSON, *To Celia*.

15
It's a miserable business, waiting till thirst has you by the throat before you dig the well. (Miserum est opus, Igitur demum fodere puteam, ubi sitis fauces tenet.)
PLAUTUS, *Mostellaria*, l. 379. (Act ii, sc. 1.)

16
When they are thirsty, fools would fain have drink.
SHAKESPEARE, *Love's Labour's Lost*. Act v, sc. 2, l. 372.

17
The thirsty drink in silence. (Οἱ διψῶντες σιωπῇ πινουσι.)
UNKNOWN. A Greek proverb.

THOREAU, HENRY DAVID

18
Masterful in genius was he, and unique,
Patient, sagacious, tender, frolicsome—

This Concord Pan.
AMOS BRONSON ALCOTT, *Thoreau.*

We, sighing, said, "Our Pan is dead;
His pipe hangs mute beside the river." . . .
Then from the flute untouched by hands,
There came a low, harmonious breath:
"For such as he there is no death;
His life the eternal life commands."
LOUISA MAY ALCOTT, *Thoreau's Flute.*

1
Thoreau's quality is very penetrating and contagious; reading him is like eating onions—one must look out or the flavor will reach his own page.
JOHN BURROUGHS, *Journal,* 1878.

2
[Thoreau's] father was a manufacturer of lead-pencils, and Henry applied himself for a time to this craft, believing he could make a better pencil than was then in use. After completing his experiments, he exhibited his work to chemists and artists in Boston, and having obtained their certificates to its excellence and to its equality with the best London manufacture, he returned home contented. His friends congratulated him that he had now opened his way to fortune. But he replied that he should never make another pencil. "Why should I? I would not do again what I have done once."
EMERSON, *Lectures and Biographical Studies: Thoreau.*

He was a protestant *à outrance,* and few lives contain so many renunciations. He was bred to no profession; he never married; he lived alone; he never went to church; he never voted; he refused to pay a tax to the State; he ate no flesh, he drank no wine, he never knew the use of tobacco; and, though a naturalist, he used neither trap nor gun. He chose, wisely no doubt for himself, to be the bachelor of thought and Nature.
EMERSON, *Lectures and Biographical Sketches: Thoreau.*

3
I love Henry, but I cannot like him; and as for taking his arm, I should as soon think of taking the arm of an elm-tree.
EMERSON, *Lectures and Biographical Sketches: Thoreau.* Quoting a friend of Thoreau.

4
Whatever question there may be of his talent, there can be none, I think, of his genius. It was a slim and crooked one, but it was eminently personal. He was unperfect, unfinished, inartistic; he was worse than provincial—he was parochial.
HENRY JAMES, *Hawthorne.* Ch. iv, p. 94. (Referring to Thoreau.)

THOUGHT

See also Mind

I—Thought: Definitions

5
Men's thoughts are much according to their inclination, their discourse and speeches according to their learning and infused opinions.
FRANCIS BACON, *Essays: Of Custom and Education.*

6
And inasmuch as feeling, the East's gift,
Is quick and transient—comes, and lo, is gone,
While Northern thought is slow and durable.
ROBERT BROWNING, *Luria.* Act v.

7
Thought is valuable in proportion as it is generative.
BULWER-LYTTON, *Caxtoniana.* Essay 14.

8
The blight of life—the demon Thought.
BYRON, *Childe Harold.* Canto i, st. 84.

9
It is the *Thought* of man; the true thaumaturgic virtue; by which man works all things whatsoever. All that he does, and brings to pass, is the vesture of a Thought.
CARLYLE, *On Heroes and Hero-Worship: The Hero as Man of Letters.*

10
One thought includes all thought, in the sense that a grain of sand includes the universe.
S. T. COLERIDGE, *Additional Table Talk: Thought.*

11
Our thought is the key which unlocks the doors of the world. There is something in us which corresponds to that which is around us, beneath us, and above us.
SAMUEL MCCHORD CROTHERS. (NEWTON, *My Idea of God,* p. 211.)

12
The art of meditation may be exercised at all hours, and in all places; and men of genius, in their walks, at table, and amidst assemblies, turning the eye of the mind inwards, can form an artificial solitude; retired amidst a crowd, calm amidst distraction, and wise amidst folly.
ISAAC D'ISRAELI, *Literary Character.* Ch. 11.

13
Man carries the world in his head, the whole astronomy and chemistry suspended in a thought.
EMERSON, *Essays, Second Series: Nature.*

Thought makes everything fit for use. The vocabulary of an omniscient man would embrace words and images excluded from polite conversation.
EMERSON, *Essays, Second Series: The Poet.*

14
Nothing in the universe so solid as a thought.
EMERSON, *Journals,* 1864.

As certainly as water falls in rain on the tops of mountains and runs down into valleys, plains and pits, so does thought fall first on the best minds, and run down, from class to class, until it reaches the masses, and works revolutions.
EMERSON, *Lectures and Biographical Sketches: The Man of Letters.*

1
A rush of thoughts is the only conceivable prosperity that can come to us.
EMERSON, *Letters and Social Aims: Inspiration.*

It takes a great deal of elevation of thought to produce a very little elevation of life.
EMERSON, *Journals*. Vol. iv, p. 441.

2
The senses collect the surface facts of matter. . . . It was sensation; when memory came, it was experience; when mind acted, it was knowledge; when mind acted on it as knowledge, it was thought.
EMERSON, *Letters and Social Aims: Poetry and Imagination.*

3
Thought is the property of him who can entertain it and of him who can adequately place it.
EMERSON, *Representative Men: Shakespeare.*

4
Thought, the gaseous ashes of burned-out thinking, the excretion of mental respiration.
O. W. HOLMES, *The Professor at the Breakfast-Table*. Ch. 1.

5
Thinkers help other people to think, for they formulate what others are thinking. No person writes or thinks alone—thought is in the air, but its expression is necessary to create a tangible Spirit of the Times.
ELBERT HUBBARD, *Pig-Pen Pete: The Bee.*

6
In the sunshine, by the shady verge of woods, by the sweet waters where the wild dove sips, there alone will thought be found.
RICHARD JEFFERIES, *Pigeons at the British Museum.*

If any imagine they will find thought in many books, certainly they will be disappointed. Thought dwells by the stream and the sea, by the hill and in the woodland, in the sunlight and free wind.
RICHARD JEFFERIES, *Pigeons at the British Museum.*

7
The thoughts that come often unsought, and, as it were, drop into the mind, are commonly the most valuable of any we have.
LOCKE, *Letter to Samuel Bold*, 16 May, 1699.

Lights by mere chance upon some happy thought.
JOHN OLDHAM, *An Ode on St. Cecilia's Day.*

Unthought-like thoughts that are the souls of thought.
EDGAR ALLAN POE, *To ——*, l. 12.

Thoughts that have tarried in my mind, and peopled its inner chambers.
M. F. TUPPER, *Proverbial Philosophy:* Ser. i, *Prefatory.*

8
Great thoughts, great feelings came to them,
Like instincts, unawares.
RICHARD MONCKTON MILNES, *The Men of Old.*

Grand Thoughts that never can be wearied out,
Showing the unreality of Time.
RICHARD MONCKTON MILNES, *To Charles Lamb.*

9
No thought without phosphorus. (Ohne Phosphor kein Gedanke.)
JACOB MOLESCHOTT, *Lehre der Nahrungsmittel*, ii, 1, 4.

Who knows whether it is not true that phosphorus and mind go together? (Qui sait si l'on ne verra pas que le phosphore et l'esprit vont ensemble?)
HENRI BEYLE (STENDHAL), *Histoire de la Peinture en Italie*. Ch. 91.

10
It is thought, and thought alone, that divides right from wrong; it is thought, and thought only, that elevates or degrades human deeds and desires.
GEORGE MOORE, *Impressions: Turgenieff.*

11
Man is but a reed, the weakest thing in nature, but he is a thinking reed. (Un roseau pensant.)
BLAISE PASCAL, *Pensées*. Pt. i, art. iv, No. 6.

You are more than the Earth, tho' you are such a dot:
You can love and think, and the Earth cannot!
WILLIAM BRIGHTY RANDS, *The World.*

Though man a thinking being is defined,
Few use the grand prerogative of mind.
How few think justly of the thinking few!
How many never think, who think they do!
JANE TAYLOR, *Prejudice.*

12
Good thoughts, even if they are forgotten, do not perish. (Bene cogitata si excidunt non occidunt.)
PUBLILIUS SYRUS, *Sententiæ*. No. 81.

Thought alone is eternal.
OWEN MEREDITH, *Lucile*. Pt. ii, canto 6.

13
Lull'd in the countless chambers of the brain,
Our thoughts are link'd by many a hidden chain.
ROGERS, *Pleasures of Memory*. Pt. i, l. 171.

14
At Learning's fountain it is sweet to drink,
But 't is a nobler privilege to think.
J. G. SAXE, *The Library*, l. 31.

15
What a man *thinks* in his spirit in the world, that he *does* after his departure from the world when he becomes a spirit.
SWEDENBORG, *Divine Providence*. Sec. 101.

Thought from the eye closes the understanding, but thought from the understanding opens the eye.
SWEDENBORG, *Divine Love and Wisdom*. Sec. 46.

16
To think is to converse with oneself.
UNAMUNO, *The Tragic Sense of Life*, p. 91.

17
Thought depends absolutely on the stomach, but in spite of that, those who have the best stomachs are not the best thinkers.
VOLTAIRE, *Letter to d'Alembert*, 20 Aug., 1770.

One of their [Continental] philosophers has lately discovered that "as the liver secretes bile, so does the brain secrete thought," which astonishing discovery Dr. Cabanis . . . has pushed into his minutest developments. . . Thought, he is inclined to hold, is still secreted by the brain; but then, poetry and religion (and it is really worth knowing) are "a product of the smaller intestines."
THOMAS CARLYLE, *Signs of the Times.*

1
Human thought is the process by which human ends are ultimately answered.
DANIEL WEBSTER, *Address,* on Laying the Corner-stone of Bunker Hill Monument.

2
Thoughts shut up want air
And spoil, like bales unopen'd to the sun.
YOUNG, *Night Thoughts.* Night ii, l. 466.

II—Thought: Apothegms

3
The cobbler puts off his considering cap.
ROBERT ARMIN, *Foole upon Foole,* p. 40. (1605)

And now I'll put on my considering cap.
JOHN FLETCHER, *Loyal Subject.* Act ii, sc. 1. (1618)

4
The kings of modern thought are dumb.
MATTHEW ARNOLD, *The Grande Chartreuse,* l. 116.

5
Great thoughts, like great deeds, need
No trumpet.
P. J. BAILEY, *Festus: Home.*

6
One thought fills immensity.
WILLIAM BLAKE, *Proverbs of Hell.*

7
Stung by the splendour of a sudden thought.
ROBERT BROWNING, *A Death in the Desert,* l. 59.

8
Stark-naked thought is in request enough.
ROBERT BROWNING, *Transcendentalism.*

9
Full thoughts cause long parentheses.
DUKE OF BUCKINGHAM, *Letter to James I,* 1622.

10
Thought once awakened does not again slumber.
CARLYLE, *Heroes and Hero-Worship.* Lecture 1.

11
Perish that thought!
CIBBER, *Richard III* (altered). Act v, sc. 3.

12
In indolent vacuity of thought.
COWPER, *The Task.* Bk. iv, l. 297.

He trudg'd along, unknowing what he sought,
And whistled as he went, for want of thought.
DRYDEN, *Cymon and Iphigenia,* l. 84.

13
Things that do almost mock the grasp of thought.
DANTE, *Purgatorio.* Canto xxix, l. 41. (Cary, tr.)

14
Will change the pebbles of our puddly thought
To Orient pearls.
DU BARTAS, *Devine Weekes and Workes.* Wk. ii, day 3. (Sylvester, tr.)

15
Our thoughts are often worse than we are.
GEORGE ELIOT, *Mr. Gilfil's Love Story.*

16
He never is alone that is accompanied with noble thoughts.
FLETCHER, *Love's Cure.* Act iii, sc. 3. See 1874:4.

My own thoughts Are my companions.
LONGFELLOW, *The Masque of Pandora.* Pt. iii.

Sell your clothes and keep your thoughts. God will see that you do not want society. If I were confined to a corner of a garret all my days, like a spider, the world would be just as large to me while I had my thoughts about me.
H. D. THOREAU, *Walden: Conclusion.*
See also SOLITUDE AND LONELINESS.

17
A penny for your thought.
JOHN HEYWOOD, *Proverbs.* Pt. ii, ch. 4. (1546); JOHN LYLY, *Euphues.* (1579); ROBERT GREENE, *Friar Bacon.* Sc. 6. (1594)

A penny for your thoughts.
SWIFT, *Polite Conversation: Introduction.*

18
For my thoughts are not your thoughts, neither are your ways my ways.
Old Testament: Isaiah, lv, 8.

19
The glow of one warm thought is to me worth more than money.
THOMAS JEFFERSON, *Writings.* Vol. iv, p. 23.

20
In the interchange of thought, use no coin but gold and silver. (N'usez que de pièces d'or et d'argent dans le commerce de la parole.)
JOUBERT, *Pensées.* No. 117.

21
It was an holy and good thought.
Apocrypha: II Maccabees, xii, 45.

22
Our new thoughts have thrilled dead bosoms.
GEORGE MEREDITH, *Richard Feverel.* Ch. 1.

23
Annihilating all that's made
To a green thought in a green shade.
ANDREW MARVELL, *The Garden.*

24
I come from nothing; but from where
Come the undying thoughts I bear?
ALICE MEYNELL, *A Song of Derivations.*

25
Then feed on thoughts, that voluntary move
Harmonious numbers.
MILTON, *Paradise Lost.* Bk. iii, l. 37.

26
Still are the thoughts to memory dear.
SCOTT, *Rokeby.* Canto i, st. 33. *See also* MEMORY: ITS SWEETNESS.

1
Their thoughts do hit The roofs of palaces.
SHAKESPEARE, *Cymbeline*. Act iii, sc. 3, l. 83.

2
As swift
As meditation, or the thoughts of love.
SHAKESPEARE, *Hamlet*. Act i, sc. 5, l. 29.

And, like a passing thought, she fled
In light away.
BURNS, *The Vision*, l. 275.

3
In the quick forge and working-house of thought.
SHAKESPEARE, *Henry V*. Act v, *Prologue*, l. 23.

4
My thoughts are whirled like a potter's wheel.
SHAKESPEARE, *I Henry VI*. Act i, sc. 5, l. 19.

5
Dive, thoughts, down to my soul.
SHAKESPEARE, *Richard III*. Act i, sc. 1, l. 41.

6
There's more in your head than the comb will take out.
BERNARD SHAW, *John Bull's Other Island*. Act iii.

7
Things breed thoughts.
M. F. TUPPER, *Proverbial Philosophy: Of Things*.

8
When a thought is too weak to be expressed simply, it is a proof that it should be rejected. (Lorsqu'une pensée est trop faible pour porter une expression simple, c'est la marque pour la rejeter.)
VAUVENARGUES, *Réflexions*. No. 3.

Great thoughts come from the heart. (Les grandés pensées viennent du cœur.)
VAUVENARGUES, *Réflexions*. No. 127.

9
All her innocent thoughts
Like rose-leaves scattered.
JOHN WILSON, *On the Death of a Child*.

10
He that will not command his thoughts . . . will soon lose the command of his actions.
THOMAS WILSON, *Sacra Privata*, p. 153.

11
Thoughts too deep to be expressed,
And too strong to be suppressed.
GEORGE WITHER, *Mistress of Philarete*.

12
How oft the noon, how oft the midnight, bell
(That iron tongue of death!) with solemn knell,
On folly's errands as we vainly roam,
Knocks at our hearts, and finds our thoughts from home.
YOUNG, *Love of Fame*. Sat. v, l. 93.

13
Thought, busy thought! too busy for my peace!
YOUNG, *Night Thoughts*. Night i, l. 223.

III—Thought and Life

14
To live is to think. (Vivere est cogitare.)
CICERO, *Tusculanarum Disputationum*. Bk. v, ch. 38, sec. 111.

I think, therefore I am. (Je pense, donc je suis.)
DESCARTES, *Principes de la Philosophie*. Bk. i, sec. 7. The Latin is: Cogito, ergo sum.

15
Life will be lengthened while growing, for
Thought is the measure of life.
C. G. LELAND, *The Return of the Gods*, l. 85.

16
Live and think.
SAMUEL LOVER, *Father Roach*.

17
Life is thought. ('Ο βίος, ὑπόληψις.)
MARCUS AURELIUS, *Meditations*. Bk. iv, sec. 3.

18
As he thinketh in his heart, so is he.
Old Testament: Proverbs, xxiii, 7.

19
But thought 's the slave of life, and life time's fool.
SHAKESPEARE, *I Henry IV*. Act v, sc. 4, l. 81.

IV—Thought: Its Power

See also Mind: Its Power

20
The power of thought—the magic of the Mind.
BYRON, *The Corsair*. Canto i, st. 8.

A wrong'd thought Will break a rib of steel.
GEORGE CHAPMAN, *Charles, Duke of Byron*. Act i, sc. 1.

21
The revelation of Thought takes man out of servitude into freedom.
EMERSON, *Conduct of Life: Fate*.

Every thought which genius and piety throw into the world, alters the world.
EMERSON, *Essays, Second Series: Politics*.

Great men are they who see that spiritual is stronger than any material force, that thoughts rule the world.
EMERSON, *Letters and Social Aims: Progress of Culture*.

22
What shame is there, but thinking makes it so?
EURIPIDES, *Æolus*. Frag. xix.

Nothing is miserable but what is thought so, and contrariwise, every estate is happy if he that bears it be content. (Nihil est miserum nisi cum putes contraque beata sors omnis est æquanimitate tolerantis.)
BOETHIUS, *Philosophiæ Consolationis*. Bk. ii, sec. 4, l. 64.

Nothing is a misery,
Unless our weakness apprehend it so.
BEAUMONT AND FLETCHER, *The Honest Man's Fortune*. Act i, sc. 1.

Man is only miserable so far as he thinks himself so. (Tanto è miser l'uom quant' ei si riputa.)
SANNAZARO, *Ecloga Octava*.

A man is as miserable as he thinks he is. (Tam miser est quisque quam credidit.)
SENECA, *Epistulæ ad Lucilium*. Epis. 78, sec. 14.

There is nothing either good or bad, but thinking makes it so.
SHAKESPEARE, *Hamlet*. Act ii, sc. 2, l. 256.

And he that knoweth what is what
Saith he is wretched that weens him so.
WYATT, *Despair Counselleth the Deserted Love.*

1 It's what you think that makes the world
Seem sad or gay to you;
Your mind may color all things gray,
Or make them radiant hue.
GRENVILLE KLEISER, *The Bridge You'll Never Cross.*

2 A thought often makes us hotter than a fire.
LONGFELLOW, *Drift-Wood: Table-Talk.*

Thoughts so sudden, that they seem
The revelations of a dream.
LONGFELLOW, *Tales of a Wayside Inn*. Pt. i, *Prelude*, l. 233.

3 All thoughts that mould the age begin
Deep down within the primitive soul.
J. R. LOWELL, *An Incident in a Railroad Car.*

4 Thought can wing its way
Swifter than lightning-flashes or the beam
That hastens on the pinions of the morn.
JAMES GATES PERCIVAL, *Sonnet*

Thought hath good legs.
JOHN RAY, *English Proverbs.*

5 As thought by thought is piled, till some great truth
Is loosened, and the nations echo round,
Shaken to their roots: as do the mountains now.
SHELLEY, *Prometheus Unbound*. Act ii, sc. 3, 40

6 Thoughts are mightier than strength of hand.
SOPHOCLES, *Fragments*. No. 584.

7 But thought and faith are mightier things than time
Can wrong,
Made splendid once with speech, or made sublime
By song.
SWINBURNE, *The Interpreters*. St. 4.

V—Thought and Act

See also Word and Deed

8 Thought is the soul of act.
ROBERT BROWNING, *Sordello*. Bk. v.

The ancestor of every action is a thought.
EMERSON, *Essays, First Series: Spiritual Laws.*

Thought is the seed of action.
EMERSON, *Society and Solitude: Art.*

9 In all men, thought and action start from a single source, namely feeling. (Πᾶσιν ἀνθρώποις μία ἀρχή, καθάπερ τοῦ συγκαταθέσθαι τὸ παθεῖν.)
EPICTETUS, *Discourses*. Bk. i, ch. 18, sec. 1.

10 If men would think more, they would act less.
LORD HALIFAX, *Works*, p. 254.

11 Great thoughts reduced to practice become great acts.
WILLIAM HAZLITT, *Table Talk: On Thought and Action.*

12 And what he greatly thought, he nobly dared.
HOMER, *Odyssey*. Bk. ii, l. 312. (Pope, tr.)

And what they dare to dream of, dare to do.
J. R. LOWELL, *Commemoration Ode*. St. 3.

Men of thought, be up and stirring
Night and day:
Sow and seed—withdraw the curtain—
Clear the way.
CHARLES MACKAY, *Clear the Way.*

13 Be great in act, as you have been in thought.
SHAKESPEARE, *King John*. Act v, sc. 1, l. 45.

The very firstlings of my heart shall be
The firstlings of my hand. And even now,
To crown my thoughts with acts, be it thought and done.
SHAKESPEARE, *Macbeth*. Act iv, sc. 1, l. 147.

14 Strange thoughts beget strange deeds.
SHELLEY, *The Cenci*. Act iv, sc. 4, l. 134.

VI—Thought: Freedom of Thought

See also Speech: Freedom of Speech

15 Thoughts are free from toll.
WILLIAM CAMDEN, *Remains*, p. 332. (1605)

You have no right to erect your toll-gate upon the highways of thought.
R. G. INGERSOLL, *The Ghosts.*

Thoughts are toll-free but not hell-free. (Gedanken sind zollfrei, aber nicht Höllenfrei.)
UNKNOWN. A German proverb.

16 Thought is free. (Liberæ sunt enim nostræ cogitationes.)
CICERO, *Pro Milone*. Ch. xxix, sec. 79.

I have heard said that thought is free.
JOHN GOWER, *Confessio Amantis*. Bk. v, l. 4485. (c. 1390)

Thought is frank and free.
SKELTON, *Philip Sparrow*, l. 1201. (c. 1520)

17 So far as a man thinks, he is free.
EMERSON, *Conduct of Life: Fate.*

18 Our thoughts and our conduct are our own.
FROUDE, *Short Studies: Education.*

19 Every man who expresses an honest thought is a soldier in the army of intellectual liberty.
R. G. INGERSOLL, *Interview on Talmadge.*

20 And I honor the man who is willing to sink

Half his present repute for the freedom to
think.

J. R. LOWELL, *A Fable for Critics*, l. 1067.

1
It is clear that thought is not free if the profession of certain opinions makes it impossible to earn a living.

BERTRAND RUSSELL, *Sceptical Essays*, p. 152.

2
Flout 'em and scout 'em, And scout 'em and flout 'em; Thought is free.

SHAKESPEARE, *The Tempest*. Act iii, sc. 2, l. 132.

Thought is free.

SHAKESPEARE, *Twelfth Night*. Act i, sc. 3, l. 73.

3
Oh, the fetterless mind! how it wandereth
free
Through the wildering maze of Eternity!

HENRY SMITH, *Thought*.

4
The happiness of the times being extraordinary, when it was lawful to think what you wished, and to say what you thought. (Rara temporum felicitate, ubi sentire quæ velis, et quæ sentias dicere licet.)

TACITUS, *History*. Bk. i, sec. 1.

VII—Thought: First and Second Thoughts

See also Reflection

5
First thoughts are not always the best. (Sempre il miglior non è il parer primiero.)

ALFIERI, *Don Garzia*. Act iii, sc. 1.

The first thought is often the best.

BISHOP JOSEPH BUTLER, *Sermons*. No. 7.

6
Generally youth is like the first cogitations, not so wise as the second.

FRANCIS BACON, *Essays: Youth and Age*.

7
Second thoughts are wisest. (Αἱ δεύτεραί πως φροντίδες σοφώτεραι.)

EURIPIDES, *Hippolytus*, l. 436.

For second thoughts, as they say, are always the wisest. (Posteriores enim cogitationes, ut aiunt, sapientiores solent esse.)

CICERO, *Philippicæ*. No. xii, sec. 5.

Second thoughts are best.

DRYDEN, *Spanish Friar*. Act ii, sc. 2. (1681)

The second thoughts are ever the best.

GUAZZO, *Civil Conversations*. Fo. 23. (1586)

8
Their own sober and second thoughts.

MATTHEW HENRY, *Commentaries: Job*, vi, 29. (1708)

9
He thinks not well that thinks not again.

GEORGE HERBERT, *Jacula Prudentum*.

10
Men's first thoughts in this matter are generally better than their second; their natural notions better than those refin'd by study, or consultation with casuists.

EARL OF SHAFTESBURY, *Characteristics: Essay on the Freedom of Wit and Humour*. Sec. i.

It is often said that second thoughts are best. So they are in matters of judgment, but not in matters of conscience. In matters of duty, first thoughts are commonly best. They have more in them of the voice of God.

CARDINAL JOHN HENRY NEWMAN.

11
Second thoughts oftentimes are the very worst of all thoughts.

WILLIAM SHENSTONE, *Detached Thoughts on Men and Manners*.

VIII—Thought and Speech

12
To speak as the common people do, to think as wise men do.

ROGER ASCHAM, *Dedication to All the Gentlemen and Yoemen of England*. (1545)

Prescribe it well, loquendum ut vulgas, sentiendum ut sapientes.

BACON, *Advancement of Learning*, ii, 14. (1605) Quoting Aristotle.

13
Think to-day and speak to-morrow.

H. G. BOHN, *Hand-Book of Proverbs*, p. 528.

See also under SPEECH.

14
Thought is often bolder than speech.

BENJAMIN DISRAELI, *Ixion in Heaven*. Pt. ii, 3.

15
One may think that dares not speak.

THOMAS FULLER, *Gnomologia*. No. 3783.

16
Thoughts that breathe, and words that burn.

THOMAS GRAY, *Progress of Poesy*. Pt. iii, st. 3.

17
Your thoughts close and your countenance loose.

GEORGE HERBERT, *Jacula Prudentum*.

Say nothing but think the more.

GEORGE HERBERT, *Jacula Prudentum*.

Think much, speak little, write less.

JOHN RAY, *English Proverbs*.

18
Why can't somebody give us a list of things that everybody thinks and nobody says, and another list of things that everybody says and nobody thinks?

O. W. HOLMES, *Professor at the Breakfast-Table*. Ch. vi.

19
Though he says nothing, he pays it with thinking, like the Welshman's jackdaw.

JOHN RAY, *English Proverbs*.

But some a different notion had,
And at each other winking,
Observ'd that though he little said,
He paid it off with thinking.

WILLIAM COWPER, *Of Himself*. St. 3.

20
Just at the age 'twixt boy and youth,
When thought is speech, and speech is truth.

SCOTT, *Marmion:* Canto ii, *Introduction* l. 110.

Thoughts, from the tongue that slowly part,
Glance quick as lightning through the heart.

SCOTT, *Rokeby*. Canto i, st. 19.

21 Give thy thoughts no tongue,

Nor any unproportion'd thought his act.
Shakespeare, *Hamlet*. Act i, sc. 3, l. 59.

Speak to me as to thy thinkings,
As thou dost ruminate, and give thy worst of thoughts
The worst of words.
Shakespeare, *Othello*. Act iii, sc. 3. l. 131.

1
He gave man speech, and speech created thought,
Which is the measure of the universe.
Shelley, *Prometheus Unbound*. Act ii, sc. 4, l. 72.

2
And Thought leapt out to wed with Thought
Ere Thought could wed itself with Speech.
Tennyson, *In Memoriam*. Pt. xxiii, st. 4.

IX—Thought: Thinking

3
Upon the cunning loom of thought
We weave our fancies, so and so.
T. B. Aldrich, *Cloth of Gold: Proem.*

4
As soon as you can say what you think, and not what some other person has thought for you, you are on the way to being a remarkable man.
J. M. Barrie, *Tommy and Grizel*, p. 22.

5
He thought as a sage, though he felt as a man.
James Beattie, *The Hermit*, l. 8.

6
And many a thought did I build up on thought,
As the wild bee hangs cell to cell.
Robert Browning, *Pauline*, l. 439.

Ah thought which saddens while it soothes!
Robert Browning, *Pictor Ignotus*, l. 3.

7
Among them, but not of them; in a shroud
Of thoughts which were not their thoughts.
Byron, *Childe Harold*. Canto iii, st. 113.

My thoughts and I were of another world.
Ben Jonson, *Every Man Out of His Humour*. Act iii, sc. 3.

8
Whatsoe'er thy birth,
Thou wert a beautiful thought, and softly bodied forth.
Byron, *Childe Harold*. Canto iv, st. 115.

9
And o'er that fair, broad brow were wrought
The intersected lines of thought.
Byron, *Parisina*. St. 20.

10
Never did I see such apparatus got ready for thinking, and so little thought.
Thomas Carlyle, *Essays: Coleridge*.

11
Nay, in every epoch of the world, the great event, parent of all others, is it not the arrival of a Thinker in the world?
Carlyle, *Heroes and Hero-Worship*. Lecture 1.

Beware when the great God lets loose a thinker on this planet.
Emerson, *Essays, First Series: Circles*.

12
Perhaps 'tis pretty to force together
Thoughts so all unlike each other;
To mutter and mock a broken charm,
To dally with wrong that does no harm.
S. T. Coleridge, *Christabel*. Pt. ii, l. 666.

13
In the book of poetry are three hundred pieces, but the design of them all may be embraced in that one sentence, "Have no depraved thoughts."
Confucius, *Analects*.

I pray thee, O God, that I may be beautiful within.
Socrates.

14
Stand porter at the door of thought. Admitting only such conclusions as you wish realized in bodily results, you will control yourself harmoniously.
Mary Baker Eddy, *Science and Health*, p. 392.

15
Nothing is too sacred to be thought about.
Ernest Crosby. (*Cosmopolitan*, Dec., 1905.)

16
If we chance to fix our thoughts elsewhere,
Though our eyes open be, we cannot see.
Sir John Davies, *Nosce Teipsum*. Sec. ii, st. 15. *See also* Absence of Mind.

17
The profound thinker always suspects that he is superficial.
Benjamin Disraeli, *Contarini Fleming*. Pt. iv, ch. 5.

18
The happiest person is the person who thinks the most interesting thoughts.
Timothy Dwight, *Happiness*.

19
Concentration is the secret of strength in politics, in war, in trade, in short, in all management of human affairs.
Emerson, *Conduct of Life: Power*.

Think alone, and all places are friendly and sacred.
Emerson, *Nature, Addresses and Lectures: Literary Ethics*.

20
There are thoughts that moan from the soul of the pine
And thoughts in a flower bell curled;
And the thoughts that are blown with scent of the fern
Are as new and as old as the world.
Sam Walter Foss, *The Bloodless Sportsman*.

21
He is a fool that thinks not that another thinks.
George Herbert, *Jacula Prudentum*.

22
A moment's thinking is an hour in words.
Thomas Hood, *Hero and Leander*. St. 41.

1
He, whose thoughts differing not in shape, but dress,
What others feel more fitly can express.
O. W. HOLMES, *Poetry: A Metrical Essay.* St. 7.

2
But men at whiles are sober
And think by fits and starts,
And if they think, they fasten
Their hands upon their hearts.
A. E. HOUSMAN, *Could Man Be Drunk Forever.*

3
He had a wonderful talent for packing thought close, and rendering it portable.
MACAULAY, *Essays: Mackintosh's History of the Revolution.*

4
I have some naked thoughts that rove about
And loudly knock to have their passage out.
MILTON, *At a Vacation Exercise,* l. 23.

5
His thoughts have a high aim, though their dwelling be in the vale of a humble heart.
MONTAIGNE, *Essays.*

High-erected thoughts seated in the heart of courtesy.
SIR PHILIP SIDNEY, *Arcadia.* Bk. i, sec. 2.

His high-erected thoughts look'd down upon
The smiling valley of his fruitful heart.
DANIEL WEBSTER, *A Monumental Column.*

6
It is thy very energy of thought
Which keeps thee from thy God.
JOHN HENRY NEWMAN, *Dream of Gerontius.* l. 363.

7
If I have done the public any service, it is due to patient thought.
SIR ISAAC NEWTON, *Remark to Dr. Bentley.*

8
There needs but thinking right and meaning well.
POPE, *An Essay on Man.* Epis. iv, l. 32.

It is too difficult to think nobly when one only thinks to get a living. (Il est trop difficile de penser noblement quand on ne pense que pour vivre.)
ROUSSEAU, *Confessions.* Bk. ii, ch. 9.

9
On the sudden
A Roman thought hath struck him.
SHAKESPEARE, *Antony and Cleopatra.* Act i, sc. 2, l. 86.

I am afraid His thinkings are below the moon.
SHAKESPEARE, *Henry VIII.* Act iii, sc. 2, l. 133.

I do begin to have bloody thoughts.
SHAKESPEARE, *The Tempest.* Act iv, sc. 1, l. 220.

Sudden a thought came like a full-blown rose,
Flushing his brow.
KEATS, *The Eve of St. Agnes.* St. 16.

10
Yond Cassius has a lean and hungry look;
He thinks too much: such men are dangerous.
SHAKESPEARE, *Julius Cæsar.* Act i, sc. 2, l. 194.

11
Divinely bent to meditation;
And in no worldly suit would he be moved,
To draw him from his holy exercise.
SHAKESPEARE, *Richard III.* Act iii, sc. 7, l. 62.

Happy the heart that keeps its twilight hour,
And, in the depths of heavenly peace reclined,
Loves to commune with thoughts of tender power,—
Thoughts that ascend, like angels beautiful,
A shining Jacob's-ladder of the mind!
PAUL HAMILTON HAYNE, *Sonnets.* No. ix.

12
If I could think how these my thoughts to leave,
Or thinking still, my thoughts might have good end;
If rebel sense would reason's law receive,
Or reason foil'd would not in vain contend;
Then might I think what thoughts were best to think;
Then might I wisely swim, or gladly sink.
SIR PHILIP SIDNEY, *Sonnet.*

13
Break, break, break,
On thy cold gray stones, O Sea!
And I would that my tongue could utter
The thoughts that arise in me.
TENNYSON, *Break, Break, Break.*

14
Wrapt in thought as in a veil.
JAMES THOMSON, *The City of Dreadful Night.* Pt. ii.

15
And yet, as angels in some brighter dreams
Call to the soul when man doth sleep,
So some strange thoughts transcend our wonted dreams,
And into glory peep.
HENRY VAUGHAN, *Ascension Hymn.*

Thoughts whose very sweetness yieldeth proof
That they were born for immortality.
WORDSWORTH, *Inside of King's College Chapel.* Sonnet i.

16
I heard a thousand blended notes,
While in a grove I sate reclined,
In that sweet mood when pleasant thoughts
Bring sad thoughts to the mind.
WORDSWORTH, *Lines Written in Early Spring.*

Yet sometimes, when the secret cup
Of still and serious thought went round,
It seemed as if he drank it up—
He felt with spirit so profound.
WORDSWORTH, *Matthew.* St. 7.

X—Thought: Its Difficulty

17
To the vast majority of mankind nothing is more agreeable than to escape the need for mental exertion. . . . To most people nothing is more troublesome than the effort of thinking.
JAMES BRYCE, *Studies in History and Jurisprudence: Obedience.*

1
There is no expedient to which a man will not go to avoid the real labor of thinking.
THOMAS A. EDISON. Posted on signs about the Edison laboratories.

2
What is the hardest task in the world? To think.
EMERSON, *Essays, First Series: Intellect.*

Thinking is the hardest work there is, which is the probable reason why so few engage in it.
HENRY FORD, *Interview*, Feb., 1929.

3
I never could find any man who could think for two minutes together.
SYDNEY SMITH, *Sketches of Moral Philosophy.* Lecture 19.

Though man a thinking being is defined,
Few use the great prerogative of mind;
How few think justly of the thinking few,
How many never think who think they do!
JANE TAYLOR, *Essay on Morals and Manners.* St. 45.

XI—Thought: Its Futility

4
The extra calories needed for one hour of intense mental effort would be completely met by the eating of one oyster cracker or one half of a salted peanut.
FRANCIS G. BENEDICT, *The Energy Requirements of Intense Mental Effort.*

5
Thought is the work of brain and nerve, in small-skulled idiot poor and mean;
In sickness sick, in sleep asleep, and dead when Death lets drop the scene.
SIR RICHARD BURTON, *Kasîdah.* Pt. vii, st. 13.

6
Why should I disparage my parts by thinking what to say? None but dull rogues think.
CONGREVE, *The Double-Dealer.* Act iv, sc. 2.

7
Do not craze yourself with thinking, but go about your business anywhere. Life is not intellectual and critical, but sturdy.
EMERSON, *Essays, Second Series: Experience.*

8
A man may dwell so long upon a thought that it may take him prisoner.
LORD HALIFAX, *Works*, p. 249.

9
He that thinks amiss concludes worse.
GEORGE HERBERT, *Jacula Prudentum.*

10
And which of you with taking thought can add to his stature one cubit?
New Testament: Luke, xii, 25.

11
"I think till I weary of thinking,"
Said the sad-eyed Hindu king.
ALFRED LYALL, *Meditations of a Hindu Prince.*

12
Wise wretch! with pleasures too refin'd to please;
With too much spirit to be e'er at ease;
With too much quickness ever to be taught;
With too much thinking to have common thought.
POPE, *Moral Essays.* Epis. ii, l. 95.

13
I think that naught is worth a thought
And I'm a fool for thinking.
W. M. PRAED, *Chant of the Brazen Head.* St. 6.

14
Drown consideration.
SHAKESPEARE, *Antony and Cleopatra,* iv, 2, 45.

Make not your thoughts your prisons.
SHAKESPEARE, *Antony and Cleopatra,* v, 2, 185.

You do unbend your noble strength, to think
So brainsickly of things.
SHAKESPEARE, *Macbeth.* Act ii, sc. 2, l. 45.

15
Thinking is but an idle waste of thought,
And nought is everything, and everything is nought.
HORACE AND JAMES SMITH, *Cui Bono.* St. 8.

16
Men suffer from thinking more than anything else.
LEO TOLSTOY, *Sevastopol.*

17
Beauty ends where an intellectual expression begins. Intellect destroys the harmony of any face. The moment one sits down to think, one becomes all nose.
WILDE, *The Picture of Dorian Gray.* Ch. 1.

THREAT

18
Threats without power are like powder without ball.
NATHAN BAILEY, *Dictionary: Definition.*

19
If it is not right to hurt, it is neither right nor wise to menace.
EDMUND BURKE, *Speech,* House of Commons, 1773.

20
Do not use threats to anyone, for that is womanish.
CHILON. (DIOGENES LAERTIUS, *Chilon.* Sec. 3.)

21
To freemen, threats are impotent. (Nulla enim minantis auctoritas apud liberos est.)
CICERO, *Epistolæ ad Familiares.* Bk. xi, epis. 3.

22
Many a one threatens while he quakes for fear.
W. G. BENHAM, *Proverbs,* p. 807. After the French, "Tel menace qui a grand peur." The Dutch say, "Dreigers vechten niet" (Threateners don't fight).

23
Truly you had the look of one threatening many and excellent things. (Atqui voltus erat multa et præclara minantis.)
HORACE, *Satires.* Bk. ii, sat. 3, l. 9.

24
He threatens many that hath injured one.
BEN JONSON, *Fall of Sejanus.* Act ii.

25
Nor think thou with wind
Of aery threats to awe whom yet with deeds
Thou canst not.
MILTON, *Paradise Lost.* Bk. vi, l. 282.

1
Even though I should live to extreme old age, the time would be short for enduring what you threaten me with. (Etsi pervivo usque ad summam ætatem, tamen Breve spatium est perferundi quæ minitas mihi.)

Plautus, *Captivi*, l. 742. (Act iii, sc. 5.)

2
Threatened folks live long.

Henry Porter, *Two Angry Women.* (1599)

The proverb says that threatened men live long.

Dickens, *Edwin Drood.* Ch. 14.

There are more men threatened than stricken.

George Herbert, *Jacula Prudentum.* The Dutch say, "Van dreigen sterft man neit" (A man does not die of threats).

3
There is no terror, Cassius, in your threats,
For I am arm'd so strong in honesty
That they pass by me as the idle wind,
Which I respect not.

Shakespeare, *Julius Cæsar.* Act iv, sc. 3, l. 66.

Before I be convict by course of law,
To threaten me with death is most unlawful.

Shakespeare, *Richard III.* Act i, sc. 4, l. 192.

4
I'll make a sop o' the moonshine of you.

Shakespeare, *King Lear.* Act ii, sc. 2, l. 34.

I will tread this unbolted villain into mortar, and daub the walls of a jakes with him.

Shakespeare, *King Lear.* Act ii, sc. 2, l. 70.

If ever henceforth thou
These rural latches to his entrance open,
Or hoop his body more with thy embraces,
I will devise a death as cruel for thee
As thou art tender to 't.

Shakespeare, *Winter's Tale.* Act iv, sc. 4, l. 447.

THRIFT

See also Economy

I—Thrift: Apothegms

5
Wise men say
Keep somewhat till a rainy day.

Nicholas Breton, *Works.* Vol. i, p. 29. (1582)

Laying up in store for themselves a good foundation against the time to come.

New Testament: I Timothy, vi, 19.

6
As great a craft is keep well as win.

Chaucer, *Troilus and Criseyde.* Bk. iii, l. 1634.

Nor is it less a virtue to take care of property than to acquire it. In the latter, there is chance; the former demands skill. (Noc minor est virtus quam quærere, parta tueri: Casus inest illic; hoc erit artis opus.)

Ovid, *Ars Amatoria.* Bk. ii, l. 13.

7
Annual income twenty pounds, annual expenditure nineteen nineteen six, result happiness. Annual income twenty pounds, annual expenditure twenty pounds ought and six, result misery.

Dickens, *David Copperfield.* Ch. 12.

8
A shilling spent idly by a fool, may be picked up by a wiser person.

Benjamin Franklin, *Letter to Benjamin Vaughan*, 26 July, 1784.

Spare and have is better than spend and crave.

Benjamin Franklin, *Poor Richard*, 1758.

For age and want save while you may,
No morning sun lasts a whole day.

Benjamin Franklin, *The Way to Wealth.*

9
If you put nothing into your purse, you can take nothing out.

Thomas Fuller, *Gnomologia.* No. 2781.

'Tis not all saved that's put in the purse.

John Clarke, *Parœmiologia*, p. 45.

All is not gain that is got into the purse.

Sterne, *Tristram Shandy.* Bk. iii, ch. 30.

10
Thrift is the philosopher's stone.

Thomas Fuller, *Gnomologia.* No. 5040.

Get what you can, and what you get hold;
'Tis the stone that will turn all your lead into gold.

Benjamin Franklin, *The Way to Wealth.*

11
Know when to spend and when to spare,
And you need not be busy; you'll never be bare.

Thomas Fuller, *Gnomologia.* No. 6437.

Who more than he is worth doth spend,
E'en makes a rope his life to end.

H. G. Bohn, *Handbook of Proverbs*, p. 567.

He who spends all he gets is on his way to beggary.

Samuel Smiles, *Thrift*, p. 172.

12
Worldly wealth he cared not for, desiring only to make both ends meet.

Thomas Fuller, *Worthies of England.* (1662)

Tho' he had a good estate, hardly making both ends meet.

Richardson, *Clarissa Harlowe*, iv, 137.

13
Live with a thrifty, not a needy fate;
Small shots paid often waste a vast estate.

Robert Herrick, *Hesperides.* No. 28.

14
He who adds to what he has will keep off bright-eyed hunger; for if you add only a little to a little and do this often, soon that little will become great. (Σμικρὸν ἐπι σμικρῷ.)

Hesiod, *Works and Days*, l. 361. *See also under* Trifles.

15
When thrift and you fell first at a fray,
You played the man and made thrift run away.

John Heywood, *Proverbs.* Pt. i, ch. 11.

16
Even as the tiny, hard-working ant drags all she can with her mouth, and adds it to the heap she is building, because she is not heedless of the morrow.

Horace, *Satires.* Bk. i, sat. 1, l. 32.

1
Resolve not to be poor: whatever you have, spend less.

SAMUEL JOHNSON. (BOSWELL, *Life*, iv, 157.)

Do not discourage your children from hoarding, if they have a taste to it; whoever lays up his penny rather than part with it for a cake, at least is not the slave of gross appetite.

SAMUEL JOHNSON, *Miscellanies*. Vol 1, p. 251.

2
If you spend a thing you can not have it. (Non tibi illud apparere si sumas potest.)

PLAUTUS, *Trinummus*. Act ii, sc. 4, l. 12. *See also under* POSSESSIONS.

3
Of saving cometh having.

JOHN RAY, *English Proverbs*, p. 139.

Saving is getting.

TORRIANO, *Piazza Universale*, p. 265.

3a
Sparing is the first gaining.

JOHN SANDFORD, *Hours of Recreation*, 212. (1572)

The first gain or profit is to spare.

JOHN FLORIO, *First Fruites*, 30. (1578)

4
As my canny subjects in Scotland say, If you keep a thing seven years, you are sure to find a use for it at last.

SCOTT, *Woodstock*. Ch. 28. King Charles II to Dr. Rochecliffe.

5
Thrift, thrift, Horatio! the funeral baked meats
Did coldly furnish forth the marriage tables.

SHAKESPEARE, *Hamlet*. Act i, sc. 2, l. 180.

6
What piles of wealth hath he accumulated
To his own portion! . . . How, i' the name of thrift
Does he rake this together?

SHAKESPEARE, *Henry VIII*. Act iii, sc. 2, l. 107.

7
Have more than thou showest,
Speak less than thou knowest,
Lend less than thou owest, . . .
And thou shalt have more
Than two tens to a score.

SHAKESPEARE, *King Lear*, i, 4, 131. See 1931:1.

8
Their thrift waxes thin
That spend more than they win.

UNKNOWN, *How the Good Wife*, l. 100. (c. 1460)

II—Thrift: Pins and Pennies

9
A pin a day is a groat a year.

JOSEPH ADDISON, *The Spectator*. No. 295.

A penny saved is two pence clear,
A pin a day's a groat a year.

BENJAMIN FRANKLIN, *Necessary Hints to Those that Would be Rich*.

He that will not stoop for a pin will never be worth a pound.

SIR WILLIAM COVENTRY, to Charles II. (PEPYS, *Diary*, 3 Jan., 1668.)

See a pin and pick it up,
All the day you'll have good luck;
See a pin and let it lie,
You'll want a pin before you die.

UNKNOWN, *Old Nursery Rhyme*. (*Notes and Queries*. Ser. iv, vol. 10, p. 477.)

10
Who will not lay up a penny
Shall never have many.

THOMAS FULLER, *Gnomologia*. No. 6383.

A penny spared is twice got.

GEORGE HERBERT, *Jacula Prudentum*.

Penny and penny laid up will be many.

JOHN RAY, *English Proverbs*, p. 130.

11
Take care of the pence, and the pounds will take care of themselves.

WILLIAM LOWNDES, Secretary of Treasury under William III.

I knew once a very covetous, sordid fellow who used to say, "Take care of the pence, for the pounds will take care of themselves."

LORD CHESTERFIELD, *Letters*. 6 Nov., 1747; also 5 Feb., 1750. Quoting Lowndes.

12
A penny in the purse is better than a friend at court.

SAMUEL SMILES, *Thrift*, p. 126. Quoted as "a true saying."

13
A penny sav'd 's a penny got.

WILLIAM SOMERVILLE, *The Sweet-Scented Miser*, l. 30.

He abounds in frugal maxims, . . . "A penny saved is a penny got."

RICHARD STEELE, *The Spectator*. No. 2.

"A penny savèd is a penny got"—
Firm to this scoundrel maxim keepeth he.

THOMSON, *Castle of Indolence*. Canto i, st. 50.

A penny well sav'd is as good as one earn'd.

UNKNOWN. (*Roxburghe Ballads*, vi, 349. c. 1686)

14
It was said of old Sarah, Duchess of Marlborough, that she never puts dots over her *i's*, to save ink.

HORACE WALPOLE, *Letter to Sir Horace Mann*, 4 Oct., 1785.

THRONE

See also King

15
Emulous always of the nearest place
To any throne except the throne of grace.

COWPER, *Hope*, l. 238.

16
The legs of the throne are the plough and the oar, the anvil and the sewing-machine.

EMERSON, *Journals*, 1857.

17
Forbade to wade through slaughter to a throne.

THOMAS GRAY, *Elegy Written in a Country Church-yard*. St. 17.

1
And in mercy shall the throne be established.
Old Testament: Isaiah, xvi, 5.

2
The throne is but a piece of gilded wood covered with velvet.
NAPOLEON BONAPARTE. (THIERS, *Consulate and Empire.* Bk. li.)

3
There is something behind the throne greater than the King himself.
WILLIAM PITT, EARL OF CHATHAM, *Speech,* 2 March, 1770. (*Chatham Correspondence;* MAHON, *History of England,* v, 258.) Hence the phrase, "The power behind the throne."

And lives to clutch the golden keys,
To mould a mighty state's decrees,
And shape the whisper of the throne.
TENNYSON, *In Memoriam.* Pt. lxiv, st. 3.

4
No throne without thorn.
W. G. BENHAM, *Proverbs,* p. 816.

A doubtful throne is ice on summer seas.
TENNYSON, *The Coming of Arthur,* l. 247.

5
In that fierce light which beats upon a throne.
TENNYSON, *Idylls of the King: Dedication,* l. 26.

6
Methought I saw the footsteps of a throne.
WORDSWORTH, *Miscellaneous Sonnets.* Pt. i, 29.

THRUSH

7
Hark, where my blossomed pear-tree in the hedge
Leans to the field and scatters on the clover
Blossoms and dewdrops—at the bent spray's edge—
That's the wise thrush: he sings each song twice over
Lest you should think he never could recapture
The first fine careless rapture!
R. BROWNING, *Home Thoughts from Abroad.*

8
No voice awoke. Dwelling sedate, apart,
Only the thrush, the thrush that never spoke,
Sang from her bursting heart.
LAURA BENÉT, *The Thrush.*

9
God's poet, hid in foliage green,
Sings endless songs, himself unseen;
Right seldom come his silent times.
Linger, ye summer hours, serene!
Sing on, dear Thrush, amid the limes!
MORTIMER COLLINS, *My Thrush.*

10
Through the wood's full strains I hear
Thy monotone deep and clear,
Like a sound amid sounds most fine.
DINAH M. M. CRAIK, *A Rhyme About Birds.*

11
The full notes clearer grow;
Hark, what a torrent gush!
They pour, they overflow—
Sing on, sing on, O thrush!
AUSTIN DOBSON, *Ballad of the Thrush.*

12
An agèd thrush, frail, gaunt, and small,
In blast-beruffled plume,
Had chosen thus to fling his soul
Upon the growing gloom. . . .
And I could think there trembled through
His happy good-night air
Some blessèd Hope, whereof he knew
And I was unaware.
THOMAS HARDY, *The Darkling Thrush.*

13
Full lasting is the song, though he,
The singer, passes: lasting too,
For souls not lent in usury,
The rapture of the forward view.
GEORGE MEREDITH, *The Thrush in February.*

14
A voice peals in this end of night
A phrase of notes resembling stars,
Single and spiritual notes of light.
What call they at my window-bars?
The South, the past, the day to be,
An ancient infelicity.
ALICE MEYNELL, *A Thrush Before Dawn.*

15
O thrush, your song is passing sweet,
But never a song that you have sung
Is half so sweet as thrushes sang
When my dear love and I were young.
WILLIAM MORRIS, *Other Days.*

16
In the gloamin' o' the wood
The throssil whusslit sweet.
WILLIAM MOTHERWELL, *Jeanie Morrison.*

The throstle with his note so true.
SHAKESPEARE, *A Midsummer-Night's Dream.* Act iii, sc. 1, l. 130.

Sing clear, O throstle,
Thou golden-tongued apostle
And little brown-frocked brother
Of the loved Assisian!
T. A. DALY, *To a Thrush.*

17
At earliest dawn, his thrilling pipe was heard;
And, when the light of evening died away,
That blithe and indefatigable bird
Still his redundant song of joy and love preferred.
ROBERT SOUTHEY, *A Tale of Paraguay: Dedication.* St. 4.

18
Sing, sweet thrushes, forth and sing!
Meet the moon upon the lea.
THOMAS TOD STODDART, *The Angler's Trysting-Tree.*

19
Hush! With sudden gush
As from a fountain sings in yonder bush
The Hermit Thrush.
JOHN BANISTER TABB, *Overflow.*

20
Blow softly, thrush, upon the hush
That makes the least leaf loud,
Blow, wild of heart, remote, apart
From all the vocal crowd,

Apart, remote, a spirit note
That dances meltingly afloat,
Blow faintly, thrush!
JOSEPH RUSSELL TAYLOR, *Blow Softly, Thrush.*

1
When rosy plumelets tuft the larch,
And rarely pipes the mounted thrush.
TENNYSON, *In Memoriam.* Pt. xci.

2
Oh, hark to the brown thrush! hear how he sings!
How he pours the dear pain of his gladness!
What a gush! and from out what golden springs!
What a rage of how sweet madness!
DAVID ATWOOD WASSON, *Joy-Month.*

3
And hark! how blithe the throstle sings!
He, too, is no mean preacher:
Come forth into the light of things,
Let Nature be your teacher.
WORDSWORTH, *The Tables Turned.*

At the corner of Wood Street, when daylight appears,
Hangs a thrush that sings loud, it has sung for three years.
WORDSWORTH, *The Reverie of Poor Susan.*

THUNDER

See also Lightning

4
And hark to the crashing, long and loud,
Of the chariot of God, in the thunder-cloud!
W. C. BRYANT, *The Hurricane.*

5
From peak to peak the rattling crags among
Leaps the live thunder!
BYRON, *Childe Harold.* Canto iii, st. 92.

6
Loud roared the dreadful thunder,
The rain a deluge showers.
ANDREW CHERRY, *The Bay of Biscay.*

7
Heaven's great artillery.
RICHARD CRASHAW, *The Flaming Heart,* l. 56.

And heaven's artillery thunder in the skies.
SHAKESPEARE, *The Taming of the Shrew.* Act i, sc. 2, l. 205.

8
They steal my thunder.
JOHN DENNIS. *See under* PLAGIARISM.

9
The thunderbolt strikes on an inch of ground, but the light of it fills the horizon.
EMERSON, *Journals,* 1865.

10
The thunder hath but its clap.
THOMAS FULLER, *Gnomologia.* No. 4793.

11
Winter's thunder Is the world's wonder.
J. O. HALLIWELL, *Nature Songs.*

12
The god hurls his thunderbolt against the loftiest building.
HERODOTUS *History.* Bk. vii, ch. 10, sec. 5. *See also* GREATNESS: ITS PENALTIES.

13
Thy thunder, conscious of the new command,
Rumbles reluctant o'er our fallen house.
KEATS, *Hyperion,* Bk. i, l. 60.

14
Men thy bold deeds shall tell,
Old Heart of Oak,
Daring Dave Farragut,
Thunderbolt stroke!
WILLIAM TUCKER MEREDITH, *Farragut*

15
Their rising all at once was as the sound
Of thunder heard remote.
MILTON, *Paradise Lost.* Bk. ii, l. 476.

16
A senseless thunderbolt. (Brutum fulmen.)
PLINY, *History.* Bk. ii, ch. 43, sec. 113.

17
He never embraced his wife unless it thundered loudly, and it was a pleasantry of his to remark that he was a happy man when it thundered.
PLUTARCH, *Lives: Marcus Cato.* Ch. 17, sec. 7. Of Cato.

18
To tear with thunder the wide cheeks o' the air.
SHAKESPEARE, *Coriolanus.* Act v, sc. 3, l. 151.

Rumble thy bellyfull.
SHAKESPEARE, *King Lear.* Act iii, sc. 2, l. 14.

19
What is the cause of thunder?
SHAKESPEARE, *King Lear.* Act iii, sc. 4, l. 160. The crazed Lear asks the fool a question which still remains unanswered.

Father very often wonders
When it lightens why it thunders,
And he wonders, when it brightens,
When it thunders why it lightens.
GUY BOAS, *Speculation.*

20
To stand against the deep dread-bolted thunder?
In the most terrible and nimble stroke
Of quick, cross lightning?
SHAKESPEARE, *King Lear.* Act iv, sc. 7, l. 33.

21
Are there no stones in heaven
But what serve for the thunder?
SHAKESPEARE, *Othello.* Act v, sc. 2, l. 234.

22
As loud As thunder when the clouds in autumn crack.
SHAKESPEARE, *The Taming of the Shrew.* Act i, sc. 2, l. 96.

23
If it should thunder as it did before,
I know not where to hide my head.
SHAKESPEARE, *The Tempest.* Act ii, sc. 2, l. 22.

24
The thunder, That deep and dreadful organ-pipe.
SHAKESPEARE, *The Tempest.* Act iii, sc. 3, l. 97.

The dread rattling thunder.
SHAKESPEARE, *The Tempest.* Act v, sc. 1, l. 44.

1
All the heavens
Open'd and blazed with thunder such as seem'd
Shoutings of all the sons of God.
TENNYSON, *The Holy Grail*, l. 507.

2
It is the flash which appears, the thunderbolt will follow. (C'est l'éclair qui paraît, la foudre va partir.)
VOLTAIRE, *Oreste*. Act ii, sc. 7.

TIBER, see under Rome

TIDE

3
Now the great winds shorewards blow,
Now the salt tides seawards flow;
Now the wild white horses play,
Champ and chafe and toss in the spray.
MATTHEW ARNOLD, *The Forsaken Merman*, l. 4.

4
Now morn has come,
And with the morn the punctual tide again.
SUSAN COOLIDGE, *Flood-Tide*.

5
The tide turns at low water as well as at high.
HAVELOCK ELLIS, *Impressions and Comments*. Ser. i, p. 103.

6
The ebb will fetch off what the tide brings in.
THOMAS FULLER, *Gnomologia*. No. 4495.

The tide will fetch away what the ebb brings.
JOHN RAY, *English Proverbs*, p. 26.

7
The tide tarries no man.
JOHN LYDGATE, *Fall of Princes*. Bk. iii, l. 2801. (c. 1440)

Hoist up sail while gale doth last,
Tide and wind stay no man's pleasure.
ROBERT SOUTHWELL, *St. Peter's Complaint*.

Tide bides no man.
JOHN RAY, *English Proverbs*.

Ebb and flood wait for no man. (Ebbe und Fluth warten auf Niemand.
UNKNOWN. A German proverb.

See also TIME AND TIDE.

8
The western tide crept up along the sand,
And o'er and o'er the sand,
And round and round the sand,
As far as eye could see.
The rolling mist came down and hid the land:
And never home came she.
CHARLES KINGSLEY, *The Sands of Dee*. St. 2.

The tide rises, the tide falls,
The twilight darkens, the curlew calls;
Along the sea-sands damp and brown
The traveller hastens toward the town,
And the tide rises, the tide falls.
LONGFELLOW, *The Tide Rises, the Tide Falls*.

9
A single breaker may recede; but the tide is evidently coming in.
MACAULAY, *Essays: Southey's Colloquies*.

10
No animal dies except upon a receding tide. (Nullum animal nisi æstu recedente expirare.)
PLINY, *Historia Naturalis*. Bk. ii, ch. 101.

11
A' parted even just between twelve and one, even at the turning o' the tide.
SHAKESPEARE, *Henry V*. Act ii, sc. 3, l. 12.

"People can't die along this coast," said Mr. Peggotty, "except when the tide's pretty nigh out. They can't be born, unless it's pretty nigh in—not properly born, till flood. He's a-going out with the tide."
DICKENS, *David Copperfield*. Ch. 30.

Pliny hath an odd and remarkable passage concerning the death of men and animals upon the recess of ebb of the sea.
SIR THOMAS BROWNE, *Letters*. No. 7.

12
Down beyond the haven the tide comes with a shout.
WILLIAM SHARP, *An Old Tale of Three*.

13
No motion but the moving tide, a breeze,
Or merely silent Nature's breathing life.
WORDSWORTH, *Elegiac Stanzas, Suggested by a Picture of Peele Castle in a Storm*, l. 27.

14
Tide flowing is fear'd, for many a thing,
Great danger to such as be sick, it doth bring;
Sea ebb, by long ebbing, some respite doth give,
And sendeth good comfort to such as shall live.
THOMAS TUSSER, *Five Hundred Points of Good Husbandry*. Ch. 14.

TIGER

15
Tiger! Tiger! burning bright
In the forests of the night,
What immortal hand or eye,
Could frame thy fearful symmetry?
WILLIAM BLAKE, *The Tiger*. St. 1.

16
If a man proves too clearly and convincingly to himself that the tiger is an optical illusion —well, he will find out that he is wrong. The tiger will himself intervene in the discussion.
G. K. CHESTERTON, *Illusions*.

17
When did the tiger's young ones teach the dam?
SHAKESPEARE, *Titus Andronicus*. Act ii, sc. 3, 142.

18
Tigers, of course, have solitary habits
And haunt where brown and yellow leaves are strown.
They're not companionable beasts like rabbits
And much prefer to eat their meals alone.
W. C. SMITH, *A Heretic*.

The Tiger, on the other hand, is kittenish and mild:
He makes a pretty playfellow for any little child;
And mothers of large families (who claim to common sense)

Will find a Tiger well repay the trouble and expense.
HILAIRE BELLOC, *The Tiger.*

Or if some time when roaming round,
A noble wild beast greets you,
With black stripes on a yellow ground,
Just notice if he eats you.
This simple rule may help you learn
The Bengal Tiger to discern.
CAROLYN WELLS, *How to Tell Wild Animals.*

1
Shun the companionship of the tiger. (Tigridis evita sodalitatem.)
UNKNOWN. A Latin proverb.

1a
The tiger on the plain is insulted by the dogs. ('Hu lo 'ping yang pei 'chüan 'chi.)
UNKNOWN. A Chinese proverb.

In painting a tiger, one can paint the skin, but not the bones. ('Hua 'hu 'hua 'pi nan 'huaku.)
UNKNOWN. A Chinese proverb.

TIME

See also Day, Hour, Minute, Year

I—Time: Definitions

2
Time which is the author of authors.
BACON, *Advancement of Learning.* Bk. i.

3
Time is the greatest innovator.
FRANCIS BACON, *Essays: Of Innovations.*

It were good therefore, that men in their innovations would follow the example of time itself, which indeed innovateth greatly, but quietly and by degrees scarce to be perceived.
FRANCIS BACON, *Essays: Of Innovations.*

4
Wherever anything lives, there is, open somewhere, a register in which time is being inscribed.
HENRI BERGSON, *Creative Evolution.* Ch. 1.

5
That great mystery of TIME, were there no other; the illimitable, silent, never-resting thing called Time, rolling, rushing on, swift, silent, like an all-embracing ocean-tide, on which we and all the Universe swim like exhalations, like apparitions which *are,* and then *are not:* this is forever very literally a miracle; a thing to strike us dumb,—for we have no word to speak about it.
CARLYLE, *Heroes and Hero-Worship.* Lecture 1.

6
Old Time, that greatest and longest established spinner of all! . . . His factory is a secret place, his work is noiseless, and his Hands are mutes.
DICKENS, *Hard Times.* Bk. i, ch. 14.

7
Time, to the nation as to the individual, is nothing absolute; its duration depends on the rate of thought and feeling.
JOHN WILLIAM DRAPER, *History of the Intellectual Development of Europe.* Vol. i, ch. 1.

8
Time dissipates to shining ether the solid angularity of facts.
EMERSON, *Essays, First Series: History.*

The surest poison is time.
EMERSON, *Society and Solitude: Old Age.*

9
Time is itself an element. (Die Zeit ist selbst ein Element.)
GOETHE, *Sprüche in Prosa.* Pt. iii.

Time is a noiseless file.
GEORGE HERBERT, *Jacula Prudentum.*

Time is the rider that breaks youth.
GEORGE HERBERT, *Jacula Prudentum.*

10
Made, bitter-sweet, from fruits of life
There is a wine;
It quenches every human thirst—
We call it Time.
JEAN HERRICK, *Time.*

11
Old Time, in whose bank we deposit our notes,
Is a miser who always wants guineas for groats;
He keeps all his customers still in arrears
By lending them minutes and charging them years.
O. W. HOLMES, *Our Banker.* St. 1.

12
What is time? The shadow on the dial, the striking of the clock, the running of the sand, day and night, summer and winter, months, years, centuries—these are but arbitrary and outward signs, the measure of Time, not Time itself. Time is the Life of the soul.
LONGFELLOW, *Hyperion.* Bk. ii, ch. 6.

13
Time is not progress, but amount;
One vast accumulating store,
Laid up, not lost!
JAMES MONTGOMERY, *Time.* St. 3.

14
For the just, Time is the best of champions. (Ἀνδρῶν δικαίων χρόνος σωτὴρ ἄριστος.)
PINDAR, *Fragments.* No. 159.

Time brings everything. (Αἰὼν πάντα φερει.)
PLATO. (*Greek Anthology.* Bk. ix, epig. 51.)

15
Time is the soul of the world.
PYTHAGORAS. (PLUTARCH, *Platonic Questions,* viii, 4.)

Time is man's angel. (Des Menschen Engel ist die Zeit.)
SCHILLER, *Theklas Monolog,* v, 11.

16
Old Time the clock-setter, that bald sexton Time.
SHAKESPEARE, *King John.* Act iii, sc. 1, l. 324.

That old common arbitrator, Time.
SHAKESPEARE, *Troilus and Cressida.* Act iv, sc. 5, l. 225.

That old bald cheater, Time.
BEN JONSON, *The Poetaster.* Act i, sc. 1.

1
Time is a gentle deity. (Χρόνος γάρ εὐμαρὴς θεός.)
SOPHOCLES, *Electra*, l. 179.

Time is the nurse and breeder of all good.
SHAKESPEARE, *The Two Gentlemen of Verona*. Act iii, sc. 1, l. 243.

II—Time: Apothegms

2
Ever-aging Time teaches all things. (Ἐκδιδάσκει πάνθ' ὁ γηράσκων χρόνος.)
ÆSCHYLUS, *Prometheus Bound*, l. 982.

Time, young man, has taught us both a lesson.
THEMISTOCLES, to Antiphales. (PLUTARCH, *Lives: Themistocles*.)

Wait, thou child of hope, for Time shall teach thee all things.
M. F. TUPPER, *Of Good in Things Evil*.

3
Time is one's best friend, teaching best of all the wisdom of silence.
A. B. ALCOTT, *Table Talk: Learning*.

The grand instructor, Time.
EDMUND BURKE, *Letter*, 26 May, 1799.

4
To choose time, is to save time.
FRANCIS BACON, *Essays: Of Despatch*.

He who gains time gains everything.
BENJAMIN DISRAELI, *Tancred*. Bk. iv, ch. 3.

Who hath time hath life.
JOHN FLORIO, *First Fruites*. Fo. 28.

Who hath time, and tarrieth for time, loseth time.
JOHN FLORIO, *First Fruites*. Fo. 28.

5
Time whereof the memory of man runneth not to the contrary.
BLACKSTONE, *Commentaries*. Vol. i, bk. 1, ch. 18.

6
Time eateth away at many an old delusion.
ROBERT BRIDGES, *Testament of Beauty*, l. 599.

7
There is no antidote against the opium of Time.
SIR THOMAS BROWNE, *Hydriotaphia*. Ch. v, 6.

8
Why should we break up
Our snug and pleasant party?
Time was made for slaves,
But never for us so hearty.
J. B. BUCKSTONE, *Billy Taylor*. (1830)

9
The silent touches of time.
EDMUND BURKE, *Letter to Matthew Smith*.

10
Time ripens all things. No man is born wise.
CERVANTES, *Don Quixote*. Pt. ii, ch. 33.

All in good time.
CERVANTES, *Don Quixote*. Pt. ii, ch. 36.

11
I count my time by times that I meet thee.
R. W. GILDER, *The New Day*. Pt. iv, Sonnet 6.

12
You cannot fight against the future. Time is on our side.
GLADSTONE, *Speech on Reform Bill*, 1866.

Time and I against any two.
JOHN ARBUTHNOT, *History of John Bull: Postscript*. (1712) A Spanish proverb, quoted by Cardinal Mazarin during the minority of Louis XIV.

Time and I are the two mightiest monarchs.
PHILIP II OF SPAIN.

13
Thus at Time's humming loom I ply. (So schaff' ich am sausenden Webstuhl der Zeit.)
GOETHE, *Faust*. Pt. i, sc. 1, l. 156.

14
My inheritance how lordly wide and fair:
Time is my fair seed-field, to Time I'm heir.
(Mein Erbteil wie herrlich, weit und breit:
Die Zeit ist mein Besitz, mein Acker ist die Zeit.)
GOETHE, *West-östlicher Divan: Buch der Sprüche*. (Carlyle, tr., *Chartism*, ch. 6.)

My inheritance how wide and fair:
Time is my estate; to Time I'm heir.
(Mein Vermächtniss, wie herrlich weit und breit!
Die Zeit ist mein Vermächtniss, mein Acker ist die Zeit.)
GOETHE, *Wilhelm Meister's Travels*. Used as motto by Carlyle for *Sartor Resartus*.

15
Time is . . . Time was . . . Time is past.
ROBERT GREENE, *The Honourable Historie of Friar Bacon*, xi, 55. (1589)

I must speak to you as Friar Bacon's head spake, . . . *Time is*, and then *Time was*, and *Time would never be*.
FRANCIS BACON, *Apologie*, iii, 152. (1603)

16
But Time was dumb within that Mansion old.
THOMAS HOOD, *The Haunted House*.

17
And panting Time toil'd after him in vain.
SAMUEL JOHNSON, *Prologue on Opening the Drury Lane Theatre*.

18
Time, that aged nurse,
Rock'd me to patience.
KEATS, *Endymion*. Bk. i, l. 705.

19
O aching time! O moments big as years!
KEATS, *Hyperion*. Bk. i, l. 64.

20
The incalculable Up and Down of Time.
SIDNEY LANIER, *Clover*.

21
Oh, glory, that we wrestle
So valiantly with Time!
RICHARD MONCKTON MILNES, *The Eld*.

22
Time will run back and fetch the age of gold.
MILTON, *On the Morning of Christ's Nativity*, l. 135. *See also under* AGE, THE.

23
Time hath a taming hand.
JOHN HENRY NEWMAN, *Persecution*.

24
Be ruled by time, the wisest counsellor of all. (Σύμβουλον ἀναμείνας χρόνον.)
PERICLES. (PLUTARCH, *Pericles*. Ch. 18, sec. 2.)

1
How goes the enemy?

FREDERIC REYNOLDS, *The Will*. Act i, sc. 1. Said by Mr. Ennui, the "time-killer."

George: How goes the enemy?
Lucifer: What can he mean?
Festus: He asks the hour.

P. J. BAILEY, *Festus: A Large Party*.

2
Who knows what may be slumbering in the background of time! (O, wer weiss Was in der Zeiten Hintergrunde schlummert.)

SCHILLER, *Don Carlos*. Act i, sc. 1, l. 44.

3
Oh, how much good time you lose over a bad matter! (O quam bonum tempus in re mala perdis!)

SENECA, *De Ira*. Bk. iii, sec. 28.

Time elaborately thrown away.

YOUNG, *The Last Day*. Bk. i, l. 206.

4
Nothing is ours except time. (Omnia aliena sunt, tempus tantum nostrum est.)

SENECA, *Epistulæ ad Lucilium*. Epis. i, sec. 3.

5
Thus the whirligig of time brings in his revenges.

SHAKESPEARE, *Twelfth Night*. Act v, sc. 1, l. 385.

6
Nick of Time!

SIR JOHN SUCKLING, *The Goblins*. Act v.

I'm just come in the nick!

SHERIDAN, *The Rivals*. Act iv, sc. 3.

7
I see that time divided is never long, and that regularity abridges all things.

MADAME DE STAËL. (STEVENS, *Life of Madame de Staël*. Ch. 38.)

8
To wind the mighty secrets of the past,
And turn the key of time.

HENRY KIRKE WHITE, *Time*, l. 249. *See also under* PAST.

9
Delivered from the galling yoke of time.

WORDSWORTH, *Laodamia*, l. 161. This line appeared in the editions of 1815 and 1820, but not in later ones.

10
The unimaginable touch of Time.

WORDSWORTH, *Sonnet: Mutability*.

III—Time: A Time for All Things

11
A time to love, and a time to wed, and a time to seek rest. (Ὥρη ἐρᾷν, ὥρη δὲ γαμεῖν, ὥρη δὲ πεπαῦσθαι.)

DIONYSIUS. (*Greek Anthology*. Bk. x, epig. 38.) Though credited to Dionysius in the *Anthology*, this line was really spoken by Timon of Dionysius of Heraclea, a Stoic philosopher who deserted to the Epicureans in his old age. It was preceded by the punning line, "Now when it is time for him to set, he begins to seek pleasure." (Ἡνίκ' ἐχρῆν δύνειν, νῦν ἄρχεται ἡδύνεσθαι.)

To every thing there is a season, and a time to every purpose under the heaven:
A time to be born, and a time to die; a time to plant, and a time to pluck up that which is planted;
A time to kill, and a time to heal; a time to break down, and a time to build up;
A time to weep, and a time to laugh; a time to mourn, and a time to dance; . . .
A time to get, and a time to lose; a time to keep, and a time to cast away;
A time to rend, and a time to sew; a time to keep silence, and a time to speak;
A time to love, and a time to hate; a time of war, and a time of peace.

Old Testament: Ecclesiastes, iii, 1–8.

Of a Monday I drive the coach, of a Tuesday I drive the plough, on Wednesday I follow the hounds, a Thursday I dun the tenants, on Friday I go to market, on Saturday I draw warrants, and a Sunday I draw beer.

FARQUHAR, *The Beaux' Stratagem*. Act iii, sc. 3

For holy offices I have a time; a time
To think upon the part of business which
I bear i' the state; and nature does require
Her times of preservation.

SHAKESPEARE, *Henry VIII*. Act iii, sc. 2, l. 144.

12
But all thing hath time.

WILLIAM LANGLAND, *Richard the Redeless*. Pt. iii, l. 278. (c. 1399)

Everything has time.

GEORGE CHAPMAN, *All Fools*. Act v, sc. 2.

Everything hath its time, and that time must be watch'd.

THOMAS FULLER, *Gnomologia*. No. 1466.

13
There's a time for all things.

SHAKESPEARE, *The Comedy of Errors*. Act ii, sc. 2, l. 65.

There is a time for some things, and a time for all things; a time for great things and a time for small things.

CERVANTES, *Don Quixote*, Pt. ii, ch. 35.

IV—Time: A River

14
Time's waters will not ebb nor stay.

JOHN KEBLE, *Christian Year: First Sunday after Christmas*.

15
Time is a river of passing events, aye, a rushing torrent. (Ποταμός τις ἐκ τῶν γινομένων καὶ ῥεῦμα βίαιον ὁ αἰών.)

MARCUS AURELIUS, *Meditations*. Bk. iv, sec. 43.

Time is a flowing river. Happy those who allow themselves to be carried, unresisting, with the current. They float through easy days. They live, unquestioning, in the moment.

CHRISTOPHER MORLEY, *Where the Blue Begins*, p. 81.

16
The stream of time glides smoothly on and is past before we know. (Labitur occulte fallitque, volubilis ætas.)

OVID, *Amores*. Bk. i, eleg. 8, l. 49.

Time glides by with constant movement, not unlike a stream. For neither can a stream stay its course, nor can the fleeting hour. (Adsiduo labuntur tempora motu, Non secus ac flumen; neque enim consistere flumen Nec levis hora potest.)
OVID, *Metamorphoses*. Bk. xv, l. 179.

1
A wonderful stream is the River Time,
As it runs through the realm of Tears,
With a faultless rhythm, and a musical rhyme,
And a broader sweep, and a surge sublime,
. As it blends with the Ocean of Years.
BENJAMIN FRANKLIN TAYLOR, *The Long Ago.*

2
The forward-flowing tide of time.
TENNYSON, *Recollections of the Arabian Nights*, l. 4.

3
Time, like an ever-rolling stream,
Bears all its sons away;
They fly forgotten, as a dream
Dies at the opening day.
ISAAC WATTS, *O God, Our Help in Ages Past.*

V—Time and Truth

4
The inseparable propriety of time, which is ever more and more to disclose truth.
BACON, *Advancement of Learning*. Bk. ii.

Time trieth truth in every doubt.
JOHN HEYWOOD, *Proverbs*. Pt. ii, ch. 5. (1546)

Time tries the troth in everything.
THOMAS TUSSER, *Five Hundred Points of Good Husbandry: Author's Epistle*. Ch. 1.

5
Time stands with impartial law. (Æquo stat fœdare tempus.)
MANILIUS, *Astronomica*, iii, 360.

Time is the old justice that examines all such offenders, and let Time try.
SHAKESPEARE, *As You Like It*. Act iv, sc. 1, l. 203.

6
O Time! whose verdicts mock our own,
The only righteous judge art thou!
THOMAS WILLIAM PARSONS, *On a Bust of Dante.*

7
See to it lest you try aught to conceal:
Time sees and hears all, and will all reveal.
SOPHOCLES, *Fragments*. No. 280.

Time shall unfold what plaited cunning hides.
SHAKESPEARE, *King Lear*. Act i, sc. 1, l. 283.

Time and chance reveal all secrets.
MARY DE LA RIVIERE MANLEY, *New Atlantis*. Pt. ii, l. 230.

8
The wisest thing is Time, for it brings everything to light. (Σοφώτατον χρόνος, ἀνευρίσκει γὰρ πάντα.)
THALES. (DIOGENES LAERTIUS, *Thales*. Bk. i, sec. 35.)

Time will bring to light whatever is hidden; it will cover up and conceal what is now shining in splendor. (Quidquid sub terra est, in apricum proferet ætas; Defodiet condetque nitentia.)
HORACE, *Epistles*. Bk. i, epis. 6, l. 24.

VI—Time: Its Flight

9
Alas! how swift the moments fly!
How flash the years along!
Scarce here, yet gone already by,
The burden of a song.
See childhood, youth, and manhood pass,
And age with furrowed brow;
Time was—Time shall be—drain the glass—
But where in Time is now?
JOHN QUINCY ADAMS, *The Hour Glass.*

10
For though we sleep or wake, or roam, or ride,
Aye fleets the time, it will no man abide.
CHAUCER, *The Clerkes Tale*, l. 118.

Bide for time who will, for time will no man bide.
JOHN SKELTON, *Works*. Vol. i, p. 137.

Time nor tide tarrieth no man.
ROBERT GREENE, *Disputations*, p. 22. (1592)

Time and tide stayeth for no man.
RICHARD BRATHWAITE, *English Gentleman*, p. 189. (1630)

For the next inn he spurs amain,
In haste alights, and skuds away,
But time and tide for no man stay.
W. C. SOMERVILLE, *Sweet-Scented Miser*, l. 98.

Nae man can tether time or tide.
BURNS, *Tam o' Shanter*, l. 67.

See also under TIDE.

11
No! no arresting the vast wheel of Time,
That round and round still turns with onward might,
Stern, dragging thousands to the dreadful night
Of an unknown hereafter.
CHARLES COWDEN CLARKE, *The Course of Time.*

12
Swift, speedy Time, feathered with flying hours.
SAMUEL DANIEL, *Sonnets to Delia*. No. xxxix.

Time is a feathered thing,
And, whilst I praise,
The sparkling of thy looks, and call them rays,
Takes wing.
JASPER MAYNE, *Time.*

13
Whether we wake or we sleep,
Whether we carol or weep,
The Sun with his Planets in chime,
Marketh the going of Time.
EDWARD FITZGERALD, *Chronomoros.*

14
You may delay, but time will not.
BENJAMIN FRANKLIN, *Poor Richard*, 1758.

15
Time flies over us, but leaves its shadow behind.
HAWTHORNE, *The Marble Faun*. Ch. 24.

1
Where's the use of sighing?
Sorrow as you may,
Time is always flying—
Flying!—and defying
Men to say him nay.
WILLIAM ERNEST HENLEY, *Villanelle.*

2
Thursday come, and the week is gone.
GEORGE HERBERT, *Jacula Prudentum.*

3
I made a posy, while the day ran by:
Here will I smell my remnant out, and tie
My life within this band.
But time did beckon to the flowers, and they
By noon most cunningly did steal away,
And wither'd in my hand.
GEORGE HERBERT, *Life.*

4
Time, you old gipsy man,
Will you not stay,
Put up your caravan
Just for one day?
RALPH HODGSON, *Time, You Old Gipsy Man.*

5
Alas, O Postumus, the years glide swiftly by!
No piety delays the wrinkles, nor advancing age,
Nor the invincible hand of Death.
(Eheu fugaces, Postume, Postume,
Labuntur anni, nec pietas moram
Rugis et instanti senectæ
Adferet indomitæque morti.)
HORACE, *Odes.* Bk. ii, ode 14, l. 1.

What Horace says is, *Eheu fugaces,*
Anni labuntur, Postume, Postume!
Years glide away and are lost to me, lost to me!
R. H. BARHAM, *Epigram: Eheu Fugaces.*

6
Even while we speak, envious Time has fled.
(Dum loquimur, fugerit invidia ætas.)
HORACE, *Odes.* Bk. i, ode ii, l. 7.

While I am speaking, the hour flies. (Dum loquor, hora fugit.)
OVID, *Amores.* Bk. i, eleg. 11, l. 15.

Time flies and draws us with it. The moment in which I am speaking is already far from me.
(Le temps fuit, et nous traîne avec soi:
Le moment où je parle est déjà loin de moi.)
BOILEAU, *Épîtres.* No. iii, l. 47.

Even now, while I write, time steals on our youth,
And a moment's cut off from thy friendship and truth.
JOHN HERVEY, *To a Friend.*

Just while we talk the jealous hours
Are bringing near the hearse and flowers.
ALBERT FOX, JR., *Time.*

7
O for an engine to keep back all clocks.
BEN JONSON, *The New Inn.* Act iv, sc. 3.

I never had a watch nor any other mode of keeping time in my possession, nor ever wish to learn how time goes. . . . When I am in a town, I can hear the clock; and when I am in the country, I can listen to the silence.
WILLIAM HAZLITT, *On a Sun-Dial.*

A handful of red sand from the hot clime
Of Arab deserts brought,
Within this glass becomes the spy of Time,
The minister of Thought.
LONGFELLOW, *Sand of the Desert in an Hour-Glass.* St. 1.

8
The noiseless foot of Time steals swiftly by,
And, ere we dream of manhood, age is nigh!
JUVENAL, *Satires.* Sat. ix, l. 182. (Gifford, tr.)

We are old, and on our quick'st decrees
The inaudible and noiseless foot of Time
Steals ere we can effect them.
SHAKESPEARE, *All's Well that Ends Well.* Act v, sc. 3, l. 39.

Nought treads so silent as the foot of Time.
YOUNG, *Love of Fame.* Sat. v, l. 497.

9
Time's horses gallop down the lessening hill.
RICHARD LE GALLIENNE, *Time Flies.*

10
Time! what an empty vapor 'tis!
And days, how swift they are.
ABRAHAM LINCOLN, *Time.*

11
But at my back I always hear
Time's wingèd chariot hurrying near.
ANDREW MARVELL, *To His Coy Mistress.*

12
However we pass Time, he passes still,
Passing away whatever the pastime,
And, whether we use him well or ill,
Some day he gives us the slip for the last time.
OWEN MEREDITH, *The Dead Pope.*

13
Ah, well! when time is flown, how it fled
It is better neither to ask nor tell.
Leave the dead moments to bury their dead.
OWEN MEREDITH, *The Wanderer: Two Out of the Crowd.* St. 17. *See also under* PAST.

14
Time slips by, and we grow old with the silent years; there is no bridle can curb the flying days. (Tempora labuntur, tacitisque senescimus annis, Et fugiunt freno non remorante dies.)
OVID, *Fasti.* Bk. vi, l. 771.

Mourn the swiftness of time. We sit and we sleep, toiling or taking our delight, and time is ever advancing, bringing to each the end of life.
PALLADAS. (*Greek Anthology.* Bk. x, epig. 81.)

15
The happier the time, the more quickly it passes. (Tanto brevius omne quanto felicius tempus.)
PLINY THE YOUNGER, *Epistles.* Bk. viii, epis. 14, sec. 4.

The clock does not strike for the happy. (Die Uhr schlägt keinem Glücklichen.)
SCHILLER, *Piccolomini.* Act iii, sc. 3.

1
Time. like a flurry of wild rain,
Shall drift across the darkened pane!
CHARLES G. D. ROBERTS, *The Unsleeping*.

2
Time flies on restless pinions—constant never.
Be constant—and thou chainest time forever.
SCHILLER, *Epigram*.

3
All past time is lost time; the very day which we are now spending is shared between ourselves and death. (Quicquid transit temporis, perit; hunc ipsum, quem agimus, diem cum morte dividimus.)
SENECA, *Epistulæ ad Lucilium*. Epis. xxiv, 20.

4
Infinitely swift is the flight of time, as they see who look back at it. (Infinita est velocitas temporis, quæ magis apparet respicientibus.)
SENECA, *Epistulæ ad Lucilium*. Epis. xlix, 2.

Note the rapidity of Time—that swiftest of things. (Respice celeritatem rapidissimi temporis.)
SENECA, *Epistulæ ad Lucilium*. Epis. xcix, 7.

5
Time rolls swiftly ahead, and rolls us with it. (Agit nos agiturque velox dies.)
SENECA, *Epistulæ ad Lucilium*. Epis. cviii, 24.

The wheel of time rolls downward through various changes. (Per varios præceps casus rota volvitur.)
SILIUS ITALICUS, *Punica*. Bk. vi, l. 121.

Time rolls his ceaseless course.
SCOTT, *The Lady of the Lake*. Canto iii, st. 1.

6
The inconstant hour flies on double wings. (Volat ambiguis mobilis alis Hora.)
SENECA, *Hippolytus*, l. 1141.

Time's fatal wings do ever forward fly;
To every day we live, a day we die.
CAMPION, *Divine and Moral Songs*. No. 17.

Time, as he passes us, has a dove's wing,
Unsoil'd, and swift, and of a silken sound.
COWPER, *The Task*. Bk. iv, l. 211.

7
See the minutes, how they run,
How many make the hour full complete;
How many hours bring about the day;
How many days will finish up the year;
How many years a mortal man may live.
SHAKESPEARE, *III Henry VI*. Act ii, sc 5, l. 25.

So minutes, hours, days, months, and years,
Pass'd over to the end they were created,
Would bring white hairs unto a quiet grave.
Ah, what a life were this! how sweet! how lovely!
SHAKESPEARE, *III Henry VI*. Act ii, sc. 5, l. 38.

8
Time is like a fashionable host
That slightly shakes his parting guest by the hand,
And with his arms outstretch'd, as he would fly,
Grasps in the comer: welcome ever smiles,
And farewell goes out sighing.
SHAKESPEARE, *Troilus and Cressida*, iii, 3, 165.

9
Too late I staid, forgive the crime,—
Unheeded flew the hours;
How noiseless falls the foot of Time
That only treads on flow'rs! . . .
Ah! who to sober measurement
Time's happy swiftness brings,
When birds of Paradise have lent
Their plumage for his wings?
WILLIAM ROBERT SPENCER, *To the Lady Anne Hamilton*.

10
Go to my love, where she is careless laid
Yet in her winter's bower, not well awake;
Tell her the joyous time will not be staid,
Unless she do him by the forelock take.
SPENSER, *Amoretti*. Sonnet lxx. *See also under* OPPORTUNITY.

11
I hate all times, because all times do fly
So fast away, and may not stayèd be,
But as a speedy post that passeth by.
EDMUND SPENSER, *Daphnaïda*, l. 411.

12
Let us alone. Time driveth onward fast,
And in a little while our lips are dumb.
Let us alone. What is it that will last?
All things are taken from us, and become
Portions and parcels of the dreadful past.
Let us alone.
TENNYSON, *The Lotos-Eaters*, l. 43.

13
Our time is a very shadow that passeth away.
Apocrypha: Wisdom of Solomon, ii, 5.

14
God stands winding His lonely horn,
And time and the world are ever in flight;
And love is less kind than the grey twilight,
And hope is less clear than the dew of the morn.
W. B. YEATS, *Into the Twilight*.

15
How swift the shuttle flies, that weaves thy shroud!
YOUNG, *Night Thoughts*. Night iv, l. 809.

Time flies like a weaver's shuttle. (Jih tzŭ ju so.)
UNKNOWN. A Chinese proverb.

16
Laurel-crowned Horatius,
True, how true thy saying:
Swift as wind flies over us
Time, devouring, slaying.
(Lauriger Horatius,
Quam dicisti verum:
Fugit Euro citius
Tempus edax rerum.)
UNKNOWN, *Lauriger Horatius*. (Symonds, tr.)

VII—Time: Its Delay

17
Time goes, you say? Ah no!
Alas, Time stays, *we* go.
AUSTIN DOBSON, *The Paradox of Time*.

1
One would think that time stood still, so slowly does it move. (Stare putes, adeo procedunt tempora tarde.)
OVID, *Tristia*. Bk. v, eleg. 10, l. 5.

2
The small intolerable drums
Of Time are like slow drops descending.
E. A. ROBINSON, *The Poor Relation.*

3
Threefold the stride of Time, from first to last:
Loitering slow, the Future creepeth—
Arrow-swift, the Present sweepeth—
And motionless forever stands the Past.
(Dreifach ist der Schritt der Zeit:
Zögernd kommt die Zukunt hergezogen,
Pfeilschnell ist das Jetzt entflogen,
Ewig still steht die Vergangenheit.)
SCHILLER, *Sprüche des Confucius.*

4
The lazy foot of Time.
SHAKESPEARE, *As You Like It.* Act iii, sc. 2, 322.

5
Time travels in divers paces with divers persons. I'll tell you who Time ambles withal, who Time trots withal, who Time gallops withal, and who he stands still withal.
SHAKESPEARE, *As You Like It.* Act iii, sc. 2, 326.

What a devil hast thou to do with the time of the day? Unless hours were cups of sack and minutes capons and clocks the tongues of bawds and dials the signs of leaping-houses and the blessed sun himself a fair hot wench in flame-coloured taffeta, I see no reason why thou shouldst be so superfluous to demand the time of the day.
SHAKESPEARE, *I Henry IV.* Act i, sc. 2, l. 6.

6
Time, that takes survey of all the world,
Must have a stop.
SHAKESPEARE, *I Henry IV.* Act v, sc. 4, l. 82.

Time goes on crutches till love have all his rites.
SHAKESPEARE, *Much Ado About Nothing.* Act ii, sc. 1, l. 372.

7
Time has fallen asleep in the afternoon sunshine.
ALEXANDER SMITH, *Dreamthorp.* Ch. 1.

8
For Time would, with us, 'stead of sand,
Put filings of steel in his glass,
To dry up the blots of his hand,
And spangle life's page as they pass.
HORACE AND JAMES SMITH, *The Beautiful Incendiary.* St. 12.

9
What a foolish thing is time! And how foolish is man, who would be as angry if time stopped, as if it passed!
SWIFT, *Letter to Vanessa,* 7 Aug., 1722.

Give me no changeless hours, for I know
Moments of earth are sweeter that they go.
HERVEY ALLEN, *Moments.*

VIII—Time: Its Value

10
The greatest sacrifice is the sacrifice of time.
ANTIPHON. (PLUTARCH, *Lives: Antony.*)

11
Time is the measure of business, as money is of wares.
FRANCIS BACON, *Essays: Despatch.*

Time, O my friend, is money! Time wasted can never conduce to money well managed.
BULWER-LYTTON, *Caxtoniana.* Essay 21.

Time is money.
BULWER-LYTTON, *Money.* Act iii, sc. 3.

Remember that time is money.
BENJAMIN FRANKLIN, *Advice to a Young Tradesman.*

12
It [the value of time] is in everybody's mouth, but in few people's practice.
LORD CHESTERFIELD, *Letters,* 11 Dec., 1747.

13
It is the wisest who grieve most at loss of time. (Chè perder tempo a chi più sa più spiace.)
DANTE, *Purgatorio.* Canto iii, l. 78.

14
Dost thou love life? Then do not squander time, for that's the stuff life is made of.
BENJAMIN FRANKLIN, *Poor Richard,* 1758.

15
Pick my left pocket of its silver dime,
But spare the right,—it holds my golden time!
O. W. HOLMES, *A Rhymed Lesson,* l. 324.

16
To the true teacher, time's hour-glass should still run gold-dust.
DOUGLAS JERROLD, *Jerrold's Wit: Time.*

17
Nothing is so dear and precious as time.
RABELAIS, *Works.* Bk. v, ch. 5.

18
Time is the one loan which even a grateful recipient cannot repay. (Qui tempus accepit, cum interum hoc unum est, quod ne gratus quidem potest reddere.)
SENECA, *Epistulæ ad Lucilium.* Epis. i, sec. 3.

19
Save your time. (Tempori parce.)
SENECA, *Epistulæ ad Lucilium.* Epis. lxxxviii, sec. 39. Quoted as an old saw.

20
Time is the most valuable thing a man can spend. (*Συνεχές τε ἔλεγε πολυτελὲς ἀνάλωμα εἶναι τὸν χρόνον.*)
THEOPHRASTUS. (DIOGENES LAERTIUS, *Theophrastus.* Bk. v, sec. 40.)

An inch of time cannot be bought by an inch of gold. ('Tsun chin nan mai 'tsun kuang yin.)
UNKNOWN. A Chinese proverb.

IX—Time: Lost Time Never Returns

21
Well can Senek, and many a philosopher
Bewailen time, more than gold in coffre.
"For loss of cattle may recovered be,
But loss of time shendeth us," quoth he.
It will not come again, withouten drede,

No more than will Malkin's maidenhead.
CHAUCER, *Introduction to the Man of Law's Prologue*, l. 25. Shendeth: ruins. For "Malkin's maidenhead" *see under* MAID.

For time y-lost, this knowen ye,
By no way may recovered be.
CHAUCER, *The Hous of Fame*. Bk. iii, l. 167.

For time y-lost may not recovered be.
CHAUCER, *Troilus and Criseyde*. Bk. iv, l. 1283.

Men may recover loss of good,
But so wise man yet never stood
Which may recover time y-lore.
JOHN GOWER, *Confessio Amantis*. Bk. iv, l. 1382. (c. 1390)

Time departed, again men may not call.
LYDGATE, *Fall of Princes*. Bk. iii, l. 2811. (1440)

1
I hope you employ your whole time, which few people do . . . a thing so precious as time, and so irrecoverable when lost.
LORD CHESTERFIELD, *Letters*, 9 Dec., 1746.

2
Hours and days, and months and years go by, nor does past time ever return. (Horæ cedunt et dies et menses et anni, nec præteritum tempus umquam revertitur.)
CICERO, *De Senectute*. Ch. xix, sec. 69.

Neither will the wave which has passed be called back, nor can the hour which has gone return. (Nec quæ præteriit, iterum revocabitur unda, Nec quæteriit, hora redire potest.)
OVID, *Ars Amatoria*. Bk. iii, l. 63.

Remember that lost time does not return. (Memento . . . perditum non redit tempus.)
À KEMPIS, *De Imitatione Christi*. Pt. i, ch. 25.

Time flies away, and cannot be restored. (Fugit inreparabile tempus.)
VERGIL, *Georgics*. Bk. iii, l. 284.

3
Lost time is never found again.
BENJAMIN FRANKLIN, *Poor Richard*, 1748.

4
Man cannot call the brimming instant back;
Time's an affair of instants spun to days;
If man must make an instant gold, or black,
Let him, he may, but Time must go his ways.
Life may be duller for an instant's blaze.
Life's an affair of instants spun to years,
Instants are only cause of all these tears.
JOHN MASEFIELD, *The Widow in the Bye Street*. Pt. v, st. 27.

Who can undo
What time hath done? who can win back the wind?
Beckon lost music from a broken lute?
Renew the redness of a last year's rose?
Or dig the sunken sunset from the deep?
OWEN MEREDITH, *Orval*. Epoch ii, sc. 1.

5
Would'st thou live long? keep Time in high esteem:
Whom gone, if thou canst not recall, redeem.
FRANCIS QUARLES, *Hieroglyphics of the Life of Man*. Epig. 6.

6
Onward the chariot of the Untarrying moves;
Nor day divulges him nor night conceals;
Thou hearest the echo of unreturning hooves
And thunder of irrevocable wheels.
WILLIAM WATSON, *Epigrams*. No. xvii.

X—Time: Its Use

7
As good have no time, as make no good use of it.
THOMAS FULLER, *Gnomologia*. No. 686.

He that has most time has none to lose.
THOMAS FULLER, *Gnomologia*. No. 2141.

8
He that hath time and looketh for a better time, loseth time. Time comes that he repents himself of time.
GEORGE HERBERT, *Jacula Prudentum*.

By losing present time, we lose all time.
W. G. BENHAM, *Proverbs*, p. 746.

9
No person will have occasion to complain of the want of time who never loses any.
THOMAS JEFFERSON, *Letter to His Daughter*, 5 May, 1787.

10
Those who make the worst use of their time most complain of its shortness.
LA BRUYÈRE, *Les Caractères: Des Jugements*. *See also under* IDLENESS.

11
Take time in time, ere time be tint,
For time will not remain.
ALEXANDER MONTGOMERIE, *Cherrie and Sloe*. St. 36.

Take time when time is, for time is ay mutable.
JOHN SKELTON, *Works*. Vol. i, p. 137.

12
Employ your time; Time glides on with speedy foot. (Utendum est ætate; cito pede labitur ætas.)
OVID, *Ars Amatoria*. Bk. iii, l. 65.

Catch then, oh catch the transient hour;
Improve each moment as it flies!
Life's a short Summer, man a flower;
He dies—alas! how soon he dies!
SAMUEL JOHNSON, *Winter: An Ode*.

The Seconds that tick as the clock moves along
Are Privates who march with a spirit so strong.
The Minutes are Captains. The Hours of the day
Are Officers brave, who lead on to the fray.
So, remember, when tempted to loiter and dream
You've an army at hand; your command is supreme;
And question yourself, as it goes on review—
Has it helped in the fight with the best it could do?
PHILANDER JOHNSON, *Each Man's Army*. Selected by Admiral Samuel MacGowan to be distributed to the men under his command during the World War. (*Everybody's Magazine*, May, 1920, p. 36.)

1
He briskly and cheerfully asked him how a man should kill time.
RABELAIS, *Works*. Bk. iv, ch. 63.

2
Ordinary people think merely how they will *spend* their time; a man of intellect tries to *use* it.
SCHOPENHAUER, *Aphorisms on the Wisdom of Life*.

3
The clock upbraids me with a waste of time.
SHAKESPEARE, *Twelfth Night*. Act iii, sc. 1, l. 141.

The time best employed is that which one wastes. (Le temps le mieux employé est celui qu'on perd.)
CLAUDE TELLIER. (Quoted by AUSTIN DOBSON, *A Dialogue from Plato*.)

4
What greater crime than loss of time?
THOMAS TUSSER, *Five Hundred Points of Good Husbandry: January's Abstract*.

5
Ease from this noble miser of his time
No moment steals; pain narrows not his cares.
WORDSWORTH, *Sonnet: Alfred*.

6
We take no note of time But from its loss.
YOUNG, *Night Thoughts*. Night i, l. 55.

Spendthrifts of inestimable time.
YOUNG, *Night Thoughts*. Night ii, l. 273.

7
Time wasted is existence, us'd is life.
YOUNG, *Night Thoughts*. Night ii, l. 150.

Time destroy'd
Is suicide, where more than blood is spilt.
Time flies, death urges, knells call, heaven invites,
Hell threatens.
YOUNG, *Night Thoughts*. Night ii, l. 290.

8
In time take time while time doth last,
For time is no time when time is past.
UNKNOWN. Written on the title page of his account book by Nicholas Stone, mason to James I.

XI—Time: Gather Ye Rosebuds

See Also Life and Living; Opportunity

9
Gather the roses, maiden, while the blooms are fresh and youth is fresh, and be mindful that in like fashion your lifetime hastes away. (Collige, virgo, rosas, dum flos novus et nova pubes,
Et memor esto ævum sic properare tuum.)
AUSONIUS [?], *De Rosis Nascentibus*, l. 49.

And sport, sweet maid, in season of these years,
And learn to gather flowers before they wither.
SAMUEL DANIEL, *Sonnets to Delia*. No. xlviii.

10
Gather roses while they bloom,
To-morrow is yet far away!
(Pflücke Rosen, weil sie blühn,
Morgen ist nicht heut!)
JOHAN GLEIM, *Benutzung der Zeit*.

11
Gather ye Rose-buds while ye may,
Old Time is still aflying:
And this same flower that smiles to-day,
To-morrow will be dying. . . .

Then be not coy, but use your time,
And while ye may, go marry:
For having lost but once your prime,
You may for ever tarry.
ROBERT HERRICK, *To the Virgins, to Make Much of Time*.

12
If you let slip time, like a neglected rose,
It withers on the stalk with languish'd head.
MILTON, *Comus*, l. 743.

13
Pluck the grapes hanging from the well-stocked vines. (Carpite de plenis pendentes vitibus uvas.)
OVID, *Amores*. Bk. i, eleg. 10, l. 55.

Pluck the flower. (Carpite florem.)
OVID, *Ars Amatoria*. Bk. iii, l. 79.

While you are upon earth, enjoy the good things that are here.
JOHN SELDEN, *Table-Talk: Pleasure*.

14
Make haste nor wait the coming hours; he who is unready today will be more so to-morrow. (Sed propera, nec te venturas differ in horas; Qui non est hodie, cras minus aptus erit.)
OVID, *Remediorum Amoris*, l. 93.

15
Sweet lady mine! while yet 'tis time,
Requite my passion and my truth,
And gather in their blushing prime
The roses of your youth.
RONSARD, *Lines to His Mistress*. (Thackeray, tr.)

16
Make use of time, let not advantage slip;
Beauty within itself should not be wasted:
Fair flowers that are not gather'd in their prime,
Rot and consume themselves in little time.
SHAKESPEARE, *Venus and Adonis*, l. 129.

17
Gather therefore the rose whilest yet is prime,
For soon comes age, that will her pride deflower.
SPENSER, *Faerie Queene*. Bk. ii, canto 12, st. 75.

18
Life let us cherish, while yet the taper glows,
And the fresh flow'ret pluck ere it close.
JOHANN USTERI, *Life Let Us Cherish*.

19
Let us crown ourselves with rose-buds, before they be withered.
Apocrypha: Wisdom of Solomon, ii, 8. (Coronemus nos rosis, antequam marcescant.—*Vulgate: Liber Sapientiæ*, ii, 8.)

20
Therefore fear not to assay
To gather, ye that may,

The flower that this day
Is fresher than the next.

Sir Thomas Wyatt, *That the Season of Enjoyment Is Short.*

XII—Time: The Consoler

1

Backward, turn backward, O Time, in your flight,
Make me a child again just for to-night!

Elizabeth Akers Allen, *Rock Me to Sleep.* Fraudulently claimed by Alexander M. W. Ball. (See Stevenson, *Famous Single Poems.*)

Backward, flow backward, O tide of the years!
I am so weary of toil and of tears—
Toil without recompense, tears all in vain—
Take them and give me my childhood again!
I have grown weary of dust and decay,
Weary of flinging my soul-wealth away,
Weary of sowing for others to reap;
Rock me to sleep, mother—rock me to sleep!

Elizabeth Akers Allen, *Rock Me to Sleep.*

2

Time, so complain'd of,
Who to no one man
Shows partiality,
Brings round to all men
Some undimm'd hours.

Matthew Arnold, *Consolation,* l. 71.

3

O Time! the beautifier of the dead,
Adorner of the ruin, comforter
And only healer when the heart hath bled—
Time! the corrector where our judgments err,
The test of truth, love,—sole philosopher,
For all beside are sophists, from thy thrift
Which never loses though it doth defer—
Time, the avenger! unto thee I lift
My hands, and eyes, and heart, and crave of thee a gift.

Byron, *Childe Harold.* Canto iv, st. 130.

4

There is no remembrance which time does not obliterate, nor pain which death does not end. (No ay memoria à quien el tiempo no acabe, ni dolor que nuerte no le consuma.)

Cervantes, *Don Quixote.* Pt. iii, ch. 1.

As time him hurt, a time doth him cure.

Chaucer, *Troilus and Criseyde,* v, 350.

5

To things immortal, Time can do no wrong,
And that which never is to die, for ever must be young.

Abraham Cowley, *To Mr. Hobbes.*

6

See! Time has touch'd me gently in his race,
And left no odious furrows in my face.

Crabbe, *Tales of the Hall.* Bk. xvii, st. 3.

Touch us gently, Time!
Let us glide down thy stream
Gently,—as we sometimes glide
Through a quiet dream.

Bryan Waller Procter, *Touch Us Gently.*

I recognize that face,
Though Time has touched it in his flight.

Longfellow, *The Golden Legend.* Pt. iv, l. 11.

Time has laid his hand
Upon my heart, gently, not smiting it,
But as a harper lays his open palm
Upon his harp, to deaden its vibrations.

Longfellow, *The Golden Legend.* Pt. iv, *The Cloisters,* l. 77.

7

Softened by Time's consummate plush,
How sleek the woe appears
That threatened childhood's citadel
And undermined the years!

Emily Dickinson, *Poems.* Pt. i, No. 138.

Look back on time with kindly eyes,
He doubtless did his best;
How softly sinks his trembling sun
In human nature's west!

Emily Dickinson, *Poems.* Pt. iv, No. 8.

8

Time is a test of trouble,
But not a remedy.
If such it prove, it prove too
There was no malady.

Emily Dickinson, *Poems.* Pt. iv, No. 85.

9

Time will bring healing. (Χρόνος μαλάξει.)

Euripides, *Alcestis,* l. 1085.

Time eases many a smart. (Multa vestutas Lenit.)

Ovid, *Ars Amatoria.* Bk. ii, l. 647.

Time is generally the best medicine. (Temporis ars medicina fere est.)

Ovid, *Remediorum Amoris,* l. 131.

Time takes away the grief of men. (Dies adimit ægritudinem hominibus.)

Erasmus, *Adagia.*

Time is an herb that cures all diseases.

Benjamin Franklin, *Poor Richard,* 1738.

10

Hush—'tis the lullaby Time is singing—
Hush, and heed not, for all things pass.

Andrew Lang, *Scythe Song.*

11

Time and reflection cure all ills.

George Lillo, *London Merchant.* Act v, sc. 2.

Time and thinking tame the strongest grief.

W. C. Hazlitt, *English Proverbs,* p. 405.

12

Time, sovereign physician of our passions. (Le temps . . . souverain médecin de nos passions.)

Montaigne, *Essays.* Bk. iii, ch. 4.

Time is the great physician.

Benjamin Disraeli, *Henrietta Temple.* Bk. vi, ch. 9.

13

Time softly there
Laughs through the abyss of radiance with the gods.

William Vaughn Moody, *Fire-Bringer.* Act i.

14

See how time makes all grief decay.

Adelaide Ann Procter, *Life in Death.* *See also under* Grief.

15

Time consecrates;
What is grey with age becomes religion.

Schiller, *Die Piccolomini.* Act iv, sc. 4. (Coleridge, tr.)

1
That saying which I hear commonly repeated, —that time assuages sorrow.
TERENCE, *Heauton Timorumenos.* Act iii, sc. 1, l. 12. *See also under* SORROW.

2
Time passes, Time the consoler, Time the anodyne.
THACKERAY, *Sketches in London: Pleasures of Being a Fogy.*

XIII—Time: The Destroyer

3
Time dissolves all things, and makes them old. (Κατατήκει ὁ χρόνος, καὶ γηράσκει πάντα.)
ARISTOTLE, *Physica.* Bk. iv, ch. 12, sec. 12.

What's not destroy'd by Time's devouring hand?
Where's Troy, and where's the Maypole in the Strand?
JAMES BRAMSTON, *Art of Politics.*

Time destroys the groundless conceits of men. (Opinionum enim commenta delet dies.)
CICERO, *De Natura Deorum.* Bk. ii, ch. 2, sec. 5.

What does not destructive time destroy? (Damnosa quid non imminuit dies?)
HORACE, *Odes.* Bk. iii, ode 6, l. 45.

Time that devours all things. (Tempus edax rerum.)
OVID, *Metamorphoses.* Bk. xv, l. 234.

Time conquers all, and we must Time obey.
POPE, *Pastorals: Winter,* l. 88.

4
How many noble thoughts,
How many precious feelings of man's heart,
How many loves, how many gratitudes,
Do twenty years wear out, and see expire!
MATTHEW ARNOLD, *Merope,* l. 177.

5
Alas! how the soul sentimental it vexes,
That thus on our labours stern Chronos should frown,
Should change our soft liquids to izzards and Xes,
And turn true-love's alphabet all upside down!
R. H. BARHAM, *The Poplar.*

6
Out upon Time! it will leave no more
Of the things to come than the things before!
Out upon Time! who for ever will leave
But enough of the past for the future to grieve.
BYRON, *The Siege of Corinth.* St. 18.

7
The rust will find the sword of fame,
The dust will hide the crown;
Ay, none shall nail so high his name
Time will not tear it down.
JOHN VANCE CHENEY, *The Happiest Heart.*

8
Time . . . with his silent sickle.
DRYDEN, *Astræa Redux,* l. 110.

You talk of the scythe of Time, and the tooth of Time: I tell you Time is scytheless and toothless; it is we who gnaw like the worm, we who smite like the scythe.
RUSKIN, *A Joy Forever.* Lecture ii, p. 83.

9
Each passing year robs us of some possession. (Singula de nobis anni prædantur euntes.)
HORACE, *Epistles.* Bk. ii, epis. 2, l. 55.

10
Time's corrosive dew-drop eats
The giant warrior to a crust
Of earth in earth and rust in rust.
F. T. PALGRAVE, *A Danish Barrow.*

11
Man yields to death; and man's sublimest works
Must yield at length to Time.
THOMAS LOVE PEACOCK, *Time,* l. 56.

Time is lord of thee:
Thy wealth, thy glory, and thy name are his.
THOMAS LOVE PEACOCK, *Time,* l. 71.

12
Before my breath, like blazing flax,
Man and his marvels pass away;
And changing empires wane and wax,
Are founded, flourish, and decay.
SCOTT, *The Antiquary.* Ch. 11.

13
Cormorant devouring Time.
SHAKESPEARE, *Love's Labour's Lost.* Act i, sc. 1, l. 4.

Devouring Time, . . . Swift-footed Time, . . .
Yet, do thy worst, old Time.
SHAKESPEARE, *Sonnets.* No. xix.

The tooth of time.
EDWARD YOUNG, *The Statesman's Creed.*

14
Time's the king of men,
He's both their parent, and he is their grave,
And gives them what he will, not what they crave.
SHAKESPEARE, *Pericles.* Act ii, sc. 3, l. 45.

15
Mis-shapen Time, copesmate of ugly Night,
Swift subtle post, carrier of grisly care,
Eater of youth, false slave to false delight,
Base watch of woes, sin's pack-horse, virtue's snare;
Thou nursest all and murder'st all that are.
SHAKESPEARE, *The Rape of Lucrece,* l. 925.

Time's glory is to calm contending kings,
To unmask falsehood and bring truth to light,
To stamp the seal of time in aged things,
To wake the morn and sentinel the night,
To wrong the wronger till he render right,
To ruinate proud buildings with thy hours,
And smear with dust their glittering golden towers.
SHAKESPEARE, *The Rape of Lucrece,* l. 939.

16
Time hath, my lord, a wallet at his back,
Wherein he puts alms for oblivion,
A great-sized monster of ingratitudes:
These scraps are good deeds past; which are devour'd

As fast as they are made, forgot as soon
As done.

SHAKESPEARE, *Troilus and Cressida*. Act iii, sc. 3, l. 145.

Beauty, wit,
High birth, vigour of bone, desert in service,
Love, friendship, charity, are subjects all
To envious and calumniating time.

SHAKESPEARE, *Troilus and Cressida*. Act iii, sc. 3, l. 171.

1
Unfathomable Sea, whose waves are years;
Ocean of Time, whose waters of deep woe
Are brackish with the salt of human tears!
Thou shoreless flood, which in thy ebb and flow
Claspest the limits of mortality!
And sick of prey, yet howling on for more,
Vomitest thy wrecks on its inhospitable shore;
Treacherous in calm, and terrible in storm,
Who shall put forth on thee,
Unfathomable Sea?

SHELLEY, *Time*.

2
Ever eating, never cloying,
All-devouring, all-destroying,
Never finding full repast,
Till I eat the world at last.

SWIFT, *On Time*.

3
In vain men tell us time can alter
Old loves or make old memories falter.

A. C. SWINBURNE, *Age and Song*.

XIV—Time and Eternity

4
He said, "What's time? Leave Now for dogs and apes!
Man has Forever."

ROBERT BROWNING, *A Grammarian's Funeral*.

Fool! All that is, at all,
Lasts ever, past recall;
Earth changes, but thy soul and God stand sure:
What entered into thee,
That was, is, and shall be:
Time's wheel runs back nor stops: Potter and clay endure.

ROBERT BROWNING, *Rabbi Ben Ezra*. St. 27.

5
Behind, he hears Time's iron gates close faintly, . . .
For he has reached the city of the saintly,
The New Jerusalem.

JAMES D. BURNS. *The Vision of Prophecy: Poem of a Death Believer*.

Time for him had merged itself into eternity; he was, as we say, no more.

THOMAS CARLYLE, *Characteristics*.

His time's forever, everywhere his place.

ABRAHAM COWLEY, *Friendship in Absence*.

6
Mere by-blows are the world and we,
And time, within eternity,
A sheer anachronism.

JOHN DAVIDSON, *Queen Elizabeth's Day*.

7
Somewhat back from the village street
Stands the old-fashioned country-seat.
Across its antique portico
Tall poplar-trees their shadows throw;
And from its station in the hall
An ancient timepiece says to all,—
"Forever—never!
Never—forever!"

LONGFELLOW, *The Old Clock on the Stairs*.

The horologe of Eternity
Sayeth this incessantly,—
"Forever—never!
Never—forever!"

LONGFELLOW, *The Old Clock on the Stairs*.

8
Day and night,
Seed-time and harvest, heat and hoary frost
Shall hold their course, till fire purge all things new.

MILTON, *Paradise Lost*. Bk. xi, l. 894.

9
Time is Eternity begun.

JAMES MONTGOMERY, *A Mother's Love*. St. 8.

See also under ETERNITY.

10
Time was created as an image of eternity. (Χρόνον τε γενέσθαι εἰκόνα τοῦ ἀϊδίου.)

PLATO. (DIOGENES LAERTIUS, *Plato*. Bk. iii, sec. 73.)

Time is a child of eternity, and resembles its parent as much as it can.

DEAN W. R. INGE. (MARCHANT, *Wit and Wisdom of Dean Inge*. No. 33.)

11
Make use of time if thou lov'st eternity.

FRANCIS QUARLES, *Enchiridion*.

12
"Time restores all things." Wrong! Time restores many things, but eternity restores all.

JOSEPH ROUX, *Meditations of a Parish Priest: Time, Life, Death, The Future*. No. 8.

13
I dimly guess what Time in mists confounds;
Yet ever and anon a trumpet sounds
From the hid battlements of Eternity;
Those shaken mists a space unsettle, then
Round the half-glimpsèd turrets slowly wash again.

FRANCIS THOMPSON, *Hound of Heaven*, l. 143.

14
Time is eternity;
Pregnant with all eternity can give;
Pregnant with all that makes archangels smile.
Who murders Time, he crushes in the birth
A power ethereal, only not ador'd.

YOUNG, *Night Thoughts*. Night ii, l. 107.

XV—Time and Man

15
When Time shall turn those amber locks to grey,

My verse again shall gild and make them gay.
MICHAEL DRAYTON, *Henry Howard, Earl of Surrey, to the Lady Geraldine*, l. 123.

Time has . . . changed the auburn hair to white.
LONGFELLOW, *The Golden Legend*. Pt. iv, *The Chapel*, l. 12.

His golden locks Time hath to silver turn'd;
O Time too swift, O swiftness never ceasing!
GEORGE PEELE, *Polyhymnia*.

Time wastes too fast: . . . everything presses on—whilst thou art twisting that lock, see, it grows grey!
STERNE, *Tristram Shandy*. Bk. ix, ch. 8.

Time flies, my pretty one! . . . Now, even as thou twinest that brown curl on that finger—see! it grows grey!
FREDERICK LOCKER-LAMPSON, *My Confidences*.

1
Alas! it is not till time, with reckless hand, has torn out half the leaves from the Book of Human Life, to light the fires of passion with, from day to day, that man begins to see that the leaves which remain are few in number.
LONGFELLOW, *Hyperion*. Bk. iv, ch. 8.

2
Time, eftsoon will tumble
All of us together like leaves in a gust,
Humbled indeed down into the dust.
JOAQUIN MILLER, *Fallen Leaves*. St. 5.

3
Let time that makes you homely, make you sage.
THOMAS PARNELL, *Elegy to an Old Beauty*. l. 35.

4
Years following years steal something ev'ry day.
At last they steal us from ourselves away.
POPE, *Imitations of Horace: Epistles*. Bk. ii, epis. 2, l. 72.

5
Even such is Time, that takes in trust
Our youth, our joys, our all we have,
And pays us but with earth and dust;
Who in the dark and silent grave,
When we have wander'd all our ways,
Shuts up the story of our days;
But from this earth, this grave, this dust,
My God shall raise me up, I trust.
SIR WALTER RALEIGH, *The Conclusion*. Written the night before his death. Found in his Bible in the Gate-house at Westminster.

6
Poets and kings are but the clerks of Time,
Tiering the same dull webs of discontent,
Clipping the same sad alnage of the years.
EDWIN ARLINGTON ROBINSON, *The Clerks*.

7
Time doth transfix the flourish set on youth
And delves the parallels in beauty's brow.
SHAKESPEARE, *Sonnets*. No. lx.

8
O, how shall summer's honey breath hold out
Against the wreckful siege of battering days,
When rocks impregnable are not so stout,
Nor gates of steel so strong, but Time decays?
O fearful meditation! where, alack,
Shall Time's best jewel from Time's chest lie hid?
Or what strong hand can hold his swift foot back?
Or who his spoil of beauty can forbid?
SHAKESPEARE, *Sonnets*. No. lxv.

XVI—Time: The Times

See also under Age, The

9
All times are not alike. (No son todos los Tiempos unos.)
CERVANTES, *Don Quixote*. Pt. ii, ch. 35.

10
Can ye not discern the signs of the times?
New Testament: Matthew, xvi, 3.

11
Be a child o' the time.
SHAKESPEARE, *Antony and Cleopatra*. Act ii, sc. 7, l. 105.

The time is out of joint.
SHAKESPEARE, *Hamlet*. Act i, sc. 5, l. 189.

12
The times are big with tidings.
ROBERT SOUTHEY, *Roderick*. Sec. 20, l. 1.

TIMIDITY

See also Cowardice, Indecision

13
Bashfulness is an ornament to youth, but a reproach to old age.
ARISTOTLE. (MONTAIGNE, *Essays*. Bk. iii, ch. 5.)

Bashfulness and apathy are a tough husk in which a delicate organization is protected from premature ripening.
EMERSON, *Essays, First Series: Friendship*.

14
I went darkling, and whistling to keep myself from being afraid.
DRYDEN, *Amphitryon*. Act iii, sc. 1.

15
He that observeth the wind shall not sow; and he that regardeth the clouds shall not reap.
Old Testament: Ecclesiastes, xi, 4.

16
Faint-hearted men never erect a trophy. ('Αλλ' *οἱ γὰρ ἀθυμοῦντες ἄνδρες οὔποτε Τρόπαιον ἐστήσαντο*.)
EUPOLIS, *Fragment*.

The timid never set up a trophy. (Timidi nunquam statuerunt trophæum.)
ERASMUS, *Adagia*.

Great empires are not maintained by timidity. (Non enim ignavia magna imperia contineri.)
TACITUS, *Annals*. Bk. xv, sec. 1.

17
Great bashfulness is oftener the effect of pride than of modesty.
LORD HALIFAX, *Works*, p. 245.

No cause more frequently produces bashfulness than too high an opinion of our own importance.
SAMUEL JOHNSON, *The Rambler*. No. 159.

1
Refusing to accept as great a share
Of hazard as of honour.
MILTON, *Paradise Lost*. Bk. ii, l. 452.

2
Ah, the folly of entrusting a weighty venture to a timid heart! (Nam ea stultiast, facinus magnum timido cordi credere.)
PLAUTUS, *Pseudolus*, l. 577. (Act ii, sc. 1.)

3
The timid man calls himself cautious, the sordid man thrifty. (Timidus se vocat cautum, parcum sordidus.)
PUBLILIUS SYRUS, *Sententiæ*. No. 689.

The timid sees dangers which do not even exist. (Pericla timidus etiam quæ non sunt videt.)
PUBLILIUS SYRUS, *Sententiæ*. No. 491.

4
Bashfulness is an enemy to poverty.
JOHN RAY, *English Proverbs*, p. 2.

Poverty has no greater foe than bashfulness.
GEORGE HERBERT, *Jacula Prudentum*.

5
To the timid and hesitating everything is impossible because it seems so.
SCOTT, *Rob Roy*. Ch. 16.

6
Who timidly requests invites refusal. (Qui timide rogat Docet negare.)
SENECA, *Hippolytus*, l. 593.

To get thine ends, lay bashfulness aside;
Who fears to ask, doth teach to be deny'd.
ROBERT HERRICK, *No Bashfulness in Begging*.

He teaches to deny that faintly prays.
FRANCIS QUARLES, *A Feast for Worms*. Sec. 7.

7
But I am pigeon-liver'd, and lack gall.
SHAKESPEARE, *Hamlet*. Act ii, sc. 2, l. 604.

Sure he is a pigeon, for he has no gall.
THOMAS DEKKER, *The Honest Whore*. Pt. i, act i, sc. 5.

Milk-liver'd man!
That bear'st a cheek for blows, a head for wrongs:
Who hast not in thy brows an eye discerning
Thine honour from thy suffering.
SHAKESPEARE, *King Lear*. Act iv, sc. 2, l. 50.

Thou wilt be as valiant as the wrathful dove or most magnanimous mouse.
SHAKESPEARE, *II Henry IV*. Act iii, sc. 2, l. 170.

8
The attempt and not the deed Confounds us.
SHAKESPEARE, *Macbeth*. Act ii, sc. 2, l. 11.

9
O, these flaws and starts,
Impostors to true fear, would well become
A woman's story at a winter's fire,
Authorized by her grandam.
SHAKESPEARE, *Macbeth*. Act iii, sc. 4, l. 63.

10
Tommy's tears and Mary's fears
Will make them old before their years.
UNKNOWN, *Old Nursery Rhyme*.

TITLES

See also Ancestry, Honors, Nobility

11
All titles terminate in prescription.
EDMUND BURKE, *Letter to Richard Burke*.

Prescription is the most solid of all titles.
EDMUND BURKE, *Speech*, 7 May, 1782.

12
I have henceforward the privilege of adding to my name the honourable title of A double S.
GEORGE COLMAN THE YOUNGER, *The Heir-at-Law*. Act i, sc. 1.

There was one also for me from Mr. Blackburne; who with his own hand superscribes it to S. P., Esq., of which God knows I was not a little proud.
SAMUEL PEPYS, *Diary*, 25 March, 1660.

The College has konfired upon me the honery title of T. K., of which I'm suffishuntly prowd.
ARTEMUS WARD, *Artemus Ward His Book: Oberlin*.

13
Rank is a great beautifier.
BULWER-LYTTON, *The Lady of Lyons*. Act ii, sc. 1.

Oh! a Baronet's rank is exceedingly nice,
But the title's uncommonly dear at the price!
W. S. GILBERT, *Ruddigore*. Act ii.

14
Princes and lords are but the breath of kings.
BURNS, *The Cotter's Saturday Night*, l. 165.

A prince can mak a belted knight,
A marquis, duke, and a' that;
But an honest man's aboon his might,
Guid faith, he maunna fa' that!
BURNS, *For a' That and a' That. See also under* GENTLEMAN.

The rank is but the guinea's stamp,
The Man's the gowd for a' that.
BURNS, *For a' That and a' That*.

Honours, like impressions upon coin, may give an ideal and local value to a bit of base metal; but gold and silver will pass all the world over without any other recommendation than their own weight.
LAURENCE STERNE, *Tristram Shandy:* Bk. ix, *Dedication*. The sentence which is said to have inspired Burns's lines.

15
To lead or brass, or some such bad
Metal, a prince's stamp may add
That value, which it never had;
But to the pure refined ore
The stamp of kings imparts no more
Worth than the metal held before.
THOMAS CAREW, *To T. H., A Lady Resembling My Mistress*.

16
Proud of the title, as the Living Skeleton said ven they showed him.
DICKENS, *Pickwick Papers*. Ch. 15.

1
A successive title, long and dark,
Drawn from the mouldy rolls of Noah's Ark.
DRYDEN, *Absalom and Achitophel*. Pt. i, l. 301.

2
Such is their [the monarchs of Europe] passion for a long list of these splendid trifles, that I have known a German Prince with more titles than subjects, and a Spanish nobleman with more names than shirts.
GOLDSMITH, *Citizen of the World*. Letter cxx.

3
A king may spill, a king may save;
A king may make of lord a knave;
And of a knave a lord also.
JOHN GOWER, *Confessio Amantis*. Bk. vii, l. 1895.

4
Empty phrases and frivolities,
As common as gold lace upon the collar
Of an obsequious lackey.
LONGFELLOW, *Michael Angelo*. Pt. i, sec. 2.

5
For titles do not reflect honor on men, but rather men on their titles. (Perchè non i titoli illustrano gli uomini, ma gli uomini i titoli.)
MACHIAVELLI, *Dei Discorsi*. Pt. iii, sec. 38.

Titles of honour add not to his worth,
Who is himself an honour to his titles.
JOHN FORD, *The Lady's Trial*. Act i, sc. 3, l. 30.

He being pure and tried gold; and any stamp
Of grace, to make him current to the world,
The duke is pleased to give him, will add honour
To the great bestower.
PHILIP MASSINGER, *The Great Duke of Florence*. Act i, sc. 1.

6
Stuck o'er with titles, and hung round with strings,
That thou mayst be by kings, or whores of kings.
POPE, *Essay on Man*. Epis. iv, l. 205.

7
Known men are greater than mere noblemen. (Noti magis quam nobiles sunt.)
SENECA, *De Beneficiis*. Bk. iii, sec. 28.

An earl by right, by courtesy a man.
ALFRED AUSTIN, *The Season*.

8
Knighthoods and honours, borne
As I wear mine, are titles but of scorn.
SHAKESPEARE, *Cymbeline*. Act v, sc. 2, l. 6.

What think you of a duchess? have you limbs
To bear that load of title?
SHAKESPEARE, *Henry VIII*. Act ii, sc. 3, l. 38.

Now does he feel his title
Hang loose about him, like a giant's robe
Upon a dwarfish thief.
SHAKESPEARE, *Macbeth*. Act v, sc. 2, l. 20.

9
Nor never title yet so mean could prove,
But there was eke a mind which did that title love.
WILLIAM SHENSTONE, *The Schoolmistress*. St. 9.

10
Of the king's creation you may be; but he who makes a count, ne'er made a man.
THOMAS SOUTHERNE, *Sir Anthony Love*. Act ii, sc. 1.

11
Virtue is honour, and the noblest titles
Are but the public stamps set on the ore
To ascertain its value to mankind.
GILBERT WEST, *Institution of the Garter*, l. 335.

I weigh the man, not his title; 'tis not the king's stamp can make the metal better or heavier.
WYCHERLEY, *The Plain-Dealer*. Act i, sc. 1.

12
Rank is a farce: if people Fools will be,
A Scavenger and King 's the same to me.
JOHN WOLCOT, *Peter's Prophecy*. Title page.

13
Titles are marks of honest men, and wise;
The fool, or knave, that wears a title, lies.
YOUNG, *Love of Fame*. Sat. i, l. 145.

TOBACCO

I—Tobacco: Its Delights

14
By thee protected, and thy sister beer,
Poets rejoice, nor think the bailiff near.
ISAAC H. BROWNE, *The Oxford Sausage*.

15
The man who smokes, thinks like a sage and acts like a *Samaritan!*
BULWER-LYTTON, *Night and Morning*. Bk. i, ch. 6.

He who doth not smoke hath either known no great griefs, or refuseth himself the softest consolation, next to that which comes from heaven.
BULWER-LYTTON, *What Will He Do With It?* Bk. i, ch. 6.

16
Tobacco, divine, rare, superexcellent tobacco, which goes far beyond all the panaceas, potable gold, and philosopher's stones, a sovereign remedy to all diseases; . . . but as it is commonly abused by most men, which take it as tinkers do ale, 'tis a plague, a mischief, a violent purger of goods, lands, health; hellish, devilish and damned tobacco, the ruin and overthrow of body and soul.
ROBERT BURTON, *Anatomy of Melancholy*. Pt. ii, sec. iv, mem. 2, subs. 1.

17
I have a liking old
For thee, though manifold
Stories, I know, are told,
Not to thy credit;
How one (or two at most)
Drops make a cat a ghost—
Useless, except to roast—
Doctors have said it. . . .

Cats may have had their goose
Cooked by tobacco juice;
Still why deny its use
Thoughtfully taken?
We're not as tabbies are:

Smith, take a fresh cigar!
Jones, the tobacco-jar!
Here's to thee, Bacon!
C. S. CALVERLEY, *Ode to Tobacco*.

1
I smoke like a furnace.
W. S. GILBERT, *Trial by Jury*.

A German, Who smoked like a chimney.
R. H. BARHAM, *The Lay of St. Odille*. St. 3.

2
What a blessing this smoking is! perhaps the greatest that we owe to the discovery of America.
HELPS, *Friends in Council*. Ser. ii, ch. 1.

3
Tobacco is a dirty weed: I like it.
It satisfies no normal need: I like it.
It makes you thin, it makes you lean,
It takes the hair right off your bean;
It's the worst darn stuff I've ever seen:
I like it.
GRAHAM HEMMINGER, *Tobacco*. (Penn State *Froth*, Nov., 1915, p. 19.)

4
When all things were made none was made better than this; to be a lone man's companion, a bachelor's friend, a hungry man's food, a sad man's cordial, a wakeful man's sleep, and a chilly man's fire, Sir; while for stanching of wounds, purging of rheum, and settling of the stomach, there's no herb like unto it under the canopy of heaven.
CHARLES KINGSLEY, *Westward Ho*. Ch. 7, second paragraph from end. Salvation Yeo's tribute to tobacco.

5
For I hate, yet love, thee so,
That, whichever thing I show,
The plain truth will seem to be
A constrain'd hyperbole,
And the passion to proceed
More from a mistress than a weed.
CHARLES LAMB, *A Farewell to Tobacco*, l. 11.

Thou in such a cloud dost bind us,
That our worst foes cannot find us,
And ill fortune, that would thwart us,
Shoots at rovers, shooting at us;
While each man, through thy height'ning steam,
Does like a smoking Etna seem.
CHARLES LAMB, *A Farewell to Tobacco*, l. 28.

For thy sake, Tobacco, I
Would do anything but die.
CHARLES LAMB, *A Farewell to Tobacco*, l. 122.

6
Tobacco has been my evening comfort and my morning curse for these five years.
LAMB, *Letter to Wordsworth*, 28 Sept., 1805.

8
Tobacco, charmer of my mind,
When like the meteor's transient gleam,
Thy substance gone to air I find,
I think, alas! my life's the same.
(Tabac! dont mon âme est ravie,
Lorsque je te vois te perdre en l'air,
Aussi promptement q'un éclair,
Je vois l'image de ma vie.)
MISSON, *Memoirs of Travels in England*.

9
When smoking began to go out of fashion, learning began to go out of fashion also.
RICHARD PORSON. (WATSON, *Life*.)

The Elizabethan age might be better named the beginning of the smoking era.
J. M. BARRIE, *My Lady Nicotine*. Ch. 14.

10
Divine tobacco.
SPENSER, *Faerie Queene*. Bk. iii, canto v, st. 32.

11
It is not for nothing that this "ignoble tabagie," as Michelet calls it, spreads over all the world. Michelet rails against it because it renders you happy apart from thought or work; to provident women this will seem no evil influence in married life. Whatever keeps a man in the front garden, whatever checks wandering fancy and all inordinate ambition, whatever makes for lounging and contentment, makes just so surely for domestic happiness.
R. L. STEVENSON, *Virginibus Puerisque*. Pt. i.

12
The Indian weed withered quite,
Greene at none, cut downe at night,
Shewes thy decay, all flesh is hay,
Thus thinke, then drinke *Tobacco*. . . .

And when the smoake ascends on high,
Thinke, thou behold'st the vanitie
Of worldly stuffe gone with a puffe:
Thus thinke, then drinke *Tobacco*.

And when the Pipe grows foule within,
Thinke on thy soule defil'd with sinne,
And then the fire it doth require,
Thus thinke, then drinke *Tobacco*.

The ashes that are left behinde,
May serue to put thee still in minde,
That vnto dust, returne thou must,
Thus thinke, then drinke *Tobacco*.
THOMAS JENNER, *Tobacco*. From *The Soules Solace; or Thirtie and one Spirituall Emblems*. Emblem 31. (1626) These verses, often parodied, have been variously ascribed to Robert Wisdom, John Erskine, and George Wither, who was really a strong opponent of smoking, as a "thing full of barbarism and shame." The "withered" (then pronounced witherèd) in the first line is a punning reference to Wither's bitter attack on tobacco in *Abuses Stript and Whipt*. (1613) Wither wrote a reply with the counter-refrain, "Thus thinke, drinke no *Tobacco*." "Drink tobacco" means to drink in or smoke it.

Tobacco's but an Indian weed,
Grows green at morn, cut down at eve;
It shows our decay, we are but clay.
Think on this when you smoak Tobacco.
SCOTT, *Rob Roy*. Quoted as an old song.

1
Am I not—a smoker and a brother?
UNKNOWN. (*Smoker's Guide*. Ch. 4.)

II—Tobacco: Its Faults

2
It's all one thing—both tend into one scope—
To live upon Tobacco and on Hope,
The one's but smoke, the other is but wind.
SIR ROBERT AYTOUN, *Sonnet on Tobacco*.

3
Pernicious weed! whose scent the fair annoys,
Unfriendly to society's chief joys,
Thy worst effect is banishing for hours
The sex whose presence civilizes ours.
COWPER, *Conversation*, l. 251.

Tobacco, an outlandish weed,
Doth in the land strange wonders breed;
It taints the breath, the blood it dries,
It burns the head, it blinds the eyes;
It dries the lungs, scourgeth the lights,
It 'numbs the soul, it dulls the sprites;
It brings a man into a maze,
And makes him sit for others' gaze;
It mars a man, it mars a purse,
A lean one fat, a fat one worse;
A white man black, a black man white,
A night a day, a day a night;
It turns the brain like cat in pan,
And makes a Jack a gentleman.
FREDERICK WILLIAM FAIRHOLT, *Tobacco*.

Neither do thou lust after that tawney weed tobacco.
BEN JONSON, *Bartholomew Fair*. Act ii, sc. 1.

4
Tobacco is the tomb of love.
BENJAMIN DISRAELI, *Sybil*. Bk. i, ch. 16.

5
Let us take the air, in a tobacco trance,
Admire the monuments,
Discuss the late events,
Correct our watches by the public clocks,
Then sit for half an hour and drink our bocks.
T. S. ELIOT, *Portrait of a Lady*.

6
The scatterbrain, Tobacco. Yet a man of no conversation should smoke.
EMERSON, *Journals*, 1866.

7
A branch of the sin of drunkenness, which is the root of all sins.
JAMES I OF ENGLAND, *A Counterblast to Tobacco*.

Herein is not only a great vanity, but a great contempt of God's good gifts, that the sweetness of man's breath, being a good gift of God, should be wilfully corrupted by this stinking smoke. . . . A custom loathsome to the eye, hateful to the nose, harmful to the brain, dangerous to the lungs, and in the black, stinking fume thereof nearest resembling the horrible Stygian smoke of the pit that is bottomless.
JAMES I OF ENGLAND, *A Counterblast to Tobacco*.

8
The tobacco business is a conspiracy against womanhood and manhood. It owes its origin to that scoundrel, Sir Walter Raleigh, who was likewise the founder of American slavery.
DR. JOHN HARVEY KELLOGG, *Tobacco*.

9
Tobacco hic,
If a man be well it will make him sick.
JOHN RAY, *English Proverbs*, 296. (1678)

Tobacco hic,
Will make you well if you be sick.
J. O. HALLIWELL, *Popular Rhymes*, 180.

10
Ods me, I marle what pleasure or felicity they have in taking this roguish tobacco! it's good for nothing but to choke a man, and fill him full of smoke and embers.
BEN JONSON, *Every Man in His Humour*. Act iii, sc. 2.

11
I have a faint recollection of pleasure derived from smoking dried lily-stems, before I was a man. I have never smoked anything more noxious.
H. D. THOREAU. (EMERSON, *Thoreau*.)

III—Tobacco: The Pipe

12
For this you've my word, and I never yet
broke it.
So put that in your pipe, my Lord Otto, and
smoke it.
R. H. BARHAM, *The Lay of St. Odille*. St. 14.

13
Little tube of mighty pow'r,
Charmer of an idle hour.
ISAAC HAWKINS BROWNE, *A Pipe of Tobacco*.

14
The pipe, with solemn interposing puff,
Makes half a sentence at a time enough;
The dozing sages drop the drowsy strain,
Then pause, and puff—and speak, and pause
again.
COWPER, *Conversation*, l. 245.

15
With what a genius for administration
We rearrange the rumbling universe,
And map the course of man's regeneration,
Over a pipe.
WILLIAM ERNEST HENLEY, *Inter Sodales*.

16
Tobacco is a traveler,
Come from the Indies hither;
It passed sea and land
Ere it came to my hand,
And 'scaped the wind and weather.

Tobacco's a musician,
And in a pipe delighteth;
It descends in a close.
Through the organ of the nose,
With a relish that inviteth.
BARTEN HOLIDAY, *Texnotamia*. (1630)

1
Certain things are good for nothing until they have been kept a long while; and some are good for nothing until they have been long kept and *used*. Of the first, wine is the illustrious and immortal example. Of those which must be kept and used I will name three,—meerschaum pipes, violins, and poems. The meerschaum is but a poor affair until it has burned a thousand offerings to the cloud-compelling deities. . . . The fire is lighted in its central shrine, and gradually the juices which the broad leaves of the Great Vegetable had sucked up from an acre and curdled into a drachm are diffused through its thirsting pores.

O. W. Holmes, *The Autocrat of the Breakfast-Table*. Ch. 5.

2
May be the truth is, that one pipe is wholesome, two pipes toothsome, three pipes noisome, four pipes fulsome, five pipes quarrelsome; and that's the sum on't.

Lamb, *Letter to Coleridge*, 13 April, 1803.

3
With pipe and book at close of day,
Oh, what is sweeter? mortal say.
It matters not what book on knee,
Old Isaak or the Odyssey,
It matters not meerschaum or clay.

Richard Le Gallienne, *With Pipe and Book*.

4
Still let us puff, puff; be life smooth, be it rough,
Such enjoyment we'er ever in lack o':
The more peace and good-will will abound as we fill
A jolly good pipe of Tobacco!

John Usher, *The Pipe of Tobacco*.

5
Contented I sit with my pint and my pipe,
Puffing sorrow and care far away,
And surely the brow of grief nothing can wipe,
Like smoking and moist'ning our clay; . . .
For tho' at my simile many may joke,
Man is but a pipe—and his life but smoke.

Unknown, *Content and a Pipe*.

IV—Tobacco: Cigar and Cigarette

6
The sweet post-prandial cigar.

Robert Buchanan, *De Berney*.

7
Sublime tobacco! which from east to west,
Cheers the tar's labour or the Turkman's rest;
Which on the Moslem's ottoman divides
His hours, and rivals opium and his brides;
Magnificent in Stamboul, but less grand,
Though not less loved, in Wapping or the Strand;
Divine in hookas, glorious in a pipe,
When tipp'd with amber, mellow, rich, and ripe; . . .
Yet thy true lovers more admire by far
Thy naked beauties—Give me a cigar!

Byron, *The Island*. Canto ii, st. 19.

8
Some sigh for this and that,
My wishes don't go far,
The world may wag at will,
So I have my cigar.

Thomas Hood, *The Cigar*. St. 1.

They tell me Nancy Low
Has married Mr. R.;
The jilt! but I can live,
So I have my cigar.

Thomas Hood, *The Cigar*. St. 14.

9
For Maggie has written a letter to give me my choice between
The wee little whimpering Love and the great god Nick o' Teen.

Kipling, *The Betrothed*.

A million surplus Maggies are willing to bear the yoke;
And a woman is only a woman, but a good Cigar is a Smoke.

Rudyard Kipling, *The Betrothed*.

Woman in this scale, the weed in that, Jupiter, hang out thy balance, and weigh them both; and if thou give the preference to woman, all I can say is, the next time Juno ruffles thee—O Jupiter, try the weed.

Bulwer-Lytton, *What Will He Do With It?* Bk. i, ch. 6.

A maid unto her lover sternly said:
"Forego the Indian weed before we wed,
For smoke take flame; I'll be that flame's bright fanner;
To have your Anna, give up your Havana."
The wretch, when thus she brought him to the scratch,
Lit the cigar and threw away the match.

Unknown, *It Ended in Smoke*.

10
What this country really needs is a good five cent cigar.

Thomas R. Marshall, *Remark*, while presiding over the U. S. Senate during a debate on the needs of the country.

The light ones may be killers,
And the dark ones may be mild;
Not the wrappers, but the fillers,
Make cigars or women wild.

Keith Preston, *Popular Fallacies*.

11
Yes, social friend, I love thee well,
In learned doctors' spite;
Thy clouds all other clouds dispel,
And lap me in delight.

Charles Sprague, *To My Cigar*.

12
It was my last cigar, it was my last cigar;
I breath'd a sigh to think, in sooth,
It was my last cigar.

Unknown, *My Last Cigar*. A popular college song for many years. A parody, *My First Cigar*, was written as long ago as 1867, by W. C. Rommel, then a student at Princeton.

1
A cigarette is the perfect type of a perfect pleasure. It is exquisite, and it leaves one unsatisfied. What more can you want?

OSCAR WILDE, *Picture of Dorian Gray*. Ch. 6.

TODAY

I—Today

See also Present

1a
There is left for myself then but one day in the week—today. Any man can fight the battles of today. Any woman can carry the burdens of just one day. Any man can resist the temptations of today. Oh, friends, it is only when we willfully add the burdens of those two awful eternities, yesterday and tomorrow, such burdens as only the mighty God can sustain, that we break down. It isn't the experience of today that drives men mad. It is the remorse for something that happened yesterday, and the dread of what tomorrow may disclose.

ROBERT J. BURDETTE, *The Golden Day*.

2
Out of Eternity the new Day is born;
Into Eternity at night will return.

THOMAS CARLYLE, *To-day*.

3
To those leaning on the sustaining infinite, to-day is big with blessings.

MARY B. EDDY, *Science and Health: Preface*, p. vii.

4
Rise! for the day is passing,
And you lie dreaming on;
The others have buckled their armour,
And forth to the fight are gone:
A place in the ranks awaits you,
Each man has some part to play;
The Past and the Future are nothing,
In the face of the stern To-day.

ADELAIDE ANN PROCTER, *Now*. St. 1.

5
The obscurest epoch is to-day.

R. L. STEVENSON, *Ethical Studies*, p. 113.

6
To-day is yesterday's pupil.

THOMAS FULLER, *Gnomologia*, No. 5153.

7
Our to-days and yesterdays
Are the blocks with which we build.

LONGFELLOW, *The Builders*. St. 3.

8
To-day is always different from yesterday.

ALEXANDER SMITH, *Dreamthorp: Books and Gardens*.

9
Life greatens in these later years,
The century's aloe flowers to-day!

J. G. WHITTIER, *Snow-Bound*, l. 738.

10
Listen to the Exhortation of the Dawn!
Look to this Day, for it is Life—
The very Life of Life!
In its brief course lie all the Verities
And Realities of your Existence:
The Bliss of Growth,
The Glory of Action,
The Splendor of Beauty;
For Yesterday is but a Dream,
And To-morrow is only a Vision;
But To-day well lived
Makes every Yesterday a Dream of Happiness,
And every To-morrow a Vision of Hope.
Look well, therefore, to this day!
Such is the Salutation of the Dawn.

UNKNOWN, *The Salutation of the Dawn*. From the Sanscrit.

II—Today and Tomorrow

See also Present and Future

12
Light to-morrow with to-day!

E. B. BROWNING, *Romance of Swan's Nest*. St. 9.

Build a little fence of trust
Around to-day;
Fill the space with loving work,
And therein stay;
Look not through the sheltering bars
Upon to-morrow;
God will help thee bear what comes
Of joy or sorrow.

MARY FRANCES BUTTS, *Trust*.

13
The rule is, jam to-morrow and jam yesterdays—but never jam to-day.

CARROLL, *Through the Looking-Glass*. Ch. 3.

14
What's lost today may be won tomorrow.

CERVANTES, *Don Quixote*. Pt. i, ch. 7.

15
Give me to-day, and take to-morrow. (*Δίδου μοι τὴν σήμερον, καὶ λάμβανε τὴν αὔριον.*)

ST. CHRYSOSTOM. A proverb condemned by him.

16
To-day is ours; what do we fear?
To-day is ours; we have it here.
Let's treat it kindly, that it may
Wish, at least, with us to stay.
Let's banish business, banish sorrow;
To the gods belongs to-morrow.

ABRAHAM COWLEY, *The Epicure*, l. 7.

17
If today will not, tomorrow may.

THOMAS FULLER, *Gnomologia*. No. 2725.

18
Oh, to be wafted away
From this black Aceldama of sorrow,
Where the dust of an earthy to-day,
Is the earth of a dusty to-morrow.

W. S. GILBERT, *Patience*. Act i.

19
Reap the harvest of to-day; trust to-morrow as little as may be. (Carpe diem, quam minimum credula postero.)

HORACE, *Odes*. Bk. i, ode 11, l. 8. *See also* LIFE AND LIVING.

20
Here's in the teeth of to-morrow
To the glory of to-day!

RICHARD HOVEY, *At the End of the Day*.

1
Live for to-day! To-morrow's light
To-morrow's cares shall bring to sight;
Go sleep, like closing flowers at night.
And heaven thy morn will bless.
JOHN KEBLE, *Live for To-day.*

2
I've shut the door on yesterday
And thrown the key away—
To-morrow holds no fears for me,
Since I have found to-day.
VIVIAN YEISER LARAMORE, *To-day.*

3
But bear to-day whate'er To-day may bring;
'Tis the one way to make To-morrow sing.
RICHARD LE GALLIENNE, *In Her Diary.*

4
Build to-day, then, strong and sure,
With a firm and ample base;
And ascending and secure
Shall to-morrow find its place.
LONGFELLOW, *The Builders.* St. 8.

The moon will wax, the moon will wane,
The mist and cloud will turn to rain,
The rain to mist and cloud again,
To-morrow be to-day.
LONGFELLOW, *Kéramos,* l. 35.

6
Ah, my Belovèd, fill the Cup that clears
TO-DAY of past Regrets and future Fears:
To-morrow?—Why, To-morrow I may be
Myself with Yesterday's Sev'n Thousand Years.
OMAR KHAYYÁM, *Rubáiyát,* 20. (Fitzgerald, tr.)

7
This day was yesterday to-morrow nam'd:
To-morrow shall be yesterday proclaim'd:
To-morrow not yet come, not far away,
What shall to-morrow then be call'd? To-day.
JOHN OWEN, *To-Day and To-Morrow,* iii, 50.

8
One to-day is worth two to-morrows.
FRANCIS QUARLES, *Enchiridion,* iv, 95; BENJAMIN FRANKLIN, *Poor Richard,* 1758.

9
Lay hold of today's task, and you will not depend so much upon tomorrow's. (Sic fiet, ut minus ex crastino pendeas, si hodierno manum injeceris.)
SENECA, *Epistulæ ad Lucilium.* Epis. i, sec. 2.

10
Where art thou, beloved To-morrow?
When young and old, and strong and weak,
Rich and poor, through joy and sorrow,
Thy sweet smiles we ever seek,—
In thy place—ah! well-a-day!
We find the thing we fled—To-day!
SHELLEY, *To-Morrow.*

11
What hapt today to me, tomorrow may to you.
SPENSER, *Faerie Queene,* vi, i, 41. (1596)

Today for thee and tomorrow for me.
CERVANTES, *Don Quixote.* Pt. ii, ch. 65. (1615)

Ille hodie, ego cras: that is, He to-day, I to-morrow.
UNKNOWN, *Ancrene Riwle,* 278. (c. 1200)

An old hempen proverb, Hodie tibi, cras mihi. [Today it is your turn, tomorrow mine.]
MARLOWE, *Jew of Malta,* iv, 4, (1592)

I today, you tomorrow. (Hodie mihi, cras tibi.)
JOHN CLARKE, *Paræmilogia,* 124. (1639)

What is not today, will be tomorrow. (Quod hodie non est, cras erit.)
PETRONIUS, *Satyricon.* Ch. 45.

12
Today at good cheer, tomorrow on the bier.
C. H. SPURGEON, *Ploughman's Pictures,* p. 67.

Today a man in gold, tomorrow closed in clay.
UNKNOWN, *Antique Repertory,* iv, 398. (c. 1500)

13
Who can say why To-day,
To-morrow will be yesterday?
TENNYSON, *Song.*

14
To-morrow, to-morrow, not to-day,
Hear the lazy people say.
(Morgen, Morgen, nur nicht heute;
Sprechen immer träge Leute.)
WEISSE, *Der Aufschub.*

15
To-morrow is a satire on to-day,
And shows its weakness.
YOUNG, *The Old Man's Relapse,* l. 6.

16
This little strip of night
'Twixt night and night,
Let me keep bright
Today! . . .
And if Tomorrow shall be sad,
Or never come at all, I've had
At least—Today!
UNKNOWN, *Today.*

17
Some say "to-morrow" never comes,
A saying oft thought right;
But if to-morrow never came,
No end were of "to-night."
The fact is this, time flies so fast,
That e'er we've time to say
"To-morrow's come," presto! behold!
"To-morrow" proves "To-day."
UNKNOWN, *To-morrow Never Comes.* (*Notes and Queries.* Ser. iv, vol. 12.)

TOIL, see Labor

TOLERANCE

18
He knows not how to wink at human frailty,
Or pardon weakness that he never felt.
ADDISON, *Cato.* Act v, sc. 4.

A man 's capable of understanding . . . how the ether vibrates, and what's going on in the sun—but how any other man can blow his nose differently from him, that he's incapable of understanding.
TURGENEV, *Fathers and Children.* Ch. 23.

19
I know not what record of sin awaits me in

the other world, but this I know, that I was never mean enough to despise a man because he was ignorant, or because he was poor—or because he was black.

JOHN ALBION ANDREW, *Address,* at Martha's Vineyard, Mass., 10 Aug., 1862.

1
Toleration is good for all or it is good for none.

BURKE, *Speech,* House of Commons, 1773.

2
Then gently scan your brother man,
Still gentler sister woman;
Tho' they may gang a kennin wrang,
To step aside is human.

ROBERT BURNS, *Address to the Unco Guid.*

3
Like feather bed betwixt a wall
And heavy brunt of cannon ball.

BUTLER, *Hudibras.* Pt. i, canto ii, l. 872.

4
I have seen gross intolerance shown in support of toleration.

S. T. COLERIDGE, *Biographia Literaria.* Ch. 10.

Intolerant only of intolerance.

UNKNOWN, *Mr. Buckle and the East.* (This is an article in *Fraser's Magazine* for August, 1863, signed "I.S.S.G.")

5
He preached upon "breadth" till it argued him narrow,—
The broad are too broad to define.

EMILY DICKINSON, *Poems.* Pt. i, No. 64.

Broadmindedness is the result of flattening high-mindedness out.

GEORGE SAINTSBURY.

6
Give to every other human being every right that you claim for yourself.

R. G. INGERSOLL, *Limitations of Toleration.*

7
Wise with the history of its own frail heart,
With reverence and sorrow, and with love,
Broad as the world for freedom and for man.

J. R. LOWELL, *Prometheus,* l. 216.

Ready to settle Freewill by a vote,
But largely liberal to its private moods.

J. R. LOWELL, *Under the Old Elm.*

8
He maketh his sun to rise on the evil and on the good, and sendeth rain on the just and on the unjust.

New Testament: Matthew, v, 45.

9
Though all society is founded on intolerance, all improvement is founded on tolerance.

BERNARD SHAW, *Saint Joan: Preface.*

10
Let your precept be, "Be easy."

RICHARD STEELE, *The Spectator* No. 196.

11
This Laodicean cant of tolerance.

MRS. HUMPHRY WARD, *Robert Elsmere.* Bk. ii, ch. 12.

TOMB, see Grave, Monument

TOMORROW

See also Future; Today and Tomorrow

12
Who knows aright of tomorrow's fortune? (*Δαίμονα τίς δ' εὖ οἶδε τὸν αὔριον.*)

CALLIMACHUS, *Epigrams.* No. 16.

It is doubtful what fortune tomorrow will bring. (Posteraque in dubio est fortunam quam vehat ætas.)

LUCRETIUS, *De Rerum Natura.* Bk. iii, l. 1085.

It is not lawful to know what the morrow will bring forth. (Quid crastina volveret aetas Scire nefas homini.)

STATIUS, *Thebais.* Bk. iii, l. 562.

See also FUTURE: KNOWLEDGE OF.

13
As much to the purpose as "Tomorrow I found a horseshoe."

CERVANTES, *Don Quixote.* Pt. ii, ch. 43.

14
Put not off till to-morrow; for the morrow never comes to completion. (*Μὴ εἰς τὴν αὔριον ἀναβάλλου· ἡ γὰρ αὔριον οὐδέποτε λαμβάνει τέλος.*)

ST. CHRYSOSTOM, *Adagia. See* PROCRASTINATION.

15
And blithe as the lark that each day hails the dawn,
Look forward with hope for To-morrow.

JOHN COLLINS, *To-morrow.* St. 1.

16
To-morrow!
'Tis a sharper—who stakes his penury
Against thy plenty—takes thy ready cash,
And pays thee naught but wishes, hopes, and promises.

NATHANIEL COTTON, *To-Morrow.*

Trust on and think To-morrow will repay;
To-morrow's falser than the former day;
Lies worse; and while it says, we shall be blest
With some new Joys, cuts off what we possest.

DRYDEN, *Aureng-Zebe.* Act iv, sc. 1.

To-morrow and to-morrow cheat our youth.
In riper age, to-morrow still we cry,
Not thinking that the present age we die,
Unpractis'd all the good we have design'd:
There's no to-morrow to a willing mind.

COUNTESS OF WINCHILSEA, *No To-Morrow.*

To-morrow is an old deceiver, and his cheat never grows stale.

SAMUEL JOHNSON, *Letters.* Vol. i, p. 221.

17
To-morrow is, ah, whose?

DINAH M. M. CRAIK, *Between Two Worlds.*

18
Ever from one who comes to-morrow
Men wait their good and truth to borrow.

EMERSON, *Considerations by the Way.*

19
And evermore he said, "To-morrow."

JOHN GOWER, *Confessio Amantis.* Bk. iv, l. 9.

"To-morrow we will open," I replied,
And when the morrow came I answered still,
"To-morrow."

LONGFELLOW, *To-morrow.* (*Mañana.*)

20
With the bitter past I will deck to-morrow.

HELEN HUNTINGTON, *The Wayfarer.*

1
Far off I heard the crowing of the cocks,
And through the opening door that time unlocks
Feel the fresh breathing of To-morrow creep.
LONGFELLOW, *To-morrow.*

To-morrow! the mysterious, unknown guest,
Who cries to me: "Remember Barmecide,
And tremble to be happy with the rest."
And I make answer: "I am satisfied;
I dare not ask; I know not what is best;
God hath already said what shall betide."
LONGFELLOW, *To-morrow.*

2
To-morrow never yet
On any human being rose or set.
WILLIAM MARSDEN, *What Is Time?*

3
Tomorrow is the ambushed walk avoided by the circumspect. Tomorrow is the fatal rock on which a million ships are wrecked.
WALT MASON, *Tomorrow.*

4
Tell me, Postumus, when does that tomorrow of yours come? (Dic mihi, cras istud, Postume, quando venit?)
MARTIAL, *Epigrams.* Bk. v, ep. 59.

Tomorrow comes never.
JOHN RAY, *English Proverbs,* 343. (1678)

Tomorrow never comes.
GEORGE COLMAN THE YOUNGER, *Man and Wife.* Act iii. (1769)

5
Take therefore no thought for the morrow: for the morrow shall take thought for the things of itself. Sufficient unto the day is the evil thereof.
New Testament: Matthew, vi, 34.

7
Then hasten we, maid To twine our braid,
To-morrow the dreams and flowers will fade.
THOMAS MOORE, *Lalla Rookh: The Light of the Harem,* l. 380.

8
When tomorrow comes, yesterday's tomorrow will have been already spent, and another morrow will be eating away our years, each just beyond our grasp. (Cum lux altera venit, Jam cras hesternum consumpsimus; ecce aliud cras Egerit hos annos et semper paulum erit ultra.)
PERSIUS, *Satires.* Sat. v, l. 67.

9
Boast not thyself of tomorrow; for thou knowest not what a day may bring forth.
Old Testament: Proverbs, xxvii, 1.

10
My country is not yesterday. My country is tomorrow.
ROMAIN ROLLAND, *Broaden, Europe, or Die.* (*Nation,* 22 Apr., 1931.)

The present day has no value for me except as the eve of to-morrow; it is with the morrow that my spirit wrestles.
METTERNICH.

11
The woman named Tomorrow
sits with a hairpin in her teeth
and takes her time
and does her hair the way she wants it.
CARL SANDBURG, *Four Preludes.*

12
No one has found the gods so kind that he can promise himself a tomorrow. (Nemo tam divos habuit faventes, Crastinum ut posset sibi polliceri.)
SENECA, *Thyestes,* l. 619.

13
To-morrow, and to-morrow, and to-morrow,
Creeps in this petty pace from day to day
To the last syllable of recorded time.
SHAKESPEARE, *Macbeth.* Act v, sc. 5, l. 19.

14
A Man he seems of cheerful yesterdays
And confident to-morrows.
WORDSWORTH, *The Excursion.* Bk. vii, l. 557.

15
To-morrow is a new day.
UNKNOWN, *Calisto and Melibœa.* (HAZLITT, *Old Plays,* i, 86. c. 1520)

TONGUE

See also Woman: Her Tongue

I—Tongue: Apothegms

16
What among men is both good and bad? The tongue.
ANACHARSIS. (DIOGENES LAERTIUS, *Anacharsis.* Sec. 5.)

Train thy tongue to say, "I do not know," lest thou be entrapped into falsehood.
Babylonian Talmud: Berachoth, p. 9b.

17
When a man dies, the last thing that moves is his heart; in a woman her tongue.
GEORGE CHAPMAN, *Widow's Tears.* Act iv, sc. 2.

When men and women die, as poets sung,
His heart's the last part moves,—her last, the tongue.
BENJAMIN FRANKLIN, *Poor Richard,* 1739.

18
Let not your tongue outrun your thought. (Τὴν γλῶτταν μὴ προτρέχειν τοῦ νοῦ.)
CHILON. (DIOGENES LAERTIUS, *Chilon.* Sec. 3.)

Let not thy tongue run away with thy brains.
THOMAS FULLER, *Gnomologia.* No. 3190.

Your tongue runs before your wit.
SWIFT, *Polite Conversation.* Dial. 1.

19
If the tongue had not been framed for articulation, man would still be a beast in the forest.
EMERSON, *Representative Men: Plato.*

20
The tongue has sworn it, but the mind is unsworn. (Ἡ γλῶσσ' ὀμώμοχ', ἡ δὲ φρὴν ἀνώμοτος.)
EURIPIDES, *Hippolytus,* l. 612. *See also* SPEECH: CANDID AND DECEITFUL.

1
A slip of the foot may be soon recovered; but that of the tongue perhaps never.
THOMAS FULLER, *Gnomologia*. No. 403.

A Slip of the Foot you may soon recover,
But a Slip of the Tongue you may never get over.
BENJAMIN FRANKLIN, *Poor Richard*, 1747.

Better the feet slip than the tongue.
GEORGE HERBERT, *Jacula Prudentum*.

2
The tongue is the rudder of our ship.
THOMAS FULLER, *Gnomologia*. No. 4798.

3
The greatest of man's treasures is the tongue. (*Γλώσσης τοι θησαυρὸς ἐν ἀνθρώποισιν ἄριστος.*)
HESIOD, *Works and Days*, l. 719.

4
Though wickedness be sweet in his mouth, though he hide it under his tongue.
Old Testament: Job, xx, 12.

He rolls it under his tongue as a sweet morsel.
MATTHEW HENRY, *Commentaries: Psalms*, xxxi.

5
The tongue can no man tame; it is an unruly evil.
New Testament: James, iii, 8.

The tongue is a wild beast; once let loose it is difficult to chain.
GRACIAN.

I should think your tongue had broken its chain!
LONGFELLOW, *The Golden Legend*. Pt. iv.

6
A fool's treasure is in his tongue. (Istic est thesaurus stultis in lingua situs.)
PLAUTUS, *Pœnulus*, l. 625. (Act iii, sc. 3.)

7
My tongue is the pen of a ready writer.
Old Testament: Psalms, xlv, 1.

8
The strife of tongues.
Old Testament: Psalms, xxxi, 20.

9
Tongues I'll hang on every tree.
SHAKESPEARE, *As You Like It*. Act iii, sc. 2, l. 135.

10
You shall never take her without her answer, unless you take her without her tongue.
SHAKESPEARE, *As You Like It*. Act iv, sc. 1, l. 174. A proverbial saying.

For lack of answer none of them shall die.
CHAUCER, *Marchantes Tale*, l. 1027.

11
My tongue, though not my heart, shall have his will.
SHAKESPEARE, *The Comedy of Errors*. Act iv, sc. 2, l. 18.

12
As poisonous-tongued as handed.
SHAKESPEARE, *Cymbeline*. Act iii, sc. 2, l. 4.

Tongues spit their duties out, and cold hearts freeze
Allegiance in them.
SHAKESPEARE, *Henry VIII*. Act i, sc. 2, l. 61.

13
You have a glib tongue. (*Γλώσση σὺ δεινός.*)
SOPHOCLES, *Œdipus Coloneus*, l. 806.

14
Their secrets lay at their tongues' end.
RICHARD TARLTON, *News Out of Purgatory*, p. 69. (1590)

Having always at her tongue's end that excellent proverb.
HENRY FIELDING, *Amelia*. Bk. xii, ch. 7.

15
The windy satisfaction of the tongue. (*Κακὸν δ' ἀνεμώλια βάζειν.*)
HOMER, *Odyssey*. Bk. iv, l. 837. (Pope, tr.)

II—Tongue: Its Use

16
My son, keep well thy tongue and keep thy friend.
A wicked tongue is worse than a fiend. . . .
The first virtue, son, if thou wilt learn,
Is to restrain and keep well thy tongue.
CHAUCER, *The Maunciples Tale*, l. 215.

17
A quiet tongue makes a wise head.
THOMAS COGAN, *John Buncle, Junior*, i, 238.

18
It hurteth not the tongue to give fair words.
JOHN HEYWOOD, *Proverbs*. Pt. i, ch. 9.

Fair words never hurt the tongue.
GEORGE CHAPMAN, *Eastward Hoe*. Act iv, sc. 1.

19
Sweet Benjamin, since thou art young,
And hast not yet the use of tongue,
Make it thy slave, while thou art free;
Imprison it, lest it do thee.
JOHN HOSKINS, *To His Son*, from the Tower.

20
Since word is thrall, and thought is free,
Keep well thy tongue, I counsel thee.
JAMES I OF SCOTLAND. *Ballad of Good Counsel*. Quoted by Scott, *Fair Maid of Perth*. Ch. 25.

21
Keep thy tongue from evil, and thy lips from speaking guile.
Old Testament: Psalms, xxxiv, 13.

Give not thy tongue too great a liberty, lest it take thee prisoner. A word unspoken is, like the sword in thy scabbard, thine: if vented, thy sword is in another's hand; if thou desire to be held wise, be so wise as to hold thy tongue.
FRANCIS QUARLES, *Enchiridion*. Cent. iii, 32.

22
My tongue will tell the anger of my heart:
Or else my heart concealing it will break.
SHAKESPEARE, *The Taming of the Shrew*. Act iv, sc. 3, l. 77.

The heart hath treble wrong
When it is barr'd the aidance of the tongue.
SHAKESPEARE, *Venus and Adonis*, l. 329.

III—Tongue: Its Abuse

23
Letting the rank tongue blossom into speech.
ROBERT BROWNING, *Caliban Upon Setebos*, l. 23.

1
A clapper-tongue wad deave a miller.
BURNS, *Sic a Wife as Willie Had.*

2
But still his tongue ran on, the less
Of weight it bore, with greater ease.
BUTLER, *Hudibras*. Pt. iii, canto 2, l. 443.

3
Flippant fluency of tongue.
COWPER, *Table Talk*, l. 147.

4
The tongue offends and the ears get the cuffing.
BENJAMIN FRANKLIN, *Poor Richard*, 1757. *See also under* EARS.

5
His tongue is as cloven as the devil's foot.
THOMAS FULLER, *Gnomologia*. No. 2516.

6
Foolish tongues talk by the dozen.
GEORGE HERBERT, *Jacula Prudentum*.
See also FOOL: THE FOOL'S TONGUE.

Not if I had ten tongues and ten mouths. (Οὐδ' εἴ μοι δέκα μὲν γλῶσσαι, δέκα δὲ στόματ' εἶεν.)
HOMER, *Iliad*. Bk. ii, l. 489.

7
Many a man's tongue shakes out his master's undoing.
SHAKESPEARE, *All's Well that Ends Well*. Act ii, sc. 4, l. 24. *See also under* SERVANT.

8
Be not thy tongue thy own shame's orator.
SHAKESPEARE, *The Comedy of Errors*. Act iii, sc. 2, l. 10.

9
Why, what a wasp-stung and impatient fool
Art thou to break into this woman's mood,
Tying thine ear to no tongue but thine own.
SHAKESPEARE, *I Henry IV*. Act i, sc. 3, l. 236.

One whom the music of his own vain tongue
Doth ravish like enchanting harmony.
SHAKESPEARE, *Love's Labour's Lost*. Act i, sc. 1, l. 167.

10
Is there a tongue, like Delia's o'er her cup,
That runs for ages without winding up?
YOUNG, *Love of Fame*. Sat. i, l. 280.

With skill she vibrates her eternal tongue,
For ever most divinely in the wrong.
YOUNG, *Love of Fame*. Sat. vi, l. 105.

11
Such men's tongues go ever on wheels.
UNKNOWN, *Partonope*, 420. (c. 1450)

Thy tongue runs upon wheels this morning.
SWIFT, *Polite Conversation*. Dial. 1.

IV—Tongue: The Persuasive Tongue

12
The magic of the tongue is the most dangerous of all spells.
BULWER-LYTTON, *Eugene Aram*. Bk. i, ch. 7.

Adding once more the music of the tongue
To the sweet speech of her alluring eyes.
SIR JOHN DAVIES, *Orchestra*. St. 97.

13
He who has no hands
Perforce must use his tongue;
Foxes are so cunning
Because they are not strong.
R. W. EMERSON, *Orator*.

A good tongue is a good weapon.
THOMAS FULLER, *Gnomologia*. No. 180.

14
Pliant is the tongue of mortals, numberless the words within it. (Στρεπτὴ δὲ γλῶσσ' ἐστὶ βροτῶν, πολέες δ' ἔνι μῦθοι.)
HOMER, *Iliad*. Bk. xx, l. 248.

15
How like an angel speaks the tongue of woman,
When pleading in another's cause her own!
LONGFELLOW, *Spanish Student*. Act iii, sc. 5.

16
A gentle tongue is a tree of life. (Lingua placabilis, lignum vitæ.)
Old Testament: Proverbs, xv, 4. The Vulgate version. The Bible version is, "A wholesome tongue is a tree of life."

17
In her tongue is the law of kindness.
Old Testament: Proverbs, xxxi, 26.

And of thy tongue the infinite graciousnesse.
CHAUCER, *Legend of Good Women: Hypsipyle and Medea*, l. 308.

You have sae saft a voice and slid a tongue,
You are the darling of baith auld and young.
ALLAN RAMSAY, *Eclogue*.

18
For these fellows of infinite tongue, that can rhyme themselves into ladies' favours, they do always reason themselves out again.
SHAKESPEARE, *Henry V*. Act v, sc. 2, l. 162.

He hath a witchcraft . . . in 's tongue.
SHAKESPEARE, *Henry VIII*. Act iii, sc. 2, l. 18.

You play the spaniel,
And think with wagging of your tongue to win me.
SHAKESPEARE, *Henry VIII*. Act v, sc. 3, l. 126.

19
O, that my tongue were in the thunder's mouth!
Then with a passion would I shake the world.
SHAKESPEARE, *King John*. Act iii, sc. 4, l. 38.

A still-soliciting eye, and such a tongue
As I am glad I have not.
SHAKESPEARE, *King Lear*. Act i, sc. 1, l. 234.

20
So on the tip of his subduing tongue
All kinds of arguments and question deep,
All replication prompt, and reason strong,
For his advantage still did wake and sleep;
To make the weeper laugh, the laugher weep,
He had the dialect and different skill,
Catching all passions in his craft of will.
SHAKESPEARE, *A Lover's Complaint*, l. 120.

21
Your tongue's sweet air
More tuneable than lark to shepherd's ear.

When wheat is green, when hawthorn buds appear.
SHAKESPEARE, *A Midsummer-Night's Dream.* Act i, sc. 1, l. 183.

My tongue should catch your tongue's sweet melody.
SHAKESPEARE, *A Midsummer-Night's Dream.* Act i, sc. 1, l. 189.

1
She that was ever fair and never proud,
Had tongue at will and yet was never loud.
SHAKESPEARE, *Othello.* Act ii, sc. 1, l. 149.

2
His tongue is now a stringless instrument.
SHAKESPEARE, *Richard II.* Act ii, sc. 1, l. 149.

The tongue which set the table in a roar,
And charm'd the public ear, is heard no more;
Clos'd are those eyes, the harbingers of wit,
Which spake before the tongue, what Shakespeare writ.
DAVID GARRICK, *Epitaph on James Quin.*

3
There is no tongue that moves, none, none i' the world,
So soon as yours could win me.
SHAKESPEARE, *Winter's Tale.* Act i, sc. 2, l. 20.

4
And oft his smooth and bridled tongue
Would give the lie to his flushing cheek.
SHELLEY, *Rosalind and Helen*, l. 252.

5
This rogue's tongue is well hung.
SWIFT, *Polite Conversation.* Dial. 1.

6
All the state-wielding magic of his tongue.
JAMES THOMSON, *Liberty.* Pt. iii, l. 468.

7
Excellent with his tongue, but his right hand remiss in the battle. (Lingua melior, sed frigida bello Dextera.)
VERGIL, *Æneid.* Bk. xi, l. 338. *See also* WORD AND DEED.

V—Tongue: Its Sharpness

8
The stroke of the whip maketh marks in the flesh: but the stroke of the tongue breaketh the bones. Many have fallen by the edge of the sword: but not so many as have fallen by the tongue.
Apocrypha: Ecclesiasticus, xxviii, 17, 18.

The tongue breaketh bone,
Though itself have none.
UNKNOWN, *Proverbs of Alfred*, l. 425. (c. 1275)

The tongue breaketh bone, although the tongue itself have none.
JOHN WYCLIFFE, *Works.* Vol. ii, p. 44. (1380)

9
A soft tongue may strike hard.
BENJAMIN FRANKLIN, *Poor Richard*, 1744.

10
The tongue is no edge tool, but yet it will cut.
JOHN HEYWOOD, *Proverbs.* Pt. i, ch. 10.

The tongue is not steel, yet it cuts.
GEORGE HERBERT, *Jacula Prudentum.*

11
A tart temper never mellows with age, and a sharp tongue is the only edged tool that grows keener with constant use.
WASHINGTON IRVING, *Rip Van Winkle.*

12
The tongue is a sharper weapon than the sword. (῞Οπλον τοι λόγος ἀνδρὶ τομώτερόν ἐστι σιδήρου.)
PHOCYLIDES, *Sententiæ.* No. 124.

The tongues of mocking wenches are as keen
As is the razor's edge invisible,
Cutting a smaller hair than may be seen
Above the sense of sense.
SHAKESPEARE, *Love's Labour's Lost.* Act v, sc. 2, l. 256.

13
For she had a tongue with a tang.
SHAKESPEARE, *The Tempest.* Act ii, sc. 2, l. 52.

VI—Tongue: Holding the Tongue

See also Silence

14
With good and gentle-humoured hearts
I choose to chat where'er I come,
Whate'er the subject be that starts;
But if I get among the glum
I hold my tongue to tell the troth
And keep my breath to cool my broth.
JOHN BYROM, *Careless Content.* St. 3.

15
Regard it as the first of virtues to restrain the tongue; he is nearest to a God who knows how to be silent when occasion requires. (Virtutum primam esse puto compescere linguam; Proximus ille Deo est qui scit ratione tacere.)
DIONYSIUS CATO, *Disticha de Moribus.* Bk. i, No. 3.

16
I prefer tongue-tied knowledge to ignorant loquacity. (Malim equidem indisertam prudentiam quam stultam loquacitatem.)
CICERO, *De Oratore.* Bk. iii, sec. 142.

17
Men are born with two eyes, but with one tongue, in order that they should see twice as much as they say; but, from their conduct, one would suppose that they were born with two tongues and one eye; for those talk the most who have observed the least.
C. C. COLTON, *Lacon.* Pt. i, No. 112. *See also under* EARS.

18
Lo, I am silent and I curb my tongue. (Ἰδοὺ σιωπῶ κἀπιλάζυμαι στόμα.)
EURIPIDES, *Andromache*, l. 250.

19
He that knows not how to hold his tongue, knows not how to talk.
THOMAS FULLER, *Gnomologia.* No. 2210.

He cannot speak well that cannot hold his tongue.
THOMAS FULLER, *Gnomologia.* No. 1820.

20
My tongue within my lips I rein;

For who talks much must talk in vain.
John Gay, *Fables: Introduction*. Pt. i, l. 57.

1
Suffer thy legs, but not thy tongue, to walk:
God, the most Wise, is sparing of His talk.
Robert Herrick, *Silence*.

2
Hold your tongue! (Favete linguis.)
Horace, *Odes*. Bk. iii, ode 1, l. 2.

3
"They are fools who kiss and tell"—
Wisely has the poet sung.
Man may hold all sorts of posts
If he 'll only hold his tongue.
Rudyard Kipling, *Pink Dominoes*.

4
Whatsoever else shall hap to-night.
Give it an understanding, but no tongue.
Shakespeare, *Hamlet*. Act i, sc. 2, l. 249.

Yes, forsooth, I will hold my tongue; so your face bids me, though you say nothing. Mum, mum.
Shakespeare, *King Lear*. Act i, sc. 4, l. 214.

5
Sweet, bid me hold my tongue,
For in this rapture I shall surely speak
The thing I shall repent.
Shakespeare, *Troilus and Cressida*. Act iii, sc. 2, l. 137.

6
You possess also the art of holding your tongue! Ah, you have all the talents for pleasing!
(Vous possédez aussi l'art de vous taire!
Ah! vous avez tous les talents de plaire.)
Voltaire, *La Prude*. Act iii, sc. 2.

7
I shall keep my tongue between my teeth.
Walker, *Parœmiologia*, 18. (1672)

If he does not keep his tongue between his teeth, I'll give him a chuck o' the chin.
Colley Cibber, *Rival Fools*. Act ii.

Keep tongue betwixt teeth!
Scott, *Kenilworth*. Ch. 7.

TOOTH

I—Tooth: Apothegms

8
I hope you take great care of your mouth and teeth, and that you clean them well every morning with a sponge and tepid water, with a few drops of arquebusade water dropped into it; besides washing your mouth carefully after every meal, I do insist upon your never using any of those sticks, or any hard substance whatsoever, which always rub away the gums, and destroy the varnish of the teeth.
Lord Chesterfield, *Letters*, 15 Feb., 1754.

9
Some ask'd how pearls did grow, and where?
Then spoke I to my girl,
To part her lips, and show'd them there
The quarelets of pearl.
Robert Herrick, *The Rock of Rubies*.

Delicate little pearl-white wedges,
All transparent at the edges.
Bailey, *Festus: A Large Party*.

Those cherries fairly do enclose
Of orient pearl a double row,
Which, when her lovely laughter shows,
They look like rosebuds fill'd with snow.
Unknown. (*An Howre's Recreation in Musike.*)

10
The best of friends fall out, and so
His teeth had done some years ago.
Thomas Hood, *A True Story*, l. 17.

11
What a word has passed the barrier of your teeth. (Ποῖόν σε ἔπος φύγεν ἕρκος ὀδόντων.)
Homer, *Iliad*. Bk. iv, l. 350.

The teeth form a barrier to check wanton words.
Aulus Gellius, *Noctes Atticæ*. Bk. i, ch. 15, sec. 3. Quoting Homer.

It was excellently said of that philosopher, that there was a wall or parapet of teeth set in our mouth, to restrain the petulancy of our words.
Ben Jonson, *Explorata: Lingua Sapientis*.

12
There shall be weeping and gnashing of teeth.
New Testament: Matthew, xxii, 13.

13
I am escaped with the skin of my teeth.
Old Testament: Job, xix, 20. Often incorrectly quoted, "I have escaped by the skin of my teeth."

14
Thais has black, Læcania white teeth; what is the reason? Thais has her own, Læcania ones she bought.
Martial, *Epigrams*. Bk. v, epig. 43.

Thais her teeth are black and nought,
Lecania's white are grown:
But what's the reason? these are bought,
The other wears her own.
Martial, *Epigrams*. Bk. v, 43. (Fletcher, tr.)

15
By Isis, I will give thee bloody teeth.
Shakespeare, *Antony and Cleopatra*. Act i, sc. 5, l. 70.

16
In the spite of his teeth.
John Skelton, *Why Come Ye Not to Court*. l. 940.

In spite of my teeth.
Thomas Middleton, *A Trick to Catch the Old One*. Act i, sc. 2.

17
With tooth and nail. (Manibus pedibusque.)
Terence, *Andria*, l. 161.

Defended with tooth and nail.
James Calfhill, *Answer to Martial*, l. 228. (1565)

With tooth and nail.
Du Bartas, *Devine Weekes and Workes*. Week i, day 2.

II—Tooth: The Aching Tooth

18
An aching tooth is better out than in.

To lose a rotten member is a gain.
RICHARD BAXTER, *Hypocrisy.*

1
My curse upon your venom'd stang,
That shoots my tortur'd gooms alang,
An' thro' my lug gies monie a twang
Wi' gnawing vengeance,
Tearing my nerves wi' bitter pang,
Like racking engines!
BURNS, *Address to the Toothache.* St. 1.

2
The tongue is ever turning to the aching tooth.
THOMAS FULLER, *Gnomologia.* No. 4796.
FRANKLIN, *Poor Richard,* 1746.

3
Of all our pains, since man was curst,
I mean of body, not the mental,
To name the worst, among the worst,
The dental sure is transcendental;
Some bit of masticating bone,
That ought to help to clear a shelf:
But lets its proper work alone,
And only seems to gnaw itself.
THOMAS HOOD, *A True Story,* l. 1.

One tooth he had with many fangs,
That shot at once as many pangs, . . .
One touch of that extatic stump
Could jerk his limbs, and make him jump.
THOMAS HOOD, *A True Story,* l. 27.

4
Who hath aching teeth hath ill tenants.
JOHN RAY, *English Proverbs,* p. 26.

5
What! sigh for the toothache?
SHAKESPEARE, *Much Ado About Nothing.* Act iii, sc. 2, l. 23.

For there was never yet philosopher
That could endure the toothache patiently.
SHAKESPEARE, *Much Ado About Nothing.* Act v, sc. 1, l. 35.

Being troubled with a raging tooth,
I could not sleep.
SHAKESPEARE, *Othello.* Act iii, sc. 3, l. 414.

TOWN, see Village

TORTURE, see Suffering

TRADE, see Commerce

TRANQUILLITY, see Quiet

TRAVEL

See also Wanderlust

I—Travel: Apothegms

6
Always somebody goin' away,
Somebody gettin' home.
JOHN JOY BELL, *On the Quay.*

7
He travels safest in the dark night who travels lightest.
HERNANDO CORTEZ. (PRESCOTT, *Conquest of Mexico.* Bk. v, ch. 3.)

8
The world is his who has money to go over it.
EMERSON, *Conduct of Life: Wealth.*

9
I have been a stranger in a strange land.
Old Testament: Exodus, ii, 22.

10
If you will be a traveller, have always the eyes of a falcon, the ears of an ass, the face of an ape, the mouth of a hog, the shoulder of a camel, the legs of a stag, and see that you never want two bags very full, that is one of patience and another of money.
JOHN FLORIO, *Second Frutes.* Fo. 93. (1591)

A traveller must have the back of an ass to bear all, a tongue like the tail of a dog to flatter all, the mouth of a hog to eat what is set before him, the ear of a merchant to hear all and say nothing.
THOMAS NASHE, *Works,* v, 141. There are many variations of this saying, which is included in most of the collections of proverbs.

11
Know most of the rooms of thy native country before thou goest over the threshold thereof.
THOMAS FULLER, *The Holy and Profane States: Of Travelling.* Maxim 4.

A wise traveler never despises his own country. (Un viaggiatore prudente non disprezza mai il suo paese.)
GOLDONI, *Pamela.* Act i, 16.

12
A gentleman ought to travel abroad, but dwell at home.
THOMAS FULLER, *Gnomologia.* No. 127.

The fool wanders, the wise man travels.
THOMAS FULLER, *Gnomologia.* No. 4540.

Travel makes a wise man better, but a fool worse.
THOMAS FULLER, *Gnomologia.* No. 5272.

13
A man who leaves home to mend himself and others is a philosopher; but he who goes from country to country, guided by the blind impulse of curiosity, is only a vagabond.
GOLDSMITH, *The Citizen of the World.* No. 7.

Remote, unfriended, melancholy, slow,
Or by the lazy Scheldt, or wandering Po.
GOLDSMITH, *The Traveller,* l. 1.

14
I journeyed fur, I journeyed fas'; I glad I
foun' de place at las'!
JOEL CHANDLER HARRIS, *Nights with Uncle Remus.* Ch. 35.

15
I should like to spend the whole of my life in traveling abroad, if I could anywhere borrow another life to spend afterwards at home.
HAZLITT, *Table-Talk: On Going a Journey.*

16
Slackness breeds worms; but the sure traveller,
Though he alight sometimes, still goeth on.
GEORGE HERBERT, *The Church-Porch.* St. 57.

I am like the Huma bird that never lights, being

always in the cars as he is always on the wing.
O. W. HOLMES, *Autocrat of the Breakfast-Table*. Ch. 1.

1
He saw the cities of many men and knew their manners. (Πολλῶν δ' ἀνθρώπων ἴδεν ἄστεα καὶ νόον ἔγνω.)
HOMER, *Odyssey*. Bk. i, l. 3.

Wand'ring from clime to clime, observant strayed,
Their manners noted, and their states surveyed.
HOMER, *Odyssey*. Bk. i, l. 5. (Pope, tr.)

He had wisely seen the world at home and abroad.
SIR THOMAS BROWNE, *To a Friend*. Sec. 24.

2
Who saw the manners of many men and their cities. (Qui mores hominum multorum vidit et urbes.)
HORACE, *Ars Poetica*, l. 142.

He was a careful observer of the cities and customs of many men. (Multorum providus urbes Et mores hominum inspexit.)
HORACE, *Epistles*. Bk. i, epis. 2, l. 19. Of Ulysses.

He delighted to wander in unknown lands, to see strange rivers, his eagerness making light of toil. (Ignotis errare locis, ignota videre Flumina gaudebat, studio minuente laborem.)
OVID, *Metamorphoses*. Bk. iv, l. 294.

For always roaming with a hungry heart,
Much have I seen and known,—cities of men
And manners, climates, councils, governments.
TENNYSON, *Ulysses*, l. 12.

3
The wonders of each region view,
From frozen Lapland to Peru.
SOAME JENYNS, *Epistle to Lord Lovelace. See also under* OBSERVATION.

4
From going to and fro in the earth, and from walking up and down in it.
Old Testament: Job, i, 7.

5
As the Spanish proverb says, "He who would bring home the wealth of the Indies, must carry the wealth of the Indies with him." So it is in traveling; a man must carry knowledge with him, if he would bring home knowledge.
SAMUEL JOHNSON. (BOSWELL, *Life*, 1778.) The proverb is inscribed on the façade of the Union Station at Washington, D. C.

6
Down to Gehenna or up to the Throne,
He travels the fastest who travels alone.
KIPLING, *The Winners. See also under* MARRIAGE AND CELIBACY.

7
He travels best that knows When to return.
MIDDLETON, *The Old Law*. Act iv, sc. 2.

8
Sir Drake whom well the world's end knew
Which thou did'st compass round,
And whom both Poles of heaven once saw
Which North and South do bound,
The stars above would make thee known,
If men here silent were;
The sun himself cannot forget
His fellow traveller.
JOHN OWEN, *Epigram on Sir Francis Drake*.

9
We sack, we ransack to the utmost sands
Of native kingdoms, and of foreign lands:
We travel sea and soil; we pry, and prowl,
We progress, and we prog from pole to pole.
FRANCIS QUARLES, *Divine Emblems*. Bk. ii, emb. 2.

10
There is a great difference between travelling to see countries or to see peoples. (Il y a bien de la différence entre voyager pour voir du pays ou pour voir des peuples.)
ROUSSEAU, *Émile*. Bk. v.

11
I think there is a fatality in it—I seldom go to the place I set out for.
STERNE, *A Sentimental Journey: The Address: Versailles*.

12
I pity the man who can travel from Dan to Beersheba, and cry, " 'Tis all barren!"
STERNE, *A Sentimental Journey: In the Street: Calais*, iii.

From Dan even to Beersheba.
Old Testament: Judges, xx, 1.

13
For my part, I travel not to go anywhere, but to go. I travel for travel's sake. The great affair is to move.
R. L. STEVENSON, *Travels With a Donkey*.

To travel hopefully is a better thing than to arrive.
R. L. STEVENSON, *Virginibus Puerisque: El Dorado*.

14
I always like to begin a journey on Sundays, because I shall have the prayers of the Church to preserve all that travel by land or by water.
SWIFT, *Polite Conversation*. Dial. ii.

15
As light and the day are free to all men, so nature has left all lands open to brave men. (Quomodo lucem diemque omnibus hominibus, ita omnes terras fortibus viris natura aperuit.)
TACITUS, *History*. Bk. iv, sec. 64.

II—Travel: Its Wisdom

16
The traveled mind is the catholic mind educated from exclusiveness and egotism.
AMOS BRONSON ALCOTT, *Table Talk: Travel*.

Traveling is no fool's errand to him who carries his eyes and itinerary along with him.
AMOS BRONSON ALCOTT, *Table Talk: Travel*.

17
Travel, in the younger sort, is a part of education; in the elder, a part of experience. He that travelleth into a country, before he hath some entrance into the language, goeth to school, and not to travel.
FRANCIS BACON, *Essays: Of Travel*.

Let him sequester himself from the company of his countrymen, and diet in such places where there is good company of the nation where he travelleth.

FRANCIS BACON, *Essays: Of Travel.*

1
Young men should travel, if but to amuse
Themselves.

BYRON, *Don Juan.* Canto ii, st. 16.

2
If a shower approach,
You find safe shelter in the next stage-coach.
There, prison'd in a parlour snug and small,
Like bottled wasps upon a southern wall,
The man of bus'ness and his friends compress'd,
Forget their labours.

COWPER, *Retirement,* l. 491.

3
Travel teaches toleration.

BENJAMIN DISRAELI, *Contarini Fleming.* Pt. v, ch. 7.

Virtue and vice, happiness and misery, are much more equally distributed to nations than those are permitted to suppose who have never been from home, and who believe, like the Chinese, that their residence is the center of the world, of light, of privilege, and of enjoyment.

AMASSA DELANO, *Narrative of Voyages,* p. 256.

Go far—too far you cannot, still the farther
The more experience finds you: And go sparing;—
One meal a week will serve you, and one suit,
Through all your travels; for you'll find it certain,
The poorer and the baser you appear,
The more you look through still.

JOHN FLETCHER, *The Woman's Prize.* Act iv, sc. 5, l. 199.

4
He that travels much knows much.

THOMAS FULLER, *Gnomologia.* No. 2335.

He who never leaves his country is full of prejudices. (Chi non esce dal suo paese, vive pieno di pregiudizi.)

GOLDONI, *Pamela.* Act i.

5
Travelling makes a man wiser, but less happy.

THOMAS JEFFERSON, *Writings.* Vol. vi, p. 31.

6
The use of travelling is to regulate imagination by reality, and instead of thinking how things may be, to see them as they are.

SAMUEL JOHNSON. (PIOZZI, *Johnsoniana.* No. 154.)

7
The country, your companions, and the length of your journey will afford a hundred compensations for your toil. (Centum solatia curæ Et rus, et comites, et via longa dabit.)

OVID, *Remediorum Amoris,* l. 242.

8
Leave thy home, O youth, and seek out alien shores: a larger range of life is ordained for thee. (Linqua tuas sedes alienque litora quære, O junevis: major rerum tibi nascitur ordo.)

PETRONIUS, *Fragments.* No. 79.

9
Of journeying the benefits are many: the freshness it bringeth to the heart, the seeing and hearing of marvellous things, the delight of beholding new cities, the meeting of unknown friends, the learning of high manners.

SADI, *Gulistan.* Ch. iii, tale 28.

10
Voyage, travel, and change of place impart vigour. (Vectatio, iterque, et mutata regio vigorem dabunt.)

SENECA, *De Tranquillitate Animi.* Sec. 17.

11
Crowns in my purse I have and goods at home,
And so am come abroad to see the world.

SHAKESPEARE, *The Taming of the Shrew.* Act i, sc. 2, l. 57.

12
Home-keeping youth have ever homely wits. . . .
I rather would entreat thy company
To see the wonders of the world abroad
Than, living dully sluggardized at home,
Wear out thy youth with shapeless idleness.

SHAKESPEARE, *The Two Gentlemen of Verona.* Act i, sc. 1, l. 2.

13
Mankind are always happier for having been happy. . . . A man is the happier for life from having made once an agreeable tour.

SYDNEY SMITH, *Sketches of Moral Philosophy.* Lecture 22.

III—Travel: Its Folly

14
And men go abroad to admire the heights of mountains, the mighty billows of the sea, the long courses of rivers, the vast compass of the ocean, and the circular motion of the stars, and yet pass themselves by.

ST. AUGUSTINE, *Confessions.* Bk. x, ch. 8.

Why seek Italy,
Who cannot circumnavigate the sea
Of thoughts and things at home?

EMERSON, *The Day's Ration.*

15
Travelling is the ruin of all happiness. There's no looking at a building here, after seeing Italy.

FANNY BURNEY, *Cecilia.* Bk. ii, ch. 6.

16
Those who travel heedlessly from place to place, observing only their distance from each other, and attending only to their accommodation at the inn at night, set out fools, and will certainly return so.

LORD CHESTERFIELD, *Letters,* 30 Oct., 1747.

How much a dunce that has been sent to roam,
Excels a dunce that has been left at home.

COWPER, *The Progress of Error,* l. 415.

If an ass goes travelling, he'll not come home a horse.

THOMAS FULLER, *Gnomologia*. No. 2668.

The fool that far is sent,
Some wisdom to attain,
Returns an idiot, as he went,
And brings the fool again.

GEOFFREY WHITNEY, *Emblems*, 178. (1586)

1 In travelling
I shape myself betimes to idleness
And take fools' pleasure.

GEORGE ELIOT, *The Spanish Gypsy*. Bk. i.

2 There are three wants which never can be satisfied: that of the rich, who wants something more; that of the sick, who wants something different; and that of the traveller, who says, "Anywhere but here."

EMERSON, *Conduct of Life: Considerations by the Way*.

It is for want of self-culture that the superstition of Travelling, whose idols are Italy, England, Egypt, retains its fascination for all educated Americans. They who made England, Italy, or Greece venerable in the imagination, did so by sticking fast where they were. . . . The soul is no traveller; the wise man stays at home. . . . Travelling is a fool's paradise.

EMERSON, *Essays, First Series: Self-Reliance*.

3 Some minds improve by travel, others, rather,
Resemble copper wire, or brass,
Which get the narrower by going farther!

THOMAS HOOD, *Ode to Rae Wilson*, l. 229.

4 They change their clime, not their disposition, who run beyond the sea. (Cælum, non animam mutant, qui trans mare currunt.)

HORACE, *Epistles*. Bk. i, epis. 11, l. 27.

If a goose flies across the sea, there comes back a quack-quack.

UNKNOWN. A German proverb.

5 Each blames the place he lives in; but the mind
Is most in fault, which ne'er leaves self behind.
(Stultus uterque locum immeritum causatur inique:
In culpa est animus, qui se non effugit umquam.)

HORACE, *Epistles*. Bk. i, epis. 14, l. 12. (Conington, tr.)

It serves you right! You travelled with yourself. (Non immerito hoc tibi evenit; tecum enim peregrinabaris.)

SOCRATES, to a man who complained that he had received no benefit from his travels. (SENECA, *Epistulæ ad Lucilium*. Epis. civ, sec. 7.)

6 Your land, and home, and pleasant wife must be left behind. (Linquenda tellus, et domus, et placens Uxor.)

HORACE, *Odes*. Bk. ii, ode 14, l. 21.

His house, his home, his heritage, his lands,
The laughing dames in whom he did delight,
Whose large blue eyes, fair locks, and snowy hands,
Might shake the saintship of an anchorite,
And long had fed his youthful appetite;
His goblets brimm'd with every costly wine,
And all that mote to luxury invite,
Without a sigh he left, to cross the brine,
And traverse Paynim shores, and pass earth's central line.

BYRON, *Childe Harold*. Canto i, st. 11.

7 Why do we in our short term of life strive with might and main for so many things? Why do we change for lands warmed by another sun? (Quid brevi fortes jaculamur ævo Multa? Quid terras alio calentes Sole mutamus?)

HORACE, *Odes*. Bk. ii, ode 16, l. 17.

8 Fools are aye fond o' flittin', and wise men o' sittin'.

JOHN RAY, *Proverbs: Scottish*.

9 Everywhere is nowhere. When a person spends all his time in foreign travel, he ends by having many acquaintances, but no friends. (Nusquam est, qui ubique est.)

SENECA, *Epistulæ ad Lucilium*. Epis. ii, sec. 2.

What profit is there in crossing the sea and in going from one city to another? If you would escape your troubles, you need not another place but another personality. Perhaps you have reached Athens, or perhaps Rhodes; choose any state you fancy, how does it matter what its character may be? You will be bringing to it your own.

SENECA, *Epistulæ ad Lucilium*. Epis. civ, sec. 8.

What benefit has travel of itself ever been able to give anyone? . . . Travelling cannot give us judgment, or shake off our errors; it merely holds our attention for a moment by a certain novelty.

SENECA, *Epistulæ ad Lucilium*. Epis. civ, sec. 13.

10 Ay, now am I in Arden: the more fool I; when I was at home, I was in a better place: but travellers must be content.

SHAKESPEARE, *As You Like It*. Act ii, sc. 4, l. 15.

11 See one promontory, one mountain, one sea, one river, and see all.

SOCRATES. (BURTON, *Anatomy of Melancholy*. Pt. i, sec. ii, mem. 4, subs. 7.)

What canst thou see elsewhere which thou seest not here? Behold the heavens and the earth, and all the elements; for of these are all things made.

THOMAS À KEMPIS, *De Imitatione Christi*. Pt. i, ch. 20.

12 There's nothing under heav'n so blue
That's fairly worth the travelling to.

R. L. STEVENSON, *A Song of the Road*.

1
He need not go away from home for instruction. (Domi habuit unde disceret.)
TERENCE, *Adelphi*, l. 413. (Act iii, sc. 3.)

2
It is not worth while to go round the world to count the cats in Zanzibar.
H. D. THOREAU, *Walden: Conclusion.*

3
He travelled here, he travelled there;—
But not the value of a hair
Was head or heart the better.
WORDSWORTH, *Peter Bell*. Pt. i, l. 238.

IV—Travel: Travellers' Tales

4
There three sorts be Of people lying, which may themselves defend In lying, for they have authority to lie: the first is pilgrims that have great wonders seen In strange countries; such may say what they will.
ALEXANDER BARCLAY, *Ship of Fools*, ii, 68. (1508)

Travellers, poets and liars are three words all of one signification.
RICHARD BRATHWAITE, *English Gentleman*, 77.

5
Travellers . . . have liberty to utter what lies they list.
THOMAS DELONEY, *Gentle Craft*. Pt. ii, ch. 6. (c. 1598)

If he has been a traveller, he certainly says true, for he may lie by authority.
DRYDEN AND LEE, *Duke of Guise*. Act iv, sc. 4.

6
The sundry contemplation of my travels, in which my often rumination wraps me in a most humorous sadness.
SHAKESPEARE, *As You Like It*. Act iv, sc. 1, l. 18.

Farewell, Monsieur Traveller: look you lisp and wear strange suits, disable all the benefits of your own country, be out of love with your nativity and almost chide God for making you that countenance you are, or I will scarce think you have swam in a gondola.
SHAKESPEARE, *As You Like It*. Act iv, sc. 1, l. 32.

7
My travels' history:
Wherein of antres vast and deserts idle,
Rough quarries, rocks and hills whose heads touch heaven,
It was my hint to speak; . . .
And of the Cannibals that each other eat,
And Anthropophagi and men whose heads
Do grow beneath their shoulders.
SHAKESPEARE, *Othello*. Act i, sc. 3, l. 139.

8
Travellers ne'er did lie,
Though fools at home condemn 'em.
SHAKESPEARE, *The Tempest*. Act iii, sc. 3, l. 26.

9
They told of prodigies, as one who has returned from far countries, the force of whirlwinds, and unheard-of birds, monsters of the deep, uncertain combinations of men and beasts—things seen, or believed through fear. (Ut quis ex longinquo revenerat, miracula narrabant, vim turbinum, et inauditas volucres, monstra maris, ambiguas hominum et beluarum formas; visa, sive ex metu credita.)
TACITUS, *Annals*. Bk. ii, sec. 24.

TREACHERY

See also Deceit

9a
They sold the righteous for silver, the poor for a pair of shoes.
Old Testament: Amos, ii, 6.

10
You too, my child! (Καὶ σὺ τέκνον.)
JULIUS CÆSAR, as Marcus Brutus stabbed him. (SUETONIUS, *Lives: The Deified Julius*. Ch. 82, sec. 3. Suetonius says that Cæsar uttered these words in Greek.)

Et tu, Brute! Then fall, Cæsar!
SHAKESPEARE, *Julius Cæsar*. Act iii, sc. 1, l. 77.

This was the most unkindest cut of all.
SHAKESPEARE, *Julius Cæsar*. Act iii, sc. 2, l. 187.

11
The smiler with the knife under the cloak.
CHAUCER, *The Knightes Tale*, l. 1141.

The rascal takes to flight and leaves me under the knife. (Fugit improbus, ac me Sub cultro linquit.)
HORACE, *Satires*. Bk. i, sat. 9, l. 73.

O noble hearts and simple, beware of treacherous blades! (Simplex nobilitas, perfida tela cave!)
OVID, *Fasti*. Bk. ii, l. 226.

Take heed of him that by the back thee claweth.
THOMAS WYATT, *Of the Feigned Friend*.

12
There are no acts of treachery more deeply concealed than those which lie under the pretence of duty, or under some profession of necessity. (Nullæ sunt occultiores insidiæ quam eæ quæ latent in simulatione officii, aut in aliquo necessitudinis nomine.)
CICERO, *In Verrem*. No. i, ch. 15, sec. 39.

13
Away with your double tongued treachery. (Removete bilingues Insidias.)
CLAUDIAN, *De Bello Gildonico*, l. 284.

14
The silence of a friend commonly amounts to treachery.
WILLIAM HAZLITT, *Characteristics*. No. 15.

15
I will forbid the man who has betrayed the sacred rites of Ceres to abide beneath the same roof or to unmoor with me the fragile bark. (Vetabo, qui Cereris sacrum Vulgarit arcanæ, sub îsdem Sit trabibus fragilemque mecum Solvat phaselon.)
HORACE, *Odes*. Bk. iii, ode 2, l. 26.

He who betrays his friend, shall never be
Under one roof, or in one ship with me.
SWIFT, *Imitations of Horace: Odes*, iii, 2.

16
More men are guilty of treachery through weakness than through any studied design to betray. (L'on fait plus souvent des trahisons

par faiblesse que par un dessein formé de trahir.)

La Rochefoucauld, *Maximes*. No. 120.

1
Treachery, though at first very cautious, in the end betrays itself. (Ipsa se fraus, etiamsi initio cautior fuerit, detegit.)

Livy, *History*. Bk. xliv, sec. 15.

2
He . . . felt toward those whom he had deserted that peculiar malignity which has, in all ages, been characteristic of apostates.

Macaulay, *History of England*. Ch. 1.

3
And forthwith he came to Jesus, and said, Hail, Master; and kissed him.

New Testament: Matthew, xxvi, 49.

But Jesus said unto him, Judas, betrayest thou the Son of man with a kiss?

New Testament: Luke, xxii, 48.

Judas had given them the slip.

Matthew Henry, *Commentaries: Matt.*, xxii.

To say the truth, so Judas kiss'd his master,
And cried "all hail!" when as he meant all harm.

Shakespeare, *III Henry VI*. Act v, sc. 7, l. 33.

We dipped our hands in the dish together.
I kissed the face I loved so well.
And here is a halter that will tether
Another ass in the fields of hell.

James L. Duff, *Iscariot*.

4
Dirty work at the crossroads!

Walter Melville, *No Wedding Bells for Him*.

5
Hast thou betray'd my credulous innocence
With vizor'd falsehood, and base forgery?

Milton, *Comus*, l. 697.

6
Punic faith. (Punica fides.)

Sallust, *Jugurtha*. Ch. 108, sec. 3. Applied by the Romans to the Carthaginians, whom they accused of breaking faith with them. Attic faith, Fides Attica, was inviolable faith, the very opposite of Punic faith.

Our Punic faith
Is infamous, and branded to a proverb.

Addison, *Cato*. Act ii, sc. 3.

7
He never counted him a man,
Would strike below the knee.

Scott, *The Lay of the Last Minstrel*. Canto iii, st. 17.

8
I am falser than vows made in wine.

Shakespeare, *As You Like It*. Act iii, sc. 5, l. 73.

Ever double Both in his words and meaning.

Shakespeare, *Henry VIII*. Act iv, sc. 2, l. 38.

He is composed and framed of treachery.

Shakespeare, *Much Ado About Nothing*. Act v, sc. 1, l. 256.

9
And wilt thou still be hammering treachery,
To tumble down thy husband and thyself
From top of honour to disgrace's feet?

Shakespeare, *II Henry VI*. Act i, sc. 2, l. 47.

10
The net has fall'n upon me! I shall perish
Under device and practice.

Shakespeare, *Henry VIII*. Act i, sc. 1, l. 203.

11
It is the bright day that brings forth the adder.

Shakespeare, *Julius Cæsar*. Act ii, sc. 1, l. 14.

12
Such protection as vultures give to lambs.

Sheridan, *Pizarro*. Act ii, sc. 2.

13
Betrayers are hated even by those whom they benefit. (Proditores, etiam iis quos anteponunt, invisi sunt.)

Tacitus, *Annals*. Bk. i, l. 58.

TREASON

I—Treason: Apothegms

14
Treason hath blister'd heels, dishonest things
Have bitter rivers, though delicious springs.

George Chapman, *Charles, Duke of Byron*. Act i, sc. 1.

15
And to talk treason for his daily bread.

Dryden, *Absalom and Achitophel*. Pt. ii, l. 351.

Treason is not own'd when 'tis descried;
Successful crimes alone are justified.

Dryden, *The Medal*, l. 207.

16
Rebellion must be managed by many swords; treason to his prince's person may be with one knife.

Thomas Fuller, *The Holy and the Profane State: The Traitor*.

17
Treason doth never prosper, what's the reason?
For if it prosper, none dare call it Treason.

Sir John Harington, *Of Treason*. (*Epigrams*. Bk. iv, epig. 259.)

18
Cæsar had his Brutus; Charles the First, his Cromwell; and George the Third ["Treason!" cried the Speaker]—*may profit by their example*. If *this* be treason, make the most of it.

Patrick Henry, *Speech in the Virginia Convention*, 1765.

I first drew in New England's air, and from her hardy breast
Sucked in the tyrant-hating milk that will not let me rest;
And if my words seem treason to the dullard and the tame,
'Tis but my Bay-State dialect,—our fathers spake the same.

J. R. Lowell, *On the Capture of Fugitive Slaves near Washington*. St. 2.

19
The labyrinths of treason.

Samuel Johnson, *Irene*.

20
I think lightly of what is called treason against a government. That may be your duty today, or mine. But treason against the peo-

ple, against mankind, against God, is a great sin not lightly to be spoken of.

THEODORE PARKER, *Speech on the Mexican War*, 1846.

1
Treason is but trusted like the fox,
Who, ne'er so tame, so cherish'd and lock'd up,
Will have a wild trick of his ancestors.

SHAKESPEARE, *I Henry IV*. Act v, sc. 2, l. 9.

Treason and murder ever kept together,
As two yoke-devils sworn to either's purpose,
Working so grossly in a natural cause,
That admiration did not hoop at them.

SHAKESPEARE, *Henry V*. Act ii, sc. 2, l. 105.

By treason's tooth bare-gnawn and canker-bit.

SHAKESPEARE, *King Lear*. Act v, sc. 3, l. 122.

2
Some guard these traitors to the block of death,
Treason's true bed and yielder up of breath.

SHAKESPEARE, *II Henry IV*. Act iv, sc. 2, l. 122.

3
The purest spring is not so free from mud,
As I am clear from treason to my sovereign.

SHAKESPEARE, *II Henry VI*. Act iii, sc. 1, l. 101.

II—Treason: To Hate the Traitor but Love the Treason

4
Princes in this case
Do hate the traitor, though they love the treason.

SAMUEL DANIEL, *Tragedy of Cleopatra*, iv, 1.

This principle is old, but true as fate,
Kings may love treason, but the traitor hate.

THOMAS DEKKER, *I The Honest Whore*, iv, 4.

5
Hate then the traitor, but yet love the treason.

DRYDEN AND LEE, *Duke of Guise*. Act iii, sc. 1.

Treason is loved of many, but the traitor is hated of all.

ROBERT GREENE, *Pandosto*.

6
For while the treason I detest,
The traitor still I love.

JOHN HOOLE, *Metastatio*. Act i, sc. 5.

Though I love the treason, I hate the traitor.

SAMUEL PEPYS, *Diary*, 7 March, 1667.

7
He loved treachery but hated a traitor. (Φιλεῖν μὲν προδοσίαν, προδότην δὲ μισεῖν.)

PLUTARCH, *Lives: Romulus*. Ch. 17, sec. 3. Of Cæsar. *See also under* SIN.

Traitors are hated even by those whom they prefer. (Proditores etiam iis quos anteponunt invisi sunt.)

TACITUS, *Annals*. Bk. i, sec. 58.

O sir! I love the fruit that treason brings,
But those that are the traitors, them I hate.

ROBERT GREENE, *Selimus*, l. 2122. (1594)

III—Treason: The Traitor

8
Is there not some chosen curse,
Some hidden thunder in the stores of Heav'n,
Red with uncommon wrath, to blast the man
Who owes his greatness to his country's ruin?

ADDISON, *Cato*. Act i, sc. 1, l. 21.

Oh for a tongue to curse the slave
Whose treason, like a deadly blight,
Comes o'er the councils of the brave
And blasts them in their hour of might!

MOORE, *Lalla Rookh: The Fire-Worshippers*. Pt. ii, l. 476.

9
A traitor to his country commits equal treason against mankind.

JOHN A. ANDREW, *Address*, Massachusetts Legislature, 3 Jan., 1862.

10
For pantisocracy he once had cried
Aloud, a scheme less moral than 't was clever;
Then grew a hearty anti-jacobin—
Had turn'd his coat—and would have turn'd his skin.

BYRON, *The Vision of Judgment*. St. 97. Referring to Robert Southey.

Just for a handful of silver he left us,
Just for a riband to stick in his coat.

ROBERT BROWNING, *The Lost Leader*. Referring to Wordsworth.

The nation looked upon him as a deserter, and he shrunk into insignificancy and an Earldom.

LORD CHESTERFIELD, *Character of Pulteney*.

11
No wise man ever thought that a traitor should be trusted. (Nemo unquam sapiens proditori credendum putavit.)

CICERO, *In Verrem*. No. ii, ch. 1, sec. 15.

12
The man who pauses on the paths of treason,
Halts on a quicksand; the first step engulfs him.

AARON HILL, *Henry V*. Act i, sc. 1.

13
The unsuccessful strugglers against tyranny have been the chief martyrs of treason laws in all countries.

THOMAS JEFFERSON, *Writings*. Vol. viii, p. 332.

14
No religion binds men to be traitors.

BEN JONSON, *Catiline*. Act iii, sc. 2.

15
The traitor to Humanity is the traitor most accursed;
Man is more than Constitutions; better rot beneath the sod,
Than be true to Church and State while we are doubly false to God!

J. R. LOWELL, *On the Capture of Certain Fugitive Slaves near Washington*. St. 5.

Write on my gravestone: "Infidel, Traitor."—infidel to every church that compromises with wrong; traitor to every government that oppresses the people.

WENDELL PHILLIPS.

16
He looked upon his people, and a tear was in his eye.
He looked upon the traitors, and his glance was stern and high.

MACAULAY, *Ivry*.

1 Though those that are betray'd
Do feel the treason sharply, yet the traitor
Stands in worse case of woe.
SHAKESPEARE, *Cymbeline*. Act iii, sc. 4, l. 87.

2
An arrant traitor as any is in the universal world, or in France, or in England!
SHAKESPEARE, *Henry V*. Act iv, sc. 8, l. 10.

A subtle traitor needs no sophister.
SHAKESPEARE, *II Henry VI*. Act v, sc. 1, l. 191.

A kind of puppy To the old dam, treason.
SHAKESPEARE, *Henry VIII*. Act i, sc. 1, l. 175.

A giant traitor.
SHAKESPEARE, *Henry VIII*. Act i, sc. 2, l. 199.

3
Maugre thy strength, youth, place, and eminence,
Despite thy victor sword and fire-new fortune,
Thy valour and thy heart, thou art a traitor; . . .
And, from the extremest upward of thy head
To the descent and dust below thy foot,
A most toad-spotted traitor.
SHAKESPEARE, *King Lear*. Act v, sc. 3, l. 131.

Son: What is a traitor?
Lady Macduff: Why, one that swears and lies.
SHAKESPEARE, *Macbeth*. Act iv, sc. 2, l. 46.

4 Live loathed and long,
Most smiling, smooth, detested parasites,
Courteous destroyers, affable wolves, meek bears,
You fools of fortune, trencher-friends, time's flies.
SHAKESPEARE, *Timon of Athens*. Act iii, sc. 6, l. 103.

5
It [traitor] does not mean in England what it does in France. In your language traitor means betrayer. . . . In our country it means simply one who is not wholly devoted to our English interests.
BERNARD SHAW, *Saint Joan*. Sc. 4.

6
Your sweet faces make good fellows fools
And traitors.
TENNYSON, *Geraint and Enid*, l. 399.

TREE

See also Wood

I—Tree: Apothegms

7
Generations pass while some trees stand, and old families last not three oaks.
SIR THOMAS BROWNE, *Hydriotaphia*. Ch. v, sec. 6.

8
A bird's weight can break the infant tree
Which after holds an aery in its arms.
ROBERT BROWNING, *Luria*. Act iv.

9
The tree of life.
Old Testament: Genesis, ii, 9; *Proverbs*, xiii. 12; *Proverbs*, xv, 4. (Lignum vitæ.—*Vulgate*.)

And on the Tree of Life,
The middle tree and highest there that grew.
MILTON, *Paradise Lost*. Bk. iv, l. 194.

And all amid them stood the Tree of Life,
High eminent, blooming ambrosial fruit
Of vegetable gold.
MILTON, *Paradise Lost*. Bk. iv, l. 218.

10
The tree that God plants no winds hurt it.
GEORGE HERBERT, *Jacula Prudentum*.

If the roots are deep, no fear that the wind will uproot the tree. (Kên shên pu 'pa fêng yao tung.)
UNKNOWN. A Chinese proverb.

11
Great trees are good for nothing but shade.
GEORGE HERBERT, *Jacula Prudentum*.

Great trees give more shade than fruit. (Gli arberi grandi fanno più ombra che frutto.)
UNKNOWN. An Italian proverb.

He that betaketh him to a good tree hath good shade.
EMERSON, *Journals*, 1866.

Those trees in whose dim shadow
The ghastly priest doth reign,—
The priest who slew the slayer,
And shall himself be slain.
MACAULAY, *The Battle of Lake Regillus*. St. 10.

12
For if they do these things in a green tree, what shall be done in the dry?
New Testament: Luke, xxiii, 31.

13
The tree is known by his fruit.
New Testament: Matthew, xii, 33.

You shall know that fruit by the tree.
WILLIAM BULLEIN, *Dialogue*, 86. (1564)

A tree is known by the fruit, and not by the leaves.
JOHN RAY, *English Proverbs*, p. 11.

Only at trees bearing fruit do people throw stones.
W. G. BENHAM, *Proverbs*, p. 825.

He is a fool who looks at the fruit of lofty trees, but does not measure their height. (Stultus est qui fructus magnarum arborum spectat, altitudinem non metitur.)
QUINTUS CURTIUS RUFUS, *De Rebus Gestis Alexandri Magni*. Bk. vii, sec. 8.

14
The highest and most lofty trees have the most reason to dread the thunder.
CHARLES ROLLIN, *Ancient History*. Bk. vi, ch. 2, sec. 1. *See also* GREATNESS: ITS PENALTIES.

15
Jock, when ye hae naething else to do, ye may be aye sticking in a tree; it will be growing, Jock, when ye're sleeping.
SCOTT, *The Heart of Midlothian*. Ch. 8.

16
But, poor old man, thou prunest a rotten tree,
That cannot so much as a blossom yield
In lieu of all thy pains and husbandry.
SHAKESPEARE, *As You Like It*. Act ii, sc. 3, l. 63.

17
Trees do not delight all persons. (Non omnes arbusta juvant.)
VERGIL, *Eclogues*. No. iv, l. 2.

II—Tree: As the Twig Is Bent

1
As long as the twig is gentle and pliant . . .
With small force and strength it may be bent.
THOMAS INGELEND, *The Disobedient Child,* 56.

I will bend the tree while it is a wand.
THOMAS LODGE, *Rosalynde,* 18.

Young twigs are sooner bent than old trees.
JOHN LYLY, *Euphues and His England.*

Tender twigs are bent with ease,
Aged trees do break with bending.
ROBERT SOUTHWELL, *Loss in Delay.*

2
By compliance is the curved bough bent away from the tree. (Flectitur obsequio curvatus ab arbore ramus.)
OVID, *Ars Amatoria.* Bk. ii, l. 179.

3
Just as the twig is bent, the tree 's inclin'd.
POPE, *Moral Essays.* Epis. i, l. 150.

4
An old tree is hard to straighten. (Vieil arbre est mal à redresser.)
UNKNOWN. A French proverb.

III—Tree: Planting the Tree

5
What do we plant when we plant the tree?
We plant the ship that will cross the sea,
We plant the mast to carry the sails,
We plant the planks to withstand the gales—
The keel, the keelson, and beam and knee—
We plant the ship when we plant the tree.
HENRY ABBEY, *What Do We Plant?*

What do we plant when we plant the tree?
A thousand things that we daily see.
We plant the spire that out-towers the crag,
We plant the staff for our country's flag,
We plant the shade from the hot sun free;
We plant all these when we plant the tree.
HENRY ABBEY, *What Do We Plant?*

6
Come, let us plant the apple-tree.
Cleave the tough greensward with the spade;
Wide let its hollow bed be made;
There gently lay the roots, and there
Sift the dark mould with kindly care.
BRYANT, *The Planting of the Apple-Tree.*

What plant we in this apple-tree?
Buds, which the breath of summer days
Shall lengthen into leafy sprays;
Boughs where the thrush, with crimson breast,
Shall haunt, and sing, and hide her nest;
We plant. upon the sunny lea,
A shadow for the noontide hour,
A shelter from the summer shower,
When we plant the apple-tree.
BRYANT, *The Planting of the Apple-Tree.*

7
What does he plant who plants a tree?
He plants the friend of sun and sky;
He plants the flag of breezes free;
The shaft of beauty, towering high;
He plants a home to heaven anigh
For song and mother-croon of bird
In hushed and happy twilight heard—
The treble of heaven's harmony—
These things he plants who plants a tree.
H. C. BUNNER, *The Heart of the Tree.*

8
He who plants a tree Plants a hope.
Rootlets up through fibres blindly grope; . . .
So man's life must climb
From the clods of time
Unto heavens sublime.
Canst thou prophesy, thou little tree,
What the glory of thy boughs shall be?
LUCY LARCOM, *Plant a Tree.*

He who plants a tree, He plants love.
Tents of coolness spreading out above
Wayfarers he may not live to see.
Gifts that grow are best;
Hands that bless are blest;
Plant: Life does the rest!
Heaven and earth help him who plants a tree,
And his work its own reward shall be.
LUCY LARCOM, *Plant a Tree.*

9
He that planteth a tree is the servant of God,
He provideth a kindness for many generations,
And faces that he hath not seen shall bless him.
HENRY VAN DYKE, *The Friendly Trees.*

IV—Tree: Its Fall

10
The tree will wither long before it fall.
BYRON, *Childe Harold.* Canto iii, st. 32.

Trees do not die of age: they only spread
Their branches still more proudly—and are dead.
MARION STROBEL, *Trees.*

11
O leave this barren spot to me!
Spare, woodman, spare the beechen tree.
THOMAS CAMPBELL, *The Beech-Tree's Petition.*

Woodman, spare that tree!
Touch not a single bough!
In youth it sheltered me,
And I'll protect it now.
GEORGE POPE MORRIS, *The Oak.* First printed in *The New York Mirror,* N. Y., 7 Jan., 1837.

12
In the place where the tree falleth, there it shall be.
Old Testament: Ecclesiastes, xi, 3.

Wheresoever the tree falleth . . . there it shall rest.
HUGH LATIMER, *Seven Sermons,* 118.

When the tree is fallen all go with their hatchets.
GEORGE HERBERT, *Jacula Prudentum.*

13
And garnished with trees that a man might cut down,
Instead of his own expenses.
THOMAS HOOD, *Miss Kilmansegg; Her Honeymoon.*

1 Ancient trees falling while all was still
Before the storm, in the long interval
Between the gathering clouds and that light breeze
Which Germans call the Wind's bride.

C. G. LELAND, *The Fall of the Trees.*

2
The ax is laid unto the root of the trees.

New Testament: Matthew, iii, 10; *Luke,* iii, 9.

The tree falls not at the first stroke.

JOHN RAY, *Proverbs: Scottish.*

V—Trees: Their Beauty

3
To-day I have grown taller from walking with the trees.

KARLE WILSON BAKER, *Good Company.*

4
I'll lie here and learn How, over their ground,
Trees make a long shadow And a light sound.

LOUISE BOGAN, *Knowledge.*

5
They say that trees were only practice work
When God made sure his hand
Before he passed to cows and men.
I cannot think that true,
Else there would surely sometimes be
An ugly tree.

AVIS D. CARLSON, *Trees.*

6
The very leaves live for love and in his season every happy tree experiences love's power. (Vivunt in Venerem frondes omnisque vicissim Felix arbor amat.)

CLAUDIAN, *De Nuptiis Honorii Augusti,* l. 65.

7
No tree in all the grove but has its charms,
Though each its hue peculiar.

COWPER, *The Task.* Bk. i, l. 307.

8
I think that I shall never see
A poem lovely as a tree.

A tree whose hungry mouth is pressed
Against the earth's sweet flowing breast. . . .

Poems are made by fools like me,
But only God can make a tree.

JOYCE KILMER, *Trees.*

I think that I shall never see
A billboard lovely as a tree.
Perhaps, unless the billboards fall,
I'll never see a tree at all.

OGDEN NASH, *Song of the Open Road.*

"Did you ever see a poem as lovely as this tree?"

ADDIE M. PROCTOR, *Helping God to Make a Tree.*

Any fool can destroy trees. . . . It took more than three thousand years to make some of the trees in these Western woods, . . . Through all the wonderful, eventful centuries since Christ's time --and long before that—God has cared for these trees, saved them from drought, disease, avalanches, and a thousand straining, leveling tempests and floods; but he cannot save them from fools,—only Uncle Sam can do that.

JOHN MUIR, *The American Forests.* (*Atlantic Monthly,* vol. lxxx, p. 157.)

9
And he spake of trees, from the cedar tree that is in Lebanon even unto the hyssop that springeth out of the wall.

Old Testament: 1 Kings, iv, 33.

10
Fair trees! where'er your barks I wound,
No name shall but your own be found.

ANDREW MARVELL, *The Garden.*

11
Cedar, and pine, and fir, and branching palm,
A sylvan scene, and as the ranks ascend
Shade above shade, a woody theatre
Of stateliest view.

MILTON, *Paradise Lost.* Bk. iv, l. 139.

12
A tree is a nobler object than a prince in his coronation robes.

ALEXANDER POPE, *Table-Talk.*

13
Under the greenwood tree
Who loves to lie with me,
And turn his merry note
Unto the sweet bird's throat,
Come hither, come hither, come hither:
Here shall he see No enemy
But winter and rough weather.

SHAKESPEARE, *As You Like It.* Act ii, sc. 5, l. 1.

14
The trees were gazing up into the sky,
Their bare arms stretched in prayer for the snows.

ALEXANDER SMITH, *A Life-Drama.* Sc. 2.

15
Much can they praise the trees so straight and high,
The sailing pine, the cedar proud and tall,
The vine-prop elm, the poplar never dry,
The builder oak, sole king of forests all,
The aspin good for staves, the cypress funeral,
The laurel, meed of mighty conquerors
And poets sage, the fir that weepest still,
The willow worn of forlorn paramours,
The yew obedient to the bender's will,
The birch for shafts, the sallow for the mill,
The myrrh sweet-bleeding in the bitter wound,
The warlike beech, the ash for nothing ill,
The fruitful olive, and the platane round,
The carver holme, the maple seldom inward sound.

SPENSER, *Faerie Queene.* Bk. i, canto i, st. 8.

16
Many a tree is found in the wood,
And every tree for its use is good;
Some for the strength of the gnarled root,
Some for the sweetness of flower or fruit.

HENRY VAN DYKE, *Salute the Trees.*

17
A brotherhood of venerable trees.

WORDSWORTH, *Memorials of a Tour in Scotland.* No. 12.

VI—Trees: Aspen to Poplar

See also Oak, Orange, Palm, Pine

1
Right as an aspes leaf she gan to quake.
CHAUCER, *Troilus and Criseyde*. Bk. iii, l. 1200.

And the wind, full of wantonness, wooes like a lover
The young aspen-trees till they tremble all over.
THOMAS MOORE, *Lalla Rookh: The Light of the Harem*.

Beneath a shivering canopy reclined,
Of aspen leaves that wave without a wind,
I love to lie, when lulling breezes stir
The spiry cones that tremble on the fir.
JOHN LEYDEN, *Noontide*.

How I shake. . . . In very truth do I, an 'twere an aspen leaf.
SHAKESPEARE, *II Henry IV*. Act ii, sc. 4, l. 116.

2
Spreading himself like a green bay tree.
Old Testament: Psalms, xxxvii, 35.

3
No tree has so fair a bole and so handsome an instep as the beech.
H. D. THOREAU, *Journal*. (EMERSON, *Thoreau*.)

4
The birch, most shy and ladylike of trees.
J. R. LOWELL, *An Indian-Summer Reverie*. St. 8.

5
Loveliest of trees, the cherry now
Is hung with bloom along the bough,
And stands about the woodland ride
Wearing white for Eastertide.
A. E. HOUSMAN, *A Shropshire Lad*, p. 3.

Sweet is the air with the budding haws, and the valley stretching for miles below
Is white with blossoming cherry-trees, as if just covered with lightest snow.
LONGFELLOW, *The Golden Legend*. Pt. iv.

My faith is all a doubtful thing,
Wove on a doubtful loom,
Until there comes each showery Spring
A cherry tree in bloom.
DAVID MORTON, *Symbol*.

6
The chestnuts, lavish of their long-hid gold,
To the faint Summer, beggared now and old,
Pour back the sunshine hoarded 'neath her favoring eye.
J. R. LOWELL, *An Indian-Summer Reverie*. St. 10.

7
Dark tree! still sad when others' grief is fled,
The only constant mourner o'er the dead!
BYRON, *The Giaour*, l. 286. The cypress.

8
And the great elms o'erhead
Dark shadows wove on their aërial looms
Shot through with golden thread.
LONGFELLOW, *Hawthorne*. St. 2.

Under the shady roof
Of branching elm star-proof.
MILTON, *Arcades*. l. 88.

9
I remember, I remember
The fir-trees dark and high;
I used to think their slender tops
Were close against the sky.
THOMAS HOOD, *I Remember, I Remember*.

In a drear-nighted December,
Too happy, happy tree,
Thy branches ne'er remember
Their green felicity.
KEATS, *Stanzas*, l. 1.

10
The hemlock's nature thrives on cold;
The gnash of northern winds
Is sweetest nutriment to him,
His best Norwegian wines.
EMILY DICKINSON, *Poems*. Pt. ii, No. 81.

11
O Reader! hast thou ever stood to see
The Holly Tree?
The eye that contemplates it well perceives
Its glossy leaves
Order'd by an intelligence so wise
As might confound the Atheist's sophistries.
SOUTHEY, *The Holly Tree*. St. 1.

12
The laurel-tree grew large and strong,
Its roots went searching deeply down;
It split the marble walls of Wrong,
And blossomed o'er the Despot's crown.
RICHARD HENGIST HORNE, *The Laurel Seed*.

13
The chestnut's proud, and the lilac's pretty,
The poplar's gentle and tall,
But the plane tree's kind to the poor dull city—
I love him best of all!
EDITH NESBIT, *Child's Song in Spring*.

14
God wrote his loveliest poem on the day
He made the first tall silver poplar tree.
GRACE NOLL CROWELL, *Silver Poplars*.

How gently rock yon poplars high
Against the reach of primrose sky
With heaven's pale candles stored.
JEAN INGELOW, *Supper at the Mill: Song*.

I resemble a poplar, that tree which, even when old, still looks young. (Je ressemble au peuplier, cet arbre qui a toujours l'air jeune, même quand il est vieux.)
JOUBERT, *Pensées*. No. 9.

TRICKERY

See also Deceit, Treachery

15
She had a thousand jadish tricks,
Worse than a mule that flings and kicks.
BUTLER, *Hudibras*. Pt. i, canto 3, l. 331.

16
In trickery, evasion, procrastination, spoliation, botheration, under false pretenses of all sorts, there are influences that can never come to good.
DICKENS, *Bleak House*. Ch. 1.

I know their tricks and their manners.
DICKENS, *Our Mutual Friend*. Bk. ii, ch. 1.

1
Which I wish to remark—
And my language is plain,—
That for ways that are dark
And for tricks that are vain,
The heathen Chinee is peculiar.
BRET HARTE, *Plain Language from Truthful James.*

2
Boy of a hundred tricks. (Centum puer artium.)
HORACE, *Odes*. Bk. iv, ode 1, l. 15.

Has monkey-tricks a full thousand. ('Hou hsi 'chêng 'chien pên.)
UNKNOWN. A Chinese proverb.

3
Remember that all tricks are either knavish or childish.
SAMUEL JOHNSON. (BOSWELL, *Life*, 1779.)

4
A trick to catch the old one.
THOMAS MIDDLETON. Title of play, 1608.

5
You fear some trick. (Captiones metuis.)
PLAUTUS, *Asinaria*, l. 790. (Act iv, sc. 1.)

6
He hath as many tricks as a dancing bear.
JOHN RAY, *English Proverbs*, p. 163.

You have more tricks than a dancing bear.
SWIFT, *Polite Conversation*. Dial. i.

7
I know a trick worth two of that.
SHAKESPEARE, *I Henry IV*. Act ii, sc. 1, l. 41.

8
At this instant He bores me with some trick.
SHAKESPEARE, *Henry VIII*. Act i, sc. 1, l. 27.

He coasts
And hedges his own way. But in this point
All his tricks founder.
SHAKESPEARE, *Henry VIII*. Act iii, sc. 2, l. 38.

These are unsightly tricks.
SHAKESPEARE, *King Lear*. Act ii, sc. 4, l. 159.

9 I have within my mind
A thousand raw tricks of these bragging Jacks,
Which I will practise.
SHAKESPEARE, *Merchant of Venice*, iii, 4, 76.

If I be served such another trick, I'll have my brains ta'en out and buttered, and give them to a dog for a new-year's gift.
SHAKESPEARE, *Merry Wives of Windsor*, iii, 5, 7.

TRIFLES

I—Trifles: Apothegms

10
Always the gods give small things to the small. (*Αἰεὶ τοῖς μικκοῖς μικκὰ διδοῦσι θεοί.*)
CALLIMACHUS, *Fragmenta Incertæ*. No. 47.

11
For the proverb saith that many small maken a great.
CHAUCER, *The Persones Tale*. Sec. 21. (1386)

Many littles make a much. (Muchos pocos hacen un Mucho.)
CERVANTES, *Don Quixote*. Pt. ii, ch. 7.

Many a little, by little and little maketh a mickle.
GABRIEL HARVEY, *Works*. Vol. ii, p. 311. (1593)

Many a little makes a mickle.
BENJAMIN FRANKLIN, *Poor Richard*, 1758.

Within a while, great heaps grow of a tittle.
CHRISTOPHER MARLOWE, *Ovid's Elegies*. No. viii, l. 90.

Many little things will make a mighty heap. (De multis grandis acervus erit.)
OVID, *Remediorum Amoris*, l. 424.

There will grow from straws a mighty heap. (Postmodo de stipula grandis acervus erit.)
OVID, *Amores*. Bk. i, eleg. 8, l. 90.

See also under THRIFT.

12
Practise yourself in little things. (*Ἀπὸ τῶν μικροτάτων.*)
EPICTETUS, *Discourses*. Bk. iv, ch. 1, sec. 111.

13
Small things are best: Grief and unrest
To rank and wealth are given;
But little things On little wings
Bear little souls to Heaven.
F. W. FABER, *Written in a Little Lady's Little Album.*

14
If we take a farthing from a thousand pounds, it will be a thousand pounds no longer.
GOLDSMITH, *The Citizen of the World*. No. 27.

15
To a philosopher no circumstance, however trifling, is too minute.
GOLDSMITH, *The Citizen of the World*. No. 30.

There is nothing, Sir, too little for so little a creature as man. It is by studying little things that we attain the great art of having as little misery and as much happiness as possible.
SAMUEL JOHNSON. (BOSWELL, *Life*, i, 433.)

16
A little Saint best fits a little Shrine,
A little Prop best fits a little Vine,
As my small Cruse best fits my little Wine.
ROBERT HERRICK, *A Ternarie of Littles.*

17
I see day at this little hole.
JOHN HEYWOOD, *Proverbs*. Pt. i, ch. 10.

I perceive you can spy day at a little hole.
THOMAS DELONEY, *Gentle Craft*. Pt. ii, ch. 2.

As daylight can be seen through very small holes, so little things will illustrate a person's character.
SAMUEL SMILES, *Self-Help*, p. 391.

18
The journey of a thousand miles begins with one step.
LAO-TSZE, *The Simple Way*. No. 64.

All difficult things have their origin in that which is easy, and great things in that which is small.
LAO-TSZE, *The Simple Way*.

1
For precept must be upon precept, precept upon precept; line upon line, line upon line; here a little, and there a little.

Old Testament: Isaiah, xxviii, 10.

2
These are small things, but it was by not despising those small things that our ancestors accomplished this very great thing. (Parva sunt hæc; sed parva ista non contemnendo majores nostri maximam hanc rem fecerunt.)

LIVY, *History*. Bk. vi, sec. 41.

3
If great things are simple to understand and easy to explain, little things demand an elaboration of detail.

GEORGE MOORE, *Impressions*.

4
Men are led by trifles.

NAPOLEON BONAPARTE, *Sayings of Napoleon*.

5
Things which are not of value singly, are useful collectively. (Quæ non prosunt singula, multa juvant.)

OVID, *Remediorum Amoris*, l. 420.

6
Trifles console us because trifles distress us. (Peu de chose nous consol, parce que peu de chose nous afflige.)

PASCAL, *Pensées*. Ch. xxiv, No. 11.

7
My copper-lamps, at any rate
For being true antique, I bought:
Yet wisely melted down my plate,
On modern models to be wrought:
And trifles I alike pursue,
Because they're old, because they're new.

MATTHEW PRIOR, *Alma*. Canto iii, l. 358.

8
Trifles, light as air.

SHAKESPEARE, *Othello*. Act iii, sc. 3, l. 322.

A snapper-up of unconsidered trifles.

SHAKESPEARE, *Winter's Tale*. Act iv, sc. 3, l. 26.

9
Little live, great pass.
Jesus Christ and Barabbas
Were found the same day.
This died, that went his way.

C. H. SORLEY, *All the Hills and Vales Along*.

10
For who hath despised the day of small things?

Old Testament: Zechariah, iv, 10.

II—Trifles: Pin-Pricks

11
Strokes of the sword, gentlemen, strokes of the sword! Not pin-pricks! (Des coups d'épée, messieurs, des coups d'épée! Mais pas de coups d'épingle!)

DAUDET, *Tartarin de Tarascon*. Pt. i, ch. 11.

12
I love to dream, but do not wish
To have a pin prick rouse me.
(J'aime à rêver, mais ne veux pas
Qu'à coups d'épingle on me réveille.)

JACQUES DELILLE, *La Conversation*.

13
Policy of pin pricks. (Coups d'épingle.)

LOUIS MARIE DE LA HAYE, *Lettres*.

14
For the maintenance of peace, nations should avoid the pin-pricks which forerun cannon-shots.

NAPOLEON to Czar Alexander, *Interview*, Tilsit, 22 June, 1807.

We are tortured to death by pin-point wounds

NAPOLEON. (LADY MALCOLM, *Diary of St Helena*.)

15
It is never the pin pricks which decide the fortune of states. (Ce ne sont jamais les coups d'épingle qui décident de la fortune des États.)

DE VERGENNES, *Letter to D'Angiviller*, 11 Aug., 1777.

III—Trifles: Their Importance

16
Small matters win great commendation.

FRANCIS BACON, *Essays: Of Ceremonies*.

17
Oh, the little more, and how much it is!
And the little less, and what worlds away!

ROBERT BROWNING, *By the Fireside*.

18
We find great things are made of little things,
And little things go lessening, till at last
Comes God behind them.

ROBERT BROWNING, *Mr. Sludge "The Medium,"* l. 1141.

Say not "a small event"! Why "small"?
Costs it more pain than this, ye call
A "great event" should come to pass
From that?

ROBERT BROWNING, *Pippa Passes: Introduction*.

19
Little drops of water, Little grains of sand,
Make the mighty ocean And the pleasant land.
So the little moments, Humble tho' they be,
Make the mighty ages Of Eternity!

So our little errors Lead the soul away
From the paths of virtue, Far in sin to stray.
Little deeds of kindness, Little words of love,
Help to make earth happy Like the Heaven above!

JULIA FLETCHER CARNEY, *Little Things*. This poem has been erroneously attributed to Ebenezer Cobham Brewer, Daniel Clement Colesworthy, Charles Mackay, and Mrs. Frances S. Osgood. It was written by Mrs. Carney in 1845.

Little drops of water poured into the milk, give the milkman's daughter lovely gowns of silk. Little grains of sugar mingled with the sand, make the grocer's assets swell to beat the band.

WALT MASON, *Little Things*.

20
He that shuns trifles must shun the world.

GEORGE CHAPMAN, *Hero and Leander: Epistle Dedicatory*.

1
Alas! by what slight means are great affairs brought to destruction. (Eheu quam brevibus pereunt ingentia fatis!)

CLAUDIAN, *In Rufinum*. Bk. ii, l. 49.

What mighty contests rise from trivial things.

POPE, *Rape of the Lock*. Canto i, l. 2.

2
An acorn one day proves an oak.

RICHARD CORBET, *Poems*. (c. 1630) (CHALMERS, v, 584.)

The greatest oaks have been little acorns.

THOMAS FULLER, *Gnomologia*. No. 4576. (1732)

The lofty oak from a small acorn grows.

LEWIS DUNCOMBE, *De Minimis Maxima*.

Large streams from little fountains flow,
Tall oaks from little acorns grow.

DAVID EVERETT, *Lines Written for a School Declamation.*

The mighty oak from an acorn towers;
A tiny seed can fill a field with flowers;
One bell alone tolls out the death of kings;
In every Sussex skylark Shelley sings.

CHARLES DALMON, *Much in Little.*

3
From little spark may burst a mighty flame.

DANTE, *Paradiso*. Canto i, l. 34.

From small fires comes oft not small mishap.

GEORGE HERBERT, *Artillerie*, l. 4.

4
He that contemneth small things shall fall by little and little.

Apocrypha: Ecclesiasticus, xix, 1.

He that despiseth small things will perish by little and little.

EMERSON, *Essays, First Series: Prudence.*

5
Many little leaks may sink a ship.

THOMAS FULLER, *The Holy and the Profane State: The Good Servant.*

Many strokes overthrow the tallest oaks.

JOHN LYLY, *Euphues*, p. 81.

Little strokes fell great Oaks.

BENJAMIN FRANKLIN, *Poor Richard*, 1750.

Many strokes, though with a little axe,
Hew down and fell the hardest-timber'd oak.

SHAKESPEARE, *III Henry VI*. Act ii, sc. 1, l. 54.

By conscientious indentation
The beaver bevels down the tree.

CHRISTOPHER MORLEY, *The Epigram.*

6
It's just the little homely things,
The unobtrusive friendly things,
The "won't-you-let-me-help-you" things
That make our pathway light.

GRACE HAINES, *Those Little Things.*

7
For want of a nail the shoe is lost, for want of a shoe the horse is lost, for want of a horse the rider is lost.

GEORGE HERBERT, *Jacula Prudentum.*

For the want of a nail the shoe was lost,
For the want of a shoe the horse was lost,
For the want of a horse the rider was lost,
For the want of a rider the battle was lost,
For the want of a battle the kingdom was lost—
And all for want of a horseshoe-nail.

BENJAMIN FRANKLIN, *Poor Richard*, 1758.

8
Great businesses turn on a little pin.

GEORGE HERBERT, *Jacula Prudentum.*

Great engines turn on small pivots.

H. G. BOHN, *Hand-Book of Proverbs*, 366.

The massive gates of Circumstance
Are turned upon the smallest hinge,
And thus some seeming pettiest chance
Oft gives our life its after-tinge.
The trifles of our daily lives,
The common things scarce worth recall,
Whereof no visible trace survives,
These are the mainsprings, after all.

UNKNOWN, *Trifles*. (*Harper's Weekly*, 30 May, 1863.)

9
Even by small things are great ends helped. (Parvis quoque rebus magna juvari.)

HORACE, *Epistles*. Bk. ii, epis. 1, l. 125.

There is naught that may not serve the need of mortal men, and in adversity despised things help us. (Nam nihil est, quod non mortalibus afferat usum; Rebus in adversis quæ jacuere juvant.)

PETRONIUS, *Fragments*. No. 80.

Insects
Have made the lion mad ere now; a shaft
I' the heel o'erthrew the bravest of the brave.

BYRON, *Marino Faliero*. Act. v, sc. 1.

Few are so small or weak, I guess,
But may assist us in distress,
Nor shall we ever, if we're wise,
The meanest, or the least despise.

JEFFREYS TAYLOR, *The Lion and the Mouse.*

10
A little one shall become a thousand, and a small one a strong nation.

Old Testament: Isaiah, lx, 22.

11
The mighty are brought low by many a thing
Too small to name. Beneath the daisy's disk
Lies hid the pebble for the fatal sling.

HELEN HUNT JACKSON, *Danger.*

12
Events of great consequence often spring from trifling circumstances. (Ex parvis sæpe magnarum momenta rerum pendent.)

LIVY, *History*. Bk. xxvii, sec. 9.

13
Alas, how easily things go wrong!
A sigh too much, or a kiss too long,
And there follows a mist and a weeping rain,
And life is never the same again.

GEORGE MACDONALD, *Phantastes: Down the Lane.*

One dark cloud can hide the sunlight;
Loose one string, the pearls are scattered;
Think one thought, a soul may perish;
Say one word, a heart may break.

ADELAIDE ANN PROCTER, *Philip and Mildred.*

Since trifles make the sum of human things,
And half our misery from our foibles springs;
Since life's best joys consist in peace and ease;
And though but few can serve yet all may please;
O! let th' ungentle spirit learn from hence,
A small unkindness is a great offence.
To spread large bounties though we wish in vain
Yet all may shun the guilt of giving pain.
HANNAH MORE, *Sensibility*, l. 293.

1
It's not much, but every little helps.
JOHN O'KEEFFE, *Wild Oats*. Act v, sc. 3.

Every little helps, as the sow said, when she snapped at a gnat.
C. H. SPURGEON, *John Ploughman*. Ch. 19.

2
Great floods have flown From simple sources.
SHAKESPEARE, *All's Well that Ends Well*. Act ii, sc. 1, l. 142.

Rivers from bubbling springs
Have rise at first, and great from abject things.
THOMAS MIDDLETON, *The Mayor of Queenborough*. Act ii, sc. 3.

3
Trifles make up the happiness or the misery of mortal life.
ALEXANDER SMITH, *Dreamthorp: Men of Letters*.

A trifle makes a dream, a trifle breaks.
TENNYSON, *Sea Dreams*, l. 140.

4
No rock so hard but that a little wave
May beat admission in a thousand years.
TENNYSON, *The Princess*. Pt. iii, l. 138. *See also under* WATER.

5
The dangerous bar in the harbour's mouth is only grains of sand.
M. F. TUPPER, *Proverbial Philosophy: Of Trifles*.

6
Think nought a trifle, though it small appear;
Small sands the mountain, moments make the year
And trifles life. Your care to trifles give,
Or you may die, before you truly live.
YOUNG, *Love of Fame*. Satire vi, l. 204.

IV—Trifles: Their Unimportance

7
Seeks painted trifles and fantastic toys.
MARK AKENSIDE, *The Virtuoso*. St. 10.

Been grieved for trifles, and amused with toys.
JAMES BEATTIE, *Epitaph, Intended for Himself*.

8
This is a gimcrack
That can get nothing but new fashions on you.
BEAUMONT AND FLETCHER, *The Elder Brother*. Act iii, sc. 3.

9
We must not stand upon trifles.
CERVANTES, *Don Quixote*. Pt. i, ch. 30.

Come, gentlemen, we sit too long on trifles.
SHAKESPEARE, *Pericles*. Act ii, sc. 3, l. 92.

10
Small things befit a small man. (Parvum parva decent.)
HORACE, *Epistles*. Bk. i, epis. 7, l. 44.

Frivolous minds are won by trifles. (Parva leves capiunt animos.)
OVID, *Ars Amatoria*. Bk. i, l. 159.

Little things affect little minds.
BENJAMIN DISRAELI, *Sybil*. Bk. iii, ch. 2.

These little things are great to little man.
GOLDSMITH, *The Traveller*, l. 42.

Small things make base men proud.
SHAKESPEARE, *II Henry VI*. Act iv, sc. 1, 106.

11
Those who concern themselves too much with little things usually become incapable of great ones. (Ceux qui s'appliquent trop aux petites choses deviennent ordinairement incapables des grandes.)
LA ROCHEFOUCAULD, *Maximes*. No. 41.

12
It is degrading to make difficulties of trifles. (Turpe est difficiles habere nugas.)
MARTIAL, *Epigrams*. Bk. ii, epig. 86.

They made light of it.
New Testament: Matthew, xxii, 5.

At ev'ry trifle scorn to take offence;
That always shows great pride or little sense.
POPE, *An Essay on Criticism*. Pt. ii, l. 186.

13
Small to greater matters must give way.
SHAKESPEARE, *Antony and Cleopatra*. Act ii, sc. 2, l. 11.

14
By great efforts obtain great trifles. (Magno jam conatu magnas nugas.)
TERENCE, *Heauton Timorumenos*, l. 621. (Act iv, sc. 1.)

15
The discovery of the little planet beyond Neptune is interesting, but is of the same relative importance that a dime found in the vest pocket of last year's winter suit bears to the French national debt.
WILLIAM ALLEN WHITE, *Editorial, Emporia Gazette*.

16
Don't make tragedies of trifles,
Don't shoot butterflies with rifles—
Laugh it off!
UNKNOWN, *Laugh It Off*.

TROUBLE

I—Trouble: Apothegms

17
Pack up your troubles in your old kit-bag,
And smile, smile, smile.
GEORGE ASAF. Title and refrain of song written in 1915, and popular with the British soldiers during World War I.

Build for yourself a strong-box,
Fashion each part with care;
Fit it with hasp and padlock;
Put all your troubles there.

Hide therein all your failures,
  And each bitter cup you quaff,
Lock all your heartaches within it,
  Then sit on the lid and laugh.

J. V. DANNER, *Sit on the Lid and Laugh.*

Wink and shut their apprehensions up.

JOHN MARSTON, *Antonio's Revenge: Prologue.*

1
Trouble rides behind and gallops with him. (Le chagrin monte en croupe et galope avec lui.)

BOILEAU, *Épîtres*, v, 44.

2
Where everything is bad it must be good to know the worst.

F. H. BRADLEY, *Appearance and Reality*. Ch. 15.

3
Whether the pleasure of making a daisy-chain would be worth the trouble of getting up and picking the daisies.

LEWIS CARROLL, *Alice's Adventures in Wonderland*, p. 2.

4
This peck of troubles.

CERVANTES, *Don Quixote*. Pt. ii, ch. 53.

The said George . . . told him that Mr. More was in a peck of troubles.

UNKNOWN, *Archæologia*, xxv, 97. (c. 1535)

5
You will soon be delivered from all your troubles.

CLEONICE, to Cimon, the enigmatic prophecy of his spirit foretelling his death. (PLUTARCH, *Lives: Cimon.*)

6
Oh, a trouble's a ton, or a trouble's an ounce,
  Or a trouble is what you make it,
And it isn't the fact that you're hurt that counts,
  But only how did you take it?

EDMUND VANCE COOKE, *How Did You Die?*

7
In trouble to be troubled
Is to have your trouble doubled.

DEFOE, *Further Adventures of Robinson Crusoe.*

8
Sweet is the remembrance of troubles when you are in safety. (Ἡδύ τοι σωθέντα μεμνῆσθαι πόνων.)

EURIPIDES, *Andromeda*. Fragment.

The memory of past troubles is pleasant. (Jucunda memoria est præteritorum malorum.)

CICERO, *De Finibus*. Bk. ii, ch. 32, sec. 105.

See also under MEMORY.

9
Women like to sit down with trouble as if it were knitting.

ELLEN GLASGOW, *The Sheltered Life*, p. 213.

10
Trouble runs off him like water from a duck's back.

W. G. BENHAM, *Proverbs*, p. 863.

11
"Law, Brer Tarrypin," sez Brer Fox, sezee, "you ain't see no trouble yit. Ef you wanter see sho' nuff trouble, you des oughter go 'longer me; I'm de man w'at kin show yer trouble," sezee.

J. C. HARRIS, *Nights with Uncle Remus*. Ch. 17.

12
The troubles of our proud and angry dust
  Are from eternity, and shall not fail.
Bear them we can, and if we can we must.
  Shoulder the sky, my lad, and drink your ale.

A. E. HOUSMAN, *Last Poems*. No. 9.

13
Man is born unto trouble, as the sparks fly upward.

Old Testament: Job, v, 7. (Homo nascitur ad laborem, et avis ad volatum.—*Vulgate.*)

14
He [an old servant] saves me trouble, and that is a saving I would rather buy dear than any other. Beyond meat and drink, it is the only use I have ever discovered for money.

J. R. LOWELL, *Letter*, 1873.

15
Be merry, think upon the lives of men,
And with what troubles threescore years and ten
Are crowded oft, yea, even unto him
Who sits at home, nor fears for life and limb.

WILLIAM MORRIS, *Life and Death of Jason*. Bk. x, l. 101.

16
Let each turn his mind to his own troubles. (Ad mala quisque animum referat sua.)

OVID, *Remediorum Amoris*, l. 559.

The wise man thinks about his troubles only when there is some purpose in doing so; at other times he thinks about other things.

BERTRAND RUSSELL, *The Conquest of Happiness*, p. 71.

17
Of our troubles we must seek some other cause than God.

PLATO, *The Republic*. Bk. ii, sec. 19.

18
I praise you when you regard the trouble of your friend as your own. (Laudo, malum cum amici tuum ducis malum.)

PLAUTUS, *Captivi*, l. 151. (Act i, sc. 2.)

19
Swifter come the things unwelcome, swifter far than things we crave. (Nimio celerius Veniet quod noles quam illud, quod cupide petas.)

PLAUTUS, *Mostellaria*, l. 73. (Act i, sc. 1.)

20
Forgetting trouble is the way to cure it. (Injuriarum remedium est oblivio.)

PUBLILIUS SYRUS, *Sententiæ*. No. 250. *See also under* INJURY.

21
To take arms against a sea of troubles.

SHAKESPEARE, *Hamlet*. Act iii, sc. 1, l. 59.

22
Double, double toil and trouble;
Fire burn, and cauldron bubble.

SHAKESPEARE, *Macbeth*. Act iv, sc. 1, l. 10.

1
This I ever held worse than all certitude,
To know not what the worst ahead might be.
SWINBURNE, *Marino Faliero*. Act v.

2
I 'll not willingly offend,
Nor be easily offended;
What 's amiss I 'll strive to mend,
And endure what can't be mended.
ISAAC WATTS, *Good Resolutions*.

2a
Shut your doors and sit in your house, yet trouble will fall from the skies. (Pi mên wu li tso 'huo 'tien shang lai.)
UNKNOWN. A Chinese proverb.

3
I survived that trouble so likewise may I survive this.
UNKNOWN, *Complaint of Deor*. Pt. ii, st. 7. (c. 900)

II—Trouble: Never Trouble Trouble

See also Worry

4
I would far rather be ignorant than wise in the foretelling of evil. (Θέλω δ' ἄιδρις μᾶλλον ἢ σοφὸς κακῶν εἶναι.)
ÆSCHYLUS, *The Suppliants*, l. 453.

5
There are times when we cannot see one step ahead of us, but five years later we are eating and sleeping somewhere.
CHRYSIS, *The Woman of Andros*. (c. 300 B.C.)

I see not a step before me as I tread on another year;
But I 've left the Past in God's keeping,—the Future His mercy shall clear;
And what looks dark in the distance may brighten as I draw near.
MARY GARDINER BRAINARD, *Not Knowing*.

6
Let's fear no storm, before we feel a show'r.
MICHAEL DRAYTON, *Barons' Wars*. Bk. iii, l. 55.

7
Let your trouble tarry till its own day comes.
THOMAS FULLER, *Gnomologia*. No. 3200.

Never trouble trouble till trouble troubles you.
UNKNOWN. (*Folk-Lore Journal*, ii, 280.)

Better never trouble Trouble
Until Trouble troubles you;
For you only make your trouble
Double-trouble when you do;
And the trouble—like a bubble—
That you're troubling about,
May be nothing but a cipher
With its rim rubbed out.
DAVID KEPPEL, *Trouble*.

Don't you trouble trouble till trouble troubles you.
Don't you look for trouble, let trouble look for you.
MARK GUY PEARSE, *Don't Trouble*.

8
If pleasures are greatest in anticipation, just remember that this is also true of trouble.
ELBERT HUBBARD, *Epigrams*.

From a distance it is something; and nearby it is nothing. (De loin, c'est quelque chose; et de près, ce n'est rien.)
LA FONTAINE, *Fables*. Bk. iv, fab. 10.

Sorrows are like thunderclouds—in the distance they look black, over our heads scarcely gray (Die Leiden sind wie die Gewitterwolken; in der Ferne sehen sie schwartz aus, über uns kaum grau.)
JEAN PAUL RICHTER, *Hesperus*. Ch. 14.

Trouble has a trick of coming butt end first;
Viewed approaching, then you've seen it at its worst.
Once surmounted, straight it waxes ever small,
And it tapers till there's nothing left at all.
So, whene'er a difficulty may impend,
Just remember you are facing the butt end;
And that, looking back upon it, like as not,
You will marvel at beholding just a dot!
EDWIN L. SABIN, *Trouble's Strong Front*.

9
Don't cross the bridge till you come to it,
Is a proverb old, and of excellent wit.
LONGFELLOW, *The Golden Legend*. Pt. vi.

10
You are hunting for a knot in a bulrush: i. e., looking for a difficulty where none exists. (In scirpo nodum quæris.)
PLAUTUS, *Menæchmi*, l. 247. (Act ii, sc. 1.)
TERENCE, *Andria*. Act v, sc. 5, l. 38. A proverb.

11
What does it avail to run out to meet your suffering? (Quid juvat dolori suo occurrere?)
SENECA, *Epistulæ ad Lucilium*. Epis. xiii, 10.

Peace, brother, be not over-exquisite
To cast the fashion of uncertain evils;
For grant they be so, while they rest unknown,
What need a man forestall his date of grief,
And run to meet what he would most avoid?
MILTON, *Comus*, l. 359.

12
It is indeed foolish to be unhappy now because you may be unhappy at some future time. (Est sine dubio stultum, quia quandoque sis futurus miser, esse jam miserum.)
SENECA, *Epistulæ ad Lucilium*. Epis. xxiv, 1.

Full of misery is the mind anxious about the future and wretched in anticipation of wretchedness. (Calamitosus est animus futuri anxius et ante miserias miser.)
SENECA, *Epistulæ ad Lucilium*. Epis. xcviii, 6.

What madness to anticipate one's troubles. . . . He suffers more than is necessary, who suffers before it is necessary. (Quæ ista dementia est malum suum antecedere? . . . Plus dolet quam necesse est, qui ante dolet quam necesse est.)
SENECA, *Epistulæ ad Lucilium*. Epis. xcviii, 8.

13
You lay out too much pains
For purchasing but trouble.
SHAKESPEARE, *Cymbeline*. Act ii, sc. 3, l. 92.

III—Trouble and Imagination

See also Worry

14
Why wilt thou add to all the griefs I suffer

Imaginary ills, and fancy'd tortures?
JOSEPH ADDISON, *Cato*. Act iv, sc. 1.

Were a man's sorrows and disquietudes summed up at the end of his life, it would generally be found that he had suffered more from the apprehension of such evils as never happened to him, than from those evils which had really befallen him.
ADDISON, *The Spectator*. No. 505.

1
Supposition is greater than truth. (Opinio veritate major.)
FRANCIS BACON, *Letter to Lord Essex*, 1596. Quoted as a proverb.

2
But human bodies are sic fools,
For a' their colleges and schools,
That when nae real ills perplex them,
They mak enow themsels to vex them.
ROBERT BURNS, *The Twa Dogs*, l. 195.

3
Why should we shrink from what we cannot shun?
Each hath his pang, but feeble sufferers groan
With brain-born dreams of evil all their own.
BYRON, *Childe Harold*. Canto ii, st. 7.

4
Ye fearful saints, fresh courage take,
The clouds ye so much dread
Are big with mercy, and shall break
In blessings on your head.
COWPER, *Light Shining out of Darkness*.

5
What we anticipate seldom occurs.
BENJAMIN DISRAELI, *Henrietta Temple*. Bk. ii, ch. 4.

I say the very things that make the greatest stir
An' the most interestin' things, are things that didn't occur.
SAM WALTER FOSS, *Things That Didn't Occur*.

6
Some of your griefs you have cured,
And the sharpest you still have survived;
But what torments of pain you endured
From evils that never arrived!
EMERSON, *Conduct of Life: Considerations by the Way*. A translation of "an old French verse."

I have had many troubles in my life, but the worst of them never came.
JAMES A. GARFIELD, *Remark in Conversation*.

How much pain have cost us the evils which have never happened.
THOMAS JEFFERSON, *Writings*. Vol. xvi, p. 111.

Let us be of good cheer, however, remembering that the misfortunes hardest to bear are those which never come.
J. R. LOWELL, *Democracy and Addresses*.

7
Borrow trouble for yourself, if that's your nature, but don't lend it to your neighbours.
KIPLING, *Rewards and Fairies: Cold Iron*.

8
Apprehensions are greater in proportion as things are unknown. (Major ignotarum rerum est terror.)
LIVY, *History*. Bk. xxviii, sec. 44.

9
You suffer no dread thing but in your fancy.
MENANDER. (PLUTARCH, *Morals: On Contentedness*. Sec. 17.)

10
To such as fear is trouble ever dead?
WILLIAM MORRIS, *The Earthly Paradise: Bellerophon in Lycia*, l. 2230.

11
He that seeks trouble never misses.
GEORGE HERBERT, *Jacula Prudentum*.

Never meet trouble half way.
W. G. BENHAM, *Proverbs*, p. 815.

I can't see the use of . . . trying to meet troubles half way.
HUTCHESON, *Crown and Anchor*. Ch. 16.

The Irish say, "Never go down a lane to meet trouble. It comes up the highroad on horseback."
HELEN MILLER, *Sheridan Road*, p. 157.

12
There are more things, Lucilius, to frighten than to injure us; we suffer more in imagination than in reality. (Plura sunt, Lucili, quæ nos terrent, quam quæ premunt, et sæpius opinione quam re laboramus.)
SENECA, *Epistulæ ad Lucilium*. Epis. xiii, 4.

13
Though life is made up of mere bubbles,
'Tis better than many aver,
For while we've a whole lot of troubles,
The most of them never occur.
NIXON WATERMAN, *Shreds and Patches*.

TROY

See also Helen of Troy

14
Troy owes to Homer what whist owes to Hoyle
BYRON, *Don Juan*. Canto iii, st. 90.

15
Troy was not took in a day.
THOMAS FULLER, *Gnomologia*. No. 5278.

16
There will be a day when sacred Ilium shall be no more. ("Εσσεται ἦμαρ ὅτ' ἄν ποτ' ὀλώλῃ Ἴλιος ἱρή.)
HOMER, *Iliad*. Bk. iv, l. 164; bk. vi, l. 448.

The day shall come, the great avenging day
Which Troy's proud glories in the dust shall lay,
When Priam's powers and Priam's self shall fall,
And one prodigious ruin swallow all.
HOMER, *Iliad*. Bk. iv, l. 196. (Pope, tr.)

17
Some time let gorgeous Tragedy
In sceptred pall come sweeping by,
Presenting Thebes, or Pelops' line,
Or the tale of Troy divine.
MILTON, *Il Penseroso*, l. 97.

18
Now are empty fields where Troy was, and the soil ready for sickle and fat with Phrygian blood, brings forth abundantly. (Jam seges est ubi Troja fuit, resecandaque falce

Luxuriat Phrygio sanguine pinguis humus.)
Ovid, *Heroides*. Epis. i, l. 53.

1
Troy fell because Cassandra was not believed. (Cassandræ quia non creditum, ruit Ilium.)
Phædrus, *Fables*. Bk. iii, fab. 10, l. 4.

The Trojans became wise too late. (Sero sapiunt Phryges.)
H. T. Riley, *Dict. of Latin Quotations*, 418.

Had doting Priam check'd his son's desire,
Troy had been bright with fame and not with fire.
Shakespeare, *The Rape of Lucrece*, l. 1490.

2
Like a Sinon, take another Troy.
Shakespeare, *III Henry VI*. Act iii, sc. 2, l. 190.

3
Cloud-kissing Ilion.
Shakespeare, *The Rape of Lucrece*, l. 1370.

4
That baleful burning night
When subtle Greeks surprised King Priam's
Troy.
Shakespeare, *Titus Andronicus*. Act v, sc. 3, 83.

After seven years siege yet Troy walls stand.
Shakespeare, *Troilus and Cressida*, i, 3, 12.

Troy must not be, nor goodly Ilion stand;
Our firebrand brother, Paris, burns us all.
Shakespeare, *Troilus and Cressida*, ii, 2, 109.

5
By trying, the Greeks got into Troy. (Ἐς Τρόιαν πειρώμενοι ἦνθον Ἀχαιοί.)
Theocritus, *Idylls*. No. xv, l. 64.

6
We were Trojans; Troy was. (Fuimus Troes; fuit Ilium.)
Vergil, *Æneid*. Bk. ii, l. 325.

We have been Trojans: Troy has been:
She sat, but sits no more, a queen.
Vergil, *Æneid*. Bk. ii, l. 325. (Conington, tr.)

7
I am on the side of the Trojans. They fought for a woman.
Oscar Wilde, *Picture of Dorian Gray*. Ch. 17.

TRUST

I—Trust: Apothegms

8
The greatest trust between man and man is the trust of giving counsel.
Francis Bacon, *Essays: Of Counsel*.

9
Do not trust all men, but trust men of worth; the former course is silly, the latter a mark of prudence.
Democritus, *Ethica*. Frag. 224.

It is equally an error to trust all men or no man. (Utrumque enim vitium est, et omnibus credere et nulli.)
Seneca, *Epistulæ ad Lucilium*. Epis. iii, sec. 4.

10
Cast the spear and leave the rest to Jove.
Homer, *Iliad*. Bk. xvii, l. 622. (Bryant, tr.)

11
We are inclined to believe those whom we do not know, because they have never deceived us.
Samuel Johnson, *The Idler*. No. 8.

12
Men are able to trust one another, knowing the exact degree of dishonesty they are entitled to expect.
Stephen Leacock, *The Woman Question*.

13
To be trusted is a greater compliment than to be loved.
George Macdonald, *Marquis of Lossie*. Ch. 4.

Those who trust us, educate us.
George Eliot, *Daniel Deronda*.

14
That, in tracing the shade, I shall find out
the sun,
Trust to me!
Owen Meredith, *Lucile*. Pt. ii, canto vi, st. 15.

15
Trust follows his words. (Dicta fides sequitur.)
Ovid, *Fasti*. Bk. vi, l. 55.

16
So far will I trust thee.
Shakespeare, *I Henry IV*. Act ii, sc. 3, l. 116.

My life upon her faith!
Shakespeare, *Othello*. Act i, sc. 3, l. 295.

Though men may not like me, they always trust my word.
Alfred Sutro, *A Marriage Has Been Arranged*.

Let chance what will, I trust thee to the death.
Tennyson, *The Coming of Arthur*, l. 133.

Trust me not at all, or all in all.
Tennyson, *Merlin and Vivien*, l. 396.

17
Do you fear to trust the word of a man whose honesty you have seen in business? (Quois tu fidem in pecuniæ perspexeris, Verere verba ei credere?)
Terence, *Phormio*, l. 60. (Act i, sc. 2.)

18
He who mistrusts most should be trusted least. (Πᾶς μὲν ἄπιστος ἀπιστεῖ.)
Theognis, *Sententiæ*. (Spenser, *Shepheardes Calender: May: Palinode's Emblem*.)

19
Trust . . . in the living God.
New Testament: I Timothy, vi, 17.

And this be our motto, "In God is our trust."
Francis Scott Key, *The Star-Spangled Banner*.

In one, no object of our sight,
Immutable, and infinite,
Who can't be cruel, or unjust,
Calm and resigned, I fix my trust.
Matthew Green, *The Spleen*, l. 782.

20
Whether in peace or war, in thee shall be my chiefest trust in deed and word. (Seu pacem seu bella geram, tibi maxima rerum Verborumque fides.)
Vergil, *Æneid*. Bk. ix, l. 279.

Public office a public trust, *see* Politics, sec. xi.

21
From whom I trust may God defend me;

From whom I trust not, I defend myself.
(Da chi ma fido mi guardi Iddio;
Da chi non mi fido mi guarderò i.)
UNKNOWN. An Italian proverb. *See under* FRIEND.

II—Trust: Its Wisdom

1
Grow wise, trust woman, doubt not man.
THOMAS BAILEY ALDRICH, *Nourmadee*. St. 10.

2
Who would not rather trust and be deceived?
ELIZA COOK, *Love On*.

Better trust all, and be deceived
And weep that trust and that deceiving,
Than doubt one heart that if believed
Had blessed one's life with true believing.
FRANCES ANNE KEMBLE, *Faith*.

It is better to suffer wrong than to do it, and happier to be sometimes cheated than not to trust.
SAMUEL JOHNSON, *The Rambler*. No. 79.

3
Trusting often makes fidelity.
THOMAS FULLER, *Gnomologia*. No. 5292.

Trust begets truth.
W. G. BENHAM, *Proverbs*, p. 748.

Trust men and they will be true to you; treat them greatly, and they will show themselves great.
EMERSON, *Essays, First Series: Prudence*.

4
O holy trust! O endless sense of rest!
Like the beloved John
To lay his head upon the Saviour's breast,
And thus to journey on!
LONGFELLOW, *Hymn for My Brother's Ordination*. St. 5.

4a
And trust that out of night and death shall rise
The dawn of ampler life; . . .
"I saw the powers of Darkness put to flight,
I saw the Morning break."
OWEN SEAMAN, *Between Midnight and Morning*. Of King Albert of Belgium.

III—Trust: Its Folly

See also Distrust

5
Never trust a man who speaks well of everybody.
CHURTON COLLINS, *Aphorisms*.

6
He who trusteth not is not deceived.
THOMAS FULLER, *Gnomologia*. No. 2406.

Trust me, but look to thyself.
THOMAS FULLER, *Gnomologia*. No. 5288.

Trust, but not too much.
GEORGE HERBERT, *Jacula Prudentum*.

It is better never to trust anybody.
HENRIK IBSEN, *Enemy of the People*. Act ii.

The word is "Pitch and Pay": Trust none.
SHAKESPEARE, *Henry V*. Act ii, sc. 3, l. 51.

7
Thou trustest in the staff of this broken reed.
Old Testament: Isaiah, xxxvi, 6.

8
Trust him no further than you can throw him.
THOMAS FULLER, *Gnomologia*. No. 5286.

I'll trust never a Duke on the world further than I can see him.
UNKNOWN, *True Tragedy of Richard Third*, 17. (1594)

9
Trust slayeth many a man, the wise man saith.
WILLIAM MORRIS, *The Earthly Paradise: Bellerophon in Lycia*, l. 2902.

10
If you trust before you try,
You may repent before you die.
JOHN RAY, *English Proverbs*.

Trust not before you try,
For under cloak of great good-will
Doth feignèd friendship lie.
GEORGE TURBERVILLE, *Of Light Belief*, l. 1.

11
Trust not to rotten planks.
SHAKESPEARE, *Antony and Cleopatra*, iii, 7, 63.

12
He that trusts to you,
Where he should find you lions, finds you hares;
Where foxes, geese.
SHAKESPEARE, *Coriolanus*. Act i, sc. 1, l. 174.

13
Trust not him that once hath broken faith.
SHAKESPEARE, *III Henry VI*. Act iv, sc. 4, l. 30.

14
Albany: Well, you may fear too far.
Goneril: Safer than trust too far.
SHAKESPEARE, *King Lear*. Act i, sc. 4, l. 351.

15
He's mad that trusts in the tameness of a wolf, a horse's health, a boy's love, or a whore's oath.
SHAKESPEARE, *King Lear*. Act iii, sc. 6, l. 19.

Trust not a horse's heel, nor a dog's tooth.
JOHN RAY, *English Proverbs*.

16
Immortal gods, I crave no pelf;
I pray for no man but myself:
Grant I may never prove so fond,
To trust man on his oath or bond;
Or a harlot, for her weeping;
Or a dog, that seems a-sleeping;
Or my friends, if I should need 'em.
SHAKESPEARE, *Timon of Athens*. Act i, sc. 2, 63.

Three things a wise man will not trust,
The wind, the sunshine of an April day,
And woman's plighted faith.
SOUTHEY, *Madoc in Aztlan*. Pt. xxiii, l. 51.

IV—Trust: The Trusts

17
Trust.
SAMUEL C. T. DODD introduced this word, as referring to a combination of capital, into the language in 1882, while acting as attorney for John D. Rockefeller.

This is the original trust.
UNKNOWN, *Report of Committee*, N. Y. State Senate, after investigation of the Standard Oil Company, in 1888.

We declare our opposition to all combinations of capital, organized as trusts or otherwise.
Republican Platform, 1888.

The interests of the people are betrayed when Trusts and combinations are permitted to exist.
Democratic Platform, 1888.

Earnest attention should be given to those combinations of capital commonly called Trusts.
BENJAMIN HARRISON, *Message to Congress*, 3 Dec., 1889.

1
Trusts are largely private affairs.
JAMES G. BLAINE, *Speech*, Portland, Me., opening Harrison campaign in 1888.

2
Undigested securities.
J. PIERPONT MORGAN, *Interview, N. Y. Times*, 30 March, 1903, referring to a mass of securities issued to inflate and water the capitalization of trusts and combinations, promoted and floated in 1901.

3
An indefinable something is to be done, in a way nobody knows how, at a time nobody knows when, that will accomplish nobody knows what. That, as I understand it, is the program against the trusts.
THOMAS B. REED. (W. A. ROBINSON, *Life*.)

4
The System.
LINCOLN STEFFENS. A term invented to describe the super-community of interest which he found between trusts.

The Octopus.
FRANK NORRIS. Title of novel describing the workings of "the system."

Special privilege.
ROBERT M. LA FOLLETTE, *Speech*, U. S. Senate, referring to the trusts.

5
The mother of trusts.
WOODROW WILSON, in 1898, referring to New Jersey, because her laws authorized the creation of "holding-corporations."

6
The Mother of Trusts.
JESSE HARDESTY. Title of book. Mr. Hardesty named railroad rebates as the maternal parent.

The mother of all trusts is the customs tariff law.
HENRY O. HAVEMEYER, while testifying before the industrial commission in 1899.

I made the first speech in favor of organizing industrial consolidations in the eighties. Later the Chicago newspapers gave me the title of "Father of Trusts."
CHARLES R. FLINT, *Memories of an Active Life*.

7
Monopolies are odious, contrary to the spirit of free government and the principles of commerce and ought not to be suffered.
Maryland Declaration of 1776, referring to grants of monopoly by royal decree.

8
A power has risen up in the government greater than the people themselves, consisting of many and various and powerful interests . . . held together by the cohesive power of the vast surplus in the banks.
J. C. CALHOUN, *Speech*, U. S. Senate, 27 May, 1836.

9
The Seven Sisters.
Seven laws drawn up by Woodrow Wilson, as Governor of New Jersey, to end the state's statutory benevolence to the trusts.

New Jersey was regularly in the business of selling not only indulgence but absolution.
LINCOLN STEFFENS, *New Jersey and the Trusts.*

TRUTH

See also Beauty and Truth

I—Truth: Definitions

10
Truth is inclusive of all the virtues, is older than sects or schools, and, like charity, more ancient than mankind.
AMOS BRONSON ALCOTT, *Table Talk: Discourse.*

Yet the deepest truths are best read between the lines, and, for the most part, refuse to be written.
AMOS BRONSON ALCOTT, *Concord Days: June.*

11
Truth is the secret of eloquence and of virtue, the basis of moral authority; it is the highest summit of art and life.
AMIEL, *Journal*, 17 Dec., 1854.

12
Another poet, whose name I have forgotten, called Truth the daughter of Time. (Veritatem Temporis filiam.)
AULUS GELLIUS, *Noctes Atticæ*. Bk. xii, ch. 11.

'Tis not antiquity, nor author,
That makes truth Truth, altho' Time's daughter.
BUTLER, *Hudibras*. Pt. ii, canto 3, l. 663.

13
Truth is within ourselves: it takes no rise
From outward things, whate'er you may believe.
There is an inmost centre in us all,
Where truth abides in fulness.
ROBERT BROWNING, *Paracelsus*. Pt. i.

14
Truth makes on the ocean of nature no one track of light—every eye looking on finds its own.
BULWER-LYTTON, *Caxtoniana*. Essay xiv.

15
Truth is the shattered mirror strown
In myriad bits; while each believes his little bit the whole to own.
SIR RICHARD BURTON, *Kasîdah*. Pt. vi, st. 1.

16
Truth in person doth appear
Like words congeal'd in northern air.
BUTLER, *Hudibras*. Pt. i, canto 1, l. 147.

17
Truth ever lovely—since the world began
The foe of tyrants, and the friend of man.
CAMPBELL, *The Pleasures of Hope*. Pt. ii, l. 347.

18
Truth is the highest thing that man may keep
CHAUCER, *The Frankeleyns Tale*, l. 751.

Truth is man's proper good, and the only immortal thing was given to our mortality to use.

Ben Jonson, *Explorata: Veritas Proprium Hominis.*

1

Truth is the object of philosophy, but not always of philosophers.

Churton Collins, *Aphorisms*, 102.

2

Truth is truest poesy.

Abraham Cowley, *Davideis.* Bk. i, l. 41.

It's deadly commonplace, but, after all, the commonplaces are the great poetic truths.

R. L. Stevenson, *Weir of Hermiston.*

3

"It is," says Chadband, "the ray of rays, the sun of suns, the moon of moons, the star of stars. It is the light of Terewth."

Dickens, *Bleak House.* Ch. 25.

4

Truth is the summit of being; justice is the application of it to affairs.

Emerson, *Essays, Second Series: Character.*

Truth, whose centre is everywhere and its circumference nowhere, whose existence we cannot disimagine; the soundness and health of things, against which no blow can be struck but it recoils on the striker.

Emerson, *Letters and Social Aims: Progress of Culture.*

5

Truth, sir, is a profound sea, and few there be who dare wade deep enough to find out the bottom on't.

Farquhar, *The Beaux' Stratagem.* Act v, sc. 1.

6

Truth is for other worlds, and hope for this;
The cheating future lends the present's bliss.

O. W. Holmes, *The Old Player.*

Veracity is a plant of paradise, and the seeds have never flourished beyond the walls.

George Eliot, *Romola.*

7

History warns us that it is the customary fate of new truths to begin as heresies and to end as superstitions.

Thomas Henry Huxley, *Science and Culture: Origin of Species.*

All great truths begin as blasphemies.

Bernard Shaw, *Annajanska.*

What everybody echoes . . . as true today, may turn out to be falsehood tomorrow, mere smoke of opinion.

H. D. Thoreau, *Walden.* Ch. 1.

8

Veracity is the heart of morality.

T. H. Huxley, *Universities Actual and Ideal.*

9

Truth, sir, is a cow, which will yield skeptics no more milk; so they have gone to milk the bull.

Samuel Johnson. (Boswell, *Life.*)

10

Teach it to the simple, the learned know it
well:
Truth is treasure, the best tried on earth.

William Langland, *Piers Plowman.* Pt. ii.

When all treasures are tried, Truth is the best. . . .
For he who is True with his tongue, True with his hands
Working True works therewith, and wishing ill to none,
He is a god, the gospel says, in earth and heaven.

William Langland, *Piers Plowman.* Pt. ii.

11

Truth is the strong compost in which beauty may sometimes germinate.

Christopher Morley, *Inward Ho.*

Truth is not a diet But a condiment.

Christopher Morley, *Veritas vos Damnabit.*

12

Truth is a fair and durable thing. (Καλὸν μὲν ἡ ἀλήθεια καὶ μόνιμον.)

Plato, *Laws*, 663. (Diogenes Laertius, *Plato.* Sec. 40.)

Truth is the pleasantest of sounds. (Εἶναί τε ἥδιον τῶν ἀκουσμάτων τὴν ἀλήθειαν.)

Plato. (Diogenes Laertius, *Plato.* Sec. 40.)

13

Truth is a jewel which should not be painted over; but it may be set to advantage and shown in a good light.

George Santayana, *Life of Reason*, iv, 105.

14

Truth is eternal, and the son of heaven.

Swift, *Ode: Dr. Wm. Sancroft.*

15

Truth is that which a man troweth.

John Horne Tooke, *Diversions of Purley.*

16

There are truths which are not for all men, nor for all times.

Voltaire, *Letter to Cardinal de Bernis*, 23 April, 1764.

Truths are fruits which should only be plucked when quite ripe.

Voltaire, *Letter to the Countess de Barcewitz*, 24 Dec., 1761.

17

Pure truth hath no man seen nor e'er shall know. (Καὶ τὸ μὲν σαφὲς οὔτις ἀνὴρ ἴδεν οὐδέ τις ἔσται εἰδώς.)

Xenophanes, *Fragments.* No. 34.

Pure truth cannot be assimilated by the crowd; it must be communicated by contagion.

Amiel, *Journal*, 26 Oct., 1875.

If God should hold enclosed in his right hand all truth, and in his left hand only the ever-active impulse after truth, although with the condition that I must always and forever err, I would with humility turn to his left hand and say, "Father, give me this: pure truth is for thee alone."

Lessing, *Anti-Götze.*

No human being is constituted to know the truth, the whole truth, and nothing but the truth; and even the best of men must be content with fragments, with partial glimpses, never the full fruition.

William Osler. *The Student Life.*

II—Truth: Apothegms

1
Truth has not such an urgent air. (La vérité n'a point cet air impétueux.)
BOILEAU, *L'Art Poétique*. Pt. i, l. 198.

2
A man may be in as just possession of truth as of a city, and yet be forced to surrender.
SIR THOMAS BROWNE, *Religio Medici*. Pt. i, sec. 6.

3
Why with old truth needs new truth disagree?
ROBERT BROWNING, *Red Cotton Night-cap Country*. Bk. ii.

4
The Truth may stretch but will not break. (La Verdad adelgaza y no quiebra.)
CERVANTES, *Don Quixote*. Pt. ii, ch. 17.

5
Full oft in game a sooth I have heard said.
CHAUCER, *The Monkes Tale: Prologue*, l. 76.

Many a true word hath been spoken in jest.
UNKNOWN, *Roxburghe Ballads*, vii, 366. (c. 1665)

6
Truths turn into dogmas the moment they are disputed.
G. K. CHESTERTON, *Heretics*. *See also under* DOCTRINE.

7
The greatest friend of truth is Time, her greatest enemy is Prejudice, and her constant companion is Humility.
C. C. COLTON, *Lacon*. Vol. i, No. 159.

8
Truth has rough flavours if we bite it through.
GEORGE ELIOT, *Armgart*. Sc. 2.

9
Face to face the truth comes out.
THOMAS FULLER, *Gnomologia*. No. 1485.

Face to face the truth comes out apace.
EDWARD FITZGERALD, *Polonius*, l. 59.

10
He who sees the truth, let him proclaim it, without asking who is for it or who is against it.
HENRY GEORGE, *The Land Question*. Ch. 3.

11
Truth like a torch, the more 'tis shook, it shines.
SIR WILLIAM HAMILTON, *Discussions on Philosophy: Title Page*.

When by night the frogs are croaking, kindle but a torch's fire;
Ha! how soon they all are silent! Thus Truth silences the liar.
FRIEDRICH VON LOGAU, *Truth*. (Longfellow, tr.)

12
Truth, when witty, is the wittiest of all things.
J. C. AND A. W. HARE, *Guesses at Truth*.

The well of true wit is truth itself.
GEORGE MEREDITH, *Diana of the Crossways*. Ch. 1.

13
In fact, there's nothing that keeps its youth,
So far as I know, but a tree and truth.
O. W. HOLMES, *The Deacon's Masterpiece*.

14
Truth is tough. It will not break, like a bubble, at a touch; nay, you may kick it about all day, like a foot-ball, and it will be round and full at evening.
O. W. HOLMES, *The Professor at the Breakfast-Table*. Ch. v.

You know what that witty and eloquent old Dr. Oliver Wendell Holmes once said. He said, "You needn't fear to handle the truth roughly; she is no invalid." The truth is the most robust and indestructible and formidable thing in the world.
WOODROW WILSON, *Address*, Tacoma, Wash., 13 Sept., 1919.

15
When speculation has done its worst, two and two still make four.
SAMUEL JOHNSON, *The Idler*, No. 36.

16
The dignity of truth is lost
With much protesting.
BEN JONSON, *Catiline*. Act iii, sc. 2.

Truth often suffers more by the heat of its defenders than from the arguments of its opposers.
WILLIAM PENN, *Fruits of Solitude*.

17
What is true by lamplight is not always true by sunlight. (Ce qui est vrai à la lampe n'est pas toujours vrai au soleil.)
JOUBERT, *Pensées*. No. 152.

It is even easier to be mistaken about the true than the beautiful. (Il est encore plus facile de se tromper sur le vrai que sur le beau.)
JOUBERT, *Pensées*. No. 164.

18
We always weaken whatever we exaggerate. (On affaiblit toujours tout ce qu'on exagère.)
LA HARPE, *Mélanie*. Act i, sc. 1.

19
Truth is often eclipsed but never extinguished. (Veritatem laborare nimis sæpe, extingui nunquam.)
LIVY, *History*. Bk. xxii, sec. 39.

20
The mask is torn off, while the reality remains. (Eripitur persona, manet res.)
LUCRETIUS, *De Rerum Natura*. Bk. iii, sec. 58.

Reality, however, has a sliding floor.
EMERSON, *Journals*. Vol. x, p. 365.

21
As true as I live.
MIDDLETON, *The Family of Love*. Act v, sc. 3.

22
Truth needs not the foil of rhetoric.
MIDDLETON, *The Family of Love*. Act v, sc. 3.

23
Truth is as impossible to be soiled by any outward touch as the sunbeam.
MILTON, *The Doctrine and Discipline of Divorce*. *See also under* SUN.

1
Truth for authority, not authority for truth.
LUCRETIA MOTT. Her motto. (HIBBEN, *The Peerless Leader*. p. 100).

2
Truth alone wounds.
NAPOLEON BONAPARTE. (O'MEARA, *Napoleon in Exile*, 14 March, 1817.)

3
Let others write for glory or reward;
Truth is well paid when she is sung and heard.
THOMAS OVERBURY, *Elegy on Lord Effingham*.

4
We know the truth, not only by the reason, but also by the heart.
BLAISE PASCAL, *Pensées*. Sec. iv, No. 282.

5
Everything is true. (Πάντ' εἶναι ἀληθῆ.)
PROTAGORAS. (DIOGENES LAERTIUS, *Protagoras*. Bk. ix, sec. 51.)

6
Truth scorns delay. (Veritas odit moras.)
SENECA, *Œdipus*, l. 850.

7
Time discovers truth. (Veritatem dies aperit.)
SENECA, *De Ira*. Bk. ii, sec. 22.

Time reveals all things. (Tempus omnia revelat.)
ERASMUS, *Adagia*.

Time discloseth all things. Nothing is covered, but shall be revealed; nothing is hid, that shall not be known, saith Christ.
TAVERNER, *Proverbs of Erasmus*, 37. (1539)

Truth is armed
And can defend itself. It must out, madam.
MASSINGER, *The Maid of Honour*. Act v, sc. 1.

Truth will come to light.
SHAKESPEARE, *The Merchant of Venice*. Act ii, sc. 2, l. 83. *See also under* MURDER.

8
Is not the truth the truth?
SHAKESPEARE, *I Henry IV*. Act ii, sc. 4, l. 254.

Truth is truth To the end of reckoning.
SHAKESPEARE, *Measure for Measure*, v, 1, 45.

Truth is for ever truth.
LEIGH HUNT, *Hero and Leander*. Canto i.

Nothing is truer than the truth. (Vero nihil verius.)
UNKNOWN, *Motto of the De Veres*.

9
They breathe truth that breathe their words in pain.
SHAKESPEARE, *Richard II*. Act ii, sc. 1, l. 8.

Truth sits upon the lips of dying men.
MATTHEW ARNOLD, *Sohrab and Rustum*, l. 656.

I like a look of agony,
Because I know it's true;
Men do not sham convulsion,
Nor simulate a throe.
EMILY DICKINSON, *Poems*. Pt. iv, No. 12.

10
And simple truth miscall'd simplicity,
And captive good attending captain ill.
SHAKESPEARE, *Sonnets*. No. lxvi.

O wither'd truth!
SHAKESPEARE, *Troilus and Cressida*, v, 2, 46.

11
Truth in spirit, not truth to letter, is the true veracity.
R. L. STEVENSON, *Truth of Intercourse*.

12
Truth is the most valuable thing we have. Let us economize it.
MARK TWAIN, *Pudd'nhead Wilson's Calendar*.

13
Wrapping truth in darkness. (Obscuris vera involvens.)
VERGIL, *Æneid*. Bk. vi, l. 100.

14
But not for golden fancies iron truths make room.
WILLIAM WATSON, *The Hope of the World*.

15
The longest sword, the strongest lungs, the most voices, are false measures of truth.
BENJAMIN WHICHCOTE, *Sermons*.

16
Truths that wake, to perish never.
WORDSWORTH, *Intimations of Immortality*, ix.

III—Truth: The Naked Truth

17
Craft must have clothes, but truth loves to go naked.
THOMAS FULLER, *Gnomologia*. No. 1200.

Truth's best ornament is nakedness.
THOMAS FULLER, *Gnomologia*. No. 5314.

18
The naked truth. (Nuda Veritas.)
HORACE, *Odes*. Bk. i, ode 24, l. 7.

19
The truth, naked and unashamed, is always unpleasant.
JAMES HUNEKER, *Iconoclasts*, p. 188.

20
The truth shows best being naked.
JOHN TAYLOR THE WATER-POET, *Watermens Suit*. (c. 1613)

Naked Truth needs no shift.
WILLIAM PENN. Title of a Broadside. (1674)

Mere white truth in simple nakedness.
TENNYSON, *Balin and Balan*, l. 509.

22
Because a cold rage seizes one at whiles
To show the bitter old and wrinkled truth
Stripped naked of all vesture that beguiles,
False dreams, false hopes, false masks and modes of youth.
JAMES THOMSON, *The City of Dreadful Night: Proem*. St. 2.

IV—Truth Lies at the Bottom of a Well

23
Of truth we know nothing, for truth is in a well. ('Ετεῇ δὲ οὐδὲν ἴδμεν· ἐν βυθῷ γὰρ ἡ ἀλήθεια.)
DEMOCRITUS. (DIOGENES LAERTIUS, *Pyrrho*. Bk. ix, sec. 72.)

Nature has buried truth at the bottom of the sea.
DEMOCRITUS. (CICERO, *Academicarum Quæstionum*. Bk. ii, sec. 10.)

Democritus quasi in puteo quodam sic alta, ut fundus sit nullus, veritatem jacere demersam.
LACTANTIUS, *Institutes*, iii, 28.

We are born to inquire after truth; it belongs to a greater power to possess it. It is not, as Democritus said, hid in the bottom of the deeps, but rather elevated to an infinite height in the divine knowledge.

MONTAIGNE, *Essays*. Bk. iii, ch. 8.

Let us seek the solution of these doubts at the bottom of the inexhaustible well, where Heraclitus says that truth is hidden.

RABELAIS, *Works*. Bk. i, ch. 18.

Truth, which wise men say, doth lie in a well.

SIR THOMAS BROWNE, *Pseudodoxia Epid.*, i, 5.

It is an old saying that Truth lies in a well, but the misfortune is, that some men will use no chain to draw her up.

C. C. COLTON, *Lacon*. Vol. i, No. 250.

Truth keeps the bottom of her well.

JOAQUIN MILLER, *Song of the South*. Sec. iii, pt. 2.

1
Truth is always at the bottom of a grave.

JAMES HUNEKER, *Iconoclasts*, p. 63.

2
Truth lies wrapped up and hidden in the depths. (Involuta veritas in alto latet.)

SENECA, *De Beneficiis*. Bk. vii, sec. 1.

3
Truth, they say, lies in a well,
Why, I vow, I ne'er could see;
Let the water-drinkers tell,
There it always lay for me.

SHERIDAN, *The Duenna*. Act iii, sc. 1.

4
Whilst the unlearned . . . were all busied in getting down to the bottom of the well, where Truth keeps her little court.

STERNE, *Tristram Shandy*. Bk. iv, pt. 1.

5
The sages say, Dame Truth delights to dwell
(Strange Mansion!) in the bottom of a well:
Questions are then the Windlass and the Rope
That pull the grave old Gentlewoman up.

JOHN WOLCOT, *Birthday Ode*.

We never see the stars
Till we can see naught but them. So with truth.
And yet if one would look down a deep well,
Even at noon, we might see those same stars.

P. J. BAILEY, *Festus: Water and Wood*.

Truth, after all, wears a different face to everybody, and it would be too tedious to wait till all were agreed. She is said to lie at the bottom of a well, for the very reason, perhaps, that whoever looks down in search of her sees his own image at the bottom, and is persuaded not only that he has seen the Goddess, but that she is far better-looking than he had imagined.

J. R. LOWELL, *Democracy*.

V—Truth Is Mighty and Will Prevail

6
Great is truth, and it prevaileth. (Magna est veritas, et prævalet.)

Biblia Sacra Vulgatæ Editionis: III Esdras, iv, 41. The *Vulgate* is the Latin version of the Bible completed by Saint Jerome in 405, of which the Gutenberg (or Mazarin) Bible (1456) was the first printed edition, as it was also the first important book printed from movable type. The Clementine text, a recension made by order of Pope Clement VIII, and completed in 1605, is the authorized text of the Roman Catholic Church, of which the Douai version, completed in 1609, is the authorized English text. All of these include the books which were placed in the *Apocrypha* by the editors of the "Authorized" or Protestant version in 1611. Among them was *III Esdras*, which, in the *Apocrypha*, is *I Esdras*. Popular usage has substituted the future, *prævalebit*, "will prevail," for the present, *prævalet*, as given in the *Vulgate* version, but it is without authority. However, the quotation is almost always given, "Truth is mighty and will prevail."

Great is Truth, and mighty above all things.

Apocrypha: I Esdras, iv, 41. (1611)

Truth, by its own sinews, will prevail.

DRYDEN, *Religio Laici*, l. 349.

Truth in the end shall prevail.

ULPIAN FULWELL, *Ars Adulandi*. E 4. (c. 1580)

7
And fierce though the fiends may fight, and long though the angels hide,
I know that truth and right have the universe on their side.

WASHINGTON GLADDEN, *Ultima Veritas*.

8
The truth is great, and shall prevail,
When none cares whether it prevail or not.

COVENTRY PATMORE, *Magna Est Veritas*.

9
Truth will ultimately prevail where there is pains taken to bring it to light.

GEORGE WASHINGTON, *Maxims*.

VI—Truth Shall Make You Free

10
Where Truth deigns to come,
Her sister Liberty will not be far.

MARK AKENSIDE, *Pleasures of the Imagination*. Bk. i, l. 23.

11
He is the freeman whom the truth makes free,
And all are slaves beside.

COWPER, *The Task*. Bk. v, l. 733.

12
Ye shall know the truth, and the truth shall make you free.

New Testament: John, viii, 32.

13
Truth and, by consequence, liberty, will always be the chief power of honest men.

MADAME DE STAËL, *Letter to General Moreau*.

14
If the truth shall have made thee free, thou shalt not care for the vain words of men.

À KEMPIS, *De Imitatione Christi*. Bk. iii, ch. 4.

VII—Truth: Its Power

15
What governs men is the fear of truth.

AMIEL, *Journal*, 1 March, 1869.

17
Truth is the strong thing. Let man's life be true!

ROBERT BROWNING, *In a Balcony*, l. 233.

18
Truth tramples on the lie as oil on water.

CERVANTES, *Don Quixote*. Pt. ii, ch. 10.

Truth and oil are even above.
GEORGE HERBERT, *Jacula Prudentum.*

1
Great is the power of truth. (A magna vis veritas.)
CICERO, *Pro Cœlio Rufo.* Sec. 26.

I am conquered by truth. (Vincer veris.)
ERASMUS, *Diluculum.*

Truth, Life, and Love are a law of annihilation to everything unlike themselves, because they declare nothing but God.
MARY BAKER EDDY, *Science and Health,* p. 243.

2
Above all things truth beareth away the victory.
Apocrypha: I Esdras, iii, 12.

As for the truth, it endureth, and is always strong; it liveth and conquereth for evermore.
Apocrypha: I Esdras, iv, 38.

3
It is right to yield to the truth. (Liceat concedere veris.)
HORACE, *Satires.* Bk. ii, sat. 3, l. 305.

4
You show that truth can ne'er decay,
Whatever fate befalls;
I, that the myrtle and the bay
Shoot fresh on ruined walls.
WALTER SAVAGE LANDOR, *In After Time.*

5
No power can die that ever wrought for Truth;
Thereby a law of Nature it became,
And lives unwithered in its blithesome youth,
When he who called it forth is but a name.
J. R. LOWELL, *Elegy on the Death of Dr. Channing.* Inscribed beneath Lowell's bust in the Hall of Fame.

Get but the truth once uttered, and 't is like
A star new-born, that drops into its place,
And which, once circling in its placid round,
Not all the tumult of the earth can shake.
J. R. LOWELL, *A Glance Behind the Curtain,* l. 173.

Put golden padlocks on Truth's lips, be callous as ye will,
From soul to soul, o'er all the world, leaps one electric thrill.
J. R. LOWELL, *On the Capture of Certain Fugitive Slaves Near Washington.*

6
Methinks the truth should live from age to age,
As 'twere retail'd to all posterity,
Even to the general all-ending day.
SHAKESPEARE, *Richard III.* Act iii, sc. 1, l. 76.

7
The truth is always the strongest argument
SOPHOCLES, *Phædra.* Frag. 737.

VIII—Truth: Love of Truth

8
Though both [Plato and truth] are dear to me, it is a sacred duty to put truth first. ('Αμφοῖν γαρ ὄντοιν φίλοιν ὅσιον προτιμᾶν τὴν ἀλήθειαν.)
ARISTOTLE, *Nicomachean Ethics.* Bk. i, ch 6, sec. 1.

Plato is dear to me, but dearer still is truth. (Amicus Plato, sed magis amica veritas.)
ARISTOTLE. (CERVANTES, *Don Quixote.* Pt. ii, ch. 51.)

Socrates is dear to me, but dearer still is truth.
ARISTOTLE. (AMMONIUS, *Aristotelis Vita,* 399.)

If you will take my advice, you will think little of Socrates, and a great deal more of truth.
SOCRATES. (PLATO, *Phædo.* Sec. 40.)

9
Arm thyself for the truth!
BULWER-LYTTON, *The Lady of Lyons.* Act v, sc. 1.

Wherever the truth is injured, defend it.
EMERSON, *Journals.* Vol. iii, p. 269.

Stake life upon the truth. (Vitam inpendere vero.)
JUVENAL, *Satires.* Sat. iv, l. 91. The motto of Rousseau.

10
Truth! though the Heavens crush me for following her.
CARLYLE, *Sartor Resartus.* Bk. ii, ch. 7.

11
Remember, then, as long as you live, that nothing but strict truth can carry you through the world, with either your conscience or your honour unwounded.
LORD CHESTERFIELD, *Letters,* 21 Sept., 1747.

12
For truth has such a face and such a mien
As to be lov'd needs only to be seen.
DRYDEN, *The Hind and Panther.* Pt. i, l. 33.

13
He that feeds men serveth few;
He serves all who dares be true.
EMERSON, *The Celestial Love.*

14
Nothing shall warp me from the belief that every man is a lover of truth.
EMERSON, *Essays, Second Series: New England Reformers.*

15
In proportion as we perceive and embrace the truth do we become just, heroic, magnanimous, divine.
WILLIAM LLOYD GARRISON, *Free Speech and Free Inquiry.*

16
The contemplation of truth and beauty is the proper object for which we were created, which calls forth the most intense desires of the soul, and of which it never tires.
WILLIAM HAZLITT, *Criticisms on Art.* Vol. i, p. 2.

To love truth for truth's sake is the principal part of human perfection in this world, and the seed-plot of all other virtues.
JOHN LOCKE, *Letter to Anthony Collins, Esq.,* 29 Oct., 1703.

17
I do not fear to follow out the truth,
Albeit along the precipice's edge.
J. R. LOWELL, *A Glance behind the Curtain,* l. 251

They must upward still, and onward, who would keep abreast of Truth.
J. R. LOWELL, *The Present Crisis*, l. 87.

1
Servant of God, well done! well hast thou fought
The better fight, who single hast maintain'd
Against revolted multitudes the cause
Of truth.
MILTON, *Paradise Lost*. Bk. vi, l. 29.

Gentlest and bravest in the battle-brunt—
The Champion of the Truth.
JAMES RYDER RANDALL, *John Pelham*.

Who never sold the truth to serve the hour,
Nor palter'd with Eternal God for power.
TENNYSON, *Ode on the Death of the Duke of Wellington*, l. 179.

2
When truth or virtue an affront endures,
Th' affront is mine, my friend, and should be yours.
POPE, *Epilogue to Satires*. Dial. i, l. 199.

3
Farewell then, verse, and love, and ev'ry toy,
The rhymes and rattles of the man or boy;
What right, what true, what fit, we justly call,
Let this be all my care—for this is all.
POPE, *Imitations of Horace: Epistles*. Bk. i, epis. 1, l. 17.

And in the light of truth thy Bondman let me live!
WORDSWORTH, *Ode to Duty*, l. 56.

4
Who tells me true, though in his tale lie death,
I hear him as he flatter'd.
SHAKESPEARE, *Antony and Cleopatra*. Act i, sc. 2, l. 102.

5
All fear of the world or consequence is swallowed up in a manly anxiety to do Truth justice.
H. D. THOREAU, *Journal*, 13 Feb., 1838.

6
Truth before peace. That is my watchword.
MIGUEL DE UNAMUNO, *Essays and Soliloquies*, p. 138.

7
It is one thing to wish to have truth on our side, and another to wish sincerely to be on the side of truth.
RICHARD WHATELY, *On the Love of Truth*.

It is a dangerous grieving of the Spirit when, instead of drawing ourselves to the Spirit, we labour to draw the Spirit to us.
RICHARD SIBBES, *Fountain Sealed*. (c. 1630)

8
Or shall we say
That, like the Red-cross Knight, they urge their way,
To lead in memorable triumph home
Truth, their immortal Una?
WORDSWORTH, *Ecclesiastical Sonnets*. Pt. i, No. 25.

IX—Truth: Its Virtues

9
No pleasure is comparable to the standing upon the vantage-ground of Truth.
FRANCIS BACON, *Essays: Of Truth*.

Certainly it is heaven upon earth to have a man's mind . . . turn upon the poles of truth.
FRANCIS BACON, *Essays: Of Truth*.

Is truth ever barren?
BACON, *Cogitationes de Scientia Humana*.

10
For truth is precious and divine;
Too rich a pearl for carnal swine.
BUTLER, *Hudibras*. Pt. ii, canto 2, l. 257.

All truth is precious, if not all divine.
COWPER, *Charity*, l. 331.

For truth is unwelcome, however divine.
COWPER, *The Flatting Mill*, l. 23.

Time is precious, but truth is more precious than time.
BENJAMIN DISRAELI, *Speech*, Aylesbury, 11 Sept., 1865.

11
Truth shall restore the light by Nature given,
And, like Prometheus, bring the fire of Heaven! . . .
What! are thy triumphs, sacred Truth, belied?
Why then hath Plato lived—or Sidney died?
CAMPBELL, *The Pleasures of Hope*. Pt. i, l. 415.

12
Individuals may perish; but truth is eternal.
JOSEPH GERRALD, *Speech*, when under arrest, Jan., 1794.

13
But there are seven sisters ever serving Truth,
Porters of the Posterns; one called Abstinence,
Humility, Charity, Chastity be the chief maidens there;
Patience and Peace help many a one;
Lady Almsgiving lets in full many.
WILLIAM LANGLAND, *Piers Plowman*. Pt. viii.

14
There is no veil like light—no adamantine armour against hurt like the truth.
GEORGE MACDONALD, *Marquis of Lossie*. Ch. 71.

Truth, a constant mistress, that
Ever protects her servants.
PHILIP MASSINGER, *The Great Duke of Florence*. Act iii, sc. 1.

15
In the mountains of truth, you never climb in vain.
NIETZSCHE, *Human All too Human*, i, 358.

16
Truth never yet fell dead in the streets; it has such affinity with the soul of man, the seed however broadcast will catch somewhere and produce its hundredfold.
THEODORE PARKER, *A Discourse of Matters Pertaining to Religion*.

1
If I had a device, it would be the True. the True only, leaving the Beautiful and the Good to settle matters afterwards as best they could.
SAINTE-BEUVE, *Letter to Duruy*, 9 Dec., 1865.

2
Truth hath a quiet breast.
SHAKESPEARE, *Richard II*. Act i, sc. 3, l. 96.

Truth needs no colour, with his colour fix'd;
Beauty no pencil, beauty's truth to lay;
But best is best, if never intermix'd.
SHAKESPEARE, *Sonnets*. No. ci.

X—Truth: Its Dangers

3
Truth is often attended with danger. (Pericula veritati sæpe contigua.)
AMMIANUS MARCELLINUS, *History*. Bk. xxvi, sec. 1.

4
Truth breeds hatred. (Veritas odium parit.)
BIAS. (AUSONIUS [?], *Ludus Septem Sapientum*. Sec. 8, l. 3.) Quoted by Terence, *Andria*, l. 68.

Truth is a narrow lane all full of quags,
Leading to broken heads, abuse, and rags.
JOHN WOLCOT, *More Lyric Odes*. No. 9.

5
The artlessness of unadorned truth, however sure in theory of extorting admiration, rarely in practice fails inflicting pain and mortification.
FANNY BURNEY, *Camilla*. Bk. iv, ch. 8.

6
I never saw any good that came of telling truth.
DRYDEN, *Amphitryon*. Act. iii, sc. 1.

7
God offers to every mind its choice between truth and repose. Take which you please,—you can never have both.
EMERSON, *Essays, First Series: Intellect*.

Truth stood on one side and Ease on the other; it has often been so.
THEODORE PARKER, *A Discourse of Matters Pertaining to Religion*.

8
Follow not truth too near the heels, lest it dash out thy teeth.
GEORGE HERBERT, *Jacula Prudentum*. (1640)

9
Nobody has a right to put another under such a difficulty, that he must either hurt the person by telling the truth, or hurt himself by telling what is not true.
SAMUEL JOHNSON. (BOSWELL, *Life*, 1778.)

Every man has a right to utter what he thinks truth, and every man has a right to knock him down for it.
SAMUEL JOHNSON. (BOSWELL, *Life*.)

10
Now comes the pain of truth, to whom 't is pain;
O folly! for to bear all naked truths,
And to envisage circumstance, all calm,
That is the top of sovereignty.
KEATS, *Hyperion*. Bk. ii, l. 202.

11
Not a truth has to art or to science been given,
But brows have ached for it, and souls toil'd and striven;
And many have striven, and many have fail'd,
And many died, slain by the truth they assail'd.
OWEN MEREDITH, *Lucile*. Pt. ii, canto 6, st. 1.

The smallest atom of truth represents some man's bitter toil and agony; for every ponderable chunk of it there is a brave truth-seeker's grave upon some lonely ash-dump and a soul roasting in hell.
H. L. MENCKEN, *Prejudices*. Ser. iii, p. 274.

12
Truth . . . never comes into the world but like a bastard, to the ignominy of him that brought her forth.
JOHN MILTON, *Works*. Vol. i, p. 276.

Still rule those minds on earth
At whom sage Milton's wormwood words were hurled:
Truth like a bastard comes into the world
Never without ill-fame to him who gives her birth.
THOMAS HARDY, *Lausanne: In Gibbon's Old Garden*.

13
Hard are the ways of truth, and rough to walk.
MILTON, *Paradise Regained*. Bk. i, l. 478.

14
And oftentimes, to win us to our harm,
The instruments of darkness tell us truths,
Win us with honest trifles, to betray 's
In deepest consequence.
SHAKESPEARE, *Macbeth*. Act i, sc. 3, l. 123.

15
I am very fond of truth, but not at all of martyrdom.
VOLTAIRE, *Letter to d'Alembert*, Feb., 1776.

XI—Truth: The Search for Truth

16
And much they grope for Truth, but never hit, . . .
Yet deem they darkness light and their vain blunders wit.
JAMES BEATTIE, *The Minstrel*. Bk. i, st. 51.

17
It is the modest, not the presumptuous, inquirer who makes a real and safe progress in the discovery of divine truths.
VISCOUNT BOLINGBROKE, *Letter to Mr. Pope*.

18
I promised, if you'd watch a dinner out,
We'd see truth dawn together?—truth that peeps
Over the glasses' edge when dinner's done,
And body gets its sop and holds its noise

And leaves soul free a little.
ROBERT BROWNING, *Bishop Blougram's Apology.*

1
Every man seeks for truth, but God only knows who has found it.
LORD CHESTERFIELD, *Letters*, 21 Sept., 1747.

And diff'ring judgments serve but to declare,
That Truth lies somewhere, if we knew but where.
COWPER, *Hope*, l. 423.

Who dares
To say that he alone has found the truth?
LONGFELLOW, *John Endicott*. Act ii, sc. 3.

2
The search after truth, and its eager pursuit, are peculiar to man. (Hominis est propria veri inquisitio atque investigatio.)
CICERO, *De Officiis*. Bk. i, ch. 4, sec. 13.

Nature has planted in our minds an insatiable longing to see truth. (Natura inest in mentibus nostris insatiabilis quædam cupiditas veri videndi.)
CICERO, *Tusculanarum Disputationum*. Bk. i, ch. 19, sec. 44.

3
Truths that the learn'd pursue with eager thought
Are not important always as dear-bought.
COWPER, *Tirocinium*, l. 73.

4
One truth discovered is immortal, and entitles its author to be so: for, like a new substance in nature, it cannot be destroyed.
WILLIAM HAZLITT, *The Spirit of the Age: Jeremy Bentham.*

The man who finds a truth lights a torch.
R. G. INGERSOLL, *The Truth.*

5
Truth and seemliness are my study and pursuit, and to that am I wholly given. (Quid verum atque decens curo et rogo et omnis in hoc sum.)
HORACE, *Epistles*. Bk. i, epis. 1, l. 11.

To seek for truth in the groves of Academe. (Inter silvas Academi quærere verum.)
HORACE, *Epistles*. Bk. ii, epis. 2, l. 45.

6
Pilate saith unto him, What is truth? And when he had said this, he went out again unto the Jews.
New Testament: John, xviii, 38.

Pilate asked, *Quid est veritas?* And then some other matter took him in the head, and so up he rose and went his way before he had his answer.
LANCELOT ANDREWES, BISHOP OF WINCHESTER, *Sermons: Of the Resurrection.* (1613)

What is truth? said jesting Pilate; and would not stay for an answer.
FRANCIS BACON, *Essays: Of Truth.*

But what is truth? 'twas Pilate's question, put
To Truth itself, that deign'd him no reply.
COWPER, *The Task*. Bk. iii, l. 270.

7
There are great truths that pitch their shining tents
Outside our walls, and though but dimly seen
In the gray dawn, they will be manifest
When the light widens into perfect day.
LONGFELLOW, *Michael Angelo:* Pt. iv, *In the Coliseum.*

8
I seek the truth, whereby no man was ever harmed. (Ζητῶ γὰρ τὴν ἀλήθειαν, ὑφ' ἧς οὐδεὶς πώποτε ἐβλάβη.)
MARCUS AURELIUS, *Meditations*. Bk. vi, sec. 21.

9
Man with his burning soul
Has but an hour of breath
To build a ship of Truth
In which his soul may sail,
Sail on the sea of death;
For death takes toll
Of beauty, courage, youth,
Of all but Truth.
JOHN MASEFIELD, *Truth*. St. 1.

10
O sir, the truth, the truth! is 't in the skies,
Or in the grass, or in this heart of ours?
But O the truth, the truth! the many eyes
That look on it! the diverse things they see,
According to their thirst for fruit or flowers!
Pass on: it is the truth seek we.
GEORGE MEREDITH, *A Ballad of Fair Ladies in Revolt*. St. 16.

Truths which transcend the searching schoolmen's vein
And half had staggered that stout Stagirite.
CHARLES LAMB, *Written at Cambridge*. Stagirite, *i.e.* Aristotle, born at Stagira.

11
Truths would you teach, or save a sinking land?
All fear, none aid you, and few understand.
POPE, *Essay on Man*. Epis. iv, l. 265.

12
While we are examining into everything, we sometimes find truth where we least expect it. (Dum omnia quærimus, aliquando ad verum, ubi minime expectavimus, pervenimus.)
QUINTILIAN, *De Institutione Oratoria*. Bk. xii, ch. 8, sec. 3.

13
As painfully to pore upon a book,
To seek the light of truth; while truth the while
Doth falsely blind the eyesight of his look.
SHAKESPEARE, *Love's Labour's Lost*. Act i, sc. 1, l. 74.

But wonder on, till truth make all things plain.
SHAKESPEARE, *A Midsummer-Night's Dream.* Act v, sc. 1, l. 129.

14
The golden guess
Is morning-star to the full round of truth.
TENNYSON, *Columbus*, l. 42.

1
Who seeks for truth should be of no country.
VOLTAIRE, *Réponse, à un Académicien.*

XII—Truth: Truth-telling

2
Simple are the words of truth. (Ἁπλᾶ γάρ ἐστι τῆς ἀληθείας ἔπη.)
ÆSCHYLUS, *Œlon Krisis.* Frag. 92.

The language of truth is simple. (Ἁπλοῦς ὁ μῦθος τῆς ἀληθείας ἔφυ.)
EURIPIDES, *Phœnissæ*, l. 469. Quoted by Seneca (*Epistulæ ad Lucilium*, xlix, 4): Veritatis simplex oratio est.

The words of truth are always paradoxical.
LAO-TSZE, *The Simple Way.* No. 78.

The language of truth is unadorned and always simple. (Veritatis absolutus sermo ac semper est simplex.)
AMMIANUS MARCELLINUS, *History.* Bk. xiv, 10.

3
Truth can never be told so as to be understood, and not be believ'd.
WILLIAM BLAKE, *Proverbs of Hell.*

4
Think truly, and thy thoughts
Shall the world's famine feed.
Speak truly, and each word of thine
Shall be a fruitful seed.
Live truly, and thy life shall be
A great and noble creed.
HORATIUS BONAR, *Be True.*

5
Truth never hurts the teller.
ROBERT BROWNING, *Fifine at the Fair.* Sec. 32.

6
For fools and mad men tell commonly truth.
ROBERT BURTON, *Anatomy of Melancholy.* Pt. ii, sec. 3, mem. 8.

Wilt thou be my fool? for fools, they say, will tell truth.
PHILIP MASSINGER, *Very Woman.* Act iii, sc. 1.

Children and fools speak true.
JOHN LYLY, *Endymion*, iv, 2.

Fools and babes tell true.
SAMUEL ROWLANDS, *More Knaves Yet*, 36.

7
The fewer the voices on the side of truth, the more distinct and strong must be your own.
WILLIAM ELLERY CHANNING, *Charge on Ordination of Rev. J. S. Dwight.*

Then to side with Truth is noble when we share her wretched crust,
Ere her cause bring fame and profit, and 't is prosperous to be just;
Then it is the brave man chooses, while the coward stands aside,
Doubting in his abject spirit, till his Lord is crucified.
J. R. LOWELL, *The Present Crisis.* St. 11.

8
No man speaks the truth or lives a true life two minutes together.
EMERSON, *Journals.* Vol. iii, p. 455.

When what should be the greatest truths flat out into shallow truisms, then we are all sick.
EMERSON, *Journals.* Vol. iv, p. 30.

9
Wherefore putting away lying, speak every man truth with his neighbour.
New Testament: Ephesians, iv, 25.

The highest compact we can make with our fellow is,—Let there be truth between us two forevermore.
EMERSON, *Conduct of Life: Behavior.*

10
Her taste exact For faultless fact
Amounts to a disease.
W. S. GILBERT, *The Mikado.* Act ii.

11
"Did I say so?" replied he, coolly; "to be sure, if I said so, it was so."
GOLDSMITH, *The Citizen of the World.* No. 54

12
An honest man speaks the truth, *though* it may give offence; a vain man, *in order that* it may.
WILLIAM HAZLITT, *Characteristics.* No. 387.

13
What forbids one to speak truth laughingly? (Quamquam ridentem dicere verum Quid vetat?)
HORACE, *Satires.* Bk. i, sat. 1, l. 24.

My way of joking is to tell the truth. It 's the funniest joke in the world.
BERNARD SHAW, *John Bull's Other Island.* Act ii.

14
You have no business with consequences; you are to tell the truth.
SAMUEL JOHNSON. (BOSWELL, *Life*, 1784.)

15
Say the truth and shame the devil.
HUGH LATIMER, *Sermons*, p. 506. (1552)

I will tell truth, and shame the fiend.
BEN JONSON, *The Devil Is an Ass.* Act v, sc. 5.

Speak the truth and shame the Devil.
RABELAIS, *Works:* Bk. v, *Author's Prologue.*

O, while you live, tell truth and shame the devil!
SHAKESPEARE, *I Henry IV.* Act iii, sc. 1, l. 62. See also l. 59 of the same scene.

What, can the devil speak true?
SHAKESPEARE, *Macbeth.* Act i, sc. 3, l. 107.

16
'Tis always best to tell the truth. (Ἀεὶ κράτιστόν ἐστι τἀληθῆ λέγειν.)
MENANDER, *Upobolimaios.* Frag. 487.

The truth is ever best. (Ὀρθὸν ἀλήθει' ἀεί.)
SOPHOCLES, *Antigone*, l. 1195.

It is always the best policy to speak the truth, unless of course you are an exceptionally good liar.
JEROME K. JEROME, *The Idler*, Feb., 1892.

HONESTY THE BEST POLICY, *see under* HONESTY.

17
When affection only speaks,
Truth is not always there.
MIDDLETON AND MASSINGER, *The Old Law.* Act iv, sc. 2.

1
You shall hear from me nothing but the truth. (Πᾶσαν την ἀλήθειαν.)
PLATO, *Apologia of Socrates.* Sec. 1.

I have learned to tell the truth. (Vera didici dicere.)
PLAUTUS, *Amphitruo,* l. 686. (Act i, sc. 2.)

Speak no more than the truth, utter no less.
JOHN LYLY, *Euphues and His England,* p. 329. (1580)

Let us see . . . how far he saith truth, the whole truth, and nothing but the truth.
PETER HEYLYN, *Animadversions.* (1659)

I speak truth, not so much as I would, but as much as I dare; and I dare a little the more as I grow older.
MONTAIGNE, *Essays.* Bk. iii, ch. 2.

Speaking truth is like writing fair, and only comes by practice.
RUSKIN, *Seven Lamps of Architecture,* ii, 1.

2
Twirling my wit as it were my mustache,
The while I pass among the crowd, I make
Bold truths ring out like spurs.
EDMOND ROSTAND, *Cyrano de Bergerac.* Act i, sc. 4.

3
O, never say hereafter
But I am truest speaker.
SHAKESPEARE, *Cymbeline.* Act v, sc. 5, l. 375.

We will answer all things faithfully.
SHAKESPEARE, *Merchant of Venice,* v, 1, 299.

4
Truth-teller was our England's Alfred named.
TENNYSON, *Ode on the Death of the Duke of Wellington,* l. 188.

5
It takes two to speak truth—one to speak and another to hear.
THOREAU, *A Week on the Concord and Merrimack Rivers: Wednesday.*

6
A faithful saying, and worthy of all acceptation.
New Testament: I Timothy, i, 15.

7
There was things which he stretched, but mainly he told the truth.
MARK TWAIN, *Huckleberry Finn.* Ch. 1.

8
When in doubt, tell the truth.
MARK TWAIN, *Pudd'nhead Wilson's Calendar.*

Tell the truth or trump—but get the trick.
MARK TWAIN, *Pudd'nhead Wilson's Calendar.*

XIII—Truth: Not Always to Be Told

9
All things to all men only fools will tell,
Truth profits none but those that use it well.
J. S. BLACKIE, *The Wise Men of Greece: Pythagoras.*

10
'Tis real humanity and kindness to hide strong truths from tender eyes.
LORD SHAFTESBURY, *Characteristics.* Vol. i, 63.

So, minds at first must be spoon-fed with truth.
ROBERT BROWNING, *A Death in the Desert.*

11
That truth should be silent I had almost forgot.
SHAKESPEARE, *Antony and Cleopatra,* ii, 2, 110.

Truth's a dog must to kennel; he must be whipped out, when Lady the brach may stand by the fire and stink.
SHAKESPEARE, *King Lear.* Act i, sc. 1, l. 124.

12
Truth telling is not compatible with the defence of the realm.
BERNARD SHAW, *Heartbreak House: Preface.*

13
All soothes be not to say.
THOMAS USK, *Testament of Love.* (c. 1387)

All truths are not to be told.
GEORGE HERBERT, *Jacula Prudentum.*

For truth itself has not the privilege to be spoken at all times and in all sorts.
MONTAIGNE, *Essays.* Bk. iii, ch. 13.

XIV—Truth and Falsehood

See also Error and Truth

14
Use not to lie, for that is unhonest; speak not every truth, for that is unneedful; yes, in time and place, a harmless lie is a great deal better than a hurtful truth.
ROGER ASCHAM, *Letter to Mr. Howe.* (1550)

'T is not enough your counsel still be true:
Blunt truths more mischief than nice falsehoods do.
POPE, *Essay on Criticism.* Pt. iii, l. 13.

A truth that's told with bad intent
Beats all the lies you can invent.
WILLIAM BLAKE, *Auguries of Innocence.*

15
Truth may perhaps come to the price of a pearl, that sheweth best by day; but it will not rise to the price of a diamond, or carbuncle, that sheweth best in varied lights. A mixture of a lie doth ever add pleasure.
FRANCIS BACON, *Essays: Of Truth.*

16
Be so true to thyself, as thou be not false to others.
FRANCIS BACON, *Essays: Of Wisdom for a Man's Self.* (1597)

To thine own self be true,
And it must follow, as the night the day,
Thou canst not then be false to any man.
SHAKESPEARE, *Hamlet.* Act i, sc. 3, l. 78. (1600)

The first great work, task perform'd by few,
Is, that yourself may to yourself be true.
WENTWORTH DILLON, *An Essay on Translated Verse,* l. 71.

17
Sow truth, if thou the truth wouldst reap:
Who sows the false shall reap the vain.
HORATIUS BONAR, *He Liveth Long Who Liveth Well.*

1
There is truth in falsehood, falsehood in truth.
ROBERT BROWNING, *A Soul's Tragedy*. Act ii.

What does the world, told truth, but lie the more?
ROBERT BROWNING, *The Ring and the Book*. Pt. x, l. 673.

2
And, after all, what is a lie? 'Tis but
The truth in masquerade.
BYRON, *Don Juan*. Canto xi, st. 37.

Truth is only falsehood well disguised.
FARQUHAR, *The Constant Couple*. Act iii, sc. 4.

3
The truth is bitter and disagreeable to fools; but falsehood is sweet and acceptable. (Τὸ μὲν ἀληθὲς πικρόν ἐστι καὶ ἀηδὲς τοῖς ἀνοήτοις· τὸ δὲ ψεῦδος γλυκὺ καὶ προσηνές.)
ST. CHRYSOSTOM, *Adagia*.

4
Falsehood is so near to truth that a wise man would do well not to trust himself on the narrow edge. (Ita enim finitima sunt falsa veris ut in præcipitem locum non debeat se sapiens committere.)
CICERO, *Academicarum Quæstionum*. Bk. ii, sec. 21.

He who has once deviated from the truth, usually commits perjury with as little scruple as he would tell a lie.
CICERO, *Pro Quinto Roscio Comœdo*. Sec. 20.

5
Ever to that truth,
Which but the semblance of a falsehood wears,
A man, if possible, should bar his lip.
(Sempre a quel ver ch' ha faccia di menzogna
De' l' uom chiuder le labbra.)
DANTE, *Inferno*. Canto xvi, l. 124.

6
For how can that be false, which every tongue
Of every mortal man affirms for true?
SIR JOHN DAVIES, *Nosce Teipsum*. Sec. 32, st. 55.

7
Some truth there was, but dashed and brewed with lies,
To please the fools, and puzzle all the wise.
Succeeding times did equal folly call,
Believing nothing, or believing all.
DRYDEN, *Absalom and Achitophel*. Pt. i, l. 114.

8
Falsehood is so easy, truth so difficult.
GEORGE ELIOT, *Adam Bede*. Ch. 17.

9
Truth is beautiful. Without doubt; and so are lies.
EMERSON, *Journals*. Vol. iii, p. 437.

10
Half the truth is often a great lie.
BENJAMIN FRANKLIN, *Poor Richard*, 1758.

Half-truths to which men are accustomed are so much easier to pass than the golden mintage they rarely encounter!
CHRISTOPHER MORLEY, *Religio Journalistici*, p. 32.

Truths would be tales
Where now half truths be truths.
SHAKESPEARE, *Antony and Cleopatra*. Act ii, sc. 2, l. 136.

That a lie which is half a truth is ever the blackest of lies,
That a lie which is all a lie may be met and fought with outright,
But a lie which is part a truth is a harder matter to fight.
TENNYSON, *The Grandmother*. St. 8.

11
The art of lying is the strongest acknowledgment of the force of truth.
WILLIAM HAZLITT, *Table Talk: On Patronage and Puffing*.

12
He that trusts in a lie shall perish in truth.
GEORGE HERBERT, *Jacula Prudentum*.

13
We know how to speak many things which are false as if they were true. (Ἴδμεν ψεύδεα πολλὰ λέγειν ἐτύμοισιν ὁμοῖα.)
HESIOD, *Theogony*, l. 27.

14
Urge him with truth to frame his fair replies;
And sure he will; for Wisdom never lies.
HOMER, *Odyssey*. Bk. iii, l. 25. (Pope, tr.)

15
Telling the truth to people who misunderstand you is generally promoting falsehood.
ANTHONY HOPE, *Dolly Dialogues*. No. 14.

16
To distinguish the false from the true. (Vero distinguere falsum.)
HORACE, *Epistles*. Bk. i, epis. 10, l. 29.

I would I could as easily discover the true as I can expose the false. (Utinam tam facile vera invenire possim, quam falsa convincere.)
CICERO, *De Natura Deorum*. Bk. i, ch. 32, sec. 91.

17
A man had rather have a hundred lies told of him, than one truth which he does not wish should be told.
SAMUEL JOHNSON. (BOSWELL, *Life*. 1773.)

18
I reckon there's more things told than are true,
And more things true than are told!
RUDYARD KIPLING, *Rewards and Fairies: The Ballad of Minepit Shaw*.

19
Man is ice for truth, fire for falsehood.
(L'homme est de glace aux verités;
Il est de feu pour les mensonges.)
LA FONTAINE, *Fables*.

20
Some falsehood mingles with all truth.
LONGFELLOW, *The Golden Legend*. Pt. ii.

21
The nimble lie

Is like the second-hand upon a clock;
We see it fly, while the hour-hand of truth
Seems to stand still, and yet it moves unseen,
And wins at last, for the clock will not strike
Till it has reached the goal.
LONGFELLOW, *Michael Angelo*. Pt. iii, sec. 5.

But a lie, whatever the guise it wears,
Is a lie, as it was of yore.
And a truth that has lasted a million years
Is good for a million more!
TED OLSON, *Things That Endure*.

1
Who speaks the truth stabs Falsehood to the heart,
And his mere word makes despots tremble more
Than ever Brutus with his dagger could.
J. R. LOWELL, *L'Envoi*, l. 100.

2
Once to every man and nation comes the moment to decide,
In the strife of Truth with Falsehood, for the good or evil side.
J. R. LOWELL, *The Present Crisis*. St. 5.

3
Against truth falsehood hath no might.
JOHN LYDGATE, *The Story of Thebes*. Pt. ii.

Let Truth and Falsehood grapple: who ever knew Truth put to the worse in a free and open encounter?
MILTON, *Areopagitica*.

4
An innocent truth can never stand in need
Of a guilty lie.
MASSINGER, *Emperor of the East*. Act v, sc. 3.

Truth never was indebted to a lie.
YOUNG, *Night Thoughts*. Night viii, l. 587.

5
For lying is thy sustenance, thy food;
Yet thou pretend'st to truth.
MILTON, *Paradise Regained*. Bk. i, l. 429.

6
For oh, 't was nuts to the Father of Lies,
(As this wily fiend is nam'd in the Bible)
To find it settled by laws so wise
That the greater the truth, the worse the libel!
THOMAS MOORE, *A Case of Libel*, l. 61.

The greater the truth the greater the libel.
LORD ELLENBOROUGH seems to have originated this saying, about 1789. Robert Burns, in some lines written at Stirling, attributed it to Lord Mansfield.

7
I love the truth and wish to have it always spoken to me: I hate a liar. (Ego verum amo, verum volo mihi dici; mendacem odi.)
PLAUTUS, *Mostellaria*, l. 181. (Act i, sc. 3.)

8
The dull flat falsehood serves for policy;
And in the cunning truth itself 's a lie.
ALEXANDER POPE, *Moral Essays*. Epis. i, l. 67.

9
Tell a lie, and find the truth.
JOHN RAY, *English Proverbs*, 75.

10
False things may be imagined, and false things composed; but only truth can be invented.
JOHN RUSKIN, *Modern Painters*. Bk. i, pt. 8, ch. 4, sec. 23.

11
They spake truth once—but all the rest was lies,
Lived for an hour—then for all time were dead.
MARGARET SACKVILLE, *Resurrection*.

12
I pull in resolution, and begin
To doubt the equivocation of the fiend
That lies like truth.
SHAKESPEARE, *Macbeth*. Act v, sc. 5, l. 42.

13
Falsehood flies and truth comes limping after it, so that when men come to be undeceived it is too late.
SWIFT, *The Examiner*. No. 15.

A lie travels round the world while Truth is putting on her boots.
C. H. SPURGEON, *Truth and Falsehood*.

A lie travels by the Marconi route, while Truth goes by slow freight and is often ditched at the first water-tank.
ELBERT HUBBARD, *Epigrams*.

14
Truth is strengthened by observation and delay, falsehood by haste and uncertainty. (Veritas visu et mora, falsa festinatione et incertis valescunt.)
TACITUS, *Annals*. Bk. ii, sec. 39.

15
Falsehoods which we spurn to-day
Were the truths of long ago.
WHITTIER, *Calef in Boston*. St. 4.

XV—Truth and Fiction

See also Fiction

16
Fiction lags after truth, invention is unfruitful, and imagination cold and barren.
EDMUND BURKE, *Thoughts on the Cause of the Present Discontents*.

17
'Tis strange—but true; for truth is always strange,—
Stranger than fiction.
BYRON, *Don Juan*. Canto xiv, st. 101.

Truth is stranger than fiction—to some people, but I am measurably familiar with it.
MARK TWAIN, *Pudd'nhead Wilson's New Calendar*.

18
Truth, fact, is the life of all things; falsity, "fiction," or whatever it may call itself, is certain to be the death.
CARLYLE, *Latter-Day Pamphlets*. No. 8.

19
When fiction rises pleasing to the eye,
Men will believe, because they love the lie;
But Truth herself, if clouded with a frown,

Must have some solemn proof to pass her down.

CHARLES CHURCHILL, *Epistle to Hogarth,* l. 291.

1
I love truth. I believe humanity has need of it. But assuredly it has much greater need still of the untruth which flatters it, consoles it, gives it infinite hopes. (J'aime la vérité. Je crois que l'humanité en a besoin; mais, certes, elle a bien plus grand besoin encore du mensonge qui la flatte, la console, lui donne des espérances infinies.)

ANATOLE FRANCE, *La Vie en Fleur.*

2
Never will the imagination approach the improbabilities and the antitheses of truth.

EDMOND AND JULES DE GONCOURT, *Journal.* Vol. ii, p. 9.

At times truth may not seem probable. (Le vrai peut quelquefois n'être pas vraisemblable.)

BOILEAU, *L'Art Poétique.* Pt. iii, l. 48.

3
And Truth severe, by fairy Fiction drest.

THOMAS GRAY, *The Bard,* l. 127.

4
Fictions meant to please should be very close to truth. (Ficta voluptatis causa sint proxima veris.)

HORACE, *Ars Poetica,* l. 338.

5
If this were played upon a stage now, I could condemn it as an improbable fiction.

SHAKESPEARE, *Twelfth Night.* Act iii, sc. 4, l. 140.

6
There is nothing so powerful as truth, and often nothing so strange.

DANIEL WEBSTER, *Speech: Murder of Captain White.*

7
Nothing can satisfy, but what confounds;
Nothing, but what astonishes, is true.

YOUNG, *Night Thoughts.* Night ix, l. 836.

TURKEY AND THE TURKS

8
Know ye the land where the cypress and myrtle
Are emblems of deeds that are done in their clime,
Where the rage of the vulture, the love of the turtle
Now melt into sorrow, now madden to crime? . . .
Where the virgins are soft as the roses they twine,
And all save the spirit of man is divine?

BYRON, *The Bride of Abydos.* Canto i, st. 1.

9
The unspeakable Turk should be immediately struck out of the question.

CARLYLE, *Letter to a Meeting at St. James's Hall,* 1876.

10
Let the Turks carry away their abuses in the only possible manner, namely by carrying off themselves. Their zaptiehs and their mudirs, their bimbashes and their yuzbashis, their kaimekans and their pashas,—one and all, bag and baggage, shall, I hope, clear out from the province they have desolated and profaned.

GLADSTONE, *Speech,* 7 May, 1877, on the occupation of Bulgaria by Turkey.

Come, shepherd, let us make an honourable retreat; though not with bag and baggage, yet with scrip and scrippage.

SHAKESPEARE, *As You Like It.* Act iii, sc. 2, l. 169.

10a
At midnight, in his guarded tent,
The Turk was dreaming of the hour
When Greece, her knee in suppliance bent,
Should tremble at his power.

FITZ-GREENE HALLECK, *Marco Bozzaris.*

11
One of that saintly murderous brood
To carnage and the Koran given.

THOMAS MOORE, *Lalla Rookh: The Fire-Worshippers.*

12
[The Ottoman Empire] has the body of a sick old man, who tried to appear healthy, although his end was near.

SIR THOMAS ROE, *Ambassador to Constantinople,* 1621. (BUCHANAN, *Letters,* p. 375.)

[The Ottoman Empire] whose sick body was not supported by a mild and regular diet, but by a powerful treatment, which continually exhausted it.

MONTESQUIEU, *Persian Letters.* Bk. i, No. 19.

We have on our hands a sick man,—a very sick man.

NICHOLAS I OF RUSSIA, *Conversation with Sir George Hamilton Seymour,* 1853. (*Blue Book,* 1854.) Hence "The sick man of Europe," as referring to the Turk.

13
I would send them to the Turk, to make eunuchs of.

SHAKESPEARE, *All's Well that Ends Well.* Act ii, sc. 3, l. 94.

Go to Constantinople and take the Turk by the beard.

SHAKESPEARE, *Henry V.* Act v, sc. 2, l. 222.

In woman, out-paramoured the Turk.

SHAKESPEARE, *King Lear.* Act iii, sc. 4, l. 94.

An you be not turned Turk, there's no more sailing by the star.

SHAKESPEARE, *Much Ado About Nothing.* Act iii, sc. 4, l. 57.

14
The Sublime Porte. (Bab-i-ali.)
The official title of the central office of the Ottoman empire under the sultans.

The lofty gate of the royal tent.

MAHOMET II, referring to the ancient place of audience. The Italians translated the phrase "La porte sublima." (CREASY, *History of the Ottoman Turks,* p. 96.)

TWILIGHT

See also Evening, Sunset

1
Whilst twilight's curtain, spreading far,
Was pinnèd with a single star.
MACDONALD CLARKE, *Death in Disguise*, l. 227.

Now twilight lets her curtain down
And pins it with a star.
LYDIA MARIA CHILD. When Macdonald Clarke died in 1842, Mrs. Child wrote an appreciation of his work, in which she misquoted his lines as above, and the misquotation became the more widely accepted rendering.

Day hath put on his jacket, and around
His burning bosom buttoned it with stars.
O. W. HOLMES, *Evening: By a Tailor*, l. 1.

Night was drawing and closing her curtain.
RICHTER, *Flower, Fruit, and Thorn Pieces*. Bk. i, ch. 2.

1a
How lovely are the portals of the night,
When stars come out to watch the daylight die.
THOMAS COLE, *Twilight*.

The lengthening shadows wait
The first pale stars of twilight.
O. W. HOLMES, *Even-Song*. St. 6.

2
Parlòur twilight: such a gloom
Suits well the thoughtful or unthinking mind.
COWPER, *The Task*. Bk. iv, l. 278.

3
Spirit of Twilight, through your folded wings
I catch a glimpse of your averted face,
And rapturous on a sudden, my soul sings
"Is not this common earth a holy place?"
OLIVE CUSTANCE, *Twilight*.

4
From that high mount of God, whence light and shade
Spring both, the face of brightest Heav'n had chang'd
To grateful twilight.
MILTON, *Paradise Lost*. Bk. v, l. 640.

Disastrous twilight.
MILTON, *Paradise Lost*. Bk. i, l. 597.

5
Our lady of the twilight,
She hath such gentle hands,
So lovely are the gifts she brings
From out the sunset-lands,
So bountiful, so merciful,
So sweet of soul is she;
And over all the world she draws
Her cloak of charity.
ALFRED NOYES, *Our Lady of the Twilight*.

6
When I was young the twilight seemed too long.
A. MARY F. ROBINSON, *Twilight*.

7
Twilight's soft dews steal o'er the village-green,
With magic tints to harmonize the scene.
Still'd is the hum that thro' the hamlet broke,
When round the ruins of their ancient oak
The peasants flock'd to hear the minstrel play,
And games and carols closed the busy day.
SAMUEL ROGERS, *Pleasures of Memory*. Pt. i, l. 1.

8
Twilight, a timid fawn, went glimmering by,
And Night, the dark-blue hunter, followed fast.
GEORGE WILLIAM RUSSELL, *Refuge*.

Dusk wraps the village in its dim caress;
Each chimney's vapour, like a thin grey rod,
Mounting aloft through miles of quietness,
Pillars the skies of God.
GEORGE WILLIAM RUSSELL, *Dusk*.

9
Twilight, ascending slowly from the east,
Entwined in duskier wreaths her braided locks
O'er the fair front and radiant eyes of day:
Night followed, clad with stars.
SHELLEY, *Alastor*, l. 337.

TYRANNY

10
Of all the tyrants that the world affords,
Our own affections are the fiercest lords.
WILLIAM ALEXANDER, *Julius Cæsar*.

Think'st thou there is no tyranny but that
Of blood and chains? The despotism of vice,
The weakness and the wickedness of luxury,
The negligence, the apathy, the evils
Of sensual sloth—produce ten thousand tyrants,
Whose delegated cruelty surpasses
The worst acts of one energetic master,
However harsh and hard in his own bearing.
BYRON, *Sardanapalus*. Act i, sc. 2, l. 113.

The worst tyrants are those which establish themselves in our own breasts.
W. E. CHANNING, *Spiritual Freedom*.

11
A usurper always distrusts the whole world. (Usurpator diffida Di tutti sempre.)
ALFIERI, *Polinice*. Act iii, sc. 2.

The tyrant now
Trusts not to men: nightly within his chamber
The watch-dog guards his couch, the only friend
He now dare trust.
JOANNA BAILLIE, *Ethwald*. Pt. ii, act v, sc. 3.

Only tyrants need always be in fear. (Il n'appartient qu'aux tyrans d'être toujours en crainte.)
HENRY IV OF FRANCE. (HARDOUIN DE PEREFIXE.)

Fear, that reigns with the tyrant.
LONGFELLOW, *Evangeline*. Pt. i, l. 35.

Tyrants' fears
Decrease not, but grow faster than the years.
SHAKESPEARE, *Pericles*. Act i, sc. 2, l. 84.

12
For tyrants make man good beyond himself:
Hate to their rule, which else would die away,
Their daily-practis'd chafings keep alive.
MATTHEW ARNOLD, *Merope*, l. 42.

13
All oppressors . . . attribute the frustration of their desires to the want of sufficient rig-

our. Then they redouble the efforts of their impotent cruelty.

EDMUND BURKE, *Impeachment of Warren Hastings,* 16 Feb., 1788.

I impeach him in the name of the people of India, whose rights he has trodden under foot, and whose country he has turned into a desert. Lastly, in the name of human nature itself, in the name of both sexes, in the name of every age, in the name of every rank, I impeach the common enemy and oppressor of all.

EDMUND BURKE, *Impeachment of Warren Hastings: Peroration.* This is the version given by Macaulay in his essay on Warren Hastings. It is much swifter and more brilliant than the original, and hence has become more familiar.

1
The tyranny of a multitude is a multiplied tyranny.

EDMUND BURKE, *Letter to Thomas Mercer,* 26 Feb., 1790. *See also under* PEOPLE.

2
A tyrant is the best sacrifice to Jupiter, as the ancients held.

ROBERT BURTON, *Anatomy of Melancholy.* Pt. ii, sec. iii, mem. 1, subs. 1.

3
Can despots compass aught that hails their sway?
Or call with truth one span of earth their own,
Save that wherein at last they crumble bone by bone?

BYRON, *Childe Harold.* Canto i, st. 42.

Here all the mighty troublers of the earth,
Who swam to sov'reign rule through seas of blood;
Th' oppressive, sturdy, man-destroying villains,
Who ravag'd kingdoms, and laid empires waste. . . .
Now, like a storm that's spent, Lie hush'd.

ROBERT BLAIR, *The Grave,* l. 208.

4
Tyranny Is far the worst of treasons.

BYRON, *The Two Foscari.* Act ii, sc. 1.

5
Is there no tyrant but the crowned one? (N'est-on jamais tyran qu'avec un diadème?)

ANDRÉ CHÉNIER, *Caius Gracchus.*

6
I deem the tyrant happy who dies a natural death.

CHILON. (DIOGENES LAERTIUS, *Chilon.* Sec. 5.)

Tremble, ye tyrants, for ye can not die. (Tremblez, tyrans, vous êtes immortels.)

JACQUES DELILLE, *L'Immortalité de l'Âme.*

How hard the tyrants die!

ELBERT HUBBARD, *Epigrams.*

The strangest thing I ever saw was an aged tyrant.

THALES. (DIOGENES LAERTIUS, *Thales.* Sec. 36.)

7
Tyrant, step from the throne, and give place to thy master. (Tyran, descends du trône et fais place à ton maître.)

CORNEILLE, *Heraclius.* Act i, sc. 2.

8
He who allows oppression shares the crime.

ERASMUS DARWIN, *The Botanic Garden.* Pt. ii, canto 3, l. 458.

9
Nature has left this tincture in the blood,
That all men would be tyrants if they could.

DANIEL DEFOE, *The Kentish Petition: Addenda,* l. 11.

Slaves would be tyrants if the chance were theirs.

VICTOR HUGO, *The Vanished City.*

There are few minds to which tyranny is not delightful.

SAMUEL JOHNSON, *Letters.* Vol. ii, p. 110.

10
O slavish man! will you not bear with your own brother, who has God for his Father, as being a son from the same stock, and of the same high descent? But if you chance to be placed in some superior station, will you presently set yourself up for a tyrant?

EPICTETUS, *Discourses.* Bk. i, ch. 13, sec. 3.

11
A state has no worse foe than a tyrant, under whom can be no common laws; but one ruler, keeping the law in his own hands, so that equality perishes.

EURIPIDES, *Suppliants,* l. 429.

Where law ends, tyranny begins.

WILLIAM PITT, *Speech,* 9 Jan., 1770.

To live by one man's will became the cause of all men's misery.

RICHARD HOOKER, *Ecclesiastical Polity.* Bk. i, ch. 10, sec. 5.

12
Tyrants commonly cut off the stairs by which they climb unto their thrones . . . for fear that, if they still be left standing, others will get up the same way.

THOMAS FULLER, *Worthies of England.* Ch. 23.

13
Some village Hampden, that, with dauntless breast,
The little tyrant of his fields withstood.

THOMAS GRAY, *Elegy Written in a Country Church-yard,* l. 57.

14
One tyrant helps another tyrant. (Τύραννος γὰρ 'εὼν τυράννῳ συγκατεργάσεται.)

HERODOTUS, *History.* Bk. viii, sec. 142.

15
'Twixt kings and tyrants there's this difference known:
Kings seek their subjects' good, tyrants their own.

ROBERT HERRICK, *Kings and Tyrants.*

16
Men are still men. The despot's wickedness
Comes of ill teaching, and of power's excess,—

Comes of the purple he from childhood wears.
VICTOR HUGO, *The Vanished City.*

1 And he looked for judgment, but behold oppression; for righteousness, but behold a cry.
Old Testament: Isaiah, v, 7.

Oppression, and Sword-law.
MILTON, *Paradise Lost.* Bk. xi, l. 668.

2 Resistance to tyrants is obedience to God.
THOMAS JEFFERSON, *Epigram*, found among his papers after his death.

The time to guard against corruption and tyranny is before they shall have gotten hold of us. It is better to keep the wolf out of the fold than to trust to drawing his teeth and claws after he shall have entered.
THOMAS JEFFERSON, *Writings.* Vol. ii, p. 163.

3 I have sworn upon the altar of God eternal hostility against every form of tyranny over the mind of man.
THOMAS JEFFERSON, *Letter to Benjamin Rush*, 23 Sept., 1800. Inscribed inside Jefferson monument at Washington.

He who endeavors to control the mind by force is a tyrant, and he who submits is a slave.
R. G. INGERSOLL, *Some Mistakes of Moses.*

Whatever crushes individuality is despotism, by whatever name it may be called.
JOHN STUART MILL, *On Liberty.* Ch. 3.

4 A country governed by a despot is an inverted cone.
SAMUEL JOHNSON. (BOSWELL, *Life*, iii, 283.)

5 What is more cruel than a tyrant's ear? (Quid violentius aure tyranni?)
JUVENAL, *Satires.* Sat. iv, l. 86.

6 Despotism sits nowhere so secure as under the effigy and ensigns of Freedom.
W. S. LANDOR, *Imaginary Conversations: Lacy and Cura Merino.*

Every tyrant who has lived has believed in freedom—for himself.
ELBERT HUBBARD, *The Philistine.* Vol. xi, p. 61.

7 Under a tyranny, freedom is destroyed by freedom of speech; a semblance of freedom is retained by silent acquiescence.
LUCAN, *De Bello Civili.* Bk. iii, l. 145.

Fortunate are the nations whom destiny has kept continuously under tyrants.
LUCAN, *De Bello Civili.* Bk. vii, l. 442.

8 Your petty tyrant's insolence I hate;
If wrong be done me, be it from the great.
(*'Εμὲ δ' ἀδικείτω πλούσιος καὶ μὴ πενης·*
ῥᾷον φέρειν γὰρ κρειττόνων τυραννίδα.)
MENANDER, *Fragments.* Frag. 688.

9 Tyranny must be,
Though to the tyrant thereby no excuse.
MILTON, *Paradise Lost.* Bk. xii, l. 95.

10 To exercise authority with cruel claws. (Exercere imperium sævis unguibus.)
PHÆDRUS, *Fables.* Bk. i, fab. 31, l. 12.

11 Oppression is but another name for irresponsible power.
WILLIAM PINKNEY, *Speech*, 15 Feb., 1820.

12 The despot's heel is on thy shore,
Maryland!
JAMES RYDER RANDALL, *My Maryland.*

13 There is no tyranny so hateful as a vulgar and anonymous tyranny. . . . Such a headless people has the mind of a worm and the claws of a dragon.
GEORGE SANTAYANA, *The Life of Reason.* Vol. ii, p. 127.

14 How fine this tyrant
Can tickle where she wounds!
SHAKESPEARE, *Cymbeline.* Act i, sc. 1, l. 84.

15 For how can tyrants safely govern home,
Unless abroad they purchase great alliance?
SHAKESPEARE, *III Henry VI.* Act iii, sc. 3, l. 69.

16 This tyrant, whose sole name blisters our tongues,
Was once thought honest: you loved him well.
SHAKESPEARE, *Macbeth.* Act iv, sc. 3, l. 12.

17 Great tyranny! lay thou thy basis sure,
For goodness dare not check thee!
SHAKESPEARE, *Macbeth.* Act iv, sc. 3, l. 32.

18 O nation miserable,
With an untitled tyrant bloody-scepter'd
When shalt thou see thy wholesome days again?
SHAKESPEARE, *Macbeth.* Act iv, sc. 3, l. 103.

19 This is Ercle's vein, a tyrant's vein.
SHAKESPEARE, *A Midsummer-Night's Dream.* Act i, sc. 2, l. 42.

20 But thou know'st this,
'Tis time to fear when tyrants seem to kiss.
SHAKESPEARE, *Pericles.* Act i, sc. 2, l. 78.

For what is he they follow? truly, gentlemen,
A bloody tyrant, and a homicide:
One raised in blood, and one in blood establish'd; . . .
A base foul stone, made precious by the foil
Of England's chair, where he is falsely set;
One that hath ever been God's enemy.
SHAKESPEARE, *Richard III.* Act v, sc. 3, l. 245.

21 Every despot must have one disloyal subject to keep him sane.
BERNARD SHAW, *Plays, Pleasant and Unpleasant: Preface.*

22 Fear not the tyrants shall rule forever,
Or the priests of the bloody faith;
They stand on the brink of that mighty river,
Whose waves they have tainted with death.
SHELLEY, *Rosalind and Helen*, l. 894.

This hand is hostile only to tyrants, and draws the sword only to attain placid quiet under liberty. (Manus hæc inimica tyrannis Ense petit placidam sub libertate quietam.)

ALGERNON SIDNEY. Written in the album of the University of Copenhagen. The first line, at least, was not original. (*Notes and Queries*, 10 March, 1866.) The second line was adopted as the motto of the State of Massachusetts.

This hand, to tyrants ever sworn the foe,
For Freedom only deals the deadly blow;
Then sheathes in calm repose the vengeful blade
For gentle peace in Freedom's hallowed shade.

JOHN QUINCY ADAMS, *Written in an Album*, 1842. A free translation of Sidney's lines.

With reasonable men, I will reason; with humane men I will plead; but to tyrants I will give no quarter, nor waste arguments where they will certainly be lost.

WILLIAM LLOYD GARRISON, *Life*. Vol. i.

2
Tyranny is a lovely eminence, but there is no way down from it.

SOLON. (PLUTARCH, *Lives: Solon*. Sec. 14.)

3
Tyrants are a money-loving race. (Τὸ δ' ἐκ τυράννων αἰσχροκέρδειαν φιλεῖ.)

SOPHOCLES, *Antigone*, l. 1056.

4
He that roars for liberty
Faster binds a tyrant's power;
And the tyrant's cruel glee
Forces on the freer hour.

TENNYSON, *The Vision of Sin*. Pt. iv, st. 17.

5
Clever tyrants are never punished. (Les habiles tyrans ne sont jamais punis.)

VOLTAIRE, *Mérope*. Act v, sc. 5.

A company of tyrants is inaccessible to all seductions.

VOLTAIRE, *Philosophical Dictionary: Tyranny*.

6
The sovereign is called a tyrant who knows no laws but his caprice.

VOLTAIRE, *Philosophical Dictionary: Tyranny*.

7
Still have I found, where Tyranny prevails,
That virtue languishes and pleasure fails.

WORDSWORTH, *Descriptive Sketches, During a Pedestrian Tour Among the Alps*, l. 597.

8
Despotism tempered by assassination, that is our Magna Charta.

A Russian noble to Count Münster, on the assassination of Emperor Paul I in 1800.

A Despotism tempered by Dynamite.

W. S. GILBERT, *Utopia, Limited*. Act i.

U

UMBRELLA

9
The rain it raineth on the just
And also on the unjust fella;
But chiefly on the just, because
The unjust steals the just's umbrella.

SIR GEORGE FERGUSON BOWEN. (SICHEL, *Sands of Time*, p. 82.) Also attributed to "Cynicus," said to have been a Mr. Robertson, of Fifeshire, Scotland, and to Dean Swift.

Rainy days will surely come:
Take your friend's umbrella home.

UNKNOWN, *For a Rainy Day*.

10
We bear our shades about us; self-depriv'd
Of other screen, the thin umbrella spread,
And range an Indian waste without a tree.

COWPER, *The Task*. Bk. i, l. 259.

11
I can't tell its name, but I can tell its history. Strangers take it away.

EMERSON, in 1871, when his memory for words was failing. (CABOT, *A Memoir of Ralph Waldo Emerson*, p. 652.)

12
Let Persian dames the umbrella's ribs display,
To guard their beauties from the sunny ray;
Or sweating slaves support the shady load,
When eastern monarchs show their state abroad;
Britain in winter only knows its aid,
To guard from chilly showers the walking maid.

JOHN GAY, *Trivia*. Bk. i, l. 213.

13
"Where is my toadstool?" loud he lamented.
—And that's how umbrellas were first invented!

OLIVER HERFORD, *The Elf and the Dormouse*.

14
It is the habitual carriage of the umbrella that is the stamp of Respectability. The umbrella has become the acknowledged index of social position.

J. W. FERRIER AND R. L. STEVENSON, *The Philosophy of Umbrellas*.

Umbrellas, like faces, acquire a certain sympathy with the individual who carries them.

J. W. FERRIER AND R. L. STEVENSON, *The Philosophy of Umbrellas*.

15
The inseparable gold umbrella which in that country [Burma] as much denotes the grandee as the star or garter does in England.

J. W. PALMER, *Up and Down the Irrawadde*.

UNBELIEF, see Atheism

UNCERTAINTY, see Certainty, Doubt

UNDERSTANDING

See also Mind

1
This devil of a man [Raymond Poincaré] is the opposite of Briand: the latter knows nothing and understands everything; the other knows everything and understands nothing. (Ce diable d'homme est le contraire de Briand: ce dernier ne sait rien et comprend tout; l'autre sait tout et ne comprend rien.)

GEORGES CLEMENCEAU, in a conversation with friends, as reported by *Les Annales*, which added that the wise-crack was well known. (Elle est bien connue, cette lézarde contre M. Poincaré.)

1a
Shut up your mouth and chew the cud of understanding.

CONGREVE, *Love for Love*. Act i, sc. 1.

2
I shall light a candle of understanding in thine heart, which shall not be put out.

Apocrypha: II Esdras, xiv, 25.

3
It is better to understand little than to misunderstand a lot.

ANATOLE FRANCE, *Revolt of the Angels*. Ch. 1.

4
When Fate destines one to ruin, it begins by blinding the eyes of his understanding.

JAMES FRASER, *Short History of the Emperors of the Moghol Race*, p. 57. (1742) *See also* MADNESS: WHOM THE GODS DESTROY.

5
Understanding is the wealth of wealth.

W. G. BENHAM, *Proverbs*, p. 865. Arabic.

6
What we do not understand we do not possess. (Was man nicht versteht, besitzt man nicht.)

GOETHE, *Sprüche in Prosa*.

7
The improvement of the understanding is for two ends: first, for our own increase of knowledge; secondly, to enable us to deliver and make out that knowledge to others.

JOHN LOCKE, *Some Thoughts Concerning Reading and Study: Appendix B*.

8
He gives us the very quintessence of perception.

J. R. LOWELL, *My Study Window: Coleridge*.

9
Each might his sev'ral province well command,
Would all but stoop to what they understand.

POPE, *Essay on Criticism*. Pt. i, l. 66.

10
With all thy getting get understanding.

Old Testament: Proverbs, iv, 7.

11
I have more understanding than all my teachers: for thy testimonies are my meditation.

Old Testament: Psalms, cxix, 99.

12
Give it an understanding but no tongue.

SHAKESPEARE, *Hamlet*. Act i, sc. 2, l. 250. *See also under* SECRECY.

13
Comprehension must be the soil in which grow all the fruits of friendship.

WOODROW WILSON, *Address*, Mobile, Ala., 1913.

UNITED STATES, see America

UNITY

See also Brotherhood

13a
All for one, one for all. (Tous pour un, un pour tous.)

ALEXANDRE DUMAS, *Les Trois Mousquetaires*. Ch. 9. Dictated by D'Artagnan, and repeated by his three friends.

14
A threefold cord is not quickly broken.

Old Testament: Ecclesiastes, iv, 12.

Strength, silence, simpleness, of these three strands
They twist the cable shall the world hold fast
To where its anchors clutch the bed-rock of the Past.

J. R. LOWELL, *On a Bust of General Grant*.

15
One Lord, one faith, one baptism, one God and Father of all, who is above all, and through all, and in you all.

New Testament: Ephesians, iv, 5, 6.

16
We must quit ourselves like men, and strive
To aid our cause, although we be but two.
Great is the strength of feeble arms combined,
And we can combat even with the brave.

HOMER, *Iliad*. Bk. xiii, l. 290. (Bryant, tr.)

Two are an army against one. (Duo sunt exercitus uni.)

UNKNOWN, *Ysengrimus*, ii, 311.

17
We are born for coöperation, as are the feet, the hands, the eyelids, and the upper and lower jaws.

MARCUS AURELIUS, *Meditations*. Bk. ii, sec. 1.

18
He that is not with me is against me.

New Testament: Matthew, xii, 30.

He that is not against us is for us.

New Testament: Luke, ix, 50.

19
Our hearts, my love, were form'd to be
The genuine twins of Sympathy,
They live with one sensation:
In joy or grief, but most in love,
Like chords in unison they move,
And thrill with like vibration.

THOMAS MOORE, *Sympathy: To Julia*.

20
Finally, be ye all of one mind.

New Testament: I Peter, iii, 8.

I would we were all of one mind and one mind good.

SHAKESPEARE, *Cymbeline*. Act v, sc. 4, l. 212.

21
Scilurus on his death-bed, being about to leave fourscore sons surviving, offered a bundle of darts to each of them, and bade them

break them. When all refused, drawing the darts out one by one, he easily broke them,—thus teaching his sons that if they held together they would continue strong; but if they were divided they would become weak.
PLUTARCH, *Apothegms of Kings and Great Commanders: Scilurus.*

All your strength is in your union,
All your danger is in discord.
LONGFELLOW, *Hiawatha.* Bk. i, l. 113.

1
Union gives strength to the humble. (Auxilia humilia firma consensus facit.)
PUBLILIUS SYRUS, *Sententiæ.* No. 4.

Strength united is the greater. (Vis unita fortior.)
Motto of Earls of Mountcashell. (Quoted by BACON, *Table of Colours,* 5.)

United we stand, divided we fall!
G. P. MORRIS, *The Flag of Our Union,* l. 3.
See also AMERICA: UNION.

2
We are one people and will act as one. (Wir sind ein Volk, und einig wollen wir handeln.)
SCHILLER, *Wilhelm Tell.* Act ii, sc. 2, l. 258.

3
Behold, how good and how pleasant it is for brethren to dwell together in unity.
Old Testament: Psalms, cxxxiii, 1.

So we grew together,
Like to a double cherry, seeming parted,
But yet a union in partition;
Two lovely berries moulded on one stem;
So, with two seeming bodies, but one heart;
Two of the first, like coats in heraldry,
Due but to one and crowned with one crest.
SHAKESPEARE, *A Midsummer-Night's Dream.* Act iii, sc. 2, l. 208.

4
Whatever the issue, we shall share one common danger, one safety. (Quo res cumque cadent, unum et commune periculum, Una salus ambobus erit.)
VERGIL, *Æneid.* Bk. ii, l. 709.

United thoughts and counsels, equal hope,
And hazard in the glorious enterprise.
MILTON, *Paradise Lost.* Bk. i, l. 88.

UNIVERSE

See also God and the Universe

5
Had I been present at the creation, I would have given some useful hints for the better ordering of the universe.
ALFONSO X, THE WISE. Of Ptolemy's astronomy.

This saying of Alphonso about Ptolemy's astronomy, "that it seemed a crank machine; that it was pity the Creator had not taken advice," is still remembered by mankind—this and no other of his many sayings.
CARLYLE, *Frederick the Great.* Bk. ii, ch. 7.

There is a crack in everything God has made.
EMERSON, *Essays, First Series: Compensation.*

Ah Love! could you and I with Him conspire
To grasp this sorry Scheme of Things entire,
Would we not shatter it to bits—and then
Re-mould it nearer to the Heart's Desire?
OMAR KHAYYÁM, *Rubáiyát,* 99. (Fitzgerald, tr.)

O me! for why is all around us here
As if some lesser god had made the world,
But had not force to shape it as he would?
TENNYSON, *The Passing of Arthur,* l. 13.

Had you the world on your chessboard, you could not fit all to your mind.
GEORGE HERBERT, *Jacula Prudentum.*

6
Taken as a whole, the universe is absurd.
WALTER BAGEHOT, *Literary Studies.* Vol. i, p. 36.

7
Of the "real" universe we know nothing, except that there exist as many versions of it as there are perceptive minds. Each man lives alone in his private universe.
GERALD BULLETT, *Dreaming.*

8
The whole universe is one commonwealth of which both gods and men are members. (Universus his mundus sit una civitas communis deorum atque hominum existimanda.)
CICERO, *De Legibus.* Bk. i, ch. 7, sec. 23.

9
A grain of sand includes the universe.
S. T. COLERIDGE, *Additional Table Talk: Thought.*

To see the world in a grain of sand.
WILLIAM BLAKE, *Auguries of Innocence.*

10
The whole creation is made of hooks and eyes, of bitumen, of sticking-plaster . . . it coheres in a perfect ball.
EMERSON, *Conduct of Life: Worship.*

11
The universe is not composed of newts only; it has its Newtons.
HARRY EMERSON FOSDICK, *Easter Sermon.*

12
The universe can best be pictured as consisting of pure thought, the thought of what for want of a better word we must describe as a mathematical thinker.
SIR JAMES JEANS, *Rede Memorial Lecture,* Cambridge, 4 Nov., 1930.

13
Space is the stature of God. (L'espace est la stature de Dieu.)
JOUBERT, *Pensées.* No. 183.

14
Every mortal man of us holds stock in the only public debt that is absolutely sure of payment, and that is the debt of the Maker of this Universe to the Universe he has made.
J. R. LOWELL, *On a Certain Condescension in Foreigners.*

15
The sum total of all sums total is eternal. (Summarum summa est æternum.)
LUCRETIUS, *De Rerum Natura.* Bk. iii, l. 817; bk. v, l. 362. Lucretius refers to the universe.

But how can finite grasp Infinity?
DRYDEN, *Hind and the Panther.* Pt. i, l. 105.

16
The Universe—mutation. (Ὁ κόσμος, ἀλλοίωσις.)
MARCUS AURELIUS, *Meditations.* Bk. iv, sec. 3.

1
All that is in tune with thee. O Universe, is in tune with me! (Πᾶν μοι συναρμόζει, ὅ σοὶ εὐάρμοστον ἐστιν, ὦ κόσμε.)

MARCUS AURELIUS, *Meditations*. Bk. iv, sec. 23.

In Tune with the Infinite.

RALPH WALDO TRINE. Title of book.

2
One Universe made up of all things; and one God in it all, and one principle of Being, and one Law, one Reason shared by all thinking creatures, and one Truth.

MARCUS AURELIUS, *Meditations*. Bk. vii, sec. 9.

3
With centric and eccentric scribbl'd o'er,
Cycle and epicycle, orb in orb.

MILTON, *Paradise Lost*. Bk. viii, l. 83.

4
Nothing exists of all this which seems to exist except the universe alone. (Ex his, quæ videntur, nihil esse uno excepto universo.)

PARMENIDES. (SENECA, *Epistulæ ad Lucilium*. Epis. lxxxviii, sec. 44.)

5
It is an infinite sphere whose centre is everywhere, its circumference nowhere. (C'est une sphère infinie dont le centre est partout, la circonférence nulle part.)

BLAISE PASCAL, *Pensées*. Sec. ii, No. 72. Referring to the universe.

The intellectual sphere, which is everywhere the centre, and which has no circumference and which we call God.

RABELAIS, *Works*. Bk. ii, ch. 47.

6
The universe is full of magical things, patiently waiting for our wits to grow sharper.

EDEN PHILLPOTTS, *A Shadow Passes*.

7
Thro' worlds unnumber'd tho' the God be known,
'T is ours to trace him only in our own.
He who thro' vast immensity can pierce,
See worlds on worlds compose one universe,
Observe how system into system runs,
What other planets circle other suns,
What varied being peoples every star.

POPE, *Essay on Man*. Epis. i, l. 21.

8
The universe, as far as we can observe it, is a wonderful and immense engine; its extent, its order, its beauty, its cruelty make it alike impressive. If we dramatize its life and conceive its spirit, we are filled with wonder, terror, and amusement, so magnificent is that spirit, so prolific, inexorable, grammatical and dull.

GEORGE SANTAYANA, *Little Essays*, p. 85.

Great is this organism of mud and fire, terrible this vast, painful, glorious experiment.

GEORGE SANTAYANA, *Little Essays*, p. 86.

9
The universe is a thought of God.

SCHILLER, *Essays: Æsthetical and Philosophical*. Letter 4.

10
This goodly frame, the earth, seems to me a sterile promontory; this most excellent canopy the air, look you, this brave o'erhanging firmament, this majestical roof fretted with golden fire, why, it appears no other thing to me than a foul and pestilent congregation of vapours.

SHAKESPEARE, *Hamlet*. Act ii, sc. 2, l. 310.

11
When I view the universe as a whole, I admit that it is a marvelous structure; and what is more, I insist that it is of what I may call an intelligent design. . . . There is really very little difference between my own thoughts about the matter and the thoughts of a Fundamentalist.

W. F. G. SWANN, *The Architecture of the Universe*.

12
One God, one law, one element,
And one far-off divine event,
To which the whole creation moves.

TENNYSON, *In Memoriam: Conclusion*.

13
This truth within thy mind rehearse,
That in a boundless universe
Is boundless better, boundless worse.

TENNYSON, *The Two Voices*, l. 25.

14
Let your soul stand cool and composed before a million universes.

WALT WHITMAN, *Song of Myself*. Sec. 48.

UNIVERSITY

15
Universities incline wits to sophistry and affectation.

BACON, *Interpretation of Nature*. Ch. 26.

They learn nothing there [at the universities of Europe] but to believe; first, to believe that others know that which they know not; and after, that themselves know that which they know not.

BACON, *Cogitationes de Scientia Humana*.

16
Universities where individualism is dreaded as nothing else, wherein manufactories of patent drama, business schools and courses for the propagation of fine embroidery are established on the order of the monied.

THOMAS BEER, *The Mauve Decade*, p. 207.

17
The true University of these days is a Collection of Books.

CARLYLE, *Heroes and Hero-Worship: The Hero as Man of Letters*.

18
And solid learning never falls
Without the verge of College walls.

CHARLES CHURCHILL, *The Ghost*. Bk. i, l. 83.

19
A university should be a place of light, of liberty, and of learning.

BENJAMIN DISRAELI, *Speech*, House of Commons, 11 March, 1873.

1
Ye can lade a man up to th' university, but ye can't make him think.
FINLEY PETER DUNNE, *Mr. Carnegie's Gift.*

2
Colleges hate geniuses, just as convents hate saints.
EMERSON, *Uncollected Lectures: Public and Private Education.*

3
A university—an institution consciously devoted to the pursuit of knowledge, the solution of problems, the critical appreciation of achievement, and the training of men at a really high level.
ABRAHAM FLEXNER, *Universities*, p. 42.

4
A pine bench, with Mark Hopkins at one end of it and me at the other, is a good enough college for me!
JAMES ABRAM GARFIELD, *Address*, at a Williams College alumni dinner, at Delmonico's, New York, 28 Dec., 1871. (WASHINGTON GLADDEN, *Recollections*, p. 73.) Differing versions of Garfield's speech are given in Hinsdale's *President Garfield and Education*, p. 43; the *Williams Vidette*, 27 Jan., 1872, and the *Williams Review*, 5 Feb., 1872. (See STEVENSON, *Famous Single Poems*, rev. ed., ch. 19.) A movement had been started to provide new buildings for the college, and Garfield, who had been a student there under Mark Hopkins, contended that a distinguished and well-paid faculty was far more essential. His words are usually quoted, "A university is a student on one end of a log and Mark Hopkins on the other." Abraham Flexner in *Universities* (p. 151), attributes the saying to Hopkins himself, as, "The ideal college consists of a log of wood with an instructor at one end and a student at the other"; but it has not been found in Hopkins's works, and evidently derives from Garfield, who, in turn, was echoing Hopkins's own disdain of apparatus of any kind, even of books. In his *Lectures on Moral Science* (p. 39), he says that, for this subject at least, "no learning is needed, no science, no apparatus, no information from distant countries." See also APPENDIX, p. 2297:3.

6
A college degree does not lessen the length of your ears: it only conceals it.
ELBERT HUBBARD, *Epigrams.*

7
Colleges are places where pebbles are polished and diamonds are dimmed.
R. G. INGERSOLL, *Abraham Lincoln.*

8
He is piping hot from the university. He smells of buttered loaves yet
THOMAS MIDDLETON, *Your Five Gallants.*

10
I am undone! while I play the good husband at home, my son and my servant spend all at the university.
SHAKESPEARE, *Taming of the Shrew*, v, 1, 71.

11
A fool's brain digests philosophy into folly, science into superstition, and art into pedantry. Hence University education.
BERNARD SHAW, *Maxims for Revolutionists.*

12
The King, observing with judicious eyes
The state of both his universities,
To one he sent a regiment; for why?
That learnèd body wanted loyalty:
To th' other he sent books, as well discerning
How much that loyal body wanted learning.
DR. JOSEPH TRAPP, *Epigram*, when George I, in 1715, sent a regiment to Oxford, and donated Bishop Ely's library to Cambridge.

The King to Oxford sent a troop of horse,
For Tories own no argument but force;
With equal skill to Cambridge books he sent,
For Whigs admit no force but argument.
SIR WILLIAM BROWNE, *Riposte to Dr. Trapp.*

Isis and Cam, to patient science dear!
WORDSWORTH, *Ecclesiastical Sonnets*. Pt. iii, 42.

13
It is . . . a small college, and yet there are those that love it.
DANIEL WEBSTER, *Argument*, when presenting Dartmouth College case to Supreme Court. Quoted by Chauncey A. Goodrich in letter to Rufus Choate. (QUINT, *Story of Dartmouth.*)

14
We have let the idea of freedom under self-respect go to seed in our colleges and are turning out too many hard-boiled, hard-hearted hard-headed dumb-bells.
WILLIAM ALLEN WHITE, *Editorial*, *Emporia Gazette.*

15
Alma mater. (Bounteous, or fostering, mother.)
A name given by the Romans to Ceres and Cybele, and applied in England and America to universities in relation to their students.

A stony-hearted step-mother.
MILTON, referring to the university. (BIRRELL, *Obiter Dicta*. Ser. ii.) De Quincey (*Confessions of an English Opium Eater*. Pt. i) uses the same phrase with reference to Oxford Street, London.

UNKINDNESS

See also Cruelty

16
As "unkindness has no remedy at law," let its avoidance be with you a point of honor.
HOSEA BALLOU, *MS. Sermons.*

17
Unkindness blunts it more than marble hard.
SHAKESPEARE, *Comedy of Errors*. Act ii, sc. 1, 93.

Sharp-tooth'd unkindness.
SHAKESPEARE, *King Lear*. Act ii, sc. 4, l. 137.

18
I hope that we shall drink down all unkindness.
SHAKESPEARE, *Merry Wives of Windsor*, i, 1, 204.

19
Unkindness may do much;
And his unkindness may defeat my life,
But never taint my love.
SHAKESPEARE, *Othello*. Act iv, sc. 2, l. 159.

1
None can be call'd deform'd but the unkind.
SHAKESPEARE, *Twelfth Night*. Act iii, sc. 4, l. 402.

USE

2
Use makes men ready. (Usus promptos facit.)
FRANCIS BACON, *Short Notes for Civil Conversation: Conclusion*.

Use is second nature.
W. G. BENHAM, *Proverbs*, p. 865.

How use doth breed a habit in a man!
SHAKESPEARE, *The Two Gentlemen of Verona*. Act v, sc. 4, l. 1. *See also under* HABIT.

3
The richest of all Lords is Use.
EMERSON, *Conduct of Life: Considerations by the Way*.

In all human action those faculties will be strong which are used.
EMERSON, *Conduct of Life: Culture*.

4
Things at first hard and rough, are by use made tender and gentle.
BEN JONSON, *Explorata: De Orationis Dignitate*.

5
Metal shines with use. (Æra nitent usu.)
OVID, *Amores*. Bk. i, eleg. 8, l. 51.

The used key is always bright.
BENJAMIN FRANKLIN, *The Way to Wealth*.

6
The iron ring is worn out by constant use. (Ferreus assiduo consumitur anulus usu.)
OVID, *Ars Amatoria*. Bk. i, l. 473. *See also under* PERSEVERANCE.

7
'T is use alone that sanctifies expense.
POPE, *Moral Essays*. Epis. iv, l. 179.

8
Nothing in itself is good or evil,
But only in its use.
SOUTHEY, *Thalaba*, l. 269.

In the use,
Not in the bare possession lies the merit.
GILBERT WEST, *Institution of the Garter*, l. 461.

9
With this for motto, "Rather use than fame."
TENNYSON, *Merlin and Vivien*, l. 478.

USEFULNESS

10
Usefulness and baseness cannot exist in the same thing. (In eadem re utilitas et turpitudo esse non potest.)
CICERO, *De Officiis*. Bk. iii, ch. 8, sec. 35.

11
Be useful where thou livest, that they may
Both want, and wish, thy pleasing presence still.
GEORGE HERBERT, *The Church-Porch*. St. 55.

12
Unless what we do is useful, glory is vain. (Nisi utile est quod facimus, stulta est gloria.)
PHÆDRUS, *Fables*. Bk. iii, fab. 17, l. 12.

13
To everything its use. (Sua cuique utilitas.)
TACITUS, *History*. Bk. i, sec. 15.

Everything in the world is good for something.
DRYDEN, *The Spanish Friar*. Act iii, sc. 2.

Sensible people find nothing useless. (Il n'est rien d'inutile aux personnes de sens.)
LA FONTAINE, *Fables*. Bk. v, fab. 19.

V

VAGABOND

See also Wanderlust

14
From their folded mates they wander far,
Their ways seem harsh and wild:
They follow the beck of a baleful star,
Their paths are dream-beguiled.
RICHARD BURTON, *Black Sheep*.

15
Let us have no meandering.
DICKENS, *David Copperfield*. Ch. 1.

16
Are you not scared by seeing that the gypsies are more attractive to us than the Apostles?
EMERSON, *Journals*. Vol. vi, p. 184.

17
His house was known to all the vagrant train.
GOLDSMITH, *The Deserted Village*, l. 149.

18
They were strangers and pilgrims on the earth.
New Testament: Hebrews, xi, 13.

19
Whose furthest footstep never strayed
Beyond the village of his birth,
Is but a lodger for the night
In this old wayside inn of earth.
To-morrow he shall take his pack,
And set out for the ways beyond,
On the old trail from star to star,
An alien and a vagabond.
RICHARD HOVEY, *More Songs from Vagabondia: Envoy*.

20
A hobo is a man who builds palaces and lives in shacks,
He builds Pullmans and rides the rods, . . .
He reaps the harvest and stands in the bread line.
GODFREY IRWIN, *American Tramp and Underworld Slang*.

21
Friends and loves we have none, nor wealth, nor blest abode.
JOHN MASEFIELD, *The Seekers*. See 2103:1.

An ardent throng, we have wandered long,
We have searched the centuries through,
In flaming pride, we have fought and died,
To keep its memory true.
We fight and die, but our hopes beat high,
In spite of the toil and tears,

For we catch the gleam of our vanished dream
Down the path of the Untrod Years.
WILMA KATE MCFARLAND, *The Untrod Years.*

O canny sons of Jacob, to fret and toiling tied,
We grudge you not the birthright for which your father lied;
We own the right of roaming, and the world is wide.
BERTHA RUNKLE, *Songs of the Sons of Esau.*

O the Raggedy Man! He works fer Pa;
An' he's the goodest man you ever saw!
JAMES WHITCOMB RILEY, *The Raggedy Man.*

1
You shall comprehend all vagrom men.
SHAKESPEARE, *Much Ado About Nothing.* Act iii, sc. 3, l. 26.

2
Nature makes us vagabonds, the world makes us respectable.
ALEXANDER SMITH, *Dreamthorp: On Vagabonds.* See also APPENDIX.

3
I will sing, I will go, and never ask me why
I was born a rover and a passer-by.
RIDGELY TORRENCE, *Eye-Witness.*

I seem to myself like water and sky,
A river and a rover and a passer-by.
RIDGELY TORRENCE, *Eye-Witness.*

4
Wanderers of the street, to whom is dealt
The bread which without industry they find.
WORDSWORTH, *Poems Dedicated to National Independence.* Pt. ii, No. 13.

4a
Oh, why don't you work like other men do?
How the hell can I work when there's no work to do?
Hallelujah, I'm a bum, hallelujah, bum again,
Hallelujah, give us a hand-out to revive us again.
UNKNOWN, *Hallelujah, I'm a Bum.* There are several versions of this song.

This old song, heard at the water tanks of railroads in Kansas in 1897 and from harvest hands who worked in the wheat fields of Pawnee County, was picked up later by the I. W. W.'s, who made verses of their own for it and gave it wide fame.
CARL SANDBURG, *The American Songbag,* p. 184.

VALENTINE

5
How different from our dreary fashion
Of playing little games with passion,
The flippant and ironic mode
Of using love as episode,
Of chinning to the fourteenth line
To make a trivial valentine.
JOSEPH AUSLANDER, *Letter to Emily Dickinson.*

6
For this was on St. Valentine's day,
When every fowl cometh there to choose his mate.
CHAUCER, *The Parlement of Foules,* l. 309.

When you hear the birds call for their mates,
Ask if it be St. Valentine, their coupling day.
BEAUMONT AND FLETCHER, *Thierry and Theodoret.* Act iii, sc. 1.

Saint Valentine is past;
Begin these wood-birds but to couple now?
SHAKESPEARE, *A Midsummer-Night's Dream.* Act iv, sc. 1, l. 143.

Upon Friday is Saint Valentine's Day, and every bird chooseth him a mate.
UNKNOWN, *Paston Letters,* iii, 169.

7
Muse, bid the Morn awake!
Sad Winter now declines,
Each bird doth choose a mate;
This day 's Saint Valentine's.
MICHAEL DRAYTON, *To His Valentine.*

8
Last Valentine, the day when birds of kind
Their paramours with mutual chirpings find.
JOHN GAY, *Shepherd's Week: Thursday,* l. 37.

9
Oft have I heard both youths and virgins say,
Birds choose their mates, and couple too, this day:
But by their flight I never can devine
When I shall couple with my Valentine.
ROBERT HERRICK, *To His Valentine.*

10
Oh, if it be to choose and call thee mine,
Love, thou art every day my Valentine!
THOMAS HOOD, *For the Fourteenth of February.*

11
Hail to thy returning festival, old Bishop Valentine! Great is thy name in the rubric, thou venerable Archflamen of Hymen! Immortal Go-between; who and what manner of person art thou? Art thou but a *name,* typifying the restless principle which impels poor humans to seek perfection in union? or wert thou indeed a mortal prelate, with thy tippet and thy rochet, thy apron on, and decent lawn sleeves? Mysterious personage! like unto thee, assuredly, there is no other mitred father in the calendar.
CHARLES LAMB, *Essays of Elia: Valentine's Day.*

Thou comest attended with thousands and ten thousands of little Loves. . . . Singing Cupids are thy choristers and thy precentors; and instead of the crosier, the mystical arrow is borne before thee. . . .

This is the day on which those charming little missives, ycleped Valentines, cross and inter-cross each other at every street and turning. The weary and all forespent twopenny postman sinks beneath a load of delicate embarrassments, not his own. . . . In these little visual interpretations, no emblem is so common as the *heart*—that little three-cornered exponent of all our hopes and fears,—the bestuck and bleeding heart. . . .

Good-morrow to my Valentine, sings poor Ophelia, and no better wish, but with better auspices, we wish to all faithful lovers, who are not too wise to despise old legends, but are content to rank themselves humble diocesans of old Bishop Valentine and his true church.
CHARLES LAMB, *Essays of Elia: Valentine's Day.*

12
Called out in the morning by Mr. Moore,

whose voice my wife hearing in my dressing-chamber with me, got herself ready, and came down and challenged him for her valentine.

SAMUEL PEPYS, *Diary*, 14 Feb., 1660. It was a common practice in England to choose a sweetheart or special friend for the ensuing year, on St. Valentine's day, and the lady in the case of course expected a gift. (*See Paston Letters*, ii, 24.)

Here Mrs. The. shewed me my name upon her breast as her Valentine, which will cost me 20s.

SAMUEL PEPYS, *Diary*, 3 March, 1663.

By and by comes Mrs. Pierce, with my name in her bosom for her Valentine, which will cost me money.

SAMUEL PEPYS, *Diary*, 15 Feb., 1666.

1
To-morrow is Saint Valentine's day,
All in the morning betime.
And I a maid at your window,
To be your Valentine.

SHAKESPEARE, *Hamlet*. Act iv, sc. 5, l. 48.

2
The rose is red, the violet's blue,
Pinks are sweet, and so are you.

UNKNOWN, *A Rhyme for St. Valentine's Day*. The American version is usually, "Sugar is sweet, and so are you."

I claim there ain't Another Saint
As great as Valentine.

OGDEN NASH, *I Always Say a Good Saint is No Worse than a Bad Cold*.

VALOR

See also Courage

3
Immod'rate valour swells into a fault.

JOSEPH ADDISON, *Cato*. Act ii, sc. 1.

4
Valour's a mouse-trap, wit a gin,
Which women oft are taken in.

BUTLER, *Hudibras*. Pt. i, canto 3, l. 391.

He that is valiant, and dares fight,
Though drubbed, can lose no honour by 't.

BUTLER, *Hudibras*. Pt. i, canto 3, l. 1041.

5
Never had valour, no not ours, before
Done aught like this upon the land or main:
Where not to be o'ercome was to do more
Than all the conquests former kings did gain.

DRYDEN, *Annus Mirabilis*. St. 80.

6
Valor consists in the power of self-recovery.

EMERSON, *Essays, First Series: Circles*.

7
'Tis still observed those men most valiant are
Who are most modest ere they came to war.

EMERSON, *Society and Solitude: Courage*. Quoted.

Wherever valour true is found,
True modesty will there abound.

W. S. GILBERT, *Yeomen of the Guard* Act i.

8
Our valours are our best gods.

JOHN FLETCHER, *Bonduca*.

9
A sad wise valour is the brave complexion,
That leads the van, and swallows up the cities.

GEORGE HERBERT, *The Church-Porch*. St. 42.

10
Valour that parleys is near yielding.

GEORGE HERBERT, *Jacula Prudentum*.

11
All honor to you in your valor, as says the godlike phrase of Cato. (Macte Virtute esto, inquit sententia diva Catonis.)

HORACE, *Satires*. Bk. i, sat. 2, l. 31.

12
Fear to do base unworthy things, is valour;
If they be done to us, to suffer them
Is valour too.

BEN JONSON, *The New Inn*. Act iv, sc. 3.

I never thought an angry person valiant. . . .
No man is valianter by being angry,
But he that could not valiant be without.

BEN JONSON, *The New Inn*. Act iv, sc. 3.

That valour lies in the eyes o' the lookers on,
And is called valour with a witness.

BEN JONSON, *The New Inn*. Act iv, sc. 3.

The things true valour 's exercised about
Are poverty, restraint, captivity,
Banishment, loss of children, long disease:
The least is death. . . . So a mind affecting
Or undertaking dangers for ambition, . . .
Deserves the name of daring, not of valour.
And over-daring is as great a vice
As over-fearing. . . . A valiant man
Ought not to undergo, or tempt a danger,
But worthily, and by selected ways:
He undertakes with reason, not by chance.
His valour is the salt to his other virtues,
They are all unseasoned without it.

BEN JONSON, *The New Inn*. Act iv, sc. 3.

13
Rivalry in valor spurred them on. (Stimulos dedit æmula virtus.)

LUCAN, *De Bello Civili*. Bk. i, l. 120.

14
More childish valorous than manly wise.

CHRISTOPHER MARLOWE, *Tamburlane*. Pt. i, act iv, sc. 1.

15
Instead of rage
Deliberate valour breath'd, firm and unmov'd
With dread of death to flight or foul retreat.

MILTON, *Paradise Lost*. Bk. i, l. 553.

No thought of flight,
None of retreat, no unbecoming deed
That argued fear; each on himself relied,
As only in his arm the moment lay
Of victory.

MILTON, *Paradise Lost*. Bk. vi, l. 236.

16
In vain doth valour bleed
While Avarice and Rapine share the land.

MILTON, *Sonnet: To the Lord General Fairfax*.

17
Valor has its limits, like the other virtues. (La vaillance a ses limites, comme les autres vertus.)

MONTAIGNE, *Essays*. Bk. i, ch. 14.

18
You will find many men most unjust, most

impious, most intemperate, and most ignorant, yet extremely valorous.
PLATO, *Protagoras*. Sec. 349.

Valour, destitute of other virtues, cannot render a man worthy of any true esteem. . . . A man may be very valiant, and yet impious and vicious.
DRYDEN, *Æneid: Dedication.*

1 Valour grows by daring, fear by holding back. (Audendo virtus crescit, tardando timor.)
PUBLILIUS SYRUS, *Sententiæ*. No. 43.

2 Mindful of the valor of former days. (Pristinæ virtutis memores.)
SALLUST, *Catilina*. Ch. 60, sec. 3.

3 When Prussia hurried to the field,
And snatch'd the spear, but left the shield!
SCOTT, *Marmion:* Canto iii, *Introduction*, l. 63.

Then rush'd to meet the insulting foe:
They took the spear, but left the shield.
PHILIP FRENEAU, *To the Memory of the Brave Americans Who Fell at Eutaw Springs.*

4 When valour preys on reason,
It eats the sword it fights with.
SHAKESPEARE, *Antony and Cleopatra*. Act iii, sc. 13, l. 199.

He that loves himself
Hath not essentially but by circumstance
The name of valour.
SHAKESPEARE, *II Henry VI*. Act v, sc. 2, l. 38.

5 What valour were it, when a cur doth grin,
For one to thrust his hand between his teeth,
When he might spurn him with his foot away?
SHAKESPEARE, *III Henry VI*. Act i, sc. 4, l. 56.

He 's truly valiant that can suffer wisely
The worst that man can breathe, and make his wrongs
His outsides, to wear them like his raiment, carelessly;
And ne'er prefer his injuries to his heart
To bring it into danger.
SHAKESPEARE, *Timon of Athens*. Act iii, sc. 5, l. 31.

6 Virtue is of so little regard in these costermonger times that true valour is turned bearherd.
SHAKESPEARE, *II Henry IV*. Act i, sc. 2, l. 191.

7 My valour is certainly going!—it is sneaking off!—I feel it oozing out, as it were, at the palms of my hands.
SHERIDAN, *The Rivals*. Act v, sc. 3.

8 Valor, gradually overpowered by the delicious poison of sloth, grows torpid. (Blandoque veneno Desidiæ virtus paullatim evicta senescit.)
SILIUS ITALICUS, *Punica*. Bk. iii, l. 580.

9 In valor there is hope. (Spes in virtute.)
TACITUS, *Annals*. Bk. ii, sec. 20.

10 Valor is of no service, chance rules all, and the bravest often fall by the hands of cowards. (Nihil prodesse virtus, fors cuncta turbare, et ignavorum sæpe telis fortissimi cadere.)
TACITUS, *History*. Bk. iv, sec. 29.

11 Sometimes valor returns even to the hearts of the conquered. (Quondam etiam victis redit in præcordia virtus.)
VERGIL, *Æneid*. Bk. ii, l. 367.

12 Now, Æneas, there is need of valor, and of a stout heart. (Nunc animis opus, Ænea, nunc pectore firmo.)
VERGIL, *Æneid*. Bk. vi, l. 261.

13 The valiant to the valiant, the wise to the wise. ("Αλκιμοι ἀλκήεντα, σοφοὶ σοφόν.)
UNKNOWN, *Epigram on the Statue of an Athlete in the Hippodrome at Constantinople.* (*Greek Anthology*. Bk. xvi, No. 339.)

14 Valor flourishes by a wound. (Virescit vulnere virtus.)
UNKNOWN, *Motto of Earls of Galloway.*

VANITY

See also Boasting; Conceit; Egotism; Self-Love; Virtue and Vanity

I—Vanity: Definitions

15 In heaven I yearn for knowledge, account all else inanity;
On earth I confess an itch for the praise of fools—that's vanity.
ROBERT BROWNING, *Solomon and Balkis.*

16 The sixth insatiable sense.
CARLYLE, *The French Revolution*. Pt. i, bk. 2, ch. 2. Quoting a proverb referring to vanity.

17 Vanity is the more odious and shocking to everybody, because everybody, without exception, has vanity; and two vanities can never love one another.
LORD CHESTERFIELD, *Letters*, 14 Jan., 1766.

18 Vanity finds in self-love so powerful an ally that it storms, as it were by a *coup de main*, the citadel of our heads, where, having blinded the two watchmen, it readily descends into the heart.
C. C. COLTON, *Lacon*. Vol. i, No. 291.

19 Vanity is the mother, and affectation is the darling daughter; vanity is the sin, and affectation is the punishment; the first may be called the root of self-love, the other the fruit.
LORD HALIFAX, *Works*, p. 38.

20 Vainglory's a worm which the very best action

Will taint, and its soundness eat through.
CHARLES AND MARY LAMB, *Charity.*

1
Triumph, that insulting vanity.
MILTON, *Paradise Regained.* Bk. iv, l. 138.

For men, with Roman pride, above
The conquest, do the triumph love:
Nor think a perfect victory gained,
Unless they through the streets their captive lead enchained.
ABRAHAM COWLEY, *Dialogue.*

2
Cruelty was the vice of the ancient, vanity is that of the modern world. Vanity is the last disease.
GEORGE MOORE, *Impressions: Mummer-Worship.*

3
We do not content ourselves with the life we have in ourselves; we desire to live an imaginary life in the minds of others, and for this purpose we endeavor to shine.
PASCAL, *Pensées.* Sec. ii, No. 147.

4
Verily every man at his best state is altogether vanity.
Old Testament: Psalms, xxxix, 5.

Surely men of low degree are vanity, and men of high degree are a lie: to be laid in the balance, they are altogether lighter than vanity.
Old Testament: Psalms, lxii, 9.

5
Vanity is the pride of Nature.
W. G. BENHAM, *Proverbs,* p. 865.

6
The highest form of vanity is love of fame.
GEORGE SANTAYANA, *Little Essays,* p. 22.

The meaning of the word vanity never crosses the vulgar heart.
GEORGE SANTAYANA, *Little Essays,* p. 82.

7
It is not vain-glory for a man and his glass to confer in his own chamber.
SHAKESPEARE, *Cymbeline.* Act iv, sc. 1, l. 8.

8
Vanity the puppet's part.
SHAKESPEARE, *King Lear.* Act ii, sc. 2, l. 39.

9
Light vanity, insatiate cormorant,
Consuming means, soon preys upon itself.
SHAKESPEARE, *Richard II.* Act ii, sc. 1, l. 38.

10
Vanity bids all her sons be generous and brave, and her daughters chaste and courteous.
LAURENCE STERNE, *Sermons.* No. 17.

11
To be vain is rather a mark of humility than pride. . . . Whoever desires the character of a proud man ought to conceal his vanity.
JONATHAN SWIFT, *Works.* Vol. iii, p. 405.

II—Vanity: Apothegms

12
Pampered vanity is a better thing perhaps than starved pride.
JOANNA BAILLIE, *The Election.* Act ii, sc. 2.

13
It pleasures him to stoop for buttercups.
E. B. BROWNING, *Aurora Leigh.* Bk. iv, l. 212.

14
And the name of that town is Vanity; and at the town there is a fair kept, called Vanity Fair.
JOHN BUNYAN, *The Pilgrim's Progress.* Pt. i.

It beareth the name of Vanity Fair, because the town where 'tis kept is "lighter than vanity."
BUNYAN, *The Pilgrim's Progress.* Pt. i. Bunyan is quoting Psalm lxii, 9.

There is a great quantity of eating and drinking, making love and jilting, laughing and the contrary, smoking, cheating, fighting, dancing and fiddling; there are bullies pushing about, bucks ogling the women, knaves picking pockets. . . . Yes, this is Vanity Fair; not a moral place certainly; nor a merry one, though very noisy.
THACKERAY, *Vanity Fair: Before the Curtain.* (1848)

15
There is no living in the world without a complaisant indulgence for people's weaknesses, and innocent, though ridiculous, vanities.
LORD CHESTERFIELD, *Letters,* 16 Oct., 1747.

You will easily discover every man's prevailing vanity by observing his favourite topic of conversation; for every man talks most of that which he has most a mind to be thought to excel in.
LORD CHESTERFIELD, *Letters,* 16 Oct., 1747

16
It is not to be imagined in how many ways vanity defeats its own purpose.
LORD CHESTERFIELD, *Letters,* 17 May, 1750.

17
Vanity, like murder, will out.
HANNAH COWLEY, *The Belle's Stratagem.* Act i, sc. 4.

18
What dotage will not vanity maintain?
What web too weak to catch a modern brain?
COWPER, *Expostulation,* l. 628.

19
Vain men will speak well of him that does ill.
OLIVER CROMWELL, *Letter to Richard Mayor,* July, 1651.

20
He that loveth silver shall not be satisfied with silver; nor he that loveth abundance with increase: this is also vanity.
Old Testament: Ecclesiastes, v, 10.

21
Vanity is as ill at ease under indifference as tenderness is under a love which it cannot return.
GEORGE ELIOT, *Daniel Deronda.* Bk. i, ch. 10.

22
Everybody hath not wit enough to act out of interest, but everybody hath little enough to do it out of vanity.
LORD HALIFAX, *Works,* p. 241.

23
The vain man makes a merit of misfortune, and triumphs in his disgrace.
WILLIAM HAZLITT, *Characteristics.* No. 113.

1
An ounce of vanity spoils a hundred weight of merit. (Une once de vanité gâte une quintal de mérite.)

WILLIAM GURNEY BENHAM, *Quotations, Proverbs, and Household Words*, p. 736. Citing a French proverb.

3
No man sympathizes with the sorrows of vanity.

SAMUEL JOHNSON, *Works*. Vol. iv, p. 53.

4
What makes the vanity of other people insupportable is that it wounds our own. (Ce qui nous rend la vanité des autres insupportable, c'est qu'elle blesse la nôtre.)

LA ROCHEFOUCAULD, *Maximes*. No. 389.

Vanity causes us to do more things against our inclination than reason does. (La vanité nous fait faire plus de choses contre notre goût que la raison.)

LA ROCHEFOUCAULD, *Maximes*. No. 467.

5
No vain man matures, he makes too much
new wood;
His blooms are too thick for the fruit to be
good;
'Tis the modest man ripens, 't is he that
achieves,
Just what's needed of sunshine and shade he
receives.

J. R. LOWELL, *A Fable for Critics*, l. 978.

6
And not a vanity is given in vain.

POPE, *Essay on Man*. Epis. ii, l. 290.

7
Ignobly vain and impotently great.

POPE, *Prologue to Addison's Cato*, l. 29.

8
Where doth the world thrust forth a vanity . . .
That is not quickly buzz'd into his ears?

SHAKESPEARE, *Richard II*. Act ii, sc. 1, l. 24.

Hoy-day, what a sweep of vanity comes this way!

SHAKESPEARE, *Timon of Athens*. Act i, sc. 2, l. 137.

9
Vanity dies hard; in some obstinate cases it outlives the man.

R. L. STEVENSON, *Prince Otto*.

10
Life without vanity is almost impossible.

LEO TOLSTOY, *The Kreutzer Sonata*. Ch. 23.

Let us thank God for imparting to us poor weak mortals the inestimable blessing of vanity.

THACKERAY, *Character Sketches: The Artist*.

11
He had only one vanity; he thought he could give advice better than any other person.

MARK TWAIN, *The Man that Corrupted Hadleyburg*. Ch. 1.

12
Meek Nature's evening comment on the
shows
That for oblivion take their daily birth
From all the fuming vanities of earth!

WORDSWORTH, *Sonnet: Sky-Prospect*.

13
Vain is the world; but only to the vain.

YOUNG, *Night Thoughts*. Night iii, l. 420.

III—Vanity: Vanity of Vanities

14
Vanity of vanities; all is vanity.

Old Testament: Ecclesiastes, i, 2; xii, 8. (Vanitas vanitatum et omnis vanitas.—*Vulgate*.)

All is vanity and vexation of spirit.

Old Testament: Ecclesiastes, i, 14.

The pomps and vanity of this wicked world.

Book of Common Prayer: Catechism.

15
Ecclesiastes said that "all is vanity"—
Most modern preachers say the same, or
show it
By their examples of true Christianity;
In short, all know, or very soon may know
it.

BYRON, *Don Juan*. Canto vii, st. 6.

16
At all times, but especially now, it is pertinent to say, "Vanity of vanities, all is vanity."

ST. JOHN CHRYSOSTOM, *Vanity of Vanities*. Vol. ii, p. 381.

17
"Vanitas vanitatum" has rung in the ears
Of gentle and simple for thousands of years;
The wail still is heard, yet its notes never
scare
Either simple or gentle from Vanity Fair.

FREDERICK LOCKER-LAMPSON, *Vanity Fair*.

18
And the grasshopper
Shall be a burden, and desire shall fail,
Because man goeth unto his long home.
Vanity of Vanities, saith the Preacher; all
Is vanity.

LONGFELLOW, *Michael Angelo*. Pt. iii, sc. 2.

19
Oh, Vanity of Vanities!
How wayward the decrees of Fate are;
How very weak the very wise,
How very small the very great are!

THACKERAY, *Vanitas Vanitatum*.

IV—Vanity: In Women

20
And by my grave you'd pray to have me
back
So I could see how well you looked in black.

MARCO CARSON, *To Any Woman*.

21
Feminine vanity; that divine gift which makes woman charming.

BENJAMIN DISRAELI, *Tancred*. Bk. ii, ch. 8.

22
Vanity ruins more women than love.

MADAME DU DEFFAND, *Letter to Voltaire*.

23
Why does the blind man's wife paint herself?

BENJAMIN FRANKLIN, *Poor Richard*, 1736.

1
How many saucy airs we meet,
From Temple Bar to Aldgate Street!

JOHN GAY, *Fables: The Barley-Mow and the Dunghill*, l. 1.

2
Vain? Let it be so! Nature was her teacher.
What if a lovely and unsistered creature
Loved her own harmless gift of pleasing feature?

O. W. HOLMES, *Iris, Her Book.*

3
"Odious! in woollen! 't would a saint provoke"
(Were the last words that poor Narcissa spoke);
"No, let a charming chintz and Brussels lace
Wrap my cold limbs, and shade my lifeless face:
One would not, sure, be frightful when one's dead—
And—Betty—give this cheek a little red."

POPE, *Moral Essays*. Epis. i, l. 245. Narcissa was Mrs. Oldfield, the actress.

Here files of pins extend their shining rows,
Puffs, powders, patches, bibles, billet-doux.

POPE, *The Rape of the Lock*. Canto i, l. 137.

4
There was never yet fair woman but she made mouths in a glass.

SHAKESPEARE, *King Lear*. Act iii, sc. 2, l. 36.

5
Call in your black man, and titivate a bit.

THACKERAY, *The Virginians*. Ch. 48. To spruce up, complete the toilette. Arnold Bennett was fond of the word.

6
She keeps on being queenly in her own room with the door shut.

EDITH WHARTON, *The House of Mirth*, p. 302.

VARIETY

7
Variety's the very spice of life,
That gives it all its flavour.

COWPER, *The Task*. Bk. ii, l. 606.

8
Variety is the soul of pleasure.

APHRA BEHN, *The Rover*. Act ii, sc. 1, l. 1.

Enchanting spirit, dear Variety!

ROBERT BLOOMFIELD, *The Farmer's Boy: Spring*, l. 290.

Variety, which all the rest endears.

SIR JOHN DENHAM, *Cooper's Hill*, l. 228.

Variety is the mother of Enjoyment.

BENJAMIN DISRAELI, *Vivian Grey*. Bk. v, ch. 4.

9
Variety is sweet in all things. (Μεταβολὴ πάντων γλυκύ.)

EURIPIDES, *Orestes*, l. 234.

10
Variety 's the source of joy below,
From whence still fresh-revolving pleasures flow.

JOHN GAY, *Epistles: To Bernard Lintot.*

The great source of pleasure is variety.

SAMUEL JOHNSON, *Lives of the Poets: Butler*

Variety alone gives joy;
The sweetest meats the soonest cloy.

MATTHEW PRIOR, *Turtle and Sparrow*, l. 234.

11
To make Uniformity amidst Variety the occasion of pleasure.

FRANCIS HUTCHESON THE ELDER, *Inquiry into the Original of Our Ideas of Beauty*. Treatise ii, sec. 8.

For variety of mere nothings gives more pleasure than uniformity of something. (Weil Verschiedenheit des Nichts mehr ergötzt, als Einerleiheit des Etwas.)

JEAN PAUL RICHTER, *Levana*. Frag. 5.

12
Variety, that is my motto. (Diversité, c'est ma devise.)

LA FONTAINE, *Fables: Le Paté d'Anguille.*

13
To sing the same tune as the saying is, is in everything cloying and offensive; but men are generally pleased with variety.

PLUTARCH, *Of the Training of Children.*

14
No pleasure endures unseasoned by variety. (Jucundum nil est, nisi quod reficit varietas.)

PUBLILIUS SYRUS, *Sententiæ*. No. 406. Quoted by FRANCIS BACON, *Ornamenta Rationalia*. No. 19.

When our old Pleasures die,
Some new One still is nigh;
Oh! fair Variety!

NICHOLAS ROWE, *Ode for the New Year.*

15
They are the weakest-minded and the hardest hearted men, that most love variety and change.

JOHN RUSKIN, *Modern Painters*. Bk. ii, pt. ii, ch. 6, sec. 7.

16
Age cannot wither her, nor custom stale
Her infinite variety: other women cloy
The appetites they feed; but she makes hungry
Where most she satisfies: for vilest things
Become themselves in her; that the holy priests
Bless her when she is riggish.

SHAKESPEARE, *Antony and Cleopatra*. Act ii, sc. 2, l. 240.

VENGEANCE, see Revenge

VENICE

17
The gods returned to earth when Venice broke
Like Venus from the dawn-encircled sea.
Wide laughed the skies with light when Venice woke
Crowned of antiquity.

WILLIAM ROSE BENÉT, *Gaspara Stampa.*

18
I stood in Venice, on the Bridge of Sighs,
A palace and a prison on each hand;

I saw from out the wave her structures rise
As from the stroke of the enchanter's wand:
A thousand years their cloudy wings expand
Around me, and a dying Glory smiles
O'er the far times, when many a subject land
Look'd to the wingèd Lion's marble piles,
Where Venice sate in state, throned on her
hundred isles!

BYRON, *Childe Harold*. Canto iv, st. 1.

She looks a sea Cybele, fresh from ocean,
Rising with her tiara of proud towers
At airy distance, with majestic motion,
A ruler of the waters and their powers.

BYRON, *Childe Harold*. Canto iv, st. 2.

In Venice Tasso's echoes are no more,
And silent rows the songless gondolier;
Her palaces are crumbling to the shore,
And music meets not always now the ear;
Those days are gone, but Beauty still is here;
States fall, arts fade, but Nature doth not die,
Nor yet forget how Venice once was dear,
The pleasant place of all festivity,
The revel of the earth, the masque of Italy!

BYRON, *Childe Harold*. Canto iv, st. 3.

1
O happy streets! to rumbling wheels unknown,
No carts, no coaches, shake the floating town!

JOHN GAY, *Trivia*. Bk. i, l. 99.

2
White swan of cities, slumbering in thy nest
So wonderfully built among the reeds
Of the lagoon, that fences thee and feeds,
As sayeth thy old historian and thy guest!

LONGFELLOW, *Venice*.

3
Be thou perpetual! (Esto perpetua!)

PIETRO SARPI, *Dying Apostrophe to Venice*, 15 Jan., 1623.

4
Many a time and oft
In the Rialto you have rated me.

SHAKESPEARE, *Merchant of Venice*, i, 3, 108.

5
Once did She hold the gorgeous east in fee;
And was the safeguard of the west: the
worth
Of Venice did not fall below her birth,
Venice, the eldest Child of Liberty.
She was a maiden City, bright and free;
No guile seduced, no force could violate;
And, when she took unto herself a Mate,
She must espouse the everlasting Sea. . . .
Men are we, and must grieve when even the
Shade
Of that which once was great is passed away

WORDSWORTH, *On the Extinction of the Venetian Republic*

VENUS

6
Is Venus odious to brides? Or do they mock the joy of their parents with false tears? (Estne novis nuptis odio Venus atque parentum Frustrantur falsis gaudia lacrimulis?)

CATULLUS, *Odes*. No. lxiv, l. 15.

7
Venus will not charm so much without her attendant Graces, as they will without her.

LORD CHESTERFIELD, *Letters*, 18 Nov., 1748.

8
Wot's the good o' callin' a young 'ooman a Wenus or a angel, Sammy?

CHARLES DICKENS, *Pickwick Papers*. Ch. 33.

8a
Now the Graces are four and the Venuses two,
And ten is the number of Muses;
For a Muse and a Grace and a Venus are you,
My dear little Molly Trefusis!

AUSTIN DOBSON, *Molly Trefusis*. See 820:2.

9
Creator Venus, genial pow'r of Love,
The bliss of men below, and gods above,
Beneath the sliding sun thou runn'st thy race,
Dost fairest shine, and best become thy place.
For thee the winds their eastern blasts forbear,
Thy month reveals the spring, and opens all
the year.
Thee, Goddess, thee the storms of winter fly,
Earth smiles with flow'rs renewing; laughs
the sky.

DRYDEN, *Palamon and Arcite*. Bk. iii, l. 129.

10
Venus, thy eternal sway
All the race of men obey.

EURIPIDES, *Iphigenia at Aulis*, l. 545.

11
Venus . . . that made herself as common as a barber's chair.

STEPHEN GOSSON, *Schoole of Abuse*, 66. (1579)

Venus, a notorious strumpet, as common as a barber's chair.

ROBERT BURTON, *Anatomy of Melancholy*. Pt. i, sec. 4, mem. 1. *See also under* BARBER.

12
But she that is the source and well
Of weal or woe.

JOHN GOWER, *Confessio Amantis*. Bk. iv, l. 147.

13
Golden Aphrodite the Cyprian, who stirs up sweet passion in the gods and subdues the tribes of mortal men and birds that fly in the air and all the many creatures that the dry land rears, and all that the sea: all these love the deeds of rich-crowned Cytherea.

HOMER [?], *The Homeric Hymns*. No. v, l. 1.

14
Cruel mother of the Cupids. (Mater sæva Cupidinum.)

HORACE, *Odes*. Bk. i, ode 19; bk. iv, ode 1.

Venus, who loves to force, with cruel humor, ill-mated minds and bodies beneath her brazen yoke. ([Venus] cui placet impares Formas atque animos sub juga aënea Sævo mittere cum joco.)

HORACE, *Odes*. Bk. i, ode 33, l. 10.

15
Thou, O Venus, art sole mistress of the nature of things, and without thee nothing rises

up into the divine realms of life, nothing grows to be lovely or glad.

LUCRETIUS, *De Rerum Natura*. Bk. i, sec. 1. (Munro, tr.)

1
Venus smiles not in a house of tears.

SHAKESPEARE, *Romeo and Juliet*. Act. iv. sc. 1, l. 8.

2
Lo, this is she that was the world's delight;
The old grey years were parcels of her might;
The strewings of the ways wherein she trod
Were the twain seasons of the day and night.

SWINBURNE, *Laus Veneris*. St. 3.

Lo, she was thus when her clear limbs enticed
All lips that now grow sad with kissing Christ.

SWINBURNE, *Laus Veneris*. St. 4.

Behold, my Venus, my soul's body, lies
With my love laid upon her garment-wise,
Feeling my love in all her limbs and hair
And shed between her eyelids through her eyes.

SWINBURNE, *Laus Veneris*. St. 8.

VICE

See also Sin, Wickedness

I—Vice: Apothegms

3
We make a ladder of our vices, if we trample those same vices underfoot. (De vitiis nostris scalam nobis facimus, si vitia ipsa calcamus.)

ST. AUGUSTINE, *Sermons: De Ascensione*.

Saint Augustine! well hast thou said,
That of our vices we can frame
A ladder, if we will but tread
Beneath our feet each deed of shame!

LONGFELLOW, *The Ladder of St. Augustine*.

I hold it truth, with him who sings
To one clear harp in divers tones,
That men may rise on stepping-stones
Of their dead selves to higher things.

TENNYSON, *In Memoriam*. Pt. i, st. 1. The reference is to Goethe.

It may be stated, on the highest authority, that the special passage alluded to cannot be identified, but *it is Goethe's creed*.

ALFRED GATTY, *A Key to Tennyson's In Memoriam*.

4
Vice itself lost half its evil, by losing all its grossness.

EDMUND BURKE, *Reflections on the Revolution in France*.

5
The world can ill spare any vice which has obtained long and largely among civilized people.

SAMUEL BUTLER THE YOUNGER, *Note-books*.

6
Vice, that digs her own voluptuous tomb.

BYRON, *Childe Harold*. Canto i, st. 2.

Ah, Vice! how soft are thy voluptuous ways!

BYRON, *Childe Harold*. Canto i, st. 66.

Vice must have variety.

BYRON, *Marino Faliero*. Act ii, sc. 1.

7
I hate him that my vices telleth me.

CHAUCER, *Wife of Bath's Prologue*, l. 662.

8
Our faith comes in moments; our vice is habitual.

EMERSON, *Essays, First Series: The Over-Soul*.

Men wish to be saved from the mischiefs of their vices, but not from their vices.

EMERSON, *Essays, Second Series: Experience*.

9
As crabs, goats, scorpions, the balance and the waterpot, lose all their meanness when hung as signs in the zodiac, so I can see my own vices without heat in the distant persons of Solomon, Alcibiades, and Catiline.

EMERSON, *Essays, First Series: History*.

10
Men of their own worse nature making gods
To serve the very vices that suggest them.

EDWARD FITZGERALD, *The Mighty Magician*.

11
Let thy vices die before thee.

BENJAMIN FRANKLIN, *Poor Richard*, 1738.

What maintains one vice would bring up two children.

BENJAMIN FRANKLIN, *Poor Richard*, 1758.

12
Vices are learned without a master.

THOMAS FULLER, *Gnomologia*. No. 5361.

13
The vices are never so well employed as in combatting one another.

WILLIAM HAZLITT, *Characters of Shakespeare's Plays*, p. 39.

14
There is a division of labour, even in vice. Some persons addict themselves to the speculation only, others to the practice.

WILLIAM HAZLITT, *Dramatic Literature of the Age of Elizabeth*, p. 144.

15
Fools, in avoiding vice, run to the opposite extreme. (Dum vitant stulti vitia, in contraria currunt.

HORACE, *Satires*. Bk. i, sat. 2, l. 24.

16
A portion of mankind glory in their vices and keep to their purpose. (Pars hominum vitiis gaudet constanter et urget Propositum.)

HORACE, *Satires*. Bk. ii, sat. 7, l. 6.

17
There are certain rudiments in vice. (Sunt quædam vitiorum elementa.)

JUVENAL, *Satires*. Sat. xiv, l. 123.

18
A vice is a failure of desire.

GERALD STANLEY LEE, *Crowds*. Bk. iv, ch. 13.

19
When our vices leave us, we flatter ourselves with the credit of having left them. (Quand les vices nous quittent, nous nous flattons de la créance que c'est nous qui les quittons.)

LA ROCHFOUCAULD, *Maximes*. No. 192.

20
My life's a statement of the sum

Of vice indulged, or overcome.
JOHN MASEFIELD, *A Creed.*

1
The vices of the world's nobler half in this day are feminine.
GEORGE MEREDITH, *Diana of the Crossways.* Ch. 1.

2
A man must either imitate the vicious or hate them.
MONTAIGNE, *Essays.* Bk. i, ch. 38.

3
The vice which offends no one is not really vice. (Il n'est vice veritablement vice qui n'offense.)
MONTAIGNE, *Essays.* Bk. iii, ch. 2.

4
Vice should not correct sin.
WILLIAM PENN, *Fruits of Solitude.* No. 45.

5
Vice is a monster of so frightful mien,
As to be hated needs but to be seen;
Yet seen too oft, familiar with her face,
We first endure, then pity, then embrace.
POPE, *Essay on Man.* Epis. ii, l. 217.

Shame checks our first attempts; but then 'tis prov'd
Sins first dislik'd, are after that belov'd.
ROBERT HERRICK, *Sins Loathed, and Yet Belov'd.*

6
The heart resolves this matter in a trice,
"Men only feel the smart, but not the vice."
POPE, *Imitations of Horace: Epistles.* Bk. ii, epis. 2, l. 216.

7
We bear with accustomed vices; we reprove those that are new. (Consueta vitia ferimus, nova reprendimus.)
PUBLILIUS SYRUS, *Sententiæ.* No. 97.

8
All that gives gloss to sin, all gay
Light folly, passed with youth away,
But rooted stood, in manhood's hour,
The weeds of vice without their power.
SCOTT, *Rokeby.* Canto i, st. 9.

9
All vices are less serious when they are open. (Omnia enim vitia in operto leniora sunt.)
SENECA, *Epistulæ ad Lucilium.* Epis. lvi, 10.

Vice is nourished and kept alive by concealment. (Alitur vitium vivitque tegendo.)
VERGIL, *Georgics.* Bk. iii, l. 454.

10
They are the vices of mankind, not of the times. (Hominum sunt ista, non temporum.)
SENECA, *Epistulæ ad Lucilium.* Epis. xcvii, sec. 1. Referring to luxury and the neglect of good manners.

Vices of the time; vices of the man. (Vitia temporis: vitia hominis.)
FRANCIS BACON, *Humble Submission and Supplication to the Lords of Parliament.* (1621)

And lash the Vice and Follies of the Age.
SUSANNAH CENTLIVRE, *The Man's Bewitched: Prologue.*

All sects, all ages smack of this vice.
SHAKESPEARE, *Measure for Measure.* Act ii, sc. 2, l. 5. Of lechery.

But think
What 'tis to cram a maw or clothe a back
From such a filthy vice.
SHAKESPEARE, *Measure for Measure.* Act iii, sc. 2, l. 24. Referring to lechery.

11
I can show you many men who have not been harmed by their vices, and not a few who have even been helped by them. (Multos tibi dabo, quibus vitia non nocuerint, quosdam, quibus profuerint.)
SENECA, *Epistulæ ad Lucilium.* Epis. cxiv, 12.

There is no man who is not at some time indebted to his vices, as no plant that is not fed from manures.
EMERSON, *Conduct of Life: Considerations by the Way.*

12
No vice remains within its limits. (Nullam intra se manet vitium.)
SENECA, *Epistulæ ad Lucilium.* Epis. xcv, 33.

The road to vice is not only downhill, but steep. (Non pronum est tantum ad vitia, sed præceps.)
SENECA, *Epistulæ ad Lucilium.* Epis. xcvii, 10.

13
He loves the vice for its own sake. (Qui ipsum vitium ament.)
SENECA, *Epistulæ ad Lucilium.* Epis. cxiv, 11.

Did you perceive how he laughed at his vice?
SHAKESPEARE, *Othello.* Act iv, sc. 1, l. 181.

14
Why dost thou converse with that trunk of humours, that bolting-hutch of beastliness, . . . that reverend vice, that grey iniquity, that father ruffian, that vanity in years?
SHAKESPEARE, *I Henry IV.* Act ii, sc. 4, l. 495.

Corrupt and tainted with a thousand vices.
SHAKESPEARE, *I Henry VI.* Act v, sc. 4, l. 45.

15
Through tatter'd clothes small vices do appear;
Robes and furr'd gowns hide all.
SHAKESPEARE, *King Lear.* Act iv, sc. 6, l. 168.

16
The gods are just, and of our pleasant vices
Make instruments to plague us.
SHAKESPEARE, *King Lear.* Act v, sc. 3, l. 170.

Vice is its own punishment.
THOMAS FULLER, *Gnomologia.* No. 5534.

17
Vice repeated is like the wandering wind,
Blows dust in others' eyes, to spread itself.
SHAKESPEARE, *Pericles.* Act i, sc. 1, l. 96.

18
They will be vanquished by their vices as easily as by force of arms. (Haud minus facile vitiis quam armis vincentur.)
TACITUS, *Germania.* Sec. 23.

19
If every year we rooted out one vice, we should soon become perfect men.
THOMAS À KEMPIS, *De Imitatione Christi.* Pt. i, ch. 11.

II—Vice and Virtue

See also Good and Evil

1
Where vices pay, the man of virtue is the sinner. (Cum vitia prosunt, peccat qui recte facit.)

Publilius Syrus, *Sententiæ*. No. 113.

Vice gets more in this vicious world Than piety.

Beaumont and Fletcher, *Love's Cure*. Act iii, sc. 1.

Vice never yields the fruits of virtue.

W. E. Channing, *The Working Classes*.

2
Put no new names or notions upon authentic virtues and vices.

Sir Thomas Browne, *Christian Morals*. Pt. i, sec. 12.

That vice may be uneasy and even monstrous unto thee, let iterated good acts and long-confirmed habits make virtue almost natural, or a second nature in thee.

Sir Thomas Browne, *Christian Morals*. Pt. i, sec. 9.

3
Virtue will catch as well as vice, by contact.

Edmund Burke, *Letter to the Sheriffs of Bristol.*

Men imagine that they communicate their virtue or vice only by overt actions, and do not see that virtue or vice emit a breath every moment.

Emerson, *Essays, First Series: Self-Reliance.*

4
Virtue must be the happiness, and vice the misery of every creature.

Joseph Butler, *Analogy of Religion: Introduction.*

5
To sanction Vice, and hunt Decorum down.

Byron, *English Bards and Scotch Reviewers*, l. 621.

6
This maxim's into common favour grown,—
Vice is no longer vice, unless 'tis known.
Virtue indeed may barefaced take the field;
But vice is virtue when 'tis well conceal'd.
Should raging passion drive thee to a whore,
Let Prudence lead thee to a postern door;
Stay out all night, but take especial care
That Prudence bring thee back to early prayer.
As one with watching and with study faint,
Reel in a drunkard, and reel out a saint. . . .
Vice must be vice, virtue be virtue still,
Though thousands rail at good and practise ill.

Charles Churchill, *Night*, l. 315. *See also* Sin: The Eleventh Commandment.

Ne'er blush'd, unless, in spreading vice's snares,
She blunder'd on some virtue unawares.

Charles Churchill, *The Rosciad*, l. 137.

7
Vice stings us even in our pleasures, but virtue consoles us even in our pains.

C. C. Colton, *Lacon*. Vol. i, No. 296.

The martyrs to vice far exceed the martyrs to virtue, both in endurance and in number. So blinded are we by our passions that we suffer more to be damned than to be saved

C. C. Colton, *Lacon*. Vol. i, No. 391.

8
Virtue and vice had bound'ries in old time
Not to be pass'd.

Cowper, *The Task*. Bk. iii, l. 75.

9
Virtue in distress, and vice in triumph
Make atheists of mankind.

Dryden, *Cleomenes*. Act iv, sc. 1.

10
There is no virtue which is final; all are initial. The virtues of society are the vices of the saint.

Emerson, *Essays, First Series: Circles.*

11
Search others for their virtues, thyself for thy vices.

Benjamin Franklin, *Poor Richard*, 1738.

12
Vice makes virtue shine.

Thomas Fuller, *Gnomologia*. No. 5356.

13
To scatter plenty o'er a smiling land,
And read their history in a nation's eyes,
Their lot forebade: nor circumscrib'd alone
Their growing virtues, but their crimes confin'd;
Forbade to wade through slaughter to a throne,
And shut the gates of mercy on mankind.

Thomas Gray, *Elegy Written in a Country Church-yard*, l. 63.

14
Every vice hath a cloak and creepeth in under the mask of a virtue.

Gabriel Harvey, *Letter Book.*

Would you wrap up vice with virtuous words? (Verbisque decoris Obvolvas vitium?)

Horace, *Satires*. Bk. ii, sat. 7, l. 41.

15
To flee vice is the beginning of virtue. (Virtus est vitium fugere.)

Horace, *Epistles*. Bk. i, epis. 1, l. 41.

'T is the first virtue vices to abhor.

Pope, *Imitations of Horace: Epistles*. Bk. i, epis. 1, l. 65.

Learning virtue means unlearning vice. (Virtutes discere vitia dediscere est.)

Seneca, *Epistulæ ad Lucilium*. Epis. 1, sec. 7.

16
The good hate vice because they love virtue. (Oderunt peccare boni virtutis amore.)

Horace, *Epistles*. Bk. i, epis. 16, l. 52.

17
Men do not vary much in virtue: their vices only are different.

Elbert Hubbard, *Epigrams.*

18
If he does really think that there is no distinction between virtue and vice, why, sir.

when he leaves our houses let us count our spoons.

SAMUEL JOHNSON. (BOSWELL, *Life*, 1763.)

1
Neither our virtues nor our vices are our own.

SAMUEL JOHNSON, *The Rambler*. No. 180.

2
Virtue is never aided by a vice.

BEN JONSON, *The New Inn*. Act iv, sc. 3.

3
Our virtues are most frequently but vices in disguise. (Nos vertus ne sont le plus souvent que des vices déguisés.)

LA ROCHEFOUCAULD, *Maximes*. Preface of the fifth edition. The epigram which is the key to La Rochefoucauld's system.

We do not despise all those who have vices, but those who have no virtues. (On ne méprise pas tous ceux qui ont des vices, mais on méprise tous ceux qui n'ont aucune vertu.)

LA ROCHEFOUCAULD, *Maximes*. No. 186.

4
God sure esteems the growth and completing of one virtuous person, more than the restraint of ten vicious.

MILTON, *Areopagitica*.

5
Great men's vices are esteemed as virtues.

SHACKERLEY MARMION, *Holland's Leaguer*. Act i, sc. 1.

6
I prefer an accommodating vice to an obstinate virtue. (J'aime mieux un vice commode Qu'une fatigante vertu.)

MOLIÈRE, *Amphitryon*. Act i, sc. 4, l. 52.

7
Virtue I grant you, is an empty boast;
But shall the dignity of Vice be lost?

POPE, *Epilogue to Satires*. Dial. i, l. 113.

Fools! who from hence into the notion fall
That Vice or Virtue there is none at all.
If white and black blend, soften, and unite
A thousand ways, is there no black or white?

POPE, *Essay on Man*. Epis. ii, l. 211.

8
Count all th' advantage prosp'rous vice attains,
'T is but what virtue flies from and disdains.

POPE, *Essay on Man*. Epis. iv, l. 89.

"But sometimes virtue starves, while vice is fed."
What then? Is the reward of virtue bread?

POPE, *Essay on Man*. Epis. iv, l. 149.

9
As virtue has its degrees, so has vice. (Ainsi que la vertu, le crime a son degrés.)

RACINE, *Phèdre*. Act iv, sc. 2.

10
Locman, the sage, being asked, where he learned virtue, he answered, "Of the vicious, for they taught me what to shun."

SADI, *The Gulistan*. Pt. ii, No. 21.

11
Virtue is according to nature; vices are hostile and dangerous. (Virtus secundum naturam est: vitia inimica et infesta sunt.)

SENECA, *Epistulæ ad Lucilium*. Epis. 50, sec. 9

12
Our virtues would be proud if our faults whipped them not; and our crimes would despair if they were not cherished by our virtues.

SHAKESPEARE, *All's Well that Ends Well*. Act iv, sc. 3, l. 84.

Apparel vice like virtue's harbinger.

SHAKESPEARE, *The Comedy of Errors*. Act iii, sc. 2, l. 12.

13
In the fatness of these pursy times,
Virtue itself of vice must pardon beg.

SHAKESPEARE, *Hamlet*. Act iii, sc. 4, l. 154.

14
There is no vice so simple, but assumes
Some mark of virtue on his outward parts.

SHAKESPEARE, *The Merchant of Venice*. Act iii, sc. 2, l. 81.

His vice; 'tis to his virtue a just equinox,
The one as long as the other.

SHAKESPEARE, *Othello*. Act ii, sc. 3, l. 127.

So smooth he daub'd his vice with show of virtue.

SHAKESPEARE, *Richard III*. Act iii, sc. 5, l. 29.

15
Virtue itself turns vice, being misapplied;
And vice sometimes by action dignified.

SHAKESPEARE, *Romeo and Juliet*. Act ii, sc. 3, l. 21

O, what a mansion have those vices got
Which for their habitation chose out thee,
Where beauty's veil doth cover every blot,
And all things turn to fair that eyes can see!

SHAKESPEARE, *Sonnets*. No. 95.

16
Could you hurt me, sweet lips, though I hurt you?
Men touch them, and change in a trice
The lilies and languors of virtue
For the roses and raptures of vice.

SWINBURNE, *Dolores*.

17
The virtues of the heathen, being devoid of grace, can only be looked upon as splendid vices. (Splendida vitia.)

TERTULLIAN, *De Carne Christi*.

The greatest virtues are only splendid sins. (Splendida vitia.)

ST. AUGUSTINE, *Confessions*.

18
We are double-edged blades, and every time we whet our virtue the return stroke straps our vice.

H. D. THOREAU, *Journal*, 8 Feb., 1841

19
Betwixt two vices every virtue lies.

WILLIAM WHITEHEAD, *On Ridicule*.

III—Vice and Virtue: The Two Natures

See also Faults: Their Virtue

20
His virtues he so mingled with his crimes

As would confound their choice to punish one
And not reward the other.
DRYDEN, *All for Love*. Act iii, sc. 1.

He redeemed his vices with his virtues. There was ever more in him to be praised than to be pardoned.
BEN JONSON, *Explorata: Of Augustus Cæsar*.

1
Virtue, when a matter of expediency, is the virtue of vice. (La vertu par calcul est la vertu du vice.)
JOUBERT, *Pensées*. No. 132.

2
In the intercourse of life, we please more often by our vices than by our virtues. (Nous plaisons plus souvent dans le commerce de la vie par nos défauts que par nos bonnes qualités.)
LA ROCHEFOUCAULD, *Maximes*. No. 90.

3
Vices enter into the composition of virtues as poisons enter into the composition of remedies; prudence mixes and tempers them, and uses them to good purpose against the ills of life.
LA ROCHEFOUCAULD, *Maximes*. No. 182.

I find that the best virtue I have has in it some tincture of vice.
MONTAIGNE, *Essays*. Bk. ii, ch. xx.

The diff'rence is too nice
Where ends the virtue or begins the vice.
POPE, *Essay on Man*. Epis. ii, l. 209.

4
I delight in the law of God after the inward man: but I see another law in my members, warring against the law of my mind, and bringing me into captivity to the law of sin.
New Testament: Romans, vii, 22, 23.

5
Vices creep into our hearts under the name of virtues. (Vitia nobis sub virtutum nomine obrepunt.)
SENECA, *Epistulæ ad Lucilium*. Epis. xlv, sec. 7.

There are vices which are next door to virtues. (Sunt virtutibus vitia confinia.)
SENECA, *Epistulæ ad Lucilium*. Epis. cxx, sec. 8.

6
He conquered by weapons, but was conquered by his vices. (Armis vicit, vitiis victus est.)
SENECA, *Epistulæ ad Lucilium*. Epis. li, sec. 6. Referring to Hannibal.

Hannibal, as he had mighty virtues, so had he many vices. . . . He had two distinct persons in him.
ROBERT BURTON, *Anatomy of Melancholy: Democritus to the Reader*.

Man is not truly one, but truly two.
R. L. STEVENSON, *Dr. Jekyll and Mr. Hyde*.

I feel two natures struggling within me.
GEORGE GREY BARNARD. Title of statuary group.

7
Vices are so intertwined with virtues that they drag the virtues along with them. (Vitia virtutibus inmissa sunt, ut illas secum tractura sint.)
SENECA, *Epistulæ ad Lucilium*. Epis. cxiv, 13.

8
Some rise by sin, and some by virtue fall.
SHAKESPEARE, *Measure for Measure*. Act ii, sc. 1, l. 38.

9
Virtue that transgresses is but patched with sin; and sin that amends is but patched with virtue.
SHAKESPEARE, *Twelfth Night*. Act i, sc. 5, l. 52.

10
Here follow her vices. Close at the heels of her virtues.
SHAKESPEARE, *The Two Gentlemen of Verona*. Act iii, sc. 1, l. 324.

11
His crimes forgive! forgive his virtues, too!
YOUNG, *Night Thoughts*. Night ix, l. 2312.

VICTORIA, QUEEN

12
'Ave you 'eard o' the Widow at Windsor
With a hairy gold crown on 'er 'ead?
She 'as ships on the foam—she 'as millions at 'ome,
An' she pays us poor beggars in red.
RUDYARD KIPLING, *The Widow at Windsor*.

Walk wide o' the Widow at Windsor,
For 'alf o' Creation she owns:
We 'ave bought 'er the same with the sword an' the flame,
An' we've salted it down with our bones.
RUDYARD KIPLING, *The Widow at Windsor*.

13
An oval, placid woman who assuaged men's lives;
Her comely hands wrought forth a century
Of oval, placid women who engaged, as wives,
In broideries and tea.
RUTH MASON RICE, *Victoria*.

14
Her court was pure; her life serene;
God gave her peace; her land reposed;
A thousand claims to reverence closed
In her as Mother, Wife, and Queen.
TENNYSON, *To the Queen*. St. 7.

An age wanting in moral grandeur and spiritual health.
MATTHEW ARNOLD, *Sohrab and Rustum: Preface*.

Blessed period of peace and prosperity, port and progeny and domesticity *in excelsis* from Buckingham Palace to Bloomsbury Square and brand-new Bayswater. Despite its limitations, it was a good, solid, happy time of English life at its best.
S. M. ELLIS, *Mainly Victorian*. Referring to the Victorian era.

15
There are no Victorias in the twentieth century who have the right to say "We are not amused."
UNKNOWN. (*Saturday Review*, 7 Feb., 1931.)
See under AMUSEMENT *for the quotation.*

VICTORY

See also Conqueror, Success

I—Victory: Apothegms

1
I will not steal a victory. (Οὐ κλέπτω τὴν νίκην.)

ALEXANDER, when advised to surprise the Persian army in the dark. (PLUTARCH, *Lives: Alexander*. Ch. 31, sec. 7.)

2
Though Victory fruit of skill or fortune be,
To conquer always is a glorious thing.
(Fù il vincer sempre mai laudabil cosa,
Vincasi o per fortune, o per ingegno.)

ARIOSTO, *Orlando Furioso*. Canto xv, st. 1.

3
He conquers twice, who upon victory overcomes himself. (Bis vincit, qui se vincit in victoria.)

FRANCIS BACON, *Ornamenta Rationalia*. No. 3. Quoting PUBLILIUS SYRUS.

4
You know how to conquer, Hannibal, but you know not how to utilize victory. (Vincere scis Hannibal; victoria uti nescis.)

MAHARBAL, *Remark*, to Hannibal, after the battle of Cannae, when Hannibal delayed pursuit of the fleeing enemy. Maharbal was commander of the Carthaginian cavalry. (LIVY, *History*. Bk. xxii, sec. 51.)

6
Kings may be blest, but Tam was glorious,
O'er a' the ills o' life victorious!

BURNS, *Tam o' Shanter*, l. 57.

7
Mine is the victory. (Ἐμὴ ἡ νίκη.)

GAIUS MARIUS. (PLUTARCH, *Lives: Gaius Marius*. Ch. 26, sec. 2.)

8
You have vanquished victory itself. (Ipsam victoriam vicisse videris.)

CICERO, *Pro Marcello*. Ch. iv, sec. 12. By mercy to the conquered.

That even in thy victory thou show,
Mortal, the moderation of a man.

MATTHEW ARNOLD, *Merope*, l. 2027.

9
The allies floated to victory on a sea of oil.

EARL CURZON OF KEDLESTON. (ROSE, *Evolution of the Oil Industry*.)

10
In many a war it has been the vanquished, not the victor, who has carried off the finest spoils.

HAVELOCK ELLIS, *The Soul of Spain*, p. 8.

11
Let the victory fall where it will, we are on that side.

EMERSON, *Essays, Second Series: Nature*.

12
War engenders war, and victory defeat. Victory is a Spirit.

ANATOLE FRANCE, *Revolt of the Angels*. Ch. 35.

Victory is a thing of the will.

GEN. FERDINAND FOCH. His favorite maxim.

13
A Cadmean victory. (Καδμεία νίκη.)

HERODOTUS. *History*. Bk. i, sec. 166. Referring to the internecine strife of the Sparti, who sprang up from the dragon's teeth sown by Cadmus. A victory which involves one's own ruin.

Another such victory over the Romans, and we are undone. (Ἂν ἔτι μίαν μάχην Ῥωμαίους νικήσωμεν, ἀπολούμεθα παντελῶς.)

PYRRHUS, King of Epirus, referring to his dearly bought victory at Asculum, 280 B.C. (PLUTARCH, *Lives: Pyrrhus*. Ch. 21, sec. 9.) Hence a "Pyrrhic victory," which costs the victor more than the vanquished.

Even victors are by victories undone.

DRYDEN, *Epistle to John Driden*, l. 164.

14
In one short hour's space comes swift death, or joyful victory. (Horæ Memento cita mors venit, aut victoria læta.)

HORACE, *Satires*. Bk. i, sat. 1, l. 7.

A crown, or else a glorious tomb!
A sceptre, or an earthly sepulchre!

SHAKESPEARE, *III Henry VI*. Act i, sc. 4, l. 17.

Either victory, or else a grave.

SHAKESPEARE, *III Henry VI*. Act ii, sc. 2, l. 174.

Westminster Abbey, or Victory.

HORATIO NELSON, at the battle off Cape St. Vincent. (SOUTHEY, *Life of Nelson*. Vol. i, ch. 4.)

"A peerage or Westminster Abbey!" cried Nelson, in his bright, boyish, heroic manner.

STEVENSON, *Virginibus Puerisque: Æs Triplex*.

15
Beware of rashness, but with energy and sleepless vigilance go forward and give us victories.

ABRAHAM LINCOLN, *Letter to Major-General Joseph Hooker*, 25 Jan., 1863.

16
The victorious cause pleased the gods, but the victory pleased Cato. (Victrix causa Diis placuit, sed victa Catoni.)

LUCAN, *De Bello Civili*. Bk. i, l. 118.

17
Be ashamed to die until you have won some victory for humanity.

HORACE MANN, *Commencement Address*, Antioch College, 1859. The concluding sentence of his last commencement address. He died a few weeks later. (*Dict. Amer. Biog.*, xii, 243.)

18
Odds blood, hammer and tongs, long as I've been to sea,
I've fought 'gainst every odds—but I've gained the victory.

FREDERICK MARRYAT, *The Captain Stood on the Carronade*.

19
Woe to the vanquished! (Væ Victis!)

PLAUTUS, *Pseudolus*, l. 1317. (Act v, sc. 2.) A proverbial saying since the day (c. 390 B.C.) when Brennus, leader of the Gauls, entered Rome, and consented to depart upon payment of 2000 talents, but when reproached with deceit, threw his sword into the scale with the cry of, "Væ victis!"

Woe to the conq'ering, not the conquer'd host.

BYRON, *Childe Harold*. Canto i, st. 25.

1
Many a victory has been and will be suicidal to the victors.
PLATO, *Laws*. Sec. 641.

2
Victory does not like rivalry. (Rivalitatem non amat victoria.)
PUBLILIUS SYRUS, *Sententiæ*. No. 623.

Victory is always where there is unanimity. (Ibi semper est victoria, ubi concordia est.)
PUBLILIUS SYRUS, *Sententiæ*. No. 319.

3
I would rather that fortune should afflict me, than that I should have cause to be ashamed of victory. (Malo me fortunæ pœniteat, quam victoriæ pudeat.)
QUINTUS CURTIUS RUFUS, *De Rebus Gestis Alexandri Magni*. Bk. iv, sec. 13.

4
With dying hand, above his head,
He shook the fragment of his blade,
And shouted "Victory!—
Charge, Chester, charge! On, Stanley, on!"
Were the last words of Marmion.
SCOTT, *Marmion*. Canto vi, st. 32.

5
Victory follows me, and all things follow victory. (La victoire me suit, et tout suit la victoire.)
MADAME DE SCUDÉRY, *Tyrannic Love*.

6
All the gods go with you! upon your sword
Sit laurel victory! and smooth success
Be strew'd before your feet!
SHAKESPEARE, *Antony and Cleopatra*, i, 3, 99.

7
Brings a victory in his pocket.
SHAKESPEARE, *Coriolanus*. Act ii, sc. 1, l. 135.

8
To whom God will, there be the victory!
SHAKESPEARE, *III Henry VI*. Act ii, sc. 5, l. 15.

Thus far our fortune keeps an upward course,
And we are graced with wreaths of victory.
SHAKESPEARE, *III Henry VI*. Act v, sc. 3, l. 1.

She shall give the day,
And kiss him with a glorious victory.
SHAKESPEARE, *King John*. Act ii, sc. 1, l. 294.

9
Open your gates and give the victors way.
SHAKESPEARE, *King John*. Act ii, sc. 1, l. 324.

A victory is twice itself when the achiever brings home full numbers.
SHAKESPEARE, *Much Ado About Nothing*, i, 1, 8.

10
"But what good came of it at last?"
Quoth little Peterkin.
"Why that I cannot tell," said he:
"But 't was a famous victory."
SOUTHEY, *The Battle of Blenheim*. l. 63.

11
They preferred victory to peace. (Victoriam malle quam pacem.)
TACITUS, *History*. Bk. iii, sec. 60.

The pride of victory is apt to corrupt even the greatest generals. (Rebus secundis etiam egregios duces insolescere.)
TACITUS, *History*. Bk. ii, sec. 7.

II—Victory and Defeat

See also Success and Failure

12
As victory is silent, so is defeat.
CARLYLE, *French Revolution*. Vol. i, bk. ii, ch. 1.

13
Not one of all the purple host
Who took the flag to-day
Can tell the definition
So clear, of victory,
As he, defeated, dying,
On whose forbidden ear
The distant strains of triumph
Break, agonized and clear.
EMILY DICKINSON, *Poems*. Pt. i, No. 1.

14
The greatest victory is defeat.
HENRIK IBSEN, *Brand*. Act iii.

Victory and defeat are each of the same price.
THOMAS JEFFERSON.

15
Shout "Victory, victory, victory ho!"
I say, 'tis not always with the hosts that win!
I say that the victory, high or low,
Is given the hero who grapples with sin,
Or legion or single, just asking to know
When duty fronts death in his Alamo.
JOAQUIN MILLER, *The Defense of the Alamo*.

The ground they gained, but we The victory.
GEORGE H. CALVERT, *Bunker Hill*.

16
There are some defeats more triumphant than victories.
MONTAIGNE, *Essays*. Bk. i, ch. 32.

17
Why, victor, dost thou exult? This victory will be your ruin. (Quid, victor, gaudes? Hæc te victoria perdet.)
OVID, *Fasti*. Bk. ii, l. 811.

18
Speak, History! who are Life's victors? Unroll thy long annals and say,
Are they those whom the world called the victors,—who won the success of a day?
The martyrs, or Nero? The Spartans, who fell at Thermopylæ's tryst,
Or the Persians and Xerxes? His judges, or Socrates? Pilate, or Christ?
WILLIAM WETMORE STORY, *Io Victis*.

They only the victory win
Who have fought the good fight and have vanquished the demon that tempts us within;
Who have held to their faith unseduced by the prize that the world holds on high;
Who have dared for a high cause to suffer, resist, fight, if need be, to die.
WILLIAM WETMORE STORY, *Io Victis*.

19
Between victor and vanquished a sincere coalition can never succeed. (Victores victosque numquam solida fide coalescere.)
TACITUS, *History*. Bk. ii, sec. 7.

Victor from vanquish'd issues at the last,
And overthrower from being overthrown.
TENNYSON, *Gareth and Lynette*, l. 1230.

1
O vanquisher, whosoever thou art, not long shalt thou exult, nor shall I be unavenged; thee also a like fate awaits. (Non me, quicumque es, inulto Victor, nec longum lætabere: te quoque fata Prospectant paria.)

VERGIL, *Æneid*. Bk. x, l. 739.

2
Nothing except a battle lost can be half so melancholy as a battle won.

DUKE OF WELLINGTON, *Despatch*, 1815.

Madam, there is nothing so dreadful as a great victory—excepting a great defeat.

DUKE OF WELLINGTON, *Remark*, to a lady expressing passionate wish to see a great victory. Wellington borrowed it from D'Argenson. (See Grimm's *Mémoires*.)

VILLAGE

3
There is more harm in the village than is dreamt of (Hay mas mal en el aldegüela que se suena.)

CERVANTES, *Don Quixote*. Pt. i, ch. 46.

4
The villager, born humbly and bred hard,
Content his wealth, and poverty his guard.

CHARLES CHURCHILL, *Gotham*. Bk. iii, l. 117.

5
If you would be known, and not know, vegetate in a village; if you would know, and not be known, live in a city.

C. C. COLTON, *Lacon*. Pt. i, No. 334.

6
Sweet Auburn! loveliest village of the plain,
Where health and plenty cheer'd the labouring swain,
Where smiling spring its earliest visit paid,
And parting summer's lingering blooms delay'd.

OLIVER GOLDSMITH, *The Deserted Village*, l. 1.

How often have I loiter'd o'er thy green,
Where humble happiness endear'd each scene;
How often have I paus'd on every charm,
The shelter'd cot, the cultivated farm,
The never-failing brook, the busy mill,
The decent church that topp'd the neighbouring hill,
The hawthorn bush, with seats beneath the shade,
For talking age and whisp'ring lovers made!

OLIVER GOLDSMITH, *The Deserted Village*, l. 7.

7
A little one-eyed, blinking sort o' place.

HARDY, *Tess of the D'Urbervilles*. Ph. i, ch. 1.

This poor little one-horse town.

MARK TWAIN, *The Undertaker's Story*.

8
A small country town is not the place in which one would choose to quarrel with a wife; every human being in such places is a spy

SAMUEL JOHNSON, *Letters*. Vol. i, p. 107.

A village is a hive of glass,
Where nothing unobserved can pass.

C. H. SPURGEON, *Salt-Cellars*.

9
Country in town. (Rus in urbe.)

MARTIAL, *Epigrams*. Bk. xii, ep. 57, l. 12.

10
Small town, great renown. (Petite ville, grand renom.)

RABELAIS, *Works*. Bk. ii, ch. 35. Of Chinon, Rabelais' native town. *See also* AMBITION.

11
In every village marked with little spire,
Embowered in trees, and hardly known to fame.

WILLIAM SHENSTONE, *The Schoolmistress*. St. 2.

And villages embosomed soft in trees.

THOMSON, *The Seasons: Spring*, l. 954.

12
They take the rustic murmur of their bourg
For the great wave that echoes round the world.

TENNYSON, *The Marriage of Geraint*, l. 419.

VILLAIN AND VILLAINY

See also Knave

I—Villain

12a
Villain of the deepest dye! thy hellish machinations I defy! me life you may gain in this wild endeavor, but me spotless honor, hardly ev—never! never! And the villain still pursued her.

MILTON NOBLES, *The Phœnix*. Act i, sc. 3. Carroll Graves, one of the characters, is writing a chapter of a story.

13
The greatest scoundrel that walks on two legs. (Omnium bipedum nequissimus.)

PLINY THE YOUNGER, *Epistles*. Bk. i, epis. 5.

A wretch, a villain, lost to love and truth.

BURNS, *The Cotter's Saturday Night*, l. 83.

Calm, thinking villains, whom no faith could fix,
Of crooked counsels and dark politics.

POPE, *The Temple of Fame*, l. 410.

One Pinch, a hungry lean-faced villain,
A mere anatomy.

SHAKESPEARE, *Comedy of Errors*. Act v, 1, 237.

With foreheads villainous low.

SHAKESPEARE, *The Tempest*. Act iv, sc. 1, 250.

Thou lowest scoundrel of the scoundrel kind,
Extract of all the dregs of all mankind.

THOMAS SHERIDAN, *Satire on Mr. Fairbrother*.

14
O villain, villain, smiling, damned villain!

SHAKESPEARE, *Hamlet*, i, 5, 106. *See under* SMILE.

15
As if we were villains by necessity; fools by heavenly compulsion.

SHAKESPEARE, *King Lear*. Act i, sc. 2, l. 132. *See also* KNAVE AND FOOL.

16
I would not be the villain that thou think'st,
For the whole space that 's in the tyrant's grasp,
And the rich East to boot.

SHAKESPEARE, *Macbeth*. Act iv, sc. 3, l. 35.

I like not fair terms and a villain's mind.
SHAKESPEARE, *The Merchant of Venice*. Act i, sc. 3, l. 180.

1
When rich villains have need of poor ones, poor ones may make what price they will.
SHAKESPEARE, *Much Ado About Nothing*. Act iii, sc. 3, l. 121.

2
Villain and he be many miles asunder.
SHAKESPEARE, *Romeo and Juliet*. Act iii, sc. 5, l. 82.

3
Barring that natural expression of villainy which we all have, the man looked honest enough.
MARK TWAIN, *A Mysterious Visit*.

4
One low churl, compact of thankless earth,
The fatal byword of all years to come.
TENNYSON, *Godiva*, l. 66.

5
The world does not contain a scoundrel of however deep a dye who, if he only made a thorough search, would not discover another scoundrel in some respects worse than himself.
TOLSTOY, *The Kreutzer Sonata*. Ch. x.

II—Villainy

6
Where villainy goes before, vengeance follows after.
THOMAS FULLER, *Gnomologia*. No. 5681.

And though the villain 'scape awhile, he feels
Slow vengeance, like a bloodhound at his heels.
SWIFT, *Imitations of Horace*. Bk. iii, ode 2, l. 21.

7
Villainy was an object of wonder in that age.
(Improbitas illo fuit admirabilis ævo.)
JUVENAL, *Satires*. Sat. xiii, l. 53.

8
Ah, this thou should'st have done,
And not have spoke on 't! In me 't is villainy;
In thee, 't had been good service.
SHAKESPEARE, *Antony and Cleopatra*. Act ii, sc. 7, l. 79.

O villainy! Ho! let the door be lock'd:
Treachery! Seek it out.
SHAKESPEARE, *Hamlet*. Act v, sc. 2, l. 322.

The villainy you teach me, I will execute, and it shall go hard but I will better the instruction.
SHAKESPEARE, *The Merchant of Venice*. Act iii, sc. 1, l. 74.

9
There 's nothing level in our cursed natures,
But direct villany.
SHAKESPEARE, *Timon of Athens*. Act iv, sc. 3, l. 19.

VIOLET

10
Deep violets, you liken to
The kindest eyes that look on you,
Without a thought disloyal.
E. B. BROWNING, *A Flower in a Letter*. St. 4.

11
Again the violet of our early days
Drinks beauteous azure from the golden sun,
And kindles into fragrance at his blaze.
EBENEZER ELLIOTT, *Spring*.

12
Cold blows the wind against the hill,
And cold upon the plain;
I sit me by the bank, until
The violets come again.
RICHARD GARNETT, *Violets*.

13
Welcome, maids of honour,
You do bring
In the Spring,
And wait upon her.

She has virgins many,
Fresh and fair;
Yet you are
More sweet than any
ROBERT HERRICK, *To Violets*.

14
Those veiled nuns, meek violets.
THOMAS HOOD, *The Plea of the Midsummer Fairies*, l. 318.

The violet is a nun.
THOMAS HOOD, *Flowers*, l. 6.

15
Love dropp'd eyelids and a kiss,—
Such our breath and blueness is.
LEIGH HUNT, *Violets*.

16
Violets!—deep-blue violets!
April's loveliest coronets!
There are no flowers grow in the vale,
Kissed by the dew, wooed by the gale,—
None by the dew of the twilight wet,
So sweet as the deep-blue violet.
LETITIA ELIZABETH LANDON, *The Violet*.

17
The violet of an unforgotten hour.
RICHARD LE GALLIENNE, *Adoration*.

18
Violet! sweet violet!
Thine eyes are full of tears;
Are they wet
Even yet
With the thought of other years?
Or with gladness are they full,
For the night so beautiful?
J. R. LOWELL, *Song*.

Winds wander, and dews drip earthward;
Rain falls, suns rise and set,
Earth whirls, and all but to prosper
A poor little violet.
J. R. LOWELL, *The Changeling*. St. 6.

19
The violets were past their prime,
Yet their departing breath
Was sweeter, in the blast of death,
Than all the lavish fragrance of the time.
JAMES MONTGOMERY, *The Adventure of a Star*, l. 37.

1
Shrinking as violets do in summer's ray.
THOMAS MOORE, *Lalla Rookh: The Veiled Prophet of Khorassan*, l. 294.

2
The violet thinks, with her timid blue eye,
To pass for a blossom enchantingly shy.
FRANCES S. OSGOOD, *Garden Gossip*.

3
You are brief, and frail, and blue—
Little sisters, I am, too.
You are heaven's masterpieces—
Little loves, the likeness ceases.
DOROTHY PARKER, *Sweet Violets*.

4
You pretty daughters of the Earth and Sun.
SIR WALTER RALEIGH, *The Shepherd to the Flowers*.

5
A violet in the youth of primy nature,
Forward, not permanent, sweet, not lasting,
The perfume and suppliance of a minute.
SHAKESPEARE, *Hamlet*. Act i, sc. 3, l. 7.

6 Lay her i' the earth:
And from her fair and unpolluted flesh,
May violets spring!
SHAKESPEARE, *Hamlet*. Act v, sc. 1, l. 261.

And from his ashes may be made
The violet of his native land.
TENNYSON, *In Memoriam*. Sec. xviii, st. 1.

7 Who are the violets now
That strew the green lap of the new come spring?
SHAKESPEARE, *Richard II*. Act v, sc. 2, l. 46.

8 Violets dim,
But sweeter than the lids of Juno's eyes
Or Cytherea's breath.
SHAKESPEARE, *Winter's Tale*. Act iv, sc. 4, l. 120.

9
Oh! faint delicious spring-tide violet,
Thine odor like a key,
Turns noiselessly in memory's wards to let
A thought of sorrow free.
W. W. STORY, *The Violet*.

The smell of violets, hidden in the green,
Pour'd back into my empty soul and frame
The times when I remember to have been
Joyful and free from blame.
TENNYSON, *A Dream of Fair Women*. St. 20.

10
In this secluded shrine,
O miracle of grace,
No mortal eye but mine
Hath looked upon thy face. . . .
Whereof—as shade to shade
Is wedded in the sun—
A moment's glance hath made
Our souls forever one.
JOHN BANISTER TABB, *To a Wood-Violet*.

11
Then let me to the valley go,
This pretty flower to see,
That I may also learn to grow
In sweet humility.
JANE TAYLOR, *The Violet*.

12
Banks that slope to the southern sky,
Where languid violets love to lie.
SARAH H. WHITMAN, *Wood Walks in Spring*.

13
A violet, by a mossy stone
Half hidden from the eye!
Fair as a star, when only one
Is shining in the sky.
WORDSWORTH, *She Dwelt Among the Untrodden Ways*.

VIRGINIA

13a
Carry me back to old Virginny,
There's where the cotton and the corn and taters grow.
JAMES A. BLAND, *Carry Me Back to Old Virginny*.

14
I am not a Virginian, but an American.
PATRICK HENRY, *Speech*, Continental Congress, 5 Sept., 1774.

15
The good Old Dominion, the mother of us all.
THOMAS JEFFERSON, *Thoughts on Lotteries*.

16
The man who, in the old world, would be dubbed a viscount or a baron, was known in the Old Dominion as an F.F.V.
RAE, *Westward by Rail*, 311. F.F.V.: First Families of Virginia; also Fast Flying Virginian.

Mr. Floyd [John B. Floyd, of Virginia] as everybody knows, is an F.F.V., and the soul of honor accordingly.
UNKNOWN. (*Harper's Weekly*, 11 April, 1857.)

17
Sic semper tyrannis. (Thus always with tyrants.)
Motto of Virginia, adopted October, 1779. The words uttered by John Wilkes Booth when he shot President Lincoln, April 14, 1865.

VIRGINS AND VIRGINITY, see Chastity

VIRTUE

See also Goodness, Vice and Virtue

I—Virtue: Definitions

18
Virtue and sense are one.
JOHN ARMSTRONG, *Art of Preserving Health*. Bk. iv, l. 265.

One's outlook is a part of his virtue.
A. B. ALCOTT, *Concord Days: April Outlook*.

19
Virtue is like a rich stone, best plain set.
FRANCIS BACON, *Essays: Of Beauty*.

Virtue, being a transcendent gem, is better set without much gold and ornament.
BACON, *De Augmentis Scientiarum*. Pt. i, bk. 6.

Virtue is like precious odours,—most fragrant when they are incensed, or crushed.
FRANCIS BACON, *Essays: Of Adversity*.
See also under ADVERSITY.

20
As in nature things move violently to their

place, and calmly in their place, so virtue in ambition is violent, in authority settled and calm.

FRANCIS BACON, *Essays: Of Great Place.*

1
Virtue has always been conceived of as victorious resistance to one's vital desire to do this, that or the other.

JAMES BRANCH CABELL, *Beyond Life*, p. 114.

2
In our dispositions the seeds of the virtues are implanted by nature. (Sunt enim ingeniis nostris semina innata virtutum.)

CICERO, *Tusculanarum Disputationum*. Bk. iii, ch. 1.

Does wisdom beget virtue, or is it a gift of Nature? (Virtutem doctrina paret Naturane donet?)

HORACE, *Epistles*. Bk. i, epis. 18, l. 100.

Although virtue receives some of its excellencies from nature, yet it is perfected by education. (Virtus, etiamsi quosdam impetus a natura sumit, tamen perficienda doctrina est.)

QUINTILIAN, *De Institutione Oratoria*. Bk. xii, ch. 2, sec. 1.

3
Virtue is a habit of the mind, consistent with nature and moderation and reason.

CICERO, *De Inventione Rhetorica*. Bk. ii, sec. 53.

4
Is virtue a thing remote? I wish to be virtuous, and lo! virtue is at hand.

CONFUCIUS, *Analects*. Bk. vii, ch. 29.

5
We fancy it rhetoric when we speak of eminent virtue. We do not yet see that virtue is Height.

EMERSON, *Essays, First Series: Self-Reliance.*

Virtue is the adherence in action to the nature of things, and the nature of things makes it prevalent. It consists in a perpetual substitution of being for seeming, and with sublime propriety God is described as saying, I AM.

EMERSON, *Essays, First Series: Spiritual Laws.*

6
Virtue is a mean between vices, remote from both extremes. (Virtus est medium vitiorum et utrimque reductum.)

HORACE, *Epistles*. Bk. i, epis. 18, l. 9.

7
Can you suppose that virtue consists of words merely? (Virtutem verba putas?)

HORACE, *Epistles*. Bk. i, epis. 6, l. 31.

Virtue's but a word; Fortune rules all.

MASSINGER, *The Bashful Lover*. Act iv, sc. 1.

8
Virtue is often merely local.

SAMUEL JOHNSON, *The Idler*. No. 53.

So much are the modes of excellence settled by time and place, that men may be heard boasting in one street of that which they would anxiously conceal in another.

SAMUEL JOHNSON. *The Rambler*. No. 201

9
Wisdom is knowing what to do next; virtue is doing it.

DAVID STARR JORDAN, *The Philosophy of Despair*, p. 37.

10
Virtue is the health of the soul. It gives a flavor to the smallest leaves of life. (La vertu est la santé de l'âme. Elle fait trouver de la saveur aux moindres feuilles de la vie.)

JOUBERT, *Pensées*. No. 131.

Virtue is to the soul what health is to the body. (La sagesse est à l'âme ce que la santé est pour le corps.)

LA ROCHEFOUCAULD, *Maximes Posthumes*. No. 541.

11
Virtue is an angel, but she is a blind one, and must ask of Knowledge to show her the pathway that leads to her goal.

HORACE MANN, *A Few Thoughts for a Young Man.*

12
Virtue is the fount whence honour springs.

MARLOWE, *Tamburlane*. Pt. i, act v, sc. 2.

13
Virtue is harmony. (Τήν τ' ἀρετὴν ἁρμονίαν.)

PYTHAGORAS. (DIOGENES LAERTIUS, *Pythagoras*. Bk. viii, sec. 33.)

14
Virtue is beauty; but the beauteous evil
Are empty trunks o'erflourish'd by the devil.

SHAKESPEARE, *Twelfth Night*. Act iii, sc. 4, l. 403.

15
Virtue consists, not in abstaining from vice, but in not desiring it.

BERNARD SHAW, *Maxims for Revolutionists.*

16
Virtue, the greatest of all monarchies.

SWIFT, *To the Hon. Sir William Temple.*

17
What, what is virtue, but repose of mind?
A pure ethereal calm that knows no storm,
Above the reach of wild ambition's wind,
Above those passions that this world deform.

JAMES THOMSON, *The Castle of Indolence*. Canto i, st. 16.

18
Virtue 's a stronger guard than brass.

EDMUND WALLER, *Epigram Upon the Golden Medal*, l. 14.

II—Virtue: Apothegms

19
It is not enough merely to possess virtue, as if it were an art; it should be practised. (Nec vero habere virtutem satis est, quasi artem aliquam, nisi utare.)

CICERO, *De Republica*. Ch. i, sec. 2.

Virtue is not left to stand alone. *He who practices it* will have neighbors.

CONFUCIUS, *Analects*. Bk. iv, ch. 25.

Virtue, if not in action, is a vice;
And when we move not forward, we go backward.

MASSINGER, *The Maid of Honour*. Act i, sc. 1.

I cannot praise a fugitive and cloistered virtue, unexercised and unbreathed, that never sallies out and sees her adversary, but slinks out of the race where that immortal garland is to be run for, not without dust and heat.

MILTON, *Areopagitica*.

1
It is the stain and disgrace of the age to envy virtue. (Est hæc sæculi labes quædam et macula virtuti invidere.)

CICERO, *Pro L. Cornelio Balbo*. Sec. 6.

A man that hath no virtue in himself, ever envieth virtue in others.

FRANCIS BACON, *Essays: Of Envy*.

2
Virtue when concealed hath no value. (Vile latens virtus.)

CLAUDIAN, *Panegyricus de Quarto Consulatu Honorii Augusti*, l. 222.

Is it a world to hide virtues in?

SHAKESPEARE, *Twelfth Night*. Act i, sc. 3, l. 140.

3
Ye were not formed to live the life of brutes,
But virtue to pursue, and knowledge high.
(Fatti non foste a viver come bruti,
Ma per seguir virtute e conoscenza.)

DANTE, *Inferno*. Canto xxvi, l. 119.

4
The highest virtue is always against the law.

EMERSON, *Conduct of Life: Worship*.

5
All the devils respect virtue.

EMERSON, *Essays, First Series: Spiritual Laws*.

6
Hast thou virtue? acquire also the graces and beauties of virtue.

BENJAMIN FRANKLIN, *Poor Richard*, 1733.

Sell not virtue to purchase wealth, nor liberty to purchase power.

BENJAMIN FRANKLIN, *Poor Richard*, 1738.

7
The greatest offence against virtue is to speak ill of it.

WILLIAM HAZLITT, *Essays: On Cant*.

8
Virtue best loves those children that she beats.

ROBERT HERRICK, *Hesperides*. No. 822.

9
We hate Virtue while it lives, and mourn it only when it is snatched from sight. (Virtutem incolumem odimus, Sublatam ex oculis quærimus.)

HORACE, *Odes*. Bk. iii, ode xxiv, l. 31.

Friendly to Virtue alone and to its friends. (Uni æquus Virtuti atque ejus amicis.)

HORACE, *Satires*. Bk. ii, sat. 1, l. 70.

10
Where does virtue go to lodge? (Où la vertu va-t-elle se nicher?)

MOLIÈRE, *Remark*, when shown the cots in a prison.

11
No way is barred to virtue. (Invia virtuti nulla est via.)

OVID, *Metamorphoses*. Bk. xiv, l. 113.

Nature has placed nothing so high that virtue can not reach it. (Nihil tam alte natura constituit quo virtus non possit eniti.)

QUINTUS CURTIUS RUFUS, *De Rebus Gestis Alexandri Magni*. Bk. vii, ch. 11, sec. 10.

12
The virtue which lies hidden unrecognized in times of prosperity, asserts itself in adversity. (Quæ latet inque bonis cessat non cognita rebus, Apparet virtus arguiturque malis.)

OVID, *Tristia*. Bk. iv, eleg. 3, l. 79. *See also* PROSPERITY AND ADVERSITY.

13
Let them [the wicked] look on virtue and pine away because they have lost her. (Virtutem videant intabescantque relicta.)

PERSIUS, *Satires*. Sat. iii, l. 38.

14
Virtue, if she could be seen, would win great love and affection.

PLATO. (BACON, *Advancement of Learning*. Bk. ii.)

15
Conquer by means of virtue. (Vincite Virtute vera.)

PLAUTUS, *Casina: Prologue*, l. 87.

16
Virtue, like a strong and hardy plant, takes root in any place, if she finds there a generous nature and a spirit that shuns no labor.

PLUTARCH, *Lives: Demosthenes*. Sec. 1.

17
To virtue no way ever happens ill.

FRANCIS ROUS, *Thule*.

18
Assume a virtue, if you have it not.

SHAKESPEARE, *Hamlet*. Act iii, sc. 4, l. 160.

19
Virtue may be gay, yet with dignity. (Hilarisque tamen cum pondere virtus.)

STATIUS, *Sylvarum*. Bk. ii, sec. 3, l. 65.

20
Stay, Worldling, stay; whither away so fast?
Hark, hark awhile to Virtue's counsels current!

JOSHUA SYLVESTER, *Spectacles*.

21
Learn virtue and true labor from me, O youth; fortune from others. (Disce, puer, virtutem ex me, verumque laborum; Fortunam ex aliis.)

VERGIL, *Æneid*. Bk. xii, l. 435.

22
Virtue debases itself in justifying itself. (La vertu s'avilit à se justifier.)

VOLTAIRE, *Œdipe*. Act i, sc. 4.

III—Virtue: Its Beauty

23
The chief good is the exercise of virtue in a perfect life.

ARISTOTLE. (DIOGENES LAERTIUS, *Aristotle*. Bk. v, sec. 30.)

24
Virtue alone is the unerring sign of a noble

soul. (La vertu d'un cœur noble est la marque certaine.)
BOILEAU, *Satires*. No. v, l. 42.

1
Virtue is not malicious; wrong done her
Is righted even when men grant they err.
CHAPMAN, *Monsieur D'Olive*. Act i, sc. 1, l. 127.

2
Virtue loves herself, for she best knows herself and realizes how lovable she is. (Amans sui virtus, optime enim se ipsa novit quamque sit intellegit.)
CICERO, *De Amicitia*. Ch. xxvi, sec. 98.

3
The only amaranthine flower on earth
Is virtue.
COWPER, *The Task*. Bk. iii, l. 268.

4
And virtue, tho' in rags, will keep me warm.
DRYDEN, *Imitations of Horace*. Bk. iii, 29, 87.

He is ill clothed who is bare of virtue.
BENJAMIN FRANKLIN, *Poor Richard*, 1733.

Rags are royal raiment when worn for virtue's sake.
BARTLEY T. CAMPBELL, *The White Slave*. Act iii.

5
For virtue which alone is free, cannot be brought into subjection. (Virtus enim servire non potest, quæ sola libera est.)
JEROME OSORIUS, *De Gloria*. Bk. i, ch. 7.

6
Virtue, dear friend, needs no defence,
The surest guard is innocence:
None knew, till guilt created fear,
What darts or poison'd arrows were.
(Integer vitæ scelerisque purus
Non eget Mauris jaculis neque arcu
Nec venenatis gravida sagittis,
Fusce, pharetra.)
HORACE, *Odes*. Bk. i, ode 22, st. 1. (Dillon, tr.)

7
Though men may falter, it is Virtue's strength
To be indelible: our smallest good
By our worst evil cannot be undone.
R. U. JOHNSON, *The Voice of Webster*.

8
With virtue and quietness one may conquer the world.
LAO-TSZE, *The Simple Way*. No. 45.

9
Virtue could see to do what virtue would
By her own radiant light, though sun and moon
Were in the flat sea sunk.
MILTON, *Comus*, l. 373.

Virtue gives herself light, through darkness for to wade.
SPENSER, *Faerie Queene*. Bk. i, canto i, st. 12.

10
Whatsoever things are true, whatsoever things are honest, whatsoever things are just, whatsoever things are pure, whatsoever things are lovely, whatsoever things are of good report: if there be any virtue, and if there be any praise, think on these things.
New Testament: Philippians, iv, 8.

11
Divinity has three elements of superiority, incorruption, power, and virtue, and the most reverend and divinest of these is virtue; for in fundamental justice nothing participates except through the exercise of intelligent reasoning powers.
PLUTARCH, *Lives: Aristides*. Ch. 6, sec. 2.

12
Virtue, the most pleasing and valuable possession in the world. ('Αρετήν, ἧς κτῆμα μεῖζον οὐδὲν οὐδ' ἥδιον.)
PLUTARCH, *Lives: Solon*. Sec. 7.

In virtue are riches. (In virtute divitiæ.)
CICERO, *Paradoxa*, vi, 2.

Silver and gold are not the only coin; virtue too passes current all over the world.
EURIPIDES, *Œdipus*. Frag. 546.

Of less worth than gold is silver, than virtue gold. (Vilius argentum est auro, virtutibus aurum.)
HORACE, *Epistles*. Bk. i, epis. 1, l. 52.

13
Virtue is bold, and goodness never fearful.
SHAKESPEARE, *Measure for Measure*. Act iii, sc. 1, l. 215.

14
Virtue is doubly pleasing in one whose form is beautiful. (Gratior et pulchro veniens in corpore virtus.)
VERGIL, *Æneid*. Bk. v, l. 344.

15
Virtue, not rolling suns, the mind matures.
YOUNG, *Night Thoughts*. Night v, l. 772.

IV—Virtue: Its Difficulty

16
There is no road or ready way to virtue.
SIR THOMAS BROWNE, *Religio Medici*. Pt. i, sec. 55.

17
How far from easy is virtue! How difficult is even a continual pretence of virtue! (Quam non est facilis virtus! Quam vero difficilis ejus diuturna simulatio.)
CICERO, *Epistolæ ad Atticum*. Bk. viii, epis. 1.

18
Virtue proceeds through toil. ('Α δ' ἀρετὰ βαίνει διὰ μόχθων.)
EURIPIDES, *Heraclidæ*, l. 625.

Between us and Virtue the gods placed sweat: long and steep is the path that leads to her; but when a man has reached the top, then is she easy to reach.
HESIOD, *Works and Days*, l. 289.

The steep path of virtue. (Virtutis viam arduæ.)
HORACE, *Odes*. Bk. iii, ode 24, l. 44.

19
Virtue requires a rough and stormy passage; she will have either outward difficulties to wrestle with . . . or internal difficulties.
MONTAIGNE, *Essays*. Bk. ii, ch. 11.

Virtue is the roughest way,
But proves at night a bed of down.
SIR HENRY WOTTON, *On the Imprisonment of the Earl of Essex*.

1
Virtue is nothing if not difficult. (Sed nulla, nisi ardua, virtus.)
OVID, *Ars Amatoria*. Bk. ii, l. 537.

2
Virtue itself 'scapes not calumnious strokes.
SHAKESPEARE, *Hamlet*. Act i, sc. 3, l. 38.

'T is but the fate of place, and the rough brake
That virtue must go through.
SHAKESPEARE, *Henry VIII*. Act i, sc. 2, l. 75.

My heart laments that virtue cannot live
Out of the teeth of emulation.
SHAKESPEARE, *Julius Cæsar*. Act ii, sc. 3, l. 13.

3
Virtue struggles after fame, regardless of the adverse heights. (Perque aspera dura Nititur ad laudem virtus interrita clivo.)
SILIUS ITALICUS, *Punica*. Pt. iv, l. 605.

4
It is easy enough to be prudent,
When nothing tempts you to stray;
When without or within no voice of sin
Is luring your soul away;
But it's only a negative virtue
Until it is tried by fire,
And the life that is worth the honor of earth,
Is the one that resists desire.
ELLA WHEELER WILCOX, *Worth While*.

V—Virtue: Its Rewards

5
Virtue is its own reward. (Officii fructus sit ipsum officium.)
CICERO, *De Finibus*. Bk. ii, sec. 73.

Virtue is its own reward. (Ipsa quidem Virtus pretium sibi.)
CLAUDIAN, *Panegyricus Dictus Manlio Theodoro Consuli*, l. 1.

Virtue, sir, is its own reward.
DRYDEN, *The Assignation*. Act iii, sc. 1. Also *Tyrannic Love*, ii, 3; HOME, *Douglas*, iii, 1; PRIOR, *Imitations of Horace*, iii, 2; etc.

The only reward of virtue is virtue.
EMERSON, *Essays, First Series: Friendship*.

Yet why should learning hope success at court?
Why should our patriots' virtues cause support?
Why to true merit should they have regard?
They know that virtue is its own reward.
JOHN GAY, *Epistle to Paul Methuen*, l. 39.

Virtue herself is her own fairest reward. (Ipsa quidem virtus sibimet pulcherrima merces.)
SILIUS ITALICUS, *Punica*. Bk. xiii, l. 663.

Virtue is its own reward. There's a pleasure in doing good which sufficiently pays itself.
SIR JOHN VANBRUGH, *The Relapse*. Act v, sc. 1.

6
Honor is the reward of virtue. (Honor est præmium virtutis.)
CICERO, *Philippicæ*. No. iv, sec. 81.

In virtue there are many grades, and the highest glory is won by the highest virtue. (In virtute multi sunt adscensus, ut is gloria maxime excellat, qui virtute plurimum præstet.)
CICERO, *Pro Cnæo Plancio*. Ch. xxv, sec. 60.

Only virtue wins eternal Fame.
PETRARCH, *The Triumph of Fame*. Pt. i, l. 183.

7
For blessings ever wait on virtuous deeds,
And though a late, a sure reward succeeds.
CONGREVE, *The Mourning Bride*. Act v, sc. 12.

8
Either virtue is an empty name, or the wise man rightly seeks it as his glory and reward. (Aut virtus nomen inane est, Aut decus et pretium recte petit experiens vir.)
HORACE, *Epistles*. Bk. i, epis. 17, l. 41.

9
Virtue may be assail'd, but never hurt,
Surpris'd by unjust force, but not enthrall'd,
Yea, even that which mischief meant most harm,
Shall in the happy trial prove most glory.
MILTON, *Comus*, l. 589.

10
Not among many thousands will you find
One man who considers virtue its own reward.
(Nec facile invenias multis in milibus unum,
Virtutem pretium qui putet esse sui.)
OVID, *Epistulæ ex Ponto*. Bk. ii, epis. 3, l. 11.

When the prizes fall to the lot of the wicked, you will not find many who are virtuous for virtue's sake.
SALLUST, *History*. Bk. i, frag.

11
Virtue will not be followed except for her own sake. (La vertu ne veult estre suyvie que pour elle mesme.)
MONTAIGNE, *Essays*. Bk. ii, ch. 1.

12
In your opinion virtue requires no reward and is to be sought for itself. (Judice te mercede caret per seque petenda est.)
OVID, *Epistulæ ex Ponto*. Bk. ii, epis. 3, l. 35.

Beauty, goodness, justice, and the like, each exists in and for itself.
PLATO. (DIOGENES LAERTIUS, *Plato*. Bk. iii, 13.)

O let us still the secret joy partake,
To follow virtue even for virtue's sake.
POPE, *Temple of Fame*, l. 364.

13
You ask what I seek from virtue? Itself. For virtue has nothing better to give; its value is in itself.
SENECA, *De Vita Beata*. Ch. ix, sec. 4.

14
One should seek virtue for its own sake, and not from hope or fear, or any external motive. It is in virtue that happiness consists, for virtue is the state of mind which tends to make the whole of life harmonious.
ZENO. (DIOGENES LAERTIUS, *Zeno*. Bk. vii, 89.)

VI—Virtue and Happiness

15
Here will I hold. If there's a Power above
(And that there is all nature cries aloud
Through all her works), he must delight in virtue;

And that which he delights in must be happy.
ADDISON, *Cato*. Act v, sc. 1. Inscribed by Franklin on his book of virtues.

1
Virtue, the strength and beauty of the soul,
Is the best gift of Heaven: a happiness
That even above the smiles and frowns of fate
Exalts great Nature's favourites.
JOHN ARMSTRONG, *Art of Preserving Health*. Bk. iv, l. 284.

2
Neither can the virtues exist without happy life, nor happy life without the virtues. (Nec enim virtutes sine beata vita cohærere possunt nec illa sine virtutibus.)
CICERO, *Tusculanarum Disputationum*. Bk. v, ch. 28, sec. 80.

3
Well may your hearts believe the truths I tell:
'Tis virtue makes the bliss, where'er we dwell.
WILLIAM COLLINS, *Persian Eclogues*. No. i, l. 5.

Virtue alone is happiness below.
GEORGE CRABBE, *The Borough*. Letter xvi.

4
You may be more happy than princes, if you will be more virtuous.
BENJAMIN FRANKLIN, *Poor Richard*, 1738.

Be in general virtuous, and you will be happy.
BENJAMIN FRANKLIN, *On Early Marriages*.

Virtue and Happiness are Mother and Daughter.
BENJAMIN FRANKLIN, *Poor Richard*, 1746.

5
Shall ignorance of good and ill
Dare to direct the eternal will?
Seek virtue, and, of that possest,
To Providence resign the rest.
JOHN GAY, *Fables: The Father and Jupiter*.

6
You wish to live rightly (and who does not?); since Virtue alone can achieve this, boldly drop trifles and scorn delights.
HORACE, *Epistles*. Bk. i, epis. 6, l. 29.

Nor can you suppose that anyone is happy but the man who is wise and good. (Neve putes alium sapiente bonoque beatum.)
HORACE, *Epistles*. Bk. i, epis. 16, l. 20.

And if the Wise be the happy man, as these sages say, he must be virtuous too; for without virtue happiness cannot be.
THOMAS JEFFERSON, *Writings*. Vol. xiv, p. 405.

7
Through virtue lies the one and only road to a life of peace. (Tranquillæ per virtutem patet unica vitæ.)
JUVENAL, *Satires*. Sat. x, l. 364.

8
Mortals that would follow me,
Love virtue; she alone is free;
She can teach ye how to climb
Higher than the sphery chime;
Or if virtue feeble were,
Heav'n itself would stoop to her.
MILTON, *Comus*, l. 1018.

9
Virtue of herself is sufficient for happiness.
PLATO. (DIOGENES LAERTIUS, *Plato*. Bk. iii, 13.)

10
Virtue may choose the high or low degree,
'T is just alike to Virtue and to me;
Dwell in a monk, or light upon a king,
She 's still the same belov'd, contented thing.
POPE, *Epilogue to the Satires*. Dial. i, l. 137.

What nothing earthly gives or can destroy,
The soul's calm sunshine and the heartfelt joy,
Is Virtue's prize.
POPE, *Essay on Man*. Epis. iv, l. 167.

Know then this truth (enough for man to know),
"Virtue alone is happiness below."
POPE, *Essay on Man*. Epis. iv, l. 309.

11
Be virtoous & you'll be happy!
ARTEMUS WARD, *Fourth of July Oration*.

Be virtuous and you will be eccentric.
MARK TWAIN, *Mental Photographs*.

Be good and you will be lonesome.
MARK TWAIN, *Following the Equator*. Caption of author's photograph used as frontispiece.

VII—Virtue and Immortality

12
Virtue never grows old.
GEORGE HERBERT, *Jacula Prudentum*.

13
Virtue treads paths that end not in the grave;
No ban of endless night exiles the brave.
J. R. LOWELL, *Commemoration Ode*.

14
He who dies for virtue does not perish. (Qui per virtutem periit, at non interit.)
PLAUTUS, *Captivi*, l. 690. (Act iii, sc. 5.)

For virtue will endure to posterity; envy will not reach them. (Ad posteros enim virtus durabit non perveniet invidia.)
QUINTILIAN, *De Institutione Oratoria*. Bk. iii, ch. 1.

15
The renown which riches or beauty confer is fleeting and frail; virtue remains bright and eternal. (Divitiarum et formæ gloria fluxa atque fragile est; virtus clara æternaque habetur.)
SALLUST, *Catilina*. Ch. i, sec. 4.

16
Virtue lives beyond the grave. (Vivit post funera virtus.)
TIBERIUS CÆSAR. (BORBONIUS, *Lives: Tiberius*.)

Virtue shall live even after the funeral.
(Vivet etiam post funera virtus.)
SIR DAVID LINDSAY, *Works: Motto on Title-page*, 1578. Inscribed on monument of Thomas Linacre, Old Saint Paul's Church, London, 1557.

17
Glory's voice is impotent to pierce
The silence of the tomb; but virtue blooms
Even on the wreck of life, and mounts the skies.
HENRY KIRKE WHITE, *Inscription for a Monument to the Memory of Cowper*, l. 20.

1
Virtue alone outbuilds the Pyramids;
Her monuments shall last, when Egypt's fall.
YOUNG, *Night Thoughts*. Night vi, l. 312.

VIII—Virtue and Nobility

See also Ancestry

2
Blood is an inheritance, virtue an acquisition.
CERVANTES, *Don Quixote*. Pt. ii, ch. 42.

3
'Tis virtue, and not birth, that makes us noble;
Great actions speak great minds, and such should govern.
JOHN FLETCHER, *The Prophetess*. Act ii, sc. 3.

4
Virtue and a trade are the best portion for children.
GEORGE HERBERT, *Jacula Prudentum*.

5
Virtue alone is true nobility. (Nobilitas sola est atque unica virtus.)
JUVENAL, *Satires*. Sat. viii, l. 20.

Oh! might we all our lineage prove,
Give and forgive, do good and love.
JOHN KEBLE, *The Christian Year: Second Sunday after Trinity*.

6
Birth is nothing where virtue is not. (La naissance n'est rien où la vertu n'est pas.)
MOLIÈRE, *Don Juan*. Act iv, sc. 6.

7
When we are planning for posterity, we ought to remember that virtue is not hereditary.
THOMAS PAINE, *Common Sense*. Ch. 4.

If there be no nobility of descent, all the more indispensable is it that there should be nobility of ascent—a character in them that bear rule, so fine and high and pure, that as men come within the circle of its influence they involuntarily pay homage to that which is the one preëminent distinction, the Royalty of Virtue.
HENRY CODMAN POTTER, *Address*, 30 April, 1889.

8
To virtue's humblest son let none prefer
Vice, though descended from the Conqueror.
YOUNG, *Love of Fame*. Sat. i, l. 141.

IX—Virtue: The Virtuous Man

9
Virtuous and wise he was, but not severe;
He still remembered that he once was young.
JOHN ARMSTRONG, *Art of Preserving Health*. Bk. iv, l. 226.

His virtues were his arts.
EDMUND BURKE, *Inscription for the Tomb of the Marquis of Rockingham*.

To Berkley ev'ry virtue under Heav'n.
POPE, *Epilogue to the Satires*. Dial. ii, l. 73.

10
In virtues nothing earthly could surpass her,
Save thine "incomparable oil," Macassar!
BYRON, *Don Juan*. Canto i, st. 17.

She's all thet's honest, honnable, an' fair,
An' when the vartoos died they made her heir.
J. R. LOWELL, *Biglow Papers*. Ser. i, No. 2.

The temple of virtue was she.
SHAKESPEARE, *Cymbeline*. Act v, sc. 5, l. 220.

11
What to one man is the virtue which he has sunk below the possibility of aspiring to, is to another the backsliding by which he forfeits his spiritual crown.
GEORGE ELIOT, *Felix Holt*.

12
Speak to his heart, and the man becomes suddenly virtuous.
EMERSON, *Essays, First Series: The Over-Soul*.

13
I wrap myself in my virtue. (Mea virtute me involvo.)
HORACE, *Odes*. Bk. iii, ode 29, l. 55.

14
His virtues walk'd their narrow round,
Nor made a pause, nor left a void;
And sure th' Eternal Master found
The single talent well employ'd.
SAMUEL JOHNSON, *On the Death of Mr. Robert Levet*.

15
Men of most renowned virtue have sometimes by transgressing most truly kept the law.
MILTON, *Tetrachordon*.

16
'T is thus the mercury of man is fix'd,
Strong grows the virtue with his nature mix'd.
POPE, *Essay on Man*. Epis. ii, l. 177.

17
Fairest Cordelia, that art most rich, being poor;
Most choice, forsaken; and most loved, despised!
Thee and thy virtues here I seize upon.
SHAKESPEARE, *King Lear*. Act i, sc. 1, l. 253.

18
His virtues
Will plead like angels, trumpet-tongued, against
The deep damnation of his taking-off.
SHAKESPEARE, *Macbeth*. Act i, sc. 7, l. 18.

19
A man of antique virtue. (Homo . . . antiqua virtute.)
TERENCE, *Adelphi*, l. 442.

X—Virtue: Its Faults

See also Faults: Their Virtues

20
Curse on his virtues! they've undone his country.
JOSEPH ADDISON, *Cato*. Act iv, sc. 4.

21
That virtue which depends on opinion, looks to secrecy alone, and could not be trusted in a desert.
C. C. COLTON, *Lacon*. Vol. i, No. 466.

1
O Virtue! I have followed thee through life, and I find thee at last but a shade.
EURIPIDES. (EMERSON, *Essays, First Series: Heroism.*)

2
The virtue which requires to be ever guarded is scarcely worth the sentinel.
GOLDSMITH, *The Vicar of Wakefield*. Ch. 5.

3
Virtue seldom walks forth without Vanity at her side.
W. G. BENHAM, *Proverbs*, p. 866.

Virtue would not go so far if vanity did not keep it company. (La vertu n'irait pas si loin si la vanité ne lui tenait compagnie.)
LA ROCHEFOUCAULD, *Maximes*. No. 200.

4
Some of 'em [virtues] like extinct volcanoes, with a strong memory of fire and brimstone.
DOUGLAS JERROLD, *The Catspaw*. Act iii, sc: 1.

5
Virtues lose themselves in self-interest, as streams lose themselves in the sea. (Les vertus se perdent dans l'intérêt, comme les fleuves se perdent dans la mer.)
LA ROCHEFOUCAULD, *Maximes*. No. 171.

6
Be virtuous: not too much; just what's correct:
Excess in anything is a defect.
(Faut d'la vertu, pas trop n'en faut,
L'excès en tout est un défaut.)
J. M. B. MONVEL, *Erreur d'un Moment*.

7
I am not impressed by external devices for the preservation of virtue in men or women. Marriage laws, the police, armies and navies are the mark of human incompetence.
DORA RUSSELL, *The Right to Be Happy*, p. 241.

8
Virtue withers away if it has no opposition. (Marcet sine adversario virtus.)
SENECA, *De Providentia*. Sec. 2.

9
He was a fool, For he would needs be virtuous.
SHAKESPEARE, *Henry VIII*. Act ii, sc. 2, l. 133.

Virtue finds no friends.
SHAKESPEARE, *Henry VIII*. Act iii, sc. 1, l. 126.

Virtue! a fig! 'tis in ourselves that we are thus or thus.
SHAKESPEARE, *Othello*. Act i, sc. 3, l. 322.

10
Virtue often trips and falls on the sharp-edged rock of poverty.
EUGÈNE SUE, *The Mysteries of Paris*. Ch. 1.

11
Come down and redeem us from virtue,
Our Lady of Pain.
SWINBURNE, *Dolores*.

XI—Virtue: Its Rarity

12
Many wish not so much to be virtuous, as to seem to be. (Virtute enim ipsa non tam multi præditi esse quam videri volunt.)
CICERO, *De Amicitia*. Ch. xxvi, sec. 98.

And he by no uncommon lot
Was fam'd for virtues he had not.
COWPER, *To the Rev. William Bull*, l. 19.

13
There are no two things so much talked of, and so seldom seen, as virtue and the funds.
C. C. COLTON, *Lacon*. Vol. i, No. 312.

Let those who would affect singularity with success, first determine to be very virtuous, and they will be sure to be very singular.
C. C. COLTON, *Lacon*. Vol. i, No. 461.

14
Virtue engages his assent,
But Pleasure wins his heart.
WILLIAM COWPER, *Human Frailty*, l. 12.

Most men admire
Virtue, who follow not her lore.
MILTON, *Paradise Regained*. Bk. i, l. 482.

15
Virtues are, in the popular estimate, rather the exception than the rule. There is the man *and* his virtues.
EMERSON, *Essays, First Series: Self-Reliance*.

16
If it is usual to be deeply moved by rare things, why are we so little moved by virtue? (S'il est ordinaire d'être vivement touché des choses rares, pourquoi le somme-nous si peu de la vertu?)
LA BRUYÈRE, *Les Caractères*. Pt. i, No. 25.

Virtue was always in a minority on the earth. (La vertu fut toujours en minorité sur la terre.)
ROBESPIERRE.

VISION

See also Ghost

17
Sometimes he thinks that Heaven the vision sent,
And ordered all the pageants as they went;
Sometimes, that only 'twas wild Fancy's play,
The loose and scattered relics of the day.
ABRAHAM COWLEY, *Davideis*. Bk. ii, l. 789.

18
Golden hours of vision come to us in this present life, when we are at our best, and our faculties work together in harmony.
CHARLES FLETCHER DOLE, *The Hope of Immortality*.

Forward, on the same old journey, let us follow where she leads,
Let us chase the beckoning glory of the Vision that Recedes.
SAM WALTER FOSS, *The Vision that Recedes*.

19
Visions of glory, spare my aching sight!
THOMAS GRAY, *The Bard*, l. 107.

20
Write the vision, and make it plain upon tables, that he may run that readeth it.
Old Testament: Habakkuk, ii, 2.

1
Do I sleep? do I dream?
Do I wonder and doubt?
Are things what they seem?
Or is visions about?
BRET HARTE, *Further Language from Truthful James*, l. 1.

Is this a vision? is this a dream? do I sleep?
SHAKESPEARE, *Merry Wives of Windsor*, iii, 5, 142.

2
I have multiplied visions, and used similitudes.
Old Testament: Hosea, xii, 10.

3
And it shall come to pass afterward, that I will pour out my Spirit upon all flesh; and your sons and your daughters shall prophesy, your old men shall dream dreams, your young men shall see visions.
Old Testament: Joel, ii, 28; *Acts*, ii, 17.

The people's prayer, the glad diviner's theme,
The young men's vision, and the old men's dream!
DRYDEN, *Absalom and Achitophel*. Pt. i, l. 238.

Thy wife hath dream'd, thy mother hath seen visions.
SHAKESPEARE, *Troilus and Cressida*, v, 3, 63.

4
Was it a vision, or a waking dream?
Fled is that music:—do I wake or sleep?
KEATS, *Ode to a Nightingale*. St. 8.

True to a vision, steadfast to a dream.
STEPHEN PHILLIPS, *Ulysses*. Act i, sc. 1.

5
Ah splendid Vision, golden time,
An end of hunger, cold, and crime,
An end of rent, an end of rank,
An end of balance at the bank!
ANDREW LANG, *The New Millennium*.

6
It is a dream, sweet child! a waking dream,
A blissful certainty, a vision bright,
Of that rare happiness, which even on earth
Heaven gives to those it loves.
LONGFELLOW, *Spanish Student*. Act iii, sc. 5.

7
I took it for a faëry vision
Of some gay creatures of the element
That in the colours of the rainbow live
And play i' th' plighted clouds.
MILTON, *Comus*, l. 298.

8
My thoughts by night are often filled
With visions false as fair:
For in the past alone I build
My castles in the air.
THOMAS LOVE PEACOCK, *Castles in the Air*.

Hence the fool's paradise, the statesman's scheme,
The air-built castle, and the golden dream,
The maid's romantic wish, the chemist's flame,
And poet's vision of eternal fame.
POPE, *Dunciad*. Bk. iii, l. 9.

See also under CASTLE.

9
Where there is no vision, the people perish.
Old Testament: Proverbs, xxix, 18.

10
'T was but a bolt of nothing, shot at nothing,
Which the brain makes of fumes: our very eyes
Are sometimes like our judgements, blind.
SHAKESPEARE, *Cymbeline*. Act iv, sc. 2, l. 300.

Alas! How is 't with you,
That you do bend your eye on vacancy
And with the incorporal air do hold discourse?
SHAKESPEARE, *Hamlet*. Act iii, sc. 4, l. 116.

11
Is this a dagger which I see before me,
The handle toward my hand? Come, let me clutch thee.
I have thee not, and yet I see thee still.
Art thou not, fatal vision, sensible
To feeling as to sight? or art thou but
A dagger of the mind, a false creation,
Proceeding from the heat-oppressed brain?
SHAKESPEARE, *Macbeth*. Act ii, sc. 1, l. 33.

The air-drawn dagger.
SHAKESPEARE, *Macbeth*. Act iii, sc. 4, l. 62.

12
Our revels now are ended. These our actors,
As I foretold you, were all spirits and
Are melted into air, into thin air:
And, like the baseless fabric of this vision,
The cloud-capp'd towers, the gorgeous palaces,
The solemn temples, the great globe itself,
Yea, all which it inherit, shall dissolve
And, like this insubstantial pageant faded,
Leave not a rack behind.
SHAKESPEARE, *The Tempest*. Act iv, sc. 1, l. 148. (1611)

The cloud capt Tow'rs
The Gorgeous Palaces,
The Solemn Temples,
The Great Globe itself,
Yea all which it Inherit,
Shall dissolve
And like the baseless Fabrick of a Vision
Leave not a wreck behind.
Inscription, on tablet in the left hand of the statue of Shakespeare in Westminster Abbey.

Those golden palaces, those gorgeous halls,
With furniture superfluously fair;
Those stately courts, those sky-encount'ring walls
Evanish all—like vapours in the air.
SIR WILLIAM ALEXANDER, *Illusion*. (1615)

13
What stately vision mocks my waking sense?
Hence, dear delusion, sweet enchantment, hence!
HORACE AND JAMES SMITH, *An Address Without a Phœnix*, l. 1.

Ah me! the vision has vanished,
The music has died away.
WILLIAM WETMORE STORY, *Cleopatra*.

14
Vision is the art of seeing things invisible.
SWIFT, *Thoughts on Various Subjects*.

15
Perfect blessedness, which consists in a vision

of God. (Beatitudinem perfectam, quæ in Dei visione consistit.)

St. Thomas Aquinas, *Summa Theologie.* Hence "beatific vision."

1
But Shapes, that come not at an earthly call,
Will not depart when mortal voices bid;
Lords of the visionary eye whose lid,
Once raised, remains aghast, and will not fall!

Wordsworth, *Dion.* St. 5.

To whom, in vision clear,
The aspiring heads of future things appear,
Like mountain-tops whose mists have rolled away.

Wordsworth, *Poems Dedicated to National Independence.* Pt. ii, No. 43.

VOICE

See also Speech

I—Voice: Apothegms

2
There is no index of character so sure as the voice.

Benjamin Disraeli, *Tancred.* Bk. ii, ch. 1.

A man's style is his mind's voice. Wooden minds, wooden voices.

Emerson, *Journals,* 1872.

3
The voice which speaks in conformity with our dearest hopes will always be listened to.

Émile Gaboriau, *File 113.* Ch. 10.

4
The voice is Jacob's voice, but the hands are the hands of Esau.

Old Testament: Genesis, xxvii, 22.

5
The voice of him that crieth in the wilderness.

Old Testament: Isaiah, xl, 3.

The voice of one crying in the wilderness.

New Testament: Matthew, iii, 3; *Mark,* i, 3; *Luke,* iii, 4; *John,* i, 23. (Vox clamantis in deserto.—*Vulgate.*)

6
A still small voice.

Old Testament: I Kings, xix, 12.

The still small voice is wanted.

Cowper, *The Task.* Bk. v, l. 685.

Inexorable conscience holds his court,
With still, small voice the plot of guilt alarms.

Erasmus Darwin, *Mores Concluded.*

The still small voice of gratitude.

Thomas Gray, *Ode for Music,* l. 64.

A still small voice spake unto me.

Tennyson, *The Two Voices,* l. 1.

7
The living voice moves. (Viva vox adficit.)

Pliny, *Epistles.* Bk. ii, epis. 3. Meaning that what they hear affects men more deeply than what they read.

The spoken voice perishes; the written word remains. (Vox audita perit, litera scripta manet.)

William Caxton. Quoted.

8
All voice and nothing else. (Φωνὰ τύ τις ἐσσι καὶ οὐδὲν ἄλλο.)

Plutarch, *Moralia: Laconic Apothegms.* Sec. 233A. The context is, "A man plucked a nightingale and finding almost no meat, said, 'It's all voice you are, and nothing else.'" The Latin is, "Vox et praeterea nihil."

9
The voice is nothing but beaten air. (Vox nihil aliud quam ictus aer.)

Seneca, *Naturales Questiones.* Bk. ii, sec. 29.

10
My voice stuck in my throat. (Vox faucibus hæsit.)

Vergil, *Æneid.* Bk. ii, l. 774; bk. iii, l. 48; bk. iv, l. 280.

Vox Populi, Vox Dei, *see under* People.

II—Voice: Good and Bad

11
The thrilling, solemn, proud, pathetic voice.

E. B. Browning, *Aurora Leigh.* Bk. ix, l. 196.

The thrilling, tender, proud, pathetic voice.

E. B. Browning, *Aurora Leigh.* Bk. ix, l. 206.

The thrilling, solemn voice, so passionless.

E. B. Browning, *Aurora Leigh.* Bk. ix, l. 248.

12
Quiet, priestlike voice,
Too used to syllable damnations round
To make a natural emphasis worth while.

E. B. Browning, *Aurora Leigh.* Bk. iv, l. 635.

I am sad-voiced as the turtle
Which Anacreon used to feed.

E. B. Browning, *Wine of Cyprus.* St. 6.

13
His voice in one dull, deep, unvaried sound,
Seems to break forth from caverns underground.

Charles Churchill, *The Rosciad,* l. 567.

His voice no touch of harmony admits,
Irregularly deep, and shrill by fits.
The two extremes appear like man and wife,
Coupled together for the sake of strife.

Charles Churchill, *The Rosciad,* l. 1003.

14
Let me hear
Thy voice—my own affrights me with its echoes.

Congreve, *The Mourning Bride.* Act ii, sc. 1.

15
His voice is soft as is the upper air,
Or dying lovers' words.

Dryden, *The Rival Ladies.* Act i, sc. 3.

16
At some glad moment was it nature's choice
To dower a scrap of sunset with a voice?

Edgar Fawcett, *To an Oriole.*

17
I love to hear thine earnest voice,
Wherever thou art hid.

O. W. Holmes, *To an Insect.*

18
When from his breast his mighty voice went

forth. ('Αλλ' ὅτε δὴ ὄπα τε μεγάλην ἐκ στήθεος εἶν.)
HOMER, *Iliad*. Bk. iii, l. 221.

1
He ceas'd; but left so pleasing on the ear
His voice, that list'ning still they seemed to hear.
HOMER, *Odyssey*. Bk. xiii, l. 1. (Pope, tr.)

The voice so sweet, the words so fair,
As some soft chime had stroked the air;
And though the sound were parted thence,
Still left an echo in the sense.
BEN JONSON, *Eupheme*. Pt. iv, st. 10.

The angel ended, and in Adam's ear
So charming left his voice, that he a while
Thought him still speaking, still stood fix'd to hear.
MILTON, *Paradise Lost*. Bk. viii, l. 1.

He ceased; but still their trembling ears retained
The deep vibrations of his witching song.
JAMES THOMSON, *The Castle of Indolence*. Canto i, st. 20.

See also under ORATORY.

2
The tuneful voice, the eye that spoke the mind,
Are gone, nor leave a single trace behind.
ROBERT LLOYD, *The Actor*.

I am listening for the voices
Which I heard in days of old.
CAROLINE NORTON, *The Lonely Harp*.

But O for the touch of a vanish'd hand,
And the sound of a voice that is still!
TENNYSON, *Break, Break, Break*, l. 11.

3
The melting voice through mazes running,
Untwisting all the chains that tie
The hidden soul of harmony.
MILTON, *L'Allegro*, l. 142.

That voice . . . heard so oft
In worst extremes, and on the perilous edge
Of battle.
MILTON, *Paradise Lost*. Bk. i, l. 274.

4
His voice as the sound of many waters.
New Testament: Revelation, i, 15.

His voice was propertied
As all the tuned spheres.
SHAKESPEARE, *Antony and Cleopatra*. Act v, sc. 2, l. 83.

5
I thank you for your voices: thank you:
Your most sweet voices.
SHAKESPEARE, *Coriolanus*. Act ii, sc. 3, l. 179.

6
For my voice, I have lost it with halloing and singing of anthems.
SHAKESPEARE, *II Henry IV*. Act i, sc. 2, l. 212.

7
I'll speak in a monstrous little voice.
SHAKESPEARE, *A Midsummer-Night's Dream*. Act i, sc. 2, l. 54.

I will aggravate my voice so that I will roar you as gently as any sucking dove; I will roar you as 't were any nightingale.
SHAKESPEARE, *A Midsummer-Night's Dream*. Act i, sc. 2, l. 85.

8
O, good my lord, tax not so bad a voice
To slander music any more than once.
SHAKESPEARE, *Much Ado About Nothing*. Act ii, sc. 3, l. 46.

9
With a voice that, like a bell
Toll'd by an earthquake in a trembling tower,
Rang ruin.
TENNYSON, *The Princess*. Canto vi, l. 311.

10
Vocal velvet.
RICHARD GRANT WHITE, characterizing the voice of Pauline Markham. (MARKS, *They All Sang*, p. 53.)

11
A clear sonorous voice, inaudible
To the vast multitude.
WORDSWORTH, *The Excursion*. Bk. ix, l. 89.

A voice so thrilling ne'er was heard
In spring-time from the Cuckoo-bird,
Breaking the silence of the seas
Among the farthest Hebrides.
WORDSWORTH, *The Solitary Reaper*, l. 13.

12
Two voices are there; one is of the sea,
One of the mountains; each a mighty Voice,
In both from age to age thou didst rejoice,
They were thy chosen music, Liberty!
WORDSWORTH, *Poems Dedicated to National Independence*. Pt. i, No. 12.

III—Voice in Women

13
Her voice changed like a bird's:
There grew more of the music and less of the words.
ROBERT BROWNING, *The Flight of the Duchess*. St. 15.

And her voice was the warble of a bird,
So soft, so sweet, so delicately clear,
That finer, simpler music ne'er was heard;
The sort of sound we echo with a tear,
Without knowing why—an overpowering tone,
Whence melody descends, as from a throne.
BYRON, *Don Juan*. Canto ii, st. 151.

14
The devil hath not, in all his quiver's choice,
An arrow for the heart like a sweet voice.
BYRON, *Don Juan*. Canto xv, st. 13.

For it stirs the blood in an old man's heart,
And makes his pulses fly,
To catch the thrill of a happy voice,
And the light of a pleasant eye.
N. P. WILLIS, *Saturday Afternoon*.

15
Then read from the treasured volume
The poem of thy choice,
And lend to the rhyme of the poet
The beauty of thy voice.
LONGFELLOW, *The Day Is Done*. St. 10.

Oh, there is something in that voice that reaches
The innermost recesses of my spirit!
LONGFELLOW, *The Divine Tragedy: The First Passover*. Pt. vi.

Thy voice Is a celestial melody.
LONGFELLOW, *Masque of Pandora*. Pt. v, l. 2.

Her silver voice
Is the rich music of a summer bird,
Heard in the still night, with its passionate cadence.
LONGFELLOW, *The Spirit of Poetry*, l. 55.

1
How sweetly sounds the voice of a good woman!
It is so seldom heard, that, when it speaks,
It ravishes all senses.
MIDDLETON, *The Old Law*. Act iv, sc. 2.

2
Her voice, whate'er she said, enchanted;
Like music to the heart it went.
SAMUEL ROGERS, *Jacqueline*. Pt. i, l. 80.

Her voice was like the voice the stars
Had when they sang together.
D. G. ROSSETTI, *The Blessed Damozel*. St. 10.

3
Her voice was ever soft,
Gentle, and low, an excellent thing in woman.
SHAKESPEARE, *King Lear*. Act v, sc. 3, l. 272.

4
Silence, beautiful voice!
Be still, for you only trouble the mind
With a joy in which I cannot rejoice,
A glory I shall not find.
TENNYSON, *Maud*, l. 180.

VOLTAIRE

5
Voltaire and Shakespeare! *He* was all
The other feigned to be.
The flippant Frenchman speaks: I weep;
And Shakespeare weeps with me.
MATTHIAS CLAUDIUS, *A Comparison*.

6
Built God a church, and laugh'd his word to scorn,
Skilful alike to seem devout and just,
And stab religion with a sly side-thrust.
COWPER, *Retirement*, l. 688.

Just knows, and knows no more, her Bible true—
A truth the brilliant Frenchman never knew.
COWPER, *Truth*, l. 328.

7
He is like the false Amphitryon; although a stranger, it is always he who has the air of being master of the house.
DUBUC. (EMERSON, *Quotation and Originality*.)

8
Voltaire was an apostle of Christian ideas; only the names were hostile to him, and he never knew it otherwise. He was like the son of the vine-dresser in the Gospel, who said No, and went; the other said Yea, and went not.
EMERSON, *Lectures and Biographical Sketches: Character*.

9
Jesus wept: Voltaire smiled.
VICTOR HUGO, *Address*, centenary of Voltaire's death, 30 May, 1878.

10
Here lies the child spoiled by the world which he spoiled. (Ci gît l'enfant gâté du monde qu'il gâta.)
BARONNE DE MONTOLIEU, *Epitaph on Voltaire*.

11
Thou art so witty, profligate, and thin,
Thou seem'st a Milton with his Death and Sin.
EDWARD YOUNG, *Epigram on Voltaire*. Referring to Voltaire's severe criticism of Milton's allegorical description of Death and Sin. (DORAN, *Life of Young*.)

VOTE AND VOTING

12
I consider biennial elections as a security that the sober, second thought of the people shall be law.
FISHER AMES, *Speech*, Jan., 1788.

13
It is hard in all causes, but especially in religion, when voices shall be numbered and not weighed.
FRANCIS BACON, *Of Church Controversies*.

Universal suffrage is the government of a house by its nursery.
BISMARCK, *Saying*.

14
The notion that a man's liberty consists in giving his vote at election-hustings, and saying, "Behold, now, I too have my twenty-thousandth part of a Talker in our National Palaver."
THOMAS CARLYLE, *Past and Present*. Bk. iii, ch. 13.

15
No method of voting can be better than that of open declaration. (Nihil ut fuerit in suffragiis voce melius.)
CICERO, *De Legibus*. Bk. iii, ch. 15, sec. 33.

We need the faith to go a path untrod,
The power to be alone and vote with God.
EDWIN MARKHAM, *The Need of the Hour*.

16
A straw vote only shows which way the hot air blows.
O. HENRY. (*New American Literature*, p. 170.)

17
The freeman casting, with unpurchased hand,
The vote that shakes the turrets of the land.
O. W. HOLMES, *Poetry, a Metrical Essay*, l. 83.

A weapon that comes down as still
As snowflakes fall upon the sod;
But executes a freeman's will,
As lightning does the will of God;
And from its force, nor doors nor locks
Can shield you; 'tis the ballot-box.
JOHN PIERPONT, *A Word from a Petitioner*.

18
I am not one to hunt for the votes of a fickle public at the cost of suppers and gifts of

worn-out clothes. (Non ego ventosæ plebis suffragia venor Impensis cenarum et tritæ munere vestis.)

HORACE, *Epistles*. Bk. i, epis. 19, l. 37.

1
The right of election is the very essence of the constitution.

JUNIUS, *Letters*. No. 11, 24 Apr., 1769.

2
Among free men there can be no successful appeal from the ballot to the bullet.

ABRAHAM LINCOLN. (E. J. YOUNG, *The Lesson of the Hour: Magazine of History*. No. 43.)

I go for all sharing the privileges of the government who assist in bearing its burdens. Consequently I go for admitting all whites to the right of suffrage who pay taxes or bear arms, by no means excluding females.

ABRAHAM LINCOLN, *Letter*, 1836.

3
Is virtue verily found in voices?
Or is wisdom won when all win votes?

SWINBURNE, *A Word from the Psalmist*. St. 3.

Is a vote a coat? will franchise feed you,
Or words be a roof against the rain?

SWINBURNE, *A Word from the Psalmist*. St. 4.

4
All forward-looking minds know that, sooner or later, the chief public question in this country will be woman's claim to the ballot.

THEODORE TILTON. (*Independent*, 18 Jan., 1866.)

5
As long as I count the votes, what are you going to do about it?

WILLIAM MARCY TWEED, of the ballot in New York City, in November, 1871.

More men have been elected between Sundown and Sunup, than ever were elected between Sunup and Sundown.

WILL ROGERS, *The Illiterate Digest*, p. 152.

6
The votes of veering crowds are not
The things that are more excellent.

WILLIAM WATSON, *Things That Are More Excellent*.

7
Democracy's ceremonial, its feast, its great function, is the election.

H. G. WELLS, *Democracy*.

8
Your telegram received. I would feel deeply mortified to have you or anyone like you vote for me. Since you have access to many disloyal citizens and I have not, I will ask you to convey this message to them.

WOODROW WILSON. Answer to telegram from Jeremiah O'Leary, in campaign of 1916, threatening Wilson with the loss of pro-German votes.

VOW

See also Oath

9
Better is it that thou shouldest not vow, than that thou shouldest vow and not pay.

Old Testament: Ecclesiastes, v, 5.

10
Vow me no vows.

JOHN FLETCHER, *Wit without Money*. Act iv, sc. 4.

11
Oh why should vows so fondly made,
Be broken ere the morrow?

JAMES HOGG, *The Broken Heart*. *See also* LOVE: ITS PERJURIES.

12
A vow is a horrible thing, it is a snare for sin.

SAMUEL JOHNSON. (BOSWELL, *Life*, iii, 357.)

13
He who breaks a resolution is a weakling;
He who makes one is a fool.

F. M. KNOWLES, *A Cheerful Year Book*.

14
Vows with so much passion, swears with so much grace,
That 'tis a kind of Heaven to be deluded by him.

NATHANIEL LEE, *The Rival Queens*. Act i, sc. 1.

15
Ease would recant
Vows made in pain, as violent and void.

MILTON, *Paradise Lost*. Bk. iv, l. 96.

16
For priests will allow of a broken vow,
For penance or for gold.

SCOTT, *Bridal of Triermain*. Canto ii, st. 17.

17
These mouth-made vows
Which break themselves in swearing.

SHAKESPEARE, *Antony and Cleopatra*. Act i, sc. 3, l. 30.

18
Men's vows are women's traitors.

SHAKESPEARE, *Cymbeline*. Act iii, sc. 4, l. 56.

Ay, springes to catch woodcocks. I do know,
When the blood burns, how prodigal the soul
Lends the tongue vows.

SHAKESPEARE, *Hamlet*. Act i, sc. 3, l. 115.

Vows were ever brokers to defiling.

SHAKESPEARE, *A Lover's Complaint*, l. 173.

19
By all the vows that ever men have broke,
In number more than ever women spoke.

SHAKESPEARE, *A Midsummer-Night's Dream*. Act i, sc. 1, l. 175.

You put me off with limber vows.

SHAKESPEARE, *Winter's Tale*. Act i, sc. 2, l. 47.

20
The vow that binds too strictly snaps itself.

TENNYSON, *The Last Tournament*, l. 652.

VULGARITY

See also People

21
Vulgarity is an inadequate conception of the art of living.

MANDELL CREIGHTON, *Life and Letters*.

22
A thing is not vulgar merely because it is common.

WILLIAM HAZLITT, *Table-Talk: On Vulgarity*.

1
If a person has no delicacy, he has you in his power.
HAZLITT, *Literary Remains.* Vol. ii, p. 258.

2
Vulgarity is the eighth sin . . . and worse than all the others put together, since it perils your salvation in *this* world.
J. R. LOWELL, *On a Certain Condescension in Foreigners.*

3
Vulgarity is setting store by "the things that are seen."
SYDNEY, LADY MORGAN, *Diary,* 12 Sept., 1818.

Vulgarity is only in concealment of truth, or affectation.
JOHN RUSKIN, *Modern Painters.* Bk. ii, pt. ii, ch. 6, sec. 7.

The higher a man stands, the more the word "vulgar" becomes unintelligible to him.
JOHN RUSKIN, *Modern Painters.* Bk. iii, pt. iv, ch. 7, sec. 9.

4
So must the writer, whose productions should
Take with the vulgar, be of vulgar mould.
EDMUND WALLER, *To Mr. Killigrew.*

5
Vulgarity is simply the conduct of other people.
OSCAR WILDE, *An Ideal Husband.* Act iii.

6
One should absorb the colour of life, but one should never remember its details. Details are always vulgar.
OSCAR WILDE, *The Picture of Dorian Gray.* Ch. 8.

W

WAITING

7
Serene I fold my hands and wait.
JOHN BURROUGHS, *Waiting.*

For evermore I wait, and longer too.
ROBERT HENRYSON, *The Town and Country Mouse.*

But the waiting time, my brothers,
Is the hardest time of all.
SARAH DOUDNEY, *The Hardest Time of All.*

8
Who longest waits of all most surely wins.
HELEN HUNT JACKSON, *The Victory of Patience.*

9
Learn to labor and to wait.
LONGFELLOW, *A Psalm of Life.*

10
She knew the life-long martyrdom,
The weariness, the endless pain
Of waiting for some one to come
Who nevermore would come again.
LONGELLOW, *Vittoria Colonna.* St. 6.

11
They also serve who only stand and wait.
MILTON, *Sonnet: On His Blindness.*

12
Stulkeley: There is only one thing to be done.
Woodhouse: What's that?
Stulkeley: To wait and see.
Woodhouse: Wait and see!
Stulkeley: Wait and see what happens.
A. W. PINERO, *Preserving Mr. Panmure.* Act iii.

13
Everything comes to those who can wait. (Tout vient à point qui peut attendre.)
RABELAIS, *Works.* Bk. iv, ch. 48. (1548)

Everything comes if a man will only wait.
BENJAMIN DISRAELI, *Tancred.* Bk. iv, ch. 8.

All things come round to him who will but wait.
LONGFELLOW, *Tales of a Wayside Inn: The Student's Tale.* Last line, quoted.

Everything comes to him who hustles while he waits.
THOMAS A. EDISON. (*Golden Book,* Apr., 1931.)

Alas! all things come too late for those who wait.
JAMES HUNEKER, *Chopin,* p. 77.

Ah, "all things come to those who wait,"
(I say these words to make me glad),
But something answers, soft and sad,
"They come, but often come too late."
MARY MONTGOMERIE SINGLETON, *Tout Vient à Qui Sait Attendre.*

14
Patient waiters are no losers.
W. G. BENHAM, *Proverbs,* p. 824.

15
Although I enter not,
Yet round about the spot
Ofttimes I hover;
And near the sacred gate
With longing eyes I wait,
Expectant of her.
THACKERAY, *At the Church Gate.*

WALKING

16
They wha canna walk right are sure to come to wrang,
Creep awa', my bairnie, creep afore ye gang.
JAMES BALLANTINE, *Creep Afore Ye Gang.*

17
Never walk fast in the streets, which is a mark of vulgarity . . . though it may be tolerable in a tradesman.
LORD CHESTERFIELD, *Letters.*

18
I nauseate walking; 'tis a country diversion; I loathe the country.
CONGREVE, *The Way of the World.* Act iv, sc. 2

19
Why then do you walk around as though you had swallowed a spit? (Τί οὖν ἡμῖν ὀβελίσκον καταπιὼν περιπατεῖς.)
EPICTETUS, *Discourses.* Bk. i, ch. 21, sec. 2.

1
Before supper walk a little; after supper do the same. (Sub cœnam paulisper inambula; cœnatus idem facito.)

ERASMUS, *De Ratione Studii. See under* HEALTH.

1a
And auld shanks-naig wad tire, I dread,
To pace to Berwick.

ROBERT FERGUSSON, *Poems*, p. 333. (1773)

I'd rather . . . ride on Shanks's mare.

SAMUEL BISHOP, *Poetical Works*, i, 204. (1795)

The humblest conveyances known as 'Shanks's mare,' and the 'Marrowbone Stage.'

G. A. SALA, *Twice Round the Clock*, p. 87. (1859)

2
Walk with stretched forth necks and wanton eyes, walking and mincing as they go.

Old Testament: Isaiah, iii, 16.

3
Walking is the best possible exercise. Habituate yourself to walk very far. The Europeans value themselves on having subdued the horse to the uses of man; but I doubt whether we have not lost more than we have gained, by the use of this animal.

THOMAS JEFFERSON, *Writings*. Vol. v, p. 84.

4
And so to tread
As if the wind, not she. did walk;
Nor prest a flower, nor bow'd a stalk.

BEN JONSON, *Masques: The Vision of Delight*.

She walks the way primroses go.

ALINE KILMER, *Experience*.

I love that beauty should go beautifully.

TENNYSON, *Geraint and Enid*, l. 679.

5
I'll fetch a turn about the garden.

SHAKESPEARE, *Cymbeline*. Act i, sc. 1, l. 81.

Come, you and I must walk a turn together.

SHAKESPEARE, *Henry VIII*. Act v, sc. 1, l. 93.

6
I grant I never saw a goddess go;
My mistress, when she walks, treads on the ground.

SHAKESPEARE, *Sonnets*. No. cxxx.

7
Every walk is a sort of crusade, preached by some Peter the Hermit in us, to go forth and reconquer this Holy Land from the hands of the Infidels.

THOREAU, *Walking*. Explaining the fanciful derivation of saunter from *à la Sainte Terre*.

Solvitur ambulando [it is solved by walking]—the motto of the philosophic tramp.

F. W. MAITLAND, *Leslie Stephen*. Ch. 17.

WANDERLUST

See also Travel, Vagabond

8
The ships are lying in the bay,
The gulls are swinging round their spars;
My soul as eagerly as they
Desires the margin of the stars.

ZOË AKINS, *The Wanderer*.

9
Oh, which were best, to roam or rest?
The land's lap or the water's breast?

ROBERT BROWNING, *In a Gondola*.

10
I will take my pipes and go now, for the bees upon the sill
Are singing of the summer that is coming from the stars.

DONN BYRNE, *To the World's Edge*.

11
Again let us dream where the land lies sunny
And live, like the bees, on our hearts' old honey.
Away from the world that slaves for money—
Come, journey the way with me.

MADISON CAWEIN, *Song of the Road*.

12
And smalle foules maken melody,
That sleepen alle night with open eye,
(So pricketh them nature in their corages:)
Then longen folk to go on pilgrimages.

CHAUCER, *Canterbury Tales: Prologue*, l. 9.

13
We travel not for trafficking alone;
By hotter winds our fiery hearts are fanned:
For lust of knowing what should not be known.
We take the Golden Road to Samarkand.

JAMES ELROY FLECKER. *Hassan*. Act v. sc. 2.

We are the Pilgrims, master; we shall go
Always a little further: it may be
Beyond that last blue mountain barred with snow,
Across that angry or that glimmering sea.

JAMES ELROY FLECKER, *Hassan*. Act v, sc. 2.

14
Beyond the East the sunrise, beyond the West the sea,
And East and West the wander-thirst that will not let me be.

GERALD GOULD, *Wander-Thirst*.

15
Where forlorn sunsets flare and fade
On desolate sea and lonely sand,
Out of the silence and the shade
What is the voice of strange command
Calling you still, as friend calls friend
With love that cannot brook delay,
To rise and follow the ways that wend
Over the hills and far away? . . .
From faded hopes and hopes agleam,
It calls you, calls you night and day
Beyond the dark into the dream
Over the hills and far away.

W. E. HENLEY, *Rhymes and Rhythms*. No. 1. *See also under* HILLS.

Till a voice, as bad as Conscience, rang interminable changes
On one everlasting Whisper day and night repeated—so:
"Something hidden. Go and find it. Go and look behind the Ranges—
Something lost behind the Ranges. Lost and waiting for you. Go!"

RUDYARD KIPLING, *The Explorer*. St. 2.

16
I am fevered with the sunset,

I am fretful with the bay,
For the wander-thirst is on me
And my soul is in Cathay.
RICHARD HOVEY, *The Sea Gypsy.*

There's a schooner in the offing,
With her topsails shot with fire,
And my heart has gone aboard her
For the Islands of Desire.

I must forth again to-morrow!
With the sunset I must be
Hull down on the trail of rapture
In the wonder of the Sea.
RICHARD HOVEY, *The Sea Gypsy.*

1
Drop anchor anywhere and the anchor will drag—that is, if your soul is a limitless, fathomless sea, and not a dogpound.
ELBERT HUBBARD, *Epigrams.*

2
Upon the road to Romany
It 's stay, friend, stay!
There 's lots o' love and lots o' time
To linger on the way;
Poppies for the twilight,
Roses for the noon,
It 's happy goes as lucky goes,
To Romany in June.
WALLACE IRWIN, *From Romany to Rome.*

3
The white moth to the closing bine,
The bee to the opened clover,
And the gipsy blood to the gipsy blood
Ever the wide world over.
RUDYARD KIPLING, *The Gipsy Trail.* St. 1.

The pied snake to the rifted rock,
The buck to the stony plain,
And the Romany lass to the Romany lad,
And both to the road again.
RUDYARD KIPLING, *The Gipsy Trail.* St. 5.

Follow the Romany patteran
Sheer to the Austral Light,
Where the besom of God is the wild South wind,
Sweeping the sea-floors white.
RUDYARD KIPLING, *The Gipsy Trail.* St. 8.

In the days when we were gypsying,
A long time ago.
EDWIN RANSFORD, *Gypsying.*

What care I for my house and my land?
What care I for my money, O?
What care I for my new-wedded lord?
I'm off with the wraggle-taggle gipsies, O.
UNKNOWN, *The Wraggle-Taggle Gipsies.*

4
The wild hawk to the wind-swept sky,
The deer to the wholesome wold,
And the heart of a man to the heart of a maid,
As it was in the days of old.
RUDYARD KIPLING, *The Gipsy Trail.* St. 11.

The hawk unto the open sky,
The red deer to the wold;
The Romany lass for the Romany lad,
As in the days of old.
FREDERIC EDWARD WEATHERLY. (Cited in *N. Y. Times Book Review* as antedating Kipling.)

5
You have heard the beat of the off-shore wind,
And the thresh of the deep-sea rain;
You have heard the song—how long? how long?
Pull out on the trail again!
RUDYARD KIPLING, *The Long Trail.* St. 1.

Her plates are flaked by the sun, dear lass,
And her ropes are taut with the dew,
For we're booming down on the old trail, our own trail, the out trail,
We're sagging south on the Long Trail—the trail that is always new.
RUDYARD KIPLING, *The Long Trail.* St. 7.

The Lord knows what we may find, dear lass,
And The Deuce knows what we may do—
But we're back once more on the old trail, our own trail, the out trail,
We're down, hull-down, on the Long Trail—the trail that is always new!
RUDYARD KIPLING, *The Long Trail.* St. 10.

6
I'm the ramblin' son with the nervous feet
That never was made for a steady beat.
I had many a job—for a little while;
I've been on the bum, and I've lived in style,
But there was the road windin' mile after mile,
And nothing to do but go.
H. H. KNIBBS, *Nothing To Do But Go.*

7
The loose foot of the wanderer
Is curst as well as blest!
It urges ever, ever on
And never gives him rest. . . .
No maid will ever hold him long
Tho' she be trim and fair—
He urges ever, ever on
With star-dust in his hair.
HESPER LE GALLIENNE, *The Wanderer.*

8
I must go down to the seas again, to the lonely sea and the sky,
And all I ask is a tall ship and a star to steer her by,
And the wheel's kick and the wind's song and the white sail's shaking,
And a grey mist on the sea's face and a grey dawn breaking.
JOHN MASEFIELD, *Sea-Fever.* St. 1.

I must go down to the seas again to the vagrant gypsy life,
To the gull's way and the whale's way where the wind's like a whetted knife;
And all I ask is a merry yarn from a laughing fellow-rover,
And quiet sleep and a sweet dream when the long trick's over.
JOHN MASEFIELD, *Sea-Fever.* St. 3.

I must go; the sea has called me
As a mistress to her swain;
From the immemorial tumult

I shall drink of peace again.
F. O'NEILL GALLAGHER, *Sea Madness.*

1
Friends and loves we have none, nor wealth nor blest abode,
But the hope of the City of God at the other end of the road.
Not for us are content, and quiet, and peace of mind,
For we go seeking a city that we shall never find.
JOHN MASEFIELD, *The Seekers.* St. 1.

It's the white road westwards is the road I must tread
To the green grass, the cool grass, and rest for heart and head,
To the violets and the brown brooks and the thrushes' song
In the fine land, the west land, the land where I belong.
JOHN MASEFIELD, *The West Wind.*

2
It's little I know what's in my heart,
What's in my mind it's little I know,
But there's that in me must up and start,
And it's little I care where my feet go.
EDNA ST. VINCENT MILLAY, *Departure.*

3
Better sit still where born, I say,
Wed one sweet woman and love her well,
Love and be loved in the old East way,
Drink sweet waters, and dream in a spell,
Than to wander in search of the Blessed Isles,
And to sail the thousands of watery miles
In search of love, and find you at last
On the edge of the world, and a curs'd outcast.
JOAQUIN MILLER, *Pace Implora.*

4
Let us probe the silent places,
Let us seek what luck betide us.
ROBERT W. SERVICE, *Call of the Wild.*

5
Wealth I ask not, hope nor love,
Nor a friend to know me;
All I ask, the heavens above,
And the road below me.
R. L. STEVENSON, *The Vagabond.*

I cannot rest from travel; I will drink
Life to the lees.
ALFRED TENNYSON, *Ulysses,* l. 6.

Afoot and light-hearted I take to the open road,
Healthy, free, the world before me,
The long brown path before me leading wherever I choose.
Henceforth I ask not good-fortune, I myself am good-fortune,
Henceforth I whimper no more, postpone no more, need nothing,
Done with indoor complaints, libraries, querulous criticisms,
Strong and content I travel the open road.
WALT WHITMAN, *Song of the Open Road.*

6
I looked in his eyes and I read the news;
His heart was having the railroad blues.
Oh, the railroad blues will cost you dear,
Keeps you moving on for something that you don't see here.
RIDGELY TORRENCE, *Eye-Witness.*

7
So let the way wind up the hill or down,
O'er rough or smooth, the journey will be joy,
Still seeking what I sought when but a boy.
HENRY VAN DYKE, *Three Best Things.*

WANT AND WANTS

I—Want

See also Poverty

8
Want passed for merit at her open door.
DRYDEN, *Eleonora,* l. 32.

9
Want is a bitter and a hateful good,
Because its virtues are not understood;
Yet many things, impossible to thought,
Have been by need to full perfection brought.
DRYDEN, *The Wife of Bath,* l. 473. *See also* ADVERSITY: A BLESSING.

10
Want is a growing giant whom the coat of
Have was never large enough to cover.
EMERSON, *Conduct of Life: Wealth.*

11
We shall never solve the paradox of want in the midst of plenty by doing away with plenty.
OGDEN MILLS, *Speech,* New York, 21 March, 1934.

12
Bad is want which is born of plenty. (Mala est inopia, ex copia quæ nascitur.)
PUBLILIUS SYRUS, *Sententiæ.* No. 411.

13
Where nothing wants that want itself doth seek.
SHAKESPEARE, *Love's Labour's Lost.* Act iv, sc. 3, l. 237.

14
Wit's whetstone, Want, there made us quickly learn.
JOHN TAYLOR, *The Penniless Pilgrimage,* l. 211.

II—Wants

See also Wishes

15
I want what I want when I want it.
HENRY BLOSSOM. Title of one of the song successes of *Mlle. Modiste.* (1905)

16
Our real wants in a small compass lie.
CHARLES CHURCHILL, *Independence,* l. 465.

All our wants, beyond those which a very moderate income will supply, are purely imaginary.
HENRY ST. JOHN, *Letter to Swift,* 17 March, 1719.

Their wants but few, their wishes all confin'd.
GOLDSMITH, *The Traveller,* l. 210.

Man's rich with little, were his judgment true;
Nature is frugal, and her wants are few.
YOUNG, *Love of Fame*. Sat. v, l. 167.
See also MODERATION: ITS VIRTUES.

1
Little I ask: my wants are few;
I only wish a hut of stone,
(A *very plain* brown stone will do,)
That I may call my own;—
And close at hand is such a one,
In yonder street that fronts the sun.
O. W. HOLMES, *Contentment*. St. 1.

I care not much for gold or land;—
Give me a mortgage here and there,—
Some good bank-stock, some note of hand,
Or trifling railroad share,—
I only ask that Fortune send
A *little* more than I shall spend.
O. W. HOLMES, *Contentment*. St. 3.

Thus humble let me live and die,
Nor long for Midas' golden touch;
If Heaven more generous gifts deny,
I shall not miss them *much*,—
Too grateful for the blessing lent
Of simple tastes and mind content!
O. W. HOLMES, *Contentment*. St. 12.

I'd rather be handsome than homely;
I'd rather be youthful than old;
If I can't have a bushel of silver
I'll do with a barrel of gold.
JAMES JEFFREY ROCHE, *Contentment*.

2
Those who want much are always much in need. (Multa petentibus Desunt multa.)
HORACE, *Odes*. Bk. ii, ode 16, l. 42.

3
Things three, no more; but three are needful.
The one is clothing, to save thee from chill,
The one is meat, for thy health's sake,
The third is drink when thou driest.
LANGLAND, *Piers Plowman*. Passus i, l. 20.

4
That mortal wants least who desires least. (Is minimum eget mortalis, qui minimum cupit.)
PUBLILIUS SYRUS, *Sententiæ*. No. 316.

5
He that wants money, means and content is without three good friends.
SHAKESPEARE, *As You Like It*. Act iii, sc. 2, l. 26.

6
As long as I have a want, I have a reason for living. Satisfaction is death.
BERNARD SHAW, *Overruled*, p. 79.

7
My belief is that to have no wants is divine; to have as few as possible comes next to the divine. (*'Εγω δὲ νομίζω τὸ μὲν μηδενὸς δεῖσθαι θεῖον εἶναι*.)
SOCRATES, *Cyropædia*, viii, 3, 40. (Quoted by Xenophon, *Memorabilia*, i, 6, 10; Diogenes Laertius, *Socrates*. Sec. 10.)

Not much is wanted nor for long. (Nec multo opus est nec diu.)
SENECA.

8
The stoical scheme of supplying our wants by lopping off our desires, is like cutting off our feet, when we want shoes.
SWIFT, *Thoughts on Various Subjects*.

9
A thousand wants Gnarr at the heels of men.
TENNYSON, *In Memoriam*. Pt. xcviii.

10
In this world there are only two tragedies. One is not getting what one wants, and the other is getting it. The last is the real tragedy.
OSCAR WILDE, *Lady Windermere's Fan*. Act iii.

11
Man wants but little, nor that little long.
YOUNG, *Night Thoughts*. Night iv, l. 118. (1742)

Man wants but little here below,
Nor wants that little long.
GOLDSMITH, *Vicar of Wakefield*: Ch. 8, *The Hermit*. (1766)

"Man wants but little here below
Nor wants that little long,"
'Tis not with me exactly so;
But 'tis so in the song.
My wants are many, and, if told,
Would muster many a score;
And were each wish a mint of gold,
I still should long for more.
JOHN QUINCY ADAMS, *The Wants of Man*.

Man wants but little drink below,
But wants that little strong.
O. W. HOLMES, *A Song of Other Days*.

WANTONNESS

See also Love and Lust; Whore

12
Lewd fellows of the baser sort.
New Testament: Acts, xvii, 5.

13
Yet, while the Titian's Venus lies at rest,
A man looks.
ROBERT BROWNING, *Any Wife to Any Husband*.

The foulest, the vilest, the obscenest picture the world possesses—Titian's Venus. It isn't that she is naked and stretched out on a bed—no, it is the attitude of one of her arms and hand. . . . Without any question it was painted for a bagnio and was probably refused because it was a trifle too strong.
MARK TWAIN, *A Tramp Abroad*.

14
The sword I forsook for the sake of the church;
He ventured the soul, and I risked the body—
'Twas then I proved false to my sodger laddie.
ROBERT BURNS, *The Jolly Beggars*.

Wantonness for evermair,
Wantonness has been my ruin.
Yet for a' my drool and care
It's wantonness for evermair.
I hae lo'ed the Black, the Brown;
I hae lo'ed the Fair, the Gowden!
A' the colours in the town—

I hae won their wanton favour.
ROBERT BURNS, *Wantonness for Evermair.*

1
Unbridled wantonness caused unbridled desire. (Libido effrenata effrenatam appetentiam efficit.)
CICERO, *Tusculanarum Disputationum.* Bk. iv, ch. 7, sec. 15.

2
A jut with her bum would stir an anchoret.
CONGREVE, *Love for Love.* Act i, sc. 2.

3
Let not his hand within your bosom stray,
And rudely with your pretty bubbies play.
DRYDEN, *Imitations of Ovid: Amores.* Bk. i, eleg. 4, l. 45.

Her nipples red as cherries.
TIMOTHY KENDALL, *Flower of Epigrams,* 292. (1577)

Graze on my lips, and if those hills be dry,
Stray lower, where the pleasant fountains lie.
SHAKESPEARE, *Venus and Adonis,* l. 233.

They pressed
The yielding marble of her snowy breast.
EDMUND WALLER, *Of Her Passing Through a Crowd,* l. 11.

4
Bred only and completed to the taste
Of lustful appetence, to sing, to dance,
To dress, and troll the tongue, and roll the eye.
MILTON, *Paradise Lost.* Bk. xi, l. 614.

5
Lord! when you have enough, what need you care
How merrily soever others fare?
Tho' all the day I give and take delight,
Doubt not sufficient will be left at night.
'Tis but a just and rational desire
To light a taper at a neighbour's fire.
POPE, *The Wife of Bath: Prologue,* l. 134.

For 't is as sure as cold engenders hail,
A liquorish mouth must have a lecherous tail.
POPE, *The Wife of Bath: Prologue,* l. 217.

6
Is this that haughty, gallant, gay Lothario?
NICHOLAS ROWE, *The Fair Penitent.* Act v, sc. 1.

7
You think none but your sheets are privy to your wishes.
SHAKESPEARE, *Antony and Cleopatra,* Act i, sc. 2, l. 41.

Leave thy lascivious wassails.
SHAKESPEARE, *Antony and Cleopatra.* Act i, sc. 4, l. 56.

I take no pleasure In aught an eunuch has.
SHAKESPEARE, *Antony and Cleopatra.* Act i, sc. 5, l. 9.

8
But all the charms of love,
Salt Cleopatra, soften thy waned lip!
Let witchcraft join with beauty, lust with both.
SHAKESPEARE, *Antony and Cleopatra.* Act ii, sc. 1, l. 20.

This amorous surfeiter.
SHAKESPEARE, *Antony and Cleopatra.* Act ii, sc. 1, l. 33.

9
You have tasted her in bed.
SHAKESPEARE, *Cymbeline.* Act ii, sc. 4, l. 57.

When the brown wench
Lay kissing in your arms.
SHAKESPEARE, *Henry VIII.* Act iii, sc. 2, l. 295.

In woman out-paramoured the Turk.
SHAKESPEARE, *King Lear.* Act iii, sc. 4, l. 94.

10
What was thy cause? Adultery?
Thou shalt not die: die for adultery? No!
The wren goes to 't, and the small gilded fly
Does lecher in my sight. Let copulation thrive.
SHAKESPEARE, *King Lear.* Act iv, sc. 6, l. 111.

11
There's no bottom, none,
In my voluptuousness: your wives, your daughters,
Your matrons and your maids, could not fill up
The cistern of my lust.
SHAKESPEARE, *Macbeth.* Act iv, sc. 3, l. 60.

We have willing dames enough.
SHAKESPEARE, *Macbeth.* Act iv, sc. 3, l. 73.

12
He hath not yet made wanton the night with her; and she is sport for Jove. . . . I'll warrant her, full of game.
SHAKESPEARE, *Othello.* Act ii, sc. 3, l. 16.

As prime as goats, as hot as monkeys,
As salt as wolves in pride.
SHAKESPEARE, *Othello.* Act iii, sc. 3, l. 403.

13
Since I have taken such pains to bring you together, let all pitiful goers-between be called to the world's end after my name; call them all Pandars; . . . all brokers-between Pandars.
SHAKESPEARE, *Troilus and Cressida.* Act iii, sc. 2, l. 207.

14
His dunghill thoughts, which do themselves enure
To dirty dross, no higher dare aspire,
Nor can his feeble earthly eyes endure
The flaming light of that celestial fire.
SPENSER, *An Hymn in Honour of Love,* l. 183. Referring to lust.

15
For always thee the fervid languid glories
Allured of heavier seas and mightier skies;
Thine ears knew all the wandering watery sighs
Where the sea sobs round Lesbian promontories.
SWINBURNE, *Ave Atque Vale.* St. 2. Referring to Charles Baudelaire.

WAR

See also Soldier

I—War: Definitions

A meditation on the conduct of political societies made old Hobbes imagine that war was the state of nature.
EDMUND BURKE, *Vindication of Natural Society.*

Hobbes clearly proves that every creature
Lives in a state of war by nature.
SWIFT, *Poetry: A Rhapsody.*

2
War is pusillanimously carried out in this degenerate age; quarter is given; towns are taken and the people spared: even in a storm, a woman can hardly hope for the benefit of a rape.
LORD CHESTERFIELD, *Letters*, 12 Jan., 1757.

3
O great corrector of enormous times,
Shaker of o'er-rank states, thou grand decider
Of dusty and old titles, that heal'st with blood
The earth when it is sick, and cure'st the world
O' the pleurisy of people.
JOHN FLETCHER, *Two Noble Kinsmen.* Act v, sc. 1.

4
War's a brain-spattering, windpipe-slitting art,
Unless her cause by right be sanctified.
BYRON, *Don Juan.* Canto ix, st. 4.

Carnage, so Wordsworth tells you, is God's daughter.
BYRON, *Don Juan.* Canto viii, st. 9.

But Thy most dreaded instrument,
In working out a pure intent,
Is Man—arrayed for mutual slaughter,
Yea, Carnage is thy daughter.
WORDSWORTH, *Ode*, 1815. St. 4. Changed in later editions.

5
All battle is well said to be Misunderstanding.
CARLYLE, *French Revolution.* Pt. iii, bk. 3, ch. 2.

6
In war events of importance are the result of trivial causes. (In bello parvis momentis magni casus intercedunt.)
CÆSAR, *De Bello Gallico.* Bk. i, sec. 21. *See also under* TRIFLES.

7
The art of war, which I take to be the highest perfection of human knowledge.
DANIEL DEFOE, *The History of Projects: Introduction.*

Our wearisome pedantic art of war,
By which we prove retreat may be success,
Delay best speed, half loss, at times, whole gain.
ROBERT BROWNING, *Luria.* Act i.

8
War is the trade of kings.
DRYDEN, *King Arthur.* Act ii, sc. 2.

9
Military glory—that attractive rainbow that rises in showers of blood, that serpent's eye that charms to destroy.
ABRAHAM LINCOLN, *Speech Against the War with Mexico*, House of Representatives, 12 Jan., 1848.

From rank showers of blood,
And the red light of blazing roofs, you build
The Rainbow Glory, and to shuddering Conscience
Cry,—Lo, the Bridge to Heaven!
BULWER-LYTTON, *Richelieu.* Act i, sc. 2.

10
When he drew the sword, he threw away the scabbard. . . . He knew that the essence of war is violence, and that moderation in war is imbecility.
MACAULAY, *Essays: Lord Nugent's Memorials of Hampden.* Referring to John Hampden.

11
War should be the only study of a prince. He should consider peace only as a breathing-time, which gives him leisure to contrive, and furnishes ability to execute, military plans.
MACHIAVELLI, *The Prince.*

And by a prince, he means every sort of state, however constituted.
BURKE, *Vindication of Natural Society.*

12
Two armies are two bodies which meet and try to frighten each other.
NAPOLEON I, *Sayings of Napoleon.*

13
It is the province of kings to cause war, and of God to end it. (Penes Reges est inferre bellum, penes autem Deum terminare.)
CARDINAL POLE, to Henry VIII. (*Notes and Queries*, 27 Jan., 1917.)

14
War should be long in preparing in order that you may conquer the more quickly. (Diu apparadum est bellum, ut vincas celerius.)
PUBLILIUS SYRUS, *Sententiæ.* No. 145.

15
The right of war, let him take who take can. (Droit de guerre, Qui potest capere, capiat.)
RABELAIS, *Works.* Bk. ii, ch. 26.

It is war's prize to take all vantage.
SHAKESPEARE, *III Henry VI.* Act i, sc. 4, l. 59; SCHILLER, *Wallenstein's Tod.* Act i, sc. 4.

ALL FAIR IN LOVE AND WAR, *see under* LOVE.

16
War, the needy bankrupt's last resort.
NICHOLAS ROWE, *Pharsalia.* Bk. i, l. 343.

17
Qualities of mind avail most in war. (In bello plurumum ingenium posse.)
SALLUST, *Catiline.* Ch. ii, sec. 2.

An army is of little value in the field unless there are wise counsels at home. (Parvi enim sunt foris arma, nisi est consilium domi.)
CICERO, *De Officiis.* Bk. i, ch. 22, sec. 76.

Yield, ye arms, to the toga. (Cedant arma togæ.)
CICERO, *De Officiis.* Bk. i, ch. 22, sec. 77.

18
It is always easy to begin a war, but very

difficult to stop one, since its beginning and end are not under the control of the same man. Anyone, even a coward, can commence a war, but it can be brought to an end only with the consent of the victors.

SALLUST, *Jugurtha*. Sec. 83.

Your breath first kindled the dead coal of wars . . .
And brought in matter that should feed this fire;
And now 'tis far too huge to be blown out
With that same weak wind which enkindled it.

SHAKESPEARE, *King John*. Act v, sc. 2, l. 83.

1

Military service produces moral imbecility, ferocity and cowardice, and the defence of nations must be undertaken by the civil enterprise of men enjoying all the rights and liberties of citizenship

BERNARD SHAW, *John Bull's Other Island: Preface*.

There is only one virtue, pugnacity; only one vice, pacifism. That is an essential condition of war.

SHAW, *Heartbreak House: Introductory*.

2

War is the statesman's game, the priest's delight,
The lawyer's jest, the hired assassin's trade.

SHELLEY, *Queen Mab* Pt. iv. l. 168.

War, that mad game the world so loves to play.

SWIFT, *Ode to Sir William Temple*.

But war 's a game, which, were their subjects wise,
Kings would not play at.

COWPER, *The Task*. Bk. v, l. 187.

3

Warfare seems to signify blood and iron. (Cædes videtur significare sanguinem et ferrem.)

QUINTILIAN, *Declamationes*, 360.

It is not by speeches and resolutions that the great questions of the time are decided . . . but by iron and blood. (Eisen und Blut.)

BISMARCK, *Speech*, in the Prussian House of Delegates, 30 Sept., 1862.

Not with dreams but with blood and iron,
Shall a nation be moulded at last.

SWINBURNE, *A Word for the Country*.

4

Gold and riches, the chief causes of wars. (Aurum et opes, præcipuæ bellorum causæ.)

TACITUS, *History*. Bk. iv, sec. 74.

War seldom enters but where wealth allures.

DRYDEN, *Hind and the Panther*. Pt. ii, l. 706.

War is the child of pride, and pride the daughter of riches.

SWIFT, *The Battle of the Books*. Quoted as "an almanac saying."

Their seducers have wished war . . . for the loaves and fishes which arise out of war expenses.

THOMAS JEFFERSON, *Writings*. Vol. iv, p. 300. Paraphrasing *John*, vi, 26.

"Stroll down Fifth Avenue and observe the luxuries demanded by women, and you will understand why wars are waged," was the gist of a recent statement by an American general, discussing commodities for which our merchants scour the earth.

CARLETON BEALS, *The Drag-Net of War*. (*Scribner's Magazine*, June, 1931.)

II—War: Apothegms

5

The joys of battle. (Certaminis gaudia.)

ATTILA, at the battle of Chalons. (JORDANUS OF RAVENNA, *De Getarum Origine*. Ch. 39.)

6

Carry on, carry on, for the men and boys are gone,
But the furrow shan't lie fallow while the women carry on.

JANET BEGBIE, *Carry On*.

7

Better pointed bullets than pointed speeches. (Lieber Spitzkugeln als Spitzreden.)

BISMARCK, *Speech*, during the Hesse-Cassel insurrection of 1850.

8

It is magnificent, but it is not war. (C'est magnifique, mais ce n'est pas la guerre.)

GENERAL PIERRE BOSQUET, watching the charge of the Light Brigade at Balaklava, 28 Oct., 1854.

A feat of chivalry, fiery with consummate courage, and bright with flashing valour.

DISRAELI, *Speech*, House of Commons, 15 Dec., 1855.

9

War never leaves where it found a nation.

EDMUND BURKE, *Letters on a Regicide Peace*. No. 1.

Red Battle stamps his foot, and nations feel the shock.

BYRON, *Childe Harold*. Canto i, st. 38.

10

War, war is still the cry, "War even to the knife."

BYRON, *Childe Harold*. Canto i, st. 86.

War even to the knife. (Guerra al cuchillo.)

JOSÉ DE PALAFOX, Governor of Saragossa, when summoned to surrender by the French, in 1808.

We made war to the end—to the very end of the end.

GEORGES CLEMENCEAU, *Message to the American People*, Sept., 1918.

11

Brave Broglie, "with a whiff of grapeshot (*salve de canons*)," if need be, will give quick account of it.

CARLYLE, *French Revolution*. Pt. i, bk. 5, ch. 3.

The whiff of grapeshot can, if needful, become a blast and tempest.

CARLYLE, *French Revolution*. Pt. i, bk. 5, ch. 3.

Singular: in old Broglie's time, six years ago, this Whiff of Grapeshot was promised; but it could not be given then. . . . Now, however, the time is come for it, and the man [Napoleon]; and behold, you have it.

CARLYLE, *French Revolution*. Pt. i, bk. 7, ch. 7.

1
Carthage must be destroyed. (Delenda est Carthago.)

Marcus Cato. Cato's hatred and fear of Carthage was such that he concluded every speech, every letter and every conversation with the words, *Ceterum censeo, Carthaginem esse delendam*, "In my opinion, Carthage must be destroyed." (*Δοκεῖ δέ μοι καὶ Καρχηδόνα μὴ εἶναι*.) (Plutarch, *Lives: Marcus Cato*. Ch. 27, sec. 1.) Publius Scipio Nasica always countered with, "In my opinion, Carthage must be spared."

2
War to the castle, peace to the cabin! (Guerre aux châteaux, paix aux chaumières!)

Sebastian Chamfort, *mot d'ordre* during French Revolution, promulgated by Cambon

3
And 'mid this tumult Kubla heard from far
Ancestral voices prophesying war!

S. T. Coleridge, *Kubla Khan*, l. 29.

4
The flames of Moscow were the aurora of the liberty of the world.

Benjamin Constant, *Esprit de Conquête: Preface*. (1813)

5
The battle is lost, but there is time to gain another.

Marshal Louis Charles Desaix, to Napoleon, who thought at four o'clock in the afternoon, that the battle of Marengo was lost. Desaix's division saved the day, though, in the advance, he was shot through the heart. Napoleon had him buried at the summit of the St Bernard Pass, saying, "His tomb shall have the Alps for its pedestal." (O'Meara, *Napoleon in Exile*.)

My centre is giving way, my right retreats, situation excellent, I am attacking. (Mon centre cède, ma droite recule, situation excellente, j'attaque.)

Gen. Ferdinand Foch, *Report*, to Marshal Joffre, at second battle of the Marne, July, 1918.

6
They brought the elephant of Asia to convey the artillery of Europe to dethrone one of the kings of Africa, and to hoist the standard of St. George upon the mountains of Rasselas.

Benjamin Disraeli, *Speech*, House of Commons, 1868, moving a vote of thanks to Sir Robert Napier's army after the Abyssinian campaign.

7
By the rude bridge that arched the flood,
 Their flag to April's breeze unfurled,
Here once the embattled farmers stood,
 And fired the shot heard round the world.

Emerson, *Hymn: Sung at the Completion of the Concord Monument, April 19, 1836*. First printed in a broadside distributed at the exercises.

The cannon will not suffer any other sound to be heard for miles and for years around it.

Emerson, *Journals*, 1864.

8
The War-god loathes those who hesitate (*Ἄρης στυγεῖ μέλλοντας*)

Euripides, *Herakleidai*, l. 722. *See also under* Hesitation

The less they spared themselves in battle, the safer they would be. (Quanto sibi in proelio minus pepercissent, tanto tutiores fore.)

Sallust, *Jugurtha*. Ch. cvii, sec. 1. Quoting Sulla.

But cautious Queensberry left the war,
Th' unmanner'd dust might soil his star;
 Besides, he hated bleeding.

Robert Burns, *Second Epistle to Robert Graham*. l. 55.

He Who Fights and Runs Away, *see under* Discretion.

9
I hate war, for it spoils conversation.

Fontanelle. (Emerson, *Miscellanies: War*.)

10
Every position must be held to the last man; there must be no retirement. With our backs to the wall, and believing in the justice of our cause, each one of us must fight on to the end.

Field-Marshal Sir Douglas Haig, *Order of the Day*, 12 April, 1918.

11
Gentlemen of the French Guard, fire first!

Lord Charles Hay, lieutenant of the First Grenadier Guards, at the battle of Fontenoy, 30 April, 1745. Comte d'Auteroches, commanding the French Guards, is said to have replied, "Sir, the French Guards never fire first; please to fire yourselves." (Fournier, *L'Esprit dans L'Histoire*.) The story is probably a fabrication.

12
Force and fraud are in war the two cardinal virtues.

Thomas Hobbes, *Leviathan*. Pt. i, ch. 13.

13
Establish the eternal truth that acquiescence under insult is not the way to escape war.

Thomas Jefferson, *Writings*. Vol. ix, p. 308. *See also under* Preparedness.

14
There is no such thing as an inevitable war. If war comes it will be from failure of human wisdom

Bonar Law, *Speech*, July, 1914.

15
In war it is not permitted to make a mistake twice.

Lamarchus. (Plutarch, *Apothegms*. No. 186.)

16
It was but chance of war.

Sir David Lindsay, *History and Testament of Squire Meldrum*, l. 1832. (1550)

 The chance of war
Is equal, and the slayer oft is slain.

Homer, *Iliad*. Bk. xviii, l. 388. (Bryant, tr.)

The chance of war.

Shakespeare, *Cymbeline*. Act v, sc. 5, l. 75. (1610)

The fortune of war.

Attributed to Reis Dragut, 16th century Barbary corsair, while serving as a galley-slave.

1
Here I am and here I stay. (J'y suis, et j'y reste.)

MARSHAL MACMAHON, after he had taken the Malakof fortress by assault, during the siege of Sebastopol, 8 Sept., 1855, and been warned that the fort might be blown up. A letter from General Biddulph to Germain Bapst states that MacMahon uttered the phrase to him. (*L'Éclair*, May, 1908.) Gabriel Hanotaux (*Contemporary France*) states that MacMahon denied this. The Marquis de Castellane (*Revue Hebdomadaire*, May, 1908) asserts that he himself coined the phrase during a speech in the National Assembly and attributed it to MacMahon. (See also *Notes and Queries*, 15 July, 1911.) Used by Victor Emmanuel at the occupation of Rome by the Italian army, Sept., 1870.

2
Wars and rumours of wars.

New Testament: Matthew, xxiv, 6.

3
For what can war but endless war still breed?

MILTON, *Sonnets: To Lord Fairfax*.

4
They shall not pass. (Ils ne passeront pas.)

GENERAL PÉTAIN, at the battle of Verdun, Feb., 1916. The phrase, an echo of the old Garibaldian battle-cry, became a slogan for the entire French nation. (N. Y. *Times*, 6 May, 1917.) It has been claimed for Gen Nivelle.)

Thou shalt not pass.

Old Testament: Numbers, xx, 18.

You may not pass, you must return.

SHAKESPEARE, *Coriolanus*. Act v, sc. 2, l. 5.

They shall not pass till the stars be darkened:
Two swords crossed in front of the Hun;
Never a groan but God has harkened,
Counting their cruelties one by one.

KATHARINE LEE BATES, *Crossed Swords*.

They shall not pass, tho' battleline
May bend, and foe with foe combine,
Tho' death rain on them from the sky
Till every fighting man shall die,
France shall not yield to German Rhine.

ALICE M. SHEPARD, *They Shall Not Pass*.

5
The bird of war is not the eagle but the stork.

CHARLES FRANCIS POTTER, *Speech*, at Senate hearing on birth control bill, 1931.

6
The notable ferocity of non-combatants.

ARTHUR RIMBAUD, *Letter to Izambard*.

War hath no fury like a non-combatant.

C. E. MONTAGUE, *Disenchantment*.

7
I feel an army in my fist. (Ich fühle eine Armee in meiner Faust.)

SCHILLER, *Die Räuber*. Act ii, sc. 3.

Can I summon armies from the earth?
Or grow a cornfield on my open palm?
(Kann ich Armeen aus der Erde stampfen?
Wächst mir ein Kornfeld in der flachen Hand?)

SCHILLER, *Jungfrau von Orleans*. Act i, sc. 3.

8
Whose ponderous grate and massy bar
Had oft rolled back the tide of war.

SCOTT, *Lay of the Last Minstrel: Intro.*, l. 33.

9
Worse than war is the fear of war. (Pejor est bello timor ipse belli.)

SENECA, *Thyestes*, l. 572.

10
All was lost, But that the heavens fought.

SHAKESPEARE, *Cymbeline*. Act v, sc. 3, l. 3.

There is war in the skies!

OWEN MEREDITH, *Lucile*. Pt. i, canto 4, st. 12.

11
And Cæsar's spirit, ranging for revenge,
With Até by his side come hot from hell,
Shall in these confines with a monarch's voice
Cry "Havoc," and let slip the dogs of war.

SHAKESPEARE, *Julius Cæsar*. Act iii, sc. 1, l. 270.

The punishment of him that crieth havoc, and of them that followeth him. (Item si quis inventus fuerit qui clamorem inciperit qui vocatur havok.)

UNKNOWN, *The Office of the Constable and Marshall in Time of War*. (c. 1375) To cry "Havoc!" was to give the command to massacre without quarter.

12
Horribly stuff'd with epithets of war.

SHAKESPEARE, *Othello*. Act i, sc. 1, l. 14.

13
Pride, pomp, and circumstance of glorious war!

SHAKESPEARE, *Othello*. Act iii, sc. 3, l. 354.

Battle's magnificently stern array!

BYRON, *Childe Harold*. Canto iii, st. 28.

14
Grim-visaged war hath smooth'd his wrinkled front.

SHAKESPEARE, *Richard III*. Act i, sc. 1, l. 9.

15
If God gave the hand, let not Man withhold the sword. All have the right to fight: none have the right to judge. To Man the weapon: to Heaven the victory. Peace shall not prevail save with a sword in her hand. Nothing is ever done in this world until men are prepared to kill each other if it is not done.

BERNARD SHAW, *Major Barbara*. Act iii. The Undershaft mottoes for their munitions plant.

16
There is many a boy here today who looks on war as all glory, but, boys, it is all hell. You can bear this warning voice to generations yet to come. I look upon war with horror.

WILLIAM TECUMSEH SHERMAN, *Address*, before a G. A. R. convention at Columbus, Ohio, 11 Aug., 1880. It was no doubt from this extempore speech that somebody coined the epigram, "War is hell," which Sherman could never remember having uttered. (*See* Lewis, *Sherman, Fighting Prophet*.) Various persons have asserted that they heard the phrase spoken by Sherman at other places, but no real evidence that it was has ever been discovered.

War is hell when you're getting licked!

BRIGADIER-GENERAL HENRY J. O'REILLY (*Outlook*, 28 Oct., 1931) asserts that this is what Sherman really said, and is confirmed by Col. J. R. M. Taylor, but without convincing evidence.

You cannot qualify war in harsher terms than I will. War is cruelty, and you cannot refine it.

WILLIAM TECUMSEH SHERMAN, *Memoirs*, ii, 126.

This is the soldier brave enough to tell
The glory-dazzled world that War is hell:
Lover of peace, he looks beyond the strife,
And rides through hell to save his country's life.

HENRY VAN DYKE, *Saint-Gaudens' Equestrian Statue of General Sherman*. This quatrain was not used by the sculptor because Sherman's coining of the phrase was thought not to be sufficiently authenticated.

O war! thou son of hell!

SHAKESPEARE, *II Henry VI*. Act v, sc. 2, l. 33.

1
We wage no war with women nor with Priests.

SOUTHEY, *Madoc in Wales*. Pt. xv, l. 65.

2
A wise man should try everything before resorting to arms. (Omnia prius experiri, quam armis sapientem decet.)

TERENCE, *Eunuchus*, l. 789. (Act iv, sc. 7.)

3
Arms and the man I sing, who, forced by fate,
And haughty Juno's unrelenting hate.
(Arma virumque cano, Troiæ qui primus ab oris
Italiam fato profugus . . . sæva memorem
Junonis ob iram.)

VERGIL, *Æneid*. Bk. i, l. 1. (Dryden, tr.)

4
Mad I take arms, yet little reason is there in arms. (Arma amens capio; nec sat rationis in armis.)

VERGIL, *Æneid*. Bk. ii, l. 314.

5
Mars, unscrupulous god of war, rages throughout the world. (Sævit toto Mars impius orbe.)

VERGIL, *Georgics*. Bk. i, l. 511.

The question of war has become the main preoccupation of humanity.

WILLIAM BOLITHO, *Twelve Against the Gods: Woodrow Wilson*, p. 342.

But what most showed the vanity of life
Was to behold the nations all on fire.

THOMSON, *Castle of Indolence*. Canto i, st. 55.

6
Three Nations of French Indians had taken up the hatchet.

GEORGE WASHINGTON, *Journal*. Vol. i, p. 21.

7
The war, then, must go on. We must fight it through.

DANIEL WEBSTER, *Supposed Speech of John Adams*.

8
They went to war against a preamble, they fought seven years against a declaration.

DANIEL WEBSTER, *Speech on the Presidential Protest*, 17 May, 1834.

9
A great country cannot wage a little war.

DUKE OF WELLINGTON. (FRANCIS, *Maxims and Opinions of Wellington*, p. 390.)

Of old, between two nations was great war:
Its cause no mortal knew; nor when begun;
Therefore they combated so much the more,
The sire his sword bequeathing to his son.

AUBREY DE VERE, *Infant Bridal*. Pt. i, sec. 1.

10
As long as war is regarded as wicked it will always have its fascinations. When it is looked upon as vulgar, it will cease to be popular.

OSCAR WILDE, *The Critic as Artist*.

11
Every bullet has its billet.

WILLIAM III, *Saying*.

King William . . . would often say to his soldiers that "every ball had its billet."

STERNE, *Tristram Shandy*. Bk. viii, ch. 19.

He never received a wound. So true is the old saying of King William, that "every bullet has its billet."

JOHN WESLEY, *Journal*, 6 June, 1765.

Sufficeth this to prove my theme withal,
That every bullet hath a lighting place.

GEORGE GASCOIGNE, *Fruits of War*.

Every shot has its commission, d'ye see?

SMOLLETT, *The Reprisal*. Act iii, sc. 8.

What argufies pride and ambition?
Soon or late death will take us in tow:
Each bullet has got its commission,
And when our time's come we must go.

CHARLES DIBDIN, *The Benevolent Tar*.

12
It is not an army that we must train for war; it is a nation.

WOODROW WILSON, *Speech*, 12 May, 1917.

The war to end war.

H. G. WELLS. Claimed by him in *Liberty*, 29 Dec., 1934, p. 4. Usually credited to Woodrow Wilson.

13
No man's land.

UNKNOWN, *Chronicles of Edward I*. Rolls i, 291. (1320) A phrase used to indicate waste ground between two kingdoms. Hence its use in the World War.

There happened so grievous a pestilence in London, that . . . the dead might seem to justle one another. . . . Whereupon this bishop [Ralph de Stratford, d. 1354] bought ground near Smithfield. It was called *No-man's-land*, . . . as designed and consecrated for the general sepulture of the deceased.

THOMAS FULLER, *Worthies of England*, iii, 227. (1662)

This was a kind of border that might be called no man's land.

DANIEL DEFOE, *Robinson Crusoe*, ii, 563. (The most famous No Man's Land in the United States was a strip of territory 35 miles wide and 167 miles long ceded to the Government by Texas in 1850, and without form of government until incorporated with Oklahoma in 1890. It was the refuge of outlaws and hostile Indians.)

The General came in a new tin hat
To the shell-torn front where the war was at.
With a faithful aide at his good right hand,
He made his way to No-Man's-Land
ARTHUR GUITERMAN, *Pershing at the Front.*

III—War: Its Virtues

1 My voice is still for war.
Gods! can a Roman senate long debate
Which of the two to choose, slav'ry or death?
ADDISON, *Cato.* Act ii, sc. 1.

My sentence is for open war.
MILTON, *Paradise Lost.* Bk. ii, l. 51.

2
War is a biological necessity of the first importance, a regulative element in the life of mankind which cannot be dispensed with. . . . But it is not only a biological law but a moral obligation and, as such, an indispensable factor in civilization.
BERNHARDI, *Germany and the Next War.* Ch. 1.

The inevitableness, the idealism, and the blessing of war, as an indispensable and stimulating law of development, must be repeatedly emphasized.
BERNHARDI, *Germany and the Next War.* Ch. 1.

3
Know that relentless strife
Remains, by sea and land,
The holiest law of life. . . .
From fear in every guise,
From sloth, from love of pelf,
By war's great sacrifice
The world redeems itself.
JOHN DAVIDSON, *War Song.*

4
You may think there are greater things than war. I do not; I worship the Lord of Hosts.
BENJAMIN DISRAELI, *Coningsby.* Bk. iii, ch. 1.

5
War educates the senses, calls into action the will, perfects the physical constitution, brings men into such swift and close collision in critical moments that man measures man.
EMERSON, *Miscellanies: War.*

6
War is delightful to those who have had no experience of it. (Dulce bellum inexpertis.)
ERASMUS, *Adagia.* Chil. iv, cent. 1, No. 1.

How sweet war is to such as know it not.
GEORGE GASCOIGNE, *Posies,* 147. (1575)

7
Rash combat oft immortalizes man.
If he should fall, he is renowned in song.
(Der rasche Kampf verewigt einen Mann,
Er falle gleich, so preiset ihn das Lied.)
GOETHE, *Iphigenia auf Tauris.* Act v, sc. 6, l. 43.

8
Terrible as is war, it yet displays the spiritual grandeur of man daring to defy his mightiest hereditary enemy—Death.
HEINE, *Wit, Wisdom, and Pathos.*

9
Life's sovereign moment is a battle won.
O. W. HOLMES, *The Banker's Secret.*

The spice of life is battle.
R. L. STEVENSON, *Memories and Portraits: Talk and Talkers.*

Being ready, hope for the battle. (Pugnam sperate parati.)
VERGIL, *Æneid.* Bk. ix, l. 158.

10
To those to whom war is necessary it is just; and a resort to arms is righteous for those to whom no other hope remains. (Justum est bellum, quibus necessarium; et pia arma, quibus nulla nisi in armis relinquitur opes.)
LIVY, *History.* Bk. ix, sec. 1.

Wars are just to those to whom they are necessary. (Justa bella quibus necessaria.)
EDMUND BURKE, *Reflections on the Revolution in France.*

Ye say, a good cause will hallow even war? I say unto you: a good war halloweth every cause. War and courage have done more great things than charity.
FRIEDRICH NEITZSCHE, *Thus Spake Zarathustra: Of War and Warriors.*

The arms are fair,
When the intent of bearing them is just.
SHAKESPEARE, *I Henry IV.* Act v, sc. 2, l. 88.

11
Not but wut abstract war is horrid,
I sign to thet with all my heart,—
But civilysation *doos* git forrid
Sometimes upon a powder-cart.
J. R. LOWELL, *Biglow Papers.* Ser. i, No. 7.

12
War is the only sport that is genuinely amusing. And it is the only sport that has any intelligible use.
H. L. MENCKEN, *Prejudices.* Ser. v, p. 28.

13
To overcome in battle, and subdue
Nations, and bring home spoils with infinite
Man-slaughter, shall be held the highest pitch
Of human glory.
MILTON, *Paradise Lost.* Bk. xi, l. 687.

14
A really great people, proud and high-spirited, would face all the disasters of war rather than purchase that base prosperity which is bought at the price of national honor.
THEODORE ROOSEVELT, *Speech,* Harvard University, 23 Feb., 1907.

15
To the wars, my boy, to the wars!
He wears his honour in a box unseen,
That hugs his kicky-wicky here at home.
SHAKESPEARE, *All's Well that Ends Well.* Act ii, sc. 3, l. 295.

He that is truly dedicate to war
Hath no self-love.
SHAKESPEARE, *II Henry VI.* Act v, sc. 2, l. 37.

16
I drew this gallant head of war,
And cull'd these fiery spirits from the world,
To outlook conquest and to win renown
Even in the jaws of danger and of death.
SHAKESPEARE, *King John.* Act v, sc. 2, l. 113.

I do not advise you to work, but to fight. I do not advise you to conclude peace, but to conquer. Let your work be a fight, your peace a victory!
FRIEDRICH NEITZSCHE, *Thus Spake Zarathustra: Of War and Warriors.*

1
War is elevating, because the individual disappears before the great conception of the state. . . . What a perversion of morality to wish to abolish heroism among men!
TREITSCHKE, *Politics.* Vol. i, p. 74.

God will see to it that war always recurs as a drastic medicine for the human race.
TREITSCHKE, *Politics.* Vol. i, p. 76.

A thousand touching traits testify to the sacred power of the love which a righteous war awakes in noble nations.
TREITSCHKE, *German History.* Vol. i, p. 482.

2
From the blood of battlefields spring daisies and buttercups.
ISRAEL ZANGWILL, *The Melting-Pot.* Act iv.

How that red rain hath made the harvest grow.
BYRON, *Childe Harold.* Canto iii, st. 17.

IV—War: Its Horrors

3
Hence bloody wars at first began,
The artificial plague of man,
That from his own invention rise,
To scourge his own iniquities.
SAMUEL BUTLER, *Satire Upon the Weakness and Misery of Man,* l. 105.

4
War in fact is becoming contemptible, and ought to be put down by the great nations of Europe, just as we put down a vulgar mob.
MORTIMER COLLINS, *Thoughts in My Garden.*

5
War lays a burden on the reeling state.
COWPER, *Expostulation,* l. 306.

6
Hence jarring sectaries may learn
Their real interest to discern;
That brother should not war with brother,
And worry and devour each other.
COWPER, *The Nightingale and Glow-Worm.*

7
The angel, Pity, shuns the walks of war!
ERASMUS DARWIN, *The Loves of the Plants.* Canto iii, l. 298.

8
War, he sung, is toil and trouble.
DRYDEN, *Alexander's Feast,* l. 99.

9
War gratifies, or used to gratify, the combative instinct of mankind, but it gratifies also the love of plunder, destruction, cruel discipline, and arbitrary power.
C. W. ELIOT, *Five American Contributions to Civilization.*

10
War, to sane men at the present day, begins to look like an epidemic insanity, breaking out here and there like the cholera or influenza, infecting men's brains instead of their bowels.
EMERSON, *Miscellanies: War.*

11
I find a hundred thousand sorrows touching my heart, and there is ringing in my ears like an admonition eternal, an insistent call, "It must not be again!"
WARREN G. HARDING, *Address,* Hoboken, over the bodies of the dead of the A. E. F.

12
War is death's feast.
GEORGE HERBERT, *Jacula Prudentum.*

Yes; quaint and curious war is!
You shoot a fellow down
You'd treat if met where any bar is,
Or help to half-a-crown.
THOMAS HARDY, *The Man He Killed.*

13
When war begins, then hell openeth.
GEORGE HERBERT, *Jacula Prudentum.* The Italians say, "Guerra cominciata, inferno scatenato" (War begun, hell let loose).

A day of battle is a day of harvest for the devil.
WILLIAM HOOK, *Sermon,* Taunton, Mass., 1640.

He that preaches war is the devil's chaplain.
JOHN RAY, *English Proverbs,* p. 27.

14
Curs'd is the man and void of law and right,
Unworthy property, unworthy light,
Unfit for public rule, or private care;
That wretch, that monster, that delights in war.
HOMER, *Iliad.* Bk. ix, l. 87. (Pope, tr.)

To gratify stern ambition's whims,
What hundreds and thousands of precious limbs
On a field of battle we scatter.
THOMAS HOOD, *Miss Kilmansegg: Her Fame.*

15
Wars hateful to mothers. (Bellaque matribus Detestata.)
HORACE, *Odes.* Bk. i, ode 1, l. 23.

Mother whose heart hung humble as a button
On the bright splendid shroud of your son,
Do not weep.
War is kind.
STEPHEN CRANE, *War Is Kind.*

16
Among the calamities of war may be justly numbered the diminution of the love of truth by the falsehoods which interest dictates and credulity encourages. A peace will equally leave the warrior and the relater of wars destitute of employment; and I know not whether more is to be dreaded from streets filled with soldiers accustomed to plunder, or from garrets filled with scribblers accustomed to lie.
SAMUEL JOHNSON, *The Idler.* No. 30.

The first casualty when war comes is truth.
HIRAM JOHNSON, *Speech,* U. S. Senate.

No one has ever succeeded in keeping nations at war except by lies.
SALVADOR DE MADARIAGA.

Lies were the stuff from which armies built morale.
DANIEL V. POLING.

In war opinion is nine parts in ten.
SWIFT, *Letter to Stella,* 7 Jan., 1711.

1
Art, thou hast many infamies,
But not an infamy like this.
O snap the fife and still the drum,
And show the monster as she is.
RICHARD LE GALLIENNE, *The Illusion of War.*

2
Ez fer war, I call it murder,—
There you hev it plain an' flat;
I don't want to go no furder
Than my Testyment fer that;
God hez sed so plump an' fairly,
It 's ez long ez it is broad,
An' you've gut to git up airly
Ef you want to take in God.
J. R. LOWELL, *The Biglow Papers.* Ser. i, No. 1.

We kind o' thought Christ went agin war an' pillage.
J. R. LOWELL, *The Biglow Papers.* Ser. i, No. 3.

3
When after many battles past,
Both tir'd with blows, make peace at last,
What is it, after all, the people get?
Why! taxes, widows, wooden legs, and debt.
FRANCIS MOORE, *Almanac: Monthly Observations for 1829,* p. 23.

Ye that follow the vision
Of the world's weal afar,
Have ye met with derision
And the red laugh of war?
ALFRED NOYES, *Love Will Find Out the Way.*

I hate that drum's discordant sound
Parading round and round and round:
To me it talks of ravaged plains,
And burning towns, and ruined swains,
And mangled limbs, and dying groans,
And widows' tears, and orphans' moans;
And all that misery's hand bestows
To fill the catalogue of human woes.
JOHN SCOTT, *Ode on Hearing the Drum.*

4
Dying is more honorable than killing. (Quanto honestius mori discunt homines quam occidere.)
SENECA, *Epistulæ ad Lucilium.* Epis. lxx, 27.

We check manslaughter and isolated murders; but what of war and the much-vaunted crime of slaughtering whole peoples? . . . Deeds which would be punished by loss of life when committed in secret, are praised by us because uniformed generals have carried them out.
SENECA, *Epistulæ ad Lucilium.* Epis. xcv, 30.

One to destroy, is murder by the law,
And gibbets keep the lifted hand in awe;
To murder thousands takes a specious name,
War's glorious art, and gives immortal fame.
YOUNG, *Love of Fame.* Sat. vii, l. 55.

5
He is come to open
The purple testament of bleeding war.
SHAKESPEARE, *Richard II.* Act iii, sc. 3, l. 93.

Follow thy drum;
With man's blood paint the ground, gules, gules;
Religious canons, civil laws are cruel;
Then what should war be?
SHAKESPEARE, *Timon of Athens.* Act iv, sc. 3, l. 58.

6
In the arts of life man invents nothing; but in the arts of death he outdoes Nature herself, and produces by chemistry and machinery all the slaughter of plague, pestilence, and famine.
BERNARD SHAW, *Man and Superman.* Act iii.

7
Let the gulled fool the toils of war pursue,
Where bleed the many to enrich the few.
WILLIAM SHENSTONE, *The Judgment of Hercules,* l. 158.

8
Terrible as an army with banners.
Old Testament: Song of Solomon, vi, 4; vi, 10

9
The children born of thee are sword and fire,
Red ruin, and the breaking up of laws.
TENNYSON, *Guinevere,* l. 421.

Wild War, who breaks the converse of the wise.
TENNYSON, *The Third of February.*

10
War! horrible war! (Bella! horrida bella!)
VERGIL, *Æneid.* Bk. vi, l. 86.

Away with themes of war! Away with war itself!
Hence from my shuddering sight to never more return that show of blacken'd, mutilated corpses!
That hell unpent and raid of blood, fit for wild tigers or for lop-tongued wolves, not reasoning men.
WALT WHITMAN, *Song of the Exposition.* Pt. vii.

11
Militarism does not consist in the existence of any army, nor even in the existence of a very great army. Militarism is a spirit. It is a point of view. It is a system. It is a purpose. The purpose of militarism is to use armies for aggression.
WOODROW WILSON, *Speech,* West Point, 13 June, 1916.

12
A commonplace against war; the easiest of all topics.
EDMUND BURKE, *Observations on a Publication, "The Present State of the Nation."*

V—War: Civil War

13
From hence, let fierce contending nations know,
What dire effects from civil discord flow.
ADDISON, *Cato.* Act v, sc. 4.

14
All things are wretched in civil wars. (Omnia sunt misera in bellis civilibus.)
CICERO, *Epistolæ ad Familiares.* Bk. iv, epis. 9.

The wounds of civil war are deeply felt. (Alta sedent civilis volnera dextræ.)
LUCAN, *De Bello Civili*. Bk. i, l. 32.

1
Any sort of peace with our fellow-citizens seems to me preferable to civil war. (Mihi enim omnis pax cum civibus, bello civili utilior videbatur.)
CICERO, *Philippicæ*. No. ii, ch. 15, sec. 37.

2
Did you choose to wage wars which could win no triumph? i. e. civil wars. (Bella geri placuit nullos habitura triumphos?)
LUCAN, *De Bello Civili*. Bk. i, l. 12.

Make us foes of every nation, but prevent a civil war. (Omnibus hostes reddite nos populis: civile avertite bellum.)
LUCAN, *De Bello Civili*. Bk. ii, l. 52.

3
She saw her sons with purple death expire,
Her sacred domes involv'd in rolling fire,
A dreadful series of intestine wars,
Inglorious triumphs, and dishonest scars.
POPE, *Windsor Forest*, l. 323.

4
Civil dissension is a viperous worm
That gnaws the bowels of the commonwealth.
SHAKESPEARE, *I Henry VI*. Act iii, sc. 1, l. 72.

VI—War: Its Sinews

5
Money is the sinews of war. (Πλοῦτον νεῦρα τοῦ πολέμου'.)
LIBANIUS, *Orations*. No. 46.

Endless money forms the sinews of war. (Nervi belli pecuniam infinitam.)
CICERO, *Philippicæ*. No. v, ch. 2, sec. 5.

Victuals and ammunition and money too are the sinews of war.
JOHN FLETCHER, *The Fair Maid of the Inn*.

The sinews of war are those two metals (gold and silver).
ARTHUR HULL, *Memorial*, to Robert Cecil, 28 Nov., 1600.

Money is the sinew of the war.
MASSINGER, *The Duke of Milan*. Act iii, sc. 1.

Gold is the glue, sinews and strength of war.
GEORGE PEELE, *Battle of Alcazar*. Act i, sc. 2. (1594)

Coin is the sinews of war. (Les nerfs des batailles sont des pécunes.)
RABELAIS, *Works*. Bk. i, ch. 46.

6
Money is the sinews of success. (Τὸν πλοῦτον νεῦρα πραγμάτων.)
BION. (DIOGENES LAERTIUS, *Bion*. Bk. iv, 48.)

He who first called money the sinews of affairs would seem to have spoken with special reference to the affairs of war. (Νεῦρα τῶν πραγμάτων.)
PLUTARCH, *Lives: Cleomenes*. Ch. 27.

7
Suppose your sinews of war quite broken; I mean your military chest insolvent.
CARLYLE, *Sartor Resartus*. Bk. ii, ch. 3.

8
Money is the sinew of love as well as of war.
THOMAS FULLER, *Gnomologia*. No. 3442.

9
Money, more money, always money. (De l'argent, encore de l'argent, et toujours de l'argent.)
MARSHAL DE TRIVULCE, when François I asked him what he needed to make war.

War demands three things,—gold, gold, gold.
LAZARUS VON SCHWENDI. (MONTECUCULI, *Memoirs*.)

10
War is a matter not so much of arms as of expenditure, through which arms may be made of service.
THUCYDIDES, *History*. Bk. i, ch. 83, sec. 2.

11
Fight thou with shafts of silver and thou shalt conquer all things.
Response of the Delphian Oracle to Philip of Macedon, when he asked how he might be victorious in war. (PLUTARCH, *Apothegms*.)

Fight thou with shafts of silver and o'ercome,
When no force else can get the masterdom.
ROBERT HERRICK, *Money Gets the Mastery*.

Silver bullets.
DAVID LLOYD GEORGE, *Speech*, 1914, referring to the war with Germany.

Not Philip, but Philip's gold, took the cities of Greece.
PLUTARCH, *Lives: Paulus Æmilius*. Quoted as "a common saying." *See also* GOLD: ITS POWER.

12
Neither is money the sinews of war, as it is trivially said.
BACON, *Essays: Of Kingdoms and Estates*.

VII—War: The Big Battalions

13
God is generally for the big squadrons against the little ones. (Dieu est ordinaire pour les gros escadrons contre les petits.)
ROGER, COMTE DE BUSSY-RABUTIN, *Letters*, 18 Oct., 1677.

I have always noticed that God is on the side of the big battalions. (J'ai toujours vu Dieu du coté des gros bataillons.)
MARSHAL DE LA FERTÉ-SENNETERRE, *Remark*, to Anne of Austria. (BOURSAULT, *Lettres Nouvelles*, p. 384.)

Providence is always on the side of the big battalions. (La Fortune est toujours pour les gros bataillons.)
MADAME DE SÉVIGNÉ, *Letter to Her Daughter, Madame de Grignan*, 22 December, 1673.

It is said that God is always on the side of the big battalions. (On dit que Dieu est toujours pour les gros bataillons.)
VOLTAIRE, *Letter to M. le Riche*, 6 Feb., 1770.

As regards Providence, he cannot shake off the belief that in war, God is on the side of the big battalions, which at present are in the enemy's camp.
EDUARD ZELLER, *Frederick the Great as Philos-*

opher, referring to a letter written by Frederick to the Duchess of Gotha, 8 May, 1760. (*See* CARLYLE, *Frederick the Great*, v, 606.)

1
Providence is always on the side of the last reserve.

NAPOLEON I, *Sayings of Napoleon.*

2
The winds and waves are always on the side of the ablest navigators.

EDWARD GIBBON, *Decline and Fall of the Roman Empire*. Ch. 68.

3
The gods are on the side of the stronger. (Deos fortioribus adesse.)

TACITUS, *History*. Bk. iv, sec. 17.

Wise men and God are on the strongest side.

SIR CHARLES SEDLEY, *Death of Marc Antony*. Act iv, sc. 2.

4
We are glad to have God on our side to maul our enemies, when we cannot do the work ourselves.

DRYDEN. (INGE, *Wit and Wisdom: Preface.*)

5
O God, assist our side: at least, avoid assisting the enemy, and leave the rest to me.

PRINCE LEOPOLD OF ANHALT-DESSAU, before his last battle. ("Prayer mythically true; mythically, not otherwise."—CARLYLE, *Life of Frederick the Great*. Bk. xv, ch. 14.)

6
It is more important to know that we are on God's side.

ABRAHAM LINCOLN, *Retort*, to a deputation of Southerners during the Civil War, whose spokesman had remarked, "We trust, Sir, that God is on our side."

7
When 'tis an aven thing in th' prayin', may th' best man win . . . an' th' best man will win.

FINLEY PETER DUNNE, *On Prayers for Victory*.

8
Hence it happened that all the armed prophets conquered, all the unarmed perished. (Di qui nacque che tutti li profeti armati vinsero, e li disarmati rovinarono.)

MACHIAVELLI, *Il Principe*. Ch. 6.

VIII—War: The Glory of Battle

9
O proud was our army that morning,
That stood where the pine darkly towers,
When Sherman said: "Boys, you are weary;
This day fair Savannah is ours!"
Then sang we a song for our chieftain
That echoed o'er river and lea,
And the stars in our banner shone brighter
When Sherman marched down to the sea.

SAMUEL H. M. BYERS, *Song of Sherman's March to the Sea*.

10
The Assyrian came down like the wolf on the fold,
And his cohorts were gleaming in purple and gold;
And the sheen of their spears was like stars on the sea,
When the blue wave rolls nightly on deep Galilee.

BYRON, *The Destruction of Sennacherib*.

11
The combat deepens. On, ye brave,
Who rush to glory, or the grave!
Wave, Munich! all thy banners wave,
And charge with all thy chivalry!

THOMAS CAMPBELL, *Hohenlinden*. St. 7.

12
Conscience avaunt, Richard's himself again:
Hark! the shrill trumpet sounds, to horse, away,
My soul's in arms, and eager for the fray.

CIBBER, *Richard III* (altered). Act v, sc. 3.

My soul is up in arms, ready to charge.

CONGREVE, *The Mourning Bride*. Act iii, sc. 2.

13
In every heart
Are sown the sparks that kindle fiery war.

COWPER, *The Task*. Bk. v, l. 205.

A steed, a steed of matchless speed!
A sword of metal keen!
All else to noble hearts is dross,
All else on earth is mean.

ROBERT CUNNINGHAME-GRAHAM, *Cavalier's Song*.

Death's couriers, Fame and Honour, call
Us to the field again.

ROBERT CUNNINGHAME-GRAHAM, *Cavalier's Song*.

14
They now to fight are gone,
Armour on armour shone,
Drum unto drum did groan,
To hear was wonder;
That with the cries they make
The very earth did shake,
Trumpet to trumpet spake,
Thunder to thunder.

MICHAEL DRAYTON, *Ballad of Agincourt*. St. 8.

"Forward, the Light Brigade!"
Was there a man dismay'd?
Not tho' the soldier knew
Some one had blunder'd.
Theirs not to make reply,
Theirs not to reason why,
Theirs but to do and die.
Into the valley of Death
Rode the six hundred.

TENNYSON, *The Charge of the Light Brigade*.

Cannon to right of them,
Cannon to left of them,
Cannon in front of them
Volley'd and thunder'd;
Storm'd at with shot and shell,
Boldly they rode and well,
Into the jaws of Death,
Into the mouth of hell

Rode the six hundred.
TENNYSON, *The Charge of the Light Brigade.*

Jaws of death.
DU BARTAS, *Devine Weekes and Workes.* Wk. iv, day 1; SHAKESPEARE, *Twelfth Night.* Act iii, sc. 4, l. 394.

1
Give us this day good heart, good enemies,
Good blows o' both sides.
JOHN FLETCHER, *Bonduca.* Act iii, sc. 1.

2
To arms! cried Mortimer, and couch'd his quivering lance.
THOMAS GRAY, *The Bard,* l. 14.

Then above all the shooting and shots
Rang his voice: "Put Watts into 'em! Boys, give 'em Watts!"
BRET HARTE, *Caldwell of Springfield.*

3
Hark! I hear the tramp of thousands,
And of armèd men the hum;
Lo! a nation's hosts have gathered
Round the quick alarming drum,—
Saying, "Come, Freemen, come!
Ere your heritage be wasted," said the quick alarming drum.
BRET HARTE, *Reveillé.* St. 1.

4
Good at the battle cry. (Βοὴν ἀγαθός.)
HOMER, *Iliad.* Bk. ii, l. 408. Frequently repeated.

5
Our business in the field of fight
Is not to question, but to prove our might.
HOMER, *Iliad.* Bk. xx, l. 304. (Pope, tr.)

For bragging-time was over, and fighting-time was come.
HENRY NEWBOLT, *Hawke.*

6
Posterity, thinned by the crimes of its ancestors, shall hear of those battles. (Audiet pugnas, vitio parentum Rara juventus.)
HORACE, *Odes.* Bk. i, ode 2, l. 23.

7
Suffer me to follow the camp. (Da mihi castra sequi.)
LUCAN, *De Bello Civili.* Bk. ii, l. 348.

8
Am I deceived, or was there a clash of arms? I am not deceived, it was the clash of arms; Mars approaches, and, approaching, gave the sign of war. (Fallor, an arma sonant? Non fallimur, arma sonabant; Mars venit, et veniens bellica signa dedit.)
OVID, *Fasti.* Bk. v, l. 549.

He saith among the trumpets, Ha, ha; and he smelleth the battle afar off, the thunder of the captains, and the shouting.
Old Testament: Job, xxxix, 25.

Oh, wherefore come ye forth, in triumph from the North,
With your hands, and your feet, and your raiment all red?
And wherefore doth your rout send forth a joyous shout?
And whence be the grapes of the wine-press that ye tread?
MACAULAY, *The Battle of Naseby.* St. 1.

March to the battlefield,
The foe is now before us;
Each heart is Freedom's shield,
And heaven is shining o'er us.
B. E. O'MEARA, *March to the Battlefield.*

9
Stand! the ground's your own, my braves!
Will ye give it up to slaves?
JOHN PIERPONT, *Warren's Address.*

Leaden rain and iron hail
Let their welcome be!
JOHN PIERPONT, *Warren's Address.*

From the Rio Grande's waters to the icy lakes of Maine,
Let all exult, for we have met the enemy again.
Beneath their stern old mountains we have met them in their pride,
And rolled from Buena Vista back the battle's bloody tide.
GENERAL ALBERT PIKE, *Battle of Buena Vista.*

10
Once more unto the breach, dear friends, once more;
Or close the wall up with our English dead.
In peace there's nothing so becomes a man
As modest stillness and humility:
But when the blast of war blows in our ears,
Then imitate the action of the tiger,
Stiffen the sinews, summon up the blood. . . .
Now set the teeth and stretch the nostril wide;
Hold hard the breath and bend up every spirit
To his full height!
SHAKESPEARE, *Henry V.* Act iii, sc. 1, l. 1.

Fight, gentlemen of England! fight, bold yeomen!
Draw, archers, draw your arrows to the head!
Spur your proud horses hard, and ride in blood;
Amaze the welkin with your broken staves!
SHAKESPEARE, *Richard III.* Act v, sc. 3, l. 338.

Let the only walls the foe shall scale
Be ramparts of the dead!
PAUL HAMILTON HAYNE, *Vicksburg.*

11
When the hurly-burly's done,
When the battle's lost and won.
SHAKESPEARE, *Macbeth.* Act i, sc. 1, l. 3.

The tumult and the shouting dies,
The captains and the kings depart.
RUDYARD KIPLING, *Recessional.*

12
Who asks whether the enemy were defeated by strategy or valor? (Dolus an virtus, quis in hoste requirat?
VERGIL, *Æneid.* Bk. ii, l. 390.

IX—War: The Terror of Battle

13
Hand to hand, and foot to foot:
Nothing there, save death, was mute;

Stroke, and thrust, and flash, and cry
For quarter, or for victory,
Mingle there with the volleying thunder.
BYRON, *The Siege of Corinth.* St. 24.

His trusty warriors, few but undismayed;
Firm-paced and slow, a horrid front they form,
Still as the breeze, but dreadful as the storm;
Low murmuring sounds along their banners fly,
Revenge, or death—the watch-word and reply;
Then pealed the notes, omnipotent to charm,
And the loud tocsin tolled their last alarm!
CAMPBELL, *The Pleasures of Hope.* Pt. i, l. 366.

1
For justice guides the warrior's steel,
And vengeance strikes the blow.
J. R. DRAKE, *To the Defenders of New Orleans.*

2
Earth was the meadow, he the mower strong.
VICTOR HUGO, *La Légende des Siècles.*

3
Now deeper roll the maddening drums,
And the mingling host like ocean heaves:
While from the midst a horrid wailing comes,
And high above the fight the lonely bugle grieves.
GRENVILLE MELLEN, *Ode on the Celebration of the Battle of Bunker Hill,* 17 June, 1825. Mellen's only important poem, which gave him the sobriquet of "The Singer of One Song."

4
Arms on armour clashing bray'd
Horrible discord, and the madding wheels
Of brazen chariots rag'd; dire was the noise
Of conflict.
MILTON, *Paradise Lost.* Bk. vi, l. 209.

5
To the fire-eyed maid of smoky war
All hot and bleeding will we offer them.
SHAKESPEARE, *I Henry IV.* Act iv, sc. 1, l. 114.

6
From camp to camp, through the foul womb of night,
The hum of either army stilly sounds, . . .
Steed threatens steed, in high and boastful neighs
Piercing the night's dull ear; and from the tents
The armourers, accomplishing the knights,
With busy hammers closing rivets up,
Give dreadful note of preparation.
SHAKESPEARE, *Henry V.* Act iv: *Prologue,* l. 4.

With clink of hammers closing rivets up.
CIBBER, *Richard III* (altered). Act v, sc. 3.

7
Make all our trumpets speak; give them all breath,
Those clamorous harbingers of blood and death.
SHAKESPEARE, *Macbeth.* Act v, sc. 6, l. 9.

Let's march without the noise of threatening drum.
SHAKESPEARE, *Richard II.* Act iii, sc. 3, l. 51.

Thus far into the bowels of the land
Have we march'd on without impediment.
SHAKESPEARE, *Richard III.* Act v, sc. 2, l. 3.

8
Put in their hands thy bruising irons of wrath,
That they may crush down with heavy fall
The usurping helmets of our adversaries!
SHAKESPEARE, *Richard III.* Act v, sc. 3, l. 110.

9
Then more fierce
The conflict grew; the din of arms, the yell
Of savage rage, the shriek of agony,
The groan of death, commingled in one sound
Of undistinguish'd horrors.
SOUTHEY, *Madoc in Aztlan.* Pt. ii, sec. 15, l. 170.

God of battles, was ever a battle like this in the world before?
TENNYSON, *The Revenge,* l. 62.

10
They came with banner, spear, and shield;
And it was proved in Bosworth-field,
Not long the Avenger was withstood—
Earth helped him with the cry of blood.
WORDSWORTH, *Song at the Feast of Brougham Castle,* l. 24.

X—War: Cannon

11
The cannon's breath
Wings the far hissing globe of death.
BYRON, *The Siege of Corinth.* St. 2.

Three hundred cannon threw up their emetic,
And thirty thousand muskets flung their pills.
BYRON, *Don Juan.* Canto viii, st. 12.

Iron-sleet of arrowy shower
Hurtles in the darken'd air.
THOMAS GRAY, *The Fatal Sisters.*

12
The last argument of kings. (Ultima ratio regum.)
LOUIS XV OF FRANCE ordered this engraved on his cannon. It was ordered removed by the National assembly, 19 Aug., 1790. Its use as a motto for cannon dates back to 1613. (BÜCHMANN, *Geflügelte Worte,* p. 476.)

The last argument of kings. (Ultima razon de reges.)
CALDERON, referring to war.

Don't forget your great guns, which are the most respectable arguments of the rights of kings.
FREDERICK THE GREAT, *Letter to His Brother, Prince Henry,* 21 April, 1759.

There are no manifestoes like cannon and musketry.
DUKE OF WELLINGTON, *Maxims and Table-Talk.*

13
And silence broods like spirit on the brae,
A glimmering moon begins, the moonlight runs
Over the grasses of the ancient way
Rutted this morning by the passing guns.
JOHN MASEFIELD, *August 14.*

14
'Tis a principle of war that when you can use the lightning 'tis better than cannon.
NAPOLEON I, *Sayings of Napoleon.*

1
The terrible rumble, grumble and roar
Telling the battle was on once more—
And Sheridan twenty miles away!

THOMAS BUCHANAN READ, *Sheridan's Ride*.

2
The cannons have their bowels full of wrath,
And ready mounted are they to spit forth
Their iron indignation 'gainst your walls.

SHAKESPEARE, *King John*. Act ii, sc. 1, l. 210.

3 It was great pity, so it was,
That villanous saltpetre should be digg'd
Out of the bowels of the harmless earth,
Which many a good tall fellow had destroy'd
So cowardly.

SHAKESPEARE, *I Henry IV*. Act i, sc. 3, l. 59.

As when that devilish iron engine, wrought
In deepest hell, and fram'd by fury's skill,
With windy nitre and quick sulphur fraught,
And ramm'd with bullet round, ordain'd to kill,
Conceiveth fire, the heavens it doth fil:
With thundering noise, and all the air doth choke,
That none can breathe, nor see, nor hear at will,
Through smouldry cloud of duskish stinking smoke,
That th' onely breath him daunts, who hath escap'd the stroke.

SPENSER, *Faerie Queene*. Bk. i, canto 7, st. 13.

XI—War and Peace

See also Peace: Its Faults

4
War must be for the sake of peace, business for the sake of leisure, things necessary and useful for the sake of things noble. (Πόλεμον μὲν εἰρήνης χάριν.)

ARISTOTLE, *Politics*. Bk. vii, ch. 13, sec. 8.

War should be undertaken in such a way as to show that its only object is peace. (Bellum autem ita suscipiatur, ut nihil aliud nisi pax quæsita videatur.)

CICERO, *De Officiis*. Bk. i, ch. 23, sec. 80.

The only excuse for war is that we may live in peace unharmed. (Quare suscipienda quidem bella sunt ob eam causam, ut sine injuria in pace vivatur.)

CICERO, *De Officiis*. Bk. i, ch. 11, sec. 35.

5
He who did well in war just earns the right
To begin doing well in peace.

ROBERT BROWNING, *Luria*. Act ii, l. 354.

6
There's but the twinkling of a star
Between a man of peace and war.

BUTLER, *Hudibras*. Pt. ii, canto 3, l. 957.

7
Most people believe the achievements of war more important than those of peace, but this is a mistake. (Cum plerique arbitrentur res bellicas majores esse quam urbanas, minuenda est hæc opinio.)

CICERO, *De Officiis*. Bk. i, ch. 22, sec. 74.

Fame may be won in peace as well as in war. (Vel pace vel bello clarum fieri licet.)

SALLUST, *Catiline*. Ch. iii, sec. 1.

But the real and lasting victories are those of peace, and not of war.

EMERSON, *Conduct of Life: Worship*.

Life may be given in many ways,
And loyalty to Truth be sealed
As bravely in the closet as the field.

J. R. LOWELL, *Commemoration Ode*. St. 5.

Peace hath her victories,
No less renown'd than war.

MILTON, *Sonnet: To the Lord General Cromwell*.

But dream not helm and harness
The sign of valor true;
Peace hath higher tests of manhood
Than battle ever knew.

WHITTIER, *The Hero*. St. 19.

8
I cease not to advocate peace; even though unjust it is better than the justest war. (Equidem pacem hortari non desino; quæ vel injusta utilior est quam justissimum bellum.)

CICERO, *Epistolæ ad Atticum*. Bk. vii, epis. 14.

It hath been said that an unjust peace is to be preferred before a just war.

SAMUEL BUTLER, *Speech in the Rump Parliament*.

A disadvantageous peace is better than the most just war.

ERASMUS, *Colloquies*.

There never was a good war or a bad peace.

BENJAMIN FRANKLIN, *Letter to Quincy*, 11 Sept., 1773.

9
Peace is better than war, because in peace the sons bury their fathers, but in war the fathers bury their sons.

CRŒSUS, to Cambyses. (BACON, *Apothegms*. No. 149.)

10
War makes thieves and peace hangs them.

GEORGE HERBERT, *Jacula Prudentum*.

11
It is a general rule of reason, That every man ought to endeavour Peace, as far as he has hope of obtaining it; and when he cannot obtain it, that he may seek and use all helps and advantages of War.

THOMAS HOBBES, *Leviathan*. Pt. i, ch. 14.

Oh! if I were Queen of France, or, still better, Pope of Rome,
I would have no fighting men abroad, no weeping maids at home;
All the world should be at peace; or if kings must show their might,
Why, let them who make the quarrels be the only ones to fight.

CHARLES JEFFRIES, *Jeannette and Jeannot*.

12
Let not him that girdeth on his harness boast himself as he that putteth it off.

Old Testament: I Kings, xx, 11.

13
You need only a show of war to have peace. (Ostendite modo bellum, pacem habebitis.)

LIVY, *History*. Bk. vi, ch. 18, sec. 7.

1
He preferred war to peace, but even when armed he loved peace. (Prætulit arma togæ, sed pacem armatus amavit.)

LUCAN, *De Bello Civili.* Bk. ix, l. 199.

2
Ye shall love peace as a means to new wars, and the short peace better than the long.

FRIEDRICH NIETZSCHE, *Thus Spake Zarathustra: Of War and Warriors.*

3
Invincible in peace and invisible in war.

GEN. E. F. NOYES, referring to Blaine, Conkling and Cameron, during Hayes campaign for president. (NEVINS, *Cleveland,* p. 176.)

4
Would you end war? Create great Peace.

JAMES OPPENHEIM, *War and Laughter.* No. 4.

5
"Go, with a song of peace," said Fingal; "go, Ullin, to the king of swords. Tell him that we are mighty in war; that the ghosts of our foes are many."

OSSIAN, *Carthon,* l. 269.

6
I am for peace: but when I speak, they are for war.

Old Testament: Psalms, cxx, 7.

I labour for peace, but when I speak unto them thereof, they make them ready to battle.

Book of Common Prayer: Psalter. Ps., cxx, 6.

7
Peace makes plenty, plenty makes pride.
Pride breeds quarrel, and quarrel brings war:
War brings spoil, and spoil poverty,
Poverty patience, and patience peace:
So peace brings war, and war brings peace.

GEORGE PUTTENHAM, *The Arte of English Poesie,* l. 217. (1589)

Plenty breeds Pride; Pride, Envy; Envy, War;
War, Poverty; Poverty, humble Care;
Humility breeds Peace, and Peace breeds Plenty;
Thus round the World doth roll alternately.

ROBERT HAYMAN, *Quodlibets: The World's Whirlegigge.* (1630)

Poverty begets Effort; Effort begets Success; Success begets Wealth; Wealth begets Pride; Pride begets Strife; Strife begets War; War begets Poverty; Poverty begets Peace; Peace, born of Poverty, begets Effort; Effort again begets Success, and the round continues s before.

ST. CADOC. (*Myvrian Archæology of Wales.*)

Second Servant: This peace is nothing, but to rust iron, increase tailors, and breed ballad-makers.
First Servant: Let me have war, say I; it exceeds peace as far as day does night; it's spritely, waking, audible, and full of vent. Peace is a very apoplexy, lethargy; mulled, deaf, sleepy, insensible; a getter of more bastard children than war's a destroyer of men.
Second Servant: 'Tis so: and as war, in some sort, may be said to be a ravisher, so it cannot be denied but peace is a great maker of cuckolds.
First Servant: Ay, and it makes men hate one another.
Third Servant: Reason; because they then less need one another. The wars for my money.

SHAKESPEARE, *Coriolanus.* Act iv, sc. 5, l. 234.

I arraign you, war, and charge you to be man's enemy;
Yet in so accusing you, I beg that clemency be shown,
For you are a hideous reality only because of man's spiritual frailties.
Man, while yet invoking your aid, has called you the enemy of peace;
Yet that peace which he craves is, in truth, progress's most bitter foe.

YATES STIRLING, JR., *Arraignment of War.*

8
None save the victor exchanges war for peace. (Nemo nisi victor pace bellum mutavit.)

SALLUST, *Catiline.* Ch. lviii, sec. 16.

Ne'er was a war did cease,
Ere bloody hands were wash'd, with such a peace.

SHAKESPEARE, *Cymbeline.* Act v, sc. 5, l. 484.

9
Now for the bare-pick'd bone of majesty
Doth dogged war bristle his angry crest
And snarleth in the gentle eyes of peace.

SHAKESPEARE, *King John.* Act iv, sc. 3, l. 148.

10
To reap the harvest of perpetual peace
By this one bloody trial of sharp war.

SHAKESPEARE, *Richard III.* Act v, sc. 2, l. 15.

We'll grasp firm hands and laugh at the old pain
When it is peace. But until peace, the storm,
The darkness and the thunder and the rain.

CHARLES SORLEY, *When It Is Peace.*

11
The drums of war, the drums of peace,
Roll through our cities without cease,
And all the iron halls of life
Ring with the unremitting strife.

R. L. STEVENSON, *The Woodman.*

12
It was rather a cessation of war than a beginning of peace. (Bellum magis desierat, quam pax cœperat.)

TACITUS, *History.* Bk. iv, sec. 1.

13
There is no safety in war; we entreat thee for peace. (Nulla salus bello; pacem te poscimus.)

VERGIL, *Æneid.* Bk. xi, l. 362.

XII—War and Death

See also Soldier: How Sleep the Brave

14
War is not sparing of the brave, but of cowards. (Ἄρης δ' οὐκ ἀγαθῶν φείδεται, ἀλλὰ κακῶν.)

ANACREON, *Epigram.* (*Greek Anthology.* Bk. vii, No. 160.)

War loves to seek its victims in the young.

SOPHOCLES, *Scyrii.* Frag. 507.

War for his meals loves dainty food;
He spares the bad and takes the good.

D'ARCY WENTWORTH THOMPSON, *Sales Attici.*

1
Rider and horse . . . in one red burial blent!
BYRON, *Childe Harold*. Canto iii, st. 28.

Fiercely stand, or fighting fall.
BYRON, *The Siege of Corinth*. St. 25.

2
Few, few shall part where many meet!
The snow shall be their winding-sheet
And every turf beneath their feet
Shall be a soldier's sepulchre.
THOMAS CAMPBELL, *Hohenlinden*. St. 8.

Shall victor exult, or in death be laid low,
With his back to the field and his feet to the foe,
And leaving in battle no blot on his name,
Look proudly to heaven from the death-bed of fame.
THOMAS CAMPBELL, *Lochiel's Warning*.

Another's sword has laid him low—
Another's and another's;
And every hand that dealt the blow—
Ay me! it was a brother's!
THOMAS CAMPBELL, *O'Connor's Child*. St. 10.

3
So ends the bloody business of the day.
HOMER, *Odyssey*. Bk. xxii, l. 516. (Pope, tr.)

The battle ends when the enemy is down. (Pugna suum finem, cum jacet hostis, habet.)
OVID, *Tristia*. Bk. iii, eleg. 5, l. 34.

4
Weave no more silks, ye Lyons looms,
To deck our girls for gay delights!
The crimson flower of battle blooms,
And solemn marches fill the nights.
JULIA WARD HOWE, *Our Orders*.

5
Doughboys were paid a whole dollar a day
and received free burial under the clay.
And movie heroes are paid even more
shooting one another in a Hollywood war.
ALFRED KREYMBORG, *What Price Glory?*

6
For the man who should loose me is dead,
Fighting with the Duke in Flanders,
In a pattern called a war.
Christ! What are patterns for?
AMY LOWELL, *Patterns*.

7
Wut's words to them whose faith an' truth
On War's red techstone rang true metal,
Who ventered life an' love an' youth
For the gret prize o' death in battle?
J. R. LOWELL, *Biglow Papers*. Ser. ii, No. 10.

8
Remember, men of guns and rhymes,
And kings who kill so fast,
That men you kill too many times
May be too dead at last.
ROSE O'NEILL, *When the Dead Men Die*.

9
There are few die well that die in a battle.
SHAKESPEARE, *Henry V*. Act iv, sc. 1, l. 148.

10
I bear in my hand war and death. (Bella manu letumque gero.)
VERGIL, *Æneid*. Bk. vii, l. 455.

WARNING

11
I know the warning song is sung in vain,
That few will hear, and fewer heed the strain.
COWPER, *Expostulation*, l. 724.

12
Enter, but this warning hear:
He forth again departs who looks behind.
DANTE, *Purgatorio*. Canto ix, l. 124. (Cary, tr.)

13
Once warned, twice armed.
THOMAS HOWELL, *H. His Devises*, 15. (1581)

He that is warned is half armed.
HILL, *Commonplace-Book*, 132.

But they that are warnèd are in time,
Half armed are 'gainst dangerous crime.
COLLMANN, *Ballads and Broadsides*, 194.

14
Am I unable to look out, when I've been forewarned? (Egon ut cavere nequeam, cui prædicitur?)
PLAUTUS, *Pseudolus*, l. 516. (Act i, sc. v.)

Forewarned, forearmed. (Præmonitus, præmunitus.)
UNKNOWN. A Latin proverb.

15
Beware the ides of March.
SHAKESPEARE, *Julius Cæsar*. Act i, sc. 2, l. 23.

Cæsar: The ides of March are come.
Soothsayer: Ay, Cæsar; but not gone.
SHAKESPEARE, *Julius Cæsar*. Act iii, sc. 1, l. 1.

A certain seer warned Cæsar to be on his guard against a great peril on the day of the month of March which the Romans call the Ides; and when that day had come and Cæsar was on his way to the senate-house, he greeted the seer with a jest and said: "Well, the Ides of March are come," and the seer said to him softly: "Aye, they are come, but they are not gone." ("Αἱ μὲν δὴ Μάρτιαι Εἶδοὶ πάρεισιν." "Ναὶ πάρεισιν, ἀλλ' οὐ παρεληλύθασι.")
PLUTARCH, *Lives: Cæsar*. Ch. 63, sec. 3.

16
On a buoy in the storm it floated and swung,
And over the waves its warning rung.
When the rock was hid by the surge's swell,
The mariners heard the warning bell.
SOUTHEY, *The Inchcape Rock*, l. 11.

How like the leper, with his own sad cry
Enforcing his own solitude, it tolls!
That lonely bell set in the rushing shoals,
To warn us from the place of jeopardy!
C. T. TURNER, *The Buoy Bell*.

17
Beware, I am here. (Cave, adsum.)
WILHELM II OF GERMANY (then Prince Wilhelm) is said to have written this on a photograph which he presented to Bismarck in 1884.

18
Stop—Look—Listen!
RALPH R. UPTON. *Warning Slogan*, devised in 1912, when Upton was safety lecturer for the Puget Sound Power Company, Seattle, Wash. The older signs at railroad crossings read "Look Out for the Engine."

1
No man provokes me with impunity. (Nemo me impune lacessit.)
Motto of the Order of the Thistle.

WASHING

See also Cleanliness

2
All will come out in the washing. (Todo saldrá en la colada.)
CERVANTES, *Don Quixote*. Pt. i, ch. 20.

And it all goes into the laundry,
But it never comes out in the wash,
'Ow we're sugared about by the old men
('Eavy-sterned amateur old men!)
RUDYARD KIPLING, *Stellenbosh*.

3
What worship, for example, is there not in mere washing!
CARLYLE, *Past and Present*. Ch. 15.

4
For washing his hands none sell his lands.
GEORGE HERBERT, *Jacula Prudentum*.

I will wash my hands and wait upon you.
JOHN RAY, *English Proverbs*, p. 353.
See also under HEALTH: ITS PRESERVATION.

5
I wash, wring, brew, bake, scour, dress meat and drink.
SHAKESPEARE, *Merry Wives of Windsor*, i, 4, 101.

6
They that wash on Monday have all the week to dry;
They that wash on Tuesday have let a day go by;
They that wash on Wednesday are not so much to blame;
They that wash on Thursday wash for very shame;
They that wash on Friday wash in fearful need;
They that wash on Saturday are filthy sluts indeed.
UNKNOWN. (*Notes and Queries*, vii, v, 180.)

Always washing, and never getting finished.
HARDY, *Tess of the D'Urbervilles*. Ph. i, ch. 4.

WASHINGTON, GEORGE

7
These are high times when a British general is to take counsel of a Virginia buckskin.
GENERAL EDWARD BRADDOCK, in rejecting George Washington's advice, 1755. (C. F. HOFFMAN, *Winter in Far West*, i, 67.)

8
Simple and brave, his faith awoke
Ploughmen to struggle with their fate;
Armies won battles when he spoke,
And out of Chaos sprang the state.
ROBERT BRIDGES (DROCH), *Washington*.

9
Where may the wearied eye repose
When gazing on the great;
Where neither guilty glory glows,
Nor despicable state?
Yes—one—the first—the last—the best—
The Cincinnatus of the West,
Whom envy dared not hate,
Bequeathed the name of Washington,
To make man blush there was but one!
BYRON, *Ode to Napoleon Bonaparte*. St. 19.

While Washington 's a watchword, such as ne'er
Shall sink while there's an echo left to air.
BYRON, *The Age of Bronze*. St. 5.

Washington,
Whose every battle-field is holy ground,
Which breathes of nations saved, not worlds undone.
BYRON, *Don Juan*. Canto viii, st. 5.

10
Washington! Here is a fine, fearless, placid man, perfectly well seated in the center of his soul, direct and pure. . . . He could smile, drink, make love. . . . He paraphrased Horace: "Carpe diem, carpe noctem." . . . To conquer and to make love.
JOSEPH DELTEIL, *Lafayette*, p. 61.

11
The character, the counsels, and example of our Washington . . . will guide us through the doubts and difficulties that beset us; they will guide our children and our children's children in the paths of prosperity and peace, while America shall hold her place in the family of nations.
EDWARD EVERETT, *Speech: Washington Abroad and at Home*, 5 July, 1858.

No gilded dome swells from the lowly roof to catch the morning or evening beam; but the love and gratitude of united America settle upon it in one eternal sunshine. While it stands, the latest generations of the grateful children of America will make this pilgrimage to it as to a shrine; and when it shall fall, if fall it must, the memory and the name of Washington shall shed an eternal glory on the spot.
EDWARD EVERETT, *Oration on the Character of Washington*. Referring to Mount Vernon.

12
Here you would know, and enjoy, what posterity will say of Washington. For a thousand leagues have nearly the same effect with a thousand years.
BENJAMIN FRANKLIN, *Letter to Washington*, 5 March, 1780. *See also under* FOREIGNERS.

13
He comes!—the Genius of these lands—
Fame's thousand tongues his worth confess,
Who conquered with his suffering bands,
And grew immortal by distress.
PHILIP FRENEAU, *Occasioned by General Washington's Arrival at Philadelphia*.

O Washington!—thrice glorious name,
What due rewards can man decree—
Empires are far below thy aims,
And sceptres have no charms for thee.
PHILIP FRENEAU, *Occasioned by General Washington's Arrival at Philadelphia*.

1
Washington is now only a steel engraving. About the real man who lived and loved and hated and schemed, we know but little.

ROBERT G. INGERSOLL, *Lincoln.*

2 His character was, in its mass, perfect.

THOMAS JEFFERSON, *Letter to Dr. Walter Jones,* 2 Jan., 1814. *See* 2299d:7.

3
Were an energetic and judicious system to be proposed with your signature it would be a circumstance highly honorable to your fame . . . and doubly entitle you to the glorious republican epithet, The Father of your Country.

HENRY KNOX, *Letter to Washington,* 19 March, 1787. (See FORD, *Washington's Writings.* Vol. xi, p. 275.) However, "Father of His Country" as applied to Washington, was probably first used on a German calendar published in 1779 at Lancaster, Pa., by a printer named Francis Baily, where Washington was referred to as "Des Landes Vater." Cicero was perhaps the first of a long line of men so called. *See* 647:4.

The Father of his Country—We celebrate Washington!

UNKNOWN, *Editorial, Pennsylvania Packet,* 9 July, 1789, p. 284.

Every countenance seemed to say, "Long live George Washington, the Father of the People."

UNKNOWN, *Article, Pennsylvania Packet,* 21 April, 1789, describing Washington's election to the Presidency.

4
A nobleness to try for,
A name to live and die for.

G. P. LATHROP, *The Name of Washington.*

5
A citizen, first in war, first in peace, and first in the hearts of his countrymen.

COLONEL HENRY (LIGHT-HORSE HARRY) LEE, *Resolutions Adopted by the Congress on the Death of Washington,* 19 Dec., 1799. These were the concluding words of the resolutions, which were written by Lee and introduced in the House of Representatives by John Marshall. They are often wrongly ascribed to Marshall because he read them and moved their adoption. (*Journal of the House of Representatives,* 6 Cong., 1 sess., p. 45; *Annals of Congress,* 6 Cong., 1 sess., col. 204.) The phrase was repeated by Lee in his memorial oration at Philadelphia, 26 Dec., 1799. Marshall, in his *Life of Washington* (vol. v, p. 765), quotes the resolutions, perhaps from memory, and erroneously gives the last clause as "first in the hearts of his fellow citizens." He states in a footnote that the resolutions were prepared by Lee. (See STEVENSON, *Famous Single Poems.* Rev. ed., ch. 19.)

6
Washington is the mightiest name of earth—long since mightiest in the cause of civil liberty, still mightiest in moral reformation. On that name no eulogy is expected. It cannot be. To add brightness to the sun or glory to the name of Washington is alike impossible. Let none attempt it. In solemn awe pronounce the name, and in its naked deathless splendor leave it shining on.

ABRAHAM LINCOLN, *Address,* Springfield, Ill., 22 Feb., 1842.

7 The purely great
Whose soul no siren passion could unsphere,
Then nameless, now a power and mixed with fate.

J. R. LOWELL, *Under the Old Elm.* Pt. i, sec. 1.

Firmly erect, he towered above them all,
The incarnate discipline that was to free
With iron curb that armed democracy.

J. R. LOWELL, *Under the Old Elm.* Pt. iii, sec. 1.

What figure more immovably august
Than that grave strength so patient and so pure,
Calm in good fortune, when it wavered, sure,
That mind serene, impenetrably just,
Modelled on classic lines so simple they endure?
That soul so softly radiant and so white
The track it left seems less of fire than light.

J. R. LOWELL, *Under the Old Elm.* Pt. v, sec. 2.

Soldier and statesman, rarest unison;
High-poised example of great duties done
Simply as breathing, a world's honors worn
As life's indifferent gifts to all men born; . . .
Not honored then or now because he wooed
The popular voice, but that he still withstood;
Broad-minded, higher-souled, there is but one
Who was all this and ours, and all men's—WASHINGTON.

J. R. LOWELL, *Under the Old Elm.* Pt. v, sec. 3.

As to pay, sir, I beg leave to assure the Congress that as no pecuniary consideration could have tempted me to accept this arduous employment at the expense of my domestic ease and happiness, I do not wish to make any profit from it.

GEORGE WASHINGTON, *Statement to Congress on his Appointment as Commander-in-Chief,* 16 June, 1775.

8
Oh, Washington! thou hero, patriot sage,
Friend of all climes, and pride of every age!

THOMAS PAINE, *Washington.*

9
Sit down, Mr. Washington; your modesty is equal to your valor, and that surpasses the power of any language that I possess.

SPEAKER ROBINSON, of the Virginia House of Burgesses, to Washington, in 1759, when the latter attempted to reply to the thanks of the House, but was unable to utter a word.

10
His work well done, the leader stepped aside,
Spurning a crown with more than kingly pride,
Content to wear the higher crown of worth,
While time endures, First Citizen of Earth.

JAMES JEFFREY ROCHE, *Washington.*

11
A Pharos in the night, a pillar in the dawn,
By his inspiring light may we fare on!

CLINTON SCOLLARD, *At the Tomb of Washington.*

1
The indignant land Where Washington hath left
His awful memory, A light for after-times.
SOUTHEY, *Ode Written during the War with America, 1814.*

2
The prevailin' weakness of most public men is to Slop Over! . . . G. Washington never slopt over.
ARTEMUS WARD, *Fourth of July Oration.*

3
Washington is in the clear upper sky.
DANIEL WEBSTER, *Eulogy on Adams and Jefferson,* 2 Aug., 1826.

Washington—a fixed star in the firmament of great names, shining without twinkling or obscuration, with clear, beneficent light.
DANIEL WEBSTER, *Eulogy,* 2 Aug., 1826.

3a
"George," said his father, "do you know who killed that beautiful little cherry tree yonder in the garden?" . . . Looking at his father with the sweet face of youth brightened with the inexpressible charm of all-conquering truth, he bravely cried out, "I can't tell a lie. Pa; you know I can't tell a lie. I did cut it with my hatchet."
MASON LOCKE WEEMS, *The Life and Memorable Actions of George Washington.* Ch. 1 (1800) Usually quoted, "I did it with my little hatchet." The story, of course, is one of Weems's many embroideries.

4
The indomitable heart and arm—proofs of the never-broken line,
Courage, alertness, patience, faith, the same —e'en in defeat defeated not, the same.
WALT WHITMAN, *Washington's Monument.*

5
Thank God! the people's choice was just,
The one man equal to his trust,
Wise beyond lore, and without weakness good,
Calm in the strength of flawless rectitude!
J. G. WHITTIER, *The Vow of Washington.*

6
The crude commercialism of America, its materialising spirit . . . are entirely due to the country having adopted for its national hero a man who was incapable of telling a lie.
OSCAR WILDE, *The Decay of Lying.*

7
Washington, the brave, the wise, the good,
Supreme in war, in council, and in peace,
Valiant without ambition, discreet without fear,
Confident without presumption.
In disaster, calm; in success, moderate; in all, himself.
The hero, the patriot, the Christian.
The father of nations, the friend of mankind,
Who, when he had won all, renounced all,
And sought in the bosom of his family and of nature, retirement.
And in the hope of religion, immortality.
UNKNOWN, *Inscription on Washington's Tomb.*

WASTE

8
Since milk, though spilt and spoilt, does marble good,
Better be down on knees and scrub the floor,
Than sigh, "the waste would make a syllabub!"
BROWNING, *Ring and the Book.* Pt. vii, l. 505.

9
Our wasted oil unprofitably burns,
Like hidden lamps in old sepulchral urns.
COWPER, *Conversation,* l. 357. A reference to the lamp which burned for fifteen hundred years in the tomb of Cicero's daughter, Tullia.

Dim lights of life, that burn a length of years
Useless, unseen, as lamps in sepulchres.
POPE, *Elegy to the Memory of an Unfortunate Lady,* l. 19.

We waste our lights in vain, like lamps by day.
SHAKESPEARE, *Romeo and Juliet.* Act i, sc. 4, l. 45.

10
Wilful waste brings woeful want.
THOMAS FULLER, *Gnomologia.* No. 5755.

He that keeps nor crust nor crum,
Weary of all, shall want some.
SHAKESPEARE, *King Lear.* Act i, sc. 4, l. 217.

And wilful waste, depend upon 't,
Brings, almost always, woeful want!
ANN TAYLOR, *The Pin.*

For wilful waste makes woeful want,
And I may live to say,
Oh! how I wish I had the bread
That once I threw away!
UNKNOWN, *The Crust of Bread.*

11
Waste brings woe.
ROBERT GREENE, *Sonnet.*

12
The plea of waste not, want not.
HARDY, *Under the Greenwood Tree.* Ch. 8.

Waste not, want not is a law of nature.
JOHN PLATT, *Economy,* p. 22.

The following words were written . . . over the chimneypiece in his uncle's spacious kitchen—'Waste not, want not.'
MARIA EDGEWORTH, *Parent's Assistant,* 232.

Waste not want not is my doctrine.
CHARLES KINGSLEY, *Westward Ho!* Ch. 8.

13
Wherefore do ye spend money for that which is not bread? and your labour for that which satisfieth not?
Old Testament: Isaiah, lv, 2.

To what purpose is this waste?
New Testament: Matthew, xxvi, 8.

14
Wasted his substance with riotous living.
New Testament: Luke, xv, 13.

15
Waste is not grandeur.
WILLIAM MASON, *English Garden.* Bk. ii, l. 20.

16
The waste of plenty is the resource of scarcity.
T. L. PEACOCK, *Melincourt.* Ch. 24.

1
I have lost both my oil and my work: i. e., both time and trouble. (Oleum et operam perdidi.)

Plautus, *Pœnulus*, l. 332. (Act i, sc. 2.) A proverbial expression used also by Plautus in *Casina*, ii, 3.

The work perishes fruitlessly. (Opera nequidquam perit.)

Phædrus, *Fables*. Bk. ii, fab. 5, l. 24.

2
Spare at the spigot and let out at the bunghole.

John Ray, *English Proverbs*, p. 193.

3
I am now about no waste, I am about thrift.

Shakespeare, *The Merry Wives of Windsor*. Act i, sc. 3, l. 47.

4
You waste the treasure of your time.

Shakespeare, *Twelfth Night*. Act ii, sc. 5, l. 85.

The clock upbraids me with the waste of time.

Shakespeare, *Twelfth Night*. Act iii, sc. 1, l. 141.

5
He knows how to squander, but not to bestow. (Perdere iste sciet, donare nesciet.)

Tacitus, *History*. Bk. i, sec. 30.

6
A nice wife and a back door
Maketh ofttimes a rich man poor.

Unknown, *Proverbs of Good Counsel*. No. 8.

WATCH

7
You own a watch, the invention of the mind,
Though for a single motion 'tis designed,
As well as that which is with greater thought
With various springs, for various motions, wrought.

Sir Richard Blackmore, *The Creation*. Bk. iii. *See also* God and the Watchmaker.

8
And I had lent my watch last night to one
That dines to-day at the sheriff's.

Ben Jonson, *The Alchemist*. Act i, sc. 1.

9
It strikes! one, two,
Three, four, five, six. Enough, enough, dear watch,
Thy pulse hath beat enough. Now sleep and rest;
Would thou could'st make the time to do so too;
I'll wind thee up no more.

Ben Jonson, *Staple of News*. Act i, sc. 1.

10
Ever out of frame,
And never going aright, being a watch,
But being watch'd that it may still go right!

Shakespeare, *Love's Labour's Lost*. Act iii, sc. 1, l. 193.

And perchance wind up my watch.

Shakespeare, *Twelfth Night*. Act ii, sc. 5, 67.

WATER

I—Water: Apothegms

11
You must not pump spring-water unawares
Upon a gracious public full of nerves.

E. B. Browning, *Aurora Leigh*. Bk. iii, l. 72.

12
We never know the worth of water till the well is dry.

Thomas Fuller, *Gnomologia*. No. 5451.

We never miss the water till the well runs dry.

Burne, *Shropshire Folk-Lore*, 590.

You never miss the water till the well runs dry.

Rowland Brown. A song for many years a minstrel favorite.

When the well's dry, we know the worth of water.

Benjamin Franklin, *Poor Richard*, 1746.

Till taught by pain,
Men really know not what good water's worth.

Byron, *Don Juan*. Canto ii, st. 84.

13
The world turns softly
Not to spill its lakes and rivers,
The water is held in its arms
And the sky is held in the water.
What is water, That pours silver,
And can hold the sky?

Hilda Conkling, *Water*.

14
The conscious water saw its God and blushed. (Nympha pudica Deum vidit, et erubuit.)

Richard Crashaw, *Epigrammata Sacra: Aquæ in Vinum Versæ*. *See under* Miracle.

15
Take the proverb to thine heart,
Take, and hold it fast—
"The mill cannot grind
With the water that is past."

Sarah Doudney, *The Lesson of the Water-Mill*. *See also under* Mill.

16
The water that comes from the same spring cannot be fresh and salt both.

Thomas Fuller, *Gnomologia*. No. 4817.

17
Unstable as water, thou shalt not excel.

Old Testament: Genesis, xlix, 4.

18
Whom your fair speeches might have made believe
That water could be carried in a sieve.

Sir John Harington, *Orlando Furioso*. Canto xxxii, st. 39.

19
In smooth water God help me; in rough water I will help myself.

George Herbert, *Jacula Prudentum*. *See also under* Trust.

20
The noblest of the elements is water. (Ἄριστον μὲν ὕδωρ.)

Pindar, *Olympian Odes*. Ode i, l. 1.

21
The water will tell you, said the guide, when

the travelers asked him how deep the water was.
PLATO, *Theætetus*. Sec. 200.

1 The noise of many waters.
Old Testament: Psalms, xciii, 4.

2 Foul water will quench fire.
JOHN RAY, *English Proverbs*.

Dirty water does not wash clean.
W. C. BENHAM, *Proverbs*, p. 752. The Italian form is, "Acqua torbida non lava."

Water washes everything. (A agoa tudo lava.)
UNKNOWN. A Portuguese proverb.

3 He seeks water in the sea.
JOHN RAY, *English Proverbs*, 75.

To carry water to the sea. (Wasser in's Meer tragen.)
UNKNOWN. A German proverb.

See also under COAL.

4 As water spilt on the ground, which cannot be gathered up again.
Old Testament: II Samuel, xiv, 14.

5 Court holy-water in a dry house is better than this rain-water out o' door.
SHAKESPEARE, *King Lear*. Act iii, sc. 2, l. 10.

6 Love's fire heats water. water cools not love.
SHAKESPEARE, *Sonnets*. No. cliv.

7 Where least expected water breaks forth. (Dove non si credo, l'acqua rompe.)
UNKNOWN. An Italian proverb.

8 Better it is to calm the troubled waters. (Motos præstat componere fluctus.)
VERGIL, *Æneid*. Bk. i, l. 135.

Pouring oil on troubled water.
BEDE, *Historia Ecclesiastica*. Bk. iii, ch. 15. *See under* SEA IN STORM.

II—Water as a Drink

9 When water chokes you, what are you to drink to wash it down? ("Οταν τὸ ὕδωρ πνίγῃ, τί δεῖ ἐπιπίνειν.)
ARISTOTLE, *Nicomachean Ethics*. Bk. vii, ch. 2, sec. 10. Referred to as a proverb.

10 The wise man of Miletus [Thales] thus declared
The first of things is water.
J. S. BLACKIE, *The Wise Men of Greece: Pythagoras*.

Oh! I have gazed into my foaming glass,
And wished that lyre could yet again be strung
Which once rang prophet-like through Greece, and taught her
Misguided sons that the best drink was water.
C. S. CALVERLEY, *Beer*. St. 8.

11 A cup of cold Adam from the next purling stream.
TOM BROWN, *Works*. Vol. iv, p. 11.

Here's to old Adam's crystal ale,
Clear sparkling and divine,
Fair H_2O, long may you flow,
We drink your health (in wine).
OLIVER HERFORD, *Toast: Adam's Crystal Ale*.

We'll drink Adam's ale, and we get it pool measure.
THOMAS HOOD, *Drinking Song*.

A Rechabite poor Will must live,
And drink of Adam's ale.
MATTHEW PRIOR, *The Wandering Pilgrim*.

Adam's ale—about the only gift that has descended undefiled from the Garden of Eden! Nature's common carrier—not created in the rottenness of fermentation, not distilled over guilty fires!
EMERY A. STORRS, *Water*.

12 No poison bubbles on its brink; no blood stains its limpid glass; . . . beautiful, pure, blessed and glorious, forever the same, sparkling, pure water!
JOHN B. GOUGH, *Toast to Water*.

13 They drank the water clear,
Instead of wine, but yet they made good cheer.
ROBERT HENRYSON, *The Town and Country Mouse*.

14 No verses can please long, or live, which are written by water drinkers. (Nulla placere diu nec vivere carmina possunt, Quæ scribuntur aquæ potoribus.)
HORACE, *Epistles*. Bk. i, epis. 19, l. 2.

15 Now to rivulets from the mountains
Point the rods of fortune-tellers;
Youth perpetual dwells in fountains,—
Not in flasks, and casks, and cellars.
LONGFELLOW, *Drinking Song*. St. 8.

16 I'm very fond of water;
It ever must delight
Each mother's son and daughter,
When qualified aright.
CHARLES NEAVES, *I'm Very Fond of Water*.

Pure water is the best of gifts that man to man can bring,
But who am I that I should have the best of anything?
Let princes revel at the pump, let peers with ponds make free,
Whiskey, or wine, or even *beer* is good enough for me.
UNKNOWN. (*Spectator*, 31 July, 1920.) Attributed to Lord Neaves, and also to G. W. E. Russell. (For other versions see *Notes and Queries*, 23 Oct., 1897.)

17 Here's that which is too weak to be a sinner,
honest water which ne'er left man i' the mire.
SHAKESPEARE, *Timon of Athens*. Act i, sc. 2, 58.

18 'Tis a little thing
To give a cup of water; yet its draught

Of cool refreshment, drained by fevered lips,
May give a shock of pleasure to the frame
More exquisite than when nectarian juice
Renews the joy of life in happiest hours.
THOMAS NOON TALFOURD, *Ion*. Act i, sc. 2.

1
The old oaken bucket, the iron-bound bucket,
The moss-covered bucket that hangs in the well!
SAMUEL WOODWORTH, *The Bucket*.

How sweet from the green mossy brim to receive it,
As poised on the curb it inclined to my lips!
Not a full blushing goblet would tempt me to leave it,
The brightest that beauty or revelry sips.
SAMUEL WOODWORTH, *The Bucket*.

WATER, WATER EVERYWHERE, *see under* THIRST.

III—Water: Still Waters

2
Take heed of still waters, they quick pass away.
GEORGE HERBERT, *Jacula Prudentum*.

3
Deep waters noiseless are; and this we know,
That chiding streams betray small depths below.
ROBERT HERRICK, *To His Mistress*.

Passions are likened best to floods and streams:
The shallow murmur, but the deep are dumb.
SIR WALTER RALEIGH, *The Silent Lover*.

The deepest rivers make least din,
The silent soul doth most abound in care.
EARL OF STIRLING, *Aurora: Song*. (1604)

See also GRIEF: SILENT AND VOCAL.

4
But there is not, as they say, any worse water than water that sleeps. (Mais il n'est, comme on dit, pire eau que l'eau qui dort.)
MOLIÈRE, *Tartuffe*. Act i, sc. 1.

Have a care of a silent dog and still water. (Cave tibi a cane muto et aqua silenti.)
UNKNOWN. A Latin proverb.

5
The deepest rivers flow with the least sound. (Altissima quæque flumina minimo sono labuntur.)
QUINTUS CURTIUS RUFUS, *De Rebus Gestis Alexandri Magni*. Bk. vii, ch. 4. (c. A.D. 50)

Smooth waters been oft sithes deep.
JOHN LYDGATE, *Minor Poems*, p. 186. (c. 1430)

Water runneth smoothest where it is deepest.
JOHN LYLY, *Sapho and Phao*. Act ii, sc. 4. (1584)

Smooth runs the water where the brook is deep.
SHAKESPEARE, *II Henry VI*, iii, 1, 53. (1590)

6
Shallow brooks murmur most, deep silent slide away.
SIR PHILIP SIDNEY, *Arcadia: Thirsis and Dorus*. (1590)

Still waters are the deepest, but the shallowest brooks brawl the most.
C. H. SPURGEON, *John Ploughman*. Ch. 6.

IV—Water: Water and Rock

7
The unceasing drop of water, as they say,
Will wear a channel in the hardest stone.
BION SMYRNÆUS, *Fragments*. No. 2.

By constant dripping a drop of water hollows out a rock. (Πέτρην κοιλαίνει ῥανὶς ὕδατος ἐνδελεχείῃ.)
CHŒRILUS OF SAMOS, *Fragments*. No. 9.

Not by strength but by constant falling does the drop hollow out the stone. (Gutta cavet lapidem non vi, sed sæpe cadendo.)
GARIOPONTUS, *Passionarius*, i, 17. (c. 1050); RICHARD, Monk of St. Victor, Paris, *Adnotationes Mysticæ in Psalmos*. (c 1165) See Migne, *Patrologia Latina*. Vol. cxcvi, p. 389. Quoted by Galen (Vol. viii, p. 27): "Gutta cavat lapidem sæpe cadentis aquæ."

8
The fall of dropping water wears away the stone. (Stillicidi casus lapidem cavat.)
LUCRETIUS, *De Rerum Natura*. Bk. i, sec. 314.

9
The soft drops of rain pierce the hard marble.
JOHN LYLY, *Euphues*, p. 81.

10
What is harder than rock, or softer than water? Yet soft water hollows out hard rock. Only persevere. (Quid magis est saxo durum, quid mollidus unda? Dura tamen molli saxa caventur aqua. Persta modo.)
OVID, *Ars Amatoria*. Bk. i, l. 475.

Stones are hollowed out by the constant dropping of water. (Caducis Percussu crebro saxa cavantur aquis.)
OVID, *Epistulæ ex Ponto*. Bk. ii, epis. 7, l. 39.

Drops of water hollow out a stone; a ring is worn thin by use. (Gutta cavat lapidem, consumitur anulus usu.)
OVID, *Epistulæ ex Ponto*. Bk. iv, epis. 10, l. 5.

11
Water continually dropping wears hard rocks hollow. (Σταγόνες ὕδατος πέτρας κοιλαίνουσι.)
PLUTARCH, *Of the Training of Children*. Sec. 4.

The waters wear the stones.
Old Testament: Job, xiv, 19.

12
No rock so hard but that a little wave
May beat admission in a thousand years.
TENNYSON, *The Princess*. Pt. iii, l. 138.

12a
How many men Have come and gone
Where you see a path Worn smooth in stone?
JOHN FRAZIER VANCE, *How Many Men?* (*Scribner's Magazine*, Sept., 1928.)

WATERLOO

13
The battle of Waterloo and its results appeared to me to put back the clock of the world six degrees.
ROBERT HALL. (GREGORY, *Life*. Note A.)

1
Every man meets his Waterloo at last.
WENDELL PHILLIPS, *Speech on John Brown*, 1 Nov., 1859.

When the first just and friendly man appeared on the earth, from that day a fatal Waterloo was visible for all men of pride and fraud and blood.
CHARLES FLETCHER DOLE, *The Coming People.*

2
John Bull was beat at Waterloo!
They'll swear to that in France.
WINTHROP MACKWORTH PRAED, *Waterloo.*

3
So great a soldier taught us there
What long-enduring hearts could do
In that world-earthquake, Waterloo!
TENNYSON, *Ode on the Death of the Duke of Wellington*, l. 131.

4
Up, Guards, and at 'em!
Attributed to the DUKE OF WELLINGTON, at the crisis of the battle of Waterloo. Also quoted, "Up, Guards, make ready."

What I must have said was, "Stand up, Guards!" and then gave the order to attack.
DUKE OF WELLINGTON, *Letter to J. W. Croker*, answering a letter written 14 March, 1852. (J. W. CROKER, *Memoirs*, p. 544.)

The Guard dies, but never surrenders. (Le garde meurt et ne se rend pas.)
GENERAL PIERRE DE CAMBRONNE, *Reply*, attributed to him when surrounded and summoned to surrender by the British during the retreat from Waterloo. Afterwards denied by him. What he probably did say was, "Merde, je ne me rends pas" (hence the "mot de Cambronne"). He did surrender and lived for twenty-seven years afterwards.

5
The battle of Waterloo was won here.
DUKE OF WELLINGTON, *Remark*, while watching a cricket match at Eton. Usually quoted, "The battle of Waterloo was won on the playing-field of Eton." See WILLIAM SELWYN, WATERLOO. The present seventh Duke denies that Wellington ever said this.

WEAKNESS

7
The cord breaketh at last by the weakest pull.
FRANCIS BACON, *Essays: Of Seditions.*

8
The concessions of the weak are the concessions of fear.
EDMUND BURKE, *Conciliation with America.*

9
People in general will much better bear being told of their vices and crimes than of their failings and weaknesses.
LORD CHESTERFIELD, *Letters*, 26 Nov., 1749.

11
Weakened and wasted to skin and bone.
DU BARTAS, *Devine Weekes and Workes.* Week ii, day 4. (Sylvester, tr.)

12
All hands shall be feeble, and all knees shall be weak as water.
Old Testament: Ezekiel, vii, 17.

Yesterday I was firm as a rock, today I'm as weak as water again.
A. W. PINERO, *Gay Lord Quex.* Act iv.

13
Amiable weakness.
FIELDING, *Tom Jones.* Bk. x, ch. 8.

Amiable weakness of human nature.
GIBBON, *Decline and Fall of the Roman Empire.* Ch. 14.

It was an amiable weakness.
SHERIDAN, *School for Scandal.* Act v, sc. 1.

See also FAULTS: THEIR VIRTUES.

14
Weak things united become strong.
FULLER, *Gnomologia.* No. 5460. *See also* UNITY.

15
And the weak soul, within itself unblest,
Leans for all pleasure on another's breast.
GOLDSMITH, *The Traveller*, l. 271.

16
When you know the weakness of a man whom you want to please, you must be very clumsy if you do not succeed. (Quand on connoît le défaut d'un homme à qui l'on veut plaire, il faut être bien maladroit pour n'y pas réussir.)
LE SAGE, *Gil Blas.* Bk. viii, ch. 2. *See also* FAULT.

17
There are two kinds of weakness, that which breaks and that which bends.
J. R. LOWELL, *Among My Books: Shakespeare Once More.*

Soft-heartedness, in times like these,
Shows sof'ness in the upper story!
J. R. LOWELL, *Biglow Papers.* Ser. ii, No. 7.

18
To be weak is miserable, Doing or suffering.
MILTON, *Paradise Lost.* Bk. i, l. 157.

If to be weak is to be wretched—miserable,
As the lost angel by a human voice
Hath mournfully pronounced.
WORDSWORTH, *The Excursion.* Bk. v, l. 318.

19
Fine by defect, and delicately weak.
POPE, *Moral Essays.* Epis. ii, l. 43.

20
Every man has his weak side.
JOHN RAY, *English Proverbs.*

Men's weaknesses are often necessary to the purposes of life.
MAURICE MAETERLINCK, *Joyzelle.* Act ii.

21
Man but a rush against Othello's breast,
And he retires.
SHAKESPEARE, *Othello.* Act v, sc. 2, l. 270.

22
What 'twas weak to do
'Tis weaker to lament, once being done.
SHELLEY, *The Cenci.* Act v, sc. 3.

23
In a just cause the weak o'ercome the strong. (Τοῖς τοι δικαίοις χὠ βραχὺς νικᾷ μέγαν.)
SOPHOCLES, *Œdipus Coloneus*, l. 880.

Throughout all past time, there has been a ceaseless devouring of the weak by the strong.
HERBERT SPENCER, *First Principles.*

See also MIGHT AND RIGHT.

1
The weak brother is the worst of mankind.
R. L. STEVENSON, *Crabbed Age and Youth.*

2
Weakness to be wroth with weakness! woman's pleasure, woman's pain—
Nature made them blinder motions bounded in a shallower brain.
TENNYSON, *Locksley Hall,* l. 149.

3
The weakest goeth ever to the wall.
UNKNOWN. *Two Coventry Plays,* p. 47. (1534)

Howsoever the cause go, the weakest is thrust to the wall.
ROBERT GREENE, *Works.* Vol. xi, p. 252. (1585)

The weakest goes to the wall.
SHAKESPEARE, *Romeo and Juliet.* Act i, sc. 1, l. 18. (1592)

WEALTH, see Riches

WEATHER

I—Weather: Apothegms

4
And altogether it's very bad weather,
And an unpleasant sort of a night!
R. H. BARHAM, *The Nurse's Story.*

5
To talk of the weather, it's nothing but folly,
For when it rains on the hill, it shines in the valley.
DENHAM, *Proverbs,* 17.

Change of weather is the discourse of fools.
JAMES HOWELL, *Proverbs.* Pt. ii. (1659)

When two Englishmen meet, their first talk is of the weather.
SAMUEL JOHNSON, *The Idler.* No. 11.

6
We will not woo foul weather all too soon,
Or nurse November on the lap of June.
THOMAS HOOD, *The Plea of the Midsummer Fairies,* l. 827.

7
Oh, what a blamed uncertain thing
This pesky weather is!
It blew and snew and then it thew
And now, by jing, it's friz!
PHILANDER JOHNSON, *Shooting Stars.*

First it rained, and then it snew,
Then it friz, and then it thew,
And then it friz again.
UNKNOWN. An old jingle.

8
The weather and my mood have little connection. I have my foggy and my fine days within me.
PASCAL, *Pensées.* Sec. ii, No. 107.

9
It hain't no use to grumble and complane,
It's jest as easy to rejoice;
When God sorts out the weather and sends rain,
Why rain's my choice.
JAMES WHITCOMB RILEY, *Wet-Weather Talk.*

10
I tax not you, you elements, with unkindness.
SHAKESPEARE, *King Lear.* Act iii, sc. 2, l. 16.

11
Many can brook the weather that love not the wind.
SHAKESPEARE, *Love's Labour's Lost,* iv, 2, 34.

12
The weather is beautiful; but as Noodle says (with his eyes beaming with delight), "We shall suffer for this, sir, by-and-by."
SYDNEY SMITH, *Letter to Sir George Phillips,* 22 Dec., 1836.

13
Plaguy twelve-penny weather.
SWIFT, *Letter to Stella,* 26 Oct., 1710.

Shilling weather.
JOHN GAY, *Letter to Swift,* meaning weather where chair-hire or coach-hire was necessary.

14
There is a sumptuous variety about New England weather that compels the stranger's admiration—and regret. . . . In the Spring I have counted one hundred and thirty-six different kinds of weather inside of twenty-four hours.
MARK TWAIN, *New England Weather: Speech at Dinner of New England Society,* New York, 22 Dec., 1876.

14a
Everybody talks about the weather, but nobody does anything about it.
CHARLES DUDLEY WARNER, *Editorial,* Hartford, Conn., *Courant,* c. 1890. Often attributed to Mark Twain.

I guess it's no use; they still believe Mark Twain said it, despite all my assurances that it was Warner.
CHARLES HOPKINS CLARK, Editor of the *Courant.*

II—Weather: Some Omens

15
A dry March and a dry May portend a wholesome summer, if there be a showering April between.
BACON, *Sylva Sylvarum.* Cent. ix, sec. 807.

16
Fair weather cometh out of the north.
Old Testament: Job, xxxvii, 22.

17
When it is evening, ye say, It will be fair weather: for the sky is red. And in the morning, It will be foul weather today for the sky is red and lowering.
New Testament: Matthew, xvi, 2–3.

Evening red and morning grey
Will speed a traveller on his way;
But evening grey and morning red
Will pour down rain upon his head.
DENHAM, *Proverbs,* 8.

The evening red, and the morning grey,
Is the sign of a fair day.
MILLS, *Essay on Weather,* 34.

18
A sunshiny shower
Won't last half an hour.

Rain before seven,
Fair by eleven.
The South wind brings wet weather,
The North wind wet and cold together;
The West wind always brings us rain,
The East wind blows it back again.
March winds and April showers
Bring forth May flowers.
Rainbow at night is the sailor's delight;
Rainbow at morning, sailors, take warning.

UNKNOWN, *Old Nursery Rhymes.*

1
The South wind brings wet weather,
The North wind wet and cold together;
The West wind always brings us rain.
The East wind blows it back again.
If the sun in red doth set
The next day surely will be wet;
If the sun doth set in grey,
The next will be a rainy day.

UNKNOWN, *Lines by a Pessimist.*

WEBSTER, DANIEL

2
Men hang out their signs indicative of their respective trades. Shoemakers hang a gigantic shoe; jewelers a monster watch; even the dentist hangs out a gold tooth; but up in Franconi Mountains God Almighty has hung out a sign to show that in New England He makes men.

DANIEL WEBSTER, referring to the Great Stone Face.

3
Mrs. Hawthorne could not bring herself quite to believe that he [Webster] was not as great as he looked; but Hawthorne had formed a somewhat different opinion. This opinion is set forth, by the by, in the story of "The Great Stone Face."

JULIAN HAWTHORNE, *Hawthorne and His Wife.* Vol. i, p. 476.

But now, again, there were reports and many paragraphs in the newspapers, affirming that the likeness of the Great Stone Face had appeared upon the broad shoulders of a certain eminent statesman. . . . Instead of the rich man's wealth and the warrior's sword, he had but a tongue; and it was mightier than both together. So wonderfully eloquent was he, that whatever he might choose to say, his auditors had no choice but to believe him; wrong looked like right, and right like wrong; for when it pleased him, he could make a kind of illuminated fog with his mere breath, and obscure the natural daylight with it. His tongue, indeed, was a magic instrument; sometimes it rumbled like thunder; sometimes it warbled like the sweetest music.

NATHANIEL HAWTHORNE, *The Great Stone Face.*

Such a figure, such an intellect, such a heart, were certainly never combined before to save the world. . . . The front of Jove, the regal, commanding air which cleared a path before him, the voice of thunder and music, the unfathomable eye—all these external signs said, "Here is a Great Man!"

SOPHIA PEABODY HAWTHORNE. (JULIAN HAWTHORNE, *Hawthorne and His Wife.* Vol. i, p. 476.)

4
How will this look in history?

DANIEL WEBSTER, on receiving a telegram announcing the 57th ballot, Scott 159, Fillmore 112, Webster 21, at the convention of 1852.

5
Have I—wife, son, doctor, friends, are you all there?—have I, on this occasion, said anything unworthy of Daniel Webster?

DANIEL WEBSTER, reported as his last words. (FUESS, *Daniel Webster;* ADAMS, *The Godlike Daniel.*) More probably his last words were, "I still live," possibly a reference to the doctor's order to an attendant, "If he is alive in an hour, give him some brandy."

6
Thirty years ago, when Mr. Webster at the bar or in the Senate filled the eyes and minds of young men, you might often hear cited as Mr. Webster's three rules: first, never to do to-day what he could defer till to-morrow; secondly, never to do himself what he could make another do for him; and, thirdly, never to pay any debt today. Well, they are none the worse for being already told, in the last generation, of Sheridan; and we find in Grimm's *Mémoires* that Sheridan got them from the witty D'Argenson.

EMERSON, *Letters and Social Aims: Quotation and Originality.*

7
I would not attempt to vie with the honorable gentleman from Massachusetts in a field where every nigger is his peer and every billy-goat his master.

JOHN RANDOLPH OF ROANOKE, of Daniel Webster, who, Randolph believed, had accused him of impotence. (ADAMS, *The Godlike Daniel*, p. 169.) The fact of Randolph's impotence was verified after his death.

8
Daniel Webster struck me much like a steam-engine in trousers.

SYDNEY SMITH. (LADY HOLLAND, *Memoir.* Ch. 9. Vol. i, p. 265.)

God Almighty never created a man half as wise as he looks.

THOMAS CARLYLE, referring to Webster.

God is only the president of the day, and Webster is his orator.

H. D. THOREAU, *Walden: Conclusion.*

9
So fallen! so lost! the light withdrawn
Which once he wore!
The glory from his gray hairs gone
For evermore!

WHITTIER, *Ichabod.*

Thou,
Whom the rich heavens did so endow
With eyes of power and Jove's own brow, . . .

New England's stateliest type of man,
In port and speech Olympian;
Whom no one met, at first. but took
A second awed and wondering look.
WHITTIER, *The Lost Occasion.*

WEDDING, see Marriage: Wedding Day

WEED

1
Call us not weeds; we are flowers of the sea.
E. L. AVELINE, *The Mother's Fables.*

Still must I on, for I am as a weed,
Flung from the rock, on Ocean's foam, to sail
Where'er the surge may sweep.
BYRON, *Childe Harold.* Canto iii, st. 2.

2
The flowers are loved, the weeds are spurned,
But for them both the suns are burned;
And when, at last, they fail the day,
The long night folds them all away.
JOHN VANCE CHENEY, *Weeds and Flowers.*

3
Turning our seed-wheat-kennel tares,
To burn-grain thistle, and to vapory darnel,
Cockle, wild oats, rough burs, corn-cumbring tares.
DU BARTAS, *Devine Weekes and Workes.* Week ii, day 3. (Sylvester, tr.)

Nothing teems
But hateful docks, rough thistles, kecksies, burs,
Losing both beauty and utility.
SHAKESPEARE, *Henry V.* Act v, sc. 2, l. 51.

Bur-docks, hemlock, nettles, cuckoo-flowers,
Darnel, and all the idle weeds that grow
In our sustaining corn.
SHAKESPEARE, *King Lear.* Act iv, sc. 4, l. 4.

4
What I thought was a flower is only a weed, and is worthless.
LONGFELLOW, *Courtship of Miles Standish.* Pt. vii.

5
A weed is no more than a flower in disguise,
Which is seen through at once, if love give a man eyes.
J. R. LOWELL, *A Fable for Critics,* l. 97.

To win the secret of a weed's plain heart
Reveals some clue to spiritual things.
J. R. LOWELL, *Sonnets.* No. 25.

6
The richest soil, if uncultivated, produces the rankest weeds.
PLUTARCH, *Lives: Coriolanus.* Ch. 1, sec. 2.

Most subject is the fattest soil to weeds.
SHAKESPEARE, *II Henry IV.* Act iv, sc. 4, l. 54.

7
He that bites on every weed must needs light on poison.
JOHN RAY, *English Proverbs.*

One ill weed mars a whole mess of pottage.
JOHN RAY, *English Proverbs.*

The weed o'ergaes the corn.
JOHN RAY, *Proverbs: Scottish.*

8
Now 'tis the spring, and weeds are shallow-rooted;
Suffer them now, and they 'll o'ergrow the garden
And choke the herbs for want of husbandry.
SHAKESPEARE, *II Henry VI.* Act iii, sc. 1, l. 31.

The noisome weeds, which without profit suck
The soil's fertility from wholesome flowers.
SHAKESPEARE, *Richard II.* Act iii, sc. 4, l. 38.

9
O thou weed,
Who art so lovely fair and smell'st so sweet
That the sense aches at thee, would thou hadst ne'er been born!
SHAKESPEARE, *Othello.* Act iv, sc. 2, l. 67.

10
"Ay," quoth my uncle Gloucester,
"Small herbs have grace, great weeds do grow apace:"
And since, methinks, I would not grow so fast,
Because sweet flowers are slow and weeds make haste.
SHAKESPEARE, *Richard III.* Act ii, sc. 4, l. 12.

You said that idle weeds are fast in growth.
SHAKESPEARE, *Richard III.* Act iii, sc. 1, l. 103.

11
The summer's flower is to the summer sweet,
Though to itself it only live and die,
But if that flower with base infection meet,
The basest weed outbraves his dignity:
For sweetest things turn sourest by their deeds;
Lilies that fester smell far worse than weeds.
SHAKESPEARE, *Sonnets.* No. xciv.

12
Once in a golden hour
I cast to earth a seed.
Up there came a flower,
The people said, a weed.
TENNYSON, *The Flower.*

13
Evil weed is soon grown.
UNKNOWN. (HULME, *Proverb Lore.* c. 1490)

Ill weed groweth fast.
JOHN HEYWOOD, *Proverbs.* Pt. i, ch. 10. (1546)

An ill weed grows apace.
GEORGE CHAPMAN, *An Humourous Day's Mirth.* (1599)

Great weeds grow apace.
BEAUMONT AND FLETCHER, *The Coxcomb.* Act iv, sc. 4. (1612)

How soon prospers the vicious weed!
PHINEAS FLETCHER, *Apollyonist.* Canto iii, st. 4. (1633)

WEEPING, see Tears

WELCOME, see Hospitality

WELLINGTON, DUKE OF

See also Waterloo

14
The Duke of Wellington brought to the post of first minister immortal fame; a quality of success which would almost seem to include all others.
BENJAMIN DISRAELI, *Sybil.* Bk. i, ch. 3.

1
No more, surveying with an eye impartial
The long line of the coast,
Shall the gaunt figure of the old Field Marshal
Be seen upon his post!
LONGFELLOW, *The Warden of the Cinque Ports.*

1a
Great Chieftain, who takest such pains
To prove—what is granted, *nem. con.*—
With how mod'rate a portion of brains
Some heroes contrive to get on.
THOMAS MOORE, *Dog-Day Reflections.* St. 8.

2
The last great Englishman is low.
TENNYSON, *Ode on the Death of the Duke of Wellington,* l. 18.

Foremost captain of his time,
Rich in saving common-sense,
And, as the greatest only are,
In his simplicity sublime.
O good grey head that all men knew,
O voice from which their omens all men drew,
O iron nerve to true occasion true,
O fallen at length that tower of strength
Which stood four-square to all the winds that blew! . . .
For this is England's greatest son,
He that gain'd a hundred fights,
Nor ever lost an English gun. . . .
O saviour of the silver-coasted isle. . . .
Ashes to ashes, dust to dust;
He is gone who seem'd so great.—
Gone; but nothing can bereave him
Of the force he made his own
Being here, and we believe him
Something far advanced in State,
And that he wears a truer crown
Than any wreath that man can weave him.
Speak no more of his renown,
Lay your earthly fancies down,
And in the vast cathedral leave him,
God accept him, Christ receive him.
TENNYSON, *Ode on the Death of the Duke of Wellington,* ll. 31, 95, 136, 270.

3
But one thing is needful.
New Testament: Luke, x, 42. (Porro unum est necessarium.—*Vulgate.*) Motto of the Duke of Wellington. Also: Virtute fortuna comes, "Good fortune is the companion of valour."

WEST

See also East

4
Odd, how all dying things turn to the West, the region of questions? So mourners on the Nile consigned the mummied citizen to the mercies of the West and soldiers of the recent muddy mess in upper France "went West" to join Hiawatha, King Arthur and the ecstatic nun Petronilla who saw God descending from the West in the shape of a fish-hook to lift her virgin soul into bliss.
THOMAS BEER, *The Mauve Decade,* p. 244.

You who went West . . . shall take your rest
In the soft sweet glooms Of twilight rooms.
FORD MADOX HUEFFER, *One Day's List.*

5
Out where the handclasp's a little stronger,
Out where the smile dwells a little longer,
That's where the West begins.
ARTHUR CHAPMAN, *Out Where the West Begins.*

6
Olivia: There lies your way, due west.
Viola: Then westward-ho!
SHAKESPEARE, *Twelfth Night.* Act iii, sc. 1, l. 145.

Westward Ho!
CHARLES KINGSLEY. Title of novel.

7
Go West, young man, go West!
JOHN L. B. SOULE, *Editorial, Terre Haute* (Ind.) *Express,* 1851.

Go West, young man.
HORACE GREELEY, *Letter to W. H. Verity,* 1854.

Go West, young man, and grow up with the country.
HORACE GREELEY, *Hints toward Reform.*

WESTMINSTER ABBEY

8
Here's an acre sown indeed
With the richest, royalest seed.
FRANCIS BEAUMONT, *On Westminster Abbey.*

10
In that temple of silence and reconciliation where the enmities of twenty generations lie buried, in the Great Abbey which has during many ages afforded a quiet resting-place to those whose minds and bodies have been shattered by the contentions of the Great Hall.
MACAULAY, *Essays: Warren Hastings.*

11
Along the walls where speaking marbles show
What worthies form the hallowed mold below;
Proud names, who once the reins of empire held;
In arms who triumphed, or in arts excelled.
THOMAS TICKELL, *To the Earl of Warwick.*

WHEEL

12
Like him in Æsop, he whipped his horses withal, and put his shoulder to the wheel.
ROBERT BURTON, *Anatomy of Melancholy.* Pt. ii, sec. 1, mem. 2.

13
Their appearance and their work were as it were a wheel in the middle of a wheel.
Old Testament: Ezekiel, i, 16.

As if a wheel had been in the midst of a wheel.
Old Testament: Ezekiel, x, 10.

As a wheel within a wheel.
BERNARD MANDEVILLE, *Virgin Unmask'd: Preface.* (1709)

Wheels within wheels.
ROGER NORTH, *Lives of the Norths.* Vol. i, p. 306. (1740)

"And a bird-cage, sir," said Sam. "Veels vithin veels, a prison in a prison."
DICKENS, *Pickwick Papers.* Ch. 40.

1
The worst wheel of the cart makes the most noise.

BENJAMIN FRANKLIN, *Poor Richard*, 1737.

I hate to be a kicker, I always long for peace,
But the wheel that does the squeaking is the one
that gets the grease.

UNKNOWN, *The Kicker.*

Call upon the wheels, master, call upon the wheels,
Steel is beneath your hand, stone beneath your
heels— . . .
Men of tact that arbitrate, slow reform that
heals—
Save the stinking grease, master, save it for the
wheels.

G. K. CHESTERTON, *The Song of the Wheels.*

2
I want to see the wheels go round.

JOHN HABBERTON, *Helen's Babies*, p. 11.

3
The wheel has come full circle.

SHAKESPEARE, *King Lear*. Act v, sc. 3, l. 174.

4
I'll put a spoke in your cart.

UNKNOWN, *Weakest to the Wall*, l. 848. (1600)

I shall put a spoke in her rising Wheel of Fortune.

APHRA BEHN, *Roundheads*. Act v, sc. 2.

I'll put a spoke among your wheels.

JOHN FLETCHER, *The Mad Lover*. Act iii, sc. 5.

For WHEEL OF FORTUNE, *see under* FORTUNE.

WHITMAN, WALT

5
We go to Whitman for his attitude toward life and the universe; we go to stimulate and fortify our souls; in short for his cosmic philosophy incarnated in a man.

JOHN BURROUGHS, *The Last Harvest.*

W. W. is the Christ of the modern world—he alone redeems it, justifies it, shows it divine.

JOHN BURROUGHS, *Entry in Journal on Death of Whitman.*

6
As Cæsar Augustus found a Rome of brick and left it a Rome of marble, so Walt Whitman found the everyday world around us a world of familiar substance and left it a world aureoled in mystery.

BENJAMIN DE CASSERES, *Philistine*. Vol. xxv, p. 172.

7
He was integrated into life,
He was a member of life,
He was harmonized, orchestrated, identified
with the program of being.

ZONA GALE, *Walt Whitman.*

8
The American poet Whitman
Did little to assist the razor industry,
But he erected a plausible philosophy
Of indolence,
Which, without soft concealments,
He called *Loafing*. . . .
He was deficient in humour,
But he had a good time.

CHRISTOPHER MORLEY, *A Happy Life.*

9
Walt Whitman, you enigma,
You egoist, who flaunt yourself
Naked to the world,
You many-sided one;
You preacher of beauty In halting lines
That sweep one before their flood
And bore one to death.

LINCOLN REIS, *Walt Whitman.*

10
Into "the troughs of Zolaism," as Lord Tennyson calls them (a phrase which bears rather unduly hard on the quadrupedal pig), I am happy to believe that Mr. Whitman has never dipped a passing nose: he is a writer of something occasionally like English, and a man of something occasionally like genius. . . . Under the dirty clumsy claws of a harper whose plectrum is a muck-rake any tune will become a chaos of discords.

A. C. SWINBURNE, *Whitmania.*

11
Democracy's divine protagonist.

FRANCIS HOWARD WILLIAMS, *Walt Whitman.*

WHITTIER, JOHN GREENLEAF

12
Great master of the poet's art!
Surely the sources of thy powers
Lie in that true and tender heart
Whose every utterance touches ours.

PHŒBE CARY, *John Greenleaf Whittier.*

Thou hast battled for the right
With many a brave and trenchant word,
And shown us how the pen may fight
A mightier battle than the sword.

PHŒBE CARY, *John Greenleaf Whittier.*

13
So long as liberty is loved,
And bud and blossom blown,
And simple thought and aim approved,
And honest life is known,
So long shall Whittier lift his face
O'er some of larger view,
And keep 'mid greater names his place,
Because his heart was true.

JOHN CAMERON GRANT, *John Greenleaf Whittier.*

14
The clear sweet singer with the crown of snow
Not whiter than the thoughts that housed
below.

J. R. LOWELL, *Epistle to George William Curtis: Postscript*, 1887.

15
Prophet and priest he stood
In the storm of embattled years;
The broken chain was his harp's refrain,
And the peace that is balm for tears.

MARGARET SANGSTER, *John Greenleaf Whittier.*

16
Gracious thine age, thy youth was strong,

For Freedom touched the tongue with fire;
To sing the right and fight the wrong
Thine equal hand held bow or lyre.
WILLIAM HAYES WARD, *To John Greenleaf Whittier.*

1
Some blamed him, some believed him good,
The truth lay doubtless 'twixt the two;
He reconciled as best he could
Old faith and fancies new.

In him the grave and playful mixed,
And wisdom held with folly truce,
And Nature compromised betwixt
Good fellow and recluse.
WHITTIER, *My Namesake.* Of himself.

2
Making his rustic reed of song
A weapon in the war with wrong,
Yoking his fancy to the breaking plough
That beam-deep turned the soil
For Truth to spring and grow.
WHITTIER. Inscribed beneath his bust in the Hall of Fame.

WHORE

3
She cries whore first, brings him upon his knees for her fault; and a piece of plate, or a new petticoat, makes his peace again.
APHRA BEHN, *The Town Fop.* Act iv, sc. 3.

4
The harlot's cry from street to street
Shall weave old England's winding-sheet.
The winner's shout, the loser's curse,
Dance before dead England's hearse.
WILLIAM BLAKE, *Auguries of Innocence.*

5
For no man tells his son the truth
For fear he speak of sin;
And every man cries, "Woe, alas!"
And every man goes in.
DANA BURNET, *Sisters of the Cross of Shames.*

6
Sampson with his strong Body, had a weak Head, or he would not have laid it in a Harlot's lap.
BENJAMIN FRANKLIN, *Poor Richard,* 1756.

7
The naughtipacks or offscourings of men.
ARTHUR GOLDING, *Calvin on the Psalms.*

I never heard she was a naughty pack.
SWIFT, *Polite Conversation.* Dial. i.

8
In silk and scarlet walks many a harlot.
W. C. HAZLITT, *English Proverbs,* 234.

Wanton look and twinkling,
Laughing and tickling,
Open breast and singing,
These without lying
Are tokens of whoring.
W. C. HAZLITT, *English Proverbs,* 447.

9
As common as the pavement to every man that walketh.
LANGLAND, *Piers Plowman: Lady Meed.*

A common stale.
SHAKESPEARE, *Much Ado About Nothing.* Act iv, sc. 1, l. 65.

10
Once a whore, and ever a whore.
HENRY PARROT, *Laquei Ridiculosi.* Bk. ii, epig. 121. (1613)

11
In common justice, Sir, there's no man
That makes the whore, but keeps the woman.
MATTHEW PRIOR, *Epistle to Fleetwood Shepherd.* No. 2.

12
And thought the nation ne'er would thrive
Till all the whores were burnt alive.
MATTHEW PRIOR, *Paulo Purganti.*

13
For the lips of a strange woman drop as a honeycomb, and her mouth is smoother than oil: But her end is bitter as wormwood, sharp as a two-edged sword. Her feet go down to death; her steps take hold on hell.
Old Testament: Proverbs, v, 3–5.

14
A young whore, an old saint.
JOHN RAY, *English Proverbs,* 155. *See also under* SAINT.

15
Broad-fronted Cæsar,
When thou wast here above the ground, I was
A morsel for a monarch.
SHAKESPEARE, *Antony and Cleopatra.* Act i, sc. 5, l. 29.

I am not a slut, though I thank the gods I am foul.
SHAKESPEARE, *As You Like It.* Act iii, sc. 3, l. 39.

I have heard I am a strumpet; and mine ear,
Therein false struck, can take no greater wound,
Nor tent to bottom that.
SHAKESPEARE, *Cymbeline.* Act iii, sc. 4, l. 116.

16
No, he hath enjoy'd her:
She hath bought the name of whore thus dearly. . . .
She hath been colted by him.
SHAKESPEARE, *Cymbeline.* Act ii, sc. 4, l. 127.

This is a brave night to cool a courtesan.
SHAKESPEARE, *King Lear.* Act iii, sc. 2, l. 79.

17
Ever your fresh whore and your powder'd bawd.
SHAKESPEARE, *Measure for Measure.* Act iii, sc. 2, l. 61.

18
Your whores, sir, being members of my occupation, used painting.
SHAKESPEARE, *Measure for Measure.* Act iv, sec. 2, l. 39.

For she that paints will doubtless be a whore.
EDWARD WARD, *London Spy,* 420.

A woman that paints puts up a bill that she is to let.
THOMAS FULLER, *Gnomologia.* No. 481.
See also FACE: PAINTED.

1
Leonato's Hero, your Hero, every man's Hero.
SHAKESPEARE, *Much Ado About Nothing*. Act iii, sc. 2, l. 109.

Your Cleopatra, Dolabella's Cleopatra, every man's Cleopatra!
DRYDEN, *All for Love*. Act iv, sc. 1.

A housewife that by selling her desires
Buys herself bread and clothes.
SHAKESPEARE, *Othello*. Act iv, sc. 1, l. 95.

2
Was this fair paper, this most goodly book,
Made to write "whore" upon?
SHAKESPEARE, *Othello*. Act iv, sc. 2, l. 71.

3
If to preserve this vessel for my lord
From any other foul unlawful touch
Be not to be a strumpet, I am none.
SHAKESPEARE, *Othello*. Act iv, sc. 2, l. 83.

I cannot say "whore":
It doth abhor me now I speak the word;
To do the act that might the addition earn
Not the world's mass of vanity could make me.
SHAKESPEARE, *Othello*. Act iv, sc. 2, l. 161.

4
This is the fruit of whoring.
SHAKESPEARE, *Othello*. Act v, sc. 1, l. 116.

Be whores still;
And he whose pious breath seeks to convert you,
Be strong in whore, allure him, burn him up.
SHAKESPEARE, *Timon of Athens*. Act iv, sc. 3, l. 139.

5
[Grafton thought] the world should be postponed to a whore and a horse race.
HORACE WALPOLE, *Letter to Henry Seymour Conway*, 16 June, 1768.

6
When dying sinners, to blot out their score,
Bequeath the church the leavings of a whore.
YOUNG, *Love of Fame*. Sat. i, l. 23.

7
The whore is proud her beauties are the dread
Of peevish virtue, and the marriage-bed.
YOUNG, *Love of Fame*. Sat. i, l. 67.

8
Who drives an ass and leads a whore,
Hath pain and sorrow evermore.
UNKNOWN. (*Poor Robin Almanac*, July, 1736.)

WICKEDNESS

See also Crime, Evil, Sin, Vice

9
The fine Felicity and flower of wickedness.
BROWNING, *The Ring and the Book: The Pope*, l. 590.

10
God bears with the wicked, but not forever.
CERVANTES, *Don Quixote*. Pt. ii, ch. 40. *See also under* RETRIBUTION.

11
A wicked man is his own hell.
THOMAS FULLER, *Gnomologia*. No. 460.

12
For never, never wicked man was wise.
HOMER, *Odyssey*. Bk. ii, l. 320. (Pope, tr.)

13
Ye have ploughed wickedness, ye have reaped iniquity.
Old Testament: Hosea, x, 13.

14
There is no peace, saith the Lord, unto the wicked.
Old Testament: Isaiah, xlviii, 22.

Let the wicked forsake his way, and the unrighteous man his thoughts.
Old Testament: Isaiah, lv, 7.

15
Though wickedness be sweet in his mouth, though he hide it under his tongue.
Old Testament: Job, xx, 12.

My lips shall not speak wickedness, nor my tongue utter deceit.
Old Testament: Job, xxvii, 4.

16
How oft is the candle of the wicked put out! and how oft cometh their destruction upon them! . . . They are as stubble before the wind, and as chaff that the storm carrieth away.
Old Testament: Job, xxi, 17, 18.

17
No man ever became extremely wicked all at once. (Nemo repente fuit turpissimus.)
JUVENAL, *Satires*. Sat. ii, l. 83.

There is a method in man's wickedness,—
It grows up by degrees.
BEAUMONT AND FLETCHER, *A King and No King*. Act v, sc. 4.

18
The world loves a spice of wickedness.
LONGFELLOW, *Hyperion*. Ch. vii, bk. 1.

19
He that has light within his own clear breast
May sit i' the centre, and enjoy bright day,
But he that hides a dark soul and foul thoughts
Benighted walks under the mid-day sun;
Himself is his own dungeon.
MILTON, *Comus*, l. 381.

20
All wickedness is weakness; that plea, therefore,
With God or man will gain thee no remission.
MILTON, *Samson Agonistes*, l. 834.

All wickedness comes of weakness. (Toute méchanceté vient de faiblesse.)
ROUSSEAU, *Émile*. Bk. i.

21
The success of the wicked entices many more. (Successus improborum plures allicit.)
PHÆDRUS, *Fables*. Bk. ii, fab. 3, l. 7.

He who renders succour to the wicked, grieves for it after a time. (Qui fert malis auxilium, post tempus dolet.)
PHÆDRUS, *Fables*. Bk. iv, fab. 18, l. 1.

22
The wicked flee when no man pursueth: but the righteous are bold as a lion.
Old Testament: Proverbs, xxviii, 1.

1
I have seen the wicked in great power, and spreading himself like a green bay tree. Yet he passed away, and, lo, he was not: yea, I sought him, but he could not be found.

Old Testament: Psalms, xxxvii, 35, 36.

2
No one is so wicked as to wish to appear wicked.

QUINTILIAN, *De Institutione Oratoria.* Bk. iii, ch. 8, sec. 44.

3
The happiness of the wicked glides away like a stream. (Le bonheur des méchants comme un torrent s'écoule.)

RACINE, *Athalie.* Act ii, sc. 7.

4
As saith the proverb of the ancients, Wickedness proceedeth from the wicked.

Old Testament: I Samuel, xxiv, 13. David to Saul. Sometimes referred to as the oldest of all proverbs.

5
The safe way to wickedness is always through wickedness. (Per scelera semper sceleribus tutum est iter.)

SENECA, *Agamemnon,* l. 115.

6
The sun shines even on the wicked. (Et sceleratis sol oritur.)

SENECA, *De Beneficiis.* Bk. iii, sec. 25.

7
And now am I, if a man should speak truly, little better than one of the wicked.

SHAKESPEARE, *I Henry IV.* Act i, sc. 2, l. 105.

8
What rein can hold licentious wickedness
When down the hill he holds his fierce career?

SHAKESPEARE, *Henry V.* Act iii, sc. 3, l. 22.

9
Oh, how cowardly wickedness always is! (O semper timidum scelus!)

STATIUS, *Thebais.* Bk. ii, l. 489.

10
'Cause I's wicked,—I is. I's mighty wicked, anyhow, I can't help it.

HARRIET BEECHER STOWE, *Uncle Tom's Cabin.* Ch. 20.

11
The wicked are wicked, no doubt, and they go astray and they fall, and they come by their deserts; but who can tell the mischief which the very virtuous do?

THACKERAY, *The Newcomes.* Bk. i, ch. 20.

12
God himself cannot procure good for the wicked.

WELSH TRIAD. (EMERSON, *Poetry and Imagination.*)

WICKLIFFE, JOHN

13
Thus this brook hath conveyed his ashes into Avon, Avon into Severn, Severn into the narrow seas, they into the main ocean. And thus the ashes of Wickliffe are the emblem of his doctrine, which now is dispersed all the world over.

THOMAS FULLER, *Church History.* Sec. ii, bk. iv, par. 53. By order of the Council of Constance, the body of John Wickliffe was exhumed in 1428, burned to ashes, and the ashes thrown into a neighboring brook called the Swift.

What Heraclitus would not laugh, or what Democritus would not weep? . . . For though they digged up his body, burned his bones, and drowned his ashes, yet the word of God and truth of his doctrine, with the fruit and success thereof, they could not burn.

JOHN FOXE, *Book of Martyrs.* Vol. i, p. 606.

14
As thou these ashes, little brook, wilt bear
Into the Avon, Avon to the tide
Of Severn, Severn to the narrow seas,
Into main ocean they, this deed accursed
An emblem yields to friends and enemies
How the bold teacher's doctrine, sanctified
By truth, shall spread, throughout the world
dispersed.

WORDSWORTH, *Ecclesiastical Sonnets: Wickliffe.*

15
The Avon to the Severn runs,
The Severn to the sea;
And Wickliffe's dust shall spread abroad
Wide as the waters be.

UNKNOWN. (Quoted by Daniel Webster, *Address Before the Sons of New Hampshire,* 1849; and by Rev. John Cumming, *Voices of the Dead.*)

WIDOW

I—Widow: Apothegms

16
These widows, sir, are the most perverse creatures in the world.

ADDISON, *The Spectator.* No. 335.

"And be very careful o' widders all your life, 'specially if they've kept a public-house, Sammy."

DICKENS, *Pickwick Papers.* Ch. 20.

17
There's Lucinda wears the willow garland for you.

NATHANIEL FIELD, *Woman's a Weathercock.* Act i. (1612)

Great pity 'twas that one so prim
Should ever wear the willow.

JOHN FARMER, *Musa Pedestris,* 46.

Tell him, in hope he 'll prove a widower shortly,
I 'll wear the willow garland for his sake.

SHAKESPEARE, *III Henry VI.* Act iii, sc. 3, l. 227.

18
Sorrow for a husband is like a pain in the elbow, sharp and short.

THOMAS FULLER, *Gnomologia.* No. 4231.

And here do I see what creatures widows are in weeping for their husbands and then presently leaving off; but I cannot wonder at it, the cares of the world taking place of all other passions.

SAMUEL PEPYS, *Diary,* 17 Oct., 1667.

1
We'll play at widows, and we'll pass our time
Railing against the perfidy of man.

W. S. Gilbert, *Pygmalion and Galatea*. Act iii, sc. 1.

2
A widow of doubtful age will marry almost any sort of a white man.

Horace Greeley, *Letter to Dr. Rufus Griswold.*

3
Who marries a widow and two daughters marries three thieves.

W. G. Benham, *Proverbs*, p. 875.

4
On Margate beach, where the sick one roams,
And the sentimental reads;
Where the maiden flirts, and the widow comes—
Like the ocean—to cast her weeds.

Thomas Hood, *The Mermaid of Margate.*

5
Be wary how you marry one that hath cast her rider, I mean a widow.

James Howell, *Proverbs: Letter of Advice.*

You must also be wary how you marry a widow, for so you will be subject to have a death's head put often in your dish.

James Howell, *Familiar Letters*. Vol. ii, p. 666.

6
I caused the widow's heart to sing for joy.

Old Testament: Job, xxix, 13.

7
One can, with dignity, be wife and widow but once. (On n'est, avec dignité, épouse et veuve qu'une fois.)

Joubert, *Pensées*. No. 100. *See also* Marriage: Second Marriage.

8
To marry a widow, in slang, means to make one's fortune, but it doesn't always work that way. (Épouser une veuve, en bon français, signifie faire sa fortune: il n'opère pas toujours ce qu'il signifie.)

La Bruyère, *Les Caractères*. Pt. iii, No. 72.

9
Did ye hear of the Widow Malone, Ohone!
Who lived in the town of Athlone, Alone?
Oh! she melted the hearts
Of the swains in them parts,
So lovely the Widow Malone.

Samuel Lover, *The Widow Malone.*

To be poking the fire all alone is a sin,
Och hone! Widow Machree.
Sure the shovel and tongs
To each other belongs,
While the kettle sings songs
Full of family glee;
Yet alone with your cup,
Like a hermit, you sup,
Och hone! Widow Machree.

Samuel Lover, *Widow Machree*. St. 3.

10
The shameless Chloe placed on the tombs of her seven husbands the inscription. "The work of Chloe." How could she have expressed herself more plainly?

Martial, *Epigrams*. Bk. ix, ep. 15.

This turf has drank a widow's tear;
Three of her husbands slumber here.

Unknown, *Epitaph in Staffordshire.*

11
From thousands of our undone widows
One may derive some wit.

Middleton, *A Trick to Catch the Old One*, i, 2.

12
And I'd rather be bride to a lad gone down
Than widow to one safe home.

Edna St. Vincent Millay, *Keen.*

13
No crafty widows shall approach my bed;
Those are too wise for bachelors to wed.

Pope, *January and May*, l. 107.

14
Marilla W. Ricker has often told us that widows are divided into two classes—the bereaved and relieved. She forgot the deceived—the grass widows.

Victor Robinson, *William Godwin.* (*The Truth Seeker*, 6 Jan., 1906.)

15
For a yeoman of Kent, with his yearly rent,
There was never a widow could say him nay.

Scott, *Ivanhoe* Ch. 40.

16
A married man can do anything he likes if his wife don't mind. A widower can't be too careful.

Bernard Shaw, *Misalliance*, p. 54.

17
A widow must be a mourner.

Jeremy Taylor, *Holy Living*. Ch. ii, sec. 3.

Widowhood is pitiable in its solitariness and loss, but amiable and comely when it is adorned with gravity and purity, and not sullied with remembrances of the passed licence, nor with present desires of returning to a second bed.

Jeremy Taylor, *Holy Living*. Ch. ii, sec. 3.

II—Widow: Wooing a Widow

See also Wooing

18
Do, but dally not, that's the widow's phrase.

Lodowick Barry, *Ram-Alley*. Act ii. (1611)

He that will woo a widow must not dally,
He must make hay while the sun doth shine;
He must not stand with her, shill I, shall I,
But boldly say, Widow, thou must be mine.

Unknown, *Cupid's Solicitor for Love.*

19
A good occasion of courtship is when the widow returns from the funeral.

H. G. Bohn, *Hand-Book of Proverbs*, 288.

Marry a widow before she leaves mourning.

George Herbert, *Jacula Prudentum.*

20
Honour is like a widow, won
With brisk attempt and putting on;
With ent'ring manfully, and urging,
Not slow approaches, like a virgin.

Butler, *Hudibras*. Pt. i, canto 1, l. 913. (1663)

Fortune is like a widow won,
And truckles to the bold alone.
WILLIAM SOMERVILLE, *The Fortune-Hunter*. Canto ii (1735)

He that will woo a widow must take time by the forelock.
THOMAS DELONEY, *Jack of Newberry*. Ch. 11. (c. 1597)

This is the way to have a widowhood,
By getting to her bed.
NATHANIEL FIELD, *Amends for Ladies*. Act iv, sc. 1. (1618)

1
He that woos a maid must come seldom in her sight,
But he that woos a widow must woo her day and night.
JOHN RAY, *English Proverbs*, 49. (1670)

He that would woo a maid must feign, lie, and flatter,
But he that woos a widow must down with his britches and at her.
NATHANIEL SMITH, *Quakers Spiritual Court*, 13. (1669)

2
He'll have a lusty widow now,
That shall be woo'd and wedded in a day.
SHAKESPEARE, *Taming of the Shrew*, iv, 2, 50.

WIFE

See also Husband, Marriage

I—Wife: Apothegms

3
Wives are young men's mistresses, companions for middle age, and old men's nurses.
FRANCIS BACON, *Essays: Of Marriage and Single Life*. (Quoted by Burton, *Anatomy of Melancholy*, iii, 2, 5.)

4
Every man who is high up loves to think he has done it all himself; and the wife smiles, and lets it go at that. It's only our joke. Every woman knows that.
BARRIE, *What Every Woman Knows*. Act iv.

5
Think you, if Laura had been Petrarch's wife,
He would have written sonnets all his life?
BYRON, *Don Juan*. Canto iii, st. 8.

6
Cæsar's wife must be above suspicion.
JULIUS CÆSAR. (PLUTARCH, *Lives: Julius Cæsar*. Sec. 10.) *For full quotation see* CÆSAR.

He makes a false wife that suspects a true.
NATHANIEL FIELD, *Amends for Ladies*. Act i, sc. 1.

7
Perhaps the wife of a patient man must have her quota of patience, too!
EDMUND VANCE COOKE, *From the Book of Extenuations: Job*.

8
When singleness is bliss, it's folly to be wives.
BILL COUNSELMAN, *Ella Cinders*.

9
Lord of yourself, uncumbered with a wife.
DRYDEN, *Epistle to John Driden*, l. 18.

10
Flesh of thy flesh, nor yet bone of thy bone.
DU BARTAS, *Devine Weekes and Workes*. Week ii, day 4.

11
And the Lord God said, It is not good that the man should be alone; I will make him an help meet for him.
Old Testament: Genesis, ii, 18.

This woman, whom thou mad'st to be my help,
And gav'st me as thy perfect gift, so good,
So fit, so acceptable, so divine.
MILTON, *Paradise Lost*. Bk. x, l. 137.

12
All are good maids, but whence come the bad wives?
THOMAS FULLER, *Gnomologia*. No. 499.

13
The wife is the key of the house.
THOMAS FULLER, *Gnomologia*. No. 4828.

14
She 's my own lawfully begotten wife,
In wedlock.
BEN JONSON, *The New Inn*. Act iv, sc. 3.

15
Nothing will so endear you to your friend as a barren wife. (Jucundum et carum sterilis facit uxor amicum.)
JUVENAL, *Satires*. Sat. v, l. 140. Meaning that it is the childless who are courted for their money.

16
The rich woman who marries a money-loving husband is as good as unmarried. (Vidua est, locuples quæ nupsit avaro.)
JUVENAL, *Satires*. Sat. vi, l. 141.

I know well the advice and warnings of my old friends: "Put on a lock and keep your wife indoors." Yes, and who will ward the warders? (Quis custodiet ipsos custodes?)
JUVENAL, *Satires*. Sat. vi, l. 347, 396. (O 31)

If those who wield the Rod forget,
'Tis truly—Quis custodiet?
AUSTIN DOBSON, *The Poet and the Critics*.

17
Maids must be wives and mothers to fulfil
The entire and holiest end of woman's being.
FRANCES ANNE KEMBLE, *Woman's Heart*.

18
Best image of myself and dearer half.
MILTON, *Paradise Lost*. Bk. v, l. 95.

Andromache! my soul's far better part.
HOMER, *Iliad*. Bk. vi, l. 624. (Pope, tr.)

My dear, my better half (said he), I find I now must leave thee.
SIR PHILIP SIDNEY, *Arcadia*. Bk. iii.

These fair helpmates are as convivial as their worser halves.
WILLIAM HONE, *Every-Day Book*, ii, 388. (1826)

19
No one can constantly sleep with his wife and take heartfelt pleasure in it.
NICHARCHUS. (*Greek Anthology*, Bk. xi, epig. 7.)

A wife is a burden imposed by law, and should be loved like one's fortune. But I do not wish to love even my fortune forever. (Uxor, legis onus, debet quasi census amari. Nec censum vellem semper amare meum.)

PETRONIUS, *Fragments*. No. 78.

When it's their wives, their youth is past. (Ubi ad uxores ventumst, tum fiunt senes.)

TERENCE, *Phormio*, l. 1010. (Act v, sc. 8.)

1
Never may I have dealings with other men's wives. (Nil fuerit mi cum uxoribus umquam alienis.)

ORIGO, *Marsœus*. (HORACE, *Satires*, i, 2, 57.)

2
Giving honour unto the wife, as unto the weaker vessel.

New Testament: I Peter, iii, 7.

I must comfort the weaker vessel, as doublet and hose ought to show itself courageous to petticoat.

SHAKESPEARE, *As You Like It*. Act ii, sc. 4, 4.

Women, being the weaker vessels, are ever thrust to the wall.

SHAKESPEARE, *Romeo and Juliet*. Act i, 1, 20.

3
The consorts of men bear divine names, being called first Virgins, then Brides, and then Mothers. (Κόρας, Νύμφας, Μητέρας.)

PYTHAGORAS, alluding to the Nymphs, and the heavenly pair, mother and daughter, Demeter and Persephone. (DIOGENES LAERTIUS, *Pythagoras*. Sec. 11.)

4
I think every wife has a right to insist upon seeing Paris.

SYDNEY SMITH, *Letter to Countess Grey*, 11 Sept., 1835.

5
An ideal wife is any woman who has an ideal husband.

BOOTH TARKINGTON, *Looking Forward*, p. 97.

6
A man whose wife was no better than she should be.

UNKNOWN, *Pasquils Jests*, 35. (1604)

II—Wife: Her Choice

See also Marriage: Advice

7
I want (who does not want?) a wife,
Affectionate and fair,
To solace all the woes of life,
And all its joys to share;
Of temper sweet, of yielding will,
Of firm yet placid mind,
With all my faults to love me still,
With sentiment refin'd.

JOHN QUINCY ADAMS, *Man Wants But Little*.

I want a girl just like the girl that married dear old dad.

WILLIAM DILLON. Title and refrain of popular song. (1911) Music by Harry von Tilzer.

8
And while the wicket falls behind
Her steps, I thought if I could find
A wife I need not blush to show
I've little further now to go.

WILLIAM BARNES, *Not Far to Go*.

9
To take a wife merely as an agreeable and rational companion, will commonly be found to be a grand mistake.

LORD CHESTERFIELD, *Letters*, 12 Oct., 1765.

10
A fair wife without a fortune is a fine house without furniture.

THOMAS FULLER, *Gnomologia*. No. 91.

Why am I unwilling to marry a rich wife? Do you ask? I will not be given in marriage to my wife. (Uxorem quare locupletem ducere nolim Quæritis? Uxori nubere nolo meæ.)

MARTIAL, *Epigrams*. Bk. viii, epig. 12.

See also under DOWRY.

11
A wife is not to be chosen by the eye only. Choose a wife rather by your ear than your eye.

THOMAS FULLER, *Gnomologia*. No. 1107.

He has great need of a wife that marries mamma's darling.

THOMAS FULLER, *Gnomologia*. No. 1872.

12
Good sense without vanity, a penetrating judgment without a disposition to satire, with about as much religion as my William likes, struck me with a wish that she was my William's wife.

HANNAH GODWIN, *Letter to her Brother William*, recommending Miss Gay.

13
In choosing a wife and buying a sword we ought not to trust another.

GEORGE HERBERT, *Jacula Prudentum*. No. 486.

14
The best or worst thing to man, for this life,
Is good or ill choosing his good or ill wife.

JOHN HEYWOOD, *Proverbs*. Pt. i, ch. 2.

When it shall please God to bring thee to man's estate, use great providence and circumspection in choosing thy wife; for thence will spring all thy future good or evil: and it is an action of life, like unto a stratagem of war, wherein a man can err but once.

LORD BURGHLEY, *Ten Precepts to His Son*.

The sum of all that makes a just man happy
Consists in the well-choosing of his wife:
And there, well to discharge it, does require
Equality of years, of birth, of fortune;
For beauty being poor and not cried up
By birth or wealth, can truly mix with neither.
And wealth, when there's such difference in years,
And fair descent, must make the yoke uneasy.

PHILIP MASSINGER, *A New Way to Pay Old Debts*. Act iv, sc. 1.

I fear that in the election of a wife,
As in a project of war, to err but once
Is to be undone for ever.

THOMAS MIDDLETON, *Anything for a Quiet Life*. Act i, sc. 1.

15
Who will have a handsome wife, let him

choose her upon Saturday, and not upon Sunday, viz. when she is in her fine clothes.
JAMES HOWELL, *Proverbs: Span.-Eng.*, ii.

1
Some cunning men choose fools for their wives, thinking to manage them, but they always fail.
SAMUEL JOHNSON. (BOSWELL, *Life*, v, 226.)

2
If you have the good luck to find a modest wife, you should prostrate yourself before the Tarpeian threshold, and sacrifice a heifer with gilded horns to Juno.
JUVENAL, *Satires*. Sat. vi, l. 47.

3
Let me have a wife not too lettered. (Sit non doctissima conjunx.)
MARTIAL, *Epigrams*. Bk. ii, epig. 90.

Most intolerable of all is the woman who, as soon as she has sat down at dinner, commends Vergil, pardons the dying Dido, and pits the poets against each other.
JUVENAL, *Satires*. Sat. vi, l. 434.

A man is in general better pleased when he has a good dinner upon his table, than when his wife talks Greek.
SAMUEL JOHNSON, *Miscellanies*. Vol. ii, p. 11.

Good wives and private soldiers should be ignorant.
WYCHERLEY, *The Country Wife*. Act i.
See also WOMAN: HER MIND.

4
Better, however, that your wife should be musical than that she should be rushing boldly about the city, attending men's meetings.
JUVENAL, *Satires*. Sat. vi, l. 398.

5
What, in the devil's name, can you want with a young wife, who have one foot in flannels, and the other in the grave?
THOMAS LOVE PEACOCK, *Maid Marian*. Ch. 13.
See also MARRIAGE: DECEMBER AND MAY.

6
Horses (thou say'st) and asses men may try,
And ring suspected vessels ere they buy;
But wives, a random choice, untried they take,
They dream in courtship, but in wedlock wake.
POPE, *Wife of Bath: Prologue*, l. 100.

7
The more a man knows, and the farther he travels, the more likely he is to marry a country girl.
BERNARD SHAW, *John Bull's Other Island*. Act ii.

8
Go down the ladder when thou choosest a wife, up when thou chooseth a friend.
Talmud: Jebamoth, p. 63a.

9
Oh, give me a woman of my race
As well controlled as I,
And let us sit by the fire,
Patient till we die!
ANNA WICKHAM, *The Tired Man*.

III—Wife: A Blessing

10
Nothing is better than a well-dispositioned wife. (Nihil est superius quam benigna conjuge.)
ALBERTANO OF BRESCIA, *Liber Consolationis*. Ch. 5.

That sovereign bliss, a wife.
DAVID MALLETT, *Cupid and Hymen*.

11
Without thee I am all unblessed,
And wholly blessed in thee alone.
G. W. BETHUNE, *To My Wife*.

In thy face have I seen the eternal.
BARON CHRISTIAN VON BUNSEN, *To His Wife*, when dying at Bonn. (*Life of Baron Bunsen*, ii, 389.)

12
I hae a wife o' my ain.
BURNS, *I Hae a Wife*.

She is a winsome wee thing,
She is a handsome wee thing,
She is a lo'esome wee thing,
This sweet wee wife o' mine!
BURNS, *My Wife's a Winsome Wee Thing*.

13
No happiness is like unto it, no love so great as that of man and wife, no such comfort as a sweet wife. (Placens uxor.)
ROBERT BURTON, *Anatomy of Melancholy*. Pt. iii, sec. 2, mem. 1, subs. 2. Quoting Horace.

Be thou the rainbow to the storms of life,
The evening beam that smiles the clouds away,
And tints to-morrow with prophetic ray!
BYRON, *The Bride of Abydos*. Canto i, st. 20.

14
It was an opinion of I know not what sage man, that there was but one good woman in the world, and his advice was, that every married man should think that his wife was she.
CERVANTES, *Don Quixote*. Pt. ii, ch. 22.

'Tis a saying, there is but one good wife in the world, and every man enjoys her.
JOHN DUNTON, *Athenian Sport*, p. 333.

15
This flower of wifely patience.
CHAUCER, *The Clerkes Tale*, l. 863.

16
What is there in the vale of life
Half so delightful as a wife,
When friendship, love, and peace combine
To stamp the marriage bond divine?
COWPER, *Love Abused*, l. 1.

17
Thy wife is a constellation of virtues; she's the moon, and thou art the man in the moon.
CONGREVE, *Love for Love*. Act ii, sc. 1.

A meek spouse on whom he could depend.
CRABBE, *Tales: The Gentleman Farmer*, l. 368.

18
The wife of thy bosom.
Old Testament: Deuteronomy, xiii, 6.

1
Blessed is the man that hath a virtuous wife. for the number of his days shall be double A virtuous woman rejoiceth her husband, and he shall fulfil the years of his life in peace. A good wife is a good portion.
Apocrypha: Ecclesiasticus, xxvi, 1–3.

2
Man's best possession is a sympathetic wife.
EURIPIDES, *Antigone*. Frag. 164.

Man's best possession is a loving wife.
ROBERT BURTON, *Anatomy of Melancholy*. Pt. iii, sec. ii, mem. 5, subs. 5.

3
Next to no wife, a good wife is best.
THOMAS FULLER, *The Holy State: Marriage.*

She will tend him, nurse him, mend him,
Air his linen dry his tears;
Bless the thoughtful fates that send him
Such a wife to soothe his years!
W. S. GILBERT, *The Sorcerer*. Act ii.

4
The world's great Author did create
The sex to fit the nuptial state,
And meant a blessing in a wife
To solace the fatigues of life;
And old inspired times display,
How wives could love, and yet obey.
MATTHEW GREEN, *The Spleen*, l. 258.

5
Busk thee, busk thee, my bonny bonny bride,
Busk thee, busk thee, my winsome marrow.
SIR WILLIAM HAMILTON, *The Braes of Yarrow*. (PERCY, *Reliques*. Ser. ii, bk. 3, No. 24.)

The gallant youth, who may have gained,
Or seeks, a "winsome marrow."
WORDSWORTH, *Yarrow Revisited*, l. 1.

6
A sweeter woman ne'er drew breath
Than my sonne's wife, Elizabeth.
JEAN INGELOW, *The High Tide on the Coast of Lincolnshire.*

7
He knew whose gentle hand was at the latch,
Before the door had given her to his eyes.
KEATS, *Isabella*. St. 3.

8
No angel she; she hath no budding wings;
No mystic halo circles her bright hair;
But lo! the infinite grace of little things,
Wrought for dear love's sake, makes her very fair.
JAMES B. KENYON, *A Wife.*

9
When I upon thy bosom lean,
Enraptured I do call thee mine,
I glory in those sacred ties
That made us ane wha ance were twain.
JOHN LAPRAIK, *Song*. An adaptation of an anonymous poem, *Lines Addressed by a Husband to His Wife,* which appeared in the *Weekly Magazine,* 14 Oct., 1773.

10
Sail forth into the sea of life,
O gentle, loving, trusting wife,
And safe from all adversity
Upon the bosom of that sea
Thy comings and thy goings be!
For gentleness and love and trust
Prevail o'er angry wave and gust;
And in the wreck of noble lives
Something immortal still survives!
LONGFELLOW, *The Building of the Ship*, l. 368.

But thou dost make the very night itself
Brighter than day.
LONGFELLOW, *The Divine Tragedy: The First Passover*. Pt. iii, l. 133.

11
Heaven deprives me of a wife who never caused me any other grief than that of her death. (Le ciel me prive d'une épouse qui ne m'a jamais donné d'autre chagrin que celui de sa mort.)
LOUIS XIV, on the death of the Queen.

She never did any wrong, unless in the fact that she died. (Nihil unquam peccavit, nisi quod mortua est.)
UNKNOWN, *Inscription on a Wife's Tomb at Rome.*

12
How much the wife is dearer than the bride.
GEORGE LYTTELTON, *An Irregular Ode.*

13
My fairest, my espous'd, my latest found,
Heaven's last best gift, my ever new delight!
MILTON, *Paradise Lost*. Bk. v, l. 18.

Thy likeness, thy fit help, thy other self,
Thy wish, exactly to thy heart's desire.
MILTON, *Paradise Lost*. Bk. viii, l. 450.

Neither her outside form'd so fair, nor aught
In procreation common to all kinds
(Though higher of the genial bed by far
And with mysterious reverence I deem)
So much delights me, as those graceful acts,
Those thousand decencies that daily flow
From all her words and actions, mix'd with love
And sweet compliance, which declare unfeign'd
Union of mind, or in us both one soul.
MILTON, *Paradise Lost*. Bk. viii, l. 596.

14
Love, sweetness, goodness, in her person shin'd.
MILTON, *Sonnets: On His Deceased Wife.*

15
A virtuous woman is a crown to her husband.
Old Testament: Proverbs, xii, 4.

Whoso findeth a wife findeth a good thing.
Old Testament: Proverbs, xviii, 22.

A prudent wife is from the Lord.
Old Testament: Proverbs, xix, 14.

All other goods by Fortune's hand are given;
A wife is the peculiar gift of heaven.
POPE, *January and May*, l. 51.

16
A good wife and health, are a man's best wealth.
H. G. BOHN, *Handbook of Proverbs*, p. 289. A variant is, "A cheerful wife is the joy of life."

17
His house she enters, there to be a light,

Shining within, when all without is night;
A guardian angel o'er his life presiding,
Doubling his pleasures, and his cares dividing.
SAMUEL ROGERS, *Human Life*, l. 349.

1
The partner of my soul,
My wife, the kindest, dearest, and the truest,
That ever wore the name.
NICHOLAS ROWE, *Royal Convert*. Act ii, sc. 1.

2
He counsels a divorce; a loss of her
That, like a jewel, has hung twenty years
About his neck, yet never lost her lustre.
SHAKESPEARE, *Henry VIII*. Act ii, sc. 2, l. 31.

That man i' the world who shall report he has
A better wife, let him in nought be trusted,
For speaking false in that: thou art, alone,
If thy rare qualities, sweet gentleness,
Thy meekness saint-like, wife-like government,
Obeying in commanding, and thy parts
Sovereign and pious else, could speak thee out.
SHAKESPEARE, *Henry VIII*. Act ii, sc. 4, l. 134.

You are my true and honourable wife,
As dear to me as are the ruddy drops
That visit my sad heart.
SHAKESPEARE, *Julius Cæsar*. Act ii, sc. 1, l. 288.

Dear as the light that visits these sad eyes,
Dear as the ruddy drops that warm my heart.
THOMAS GRAY, *The Bard*, l. 40.

3
O ye gods,
Render me worthy of this noble wife!
SHAKESPEARE, *Julius Cæsar*. Act ii, sc. 1, l. 302.

4
My wife! my wife! what wife? I have no wife.
O, insupportable! O heavy hour!
Methinks it should be now a huge eclipse
Of sun and moon.
SHAKESPEARE, *Othello*. Act v, sc. 2, l. 97.

The gentle lady married to the Moor,
And Heavenly Una with her milk-white lamb.
WORDSWORTH, *Personal Talk*. No. 3.

What is there left but sorrow, for a man alone in the world, his wife gone?
UNKNOWN, *Epigram*. (*Greek Anthology*. Bk. vii, No. 340.)

5
What nearer debt in all humanity
Than wife is to the husband?
SHAKESPEARE, *Troilus and Cressida*. Act ii, sc. 2, l. 175.

6
Of earthly goods, the best is a good wife;
A bad, the bitterest curse of human life.
(Γυναικὸς οὐδὲ χρημ' ανὴρ ληΐζεται
Εσθλῆς ἄμεινον, οὐδὲ ῥίγιον κακῆς.)
SIMONIDES, *Epigram*. Frag. 7.

A man's best fortune or his worst is a wife.
JOHN RAY, *English Proverbs*, 28.

7
Trusty, dusky, vivid, true,
With eyes of gold and bramble-dew,
Steel-true and blade-straight
The great Artificer made my mate.
R. L. STEVENSON, *My Wife*.

Teacher, tender comrade, wife,
A fellow-farer true through life,
Heart-whole and soul-free,
The august Father gave to me.
R. L. STEVENSON, *My Wife*.

8
A courage to endure and to obey;
A hate of gossip parlance, and of sway,
Crown'd Isabel, thro' all her placid life,
The queen of marriage, a most perfect wife.
TENNYSON, *Isabel*. St. 2.

9
My wife is one of the best wimin on this continent, altho' she isn't always gentle as a lamb, with mint sauce.
ARTEMUS WARD, *A War Meeting*.

10
The world well tried—the sweetest thing in life
Is the unclouded welcome of a wife.
N. P. WILLIS, *The Lady Jane*. Canto ii, st. 11.

11
She gave me eyes, she gave me ears;
And humble cares, and delicate fears;
A heart, the fountain of sweet tears;
And love, and thought, and joy.
WORDSWORTH, *The Sparrow's Nest*. Referring to his wife.

IV—Wife: A Curse

12
What is it, then, to have, or have no wife,
But single thraldom, or a double strife?
FRANCIS BACON, *The World*.

13
I have a wife, the worste that may be;
For though the fiend to her y-coupled were,
She would him overmatch, I dare well swear.
CHAUCER, *The Marchantes Tale: Prologue*, l. 6.

14
What rugged ways attend the noon of life!
Our sun declines, and with what anxious strife,
What pain, we tug that galling load, a wife!
CONGREVE, *The Old Batchelor*. Act v, sc. 15.

Lord Erskine, at women presuming to rail,
Calls a wife a tin canister tied to one's tail;
While fair Lady Anne, as the subject he carries on,
Feels hurt at his lordship's degrading comparison.
Yet wherefore degrading? Considered aright,
A canister 's useful, and polish'd, and bright;
And should dirt its original purity hide,
That 's the fault of the puppy to whom it is tied.
MATTHEW GREGORY LEWIS, *Impromptu on Lord Erskine's Simile*. (See *Life and Correspondence of M. G. Lewis*, vol. ii, p. 2.) Often attributed to Richard Brinsley Sheridan.

15
Strange that God hath given to men
Salves for the venom of all creeping pests,
But none hath ever yet devised a balm
For venomous woman, worse than fire or viper.
EURIPIDES, *Andromache*, l. 269.

Man has found remedies against all poisonous creatures, but none was yet found against a bad wife.

RABELAIS, *Works*. Bk. iv, ch. 65. Quoting Euripides.

1
He that takes a wife takes care.

BENJAMIN FRANKLIN, *Poor Richard*, 1736.

He that hath a wife, hath strife.

JOHN RAY, *English Proverbs*.

2
One wife is too much for most husbands to hear,
But two at a time there's no mortal can bear.

JOHN GAY, *The Beggar's Opera*. Act iii, sc. 11.

3
Roy's wife of Aldivalloch,
Wat ye how she cheated me
As I cam o'er the braes of Balloch?

MRS. ELIZABETH GRANT, *Roy's Wife*.

4
The only comfort of my life
Is that I never yet had wife.

ROBERT HERRICK, *His Comfort*.

Suspicion, Discontent, and Strife,
Come in for Dowry with a wife.

ROBERT HERRICK, *Single Life Most Secure*.

Being married to those sleepy-souled women is just like playing at cards for nothing: no passion is excited and the time is filled up. I do not, however, envy a fellow one of those honeysuckle wives for my part, as they are but creepers at best and commonly destroy the tree they so tenderly cling about.

SAMUEL JOHNSON. (MRS. PIOZZI, *Johnsoniana*.)

I would not marry her, though she were endowed with all that Adam had left him before he transgressed: she would have made Hercules have turned spit, yea, and have cleft his club to make the fire too. . . . I would to God some scholar would conjure her; for certainly, while she is here, a man may live as quiet in hell as in a sanctuary.

SHAKESPEARE, *Much Ado About Nothing*. Act ii, sc. 1, l. 258.

5
Is any dignity in a wife, any beauty, worth the cost, if she is forever reckoning up her merits against you? (Quæ tanti gravitas, quæ forma, ut se tibi semper Imputet?)

JUVENAL, *Satires*. Sat. vi, l. 178.

The better the man, the more desirable as a husband, the less good will he get out of his wife. (Igitur longe minus utilis illi Uxor, quisquis erit bonus optandusque maritus.)

JUVENAL, *Satires*. Sat. vi, l. 211.

6
Give up all hope of peace so long as your mother-in-law is alive. (Desperanda tibi salva concordia socru.)

JUVENAL, *Satires*. Sat. vi, l. 231.

7
With quarrels let wives pursue husbands and husbands wives; this befits wives; the dowry of a wife is quarreling. (Lite fugent nuptæque viros, nuptasque mariti; Hoc decet uxores; dos est uxoria lites.)

OVID, *Ars Amatoria*. Bk. ii, l. 153.

8
He who is cursed with an ugly wife sees darkness when he lights the evening lamp.

PALLADAS. (*Greek Anthology*. Bk. xi, epig. 287.)

The husband of the ugly wife
Is better blinded all his life.

SADI, *The Gulistan*. Pt. ii, No. 45. (Arnold, tr.)

9
Every one of you hath his particular plague, and my wife is mine; and he is very happy who hath this only.

PITTACUS. (PLUTARCH, *On the Tranquillity of the Mind*.)

But what so pure, which envious tongues will spare?
Some wicked wits have libell'd all the fair.
With matchless impudence they style a wife
The dear-bought curse and lawful plague of life;
A bosom-serpent, a domestic evil,
A night-invasion and a midday-devil.
Let not the wise these sland'rous words regard,
But curse the bones of ev'ry living bard.

POPE, *January and May*, l. 43.

10
To please a wife, when her occasions call,
Would busy the most vigorous of us all.
And trust me, sir, the chastest you can choose,
Will ask observance, and exact her dues.

POPE, *January and May*, l. 210.

11
A modernist married a fundamentalist wife,
And she led him a catechism and dogma life.

KEITH PRESTON, *Marital Tragedy*.

12
In a wife's lap, as in a grave,
Man's airy notions mix with earth.

A. T. QUILLER-COUCH, *The Splendid Spur*.

13
Who hath a fair wife needs more than two eyes.

JOHN RAY, *English Proverbs*.

A fellow almost damn'd in a fair wife.

SHAKESPEARE, *Othello*. Act i, sc. 1, l. 21.

14
'Tis reason a man that will have a wife should be at the charge of all her trinkets, and pay all the scores she sets him on. He that will keep a monkey, 'tis fit he should pay for the glasses she breaks.

JOHN SELDEN, *Table-Talk: Wife*.

15
As for my wife,
I would you had her spirit in such another;
The third o' the world is yours; which with a snaffle
You may pace easy, but not such a wife.

SHAKESPEARE, *Antony and Cleopatra*. Act ii, sc. 2, l. 61.

1
A light wife doth make a heavy husband.
SHAKESPEARE, *Merchant of Venice*, v, 1, 130.

It is a common thing To have a foolish wife.
SHAKESPEARE, *Othello*. Act iii, sc. 3, l. 302.

2
Richard Penlake was a cheerful man,
Cheerful and frank and free,
But he led a sad life with Rebecca his wife,
For a terrible shrew was she.
SOUTHEY, *St. Michael's Chair*. St. 2.

A proverb look in mind ye keep,
As good a shrew as is a sheep
For you to take to wive.
THOMAS TUSSER, *Five Hundred Points of Good Husbandry*, l. 157.

3
I hold that man the worst of public foes
Who either for his own or children's sake,
To save his blood from scandal, lets the wife
Whom he knows false, abide and rule the house. . . .
She like a new disease, unknown to men,
Creeps, no precaution used, among the crowd,
Makes wicked lightnings of her eyes and saps
The fealty of our friends, and stirs the pulse
With devil's leaps, and poisons half the young.
TENNYSON, *Guinevere*, l. 509.

4
My wife's gone to the country,
Hurrah! Hurrah!
She thought it best; I need a rest,
That's why she went away.
GEORGE WHITING AND IRVING BERLIN, *My Wife's Gone to the Country*. (1909)

4a
The clog of all pleasure, the luggage of life,
Is the best can be said for a very good wife.
JOHN WILMOT, EARL OF ROCHESTER, *On a Wife*.

5
Many a man singeth when he home bringeth
His young wife;
If he knew what he brought, weepen he mought,
Or all his life sigheth.
UNKNOWN, *Proverbs of Alfred*. (c. 1300)

V—Wife: Her Behavior

6
It is not a wife's part to be her husband's judge.
HENRIK IBSEN, *Ghosts*. Act i.

7
My author and disposer, what thou bidd'st,
Unargu'd I obey; so God ordains;
God is thy law, thou mine: to know no more
Is woman's happiest knowledge and her praise.
MILTON, *Paradise Lost*. Bk. iv, l. 635.

For nothing lovelier can be found
In woman, than to study household good,
And good works in her husband to promote.
MILTON, *Paradise Lost*. Bk. ix, l. 232.

The wife, where danger or dishonour lurks,
Safest and seemliest by her husband stays;
Who guards her, or with her the worst endures.
MILTON, *Paradise Lost*. Bk. ix, l. 267.

8
Therefore God's universal law
Gave to the man despotic power
Over his female in due awe,
Nor from that right to part an hour,
Smile she or lour.
MILTON, *Samson Agonistes*, l. 1053.

There's nothing situate under heaven's eye
But hath his bound, in earth, in sea, in sky:
The beasts, the fishes, and the winged fowls,
Are their males' subjects and at their controls:
Men, more divine, the masters of all these,
Lords of the wide world and wild watery seas,
Indued with intellectual sense and souls,
Of more pre-eminence than fish and fowls,
Are masters to their females, and their lords:
Then let your will attend on their accords.
SHAKESPEARE, *The Comedy of Errors*. Act ii, sc. 1, l. 16.

9
A good wife should be as a looking-glass to represent her husband's face and passion; if he be pleasant, she should be merry; if he laugh, she should smile; if he look sad, she should participate of his sorrow.
PLUTARCH, *Moralia: Advice to a Bride*. Sec. 140A. (c. A.D. 95)

I have been to you a true and humble wife,
At all times to your will comformable;
Ever in fear to kindle your dislike,
Yea, subject to your countenance, glad or sorry
As I saw it inclined. . . .
I have been your wife, in this obedience,
Upward of twenty years, and have been blest
With many children by you.
SHAKESPEARE, *Henry VIII*. Act ii, sc. 4, l. 23.

10
She looketh well to the ways of her household, and eateth not the bread of idleness.
Old Testament: Proverbs, xxxi, 27.

11
A virtuous wife rules her husband by obeying him. (Casta ad virum matrona parendo imperat.)
PUBLILIUS SYRUS, *Sententiæ*. No. 105.

She commandeth her husband, in any equal matter, by constant obeying him.
THOMAS FULLER, *The Holy and the Profane State: The Good Wife*.

She who ne'er answers till a husband cools,
Or, if she rules him, never shows she rules.
Charms by accepting, by submitting sways,
Yet has her humour most when she obeys.
POPE, *Moral Essays*. Epis. ii, l. 261.

The cunning wife makes her husband her apron.
JOHN RAY, *English Proverbs*, p. 29.

12
It's a good horse that never stumbles,
And a good wife that never grumbles.
JOHN RAY, *English Proverbs*.

The wife that expects to have a good name
Is always at home, as if she were lame.
JOHN RAY, *English Proverbs*.

See also WOMAN AND THE HOME.

1
Come, I will fasten on this sleeve of thine:
Thou art an elm, my husband, I, a vine.
SHAKESPEARE, *The Comedy of Errors*. Act ii, sc. 2, l. 175.

Happy in this, she is not yet so old
But she may learn; happier than this,
She is not bred so dull but she can learn;
Happiest of all is that her gentle spirit
Commits itself to yours to be directed.
SHAKESPEARE, *The Merchant of Venice*. Act iii, sc. 2, l. 162.

2
Wives may be merry and yet honest too:
We do not act that often jest and laugh;
'Tis old, but true, Still swine eats all the draff.
SHAKESPEARE, *The Merry Wives of Windsor*. Act iv, sc. 2, l. 105.

3
Such duty as the subject owes the prince
Even such a woman oweth to her husband;
And when she is froward, peevish, sullen, sour,
And not obedient to his honest will,
What is she but a foul contending rebel
And graceless traitor to her loving lord?
I am ashamed that women are so simple
To offer war when they should kneel for peace,
Or seek for rule, supremacy, and sway,
When they are bound to serve, love and obey.
SHAKESPEARE, *The Taming of the Shrew*. Act v, sc. 2, l. 155.

4
That wife alone unsullied credit wins,
Whose virtues can atone her husband's sins,
Thus, while the man has other nymphs in view,
It suits the woman to be doubly true.
SHERIDAN, *A Trip to Scarborough*. Act iii, sc. 3.

VI—Wife: The Unwilling Wife

5
I owe a duty where I cannot love.
APHRA BEHN, *Abdelazer*. Act iii, sc. 3.

6
O wretched is the dame, to whom the sound,
"Your lord will soon return," no pleasure brings.
MATURIN, *Bertram*. Act ii, sc. 5.

7
As a captive I shall follow my captor, and not as a wife a husband. (Victorem captiva sequar, non nupta maritum.)
OVID, *Heroides*. Epis. iii, l. 69.

8
An unwilling woman given to a man in marriage is not his wife but his enemy. (Hostis est uxor invita quæ ad virum numtum datur.)
PLAUTUS, *Stichus* Act i. sc. 2, l. 84.

For what is wedlock forced but a hell,
An age of discord and continual strife?
Whereas the contrary bringeth bliss,
And is a pattern of celestial peace.
SHAKESPEARE, *I Henry VI*. Act v, sc. 5, l. 62.

9
But who may have a more ungracious life
Than a child's bird and a knave's wife?
JOHN SKELTON, *Garlande of Laurell*, l. 1452.

VII—Wife: Her Control

10
Avoid being affectionate to your wife or quarreling with her in the presence of strangers: the one savors of folly, the other of madness.
CLEOBULUS. (DIOGENES LAERTIUS, *Cleobulus*. Sec. 5.)

11
What a pity it is that nobody knows how to manage a wife, but a bachelor.
GEORGE COLMAN THE ELDER, *The Jealous Wife*. Act iv, sc. 1. (1761)

Every man can rule an ill wife but him that has her.
JOHN RAY, *Proverbs: Scottish*.

12
If you give your wife a yard, she'll take an ell.
THOMAS DEKKER, *The Honest Whore*. Pt. ii, act ii, sc. 2.

13
He knows little who will tell his wife all he knows.
THOMAS FULLER, *The Holy and the Profane State: The Good Husband*.

He that tells his wife news is but newly married.
GEORGE HERBERT, *Jacula Prudentum*.

Who, like a fondling, to his wife tells news,
He hath not yet worn out his marriage shoes.
R. WATKYNS, *Flamma Sine Fumo*.

No man should have a secret from his wife. She invariably finds it out.
OSCAR WILDE, *An Ideal Husband*. Act ii.

14
First get absolute conquest over thyself, and then thou wilt easily govern thy wife.
THOMAS FULLER, *Intro. ad Prudentiam*, ii, 26.

15
Who lets his wife go to every feast, and his horse drink at every water, shall have neither good wife nor good horse.
GEORGE HERBERT, *Jacula Prudentum*.

16
He knocked at his wife's head, until
It opened unto him.
THOMAS HOOD, *Tim Turpin*.

17
Fasten the bolt; restrain her; but who shall keep the keepers themselves? The wife is cunning, and begins with them. (Pone seram, cohibe. Sed quis custodiet ipsos Custodes? Cauta est et ab illis incipit uxor.)
JUVENAL, *Satires*. Sat. vi, l. 347.

I do think it is their husbands' faults
If wives do fail. . . . Let husbands know
Their wives have sense like them: they see and smell
And have their palates both for sweet and sour,
As husbands have.
SHAKESPEARE, *Othello*. Act iv, sc. 3, l. 87.

1
Nay, look not big, nor stamp, nor stare, nor fret;
I will be master of what is mine own;
She is my goods, my chattels; she is my house,
My household stuff, my field, my barn,
My horse, my ox, my ass, my any thing;
And here she stands, touch her whoever dare.
SHAKESPEARE, *Taming of the Shrew*, iii, 2, 230.

Why, man, she is mine own,
And I as rich in having such a jewel
As twenty seas, if all their sand were pearl,
The water nectar and the rocks pure gold.
SHAKESPEARE, *The Two Gentlemen of Verona*. Act ii, sc. 4, l. 168.

2
Should all despair
That have revolted wives, the tenth of mankind
Would hang themselves.
SHAKESPEARE, *Winter's Tale*. Act i, sc. 2, l. 198.

2a
Every evil, but not an evil wife.
Babylonian Talmud: Shabbath, fo. 11a.

3
Who, for his business, from his wife will run,
Takes the best care to have her business done.
WYCHERLEY, *The Country Wife*. Act ii.

4
Break her betimes, and bring her under by force,
Or else the grey mare will be the better horse.
UNKNOWN, *Marriage of Wit and Science*, ii, 1. (1570)

Look you! The grey mare
Is ill to live with, when her whinny shrills
From tile to scullery, and her small good-man
Shrinks in his arm-chair while the fires of hell
Mix with his hearth.
TENNYSON, *The Princess*. Pt. v, l. 441.

GRAY MARE THE BETTER HORSE, *see under* HORSE.

VIII—Wife: The Breeches and the Crowing Hen

5
"And now, Madam," I addressed her, "we shall try who shall get the breeches."
ANTONIUS MUSA BRASSAVOLUS, *My Wife and I*. 1540. (William Beloe, tr.)

I saw many women using hard words to their husbands: some striving for the breeches.
ROBERT GREENE, *Works*, xi, 219. (1592)

I am sure his wife wore the breeches.
SIR JOHN HARINGTON, *Metamorphosis of Ajax*, 63. (1596)

Children rule, old men go to school, women wear the breeches.
ROBERT BURTON, *Anatomy of Melancholy: Democritus to the Reader*. (1621)

6
Since you have given us the character of a wife who wears the breeches, pray say something of a husband that wears the petticoat.
ADDISON, *The Spectator*. No. 482. (1712)

7
You must not look to be my master, sir,
Nor talk in th' house as though you wore the breeches.
JOHN FLETCHER, *Rule a Wife and Have a Wife*. Act ii. (1624)

8
For of all wise words of tongue or pen,
The wisest are these: "Leave pants to men."
S. E. KISER, *Maud Muller A-Wheel*.

9
Between Adam and me the great difference is,
Though a paradise each has been forced to resign,
That he never wore breeches till turned out of his,
While, for want of my breeches, I'm banished from mine.
THOMAS MOORE, *Upon Being Obliged to Leave a Pleasant Party from the Want of a Pair of Breeches to Dress for Dinner In*.

10
'Tis a thing to me extremely displeasing
When the hen talks and the cock is silent.
(C'est chose qui me moult deplaist,
Quand poule parle et coq se taist.)
GUILLAUME DE LORRIS, *Roman de la Rose*. (c. 1250)

They are sorry houses where the hens crow and the cock holds his peace.
JOHN FLORIO, *First Fruites*. Fo. 33 (1578)

Ill thrives the hapless family that shows
A cock that's silent and a hen that crows.
FRANCIS QUARLES, *History of Queen Esther*. Sec. 3. (1630)

Ill thrives that hapless family that shows
A cock that's silent, and a hen that crows:
I know not which live more unnatural lives,
Obeying husbands, or commanding wives.
BENJAMIN FRANKLIN, *Poor Richard*, 1734.

11
A whistling woman and a crowing hen
Is neither fit for God nor men.
UNKNOWN. (*Notes and Queries*, i, ii, 164.)

Whistling girls and crowing hens
Will surely come to some bad ends.
UNKNOWN. A Cornwall proverb.

Girls that whistle and hens that crow
Will always have fun, wherever they go.
UNKNOWN. A modern variation.

12
As the goodman saith, so say we;
As the goodwife saith, so it must be.
UNKNOWN. (CHEALES, *Proverbial Folk-Lore*, 7.)

It's my old girl that advises. She has the head. But I never own to it before her. Discipline must be maintained.
DICKENS, *Bleak House*. Ch. 27.

13
Wilhelmus . . . submitted at home to a species of government neither laid down in Aristotle or Plato; in short, it partook of

the nature of a pure, unmixed tyranny, . . . petticoat government.

WASHINGTON IRVING, *Knickerbocker's History of New York*. Ch. 4.

There was one species of despotism under which he had long groaned, and that was petticoat government.

WASHINGTON IRVING, *Rip Van Winkle*.

1
The wife rules the roast. (Regnat poscitque maritum.)

JUVENAL, *Satires*. Sat. vi, l. 149.

2
He had by heart the whole detail of woe
Xantippe made her good man undergo;
How oft she scolded in a day he knew,
How many pisspots on the sage she threw—
Who took it patiently, and wiped his head:
"Rain follows thunder," that was all he said.

POPE, *The Wife of Bath: Prologue*, l. 387.

Socrates . . . by all accounts undoubted head of the sect of the hen-pecked.

RICHARD STEELE, *The Spectator*. No. 479. (1712)

3
Seeing how you resemble each other, vilest of wives, vilest of husbands, I wonder you don't agree! (Cum sitis similes paresque vita, Uxor pessima, pessimus maritus, Miror non bene convenire vobis.)

MARTIAL, *Epigrams*. Bk. viii, epig. 35.

IX—Wife: The Curtain Lecture

4
He was then lying under the discipline of a curtain lecture.

JOSEPH ADDISON, *The Tatler*. No. 243. (1710)

Yes, she may toss her head and hector,
But she shall have a curtain lecture.

WILLIAM COMBE, *Dr. Syntax in Search of a Wife*. Canto xxxiv, l. 579. (1821)

Curtain-lectures made a restless night.

POPE, *Wife of Bath*, l. 165. (1717)

For which I have had already two curtain-lectures and a black and blue eye.

FRANCIS QUARLES, *Virgin Widow*, ii. (1649)

A Curtain Lecture; as it is read by a Country Farmer's Wife to her Good Man.

UNKNOWN. Title of book published 1638.

Mrs. Caudle's Curtain Lectures.

DOUGLAS JERROLD. Title of book. (1846)

5
Woman, wakeful woman's never weary,
Above all, when she waits to thump her deary.

R. H. BARHAM, *The Ghost*.

6
If in your censure you prove sweet to me,
I little care, believe 't, how sour you be.

RICHARD BRATHWAITE, *A Boulster Lecture: Dedication*. (1640)

7
Curs'd be the man, the poorest wretch in life,
The crouching vassal, to the tyrant wife! . . .
Who must to her his dear friend's secret tell;
Who dreads a curtain lecture worse than hell.
Were such the wife had fallen to my part,
I'd break her spirit or I'd break her heart.

BURNS, *The Henpeck'd Husband*.

8
The wife was pretty, trifling, childish, weak;
She could not think, but would not cease to speak.

GEORGE CRABBE, *Tales: The Struggles of Conscience*.

9
For me, I neither know nor care
Whether a Parson ought to wear
A black dress or a white dress;
Fill'd with a trouble of my own,—
A Wife who preaches in her gown,
And lectures in her night-dress!

THOMAS HOOD, *The Surplice Question*.

She shakes the curtains with her kind advice.

YOUNG, *Love of Fame*. Sat. v, l. 79.

10
The bed that holds a wife is never free from wrangling; no sleep is to be got there! (Semper habet lites alternaque jurgia lectus In quo nupto jacet; minimum dormitur in illo.)

JUVENAL, *Satires*. Sat. vi, l. 268.

11
I find my wife has something in her gizzard that only wants an opportunity of being provoked to bring up.

SAMUEL PEPYS, *Diary*, 17 June, 1668.

12
The contentions of a wife *are* a continual dropping.

Old Testament: Proverbs, xix, 13.

A continual dropping in a very rainy day and a contentious woman are alike.

Old Testament: Proverbs, xxvii, 15.

13
My lord shall never rest;
I 'll watch him, tame and talk him out of patience:
His bed shall seem a school, his board a shrift.

SHAKESPEARE, *Othello*. Act iii, sc. 3, l. 22.

14
It is well within the order of things
That man should listen when his mate sings;
But the true male never yet walked
Who liked to listen when his mate talked.

ANNA WICKHAM, *The Affinity*.

I would be married to a full man,
As would all women since the world began;
But from a wealth of living I have proved
I must be silent, if I would be loved.

ANNA WICKHAM, *The Affinity*.

X—Wife: Deliverance

15
"What? rise again with *all* one's bones,"
Quoth Giles, "I hope you fib:

I trusted, when I went to Heaven,
To go without my rib."
S. T. COLERIDGE, *Epigram.*

1
Oh! 'tis a precious thing, when wives are dead,
To find such numbers who will serve instead:
And in whatever state a man be thrown,
'Tis that precisely they would wish their own.
GEORGE CRABBE, *Tales: The Learned Boy*, l. 17.

2
Here lies my wife: here let her lie!
Now she's at rest, and so am I.
DRYDEN, *Suggested Epitaph.*

3
Down Theseus went to hell, Pirith his friend to find:
O that wives in these our days were to their mates as kind!
NICHOLAS GRIMALD, *Of Friendship.*

Lycoris has buried all the female friends she had, Fabianus: would she were the friend of my wife! (Omnes quas habuit, Fabiane, Lycoris amicas Extulit. Uxori fiat amica meæ.)
MARTIAL, *Epigrams.* Bk. iv, epig. 24.

Already, Phileros, your seventh wife is being buried in your field. No man's field brings him greater profit than yours, Phileros. (Septima jam, Phileros, tibi conditur uxor in agro. Plus nulli, Phileros, quam tibi reddit ager.)
MARTIAL, *Epigrams.* Bk. x, epig. 43.

4
A dead wife under the table is the best goods in a man's house.
SWIFT, *Polite Conversation.* Dial. i.

WILDE, OSCAR

5
I heard his golden voice and marked him trace
Under the common thing the hidden grace,
And conjure wonder out of emptiness,
Till mean things put on beauty like a dress
And all the world was an enchanted place.
ALFRED BRUCE DOUGLAS, *The Dead Poet.*

6
A delicate design that lay like lace
Upon the purple velvet of disgrace.
JOHN MACY, *Couplets in Criticism: Wilde.*

7
What has Oscar in common with art? except that he dines at our tables and picks from our platters the plums for the puddings he peddles in the provinces. Oscar . . . has the courage of the opinions . . . of others.
JAMES MCNEILL WHISTLER, *The* (London) *World*, 17 Nov., 1886.

As for borrowing Mr. Whistler's ideas about art, the only thoroughly original ideas I have ever heard him express have had reference to his own superiority as a painter over painters greater than himself.
OSCAR WILDE, *Truth*, 9 Jan., 1890.

Oscar, bourgeois malgré lui.
JAMES MCNEIL WHISTLER, of Oscar Wilde.

WILHELM II

See also Germany

8
To see the Kaiser's epitaph
Would make a weeping willow laugh.
OLIVER HERFORD, *The Laughing Willow.*

9
Did the skies the Lord dressed in Prussian blue
Make the Kaiser dream that He was Prussian too?
ALFRED KREYMBORG, *God Complex.*

10
Der Kaiser auf der Vaterland
Und Gott on high, all dings gommand,
Ve two. ach, don'd you understandt?
Meinself—und Gott. . . .
Gott pulls mit me und I mit him—
Meinself—und Gott.
ALEXANDER MACGREGOR ROSE, *Kaiser & Co.* Written for the Toronto *Herald*, in 1897, and signed A. M. R. Gordon, by which name Rose was known at the time. He had been minister of the Free Church, at Orkney, Scotland, and was shipped off to America because of intemperance. Erroneously attributed to Rodney Blake, pseudonym of W. M. Clemens. Recited by Captain J. B. Coghlan at the Union League Club, N. Y., 21 April, 1899, causing an international incident. (See STEVENSON, *Famous Single Poems.*)

11
This was the "Day" foretold by yours and you
In whispers here, and there with beery clamours—
You and your rat-hole spies and blustering crew
Of loud Potsdamers.
And lo, there dawns another, swift and stern,
When on the wheels of wrath, by Justice' token,
Breaker of God's own Peace, you shall in turn
Yourself be broken.
SIR OWEN SEAMAN, *Dies Iræ: To the German Kaiser. Punch*, 19 Aug., 1914.

12
Thou Blot
On the fair script of Time, thou sceptred Smear
Across the Day.
WILLIAM WATSON, *To the German Emperor after the Sack of Louvain.*

13
Remember the German people are the chosen of God. On me, the German Emperor, the spirit of God has descended. I am His sword, His weapon, and His vicegerent.
WILHELM II, *Address*, to his soldiers, as they started for the front, 4 Aug., 1914. (New York *Times, Current History of the War*, i, 341.)

WILL

I—Will: Apothegms

1
Will without power is like children playing at soldiers.
GEORGE CANNING, *The Rovers*. Act iv.

Wilful will do't, that's the word.
CONGREVE, *The Way of the World*. Act iv, sc. 2.

2
Here vigor fail'd the towering fantasy:
But yet the will roll'd onward, like a wheel
In even motion, by the Love impell'd,
That moves the sun in Heaven and all the stars.
DANTE, *Paradiso*. Canto xxxiii. (Cary, tr.)

A breath of will blows eternally through the universe of souls in the direction of the Right and Necessary.
EMERSON, *Conduct of Life: Fate*.

3
'T is what you will,—or will be what you would.
DU BARTAS, *Devine Weekes and Workes*. Week i, day 3. (Sylvester, tr.)

He who is firm in will molds the world to himself. (Aber wer fest auf dem Sinne beharrt, der bildet die Welt sich.)
GOETHE, *Hermann und Dorothea*. Pt. ix, l. 303.

With will one can do anything.
SAMUEL SMILES, *Self-Help*. Ch. 7.

All Life needs for life is possible to will.
TENNYSON, *Love and Duty*, l. 82.

4
The education of the will is the object of our existence.
EMERSON, *Society and Solitude: Courage*.

5
There is nothing good or evil save in the will. ("Οτι ἔξω τῆς προαιρέσεως οὐδέν ἐστιν οὔτε αγαθὸν οὔτε κακὸν.)
EPICTETUS, *Discourses*. Bk. iii, ch. 10, sec. 18.

6
To him that will, ways are not wanting.
GEORGE HERBERT, *Jacula Prudentum*. No. 726. (1640)

I fall back on my favourite proverb, "Where there's a will there's a way."
BULWER-LYTTON, *The Caxtons*. Pt. xviii, ch. 5. The French form of the proverb is, "Vouloir c'est pouvoir."

When there's a will there's a way.
BERNARD SHAW, *Fanny's First Play: Preface*.

In idle wishes fools supinely stay;
Be there a will, and wisdom finds a way.
GEORGE CRABBE, *The Birth of Flattery*.

7
Where your will is ready, your feet are light.
GEORGE HERBERT, *Jacula Prudentum*. No. 444.

A willing heart adds feather to the heel.
JOANNA BAILLIE, *De Montfort*. Act iii, sc. 2.

8
Will will have will though will woe win.
JOHN HEYWOOD, *Proverbs*. Pt. i, ch. 11.

Will is the cause of woe.
JOHN RAY, *English Proverbs*.

9
I will this, I command this: let my will be the voucher for the deed. (Hoc volo, sic jubeo, sit pro ratione voluntas.)
JUVENAL, *Satires*. Sat. vi, l. 223.

We'll take the will for the deed.
RABELAIS, *Works*. Bk. iv, ch. 49.

The will for deed I do accept.
DU BARTAS, *Devine Weekes and Workes*. Week ii, day 3. (Sylvester, tr.)

You must take the will for the deed.
SWIFT, *Polite Conversation*. Dial. ii; COLLEY CIBBER, *The Rival Fools*. Act iii.

10
Will thou, or will thou not, we will have our will.
LANGLAND, *Piers Plowman*. Passus ix, l. 153.

11
A tender heart; a will inflexible.
LONGFELLOW, *John Endicott*. Act iii, sc. 2.

12
Not my will, but thine, be done.
New Testament: Luke, xxii, 42. *See also under* RESIGNATION.

13
The man who has the will to undergo all labor may win to any goal. (Ὁ πάντα βουληθεὶς ἂν ἄνθρωπος πονεῖν παν ἄν γένοιτο.)
MENANDER, *Fragments*. No. 539.

14
The unconquerable will.
MILTON, *Paradise Lost*. Bk. i, l. 106.

The star of the unconquered will,
He rises in my breast,
Serene, and resolute, and still,
And calm, and self-possessed.
LONGFELLOW, *The Light of Stars*. St. 7.

15
Even though the power be wanting, yet the will is praiseworthy. (Ut desint vires, tamen est laudanda voluntas.)
OVID, *Epistulæ ex Ponto*. Bk. iii, epis. 4, l. 79.

Let not thy Will roar, when thy Power can but whisper.
FULLER, *Introductio ad Prudentiam*, i, 14.

16
Our wills and fates do so contrary run
That our devices still are overthrown.
SHAKESPEARE, *Hamlet*. Act iii, sc. 2, l. 221.

At war 'twixt will and will not.
SHAKESPEARE, *Measure for Measure*, ii, 2, 33.

My will enkindled by mine eyes and ears,
Two traded pilots 'twixt the dangerous shores
Of will and judgement.
SHAKESPEARE, *Troilus and Cressida*, ii, 2, 63

He wants wit that wants resolved will.
SHAKESPEARE, *The Two Gentlemen of Verona*. Act ii, sc. 6, l. 12.

17
What he will he does, and does so much
That proof is call'd impossibility.
SHAKESPEARE, *Troilus and Cressida*, v, 5, 28.

1
Will was his guide, and grief led him astray.
SPENSER, *Faerie Queene*. Bk. i, canto i, st. 12.

2
O, well for him whose will is strong!
He suffers, but he will not suffer long;
He suffers, but he cannot suffer wrong.
TENNYSON, *Will*, l. 1.

And I compel all creatures to my will.
TENNYSON, *Geraint and Enid*, l. 672.

Peggy has a whim of iron.
OLIVER HERFORD, referring to his wife, and explaining that the atrocious hat he was wearing was a whim of hers.

3
Nothing is so easy but it is difficult if you do it against your will. (Nullast tam facilias res quin difficilis siet, Quam invitus facias.)
TERENCE, *Heauton Timorumenos*, l. 805.

Nothing is troublesome that we do willingly.
THOMAS JEFFERSON, *Writings*. Vol. xvi, p. 111

4
For though with judgement we on things reflect,
Our will determines, not our intellect.
EDMUND WALLER, *Divine Love*. Canto i, l. 39.

5
The Will is the Man.
JOHN WILSON, *Noctes Ambrosianæ*. No. 29.

II—Will: Free Will

6
Where we are free to act, we are also free to refrain from acting, and where we are able to say No we are also able to say Yes. (Καὶ ἐν οἷς τὸ μή, καὶ τὸ ναί.)
ARISTOTLE, *Nicomachean Ethics*. Bk. iii, ch. 5, sec. 2.

7
No one can rob us of our free will. (Ληστὴς προαιρέσεως οὐ γίνεται.)
EPICTETUS, *Discourses*. Bk. iii, ch. 22, sec. 105.

The commander of the forces of a large State may be carried off, but the will of even a common man cannot be taken from him.
CONFUCIUS, *Analects*. Bk. ix, ch 25.

The will cannot be compelled. (Voluntas non potest cogi.)
UNKNOWN. A Latin proverb.

8
To deny the freedom of the will is to make morality impossible.
J. A. FROUDE, *Short Studies: Calvinism*.

9
All theory is against the freedom of the will, all experience for it.
SAMUEL JOHNSON. (BOSWELL, *Life*. 1778.)

Say not the will of man is free
Within the limits of his soul—
Who from his heritage can flee?
Who can his destiny control?
DONALD A. MACKENZIE, *Free Will*.

10
Good he made thee, but to persevere
He left it in thy power, ordain'd thy will
By nature free, not over-ruled by Fate
Inextricable, or strict necessity.
MILTON, *Paradise Lost*. Bk. v, l. 525.

And binding Nature fast in Fate,
Left free the human Will.
POPE, *Universal Prayer*. St. 3.

11
The only way of setting the will free is to deliver it from wilfulness.
J. C. AND A. W. HARE, *Guesses at Truth*.

12
Our wills are ours, we know not how;
Our wills are ours, to make them thine.
TENNYSON, *In Memoriam: Introduction*. St. 4.

WILLOW

13
In the misty twilight
You can see their hair,
Weeping water maidens
That were once so fair.
WALTER PRICHARD EATON, *The Willows*.

14
Willow, in thy breezy moan,
I can hear a deeper tone;
Through thy leaves come whispering low,
Faint sweet sounds of long ago—
Willow, sighing willow!
FELICIA DOROTHEA HEMANS, *Willow Song*.

15
Willows are weak, yet they bind other wood.
GEORGE HERBERT, *Jacula Prudentum*.

The wind sways the willow. (Fêng 'chui liu.)
UNKNOWN. A Chinese proverb.

16
Thou art to all lost love the best,
The only true plant found,
Wherewith young men and maids distrest,
And left of love, are crown'd.

When once the lover's rose is dead,
Or laid aside forlorn,
Then willow-garlands, 'bout the head,
Bedewed with tears, are worn.
ROBERT HERRICK, *To the Willow-Tree*.

17
We hanged our harps upon the willows in the midst thereof.
Old Testament: Psalms, cxxxvii, 2.

18
To the brook and the willow that heard him complain,
Ah willow, willow,
Poor Colin sat weeping and told them his pain;
Ah willow, willow; ah willow, willow.
NICHOLAS ROWE, *Song: Ah Willow*.

On a tree by a river a little tom-tit
Sang, "Willow, titwillow, titwillow!"
And I said to him, "Dicky-bird, why do you sit
Singing, 'Willow, titwillow, titwillow'?"
W. S. GILBERT, *The Mikado*. Act ii.

Phillis hath forsaken me,
Which makes me wear the willow-tree.
UNKNOWN, *The Willow-Tree*. (PERCY, *Reliques*. Ser. iii, bk. ii, No. 9.)

1
Know ye the willow-tree Whose grey leaves quiver,
Whispering gloomily To yon pale river?
Lady, at even-tide Wander not near it:
They say its branches hide A sad lost spirit!
W. M. THACKERAY, *The Willow-Tree.*

2
My mother had a maid call'd Barbara:
She was in love, and he she loved proved mad
And did forsake her: she had a song of 'willow;'
An old thing 'twas, but it express'd her fortune,
And she died singing it.
SHAKESPEARE, *Othello.* Act iv, sc. 3, l. 26.

The poor soul sat sighing by a sycamore tree,
Sing all a green willow;
Her hand on her bosom, her head on her knee,
Sing willow, willow, willow:
The fresh streams ran by her, and murmur'd her moans;
Sing willow, willow, willow;
Her salt tears fell from her, and soften'd the stones;
Sing willow, willow, willow.
SHAKESPEARE, *Othello.* Act iv, sc. 3, l. 41.

A poor soul sat sighing under a sycamore tree;
O willow, willow, willow!
With his hand on his bosom, his head on his knee:
O willow, willow, willow!
Sing, O the green willow shall be my garland.
UNKNOWN, *A Lover's Complaint Being Forsaken of His Love.* (PERCY, *Reliques.* Ser. i, bk. ii, No. 8.)

All a green willow is my garland.
JOHN HEYWOOD, *The Green Willow.*

WILSON, WOODROW

3
And if he failed in part,
Only the years are strong
With patience that waits long;
With wisdom that sees far.
The years shall right the balance tilted wrong,
The years shall set upon his brows a star.
ADA ALDEN, *Ave.*

4
I served Woodrow Wilson for five years. He is standing at the throne of a God whose approval he won and has received. As he looks down from there, I say to him: "I did my best. I am doing it now. You are still the captain of my soul."
NEWTON D. BAKER, *Speech,* Democratic Convention, 28 June, 1924.

5
He was sole out-post for that world-old hope
Humanity can never quite release:
He gave his heart, his life, his soul, to hold
Our eyes upon the gleam of lasting peace.
S. OMAR BARKER, *Woodrow Wilson.*

6
Spirit long shaping for sublime endeavor,
A Sword of God, the gleaming metal came
From stern Scotch ancestry, where whatsoever
Was true, was pure, was noble, won acclaim.
KATHARINE LEE BATES, *Woodrow Wilson.*

Here is the man who imposed himself as the supreme head of the continental empire of the United States. Who, further, handled that colossal power as if it were a sword in his hand. . . . With this and the power of his thought he ends the war. And then in person he sets out to save humanity by ending war for ever. . . . Wilson adventured for the whole of the human race. Not as a servant, but as a champion. . . . In Wilson, the whole of mankind breaks camp, sets out from home and wrestles with the universe and its gods.
WILLIAM BOLITHO, *Twelve Against the Gods: Woodrow Wilson,* p. 332.

8
Beleaguered Liberty takes heart again,
Hearing afar the rescuing bugles blow;
And even in the strongholds of the foe
His name becomes the whispered hope of men.
ROBERT UNDERWOOD JOHNSON, *The Leader.*

9
What is the thing about his face
That makes me dream of something dim—
A crucifix at some torn place
And the shell-scarred face of Him?
HUBERT KELLEY, *The Warrior Passes.*

10
Byzantine Logothete.
THEODORE ROOSEVELT, referring to Woodrow Wilson, at the time of the latter's many notes to Germany, 1915–17. The officials of Byzantium were called Logothetes. Instead of defending the Empire against the barbarians, they wrote notes to them and were eventually conquered. See BURY, *History of the Later Roman Empire;* N. Y. *Tribune,* 13 Dec., 1915.

11
To Woodrow Wilson, the apparent failure, belongs the undying honour, which will grow with the growing centuries, of having saved the "little child that shall lead them yet."
GEN. JAN CHRISTIAAN SMUTS, *Letter,* 8 Jan., 1921. (N. Y. *Evening Post,* March 2, 1921.)

It was the human spirit itself that failed at Paris. . . . It was not Wilson who failed there, but humanity itself. It was not the statesmen that failed, so much as the spirit of the peoples behind them.
GENERAL JAN SMUTS, *Letter,* 8 Jan., 1921.

I had to deal in the peace conference with two men, one of whom thought he was Napoleon and the other Jesus Christ.
GEORGES CLEMENCEAU, referring to Lloyd George and Woodrow Wilson.

No man ever more fully exemplified the adage that the pen is mightier than the sword.
MARK SULLIVAN, of Wilson. (*Our Times,* v, 274.)

WIND

I—Wind: Apothegms

1
The wench has shot him between wind and water.
BEAUMONT AND FLETCHER, *Philaster*, iv, 1. (1608)

Sea-fights are more bloody . . . since guns came up, whose shot betwixt wind and water . . . is commonly observed mortal.
THOMAS FULLER, *Holy War*, iv, 24. (1639)

We'll strike 'Twixt wind and water.
BULWER-LYTTON, *Richelieu*. Act ii, sc. 2.

2
While the battle rages loud and long,
And the stormy winds do blow.
CAMPBELL, *Ye Mariners of England.*

When the stormy winds do blow.
MARTIN PARKER, *Ye Gentlemen of England.*

But sailors were born for all weathers,
Great guns let it blow high or low.
CHARLES DIBDIN, *The Tar for All Weathers.*

It blows great guns indeed.
DICKENS, *Barnaby Rudge*. Ch. 23.

3
What manner winds guideth you now here?
CHAUCER, *Troilus and Criseyde*. Bk. ii, l. 1105. (1374)

Falstaff: What wind blew you hither, Pistol?
Pistol: Not the ill wind which blows no man to good.
SHAKESPEARE, *II Henry IV*, v, 3, 89. (1597)

4
To tell him tidings how the wind was went.
CHAUCER, *Tale of Gamelyn*, l. 703. (c. 1380)

I know, and knew, which way the wind blew and will blow.
JOHN HEYWOOD, *Proverbs*, ii, 9. (1546)

Is it as plainly in our living shown,
By slant and twist, which way the wind hath blown?
ADELAIDE CRAPSEY, *On Seeing Weather-Beaten Trees.*

Take a straw and throw it up into the air, you may see by that which way the wind is.
JOHN SELDEN, *Table-Talk: Ballads and Libels.*

5
The way of the Wind is a strange, wild way.
INGRAM CROCKETT, *The Wind.*

6
What, husband (quoth she), is the wind at that door?
THOMAS DELONEY, *Thomas of Reading*. Ch. 3. (1600)

Sits the wind in that corner?
SHAKESPEARE, *Much Ado About Nothing*. Act ii, sc. 3, l. 102. (1598)

Which way does the wind set now?
DAVID GARRICK, *Neck or Nothing*. Act i, sc. 2.

7
He that will use all winds, must shift his sail.
JOHN FLETCHER, *Faithful Shepherdess*. Act i.

To a crazy ship all winds are contrary.
GEORGE HERBERT, *Jacula Prudentum.*

Thus far we run before the wind.
ARTHUR MURPHY, *The Apprentice*. Act v, sc. 1.

8
Can any wind blow rough upon a blossom
So fair and tender?
JOHN FLETCHER, *The Pilgrim*. Act i, sc. 1.

9
High winds blow on high hills.
THOMAS FULLER, *Gnomologia*. No. 2502. *See also* GREATNESS: ITS PENALTIES.

10
A little wind kindles, much puts out the fire.
GEORGE HERBERT, *Jacula Prudentum. See also under* FIRE.

11
An ill wind that bloweth no man good—
The blower of which blast is she.
JOHN HEYWOOD, *Song Against Idleness.* (c. 1540)

Yet true it is as cow chews cud,
And trees at spring do yield forth bud,
Except wind stands as never it stood,
It is an ill wind turns none to good.
THOMAS TUSSER, *Five Hundred Points of Good Husbandry*. Ch. 12. (1557)

Ill blows the wind that profits nobody.
SHAKESPEARE, *III Henry VI*. Act ii, sc. 5, l. 55. (1590)

12
For they have sown the wind, and they shall reap the whirlwind.
Old Testament: Hosea, viii, 7. (Ventum seminabant et turbinem metent.—*Vulgate.*) *See also under* RETRIBUTION.

13
'Tis the old wind in the old anger.
A. E. HOUSMAN, *On Wenlock Edge.*

14
He stayeth his rough wind in the day of the east wind.
Old Testament: Isaiah, xxvii, 8.

The wind's in the east. . . . I am always conscious of an uncomfortable sensation now and then when the wind is blowing in the east.
DICKENS, *Bleak House*. Ch. 6.

But certain winds will make men's temper bad.
GEORGE ELIOT, *The Spanish Gypsy*. Bk. i.

15
The wind bloweth where it listeth.
New Testament: John, iii, 8.

16
The felon winds.
MILTON, *Lycidas*, l. 91.

17
It is folly to complain of the fickleness of the wind. (Stultum est venti de levitate queri.)
OVID, *Heroides*. Epis. xxi, l. 76.

18
To strive with the winds. (Cum ventis litigare.)
PETRONIUS ARBITER, *Satyricon*. Sec. 83.

19
Yea, he did fly upon the wings of the wind.
Old Testament: Psalms, xviii, 10.

Who walketh upon the wings of the wind.
Old Testament: Psalms, civ, 3.

On wings of winds came flying all abroad.
POPE, *Epistle to Dr. Arbuthnot*, l. 218.

1
They who plough the sea do not carry the winds in their hands.
PUBLILIUS SYRUS, *Sententiæ*. No. 759.

The pilot cannot mitigate the billows or calm the winds.
PLUTARCH, *Of the Tranquillity of the Mind.*

2
The wind from the Kingdom of Heaven has blown over the world, and shall blow for centuries yet.
GEORGE WILLIAM RUSSELL, *The Economics of Ireland*, p. 23.

3
You can't catch the wind in a net.
C. H. SPURGEON, *Ploughman's Pictures*, p. 97.

4
Here in his vast cavern, Æolus, their king, curbs by his authority the struggling winds and the roaring gales. (Hic vasto rex Æolus antro Luctantis ventos tempestatesque sonoras Imperio premit.)
VERGIL, *Æneid*. Bk. i, l. 53.

II—Wind: Description

5
The hushed winds wail with feeble moan
Like infant charity.
JOANNA BAILLIE, *Orra*. Act iii, sc. 1.

6
Blow, Boreas, foe to human kind!
Blow, blustering, freezing, piercing wind!
Blow, that thy force I may rehearse,
While all my thoughts congeal to verse!
JOHN BANCKS, *To Boreas.*

Cease, rude Boreas! blustering railer!
G. A. STEVENS, *The Storm.*

7
The wind
Sweeps the broad forest in its summer prime,
As when some master-hand exulting sweeps
The keys of some great organ.
BRYANT, *Among the Trees*, l. 63.

8
Wind of the sunny south! oh, still delay
In the gay woods and in the golden air,
Like to a good old age released from care,
Journeying. in long serenity, away.
BRYANT, *October*, l. 5.

And the South Wind—he was dressed
With a ribbon round his breast
That floated, flapped, and fluttered
In a riotous unrest,
And a drapery of mist
From the shoulder to the wrist
Floating backward with the motion of the waving hand he kissed.
JAMES WHITCOMB RILEY, *The South Wind and the Sun.*

9
Where hast thou wandered, gentle gale, to find
The perfumes thou dost bring?
BRYANT, *May Evening*. St. 4.

The faint old man shall lean his silver head
To feel thee; thou shalt kiss the child asleep.
BRYANT, *Evening Wind*. St. 4.

10
A breeze came wandering from the sky,
Light as the whispers of a dream;
He put the o'erhanging grasses by,
And softly stooped to kiss the stream,
The pretty stream, the flattered stream,
The shy, yet unreluctant stream.
BRYANT, *The Wind and Stream*. St. 2.

As winds come lightly whispering from the west,
Kissing, not ruffling the blue deep's serene.
BYRON, *Childe Harold*. Canto ii, st. 70.

The winds with wonder whist,
Smoothly the waters kist.
MILTON, *On the Morning of Christ's Nativity*, l. 64.

Mildly and soft the western breeze
Just kissed the lake, just stirred the trees.
SCOTT, *The Lady of the Lake*. Canto iii, st. 2.

11
There paused to shut the door
A fellow called the Wind,
With mystery before,
And reticence behind.
BLISS CARMAN, *At the Granite Gate.*

12
The wind is awake, pretty leaves, pretty leaves,
Heed not what he says, he deceives, he deceives;
Over and over To the lowly clover
He has lisped the same love (and forgotten it, too),
He'll be lisping and pledging to you.
JOHN VANCE CHENEY, *The Way of It.*

13
Loud wind, strong wind, sweeping o'er the mountains,
Fresh wind, free wind, blowing from the sea,
Pour forth thy vials like streams from airy fountains,
Draughts of life to me.
DINAH MARIA MULOCK CRAIK, *North Wind.*

14
The winds that never moderation knew,
Afraid to blow too much, too faintly blew;
Or out of breath with joy, could not enlarge
Their straighten'd lungs.
DRYDEN, *Astræa Redux*, l. 242.

15
The wind moans, like a long wail from some despairing soul shut out in the awful storm!
W. H. GIBSON, *Pastoral Days: Winter.*

Have you heard the wind go "Yo-o-o-o"?
'Tis a pitiful sound to hear.
EUGENE FIELD, *The Night Wind.*

Perhaps the wind
Wails so in winter for the summer's dead,
And all sad sounds are nature's funeral cries
For what has been and is not.
GEORGE ELIOT, *The Spanish Gypsy*. Bk. i.

1

No stir of air was there,
Not so much life as on a summer's day
Robs not one light seed from the feather'd grass,
But where the dead leaf fell, there did it rest.
KEATS, *Hyperion*. Bk. i, l. 7.

Nought but a lovely sighing of the wind
Along the reedy stream; a half-heard strain,
Full of sweet desolation—balmy pain.
KEATS, *I Stood Tip-toe Upon a Little Hill.*

So near to mute the zephyrs flute
That only leaflets dance.
GEORGE MEREDITH, *Outer and Inner*. St. 1.

2

I hear the wind among the trees
Playing celestial symphonies;
I see the branches downward bent,
Like keys of some great instrument.
LONGFELLOW, *A Day of Sunshine*. St. 3.

Chill airs and wintry winds! my ear
Has grown familiar with your song;
I hear it in the opening year,
I listen, and it cheers me long.
LONGFELLOW, *Woods in Winter*. St. 7.

It's a warm wind, the west wind, full of birds' cries;
I never hear the west wind but tears are in my eyes.
For it comes from the west lands, the old brown hills.
And April's in the west wind, and daffodils.
JOHN MASEFIELD, *The West Wind.*

3

While rocking winds are piping loud,
Or usher'd with a shower still,
When the gust hath blown his fill,
Ending on the rustling leaves,
With minute drops from off the eaves.
MILTON, *Il Penseroso*, l. 126.

4

Never does a wilder song
Steal the breezy lyre along,
When the wind in odours dying
Woos it with enamour'd sighing.
THOMAS MOORE, *To Rosa.*

5

Mournfully, oh, mournfully,
The midnight wind doth sigh,
Like some sweet plaintive melody
Of ages long gone by.
WILLIAM MOTHERWELL, *The Midnight Wind.*

The wind was a torrent of darkness among the gusty trees.
ALFRED NOYES, *The Highwayman.*

6

Who has seen the wind?
Neither you nor I:
But when the trees bow down their heads,
The wind is passing by.
CHRISTINA ROSSETTI, *Who Has Seen the Wind?*

7

The gypsy wind goes down the night;
I hear him lilt his wander-call,
And to the old divine delight
Am I athrall.
CLINTON SCOLLARD, *The Gypsy Wind.*

8

The swiftest harts have posted you by land;
And winds of all the corners kiss'd your sails,
To make your vessel nimble.
SHAKESPEARE, *Cymbeline*. Act ii, sc. 4, l. 27.

9

Hamlet: The air bites shrewdly; it is very cold.
Horatio: It is a nipping and an eager air.
SHAKESPEARE, *Hamlet*. Act i, sc. 4, l. 1.

10

The southern wind
Doth play the trumpet to his purposes,
And by his hollow whistling in the leaves
Foretells a tempest and a blustering day.
SHAKESPEARE, *I Henry IV*. Act v, sc. 1, l. 3.

We shall be winnow'd with so rough a wind
That even our corn shall seem as light as chaff,
And good from bad find no partition.
SHAKESPEARE, *II Henry IV*. Act iv, sc. 1, l. 194.

Blow, winds, and crack your cheeks! rage! blow!
SHAKESPEARE, *King Lear*. Act iii, sc. 2, l. 1.

11

A fresher gale
Begins to wave the wood and stir the stream,
Sweeping with shadowy gust the fields of corn,
While the quail clamours for his running mate.
THOMSON, *The Seasons: Summer*, l. 1654.

Wild as the winds, across the howling waste
Of mighty waters.
THOMSON, *The Seasons: Winter*, l. 165.

12

I hear the little children of the wind
Crying solitary in lonely places.
WILLIAM SHARP, *Little Children of the Wind.*

13

O wild West Wind, thou breath of Autumn's being,
Thou, from whose unseen presence the leaves dead
Are driven, like ghosts from an enchanter fleeing,
Yellow, and black, and pale, and hectic red,
Pestilence-stricken multitudes.
SHELLEY, *Ode to the West Wind*. Sec. 1.

O thou
Who chariotest to their dark wintry bed
The wingèd seeds, where they lie cold and low,
Each like a corpse within its grave, until
Thine azure sister of the Spring shall blow
Her clarion o'er the dreaming earth.
SHELLEY, *Ode to the West Wind*. Sec. 1.

1
A wind arose among the pines; it shook
The clinging music from their boughs, and then
Low, sweet, faint sounds, like the farewell
of ghosts,
Were heard: OH, FOLLOW, FOLLOW, FOLLOW
ME!

SHELLEY, *Prometheus Unbound*. Act ii, sc. 1, 156.

And wind, that grand old harper, smote
His thunder-harp of pines.

ALEXANDER SMITH, *A Life Drama*. Sc. 2.

A wind arose and rush'd upon the South,
And shook the songs, the whispers, and the shrieks
Of the wild woods together; and a Voice
Went with it, "Follow, follow, thou shalt win."

TENNYSON, *The Princess*. Pt. i, l. 96.

2
Sweet and low, sweet and low,
Wind of the western sea,
Low, low, breathe and blow,
Wind of the western sea!

TENNYSON, *The Princess*. Pt. ii, l. 456.

3
Do ye now dare, O winds, without command of mine, to mingle earth and sky, and raise confusion thus?
(Jam cælum terramque meo sine numine, venti,
Miscere et tantas audetis tollere moles?)

VERGIL, *Æneid*. Bk. i, l. 133. Neptune is addressing the winds, which Æolus, at the request of Juno, has loosed against the Trojan fleet.

WINDOW

4
Each window like a pill'ry appears,
With heads thrust thro' nail'd by the ears.

BUTLER, *Hudibras*. Pt. ii, canto iii, l. 391.

5
From a window richly peint
With lives of many divers saint.

CHAUCER, *Chaucer's Dream*, l. 1847.

And diamonded with panes of quaint device
Innumerable, of stains and splendid dyes.

KEATS, *Eve of St. Agnes*. St. 24.

And storied windows richly dight,
Casting a dim religious light.

MILTON, *Il Penseroso*, l. 159.

Rich windows that exclude the light,
And passages that lead to nothing.

THOMAS GRAY, *A Long Story*, l. 7.

6
"Tehee!" quod she, and clapt the window to.

CHAUCER, *The Milleres Tale*, l. 554.

7
Better keep yourself clean and bright: you are the window through which you must see the world.

BERNARD SHAW, *Maxims for Revolutionists*.

WINE

See also Drinking

I—Wine: Apothegms

8
Bronze is the mirror of the form; wine, of the heart.

ÆSCHYLUS, *Fragments*. No. 384.

9
Well, my dear fellow, what did you expect—champagne?

GROVER CLEVELAND, to John Finley, who complained there was water in the cellar of a house he had rented from Cleveland. (FINLEY, *Cleveland. Scribner's Magazine*, April, 1927.)

10
Drink wine and have the gout; drink none and have the gout.

THOMAS COGAN, *Haven of Health: Dedication*. (1588)

The unearned increment of my grandfather's Madeira.

JAMES RUSSELL LOWELL, to Judge Hoar, commiserating with him on his sufferings with the gout.

11
Fan the sinking flame of hilarity with the wing of friendship; and pass the rosy.

DICKENS, *The Old Curiosity Shop*. Ch. 7.

12
"It wasn't the wine," murmured Mr. Snodgrass, in a broken voice. "It was the salmon."

DICKENS, *Pickwick Papers*. Ch. 8.

13
"I rather like bad wine," said Mr. Mountchesney; "one gets so bored with good wine."

BENJAMIN DISRAELI, *Sybil*. Bk. i, ch. 1.

14
Wine by the savour and bread by the heat.

JOHN FLORIO, *First Fruites*. Fo. 29.

15
Wine's old prophetic aid.

MATTHEW GREEN, *The Spleen*, l. 326.

16
You cannot know wine by the barrel.

GEORGE HERBERT, *Jacula Prudentum*.

The wine in the bottle does not quench thirst.

GEORGE HERBERT, *Jacula Prudentum*.

Wine ever pays for his lodging.

GEORGE HERBERT, *Jacula Prudentum*.

Milk says to wine, "Welcome, friend."

GEORGE HERBERT, *Jacula Prudentum*.

17
Can name his claret—if he sees the cork.

O. W. HOLMES, *The Banker's Secret*.

18
The Gentleman did take a drop too much,
(Tho' there are many such)
And took more Port than was exactly portable.

THOMAS HOOD, *The Green Man*, l. 12.

19
You appear to have emptied your wine-cellar into your bookseller.

THEODORE HOOK, to a friend who made his publisher drunk at dinner.

20
Drunken, but not with wine.

Old Testament: Isaiah, li, 21.

Wine is one thing, drunkenness another. (Aliud vinum, aliud ebrietas.)

ROBERT BURTON, *Anatomy of Melancholy*. Quoted.

No nation is drunken where wine is cheap; and none sober where the dearness of wine substitutes ardent spirits as the common beverage.
THOMAS JEFFERON, *Writings*. Vol. xv, p. 179.

1
I have trodden the wine press alone.
Old Testament: Isaiah, lxiii, 3.

2
A jar of wine so priceless did not deserve to die. (Amphora non meruit tam pretiosa mori.)
MARTIAL, *Epigrams*. Bk. i, epig. 18.

This wine should be eaten, it is too good to be drunk.
SWIFT, *Polite Conversation*. Dial. ii.

3
Let Nepos serve Cæretan, you will imagine it Setine. He does not serve it to a crowd: with three guests he drinks it. (Cæretana Nepos ponat, Setina putabis. Non ponit turbæ, cum tribus illa bibit.)
MARTIAL, *Epigrams*. Bk. xiii, epig. 124.

When you ask one friend to dine,
Give him your best wine!
When you ask two,
The second best will do!
H. W. LONGFELLOW. (BRANDER MATTHEWS, *Recreations of an Anthologist*, p. 117.)

3a
Season the wood never so well, the wine will taste of the cask.
JOHN LYLY, *Euphues*, p. 41. (1579)

4
Neither do men put new wine into old bottles: else the bottles break, and the wine runneth out, and the bottles perish: but they put new wine into new bottles, and both are preserved.
New Testament: Matthew, ix, 17.

5
The gadding vine.
MILTON, *Lycidas*, l. 40.

The mantling vine.
MILTON, *Paradise Lost*. Bk. iv, l. 258.

6
Lords are lordliest in their wine.
MILTON, *Samson Agonistes*, l. 1418.

7
The master's wine is in the butler's gift. (Vinum dominicum ministratoris gratia est.)
PETRONIUS, *Satyricon*. Sec. 31.

8
Give, in return for old wine, a new song. (Redde cantionem, veteri pro vino, novam.)
PLAUTUS, *Stichus*. Act v, sc. 6, l. 8.

What were revel without wine?
What were wine without a song?
STEPHEN PHILLIPS, *Ulysses*. Act iii, sc. 2.

9
It has become quite a common proverb that in wine there is truth. (In vino veritas.)
PLINY, *Historia Naturalis*. Bk. xiv, sec. 14.

10
You need not hang up the ivy-branch over the wine that will sell. (Vino vendibili suspensa hedera nihil opus.)
PUBLILIUS SYRUS, *Sententiæ*. No. 968.

Wine that is salable and good needeth no bush or garland of yew to be hanged before.
RICHARD TAVERNER, *Proverbs*. Fo. 42. (1539)

Things of greatest profit are set forth with least price. Where the wine is neat, there needeth no ivy-bush.
JOHN LYLY, *Euphues*. (1579)

Good wine needs no bush.
SHAKESPEARE, *As You Like It: Epilogue*. (1599)

I hang no ivy out to sell my wine;
The nectar of good wits will sell itself.
ROBERT ALLOTT, *England's Parnassus: Sonnet to the Reader*. (1600)

11
Counsels in wine seldom prosper.
JOHN RAY, *English Proverbs*.

Take counsel in wine, but resolve afterwards in water.
BENJAMIN FRANKLIN, *Poor Richard*, 1733.

12
I question if keeping it does it much good
After ten years in bottle, and three in the wood.
R. H. BARHAM, *Ingoldsby Legends: The Wedding-Day*. Quoted approvingly by GEORGE SAINTSBURY, *Notes for a Cellar-Book*.

13
A cup of hot wine with not a drop of allaying Tiber in 't.
SHAKESPEARE, *Coriolanus*. Act ii, sc. 1, l. 52.

When flowing cups pass swiftly round
With no allaying Thames.
RICHARD LOVELACE, *To Althea from Prison*.

14
If sack and sugar be a fault, God help the wicked!
SHAKESPEARE, *I Henry IV*. Act ii, sc. 4, l. 517.

O monstrous! but one half-penny-worth of bread to this intolerable deal of sack!
SHAKESPEARE, *I Henry IV*. Act ii, sc. 4, l. 591.

If I had a thousand sons, the first humane principle I would teach them should be, to forswear thin potations and to addict themselves to sack.
SHAKESPEARE, *II Henry IV*. Act iv, sc. 3, l. 134.
Sack was the term applied to the strong white wines imported from Spain and the Canaries. They were often sweetened and mixed with eggs and other ingredients to make a kind of punch.

We care not for money, riches, nor wealth;
Old sack is our money, old sack is our wealth.
THOMAS RANDOLPH, *The Praise of Old Sack*.

15
A man cannot make him laugh;—but that's no marvel; he drinks no wine.
SHAKESPEARE, *II Henry IV*. Act iv, sc. 3, l. 95.

16
Give me a bowl of wine.
In this I bury all unkindness.
SHAKESPEARE, *Julius Cæsar*. Act iv, sc. 3, l. 158.

Give me a bowl of wine:
I have not that alacrity of spirit,
Nor cheer of mind, that I was wont to have.
SHAKESPEARE, *Richard III*. Act v, sc. 3, l. 72.

Come and crush a cup of wine.
SHAKESPEARE, *Romeo and Juliet*. Act i, sc. 2, l. 86.

Cassio: Every inordinate cup is unblessed and the ingredient is a devil.
Iago: Come, come, good wine is a good familiar creature, if it be well used; exclaim no more against it.
SHAKESPEARE, *Othello*. Act ii, sc. 3, l. 311.

1
The vines of France and milk of Burgundy.
SHAKESPEARE, *King Lear*. Act i, sc. 1, l. 86.

The foaming grape of eastern France.
TENNYSON, *In Memoriam: Conclusion*. St. 20.

The red grape in the sunny lands of song.
BYRON, *Don Juan*. Canto xiii, st. 76.

2
The best wine, . . . that goeth down sweetly, causing the lips of those that are asleep to speak.
Old Testament· Song of Solomon, vii, 9.

Wine is wont to show the mind of man.
THEOGNIS, *Sententiæ*, l. 500.

A man will be eloquent if you give him good wine.
EMERSON, *Representative Men: Montaigne*.

3
He has had a smack of every sort of wine, from humble port to Imperial Tokay.
TOWNLEY, *High Life Below Stairs*. Act ii.

Old Simon the cellarer keeps a rare store
Of Malmsey and Malvoisie.
W. A. BELLAMY, *Simon the Cellarer*.

Your best barley-wine, the good liquor that our honest forefathers did use to drink of.
IZAAK WALTON, *The Compleat Angler*. Ch. 5.

Grudge myself good wine? as soon grudge my horse corn.
THACKERAY.

II—Wine: Its Virtues

4
The very best of vineyards is the cellar.
BYRON, *Don Juan*. Canto xiii, st. 76.

Sweet is old wine in bottles, ale in barrels.
BYRON, *Sweet Things*. St. 5.

5
Long life to the grape! for when summer is flown,
The age of our nectar shall gladden our own.
BYRON, *Fill the Goblet Again*.

5a
To old men, wine is as suck to young children, and is therefore called of some *Lac senum*.
THOMAS COGAN, *Haven of Health*, 244. (1584)

6
Bring me wine, but wine which never grew
In the belly of the grape,
Or grew on vine whose tap-roots, reaching through
Under the Andes to the Cape,
Suffer no savor of the earth to scape.
EMERSON, *Bacchus*. St. 1.

Wine which Music is,—
Music and wine are one.
R. W. EMERSON, *Bacchus*. St. 6.

7
From wine what sudden friendship springs!
JOHN GAY, *Fables* Pt. ii, No. 6.

8
Fill every beaker up, my men, pour forth the cheering wine:
There's life and strength in every drop,—thanksgiving to the vine!
ALBERT GORTON GREENE, *Baron's Last Banquet*.

9
On turnpikes of wonder wine leads the mind forth,
Straight, sidewise, and upward, west, southward, and north.
HAFIZ. (EMERSON, *Persian Poetry*.)

10
Wine is like rain: when it falls on the mire it but makes it the fouler,
But when it strikes the good soil wakes it to beauty and bloom.
JOHN HAY, *Distichs*.

11
"I am beauty and love;
I am friendship, the comforter;
I am that which forgives and forgets."
The Spirit of Wine
Sang in my heart, and I triumphed
In the savour and scent of his music,
His magnetic and mastering song.
W. E. HENLEY, *The Spirit of Wine*.

12
Sparkling and bright in liquid light
Does the wine our goblets gleam in;
With hue as red as the rosy bed
Which a bee would choose to dream in.
Then fill to-night, with hearts as light
To loves as gay and fleeting
As bubbles that swim on the beaker's brim
And break on the lips while meeting.
CHARLES HOFFMAN, *Sparkling and Bright*.

This song of mine
Is a Song of the Vine
To be sung by the glowing embers
Of wayside inns,
When the rain begins
To darken the drear Novembers.
LONGFELLOW, *Catawba Wine*. St. 1.

Sing! Who sings
To her who weareth a hundred rings?
Ah, who is this lady fine?
The Vine, boys, the Vine!
The mother of the mighty Wine,
A roamer is she O'er wall and tree,
And sometimes very good company.
BRYAN WALLER PROCTER, *A Bacchanalian Song*.

13
With crimson juice the thirsty southern sky
Sucks from the hills where buried armies lie,
So that the dreamy passion it imparts
Is drawn from heroes' bones and lovers' hearts.
O. W. HOLMES, *The Banker's Secret*, l. 127.

Wines that, heaven knows when,
Had suck'd the fire of some forgotten sun,
And kept it thro' a hundred years of gloom.
TENNYSON, *The Lover's Tale*, l. 192.

14
O Varus, plant no tree in preference to the

sacred vine. (Nullam, Vare, sacra vite prius severis arborem.)
HORACE, *Odes*. Bk. i, ode 18, l. 1.

1
Now drown care in wine. (Nunc vino pellite curas.)
HORACE, *Odes*. Bk. i, ode 7, l. 32.

Dispel the chill, piling high the logs upon the fire, and pour out with generous hand the four year old wine from the Sabine jar.
(Dissolve frigus ligna super foco
Large reponens atque benignius
Deprome quadrimum Sabina.)
HORACE, *Odes*. Bk. i, ode 9, l. 5.

When Horace wrote his noble verse,
His brilliant, glowing line,
He must have gone to bed the worse
For good Falernian wine.
No poet yet could praise the rose
In verse that so serenely flows
Unless he dipped his Roman nose
In good Falernian wine.
THEODORE MAYNARD, *A Tankard of Ale*.

2
Nor are cankering cares dispelled except by Bacchus' gift. (Neque Mordaces aliter diffugiunt sollicitudines.)
HORACE, *Odes*. Bk. i, ode 18, l. 4.

Bacchus opens the gate of the heart. (Aperit præcordia Liber.)
HORACE, *Satires*. Bk. i, sat. 4, l. 89.

Bacchus scatters carking cares. (Dissipat Evhius curas edaces.)
HORACE, *Odes*. Bk. ii, ode 11, l. 17.

Come, thou monarch of the vine,
Plumpy Bacchus with pink eyne!
In thy fats our cares be drown'd,
With thy grapes our hairs be crown'd:
Cup us, till the world go round.
SHAKESPEARE, *Anthony and Cleopatra*. Act ii, sc. 7, l. 120.

Bacchus, ever fair and ever young.
DRYDEN, *Alexander's Feast*, l. 54.

Bacchus, that first from out the purple grape,
Crush'd the sweet poison of misused wine.
MILTON, *Comus*, l. 46.

He turn'd a fruit to an enchantment
Which cheers the sad, revives the old, inspires
The young, makes Weariness forget his toil,
And Fear her danger; opens a new world
When this, the present, palls.
BYRON, *Sardanapalus*. Act i, sc. 2.

3
Mighty to inspire new hopes and powerful
To drown the bitterness of cares.
(Spes donare novas largus amaraque
Curarum eluere efficax.)
HORACE, *Odes*. Bk. iv, ode 12, l. 19.

Drown'd all in Rhenish and the sleepy mead.
JOHN KEATS, *The Eve of St. Agnes*. St. 39.

4
For fifty years the liquid joy has been curbed within these ribs of oak waiting to touch the lips of man.
R. G. INGERSOLL, *Works*. Vol. vii, p. 348.

5
But that which most doth take my Muse and me,
Is a pure cup of rich Canary wine,
Which is the Mermaid's now, but shall be mine.
BEN JONSON, *Epigrams:* No. 101, *Inviting a Friend to Supper*.

6
Wine it is the milk of Venus,
And the poet's horse accounted:
Ply it and you all are mounted.
BEN JONSON, *Verses Placed Over the Door at the Entrance into the Apollo Room at the Devil Tavern*.

7
O for a beaker full of the warm South,
Full of the true, the blushful Hippocrene.
JOHN KEATS, *Ode to a Nightingale*. St. 2.

8
When thirsty grief in Wine we steep,
When healths and draughts go free,
Fishes that tipple in the deep,
Know no such liberty.
RICHARD LOVELACE, *To Althea, from Prison*.

9
Attic honey, thicken the nectar-like Falernian. Such drink deserves to be mixed by Ganymede. (Attica nectareum turbatis mella Falernum. Misceri decet hoc a Ganymede merum.)
MARTIAL, *Epigrams*. Bk. xiii, epig. 108. To blend with honey, the wine had to be old. (PLINY, *Historia Naturalis*, xiv, 8.)

10
Note the superiority of wine over Venus! I may say the magnanimity of wine; our jealousy turns on him that will not share!
GEORGE MEREDITH, *The Egoist*. Ch. 19.

An aged Burgundy runs with a beardless Port. I cherish the fancy that Port speaks the sentences of wisdom, Burgundy sings the inspired Ode.
GEORGE MEREDITH, *The Egoist*. Ch. xx.

11
As with new wine intoxicated both,
They swim in mirth, and fancy that they feel
Divinity within them breeding wings
Wherewith to scorn the earth.
MILTON, *Paradise Lost*. Bk. ix, l. 1008.

12
Wine to the poet is a wingèd steed:
Those who drink water gain but little speed.
(Οἶνος τοι χαρίεντι πέλει ταχὺς ἵππος ἀοιδῷ·
ὕδωρ δὲ πίνων οὐδὲν ἂν τέκοις σοφόν.)
NICÆNETUS. (*Greek Anthology*. Bk. xiii, epig. 29.)

13
Perplext no more with Human or Divine,
To-morrow's tangle to the winds resign,
And lose your fingers in the tresses of
The Cypress-slender Minister of Wine.
OMAR KHAYYÁM, *Rubáiyát*. St. 41. (Fitzgerald, tr.)

Better be jocund with the fruitful Grape
Than sadden after none, or bitter Fruit.
OMAR KHAYYÁM, *Rubáiyát*. St. 54. (Fitzgerald, tr.)

You know, my Friends, with what a brave Carouse
I made a second marriage in my house;
Divorced old barren Reason from my Bed,
And took the Daughter of the Vine to spouse.
OMAR KHAYYÁM, *Rubáiyát*. St. 55. (Fitzgerald, tr.)

The Grape that can with Logic absolute
The Two-and-Seventy jarring Sects confute:
The sovereign Alchemist that in a trice
Life's leaden metal into Gold transmute.
OMAR KHAYYÁM, *Rubáiyát*. St. 59. (Fitzgerald, tr.)

And much as Wine has play'd the Infidel,
And robb'd me of my Robe of Honour—Well,
I wonder often what the Vintners buy
One half so precious as the stuff they sell.
OMAR KHAYYÁM, *Rubáiyát*. St. 95. (Fitzgerald, tr.)

1
O sweet essence! How good, I should say, were your former contents, when the remains of them smell so delicious! (O suavis anima, quale in te dicam bonum Ante hac fuisse; tales cum sint reliquiæ!)
PHÆDRUS, *Fables*. Bk. iii, fab. 1, l. 5. The ass to the empty wine-jar.

2
Wine whets the wit, improves its native force,
And gives a pleasant flavour to discourse.
JOHN POMFRET, *The Choice*, l. 55.

3
So will I pass the night with wine-cup and with song,
Till dawn shall cast its rays upon my wine.
(Sic noctem patera, sic ducam carmine, donec
Iniciat radios in mea vina dies.)
PROPERTIUS, *Elegies*. Bk. iv, eleg. 6, l. 85.

4
Wine that maketh glad the heart of man.
Old Testament: Psalms, civ, 15. (Vinum bonum lætificet cor hominis.—*Vulgate*.)

5
Day and night my thoughts incline
To the blandishments of wine,
Jars were made to drain, I think;
Wine, I know, was made to drink.
R. H. STODDARD, *A Jar of Wine.*

6
Drink no longer water, but use a little wine for thy stomach's sake.
New Testament: I Timothy, v, 23.

7
Wine fills the veins, and healths are understood
To give our friends a title to our blood.
EDMUND WALLER, *For Drinking of Healths*, l. 21. *See also* DRINKING: HEALTHS.

8
Corn shall make the young men cheerful, and new wine the maids.
Old Testament: Zechariah, ix, 17.

III—Wine: Its Faults

9
Wine in excess keeps neither secrets nor promises.
CERVANTES, *Don Quixote*. Pt. ii, ch. 43.

10
Wine hath drowned more men than the sea.
THOMAS FULLER, *Gnomologia*.

So Noah, when he anchor'd safe on
The mountain's top, his lofty haven,
And all the passengers he bore
Were on the new world set ashore,
He made it next his chief design
To plant and propagate a vine,
Which since has overwhelm'd and drown'd
Far greater numbers, on dry ground,
Of wretched mankind, one by one,
Than all the flood before had done.
BUTLER, *Satire Upon Drunkenness*, l. 105.

And Noah he often said to his wife when he sat down to dine,
"I don't care where the water goes if it doesn't get into the wine."
G. K. CHESTERTON, *The Flying Inn.*

It was a wet world—and I gave it wine.
EDMUND VANCE COOKE, *From the Book of Extenuations: Noah.*

11
Wine turns a man inside outwards.
THOMAS FULLER, *Gnomologia.*

Wine makes all sorts of creatures at table.
GEORGE HERBERT, *Jacula Prudentum.*

12
Inflaming wine, pernicious to mankind,
Unnerves the limbs, and dulls the noble mind.
HOMER, *Iliad*. Bk. vi, l. 330. (Pope, tr.)

And wine can of their wits the wise beguile,
Make the sage frolic, and the serious smile.
HOMER, *Odyssey*. Bk. xiv, l. 520. (Pope, tr.)

13
He rails bitterly against Bacchus, and swears there's a devil in every berry of his grape.
JAMES HOWELL, *Familiar Letters*. Bk. ii, No. 3.

There is a devil in every berry of the grape.
The Koran. Ch. 2.

O thou invisible spirit of wine, if thou hast no name to be known by, let us call thee devil!
SHAKESPEARE, *Othello*. Act ii, sc. 3, l. 283.

14
Wine makes a man better pleased with himself. . . . But the danger is, that while a man grows better pleased with himself, he may be growing less pleasing to others. Wine gives a man nothing. . . . It only puts in motion what had been locked up in frost.
SAMUEL JOHNSON. (BOSWELL, *Life*, 28 April, 1778.)

15
Their sinfulness is greater than their use.
The Koran. Ch. 2. Of wine and gambling.

16
And when night
Darkens the streets, then wander forth the sons
Of Belial, flown with insolence and wine.
MILTON, *Paradise Lost*. Bk. i, l. 500.

1
That's the great evil in wine: it catches you by the feet, it's a cunning wrestler. (Magnum hoc vitium vino est: Pedes captat primum, luctator doloust.)

PLAUTUS, *Pseudolus*, l. 1250. (Act v, sc. 1.)

2
Wine is a mocker, strong drink is raging.

Old Testament: Proverbs, xx, 1.

Who hath woe? who hath sorrow? who hath contentions? who hath babbling? who hath wounds without cause? who hath redness of eyes? They that tarry long at the wine.

Old Testament: Proverbs, xxiii, 29, 30.

Look not thou upon the wine when it is red, when it giveth his colour in the cup. . . . At the last it biteth like a serpent, and stingeth like an adder.

Old Testament: Proverbs, xxiii, 31, 32.

Take especial care that thou delight not in wine; for there never was any man that came to honour or preferment that loved it; for it transformeth a man into a beast, decayeth health, poisoneth the breath, destroyeth natural heat, deformeth the face, rotteth the teeth, and maketh a man contemptible.

SIR WALTER RALEIGH, *Instructions to His Son.*

3
But the wine is bright at the goblet's brim,
Though the poison lurk beneath.

D. G. ROSSETTI, *The King's Tragedy*. St. 61.

4
Wine kindles wrath. (Vinum incendit iram.)

SENECA, *De Ira*. Bk. ii, sec. 19.

IV—Wine and Love

5
What fool is he that shadows seeks,
And may the substance gain!
Then if thou'lt have me love a lass,
Let it be one that's kind,
Else I'm a servant to the glass
That's with Canary lined.

ALEXANDER BROME, *The Resolve.*

6
Where there is no wine there is no love. (Οἴνου δὲ μηκέτ' ὄντος οὐκ ἔστιν Κύπρις.)

EURIPIDES, *Bacchæ*, l. 773.

7
A generous bottle and a lovesome she,
Are th' only joys in nature next to thee.

THOMAS OTWAY, *Epistle to Mr. Duke.*

8
Wine gives courage and makes men apt for passion. (Vina parant animos, faciuntque caloribus aptos.)

OVID, *Ars Amatoria*. Bk. i, l. 227.

Wine prepares the heart for love, unless you take too much. (Vina parant animum veneri, nisi plurima sumas.)

OVID, *Remediorum Amoris*, l. 805.

What man can pretend to be a believer in love, who is an abjurer of wine? 'T is the test by which the lover knows his own heart. Fill a dozen bumpers to a dozen beauties, and she that floats atop is the maid that has bewitched you.

SHERIDAN, *School for Scandal*. Act iii, sc. 3.

Bacchus and Phœbus are by Jove allied,
And each by other's timely heat supplied.

EDMUND WALLER, *Drinking of Healths*, l. 17.

9
Often have I sought to banish love's pain with wine, but grief turned all the wine to tears. (Sæpe ego temptavi curas depellere vino;
At dolor in lacrimas verteret omne merum.)

TIBULLUS, *Elegies*. Bk. i, eleg. 5, l. 37.

Weep on, weep on, my pouting vine!
Heav'n grant no tears, but tears of wine.

THOMAS MOORE, *Anacreontic: Press the Grape.*

10
Wine gives us liberty, love takes it away.
Wine makes us princes, love makes us beggars.

WYCHERLEY, *The Country Wife*. Act i.

V—Wine and Women

10a
This is wisdom: to love wine,
Beauty, and the spring divine;
That is enough. The rest is vain.
(C'est la sagesse: aimer le vin,
La beauté, le printemps divin;
Cela suffit. La reste est vain.)

THÉODORE DE BANVILLE, *C'est la Sagesse.*

11
I may not here omit those two main plagues and common dotages of human kind, wine and women, which have infatuated and besotted myriads of people; they go commonly together.

ROBERT BURTON, *Anatomy of Melancholy*. Pt. i, sec. 2, mem. 3, subs. 13.

12
Few things surpass old wine; and they may preach
Who please,—the more because they preach in vain,—
Let us have wine and women, mirth and laughter,
Sermons and soda-water the day after.

BYRON, *Don Juan*. Canto ii, st. 178.

13
Women and wine do make a man
A doting fool all that they can.

EVANS, *Revised Withals Dictionary*. (1586)

14
Women, wine, and dice
Will bring a man to lice.

JOHN FLORIO, *Second Frutes*, Fo. 73.

Women and wine, game and deceit,
Make the wealth small and the wants great.

FULLER, *Gnomologia*. No. 6416. See also 753:16.

16
Wine and women into apostasie
Cause wise men to fall.

UNKNOWN, *The Remedy of Love*. (c. 1532)

17
Wine and wenches empty men's purses.

JOHN RAY, *English Proverbs.*

Love of a woman and a bottle of wine
Are sweet for a season, but last for a time.

JOHN RAY, *English Proverbs*, p. 55.

1
Who loves not women, wine, and song,
Remains a fool his whole life long.
(Wer nicht liebt Weiber, Wein, und Gesang,
Der bleibt ein Narr sein Leben lang.)

JOHN HENRY VOSS, who included it in a collection of his poems. (REDLICH, *Die Poetischen die Geisterkelter.*) Usually ascribed to Martin Luther, but without the slightest warrant, except a passage in his *Table-Talk* (No. 728). Its first appearance in literature was in 1775, in *Der Wandsbecker Bote,* of Matthias Claudius, who incorporated it as a toast. Ascribed to Luther by Th. Weyler, who changed "Weiber," women, to "Weib," wife, to make it a little more decorous. (See BÜCHMANN, *Geflügelte Worte.*)

Then sing, as Martin Luther sang,
As Doctor Martin Luther sang:
"Who loves not wine, woman, and song,
He is a fool his whole life long!"

W. M. THACKERAY, *A Credo.* St. 1.

Thou art in danger, Cincius, on my word,
To die ere thou hast lived, which were absurd.
Open thine ears to song, thy throat to wine,
Thy arms unto that pretty wife of thine.
Philosophy, I have nowise forgot,
Is deathless, but philosophers are not.

RICHARD GARNETT, *Epigram.* (After Argentarius.)

In the order named these are the hardest to control: Wine, Women and Song.

FRANKLIN P. ADAMS, *The Ancient Three.*

One of the oldest and quietest roads to contentment lies through the conventional trinity of wine, woman and song.

REXFORD GUY TUGWELL, *Address,* Woman's National Democratic Club, Washington, D. C., May, 1934.

2
Women, money and wine have their pleasure and their poison. (Femme, argent et vin, Ont leur bien et leur venin.)

UNKNOWN. A French proverb.

3
Baths, wine, and Venus bring decay to our bodies,
But baths, wine, and Venus make life worth living.
(Balnea, vina, Venus corrumpunt corpora nostra,
Sed vitam faciunt balnea, Vina, Venus.)

UNKNOWN, *Epitaph.* (GRUTER, *Monumenta.*)

WINKING

4
There's a time to wink as well as to see.

BENJAMIN FRANKLIN, *Poor Richard,* 1747.

5
Bean-pods are noisiest when dry,
And you always wink with your weakest eye.

BRET HARTE, *The Tale of a Pony.*

6
He that winketh with eye and looketh with the other
I will not trust him though he were my brother.

JOHN HEYWOOD, *Proverbs.* Pt. i, ch. 11.

7
Wink and shut their apprehensions up.

JOHN MARSTON, *Antonio's Revenge: Prologue.*

8
Hard must he wink that shuts his eyes from heaven.

FRANCIS QUARLES, *Feast for Worms.* Sec. iii, 3.

9
You may wink and choose.

JOHN RAY, *English Proverbs,* p. 216.

10
Although I wink I am not blind.

CLEMENT ROBINSON, *Handful of Pleasant Delites.* (1585)

11
I will wink on her to consent, my lord, if you will teach her to know my meaning.

SHAKESPEARE, *Henry V.* Act v, sc. 2, l. 333.

Wink each at other; hold the sweet jest up.

SHAKESPEARE, *A Midsummer-Night's Dream.* Act iii, sc. 2, l. 239.

12
When most I wink, then do mine eyes best see.

SHAKESPEARE, *Sonnets.* No. xliii.

13
A wink's as good as a nod with some folks.

DOROTHY WORDSWORTH, *Journal.* Vol. i, p. 129. (1802)

A nod is as good as a wink.

SCOTT, *The Fortunes of Nigel.* Ch. 25. (1822)

WINTER

14
O Winter! bar thine adamantine doors:
The north is thine; there hast thou built thy dark,
Deep-founded habitation. Shake not thy roofs,
Nor bend thy pillars with thine iron car.

WILLIAM BLAKE, *To Winter.*

O Winter, ruler of th' inverted year, . . .
I crown thee king of intimate delights,
Fire-side enjoyments, home-born happiness,
And all the comforts that the lowly roof
Of undisturb'd retirement, and the hours
Of long uninterrupted ev'ning, know.

COWPER, *The Task.* Bk. iv, l. 120.

See, Winter comes to rule the varied year,
Sullen and sad, with all his rising train—
Vapours, and clouds, and storms.

THOMSON, *The Seasons: Winter,* l. 1.

15
Nor from the perfect circle of the year
Can even Winter's crystal gems be spared.

CHRISTOPHER PEARSE CRANCH, *December.*

16
Hence, rude Winter; crabbed old fellow,
Never merry, never mellow!
Well-a-day! in rain and snow
What will keep one's heart aglow?

ALFRED DOMETT, *A Glee for Winter.*

17
But winter ling'ring chills the lap of May.

GOLDSMITH, *The Traveller,* l. 172.

Winter lingered so long in the lap of Spring, that it occasioned a great deal of talk.

BILL NYE, *Spring.*

1
Sharp winter is now loosened. (Solvitur acris hiems.)
HORACE, *Odes*. Bk. i, ode 4, l. 1.

The sluggish winter returns to us. (Bruma recurrit iners.)
HORACE, *Odes*. Bk. iv, ode 7, l. 12.

2
His breath like silver arrows pierced the air,
The naked earth crouched shuddering at his feet,
His finger on all flowing waters sweet
Forbidding lay—motion nor sound was there:—
Nature lay frozen dead,—and still and slow,
A winding sheet fell o'er her body fair,
Flaky and soft, from his wide wings of snow.
FRANCES ANNE KEMBLE, *Winter*, l. 9.

3
Oh the long and dreary Winter!
Oh the cold and cruel Winter!
LONGFELLOW, *The Song of Hiawatha*. Pt. xx.

Drag on, long night of winter, in whose heart,
Nurse of regret, the dead spring yet has part!
WILLIAM MORRIS, *The Earthly Paradise: Fostering of Aslang: Conclusion.*

Late February days; and now, at last,
Might you have thought that Winter's woe was past;
So fair the sky was and so soft the air.
WILLIAM MORRIS, *The Earthly Paradise: February.*

4
Old Winter sad, in snow y-clad,
Is making a doleful din;
But let him howl till he crack his jowl,
We will not let him in. . . .

Come, lads, let's sing, till the rafters ring;
Come, push the can about;—
From our snug fireside this Christmas-tide
We'll keep old Winter out.
THOMAS NOEL, *Old Winter.*

5
Now there is frost upon the hill
And no leaf stirring in the wood;
The little streams are cold and still;
Never so still has winter stood.
GEORGE O'NEIL, *Where It Is Winter.*

6
But see, Orion sheds unwholesome dews;
Arise, the pines a noxious shade diffuse;
Sharp Boreas blows, and Nature feels decay,
Time conquers all, and we must Time obey.
POPE, *Pastorals: Winter*, l. 85.

7
A green winter makes a fat churchyard.
JOHN RAY, *English Proverbs*, 42. (1670)

8
Here feel we but the penalty of Adam,
The seasons' difference, as the icy fang
And churlish chiding of the winter's wind,
Which, when it bites and blows upon my body,
Even till I shrink with cold, I smile and say,
"This is no flattery."
SHAKESPEARE, *As You Like It*. Act ii, sc. 1, l. 5.

Quake in the present winter's state and wish
The warmer days would come.
SHAKESPEARE, *Cymbeline*. Act ii, sc. 4, l. 5.

Winter tames man, woman and beast.
SHAKESPEARE, *The Taming of the Shrew*. Act iv, sc. 1, l. 24.

9
Winter's not gone yet, if the wild-geese fly that way.
SHAKESPEARE, *King Lear*. Act ii, sc. 4, l. 46.

10
When icicles hang by the wall,
And Dick the shepherd blows his nail,
And Tom bears logs into the hall,
And milk comes frozen home in pail,
When blood is nipp'd and ways be foul,
Then nightly sings the staring owl,
Tu-whit;
Tu-who, a merry note,
While greasy Joan doth keel the pot.
SHAKESPEARE, *Love's Labour's Lost*. Act v, sc. 2, l. 922.

When all aloud the wind doth blow,
And coughing drowns the parson's saw,
And birds sit brooding in the snow,
And Marian's nose looks red and raw,
When roasted crabs hiss in the bowl,
Then nightly sings the staring owl.
SHAKESPEARE, *Love's Labour's Lost*. Act v, sc. 2, l. 931.

11
Winter, which being full of care
Makes summer's welcome thrice more wish'd, more rare.
SHAKESPEARE, *Sonnets*. No. lvi.

A sad tale's best for winter;
I have one of sprites and goblins.
SHAKESPEARE, *Winter's Tale*. Act ii, sc. 1, l. 25.

12
Be like the sun and the meadow, which are not in the least concerned about the coming winter.
BERNARD SHAW, *An Unsocial Socialist*. Ch. 5.

13
If Winter comes, can Spring be far behind?
SHELLEY, *Ode to the West Wind.*

Lastly came Winter, clothed all in frieze,
Chattering his teeth for cold that did him chill,
Whilst on his hoary beard his breath did freeze,
And the dull drops, that from his purpled bill
As from a limbeck did adown distill.
SPENSER, *Faerie Queene*. Bk. vii, canto 7, st. 31.

14
Thus Winter falls,
A heavy gloom oppressive o'er the world,
Through Nature shedding influence malign,
And rouses up the seeds of dark disease.
THOMSON, *The Seasons: Winter*, l. 57.

Dread Winter spreads his latest glooms,
And reigns tremendous o'er the conquered year.
How dead the vegetable kingdom lies!

How dumb the tuneful! Horror wide extends
His desolate domain.
THOMSON, *The Seasons: Winter*, l. 1024.

1
Such a winter eve. Now for a mellow fire, some old poet's page, or else serene philosophy.
H. D. THOREAU, *Journal*.

2
Winter eateth what summer getteth.
UNKNOWN, *Good Wyfe Wold a Pylgremage*, l. 155. (1460)

Winter draws out what summer laid in.
THOMAS FULLER, *Gnomologia*. No. 5753.

WISDOM

See also Knowledge and Wisdom; Learning; Fools and Wise Men

I—Wisdom: Definitions

3
Wisdom cometh by suffering. (Τὸν πάθει μάθος θέντα κυρίως ἔχειν.)
ÆSCHYLUS, *Agamemnon*, l. 177.

Justice turns her scale, so that wisdom cometh at the price of suffering. (Δίκα δὲ τοῖς μὲν παθοῦσιν μαθεῖν ἐπιρρέπει.)
ÆSCHYLUS, *Agamemnon*, l. 250.

Who knows useful things, not many things, is wise. (Ὁ χρήσιμ' εἰδώς, οὐχ ὁ πόλλ' εἰδώς, σοφός.)
ÆSCHYLUS, *Fragments*. Frag. 218.

This is the mark of men just and wise as well—even in calamity not to cherish anger against the gods.
ÆSCHYLUS [?], *Fragments*. Frag. 240.

4
Wisdom consists in rising superior both to madness and to common sense, and in lending oneself to the universal illusion without becoming its dupe.
AMIEL, *Journal*, 11 Dec., 1872.

5
Many are wise in their own ways, that are weak for government or counsel.
BACON, *Advancement of Learning*. Bk. ii.

To be wise by rule and by experience are utterly opposite principles; so that he who is used to the one is unfit for the other.
BACON, *De Augmentis Scientiarum*. Pt. i, bk. 6.

6
It hath been an opinion that the French are wiser than they seem, and the Spaniards seem wiser than they are; but howsoever it be between nations, certainly it is so between man and man.
BACON, *Essays: Of Seeming Wise*.

The Italians are wise before the deed; the Germans in the deed; the French after the deed.
GEORGE HERBERT, *Jacula Prudentum*.

Ask, who is wise?—You'll find the self-same man
A sage in France, a madman in Japan;
And *here* some head beneath a mitre swells,
Which *there* had tingled to a cap and bells.
THOMAS MOORE, *The Sceptic*, l. 17.

7
Wisdom is the knowledge of things human and divine and of the causes by which those things are controlled. (Sapientia est, . . . rerum divinarum et humanarum causarumque, quibus eæ res continentur, scientia.)
CICERO, *De Officiis*. Bk. ii, ch. 2, sec. 5.

They call him the wisest man to whose mind that which is required at once occurs. (Sapientissimum esse dicunt eum, cui, quod opus sit, ipsi veniat in mentem.)
CICERO, *Pro Cluentio*. Ch. 31, sec. 84.

The wise man does nothing of which he can repent, nothing against his will, but does everything nobly, consistently, soberly, rightly.
CICERO, *Tusculanarum Disputationum*. Bk. v, ch. 28, sec. 81.

8
There is this difference between happiness and wisdom: he that thinks himself the happiest man, really is so; but he that thinks himself the wisest is generally the greatest fool.
C. C. COLTON, *Lacon*. Vol. i, No. 326.

9
In wisdom's ranks he stands the first,
Who stands prepared to meet the worst.
NATHANIEL COTTON, *When Dangers*.

Extremes of fortune are true wisdom's test,
And he's of men most wise who bears them best.
RICHARD CUMBERLAND, *Philemon*.

10
Wisdom and goodness are twin-born, one heart
Must hold both sisters, never seen apart.
COWPER, *Expostulation*, l. 634.

Wisdom is only found in truth. (Die Weisheit ist nur in der Wahrheit.)
GOETHE, *Sprüche in Prosa*. Pt. iii.

Wisdom without honesty is mere craft and cozenage.
BEN JONSON, *Explorata: Vita Recta*.

11
To finish the moment, to find the journey's end in every step of the road, to live the greatest number of good hours, is wisdom.
EMERSON, *Essays, Second Series: Experience*.

The invariable mark of wisdom is to see the miraculous in the common.
EMERSON, *Nature, Addresses, and Lectures: Prospects*.

Raphael paints wisdom, Handel sings it, Phidias carves it, Shakespeare writes it, Wren builds it, Columbus sails it, Luther preaches it, Washington arms it, Watt mechanizes it.
EMERSON, *Society and Solitude: Art*.

12
He is a wise man who does not grieve for the things which he has not, but rejoices for those which he has.
EPICTETUS, *Fragments*. No. cxxix.

13
Wisdom is full of pity; and thereby

Men pay for too much wisdom with much pain.

EURIPIDES, *Electra*, l. 294. (Murray, tr.)

1
He is not wise to me who is wise in words only, but he who is wise in deeds. (Non mihi sapit qui sermone, sed qui factis sapit.)

ST. GREGORY, *Agrigent. See also* WORD AND DEED.

2
He that has grown to wisdom hurries not,
But thinks and weighs what wisdom bids him do.

GUINICELLI, *Of Moderation and Tolerance.*

3
The mark of wisdom is to read aright the present, and to march with the occasion.

HOMER. (*Contest of Hesiod and Homer*. Sec. 321.)

Wisdom sails with wind and tide.

JOHN FLORIO, *Second Frutes*. Fo. 97.

4
To flee from folly is the beginning of wisdom. (Sapientia prima Stultitia caruisse.)

HORACE, *Epistles*. Bk. i, epis. 1, l. 41.

5
The wisdom of mankind creeps slowly on,
Subject to every doubt that can retard
Or fling it back upon an earlier time.

RICHARD HENGIST HORNE, *Orion*. Bk. iii, canto ii.

6
Wisdom denotes the pursuing of the best ends by the best means.

FRANCIS HUTCHESON THE ELDER, *Inquiry into the Original of Our Ideas of Beauty and Virtue*. Tr. ii, sec. 5.

7
The wisdom of the wise is an uncommon degree of common sense.

DEAN W. R. INGE. (MARCHANT, *Wit and Wisdom of Dean Inge*. No. 173.)

8
Wisdom is the conqueror of fortune. (Victrix fortunæ sapientia.)

JUVENAL, *Satires*. Sat. xiii, l. 20.

A wise man is out of the reach of fortune.

SIR THOMAS BROWNE, *Religio Medici*. Pt. i, sec. 52. Cited as "that insolent paradox."

A wise man turns chance into good fortune.

THOMAS FULLER, *Gnomologia*. No. 475.

9
Wisdom first teaches what is right. (Prima docet rectum sapientia.)

JUVENAL, *Satires*. Sat. xiii, l. 189.

10
Wisdom is to the soul what health is to the body. (La sagesse est à l'âme ce que la santé est pour le corps.)

LA ROCHEFOUCAULD, *Maximes Posthumes*, 541.

11
The wise man does not lay up treasure.

LAO-TSZE, *The Simple Way*. No. 81.

12
Wise men are those who drink old wine and see old plays. (Qui utuntur vino vetere sapientis puto Et qui libenter veteres spectant fabulas.)

PLAUTUS, *Casina: Prologue*, l. 5.

13
Wisdom, which is the only liberty. (Sapientia, quæ sola libertas est.)

SENECA, *Epistulæ ad Lucilium*. Epis. 37, sec. 4.

Wisdom is the perfect good of the human mind; philosophy is the love of wisdom and the endeavor to attain it. (Sapientia perfectum bonum est mentis humanæ. Philosophia sapientiæ amor est et adfectatio.)

SENECA, *Epistulæ ad Lucilium*. Epis. 89, sec. 4.

Chief Good is to live in agreement and harmony with nature.

CICERO, *De Finibus*. Bk. iii, ch. 9, sec. 31.

14
Wisdom is a hen, whose cackling we must value and consider because it is attended with an egg; but, then, lastly, it is a nut, which, unless you choose with judgement, may cost you a tooth, and pay you with nothing but a worm.

SWIFT, *A Tale of a Tub: Introduction.*

15
True wisdom consists not only in seeing what is before your eyes, but in foreseeing what is to come. (Istuc est sapere, non quod ante pedes modest Videre sed etiam illa quae futura sunt Prospicere.)

TERENCE, *Adelphi*, l. 386. (Act iii, sc. 3.)

To know
That which before us lies in daily life,
Is the prime wisdom; what is more is fume.

MILTON, *Paradise Lost*. Bk. viii, l. 192.

16
A man is wise with the wisdom of his time only, and ignorant with its ignorance.

H. D. THOREAU, *Journal*, 31 Jan., 1853.

Whatever of past or present wisdom has published itself to the world, is palpable falsehood till it come and utter itself by my side.

H. D. THOREAU, *Journal*, 4 Aug., 1838.

The wisest man preaches no doctrines; he has no scheme; he sees no rafter, not even a cobweb, against the heavens. It is clear sky.

THOREAU, *A Week on the Concord and Merrimack Rivers*, p. 60.

17
Wisdom is to science what death is to life, or, if you prefer it, wisdom is to death what science is to life.

MIGUEL DE UNAMUNO, *Essays and Soliloquies*, p. 55.

18
Wisdom is not finally tested in the schools,
Wisdom cannot be pass'd from one having it to another not having it,
Wisdom is of the soul, is not susceptible of proof, is its own proof.

WALT WHITMAN, *Song of the Open Road*. Sec. 6.

1
The clouds may drop down titles and estates;
Wealth may seek us; but wisdom must be
sought.
YOUNG, *Night Thoughts*. Night viii, l. 620.

II—Wisdom: Apothegms

2
The wise learn many things from their foes. (Ἀπ' ἐχθρῶν πολλὰ μανθάνουσιν οἱ σοφοί.)
ARISTOPHANES, *The Birds*, l. 376.

3
Some deemed him wondrous wise, and some
believed him mad.
JAMES BEATTIE, *The Minstrel*. Bk. i, l. 144.

4
I carry all my effects with me.
BIAS, one of the Seven Wise Men of Greece, during the siege of Priene. (Omnia mecum porto mea.—CICERO, *Paradoxa*, i, 1.) Bias referred to his wisdom, but Mlle. Fanny Bias, an opera singer, on leaving Paris, pointed to her face and figure, as she said, "Like my illustrious ancestor, omnia mea mecum porto." (LAROUSSE, *Fleurs Historiques*.)

5
You are the men, and wisdom shall die with you.
ROBERT BROWNING, *Christmas-Eve*. Canto ii.

The assembled souls of all that men held wise.
SIR WILLIAM D'AVENANT, *Gondibert*. Bk. ii, canto 5, st. 37.

6
With a perfect distrust of my own abilities, . . . and a profound reverence for the wisdom of our ancestors.
EDMUND BURKE, *Speech on Conciliation with America*, 22 March, 1775. Lord Brougham states that Sir Francis Bacon was the first user of the phrase, but it has not been found in his works.

7
I love wisdom more than she loves me.
BYRON, *Don Juan*. Canto vi, st. 63.

8
There is often wisdom under a shabby cloak. (Sæpe est etiam sub palliolo sordido sapientia.)
CÆCILIUS STATIUS. (CICERO, *Tusculanarum Disputationum*. Bk. iii, ch. 23, sec. 56.)

9
The greatest clerks be not the wisest men.
CHAUCER, *The Reves Tale*, l. 4051. Also HEYWOOD, *Proverbs*, ii, 5.

10
Be wiser than other people if you can; but do not tell them so.
LORD CHESTERFIELD, *Letters*, 19 Nov., 1745.

Never seem wiser nor more learned than the people you are with.
LORD CHESTERFIELD, *Letters*, 22 Feb., 1748.

It is not wise to be wiser than is necessary. (Ce n'est pas être sage D'être plus sage qu'il ne le faut.)
PHILIPPE QUINAULT, *Armide*.

11
If Wisdom be attainable, let us not only win but enjoy it. (Sive enim ad sapientiam pervenire potest, non paranda nobis solum ea sed fruenda etiam est.)
CICERO, *De Finibus*. Bk. i, ch. 1, sec. 3.

12
A sadder and a wiser man,
He rose the morrow morn.
S. T. COLERIDGE, *The Ancient Mariner*. Pt. vii.

13
A wise man, like the moon, only shows his bright side to the world.
CHURTON COLLINS, *Aphorisms*.

14
Some people are suffering from lack of work, some from lack of water, many more from lack of wisdom.
CALVIN COOLIDGE, *Calvin Coolidge Says*, 1931.

15
Learn in us not to think of men above that which is written.
New Testament: I Corinthians, iv, 6. ("Not to be wise above that which is written." SCHOLEFIELD, *Hints for an Improved Translation of the New Testament*.)

16
It seems the part of wisdom.
COWPER, *The Task*. Bk. iv, l. 336.

17
We are wiser than we know.
EMERSON, *Essays, First Series: The Over-Soul*.

18
I hate a wise man for himself unwise. (Μισῶ σοφιστήν, ὅστις οὐδ' αὑτῷ σοφός.)
EURIPIDES, *Fragments*. No. 930. (PLUTARCH, *Lives: Alexander*. Ch. 53, sec. 2.)

In vain is the wise man wise who is not wise for himself. (Nequiquam sapere sapientem, qui ipse sibi prodesse non quiret.)
ENNIUS. (CICERO, *De Officiis*. Bk. iii, ch. 15, sec. 62.)

That wise man I cannot abide
That for himself cannot provide.
MONTAIGNE, *Essays*. Bk. i, ch. 24.

See also under ADVANTAGE.

19
Some wisdom must thou learn from one who's wise. (Σοφοῦ παρ' ἀνδρὸς χρὴ σοφόν τι μανθάνειν.)
EURIPIDES, *Rhesus*, l. 206.

Who with the wise consorts will wise become. (Σοφοῖς ὁμιλῶν καὐτὸς ἐκβήσῃ σοφός.)
MENANDER, *Monostikoi*. No. 475.

Unless you grow wise of yourself you will listen in vain to the wise. (Nisi per te sapias, frustra sapientem audias.)
PUBLILIUS SYRUS, *Sententiæ*. No. 464.

20
A wise man is a great wonder.
THOMAS FULLER, *Gnomologia*. No. 472.

No man is born wise or learned.
THOMAS FULLER, *Gnomologia*. No. 3599.

21
As wise as a man of Gotham.
THOMAS FULLER, *Worthies of England*. Vol. ii, p. 569. (1662)

Three wise men of Gotham went to sea in a bowl:
If the bowl had been stronger, my tale had been longer.
UNKNOWN. (HALLIWELL, *Nursery Rhymes.*)

On the borders of that island he found Gotham, where the wise men live; the same who dragged the pond because the moon had fallen into it.
CHARLES KINGSLEY, *Water Babies.* Ch. 8.

1
They say that the lady from Philadelphia who is staying in town is very wise. Suppose I go ask her what is best to be done.
LUCRETIA P. HALE, *Peterkin Papers.* Ch. 1.

2
He that is not handsome at twenty, nor strong at thirty, nor rich at forty, nor wise at fifty, will never be handsome, strong, rich, or wise.
GEORGE HERBERT, *Jacula Prudentum.*

3
In youth and beauty wisdom is but rare!
HOMER, *Odyssey.* Bk. vii, l. 379. (Pope, tr.)

Days should speak, and multitude of years should teach wisdom.
Old Testament: Job, xxxii, 7.

Happy those
Who in the after-days shall live, when Time
Hath spoken, and the multitude of years
Taught wisdom to mankind!
SOUTHEY, *Joan of Arc.* Bk. i, l. 181.

The man of wisdom is the man of years.
YOUNG, *Night Thoughts.* Night v, l. 775.

Not by age, but by capacity is wisdom attained. (Non ætate, verum ingenio, adipiscitur sapientia.)
PLAUTUS, *Trinummus.* Act ii, sc. 2.

4
Dare to be wise. (Sapere aude.)
HORACE, *Epistles.* Bk. i, epis. 2, l. 40.

5
An abnormally wise man. (Abnormis sapiens.)
HORACE, *Satires.* Bk. ii, sat. 2, l. 3.

All wisdom's armory this man could wield.
GEORGE MEREDITH, *The Sage Enamoured.*

No one could be so wise as Thurlow looked.
CHARLES JAMES FOX. (CAMPBELL, *Lives of the Lord Chancellors.* Vol. v, p. 661.) Said also by Carlyle of Webster.

You look wise. Pray correct that error.
CHARLES LAMB, *Essays of Elia: All Fools' Day.*

6
Woe unto them that are wise in their own eyes, and prudent in their own sight!
Old Testament: Isaiah, v, 21. *See also under* VANITY.

7
He taketh the wise in their own craftiness.
Old Testament: Job, v, 13.

8
Deign on the passing world to turn thine eyes,
And pause awhile from letters, to be wise.
SAMUEL JOHNSON, *Vanity of Human Wishes,* l. 155.

9
It is easier to be wise for others than for one's self. (Il est plus aisé d'être sage pour les autres que de l'être pour soi-même.)
LA ROCHEFOUCAULD, *Maximes.* No. 132.

10
Ripe in wisdom was he, but patient and simple and childlike.
LONGFELLOW, *Evangeline.* Pt. i, sec. 3, l. 11.

His form was ponderous, and his step was slow;
There never was so wise a man before;
He seemed the incarnate "Well, I told you so!"
LONGFELLOW, *The Birds of Killingworth.* St. 9.

But wise and wary was that noble pere.
SPENSER, *Faerie Queene.* Bk. i, canto viii, st. 7.

11
Whoever is not too wise is wise. (Quisquis plus justo non sapit, ille sapit.)
MARTIAL, *Epigrams.* Bk. xiv, epig. 210.

12
Be ye therefore wise as serpents, and harmless as doves.
New Testament: Matthew, x, 16.

Now will I show myself to have more of the serpent than the dove; that is, more knave than fool.
MARLOWE, *The Jew of Malta.* Act ii.

13
The Athenians do not mind a man being clever, provided he does not impart his wisdom to others.
PLATO, *Euthyphro.* Sec. 3.

"I knew that before you were born." Let him who would instruct a wiser man consider this as said to himself.
PHÆDRUS, *Fables.* Bk. ii, fab. 9, l. 4.

14
No man is wise enough by himself. (Nemo solus satis sapit.)
PLAUTUS, *Miles Gloriosus,* l. 885. (Act iii, sc. 3.)

It becomes all wise men to confer and converse. (Omnes sapientes decet conferre et fabulari.)
PLAUTUS, *Rudens.* Act ii, sc. 3, l. 8.

15
No one is wise at all times. (Nemo mortalium omnibus horis sapit.)
PLINY THE ELDER, *Historia Naturalis.* Bk. vii, ch. 41, sec. 2.

The wisest man sometimes acts weakly, and the weakest sometimes wisely.
LORD CHESTERFIELD, *Letters,* 26 April, 1748.

A wise man is not wise in everything. (Un personnage sçavant n'est pas sçavant par tout.)
MONTAIGNE, *Essays.* Bk. iii, ch. 2.

16
Wisdom crieth without; she uttereth her voice in the streets.
Old Testament: Proverbs, i, 20.

Wisdom cries out in the streets and no man regards it.
SHAKESPEARE, *I Henry IV.* Act i, sc. 2, l. 99.

17
So teach us to number our days, that we may apply our hearts unto wisdom.
Old Testament: Psalms, xc, 12.

Teach me my days to number, and apply
My trembling heart to wisdom.
YOUNG, *Night Thoughts*. Night ix, l. 1311.

1
All things that pass
Are wisdom's looking-glass.
CHRISTINA ROSSETTI, *Passing and Glassing*.

2
The wise man is his own best assistant.
SCOTT, *Fortunes of Nigel*. Ch. 22.

3
No man was ever wise by chance. (Nulli sapere casu obtigit.)
SENECA, *Epistulæ ad Lucilium*. Epis. 76, sec. 6.

4
I would you would make good use of that wisdom,
Whereof I know you are fraught.
SHAKESPEARE, *King Lear*. Act i, sc. 4, l. 240.

5
Wisdom and goodness to the vile seem vile.
SHAKESPEARE, *King Lear*. Act iv, sc. 2, l. 38.

Cleverness and stupidity are generally in the same boat against wisdom.
J. A. SPENDER, *The Comments of Bagshot*. Ch. 11.

6
He hath a wisdom that doth guide his valour
To act in safety.
SHAKESPEARE, *Macbeth*. Act iii, sc. 1, l. 53.

He speaks sense.
SHAKESPEARE, *The Merry Wives of Windsor*. Act ii, sc. 1, l. 129. *See also under* SENSE.

7
Some folks are wise, and some are otherwise.
SMOLLETT, *Roderick Random*. Ch. 6. Quoting a proverb.

Some are weather-wise, some are otherwise.
BENJAMIN FRANKLIN, *Poor Richard*, 1735.

8
Sciences may be learned by rote, but wisdom not.
STERNE, *Tristram Shandy*. Bk. v, ch. 32.

9
Wearing his wisdom lightly, like the fruit
Which in our winter woodland looks a flower.
TENNYSON, *A Dedication*. The reference is to the fruit of the Spindle-tree.

10
The children of this world are in their generation wiser than the children of light.
New Testament: Luke, xvi, 8.

11
Full as an egg of wisdom, thus I sing.
JOHN WOLCOT, *Subjects for Painters: The Gentleman and His Wife*.

12
Wisdom is ofttimes nearer when we stoop
Than when we soar.
WORDSWORTH, *The Excursion*. Bk. iii, l. 231.

Be wise;
Soar not too high to fall; but stoop to rise.
MASSINGER, *Duke of Milan*. Act i, sc. 2, l. 45.

13
It takes a wise man to recognize a wise man. (Σοφὸν γὰρ εἶναι δεῖ τὸν ἐπιγνωσόμενον τὸν σοφόν.)
XENOPHANES. (DIOGENES LAERTIUS, *Xenophanes*. Bk. ix, sec. 20.)

14
But who in heat of blood was ever wise?
YOUNG, *Love of Fame*. Sat. iii, l. 152.

III—Wisdom: Its Value

15
Make wisdom your provision for the journey from youth to old age, for it is a more certain support than all other possessions.
BIAS. (DIOGENES LAERTIUS, *Bias*. Bk. i, sec. 88.)

16
The true Sovereign is the Wise Man.
CARLYLE, *Essays: On the Death of Goethe*.

17
And be ye wise, as ye be fair to see,
Well in the ring then is the ruby set.
CHAUCER, *Troilus and Criseyde*. Bk. ii, l. 584.

18
But they whom truth and wisdom lead
Can gather honey from a weed.
COWPER, *The Pine-Apple and the Bee*, l. 35.

19
Wisdom giveth life to them that have it.
Old Testament: Ecclesiastes, vii, 12.

20
Go where he will, the wise man is at home,
His hearth the earth—his hall the azure dome.
R. W. EMERSON, *Woodnotes*. Pt. iii.

21
Wisdom makes but a slow defence against trouble, though at last a sure one.
GOLDSMITH, *The Vicar of Wakefield*. Ch. 21.

Sorrow can wait,
For there is magic in the calm estate
Of grief; lo, where the dust complies
Wisdom lies.
GLADYS CROMWELL, *Folded Power*.

22
This task, this pursuit [of wisdom] let us speed, small and great, if we would live dear to our country and to ourselves. (Hoc opus, hoc studium, parvi properemus et ampli, Si patriæ volumus, si nobis vivere cari.)
HORACE, *Epistles*. Bk. i, epis. 3, l. 28.

Defer not till to-morrow to be wise,
To-morrow's sun on thee may never rise.
WILLIAM CONGREVE, *Letter to Cobham*.

Be wise to-day; 'tis madness to defer;
Next day the fatal precedent will plead;
Thus on, till wisdom is push'd out of life.
YOUNG, *Night Thoughts*. Night i, l. 390.

23
The price of wisdom is above rubies.
Old Testament: Job, xxviii, 18.

Wisdom is better than rubies.
Old Testament: Proverbs, viii, 11.

24
Nothing is sweeter than to dwell in the serene temples of the wise, well fortified by learn-

ing. (Nil dulcius est, bene quam munita tenere
Edita doctrina sapientum templa serena.)
LUCRETIUS, *De Rerum Natura*. Bk. ii, l. 7.

So, from this glittering world with all its fashion,
Its fire and play of men, its stir, its march,
Let me have wisdom, Beauty, wisdom and passion,
Bread to the soul, rain where the summers parch.
Give me but these, and though the darkness close
Even the night will blossom as the rose.
JOHN MASEFIELD, *On Growing Old*.

1 Wisdom is justified of her children.
New Testament: Matthew, xi, 19; *Luke*, vii, 35.

2 Be famous then
By wisdom; as thy empire must extend,
So let extend thy mind o'er all the world.
MILTON, *Paradise Regained*. Bk. iv, l. 221.

2a May I reckon the wise to be wealthy. (Πλούσιον δὲ νομίζοιμι τὸν σοφόν.)
PLATO, *Phædrus*. The prayer with which Socrates concludes the dialogue.

Wisdom is the wealth of the wise.
W. G. BENHAM, *Proverbs*, p. 876.

3 Think, to be happy; to be great, be wise:
Content of spirit must from science flow,
For 'tis a godlike attribute to know.
MATTHEW PRIOR, *Solomon*. Bk. i, l. 41.

4 Wisdom is the principal thing; therefore get wisdom: and with all thy getting get understanding.
Old Testament: Proverbs, iv, 7.

A wise man is strong; yea, a man of knowledge increaseth strength.
Old Testament: Proverbs, xxiv, 5.

Wisdom is always an overmatch for strength.
PHÆDRUS, *Fables*. Bk. i, fab. 13.

6 Wisdom and fortune combating together,
If that the former dare but what it can,
No chance may shake it.
SHAKESPEARE, *Antony and Cleopatra*, iii, 13, 79.

7 She that in wisdom never was so frail
To change the cod's head for the salmon's tail.
SHAKESPEARE, *Othello*. Act ii, sc. 1, l. 155.

8 To wisdom he's a fool that will not yield.
SHAKESPEARE, *Pericles*. Act ii, sc. 4, l. 54.

9 By Wisdom wealth is won;
But riches purchased wisdom yet for none.
BAYARD TAYLOR, *The Wisdom of Ali*.

10 How great a thing is wisdom! I never come near you but I go away wiser. (Quanti est sapere! Numquam accedo, quin abs te abeam doctior.)
TERENCE, *Eunuchus*, l. 791. (Act iv, sc. 7.)

11 Wisdom alone is true ambition's aim,
Wisdom the source of virtue, and of fame,
Obtained with labour, for mankind employed,
And then, when most you share it, best enjoyed.
WILLIAM WHITEHEAD, *On Nobility*.

12 Wisdom is the gray hair unto men, and an unspotted life is old age.
Apocrypha: Wisdom of Solomon, iv, 9.

Wisdom is glorious and never fadeth away: yes, she is easily seen of them that love her, and found of such as seek her.
Apocrypha: Wisdom of Solomon, vi, 12.

13 Wisdom, the sole artificer of bliss.
YOUNG, *Love of Fame*. Satire vi, l. 94.

Can gold calm passion, or make reason shine?
Can we dig peace, or wisdom, from the mine?
Wisdom to gold prefer; for 'tis much less
To make our fortune than our happiness.
YOUNG, *Love of Fame*. Satire vi, l. 291.

Wisdom, tho' richer than Peruvian mines,
And sweeter than the sweet ambrosial hive,
What is she, but the means of happiness?
YOUNG, *Night Thoughts*. Night ii, l. 498.

But wisdom, awful wisdom! which inspects,
Discerns, compares, weighs, separates, infers,
Seizes the right, and holds it to the last.
YOUNG, *Night Thoughts*. Night viii, l. 1247.

IV—Wisdom: Its Emptiness

14 The wisdom of this world is foolishness with God.
New Testament: I Corinthians, iii, 19.

15 Some people are more nice than wise.
COWPER, *Mutual Forbearance*, l. 20.

God never meant that man should scale the heavens
By strides of human wisdom.
COWPER, *The Task*. Bk. iii, l. 221.

16 In much wisdom is much grief.
Old Testament: Ecclesiastes, i, 18.

17 They who travel in pursuit of wisdom walk only in a circle, and, after all their labour, at last return to their pristine ignorance.
GOLDSMITH, *The Citizen of the World*. No. 37.

To say the truth, I was tired of being always wise.
GOLDSMITH, *The Vicar of Wakefield*. Ch. 10.

18 Wisdom's sullen pomp.
MATTHEW GREEN, *The Spleen*, l. 216.

19 How prone to doubt, how cautious are the wise!
HOMER, *Odyssey*. Bk. xiii, l. 375. (Pope, tr.)

20 Wisdom and wit now is not worse a kerse.
WILLIAM LANGLAND, *Piers Plowman: The Vision of Do-Well*. Kerse is Middle English for cress.

1
Vain wisdom all and false philosophy.
MILTON, *Paradise Lost.* Bk. ii, l. 565.

2
Tell wisdom she entangles
Herself in overwiseness.
SIR WALTER RALEIGH, *The Lie.*

3
O world, thou choosest not the better part!
It is not wisdom to be only wise,
And on the inward vision close the eyes,
But it is wisdom to believe the heart.
GEORGE SANTAYANA, *O World.*

Oh, thriftlessness of dream and guess!
Oh, wisdom which is foolishness!
Why idly seek from outward things
The answer inward silence brings?
WHITTIER, *Questions of Life.*

4
Take thy balance if thou be so wise,
And weigh the wind that under heaven doth blow:
Or weigh the light that in the east doth rise;
Or weigh the thought that from man's mind doth flow.
SPENSER, *Faerie Queene.* Bk. v, canto ii, st. 43.

5
Thy wisdom all can do, but—make thee wise.
YOUNG, *Night Thoughts.* Night viii, l. 1415.

V—Wisdom and Ignorance

6
The wisest man is he who does not fancy that he is so at all. (Le plus sage est celui qui ne pense point l'être.)
BOILEAU, *Satires.* Sat. i, l. 46.

You read of but one wise man, and all that he knew was that he knew nothing.
CONGREVE, *The Old Batchelor.* Act i, sc. 1.

7
The wise know too well their weakness to assume infallibility; and he who knows most, knows best how little he knows.
THOMAS JEFFERSON, *Writings.* Vol. xviii, p. 129.

8
For only by unlearning Wisdom comes.
J. R. LOWELL, *The Parting of the Ways.* St. 8.

9
And Wisdom cries, "I know not anything";
And only Faith beholds that all is well.
SIDNEY LYSAGHT, *A Lesson,* l. 102.

11
That man is wisest who, like Socrates, realizes that his wisdom is worthless. (Ὅτι οὗτος ὑμῶν σοφώτατός ἐστιν, ὅστις ὥσπερ Σωκράτης ἔγνωκεν ὅτι οὐδενὸς ἄξιός ἐστι τῇ ἀληθείᾳ πρὸς σοφίαν.)
PLATO, *Apology of Socrates.* Sec. 23B.

The first and wisest of them all profess'd
To know this only, that he nothing knew.
MILTON, *Paradise Regained.* Bk. iv, l. 293.

Socrates . . .
Whom, well inspir'd, the oracle pronounc'd
Wisest of men.
MILTON, *Paradise Regained.* Bk. iv, l. 274.

What is it to be wise?
'T is but to know how little can be known,
To see all others' faults, and feel our own.
POPE, *Essay on Man.* Epis. iv, l. 260.
See also under SELF-KNOWLEDGE.

12
He bids fair to grow wise who has discovered that he is a fool. (Non pote non sapere, qui se stultum intellegit.)
PUBLILIUS SYRUS, *Sententiæ.* No. 598.

13
For when I dinna clearly see,
I always own I dinna ken,
And that's the way with wisest men.
ALLAN RAMSAY, *The Clock and the Dial.*

14
The doorstep to the temple of wisdom is a knowledge of our own ignorance.
CHARLES HADDEN SPURGEON, *Gleanings among the Sheaves: The First Lesson.*

15
One may almost doubt if the wisest man has learned anything of absolute value by living.
H. D. THOREAU, *Walden.* Ch. 1.

16
Disasters, do the best we can,
Will reach both great and small;
And he is oft the wisest man
Who is not wise at all.
WORDSWORTH, *The Oak and the Broom.* St. 7.

VI—Wisdom, After the Event

17
The wise man must be wise before, not after, the event. (Οὐ μετανοεῖν, ἀλλὰ προνοεῖν χρὴ τὸν ἄνδρα τὸν σοφόν.)
EPICHARMUS, *Fabulæ Incertæ.* Frag. 5.

18
After the event, even a fool is wise. (Ῥεχθὲν δέ τε νήπιος ἔγνω.)
HOMER, *Iliad.* Bk. xvii, l. 32.

He is a fool
Who only sees the mischiefs that are past.
HOMER, *Iliad.* Bk. xvii, l. 32. (Bryant, tr.)

You are wise after the event. (Οἴμ' ὡς ἔοικας ὀψὲ τὴν δίκην ἰδεῖν.)
SOPHOCLES, *Antigone,* l. 1270.

Their hindsight was better than their foresight.
HENRY WARD BEECHER [?].

If a man had half as much foresight as he has twice as much hindsight, he'd be a lot better off.
ROBERT J. BURDETTE, *Hawkeyes.* Sometimes quoted, "If our foresight were as good as our hindsight, we'd be better off a damn sight."

19
Away, thou strange justifier of thyself, to be wiser than thou wert, by the event.
BEN JONSON, *The Silent Woman.* Act ii, sc. 2.

20
The event is the schoolmaster of fools. (Eventus stultorum magister est.)
LIVY, *History.* Bk. xx, sec. 39.

21
To protect the booty when it is too late. (Post tempus prædæ præsidium parem.)
PLAUTUS, *Asinaria,* l. 394. (Act ii, sc. 2.)

When the great steed
Is stole, then he taketh heed
And maketh the stable-door fast.
JOHN GOWER, *Confessio Amantis*. Bk. iv, l. 901. (c. 1390)

It was not time to shut the stable when the horses be lost and gone.
WILLIAM CAXTON, *Æsop*, ii, 245. (1484)

It is too late to shut the stable door when the steed is stolen.
JOHN LYLY, *Euphues*, p. 37. (1579)

When the horse has been stolen, the fool shuts the stable. (Quant le cheval est emblé dounke ferme fols l'estable.)
UNKNOWN, *Les Proverbes de Vilain*.

1
So that we may not be like the Athenians, who never consulted except after the event done. (Afin que ne semblons es Atheniens, qui ne consultoient jamais sinon après le cas faict.)
RABELAIS, *Works*. Bk. ii, ch. 24.

2
Nine-tenths of wisdom is being wise in time.
THEODORE ROOSEVELT, *Speech*, Lincoln, Neb., 14 June, 1917.

3
The men who were yesterday so cautious and prudent, were now, after the event, ready and vainglorious. (Atque illi modo cauti ac sapientes prompti post eventum ac magniloqui erant.)
TACITUS, *Agricola*. Ch. 27.

WISH

See also Wants

4
Every wish Is like a prayer—with God.
E. B. BROWNING, *Aurora Leigh*. Bk. ii, l. 955.

5
Men easily believe what they wish to believe. (Libenter homines id quod volunt credunt.)
CÆSAR, *De Bello Gallico*. Bk. iii, sec. 18.

What he wishes he also believes.
QUINTILIAN, *De Institutione Oratoria*. Bk. vi, sec. 5.

What most we wish, with ease we fancy near.
YOUNG, *Love of Fame*. Sat. iii, l. 274.

What ardently we wish, we soon believe.
YOUNG, *Night Thoughts*. Night vii, l. 1311.

6
All her commands were gracious, sweet requests.
How could it be then, but that her requests
Must need have sounded to me as commands?
S. T. COLERIDGE, *Zapolya*. Pt. ii, act i, sc. 1.

7
Yearn not for soft things, lest thou earn the hard. (Μὴ τὰ μαλακὰ μῶσο, μὴ τὰ σκλήρ' ἔχῃς.)
EPICHARMUS. (XENOPHON, *Memorabilia*. Bk. ii, ch. 1, sec. 20.)

Don't ask for what you'll wish you hadn't got. (Postea noli rogare, quod inpetrare nolueris.)
SENECA, *Epistulæ ad Lucilium*. Epis. xcv, sec. 2. Quoted as a common saying.

8
If a man could have half his wishes he would double his Troubles
BENJAMIN FRANKLIN, *Poor Richard*, 1752.

9
What one has wished for in youth, in old age one has in abundance. (Was man in der Jugend wünscht, hat man im Alter die Fülle.)
GOETHE, *Wahrheit und Dichtung:* Pt. ii, *Motto*.

10
Most men let their wishes run away with them. They have no mind to stop them in their career, the motion is so pleasing.
LORD HALIFAX, *Works*, p. 248.

11
The evil wish is most evil to the wisher. (Δὲ κακὴ βουλὴ τῷ βουλεύσαντι κακίστη.)
HESIOD, *Works and Days*, l. 266.

12
Pious wishes. (Pia desideria.)
HERMANN HUGO. Title of book published at Antwerp, 1627.

13
I wish I knew the good of wishing.
H. S. LEIGH, *A Day for Wishing*.

14
Not what we wish but what we want.
JAMES MERRICK, *Hymn*.

15
You have wished it so, you have wished it so, George Dandin, you have wished it so. (Vous l'avez voulu, vous l'avez voulu, George Dandin, vous l'avez voulu.)
MOLIÈRE, *George Dandin*. Act i, sc. 7.

16
What are you doing, unhappy one? You are losing our good wishes. (Quid facis, infelix? Perdis bona vota!)
OVID, *Amores*. Bk. iii, eleg. 2, l. 71.

17
You should wish as we wish. (Bebetis velle quæ velimus.)
PLAUTUS, *Amphitruo: Prologue*, l. 39.

You have your wish. (Ergo sunt quæ exoptas.)
PLAUTUS, *Asinaria*, l. 847. (Act v, sc. 1.)

18
If wishes were butter cakes, beggars might bite.
JOHN RAY, *English Proverbs*, p. 143.

If wishes were horses, beggars would ride.
H. G. BOHN, *Handbook of Proverbs*, p. 419.

19
Wishers were ever fools.
SHAKESPEARE, *Antony and Cleopatra*. Act iv, sc. 15, l. 37.

20
Your heart's desires be with you!
SHAKESPEARE, *As You Like It*. i, 2, 211.

21
Thy wish was father, Harry, to that thought.
SHAKESPEARE, *II Henry IV*. Act iv, sc. 5, l. 93.

1
Wisheth, poor starveling elf! his paper kite
may fly.
William Shenstone, *The Schoolmistress.*

2
Now am I a tin whistle
Through which God blows,
And I wish to God I were a trumpet
—But why, God only knows.
J. C. Squire, *A Fresh Morning.*

3
Wishers and woulders ben small house holders.
John Stanbridge, *Vulgaria*.C6.(c. 1520) Quoted by John Heywood, *Proverbs*, i, 11 (1546), and frequently thereafter.

Wishers and woulders are never good householders.
John Ray, *English Proverbs.*

Wishes never can fill a sack.
Torriano, *Italian Proverbs*, 29. (1666)

4
As you cannot do what you wish, you should wish what you can do. (Quoniam non potest id fieri quod vis, id velis quod possit.)
Terence, *Andria*, l. 305. (Act ii, sc. 1.)

When what you wish does not happen, wish for what does happen.
Unknown. An Arabic proverb.

5
Take this in good part, whatsoever thou be,
And wish me no worse than I wish unto thee.
Thomas Tusser, *Five Hundred Points of Good Husbandry: Think on the Poor.*

6
We cannot wish for that we know not. (On ne peut désirer ce qu'on ne connaît pas.)
Voltaire, *Zaïre.* Act i, sc. 1.

7
I would it were not as I think;
I would I thought it were not.
Sir Thomas Wyatt, *A Lament.*

O, that I were where I would be,
Then would I be where I am not;
For where I am I would not be,
And where I would be I can not.
A. T. Quiller-Couch, *The Ship of Stars.* Ch. 12. Quoted.

8
Wishing, of all employments, is the worst;
Philosophy's reverse, and health's decay! . . .
Wishing is an expedient to the poor.
Wishing, that constant hectic of a fool.
Young, *Night Thoughts.* Night iv, l. 71.

9
Like our shadows,
Our wishes lengthen as our sun declines.
Young, *Night Thoughts.* Night v, l. 661.

Thy fickle wish is ever on the wing.
Young, *Night Thoughts.* Night viii, l. 917.

WIT

I—Wit: Definitions

10
Wit without an employment is a disease.
Burton, *Anatomy of Melancholy.* Pt. i, sec. ii, mem. 2, subs. 6.

11
A witty thing never excited laughter; it pleases only the mind, and never distorts the countenance.
Lord Chesterfield, *Letters*, 9 March, 1748.

True wit never made us laugh.
Emerson, *Letters and Social Aims: Social Aims.*

He is always laughing, for he has an infinite deal of wit.
Joseph Addison, *The Spectator.* No. 475.

I can't say whether we had more wit amongst us now than usual, but I am certain we had more laughing, which answered the end as well.
Goldsmith, *The Vicar of Wakefield.* Ch. 32.

12
If you have wit, use it to please, and not to hurt: you may shine like the sun in the temperate zones, without scorching.
Lord Chesterfield, *Letters*, 5 Sept., 1748.

If God gives you wit . . . wear it like your sword in the scabbard, and do not brandish it to the terror of the whole company. . . . A wise man will live as much within his wit as his income.
Lord Chesterfield, *Letters*, 21 July, 1752.

I have too thoughtful a wit: like a penknife in too narrow a sheath, too sharp for its body.
George Herbert. (Walton, *Life of Herbert.*)

13
Wit is so shining a quality that everybody admires it; most people aim at it, all people fear it, and few love it except in themselves.
Lord Chesterfield, *Letters*, 21 July, 1752.

14
A wit should no more be sincere than a woman constant; one argues a decay of parts, as t'other of beauty.
Congreve, *The Way of the World.* Act i, sc. 6.

15
Thus reputation is a spur to wit,
And some wits flag through fear of losing it.
Cowper, *Table Talk*, l. 520.

16
Wit makes its own welcome, and levels all distinctions. No dignity, no learning, no force of character, can make any stand against good wit.
Emerson, *Letters and Social Aims: The Comic.*

17
Nothing more smooth than glass, yet nothing
more brittle;
Nothing more fine than wit, yet nothing more
fickle.
Thomas Fuller, *Gnomologia.* No 6472.

18
There must be more malice than love in the hearts of all wits.
B. R. Haydon, *Table Talk.*

19
Wit is the salt of conversation, not the food.
William Hazlitt, *Lectures on the English Comic Writers.* Lecture i.

Those who cannot miss an opportunity of saying a good thing . . . are not to be trusted with the management of any great question.
WILLIAM HAZLITT, *Characteristics*, p. 59.

1
Wit's an unruly engine, wildly striking
Sometimes a friend, sometimes the engineer.
Hast thou the knack? pamper it not with liking:
But if thou want it, buy it not too dear.
Many affecting wit beyond their power,
Have got to be a dear fool for an hour.
GEORGE HERBERT, *The Church-Porch*. St. 41.

2
Wit is the clash and reconcilement of incongruities; the meeting of extremes round a corner.
LEIGH HUNT, *Wit and Humour*.

3
Wit, at its best, consists in the terse intrusion into an atmosphere of serene mental habit of some uncompromising truth.
PHILANDER JOHNSON, *Colyumists' Confessional*. (*Everybody's Magazine*, May, 1920.)

4
Ev'n wit's a burthen, when it talks too long.
JUVENAL, *Satires*. Sat. vi, l. 573. (Dryden, tr.)

A man does not please long when he has only one species of wit. (On ne plaît pas longtemps quand on n'a qu'une sorte d'esprit.)
LA ROCHEFOUCAULD, *Maximes*. No. 413.

One wit, like a knuckle of ham in soup, gives a zest and flavour to the dish, but more than one serves only to spoil the pottage.
SMOLLETT, *Humphrey Clinker*.

5
Wit is nothing worth till it be dear bought.
HENRY MEDWALL, *Nature*. Pt. ii, l. 1292. (c. 1500)

It hath been an old said saw . . . that wit is better if it be the dearer bought.
JOHN LYLY, *Euphues*, p. 34.

Bought wit is best, but may cost too much.
THOMAS FULLER, *Gnomologia*. No. 1011.

Bought wit is dear.
GEORGE GASCOIGNE, *Posies*.

6
Impromptu is truly the touchstone of wit. (L'impromptu est justement la pierre de touche de l'esprit.)
MOLIÈRE, *Les Précieuses Ridicules*. Sc. ix, l. 152.

7
Raillery is a mode of speaking in favor of one's wit at the expense of one's better nature. (La raillerie est un discours en faveur de son esprit contre son bon naturel.)
MONTESQUIEU, *Pensées Diverses*.

8
Wit is the most rascally, contemptible, beggarly thing on the face of the earth.
ARTHUR MURPHY, *The Apprentice*.

9
Wit when temperate is pleasing, when unbridled it offends. (Temperatæ suaves sunt argutiæ: Immodicæ offendunt.)
PHÆDRUS, *Fables*. Bk. v, fab. 5, l. 41.

10
For wit and judgment often are at strife,
Tho' meant each other's aid, like man and wife.
POPE, *Essay on Criticism*. Pt. i, l. 82.

11
True wit is nature to advantage dress'd,
What oft was thought, but ne'er so well express'd.
POPE, *Essay on Criticism*. Pt. ii, l. 97. (1711)

Madame de Sévigné said the same thing: "C'est ce qu'on a toujours pensé, ce qu'on n'a jamais si bien dit," in *Letters*, No. 1289, written in 1690 but published after 1711.

So modest plainness sets off sprightly wit:
For works may have more wit than does them good,
As bodies perish thro' excess of blood.
POPE, *Essay on Criticism*. Pt. ii, l. 102.

12
If faith itself has diff'rent dresses worn,
What wonder modes in wit should take their turn?
Oft, leaving what is natural and fit,
The current folly proves the ready wit;
And authors think their reputation safe,
Which lives as long as fools are pleas'd to laugh.
POPE, *Essay on Criticism*. Pt. ii, l. 246.

13
Wit is folly unless a wise man hath the keeping of it
JOHN RAY, *English Proverbs*, p. 174.

14
Wit, like tierce claret, when 't begins to pall,
Neglected lies, and 's of no use at all,
But, in its full perfection of decay,
Turns vinegar, and comes again in play.
CHARLES SACKVILLE, *To Mr. Edward Howard*.

15
Wit and wisdom are born with a man.
JOHN SELDEN, *Table-Talk: Learning*.

16
Thou know'st we work by wit, and not by witchcraft;
And wit depends on dilatory time.
SHAKESPEARE, *Othello*. Act ii, sc. 3, l. 378.

17
There's no possibility of being witty without a little ill-nature; the malice of a good thing is the barb that makes it stick.
SHERIDAN, *The School for Scandal*. Act i, sc. 1.

Nae wut without a portion o' impertinence.
JOHN WILSON, *Noctes Ambrosianæ*.

18
Surprise is so essential an ingredient of wit that no wit will bear repetition;—at least the original electrical feeling produced by any piece of wit can never be renewed.
SYDNEY SMITH, *Lectures on Moral Philosophy*, No. 10.

19
Wit consists in knowing the resemblance of things which differ, and the difference of things which are alike.
MADAME DE STAËL, *Germany*. Pt. iii, ch. 8.

1
It is with wits as with razors, which are never so apt to cut those they are employed on as when they have lost their edge.
SWIFT, *Tale of a Tub: Author's Preface.*

As in smooth oil the razor best is whet,
So wit is by politeness sharpest set:
Their want of edge from their offence is seen;
Both pain us least when exquisitely keen.
YOUNG, *Love of Fame.* Sat. ii, l. 119.

Don't put too fine a point to your wit, for fear it should get blunted.
CERVANTES, *Exemplary Novels: Little Gypsy.*

2
Wit rules the heavens, discretion guides the skies.
TASSO, *Gerusalemme.* Bk. x, st. 20.

3
Backstair wit. (Esprit de l'escalier.)
M. DE TRÉVILLE. (PIERRE NICOLE, *King's English,* p. 32, note.)

I never have any wit until I am below stairs. (Je n'ai jamais d'esprit qu'au bas de l'escalier.)
LA BRUYÈRE, according to J. J. Rousseau.

4
Lucian, well skill'd in scoffing, this has writ:
Friend, that's your folly which you think your wit;
This you vent oft, void both of wit and fear,
Meaning another, when yourself you jeer.
IZAAK WALTON, *The Compleat Angler.* Ch. 1.

5
Wit is more necessary than beauty; and I think no young woman ugly that has it, and no handsome woman agreeable without it.
WYCHERLEY, *The Country Wife.* Act i, sc. 1.

6
Against their wills what numbers ruin shun,
Purely through want of wit to be undone!
Nature has shown, by making it so rare,
That wit 's a jewel which we need not wear.
YOUNG, *Epistle to Mr. Pope.* Epis. ii, l. 80.

7
Wit, how delicious to man's dainty taste!
'T is precious, as a vehicle of sense;
But, as its substitute, a dire disease.
YOUNG, *Night Thoughts.* Night viii, l. 1232.

Wit, widow'd of good sense, is worse than nought.
YOUNG, *Night Thoughts.* Night viii, l. 1264.

8
There is nothing breaks so many friendships as a difference of opinion as to what constitutes wit.
ELBERT HUBBARD, *Epigrams.*

II—Wit: Apothegms

9
Melancholy men of all others are most witty.
ARISTOTLE. (BURTON, *Anatomy of Melancholy,* i, iii, 1, 3.)

10
All this is but a web of the wit; it can work nothing.
FRANCIS BACON, *Essays: Of Empire.*

11
I can say a neat thing myself if they will give me time.
J. M. BARRIE, *Farewell, Miss Julie Logan,* p. 16.

12
An ounce of wit is worth a pound of sorrow.
RICHARD BAXTER, *Of Self-Denial.*

13
What silly people wits are! (Que les gens d'esprit sont bêtes.)
BEAUMARCHAIS, *Barbier de Séville.* Act i, sc. 1.

14
Great wits and valours, like great states,
Do sometimes sink with their own weights.
BUTLER, *Hudibras.* Pt. ii, canto 1, l. 269.

15
Here lies a king that ruled, as he saw fit,
The universal monarchy of wit.
THOMAS CAREW, *Elegy Upon Dr. Donne.*

Her wit was more than man, her innocence a child.
DRYDEN, *Elegy on Anne Killigrew,* l. 70.

As a wit, if not first, in the very first line.
GOLDSMITH, *Retaliation,* l. 96.

Of Manners gentle, of Affections mild;
In Wit a man; Simplicity, a child.
POPE, *Epitaph on Mr. Gay.*

16
Good wits jump; a word to the wise is enough.
CERVANTES, *Don Quixote.* Pt. ii, ch. 37.

See how good wits jump.
DAVID GARRICK, *Correspondence.* Vol. ii, p. 94.

Ah, where thy legs, that witty pair!
For "great wits jump"—and so did they.
THOMAS HOOD, *To Grimaldi.*

Great wits jump together. (Les beaux esprits rencontrent.)
Pointed out by *Notes and Queries* (vi, x, 216) to be the same epigram.

17
Thou hast wit at will.
GEORGE CHAPMAN, *May-Day.* Act iv, sc. 3.

She's very handsome, and has wit at will.
SWIFT, *Polite Conversation.* Dial. i.

18
Wit to persuade and beauty to delight.
SIR JOHN DAVIES, *Orchestra.* St. 5.

19
Wit will shine
Through the harsh cadence of a rugged line.
DRYDEN, *To the Memory of Mr. Oldham.*

20
Good wits, you know, have short memories.
DRYDEN, *Sir Martin Mar-All.* Act iv, sc. 1.

Great wits have short memories.
SWIFT, *Works.* Vol. ix, p. 191.

21
And leave thy peacock wit behind.
EMERSON, *Woodnotes.* Pt. ii.

22
It is wit to pick a lock and steal a horse, but it is wisdom to let them alone.
THOMAS FULLER, *Gnomologia.* No. 3031.

1
Wit is news only to ignorance.
GEORGE HERBERT, *The Church-Porch*. St. 39.

2
So many heads so many wits.
JOHN HEYWOOD, *Proverbs*. Pt. i, ch. 3. *See also under* OPINION.

3
This man I thought had been a Lord among wits, but, I find, he is only a wit among Lords.
SAMUEL JOHNSON, referring to Lord Chesterfield. (BOSWELL, *Life*, 1754.)

He was a rake among scholars, and a scholar among rakes.
MACAULAY, *Essays: Aikin's Life of Addison*. Referring to Richard Steele.

A man of the world amongst men of letters, a man of letters amongst men of the world.
MACAULAY, *Essays: Sir William Temple*.

A wit with dunces, and a dunce with wits.
POPE, *The Dunciad*. Bk. iv, l. 90.

4
Plagued with an itching leprosy of wit.
BEN JONSON, *Every Man Out of His Humour: Induction*, l. 66.

5
A man of wit would often be at a loss, were it not for the company of fools. (Un homme d'esprit serait souvent bien embarrassé sans la compagnie des sots.)
LA ROCHEFOUCAULD, *Maximes*. No. 140.

There are no fools so troublesome as those who have wit. (Il n'y a point de sots si incommodes que ceux qui ont de l'esprit.)
LA ROCHEFOUCAULD, *Maximes*. No. 451.

6
Wit sometimes enables us to act rudely with impunity. (L'esprit nous sert quelquefois hardiment à faire des sottises.)
LA ROCHEFOUCAULD, *Maximes*. No. 415.

Great wits sometimes may gloriously offend,
And rise to faults true critics dare not mend;
From vulgar bounds with brave disorder part,
And snatch a grace beyond the reach of art.
POPE, *Essay on Criticism*. Pt. i, l. 152.

Rudeness is a sauce to his good wit,
Which gives men stomach to digest his words
With better appetite.
SHAKESPEARE, *Julius Cæsar*. Act i, sc. 2, l. 304.

7
In the midst of the fountain of wit, something bitter arises, which poisons every flower. (Medio de fonte leporum, Surgit amari aliquid quod in ipsis floribus angat.)
LUCRETIUS, *De Rerum Natura*. Bk. iv, l. 1133.

Full from the fount of Joy's delicious springs
Some bitter o'er the flowers its bubbling venom flings.
BYRON, *Childe Harold*. Canto i, st. 82.

8
Enjoy your dear wit and gay rhetoric,
That hath so well been taught her dazzling fence.
MILTON, *Comus*, l. 790.

9
Whose wit, in the combat, as gentle as bright,
Ne'er carried a heart-stain away on its blade.
THOMAS MOORE, *Lines on the Death of Sheridan*, l. 43.

And wit that loved to play, not wound.
SCOTT, *Marmion:* Canto i, *Introduction*, l. 134.

And wit its honey lent without the sting.
JAMES THOMSON, *To the Memory of Lord Talbot*, l. 258.

10
Regard not then if wit be old or new,
But blame the false, and value still the true.
POPE, *Essay on Criticism*. Pt. ii, l. 206.

11
They reel to and fro, and stagger like a drunken man, and are at their wit's end.
Old Testament: Psalms, cvii, 27.

When they were driven to their wits' end.
JOHN LYDGATE, *Assembly of Gods*. St. 238. (c. 1420)

We both be at our wits' end.
JOHN HEYWOOD, *Proverbs*. Pt. i, ch. 8. (1546)

12
All the wit in the world is not in one head.
W. G. BENHAM, *Proverbs*, p. 733.

13
Generally speaking there is more wit than talent in this world. Society swarms with witty people who lack talent.
DE RIVAROL, *On Madame de Staël*.

14
Wit that can call forth smiles even from mourners. (Facetias, quæ risum evocare lugentibus.)
SENECA, *Epistulæ ad Lucilium*. Epis. xxix, 5.

15
I shall ne'er be ware of mine own wit till I break my shins against it.
SHAKESPEARE, *As You Like It*. Act ii, sc. 4, l. 60.

You have a nimble wit; I think 't was made of Atalanta's heels.
SHAKESPEARE, *As You Like It*. Act iii, sc. 2, l. 293.

Thy wit shall ne'er go slip-shod.
SHAKESPEARE, *King Lear*. Act i, sc. 5, l. 11.

Your wit's too hot, it speeds too fast, 'twill tire.
SHAKESPEARE, *Love's Labour's Lost*. Act ii, sc. 1, l. 120.

Sir, your wit ambles well; it goes easily.
SHAKESPEARE, *Much Ado About Nothing*. Act v, sc. 1, l. 159.

Thy wit is as quick as the greyhound's mouth; it catches.
SHAKESPEARE, *Much Ado About Nothing*. Act v, sc. 2, l. 11.

Thy wit is a very bitter sweeting: it is a most sharp sauce.
SHAKESPEARE, *Romeo and Juliet*. Act ii, sc. 4, l. 83.

A man that had a wife with such a wit, he might say, "Wit, whither wilt?"
SHAKESPEARE, *As You Like It*. Act iv, sc. 1, l. 167.

1
Make the doors upon a woman's wit and it will out at the casement; shut that and 'twill out at the key-hole; stop that, 't will fly with the smoke out at the chimney.
SHAKESPEARE, *As You Like It*. Act iv, sc. 1, l. 163.

2
I am not only witty in myself, but the cause that wit is in other men.
SHAKESPEARE, *II Henry IV*. Act i, sc. 2, l. 11.

Your wit makes others witty. (Votre esprit en donne aux autres.)
CATHERINE II, *Letter to Voltaire*.

It is having in some measure a sort of wit to know how to use the wit of others.
STANISLAUS, KING OF POLAND, *Maxims and Moral Sentences*.

It is by such encounters that wits become acquainted. (Les beaux esprits lernen einander durch dergleichen rencontre erkennen.)
ANDREAS GRYPHIUS, *Horribilicribfox*. Act iv, 7.

3
His eye begets occasion for his wit;
For every object that the one doth catch,
The other turns to a mirth-moving jest.
SHAKESPEARE, *Love's Labour's Lost*. Act ii, sc. 1, l. 69.

This fellow pecks up wit, as pigeons pease,
And utters it again when God doth please:
He is wit's pedler, and retails his wares
At wakes and wassails, meetings, markets, fairs;
And we that sell by gross, the Lord doth know,
Have not the grace to grace it with such show.
SHAKESPEARE, *Love's Labour's Lost*. Act v, sc. 2, l. 315.

What a wit-snapper are you!
SHAKESPEARE, *The Merchant of Venice*. Act iii, sc. 5, l. 55.

4
Wilt thou show the whole wealth of thy wit in an instant?
SHAKESPEARE, *The Merchant of Venice*. Act iii, sc. 5, l. 61.

Repair thy wit, good youth, or it will fall
To cureless ruin.
SHAKESPEARE, *The Merchant of Venice*. Act iv, sc. 1, l. 141.

5
He doth indeed show some sparks that are like wit.
SHAKESPEARE, *Much Ado About Nothing*. Act ii, sc. 3, l. 194.

Wit now and then, struck smartly, shows a spark.
COWPER, *Table Talk*, l. 663.

6
There's a skirmish of wit between them.
SHAKESPEARE, *Much Ado About Nothing*. Act i, sc. 1, l. 64.

To leave this keen encounter of our wits,
And fall somewhat into a slower method.
SHAKESPEARE, *Richard III*. Act i, sc. 2, l. 115.

7
He . . . turn'd your wit the seamy side without.
SHAKESPEARE, *Othello*. Act iv, sc. 2, l. 146.

8
Katharina: Where did you study all this goodly speech?
Petruchio: It is extempore, from my mother-wit.
SHAKESPEARE, *The Taming of the Shrew*. Act ii, sc. 1, l. 264.

From jigging veins of rhyming mother wits.
MARLOWE, *Tamburlaine the Great: Prologue*, l. 1.

9
Look, he 's winding up the watch of his wit; by and by it will strike.
SHAKESPEARE, *The Tempest*. Act ii, sc. 1, l. 12.

10
I am a great eater of beef, and I believe that does harm to my wit.
SHAKESPEARE, *Twelfth Night*. Act i, sc. 3, l. 89.

11
For what says Quinapalus? "Better a witty fool than a foolish wit."
SHAKESPEARE, *Twelfth Night*. Act i, sc. 5, l. 39. "Quinapalus" is an imaginary author.

I am a fool, I know it: and yet, heav'n help me,
I'm poor enough to be a wit.
CONGREVE, *Love for Love*. Act i, sc. 1.

His wit ran him out of his money, and now his poverty has run him out of his wits.
CONGREVE, *Love for Love*. Act v, sc. 2.

For though he is a wit, he is no fool.
YOUNG, *Love of Fame*. Sat. ii, l. 106.

12
Of course it's all tommy rot; but it's so brilliant, you know! How the dickens do you think of such things?
G. B. SHAW, *John Bull's Other Island*. Act i.

III—Wit: Lack of Wit

13
We grant, although he had much wit,
H' was very shy of using it,
As being loth to wear it out,
And therefore bore it not about;
Unless on holy days or so,
As men their best apparel do.
BUTLER, *Hudibras*. Pt. i, canto 1, l. 45.

14
He says but little, and that little said
Owes all its weight, like loaded dice, to lead.
His wit invites you by his looks to come,
But when you knock it never is at home.
COWPER, *Conversation*, l. 301.

You beat your pate, and fancy wit will come:
Knock as you please, there 's nobody at home.
POPE, *Epigram: An Empty House*.

15
Men of quality are above wit.
JOHN CROWNE, *Sir Courtly Nice*.

16
Who can prove
Wit to be witty when with deeper ground

Dulness intuitive declares wit dull?
GEORGE ELIOT, *A College Breakfast-party.*

1
Of all wit's uses the main one
Is to live well with who has none.
R. W. EMERSON, *Life.*

2
Their heads sometimes so little that there is no room for wit; sometimes so long, that there is no wit for so much room.
THOMAS FULLER, *The Holy and Profane State.* Bk. iv, ch. 12.

3
Some of them are half-wits,
Two to a wit, there are a set of them.
BEN JONSON, *The Staple of News.* Act i, sc. 1.

4
He must be a dull Fellow indeed, whom neither Love, Malice, nor Necessity, can inspire with Wit.
LA BRUYÈRE, *Les Caractères.* Pt. iv.

5
No one shall have wit save we and our friends.
(Nul n'aura de l'esprit, hors nous et nos amis.)
MOLIÈRE, *Les Femmes Savantes.* Act iii, sc. 2.

6
Want o' wit is waur than want o' siller.
JOHN RAY, *Proverbs: Scottish.*

7
They have a plentiful lack of wit.
SHAKESPEARE, *Hamlet.* Act ii, sc. 2, l. 202.

What a pretty thing man is when he goes in his doublet and hose and leaves off his wit.
SHAKESPEARE, *Much Ado About Nothing.* Act v, sc. 1, l. 210.

Methinks sometimes I have no more wit than a Christian or an ordinary man has.
SHAKESPEARE, *Twelfth Night.* Act i, sc. 3, l. 88.

WITCH, WITCHCRAFT

8
I have ever believed, and do now know, that there are Witches: they that are in doubt of these . . . are obliquely and upon consequence a sort, not of Infidels, but Atheists.
SIR THOMAS BROWNE, *Religio Medici.* Pt. i, sec. 30.

9
And, vow! Tam saw an unco sight!
Warlocks and witches in a dance: . . .
Coffins stood round, like open presses,
That shaw'd the dead in their last dresses;
And, by some devilish cantraip sleight,
Each in its cauld hand held a light:
BURNS, *Tam o' Shanter,* l. 114.

10
[Witches] steal young children out of their cradles, *ministerio dæmonum,* and put deformed in their rooms, which we call changelings.
ROBERT BURTON, *Anatomy of Melancholy.* Pt. i, sec. ii, mem. 1, subs. 3.

11
I tell thee, that is Mambrino's helmet.
CERVANTES, *Don Quixote.* Pt. i, ch. 7. A helmet of pure gold which rendered the wearer invisible.

12
They that burn you for a witch lose all their coals.
THOMAS FULLER, *Gnomologia.* No. 4974.

They who see the Flying Dutchman never, never reach the shore.
JOHN BOYLE O'REILLY, *The Flying Dutchman.*

13
They are neither man nor woman—
They are neither brute nor human,
They are Ghouls!
EDGAR ALLAN POE, *The Bells.*

14
An' all us other children, when the supper things is done,
We set around the kitchen fire an' has the mostest fun
A-list'nin' to the witch tales 'at Annie tells about
An' the gobble-uns 'at gits you
Ef you Don't Watch Out!
JAMES WHITCOMB RILEY, *Little Orphant Annie.*

15
This is the foul fiend Flibbertigibbet. He begins at curfew, and walks till the first cock. He . . . squints the eye and makes the harelip.
SHAKESPEARE, *King Lear.* Act iii, sc. 4, l. 120.

16
Aroint thee, witch, aroint thee!
SHAKESPEARE, *King Lear.* Act iii, sc. 4, l. 129.

17
What are these,
So wither'd, and so wild in their attire;
That look not like the inhabitants o' th' earth,
And yet are on 't?
SHAKESPEARE, *Macbeth.* Act i, sc. 1, l. 33.

The earth hath bubbles, as the water has,
And these are of them.
SHAKESPEARE, *Macbeth.* Act i, sc. 3, l. 79.

Saw you the weird sisters?
SHAKESPEARE, *Macbeth.* Act iv, sc. 1, l. 136.

18
I'll charm the air to give a sound,
While you perform your antic round.
SHAKESPEARE, *Macbeth.* Act iv, sc. 1, l. 129.

19
The foul witch Sycorax.
SHAKESPEARE, *The Tempest.* Act i, sc. 2, l. 258.

Giving up witchcraft is giving up of Bible.
JOHN WESLEY, *Journal,* 1768. *See* 2298i:2.

WOE

See also Misery, Misfortune, Sorrow

20
Here is woe's self, and not the mask of woe.
THOMAS BAILEY ALDRICH, *Andromeda.*

21
But we are all the same—the fools of our own woes!
MATTHEW ARNOLD, *Empedocles on Etna,* l. 166.

I have been cunning in mine overthrow,
The careful pilot of my proper woe.
BYRON, *Epistle to Augusta*, l. 24.

1
Lost, lost! one moment knelled the woe of years.
ROBERT BROWNING, *Childe Roland to the Dark Tower Came*. St. 33.

2
O sudden woe, that ever art successor
To worldly bliss!
CHAUCER, *Tale of the Man of Lawe*, l. 323.

Hard fate of man, on whom the heavens bestow
A drop of pleasure for a sea of woe.
SIR WILLIAM JONES, *Laura*.
See also under COMPENSATION.

3
So great an Iliad of woes threatens us. (Tanta malorum impendet Ilias.)
CICERO, *Epistolæ ad Atticum*. Bk. viii, sec. 11.

An Iliad of woes.
THOMAS DE QUINCEY, *Confessions of an English Opium-Eater*. Pt. ii.

4
Thus do extremest ills a joy possess,
And one woe makes another woe seem less.
MICHAEL DRAYTON, *England's Heroical Epistles*.

5
Sure there's a lethargy in mighty woe,
Tears stand congeal'd and cannot flow, . . .
Like Niobe we marble grow
And petrify with grief.
JOHN DRYDEN, *Threnodia Augustalis*, l. 2.

6
In all the sad variety of woe.
WILLIAM GIFFORD, *The Baviad*.

Led thro' a safe variety of woe.
POPE, *Eloisa to Abelard*, l. 36.

7
In the bitter waves of woe,
Beaten and tossed about
By the sullen winds which blow
From the desolate shores of doubt.
WASHINGTON GLADDEN, *Ultima Veritas*.

8
Through horrid tracts with fainting steps they go,
Where wild Altama murmurs to their woe.
GOLDSMITH, *The Deserted Village*, l. 343.

9
Grief tears his heart, and drives him to and fro,
In all the raging impotence of woe.
HOMER, *Iliad*. Bk. xxii, l. 526. (Pope, tr.)

Long exercised in woes.
HOMER, *Odyssey*. Bk. i, l. 2. (Pope, tr.)

Aghast I stood, a monument of woe.
HOMER, *Odyssey*. Bk. xii, l. 311. (Pope, tr.)

10
And her woe began to run afresh,
As if she'd said Gee woe!
THOMAS HOOD, *Faithless Sally Brown*.

11
For in my life I never saw a man so full of woe.
HENRY HOWARD, *Complaint of a Dying Lover*, l. 26.

I was not always a man of woe.
SCOTT, *Lay of the Last Minstrel*. Canto ii, st. 12.

12
When our heads are bowed with woe,
When our bitter tears o'erflow.
H. H. MILMAN, *Hymn: When Our Heads*.

13
O'er woes long wept Oblivion softly lays
Her shadowy veil.
PINDAR, *Olympian Odes*. Ode ii, l. 34. (Abraham Moore, tr.)

14
So perish all whose breast ne'er learn'd to glow
For others' good, or melt at others' woe.
POPE, *Elegy to the Memory of an Unfortunate Lady*, l. 45.

What sorrow was, thou bad'st her know,
And from her own she learn'd to melt at others' woe.
THOMAS GRAY, *Hymn to Adversity*, l. 15.

15
The well-sung woes will soothe my pensive ghost;
He best can paint them who shall feel them most.
POPE, *Eloisa to Abelard*, l. 365.

16
Lift not the festal mask!—enough to know,
No scene of mortal life but teems with mortal woe.
SCOTT, *The Lord of the Isles*. Canto ii, st. 1.

17
'Tis not alone my inky cloak, good mother,
Nor customary suits of solemn black,
Nor windy suspiration of forced breath,
No, nor the fruitful river in the eye,
Nor the dejected 'haviour of the visage,
Together with all forms, moods, shapes of grief,
That can denote me truly; these indeed seem,
For they are actions that a man might play,
But I have that within which passeth show;
These but the trappings and the suits of woe.
SHAKESPEARE, *Hamlet*. Act i, sc. 2, l. 76.

My grief lies all within;
And these external manners of laments
Are merely shadows to the unseen grief
That swells with silence in the tortured soul.
SHAKESPEARE, *Richard II*. Act iv, sc. 1, l. 295.

Beholding this, I weep and waste within,
And to myself bewail the unhallowed feast.
SOPHOCLES, *Electra*, l. 282.

18
The man that makes his toe
When he his heart should make
Shall of a corn cry woe,
And turn his sleep to wake.
SHAKESPEARE, *King Lear*. Act iii, sc. 2, l. 31.

1
As often shrieking undistinguished woe
In clamours of all size, both high and low
SHAKESPEARE, *A Lover's Complaint*, l. 20.

O, what a sympathy of woe is this,
As far from help as Limbo is from bliss.
SHAKESPEARE, *Titus Andronicus*. Act iii, sc. 1, l. 148.

2
All these woes shall serve
For sweet discourses in our time to come.
SHAKESPEARE, *Romeo and Juliet*. Act iii, sc. 5, l. 52. *See also under* MEMORY.

3
Woe, woe, and woe upon woe! (Πόνος πόνῳ πόνον φέρει.)
SOPHOCLES, *Ajax*, l. 866. Sometimes translated, "Toil, toil, and toil on toil!"

And woe succeeds to woe.
HOMER, *Iliad*. Bk. xvi, l. 139. (Pope, tr.)

Pain after pain, and woe succeeding woe.
S. T. COLERIDGE, *On Receiving an Account that His Only Sister's Death Was Inevitable.*

When one is past, another care we have;
Thus woe succeeds a woe, as wave a wave.
ROBERT HERRICK, *Sorrows Succeed.*

One woe doth tread upon another's heel,
So fast they follow.
SHAKESPEARE, *Hamlet*. Act iv, sc. 7, l. 164.

Woes cluster; rare are solitary woes;
They love a train, they tread each other's heel.
YOUNG, *Night Thoughts*. Night iii, l. 63.

4
Shame followed shame—and woe supplanted woe
Is this the only change that time can show?
WORDSWORTH, *Poems Dedicated to National Independence*. Pt. i, No. 28.

WOLF

See also Sheep and Wolf

5
This ravening fellow has a wolf in 's belly.
BEAUMONT AND FLETCHER, *Women Pleased*. Act i, sc. 2.

6
Who is bred among wolves will learn to howl.
JOHN FLORIO, *Second Frutes*, Fo. 57. (1591)

7
Wolves lose their teeth but not their nature.
THOMAS FULLER, *Gnomologia*. No. 5802.

Wolves lose their teeth but not their memory.
JOHN RAY, *English Proverbs*.

8
A wolf will never make war against another wolf.
GEORGE HERBERT, *Jacula Prudentum*.

It is a hard winter when one wolf eats another.
JOHN LYLY, *Euphues*, p. 78. (1579)

9
The wolf must die in his own skin.
GEORGE HERBERT, *Jacula Prudentum*.

10
Gaunt was he as a wolf of Languedoc.
THOMAS HOOD, *The Plea of the Midsummer Fairies*, l. 145.

11
The Boy . . . would be crying *a Wolf, a Wolf*, when there was none.
SIR ROGER L'ESTRANGE, *Fables*. No. 360. (1692)

They say the false cry of wolf made the neighbours not regard the cry when the wolf came in earnest.
NORTH, *Examen*, p. 315. (1740)

You've cried "Wolf!" till, like the shepherd youth, you're not believed when you do speak the truth.
JAMES ROBINSON PLANCHÉ, *Extravaganza*, ii, 288.

12
The wolf in the tale. (Lupus in sermone.)
PLAUTUS, *Stichus*. Act ii, sc. 6. *See also* TERENCE *under* DEVIL.

13
The Wolf never wants for a Pretence against a Lamb.
THOMAS FULLER, *Gnomologia*. No. 4839.

14
Who's afraid of the big bad wolf?
ANN RONELL. Popular song used in connection with Walt Disney's *Three Little Pigs*. (1933)

15
He who a wolf-cub kept, the beast to tame,
Was torn to pieces when to wolf it came.
SADI, *Gulistan*. Ch. iii, tale 5. (Arnold, tr.)

16
The wolf doth grin before he barketh.
SHAKESPEARE, *Venus and Adonis*, l. 459.

17
The wolf from the door.
JOHN SKELTON, *Colyn Cloute*, l. 153. (c. 1500)

That we may live out of debt and danger, and drive the wolf from the door.
DELONEY, *Gentle Craft*. Pt. i, ch. 9. (1597)

Though home be but homely and never so poor,
Yet let us keep, warily, the wolf from the door.
UNKNOWN. (*Roxburghe Ballads*, i, 167.)

18
I've got a wolf by the ears, as they say: I can't let go and can't hold on. (Id quod aiunt, auribus teneo lupum: Nam neque quo pacto a me amittam neque uti Retineam scio.)
TERENCE, *Phormio*, l. 506. (Act iii, sc. 2)

Holding a wolf by the ears. (Ut sæpe lupum se auribus tenere diceret.)
TIBERIUS. (SUETONIUS, *Tiberius*. Ch. 25, sec. 1.)

They had but a wolf by the ears, whom they could neither well hold, nor might safely let go.
WILLIAM LAMBARDE, *Perambulation of Kent*, 418. (1576)

19
There is a wolf in a lamb's skin.
UNKNOWN, *Wisdom*. Sc. iii, st. 61. (c. 1460)

She is perchance
A wolf or goat within a lammys skin.
ALEXANDER BARCLAY, *The Shyp of Folys*. (1508)

There is the meekness of the clergyman. There spoke the wolf in sheep's clothing.
FIELDING, *Amelia*. Bk. ix, ch. 9.

20
To tame the wolf you must marry him. (Pour ranger le loup, il faut le marier.)
UNKNOWN. A French proverb.

WOMAN

See also Age: Age in Women; Dress for Women; Faults in Women; Flattery and Women; Jealousy and Women; Man and Woman; Modesty in Woman; Scandal and Women; Smile: Women's Smiles; Tears of Women; Vanity in Woman; Voice in Woman; Wine and Woman

I—Woman: Definitions

1
The weaker sex, to piety more prone.
WILLIAM ALEXANDER, *Doomsday: The Fifth Hour*. St. 55.

WEAKER VESSEL, *see* WIFE: APOTHEGMS.

2
A woman is but an animal, and an animal not of the highest order.
EDMUND BURKE, *Reflections on the Revolution in France.* Burke is quoting the opinions of the revolutionists.

3
Women are only children of a larger growth.
LORD CHESTERFIELD, *Letters,* 5 Sept., 1748.

Women who are either indisputably beautiful, or indisputably ugly, are best flattered upon the score of their understandings; but those who are in a state of mediocrity, are best flattered upon their beauty, or at least their graces; for every woman who is not absolutely ugly thinks herself handsome.
LORD CHESTERFIELD, *Letters,* 5 Sept., 1748.

Women are to be talked to as below men, and above children.
LORD CHESTERFIELD, *Letters,* 20 Sept., 1748.

4
What is woman? only one of Nature's agreeable blunders.
HANNAH COWLEY, *Who's the Dupe?* Act ii, 2.

5
Women are door-mats and have been,—
The years those mats applaud,—
They keep their men from going in
With muddy feet to God.
MARY CAROLYN DAVIES, *Door-Mats.*

6
A lady is one who never shows her underwear unintentionally.
LILIAN DAY, *Kiss and Tell.*

6a
Mark her majestic fabric: she 's a temple
Sacred by birth, and built by hands divine;
Her soul 's the deity that lodges there:
Nor is the pile unworthy of the god.
DRYDEN, *Don Sebastian.* Act ii, sc. 1.

7
Women are like pictures; of no value in the hands of a fool till he hears men of sense bid high for the purchase.
FARQUHAR, *The Beaux' Stratagem.* Act ii, sc. 1.

8
Woman, I tell you, is a microcosm, and rightly to rule her requires as great talents, as to govern a state.
SAMUEL FOOTE, *The Devil upon Two Sticks.* Act i, sc. 1.

9
Are women books? says Hodge, then would mine were
An Almanack, to change her every year.
BENJAMIN FRANKLIN, *Poor Richard,* 1737.

10
Women are silver dishes into which we put golden apples.
GOETHE, *Conversations with Eckermann.*

11
No woman gives us the radiant dream that lurks beneath the word Woman.
ÉMILE HENNEQUIN, *Pastels in Prose,* p. 203.

12
The hydrogen derivatives.
O. HENRY, *Man About Town.*

13
Women were created for the comfort of men.
HOWELL, *Familiar Letters: To Sergeant D.*

God made the woman for the use of man,
And for the good and increase of the world.
TENNYSON, *Edwin Morris,* l. 91.

Women were made to give our eyes delight.
YOUNG, *Love of Fame.* Satire vi, l. 224.

Women! Help Heaven! men their creations mar
In profiting by them.
SHAKESPEARE, *Measure for Measure,* ii, 4, 127.

14
I expect that woman will be the last thing civilized by man.
GEORGE MEREDITH, *Richard Feverel.* Ch. 1.

A woman is a foreign land,
Of which, though there he settle young
A man will ne'er quite understand
The customs, politics, and tongue.
COVENTRY PATMORE, *The Angel in the House: The Foreign Land.*

15
A child of our grandmother Eve, a female; or, for thy more sweet understanding, a woman.
SHAKESPEARE, *Love's Labour's Lost.* Act i, sc. 1, l. 266.

16
Woman . . . the female of the human species, and not a different kind of animal.
BERNARD SHAW, *Saint Joan: Preface.*

17
A set of phrases learned by rote;
A passion for a scarlet coat.
SWIFT, *The Furniture of a Woman's Mind.*

A nobler yearning never broke her rest
Than but to dance and sing, be gaily drest.
TENNYSON, *Three Sonnets to a Coquette.* No. 2.

18
"Describe us as a sex," was her challenge.
"Sphinxes without secrets."
OSCAR WILDE, *Picture of Dorian Gray.* Ch. 17.

II—Woman: Apothegms

19
The woman that deliberates is lost.
JOSEPH ADDISON, *Cato.* Act iv, sc. 1.

20
When a woman ceases to alter the fashion of

her hair, you guess that she has passed the crisis of her experience.

MARY AUSTIN, *The Land of Little Rain.*

1

Here's to woman! Would that we could fall into her arms without falling into her hands.

AMBROSE BIERCE. His favorite toast. [GRATTAN, *Bitter Bierce*, p. 55.]

More bitter than death the woman
(Beside me still she stands)
Whose heart is snares and nets,
And whose hands are bands.

MORRIS BISHOP, *Ecclesiastes.* See 2187:7.

2

A handsome woman would have been English to the neck, French to the waist, and Dutch below.

JOHN BULWER, *Anthropomet.*, p. 228. (1650)

Down from the waist they are Centaurs,
Though women all above.

SHAKESPEARE, *King Lear.* Act iv, sc. 6, l. 126.

3

'Twas a strange riddle of a lady.

BUTLER, *Hudibras.* Pt. i, canto iii, l. 337.

For 'tis in vain to think or guess
At women by appearances.

BUTLER, *Hudibras.* Pt. iii, canto i, l. 725.

Who is 't can read a woman?

SHAKESPEARE, *Cymbeline.* Act v, sc. 5, l. 47.

4

There is a tide in the affairs of women
Which, taken at the flood, leads—God knows where.

BYRON, *Don Juan.* Canto vi, st. 2.

5

"Petticoat influence" is a great reproach. . . .
I for one venerate a petticoat—
A garment of a mystical sublimity,
No matter whether russet, silk, or dimity.

BYRON, *Don Juan.* Canto xiv, st. 26. PETTICOAT GOVERNMENT, *see* WIFE: THE CROWING HEN.

I your angels don't like,—I love women.

CHARLES DIBDIN, *Nature and Nancy.*

6

No lady is ever a gentleman.

J. B. CABELL, *Something About Eve*, p. 25.

7

Do the women in their country never bear children?

JULIUS CÆSAR, when he saw some wealthy foreign women in Rome carrying dogs and monkeys in their arms. (PLUTARCH, *Lives: Pericles.* Ch. 1, sec. 1.)

8

The man who strikes his wife or child lays violent hands upon the holiest of holy things.

MARCUS CATO. (PLUTARCH, *Lives: Marcus Cato.* Ch. 20, sec. 2.)

The man that lays his hand on woman,
Save in the way of kindness, is a wretch
Whom 'twere gross flattery to name a coward.

JOHN TOBIN, *The Honeymoon.* Act ii, sc. 1.

9

What attracts us in a woman rarely binds us to her.

CHURTON COLLINS, *Aphorisms.* No. 101.

10

A nut tree, an ass and a woman are bound together by the same law: None of the three will do well if the blows cease. (Nux, asinus, mulier, simili sunt lege legati: Hæc tria nil recta faciunt, si verbera cessent.)

COGNATUS, *Adagia.* c. 1560. (GRYNÆUS, *Adagia*, p. 484. *Notes and Queries.* Ser. x, 9, 298.)

A woman, a dog, and a walnut-tree,
The more you beat 'em the better they be.

THOMAS FULLER, *Gnomologia.* No. 6404.

A woman, an ass, and a walnut-tree,
Bring the more fruit the more beaten they be.

GUAZZO, *Civil Conversation.* Fo. 139. (1586)

A nut, a woman and an ass are alike:
These three do nothing right except you strike.

THOMAS NASHE, *Works.* Vol. iii, p. 110.

It is said that an ass, a walnut-tree and a woman asketh much beating before they be good.

LEONARD WRIGHT, *Display of Dutie*, p. 24. (1589)

Love well, whip well.

BENJAMIN FRANKLIN, *Poor Richard*, 1733.

11

O fat white woman whom nobody loves,
Why do you walk through the fields in gloves?

FRANCES CORNFORD, *To a Fat Lady Seen From the Train.*

O fat white woman whom nobody shoots,
Why do you walk through the fields in boots?

A. E. HOUSMAN.

12

O Mrs. Higden, Mrs. Higden, you was a woman and a mother, and a mangler in a million million.

DICKENS, *Our Mutual Friend.* Ch. ix.

13

The only useless life is woman's.

BENJAMIN DISRAELI, *Coningsby.* Bk. iv, ch. 15.

14

Some, ladies wed, some love, and some adore them;
I like their wanton sport, then care not for them!

WILLIAM DRUMMOND, *Pamphilus.*

WOMEN ENJOYED, *see* LOVE: ITS FRUITION.

15

The happiest women, like the happiest nations, have no history.

GEORGE ELIOT, *The Mill on the Floss.* Bk. vi, ch. 3.

16

Dally not with other folks' women or money.

BENJAMIN FRANKLIN, *Poor Richard*, 1757.

18

The Eternal Feminine draws us upward. (Das Ewig-Weibliche zieht uns hinan.)

GOETHE, *Faust.* Act ii, sc. 5.

La Féminine Eternel Nous attire au ciel.

GOETHE, *Faust*, ii, 5. (French tr. by H. Blaze de Bury.)

The Woman Soul leadeth us Upward and on.

GOETHE, *Faust*, ii, 5. (Bayard Taylor, tr.)

19

"For shame, fond youth, thy sorrows hush,

And spurn the sex." he said.
GOLDSMITH, *A Ballad.* (*Vicar of Wakefield.* Ch. 8.)

Take heed of a young wench, a prophetess, and a Latin-bred woman.
GEORGE HERBERT, *Jacula Prudentum.*

1
Women and music should never be dated.
GOLDSMITH, *She Stoops to Conquer.* Act iii.

2
Mills and women ever want something.
GUAZZO, *Civil Conversation,* 137. (Pettie, tr.)

To furnish a ship requireth much trouble,
But to furnish a woman the charges are double.
JOHN MANNINGHAM, *Diary,* p. 12. (1602)

See also under DRESS.

3
The plain ones be as safe as churches.
THOMAS HARDY, *Tess.* Ch. 14.

4
A woman hath nine lives like a cat.
JOHN HEYWOOD, *Proverbs.* Pt. ii, ch. 4. (1546)

A cat has nine lives, and a woman has nine cats' lives.
THOMAS FULLER, *Gnomologia.*

5
A thing far fetched is good for ladies.
HILL, *Commonplace-Book,* 132. (c. 1500)

Dear bought and far fetched are dainties for ladies.
JOHN HEYWOOD, *Proverbs.* Pt. i, ch. 11.

Things far-fetched and dear-bought are good for ladies.
MONTAIGNE, *Essays.* Bk. iii, ch. 5.

Far-fetched and dear-bought, as the proverb rehearses,
Is good, or was held so, for ladies.
A. C. SWINBURNE, *A Singing Lesson.*

6
Nature is in earnest when she makes a woman.
O. W. HOLMES, *The Autocrat of the Breakfast-Table.* Ch. 12.

7
A woman and a cherry paint themselves for their own hurt.
JAMES HOWELL, *Proverbs: Span.-Eng.,* 18. *See also* FACE: PAINTED.

8
In that day seven women shall take hold of one man.
Old Testament: Isaiah, iv, 1.

9
As the faculty of writing has been chiefly a masculine endowment, the reproach of making the world miserable has been always thrown upon the women.
SAMUEL JOHNSON, *The Rambler.* No. 18.

10
When a woman means mischief, if she but look upon her apron-strings the devil will help her presently.
JOHN LACY, *Dumb Lady.* Act i.

11
"My officious friend," said I, "he that does not love a woman sucked a sow."
SIR ROGER L'ESTRANGE, *Quevedo's Visions,* 144. (1667)

He that hates woman sucked a sow.
SWIFT, *Polite Conversation.* Dial. i.

12
One woman drives out another so quickly in Paris, when one is a bachelor.
GUY DE MAUPASSANT, *All Over.*

13
Women are not altogether in the wrong when they refuse the rules of life prescribed in the world, forsomuch as only men have established them without their consent.
MONTAIGNE, *Essays.* Bk. iii, ch. 5.

14
Women have no rank. (Les femmes n'ont pas de rang.)
NAPOLEON I, *Sayings of Napoleon.*

The only rank which elevates a woman is that which a gentle spirit bestows upon her.
A. W. PINERO, *Sweet Lavender.* Act iii.

There's no social differences—till women come in.
H. G. WELLS, *Kipps.* Bk. ii, ch. 4.

15
Wit and woman are two frail things, and both the frailer by concurring.
THOMAS OVERBURY, *News from Court;* SIR HENRY WOTTON, *Table-Talk.*

Pretty, witty Nell.
SAMUEL PEPYS, *Diary,* 3 April, 1665. Referring to Nell Gwynne.

16
An artful woman makes a modern saint.
MATTHEW PRIOR, *Epigrams: The Modern Saint.*

17
A woman's work and washing of dishes is never at an end.
JOHN RAY, *English Proverbs.* (1670)

When Darby saw the setting sun
He swung his scythe, and home he run,
Sat down, drank off his quart and said,
"My work is done, I'll go to bed."
"My work is done!" retorted Joan,
"My work is done! Your constant tone,
But hapless woman ne'er can say
'My work is done' till judgment day."
ST. JOHN HONEYWOOD, *Darby and Joan.*

Some respite to husbands the weather may send,
But housewives' affairs have never an end.
THOMAS TUSSER, *Book of Housewifery: Preface.*

Man's work lasts till set of sun;
Woman's work is never done.
UNKNOWN. (*Roxburghe Ballads,* iii, 302. c. 1655.)

18
Women and princes must trust somebody.
JOHN SELDEN, *Table-Talk: Women.*

Women, like princes, find few real friends:
All who approach them their own ends pursue;
Lovers and ministers are seldom true.
GEORGE LYTTELTON, *Advice to a Lady.*

19
One that was a woman, sir; but, rest her soul, she's dead.
SHAKESPEARE, *Hamlet.* Act v, sc. 1, l. 146.

Iago: She was a wight, if ever such wight were,—
Desdemona: To do what?
Iago: To suckle fools and chronicle small beer.
Desdemona: O most lame and impotent conclusion!

SHAKESPEARE, *Othello*. Act ii, sc. 1, l. 159.

1
A poor lone woman.

SHAKESPEARE, *II Henry IV*. Act ii, sc. 1, l. 35.

I grant I am a woman; but withal,
A woman that Lord Brutus took to wife:
I grant I am a woman; but withal
A woman well-reputed; Cato's daughter.

SHAKESPEARE, *Julius Cæsar*. Act ii, sc. 1, l. 292.

2
Like all young men, you greatly exaggerate the difference between one young woman and another.

BERNARD SHAW, *Major Barbara*. Act iii.

3
Women and linen show best by candle-light.

SWIFT, *Polite Conversation* Dial. iii.

Neither a woman nor linen choose thou by a candle.

JOHN FLORIO, *First Fruites,* Fo. 32.

4
Henceforth I blot all women out of my mind. I am sick of these everyday beauties. (Deleo omnes dehinc ex animo mulieres: Tædet cottidianarum harum formarum.)

TERENCE, *Eunuchus*, l. 295. (Act ii, sc. 3.)

Though nowadays he's not so much for women.
"So few of them," he says, "are worth the guessing."

E. A. ROBINSON, *Ben Jonson Entertains a Man from Stratford.*

5
What was that pretty bit of muslin hanging on your arm—who was she?

THACKERAY, *Pendennis*. Ch. 1.

6
The man in the moon isn't half as interesting as the lady in the sun.

MRS. JENELL TILTON, *Pathfinder* No. 1866.

I never expected to see the day when the girls would get sunburned in the places they do now.

WILL B. ROGERS. (*The Pathfinder* No. 1866.)

7
Woman, God bless her by that name, for it is a far nobler name than lady.

WALTER VON DER VOGELWEIDE, *Woman and Lady*. (WALSH, *Golden Treasury of Medieval Literature*, p. 109.)

Give us that grand word "woman" once again,
And let's have done with "lady"; one's a term
Full of fine force, strong, beautiful and firm,
Fit for the noblest use of tongue or pen;
And one's a word for lackeys.

ELLA WHEELER WILCOX, *Woman.*

8
The female woman is one of the greatest institooshuns of which this land can boste.

ARTEMUS WARD, *Woman's Rights.*

She was born to make hash of men's buzzums.

ARTEMUS WARD, *Piccolomini.*

9
Many a woman has a past; but I am told she has at least a dozen, and that they all fit.

OSCAR WILDE, *Lady Windermere's Fan.* Act i.

A woman with a past has no future.

OSCAR WILDE.

A young man with a very good past. (Un jeune homme d'un bien beau passé.)

HEINE, of Alfred de Musset. (SWINBURNE, *Miscellanies*, p. 233.)

10
Oh! no one. No one in particular. A woman of no importance.

OSCAR WILDE, *A Woman of No Importance.* Act i.

11
All men are married women's property. That is the only true definition of what married women's property really is.

OSCAR WILDE, *A Woman of No Importance.* Act ii.

11a
A woman of sixty, the same as a girl of six, runs to the sound of the timbrel.

Babylonian Talmud: Moéd Katan, p. 9b.

III—Woman: Her Creation

See also under Adam

12
God, when he made the first woman . . . made her not of the head of Adam, for she should not climb to great lordship; . . . also certes, God made not woman of the foot of Adam, for she should not be holden too low; for she can not patiently suffer; but God made woman of the rib of Adam, for woman should be fellow unto man.

CHAUCER, *The Persones Tale*. Sec. 79.

That the woman was made of a rib out of the side of Adam; not out of his feet to be trampled upon by him, but out of his side to be equal with him, under his arm to be protected, and near his heart to be loved.

MATTHEW HENRY, *Note on Genesis,* ii, 21, 22.

The woman was not taken
From Adam's head, we know,
To show she must not rule him—
'Tis evidently so.
The woman she was taken
From under Adam's arm,
So she must be protected
From injuries and harm.

ABRAHAM LINCOLN, *Adam and Eve's Wedding Song*. Written for Sarah Haggard on her marriage to Aaron Grigsby.

Not from his head was woman took,
As made her husband to o'erlook;
Not from his feet, as one designed
The footstool of the stronger kind;
But fashioned for himself, a bride;
An equal, taken from his side.

CHARLES WESLEY, *Short Hymns on Select Passages of the Holy Scriptures.*

She was not made out of his head, Sir,
To rule and to govern the man;

Nor was she made out of his feet, Sir,
  By man to be trampled upon. . . .
But she did come forth from his side, Sir,
  His equal and partner to be;
And now they are coupled together,
  She oft proves the top of the tree.

UNKNOWN. (DIXON, *Ballads and Songs of the Peasantry of England.*)

Reason and religion teach us that we too are primary existences, that it is for us to move in the orbit of our duty around the holy center of perfection, the companions not the satellites of men.

EMMA WILLARD. Inscribed beneath her bust in Hall of Fame.

1
You see, dear, it is not true that woman was made from man's rib; she was really made from his funny bone.

BARRIE, *What Every Woman Knows.* Act iii.

2
Woman, they say, was only made of man:
Methinks 'tis strange they should be so unlike!
It may be all the best was cut away,
To make the woman, and the naught was left
Behind with him.

BEAUMONT AND FLETCHER, *Scornful Lady,* iii, 2.

3
Auld Nature swears, the lovely dears
  Her noblest work she classes, O:
Her prentice han' she tried on man,
  An' then she made the lasses, O.

BURNS, *Green Grow the Rashes.*

Our sex, you know, was after yours designed:
The last perfection of the Maker's mind:
Heaven drew out all the gold for us, and left
  your dross behind.

DRYDEN, *Amphitryon: Prologue.*

Man was made when Nature was but an apprentice, but woman when she was a skilful mistress of her art.

EDWARD SHARPHAM, *Cupid's Whirligig.* (1607)

I have always said it: Nature meant woman to be her masterpiece. (Ich hab' es immer gesagt: das Weib wollte die Natur zu ihrem Meisterstücke machen.)

LESSING, *Emilia Galotti.* Act v, sc. 7.

4
To chase the clouds of life's tempestuous hours,
To strew its short but weary way with flow'rs,
New hopes to raise, new feelings to impart,
And pour celestial balsam on the heart;
For this to man was lovely woman giv'n,
The last, best work, the noblest gift of Heav'n.

T. L. PEACOCK, *The Vision of Love,* l. 1.

5
He beheld his own rougher make softened into sweetness, and tempered with smiles; he saw a creature who had, as it were, Heaven's second thought in her formation.

STEELE, *The Christian Hero.* Of Adam's first sight of Eve.

6
The man is, as a first creation, genuine;
The woman is the clearer, softer, and diviner,
For he was from the inorganic dirt unfolded,
But she came forth from clay which life before had moulded.

UNKNOWN, *Woman.* (From the Persian.)

IV—Woman: Good and Bad

7
Woman is the salvation or destruction of the family She carries its destinies in the folds of her mantle.

AMIEL, *Journal,* 11 Dec., 1872.

8
Woman brings to man his greatest blessing and his greatest plague. (*Γυνὴ κώφέλειαν καὶ νόσον ἀνδρὶ φέρει μεγίσταν.*)

EURIPIDES, *Alcmæon.*

There is no worse evil than a bad woman; and nothing has ever been created better than a good one.
(*Τῆς μὲν κακῆς κάκιον οὔτι γίγνεται
Γυναικός· ἐσθλῆς δ' οὐδὲν εἰς ὑπερβολὴν
Πέφυκ' ἄμεινον.*)

EURIPIDES, *Melanippe Desmotis.*

9
Women are ever in extremes; they are either better or worse than men.

LA BRUYÈRE, *Les Caractères: Des Femmes.*

10
There's no such thing as picking out the best woman; it's only a question of comparative badness. (Nam optuma nulla potest eligi; Alia alia pejor est.)

PLAUTUS, *Aulularia,* l. 139. (Act ii, sc. 1.)

This woman is a bad piece of goods. (Mala mers, era, hæc et callida est.)

PLAUTUS, *Cistellaria,* l. 707. (Act iv, sc. 2.)

11
And yet believe me, good as well as ill,
Woman 's at best a contradiction still.
Heav'n, when it strives to polish all it can
Its last best work, but forms a softer man.

POPE, *Moral Essays.* Epis. ii, l. 269.

The soft, unhappy sex.

APHRA BEHN, *The Wandering Beauty.*

12
O Woman! in our hours of ease
Uncertain, coy, and hard to please,
And variable as the shade
By the light quivering aspen made;
When pain and anguish wring the brow,
A ministering angel thou!

SCOTT, *Marmion.* Canto vi, st. 30.

We women seldom fail at a pinch.

BEN JONSON, *Bartholomew Fair.* Act i.

'Twas ever thus, when in life's storm
  Hope's star to man grows dim,
An angel kneels, in woman's form,
  And breathes a prayer for him.

GEORGE POPE MORRIS, *Pocahontas.*

The soul's armour is never well set to the heart unless a woman's hand has braced it.

RUSKIN, *Sesame and Lilies: Of Queens' Gardens.*

13
A man gains no possession better than a good

woman, nothing more horrible than a bad one. (Γυναικὸς οὐδέ χρημ' ἀνὴρ ληΐζεται Ἐσθλῆς ἄμεινον, οὐδὲ ῥίγιον κακῆς.)

SIMONIDES, *Iambics*. No. 7.

1
Daphne knows, with equal ease,
How to vex and how to please;
But the folly of her sex
Makes her sole delight to vex.

SWIFT, *Daphne*, l. 1.

Lose not time to contradict her,
Nor endeavour to convict her. . . .
Only take this rule along,
Always to advise her wrong,
And reprove her when she's right;
She may then grow wise for spite.

SWIFT, *Daphne*, l. 29.

2
Wicked women bother one. Good women bore one. That is the only difference between them.

OSCAR WILDE, *Lady Windermere's Fan*. Act iii.

I find that, ultimately, there are only two kinds of women, the plain and the coloured.

OSCAR WILDE, *The Picture of Dorian Gray*. Ch. 4; *A Woman of No Importance*. Act iii.

The world is perfectly packed with good women. To know them is a middle-class education.

OSCAR WILDE, *Lady Windermere's Fan*. Act iii.

Oh, there was a woman-hater hated women all he could,
And he built himself a bungle in a dingle in the wood;
Here he lived and said of ladies things I do not think he should,
"If they 're good, they 're not good-looking; if good-looking, they 're not good."

CLARE KUMMER, *In the Dingle-Dongle Bell.*

V—Woman: Saint Abroad, Devil at Home

3
A woman is a fury and a hurtful spirit in the house, an angel in the church, an ape in the bed, a mule unbridled in the field, and a goat in the garden.

BERCHER, *Nobility of Women*, 127. (1559)

We limit the comely parts of a woman to consist in four points: that is to be a shrew in the kitchen, a saint in the church, an angel at the board, and an ape in the bed, as the Chronicle reports by Mistress Shore, paramour to King Edward the Fourth.

GEORGE PUTTENHAM, *English Poesie*, 299. (1589)

According to that wise saying, women be saints in the church, angels in the street, devils in the kitchen, and apes in your bed.

THOMAS MIDDLETON, *Blurt, Master-Constable*. Act iii, sc. 3. (1602)

You are pictures out of doors,
Bells in your parlours, wild-cats in your kitchens,
Saints in your injuries, devils being offended,
Players in your housewifery, and housewives in your beds.

SHAKESPEARE, *Othello*. Act ii, sc. 1, l. 110. (1604)

4
At home like devils they be,
Abroad like angels pure.

EDWARD MORE, *Defence of Women*, l. 474. (1560)

5
God save us all from wives who are angels in the street, saints in the church, and devils at home.

C. H. SPURGEON, *John Ploughman*. Ch. 13.

They are all saints abroad, but ask their maids what they are at home.

C. H. SPURGEON, *Ploughman's Pictures*, 67.

6
Women are in churches, saints; abroad, angels; at home, devils.

GEORGE WILKINS, *The Miseries of Enforced Marriage*. Act i.

As holy as saints in church they be,
And in street as angels they were,
At home, for all their hypocrisy,
A devilish life they lead all the year.

UNKNOWN, *School House of Women*, l. 658. (1542)

7
A woman is an angel at ten, a saint at fifteen, a devil at forty, and a witch at fourscore.

UNKNOWN, *Swetnam, Woman-Hater*. (1620)

VI—Woman: A Blessing

See also Beauty in Women.

8
Loveliest of women! Heav'n is in thy soul,
Beauty and virtue shine for ever round thee,
Bright'ning each other: thou art all divine.

ADDISON, *Cato*. Act iii, sc. 2.

9
Where women are, the better things are implied if not spoken.

A. B. ALCOTT, *Table Talk: Conversation.*

10
Not she with trait'rous kiss her Saviour stung,
Not she denied Him with unholy tongue;
She, while apostles shrank, could dangers brave,
Last at the cross and earliest at the grave.

EATON STANNARD BARRETT, *Woman*. Pt. i, l. 141.

11
There's a woman like a dewdrop, she's so purer than the purest;
And her noble heart's the noblest, yes, and her sure faith's the surest.

ROBERT BROWNING, *Blot in the 'Scutcheon*, i, 3.

12
Dear, dead women, with such hair, too—what's become of all the gold
Used to hang and brush their bosoms? I feel chilly and grown old.

ROBERT BROWNING, *A Toccata of Galuppi's.*

Round and round, like a dance of snow
In a dazzling drift, as its guardians, go
Floating the women faded for ages,
Sculptured in stone, on the poet's pages.
Then follow women fresh and gay,
Living and loving and loved to-day.

ROBERT BROWNING, *Women and Roses.*

All loved and lovely women dear to rhyme:
Thais, Cassandra, Helen and their fames,
Burn like tall candles through forgotten time,
Lighting the Past's dim arras with their names.
DAVID MORTON, *Immortals.*

Women, who were summer in men's hearts.
JOHN MASEFIELD, *Sonnets.* No. xviii. See 1745:8.

1
To see her is to love her
And love but her for ever;
For Nature made her what she is,
And never made anither!
BURNS, *Bonie Leslie.*

To know her was to love her.
SAMUEL ROGERS, *Jacqueline.* St. i.

2
There's nought but care on every hand,
In every hour that passes, O:
What signifies the life o' man,
And 't were na for the lasses, O.
ROBERT BURNS, *Green Grow the Rashes.*

3
There is something in a woman beyond all human delight; a magnetic virtue, a charming quality, an occult and powerful motive.
ROBERT BURTON, *Anatomy of Melancholy.* Pt. iii, sec. 2, mem. i, subs. 2. After Fonseca.

More royalty in woman's honest heart
Than dwells within the crowned majesty
And sceptered anger of a hundred kings!
BULWER-LYTTON, *Richelieu.* Act iii, sc. 1.

Soft as the memory of buried love,
Pure as the prayer which childhood wafts above.
BYRON, *The Bride of Abydos.* Canto i, st. 6.

She was the rainbow to thy sight!
Thy sun—thy heaven—of lost delight!
CAMPBELL, *Gertrude of Wyoming.* Pt. iii, st. 36.

4
Without the smile from partial beauty won,
Oh! what were man?—a world without a sun!
CAMPBELL, *The Pleasures of Hope.* Pt. ii, l. 23.

The world was sad; the garden was a wild;
And man, the hermit, sigh'd—till woman smiled!
CAMPBELL, *The Pleasures of Hope.* Pt. ii, l. 37.

If the heart of a man is depressed with cares,
The mist is dispell'd when a woman appears.
JOHN GAY, *The Beggar's Opera.* Act ii, sc. 1.

5
For with affections warm, intense, refined,
She mixed such calm and holy strength of mind.
That, like Heaven's image in the smiling brook,
Celestial peace was pictured in her look.
THOMAS CAMPBELL, *Theodric,* l. 188.

A mind at peace with all below,
A heart whose love is innocent!
BYRON, *She Walks in Beauty.*

She was a queen of noble Nature's crowning,
A smile of hers was like an act of grace.
HARTLEY COLERIDGE, *The Solitary-Hearted.*

Women may be whole oceans deeper than we are, but they are also a whole paradise better. She may have got us out of Eden, but as a compensation she makes the earth very pleasant.
JOHN OLIVER HOBBES, *Ambassador.* Act iii.

6
The most precious possession that ever comes to a man in this world is a woman's heart.
J. G. HOLLAND, *Lessons in Life: Perverseness.*

Do you know you have asked for the costliest thing
Ever made by the Hand above—
A woman's heart, and a woman's life,
And a woman's wonderful love?
MARY T. LATHROP, *A Woman's Answer to a Man's Question.*

7
If it was woman who put man out of Paradise, it is still woman, and woman only, who can lead him back.
ELBERT HUBBARD, *Epigrams.*

The Woman tempted me—and tempts me still!
Lord God, I pray You that she ever will!
E. V. COOKE, *Book of Extenuations: Adam.*

8
And where she went, the flowers took thickest root,
As she had sow'd them with her odorous foot.
BEN JONSON, *The Sad Shepherd.* Act i, sc. 1.

Her face betokened all things dear and good,
The light of somewhat yet to come was there
Asleep, and waiting for the opening day,
When childish thoughts, like flowers, would drift away.
JEAN INGELOW, *Margaret in the Xebec.* St. 57.

9
Without women the beginning of our life would be deprived of assistance, the middle portion of pleasure, and the end of consolation. (Sans les femmes le commencement de notre vie seroit privé de secours, le milieu de plaisirs, et le fin de consolation.)
VICTOR J. E. JOUY, *Maximes.*

10
There in the fane a beauteous creature stands,
The first best work of the Creator's hands,
Whose slender limbs inadequately bear
A full-orbed bosom and a weight of care;
Whose teeth like pearls, whose lips like cherries, show,
And fawn-like eyes still tremble as they glow.
KALIDASA, *Sakoontalâ.* (Williams, tr.)

11
A Lady with a Lamp shall stand
In the great history of the land,
A noble type of good,
Heroic womanhood.
LONGFELLOW, *Santa Filomena.* St. 10.

When all the medical officers have retired for the night, and silence and darkness have settled down upon those miles of prostrate sick, she [Florence Nightingale] may be observed alone, with a little lamp in her hand, making her solitary rounds.
MACDONALD, *Letter* to the London *Times,* when leaving Scutari. (*Pictorial History of the Russian War,* p. 310.)

12
'T was kin' o' kingdom-come to look
On sech a blessed cretur.
J. R. LOWELL, *The Courtin'.* St. 7.

For she was jes' the quiet kind
Whose naturs never vary,
Like streams that keep a summer mind
Snowhid in Jenooary.

J. R. LOWELL, *The Courtin'*. St. 22.

1
Ah, there's many a beam from the fountain of day
That, to reach us unclouded, must pass, on its way,
Through the soul of a woman.

J. R. LOWELL, *A Fable for Critics*, l. 1425.

Earth's noblest thing, a Woman perfected.

J. R. LOWELL, *Irene*, l. 62.

2
A little, tiny, pretty, witty, charming darling she. (Parvula, pumilio, chariton mia tota merum sal.)

LUCRETIUS. *De Rerum Natura*. Bk. iv, l. 1158.

She is pretty to walk with,
And witty to talk with,
And pleasant too, to think on.

SIR JOHN SUCKLING, *The Discontented Colonel*, Act ii, sc. 1.

Airy, fairy Lilian.

TENNYSON, *Lilian*.

A rosebud set with little wilful thorns,
And sweet as English air could make her, she!

TENNYSON, *The Princess: Prologue*, l. 153.

3
She walks—the lady of my delight—
A shepherdess of sheep.
Her flocks are thoughts. She keeps them white;
She guards them from the steep;
She feeds them on the fragrant height,
And folds them in for sleep.

ALICE MEYNELL, *The Shepherdess*.

My sheep are thoughts, which I both guide and serve.

SIR PHILIP SIDNEY, *The Arcadia*. Bk. ii.

4
A bevy of fair women, richly gay
In gems and wanton dress.

MILTON, *Paradise Lost*. Bk. xi, l. 578.

Fair ladies, you drop manna in the way
Of starved people.

SHAKESPEARE, *Merchant of Venice*, v, 1, 294.

5
When I approach
Her loveliness, so absolute she seems
And in herself complete, so well to know
Her own, that what she wills to do or say,
Seems wisest, virtuousest, discreetest, best.

MILTON, *Paradise Lost*. Bk. viii, l. 546.

O fairest of creation! last and best
Of all God's works! creature in whom excell'd
Whatever can to sight or thought be form'd,
Holy, divine, good, amiable, or sweet!

MILTON, *Paradise Lost*. Bk. ix, l. 896.

6
O woman! lovely woman! Nature made thee
To temper man: we had been brutes without you.

THOMAS OTWAY, *Venice Preserved*. Act i, sc. 1.

Without women the world would be like a palette set in the raw umber and white. Women are the colouring matter, the glaze the old painters used.

GEORGE MOORE, *Ave*, p. 169.

7
I fill this cup to one made up
Of loveliness alone,
A woman, of her gentle sex
The seeming paragon;
To whom the better elements
And kindly stars have given
A form so fair, that, like the air,
'Tis less of earth than heaven.

EDWARD COOTE PINKNEY, *A Health*.

Her very tone is music's own,
Like those of morning birds,
And something more than melody
Dwells ever in her words.

EDWARD COOTE PINKNEY, *A Health*.

Come to the festal board to-night,
For bright-eyed beauty will be there,
Her coral lips in nectar steeped,
And garlanded her hair.

UNKNOWN, *The Festal Board*. (*McGuffey's Third Reader*, p. 217.)

8
Here rests a Woman, good without pretence,
Bless'd with plain Reason and with sober Sense.

POPE, *Epitaph on Mrs. Corbet*.

The age of a woman doesn't mean a thing. The best tunes are played on the oldest fiddles.

SIGMUND Z. ENGEL, love pirate, *Retort*, when asked why he concentrated on older women. He himself was eighty years old. See *News Week*, 4 July, 1949, p. 40.

9
Honor women! they entwine and weave
Heavenly roses in our earthly life.
(Ehret die Frauen! sie flechten und weben
Himmlische Rosen in's irdische Leben.)

SCHILLER, *Würde der Frauen*.

10
She is a gallant creature, and complete
In mind and feature.

SHAKESPEARE, *Henry VIII*. Act iii, sc. 2, l. 49.

She in beauty, education, blood,
Holds hand with any princess of the world.

SHAKESPEARE, *King John*. Act ii, sc. 1, l. 493.

Who is Silvia? what is she,
That all our swains commend her?
Holy, fair, and wise is she;
The heaven such grace doth lend her,
That she must admired be.

SHAKESPEARE, *The Two Gentlemen of Verona*. Act iv, sc. 2, l. 39.

11
She is her self of best things the collection.

SIR PHILIP SIDNEY, *Arcadia: Thyrsis and Dorus*.

12
O Woman, you are not merely the handiwork of God, but also of men; these are ever endowing you with beauty from their hearts. . . . You are one half woman and one half dream.

RABINDRANATH TAGORE, *The Gardener*. No. 59.

1
O miracle of noble womanhood!
TENNYSON, *The Princess: Prologue*, l. 48.

Scarce of earth nor all divine.
TENNYSON, *Adeline*, l. 3.

2
Amoret! as sweet and good
As the most delicious food,
Which, but tasted, does impart
Life and gladness to the heart.
EDMUND WALLER, *To Amoret*, l. 39.

How small a part of time they share
That are so wondrous sweet and fair!
EDMUND WALLER, *Go, Lovely Rose*, l. 19.

3
O! what's a table richly spread,
Without a woman at its head?
THOMAS WARTON, *The Progress of Discontent.*

Now in hot, now in cold,
Full woeful is the household
That wants a woman.
UNKNOWN. (*Towneley Plays.* No. 13, l. 419. c. 1388)

4
How all her care was but to be fair,
And all her task to be sweet.
WILLIAM WATSON, *The Heart of the Rose.*

5
The sweetest woman ever Fate
Perverse denied a household mate,
Who, lonely, homeless, not the less
Found peace in love's unselfishness. . . .
Through years of toil and soil and care,
From glossy tress to thin gray hair,
All unprofaned she held apart
The virgin fancies of the heart.
WHITTIER, *Snow-Bound*, l. 352.

A woman tropical, intense,
In thought and act, in soul and sense,
She blended in a like degree
The vixen and the devotee.
WHITTIER, *Snow-Bound*, l. 531. Referring to Harriet Livermore.

6
Angels listen when she speaks;
She's my delight, all mankind's wonder;
But my jealous heart would break
Should we live one day asunder.
JOHN WILMOT, *My Dear Mistress Has a Heart.*

7
She was a Phantom of delight
When first she gleamed upon my sight;
A lovely Apparition sent
To be a moment's ornament;
Her eyes as stars of Twilight fair;
Like Twilight's, too, her dusky hair;
But all things else about her drawn
From May-time and the cheerful Dawn.
WORDSWORTH, *She Was a Phantom of Delight.*

I saw her upon nearer view,
A Spirit, yet a Woman too! . . .
A Creature not too bright or good
For human nature's daily food;
For transient sorrows, simple wiles,
Praise, blame, love, kisses, tears, and smiles.
And now I see with eye serene
The very pulse of the machine; . . .
A perfect Woman, nobly planned,
To warn, to comfort, and command;
And yet a Spirit still, and bright
With something of angelic light.
WORDSWORTH, *She Was a Phantom of Delight.*

'T is hers to pluck the amaranthine flower
Of Faith, and round the sufferer's temples bind
Wreaths that endure affliction's heaviest shower,
And do not shrink from sorrow's keenest wind.
WORDSWORTH, *Weak Is the Will of Man.*

8
But Woman is rare beyond compare,
The poets tell us so;
How little they know of Woman
Who only women know!
CAROLYN WELLS, *Woman.*

VII—Woman: A Curse

9
The wicked woman, full of subtlety,
Worse than a fox in crafty hardihood.
ARIOSTO, *Orlando Furioso.* Canto xvi, st. 13.

10
There is nothing in the world worse than a woman
By nature shameless—save some other woman.
(*'Αλλ' οὐ γάρ ἐστιτῶν αναισχύντων φύσει γυναικῶν οὐδὲν κάκιον εἰς ἄπαντα πλὴν ἄρ' εἰ γυναῖκες.*)
ARISTOPHANES, *Thesmophoriazusæ*, l. 531.

A shameless woman is the worst of men.
YOUNG, *Love of Fame.* Sat. v, l. 468.

A man shall walk behind a lion rather than behind a woman.
Babylonian Talmud: Berachoth, fo. 61a.

11
Oh the gladness of her gladness when she's glad,
And the sadness of her sadness when she's sad,
But the gladness of her gladness,
And the sadness of her sadness
Are as nothing, Charles,
To the badness of her badness when she's bad.
J. M. BARRIE, *Rosalind.* Quoted.

Oh, the shrewdness of her shrewdness when she's shrewd,
And the rudeness of her rudeness when she's rude;
But the shrewdness of her shrewdness and the rudeness of her rudeness,
Are as nothing to her goodness when she's good.
UNKNOWN, *A Libel Answered.*

12
There is no other purgatory but a woman.
BEAUMONT AND FLETCHER, *Scornful Lady.* Act iii.

Women are the gate of hell.
ST. JEROME.

Were 't not for gold and women, there would be no damnation.
CYRIL TOURNEUR, *Revenger's Tragedy.* Act ii, sc. 1.

13
Oh, woman, woman! thou shouldst have few sins
Of thine own to answer for! Thou art the author

Of such a book of follies in a man,
That it would need the tears of all the angels
To blot the record out!
BULWER-LYTTON, *The Lady of Lyons*. Act v, sc. 1.

1
Women are not a hobby—they're a calamity.
ALEXANDER BRAILOWSKY, *Interview at Minneapolis*, 1931.

2
From Adam's wife, that proved a curse,
Though God had made her for a blessing,
All women born are so perverse
No man need boast their love possessing.
ROBERT BRIDGES [DROCH], *Triolet*.

3
The world is full of women, and the women full of wile.
GELETT BURGESS, *Willy and the Lady*.

4
A woman (tho' the phrase may seem uncivil)
As able—and as cruel—as the Devil!
BURNS, *Scots Prologue for Mrs. Sutherland*, l. 27. Referring to Queen Elizabeth.

5
Pricking her fingers with those cursèd pins,
Which surely were invented for our sins,
Making a woman like a porcupine,
Not to be rashly touch'd.
BYRON, *Don Juan*. Canto vi, st. 61.

6
There's no music when a woman is in the concert.
DEKKER, *II The Honest Whore*. Act iv, sc. 1.

7
And I find more bitter than death the woman, whose heart is snares and nets, and her hands as bands.
Old Testament: Ecclesiastes, vii, 26.

All wickedness is but little to the wickedness of a woman.
Apocrypha: Ecclesiasticus, xxv, 19.

Woman—a foe to friendship, an unescapable punishment, a necessary evil.
ST. CHRYSOSTOM.

8
There is no evil so terrible as a woman. (Οὐδὲν οὕτω δεινὸν, ὡς γυνὴ, κακόν.)
EURIPIDES, *Fragment*.

9
Oh, woman, perfect woman! what distraction
Was meant to mankind when thou wast made a devil!
What an inviting hell invented.
JOHN FLETCHER, *Monsieur Thomas*. Act iii, sc. 1.

10
'Tis woman that seduces all mankind;
By her we first were taught the wheedling arts.
JOHN GAY, *The Beggar's Opera*. Act i, sc. 2.

11
When toward the Devil's House we tread,
Woman's a thousand steps ahead.
(Denn geht es zu des Bösen Haus
Das Weib hat tausend Schritt voraus.)
GOETHE, *Faust*. Pt. i, sc. 21, l. 147.

Women's feet run still astray
If to ill they know the way.
WILLIAM HABINGTON, *Castara*.

12
Mankind, from Adam, have been women's fools;
Women, from Eve, have been the devil's tools:
Heaven might have spar'd one torment when we fell;
Not left us women, or not threatened hell.
GEORGE GRANVILLE, *The She-Gallants*.

Of all the plagues with which the world is curst,
Of every ill, a woman is the worst.
GEORGE GRANVILLE, *British Enchanters*. Act ii, 1.

13
He seldom errs
Who thinks the worst he can of womankind.
JOHN HOME, *Douglas*. Act ii, sc. 3.

14
O woman, woman, when to ill thy mind
Is bent, all hell contains no fouler fiend.
HOMER, *Odyssey*. Bk. xi, l. 531. (Pope, tr.)

What mighty woes
To thy imperial race from woman rose.
HOMER, *Odyssey*. Bk. xi, l. 541. (Pope, tr.)

15
Nothing is more unbearable than a woman of wealth. (Intolerabilius nihil est quam femina dives.)
JUVENAL, *Satires*. Sat. vi, l. 460.

16
I met a lady in the meads,
Full beautiful—a faery's child;
Her hair was long, her foot was light,
And her eyes were wild. . . .

She took me to her elfin grot,
And there she wept, and sigh'd full sore,
And there I shut her wild, wild eyes
With kisses four. . . .

I saw pale kings, and princes too,
Pale warriors, death-pale were they all:
They cried—"La Belle Dame sans Merci
Hath thee in thrall!"
KEATS, *La Belle Dame Sans Merci*.

17
When the Himalayan peasant meets the he-bear in his pride,
He shouts to scare the monster, who will often turn aside.
But the she-bear thus accosted rends the peasant tooth and nail.
For the female of the species is more deadly than the male.
RUDYARD KIPLING, *The Female of the Species*.

But when hunter meets with husband, each confirms the other's tale—
The female of the species is more deadly than the male.
RUDYARD KIPLING, *The Female of the Species*.

And as seen from any angle, 'twas a wisely ordered plan,
For the female of the species is the mother of the man.
LEO J. RABBETTE, *The Female of the Species: A Reply*. One of many replies to Kipling's poem.

18
Oh, the years we waste and the tears we waste

And the work of our head and hand
Belong to the woman who did not know
(And now we know that she never could know)
And did not understand!
RUDYARD KIPLING, *The Vampire.*

Somewhere she waits to make you win, your soul in her firm white hands—
Somewhere the gods have made for you the Woman Who Understands.
EVERARD JACK APPLETON, *The Woman Who Understands.*

1
Nature doth paint them further to be weak, frail, impatient, feeble and foolish; and experience hath declared them to be unconstant, variable, cruel, and lacking the spirit of counsel.
JOHN KNOX, *The First Blast of the Trumpet Against the Monstrous Regiment of Women.*

2
"Now women are troublesome cattle to deal with mostly," said Goggins.
SAMUEL LOVER, *Handy Andy.* Ch. 36.

Lor', but women's rum cattle to deal with,
The first man found that to his cost,
And I reckon it's just through a woman
The last man on earth'll be lost.
G. R. SIMS, *Moll Jarvis o' Morley.*

3
A cunning woman is a knavish fool.
GEORGE LYTTELTON, *Advice to a Lady.*

4
There is more death in women than we think.
JOHN MASEFIELD, *The Widow in the Bye Street.* Pt. ii, l. 171.

5
All women be evils, yet necessary evils.
BRIAN MELBANCKE, *Philotimus.* (1583) A rendering of the Latin proverb, "Malum est Mulier, sed necessarium malum," a translation of the Greek of Menander.

As for the women, though we scorn and flout 'em,
We may live with, but cannot live without 'em.
FREDERIC REYNOLDS, *The Will.* Act i, sc. 1.

See also under CHARACTER.

6
Nothing is worse than a woman, even a good one. (Οὐδὲν γυναικὸς χεῖρον, οὐδὲ τῆς καλῆς.)
MENANDER. (*Greek Anthology.* Bk. xi, epig. 286.)

There are many wild beasts on land and in the sea, but the beastliest of all is woman. (Πολλῶν κατὰ γῆν καὶ κατὰ θάλατταν θηρίων ὄντων, μέγιστόν ἐστι θηρίον γυνή.)
MENANDER, *Upobolimaios.* Frag. 488.

Her dove-like eyes turn'd to coals of fire,
Her beautiful nose to a terrible snout,
Her hands to paws, with nasty great claws,
And her bosom went in and her tail came out.
R. H. BARHAM, *A Lay of St. Nicholas.*

7
O why did God,
Creator wise, that peopl'd highest Heaven
With spirits masculine, create at last
This novelty on earth, this fair defect
Of nature, and not fill the world at once
With men as angels without feminine,
Or find some other way to generate
Mankind? This mischief had not then befall'n.
MILTON, *Paradise Lost.* Bk. x, l. 888.

What mighty ills have not been done by woman!
Who was 't betray'd the Capitol? A woman.
Who lost Mark Antony the world? A woman.
Who was the cause of a long ten years' war,
And laid at last old Troy in ashes? Woman,
Destructive, damnable, deceitful woman!
THOMAS OTWAY, *The Orphan.* Act iii, sc. 1.

Find out some song that describes
Women's hypocrisies, their subtle wiles,
Betraying smiles, feign'd tears, inconstancies;
Their painted outsides, and corrupted minds,
The sum of all their follies, and their falsehoods.
THOMAS OTWAY, *The Orphan.* Act iii, sc. 1.

8
Ah, wasteful woman, she who may
On her sweet self set her own price,
Knowing man cannot choose but pay,
How has she cheapen'd Paradise;
How given for nought her priceless gift,
How spoil'd the bread and spill'd the wine,
Which, spent with due, respective thrift,
Had made brutes men, and men divine.
COVENTRY PATMORE, *The Angel in the House:* Canto iii, *Unthrift.*

9
Every woman is a source of annoyance, but she has two good seasons, the one in her bridal chamber and the other in her grave. (Πᾶσα γυνὴ χόλος ἐστίν· ἔχει δ' ἀγαθὰς δύω ὥρας, τὴν μίαν ἐν θαλάμῳ, τὴν μίαν ἐν θανάτῳ.)
PALLADAS. (*Greek Anthology.* Bk. xi, epig. 381.)

With a wife are two days of pleasure; the first is the joy of the marriage day and night; the second to be at the wife's sepulture.
THOMAS INGELAND, *The Disobedient Child,* 32. (c. 1560)

Although all womankind be nought, yet two good days hath she:
Her marriage day, and day of death, when all she leaves to thee.
TIMOTHY KENDALL, *Flower of Epigrams,* 143.

In every marriage two things are allowed,
A wife in wedding-sheets and in a shroud;
How can a marriage state then be accurst,
Since the last day's as happy as the first?
UNKNOWN, *Agreeable Companion,* 44. (1745)

10
Women are one and all a set of vultures. (Mulier quæ mulier milvinum genus.)
PETRONIUS, *Satyricon.* Sec. 42.

11
Women are worthless wares. (Mala mulier mers est.)
PLAUTUS, *Miles Gloriosus,* l. 894. (Act iii, sc. 3.)

Two women are worse than one. (Mulieres duas pejores esse quam unam.
PLAUTUS, *Curculio,* l. 592. (Act v, sc. 1.) Quoted as a saying from an ancient poet.

He who can avoid women, let him avoid them. (Qui potest mulieres vitare, vitet.)
PLAUTUS, *Stichus*. Act i, sc. 2.

A woman finds it much easier to do ill than well. (Mulieri nimio male facere melius est onus, quam bene.)
PLAUTUS, *Truculentus*. Act ii, sc. 5, l. 17.

1
Give God thy broken heart, He whole will make it:
Give woman thy whole heart, and she will break it.
EDMUND PRESTWICH, *The Broken Heart*.

2
Weal and women cannot pan,
But woe and women can.
JOHN RAY, *English Proverbs*, 355.

3
Amongst women (some will say) there is but two faults, and those are, they can neither do nor say well.
BARNABE RICH, *Faultes*. Fo. 23. (1606)

Men have many faults;
Poor women have but two:
There's nothing good they say,
And nothing right they do.
UNKNOWN, *Women's Faults*.

4
Parasite women.
THEODORE ROOSEVELT, *Metropolitan Magazine*, May, 1916; also *Foes of Our Own Household*.

5
Because of their vices, women have ceased to deserve the privileges of their sex; they have put off their womanly nature and are therefore condemned to suffer the diseases of men.
SENECA, *Epistulæ ad Lucilium*. Epis. xcv, 21.

6
There's no motion
That tends to vice in man, but I affirm
It is the woman's part: be it lying, note it,
The woman's; flattering, hers; deceiving, hers;
Lust and rank thoughts, hers; revenges, hers;
Ambitions, covetings, change of prides, disdain,
Nice longings, slanders, mutability,
All faults that may be named, nay, that hell knows,
Why, hers, in part or all; but rather, all;
For even to vice
They are not constant, but are changing still
One vice, but of a minute old, for one
Not half so old as that.
SHAKESPEARE, *Cymbeline*. Act ii, sc. 5, l. 20.

You jig, you amble, and you lisp, and nickname God's creatures, and make your wantonness your ignorance. Go to, I'll no more on 't; it hath made me mad.
SHAKESPEARE, *Hamlet*. Act iii, sc. 1, l. 151.

So curses all Eve's daughters, of what complexion soever.
SHAKESPEARE, *The Merry Wives of Windsor*. Act iv, sc. 2, l. 24.

7
Beautiful tyrant! fiend angelical!
SHAKESPEARE, *Romeo and Juliet*. Act iii, sc. 2, l. 75.

Her only fault, and that is faults enough,
Is that she is intolerable curst
And shrewd and froward, so beyond all measure
That, were my state far worser than it is,
I would not wed her for a mine of gold.
SHAKESPEARE, *The Taming of the Shrew*. Act i, sc. 2, l. 88.

8
Is folly then so old? Why, let me see,—
About what time of life may folly be?
Oh! she was born, by nicest calculation,
One moment after woman's first creation.
W. R. SPENCER, *Fashionable Friends: Prologue*.

9
The women were proposed to be taxed according to their beauty and skill in dressing, . . . but constancy, charity, good sense, and good nature were not rated, because they would not bear the charge of collecting.
SWIFT, *Gulliver's Travels: Voyage to Laputa*.

10
There are some meannesses which are too mean even for man—woman, lovely woman alone, can venture to commit them.
THACKERAY, *A Shabby Genteel Story*. Ch. 3.

In point of morals the average woman is, even for business, too crooked.
STEPHEN LEACOCK, *The Woman Question*.

11
Regard the society of women as a necessary unpleasantness of social life, and avoid it as much as possible.
LEO TOLSTOY, *Diary*.

A woman without a laugh in her . . . is the greatest bore in existence.
THACKERAY, *Sketches*. Pt. iii.

12
Most women have small waists the world throughout,
But their desires are thousand miles about.
CYRIL TOURNEUR, *The Revengers*. Act v.

13
Woman is man's confusion. (Mulier est hominis confusio.)
VINCENT OF BEAUVAIS, *Speculum Majus*. Sec. 346.

Mulier est hominis confusio;
Madame, the sentence of this Latin is,
Woman is man's joy and all his bliss.
CHAUCER, *The Nonne Preestes Tale*, l. 344. A humorous mistranslation.

14
Forbear to attribute to all women the guilt of a few. Let each be judged on her own merits. (Parcite paucarum diffundere crimen in omnes; Spectetur meritis quæque puella suis.)
OVID, *Ars Amatoria*. Bk. iii, l. 9.

15
I thank God I am not a woman, to be touched

with so many giddy offences as he hath generally taxed their whole sex withal.
SHAKESPEARE, *As You Like It*. Act iii, sc. 2, l. 366.

VIII—Woman: Her Nature

1
Divination seems heightened and raised to its highest power in woman.
AMOS BRONSON ALCOTT, *Concord Days: August.*

But there's wisdom in women, of more than they have known,
And thoughts go blowing through them, are wiser than their own.
RUPERT BROOKE, *There's Wisdom in Women.*

Oh, there are many things that women know,
That no one tells them, no one needs to tell.
ROSELLE MERCIER MONTGOMERY, *Ulysses Returns.*

2
Forgetting is Woman's First and Greatest Art.
RICHARD ALDINGTON, *The Colonel's Daughter*, p. 138.

3
With women the heart argues, not the mind.
MATTHEW ARNOLD, *Merope*, l. 341.

Ay, me, how weak a thing
The heart of woman is!
SHAKESPEARE, *Julius Cæsar*. Act ii, sc. 4, l. 39.

4
Poets, beware! never compare
Women to aught in earth or in air.
THOMAS HAYNES BAYLY, *Song.*

5
Yet when I hold her best, she's but a woman,
As full of frailty as of faith; a poor slight woman,
And her best thoughts but weak fortifications.
BEAUMONT AND FLETCHER, *The Little French Lawyer*. Act ii, sc. 2.

With my frailty don't upbraid me,
I am woman as you made me;
Causeless doubting or despairing,
Rashly trusting, idly fearing.
If obtaining, Still complaining;
If consenting, Still repenting.
WILLIAM CONGREVE, *Semele to Jupiter.*

Women are never stronger than when they arm themselves with their weaknesses.
MADAME DU DEFFAND, *Letter to Voltaire.*

6
Women have no wilderness in them,
They are provident instead,
Content in the tight hot cell of their hearts
To eat dusty bread.
LOUISE BOGAN, *Women.*

7
Most illogical
Irrational nature of our womanhood,
That blushes one way, feels another way,
And prays, perhaps, another!
E. B. BROWNING, *Aurora Leigh*. Bk ii, l. 701.

We're all so,—made so—'tis our woman's trade
To suffer torment for another's ease.
E. B. BROWNING, *Aurora Leigh*. Bk. vii, l. 222.

8
The souls of women are so small,
That some believe they've none at all;
Or if they have, like cripples, still
They've but one faculty, the will.
SAMUEL BUTLER, *Miscellaneous Thoughts*, l. 386.

Women have no souls, this saying is not new.
LEWIS WAGER, *Repentance of Marie Magdalene.* (1566)

9
Woman is made of glass. (Es de vidrio la mujer.)
CERVANTES, *Don Quixote*. Pt. i, ch. 33.

10
Women of kind desiren liberty,
And not to be constrained as in a thrall.
CHAUCER, *The Frankeleyns Tale*, l. 40.

There are only three things in the world that women do not understand: and they are Liberty, Equality and Fraternity.
G. K. CHESTERTON, *On Women.*

11
O silly woman, full of innocence,
Full of pity, of truth, and conscience,
What maketh you to men to trusten so?
CHAUCER, *Legend of Good Women: Dido*, l. 331.

Women do not look so closely. They are easily caught by a birdlime of words.
ALPHONSE DAUDET, *The Credo of Love.*

A woman, no less than the populace, a grave judge or a chosen senate, will surrender, defeated, to eloquence. (Quam populus judexque gravis lectusque senatus, Tam dabit eloquio victa puella manus.)
OVID, *Ars Amatoria*. Bk. i, l. 461.

Nor was it hard to move the lady's mind;
When fortune favours, still the fair are kind.
POPE, *January and May*, l. 303.

With the easy credulity of women. (Facili fæminarum credulitate.)
TACITUS, *Annales*. Bk. xiv, sec. 4.

What cannot a neat knave with a smooth tale
Make a woman believe?
JOHN WEBSTER, *The Duchess of Malfi*. Act i, sc. 2.

12
A woman who is confuted is never convinced.
CHURTON COLLINS, *Aphorisms.*

Women have always some mental reservation. (Les femmes ont toujours quelque arrière-pensée.)
DESTOUCHES, *Le Dissipateur*. Act v, sc. 9.

13
You are a woman, you must never speak what you think; your words must contradict your thoughts, but your actions may contradict your words.
CONGREVE, *Love for Love*. Act ii, sc. 11.

She's all sail and no ballast. . . . A fine lady is

angry without a cause, and pleased without reason.

FARQUHAR, *Sir Harry Wildair*. Act i, sc. 1.

She will play with reason and discourse,
And well she can persuade.

SHAKESPEARE, *Measure for Measure*. Act i, sc. 2, l. 190.

1
Glory and empire are to female blood
More tempting dangerous rivals than a god.

JOHN CROWNE, *The Destruction of Jerusalem*. Pt. i, act iii, sc. 2.

2
What soft, cherubic creatures
These gentlewomen are!
One would as soon assault a plush
Or violate a star.
Such dimity convictions.

EMILY DICKINSON, *Poems*. Pt. i, No. 130.

3
Women are not compris'd in our laws of friendship; they are feræ naturæ.

DRYDEN, *The Mock Astrologer*. Act iv. Feræ naturæ, the legal term for animals living in a wild state.

4
A woman's hopes are woven of sunbeams; a shadow annihilates them.

GEORGE ELIOT, *Felix Holt*. Ch. 1.

5
You will find many excuses, for you are a woman. (Πολλὰς ἂν εὕροις μηχανάς· γυνὴ γὰρ εἶ.)

EURIPIDES, *Andromache*, l. 85.

What could a woman's head contrive
Which it would not know how to excuse?
(Was hätt ein Weiberkopf erdacht, das er
Nicht zu beschönen wüsste?)

LESSING, *Nathan der Weise*. Pt. iii.

Women are never without an excuse.

GEORGE PETTIE, *Pallace*, ii, 157. (1576)

6
'Tis woman's nature to bear her ills on lip and tongue with mournful pleasure.

EURIPIDES, *Andromache*, l. 94.

Those women who grieve least make the most lamentation. (Jactantius mœrent, quæ minus dolent.)

TACITUS, *Annales*. Bk. ii, sec. 77.

But woman's grief is like a summer storm,
Short as it violent is.

JOANNA BAILLIE, *Basil*. Act v, sc. 3.

7
Pride is the life of a woman, and flattery is our daily bread.

FARQUHAR, *The Beaux' Stratagem*. Act iv, sc. 2.

What woman can resist the force of praise?

JOHN GAY, *Trivia*. Bk. i, l. 260.

What female heart can gold despise?
What cat's averse to fish?

THOMAS GRAY, *On the Death of a Favourite Cat*.

A woman's mind is affected by the meanest gifts. (Parvis mobilis rebus animus muliebris.)

LIVY, *Annales*. Bk. vi, sec. 34.

Fond of dress and change and praise,
So mere a woman in her ways.

D. G. ROSSETTI, *Jenny*.

How easy is it for the proper-false
In women's waxen hearts to set their forms!

SHAKESPEARE, *Twelfth Night*. Act ii, sc. 2, l. 30.

8
With women one should never venture to joke. (Mit Frauen soll man sich nie unterstehn zu scherzen.)

GOETHE, *Faust*. The advice of Mephistopheles.

9
Women forgive injuries, but never forget slights.

T. C. HALIBURTON (SAM SLICK), *The Old Judge*. Ch. 15.

10
No fault in woman to make show
Of largeness, when they're nothing so;
When true it is, the outside swells
With inward buckram, little else.

ROBERT HERRICK, *No Fault in Women*.

11
Nothing agreeth worse
Than a lady's heart and a beggar's purse.

JOHN HEYWOOD, *Proverbs*. Pt. i, ch. 10.

12
A woman dares all things when she loves or hates. (Audax est ad omnia, quæ amat vel odit, femina.)

ST. JEROME, *Epistles: Valerius to Rufinus*. Considered spurious.

When greater perils men environ,
Then women show a front of iron;
And, gentle in their manner, they
Do bold things in a quiet way.

THOMAS DUNN ENGLISH, *Betty Zane*.

When danger comes in an honorable way, a woman's heart grows chill with fear; but if she is doing a bold bad thing her courage never fails.

JUVENAL, *Satires*. Sat. vi, l. 94.

What wilt not woman, gentle woman, dare
When strong affection stirs her spirit up?

ROBERT SOUTHEY, *Madoc*. Pt. ii, canto 2, l. 125.

13
Women commonly eat more sparingly, and are less curious in their choice of meat; but if once you find a woman gluttonous, expect from her very little virtue.

SAMUEL JOHNSON, *Letters*. Vol. ii, p. 323.

14
She knifed me one night 'cause I wished she
was white,
And I learned about women from 'er!

RUDYARD KIPLING, *The Ladies*.

15
There is a false modesty which is vanity; a false glory which is levity; a false grandeur which is meanness; a false virtue which is hypocrisy; and a false wisdom which is prudery.

LA BRUYÈRE, *Les Caractères: Des Femmes*.

16
As soon as a woman begins to be ashamed of what she ought not, she will not be ashamed

of what she should. (Næ simul pudere quod non oportet cœperit; quod oportet non pudebit.)
LIVY, *Annals*. Bk. xxxiv, sec. 4.

1
The life of woman is full of woe,
Toiling on and on and on,
With breaking heart, and tearful eyes,
And silent lips, and in the soul
The secret longings that arise,
Which this world never satisfies!
Some more, some less, but of the whole
Not one quite happy, no, not one!
LONGFELLOW, *The Golden Legend*. Pt. ii.

2
All women are ambitious naturally.
MARLOWE, *Hero and Leander*. Sestiad i, l. 428.

3
Feminine policy has a mysterious method; it is better to leave it to them. (La police feminine a un train mysterieux; il faut le leur quitter.)
MONTAIGNE, *Essays*. Bk. iii, ch. 5.

4
A woman with a passion for buying. (Ad dominam . . . emacem.)
OVID, *Ars Amatoria*. Bk. i, l. 421.

And life made wretched out of human ken,
And miles of shopping women served by men.
JOHN MASEFIELD, *Biography*. St. 7.

5
However ugly she may be, every woman is pleased with her own looks. (Pessima sit, nulli non sua forma placet.)
OVID, *Ars Amatoria*. Bk. i, l. 614.

Haughtiness is natural in the fair, and pride waits on beauty. (Fastus inest pulchris, sequiturque superbia formam.)
OVID, *Fasti*. Bk. i, l. 419.

As is the body, so is the soul of tender women frail. (Ut corpus, teneris ita mens infirma puellis.)
OVID, *Heroides*. Epis. xix, l. 7.

6
Regret is a woman's natural food—she thrives upon it.
A. W. PINERO, *Sweet Lavender*. Act iii.

7
Woman indeed was born of delay itself. (Mulier profecto nata est ex ipsa mora.)
PLAUTUS, *Miles Gloriosus*, l. 1292. (Act iv, sc. 7.)

Women have many faults, but the worst of them all is that they are too pleased with themselves and take too little pains to please the men. (Multa mulierum sunt vitia, sed hoc e multis maxumumst, Quom sibi nimis placent minusque addunt operam, uti placeant viris.)
PLAUTUS, *Pœnulus*, l. 1203. (Act v, sc. 4.)

8
Nothing so true as what you once let fall,
"Most women have no characters at all,"
Matter too soft a lasting mark to bear,
And best distinguish'd by black, brown, or fair.
POPE, *Moral Essays*. Epis. ii, l. 1.

In men, we various ruling passions find;
In women two almost divide the kind;
Those only fix'd, they first or last obey,
The love of pleasure, and the love of sway.
POPE, *Moral Essays*. Epis. ii, l. 207.

Pleasures the sex, as children birds, pursue,
Still out of reach, yet never out of view.
POPE, *Moral Essays*. Epis. ii, l. 231.

Heav'n gave to woman the peculiar grace
To spin, to weep, and cully human race.
POPE, *The Wife of Bath's Prologue*, l. 160.

9
A woman who meditates alone meditates evil. (Mulier cum sola cogitat, male cogitat.)
PUBLILIUS SYRUS, *Sententiæ*. No. 369.

10
Such, Polly, are your sex—part truth, part fiction;
Some thought, much whim, and all a contradiction.
RICHARD SAVAGE, *To a Young Lady*.

11
If ladies be but young and fair,
They have the gift to know it.
SHAKESPEARE, *As You Like It*. Act ii, sc. 7, l. 37.

'Tis beauty that doth oft make women proud; . . .
'Tis virtue that doth make them most admired; . . .
'Tis government that makes them seem divine.
SHAKESPEARE, *III Henry VI*. Act i, sc. 4, l. 128.

There was never yet fair woman but she made mouths in a glass.
SHAKESPEARE, *King Lear*. Act iii, sc. 2, l. 35.

Complacencies of the peignoir, and late
Coffee and oranges in a sunny chair.
WALLACE STEVENS, *Sunday Morning*.

12
A woman moved is like a fountain troubled,
Muddy, ill-seeming, thick, bereft of beauty;
And while it is so, none so dry or thirsty
Will deign to sip or touch one drop of it.
SHAKESPEARE, *The Taming of the Shrew*. Act v, sc. 2, l. 142.

Why are our bodies soft and weak and smooth,
Unapt to toil and trouble in the world,
But that our soft conditions and our hearts
Should well agree with our external parts?
SHAKESPEARE, *The Taming of the Shrew*. Act v, sc. 2, l. 165.

For women are as roses, whose fair flower
Being once display'd, doth fall that very hour.
SHAKESPEARE, *Twelfth Night*. Act ii, sc. 4, l. 39.

13
In the beginning, said a Persian poet—Allah took a rose, a lily, a dove, a serpent, a little honey, a Dead Sea apple, and a handful of clay. When he looked at the amalgam—it was a woman.
WILLIAM SHARP. (*Portfolio*, July, 1894, p. 6.)

1 No woman will deny herself the romantic luxury of self-sacrifice and forgiveness when they take the form of doing something agreeable.

BERNARD SHAW, *Fanny's First Play*. Act iii.

2 For a woman glory can only be a splendid mourning for lost happiness. (La gloire ne saurait être pour une femme qu'un deuil éclatant du bonheur.)

MADAME DE STAËL, *Pensées Détachées*.

3 How foolish and miserably superstitious all we women are! (Ut stultæ et misere omnes sumus Religiosæ!)

TERENCE, *Heauton Timorumenos*, l. 649. (Act iv, sc. 1.)

4 I have to thank God I'm a woman,
For in these ordered days a woman only
Is free to be very hungry, very lonely.

ANNA WICKHAM, *The Affinity*.

Love and grief and motherhood,
Fame and mirth and scorn—
These are all shall befall
Any woman born.

MARGARET WIDDEMER, *A Cyprian Woman*.

I was, being human, born alone;
I am, being woman, hard beset;
I live by squeezing from a stone
The only nourishment I get.

ELINOR WYLIE, *Let No Charitable Hope*.

5 Often change doth please a woman's mind.

SIR THOMAS WYATT, *The Deserted Lover*.

6 Whate'er she is, she 'll not appear a saint.

YOUNG, *Love of Fame*. Sat. vi, l. 72.

IX—Woman: Her Mind

See also Wife: Her Choice

7 Spell well, if you can.

COUNTESS DOWAGER OF CARLISLE, *Thoughts*, p. 116.

But 'twill appear, in spite of all enditing,
A woman's way to charm is not by writing.

ANNE FINCH, COUNTESS OF WINCHILSEA, *Aristomenes: Prologue*, l. 31.

Cécile: Do you think it wrong for a girl to know Latin?
Pierre: Not if she can cook a hare or a partridge as well as Mademoiselle Auclaire! She may read all the Latin she pleases.

WILLA CATHER, *Shadows on the Rock*.

8 Women, in my observation, have little or no difference in them, but as they are or are not distinguished by education.

DANIEL DEFOE, *The History of Projects: Of Academies*.

9 A wise woman is twice a fool.

ERASMUS, *Colloquies*.

When an ass climbeth a ladder you may find wisdom in women.

THOMAS FULLER, *Gnomologia*. No. 5546.

10 I hate a learned woman. May there never be in my abode a woman knowing more than a woman ought to know. (Σοφὴν δὲ μισῶ. Μὴ γὰρ ἔν γ'ἐμοῖς δόμοις Εἴη φρονοῦσα πλεῖον ἢ γυναῖκα χρή.)

EURIPIDES, *Hippolytus*, l. 640.

I hate a woman who is forever poring over the *Grammar* of Palæmon, who observes all the rules and laws of language, who quotes from ancient poets that I never heard of, and corrects her unlettered friends for slips of speech that no man need trouble about: let husbands at least be permitted to make slips in grammar!

JUVENAL, *Satires*. Sat. vi, l. 451.

Men hate learned women.

TENNYSON, *The Princess*. Pt. ii, l. 442.

'Tis pity learned virgins ever wed.

BYRON, *Don Juan*. Canto i, st. 22.

11 The brain-women never interest us like the heart-women; white roses please less than red.

O. W. HOLMES, *The Professor at the Breakfast-Table*. Ch. 6.

12 He who teaches a woman letters feeds more poison to a frightful asp. (Γυναῖχ' ὁ διδάσκων γράμματ' ἀσπίδι δὲ φοβερᾷ προσποτίζει φάρμακον.)

MENANDER, *Fragments*. No. 702.

13 When you educate a man you educate an individual; when you educate a woman you educate a whole family.

DR. CHARLES D. MCIVER, *Address*, North Carolina College for Women.

14 She can be as wise as we,
And wiser when she wishes.

GEORGE MEREDITH, *Marian*. St. 1.

15 A witty woman is a treasure; a witty beauty is a power.

GEORGE MEREDITH, *Diana of the Crossways*.

I know a thing that 's most uncommon;
(Envy, be silent and attend!)
I know a reasonable woman,
Handsome and witty, yet a friend.

POPE, *On a Certain Lady at Court*.

Make the door upon a woman's wit, and it will out at the casement.

SHAKESPEARE, *As You Like It*. Act iv, sc. 1, l. 162.

16 A learned woman is not of much account in the world. A clever woman rules as much of it as lies in her neighbourhood—that is tc say, as much as she cares to rule.

H. S. MERRIMAN, *The Sowers*. Ch. 7.

17 I'd as lief your little head
Should be cumbered up with lead

As with learning, live or dead,
Or with brains.
RICHARD MONCKTON MILNES, *To Doris.*

1
If a young lady has that discretion and modesty, without which all knowledge is little worth, she will never make an ostentatious parade of it, because she will rather be intent on acquiring more, than on displaying what she has.
HANNAH MORE, *Thoughts on Conversation.*

2
So I wonder a woman, the Mistress of Hearts,
Should descend to aspire to be Master of Arts;
A Ministering Angel in woman we see,
And an angel need covet no other Degree.
CHARLES NEAVES, *O Why Should a Woman Not Get a Degree?*

3
Be to her virtues very kind;
Be to her faults a little blind;
Let all her ways be unconfin'd;
And clap your padlock—on her mind.
MATTHEW PRIOR, *An English Padlock*, l. 78. (c. 1700) Quoted by Bickerstaffe, *The Padlock*. Act ii, sc. 3.

4
A blue-stocking is the scourge of her husband, children, friends, servants, and every one. (Une femme bel-esprit est le fléau de son mari, de ses enfants, de ses amis, de ses valets, de tout le monde.)
ROUSSEAU, *Émile*. Bk. i, ch. 5.

Every blue-stocking will remain a spinster as long as there are sensible men on the earth. (Toute fille lettrée restera fille toute sa vie, quand il n'y aura que des hommes sensés sur la terre.)
ROUSSEAU, *Émile*. Bk. i, ch. 5.

I always thought a tinge of blue
Improved a charming woman's stocking.
R. M. MILNES, *Four Lovers*. Pt. ii.

5
She was a woman of no mean endowments: she could write verses, bandy jests, and use language which was modest, or tender, or wanton; in fine, she was possessed of a high degree of wit and charm.
SALLUST, *Catiline*. Ch. 25. Of Sempronia.

A woman of charm is as rare as a man of genius.
SALVADOR DE MADARIAGA, *Americans Are Boys.*

6
Seek me a woman that hath a familiar spirit.
Old Testament: I Samuel, xxviii, 7.

7
Most learned of the fair, most fair of the learned.
JACOPO SANNAZARO, *Inscription to Cassandra Marchesia*, in an edition of the latter's poems. (GRESWELL, *Memoirs of Politian.*)

8
Women have great talent, but no genius, for they always remain subjective.
SCHOPENHAUER, *The World as Will and Idea.*

9
If her breath were as terrible as her terminations, there were no living near her; she would infect to the north star.
SHAKESPEARE, *Much Ado About Nothing*. Act ii, sc. 1, l. 256.

For there be women, fair as she,
Whose verbs and nouns do more agree.
BRET HARTE, *Mrs. Judge Jenkins.*

10
Men call you fair, and you do credit it,
For that yourself ye daily such do see:
But the true fair, that is the gentle wit
And virtuous mind, is much more praised of me.
EDMUND SPENSER, *Amoretti*. Sonnet lxxix.

11
Enthusiasm about art is become a function of the average female being, which she performs with precision and a sort of haunting sprightliness.
R. L. STEVENSON, *Virginibus Puerisque*. Ch. 1.

12
She look'd as grand as doomsday and as grave!
TENNYSON, *The Princess*. Pt. i, l. 185.

For she was crammed with theories out of books.
TENNYSON, *The Princess: Conclusion*, l. 35.

13
In the East, women religiously conceal that they have faces; in the West, that they have legs. In both cases they make it evident that they have but little brains.
H. D. THOREAU, *Journal*, 31 Jan., 1852.

14
Very learned women are to be found, in the same manner as female warriors; but they are seldom or never inventors.
VOLTAIRE, *Philosophical Dictionary: Women.*

We issued gorged with knowledge, and I spoke:
"Why, sirs, they do all this as well as we."
"They hunt old trails," said Cyril, "very well;
But when did woman ever yet invent?"
TENNYSON, *The Princess*. Pt. ii, l. 366.

15
There is nothing in the whole world so unbecoming to a woman as a nonconformist conscience.
OSCAR WILDE, *Lady Windermere's Fan*. Act ii.

16
Ladies supreme among amusements reign;
By nature born to soothe, and entertain.
Their prudence in a share of folly lies:
Why will they be so weak, as to be wise?
YOUNG, *Love of Fame*. Satire vi, l. 190.

X—Woman: Her Power

17
Let men say whate'er they will
Woman, woman, rules them still.
ISAAC BICKERSTAFFE, *The Sultan*. Act ii, sc. 1.

As Father Adam first was fool'd,
A case that's still too common,
Here lies a man a woman rul'd:

The Devil ruled the woman.
ROBERT BURNS, *Epitaph on a Hen-Pecked Country Squire.*

Disguise our bondage as we will,
'Tis woman, woman rules us still.
THOMAS MOORE, *Sovereign Woman.*

Beshrew my heart, but it is wond'rous strange;
Sure there is something more than witchcraft in them,
That masters ev'n the wisest of us all.
NICHOLAS ROWE, *Jane Shore.* Act iv, sc. 1.

Why, this it is, when men are ruled by women.
SHAKESPEARE, *Richard III.* Act i, sc. 1, l. 62.

1
Women wear the breeches.
ROBERT BURTON, *Anatomy of Melancholy: Democritus to the Reader. See also under* WIFE: BREECHES AND CROWING HEN.

2
Women, you know, do seldom fail
To make the stoutest men turn tail.
BUTLER, *Hudibras.* Pt. iii, canto 1, l. 1081.

3
She was his life,
The ocean to the river of his thoughts,
Which terminated all.
BYRON, *The Dream,* l. 56.

And, like a lily on a river floating,
She floats upon the river of his thoughts!
LONGFELLOW, *Spanish Student.* Act ii, sc. 3.

River of his thought.
DANTE, *Purgatorio.* Canto xiii, l. 88.

4
Whoe'er she be,
That not impossible She,
That shall command my heart and me.
RICHARD CRASHAW, *Wishes to His (Supposed) Mistress.*

5
What all your sex desire is Sovereignty.
DRYDEN, *Wife of Bath's Tale,* l. 279.

6
Our sex still strikes an awe upon the brave,
And only cowards dare affront a woman.
FARQUHAR, *The Constant Couple.* Act v, sc. 1.

7
A noble man is led far by woman's gentle words. (Ein edler Mann wird durch ein gutes Wort Der Frauen weit geführt.)
GOETHE, *Iphigenia auf Tauris.* Act i, sc. 2, l. 162.

God in his harmony has equal ends
For cedar that resists and reed that bends;
For good it is a woman sometimes rules.
VICTOR HUGO, *Eviradnus.* Pt. v.

8
Nature has given women so much power that the law has very wisely given them little.
SAMUEL JOHNSON, *Letters.* Vol. i, p. 104.

9
For them the Ceylon diver held his breath,
And went all naked to the hungry shark;
For them his ears gush'd blood; for them in death,
The seal on the cold ice with piteous bark
Lay full of darts; for them alone did seethe
A thousand men in troubles wide and dark.
KEATS, *Isabella.* St. 15.

10
Never any good came out of female domination. God created Adam master and lord of living creatures, but Eve spoiled all.
MARTIN LUTHER, *Table-Talk.* No. 727.

11
Better the devil's than a woman's slave.
MASSINGER, *Parliament of Love.* Act ii, sc. 2.

12
She can flourish staff or pen,
And deal a wound that lingers;
She can talk the talk of men,
And touch with thrilling fingers.
GEORGE MEREDITH, *Marian.* St. 1.

13
My only books Were woman's looks,
And folly's all they've taught me.
THOMAS MOORE, *The Time I've Lost in Wooing.*

The virtue of her lively looks
Excels the precious stone;
I wish to have none other books
To read or look upon.
UNKNOWN. (*Songs and Sonnets.* 1557.)

14
When loving woman wants her way,
God hesitates to say her nay.
ARTHUR WILLIAM RYDER, *When Woman Wills.*

15
They would have all men bound and thrall
To them, and they for to be free.
ALEXANDER SCOTT, *Of Womankind.*

16
Her sighs will make a battery in his breast;
Her tears will pierce into a marble heart;
The tiger will be mild whiles she doth mourn;
And Nero will be tainted with remorse,
To hear and see her plaints.
SHAKESPEARE, *III Henry VI.* Act iii, sc. 1, l. 37.

He will not manage her, although he mount her.
SHAKESPEARE, *Venus and Adonis,* l. 598.

17
Woman reduces us all to the common denominator.
BERNARD SHAW, *Great Catherine.* Sc. 1.

18
"One moral's plain," cried I, "without more fuss;
Man's social happiness all rests on us:
Through all the drama—whether damn'd or not—
Love gilds the scene, and women guide the plot."
SHERIDAN, *The Rivals: Epilogue.*

19
It is said of the horses in the vision, that "their power was in their mouths and in their tails." What is said of horses in the vision, in reality may be said of women.
SWIFT, *Thoughts on Various Subjects.*

1
Let our weakness be what it will, mankind will still be weaker; and whilst there is a world, 'tis woman that will govern it.
VANBRUGH, *The Provok'd Wife*. Act iii, sc. 3.

Ladies whose smile embroiled the world.
WILLIAM WATSON, *Father of the Forest*, i, 5.

2
The history of women is the history of the worst form of tyranny the world has ever known. The tyranny of the weak over the strong. It is the only tyranny that lasts.
OSCAR WILDE, *Woman of No Importance*, iii.

XI—Woman: Her Advice

3
Woman's counsel is either too dear or too cheap. (Consilium feminile nimis carum aut nimis vile.)
ALBERTANO OF BRESCIA, *Liber Consolationis*. Cited as a common saying.

The counselling of women is either too dear, or else too little of price.
CHAUCER, *Tale of Melibeus*. Sec. 15, l. 2285.

4
Ah! gentle dames, it gars me greet,
To think how monie counsels sweet,
How monie lengthen'd, sage advices,
The husband frae the wife despises!
BURNS, *Tam o' Shanter*, l. 33.

5
The best counsel is that of woman. (El primer consejo Ha de ser de la muger.)
CALDERON, *El Médico de su Honra*. Act i, sc. 2.

She generally gave herself very good advice (though she very seldom followed it).
CARROLL, *Alice's Adventures in Wonderland*, 1.

6
A woman's advice has little value, but he who won't take it is a fool.
CERVANTES, *Don Quixote*. Pt. ii, ch. 7.

7
Let no man value at a little price
A virtuous woman's counsel; her wing'd spirit
Is feather'd oftentimes with heavenly words.
CHAPMAN, *The Gentleman Usher*. Act iv, sc. 1.

8
Woman been wise in short avysement.
CHAUCER, *Troilus and Criseyde*. Bk. iv, l. 936.

9
For women, with a mischief to their kind,
Pervert, with bad advice, our better mind.
DRYDEN, *The Cock and the Fox*, l. 555.

A woman's counsel brought us first to woe,
And made her man his paradise forego,
Where at heart's ease he liv'd; and might have been
As free from sorrow as he was from sin.
DRYDEN, *The Cock and the Fox*, l. 557.

10
Take the first advice of a woman and not the second. (Primo dede mulieris consilio, secundo noli.)
GILBERTUS NOXERANUS. (GRYNÆUS, *Adagia*, p. 130.)

Take the first advice of a woman, and not the second (Prends le premier conseil d'une femme, et non le second), for in processes of reasoning, out of which the second counsels spring, women may and will be inferior to us.
RICHARD CHEVENIX TRENCH, *Proverbs and Their Lessons*, iv, 89.

11
Would men but follow what the sex advise,
All things would prosper, all the world grow wise.
POPE, *January and May*, l. 67.

12
Women beat men in evil counsel. (Malo in consilio feminæ vincunt viros.)
PUBLILIUS SYRUS, *Sententiæ*. No. 358.

13
Woman's counsel is fatal counsel.
UNKNOWN, *Proverbs of Alfred*, l. 375 (c. 1250)

Woman's counsel is full often fatal.
CHAUCER, *Nonne Preestes Tale*, l. 436.

Yet a woman's advice helps at the last.
UNKNOWN. (*Towneley Plays*. No. xiii, 342. 1388.)

XII—Woman: Her Falseness

14
More false than fair.
ARIOSTO, *Orlando Furioso*. Canto vi, st. 14.

Unchaste and false as ever water went.
ARIOSTO, *Orlando Furioso*, xvi, 14. (Harington, tr.)

She was false as water.
SHAKESPEARE, *Othello*, v, 2, 134. (1604)

As false as fair.
JOHN HEYWOOD, *Proverbs*. Pt. ii, ch. 9. (1546)

As false as hell.
THOMAS D'URFEY, *Virtuous Wife*. Act iv, sc. 3. (1680)

As false as the devil.
JOHN CLARKE, *Parœmiologia*, 139. (1639)

15
Woman's love is writ in water!
Woman's faith is traced on sand!
W. E. AYTOUN, *Charles Edward at Versailles*, l. 201.

This record will for ever stand,
"Woman, thy vows are traced in sand."
BYRON, *To Woman*, l. 21.

Woman's faith, and woman's trust—
Write the characters in dust.
SCOTT, *The Betrothed*. Ch. 20.

16
But when I trust a wild fool, and a woman,
May I lend gratis, and build hospitals.
BEAUMONT AND FLETCHER, *Scornful Lady*, iii.

Trust a woman?
I'll trust the devil first; for he dare be
Better than 's word sometime.
JOHN FLETCHER, *The Chances*. Act ii, sc. 1.

A woman's oaths are wafers, break with making.
JOHN FLETCHER, *The Chances*. Act ii, sc. 1.

17
Believe a woman or an epitaph.

Or any other thing that's false.
BYRON, *English Bards and Scotch Reviewers*, l. 78.

1
Women I know are dressed in rags,
Women I know in lace,
And one in a dusky robe of gold
With a hooded cloak of mace;
But every robe and every rag
Is a secret hiding place.
ESTHER LILIAN DUFF, *Not Three—But One.*

2
A woman-friend! He that believes that weakness
Steers in a stormy night without a compass.
JOHN FLETCHER, *Women Pleased.* Act ii, sc. 1.

Who to a woman trusts his peace of mind,
Trusts a frail bark, with a tempestuous wind.
GEORGE GRANVILLE, *The British Enchanters.* Act ii, sc. 1.

Who trusts himself to women, or to waves,
Should never hazard what he fears to lose.
JOHN OLDMIXON, *Governor of Cyprus.*

3
Her promise of friendship for any avail
Is as sure to hold as an eel by the tail.
JOHN HEYWOOD, *Proverbs.* Pt. i, ch. 10.

He that hath a woman hath an eel by the tail.
BEAUMONT AND FLETCHER, *Scornful Lady.* Act ii, sc. 1.

A woman and a wet eel both have slippery tails.
JAMES SHIRLEY, *Arcadia.* Act v, sc. 1.

4
As false
As air, as water, wind, or sandy earth,
As fox to lamb, as wolf to heifer's calf,
Pard to the hind, or stepdame to her son;
Yea, let them say, to stick the heart of falsehood,
As false as Cressid.
SHAKESPEARE, *Troilus and Cressida.* Act iii, sc. 2, l. 198.

5
Women have tongues of craft, and hearts of guile,
They will, they will not; fools that on them trust;
For in their speech is death, hell in their smile.
(Femina è cosa garrula e fallace:
Vuole e disvuole, è folle uom chi sen fida,
Sí tra sé volge.)
TASSO, *Jerusalem Delivered.* Canto xix, st. 84.

6
Commit thy ship unto the wind,
But not to faith of womankind;
For there's more credit in a wave
Than any faith that women have.
UNKNOWN, *Woman's Unfaith.* (c. 1693)

7
False, but, however false, beloved still. (Perfida, sed. quamvis perfida, cara tamen.)
TIBULLUS, *Odes.* Bk. iii, ode 6, l. 56.

XIII—Woman: Her Fickleness and Inconstancy

See also Coquetry

8
Thy favours are but like the wind,
That kisseth everything it meets.
SIR ROBERT AYTON, *I Do Confess.*

Thy favours are the silly wind,
That kisses ilka thing it meets.
BURNS, *I Do Confess Thou Art Sae Fair.* A paraphrase of Ayton.

9
She's as inconstant as the seas and winds,
Which ne'er are calm but to betray adventurers.
APHRA BEHN, *The Forced Marriage.* Act i, sc. 1.

10
Their tricks an' craft hae put me daft,
They've ta'en me in, and a' that;
But clear your decks, an' Here's the sex!
I like the jads for a' that.
BURNS, *The Jolly Beggars.* Air vii.

An' fareweel, dear, deluding Woman,
The joy of joys!
BURNS, *Epistle to James Smith.* St. 14.

O thou delicious, damned, dear, destructive woman!
CONGREVE, *The Old Batchelor.* Act iii, sc. 2.

11
The fault was Nature's fault, not thine,
Which made thee fickle as thou art.
BYRON, *To a Youthful Friend,* l. 15.

12
And every century
Spawn divers queens who die with Antony
But live a great while first with Julius.
JAMES BRANCH CABELL, *Retractions.*

13
Lo, which sleights and subtleties
In women been!
CHAUCER, *The Marchantes Tale: Epilogue,* l. 3.

The wiles and guiles that women work,
Dissembled with an outward show,
The tricks and toys that in them lurk,
The cock that treads them shall not know.
SHAKESPEARE [?], *The Passionate Pilgrim,* l. 335.

14
Dust is lighter than a feather,
And the wind more light than either:
But a woman's fickle mind
More than feather, dust, or wind.
(Quid pluma levius?—Pulvis. Quid pulvere? Ventus.
Quid vento? Mulier. Quid muliere? Nihil.)
WALTER DAVISON, *Poetical Rhapsody.* (1602) Davison quotes the Latin as *Incerti Auctoris.*

What is lighter than the wind? a feather.
What is lighter than a feather? fire.
What lighter than fire? a woman.
What lighter than a woman? Nothing.
(Vente quid levius? fulgur. Quid fulgure? flamma.
Flamma quid? mulier. Quid mulier? nihil.)
UNKNOWN. (*Harleian MS.* Fo. 47, No. 3362.)

Pray, what is lighter than a feather?

Dust, my friend, in summer weather.
What 's lighter than the dust, I pray?
The wind that blows them both away.
What is lighter than the wind?
The lightness of a woman's mind.
And what is lighter than the last?
Ah, now, my friend, you have me fast!
UNKNOWN. (*Notes and Queries,* 11 Aug., 1866.)

A woman often is but a feather in the wind. (Une femme souvent N'est qu'une plume au vent.)
VICTOR HUGO, *Le Roi S'Amuse.* Act iv, sc. 2. (1832)

Woman is as fickle as a feather in the wind. (La donna è mobile Qual piuma al vento.)
F. M. PIAVE. (VERDI, *Rigoletto.*) Piave wrote the libretto. (1851)

1
Woman often changes; foolish the man who trusts her. (Souvent femme varie; Bien fol est qui s'y fie.)
FRANÇOIS I OF FRANCE. Written by him with his ring on a window of the château of Chambord. Sometimes quoted, "Tout femme varie." (THÉOPHILE, *Essai sur Divers Arts;* BRANTÔME, *Œuvres,* vii, 395.)

2
He ploughs in sand, and sows against the wind,
That hopes for constant love of woman kind.
THOMAS FULLER, *Medicina Gymnastica.* Vol. x, p. 7.

He ploughs the waves, and sows the sand,
And seeks to gather the wind in a net,
Whose hopes on the heart of a woman are set.
(Ne l'onde solca, e ne l'arena semina,
E'l vago vento spera in rete accogliere
Chi sue speranze fonda in cor di femina.)
JACOPO SANNAZARO, *Ecloga Octava.*

He waters, plows, and soweth in the sand,
And hopes the flick'ring wind with net to hold,
Who hath his hopes laid upon woman's hand.
SIR PHILIP SIDNEY, *Arcadia.* Bk. ii.

See also under FUTILITY.

3
Whimsey, not reason, is the female guide.
GEORGE GRANVILLE, *The Vision,* l. 81.

Women, giddy women!
In her the blemish of your sex you prove,
There is no reason for your hate or love.
MASSINGER, *A Very Woman.* Act v, sc. 2.

4
What is there in this vile earth that more commendeth a woman than constancy?
JOHN LYLY, *Euphues and His England.*

5
There is no accounting for the actions of a woman.
NAPOLEON I. (O'MEARA, *Napoleon in Exile.*)

6
How many pictures of one nymph we view,
And how unlike each other, all how true!
Arcadia's countess here, in ermined pride,
Is there, Pastora by a fountain side:
Here Fannia, leering on her own good man,
And there a naked Leda with a swan. . . .
Whether the charmer sinner it, or saint it,
If folly grow romantic, I must paint it.
Come then, the colours and the ground prepare;
Dip in the rainbow, trick her off in air;
Choose a firm cloud before it fall, and in it
Catch, ere she change, the Cynthia of this minute.
POPE, *Moral Essays.* Epis. ii, l. 5.

Papilia, wedded to her am'rous spark,
Sighs for the shades—"How charming is a park!"
A park is purchased; but the Fair he sees
All bathed in tears— "Oh, odious, odious trees!"
POPE, *Moral Essays.* Epis. ii, l. 37.

Ladies, like variegated tulips show;
'Tis to their changes half their charms they owe;
Fine by defect, and delicately weak,
Their happy spots the nice admirer take.
POPE, *Moral Essays.* Epis. ii, l. 41.

She went from Op'ra, Park, Assembly, Play,
To morning walks, and prayers three hours a day;
To part her time 'twixt reading and Bohea,
To muse, and spill her solitary tea;
Or o'er cold coffee trifle with the spoon,
Count the slow clock, and dine exact at noon.
POPE, *Epistle to Mrs. Teresa Blount on Leaving Town,* l. 13.

To give the sex their due,
They scarcely are to their own wishes true;
They love, they hate, and yet they know not why;
"Constant in nothing but inconstancy."
POPE. Quoting Richard Barnfield. *See under* FORTUNE.

7
No, no, I'll love no more; let him who can
Fancy the maid who fancies every man;
In some lone place I'll find a gloomy cave,
There my own hands shall dig a spacious grave:
Then all unseen I'll lay me down and die
Since woman's constancy is—all my eye.
WILLIAM BARNES RHODES, *Bombastes Furioso.*

8
The vows of women
Of no more bondage be, to where they are made,
Than they are to their virtues; which is nothing.
SHAKESPEARE, *Cymbeline.* Act ii, sc. 4, l. 110.

They are not constant, but are changing still.
SHAKESPEARE, *Cymbeline.* Act ii, sc. 5, l. 30.

Hamlet: Is this a prologue, or the posy of a ring?
Ophelia: 'T is brief, my lord.
Hamlet: As woman's love.
SHAKESPEARE, *Hamlet.* Act iii, sc. 2, l. 162.

9
Constant you are; But yet a woman.
SHAKESPEARE, *1 Henry IV.* Act ii, sc. 3, l. 111.

10
Look to her, Moor; if thou hast eyes to see:

She has deceived her father, and may thee.
SHAKESPEARE, *Othello*. Act i, sc. 3, l. 293.

Framed to make women false.
SHAKESPEARE, *Othello*. Act i, sc. 3, l. 404.

1
The fickleness of the woman I love is only equalled by the infernal constancy of the women who love me.
BERNARD SHAW, *The Philanderer*. Act ii.

2
Yet do not my folly reprove;
She was fair—and my passion begun:
She smiled—and I could not but love;
She is faithless—and I am undone.
WILLIAM SHENSTONE, *Pastoral Ballad*. Pt. iv.

3
I know the nature of women: they won't when you would; when you won't, they long for it all the more. (Novi ingenium mulerium: Nolunt ubi velis, ubi nolis cupiunt ultro.)
TERENCE, *Eunuchus*, l. 812. (Act iv, sc. 7.)

When I say that I know women, I mean I know that I don't know them. Every single woman I ever knew is a puzzle to me, as, I have no doubt, she is to herself.
THACKERAY, *Mr. Brown's Letters*.

4
A fickle and changeful thing is woman ever. (Varium et mutabile semper Femina.)
VERGIL, *Æneid*. Bk. iv, l. 569.

My lord, you know what Virgil sings—
Woman is various and most mutable.
TENNYSON, *Queen Mary*. Act iii, sc. 6, l. 77.

5
Shall I, wasting in despair,
Die because a woman's fair?
Or make pale my cheeks with care
'Cause another's rosy are?
Be she fairer than the day,
Or the flow'ry meads in May,
If she think not well of me,
What care I how fair she be?
GEORGE WITHER, *The Lover's Resolution*.

Be she meeker, kinder, than
Turtle-dove or pelican,
If she be not so to me,
What care I how kind she be?
GEORGE WITHER, *The Lover's Resolution*.

If she undervalue me,
What care I how fair she be?
SIR WALTER RALEIGH [?], *His Further Resolution*.

6
O faithless world, and thy most faithless part,
A woman's heart!
The true shop of variety, where sits
Nothing but fits
And fevers of desire, and pangs of love,
Which toys remove.
SIR HENRY WOTTON, *The World*.

7
Why should I sing of woman
And the softness of night,
When the dawn is loud with battle
And the day's teeth bite,
And there's a sword to lay my hand to
And a man's fight?
W. H. WRIGHT, *Song Against Women*.

I fear no power a woman wields
While I can have the woods and fields.
ERNEST MCGAFFEY, *Song*.

8
Woman's love is but a blast,
And turneth like the wind.
SIR THOMAS WYATT, *The Careful Lover Complaineth*.

XIV—Woman: Her Tongue

8a
Ten measures of speech descended on the world; women took nine and men one.
Babylonian Talmud: Kiddushin, fo. 49b.

9
As men
Do walk a mile, women should talk an hour,
After supper: 'tis their exercise.
BEAUMONT AND FLETCHER, *Philaster*. Act ii, sc. 4.

The pleasure of talking is the inextinguishable passion of a woman, coeval with the act of breathing.
LE SAGE, *Gil Blas*. Bk. vii, ch. 7.

10
I have but one simile, and that's a blunder,
For wordless woman, which is silent thunder.
BYRON, *Don Juan*. Canto vi, st. 57.

11
I am a woman, needs must I speak.
CHAUCER, *The Marchantes Tale*, l. 1061.

Do you not know I am a woman? when I think, I must speak.
SHAKESPEARE, *As You Like It*. Act iii, sc. 2, l. 263.

12
Let your women keep silence in the churches.
New Testament: I Corinthians, xiv, 34.

13
The sweetest noise on earth, a woman's tongue;
A string which hath no discord.
BRYAN W. PROCTER, *Rafaelle and Fornarina*. Sc. 2.

14
The old proverb, Many women, many words.
THOMAS DELONEY, *Thomas of Reading*. Ch. 12. (c. 1600)

Geese with geese and women with women.
THOMAS FULLER, *Gnomologia* No. 1645.

15
Thus through a woman was the secret known;
Tell us, and in effect you tell the town.
DRYDEN, *Wife of Bath's Tale*, l. 201.

A free-tongued woman,
And very excellent at telling secrets.
MIDDLETON AND MASSINGER, *The Old Law*. Act iv, sc. 2.

How hard it is for women to keep counsel!
SHAKESPEARE, *Julius Cæsar*. Act ii, sc. 4, l. 9.

16
Half the sorrows of women would be averted if they could repress the speech they know to

be useless—nay, the speech they have resolved not to utter.

GEORGE ELIOT, *Felix Holt*. Ch. 2.

1
I am very fond of the company of ladies. I like their beauty, I like their delicacy, I like their vivacity, and I like their *silence*.

SAMUEL JOHNSON. (SEWARD, *Johnsoniana*, 617.)

Silence in woman is like speech in man,
Deny 't who can.

BEN JONSON, *Epicœne*. Act ii, sc. 2.

2
Such a clatter of words pours from her tongue that you would think all the pots and bells were being clashed together. (Verborum tanta cadit vis, Tot pariter pelves ac tintinnabula dicas Pulsari.)

JUVENAL, *Satires*. Sat. vi, l. 440.

I know that we women are all justly accounted chatterboxes; and then there is that old proverb, "Never now, nor in any age, such a wonder as a dumb woman." (Nam multum loquaces merito omnes habemur, Nec mutam profecto repertam ullum esse Aut hodie dicunt mulierem aut ullo in sæclo.)

PLAUTUS, *Aulularia*, l. 124. (Act ii, sc. 1.)

3
High flights she had, and wit at will;
And so her tongue lay seldom still:
For in all visits who but she
To argue, or to repartee?

MATTHEW PRIOR, *Hans Carvel*, l. 5.

4
It is better to dwell in a corner of the housetop than with a brawling woman in a wide house.

Old Testament: Proverbs, xxi, 9.

5
One tongue is enough for a woman.

JOHN RAY, *English Proverbs*, 59. This proverb is sometimes ascribed to John Milton, because he used it when asked if he intended to teach his daughters Greek and Latin.

You wished me to a wife, fair, rich and young,
That had the Latin, French and Spanish tongue.
I thank't, and told you I desir'd none such,
And said, One language may be tongue too much.
Then love I not the learned? yes, as my life;
A learned mistress, not a learned wife.

SIR JOHN HARINGTON, *Of Women Learned in the Tongues*. (*Epigrams*. Bk. iv, epig. 261.)

6
And the lady shall say her mind freely, or the blank verse shall halt for 't.

SHAKESPEARE, *Hamlet*. Act ii, sc. 2, l. 338.

Think you a little din can daunt mine ears?
Have I not in my time heard lions roar?
Have I not heard the sea puff'd up with winds
Rage like an angry boar chafed with sweat?
Have I not heard great ordnance in the field,
And heaven's artillery thunder in the skies?
Have I not in a pitched battle heard
Loud 'larums, neighing steeds, and trumpets' clang?
And do you tell me of a woman's tongue,
That gives not half so great a blow to hear
As will a chestnut in a farmer's fire?

SHAKESPEARE, *The Taming of the Shrew*. Act i, sc. 2, l. 200.

I will board her, though she chide as loud
As thunder when the clouds in autumn crack.

SHAKESPEARE, *The Taming of the Shrew*. Act i, sc. 2, l. 95.

Say that she rail; why then I'll tell her plain
She sings as sweetly as a nightingale:
Say that she frown; I'll say she looks as clear
As morning roses newly wash'd with dew:
Say she be mute and will not speak a word;
Then I'll commend her volubility,
And say she uttereth piercing eloquence.

SHAKESPEARE, *The Taming of the Shrew*. Act ii, sc. 1, l. 171.

7
To be slow in words is a woman's only virtue.

SHAKESPEARE, *The Two Gentlemen of Verona*. Act iii, sc. 1, l. 338.

8
Grief hath two tongues, and never woman yet
Could rule them both without ten women's wit.

SHAKESPEARE, *Venus and Adonis*, l. 1007.

9
Silence gives grace to woman. (Γυναιξὶ κόσμον ἡ σιγὴ φέρει.)

SOPHOCLES, *Ajax*, l. 293.

A silent woman is always better than a talkative one. (Tacitast melior mulier semper quam loquens.)

PLAUTUS, *Rudens*, l. 1114. (Act iv, sc. 4.)

Silence is the best ornament of a woman.

JOHN RAY, *English Proverbs*, p. 24.

10
Yet will the woman have the last word.

UNKNOWN, *School House of Women*, l. 76. (1542)

Whilst women strive for the last word.

FULLER, *Church History of Britain*, ix, 3.

XV—Woman: Her Untruthfulness

11
Now what I love in women is, they won't
Or can't do otherwise than lie, but do it
So well, the very truth seems falsehood to it.

BYRON, *Don Juan*. Canto xi, st. 36.

12
For half so boldly can there no man
Swear and lyen as a woman can.

CHAUCER, *Wife of Bath's Prologue*, l. 227.

For never was it given to mortal man
To lie so boldly as we women can.

POPE, *Wife of Bath's Prologue*, l. 62.

13
Deceit, weeping, spinning, God hath give
To women kindly, while they may live.

CHAUCER, *Wife of Bath's Prologue*, l. 401. A rendering of a medieval proverb: "Fallere flere, nere, Dedit deus in muliere."

1
Hang art, madam! and trust to nature for dissembling.

CONGREVE, *The Old Batchelor*. Act iii, sc. 1.

2
Women never confess; even when they seemingly resign themselves to such a course, they are never sincere. . . . A woman scoffs at evidence. Show her the sun, tell her it is daylight, at once she will close her eyes and say to you, "No, it is night."

ÉMILE GABORIAU, *Monsieur Lecoq*. Ch. 10.

When a woman writes her confession she is never further from the truth.

JAMES HUNEKER, *Pathos of Distance*, p. 58.

3
O woman! thou wert fashioned to beguile:
So have all sages said, all poets sung.

JEAN INGELOW, *The Four Bridges*. St. 68.

4
There's no effrontery like that of a woman caught in the act; her very guilt inspires her with wrath and insolence. (Nihil est audacius illis Deprensis: iram atque animos a crimine sumunt.)

JUVENAL, *Satires*. Sat. vi, l. 284.

5
Talk to me tenderly, tell me lies;
I am a woman and time flies.

VIVIAN YEISER LARAMORE, *Talk to Me Tenderly*.

6
Women were liars since the world began.

MASEFIELD, *The Widow in the Bye Street*.

7
I open an old book, and there I find,
That "Women still may love whom they deceive."

GEORGE MEREDITH, *Modern Love*. St. 14.

O woman, born first to believe us;
Yea, also born first to forget;
Born first to betray and deceive us,
Yet first to repent and regret!

JOAQUIN MILLER, *Charity*. St. 11.

Wisest men
Have err'd, and by bad women been deceiv'd;
And shall again, pretend they ne'er so wise.

MILTON, *Samson Agonistes*, l. 210.

8
There are three things that are not to be credited, a woman when she weeps, a merchant when he swears, nor a drunkard when he prays.

BARNABE RICH, *My Lady's Looking Glass*, 34. (1616)

9
A very honest woman, but something given to lie.

SHAKESPEARE, *Antony and Cleopatra*. Act v, sc. 2, l. 252.

XVI—Woman: Her Virtue

See also Chastity; Love: Not Wisely But Too Well

10
Nothing is so delicate as the reputation of a woman; it is at once the most beautiful and most brittle of all human things.

FANNY BURNEY, *Evelina*. Letter 39.

11
Cease, ye prudes, your envious railing!
Lovely Burns has charms: confess!
True it is she had ae failing:
Had ae woman ever less?

ROBERT BURNS, *Under the Portrait of Miss Burns*.

She had all the virtues but one.

GEORGE DU MAURIER, *Trilby*, p. 51.

12
The woman who is resolved to be respected can make herself so even amidst an army of soldiers. (La mujer que se determina á ser honrada entre un ejército de soldados lo puede ser.)

CERVANTES, *La Gitanilla*.

13
A man with a bad heart has been sometimes saved by a strong head; but a corrupt woman is lost forever.

S. T. COLERIDGE, *Table-Talk*.

14
Still for all slips of hers
One of Eve's family.

THOMAS HOOD, *The Bridge of Sighs*.

All that remains of her
Now is pure womanly.

THOMAS HOOD, *The Bridge of Sighs*.

15
The trav'ller, if he chance to stray,
May turn uncensured to his way;
Polluted streams again are pure,
And deepest wounds admit a cure;
But woman no redemption knows;
The wounds of honour never close.

EDWARD MOORE, *Fables*. No. 15.

16
By no art can chastity, once injured, be made whole. (Nulla reparabilis arte Læsa pudicitia est.)

OVID, *Heroides*. Epis. v, l. 103.

When lovely woman stoops to folly,
And finds too late that men betray,
What charm can soothe her melancholy?
What art can wash her guilt away?

The only art her guilt to cover,
To hide her shame from every eye,
To give repentance to her lover,
And wring his bosom, is—to die.

GOLDSMITH, *Song*. (*Vicar of Wakefield*. Ch. 24.)

And one false step entirely damns her fame.
In vain with tears the loss she may deplore,
In vain look back on what she was before;
She sets like stars that fall, to rise no more.

NICHOLAS ROWE, *Jane Shore*. Act i.

But the sin forgiven by Christ in heaven
By man is curst alway!

N. P. WILLIS, *Unseen Spirits*.

17
She made it plain that human passion

Was order'd by predestination;
That if weak women went astray,
Their stars were more in fault than they.
MATTHEW PRIOR, *Hans Carvel*, l. 9.

1
As a jewel of gold in a swine's snout, so is a fair woman which is without discretion.
Old Testament: Proverbs, xi, 22.

2
Women are not
In their best fortunes strong; but want will perjure
The ne'er touch'd vestal.
SHAKESPEARE, *Antony and Cleopatra*. Act iii, sc. 12, l. 29.

Though flattery fail,
Presents with female virtue must prevail.
JOHN GAY, *Trivia*. Bk. i, l. 279.

3
Frailty, thy name is woman!
SHAKESPEARE, *Hamlet*. Act i, sc. 2, l. 146.

4
O, she is fallen
Into a sea of ink, that the wide sea
Hath drops too few to wash her clean again.
SHAKESPEARE, *Much Ado About Nothing*. Act iv, sc. 1, l. 141.

Death is the fairest cover for her shame.
SHAKESPEARE, *Much Ado About Nothing*. Act iv, sc. 1, l. 117.

XVII—Woman: A Woman's No

See also Wooing: Faint Heart and Fair Lady

5
"Yes," I answered you last night;
"No," this morning, sir, I say:
Colours seen by candle-light
Will not look the same by day.
E. B. BROWNING, *The Lady's "Yes."*

And her *yes*, once said to you,
SHALL be Yes for evermore.
E. B. BROWNING, *The Lady's Yes*.

6
A little while she strove, and much repented,
And whispering "I will ne'er consent"—consented.
BYRON, *Don Juan*. Canto i, st. 117.

But yet she listen'd—'tis enough,
Who listens once will listen twice;
Her heart, be sure, is not of ice,
And one refusal no rebuff.
BYRON, *Mazeppa*, l. 278.

7
Between a woman's Yes and No
There is not room for a pin to go.
(Entre el Si y el No de la mujer,
No me atreveria yo á poner una punta de alfiler.)
CERVANTES, *Don Quixote*.

8
Take not the first refusal ill:
Tho' now she won't, anon she will.
THOMAS D'URFEY, *A Song Set by Mr. Berenclow*.

Never take No for an answer.
J. F. MITCHELL. Title and refrain of a popular song. (1886)

9
The swain did woo; but she was nice;
Following fashion, nayed him twice.
ROBERT GREENE, *The Shepherd's Ode*.

10
Maids' nays are nothing, they are shy,
But to desire what they deny.
ROBERT HERRICK, *Maid's Nays Are Nothing*.

The lass saith no, and would full fain:
And this is Love, as I hear saine.
SIR WALTER RALEIGH, *What Is Love?*

Maids, in modesty, say "No" to that
Which they would have the profferer construe "Ay."
SHAKESPEARE, *The Two Gentlemen of Verona*. Act i, sc. 2, l. 55.

11
To say why gals acts so or so,
Or don't, 'ould be persumin';
Mebby to mean *yes* an' say *no*
Comes nateral to women.
J. R. LOWELL, *The Courtin'*.

12
Woman's behaviour is a surer bar
Than is their No! That fairly doth deny
Without denying. Thereby kept they are
Safe even from hope. In part to blame is she
Which hath without consent been only tried.
He comes too near that comes to be denied.
SIR THOMAS OVERBURY, *A Wife*. St. 36.

While vain coquets affect to be pursued,
And think they're virtuous if not grossly lewd,
Let this great maxim be my virtue's guide:
In part she is to blame that has been try'd—
He comes too near, that comes to be deny'd.
LADY MARY WORTLEY MONTAGU, *The Lady's Resolve*.

13
Make denials Increase your services.
SHAKESPEARE, *Cymbeline*. Act ii, sc. 3, l. 53.

14
Have you not heard it said full oft,
A woman's nay doth stand for nought?
SHAKESPEARE [?], *Passionate Pilgrim*, l. 339.

Take no repulse, whatever she doth say;
For, "get you gone," she doth not mean, "away."
SHAKESPEARE, *The Two Gentlemen of Verona*. Act iii, sc. 1, l. 100.

15
Play the maid's part, still answer nay, and take it.
SHAKESPEARE, *Richard III*. Act iii, sc. 7, l. 51.

16
No is no negative in a woman's mouth.
SIR PHILIP SIDNEY, *Arcadia*. Bk. iii.

17
I have not skill
From such a sharp and waspish word as "No"
To pluck the sting.
HENRY TAYLOR, *Philip Van Artevelde*. Act i, sc. 2.

18
When Venus said "Spell no for me,"

"N-O," Dan Cupid wrote with glee,
  And smiled at his success:
"Ah, child," said Venus, laughing low,
"We women do not spell it so,
  We spell it Y-E-S."
CAROLYN WELLS, *The Spelling Lesson*.

XVIII—Woman: A Woman's Reason

1
It is a woman's reason to say I will do such a thing because I will.
JEREMIAH BURROUGHES, *On Hosea*. Vol. iv. (1652)

A woman's reason—because it is so.
GEORGE FARQUHAR, *The Recruiting Officer*. Act iv, sc. 3.

Women's reasons; they would not because they would not.
JOHN LYLY, *Love's Metamorphosis*, iv, 1.

Besides, I have a woman's reason, I will not dance, because I will not dance.
THOMAS MIDDLETON, *Blurt, Master-Constable*. Act i, sc. 1.

2
Shall I lose
The privilege of my sex, which is my will,
To yield a reason like a man?
MASSINGER, *A Very Woman*. Act i, sc. 1.

3
Woman's reason is in the milk of her breasts.
GEORGE MEREDITH, *Richard Feverel*. Ch. 43.

4
If a man should importune me to give a reason why I loved him, I find it could no otherwise be expressed than by making answer, Because it was he; because it was I.
MONTAIGNE, *Essays*. Bk. i, ch. 27.

5
He may go forward like a stoic Roman
Where pangs and terrors in his pathway lie—
Or, seizing the swift logic of a woman,
Curse God and die.
E. A. ROBINSON, *The Man Against the Sky*.

He owns her logic of the heart,
And wisdom of unreason.
WHITTIER, *Among the Hills*.

6
I have no other but a woman's reason:
I think him so, because I think him so.
SHAKESPEARE, *The Two Gentlemen of Verona*. Act i, sc. 2, l. 23.

7
You sometimes have to answer a woman according to her womanishness, just as you have to answer a fool according to his folly.
BERNARD SHAW, *An Unsocial Socialist*. Ch. 18.

XIX—Woman: A Woman's Vengeance

8
The fool that willingly provokes a woman
Has made himself another evil angel,
And a new hell, to which all other torments
Are but mere pastime.
BEAUMONT AND FLETCHER, *Cupid's Revenge*. Act iii.

9
Women do most delight in revenge.
SIR THOMAS BROWNE, *Christian Morals*. Pt. iii, sec. 12.

Sweet is revenge—especially to women.
BYRON, *Don Juan*. Canto i, st. 124.

And their revenge is as the tiger's spring,
Deadly, and quick, and crushing.
BYRON, *Don Juan*. Canto ii, st. 199.

No vengeance like a woman's.
GEORGE GRANVILLE, *The British Enchanters*. Act v, sc. 2.

Not ev'n the soldier's fury, rais'd in war,
The rage of tyrants, when defiance stings 'em!
The pride of priests, so bloody when in power!
Are half so dreadful as a woman's vengeance.
RICHARD SAVAGE, *Sir Thomas Overbury*.

10
I've seen your stormy seas and stormy women,
And pity lovers rather more than seamen.
BYRON, *Don Juan*. Canto vi, st. 53.

And her brow clear'd, but not her troubled eye;
The wind was down, but still the sea ran high.
BYRON, *Don Juan*. Canto vi, st. 110.

And femininely meaneth furiously,
Because all passions in excess are female.
BYRON, *Sardanapalus*. Act iii, sc. 1.

11
We shall find no fiend in hell can match the fury of a disappointed woman,—scorned, slighted, dismissed without a parting pang.
COLLEY CIBBER, *Love's Last Shift*. Act iv, sc. 1. (1696)

Heav'n has no rage like love to hatred turn'd,
Nor hell a fury like a woman scorn'd.
WILLIAM CONGREVE, *The Mourning Bride*. Act iii, sc. 8. Concluding lines. (1697)

Is any Panther's, Lioness's rage
So furious, any Torrent's fall so swift
As a wrong'd woman's hate?
NATHANIEL LEE, *The Rival Queens*. Act i, sc. 1. (1677)

A slighted woman knows no bounds.
VANBRUGH, *The Mistake*. Pt. i, act ii, sc. 1. (1705)

Oh, woman wronged can cherish hate
More deep and dark than manhood may!
WHITTIER, *Mogg Megone*. Pt. i, st. 21.

12
To work a fell revenge a man's a fool,
If not instructed in a woman's school.
JOHN FLETCHER, *Spanish Curate*. Act v, sc. 1.

13
Revenge, we find,
Ever the pleasure of a petty mind,
And hence so dear to poor weak womankind.
(Quippe minuti
Semper et infirmi est animi exiguique voluptas
Ultio. Continuo sic collige, quod vindicta
Nemo magis gaudet quam femina.)
JUVENAL, *Satires*. Sat. xiii, l. 189.

Then, my boy, beware of Daphne. Learn a lesson from the rat:

What is cunning in the kitten may be cruel in the cat.
ROBERT UNDERWOOD JOHNSON, *Daphne*.

1
Offend her, and she knows not to forgive;
Oblige her, and she'll hate you while you live.
POPE, *Moral Essays*. Epis. ii, l. 137.

2
I am a woman! nay, a woman wrong'd!
And when our sex from injuries take fire,
Our softness turns to fury—and our thoughts
Breathe vengeance and destruction.
RICHARD SAVAGE, *Sir Thomas Overbury*.

3
What an enraged woman can accomplish!
(Quid femina possit.)
VERGIL, *Æneid*. Bk. v, l. 6.

4
Women and elephants never forget an injury.
H. H. MUNRO (SAKI), *Reginald on Besetting Sins*

Prince, a precept I'd leave for you,
Coined in Eden, existing yet:
Skirt the parlor, and shun the zoo—
Women and elephants never forget.
DOROTHY PARKER, *Ballade of Unfortunate Mammals*.

XX—Woman: A Woman's Will

5
He is a fool who thinks by force or skill
To turn the current of a woman's will.
CALDERON, *Adventures of Five Hours*. Act v, sc. 3, l. 483. (Samuel Tuke, tr.)

Where is the man who has the power and skill
To stem the torrent of a woman's will?
For if she will, she will, you may depend on't;
And if she won't, she won't; so there's an end on't.
UNKNOWN, *Inscription*, on pillar, Dane John Field, Canterbury, Eng. (*London Examiner*, 31 May, 1829.)

6
She is one of them to whom God bade ho;
She will all have, and will right nought forego.
JOHN HEYWOOD, *Proverbs*. Pt. i, ch. 11.

7
First, then, a woman will, or won't,—depend on't;
If she will do't, she will; and there's an end on't.
But, if she won't, since safe and sound your trust is,
Fear is affront: and jealousy injustice.
AARON HILL, *Zara: Epilogue*.

8
Man has his will—but woman has her way!
O. W. HOLMES, *Prologue*. (*Autocrat of the Breakfast-Table*. Ch. 2.)

9
Women because they cannot have their wills when they die, they will have their wills while they live.
JOHN MANNINGHAM, *Diary*, p. 92. (1602)

Men, dying, make their wills, but wives
Escape a task so sad;
Why should they make what all their lives
The gentle dames have had?
J. G. SAXE, *Woman's Will*.

10
Thus it shall befall
Him, who to worth in women overtrusting,
Lets her will rule; restraint she will not brook;
And left to herself, if evil thence ensue,
She first his weak indulgence will accuse.
MILTON, *Paradise Lost*. Bk. ix, l. 1182.

11
What I will, I will, and there an end.
SHAKESPEARE, *Two Gentlemen of Verona*, i, 3, 65.

12
Many men have many minds,
But women have but two,
Everything would they have,
And nothing would they do.
UNKNOWN, *Women's Minds*. (*Notes and Queries*. Ser. iii, vol. 8, p. 494.)

XXI—Woman and the Home

13
The works of women are symbolical.
We sew, sew, prick our fingers, dull our sight,
Producing what? A pair of slippers, sir,
To put on when you're weary.
E. B. BROWNING, *Aurora Leigh*. Bk. i, l. 466.

Dusting, darning, drudging, nothing is great or small,
Nothing is mean or irksome, love will hallow it all.
WALTER CHALMERS SMITH, *Hilda Among the Broken Gods*. Bk. ii.

14
She was so diligent, with-outen sloth,
To serve and pleasen everich in that place,
That all her loved that looked upon her face.
CHAUCER, *Tale of the Man of Lawe*, l. 432.

Her natural turn is grave and domestic; and she seems to have been raised by her aunts à la grace, instead of being raised in a hot bed, as most young ladies are of late.
LORD CHESTERFIELD, *Letters*, 30 Sept., 1757.

In her very style of looking
There was cognisance of cooking!
From her very dress were peeping
Indications of housekeeping!
ROBERT BUCHANAN, *White Rose and Red*.

15
Her best and safest club is the home. . . . Sensible and responsible women do not want to vote. The relative positions to be assumed by man and woman in the working out of our civilization were assigned long ago by a higher intelligence than ours.
GROVER CLEVELAND. (*Ladies' Home Journal*, April and October, 1905.)

16
When housewives all the house forsake,
And leave good men to brew and bake,
Withouten guile, then be it said,
That house doth stand upon its head.
CONGREVE, *Love for Love*. Act ii, sc. 3. Quoted as by "Messahalah the Arabian."

1
A woman should be good for everything at home, but abroad good for nothing.
EURIPIDES, *Meleager*. Frag. 525.

The woman and the hen by gadding about soon got lost.
CERVANTES, *Don Quixote*. Pt. ii, ch. 49.

The house goes mad when women gad.
SCOTT, *Fortunes of Nigel*. Ch. 4.

2
A dishonest woman cannot be kept in, and an honest one will not out.
THOMAS FULLER, *Gnomologia*. No. 76.

She will stay at home, perhaps, if her leg be broke.
THOMAS FULLER, *Gnomologia*. No. 4150.

A woman is to be from her house three times:
When she is christened, married, and buried.
THOMAS FULLER, *Gnomologia*. No. 480.

3
A wife, domestic, good, and pure,
Like snail, should keep within her door;
But not, like snail, with silver track,
Place all her wealth upon her back.
W. W. HOW, *Good Wives*.

Appeles us'd to paint a good housewife upon a snail, which intimated that she would be as slow from gadding abroad, and when she went she should carry her house upon her back; that is, she should make all sure at home.
JAMES HOWELL, *Parly of Beasts*, p. 58. (1660)

Phidias made the statue of Venus at Elis with one foot upon the shell of a tortoise, to signify two great duties of a virtuous woman, which are to keep home and be silent.
W. DE BRITAINE, *Human Prudence*, p. 134.

All virtuous women, like tortoises, carry their house on their heads, and their chappel in their heart, and their danger in their eye, and their souls in their hands, and God in all their actions.
JEREMY TAYLOR, *Life of Christ*. Pt. i, bk. ii, ch. 4.

4
The foot on the cradle, the hand on the distaff, a sign of a good housewife.
JAMES HOWELL, *Proverbs*, 2. (1659)

5
A hearth is no hearth unless a woman sit by it.
RICHARD JEFFERIES, *The Field-Play*. *See also under* HOME.

6
A woman, the more curious she is about her face, is commonly the more careless about her house.
BEN JONSON, *Explorata: Munda et Sordida*.

Ladies grow handsome by looking at themselves in the glass.
HAZLITT, *The Plain Speaker*. Vol ii, p 52.

7
You married that thin-flanked woman, as white and as stale as a bone.
An' she gave you your social nonsense; but where's that kid o' your own?
I've seen your carriages blocking the half o' the Cromwell Road,
But never the doctor's brougham to help the missus unload.
RUDYARD KIPLING, *The "Mary Gloster."*

8
Seek to be good, but aim not to be great;
A woman's noblest station is retreat.
GEORGE LYTTELTON, *Advice to a Lady*.

Be plain in dress, and sober in your diet;
In short, my deary, kiss me! and be quiet.
MARY WORTLEY MONTAGU, *In Summary of Lord Lyttleton's "Advice to a Lady."*

9
To give Society its highest taste;
Well-ordered home man's best delight to make;
And, by submissive wisdom, modest skill,
With every gentle, care-eluding art,
To raise the virtues, animate the bliss, . . .
And sweeten all the toils of human life:
This be the female dignity and praise!
THOMSON, *The Seasons: Autumn*, l. 602.

10
But give me the fair one, in country or city,
Whose home and its duties are dear to her heart.
SAMUEL WOODWORTH, *The Needle*.

10a
The three virtues of a woman are to obey the father, to obey the husband, to obey the son. ('Tsung fu, 'tsung fu, 'tsung tzŭ.)
UNKNOWN. A Chinese proverb.

XXII—Woman and Woman

11
Gayer insects fluttering by
Ne'er droop the wing o'er those that die,
And lovelier things have mercy shown
To every failing but their own,
And every woe a tear can claim,
Except an erring sister's shame.
BYRON, *The Giaour*, l. 416.

12
A woman should always stand by a woman. (*Γυναῖκα γὰρ δὴ συμπονεῖν γυναικὶ χρή.*)
EURIPIDES, *Helen*, l. 329.

Woman is woman's natural ally.
EURIPIDES, *Alope*. Frag. 109.

13
To cheat a man is nothing; but the woman must have fine parts, indeed, who cheats a woman.
JOHN GAY, *The Beggar's Opera*. Act ii, sc. 1.

14
It's a very venerable and useful superstition that one woman is perfectly safe if another woman is pretending to look after her.
HENRY ARTHUR JONES, *The Triumph of the Philistines*. Act. i.

15
One woman reads another's character
Without the tedious trouble of deciphering.
BEN JONSON, *New Inn*. Act iv, sc. 4.

16
No friendship is so cordial or so delicious as

that of girl for girl; no hatred so intense and immovable as that of woman for woman.

W. S. LANDOR, *Imaginary Conversations: Epicurus, Leontion and Ternissa.*

1
Two women placed together makes cold weather.

SHAKESPEARE, *Henry VIII.* Act i, sc. 4, l. 22.

2
The woman is so hard Upon the woman.

TENNYSON, *The Princess.* Pt. vi, l. 205.

3
Two women in one house,
Two cats and one mouse,
Two dogs and one bone,
May never accord in one.

UNKNOWN, *Woman and Woman.* (*Reliq. Antiquæ,* i, 233.)

XXIII—Woman: Find the Woman

4
Find the woman. (Cherchez la femme.)

ALEXANDRE DUMAS, PÈRE, *Les Mohicans de Paris.* Bk. iii, ch. 10. Used several times in the novel, and in Act iii, sc. 7 of the play. Attributed to Joseph Fouché, Minister of Police under Napoleon. Sometimes the expression takes the form, "Où est la femme?" (in German, "Wo ist sie?" or "Wie heiszt sie?"): "Where is the woman?"

"Look for the woman"—it was Solomon who first said it.

ÉMILE GABORIAU, *Other People's Money.* Ch. 29.

5
Tell me the cause: I know there is a woman in't.

JOHN FLETCHER, *Humorous Lieutenant.* Act iv, sc. 2.

They talk about a woman's sphere,
As though it had a limit.
There's not a place in earth or heaven,
There's not a task to mankind given. . . .
Without a woman in it.

KATE FIELD, *Woman's Spirit.*

6
And when a lady's in the case,
You know all other things give place.

JOHN GAY, *The Hare and Many Friends.*

In all the woes that curse our race
There is a lady in the case.

W. S. GILBERT, *Fallen Fairies.*

A woman doth the mischief brew
In nineteen cases out of twenty.

W. S. GILBERT, *Fallen Fairies.*

7
There never was a case in which the quarrel was not started by a woman. (Nulla ferre causa est in qua non femina litem Moverit.)

JUVENAL, *Satires.* Sat. vi, l. 242.

You forget there is a woman in this case. That is so all the world over.

GEORGE EBERS, *Uarda.* Bk. ii, ch. 14.

8
Such a plot must have a woman in it.

SAMUEL RICHARDSON, *Sir Charles Grandison.* Vol. i, letter 24.

9
There is not a war in the world, no, nor an injustice, but you women are answerable for it; not in that you have provoked, but in that you have not hindered.

RUSKIN, *Sesame and Lilies: Of Queens' Gardens.*

10
The leader in the deed a woman. (Dux femina facti.)

VERGIL, *Æneid.* Bk. i, l. 364.

11
There is no mischief, but a woman is at one end of it.

UNKNOWN, *Wit Restor'd,* 150. (1658)

There is no mischief done but a woman is one.

JOHN RAY, *English Proverbs.*

XXIV—Woman and Love

See also Love in Man and Woman

12
Women wish to be loved without a why or a wherefore; not because they are pretty, or good, or well-bred, or graceful, or intelligent, but because they are themselves.

AMIEL, *Journal,* 17 March, 1868.

13
A woman can be anything that the man who loves her would have her be.

J. M. BARRIE, *Tommy and Grizel,* p. 31.

As a man thinketh, so is she.

ELBERT HUBBARD, *Epigrams.*

A woman, like the Koh-i-noor,
Mounts to the price that's put on her.

COVENTRY PATMORE, *The Angel in the House: The Koh-i-noor.*

A woman who is loved always has success.

VICKI BAUM, *Grand Hotel,* p. 132.

14
If I ever really love it will be like Mary Queen of Scots, who said of her Bothwell that she could follow him round the world in her nighty.

J. M. BARRIE, *What Every Woman Knows.* Act ii.

THROUGH THICK AND THIN, *see under* PROVERBS.

15
A compliment for a woman in love is like a sudden warmth falling around her—it is intoxication—it is like strong wine, one grows drunk with it.

HENRY BERNSTEIN, *The Thief.* Act ii.

A woman . . . always feels herself complimented by love, though it may be from a man incapable of winning her heart, or perhaps even her esteem.

ABEL STEVENS, *Life of Madame de Staël.* Ch. 3.

The heart of woman tastes no truer joy,
Is never flatter'd with such dear enchantment—
'Tis more than selfish vanity—as when
She hears the praises of the man she loves.

JAMES THOMSON, *Tancred and Sigismunda.* Act i, sc. 1.

16
For women (I am a woman now like you)

There is no good of life but love.
ROBERT BROWNING, *In a Balcony.*

1
All women love great men
If young or old; it is in all the tales.
ROBERT BROWNING, *In a Balcony.*

Such great achievements cannot fail
To cast salt on a woman's tail.
BUTLER, *Hudibras.* Pt. ii, canto 1, l. 277.

I love you for the sake of what you are,
And not of what you do.
JEAN INGELOW, *Honours.* Pt. i, st. 43.

Intellect may subdue women—make slaves of them; and they worship beauty perhaps as much as you do. But they only love forever and are mated when they meet a noble nature.
GEORGE MEREDITH, *Richard Feverel.* Ch. 13.

It is always interesting, in the case of a great man, to know how he affected the women of his acquaintance.
JOHN MORLEY, *Burke,* p. 116.

Mrs. Allonby: We women adore failures. They lean on us.
Lord Illingworth: You worship successes. You cling to them.
Mrs. Allonby: We are the laurels to hide their baldness.
OSCAR WILDE, *A Woman of No Importance.* Act i.

2
And all because a lady fell in love.
BYRON, *Don Juan.* Canto iv, st. 51.

So loving and so lovely.
BYRON, *Don Juan.* Canto ii, st. 193.

If women could be fair and yet not fond.
EDWARD DE VERE, *Woman's Changeableness.*

3
Why did she love him? Curious fool!—be still—
Is human love the growth of human will?
BYRON, *Lara.* Canto ii, st. 22.

4
There are women whose talent it is to serve.
And some are great lovers.
JOHN DRINKWATER, *Mary Stuart.*

5
The hearts of women sicken for love more than do the hearts of men, but honor curbs desire.
EURIPIDES, *Andromache,* l. 220.

Every woman loves more than a man loves, but out of shame she hides the sting of love, although she be mad for it. (*Πᾶσα γυνὴ φιλέει πλέον ἀνέρος· αἰδομένη δὲ κεύθει κέντρον ἔρωτος, ἐρωμανέουσα καὶ αὐτή.*)
NONNUS, *Dionysius,* xlii, 209. (*Greek Anthology.* Bk. x, epig. 120.)

6
How a little love and conversation improve a woman!
FARQUHAR, *The Beaux' Stratagem.* Act iv, sc. 2.

7
A curse attends that woman's love
Who always would be pleasing.
JOHN GAY, *The Beggar's Opera.* Act ii, sc. 2.

8
"I love you" is all the secret that many, nay, most women have to tell. When that is said, they are like China-crackers on the morning of the fifth of July.
O. W. HOLMES, *The Professor at the Breakfast-Table.* Ch. 8.

9
And beaux were turn'd to flambeaux where she came.
THOMAS HOOD, *Bianca's Dream,* l. 12.

10
How could I tell I should love thee to-day
Whom that day I held not dear?
How could I know I should love thee away
When I did not love thee anear?
JEAN INGELOW, *Supper at the Mill.*

11
Never will you find a woman who spares the man who loves her; for though she be herself aflame, she delights to torment him. (Nullum invenies quæ parcat amanti; Ardeat ipsa licet, tormentis gaudet amantis.)
JUVENAL, *Satires.* Sat. vi, l. 208.

Nowhere in stone, paint, or poem is a lady in my line portrayed as using a lover well. (Nam neque fictum usquamst neque pictum necque scriptum in poematis Ubi lena bene agat cum quiquam amante.)
PLAUTUS, *Asinaria,* l. 174. (Act i, sc. 3.)

The woman that spares her lover spares herself too little. (Quæ amanti parcet, eadem sibi parcet parum.)
PLAUTUS, *Asinaria,* l. 177. (Act i, sc. 3.)

Womankind more joy discovers
Making fools, than keeping lovers.
JOHN WILMOT, *A Dialogue on the Coquetry of Women,* l. 71.

12
Men love us, or they need our love.
JOHN KEBLE, *The Christian Year: 7th Sunday after Trinity.*

13
One can find women who have never had one love affair, but it is rare indeed to find any who have had only one. (On peut trouver des femmes qui n'ont jamais eu de galanterie, mais il est rare d'en trouver qui n'en aient jamais eu qu'une.)
LA ROCHEFOUCAULD, *Maximes.* No. 73.

Women in love pardon great indiscretions more easily than little infidelities. (Les femmes qui aiment pardonnent plus aisément les grandes indiscrétions que les petites infidélités.)
LA ROCHEFOUCAULD, *Maximes.* No. 429.

A lover without indiscretion is no lover at all.
THOMAS HARDY, *Hand of Ethelberta.* Ch. 20.

14
How unhappy the woman who is in love and virtuous at the same time! (Qu'une femme est à plaindre, quand elle a tout ensemble de l'amour et de la vertu!)
LA ROCHEFOUCAULD, *Maximes Posthumes,* 548.

1 It is better to poison her with the sweet bait of love.
JOHN LYLY, *Euphues.*

Steal love's sweet bait from fearful hooks.
SHAKESPEARE, *Romeo and Juliet:* Act ii, *Prologue,* l. 8.

2 Women hate revolutions and revolutionists. They like men who are docile, and well-regarded at the bank, and never late at meals.
H. L. MENCKEN, *Prejudices.* Ser. iv, p. 252.

3 The great ambition of women, believe me, is to inspire love. (La grande ambition des femmes est, croyez-moi, d'inspirer de l'amour.)
MOLIÈRE, *Le Sicilien.* Sc. 6, l. 39.

4 All women can be caught; spread but your nets and you will catch them. (Cunctas Posse capi; capies, tu modo tende plagas.)
OVID, *Ars Amatoria.* Bk. i, l. 269.

Every woman thinks herself lovable. (Sibi quæque videtur amanda.)
OVID, *Ars Amatoria.* Bk. i, l. 613.

5 Whether they give or refuse, it delights women to have been asked. (Quæ dant, quæque negant, gaudent tamen esse rogatæ.)
OVID, *Ars Amatoria.* Bk. i, l. 345.

Women often wish to give unwillingly what they really like to give. (Quod juvat, invitæ sæpe dedisse volunt.)
OVID, *Ars Amatoria.* Bk. i, l. 674.

6 'Tis never for their wisdom that one loves the wisest, or for their wit that one loves the wittiest; 'tis for benevolence and virtue and honest fondness one loves people; the other qualities make one proud of loving them, too.
HESTER LYNCH PIOZZI, *Letter to Fanny Burney,* 1781.

7 Oh! say not Woman's love is bought
With vain and empty treasure!
Oh! say not Woman's heart is caught
By ev'ry idle pleasure!
When first her gentle bosom knows
Love's flame, it wanders never,
Deep in her heart the passion glows;
She loves, and loves for ever!
ISAAC POCOCK, *Song.* From a musical entertainment, *The Heir of Vironi,* produced at Covent Garden, London, 27 Feb., 1817. Often wrongly ascribed to Thomas Love Peacock.

8 There swims no goose so grey, but soon or late
She finds some honest gander for her mate.
POPE, *Wife of Bath's Prologue,* l. 98.

This I set down as a positive truth. A woman with fair opportunities and without a positive hump, may marry whom she likes.
THACKERAY, *Vanity Fair.* Ch. 4.

Any woman will love any man that bothers her enough.
HENRY WALLACE PHILLIPS, *Mr. Scroggs.*

9 How quaint an appetite in woman reigns!
Free gifts we scorn, and love what costs us pains.
Let men avoid us, and on them we leap;
A glutted market makes provision cheap.
POPE, *Wife of Bath's Prologue,* l. 259.

No woman ever hates a man for being in love with her, but many a woman hates a man for being a friend to her.
POPE, *Thoughts on Various Subjects.*

10 She should be humble, who would please;
And she must suffer, who can love.
MATTHEW PRIOR, *Chloe Jealous.* St. 5.

11 Let not the creaking of shoes nor the rustling of silks betray thy poor heart to woman.
SHAKESPEARE, *King Lear.* Act iii, sc. 4, l. 97.

12 Every woman who hasn't any money is a matrimonial adventurer.
BERNARD SHAW, *Heartbreak House.* Act ii.

Vitality in a woman is a blind fury of creation.
BERNARD SHAW, *Man and Superman.* Act i.

13 They say there are sixty-seven different ways in which a woman can like a man.
ALFRED SUTRO, *The Walls of Jericho.* Act i.

14 Shepherd, be advised by me,
Cast off grief and willow-tree:
For thy grief brings her content;
She is pleased if thou lament.
UNKNOWN, *The Willow Tree.* (Old Ballad.)

WONDER

15 Wonder—which is the seed of knowledge.
FRANCIS BACON, *Advancement of Learning.*

Men love to wonder and that is the seed of our science.
EMERSON, *Society and Solitude: Works and Days.*

Wonder is the foundation of all philosophy. (L'admiration est fondement de toute philosophie.)
MONTAIGNE, *Essays.* Bk. iii, ch. 11.

Wonder is the feeling of a philosopher, and philosophy begins in wonder.
SOCRATES. (PLATO, *Theætetus.* Sec. 155.)

16 Has a man done wondering at women?—there follow men, dead and alive, to wonder at. Has he done wondering at men?—there's God to wonder at.
ROBERT BROWNING, *Pippa Passes.* Pt. i.

17 The man who cannot wonder, who does not habitually wonder (and worship), . . . is

but a pair of spectacles, behind which there is no Eye.

CARLYLE, *Sartor Resartus*. Bk. i, ch. 10.

1
How great is the wonder of heavenly and earthly things! (Quanta sit admirabilitas cœlestium rerum atque terrestrium.)

CICERO, *De Natura Deorum*. Bk. ii, sec. 36.

2
To wonder at nothing when it happens: to consider nothing impossible before it has come to pass. (Nihil admirari cum acciderit, nihil, ante quam evenerit, non evenire posse arbitrari.)

CICERO, *Tusculanarum Disputationum*. Bk. iii, ch. 14, sec. 30. Cicero refers to this attitude of mind as the ideal of wisdom.

NIL ADMIRARI, *see under* ADMIRATION.

3
And Katterfelto, with his hair on end
At his own wonders, wond'ring for his bread.

COWPER, *The Task*. Bk. iv, l. 86.

I've made bread from the bump of wonder:
That's my business, and there's my tale.

GEORGE MEREDITH, *Juggling Jerry*.

4
Long stood the noble youth oppress'd with awe
And stupid at the wondrous things he saw,
Surpassing common faith, transgressing nature's law.

DRYDEN, *Theodore and Honoria*, l. 217.

5
Wonder is the daughter of ignorance.

JOHN FLORIO, *First Fruites*. Fo. 32. (1578)

"Wonderful!" I ejaculated.
"Common-place," said Holmes.

A. CONAN DOYLE, *A Study in Scarlet*, p. 16. (1887) A colloquy in the first Sherlock Holmes tale, and repeated with variations many times in later ones.

6
Wonders will never cease.

DAVID GARRICK, *Correspondence*. Vol. ii, p. 174.

The world will never starve for want of wonders; but only for want of wonder.

G. K. CHESTERTON, *Tremendous Trifles*.

7
On account of that wonderful event, a nine days' solemn feast was celebrated by the Romans. (Romanis quoque ab eodem prodigio novendiale sacrum publice susceptum est.)

LIVY, *History*. Bk. i, sec. 31.

A wonder last but nine night never in town.

CHAUCER, *Troilus*. Bk. iv, l. 588. (c. 1374)

This wonder (as wonders last) lasted nine days.

JOHN HEYWOOD, *Proverbs*. Pt. ii, ch. 1. (1546)

Edward: You 'ld think it strange if I should marry her. . . .
Gloucester: That would be ten days' wonder at the least.
Clarence: That's a day longer than a wonder lasts.

SHAKESPEARE, *III Henry VI*. Act iii, sc. 2, l. 112.

No wonder lasts more than three days. (Niuna maraviglia dura più che tre giorni.)

UNKNOWN. An Italian proverb.

8
Things too wonderful for me, which I knew not.

Old Testament: Job, xlii, 3.

There be three things which are too wonderful for me, yea, four which I know not: The way of an eagle in the air; the way of a serpent upon a rock; the way of a ship in the midst of the sea; and the way of a man with a maid.

Old Testament: Proverbs, xxx, 18, 19.

There be triple ways to take, of the eagle or the snake,
Or the way of a man with a maid.

RUDYARD KIPLING, *The Long Trail*.

There be three things full hard to be known which way they will draw. The first is of a bird sitting upon a bough. The second is of a vessel in the sea. And the third is the way of a young man.

UNKNOWN. (*Reliq. Antiquæ*, i, 233. 1417)

9
Nay, I'll speak that Which you will wonder at.

SHAKESPEARE, *All's Well that Ends Well*. Act iv, sc. 1, l. 94.

I am to discourse wonders.

SHAKESPEARE, *A Midsummer-Night's Dream*. Act iv, sc. 2, l. 29.

10
O wonderful, wonderful, and most wonderful wonderful! and yet again wonderful, and after that, out of all hooping!

SHAKESPEARE, *As You Like It*. Act iii, sc. 2, l. 201.

O day and night, but this is wondrous strange!

SHAKESPEARE, *Hamlet*. Act i, sc. 5, l. 164.

There is something in this more than natural, if philosophy could find it out.

SHAKESPEARE, *Hamlet*. Act ii, sc. 2, l. 385.

Can such things be,
And overcome us like a summer's cloud,
Without our special wonder?

SHAKESPEARE, *Macbeth*. Act iii, sc. 4, l. 110.

11
Whilst I am bound to wonder, I am bound
To pity too.

SHAKESPEARE, *Cymbeline*. Act i, sc. 4, l. 81.

'Twas strange, 'twas passing strange;
'Twas pitiful, 'twas wondrous pitiful.

SHAKESPEARE, *Othello*. Act i, sc. 3, l. 160.

12
This man so complete
Who was enroll'd 'mongst wonders.

SHAKESPEARE, *Henry VIII*. Act i, sc. 2, l. 118.

13
You shall see wonders.

SHAKESPEARE, *The Merry Wives of Windsor*. Act v, sc. 1, l. 13.

I am . . . attired in wonder.

SHAKESPEARE, *Much Ado About Nothing*. Act iv, sc. 1, l. 146.

Here is a wonder, if you talk of a wonder.

SHAKESPEARE, *The Taming of the Shrew*. Act v, sc. 2, l. 106.

Wonder and amazement Inhabits here.

SHAKESPEARE, *The Tempest*. Act v, sc. 1, l. 104.

1
I do not envy, but I rather wonder. (Non equidem invideo; miror magis.)
VERGIL, *Eclogues*. No. i, l. 11.

2
There's something in a flying horse,
There's something in a huge balloon;
But through the clouds I'll never float
Until I have a little Boat,
Shaped like the crescent moon.
WORDSWORTH, *Peter Bell: Prologue*, l. 1.

3
We nothing know, but what is marvellous;
Yet what is marvellous. we can't believe.
YOUNG, *Night Thoughts*. Night vii, l. 1423.

Nothing can satisfy, but what confounds;
Nothing, but what astonishes, is true.
YOUNG, *Night Thoughts*. Night ix, l. 836.

4
Wonder is involuntary praise.
YOUNG, *The Revenge*. Act iii, sc. 1.

WOODS

I—Woods: Apothegms

5
He that fears leaves, let him not go into the wood.
GEORGE HERBERT, *Jacula Prudentum*.

6
Ye cannot see the wood for trees.
JOHN HEYWOOD, *Proverbs*. Pt. ii, ch. 4. (1546)

7
It is foolish to carry timber to the wood. (In silvam non ligna feras insanius.)
HORACE, *Satires*. Bk. i, sat. 10, l. 34.

8
This is the forest primeval.
LONGFELLOW, *Evangeline*, l. 1.

9
In a moment the ashes are made, but a forest is a long time growing. (Momento fit cinis: diu sylva.)
SENECA, *Naturales Quæstiones*. Bk. iii, sec. 27.

10
Who can impress the forest, bid the tree
Unfix his earth-bound root?
SHAKESPEARE, *Macbeth*. Act iv, sc. 1, l. 95.

11
Don't boast until you see the enemy dead. (Μήπω μέγ' εἴπῃς πρὶν τελευτήσαντ' ἴδῃς.)
SOPHOCLES. (CICERO, *Epistolæ ad Atticum*. Bk. iv, epis. 8.)

We are not yet out of the wood.
MADAME D'ARBLAY, *Diary*. Vol. iii, p. 473.

12
Woods have tongues As walls have ears.
TENNYSON, *Balin and Balan*, l. 522.

13
Even the gods dwelt in the woods. (Habitarunt di quoque sylvas.)
VERGIL, *Eclogues*. No. ii, l. 60.

[A wood] made sacred by the religious mysteries of our fathers, and by ancient awe. (Auguriis patrum et prisca formidine sacram.)
TACITUS, *Germania*. Sec. 39.

The groves were God's first temples.
BRYANT, *A Forest Hymn*.

14
Again, ye woods, farewell. (Ipsæ rursus concedite silvæ.)
VERGIL, *Eclogues*. No. x, l. 63.

15
The woods are full of them.
ALEXANDER WILSON, *American Ornithology: Preface*. (1808) Quoting the story of a boy returning from gathering wild-flowers.

16
Chop your own wood and it will warm you twice.
UNKNOWN. *Motto over Henry Ford's Fireplace, Dearborn, Mich.*

II—Woods: Description

17
This forest looks the way
Nightingales sound.
GRACE HAZARD CONKLING, *Frost on a Window*.

18
In the midway of this our mortal life,
I found me in a gloomy wood astray,
Gone from the path direct.
(Nel mezzo del cammin di nostra vita
Mi ritrovai per una selva oscura,
Che la diritta via era smarrita.)
DANTE, *Inferno*. Canto i, l. 1.

19
As oft as on the earth I've lain
I've died and come to life again
For only men who are brave and good
Can come out changeless from a wood.
MARY CAROLYN DAVIES, *Out of the Earth*.

20
At the gates of the forest, the surprised man of the world is forced to leave his city estimates of great and small, wise and foolish. The knapsack of custom falls off his back.
EMERSON, *Essays, Second Series: Nature*.

When a lady rallied Adam Smith on his plain dress, he pointed to his well-bound library, and said, "You see, Madame, I am a beau in my books." The farmer in this month [October] is very patient of his coarse attire, and thinks, "at least, I am a beau in my woods."
EMERSON, *Journals*, October, 1864.

The woods appear
With crimson blotches deeply dashed and crossed,—
Sign of the fatal pestilence of Frost.
BAYARD TAYLOR, *Mon-da-Min*. St. 38.

21
To linger silent among the healthful woods, musing on such things as are worthy of a wise and good man. (Tacitum silvas inter reptare salubres, Curantem quicquid dignum sapiente bonoque est.)
HORACE, *Epistles*. Bk. i, epis. 4, l. 4.

22
The perplex'd paths of this drear wood,
The nodding horror of whose shady brows
Threats the forlorn and wand'ring passenger.
MILTON, *Comus*, l. 38.

1
Thick as autumnal leaves that strow the brooks
In Vallombrosa, where th' Etrurian shades
High over-arch'd imbow'r.
MILTON, *Paradise Lost*. Bk. i, l. 302.

Groves whose rich trees wept odorous gums and balm.
MILTON, *Paradise Lost*. Bk. iv, l. 248.

A pillar'd shade
High overarch'd, and echoing walks between.
MILTON, *Paradise Lost*. Bk. ix, l. 1106.

1a
The forests of America, however slighted by man, must have been a great delight to God; for they were the best he ever planted.
JOHN MUIR, *The American Forests*. (*Atlantic Monthly*, vol. lxxx, p. 145.)

2
Hath not old custom made this life more sweet
Than that of painted pomp? Are not these woods
More free from peril than the envious court?
SHAKESPEARE, *As You Like It*. Act ii, sc. 1, l. 2.

Under the shade of melancholy boughs,
Lose and neglect the creeping hours of time.
SHAKESPEARE, *As You Like It*. Act ii, sc. 7, 111.

Unfrequented woods
I better brook than flourishing peopled towns.
SHAKESPEARE, *The Two Gentlemen of Verona*. Act v, sc. 4, l. 2.

3
The ruthless, vast, and gloomy woods.
SHAKESPEARE, *III Henry VI*. Act iv, sc. 1, l. 53.

With shadowy forests and with champains rich'd.
SHAKESPEARE, *King Lear*. Act i, sc. 1, l. 65.

4
Good is an Orchard, the Saint saith,
To meditate on life and death.
KATHARINE TYNAN, *Of an Orchard*.

5
The woods please us above all things. (Nobis placeant ante omnia sylvæ.)
VERGIL, *Eclogues*. No. ii, l. 62.

In such green palaces the first kings reign'd,
Slept in their shades, and angels entertain'd;
With such old counsellors they did advise,
And, by frequenting sacred groves, grew wise.
EDMUND WALLER, *On St. James' Park*, l. 71.

6
One impulse from a vernal wood
May teach you more of man,
Of moral evil and of good,
Than all the sages can.
WORDSWORTH, *The Tables Turned*. St. 6.

There is a spirit in the woods.
WORDSWORTH, *Nutting*, l. 56.

WOOING

See also Widow: Wooing a Widow

I—Wooing: Definitions and Apothegms

7
Men who do not make advances to women are apt to become victims to women who make advances to them.
WALTER BAGEHOT, *Biographical Studies*, p. 314.

8
Blessed is the wooing that is not long a-doing.
ROBERT BURTON, *Anatomy of Melancholy*. Pt. iii, sec. 2, mem. 6, subs. 5.

Thrice happy is that wooing
That is not long a-doing.
UNKNOWN. (*Paradise of Daintie Devices*. 1576.)

"Thrice happy's the wooing that's not long a-doing!"
So much time is saved in the billing and cooing.
R. H. BARHAM, *Sir Rupert the Fearless*.

9
Why don't the men propose, mamma?
Why don't the men propose?
T. H. BAYLY, *Why Don't the Men Propose?*

10
Why did not you pinch a flower
In a pellet of clay and fling it?
Why did not I put a power
Of thanks in a look, or sing it?
ROBERT BROWNING, *Youth and Art*.

11
Had sigh'd to many though he loved but one.
BYRON, *Childe Harold*. Canto i, st. 5.

And, oh! he had that merry glance
That seldom lady's heart resists.
Lightly from fair to fair he flew,
And loved to plead, lament, and sue—
Suit lightly won, and short-lived pain,
For monarchs seldom sigh in vain.
SCOTT, *Marmion*. Canto v, st. 9.

12
Barkis is willin'!
DICKENS, *David Copperfield*. Ch. 1.

"When a man says he's willin'," said Mr. Barkis, "it's as much as to say, that man's a-waitin' for a answer."
DICKENS, *David Copperfield*. Ch. 8.

13
The wooing was a day after the wedding.
THOMAS FULLER, *Gnomologia*. No. 4840.

He gave me an Italian glance and made me his.
W. S. GILBERT, *Ruddigore*. Act i. *See also* EYES AND LOVE.

14
Sure, I said, heav'n did not mean,
Where I reap thou shouldst but glean,
Lay thy sheaf adown and come,
Share my harvest and my home.
THOMAS HOOD, *Ruth*. St. 5.

Come live in my heart and pay no rent.
LOVER, *Vourneen! When Your Days Were Bright*.

15
Love is uniform, but courtship is perpetually varying: the different arts of gallantry, which beauty has inspired, would of themselves be sufficient to fill a volume.
SAMUEL JOHNSON, *The Adventurer*. No. 95.

16
If I am not worth the wooing, I surely am not worth the winning.
LONGFELLOW, *Courtship of Miles Standish*. Pt. iii.

17
Archly the maiden smiled, and, with eyes overrunning with laughter,

Said, in a tremulous voice, "Why don't you speak for yourself, John?"
LONGFELLOW, *The Courtship of Miles Standish*. Pt. iii, conclusion.

I wooed the blue-eyed maid,
Yielding, yet half afraid,
And in the forest's shade
Our vows were plighted.
LONGFELLOW, *The Skeleton in Armor.*

1
Erelong the time will come, sweet Preciosa,
When that dull distance shall no more divide us;
And I no more shall scale thy wall by night
To steal a kiss from thee, as I do now.
LONGFELLOW, *The Spanish Student*. Act i, sc. 3.

2
Her virtue and the conscience of her worth,
That would be woo'd, and not unsought be won.
MILTON, *Paradise Lost*. Bk. viii, l. 502.

3
The time I've lost in wooing,
In watching and pursuing
The light that lies
In woman's eyes,
Has been my heart's undoing.
THOMAS MOORE, *The Time I've Lost in Wooing.*

The heart of the wooer is warm, but warmer the heart of the wooing.
RICHARD REALF, *Indirection.*

4
I touch her, like my beads, with devout care,
And come unto my courtship as my prayer.
THOMAS RANDOLPH, *A Devout Lover.*

5
It was a happy age when a man might have wooed his wench with a pair of kid leather gloves, a silver thimble, or with a tawdry lace; but now a velvet gown, a chain of pearl, or a coach with four horses will scarcely serve the turn.
BARNABE RICH, *My Lady's Looking Glass.*

6
Afraid he would now, and now, and now, pop the question; which he had not the courage to put.
SAMUEL RICHARDSON, *Sir Charles Grandison*, vi, xx, 101.

7
And frame love ditties passing rare,
And sing them to a lady fair.
SCOTT, *Marmion*. Canto i, st. 7.

8
Most fair,
Will you vouchsafe to teach a soldier terms
Such as will enter at a lady's ear
And plead his love-suit to her gentle heart?
SHAKESPEARE, *Henry V*. Act v, sc. 2, l. 98.

I was not born under a rhyming planet, nor I cannot woo in festival terms.
SHAKESPEARE, *Much Ado About Nothing*, v, 2, 41.

Now, as I said before, I was never a maker of phrases.
I can march up to a fortress and summon the place to surrender,
But march up to a woman with such a proposal, I dare not.
I'm not afraid of bullets, nor shot from the mouth of a cannon,
But of a thundering "No!" point-blank from the mouth of a woman,
That I confess I'm afraid of, nor am I ashamed to confess it!
LONGFELLOW, *Courtship of Miles Standish*. Pt. ii.

9
She 's beautiful and therefore to be woo'd:
She is a woman, therefore to be won.
SHAKESPEARE, *I Henry VI*. Act v, sc. 3, l. 78.

She is a woman, therefore may be woo'd;
She is a woman, therefore may be won.
SHAKESPEARE, *Titus Andronicus*, ii, 1, 82.

Was ever woman in this humour woo'd?
Was ever woman in this humour won?
SHAKESPEARE, *Richard III*. Act i, sc. 2, l. 228.

For nature framed all women to be won.
TASSO, *Jerusalem Delivered*. Bk. ii, st. 15.

10
Be merry, and employ your chiefest thoughts
To courtship and such fair ostents of love
As shall conveniently become you there.
SHAKESPEARE, *The Merchant of Venice*. Act ii, sc. 8, l. 43.

You have brought her into such a canaries as 'tis wonderful.
SHAKESPEARE, *The Merry Wives of Windsor*. Act ii, sc. 2, l. 61.

11
If you were men, as you are men in show,
You would not use a gentle lady so;
To vow and swear and superpraise my parts,
When I am sure you hate me with your hearts.
SHAKESPEARE, *A Midsummer-Night's Dream*. Act iii, sc. 2, l. 151.

12
She wish'd she had not heard it, yet she wish'd
That heaven had made her such a man: she thank'd me,
And bade me, if I had a friend that loved her,
I should but teach him how to tell my story,
And that would woo her.
SHAKESPEARE, *Othello*. Act i, sc. 3, l. 162.

13
Gentle thou art and therefore to be won,
Beauteous thou art, therefore to be assailed:
And when a woman woos, what woman's son
Will sourly leave her till she have prevailed?
SHAKESPEARE, *Sonnets*. No. xli.

14
Women are angels, wooing:
Things won are done, joy's soul lies in the doing.
That she belov'd knows nought that knows not this:
Men prize the thing ungain'd more than it is.
SHAKESPEARE, *Troilus and Cressida*, i, 2, 312.

Our kindred, though they be long ere they are wooed, they are constant being won: they are burs, I can tell you; they'll stick where they are thrown.
SHAKESPEARE, *Troilus and Cressida*. Act iii, sc. 2, l. 118.

1
There is a young lady I have set my heart on; though whether she is a-goin' to give me hern, or give me the mitten, I ain't quite satisfied.
SAM SLICK, *Human Nature*, p. 90.

2
The weather is usually fine when people are courting.
R. L. STEVENSON, *Virginibus Puerisque*. Pt. iii.

3
I thought to undermine the heart
By whispering in the ear.
SIR JOHN SUCKLING, *'Tis Now, Since I Sat Down Before*.

4
Or sighed and looked unutterable things.
THOMSON, *The Seasons: Summer*, l. 1188.

II—Wooing: Its Delights

5
All soft and sweet the maid appears,
With looks that know no art,
And though she yields with trembling fears,
She yields with all her heart.
APHRA BEHN, *The Emperor of the Moon*. Act iii, sc. 3.

6
Much ado there was, God wot!
He would love and she would not.
She said, Never was man true;
He said, None was false to you.
He said, He had lov'd her long;
She said, Love should have no wrong.
Coridon would kiss her then;
She said, Maids must kiss no men
Till they did for good and all.
NICHOLAS BRETON, *Phillida and Coridon*.

But 'neath yon crimson tree,
Lover to listening maid might breathe his flame,
Nor mark, within its roseate canopy,
Her blush of maiden shame.
BRYANT, *Autumn Woods*.

7
Duncan Gray cam here to woo
(Ha, ha, the wooing o't!)
On blythe Yule-Night when we were fou
(Ha, ha, the wooing o't!).
Maggie coost her head fu' high,
Look'd asklent and unco skeigh,
Gart poor Duncan stand abeigh—
Ha. ha! the wooing o't!
BURNS, *Duncan Gray*.

He kin o' l'itered on the mat,
Some doubtfle o' the sekle,
His heart kep' goin' pity-pat,
But hern went pity Zekle.
LOWELL, *The Courtin'*. St. 15.

He stood a spell on one foot fust,
Then stood a spell on t'other,
An' on which one he felt the wust
He couldn't ha' told ye nuther.
J. R. LOWELL, *The Courtin'*. St. 19.

8
With a hey, Dolly! ho, Dolly!
Dolly shall be mine,
Before the spray is white with May,
Or blooms the eglantine.
AUSTIN DOBSON, *The Milkmaid*.

9
What is the greatest bliss
That the tongue o' man can name?
'Tis to woo a bonnie lassie
When the kye comes hame.
JAMES HOGG, *When the Kye Comes Hame*.

My Peggy is a young thing,
And I'm na very auld,
Yet weel I like to meet her at
The wauking o' the fauld.
ALLAN RAMSAY, *My Peggy*.

O ruddier than the cherry!
O sweeter than the berry!
O nymph more bright
Than moonshine night,
Like kidlings, blithe and merry!
Ripe as the melting cluster!
No lily has such lustre;
Yet hard to tame
As raging flame,
And fierce as storms that bluster!
JOHN GAY, *Acis and Galatea*. Pt. ii.

10
I sat with Doris, the Shepherd maiden;
Her crook was laden with wreathèd flowers;
I sat and wooed her through sunlight wheeling,
And shadows stealing for hours and hours.
ARTHUR JOSEPH MUNBY, *Pastoral*.

11
Wooed, and married, and a',
Married, and wooed, and a'!
And was she nae very weel aff
That was wooed, and married, and a'?
ALEXANDER ROSS, *Wooed and Married and A'*.

12
A heaven on earth I have won by wooing thee.
SHAKESPEARE, *All's Well that Ends Well*. Act iv, sc. 2, l. 66.

Wooing thee, I found thee of more value
Than stamps in gold or sums in sealed bags;
And 'tis the very riches of thyself
That now I aim at.
SHAKESPEARE, *The Merry Wives of Windsor*. Act iii, sc. 4, l. 15.

III—Wooing: Advice

13
Woo the fair one when around
Early birds are singing;
When o'er all the fragrant ground
Early herbs are springing:
When the brookside, bank, and grove
All with blossom laden,

Shine with beauty, breathe of love,
  Woo the timid maiden.
  BRYANT, *Love's Lessons.*

1
She that with poetry is won,
Is but a desk to write upon;
And what men say of her they mean
No more than on the thing they lean.
  BUTLER, *Hudibras.* Pt. ii, canto 1, l. 591.

2
Maidens, like moths, are ever caught by glare,
And Mammon wins his way where seraphs might despair.
  BYRON, *Childe Harold.* Canto i, st. 9.

The miller, he hecht her a heart leal and loving;
The laird did address her wi' matter mair moving:
A fine pacing-horse, wi' a clear, chainèd bridle,
A whip by her side, and a bonie side-saddle!
  ROBERT BURNS, *Meg o' the Mill.*

3
He that will win his dame must do
As love does when he draws his bow;
With one hand thrust the lady from,
And with the other pull her home.
  BUTLER, *Hudibras.* Pt. ii, canto 1, l. 449.

4
A man shall win us best with flattery.
  CHAUCER, *Wife of Bath's Tale,* l. 76.

Have you not found out that every woman is infallibly to be gained by every sort of flattery, and every man by one sort or other?
  LORD CHESTERFIELD, *Letters,* 16 March, 1752.

The firmest purpose of a woman's heart
To well-timed, artful flattery may yield.
  GEORGE LILLO, *Elmerick.*

5
He behaved as most professed admirers do. Said some civil things of my face, talked much of his want of merit, and the greatness of mine; mentioned his heart, gave a short tragedy speech, and ended with pretended rapture.
  GOLDSMITH, *She Stoops to Conquer.* Act v, 1.

6
If doughty deeds my lady please,
  Right soon I'll mount my steed;
And strong his arm and fast his seat,
  That bears frae me the meed. . . .
Then tell me how to woo thee, Love,
  O tell me how to woo thee!
For thy dear sake nae care I'll take,
  Tho' ne'er another trow me.
  ROBERT CUNNINGHAME-GRAHAM, *Tell Me How to Woo Thee.*

7
But, alas! alas! for the Woman's fate,
Who has from a mob to choose a mate
  'Tis a strange and painful mystery!
But the more the eggs, the worse the hatch;
The more the fish, the worse the catch;
The more the sparks, the worse the match;
  Is a fact in Woman's history.
  THOMAS HOOD, *Miss Kilmansegg: Her Courtship.* St. 7.

8
The surest way to hit a woman's heart is to take aim kneeling.
  DOUGLAS JERROLD, *The Way to a Woman's Heart.*

9
If I speak to thee in friendship's name,
  Thou think'st I speak too coldly;
If I mention Love's devoted flame,
  Thou say'st I speak too boldly.
  THOMAS MOORE, *How Shall I Woo?*

10
Frivolous minds are won by trifles: many have found useful the deft arranging of a cushion; it has helped, too, to stir the air with a light fan, or to set a stool beneath a dainty foot. (Parva leves capiunt animos.)
  OVID, *Ars Amatoria.* Bk. i, l. 159.

Employ soft flatteries, and words which delight the ear. (Blanditias molles, auremque juvantia verba Adfer.)
  OVID, *Ars Amatoria.* Bk. ii, l. 159.

If you can, truly; if not, at any rate readily. (Si poteris, vere; si minus, apta tamen.)
  OVID, *Ars Amatoria.* Bk. i, l. 228.

11
Do not begin your wooing with the maid. (Non tibi ab ancilla est incipienda venus.)
  OVID, *Ars Amatoria.* Bk. i, l. 386.

Who could not win the mistress wooed the maid.
  POPE, *Essay on Criticism.* Pt. i, l. 106.

Well, I will love, write, sigh, pray, sue, and groan:
Some men must love my lady and some Joan.
  SHAKESPEARE, *Love's Labour's Lost.* Act iii, sc. 1, l. 206.

12
He that would the daughter win,
Must with the mother first begin.
  JOHN RAY, *English Proverbs.*

13
Friendship is constant in all other things
Save in the office and affairs of love:
Therefore all hearts in love use their own tongues;
Let every eye negotiate for itself
And trust no agent.
  SHAKESPEARE, *Much Ado About Nothing.* Act ii, sc. 1, l. 182.

14
If thou dost love, pronounce it faithfully.
Or if thou think'st I am too quickly won,
I'll frown and be perverse and say thee nay,
So thou wilt woo: but else, not for the world.
  SHAKESPEARE, *Romeo and Juliet.* Act ii, sc. 2, l. 94.

15
Win her with gifts, if she respect not words;
Dumb jewels often in their silent kind
More than quick words do move a woman's mind.
  SHAKESPEARE, *The Two Gentlemen of Verona.* Act iii, sc. 1, l. 89.

Flatter and praise, commend, extol their graces;
Though ne'er so black, say they have angels' faces.

That man that hath a tongue, I say, is no man,
If with his tongue he cannot win a woman.
SHAKESPEARE, *The Two Gentlemen of Verona.* Act iii, sc. 1, l. 102.

Say that upon the altar of her beauty
You sacrifice your tears, your sighs, your heart:
Write till your ink be dry and with your tears
Moist it again, and frame some feeling line.
SHAKESPEARE, *The Two Gentlemen of Verona.* Act iii, sc. 2, l. 73.

Giving presents to a woman to secure her love, is as vain as endeavouring to fill a sieve with water.
EDWARD WARD, *Female Policy*, 23. (1716)

1
For courtesy wins woman all as well
As valour may.
TENNYSON, *The Last Tournament*, l. 702.

Perhaps if you address the lady
Most politely, most politely—
Flatter and impress the lady,
Most politely, most politely—
Humbly beg and humbly sue—
She may deign to look on you.
W. S. GILBERT, *Princess Ida.* Act i.

IV—Wooing: Faint Heart and Fair Lady

2
And let us mind, faint heart ne'er wan
A lady fair:
Wha does the utmost that he can
Will whyles do mair.
BURNS, *Epistle to Dr. Blacklock.*

Remember the old saying, "Faint heart never won fair lady."
CERVANTES, *Don Quixote.* Pt. ii, ch. 10.

Ah fool! faint heart fair lady ne'er could win.
PHINEAS FLETCHER, *Britain's Ida.* Canto v, st. 1. Sometimes wrongly attributed to Edmund Spenser.

Then have amongst ye once again,
Faint hearts fair ladies never win.
UNKNOWN, *A Proper Ballad in Praise of My Lady Marquess.* (1569)

Faint heart, hath been a common phrase,
Fair lady never wives.
UNKNOWN, *The Rocke of Regard.* (1576)

3
Brisk confidence still best with woman copes;
Pique her and soothe in turns, soon passion crowns thy hopes.
BYRON, *Childe Harold.* Canto ii, st. 34.

Thus the Soldier arm'd with Resolution
Told his soft Tale, and was a thriving Wooer.
CIBBER, *Richard III* (altered). Act ii, sc. 1.

4
But as men say, Where heart is failed,
There shall no castle be assailed.
JOHN GOWER, *Confessio Amantis.* Bk. v, l. 6573. (c. 1390)

Come not cringing to sue me!
Take me with triumph and power,
As a warrior storms a fortress!
I will not shrink or cower.
Come, as you came in the desert
Ere we were women and men,
When the tiger passions were in us,
And love as you loved me then!
WILLIAM WETMORE STORY, *Cleopatra.*

From the Desert I come to thee
On a stallion shod with fire,
And the winds are left behind
In the speed of my desire.
BAYARD TAYLOR, *Bedouin Song.*

5
To get thine ends, lay bashfulness aside;
Who fears to ask, doth teach to be deny'd.
ROBERT HERRICK, *No Bashfulness in Begging.*

6
I'll woo her as the lion woos his brides.
JOHN HOME, *Douglas.* Act i, sc. 1.

I now will court her in the conqueror's style;
"Come, see, and overcome."
MASSINGER, *The Maid of Honour.* Act ii, sc. 1.

7
The adventurous lover is successful still.
POPE, *Prologue for Mr. D'Urfey's Last Play.*

A pressing lover seldom wants success,
Whilst the respectful, like the Greek, sits down
And wastes a ten years' siege before one town.
NICHOLAS ROWE, *To the Inconstant: Epilogue*, l. 18.

8
He her chamber-window will ascend
And with a corded ladder fetch her down.
SHAKESPEARE, *The Two Gentlemen of Verona.* Act iii, sc. 1, l. 39.

He that climbs the tall tree has won right to the fruit,
He that leaps the wide gulf should prevail in his suit.
SCOTT, *The Talisman.* Ch. 26.

Ah, me! it was he that won her
Because he dared to climb!
THOMAS BAILEY ALDRICH, *Nocturne.*

9
Never give her o'er;
For scorn at first makes after-love the more.
If she do frown, 'tis not in hate of you,
But rather to beget more love in you:
If she do chide, 'tis not to have you gone,
For why, the fools are mad, if left alone.
SHAKESPEARE, *The Two Gentlemen of Verona.* Act iii, sc. 1, l. 94.

Foul words and frowns must not repel a lover;
What though the rose have prickles, yet 'tis pluck'd.
SHAKESPEARE, *Venus and Adonis*, l. 573.

He that after ten denials
Dares attempt no further trials,
Hath no warrant to acquire
The dainties of his chaste desire.
SIR PHILIP SIDNEY, *Wooing Stuff.*

10
Bring therefore all the forces that ye may,
And lay incessant battery to her heart;
Plaints, prayers, vows, ruth, sorrow, and dismay;
Those engines can the proudest love convert.

And, if those fail, fall down and die before her;
So dying live, and living do adore her.
EDMUND SPENSER, *Amoretti*. Sonnet xiv.

V—Wooing: Pursuer and Pursued

1
While I am I, and you are you,
So long as the world contains us both,
Me the loving and you the loth,
While the one eludes, must the other pursue.
ROBERT BROWNING, *Life in a Love*.

In fact, 'tis the season of billing and cooing,
Amorous flying and fond pursuing.
ROBERT BUCHANAN, *Fine Weather on the Digentia*. Pt. i, st. 1.

2
'Tis leap year, lady, and therefore very good to enter a courtier.
GEORGE CHAPMAN, *Bussy d'Ambois*. Act i, sc. 1. (1608) The custom of women proposing in leap year is said to have originated from a law passed in Scotland in 1228; another legend attributes it to St. Patrick.

Alas! to seize the moment
When heart inclines to heart,
And press a suit with passion,
Is not a woman's part.

If man come not to gather
The roses where they stand,
They fade among their foliage;
They cannot seek his hand.
BRYANT, *Song*. From the Spanish of Iglesias.

What then in love can woman do?
If we grow fond they shun us;
And when we fly them, they pursue,
And leave us when they've won us.
JOHN GAY, *The Beggar's Opera*. Act iii, sc. 8.

We cannot fight for love, as men may do;
We should be woo'd and were not made to woo.
SHAKESPEARE, *A Midsummer-Night's Dream*. Act ii, sc. 1, l. 241.

Though I lov'd you well, I woo'd you not;
And yet, good faith, I wish'd myself a man,
Or that we women had men's privilege
Of speaking first.
SHAKESPEARE, *Troilus and Cressida*. Act iii, sc. 2, l. 134.

3
Most complying, When denying,
And to be follow'd only flying.
WILLIAM CONGREVE, *Simile to Jupiter*.

4
Flee it [love], and it will flee thee,
Follow it, and it will follow thee.
THOMAS HOWELL, *H. His Devises*, 64. (1581)

I have pursued her as love hath pursued me; which hath been on the wing of all occasions. . . .
And that hath taught me to say this:
"Love like a shadow flies when substance love pursues;
Pursuing that that flies, and flying what pursues."
SHAKESPEARE, *The Merry Wives of Windsor*. Act ii, sc. 2, l. 208. (1600)

5
Follow a shadow, it still flies you,
Seem to fly it, it will pursue:
So court a mistress, she denies you;
Let her alone, she will court you.
Say are not women truly, then,
Styled but the shadows of us men?
BEN JONSON, *That Women Are but Men's Shadows*.

Flee, and she follows; follow, and she'll flee;
Than she there's none more coy; there's none more fond than she.
FRANCIS QUARLES, *Emblems*. Bk. i, No. 4.

6
Coy Hebe flies from those that woo,
And shuns the hands would seize upon her;
Follow thy life, and she will sue
To pour for thee the cup of honor.
J. R. LOWELL, *Hebe*. St. 7.

7
You pursue, I fly; you fly, I pursue. Such is my mind. (Insequeris, fugio; fugis, insequor; hæc mihi mens est.)
MARTIAL, *Epigrams*. Bk. v, epig. 83.

8
'Tis the quarry that flees that the hunter follows; what he takes he leaves behind, and ever strains to the prey ahead. (Venator sequitur fugienta; sapta relinquit Semper et inventis ulteriora petit.)
OVID, *Amores*. Bk. ii, eleg. 9, l. 9.

Many women desire what flees them; they hate what is too forward. (Quod refugit, multæ cupiunt: odere quod instat.)
OVID, *Ars Amatoria*. Bk. i, l. 717.

9
Ah, whither shall a maiden flee,
When a bold youth so swift pursues,
And siege of tenderest courtesy,
With hope perseverant, still renews?
COVENTRY PATMORE, *The Angel in the House:* Canto xii, *The Chase*.

10
You think that you are Ann's suitor; that you are the pursuer and she the pursued; that it is your part to woo, to persuade, to prevail, to overcome. Fool: it is you who are the pursued, the marked-down quarry, the destined prey.
BERNARD SHAW, *Man and Superman*. Act ii.

Pursued man loves to think himself pursuer.
EDMUND VANCE COOKE, *From the Book of Extenuations: Ruth*.

A man always chases a woman until she catches him.
UNKNOWN. (Columnist in El Paso *Times*.)

11
My love is male and proper-man
And what he'd have he'd get by chase,
So I must cheat as women can
And keep my love from off my face.
'Tis folly to my dawning, thrifty thought
That I must run, who in the end am caught.
ANNA WICKHAM, *The Contemplative Quarry*.

VI—Wooing and Repenting

1
Of her scorn the maid repented,
And the shepherd of his love.

ANNA LETITIA BARBAULD, *Leave Me, Simple Shepherd.*

2
And she, she lies in my hand as tame
As a late pear basking over the wall;
Just a touch to try and off it came;
'Tis mine—can I let it fall?

ROBERT BROWNING, *A Light Woman.*

That you're in a terrible taking,
By all these sweet oglings I see,
But the fruit that will fall without shaking,
Indeed is too mellow for me.

LADY MARY WORTLEY MONTAGU, *To a Lady Making Love.*

3
For this is a sort of engagement, you see,
Which is binding on you but not binding on me.

WILLIAM ALLEN BUTLER, *Nothing to Wear.*

4
I'm jilted, forsaken, outwitted;
Yet think not I'll whimper or bawl—
The lass is alone to be pitied
Who ne'er has been courted at all; . . .
What though at my heart he has tilted,
What though I have met with a fall?
Better be courted and jilted
Then never be courted at all.

THOMAS CAMPBELL, *The Jilted Nymph.*

Never wedding, ever wooing,
Still a love-lorn heart pursuing,
Read you not the wrong you're doing
In my cheek's pale hue?
All my life with sorrow strewing—
Wed, or cease to woo.

THOMAS CAMPBELL, *The Maid's Remonstrance.*

5
It's better to change your attitude an' pay some heart balm than to be dug up later an' analyzed.

KIN HUBBARD, *Abe Martin's Broadcast*, p. 85.

6
A fool there was and he made his prayer
(Even as you and I!)
To a rag and a bone and a hank of hair
(We called her the woman who did not care)
But the fool he called her his lady fair—
(Even as you and I!)

RUDYARD KIPLING, *The Vampire.* St. 1. Written to accompany the description of Burne-Jones's picture, "The Vampire," in the catalogue of the 1897 summer exhibition of the New Gallery, London.

7
Ye shall know my breach of promise.

Old Testament: Numbers, xiv, 34.

Chops and Tomato sauce. Yours, Pickwick. Chops! Gracious heavens! and Tomato sauce! Gentlemen, is the happiness of a sensitive and confiding female to be trifled away by such shallow artifices as these?

DICKENS, *Pickwick Papers.* Ch. 34.

Thou didst swear to me upon a parcel-gilt goblet, sitting in my Dolphin-chamber, at the round table, by a sea-coal fire, on Wednesday in Wheeson week, when the prince broke thy head for liking his father to a singing-man of Windsor, thou didst swear to me then, as I was washing thy wound, to marry me, and make me my lady thy wife. Canst thou deny it?

SHAKESPEARE, *II Henry IV.* Act ii, sc. 1, l. 93.

8
Who wooed in haste, and means to wed at leisure.

SHAKESPEARE, *Taming of the Shrew*, iii, 2, 11.

WORDS

See also Language, Speech

I—Words: Definitions

9
Words are the physicians of a mind diseased.
(᾽Οργῆς νοσούσης εἰσιν ἰατροὶ λόγοι.)

ÆSCHYLUS, *Prometheus, Bound*, l. 380.

The spoken word is man's physician in grief.
(Λύτης ἰατρός ἐστιν ἀνθρώποις λόγος.)

MENANDER, *Fragments.* No. 559.

10
Words are the tokens current and accepted for conceits, as moneys are for values.

BACON, *Advancement of Learning.* Bk. ii.

Words are wise men's counters, they do but reckon by them; but they are the money of fools.

THOMAS HOBBES, *Leviathan.* Pt. i, ch. 4.

11
All words are pegs to hang ideas on.

HENRY WARD BEECHER, *Proverbs from Plymouth Pulpit: Human Mind.*

12
Slang has no country, it owns the world. . . It is the voice of the god that dwells in the people.

RALCY HUSTED BELL, *The Mystery of Words.*

Dialect words—those terrible marks of the beast to the truly genteel.

THOMAS HARDY, *Mayor of Casterbridge.* Ch. 20.

13
For what are the voices of birds
Ay, and of beasts—but words, our words,
Only so much more sweet?

ROBERT BROWNING, *Pippa Passes.* Pt. iv.

14
Articulate words are a harsh clamor and dissonance. When man arrives at his highest perfection, he will again be dumb!

HAWTHORNE, *American Note-Books*, April, 1841.

15
A word is not a crystal, transparent and unchanging, it is the skin of a living thought and may vary greatly in color and content according to the circumstances and time in which it is used.

JUSTICE O. W. HOLMES, *Decision.* (*Towne v. Eisner*, 245 U.S. 418.)

Life and language are alike sacred. Homicide and *verbicide*—that is, violent treatment of a word with fatal results to its legitimate meaning, which is its life—are alike forbidden.

HOLMES, *Autocrat of the Breakfast-Table.* Ch. 1.

1
Words are the soul's ambassadors, who go
Abroad upon her errands to and fro.
JAMES HOWELL, *Of the Strange Vertu of Words.*

2
Sincere words are not grand.
LAO-TSZE, *The Simple Way.* No. 81.

2a
We should have a great many fewer disputes in the world if words were taken for what they are, the signs of our ideas only, and not for things themselves.
JOHN LOCKE, *Essay on the Human Understanding.* Pt. iii, ch. 10.

3
Things were first made, then words.
SIR THOMAS OVERBURY, *A Wife.*

As shadows attend substances, so words follow upon things.
RICHARD CHENEVIX TRENCH, *Study of Words.*

5
Out, idle words, servants to shallow fools!
Unprofitable sounds, weak arbitrators!
SHAKESPEARE, *The Rape of Lucrece.* St. 146.

Weasel words are words that suck all the life out of the words next to them, just as a weasel sucks an egg and leaves the shell.
STEWART CHAPLIN, *The Stained-Glass Political Platform.* (*Century Mag.*, June, 1900, p. 305.)

One of our defects as a nation is a tendency to use what have been called "weasel words." When a weasel sucks an egg, the meat is sucked out of the egg; and if you use a "weasel word" after another there is nothing left of the other.
THEODORE ROOSEVELT, *Speech,* at St. Louis, Mo., 31 May, 1916.

II—Words: Apothegms

6
Words of truth and soberness.
New Testament: Acts, xxvi, 25.

Words pregnant with celestial fire.
COWPER, *Boadicea.* St. 9.

Some heart once pregnant with celestial fire.
THOMAS GRAY, *Elegy Written in a Country Church-yard.* St. 12.

Large, divine and comfortable words.
TENNYSON, *The Coming of Arthur,* l. 267.

7
No words suffice the secret soul to show,
For Truth denies all eloquence to Woe.
BYRON, *The Corsair.* Canto iii, st. 22. *See also* GRIEF: SILENT AND VOCAL.

8
Words that weep and tears that speak.
ABRAHAM COWLEY, *The Prophet.* St. 2.

Words that weep, and strains that agonise.
DAVID MALLET, *Amyntor and Theodora,* ii, 306.

Strains that sigh and words that weep.
DAVID MALLET, *Funeral Hymn,* l. 23.

OF ALL SAD WORDS, *see under* REGRET.

9
Religion! what treasure untold
Resides in that heavenly word!
COWPER, *Verses Supposed to Have Been Written by Alexander Selkirk.*

I have found great support in that heavenly word, Mesopotamia.
UNKNOWN. Supposed to have been said by an old woman to her pastor. (BREWER, *Dictionary of Phrase and Fable.*)

He could make men laugh or cry by pronouncing the word Mesopotamia.
DAVID GARRICK, of George Whitefield, the famous Methodist preacher. (FRANCIS JACOX, *Notes and Queries.* Ser. xi, vol. i, p. 458.)

Alice had not the slightest idea what Latitude was, or Longitude either, but she thought they were nice grand words to say.
LEWIS CARROLL, *Alice's Adventures in Wonderland.* Ch. 1.

10
I am not a man scrupulous about words or names or such things.
OLIVER CROMWELL, *Speech,* 13 April, 1657.

11
A word in earnest is as good as a speech.
DICKENS, *Bleak House.* Ch. 6.

12
The words of the wise are as goads.
Old Testament: Ecclesiastes, xii, 11.

Her words y-clad with wisdom's majesty.
SHAKESPEARE, *II Henry VI.* Act i, sc. 1, l. 33.

13
Good words anoint a man, ill words kill a man.
JOHN FLORIO, *First Fruites.* Fo. 31. (1578)

Good words are worth much and cost little.
GEORGE HERBERT, *Jacula Prudentum.*

14
Better one living word than a hundred dead.
W. G. BENHAM, *Quotations,* p. 743b.

15
To make dictionaries is dull work.
SAMUEL JOHNSON, *Dictionary: Dull.*

Dictionaries are like watches; the worst is better than none, and the best cannot be expected to go quite true.
SAMUEL JOHNSON. (PIOZZI, *Johnsoniana,* 178.)

16
By thy words thou shalt be condemned.
New Testament: Matthew, xii, 37.

17
You actually snatch the words from my mouth. (Tu quidem ex ore orationem mihi eripis.)
PLAUTUS, *Mercator,* l. 176. (Act i, sc. 2.)

18
A word to the wise is sufficient. (Dictum sapienti sat est.)
PLAUTUS, *Persa,* l. 729. (Act iv, sc. 7.)

To a man of understanding only a word is necessary. (À bon entendeur ne faut qu'une parole.)
RABELAIS, *Works.* Pt. ii, bk. 5, ch. 7.

A word is enough for the wise. (Dictum sapienti sat est.)
TERENCE, *Phormio,* l. 541. (Act iii, sc. 3.)

To the intelligent man a word is enough. (Intelligenti satis dictum est.)
À KEMPIS, *De Imitatione Christi.* Pt. iii, ch. 34.

Presto, Go to, a word to the wise; away, fly.
BEN JONSON, *The Case Is Altered*. Act i, sc. 1.

A word to the wise is enough.
SIR JOHN VANBRUGH, *Æsop*. Act iii, sc. 1.

Send the wise and say nothing.
CHAUCER, *Milleres Tale*, l. 412.

1 We're pouring our words into a sieve. (In pertusum ingerimus dicta dolium.)
PLAUTUS, *Pseudolus*, l. 369. (Act i, sc. 3.)

2 These words did not come from the edge of the lips. (Non a summis labris ista venerunt.)
SENECA, *Epistulæ ad Lucilium*. Epis. x, sec. 3.

3 He words me, girls, he words me.
SHAKESPEARE, *Antony and Cleopatra*, v, 2, 191.

4 Answer me in one word.
SHAKESPEARE, *As You Like It*. Act iii, sc. 2, l. 237.

Celia: Not a word?
Rosalind: Not one to throw at a dog.
SHAKESPEARE, *As You Like It*. Act i, sc. 3, l. 2.

5 Familiar in his mouth as household words.
SHAKESPEARE, *Henry V*. Act iv, sc. 3, l. 52.

6 The words of Mercury are harsh after the songs of Apollo.
SHAKESPEARE, *Love's Labour's Lost*. Act v, sc. 2, l. 940.

7 Madam, you have bereft me of all words.
Only my blood speaks to you in my veins.
SHAKESPEARE, *The Merchant of Venice*. Act iii, sc. 2, l. 177.

8 I understand a fury in your words,
But not the words.
SHAKESPEARE, *Othello*. Act iv, sc. 2, l. 32.

9 A fool and his words are soon parted.
WILLIAM SHENSTONE, *On Reserve*.

10 Before I eat these words, I will make thee eat a piece of my blade.
RICHARD STANYHURST, *Description of Ireland*. Fo. 20. (1577)

I'll make you eat your words before I've done.
EDWARD WARD, *Nuptial Dialogues*, i, 353.

I'll make you eat your words.
UNKNOWN, *Play of Stuckley*, l. 428. (c. 1600)

11 What need is there for words? (Quid opus est verbis?)
TERENCE, *Andria*, l. 165. (Act i, sc. 1.)

12 It is the man determines what is said, not the words.
H. D. THOREAU, *Journal*, 11 July, 1840.

13 A word in your ear.
VANBRUGH AND CIBBER, *The Provok'd Husband*. Act iv, sc. 1.

14 Briticism.
RICHARD GRANT WHITE, *Galaxy*, March, 1868.

The word Americanism, which I have coined, . . . is exactly similar in its formation and signification to the word Scotticism.
JOHN WITHERSPOON. *The Druid*, No. 5. (1781)
It was Witherspoon who coined the word Americanism, and at once the English guardians of the sacred vessels began employing it as a general synonym for vulgarism and barbarism.—H. L. MENCKEN, *The American Language*, p. 49.

III—Words: Their Power

15 Words provoke to senseless wrath. (Ὀργῆς ματαίας εἰσὶν αἴτιοι λόγοι.)
ÆSCHYLUS [?], *Fragments*. Frag. 260.

16 By words the mind is excited and the spirit elated.
ARISTOPHANES, *The Birds*, l. 1445.

17 Words, as a Tartar's bow, do shoot back upon the understanding of the wisest, and mightily entangle and pervert the judgement.
BACON, *Advancement of Learning*. Bk. ii.

18 A very great part of the mischiefs that vex this world arises from words.
EDMUND BURKE, *Letter*. (c. 1795)

19 Words, words that gender things!
SIR RICHARD BURTON, *Kasîdah*. Pt. vii, st. 4.

But words are things; and a small drop of ink,
Falling, like dew, upon a thought, produces
That which makes thousands, perhaps millions, think.
BYRON, *Don Juan*. Canto iii, st. 88.

Words lead to things; a scale is more precise,—
Coarse speech, bad grammar, swearing, drinking, vice.
O. W. HOLMES, *A Rhymed Lesson*, l. 374.

20 High Air-castles are cunningly built of Words, the Words well bedded also in good Logic-mortar; wherein, however, no Knowledge will come to lodge.
CARLYLE, *Sartor Resartus*. Bk. i, ch. 8.

Intellect can raise,
From airy words alone, a Pile that ne'er decays.
WORDSWORTH, *Inscriptions*. No. 4.

Word by word the book is made. (Mot à mot on fait les gros livres.)
UNKNOWN. A French proverb.

21 How strong an influence works in well-placed words.
CHAPMAN, *The Gentleman Usher*. Act iv, sc. 1.

22 Without knowing the force of words, it is impossible to know men.
CONFUCIUS, *Analects*. Bk. xx, ch. 3.

For one word a man is often deemed to be wise, and for one word he is often deemed to be foolish. We should be careful indeed what we say.
CONFUCIUS, *Analects*. Bk. xix, ch. 25.

1 With words we govern men.
BENJAMIN DISRAELI, *Contarini Fleming*, i, 21.

Syllables govern the world.
JOHN SELDEN, *Table-Talk: Power, State.*

2 Words are, of course, the most powerful drug used by mankind.
RUDYARD KIPLING, *Speech*, 14 Feb., 1923.

The masterless man, . . . afflicted with the magic of the necessary words . . . Words that may become alive and walk up and down in the hearts of the hearers.
RUDYARD KIPLING, *Speech*, Royal Academy Banquet. London, 1906.

3 Heaven and earth shall pass away, but my words shall not pass away.
New Testament: Matthew, xxiv, 35.

Words are the only things that last forever.
HAZLITT, *Table Talk: On Thought and Action.*

Every word man's lips have uttered
Echoes in God's skies.
ADELAIDE ANN PROCTER, *Words.*

4 Loyal words have the secret of healing grief. (Λύπην γὰρ εὔνους οἶδε θεραπεύειν λογος.)
MENANDER, *Fragments*. No. 591.

A word in season spoken
May calm the troubled breast.
CHARLES JEFFERYS, *A Word in Season.*

Apt words have power to suage
The tumors of a troubl'd mind.
MILTON, *Samson Agonistes*, l. 184.

Good words cool more than cold water.
JOHN RAY, *English Proverbs.*

Kind words are benedictions.
FREDERICK SAUNDERS, *Stray Leaves: Smiles and Tears.*

5 A word spoken in due season, how good is it!
Old Testament: Proverbs, xv, 23.

A word fitly spoken is like apples of gold in pictures of silver.
Old Testament: Proverbs, xxv, 11.

6 Often a single word betrays a great design. (Souvent d'un grand dessein un mot nous fait juger.)
RACINE, *Athalie*. Act ii, sc. 6.

7 Words should be scattered like seed; no matter how small the seed may be, if it has once found favorable ground, it unfolds its strength.
SENECA, *Epistulæ ad Lucilium*. Epis. 38, sec. 2.

8 Words distract me more than noises, for words demand attention.
SENECA, *Epistulæ ad Lucilium*. Epis. 56, sec. 4.

9 A Daniel, still say I, a second Daniel!
I thank thee, Jew, for teaching me that word.
SHAKESPEARE, *Merchant of Venice*, iv, 1, 340.

I thank thee, Roderick, for the word!
It nerves my heart, it steels my sword.
SCOTT, *The Lady of the Lake*. Canto v, st. 14.

10 How long a time lies in one little word!
Four lagging winters and four wanton springs
End in a word: such is the breath of kings.
SHAKESPEARE, *Richard II*. Act i, sc. 3, l. 213.

11 Such words would have robbed me of my certainty that stars shine in the skies and that streams run downwards. (Illis eriperes verbis mini sidera cæli Lucere et pronas fluminis esse vias.)
TIBULLUS, *Odes*. Bk. i, ode 9, l. 35.

IV—Words: Their Weakness

12 Words, phrases, fashions pass away;
But truth and nature live through all.
BERNARD BARTON, *Stanzas on Bloomfield.*

Words writ in waters.
CHAPMAN, *Revenge for Honour*. Act v, sc. 2.

13 Words and feathers are tossed by the wind.
JOHN RAY, *English Proverbs.*

14 And their words seemed to them as idle tales.
New Testament: Luke, xxiv, 11.

15 To recount almighty works,
What words or tongue of seraph can suffice?
MILTON, *Paradise Lost*. Bk. vii, l. 112.

16 Fair words fat few.
JOHN LYLY, *Euphues and His England*, p. 476. (1580)

Fair words fill not the belly.
THOMAS FULLER, *Gnomologia*. No. 1491. (1732)

Fair words butter no parsnips, verba non alunt familiam.
JOHN CLARKE, *Parœmiologia*, 12. (1639) ARTHUR MURPHY, *The Citizen*, i, 2. (1795)

Fair words butter no cabbage.
WYCHERLEY, *Plain Dealer*. Act v, sc. 3. (1674)

17 Words don't chink. (Dicta non sonant.)
PLAUTUS, *Pseudolus*, l. 308. (Act i, sc. 3.)

Good words fill not a sack.
JOHN RAY, *English Proverbs*, 220. (1678)

18 But words are words; I never yet did hear
That the bruis'd heart was pierced through the ear.
SHAKESPEARE, *Othello*. Act i, sc. 3, l. 218.

19 Words are grown so false, I am loath to prove reason with them.
SHAKESPEARE, *Twelfth Night*. Act iii, sc. 1, l. 28

20 My words are only words, and moved
Upon the topmost froth of thought.
TENNYSON, *In Memoriam*. Pt. lii, st. 1.

21 What signifies a few foolish angry words?
They don't break bones, nor give black eyes.
GEORGE VILLIERS, *The Militant Couple.*

Words will build no walls. (Λόγοισι προάγει . . . ἔργοισι δ' οὐδὲ κινεῖ.)

UNKNOWN. (KOCK, *Com. Att. Frag.*, i, 100.) A line from an old play quoted by Cratinus in ridicule of the delay shown by Pericles in building a wall about Athens. (PLUTARCH, *Lives: Pericles*, 13, 5.)

1
What is word but wind?

UNKNOWN, *Ancrene Riwle*, 122. (c. 1220)

Word is but wind; leave word and take the deed.

JOHN LYDGATE, *Secrees*, 39. (c. 1450)

'Tis not *Good words* that can a man maintain;
Words are but wind; and wind is all but vain.

RICHARD BARNFIELD, *The Complaint of Poetrie*. (1598)

Tempestuous winds of words.

MASSINGER, *The Maid of Honour*. Act i, sc. 1.

Words are but wind, but blows unkind.

JOHN RAY, *English Proverbs*.

WORD AND A BLOW, *see under* ARGUMENT.

2
Fair words enough a man shall find;
They be good cheap: they cost right nought;
Their substance is but only wind.

SIR THOMAS WYATT, *Of Dissembling Words*.

V—Words: Their Use

See also Style; Writing: The Manner

3
The noisomeness of far-fetched words. (Reconditorum verborum fetoribus.)

AUGUSTUS. (SUETONIUS, *Twelve Cæsars: Augustus*. Sec. 86.)

4
"Correct my manners or my waggeries,
But though my accent's not the berries,
Spare my pronunciation's vagaries . . ."
To that she merely said, "Vagaries!"

MORRIS BISHOP, *Why and How I Killed My Wife*.

5
Well, "slithy" means "lithe and slimy." . . . You see it's like a portmanteau—there are two meanings packed up into one word.

LEWIS CARROLL, *Through the Looking-Glass*. Ch. 6. Hence "portmanteau word," a word formed by combining the elements of two other words.

Pennyboy: Emissaries? stay, there's a fine new word, Tom;
Pray God it signify anything! what are emissaries?
Thomas: Men employed outward, that are sent abroad
To fetch in the commodity.

BEN JONSON, *The Staple of News*. Act i, sc. 1.

I will maintain the word with my sword to be a good soldier-like word, and a word of exceeding good command, by heaven. Accommodated: that is, when a man is, as they say, accommodated; or, when a man is, being, whereby, a' may be thought to be accommodated; which is an excellent thing.

SHAKESPEARE, *II Henry IV*. Act iii, sc. 2, l. 82.

6
"The question is," said Alice, "whether you *can* make words mean so many different things."
"The question is," said Humpty Dumpty, "which is to be master—that's all."

LEWIS CARROLL, *Through the Looking-Glass* Ch. 6.

7
Words are the dress of thoughts; which should no more be presented in rags, tatters, and dirt, than your person should.

LORD CHESTERFIELD, *Letters*, 25 Jan., 1750.

8
Philologists who chase
A panting syllable through time and space,
Start it at home, and hunt it in the dark
To Gaul, to Greece, and into Noah's ark.

COWPER, *Retirement*, l. 691.

And torture one poor word ten thousand ways.

DRYDEN, *Mac Flecknoe*, l. 208.

How many quarrels, how many important ones, have been caused by doubt as to the meaning of this single syllable, "Hoc." (Combien de querelles, et combien importantes, a produit au monde le doute du sens de cette syllabe, "Hoc.")

MONTAIGNE, *Essays*. Bk. ii, ch. 12. Referring to the controversies on transubstantiation, "Hoc est corpus meum."

Imperious some a classic fame demand
For heaping up, with a laborious hand,
A waggon-load of meanings for one word.

YOUNG, *Love of Fame*. Sat. i, l. 85.

Each wight who reads not, and but scans and spells,
Each word-catcher that lives on syllables.

POPE, *Epistle to Dr. Arbuthnot*, l. 165.

9
The little *and*, the tiny *if*,
The ardent *ahs* and *ohs*,
They haunt the lanes of poesy,
The boulevards of prose.

NATHALIA CRANE, *Alliances*.

10
He had used the word in its Pickwickian sense . . . he had merely considered him a humbug in a Pickwickian point of view.

DICKENS, *Pickwick Papers*. Ch. 1. A paraphrase of a quarrel between Brougham and Canning in the House of Commons, 17 April, 1823.

"Do you spell it with a *'V'* or a *'W'?*" inquired the judge.
"That depends upon the taste and fancy of the speller, my Lord," replied Sam.

DICKENS, *Pickwick Papers*. Ch. 34.

"Put it down a we, my Lord, put it down a we."

DICKENS, *Pickwick Papers*. Ch. 34.

11
As long as words a diff'rent sense will bear
And each may be his own interpreter,
Our airy faith will no foundation find,
The word's a weathercock for ev'ry wind.

DRYDEN, *The Hind and Panther*. Pt. i, l. 462

1
There is no choice of words for him who clearly sees the truth. . . . Any word, every word in language, every circumstance, becomes poetic in the hands of a higher thought.

EMERSON, *Letters and Social Aims: Poetry and Imagination.*

2
Grant me some wild expressions, Heavens, or I shall burst. . . . Words, words, or I shall burst.

FARQUHAR, *The Constant Couple.* Act v, sc. 3.

3
And don't confound the language of the nation
With long-tailed words in osity and ation.

J. HOOKHAM FRERE, *The Monks and the Giants.* Canto i, l. 6.

While words of learned length and thund'ring sound
Amazed the gazing rustics rang'd around.

GOLDSMITH, *The Deserted Village,* l. 213.

Words a foot-and-a-half long. (Sesquipedalia verba.)

HORACE, *Ars Poetica,* l. 96.

Physicians deafen our ears with the honorificabilitudinitatibus of their heavenly Panochœa, their sovereign guiacum.

THOMAS NASHE, *Lenten Stuff.* (1599)

Thou art not so long by the head as honorificabilitudinitatibus.

SHAKESPEARE, *Love's Labour's Lost.* Act v, sc. 1, l. 44. (1594)

The iron age returned to Erebus,
And Honorificabilitudinitatibus
Thrust out the kingdom by the head and shoulders.

BEAUMONT AND FLETCHER, *The Mad Lover.* This word is said to have first appeared in 1548 in a volume entitled *The Complaynt of Scotland.* It was no doubt a stock example of the longest Latin word.

4
Harsh words, though pertinent, uncouth appear;
None please the fancy who offend the ear.

GARTH, *The Dispensary.* Canto iv, l. 204.

5
I had always imagined that Cliché was a suburb of Paris, until I discovered it to be a street in Oxford.

PHILIP GUEDALLA, *Some Historians.*

6
I hate to see a load of band-boxes go along the street, and I hate to see a parcel of big words without anything in them.

WILLIAM HAZLITT, *Table Talk,* ii, 190.

7
Some scurvy quaint collection of fustian phrases, and uplandish words.

THOMAS HEYWOOD, *Faire Maide of the Exchange.* Act ii, sc. 2.

8
Sorrowful words become the sorrowful, angry words the passionate, jesting words the merry, and solemn words the grave. (Tristia mæstum Voltum verba decent, iratum plena minarum, Ludentem lasciva, severum seria dictu.)

HORACE, *Ars Poetica,* l. 105.

9
How forcible are right words!

Old Testament: Job, vi, 25.

Hold fast the form of sound words.

New Testament: II Timothy, i, 13.

10
The study of words is the first distemper of learning.

BEN JONSON, *Explorata: Notæ.* Quoting Bacon.

11
His words were simple words enough,
And yet he used them so,
That what in other mouths was rough
In his seemed musical and low.

J. R. LOWELL, *The Shepherd of King Admetus.*

12
How many honest words have suffered corruption since Chaucer's days!

THOMAS MIDDLETON, *No Wit, No Help, Like a Woman's.* Act ii, sc. 1.

13
His words, . . . like so many nimble and airy servitors, trip about him at command.

MILTON, *Apology for Smectymnuus.*

High words, that bore
Semblance of worth, not substance.

MILTON, *Paradise Lost.* Bk. i, l. 528.

Words repeated again have as another sound, so another sense.

MONTAIGNE, *Essays.* Bk. iii, ch. 12.

14
To bring in a new word by the head and shoulders, they leave out the old one.

MONTAIGNE, *Essays:* Bk. iii, ch. 5.

The third refinement observable in the letter I send you consists of the choice of certain words invented by some pretty fellows, such as *banter, bamboozle,* . . . and *kidney* . . . some of which are now struggling for the vogue, and others are in possession of it.

SWIFT, *The Tatler,* 28 Sept., 1710.

15
I almost had forgotten
That words were meant for rhyme:
And yet how well I knew it—
Once upon a time!

CHRISTOPHER MORLEY, *I Almost Had Forgotten.*

16
In words as fashions the same rule will hold,
Alike fantastic if too new or old:
Be not the first by whom the new are tried,
Nor yet the last to lay the old aside.

POPE, *Essay on Criticism.* Pt. ii, l. 133.

Command old words, that long have slept, to wake,

Words that wise Bacon, or brave Raleigh spake.
POPE, *Imitations of Horace: Epistles*. Bk. ii, epis. 2, l. 167.

So all my best is dressing old words new.
SHAKESPEARE, *Sonnets*. No. lxxvi.

1
Clearness is the most important matter in the use of words. (Perspicuitas in verbis præcipuam habet proprietatem.)
QUINTILIAN, *De Institutione Oratoria*. Bk. vii, ch. 2, sec. 1.

2
We tie knots and bind up words in double meanings, and then try to untie them. (Nectimus nodos et ambiguam significationem verbis inligamus ac deinde dissolvimus.)
SENECA, *Epistulæ ad Lucilium*. Epis. xlv, sec. 5.

3
Do not play in wench-like words with that
Which is so serious.
SHAKESPEARE, *Cymbeline*. Act iv, sc. 2, l. 230.

4
Your words,
Domestics to you, serve your will as 't please
Yourself pronounce their office.
SHAKESPEARE, *Henry VIII*. Act ii, sc. 4, l. 113.

5
Few words, but to effect.
SHAKESPEARE, *King Lear*. Act iii, sc. 1, l. 52.

6
I have words
That would be howl'd out in the desert air,
Where hearing should not latch them.
SHAKESPEARE, *Macbeth*. Act iv, sc. 3, l. 193.

7
The fool hath planted in his memory
An army of good words; and I do know
A many fools, that stand in better place,
Garnish'd like him, that for a tricksy word
Defy the matter.
SHAKESPEARE, *The Merchant of Venice*. Act iii, sc. 5, l. 71.

His very words are a fantastical banquet, just so many strange dishes.
SHAKESPEARE, *Much Ado About Nothing*. Act ii, sc. 3, l. 21.

I moralise two meanings in one word.
SHAKESPEARE, *Richard III*. Act iii, sc. 1, l. 83.

8
They that dally nicely with words may quickly make them wanton.
SHAKESPEARE, *Twelfth Night*. Act iii, sc. 1, l. 16.

9
The arts Babblative and Scribblative.
ROBERT SOUTHEY, *Colloquies on the Progress and Prospects of Society*.

10
All the charm of all the Muses often flowering in a lonely word.
TENNYSON, *To Virgil*. St. 3.

Wild words wander here and there;
God's great gift of speech abused.
TENNYSON, *A Dirge*. St. 7.

11
Cunning, I trow, to war with words.
TIMON, *Fragments*, No. 47. Referring to Protagoras. (DIOGENES LAERTIUS, *Protagoras*. Bk. ix, sec. 51.)

12
Some of his words were not Sunday-school words. . . . Some of those old American words do have a kind of a bully swing to them.
MARK TWAIN, *A Tramp Abroad*. Ch. 20.

13
You phrase tormenting fantastic chorus,
With strangest words at your beck and call.
WILLIAM WATSON, *Orgy on Parnassus*.

Would you repeat that again, sir, for it soun's sae sonorous that the words droon the ideas?
JOHN WILSON, *Noctes Ambrosianiæ*. Ch. 27.

14
Choice word and measured phrase, above the reach
Of ordinary men.
WORDSWORTH, *Resolution and Independence*. St. 14.

VI—Words: Sweet Words

15
Words of affection, howsoe'er express'd,
The latest spoken still are deem'd the best.
JOANNA BAILLIE, *Address to Miss Agnes Baillie on Her Birthday*, l. 126.

Words that will solace him while life endures.
THOMAS CAMPBELL, *Theodric*, l. 565.

Speaking words of endearment where words of comfort availed not.
LONGFELLOW, *Evangeline*. Pt. i, sec. 5, l. 43.

16
Fair words never hurt the tongue.
GEORGE CHAPMAN, *Eastward Hoe*. Act iv, sc. 1.

Soft words hurt not the mouth.
GEORGE HERBERT, *Jacula Prudentum*.

Soft words win hard hearts.
W. G. BENHAM, *Proverbs*, p. 835.

17
Fair words make me look to my purse.
GEORGE HERBERT, *Jacula Prudentum*.

18
Words sweet as honey from his lips distill'd.
HOMER, *Iliad*. Bk. i, l. 332. (Pope, tr.)

The words of his mouth were smoother than butter, but war was in his heart: his words were softer than oil, yet were they drawn swords.
Old Testament: Psalms, lv, 21.

See also under SPEECH.

19
The time will come when three words, uttered with charity and meekness, shall receive a far more blessed reward than three thousand volumes written with disdainful sharpness and wit.
RICHARD HOOKER, *Ecclesiastical Polity*.

20
No simple word
That shall be uttered at our mirthful board,
Shall make us sad next morning; or affright
The liberty that we'll enjoy to-night.
BEN JONSON, *Epigrams*. No. 101.

21
Smooth words in place of gifts. (Dicta docta pro datis.)
PLAUTUS, *Asinaria*, l. 525. (Act iii, sc. 1.)

So spake those wary foes, fair friends in look,

And so in words great gifts they gave and took,
And had small profit, and small loss thereby.
WILLIAM MORRIS, *Life and Death of Jason*. Bk. viii, l. 379.

1
Smooth words make smooth ways.
W. G. BENHAM, *Proverbs*, p. 835.

Soft words break no bones.
JOHN RAY, *English Proverbs*.

Fair words break never bone,
Foul words break many ane.
JOHN RAY, *Proverbs: Scottish*.

2
His plausive words
He scatter'd not in ears, but grafted them,
To grow there and to bear.
SHAKESPEARE, *All's Well that Ends Well*. Act i, sc. 2, l. 53.

Whose words all ears took captive.
SHAKESPEARE, *All's Well that Ends Well*. Act v, sc. 3, l. 17.

Let not his smoothing words Bewitch your hearts.
SHAKESPEARE, *II Henry VI*. Act i, sc. 1, l. 156.

VII—Words: Bitter Words

3
A blow with a word strikes deeper than a blow with a sword.
ROBERT BURTON, *Anatomy of Melancholy*. Pt. i, sec. ii, mem. 4, subs. 4. Quoted as an old saying.

Sharp words make more wounds than surgeons can heal.
THOMAS CHURCHYARD, *Mirror of Man*. Sig. A4. (1594)

An acute word cuts deeper than a sharp weapon.
THOMAS FULLER, *Gnomologia*. No. 575.

More sharp word than sword.
UNKNOWN, *Ancrene Riwle*, 74. (c. 1220)

4
Your little words are hard and cold,
You try to use them in a sling
As David did to slay the bold
Goliath—but they only sting!
MAY BRINKLEY, *Pebbles*.

5
Religion, freedom, vengeance, what you will—
A word 's enough to raise mankind to kill.
BYRON, *Lara*. Canto ii, l. 222.

A single little word can strike him dead. (Ein Wörtlein kann ihn fällen.)
LUTHER, *Table-Talk*. No. 430. Referring to the Pope.

6
She dealt her pretty words like blades,
As glittering they shone,
And every one unbared a nerve
Or wantoned with a bone.
EMILY DICKINSON, *Poems*. Pt. v, No. 29.

7
Whatsoever word thou speaketh, that shalt thou also hear. (*Ὀπποῖόν κ' εἴπησθα ἔπος, τοῖόν κ' ἐπακούσαις*)
HOMER, *Iliad*. Bk. xx, l. 250. *See also* RETRIBUTION.

8
I'll sauce her with bitter words.
SHAKESPEARE, *As You Like It*. Act iii, sc. 5, l. 69.

These are but wild and whirling words, my lord
SHAKESPEARE, *Hamlet*. Act i, sc. 5, l. 133.

Here are a few of the unpleasant'st words
That ever blotted paper!
SHAKESPEARE, *Merchant of Venice*, iii, 2, 254.

These words are razors to my wounded heart.
SHAKESPEARE, *Titus Andronicus*. Act i, sc. 1, 314.

9
Thy words are like a cloud of wingèd snakes.
SHELLEY, *Prometheus Unbound*. Act i, l. 632.

10
From sharp words and wits men pluck no fruit;
And gathering thorns they shake the tree at root.
SWINBURNE, *Atalanta in Calydon: Chorus*.

VIII—Words: Verbosity

See also Speech: Loquacity; Talk: Loquacity

11
See how your words come from you in a crowd!
ROBERT BROWNING, *A Soul's Tragedy*. Act i.

What so wild as words are?
ROBERT BROWNING, *A Woman's Last Word*.

Words like wildfire.
SHAKESPEARE, *The Rape of Lucrece*. St. 217.

12
What is so insane as the empty sound of words, however well-chosen and elegant, if there is no foundation of sense or sagacity? (Quid enim est tam furiosum quam verborum vel optimorum atque arnatissimorum sonitus inanis, nulla subjecta sententia nec scientia?)
CICERO, *De Oratore*. Bk. i, sec. 51.

What is so furious and Bethlem-like as a vain sound of chosen and excellent words?
BEN JONSON, *Explorata: Lingua Sapientis*.

13
A barren superfluity of words.
GARTH, *The Dispensary*. Canto ii, l. 95.

A meaningless torrent of words. (Inanis verborum torrens.)
QUINTILIAN, *De Institutione Oratoria*. Bk. x, ch. 7, sec. 23.

14
Do not go forth on the gale with every sail set into an ocean of words.
HIPPIAS. (PLATO, *Protagoras*. Sec. 338.)

15
He multiplieth words without knowledge.
Old Testament: Job, xxxv, 16.

Who is this that darkeneth counsel by words without knowledge?
Old Testament: Job, xxxviii, 2.

In a multitude of words there will certainly be error. (Yen to pi shih.)
UNKNOWN. A Chinese proverb.

1
A glutton of words.
LANGLAND, *Piers the Plowman*. Passus i, l. 139.

2
He can compress the most words into the smallest ideas of any man I ever met.
ABRAHAM LINCOLN, of a fellow lawyer. (Gross, *Lincoln's Own Stories*, p. 36.)

3
The world pays itself with words; there is little plumbing of the depths of things. (Le monde se paye de paroles; peu approfondissement les choses.)
BLAISE PASCAL, *Lettres Provinciales*, ii.

4
Words are like leaves, and where they most abound,
Much fruit of sense beneath is rarely found.
POPE, *Essay on Criticism*. Pt. ii, l. 109.

Putting all his words together,
'Tis three blue beans in one blue bladder.
MATTHEW PRIOR, *Alma*. Canto i, l. 27.

5
He that uses many words for the explaining any subject, doth, like the cuttle fish, hide himself for the most part in his own ink.
JOHN RAY, *On the Creation*.

6
Words enough, but little wisdom. (Satis eloquentiæ, sapientiæ parum.)
SALLUST, *Catiline*. Ch. 5, sec. 5.

Words, words, mere words, no matter from the heart.
SHAKESPEARE, *Troilus and Cressida*, v, 3, 108.

A fine volley of words, gentlemen, and quickly shot off.
SHAKESPEARE, *The Two Gentlemen of Verona*. Act ii, sc. 4, l. 33.

The artillery of words.
SWIFT, *Ode to Sancroft*, l. 13.

7
Zounds! I was never so bethump'd with words
Since I first call'd my brother's father dad.
SHAKESPEARE, *King John*. Act ii, sc. 2, l. 466.

I was ne'er so thrummed since I was a gentleman.
DEKKER, *The Honest Whore*. Act iv, sc. 2.

8
Thou wilt be like a lover presently
And tire the hearer with a book of words.
SHAKESPEARE, *Much Ado About Nothing*, i, 1, 309.

Discourse fustian with one's own shadow.
SHAKESPEARE, *Othello*. Act ii, sc. 3, l. 282.

This helpless smoke of words.
SHAKESPEARE, *The Rape of Lucrece*. St. 147.

You cram these words into my ears against
The stomach of my sense.
SHAKESPEARE, *The Tempest*. Act ii, sc. 1, l. 106.

9
He utters empty words, sound without thought. (Dat inania verba, Dat sine mente sonum.)
VERGIL, *Æneid*. Bk. x, l. 639.

10
You who possessed the talent of speaking much without saying anything.
VOLTAIRE, *Sur la Carrousell de l'Impératrice de Russie*. Referring to Pindar.

11
Why should I spare words? They cost nothing. (Quare verbis parcem? Gratuita sunt.)
SENECA, *Epistulæ ad Lucilium*. Epis. xxix, 2.

IX—Words: Reticence

See also Silence

12
Our words are our own if we keep them within.
ALEXANDER BROME. (*Roxburghe Ballads*, viii, 109.)

13
A word that is not spoken never does any mischief.
CHARLES A. DANA, *The Making of a Newspaper Man*. Maxim 4.

14
Be not rash with thy mouth; . . . let thy words be few.
Old Testament: Ecclesiastes, v, 2.

When looks were fond and words were few.
ALLAN CUNNINGHAM, *Poet's Bridal-day Song*.

15
Few words, but proceeding from a heart filled with truth. (Pauca Verba sed a pleno venientia pectore veri.)
LUCAN, *De Bello Civili*. Bl. ix, l. 188.

16
He that hath knowledge spareth his words.
Old Testament: Proverbs, xvii, 27.

As it is the mark of great minds to be able to say much in few words, so it is the mark of little ones to speak much and to say nothing. (Comme c'est le caractère des grands esprits de faire entendre en peu de paroles beaucoup de choses, les petits esprits, au contraire, ont le don de beaucoup parler, et de ne rien dire.)
LA ROCHEFOUCAULD, *Maximes*. No. 142.

16a
Tower of ivory. (Tour d'ivoire.)
CHARLES-AUGUSTIN SAINTE-BEUVE, *Pensées d'Août: À M. Villemain*. St. 3. (1837) Sainte-Beuve compares Victor Hugo to a feudal baron with his armor on ready to fight, and then says of Alfred de Vigny:
Et Vigny, plus secret,
Comme en sa tour d'ivoire, avant midi, rentrait.

17
Men of few words are the best men.
SHAKESPEARE, *Henry V*. Act iii, sc. 2, l. 39.

I know thou'rt full of love and honesty,
And weigh'st thy words before thou givest them breath.
SHAKESPEARE, *Othello*. Act iii, sc. 3, l. 118.

18
Deep in my heart subsides the infrequent word,
And there dies slowly throbbing like a wounded bird.
FRANCIS THOMPSON, *Her Portrait*. St. 3

X—Words: Their Beauty

1

What things have we seen
Done at the Mermaid! heard words that have
been
So nimble and so full of subtile flame
As if that every one from whence they came
Had meant to put his whole wit in a jest,
And resolved to live a fool the rest
Of his dull life.

FRANCIS BEAUMONT, *Letter to Ben Jonson.*

God wove a web of loveliness,
Of clouds and stars and birds,
But made not any thing at all
So beautiful as words.

ANNA HEMPSTEAD BRANCH, *Her Words.*

2

My words are little jars
For you to take and put upon a shelf.
Their shapes are quaint and beautiful,
And they have many pleasant colours and
lustres
To recommend them.
Also the scent from them fills the room
With sweetness of flowers and crushed grasses.

AMY LOWELL, *A Gift.*

Such little, puny things are words in rhyme:
Poor feeble loops and strokes as frail as hairs;
You see them printed here, and mark their chime,
And turn to your more durable affairs.
Yet on such petty tools the poet dares
To run his race with mortar, bricks and lime,
And draws his frail stick to the point, and stares
To aim his arrow at the heart of Time.

CHRISTOPHER MORLEY, *Quickening.*

3

Words, like fine flowers, have their colours too.

ERNEST RHYS, *Words.*

4

I love smooth words, like gold-enameled fish
Which circle slowly with a silken swish,
And tender ones, like downy-feathered birds:
Words shy and dappled, deep-eyed deer in
herds.

ELINOR WYLIE, *Pretty Words.*

XI—Words: Their Finality

5

A word once spoken revoked can not be.

ALEXANDER BARCLAY, *Shyp of Folys*, p. 108. (1509)

Boys flying kites haul in their white winged birds.
You can't do that way when you're flying words.
"Careful with fire," is good advice we know;
"Careful with words," is ten times doubly so.
Thoughts unexpressed may sometimes fall back
dead;
But God Himself can't kill them when they're
said.

WILL CARLETON, *First Settler's Story*. St. 21.

6

A word spoken is an arrow let fly.

THOMAS FULLER, *Gnomologia*. No. 486.

The arrow belongs not to the archer when it has once left the bow; the word no longer belongs to the speaker when it has once passed his lips.

HEINE, *Religion and Philosophy: Preface.*

7

Winged words. (Ἔπεα πτερόεντα.)

HOMER, *Iliad*. Bk. xx, l. 331. This phrase occurs 46 times in the *Iliad* and 58 times in the *Odyssey*.

Winged words. (Geflügelte Worte.)

GEORGE BÜCHMANN. Title of his book on proverbs and famous phrases.

Our words have wings, but fly not where we would.

GEORGE ELIOT, *The Spanish Gypsy*. Bk. iii.

8

It is as easy to recall a stone thrown violently from the hand as a word which has left your tongue. (Οὔτ' ἐκ χερὸς μεθέντα καρτερὸν λίθον ῥᾷον κατασχεῖν, οὔτ' ἀπὸ γλώσσης λόγον.)

MENANDER, *Fragments*. Frag. 1092K.

The word once spoken flies beyond recall. (Semel emissum volat irrevocabile verbum.)

HORACE, *Epistles*. Bk. i, epis. 18, l. 71.

The written word, unpublished, can be destroyed, but the spoken word can never be recalled. (Delere licebit Quod non edideris; nescit vox missa reverti.)

HORACE, *Ars Poetica*, l. 389.

9

Look out how you use proud words.
When you let proud words go, it is not easy
to call them back.

CARL SANDBURG, *Primer Lesson.*

10

O! many a shaft, at random sent,
Finds mark the archer little meant!
And many a word at random spoken
May soothe or wound a heart that's broken!

SCOTT, *Lord of the Isles*. Canto v, st. 18.

XII—Word and Deed

See also Example and Precept; Preaching and Practice

11

There is no man but speaketh more honestly than he can do or think.

BACON, *Advancement of Learning*. Bk. ii.

12

Do as we say, and not as we do. (Faites ce que nous disons, et ne faites pas ce que nous faisons.)

BOCCACCIO, *Decameron*. Day iii, tale 7. (French translation by Sabatier de Castres.)

Do you that good which I say, but not that ill which I do.

JAMES MABBE, *Celestina*, p. 27. (1631)

The common saying of "Do as I say, not as I do," is usually reversed in the actual experience of life.

SAMUEL SMILES, *Self-Help*. Ch. 12.

13

I see that saying and doing are two things, and hereafter I shall better observe this distinction.

JOHN BUNYAN, *The Pilgrim's Progress*. Pt. i.

Saying and doing are two things.
MATTHEW HENRY, *Commentaries: Matthew*, xxi; JOHN HEYWOOD, *Proverbs*, ii, 5.

Saying is one thing, doing another. (Le dire est autre chose que le faire.)
MONTAIGNE, *Essays*. Bk. ii, ch. 31.

Without doubt it is a delightful harmony when doing and saying go together. (C'est sans doubte une belle harmonie, quand le faire et le dire vont ensemble.)
MONTAIGNE, *Essays*. Bk. ii, ch. 31.

1
This, young man, is harder for me to say than to do.
JULIUS CÆSAR, to Metellus. (PLUTARCH, *Lives: Cæsar*.)

Such things are easier said than done, I see. (Magis istuc percipimus lingua dici, quam factis fore.)
PLAUTUS, *Asinaria*, l. 162. (Act i, sc. 3.)

Easier said than done. (Id dictu quam re, ut pleraque, facilius.)
LIVY, *History*. Bk. xxxi, sec. 38.

That is . . . sooner said than done.
JOHN HEYWOOD, *Proverbs*. Pt. ii, ch. 5. (1546)

2
A controversy that affords
Actions for arguments, not words.
BUTLER, *Hudibras*. Pt. i, canto 1, l. 871.

3
It's a long step from saying to doing.
CERVANTES, *Don Quixote*. Pt. ii, ch. 34.

4
Plato saith, who-so that can him read,
The words must be cousin to the deed.
CHAUCER, *Canterbury Tales: Prologue*, l. 741.

The wise Plato saith, as ye may read,
The word must needs accorde with the deed.
CHAUCER, *Maunciples Tale*, l. 205.

5
His deeds do not agree with his words. (Facta ejus cum dictis discrepant.)
CICERO, *De Finibus*. Bk. ii, sec. 30.

Let deeds correspond with words. (Dictis facta suppetant.)
PLAUTUS, *Pseudolus*, l. 108. (Act i, sc. 1.)

Thy actions to thy words accord.
MILTON, *Paradise Regained*. Bk. iii, l. 9.

6
Say well and do well, end with a letter,
Say well is good, but do well is better.
JOHN CLARKE, *Paræmiologia*, 194.

7
Though language forms the preacher,
'Tis "good works" make the man.
ELIZA COOK, *Good Works*.

8
Good words and ill deeds deceive wise and fools.
JOHN DAVIES, *Scourge of Folly*, 46. (1611)

That you can speak so well, and do so ill!
MASSINGER, *The Fatal Dowry*. Act iv, sc. 4.

What pity 'tis, one that can speak so well,
Should, in his actions, be so ill.
MASSINGER, *Parliament of Love*. Act iii, sc. 3.

9
Feeble deeds are vainer far than words.
BENJAMIN DISRAELI, *Sybil*. Bk. iv, ch. 3.

10
Go put your creed into the deed,
Nor speak with double tongue.
RALPH WALDO EMERSON, *Ode: Concord*.

Words and deeds are quite indifferent forms of the divine energy. Words are also actions, and actions are a kind of words.
EMERSON, *Essays, Second Series: The Poet*.

11
Never should this thing have been,
That words with men should more avail than deeds.
('Ανθρώποισιν οὐκ ἐχρῆν ποτε
τῶν πραγμάτων τὴν γλῶσσαν ἰσχύειν πλέον.)
EURIPIDES, *Hecuba*, l. 1187.

12
Deeds not words.
FLETCHER, *The Lover's Progress*. Act iii, sc. 6.

For now the field is not far off
Where we must give the world a proof
Of deeds, not words.
BUTLER, *Hudibras*. Pt. i, canto i, l. 867.

13
Deeds are males, words are females.
JOHN FLORIO, *First Fruites*. Fo. 32. (1578) "Le parole son femmine, i fatti son maschi" has a point in Italian which it lacks in English.

They say in Italy, that deeds are men, and words are but women.
JAMES HOWELL, *Familiar Letters*. Bk. i, sec. 5, letter 21.

Words are women, deeds are men.
GEORGE HERBERT, *Jacula Prudentum*. (1640) In frequent use thereafter.

I am not yet so lost in lexicography as to forget that words are the daughters of the earth, and that things are the sons of heaven.
SAMUEL JOHNSON, *Dictionary of the English Language: Preface*.

Words are the daughters of earth, and deeds are the sons of heaven.
SIR WILLIAM JONES. Translating a Hindoo proverb.

Words are men's daughters, but God's sons are things.
SAMUEL MADDEN, *Boulter's Monument*. Said to have been inserted by Dr. Johnson.

14
Well done is better than well said.
BENJAMIN FRANKLIN, *Poor Richard*, 1737.

Saying and doing have quarrelled and parted.
BENJAMIN FRANKLIN, *Poor Richard*, 1756.

15
Good words without deeds are rushes and reeds.
THOMAS FULLER, *Gnomologia*. No. 6247.

16
If you'd pooh-pooh this monarch's plan,
Pooh-pooh it;
But when he says he'll hang a man
He'll do it.
W. S. GILBERT, *Princess Ida*. Act ii.

1
It is as folk do, and not as folk say.
JOHN HEYWOOD, *Proverbs*. Pt. ii, ch. 5. (1546)

2
An acre of performance is worth the whole Land of Promise.
JAMES HOWELL, *Familiar Letters*. Bk. iv, 33.

3
A man of words and not of deeds
Is like a garden full of weeds.
JAMES HOWELL, *Proverbs*, 20; HALLIWELL, *Nursery Rhymes*. No. 166.

4
Deeds are better things than words are,
Actions mightier than boastings.
LONGFELLOW, *The Song of Hiawatha*. Pt. ix.

5
And I am tired of the cruelty of men,
With their words like gods and their deeds like lice.
MARIE LUHRS, *Ennui of an Empress*.

6
Trust on the deed and not in gay speeches.
JOHN LYLY, *Secreta Secretorum*.

7
The smallest actual good is better than the most magnificent promises of impossibilities.
MACAULAY, *Essays: Lord Bacon*.

8
It seems to me to be common sense to look at what is done, and not to what is said. (Acta exteriora indicant interiora secreta.)
SIR JAMES MARTIN, *Caine v. Coulson*. (1 H & C. 764.)

9
All words, And no performance.
MASSINGER, *Parliament of Love*. Act iv, sc. 2.

You have said,
Gallants, so much, and hitherto done so little,
That, till I learn to speak, and you to do,
I must take time to thank you.
MASSINGER, *The Picture*. Act ii, sc. 2.

10
Great talkers are never great doers.
THOMAS MIDDLETON, *Blurt*. Act i, sc. 1.

Speaking much is also a sign of vanity; for he that is lavish of words is a niggard in deed.
SIR WALTER RALEIGH, *Instructions to His Son*. Ch. 4.

Talkers are no good doers; be assured
We come to use our hands and not our tongues.
SHAKESPEARE, *Richard III*. Act i, sc. 3, l. 352.

11
Just deeds are the best answer to injurious words.
MILTON, *Observations upon the Articles of Peace with the Irish Rebels*.

12
Some men never spake a wise word, yet do wisely; some on the other side do never a wise deed, and yet speak wisely.
SIR THOMAS OVERBURY, *Crumms Fal'n from King James Talk*.

13
No need of words; trust deeds. (Non opus est verbis, credite rebus.)
OVID, *Fasti*. Bk. ii. l. 734.

Begin to supplement your promises with deeds. (Incipe pollicitis addere facta tuis.)
OVID, *Amores*. Bk. ii, eleg. 16, l. 48.

14
What then does it signify that you are generous in talk, if, when it comes to the point, your help has died out? (Quid te igitur retulit Beneficium esse oratione, si ad rem auxilium emortuum est?)
PLAUTUS, *Epidicus*. Act i, sc. 2, l. 14.

"He wishes well" is worthless, unless the deed go with it. (Nequam illud verbum est, Bene vult, nisi qui benefacit.)
PLAUTUS, *Trinummus*. Act ii, sc. 4.

15
A word spoken in season is like an apple of silver, and actions are more precious than words.
JOHN PYM, *Debate on a Message from Charles I*, 1628.

16
It is not as far from the heart to the mouth, as it is from the mouth to the hand.
JOSEPH ROUX, *Meditations of a Parish Priest*. Pt. iv, No. 56.

17
Men's words are ever bolder than their deeds.
SCHILLER, *Die Piccolomini*. Act i, sc. 4. (Coleridge, tr.)

18
Prove your words by your deeds. (Verba res proba.)
SENECA, *Epistulæ ad Lucilium*. Epis. xx, sec. 1.

19
Ill deeds are doubled with an evil word.
SHAKESPEARE, *The Comedy of Errors*, iii, 2, 20.

20
Have not I
An arm as big as thine? a heart as big?
Thy words, I grant, are bigger, for I wear not
My dagger in my mouth.
SHAKESPEARE, *Cymbeline*. Act iv, sc. 2, l. 76.

I profess not talking: only this—
Let each man do his best.
SHAKESPEARE, *I Henry IV*. Act v, sc. 2, l. 92.

I have no words: My voice is in my sword.
SHAKESPEARE, *Macbeth*. Act v, sc. 8, l. 6.

21
And ever may your highness yoke together,
As I will lend you cause, my doing well
With my well saying.
SHAKESPEARE, *Henry VIII*. Act iii, sc. 2, l. 150.

'T is a kind of good deed to say well,
And yet words are no deeds.
SHAKESPEARE, *Henry VIII*. Act iii, sc. 2, l. 153.

Your large speeches may your deeds approve,
That good effects may spring from words of love.
SHAKESPEARE, *King Lear*. Act i, sc. 1, l. 187.

So well thy words become thee as thy wounds;
They smack of honour both.
SHAKESPEARE, *Macbeth*. Act i, sc. 2, l. 43.

22
Your words and performances are no kin together.
SHAKESPEARE, *Othello*. Act iv, sc. 2, l. 85.

Words pay no debts, give her deeds.
SHAKESPEARE, *Troilus and Cressida*, v, 3, 58.

1
Words are but holy as the deeds they cover.
SHELLEY, *The Cenci*. Act ii, sc. 2.

2
You do the deeds,
And your ungodly deeds find me the words.
(Σὺ γὰρ ποεῖς
Τοὔργον· τὰ δ' ἔργα τοὺς λόγους εὑρίσκεται.)
SOPHOCLES, *Electra*, l. 624.

3
Such distance is between high words and deeds!
In proof, the greatest vaunter seldom speeds.
ROBERT SOUTHWELL, *St. Peter's Complaint*.

4
Every recreant who proved his cowardice in the hour of danger, was afterwards boldest in words and tongue.
TACITUS, *Annals*. Bk. iv, sec. 62.

Not one of those men who in words are valiant,
And when it comes to action skulk away.
SCHILLER, *Die Piccolomini*. Act iv, sc. 4. (Coleridge, tr.)

5
Thy leaf has perish'd in the green,
And, while we breathe beneath the sun,
The world which credits what is done
Is cold to all that might have been.
TENNYSON, *In Memoriam*. Pt. lxxv, st. 4.

6
Done and said. (Factis et dictis.)
TERENCE, *Eunuchus*, l. 941. (Act v, sc. 3.)

7
A slender acquaintance with the world must convince every man that actions, not words, are the true criterion.
GEORGE WASHINGTON, *Social Maxims: Friendship*.

8
God blesses still the generous thought,
And still the fitting word He speeds,
And Truth, at His requiring taught,
He quickens into deeds.
WHITTIER, *Channing*. St. 23.

Each crisis brings its word and deed.
WHITTIER, *The Lost Occasion*, l. 58.

9
On wings of deeds the soul must mount!
When we are summoned from afar,
Ourselves, and not our words, will count—
Not what we said, but what we are!
WILLIAM WINTER, *George Fawcett Rowe*.

10
To harps preferring swords,
And everlasting deeds to burning words!
WORDSWORTH, *Ecclesiastical Sonnets*. Pt. i, No. 10.

11
Every word is vain that is not completed by deed. (Πᾶς λόγος ἐστὶ μάταιος ο μὴ τετελεσμένος ἔργῳ.)
UNKNOWN. (*Greek Anthology*. Bk. x, epig. 109.)

Can talk, but not do. (Nêng shuo pu nêng hsing.)
UNKNOWN. A Chinese proverb.

12
Say well is good, but do well is better;
Do well seems the spirit, say well is the letter.
UNKNOWN, *Saying and Doing*.

XIII—Word and Bond

13
No less flattering in her word,
That purely, her simple record
Was found as true as any bond.
CHAUCER, *Book of the Duchesse*, l. 935.

His word is as good as his bond.
FRANCIS LENTON, *Characterismi*. (1631)

Your word is as good as the Bank, sir.
HOLCROFT, *Road to Ruin*. Act i, sc. 3, l. 235.

His words are bonds, his oaths are oracles.
SHAKESPEARE, *The Two Gentlemen of Verona*. Act ii, sc. 7, l. 75.

14
He who lightly assents will seldom keep his word.
LAO-TSZE, *The Simple Way*. No. 63.

15
An honest man's word is as good as his bond.
JOHN RAY, *English Proverbs*, 103. (1670)

Every honest man is as good as his word.
GEORGE LILLO, *Silvia*. Act i, sc. 9.

16
Dearer is love than life, and fame than gold;
But dearer than them both your faith once plighted hold.
SPENSER, *Faerie Queene*. Bk. v, canto xi, st. 63.

To honour his own word as if his God's.
TENNYSON, *Guinevere*, l. 469.

WORDSWORTH, WILLIAM

17
Time may restore us in his course
Goethe's sage mind and Byron's force;
But where will Europe's latter hour
Again find Wordsworth's healing power?
MATTHEW ARNOLD, *Memorial Verses*.

18
No poet ever took himself more seriously than did William Wordsworth; however wide his outlook, he lived as a sectary in a closed system, and imagined that whatever he happened to think was of primary importance.
ROBERT BRIDGES, *Collected Essays*. Vol. ii.

19
Just for a handful of silver he left us,
Just for a riband to stick in his coat—
Found the one gift of which fortune bereft us,
Lost all the others she lets us devote.
ROBERT BROWNING, *The Lost Leader*. Wordsworth's acceptance of the laureateship and a pension had seemed a defection from the Liberal cause.

20
That mild apostate from poetic rule,
The simple Wordsworth, framer of a lay
As soft as evening in his favourite May, . . .
Who, both by precept and example, shows
That prose is verse, and verse is merely prose.
BYRON, *English Bards, Scotch Reviewers*, l. 236.

Yet not to vulgar Wordsworth let us stoop,
The meanest object of the lowly group,
Whose verse, of all but childish prattle void,
Seems blessed harmony to Lamb and Lloyd.
BYRON, *English Bards, Scotch Reviewers*, l. 903.

Let simple Wordsworth chime his childish verse.
BYRON, *English Bards, Scotch Reviewers*, l. 917.

1
One finds also a kind of sincerity in his speech. But for prolixity, thinness, endless dilution, it excels all the other speech I have heard from mortals.
THOMAS CARLYLE, *Essays: Wordsworth.*

2
Is Wordsworth a bell with a wooden tongue?
R. W. EMERSON, *Journals*, 1863.

3
This will never do!
FRANCIS LORD JEFFREY, *Review*, of Wordsworth's *Excursion*. (*Edinburgh Review.*)

Although Jeffrey completely failed to recognize Wordsworth's real greatness, he was yet not wrong in saying of the *Excursion* as a work of poetic style, "This will never do!"
MATTHEW ARNOLD, *Poems of William Wordsworth: Preface.*

4
A modern Moses who sits on Pisgah with his back obstinately turned to that promised land, the Future; he is only fit for those old maid tabbies, the Muses.
DOUGLAS JERROLD, *Review of Wordsworth's Poems.*

5
To William Wordsworth, true philosopher and inspired poet, who, by the special gift and calling of Almighty God, whether he sang of man or of nature, failed not to lift up men's hearts to holy things.
JOHN KEBLE, *Lectures on Poetry: Dedication.*

6
Wordsworth in sonnet is a classic too
And on that grass plot sits at Milton's side.
W. S. LANDOR, *To the Author of Festus.*

7
We are not called upon to place great men of his stamp as if they were collegians in a class-list.
JOHN MORLEY, *Miscellanies: Introduction to Wordsworth.*

8
To his own self not always just,
Bound in the bonds that all men share,—
Confess the failings as we must,
The lion's mark is always there!
Nor any song so pure, so great,
Since his, who closed the sightless eyes,
Our Homer of the war in Heaven,
To wake in his own Paradise.
FRANCIS TURNER PALGRAVE, *Wordsworth.*

9
This laurel greener from the brows
Of him that utter'd nothing base.
TENNYSON, *To the Queen.*

10
Wordsworth, thy music like a river rolls
Among the mountains, and thy song is fed
By living springs far up the watershed.
HENRY VAN DYKE, *Wordsworth.*

11
What hadst thou that could make such large amends
For all thou hadst not, and thy peers possessed,
Motion and fire, swift means to radiant ends?
Thou hadst, for weary feet, the gift of rest.
WILLIAM WATSON, *Wordsworth's Grave*, ii, 3.

No word-mosaic artificer, he sang
A lofty song of lowly weal and dole.
Right from the heart, right to the heart it sprang,
Or from the soul leapt instant to the soul.
WILLIAM WATSON, *Wordsworth's Grave*, iii, 3.

12
He [Wordsworth] found in stones the sermons he had already hidden there.
OSCAR WILDE, *The Decay of Lying.*

WORK

See also Labor

I—Work: Apothegms

13
The real essence of work is concentrated energy.
WALTER BAGEHOT, *Biographical Studies*, p. 370.

14
To youth I have but three words of counsel —Work, work, work.
BISMARCK, *Sayings of Bismarck.*

It is the great modern maxim: Work, always work, and yet more work. (C'est la grande formule moderne: Du travail, toujours travail, et encore du travail.)
GAMBETTA, *Speech*, at banquet to General Hoche, 24 June, 1872.

15
The faltering, restless hand of Hack,
And the tireless hand of Hew.
BLISS CARMAN, *Hack and Hew.*

15a
I . . . worked away like a galley-slave.
FREDERICK CHAMIER, *Tom Bowling.* Ch. 2. (1841)

Lord Wharton . . . is working like a horse.
SWIFT, *Journal to Stella*, 9 Sept., 1710.

After having worked like horses, don't set about to fight like dogs.
MARIA EDGEWORTH, *Parent's Assistant*, 309. (1796)

16
The more one works, the more willing one is to work.
LORD CHESTERFIELD, *Letters*, 17 Sept., 1757.

It is working that makes a workman.
THOMAS FULLER, *Gnomologia*. No. 3034.

Think of ease, but work on.
GEORGE HERBERT, *Jacula Prudentum.*

I go on working for the same reason that a hen goes on laying eggs.
H. L. MENCKEN. (DURANT, *On the Meaning of Life*, p. 30.)

1
Now, by St. Paul, the work goes bravely on.
CIBBER, *Richard III* (altered). Act iii, sc. 1.

2
Of the professions it may be said that soldiers are becoming too popular, parsons too lazy, physicians too mercenary, and lawyers too powerful.
C. C. COLTON, *Lacon*. Vol. i, No. 279.

3
Every man's work shall be made manifest.
New Testament: I Corinthians, iii, 13.

4
The grinders cease because they are few.
Old Testament: Ecclesiastes, xii, 3.

When a great many people are unable to find work, unemployment results.
CALVIN COOLIDGE, in his syndicated daily article. (STANLEY WALKER, *City Edi.or*, p. 131)

5
His sole concern with work was considering how he might best avoid it.
ANATOLE FRANCE, *Revolt of the Angels*. Ch. 1.

I like work; it fascinates me. I can sit and look at it for hours.
JEROME K. JEROME, *Three Men in a Boat*. Ch. 15.

An' never hed a relative thet done a stroke o' work.
J. R. LOWELL, *Biglow Papers*. Ser. ii, No. 1.

6
Work is no disgrace: it is idleness which is a disgrace. (Ἔργον δ' οὐδὲν ὄνειδος, ἀεργίη δέ τ' ὄνειδος.)
HESIOD, *Works and Days*, l. 311.

A workman that needeth not to be ashamed.
New Testament: II Timothy, ii, 15.

7
Run, if you like, but try to keep your breath;
Work like a man, but don't be worked to death.
O. W. HOLMES, *A Rhymed Lesson*, l. 300.

Work first and then rest.
JOHN RUSKIN, *The Seven Lamps of Architecture: The Lamp of Beauty*.

8
Light is the task when many share the toil. (Πλεόνων δέ τε ἔργον ἄμεινον.)
HOMER, *Iliad*. Bk. xii, l. 413. (Bryant, tr.)

Work divided is in that manner shortened. (Divisum sic breve fiet opus.)
MARTIAL, *Epigrams*. Bk. iv, ep. 82, l. 8.

Many hands make light work.
WILLIAM PATTEN, *Expedition into Scotland*. (1547)

9
All work and no play makes Jack a dull boy.
JAMES HOWELL, *Proverbs*, 12. (1659)

The colt that's back'd and burden'd being young,
Loseth his pride and never waxeth strong.
SHAKESPEARE, *Venus and Adonis*, l. 419.

See also under JACK.

10
By the work one knows the workman.
LA FONTAINE, *Fables: The Hornets and the Bees*. Fab. 21.

Work bears witness who does well.
JOHN RAY, *English Proverbs*.

11
The lady bearer of this says she has two sons who want to work. Set them at it if possible. Wanting to work is so rare a merit that it should be encouraged.
ABRAHAM LINCOLN, *Letter to Major Ramsay*.

12
Never is there either work without reward, nor reward without work being expended. (Nusquam nec opera sine emolumento, nec emolumentum ferme sine impensa opera est.)
LIVY, *History*. Bk. v, sec. 4.

13
A man who gets his board and lodging on this ball in an ignominious way is inevitably an ignominious man.
H. L. MENCKEN, *Prejudices*. Ser. iv, p. 200.

14
The work excelled the material. (Materiem superabat opus.)
OVID, *Metamorphoses*. Bk. ii, l. 5.

15
Finish thoroughly, he said, the work you have set yourself. (Propositum perfice, dixit, opus.)
OVID, *Remediorum Amoris*, l. 40.

When I die may I be taken in the midst of work. (Cum moriar, medium solvar et inter opus.)
OVID, *Amores*. Bk. ii, eleg. 10, l. 36. The work Ovid refers to, however, is that of love.

17
There's other work in hand.
SHAKESPEARE, *Cymbeline*. Act v, sc. 5, l. 103.

18
It will go all in your day's work.
SWIFT, *Polite Conversation*. Dial. 1.

It's all in the day's work, as the huntsman said when the lion ate him.
CHARLES KINGSLEY, *Westward Ho*. Ch. 4.

A day's work is a day's work, neither more nor less, and the man who does it needs a day's sustenance, a night's repose, and due leisure, whether he be painter or ploughman.
BERNARD SHAW, *An Unsocial Socialist*. Ch. 5.

19
If any would not work, neither should he eat.
New Testament: II Thessalonians, iii, 10. (Si quis non vult operari, nec manducet.—*Vulgate*.)

They must hunger in frost that will not work in heat.
WILLIAM CAMDEN, *Remains*, p. 333. (1605)

He that will not labour must not eat.
THOMAS DRAXE, *Biblio. Schol. Instruct.*, 109.

Though this is a fable, the moral is good:
If you live without work, you must live without food.
UNKNOWN, *The Ant and the Cricket*.

20
There is no trade or employment but the young man following it may become a hero.
WALT WHITMAN, *Song of Myself*.

II—Work: Its Necessity

1
It is the first of all problems for a man to find out what kind of work he is to do in this universe.
THOMAS CARLYLE, *Inaugural Address,* Edinburgh, 2 April, 1866.

That which each can do best, none but his Maker can teach him.
EMERSON, *Essays, First Series: Self-Reliance.*

On bravely through the sunshine and the showers,
Time hath his work to do, and we have ours.
EMERSON, *The Man of Letters: Motto.*

2
I must work the works of him that sent me, while it is day: the night cometh, when no man can work.
New Testament: John, ix, 4.

Man goeth forth unto his work and to his labour until the evening.
Old Testament: Psalms, civ, 23.

3
Hear ye not the hum of mighty workings?
KEATS, *Sonnet.* No. xiv.

4
Heirs of more than royal race,
Framed by heaven's peculiar grace
God's own work to do on earth!
JOHN KEBLE, *The Christian Year: Palm Sunday.*

5
My new-cut ashlar takes the light
Where crimson-blank the windows flare;
By my own work, before the night,
Great Overseer, I make my prayer.
RUDYARD KIPLING, *A Dedication.*

Father, I scarcely dare to pray,
So clear I see, now it is done,
How I have wasted half my day,
And left my work but just begun.
HELEN HUNT JACKSON, *A Last Prayer.*

6
But till we are built like angels—with hammer and chisel and pen,
We will work for ourself and a woman, for ever and ever, amen.
RUDYARD KIPLING, *An Imperial Rescript.*

This we learned from famous men,
Knowing not its uses,
When they showed, in daily work,
Man must finish off his work—
Right or wrong, his daily work—
And without excuses.
RUDYARD KIPLING, *A School Song.*

7
The Sons of Mary seldom bother, for they have inherited that good part;
But the Sons of Martha favour their Mother of the careful soul and the troubled heart.
And because she lost her temper once, and because she was rude to the Lord her Guest,
Her Sons must wait upon Mary's Sons, world without end, reprieve, or rest.
RUDYARD KIPLING, *The Sons of Martha.* St. 1.

And the Sons of Mary smile and are blessèd—they know the angels are on their side.
They know in them is the Grace confessèd, and for them are the Mercies multiplied.
They sit at the Feet—they hear the Word—they see how truly the Promise runs.
They have cast their burden upon the Lord, and—the Lord He lays it on Martha's Sons!
RUDYARD KIPLING, *The Sons of Martha.* St. 8.

And Jesus answered and said unto her, Martha, Martha, thou art careful and troubled about many things: But one thing is needful; and Mary has chosen that good part, which shall not be taken away from her.
New Testament: Luke, x, 41, 42.

8
Each morning sees some task begin,
Each evening sees it close;
Something attempted, something done,
Has earned a night's repose.
H. W. LONGFELLOW, *The Village Blacksmith.*

9
No man is born into the world whose work
Is not born with him; there is always work,
And tools to work withal, for those who will.
J. R. LOWELL, *A Glance Behind the Curtain,* l. 202.

10
The field, the wheel, the desk have called once more,
And we have stooped to pick the slender threads
By which we weave the patterns of our pride.
SCUDDER MIDDLETON, *Jezebel.*

11
Man hath his daily work of body or mind
Appointed.
MILTON, *Paradise Lost.* Bk. iv, l. 618.

12
The work of the world must still be done,
And minds are many though truth be one.
HENRY NEWBOLT, *The Echo.*

13
Establish thou the work of our hands upon us: yea, the work of our hands establish thou it.
Old Testament: Psalms, xc, 17.

14
Work, as though work alone thine end could gain;
But pray to God as though all work were vain.
D'ARCY WENTWORTH THOMPSON, *Sales Attici.* Paraphrasing Euripides.

15
O men, the greatest part of our work is accomplished; away with all fear as to what remains. (Maxima res effecta, viri; timor omnis abesto Quod superest.)
VERGIL, *Æneid.* Bk. xi, l. 14.

III—Work: A Blessing

See also Labor: A Blessing

16
It is work which gives flavor to life.
AMIEL, *Journal,* 21 March, 1881.

1
Don't worry and fret, faint-hearted,
The chances have just begun,
For the best jobs haven't been started,
The best work hasn't been done.
BERTON BRALEY, *No Chance.*

2 Get leave to work
In this world,—'tis the best you get at all.
E. B. BROWNING, *Aurora Leigh*. Bk. iii, l. 164.

Free men freely work:
Whoever fears God, fears to sit at ease.
E. B. BROWNING, *Aurora Leigh*. Bk. viii, l. 784.

3
Man's work is to labour and leaven—
As best he may—earth here with heaven;
'Tis work for work's sake that he's needing
ROBERT BROWNING, *Of Pacchiarotto*. St. 21.

4
Work is a grand cure for all the maladies and miseries that ever beset mankind—honest work, which you intend getting done.
THOMAS CARLYLE, *Inaugural Address*, Edinburgh, 2 April, 1866.

Genuine Work alone, what thou workest faithfully, that is eternal, as the Almighty Founder and World-Builder himself
CARLYLE, *Past and Present*. Bk. ii, ch. 17.

All work . . . is noble, work is alone noble.
CARLYLE, *Past and Present*. Bk. iii, ch. 4.

Blessed is he who has found his work; let him ask no other blessedness.
CARLYLE, *Past and Present*. Bk. iii, ch. 11.

The "wages" of every noble work do yet lie in Heaven or else nowhere.
CARLYLE, *Past and Present*. Bk. iii, ch. 12.

5
The *best* worship, however, is stout working.
THOMAS CARLYLE, *Letter to His Wife*.

The glory of a workman, still more of a master-workman, that he does his work well, ought to be his most precious possession; like the "honour of a soldier" dearer to him than life.
THOMAS CARLYLE, *Shooting Niagara*. Sec. 7.

6
Work, and your house shall be duly fed:
Work, and rest shall be won;
I hold that a man had better be dead
Than alive when his work is done.
ALICE CARY, *Work*.

Work and thou wilt bless the day
Ere the toil be done;
They that work not, can not pray,
Can not feel the sun.
God is living, working still,
All things work and move;
Work, or lose the power to will,
Lose the power to love.
J. S. DWIGHT, *Working*.

7
Honor lies in honest toil.
GROVER CLEVELAND, *Letter Accepting Nomination for President*, 18 August, 1884.

8
Night and day! night and day!
Sound the song the hours rehearse!
Work and play! work and play!
The order of the universe.
JOHN DAVIDSON, *Piper, Play*.

Give me simple laboring folk,
Who love their work,
Whose virtue is a song
To cheer God along
H D THOREAU, *A Week on the Concord and Merrimack Rivers*.

9
There is no substitute for hard work.
THOMAS A. EDISON (*Golden Book*, April, 1931.)

As a cure for worrying, work is better than whiskey.
THOMAS A. EDISON, *Interview on Prohibition*.

Hard work is the best investment a man can make.
C. M. SCHWAB, *Ten Commandments of Success*.

10
The high prize of life, the crowning fortune of a man, is to be born with a bias to some pursuit which finds him in employment and happiness.
EMERSON, *Conduct of Life: Considerations by the Way*.

Truly, one thing is sweet
Of things beneath the Sun;
This, that a man should earn his bread and eat,
Rejoicing in his work which he hath done.
JOSEPHINE PRESTON PEABODY, *The Singing Man*.

11
I look on that man as happy, who, when there is question of success, looks into his work for a reply.
EMERSON, *Conduct of Life: Worship*.

Too busy with the crowded hour to fear to live or die.
EMERSON, *Quatrains: Nature*.

The sum of wisdom is, that the time is never lost that is devoted to work.
EMERSON, *Society and Solitude: Success*.

12
The gods sell us all good things for hard work. (Τῶν πόνων πωλοῦσιν ἡμῖν πάντα τἀγαθὰ θεοί.)
EPICHARMUS. (XENOPHON, *Memorabilia*. Bk. ii, ch. 1, sec. 20.)

13
To generous souls, every task is noble. (Φεῦ τοῖσι γενναίοισιν ὡς ἅπαν καλόν.)
EURIPIDES, *Fragments*. (NAUCK, p. 671.)

14
Our best friend is ever work. (Notre meilleur ami, c'est encor le travail.)
COLLIN D'HARLEVILLE, *Mœurs du Jour*, i, 4.

15
Your work and labour of love.
New Testament: Hebrews. vi, 10.

And only the Master shall praise us, and only the Master shall blame:
And no one shall work for money, and no one shall work for fame:
But each for the joy of the working, and each, in his separate star,
Shall draw the Thing as he sees It, for the God of Things as They Are!
RUDYARD KIPLING, *The Seven Seas: L'Envoi*.

1
He that works after his own manner, his head aches not at the matter.
George Herbert, *Jacula Prudentum.*

If you work for yourself you do it for your own amusement, which is all right; if you work for others, you reap nothing but ingratitude.
Guy de Maupassant, *Waiter, A Bock.*

Work is something you want to get done; play is something you just like to be doing.
Harry Leon Wilson, *The Spenders,* p. 26.

2
Any man who has a job has a chance.
Elbert Hubbard, *Epigrams.*

3
Wit can spin from work a golden robe
To queen it in.
Jean Ingelow, *Gladys and Her Island.*

4
Every child should be taught that useful work is worship and that intelligent labor is the highest form of prayer.
R. G. Ingersoll, *How to Reform Mankind.*

5
If you will let me, I will wish you in your future what all men desire—enough work to do, and strength enough to do your work.
Rudyard Kipling, *Address to Medical Students,* 1908.

6
But finding ample recompense
For life's ungarlanded expense
In work done squarely and unwasted days.
J. R. Lowell, *Under the Old Elm.*

7
In the morning, when thou art sluggish at rousing, let this thought be present: "I am rising to a man's work." ('Επὶ ἀνθρώπου ἔργον ἐγείρομαι.)
Marcus Aurelius, *Meditations.* Bk. v, sec. 1.

Give us this day our daily work.
Elbert Hubbard, *Philistine.* Vol. xxv, p. 51.

Thank God every morning when you get up that you have something to do that day which must be done whether you like it or not. Being forced to work and forced to do your best, will breed in you temperance and self-control, diligence and strength of will, cheerfulness and content, and a hundred virtues which the idle will never know.
Charles Kingsley, *Town and Country Sermons.*

8
The sick man is not to be pitied who has a remedy in his sleeve. (Le malade n'est pas à plaindre, qui a la guarison en sa manche.) *i.e.,* his arm, capable of work.
Montaigne, *Essays.* Bk. iii, ch. 3.

9
Work is the sustenance of noble minds. (Generosos animos labor nutrit.)
Seneca, *Epistulæ ad Lucilium.* Epis. xxxi, 5.

10
A piece of work
So bravely done, so rich, that it did strive
In workmanship and value.
Shakespeare, *Cymbeline.* Act ii, sc. 4, l. 72.

10a
Great is work which lends dignity to man.
Babylonian Talmud: Nedarim, p. 49b.

Flay a carcass in the market to earn thy living, and say not, "I am a great man and it is beneath my station."
Babylonian Talmud: Pesachim, p. 113a.

11
Good for the body is the work of the body, good for the soul the work of the soul, and good for either the work of the other.
H. D. Thoreau, *Journal,* 23 Jan., 1841.

12
Work is the inevitable condition of human life, the true source of human welfare.
Tolstoy, *My Religion.* Ch. 10.

IV—Work: A Curse

See also Labor: A Curse

13
And hold one another's noses to the grindstone hard.
Robert Burton, *Anatomy of Melancholy.* Pt. iii, sec. 1, mem. 3. *See also under* Business.

14
And still be doing, never done.
Butler, *Hudibras.* Pt. i, canto 1, l. 204.

15
Unravelling the web of Penelope. (Penelopæ telam retexens.)
Cicero, *Academicarum Quæstionum.* Bk. iv, ch. 29, sec. 95.

The work she plied, but, studious of delay,
Each foll'wing night revers'd the toils of day.
Homer, *Odyssey.* Bk. xxiv, l. 166. (Pope, tr.)

Thou, Sisyphus, either push or pursue the rock which must always be rolling down the hill again. (Aut petis aut urgues rediturum, Sisyphe saxum.)
Ovid, *Metamorphoses.* Bk. iv, l. 460.

16
In the sweat of thy face shalt thou eat bread.
Old Testament: Genesis, iii, 19. Frequently misquoted "in the sweat of thy brow."

Which I have earned with the sweat of my brows.
Cervantes, *Don Quixote.* Pt. i, bk. i, ch. 4.

Let us go forth and resolutely dare with sweat of brow to toil our little day.
Milton, *Tractate of Education.*

17
Work—work—work
Till the brain begins to swim;
Work—work—work
Till the eyes are heavy and dim! . . .
Stitch—stitch—stitch,
In poverty, hunger, and dirt,
Sewing at once with a double thread,
A Shroud as well as a Shirt.
Thomas Hood, *The Song of the Shirt.*

18
For men must work, and women must weep,
And there's little to earn, and many to keep,
Though the harbour bar be moaning.
Charles Kingsley, *The Three Fishers.* St. 1.

For men must work, and women must weep,
And the sooner it's over the sooner to sleep;
And good-bye to the bar and its moaning.
CHARLES KINGSLEY, *The Three Fishers*. St. 3.

1
Who first invented work, and bound the free
And holy-day rejoicing spirit down
To the ever-haunting importunity
Of business? . . . Sabbathless Satan!
CHARLES LAMB, *Sonnet: Work*. *See also under* BUSINESS.

2
Hard toil can roughen form and face,
And want can quench the eye's bright grace.
WALTER SCOTT, *Marmion*. Canto i, st. 28.

3
Work is not a good. Then what is a good? The scorning of work. (Labor bonum non est. Quid ergo est bonum? Laboris contemptio.)
SENECA, *Epistulæ ad Lucilium*. Epis. xxxi, 4.

4
As for work, we haven't any of consequence. We have the Saint Vitus' dance, and cannot possibly keep our heads still.
H. D. THOREAU, *Walden*. Ch. 2.

5
The more we work, the more we may;
It makes no difference to our pay.
UNKNOWN, *We Are the Royal Sappers*. British war song, 1915.

6
Let us be grateful to Adam, our benefactor. He cut us out of the "blessing" of idleness and won for us the "curse" of labor.
MARK TWAIN, *Pudd'nhead Wilson's Calendar*.

WORLD

See also Earth

I—World: Definitions

7
The world is a great poem, and the world's
The words it is writ in, and we souls the thoughts.
P. J. BAILEY, *Festus: Everywhere*.

8
The created world is but a small parenthesis in eternity.
SIR THOMAS BROWNE, *Christian Morals*. Pt. iii, sec. 29.

The world was made to be inhabited by beasts, but studied and contemplated by man.
SIR THOMAS BROWNE, *Religio Medici*. Pt. i, sec. 13.

The world to me is but a dream or mock-show, and we all therein but Pantaloons and Antics, to my severer contemplations.
SIR THOMAS BROWNE, *Religio Medici*. Pt. i, sec. 41.

For the world, I count it not an inn, but an hospital, and a place, not to live, but to die in.
SIR THOMAS BROWNE, *Religio Medici*. Pt. ii, sec. 11. *See also* LIFE: AN INN.

9
The severe schools shall never laugh me out of the philosophy of Hermes, that this visible world is but a picture of the invisible, wherein, as in a portrait, things are not truly, but in equivocal shapes, and as they counterfeit some more real substance in that invisible fabric.
SIR THOMAS BROWNE, *Religio Medici*. Pt. i, sec. 15.

Hath this world, without me wrought,
Other substance than my thought?
Lives it by my sense alone,
Or by essence of its own?
FREDERIC HENRY HEDGE, *Questionings*.

The visible world is but man turned inside out that he may be revealed to himself.
HENRY JAMES THE ELDER. (J. A. KELLOG, *Digest of the Philosophy of Henry James*.)

This outer world is but the pictured scroll
Of worlds within the soul;
A coloured chart, a blazoned missal-book,
Whereon who rightly look
May spell the splendours with their mortal eyes,
And steer to Paradise.
ALFRED NOYES, *The Two Worlds*.

My God, I would not live
Save that I think this gross hard-seeming world
Is our misshaping vision of the Powers
Behind the world, that make our griefs our gains.
TENNYSON, *The Sisters*, l. 223.

The true mystery of the world is the visible, not the invisible.
OSCAR WILDE, *Picture of Dorian Gray*. Ch. 2.

10
What, in fact, is the world? A glass which shines,
Which a breath has made, and which a breath can destroy.
(Quel est-il en effet? C'est un verre qui luit,
Qu'un souffle a produit, et qu'un souffle peut detruire.)
GILLES DE CAUX, *L'Horloge de Sable*. (D'ISRAELI, *Curiosities of Literature*.)

11
The world is a wheel, and it will all come round right.
BENJAMIN DISRAELI, *Endymion*. Ch. 70.

12
The world is a divine dream, from which we may presently awake to the glories and certainties of day.
EMERSON, *Nature, Addresses, and Lectures: Spirit*.

The existing world is not a dream, and cannot with impunity be treated as a dream; neither is it a disease; but it is the ground on which you stand, it is the mother of whom you were born.
EMERSON, *Nature, Addresses, and Lectures: The Conservative*.

13
Our Copernican globe is a great factory or shop of power, with its rotating constellations, times, and tides.
EMERSON, *Letters and Social Aims: Resources*.

The world is a proud place, peopled with men of positive quality, with heroes and demigods standing around us, who will not let us sleep.
EMERSON, *Society and Solitude: Books*.

1
This world's a city, full of straying streets,
And death's the market place, where each one
meets.

JOHN FLETCHER, *Two Noble Kinsmen*. Act i, sc. 5

This world's a city full of crooked streets,
Death's the market-place where all men meet;
If life were merchandise that men should buy,
The rich would always live, the poor might die.

UNKNOWN, *Epitaph to John Gadsden* (d. 1739), at Stoke Goldington, England. (SUFFLING, *Epitaphia*, p. 401.)

2
The world is a ladder for some to go up and some down.

THOMAS FULLER, *Gnomologia*. No. 4841. From the Italian, "Il monde è fatto a scale, Chi le scende, e chi le sale."

3
The world is a beautiful book, but of little use to him who cannot read it. (Il mondo è un bel libro, ma poco serve a chi non lo sa leggere.)

GOLDONI, *Pamela*. Act i, sc. 14.

The world is woman's book. (Le monde est le livre des femmes.)

ROUSSEAU.

4
The world is nothing but vanity cut out into several shapes.

LORD HALIFAX, *Works*, p. 240.

5
The world!—it is a wilderness,
Where tears are hung on every tree.

THOMAS HOOD, *Ode to Melancholy*, l. 13.

6
There are two worlds; the world that we can measure with line and rule, and the world that we feel with our hearts and imaginations.

LEIGH HUNT, *Men, Women, and Books: Fiction and Matter-of-Fact*.

7
The world, in its best state, is nothing more than a larger assembly of beings, combining to counterfeit happiness which they do not feel.

SAMUEL JOHNSON, *The Adventurer*. No. 120.

8
The world is a nettle; disturb it, it stings.
Grasp it firmly, it stings not.

OWEN MEREDITH, *Lucile*. Pt. i, canto 3, sec. 2.

Let any man once show the world that he feels
Afraid of its bark, and 'twill fly at his heels:
Let him fearlessly face it, 'twill leave him alone:
But 'twill fawn at his feet if he flings it a bone.

OWEN MEREDITH, *Lucile*. Pt. i, canto 2, st. 7.
See also BOLDNESS: ITS VIRTUES.

9
The world is but a perpetual see-saw. (Le monde n'est qu'une bransloire perenne.)

MONTAIGNE, *Essays*. Bk. iii, ch. 2.

11
The world is not a "prison house" but a kind of spiritual kindergarten where millions of bewildered infants are trying to spell God with the wrong blocks.

E. A. ROBINSON, *Letter to the Bookman*, March, 1897 (p. 7), referring to a short notice of his first book, *The Torrent and the Night Before*, by Harry Thurston Peck, which had appeared in the issue of *The Bookman* for February, 1897 (p 510), and in which Mr. Peck had said, "The world is not beautiful to him, but a prison-house."

12
The world is a looking glass, and gives back to every man the reflection of his own face. Frown at it and it will in turn look sourly upon you; laugh at it and with it, and it is a jolly kind companion.

THACKERAY, *Vanity Fair*. Ch. 2.

The world is a mirror of infinite beauty, yet no man sees it It is a Temple of Majesty, yet no man regards it. It is a region of Light and Peace, did not men disquiet it. It is the Paradise of God.

THOMAS TRAHERNE, *Centuries of Meditations*.

13
The world is but a frozen kind of gas
A transient ice we sport on, where, alas!
Diverted by the pictures in the glass,
We heed not the Realities that pass.

J. T. TROWBRIDGE, *Idealist*.

14
What is this world? A net to snare the soul.

GEORGE WHETSTONE, *The World*.

15
I have often said, and oftener think, *that this world is a comedy to those that think, a tragedy to those that feel*—a solution of why Democritus laughed and Heraclitus wept.

HORACE WALPOLE, *Letter to Sir Horace Mann*, 31 Dec., 1769.

16
The world's a prophecy of worlds to come.

YOUNG, *Night Thoughts*. Night vii, l. 16.

17
What a dark world—who knows?—
Ours to inhabit is!
One touch and what a strange
Glory might burst on us,
What a hid universe!

ISRAEL ZANGWILL, *Blind Children*.

II—World: Apothegms

18
The verdict of the world is conclusive. (Securus judicat orbis terrarum.)

SAINT AUGUSTINE, *Contra Litteras Parmeniani*, iii, 24.

19
A Mad World, My Masters.

NICHOLAS BRETON. Title of dialogue. (1603);
THOMAS MIDDLETON. Title of play. (1608)

'Tis a mad world (my masters) and in sadness
I travail'd madly in these days of madness.

JOHN TAYLOR THE WATER-POET, *Wandering to See the Wonders of the West*. (1649)

Mad world! mad kings! mad composition!

SHAKESPEARE, *King John*. Act ii, sc. 1, l. 561.

20
The world, which took but six days to make, is like to take six thousand to make out.

SIR THOMAS BROWNE, *Christian Morals*. Pt. ii, sec. 5.

1
Without, or with, offence to friends or foes,
I sketch your world exactly as it goes.
BYRON, *Don Juan*. Canto viii, st. 89.

2
I value not the world a button.
SUSANNAH CENTLIVRE, *The Wonder*. Act i, sc. 1.

3
A world where nothing is had for nothing.
ARTHUR HUGH CLOUGH, *The Bothie of Toberna-Vuolich*. Sec. 8, l. 5.

4
The world, like an accomplished hostess, pays most attention to those whom it will soonest forget.
CHURTON COLLINS, *Aphorisms*.

5
Such stuff the world is made of.
COWPER, *Hope*, l. 211.

'Tis pleasant through the loop-holes of retreat
To peep at such a world; to see the stir
Of the great Babel, and not feel the crowd.
COWPER, *The Task*. Bk. iv, l. 88.

6
And for the few that only lend their ear,
That few is all the world.
SAMUEL DANIEL, *Musophilus*. St. 97.

There was all the world and his wife.
SWIFT, *Polite Conversation*. Dial. iii. (1738)

How he welcomes at once all the world and his wife,
And how civil to folk he ne'er saw in his life!
CHRIS. ANSTEY, *New Bath Guide*, 130. (1766)

7
Come, follow me, and leave the world to its babblings. (Vien retro a me, e lascia dir le genti.)
DANTE, *Purgatorio*. Canto v, l. 13.

8
Behold the world, how it is whirlèd round,
And for it is so whirl'd is named so.
SIR JOHN DAVIES, *Orchestra*. St. 34.

9
What a world of gammon and spinnage it is, though, ain't it?
DICKENS, *David Copperfield*. Ch. 22.

10
I am a citizen of the world.
DIOGENES. (DIOGENES LAERTIUS, *Socrates*. Bk. vi, sec. 63.) *See under* COSMOPOLITANISM.

11
We must see that the world is rough and surly.
EMERSON, *Conduct of Life: Fate*.

The world is always equal to itself.
EMERSON, *Social Aims: Progress of Culture*.

12
The world is too narrow for two fools a quarrelling.
THOMAS FULLER, *Gnomologia*. No. 4844.

This world surely is wide enough to hold both thee and me.
LAURENCE STERNE, *Tristram Shandy*. Bk. ii, ch. 12

I have my beauty,—you your Art—
Nay, do not start:
One world was not enough for two
Like me and you.
OSCAR WILDE, *Her Voice*.

13
It moves, nevertheless! (E pur si muove!)
GALILEO. A phrase which he is said to have whispered to a friend as he rose from signing his recantation of his theory that "the sun is the centre of the universe, and immovable, and that the earth moves." (1615) Von Gebler (*Galileo Galilei and the Roman Curia*) doubts that he ever uttered them.

Does the world go round?
SHAKESPEARE, *Cymbeline*. Act v, sc. 5, l. 232.

Roll on, thou ball, roll on
Through pathless realms of space,
Roll on! [It rolls on.]
W. S. GILBERT, *To the Terrestrial Globe*.

Gyrate, old Top, and let who will be clever;
The mess we 're in is much too deep to solve.
Me for a quiet life while you, as ever,
Continue to revolve.
BERT LESTON TAYLOR, *To a Well-Known Globe*.

Long and long has the grass been growing,
Long and long has the rain been falling,
Long has the globe been rolling round.
WALT WHITMAN, *Song of the Exposition*. Pt. i.

14
Creation's heir, the world, the world is mine!
GOLDSMITH, *The Traveller*, l. 50.

15
If the world were good for nothing else, it is a fine subject for speculation.
WILLIAM HAZLITT, *Characteristics*. No. 302.

To understand the world, and to like it, are two things not easily to be reconciled.
LORD HALIFAX, *Works*, p. 230.

16
The world runneth on wheels.
JOHN HEYWOOD, *Proverbs*. Pt. ii, ch. 7. (1546)

They were wont to say, the world doth run on wheels.
BARNABE RICH, *Honestie of This Age*, p. 30. (1614)

17
The world belongs to those who think and act with it, who keep a finger on its pulse.
DEAN W. R. INGE. (MARCHANT, *Wit and Wisdom of Dean Inge*. No. 171.)

18
World without end.
Old Testament: Isaiah, xlv, 17.

19
It takes all sorts of people to make a world.
DOUGLAS JERROLD, *Story of a Feather*. Ch. 28. (1844)

In the world there must be of all sorts.
JOHN SKELTON, *Quixote*. Pt. ii, ch. 6. (1620)

The world has people of all sorts.
JOHN LOCKE. Quoted by Samuel Johnson. (BOSWELL, *Life*, 17 Nov., 1767.)

20
This world, where much is to be done and little to be known.
SAMUEL JOHNSON, *Prayers and Meditations: Against Inquisitive and Perplexing Thoughts*.

21
I never have sought the world; the world was not to seek me.
SAMUEL JOHNSON. (BOSWELL, *Life*, 1783.)

I have not loved the world, nor the world me;
I have not flatter'd its rank breath, nor bow'd
To its idolatries a patient knee.
BYRON, *Childe Harold*. Canto iii, st. 113.

1
The world meets nobody half-way.
LAMB, *Essays of Elia: Valentine's Day*.

2
He who imagines he can do without the world deceives himself greatly; but he who fancies that the world cannot do without him deceives himself still more. (Celui qui croit pouvoir trouver en soi-même de quoi se passer de tout le monde se trompe fort; mais celui qui croit qu'on ne peut se passer de lui se trompe encore davantage.)
LA ROCHEFOUCAULD, *Maximes*. No. 201.

Truly, this world can go on without us, if we would but think so.
LONGFELLOW, *Hyperion*. Bk. i, ch. 5.

3
The flaming ramparts of the world. (Flammantia mœnia mundi.)
LUCRETIUS, *De Rerum Natura*. Bk. i, l. 73.

4
It is a world to see.
JOHN LYLY, *Euphues*, p. 116. (1579)

It is a world to see this world.
THOMAS NASHE, *Works*. Vol. i, p. 149. (1589)

For young and old, and every manner age,
It was a world to look on her visage.
UNKNOWN, *Assembly of Ladies*, l. 539. (1475)

5
Upon the battle ground of heaven and hell
I palsied stand.
MARIE JOSEPHINE, *Rosa Mystica*, p. 231.

6
This opacous earth, this punctual spot.
MILTON, *Paradise Lost*. Bk. viii, l. 23.

7
The world was all before them.
MILTON, *Paradise Lost*. Bk. xii, l. 646.

The wide world is all before us.
BURNS, *Strathallan's Lament*.

The world is all before me.
BYRON, *Epistle to Augusta*. St. 11.

8
A world made to be lost,—
A bitter life 'twixt pain and nothing tost.
WILLIAM MORRIS, *The Earthly Paradise: The Hill of Venus*.

The world still needs
Its champion as of old, and finds him still.
LEWIS MORRIS, *The Epic of Hades: Herakles*.

9
The world where one bores oneself. (Le monde où l'on s'ennuie.)
ÉDOUARD PAILLERON. Title of play, 1881.

10
Half the world does not know how the other half lives. (La moitié du monde ne sçait comme l'autre vit.)
RABELAIS, *Works*. Pt. ii, ch. 32. Quoted by Emerson, *Manners*. How the Other Half Lives.—Title of book by JACOB A. RIIS.

11
The world is as you take it.
JOHN RAY, *English Proverbs*.

Take the world as it is, not as it ought to be. (Nimm die Welt wie sie ist, nicht wie sie sein sollte.)
UNKNOWN. A German proverb.

12
The world is much the same everywhere.
JOHN RAY, *English Proverbs*. From the French, "C'est partout comme chez nous," It is everywhere as it is at home.

13
One real world is enough.
GEORGE SANTAYANA, *Little Essays*, p. 31.

14
The world in which a man lives shapes itself chiefly by the way in which he looks at it.
ARTHUR SCHOPENHAUER, *The World as Will and Idea*.

15
You must either imitate or loathe the world. (Necesse est aut imiteris aut oderis.)
SENECA, *Epistulæ ad Lucilium*. Epis. vii, sec. 7.

16
"Thus we may see," quoth he, "how the world wags."
SHAKESPEARE, *As You Like It*. Act ii, sc. 7, l. 23.

Why, let the stricken deer go weep,
The hart ungalled play;
For some must watch, while some must sleep:
So runs the world away.
SHAKESPEARE, *Hamlet*. Act iii, sc. 2, l. 282.

You see how this world goes.
SHAKESPEARE, *King Lear*. Act iv, sc. 6, l. 151.

How goes the world, sir, now?
SHAKESPEARE, *Macbeth*. Act ii, sc. 4, l. 21.

17
Daff'd the world aside, And bid it pass.
SHAKESPEARE, *I Henry IV*. Act iv, sc. 1, l. 96.

18
Why, then the world's mine oyster,
Which I with sword will open.
SHAKESPEARE, *The Merry Wives of Windsor*. Act ii, sc. 2, l. 2.

19
I consider the world as made for me, not me for the world. It is my maxim therefore to enjoy it while I can, and let futurity shift for itself.
SMOLLETT, *Roderick Random*. Ch. 45.

20
The world knows nothing of its greatest men.
SIR HENRY TAYLOR, *I Philip van Artevelde*. Act i, sc. 5, l. 19.

The world will commonly end by making men what it thinks them.
SIR HENRY TAYLOR, *The Statesman*, p. 135.

21
One world at a time.
H. D. THOREAU, *Remark*. *See* 2298i:5.

22
'Tis a very good world to live in,
To lend, or to spend, or to give in;
But to beg, or to borrow, or to get a man's own,
It's the very worst world that ever was known.
JOHN WILMOT, EARL OF ROCHESTER, *The*

World. A slightly different version attributed to J. Bromfield appeared in the *Mirror*, 12 Sept., 1840. Quoted by Washington Irving (*Tales of a Traveller:* Pt. ii, *Motto*).

1
They most the world enjoy, who least admire.
YOUNG, *Night Thoughts*. Night viii, l. 1173.

2
Let the world pass.
UNKNOWN. (*Towneley Plays*, 201. c. 1400); NICHOLAS UDALL, *Ralph Roister Doister*. Act iii, sc. 3. (1550); DRYDEN, *The Kind Keeper*. Act v, sc. 1. (1678)

Let the wide world wind!
UNKNOWN, *Four Elements*. (HAZLITT, *Old Plays*, i, 20. 1519.)

But *moveatur terra*, let the world wag.
JOHN SKELTON, *Speke, Parrot*. St. 13. (a. 1529)

To let the world wag and take mine ease in mine inn.
JOHN HEYWOOD, *Proverbs*. Pt. i, ch. 5. (1546)

Let the world slide, let the world go;
A fig for care and a fig for woe!
JOHN HEYWOOD, *Be Merry Friends*. (c. 1560)

Let the world slide.
SHAKESPEARE, *The Taming of the Shrew: Induction*. Sc. 1, l. 6. (1594)

Let the world slip.
SHAKESPEARE, *The Taming of the Shrew: Induction*. Sc. 2, l. 146.

Do well and right, and let the world sink.
GEORGE HERBERT, *Country Parson*. Ch. 29.

3
The world is wiser than it was.
From the French, "Le monde n'est plus fat," stated by Rabelais to be a common proverb in 1533.

4
To the city and the world. (Urbi et orbi.)
Formula accompanying the proclamation of Papal rescripts; also affixed to the gates of the Vatican. (ADDIS, *Promulgation*, in *Catholic Encyclopedia*.)

III—World: A Bubble

See also Life: A Bubble; Man: A Bubble

5
The world's a bubble.
FRANCIS BACON, *The World*.

6
Happy the man who . . . gets acquainted with the world early enough to make it his bubble, at an age when most people are the bubbles of the world!
LORD CHESTERFIELD, *Letters*, 6 May, 1751.

7
Or may I think when toss'd in trouble,
This world at best is but a bubble.
MICHAEL MOOR, *Bubbles*.

8
The pleasure, honour, wealth of sea and land
Bring but a trouble;
The world itself, and all the world's command
Is but a bubble.
FRANCIS QUARLES, *Emblems*. Bk. i, No. 6.

My soul, what's lighter than a feather? Wind.
Than wind? The fire. And what than fire? The mind.
What's lighter than the mind? A thought. Than thought?
This bubble world. What than this bubble? Nought.
FRANCIS QUARLES, *Emblems*. Bk. i, No. 4. *See also under* WOMAN: HER FICKLENESS.

9
The world is full of care, and much like unto a bubble;
Women and care and care and women, and women and care and trouble.
NATHANIEL WARD, *Epigram*.

IV—World: A Stage

See also Life: A Play

10
God is the author, men are only the players. These grand pieces which are played upon earth have been composed in heaven. (Dieu est le poète, les hommes ne sont que les acteurs. Ces grandes pièces qui se jouent sur la terre ont été composées dans le ciel.)
BALZAC, *Socrate Chrétien*.

11
All our pride is but a jest;
None are worst and none are best;
Grief and joy, and hope and fear
Play their pageants everywhere:
Vain opinion all doth sway,
And the world is but a play.
THOMAS CAMPION, *Song: Whether Men Do Laugh or Weep*.

12
The world's a stage where God's omnipotence,
His justice, knowledge, love and providence,
Do act the parts.
DU BARTAS, *Devine Weekes and Workes*. Week i, day 1.

I take the world to be but as a stage,
Where net-masked men do play their personage.
DU BARTAS, *Devine Weekes and Workes: Dialogue Between Heraclitus and Democritus*.

Pythagoras said that this world was like a stage,
Whereon many play their parts; the lookers-on the sage
Philosophers are, saith he, whose part is to learn
The manners of all nations, and the good from the bad to discern.
RICHARD EDWARDS, *Damon and Pythias*.

13
If this world be a stage, what hours we give
To tedious make-up in the tiring-room.
JOHN ERSKINE, *At the Front*. Sonnet iii.

14
Shall I speak truly what I now see below?
The World is all a carcass, smoke and vanity,
The shadow of a shadow, a play
And in one word, just Nothing.
OWEN FELLTHAM, *Resolves*. (1696) A paraphrase of the Latin lines said to have been left by Lipsius, to be inscribed on his tomb.

1
The world's a theatre, the earth a stage,
Which God and nature do with actors fill.
JOHN HEYWOOD, *The Author to His Book.*

2
The world's a stage,—as Shakespeare said, one day;
The stage a world—was what he meant to say.
O. W. HOLMES, *Prologue*, l. 9.

There is that smaller world which is the stage, and that larger stage which is the world.
ISAAC GOLDBERG, *The Theatre of George Jean Nathan*, p. 3.

3
The world's a stage on which all parts are played.
MIDDLETON, *A Game of Chess.* Act v, sc. 2.

4
Is it not a noble farce wherein kings, republics, and emperors have for so many ages played their parts, and to which the vast universe serves for a theatre?
MONTAIGNE, *Essays.* Bk. ii, ch. 36.

All the world must practice stage-playing. We must play our parts duly.
MONTAIGNE, *Essays.* Bk. iii, ch. 10.

5
I hold the world but as the world, Gratiano;
A stage where every man must play a part.
SHAKESPEARE, *The Merchant of Venice.* Act i, sc. 1, l. 77.

All the world's a stage.
And all the men and women merely players:
They have their exits and their entrances;
And one man in his time plays many parts,
His acts being seven ages. At first the infant,
Mewling and puking in the nurse's arms.
And then the whining school-boy, with his satchel
And shining morning face, creeping like snail
Unwillingly to school. And then the lover,
Sighing like furnace, with a woeful ballad
Made to his mistress' eyebrow. Then a soldier,
Full of strange oaths and bearded like the pard,
Jealous in honour, sudden and quick in quarrel,
Seeking the bubble reputation
Even in the cannon's mouth. And then the justice,
In fair round belly with good capon lined,
With eyes severe and beard of formal cut,
Full of wise saws and modern instances;
And so he plays his part. The sixth age shifts
Into the lean and slipper'd pantaloon,
With spectacles on nose and pouch on side,
His youthful hose, well saved, a world too wide
For his shrunk shank; and his big manly voice,
Turning again toward childish treble, pipes
And whistles in his sound. Last scene of all,
That ends this strange eventful history,
Is second childishness and mere oblivion,
Sans teeth, sans eyes, sans taste, sans every thing.
SHAKESPEARE, *As You Like It.* Act ii, sc. 7, l 139.

The child, who by now can utter words and set firm step upon the ground, delights to play with his mates, flies into a passion and as lightly puts it aside, and changes every hour. The beardless youth, freed at last from his tutor, finds joy in horses and hounds and the grass of the sunny Campus, soft as wax for moulding to evil, peevish with his counsellors, slow to make needful provision, lavish of money, spirited, of strong desires, but swift to change his fancies. With altered aims, the age and spirit of the man seeks wealth and friends, becomes a slave to ambition. . . . Many ills encompass an old man; . . . he lacks fire and courage, is dilatory and slow to form hopes.
HORACE, *Ars Poetica*, l. 158.

6
Almost the whole world are players. (Quod fere totus mundus exerceat histrionem.)
Motto over the Door of Shakespeare's Theatre, the Globe, Bankside, London. An adaptation from Petronius. (*Frag.* 10.)

They are a nation of actors. (Natio comœda est.)
JUVENAL, *Satires.* Sat. iii, l. 100. Of the Greeks.

7
In this playhouse of infinite forms I have had my play.
RABINDRANATH TAGORE, *Gitanjali.* No. 96.

8
Life's little stage is a small eminence,
Inch-high the grave above.
YOUNG, *Night Thoughts.* Night ii, l. 360.

V—World: Its Beauty and Happiness

9
O world, as God has made it! All is beauty:
And knowing this, is love, and love is duty.
What further may be sought for or declared?
ROBERT BROWNING, *The Guardian-Angel.*

However, you're a man, you've seen the world—
The beauty and the wonder and the power,
The shapes of things, their colours, lights and shades,
Changes, surprises—and God made it all!
ROBERT BROWNING, *Fra Lippo Lippi*, l. 276.

This world's no blot for us,
Nor blank; it means intensely, and means good:
To find its meaning is my meat and drink.
ROBERT BROWNING, *Fra Lippo Lippi*, l. 313.

10
I say the world is lovely
And that loveliness is enough.
ROBERT BUCHANAN, *Artist and Model.*

11
The world is good in the lump.
GEORGE COLMAN THE YOUNGER, *The Torrent.* Act i, sc. 2.

12
Of this fair volume which we World do name,
If we the sheets and leaves could turn with care,
Of him who it corrects, and did it frame,
We clear might read the art and wisdom rare.
WILLIAM DRUMMOND, *The Book of the World.*

Let the great book of the world be your serious study; read it over and over, get it by heart, adopt its style, and make it your own.
LORD CHESTERFIELD, *Letters*, 9 July, 1750.

1
For the world is not painted or adorned, but is from the beginning beautiful; and God has not made some beautiful things, but Beauty is the creator of the universe.

EMERSON, *Essays, Second Series: The Poet.*

2
I found many who were continually wishing for beauty. I went to them with a sunset and a spray of mist, but they had already contented themselves in a shop with little painted candlesticks.

CHARLOTTE HARDIN, *Coins and Medals.*

It is not accident that wherever we point the telescope we see beauty, that wherever we look with the microscope there we find beauty. It beats in through every nook and cranny of the mighty world.

R. M. JONES. (NEWTON, *My Idea of God,* p. 61.)

The world is not respectable; it is mortal, tormented, confused, deluded for ever; but is shot through with beauty, with love, with glints of courage and laughter; and in these the spirit blooms timidly, and struggles to the light among the thorns.

GEORGE SANTAYANA, *Platonism and the Spiritual Life.*

3
There's too much beauty upon this earth
For lonely men to bear.

RICHARD LE GALLIENNE, *Ballad of Too Much Beauty.*

4
Oh, what a glory doth this world put on
For him who, with a fervent heart, goes forth
Under the bright and glorious sky, and looks
On duties well performed, and days well spent!

LONGFELLOW, *Autumn,* l. 30.

Glorious indeed is the world of God around us, but more glorious the world of God within us. There lies the Land of Song; there lies the poet's native land.

LONGFELLOW, *Hyperion.* Bk. i, ch. 8.

5
This world is full of beauty, as other worlds above;
And, if we did our duty, it might be full of love.

GERALD MASSEY, *This World Is Full of Beauty.*

6
O world, I cannot hold thee close enough!

EDNA ST. VINCENT MILLAY, *God's World.*

The world stands out on either side
No wider than the heart is wide;
Above the world is stretched the sky,—
No higher than the soul is high.

EDNA ST. VINCENT MILLAY, *Renascence.*

7
An idle poet, here and there
Looks round him, but for all the rest,
The world, unfathomably fair,
Is duller than a witling's jest.

COVENTRY PATMORE, *The Revelation.*

8
The world is full of poetry—the air
Is living with its spirit; and the waves
Dance to the music of its melodies.

J. G. PERCIVAL, *The Prevalence of Poetry.*

9
Great, wide, beautiful, wonderful World,
With the wonderful water round you curled,
And the wonderful grass upon your breast,
World, you are beautifully dressed.

W. B. RANDS, *The Wonderful World.*

10
The whole world is the temple of the immortal gods. (Totum mundum Deorum esse immortalium templum.)

SENECA, *De Beneficiis.* Bk. vii, sec. 7.

11
The world is such a happy place,
That children, whether big or small,
Should always have a smiling face,
And never, never sulk at all.

GABRIEL SETOUN, *The World's Music.*

The world is so full of a number of things,
I'm sure we should all be as happy as kings.

ROBERT LOUIS STEVENSON, *Happy Thought.*

12
The world was never less beautiful though viewed through a chink or knothole.

H. D. THOREAU, *Journal,* 16 Jan., 1838.

13
I swear the earth shall surely be complete to him or her who shall be complete,
The earth remains jagged and broken only to him or her who remains jagged and broken.

WALT WHITMAN, *Song of the Rolling Earth.* Pt. iii.

14
Not in Utopia, subterranean fields,
Or some secreted island, Heaven knows where!
But in the very world, which is the world
Of all of us,—the place where in the end
We find our happiness, or not at all!

WORDSWORTH, *French Revolution,* l. 36.

VI—World: Its Ugliness and Misery

14a
Oh, Lucius, I am sick of this bad world!
The day-light and the sun grow painful to me.

ADDISON, *Cato.* Act iv, sc. 4.

15 This restless world
Is full of chances, which by habit's power
To learn to bear is easier than to shun.

JOHN ARMSTRONG, *Art of Preserving Health.* Bk. ii, l. 453.

16
It's a weary warld, and nobody bides in 't.

J. M. BARRIE, *The Little Minister.* Ch. 4.

A brave world, sir, full of religion, knavery, and change! We shall shortly see better days.

APHRA BEHN, *The Roundheads.* Act i, sc. 1.

17
This bad, twisted, topsy-turvy world,
Where all the heaviest wrongs get uppermost.

E. B. BROWNING, *Aurora Leigh.* Bk. v, l. 981.

18 This world has been harsh and strange;
Something is wrong: there needeth a change.

ROBERT BROWNING, *Holy-Cross Day.*

1
The world is naturally averse
To all the truth it sees or hears,
But swallows nonsense, and a lie,
With greediness and gluttony.
BUTLER, *Hudibras*. Pt. iii, canto 2, l. 805.

2
'Tis but a worthless world to win or lose.
BYRON, *Childe Harold*. Canto iii, st. 40.

The world is full of strange vicissitudes.
BYRON, *Don Juan*. Canto iv, st. 51.

Well, my deliberate opinion is—it's a jolly strange world.
ARNOLD BENNETT, *The Title*. Act i.

3
Ah, World of ours, are you so grey
And weary, World, of spinning,
That you repeat the tales today
You told at the beginning?
For lo! the same old myths that made
The early "stage-successes,"
Still "hold the boards," and still are played,
"With new effects and dresses."
AUSTIN DOBSON, *The Drama of the Doctor's Window*.

4
Good-bye, proud world! I'm going home.
I am going to my own hearth-stone,
Bosomed in yon green hills alone,— . . .
A spot that is sacred to thought and God.
EMERSON, *Good-Bye*.

5
For every worldes thing is vain,
And ever go'th the wheel about. . . .
Now here, now there, now to, now fro,
Now up, now down, the world go'th so,
And ever hath done and ever shall.
JOHN GOWER, *Confessio Amantis: Prologue*, l. 560.

So go'th the world; now woe, now weal.
JOHN GOWER, *Confessio Amantis*. Bk. viii.

Well—well, the world must turn upon its axis,
And all mankind turn with it, heads or tails,
And live and die, make love and pay our taxes,
And as the veering wind shifts, shift our sails.
BYRON, *Don Juan*. Canto ii, st. 4.

6
The world is with me, and its many cares,
Its woes—its wants—the anxious hopes and fears
That wait on all terrestrial affairs— . . .
Heavens! what a wilderness the earth appears,
Where Youth, and Mirth, and Health are out of date!
THOMAS HOOD, *Sonnet*.

7
We live together in a world that is bursting with sin and sorrow.
SAMUEL JOHNSON, *Miscellanies*. Vol. i, p. 301.

The world's as ugly, ay, as Sin,—
And almost as delightful.
F. LOCKER-LAMPSON, *The Jester's Plea*.

8
Yes, Heaven is thine; but this
Is a world of sweets and sours;
Our flowers are merely—flowers,
And the shadow of thy perfect bliss
Is the sunshine of ours.
EDGAR ALLAN POE, *Israfel*.

9
O what a crocodilian world is this!
FRANCIS QUARLES, *Emblems*. Bk. i, No. 4.

O who would trust this world, or prize what's in it,
That gives and takes, and chops and changes every minute.
FRANCIS QUARLES, *Emblems*. Bk. i, No. 9.

10
O how full of briars is this working-day world!
SHAKESPEARE, *As You Like It*. Act i, sc. 3, l. 12.

How weary, stale, flat and unprofitable,
Seem to me all the uses of this world!
SHAKESPEARE, *Hamlet*. Act i, sc. 2, l. 133.

Would I were dead! if God's good will were so:
For what is in this world but grief and woe?
SHAKESPEARE, *III Henry VI*. Act ii, sc. 5, l. 19.

Vain pomp and glory of this world, I hate ye.
SHAKESPEARE, *Henry VIII*. Act iii, sc. 2, l. 365.

The world is grown so bad,
That wrens make prey where eagles dare not perch.
SHAKESPEARE, *Richard III*. Act i, sc. 3, l. 70.

11
The world is not thy friend, nor the world's law;
The world affords no law to make thee rich;
Then be not poor, but break it.
SHAKESPEARE, *Romeo and Juliet*. Act v, sc. 1, l. 72.

Ah, how the poor world is pestered with such waterflies, diminutives of nature.
SHAKESPEARE, *Troilus and Cressida*. Act v, sc. 1, l. 37.

12
A maniac world,
Homeless and sobbing through the deep she goes.
ALEXANDER SMITH, *Unrest and Childhood*.

13
Meseems the world is run quite out of square
From the first point of his appointed source;
And being once amiss grows daily worse and worse.
SPENSER, *The Faerie Queene*: Bk. v, *Introduction*. St. 1.

14
Strange the world about me lies
Never yet familiar grown—
Still disturbs me with surprise,
Haunts me like a face half known.

In this house with starry dome,
Floored with gem-like plains and seas,
Shall I never feel at home,
Never wholly be at ease?
WILLIAM WATSON, *World-Strangeness*.

15
When the fretful stir
Unprofitable, and the fever of the world

Have hung upon the beatings of my heart.
WORDSWORTH, *Lines Composed a Few Miles Above Tintern Abbey,* l. 52.

1
Let not the cooings of the world allure thee:
Which of her lovers ever found her true?
YOUNG, *Night Thoughts.* Night viii, l. 1272.

VII—World: Knowledge Of, Worldliness

2
The more a man drinketh of the world, the more it intoxicateth.
FRANCIS BACON, *Essays: Of Youth and Age.*

3
He sees that this great roundabout,
The world, with all its motley rout,
  Church, army, physic, law,
Its customs and its businesses,
Is no concern at all of his,
  And says—what says he?—Caw.
VINCENT BOURNE, *The Jackdaw.* (Cowper, tr.)

4
    Worldly in this world,
I take and like its way of life.
ROBERT BROWNING, *Bishop Blougram's Apology.*

Of the world most worldly, who never compromised himself by an ungentlemanly action, and was never guilty of a manly one.
DICKENS, *Barnaby Rudge.* Ch. 25.

5
Such is the world. Understand it, despise it, love it; cheerfully hold on thy way through it, with thy eye on highest loadstars!
CARLYLE, *Essays: Count Cagliostro.*

The true Sovereign of the world, who moulds the world like soft wax, according to his pleasure, is he who lovingly sees into the world.
CARLYLE, *Essays: Death of Goethe.*

6
Knowledge of the world is to be acquired only in the world, not in the closet.
LORD CHESTERFIELD, *Letters,* 4 Oct., 1746.

The world is a country which no one yet ever knew by description; one must travel through it oneself to be acquainted with it. . . . Courts and camps are the only places to learn the world in.
LORD CHESTERFIELD, *Letters,* 2 Oct., 1747.

The preposterous notions of a systematical man who does not know the world, tire the patience of a man who does.
LORD CHESTERFIELD, *Letters,* 27 May, 1753.

7
The world is a lively place enough, in which we must accommodate ourselves to circumstances, sail with the stream as glibly as we can, be content to take froth for substance, the surface for the depth, the counterfeit for the real coin.
DICKENS, *Barnaby Rudge.* Ch. 12.

8
Map me no maps, sir; my head is a map, a map of the whole world.
FIELDING, *Rape upon Rape.* Act i, sc. 5.

Geographers crowd into the outer edges of their maps the parts of the world which they know nothing about, adding a note, "What lies beyond is sandy desert full of wild beasts," or "blind marsh," or "Scythian cold," or "frozen sea."
PLUTARCH, *Lives: Theseus.* Ch. i, sec. 1.

So geographers, in Afric maps,
With savage pictures fill their gaps,
And o'er unhabitable downs
Place elephants for want of towns.
SWIFT, *Poetry, a Rhapsody.*

9
Unworldliness based on knowledge of the world is the finest thing on earth; but unworldliness based on ignorance of the world is less admirable.
DEAN W. R. INGE. (MARCHANT, *Wit and Wisdom of Dean Inge.* No. 172.)

10
To know the world is necessary, . . . and to know it early is convenient, if it be only that we may learn early to despise it.
SAMUEL JOHNSON, *The Idler.* No. 80.

The world will, in the end, follow only those who have despised as well as served it.
SAMUEL BUTLER THE YOUNGER, *Note-Books,* p. 365.

11
That observation which is called knowledge of the world will be found much more frequently to make men cunning than good.
SAMUEL JOHNSON, *The Rambler.* No. 4.

12
If there is one beast in all the loathsome fauna of civilization I hate and despise, it is a man of the world.
HENRY ARTHUR JONES, *The Liars.* Act i.

Man of the World (for such wouldst thou be call'd)—
And art thou proud of that inglorious style?
YOUNG, *Night Thoughts.* Night viii, l. 8.

Long ago a man of the world was defined as a man who in every serious crisis is invariably wrong.
UNKNOWN, *Armageddon—and After.* (*Fortnightly Review,* Nov., 1914, p. 736.)

13
For to admire an' for to see,
  For to be'old this world so wide—
It never done no good to me,
  But I can't drop it if I tried!
RUDYARD KIPLING, *"For to Admire."*

14
A man may know the world without leaving his own home.
LAO-TSZE, *The Simple Way.* No. 47.

15
If all the world must see the world
  As the world the world hath seen,
Then it were better for the world
  That the world had never been.
C. G. LELAND, *The World and the World.*

16
Be wisely worldly, be not worldly wise.
FRANCIS QUARLES, *Emblems.* Bk. ii. No. 2.

1
Here's three on 's are sophisticated!
SHAKESPEARE, *King Lear*. Act iii, sc. 4, l. 111.

2
You have too much respect upon the world:
They lose it that do buy it with much care.
SHAKESPEARE, *The Merchant of Venice*. Act i, sc. 1, l. 74.

The world is too much with us; late and soon,
Getting and spending, we lay waste our powers
WORDSWORTH, *Miscellaneous Sonnets*. Pt. i, No. 33.

3
The world, well known, will give our hearts to Heaven,
Or make us demons, long before we die.
YOUNG, *Night Thoughts*. Night viii, l. 379.

To know the world, not love her, is thy point.
She gives but little, nor that little, long.
YOUNG, *Night Thoughts*. Night viii, l. 1276.

VIII—World: Its Creation

4
Had you the world on your chessboard you could not fit all to your mind.
GEORGE HERBERT, *Jacula Prudentum*. No. 697.
See also under UNIVERSE.

5
Let's make the whole world over;
No, not quite all, that's true.
A few things were right to begin with,
Like God—and myself—and you.
LEONARD HINTON, *For a New Year*.

6
While the Creator great His constellations set
And the well-balanc'd world on hinges hung.
MILTON, *On the Morning of Christ's Nativity*, l. 120.

In his hand
He took the golden compasses, prepar'd
In God's eternal store, to circumscribe
This universe, and all created things:
One foot he centred, and the other turn'd
Round through the vast profundity obscure,
And said, Thus far extend, thus far thy bounds,
This be thy just circumference, O World."
MILTON, *Paradise Lost*. Bk. vii, l. 224.

Open, ye heavens, your living doors; let in
The great Creator from his work return'd
Magnificent, his six days' work, a world!
MILTON, *Paradise Lost*. Bk. vii, l. 566.

7
The world was made at one cast.
SIR ISAAC NEWTON. (EMERSON, *Uncollected Lectures: Natural Religion*.)

8
The world, harmoniously confused,
Where order in variety we see,
And where, tho' all things differ, all agree.
POPE, *Windsor Forest*, l. 14.

The world by difference is in order found.
WILLIAM ROWLEY, *The Tournament*. (c. 1630)

9
We are told that when Jehovah created the world he saw that it was good. What would he say now?
BERNARD SHAW, *Maxims for Revolutionists*.

10
The splendid discontent of God
With Chaos, made the world.
ELLA WHEELER WILCOX, *Discontent*.

11
This fine old world of ours is but a child,
Yet in the go-cart. Patience! Give it time
To learn its limbs: there is a hand that guides.
TENNYSON, *The Princess: Conclusion*, l. 77.

WORM

12
The loving worm within its clod
Were diviner than a loveless God.
ROBERT BROWNING, *Christmas-Eve*. Sec. 5.

The spirit of the worm beneath the sod
In love and worship, blends itself with God.
SHELLEY, *Epipsychidion*, l. 124.

13
Worms wind themselves into our sweetest flowers.
COWPER, *The Task*. Bk. vi, l. 831.

A worm is in the bud of youth
And at the root of age.
COWPER, *Stanzas Subjoined to the Yearly Bill of Mortality*, 1787.

14
Fear not then, thou child infirm;
There's no god dare wrong a worm.
EMERSON, *Essays, First Series: Compensation*.

15
"I do not want to be a fly,
I want to be a worm!"
CHARLOTTE P. S. GILMAN, *A Conservative*.

16
Tread on a worm and it will turn.
ROBERT GREENE, *The Worth of Wit*.

Poor worms being trampled on
Turn tail, as bidding battle to the feet
Of their oppressors.
THOMAS RANDOLPH, *The Muses' Looking-glass*. Act iii, sc. 2.

The smallest worm will turn, being trodden on.
SHAKESPEARE, *III Henry VI*. Act ii, sc. 2, l. 17.

Not only the bull strikes at its foe with curved horn; even the ewe, when hurt, resists its assailant. (Non solum taurus ferit uncis cornibus hostem,
Verum etiam instanti læsa repugnat ovis.)
PROPERTIUS, *Elegies*. Bk. ii, eleg. 5, l. 19.

17
Worms' food is fine end of our living.
JOHN LYDGATE, *Daunce of Machabree*, l. 640. (1430)

The heart and life of a mighty and triumphant emperor is but the breakfast of a silly little worm.
MONTAIGNE, *Essays*. Bk. ii, ch. 12.

When I shall dwell with worms.
SHAKESPEARE, *Henry VIII*. Act iv, sc. 2, l. 126.
See also under DEATH.

18
Your worm is your only emperor for diet;

we fat all creatures else to fat us, and we fat ourselves for maggots.

SHAKESPEARE, *Hamlet*. Act iv, sc. 3, l. 22.

1
For every worm beneath the moon
Draws different threads, and late and soon
Spins, toiling out of his own cocoon.

TENNYSON, *The Two Voices*, l. 178.

WORRY

See also Trouble

2
Don't fight with the pillow, but lay down your head
And kick every worriment out of the bed.

EDMUND VANCE COOKE, *Don't Take Your Troubles to Bed*.

3
O fond anxiety of mortal men!
How vain and inconclusive arguments
Are those, which make thee beat thy wings below!

DANTE, *Paradise*. Canto xi, l. 1. (Cary, tr.)

4
The world is wide
In time and tide,
And God is guide,
Then—do not hurry.
That man is blest
Who does his best
And leaves the rest,
Then—do not worry.

CHARLES F. DEEMS, *Epigram*, on his 70th birthday.

5
A hundred load of thought will not pay one of debts.

GEORGE HERBERT, *Jacula Prudentum*. No. 410.

6
Worry, the interest paid by those who borrow trouble.

GEORGE W. LYON. (See New York *Times Book Review*, 23 Oct., 1932, p. 27.) Appeared in *Judge*, 1 March, 1924, p. 6.

Worry is interest paid on trouble before it becomes due.

DEAN WILLIAM RALPH INGE. (*Reader's Digest*, May, 1932, p. 108.)

7
Nothing in the affairs of men is worthy of great anxiety. (Οὔτε τι τῶν ἀνθρωπίνων ἄξιον ὂν μεγάλης σπουδῆς.)

PLATO, *Republic*. Bk. x, sec. 604.

8
Suspense, the only insupportable misfortune of life.

HENRY ST. JOHN, *Letter*, 24 July, 1725.

It is a miserable thing to live in suspense; it is the life of a spider.

SWIFT, *Thoughts on Various Subjects*.

9
Tell me, sweet lord, what is 't that takes from thee
Thy stomach, pleasure, and thy golden sleep?

SHAKESPEARE, *I Henry IV*. Act ii, sc. 3, l. 43.

Some strange commotion
Is in his brain: he bites his lip, and starts;
Stops on a sudden, looks upon the ground,
Then lays his finger on his temple; straight
Springs out into fast gait; then stops again,
Strikes his breast hard, and anon he casts
His eye against the moon.

SHAKESPEARE, *Henry VIII*. Act iii, sc. 2, l. 112.

10
'Gainst minor evils let him pray,
Who fortune's favour curries,—
For one that big misfortunes slay,
Ten die of little worries.

GEORGE ROBERT SIMS, *Occasional Lines*.

WORSHIP

See also Creed, Prayer, Religion

11
He wales a portion with judicious care,
And "Let us worship God!" he says, with solemn air.

BURNS, *The Cotter's Saturday Night*. St. 12.

12
Worship is transcendent wonder.

CARLYLE, *Heroes and Hero-Worship*. Lecture 1.

Man always worships something: always he sees the Infinite shadowed forth in something finite; and indeed can and must so see it in any finite thing, once tempt him well to fix his eyes thereon.

CARLYLE, *Essays: Goethe's Works*.

Yet, if he would, man cannot live all to this world. If not religious, he will be superstitious. If he worship not the true God, he will have his idols.

THEODORE PARKER, *A Lesson for the Day*.

13
And what greater calamity can fall upon a nation than the loss of worship.

EMERSON, *Nature, Addresses, and Lectures: An Address at Cambridge*, 15 July, 1838.

14
They that worship God merely from fear,
Would worship the devil too, if he appear.

THOMAS FULLER, *Gnomologia*. No. 6419.

15
The various modes of worship which prevailed in the Roman world were all considered by the people as equally true; by the philosopher as equally false; and by the magistrate as equally useful.

EDWARD GIBBON, *Decline and Fall of the Roman Empire*. Ch. 2.

16
And learn there may be worship without words!

J. R. LOWELL, *My Cathedral*.

17
For where two or three are gathered together in my name, there am I in the midst of them.

New Testament: Matthew, xviii, 20.

18
Every one's true worship was that which he

found in use in the place where he chanced to be.

MONTAIGNE, *Essays*. Bk. ii, ch. 12. *See also under* ROME.

1

Stoop, boys: this gate
Instructs you how to adore the heavens and bows you
To morning's holy office.

SHAKESPEARE, *Cymbeline*. Act iii, sc. 3, l. 2.

WORTH

See also Deserving, Merit, Price

2

A pilot's part in calms cannot be spy'd,
In dangerous times true worth is only try'd.

WILLIAM ALEXANDER, *Doomes-day: The Fifth Hour*.

3

It is not what he has, nor even what he does, which directly expresses the worth of a man, but what he is.

AMIEL, *Journal*, 15 Dec., 1859.

He is rich or poor according to what he *is*, not according to what he *has*.

HENRY WARD BEECHER, *Proverbs from Plymouth Pulpit*.

3a

They are not worth the healthy bones of a single Pomeranian musketeer. (Die gesunden Knochen eines einzigen pommerschen Musketiers.)

BISMARCK, *Remark*, 5 Dec., 1876, referring to the Balkans, which had become engaged in a struggle with Turkey. (GEORG BÜCHMANN, *Geflügelte Worte*.) The remark is said to derive from a similar one by Frederick the Great: "No work of art is worth the bones of a Pomeranian grenadier."

4

'Tis virtue, wit, and worth, and all
That men divine and sacred call;
For what is worth, in anything,
But so much money as 't will bring?

BUTLER, *Hudibras*. Pt. ii, canto 1, l. 463.

What is the worth of anything
But for the happiness 'twill bring?

R. O. CAMBRIDGE, *Learning*, l. 23.

5

This was the penn'worth of his thought.

BUTLER, *Hudibras*. Pt. ii, canto 3, l. 57.

6

The worth of a thing is known by its want.

THOMAS D'URFEY, *Quixote*. Pt. i, act v, sc. 2.

What is not needed is dear at a farthing. (Quod non opus est. asse carum est.)

CATO, *Reliquæ*, p. 79. (SENECA, *Epistulæ ad Lucilium*. Epis. xciv, sec. 27.)

Far-fetched and little worth.

COWPER, *The Task*. Bk. i, l. 243.

7

A man passes for that he is worth. What he is engraves itself on his face in letters of light.

EMERSON, *Essays, First Series: Spiritual Laws*.

8

Of whom the world was not worthy.

New Testament: Hebrews, xi. 38.

Deserves [not] to carry the buckler unto Sampson.

SIR THOMAS BROWNE, *Religio Medici*. Pt. i, 21.

There is not one among my gentlewomen
Were fit to wear your slipper for a glove.

TENNYSON, *Geraint and Enid*, l. 621.

9

Much is she worth, and even more is made of her.

W. E. HENLEY, *In Hospital: Staff Nurse*.

10

The "value" or "worth" of a man, is, as of all other things, his price; that is to say, so much as would be given for the use of his power.

THOMAS HOBBES, *Leviathan*. Pt. i, ch. 10.

11

'Tis fortune gives us birth,
But Jove alone endues the soul with worth.

HOMER, *Iliad*. Bk. xx, l. 290. (Pope, tr.)

13

Farewell! I did not know thy worth;
But thou art gone, and now 'tis priz'd;
So angels walk'd unknown on earth,
But when they flew were recogniz'd.

THOMAS HOOD, *To an Absentee*.

I never knew the worth of him Until he died.

EDWIN ARLINGTON ROBINSON, *An Old Story*.

14

Hidden worth differs little from buried indolence. (Paulum sepultæ distat inertiæ Celata virtus.)

HORACE, *Odes*. Bk. iv, ode 9, l. 29.

15

Slow rises worth, by poverty depress'd:
But here more slow, where all are slaves to gold,
Where looks are merchandise, and smiles are sold.

SAMUEL JOHNSON, *London*, l. 177.

16

Life is continually weighing us in very sensitive scales, and telling every one of us precisely what his real weight is to the last grain of dust.

J. R. LOWELL, *On a Certain Condescension in Foreigners*.

In life's small things be resolute and great
To keep thy muscle trained: know'st thou when Fate
Thy measure takes, or when she'll say to thee,
"I find thee worthy; do this deed for me"?

J. R. LOWELL, *Sayings*.

17

Ye are worth thy weight of gold.

HENRY MEDWALL, *Nature*, l. 936. (c. 1500)

18

Things are only worth what one makes them worth. (Les choses ne valent que ce qu'on les fait valoir.)

MOLIÈRE, *Les Précieuses Ridicules*. Sc. 9, l. 278.

19

Not because you were worthy, but because I was indulgent. (Non quia tu dignus, sed quia mitis ego.)

OVID, *Heroides*. Epis. vi, l. 148.

1
Worthy things happen to the worthy. (Eveniunt digna dignis.)
PLAUTUS, *Pœnulus*, l. 1270. (Act v, sc. 4.)

2
Worth makes the man, and want of it the fellow,
The rest is all but leather or prunella.
POPE, *Essay on Man*. Epis. iv, l. 203. Quoted by Henry Wadsworth Longfellow when introduced to Nicholas Longworth, and commenting on the similarity of their names.

3
Everything is worth what its purchaser will pay for it.
PUBLILIUS SYRUS, *Sententiæ*. No. 847.

What is aught, but as 'tis valued?
SHAKESPEARE, *Troilus and Cressida*, ii, 2, 52.

4
So much is a man worth as he esteems himself.
RABELAIS, *Works*. Bk. ii, ch. 29.

5
Worth is by worth in every rank admired.
RICHARD SAVAGE, *Epistle to Aaron Hill*.

6
Great things cannot be bought for small sums. (Non potest parvo res magna constare.)
SENECA, *Epistulæ ad Lucilium*. Epis. xix, sec. 4.

7
They are worthy To inlay heaven with stars.
SHAKESPEARE, *Cymbeline*. Act v, sc. 5, l. 351.

8
I am not worth this coil that 's made for me.
SHAKESPEARE, *King John*. Act ii, sc. 1, l. 165.

Goneril: I have been worth the whistle.
Albany: You are not worth the dust which the rude wind blows in your face.
SHAKESPEARE, *King Lear*. Act iv, sc. 2, l. 29.

He has paid dear, very dear, for his whistle.
BENJAMIN FRANKLIN, *The Whistle*.

9
Let there be some more test made of my metal,
Before so noble and so great a figure
Be stamp'd upon it.
SHAKESPEARE, *Measure for Measure*, i, 1, 49.

10
They are but beggars that can count their worth.
SHAKESPEARE, *Romeo and Juliet*, ii, 6, 32.

11
For beauties that from worth arise
Are like the grace of deities,
Still present with us, though unsighted.
SIR JOHN SUCKLING, *When, Dearest, I But Think of Thee*.

12
Forgive what seem'd my sin in me;
What seem'd my worth since I began.
TENNYSON, *In Memoriam: Introduction*. St. 9.

13
All good things are cheap: all bad are very dear.
H. D. THOREAU, *Journal*, 3 March, 1841.

14
All human things
Of dearest value hang on slender strings.
EDMUND WALLER, *Of the Danger His Majesty Escaped*, l. 163.

15
There buds the promise of celestial worth.
YOUNG, *The Last Day*. Bk. iii, l. 317.

WOUNDS

See also Injuries

16
For want of timely care
Millions have died of medicable wounds.
JOHN ARMSTRONG, *Art of Preserving Health*. Bk. iii, l. 519.

18
The wound is for you, but the pain is for me. (La blessure est pour vous, la douleur est pour moi.)
CHARLES IX to Admiral Coligny, fatally wounded in massacre of St. Bartholomew.

19
To tear open a wound. (Refricare cicatricem.)
CICERO, *De Lege Agraria*. No. iii, ch. 2, sec. 4.

20
They that are afraid of wounds must not come near a battle.
JOHN CLARKE, *Parœmiologia*, 310.

One mask of brooses both blue and green.
DICKENS, *Nicholas Nickleby*. Ch. 15.

21
Bellum . . . striketh with a sting,
And leaves a scar although the wound be healed.
GEORGE GASCOIGNE, *Posies: Dulce Bellum*. (1575)

Bearing away the wound that nothing healeth,
The scar that will despite of cure remain.
SHAKESPEARE, *Rape of Lucrece*, l. 732. (1594)

Wounds once healed leave a scar behind them.
JOSEPH HALL, *Contemplations*, iii, 5. (1612)

A wound heals but the scar remains.
JOHN RAY, *English Proverbs*. (1670)

A wound, tho' cured, yet leaves behind a scar.
JOHN OLDHAM, *Satires upon the Jesuits*. No. 3. (1680)

What deep wounds ever closed without a scar?
BYRON, *Childe Harold*. Canto iii, st. 84. (1816)

22
Fools, through false shame, conceal their open wounds. (Stultorum incurata pudor malus ulcera celat.)
HORACE, *Epistles*. Bk. i, epis. 16, l. 24.

23
Wounds cannot be cured unless probed and dressed. (Vulnera, nisi sint tacta tractataque, sanari non possunt.)
LIVY, *History*. Bk. xxviii, sec. 27.

Wounds cannot be cured without searching.
FRANCIS BACON, *Essays: Of Expence*.

Many a wound must be probed till it bleeds before you are cured of your sickness.
HENRIK IBSEN, *Brand*. Act iv.

24
Of wounds and sore defeat
I made my battle stay.
WILLIAM VAUGHN MOODY, *The Fire-Bringer*.

1
Perhaps in long time a scar will form; a raw wound quivers at a touch. (Tempora ducetur longo fortasse cicatrix: Horrent admotas vulnera cruda manus.)
OVID, *Epistulæ ex Ponto*. Bk. i, epis. 3, l. 15.

2
The wounded gladiator forswears all fighting, but soon forgetting his former wound resumes his arms. (Saucius ejurat pugnam gladiator, et idem Immemor antiqui vulneris arma capit.)
OVID, *Epistulæ ex Ponto*. Bk. i, epis. 5, l. 37.

3
Too late I grasp my shield when wounded. (Sero clipeum post vulnera sumo.)
OVID, *Tristia*. Bk. i, eleg. 3, l. 35.

4
His breast was covered with honorable wounds. (Τὸ σῶμα μεστὸν ἐναντίων εἶχε.)
PLUTARCH, *Lives: Marcus Cato*. Of Cato.

All the bodies bore their wounds in front. (Omnes tamen advorsis volneribus conciderant.)
SALLUST, *Bellum Catilinæ*. Sec. 61.

Siwald: Had he his hurts before?
Ross: Ay, on the front.
Siwald: Why then, God's soldier be he!
SHAKESPEARE, *Macbeth*. Act v, sc. 8, l. 46.

His breast with wounds unnumber'd riven,
His back to earth, his face to heaven.
BYRON, *The Giaour*, l. 667.

5
A green wound is soon healed.
JOHN RAY, *English Proverbs*.

6
His cicatrice, an emblem of war, here on his sinister cheek.
SHAKESPEARE, *All's Well that Ends Well*. Act ii, sc. 1, l. 43.

A scar nobly got, or a noble scar, is a good livery of honour.
SHAKESPEARE, *All's Well that Ends Well*. Act iv, sc. 5, l. 105.

Gash'd with honourable scars,
Low in Glory's lap they lie;
Though they fell, they fell like stars,
Streaming splendour through the sky.
MONTGOMERY, *Battle of Alexandria*. St. 17.

7
With a wound I must be cured.
SHAKESPEARE, *Antony and Cleopatra*. Act iv, sc. 14, l. 78.

The wound that bred this meeting here
Cannot be cured by words.
SHAKESPEARE, *III Henry VI*. Act ii, sc. 2, l. 121.

8
Open thy gate of mercy, gracious God!
My soul flies through these wounds to seek out Thee.
SHAKESPEARE, *III Henry VI*. Act i, sc. 4, l. 177.

9
Show you sweet Cæsar's wounds, poor, poor dumb mouths,
And bid them speak for me.
SHAKESPEARE, *Julius Cæsar*. Act iii, sc. 2, l. 229.

Put a tongue
In every wound of Cæsar that should move
The stones of Rome to rise and mutiny.
SHAKESPEARE, *Julius Cæsar*. Act iii, sc. 2, l. 232.

10
His silver skin laced with his golden blood;
And his gash'd stabs look'd like a breach in nature
For ruin's wasteful entrance.
SHAKESPEARE, *Macbeth*. Act ii, sc. 3, l. 118.

Safe in a ditch he bides,
With twenty trenched gashes on his head;
The least a death to nature.
SHAKESPEARE, *Macbeth*. Act iii, sc. 4, l. 26.

11
What wound did ever heal but by degrees?
SHAKESPEARE, *Othello*. Act ii, sc. 3, l. 377.

12
Iago: What, are you hurt, lieutenant?
Cassio: Ay, past all surgery.
SHAKESPEARE, *Othello*. Act ii, sc. 3, l. 259.

Romeo: Courage, man; the hurt cannot be much.
Mercutio: No, 'tis not so deep as a well, nor so wide as a church-door; but 'tis enough, 'twill serve: ask for me tomorrow, and you shall find me a grave man. I am peppered, I warrant, for this world. A plague o' both your houses!
SHAKESPEARE, *Romeo and Juliet*, iii, 1, 100.

13
He in peace is wounded, not in war.
SHAKESPEARE, *The Rape of Lucrece*, l. 831.

The private wound is deepest.
SHAKESPEARE, *The Two Gentlemen of Verona*. Act v, sc. 4, l. 71.

14
He jests at scars that never felt a wound.
SHAKESPEARE, *Romeo and Juliet*, ii, 2, 1.

15
None can speak of a wound with skill, if he hath not a wound felt.
SIR PHILIP SIDNEY, *Arcadia*. Bk. i.

16
She cherishes the wound in her veins, and is consumed by an unseen fire. (Volnus alit venis et cæco carpitur igni.)
VERGIL, *Æneid*. Bk. iv, l. 2.

Deep in her breast still lives the secret wound. (Tacitum vivit sub pectore volnus.)
VERGIL, *Æneid*. Bk. iv, l. 67.

The wound that bleedeth inwardly is the most dangerous.
JOHN LYLY, *Euphues*, p. 63. (1579)

H' had got a hurt
O' th' inside, of a deadlier sort.
BUTLER, *Hudibras*. Pt. i, canto 3, l. 309.

17
I was wounded in the house of my friends.
Old Testament: Zechariah, xiii, 6.

WREN

18
Wrens make prey where eagles dare not perch.
SHAKESPEARE, *Richard III*. Act i, sc. 3, l. 71.

See also under EAGLE *and* 2242:10

1
And then the wren gan scippen and to
daunce.

CHAUCER [?], *The Court of Love*, l. 1372.

2
The poor wren,
The most diminutive of birds, will fight,
Her young ones in her nest, against the owl.

SHAKESPEARE, *Macbeth*. Act iv, sc. 2, l. 9.

3
Amongst the dwellings framed by birds
In field or forest with nice care,
Is none that with the little wren's
In snugness may compare.

WORDSWORTH, *A Wren's Nest*.

WRITING

See also Books, Newspapers, Plagiarism, Poets

I—Writing: Definitions

4
Writing is not literature unless it gives to the reader a pleasure which arises not only from the things said, but from the way in which they are said.

STOPFORD A. BROOKE, *Primer of English Literature*.

That writer does the most, who gives his reader the *most* knowledge, and takes from him the *least* time.

C. C. COLTON, *Lacon: Preface*.

5
Certainly the Age of Writing is the most miraculous of all things man has devised.

CARLYLE, *On Heroes and Hero-Worship: The Hero as Man of Letters*.

With the art of Writing, of which Printing is a simple, an inevitable and comparatively insignificant corollary, the true reign of miracles for mankind commenced.

CARLYLE, *On Heroes and Hero-Worship: The Hero as Man of Letters*.

6
Miscellanists are the most popular writers among every people; for it is they who form a communication between the learned and the unlearned, and, as it were, throw a bridge between those two great divisions of the public.

ISAAC D'ISRAELI, *Literary Character of Men of Genius: Miscellanists*.

There are two things which I am confident I can do very well: one is an introduction to any literary work, stating what it is to contain, and how it should be executed in the most perfect manner.

SAMUEL JOHNSON. (BOSWELL, *Life*, 1775.)

7
All writing comes by the grace of God.

EMERSON, *Essays, Second Series: Experience*.

No man can write anything who does not think that what he writes is, for the time, the history of the world.

EMERSON, *Essays, Second Series: Nature*.

The nobler the truth or sentiment, the less imports the question of authorship.

EMERSON, *Letters and Social Aims: Quotation and Originality*.

8
All great men have written proudly, nor cared to explain. They knew that the intelligent reader would come at last, and would thank them.

EMERSON, *Natural History of Intellect: Thoughts on Modern Literature*.

9
Composition is, for the most part, an effort of slow diligence and steady perseverance, to which the mind is dragged by necessity or resolution.

SAMUEL JOHNSON, *The Adventurer*. No. 138.

To write and to live are very different. Many who praise virtue do no more than praise it.

JOHNSON, *Works*. Vol. iii, p. 83. (Hawkins, ed.)

10
If the works of the great poets teach anything, it is to hold mere invention somewhat cheap. It is not the finding of a thing, but the making something out of it after it is found, that is of consequence.

J. R. LOWELL, *My Study Windows: Chaucer*.

11
The art of the pen is to rouse the inward vision. . . . That is why the poets, who spring imagination with a word or a phrase, paint lasting pictures.

GEORGE MEREDITH, *Diana of the Crossways*. Ch. 15.

II—Writing: Apothegms

12
With pen and with pencil we're learning to
say
Nothing, more cleverly, every day.

WILLIAM ALLINGHAM, *Blackberries*.

13
The reason why so few good books are written, is that so few people who can write know anything.

BAGEHOT, *Literary Studies: Shakespeare*.

14
The very dust of whose writings is gold.

RICHARD BENTLEY, *On Phalaris*. Referring to Bishop Pearson.

15
And tell prose writers, stories are so stale,
That penny ballads have a better sale.

NICHOLAS BRETON, *Pasquil*. (1600)

16
In the same hour came forth fingers of a man's hand, and wrote over against the candlestick upon the plaister of the wall of the king's palace. . . . And this is the writing that was written, MENE, MENE, TEKEL, UPHARSIN.

Old Testament: Daniel, v, 5, 25. Hence, "Writing on the wall."

1
When I want to read a book I write one.
BENJAMIN DISRAELI, *Remark*. Attributed to him in *Blackwood's* review of *Lothair*.

2
The lover of letters loves power too.
EMERSON, *Society and Solitude: Clubs*

3
Write with the learned, pronounce with the vulgar.
FRANKLIN, *Poor Richard*, 1738. See 1993:12.

Write disagreeably, if you like; as the man said of the rack, it will help me to pass an hour or two, at any rate.
MADAME DU DEFFAND, *Letters*.

4
Written with a pen of iron, and with the point of a diamond.
Old Testament: Jeremiah, xvii, 1.

5
Oh that . . mine adversary had written a book.
Old Testament: Job, xxxi, 35.

6
What I have written I have written.
New Testament: John, xix, 22. (Quod scripsi, scripsi.—*Vulgate*.) Pilate's reply to the priest who protested against the title, "Jesus of Nazareth the King of the Jews," which he had written and placed upon the cross.

7
A man may write at any time if he set himself doggedly to it.
SAMUEL JOHNSON. (BOSWELL, *Life*, 1773.)

8
No man but a blockhead ever wrote except for money.
SAMUEL JOHNSON. (BOSWELL, *Life*, 1776.)

As soon as any art is pursued with a view to money, then farewell, in ninety-nine cases out of a hundred, all hope of genuine good work
SAMUEL BUTLER THE YOUNGER, *Note-Books*, p. 171.

A man starts upon a sudden, takes Pen, Ink, and Paper, and without ever having had a thought of it before, resolves within himself he will write a Book; he has no Talent at Writing, but he wants fifty Guineas.
LA BRUYÈRE, *Les Caractères*. Ch. 15.

The impulse to create beauty is rather rare in literary men. . . . Far ahead of it comes the yearning to make money. And after the yearning to make money comes the yearning to make a noise.
H. L. MENCKEN, *Prejudices*. Ser v, p. 189.

9
No great work, or worthy of praise or memory, but came out of poor cradles.
BEN JONSON, *Explorata: De Bonis et Malis*.

10
Our literary masonry, nowadays, is well done, but our architecture is poor. (En littérature, aujourd'hui, on fait bien la maçonnerie, mais on fait mal l'architecture.)
JOUBERT, *Pensées*. No. 256.

11
Damn the age; I will write for antiquity.
CHARLES LAMB. (JERROLD, *Bon Mots by Charles Lamb*.)

12
He was the author, our hand finished it. (Invenit ille, nostra perfecit manus.)
PHÆDRUS, *Fables*. Bk. vi, l. 20.

Washington's Farewell Address was written by Alexander Hamilton. Andrew Jackson's famous proclamation on nullification, when South Carolina threatened to secede, was written by Edward Livingston. As a rule, however, Presidents have employed "ghost writers" only on the endless list of routine speeches their hard lot forced them to make. No President ever used this device to such a great extent as Coolidge.
CHARLES WILLIS THOMPSON, *Presidents I've Known*, p. 380.

13
I think this piece will help to boil thy pot.
JOHN WOLCOT, *The Bard Complimenteth Mr. West on His "Lord Nelson."* (c. 1790) The first recorded use of "pot-boiler" in this particular sense, though Sir Roger L'Estrange, in 1692, remarked in his *Fables of Æsop*, p. 305, that "Money makes the pot boil."

To employ them, as a literary man is always tempted, to keep the domestic pot a boiling.
J. R. LOWELL, *My Study Windows*, p. 139.

14
A dedication is a wooden leg.
YOUNG, *Love of Fame*. Sat. iv, l. 192.

Presumption or meanness are both too often the only articles to be found in a preface.
GEORGE CRABBE, *Inebriety: Preface*.

III—Writing: The Matter

15
Write to the mind and heart, and let the ear
Glean after what it can.
P. J. BAILEY, *Festus: Home*.

What comes from the heart goes to the heart.
S. T. COLERIDGE, *Table-Talk*. Of composition.

He that writes to himself writes to an eternal public.
EMERSON, *Essays, First Series: Spiritual Laws*.

16
'Tis mean for empty praise of wit to write,
As fopplings grin to show their teeth are white.
JOHN BROWN, *Essay on Satire*. St. 2.

17
Not pickt from the leaves of any Author, but bred amongst the weeds and tares of mine own brain.
SIR THOMAS BROWNE, *Religio Medici*. Pt. i, 36.

Some hold translations not unlike to be
The wrong side of a Turkey tapestry.
JAMES HOWELL, *Familiar Letters*. Bk. i, sec. 6, let. 27.

The greatest part of a writer's time is spent in reading, in order to write; a man will turn over half a library to make one book.
SAMUEL JOHNSON. (BOSWELL, *Life*, 1775.)

What boots all your grist? it can never be ground
Till a breeze makes the arms of the windmill go round.

J. R. LOWELL, *A Fable for Critics*, l. 83.

1
Let these describe the undescribable.

BYRON, *Childe Harold*. Canto iv, st. 53.

1a
You praise the firm restraint with which they write—
I'm with you there, of course:
They use the snaffle and the curb all right,
But where's the bloody horse?

ROY CAMPBELL, *Adamastor: On Some South African Novelists*.

2
Choose a subject, ye who write, suited to your strength. (Sumite materiam vestris, qui scribitis, æquam Viribus.)

HORACE, *Ars Poetica*, l. 38.

Dear authors! suit your topics to your strength,
And ponder well your subject and its length;
Nor lift your load, before you're quite aware
What weight your shoulders will, or will not, bear.

BYRON, *Hints from Horace*, l. 59.

3
Notes are often necessary, but they are necessary evils.

SAMUEL JOHNSON, *Shakespeare: Preface*.

4
O thou sculptor, painter, poet!
Take this lesson to thy heart:
That is best which lieth nearest;
Shape from that thy work of art.

LONGFELLOW, *Gaspar Becerra*. St. 7.

It may be glorious to write
Thoughts that will glad the two or three
High souls, like those far stars that come in sight
Once in a century;—
But better far it is to speak
One simple word, which now and then
Shall waken their free natures in the weak
And friendless sons of men.

J. R. LOWELL, *An Incident in a Railroad Car*. St. 19.

5
Thou art the cause, O reader, that I write on lighter topics, when I would prefer serious ones. (Seria cum possim, quod delectantia malim Scribere, tu causa es lector.)

MARTIAL, *Epigrams*. Bk. v, epig. 16, l. 1.

Authors hear at length one general cry,
Tickle and entertain us, or we die!

COWPER, *Retirement*, l. 707.

6
To write upon *all* is an author's sole chance
For attaining, at last, the least knowledge of *any*.

THOMAS MOORE, *Literary Advertisement*, l. 35.

7
There is no such thing as a dirty theme. There are only dirty writers.

G. J. NATHAN, *Testament of a Critic*, p. 179.

9
I'll call for pen and ink, and write my mind.

SHAKESPEARE, *I Henry VI*. Act v, sc. 3, l. 66.

10
Thus, great with child to speak, and helpless in my throes,
Biting my truant pen, beating myself for spite:
Fool! said my Muse to me, look in thy heart, and write.

SIR PHILIP SIDNEY, *Astrophel and Stella*. Sonnet i.

Look, then, into thine heart and write.

LONGFELLOW, *Voices of the Night: Prelude*. St. 19.

11
Authors—essayist, atheist, novelist, realist, rhymester, play your part,
Paint the mortal shame of nature with the living hues of art.

TENNYSON, *Locksley Hall Sixty Years After*, l. 139.

IV—Writing: The Manner

See also Style; Words: Their Use

12
Thus I set pen to paper with delight,
And quickly had my thoughts in black and white.
For having now my method by the end,
Still as I pull'd it came; and so I penn'd
It down, until at last it came to be
For length and breadth the bigness which you see.

JOHN BUNYAN, *The Pilgrim's Progress: The Author's Apology for His Book*.

Honest John [Bunyan] was the first that I know of who mixed narration and dialogue; a method of writing very engaging to the reader.

BENJAMIN FRANKLIN, *Autobiography*. Ch. 1.

13
How doth it make judicious readers smile,
When authors are detected by their style!
Though every one, who knows this author, knows
He shifts his style much oftener than his clothes.

CHARLES CHURCHILL, *The Apology*, l. 140.

14
So that the jest is clearly to be seen,
Not in the words—but in the gap between:
Manner is all in all, whate'er is writ,
The substitute for genius, sense, and wit.

COWPER, *Table Talk*, l. 540.

Though such continual zigzags in a book,
Such drunken reelings, have an awkward look.

COWPER, *Conversation*, l. 861. Condemning digressions.

By my rambling digressions I perceive myself to be grown old. I used to write more methodically. But one does not dress for private company as for a public ball.

BENJAMIN FRANKLIN, *Autobiography*. Ch. 1.

1
The ablest writer is a gardener first, and then a cook. His tasks are, carefully to select and cultivate his strongest and most nutritive thoughts, and, when they are ripe, to dress them wholesomely, and so that they may have a relish.

J. C. AND A. W. HARE, *Guesses at Truth.*

2
And since, I never dare to write
As funny as I can.

O. W. HOLMES, *The Height of the Ridiculous.*

I can't write what I feel: I'm coarse, when terse.

DON MARQUIS, *Savage Portraits.*

3
Do not seek to render word for word, like a slavish translator. (Nec verbo verbum curabis reddere fidus Interpres.)

HORACE, *Ars Poetica,* l. 133.

4
Nothing is ended with honour which does not conclude better than it began.

SAMUEL JOHNSON, *The Rambler.* No. 207.

5
Nothing is fashionable till it be deformed, and this is to write like a gentleman.

BEN JONSON, *Explorata: De Vere Argutis.*

6
In creating, the only hard thing's to begin;
A grass-blade 's no easier to make than an
oak;
If you've once found the way, you've achieved
the grand stroke.

J. R. LOWELL, *A Fable for Critics,* l 534.

The last thing one settles in writing a book is what one should put in first.

PASCAL, *Pensées.* Sec. i, No. 19.

7
Make 'em laugh; make 'em cry; make 'em wait.

CHARLES READE, *Recipe for a Successful Novel.*

8
It is ignoble to say one thing and mean another; how much more so to write one thing and mean another! (Turpe est aliud loqui, aliud sentire; quanto turpius aliud scribere, aliud sentire!)

SENECA, *Epistulæ ad Lucilium.* Epis. xxiv, 19.

V—Writing: Good and Bad

9
This writing seemeth to me . . not much better than that noise or sound which musicians make while they are in tuning their instruments; which is nothing pleasant to hear, but yet is a cause why the music is sweeter afterwards.

BACON, *Advancement of Learning.* Bk. ii.

10
It is scarcely possible for authors to be admired and at the same time to excel.

FRANCIS BACON, *De Augmentis Scientiarum: Præfatio.*

He who pleases many must have some species of merit.

JOHNSON, *Works,* ii, 279. (Hawkins, ed.)

So must the writer, whose productions should
Take with the vulgar, be of vulgar mould.

EDMUND WALLER, *To Mr. Killigrew.*

11
The weighty bullion of one sterling line,
Drawn to French wire, would thro' whole
pages shine.

WENTWORTH DILLON, *An Essay on Translated Verse.*

12
Learn to write well, or not to write at all.

JOHN DRYDEN AND JOHN SHEFFIELD, *An Essay Upon Satire,* l. 281.

13
People do not deserve to have good writing, they are so pleased with bad.

EMERSON, *Journals.* Vol. vi, p. 132.

It is very hard to go beyond your public. If they are satisfied with your poor performance, you will not easily make it better.

EMERSON, *Journals.* Vol. ix, p. 304.

14
Good writing is a kind of skating which carries off the performer where he would not go.

EMERSON, *Journals.* Vol. vii, p. 334.

15
If you wish to be a good writer, write. ("Αν θέλῃς γραφικὸς εἶναι, γράφε.)

EPICTETUS, *Discourses.* Bk. ii, ch. 18, sec. 1.

Scribendo disces scribere. [By writing you learn to write.] It is only by writing ill that you can attain to write well.

SAMUEL JOHNSON. (BOSWELL, *Life,* 16 Apr., 1763.)

Write something great. (Scribe aliquid magnum.)

MARTIAL, *Epigrams.* Bk. i, ep. 107, l. 2.

16
Let us beware of writing too well; it is the worst possible manner of writing.

ANATOLE FRANCE. (COURNOS, *Modern Plutarch,* p. 29.)

17
Knowledge is the foundation and source of good writing. (Scribendi recte sapere est et principium et fons.)

HORACE, *Ars Poetica,* l. 309.

Sound judgment is the ground of writing well:
And when philosophy directs your choice,
To proper subjects rightly understood,
Words from your pen will naturally flow.

HORACE, *Ars Poetica,* l. 342. (Dillon, tr.)

18
The Dean could write finely upon a broomstick.

SAMUEL JOHNSON, *Life of Swift.* When someone remarked that Vanessa must be an extraordinary woman to inspire Dean Swift to write so finely upon her.

19
It is the glory and merit of some men to write well, and of others not to write at all.

LA BRUYÈRE, *Les Caractères.* Ch. 1.

1
Whatever hath been written shall remain,
Nor be erased nor written o'er again,
The unwritten only still belongs to thee:
Take heed, and ponder well what that shall be.
LONGFELLOW, *Morituri Salutamus*, l. 168. *See also* WORDS: THEIR FINALITY.

2
In this manner of writing [prose], knowing myself inferior to myself . . . I have the use, as I may account, but of my left hand.
MILTON, *Reason of Church Government*: Bk. ii, *Introduction*.

Things unattempted yet in prose or rhyme.
MILTON, *Paradise Lost*. Bk. i, l. 16.

3
The p'int of good writing is knowing when to stop.
L. M. MONTGOMERY, *Anne's House of Dreams*. Ch. 24.

4
Good sense must be the certain standard still
To all that will pretend to writing well.
JOHN OLDHAM, *An Ode on St. Cecilia's Day*.

Of all those arts in which the wise excel,
Nature's chief masterpiece is writing well.
JOHN SHEFFIELD, DUKE OF BUCKINGHAM, *Essay on Poetry*, l. 1.

Such was the Muse whose rules and practice tell
"Nature's chief masterpiece is writing well."
POPE, *Essay on Criticism*. Pt. iii, l. 164. Referring to Buckingham.

5
While writing the very toil gives pleasure, and the growing work glows with the writer's heart. (Scribentem juvat ipse labor minuitque laborem, Cumque suo crescens pectore fervet opus.)
OVID, *Epistulæ ex Ponto*. Bk. iii, epis. 9, l. 21.

A fever in these pages burns
Beneath the calm they feign;
A wounded human spirit turns
Here, on its bed of pain.
MATTHEW ARNOLD, *Stanzas in Memory of the Author of Obermann*. St. 6.

The mind conceives with pain, but brings forth with delight. (L'esprit conçoit avec douleur; mais il enfante avec délices.)
JOUBERT, *Pensées*. No. 343.

6
Whoever thinks a faultless piece to see,
Thinks what ne'er was, nor is, nor e'er shall be.
In every work regard the writer's end,
Since none can compass more than they intend;
And if the means be just, the conduct true,
Applause, in spite of trivial faults, is due.
POPE, *Essay on Criticism*. Pt. ii, l. 53.

The faults of great authors are generally excellencies carried to excess.
S. T. COLERIDGE, *Miscellanies*, p. 149.

A man may be a very good author with some faults, but not with many faults.
VOLTAIRE, *Letters on the English*. No. 24.

7
Ah! friend! to dazzle let the vain design;
To raise the thought and touch the heart be thine!
POPE, *Moral Essays*. Epis. ii, l. 249.

Those write because all write, and so have still
Excuse for writing, and for writing ill.
POPE, *Satires of Dr. Donne, Versified*, ii, 27.

8
'Tis not how well an author says,
But 'tis how much, that gathers praise.
MATTHEW PRIOR, *Epistle to Fleetwood Shepherd*. No. i, l. 100.

9
Let him be kept from paper, pen, and ink;
So may he cease to write, and learn to think.
MATTHEW PRIOR, *To a Person Who Wrote Ill*.

You, for example, clever to a fault,
The rough and ready man, who write apace,
Read somewhat seldomer, think perhaps even less.
ROBERT BROWNING, *Bishop Blougram's Apology*.

Two sorts of writers possess genius: those who think, and those who cause others to think.
ROUX, *Meditations of a Parish Priest: Literature: Poets*. No. 16.

So in the way of writing without thinking,
Thou hast a strange alacrity in sinking.
CHARLES SACKVILLE, EARL OF DORSET, *To Mr. Edward Howard*.

You may know by my size that I have a kind of alacrity in sinking.
SHAKESPEARE, *Merry Wives of Windsor*, iii, 5, 12.

10
This dull product of a scoffer's pen.
WORDSWORTH, *The Excursion*. Bk. ii, l. 484.

VI—Writing: Easy Writing

11
Whate'er is well-conceived is clearly said,
And the words to say it flow with ease.
(Ce que l'on conçoit bien s'énonce clairement,
Et les mots pour le dire arrivent aisément.)
BOILEAU, *L'Art Poétique*. Pt. i, l. 153.

12
True ease in writing comes from art, not chance,
As those move easiest who have learn'd to dance.
'T is not enough no harshness gives offence;
The sound must seem an echo to the sense.
Soft is the strain when zephyr gently blows,
And the smooth stream in smoother numbers flows;
But when loud surges lash the sounding shore,
The hoarse rough verse should like the torrent roar.
When Ajax strives some rock's vast weight to throw,
The line, too, labours, and the words move slow:
Not so when swift Camilla scours the plain,
Flies o'er th' unbending corn, and skims along the main.
POPE, *Essay on Criticism*. Pt. ii, l. 162.

The Mob of Gentlemen who wrote with Ease.
POPE, *Imitations of Horace: Epistles*, ii, 1, 108

1
I argue thus: the world agrees,
That he writes well, who writes with ease:
Then he, by sequel logical,
Writes best, who never thinks at all.

MATTHEW PRIOR, *Epistle to Fleetwood Shepherd*. No. i, l. 38.

Oh that I had the art of easy writing
Which should be easy reading!

BYRON, *Beppo*. St. 51.

What is written without effort is in general read without pleasure.

SAMUEL JOHNSON, *Miscellanies*. Vol. ii, p. 309.

What is easy is seldom excellent.

SAMUEL JOHNSON, *Works*. Vol. iv, p. 134.

Ready writing makes not good writing; but good writing brings on ready writing.

BEN JONSON, *Explorata: De Stylo.*

2
You write with ease to show your breeding,
But easy writing's curst hard reading.

R. B. SHERIDAN, *Clio's Protest*. (MOORE, *Life of Sheridan*. Vol. i, p. 55.)

VII—Writing: Careful Writing

3
Hasten slowly; without losing heart,
Twenty times upon the anvil place your work.
(Hâtez-vous lentement; et, sans perdre courage,
Vingt fois sur le métier remettez votre ouvrage.)

BOILEAU, *L'Art Poétique*. Pt. i, l. 171.

4
I had not time to lick it into form, as a bear doth her young ones.

ROBERT BURTON, *Anatomy of Melancholy: Democritus to the Reader.*

Arts and sciences are not cast in a mould, but are found and perfected by degrees, by often handling and polishing, as bears leisurely lick their cubs into shape.

MONTAIGNE, *Essays*. Bk. ii, ch. 12.

He fashioned his poem after the manner of a she-bear, and gradually licked it into shape. (Carmen se more ursæ parere et lambendo demum effingere.)

SUETONIUS, *Lives: Vergil*. Sec. 23.

See also under BEAR.

5
Little do such men know the toil, the pains,
The daily, nightly racking of the brains,
To range the thoughts, the matter to digest,
To cull fit phrases, and reject the rest.

CHARLES CHURCHILL, *Gotham*. Bk. ii, l. 11.

None but an author knows an author's cares,
Or fancy's fondness for the child she bears.

COWPER, *The Progress of Error*, l. 516.

6
The men, who labour and digest things most,
Will be much apter to despond than boast;
For if your author be profoundly good,
'Twill cost you dear before he's understood.

WENTWORTH DILLON, *Essay on Translated Verse*, l. 163.

7
Writing is more and more a terror to old scribes.

EMERSON, *Journals*, 1864.

The more a man writes, the more he can write.

WILLIAM HAZLITT, *Lectures on Dramatic Literature*, p. 77.

8
Often must you turn your stylus to erase, if you hope to write something worth a second reading. (Sæpe stilum vertas, iterum quæ digna legi sint Scripturus.)

HORACE, *Satires*. Bk. i, sat. 10, l. 72.

Wordy, and too lazy to take the trouble to write well. (Garrulus atque piger scribendi ferre laborem, Scribendi recte.)

HORACE, *Satires*. Bk. i, sat. 4, l. 12.

9
That dry drudgery at the desk's dead wood.

CHARLES LAMB, *Sonnet: Work.*

A votary of the desk—a notched and cropt scrivener—one that sucks his substance, as certain sick people are said to do, through a quill.

LAMB, *Essays of Elia: Oxford in the Vacation.*

10
Much have I written, but what I thought defective I have myself given to the flames, for their revision. (Multa quidem scripsi: sed, quæ vitiosa putavi, Emendaturis ignibus ipse dedi.)

OVID, *Tristia*. Bk. iv, eleg. 10, l. 61.

11
Too much polishing weakens rather than improves a work. (Nimia cura deterit magis quam emendat.)

PLINY THE YOUNGER, *Epistles*. Bk. ix, epis. 35.

12
Let our literary compositions be laid aside for some time, that we may after a reasonable period return to their perusal, and find them, as it were, altogether new to us.

QUINTILIAN, *De Institutione Oratoria*. Bk. x, ch. 4, sec. 2.

Perhaps the greatest lesson which the lives of literary men teach us is told in a single word: Wait!

LONGELLOW, *Hyperion*. Bk. i, ch. 8.

13
Write till your ink be dry, and with your tears
Moist it again, and frame some feeling line
That may discover such integrity.

SHAKESPEARE, *The Two Gentlemen of Verona*. Act iii, sc. 2, l. 74.

14
He wrote drop by drop.

SYDNEY SMITH. Of Charles James Fox. (LADY HOLLAND, *Memoir*. Vol. i, p. 231.)

He has produced a couplet. When our friend is delivered of a couplet, with infinite labor and pain, he takes to his bed, has straw laid down, the knocker tied up, and expects his friends to call and make inquiries.

SYDNEY SMITH. (LADY HOLLAND, *Memoir*. Vol. i, p. 232.)

VIII—Writing: The Itch foı Writing

1
Of writing many books there is no end.
E. B. BROWNING, *Aurora Leigh*. Bk. i, l. 1.

2
And force them, though it was in spite
Of Nature and their stars, to write.
BUTLER, *Hudibras*. Pt. i, canto 1, l. 647.

3
There are some who write and fling books broadcast on the world as if they were fritters.
CERVANTES, *Don Quixote*. Pt. ii, ch. 3.

4
Who often reads will sometimes wish to write.
GEORGE CRABBE, *Tales: Edward Shore.*

But years hath done this wrong,
To make me write too much, and live too long.
SAMUEL DANIEL, *Philotas*, l. 106.

5
This comes of drinking asses' milk and writing.
DRYDEN, *Absalom and Achitophel*. Pt. ii, l. 395.

6
Th' unhappy man who once has trail'd a pen,
Lives not to please himself, but other men;
Is always drudging, wastes his life and blood,
Yet only eats and drinks what you think good.
DRYDEN, *Prologue to Lee's Cæsar Borgia*, l. 1.

For thee we dim the eyes, and stuff the head
With all such reading as was never read;
For thee explain a thing till all men doubt it,
And write about it, Goddess, and about it:
So spins the silk-worm small its slender store,
And labours till it clouds itself all o'er.
POPE, *The Dunciad*. Bk. iv, l. 249.

7
The fickle populace has changed its taste and burns with a craze for scribbling. (Mutavit mentem populus levis, et calet uno Scribendi studio.)
HORACE, *Epistles*. Bk. ii, epis. 1, l. 108.

8
The incurable itch of writing possesses many. (Tenet insanabile multos scribendi cacoëthes.)
JUVENAL, *Satires*. Sat. vii, l. 52.

The desire for writing grows with writing. (Crescit scribendo scribendi studium.)
ERASMUS, *Adagia*.

When once the itch of litherature comes over a man, nothing can cure it but the scratching of a pen.
SAMUEL LOVER, *Handy Andy*. Ch. 36.

If all the trees in all the woods were men,
And each and every blade of grass a pen;
If every leaf on every shrub and tree
Turned to a sheet of foolscap; every sea
Were changed to ink, and all the earth's living tribes
Had nothing else to do but act as scribes,
And for ten thousand ages, day and night,
The human race should write, and write, and write,
Till all the pens and paper were used up,
And the huge inkstand was an empty cup,
Still would the scribblers clustered round its brink
Call for more pens, more paper, and more ink.
O. W. HOLMES, *Cacoëthes Scribendi.*

9
It is foolish weakness, when you jostle poets at every corner, to spare paper already doomed to perish. (Stulta est clementia, cum tot ubique Vatibus occurras, perituræ parcere chartæ.)
JUVENAL, *Satires*. Sat. i, l. 17.

10
There is no measure or limit to this fever for writing; every one must be an author; some out of vanity to acquire celebrity and raise up a name, others for the sake of lucre and gain.
MARTIN LUTHER, *Table-Talk*. No. 911.

Who shames a scribbler? break one cobweb thro'.
He spins the slight, self-pleasing thread anew:
Destroy his fib, or sophistry,—in vain!
The creature 's at his dirty work again,
Throned in the centre of his thin designs,
Proud of a vast extent of flimsy lines.
POPE, *Epistle to Dr. Arbuthnot*, l. 89.

11
Why did I write? what sin to me unknown
Dipt me in ink, my parents', or my own?
As yet a child, nor yet a fool to fame,
I lisp'd in numbers, for the numbers came.
POPE, *Epistle to Dr. Arbuthnot*, l. 125.

Whether the darken'd room to muse invite,
Or whiten'd wall provoke the skewer to write;
In durance, exile, Bedlam, or the Mint,—
Like Lee or Budgell I will rhyme and print.
POPE, *Imitations of Horace: Satires*. Bk. ii, sat. 1, l. 97.

12
Some write, confin'd by physic; some, by debt;
Some, for 'tis Sunday; some, because 'tis wet; . . .
Another writes because his father writ,
And proves himself a bastard by his wit.
YOUNG, *Epistles to Mr. Pope*. Epis. i, l. 75.

For who can write so fast as men run mad.
YOUNG, *Love of Fame*. Sat. i, l. 286.

IX—Writing and Fame

13
I account the use that a man should seek of the publishing of his own writings before his death, to be but an untimely anticipation of that which is proper to follow a man, and not to go along with him.
FRANCIS BACON, *An Advertisement Touching a Holy War: Epistle Dedicatory.*

14
He who writes prose builds his temple to Fame in rubble; he who writes verse builds it in granite.
BULWER-LYTTON, *Caxtoniana: The Spirit of Conservatism.*

1
The book that he has made renders its author this service in return, that so long as the book survives, its author remains immortal and cannot die.

RICHARD DE BURY, *Philobiblon*. Ch. i, sec. 21.

2
Thou too hast built what will outlast all marble and metal, and be a wonder-bringing City of the mind, a Temple and Seminary, and Prophetic Mount, whereto all kindreds of the earth will pilgrim.

CARLYLE, *Sartor Resartus*. Bk. ii, ch. 8.

3
If you would not be forgotten, as soon as you are dead and rotten, either write things worth reading, or do things worth the writing.

BENJAMIN FRANKLIN, *Poor Richard*, 1738.

4
Wide as the light extends shall be the fame
Of this great work.
(Τοῦ δ' ἤτοι κλέος ἔσται ὅσον τ' ἐπικίδναται ἠώς.)

HOMER, *Iliad*. Bk. vii, l. 451. (Derby, tr.)

I have a great work in hand. (Habeo opus magnum in manibus.)

CICERO, *Academicarum Quæstionum*, i, 1, 2.

And now I have completed a work which neither the wrath of Jove, nor fire, nor sword, nor devouring age, will have power to destroy. (Jamque opus exegi, quod nec Jovis ira, nec ignis, Nec poterit ferrum, nec edax abolere vetustas.)

OVID, *Metamorphoses*. Bk. xv, l. 871.

O what an endless work have I in hand!

SPENSER, *Faerie Queene*. Bk. iv, canto xii, st. 1.

5
He that cometh in print because he would be known, is like the fool that cometh into the Market because he would be seen.

LYLY, *Euphues: To the Gentlemen Readers.*

6
By labour and intense study (which I take to be my portion in this life) joined with the strong propensity of nature, I might perhaps leave something so written to after-times, as they should not willingly let it die.

JOHN MILTON, *Reason of Church Government:* Bk. ii, *Introduction.*

7
Writing endures the years; it is through writing that you know Agamemnon, and all those who fought with or against him. (Scripta ferunt annos; scriptis Agamemnona nosti, Et quisquis contra vel simul arma tulit.)

OVID, *Epistulæ ex Ponto*. Bk. iv, epis. 8, l. 51.

8
Yield ye, bards of Rome! yield ye, singers of Greece! (Cedite Romani scriptores, cedite Grai!)

PROPERTIUS, *Elegies*. Bk. ii, eleg. 34, l. 65.

9
Literary fame is the only fame of which a wise man ought to be ambitious, because it is the only lasting and living fame.

ROBERT SOUTHEY. (FORSTER, *Life of Landor*. Bk. vii, ch. 13.)

I would rather be Charles Lamb than Charles XII. I would rather be remembered by a song than by a victory. I would rather build a fine sonnet than have built St. Paul's. . . . Fine phrases I value more than bank-notes. I have ear for no other harmony than the harmony of words.

ALEXANDER SMITH, *Dreamthorp: Men of Letters.*

10
I grant the man is vain who writes for praise.
Praise no man e'er deserved, who sought no more.

YOUNG, *Night Thoughts*. Night v, l. 3.

X—Writing: The Writer

11
The circumstance which gives authors an advantage above all these great masters, is this, that they can multiply their originals; or rather, can make copies of their works, to what number they please, which shall be as valuable as the originals themselves.

ADDISON, *The Spectator*. No. 166.

12
Writers, like teeth, are divided into incisors and grinders.

WALTER BAGEHOT, *Literary Studies: The First Edinburgh Reviewers.*

13
There is probably no hell for authors in the next world—they suffer so much from critics and publishers in this.

C. N. BOVEE, *Summaries of Thought: Authors.*

13a
One hates an author that's *all author*, fellows
In foolscap uniforms turn'd up with ink,
So very anxious, clever, fine, and jealous,
One don't know what to say to them, or think,
Unless to puff them with a pair of bellows.

BYRON, *Beppo*. St. 75.

14
That unspeakable shoeblack-seraph Army of Authors.

CARLYLE, *Essays: Boswell's Johnson.*

He, with his copy-rights and copy-wrongs, in his squalid garret, in his rusty coat; ruling (for this is what he does), from his grave, after death, whole nations and generations who would, or would not, give him bread while living,—is a rather curious spectacle!

CARLYLE, *Heroes and Hero-Worship*. Lect. v.

15
There are genuine Men of Letters, and not genuine; as in every kind there is a genuine and spurious. . . . The Hero as Man of Letters will be found discharging a function for us which is ever honourable, ever the highest; and was once well known to be the highest. He is uttering forth, in such way as he has, the inspired soul of him; all that a man, in any case, can do.

CARLYLE, *Heroes and Hero-Worship*. Lect. v.

Men of Letters are a perpetual Priesthood, from age to age, teaching all men that a God is still present in their life. . . . In the true Literary

Man there is thus ever, acknowledged or not by the world, a sacredness: he is the light of the world; the world's Priest;—guiding it, like a sacred Pillar of Fire, in its dark pilgrimage through the waste of Time.

CARLYLE, *Heroes and Hero-Worship*. Lect. v.

Literary men are . . . a perpetual priesthood.

CARLYLE, *Essays: Richter.*

1

Until you understand a writer's ignorance, presume yourself ignorant of his understanding.

S. T. COLERIDGE, *Biographia Literaria*. Ch. 12.

If you once understand an author's character, the comprehension of his writings becomes easy.

LONGFELLOW, *Hyperion*. Bk. i, ch. 5.

2

It is a hard and nice thing for a man to write of himself. It grates his own heart to say anything of disparagement, and the reader's ears to hear anything of praise from him.

ABRAHAM COWLEY, *Of Myself.*

The author who speaks about his own books is almost as bad as the mother who talks about her own children.

DISRAELI, *Speech*, 19 Nov., 1870.

But every little busy scribbler now
Swells with the praises which he gives himself;
And, taking sanctuary in the crowd,
Brags of his impudence, and scorns to mend.

HORACE, *Ars Poetica*, l. 475. (Dillon, tr.)

3

A man of letters, and of manners too!

COWPER, *The Task*. Bk. ii, l. 782.

4

How strange that men,
Who guide the plough, should fail to guide
the pen.

GEORGE CRABBE, *The Parish Register*. Pt. ii.

5

Choose an author as you choose a friend.

WENTWORTH DILLON, *Essay on Translated Verse*, l. 96.

6

'Tis a vanity common to all writers, to overvalue their own productions.

DRYDEN, *Examen Poeticum: Dedication.*

7

The writer, like the priest, must be exempted from secular labor. His work needs a frolic health; he must be at the top of his condition.

EMERSON, *Poetry and Imagination: Creation.*

Talent alone cannot make a writer. There must be a man behind the book.

EMERSON, *Representative Men: Goethe.*

8

An affected modesty is very often the greatest vanity, and authors are sometimes prouder of their blushes than of the praises that occasioned them.

FARQUHAR, *The Constant Couple: Preface.*

Nothing gives an author so much pleasure as to find his works respectfully quoted by other learned authors.

BENJAMIN FRANKLIN, *Poor Richard*, 1758.

I never saw an author in my life, saving perhaps one, that did not purr as audibly as a full-grown domestic cat on having his fur smoothed the right way by a skilful hand.

O. W. HOLMES, *The Autocrat of the Breakfast-Table*. Ch. 3.

There is nothing more dreadful to an author than neglect, compared with which reproach, hatred and opposition are names of happiness.

SAMUEL JOHNSON, *The Rambler*. No. 2.

9

No author ever spar'd a brother.

JOHN GAY, *Fables: The Elephant and the Bookseller.*

10

Whatever an author puts between the two covers of his book is public property; whatever of himself he does not put there is his private property, as much as if he had never written a word.

GAIL HAMILTON, *Country Living and Country Thinking: Preface.*

11

I don't want to be a doctor, and live by men's diseases; nor a minister to live by their sins; nor a lawyer to live by their quarrels. So I don't see there's anything left for me but to be an author.

NATHANIEL HAWTHORNE, *Remark to His Mother.*

13

The only happy author in this world is he who is below the care of reputation.

WASHINGTON IRVING, *Tales of a Traveller: Poor-Devil Author.*

14

The chief glory of every people arises from its authors.

SAMUEL JOHNSON, *Dictionary of the English Language: Preface.*

To commence author is to claim praise.

SAMUEL JOHNSON, *The Rambler*. No. 93.

Modern writers are the moons of literature; they shine with reflected light, with light borrowed from the ancients.

SAMUEL JOHNSON. (BOSWELL, *Life*, iii, 333.)

15

I never desire to converse with a man who has written more than he has read.

SAMUEL JOHNSON, *Miscellanies*. Vol. ii, p. 6.

16

He is the richest author that ever grazed the common of literature.

SAMUEL JOHNSON, of Dr. Thomas Campbell. (WHARTON, *Life*.)

17

There are two literary maladies—writer's cramp and swelled head. The worst of writer's cramp is that it is never cured; the worst of swelled head is that it never kills.

COULSON KERNAHAN, *Lecture*, Birmingham.

18

A writer owned an asterisk,
And kept it in his Den,
Where he wrote tales (which had large sales)
Of frail and erring men;

And always, when he reached the point
Where carping Censors lurk,
He called upon the Asterisk
To do his dirty work.

STODDARD KING, *The Writer and the Asterisk.*

1
Skilled equally with voice and pen
To stir the hearts or mould the minds of men.

J. R. LOWELL, *Epistle to G. W. Curtis,* l. 11.

2
But I became a writer all the same, and shall remain one until the end of the chapter, just as a cow goes on giving milk all her life, even though what appears to be her self-interest urges her to give gin.

H. L. MENCKEN. (DURANT, *On the Meaning of Life,* p. 32.)

3
Whate'er my fate is, 'tis my fate to write.

JOHN OLDHAM, *A Letter from the Country.*

4
His powers betray the author. (Prodent auctorem vires.)

OVID, *Epistulæ ex Ponto.* Bk. iv, epis. 13, l. 11.

5
A man of letters, of the kind that rich men hate. (Litteratum esse, quos odisse divites solent.)

PETRONIUS ARBITER, *Satyricon.* Sec. 83.

6
Authors, like coins, grow dear as they grow old;
It is the rust we value, not the gold.
Chaucer's worst ribaldry is learn'd by rote,
And beastly Skelton heads of houses quote;
One likes no language but the Faery Queen;
A Scot will fight for Christ's Kirk o' the Green;
And each true Briton is to Ben so civil,
He swears the Muses met him at the Devil.

POPE, *Imitations of Horace: Epistles.* Bk. ii, epis. 1, l. 35. Referring to the Devil Tavern.

7
As though I lived to write, and wrote to live.

SAMUEL ROGERS, *Italy: A Character,* l. 16.

You must not suppose, because I am a man of letters, that I never tried to earn an honest living.

BERNARD SHAW, *The Irrational Knot: Preface.*

8
Admitted into the company of paper-blurrers.

SIR PHILIP SIDNEY, *Apology for Poetry: Causes of Defect.*

9
The punishment of writers of genius exalts the credit of their writings. (Punitis ingeniis, gliscit auctoritas.)

TACITUS, *Annales.* Bk. iv, sec. 35.

10
In every author let us distinguish the man from his works.

VOLTAIRE, *A Philosophical Dictionary: Poets.*

11
An author! 'tis a venerable name!
How few deserve it, and what numbers claim!

YOUNG, *Epistles to Mr. Pope.* Epis. ii, l. 15.

Thus nature's refuse, and the dregs of men,
Compose the black militia of the pen.

YOUNG, *Epistles to Mr. Pope.* Epis. i, last lines.

Is now a scribbler, who was once a man.

YOUNG, *Love of Fame.* Sat. i, l. 84.

12
The author of "Amelia," the most singular genius which their island ever produced, whose works it has long been the fashion to abuse in public and to read in secret.

GEORGE BORROW, *The Bible in Spain.* Ch. 1.

13
To him no author was unknown,
Yet what he wrote was all his own. . . .
Horace's wit and Virgil's state
He did not steal, but emulate;
And when he would like them appear,
Their garb, but not their clothes, did wear.

SIR JOHN DENHAM, *On the Death of Mr. Abraham Cowley.*

14
Thou last great prophet of tautology.

JOHN DRYDEN, *Mac Flecknoe.* Referring to Thomas Shadwell.

15
His writing has no enthusiasms, no aspiration; contented, self-respecting and keeping the middle of the road.

EMERSON, *Representative Men: Montaigne.*

16
While he walks like Jack the Giant Killer in a coat of darkness, he may do much mischief with little strength.

SAMUEL JOHNSON, *Falkland's Islands.* Referring to "Junius."

17
Such stains there are—as when a Grace
Sprinkles another's laughing face
With nectar, and runs on.

W. S. LANDOR, *Catullus.*

18
His Nature's a glass of Champagne with the foam on 't,
As tender as Fletcher, as witty as Beaumont;
So his best things are done in the flash of the moment.

J. R. LOWELL, *A Fable for Critics,* l. 717. Of N. P. Willis.

19
Cinna writes verses 'gainst me, it is said:
But he writes nothing who is never read.
(Versiculos in me narratur scribere Cinna;
Non scribit, cujus carmina nemo legit.)

MARTIAL, *Epigrams.* Bk. iii, epig. 9.

Do you wonder, Theodorus, why it is that, despite your entreaties, I have never given you my books? I have an excellent reason: lest you should give me yours.
(Non donem tibi cur meos libellos
Oranti totiens et exigenti
Miraris, Theodore? Magna causa est:
Dones tu mihi ne tuos libellos.)

MARTIAL, *Epigrams.* Bk. v, epig. 73.

20
Poor Henry [James], he's spending eternity wandering round and round a stately park and the fence is just too high for him to peep

over and they're having tea just too far for him to hear what the countess is saying.

SOMERSET MAUGHAM, *Cakes and Ale*, p. 152.

1
Only a little more
I have to write,
Then I'll give o'er
And bid the world Good-night.

ROBERT HERRICK, *His Poetrie His Pillar*.

XI—Writing: Handwriting

2
Every man, who has the use of his eyes and of his right hand, can write whatever hand he pleases.

LORD CHESTERFIELD, *Letters*, 9 July, 1750.

3
He can't write, nor rade writing from his cradle, plase your honour; but he can make his mark equal to another, sir.

MARIA EDGEWORTH, *Love and Law* Act iii, sc. 1.

4
Phœnicia first, if fame be truly heard,
Fixed in rude characters the fleeting word.
(Phœnices primi, famæ si creditur, ausi
Mansuram rudibus vocem signare figuris.)

LUCAN, *De Bello Civili*. Bk. iii, l. 220. (King, tr.)

Cadmus brought the twenty-two or twenty-four Phœnician letters to Greece. They are called "the black daughters of Cadmus."

EMERSON, *Uncollected Lectures: Public and Private Education*. The ancient tradition was that Cadmus brought sixteen letters from Phœnicia to Greece, to which Palamedes subsequently added four more, and Simonides, still later, four others.

Thence comes to us that ingenious art
Of painting words and speaking to the eyes;
And by the differing form of figures traced,
To give color and form to thought.
(C'est de lui que nous vient cet art ingenieux
De peindre la parole at de parler aux yeux;
Et par las traits divers de figures tracées,
Donner de la couleur et du corps aux pensées.)

BRÉBŒUF, *Paraphrase of Lucan*.

5
The swifter hand doth the swift words outrun:
Before the tongue hath spoke, the hand hath done.
(Currant verba licet, manus est velocior illis:
Nondum lingua suum, dextra peregit opus.)

MARTIAL, *Epigrams: On a Shorthand Writer*. Bk. xiv, epig. 208. (Wright, tr.)

6
I wish that I had never learned to write!
(Quam vellem me nescire literas!)

EMPEROR NERO, on being asked to sign his first writ for the execution of a malefactor. (SUETONIUS, *Twelve Cæsars: Nero*. Sec. 10.)

7
Write it down in a good firm hand. (Scribas vide plane et probe.)

PLAUTUS, *Asinaria*, l. 755. (Act iv, sc. 1.)

8
Men of quality are in the wrong to undervalue, as they often do, the practise of a fair and quick hand in writing; for it is no immaterial accomplishment. (Non sest aliena res, quæ fere ab honestis negligi solet, cura bene ac velociter scribendi.)

QUINTILIAN, *De Institutione Oratoria*. Bk. i, ch. 5.

I once did hold it, as our statists do,
A baseness to write fair, and labour'd much
How to forget that learning, but, sir, now
It did me yeoman's service.

SHAKESPEARE, *Hamlet*. Act v, sc. 2, l. 33.

9
If you give me six lines written by the hand of the most honest of men, I will find something in them which will hang him. (Qu'on me donne six lignes écrites de la main du plus honnête homme, j'y trouverai de quoi le faire pendre.)

CARDINAL RICHELIEU, *Mirame*. (1641) *See also* ÉDOUARD FOURNIER, *L'Esprit dans l'Histoire*, p. 159.

10
Clerk: Sir, I thank God that I have been so well brought up that I can write my name.
Cade: Away with him, I say! hang him with his pen and ink-horn about his neck.

SHAKESPEARE, *II Henry VI*. Act iv, sc. 2, l. 112.

To be a well-favoured man is a gift of fortune: but to write and read comes by nature.

SHAKESPEARE, *Much Ado About Nothing*. Act iii, sc. 3, l. 15.

11
I think we do know the sweet Roman hand.

SHAKESPEARE, *Twelfth Night*. Act iii, sc 4, l. 30.

12
Who'er writ it, writes a hand like a foot.

SWIFT, *Polite Conversation*. Dial. i. (1738)

WRONGS

I—Wrong, in the Sense of Injury

See also Injury; Right and Wrong

13
Some kind of wrongs there are, which flesh and blood
Cannot endure.

BEAUMONT AND FLETCHER, *The Little French Lawyer*. Act i, sc. 1.

14
The wrong was his who wrongfully complain'd.

COWPER, *Hope*, l. 321.

15
My ear is pain'd,
My soul is sick with every day's report
Of wrong and outrage with which earth is fill'd.

COWPER, *The Task*. Bk. ii, l. 5.

16
Wrongs do not leave off there where they begin,
But still beget new mischiefs in their course.

SAMUEL DANIEL, *The History of the Civil War*. Bk. iv, st. 10.

1 You cannot do wrong without suffering wrong.
EMERSON, *Essays, First Series: Compensation.*

Not the wrongs done to us harm us, only those we do to others.
H. W. LONGFELLOW. (*Bradford, Biography and the Human Heart*, p. 42.)

2 For every social wrong there must be a remedy. But the remedy can be nothing less than the abolition of the wrong.
HENRY GEORGE, *Social Problems*. Ch. 9.

3 Wrong rules the land and waiting Justice sleeps.
J. G. HOLLAND, *Wanted.*

Truth forever on the scaffold, Wrong forever on the throne.
J. R. LOWELL, *The Present Crisis*. St. 8.

4 He wrought no wrong in deed or word to any man. (Οὔτε τινὰ ῥέξας ἐξαίσιον οὔτε τι εἰπών.)
HOMER, *Odyssey*. Bk. iv, l. 690.

5 And bear unmov'd the wrongs of base mankind,
The last, and hardest, conquest of the mind.
HOMER, *Odyssey*. Bk. xiii, l. 353. (Pope, tr.)

6 A passionate wrong cries ever till judgment comes.
JOHN MASEFIELD, *The Wild Swan.*

7 Wronged me! in the nicest point—
The honour of my house.
THOMAS OTWAY, *Venice Preserved*. Act i, sc. 1.

8 By bearing old wrongs you provoke new ones. (Veterem ferendo injuriam invites novam.)
PUBLILIUS SYRUS, *Sententiæ*. No. 705.

9 Wrong has no warrant.
JOHN RAY, *English Proverbs.*

10 He hath done me wrong.
SHAKESPEARE, *I Henry VI*. Act iv, sc. 1, l. 85.

Won't you come home, Bill Bailey,
Won't you come home? . . .
I'll do de cooking, darling,
I'll pay de rent;
I knows I've done you wrong.
HUGHIE CANNON, *Bill Bailey*. (1902)

11 Wrongs, unspeakable, past patience,
Or more than any living man could bear.
SHAKESPEARE, *Titus Andronicus*. Act v, sc. 3, l. 126.

Wrongs unredressed, or insults unavenged.
WORDSWORTH, *The Excursion*. Bk. iii, l. 374.

12 Higher than the perfect song
For which love longeth,
Is the tender fear of wrong,
That never wrongeth.
BAYARD TAYLOR, *Improvisations*. Pt. iv.

II—Wrong: Error

See also Error; Mistake; Right and Wrong

13 You rose on the wrong side of the bed today.
RICHARD BROME, *Court-Beggar*. Act ii. (1653)

14 He knew he had the wrong end of the stick.
GABRIEL HARVEY, *Letter-Book*, p. 5. (1573)

15 Ye lean to the wrong shore.
JOHN HEYWOOD, *Proverbs*. Pt. ii, ch. 2. (1546)

Ye took the wrong way to wood and the wrong sow by the ear.
JOHN HEYWOOD, *Proverbs*. Pt. ii, ch. 9.

In the wrong box.
JOHN HEYWOOD, *Proverbs*. Pt. ii, ch. 9. (1546)

The Wrong Box.
R. L. STEVENSON. Title of novel.

16 The wrong way always seems the more reasonable.
GEORGE MOORE, *The Bending of the Bough*. Act iii.

17 I didn't come on the wrong side of the blanket.
SMOLLETT, *Humphrey Clinker*. Meaning to be illegitimate.

18 A man should never be ashamed to own he has been in the wrong, which is but saying, in other words, that he is wiser to-day than he was yesterday.
SWIFT, *Thoughts on Various Subjects.*

Y

YEAR

See also Time

I—Year: Apothegms

19 Six years—six little years—six drops of time.
MATTHEW ARNOLD, *Mycerinus*. St. 11.

20 Years have hardier tasks
Than listening to a whisper or a sigh.
STEPHEN VINCENT BENÉT, *The Golden Corpse.*

21 Lament who will, in fruitless tears,
The speed with which our moments fly;
I sigh not over vanished years,
But watch the years that hasten by.
BRYANT, *The Lapse of Time.*

22 Lib'ral in all things else, yet Nature here
With stern severity deals out the year.
COWPER, *Table Talk*, l. 207.

23 The wonderful year. (Annus mirabilis.)
JOHN DRYDEN. Title of historical poem, dealing with "the year of wonders," 1666.

1
The years teach much which the days never know.
EMERSON, *Essays, Second Series: Experience.*

All sorts of things and weather
Must be taken in together,
To make up a year.
EMERSON, *Fable.*

2
The specious panorama of a year
But multiplies the image of a day,—
A belt of mirrors round a taper's flame;
And universal Nature, through her vast
And crowded whole, an infinite paroquet,
Repeats one note.
EMERSON, *Xenophanes.*

3
A year is no contemptible portion of this mortal existence.
GIBBON, *Miscellaneous Works.* Vol. i, p. 644.

4
Years know more than books.
GEORGE HERBERT, *Jacula Prudentum.*

The year doth nothing else but open and shut.
GEORGE HERBERT, *Jacula Prudentum.*

5
Years, as they come, bring blessings in their train;
Years, as they go, take blessings back again.
(Multa ferunt anni venientes commoda secum,
Multa recedentes adimunt.)
HORACE, *Ars Poetica,* l. 175. (Conington, tr.)

From each of us each passing year takes something. (Singula de nobis anni prædantur eantes.)
HORACE, *Epistles.* Bk. ii, epis. 2, l. 55.

Years following years steal something every day.
At last they steal us from ourselves away.
HORACE, *Epistles.* Bk. ii, 2, 72. (Pope, tr.)

Welcome, thou kind deceiver!
Thou best of thieves! who, with an easy key,
Dost open life, and, unperceiv'd by us,
Ev'n steal us from ourselves.
DRYDEN, *All for Love.* Act v, sc. 1.

6
Nothing is swifter than the years. (Nihil est annis velocius.)
OVID, *Metamorphoses.* Bk. xx, l. 520.

The swift years slip and slide adown the steep;
The slow years pass; neither will come again.
WILLIAM SHARP, *End of Aodh-of-the-Songs.*

7
A thousand years in thy sight are but as yesterday when it is past, and as a watch in the night.
Old Testament: Psalms, xc, 4.

But to the dwellers in eternity
A thousand years shall as a moment be.
ABRAHAM COLES, *The Microcosm and Other Poems,* p. 289.

8
We spend our years as a tale that is told.
Old Testament: Psalms, xc, 9.

9
I will not let the years run over me like a Juggernaut car.
THOREAU, *Journal,* 25 June, 1840.

10
In masks outrageous and austere
The years go by in single file;
But none has merited my fear,
And none has quite escaped my smile.
ELINOR WYLIE, *Let No Charitable Hope.*

11
Years ago—years and years and donkey's ears, as the saying is.
E. M. WRIGHT, *Rustic Speech,* 34.

12
The years like great black oxen tread the world
And God the herdsman goads them on behind,
And I am broken by their passing feet.
W. B. YEATS, *The Countess Cathleen.* Closing lines.

After the black ox hath trodden on her toe.
BURTON, *Anatomy of Melancholy.* Pt. iii, sec. 2, memb. 5, subs. 3.i.e., when care has passed by.

I read once in an ancient and proud book
How beauty fadeth,
How stale will Helen or Leucippe grow
When custom jadeth.
"When the black ox hath trodden on her toe,"
Beauty will alter,
And love that lives on beauty, so it said,
Will fade and falter.
DUNCAN CAMPBELL SCOTT, *The Anatomy of Melancholy.*

Black Oxen.
GERTRUDE ATHERTON. Title of novel.

II—Year: New Year

13
Thou art my single day, God lends to leaven
What were all earth else, with a feel of heaven.
BROWNING, *Pippa Passes: Introduction,* l. 39.

14
Even while we sing, he smiles his last,
And leaves our sphere behind.
The good Old Year is with the past,
O be the New as kind!
BRYANT, *A Song for New-Year's Eve.*

15
The merry year is born
Like the bright berry from the naked thorn.
HARTLEY COLERIDGE, *New Year's Day.*

16
A song for the Old, while its knell is tolled,
And its parting moments fly!
But a song and a cheer for the glad New Year,
While we watch the Old Year die!
Oh! its grief and pain ne'er can come again,
And its care lies buried deep;
But what joy untold doth the New Year hold,
And what hopes within it sleep!
GEORGE COOPER, *The New Year.*

17
Who comes dancing over the snow,
His soft little feet all bare and rosy?
Open the door, though the wild winds blow,
Take the child in and make him cosy.
Take him in and hold him dear,

He is the wonderful glad New Year.
Dinah Maria Mulock Craik, *The New Year.*

1
New Year comes but once a twelvemonth.
W. E. Henley, *In Hospital: Interlude.*

2
For hark! the last chime of the dial has ceased,
And Old Time, who his leisure to cozen,
Has finish'd the Months, like the flasks at a feast,
Is preparing to tap a fresh dozen!
Hood, *Anacreontic for the New Year.* St. 1.

And ye, who have met with Adversity's blast,
And been bow'd to the earth by its fury;
To whom the Twelve Months, that have recently pass'd
Were as harsh as a prejudiced jury—
Still, fill to the Future! and join in our chime,
The regrets of remembrance to cozen,
And having obtained a New Trial of Time,
Shout in hopes of a kindlier dozen.
Hood, *Anacreontic for the New Year.* St. 3.

3
Sad, sad to think that the year is all but done.
Charles Kingsley, *The Starlings.*

4
Then sing, young hearts that are full of cheer,
With never a thought of sorrow;
The old goes out, but the glad young year
Comes merrily in to-morrow.
Emily Huntington Miller, *New Year Song.*

5
Gone! gone forever!—like a rushing wave
Another year has burst upon the shore
Of earthly being—and its last low tones,
Wandering in broken accents in the air,
Are dying to an echo.
George D. Prentice, *Flight of Years.*

6
Like yonder stars so bright and clear
That praise their Maker as they move,
And usher in the circling year.
Schiller, *Song of the Bell.* (Bowring, tr.)

7
"Orphan Hours, the Year is dead:
Come and sigh, come and weep."
"Merry Hours, smile instead,
For the Year is but asleep.
See, it smiles as it is sleeping,
Mocking your untimely weeping."
Shelley, *Dirge for the Year.*

The warm sun is failing, the bleak wind is wailing,
The bare boughs are sighing, the pale flowers are dying;
And the year
On the earth her deathbed, in a shroud of leaves dead,
Is lying.
Come, months, come away,
From November to May,
In your saddest array;
Follow the bier
Of the dead cold year,
And like dim shadows watch by her sepulchre.
Shelley, *Autumn, A Dirge.*

8
Full knee-deep lies the winter snow.
And the winter winds are wearily sighing:
Toll ye the church-bell sad and slow,
And tread softly and speak low,
For the old year lies a-dying. . . .
There's a new foot on the floor, my friend
And a new face at the door, my friend,
A new face at the door.
Tennyson, *The Death of the Old Year.*

Ring out, wild bells, to the wild sky,
The flying cloud, the frosty light:
The year is dying in the night;
Ring out, wild bells, and let him die.
Tennyson, *In Memoriam.* Pt. cvi, st. 1.

Ring out the old, ring in the new,
Ring, happy bells, across the snow:
The year is going, let him go;
Ring out the false, ring in the true.
Alfred Tennyson, *In Memoriam.* Pt. cvi, st. 2.

A spirit haunts the year's last hours
Dwelling amid these yellowing bowers.
Tennyson, *Song.*

YESTERDAY

See also Past

9
How long ago it may seem since yesterday!
J. M. Barrie, *Sentimental Tommy,* p. 312.

10
These fatuous, ineffectual yesterdays.
W. E. Henley, *Rhymes and Rhythms.* No. 13.

10a
Yesterday you were a beautiful thing
Running across the road, little white hen—
But that was then.
June Knapp, *But That Was Then.*

11
On morning wings how active springs the mind
That leaves the load of yesterday behind!
Pope, *Imitations of Horace: Satires,* ii, 2, 81.

12
And all our yesterdays have lighted fools
The way to dusty death.
Shakespeare, *Macbeth.* Act v, sc. 5, l. 22.

13
O, call back yesterday, bid time return.
Shakespeare, *Richard II.* Act iii, sc. 2, l. 69.

O God! Put back Thy universe and give me yesterday.
Henry Arthur Jones, *Silver King.*

Yesterday will not be called again.
John Skelton, *Magnyfycence,* l. 2057.

14
The tasks are done and the tears are shed.
Yesterday's errors let yesterday cover;
Yesterday's wounds, which smarted and bled,
Are healed with the healing that night has shed.
Sarah C. Woolsey, *New Every Morning.*

15
A man he seems of cheerful yesterdays
And confident to-morrows.
Wordsworth, *The Excursion.* Bk. vii, l. 557.

Cheerful Yesterdays.
T. W. Higginson. Title of autobiography.

1
Whose yesterdays look backwards with a smile
Nor, like the Parthian, wound him as they fly.
YOUNG, *Night Thoughts*. Night ii, l. 334.

O for yesterdays to come!
YOUNG, *Night Thoughts*. Night ii, l. 311.

YOUTH

See also Age and Youth; Boy; Girl

I—Youth: Definitions

2
A man that is young in years may be old in hours, if he have lost no time; but that happeneth rarely.
FRANCIS BACON, *Essays: Of Youth and Age*.

Young men are fitter to invent than to judge; fitter for execution than for counsel; and fitter for new projects than for settled business.
FRANCIS BACON, *Essays: Of Youth and Age*.

Young men, in the conduct and manage of actions, embrace more than they can hold, stir more than they can quiet, fly to the end without consideration of the means.
FRANCIS BACON, *Essays: Of Youth and Age*.

3
Youth being indeed the philosopher's rasa tabula, is apt to receive any impressure.
RICHARD BRATHWAITE, *English Gentleman*, 3. (1630)

4
Every street has two sides, the shady side and the sunny. When two men shake hands and part, mark which of the two takes the sunny side; he will be the younger man of the two.
BULWER-LYTTON, *What Will He Do With It?* Bk. ii, ch. 15.

5
Youth is to all the glad season of life; but often only by what it hopes, not by what it attains, or what it escapes.
CARLYLE, *Essays: Schiller*.

6
The young leading the young, is like the blind leading the blind; they will both fall into the ditch.
LORD CHESTERFIELD, *Letters*, 6 Nov., 1747.

Young men are apt to think themselves wise enough, as drunken men are apt to think themselves sober enough.
LORD CHESTERFIELD, *Letters*, 15 Jan., 1753.

7
The best recommendation that a young man can have is modesty, filial affection, and devotion to kindred. (Prima igitur commendatio preficiscitur a modestia cum pietate inparentes, in suos benivolentia.)
CICERO, *De Officiis*. Bk. ii, ch. 13, sec. 46.

8
Young heads are giddy, and young hearts are warm,
And make mistakes for manhood to reform.
Boys are, at best, but pretty buds unblown,
Whose scent and hues are rather guess'd than known;
Each dreams that each is just what he appears,
But learns his error in maturer years,
When disposition, like a sail unfurl'd,
Shows all its rents and patches to the world.
COWPER, *Tirocinium*, l. 444.

9
Youth, what man's age is like to be, doth show;
We may our ends by our beginnings know.
SIR JOHN DENHAM, *On Prudence*, l. 225.

10
The Youth of a Nation are the trustees of Posterity.
BENJAMIN DISRAELI, *Sybil*. Bk. vi, ch. 13.

11
"And youth is cruel, and has no remorse
And smiles at situations which it cannot see."
I smile, of course,
And go on drinking tea.
T. S. ELIOT, *Portrait of a Lady*.

12
Say, was it never heard
That wisdom might in youth be gotten,
Or wit be ripe before 'twas rotten?
EMERSON, *Fame*.

13
There is a feeling of Eternity in youth which makes us amends for everything. To be young is to be as one of the Immortals.
WILLIAM HAZLITT, *Table Talk: The Feeling of Immortality in Youth*.

14
Youth is a continual intoxication; it is the fever of reason. (La jeunesse est une ivresse continuelle: c'est la fièvre de la raison.)
LA ROCHEFOUCAULD, *Maximes*. No. 271.

15
Youth sees too far to see how near it is
To seeing farther.
E. A. ROBINSON, *Tristram*.

16
Our youth is like a rustic at the play
That cries aloud in simple-hearted fear,
Curses the villain, shudders at the fray,
And weeps before the maiden's wreathèd bier
GEORGE SANTAYANA, *The Rustic at the Play*.

17
Youth is wholly experimental.
R. L. STEVENSON, *A Letter to a Young Gentleman*.

Youth is the time to go flashing from one end of the world to the other both in mind and body; to try the manners of different nations; to hear the chimes at midnight.
R. L. STEVENSON, *Virginibus Puerisque: Crabbed Age and Youth*.

18
Youth is not a time of life; it is a state of mind.
SAMUEL ULLMAN, *From the Summit of Four Score Years*.

II—Youth: Apothegms

1
Young fellows will be young fellows.
Isaac Bickerstaffe, *Love in a Village*, ii, 9.

2
Youth will be served, every dog hath his day, and mine has been a fine one.
Borrow, *Lavengro*. Ch. 92, par. 1. (1851)

Young blood! Youth will be served!
Stephen Vincent Benét, *Young Blood*. Used as a quotation from "D'Hermonville's Fabliaux," a fabrication of Mr. Benét.

We have an old proverb, youth will have his course.
John Lyly, *Euphues*, p. 124. (1579)

Youth will have his swing.
Shackerley Marmion, *Fine Companion*. Act i, sc. 7. (1633)

When all the world is young, lad,
And all the trees are green;
And every goose a swan, lad,
And every lass a queen;
Then hey, for boot and horse, lad,
And round the world away;
Young blood must have its course, lad,
And every dog his day.
Charles Kingsley, *The Water Babies: Song*.

3
What I promised thee was in my nonage.
John Bunyan, *The Pilgrim's Progress*. Pt. i.

4
Our most important are our earliest years.
Cowper, *The Progress of Error*, l. 354.

Almost everything that is great has been done by youth.
Benjamin Disraeli, *Coningsby*. Bk. iii, ch. 1.

5
A sensual and intemperate youth delivers a worn-out body to old age. (Libidinosa etenim et intemperans adolescentia effœtum corpus tradit senectuti.)
Cicero, *De Senectute*. Sec. ix.

Youth riotously led breedeth a loathsome old age.
Cogan, *Haven of Health: Dedication*. (1588)

The excesses of our youth are drafts upon our old age, payable with interest about thirty years after date.
C. C. Colton, *Lacon: Reflections*. Pt. i, No. 76.

The majority of men employ the first portion of their life in making the other portion wretched. (La plupart des hommes emploient la première partie de leur vie à rendre l'autre misérable.)
La Bruyère, *Les Caractères: De L'Homme*.

Yet few without long discipline are sage;
And our youth only lays up sighs for age.
Young, *Love of Fame*. Sat. i, l. 193.

6
My youth may wear and waste, but it shall never rust in my possession.
William Congreve, *The Way of the World*. Act ii, sc. 1. *See also under* Rust.

7
Youth is a curse to mortals, when with youth a man hath not implanted righteousness.
Euripides, *Andromache*, l. 184.

7a
Gilded youth. (Jeunesse dorée.)
Elie Catherine Fréron, describing the French dandies of 1714. (Monsélet, *Fréron, Sa Vie*.)

8
Girls we love for what they are;
Young men for what they promise to be.
(Man liebt an dem Mädchen was es ist,
Und an dem Jüngling was er ankündigt.)
Goethe, *Die Wahrheit und Dichtung*.

9
To maids and boys I sing. (Virginibus puerisque canto.)
Horace, *Odes*. Bk. iii, ode 1, l. 4. The first two words used as the title of a book of essays by Robert Louis Stevenson.

Solemn and holy words should be read by boys and maids. (Venerandaque santaque verba A pueris debent, virginibusque legi.)
Martial, *Epigrams*. Bk. iii, epig. 69.

He is wont to be read by boys and girls. (Solet hic pueris virginibusque legi.)
Ovid, *Tristia*. Eleg. ii, l. 370.

10
I do feel
The powers of one-and-twenty, like a tide,
Flow in upon me.
Ben Jonson, *The Staple of News*. Act i, sc. 1.

When the brisk minor pants for twenty-one.
Pope, *Imitations of Horace: Epistles*. Bk. i, epis. 1, l. 38.

Lightly I vaulted up four pair of stairs,
In the brave days when I was twenty-one.
W. M. Thackeray, *The Garret*.

In my hot youth, when George the Third was king.
Byron, *Don Juan*. Canto i, st. 212.

11
The flower of youth. (Flos juventutis.)
Livy, *History*. Bk. xxxvii, ch. 12.

The flower of the young men. (Flos juvenum.)
Livy, *History*. Bk. viii, ch. 8.

Age? Sixteen. The very flower of youth. (Anni? sedecim. Flos ipsus.)
Terence, *Eunuchus*, l. 318. (Act ii, sc. 3.)

Force of juventus, hardy as lion.
John Lydgate, *Minor Poems*, p. 198. (c. 1430)

12
Youth comes but once in a lifetime.
Longfellow, *Hyperion*. Bk. ii, ch. 10.

13
Youth condemns; maturity condones.
Amy Lowell, *Tendencies in Modern American Poetry*, p. 60.

14
The atrocious crime of being a young man, which the honourable gentleman has, with such spirit and decency, charged upon me, I shall neither attempt to palliate nor deny; but content myself with wishing that I may be one of those whose follies cease with their youth, and not of those who continue ignorant in spite of age and experience.
William Pitt, *Speech*, 6 March, 1741, in reply to Walpole, the "honourable gentleman" referred to. Boswell, in his *Life* (1741), alleges that this speech was written by Dr. Johnson.

If youth be a defect, it is one that we outgrow only too soon.

J. R. LOWELL, *Address*, Cambridge, Mass., 8 Nov., 1886.

1
I confess to pride in this coming generation. You are working out your own salvation; you are more in love with life; you play with fire openly, where we did in secret, and few of you are burned!

FRANKLIN D. ROOSEVELT, *Address: Whither Bound*, at Milton Academy, May, 1926.

2
My salad days
When I was green in judgement: cold in blood.

SHAKESPEARE, *Antony and Cleopatra*, i, 5, 73.

How green you are and fresh in this old world.

SHAKESPEARE, *King John*. Act iii, sc. 4, l. 145.

The text is old, the orator too green.

SHAKESPEARE, *Venus and Adonis*, l. 806.

"He is so jolly green," said Charley.

DICKENS, *Oliver Twist*. Ch. 9.

Fresh as an angel o'er a new inn-door

BYRON, *Beppo*. St. 57.

3
He wears the rose Of youth upon him.

SHAKESPEARE, *Antony and Cleopatra*, iii, 13, 20.

We have some salt of our youth in us.

SHAKESPEARE, *Merry Wives of Windsor*, ii, 3, 50.

'Tis now the summer of your youth.
Time has not cropt the roses from your cheek,
Though sorrow long has washed them.

EDWARD MOORE, *The Gamester*. Act iii, sc. 4.

4
For though the camomile, the more it is trodden on the faster it grows, yet youth, the more it is wasted the sooner it wears.

SHAKESPEARE, *I Henry IV*. Act ii, sc. 4, l. 440.

See also ADVERSITY: A BLESSING.

5
Is in the very May-morn of his youth,
Ripe for exploits and mighty enterprises.

SHAKESPEARE, *Henry V*. Act i, sc. 2, l. 120.

The May of life blooms once and never again.
(Des Lebens Mai blüht einmal und nicht wieder.)

SCHILLER, *Resignation*. St. 2.

6
He that is more than a youth is not for me, and he that is less than man, I am not for him.

SHAKESPEARE, *Much Ado About Nothing*, ii, 1, 40.

7
He has quitted the hobbledehoy stage; he is out of his teens. (Excessit ex ephebis.)

TERENCE, *Andria*, l. 51. (Act i, sc. 1.)

Their hobbledehoy time, the years that one is neither a man nor a boy.

JOHN PALSGRAVE, *Acolastus*, D 4. (1540)

The first seven years bring up as a child,
The next to learning, for waxing too wild,
The next keep under sir hobbard de hoy,
The next a man, no longer a boy.

THOMAS TUSSER, *Hundred Good Points of Husbandry*. (1573)

I was between
A man and a boy, A hobble-de-hoy,
A fat, little, punchy concern of sixteen.

R. H. BARHAM, *Aunt Fanny*.

Hobbledehoy, neither man nor boy,
With a burden of pain and a purpose of joy,
With a heart and a hunger of human alloy,
He's a lad whom the jungle and heaven decoy.
There's a god and a devil in Hobbledehoy!

WITTER BYNNER, *Hobbledehoy*.

Being but a moonish youth.

SHAKESPEARE, *As You Like It*. Act iii, sc. 2, l. 430.

Not yet old enough for a man, nor young enough for a boy; as a squash is before 'tis a peas-cod, or a codling when 'tis almost an apple: 'tis with him in standing water, between boy and man. He is very well-favoured and he speaks very shrewishly; one would think his mother's milk were scarce out of him.

SHAKESPEARE, *Twelfth Night*. Act i, sc. 5, l. 165.

The imagination of a boy is healthy, and the mature imagination of a man is healthy; but there is a space of life between, in which the soul is in a ferment, the character undecided, the way of life uncertain, the ambition thick-sighted: thence proceeds mawkishness.

KEATS, *Endymion: Preface*.

8
The wildest colts make the best horses.

THEMISTOCLES. (PLUTARCH, *Lives: Themistocles*. Ch. 2, sec. 5.)

For young hot colts being raged, do rage the more.

SHAKESPEARE, *Richard II*. Act ii, sc. 1, l. 70.

A man whose youth has no follies, will in his maturity have no power.

MORTIMER COLLINS, *Thoughts in My Garden*, ii, 108.

For God's sake give me the young man who has brains enough to make a fool of himself.

R. L. STEVENSON, *Crabbed Age and Youth*.

And still my delight is in proper young men.

BURNS, *The Jolly Beggars*.

9
My prime of youth is but a frost of cares.

CHIDIOCK TICHBORNE, *A Lament*.

10
Let no man despise thy youth.

New Testament: I Timothy, iv, 12.

10a
It is better to be a young June-bug than an old bird of paradise.

MARK TWAIN, *Pudd'nhead Wilson's Calendar*.

See also AGE AND YOUTH.

11
Everything loses charm when one's own youth does not lend the gilding.

WALPOLE, *Letter to George Montagu*, 22 Sept., 1765.

III—Youth: Its Sweetness

12
O youth, whose hope is high,
Who dost to Truth aspire,
Whether thou live or die,
O look not back nor tire.

ROBERT BRIDGES, *Song*.

13
I felt so young, so strong, so sure of God.

E. B. BROWNING, *Aurora Leigh*. Bk. ii, l. 13.

1
O enviable, early days,
When dancing thoughtless pleasure's maze,
To care, to guilt unknown!
How ill exchang'd for riper times,
To feel the follies or the crimes,
Of others, or my own!
BURNS, *Despondency*. St. 5.

O Life! how pleasant is thy morning,
Young Fancy's rays the hills adorning!
Cold-pausing Caution's lesson scorning,
We frisk away,
Like schoolboys at th' expected warning,
To joy an' play.
BURNS, *Epistle to James Smith*. St. 15.

Oh, talk not to me of a name great in story;
The days of our youth are the days of our glory;
And the myrtle and ivy of sweet two-and-twenty
Are worth all your laurels, though ever so plenty.
BYRON, *Stanzas Written on the Road Between Florence and Pisa*.

2
In life's morning march, when my bosom was young.
THOMAS CAMPBELL, *The Soldier's Dream*, l. 14.

There is no time like the old time, when you and I were young.
O. W. HOLMES, *No Time Like the Old Time*.

3
Nought cared this body for wind or weather
When Youth and I lived in 't together.
S. T. COLERIDGE, *Youth and Age*, l. 16.

4
Rejoice, O young man, in thy youth; and let thy heart cheer thee in the days of thy youth.
Old Testament: Ecclesiastes, xi, 9.

Remember now thy Creator in the days of thy youth, while the evil days come not, nor the years draw nigh, when thou shalt say, I have no pleasure in them.
Old Testament: Ecclesiastes, xii, 1.

5
Ah, sweet is youth! (Ἁ νεότας μοι φίλον.)
EURIPIDES, *Hercules Furens*, l. 637.

Ah youth! for ever dear, for ever kind!
HOMER, *The Iliad*. Bk. xix, l. 303. (Pope, tr.)

6
Youth! youth! how buoyant are thy hopes! they turn,
Like marigolds, toward the sunny side.
JEAN INGELOW, *The Four Bridges*. St. 56.

How beautiful is youth! how bright it gleams
With its illusions, aspirations, dreams!
Book of Beginnings, Story without End,
Each maid a heroine, and each man a friend! . . .
All possibilities are in its hands,
No danger daunts it, and no foe withstands;
In its sublime audacity of faith,
"Be thou removed!" it to the mountain saith,
And with ambitious feet, secure and proud,
Ascends the ladder leaning on the cloud!
LONGFELLOW, *Morituri Salutamus*, l. 66.

7
And a verse of a Lapland song
Is haunting my memory still:
"A boy's will is the wind's will,
And the thoughts of youth are long, long thoughts."
LONGFELLOW, *My Lost Youth*. St. 1.

8
When nature pleased, for life itself was new,
And the heart promised what the fancy drew.
SAMUEL ROGERS, *Pleasures of Memory*. Pt. i, l. 19.

9
I 'll hold thee any wager,
When we are both accoutered like young men,
I 'll prove the prettier fellow of the two,
And wear my dagger with the braver grace,
And speak between the change of man and boy,
With a reed voice; and turn two mincing steps
Into a manly stride; and speak of frays,
Like a fine bragging youth.
SHAKESPEARE, *Merchant of Venice*, iii, 4, 62.

10
I must laugh and dance and sing,
Youth is such a lovely thing.
ALINE THOMAS, *A Song of Youth*.

11
Bliss was it in that dawn to be alive,
But to be young was very Heaven!
WORDSWORTH, *The Prelude*. Bk. xi, l. 108.

There was a time when meadow, grove, and stream,
The earth, and every common sight,
To me did seem
Apparelled in celestial light,
The glory and the freshness of a dream.
WORDSWORTH, *Intimations of Immortality*. St. 1.

The Youth, who daily farther from the East
Must travel, still is Nature's Priest,
And by the vision splendid
Is on his way attended.
WORDSWORTH, *Intimations of Immortality*. St. 5.

IV—Youth: Its Fleetness

12
Unthinking, idle, wild, and young,
I laugh'd and danc'd and talk'd and sung.
PRINCESS AMELIA (Daughter of George III), *Youth*.

13
Our youth we can have but to-day;
We may always find time to grow old.
BISHOP GEORGE BERKELEY, *Can Love Be Controlled by Advice?*

14
'T is not on youth's smooth cheek the blush alone, which fades so fast,
But the tender bloom of heart is gone, ere youth itself be past.
BYRON, *Stanzas for Music*.

15
Alas! the slippery nature of tender youth.
(Teneris heu lubrica moribus ætas!)
CLAUDIAN, *De Raptu Proserpina*. Bk. iii, l. 227.

1
Youth should watch joys and shoot them as they fly.
DRYDEN, *Aureng-Zebe.* Act iii, sc. 1.

2
Let's now take our time
While we're in our prime,
And old, old age is afar off:
For the evil, evil days
Will come on apace,
Before we can be aware of.
ROBERT HERRICK, *To Be Merry.*

3
Youth flies. (Fugit juventus.)
HORACE, *Epodes.* No. xvii, l. 21.

Youth now flees on feathered foot.
R. L. STEVENSON, *To Will H. Low.*

Youth is a malady of which one becomes cured a little every day.
BENITO MUSSOLINI, on his fiftieth birthday.

4
This be our solace: that it was not said
When we were young and warm and in our prime,
Upon our couch we lay as lie the dead,
Sleeping away the unreturning time.
EDNA ST. VINCENT MILLAY, *Sonnet.*

5
That Youth's sweet-scented manuscript should close!
OMAR KHAYYÁM, *Rubáiyát.* St. 96. (Fitzgerald, tr.)

6
O Youth with song and laughter,
Go not so lightly by.
Have pity—and remember
How soon thy roses die!
ARTHUR WALLACE PEACH, *O Youth With Blossoms Laden.*

7
Youth flies, as bloom forsakes the grove,
When icy winter blows:
And transient are the smiles of love,
As dew-drops on the rose.
T. L. PEACOCK, *Genius of the Thames.* St. 11.

8
The spirit of a youth
That means to be of note, begins betimes.
SHAKESPEARE, *Antony and Cleopatra,* iv, 4, 26.

Clay lies still, but blood's a rover;
Breath's a ware that will not keep.
Up, lad: when the journey's over
There'll be time enough to sleep.
A. E. HOUSMAN, *Reveillé.*

9
Then come kiss me, Sweet-and-twenty,
Youth's a stuff will not endure.
SHAKESPEARE, *Twelfth Night.* Act ii, sc. 3, l. 53.

10
There are gains for all our losses,
There are balms for all our pain;
But when youth, the dream, departs,
It takes something from our hearts,
And it never comes again.
R. H. STODDARD. *The Flight of Youth.*

11
In youth alone unhappy mortals live;
But ah! the mighty bliss is fugitive.
VERGIL, *Georgics.* Bk. iii, l. 258. (Dryden, tr.)

12
Enjoy the season of thy prime; all things soon decline: one summer turns the kid into a shaggy goat. (Τῆς ὥρας ἀπόλαυε· παρακμάζει ταχὺ πάντα· ἓν θέρος ἐξ ἐρίφου τρηχὺν ἔθηκε τράγον.)
UNKNOWN. (*Greek Anthology.* Bk. xi, epig. 51.)

Be advised, young men—whilst the morning shines, gather the flowers. (Dum aurora fulget, moniti adolescentes, flores colligite.)
UNKNOWN. A medieval aphorism.

See also TIME: GATHER YE ROSES.

13
There are worse losses than the loss of youth.
JEAN INGELOW, *The Star's Monument.*

V—Youth and Love

See also Love: Love's Young Dream

14
Youth calls for Pleasure, Pleasure calls for Love.
MARK AKENSIDE, *Love: An Elegy,* l. 90.

Youth means love.
ROBERT BROWNING, *The Ring and the Book.* Pt. i, l. 1056.

15
But they were young: Oh! what without our youth
Would love be? What would youth be without love?
BYRON, *Beppo.* St. 55.

Alas! they are so young, so beautiful.
BYRON, *Don Juan.* Canto ii, st. 192.

And both were young, and one was beautiful.
BYRON, *The Dream.* St. 2.

16
Why should a man, whose blood is warm within,
Sit like his grandsire cut in alabaster?
SHAKESPEARE, *The Merchant of Venice.* Act i, sc. 1, l. 83.

17
It is the season now to go
About the country high and low,
Among the lilacs hand in hand,
And two by two in fairy land.

The brooding boy and sighing maid,
Wholly fain and half afraid,
Now meet along the hazel'd brook
To pass and linger, pause and look.
R. L. STEVENSON, *Underwoods.* No. 4.

A year ago and blithely paired
Their rough-and-tumble play they shared;
They kissed and quarrelled, laughed and cried
A year ago at Eastertide.

With bursting heart, with fiery face,
She strove against him in the race;
He unabashed her garter saw

That now would touch her skirts with awe.
R. L. STEVENSON, *Underwoods*. No. 4.
See also SPRING AND LOVE.

1
From tavern to tavern Youth dances along
With an arm full of girl and a heart full of song.
UNKNOWN, *Youth*. (*Philistine*. Vol. x, p. 60.)

VI—Youth: Illusion and Disillusion

See also Illusion

2
They shall grow not old, as we that are left grow old:
Age shall not weary them nor the years condemn.
LAURENCE BINYON, *For the Fallen*.

O youth foregone, foregoing!
O dreams unseen, unsought!
God give you joy of knowing
What life your death has bought.
BRIAN HOOKER, *A. D. 1919*. Inscribed on tablet in Woolsey Hall, Yale University, commemorating over 200 Yale men who lost their lives in the World War.

3
What Youth deemed crystal, Age finds out was dew
Morn set a-sparkle, but which noon quick dried,
While Youth bent gazing at its red and blue,
Supposed perennial,—never dreamed the sun
Which kindled the display would quench it too.
ROBERT BROWNING, *Jochanan Hakkadosh*. St. 101.

4
Fair laughs the morn, and soft the Zephyr blows,
While proudly riding o'er the azure realm
In gallant trim the gilded vessel goes;
Youth on the prow, and Pleasure at the helm;
Regardless of the sweeping whirlwind's sway,
That, hush'd in grim repose, expects his evening-prey.
THOMAS GRAY, *The Bard*, l. 71.

5
O Memory, where is now my youth,
Who used to say that life was truth?
THOMAS HARDY, *Memory and I*.

6
Over the trackless past, somewhere,
Lie the lost days of our tropic youth,
Only regained by faith and prayer,
Only recalled by prayer and plaint,
Each lost day has its patron saint!
BRET HARTE, *The Lost Galleon*. St. 16.

7
O Youth, alas, why wilt thou not incline
And unto rulèd reason bowè thee,
Since Reason is the very straightè line
That leadeth folk into felicity?
THOMAS HOCCLEVE, *La Male Règle*. (c. 1430)

8
Youth enters the world with very happy prejudices in her own favour.
SAMUEL JOHNSON, *The Rambler*. No. 127.

9
Our youth began with tears and sighs,
With seeking what we could not find;
We sought and knew not what we sought;
We marvel, now we look behind.
ANDREW LANG, *Ballade of Middle Age*.

10
When all the illusions of his Youth were fled,
Indulged perhaps too much, cherish'd too fondly.
SAMUEL ROGERS, *Italy: Arqua*.

11
The enthusiastic and pleasing illusions of youth.
J. H. SHORTHOUSE, *John Inglesant*.

12
Ah, what shall I be at fifty
Should Nature keep me alive,
If I find the world so bitter
When I am but twenty-five?
TENNYSON, *Maud*, l. 220.

13
This I say to you.
Be arrogant!
JOHN V. A. WEAVER, *To Youth*.

Z

ZEAL

See also Enthusiasm

14
If our zeal were true and genuine we should be much more angry with a sinner than a heretic.
ADDISON, *The Spectator*. No. 185.

There is no greater sign of a general decay of virtue in a nation, than a want of zeal in its inhabitants for the good of their country.
ADDISON, *The Freeholder*. No. 5.

15
For Zeal's a dreadful termagant,
That teaches saints to tear and yant.
BUTLER, *Hudibras*. Pt. iii, canto 2, l. 677.

16
Zeal without knowledge is the sister of folly.
JOHN DAVIES OF HEREFORD, *The Scourge of Folly*, p. 42. (1611)

Zeal without knowledge is fire without light.
JOHN RAY, *English Proverbs*, p. 146. (1678)

Zeal without knowledge is a runaway horse.
W. G. BENHAM, *Proverbs*, p. 880. (1907)

Zeal is like fire, it wants both feeding and watching.
W. G. BENHAM, *Proverbs*, p. 880. (1907)

1
It is good to be zealously affected always in a good thing.
New Testament: Galatians, iv, 18.

2
I do not love a man who is zealous for nothing.
OLIVER GOLDSMITH, *Vicar of Wakefield*, expunged passage. (See BOSWELL, *Life of Johnson*, 1779.)

Blind zeal can only do harm. (Blinder Eifer schadet nur.)
LICHTWER, *Die Katzen und der Hausherr.*

The zeal of fools offends at any time,
But most of all the zeal of fools in rhyme.
POPE, *Imitations of Horace: Epistles*. Bk. ii, epis. 1, l. 406.

3
Our Hero, whose homeopathic sagacity
With an ocean of zeal mixed his drop of capacity.
J. R. LOWELL, *A Fable for Critics*, l. 370.

4
His zeal
None seconded, as out of season judg'd,
Or singular and rash.
MILTON, *Paradise Lost*. Bk. v, l. 846.

But zeal moved thee;
To please thy gods thou didst it.
MILTON, *Samson Agonistes*, l. 895.

5
Zeal then, not charity, became the guide,
And Hell was built on spite, and Heav'n on pride.
POPE, *Essay on Man*. Epis. iii, l. 261.

6
A zeal of God, but not according to knowledge.
New Testament: Romans, x, 2.

I have more zeal than wit.
POPE, *Imitations of Horace: Satires*. Bk. ii, sat. 6, l. 56.

7
We do that in our zeal our calmer moment would be afraid to answer.
SCOTT, *Woodstock*. Ch. 17.

8
But zeal is weak and ignorant, though wondrous proud,
Though very turbulent and very loud.
SWIFT, *Ode: Dr. Wm. Sancroft*.

9
Not too much zeal. (Pas trop de zèle.)
TALLEYRAND. (SAINTE-BEUVE, *Critiques et Portraits*, iii, 324.) Sometimes quoted, Surtout pas de zèle, "Above all, no zeal."

10
We are often moved with passion, and we think it to be zeal.
THOMAS À KEMPIS, *De Imitatione Christi*. Pt. ii, ch. 5.

11
Persecuting zeal . . . Hell's fiercest fiend!
JAMES THOMSON, *Liberty*. Pt. iv, l. 66.

12
Press bravely onward! not in vain
Your generous trust in human-kind;
The good which bloodshed could not gain
Your peaceful zeal shall find.
J. G. WHITTIER, *To the Reformers of England*. St. 13.

13
Zaccheus, he
Did climb the tree,
His Lord to see.
UNKNOWN, *The New England Primer*.

ZEPHYR

14
Where the light wings of Zephyr, oppress'd with perfume,
Wax faint o'er the gardens of Gúl in her bloom.
BYRON, *The Bride of Abydos*. Canto i, st. 1.

While the wanton Zephyr sings,
And in the vale perfumes his wings.
JOHN DYER, *Grongar Hill*.

15
Let Zephyr only breathe,
And with her tresses play.
WILLIAM DRUMMOND, *Song: Phœbus, Arise*, l. 35.

16
And on the balmy zephyrs tranquil rest
The silver clouds.
KEATS, *Sonnet: Oh! How I Love*.

17
Zephyr with Aurora playing,
As he met her once a-Maying,
There on beds of violets blue,
And fresh-blown roses wash'd in dew,
Fill'd her with thee, a daughter fair,
So buxom, blithe, and debonair.
MILTON, *L'Allegro*, l. 19.

A bowl of wine is wondrous good cheer
To make one blithe, buxom, and debonair.
THOMAS RANDOLPH, *The Jealous Lovers*.

18
Soft o'er the shrouds aërial whispers breathe,
That seem'd but zephyrs to the train beneath.
POPE, *The Rape of the Lock*. Canto ii, l. 57.

The balmy zephyrs, silent since her death,
Lament the ceasing of a sweeter breath.
POPE, *Winter*, l. 49.

19
As gentle
As zephyrs blowing below the violet,
Not wagging his sweet head.
SHAKESPEARE, *Cymbeline*. Act iv, sc. 2, l. 171.

APPENDIX

APPENDIX I

See also Appendix II on page 2298j.

When quotations given in the Appendix are extensions of entries in the body of the book, the page on which the entry occurs has been given, in order that the extension may be found without difficulty.

1 **60:12**

Your women shall scream like peacocks when they talk and your men neigh like horses when they laugh. You shall call 'round' 'raound,' and 'very' 'varry,' and 'news' 'noose' till the end of time. You shall be governed by the Irishman and the German, the vendors of drinks and the keepers of vile dens, that your streets may be filthy in your midst and your sewage arrangements filthier.

Rudyard Kipling, *Letter to The Pioneer Mail*, Allahabad, India, 13 Nov., 1889. These letters were afterwards collected and published in a volume called *From Sea to Sea*, but the sentences above, which have been called "Kipling's seven-fold curse on America," were omitted. They were written in resentment at the pirating of his books by American publishers. (See *The Bookman*, vol. ix, p. 429.)

2 **203:7**

I chanced upon a new book yesterday:
I opened it, and, where my finger lay
'Twixt page and uncut page, these words I read
—Some six or seven at most—and learned thereby
That you, Fitzgerald, whom by ear and eye
She never knew, "thanked God my wife was dead."

Ay, dead! and were yourself alive, good Fitz,
How to return you thanks would tax my wits:
Kicking you seems the lot of common curs—
While more appropriate greeting lends you grace:
Surely to spit there glorifies your face—
Spitting—from lips once sanctified by Hers.

Robert Browning, *To Edward Fitzgerald*. (*The Athenæum*, 13 July, 1889.)

Mrs. Browning's death is rather a relief to me, I must say. No more Aurora Leighs, thank God! A woman of real genius, I know; but what is the upshot of it all? She and her sex had better mind the kitchen and the children; and perhaps the poor. Except in such things as little novels, they only devote themselves to what men do much better, leaving that which men do worse or not at all.

Edward Fitzgerald. (W. A. Wright, *Letters and Literary Remains of Edward Fitzgerald.*)

3 **220:20**

If every man's internal care
Were written on his brow,
How many would our pity share
Who have our envy now!

The fatal secret, when reveal'd,
Of every aching breast,
Would prove that only while conceal'd
Their lot appeared the best.

(Se a ciascun l'interno affanno
Si leggesse in fronte scritto,
Quanti mai, che invidia fanno,
Ci farebbero pietà!

Si vedría che i lor nemici
Anno in seno; e si riduce
Nel parere a noi felici
Ogni lor felicità.

Pietro Metastatio, *Giuseppe Riconosciuto*. Pt. i. (*Opere*, vol. vii, p. 266. Paris, 1780)

If mental sufferings we could read
Inscribed with truth upon each brow,
With pity then our hearts would bleed,
For those whom most we envy now!

Metastatio. (Charles Burney, tr., *Memoirs of the Life and Writings of the Abate Metastatio*. Vol. i, p. 354. 1796)

If all was written on the brow,
Which inwardly gives pain,
How many who are envied now
Compassion would obtain!

For oft, concealed within the breast,
They lodge their deadliest foe;
And being thought by others blest
Is all the bliss they know.

Metastatio. (James Glassford, tr., *Select Airs from Metastatio*. In his *Miscellanea*, p. 53. 1818)

Did every outward feature show
The inward pangs of secret woe,
How oft would those our pity know,
That now our envy move.

'Twould then be seen, in many a breast,
What cruel foes their peace molest;
And those, who seem to us so blest,
As wretched then would prove.

Metastatio. (John Hoole, tr., *Dramas and Other Poems of the Abbé Pietro Metastatio: The Discovery of Joseph*. Pt. i, iii, 374. 1800)

If each man's secret, unguessed care
Were written on his brow,
How many would our pity share
Who have our envy now!

And if the promptings of each heart
  No artifice concealed,
How many trusting friends would part
  At what they saw revealed.
  METASTATIO. (UNKNOWN, *What Others May Not See.*)

1 230:6

The more it changes, the more it's the same thing. (Plus ça change, plus c'est la même chose.)

ALPHONSE KARR, *Les Guêpes; Les Femmes,* Jan., 1849. (Edition Levy, vol. vi, p. 304.) In 1875, Karr used this phrase for the title of two volumes of articles dealing with the events of 1871. The first volume was called "Plus ça change," and the second, "Plus c'est la même chose."

Of all that I have written, stories, plays, history, criticism, fantaisie, verse and prose, if I have the rare and happy fortune to be survived by anything, it will be by two little phrases, three lines in all, very light baggage. . . . One is the résumé of my political studies —of what I have read and what I have seen— written in 1848: "The more it changes, the more it's the same thing." The other is older; it may be found in the *Guêpes* of 1840: "Let us abolish the death penalty—but let the assassins begin." (De tout ce que j'ai écrit, romans, pièces de théâtre, histoire, critique, fantaisie, vers et prose, etc., si j'ai cette rare et heureuse chance que quelque chose me survive, ce sera deux petites phrases composant trois lignes à elles deux, bagage bien léger. . . . L'une est un résumé de mes études politiques—de ce que j'ai lu et de ce que j'ai vu—je l'ai écrite en 1848: "Plus ça change, plus c'est la même chose." L'autre est plus ancienne; on la trouverait dans les *Guêpes* de 1840: "Abolissons la peine de mort, mais que messieurs les assassins commencent." (Begin: *i.e.* "do it first.")

ALPHONSE KARR, *Preface to Brochure.* (1885)

Oh, tear the gate from its rotted hinge!
Burst the bars of the musty cage!
Cross the river and burn the bridge!
I am a lover of things that change.
And shall I be changed on the Ultimate Day
To become a lover of things that stay?
  GARRETT OPPENHEIM, *Metamorphosis.*

2 264:10

My faith looks up to thee,
Thou Lamb of Calvary,
  Saviour Divine!
  RAY PALMER, *The Lamb of God.*

What can I give Him,
  Poor as I am?
If I were a shepherd
  I would bring a lamb,
If I were a wise man
  I would do my part—
Yet what can I give Him?
  Give my heart.
  CHRISTINA ROSSETTI, *A Christmas Carol.*

Jesus loves me—this I know,
For the Bible tells me so.
  SUSAN WARNER, *The Love of Jesus.*

Jesus shall reign where e'er the sun
Does his successive journeys run;
His kingdom stretch from shore to shore,
Till moons shall wax and wane no more.
  ISAAC WATTS, *The Psalms of David,* 186. (1719)

Joy to the world; the Lord is come;
  Let earth receive her King:
Let every heart prepare Him room,
  And Heaven and Nature sing.
  ISAAC WATTS, *The Psalms of David,* 253. (1719)

3 467:9

I do solemnly swear by that which I hold most sacred:
That I will be loyal to the profession of medicine and just and generous to its members;
That I will lead my life and practise my art in uprightness and honor;
That into whatsoever house I shall enter, it shall be for the good of the sick to the utmost of my power, I holding myself aloof from wrong, from corruption, and from the tempting of others to vice;
That I will exercise my art solely for the cure of my patients, and will give no drug, perform no operation for a criminal purpose, even if solicited, far less suggest it;
That whatsoever I shall see or hear of the lives of men which is not fitting to be spoken, I will keep inviolably secret.
These things I do promise, and in proportion as I am faithful to this my oath may happiness and good repute be ever mine—the opposite if I shall be forsworn.

The Hippocratic Oath. This oath, which probably originated with Hippocrates, about 400 B.C., and which certainly embodies the ideals of medical ethics for which he stood, has been subject to many revisions. The version given above is that made by the late Professor John G. Curtis, of the College of Physicians and Surgeons, and is a fairly close paraphrase of the Greek. In this form it is administered at each commencement to the candidates for the degree of Doctor of Medicine at Columbia, Cornell, and other universities. For modern version see p. 2298g:5.

4 501:10

  One evening in October,
  When I was far from sober,
And dragging home a load with manly pride,
  My feet began to stutter,
  So I laid down in the gutter,
And a pig came up and parked right by my side.
  Then I warbled, "It 's fair weather
  When good fellows get together,"
Till a lady passing by was heard to say:
  "You can tell a man who boozes
  By the company he chooses."
Then the pig got up and slowly walked away.
  BENJAMIN H. BURT. (DE WOLF HOPPER, *Once a Clown, Always a Clown,* p. 237.)

5 561:3

We know no spectacle so ridiculous as the British public in one of its periodical fits of morality. In general, elopements, divorces, and family quarrels, pass with little notice. We read the scandal, talk about it for a day, and forget it. But once in six or seven years our virtue becomes outrageous. We cannot suffer the laws of religion and decency to be violated. We must make a stand against vice. We must teach libertines that the English people appreciate the importance of domestic ties. Accordingly some unfortunate man, in no respect more depraved than hundreds whose offences have been treated with lenity, is singled out as an expiatory sacrifice. If he has children, they are to be taken from him. If he has a profession, he is to be driven from it. He is cut by the higher orders, and hissed by the lower. He is, in truth, a sort of whipping-boy, by whose vicarious agonies all the other transgressors of the same class are, it is supposed, sufficiently chastised. We reflect very complacently on our own severity, and compare with great pride the high standard of morals established in England with the Parisian laxity. At length our anger is satiated. Our victim is ruined and heart-broken. And our virtue goes quietly to sleep for seven years more.

MACAULAY, *Essays: Moore's Life of Lord Byron*. Paragraph 8.

1 630:8

If a man can write a better book, preach a better sermon, or make a better mouse-trap than his neighbor, though he builds his house in the woods, the world will make a beaten path to his door.

EMERSON. (*Borrowings*, p. 38. 1889) Since the discussion of the authorship of this quotation which appears on page 630 was written, a mass of new material has come into the hands of the compiler, but none of it invalidates, or even weakens, the opinion previously set forth, that the sentence is from a lecture delivered by Ralph Waldo Emerson at San Francisco or Oakland, California, in the spring of 1871. There is some reason to believe that it is from the lecture on "Chivalry," delivered May 17th at San Francisco, for Mr. James Bradley Thayer (*A Western Journey With Mr. Emerson*, p. 121) describes it as "extemporized from certain fragments, [he] having failed to find one of his best lectures that had been brought along, but lay hidden somewhere in his trunk." An interesting detail is the recent discovery in *The Saturday Evening Post* for 20 March, 1852, of an abstract of Emerson's lecture on "Wealth," in which occurs the following: "Every man must be bought at his own price in his own place. Lawyers agree that if a man understand the law he may open his office in a pine barrel, and the people will come to him when they want law." This points straight at the "mouse-trap" three years earlier than the famous entry in the *Journals* quoted on page 630. There is nothing resembling it, however, in the lecture on "Wealth" as printed in his works. Mr. David C. Mearns, of the Library of Congress, has pointed out the amusing coincidence that Jay Gould, in his youth, was the inventor of a mouse-trap, and that in later years he was the most distinguished member of the New York church of the Rev. John R. Paxton, whose friends have claimed that he, and not Emerson, was the author of the quotation. Nothing has been discovered to substantiate this claim; and further examination also confirms the flimsiness of Elbert Hubbard's case. It is perhaps enough to point out that Hubbard's first published writing appeared in 1893 (see the article on Hubbard in the *Dictionary of American Biography*), while the "mouse-trap" appeared in 1889. For a discussion of the evidence in detail, see STEVENSON, *Famous Single Poems*, revised (1935) edition, pp. 343–381.

1a

He dwelt with the tribes of the marsh and moor,
He sate at the board of kings;
He tasted the toil of the burdened slave
And the joy that triumph brings.
But whether to jungle or palace hall
Or white-walled tent he came,
He was brother to king and soldier and slave,
His welcome was the same.

HENRY CABOT LODGE, *Eulogy on Theodore Roosevelt*, 9 Feb., 1919. The assumption has been that this stanza was quoted from a poem by some unknown author, but intensive search has failed to discover it, and it seems probable that it was original with Senator Lodge.

2 638:15

In the life of a successful farmer . . . the year flows on harmoniously, fortunately: through ploughing, seed-time, growth of grain, the yellowing of it beneath meek autumn suns and big autumn moons, the cutting of it down, riotous harvest-home, final sale, and large balance at the banker's. From the point of view of almost unvarying success, the farmer's life becomes beautiful, poetic. Everything is an aid and a help to him. Nature puts her shoulder to his wheel. He takes the winds, the clouds, the sunbeams, the rolling stars into partnership, and, asking no dividend, they let him retain the entire profits.

ALEXANDER SMITH, *Dreamthorp: Men of Letters*.

3 673:7

I pledge allegiance to the flag of the United States and to the Republic for which it stands, one nation, indivisible, with liberty and justice for all. (Originally, "my flag.")

JAMES B. UPHAM AND FRANCIS BELLAMY, *Pledge to the Flag*. On 21 July, 1892, President Benjamin Harrison, in obedience to an act of Congress, issued a proclamation recommending that October 31, the four hundredth anniversary of the discovery of America, be celebrated everywhere by suitable exercises in the schools. The National Convention of Superintendents of Education appointed a committee to conduct the entire movement, and the chairman of this committee was Francis Bellamy, representing *The Youth's Companion*, a juvenile weekly published at Boston, Mass., which had taken a leading part in promoting the celebration. Under his direction the program was prepared, including the *Pledge to the Flag*, which was first published in *The Youth's Companion* 8 Sept., 1892 (vol. lv, no. 36, p. 446). In its issue for 20 Dec., 1917 (vol. xci, no. 51, p. 722), the *Companion* printed a short account of how the pledge came to be written, stating that "in 1888 the late James B. Upham, then a member of the Perry Mason Company [publishers of *The Youth's Companion*], began the great work of rousing public opinion . . . to the opportunity of fostering patriotism by putting the Stars and Stripes over every schoolhouse in the United States. . . . Mr. Upham had already written a form of pledge very much like that which is now so well known, and with the help of other members of the firm and of members of the editorial staff the present and final form was written." This indicates that Mr. Upham was the author of the first draft of the pledge, and that Mr. Bellamy assisted in putting it into its final shape.

1 726:5

I disapprove of what you say, but I will defend to the death your right to say it.

Attributed to VOLTAIRE, by S. G. Tallentyre (E. Beatrice Hall), an English writer, in her book, *The Friends of Voltaire* (p. 199), published in England in 1906. The sentence was enclosed in quotation marks, and was supposed to have been written in a letter to Claude Adrien Helvétius, referring to his book, *De l'Esprit*, which Voltaire greatly admired. The quotation was so striking that it was widely quoted, but an exhaustive search through Voltaire's letters to Helvétius failed to disclose it, and finally Miss Tallentyre was asked where it could be found. In a letter to Mr. Harry Weinberger, of New York City, dated 20 July, 1935, she says: "I believe I did use the phrase as a description of Voltaire's attitude on Helvétius' book *On the Mind*. I did not intend to imply that Voltaire used these words verbatim, and should be surprised if they are found in any of his works. They are rather a paraphrase of Voltaire's words in the *Essay on Tolerance*, 'Think for yourselves, and let others enjoy the privilege to do so too.'" Of course Miss Tallentyre's sentence is not in any way a paraphrase of this one, but it may very fairly be held to paraphrase a passage in Voltaire's *Philosophical Dictionary* referring to Helvétius:

I liked the author of *De l'Esprit*. . . . But I have never approved either the errors of his book, or the trivial truths which he so emphatically enforced. I have, however, boldly taken his part when absurd men have condemned him for these very truths. (J'aimais l'auteur du livre *De l'Esprit*. . . . Mais je n'ai jamais approvó ni les erreurs de son livre, ni les vérités triviales qu'il débite avec emphase. J'ai pris son parti hautement quand des hommes absurdes l'ont condamné pour ces vérités mêmes.)

VOLTAIRE, *Dictionnaire Philosophique: Homme.*

2 928:13

Veterinary Surgeon: Legs queer, Sir! Do you 'ack 'im or 'unt 'im?

Proprietor of Quadruped: I hunt him sometimes; but I mostly use him as a hack.

Veterinary Surgeon: Ah, Sir, that's where it is. It ain't the 'unting as 'urts 'im, it's the 'ammer, 'ammer, 'ammer along the 'ard 'ighroad.

JOHN LEECH, *Caption*, of cartoon in London *Punch*, 31 May, 1856.

3 1063:4

God walks among the pots and pipkins.

SAINT TERESA.

Lord of the pots and pipkins, since I have no time to be
A saint by doing lovely things and vigilling with Thee,
By watching in the twilight dawn, and storming Heaven's gates,
Make me a saint by getting meals, and washing up the plates!

CECILY HALLACK, *Divine Office of the Kitchen*. The title is followed by the line, "God walks among the pots and pipkins.—Saint Teresa." The poem was composed, so Miss Hallack states, as a message to a girl friend who complained that domestic drudgery was spoiling her hands for violin playing. In some way this got twisted in the head of Dr. G. Campbell Morgan, the famous London preacher, and at a service in Westminster Chapel in the summer of 1928, he read the poem from the pulpit, announcing that it had been written by an English servant girl of nineteen. Mr. John D. Rockefeller, Sr., heard of it and was so moved by this extraordinary piety that he had some copies of the poem printed under the title, *Lord of All Pots and Pans*. ascribing it to the aforesaid servant girl, and distributed them at Lakewood, N. J., on a Sunday early in April, 1929. The legend thus started still survives. (See *Literary Digest*, 2 March, 1929, p. 36.)

4 1091:24

We have an expression in New York, when we meet a very difficult problem—"You will have to get a Philadelphia lawyer to solve that." Few people know that there is a basis of truth in the expression, for in 1735, when no New York lawyer could be obtained to defend John Peter Zenger, accused of criminal libel, because his two lawyers, James Alexander and William Smith, having challenged the jurisdiction of the court, had already been disbarred, the friends of Zenger came to Philadelphia and obtained the services of Andrew Hamilton, then eighty years of age, to go to New York without fee, and defend the action in the face of a hostile court.

HARRY WEINBERGER, *The Liberty of the Press.* Address at Independence Hall, Philadelphia, 9 March, 1934.

1 1103:12

The world has never had a good definition of the word liberty, and the American people, just now, are much in want of one. We all declare for liberty; but in using the same word we do not all mean the same thing. With some the word liberty may mean for each man to do as he pleases with himself, and the product of his labor; while with others the same word may mean for some men to do as they please with other men, and the product of other men's labor. Here are two, not only different, but incompatible things, called by the same name, liberty. And it follows that each of the things is, by the respective parties, called by two different and incompatible names—liberty and tyranny.

ABRAHAM LINCOLN, *Address,* Baltimore, Md., 18 April, 1864.

2 1242:5

Like to the falling of a Star;
Or as the flights of Eagles are.

HENRY KING (?), *Sic Vita.* Bishop Henry King's authorship of these lines, which are given in full on page 1242, has often been challenged on the ground that his *Poems,* in which they occur, were not published until 1657, whereas they had already appeared in Francis Beaumont's *Poems,* published in 1640. Nevertheless, scholars are pretty generally of the opinion that they belong to King, whose verses, after the fashion of the time, were circulated in manuscript form for many years before they were collected and printed. (See Lawrence Mason's unpublished thesis on King, in the Yale University Memorial Library.) The verses were imitated by Francis Quarles, John Philpot, Simon Wastell, and many others, Dr. Mason having unearthed fifteen poems written on this model. Here are two of them:

Like to the Bubble in the brook,
Or in a glass much like a look, . . .
Even such is Man, who lives by breath;
Is here, now there: so life, and death.

UNKNOWN, *Verses of Man's Mortality.* (SPARKES, *Crumbs of Comfort.* 1628.) Sometimes attributed to Simon Wastell.

Like to the damask Rose you see,
Or like the Blossom on the tree,
Or like the dainty Flower of May,
Or like the Morning to the day,
Or like the Sun, or like the Shade,
Or like the Gou-d that Jonas had;
Even such is Man whose thread is spun,
Drawn out and cut, and so is done.
The Rose withers, the Blossom blasteth,
The Flower fades, the Morning hasteth:
The Sun sets, the Shadow flies,
The Gourd consumes, and Man he dies.

FRANCIS QUARLES, *Hos Ego Versiculos.* (*Argalus and Parthenia.* 1629.) These lines had been printed anonymously in Sparkes' *Crumbs of Comfort,* in 1628, as the beginning of a poem of seventy-two lines. They have been attributed to Simon Wastell, but were claimed by Quarles.

There is, however, yet another piece attributed to King which has considerable interest both in itself and as illustrating a peculiarity of the time. There was still, on the one hand, a certain shyness in regard to the formal publication of poetry, and, on the other, the inveterate habit of handing about MS. copies of verses, with the result that ill-informed persons entered them in their albums, and piratical, or, at least, enterprising publishers issued them in collections, under different names. The instance at present referred to is the curious batch of similes for the shortness and instability of life sometimes entitled *Sic Vita.* . . . There can be no doubt that King was quite equal to composing . . . them; but his authorship is a question of less interest than the way in which the circumstances illustrate the manners and taste of the time.

GEORGE SAINTSBURY, *Lesser Caroline Poets.* (*Cambridge History of English Literature,* vol. vii, p. 94.)

[There is] detailed evidence to establish the overwhelming probability of Henry King's authorship, . . . as well as the reasonable probability of his priority in employing the stanzaic form involved. . . . The title may well have been taken from King's favorite Petronius, cap. 45: "sic vita truditur."

LAWRENCE MASON, *English Poems of Henry King,* p. 207, note.

What is not today, will be tomorrow: so we trudge through life. (Quod hodie non est, cras erit: sic vita truditur.)

PETRONIUS, *Satyricon.* Ch. 45. See 2021:11.

3 1398:2

Vulgar of manner, overfed,
Overdressed and underbred;
Heartless, Godless, hell's delight,
Rude by day and lewd by night;
Bedwarfed the man, o'ergrown the brute,
Ruled by Jew and prostitute;
Purple-robed and pauper-clad,
Raving, rotting, money-mad;
A squirming herd in Mammon's mesh,
A wilderness of human flesh;
Crazed with avarice, lust and rum,
New York, thy name's Delirium.

BYRON R. NEWTON, *Owed to New York.* Claimed by Mr. Newton in the N. Y. *Times Book Review,* 26 April, 1925. He states that he wrote the lines in 1906 to be read at a dinner of the staff of the N. Y. *Herald.*

4 1465:14

I vow to thee, my country—all earthly things above—
Entire and whole and perfect, the service of my love,

The love that asks no questions: the love that
 stands the test,
That lays upon the altar the dearest and the
 best:
The love that never falters, the love that pays
 the price,
The love that makes undaunted the final
 sacrifice.

CECIL SPRING-RICE, *I Vow to Thee, My Country.*

1 1491:12

My grandad, viewing earth's worn cogs,
Said things were going to the dogs;
His grandad in his house of logs
Swore things were going to the dogs;
His grandad in the Flemish bogs
Vowed things were going to the dogs;
His grandad in his old skin togs
Said things were going to the dogs.
Well, there's one thing I have to state:
Those dogs have had a good long wait.

UNKNOWN, *Going to the Dogs.* Sometimes attributed to Dr. George B. Cutten, President of Colgate University, who writes to the compiler: "No matter how much I should like to claim the authorship, my Pilgrim conscience will not permit me to do so. I got the verses from my brother, who told me that he had got them from the Boston *Post* in the early part of the century."

2 1525:2

Another of Addison's favourite companions was Ambrose Philips, a good Whig and a middling poet, who had the honour of bringing into fashion a species of composition which had been called, after his name, Namby Pamby.

MACAULAY, *Essays: Addison.*

A lady of quality . . . sends her waiting gentlewoman to namby-pamby me.

MARIA EDGEWORTH, *The Absentee.* Ch. 16.

3 1546:1

For the present, if we glance into that Assembly-Hall of theirs, it will be found, as is natural, "most irregular." . . . Rudiments of Methods disclose themselves; rudiments of Parties. There is a Right Side (Côté Droit), a Left Side (Côté Gauche); sitting on M. le President's right hand, or on his left. The Côté Droit conservative; the Côté Gauche destructive.

CARLYLE, *The French Revolution.* Bk. vi, ch. 2. Referring to the French Constituent Assembly, of July, 1789. The *Oxford Dictionary* states that "left" was first applied to persons of "more advanced or innovating" views in 1837, which was the date of publication of Carlyle's history. "Right," as applied to conservatives, goes much farther back, to Shakespeare, in fact, for in *Coriolanus,* ii, 1, 26, Menenius, who a few lines farther on described himself as a "humorous patrician," asks of the two tribunes, Sicinius and Brutus: "Do you two know how you are censured here in the city, I mean by us o' the right-hand file?" and adds that the "right-hand file," that is, the conservatives, find them fools, "ambitious for poor knaves' caps and legs."

Politics—Familiar Phrases

(*Continued from page 1556*)

4

I know, sir, that it is the habit of some gentlemen to speak with censure or reproach of the politics of New York. . . . It may be, sir, that the politicians of New York are not as fastidious as some gentlemen are as to disclosing the principles on which they act. They boldly preach what they practice. When they are not contending for victory, they avow their intention of enjoying the fruits of it. . . . They see nothing wrong in the rule that to the victor belong the spoils of the enemy.

WILLIAM L. MARCY, U. S. Senator from New York, *Speech,* during a debate in 1832, on the confirmation of Martin Van Buren as Minister to England, defending him from the attacks of Henry Clay.

5

"Vote early and vote often," the advice openly displayed on the election banners in one of our northern cities.

W. P. MILES, of South Carolina, *Speech,* House of Representatives, 31 March, 1858.

6

Mournfully I prophesy that the program of these sons of the wild jackass who now control the Senate will probably go forward to complete consummation.

GEORGE H. MOSES, *Speech,* at a dinner of New England manufacturers, Washington, D. C., 7 Nov., 1929, referring to the so-called insurgent Republicans in the U. S. Senate, Borah, Brookhart, Johnson, La Follette, Norris, Nye, Shipstead, and Wheeler. Mr. Moses was at that time Senator from New Hampshire, a rock-ribbed Republican, and was discussing the difficulty of getting any legislation for higher tariffs through the Senate, because of the coalition which the insurgent Republicans had formed with the Democratic members. He afterwards stated that he had adapted the phrase, "Sons of the wild jackass," from the *Old Testament: Jeremiah,* xiv, 6: "And the wild asses did stand in the high places, they snuffed up the wind like dragons." Senator Simeon Fess, of Ohio, called the same group "pseudo-Republicans"; Charles Francis Adams, Secretary of the Treasury, referred to them as "hybrids"; James Francis Burke, of the White House patronage committee, branded them as "pigmies"; and Senator David A. Reed, of Pennsylvania, said they were "more dangerous than Communists." All of which publicity the "insurgents" greatly enjoyed. There was a stormy debate in the Senate over the Moses utterance on the following day, 8 Nov., 1929.

1
Cradle of American liberty.
JAMES OTIS, referring to Faneuil Hall, Boston. (*See* WINSOR, *Memorial History of Boston.* Vol. ii, p. 524.) For Webster's use of the phrase, see 64:5.

2
Abstain from beans. (Ἀπέχεσθαι τῶν κυάμων.)
PYTHAGORAS. (ARISTOTLE, *On the Pythagoreans.*) According to Aristotle, this Pythagorean rule had nothing to do with politics; beans were banished from the diet because they resembled the testicles. (See DIOGENES LAERTIUS, *Pythagoras.* Bk. viii, sec. 34.) However, the same word was used for the lot by which officials at Athens were chosen. (ὁ κυάμῳ λαχών), and the phrase was given that meaning. Diogenes Laertius states that Pythagoras was captured and killed by some enemies pursuing him because he refused to cross a field of beans.

Abstain from beans. There be sundry interpretations of this symbol. But Plutarch and Cicero think beans to be forbidden of Pythagoras, because they be windy and do engender impure humours and for that cause provoke bodily lust.
RICHARD TAVERNER, *Proverbs.* Fo. 1 . (1539)

To abstain from beans, that is, not to meddle in civil affairs or business of the commonweal, for in old times the election of Magistrates was made by the pulling of beans.
JOHN LYLY, *Euphues,* p. 148. (1579)

I read a Latin proverb, 'A fabis abstineto,' (forbear beans); whereof some make a civil interpretation. 'Meddle not with the matters of state'; because anciently men cast in a bean when they gave their suffrages in public elections.
THOMAS FULLER, *Worthies of England,* ii, 225. (1662)

3
The coalition of Blifil and Black George—the combination, unheard of till then, of the puritan with the blackleg.
JOHN RANDOLPH OF ROANOKE, *Speech,* House of Representatives, 30 March, 1826. (*Register of Debates,* II, pt. i, 19 Cong., 1st session, col. 401.) Referring to the alliance of John Quincy Adams and Henry Clay. The result of this denunciation was a duel with Clay, fought on the Virginia side of the Potomac, 8 April, 1826. Clay's second shot pierced the skirt of Randolph's coat, but Randolph himself fired in the air. Blifil and Black George are disreputable characters in Fielding's *Tom Jones.*

4
Prosperity will not be obtained from the Federal government. It will come, when it comes, from the grass roots, from where it always must come.
JAMES A. REED, formerly U. S. Senator from Missouri, *Speech,* after F. D. Roosevelt's nomination as Democratic candidate for President, 1 July, 1932, appealing for party harmony. Reed repudiated Roosevelt in 1935, and campaigned against him in 1936.

The real test of party strength is down close to the grass roots.
CALVIN COOLIDGE, *Political Parties.* (1934)

Grass roots convention.
The name adopted by a convention of Midwest Republicans, which met at Springfield, Ill., in June, 1935, to discuss ways of combating the New Deal. Said to have originated with John D. M. Hamilton, of Topeka, Kansas, who became manager of the ill-fated Landon campaign in 1936.

5
Our policy is "Nothing is no good."
WILL ROGERS, *The Illiterate Digest.*

6
The whole tendency over many years has been to view the interstate commerce clause in the light of present-day civilization, although it was written into the Constitution in the horse-and-buggy days of the eighteenth century.
PRESIDENT FRANKLIN D. ROOSEVELT, at a press conference at the White House, 31 May, 1935. He was commenting on the unanimous decision of the U. S. Supreme Court in the Schechter case. rendered a few days previously, in which the National Recovery Administration had been declared unconstitutional, and suggesting that the Constitution was antiquated and must be modernized. The N. R. A., which had adopted the Blue Eagle as its emblem, had in 1933–4 been the most spectacular activity of the Roosevelt administration in attempting to regulate all the business of the country by the use of codes and penalties, but the Supreme Court ended it abruptly by ruling unanimously that the Federal Government had no constitutional right to interfere with any business not engaged in interstate commerce. The phrase "horse-and-buggy days" was seized upon by the administration's critics as an apt characterization of the peaceful era to which the country should be happy to return. (The newspaper reports of Mr. Roosevelt's remarks vary somewhat. The one used here is from the New York *Times,* 1 June, 1935.)

7
I hope that your committee will not permit doubt as to constitutionality, however reasonable, to block the suggested legislation.
PRESIDENT FRANKLIN D. ROOSEVELT, *Letter,* to Representative Samuel B. Hill, referring to the Guffey Coal Control Bill, which was being investigated by a House committee of which Mr. Hill was chairman, in July, 1935.

8
I am as strong as a bull moose and you can use me to the limit.
THEODORE ROOSEVELT, *Letter to Mark Hanna,* at opening of the campaign in 1900. (BISHOP, *Theodore Roosevelt and His Times.* Vol. i, p. 139.)

It takes more than that to kill a Bull Moose.
THEODORE ROOSEVELT, *Speech,* at Milwaukee,

Wis., on the evening of the attempt to assassinate him, 14 Oct., 1912. He had received a bullet in the chest.

Bull Moose, an emblem of the Progressive Party in 1912, originated from the statement of President Roosevelt made upon his arrival at Chicago just before the Republican convention, that he felt like a "Bull Moose."

E. C. SMITH, *Dictionary of American Politics*. The first discovered newspaper use of the term was in the New York *Tribune*, 26 June, 1912. The New York *Times* used it the following day.

I want to be a Bull Moose,
And with the Bull Moose stand
With Antlers on my forehead
And a Big Stick in my hand.

UNKNOWN, *Inscription*, on California campaign banner at Bull Moose convention, 1912.

1
I took the canal zone and let Congress debate, and while the debate goes on the canal does also.

THEODORE ROOSEVELT, referring to his action in recognizing the Republic of Panama, immediately following its secession from Colombia. (New York *Times*, 24 March, 1911.)

2
My hat's in the ring. The fight is on and I'm stripped to the buff.

THEODORE ROOSEVELT, *Newspaper Interview*, at Cleveland, Ohio, 21 Feb., 1912, while on his way to Columbus to address the State Constitutional Convention.

When a man says at breakfast in the morning, "No, thank you, I will not take any more coffee," it does not mean that he will not take any more coffee tomorrow morning, or next week, or next month, or next year.

LYMAN ABBOTT, *Editorial, The Outlook*, 17 Feb., 1912. (Vol. c, p. 338.) Mr. Abbott was arguing that Theodore Roosevelt's statement, while serving his second term as President, that he would not be a candidate for a third term, referred only to a third *consecutive* term.

Any one can issue manifestoes.

THOMAS C. PLATT, referring to Theodore Roosevelt's first message as Governor of New York, 1899, in which a number of reforms were proposed. (ALEXANDER, *Four Famous New Yorkers*, p. 326.)

3
Don't hit at all if it is honorably possible to avoid hitting; but *never* hit soft.

THEODORE ROOSEVELT. (J. B. BISHOP, *Theodore Roosevelt* Vol. ii, p. 437.)

It is no advantage to change the Barneses, the Guggenheims and the Penroses, for the Murphys, the Sullivans and the Taggarts.

THEODORE ROOSEVELT, *Speech*, in campaign against Wilson and Taft in 1912.

Dear Maria.

THEODORE ROOSEVELT, *Letter to Mrs. Bellamy Storer*, 9 Dec., 1906.

4
We fight in honorable fashion for the good of mankind; fearless of the future, unheeding of our individual fates, with unflinching hearts and undimmed eyes; we stand at Armageddon, and we battle for the Lord.

THEODORE ROOSEVELT, *Speech*, at Chicago, 17 June, 1912, on the eve of the Republican National Convention which re-nominated Taft.

We seemed to see our flag unfurled,
Our champion waiting in his place
For the last battle of the world,—
The Armageddon of the race.

J. G. WHITTIER, *Rantoul*.

And he gathered them together into a place called in the Hebrew tongue Armageddon.

New Testament: Revelation, xvi, 16. Armageddon, or Har-Magedon, meant Mount Megiddo, possibly Mount Carmel, at whose foot lay the plain of Megiddo, the scene of many battles.

5
Salamander? Call it Gerrymander.

BENJAMIN RUSSELL, *Retort*, in 1811, to Gilbert Stuart, the celebrated painter. Russell was editor of the Massachusetts *Centinel*, and had hung on the wall of his office a map showing the proposed redistricting of Essex County, which the Democratic legislature was putting through in order to give them control of the district. Russell had blocked the new district off in color, and Stuart, coming in one day and looking at the map, remarked that it resembled a monstrous animal, and took a pencil and added claws. "There," he said, "that will do for a salamander." "Salamander?" echoed Russell. "Call it Gerrymander," and coined a word which has passed into the language to describe sinuous political redistricting. The point of the retort was that the Governor of Massachusetts was named Elbridge Gerry, and it was he who was supposed to have instigated the redistricting, though, as it developed later, he was opposed to it. It should be noted that his name was pronounced with a hard "g." (See BUCKINGHAM, *Specimens of Newspaper Writing*, vol. ii, p. 91; *Dictionary of American Biography*, vol. xvi, p. 238.) Mr. John Ward Dean in an article in the *New England Historical and Genealogical Register* (vol. xlvi, p. 374), questions the attribution of the phrase to Mr. Russell, citing a contemporary statement of Samuel Batchelder, of Cambridge, to the effect that the claws were added by Elkanah Tisdale, a miniature painter, and that the name "gerrymander" was suggested by Richard Alsop, a once-noted political satirist. Another account attributes it to James Ogilvie, a lecturer on oratory.

6
I have come home to look after my fences.

JOHN SHERMAN, *Speech*, to his neighbors at Mansfield, Ohio, referring to the fences around his farm; said to be the origin of the political phrase. (See STODDARD, *As I Knew Them*, p. 161.)

1

I will not accept if nominated, and will not serve if elected.

WILLIAM TECUMSEH SHERMAN, *Telegram*, to General Henderson of Missouri, 5 June, 1884. Henderson was at the Republican National Convention at Chicago, and had repeatedly urged Sherman to accept the nomination for President, which Sherman had steadily refused to do. The telegram was in answer to a last urgent appeal. See SHERMAN, *Memoirs*, 4th edition, p. 466. This final chapter was added by members of Sherman's family after his death, and the text of the telegram as given is on the evidence of his son, Thomas. It is usually quoted, "If nominated I will not accept; if elected I will not serve." On 25 May, Sherman had written to James G. Blaine, "I will not in any event entertain or accept a nomination as candidate for President. . . . I would account myself a fool, a madman, an ass, to embark now, at sixty-five years of age, in a career that may at any moment become tempestuous." See *North Amer. Review*, Dec., 1888.

2

Hello, my old potato.

ALFRED E. SMITH, to Franklin D. Roosevelt, at the Democratic State Convention, at Albany, N. Y., 4 Oct., 1932. It was the first meeting of the two men since Roosevelt had defeated Smith for the presidential nomination at the Democratic National Convention at Chicago on 1 July, after a bitter contest, accentuated by Smith's feeling that he had been betrayed. It has been denied that Smith actually said this, but in a letter to the compiler he writes: "At the State Convention for the nomination of Governor, President Roosevelt was on the platform as I came up to place Governor Lehman's name in nomination and I said to him, 'Hello, my old potato.'"

"Well, ta ta, my turnip!" observed Mr. Waddle, and away the coaches rattled in opposite directions.

HENRY COCKTON, *Valentine Vox*. Ch. 5. (1840)

3

What a man that would be had he . . . the least knowledge of the value of red tape.

SYDNEY SMITH, referring to Sir James Mackintosh. (LADY HOLLAND, *Memoir*, p. 245.)

4

In your war of 1812, your arms on shore were covered by disaster. . . . Who first relit the fires of national glory and made the welkin ring with the shouts of victory?

SENATOR R. F. STOCKTON, *Speech*, U. S. Senate, 7 Jan., 1852, against flogging in the navy. (*Congressional Globe*, v. 21, pt. 1, p. 219, col. 3.)

5

Hanna was *a* fat-frier, not *the* fat-frier. *The* fat-frier was John P. Forster, president of the League of Young Republican Clubs. It was in 1888 that he wrote a letter suggesting 'to fry the fat out of the manufacturers,' i. e., secure campaign contributions.

HENRY L. STODDARD, *As I Knew Them*.

6

You can't beat somebody with nobody.

MARK SULLIVAN, *Our Times*, iii, 289. Quoted as an axiom of practical politics. Usually attributed to "Uncle Joe" Cannon, Speaker of the House of Representatives for many years.

One truth which they enforce is the old one that you can't beat somebody with nobody.

Editorial, N. Y. *Times*, 3 July, 1932.

7

Congressmen? In Washington they hitch horses to them.

TIMOTHY D. (BIG TIM) SULLIVAN, of New York City, announcing his decision to retire from the House of Representatives and return to the New York State Senate.

8

The Forgotten Man works and votes—generally he prays—but his chief business in life is to pay. . . . If any student of social science comes to appreciate the case of the Forgotten Man, he will become . . . a hard-hearted skeptic as regards any scheme of social amelioration. He will always want to know, Who and where is the Forgotten Man in this case, who will have to pay for it all?

WILLIAM GRAHAM SUMNER, *The Forgotten Man*. (Title essay in *The Forgotten Man and Other Essays*, 1883.)

The State cannot get a cent for any man without taking it from some other man, and this latter must be a man who has produced and saved it. The latter is the Forgotten Man.

WILLIAM GRAHAM SUMNER, *What Social Classes Owe to Each Other*. As will be seen from the above, Mr. Sumner's "forgotten man" was the taxpayer.

The Forgotten Man was never more completely forgotten than he is now. Congress does not know that he exists. The President [Warren G. Harding] suspects that there is such a person, who may turn up at the polls in November, but he is not quite sure.

FRANK I. COBB, *Editorial*, New York *World*, Sept., 1922.

These unhappy times call for the building of plans that rest upon the forgotten, the unorganized but indispensable units of economic power, for plans like those of 1917 that build from the bottom up and not from the top down, that put their faith once more in the forgotten man at the bottom of the economic pyramid.

FRANKLIN D. ROOSEVELT, *Radio Address*, 7 April, 1932. It will be noted that Mr. Roosevelt's "forgotten man" bears no resemblance to Mr. Sumner's.

The Forgotten Man is a myth.

ALFRED E. SMITH, *Editorial, The New Outlook*, October, 1932, p. 3.

9

Talking for Buncombe.

FELIX WALKER, *Speech on the Missouri Bill*,

House of Representatives, 25 Feb., 1820. Walker was a Representative from North Carolina, and Buncombe County was part of his district. He was a naïve old mountaineer, familiarly called "the old oil-jug" because of his flow of language, and toward the close of the debate on the Missouri Bill, while the House was impatiently calling for the question, he rose to speak. Several members urged him to desist, but he refused, stating that he was bound "to make a speech for Buncombe." For a full account of the incident, see the communication from Dr. William Darlington in *The Historical Magazine,* Oct., 1858. (Vol. i, no. 10, p. 311.) Dr. Darlington was a member of the House at the time and was seated near Walker when he coined the phrase. His account is partially confirmed by a passage in the *Annals of Congress* (16th Cong., 1st sess., vol. xxxvi, col. 1539) which states, under date of 25 Feb., 1820: "Mr. Walker, of North Carolina, rose then to address the Committee on the question; but the question was called for so clamorously and so perseveringly that Mr. W. could proceed no farther than to move that the Committee rise." The phrase has been erroneously attributed to John Culpepper by Joseph T. Buckingham (*Personal Memoirs and Recollections of Editorial Life,* vol. i, p. 207, footnote), but no evidence is given to prove the attribution, and while Mr. Culpepper was also a Congressman from North Carolina, Buncombe County was not in his district. One A. Wilder, writing in *Miscellaneous Notes and Queries* (Manchester, N. H.) April, 1887 (vol. iv, no. 4, p. 287), attributes the phrase to Thomas L. Clingman, but Clingman did not enter Congress until 1843, and the phrase was in use long before that, as is shown by the following:

"Talking to Bunkum!" This is an old and common saying at Washington, when a member of Congress is making one of these hum-drum and unlistened-to "long talks" which have lately become so fashionable—not with the hope of being heard in the House, but to afford an enlightened representative a pretence for sending a copy of his speech to his constituents. . . . This is cantly called "Talking to Bunkum": an "honorable gentleman" long ago, having said that he was not talking to the House, but to the people of a certain county in his district, which, in local phrase, he called "Bunkum."

UNKNOWN (*Niles' Weekly Register,* 27 Sept., 1828. Vol. xxxv, no. 889, p. 66.)

Several years ago, in Congress, the member from this immediate district [Buncombe County, N. C.] arose to address the House, without any extraordinary powers either in manner or matter to interest his audience. Many members left the hall. Very naïvely, he told those who were so kind as to remain that they might go too; for he should speak for some time, but he was only talking for Buncombe.

JOHN WHEELER, *Historical Sketches of North Carolina.* Vol. ii, p. 52. (1851)

Talk plain truth, and leave bunkum for right honorables who keep their places thereby.

CHARLES KINGSLEY, *Two Years Ago.* Ch. 25.

America too will find that caucuses, division-lists, stump-oratory, and speeches to Buncombe will not carry men to the immortal gods.

CARLYLE, *Latter-Day Pamphlets: Parliaments.*

1

Now is the time for all good men to come to the aid of the party.

CHARLES E. WELLER. A sentence devised to test the practicability of the first typewriter, constructed at Milwaukee, Wis., by Christopher Latham Sholes, in the autumn of 1867. (See WELLER, *The Early History of the Typewriter.*) Mr. Weller was a court reporter and a friend of Sholes. He says: "We were then in the midst of an exciting political campaign and it was then for the first time that the sentence was inaugurated . . . and repeated many times to test the speed of the machine." It is still in use, and *The New Yorker* (1 Feb., 1936, p. 12) states that there are also test sentences for the telephone and the telegraph. The Bell Laboratories use "Joe took father's shoe-bench out" to test the volume of its phones, and "Some settlers suggest settling southern settlements in succession" to test articulation. The Western Union uses "William Jax quickly taught five dozen Republicans" to test its teletypewriters, and for radio-telephony, the American Telephone and Telegraph Company uses "The barking dog's bark is worse than its bite."

2

Pitiless publicity.

WOODROW WILSON. His prescription for curing the ills of government. (SULLIVAN, *Our Times,* iv, 119.) See 1653:10.

They released a letter written five years earlier by Wilson to Adrian Joline, expressing the wish that "something at once dignified and effective" might be done to "knock Bryan once and for all into a cocked hat."

PAXTON HIBBEN, *The Peerless Leader,* p. 303.

3

To seek for political flaws is no use;
His opponents will find he is sound on the goose.

UNKNOWN. (Providence *Journal,* 18 June, 1857.) "Sound on the goose" meant orthodox as to opinions and sentiments, on the popular side of any discussion.

4

The Copperhead Bright Convention meets in Indianapolis today.

UNKNOWN. (Cincinnati *Gazette,* 30 July, 1862.)

A glorious sequel to the Copperhead convention.

UNKNOWN. (Cincinnati *Gazette,* 31 July, 1862.) Both references were to the Indiana Democratic convention, and are the earliest printed use of the word "copperhead" in this connection. James Ford Rhodes (*History of the United States,* iv, 224) states that the earliest use of the word he could find was in the Cincinnati *Commercial*, of 1 Oct., 1862. Albert Matthews (*Publications of the Colonial Society of Massachusetts*, xx, 207) states that he found it in the Chicago *Tribune*, for 24 Sept., 1862. (PAUL S. SMITH, *First Use of the Term Copperhead, American Historical Review*, xxxii, 799.)

Every Democrat who did not openly and actively support the Administration and the war was labelled a venomous 'copperhead,' at once a southern sympathiser and a traitor to the Union.

MILO ERWIN, *History of Williamson County, Illinois*, p. 302.

As the copperhead is a particularly poisonous snake indigenous to southern Illinois the meaning was clear.

PAXTON HIBBEN, *The Peerless Leader*, p. 25.

1

The Mysterious Stranger.

In the election of 1904, the state of Missouri for the first time appeared in the Republican column. On November 10, John T. McCutcheon published a cartoon in the Chicago *Tribune* with this caption, which instantly became famous. A fragment by Mark Twain called *The Mysterious Stranger* was published in 1916.

3 1636:8

Doctor Livingstone, I presume?

HENRY M. STANLEY to David Livingstone, when he found the latter in the heart of the African jungle, 10 Nov., 1871. Stanley's expedition had been financed by James Gordon Bennett, publisher of the New York *Herald*, and on 2 July, 1872, *The Herald* printed an account of the meeting in a "special from Central Africa." Here is its description of the crucial moment:

Preserving a calmness of exterior before the Arabs which was hard to simulate as he reached the group, Mr. Stanley said:—

"Doctor Livingstone, I presume?"

A smile lit up the features of the hale white man as he answered:—

"Yes, that is my name."

4 1636:10

"Tell it to the Marines." The time of the saying was toward eleven of the clock on an autumn morning in the year of our Lord one thousand six hundred and sixty-four; the place, the Green Park of St. James. It so befell that His light-hearted Majesty Charles the Second, with an exceedingly bored expression upon his swarthy face, was strolling in the shade with the ingenious Mr. Samuel Pepys, Secretary to the Admiralty. [Pepys tells the King an anecdote about flying fish having been seen in the waters of the Indies by the officers of a British ship. The King is incredulous and turns to a Colonel of the newly-raised Marine Regiment, who happens to be near.]

"What say you, Colonel, to a man who swears he hath seen fishes fly in the air?"

"I should say, Sire," returned the sea-soldier simply, "that the man hath sailed in southern seas. For, when Your Majesty's business carried me there of late, I did frequently observe more flying fish in one hour than the hairs of my head in number."

His Majesty glanced narrowly at the Colonel's frank, weather-beaten face. Then, with a laugh, he turned to the Secretary.

"Mr. Pepys," said he, "from the very nature of their calling, no class of our subjects can have so wide a knowledge of seas and lands as the officers and men of our loyal Marine Regiment. Henceforward ere we cast doubts upon a tale that lacketh likelihood, we will first tell it to the Marines."

W. P. DRURY, *The Tadpole of an Archangel, The Petrified Eye, and Other Naval Stories: Preface*. (1904)

The story of "Tell it to the Marines" is taken from my earliest literary crime, *The Petrified Eye*. It is a leg-pull of my youth of which I have grown a little ashamed. I seem to have forged the style of Samuel Pepys so successfully that many of our comrades have wasted time hunting thru the diary to verify my statement.

W. P. DRURY, *Letter*, to Brig.-Gen. George Richards, U. S. Marine Corps. (See N. Y. *Sun*, 4 Feb., 1931.) Mr. Drury is himself a retired Colonel of the British Marine Corps.

Song: Familiar Refrains

(*Continued from page 1883*)

5

A face behind a mask,
  A pair of dreamy eyes,
A smile that drags you downward,
  From the gates of Paradise;
Forgive, but don't forget,
  These warning words I ask,
For such a face, brought my disgrace,
  A face behind a mask.

WILL D. COBB, *A Face Behind a Mask*. (1900) Music by Ben M. Jerome. Popularized by Bettina Girard.

For I just can't make my eyes behave,
Two bad brown eyes, I am their slave;
My lips may say, "Run away from me,"
But my eyes say, "Come and play with me."

WILL D. COBB, *I Just Can't Make My Eyes Behave*. (1906) Sung with great éclat by Anna Held in *A Parisian Model*.

For a woman loves forever, but a man loves for a day;
She makes him a god for her worship, he makes her a toy for his play;
For the man is the guest at the banquet where music of love madly plays,
But the woman, 'tis ever the woman who pays.

WILL D. COBB, *It's the Woman Who Pays*. Music by Gus Edwards. (1916)

School-days, school-days, dear old golden rule days,
Readin' and 'ritin' and 'rithmetic,
Taught to the tune of a hick'ry stick;
You were my queen in calico,

I was your bashful barefoot beau,
And you wrote on my slate, I love you, Joe,
When we were a couple of kids.

WILL D. COBB, *School-Days.* (1907) Music by Gus Edwards.

Sing of joy, sing of bliss,
Home was never like this,
Yip-I-Addy-I-Ay!

WILL D. COBB, *Yip-I-Addy-I-Ay.* (1908) Music by John H. Flynn. Introduced by Blanche Ring in *The Merry Widow and the Devil.*

1
Oh, my poor Nelly Gray, they have taken you away,
And I'll never see my darling any more;
I'm sitting by the river and I'm weeping all the day,
For you've gone from the old Kentucky shore.

BENJAMIN RUSSELL HANBY, *Darling Nelly Gray.* (1856) A lament of a young negro slave for his sweetheart, which became ammunition for the abolitionists just prior to the Civil War. The Hanby home at Westerville, Ohio, has recently been acquired by the state and converted into a memorial.

2
I guess I'll have to telegraph my baby.

GEORGE M. COHAN. Title and refrain. (1898)

Over there, over there, send the word, send the word over there!
That the Yanks are coming, the Yanks are coming,
The drums rum-tumming ev'rywhere:
So prepare, say a pray'r,
Send the word, send the word to beware!
We'll be over, we're coming over,
And we won't come back till it's over, over there.

GEORGE M. COHAN, *Over There.* (1917) Cohan received public thanks from President Wilson for this song, which became the official marching song of the American army. There was, of course, an epidemic of patriotic songs when America entered the war. The following are examples:

Away he went, to live in a tent;
Over in France with his regiment.
Were you there, and tell me, did you notice?
They were all out of step but Jim.

IRVING BERLIN, *They Were All Out of Step But Jim.* (1918)

Sister Susie's sewing shirts for soldiers,
Such skill at sewing shirts our sly young sister Susie shows!
Some soldiers send epistles, say they'd sooner sleep in thistles
Than the saucy, soft, short shirts for soldiers sister Susie sews.

R. P. WESTON, *Sister Susie's Sewing Shirts for Soldiers.*(1914) Music by Herman E. Darewski. Sung by Al Jolson.

Don't try to steal the sweetheart of a soldier,
It's up to you to play a manly part:
Tho' he's over there and she's over here,
Still she's always in his heart.

ALFRED BRYAN, *Don't Try to Steal the Sweetheart of a Soldier.* (1917)

He's had no lovin' for a long, long time,
And he's got to have a lot of it now.

WILLIAM TRACEY, title and refrain of song set to music in 1919 by Maceo Pinkard, celebrating the return of the A.E.F. He'd won a lot of medals but no "lovin'."

How'ya gonna keep 'em down on the farm,
After they've seen Paree?

SAM M. LEWIS and JOE YOUNG. Title and refrain of song set to music in 1919 by Walter Donaldson. Much more realistic than Tracey's effort quoted above. For "I did not raise my boy to be a soldier," etc., see 1864:7.

3
If you lak-a-me, lak I lak-a-you
And we lak-a-both the same,
I lak-a say, this very day,
I lak-a-change your name, . . .
One live as two, two live as one
Under the bam-boo tree.

BOB COLE, *Under The Bamboo Tree.* (1902) Sung by Marie Cahill in *Sally in Our Alley.*

When you're all by your lonely,
You and your only!
Under the Yum Yum tree.

ANDREW B. STERLING, *Under the Yum Yum Tree.* (1910) Music by Harry Von Tilzer.

4
Let us bless the golden hours
With no eyes to mark,
That we pass among the maidens,
Kissing in the dark!

GEORGE COOPER, *Kissing in the Dark.* (1863) Music by Stephen Collins Foster.

Softly she murmurs, while chills o'er her creep,
"Why did they dig ma's grave so deep?"

GEORGE COOPER, *Why Did They Dig Ma's Grave so Deep?* Music by J. P. Skelly.

5
There never were two greater chums than we,
Johnny, my old friend John.

WILLIAM COURTRIGHT, *Johnny, My Old Friend John.* (1894)

6
Elsie from Chelsea, I thought of nobody elsie
But Elsie from Chelsea! Nobody elsie for me!

HARRY DACRE, *Elsie from Chelsea.* (1896)

Sweet Katie Connor,
I dote upon her.
Kate, Kate, as sure as fate, you'll have to marry me,
Or else I'll have a notion
Of diving in the ocean,
And flirting with the mermaids at the bottom of the sea!

HARRY DACRE, *Sweet Katie Connor.* (1890) Sung by Maggie Cline at Tony Pastor's Theatre, New York.

7
While the train rolled onward,
A husband sat in tears,
Thinking of the happiness
Of just a few short years;
For baby's face brings pictures of
A cherished hope that's dead,
But baby's cries can't waken her

In the baggage coach ahead.

Gussie L. Davis, *In the Baggage Coach Ahead.* (1896) Rewritten from Frank Archer's *Mother*. See 1350:21. Made famous by Imogene Comer, who sang it for the first time at Howard's Athenæum, Boston, Mass. The song is said to be founded upon an incident on a railway train of which Arnold was conductor and Davis the pullman porter.

1

So laugh, lads, and quaff, lads,
'Twill make you stout and hale;
Through all my days I'll sing the praise
Of brown October ale.

Reginald De Koven, *Brown October Ale.* (1891) From De Koven's famous light opera, *Robin Hood*. See also under Clement Scott, below.

2

Let her go, Gallagher!

William W. Delaney. Title and refrain. (1887)

3

Ev'ry little bit added to what you've got makes just a little bit more.

William A. and Lawrence M. Dillon. Title and refrain. (1907)

4

It's English you know, quite English you know,
How queer are the people, it's English you know,
We copy their ways, we pay for their plays,
It's English, quite English, so English you know.

W. S. Douglass, *Quite English.* (1885)

5

"Just tell them that you saw me," she said, "they'll know the rest;
Just tell them I was looking well, you know;
Just whisper if you get a chance to mother dear, and say,
I love her as I did long, long ago."

Paul Dresser. *Just Tell Them that You Saw Me.* (1895)

The letter that he longed for never came.

Paul Dresser. Title and refrain. (1886)

We shared with each other our joys and tears,
We were sweethearts for many years.

Paul Dresser, *We Were Sweethearts for Many Years.* (1895)

6

Arrah Wanna, on my honor I'll take care of you,
I'll be kind and true, we can love and bill and coo,
In a wigwam built of shamrocks green, we'll make those red men smile,
When you're Missus Barney, heap much Carney, from Killarney's Isle.

Jack Drislane, *Arrah Wanna.* (1906) Music by Theodore Morse.

7

But fu' real melojous music,
Dat jes' strikes yo' hea't and clings,
Jes' you stan' an' listen wif me,
When Malindy sings.

Paul Laurence Dunbar, *When Malindy Sings.*

Who dat say chicken in dis crowd?
Speak de word agin, and speak it loud.
Blame de lan'; let white folks rule it,
I'se looking for a pullet;
Who dat say chicken in dis crowd?

Paul Laurence Dunbar, *Who Dat Say Chicken?*

8

We never speak as we pass by,
Altho' a tear bedims her eye;
I know she thinks of her past life,
When we were loving man and wife.

Frank Egerton, *We Never Speak as We Pass By.* (1882) Music by Charles D. Blake.

9

Hail! Hail! the gang's all here,—
What the hell do we care,
What the hell do we care?
Hail! Hail! we're full of cheer,—
What the hell do we care, Bill!

D. A. Estrom, *Hail! Hail! the Gang's All Here.* (1897) A popular song during the war with Spain, sung to an air from W. S. Gilbert's *The Pirates of Penzance*.

10

Up in a balloon, boys, up in a balloon,
All among the little stars, sailing round the moon;
Up in a balloon, boys, up in a balloon,
It's something very jolly to be up in a balloon.

H. B. Farnie, *Up in a Balloon.* (1869)

11

Teach me to love you, I'm willing to learn.

Edgar T. Farran. Title and refrain. (1912)

12

Please don't take the baby from me,
He's all that I have now,
You'll make me so happy if you'll let him be,
I'll take care of him somehow.

Fred H. Finch, *Please Don't Take the Baby from Me.* (1904) Sung by Adelaide Ackland. Addressed to a policeman who had arrived to take the baby from its impoverished mother, "in society's name."

13

Down went McGinty to the bottom of the say,
And he must be very wet, for they haven't found him yet,
But they say his ghost comes round the docks before the break of day,
Dressed in his best suit of clothes.

Joseph Flynn, *Down Went McGinty.* First sung at Hyde & Behman's theatre, Brooklyn, N. Y., in 1889.

14

Keep the home fires burning, while your hearts are yearning,
Tho' your lads are far away they dream of home.

Mrs. Lena Guilbert Ford, *Keep the Home Fires Burning.* Theme suggested by Ivor Novello, who wrote the music. Published in 1915, and popular during the World War.

15

Say it with flowers, the fairest that grow,
Roses as red as the dawn's rosy glow, . . .
Say it with flowers from love's sweetest bowers

And you'll find her waiting, waiting for you.
Neville Fleeson, *Say It with Flowers.* (1919) Music by Albert Von Tilzer.

1
One got the kisses and kindly words,
That was her pet, Marie;
One told her troubles to bees and birds,
That one was only me!
Walter H. Ford, *Only Me.* (1894) Music by John W. Bratton.

Ev'ry Sunday down to her home we go,
All the boys and all the girls they love her so.
Always jolly, heart that is true, I know,
She is the Sunshine of Paradise Alley.
Walter H. Ford, *The Sunshine of Paradise Alley.* (1895) Suggested by the name of an alley in Philadelphia, Pa. Music by John W. Bratton. Introduced by Lottie Gilson at the Casino Roof Garden, New York City, and used also by Bessie Bonehill in *1492.*

2
Ah! may the red rose live alway,
To smile upon earth and sky!
Why should the beautiful ever weep?
Why should the beautiful die?
Stephen Collins Foster, *Ah! May the Red Rose Live Alway.* (1850)

Come where my love lies dreaming.
Stephen Collins Foster. Title and refrain. (1855)

Oh! give the stranger happy cheer,
When, o'er his cheek, the tear-drops start;
The balm that flows from one kind word
May heal the wound in a breaking heart.
Stephen Collins Foster, *Give the Stranger Happy Cheer.* (1851)

Summer will pass and skies will gray,
Keep my rose for a wintry day.
Stephen Collins Foster, *Long-Ago Day.* (1851)

Molly dear, I cannot linger;
Let me soon be gone.
Time now points with warning finger
T'wards the coming dawn.
Stephen Collins Foster, *Molly Dear, Good Night.* (1861)

For tho' nothing to another,
She was all the world to me.
Stephen Collins Foster, *She Was All the World to Me.* (1864) This song was copyrighted February 23. Foster had died ten days previously.

Wilt thou be true, though lips of scorn
Seek to revile me when I am gone?
Stephen Collins Foster, *Wilt Thou Be True?* (1864)

3
Little Ella's an angel in the skies,
Sing, merrily sing.
Stephen Collins Foster, *Little Ella's an Angel.* (1863)

Tell me of the angels, mother,
And the radiant land
Where my gentle little brother
Joined their happy band.
Stephen Collins Foster, *Tell Me of the Angels, Mother.* (1863)

Little Willie's gone to Heaven,
Praise the Lord!
All his sins have been forgiven,
Praise the Lord!
Joyful let your voices rise,
Do not come with tearful eyes,
Willie's dwelling in the skies,
Willie's gone to Heaven!
Stephen Collins Foster, *Willie's Gone to Heaven.* (1863) Foster was fond of Willie. He wrote two more songs about him, *Willie, My Brave,* and *Willie, We Have Missed You,* and composed the music for another by George Cooper, *Willie Has Gone to the War.*

4
Oh! comrades, fill no glass for me.
Stephen Collins Foster. Title and refrain. (1855)

For the dear old Flag I die,
Mother, dry your weeping eye.
Stephen Collins Foster, *For the Dear Old Flag I Die.* (1863)

Take the locket, soldier, brother,
Don't forget, give this to mother.
Stephen Collins Foster, *Give This to Mother.* (1864)

Nothing but a plain old soldier,
An old revolutionary soldier,
But I've handled a gun
Where noble deeds were done,
For the name of my commander was George Washington.
Stephen Collins Foster, *I'm Nothing But a Plain Old Soldier.* (1863)

Tell me, tell me, weary soldier,
From the rude and stirring wars,
Was my brother in the battle
Where you gain'd those noble scars?
Stephen Collins Foster, *Was My Brother in the Battle?* (1862)

5
Oh! Belle, de Lou'siana Belle,
I's gwine to marry you, Lou'siana Belle.
Stephen Collins Foster, *Lou'siana Belle.* (1847) Written for Joseph Murphy.

Down in de cornfield,
Hear dat mournful sound:
All de darkies am a-weeping,
Massa's in de cold, cold ground.
Stephen Collins Foster, *Massa's in de Cold Ground.* (1853)

Nelly Bly! Nelly Bly! bring de broom along,
We'll sweep de kitchen clean, my dear, and hab a little song.
Stephen Collins Foster, *Nelly Bly.* (1850)

I'm coming, I'm coming, for my head is bending low:
I hear those gentle voices calling, "Old Black Joe."
Stephen Collins Foster, *Old Black Joe.* (1860)

Dere was an old nigga, dey call'd him Uncle Ned,
He's dead long ago, long ago;
He had no wool on de top ob de head,
De place wha de wool ought to grow.
Stephen Collins Foster, *Old Uncle Ned.* (1848) Written for William Roark, of the "Sable Harmonists."

 APPENDIX

Oh! Susanna, don't you cry for me,
I've come from Alabama wid my banjo on my knee.

STEPHEN COLLINS FOSTER, *Oh! Susanna.* Sung for first time at Andrews' Eagle Ice Cream Saloon, Pittsburgh, Pa., by Nelson Kneass, 11 Sept., 1847, and soon a world-wide hit. Used by the Republicans in the Landon campaign of 1936.

Den come again, Susanna,
By de gas-light ob de moon;
We'll tum de old piano
When de banjo's out ob tune.

STEPHEN COLLINS FOSTER, *Ring de Banjo.* (1851)

I hear my true-lub weep,
I hear my true-lub sigh,
"Way down in Ca-i-ro
Dis nigga's gwine to die."

STEPHEN COLLINS FOSTER, *Way Down in Ca-i-ro.* (1850)

Nelly was a lady,
Last night she died,
Toll de bell for lubly Nell,
My dark Virginny bride.

STEPHEN COLLINS FOSTER, *Nelly Was a Lady.* (1849)

Edie was a lady.

DOROTHY PARKER. Caption of a review of Edith Wharton's autobiography.

1

Tell the people far and wide that better times are coming.

S. C. FOSTER, *Better Times Are Coming.* (1862)

Abraham the Joker soon will diskiver
We'll send him on a gunboat up Salt River. . . .
Sound the rally thro' the whole United States,
Little Mac and Pendleton are our candidates.

STEPHEN COLLINS FOSTER, *Little Mac.* (1864) A campaign song for Gen. George B. McClellan. "Up Salt River" dates from the Clay-Jackson campaign of 1832.

2

There's her picture on the table,
There's a baby in the cradle,
There's a husband crying bitterly alone,
There's no wife's voice to cheer,
In his sorrow to be near,
What was paradise is now a broken home.

WILL H. FOX, *The Broken Home.* (1892) Popularized by May Howard.

3

Don't judge by appearances, but by his actions more,
You never know when you may drive a good man from your door;
Clothes don't make the man, you know, some wise person wrote,
For many an honest heart may beat beneath a ragged coat.

HAWLEY FRANCK, *Many an Honest Heart May Beat Beneath a Ragged Coat.* (1901) Music by Arthur Trevelyan. Popularized by Effie Brooklyn.

4

Sweet Adeline, My Adeline,
At night, dear heart, For you I pine.
In all my dreams, Your fair face beams;
You're the flower of my heart, Sweet Adeline.

RICHARD H. GIRARD, *Sweet Adeline.* (1903) Music by Harry Armstrong. "The Old Faithful of all harmonic geysers."

5

A shady nook, a babbling brook,
Two lips where kisses dwell-o,
"Swear to be true." "I do! I do!"
Aha! the lucky fellow.

J. CHEEVER GOODWIN, *A Shady Nook.* From the comic opera, *Wang.* (1891)

For that elephant ate all night,
And that elephant ate all day,
Do what he would to get him food,
The cry was still, "More hay!"

J. CHEEVER GOODWIN, *Elephant Song* from *Wang.* (1891) See also 1558:1.

6

Two little girls in blue, lad, two little girls in blue,
They were sisters, we were brothers, and learned to love the two.

CHARLES GRAHAM, *Two Little Girls in Blue.* (1893) Inspired by Harris's *After the Ball,* and also featured by J. Aldrich Libby. See under Harris, below.

7

Just when it seemed that the end had come,
You landed me safe on the coast,
And proved you were faithful, yes, staunch and true,
Just when I needed you most.

WILLIAM BENSON GRAY, *Just When I Needed You Most.* (1900)

Oh, Mr. Austin, since I've been in Boston
Everything's been happiness without a care or pain:
My brain's been in a constant whirl
And I'll be a much wiser girl
When I go back to Saccarappa, Maine.

WILLIAM BENSON GRAY, *Oh, Mr. Austin.* (1899)

8

Ol' man river, dat ol' man river,
He must know sumpin', but don't say nothin',
He just keeps rollin', he keeps on rollin' along.

OSCAR HAMMERSTEIN, 2ND, *Ol' Man River.* (1927) Music by Jerome Kern.

9

Brother, can you spare a dime?

E. Y. HARBURG. Title and refrain. (1932)

10

Oh! Mister Johnson, turn me loose,
Got no money but a good excuse.

BEN R. HARNEY, *Mister Johnson.* (1896)

11

We shouldered arms and marched and marched away,
From Baxter street we marched to Avenue A;
The fifes and drums how sweetly they did play,
As we marched, marched, marched in the Mulligan Guard.

EDWARD HARRIGAN, *The Mulligan Guard.*

(1873) Music by David Braham. The skit of which the song was the conclusion, a satire against the numerous semi-political military organizations of the period, was first produced at the Academy of Music, Chicago, in July, 1873. The melody became famous. Kipling mentions it in *Kim* as being played by the British bands in India.

1
Many a heart is aching, if you could read them all,
Many the hopes that have vanished, after the ball.

CHARLES K. HARRIS, *After the Ball.* (1892) One of the greatest hits in the history of Tin Pan Alley. First sung by J. Aldrich Libby, a famous baritone, at a matinee of Charles Hoyt's *A Trip to Chinatown,* at the Bijou Theatre, Milwaukee, Wis.

This is the end of our sinning,
Bright though as seemed the beginning,
You long for love that is surer,
Love that to you will be purer,
I hoped you'd always be near me,
That your heart ne'er would grow weary,
Yet you leave mine sad and dreary,
Now that I'm cast aside.

CHARLES K. HARRIS, *Cast Aside.* (1895)

Just break the news to mother,
She knows how dear I love her,
And tell her not to wait for me,
For I'm not coming home.

CHARLES K. HARRIS, *Break the News to Mother.* (1897) Another of Harris's great hits, recounting the heroic death of a soldier boy while saving the flag from the disgrace of being captured by the enemy on some unnamed battle-field of the Civil War. Harris got the refrain from a line in William Gillette's *Secret Service,* where a wounded drummer-boy is brought home and says to the darky at the door, "Break the news to mother." The song was sung with great effect by Emma Carus, and was popular with American soldiers during the war with Spain.

Then comes the sad awakening,
The pangs of deep regret,
She longed to be forgiven,
She prayed that he'd forget.

CHARLES K. HARRIS, *Then Comes the Sad Awakening.* (1898) Sung by Gertrude Rutledge at Hammerstein's Victoria Roof Garden.

There'll come a time, some day
When I have passed away,
There'll be no father to guide you from day to day;
Think well of all I've said:
Honor the man you wed:
Always remember my story, there'll come a time.

CHARLES K. HARRIS, *There'll Come a Time.* (1895)

Too late, too late, alas! too late!
The words that now you speak;
Your vows so dear I dare not hear,
My love you must not seek!
Another now doth claim my vow,
Why, darling, did you wait?
Had you but told your love last night—
Alas! 'tis now too late!

CHARLES K. HARRIS, *Too Late, Alas! Too Late.* (1895)

2
Listen to the mocking bird, listen to the mocking bird,
Still singing where the weeping willows wave.

ALICE HAWTHORNE, *Listen to the Mocking Bird.* (1870)

3
There'll be a hot time in the old town tonight!

JOSEPH HAYDEN. Refrain of popular song set to music by Theodore Metz in the fall of 1896, when the McIntyre and Heath Minstrels visited Old Town, La. Adopted by the American soldiers as the unofficial melody of the War with Spain.

4
Ain't it awful, Mabel?

JOHN EDWARD HAZZARD. Title and refrain. (1908)

5
I'd leave ma happy home for you,
You're de nicest man I ever knew.

WILL A. HEELAN, *I'd Leave Ma Happy Home for You.* (1899) Music by Harry Von Tilzer.

I left my old Kentucky home for you.

WILLIAM JEROME. Title and refrain of a song set to music by Harry Von Tilzer in 1912.

I wouldn't leave my home if I were you.

ANDREW B. STERLING. Title and refrain of song set to music in 1899 by Harry Von Tilzer.

6
Dreaming, dreaming, of you, sweetheart, I am dreaming,
Dreaming of days, when you loved me best,
Dreaming of hours that have gone to rest. . . .
Dreaming.

L. S. HEISER, *Dreaming.* (1906) Music by J. Anton Dailey.

7
All coons look alike to me.

ERNEST HOGAN. Title and refrain. (1896) One of May Irwin's great hits.

8
Hello! ma baby, Hello! ma honey,
Hello! ma rag-time gal,
Send me a kiss by wire,
Baby, my heart's on fire!
If you refuse me, Honey, you'll lose me,
Then you'll be left alone; oh, baby,
Telephone and tell me I'se your own.

FRANK HOWARD, *Hello, Ma Baby.* (1899)

For his last words were, Darling, I'll meet you
When the robins nest again.

FRANK HOWARD, *When the Robins Nest Again.* Popular song, written in 1883, the title taken from a melody by Barney Fagan. Howard's real name was Martindale. "When the robins nest again" became, in the slang of the day, synonymous with never. It is so used in John Luther Long's novel, *Madame Butterfly,* and also in Puccini's opera.

With the robins I'll return.

JAMES J. WALKER. Title of lyric. (1907)

1
The Bow'ry, the Bow'ry!
They say such things, and they do strange things
On the Bow'ry, the Bow'ry!
I'll never go there any more!
CHARLES H. HOYT, *The Bowery*. (1891) Music by Percy Gaunt. Introduced by Harry Conor in *A Trip to Chinatown*, at the Madison Square Theatre, in New York City.

2
But they tell me I'm awfully clevar,
Oh so clevar, deuced clevar;
They say that they nevar, no nevar,
Met a fella so clevar before.
G. W. HUNT, *Awfully Clever*. (c. 1870)

3
Ting, ting, that's how the bells go,
Ting, ting, pretty young thing,
You be my wife, I'll buy the ring,
Servants to wait on our ting, ting, ting.
GEORGE EDWARD JACKSON, *Ting, Ting, That's How the Bell Goes*. (1885)

4
This coal black lady, She is my baby.
Don't trifle with my coal black lady.
W. T. JEFFERSON, *My Coal Black Lady*. (1896)

5
Any old place I can hang my hat is home sweet home to me.
WILLIAM JEROME. Title and refrain. (1901) Music by Jean Schwartz.

Bedelia, I want to steal ye.
WILLIAM JEROME, *Bedelia*. (1903)

He never came back, he never came back,
His dear form she never saw more,
But how happy she'll be, when his sweet face she'll see,
When they meet on that beautiful shore.
WILLIAM JEROME, *He Never Came Back*. (1891)

His sweet face she never saw more;
Each day as she strolls by the sea
She cries in despair as she offers this pray'r,
Oh, send back my darling to me.
WILLIAM JEROME, *His Sweet Face She Never Saw More*. (1892)

You needn't try to reason,
Your excuse is out of season,
Just kiss yourself good-bye.
WILLIAM JEROME, *Just Kiss Yourself Good-Bye*. (1902) Music by Jean Schwartz.

A "Jay" came to the city once, to see the funny sights,
With a little bunch of whiskers on his chin.
WILLIAM JEROME, *The Little Bunch of Whiskers on His Chin*. (1894) Music by Andrew Mack.

6
And now we are aged and gray, Maggie,
The trials of life nearly done,
Let us sing of the days that are gone, Maggie,
When you and I were young.
GEORGE W. JOHNSON, *When You and I Were Young*. (1866) Music by J. A. Butterfield.

7
Take your clothes and go.
IRVING JONES. Title and refrain. (1897)

8
Weddings make a lot of people sad,
But if you're not the groom, they're not so bad, . . .
But don't forget, folks,
That's what you get, folks,
For makin' whoopee.
GUS KAHN, *Makin' Whoopee*. (1928) Music by Walter Donaldson. "Whoopee" is said to have been used as long ago as 1450, in a play called *Mankind*. (See *Literary Digest*, vol. 107, no. 13, p. 43.) The *Oxford Dictionary* says it is of American origin, dating from 1845. Its modern vogue is largely due to Walter Winchell, newspaper columnist.

9
"Throw him down, McCloskey," was to be the battle cry,—
"Throw him down, McCloskey, you can lick him if you try."
JOHN W. KELLY, *Throw Him Down, McCloskey*. A popular song made famous by Maggie Cline in 1890. Kelly was known as "The Rolling Mill Man," and is said to have got the inspiration for the song from a barroom fight in Union Square, New York. *Maloney, the Rolling Mill Man* was a popular song of which he was the author.

10
Baby left her cradle for the golden shore,
O'er the silv'ry waters she has flown,
Gone to join the angels, peaceful ever-more;
Empty is the cradle, Baby's gone.
HARRY KENNEDY, *"Cradle's Empty, Baby's Gone."* (1880)

I had fifteen dollars in my inside pocket,
Don't you see, to me it is a warning,
Saturday night I made a call
On a friend of Tam'ny Hall
And the divil a cent I had on Sunday morning.
HARRY KENNEDY, *I Had Fifteen Dollars in My Inside Pocket*. (1885) Pat Rooney's great song.

Molly, Molly, always so jolly,
Always laughing, chock full of glee,
Living as happy as happy can be,
Molly and I and the baby.
HARRY KENNEDY, *Molly and I and the Baby*. (1892)

11
Sailor, take care! Sailor, take care!
Danger is near thee, beware! beware!
Many brave hearts are asleep in the deep,
So beware! beware!
ARTHUR J. LAMB, *Asleep in the Deep*. (1898) Music by H. W. Petrie. Introduced by John Early, with Haverly's Minstrels, at McVicker's Theatre, Chicago.

She lives in a mansion of aching hearts,
She's one of a restless throng,
The diamonds that glitter around her throat,
They speak both of sorrow and song;
The smile on her face is only a mask,
And many the tear that starts,

For sadder it seems, when of mother she dreams,
In the mansion of aching hearts.

ARTHUR J. LAMB, *The Mansion of Aching Hearts.* (1902) Music by Harry Von Tilzer.

Tell me that beautiful story only once again,
Tell me of love and its glory, tho' I know it is in vain;
Your mem'ry is always before me, with joy my soul to fill,
So tell me that beautiful story,—say that you love me still.

ARTHUR J. LAMB, *Tell Me That Beautiful Story.* (1902) Music by Albert Von Tilzer.

1
The waiter roars it through the hall,
"We don't give bread with one fishball!"

GEORGE MARTIN LANE, *The Lay of the One Fishball.* The ballad was used as the basis of a mock Italian opera, *Il Pesceballo,* by Professor Francis James Child and James Russell Lowell.

2
She's somebody's mother, boys, don't you know,
Somebody's mother, so old and so slow.

CHARLES LAWLOR and JAMES BLAKE, *She's Somebody's Mother.* (1897) An adaptation from Mary Dow Brine. See 1350:2.

3
There was I, waiting at the church,
Waiting at the church, waiting at the church,
When I found he'd left me in the lurch,
Lor, how it did upset me!
All at once he sent me round a note
Here's the very note, This is what he wrote,
Can't get away to marry you today—
My wife won't let me.

FRED W. LEIGH, *Waiting at the Church.* (1906) Music by Henry E. Pether. Sung with great success by Vesta Victoria.

4
Don't say one word against her, do not say she was untrue;
If another's won her heart she's not to blame.
This town is good, a-plenty, for the likes of me and you,
But she's a picture that deserves a better frame!

PAUL LESLIE, *A Picture That Deserves a Better Frame.* (1901)

5
Always take mother's advice,
She knows what is best for your good;
Let her kind words then suffice,
And always take mother's advice.

JENNIE LINDSAY, *Always Take Mother's Advice.* (1884)

6
I'm Captain Jinks of the Horse Marines,
I often live beyond my means;
I sport young ladies in their teens,
To cut a swell in the army.

WILLIAM LINGARD, *Captain Jinks of the Horse Marines.* (1869) Chiefly remembered for Clyde Fitch's play of the same name, in which Ethel Barrymore made her debut at the Garrick Theatre, New York City, 4 Feb., 1901. Sometimes attributed to T. Maclagen.

7
Waltz me till I'm weary, dearie, and hold me tight,
Home was never once like this, now ain't I right?

ARTHUR LONGBRAKE, *Waltz Me Till I'm Weary, Dearie.* (1910) Music by Tom Sherman. See also 360:6.

8
Whoa! Emma! whoa! Emma!
Emma, you've put me in quite a dilemma.

JAMES LONSDALE, *Whoa, Emma.* (1877) Made famous by Tony Pastor.

9
I love my wife, But oh you kid!

JIMMY LUCAS. Title and Refrain. (1909)

10
Everybody works but father, and he sits around all day,
Feet in front of the fire, smoking his pipe of clay;
Mother takes in washing, so does sister Ann,
Everybody works at our house but my old man.

CHARLES W. MCCLINTOCK, *Everybody Works but Father.* (1891) One of Lew Dockstader's hits. The song was of English origin, and was revised for American consumption by Jean Havez. Princeton students of the period made it "Henry Clay," the name of their favorite cigar.

11
I've got the time, I've got the place,
Will some one kindly introduce me to the girl?

BALLARD MACDONALD, *I've Got the Time, I've Got the Place, But It's Hard to Find the Girl.* (1910) Music by S. R. Henry. Sung by Hetty King. See 1431:5.

12
We were comrades, comrades, ever since we were boys,
Sharing each other's sorrows, sharing each other's joys,
Comrades when manhood was dawning, faithful what e'er might betide,
When danger threatened my darling old comrade was there by my side.

FELIX MCGLENNON, *Comrades.* (1887)

Oh! Uncle John! isn't it nice on Broadway?
Oh! Uncle John! here I will remain.
Oh! Uncle John, now that I've seen the Bow'ry,
Life in the country's awful slow,
And I'll never go back again!

FELIX MCGLENNON, *Oh! Uncle John.* (1895) Sung by Kittie Gilmore.

Oh! what a difference in the morning!
Don't we regret it at the dawning!
Of cash we find a lack,
And with two eyes awful black,
It's "ten days or ten dollars," in the morning!

FELIX MCGLENNON, *Oh! What a Difference in the Morning.* (1891) A Lottie Gilson hit.

13
Has anybody here seen Kelly?
Kelly from the Emerald Isle?

WILLIAM J. MCKENNA, *Has Anybody Here Seen*

Kelly? An American version of an English song, *Kelly from the Isle of Man*, by C. W. Murphy and Will Letters. Sung by Nora Bayes in *The Jolly Bachelors*, produced in 1908.

1
Only one girl in the world for me,
Only one girl has my sympathy.
DAVE MARION, *Only One Girl in the World for Me.* (1895) Sung by Julius P. Witmark.

2
Do not fear, my little darling,
And I will take you home.
Come and sit close beside me,
No more from me you shall roam,
For you were a babe in arms
When your mother left me one day;
Left me at home, deserted, alone,
And took you, my child, away.
EDWARD B. MARKS, *The Little Lost Child.* (1894) Introduced by Lottie Gilson, the "Little Magnet," it became—incredible as it may seem—one of the smash hits of the '90's.

3
Do they miss me at home, do they miss me?
'Twould be an assurance most dear
To know at this moment some lov'd one
Were saying, "I wish he were here."
CAROLINE ATHERTON MASON, *Do They Miss Me At Home?* (c. 1850) Music by Mrs. S. M. Grannis.

Little bright eyes, will you miss me,
Will you dream sweet dreams of me?
Come, my darling, sweetly kiss me,
I'll be constant still to thee.
JOHN T. RUTLEDGE, *Little Bright Eyes, Will You Miss Me?* (c. 1855)

4
"Oh! Fred! tell them to stop!" that was the cry of Maria;
But the more she said "Whoa,"
They said, "Let it go!"
And the swing went a little bit higher.
GEORGE MEEN, *Oh! Fred! Tell Them to Stop!* One of Tony Pastor's great hits half a century ago.

5
But the cat came back, couldn't stay no longer,
Yes, the cat came back the very next day;
The cat came back, thought he was a goner,
But the cat came back for it wouldn't stay away.
HARRY S. MILLER, *The Cat Came Back.* (1893)

You can't lose me, Charlie.
HARRY S. MILLER. Title and refrain. (1893)

6
I'm afraid, I'm afraid,
I can't help the feeling that's over me stealing, . . .
Some girls do, then they rue,
So nothing for me to-day.
J. F. MITCHELL, *I'm Afraid.* (1885) Popularized by Alice Clark.

7
In a cavern, in a canyon,
Excavating for a mine,
Dwelt a miner, forty-niner,
And his daughter, Clementine.
PERCY MONTROSS, *Clementine.* (1880)

8
Wild women loved that child,
And he could drive tame women wild,
Sinbad was in bad all the time.
STANLEY MURPHY, *Sinbad Was In Bad.* (1917) Music by Harry Carroll.

9
She's my sweetheart, I'm her beau,
She's my Annie, I'm her Joe,
Soon we'll marry, never to part,
Little Annie Rooney is my sweetheart.
MICHAEL NOLAN, *Little Annie Rooney.* (1890) Sung by Nolan in the English music-halls, and introduced to America by Annie Hart, "the Bowery girl," at the old London Theatre, New York City. Nolan was also the author of *I'll Whistle and Wait for Katie.*

10
There'll be no wedding bells for her,
Past are her days to love;
No one can claim her worthy hand,
Giv'n to the cause above.
GEORGE A. NORTON, *No Wedding Bells for Her.* (1898) Music by James W. Casey. This cryptic chorus refers to "a maiden pure and trusting" who "took the veil," after "a pained expression came into her fair young face" when her "idol turned to dust."

Sing me a song of the Sunny South,
One with a sweet refrain;
Sing me a song of Dixie land,
That I may be happy again.
GEORGE A. NORTON, *Sing Me a Song of the South.* (1899) Music by James W. Casey. Popularized by Will Thompson, the baritone of Primrose and Dockstader's minstrels.

11
Take me out to the ball game,
Take me out with the crowd,
Buy me some peanuts and cracker-jack,
I don't care if I never get back.
Let me root, root, root for the home team,
If they don't win it's a shame,
For it's one, two, three strikes you're out,
At the old ball game.
JACK NORWORTH, *Take Me Out to the Ball Game.* (1908) Music by Albert Von Tilzer. Popularized by Nora Bayes.

12
There was an old man and he had two sons,
He had, he had,
He lived on a ranch, so the story runs,
He did, he did.
'Twas built on the good old Queen Anne plan,
Right next to the New Jerusalem,
The vicinity, it does not matter a—bit,
Sing tra la la la la la la.
BILL NYE, *The Prodigal Son.* (1891) Sung by Thomas Q. Seabrook in *The Isle of Champagne.* Music by Josephine Gro.

13
O Heidelberg, dear Heidelberg, thy sons will ne'er forget,

The golden haze of student days is round about
us yet.
Those days of yore will come no more, while
through our manly years,
The thought of you, so good and true, will
fill our eyes with tears.

FRANK PIXLEY, *O Heidelberg*. (1902) Music by Gustave Luders. The stein song from *The Prince of Pilsen*.

1
Somewhere, Somewhere, Beautiful Isle of
Somewhere,
Land of the true, where we live anew,
Beautiful Isle of Somewhere!

JESSIE BROWN POUNDS, *Beautiful Isle of Somewhere*. (1901)

2
We'd both been there before, many a time,
many a time.

CHARLES E. PROTH. Title and refrain. (1888)

3
I care not for the stars that shine,
I dare not hope to e'er be thine,
I only know I love you,
Love me, and the world is mine.

DAVID REED, JR., *Love Me and the World Is Mine*. (1906) Music by Ernest R. Ball.

4
Shoo fly, don't bother me, shoo fly, don't
bother me,
Shoo fly, don't bother me, I belong to Company G.

BILLY REEVES, *Shoo Fly, Don't Bother Me*. (1866) Music by Jasper Ross.

5
Tramp! Tramp! Tramp! the boys are march-
ing,
Cheer up, comrades, they will come,
And beneath the starry flag
We shall breathe the air again
Of the free land in our own beloved home.

GEORGE F. ROOT, *Tramp! Tramp! Tramp!* (1862)

6
Hush, little baby, don't you cry,
You'll be an angel bye and bye.

MONROE H. ROSENFELD, *Hush, Little Baby*. (1884)

I don't care if you never come back.

MONROE H. ROSENFELD. Title and refrain of popular song. (1897)

Johnny, get your gun, get your gun today,
Pigeons a-flying all de way,
If you want to get to Heaven in de good ole way,
Johnny, get your gun, get your gun.

MONROE H. ROSENFELD, *Johnny, Get Your Gun*. (1886) An echo of an older jingle, "Johnny, get your gun and your sword and your pistol."

Take back your gold, for gold can never buy me;
Take back your bribe, and promise you'll be true;
Give me the love, the love that you'd deny me,
Make me your wife, that's all I ask of you.

MONROE H. ROSENFELD, *Take Back Your Gold*. (1897) The words are sometimes credited to Louis W. Pritzkow, a ballad reader with a popular minstrel troupe, who agreed to introduce the song on condition that his name be printed on the music as the lyricist, but Rosenfeld really wrote both words and music. The song was made famous by Imogene Comer, at the Bowdoin Theatre, Boston.

Cash, cash, cash! That's what we're looking for,
There's nothing like the good old Rhino!

MONROE H. ROSENFELD, *There's Nothing Like It*. (1887) See 1333:16.

With all her faults I love her still,
And even so till Death doth part!
No love like hers, my soul can thrill,
No other love can win my heart!
I love her still! I love her still,
With all her faults I love her still.

MONROE H. ROSENFELD, *With All Her Faults I Love Her Still*. (1888)

7
A mademoiselle from Armenteers,
She hasn't been kissed in forty years,
Hinky, dinky, par-lee-voo.

EDWARD ROWLAND, *Mademoiselle from Armentières*. "Folk song of the Great War." Stanzas were added *ad lib* by numberless volunteers.

8
Where the dear old Shannon's flowing,
Where the three-leaved Shamrock grows,
Where my heart is I am going,
To my little Irish rose.
And the moment that I meet her
With a hug and kiss I'll greet her,
For there's not a colleen sweeter
Where the River Shannon flows.

JAMES I. RUSSELL, *Where the River Shannon Flows*. (1906)

9
A sweet Tuxedo girl you see,
Queen of swell society,
Fond of fun as fond can be,
When it's on the strict Q. T.
Ta-ra-ra Boom-der-é. [Four times repeated]

HENRY J. SAYERS, *Ta-ra-ra Boom-der-é*. (1891) The French accent proved too much for the American *hoi polloi*, and the title is generally given as *Ta-ra-ra Boom-de-ay*. Sayers is said to have heard the refrain in a negro resort run by "Babe" Connors, in St. Louis, Mo. Used first in a farce comedy called *Tuxedo*, it was afterwards made a riot in England by Lottie Collins. During a lawsuit over the song, Flora Moore made affidavit that she sang it in the United States in 1884, and others dated it back to 1878. (See SPAETH, *Read 'Em and Weep*, p. 163; GOLDBERG, *Tin Pan Alley*, p. 113.) "Q. T.," it should perhaps be explained, was slang of the period for quiet.

I'm the man that wrote Ta-ra-ra, Boom-de-ay,
It has been sung in every language night and day,
I wrote it in a garret, while out with Booth and
Barrett,
I'm the man that wrote Ta-ra-ra, Boom-de-ay.

JAMES THORNTON, *I'm the Man That Wrote Ta-ra-ra, Boom-de-ay*. (1892) Sung by Thornton in *O'Dowd's Neighbors*.

1
Tell me, do you love me?
  Whisper softly, sweetly, as of old!
Tell me that you love me,
  For that's the sweetest story ever told.

R. M. STULTS, *The Sweetest Story Ever Told.* (1892)

I love you! Dearly love you!
If thou wert here I'd answer with a kiss.

R. M. STULTS, *Yes, I Love You.* (1893) "An answer to *The Sweetest Story Ever Told,*" but the answer never achieved the popularity of the question.

2
Oh, promise me that some day you and I
Will take our love together to some sky
Where we can be alone and faith renew,
And find the hollows where those flowers grew.

CLEMENT SCOTT, *Oh, Promise Me.* (1888) Music by Reginald De Koven. De Koven's opera, *Robin Hood,* opened at Chicago, 9 June, 1890, and immediately after the performance, the famous contralto, Jessie Bartlett Davis, who took the part of Alan-a-Dale, announced that she would never appear in it again, as she considered parts of the score unsuitable. In despair, De Koven chanced to remember a ballad which he had composed some time before to words by Clement Scott, and he ran it over on the piano for Miss Davis, who was delighted with it. When she sang it at the second performance the following night, it brought down the house, and was soon being sung all over the world.

3
All bound round with a woolen string.

CHARLES SEAMON. Title and refrain of popular song. (1898)

4
Mrs. Jones sat on her bed a-sighin',
Just received a message that Casey was dyin';
Said, "Go to bed, children, and hush your cryin',
'Cause you've got another papa on the Salt Lake Line."

T. LAWRENCE SEIBERT, *Casey Jones.* (1909) Adapted from an old southern ballad, whose melody was "ragged" by Eddie Newton.

5
All that I ask is love, All that I want is you;
And I swear by all the stars, I'll be forever true.

EDGAR SELDEN, *All That I Ask of You Is Love.* (1910) Music by Herbert Ingraham.

6
Yes, we have no bananas,
We have no bananas today.

FRANK SILVER (1892–1960) AND IRVING COHN (1898–1961), *Yes, We have No Bananas.* (1923)

I claim that it ["Yes, we have no bananas"] is the greatest document that has been penned in the entire History of American Literature.

WILL ROGERS, *The Illiterate Digest,* p. 77.

7
That's carrying things a step too far,
  I draw the line at that.

HARRY B. SMITH, *We Draw the Line at That.* (1884)

8
Where was Moses when the light went out?
Where was Moses? What was he about?
  Now, my little man,
  Tell me if you can,
Where was Moses when the light went out?

JOHN STAMFORD, *Where Was Moses When the Light Went Out?* (c. 1880)

9
Somebody loves me; how do I know?
Somebody's eyes have told me so!
Somebody loves me; how do I know?
Somebody told me so!

HATTIE STARR, *Somebody Loves Me.* (1893) Introduced by Josephine Sabel at Koster and Bial's music hall in New York City.

Nobody loves me, well do I know,
Don't all the cold world tell me so?

HATTIE STARR, *Nobody Loves Me.* (1894)

10
Can't you see the rain and hail am fastly falling, Alexander?
Don't you hear your lady love a-softly calling, Alexander?
Take me to your heart again and call me honey,
All I want is lovin', I don't want your money,
Alexander, tell me, don't you love your baby no more?

ANDREW B. STERLING, *Alexander.* (1904) Music by Harry Von Tilzer. The progenitor of *Alexander's Ragtime Band.* See 1369:14.

Remember there's no other
  As dear, where'er you roam,
So don't forget your mother
  And the dear old home!

ANDREW B. STERLING, *Don't Forget Your Mother.* (1899) Music by Max Dreyfus.

Down in the City of Sighs and Tears, under the white light's glare,
Down in the City of Wasted Years, you'll find your mamma there.

ANDREW B. STERLING, *In the City of Sighs and Tears.* (1902) Music by Kerry Mills.

Meet me in St. Louis, Louis,
  Meet me at the fair,
Don't tell me the lights are shining
  Any place but there.

ANDREW B. STERLING, *Meet Me in St. Louis, Louis.* (1904) Music by Kerry Mills. A by-product of the St. Louis World's fair.

Wait 'till the sun shines, Nellie,
  When the clouds go drifting by,
We will be happy, Nellie,
  Don't you sigh.

ANDREW B. STERLING, *Wait 'Till the Sun Shines, Nellie.* (1905) Music by Harry Von Tilzer. Introduced by Winona Winter.

Rufus Rastus Johnson Brown,
What you goin' to do when the rent comes 'round?

ANDREW B. STERLING, *What You Goin' to Do When the Rent Comes 'Round?* (1905) Music by Harrv Von Tilzer.

And I long to be with mother in that old log cabin room,
Way down South in dear old Georgia, where the sweet magnolias bloom.

ANDREW B. STERLING, *Where the Sweet Magnolias Bloom.* (1899) Music by Harry Von Tilzer. Popularized by Fanny Da Costa.

1
Daddy wouldn't buy me a bow-wow! bow-wow!
Daddy wouldn't buy me a bow-wow! bow-wow!
I've got a little cat,
And I'm very fond of that,
But I'd rather have a bow-wow, wow.

JOSEPH TABRAR, *Daddy Wouldn't Buy Me a Bow-Wow.* (1892) Made famous by Vesta Victoria.

2
The Moth and the Flame play'd a game, one day,
The game of a woman's heart;
And the Moth that play'd was a maid, they say,
The Flame was a bad man's art.

GEORGE TAGGART, *The Moth and the Flame.* (1898) Music by Max S. Witt. Suggested by the second act of Clyde Fitch's play of the same name. Introduced by the famous female baritone Helene Mora, at the Pleasure Palace Theatre, New York City. Fitch afterwards used the melody as incidental music to the play.

3
My sweetheart's the man in the moon,
I'm going to marry him soon,
'Twould fill me with bliss just to give him one kiss,
But I know that a dozen I never would miss;
I'll go up in a great big balloon,
And see my sweetheart in the moon,
Then behind some dark cloud, where no one is allowed,
I'll make love to the man in the moon.

JAMES THORNTON, *My Sweetheart's the Man in the Moon.* (1892) Popularized by Bonnie Thornton at Tony Pastor's Theatre, New York. Considered very daring in its day.

She may have seen better days,
When she was in her prime;
She may have seen better days,
Once upon a time.
Tho' by the way-side she fell,
She may yet mend her ways.
Some poor old mother is waiting for her
Who has seen better days.

JAMES THORNTON, *She May Have Seen Better Days.* (1894) W. H. Windom sang this in Primrose & West's minstrels. It was a surefire tear producer.

4
One thought of mother, at home, alone,
Feeble and old and gray;
One of the sweetheart, he left in town,
Happy and young and gay;
One kissed a ringlet of thin gray hair,
One kissed a lock of brown,
Bidding farewell to the Stars and Stripes,
Just as the sun went down.

LYN UDALL, *Just As the Sun Went Down.* (1898)

5
It takes a long tall brown-skin gal to make a preacher lay his Bible down.

MARSHALL WALKER. Title and refrain. (1917)

6
Come to me, sweet Marie, sweet Marie, come to me,
Not because your face is fair, love, to see,
But your soul, so pure and sweet,
Makes my happiness complete,
Makes me falter at your feet, sweet Marie.

CY WARMAN, *Sweet Marie.* (1893) Set to music by Ramon Moore, a famous ballad reader, and introduced by him in a musical comedy called *Africa,* at the Euclid Avenue Opera House, Cleveland, Ohio.

7
Baby dear, (sh) listen here, I'm afraid to come home in the dark—
Ev'ry day the papers say a robbery in the park
So I sat alone in the Y.M.C.A., singing just like a lark—
There's no place like home—but I couldn't come home in the dark.

HARRY WILLIAMS, *I'm Afraid to Come Home in the Dark.* (1907) Music by Egbert Von Alstyne.

I used to be afraid to go home in the dark,
Now I'm afraid to go at all!

HARRY H. WILLIAMS. Title and refrain. (1908)

I could hear the dull buzz of the bee,
In the blossoms as you said to me,
"With a heart that is true,
I'll be waiting for you,
In the shade of the old apple tree."

HARRY H. WILLIAMS, *In the Shade of the Old Apple Tree.* (1905) Music by Egbert Von Alstyne.

8
Papa, mama, kiss and be friends!
I love you both, I do!
Make it all up, for your daughter's sake,
Let me go home with you:
I know you'll listen to your child,
Whose heart is filled with pain;
Papa, mama, kiss and be friends,
Kiss and be friends again.

CHARLES A. WILSON, *Papa, Mama, Kiss and Be Friends.* (1899) Music by Leo E. Berliner.

1
Just another fatal wedding, just another broken heart.
W. H. WINDOM, *The Fatal Wedding.* (1893) Music by Gussie L. Davis.

2
I don't want to play in your yard,
I don't like you any more;
You'll be sorry when you see me
Sliding down our cellar door;
You can't holler down our rain-barrel,
You can't climb our apple-tree,
I don't want to play in your yard
If you won't be good to me.
PHILIP WINGATE, *I Don't Want to Play in Your Yard.* (1894) Music by H. W. Petrie. Sung by Gus Edwards.

3
"White Wings," they never grow weary,
They carry me cheerily over the sea;
Night comes, I long for my dearie,
I'll spread out my "White Wings" and sail home to thee!
BANKS WINTER, *"White Wings."* (1882) A rewrite of an earlier song of the same title by Joseph Gulick, named after a popular novel of the day by William Black—hence the quotes.

4
Father, dear father, come home with me now!
The clock in the steeple strikes one.
HENRY CLAY WORK, *Come Home, Father.* (1862) In the second verse, the clock strikes two, and in the third verse three. Meanwhile the baby has died. Widely sung for more than a quarter of a century as a withering indictment of the Demon Rum.

5
Playmates, playmates, since we were kids so high, . . .
And though we are gray and life's fading away
We're still playmates dear.
JACK YELLEN, *Playmates.* (1917) Music by Albert Crumble.

6
Linger longer, Lucy, longer linger, Loo,
How I love to linger, Lucy, linger 'longer you;
Listen while I sing, oh, promise you'll be true,
Linger longer, longer linger, linger longer, Loo.
WILLIE YOUNGE, *Linger Longer, Loo.* (1893) Music by Sidney Jones. Sung by Millie Hylton in the "gaiety burlesque," *Don Juan.*

7
I've a letter from thy sire, Baby mine,
I could read and never tire, Baby mine;
He is sailing o'er the sea,
He is coming back to me,
He is coming back to me, Baby mine.
CHARLES MACKAY, *Baby Mine.* (1901)

8
Frankie and Albert were lovers, O Lordy, how they could love.
Swore to be true to each other, true as the stars above;
He was her man, and he done her wrong.
UNKNOWN, *Frankie and Albert.* The original version of *Frankie and Johnny,* the so-called St. Louis version, relating the story of the murder of Albert, or Allen, Britt, by Frankie Baker, at St. Louis, 15 Oct., 1899. (See the St. Louis *Post-Dispatch,* 19 Oct., 1899, p. 8, col. 2.) Britt was shot on the 15th and died at the City Hospital on the night of the 18th. When he entered the hospital, he gave his occupation as job worker, and his residence as 212 Targee Street. There are more than 200 versions of this song, which has become an American classic. (See JOHN HUSTON, *Frankie and Johnny.*)

9
Once on a time there was a wood,
The funniest wood that ever you see,
Oh, the tree in the wood, and the wood in the ground,
And the green grass growing all around, all around,
And the green grass growing all around.
UNKNOWN, *The Green Grass Growing All Around.* (*American College Song Book,* 1882.) This version is that sung by the Tufts College Glee Club, arranged by C. W. Gerould.

And the green grass grew all around.
WILLIAM JEROME. Title and refrain of song set to music by Harry Von Tilzer in 1912

10
We're here because we're here,
Because we're here, because we're here;
Oh, here we are, and here we are,
And here we are again.
UNKNOWN, *Here We Are.* (Soldiers' Song, 1916)

Ten thousand dollars for the folks back home.
UNKNOWN. Sung by A.E.F. funeral parties to the tune of Chopin's *Funeral March.*

11
When a pair of red lips are upturned to your own,
With no one to gossip about it,
Do you pray for endurance to let them alone?
Well! maybe you do, but I doubt it.
UNKNOWN, *I Doubt It.* (1884) Music by Richard Mansfield.

12
Is that Mr. Reilly, can any one tell?
Is that Mr. Reilly, that owns the hotel?
Well, if that's Mr. Reilly, they speak of so highly,
Well upon my soul, Reilly, you're doing quite well.
UNKNOWN, *Is That Mr. Reilly?* (1883) See 1636:7.

13
I've been workin' on the railroad,
All the live-long day,
I've been workin' on the railroad
Just to pass the time away.
Don't you hear the whistle blowing,
Rise up so early in the morn,

Don't you hear the captain shouting:
Dinah, blow your horn.

UNKNOWN, *I've Been Workin' on the Railroad.* "The most famous standby of barber-shop agonizers." It's first known publication was in *Carmina Princetonia,* 1894. It was called *Levee Song,* and no author was given.

1
He flies through the air with the greatest of ease,
This daring young man on the flying trapeze;
His figure is handsome, all girls he can please,
And my love he purloined her away.

GEORGE LEYBOURNE, *The Man on the Flying Trapeze.* (1860) Music by Alfred Lee.

2
My Bonnie lies over the ocean,
My Bonnie lies over the sea,
My Bonnie lies over the ocean,
Oh, bring back my Bonnie to me.

UNKNOWN, *Bring Back My Bonnie to Me.* (1882)

3
Like ev'ry jolly fellow,
I takes my whiskey clear,
I'm a rambling wretch of poverty,
And the son of a gambolier.

UNKNOWN, *The Son of a Gambolier.* A popular college song of fifty years ago.

4
I blow through here; the music goes 'round and around.

WILLIAM HAROLD (RED) HODGSON, *The Music Goes 'Round and Around.* (1931) The authorship of this insane "swing" tune, which swept the country for a while, has also been credited to Eddy Farley and Mike Riley, but Hodgson seems to have the prior claim. The song is said to have been suggested by some lines in a joke book for the Ford automobile, published in 1915:
You push the first pedal down,
The wheels go 'round and around.

5
Home, home on the range,
Where the deer and the antelope play;
Where seldom is heard a discouraging word,
And the skies are not cloudy all day.

DR. BREWSTER HIGLEY, *The Western Home.* Written in 1873, the name of the song was afterwards changed to *Home on the Range,* and became very popular. It should be noted that it is not a cowboy song, for in this instance "range" has nothing to do with a cattle range or ranch, but denotes a row of townships six miles wide running north and south through a county. Higley was a Pennsylvania physician who had homesteaded near South Center, Kansas, about 1870. The music was written by Dan Kelly, a neighbor at South Center. (For history of the song see *Smith County Pioneer,* 19 Feb., 1914.) There have been many claimants to its authorship. The Paull-Pioneer Music Corporation has published a version ascribing the music to C. O. (Bob) Swartz, a prospector living near Leadville, Colorado, and the words to a number of his friends, placing the date of composition in 1885, and giving its name as *Colorado Home.* (See *The Story of Colorado Home,* by Kenneth S. Clark, which accompanies the music.) A modern version was written by Carson Robison in 1932, and in 1934 Mr. and Mrs. William Goodwin, of Tempe, Arizona, claimed it was an infringement of a song called *Arizona Home,* written by them in 1903. Both *Colorado Home* and *Arizona Home* vary slightly from Dr. Higley's *Western Home,* but evidently descended from it.

6
K-K-Katy, beautiful Katy,
You're the only g-g-g-girl that I adore,
When the m-m-m-moon shines over the cow-shed,
I'll be waiting at the k-k-k-kitchen door.

GEOFFREY O'HARA, *K-K-Katy.* (1918) Popular during the World War. There were many parodies, one being:
C-c-c-cootie, horrible cootie,
You're the only b-b-b-bug that I abhor,
When the moon shines over the bunk-house,
I'll scratch my b-b-b-back until it's sore.

7
Barney Google with his Goo Goo Googly eyes,
Barney Google had a wife three times his size,
She sued Barney for divorce,
Now he's living with his horse,
Barney Google with his Goo Goo Googly eyes.

BILLY ROSE and CON CONRAD, *Barney Google.* (1923)

8 1099:3
Then I shall be able to pull the leg of that chap Mike. He is always trying to do me.

WILLIAM BROWN CHURCHWARD, *Blackbirding in the South Pacific,* p. 215. (1888) This is the earliest use of this phrase in the sense of deceiving or humbugging which has been discovered. (See *New English Dictionary,* vi, 181.) But Thomas Hood used it in another sense in the concluding stanza of his *The Last Man,* written in 1826:

For hanging looks sweet,—but alas! in vain
My desperate fancy begs,—
I must turn my cup of sorrows quite up,
And drink it to the dregs,—
For there is not another man alive,
In the world, to pull my legs!

Hood is referring to the fact that, before the invention of the long drop in executions, the friends of a criminal were permitted to pull his legs in order to shorten his sufferings. (See *Notes and Queries,* 10th series, vii, 164, 2 March, 1907. There are a number of other communications on the same subject in *N. & Q.* for 1913.)

Jamie 's been drawing your leg (befooling you).

IAN MACLAREN, *Beside the Bonny Brier Bush,* p. 200. (1895) The phrase is used by Kipling, in his story, *The Tomb of His Ancestors.* (*McClure's Magazine,* December, 1897.)

9 1770:4a
Works with noble beginnings and grand promises often have one or two purple patches so

stitched on as to glitter far and wide. (Inceptis gravibus plerumque et magna professis Pupureus, late qui splendeat, unus et alter Adsitur pannus.)

HORACE, *De Arte Poetica*, l. 14. Macaulay is said to have popularized the phrase in referring to his *Decline and Fall of the Roman Empire*, and Maria Edgeworth used it in referring to Sir Walter Scott. See 1770:4a.

1 1924:18

I want to be a moron
And with the morons train;
A low, receding forehead,
A silly, half-baked brain.
I want to be a moron,
Because you see, gee whiz!
I like congenial spirits,
I'm lonely as it is.

CAROLYN WELLS, *A Longing*.

2 1966:17

Taxation without representation is tyranny.

JAMES OTIS, *Argument on the Illegality of the Writs of Assistance*, before the Superior Court of Massachusetts, in February, 1761. (COUSIN and HILL, *American History for Schools*, p. 155.) However, the only record of what Otis actually said is some rough notes by John Adams, which formed the basis of the first printed account of the speech, published in the *Massachusetts Spy*, 29 April, 1773. Fifty years after the event, Adams corrected his notes for William Tudor's *Life of James Otis*, and in a letter to Tudor, dated 9 June, 1818, he wrote (*Works*, x, 317): "And here he gave reins to his genius, in declamation, invective, philippic, call it what you will, against the tyranny of taxation without representation." Tudor used this paragraph in his biography (p. 77), without quotation marks, and adds, "From the energy with which he urged this position, that taxation without representation is tyranny, it came to be a common maxim in the mouth of everyone." Otis's most recent biographer, Samuel Eliot Morrison, says (*D.A.B.*, xiv, 102): "What Otis said cannot now be recovered with any exactness. . . . The phrase, 'Taxation without representation is tyranny,' which was not germane to the issue, appears only in Adams's final expansion of his notes, made about 1820." (See CANNING, *History of the United States*, iii, 5, note 1.)

For the acts passed in Parliament for encouraging trade and navigation, we humbly conceive, according to the usual sayings of the learned in the law, that the laws of England are bounded by the four seas, and do not reach America. The subjects of his majesty here being not represented in Parliament, so we have not looked at ourselves to be impeded in our trade by them.

UNKNOWN, *Declaration of the General Court of the Colony*, 2 Oct., 1678. (*Records of the Governor and Company of the Massachusetts Bay in New England*, v, 200.)

3 2069:4

It has long been my opinion that we are all educated, whether children, men or women, far more by personal influence than by books and the apparatus of schools. If I could be taken back into boyhood today, and had all the libraries and apparatus of a university, with ordinary routine professors, offered me on the one hand, and on the other a great, luminous, rich-souled man, such as Dr. Hopkins was twenty years ago, in a tent in the woods alone, I should say give me Dr. Hopkins for my college course rather than any university with only routine professors.

JAMES ABRAM GARFIELD, *Address*, before the Department of Superintendence of the National Educational Association, Washington, D. C., 11 Dec., 1877.

4 2071:2

Genius is a vagabond; Art is a vagabond; Enterprise is a Vagabond. Vagabonds have moulded the world into its present shape; they have made the houses in which we dwell, the roads on which we ride and drive, the very laws that govern us. Respectable people throng in the track of the vagabond as rooks in the track of the ploughshare. . . . Nature makes us vagabonds, the world makes us respectable.

ALEXANDER SMITH, *Dreamthorp: On Vagabonds*.

The fresh, rough, heathery parts of human nature, where the air is freshest, and where the linnets sing, is getting encroached upon by cultivated fields. Everyone is making himself and herself useful. Everyone is producing something. Everybody is clever. Everybody is a philanthropist. I don't like it. I love a little eccentricity. I respect honest prejudices. I admire foolish enthusiasm in a young head better than wise scepticism. It is high time, it seems to me, that a moral game-law was passed for the preservation of the wild and vagrant feelings of human nature.

ALEXANDER SMITH, *Dreamthorp: On Vagabonds*.

5

Russia seems undoubtedly . . . to be carrying on a process of absorption in Persia, and it is being done by what, I think, a French writer has called "peaceful penetration."

SIR EDWARD GREY. (*Parliamentary Debates*, 18 Feb., 1903.) The earliest use of the phrase "peaceful penetration" which the editor has been able to discover. Used in *The Nation* in 1913 (July 31, p. 103). In 1916 an Australian writer, A. D. McLaren, wrote a book by that title, placing the phrase in quotation marks, with no indication of its source. In common use since.

6 755:6

Tinker to Evers to Chance.

FRANKLIN P. ADAMS, *Baseball's Sad Lexicon*. Perhaps this famous line needs some elucidation. Joe Tinker, Johnny Evers and Frank

Chance were members of the Chicago Cubs, the first at shortstop, the second at second base, and the third at first base. With a runner at first base, Tinker would stop a ground hit, toss the ball to Evers on second before the runner could reach it, and Evers would whip the ball to first before the man who hit the ball could get there, making a double play which was frequently repeated.

1
This is an imitation of a Latin poem, attributed to Bonnefonius:

Semper munditias, semper, Basilissa, decores.
Semper compositas arte recente comas,
Et comptos semper cultus, unguentaque semper,
Omnia sollicita compta videre manu,
Non amo. Neglectim mihi se quæ comit amicæ
Se det; et ornatus simplicitate valet.
Vincula ne cures capitis discussa soluti,
Nec ceram in faciem: mel habet illa suum.
Fingere se semper, non est confidere amori;
Quid quod sæpe decor, cum prohibitur, adest?

The learned may find these verses among those printed at the end of the Variorum edition of Petronius. Mr. Upton imagines that there are some passages faulty in this poem: I have given it as I find it in the notes of Colomesius on some passages of Quintillian, printed in his *Opuscula;* He tells us, *Hi versus sic legendi sunt, licet alio abeat ingeniosissimus Nicolaus Heinsius ad Ovidium*. Tom. i, p. 394.

PETER WHALLEY, *Note to Ben Jonson's Epicœne,* act i, sc. 1.

2
From each according to his abilities, to each according to his needs. (Jeder nach seinen Fähigkeiten, jedem nach seinen Bedürfnissen.)

KARL MARX, *Program Kritiken. Randglossen zum Programm der Deutschen Arbeiter Partei,* p. 27. (1875) Known in English as *Critique of the Gotha Program.*

3
Rulers, Statesmen, nations are wont to be emphatically commended to the teaching which experience offers in history. But what experience and history teach is this—that peoples and governments never have learned anything from history, or acted on principles deduced from it. (Was die Erfahrung aber und die Geschichte lehren, ist dieses, das Völker und Regierungen niemals etwas aus der Geschichte gelernt.)

GEORG WILHELM FRIEDRICH HEGEL, *Philosophy of History: Introduction*. Sibree, tr. Usually quoted, "The only thing we learn from history is that we learn nothing from history."

Alas! Hegel was right when he said that we learn from history that men never learn anything from history.

BERNARD SHAW, *Heartbreak House: Preface.*

4
One can resist the invasion of armies, but not the invasion of ideas. (On résiste à l'invasion des armées; on ne résiste pas à l'invasion des idées.)

VICTOR HUGO, *Histoire d'un Crime: Conclusion: La Chute.* Ch. 10, p. 649. Édition Nationale, Paris, 1893. Vol. 36. This sentence has been variously translated. In the Atheneum Society edition, vol. xiv, p. 627, it is translated literally, "One resists the invasion of armies; one does not resist the invasion of ideas." William F. Giese, *Victor Hugo*, p. 295, renders it, "An invasion of armies can be resisted; an invasion of ideas can not be resisted." And on April 15, 1943, *The Nation* sent out a subscription circular with the sentence, "There is one thing stronger than all the armies in the world; and that is an idea whose time has come," stating that this was the closing entry in Victor Hugo's diary, who died the same night in his sleep. A talk with the circulation manager responsible for the circular elicited the information that, while he remembered using the quotation, he had no idea of its source or where he found it. A search by the Information Division of the New York Public Library disclosed no trace of any publication of Victor Hugo resembling a diary or journal. A similar search by the reference department of the Library of Congress was also unavailing, but the sentence from *Histoire d'un Crime* given above was found, and is probably the origin of the sentence quoted by *The Nation,* which has since become familiar in a more picturesque form, "Greater than the tread of mighty armies is an idea whose hour has come." Emerson, in his essay, *Civilization,* paraphrases Hugo's idea, "Gibraltar may be strong, but ideas are impregnable, and bestow on the hero their invincibility."

5
The Greeks Had a Word for It.

ZOE AKINS. Title of play produced in 1929. The word in question was *hetaera:* "irregular they were, but pleasant, even as those three errant ladies—Polaire, Schatze, and Jean—who wander cynically through Miss Akins's play." —New York *Times,* 12 Oct., 1930, sec. 8, page 4, col. 4. In a bit of dialogue which was deleted before the play was produced, one of the characters comments, "Even the Anglo-Saxons have a word for her sort, and it's usually spelt with a dash."

6 **THE NEW DEAL**

If it is reorganization, a new deal and a change you are seeking, it is Hobson's choice. I am sorry for you, but it is really vote for me or not vote at all.

WOODROW WILSON, *Address,* Camden, N.J., 24 Oct., 1910. The first known use of "new deal" in a political address by a candidate for office. See *Philadelphia Record,* 25 Oct., 1910.

I pledge you, I pledge myself, to a new deal for the American people.

Franklin Delano Roosevelt, *Speech,* to the Democratic National Convention, which had just nominated him for President, 3 June, 1932. In a letter to the present editor, dated 17 Feb., 1952, George W. Watt states, "F.D.R. told me, personally, that he took it [new deal] from W.W.'s speech at Camden." The phrase had, of course, been in use for many years, usually with reference to card-playing. "A new deal and a new bank" was used in a letter from John Rathbone to Nicholas Biddle in 1834. Charles Lever, in his novel *Roland Cashel,* ch. 13, (1849), has "Give us the cards for awhile. . . . Hurrah for a new deal." Other instances are cited in *The Historical Dictionary of American English.*

In the field of world policy, I would dedicate this nation to the policy of a good neighbor.

F. D. Roosevelt, *First Inaugural Address,* 4 March, 1933.

If I were asked to state the great objective which church and state are both demanding for the sake of every man and woman and child in this country, I would say that that great objective is a more abundant life.

F. D. Roosevelt, *Address,* before the Federal Council of the Churches of Christ, 6 Dec., 1933. He used the phrase "A more abundant life" on several subsequent occasions. On 30 March, 1939, in a talk at the Alabama Polytechnic Institute, Auburn, Ala., he said he had tried to give the Southern states "a balanced economy that will spell a higher wage scale, a greater purchasing power, and a more abundant life than they have had in all their history " Again, on 6 Nov., 1941, in an address before the Conference of the International Labor Organization, delivered in the East Room of the White House, he said, in linking world-peace to the attainment of a better world, "If that world is to be one in which peace is to prevail, there must be a more abundant life for the masses of the people of all countries."

To try to increase the security and the happiness of a larger number of people in all occupations of life; . . . to give them assurance that they are not going to starve in their old age; to give honest business a chance to go ahead and make a reasonable profit, and to give everyone a chance to earn a living.

F. D. Roosevelt, when asked what were the social objectives of his administration, the so-called New Deal, at a press conference, 7 June, 1935.

Yes, we are on our way back—not by mere chance, not by a turn of the cycle. We are coming back more surely than ever before because we planned it that way; and don't let anybody tell you differently.

F. D. Roosevelt, *Address,* at Charleston, S.C., 23 Oct., 1935. The phrase, "we planned it that way," was used with considerable effect in late 1937 by the President's opponents when the country sank back into depression.

In 1776 we sought freedom from the tyranny of a political autocracy—from the eighteenth century royalists who held special privileges from the crown. . . Since that struggle, however, man's inventive genius released new forces in our land which reordered the lives of our people. . . . Out of this modern civilization economic royalists carved new dynasties. . . . The royalists of the economic order have conceded that political freedom was the business of the Government, but they have maintained that economic slavery was nobody's business. . . . These economic royalists complain that we seek to overthrow the institutions of America.

F. D. Roosevelt, *Speech of Acceptance,* second nomination for the Presidency, Democratic National Convention, Philadelphia, Pa., 27 June, 1936.

I see one-third of a nation ill-housed, ill-clad, and ill-nourished.

F. D. Roosevelt, *Inaugural Address,* 20 Jan., 1937.

I am reminded of four definitions: A radical is a man with both feet firmly planted—in the air; a conservative is a man with two perfectly good legs who, however, has never learned to walk; a reactionary is a somnambulist walking backwards; a liberal is a man who uses his legs and his hands at the behest of his head.

F. D. Roosevelt, *Radio Broadcast,* 26 Oct., 1939.

The Executive Order I have signed today is a hold-the-line order. To hold the line we cannot tolerate further increases in general wage or salary rates except where clearly necessary to correct sub-standard living conditions.

F. D. Roosevelt, *Executive Order,* 8 April, 1943, designed to prevent inflation.

Clear everything with Sidney.

F. D. Roosevelt (?), *Remark,* to Robert Hannegan, Chairman of the Democratic National Committee, at a conference at Chicago, during the convention which nominated Mr. Roosevelt for a fourth term, June, 1944. The only contest before the convention was over the nomination of vice president, and "Sidney" was Sidney Hillman, head of the Political Action Committee of the Congress of Industrial Organizations (C.I.O.), whose support was very important to Mr. Roosevelt, and who was demanding the nomination of some one satisfactory to his organization. That Mr. Roosevelt actually said, "Clear everything with Sidney" was never admitted either by him or his advisers, but the phrase was used extensively by the Republicans during the ensuing campaign.

The first twelve years are the hardest.

F. D. Roosevelt, *Remark,* at a press conference at the White House, 19 Jan., 1945, answering a question as to his reflections on what he had accomplished during his third term as President, just drawing to a close.

For other quotations from Mr. Roosevelt's speeches see *Index of Authors* (p. 2370), and the *Index and Concordance.*

1
An ever normal granary.

HENRY A. WALLACE, explaining the phrase of the second Agricultural Adjustment Act, passed 16 Feb., 1938, fixing a "parity price" on crops, which the Government maintained.

Modern science . . . has made it technologically possible to see that all the people of the world get enough to eat. Half in fun and half seriously I said the other day to Madame Litvinoff, "The object of this war is to make sure that everybody in the world has the privilege of drinking a quart of milk a day."

HENRY A. WALLACE, *Address,* before the Free World Association, New York City. 8 May, 1942. Madame Litvinoff was the wife of the Russian Ambassador to the United States.

Much of what Mr. Wallace calls his global thinking is, no matter how you slice it, still "Globaloney."

CLARE BOOTH LUCE, *Speech,* House of Representatives, 9 Feb., 1943.

The times call for clear, lucid thinking rather than Clare Luceish thought.

BENNETT CERF, *Speech,* introducing Norman Angell, a few days after Clare Luce's speech.

2
The nine old men.

DREW PEARSON and ROBERT S. ALLEN. Title of book dealing with the Supreme Court. (1936) On 5 Feb., 1937, President Roosevelt sent to Congress a message urging reorganization of the court, upon which he was defeated.

WORLD WAR II

I—Mr. Roosevelt and the War *

3
War is a contagion.

PRESIDENT FRANKLIN DELANO ROOSEVELT, *Speech,* Chicago, 5 Oct., 1937.

The hand that held the dagger has struck it into the back of its neighbor.

F. D. ROOSEVELT, *Address,* 10 June, 1940, referring to Mussolini's declaration of war against France.

And while I am talking to you mothers and fathers, I give you one more assurance. I have said this before, but I shall say it again and again and again. Your boys are not going to be sent into any foreign wars. [For comment *see* 2298i:3]

F. D. ROOSEVELT, *Speech,* Boston, Mass., 30 Oct., 1940. This was a few days before his election for a third term, defeating Wendell Willkie. "He kept us out of war," *see* 1558:7.

We must be the great arsenal of democracy.

F. D. ROOSEVELT, *Radio Address,* 29 Dec., 1940.

The first is freedom of speech and expression—everywhere in the world. The second is freedom of every person to worship God in his own way—everywhere in the world. The third is freedom from want . . . everywhere in the world. The fourth is freedom from fear . . . anywhere in the world.

F. D. ROOSEVELT, *Message to Congress,* 6 Jan., 1941. Hailed as the "four freedoms." *See* BAIRD, *Representative American Speeches,* 1940–41, p. 185.

Aid [to democracies] will be increased—and yet again increased—until total victory has been won.

F. D. ROOSEVELT, *Speech,* at dinner of White House Correspondents' Association, Washington, 15 March, 1941.

We cannot save freedom with pitchforks and muskets alone after a dictator combination has gained control of the rest of the world.

F. D. ROOSEVELT, *Radio Broadcast,* 4 July, 1941.

We have sought no shooting war with Hitler. We do not seek it now. But neither do we want peace so much that we are willing to pay for it by permitting him to attack our naval and merchant ships while they are on legitimate business.

F. D. ROOSEVELT, *Radio Broadcast,* 11 Sept., 1941, referring to the attack on the U.S. destroyer *Greer* by a German submarine off Greenland on 4 Sept.

A new peace which will give decent people everywhere a better chance to live and prosper in security and in freedom and in faith.

F. D. ROOSEVELT. *Radio Address,* 27 Oct., 1941.

Yesterday, December 7, 1941—a date that will live in infamy—the United States of America was suddenly and deliberately attacked by naval and air forces of the Empire of Japan.

F. D. ROOSEVELT, *Message to Congress,* 8 Dec., 1941. This was the beginning of the message which asked for a declaration of war.

We are now in this war. We are in it—all the way. We are going to win the war, and we are going to win the peace that follows.

F. D. ROOSEVELT, *Radio Address,* 9 Dec., 1941, the day after the United States had declared war on Japan and the Axis powers.

The militarists of Berlin and Tokyo started this war, but the massed angered forces of common humanity will finish it.

F. D. ROOSEVELT, *Speech,* before joint session of Congress, 6 Jan., 1942.

We fight to retain a great past—and we fight to gain a greater future.

F. D. ROOSEVELT, *Annual Message to Congress,* 7 Jan., 1943.

Soon we and not our enemies will have the offensive; we, not they, will win the final battles; and we, not they, will make the final peace.

F. D. ROOSEVELT, *Radio Address,* 23 Feb., 1942.

This is the toughest war of all time.

F. D. ROOSEVELT, *Radio Address,* 7 Sept., 1942.

There can be no coasting to victory.

F. D. Roosevelt, *Address,* to closing session of the New York Herald-Tribune forum, New York City, 17 Nov., 1942.

The first crack in the Axis has come.

F. D. ROOSEVELT, *Radio Broadcast,* 28 July, 1943, referring to the invasion of Sicily.

* Other quotations from the speeches of Mr. Roosevelt will be found in the text under appropriate headings. Consult the *Index of Authors* (p. 2370), or the *Index and Concordance.*

II—Mr. Churchill and the War

1
It was for Hitler to say when the war would begin; but it is not for him or for his assistants to say when it will end. It began when he wanted it, but it will end only when we are convinced that he has had enough.

Winston Churchill, *Radio Address*, 1 Oct., 1939.

I have nothing to offer but blood, toil, tears, and sweat.

Winston Churchill, *Speech*, House of Commons, 13 May, 1940, after being commissioned by the King to form a new government. Where Mr. Churchill got the phrase is uncertain—he may, of course, have coined it, as he did so many others—but in 1611, John Donne, *An Anatomie of the World: The First Anniversary*, l. 430, wrote,

" 'Tis in vain to dew, or mollifie
It with thy teares, or sweat, or blood."

We shall fight on beaches, landing grounds, in fields, in streets and on hills.

Winston Churchill, *Speech*, House of Commons, 4 June, 1940.

The battle of Britain is about to begin.

Winston Churchill, *Speech*, House of Commons, 1 July, 1940. The bombing of Britain, or "the blitz," as it was called, from the German "Blitzkrieg," meaning "lightning-war," or war conducted with lightning speed, began in August, 1940, and lasted until the end of the following May, when the Germans intensified their submarine warfare. On 5 March, 1941, A. V. Alexander, First Lord of the Admiralty, referred to this as "The Battle of the Atlantic, now opening."

Never in the field of human conflict was so much owed by so many to so few.

Winston Churchill, *Speech*, House of Commons, 20 Aug., 1940, referring to the Royal Air Force, which had beat off the German Luftwaffe during the Battle of Britain.

We do not covet anything from any nation except their respect.

Winston Churchill. *Address*, broadcast to the French people, 21 Oct., 1940.

The crafty, cold-blooded, black-hearted Italian.

Winston Churchill, *Radio Broadcast*, 9 Feb., 1941, referring to Benito Mussolini. In a speech at the Guildhall, London, 30 June, 1943, Churchill characterized Mussolini as "Their pinchbeck Caesar," and in a radio address of 22 June, 1941, he had referred to Hitler as "This bloodthirsty guttersnipe."

All his usual formalities of perfidy were observed with scrupulous technique.

Winston Churchill, *Radio Address*, 21 June, 1941, referring to Hitler's invasion of Russia.

We shall not fail or falter; we shall not weaken or tire. . . . Give us the tools, and we will finish the job.

Winston Churchill, *Broadcast Address*, 9 February, 1941, answering American critics.

If we fail, all fails, and if we fall, all will fall together.

Winston Churchill, *Speech*, House of Commons, 29 July, 1941.

One by one—that was his plan.

Winston Churchill, *Radio Address*, 24 Aug., 1941, referring to Hitler's plan of world conquest. "Divide and conquer was Hitler's strategy."—*Newsweek*, 12 Jan., 1942, p. 21. See 815:5. In 1942, the Allies set up the opposing strategy of "Unite, encircle, close in."

I am sure that at the end all will be well for us in our island home, all will be better for the world.

Winston Churchill, *Speech*, Guildhall, Hull, 7 Nov., 1941.

We shall drive on to the end, and do our duty, win or die. God helping us, we can do no other.

Winston Churchill, *Radio Address*, from London, 10 May, 1942. *See* 1227:5.

When the hour of liberation strikes in Europe, as strike it will, it will also be the hour of retribution.

Winston Churchill, *Speech*, House of Commons, 8 Sept., 1942.

Our defeats are but stepping-stones to victory, and his victories are only stepping-stones to ruin.

Winston Churchill, *Speech*, at Edinburgh, 12 Oct., 1942. Referring to Hitler.

Let me, however, make this clear, in case there should be any mistake about it in any quarter. We mean to hold our own. I have not become the King's First Minister in order to preside over the liquidation of the British Empire.

Winston Churchill, *Speech*, at the Mayor's Day Luncheon, Mansion House, London, 10 Nov., 1942.

The problems of victory are more agreeable than those of defeat, but they are no less difficult.

Winston Churchill, *Speech*, House of Commons, 11 Nov., 1942, referring to the victorious end of the African campaign.

I believe it was Bismarck who said in the closing years of his life that a dominating fact in the modern world was that the people of Britain and of the United States spoke the same language.

Winston Churchill, *Speech*, House of Commons, 11 Feb., 1943. Quoted again in his speech at Harvard University, 6 Sept., 1943.

Difficulties mastered are opportunities won.

Winston Churchill, *Radio Broadcast*, 21 March, 1943.

I can imagine that some time next year—but it may well be the year after—we might beat Hitler, by which I mean beat him and his powers of evil into death, dust, and ashes.

Winston Churchill, *Radio Broadcast*, 21 March, 1943.

By its sudden collapse, the proud German army has once again proved the truth of the saying, "The Hun is always either at your throat or at your feet."

Winston Churchill, *Speech*, to the U. S. Congress, 19 May, 1943.

It is a poor heart that never rejoices.

Winston Churchill, *Speech*, to the U. S. Congress, 19 May, 1943. Quoting an old proverb.

We shall continue to operate on the Italian donkey at both ends, with a carrot and with a stick.
WINSTON CHURCHILL, *Press Conference,* 25 May, 1943.

I quote the words of your great general, Nathan Bedford Forrest, the eminently successful Confederate leader. Asked the secret of his victories, Forrest said, "I git thar fustest with the mostest men."
WINSTON CHURCHILL, *Press Conference,* 25 May, 1943.

Brighter and solid prospects lie before us.
WINSTON CHURCHILL, *Speech,* House of Commons, June, 1943, after his return from a tour of the North African front.

We seek no profit, we covet no territory or aggrandisement. We expect no reward and we will accept no compromise.
WINSTON CHURCHILL, *Speech,* Guildhall, London, 30 June, 1943.

The time has come for you to decide whether Italians shall die for Mussolini and Hitler, or live for Italy and for civilization.
WINSTON CHURCHILL and F. D. ROOSEVELT, *Joint Message,* to the Italian people, 16 July, 1943

The keystone of the Fascist arch has crumbled.
WINSTON CHURCHILL, *Speech,* House of Commons, 27 July, 1943, referring to the overthrow of Mussolini by the Italian Fascists two days earlier.

The price of greatness is responsibility.
WINSTON CHURCHILL, *Address,* Harvard University, 6 Sept., 1943.

The empires of the future are empires of the mind.
WINSTON CHURCHILL, *Speech,* at Harvard University, 16 Sept., 1943. *See also* 2299b:1.

III—General MacArthur and the War

1
Only those are fit to live who are not afraid to die.
GENERAL DOUGLAS MACARTHUR, *Address,* to the Filipino air force, July 31, 1941. *See* CONSIDINE, *MacArthur the Magnificent,* p. 9.

I shall return.
GENERAL DOUGLAS MACARTHUR, to his fellow officers as he boarded a small patrol boat to leave the Philippines for Australia, 11 March, 1942.

I came through and I shall return.
GENERAL DOUGLAS MACARTHUR, *Pledge,* upon reaching Australia from Bataan, 17 March, 1942. A few days later, on his arrival at Melbourne, MacArthur added, "I shall keep a soldier's faith." *See* CONSIDINE, *MacArthur the Magnificent,* p. 126.

America's Holy Grail lies on Corregidor.
GENERAL DOUGLAS MACARTHUR, *Statement,* on the first anniversary of the surrender of the fortress in Manila Bay, 8 May, 1943.

The inescapable price of liberty is an ability to preserve it from destruction.
GENERAL DOUGLAS MACARTHUR, to President Quezon of the Philippines. *See* MILLER, *MacArthur,* p. 192. *See also* 2299c:6.

IV—Miscellaneous

2
Hell, we haven't started to fight. Our artillery hasn't been overrun yet.
GENERAL TERRY ALLEN, at the invasion of Sicily, July, 1943. Reminiscent of John Paul Jones. *See* 62:7.

3
Hitler has missed the bus.
SIR NEVILLE CHAMBERLAIN, *Speech,* 4 April, 1940, referring to Hitler's invasion of Norway.

4
There are no atheists in the fox-holes.
REV. WILLIAM THOMAS CUMMINGS, *Sermon,* on Bataan, Philippine Islands, March, 1942. Father Cummings was an army chaplain. *See* ROMULO, *I Saw the Fall of the Philippines,* p. 263. Claimed also for Col. W. J. Clear.

5
France has lost a battle. But France has not lost the war.
GENERAL CHARLES DEGAULLE, *Remark,* to Winston Churchill. 17 June, 1940, the day of his arrival in London after the fall of France.

6
The eyes of the world are upon you. The hopes and prayers of liberty-loving people everywhere march with you.
GENERAL DWIGHT EISENHOWER, to his troops as the invasion of Normandy started, 6 June, 1944 American infantrymen had given themselves the name of GI Joes—GI meaning Government Issue, referring to all the articles issued from the Quartermaster's supplies. "GI Turkey" was corned beef, "GI Cocktail" was a dose of salts, and so on.

7
Praise the Lord and pass the ammunition.
LIEUTENANT COMMANDER HOWELL FORGY, navy chaplain, to a chain of men passing ammunition aboard his cruiser at Pearl Harbor. 7 Dec., 1941. Attributed also to Fleet Chaplain William B. Maguire, who denied it.

8
Guns will make us powerful; butter will only make us fat.
FIELD MARSHALL HERMANN GOERING, *Radio Broadcast,* July, 1936. Perhaps the most famous gun to come out of the war on the American side was the so-called "Bazooka," an anti-tank gun using rocket propulsion, and operated by two men. The most famous vehicle was the "jeep," a quarter-ton pygmy truck, which supposedly got its name from the initials GP (general purpose) painted on the back of the early models. On 22 Feb., 1941, one of these trucks gave an exhibition by climbing the steps of the Capitol at Washington, and when a reporter asked its driver what he called the vehicle, the driver answered, "Why, I call it a jeep. Everybody does."

9
We have a phrase in English, "straight from the horse's mouth."
JOSEPH CLARK GREW, *Address,* delivered in Tokyo, 19 Oct., 1939. This was the opening

sentence of the address, which came to be known as "The horse's mouth speech," in which Mr. Grew, the United States Ambassador to Japan indicated clearly the feeling of the American government and people toward the militaristic government of Japan.

There is not sufficient room in the area of the Pacific Ocean for a peaceful America . . . and a swashbuckling Japan.

JOSEPH C. GREW, *Radio Broadcast*, from Washington, D.C., 30 Aug., 1942.

1

The lamps are going out all over Europe; we shall not see them lit again in our lifetime.

VISCOUNT GREY OF FALLODEN, at the outbreak of the first World War, 3 Aug., 1914. See his *Twenty-five Years*, vol. ii, p. 20.

2

We are the ultimate hope and sanctuary of human liberty.

HERBERT HOOVER, *Address*, to Pennsylvania Society of New York, 21 Dec., 1940.

3

It is better to die on your feet than to live on your knees.

DOLORES IBARRURI, (LA PASIONARIA), *Speech*, at Paris, 3 Sept., 1936. The phrase has been claimed for Emiliano Zapata (*See* GUNTHER, *Inside Latin America*, p. 63), but PINCHON, *Zapata the Unconquerable*, p. 44, quotes Zapata as saying, "Better a fighting death than a slave's life." The attribution to La Pasionaria is by *American Notes and Queries*.

4

In this tragic hour when you too are assailed by the treacherous aggressor, the people of China renew their gratitude to the people of the United States for the understanding and help that have been given us. To our now common battle we offer all we are and all we have to stand with you until the Pacific and the world are freed from the curse of brute force and endless perfidy.

CHIANG KAI-SHEK, *Message*, to President Roosevelt, 9 Dec., 1941.

America is not only the cauldron of democracy, but the incubator of democratic principles.

MADAME CHIANG KAI-SHEK, *Speech*, House of Representatives, 18 Feb., 1943.

5

A bloody monument to divided responsibility.

COLONEL HIGH J. KNERR, referring to the Japanese attack on Pearl Harbor, 7 Dec., 1941. See *American Mercury*, June, 1942, p. 648. The result was a demand for the integration of army, navy and air force under one command, which was recommended by President Truman in a message to Congress, 19 Dec., 1945.

6

Sighted sub. Sank same.

DONALD FRANCIS MASON, *Radio Message*, to U.S. Navy Department, 26 February, 1942.

Scratch one flat-top.

LIEUTENANT COMMANDER ROBERT E. DIXON, *Radio Message*, to his carrier after sinking Japanese carrier off Misima Island during the battle of the Coral Sea, 7 May, 1942. *See* JOHNSTON, *Queen of the Flat-Tops*, p. 181. In the battle of Midway, May, 1943, the last message radioed by a PBY pilot was, "Sighted aircraft carrier. Am trailing same. Notify next of kin."

This is it, chaps.

BRENDEN (PADDY) FINUCANE, *Radio Message*, to his squadron, as his plane collapsed into the English Channel, 11 Nov., 1942.

Take her down.

COMMANDER HOWARD W. GILMORE, *Order*, to the crew of his submarine the *Growler*, during a battle against a Japanese squadron in the south Pacific, in February, 1943, as he lay mortally wounded on her deck, knowing that the delay in getting him safely into the submarine might mean its destruction.

7

The fifth column.

GENERAL EMILIO MOLA, *Radio Address*, when he was leading four columns of troops against Madrid in 1938. The "fifth column" consisted of the Franco sympathizers within the city, and the term came to be applied to all secret sympathizers and supporters of the enemy, engaged in sabotage, espionage and other subversive activities within defense lines. See *Webster's New International Dictionary*, 1943, p.c. Early in 1942, the term "Sixth column" was applied by Colonel Richard C. Patterson, Jr., New York State Chairman of the Defense Savings Staff, to gossipers and rumor mongers, and was adopted by President Roosevelt in a broadcast on 24 March, 1942. In July, 1942, "Seventh column" was applied to strikers or careless workers in war industries.

8

The Rome-Berlin axis.

BENITO MUSSOLINI, *Speech*, at Milan, 2 Nov., 1936. For definition see *Webster's New International Dictionary*, 1943, p. xcvii.

9

The former allies have blundered in the past by offering Germany too little, and offering even that too late, until finally Nazi Germany has become a menace to all mankind.

ALLAN NEVINS, *Germany Disturbs the Peace*. In *Current History*, May, 1935, p. 178.

It is the old trouble—too late. . . . It is always too late, or too little, or both, and that is the road to disaster.

DAVID LLOYD GEORGE, *Speech*, House of Commons, March, 1940, the day after Finland fell.

10

We shall attack and attack until we are exhausted, and then we shall attack again.

MAJOR GENERAL GEORGE S. PATTON, JR., *Slogan*, to the American troops under his command, before sailing for North Africa, 15 Nov., 1942 In the preceding August, General Sir Harold R. L. G. Alexander gave his British troops a somewhat similar slogan, "Attack, attack, and attack again, even when you are on the defensive." See *Newsweek*, 31 Aug.,

1942. p. 25. "Back the attack" was selected as the slogan of the fifth War Loan drive, in June, 1944.

1

In a few minutes I am going out to prepare the tomorrows that sing. (Je vais préparer tout à l'heure les lendemains qui chantent.)

COMMUNIST DEPUTY GABRIEL PERI, *Letter,* just before his execution by the Nazis, July, 1942. See *New York Times Magazine,* 11 April, 1943, p. 15.

2

The Grumlin does the same job of sabotage on the home front that the Gremlin does to the airplanes of our pilots fighting the Axis.

SAMUEL RAYBURN, Speaker of the House of Representatives, *Speech,* at East Texas State Teachers College, 5 Aug., 1943. "Gremlins" was the name to the perverse imps who made things go wrong with airplanes during World War II. The first one was supposed to have been born in a beer bottle in 1923. See *Newsweek,* 7 Sept., 1942.

3

Bataan has fallen, but the spirit that made it stand—a beacon to all the liberty-loving peoples of the world—cannot fall!

LIEUTENANT NORMAN REYES, *Radio Report,* of the fall of Bataan, sent from a tunnel in the rock fortress of Corregidor, 9 April, 1942. *See* ROMULO, *I Saw the Fall of the Philippines,* p. 302

4

The Seabees are always happy to welcome the Marines.

LIEUTENANT BOB RYAN, greeting to the Marines as they landed at Segi, New Georgia, Sept., 1943. "Seabees" was the nickname of the Construction Battalion of the U. S. Navy. Supposed to land with or just after the Marines, they had somehow managed to land first at Segi.

5

God bless America.

IRVING BERLIN. Title of song. First sung in public by Kate Smith in a radio broadcast on Armistice Day, 11 Nov., 1938.

There'll always be an England.

ROSS PARKER and HUGHIE CHARLES. Title of song written in March, 1939, and immensely popular with the English after the outbreak of the war six months later. *See* 2298m:11.

We'll hang out the washing on the Siegfried line.

UNKNOWN. Title of popular British song soon after the start of the war, September, 1939.

The last time I saw Paris.

OSCAR HAMMERSTEIN, II. Title of lyric, from the moving picture, *Lady be Good.* (1940) Title of book of reminiscences of Paris by Elliot Paul

All Out for America.

JOHN ADAMS. Title of marching song of the U.S.A. Music by Mayhew Lake. (c. 1941)

6

Expedience and justice frequently are not even on speaking terms.

ARTHUR H. VANDENBERG, *Speech,* in U. S. Senate, 8 March, 1945, referring to the decision made at Yalta by Roosevelt, Churchill and Stalin to cede eastern Poland to Russia.

7

Suppose you're a sergeant machine-gunner, and your army is retreating and the enemy advancing. The captain takes you to a machine gun covering the road. "You're to stay here and hold this position," he tells you. "For how long?" you ask. "Never mind," he answers, "just hold it." Then you know you're expendable. In a war anything can be expendable—money or gasoline or equipment or most usually men. They are expending you and that machine gun to get time.

W. L. WHITE, *They Were Expendable,* p. 3.

8

The people of Germany are just as responsible for Hitler as the people of Chicago are for the Chicago Tribune.

ALEXANDER WOOLLCOTT, his last words before collapsing at the microphone, 23 Jan., 1943, where he was taking part in a "People's Platform" program on the subject "Is Germany incurable?" He died a few hours later.

9

China incident.

The Japanese-coined phrase for the "incident" which started the attack upon China on the night of 7 July, 1937, when the Japanese held large-scale military maneuvres near Lukouchaio and alleged afterwards that one of their men was missing. See *China Handbook,* 1937–1943, p 350.

10

South America becomes very quisling conscious.

UNKNOWN, *Time,* 24 May, 1940, p. 40. A new word for a traitor or collaborator with the enemy, deriving from Vidkun Quisling, head of the Norwegian Nazi party, who was appointed head of the Nazi-sponsored government after the German invasion of Norway in April, 1940. He was condemned to death as a traitor and executed on 24 October, 1945. All of the Allied governments had their Quislings. The outstanding French one was Pierre Laval, executed in November, 1945. The most famous British one was "Lord Haw Haw," the microphone name of William Joyce, an American who had gone to Germany on a British passport and began broadcasting German propaganda from Berlin soon after the start of the war. He was captured by the British shortly after the German surrender and executed in London, 3 January, 1946. On 26 July, 1943, the District of Columbia Federal Grand Jury indicted eight Americans living abroad for treason, including Frederick Wilhelm Kaltenbach, known as "The American Lord Haw-Haw"; Douglas Chandler, one-time Baltimore columnist, whose mike name was "Paul Revere"; Edward Leo Delaney, known as E. D. Ward; and Ezra Pound, the well-known poet, all of them for broadcasting enemy propaganda, Pound from Italy and the others from Germany. In a letter to the compiler the Department of Justice states that Kaltenbach died in Germany prior to the end of the war; Pound was declared mentally incapable to stand trial and was confined in St. Elizabeth's Hospital, Washington, D.C., and finally released, Apr., 1958; Chandler and Robert H. Best were convicted and sentenced to life imprisonment; the case against Delaney was presented to a New York grand jury, which voted a no true bill. Two others of those indicted were Constance Drexell and Jane Anderson, but both indictments were dismissed. Jane Anderson was never apprehended. By January, 1950, there were twelve such convictions, the latest being that of H. J. Burgman, of Hokah, Minn.

1

I said to a man who stood at the gate of the year: "Give me a light that I may tread safely into the unknown." And he replied, "Go out into the darkness and put your hand into the hand of God. That shall be to you better than a light and safer than a known way."

MINNIE L. HASKINS, *The Desert: Introduction.* (c. 1920) Quoted by King George VI, of England, Christmas Day broadcast, 1939. *The Desert* was a small volume of verse published privately by its author, a teacher in the London School of Economics. See *Time,* 8 Jan., 1940. *See also* 2300n:3.

2

A shadow has fallen upon the scenes so lately lighted by the Allied victory. From Stettin in the Baltic to Trieste in the Adriatic, an iron curtain has descended across the continent.

WINSTON CHURCHILL, *Address,* at Westminster College, Fulton, Mo., 5 March, 1946. It was this use of the phrase by Churchill which popularized it, but it had been used in the same connection forty years earlier:

Redwood had still imperfectly apprehended the fact that an iron curtain had dropped between him and the outer world.

H. G. WELLS, *The Food of the Gods.* Bk. iii, ch. 4, pt. 1. (1904) Repeated in pt. 3.

Mexico . . . with a deep rooted grievance, and an iron curtain at its frontier.

GEORGE M. CRILE, *A Mechanistic View of War and Peace.* Ch. 4, p. 69. (1915) The phrase perhaps derives from the iron curtain formerly lowered in larger theatres to prevent fire spreading from stage to audience.

3

Are you in earnest? seize this very minute—
What you can do, or dream you can, begin it,
Boldness has genius, power, and magic in it.
Only engage, and then the mind grows heated—
Begin it, and the work will be completed!
(Das Mögliche soll der Entschluss
Beherzt sogleich beim Schopfe fassen;
Er will es dann nicht fahren lassen,
Und wirket weiter, weil er muss.)

JOHANN WOLFGANG VON GOETHE, *Faust: Vorspiel auf dem Theater,* l. 227. (1806) As translated by JOHN ANSTER, *Faustus, A Dramatic Mystery: Prelude at the Theatre,* l. 303. (1835) It will be noted that Anster's translation is a very free one—really a paraphrase, or, as some one has said, the translation of a poet by a poet. Later renderings, while usually more literal, are much less successful as poetry. Here is that of James Adey Birds (London, Longmans, 1880, p. 94):

Resolve, and in your own selves trust,
Grasp by the forelock what you've got,
And take heed ye loose it not;
But work away because you must.

And here is George Madison Priest's latest revision of his translation of the same passage (New York, Knopf, 1941, p. 10):

With resolution seize the possible straightway
By forelock and with quick, courageous trust;
Then holding fast you will not let it further fly
And you will labour on because you must.

John Anster was an Irishman, born at Charleville, County Cork, in 1793. After publishing one or two small volumes of verse, he began his translation of Goethe, and in 1820 translations of various passages appeared in *Blackwood's Magazine,* being the first rendering into English of any part of *Faust.* The complete translation of the first part appeared in 1835, and that of the second part not until 1864, three years before Anster's death.

4

"Oh, what a superior man!" said Candide to himself. "What a prodigious genius is this Pococurante! Nothing can please him." (Oh! quel homme supérieur! disait Candide entre ses dents; quel grand génie que se Pococurante! Rien ne peut lui plaire.)

VOLTAIRE, *Candide.* Ch. 25. (1758) The entire chapter is devoted to a description of Candide's visit to the home of the "Noble Venitien," Pococurante (Ital., *poco curante,* little caring), who detested Raphael, Homer, Vergil, Horace, Cicero and Milton, as well as music and the theatre. The saying is quoted by *Fortune* (Nov., 1948, p. 204) in referring to John L. Lewis.

Mr. Trotter, it is easy for you to play the pococurantist.

GEORGE BERNARD SHAW, *Fanny's First Play: Epilogue.* (1911) Used here in the sense of taking nothing seriously, of being indifferent to matters of importance.

5

The modernization of the Hippocratic Oath by the World Medical Association, known as the Declaration of Geneva (1948), is worthy of note. It runs: "Now being admitted to the profession of medicine. I solemnly pledge to consecrate my life to the service of humanity. I will give respect and gratitude to my deserving teachers. I will practice medicine with conscience and dignity. The health and life of my patients will be my first consideration. I will hold in confidence all that my patient confides in me. I will maintain the honor and noble traditions of the medical profession. My colleagues will be my brothers. I will not permit consideration of race, religion, nationality, party politics or social standing to intervene between my duty and my patient. I will maintain the utmost respect for human life from its conception. Even under threat I will not use my knowledge contrary to the laws of humanity. These promises I make freely and upon my honor.

1
If I should ever be in England's thought
After I die,
Say, "There were many things he might have bought
And did not buy!
Unhonoured by his fellows, he grew old
And trod the path to Hell,
But there were many things he might have sold,
And did not sell!"

THOMAS W. H. CROSLAND, *Epitaph.*

2
Climb high. Climb far,
Your goal the sky, Your aim the star.

ALBERT HOPKINS (?), *Inscription*, on Hopkins Gate, Williams College. Found among the papers of Prof. Hopkins after his death, copied perhaps from some unknown source.

3
Cold war.

HERBERT BAYARD SWOPE. In a letter to the compiler, Mr. Swope writes: "I have been using the phrase 'cold war,' as B. M. Baruch and others will confirm, since 1945, several months before the death of President Roosevelt. I put it in writing in one or two letters in 1946. . . . I put it in a speech that Baruch made to the South Carolina legislature on the unveiling of his portrait there by the State, 16 April, 1947." This was the first public use of the phrase.

Let us not be deceived—we are today in the midst of a cold war.

BERNARD M. BARUCH, *Speech*, before South Carolina Legislature, 16 April, 1947.

In the interview, which was brief, Baruch said he was the first person to use the phrase "cold war." He said it was suggested to him by Herbert Bayard Swope, former editor of the defunct New York *World*.

Interview, with Mr. Baruch in Boston *Globe*, 1 April, 1949.

4
When I joined the army, even before the turn of the century, it was the fulfillment of all my boyish hopes and dreams. . . . I still remember the refrain of one of the most popular barracks ballads of that day, which proclaimed most proudly that old soldiers never die; they just fade away. And like the old soldier of that ballad, I now close my military career and just fade away.

GENERAL OF THE ARMY DOUGLAS MACARTHUR, *Address*, before a joint meeting of the United States Congress, Washington, D.C., 19 April, 1951.

The ballad General MacArthur referred to derives from a gospel hymn, "Kind Words Can Never Die," written about 1855 by "Sister" Abby Hutchinson, a member of a well-known group of evangelists who toured the country for over thirty years in the middle of the last century. The first stanza is as follows:

Kind words can never die,
Cherished and blest,
God knows how deep they lie,
Lodged in the breast;
Like childhood's simple rhymes,
Said o'er a thousand times,
Go through all years and climes,
The heart to cheer.
Chorus: Kind words can never die, never die, never die,
Kind words can never die, no never die.

There are three additional stanzas, "Childhood can never die," "Sweet tho'ts can never die," and "Our souls can never die." The version given here is taken from "Woman in Sacred Song," p. 457, published by D. Lothrop & Company in 1885.

In 1858 the chorus was added when the hymn was set to music by Horace Waters. Whether it was written by Waters or by Miss Hutchinson is uncertain, but it was this chorus which furnished the inspiration for "Old Soldiers Never Die."

The Hutchinsons toured the Union Camps widely during the Civil War, much as the USO entertainers do today, and the chorus was soon picked up by the soldiers and parodied in various ways, most of them extremely bawdy. There is an impression that it is of English origin, due probably to the fact that it first appeared in print, so far as known, in an English book, "Tommy's Tunes," page 58, published in London in 1917, which gives two stanzas:

Old soldiers never die, never die, never die,
Old soldiers never die, they always fade away.
This rain will never stop, never stop, never stop,
This rain will never stop—No, no, no, no, no.

It was sung by British soldiers during the first World War, usually as "They simply fade away." But General MacArthur's memory was correct, for the West Point version is "They just fade away." There is a legend at West Point that it was written by General Charles P. Summerall, who graduated in 1892, eight years before General MacArthur became a cadet, but, as Mr. Richard S. Hill, reference librarian of the Music Division of the Library of Congress writes to the compiler, "I would be profoundly suspicious of any attribution to any person living or dead, but particularly suspicious of any attribution to a General. Soldier songs rarely grow that way."

1
The stairway of time ever echoes with the wooden shoe going up and the polished boot coming down.

JACK LONDON, *What Life Means to Me*. In *Cosmopolitan Magazine*, March, 1906. See also Carl Sandburg's *The People*, 1936. The origin of this saying is of course much older, and in various versions it has been attributed to Voltaire, Balzac, Hugo, and others, but the present editor has been unable to find it in their works. One version is "History is silver slippers walking down the steps and wooden clogs climbing up." The same idea as that of the Lancashire proverb, cited by *Notes and Queries*, (4th ser., vii, 472. 1871) "Clogs to clogs is only three generations," or by the American "Three generations from shirtsleeves to shirtsleeves."

2
In 1768, we find in Protestant England John Wesley standing firmly for witchcraft, and uttering his famous declaration, "The giving up of witchcraft is in effect the giving up of the Bible."

ANDREW DICKSON WHITE, *A History of the Warfare of Science with Theology*. Vol. i, p. 363. (1896) In a footnote Mr. White enumerates statements from Increase Mather, Cotton Mather, Deodat Lawson, and many others, indicating a belief in witchcraft.

I cannot give up to all the Deists in Great Britain the existence of witchcraft, 'till I give up the credit of all history, sacred and profane.

JOHN WESLEY, *Journal*, 23 May, 1776.

3
In almost all of his other addresses in which FDR promised not to send American boys to fight in foreign wars he added the phrase "except in case of attack," or "unless we are attacked," but he did not use this phrase in his speech at Boston. Here is what Sam Rosenman has to say about it in his *Working With Roosevelt*, p. 242: "Every time the President had made this statement before Boston—and every time thereafter—he added to it the words he himself had so carefully added to the foreign policy plank: 'Except in case of attack.' I suggested that he add the same words this time but he suddenly got stubborn about it—I could not understand why. 'It's not necessary,' he said. 'If we're attacked it's no longer a foreign war.' " (*See* 2298b:3)

4
I had become one of the notorieties of the metropolis of the world. . . . You could not take up a newspaper, English, Scotch, or Irish, without finding in it one or more references to the "vest-pocket million pounder" and his latest doings and sayings. At first, in these mentions, I was at the bottom of the personal-gossip column; next, I was listed above the knights, next above the barons, and so on, . . . until I reached the highest altitude possible, and there I remained, taking precedence of all dukes not royal, and of all ecclesiastics except the Primate of all England.

MARK TWAIN, *The Million Pound Banknote*. (1893) Probably the first use of "gossip column."

5
One world at a time.

HENRY DAVID THOREAU, *Remark*, shortly before his death in 1862, to Parker Pillsbury, "who would fain talk with Thoreau in this last winter concerning the next world." (F. B. SANBORN, *Henry D. Thoreau*, p. 314. 1882.) Parker Pillsbury, anti-slavery orator, was an old friend of Thoreau. Brooks Atkinson, who refers to "the pontifical Frank Sanborn, sole custodian of Thoreau," says the visitor was William Ellery Channing, Thoreau's "closest friend." (*Walden and Other Writings of Thoreau*.)

When a pious visitor inquired sweetly, "Henry, have you made your peace with God?" he replied, "We have never quarrelled."

J. BROOKS ATKINSON, *Henry Thoreau, the Cosmic Yankee*, p. 29. (1927)

6
My grandfather, William H. Vanderbilt, had, considering his numerous philanthropic gifts, an unmerited reputation for indifference to the welfare of others. It was, as is often the case, founded on a remark shorn of its context. This is the version of the "public be damned" story that was given me by a friend of the family. Mr. Vanderbilt was on a business trip and, after a long and arduous day, had gone to his private car for a rest. A swarm of reporters arrived asking to come on board for an interview. Mr. Vanderbilt sent word that he was too tired and did not wish to give an interview, but would receive one representative of the press for a few minutes. A young man arrived saying, "Mr. Vanderbilt, *your* public *demands* an interview." This made Mr. Vanderbilt laugh, and he answered, "Oh, *my* public be damned!" In due course the young man left and next morning his article appeared in the paper with a large headline reading, "Vanderbilt Says 'The Public be Damned.' "

CONSUELO VANDERBILT BALSAN, *The Glitter and the Gold*, p. 3. (1952) *See* 1480:10.

7
In his *Working With Roosevelt*, pp. 90–91, Sam Rosenman states that Roosevelt had been reading Thoreau at the time he was preparing his inaugural address, and that in all probability Tho eau's sentence had struck him as given in 655:15, and that he paraphrased it in his inaugural address.

However, on page 71, Mr. Rosenman seems to claim credit for the phrase, as does Raymond Mo ey (*After Seven Years*, p. 23). Cyril Clemens, in *St. Louis Post Dispatch*, 31 May, 1952, records an interview with Roosevelt in which the latter stated that he got the phrase from Mark Twain's *A Connecticut Yankee in King Arthur's Court*. Probably by that time he had forgotten where he did get it. *See also* 2298:6.

1
It was now the Virginian's turn to bet, or leave the game, and he did not speak at once. Therefore Trampas spoke. "Your bet, you son-of-a- . . . . . ."

The Virginian's pistol came out, and his hand lay on the table, holding it unaimed. And with a voice as gentle as ever, the voice that sounded almost like a caress, but drawling a little more than usual, . . . he issued his orders to the man Trampas:—

"When you call me that, *smile!*" and he looked at Trampas across the table.

Yes, the voice was gentle. But in my ears it seemed as if somewhere the bell of death was ringing; and silence, like a stroke, fell on the large room.

OWEN WISTER, *The Virginian*. Ch. ii, p. 28. (1902) *See* 1852:13.

APPENDIX II

ACT, ACTION

2
It is better to be making the news than taking it; to be an actor rather than a critic.

WINSTON CHURCHILL, *The Story of the Malakand Field Force*. (1898)

3
Lyndon acts like there was never going to be a tomorrow.

CLAUDIA T. (MRS. LYNDON B.) JOHNSON, referring to her husband. (*New York Times Magazine*, 29 Nov., 1964, p. 28)

4
Let's get this thing airborne.

LYNDON B. JOHNSON, to subordinates aboard the presidential plane in Dallas, 22 Nov., 1963, a few minutes after he was sworn into office in the conference room of the same plane, following the assassination of John F. Kennedy. The order directed an immediate return to Washington, D.C. (H. A. ZEIGER, *Lyndon B. Johnson: Man and President*, p. 10)

ACTING

5
For an actress to be a success she must have the face of Venus, the brains of Minerva, the grace of Terpsichore, the memory of Macaulay, the figure of Juno, and the hide of a rhinoceros.

ETHEL BARRYMORE. (GEORGE JEAN NATHAN, *The Theatre in the Fifties*, 1953)

6
His life was what the marquees describe as a "continuous performance."

JOHN MASON BROWN, *The Portable Woollcott: Introduction*. Referring to ALEXANDER WOOLLCOTT.

7
An actor is totally vulnerable. He's vulnerable from head to toe, his total personality is exposed to critical judgment—his intellect, his bearing, his diction, his whole appearance. In short, his ego. Actors want to be admired. They want very much to be at their best. And, mind you, our emotions are always near the surface. We, in this profession, have been blessed or cursed with vivid imaginations. Nor are we known for our thick skins.

ALEC GUINNESS. (*New York Times Magazine*, 17 May, 1964, p. 20)

8
Too lined for Hamlet, on the whole;
For tragic Lear, too coarsely built,
Himself becomes his favorite role,
Played daily to the hilt.

PHYLLIS MCGINLEY, *The Love Letters of Phyllis McGinley: The Old Actor*.

9
A little ham is an asset to the actor. It contributes to his color and charm. But an all-out ham can be as obnoxious as a drunk on a roller-coaster. Ham is not peculiar to actors. All the theatre's workers are infected.

RICHARD MANEY, *Fanfare*, p. 274. (1957)

10
Actors are like politicians, and politicians are like actors. They both spend time each day contemplating their image. They both have a desire to be loved.

GORE VIDAL, *Interview*, New York *Times*, 6 Oct., 1963.

ADVERTISING

11
Good times, bad times, there will always be advertising. In good times, people want to advertise; in bad times, they have to.

BRUCE BARTON. (*Town & Country*, Feb., 1955)

12
Who's kidding whom? What's the difference between Giant and Jumbo? Quart and *full* quart? Two-ounce and *big* two-ounce? What does Extra Long mean? What's a *tall* 24-inch? And what busy shopper can tell?

MARYA MANNES. (*Life*, 12 June, 1964, p. 64)

13
You wouldn't tell lies to your own wife. Don't tell them to mine. Do as you would be done by. If you tell lies about a product, you will

be found out—either by the Government, which will prosecute you, or by the consumer, who will punish you by not buying your product a second time.

DAVID OGILVY, *Confessions of an Advertising Man,* ch. 5. (1963)

1
The Hidden Persuaders.

VANCE PACKARD, Title of book (1955).

2
Half the money I spend on advertising is wasted, and the trouble is I don't know which half.

JOHN WANAMAKER, paraphrasing a statement originally made by the first Lord Leverhulme. (DAVID OGILVY, *Confessions of an Advertising Man,* ch. 3)

AGE

3
To me, old age is always fifteen years older than I am.

BERNARD M. BARUCH, on his 85th birthday, Aug., 1955.

4
The best part of the art of living is to know how to grow old gracefully.

ERIC HOFFER, *The Passionate State of Mind,* p. 136. (1954) *See also* 26: 13.

5
Our machines have now been running seventy or eighty years, and we must expect that worn as they are, here a pivot, there a wheel, now a pinion, next a spring, will be giving way; and however we may tinker them up for a while, all will at length surcease motion.

THOMAS JEFFERSON, *Letter to John Adams,* 5 July, 1814.

6
I heard once a very old friend, who had troubled himself with neither poets nor philosophers, say that he was tired of pulling off his shoes and stockings at night, and putting them on again in the morning. The wish to stay here is thus gradually extinguished.

THOMAS JEFFERSON, *Letter to Abigail Adams,* 11 Jan., 1817.

The future is but dressing and undressing.

JAMES BRANCH CABELL, *Jurgen,* p. 30. (1919)

7
I promise to keep on living as though I expected to live forever. Nobody grows old by merely living a number of years. People grow old only by deserting their ideals. Years may wrinkle the skin, but to give up interest wrinkles the soul.

GENERAL DOUGLAS MACARTHUR, *Address,* at the dedication of the MacArthur Monument, Los Angeles, 26 Jan., 1955.

8
Oh hell, another birthday.

SOMERSET MAUGHAM, on his 91st birthday, Jan., 1965.

9
Pick the right grandparents, don't eat or drink too much, be circumspect in all things, and take a two-mile walk every morning before breakfast.

HARRY S TRUMAN, Comment to reporters on the prescription for reaching the age of 80. Spoken in Washington, D.C., on his own 80th birthday, 8 May, 1964.

AMBITION

10
Too many people have gone in for this senseless chasing of rainbows. How many rainbows does one need?

FREDERICK LOEWE, *Interview,* New York *Times,* 1 Oct., 1964. He was surveying a career during which he composed the music for *My Fair Lady, Brigadoon,* and *Camelot.*

11
The Status Seekers.

VANCE PACKARD, Title of book (1959), which helped to popularize the terms "status" and "status symbol."

AMERICA

12
I do not think America is a good place in which to be a genius. A genius can never expect to have a good time anywhere, if he is a genuine article, but America is about the last place in which life will be endurable at all for an inspired writer of any kind.

SAMUEL BUTLER, *Notebooks,* p. 257. (c. 1890)

13
Great Mother of a mighty race,
All earth shall be thy dwelling-place;
Democracy, thy holy name
Shall set the continents aflame,
Shall thrill the islands of the sea,
And keep thy children ever free.

WILLIAM MILL BUTLER, *Democracy.* (1918)

14
The world is not a big Red sea in which this country is being scuttled, but a vast arena of political upheaval, in which the quest for freedom, ever stronger, has overthrown the colonial empires of the past. It isn't a tidy world, nor is it a secure one. But it is one for which the United States set the revolutionary example.

FRANK CHURCH, *Speech,* in U.S. Senate, 12 Jan., 1965.

15
During toasts at dinner [April 13, 1830], Jackson sat impassive, giving no hint of his mind. Finally, he rose. He looked fixedly at Calhoun. He paused briefly. Then he proposed the most dramatic, as it is the most historic, toast in American history: "Our Federal Union. It must and shall be preserved."

DAVID L. COHN, *The Fabulous Democrats,* p. 45. (1956) *See also* 57:8.

16
There can be no such thing as a state's right to default on a national duty.

LEROY COLLINS, *Address,* to the Greater Columbia (S.C.) Chamber of Commerce, 3 Dec., 1963.

1
When I was in Paris last week, I said that . . . the United States would have to undertake an agonizing reappraisal of basic foreign policy in relation to Europe. This statement, I thought, represented a self-evident truth.

JOHN FOSTER DULLES, *Speech,* before National Press Club, Washington, 22 Dec., 1953.

It was to achieve the indispensable goal of rearming Germany that Dulles made one of his most criticized statements: his blunt warning that the U.S. would be forced to make an "agonizing reappraisal" of its foreign policy if France continued to block the establishment of the European Defense Community.

JAMES SHEPLEY, "How Dulles Averted War." (*Life,* 16 Jan., 1956, p. 70.)

2
The broad goal of our foreign policy is to enable the people of the United States to enjoy in peace the blessings of liberty.

JOHN FOSTER DULLES, *Address,* before the Foreign Policy Association, New York, 16 Feb., 1955.

3
We recognize and accept our own deep involvement in the destiny of men everywhere.

DWIGHT D. EISENHOWER, *Second Inaugural Address,* 21 Jan., 1957.

4
To be effective in the nation's rightful role as a Free World leader, our people and their government should always, in my view, display a spirit of firmness without truculence, conciliation without appeasement, confidence without arrogance.

DWIGHT D. EISENHOWER, *The White House Years: Mandate for Change 1953–1956.*

5
The United States—bounded on the north by the Aurora Borealis, on the south by the procession of the equinoxes, on the east by primeval chaos, and on the west by the Day of Judgment.

JOHN FISKE, *Toast,* at a dinner in Boston.

6
The American system of rugged individualism.

HERBERT CLARK HOOVER, *Speech,* New York City, 22 Oct., 1928; *The New Day,* p. 154. (1934)

While I can make no claim for having introduced the term "rugged individualism," I should be proud to have invented it.

HERBERT CLARK HOOVER, *The Challenge to Liberty,* Ch. v. (1934) *See* 978:15.

7
It cannot be to our interest that all Europe be reduced to a single monarchy.

THOMAS JEFFERSON, *Letter to Thomas Lieper,* 1 Jan., 1814.

8
Our first and fundamental maxim should be never to entangle ourselves in the broils of Europe. Our second, never to suffer Europe to intermeddle with cis-Atlantic affairs.

THOMAS JEFFERSON, *Letter to James Monroe,* 24 Oct., 1823. The letter which led to the adoption of the Monroe Doctrine. And of course "This country ought never to seek alliances, it ought to grant them." *See* 59:2.

9
I am a yes man for everything that is American. I am a yes man for anything that will aid in the defense of this republic. I am a yes man to the Commander-in-Chief, as every good soldier should be in time of emergency.

LYNDON B. JOHNSON, during his unsuccessful campaign, in 1941, to succeed Morris Sheppard as Democratic Senator from Texas. During this special primary election, caused by Sheppard's death, the opponents of Johnson accused him of being a "yes man" to the Roosevelt administration. (BOOTH MOONEY, *The Lyndon Johnson Story*)

10
I am a free man, an American, a United States Senator, and a Democrat, in that order.

I am also a liberal, a conservative, a Texan, a taxpayer, a rancher, a businessman, a consumer, a parent, a voter, and not as young as I used to be nor as old as I expect to be—and I am all these things in no fixed order.

I am unaware of any descriptive word in the second paragraph which qualifies, modifies, amends, or is related by hyphenation to the terms listed in the first paragraph. In consequence, I am not able—nor even the least interested in trying—to define my political philosophy by the choice of a one-word or two-word label. This may be against the tide, but, if so, the choice is deliberate.

LYNDON B. JOHNSON, *My Political Philosophy* (published originally in 1958 in *The Texas Quarterly* of the University of Texas, as a copyrighted article).

11
First, I believe every American has something to say and, under our system, a right to an audience.

Second, I believe there is always a national answer to each national problem, and, believing this, I do not believe that there are necessarily two sides to every question.

Third, I regard achievement of the full potential of our resources—physical, human, and otherwise—to be the highest purpose of governmental policies next to the protection of those rights we regard as inalienable.

Fourth, I regard waste as the continuing enemy of our society and the prevention of waste—waste of resources, waste of lives, or waste of opportunity—to be the most dynamic of the responsibilities of our Government.

LYNDON B. JOHNSON, *My Political Philosophy* (published originally in 1958 in *The Texas Quarterly* of the University of Texas, as a copyrighted article).

1
These are the United States—a united people with a united purpose. Our American unity does not depend upon unanimity. We have differences, but now, as in the past, we can derive from those differences strength, not weakness; wisdom, not despair.

LYNDON B. JOHNSON, *Address,* to joint session of Congress, 27 Nov., 1963—his first major speech after his accession to the presidency.

2
This Administration here and now declares unconditional war on poverty in America.

LYNDON B. JOHNSON, *State of the Union Message,* 8 Jan., 1964.

3
In short, we must be constantly prepared for the worst and constantly acting for the best —strong enough to win a war and wise enough to prevent one.

LYNDON B. JOHNSON, *State of the Union Message,* 8 Jan., 1964.

4
The people in this country have more blessed hopes than bitter victories. The people of this country and the world expect more from their leaders than just a show of brute force. And so our hope and our purpose is to employ reasoned agreement instead of ready aggression, to preserve our honor without a world in ruins, to substitute if we can understanding for retaliation.

LYNDON B. JOHNSON, *Address,* in Washington, D.C., 24 Mar., 1964.

5
My most fervent prayer is to be a President who can make it possible for every boy in this land to grow to manhood by loving his country—instead of dying for it.

LYNDON B. JOHNSON, *Address,* in Washington, D.C., 24 Mar., 1964.

6
We have voted as many, but tonight we must face the world as one.

LYNDON B. JOHNSON, *Speech,* in Austin, Texas, 4 Nov., 1964, the day after his victory over Barry M. Goldwater in the presidential election.

7
This, then, is the state of the union: free and restless, growing and full of hope. So it was in the beginning. So it shall always be, while God is willing, and we are strong enough to keep the faith.

LYNDON B. JOHNSON, *State of the Union Message,* 4 Jan., 1965.

8
The Great Society asks not how much, but how good; not only how to create wealth, but how to use it; not only how fast we are going, but where we are headed. It proposes as the first test for a nation: the quality of its people.

LYNDON B. JOHNSON, *State of the Union Message,* 4 Jan., 1965.

9
Here is our difference with the Communists —and our strength. They would use their skills to forge new chains of tyranny. We would use ours to free men from the bonds of the past.

LYNDON B. JOHNSON, *Message to Congress,* 14 Jan., 1965. He was contrasting the rival systems' goals in foreign aid.

10
For this is what America is all about. It is the uncrossed desert and the unclimbed ridge. It is the star that is not reached and the harvest that's sleeping in the unplowed ground.

LYNDON B. JOHNSON, *Inaugural Address,* 20 Jan., 1965.

11
In these circumstances it is clear that the main element of any United States policy toward the Soviet Union must be that of a long-term, patient but firm and vigilant containment of Russian expansive tendencies.

GEORGE KENNAN, "The Sources of Soviet Conduct"; *Foreign Affairs,* July, 1947. The first use of "containment" as a label for American policy after World War II. The article was published anonymously, but the editors of *Foreign Affairs* and the author later confirmed Kennan's origin of the term.

12
Let the word go forth from this time and place, to friend and foe alike, that the torch has been passed to a new generation of Americans—born in this century, tempered by war, disciplined by a hard and bitter peace, proud of our ancient heritage—and unwilling to witness or permit the slow undoing of those human rights to which this nation has always been committed, and to which we are committed today at home and around the world.

JOHN F. KENNEDY, *Inaugural Address,* 20 Jan., 1961.

13
To our sister republics south of our border, we offer a special pledge—to convert our good words into good deeds—in a new alliance for progress—to assist free men and free governments in casting off the chains of poverty.

JOHN F. KENNEDY, *Inaugural Address,* 20 Jan., 1961.

14
And so, my fellow Americans: ask not what your country can do for you—ask what you can do for your country. My fellow citizens

of the world: ask not what America will do for you, but what together we can do for the freedom of man.

JOHN F. KENNEDY, *Inaugural Address*, 20 Jan., 1961.

1
A Nation of Immigrants.

JOHN F. KENNEDY, Title of book, published posthumously (1964).

2
Whether you like it or not, history is on our side. We will bury you.

NIKITA S. KHRUSHCHEV, Statement at a Kremlin diplomatic reception, 26 Nov., 1956.

The words "We will bury capitalism" should not be taken literally as indicating what is done by ordinary gravediggers who carry a spade and dig graves and bury the dead. What I had in mind was the outlook for the development of human society. Socialism will inevitably succeed capitalism.

NIKITA S. KHRUSHCHEV, Statement to civic authorities in Los Angeles, 19 Sept., 1959. (*Conquest Without War*, p. 49)

We face in Communist hostility and expansionism a formidable force, whether Mr. Khrushchev and Mr. Mao Tse-tung pull together or apart. They disagree so far only on whether capitalism should be peacefully or violently buried. They are both for the funeral.

ADLAI E. STEVENSON, "The Hard Kind of Patriotism"; *Harper's Magazine*, July, 1963.

We intend to bury no one—and we do not intend to be buried.

LYNDON B. JOHNSON, *State of the Union Message*, 8 Jan., 1964.

3
We consider that the Monroe Doctrine has outlived its time; has died, so to say, a natural death.

NIKITA S. KHRUSHCHEV, News Conference in the Kremlin, 12 July, 1960.

4
It is true that America produces and consumes more cars, soap, and bathtubs than any other nation, but we live among these objects rather than by them. Americans build skyscrapers; Le Corbusier worships them. Ehrenburg, our Soviet critic, fell in love with the Check-O-Mat in American railway stations, writing home paragraphs of song to this gadget—while deploring American materialism. When an American heiress wants to buy a man, she at once crosses the Atlantic. The only really materialistic people I have ever met have been Europeans.

MARY MCCARTHY, *Perspective* (1953).

5
There is a small articulate minority in this country which advocates changing our national symbol which is the eagle to that of the ostrich and withdrawing from the UN.

ELEANOR ROOSEVELT, *Speech*, at the Democratic national convention, Chicago, 23 July, 1952.

6
America is a "happy-ending" nation.

DORE SCHARY, *Address*, to the Harvard Club of Los Angeles. (Quoted by Louis Kronenberger as a foreword to his *Company Manners*.)

7
President Johnson has directed me to affirm to this Assembly that there will be no "Johnson policy" toward the United Nations—any more than there was a "Kennedy policy." There was—and is—only a United States policy, and that . . . outlasts violence and outlives men.

ADLAI E. STEVENSON, *Address*, to the United Nations General Assembly, 26 Nov., 1963, four days after the death of Mr. Kennedy.

8
Since many [settlers in America] were escaping from tyranny . . . it is not surprising that the Americans do not love the machinery of government. So they have deliberately created a system of government which will permit each of them to do what he likes to a degree unknown elsewhere in the world.

STEPHEN JAMES LAKE TAYLOR (BARON TAYLOR of HARLOW), "Deep Analysis of the American Mind"; *New York Times Magazine*, 23 Feb., 1964.

ARCHITECTURE

9
Architecture is the art of how to waste space.

PHILIP JOHNSON. (New York *Times*, "Ideas and Men," 27 Dec., 1964, p. 9E) *See* 94:10.

10
Everything betrays us as a bunch of catchpenny materialists devoted to a blatant, screeching insistence on commercialism. If you look around you, and you give a damn, it makes you want to commit suicide.

EDWARD DURELL STONE, *Interview*, New York *Times*, 27 Aug., 1964.

ART AND ARTISTS

11
What is the public's responsibility to the arts? You have to learn to distinguish good from bad, support the good and write your congressman. He may not be able to read your letters, but he can count them.

AGNES DE MILLE. (*Life*, 15 Nov., 1963)

12
Is adversity in the arts ennobling? I doubt it. I struggled fifteen years before I made any success. It didn't make me a better person, it just made me hungry.

AGNES DE MILLE. (*Life*, 15 Nov., 1963)

13
America has not always been kind to its artists and scholars. Somehow the scientists always seem to get the penthouse while the arts and humanities get the basement.

LYNDON B. JOHNSON, *Speech*, upon signing the Arts and Humanities Act of 1965, 29 Sept., 1965.

1
I look forward to an America which will reward achievement in the arts as we reward achievement in business or statecraft.

JOHN F. KENNEDY, *Address,* at Amherst College, Amherst, Mass., 26 Oct., 1963.

2
I see little of more importance to the future of our country and our civilization than full recognition of the place of the artist. If art is to nourish the roots of our culture, society must set the artist free to follow his vision wherever it takes him.

JOHN F. KENNEDY, *Address,* at Amherst College, Amherst, Mass., 26 Oct., 1963.

3
Literature plays an important role in our country, helping the Party to educate the people correctly, to instill in them advanced, progressive ideas by which our Party is guided. And it is not without reason that writers in our country are called engineers of the human soul.

NIKITA S. KHRUSHCHEV, Interview with HENRY SHAPIRO of the United Press, 14 Nov., 1957.

We must never forget that art is not a form of propaganda, it is a form of truth. . . . In free society art is not a weapon and it does not belong to the sphere of polemics and ideology. Artists are not engineers of the soul.

JOHN F. KENNEDY, *Address,* at Amherst College, Amherst, Mass., 26 Oct., 1963.

4
The arts are always in trouble. It is their nature to be in trouble.

ARCHIBALD MACLEISH, Statement marking the 50th anniversary of the American Society of Composers, Authors and Publishers (ASCAP); New York *Times,* 16 Feb., 1964.

5
Artists don't see the world the way it wants to be seen and the world reciprocates.

ARCHIBALD MACLEISH, Statement marking the 50th anniversary of the American Society of Composers, Authors and Publishers (ASCAP); New York *Times,* 16 Feb., 1964.

6
Jesus Christ is not a man of a certain period; he is living. It is the same thing for a work of art: Its fundamental character resides in this mysterious survival.

ANDRÉ MALRAUX, *Address,* to French Parliament, 9 Nov., 1963.

7
The artist of today says to the public: If you don't understand this you are dumb. I maintain that you are not. If you have to go the whole way to meet the artist, it's his fault.

MARYA MANNES. (*Life,* 12 June, 1964)

8
The question no longer is whether there should be government support of the arts. The question is the extent of that support.

NELSON A. ROCKEFELLER. (New York *Times,* "Ideas and Men," 30 May, 1965, p. 11E)

BELL

9
Nunc lento sonitu dicunt, Moriaris. Now, this Bell tolling softly for another, saies to me, Thou must die. . . . Any man's *death* diminishes *me,* because I am involved in *Mankinde;* And therefore never send to know for whom the *bell* tolls; It tolls for *thee.*

JOHN DONNE, *Devotions.* No. xvii. (c. 1623) *For Whom the Bell Tolls* is the title of a novel by Ernest Hemingway. (1940)

10
Gay go up and gay go down,
To ring the bells of London Town.

Bulls'-eyes and targets,
Say the bels of Saint Marg'ret's.
Brickbats and tiles,
Say the bells of Saint Giles'.
Half-pence and farthings,
Say the bells of Saint Martin's.
Oranges and Lemons,
Say the bells of Saint Clement's. . . .
You owe me ten shillings,
Say the bells of Saint Helen's.
When will you pay me?
Say the bells at Old Bailey.
When I grow rich,
Say the bells of Shoreditch.
Pray, when will that be?
Say the bells of Stepney.
I'm sure I don't know,
Says the great bell at Bow.
Here comes a candle to light you to bed,
And here comes a chopper to chop off your head.

UNKNOWN, *The Bells of London.* James O. Halliwell, in his *Nursery Rhymes of England,* p. 61 (1843), says that these jingles were used in a children's game in which sides were chosen, followed by a tug of war. Katherine Thomas, in her *The Real Personages of Mother Goose,* has a fascinating chapter (xiii) dealing with the couplets and pointing out their hidden meanings, many of them political, satirizing Charles II and his winsome mistress, Nell Gwynne, the enchanting orange girl of Drury Lane, whose ashes lie today in the churchyard crypt of Saint-Martin's-in-the-Fields. Many of London's churches were destroyed during World War II, but most of them have been rebuilt and their bells are ringing again. St. Clement's, for example, rang in January, 1957, for the first time in sixteen years.

BOY AND BOYHOOD

11
I was born in a very fortunate age. The term "juvenile delinquent" wasn't thought of. We were just known as pests.

REV. JOHN CARMEL HEENAN, Archbishop of Westminster. (*The Reader's Digest,* Dec., 1963, p. 205)

12
A boy has two jobs. One is just being a boy. The other is growing up to be a man.

HERBERT HOOVER, *Speech,* 21 May, 1956, marking the 50th anniversary of the Boys' Clubs of America.

BROTHER AND BROTHERHOOD

1
To live is good. To live vividly is better. To live vividly together is best.

MAX EASTMAN. (*The Reader's Digest,* Dec., 1963, p. 205)

2
The world has narrowed to a neighborhood before it has broadened to brotherhood.

LYNDON B. JOHNSON, *Address,* at a luncheon in New York City, 17 Dec., 1963, attended by United Nations officials.

3
In the final analysis, our most basic common link is that we all inhabit this small planet. We all breathe the same air. We all cherish our children's future. And we are all mortal.

JOHN F. KENNEDY, *Address,* at American University, Washington, D.C., 10 June, 1963.

4
We must learn to live together as brothers or perish together as fools.

REV. MARTIN LUTHER KING, JR., *Address,* in St. Louis, 22 Mar., 1964, referring specifically to racial integration.

5
The brotherhood of man under the fatherhood of God.

NELSON A. ROCKEFELLER, Slogan coined during his unsuccessful campaign for the Republican presidential nomination in 1964.

6
We can truly begin to perceive the meaning of our great propositions—of liberty and equality—if we see them as part of the patrimony of all men. We shall not love our corner of the planet less for loving the planet too, and resisting with all our skill and passion the dangers that would reduce it to smoldering ashes.

ADLAI E. STEVENSON, "The Hard Kind of Patriotism"; *Harper's Magazine,* July, 1963.

BUSINESS

7
Don't speculate unless you can make it a full-time job. Beware of barbers, beauticians, waiters—or anyone—bringing gifts of "inside" information or "tips." . . . Don't try to buy at the bottom and sell at the top. This can't be done—except by liars.

BERNARD M. BARUCH, *Baruch: My Own Story,* ch. 19.

8
My father always told me that all businessmen were sons-of-bitches, but I never believed it till now!

Attributed to JOHN F. KENNEDY, supposedly his off-the-record reaction, as President, to steel producers' raising of prices, which Kennedy viewed as a threat to the economy. At a press conference, 9 May, 1962, just a month after the remark supposedly was made, Kennedy challenged its accuracy. He said that neither his father nor he put all businessmen in such a category, and otherwise sought to be conciliatory, since the companies had rescinded the price rises. Nevertheless, the incident led to widespread charges of an anti-business administration.

9
When a President said that "the business of America is business," he told us something about the degree to which a standard of living can do stand-in duty for a way of life.

ADLAI E. STEVENSON, "The Hard Kind of Patriotism"; *Harper's Magazine,* July, 1963. The words he quoted were spoken by Calvin Coolidge in 1925.

10
Businessmen don't elect Presidents, anyway. The common people elect them. I proved that back in 1948.

HARRY S TRUMAN, Press Conference in New York City, 9 Jan., 1964.

11
For many years I thought what was good for our country was good for General Motors, and vice versa.

CHARLES ERWIN WILSON, Testimony before the Senate Armed Services Committee, Jan., 1953, after he was nominated by President Eisenhower to be Secretary of Defense. This was one of the most controversial statements of one of the most controversial men in the Eisenhower cabinet, largely because it was misquoted. Wilson, a former officer of General Motors and still a large stockholder in the company when his name went to the Senate committee for approval, was questioned closely by Senators who feared the possibility of a conflict of interest. He was asked whether he could make a decision in the interest of the United States and adverse to General Motors, if the necessity arose. He replied, "I could. I cannot conceive of [such a situation] because for many years I thought what was good for our country was good for General Motors, and vice versa." But his critics quoted him as having said, "What's good for General Motors is good for the country." Subsequently a transcript of the testimony established the actual words.

CAT

12
I cannot agree that it should be the declared public policy of Illinois that a cat visiting a neighbor's yard or crossing the highway is a public nuisance. It is in the nature of cats to do a certain amount of unescorted roaming . . . to escort a cat abroad on a leash is against the nature of the owner. Moreover, cats perform useful service, particularly in the rural areas. The problem of the cat vs. the bird is as old as time. If we attempt to resolve it by legislation, who knows but what we may be called upon to take sides as well in the age-old problems of dog vs. cat, bird

vs. bird, or even bird vs. worm. In my opinion, the State of Illinois and its local governing bodies already have enough to do without trying to control feline delinquency.

ADLAI E. STEVENSON, Message to the Illinois Senate, 23 Apr., 1949, explaining his refusal, as Governor, to approve a b'll that would have punished owners who permitted cats to run at large. One of the most quoted of Stevenson's writings.

CHANGE

1
We do not fear this world of change.

DWIGHT D. EISENHOWER, *Second Inaugural Address*, 21 Jan., 1957.

2
We must change to master change.

LYNDON B. JOHNSON, *State of the Union Message*, 12 Jan., 1966.

3
Change means the unknown. . . . It means, too many people cry, insecurity. Nonsense! No one from the beginning of time has had security.

ELEANOR ROOSEVELT. (ARCHIBALD MACLEISH, "Tribute to a 'Great American Lady'"; *New York Times Magazine*, 3 Nov., 1963, p. 119)

CHILDREN

4
Children are our most valuable natural resource.

HERBERT HOOVER, Remark made by him many times.

5
Do not be afraid of having many children. This world has not been created to be a cemetery.

POPE JOHN XXIII. (New York *Times*, 30 Dec., 1959)

6
Our irrational contemporary Western impatience and our blind adulation of speed for speed's sake are making havoc, today, of the education of our children. We force their growth as if they were chicks in a pullet factory. We drive them into a premature awareness of sex even before physical puberty has overtaken them. In fact, we deprive our children of the human right of having a childhood.

ARNOLD J. TOYNBEE, "Why I Dislike Western Civilization"; *New York Times Magazine*, 10 May, 1964, p. 32.

CIVILIZATION

7
All civilization has from time to time become a thin crust over a volcano of revolution.

HAVELOCK ELLIS, *Little Essays of Love and Virtue*. Ch. vii.

8
Civilization begins at home.

HENRY JAMES, *Siege of London*. Ch. v. (1883)

9
I view great cities as penitential to the morals, the health, and the liberties of man.

THOMAS JEFFERSON, *Letter to Benjamin Rush*, 23 Sept., 1800.

10
This nation, the Soviet Union and the world are destined to live for a long time with feet dangling over the grave that beckons to the human civilization which is our common heritage. Against that immense void of darkness, this treaty is a feeble candle. It is a flicker of light where there had been no light.

MIKE MANSFIELD, Comment on the nuclear test-ban treaty of 1963 in September of that year.

11
Human beings do not carry civilization in their genes. All that we do carry in our genes are certain capacities—the capacity to learn to walk upright, to use our brains, to speak, to relate to our fellow men, to construct and use tools, to explore the universe, and to express that exploration in religion, in art, in science, in philosophy.

MARGARET MEAD, "Human Nature Will Flower, If—"; *New York Times Magazine*, 19 Apr., 1964, p. 97.

12
What a bore one's own native civilization is. It is dull just because it is familiar.

ARNOLD J. TOYNBEE, "Why I Dislike Western Civilization"; *New York Times Magazine*, 10 May, 1964, p. 15.

13
Disinterested intellectual curiosity is the life blood of real civilization.

GEORGE MACAULAY TREVELYAN, *English Social History: Preface*. (1942)

CONSERVATISM

14
The current political movement that describes itself as conservative is not conservative but by every test reactionary. The reactionary-conservative thinks primarily in terms of the past, of a world in which the problems confronting him were fewer and simpler, of conditions which will never return. The liberal understands that factors exist today which were not present yesterday and knows that neither wishful thinking nor meaningless oratory will remove them.

HARRY J. CARMAN, *Letter* to the St. Louis *Post-Dispatch*, published 10 Aug., 1964. Carman was writing as chairman of the American Liberal Association.

15
A conservative, briefly, has a philosophy based upon the proven values of the past. When we seek answers for the problems of today we look to the past to see if those problems existed. Generally, they have. So

we ask: What was the answer? Did it work? If it did, let us try it again.

BARRY M. GOLDWATER. ("Goldwater Defines Conservatism"; *New York Times Magazine,* 24 Nov., 1963, p. 122)

1
My idea of a conservative is one who desires to retain the wisdom and the experience of the past and who is prepared to apply the best of that wisdom and experience to meet the changes which are inevitable in every new generation. The term "liberal" came to the United States in its political sense from England during the 19th century. As defined by them at that time, a liberal would be the conservative of today. . . . The conservative is the true liberal.

HERBERT HOOVER, 1962. ("Herbert Hoover in His Own Words"; compiled and edited by LOUIS P. LOCHNER; *New York Times Magazine,* 9 Aug., 1964, p. 15)

2
To defend every abuse, every self-interest, every encrusted position of privilege in the name of love of country—when in fact it is only love of the status quo—that indeed is the lie in the soul to which any conservative society is prone.

ADLAI E. STEVENSON, "The Hard Kind of Patriotism"; *Harper's Magazine,* July, 1963.

CONSTITUTION

3
No person . . . shall be compelled in any criminal case to be a witness against himself.

Bill of Rights, Article v. (25 Sept., 1789) Submitted by the First Congress at its first session. The section that many persons have invoked to escape testifying when on the witness stand.

4
Whenever the Constitution comes between men and the virtue of the white women of South Carolina, I say—to hell with the Constitution.

COLE L. BLEASE, *Public Statement,* as Governor of South Carolina. (1911)

5
In essence, the Constitution is not a literary composition, but a way of ordering society, adequate for imaginative statesmanship, if judges have imagination for statesmanship.

FELIX FRANKFURTER.

6
Reassertion of the fundamental character of the Constitution, not as a treaty between the States, but rather as a charter emanating directly from the people, is ever necessary in the face of assertions, made even to this day, that the States, or rather their legislatures, are to be the final judges of their own powers and those of the national government. . . . These echoes of nullification are denied by the Constitution itself and by our national experience. They have no place in our day when our unity as a people is indispensable for survival.

ARTHUR J. GOLDBERG, *Address,* to the American Bar Association, Chicago, Aug., 1963.

7
These decisions give support to a current mistaken view of the Constitution and the constitutional function of this Court. This view, in a nutshell, is that every major social ill in this country can find its cure in some constitutional "principle," and that this Court should "take the lead" in promoting reform when other branches of government fail to act. The Constitution is not a panacea for every blot upon the public welfare, nor should this Court, ordained as a judicial body, be thought of as a general haven for reform movements. This Court, limited in function, does not serve its high purpose when it exceeds its authority, even to satisfy justified impatience with the slow workings of the political process.

JOHN MARSHALL HARLAN, of the U.S. Supreme Court, in dissenting in legislative reapportionment cases during the term of 1963–64.

8
The Constitution is what the judges say it is.

CHARLES EVANS HUGHES, *Speech,* at Elmira, N.Y., 3 May, 1907.

9
Some men look at Constitutions with sactimonious reverence, and deem them like the ark of the covenant, too sacred to be touched. . . . Let us provide in our constitution for its revision at stated periods.

THOMAS JEFFERSON, *Letter to Samuel Kercheval,* 12 July, 1818.

10
Our basic law—the Constitution—is distinctive among the basic law of all nations, even the free nations of the West, in that it prescribes no national dogma: economic, social, or religious.

LYNDON B. JOHNSON, *My Political Philosophy.* Published originally in 1958 as a copyrighted article in *The Texas Quarterly* of the University of Texas.

11
It is the genius of our Constitution that under its shelter of enduring institutions and rooted principles there is ample room for the rich fertility of American political invention.

LYNDON B. JOHNSON, *State of the Union Message,* 12 Jan., 1966.

12
We hold that the Constitution follows the flag, and denounce the doctrine that an Executive or Congress deriving their existence and their powers from the Constitution can exercise lawful authority beyond it, or in violation of it. We assert that no nation can long endure half republic and half empire, and we warn the American people that imperialism

abroad will lead quickly and inevitably to despotism at home.

Platform of the Democratic Party, adopted at the National Convention at Kansas City, Mo., 5 July, 1900, concluding sentences of the first paragraph. See *Official Proceedings of the Democratic National Convention* [of 1900], Chicago, McClellan Printing Company. Also *U.S. Congress, House, Platforms of the Two Great Political Parties, 1856–1932,* p. 105. Washington, 1932. So far as known this is the origin of the phrase, but who coined it is unknown. The platform committee consisted of one member from each state. The compiler is indebted to Miss Ellen F. Watson, of the Reference Department of the Enoch Pratt Free Library of Baltimore, Md., and to Mr. Henry J. Dubester, Chief of the General Reference Division of the Library of Congress, for tracing this elusive quotation to its source.

No matter whether th' Constitution follows th' flag or not, th' Supreme Coort follows th' iliction returns.

FINLEY PETER DUNNE, *Mr. Dooley's Opinions: The Supreme Court's Decisions.* (1900) It will be noted that Mr. Dooley had just read the platform.

While the Democratic party had fought the presidential campaign on the issue of anti-imperialism, in accepting its defeat it was insistent that, as "the Constitution follows the flag," its benefits must be extended to the people of our newly-acquired possessions.

HENRY F. WOODS, *American Sayings,* p. 73. (1950)

COURAGE

1

Courage is like love: it must have hope to nourish it. (*Le courage est comme l'amour: il vent de l'espérance pour nourriture.*)

NAPOLEON BONAPARTE, *Epigram.* See GUILLON, *Napoléon,* p. 280.

2

I have a disastrous cold, but it is a cold in the head and not in the feet.

ALEC DOUGLAS-HOME, *Speech,* at a Foreign Press Association luncheon in London, Apr., 1964. As Britain's prime minister, he was replying to taunts by the opposition (Labour party) that his refusal to call an immediate general election signified lack of confidence in his own (Conservative) party.

3

Here comes Courage! that seized the lion absent, and ran away from the present mouse.

BENJAMIN FRANKLIN, *Poor Richard's Almanac,* 1775.

4

I'd rather give my life than be afraid to give it.

LYNDON B. JOHNSON, *Reply,* to Secret Service agents who had advised him against joining the funeral procession for John F. Kennedy, 25 Nov., 1963. Johnson thus joined the procession of marchers on foot instead of going to St. Matthew's Cathedral, in Washington, D.C., in a guarded limousine, as the agents requested. (New York *Herald Tribune* and St. Louis *Post-Dispatch,* 26 Nov., 1963; also quoted by DOUGLAS B. CORNELL of Associated Press, 17 Apr., 1964)

5

The courage of life is often a less dramatic spectacle than the courage of a final moment; but it is no less than a magnificent mixture of triumph and tragedy. A man does what he must—in spite of personal consequences, in spite of obstacles and dangers and pressures—and that is the basis of all human morality.

JOHN F. KENNEDY, *Profiles in Courage.* (1955)

6

Give me the serenity to accept
  what cannot be changed.
Give me the courage to change
  what can be changed.
The wisdom to know one from the other.

REINHOLD NIEBUHR. (In *The Way of Light: A Manual of Praise, Prayer and Meditation,* 1933)

7

Courage is doing what you're afraid to do. There can be no courage unless you're scared.

EDWARD V. (EDDIE) RICKENBACKER. (PEGGY STREIT, "What Is Courage?"; *New York Times Magazine,* 24 Nov., 1963, p. 30)

8

The brave live on. (*Vivunt fortes.*)

SENECA, *Hercules Oetœus,* 1. 1984. (c. A.D. 60) It is the cowards who are slain in battle as they turn to run away.

CRITICISM

9

A thick skin is a gift from God.

KONRAD ADENAUER. (New York *Times,* 30 Dec., 1959)

10

This is the kind of thing that comes to you when you've outlived your critics.

THOMAS HART BENTON, Remark at a dinner marking his 75th birthday, 15 Apr., 1964.

11

The greatest corrective known to man is criticism with good will. We have lost the art of cross-criticism in the daily media. It was better in the days when publishers went out and horsewhipped each other when they differed on important issues.

MORRIS ERNST, *Speech,* in St. Louis, 16 July, 1964.

12

Criticism is no doubt good for the soul but we must beware that it does not upset our confidence in ourselves.

HERBERT HOOVER, Statement on his 90th birthday, 10 Aug., 1964.

13

Mediocrity is more dangerous in a critic than in a writer.

EUGÈNE IONESCO. (New York *Times,* "Ideas and Men," 13 Mar., 1966, p. 11–E)

1
The men who create power make an indispensable contribution to the nation's greatness. But the men who question power make a contribution just as indispensable, especially when that questioning is disinterested.

JOHN F. KENNEDY, *Address,* at Amherst College, Amherst, Mass., 26 Oct., 1963.

2
There will always be dissident voices heard in the land, expressing opposition without alternatives, finding fault but never favor, perceiving gloom on every side and seeking influence without responsibility. Those voices are inevitable.

JOHN F. KENNEDY, *Speech,* prepared for delivery in Dallas, Tex., 22 Nov., 1963, the day of his assassination.

3
Let posterity choose. I have done my work.

SOMERSET MAUGHAM, Reply to the query: "Where will posterity place you among writers?" Spoken in Jan., 1964, on his 90th birthday.

4
You won't have Nixon to kick around any more.

RICHARD M. NIXON, Press Conference, 7 Nov., 1962, the morning after the election in which he unsuccessfully sought to unseat Edmund G. (Pat) Brown as governor of California. Nixon called the press conference "my last," and used it to assail some elements of the press that, he said, were unfair to him. Later he regretted the outburst; at a Gridiron Club dinner in Washington, D.C., in April, 1964, he was quoted thus: "I hope that a man can lose his temper once in 16 years and be forgiven for it."

5
I dance to please myself. I am my most critical audience. If you try to please everybody, there is no originality.

RUDOLF NUREYEV, *Interview,* St. Louis *Post-Dispatch,* 21 Jan., 1964.

6
When they praise me, it bores me; when they pan me, it annoys me.

ARTUR RUBINSTEIN. (*New York Times Magazine,* 26 Jan., 1964)

7
A critic is a man who knows the way but can't drive the car.

KENNETH TYNAN. (*New York Times Magazine,* 9 Jan., 1966, p. 27)

8
Self-criticism is a mark of social maturity.

GORE VIDAL, *Article,* New York *Times* drama section, 5 Apr., 1964.

DANGER

9
To be alive at all involves some risk.

HAROLD MACMILLAN, Comment, while he was British prime minister. (New York *Times,* 30 Dec., 1959)

10
The most dangerous situation that humanity has ever faced in all history.

HAROLD C. UREY, *One World or None,* ch. 2. (1946) Referring to the possibility of atomic warfare.

DEATH

11
It is time for me to become an apprentice once more. I am not certain in which direction, but somewhere, sometime, soon.

LORD BEAVERBROOK, *Speech,* in London, 25 May, 1964, at a party in honor of his 85th birthday. This exit line, an allusion to death, was quite prophetic; he died 9 June, 1964.

12
He cannot read his tombstone when he's dead.

BERTON BRALEY, *Do It Now.*

13
Death is only a larger kind of going abroad.

SAMUEL BUTLER, *Notebooks,* p. 144.

14
To die is to leave off dying and do the thing once for all.

SAMUEL BUTLER, *Notebooks,* p. 255.

15
I am ready to meet my Maker. Whether my Maker is prepared for the great ordeal of meeting me is another matter.

WINSTON CHURCHILL, Comment, 30 Nov., 1949.

16
I am bored with it all.

WINSTON CHURCHILL, Last words to his family, spoken to his son-in-law, Christopher Soames, 15 Jan., 1965. Although death did not come until 24 Jan., Churchill was unconscious most of the time. Reported by the London *Evening Standard,* on what it termed excellent authority.

17
I am not too bad, but rest assured, one of these days I will not fail to die.

CHARLES DE GAULLE, Press Conference in Paris, 4 Feb., 1965. This was his reply to a query about his health, from a reporter for *L'Aurore,* a strongly anti-Gaullist Paris newspaper.

18
A craven fear of death is entering the American consciousness; so much so that many recently felt that honoring the chief despot himself was the price we had to pay to avoid nuclear destruction.

BARRY M. GOLDWATER, *The Conscience of a Conservative* (Macfadden ed., 1961), p. 90.

19
The problem is not the death of one man—the problem is the life of this organization.

JOHN F. KENNEDY, Statement upon the death of Dag Hammarskjöld, Sept., 1961. On 26 Nov., 1963, at a memorial service for Kennedy at the United Nations, Adlai E. Stevenson quoted Kennedy's statement in rededicating the continuing work of the UN, of which Hammarskjöld was secretary general.

1
A piece of each of us died at that moment.
MIKE MANSFIELD, Eulogy on John F. Kennedy, 24 Nov., 1963.

2
A flame kindled of human decency, courage and dedication does not die.
MIKE MANSFIELD, Eulogy on John F. Kennedy, spoken in the U.S. Senate, 11 Dec., 1963.

3
There is a calm for those who weep,
A rest for weary pilgrims found,
They softly lie and sweetly sleep
Low in the ground.

The storm that wrecks the winter sky
No more disturbs their sweet repose,
Than summer evening's latest sigh
That shuts the rose.

JAMES MONTGOMERY, *The Grave.* Stanzas i and ii. (1804)

4
One should die proudly when it is no longer possible to live proudly.
FRIEDRICH NIETZSCHE, *The Twilight of the Idols.* (c. 1885)

To die with honor when one can no longer live with honor.
JOHN LUTHER LONG, *Madame Butterfly.* Inscription on Samurai sword. *See also* 1149:7.

5
A good Christian owes two things to his dead: an act of gratitude, for all we have comes from them, and an act of charity.
POPE PAUL VI, *Address,* at the Rome city cemetery on All Souls' Day, 2 Nov., 1963.

DIPLOMACY

6
In dealing with the Communists, remember that in their mind what is secret is serious, and what is public is merely propaganda.
CHARLES E. BOHLEN. (JAMES RESTON, Washington Column, New York *Times,* 2 Jan., 1966. Quoted as "Bohlen's law," the maxim of a veteran American career diplomat.)

7
The only summit meeting that can succeed is one that does not take place.
BARRY M. GOLDWATER, *Why Not Victory?* (Macfadden ed., 1963, p. 45)

8
I wish there were some giant economy-size aspirin tablet that would work on international headaches. But there isn't. The only cure is patience with reason mixed in.
LYNDON B. JOHNSON, *Speech,* in Belleville, Ill., 21 Oct., 1964, during the presidential campaign.

9
Let us never negotiate out of fear. But let us never fear to negotiate.
JOHN F. KENNEDY, *Inaugural Address,* 20 Jan., 1961.

10
It is never too early to try; it is never too late to talk; and it is high time that many disputes on the agenda of this Assembly were taken off the debating schedule and placed on the negotiating table.
JOHN F. KENNEDY, *Address,* to the United Nations General Assembly, 20 Sept., 1963.

11
This is the devilish thing about foreign affairs: they are foreign and will not always conform to our whims.
JAMES RESTON, Washington Column, New York *Times,* 16 Dec., 1964.

12
The world is a very complicated place. I am skeptical of dealing with complicated situations in easy and dramatic phrases. Policy is not a matter of rhetoric but of right and wise conduct. When I write a sentence, I ask myself: "Is this really so?"
DEAN RUSK, (E. W. KENWORTHY, "Evolution of Our No. 1 Diplomat"; *New York Times Magazine,* 18 Mar., 1962)

13
In diplomacy, as so understood, you do not go out for unconditional surrender or even for decisive victory. You go for the settlement which is most likely to endure. You will have to go on living with the other side afterward; and though you may be the stronger today, he may be the stronger tomorrow.
WILLIAM STRANG (BARON STRANG of STONESFIELD), "New Harsh Language in Diplomacy"; *New York Times Magazine,* 15 Apr., 1962, p. 27.

DREAMS

14
The Gigantic Enterprise . . . got into the Public Prints as a Pipe Dream.
GEORGE ADE, *More Fables,* p. 190. (1900)

I don't have any pipe-dreams about the law.
E. D. BIGGERS, *Seven Keys to Baldpate.* Ch. xiii. (1913)

15
Dreams give wings to fools.
BEN SIRA, *Book of Wisdom (Ecclesiasticus).* Ch. xxxiv, l. 7. (c. 190 B.C.)

16
To believe in one's dreams is to spend all of one's life asleep.
S. G. CHAMPION, *Racial Proverbs,* p. 357. (1938) A Chinese proverb.

17
I'll nor fight with the powers of Air,
Sentry, pass him through!
Drawbridge let fall, 'tis the Lord of us all,
The Dreamer whose dreams come true!

RUDYARD KIPLING, *The Fairies' Siege.* (1901) *See also* 480:4.

There is not a dream which may not come true, if we have the energy which makes or chooses our own fate. . . . It is only the dreams of those light sleepers who dream faintly that do not come true.

ARTHUR SYMONS, *Introduction to Poems of Ernest Dowson.* (1900)

DRINKING

1
I am willing to taste any drink once.

JAMES BRANCH CABELL, *Jurgen,* p. 6. (1919)

2
Field Marshall Viscount Montgomery: I don't use either alcohol or tobacco, and I'm 100 per cent efficient.
Winston Churchill: I use both, and my efficiency is 200 per cent.

Attributed to CHURCHILL and MONTGOMERY on the occasion of their first meeting, early in World War II.

3
I have taken more out of alcohol than alcohol has taken out of me.

WINSTON CHURCHILL. (Quoted in *By Quentin Reynolds,* autobiography, and United Press International compilation of Churchill sayings, 25 Jan., 1965)

4
I have been brought up and trained to have the utmost contempt for people who get drunk.

WINSTON CHURCHILL. (Quoted in New York *Times* supplement on Churchill, published at his death, and simultaneously in a United Press International compilation of Churchill quotations, 25 Jan., 1965)

5
I saved shoe-leather by keeping one foot on the foot-rest.

O. HENRY (W. S. PORTER), *The Four Million: Memoirs of a Yellow Dog.* (1906)

6
Drink always rubbed him the right way.

O. HENRY, *The Rubaiyat of a Scotch Highball.* (1907)

7
When the mint is in the liquor and its fragrance on the glass,
It breathes a recollection that can never, never pass.

CLARENCE OUSLEY, *When the Mint is in the Liquor.* (c. 1910)

8
I'm only a beer teetotaller, not a champagne teetotaller.

BERNARD SHAW, *Candida.* Act iii. (1895)

9
Lechery, sir, it [drink] provokes, and unprovokes. It provokes the desire, but it takes away the performance.

SHAKESPEARE, *Macbeth.* Act ii, sc. 3, l. 29; the porter speaking. (1605)

EDUCATION

10
When eras die, their legacies
Are left to strange police;
Professors in New England guard
The glory that was Greece.

CLARENCE DAY, *Thoughts Without Words.* (1921) *See also* 140:6.

11
Higher education must abandon the comfortable haven of objectivity, the sterile pinnacle of moral neutrality. In our perilous world, we cannot avoid moral judgments; that is a privilege only of the uninvolved.

MILTON S. EISENHOWER, "The Need for a New American"; *The Educational Record,* Oct., 1963, p. 305.

12
Perhaps the most valuable result of all education is the ability to make yourself do the thing you have to do, when it ought to be done, whether you like it or not.

THOMAS HENRY HUXLEY, *On University Education.* (1876)

I forget who it was that recommended men for their soul's good, to do each day two things they disliked: . . . it is a precept I have followed scrupulously; for every day I have got up and I have gone to bed.

SOMERSET MAUGHAM, *The Moon and Sixpence.* Ch. ii. (1919)

13
At the desk where I sit, I have learned one great truth. The answer for all our national problems—the answer for all the problems of the world—comes down to a single word. That word is "education."

LYNDON B. JOHNSON, *Address,* before the 200th anniversary convocation, Brown University, Providence, R.I., 28 Sept., 1964.

14
The three R's of our school system must be supported by the three T's—teachers who are superior, techniques of instruction that are modern, and thinking about education which places it first in all our plans and hopes.

LYNDON B. JOHNSON, Message to Congress, on education, 12 Jan., 1965.

15
We think of schools as places where youth learns, but our schools also need to learn.

LYNDON B. JOHNSON, *Message to Congress,* on education, 12 Jan., 1965.

16
A child miseducated is a child lost.

JOHN F. KENNEDY, *State of the Union Address,* 11 Jan., 1962.

17
It might be said now that I have the best of both worlds. A Harvard education and a Yale degree.

JOHN F. KENNEDY, Comment on receiving an honorary degree from Yale University, June, 1962.

18
The specialist who is trained but uneducated, technically skilled but culturally incompetent, is a menace.

DAVID B. TRUMAN, *Address,* in Chicago to Columbia University alumni, 15 Apr., 1964.

1
Intelligence appears to be the thing that enables a man to get along without education. Education appears to be the thing that enables a man to get along without the use of his intelligence.

ALBERT EDWARD WIGGAM, *The New Decalogue of Science.* (1923)

2
We must believe the things we teach our children.

WOODROW WILSON, in an attack on the hypocrisy in the field of education. (COHN, *The Fabulous Democrats,* p. 118.)

ENGLAND

3
Our policy now can only be to sustain the fragments of what was once a glorious empire on which the sun used never to set and on which it now seldom rises.

LORD BEAVERBROOK, Comment, on his 85th birthday, May, 1964.

4
Britain today is suffering from galloping obsolescence.

ANTHONY WEDGWOOD BENN, M.P. (New York *Times,* "Ideas and Men," 16 Feb., 1964)

5
There'll always be an England
While there's a busy street,
Wherever there's a turning wheel,
A million marching feet.

HUGHIE CHARLES and ROSS PARKER, *There'll Always Be an England.* (1939)

6
I have never accepted what many people have kindly said, namely, that I inspired the nation. Their will was resolute and remorseless and, it was proved, unconquerable. It fell to me to express it, and if I found the right words, you must remember that I always earned my living by my pen and by my tongue. It was the nation and the race dwelling round the globe that had the lion's heart. I had the luck to be called upon to give the roar.

WINSTON CHURCHILL, *Address,* in 1954, marking his 80th birthday.

7
Another signal was run up upon the Victory, "England expects every man will do his duty." When Collingwood [Captain of the Royal Sovereign] saw the flutter he remarked testily, "I wish Nelson would stop signalling as we know well enough what we have to do," but when the message was reported to him cheers broke out from the ships in his line.

WINSTON CHURCHILL, *The Age of Revolution,* p. 307. (1957) *See also* 545:12.

8
England is my wife—America, my mistress. It is very good sometimes to get away from one's wife.

CEDRIC HARDWICKE. (Quoted in Associated Press obituary of Sir Cedric, datelined New York City, 6 Aug., 1964)

9
An Englishman is never so natural as when he's holding his tongue.

HENRY JAMES, *The Portrait of a Lady,* ch. x. (1881)

An Englishman is a man who lives on an island in the North Sea governed by Scotsmen.

PHILIP GUEDALLA, *Supers and Supermen.* (1920)

10
Our England is a garden, and such gardens are not made
By singing: "Oh how beautiful!" and sitting in the shade.

RUDYARD KIPLING, *The Glory of the Garden.* (1911)

11
Those white cliffs I never more must see.

THOMAS BABINGTON MACAULAY, *A Jacobite's Epitaph.* (c. 1842)

Colour has often suggested the name, as in the well-known instance of our "Albion,"—"the silver-coasted isle," as Tennyson so beautifully has called it—which had this name from the white line of cliffs which it presents to those approaching it by the narrow seas.

RICHARD CHEVENIX TRENCH, *On the Study of Words,* p. 52. (1851)

Our towns of wasted honour—
Our streets of lost delight!
How stands the old Lord Warden?
Are Dover's cliffs still white?

RUDYARD KIPLING, *The Broken Men.* (1902)

When you think about the defence of England you no longer think of the chalk cliffs of Dover. You think of the Rhine. That is where our frontier lies today.

STANLEY BALDWIN, *Speech,* House of Commons, 30 July, 1934.

I have loved England, dearly and deeply,
Since that first morning, shining and pure,
The white cliffs of Dover I saw rising steeply
Out of the sea that once made her secure.

I had no thought then of husband or lover,
I was a traveler, the guest of a week,
Yet when they pointed "the white cliffs of Dover,"
Startled I found there were tears on my cheek.

ALICE DUER MILLER, *The White Cliffs of Dover.* Stanzas i–ii. First published in *Life,* 31 March, 1944.

12
It has to be admitted that we English have sex on the brain, which is a very unsatisfactory place to have it.

MALCOLM MUGGERIDGE. (New York *Times,* "Ideas and Men," 11 Oct., 1964)

1
We always used to be noted for understatement. The difference is that in the past we never meant it.

WILLIAM PENNEY, British peer. (New York *Times,* "Ideas and Men," 22 Mar., 1964)

2
However the statement, "So Britain's monarch once uncovered sat" is not borne out in the account in *State Trials* (4th edition), which has, "After a stern looking upon the court . . . he placed himself [*i.e.,* sits in a "crimson velvet chair placed before him"] not at all moving his hat or otherwise shewing the least respect to the Court." Clarendon has it, "He . . . sat down . . . never stirring his hat . . . the judges sitting covered." *See* 864:6.

EPIGRAMS

3
An expert is one who knows more and more about less and less.

NICHOLAS MURRAY BUTLER, *Commencement Address,* Columbia University.

4
One man's gnat is another man's camel.

SAMUEL BUTLER, *Notebooks,* p. 169. (c. 1890) Quoted as having been said by Herbert Clarke.

5
People care more about being thought to have taste than about being thought either good, clever, or amiable.

SAMUEL BUTLER, *Notebooks,* p. 202.

6
When it is fair take thy greatcoat.

BENJAMIN FRANKLIN. (Attr., but source unverified.)

7
To read between the lines was easier than to follow the text.

HENRY JAMES, *The Portrait of a Lady,* ch. xiii. (1881)

8
There are more iron pots than porcelain ones.

HENRY JAMES, *The Portrait of a Lady,* ch. xix.

9
She was as honest as a pair of compasses.

HENRY JAMES, *The Portrait of a Lady,* ch. xxi.

10
Assuredly nobody will care for him who cares for nobody.

THOMAS JEFFERSON, *Letter to Maria Cosway.* (1786) *See* 1302:3

11
Only the game fish swims upstream.

JOHN TROTWOOD MOORE, *The Unafraid.* (1897)

12
Only the gamefish swims upstream,
But the sensible fish swims down.

OGDEN NASH, *When You say That, Smile.* (c. 1936) *See* 670:7

13
What I like in a good author is not what he says but what he whispers.

LOGAN PEARSALL SMITH, *Afterthoughts.* (1931)

14
Dollars cannot buy yesterday.

ADMIRAL HAROLD R. STARK, Chief of Naval Operations, referring to the $300,000,000 recommended by Secretary of the Navy Knox for improving the protection of warships against naval attack, after months of delay by the navy high command. See *Time,* 16 Dec., 1940, p. 26.

15
Building railroads from nowhere to nowhere is not a legitimate business.

COMMODORE CORNELIUS VANDERBILT, *Remark,* to President Grant during panic of 1873. (HOLBROOK, *The Age of the Moguls,* p. 55)

16
Gold is orange sucked at morn;
Silver 'tis at noon of day;
Lead when evening hours return;
And at night it doth thee slay.

UNKNOWN, Translation of Spanish proverb, dating from 27 March, 1850. (See *Notes and Queries,* Ser. x, vol. 1, p. 206, 12 March, 1904)

Fruit is gold in the morning, silver in the afternoon, lead at night.

BISHOP SHUTE BARRINGTON (?), c. 1820. (*Notes and Queries,* x, ix, p. 251)

Honey is gold in the morning, silver at noon, and lead at night.

UNKNOWN, Translation of Spanish proverb. (*Notes and Queries,* x, ii, p. 134.)

Cheese in the morning is gold, at midday silver, at night lead.

S. G. CHAMPION, *Racial Proverbs: Polish,* p. 241, No. 64.

EQUALITY

17
Equal opportunity and mutual respect are matters not only of law, but also of the human heart and spirit, and the latter are not always amenable to law.

DWIGHT D. EISENHOWER, Article written for the New York *Herald Tribune,* 25 May, 1964.

18
We have talked long enough in this country about equal rights. We have talked for a hundred years or more. It is time now to write the next chapter, and to write it in the books of law.

LYNDON B. JOHNSON, *Address,* to joint session of Congress, 27 Nov., 1963—his first major speech as President.

19
It should be clear by now that a nation can be no stronger abroad than she is at home. Only America which practices what it preaches about equal rights and social justice will be respected by those whose choice affects our future.

JOHN F. KENNEDY, *Address* (undelivered), prepared for delivery in Dallas, Tex., 22 Nov., 1963, the day of his death.

EXTREMES

1
I like to operate like a submarine on sonar. When I am picking up noise from both the left and the right, I know my course is correct.

GUSTAVO DÍAZ ORDAZ, defining a political philosophy that he brought to the post of President of Mexico in 1964. (New York Times News Service dispatch, 3 Dec., 1964)

2
People talk about the middle of the road as though it were unacceptable. Actually, all human problems, excepting morals, come into the gray areas. Things are not all black and white. There have to be compromises. The middle of the road is all of the usable surface. The extremes, right and left, are in the gutters.

DWIGHT D. EISENHOWER, *Interview, Christian Science Monitor,* Nov., 1963.

3
I would remind you that extremism in the defense of liberty is no vice. And let me remind you also that moderation in the pursuit of justice is no virtue!

BARRY M. GOLDWATER, *Speech,* at Republican national convention, San Francisco, 16 July, 1964—his speech of acceptance of the presidential nomination. This statement about extremism was the most quoted one of the campaign.

To extol extremism whether "in defense of liberty" or "in pursuit of justice" is dangerous, irresponsible and frightening. . . . I shall continue to fight extremism within the Republican party. It has no place in the party. It has no place in America.

NELSON A. ROCKEFELLER, Statement at Republican national convention, 17 July, 1964—his rebuttal of Barry M. Goldwater.

The essence of the matter is that to be an extremist is to encourage and condone the taking of the law into unauthorized private hands. It is in truth shocking that the Republican candidate for President is unconscious of this sovereign truth. For the distinction between private violence and public force is the central principle of a civilized society.

WALTER LIPPMANN, Syndicated Column, 21 July, 1964. Referring to Barry M. Goldwater.

4
In the world of the extremists there can be no solution of important issues by conciliation and consent. There must always be a winner and a loser. The conflict must always end in unconditional surrender. There is no such thing as the harmonizing of interests.

WALTER LIPPMANN, Syndicated Column, 12 Nov., 1964.

5
We in America—having given extremism, as it were, a constitutional right to exist—have been able to afford the active presence of a far Left and a far Right because we have been overwhelmingly a nation of moderates. Extremism of Left and Right, home-grown and imported, has been with us always. But the liberal-conservative, or conservative-liberal, center has been the native habitat of the vast majority of our people.

HARRY AND BONARO OVERSTREET, *The Strange Tactics of Extremism.* (1964)

FAMILIAR PHRASES

6
What this country needs is a good five-cent nickel.

FRANKLIN P. ADAMS, *The Sun Dial.* (1932) *See* 2019:10

7
Comin' in on a wing and a prayer.

HAROLD ADAMSON, Title of popular song of World War II. (1943) Echoing the radio from returning aviator.

8
In union there is strength.

AESOP, *Fables: The Bundle of Sticks.* (c. 600 B.C.)

9
Kith makes kind, as people say.

JAMES BRANCH CABELL, *Jurgen,* p. 29. (1919)

10
Rossom's Universal Robots.

KAREL CAPEK, *R. U. R.,* the play which introduced "robot" into the English language. (1920)

11
A racket's a line you adopt to make money you don't deserve.

JOHN COATES, *Time for Tea,* p. 95. (1950)

12
Me name is Mud.

CLARENCE J. DENNIS, *A Spring Song.* (1916)

13
At length one day, so runs the lay,
As the King sat on his throne,
Came crawling in a man so thin
He was simply skin and bone.
"Great Monarch," cried he, "have pity on me
Before my name is Mud,
Take back your elephant, Sire, I beg,
He's too rich for my blood."

J. CHEEVER GOODWIN, *Wang: Elephant Song.* (1891) The song made famous by De Wolf Hopper.

14
For years I have been known for saying "Include me out."

SAMUEL GOLDWYN, *Address,* to students of Balliol College, Oxford, 1 March, 1945.

ALVA JOHNSON, in *The Great Goldwyn,* quotes him as also saying, "In two words: im-possible."

15
Again she spoke, "Where is my lord, the King?"

JOHN CAMERON GRANT, first line of a six-line text, written to explain a large picture painted by Herbert Schmalz, hung at the Academy Exhibition of 1887. See *Notes and Queries,* Ser. iii, vol. iii, p. 360, July, 1917.

1
Busy as a one-armed man with the nettle-rash pasting on wall-paper.

O. HENRY, *The Gentle Grafter: The Ethics of Pig.* (1908)

2
Holy Deadlock.

ALAN PATRICK HERBERT, *Title of Novel.* (1934) Herbert was satirizing the absurdity of English divorce laws, and influencing their later modification.

3
Remember the Alamo!

GENERAL SAM HOUSTON, *Report,* on the battle of San Jacinto, March, 1836, stating, "The attack was led by the regiment commanded by Col. Sidney Sherman, whose men advanced to the attack singing the war-cry, 'Remember the Alamo,'" where the Mexicans, a month previously, had massacred 180 Americans, including Davy Crockett and James Bowie. For "Remember the Maine" *see* 66:5.

4
Of all the fish that swim or swish
In ocean's deep autocracy,
There's none possess such haughtiness
As the codfish aristocracy.

WALLACE IRWIN, *Codfish Aristocracy.* (c. 1915) *See also* 194:15.

5
A Century of Dishonor.

HELEN HUNT JACKSON, *Report,* on the treatment of the Indians by the Government and people of the United States. (1881) This report, of 457 pages, she sent at her own expense to every member of Congress, with the result that in 1883 she was appointed Special Commissioner to examine the condition of the Mission Indians of California.

6
Misfortune makes strange bedfellows.

HENRY JAMES, *The Portrait of a Lady,* ch. v. (1881)

7
There is no accounting for tastes.

HENRY JAMES, *The Portrait of a Lady,* ch. xii.

8
I don't care anything about reasons, but I know what I like.

HENRY JAMES, *The Portrait of a Lady,* ch. xxiv.

She was one of those people who say, "I don't know anything about music really, but I know what I like."

MAX BEERBOHM, *Zuleika Dobson,* ch. ix. (1911)

9
It *was* certainly better to suffer as a sheep than as a lamb. One might as well perish by the sword as by famine.

HENRY JAMES, *The Ambassadors,* p. 211.

10
You're looking, this morning, as fit as a flea.

HENRY JAMES, *The Ambassadors,* p. 219.

11
Treating her handsomely buttered no parsnips.

HENRY JAMES, *The Ambassadors,* p. 315.

12
You ain't heard nothin' yet, folks.

AL JOLSON, *Remark,* introduced by Jolson into *The Jazz Singer,* the first talking motion picture. (July, 1927)

13
The Robber Barons.

MATHEW JOSEPHSON, *Title of Book,* dealing with the Rockefellers, Morgans, Vanderbilts, et alii.

14
Hot and bothered.

RUDYARD KIPLING, *Rectorial Address,* St. Andrew's University, Scotland, 10 Oct., 1923.

15
It Can't Happen Here.

SINCLAIR LEWIS, *Title of Book.* (1935)

16
One if by land and two if by sea.

H. W. LONGFELLOW, *Paul Revere's Ride,* referring to the signal to be given Revere by lantern from the tower of North Church, Boston, 18 April, 1775. (1860)

17
Because it's there.

GEORGE MALLORY, famed Alpinist, when asked "Why do you climb this mountain?" The phrase has been the climber's answer ever since. (See *Time,* 6 July, 1953, p. 24)

18
Obey That Impulse.

THOMAS L. MASSON, *Subscription Slogan,* for the old *Life,* of which he was editor for many years. (1895)

19
Keeping up with the Joneses.

ARTHUR R. (POP) MONAND, *Title of Cartoon Strip,* which ran from 1914 to 1938. In a letter to the compiler, Mr. Monand wrote, "I originated and sold the feature to The Associated Newspapers in May of 1914. By 1920 it was being syndicated by 100 papers. The feature ran until 1938 daily and Sunday. When weary of it I retired from the cartoon field. I inventrd the phrase, and at first thought of calling it 'Keeping up with the Smiths,' but decided keeping up with the Joneses was more euphonius." Mr. Monand adds that he got the idea from his own disastrous experience in trying to keep up with his neighbors in fashionable Cedarhurst, Long Island.

"Superior people," Stuart Chase said, "lord it over their pecuniary inferiors by wasteful expenditures, whereupon the inferiors move heaven and earth to improve their status by spending to the limit themselves." This is so true that we have embodied it in an expression—keeping up with the Joneses.

STEWART H. HOLBROOK, *The Age of the Moguls,* p. 323. (1953)

All progress is based upon the universal innate desire on the part of every organism to live beyond its income.

SAMUEL BUTLER, *Notebooks*, p. 191. (c. 1890)

1
The solid South.

GENERAL JOHN SINGLETON MOSBY, *Letter*, to a former Confederate comrade, 1876.

2
Say it with flowers.

PATRICK F. O'KEEFE, *Slogan*, Society of American Florists. (1917) *See* 2285:15

3
Era of wonderful nonsense.

WESTBROOK PEGLER, *Newspaper Column*, referring to the wild stock speculation of 1929. The article was later included in Mr. Pegler's book, *'Taint Right*, under the title *Mr. Gump Himself*.

4
Profitless prosperity.

A. W. SHAW, *The Underlying Trend of Business*. (See *Magazine of Business*, Nov. 1927, p. 571, col. 1.)

5
Wall Street lays an egg.

SIME SILVERMAN, *Heading*, in *Variety*, referring to the stock market crash in 1929.

6
Nobody shoots at Santa Claus.

ALFRED E. SMITH, *Speech*, decrying the spendthrift policies of the New Deal. (1936)

7
Okie use' to mean you was from Oklahoma. Now it means you're scum.

JOHN STEINBECK, *The Grapes of Wrath*. Ch. xviii. (1939)

8
With . . . . deliberate speed.

FRANCIS THOMPSON, *The Hound of Heaven*, l. 12. *See* 794:11.

With all deliberate speed.

U.S. Supreme Court Decision, 31 May, 1955, ruling that "separate but equal" public schools for Negroes were unconstitutional, and that they should be integrated.

9
As easy as rolling off a log.

MARK TWAIN, *A Connecticut Yankee at King Arthur's Court*, p. 6. (1889)

10
I was up a stump, as you might say.

MARK TWAIN, *Connecticut Yankee*, p. 7.

11
I couldn't make head or tail of it.

MARK TWAIN, *Connecticut Yankee*, p. 10.

12
As snug as a candle in a candle-mould.

MARK TWAIN, *Connecticut Yankee*, p. 85.

13
"Go to" was their way of saying "I should smile!" or "I like that!"

MARK TWAIN, *Connecticut Yankee*, p. 381.

14
Sticks like a burr to a cow's tail.

EDWARD NOYES WESTCOTT, *David Harum*, p. 220. (1898)

15
All dressed up and nowhere to go.

WILLIAM ALLEN WHITE, *Remark*, referring to the Progressive Party after Theodore Roosevelt's retirement in 1916.

16
Over the piano was printed a notice: "Please do not shoot the pianist. He is doing his best."

OSCAR WILDE, *Impressions of America: Leadville*. (1882)

It's a pity to shoot the pianist when the piano is out of tune.

RENÉ COTY, President of the French Republic, *Remark*, referring to the confusion of French politics. (See *Time*, 4 Jan., 1957, p. 22.)

17
The Spirit of '76.

ARCHIBALD M. WILLARD, *Title of Painting*, originally exhibited at the Centennial Exhibition at Philadelphia, in 1876. It was then entitled "Yankee Doodle," but Willard afterwards retitled it "The Spirit of '76." Reproduced in thousands of copies, it shows an old man, white locks flowing, beating a drum, a soldier in the uniform of the Continental army blowing a fife, and a boy in soldier's uniform also drumming, the three marching along side by side. One of the best known works of any American artist.

FANATICISM

18
A fanatic is one who can't change his mind and won't change the subject.

WINSTON CHURCHILL. (New York *Times*, 5 July, 1954)

19
This, I believe, is the core of the democratic spirit. When we acknowledge our own fallibility, tolerance and compromise become possible and fanaticism becomes absurd.

J. WILLIAM FULBRIGHT, *Address*, in Washington, D.C., 5 Dec., 1963.

20
Fanaticism is not a characteristic of mature societies but of unstable and politically primitive societies. Nor is it an expression of strength and self-confidence.

J. WILLIAM FULBRIGHT, *Address*, Sept., 1964, during the presidential campaign.

21
The irresponsibles win elections—but always for the other party.

LYNDON B. JOHNSON. (HENRY A. ZEIGER, *Lyndon B. Johnson: Man and President*, p. 61)

22
What a price we pay for this fanaticism!

EARL WARREN, *Eulogy on John F. Kennedy*, 24 Nov., 1963.

FEAR

23
The first and great commandment is, Don't let them scare you.

ELMER DAVIS, *But We Were Born Free*. (1954)

1
Our tragedy today is a general and universal physical fear so long sustained by now that we can even bear it. There are no longer problems of the spirit. There is only the question: when will I be blown up?

WILLIAM FAULKNER, *Address*, in Stockholm, 10 Dec., 1950, on accepting the Nobel Prize in literature.

2
There is the fear that we shan't prove worthy in the eyes of someone who knows us at least as well as we know ourselves. That is the fear of God. And there is the fear of Man—fear that men won't understand us and we shall be cut off from them.

ROBERT FROST. (*Newsweek*, 11 Feb., 1963)

3
There is no panic on our agenda.

LYNDON B. JOHNSON, *Speech*, at the University of California, Los Angeles, 21 Feb., 1964.

4
You gain strength, courage and confidence by every experience in which you really stop to look fear in the face.

ELEANOR ROOSEVELT, *You Learn by Living*. (1960)

FIGHTING

5
Never give in, never give in, *never, never, never, never*—in nothing, great or small, large or petty—never give in except to convictions of honour and good sense.

WINSTON CHURCHILL, *Address*, at Harrow School, 29 Oct., 1941.

6
We're eyeball to eyeball, and the other fellow just blinked.

DEAN RUSK, *Comment*, Oct., 1962, during the crisis brought about by U.S. demands that Soviet missiles be pulled out of Cuba. Rusk had just been informed that Cuba-bound Soviet ships, carrying missiles, had turned tail at sea—the first visible indication that Russia was backing down.

7
For it is often easier to fight for principles than to live up to them.

ADLAI E. STEVENSON, *Speech*, in New York City, 27 Aug., 1952, during the presidential campaign.

8
The joy of life is a fighting chance.

NORMAN THOMAS, Television Program: *Norman Thomas: Years of Protest*, 1 Mar., 1966, WNDT, New York City.

FLATTERY

9
None are more taken by flattery than the proud.

BARUCH SPINOZA, *Ethics*. Pt. iv, Appendix 21. (1674)

10
When my friend, Judge Douglas, came to Chicago, . . . he complimented me as being a "kind, amiable and intelligent gentleman." . . . I was not very much accustomed to flattery, and it came the sweeter to me. I was rather like the Hoosier with the gingerbread, when he said he reckoned he loved it better than any other man, and got less of it.

ABRAHAM LINCOLN, *Speech*, at Ottawa, Illinois, replying to Stephen A. Douglas, 31 July, 1858. (STERN, *Life and Writings of Abraham Lincoln*, p. 468.)

FORCE

11
I hope we are learning that force is not always the answer to Communism but even can become its greatest incubator.

LEROY COLLINS, *Speech*, in San Juan, P.R., 25 May, 1965.

12
Communists only respect force. You remember the remark attributed to Stalin at the Yalta conference when he was told of the importance of the views of Pope Pius XII. "How many divisions does Pope Pius command?" Stalin asked at the time. That shows us the Communist mentality clearly.

DWIGHT D. EISENHOWER, *Interview*, New York *Times*, 9 May, 1965. (New York *Times*, 10 May, 1965)

13
Democracy will never solve its problems at the end of a billy club.

LYNDON B. JOHNSON, *Speech*, in Washington, D.C., 28 July, 1964, referring to violence caused by racial unrest.

14
Some of you have knives, and I ask you to put them up. Some of you may have arms, and I ask you to put them up. Get the weapon of nonviolence, the breastplate of righteousness, the armor of truth, and just keep marching.

REV. MARTIN LUTHER KING, JR., addressing civil-rights demonstrators in Gadsden, Ala., late in 1963. (*Time*, 3 Jan., 1964, p. 14)

FRANCE AND THE FRENCH

15
For all us Frenchmen, the rule of our epoch is to be faithful to France.

CHARLES DE GAULLE, *Speech*, in Lyons, 28 Sept., 1963, explaining France's role in world affairs.

16
It is the will of France to dispose of her own fate.

CHARLES DE GAULLE, Press Conference in Paris, 21 Feb., 1966. The statement in effect heralded the end of French commitment to the North Atlantic Treaty Organization (NATO).

17
The Fifth Republic is not the Fourth plus General de Gaulle.

ANDRÉ MALRAUX. (New York *Times*, "Ideas and Men"; 8 Dec., 1963)

FREEDOM

1
We must be ready to dare all for our country. For history does not long entrust the care of freedom to the weak or the timid.
DWIGHT D. EISENHOWER, *First Inaugural Address,* 20 Jan., 1953.

2
May the light of freedom, coming to all darkened lands, flame brightly—until at last the darkness is no more.
DWIGHT D. EISENHOWER, *Second Inaugural Address,* 21 Jan., 1957.

3
Only our individual faith in freedom can keep us free.
DWIGHT D. EISENHOWER, "Let's Be Honest with Ourselves"; *The Reader's Digest,* Dec., 1963.

4
When "freedom" is worshiped as a sublime and mystical state rather than as simply a necessary condition for human fulfillment, the faith in freedom itself ceases to express the democratic spirit and becomes something quite different; it ceases to express the conscience of a conservative and becomes instead the faith of a fanatic.
J. WILLIAM FULBRIGHT, *Speech,* Sept., 1964, during the presidential campaign. He was assailing the ideology of Barry M. Goldwater, the Republican nominee.

5
Freedom is the open window through which pours the sunlight of the human spirit and of human dignity. With the preservation of these moral and spiritual qualities and with God's grace will come further greatness for our country.
HERBERT HOOVER, Statement on his 90th birthday, 10 Aug., 1964.

6
The only struggle worthy of man's unceasing sacrifice—the struggle to be free.
LYNDON B. JOHNSON, *Speech* in New York City, 23 Feb., 1966, upon accepting the national freedom award of Freedom House.

7
In the long history of the world, only a few generations have been granted the role of defending freedom in its hour of maximum danger. I do not shrink from this responsibility—I welcome it. I do not believe that any of us would exchange places with any other people or any other generation. The energy, the faith, the devotion which we bring to this endeavor will light our country and all who serve it—and the glow from that fire can truly light the world.
JOHN F. KENNEDY, *Inaugural Address,* 20 Jan., 1961.

8
The cost of freedom is always high, but Americans have always paid it. And one path we shall never choose, and that is the path of surrender, or submission.
JOHN F. KENNEDY, *Address,* broadcast nationally, 22 Oct., 1962, during the crisis precipitated by the Soviet Union's installation of missiles in Cuba.

9
All free men, wherever they may live, are citizens of Berlin. And therefore, as a free man, I take pride in the words *Ich bin ein Berliner.*
JOHN F. KENNEDY, *Address,* at City Hall, West Berlin, 26 June, 1963.

10
What we are suffering from in modern times is the failure of the primitive liberals to see that freedom does not begin when tyranny is overthrown. Freedom is a way of life which requires authority, discipline, and government of its own kind.
WALTER LIPPMANN, Syndicated Column, 4 Aug., 1964.

11
If freedom had been the happy, simple, relaxed state of ordinary humanity, man would have everywhere been free—whereas through most of time and space he has been in chains. Do not let us make any mistake about this. The natural government of man is servitude. Tyranny is the normal pattern of government.
ADLAI E. STEVENSON, *A. Powell Davies Memorial Address,* Washington, D.C., 18 Jan., 1959. (*Contemporary Forum,* ed. by ERNEST J. WRAGE AND BARNET BASKERVILLE, p. 360)

12
We have confused the free with the free and easy.
ADLAI E. STEVENSON, *Putting First Things First: A Democratic View.* (1960)

FRIENDS

13
Until harsh experience taught him the folly of it, he was always willing to endorse a friend's note, and surely greater love hath no man than this: laying down one's life is nothing in comparison.
GAMALIEL BRADFORD, *As God Made Them: Henry Clay,* p. 63. (1921)

14
There is nothing final between friends.
WILLIAM JENNINGS BRYAN, *Reply,* as Secretary of State, 23 May, 1914, when Viscount Chinda, the Japanese Ambassador, asked him if the decision of the United States to support the law just passed by the California Legislature excluding Japanese from holding title to real estate in California was final.

15
Friendship is like money, easier made than kept.
SAMUEL BUTLER, *Notebooks,* p. 278. (c. 1890)

16
How to Win Friends and Influence People.
DALE CARNEGIE, *Title of Book.* (1938)

1
I have no trouble with my enemies. But my Goddam friends, White, they are the ones that keep me walking the floor nights.

WARREN G. HARDING, to William Allen White, 1923. See COHN, *The Fabulous Democrats,* p. 127. *See also* 733:11.

GENIUS

2
"Genius," said Dr. Moreau, "is but one of the many branches of the neurotic tree." "Genius," says Dr. Lombroso, "is a symptom of hereditary degeneration of the epileptoid variety." "The greater the genius, the greater the unsoundness," writes Dr. Nisbet.

WILLIAM JAMES, *The Varieties of Religious Experience,* p. 16. (1902) And John Foster declared, "Genius is the power of lighting one's own fire." *See also* 759:13.

3
That divine unrest, that old stinging trouble of humanity, that makes all high achievements and all miserable failures, the same that spreads wings with Icarus, the same that sent Columbus into the desolate Atlantic.

R. L. STEVENSON, *Will o' the Mill.* (c. 1887)

GOD

4
Vouchsafe, O Lord, to keep us this day without being found out!

SAMUEL BUTLER, *Notebooks,* p. 87. (c. 1890)

5
For, Lord, I was free of all Thy flowers, but I chose the world's sad roses,
And that is why my feet are torn and mine eyes are blind with sweat,
But at Thy terrible judgment-seat, when this my tired life closes,
I am ready to reap whereof I sowed, and pay my righteous debt.

ERNEST DOWSON, *Impenitentia Ultima.* (1896)

6
God obligeth no man to do more than he hath given him ability to perform.

MOHAMMED, *The Koran.* Ch. ii. (c. A.D. 630) Sale, tr.

7
Your God is one God; there is no God but he.

MOHAMMED, *The Koran.* Ch. ii. Frequently repeated.

8
Wherever ye be, God will bring you all back at the resurrection.

MOHAMMED, *The Koran.* Ch. ii.

9
We are God's and unto him shall we surely return.

MOHAMMED, *The Koran.* Ch. ii.

10
And God saw every thing that he had made, and, behold, it was very good.

Old Testament: Genesis, i, 31.

God was satisfied with his own work, and that is fatal.

SAMUEL BUTLER, *Notebooks,* p. 255. (c. 1890)

11
God is the indwelling and not the transient cause of all things.

BARUCH SPINOZA, *Ethics.* Pt. i. Prop. 18. (1674)

12
Thought is an attribute of God, or God is a thinking thing.

BARUCH SPINOZA, *Ethics.* Pt. ii. Prop. 1.

13
God buries his workmen but carries on his work.

CHARLES WESLEY, *Remark,* said to have been frequently uttered by him. See THOMAS JACKSON, *Century of Wesleyan Methodism,* p. 193. (1839)

14
In God we trust. As a matter of fact, "In God is our trust," or "In God we trust," did not become the motto of the United States until 1956, when it was adopted officially by Congress to appear on all U.S. coins as well as paper money. The motto "In God we trust" was originally used on U.S. coins in 1864 at the direction of Salmon P. Chase, Secretary of the Treasury under President Lincoln, but in 1907 it was removed from all gold coins at the insistence of President Theodore Roosevelt. This, however, aroused so much criticism, that it was restored in 1908. It now appears also on the one dollar bill. *See* 674:3.

GOOD HUMOR

15
I have mentioned good humor as one of the preservatives of our peace and tranquility. It is among the most effectual, and its effect is so well imitated and aided, artificially, by politeness, that this also becomes an acquisition of first rate value. In truth, politeness is artificial good humor.

THOMAS JEFFERSON, *Letter to His Grandson, Thomas Jefferson Randolph,* 24 Nov., 1808.

16
Good-humor is a philosophic state of mind; it seems to say to Nature that we take her no more seriously than she takes us.

ERNEST RENAN, *Feuilles Détachées,* p. 397. (c. 1880)

17
Cheerfulness can never be excessive, but always good; melancholy, on the contrary, is always evil.

BARUCH SPINOZA, *Ethics.* Pt. iv. Prop. 42 (1674)

GOVERNMENT

18
You talk about capitalism and communism and all that sort of thing, but the important thing is the struggle everybody is engaged in

to get better living conditions, and they are not interested too much in the form of government.

BERNARD BARUCH, Press Conference in New York City, 18 Aug., 1964, on the eve of his 94th birthday.

1
Socialism seeks to pull down wealth; Liberalism seeks to raise up poverty. Socialism would kill enterprise; Liberalism would rescue enterprise from the trammels of privilege and preference. . . . Socialism exalts the rule; Liberalism exalts the man. Socialism attacks capital; Liberalism attacks monopoly.

WINSTON CHURCHILL. (HENRY ANATOLE GRUNWALD, *Man of the Century;* in *Churchill: The Life Triumphant,* 1965)

2
We Republicans believe in limited government, but also in effective and humane government. We believe in keeping government as close to the people as possible—in letting each citizen do for himself what he can do for himself, then making any call for government assistance first on the local government, then on the state government, and only in the final resort on the Federal Government. But we do not shrink from a recognition that there are national problems that require national solutions.

DWIGHT D. EISENHOWER, *Article,* New York *Herald Tribune,* 25 May, 1964.

3
Our best protection against bigger government in Washington is better government in the states.

DWIGHT D. EISENHOWER, *Address,* at the National Governors' Conference, Cleveland, 8 June, 1964.

4
I fear Washington and centralized government more than I do Moscow.

BARRY M. GOLDWATER, *Speech,* in Spartanburg, S.C., 15 Sept., 1960.

5
A government that is big enough to give you all you want is big enough to take it all away.

BARRY M. GOLDWATER, *Speech,* in West Chester, Pa., 21 Oct., 1964, during the presidential campaign of that year.

6
The truth is, far from crushing the individual, government at its best liberates him from the enslaving forces of his environment.

LYNDON B. JOHNSON, *Commencement Address,* Swarthmore College, Swarthmore, Pa., 8 June, 1964.

7
Government exists to protect freedom and enlarge the opportunities of every citizen. The American government is not to be feared and attacked. It is to be helped as long as it serves its country well, and changed when it neglects its duty.

LYNDON B. JOHNSON, *Address,* in Valley Forge, Pa., 24 July, 1964.

8
Capitalism is a worn-out old mare while socialism is new, young, and full of teeming energy.

NIKITA S. KHRUSHCHEV, Statement in Tatabanya, Hungary, reported in *Pravda,* 9 Apr., 1958. (*Conquest Without War,* edited by N. H. MAGER AND JACQUES KATEL, p. 49)

9
I have never believed in the infallibility of governments. I think if a Minister is right oftener than he is wrong it is a considerable achievement.

SELWYN LLOYD. (New York *Times,* "Ideas and Men," 23 May, 1965, p. 11E)

10
I have had little experience of self-government. In fact, I am one of the most governed people in the world.

PRINCE PHILIP OF THE UNITED KINGDOM, commenting, in 1959, on his role as husband of Queen Elizabeth II.

GREATNESS

11
The fellow that does his job every day. The mother who has children and gets up and gets the breakfast and keeps them clean and sends them off to school. The fellow who keeps the streets clean—without him we wouldn't have any sanitation. The Unknown Soldier. Millions of men.

BERNARD BARUCH, Press Conference, 18 Aug., 1964, on the eve of his 94th birthday. This was his reply to a question: Who was the greatest man of Baruch's time?

12
Call to Greatness.

ADLAI E. STEVENSON, *Title of Book* (1954).

13
Life is good in America, but the good life still eludes us. Our standard of living is admittedly high, but measured by those things that truly distinguish a civilization, our living standards are hardly high at all. We have, I fear, confused power with greatness.

STEWART L. UDALL, *Commencement Address,* Dartmouth College, Hanover, N.H., 13 June, 1965.

HAPPINESS

14
Happiness Makes Up in Height for What It Lacks in Length.

ROBERT FROST, *Title of Poem.* (1942)

15
Most of the disappointments of later life could be lightened immeasurably if we could learn—and truly believe—early in life that what we confusedly call "happiness" is a direction and not a place.

SYDNEY J. HARRIS, Publishers Newspaper Syndicate. (*The Reader's Digest,* Dec., 1963, p. 205)

1
As far as the job as President goes, it's rewarding and I've given before this group the definition of happiness of the Greeks. I'll define it again: the full use of your powers along lines of excellence. I find that, therefore, the presidency provides some happiness.

JOHN F. KENNEDY, Press Conference, 31 Oct., 1963.

2
If you cannot catch a bird of paradise, better take a wet hen.

NIKITA S. KHRUSHCHEV. (*Time,* 6 Jan., 1958)

3
Happiness puts on as many shapes as discontent, and there is nothing odder than the satisfactions of one's neighbor.

PHYLLIS MCGINLEY, *The Province of the Heart: Pipeline and Sinker,* p. 79.

4
Today people who possess so many objects of so-called exterior happiness often stand in need of interior happiness, the only kind that is genuine, personal, profound and sincere.

POPE PAUL VI, Christmas message broadcast from Rome, 23 Dec., 1963. (Translation by the Vatican press office.)

5
Happiness is beneficial for the body, but it is grief that develops the powers of the mind.

MARCEL PROUST, *Remembrance of Things Past: The Past Recaptured.* (1920)

6
It is wrong to assume that men of immense wealth are always happy.

JOHN D. ROCKEFELLER, *Remark,* to his Sunday School class. (HOLBROOK, *The Age of the Moguls,* p. 134.)

7
Any man that can make a living doing what he likes is lucky, and I'm that.

CHARLES RUSSELL, *Letter to a Friend.* (1920) *See also* 2233:10.

HERO AND HEROISM

8
It was absolutely involuntary. They sank my boat.

JOHN F. KENNEDY, Reply to a small boy who had asked: "Mr. President, how did you become a war hero?" (*The Kennedy Wit,* ed. by BILL ADLER)

9
To be negative is just the other side of having a very clear idea of gallantry and beauty. I would like to see the return of the hero—I mean the man who really stands up and is counted, ethically, morally and humanly, and so becomes larger than himself.

MARYA MANNES. (*Life,* 12 June, 1964, p. 59)

HESITATION

10
On the Plains of Hesitation bleach the bones of countless millions who, at the Dawn of Victory, sat down to wait—and waiting, died.

GEORGE W. CECIL, *Advertisement, American Magazine,* March, 1923, p. 87. Mr. Cecil was a well-known copy-writer, and the ad., titled "The Warning of the Desert," was for the International Correspondence Schools, and was signed William A. Lawrence, which was Cecil's nom de plume at the time. The lines were in quotation marks. In a letter to the compiler he states that the ad. was probably written some time in 1921.

On the Plains of Hesitation bleach the bones of countless thousands who, on the eve of Victory, rested—and resting died.

ADLAI STEVENSON, *Speech,* Chicago, 3 Nov., 1952. *See* New York *Times,* 4 Nov., 1952, p. 25. In a letter to a friend, Mr. Stevenson wrote, "I had always thought that the quotation which was filed somewhere in the back of my mind came from a fairly recent writer. . . . Ensuing research seems to reveal something very like it in an advertisement of about 1920. Could it be that I saw it then, and remembered it all these years?"

HISTORY

11
History is more than the record of man's conflict with nature and himself. It is the knowledge which gives dimension to the present, direction to the future, and humility to the leaders of men. A nation, like a person, not conscious of its own past is adrift without purpose or protection against the contending forces of dissolution.

LYNDON B. JOHNSON, *Proclamation* establishing 22 Nov., 1964, the first anniversary of the death of John F. Kennedy, as "a day of national rededication."

12
I am always amazed that the people who attack me never ask the first question that a historian would ask: Is it true?

ARTHUR M. SCHLESINGER, JR., Comment, in reply to critics of his book on John F. Kennedy, *A Thousand Days* (1965). (WILLIAM V. SHANNON, "Controversial Historian of the Age of Kennedy"; *New York Times Magazine,* 21 Nov., 1965, p. 132)

13
A historian's métier is to move freely through time and space.

ARNOLD J. TOYNBEE, "Why I Dislike Western Civilization"; *New York Times Magazine,* 10 May, 1964, p. 15.

HONOR

14
A nation reveals itself not only by the men it produces but also by the men it honors, the men it remembers.

JOHN F. KENNEDY, *Address,* at Amherst College, Amherst, Mass., 26 Oct., 1963.

1
It is not the same thing if I sign myself "Jean Paul Sartre" or "Jean Paul Sartre, Nobel Prize winner."

JEAN PAUL SARTRE, Comment to reporters, in Paris, 22 Oct., 1964, explaining why he turned down the 1964 Nobel Prize in literature—in order to remain free to bring together the cultures of the capitalist and Communist nations.

2
To repay honor with dishonor.

ADLAI E. STEVENSON, Public Statement broadcast nationally just after the Democratic national convention nominated him for the presidency in July, 1952. He said in full, "I did not seek it. I did not want it. I am, however, persuaded that to shirk it, to evade it, would be to repay honor with dishonor."

3
If somebody throws a brick at me I can catch it and throw it back. But when somebody awards a decoration to me, I am out of words.

HARRY S TRUMAN, Comment upon receiving Austria's highest decoration, the Gold Grand Cross for Merit, in Washington, D.C., 7 May, 1964.

HUMILITY

4
It behooves all of us—whether in government, the academic world or in the press—to avoid that most dangerous disease, infectious omniscience.

GEORGE W. BALL, *Commencement Address,* Miami University, Oxford, Ohio, June, 1965.

5
He is a small modest man—with a great deal to be modest about.

WINSTON CHURCHILL, characterizing Clement Attlee when the latter was British prime minister.

6
Humility must always be the portion of any man who receives acclaim earned in the blood of his followers and the sacrifices of his friends.

GENERAL DWIGHT D. EISENHOWER, *Address,* in London, 12 June, 1945.

7
Why is there such a lack of grace today? There can only be one answer. The people have gotten away from humility. We must recognize it and face it. May God help us to be a humble people.

REV. WILLIAM FRANKLIN (BILLY) GRAHAM, *America's Hour of Decision.*

8
Some editors ate crow and left the feathers on.

HARRY S TRUMAN, Remark to a reporter shortly after he returned to Independence, Mo., in 1953 to become "Mr. Citizen." He was referring to the cordial reaction of newspaper editors who, during the Truman years in Washington, had been quite hostile. (ALFRED STEINBERG, *The Man from Missouri,* p. 420)

HUNGER

9
I've never known a country to be starved into democracy.

GEORGE D. AIKEN, Comment to reporters, Mar., 1964. Aiken was among the Senators who took an unfavorable view of the U.S.-sponsored economic boycott of Cuba.

10
If you feed people just with revolutionary slogans they will listen today, they will listen tomorrow, they will listen the day after tomorrow, but on the fourth day they will say: "To hell with you."

NIKITA KHRUSHCHEV, Comment, Sept., 1964. (Quoted in New York *Times,* "Ideas and Men," 4 Oct., 1964)

11
A hungry man is not a free man.

ADLAI E. STEVENSON, *Speech,* in Kasson, Minn., 6 Sept., 1952, during the presidential campaign.

IDEALS

12
An idealist without illusions.

JOHN F. KENNEDY, Self-characterization. (Quoted by Arthur M. Schlesinger, Jr., on *Meet the Press,* NBC-TV, 28 Nov., 1965)

13
Ideals are in crisis; philosophy has been replaced by calculations of immediate utility.

POPE PAUL VI, *Address,* to Roman Catholic clergy, Vatican City, 12 Feb., 1964.

IGNORANCE

14
A man must have a certain amount of intelligent ignorance to get anywhere.

CHARLES F. KETTERING, *Remark,* on his 70th birthday, 29 Aug., 1946.

15
He who neglects to drink of the spring of experience is apt to die of thirst in the desert of ignorance.

LING PO, Chinese Philosopher, *Epigram.*

16
We hear it not seldom said that ignorance is the mother of admiration. No falser word was ever spoken.

RICHARD CHEVENIX TRENCH, *On the Study of Words,* p. 2. (1851) *See* 958:3.

17
Statesmanship should quickly learn the lesson of biology as stated by Conklin, that "Wooden legs are not inherited, but wooden heads are."

ALBERT EDWARD WIGGAM, *The New Decalogue of Science.* (1923)

JEFFERSON, THOMAS

1
I think this is the most extraordinary collection of talent, of human knowledge, that has ever been gathered together at the White House—with the possible exception of when Thomas Jefferson dined alone.

JOHN F. KENNEDY. Greeting to guests at a White House dinner honoring Nobel Prize winners, 29 Apr., 1962.

JUSTICE

2
I always felt from the beginning that you had to defend people you disliked and feared as well as those you admired.

ROGER BALDWIN. (WILLIE MORRIS, "Barely Winded at Eighty"; *The New Republic*, 25 Jan., 1964)

3
Justice is my being allowed to do whatever I like. Injustice is whatever prevents my doing so.

SAMUEL BUTLER, *Notebooks*, p. 56. (c. 1890)

4
What seems just at one time in a man's life may come to seem unjust at other times. I grew up in a segregated society. It never occurred to me that this was unjust.

LEROY COLLINS, *Television Interview: Face the Nation*, 20 Dec., 1964. Speaking as director of the Community Relations Service, created by the 1964 Civil Rights Law, Collins went on to explain that he had since come to recognize the injustice of a segregated society.

5
A long line of cases shows that it is not merely of some importance, but is of fundamental importance, that justice should not only be done, but should manifestly and undoubtedly be seen to be done.

VISCOUNT C. J. HEWART, *Opinion*, in Rex *vs.* Sussex Justices. (1924)

6
Communism is the corruption of a dream of justice.

ADLAI E. STEVENSON, *Speech*, in Urbana, Ill., 1951.

7
Expedience and justice frequently are not even on speaking terms.

ARTHUR H. VANDENBERG, *Speech*, U.S. Senate, 8 March, 1945, protesting the Yalta agreement to cede Polish territory to Russia.

8
The laws of changeless justice bind
Oppressor and oppressed;
And, close as sin and suffering joined,
We march to Fate abreast.

JOHN GREENLEAF WHITTIER, *Song of the Negro Boatmen*. Quoted by Booker T. Washington, in a famous speech at Atlanta, Ga., in 1895. *See* his *Up From Slavery*.

9
You stand here convicted of seeking to corrupt the administration of justice. You stand here convicted of having tampered, really, with the very soul of this nation.

FRANK W. WILSON, U.S. District Judge, in passing sentence on James R. Hoffa, head of the Teamsters Union, for attempting to rig a Federal jury; Chattanooga, Tenn., 12 Mar., 1964.

10
When you reflect on it, the only thing that allowed the human race to stop living as animals and to start living as human beings was by adopting a set of rules—a system of justice. Maintaining a system of justice in an orderly society is essential to whatever else people accomplish.

FRANK W. WILSON, U.S. District Judge, commenting on his sentencing of James R. Hoffa, head of the Teamsters Union, 12 Mar., 1964, in Chattanooga, Tenn.

KINGS

11
On November 16 [1699] a famous scene was enacted at Versailles. Louis XIV, at his levee, presented the Spanish Ambassador to the Duke of Anjou, saying, "You may salute him as your King." The Ambassador gave vent to his celebrated indiscretion, "There are no more Pyrenees."

WINSTON CHURCHILL, *The Age of Revolution*, p. 20. (1957) The French King had just succeeded in getting the Duc d'Anjou appointed King of Spain. *See also* 1354:2.

12
There is not a single crowned head in Europe whose talents or merits would entitle him to be elected a vestryman by the people of any parish in America.

THOMAS JEFFERSON, *Letter to George Washington*, 2 May, 1788.

KISS

13
An old Spanish saying is that "a kiss without a mustache is like an egg without salt."

MADISON CAWEIN, *Nature-Notes*. (c. 1900)

14
A kiss, when all is said, what is it?
An oath that's given closer than before;
A promise more precise; the sealing of
Confessions that till then were barely
breathed;
A rosy dot placed on the i in loving;
A secret that's confided to a mouth
And not to ears; a precious moment of
Infinity that buzzes like a bee;
Communion with the fragrance flowers have;
A gentle way for heart to breathe a heart,
For soul from fervent lips to drink a soul.

(Un baiser, mais à tout prendre, qu'est-ce?
Un serment fait d'un peu plus près, une
promesse

Plus précise, un aveu qui veut se confirmer,
Un point rose qu'on met sur l'i du verbe aimer;
C'est un secret qui prend la bouche pour oreiller,
Un instant d'infini qui fait un bruit d'abeille,
Une communion ayant un goût de fleur,
Une façon d'un peu se respirer le cœur,
Et d'un peu se goûter, au bord des lèvres, l'âme!)

EDMOND ROSTAND, *Cyrano de Bergerac*. Act iii, sc. 10. (1897) Charles Renauld, tr.

1
The kiss of death.

ALFRED E. SMITH, *Speech,* referring to William Randolph Hearst's support of Ogden Mills. (1926)

LABOR

2
The dictionary is the only place where success comes before work.

ARTHUR BRISBANE, editor of the N.Y. *Evening Journal,* as quoted by Bennett Cerf.

3
It is impossible to escape from toil
O' the sudden and receive thy spiriting:
The flower must drink the nature of the soil
Before it can put forth its blossoming.

JOHN KEATS, *To Spenser,* l. 9. (1818)

4
Set me anything to do as a task, and it is inconceivable the desire I have to do something else.

BERNARD SHAW. As quoted by Gamaliel Bradford, *As God Made Them,* p. 6. (1921)

5
The law of work does seem utterly unfair, but there it is, and nothing can change it: the higher the pay in enjoyment the worker gets out of it, the higher shall be his pay in cash also.

MARK TWAIN, *A Connecticut Yankee at King Arthur's Court,* p. 269. (1889)

6
No race can prosper till it learns there is as much dignity in tilling a field as in writing a poem.

BOOKER T. WASHINGTON, *Address,* Atlanta Exposition, 18 Sept., 1895. See *Up From Slavery,* p. 220. *See also* 637:16.

LAW

7
For law is meaningless if there is no public will to observe it. And this public will, in turn, can exist only when the law is just and deserving of honor. . . . There are not enough jails, not enough policemen, not enough courts to enforce a law not supported by the people.

HUBERT H. HUMPHREY, *Speech,* in Williamsburg, Va., 1 May, 1965.

8
There is no greater wrong, in our democracy, than violent, willful disregard of law.

LYNDON B. JOHNSON, Public Statement on the rioting in Los Angeles, 15 Aug., 1965.

9
We prefer world law, in the age of self-determination, to world war in the age of mass extermination.

JOHN F. KENNEDY, *Address,* to the United Nations General Assembly, 25 Sept., 1961.

10
Despotism and anarchy prevail when a constitutional order does not exist. Both are lawless and arbitrary. Indeed, despotism may be defined as the anarchy of lawless rulers, and anarchy as the despotism of lawless crowds.

WALTER LIPPMANN, *The Public Philosophy,* bk. ii, ch. 11. (1955)

11
The atrocity of the laws prevents their execution.

MONTESQUIEU, *Spirit of Laws.* Bk. vi, ch. 13. (1748)

12
Law, the lord of all, mortals and immortals.

PINDAR, *Fragment* 169. (c. 500 B.C.) Quoted by Plato, Gorgias, 484:B; Herodotus, iii, 38; Aristides, ii, 68; Plutarch, Moralia, 780:C, and many others.

13
It is a form of anarchy to say that a person need not comply with a particular statute with which he disagrees. Ours is a government of laws, not of men, and our system cannot tolerate the philosophy that obedience to law rests upon the personal likes or dislikes of any individual citizen, whether he supports or opposes the statute in question.

RICHARD RUSSELL, *Speech,* in Rome, Ga., 15 July, 1964. He was urging Southern acceptance of the Civil Rights Law of 1964, against which he had fought hard in the Senate, before its passage.

14
Most good lawyers live well, work hard and die poor.

DANIEL WEBSTER, *Speech,* Charleston, S.C., 10 May, 1847.

15
No person shall be . . . deprived of life, liberty, or property, without due process of law.

Bill of Rights, Article v. (25 Sept., 1789) Submitted by the First Congress at its first session. The phrase, "without due process of law," is repeated in the Fourteenth Amendment to the Constitution, designed to protect the newly emancipated slaves in the enjoyment of civil rights.

16
The Seven Sisters.

Name given to the seven laws put through the New Jersey Legislature in 1913 by Woodrow Wilson, then Governor of the State, designed to tighten up the over-liberal state laws relating to corporations.

LIBERTY

1
Let every nation know, whether it wishes us well or ill, that we shall pay any price, bear any burden, meet any hardship, support any friend, oppose any foe to assure the survival and the success of liberty.

John F. Kennedy, *Inaugural Address,* 20 Jan., 1961.

2
No people in the world ever did achieve their freedom by goody-goody talk and moral suasion: it being the immutable law that all revolutions that will succeed must *begin* in blood.

Mark Twain, *A Connecticut Yankee at King Arthur's Court,* p. 164. (1889)

3
Human liberty may yet, perhaps, be obliged to repose its principal hopes on the intelligence and vigor of the Saxon race.

Daniel Webster. As quoted by Norman Hapgood, *Daniel Webster,* p. 61.

4
Liberty does not consist in mere general declarations of the rights of men. It consists in the translation of those declarations into definite action.

Woodrow Wilson, *Address,* Independence Hall, Philadelphia, 4 July, 1914. Lord Acton's definition of liberty is, "Freedom to do what one's conscience says is right."

LIES AND LYING

5
Men cannot live with a lie and not be stained by it.

Lyndon B. Johnson, *Address,* 6 Aug., 1965, upon signing the voting-rights bill of 1965. He was referring to earlier professions of equal rights for Negroes, which were nullified by severely restricting Negro suffrage.

6
If the Republicans stop telling lies about us, we will stop telling the truth about them.

Adlai E. Stevenson, *Speech,* in Bakersfield, Calif., during the 1952 presidential campaign.

LIFE

7
After all, what is human life? A vapor, a fog, a dew, a blossom, a flower, a rose, a blade of grass, a glass bubble, a tale told by an idiot, a *boule de savon,* vanity of vanities, an eternal succession of which would terrify me almost as much as annihilation.

John Adams, *Letter to Thomas Jefferson.* (1813)

I ask you, what is human life? Is it not a maimed happiness—care and weariness, weariness and care, with the baseless expectation, the strange cozenage of a brighter tomorrow? At best it is but a froward child, that must be played with and humored, to keep it quiet till it falls asleep, and then the care is over.

Ernest Renan, *Feuilles Détachées,* p. 314. (c. 1880)

8
Living seems to me in every thing a wasteful and inequitable process.

James Branch Cabell, *Jurgen,* p. 34.

9
Science, rapidly giving us the means to build a new world, does not tell us what kind of world it should be or how we as individuals and citizens can live in it. Perhaps it is . . . that the more able we are to control life, the less able we are to live it.

Milton S. Eisenhower, "The Need for a New American"; *The Educational Record,* Oct., 1963, p. 304.

10
They were born, they suffered, they died. (*Ils naquirent, ils souffrirent, ils moururent.*)

Anatole France, *Opinions of Jérôme Coignard,* ch. xvi. (1893)

11
A short life in the saddle, Lord,
Not long life by the fire.

Louise Imogen Guiney, *The Knight Errant.* (1884)

12
I have lived temperately, eating little animal food. . . . The ardent wines I cannot drink, nor do I use ardent spirits in any form. . . . I may end these egotisms therefore, by saying that my life has been so much like that of other people, that I might say with Horace, to every one *"nomine mutato, narratur fabula de te."* [Change but the name, and the tale is told of you.—Horace, Bk. i, sat. i, l. 69.]

Thomas Jefferson, *Letter to Vine Utley,* 21 March, 1819, at the age of seventy-six.

Decalogue of Canons for Observation in Practical Life: 1.—Never put off till tomorrow what you can do today; 2.—Never trouble another for what you can do yourself; 3.—Never spend your money before you have it; 4.—Never buy what you do not want because it is cheap—it will be dear to you; 5.—Pride costs us more than hunger, thirst, and cold; 6.—We never repent of having eaten too little; 7.—Nothing is troublesome that we do willingly; 8.—How much pain have cost us the evils which have never happened; 9.—Take things always by their smooth handle; 10.—When angry, count ten before you speak; if very angry, a hundred.

Thomas Jefferson, *Letter to Thomas Jefferson Smith,* 21 Feb., 1825, named after Jefferson, but no relation. Reminiscent of Mr. Meagles' "Count five-and-twenty, Tattycoram."

Avoid running at all times. Don't look back. Someone might be gaining on you.

Leroy (Satchel) Paige, *How to Stay Young.* See *Collier's,* 13 June, 1953, p. 55.

1
The good life in the good society, though attainable, is never attained and possessed once and for all. So what has been attained will again be lost if the wisdom of the good life in a good society is not transmitted.

WALTER LIPPMANN, *The Public Philosophy,* bk. ii, ch. 8. (1955)

2
It is not true that life is one damn thing after another—it's one damn thing over and over.

EDNA ST. VINCENT MILLAY. (*Letters of Edna St. Vincent Millay,* ed. by ALLEN R. MACDOUGALL) *See* p. 1116:4.

3
Life was meant to be lived, and curiosity must be kept alive. One must never, for whatever reason, turn his back on life.

ELEANOR ROOSEVELT, *The Autobiography of Eleanor Roosevelt.*

4
What good are vitamins? Eat a lobster, eat a pound of caviar—live! If you are in love with a beautiful blonde with an empty face and no brains at all, don't be afraid. Marry her! Live!

ARTUR RUBINSTEIN. ("Rubinstein Speaking"; *New York Times Magazine,* 26 Jan., 1964)

5
Keep breathing.

SOPHIE TUCKER, on the secret of achieving a long life. Spoken on her 80th birthday, 13 Jan., 1964.

6
Life imitates art far more than art imitates life.

OSCAR WILDE, *The Decay of Lying. Essays,* p. 55. (Methuen, London, 1950.)

LINCOLN, ABRAHAM

7
Lincoln's words have become the common covenant of our public life. Let us now get on with his work.

LYNDON B. JOHNSON, *Address,* at the Lincoln Memorial, Washington, D.C., 12 Feb., 1964.

LOVE

8
Love alone can lend young people rapture, however transient.

JAMES BRANCH CABELL, *Jurgen,* p. 45. (1919)

9
I can't give you anything but love, baby. (*Sed contra accipies meros amores.*)

CATULLUS, *Poems.* No. xiii. (c. 57 B.C.) Copley, tr.

10
You would have understood me had you
  waited;
I could have loved you, dear, as well as he:
Had we not been impatient, dear, and fated
  Always to disagree.

ERNEST DOWSON, *You Would Have Understood Me.* (1896)

11
A cottage, with the man one loves, is a palace.

HENRY FIELDING, *Amelia.* Bk. ii, ch. 6. (1751)

12
Every day I love you more, today more than yesterday, and much less than tomorrow. (*Chaque jour je t'aime davantage, Aujourd'hui plus que hier et bien moins que demain.*)

ROSAMONDE GERARD (MME. EDMOND ROSTAND), *L'Eternelle Chanson.* (c. 1920)

13
Perhaps true love can best be recognized by the fact that it thrives under circumstances which would blast anything else into small pieces.

ERNEST HAVEMANN, *Men, Women, and Marriage,* p. 215. (1962)

14
Mamie bloomed and bridled. . . . "Any man's nice when he's in love."

HENRY JAMES, *The Ambassadors,* p. 308. (1902)

15
Here I am, Madame, gazing whole hours at the Maison Quarrée, like a lover at his mistress. . . . This is the second time I have been in love since I left Paris. The first time was with the Diana at the Chateau de Laye-Epinaye in Beaujolais, a delicious morsel of sculpture by M. A. Slodtz. This, you will say, was in rule, to fall in love with a female beauty; but with a house it is out of all precedent.

THOMAS JEFFERSON, *Letter to the Countess Noailles de Tessé,* from Nîmes. (1785) When Jefferson submitted his design for the capitol at Richmond, Virginia, he explained that it was after the Maison Carrée at Nîmes, "which, in the opinion of all who have seen it, yields in beauty to no piece of architecture on earth." It is an adaptation of that building which is Virginia's capitol today.

16
Europeans used to say Americans were puritanical. Then they discovered that we were not puritans. So now they say that we are obsessed with sex.

MARY MCCARTHY. (*Life,* 20 Sept., 1963, p. 62)

17
Love must be as much a light as a flame.

H. D. THOREAU, *Letter to Harrison Blake.*

18
Nothing spoils a romance so much as a sense of humor in a woman.

OSCAR WILDE, *A Woman of No Importance.* Act i. (1893) *See also* 1736:7.

MAN

19
Man is the only animal that can remain on friendly terms with the victims he intends to eat until he eats them.

SAMUEL BUTLER, *Notebooks,* p. 53. (c. 1890)

1
Good and evil keep very exact accounts and the face of every man is their ledger.

JAMES BRANCH CABELL, *Jurgen*, p. 20. (1919)

2
I decline to accept the end of man.

WILLIAM FAULKNER, *Address*, in Stockholm, 10 Dec., 1950, on accepting the Nobel Prize in literature.

I believe that man will not merely endure: he will prevail. He is immortal, not because he alone among creatures has an inexhaustible voice, but because he has a soul, a spirit capable of compassion and sacrifice and endurance.

WILLIAM FAULKNER, *Address*, in Stockholm, 10 Dec., 1950, on accepting the Nobel Prize in literature.

3
It is a curious fact that when we get sick we want an uncommon doctor. If we have a construction job, we want an uncommon engineer. When we get into a war, we dreadfully want an uncommon admiral and an uncommon general. Only when we get into politics are we content with the common man.

HERBERT HOOVER. (Quoted in obituary of Hoover, New York *Times*, 21 Oct., 1964, p. 40)

4
Behind every successful man stands a surprised mother-in-law.

HUBERT H. HUMPHREY, *Speech*, during the presidential campaign of 1964. (New York *Times*, "Ideas and Men," 11 Oct., 1964, p. 13E)

5
A man in trouble *must* be possessed, somehow, of a woman.

HENRY JAMES, *The Ambassadors*, p. 211. (1902)

6
He believed that one man can make a difference, and that every man should try.

JACQUELINE KENNEDY, Television Broadcast, in memory of her husband, John F. Kennedy, 29 May, 1964. Referring specifically to Kennedy's thoughts on public service.

7
All honor to the one that in this hour
Cries to the world as from a lighted tower—
Cries for the Man Forgotten.

EDWIN MARKHAM, *The Forgotten Man*. *See* 2281:8.

8
It is a dull man who is always sure, and a sure man who is always dull.

H. C. MENCKEN, *Prejudices*. Ser. ii, ch. 1. (1920) *See also* 226:15.

9
Men are made stronger on realization that the helping hand they need is at the end of their own right arm.

SIDNEY J. PHILLIPS, *Address*, at the dedication of the Booker T. Washington Memorial Highway, near his birthplace in Virginia, July, 1953.

10
I feel sorry for men. They have more problems than women. In the first place they have to compete with women.

FRANÇOISE SAGAN. (New York *Times*, 30 Dec., 1959)

11
We are all in the gutter, but some of us are looking at the stars.

OSCAR WILDE, *Lady Windermere's Fan*. Act iii. (1892)

12
Men with a passion for anonymity.

Report of President's Committee on Administrative Management, referring to F. D. Roosevelt's assistants.

MARRIAGE

13
His wife not only edited his works but edited him.

VAN WYCK BROOKS, *The Ordeal of Mark Twain*. Ch. v. (1920)

14
Marriage is distinctly and repeatedly excluded from heaven. Is this because it is thought likely to mar the general felicity?

SAMUEL BUTLER, *Notebooks*, p. 64. (c. 1890)

15
"Home, sweet home" must surely have been written by a bachelor.

SAMUEL BUTLER, *Notebook*, p. 271. As a matter of fact, Payne *was* a bachelor, and never knew what it was to have a home after the age of thirteen, when his mother died. *See* 906:7.

16
More effort has been made to keep together that artificial collection called the human family, than any other institution.

SAMUEL BUTLER. *See* David H. Cohn, *The Fabulous Democrats*, p. 174.

17
I shall marry in haste and repeat at leisure.

JAMES BRANCH CABELL, *Jurgen*. Ch. 38. (1919)

18
Such a wife as I want . . . must be young, handsome (I lay most stress upon a good shape), sensible (a little learning will do), well bred, chaste, and tender. . . . As to religion a moderate stock will satisfy me. She must believe in God and hate a saint.

ALEXANDER HAMILTON, *Letter to John Laurens*, Dec., 1779. *See also* 2138:12.

19
How to be Happy Though Married.

REV. E. J. HARDY, *Title of Book*. (1910)

20
Marrying a man is like buying something you've been admiring for a long time in a shop window. You may love it when you get it home, but it doesn't always go with everything else in the house.

JEAN KERR, *The Snake Has All the Lines: The Ten Worst Things About a Man*, p. 121. (1960)

1
Same old slippers, same old rice,
Same old glimpse of Paradise.

W. J. LAMPTON, *June Weddings.* (c. 1900)

2
Marriage is a lot of things—an alliance, a sacrament, a comedy, or a mistake; but it is definitely not a partnership because that implies equal gain. And every right-thinking woman knows the profit in matrimony is by all odds hers.

PHYLLIS MCGINLEY, *The Province of the Heart: How to Get Along with Men,* p. 73. (1959)

3
Though he has Eden to live in,
Man cannot be happy alone.

JOSEPHINE POLLARD, *We Cannot Be Happy Alone.* (c. 1880) *See* 1874:2.

MEMORY

4
When memory keeps me company and moves to smiles or tears,
A weather-beaten object looms through the mist of years.
Behind the house and barn it stood, half a mile or more,
And hurrying feet a path had made, straight to its swinging door.
Its architecture was a type of simple classic art,
But in the tragedy of life it played a leading part,
And oft the passing traveller drove slow and heaved a sigh
To let the modest hired girl slip out with glances shy.

JAMES WHITCOMB RILEY, *The Old Backhouse.* See *Suppressed Poems by James Whitcomb Riley and Eugene Field.* (n.d.) Riley's close friends and relatives say that Riley did not write the poem. See *A Bibliography of James Whitcomb Riley,* by Anthony J. and Dorothy R. Russo, p. 351. (1944) There are six stanzas, of which the first is quoted here.

5
Memory is the diary we all carry about with us.

OSCAR WILDE, *The Importance of Being Earnest.* Act i. (1895) *See also* 1292:15.

MIND

6
Life is not a static thing. The only people who do not change their minds are incompetents in asylums, who can't, and those in cemeteries.

EVERETT M. DIRKSEN, News Conference, Washington, D.C., 1 Jan., 1965.

7
The mind need never stop growing. Indeed, one of the few experiences which never pall is the experience of watching one's own mind, and observing how it produces new interests, responds to new stimuli, and develops new thoughts, apparently without effort and almost independently of one's own conscious control.

GILBERT HIGHET, *Talents and Geniuses: The Mystery of Zen,* p. 308. (1957)

8
A democracy which despises the gifted as eggheads is a democracy which has abdicated to dictatorship.

QUINTIN HOGG, M.P. (New York *Times,* "Ideas and Men," 31 Jan., 1965, p. 9E)

9
The human mind is our fundamental resource.

JOHN F. KENNEDY, *Message to Congress,* on education, 20 Feb., 1961.

10
Those who corrupt the public mind are just as evil as those who steal from the public purse.

ADLAI E. STEVENSON, *Speech,* in Albuquerque, N. Mex., 12 Sept., 1952, during the presidential campaign.

11
Eggheads unite! You have nothing to lose but your yolks.

ADLAI E. STEVENSON, Remark during the 1952 presidential campaign, in reply to the Republican taunt of "egghead."

12
Free enterprise of the mind.

ADLAI E. STEVENSON, during the presidential campaign of 1952—his antidote to excessive zeal in hunting alleged subversives.

MONEY

13
The money that men make lives after them.

SAMUEL BUTLER, *Notebooks,* p. 223. (c. 1890)

14
Money is an essential ingredient to happiness in this world.

ALEXANDER HAMILTON, *Letter to John Laurens,* Dec., 1779.

15
In the race for money some men may come first, but man comes last.

MARYA MANNES. (*Life,* 12 June, 1964, p. 62)

16
He got some gold, dug from the mud,
Some silver crushed from stones;
But the gold was red with dead men's blood,
The silver black with groans;
And when he died he moaned aloud,
"They'll make no pocket in my shroud."

JOAQUIN MILLER, *The Dead Millionaire.* (c. 1890)

Whenever you git holt of a ten-dollar note you want to git it *into you* or *onto ye* jest 's quick 's you kin. We're here today an' gone tomorrer, and the' ain't no pocket in a shroud.

EDWARD NOYES WESTCOTT, *David Harum,* p. 204. (1898)

There's No Pocket in a Shroud.

JOHN A. JOYCE, *Title of Poem.* (c. 1900)

You Can't Take It With You.

MOSS HART and GEORGE KAUFMAN, *Title of Comedy.* (1937) All of these variations are, of course, founded upon *I Timothy*, vi, 7: "We brought nothing into this world, and it is certain we can carry nothing out." *See also* 1719:8.

1
The vagabond, when rich, is called a tourist.

PAUL RICHARD, *The Scourge of Christ*, p. 40. (1929)

2
It isn't the sum you get, it's how much you can buy with it that's the important thing; and it's that that tells whether your wages are high in fact or only high in name.

MARK TWAIN, *A Connecticut Yankee at King Arthur's Court*, p. 292. (1889)

3
It's harder to give away money than it is to make it. After all, you want it to be useful.

MAXWELL M. UPSON, upon pledging $9,000,000 in stock to Cornell University, 10 Oct., 1964.

MORALITY

4
It may well be that the middle classes are taking up the vices of their betters and also of their inferiors.

D. W. BROGAN, Comment on the scandal that rocked the administration of Harold Macmillan in Great Britain in 1963. (*Time*, 21 June, 1963, p. 25)

5
Friendly cynics and fierce enemies alike often underestimate or ignore the strong thread of moral purpose which runs through the fabric of American history.

LYNDON B. JOHNSON, *Speech*, at an American Bar Association meeting, Aug., 1964.

MUSIC

6
Composers tend to assume that everyone loves music. Surprisingly enough, everyone doesn't.

AARON COPLAND, "ASCAP and the Symphonic Composer"; *New York Times Magazine*, 16 Feb., 1964.

7
It is safe to say that no man ever went wrong, morally or mentally, while listening to a symphony.

JUSTICE JOHN J. DILLON, New York State Supreme Court, Decision, 31 Dec., 1964, granting tax exemption on a Bedford, N.Y. estate, Caramoor, used for public concerts.

8
Last year, more Americans went to symphonies than went to baseball games. This may be viewed as an alarming statistic, but I think that both baseball and the country will endure.

JOHN F. KENNEDY, Remark, at a White House Youth Concert, 6 Aug., 1962. (*The Kennedy Wit*, ed. by BILL ADLER: *The Presidency*)

9
The public of today must pay its debt to the great composers of the past by supporting the living creators of the present.

SERGE KOUSSEVITZKY. (HOWARD HANSON, "ASCAP and the Forgotten Man"; *New York Times Magazine*, 16 Feb., 1964)

10
A materialist asks of a concert audience, "What are you crying about with your Wagner and your Brahms? It is only horsehair scraping on catgut.

SIR OLIVER LODGE, *Reason and Belief*, p. 78. (1911)

The Fiddle: An instrument to tickle human ears by friction of a horse's tail on the entrails of a cat.

AMBROSE BIERCE, *The Devil's Dictionary.* (1906)

The violins have been gregarious, . . .
Producing tones both high and deep
From hair of horse on gut of sheep.

LAWRENCE MCKINNEY, *Men of Note. See also* 1369:13.

11
I'd rather people go around making noise, even idiots' noise. It's better than fighting.

PRINCE PHILIP OF THE UNITED KINGDOM, Comment to a reporter during a visit to the United States, Mar., 1966. This was his evaluation of rock-and-roll music—specifically, of a British group known as the Beatles.

12
The trouble with music appreciation in general is that people are taught to have too much respect for music; they should be taught to love it instead.

IGOR STRAVINSKY. (*New York Times Magazine*, 27 Sept., 1964)

13
I love music more than my own convenience. Actually, I love it more than myself—but it is vastly more lovable than I.

GEORGE SZELL. (*Newsweek*, 28 Jan., 1963)

NEGRO

14
Forced integration is just as wrong as forced segregation.

BARRY M. GOLDWATER, *Speech*, in Chicago, 16 Oct., 1964, during the presidential campaign.

15
We shall overcome.

ZILPHIA HORTON, PETE SEEGER, FRANK HAMILTON, and GUY CARAWAN, Title and refrain of song that became the anthem of the civil-rights movement of the 1960s. The basic song was written in the 1940s by Mrs. Horton while she was conducting a folk school in Tennessee. In the tradition of folk music, new material was added, notably by the folk singers Seeger, Hamilton, and Carawan. The song was published in 1962 with authorship credited to the four.

1
In this hour, it is not our respective races which are at stake—it is our nation. Let those who care for their country come forward, North and South, white and Negro, to lead the way through this moment of challenge and decision. The Negro says, "Now." Others say, "Never." The voice of responsible Americans—the voices of those who died here and of the great man who spoke here—their voices say, "Together." There is no other way.

LYNDON B. JOHNSON, *Memorial Day Address,* Gettysburg, Pa., 30 May, 1963.

2
Let us close the springs of racial poison. Let us pray for wise and understanding hearts. Let us lay aside irrelevant differences and make our nation whole.

LYNDON B. JOHNSON, Public Statement, 2 July, 1964, on signing the Civil Rights Act of that year.

3
The real hero of this struggle is the American Negro. His actions and protests, his courage to risk safety, and even to risk his life, have awakened the conscience of this nation. His demonstrations have been designed to call attention to injustice, designed to provoke change; designed to stir reform. He has called upon us to make good the promise of America.

LYNDON B. JOHNSON, *Address,* to joint session of Congress, on voting rights, 15 Mar., 1965.

4
Freedom is not enough. You do not take a person who for years has been hobbled by chains and liberate him, bring him up to the starting line and then say, "You're free to compete with all the others," and still justly believe that you have been completely fair.

LYNDON B. JOHNSON, *Commencement Address,* Howard University, Washington, D.C., 4 June, 1965.

5
When pioneers subdued a continent to the need of man they did not tame it for the Negro. When the Liberty Bell rang out in Philadelphia it did not toll for the Negro. When Andrew Jackson threw open the doors of democracy they did not open for the Negro. It was only at Appomattox a century ago that an American victory was also a Negro victory.

LYNDON B. JOHNSON, *Speech,* on signing the voting rights bill of 1965 in Washington, D.C., 6 Aug., 1965.

6
A rioter with a Molotov cocktail in his hands is not fighting for civil rights any more than a Klansman with a sheet on his back and mask on his face.

LYNDON B. JOHNSON, *Speech,* in Washington, D.C., 20 Aug., 1965.

7
We are confronted primarily with a moral issue. It is as old as the Scriptures and is as clear as the American Constitution.

JOHN F. KENNEDY, *Address,* televised nationally, June, 1963.

8
I ask you to look into your hearts—not in search of charity, for the Negro neither wants nor needs condescension—but for the one plain, proud and priceless quality that unites us all as Americans: a sense of justice.

JOHN F. KENNEDY, *Message to Congress,* on civil-rights legislation, 19 June, 1963.

9
Before the Pilgrims landed at Plymouth, we were here. Before the pen of Jefferson etched across the pages of history the majestic words of the Declaration of Independence, we were here. For more than two centuries, our foreparents labored in this country without wages; they made cotton "king," and they built the homes of their masters in the midst of brutal injustice and shameless humiliation—and yet out of a bottomless vitality, they continued to thrive and develop. If the inexpressible cruelties of slavery could not stop us, the opposition we now face will surely fail. We will win our freedom because the sacred heritage of our nation and the eternal will of God are embodied in our echoing demands.

REV. MARTIN LUTHER KING, JR., *Letter,* written Apr., 1963, while he was in prison in Birmingham, Ala., following his participation in civil-rights demonstrations in that city. This famous letter was in reply to a group of white clergymen who had criticized him for his part in the demonstrations.

10
I have a dream. . . . It is a dream deeply rooted in the American dream. . . . I have a dream that one day in the red hills of Georgia, sons of former slaves and the sons of former slave-owners will be able to sit down together at the table of brotherhood.

REV. MARTIN LUTHER KING, JR., *Address,* in Washington, D.C., 28 Aug., 1963. These words, spoken at the foot of Lincoln Memorial, were the high point of the memorable civil-rights "march" on Washington.

11
Segregation is on its deathbed—the question now is, how costly will the segregationists make the funeral?

REV. MARTIN LUTHER KING, JR., *Address,* at Villanova University, Villanova, Pa., 20 Jan., 1965.

1
In this and like communities, public sentiment is everything. With public sentiment, nothing can fail; without it, nothing can succeed. Consequently he who molds public sentiment goes deeper than he who enacts statutes or pronounces decisions.

ABRAHAM LINCOLN, *Speech,* at Ottawa, Illinois, 31 July, 1858. Lincoln is referring to slavery.

The wisest among my race understand that the agitation of questions of social equality is the extremest folly, and that progress in the enjoyment of all the privileges that will come to us must be the result of severe and constant struggle rather than of artificial forcing.

BOOKER T. WASHINGTON, *Address,* Atlanta Exposition, 18 Sept., 1895. See *Up From Slavery,* p. 223. *See also* 1395:11.

2
The black man in this country has been sitting on the hot stove for nearly 400 years. And no matter how fast the brainwashers and the brainwashed think they are helping him advance, it's still too slow for the man whose behind is burning on that hot stove!

MALCOLM X. (GORDON PARKS, "What Their Cry Means to Me"; *Life,* 31 May, 1963, p. 31)

3
The black man has died under the flag. His women have been raped under it. He has been oppressed, starved and beaten under it —and still after what happened in Mississippi they'll ask him to fight their enemies under it. I'll do my fighting right here at home, where the enemy looks me in the eye every day of my life. I'm not talking against the flag. I'm talking *about* it!

MALCOLM X. (GORDON PARKS, "What Their Cry Means to Me"; *Life,* 31 May, 1963, p. 31)

4
The Negro problem is not only America's greatest failure but also America's great opportunity for the future. If America should follow its own deepest convictions, its well-being at home would be increased directly. At the same time America's prestige and power abroad would rise.

GUNNAR MYRDAL, *An American Dilemma* (1944).

5
On the tenth anniversary of the Supreme Court's public school integration decision, the paradox and the tragedy of the American Negro are fairly clear. He is gaining legally but falling behind economically. He is slowly getting the rights but not the skills of a modern computerized society.

JAMES RESTON, Washington Column, New York *Times,* 15 May, 1964.

6
I believe in the brotherhood of man, not merely the brotherhood of white men but the brotherhood of all men before law.

HARRY S TRUMAN, *Speech,* in 1940, at a political rally in Sedalia, Mo. (JONATHAN DANIELS, *The Man of Independence,* p. 339)

7
I wish to make it clear that I am not appealing for social equality of the Negro. The Negro himself knows better than that, and the highest type of Negro leaders say quite frankly they prefer the society of their own people. Negroes want justice, not social relations.

HARRY S TRUMAN, *Speech,* to an audience of Negroes in Chicago, July, 1940. (JONATHAN DANIELS, *The Man of Independence,* p. 338)

8
The top dog in a world which is over half colored ought to clean his own house.

HARRY S TRUMAN. (JONATHAN DANIELS, *The Man of Independence,* 1950, p. 336)

NEW YORK CITY

9
If 1,668,172 people (out of New York's total population of 7,710,346) are to be set down in one narrow strip of land between two quiet rivers, you can hardly improve on this solid mass of buildings and the teeming organism of human life that streams through them. For better or worse, this is real.

BROOKS ATKINSON, "Critic at Large" Column, New York *Times,* 17 Mar., 1964. Referring to Manhattan.

10
It's a city where everyone mutinies but no one deserts.

HARRY HERSHFIELD, *Interview,* New York *Times,* 5 Dec., 1965.

11
There is no greenery; it is enough to make a stone sad.

NIKITA KHRUSHCHEV, Comment during a visit in Oct., 1960.

12
New York attracts the most talented people in the world in the arts and professions. It also attracts them in other fields. Even the bums are talented.

EDMUND LOVE, *Subways Are for Sleeping,* introduction. (1957)

NOSE

13
A great nose is a mark of a man affable, good, courteous, spiritual, liberal, brave, such as I am. (*Un grand nez est proprement l'indice d'un homme affable, bon, courtois, spirituel, libéral, courageux, tel que je suis.*)

EDMOND ROSTAND, *Cyrano de Bergerac,* Act i, sc. 4. (1897)

Morgan's ruby nose added to his personal fame and with some humor he once said it "would be impossible for me to appear on the streets without it." His nose, he remarked on another occasion, "was part of the American business structure."

STEWART H. HOLBROOK, *The Age of the Moguls*, p. 214. (1953) *See also* 1412:11.

OPINION

1
Insofar as it represents a genuine reconciliation of differences, a consensus is a fine thing; insofar as it represents the concealment of differences, it is a miscarriage of democratic procedure. I think we Americans tend to put too high a value on unanimity—on bipartisanship in foreign policy, on politics stopping at the water's edge, on turning a single face to the world—as if there were something dangerous and illegitimate about honest differences of opinion honestly expressed by honest men.

J. WILLIAM FULBRIGHT, *Speech*, U.S. Senate, 22 Oct., 1965.

2
Too often we . . . enjoy the comfort of opinion without the discomfort of thought.

JOHN F. KENNEDY, *Speech*, at Yale University, 1962.

OPPORTUNITY

3
We must open the doors of opportunity. But we must also equip our people to walk through those doors.

LYNDON B. JOHNSON, *Speech*, at a National Urban League conference, 10 Dec., 1964.

4
Never before has man had such capacity to control his own environment—to end thirst and hunger—to conquer poverty and disease—to banish illiteracy and massive human misery. We have the power to make this the best generation of mankind in the history of the world—or to make it the last.

JOHN F. KENNEDY, *Address*, to the United Nations General Assembly, 20 Sept., 1963.

5
There is no security on this earth; there is only opportunity.

GENERAL DOUGLAS MACARTHUR. (COURTNEY WHITNEY, *MacArthur: His Rendezvous with History*) (1955)

ORATOR AND ORATORY

6
Come on down to the speakin' tonight!

LYNDON B. JOHNSON, his familiar greeting to street crowds, amplified by a bullhorn, during the 1964 presidential campaign. (TOM WICKER, "Lyndon Johnson Is Ten Feet Tall"; *New York Times Magazine*, 23 May, 1965, p. 92)

7
In some respects a speech is like a love affair: any fool can start one, but to end it requires considerable skill.

BARON MANCROFT OF GREAT BRITAIN. (New York *Times*, "Ideas and Men," 25 July, 1965, p. 11E)

8
I sometimes marvel at the extraordinary docility with which Americans submit to speeches.

ADLAI E. STEVENSON, *Speech*, to tne American Legion, Chicago, 1950.

9
When I was a boy I never had much sympathy for a holiday speaker. He was just a kind of interruption between the hot dogs, a fly in the lemonade.

ADLAI E. STEVENSON, *Speech*, in Flint, Mich., 1952.

PAIN

10
The tree will be there long after the discomfort is gone.

JOHN F KENNEDY, Note to Prime Minister Diefenbaker of Canada, 9 June, 1961. The President suffered a back strain during a tree-planting ceremony, on a visit to Canada, and Diefenbaker had expressed his regret. (*The Kennedy Wit*, ed. by BILL ADLER: *The Presidency*)

11
Pain makes man think. Thought makes man wise. Wisdom makes life endurable.

JOHN PATRICK, *The Teahouse of the August Moon*. (1954)

12
Let's tell them [the American people] the truth, that there are no gains without pains.

ADLAI E. STEVENSON, *Speech*, at the Democratic national convention, Chicago, 26 July, 1952, upon accepting the presidential nomination.

PATRIOTISM

13
No man can be a patriot on an empty stomach.

WILLIAM C. BRANN, *The Iconoclast: Old Glory*. (c. 1890)

14
Patriotism means equipped forces and a prepared citizenry.

DWIGHT D. EISENHOWER, *First Inaugural Address*, 20 Jan., 1953.

15
I think patriotism is like charity—it begins at home.

HENRY JAMES, *The Portrait of a Lady*, ch. x. (1881)

16
I am already married to my country.

WILLIAM PITT, THE YOUNGER. (An extension of 1464:9, q.v.) Lord Stanhope in his *Life of Pitt*, ch. iv, turns down the "I am already married to my country" story as "a mere silly rumour," and adds, "I believe he never had the opportunity of refusing Mademoiselle Necker, but if he did I am sure that it was not in any such melodramatic phrase." Lord Ashbourne, on the other hand, in his

Pitt: Some Chapters of His Life and Times (1898), says there was "a rumour about a possible marriage, during Pitt's visit to France in 1783, when he and Mademoiselle Necker met at Fontainebleau. Whether Pitt ever thought of it," he adds, "we can only guess. There were many wordly reasons to make such a union suitable. She was wealthy, clever, young, attractive and Protestant, the daughter of a great French statesman," and he quotes a letter of Madame Necker to her daughter found among her papers, and written probably at the end of 1783, intended to be given her daughter after Madame Necker's death: "Je désirais que tu épousesses Mr. Pitt . . . Tu n'as pas voulu me donner cette satisfaction." [I had wished that you marry Mr. Pitt. You have not been willing to give me that satisfaction.] See *Le Salon de Madame Necker*, par le Vicomte de Haussonville, ii, 56. Wilberforce, an intimate of Pitt, in his *Sketch of Pitt*, written in 1821, says: "At Paris, in October. 1783, or immediately afterwards, it was suggested to the late Lord Camden by Mr. Walpole, a particular friend of Mr. Necker, that if Mr. Pitt should be disposed to offer his hand to Mlle. Necker, afterwards Mme. de Staël, such was the respect entertained for him by M. and Mme. Necker that he had no doubt the proposal would be accepted." The compiler is indebted for the above information to Mr. Frank A. Gibson, of Ross-on-Wye, Herefordshire, England.

1

The patriots are those who love America enough to wish to see her as a model to mankind.

ADLAI E. STEVENSON, "The Hard Kind of Patriotism"; *Harper's Magazine*, July, 1963.

Do not, therefore, regard the critics as questionable patriots. What were Washington and Jefferson and Adams but profound critics of the colonial status quo?

ADLAI E. STEVENSON, "The Hard Kind of Patriotism"; *Harper's Magazine*, July, 1963.

2

No patriots so defaced America as those who, in the name of Americanism, launched a witch-hunt which became a byword around the world. We have survived it. We shall survive John Birchism and all the rest of the superpatriots—but only at the price of perpetual and truly patriotic vigilance.

ADLAI E. STEVENSON, "The Hard Kind of Patriotism"; *Harper's Magazine*, July, 1963

3

My kind of loyalty was loyalty to one's country, not to its institutions or its officeholders.

MARK TWAIN, *A Connecticut Yankee at King Arthur's Court*, p. 100. (1899)

PEACE

4

There is no more dangerous misconception than this which misconstrues the arms race as the cause rather than a symptom of the tensions and divisions which threaten nuclear war. If the history of the past fifty years teaches us anything, it is that peace does not follow disarmament—disarmament follows peace.

BERNARD M. BARUCH, Memorandum composed for U.S. Government officials, 6 Jan., 1961, but first made public almost three years later. Quoted by Arthur Krock, "In the Nation," Column, New York *Times*, 26 Dec., 1963.

5

We seek peace, knowing that peace is the climate of freedom.

DWIGHT D. EISENHOWER, *Second Inaugural Address*, 21 Jan., 1957.

6

Peace and justice are two sides of the same coin.

DWIGHT D. EISENHOWER, News Conference, 6 Feb., 1957.

7

Peace is a blessing, and like most blessings, it must be earned.

DWIGHT D. EISENHOWER, "Let's be Honest with Ourselves"; *The Reader's Digest*, Dec., 1963.

8

I have no illusions that peace can be achieved rapidly, but I have every confidence that it is going to be possible to inch toward it, inch by agonizing inch.

ARTHUR J. GOLDBERG, *Address*, at the ceremony marking his inauguration as U.S. Ambassador to the United Nations, 26 July, 1965.

9

Nor is there such a thing as peaceful coexistence.

BARRY M. GOLDWATER. (*New York Times Magazine*, 17 Sept., 1961)

10

In this age where there can be no losers in peace and no victors in war, we must recognize the obligation to match national strength with national restraint—we must be prepared at one and the same time for both the confrontation of power and the limitation of power—we must be ready to defend the national interest and to negotiate the common interest.

LYNDON B. JOHNSON, *Address*, to a joint session of Congress, 27 Nov., 1963, his first major statement of policy after he became President.

11

President Kennedy, I am sure, would regard as his best memorial the fact that in his three years as President the world became a little safer and the way ahead became a little brighter. To the protection and the enlargement of this new hope for peace I pledge my country and its government.

LYNDON B. JOHNSON, *Address*, to the United Nations General Assembly, 17 Dec., 1963.

1
There is only one item on the agenda of this conference—it is the leading item on the agenda of mankind—and that one item is peace.

LYNDON B. JOHNSON, Message to the disarmament conference in Geneva, 21 Jan., 1964.

2
The best way to begin disarming is to begin—and the United States is ready to conclude firm agreements in these areas and to consider any other reasonable proposal.

LYNDON B. JOHNSON, Message to the disarmament conference in Geneva, 21 Jan., 1964.

3
For America today, as in Jefferson's time, peace must be our passion. It is not enough for America to be a sentinel on the frontiers of freedom. America must also be on the watchtower seeking out the horizons of peace.

LYNDON B. JOHNSON, *Speech,* at the University of California, Los Angeles, 21 Feb., 1964.

4
In other words, our guard is up but our hand is out.

LYNDON B. JOHNSON, *Speech,* at annual luncheon of the Associated Press, New York City, 20 Apr., 1964.

5
If we are to live together in peace, we must come to know each other better.

LYNDON B. JOHNSON, *State of the Union Message,* 4 Jan., 1965.

6
The mere absence of war is not peace.

JOHN F. KENNEDY, *State of the Union Message,* 14 Jan., 1963.

7
Peace is a daily, a weekly, a monthly process, gradually changing opinions, slowly eroding old barriers, quietly building new structures. And however undramatic the pursuit of peace, that pursuit must go on.

JOHN F. KENNEDY, *Address,* to the United Nations General Assembly, 20 Sept., 1963.

8
Peace does not rest in charters and covenants alone. It lies in the hearts and minds of the people. And if it is cast out there, then no act, no pact, no treaty or organization can ever hope to preserve it. So let us not rest all our hopes for peace on parchment and paper—let us strive also to build peace in the hearts and minds of our people.

JOHN F. KENNEDY, *Address,* to the United Nations General Assembly, 20 Sept., 1963.

9
Today we may have reached a pause in the cold war—but that is not a lasting peace. A test ban treaty is a milestone—but that is not the millennium. We have not been released from our obligations—we have been given an opportunity. And if we fail to make the most of this moment . . . then the shaming indictment of posterity will rightly point its finger at us all.

JOHN F. KENNEDY, *Address,* to the United Nations General Assembly, 20 Sept., 1963.

10
There is no evil in the atom; only in men's souls.

ADLAI E. STEVENSON, *Speech,* in Hartford, Conn., 18 Sept., 1952.

PEOPLE, THE

11
No one should ever give the people what they want. What if the president of a college would say, "Give the students what they want"? He would be laughed out of existence.

MORRIS ERNST, *Speech,* in St. Louis, 16 July, 1964. He was criticizing in particular the television networks' practice of "giving the public what it wants."

12
These programs will take hold and succeed only when we become determined that nothing is to take priority over people.

LYNDON B. JOHNSON, *Annual Manpower Report to Congress,* 9 Mar., 1964, requesting legislation to create jobs and train workers.

13
There is in any large-scale dispute a question of the public interest. This interest must always be overriding. But we must never delude ourselves that we are serving the public interest if at any time we suppress the legitimate rights of the conflicting parties.

LYNDON B. JOHNSON, News Conference, 11 Apr., 1964.

14
As long as I am President, this Government will not set one group against another—but will build a creative partnership between business and labor, farm areas and urban centers, consumer and producer. This is what I mean when I choose to be a President of all the people.

LYNDON B. JOHNSON, *Speech,* in Minneapolis, 27 June, 1964. "President of all the people" was often used thereafter by Johnson.

15
Son, if you are to speak for people, you must know them, and if you are to represent people, you must love them.

SAMUEL EALY JOHNSON, Advice to his son, Lyndon B. Johnson, when the elder Johnson was serving in the Texas legislature. Quoted by President Johnson during a speech in San Antonio, Tex., 8 Apr., 1966.

16
I draw strength from seeing them, and they seem to get something from seeing me.

JAWAHARLAL NEHRU, Remark, explaining his love of mingling with the Indian people. (Associated Press obituary of Nehru, 27 May, 1964)

1
Better we lose the election than mislead the people; and better we lose than misgovern the people.

ADLAI E. STEVENSON, *Speech,* at the Democratic national convention, 26 July, 1952, accepting the presidential nomination.

2
The people are wise—wiser than the Republicans think.

ADLAI E. STEVENSON, *Speech,* at the Democratic national convention, 26 July, 1952, accepting the presidential nomination.

3
Government . . . cannot be wiser than the people.

ADLAI E. STEVENSON, *Speech,* in Chicago, 29 Sept., 1952, during the presidential campaign.

4
As citizens of this democracy, you are the rulers and the ruled, the law-givers and the law-abiding, the beginning and the end.

ADLAI E. STEVENSON, *Speech,* in Chicago, 29 Sept., 1952, during the presidential campaign.

POETRY

5
Poetry is of all arts the most parochial. It cannot be translated. So, thank God, there can be no international style.

W. H. AUDEN. (New York *Times,* "Ideas and Men," 24 May, 1964)

6
The poet's voice need not merely be the record of man; it can be one of the props, the pillars, to help him endure and prevail.

WILLIAM FAULKNER, *Address,* in Stockholm, 10 Dec., 1950, upon accepting the Nobel Prize in literature.

7
I don't call myself a poet yet. It's for the world to say whether you're a poet or not. I'm one-half teacher, one-half poet and one-half farmer; that's three halves.

ROBERT FROST, Comment on his 80th birthday, Mar., 1954.

8
Poetry is a way of taking life by the throat.

ROBERT FROST. (*Vogue,* 15 Mar., 1963)

9
When power leads man toward arrogance, poetry reminds him of his limitations. When power narrows the areas of man's concern, poetry reminds him of the richness and diversity of his existence. When power corrupts, poetry cleanses.

JOHN F. KENNEDY, *Address,* at Amherst College, Amherst, Mass., 26 Oct., 1963.

10
Poetry is still the supremely inclusive speech which escapes, as if unaware of them, the strictures and reductions of the systematic logical understanding.

JOHN CROWE RANSOM, *Selected Poems* (1963).

11
It is difficult to write the proper poem nowadays because after many ages of hard prose we have come far from the primitive and natural speech of poetry.

JOHN CROWE RANSOM, *Selected Poems* (1963).

POLITICS

12
A liberal is a man who cultivates the skills that make freedom operational. He is always a man on special assignment.

MAX ASCOLI, *The Reporter,* 30 Jan., 1964.

13
I'm glad to sit in the back row. I would rather be a servant in the house of the Lord than to sit in the seats of the mighty.

SENATOR ALBEN WILLIAM BARKLEY, *Speech,* at Washington & Lee University, Lexington, Va., 30 April, 1956. A moment later he slumped to the floor dead of a heart attack, at the age of 78. (See *Time,* 14 May, 1956, p. 30.) The sentence was a skillful and apposite paraphrase of *Psalms,* 84:10: "I had rather be a doorkeeper in the house of my God, than to dwell in the tents of wickedness." And perhaps Mr. Barkley had also in mind another sentence from the *Bible* (*Luke,* i, 52): "He hath put down the mighty from their seats, and exalted them of low degree." The appositeness of the quotation stemmed from the fact that in 1944 Barkley had ridiculed F. D. Roosevelt on the Senate floor by saying, "The President cites his own experience as a timber man. I do know that he sells Christmas trees at Christmas time. But to compare these little pine bushes with a sturdy oak, gum, poplar, or spruce is like comparing a cricket to a stallion." This speech may well have locked Barkley out of the White House, for at the Democratic convention in 1944, Roosevelt, who always resented ridicule, passed up Barkley, who had every reason to expect the nomination for the Vice-Presidency, and chose Harry S Truman, then comparatively unknown. However, in 1948, three years after the death of Roosevelt, Truman, who had succeeded to the Presidency, somewhat reluctantly accepted Barkley as his running-mate, and Barkley became the beloved "Veep," as his grandchildren called him. His great chance for the Presidential nomination came in 1952 at the Democratic National Convention, but union labor leaders turned him down, ostensibly on account of his age, 74, and the nomination went to Adlai Stevenson. Deeply hurt and bitterly disappointed, Barkley retired from public life, but came back in 1954 and returned to Washington as junior Senator from Kentucky.

14
Vote for the man who promises least; he'll be the least disappointing.

BERNARD M. BARUCH. (*Meyer Berger's New York*)

15
A political leader must keep looking over his shoulder all the time to see if the boys are still there. If they aren't still there, he's no longer a political leader.

BERNARD M. BARUCH. (New York *Times* obituary of Baruch, 21 June, 1965, p. 16)

1
This party comes from the grass roots. It has grown from the soil of the people's hard necessities.

ALBERT J. BEVERIDGE, *Address*, Bull Moose Convention, Chicago, 5 August, 1912. *See* 2279:4.

2
The crime of 1873.

WILLIAM JENNINGS BRYAN, *Speech*, House of Representatives, 12 Aug., 1892, referring to the adoption of the gold standard by the United States. Bryan was advocating the adoption of the bill introduced by Representative Richard P. Bland, providing for the free and unlimited coinage of silver at a fixed ratio to gold. Hence the slogan "Sixteen to one."

The crime of '76.

The Democratic description of the election, which they contended to be fraudulent, of Rutherford B. Hayes to the Presidency over Samuel J. Tilden by one vote in the Electoral College.

3
The true liberal is liberal in human relations and conservative in his economics. He seeks to conserve a capitalistic system characterized by free enterprise and the profit motive because it is essential to liberty.

HARRY J. CARMAN, *Letter*, to the editor of the St. Louis *Post-Dispatch*, 10 Aug., 1964. Carman was chairman of the American Liberal Association at the time.

4
He held his party together by not allowing his left wing to see what his right wing was doing.

VIOLET BONHAM CARTER (LADY ASQUITH OF YARNBURY), Comment on the administration of Prime Minister Harold Macmillan, Mar., 1964

5
I go for honorable compromise wherever it can be made. Life itself is but a compromise between death and life, the struggle continuing throughout our whole existence until the great destroyer finally triumphs. . . . Let no one who is not above the frailties of our common nature disdain compromise.

HENRY CLAY, *Speech*, 8 April, 1850. (See *Works*, vi, 412.) Clay, known as the Great Compromiser, was the artificer of the Missouri Compromise of 1820, the compromise tariff of 1833, and the compromise of 1850, which he was defending in the above quotation.

6
Republicans, having taken over the government, then took over God. When the votes were counted, Mark Hanna sent a telegram indicative both of his simple faith and his comradely knowledge of God's whereabouts. He said, "God's in His heaven." The New York *Tribune*, with a private wire to heaven, said Bryan had lost "because right is right and God is God."

DAVID H. COHN, *The Fabulous Democrats*, p. 106. (1956) Hanna's telegram was, or course, a quote from Browning's *Pippa Passes* ("God's in his heaven, All's right with the world!"), which is rather surprising. It referred to the presidential election of 1896, when McKinley won over Bryan by seven million votes against six and a half million.

7
Politics is a profession; a serious, complicated, and in its true sense a noble one.

DWIGHT D. EISENHOWER, *Letter*, to Leonard V. Finder, publisher of the Manchester, N.H. *Evening Leader*, 1948. Elsewhere in the letter Eisenhower said, "My decision to remove myself completely from the political scene is definite and positive."

8
The party should be a knight in shining armor on a white charger.

DWIGHT D. EISENHOWER, *Interview*, New York *Times*, 13 Sept., 1965. Referring to the Republican party.

9
The only promise I ever made was to say: "Boys, I'll do the best I can." If you are honest and intelligent, that is the only platform you need to have.

JOHN NANCE GARNER, Interview with Carlton Wilson, United Press International, 18 Nov., 1963.

10
I will offer a choice, not an echo. This will not be an engagement of personalities. It will be an engagement of principles.

BARRY M. GOLDWATER, Public Statement, 3 Jan., 1964, announcing his candidacy for the Republican presidential nomination, which he eventually won.

11
You cannot in this game of politics fight your own party. It just doesn't work.

BARRY M. GOLDWATER, Press Conference in Scottsdale, Ariz., 4 Nov., 1964, just after he had conceded President Johnson's victory in the election. He was referring to the unwillingness of some prominent Republican candidates to support the national ticket headed by Goldwater.

12
Public office in this country has few attractions. The pecuniary emolument is so inconsiderable as to amount to a sacrifice to any man who can employ his time with advantage in any liberal profession.

ALEXANDER HAMILTON, *Autobiographic Letter*, 2 May, 1797.

13
A garden, you know, is a very useful refuge of a disappointed politician. Accordingly, I have purchased a few acres about nine miles from town, have built a house, and am cultivating a garden.

ALEXANDER HAMILTON, *Letter to Charles Cotesworth Pinckney*, 29 Dec., 1802.

1
One of the greatest tragedies would be to have two political parties made up just of the right and the left.

ALBERTIS HARRISON, Comment, Aug., 1964, during the presidental campaign of that year. He was governor of Virginia at the time.

2
Being a politician is a poor profession. Being a public servant is a noble one.

HERBERT HOOVER. (RICHARD M. KETCHUM, "Faces from the Past"; *American Heritage,* Dec., 1964, p. 31)

3
He proved that a man can be both decent and political.

HUBERT H. HUMPHREY, referring to Adlai E. Stevenson; memorial telecast on Stevenson, Columbia Broadcasting System, 19 July, 1965.

4
I am against government by crony.

HAROLD L. ICKES, *Remark,* on resigning as Secretary of the Interior, Feb., 1946, referring to President Truman's propensity toward rewarding old friends with government positions.

5
This is practical politics.

HENRY JAMES, *The Ambassadors,* p. 318. (1902) A phrase probably coined by Disraeli in 1826. *See* 1553:2.

6
The minority possess their equal rights which . . . to violate would be oppression.

GERALD W. JOHNSON, *The Lunatic Fringe,* p. 121 (1956), paraphrasing Jefferson's dictum that "The will of the majority to be rightful must be reasonable."

7
If you're in politics and you can't tell when you walk into a room who's for you and who's against you, then you're in the wrong line of work.

LYNDON B. JOHNSON. (BOOTH MOONEY, *The Lyndon Johnson Story*) (1963)

8
There are two courses open to a minority party. It can indulge in the politics of partisanship, or it can remain true to the politics of responsibility. The first course is tempting to the weak, but ultimately would be rejected by the American people. The second course is difficult but is the road upon which we can offer leadership to the American people that will be accepted.

LYNDON B. JOHNSON, *Speech,* at a Jefferson-Jackson Day dinner, New York City, shortly after he became Senate minority leader in 1953.

9
I seldom think of politics more than eighteen hours a day.

LYNDON B. JOHNSON, *Speech,* to a Texas audience in 1958. (HENRY A. ZEIGER, *Lyndon B. Johnson: Man and President,* p. 68)

10
I want to be progressive without getting both feet off the ground at the same time. . . . If I had to place a label on myself, I would want to be a progressive who is prudent.

LYNDON B. JOHNSON, *Interview,* televised nationally from Washington, D.C., 15 Mar., 1964.

11
He's a working liberal and not a talking liberal.

LYNDON B. JOHNSON, speaking admiringly of a member of his staff. (MARQUIS W. CHILDS, Column, St. Louis *Post-Dispatch,* 31 Mar., 1964)

12
I think that it is very important that we have a two-party country. I am a fellow that likes small parties, and the Republican party is about the size I like.

LYNDON B. JOHNSON, Press Conference, 21 Apr., 1964.

13
This nation, this generation, in this hour has man's first chance to build the Great Society—a place where the meaning of man's life matches the marvels of man's labor. We seek a nation where every man can seek knowledge, and touch beauty, and rejoice in the closeness of family and community. We seek a nation where every man can, in the words of our oldest promise, follow the pursuit of happiness—not just security, but achievements and excellence and fulfillment of the spirit.

LYNDON B. JOHNSON, *Speech,* on accepting the Democratic presidential nomination, 27 Aug., 1964.

14
A President's hardest task is not to do what is right, but to know what is right.

LYNDON B. JOHNSON, *State of the Union Message,* 4 Jan., 1965.

15
We stand today on the edge of a new frontier—the frontier of the 1960s—a frontier of unknown opportunities and perils—a frontier of unfulfilled hopes and threats.

JOHN F. KENNEDY, *Speech,* upon accepting the Democratic presidential nomination, July, 1960.

16
When we got into office, the thing that surprised me most was to find that things were just as bad as we'd been saying they were.

JOHN F. KENNEDY, *Speech,* at a dinner in honor of his 44th birthday, Washington, D.C., 27 May, 1961.

17
Politics is like football. If you see daylight, go through the hole.

JOHN F. KENNEDY, on the authority of Pierre Salinger, press secretary to Kennedy. (JOSEPH ALSOP, Column, New York *Herald Tribune,* 3 Apr., 1964)

1
You do not know—you cannot know—the difficulty of life of a politician. It means every minute of the day or night, every ounce of your energy. There is no rest, no relaxation. Enjoyment? A politician does not know the meaning of the word.

NIKITA S. KHRUSHCHEV, Comment to reporters at the Glen Cove, N.Y., estate of the Soviet delegation to the United Nations, Oct., 1960.

2
Politicians are the same all over. They promise to build a bridge even where there is no river.

NIKITA KHRUSHCHEV. (New York *Herald Tribune,* 22 Aug., 1963)

3
The convention is the voice, the bone and the sinews of a political party—and sometimes it even nominates an Abraham Lincoln.

FLETCHER KNEBEL "One Vote for the Convention System"; *New York Times Magazine,* 23 Aug., 1964.

4
There is no Republican way or Democratic way to clean the streets.

FIORELLO H. LA GUARDIA, while he was mayor of New York City. This was quoted by John V. Lindsay in 1965 during his successful campaign for the same post.

5
Is there a distinct and coherent political movement, . . . a political philosophy with a clear set of principles, which one might perhaps call the New Republicanism?

ARTHUR LARSON, *A Republican Looks at His Party,* ch. i, opening sentence. (1956) President Eisenhower happened to read the book, liked the phrase, New Republicanism, used it frequently thereafter, and in 1957 appointed Mr. Larson, who at the time he wrote the book had been Under Secretary of Labor, to the cabinet position of Secretary of Health, Education, and Welfare, from which, however, he was soon removed and given a position as adviser to the President.

6
With exceptions so rare that they are regarded as miracles and freaks of nature, successful democratic politicians are insecure and intimidated men. They advance politically only as they placate, appease, bribe, seduce, bamboozle, or otherwise manage to manipulate the demanding and threatening elements in their constituencies.

WALTER LIPPMANN, *The Public Philosophy,* bk. i, ch. 2. (1955)

7
The issue between the Republicans and Democrats is clearly drawn. It has been deliberately drawn by those who have been in charge of twenty years of treason.

JOSEPH MCCARTHY, *Speech,* at Charleston, W. Va., 4 Feb., 1954. He gave the title "Twenty Years of Treason" to a series of nine speeches he delivered on a nine-day tour arranged by the Republican National Committee.

8
My father was a Democrat; my mother was a Republican: I am an Episcopalian.

GEORGE C. MARSHALL, Statement during the 1952 presidential campaign, in which he maintained a neutral position.

9
Overnominated and underelected.

RICHARD M. NIXON, describing himself at a dinner in Washington, D.C., in 1965. (ROBERT J. DONOVAN, Article, *New York Times Magazine,* 25 Apr., 1965, p. 14)

10
I'm as conservative as the Constitution, as liberal as Lincoln, and as progressive as Theodore Roosevelt.

GEORGE ROMNEY, News Conference, Hartford, Conn., 23 Feb., 1965.

11
These Republican leaders have not been content with attacks on me, on my wife, or on my sons. No, not content with that, they now include my little dog, Fala.

FRANKLIN D. ROOSEVELT, *Speech,* Teamster's dinner, Washington, D.C., 23 Sept., 1944. It had been charged that the President had sent a destroyer back to the Aleutian Islands, to fetch his Scottie, Fala, at a cost of several million dollars to American taxpayers.

12
Let's face it. Let's talk sense to the American people. Let's tell them the truth, that there are no gains without pains, that we are now on the eve of great decisions, not easy decisions, like resistance when you're attacked, but a long, patient, costly struggle which alone can assure triumph over the great enemies of man—war, poverty, and tyranny—and the assaults upon human dignity which are the most grievous consequences of each.

ADLAI E. STEVENSON, *Speech,* upon accepting the presidential nomination, 26 July, 1952.

13
Even more important than winning the election is governing the nation. That is the test of a political party—the acid, final test.

ADLAI E. STEVENSON, *Speech,* of acceptance upon receiving the presidential nomination, Democratic national convention, 26 July, 1952.

14
Someone asked me . . . how I felt, and I was reminded of a story that a fellow-townsman of ours used to tell—Abraham Lincoln. They asked him how he felt once after an unsuccessful election. He said he felt like a little boy who has stubbed his toe in the dark. He said that he was too old to cry, but it hurt too much to laugh.

ADLAI E. STEVENSON, *Speech,* on election night, 5 Nov., 1952.

1
I would like most to be remembered as having contributed to a higher level of political dialogue in the United States.

ADLAI E. STEVENSON, Television Interview in London, July, 1959. This was in reply to a question about the quality he would emphasize were he able to write his own epitaph. (*Contemporary Forum*, ed. by E. J. WRAGE AND B. BASKERVILLE, p. 354)

2
The Radical Right.

TELFORD TAYLOR, *Grand Inquest:* foreword, p. 16. (1954)

The Radical Right.

Title of a collection of essays, ed. by DANIEL BELL (1963). This was an updated expansion of an earlier volume, *The New American Right* (1955), in which "radical Right" appeared, though not as a title.

3
It was in 1948, and we were holding an enthusiastic meeting [in Seattle] when some man with a great big voice cried from the galleries, "Give 'em hell, Harry!" I told him at that time, and I have been repeating it ever since, that I have never deliberately given anybody hell. I just tell the truth on the opposition—and they think it's hell.

HARRY S TRUMAN, *Mr. Citizen,* p. 149. Nevertheless, before beginning his famous whistlestop tour of 1948, Truman did say, "I'm going to give 'em hell."

4
There never was a non-partisan in politics. A man cannot be a non-partisan and be effective in a political party. When he's in any party he's partisan—he's got to be. The only way a man can act as a non-partisan is when he is in office, either as President or head of a state or county or city.

HARRY S TRUMAN, *Mr. Citizen,* p. 166.

5
I never had any falling out with him. The only trouble was, he had a lot of damn fool Republicans around him. He's a good man

HARRY S TRUMAN, Comment about Dwight D. Eisenhower, Dec., 1963.

6
Carry the battle to them. Don't let them bring it to you. Put them on the defensive. And don't ever apologize for anything.

HARRY S TRUMAN, Advice to Hubert H. Humphrey during the 1964 campaign, when Humphrey ran successfully for the Vice Presidency. (New York *Times,* 20 Sept., 1964)

7
These Dissenters were ineligible; they could not run if asked, they could not serve if elected.

MARK TWAIN, *A Connecticut Yankee at King Arthur's Court,* 1. 226. (1889) *See* 2231:1.

8
Things have come to a helluva pass
When a man can't cudgel his own jackass.

HENRY WATTERSON, *Retort,* when accused of unduly criticizing the Governor of Kentucky.

9
Tin-horn politicians.

WILLIAM ALLEN WHITE, *Editorial,* Emporia, Kansas, *Gazette,* 25 Oct., 1901.

10
A vital element in the operation of a democracy is a strong, alert and watchful opposition. That is our task for the next four years. We must constitute ourselves a vigorous, loyal and public-spirited opposition party.

WENDELL WILLKIE, *Radio Address,* 11 Nov., 1940, after his defeat for the Presidency by F. D. Roosevelt. "His Majesty's loyal opposition" is a phrase used in the British Parliament, dating from a speech by Hobhouse in the House of Commons, 10 April, 1826.

11
Keep cool with Coolidge.

Republican campaign slogan in Presidential campaign of 1924, when Calvin Coolidge, whose calm nothing could disturb, was nominated to run against John W. Davis, and won an easy victory.

12
Side tracks are rough, and they're hard to walk;
Keep in the middle of the road.

UNKNOWN, *Keep in the Middle of the Road.* Title of song c. 1870.

The principal candidate against him [Bryan] was Colonel S. F. Norton, of Chicago . . . originator of the phrase so important to the Populist politics, "Middle of the road."

UNKNOWN, *Report,* on Democratic National Convention, St. Louis, 1896. (See *Chicago Inter-Ocean,* 26 July, 1896, p. 1.) "Middle of the roaders" were referred to almost as a third party.

The middle of the road is where the white line is—and that's the worst place to drive.

ROBERT FROST, *Interview, Collier's,* 27 April, 1956, p. 42. Mr. Frost is, of course, right, though "Middle of the road" was for a time a favorite phrase of the Eisenhower administration, to describe its position.

13
"What on earth have you done?" said Christine,
"You have wrecked the whole party machine.
"To lie in the nude,
"Is not at all rude,
"But to lie in the House is obscene."

UNKNOWN, Limerick inspired by the scandal that rocked the administration of Prime Minister Harold Macmillan in June, 1963. "Christine" was Christine Keeler, who was simultaneously involved in a liaison with the British Secretary of State for War, John Profumo, and a Soviet naval attaché, thus creating the possibility of a breach of British security. Revelation of Profumo's indiscretion, and its potential consequence, was less upsetting to the British than the fact that he lied in the House of Commons by at first denying a relationship with Miss Keeler. (*Time,* 21 June, 1963, p. 24)

POVERTY

1
The wall between rich and poor is a wall of glass through which all can see.

LYNDON B. JOHNSON, *Speech,* in New York City, 20 Apr., 1964.

2
Poverty has many roots but the tap root is ignorance.

LYNDON B. JOHNSON, *Message to Congress,* on education, 12 Jan., 1965. (For the origin of "war on poverty," see AMERICA in this appendix.)

3
If a free society cannot help the many who are poor, it cannot save the few who are rich.

JOHN F. KENNEDY, *Inaugural Address,* 20 Jan., 1961.

4
There is inherited wealth in this country and also inherited poverty.

JOHN F. KENNEDY, *Address,* at Amherst College, Amherst, Mass., 26 Oct., 1963.

5
Poverty keeps together more homes than it breaks up.

H. H. MUNRO (SAKI), *The Chronicles of Clovis: Esmé.* (1911)

6
The greatest of evils and the worst of crimes is poverty.

BERNARD SHAW, *Major Barbara: Preface.* (1907)

7
I've never been poor, only broke. Being poor is a frame of mind. Being broke is only a temporary situation.

MICHAEL TODD. (*Newsweek,* 31 Mar., 1958)

POWER

8
All I have I would have given gladly not to be standing here today.

LYNDON B. JOHNSON, *Address,* to a joint session of Congress, 27 Nov., 1963, his first major address as President.

9
We often say how impressive power is. But I do not find it impressive at all. The guns and the bombs, the rockets and the warships are all symbols of human failure. They are necessary symbols. They protect what we cherish. But they are witness to human folly.

LYNDON B. JOHNSON, *Address,* at Johns Hopkins University, Baltimore, 7 Apr., 1965.

10
In the past, those who foolishly sought power by riding the back of the tiger ended up inside.

JOHN F. KENNEDY, *Inaugural Address,* 20 Jan., 1961. This recalls Winston Churchill's observation in *While England Slept:* "Dictators ride to and fro upon tigers which they dare not dismount. And the tigers are getting hungry."

11
The first principle of a civilized state is that power is legitimate only when it is under contract. Then it is, as we say, duly constituted.

WALTER LIPPMANN, *The Public Philosophy,* bk. ii, ch. 11. (1955)

12
Every man invested with power is apt to abuse it.

MONTESQUIEU, *The Spirit of Laws,* bk. ii, ch. 6. (1748)

13
Unlimited power is apt to corrupt the minds of those who possess it.

WILLIAM PITT, EARL OF CHATHAM, *Speech,* House of Lords, 9 Jan., 1770.

Power tends to corrupt, and absolute power corrupts absolutely.

LORD ACTON, *Letter to Mandell Creighton,* 3 April, 1887. Creighton was editor of *The English Historical Review,* and the letter accompanied a review of his *History of the Papacy.* The letter is in possession of Cambridge University. Gertrude Himmelfarb prints it in full in her collection of Acton's *Essays on Freedom and Power,* p. 264. (Beacon Press, 1948)

It has often been said that power corrupts. But it is perhaps equally important to realize that weakness, too, corrupts. Power corrupts the few, while weakness corrupts the many.

ERIC HOFFER, *The Passionate State of Mind,* p. 28. (1954) *See also* 1573:16.

14
Power is sweet; it is a drug, the desire for which increases with habit.

BERTRAND RUSSELL, *Came the Revolution.* See *Saturday Review Reader,* No. i, p. 128.

15
Unlimited power *is* the ideal thing when it is in safe hands.

MARK TWAIN, *A Connecticut Yankee at King Arthur's Court,* p. 73. (1889)

PRESS

16
The Wayward Press.

A. J. LIEBLING, Title of a series of articles, dealing with the lapses of American newspapers, that appeared in *The New Yorker* in the years following World War II. In 1947 a collection of such pieces by him appeared as a book, *The Wayward Pressman.*

17
A free press is not a privilege but an organic necessity in a great society. Without criticism and reliable and intelligent reporting, the government cannot govern. For there is no adequate way in which it can keep itself informed about what the people of the country are thinking and doing and wanting.

WALTER LIPPMANN, Syndicated Column, 27 May, 1965 (part of an address to the International Press Institute, London, on that date).

1
The paramount point is whether, like a scientist or a scholar, the journalist puts truth in the first place or in the second. If he puts it in the second place, he is a worshiper of the bitch goddess Success. Or he is a conceited man trying to win an argument. Insofar as he puts truth in the first place, he rises toward —I will not say into, but toward—the company of those who taste and enjoy the best things in life.

WALTER LIPPMANN, Syndicated Column, 27 May, 1965 (part of an address to the International Press Institute, London).

2
We tell the public which way the cat is jumping. The public will take care of the cat.

ARTHUR HAYS SULZBERGER, of the New York *Times*. (*Time*, 8 May, 1950)

3
Everyone thinks he can edit a newspaper—only a fool would try to edit a hundred.

ROY HERBERT THOMSON (BARON THOMSON of FLEET), Comment on his own vast, and highly successful, chain of British provincial newspapers. (New York *Times*, 15 Sept., 1965, p. 9)

4
Dictators always seek to control the press, and if they have once secured real power, they seldom find it difficult to do so.

H. R. TREVOR-ROPER, *New York Times Book Review*, 31 May, 1964.

5
Dick Outcault, the cartoonist of the *New York World*, evolved his "Yellow Kid" cartoons, and the urchin in the yellow gabardine, purchased by the Hearst interests, had taken New York's fancy. *The Press*, in duty bound, was whanging away at the Hearst sensationalism and vulgarity, when one dull day it occurred to me that our shopworn tag of "The New Journalism" could be improved upon, and I put all the vitriol of my nature into an editorial which I captioned "Yellow Kid Journalism." When the galleys came up from the pressroom the caption proved to be two letters too long for the column, and having no time to frame another, I struck out the middle word. Thus by sheer accident was created the phrase "Yellow Journalism."

POST WHEELER, *Dome of Many-Coloured Glass*, p. 97. (2 Feb., 1896) See also 1600:18.

PROPERTY

6
Property is in its nature timid and seeks protection, and nothing is more gratifying to government than to become a protector.

JOHN C. CALHOUN, *Speech*, on rechartering of Bank, 21 March, 1834. *See also* 1622:2.

7
The Duke [of Wellington] said the natural state of man was plunder. Society was based on security of property alone. It was for that object men associated; and he thought we were coming to the natural state of society very fast.

BENJAMIN ROBERT HAYDON, *Memoirs*, 1839, edited by Tom Taylor. *See also* 1167:8.

This seems to me quite tremendous; a key to sanity in the present state of the world, . . . tremendous because it blows nearly the whole of Rousseau's doctrine sky high.

FRANK A. GIBSON, *Letter to the Compiler*, Nov., 1957.

PURPOSE

8
In the name of noble purposes men have committed unspeakable acts of cruelty against one another.

J. WILLIAM FULBRIGHT, *Address*, in Washington, D.C., 5 Dec., 1963.

9
Every night before I turn out the lights to sleep I ask myself this question: Have I done everything that I can do to unite this country? Have I done everything I can to help unite the world, to try to bring peace and hope to all the peoples of the world? Have I done enough?

LYNDON B. JOHNSON, *Address*, at Johns Hopkins University, Baltimore, 7 Apr., 1965.

10
A man must have goals. There is not sufficient time, even in two terms, to achieve these goals. Almost all Presidents leave office feeling that their work is unfinished. I have a lot to do, and so little time in which to do it.

JOHN F. KENNEDY, Interview with Jim Bishop, three weeks prior to Kennedy's death. Quoted in a syndicated newspaper article by Bishop, 25 Nov., 1963, three days after Kennedy was assassinated.

REASON

11
The people of the world, I think, prefer reasoned agreement to ready attack. And that is why we must follow the Prophet Isaiah many times before we send the Marines, and say, "Come now, and let us reason together."

LYNDON B. JOHNSON, *Speech*, in Washington, D.C., 24 Mar., 1964. The quotation, from Isaiah i, 18, was one of Johnson's favorites.

12
I would rather win a convert than an argument.

LYNDON B. JOHNSON. (H. A. ZEIGER, *Lyndon B. Johnson: Man and President*, p. 65)

13
There is nothing more profitable to man than to live by the guidance of reason.

BARUCH SPINOZA, *Ethics*. Pt. iv, Prop. 35. (1674)

REFORM AND REFORMERS

1
Pride isn't one of my attributes. Either pride or disappointment or failure doesn't enter my calculations. I don't do something just because I think I'll win. It's the reformer's instinct, I suppose. It has nothing to do with doing people good. I just try to put things to rights. I tackle the things that arouse me—injustice, cruelty, unfairness.

ROGER BALDWIN. (WILLIE MORRIS, "Barely Winded at Eighty"; *The New Republic,* 25 Jan., 1964)

2
No reforms come easy; even the most obvious will have its entrenched enemies. Each one is carried to us on the bent and the weary backs of patient, dedicated men and women.

ADLAI E. STEVENSON, *Address,* in Washington, D.C., 18 Jan., 1959.

RELIGION

3
What is faith but a kind of betting or speculation after all? It should be "I bet that my Redeemer liveth."

SAMUEL BUTLER, *Notebooks,* p. 55. (c. 1890)

4
Priests are no more necessary to religion than politicians to patriotism.

JOHN HAYNES HOLMES, *The Sensible Man's View of Religion.* (1933)

5
The Church is no dead pile of stones.

CHARLES RANN KENNEDY, *The Servant in the House.* Act ii. (1908)

6
Whosoever transgresseth against you, do ye transgress against him in like manner as he hath transgressed against you.

MOHAMMED, *The Koran.* Ch. ii. (c. 630) *See* 1708:1.

REVOLUTION

7
I hope we are learning that not everyone who struggles for change is an instrument of Communism and that fundamental change does not necessarily mean Communism, just as not everyone who opposes Communism is a supporter of human freedom.

LEROY COLLINS, *Speech,* in San Juan, P.R., 25 May, 1965.

8
We welcome changes which advance the welfare of our people. Our system always needs repairs. The remedies in America are not revolution. They are, except for peace and war, mostly jobs of marginal repairs around a sound philosophy and a stout heart.

HERBERT HOOVER, 1954. (*Herbert Hoover in His Own Words,* compiled by LOUIS P. LOCHNER; *New York Times Magazine,* 9 Aug., 1964, p. 15)

9
Our "permanent revolution" is dedicated to broadening—for all Americans—the material and spiritual benefits of the democratic heritage.

LYNDON B. JOHNSON, *Speech,* in Los Angeles, 21 Feb., 1964.

10
Revolutions are not exportable.

NIKITA S. KHRUSHCHEV, *Speech,* to the 21st Congress of the Communist Party, 27 Jan., 1959.

11
The time to stop a revolution is at the beginning, not the end.

ADLAI E. STEVENSON, *Speech,* in San Francisco, 9 Sept., 1952, during the presidential campaign.

RIGHTS

12
The true Republic: men, their rights and nothing more; women, their rights and nothing less.

SUSAN B. ANTHONY, *Motto,* of her paper, *Revolution.* (1868)

13
Rights can exist only under law, not independent of it.

TOM C. CLARK, *Address,* in St. Louis, 9 Feb., 1965.

14
The sacred rights of mankind are not to be rummaged from among old parchments or musty records. They are written, as with a sunbeam, in the whole volume of human nature, by the hand of the divinity itself; and can never be erased or obscured by mortal power.

ALEXANDER HAMILTON, *The Farmer Refuted,* 5 Feb., 1775. A pamphlet, defending American liberty, written while Hamilton, aged 19, was still in college.

15
Civil wrongs do not bring civil rights. Civil disobedience does not bring equal protection under the laws. Disorder does not bring law and order.

HUBERT H. HUMPHREY AND THOMAS H. KUCHEL, Joint Statement, Apr., 1964, during Congressional debate on the civil rights bill of that year. As majority whip and minority whip of the Senate, respectively, they were speaking against demonstrations designed to secure passage of a strong bill.

16
The same revolutionary beliefs for which our forebears fought are still at issue around the globe—the belief that the rights of man come not from the generosity of the state but from the hand of God.

JOHN F. KENNEDY, *Inaugural Address,* 20 Jan., 1961.

17
The right to interfere with the rights of others is no part of academic freedom.

GRAYSON KIRK, Statement, warning against irresponsible actions by student demonstrators, June, 1965. This admonition was for students of Columbia University, of which he was president.

1
Let's put the record straight. Our concern is not for some abstract concept of "states' rights." States have no rights—only people have rights. States have responsibilities.

GEORGE ROMNEY, Testimony before the Republican platform committee, 8 July, 1964, during the party's national convention in San Francisco.

2
Government laws are needed to give us civil rights, and God is needed to make us civil.

REV. RALPH M. SOCKMAN, *Sermon,* at Riverside Church, New York City, 13 Dec., 1964.

RUSSIA

3
I cannot forecast to you the action of Russia. It is a riddle wrapped in a mystery inside an enigma.

WINSTON CHURCHILL, *Broadcast,* 1 Oct., 1939.

4
We must assume that the Soviet leaders consider their recent change of policy to be an application of the classic Communist maneuver known as "zigzag," i.e., resort to "tactics of retreat to buy off a powerful enemy and gain a respite."

JOHN FOSTER DULLES, quoting Stalin in an address shortly after returning from the Geneva conference, July, 1955.

5
They pay little attention to what we say, and prefer to read tea leaves.

NIKITA S. KHRUSHCHEV, Comment, 5 July, 1955, on journalists of the non-Communist world.

6
Those who wait for that [rejection of Communism by the Soviet Union] must wait until a shrimp learns to whistle.

NIKITA S. KHRUSHCHEV, Comment, 18 Sept., 1955.

7
Every year humanity takes a step toward Communism. Maybe not you, but at all events your grandson will surely be a Communist.

NIKITA S. KHRUSHCHEV, Comment to the British ambassador, William Hayter, June, 1956.

8
After the liquidation of classes we have a monolithic society. Therefore, why found another party? That would be like voluntarily letting someone put a flea in your shirt.

NIKITA S. KHRUSHCHEV, *Speech,* June, 1957, to a group of French socialists.

9
We are not the kind of people we have been pictured. We do not gobble up babies.

NIKITA S. KHRUSHCHEV, referring to the Russians. (New York *Times,* 30 Dec., 1959)

10
We do not sell ideas if they are not good. Ideas are not salami.

NIKITA S. KHRUSHCHEV. (New York *Herald Tribune,* 11 Feb., 1960)

11
No one is born a Communist. . . . In the Soviet Union farmers look in the barn for "their" horses even after they have given them to the collective.

NIKITA S. KHRUSHCHEV, *Speech,* in Rumania, June, 1962.

12
The enemies of Communism always dream of a failure of our economy. We say to the authors of such forgeries: You will sooner vanish as if the earth had opened and swallowed you, than see our economic failure.

NIKITA S. KHRUSHCHEV, *Speech,* in Kalinin, U.S.S.R., reported by Tass, 18 Jan., 1964.

13
Citizens of the U.S.S.R. have the right to work; the right to rest; the right to maintenance in old age; the right to education.

JOSEPH STALIN, *Constitution of the U.S.S.R.* Articles 118–121. (1930)

SCIENCE

14
Modern man worships at the temple of science, but science tells him only what is possible, not what is right.

MILTON S. EISENHOWER, "The Need for a New American"; *The Educational Record,* Oct., 1963, p. 305.

15
No national sovereignty rules in outer space. Those who venture there go as envoys of the entire human race. Their quest, therefore, must be for all mankind, and what they find should belong to all mankind.

LYNDON B. JOHNSON, News Conference, Johnson City, Tex., 29 Aug., 1965.

16
As man increases his knowledge of the heavens, why should he fear the unknown on earth? As man draws nearer to the stars, why should he not also draw nearer to his neighbor? As we push ever more deeply into the universe, probing its secrets, discovering its way, we must also constantly try to learn to cooperate across the frontiers that really divide earth's surface.

LYNDON B. JOHNSON, News Conference in Johnson City, Tex., 29 Aug., 1965.

17
Let both sides seek to invoke the wonders of science instead of its terrors. Together let us explore the stars, conquer the deserts, eradicate disease, tap the ocean depths, and encourage the arts and commerce.

JOHN F. KENNEDY, *Inaugural Address,* 20 Jan., 1961. "Both sides" refers to the United States and its allies, on one hand, and to "those nations who would make themselves our adversary," on the other.

1
The language of science is universal, and perhaps scientists have been the most international of all professions in their outlook. But the contemporary revolution in transport and communication has dramatically speeded the internationalization of science.

JOHN F. KENNEDY, *Address,* to the National Academy of Sciences, Washington, D.C., 22 Oct., 1963.

2
Science contributes to our culture in many ways, as a creative intellectual activity in its own right, as the light which has served to illuminate man's place in the universe, and as the source of understanding of man's own nature.

JOHN F. KENNEDY, *Address,* to the National Academy of Sciences, Washington, D.C., 22 Oct., 1963.

3
In the years since man unlocked the power stored up within the atom, the world has made progress, halting but effective, toward bringing that power under human control. The challenge may be our salvation. As we begin to master the destructive potentialities of modern science, we move toward a new era in which science can fulfill its creative promise and help bring into existence the happiest society the world has ever known.

JOHN F. KENNEDY, *Address,* to the National Academy of Sciences, Washington, D.C., 22 Oct., 1963.

4
In a world that sits not on a powder keg but on a hydrogen bomb, one begins to suspect that the technician who rules our world is not the master magician he thinks he is but only a sorceror's apprentice who does not know how to turn off what he turned on—or even how to avoid blowing himself up.

JOSEPH WOOD KRUTCH, *Wilderness as a Tonic; The Saturday Review,* 8 June, 1963, p. 15.

5
Science is a great game. It is inspiring and refreshing. The playing field is the universe itself.

ISIDOR I. RABI. (New York *Times,* 28 Oct., 1964, p. 38)

6
People must understand that science is inherently neither a potential for good or for evil. It is a potential to be harnessed by man to do his bidding. Man will determine its direction and its effects. Man, therefore, must understand science if he is to harness it, to live with it, to grow with it.

GLENN T. SEABORG, Interview with Alton Blakeslee of the Associated Press, 29 Sept., 1964.

7
Nature is neutral. Man has wrested from nature the power to make the world a desert or to make the deserts bloom. There is no evil in the atom; only in men's souls.

ADLAI E. STEVENSON, *Speech,* in Hartford, Conn., 18 Sept., 1952, during the presidential campaign.

8
It will free man from his remaining chains, the chains of gravity which still tie him to this planet. It will open to him the gates of heaven.

WERNHER VON BRAUN, referring to travel in outer space. (*Time,* 10 Feb., 1958)

SHIP

9
Ocean greyhound.

DAVID DRUMMOND BONE, referring to the steamer *Alaska,* first ship to cross the Atlantic in less than a week. (1881)

10
The strength of the ship is the Service,
And the strength of the Service, the ship.

RONALD ARTHUR HOPGOOD, *The Laws of the Navy.* (c. 1920)

11
A ship is always referred to as "she" because it costs so much to keep one in paint and powder.

ADMIRAL CHESTER WILLIAM NIMITZ, *Talk,* before Society of Sponsors of U.S. Navy. (13 Feb., 1940) *See also* 1813:5.

SILENCE AND SPEECH

12
Sometimes I doubt whether there is divine justice; all parts of the human body get tired eventually—except the tongue. And I feel this is unjust.

KONRAD ADENAUER. (New York *Times,* "Ideas and Men"; 16 Feb., 1964)

13
I have left unsaid much that I am sorry I did not say, but I have said little that I am sorry for having said.

SAMUEL BUTLER, *Notebooks,* p. 138. (c. 1890)

Silence is not always tact and it is tact that is golden, not silence.

SAMUEL BUTLER, *Notebooks,* p. 229.

14
"Woe unto you when all men speak well of you." Yes, and Woe unto you when you speak well of all men.

SAMUEL BUTLER, *Notebooks,* p. 260.

15
Persons in public positions—including me—miss too many chances to keep their mouths shut. I'm not passing up my chance tonight.

DWIGHT D. EISENHOWER, Comment at George Washington University, Washington, D.C., 7 June, 1964. He was attending commencement exercises at the school, and was asked to state publicly his preference for the Republican presidential nomination. This was just a month before the party's national convention.

1
Eleanor Roosevelt taught us that sometimes silence is the greatest sin.

CLAUDIA T. (MRS. LYNDON B.) JOHNSON, *Speech,* at luncheon of the Eleanor Roosevelt Memorial Foundation, New York City, 9 Apr., 1964. Referring to Mrs. Roosevelt's courage in speaking out on controversial issues.

2
You've got to know when to keep your mouth shut. The Senate's the cruelest judge in the world. A man's a fool to talk to other fellows about any subject unless he knows more about that subject than they do.

LYNDON B. JOHNSON. (HENRY A. ZEIGER, *Lyndon B. Johnson: Man and President,* p. 67)

3
The world would be much happier if men were as fully able to keep silence as they are to speak.

BARUCH SPINOZA, *Ethics.* (1674) *See* RUNES, *Road to Inner Freedom,* p. 30.

4
Famous remarks are seldom quoted correctly.

SIMEON STRUNSKY, *No Mean City,* ch. 38. (1944)

SIN

5
Oh, Lord, it is not the sins I have committed that I regret, but those which I have had no opportunity to commit.

SHEYKH GHALIB, *Prayer.* (c. 1800) Last of the great poets of the old Turkish school.

There is not any memory with less satisfaction than the memory of some temptation we resisted.

JAMES BRANCH CABELL, *Jurgen,* p. 39. (1919)

6
Sin has always been an ugly word, but it has been made so in a new sense over the last half-century. It has been made not only ugly but passé. People are no longer sinful, they are only immature or underprivileged or frightened or, more particularly, sick.

PHYLLIS MCGINLEY, *The Province of the Heart: In Defense of Sin,* p. 35. (1959)

7
For my part I believe in the forgiveness of sin and the redemption of ignorance.

ADLAI E. STEVENSON, Reply to a heckler during a United Nations Day speech in Dallas, 24 Oct., 1963. After his speech Stevenson was jostled by anti-UN pickets, struck with a sign carried by one of them, and spat upon.

8
The only deadly sin I know is cynicism.

HENRY L. STIMSON, *On Active Service in Peace and War: Introduction.* (1948)

SINCERITY

9
I am not two-faced, because if I were I would certainly be wearing the other one.

GUSTAVO DÍAZ ORDAZ, Remark that recurred in his political speeches during his successful campaign for the presidency of Mexico in 1964. It was his way of turning homeliness into advantage. (New York Times News Service dispatch, 3 Dec., 1964)

10
Sincerity is always subject to proof.

JOHN F. KENNEDY, *Inaugural Address,* 20 Jan., 1961.

11
See, talk, and feel the people. But above all be yourself in any direction. Then you'll be what you are, and represent America.

JOHN F. KENNEDY, Instruction to John Steinbeck when the novelist set out on a mission for the United States behind the Iron Curtain. Steinbeck quoted these words at a press conference in Vienna, 26 Nov., 1963, four days after Kennedy's death.

SOCIETY

12
Who Killed Society?

CLEVELAND AMORY, *Title of book* (1960).

13
The Hostess with the Mostes' on the Ball.

IRVING BERLIN, Title of song from *Call Me Madam* (1950), sung by Ethel Merman.

14
The great society is not a safe harbor . . . The great society is a place where men are more concerned with the quality of their goals than the quantity of their goods.

LYNDON B. JOHNSON, *Speech,* at the University of Michigan, Ann Arbor, Mich., 22 May, 1964—the first use of "great society" with reference to his administration.

15
In general, American social life constitutes an evasion of talking to people. Most Americans don't, in any vital sense, get together; they only do things together.

LOUIS KRONENBERGER, *Company Manners,* p. 148. (1954)

16
The name of the subspecies, then, is Exurbanite; its habitat, the Exurbs. The exurb is generally further from New York than the suburb on the same railway line. Its houses are more widely spaced and generally more various and expensive. The town center tends to quaintness and class, rather than modernity and glass, and the further one lives from the station the better.

A. C. SPECTORSKY, *The Exurbanites.* (1955)

SOLDIER

17
A man should have dinner with his friends, and the commanding general has no friends.

GENERAL CURTIS LEMAY, refusing a dinner invitation from his fellow officers. (*Look,* 2 Nov., 1965)

18
My first recollection is that of a bugle call.

GENERAL DOUGLAS MACARTHUR, recalling his

early years. (New York *Herald Tribune* obituary of MacArthur, 6 Apr., 1964, p. 12)

1
Your mission remains fixed, determined, inviolable—it is to win our wars. Everything else in your professional career is but corollary to this vital dedication.

GENERAL DOUGLAS MACARTHUR, *Address,* at the U.S. Military Academy, West Point, N.Y., 12 May, 1962.

2
My estimate of him [the American man-at-arms] was formed on the battlefield many, many years ago, and has never changed. I regarded him then as I regard him now—as one of the world's noblest figures. . . . His name and fame are the birthright of every American citizen.

GENERAL DOUGLAS MACARTHUR, *Address,* at the U.S. Military Academy, West Point, N.Y., 12 May, 1962.

3
The soldier, above all other people, prays for peace, for he must suffer and bear the deepest wounds and scars of war.

GENERAL DOUGLAS MACARTHUR, *Address,* at the U.S. Military Academy, West Point, N.Y., 12 May, 1962.

4
Today marks my final roll call with you, but I want you to know that when I cross the river my last conscious thoughts will be of The Corps, and The Corps, and The Corps.

GENERAL DOUGLAS MACARTHUR, *Address,* at the U.S. Military Academy, West Point, N.Y., 12 May, 1962.

SPEECH

5
The United States is a land of free speech. Nowhere is speech freer—not even here where we sedulously cultivate it even in its most repulsive form.

WINSTON CHURCHILL, *Speech,* in the House of Commons, 28 Sept., 1944.

6
The right to be heard does not automatically include the right to be taken seriously. To be taken seriously depends entirely upon what is being said.

HUBERT H. HUMPHREY, *Speech,* at annual congress of the National Student Association, Madison, Wis., 23 Aug., 1965.

7
Let no one ever think for a moment that national debate means national division.

LYNDON B. JOHNSON, *Commencement Address,* at National Cathedral School for Girls, Washington, D.C., 1 June, 1965.

8
The first principle of a free society is an untrammeled flow of words in an open forum.

ADLAI E. STEVENSON. (New York *Times,* 19 Jan., 1962)

STAGE

9
There's No Business Like Show Business.

IRVING BERLIN, Title of song from the musical comedy *Annie Get Your Gun* (1946).

10
A theater which depends entirely on the production of immediate smash hits is doomed. . . . The theater, once a profession, ceases to preserve that status as a business.

HAROLD CLURMAN, "Where Are the New Playwrights? 'Waiting' "; *New York Times Magazine,* 7 June, 1964, p. 26.

11
The Fabulous Invalid.

MOSS HART AND GEORGE S. KAUFMAN, Title of play (1938). The term has become synonymous with the American theater.

12
The most alarming thing about the contemporary American theater is the absolute regularity of its march toward extinction.

WALTER KERR, *How Not to Write a Play: Introduction,* p. 1 (1955).

The theatre is both the cliffhanger and the phoenix of the arts. Its swoons are deceptive. No gadget wired for sound or sight or ptomaine will ever subdue it.

RICHARD MANEY, *Fanfare,* p. 362. (1957)

So long as there is one pretty girl left on the stage, the professional undertakers may hold up their burial of the theatre.

GEORGE JEAN NATHAN. (*Theatre Arts,* July, 1958)

13
The theatre is the last free institution in the amusement world.

RICHARD MANEY, *Fanfare,* p. 362.

14
We want to create a "theater," not build one. Formal externals are not important. It is the activity within that counts.

LEE STRASBERG, Interview with PAUL GARDNER of the New York *Times,* 5 May, 1964. He was referring to the Actors Studio in New York, of which he was artistic director.

15
It is the destiny of the theater nearly everywhere and in every period to struggle even when it is flourishing.

HOWARD TAUBMAN, Article, New York *Times,* 4 Aug., 1964, p. 20.

STRENGTH

16
Our real problem is not our strength today; it is the vital necessity of action today to ensure our strength tomorrow.

DWIGHT D. EISENHOWER, *State of the Union Message,* 9 Jan., 1958.

17
The United States is a peaceful nation. And where our strength and determination are clear, our words need merely to convey conviction, not belligerence. If we are strong,

our strength will speak for itself. If we are weak, words will be no help.

JOHN F. KENNEDY, *Speech,* prepared for delivery in Dallas, 22 Nov., 1963, the day of his assassination in that city.

1
Government cannot be stronger or more tough-minded than its people. It cannot be more inflexibly committed to the task than they.

ADLAI E. STEVENSON, *Speech,* in Chicago, 29 Sept., 1952, during the presidential campaign.

SUCCESS

2
It takes twenty years to make an overnight success.

Attributed to EDDIE CANTOR. (*New York Times Magazine,* 20 Oct., 1963)

3
Sweet Smell of Success.

ERNEST LEHMAN, Title of novel and screenplay for film (1956).

4
Nothing fails like success; nothing is so defeated as yesterday's triumphant Cause.

PHYLLIS MCGINLEY, *The Province of the Heart: How to Get Along with Men,* p. 71. (1959)

TAXATION

5
The art of taxation consists in so plucking the goose as to obtain the largest possible amount of feathers with the smallest possible amount of hissing.

JEAN BAPTISTE COLBERT, *Epigram.* (c. 1665) Colbert was Minister of Finance to Louis XIV of France. The saying has been attributed also to Cardinal Mazarin, with whom it would be quite in character and under whom Colbert served. *See also* 1966:17.

It is impossible to make great largesses to the people without great extortion.

MONTESQUIEU, *The Spirit of Laws.* Bk. vii, ch. 2. (1748)

The point to remember is that what the government gives it must first take away.

JOHN S. COLEMAN, President of the Detroit Chamber of Commerce, *Address to the Chamber.*

6
Taxes are what we pay for civilized society.

JUSTICE OLIVER WENDELL HOLMES, *Opinion,* Companie de Tobaccos v. Collector. (1904)

7
The grass will grow in the streets of a hundred cities, a thousand towns; the weeds will overrun millions of farms if that protection is taken away.

HERBERT HOOVER, *Speech,* New York City, 31 Oct., 1932, in campaign for re-election, referring to the protective tariff.

THOUGHT

8
During my eighty-seven years I have witnessed a whole succession of technological revolutions. But none of them has done away with the need for character in the individual or the ability to think.

BERNARD M. BARUCH, *Baruch: My Own Story,* ch. 22. (1957)

9
We must dare to think about "unthinkable things," because when things become "unthinkable," thinking stops and action becomes mindless.

J. WILLIAM FULBRIGHT, *Speech,* in U.S. Senate, 25 Mar., 1964, urging a re-examination of what he termed stereotyped thinking about American relations with the Communist world.

10
The Power of Positive Thinking.

NORMAN VINCENT PEALE, *Title of book* (1952).

THRIFT

11
That rule which I wish to see you governed by through your whole life, of never buying anything which you have not the money in your pocket to pay for. Be assured that it gives much more pain to the mind to be in debt, than to do without any article whatever which we may seem to want.

THOMAS JEFFERSON, *Letter to His Daughter, Martha Washington,* June 14, 1787. Martha wished to borrow some money with which to buy some dresses. Jefferson advanced the money with this admonition.

12
Never spend your money before you have it.

THOMAS JEFFERSON, *Letter to Thomas Jefferson Smith,* 21 Feb., 1825. No. 3 of ten rules for a practical life.

Draw your salary before spending it.

GEORGE ADE, *Forty Modern Fables: The People's Choice.* (1901)

TRUTH AND FALSEHOOD

13
There is more truth in honest lies,
Believe me, than in half the truths.

SAMUEL BUTLER, *Notebooks,* p. 52. (c. 1890)

14
Any fool can tell the truth, but it requires a man of some sense to know how to lie well.

SAMUEL BUTLER, *Notebooks,* p. 114.

15
In all matters which concern my daughter I would have you lie like a gentleman.

JAMES BRANCH CABELL, *Jurgen,* p. 64. (1919)

16
Nothing but experience could evince the frequency of false information, or enable any man to conceive that so many groundless reports should be propagated, as every man of eminence may hear of himself.

SAMUEL JOHNSON. Quoted by RICHARD D. ALTICK, *The Scholar Adventurers,* p. 88. (1951)

1
We believe that truth is stronger than error and that freedom is more enduring than coercion.

JOHN F. KENNEDY, *Address,* to the United Nations General Assembly, 20 Sept., 1963.

2
You will find that the truth is often unpopular and the contest between agreeable fancy and disagreeable fact is unequal. For, in the vernacular, we Americans are suckers for good news.

ADLAI E. STEVENSON, *Commencement Address,* Michigan State University, East Lansing, Mich., 8 June, 1958.

UNITY

3
A mandate for unity.

LYNDON B. JOHNSON, *Speech,* in Austin, Tex., 4 Nov., 1964, in the early morning hours when election returns showed him a victor over Barry Goldwater in a landslide.

4
We come to reason, not to dominate. We do not seek to have our way, but to find a common way.

LYNDON B. JOHNSON, *Speech,* at Georgetown University, Washington, D.C., 3 Dec., 1964, referring to the United States and the North Atlantic Treaty Organization (NATO).

5
United, there is little we cannot do in a host of new cooperative ventures. Divided, there is little we can do—for we dare not meet a powerful challenge at odds and split asunder.

JOHN F. KENNEDY, *Inaugural Address,* 20 Jan., 1961. Referring to the United States and "those old allies whose cultural and spiritual origins we share."

There are no problems we cannot solve together, and very few we can solve by ourselves.

LYNDON B. JOHNSON, News Conference, Johnson City, Tex., 28 Nov., 1964, referring to members of the North Atlantic Treaty Organization (NATO).

6
Let both sides explore what problems unite us instead of belaboring those problems which divide us.

JOHN F. KENNEDY, *Inaugural Address,* 20 Jan., 1961. Referring to the United States and its allies opposed to "those nations who would make themselves our adversary."

UNIVERSE

7
The universe is not hostile, nor yet is it friendly. It is simply indifferent.

JOHN HAYNES HOLMES, *The Sensible Man's View of Religion.* (1933)

8
"I accept the universe" is reported to have been a favorite utterance of our New England transcendentalist, Margaret Fuller; and when some one repeated this phrase to Thomas Carlyle, his sardonic comment is said to have been, "Gad! she'd better."

WILLIAM JAMES, *The Varieties of Religious Experience,* p. 41. (1902)

VICTORY

9
Why Not Victory?

BARRY M. GOLDWATER, *Title of book* (1962), advocating a strongly nationalistic foreign policy.

10
Victory is no longer a truth. It is only a word to describe who is left alive in the ruins.

LYNDON B. JOHNSON, *Speech,* in New York City, 6 Feb., 1964.

VOTE AND VOTING

11
This right to vote is the basic right without which all others are meaningless. It gives people—people as individuals—control over their own destinies.

LYNDON B. JOHNSON, *Speech,* in 1957, in support of voting-rights legislation. He was speaking as Senate majority leader.

12
We preach the virtues of democracy abroad. We must practice its duties here at home. Voting is the first duty of democracy.

LYNDON B. JOHNSON, *Address,* in Washington, D.C., 11 Aug., 1964, urging registration for the elections of that year.

13
We have been awakened to justice by the sound of songs and sermons, speeches and peaceful demonstrations. But the noiseless, secret vote will thunder forth a hundred times more loudly.

LYNDON B. JOHNSON, Public Statement on passage of the voting-rights bill of 1965 by the House of Representatives, 10 July, 1965. This was designed especially to insure Negro voting.

14
The vote is the most powerful instrument ever devised by man for breaking down injustice and destroying the terrible walls which imprison men because they are different from other men.

LYNDON B. JOHNSON, *Address,* on signing the voting-rights bill of 1965, Washington, D.C., 6 Aug., 1965.

15
The secret ballot in America is the most sacred heritage which we have and that I have stood by. Even my wife doesn't know how I voted.

NELSON A. ROCKEFELLER, Reply to a reporter, shortly after the election in Nov., 1964, who asked how Rockefeller voted in the contest for the presidency. Rockefeller had bitterly opposed the Republican candidate, Barry M. Goldwater, prior to Goldwater's nomination.

1
One man, one vote.

UNKNOWN, a popular paraphrase of U.S. Supreme Court decisions of 1964. On 17 Feb., 1964, Hugo L. Black wrote the majority decision setting "equal representation for equal numbers" as the basis for representation in the U.S. House of Representatives (in short, Congressional districts within a state must be substantially equal in population). On 15 June, 1964, Earl Warren wrote the majority opinion ordering both houses of state legislatures apportioned solely on the basis of population.

WAR

2
I ordered the commander, Captain de la Place, to come forth instantly, or I would sacrifice the whole garrison; at which the Captain came immediately to the door, with his breeches in his hand, when I ordered him to deliver me the fort instantly. He asked by what authority I demanded it. I answered him, "In the name of the great Jehovah, and the Continental Congress." The authority of the Congress being very little known at that time, he began to speak again. I interrupted him and, with my drawn sword over his head, again demanded an immediate surrender of the garrison, with which he then complied.

ETHAN ALLEN, at the capture of Fort Ticonderoga, 10 May, 1775. From his own narrative. *See* DOTSON, *American Rebels*, p. 58. One cannot help suspecting a little embroidery. *See* 61:8.

3
England will fight to the last drop of blood of the Russian soldier.

BULATZEL. Russian edition during World War I. Quoted by BOTKIN, *The Real Romanoffs*, p. 117.

4
Ye hypocrites! are these your pranks?
To murder men, and give God thanks?
Desist for shame! Proceed no further:
God won't accept your thanks for Murther.

ROBERT BURNS, *On Thanksgiving for a National Victory*. The victory was probably Howe's, off Ushant, 1 June, 1794.

5
On this march I came to the conclusion that no man of any spirit and ambition would join the "Doughboys," and go afoot when he could ride a fine horse and wear spurs like a gentleman.

SAMUEL E. CHAMBERLAIN, *My Confession*. See *Life*, 23 July, 1956, p. 84: "This bit of army slang dates from the battle of Monterey [1846] when some of General William J. Worth's infantry, who had captured the Bishop's palace, baked a mixture of flour and rice in their campfire ashes."

For bread we took the corn of the fields, and, having no proper means of winnowing and grinding it, were obliged . . . to rub out the ears between our hands and pound it between stones to make dough . . . from which wretched practice we christened the place Dough Boy Hill.

RICHARD ALDINGTON, *The Duke*, an account of the first Duke of Wellington. The above quotation is from the diary of one of Wellington's soldiers in the 1812 Spanish campaign. However, "the term existed before Wellington. British soldiers used pipe clay to whiten their uniforms. Because rain made the garb soggy and gave it a doughy look, the men called themselves doughboys."—*Life*, 13 August, 1956, p. 14. *See also* 1862:13.

6
The maxim of the British people is "Business as usual."

WINSTON CHURCHILL, *Speech*, Guildhall, London, 9 Nov., 1914.

7
Victory at all costs, victory in spite of all terror, however long and hard the road may be; for without victory there is no survival.

WINSTON CHURCHILL, *Speech*, House of Commons, 13 May, 1940, on becoming Prime Minister.

8
We shall not flag or fail. We shall fight in France, we shall fight on the seas and oceans, we shall fight with confidence and growing strength in the air, we shall defend our island whatever the cost may be, we shall fight on the beaches, we shall fight on the landing grounds, we shall fight in the fields and in the streets, we shall fight in the hills; we shall never surrender.

WINSTON CHURCHILL, *Speech*, after the disaster at Dunkirk, House of Commons, 18 June, 1940. *See also* 2298c:1.

9
I am too weak for that sort of thing [to paint], but I am still strong enough to wage war.

WINSTON CHURCHILL, *Retort*, when General Charles de Gaulle, at their meeting at Marrakesh, asked him if he was still painting. *See* New York *Times*, 17 Jan., 1944, p. 3, col. 3.

10
If I were a Mexican, I would tell you, "Have you not enough room in your own country to bury your dead men? If you come into mine, I will greet you with bloody hands and welcome you to hospitable graves."

THOMAS CORWIN, *Speech*, in U.S. Senate, 11 Feb., 1846, protesting the entrance of the United States into the War with Mexico, when Lewis Cass attempted to justify it by saying, "We want room."

11
Une drôle de guerre.

ÉDOUARD DALADIER, *Speech*, Chamber of Deputies, 22 Dec., 1939. Usually translated as "A phony war."

1
All good poetry is forged slowly and patiently, link by link, with sweat and blood and tears.

LORD ALFRED DOUGLAS, *Collected Poems: Introduction.* (1919)

Their sweat, their tears, their blood bedewed the endless plain.

WINSTON CHURCHILL, *The Unknown War.* (1931) Referring to the Russian armies before the Revolution. Churchill's most famous use of the phrase was, of course, in the House of Commons, 13 May, 1940 (*See* 2298c:1), but he also used it on 8 Oct., 1940, 7 May and 2 Dec., 1941, 27 Jan. and 16 Nov., 1942, and no doubt upon other occasions.

2
Local defense must be reinforced by the further deterrent of massive retaliatory power.

JOHN FOSTER DULLES, *Speech,* to Council of Foreign Relations, 12 Jan., 1954. In the April issue of *Foreign Affairs,* Dulles explained that by "massive retaliation" he was not thinking of an attack on Moscow, but of such retaliation as would make a Communist military adventure of any size unprofitable. He repeated the phrase in a speech at Chicago, 8 Dec., 1955, in which he said, "Our capacity to retaliate must be, and is, massive in order to deter all forms of aggression." Another famous phrase occurred in his "brink of war" statement, in which he said, "You have to take chances for peace, just as you must take chances in war. The ability to get to the verge without getting into the war is a necessary art. If you try to run away from it, if you are scared to go to the brink, you are lost."

One of the great advances of our time is recognition that one of the ways to prevent war is to deter it by having the will and the capacity to use force to punish the aggressor.

JOHN FOSTER DULLES, *Address,* at Williams College, Williamstown, Mass., 6 Oct., 1956.

Even to observe neutrality you must have a strong government.

ALEXANDER HAMILTON, *Address,* in Constitutional Convention, 29 June, 1787.

3
We're ready for a fight or a frolic.

REAR ADMIRAL ROBLEY D. EVANS (FIGHTING BOB), *Remark,* 16 Dec., 1907, as the fleet under his command started on a cruise around the word, undertaken to impress Japan.

4
The enemy now demanded of us if we had struck. "If you have," said they, "why don't you haul down your pennant?" "Ay ay," said Jones, "we'll do that when we can fight no longer, but we shall see yours come down the first; for you must know that Yankees do not haul down their colors till they are fairly beaten."

NATHANIEL FANNING, *Narrative of the Adventures of an American Naval Officer Who Served under the Command of Captain John Paul Jones. See* DOTSON, *American Rebels,* p. 168. One cannot but doubt if Jones really spoke at such length under the circumstances. *See* 62:7.

5
Mon centre cède, ma droite recule, situation excellente. J'attaque! (My center is giving way, my right is in retreat, situation excellent. I attack!)

GEN. FERDINAND FOCH, *Report,* at second battle of the Marne, 1 August, 1918. *See* ASHTON, *Biography of Foch,* p. 122. (1929)

6
Out of the trenches and back to their homes by Christmas.

HENRY FORD, announcing the purpose of his peace ship, *Oscar II,* Dec., 1915, a voyage which Ford abandoned in disgust at the half-way mark and which ended in a fizzle.

7
Keep the home fires burning,
While your hearts are yearning. . . .
There's a silver lining
Through the dark clouds shining,
Turn the dark cloud inside out,
Till the boys come home.

LENA GUILBERT FORD, *Keep the Home Fires Burning.* (1915) *See also* 2285:14.

8
Make no mistake. There is no such thing as a conventional nuclear weapon.

LYNDON B. JOHNSON, *Speech,* in Detroit, 7 Sept., 1964.

9
In the future, if nuclear weapons are unleashed there will be no front and no rear.

NIKITA S. KHRUSHCHEV, *Speech,* in Moscow, Aug., 1961.

10
I would say that only a child and an idiot do not fear war—the child because he cannot yet understand, and the idiot because he has been deprived by God of this possibility.

NIKITA S. KHRUSHCHEV, *Speech,* in Kazincbarcika, Hungary, 6 Apr., 1964.

11
French and Russian they matter not,
A blow for a blow and a shot for a shot;
We love them not, we hate them not;
We hold the Weichsel and Vosges gate,
We have but one and only hate;
We love as one, we hate as one,
We have one foe and one alone,
England!
(*Was schiert uns Russe und Franzos?*
Schuss wider Schuss und Stoss um Stoss,
Wir lieben sie nicht, Wir hassen sie nicht,
Wir schützen Weichsel und Wasgaupass,—
Wir haben nur einen einzigen Hass,
Wir lieben vereint, Wir hassen vereint,
Wir haben nur einen einzigen Feind,
England!)

Ernst Lissauer, *Hassgesang Gegen England.* St. i. (1914) Barbara Henderson, tr.

At the Captain's mess, in the banquet-hall,
Sat feasting the officers, one and all—
Like a saber-blow, like the swing of a sail,
One raised his glass, held high to hail,
Sharp snapped like the stroke of a rudder's play,
Spoke three words only, "To the day!"

Ernst Lissauer, *Hassgesang Gegen England.*

"To the day!" (*Auf den Tag!*), the day, that is, when war would begin.

Twelve men of iron drinking late,
Strike hands and pledge a cup of hate:
"The Day!"

C. A. Richmond, *The Day.*

I pray that every passing hour
Your hearts may bruise and beat,
I pray that every step you take
May bruise and burn your feet.

Émile Cammaerts, *Vœux du Nouvelle An, 1915.* Lord Curzon, tr. (*Observer,* London, 10 Jan., 1915.)

For agony and spoil
Of nations beat to dust,
For poisoned air and tortured soil
And cold commanded lust,
And every secret woe
The shuddering waters saw—
Willed and fulfilled by high and low—
Let them relearn the Law.

Rudyard Kipling, *Justice.* (25 Oct., 1918)

1
In the face of this victory of United Nations arms the Communists committed one of the most offensive acts of international lawlessness of historic record by moving without any notice of belligerency elements of alien Communist forces across the Yalu River into North Korea and massing a great concentration of possible reinforcing divisions with adequate supply behind the privileged sanctuary of the adjacent Manchurian border.

Gen. Douglas MacArthur, *Communique No. 11,* 6 Nov., 1950.

United Nations forces are now being attacked from the safety of a privileged sanctuary.

Harry S Truman, *Statement,* 15 Nov., 1950. Quoted by Frazier Hunt, *The Untold Story of Douglas MacArthur,* p. 482. Mr. Hunt adds, "It was the first time that the phrase 'privileged sanctuary' had been used in a public document." But it had been coined, ten days previously, by General MacArthur in a communique which Mr. Truman had, of course, seen.

2
I shall return.

Gen. Douglas MacArthur, *Message,* on leaving Corregidor for Australia, 11 March, 1942.

I came through and I shall return.

Gen. Douglas MacArthur, *Statement,* on arriving in Australia, 20 March, 1942.

People of the Philippines, I have returned.

Gen. Douglas MacArthur, *Radio Address,* upon landing at Leyte Island, 20 Oct., 1944.

3
It is fatal to enter any war without the will to win it.

Gen. Douglas MacArthur, *Speech,* Republican National Convention, 7 July, 1952.

4
Nuclear war is not an acceptable instrument of national policy.

John J. McCloy, Public Statement, as chairman of the U.S. General Advisory Committee on Disarmament, Jan., 1964.

5
All other sovereignties, united as one strength, shall compel the submission and performance of the sentence, with damages to the suffering party, and charges to the sovereignties that obliged their submission.

William Penn, *Essay Towards the Present and Future Peace of Europe* (c. 1670). The beginning of "collective security." Penn proposed the use of force against aggression, in spite of the fact that he was a Quaker. He suggested an annual General Assembly of governmental delegates empowered to consider all international disputes. If arbitration was refused or rejected, then the punishment outlined above was to go into effect.

In the event of aggression by one government against another, following a refusal to arbitrate the dispute, "then the remaining members of the League agree to join in the forcible defense of the member thus prematurely attacked."

William Howard Taft, *Speech,* at Cleveland, 12 May, 1915. Taft was proposing a "League of Peace," and the above was the last of four points he laid down to guide it.

For over forty years American statesmen, regardless of party, have agreed that the most effective way to prevent war is to make aggression unprofitable. Theodore Roosevelt advocated this as early as 1910.

Felix Morley, "Collective Security"; in *Barron's Magazine,* 5 Feb., 1951, p. 3. For "massive retaliation," see under Dulles, above.

6
No more war, war never again.

Pope Paul VI, *Address,* to the United Nations General Assembly, 4 Oct., 1965. The Pope urged this as the aim of the UN.

7
If you wish to be brothers, let the arms fall from your hands; one cannot love while holding offensive arms.

Pope Paul VI, *Address,* to the United Nations General Assembly, 4 Oct., 1965.

8
It seems unfortunately true that the epidemic of world lawlessness is spreading. When an epidemic of physical disease starts to spread, the community . . . joins in a quarantine of the patients in order to protect the health of the community against the spread of the disease.

FRANKLIN D. ROOSEVELT, *Speech,* at Chicago, October, 1937. The famous quarantine speech.

1
First, their countries seek no aggrandizement, territorial or otherwise. Second, they desire to see no territorial changes that do not accord with the freely expressed wishes of the people concerned.

FRANKLIN D. ROOSEVELT and WINSTON CHURCHILL, *The Atlantic Charter,* on U.S.S. *Augusta,* 14 Aug., 1941.

2
Dictatorship underestimates democracy's willingness to do what it has to do.

DEAN RUSK, on resistance to aggression. (HENRY F. GRAFF, "How Johnson Makes Foreign Policy"; *New York Times Magazine,* 4 July, 1965, p. 16)

3
We shall not find it possible to learn from World War III because there would not be enough left.

DEAN RUSK, *Address,* to the American Legion national convention, Portland, Ore., 24 Aug., 1965.

4
History shows that there are no invincible armies.

JOSEPH STALIN, *Address,* on declaration of war with Germany, 3 July, 1941.

5
The War That Will End War.

H. G. WELLS, *Title of Book,* published Oct., 1914.

I launched the phrase "The War to End War"—and that was not the least of my crimes.

H. G. WELLS, *Article,* in *Liberty Magazine,* 29 Dec., 1934, p. 4.

In that derided phrase which he seems to have invented, this was "the war to end war."

GEOFFREY WEST, *H. G. Wells,* p. 204 (1930). So Wells's claim seems to be well-founded. Woodrow Wilson, so far as known, never used the exact phrase. He came nearest it in two speeches at Portland, Oregon, 9 and 15 Sept., 1919: "This was a war to make similar wars impossible," and "It was a war to put an end to wars of aggression forever." *See* 2110:12.

WASHINGTON, GEORGE

6
Ten thousand people in the streets of Philadelphia, day after day, threatened to drag Washington out of his house, and effect a revolution in government, or compel it to declare war in favor of the French Revolution and against England.

JOHN ADAMS. See *Life and Works,* vol. x, p. 47. It was this agitation that persuaded Washington to make his famous Farewell Address. *See* 59: 9.

7
We have Rudyard's word that it [*If*] was drawn from the character of Dr. Jameson whom he had known for about ten years in Africa. . . . The poem was printed as an epilogue to the story [*Brother Square Toes*] in which Washington makes an appearance.

C. E. CARRINGTON, *The Life of Rudyard Kipling,* p. 297. It was no doubt because of the mention of Washington that the poem was supposed to relate to him. This is confirmed by Sir Roderick Jones, *A Life in Reuters,* p. 42. *See* 1930:11.

8
It was not very long before I discovered that he was neither remarkable for delicacy or good temper.

ALEXANDER HAMILTON, *Letter to Philip Schuyler,* 18 Feb., 1781.

9
If virtue can secure happiness in another world, he is happy.

ALEXANDER HAMILTON, *Letter to Tobias Lear,* 2 Jan., 1800.

10
His mind was great and powerful, without being of the very first order, . . . and as far as he saw, no judgment was ever sounder. . . . He was incapable of fear, meeting personal dangers with the calmest unconcern. His integrity was most pure, his justice the most inflexible I have ever known. . . . He was, indeed, in every sense of the words, a wise, a good, and a great man. . . . His person, you know, was fine, his stature exactly what one would wish, his deportment easy, erect and noble; the best horseman of his age, and the most graceful figure that could be seen on horseback. . . . His character was, in its mass, perfect, in nothing bad, in few points indifferent; and it may truly be said that never did nature and fortune combine more perfectly to make a man great, and to place him in the same constellation with whatever worthies have merited from men an everlasting remembrance.

THOMAS JEFFERSON, *Letter to Dr. Walter Jones,* 2 Jan., 1814. In a letter to W. B. Giles, in 1795, he had said, "He errs as other men do, but errs with integrity."

11
Few men lived whose opinions were more unbiased and correct. Not that it is pretended he never felt bias. His passions were naturally strong, but his reason, generally, stronger. . . . He possessed the love, veneration, and confidence of all.

THOMAS JEFFERSON, *The Anas,* 4 Feb., 1818. See PADOVER, *The Complete Jefferson,* p. 1205.

WINE

12
Wine and women and song,
  Three things garnish our way:
Yet is day over long.
Lest we do our youth wrong,

Gather them while we may:
Wine and women and song.

ERNEST DOWSON, *Villanelle of the Poet's Road.*

1

God made Man Frail as a bubble;
God made Love, Love made Trouble.
God made the Vine; Was it a sin
That Men made Wine To drown Trouble in?

OLIVER HERFORD, *A Plea.* (1929)

2
The wines that have given such celebrity to Burgundy grow only on the Côte, an extent of about five leagues long and half a league wide. They begin at Chambertin . . . and end at Montrachet. It is remarkable that the best of each kind, of the red and white, is made at the extremities of the line.

THOMAS JEFFERSON, *Notebook,* during his journey through Burgundy in 1787. Jefferson became a real connoisseur of wines. He never drank ardent spirits.

3
Our bitterest wine is always drained from crushed ideals.

ARTHUR STRINGER, *The Devastator.* (c. 1892)

Youth can afford ideals, being vigorous enough to stand the hard knocks they earn their possessor.

JAMES BRANCH CABELL, *Jurgen,* p. 64. (1919)

WOMAN

4
Women love the lie that saves their pride, but never an unflattering truth.

GERTRUDE ATHERTON, *The Conqueror.* Bk. iii, ch. 6. (1902)

5
Most women are not as young as they are painted.

MAX BEERBOHM, *A Defence of Cosmetics.* (c. 1910)

6
Her eyes had languorously opened, and then the lids had fallen, about half way, just as the eyelids of a woman ought to do when she is being kissed properly.

JAMES BRANCH CABELL, *Jurgen,* p. 47. (1919)

7
Her face was colored tenderly and softly: it made the faces of other women seem the work of a sign-painter.

JAMES BRANCH CABELL, *Jurgen,* p. 67.

8
A woman's honor is concerned with one thing only, and it is a thing with which the honor of a man is not concerned at all.

JAMES BRANCH CABELL, *Jurgen,* p. 63.

9
She was a woman who, between courses, could be graceful with her elbows on the table.

HENRY JAMES, *The Ambassadors,* p. 212. (1902)

10
When Milly smiled it was a public event—when she didn't it was a chapter of history.

HENRY JAMES, *The Wings of the Dove,* p. 132. (1902)

11
I want to make a policy statement. I am unabashedly in favor of women.

LYNDON B. JOHNSON, *Speech,* 4 Apr., 1964, announcing a series of appointments of women to high posts in the government.

I believe a woman's place not only is in the home, but in the House and Senate and throughout the government. One thing we are insisting on is that we not have this stag government.

LYNDON B. JOHNSON, *Speech,* in Washington, D.C., 3 Mar., 1964, on awarding prizes to women for work in government.

To conclude that women are unfitted to the task of our historic society seems to me the equivalent of closing male eyes to female facts.

LYNDON B. JOHNSON, *Speech,* in Washington, D.C., 13 Apr., 1964.

12
A woman's guess is much more accurate than a man's certainty.

RUDYARD KIPLING, *Plain Tales from the Hills: Three and an Extra.* (1888)

13
The women-swamped tennis parties and tea-fights of the village.

RUDYARD KIPLING, *Soldiers Three: Only a Subaltern.* (1888) Oliver Wendell Holmes had previously described a tea-fight as "Giggle, gabble, gobble, git."

14
The blush that flies at seventeen
Is fixed at forty-nine.

RUDYARD KIPLING, *My Rival.* (1885) *See also* 172:6.

15
Although the story goes that woman was contrived from Adam's rib, I have a different theory. In her public sense, she sprang full-panoplied out of his imagination.

PHYLLIS MCGINLEY, *The Province of the Heart: Some of My Best Friends . . . ,* p. 103. (1959)

16
Women like other women fine. The more feminine she is, the more comfortable a woman feels with her own sex. It is only the occasional and therefore noticeable adventuress who refuses to make friends with us.

PHYLLIS MCGINLEY, *The Province of the Heart: Some of My Best Friends . . . ,* p. 103.

WRITING

17
He must teach himself that the basest of all things is to be afraid; and, teaching himself that, forget it forever, leaving no room in his workshop for anything but the old verities and truths of the heart, the old universal truths lacking which any story is ephemeral and doomed—love and honor and pity and pride and compassion and sacrifice.

WILLIAM FAULKNER, *Address,* in Stockholm,

10 Dec., 1950, upon receiving the Nobel Prize in literature. A statement of the writer's creed.

1
Writing, at its best, is a lonely life. Organizations for writers palliate the writer's loneliness, but I doubt if they improve his writing. He grows in public stature as he sheds his loneliness and after his work deteriorates. For he does his work alone and if he is a good enough writer he must face eternity, or the lack of it, each day.

ERNEST HEMINGWAY, *Address,* prepared for his acceptance of the Nobel Prize in literature, 10 Dec., 1954.

2
I put the words down and push them a bit.

EVELYN WAUGH. (New York *Times* and United Press International obituaries of Waugh, 11 Apr., 1966)

MISCELLANEOUS

3
Ruthlessly pricking our gonfalon bubble,
Making a Giant hit into a double,
Words that are weighty with nothing but trouble:
"Tinker to Evers to Chance."

FRANKLIN P. ADAMS, *Baseball's Sad Lexicon.* *See* 2297:6.

4
Sob, heavy world, Sob as you spin,
Mantled in mist, remote from the happy.

W. H. AUDEN, *The Age of Anxiety.* (c. 1945)

5
We'll to the woods no more,
They've cut the laurels down.
(*Nous n'irons pas aux bois, les lauriers sont coupés.*)

THÉODORE DE BANVILLE, *Les Cariatides; Les Stalactites.* (c. 1890)

6
Speed, bonnie boat, like a bird on the wing;
Onward, the sailors cry:
Carry the lad that's born to be King
Over the sea to Skye.

HARRY E. BOULTON, *Skye Boat Song.* The lad was Prince Charles Edward, the Young Pretender, whom Flora Macdonald spirited over to Skye, 27 June, 1746, after his defeat at Culloden. Boswell and Dr. Johnson met her in September, 1773, during their famous journey to the Hebrides, and Boswell says, "To see Mr. Samuel Johnson salute Miss Flora Macdonald was a wonderful romantic scene to me." She was at that time 51 years of age. *See also* 258:2.

Make no little plans: they have no magic to stir men's blood. . . . Make big plans, aim high in hope and work.

DANIEL H. BURNHAM, *Article,* in *Christian Science Monitor,* 18 Jan., 1927, p. 6. Burnham, who was an architect, is referring to his plans for the city of Chicago.

8
It is wrong to be too right.

SAMUEL BUTLER, *Notebooks,* p. 54. (c. 1890)

9
He is greatest who is most often in good men's thoughts.

SAMUEL BUTLER, *Notebooks,* p. 147.

10
It is the function of vice to keep virtue within reasonable bounds.

SAMUEL BUTLER, *Notebooks,* p. 219.

11
The course of true anything never does run smooth.

SAMUEL BUTLER, *Notebooks,* p. 220.

12
Conscience is thoroughly well-bred and soon leaves off talking to those who do not wish to hear it.

SAMUEL BUTLER, *Notebooks,* p. 250.

13
True consistency, that of the prudent and the wise, is to act in conformity with circumstances, and not to act always the same way under a change of circumstances.

JOHN C. CALHOUN, *Speech on Joint Occupancy,* 16 March, 1848.

14
Always there is a black spot in our sunshine; it is even, as I said, the *Shadow of Ourselves.*

THOMAS CARLYLE, *Sartor Resartus.* Bk. ii, sc. 2, par. 11. (1835)

15
Dictators ride to and fro upon tigers from which they dare not dismount. And the tigers are getting hungry.

WINSTON CHURCHILL, *While England Slept* (1936)

16
Yes! let the proud despise, the rich deride
These simple joys to Competence allied:
To me, they bloom, all fragrant to my heart,
Nor ask the pomp of wealth, nor gloss of art.

TIMOTHY DWIGHT, *Greenfield Hill.* (1794)

17
There is that destroyeth his own soul through bashfulness.

O.T. Apocrapha: Ecclesiasticus, xx, 22. (c. 200 B.C.)

18
Billy, in one of his nice new sashes,
Fell in the fire and burnt to ashes;
Now, although the room grows chilly,
I haven't the heart to poke poor Billy.

HARRY GRAHAM, *Ruthless Rhymes for Heartless Homes: Tender-heartedness.* (1899)

19
Self-preservation is the first principle of our nature.

ALEXANDER HAMILTON, *Full Vindication,* 15 Dec., 1774.

20
I sincerely wish ingratitude was not so natural to the human heart as it is.

ALEXANDER HAMILTON, *Letter to George Washington,* 25 March, 1783.

1
A promise must never be broken.
ALEXANDER HAMILTON, *Letter to His Son, Philip*, aged 10, 5 Dec., 1791.

2
We must make the best of those ills which cannot be avoided.
ALEXANDER HAMILTON, *Letter to Mrs. Hamilton*, 20 Feb., 1801.

3
I said to the man who stood at the gate of the year.
MINNIE LOUISE HASKINS, *The Desert: Introduction. The Desert,* a thin volume of verse, had been printed privately to aid an Indian charity, while Miss Haskins was engaged in educational work in India. The lines were given fleeting fame by King George VI, of England, who had chanced to see them on a Christmas card that had been reprinted in *The Times,* of London. Miss Haskins at the time was employed as a teacher in the London School of Economics. She died at her home in Tunbridge Wells, in February, 1957, at the age of 81. *See* 2298g:1, of which this is a continuation.

4
During the next thousand years no revolution will take place in Germany.
ADOLF HITLER, *Address,* at party rally, Sept., 1934.

5
Note how perverse is the attitude of the weak toward their benefactors. They feel generosity as oppression; they want to retaliate. They say to their benefactors, "May the day come when you shall be weak and we will send bundles to America."
ERIC HOFFER, *The Passionate State of Mind,* p. 29. (1954)

6
Rudeness is the weak man's imitation of strength.
ERIC HOFFER, *The Passionate State of Mind,* p. 138.

7
He [Daniel Drew] seems never to have denied his most celebrated piece of knavery, which he used in his cattle business for many years. As a big herd of anywhere from six hundred to a thousand head of Ohio beef approached New York City, Drew had his drovers salt them well, then, just before reaching the market place, he let them drink their fill. Cattle were sold live-weight. Drew's processing with salt and water added many tons to the average herd. "Watered stock" soon became a term in Wall Street.
STEWART H. HOLBROOK, *The Age of the Moguls,* p. 21. (1953)

8
The folks that on the first of May
Wore winter coats and hose,
Began to say, the first of June,
"Good Lord! how hot it grows!"
OLIVER WENDELL HOLMES, *The Hot Season.* (c. 1830)

9
The Bird's nest, mark it well within, without;
No tool had he that wrought, no knife to cut,
No nail to fix, no bodkin to insert,
No glue to join: his little beak was all.
JAMES HURDIS, *The Village Curate,* p. 44. (1797)

10
Europe, the great American sedative.
HENRY JAMES, *The Wings of the Dove,* p. 129. (1902)

11
I believe we may safely affirm that the inexperienced and presumptuous band of medical tyros let loose upon the world destroys more of human life in one year than all the Robin Hoods, Cartouches, and MacHeaths do in a century.
THOMAS JEFFERSON, *Letter to Jasper Wistar,* 21 June, 1807.

12
Like William James, he [Henry George] saw success as a bitch-goddess and simply did not like her company.
GERALD W. JOHNSON, *The Lunatic Fringe,* p. 111. *See also* 1931:9.

13
It is better to light one candle than to curse the darkness.
FATHER JAMES KELLER, *One Moment Please: Preface.* (1950) The motto of the Christophers. (See *N.Y. Herald Tribune,* 10 Feb., 1957.) The sentence is in quotation marks and there has been no reply to an inquiry by the compiler as to its origin. Legend says that Saint Christopher (Christ-bearer), a martyr of the third century, devoted himself, as a penance for having been a servant of the devil, to carrying pilgrims across a river where there was no bridge, and one day carried the Christ child across without knowing who He was until he reached mid-stream. Hence he is the patron saint of travellers.

What is it the Christophers say? Something about it being better to light one candle than to curse the darkness.
DAVID KARP, *Leave Me Alone,* p. 293. (1947)

14
The one dominant quality that should shine forth in everyone who would be a Christopher is Love—love of God and love of all men.
FATHER JAMES KELLER, *One Moment Please,* p. 7.

15
The meek, the terrible meek, the fierce agonizing meek, are about to enter into their inheritance.
CHARLES RANN KENNEDY, *The Terrible Meek.* (1912)

16
He became an officer and a gentleman, which is an enviable thing.
RUDYARD KIPLING, *Soldiers Three: Only a Subaltern.* (1888)

1
Ticker tape ain't spaghetti.
FIORELLO LA GUARDIA, *Speech,* to United Nations Relief and Rehabilitation Commission, 29 March, 1946.

2
People everywhere confuse
What they read in newspapers with news.
A. J. LIEBLING, *A Talkative Something or Other.* (*New Yorker,* 7 April, 1956, p. 154.)

3
By the shore of Gitchie Gumee,
By the Shining Big-Sea-Water,
At the doorway of his wigwam,
In the pleasant summer morning,
Hiawatha stood and waited.
H. W. LONGFELLOW, *The Song of Hiawatha.* Pt. xxii, l. 1. (1855)

4
The French never allow a distinguished son of France to lack a statue.
E. V. LUCAS, *Wanderings and Diversions: Zigzags in France.* (1926) *See also* 720:14.

5
He who makes a garden
Works hand in hand with God.
DOUGLAS MALLOCH, *Who Makes a Garden.* (c. 1930)

6
Opinions cannot survive if one has no chance to fight for them.
THOMAS MANN, *The Magic Mountain.* Ch. vi. (1924)

7
The world belongs to the enthusiast who keeps cool.
WILLIAM MCFEE, *Casuals of the Sea.* Bk. i, p. 14. (c. 1940)

8
As I was going up the stair
I met a man who wasn't there.
He wasn't there again today.
I wish, I wish he'd stay away.
HUGHES MEARNS, *The Psychoed.*

9
Time is a great legalizer, even in the field of morals.
H. L. MENCKEN, *A Book of Prefaces.* Ch. iv, sec. 6. (1917)

10
Coward, take my coward hand.
EVE MERRIAM, *The Coward.* Quoted by ARTHUR LAURENTS, *Home of the Brave,* p. 92.

11
How shall I know, unless I go
To China and Cathay,
Whether or not this blessed spot
Is blest in every way?
EDNA ST. VINCENT MILLAY, *To the Not Impossible Him.* (1920)

12
Knowledge humanizes mankind, and reason inclines to mildness; but prejudices eradicate every tender disposition.
MONTESQUIEU, *Spirit of Laws.* Bk. xv, ch. 3. (1748)

13
All the News That's Fit to Print.
ADOLPH S. OCHS, *Motto of the New York Times.* Ochs was publisher of the *Times,* and he and his editors had tentatively chosen this slogan, which Ochs had coined, but in the hope of getting a better one offered a prize of $100 for a slogan of not more than ten words. Richard Watson Gilder, editor of the *Century Magazine,* consented to judge the contest, but though thousands of entries were received, the one coined by Ochs was judged to be the best. It was first printed on the editorial page 25 Oct., 1896. On 10 Feb., 1897, it was put on the front page in the spot it still occupies.

14
I took Panama without consulting the Cabinet.
THEODORE ROOSEVELT, *Memoirs,* referring to the revolution 1 Nov., 1903, by which Panama became a republic.

15
Man is born free, and everywhere he is in chains. (L'homme est né libre, et partout il est dans les fers.)
JEAN-JACQUES ROUSSEAU, *Du Contrat Social,* Ch. i. The famous opening sentence.

16
I never lamented about the vicissitudes of time or complained of the turns of fortune except on the occasion when I was barefooted and unable to procure slippers. But when I entered the great mosque of Kufah with a sore heart, and beheld a man without feet, I offered thanks to the bounty of God.
SADI, *Tales from the Gulistan,* p. 130. (c. 1250)

I cried because I had no shoes, until I beheld a man who had no feet.
ROBERT KASS, *Film and TV. Catholic World,* July, 1954, p. 303. CHAMPION, *Racial Proverbs,* has "I had no shoes and I murmured, till I met a man who had no feet." Said to be the credo of Helen Keller's life.

17
There comes a time when a man is too honest to teach. It is not an honest profession.
ALFRED SLOTS, *Lazarus in Vienna,* p. 6. (1956)

18
Pride is pleasure springing from a man thinking too highly of himself.
BARUCH SPINOZA, *Ethics.* Pt. iii, def. 28. (1674)

19
Minds are not conquered by arms, but by love and generosity.
BARUCH SPINOZA. Pt. iv, Appendix 11.

20
The human mind cannot be absolutely destroyed with the body, but something of it remains which is eternal.
BARUCH SPINOZA, *Ethics.* Pt. v, prop. 23.

21
The business of the state is security for its citizens and nothing else.
BARUCH SPINOZA, *Ethics.* (1674) See RUNES, *Road to Inner Freedom,* p. 11.

Of all the tasks of government, the most basic is to protect its citizens against violence.

JOHN FOSTER DULLES, *Speech,* before the Associated Press annual luncheon, 22 April, 1957.

There can be no truer principle than this—that every individual of the community at large has an equal right to the protection of government.

ALEXANDER HAMILTON, *Address,* in Constitutional Convention, 29 June, 1787.

1
Why level downward to our dullest perception always, and praise that as common sense? The commonest sense is the sense of men asleep, which they express by snoring.

H. D. THOREAU, *Walden: Conclusion,* par. 7. (1854)

2
When he who speaks understands nothing and he who listens understands even less, that's metaphysics (Quand celui qui parle n'entend rien et celui qui écoute n'entend plus, c'est métaphysique.)

VOLTAIRE. Quoted in *The Quarterly Review,* No. 302, April, 1881.

3
Nothing can make an aristocrat but pride, knowledge, training, and the sword.

H. G. WELLS, *Tono-Bungay.* Ch. ii, ces. 8. (1908) *See also* 72:1.

4
An angel's heart, an angel's mouth,
Not Homer's, could alone for me
Hymn well the great Confederate South,
Virginia first, and Lee.

PHILIP STANHOPE WORSLEY, *R. E. Lee.* Last stanza. Quoted by JOHN WILLIAM JONES, *Reminiscences of General Robert E. Lee,* p. 78. (1875)

INDEX OF AUTHORS

SUGGESTIONS FOR USING THE INDEX OF AUTHORS

The INDEX OF AUTHORS includes the name of every person quoted in this book, together with the dates of his birth and death, and a brief characterization giving his nationality and occupation. (A blank death date indicates that the person was still living May 6, 1958, when this index was completed.) Where these biographical data are missing or incomplete, the editor will greatly appreciate information which will enable him to fill them in.

If the number of quotations from an author's works does not exceed 150, the pages on which the quotations appear are also given. If the number is in excess of 150, the name is preceded by a star. There are a few exceptions to this, the quotations from W. S. Gilbert, Thomas Jefferson, Rudyard Kipling, Bernard Shaw, Robert Louis Stevenson, H. D. Thoreau, Mark Twain, Voltaire, Walt Whitman, and Oscar Wilde being listed in full because of the special interest in their work. It was felt that to list the quotations from all authors would encumber the index unreasonably; those from such writers as Shakespeare and Pope, for example, number perhaps a thousand, and the figures listing them would occupy nearly four columns of space.

There are four ways in which the index may be used to advantage:

(1) To check the quotations from any author's work.

(2) To find a quotation where the author is remembered, but the quotation itself only indistinctly. For example, if one is searching for a quotation by Walt Whitman and all that is remembered is that it has something to do with the sea, one need only look up the quotations by Whitman between pages 1771 and 1782.

(3) To ascertain what any author has to say on any given subject. If one wishes to know what Oscar Wilde has to say about women, for instance, the Wilde quotations should be consulted for pages 2178–2208.

(4) To find a quotation whose supposed key-word cannot be turned up in the CONCORDANCE, but whose author is known. Key-words are sometimes wrongly remembered, or perhaps the editor has chosen some other word in the quotation as the most important. Again it is only necessary to check the quotations by the author in question, in the section in which the desired quotation would naturally fall.

The following abbreviations are used: b. = born; c. = circa, about; d. = died; fl. = flourished, indicating an author's period when his exact dates are not known; pseud. = pseudonym.

INDEX OF AUTHORS

See also page 2417 for index to recent additions.

ALI BEN ABOU TALEB, son-in-law of Mahomet. (c. 600–661)
735.
ALISON, SIR ARCHIBALD, English historian. (1792–1867)
720.
ALLAINVAL, LÉONOR JEAN, French dramatic poet. (c. 1700–1753)
1717.
ALLEGRI, ALESSANDRO, Italian poet. (fl. 1596)
470.
ALLEN, [MRS.] ELIZABETH AKERS, American verse-writer. (1832–1911)
540, 1048, 1857, 2011.
ALLEN, ETHAN, American revolutionary soldier. (1737–1789)
61.
ALLEN, FRED (JOHN F. SULLIVAN), American radio and screen comedian. (1894–1956)
1545.
ALLEN, FREDERICK LEWIS, American magazine editor (1890–1954)
593, 1174, 1362, 1644.
ALLEN, HERVEY, American poet and novelist. (1889–1949)
769, 2008.
ALLEN, JAMES LANE, American novelist. (1849–1925)
1083.
ALLEN, WILLIAM, American lawyer and politician, Governor of Ohio. (1803–1879)
1557.
ALLERTON, [MRS.] ELLEN PALMER, American verse-writer. (1835–1893)
131.
ALLINGHAM, WILLIAM, English poet. (1824–1889)
106, 117, 150, 186, 404, 588, 614, 676, 732, 733, 1126, 1210, 1219, 1337, 1610, 1735, 1777, 1831, 1849, 1862, 1905, 1936, 2249.
ALLOTT, ROBERT, English editor. (fl. 1600)
2155.
ALLSTON, WASHINGTON, American painter and poet. (1779–1843)
61, 624, 1447.
ALPHEIUS OF MITYLENE, Greek epigrammatist.
912.
ALPHONSO, see ALFONSO
ALTGELD, JOHN PETER, American reformer and politician, Governor of Illinois. (1847–1902)
1477.
AMBROSE, SAINT, Latin prelate, Bishop of Milan. (c. 340–397)
792, 1345, 1425, 1737, 1900.
AMELIA, PRINCESS, daughter of George III. (1783–1810)
2266.
AMES, EDWARD SCRIBNER, American clergyman and educator. (1870–)
1692.
AMES, FISHER, American statesman and orator. (1758–1808)
1379, 2098.
AMES, OAKES, American capitalist and politician. (1804–1873)
1551.
AMIEL, HENRI-FRÉDÉRIC, Swiss philosopher and critic. (1828–1881)
7, 26, 42, 101, 106, 146, 150, 280, 374, 438, 457, 475, 577, 616, 720, 761, 830, 833, 841, 854, 895, 925, 936, 977, 980, 1026, 1036, 1115, 1144, 1253, 1440, 1688, 1844, 1926, 1961, 1969, 1973, 1978, 2048, 2049, 2052, 2162, 2182, 2206, 2232, 2246.
AMMIANUS MARCELLINUS, Latin historian. (fl. 350)
127, 336, 434, 1043, 1931, 2055, 2057.
ANACHARSIS, Scythian philosopher. (fl. c. 600 B.C.)
208, 216, 426, 492, 544, 654, 726, 1026, 1085, 1306, 1326, 2023.
ANACREON, Greek amatory lyric poet. (c. 563–478 B.C.)
138, 361, 494, 1196, 2119.
ANAXAGORAS, Greek philosopher and scientist. (500–428 B.C.)
414, 892.
ANAXANDRIDES, Greek comic poet. (fl. 370 B.C.)
1267.
ANAXIMANDER, Greek physical philosopher and mathematician. (c. 611–547 B.C.)
585.
ANDERSEN, HANS CHRISTIAN, Danish poet, dramatist, novelist and writer of fairy tales. (1805–1875)
1125.
ANDERSON, ALEXANDER (pseud., SURFACEMAN), Scottish poet. (1845–1909)
1846.
ANDERSON, JUDITH, American actress, born in Australia. (1898–)
1253.
ANDERSON, MAXWELL, American playwright. (1888–1959)
436, 1046, 1187.
ANDERSON, MAXWELL, and STALLINGS, LAURENCE, American dramatists. (1888–1959), (1894–)
1640.
ANDERSON, N. D., contemporary American writer.
175.
ANDERSON, W. R., English writer on music.
582.
ANDRÉ, MAJOR JOHN, English officer executed as a spy during the American Revolution. (1751–1780)
62.
ANDREW, JOHN ALBION, Governor of Massachusetts during Civil War. (1818–1867)
2021, 2034.
ANDREWES, LANCELOT, English prelate, Bishop of Winchester. (1555–1626)
2056.
ANDREWS, JOHN, English poet. (fl. 1615)
813.
ANDRIEUX, FRANÇOIS GUILLAUME JEAN STANISLAUS, French scholar and dramatist. (1759–1833)
1040.

ANHALT-DESSAU, LEOPOLD, DUKE OF, Prussian Field-Marshal under Prince Eugène. (1676–1747)
2115.

ANNAN, ANNIE RANKIN [MRS. WILLIAM H. GLENNY], American verse-writer. (1848–1925)
362.

ANNANDALE, R. B., see LINDSAY, WALTER

ANNE OF AUSTRIA, Queen of France. (1601–1666)
1708.

ANSTEY, CHRISTOPHER, English poet. (1724–1805)
478, 892, 988, 1099, 1859.

ANSTEY, F. (pseud. of THOMAS ANSTEY GUTHRIE), English humorist. (1856–1934)
1890.

ANSTICE, JOSEPH, English classical scholar. (1808–1836)
514.

ANTHONY, EDWARD, American miscellaneous writer. (1895–)
254.

ANTIGONOUS (or ANTIGONUS) I, one of Alexander's generals, King of Sparta. (382?–301 B.C.)
897, 982, 1923.

ANTIPATER, Regent of Macedonia during the absence of Alexander the Great in Persia. (d. 319 B.C.)
913, 1565, 1771.

ANTIPHANES, Greek comic poet. (fl. 360 B.C.)
106, 820, 1783.

ANTIPHILUS OF BYZANTIUM, Greek epigrammatist.
911.

ANTIPHON, Greek orator. (480–411 B.C.)
2008.

ANTISTHENES, Greek philosopher, founder of the Cynic school. (fl. c. 400 B.C.)
1040, 1095.

ANTONINUS, MARCUS AURELIUS, see MARCUS AURELIUS

APELLES, Greek painter, favored by Alexander the Great. (fl. 325 B.C.)
1817.

APOLLONIDES, Greek epigrammatic poet, date unknown.
1874.

APOLLONIUS RHODIUS, Greek rhetorician, scholar and poet. (c. 295–215 B.C.)
815, 1117, 1972.

APOSTOLIUS, MICHAEL, Greek theologian and rhetorician. (d. 1480)
169, 1779.

APPIUS CLAUDIUS, see CLAUDIUS

APPLETON, EVERARD JOHN, American poet and newspaper columnist. (1872–1931)
611, 982, 2188.

APPLETON, THOMAS GOLD, American wit, scholar and verse-writer. (1812–1884)
144, 194, 1452.

APULEIUS, Roman satirist and philosopher. (fl. 2nd century)
134, 479, 631, 699, 849, 964.

AQUAVIVA, CLAUDIO, Italian general of the Society of Jesus. (1543–1615)
766.

AQUINAS, SAINT THOMAS, Italian philosopher and scholastical teacher; a Dominican monk. (c. 1225–1274)
181, 307, 2096.

ARATUS, Greek poet and astronomer. (c. 300–250 B.C.)
789.

ARBLAY, MADAME D', see BURNEY, FRANCES

ARBUCKLE, MACLYN, American actor. (1866–1931)
647.

ARBUTHNOT, JOHN, English physician and wit. (1667–1735)
159, 170, 546, 818, 849, 906, 1080, 1543, 2003.

ARCHER, FRANK, American railway conductor and song-writer.
1350.

ARCHESTRATUS, Greek naturalistic poet. (fl. 330 B.C.)
450.

ARCHIAS, AULUS LICINIUS, Greek poet and epigrammatist. (c. 199– ? B.C.)
206.

ARCHIDAMUS III, King of Sparta. (fl. 350 B.C.)
1803.

ARCHILOCHUS, Greek poet and satirist. (fl. 648 B.C.)
456.

ARCHIMEDES, Syracusan geometrician. (287–212 B.C.)
273, 414, 1573, 1928.

ARCHYTAS OF TARENTUM, general, mathematician and Pythagorean philosopher. (fl. c. 400 B.C.)
1511.

ARETINO, PIETRO, Italian playwright. (1492–1556)
988.

ARIOSTO, LUDOVICO, Italian poet, author of *Orlando Furioso*. (1474–1533)
438, 489, 501, 634, 787, 906, 1424, 1486, 2083, 2186, 2196.

ARIPHON THE SICYONIAN, Greek poet. (c. 550 B.C.)
871.

ARISTIDES, Greek general and statesman. (fl. 450 B.C.)
199, 544, 1106, 1822, 1867.

ARISTIPPUS, Greek philosopher, founder of the Cyrenaic school. (425?–366? B.C.)
531, 1498, 1673, 1922.

ARISTODEMUS, semi-legendary ruler of Messenia. (fl. 750 B.C.)
1332.

ARISTOPHANES, Greek comic poet and satirist. (444–380 B.C.)
27, 106, 218, 237, 281, 283, 320, 541, 970, 1051, 1249, 1437, 1441, 1531, 1808, 1876, 1899, 2164, 2186, 2219.

ARISTOTLE, Greek philosopher. (384–322 B.C.)
80, 85, 128, 146, 156, 230, 234, 242, 260, 289, 319, 423, 430, 435, 528, 648, 698, 726, 729, 738, 761, 804, 823, 845, 846, 854, 921, 1019, 1027, 1079, 1112, 1240, 1247, 1265,

Ballantine, James, English artist and miscellaneous writer. (1803–1877)
222, 256, 445, 1647, 2100.

Ballou, Hosea, American preacher, founder of Universalism. (1771–1852)
859, 865, 952, 1670, 1926, 2069.

Ballou, Maturin Murray, American journalist and writer of travel books. (1820–1895)
682.

Balzac, Honoré de, French novelist. (1799–1850)
212, 409, 462, 581, 782, 823, 861, 1000, 1124, 2239.

Bampfylde, John Codrington, English poet. (1754–1796)
1362.

Bancks, or Banks, John, English miscellaneous writer. (1709–1751)
2152.

Bancroft, George, American historian. (1800–1891)
36, 1041, 1658.

Bancroft, Richard, English prelate, Archbishop of Canterbury. (1544–1610)
272.

Bangs, Edward, American judge and reputed author of *Yankee Doodle*. (fl. 1775)
61.

Bangs, John Kendrick, American humorous writer. (1862–1922)
1017, 1018, 1499, 1776.

Banks, George Linnæus, English miscellaneous writer. (1821–1881)
1660.

Banville, Théodore de, French poet and parodist, "roi des rimes." (1823–1891)
2159.

Barbauld, Anna Letitia, English poet and miscellaneous writer. (1743–1825)
393, 403, 550, 927, 1146, 1182, 1302, 1348, 1749, 1862, 1915, 2217.

Barbour, John, Scottish poet. (1316?–1395)
88, 666, 722, 1187.

Barca, see Hamilcar

Barclay, Alexander, English poet, scholar and divine. (1475?–1552)
167, 326, 327, 699, 713, 733, 898, 1155, 1216, 1322, 1608, 1770, 1960, 2032, 2226.

Barclay, William, Scottish jurist. (1546 or 1547–1608)
1019.

Barère, Bertrand, French Jacobin revolutionist. (1755–1841)
388, 548, 899, 1104.

Baret, or Barret, John, English lexicographer. (d. 1580?)
656.

Barham, Richard Harris, English divine, author of *Ingoldsby Legends*. (1788–1845)
75, 85, 113, 195, 252, 353, 408, 417, 448, 466, 472, 501, 580, 686, 769, 819, 820, 928, 930, 1012, 1034, 1043, 1247, 1340, 1412, 1413, 1482, 1487, 1592, 1637, 1765, 1766, 1933, 1934, 1941, 2006, 2012, 2017, 2018, 2128, 2146, 2188, 2211, 2265.

Baring, Evelyn, first Earl of Cromer, English statesman and man of letters. (1841–1917)
1816.

Baring, Maurice, English poet and essayist. (1874–1945)
457.

Baring-Gould, Sabine, English clergyman and miscellaneous writer. (1834–1924)
267, 1843.

Barker, Elsa, American poet. (1869–1954)
617.

Barker, Matthew, English nonconformist divine. (1619–1698)
1243.

Barker, Squire Omar, American journalist and verse-writer. (1894–)
2150.

Barker, Thomas, English poet. (fl. 1651)
671.

Barlow, Joel, American poet, patriot and diplomatist. (1755–1812)
524, 861.

Barnard, Lady Anne, English poet. (1750–1825)
1270, 1350, 1846.

Barnard, Charlotte Alington (Claribel), English ballad-writer. (1830–1869)
1878, 1881.

Barnard, George Grey, American sculptor. (1863–1938)
1890.

Barnes, Barnabe, English poet. (1569?–1609)
309, 700.

Barnes, William, Dorsetshire poet. (1801–1886)
167, 182, 1417, 2138.

Barnfield, Richard, English poet. (1574–1627)
32, 227, 629, 713, 735, 737, 739, 762, 803, 1172, 1282, 1334, 1362, 1404, 1523, 1804, 1903, 2221.

Barr, Mary A., Scottish writer. (1852– ?)
1559.

Barr, Matthias, Scottish poet. (1831– ?)
120.

Barrett, Eaton Stannard, English poetical writer. (1786–1820)
1633, 2183.

Barrett, Lawrence Patrick, American actor. (1838–1891)
8.

Barretto, Laurence Brevoort (Larry), American miscellaneous writer. (1890–)
120.

Barrie, Sir James Matthew, Scottish novelist and dramatist. (1860–1937)
1, 94, 106, 154, 244, 284, 323, 345, 398, 501, 564, 589, 614, 658, 704, 757, 758, 778, 876, 885, 1006, 1013, 1115, 1176, 1192, 1585, 1612, 1660, 1703, 1735, 1768, 1769, 1798, 1923, 1963, 1994, 2017, 2137, 2172, 2182, 2186, 2206, 2241, 2262.

Barrington, George (real name Waldron), English pickpocket and writer; transported to Australia. (1755– ?)
1467.

BARRINGTON, BISHOP SHUTE, English divine and religious writer. (1734–1826)
746.
BARROW, ISAAC, English divine and mathematical and classical scholar. (1630–1677)
1796.
BARRY, or BARREY, LODOWICK, English dramatist. (fl. 17th century)
94, 2136.
BARRY, MICHAEL JOSEPH, Irish barrister. (1817–1889)
396, 1954.
BARTHÉLEMY, AUGUSTE MARSEILLE, French poet and politician. (1796–1867)
304
BARTHOLIN, THOMAS, Danish physician and scholar. (1616–1680)
183.
BARTLETT, WILLIAM O., American journalist. (1812–1881)
1396, 1551.
BARTOL, CYRUS AUGUSTUS, American Unitarian clergyman. (1813–1900)
722, 757, 851, 921, 1832.
BARTON, BERNARD, English poet of Quaker parentage. (1784–1849)
1788, 2220.
BARTON, BRUCE, American writer and publicist. (1886–)
294.
BASHFORD, [SIR] HENRY HOWARTH, English physician and miscellaneous writer. (1880–)
1167.
BASHFORD, HERBERT, American librarian and verse-writer. (1871–1928)
120.
BASHŌ, Japanese poet, celebrated especially for his *hokku*. (1644–1694)
1488.
BASIL, one of the four Greek doctors, Bishop of Cæsarea. (329?–379)
921.
BASSE, or BAS, WILLIAM, English poet. (d. 1653?)
1804.
BASSELIN, OLIVIER, French dyer and reputed author of *Vaux de Vire*. (c. 1400–c. 1450)
1412.
BASSETT, JOHN SPENCER, American historian. (1867–1928)
1541.
BASSUS, LOLLIUS, Greek poet. (fl. A.D. 20)
406.
BASTARD, THOMAS, English satirist and divine. (1566–1618)
539, 1810.
BATES, KATHARINE LEE, American educator and poet. (1859–1929)
51, 472, 1207, 2109, 2150.
BATES, LEWIS J., American poet. (1832– ?)
1016, 1023, 1431, 1434.
BAUDELAIRE, CHARLES, French poet. (1821–1867)
106, 828, 1232.
BAUM, VICKI, German novelist. (1888–)
628, 1011, 1262, 1503, 2206.
BAXTER, RICHARD, English divine and religious writer. (1615–1691)
363, 891, 920, 1126, 1147, 1248, 1317, 1593, 1606, 1674, 1694, 1718, 1756, 1800, 1980, 2028, 2172.
BAYARD, PIERRE DU TERRAIL, SEIGNEUR DE, French captain in the Italian campaigns of Charles VIII. (1476–1524)
259, 1281.
BAYARD, JEAN FRANÇOIS ALFRED, and DUMANOIR, PHILIPPE FRANÇOIS PINEL, French dramatists. (1796–1853), (1806–1865)
1463.
BAYLE, BERNARD, English dramatist. (fl. 1854)
1920.
BAYLE, PIERRE, French philosopher and critic. (1647–1706)
1666.
BAYLY, ADA ELLEN, see LYALL, EDNA
BAYLY, THOMAS HAYNES, English poet and miscellaneous writer. (1797–1839)
2, 124, 170, 211, 269, 317, 359, 482, 708, 739, 1288, 1370, 1375, 1485, 1647, 1722, 1743, 1747, 1774, 1878, 1959, 2190, 2211.
BEACON, JOHN, English clergyman. (fl. 1831)
1437.
BEACONSFIELD, see DISRAELI
BEADLE, J. H., American writer. (fl. 1860)
1954.
BEALS, CARLETON, American writer and lecturer. (1893–)
2107.
BEALS, EDWARD E., contemporary American economist.
1334.
BEARD, CHARLES AUSTIN, American educator and historian. (1874–1948)
1114.
BEATTIE, JAMES, Scottish poet. (1735–1803)
27, 135, 162, 238, 311, 580, 581, 617, 628, 644, 707, 715, 827, 959, 964, 1088, 1112, 1303, 1315, 1342, 1363, 1368, 1422, 1492, 1578, 1670, 1706, 1764, 1773, 1794, 1835, 1878, 1905, 1961, 1994, 2042, 2055, 2164.
BEAUMARCHAIS, PIERRE AUGUSTE CARON DE, French dramatist. (1732–1799)
163, 214, 744, 1077, 1288, 1414, 1678, 1875, 1876, 2172.
BEAUMONT, FRANCIS, English dramatist. (1584–1616)
448, 828, 2131, 2226.
* BEAUMONT, FRANCIS, and FLETCHER, JOHN, English dramatists and collaborators. (1584–1616), (1579–1625)
BEAUMONT, SIR JOHN, English poet. (1583–1627)
1403.
BEAUMONT, DR. JOSEPH, English educator and poet. (1616–1699)
42.
BEAUVAIS, JEAN B. C. M., French prelate, Bishop of Senez. (1731–1790)
1821.
BECCARIA, CESARE BONESANO, MARCHESE DI, Italian writer on crime. (1738–1794)
859, 902.

BECKER, NIKOLAUS, German poet. (1809–1845)
1716.
BECKET, THOMAS À, see THOMAS À BECKET
BECON, THOMAS, English Protestant divine and religious writer. (1512–1567)
272, 497, 589, 648, 788, 818, 875, 939, 952, 1154, 1332, 1336, 1353, 1414, 1631, 1634.
BÉCQUER, GUSTAVO ADOLPHO, Spanish poet and romance writer. (1836–1870)
385.
BEDDOES, THOMAS LOVELL, English poet and physiologist. (1803–1849)
480.
BEDE, or BÆDA (VENERABLE BEDE), Anglo-Saxon historian and scholar. (673–735)
1775.
BEDE, CUTHBERT (pseud. of EDWARD BRADLEY), English novelist. (1827–1889)
1417, 1636.
BEDINGFIELD, THOMAS, English miscellaneous writer. (? –1613)
138.
BEE, BARNARD ELLIOTT, American Confederate general. (1824–1861)
1005.
BEECHER, HENRY WARD, American Congregational clergyman and religious writer. (1813–1887)
78, 106, 235, 264, 278, 294, 362, 414, 468, 506, 682, 711, 817, 824, 979, 994, 1046, 1059, 1087, 1089, 1108, 1126, 1176, 1263, 1350, 1503, 1602, 1752, 1753, 1756, 1786, 1843, 1928, 2168, 2217, 2246.
BEECHER, THOMAS KINNICUT, American Congregational clergyman. (1824–1900)
144.
BEECHING, HENRY CHARLES, English divine and man of letters. (1859–1919)
108, 792.
BEER, THOMAS, American novelist and miscellaneous writer. (1889–1940)
1397, 1536, 2068, 2131.
BEERS, ETHEL LYNN (ETHELINDA ELIOTT), American verse-writer. (1827–1879)
65, 120, 1477.
BEETHOVEN, LUDWIG VAN, German composer. (1770–1827)
414.
BEGBIE, JANET, contemporary English poet.
2107.
BEHN, [MRS.] AFRA, APHRA, or AYFARA, English dramatist and novelist. (1640–1689)
69, 169, 351, 371, 442, 455, 751, 818, 875, 901, 949, 1070, 1117, 1176, 1180, 1182, 1197, 1204, 1207, 1208, 1269, 1284, 1292, 1462, 1469, 1564, 1567, 1639, 1694, 1828, 1831, 1945, 2076, 2132, 2133, 2144, 2182, 2197, 2213, 2241.
BEITH, MAJOR JOHN HAY, see HAY, IAN
BELL, HENRY GLASSFORD, Scottish editor and writer. (1803–1874)
1007.
BELL, JOHN JOY, Scottish poet and novelist. (1871–1934)
1813, 2028.
BELL, RALCY HUSTED, American writer. (1869–1931)
2217.
BELL, WALKER MERIWETHER, American verse-writer.
367.
BELLAMY, [MRS.] BLANCHE WILDER, American miscellaneous writer. (1852– ?)
2275.
BELLAMY, FRANCIS M., American editor and miscellaneous writer. (1856–1931)
673.
BELLAMY, W. A. No biographical data available.
2156.
BELLAY, JOACHIM DU, French poet and prose writer. (1525–1560)
1738, 1739.
BELLOC, JOSEPH HILAIRE PIERRE, English poet and miscellaneous writer. (1870–1953)
190, 328, 464, 535, 729, 879, 890, 1540, 1875, 2002.
BELLOWS, GEORGE WESLEY, American painter and illustrator. (1882–1925)
101.
BELLOY, PIERRE LAURENT BUIRETTE DE, French dramatist. (1727–1775)
471, 707, 1464.
BEN SYRA (SIRA), collector of proverbs from the Hebrew. (c. 190 B.C.)
104.
BENEDICT, FRANCIS GANO, American chemist. (1870–)
1996.
BENEŠ, EDUARD, Czech statesman. (1884–1948)
1472.
BENÉT, LAURA, contemporary American poet.
1999.
BENÉT, STEPHEN VINCENT, American poet and novelist. (1898–1943)
840, 1034, 1370, 1698, 2260, 2264.
BENÉT, WILLIAM ROSE, American poet and critic. (1886–1950)
167, 1889, 2076.
*BENHAM, W. GURNEY, English compiler.
BENJAMIN, CHARLES L., and SUTTON, GEORGE D., American song-writers.
673.
BENJAMIN, JUDAH P., United States Senator, Confederate Secretary of War. (1811–1884)
1011.
BENJAMIN, PARK, American journalist and verse-writer. (1809–1864)
76, 686, 1373, 1644.
BENNETT, ENOCH ARNOLD, English novelist and essayist. (1867–1931)
179, 219, 224, 250, 533, 558, 943, 1490, 1503, 1548, 1568, 1603, 1619, 1672, 2242.
BENNETT, HENRY, Irish poet. (1785– ?) 1463.
BENNETT, HENRY HOLCOMB, American poet and journalist. (1863–1924) 673, 1463.
BENNETT, JAMES GORDON, American journalist (1795–1872) 64.
BENNETT, JESSE LEE, American miscellaneous writer. (1885–1931) 179, 347, 531.

BENNETT, JOHN, American poet and novelist. (1865–1957)
1122, 1635.
BENNETT, WILLIAM COX, English poet. (1820–1895)
120.
BENNOCH, FRANCIS, English poet. (1812–1890)
188.
BENSERADE, ISAAC DE, French poet. (1613–1691)
141.
BENSON, ARTHUR CHRISTOPHER, English educator, scholar and poet. (1862–1925)
321, 690.
BENSON, STELLA, English novelist. (1892–1933)
149.
BENT, SILAS, American miscellaneous writer. (1882–1945)
1549, 1600, 1658.
BENTHAM, JEREMY, English jurist and utilitarian philosopher. (1748–1832)
109, 859, 874, 1655.
BENTINCK, LORD GEORGE, English statesman and sportsman. (1802–1848)
574.
BENTLEY, RICHARD, English classical scholar and critic. (1662–1742)
6, 1089, 1509, 1702, 1924, 2249.
BENTON, JOEL, American verse-writer and critic. (1832–1911)
1158.
BENTON, THOMAS HART, American statesman. (1782–1858)
1551.
BÉQUET, ÉTIENNE, French journalist and critic. (c. 1800–1838)
718.
BÉRANGER, PIERRE JEAN DE, French poet and song-writer. (1780–1857)
32, 144, 490, 550, 733, 1013, 1040, 1302, 1865.
BERCHER, JOHN, English writer. (fl. 1559)
2183.
BERGSON, HENRI, French philosopher. (1859–1941)
993, 994, 1116, 1117, 1459, 2002.
BERKELEY, BISHOP GEORGE, English prelate and metaphysical philosopher. (1685–1753)
52, 1119, 1314, 1968, 2266.
BERLIN, IRVING, American song-writer and composer. (1888–)
1369, 1729, 1881, 2143, 2284.
BERNARD, SAINT, Abbot of Clairvaux, French ecclesiastic. (1091–1153)
264, 377, 469, 594, 891, 1063, 1144, 1389, 1568, 1692.
BERNARD OF CLUNY, Benedictine monk, poet and religious writer. (fl. 12th century)
886.
BERNERS, BERNES, or BARNES, JULIANA, English writer. (1388?– ?)
261, 1037.
BERNHARDI, FRIEDRICH A. J. VON, German general and writer on military subjects. (1849–1930)
767, 2111.
BERNI, or BERNIA, FRANCESCO, Italian poet. (c. 1497–1535)
1702.
BERNSTEIN, HENRY, French dramatist. (1876–1953)
2206.
BEROALDUS, FILIPPO, Italian scholar and classical commentator. (1453–1505)
1172.
BERRY, DOROTHY, English verse-writer. (c. 1699)
1477.
BERTAUT, JEAN, French prelate and poet, Bishop of Sées. (1552–1611)
987.
BERTHELSON, JOHN, English lexicographer. (fl. 1754)
118, 1004, 1225.
BESANT, SIR WALTER, English novelist. (1836–1901)
1251.
BESANT, SIR WALTER, and RICE, JAMES, English novelists and collaborators. (1836–1901), (1843–1882)
1846.
BETHELL, RICHARD, first BARON WESTBURY, English Lord Chancellor. (1800–1873)
206, 1307.
BETHMANN-HOLLWEG, THEOBALD THEODORE FREDERIC ALFRED VON, German statesman; Imperial Chancellor from 1909–1917. (1856–1921)
767.
BETHUNE, GEORGE WASHINGTON, American Dutch Reformed clergyman and devotional writer. (1805–1862)
2139.
BETTS, CRAVEN LANGSTROTH, American poet. (1853–1941)
538, 1169.
BETTS, FRANK, contemporary English poet and miscellaneous writer.
752.
BEVERLY, MICHAEL. No biographical data available.
380.
BEYERLINCK, LAURENS, Canon of cathedral at Antwerp, Belgium. (1578–1627)
1280.
BEYLE, MARIE HENRI (STENDHAL), French novelist. (1783–1842)
1989.
BHÁSCARA, known as ACÂRYA (the learned), Indian astronomer and mathematician. (1114– ?)
1701.
BIAS, one of the Seven Sages of Greece. (fl. c. 566 B.C.)
245, 816, 970, 1247, 1248, 1323, 1336, 1548, 1561, 1972, 2055, 2164, 2166.
BIBESCŬ, PRINCESS ANTOINE (ELIZABETH ASQUITH), contemporary English novelist.
862.
BICKERSTAFFE, ISAAC, Irish dramatist. (c. 1735–c. 1812)
40, 307, 308, 311, 447, 485, 574, 921, 1265,

1302, 1308, 1407, 1742, 1817, 1876, 2194, 2264.

Bidpai, see Pilpay

Bierce, Ambrose, American journalist and satirist. (1842–1914?)
4, 18, 90, 122, 192, 226, 249, 266, 451, 567, 663, 821, 828. 874, 884, 947, 1090, 1230, 1262, 1271, 1357, 1434, 1596, 1688, 1754, 1895, 1905, 1951, 2179.

Biggers, Earl Derr, American novelist and playwright. (1884–1933)
373.

Billings, Josh (pseud. of Henry Wheeler Shaw), American humorist. (1818–1885)
113, 675, 762, 959, 1055, 1074, 1566.

Billings, William, American composer of hymn tunes. (1746–1800)
555.

Billyng, William, English writer. (c. 1680)
1348.

Binney, Horace, American lawyer and historical writer. (1780–1875)
975.

Binyon, Laurence, English poet and Orientalist. (1869–1943)
556, 1297, 2268.

Bion, Greek bucolic poet. (fl. 280 B.C.)
32, 117, 128, 623, 728, 745, 848, 892, 1022. 1265, 1332, 1412, 1621, 2114, 2126.

Bird, Robert Montgomery, American chemist, educator and scientific writer. (1867–1938)
614.

Birdseye, George, American verse-writer. (1844–1919)
317, 566.

Birrell, Augustine, English essayist and critic. (1850–1933)
77, 187, 661, 741, 899, 1165, 1428, 1448, 1515, 1531, 1558, 1672, 1740, 1937.

Bishop, Morris Gilbert, American poet. (1893–)
2179, 2221.

Bishop, Roy, English poet. (1895–)
532.

Bishop, Samuel, English poet. (1731–1795)
699, 2101.

Bismarck, Otto Eduard Leopold, Prince von, German statesman and Chancellor. (1815–1898)
255, 768, 777, 1039, 1043, 1379, 1633, 1713, 2098, 2107, 2230, 2246.

Bixby, Ammi Leander, American journalist. (1856–1934)
1360.

Björnson, Björnsterne, Norwegian poet, novelist and playwright. (1832–1910)
968.

Black, Hugh, Scottish divine and inspirational writer. (1868–1953)
737, 963.

Black, William, English novelist. (1841–1898)
1630.

Blackburn, Thomas. No biographical data available.
514.

Blackie, John Stuart, Scottish professor and man of letters. (1809–1895)
1871, 2058, 2125.

Blacklock, Thomas, blind Scottish poet. (1721–1791)
500, 703, 1115, 1194.

Blackmore, Sir Richard, English physician and miscellaneous writer. (1650?–1729)
491, 1668.

Blackmore, Richard Doddridge, English lawyer and novelist. (1825–1900)
771, 788.

Blackstone, Sir William, English jurist and legal writer. (1723–1780)
547, 844, 935, 1043, 1492, 1858, 2003.

Blaine, James Gillespie, American statesman. (1830–1893)
974, 1545, 1551, 1965, 2048.

Blair, Robert, English poet. (1699–1746)
71, 76, 136, 323, 333, 380, 382, 385, 388, 534, 628, 741, 746, 769, 802, 828, 836, 1295, 1303, 1339, 1933, 1935, 2063.

Blake, James W., American song-writer. (1862–1935)
1881, 2290.

Blake, John Lauris, American miscellaneous writer. (1788–1857)
294.

* Blake, William, English poet and painter. (1757–1827)

Blamire, Susanna, English poet. (1747–1794)
488.

Blanchard, Samuel Laman, English journalist and poet. (1804–1845)
486, 679, 690, 1317, 1811.

Blanchet, Pierre, French dramatist. (fl. 1460)
1636.

Bland, James A., American Negro song-writer. (1854–1911)
1881, 2087.

Bland, Robert, English divine and classical writer. (1779?–1825) 135.

Blanden, Charles Granger, American verse-writer. (1857–1933)
682, 1158.

Blanding, Don, American verse- and song-writer. (1894–)
1025.

Blasco y Ibáñez, Vicente, Spanish novelist. (1867–1928)
1198.

Bleecker, Ann Eliza, American verse-writer. (1752–1783)
333.

Blessington, Marguerite, Countess of, English novelist and miscellaneous writer. (1789–1849)
735, 1269, 1692.

Blind, Mathilde, English poet. Born in Germany, real name Cohen. Taken to London in 1849. (1841–1896)
252, 400, 1207.

Block, Louis James, American educator and writer. (1851–1927)
284.

BLOOMFIELD, ROBERT, English poet. (1766–1823)
469, 506, 639, 989, 1048, 1389, 1568, 1951, 2076.

BLOSSOM, HENRY, American librettist and song-writer. (1866–1919)
1881, 2103.

BLOUET, PAUL, see O'RELL, MAX

BLÜCHER, GEBHARD LEBERECHT VON, Prussian Field Marshal. (1742–1819)
1167.

BLUNT, WILFRID SCAWEN, English poet and publicist. (1840–1922)
22, 303, 905, 942, 1458, 1815.

BOAS, GUY, English educator and poet. (1896–)
2000.

BOCCACCIO, GIOVANNI, Italian novelist, poet and humanist. (1313?–1375)
658, 2226.

BODENHAM, JOHN, English writer. (fl. 1600)
952.

BODENHEIM, MAXWELL, American poet and novelist, (1893–1954)
162.

BODENSTEDT, FRIEDRICH MARTIN VON, German journalist and poet. (1819–1892)
1744.

BODINUS (BODIN), JEAN, French political philosopher and advocate. (1530–1596)
1841.

BOËTHIUS, ANCIUS MANLIUS SEVERINUS, Roman statesman and philosopher. (470?–525)
72, 453, 783, 859, 1191, 1192, 1321, 1362, 1521, 1823, 1991.

BOGAN, LOUISE [MRS. RAYMOND HOLDEN], American poet and novelist. (1897–)
1180, 2037, 2190.

BOGART, JOHN B., American newspaperman; city editor N. Y. *Sun*. (1845–1921)
1398.

* BOHN, HENRY GEORGE, English publisher and bookseller; compiler of *A Hand-Book of Proverbs* (1855), based upon Ray's and Heywood's collections. (1796–1884)

BOILEAU-DESPRÉAUX, NICHOLAS, French poet and satirist. (1636–1711)
14, 18, 42, 220, 414, 450, 583, 696, 698, 802, 867, 916, 1371, 1423, 1513, 1535, 1694, 2006, 2043, 2050, 2061, 2090, 2168, 2253, 2254.

BOKER, GEORGE HENRY, American poet. (1823–1890)
391, 725, 1158, 1172, 1868.

BOLEYN, ANNE, English queen, second wife of Henry VIII. (1507–1536)
414, 1279.

BOLINGBROKE, VISCOUNT, see ST. JOHN, HENRY

BOLITHO, WILLIAM (pseud. of WILLIAM BOLITHO RYALL), English miscellaneous writer. (1890–1930)
15, 176, 347, 499, 1085, 1253, 1262, 1986, 2110, 2150.

BONAPARTE, JEROME, brother of Napoleon I, and King of Westphalia. (1784–1860)
1741.

BONAPARTE, NAPOLEON, see NAPOLEON I

BONAR, HORATIUS, Scottish Free Church divine and poet. (1808–1889)
28, 390, 1134, 1831, 1832, 2057, 2058.

BOND, CARRIE JACOBS, American song-writer and composer. (1862–1946)
372.

BOND, WARWICK, English editor and critic.
1851.

BONER, JOHN HENRY, American editor and verse-writer. (1845–1903)
1215, 1296, 1514.

BONIFACE, JOSEPH FRANÇOIS, see SAINTINE, XAVIER

BONNARD, ABEL, French littérateur. (1883–)
726, 744, 1217.

BOORDE, or BORDE, ANDREW, English physician and traveller. (1490?–1549)
169, 501, 1606, 1769.

BOOTH, BARTON, English actor. (1681–1733)
306.

BOOTH, EDWIN THOMAS, American actor. (1833–1893)
265, 1121.

BOOTH, REV. JOHN, English compiler. (fl. 1860)
467.

BOOTH, JOHN WILKES, American actor, assassin of Abraham Lincoln. (1839–1865)
414.

BORAH, WILLIAM EDGAR, American lawyer and statesman. (1865–1940)
1967.

BORROW, GEORGE, English traveller and picaresque novelist. (1803–1881)
44, 545, 558, 845, 857, 979, 1142, 1251, 1467, 1546, 1724, 1787, 1962, 2258, 2264.

BOSQUET, PIERRE FRANÇOIS JOSEPH, French Marshal. (1810–1861)
2107.

BOSSIDY, JOHN COLLINS, American physician and verse-writer. (1860–1928)
194.

BOSSUET, JACQUES BÉNIGNE, French divine and pulpit orator. (1627–1704)
146, 545, 890.

BOSWELL, JAMES, English biographer of Dr. Samuel Johnson. (1740–1795)
725, 1797, 1875.

BOTTA, ANNE CHARLOTTE, American verse-writer. (1820–1891)
142.

BOUCICAULT, DION, English actor and dramatist. (1820?–1890)
998.

BOURCHIER, JOHN, second BARON BERNERS, English statesman and translator. (1467–1533)
564, 786, 1469.

BOURDILLON, FRANCIS WILLIAM, English poet. (1852–1921)
167, 1188.

BOURNE, VINCENT, English poet who wrote in Latin. (1695–1747)
1855, 2243.

BOVEE, CHRISTIAN NESTELL, American editor and epigrammatic writer. (1820–1904)
1832, 2256.

BOWDITCH, KATHERINE [MRS. E. W. BOWDITCH], American verse-writer. (1894–1933)
1210.
BOWDLER, DR. THOMAS, English editor of Shakespeare, in a "family" expurgated version. (1754–1825)
579.
BOWEN, SIR GEORGE FERGUSON, English colonial governor. (1821–1899)
2065.
BOWER, WALTER, Scottish Abbot and historian. (? –1449)
443.
BOWKER, RICHARD ROGERS, American editor and publisher. (1848–1934)
1305.
BOWLES, WILLIAM LISLE, English divine, poet and antiquary. (1762–1850)
723, 1537.
BOWMAN, ELMER, American song-writer.
1881.
BOWMAN, LOUISE MOREY, contemporary Canadian writer.
1210.
BOYD, ZACHARY, Scottish divine. (1585?–1653)
1014.
BOYESEN, HJALMAR HJORTH, Norwegian novelist. (1848–1895)
1048, 1194.
BOYLE, JOHN, fifth EARL OF CORK, fifth EARL OF ORRERY, second BARON MARSTON, Irish writer and translator. (1707–1762)
716.
BOYLE, HON. ROBERT, English natural philosopher and chemist, founder of the Royal Society. (1627–1691)
1263.
BOYLE, ROGER, BARON BROGHILL and first EARL OF ORRERY, Irish statesman, soldier and dramatist. (1621–1679)
1536.
BOYLE, SARAH ROBERTS, American verse-writer. (1812–1869)
822.
BOYSE, SAMUEL, English poet. (1708–1749)
792, 1295.
BRACTON, BRATTON, or BRETTON, HENRY DE, English ecclesiastic and judge. (? –1268)
1649.
BRADDOCK, EDWARD, English major-general. (1695–1755)
2121.
BRADFORD, GAMALIEL, American poet and biographical writer. (1863–1932)
797, 890.
BRADFORD, JOHN, English preacher and Protestant martyr. (1510?–1555)
1593, 1634.
BRADLEY, EDWARD, see BEDE, CUTHBERT
BRADLEY, FRANCIS HERBERT, English philosopher. (1846–1924)
1497, 2043.
BRADLEY, MARY EMILY, American verse-writer. (1835–1898)
1450.
BRADSHAW, HENRY, Benedictine monk of Chester. (c. 1450–1513)
1258, 1606.
BRADSTREET, ANNE, English Puritan poet. Settled in Massachusetts in 1630. (1612–1672)
1373, 1938.
BRAGDON, ALONZO B., American jurist. (1847– ?)
1124.
BRAGDON, CLAUDE FAYETTE, American architect. (1866–1946)
94.
BRAGG, EDWARD STUYVESANT, American legislator. (1827–1912)
279.
BRAILOWSKY, ALEXANDER, Polish pianist. (1896–)
2187.
BRAINARD, JOHN GARDINER CALKINS, American verse-writer. (1796–1828)
280, 376, 1025, 1363.
BRAINARD, MARY GARDINER, American verse-writer. (fl. 1860)
794, 2044.
BRAISTED, HARRY, American song-writer.
1034, 1881.
BRALEY, BERTON, American journalist and publicist. (1882–)
207, 484, *2233*.
BRAMAH, ERNEST (pseud. ERNEST BRAMAH SMITH), English writer. (1869?–1942)
1649, 1759.
BRAMSTON, JAMES, English poet. (1694?–1744)
490, 864, 1163, 1362, 2012.
BRANCH, ANNA HEMPSTEAD, American poet. (1875–1937)
41, 1440, *2226*.
BRANCH, MARY LYDIA BOLLES, American verse-writer. (1840–1922)
1025.
BRASSAVOLA, ANTONIO MUSA, Italian physician. (1500–1570)
2145.
BRASTON, OLIVER S., American publicist.
1497.
BRATHWAITE, RICHARD, English poet. (1588?–1673)
85, 254, 343, 849, 1014, 1085, 1168, 1348, 1753, 1822, 2005, 2032, 2146, 2263.
BRÉBŒUF, GUILLAUME DE, French poet. (1618–1661)
2259.
BRENAN, JOSEPH, American poet, born in Ireland. (1828–1857)
483.
BRENNUS, leader of the Senonian Gauls. (fl. 390 B.C.)
1955.
BRERETON, JANE, English verse-writer. (1685–1740)
694.
BRET, ANTOINE, French writer and poet. (1717–1792)
1180.

BRETON, NICHOLAS, English poet. (1545?-1626?)
68, 103, 228, 373, 541, 592, 861, 910, 920, 1332, 1729, 1960, 1997, 2213, 2236, 2249.

BREVINT, or BREVIN, DANIEL, English divine (1616-1695)
792.

BREWER, ANTONY, English dramatic writer. (fl. 1655)
923, 1300.

BREWSTER, CLARENCE S., American song-writer
1881.

BRIAND DE VALLÉE, French courtier. (fl. 1550)
489.

BRIDGES, HORACE JAMES, American writer and lecturer. (1880-)
965.

BRIDGES, MADELINE S. (MARY AINGE DE VERE), American poet. (1844-1920)
745, 1114.

BRIDGES, ROBERT, English Poet Laureate. (1844-1930)
92, 128, 143, 280, 321, 581, 599, 628, 654, 682, 798, 886, 923, 924, 954, 1188, 1227, 1376, 1383, 1522, 1537, 1677, 1905, 1914, 2003, 2229, 2265.

BRIDGES, ROBERT (DROCH), American poet and editor. (1858-1941)
2121, 2187.

BRIFFAULT, ROBERT STEPHEN, English writer on philosophy and social anthropology; later a successful novelist. (1876-1948)
303.

BRIGHT, JOHN, English orator and statesman. (1811-1889)
374, 432, 545, 706, 1069, 1240, 1551, 1555, 1934.

BRIGHT, VERNE, American educator and journalist. (1893-)
1121.

BRILLAT-SAVARIN, ANTHELME, French magistrate and writer on gastronomy. (1755-1826)
316, 450, 515, 517, 519.

BRIMLEY, GEORGE, English essayist. (1819-1857)
1547.

BRINE, [MRS.] MARY DOW, contemporary American writer of verse and juveniles.
1350.

BRINKELOW, HENRY, English satirist. (? -1546)
1081, 1633.

BRINKLEY, MAY, American journalist and verse-writer. (1898-)
2224.

BRISSOT, JEAN PIERRE, French Girondist leader and political writer. (1754-1793)
1622.

BRITAINE, WILLIAM DE, author of *The Human Prudence of William de Britaine,* first published anonymously in London in 1680. It has been asserted that John Davies of Kidwelly, a translator, was the real author. (See *Spectator,* 1 Jan., 1898.)
2205.

BROME, ALEXANDER, English poet. (1620-1666)
443, 1479, 2159, 2225.

BROME, RICHARD, English dramatist. (? -1652?)
84, 763, 914, 1176, 1178, 1354, 1668, 2260.

BROMLEY, ISAAC HILL, American journalist. (1833-1898)
1409, 1551.

BRONAUGH, ANNE, contemporary American actress and verse-writer.
1124.

BRONSTON, MILT, contemporary American journalist and verse-writer.
1136.

BRONTË, CHARLOTTE, English novelist and poet. (1816-1855)
852, 1121, 1260, 1263, 1649, 1861.

BRONTË, EMILY JANE, English novelist and poet. (1818-1848)
905, 1892.

BROOKE, CHRISTOPHER, English poet. (? -1628)
421.

BROOKE, HENRY, Irish dramatist. (1703?-1783)
725, 1825.

BROOKE, RUPERT, English poet. (1887-1915)
276, 369, 380, 385, 398, 410, 480, 556, 812, 883, 888, 967, 1192, 1200, 1210, 1220, 1403, 1666, 1754, 2190.

BROOKE, STOPFORD AUGUSTUS, English divine and man of letters. (1832-1916)
511, 877, 1136, 2249.

BROOKS, MARY ELIZABETH [MRS. JAMES GORDON BROOKS], American writer. (fl. 1828)
404.

BROOKS, PHILLIPS, American Protestant Episcopal Bishop and orator. (1835-1893)
268, 275, 514, 830, 1166, 1584, 1658.

BROOME, WILLIAM, English clergyman, poet and translator. (1689-1745)
176, 467, 774, 836, 1147, 1268, 1987.

BROTHERTON, ALICE WILLIAMS, American story- and verse-writer. (d. 1930)
188, 1983.

BROUGH, ROBERT BARNABAS, English burlesque writer. (1828-1860)
1609.

BROUGHAM, HENRY PETER, BARON BROUGHAM and VAUX, English Lord Chancellor and historical writer. (1778-1868)
159, 527, 1026, 1089, 1415, 1543, 1970.

BROUN, HEYWOOD CAMPBELL, American newspaper columnist. (1888-1939)
891.

BROWN, ABBIE FARWELL, American writer for children. (1875-1927)
614.

BROWN, ALICE, American poet and novelist. (1857-1948)
191, 683, 1939.

BROWN, JOHN, English clergyman and miscellaneous writer. (1715-1766)
16.

BROWN, JOHN, English essayist. (1810-1882)
101, 928, 1078, 1182, 2250.

BULLEIN, WILLIAM, English physician and medical writer. (d. 1576)
751, 812, 872, 935, 973, 1006, 1154, 1332, 1751, 2035.

BULLETT, GERALD, English novelist, essayist and critic. (1893–)
268, 2067.

BÜLOW, BERNHARD, PRINCE VON, German statesman and Chancellor. (1849–1929)
84, 278.

BULWER, JOHN, English physician. (fl. 1654)
1958, 2179.

BULWER-LYTTON, see LYTTON

BUNN, ALFRED, English theatrical manager and verse-writer. (1796?–1860)
478, 927, 1294, 1296.

BUNNER, HENRY CUYLER, American journalist and miscellaneous writer. (1855–1896)
22, 94, 673, 690, 1194, 1531, 1804, 2036.

BUNSEN, CHRISTIAN KARL JOSIAS, BARON, German ambassador and scholar. (1791–1860)
1227, 2139.

BUNYAN, JOHN, English allegorical writer, author of *The Pilgrim's Progress.* (1628–1688)
97, 130, 161, 190, 224, 242, 294, 319, 325, 365, 397, 412, 420, 485, 541, 621, 633, 668, 678, 773, 852, 936, 947, 973, 1077, 1354, 1475, 1476, 1593, 1598, 1632, 1672, 1727, 1742, 1826, 1830, 1847, 1926, 1952, 2074, 2226, 2251, 2264.

BUONARROTI, MICHELANGELO, see MICHELANGELO

BURCHARD, SAMUEL DICKINSON, American Presbyterian clergyman. (1812–1891)
1552.

BURDETTE, ROBERT JONES, American lecturer and humorist. (1844–1914)
1878, 2020, 2168.

BÜRGER, GOTTFRIED AUGUSTUS, German poet. (1748–1794)
375, 1210.

BURGESS, FRANK GELETT, American humorist and novelist. (1866–1951)
331, 704, 744, 1644, 1654, 2187.

BURGESS, ROBERT LOUIS, contemporary American poet.
778.

BURGHLEY, LORD; WILLIAM CECIL, BARON BURGHLEY, English statesman. (1520–1598)
68, 1862, 1875, 2138.

BURGON, JOHN WILLIAM, English divine. (1813–1888)
275.

BURGOYNE, JOHN, English dramatist and general. (1722–1792)
1652.

* BURKE, EDMUND, English statesman. (1729–1797)

BURLAMAQUI, JEAN JACQUES, Swiss publicist. (1694–1748)
1311.

BURLEIGH, WILLIAM HENRY, American journalist, reformer and verse-writer. (1812–1871)
535, 639, 950.

BURNAND, SIR FRANCIS COWLEY, English playwright and editor. (1836–1917)
1198.

BURNET, DANA, American poet. (1888–)
1813, 2133.

BURNET, GILBERT, English divine and historical writer. (1643–1715)
1089, 1122.

BURNEY, FRANCES (FANNY), MADAME D'ARBLAY, English novelist. (1752–1840)
77, 222, 361, 750, 957, 972, 1003, 1014, 1063, 1136, 1257, 1363, 1632, 1702, 1705, 1911, 2030, 2055, 2210.

BURNS, JAMES DRUMMOND, English divine and hymn-writer. (1823–1864)
414, 1464, 2013.

* BURNS, ROBERT, Scottish poet. (1759–1796)

BURR, AARON, American politician. (1756–1836)
1079, 1509, 1614.

BURR, AMELIA JOSEPHINE, American poet. (1878–)
226, 1277, 1906.

BURR, THEODOSIA [MRS. JOSEPH ALSTON], daughter of Aaron Burr. (1783–1813)
366.

BURROUGHES, or BURROUGHS, JEREMIAH, English Congregational divine. (1599–1646)
880, 2203.

BURROUGHS, JOHN, American naturalist and nature-writer. (1837–1921)
968, 974, 1188, 1782, 1797, 1988, 2132.

BURROUGHS, JOSEPH, English Baptist minister. (1685–1761)
750.

BURT, BENJAMIN HAPGOOD, American lyricist and composer; "lyric laureate of the Lambs' Club." (1876–1950)
359, 2274.

BURT, EDWARD, Scottish writer. (? –1755)
499.

BURT, MAXWELL STRUTHERS, American novelist and poet. (1882–1954)
128, 165, 321, 1074.

BURTON, HENRY. No biographical data available.
1036.

BURTON, LADY ISABEL ARUNDELL, wife of Sir Richard Burton. (1831–1896)
1060.

BURTON, JOHN, English classical scholar. (1696–1771)
157.

BURTON, RICHARD EUGENE, American educator and poet. (1861–1940)
394, 611, 1023, 2070.

BURTON, SIR RICHARD FRANCIS, English explorer and scholar. (1821–1890)
22, 229, 298, 378, 388, 412, 434, 504, 517, 585, 700, 740, 754, 797, 809, 888, 957, 960, 968, 1114, 1117, 1123, 1126, 1130, 1138, 1242, 1244, 1249, 1290, 1326, 1342, 1450, 1451, 1454, 1554, 1599, 1677, 1803, 1804, 1996, 2048, 2219.

* BURTON, ROBERT, English philosopher and humorist, author of *The Anatomy of Melancholy.* (1577–1640)

784, 809, 894, 1055, 1077, 1204, 1233, 1470, 1972, 1985, 2022, 2039.

CALPURNIUS SICULUS, TITUS, Latin poet. (c. 200)
1477.

CALVERLEY, CHARLES STUART, English poet and parodist. (1831–1884)
122, 169, 582, 906, 1118, 1409, 1878, 2017, 2125.

CALVERT, GEORGE HENRY, American essayist and verse-writer. (1803–1889)
680, 2084.

CAMBRENSIS, see GIRALDUS DE BARRI

CAMBRIDGE, RICHARD OWEN, English satirical writer. (1717–1802)
693, 743, 2246.

CAMBRONNE, PIERRE JACQUES ETIENNE DE, French general, Commander of the Old Guard at Waterloo. (1770–1842)
2127

CAMDEN, WILLIAM, English antiquary and historian. (1551–1623)
33, 95, 160, 197, 222, 223, 464, 469, 471, 564, 589, 701, 745, 788, 869, 935, 1004, 1046, 1081, 1155, 1208, 1236, 1318, 1319, 1429, 1635, 1719, 1992, 2231.

CAMERON, SIMON, American politician and diplomatist. (1799–1889)
1547, 1552.

CAMMAERTS, ÉMILE, Belgian essayist, translator, poet, living in England since 1908. (1878–1953)
2300j.

CAMOËNS, LUIS DE, Portuguese poet. (1524–1580)
1194.

CAMPBELL, BARTLEY T., American playwright. (1843–1888)
2090.

CAMPBELL, GORDON, English poet. (1886–)
881.

CAMPBELL, JOHN, first BARON CAMPBELL, English Lord Chancellor. (1779–1861)
513, 976, 1841.

CAMPBELL, JOSEPH, Irish poet. (1881–1944)
40.

CAMPBELL, ROY, British poet. (1902–)
1115, 2251.

* CAMPBELL, THOMAS, Scottish poet. (1777–1844)

CAMPBELL, TIMOTHY J., American politician. (1840–1904)
307.

CAMPION, THOMAS, English poet and musician. (? –1620)
608, 703, 809, 1150, 1182, 1706, 1887, 2239.

CAMPISTRON, JEAN GALBERT DE, French dramatist. (1656–1723)
1901.

CANE, MELVILLE, American poet. (1879–)
694.

CANNING, GEORGE, English statesman. (1770–1827)
58, 219, 285, 289, 293, 775, 824, 1099, **1467**, 1543, 1569, 1681, 1959, 2148.

CANNON, EDMUND. No biographical data.
1409.

CANNON, HUGHIE, American variety player and song-writer.
1882, 2260.

CANNON, JOSEPH GURNEY, American politician, Speaker of the House of Representatives. (1836–1926)
2281.

CANTON, WILLIAM, English poet. (1845–1926)
253, 268, 344, 1519.

CANUTE, or CNUT, called THE GREAT, King of the Danes and English. (994?–1035)
1337.

CAPDUEIL, PONS, Provençal troubadour. (fl. 1190)
789.

CAPEL, ARTHUR, first BARON CAPEL OF HADHAM, English royalist leader. (1610?–1649)
1613.

CAPEN, JOSEPH, American writer. (d. 1725)
572.

CAPGRAVE, JOHN, English theologian and historian. (1393–1464)
822.

CAPITO, or KÖPFEL, WOLFGANG FABRICIUS, German Protestant reformer. (1478–1541)
131.

CAPONE, ALPHONSE, American bootlegger. (1899–1947)
1619.

CARAFFA, CARDINAL CARLO, Italian cardinal. (1517–1561)
420.

CAREW, RICHARD, English antiquary. (1555–1620)
806.

CAREW, THOMAS, English poet. (1595?–1639?)
568, 608, 825, 826, 847, 1186, 1200, 1202, 1659, 1766, 2015, 2172.

CAREY, LADY ELIZABETH, English poet. (d. 1635)
728, 986.

CAREY, HENRY, English poet and song-writer. (? –1743)
212, 222, 400, 546, 1211, 1259, 1409, 1525, 1752, 1879, 1903.

CAREY, M. F., American song-writer.
1882.

CARLETON, EMMA NUNEMACHER, American newspaper columnist and miscellaneous writer. (1850–1925)
1702.

CARLETON, WILL, American writer of homely verse. (1845–1912)
100, 219, 888, 905, 906, 1058, 1065, 1263, 1566, 1722, 1880, 1978, 1983, 2226.

CARLETON, WILLIAM, Irish novelist. (1794–1869)
1630.

CARLIN, FRANCIS (pseud. of JAMES FRANCIS CARLIN MACDONNELL), American poet. (1881–1945)
113, 1849.

CARLISLE, COUNTESS DOWAGER OF, see HAY, LUCY

CARLISLE, EARL OF, see HOWARD, FREDERICK

CARLO ALBERTO, King of Sardinia. (1798–1849)
1916.

CAVELL, EDITH LOUISA, English nurse shot by the Germans during the World War. (1865–1915)
1467.
CAVENDISH, MARGARET, DUCHESS OF NEWCASTLE, English poet, essayist and dramatist. (1624?–1674)
1224, 1398.
CAVOUR, CAMILLO BENSO, COUNT DI, Italian statesman. (1810–1861)
271.
CAWEIN, MADISON JULIUS, American poet. (1865–1914)
135, 634, 692, 905, 1342, 1384, 1567, 1730, 1825, 1932, 2101.
CAWTHORN, JAMES, English poet. (1719–1761)
527.
CAXTON, WILLIAM, English printer, writer and translator. (1422?–1491)
172, 222, 228, 456, 988, 1000, 1051, 1157, 1281, 1649, 1823, 2096, 2169.
CAYLEY, GEORGE JOHN, English miscellaneous writer. (1826–1878)
978.
CECIL, ROBERT ARTHUR TALBOT GASCOYNE, third MARQUESS OF SALISBURY, English statesman and Prime Minister. (1830–1903)
1602.
CECIL, WILLIAM, BARON BURGHLEY, see BURGHLEY, LORD
CELANO, TOMMASO DI, Italian poet. (c. 1185–c. 1255)
377, 1025.
CELLARIUS (properly KELLAR), CHRISTOPH, German humanist and pedagogue. (1638–1707)
1915.
CELSUS, or CELLACH, SAINT, Irish prelate, Archbishop of Armagh. (1079–1129)
970.
CENTLIVRE, SUSSANAH, English actress and dramatist. (1667?–1723)
22, 323, 349, 551, 562, 696, 744, 915, 1176, 1208, 1290, 1300, 1394, 1638, 1665, 1700, 1763, 1853, 2079, 2237.
CERCIDAS OF CRETE, Greek epigrammatist. (c. 325 B.C.)
469.
* CERVANTES SAAVEDRA, MIGUEL DE, Spanish novelist and dramatist. (1547–1616)
CHADWICK, JOHN WHITE, American Unitarian clergyman, essayist and poet. (1840–1904)
62, 400.
CHALKHILL, JOHN, English poet. (fl. 1600)
1078.
CHALMERS, PATRICK REGINALD, Irish poet. (1872–1942)
472, 614, 751, 1450.
CHALMERS, STEPHEN, Scottish-born American poet. (1880–1935)
905.
CHALMERS, THOMAS, Scottish theologian. (1780–1847)
1481.
CHALONER, SIR THOMAS, THE YOUNGER, English naturalist. (1561–1615)
1895.
CHAMBERLAIN, JOHN, English letter-writer. (1553–1627)
373.
CHAMBERLAIN, JOSEPH, English statesman. (1836–1914)
323, 580, 970, 1167, 1380.
CHAMBERLAYNE, EDWARD, English historical writer. (1616–1703)
1422.
CHAMBERS, CHARLES HADDON, English journalist and playwright. (1860–1921)
274.
CHAMBERS, ROBERT, Scottish publisher and compiler. (1802–1871)
180, 579, 1265.
CHAMFORT, SEBASTIAN-ROCH-NICHOLAS DE, French epigrammatist. (1741–1794)
718, 719, 1075, 1481, 1645, 1714, 2108.
CHAMIER, FREDERICK, English novelist. (1796–1870)
2230.
CHAMPOLLION, JEAN FRANÇOIS, French Egyptologist. (1791–1832)
1563.
CHANCEL, AUSONE, see AUSONE DE CHANCEL
CHANNING, WILLIAM ELLERY, American Unitarian theologian and orator. (1780–1842)
176, 183, 575, 616, 728, 904, 963, 1061, 1123, 1165, 1472, 1508, 1979, 2057, 2062, 2080.
CHANNING, WILLIAM ELLERY, American poet. (1818–1901)
965, 1530.
CHANNING, WILLIAM HENRY, American Unitarian minister. (1810–1884) 1127.
CHAPLIN, STEWART, American writer. 2218.
CHAPMAN, ARTHUR, American poet and miscellaneous writer. (1873–1935)
2131.
* CHAPMAN, GEORGE, English poet and dramatist. (1559?–1634)
CHARLES I, King of England. (1600–1649)
323, 414, 589, 1655.
CHARLES II, King of England. (1630–1685)
244, 414, 522, 864, 1358, 1408, 1636, 1799, 1909.
CHARLES V, Holy Roman Emperor and CHARLES I of Spain. (1500–1558)
216, 711, 1044, 1315, 1750.
CHARLES IX, King of France. (1550–1574)
2247.
CHARLES XII, King of Sweden. (1682–1718)
1863.
CHARLES, DUC D'ORLÉANS, French poet. (1391–1465)
1907.
CHARLES, [MRS.] ELIZABETH RUNDLE, English novelist. (1828–1896)
1279.
CHARLEVAL, CHARLES FAUCONDE RIS DE, French versifier. (c. 1612–1693)
1196.
CHAROST, ARMAND JOSEPH DE BETHUNE DE, French economist. (1728–1800)
1711.

Charron, Pierre, French philosopher and theologian. (1541–1603)
695, 1251, 1719.

Chase, Salmon Portland, American lawyer and statesman. (1808–1873)
57, 66, 1841.

Chassebœuf, Constantin François, Comte de Volney, French traveller. (1757–1820)
1749.

Chatham, Lord, see Pitt, William, first Earl of Chatham

Chattaway, Thurland, American song-writer. (1872–)
1883.

Chatterton, Thomas, English poet. (1752–1770)
326, 333, 358, 390, 741, 784, 802, 917, 1172, 1219, 1486, 1578, 1978.

* Chaucer, Geoffrey, English poet. (1340?–1400)

Chavasse, Pye Henry, English writer. (fl. 1877)
518.

Chekhov, Anton Pavlovich, Russian dramatist and novelist. (1860–1904)
153, 865, 955.

Cheney, Gertrude Louise, American child poet. (1918–)
449.

Cheney, John Vance, American poet. (1848–1922)
117, 134, 511, 858, 1158, 1390, 1432, 1936, 1973, 2012, 2130, 2152.

Chénier, André Marie de, French poet. (1762–1794)
2, 840, 2063.

Cherry, Andrew, Irish actor and playwright. (1762–1812)
998, 1813, 2000.

Chester, Anton G. No biographical data available.
1128.

* Chesterfield, Lord; Philip Dormer Stanhope, fourth Earl of Chesterfield, English statesman, wit and letter-writer. (1694–1773)

Chesterton, Gilbert Keith, English essayist, critic, novelist and poet. (1874–1936)
44, 55, 60, 63, 106, 111, 113, 227, 261, 262, 265, 268, 340, 430, 431, 555, 562, 585, 882, 970, 999, 1068, 1142, 1167, 1235, 1238, 1318, 1361, 1434, 1490, 1540, 1658, 1673, 1688, 1691, 1734, 1747, 1926, 1982, 2001, 2050, 2132, 2158, 2190, 2209

Chettle, Henry, English dramatist. (d. 1607)
1003.

Chew, Beverly, American poet. (1850–1924)
187.

Cheyney, Edward Ralph, American poet and miscellaneous writer. (1896–)
399.

Child, [Mrs.] Lydia Maria, American miscellaneous writer. (1802–1880)
53, 761, 1654, 1983, 2062.

Chillingworth, William, English theologian. (1602–1644)
948.

Chilon, Grecian sage, one of the Seven Wise Men of Greece. (fl. c. 560 B.C.)
22, 156, 405, 447, 540, 726, 735, 750, 801, 1217, 1666, 1790, 1947, 1996, 2023, 2063.

Chivers, Thomas Holley, American verse-writer. (1809–1858)
437, 878, 1879.

Choate, Joseph Hodges, American lawyer and wit. (1832–1917)
414.

Choate, Rufus, American lawyer and orator. (1799–1858)
9, 57, 901, 974, 1079, 1552, 1658.

Chœrilus, Greek epic poet. (fl. c. 475 B.C.)
1530, 2126.

Cholmondeley, Hester H., contemporary English writer.
1605.

Chorley, Henry Fothergill, English critic and miscellaneous writer. (1808–1872)
802, 1417.

Chrisippus, Greek Stoic philosopher. (280–207 B.C.)
643, 1170.

Christina, Queen of Sweden. (1626–1689)
1253.

Christy, David, American lecturer and anti-slavery agitator. (1802– ?)
64.

Chrysis, Greek dramatist. (c. 300 B.C.)
2044.

Chrysostom, Saint John, Greek writer and Father of the Church. (c. 345–407)
241, 404, 477, 892, 1337, 1495, 1829, 1981, 2020, 2022, 2059, 2075, 2187.

Church, Benjamin, American poet and political writer. (1734–1776)
396.

Church, Francis Pharcellus, American newspaperman and editorial writer. (1839–1906)
269.

Church, Richard, English poet. (1893–)
1906.

Churchill, Charles, English satirist and poet. (1731–1764)
9, 12, 28, 88, 104, 187, 199, 217, 235, 249, 271, 285, 309, 310, 341, 343, 349, 354, 442, 456, 478, 545, 553, 564, 565, 583, 619, 623, 625, 641, 661, 696, 700, 717, 733, 757, 759, 835, 863, 872, 877, 895, 918, 1008, 1009, 1014, 1035, 1076, 1083, 1142, 1153, 1256, 1259, 1299, 1310, 1312, 1313, 1321, 1327, 1339, 1382, 1417, 1422, 1437, 1461, 1463, 1485, 1486, 1503, 1505, 1513, 1523, 1525, 1529, 1549, 1568, 1604, 1606, 1615, 1628, 1649, 1676, 1679, 1680, 1725, 1754, 1757, 1769, 1793, 1803, 1805, 1837, 1876, 1903, 1918, 1919, 1924, 1945, 1964, 1966, 1967, 2061, 2068, 2080, 2096, 2103, 2251, 2254.

Churchill, John, first Duke of Marlborough, English military leader, victor at Battle of Blenheim, 1704. (1650–1722)
1863.

CHURCHILL, RANDOLPH HENRY SPENCER, commonly known as LORD RANDOLPH CHURCHILL, English statesman. (1849–1894)
1544.

CHURCHILL, SIR WINSTON, English politician. (1620?–1688)
970.

CHURCHILL, SIR WINSTON LEONARD SPENCER, English statesman. (1874–)
1840, 2298a, 2298g.

CHURCHWARD, WILLIAM BROWN, English soldier and diplomatist. (1844–1920)
2296.

CHURCHYARD, THOMAS, English miscellaneous writer. (1520?–1604)
373, 668, 1004, 1225, 1801, 2224.

CIALDINI, ENRICO, Italian general. (c. 1814–1892)
1297.

CIBBER, COLLEY, English actor, poet and dramatist. (1671–1757)
2, 51, 79, 95, 170, 206, 299, 349, 483, 501, 509, 517, 541, 624, 641, 824, 852, 861, 862, 869, 1009, 1031, 1162, 1170, 1182, 1198, 1200, 1259, 1262, 1275, 1445, 1490, 1565, 1569, 1618, 1639, 1799, 1968, 1990, 2027, 2115, 2117, 2203, 2215, 2231.

* CICERO, MARCUS TULLIUS, Latin philosopher, statesman and orator. (106–43 B.C.)

CIVILIS, JULIUS (or CLAUDIUS), Roman commander. (fl. c. A.D. 70)
176.

CLARE, JOHN, English poet. (1793–1864)
92, 782, 989.

CLARK, ABRAHAM, American lawyer, signer of the Declaration of Independence. (1726–1794)
53, 974, 1482.

CLARK, CHAMP, American politician. (1850–1921)
1552.

CLARK, CHARLES HOPKINS, American journalist. (1848–1926)
2128.

CLARK, EDWARD BRAYTON, American journalist. (1860–)
1382.

CLARK, JOHN MAURICE, American political economist. (1884–)
1054.

CLARK, WILLIS GAYLORD, American editor, publisher and verse-writer. (1808–1841)
204.

CLARKE, CHARLES COWDEN, English writer and lecturer on Shakespeare. (1787–1877)
2005.

CLARKE, JAMES FREEMAN, American Unitarian clergyman and theological writer. (1810–1888)
1688.

* CLARKE, JOHN, English compiler; published *Paræmiologia Anglo-Latina* in 1639.

CLARKE, JOSEPH IGNATIUS CONSTANTINE, American journalist and verse-writer. (1846–1925)
999, 1895.

CLARKE, M'DONALD, American verse-writer, commonly styled "The Mad Poet" because of his eccentricities. (1798–1842)
497, 2062.

CLARKE, SAMUEL, English metaphysician. (1675–1729)
1440.

CLAUDEL, PAUL LOUIS CHARLES, French diplomatist, poet and dramatist. (1868–1955)
451, 1919.

CLAUDIANUS (CLAUDIAN), Latin poet. (fl. 365–408)
4, 16, 80, 115, 118, 383, 506, 564, 587, 657, 765, 799, 836, 855, 872, 920, 987, 1011, 1040, 1042, 1046, 1088, 1176, 1204, 1222, 1327, 1470, 1482, 1504, 1656, 1738, 1739, 1890, 2032, 2037, 2041, 2089, 2091, 2267.

CLAUDIUS CÆCUS, APPIUS, Roman censor and poet. (fl. 312 B.C.)
715, 1835.

CLAUDIUS, MATTHIAS, known as ASMUS, German poet and prose-writer. (1740–1815)
1716, 2098.

CLAY, HENRY, American statesman and orator. (1777–1852)
57, 58, 1550, 1552, 1714.

CLEANTHES, Greek Stoic philosopher. (c. 300–220 B.C.)
642.

CLEGHORN, SARAH NORCLIFFE, American poet. (1876–1959)
25, 30, 587, 1064.

CLEMENCEAU, GEORGES B. E., French journalist and statesman. (1841–1929)
795, 968, 1147, 2066, 2107, 2151.

CLEMENS, SAMUEL LANGHORNE, see TWAIN, MARK

CLEMENT I, or CLEMENS ROMANUS, Bishop of Rome. (fl. c. 90)
287.

CLEMENT II, Roman Pope; a Saxon, whose name was Suidger. (fl. 1046)

CLEMENT VII (GIULIO DE' MEDICI), Roman Pope. (1478?–1534)
1637.

CLEMMER, MARY [MRS. MARY CLEMMER HUDSON], American miscellaneous writer. (1839–1884)
1602, 1604, 1936.

CLEOBULUS, Greek poet, one of the Seven Sages. (633–564 B.C.)
336, 532, 733, 872, 1031, 1098, 1325, 1965, 2144.

CLEONICÉ, Greek maiden killed by Pausanius. (c. 476 B.C.)
2043.

CLEPHANE, ELIZABETH CECILIA, Scottish poet. (1830–1869)
1811.

CLERK, JOHN, LORD ELDIN, Scottish jurist. (1757–1832)
681.

CLESI, N. J., American song-writer.
1883.

CLEVELAND, JOHN, English Cavalier poet. (1613–1658)
139, 142, 822, 1261, 1958.

CLEVELAND, STEPHEN GROVER, twenty-second and twenty-fourth President of the United States. (1837–1908)
58, 66, 279, 431, 506, 607, 665, 815, 1061, 1081, 1086, 1543, 1549, 1550, 1551, 1717, 1965, 2154, 2204.

CLIFTON, HARRY, English song-writer. (fl. 1870)
1883.

CLIVE, ROBERT, LORD CLIVE, English Statesman. (1725–1774) 1326:1.

CLOTAIRE I, second King of the Franks. (497–561) 414.

CLOUD, VIRGINIA WOODWARD, American poet. (1880–1938) 1099.

CLOUGH, ARTHUR HUGH, English poet. (1819–1861)
5, 30, 114, 209, 249, 303, 443, 517, 612, 809, 1055, 1334, 1358, 1414, 1415, 1608, 1739, 1813, 2237.

COATES, FLORENCE EARLE, American poet. (1850–1927)
23, 203, 284, 390, 484, 612, 653, 690, 693, 722, 745, 1193, 1244, 1390, 1444, 1864.

COATES, GRACE STONE, American writer. (1881–)
1222.

COBB, FRANK IRVING, American journalist. (1869–1923)
2281.

COBB, IRVIN SHREWSBURY, American novelist and miscellaneous writer. (1876–1944)
1637.

COBB, JAMES, English dramatist. (1756–1818)
1920.

COBB, WILL D., American song-writer. (1876–1930)
360, 1233, 1375, 1454, 1883, 2283, 2284.

COBBETT, WILLIAM, English essayist, politician and agriculturist. (1762–1835)
333, 1569, 1968.

COBDEN, RICHARD, English statesman. (1804–1865)
1556, 1602.

COBLENTZ, CATHERINE CATE, contemporary American writer.
1115.

COCHRANE, ALFRED, English poet and miscellaneous writer. (1865–1948)
100.

COCKER, EDWARD, English arithmetician. (1631–1675)
1097.

COCKTON, HENRY, English humorous novelist. (1807–1853)
2281.

COCTEAU, JEAN, French poet and pamphleteer. (1891–)
42, 101, 1166, 1434, 1482, 1536.

CODRINGTON, CHRISTOPHER, English soldier. (1668–1710)
652.

COFFEY, CHARLES, English dramatist. (d. 1745)
877.

COFFIN, HENRY SLOANE, American educator and Presbyterian clergyman. (1877–1954)
783.

COGAN, THOMAS, English physician. (1545?–1607)
448, 451, 1950, 2154, 2156, 2264.

COGAN, THOMAS, English philosopher, minister and physician. (1736–1818)
88, 91, 873, 1288, 1821, 2024.

COGNATUS, see COUSIN

COGNIARD, THÉODORE and HIPPOLYTE, French dramatists. (1806–1872), (1807–1882)
1463.

COHAN, GEORGE MICHAEL, American playwright and comedian. (1878–1942)
1117, 1397, 2284.

COKE, SIR EDWARD, English jurist and legal writer. (1552–1634)
227, 249, 303, 319, 815, 935, 936, 1079, 1081, 1087, 1088, 1096, 1648, 1665, 1950.

COLBERT, JEAN BAPTISTE, French statesman and financier. (1619–1683)
1552.

COLBY, FRANK MOORE, American critic and encyclopedist. (1865–1925)
1757.

COLE, BOB, American song-writer.
2284.

COLE, HENRY, English divine, Dean of St. Paul's. (1500?–1580)
958.

COLE, SAMUEL VALENTINE, American poet. (1851–1925)
84, 1785.

COLE, THOMAS, English nonconformist divine. (1627?–1697)
2062.

COLEMAN, CHARLES WASHINGTON, American writer and librarian. (1862–)
1895.

COLERIDGE, HARTLEY, English poet and miscellaneous writer. (1796–1849)
139, 356, 393, 436, 600, 722, 1072, 1077, 1126, 1382, 1404, 1456, 1530, 1569, 1887, 1983, 2184, 2261.

COLERIDGE, MARY ELIZABETH, English poet, novelist and essayist. (1861–1907)
481, 708, 1054, 1253, 1512, 1872.

* COLERIDGE, SAMUEL TAYLOR, English poet and critic. (1772–1834)

COLES, ABRAHAM, American physician and verse-writer. (1813–1891)
52, 301, 510, 578, 605, 673, 1669, 2261.

COLLIER, JEREMY, English churchman and polemical writer. (1650–1726)
183, 1676, 1910, 1951.

COLLIER, JOHN PAYNE, English Shakespearian critic. (1789–1883)
469, 470.

COLLIER, HIRAM PRICE, American miscellaneous writer. (1860–1913)
769.

COLLIN-D'HARLEVILLE, JEAN FRANÇOIS, French comic dramatist. (1755–1806)
306, 588, 971, 1281, 1559, 2233.

COLLINGWOOD, ROBIN GEORGE, English educator and philosophical writer. (1889–1943)
722.

1944, 2011, 2013, 2020, 2049, 2074, 2218, 2257.

COWLEY, HANNAH, English dramatist. (1743–1809)
1073, 1270, 1637, 2074, 2178.

* COWPER, WILLIAM, English poet. (1731-1800)

COX, COLEMAN, contemporary American humorist.
1488.

COX, GEORGE VALENTINE, English miscellaneous writer. (1786–1875)
348.

COX, KENYON, American artist. (1856–1919)
106.

COX, SAMUEL SULLIVAN, American politician and journalist. (1824–1889)
1377, 1856.

COXE, ARTHUR CLEVELAND, American Episcopal Bishop, poet and miscellaneous writer. (1818–1896)
681.

COYLE, HENRY, American journalist and verse-writer. (1865–)
908.

COYNE, JOSEPH STIRLING, British dramatist. (1803-1868)
1917.

* CRABBE, GEORGE, English poet. (1754–1832)

CRAIG, ADAM, contemporary American compiler.
1864.

CRAIG, ALEXANDER, English poet. (1567?–1627)
220.

CRAIGIE, PEARL MARY TERESA, see HOBBES, JOHN OLIVER

CRAIK, [MRS.] DINAH MARIA MULOCK (MISS MULOCK), English novelist. (1826–1887)
116, 210, 269, 362, 390, 412, 438, 568, 582, 608, 617, 683, 708, 740, 1063, 1072, 1129, 1179, 1188, 1219, 1262, 1342, 1402, 1782, 1824, 1999, 2022, 2152, 2262.

CRAIK, GEORGE LILLIE, Scottish miscellaneous writer. (1798–1866)
1055.

CRANCH, CHRISTOPHER PEARSE, American Transcendentalist and poet. (1813–1892)
174, 661, 1242, 1435, 1906, 2160.

CRANE, FRANK, American clergyman and journalist. (1861–1928)
726.

CRANE, NATHALIA CLARA RUTH, American poet. (1913–)
324, 883, 1684, 1745, 1748, 2221.

CRANE, STEPHEN, American novelist and poet. (1871–1900)
876, 1246, 1596, 1601, 1830, 2112.

CRANFIELD, LIONEL, EARL OF MIDDLESEX, English nobleman and Master of the Royal Wardrobe. (1575–1645)
1069.

CRANMER, THOMAS, English Archbishop and statesman. (1489–1556)
414, 849, 1960.

CRAPO, WILLIAM WALLACE, American lawyer. (1830–1926)
1550.

CRAPSEY, ADELAIDE, American poet. (1878–1914)
190, 1223, 1523, 1825, 2151.

CRASHAW, RICHARD, English poet. (1613?–1649)
157, 242, 261, 371, 390, 438, 604, 610, 706, 774, 842, 847, 915, 1070, 1147, 1188, 1223, 1315, 1348, 1585, 1893, 1973, 2000, 2195.

CRASSUS, MARCUS LICINIUS, Roman general and statesman. (115–53 B.C.)
95, 1154.

CRATES, Greek actor and dramatist. (fl. c. 470 B.C.)
1186, 1826.

CRATINUS, THE YOUNGER, Greek comic poet. (fl. 400 B.C.)
1947.

CRAWFORD, ALEXANDER, Scottish poet.
1767.

CRAWFORD, LOUISA MACARTNEY, English poet. (1790–1858)
1454.

CRÉBILLON, PROSPER JOLYOT DE, French dramatic poet. (1674–1762)
800, 1150, 1478.

CREIGHTON, MANDELL, English Bishop and biographical writer. (1843–1901)
566, 901, 1494, 1547, 2099.

CRESSWELL, WALTER D'ARCY, English poet. (1896–)
1531.

CREWE-MILNES, ROBERT OFFLEY ASHBURTON, MARQUIS OF CREWE, English statesman and writer. (1858–1945)
188, 703, 887, 1693.

CRINAGORAS, Greek epigrammatist. (fl. c. 45 B.C.)
1339.

CRISPUS, CAIUS SALLUSTIUS, see SALLUST

CRITTENDEN, JOHN JORDAN, American lawyer and statesman. (1787-1863)
63.

CRITTENDEN, THOMAS LEONIDAS, American lawyer and soldier. (1819–1893)
64.

CROCKETT, DAVID, American frontiersman and politician. (1786–1836)
1657, 1725.

CROCKETT, INGRAM, American nature-writer. (1856–)
2151.

CRŒSUS, King of Lydia, proverbial for his great wealth. (fl. 560 B.C.)
2118.

CROFFUT, WILLIAM AUGUSTUS, American journalist and historian. (1836–1915)
521.

CROGHAN, GEORGE, English officer and Indian agent in America. (? –1782)
63.

CROKER, JOHN WILSON, English politician and essayist. (1780–1857)
303.

CROKER, RICHARD, American Tammany politician. (1841–1922)
970.

CROLY, GEORGE, English divine and miscellaneous writer. (1780–1860)
389, 582, 826, 945, 1157, 1306, 1342, 1797.

CROMWELL, GLADYS, American poet. (1885–1919)
2166.

CROMWELL, OLIVER, English Lord Protector. (1599–1658)
89, 414, 420, 763, 914, 1037, 1392, 1447, 1470, 1556, 1598, 1650, 1736, 1929, 2074, 2218.

CRONIN, ARCHIBALD JOSEPH, English novelist. (1896–)
642.

CROSBY, ERNEST HOWARD, American reformer and miscellaneous writer. (1856–1907)
396, 1994.

CROSLAND, THOMAS WILLIAMS HODGSON, English journalist. (1865–1924)
1769, 2298b.

CROSS, JAMES C., English playwright. (fl. 1796)
1051.

CROSS, MARY ANN EVANS, see ELIOT, GEORGE

CROSS, WILBUR LUCIUS, American educator; ex-governor of Connecticut. (1862–1948)
816.

CROTHERS, SAMUEL MCCHORD, American Unitarian clergyman and essayist. (1857–1927)
1165, 1988.

CROUCH, NATHANIEL, English miscellaneous writer under initials R. B. (1632?–1725?)
1137.

CROUSE, MARY ELIZABETH, American miscellaneous writer. (1873–)
1956.

CROWELL, GRACE NOLL [MRS. NORMAN H. CROWELL], American verse-writer. (1877–)
2038.

CROWLEY, CROLE, or CROLEUS, ROBERT, English writer, printer and divine. (1518?–1588)
1793.

CROWNE, JOHN, English dramatist. (d. 1703?)
301, 763, 1179, 1183, 1875, 2174, 2191.

CUDWORTH, RALPH, English divine and theological writer. (1617–1688)
1904.

CULLEN, COUNTEE, American Negro poet. (1903–1946)
381.

CULPEPER, NICHOLAS, English writer on astrology and medicine. (1616–1654)
141.

CUMBERLAND, RICHARD, English prelate, Bishop of Peterborough. (1631–1718)
1752.

CUMBERLAND, RICHARD, English dramatist. (1732–1811)
1144, 1332, 1979, 2162.

CUMMINGS, EDWARD ESTLIN, American artist and poet. (1894–)
1310, 1861.

CUNNINGHAM, ALLAN, Scottish miscellaneous writer. (1784–1842)
769, 905, 1776, 1778, 2225.

CUNNINGHAM, JOHN, English poet. (1729–1773)
463, 1137, 1240, 1560, 1745.

CUNNINGHAME-GRAHAM, ROBERT BONTINE, British writer and traveller. (1852–1936)
1931, 2115, 2214.

CURIO, GAIUS SCRIBONIUS, Roman statesman and orator. (? –53)
213.

CURRAN, JOHN PHILPOT, Irish judge. (1750–1817)
996, 1106, 1840, 1962.

CURTIS, GEORGE WILLIAM, American essayist. (1824–1892)
38, 77, 288, 484, 626, 870, 900, 1557, 1731, 1735.

CURTIS, JOHN GREEN, American physiologist. (1844–1913)
2274.

CURTIUS RUFUS, QUINTUS, see QUINTUS CURTIUS

CURZON, GEORGE NATHANIEL, first MARQUESS OF, (CURZON OF KEDLESTON), English statesman, Viceroy of India. (1859–1925)
2083.

CUSHMAN, CHARLOTTE, American actress. (1816–1876)
101, 795, 1910.

CUSTANCE, OLIVE ELEANOR [LADY ALFRED DOUGLAS], English poet. (1874–1944)
2062.

CUSTER, [MRS.] ELIZABETH, wife of George Armstrong Custer, Indian fighter. (1842–1933)
1862.

CUVIER, GEORGES, French naturalist. (1769–1832)
414.

CYNEWULF, OR CYNWULF, Anglo-Saxon poet. (fl. 750)
1709.

CYPRIAN, SAINT (THASCIUS CÆCILIUS CYPRIANUS), one of the great Fathers of the Church. (c. 200–258)
1740.

D

DACH, SIMON, German poet and hymn-writer. (1605–1659)
731, 1449.

DACRE, HARRY, English song-writer.
1211, 2284.

DALMON, CHARLES, English poet. (1872–)
770, 1390, 2041.

DALRYMPLE, SIR JOHN, fourth BARONET OF CRANSTOUN, Scottish jurist. (1726–1810)
1781.

DALTON, POWER (HAROLD CALEB DALTON), contemporary American poet.
291.

DALY, DANIEL, American Marine Corps gunnery-sergeant in World War. (1874–1937)
67.

DALY, JOHN. No biographical data available.
673.

DALY, THOMAS AUGUSTIN, American poet and journalist. (1871–1948)
1999.

Damascius, Neoplatonic philosopher of Damascus. (b. c. A.D. 480)
175.

Dana, Charles Anderson, American journalist. (1819–1897)
532, 1398, 1557, 1612, 2225.

Dana, John Cotton, American librarian. (1856–1929)
128.

Dana, Richard Henry, American poet and critic. (1787–1879)
252.

Dana, Richard Henry, American lawyer and miscellaneous writer. (1815–1882)
492, 1812.

D'Anchères, Daniel, French poet. (1586–?)
1624.

Dancourt, Florent Carton, French dramatist. (1661–1725)
1076.

Dane, Nathan, American lawyer and statesman. (1752–1835)
1841.

Daniel, Samuel, English poet, dramatist and historian. (1562–1619)
50, 134, 136, 179, 245, 261, 323, 327, 354, 423, 424, 445, 624, 628, 656, 681, 695, 836, 842, 1013, 1022, 1045, 1070, 1173, 1180, 1246, 1303, 1313, 1424, 1483, 1560, 1625, 1689, 1754, 1809, 1848, 1885, 1914, 1955, 2005, 2010, 2034, 2237, 2255, 2260.

Danner, J. V., contemporary American writer.
2043.

D'Annunzio, Gabriele, Italian poet and novelist. (1863–1938)
48, 1358.

Dante, Alighieri, Italian epic poet. (1265–1321)
21, 25, 74, 89, 105, 153, 170, 287, 300, 301, 325, 328, 355, 375, 420, 429, 464, 475, 582, 583, 595, 604, 623, 626, 628, 860, 889, 922, 1001, 1023, 1029, 1054, 1138, 1142, 1165, 1184, 1205, 1280, 1288, 1295, 1302, 1311, 1390, 1392, 1445, 1451, 1475, 1489, 1503, 1594, 1606, 1656, 1665, 1673, 1686, 1695, 1698, 1740, 1851, 1916, 1952, 1953, 1978, 1990, 2008, 2041, 2059, 2089, 2120, 2148, 2195, 2210, 2237, 2245.

Danton, Georges Jacques, leader in French Revolution. (1759–1794)
176, 414, 815, 1380.

D'Arcy, Hugh Antoine, publicist and writer born in Paris, France, but resident of the United States from 1872. (1843–1925)
607.

Dargan, Olive Tilford [Mrs. Pegram Dargan], contemporary American poet.
167, 1356.

D'Argenson, Marc Pierre, Comte de, French war minister. (1696–1764)
1392.

Darley, George, English poet and mathematician. (1795–1846)
1356, 1730, 1935.

Darling, Charles John, English jurist and wit. (1849–1936)
295, 1089, 1275, 1543, 1683, 1728.

Darmesteter, Madame James, see **Robinson, A. Mary F.**

Darrow, Clarence S., American lawyer and publicist. (1857–1938)
968.

Darwin, Charles Robert, English naturalist, propounder of the Darwinian theory of evolution. (1809–1882)
82, 586, 587, 965, 968.

Darwin, Erasmus, English naturalist and poet. (1731–1802)
233, 1341, 1385, 1495, 1912, 1920, 1944, 1975, 2063, 2096, 2112.

D'Aubigne, Jean Henri Merle, French theologian and historian. (1794–1872)
1741.

Daudet, Alphonse, French novelist. (1840–1897)
2040, 2190.

Daugherty, Harry Micajah, American politician. (1860–1941)
1553.

D'Avenant, Sir William, English poet and dramatist. (1606–1668)
47, 48, 180, 194, 354, 600, 670, 704, 731, 920, 968, 1072, 1301, 1505, 1564, 1730, 1843, 1921, 2164.

Davenport, Robert, English poet and dramatist. (fl. 1623)
98, 1051, 1300.

Davidson, John, British poet. (1857–1909)
211, 941, 961, 1194, 1211, 1338, 1345, 1518, 1892, 1934, 1939, 2013, 2111, 2233.

Davidson, Thomas, American miscellaneous writer.
769.

Davies, John (of Hereford), English poet and writing-master. (1565?–1618)
137, 485, 877, 1477, 2227, 2268.

Davies, Sir John, English jurist and poet. (1569–1626)
16, 104, 310, 359, 517, 600, 965, 1058, 1250, 1278, 1388, 1456, 1724, 1860, 1903, 1994, 2025, 2059, 2172, 2237.

Davies, Mary Carolyn, contemporary American poet and playwright.
202, 1417, 1435, 1444, 1908, 1909, 2178, 2210.

Davies, S. B. No biographical data available.
1232.

Davies, William Henry, English poet. (1870–1940)
50, 211, 882, 1017, 1042, 1099, 1567.

Davis, Gussie L., American Pullman porter and song-writer.
2285.

Davis, Jefferson, American statesman, soldier, President of the Confederate States. (1808–1889)
65, 367, 721.

Davis, John William, American lawyer and publicist. (1873–1955)
977.

DAVIS, RICHARD HARDING, American journalist, novelist and miscellaneous writer. (1864–1916)
142, 1398, 1636.

DAVIS, ROBERT HOBART, American editor and miscellanist. (1869–1942)
1742.

DAVIS, THOMAS OSBORNE, Irish poet and politician. (1814–1845)
933, 1868.

DAVISON, FRANCIS, English poet. (fl. 1602)
144, 436, 1885.

DAVISON, WALTER, English poet. (1581–1608?)
1208, 2197.

DAVY, WILLIAM, English lawyer, King's Sergeant. (d. 1780)
513.

DAWES, CHARLES GATES, American banker, soldier and politician. (1865–1951)
451, 891.

DAWSON, REVEREND GEORGE, English preacher, lecturer and politician. (1821–1876)
1108.

DAY, DOROTHEA, contemporary American writer.
1892.

DAY, JOHN, English dramatist. (1584?–1661?)
516, 1441, 1649, 1960, 1985.

DAY, SIR JOHN CHARLES FREDERIC SIGISMUND, English judge. (1826–1908)
681.

DAY, LILLIAN, American writer. (1893–)
2178.

DAY, THOMAS, English writer. (1748–1789)
1393.

DEBARY, ANNA BUNSTON, English poet. (1869–)
691.

DE BRITAINE, WILLIAM, see BRITAINE

DEBS, EUGENE VICTOR, American socialist advocate. (1855–1926)
202, 1235, 1902.

DE CASSERES, BENJAMIN, American dramatic critic and miscellanist. (1873–1945)
538, 2132.

DECATUR, STEPHEN, American naval commander. (1779–1820)
63.

DECHEZ, LOUIS A., French man of letters. (1808–1830)
150.

DEDEKIND, FRIEDRICH, German student. (fl. 1549)
73.

DEEMS, CHARLES FORCE, American Methodist clergyman and inspirational writer. (1820–1893)
2245.

DEFFAND, MARIE DE VICHY-CHAMROND, MADAME DU, French wit and literary hostess. (1697–1780)
146, 900, 1414, 2075, 2190, 2250.

DE FLEURY, MARIA, American essayist and verse-writer. (fl. 1804)
1733.

DEFOE, DANIEL, English journalist and novelist. (1661?–1731)
71, 126, 272, 286, 440, 444, 503, 539, 553, 560, 655, 722, 809, 844, 915, 1003, 1004, 1014, 1027, 1045, 1093, 1258, 1349, 1392, 1469, 1549, 1591, 1630, 1657, 1662, 1695, 1717, 1919, 1935, 1960, 1970, 1985, 2043, 2063, 2106, 2110, 2193.

DEKKER, THOMAS, English dramatist and pamphleteer. (1570?–1641?)
27, 77, 261, 296, 418, 424, 500, 549, 704, 842, 874, 1003, 1061, 1142, 1176, 1233, 1253, 1301, 1462, 1538, 1569, 1637, 1771, 1818, 1847, 2015, 2034, 2144, 2187, 2225.

DEKKER, THOMAS, and WEBSTER, JOHN, English dramatists and collaborators. (1570?–1641?), (1580?–1625?)
1958.

DEKOVEN, HENRY LOUIS REGINALD, American musical composer. (1861–1920)
2285.

DE LA MARE, WALTER, English poet. (1873–1956)
170, 556, 593, 756, 1742, 1844, 1912.

DELAND, MARGARET, or MARGARETTA, WADE, American poet and novelist. (1857–1945)
1792.

DELANEY, WILLIAM W., American song-writer. (1865–1930)
2285.

DELANO, AMASSA, American ship-captain and writer of travel books. (1763–1823)
2030.

DELAUNE, HENRY, English writer. (fl. 1670)
1901.

DELAVIGNE, JEAN FRANÇOIS CASIMIR, French poet and dramatist. (1793–1843)
699, 978.

DE LEON, EDWIN, American writer and diplomatist. (1828–1891)
1557.

DELILLE, JACQUES, French poet and translator. (1738–1813)
94, 729, 2040, 2063.

DELMAS, DELPHIN MICHAEL, American lawyer. (1844–1928)
1084.

DELONEY, THOMAS, English ballad-writer and pamphleteer. (1543?–1607?)
315, 549, 1191, 1332, 1818, 1821, 1900, 1949, 2032, 2039, 2137, 2151, 2177, 2199.

DELORD, TAXILE, French publicist. (1815–1877)
212.

DELTA, see MOIR, DAVID MACBETH

DELTEIL, JOSEPH, French essayist, poet and biographical writer. (1894–)
2121.

DEMACATUS, Greek dramatist.
699.

DEMADES, Greek orator and politician. (fl. 350 B.C.)
173, 1084, 1330.

DEMAREST, MARY LEE, American verse-writer. (1857–1888)
886.

DEMOCRITUS, Greek philosopher. (fl. c. 400 B.C.)
321, 1081, 1240, 1382, 1426, 1435, 1680, 1896, 2046, 2051.

DEMODOCUS, Greek epigrammatist. (fl. 350 B.C.)
1798.

DEMONAX, Greek Cynic philosopher. (fl. A.D. 150)
414, 1080.

DE MORGAN, AUGUSTUS, English mathematician. (1806–1871)
159, 679.

DE MORGAN, WILLIAM FREND, English novelist. (1839–1917)
250, 398, 770, 965, 1709.

DEMOSTHENES, Greek orator. (385–322 B.C.)
7, 179, 198, 422, 749, 1418, 1430, 1439, 1478, 1698, 1948.

DENHAM, SIR JOHN, English poet. (1615–1669)
7, 23, 29, 34, 41, 93, 97, 100, 183, 320, 438, 476, 537, 540, 617, 625, 653, 911, 934, 1007, 1021, 1031, 1045, 1150, 1249, 1529, 1532, 1571, 1617, 1934, 1937, 1983, 2076, 2258, 2263.

DENHAM, MICHAEL AISLABIE, English collector of folklore. (? –1859)
694, 1669, 2128.

DENMAN, THOMAS, second BARON DENMAN, English jurist. (1805–1894)
1081, 1087.

DENNIS, JOHN, English critic and playwright. (1657–1734)
1505, 1653.

DENTON, LYMAN W., American miscellaneous writer.
1194.

DEPEW, CHAUNCEY MITCHELL, American Senator and after-dinner speaker. (1834–1928)
449.

DE QUINCEY, THOMAS, English essayist and miscellaneous writer. (1785–1859)
502, 708, 733, 1165, 1169, 1292, 1358, 1451, 1482, 1697, 1855, 1968, 2176.

DERBY, LORD, see STANLEY

DESAIX DE VEYGOUX, LOUIS CHARLES ANTOINE, French soldier. (1768–1800)
2108.

DESCAMPS, JEAN BAPTISTE, French painter and writer. (1714–1791)
753.

DESCARTES, RENÉ, French mathematician and philosopher. (1596–1650)
1991.

DESCHAMPS, EUSTACHE (surname MOREL), French poet and fabulist. (c. 1320–1400)
729, 1121.

DESHOULIÈRES, ANTOINETTE DU LIGIER DE LA GARDE, French poet. (1638–1694)
476, 711.

DESLANDES, ANDRÉ FRANÇOIS BOUREAU, French skeptical writer. (1690–1757)
1725.

DESMOULINS, LUCIE SIMPLICE CAMILLE BENOIT, French politician and journalist. (1760–1794)
97, 165, 799, 1042.

DESPREZ, FRANK, English editor and miscellanist. (1853–1916)
724.

DESTOUCHES, PHILIPPE N., French dramatist. (1680–1754)
339, 1382, 2190.

DE TABLEY, LORD; JOHN BYRNE LEICESTER WARREN, third and last BARON DE TABLEY, English poet. (1835–1895)
1124, 1220, 1687.

DEUTSCH, BABETTE [MRS. AVRAHM YARMOLINSKY], American poet. (1895–)
40, 410.

DE VERE, SIR AUBREY, second BARONET, English poet and dramatist. (1788–1846)
956, 1104, 1831.

DE VERE, AUBREY THOMAS, Irish poet. (1814–1902)
357, 372, 603, 1188, 1293, 1598, 1747, 1846, 1886, 2110

DE VERE, MARY AINGE, see BRIDGES, MADELINE S.

DEVEREUX, ROBERT, third EARL OF ESSEX, see ESSEX, EARL OF

DEVLIN, JOSEPH. No biographical data available.
478.

DEWAR, LORD THOMAS ROBERT, first BARON DEWAR, English distiller, wit and miscellaneous writer. (1864–1930)
1263.

DEWEY, GEORGE, American admiral. (1837–1917)
66, 1557.

DEWEY, STODDARD, American newspaper correspondent. (1853–1934)
1630.

DIBDIN, CHARLES, English dramatist and songwriter. (1745–1814)
492, 495, 499, 500, 568, 635, 1003, 1009, 1177, 1188, 1321, 1503, 1778, 1780, 1805, 1866, 1973, 2110, 2151, 2179.

DIBDIN, THOMAS JOHN, English actor and dramatist. (1771–1841)
549.

* DICKENS, CHARLES, English novelist. (1812–1870)

DICKINSON, CHARLES MONROE, American journalist and verse-writer. (1842–1924)
253, 408, 1588, 1971.

DICKINSON, EMILY, American poet. (1830–1886)
71, 76, 116, 128, 130, 142, 170, 177, 183, 218, 322, 383, 386, 412, 455, 535, 593, 612, 619, 623, 729, 828, 837, 874, 875, 883, 921, 948, 962, 991, 1036, 1101, 1144, 1219, 1221, 1232, 1342, 1409, 1454, 1535, 1581, 1586, 1594, 1617, 1625, 1670, 1671, 1697, 1735, 1765, 1780, 1785, 1834, 1892, 1903, 1932, 1974, 2011, 2022, 2051, 2084, 2191, 2224.

DICKINSON, JOHN, American lawyer, patriot and statesman. (1732–1808)
56, 225.

DICKMAN, FRANKLIN J., American critic. (fl. 1849)
974.

DIDACUS STELLA, Roman general. (fl. 50 B.C.)
771.

DOLLIVER, CLARA, American verse-writer.
122.
DOMETT, ALFRED, English statesman and poet. (1811–1887)
268, 2160.
DONAHEY, ALVIN VICTOR, American politician and legislator. (1873–1946)
1553.
DONATUS, ÆLIUS, Latin grammarian and teacher of rhetoric. (fl. A.D. 360)
1507.
DONNE, JOHN, English poet and divine. (1573–1631)
40, 89, 133, 156, 173, 230, 262, 290, 369, 406, 578, 600, 610, 619, 679, 701, 909, 1101, 1195, 1200, 1208, 1213, 1221, 1243, 1331, 1486, 1735, 1792, 1802, 1831, 1843, 1889.
DOOLITTLE, HILDA ("H. D.") [MRS. RICHARD ALDINGTON], American poet. (1886–)
534.
DORION, Greek writer. (c. A.D. 150)
1920.
DORR, JULIA CAROLINE RIPLEY, American poet and novelist. (1825–1913)
31, 93, 210, 365, 683, 806, 822, 1156, 1746, 1825.
DOTEN, ELIZABETH, American verse-writer. (1829– ?)
795.
DOTY, WALTER G., American verse-writer. (1876–1920)
1488.
DOUBLEDAY, THOMAS, English poet, dramatist, radical politician and political economist. (1790–1870)
1871.
DOUDNEY, SARAH, English writer. (1843–1926)
394, 1130, 1304, 1450, 2100, 2124.
DOUGLAS, LORD ALFRED BRUCE, English poet. (1870–1945)
834, 1518, 1809, 2147.
DOUGLAS, GAWIN, or GAVIN, Scottish poet and Bishop. (1474?–1522)
161, 344, 1939.
DOUGLAS, JESSE, American humorist. (fl. 1839)
1734.
DOUGLAS, NORMAN, English novelist. (1869–1952)
506, 1028, 1086.
DOUGLAS, STEPHEN ARNOLD, American statesman, opponent of Lincoln in 1860. (1813–1861)
1553.
DOUGLAS, WILLIAM, OF FLEUGLAND, Scottish writer. (c. 1672–1748)
1211.
DOUGLASS, W. S., American song-writer.
2285.
DOUVIER, French antiquarian. (fl. 1660)
718.
DOW, DOROTHY, American poet. (1899–)
40, 134.
DOW, LORENZO, American evangelist preacher. (1777–1834)
487, 1696, 1830.
DOWDEN, EDWARD, English educator and critic. (1842–1913)
888.
DOWLING, BARTHOLOMEW, Irish poet. (1823–1863)
1868.
DOWSON, ERNEST, English poet. (1867–1900)
437, 1137, 1198, 1216.
DOWTY, A. A., American humorist. (fl. 1873)
1615, 1699.
DOYLE, SIR ARTHUR CONAN, English physician and novelist. (1859–1930)
472, 551, 2209.
DOYLE, SIR FRANCIS HASTINGS CHARLES, second BARONET, English poet. (1810–1888)
562, 1864.
DRAKE, SIR FRANCIS, English circumnavigator and admiral. (1540?–1596)
1895.
DRAKE, JOSEPH RODMAN, American poet. (1795–1820)
673, 1466, 1732, 1834, 2117.
DRAPER, JOHN WILLIAM, English chemist and historical writer. (1811–1882)
956, 2002.
DRAXE, THOMAS, English divine and compiler. (? –1618)
134, 210, 227, 267, 564, 656, 832, 917, 922, 1095, 1304, 1332, 1441, 1985, 2231.
DRAYTON, MICHAEL, English poet. (1563–1631)
3, 123, 220, 294, 441, 476, 551, 583, 670, 696, 747, 850, 868, 1015, 1038, 1098, 1203, 1225, 1252, 1261, 1307, 1319, 1359, 1373, 1398, 1454, 1477, 1530, 1532, 1572, 1630, 1632, 1705, 1805, 1980, 2014, 2044, 2071, 2115, 2176.
DRENNAN, WILLIAM, Irish poet. (1754–1820)
996.
DRESBACH, GLENN WARD, American poet. (1889–)
23.
DRESSER, PAUL, American song-writer. (1857–1911) Born Paul Dreiser.
977, 2285.
DREWRY, GUY CARLETON, American journalist and verse-writer. (1901–)
1144.
DRINKWATER, JOHN, English poet and dramatist. (1882–1937)
23, 339, 425, 610, 833, 965, 1261, 1385, 1676, 1813, 1906, 1910, 2207.
DRISCOLL, LOUISE, American poet and miscellaneous writer. (1875–)
23, 396, 1193.
DRISLANE, JACK, American song-writer.
2285.
DRIVER, CAPTAIN WILLIAM, American sea-captain. (fl. 1831)
674.
DRUMMOND, HENRY, Scottish theological writer. (1851–1897)
1828.
DRUMMOND, THOMAS, English engineer and administrator. (1797–1840)
1622.

DRUMMOND, WILLIAM, Scottish poet. (1585-1649)
268, 272, 407, 851, 892, 1127, 1133, 1135, 1355, 1374, 1404, 1844, 1873, 2179, 2240, 2269.

DRUMMOND, SIR WILLIAM, English scholar and diplomatist. (1770?-1828)
1678.

DRURY, LIEUT.-COL. WILLIAM PRICE, English soldier and miscellaneous writer. (1861-1949)
2283.

DRYDEN, CHARLES, American newspaperman. (1860-1931)
1644.

* DRYDEN, JOHN, English poet and dramatist. (1631-1700)

DRYDEN, JOHN, and CAVENDISH, WILLIAM, DUKE OF NEWCASTLE, English dramatists and collaborators. (1631-1700), (1592-1676)
761.

DRYDEN, JOHN, and LEE, NATHANIEL, English dramatists and collaborators. (1631-1700), (1653?-1692)
375, 799, 2032, 2034.

DRYDEN, JOHN, and SHEFFIELD, JOHN, first DUKE OF BUCKINGHAM, English writers and collaborators. (1631-1700), (1648-1721)
2252.

DU BARTAS, GUILLAUME SALLUSTE, French poet and soldier. (1544-1590)
126, 142, 355, 375, 387, 423, 466, 521, 602, 608, 617, 667, 670, 679, 705, 721, 849, 1031, 1072, 1133, 1181, 1251, 1284, 1388, 1389, 1400, 1639, 1642, 1677, 1903, 1949, 1990, 2027, 2116, 2127, 2130, 2137, 2148, 2239.

DUBOIS, CARDINAL GUILLAUME, French Cardinal and Minister of State. (1656-1723)
832.

DUBOSCQ-MONTANDRÉ, CLAUDE, French man of letters and pamphleteer of the Fronde. (d. c. 1690)
835.

DUBUC, GUILLAUME, French pastor and professor of theology at Lausanne. (d. 1603)
2098.

DUCK, STEPHEN, English poet. (1705-1756)
1565.

DUDEVANT, ARMANDINE LUCILE DUPIN, BARONNE, see SAND, GEORGE

DUDLEY, ROBERT, EARL OF LEICESTER, English courtier. (1532?-1588)
1084.

DUFF, ESTHER LILIAN, contemporary English poet.
1783, 2197.

DUFF, JAMES L. No biographical data available.
2033.

DUFFERIN, COUNTESS OF, see SHERIDAN, HELEN SELINA

DUFFIELD, SAMUEL AUGUSTUS WILLOUGHBY, American Presbyterian clergyman and hymn-writer. (1843-1887)
11, 278.

DUFFY, JAMES, Irish dramatist.
118.

DUGANNE, AUGUSTINE JOSEPH HICKEY, American versifier and miscellaneous writer. (1823-1884)
343, 1528.

DUKE, RICHARD, English poet and divine. (1658-1711)
1275.

DU LORENS, JACQUES, French satirical poet. (1583-1650)
1696.

DUMANOIR, PHILIPPE FRANÇOIS PINEL, see BAYARD and DUMANOIR

DUMAS, ALEXANDRE, French novelist and dramatist. (1803-1870)
73, 680, 1294, 1929, 2066, 2206.

DUMAS, ALEXANDRE, FILS, French dramatist. (1824-1895)
207.

DU MAURIER, GEORGE LOUIS PALMELLA BUSSON, French-English artist and novelist. (1834-1896)
464, 943, 1018, 1118, 1138, 1157, 1416, 1475, 2201.

DUMOURIEZ, CHARLES FRANÇOIS, French soldier and statesman. (1739-1823)
1741.

DUNBAR, PAUL LAURENCE, American Negro poet. (1872-1906)
791, 1137, 1879, 2285.

DUNBAR, WILLIAM, Scottish poet. (1465-1529)
790, 1300, 1395.

DUNCOMBE, LEWIS, English writer and translator. (1711-1730)
2041.

DUNLOP, JOHN, Scottish song-writer. (1755-1820)
731.

DUNNE, FINLEY PETER, American humorist. (1867-1936)
473, 502, 825, 852, 1026, 1028, 1286, 1431, 1439, 1473, 1612, 1658, 1741, 2069, 2115.

DUNTON, JOHN, English bookseller and satirical writer. (1659-1733)
716, 2139.

DUPANLOUP, FELIX ANTOINE PHILIBERT, French prelate and educational writer. (1802-1878)
649.

DUPIN, ANDRÉ, French lawyer and statesman. (1783-1865)
1741, 1793.

DURANT, WILLIAM JAMES (WILL), American miscellaneous writer. (1885-)
1345.

D'URFEY, THOMAS, English poet and dramatist. (1653-1723)
111, 126, 245, 390, 441, 469, 546, 671, 891, 1004, 1257, 1365, 1502, 1636, 1710, 1726, 1771, 1817, 2196, 2202, 2246.

DURYEA, WILLIAM RANKIN, American verse-writer. (fl. 1866)
908.

DWIGHT, JOHN SULLIVAN, American music critic and editor. (1813-1893)
1100, 1706, 2233.

DWIGHT, TIMOTHY, Congregational clergyman, educator and miscellaneous writer; President of Yale College. (1752–1817)
51, 1994.

DYER, SIR EDWARD, English poet and courtier. (1543–1607)
310, 751, 870, 1179, 1249, 1310, 1329.

DYER, JOHN, English poet. (1700?–1758)
463, 500, 829, 1137, 1290, 1309, 1385, 1732, 2269.

DYKES, THOMAS, English divine and religious writer. (1761–1847)
49, 1225.

DYMOKE, SIR ROBERT, English knight-banneret and sheriff. (? –1546)
1742.

E

EARLE, SIR WILLIAM, English jurist.
234.

EAST, REV. JOHN. No biographical data available.
790.

EASTMAN, ELAINE GOODALE, American poet. (1863–)
687, 689.

EATON, DORMAN BRIDGMAN, American lawyer and civil service reformer. (1823–1899)
1550.

EATON, WALTER PRICHARD, American dramatic critic and essayist. (1878–1957)
2149.

EBERS, GEORG MORITZ, German Egyptologist and novelist. (1837–1898)
2206.

ECKENRODE, HAMILTON JAMES, American historical writer. (1881–)
1551.

EDDY, MRS. MARY BAKER GLOVER, American religious leader, founder of Christian Science. (1821–1910)
278, 459, 577, 783, 870, 1057, 1188, 1285, 1306, 1583, 1693, 1827, 1830, 1831, 1994, 2020, 2053.

EDGEWORTH, MARIA, English novelist, who spent most of her life in Ireland. (1767–1849)
192, 206, 208, 254, 501, 513, 693, 747, 996, 1003, 1259, 1269, 1414, 1546, 1622, 1636, 1770, 2123, 2230, 2259, 2278.

EDISON, THOMAS ALVA, American inventor. (1847–1931)
27, 103, 560, 758, 1059, 1680, 1888, 1996, 2100, 2233

EDMAN, IRWIN, American educator and essayist. (1896–1954)
1301.

EDWARDS, DAVID, American writer. (fl. 1780)
1654.

EDWARDS, JONATHAN, American Congregational clergyman, philosopher and defender of Calvinism. (1703–1757)
589, 790, 892, 903.

EDWARDS, RICHARD, English poet and playwright. (1523?–1566)
223, 731, 928, 1197, 1282, 2239.

EDWARDS, THOMAS, English controversial writer. (1599–1647)
1827.

EDWIN, JOHN, English comedian. (1749–1790)
1139.

EGAN, MAURICE FRANCIS, American translator, novelist, editor and diplomatist. (1852–1924)
265.

EGBERT OF LIÉGE, or EGBERT VON LÜTTICH, Flemish poet, cleric and hagiographer. (fl. 1060)
667.

EGERTON, FRANK, American song-writer.
2285.

EGGLESTON, EDWARD, American itinerant Methodist preacher and novelist. (1837–1902)
890.

EHRMANN, MAX, American poet, dramatist and miscellaneous writer. (1872–1945)
1825.

EINSTEIN, ALBERT, German-Swiss physicist, propounder of the theory of relativity. (1879–1955)
53, 748, 786, 940, 961, 1012, 1058, 1126, 1472, 1765, 1969.

ELDON, LORD, see SCOTT, JOHN

ELDRIDGE, PAUL, American writer and educator. (1888–)
567.

ELEANOR OF CASTILE, Queen of England. (? –1290)
885.

ELIOT, CHARLES WILLIAM, American educator, President of Harvard University. (1834–1926)
185, 518, 535, 632, 856, 916, 968, 1497, 2112.

* ELIOT, GEORGE (pseud. of MARY ANN EVANS CROSS), English novelist and poet. (1819–1880)

ELIOT, JOHN, English scholar and Puritan preacher who came to Massachusetts in 1631 and spent the remainder of his life as missionary among the New England Indians. (1604–1690)
1316.

ELIOT, THOMAS STEARNS, poet and essayist, born in America, but a British subject since 1927. (1888–)
9, 93, 348, 694, 1676, 2018, 2263.

ELIZABETH, Queen of England. (1533–1603)
245, 262, 306, 414, 454, 622, 709, 716, 869, 1040, 1428, 1620, 1649, 1664.

ELKINS, STEPHEN BENTON, American legislator, captain of industry and Secretary of War. (1841–1911)
1568.

ELLENBOROUGH, LORD, see LAW, EDWARD

ELLERTON, EDWARD, English clergyman and founder of scholarships. (1770–1851)
378.

ELLERTON, JOHN LODGE (formerly JOHN LODGE), English amateur musical composer. (1801–1873)
394.

ELLIOT, JANE, Scottish poet. (1727–1805)
681.

ELLIOTT, CHARLOTTE, English hymn-writer. (1789–1871)
264.

ESTE, IPPOLITO D', Italian Cardinal and patron of arts. (1479–1520)
995.
ESTROM, D. A., American song-writer.
2285.
ETHELWOLD, Bishop of Winchester. (908?–984)
939.
ETHEREGE, SIR GEORGE, English dramatist. (1636–1694)
1169.
ETIENNE, or ÉSTIENNE, HENRI, French printer and scholar. (1531–1598)
23, 789, 1206.
EUCLID, Alexandrian geometrician. (fl. 300 B.C.)
528.
EUPOLIS, Greek poet. (c. 446–411 B.C.)
1096, 1490, 1898, 1962, 2014.
* EURIPIDES, Greek dramatic poet. (480–406 B.C.)
EUSDEN, LAURENCE, English Poet Laureate. (1688–1730)
766.
EUSTATHIUS, Greek Archbishop and classical commentator. (? –c. 1193)
539.
EUWER, ANTHONY, American journalist, verse-writer and illustrator. (1877–)
609.
EVANS, ABEL, English divine and poet. (1679–1737)
568.
EVANS, ARTHUR BENONI, English miscellaneous writer. (1781–1854)
137.
EVANS, DONALD, American poet. (1884–1921)
433, 1041, 1136.
EVANS, LEWIS, English controversialist. (fl. 1574)
443, 605, 2159.
EVARTS, WILLIAM MAXWELL, American statesman and Secretary of State. (1818–1901)
473, 1553.
EVE, JOSEPH, American poet. (fl. 1823)
572.
EVELYN, JOHN, English virtuoso and diarist. (1620–1706)
253, 491, 669, 920, 1232, 1806.
EVERETT, DAVID, American lawyer and journalist. (1770–1813)
1438, 2041.
EVERETT, EDWARD, American scholar, statesman and orator. (1794–1865)
57, 234, 404, 639, 1339, 2121.
EVODUS, Greek poet, date unknown.
525.
EWART, WILLIAM, English scholar and politician. (1798–1869)
111.
EWER, W. N. No biographical data available.
1466.
EYTINGE, MARGARET, American actress and poet.
120.

F

FABER, FREDERICK WILLIAM, English priest, poet and devotional writer. (1814–1863)
157, 618, 793, 1064, 1451, 1706, 1725, 1773, 2039.
FABIUS, QUINTUS FABIUS MAXIMUS VERRUCOSUS (CUNCTATOR), Roman general and statesman. (d. 203 B.C.)
198, 461, 653, 780, 1324.
FABYAN, ROBERT, English chronicler. (d. 1513)
377, 545.
FAGAN, BARNEY, American song-writer. (1850–1937)
778.
FAGNANO, ANGE. No biographical data available.
1816.
FAIRCHILD, HENRY PRATT, American social scientist. (1880–)
1924.
FAIRCHILD, LUCIUS, American Union soldier, Governor of Wisconsin, and diplomatist. (1831–1896)
353.
FAIRFAX, EDWARD, English writer and translator. (d. 1635)
487, 1437.
FAIRHOLT, FREDERICK WILLIAM, English engraver and antiquarian writer. (1814–1866)
2018.
FALCONER, WILLIAM, English poet. (1732–1769)
750, 1097, 1306, 1758, 1776, 1815, 1938, 1941.
FALKLAND, LORD, see CARY, LUCIUS
FALLERSLEBEN, HOFFMANN VON (pseud. of AUGUST HEINRICH HOFFMANN), German poet and philologist. (1798–1874)
767.
FANE, VIOLET, see SINGLETON, MARY MONTGOMERIE, BARONESS CURRIE
FANSHAWE, CATHERINE MARIA, English verse-writer. (1765–1834)
362, 1724.
FARGUS, FREDERICK JOHN, see CONWAY, HUGH
FARMER, JOHN, English composer. (fl. 1591–1601)
2135.
FARNIE, H. B., English song-writer.
2285.
FARQUHAR, GEORGE, English dramatist. (1678–1707)
27, 44, 117, 134, 169, 187, 219, 322, 350, 492, 493, 697, 760, 803, 830, 898, 917, 944, 952, 1076, 1154, 1217, 1259, 1275, 1336, 1394, 1412, 1432, 1467, 1490, 1492, 1512, 1569, 1577, 1598, 1638, 1695, 1750, 1778, 1783, 1875, 1910, 1912, 2004, 2049, 2059, 2178, 2191, 2195, 2203, 2207, 2222, 2257.
FARRAGUT, DAVID GLASGOW, American naval commander. (1801–1870)
65.
FARRAN, EDGAR T., American song-writer.
2285.
FARRAR, FREDERIC WILLIAM, English divine and devotional writer. (1831–1903)
1103, 1938.
FARRER, GEORGINA. No biographical data available.
1453.

FAUNCE, WILLIAM HERBERT PERRY, American educator. (1859–1930)
527.

FAVART, CHARLES SIMON, French dramatist. (1710–1792)
1045, 1412.

FAVORINUS, Latin rhetorician and sophist. (fl. c. A.D. 125)
653, 1352, 1575, 1580.

FAVRE, GABRIEL CLAUDE JULES, French statesman and orator. (1809–1880)
718.

FAWCETT, EDGAR, American novelist and poet. (1847–1904)
668, 822, 2096.

FAWCETT, JOHN, THE ELDER, English composer and hymn-writer. (1789–1867)
264.

FAWKES, FRANCIS, English poet and divine. (1720–1777)
1565.

FEATLEY, or FAIRCLOUGH, DANIEL, English controversialist. (1582–1645)
804.

FEINSTEIN, MARTIN, American miscellaneous writer. (1892–)
1862.

FELLTHAM, OWEN, English miscellaneous writer. (1602?–1668)
320, 331, 731, 733, 753, 1018, 1426, 1515, 1877, 2239.

FÉNELON, FRANÇOIS DE SALIGNAC DE LA MOTHE-, French writer and romanticist. (1651–1715)
244, 536, 732, 786, 1495, 1584, 1585, 1690, 1788, 1926.

FENTON, EDWARD, English captain and navigator. (? –1603)
1185.

FENTON, ELIJAH, English poet. (1683–1730)
1271.

FENTON, SIR GEOFFREY, English translator and statesman. (1539?–1608)
656, 711, 1632.

FERGUSON, CHARLES, American clergyman and economist. (1863–)
535.

FERGUSON, SIR SAMUEL, Irish poet. (1810–1886)
933, 1854.

FERGUSON, JAMES, Scottish poet. (1710–1776)
365.

FERGUSSON, JAMES, English architect and writer on architectural subjects. (1808–1886)
94, 365.

FERGUSSON, ROBERT, Scottish poet. (1750–1774)
568, 1099, 2101.

FERN, FANNY (pseud. of MRS. SARAH PAYSON PARTON), American writer of children's books. (1811–1872)
515.

FERRIAR, JOHN, English physician and writer on medical subjects. (1761–1815)
189.

FERRIER, LOUIS, French poet. (1652–1721)
645.

FERTÉ, HENRI FRANÇOIS DE LA, French Marshal. (1657–1703)
2114.

FESSENDEN, SAMUEL, American lawyer and politician. (1847–1908)
331.

FESSENDEN, WILLIAM PITT, American statesman and financier. (1806–1869)
1557.

FEUERBACH, LUDWIG ANDREAS, German philosopher. (1804–1872)
1984.

FICKE, ARTHUR DAVISON, American poet. (1883–1945)
129, 227, 1833.

FIELD, ARTHUR, contemporary American writer.
1241.

FIELD, DAVID DUDLEY, American jurist. (1805–1894)
1029, 1463.

FIELD, EUGENE, American poet and humorist. (1850–1895)
92, 185, 260, 269, 370, 408, 505, 521, 669, 928, 1017, 1304, 1475, 1519, 1673, 1847, 2152.

FIELD, MARY KATHERINE KEMBLE (KATE FIELD), American lecturer and journalist. (1838–1896)
2206.

FIELD, NATHANIEL, English actor and dramatist. (1587–1633)
1730, 2135, 2137.

FIELD, STEPHEN JOHNSON, American jurist. (1816–1899)
1020.

FIELDER, R. R. No biographical data available.
679.

FIELDING, HENRY, English novelist. (1707–1754)
9, 77, 98, 99, 124, 216, 235, 254, 265, 306, 386, 424, 440, 441, 446, 464, 479, 500, 503, 506, 517, 522, 531, 544, 549, 564, 589, 597, 659, 705, 824, 825, 844, 900, 941, 959, 989, 1020, 1031, 1184, 1258, 1263, 1267, 1274, 1279, 1315, 1322, 1331, 1334, 1382, 1414, 1440, 1564, 1591, 1601, 1649, 1663, 1664, 1721, 1724, 1851, 1910, 1925, 1959, 1968, 2243.

FIELDS, JAMES THOMAS, American publisher and essayist. (1816–1881)
124, 329, 341, 794, 907, 1227, 1447, 1778, 1815.

FIGULUS, PUBLIUS NIGIDIUS, Roman savant. (c. 98–45 B.C.)
1110, 1691.

FILICAJA, VINCENZA DA, Italian poet. (1642–1707)
1001.

FINCH, ANNE, COUNTESS OF WINCHELSEA, English poet. (1661–1720)
1912, 2022, 2193.

FINCH, FRANCIS MILES, American jurist and verse-writer. (1827–1907)
1869.

FINCH, FRED H., American song-writer.
2285.

FINK, HENRY, American song-writer.
982.

FINLAY, GEORGE, Scottish historian. (1799–1875)
163.

FINLEY, JOHN, Irish poet. (1796–1866)
1278.

FINLEY, JOHN, a journalist of Richmond, Ind. (1796–1866)
977.

FINNEY, CHARLES GRANDISON, American revivalist and educator. (1792–1875)
1594.

FIRDUSI, or FIRDAUSI, ABUL KASIM MANSUR, greatest of Persian poets. (c. 950–1020)
1801.

FIRMIN, GILES, English ejected minister and theological writer. (1614–1697)
892, 1763.

FISH, HOWARD, English poet. (c. 1819)
1792.

FISHER, JOHN, English prelate and theological writer, Bishop of Rochester. (1459–1535)
1040.

FISHER, JOHN ARBUTHNOT, first BARON FISHER, English admiral. (1841–1920)
149.

FISHER, VARDIS, American educator and miscellaneous writer. (1895–)
1145.

FISK, JAMES, American speculator. (1834–1872)
1645.

FISKE, JOHN, American essayist and historian. (1842–1901)
788.

FITCH, WILLIAM CLYDE, American playwright. (1865–1909)
603, 727, 1635, 1881.

FITZGEFFREY, HENRY, English satirical writer. (fl. 1617)
1467.

FITZGERALD, EDWARD, English poet and translator. (1809–1883)
203, 258, 709, 1139, 1417, 1590, 1734, 2005, 2050, 2078, 2273.

FITZGERALD, PERCY H., Irish writer. (1834–1925)
599.

FITZHERBERT, SIR ANTHONY, English jurist and legal writer. (1470–1538)
1729.

FITZHUGH, LAFAYETTE, American politician of the Civil War period.
1553.

FITZSIMMONS, ROBERT PROMETHEUS, pugilist and actor, born in England, came to America in 1890. (1862–1917)
837.

FLACCUS, AULUS PERSIUS, see PERSIUS

FLACCUS, QUINTUS HORATIUS, see HORACE

FLAGG, WILSON, American naturalist. (1805–1884)
174.

FLAMM, PROFESSOR OSWALD, German scientist. (1861– ?)
768.

FLAMMARION, CAMILLE, French astronomer. (1842–1925)
88.

FLANAGAN, WEBSTER, American politician, Republican leader in Texas. (1832–1924)
1549.

FLATMAN, THOMAS, English poet and miniature-painter. (1637–1688)
40, 209, 391, 1124.

FLAVEL, JOHN, English Presbyterian divine. (1630?–1691)
1430.

FLECKER, JAMES ELROY, English poet and dramatist. (1884–1915)
1055, 1531, 1611, 2101.

FLECKNOE, RICHARD, Irish poet. (d. 1678?)
216, 920, 1463, 1666, 1820.

FLEESON, NEVILLE, American song-writer. (1887–)
2286.

FLEETWOOD, WILLIAM, English divine and theological writer. (1656–1723)
542.

FLEMING, ALICE, English poet. (fl. 1900)
410.

FLEMING, CARROLL, American song-writer.
1747.

FLETCHER, ANDREW, of Saltoun, Scottish patriot. (1655–1716)
123, 215.

FLETCHER, GILES, THE YOUNGER, English poet. (1588?–1623)
263, 1173, 1405, 1670, 1950.

FLETCHER, HENRY PRATHER. American diplomatist and politician. (1873–)
451.

FLETCHER, JOHN, English dramatist. (1579–1625)
7, 217, 353, 358, 363, 380, 387, 396, 441, 454, 493, 495, 503, 517, 600, 601, 648, 742, 789, 808, 828, 858, 922, 1003, 1052, 1094, 1191, 1211, 1230, 1247, 1260, 1275, 1288, 1291, 1340, 1405, 1418, 1456, 1523, 1604, 1633, 1638, 1710, 1827, 1828, 1830, 1844, 1848, 1867, 1874, 1875, 1906, 1954, 1958, 1978, 1990, 2030, 2072, 2093, 2099, 2106, 2132, 2145, 2151, 2196, 2197, 2203, 2206, 2227, 2236.

FLETCHER, JOHN, and MASSINGER, PHILIP, English dramatists and collaborators. (1579–1625), (1583–1640)
745.

FLETCHER, PHINEAS, English poet. (1582–1650)
489, 600, 785, 815, 1016, 1135, 1173, 1184, 1191, 1200, 1539, 1580, 1786, 1849, 1903, 1935, 1950, 2130, 2215.

FLEXNER, ABRAHAM, American educator. (1866–1946)
278, 527, 528, 529, 530, 960, 2069.

FLINT, CHARLES RANLETT, American merchant and banker. (1850–1934)
2048.

FLINT, FRANK STEWART, English poet. (1885–)
1155.

FLORIAN, JEAN P. C., CHEVALIER DE, French writer. (1755–1794)
207, 1061.

* FLORIO, JOHN, English translator and lexicographer. (1553?–1625)

FLORUS, LUCIUS ANNÆUS, Latin historian. (fl. 125 B.C.)
1532.

FLYNN, JOSEPH, American song-writer.
2285.

FOCH, FERDINAND, French Marshal; commander of allied armies on the Western front in the World War. (1851–1929)
414, 977, 2083, 2108.

FOGERTY, FRANK, American song-writer.
1882.

FONTANES, LOUIS, MARQUIS DE, French legislator and poet. (1757–1821)
1485.

FONTENELLE, BERNARD LE BOUYER DE, French writer. (1657–1757)
351, 415, 1133, 1725, 2108.

FOOTE, SAMUEL, English actor and dramatist. (1720–1777)
163, 383, 667, 753, 898, 1097, 1259, 1410, 2178.

FORAKER, JOSEPH BENSON, American politician and Governor of Ohio. (1846–1917)
204.

FORBY, ROBERT, English philologist. (1759–1825)
1633.

FORD, FORD MADOX, English miscellaneous writer. (1873–1939)
2131.

FORD, HENRY, American automobile manufacturer. (1863–1947)
899, 951, 1335, 1996.

FORD, JOHN, English dramatist. (1586–1639?)
240, 429, 446, 466, 493, 582, 676, 723, 786, 837, 1022, 1173, 1187, 1274, 1278, 1291, 1415, 1500, 1713, 1958, 1960, 2016.

FORD, JOHN, and DEKKER, THOMAS, English dramatists and collaborators. (1586–1639?), (1570?–1641)
220, 1335.

FORD, [MRS.] LENA GUILBERT, American poet, killed in an air-raid in London during the World War.
282, 2285.

FORD, PAUL LEICESTER, American novelist and historical writer. (1865–1902)
721.

FORD, SIMEON, American hotel-keeper and after-dinner speaker. (1855–1933)
1768.

FORD, WALTER H., American song-writer.
2286.

FORDE, THOMAS, English satirical writer. (fl. 1660)
462, 1281.

FORDYCE, JAMES, Scottish Presbyterian divine. (1720–1796)
791.

FORMAN, SIMON, English astrologer and quack doctor. (1552–1611)
287.

FORSTER, JOHN, English historian and biographer. (1812–1876)
759, 1772.

FORTESCUE, SIR JOHN, English jurist and legal writer. (1394?–1476?)
290, 1640.

FORTUNATUS, VENANTIUS HONORIUS, SAINT, Bishop of Poitiers, Latin poet. (530–600)
514.

FOSDICK, HARRY EMERSON, American clergyman. (1878–)
131, 430, 783, 865, 966, 1103, 1117, 1245, 1263, 2067.

FOSS, SAM WALTER, American poet. (1858–1911)
56, 195, 942, 1064, 1430, 1435, 1494, 1495, 1502, 1596, 1994, 2045, 2094.

FOSTER, BIRKET, English artist. (1825–1899)
1766.

FOSTER, CHARLES, Secretary of the Treasury under President Harrison. (1828–1904)
66.

FOSTER, HON. SIR GEORGE EULAS, Canadian Minister of Trade and Commerce. (1847–1931)
545.

FOSTER, SIR MICHAEL, English jurist and writer of legal works. (1689–1763)
1611.

FOSTER, SIR ROBERT, English Lord Chief-Justice. (1589–1663)
596.

FOSTER, STEPHEN COLLINS, American song-writer. (1826–1864)
472, 907, 1034, 1454, 1978, 2286, 2287.

FOSTER, THOMAS. No biographical data available.
670.

FOSTER, THOMAS, American journalist. (fl. 1868)
275.

FOUCHÉ, JOSEPH, French administrator. (1763–1820)
337, 394.

FOUCHER, LÉON, French critic. (fl. 1860)
66.

FOULKE, WILLIAM DUDLEY, American poet and miscellaneous writer. (1848–1935)
780.

FOULKES, WILLIAM HIRAM, American Presbyterian clergyman. (1877–)
646.

FOURIER, FRANÇOIS MARIE CHARLES, French socialist and writer on economics. (1772–1837)
1472, 1902.

FOWLER, ELLEN THORNEYCROFT [MRS. A. L. FELKIN], English novelist. (1860–1929)
282.

FOX, ALBERT, JR. No biographical data available.
2006.

FOX, CHARLES JAMES, English statesman. (1749–1806)
415, 1041, 1460, 1550, 1714, 2165.

FOX, GEORGE, English founder of Society of Friends and missionary. (1624–1691)
1592.

FOX, HENRY, first BARON HOLLAND, English statesman. (1705–1774)
415, 1171.

FOX, HENRY RICHARD VASSALL, third BARON HOLLAND, English statesman and editor. (1773–1840)
1901.

FOXE, JOHN, English martyrologist. (1516–1587)
2135.

FRANC, MARTIN LE, French poet. (d. c. 1460)
780.

FRANCE, ANATOLE (pseud. of JACQUES ANATOLE THIBAULT), French novelist, dramatist and poet. (1844–1924)
133, 228, 338, 762, 1011, 1079, 1177, 1267, 1647, 1678, 1926, 2061, 2066, 2083, 2231, 2252.

FRANCIS (FRANÇOIS) I, King of France. (1494–1547)
663, 917, 1040, 1043, 2198.

FRANCIS DE SALES, SAINT, French Bishop and devotional writer. (1567–1622)
198.

FRANCK, HAWLEY, American song-writer.
2287.

FRANCK, RICHARD, English writer. (1624?–1708)
105, 363.

FRANCK, SEBASTIAN, German writer. (1499–1542)
420.

FRANK, FLORENCE KIPER [MRS. JEROME N. FRANK], contemporary American poet.
1352.

* FRANKLIN, BENJAMIN, American philosopher and statesman. (1706–1790)

FRANKLIN, KATE. No biographical data available.
819.

FRAZEE-BOWER, HELEN [MRS. W. M. BOWER], American poet. (1896–)
226.

FRASER, JAMES, English writer and collector of Oriental manuscripts. (1713–1754)
2066.

FREDERICK II, THE GREAT, King of Prussia, patron of literature. (1712–1786)
67, 170, 415, 568, 820, 832, 1241, 1252, 1437, 1597, 1610, 1693, 1863, 1939, 2117.

FREDERICK III, Emperor of the Holy Roman Empire. (1415–1493)
1630.

FREEDMAN, ANDREW, American sportsman and capitalist; owner of the New York Giants. (1861–1915)
363.

FREEMAN, EDWARD AUGUSTUS, English historian. (1823–1892)
1037.

FREEMAN, JOHN, English poet. (1880–1929)
1346.

FREEMAN, ROBERT, American clergyman and writer. (1878–1940)
201, 883, 1587.

FREEMAN, THOMAS, English epigrammatist. (fl. 1614)
551.

FREILIGRATH, FERDINAND, German poet. (1810–1876)
1221.

FRENEAU, PHILIP MORIN, American poet and journalist. (1752–1832)
49, 284, 721, 769, 1145, 1896, 2073, 2121, 2122.

FRERE, JOHN HOOKHAM, English diplomatist and miscellaneous writer. (1769–1846)
329, 437, 742, 2222.

FRÉRON, ELIE CATHARINE, French educator and miscellaneous writer. (1718–1776)
2264.

FRIEND, HENRY. No biographical data available.
746.

FRITH, JOHN, English Protestant martyr. (1503–1533)
1341.

FROHMAN, CHARLES, American theatrical manager. (1860–1915)
398.

FROISSART, JEAN, French chronicler. (1337?–1410)
560.

FROST, ROBERT, American poet. (1875–1963)
117, 152, 200, 201, 419, 612, 904, 950, 1193, 1395, 1525, 1680, 1873.

FROTHINGHAM, NATHANIEL LANGDON, American Unitarian clergyman and poet. (1793–1870)
1844.

FROTHINGHAM, RICHARD, American historian. (1812–1880)
1106.

FROUDE, JAMES ANTHONY, English historian and man of letters. (1818–1894)
1, 149, 337, 574, 575, 577, 594, 595, 653, 661, 935, 942, 958, 1027, 1080, 1083, 1118, 1244, 1324, 1345, 1407, 1424, 1459, 1497, 1531, 1684, 1689, 1792, 1794, 1832, 1874, 1992, 2149.

FULKE-GREVILLE, MRS. FRANCES MACARTNEY, English poet. (18th century)
306, 977.

FULLER, MARGARET WITTER, American poet. (1871–)
966, 1047, 1142.

* FULLER, THOMAS, English divine; historical and religious writer. (1608–1661)

* FULLER, THOMAS, English physician and compiler. (1654–1734)

FULWELL, ULPIAN, English poet. (fl. 1586)
421, 649, 821, 1442, 2052.

FULLWOOD, WILLIAM, English didactic writer. (fl. 1562)
728, 953.

G

GABORIAU, ÉMILE, French novelist. (1835–1873)
229, 328, 1000, 1254, 1438, 1712, 1948, 2096, 2201, 2206.

GAGE, THOMAS, English missionary and author. (c. 1596–1656)
1806

Gainsborough, Thomas, English painter. (1727–1788)
415.

Gaius Marius, see Marius

Galbreath, Charles Burleigh, American librarian and historian. (1858–1934)
1869.

Gale, Norman, English poet. (1862–1942)
1598.

Gale, Zona, American novelist. (1874–1938)
2132.

Galen, or Galenus, Claudius, Greek physician and medical writer. (130–201)
354.

Galerius, Gaius Valerius Maximianus, Roman Emperor. (? –311)
1925.

Gales, Richard Lawson, English poet and essayist. (1862–1927)
1260, 1957.

Galiani, Abbé Ferdinando, Italian economist. (1728–1787)
1453, 1691.

Galileo, Italian physicist and astronomer. (1564–1642)
2237.

Gallagher, F. O'Neill, contemporary Irish artist and poet.
2103.

Galsworthy, John, English novelist and dramatist. (1867–1933)
109, 378, 1011, 1079, 1587, 1750.

Galt, John, British novelist. (1779–1839)
1767.

Gambetta, Léon Michel, French lawyer, statesman and premier. (1838–1882)
1038, 2230.

Gandhi, Mohandas Karamchand (Mahatma), Hindoo leader, advocate of "non-coöperation." (1869–1948)
1118.

Gannett, William Channing, American Unitarian clergyman and devotional writer. (1840–1923)
1493, 1957.

Garden, Mary, American operatic soprano. (1877–)
1263.

Gardner, Augustus P., American soldier and sportsman. (1865–1918)
67.

Gardner, Mrs. Jack (Isabella Stewart), American social leader and art collector. (1840–1924)
1258.

Garfield, James Abram, twentieth President of the United States. (1831–1881)
65, 530, 899, 1127, 1280, 1544, 1552, 2045, 2069, 2297.

Gariopontus, medieval writer. (c. 1050)
2126.

Garland, Landon Cabell, American mathematician. (1810–1895)
1244.

Garnett, Louise Ayres [Mrs. Eugene H. Garnett], contemporary American writer and composer.
1161.

Garnett, Richard, English librarian and man of letters. (1835–1906)
451, 790, 1189, 1209, 1216, 1270, 1392, 1584, 2086, 2160.

Garrett, William. No biographical data available.
1615.

Garrick, David, English actor. (1717–1779)
219, 237, 316, 370, 375, 380, 441, 458, 542, 562, 568, 723, 753, 805, 928, 1006, 1074, 1097, 1098, 1263, 1603, 1632, 1685, 1709, 1839, 1910, 1939, 1956, 2026, 2151, 2172, 2209, 2218.

Garrison, Theodosia Pickering [Mrs. Frederick Faulks], American poet. (1874–)
241, 769, 854, 1881.

Garrison, William Lloyd, American editor and abolitionist. (1805–1879)
320, 432, 502, 1705, 1728, 1753, 1841, 1929, 2053, 2065.

Garrod, Heathcote William, English statesman and writer. (1878–)
1165, 1166.

Garstin, Crosbie, English writer. (1887–1930)
1747.

Garth, Sir Samuel, English physician and poet. (1661–1719)
220, 296, 378, 463, 467, 468, 639, 806, 918, 984, 1267, 1286, 1523, 1664, 1906, 2222, 2224.

Gascoigne, George, English poet. (1525?–1577)
141, 151, 153, 222, 362, 863, 922, 1154, 1301, 1713, 2110, 2111, 2171, 2247.

Gaskell, [Mrs.] Elizabeth Cleghorn, English novelist. (1810–1865)
821, 1564.

Gataker, Thomas, English Puritan divine and critic. (1574–1654)
1706.

Gates, Ellen M. Huntington, American verse-writer. (1835–1920)
1846.

Gatty, Alfred, English clergyman and miscellaneous writer. (1813–1903)
2078.

Gauguin, Paul, French painter (1848–1903)
102, 277, 315.

Gaultier de Lille, Philippe, Flemish poet. (d. 1201)
364.

Gautemozin, Emperor of Mexico. (c. 1520)
125.

Gautier, Pierre Jules Théophile, French poet and novelist. (1811–1872)
102, 602, 1747, 1949.

Gavarni, Paul (pseud. of Sulpice Guillaume Chevalier), French caricaturist. (1801–1866)
1239.

* Gay, John, English poet and dramatist. (1685–1732)

GAYNOR, WILLIAM JAY, American jurist, Mayor of New York City. (1849–1913)
1055, 1655.

GAYTON, EDMUND, English miscellaneous writer. (1608–1666)
145, 295, 1118, 1154, 1416, 1951.

GEDDES, WILLIAM, Scottish divine and devotional writer. (1600?–1694)
1866.

GELLERT, CHRISTIAN FÜRCHTEGOTT, German poet and moralist. (1715–1769)
1150.

GELLIUS, AULUS, Latin writer and grammarian. (117?–180?)
18, 278, 314, 457, 697, 911, 928, 930, 1022, 1117, 1362, 1824, 1964, 2027, 2048.

GENLIS, STÉPHANIE-FÉLICITÉ DU CREST DE SAINT-AUBIN, COMTESSE DE, French educator and writer of memoirs. (1746–1830)
183.

GEORGE I (GEORGE LEWIS), King of England. (1660–1727)
1537.

GEORGE II, King of England. (1683–1760)
1325, 1867.

GEORGE III (GEORGE WILLIAM FREDERICK), King of England. (1738–1820)
60, 1537.

GEORGE IV, King of England. (1762–1830)
415, 1769.

GEORGE, HENRY, American writer on political economy and sociology. (1839–1897)
230, 241, 435, 795, 1027, 1028, 1032, 1066, 1281, 1464, 1547, 1561, 1616, 1689, 1717, 1718, 1722, 1728, 1965, 1967, 2050, 2260.

GERARD, JAMES WATSON, American diplomatist, jurist, ambassador to Germany at outbreak of the World War. **(1867–1951)**
67.

GERBIER, SIR BALTHAZAR, English painter, architect and courtier. (1591?–1667)
94, 315.

GERHARDT, PAUL, German Protestant divine and hymn-writer. (1607–1676)
1122.

GERRALD, JOSEPH, English political reformer. (1763–1796)
2054.

GESSNER, SALOMON, Swiss poet and artist. (1730–1788)
1233.

GIBBON, EDWARD, English historian. (1737–1794)
1, 66, 222, 319, 638, 640, 715, 870, 902, 1088, 1185, 1590, 1616, 1675, 1695, 1711, 1860, 1874, 1903, 1926, 1957, 2115, 2127, 2245, 2261.

GIBBONS, DR. HENRY, American educator. (1808–1848)
1045.

GIBBONS, HERBERT ADAMS, American writer and publicist. (1880–1934)
752.

GIBBONS, JAMES, CARDINAL, American Roman Catholic prelate and author. (1834–1921)
53, 1683.

GIBBONS, JAMES SLOAN, American abolitionist and writer on economics. (1810–1892)
1158.

GIBBONS, THOMAS, English dissenting minister and hymn-writer. (1720–1785)
773.

GIBRAN, KAHLIL, Syrian poet, came to America in 1910. (1833–1931)
1069.

GIBSON, WILLIAM HAMILTON, American artist and writer on art subjects. (1850–1896)
93, 2152.

GIDDINGS, FRANKLIN HENRY, American sociologist. (1855–1931)
968, 1140.

GIDE, ANDRÉ, French novelist. **(1869–1951)**
156, 485, 1173, 1597.

GIFFORD, HUMPHREY, English poet. (fl. 1580)
218, 607, 706, 1726.

GIFFORD, RICHARD, English miscellaneous writer. (1725–1807)
1876.

GIFFORD, WILLIAM, English editor and critic. (1756–1826)
1240, 1408, 1525, 2176.

GIL VICENTE, Portuguese dramatist. (1485–1557)
1748.

GILBERT, FRED, English song-writer. (fl. 1892)
752.

GILBERT, SIR HUMPHREY, English navigator and explorer. (1539?–1583)
429, 885.

GILBERT, WARREN, contemporary American writer.
1254.

GILBERT, SIR WILLIAM SCHWENK, English writer of humorous verse and comic opera librettos. (1836–1911)
5, 40, 41, 68, 70, 71, 79, 83, 86, 87, 98, 148, 168, 192, 199, 207, 210, 258, 278, 282, 293, 295, 303, 313, 317, 327, 425, 427, 450, 455, 474, 490, 499, 506, 521, 522, 546, 554, 558, 574, 590, 632, 643, 648, 669, 672, 677, 692, 705, 707, 721, 778, 832, 880, 913, 936, 961, 991, 1045, 1089, 1091, 1092, 1111, 1115, 1143, 1173, 1177, 1195, 1203, 1233, 1238, 1268, 1271, 1279, 1304, 1330, 1367, 1377, 1423, 1444, 1448, 1491, 1507, 1508, 1540, 1542, 1544, 1581, 1590, 1632, 1637, 1638, 1639, 1655, 1658, 1681, 1726, 1748, 1750, 1778, 1779, 1814, 1818, 1833, 1855, 1856, 1866, 1876, 1879, 1880, 1886, 1890, 1897, 1909, 1951, 1964, 1966, 1967, 1985, 2015, 2020, 2057, 2065, 2072, 2136, 2140, 2149, 2206, 2211, 2215, 2227, 2237.

GILBERTUS NOXERANUS, French philosopher. (c. 1070–1154)
2196.

GILDER, RICHARD WATSON, American editor and poet. (1844–1909)
237, 245, 268, 383, 387, 434, 617, 876, 1034, 1075, 1151, 1211, 1373, 1396, 1535, 1745, 1746, 1807, 1864, 1883, 2003.

GILES, HENRY, English Unitarian clergyman and lecturer. Lived in the United States after 1840. (1809–1882)
1105.

GILES, HERBERT ALLEN, English professor and writer. (1845–1935)
123.

GILFILLAN, ROBERT, Scottish poet. (1798–1850)
1017.

GILLESPIE, ARTHUR, American song-writer. (1868–1914)
2.

GILLESPIE, THOMAS, Scottish educator and writer. (1777–1844)
428.

GILLILAN, STRICKLAND W., American publicist and verse-writer. (1869–1954)
12, 198, 1351, 1788.

GILLRAY, JAMES, English caricaturist. (1757–1815)
1167.

GILMAN, CHARLOTTE PERKINS STETSON, American sociological writer. (1860–1935)
304, 334, 578, 585, 611, 1249, 1462, 1597, 2244.

GILTINAN, CAROLINE [MRS. LEO P. HARLOW], American poet. (1884–)
262, 461, 756, 934, 1909.

GINSBERG, LOUIS, American poet. (1896–)
291, 773, 1103, 1519.

GIOVANNITTI, ARTURO, poet, born at Abruzzi, Italy, but a resident of New York City since 1902. (1884–)
1241.

GIRALDUS DE BARRI, called CAMBRENSIS, English topographer and writer. (1146?–1220?)
1038.

GIRARD, RICHARD H., pseud. of Richard G. Husch, American song-writer. (1876–1948)
2287.

GIRARDIN, DELPHINE GAY, MADAME DE, French novelist and miscellaneous writer. (1804–1855)
207.

GIUSTI, GIUSEPPE, Italian satiric poet. (1809–1850)
1816.

GLADDEN, WASHINGTON, American Congregational clergyman and devotional writer. (1836–1918)
1758, 2052, 2176.

GLADSTONE, WILLIAM EWART, English statesman and miscellaneous writer. (1809–1898)
301, 307, 334, 367, 527, 549, 815, 987, 998, 1235, 1371, 1553, 1727, 1793, 1919, 2003, 2061.

GLANVILL, JOSEPH, English divine and controversial writer. (1636–1680)
509, 1059.

GLAPTHORNE, HENRY, English dramatist. (fl. 1639)
442, 515, 697.

GLASGOW, ELLEN, American novelist and poet. (1874–1945)
85, 1803, 2043.

GLASS, CARTER, American statesman and Senator. (1858–1946)
1554.

GLEIM, JOHANN WILHELM LUDWIG, German poet. (1719–1803)
2010.

GLUCK, CHRISTOPH WILLIBALD, German musician and composer. (1714–1787)
1382.

GLYCON, Greek sculptor, date unknown.
695.

GLYNN, MARTIN HENRY, American politician, Governor of New York State. (1871–1924)
1558.

GODDARD, WILLIAM, English satirist. (fl. 1615)
1082.

GODFREY, ROBERT, English physicist. (fl. 1674)
804.

GODKIN, EDWIN LAWRENCE, American journalist and critic. (1831–1902)
338.

GODOLPHIN, SIDNEY, English poet. (1610–1643)
1202.

GODWIN, HANNAH, sister of English philosopher, William Godwin. (fl. 1800)
2138.

GODWIN, WILLIAM, English philosopher and novelist. (1756–1836)
723, 1108, 1166, 1675.

* GOETHE, JOHANN WOLFGANG VON, German poet. (1749–1832)

GOGARTY, OLIVER ST. JOHN, Irish writer. (1878–1957)
1864.

GOLDBERG, ISAAC, American writer and critic. (1887–1938)
1856, 2240.

GOLDING, ARTHUR, English translator from Latin and French. (1536?–1605?)
1304, 1412, 1987.

GOLDING, LOUIS, English novelist and essayist. (1895–1958)
638.

GOLDINGHAM, HENRY, English writer. (c. 1575)
1953.

GOLDONI, CARLO, Italian writer of comedies. (1707–1793)
172, 420, 1407, 1874, 1964, 2028, 2030, 2236.

GOLDRING, DOUGLAS, English poet. (1887–)
892.

* GOLDSMITH, OLIVER, English poet, essayist and dramatist. (1728–1774)

GONCOURT, EDMOND LOUIS ANTOINE HUOT DE, French novelist and dramatist. (1822–1896)
1251.

GONCOURT, EDMOND HUOT and JULES DE, French writers and collaborators. (1822–1896), (1830–1870)
182, 758, 2061.

GOOD, JOHN MASON, English physician and translator. (1764–1827)
854.

GOODALE, DORA READ, American verse-writer. (1866–)
283, 688.

GOODCHILD, JOHN ARTHUR, English writer. (1851– ?)
1352.
GOODLOE, WILLIAM CASSIUS, American politician. (1841–1889)
1554.
GOODRICH, SAMUEL GRISWOLD (PETER PARLEY), American juvenile and educational writer. (1793–1860)
615.
GOODWIN, J. CHEEVER, American librettist. (1850–1912)
536, 2287.
GOOGE, BARNABE, English poet. (1540–1594)
4, 491, 717, 1211.
GORDON, ADAM LINDSAY, Australian poet. (1833–1870)
109, 443, 517, 583, 708, 754, 929, 930, 941, 1120, 1133, 1137, 1232, 1745.
GORDON, CHARLES GEORGE, English general. (1833–1885)
506.
GORDON, ELIZABETH (MRS. GEORGE E. CANFIELD) American writer of children's books. (1865–1922)
483.
GORE-BOOTH, EVA, Irish poet. (1872–1926)
997.
GORGES, SIR ARTHUR, English poet and translator. (? –1625)
1941.
GORGIAS LEONTINUS, Greek statesman, orator and sophist. (480–380 B.C.)
98, 938.
GOSCHEN, RIGHT HON. SIR WILLIAM EDWARD, English diplomatist and statesman. (1847–1924)
545, 1554.
GOSSE, SIR EDMUND, English librarian and man of letters. (1849–1928)
130, 168, 201, 275, 445, 612, 1061, 1182, 1189, 1230, 1460.
GOSSON, STEPHEN, English divine and dramatist. (1554–1624)
218, 1305, 1326, 1505, 1633, 1640, 2077.
GOUGH, JOHN BARTHOLOMEW, American temperance lecturer. (1817–1886)
2125.
GOULD, GERALD LOUIS, English poet. (1885–1936)
159, 578, 1352, 2101.
GOULD, HANNAH FLAGG, American poet. (1789–1865)
745, 1375.
GOURMONT, RÉMY DE, French critic, essayist and novelist. (1858–1915)
1345.
GOWER, JOHN, English poet. (1325?–1408)
148, 176, 228, 260, 372, 663, 679, 727, 846, 869, 881, 886, 954, 1014, 1082, 1143, 1183, 1189, 1191, 1196, 1281, 1320, 1392, 1461, 1566, 1609, 1631, 1709, 1828, 1992, 2009, 2016, 2022, 2077, 2169, 2215, 2242.
GRACCHUS, CAIUS SEMPRONIUS, Roman statesman and orator. (c. 159–121 B.C.)
1851.
GRACIÁN Y MORALES, BALTASAR, Spanish Jesuit prose writer. (1601–1658)
1700, 2024.
GRAFTON, RICHARD, English chronicler and printer. (? –1572?)
670, 1032, 1338.
GRAHAM, CHARLES, American song-writer.
1375, 2287.
GRAHAM, GORDON. No biographical data available.
453.
GRAHAM, JAMES, first MARQUIS OF MONTROSE, English general and statesman. (1612–1650)
177, 244, 1522.
GRAHAM, ROBERT, see CUNNINGHAME-GRAHAM, ROBERT BONTINE
GRAHAME, JAMES, Scottish poet. (1765–1811)
907, 1752.
GRAINGER, JAMES, Scottish physician and poet. (1721?–1766)
803, 870, 1246.
GRANGE, JOHN, English poet. (fl. 1577)
516, 523, 600, 746, 1283, 1475, 1923.
GRANT, [MRS.] ELIZABETH, Scottish poet. (c. 1745–1814)
2142.
GRANT, JOHN CAMERON, contemporary American verse-writer.
2132.
GRANT, ULYSSES SIMPSON (originally HIRAM ULYSSES), American general and eighteenth President of the United States. (1822–1885)
65, 844, 970, 1087, 1471, 1479, 1501.
GRANVILLE, or GRENVILLE, GEORGE, BARON LANSDOWNE, English poet and dramatist. (1667–1735)
24, 139, 310, 350, 383, 399, 437, 564, 588, 623, 643, 780, 860, 1018, 1046, 1148, 1184, 1189, 1196, 1202, 1270, 1463, 1712, 1828, 1862, 2187, 2197, 2198, 2203.
GRATTAN, CLINTON HARTLEY, American writer of biography. (1902–)
1802.
GRATTAN, HENRY, Irish statesman. (1746–1820)
733.
GRAVES, ALFRED PERCEVAL, English poet. (1846–1931)
501, 1592, 1730.
GRAVES, RICHARD, THE YOUNGER, English poet and novelist. (1715–1804)
517, 643, 737.
GRAVES, ROBERT RANKE, English poet. (1895–)
614.
GRAY, ASA, American botanist. (1810–1888)
1693.
GRAY, DAVID, Scottish poet. (1838–1861)
1034.
GRAY, GEORGE. No biographical data available.
1773.
* GRAY, THOMAS, English poet. (1716–1771)
GRAY, WILLIAM BENSON, American song-writer.
2287.

GREELEY, HORACE, American journalist, founder of the New York *Tribune*. (1811–1872)
42, 58, 1324, 1602, 2131, 2136.

GREELY, MAJOR GENERAL ADOLPHUS WASHINGTON, American soldier and arctic explorer. (1844–1935)
1139.

GREEN, ANNA KATHERINE [MRS. CHARLES ROHLFS], American writer of detective stories. (1846–1935)
507.

GREEN, JOSEPH, American merchant and satirical writer. (1706–1780)
1388.

GREEN, MATTHEW, English poet. (1696–1737)
71, 118, 317, 348, 469, 485, 491, 545, 590, 593, 603, 605, 634, 662, 778, 858, 860, 864, 873, 874, 941, 955, 1013, 1074, 1079, 1104, 1148, 1329, 1363, 1398, 1505, 1510, 1515, 1542, 1583, 1601, 1653, 1683, 1761, 1776, 1795, 1894, 1910, 1953, 2046, 2140, 2154, 2167.

GREENE, ALBERT GORTON, American lawyer and writer of humorous verse. (1802–1868)
400, 2156.

GREENE, EDWARD BURNABY, English poet and translator. (d. 1788)
908.

GREENE, HOMER, American novelist and verse-writer. (1853–1940)
1289.

GREENE, ROBERT, English pamphleteer and poet. (1560?–1592)
6, 23, 133, 145, 287, 310, 427, 485, 604, 717, 784, 786, 853, 880, 932, 959, 1007, 1162, 1164, 1172, 1173, 1188, 1189, 1264, 1269, 1309, 1394, 1433, 1469, 1503, 1639, 1799, 1811, 1920, 1954, 1974, 2003, 2005, 2034, 2123, 2128, 2145, 2202, 2244.

GREENE, SARAH PRATT MCLEAN, American novelist and poet. (1856–1935)
1811.

GREENOUGH, HORATIO, American sculptor. (1805–1852)
1920.

GREENOUGH, WALTER, contemporary American journalist.
865.

GREGG, W. S. No biographical data available.
1545.

GREGORY I, SAINT (THE GREAT), Roman Pope and theological writer. (590–604)
77, 620, 1979, 2163.

GREGORY VII (HILDEBRAND), Roman Pope. (c. 1020–1085)
1032.

GREGORY NAZIANZEN (THE THEOLOGIAN), Greek Father and pulpit orator. (328–389)
391, 1406.

GRELLET, STEPHEN, American Quaker of French birth. (1773–1855)
1493.

GRESSET, JEAN BAPTISTE LOUIS DE, French poet and dramatist. (1709–1777)
1925.

GREVILLE, CHARLES CAVENDISH FULKE, English diarist. (1794–1865)
1229, 1479.

GREVILLE, SIR FULKE, first BARON BROOKE, English poet and statesman. (1554–1628)
5, 279, 564, 667, 1046, 1250, 1319.

GREY, EDWARD, VISCOUNT (GREY OF FALLODON), English statesman. (1862–1933)
1673, 2297.

GRIFFIN, GERALD, Irish dramatist, novelist and poet. (1803–1840)
1198, 1296, 1620.

GRIFFITH, WILLIAM, American editor and poet. (1876–1936)
823, 1523, 1524.

GRIGNAN, FRANÇOISE MARGUERITE, MADAME DE, French letter-writer, daughter of Madame de Sévigné. (1646– ?)
1678.

GRIMALD, or GRIMALDE, or GRIMOALD, NICHOLAS, English poet and translator. (1519–1562)
86, 730, 811, 1169, 2147.

GRIMES, JOHN, American poet. (1894–)
1759.

GRINDAL, EDMUND, English prelate, Archbishop of Canterbury. (1519?–1583)
1003.

GROSE, FRANCIS, English antiquary and draughtsman. (1731?–1791)
581.

GROSE, JOHN, English divine and compiler. (1758–1821)
1052, 1650.

GROSVENOR, GENERAL CHARLES HENRY, American soldier and politician. (1833–1917)
1112.

GROTE, HARRIET, English biographer. (1792–1878)
1541.

GROTIUS, HUGO, Dutch statesman and jurist. (1583–1645)
275, 319, 953.

GRÜN, ANASTASIUS (pseud. of ANTON ALEXANDER, GRAF VON AUERSPERG), Austrian poet. (1806–1876)
543, 1519.

GRUNDY, SYDNEY, English dramatist. (1848–1914)
280.

GRYPHIUS, ANDREAS, German poet and dramatist. (1616–1664)
2174.

GUARINI, GIOVANNI BATTISTA, Italian poet. (1538–1612)
1218, 1896.

GUAZZO, MARCO, Italian littérateur. (c. 1496–1556)
692, 802, 1056, 1993, 2179, 2180.

GUEDALLA, PHILIP, English miscellaneous writer. (1889–1944)
1984, 2222.

GUÉRIN, CHARLES, French philosophical and elegiac poet. (1873–1907)
151.

GUEST, EDGAR ALBERT, humorist and verse-writer, born in England, but long resident in the United States. (1881-)
904, 937, 1036, 1578, 1595, 1788, 1869, 1931.

GUIBERT OF NOGENT, French Benedictine theologian. (1053–1124)
1254.

GUICCIARDINI, FRANCESCO, Italian historian. (1483–1540)
452, 665, 810, 963, 1929.

GUICHARD, JEAN FRANÇOIS, French poet and dramatist. (1731–1811)
1263.

GUIDO RENI, Italian painter. (1575–1642)
1447.

GUINAN, TEXAS, American night-club hostess. (1884-1933)
721, 1631.

GUINEY, LOUISE IMOGEN, American poet. (1861–1920)
203, 439, 611, 866, 1017, 1422.

GUINICELLI, GUIDO, Italian poet. (c. 1240–c. 1276)
162, 2163.

GUITERMAN, ARTHUR, American poet. (1871–1943)
83, 108, 111, 112, 143, 168, 195, 223, 235, 300, 339, 391, 409, 586, 873, 893, 933, 1252, 1650, 1653, 1683, 1687, 1742, 1835, 1923, 1983, 2111.

GURNALL, WILLIAM, English divine and devotional writer. (1617-1679)
692, 745, 1304, 1955.

GURNEY, DOROTHY FRANCES, contemporary English poet.
756.

GUTHRIE, THOMAS ANSTEY, see ANSTEY, F.

GUYET, FRANÇOIS, French scholar and poet. (1575–1655)
671.

H

HABBERTON, JOHN, American journalist and miscellanist. (1842–1921)
2132.

HABINGTON, WILLIAM, English poet. (1605–1654)
321, 1029, 1041, 1331, 1339, 1912, 2187.

HACKWOOD, JOHN. No biographical data available.
287.

HADDON, WALTER, English writer and educator. (1516–1572)
1361.

HADRIAN, or ADRIAN (PUBLIUS ÆLIUS HADRIANUS), Roman Emperor. (76–138)
467, 1893.

HADRIANUS, JULIUS, Latin commentator. (c. 1550)
1393.

HAFIZ (pseud. of SHAMS-ED-DINMUHAMMAD), Persian poet and philosopher. (? –c. 1390)
177, 644, 711, 1520, 2156.

HAGEMAN, SAMUEL MILLER, American Presbyterian clergyman and poet. (1848–1905)
511.

HAGENBACH, KARL RUDOLF, Swiss theologian and writer. (1801–1874)
1554.

HAGGARD, SIR HENRY RIDER, English novelist. (1856–1925)
1145.

HAHNEMANN, CHRISTIAN FRIEDRICH SAMUEL, German founder of homeopathy. (1755–1843)
1285.

HAIG, DOUGLAS, first EARL, British commander in the World War. (1861–1928)
2108.

HAINES, GRACE. No biographical data available.
2041.

HAKEWILL, GEORGE, English divine and devotional writer. (1578–1649)
82, 367.

HALE, EDWARD EVERETT, American Unitarian clergyman and inspirational writer. (1822–1909)
1435.

HALE, LUCRETIA PEABODY, American writer of juvenile and educational books. (1820–1900)
1644.

HALE, SIR MATTHEW, English jurist. (1609–1676)
1086, 1752.

HALE, NATHAN, American patriot and Revolutionary officer. (1755–1776)
61.

HALE, [MRS.] SARAH JOSEPHA, American miscellaneous writer and editor of *Godey's Lady's Book* for forty years. (1788–1879)
1067.

HALÉVY, LUDOVIC, see MEILHAC, HENRY

HALIBURTON, THOMAS CHANDLER, see SLICK, SAM

HALIFAX, LORD, see SAVILE, GEORGE

HALL, AMANDA BENJAMIN [MRS. JOHN A. BROWNELL], American poet. (1890-)
1874.

HALL, CAROLYN, contemporary American poet.
668.

HALL, CHARLES ALBERT, English Minister of the New Church, writer and lecturer. (1872-)
845.

HALL, CHARLES SPRAGUE, American verse-writer. (fl. 1860)
203, 367.

HALL, EDWARD, English chronicler. (d. 1547)
785, 1638, 1685, 1798.

HALL, GEORGE, Bishop of Chester, England. (1612?–1668)
166.

HALL, GRANVILLE STANLEY, American psychologist, philosopher and educator. (1844–1924)
1176, 1692.

HALL, HAZEL, American poet. (1886–1924)
439.

HALL, JOSEPH, English divine and miscellaneous writer. (1574–1656)
185, 407, 786, 826, 858, 914, 931, 1422, 1632, 1651, 1816, 1874, 1945, 2247.

HALL, NORMAN B. No biographical data available.
165.

HALL, ROBERT, English Baptist divine and orator. (1764–1831)
499, 1446, 1464, 1676, 2126.

HALL, SHARLOT MABRIDTH, American poet and historical writer. (1870–1944)
1733.

HALL, THOMAS, English ejected minister. (1610–1665)
214, 441.

HALLACK, CECILY, contemporary English writer.
2276.

HALLECK, FITZ-GREENE, American poet. (1790–1867)
205, 207, 386, 431, 666, 740, 839, 877, 897, 1334, 1373, 1464, 1465, 2061.

HALLIWELL (afterward HALLIWELL-PHILLIPPS), JAMES ORCHARD, English biographer, scholar and librarian. (1820–1889)
1003, 2000, 2018.

HALPINE, CHARLES GRAHAM (MILES O'REILLY), American journalist, poet and humorist. (1829–1868)
367, 495, 821, 848, 1158.

HALSHAM, JOHN (pseud. of G. FORRESTER SCOTT), contemporary English writer.
472.

HAMBLEN, BERNARD. No biographical data available.
1296.

HAMERTON, PHILIP GILBERT, English art critic. (1834–1894)
707, 1148, 1280, 1673, 1861, 1871.

HAMILCAR (surnamed BARCA), Carthaginian general. (d. 229 B.C.)
2083.

HAMILTON, ALEXANDER, American statesman. (1757–1804)
62, 432, 1728.

HAMILTON, ANNA ELIZABETH, Irish poet. (1843–1875)
981.

HAMILTON, ELIZABETH, English educational writer. (1758–1816)
905.

HAMILTON, GAIL (pseud. of MARY ABIGAIL DODGE), American essayist. (1838–1896)
1, 2257.

HAMILTON, ROBERT BROWNING. No biographical data available.
1885.

HAMILTON, WILLIAM, Scottish poet. (1704–1754)
1943.

HAMILTON, SIR WILLIAM, English metaphysician. (1788–1856)
1245, 1795, 2050, 2140.

HAMLEY, SIR EDWARD BRUCE, English general. (1824–1893)
675.

HAMMERSTEIN, OSCAR, 2D, American librettist and song-writer. (1895–)
1733, 2287.

HAMMOND, [MRS.] ELEANOR PALMER, contemporary American poet.
1855.

HAMMOND, ELEANOR PRESCOTT, American writer. (1866–1933)
1729.

HAMMOND, JAMES, English poet. (1710–1742)
849, 1219, 1228.

HAMMOND, JAMES HENRY, American Senator, Governor of South Carolina. (1807–1864)
64, 878, 1841.

HAMMOND, PERCY, American dramatic critic. (1873–1936)
1099.

HAMPOLE, RICHARD ROLLE DE, see ROLLE

HANBY, BENJAMIN RUSSELL, American clergyman and song-writer. (1833–1867)
2284.

HANCOCK, JOHN, American statesman. (1737–1793)
62.

HANCOCK, WINFIELD SCOTT, American general. (1824–1886)
1965.

HANES, LEIGH BUCKNER, American lawyer and editor. (1894–)
1356.

HANFF, MINNY MAUD [MRS. RAYMOND F. AYERS], contemporary American writer of light verse and advertising. (1880–1942)
1436.

HANNA, MARCUS ALONZO (MARK), American capitalist and politician. (1837–1904)
1554, 1741.

HANNAY, PATRICK, Irish poet. (d. 1629?)
913, 1184.

HANSARD, RICHARD, English writer and traveller. (fl. 1599)
660.

HARBACH, OTTO A. (born HAUERBACH), American librettist and song-writer. (1873–)
318, 1980.

HARBURG, E. Y., American song-writer. (1896–)
2287.

HARDENBERG, FRIEDRICH LEOPOLD VON, see NOVALIS

HARDESTY, JESSE, American writer. (1842– ?)
2048.

HARDIN, CHARLOTTE, contemporary American writer.
2241.

HARDING, RUTH GUTHRIE, American poet. (1882–)
357.

HARDING, WARREN GAMALIEL, twenty-ninth President of the United States. (1865–1923)
67, 1553, 1618, 2112.

HARDINGE, GEORGE, English writer. (1743–1816)
286

HARDY, THOMAS, English poet and novelist. (1840–1928)
24, 159, 238, 250, 265, 371, 412, 439, 481, 483, 485, 492, 583, 598, 617, 634, 829, 902, 1000, 1145, 1148, 1195, 1239, 1254, 1278, 1287, 1396, 1429, 1474, 1536, 1543, 1628,

HEBER, REGINALD, English Bishop (of Calcutta) and poet. (1783–1826)
96, 264, 379, 404, 507, 612, 668, 689, 793, 887, 925, 957, 1011, 1156, 1207, 1246, 1324, 1587, 1906.

HECATO, or HECATÆUS, Greek historian and geographer. (c. 550–476 B.C.)
727, 927, 1184.

HEDGE, FREDERIC HENRY, American Unitarian clergyman and devotional writer. (1805–1890)
2235.

HEDYLUS, Greek epigrammatist.
460.

HEELAN, WILL A., American song-writer.
1271, 2288.

HEELAN, WILL A., and HELF, J. FRED, American song-writers.
1836.

HEGEL, GEORG WILHELM FRIEDRICH, German philosopher. (1770–1831)
1435, 2298.

HEGGE, ROBERT, English historical writer. (1599–1629)
463.

HEINE, HEINRICH, German poet of Jewish descent. (1797–1856)
96, 113, 157, 234, 332, 444, 483, 559, 594, 603, 782, 828, 843, 848, 869, 1011, 1047, 1102, 1206, 1241, 1334, 1378, 1450, 1593, 1680, 1906, 1959, 2111, 2181, 2226.

HEISER, L. S., American song-writer.
2288.

HELLOWES, EDWARD, English translator. (fl. 1574–1600)
891.

HELMUTH, WILLIAM TOD, American surgeon and medical writer. (1833–1902)
873.

HELPS, SIR ARTHUR, English miscellaneous writer. (1813–1875)
19, 88, 103, 158, 343, 433, 560, 662, 899, 936, 971, 1089, 1165, 1453, 1494, 1570, 1571, 1676, 1691, 1697, 1792, 1823, 1919, 2017.

HEMANS, FELICIA DOROTHEA, English poet. (1793–1835)
94, 195, 276, 379, 381, 408, 481, 551, 556, 615, 668, 683, 686, 707, 844, 883, 886, 907, 969, 1001, 1002, 1272, 1315, 1352, 1437, 1501, 1745, 1775, 1796, 1844, 1853, 1907, 1917, 1976, 2149.

HEMMINGER, GRAHAM, American journalist and publicist. (1896–)
2017.

HÉNAULT, CHARLES JEAN, French historian and dramatist. (1685–1770)
960, 1039.

HENDERSON, DANIEL, American poet and miscellaneous writer. (1880–1955)
203.

HENLEY, JOHN, English orator. (1692–1756)
1558.

HENLEY, WILLIAM ERNEST, English poet, critic and dramatist. (1849–1903)
24, 167, 223, 388, 391, 398, 426, 493, 547, 551, 1115, 1116, 1121, 1132, 1294, 1376, 1389, 1445, 1687, 1771, 1851, 1892, 1936, 1941, 1954, 2006, 2018, 2101, 2156, 2246, 2262.

HENNEQUIN, ÉMILE, French critic and journalist. (1859–1888)
2178.

HENRIETTA MARIA, Queen of England. (1609–1669)
1044.

HENRY IV OF NAVARRE, King of France. (1553–1610)
516, 647, 663, 676, 701, 853, 1453, 1693, 2062.

HENRY VIII, King of England. (1491–1547)
415, 545, 764.

HENRY, MATTHEW, English nonconformist clergyman and Bible commentator. (1662–1714)
11, 158, 172, 198, 208, 272, 285, 370, 373, 403, 528, 670, 940, 1165, 1398, 1444, 1550, 1797, 1980, 1993, 2024, 2033, 2181, 2227.

HENRY, O., see O. HENRY

HENRY, PATRICK, American patriot and orator. (1736–1799)
57, 593, 925, 1106, 1460, 2033.

HENRY, PHILIP, English nonconformist divine. (1631–1696)
403, 885.

HENRYSON, or HENDERSON, ROBERT, Scottish poet. (1430?–1506?)
1328, 2100, 2125.

HENSHALL, JAMES ALEXANDER, American physician, naturalist and writer on angling. (1836–1925)
670.

HENSHAW, JOSEPH, English Bishop and devotional writer. (1603–1679)
573.

HEPBURN, THOMAS NICOLL, see SETOUN, GABRIEL

HERACLITUS, or HERACLEITUS, Greek philosopher. (fl. 500 B.C.)
232, 234, 369, 476, 620, 758, 1306.

HERBERT OF BOSHAM, English biographer of Becket. (fl. 1162–1186)
1491.

HERBERT, SIR ALAN PATRICK, English humorist and novelist. (1890–)
528, 2298o.

HERBERT, EDWARD, first BARON HERBERT OF CHERBURY, English philosopher, historian, poet and diplomatist. (1583–1648)
365, 1139.

* HERBERT, GEORGE, English divine and poet. (1593–1633)

HERBERT, HENRY, tenth EARL OF PEMBROKE, English general. (1734–1794)
1015.

HERFORD, OLIVER, American humorist, poet and illustrator. (1863–1935)
108, 331, 532, 586, 1161, 1242, 1258, 1410, 1654, 1681, 1860, 2065, 2125, 2147, 2149.

HERNDON, WILLIAM HENRY, American lawyer, partner of Abraham Lincoln. (1818–1891)
640.

HERODAS, Greek writer of mimes. (fl. 270 B.C.)
1154, 1813.

Herodotus, Greek historian. (484–424? B.C.)
229, 564, 604, 704, 1101, 1284, 2000, 2063, 2083.

Herrick, Jean. No biographical data available.
2002.

* Herrick, Robert, English poet. (1591–1674)

Herrlossohn, Karl, German novelist and poet. (1804–1849)
1212.

Herschel, Sir John Frederick William, first Baronet, English astronomer. (1792–1871)
1792.

Herschell, Farrer, first Baron Herschell, English Lord Chancellor. (1837–1899)
1087.

Hertslet, Lewis, English librarian to the foreign office. (1787–1870)
452.

Hervey, James, English devotional writer. (1714–1758)
1587.

Hervey, John, Baron Hervey of Ickworth, English pamphleteer and memoir writer. (1696–1743)
1835, 2006.

Hervey, Thomas Kibble, English poet and critic. (1799–1859)
403, 1195, 1558, 1813.

Herwegh, Georg, German political poet. (1817–1875)
1217.

Hesiod, Greek pastoral poet. (c. 735 B.C.)
145, 227, 564, 601, 637, 727, 731, 734, 751, 773, 956, 1127, 1243, 1266, 1295, 1326, 1346, 1396, 1428, 1451, 1480, 1536, 1565, 1614, 1634, 1710, 1730, 1751, 1848, 1904, 1997, 2024, 2059, 2090, 2169, 2231.

Hewitt, Abram Stevens, American manufacturer, statesman and philanthropist. (1822–1903)
1550, 1967.

Heylyn, Peter, English ecclesiastical writer. (1600–1662)
1491, 2058.

Heyward, Du Bose, American poet and novelist. (1885–1940)
381, 857.

Heyward, Janie Screven, contemporary American poet. (d. 1939)
40, 1904.

Heywood, Jasper, English Jesuit writer and translator. (1535–1598)
1883.

Heywood, John, English epigrammatist and dramatist. (1497?–1580?)
383, 598, 607, 785, 846, 956, 1003, 1592, 1751, 2150, 2151, 2222.

Heywood, Oliver, English divine and diarist. (1630–1702)
1545.

Heywood, Thomas, English dramatist and poet. (? –1650?)
262, 375, 488, 601, 610, 631, 680, 700, 796, 869, 911, 934, 1360, 1372, 1432, 1633, 1671, 1730, 1806, 2222.

Heywood, Thomas, and Rowley, William, English dramatists and collaborators. (? –1650?), (1585–1642?)
377, 1341.

Hibbard, Grace [Helen Grace Porter], contemporary American writer.
1091.

Hibben, Paxton Pattison, American diplomatist, soldier and journalist. (1880–1928)
844, 1552, 1619, 2282, 2283.

Hickey, Emily Henrietta, Irish poet. (1845–1924)
1346, 1580, 1588.

Hickson, William Edward, English educational writer. (1803–1870)
1488.

Hicky, Daniel Whitehead, American verse-writer. (1902–)
130.

Hieronymus, see Jerome, Saint

Higginson, Ella, American poet and novelist. (1862–1940)
291, 1227.

Higginson, John, English divine. (1616–1708)
1658.

Higginson, Thomas Wentworth, American essayist and littérateur. (1823–1911)
56, 151, 211, 320, 559, 758, 830, 1717, 1735, 2262.

Higley, Brewster, American physician, author of *Home on the Range*. (fl. 1873)
2296.

Hildebrand, see Gregory VII

Hill, Aaron, English dramatist. (1685–1750)
177, 1101, 1270, 1400, 1456, 2034, 2204.

Hill, David Bennett, American lawyer and politician. (1843–1910)
431.

Hill, James Jerome, American railroad executive and financier. (1838–1916)
1930.

Hill, Rowland, English itinerant preacher. (1744–1833)
1362.

Hill, Thomas, American Unitarian clergyman and mathematician. (1818–1891)
175.

Hillard, George Stillman, American lawyer and man of letters. (1808–1879)
740, 833, 866, 1919.

Hills, Richard, English commentator. (fl. 1530)
161, 596, 939, 1392, 1713, 1738, 1810, 1857, 1954, 2120, 2180.

Hillyer, Robert Silliman, American poet and miscellaneous writer. (1895–1962)
1195, 1403, 1415.

Hilton-Turvey, Caroll Brevoort, American writer. (1880–)
1943.

Hinkson, Katherine Tynan, Irish poet and novelist. (1861–1931)
111, 162, 233, 378, 909, 1026, 1909, 2211.

Hinton, Leonard. No biographical data available.
2244.

HIPPIAS, Greek sophist. (fl. 450 B.C.)
1086, 2224.
HIPPOCRATES, Greek physician, the "Father of Medicine." (c. 460–357 B.C.)
104, 1118, 1285, 1286, 1287, 1327, 2274.
HITCHCOCK, ETHAN ALLEN, American soldier and writer on military subjects. (1798–1870)
64.
HITCHCOCK, ROSWELL DWIGHT, American educator. (1817–1887)
896, 1497, 1509, 1606, 1689, 1969.
HOAR, GEORGE FRISBIE, American lawyer and legislator. (1826–1904)
673, 1008, 1549.
HOBBES, JOHN OLIVER (pseud. of PEARL MARY TERESA CRAIGIE), American novelist and dramatist living in London. (1867–1906)
1173, 1783, 2184.
HOBBES, THOMAS, English philosopher. (1588–1679)
186, 188, 233, 299, 415, 723, 894, 961, 1045, 1057, 1087, 1089, 1100, 1169, 1292, 1428, 1470, 1676, 1678, 1700, 1740, 1764, 1787, 2108, 2118, 2217, 2246.
HOBY, SIR EDWARD, English courtier, favorite of James I. (1560–1617)
999.
HOCCLEVE, or OCCLEVE, THOMAS, English poet. (1370?–1450?)
169, 245, 302, 1056, 1480, 1872, 2268.
HOCH, EDWARD WALLIS, American politician, Governor of Kansas. (1849–1925)
1023.
HODGES, LEIGH MITCHELL, American journalist and miscellaneous writer. (1876–1954)
793, 1932.
HODGSON, RALPH, English poet. (1871–)
11, 1539, 1670, 1743, 2006.
HODGSON, WILLIAM HAROLD (RED), American entertainer and song-writer.
2296.
HOFFENSTEIN, SAMUEL, American poet and journalist. (1890–1947)
11, 577, 832, 1266, 1310, 1802, 1884.
HOFFMAN, CHARLES FENNO, American poet and story-writer. (1806–1884)
2156.
HOFFMANN, AUGUST HEINRICH, see FALLERSLEBEN, HOFFMANN VON
HOFFMANN, ERNST THEODOR AMADEUS, German novelist. (1776–1822)
94, 903.
HOGAN, ERNEST, American song-writer.
2288.
HOGARTH, WILLIAM, English painter and political caricaturist. (1697–1764)
758, 1391.
HOGG, JAMES, the Ettrick Shepherd, Scottish poet. (1770–1835)
434, 684, 730, 1072, 1189, 1235, 1386, 1852, 2099, 2213.
HOHENHEIM, PHILIPPUS THEOPHRASTUS BOMBASTUS AB (VON), see PARACELSUS
HOLCROFT, THOMAS, English dramatist. (1745–1809)
741, 1177, 1566, 1925, 1933, 2229.
HOLIDAY, BARTEN, English writer. (fl. 1630)
2019.
HOLINSHED, RAPHAEL, English chronicler. (d. 1580?)
230.
HOLLAND, LORD, see FOX, HENRY
HOLLAND, HUGH, English poet. (d. 1633)
1579, 1807.
HOLLAND, JOSIAH GILBERT, American novelist, poet and moralist. (1819–1881)
13, 84, 101, 109, 112, 121, 160, 268, 425, 762, 785, 795, 877, 882, 904, 907, 920, 951, 952, 963, 964, 1063, 1080, 1148, 1252, 1361, 1379, 1462, 1574, 1616, 1627, 1661, 1684, 1929, 2184, 2260.
HOLLAND, NORAH M., American poet. (1876–1925)
1137, 1212.
HOLLAND, SIR RICHARD, Scottish poet. (fl. 1450)
1219.
HOLMAN, JOSEPH GEORGE, English actor and dramatist. (1764–1817)
447.
HOLMES, JOHN HAYNES, American clergyman, publicist and reformer. (1879–)
583, 1270, 1345.
* HOLMES, OLIVER WENDELL, American wit, poet and novelist. (1809–1894)
HOLMES, OLIVER WENDELL, American jurist. (1841–1935)
39, 1114, 1118, 1132, 1426, 1967, 2217.
HOLMES, WILLIAM KERSLEY, English writer. (1882–) 240.
HOLT, SIR JOHN, English jurist. (1642–1710) 370.
HOLYDAY, or HOLIDAY, BARTEN, English divine and translator. (1593–1661) 1092.
HOME, F. WYVILLE, Scottish poet. (1851– ?)
292.
HOME, JOHN, Scottish dramatist. (1722–1808)
215, 231, 297, 773, 861, 921, 1352, 1778, 1812, 2187, 2215.
* HOMER, Greek epic poet. (fl. 1000 B.C.)
HONE, WILLIAM, English compiler, editor and bookseller. (1780–1842)
124, 126, 161, 281, 480, 934, 1046, 1272, 1607, 1635, 1669, 1851, 2137.
HONEIN BEN ISAAK, Arabic moralist. (c. 870)
734.
HONEYWOOD, ST. JOHN, American lawyer and poet. (1763–1798)
2180.
* HOOD, THOMAS, English poet and humorist. (1799–1845)
HOOK, THEODORE EDWARD, English novelist and wit. (1788–1841)
362, 549, 849, 1074, 1360, 1603, 1654, 2154.
HOOK, WILLIAM, English Puritan divine; Massachusetts colonist. (1600–1677)
2112.
HOOKER, JOSEPH, Union general in the American Civil War. (1814–1879)
506.
HOOKER, RICHARD, English theologian. (1554?–1600)
230, 260, 796, 817, 1083, 1589, 1649, 2063, 2223.

HOOKER, WILLIAM BRIAN, American educator and poet. (1880–1946)
121, 2268.
HOOLE, JOHN, English translator. (1727–1803)
2034.
HOOPER, ELLEN STURGIS, American verse-writer. (1816–1841)
507, 538.
HOOVER, HERBERT CLARK, thirty-first President of the United States. (1874–)
978, 1554, 1618, 1619, 1626.
HOOVER, IRWIN HOOD ("IKE"), chief usher at the White House. (1871–1933)
1553.
HOPE, ANTHONY (pseud. of ANTHONY HOPE HAWKINS), English novelist. (1863–1933)
71, 197, 568, 760, 776, 1032, 1706, 2059.
HOPE, JAMES BARRON, American lawyer and journalist. (1829–1887)
372, 1342.
HOPE, LAURENCE (pseud. of ADELA FLORENCE NICOLSON), English poet. (1865–1904)
851, 1130, 1456, 1874.
HOPE, SIR WILLIAM, English miscellaneous writer. (fl. 1692) 1750.
HOPKINS, ALBERT, American educator. (1807–1872) 2298h:2.
HOPKINS, CHARLES, English poet. (1664?–1700?)
3.
HOPKINS, ERNEST MARTIN, American educator. (1877–) 1692.
HOPKINS, JANE ELLICE, English social reformer. (1836–1904)
758.
HOPKINS, MARK, American Congregational clergyman and educator. (1802–1887)
1068, 1390, 2069.
HOPKINSON, JOSEPH, American jurist and poet. (1770–1842)
51.
HOPPER, NORA [MRS. WILFRID HUGH CHESSON], English poet. (1871–1906)
1260.
HOPWOOD, RONALD ARTHUR, English admiral. (1868–1949)
1779.
* HORACE, QUINTUS HORATIUS FLACCUS, Latin poet. (65–8 B.C.)
HORMAN, WILLIAM, English educator. (d. 1535)
326, 1394, 1469, 1634.
HORNE, RICHARD HENRY, or HENGIST, English poet. (1803–1884)
211, 309, 638, 1347, 2038, 2163.
HORNICK, P. W. VON. No biographical data available.
767.
HOROZCO, JUAN DE, Spanish dramatist.
1699.
HOSKINS, JOHN, English lawyer and wit. (1566–1638)
2024.
HOSKYNS-ABRAHALL, JOHN, English writer, churchman and educator. (1829–1891)
1735.
HOUDETOT, ALFRED D', French writer.
38.
HOUGH, WILL M., American song-writer.
1881.
HOUGHTON, LORD, see MILNES
HOUSMAN, ALFRED EDWARD, English classical scholar and poet. (1859–1936)
44, 167, 394, 628, 646, 825, 852, 880, 892, 1087, 1140, 1145, 1219, 1226, 1680, 1730, 1863, 1868, 1995, 2038, 2043, 2151, 2179, 2267.
HOUSMAN, LAURENCE, English poet. (1865–)
26, 474, 1183, 1235, 1368, 1502.
HOVELL-THURLOW, EDWARD, second BARON THURLOW, English poet. (1781–1829)
31, 1282, 1343, 1384, 1388.
HOVEY, RICHARD, American poet. (1864–1900)
45, 51, 64, 66, 368, 456, 492, 612, 725, 744, 822, 898, 933, 941, 1031, 1112, 1131, 1221, 1272, 1379, 1796, 1906, 1907, 2020, 2070, 2102.
HOW, WILLIAM WALSHAM, first bishop of Wakefield, English prelate. (1823–1897)
2205.
HOWARD, EDWARD, English dramatist. (d. 1669)
491.
HOWARD, FRANK, contemporary American song-writer.
2288.
HOWARD, FREDERICK, fifth EARL OF CARLISLE, English statesman, poet and dramatist. (1748–1825)
419, 1748.
HOWARD, HENRY, EARL OF SURREY, English courtier and poet. (1517?–1547)
3, 136, 216, 363, 602, 1209, 1818, 1907, 2176.
HOWARD, JAMES, English dramatist; brother of Sir Robert Howard. (fl. 1674)
695.
HOWARD, SIR ROBERT, English dramatist. (1626–1698)
916, 1180, 1919, 1985.
HOWARTH, [MRS.] ELLEN CLEMENTINE, American verse-writer. (1827–1899)
1296.
HOWE, EDGAR WATSON, American journalist and miscellaneous writer. (1854–1937)
246, 533, 654, 724, 1246, 1620, 1657.
HOWE, JULIA WARD, American poet and miscellaneous writer. (1819–1910)
51, 263, 674, 725, 1501, 2120.
HOWE, LOUIS MCHENRY, American politician, secretary to President F. D. Roosevelt. (1871–1936)
1542.
HOWE, MARK ANTONY DEWOLFE, American man of letters. (1864–)
628.
HOWE, NATHANIEL, American clergyman. (1764–1837)
956, 1100, 1755.
HOWELL, JAMES, English essayist and letter-writer. (1594?–1666)
3, 112, 118, 122, 126, 129, 135, 141, 146, 150, 155, 160, 177, 310, 511, 514, 520, 560,

JENYNS, SOAME, English poet and philosophical writer. (1704–1787)
359, 537, 791, 1014, 1380, 1423, 1537, 1541, 1544, 1615, 1925, 2029.

JEROME, SAINT (EUSEBIUS HIERONYMUS SOPHRONIUS), called HIERONYMUS, Latin Father and theologian. (c. 340–420)
154, 159, 444, 590, 647, 773, 954, 1134, 1154, 1191, 1721, 2186, 2191.

JEROME, JEROME KLAPKA, English humorist. (1859–1927)
294, 485, 500, 769, 954, 1122, 1177, 2057, 2231.

JEROME, WILLIAM, American song-writer. (1865–1932)
2288, 2289, 2295.

JEROME, WILLIAM, and SCHWARTZ, JEAN, American song-writers. (1865–1932), (1878–)
910.

JEROME, WILLIAM TRAVERS, American lawyer and district attorney. (1859–1934)
1084.

JERROLD, DOUGLAS WILLIAM, English humorist, journalist and dramatist. (1803–1857)
45, 185, 207, 316, 333, 352, 499, 549, 559, 615, 639, 754, 808, 859, 864, 924, 1025, 1102, 1166, 1173, 1177, 1225, 1226, 1271, 1286, 1304, 1428, 1462, 1471, 1495, 1691, 1701, 1780, 1836, 1981, 2008, 2094, 2146, 2214, 2230, 2237.

JEWEL, JOHN, Bishop of Salisbury, English divine and theologian. (1522–1571)
97, 417, 577, 583, 649, 842.

JEWETT, SARAH ORNE, American short-story writer. (1849–1909)
1884.

JOHN III, King of Poland, see SOBIESKI, JOHN

JOHN OF DAMASCUS (JOANNES DAMASCENUS), Greek theologian and hymn-writer. (c. 700–754)
514.

JOHN OF SALISBURY, Bishop of Chartres, English prelate. (? –1180)
145, 753, 1433.

JOHNSON, ANDREW, seventeenth President of the United States. (1808–1875)
1555.

JOHNSON, BILLY, American song-writer.
1882.

JOHNSON, or JONSON, CHRISTOPHER, English poet and physician. (1536?–1597)
1799.

JOHNSON, DOROTHY COOPER, contemporary American writer.
1942.

JOHNSON, GEORGE W., American minstrel and song-writer.
2289.

JOHNSON, HIRAM WARREN, American politician. (1866–1945)
2112.

JOHNSON, HOWARD, American song-writer. (1887–)
1350.

JOHNSON, HUGH S., American soldier and publicist. (1882–1942)
814, 1555.

JOHNSON, JAMES WELDON, American Negro poet and miscellaneous writer. (1871–1938)
602.

JOHNSON, LIONEL PIGOT, English critic and poet. (1867–1902)
184, 244, 791, 998, 1458, 1844.

JOHNSON, PHILANDER CHASE, American humorist and dramatic critic. (1866–1939)
45, 250, 1644, 2009, 2128, 2171.

JOHNSON, RICHARD, English writer. (1573–1659?)
200, 375, 1593.

JOHNSON, ROBERT UNDERWOOD, American editor, poet, publicist and diplomatist. (1853–1937)
34, 129, 481, 681, 909, 938, 995, 1001, 1106, 1212, 1310, 1533, 1738, 1824, 1839, 1852, 1907, 1917, 1918, 2090, 2150, 2204.

JOHNSON, (JOHN) ROSAMOND, American Negro musician and composer. (1873–)
1212.

JOHNSON, ROSSITER, American editor and essayist. (1840–1931)
1669, 1937.

* JOHNSON, SAMUEL, English lexicographer and poet. (1709–1784)

JOHNSON, "TINY," mother of Jack Johnson, pugilist.
1929.

JOHNSON, TOM LOFTIN, American inventor, steel producer and politician. (1854–1911)
1555.

JOHNSON-CORY, WILLIAM, English poet and educator. (1823–1892)
405, 1805.

JOHNSTON, MARY, American novelist. (1870–1936)
1271.

JOHNSTONE, GORDON. No biographical data available.
263.

JOHNSTONE, HENRY, LORD JOHNSTONE, Scottish poet. (1844– ?)
1797.

JOINVILLE, FRANÇOIS FERDINAND D'ORLÉANS, PRINCE DE, French soldier and writer. (1818–1900)
1829.

JONAS, ROSALIE M., contemporary American poet.
1456.

JONES, EMILY BEATRIX COURSOLLES [MRS. F. L. LUCAS], English writer. (1893–)
26.

JONES, FREDERICK SCHEETZ, American educator. (1862–1944)
194.

JONES, HENRY ARTHUR, English dramatist. (1851–1929)
561, 896, 1622, 2205, 2243, 2262.

JONES, I. EDGAR. No biographical data available.
708.

JONES, IRVING, American song-writer.
2289.

Jones, John Paul; John Paul, a Scottish adventurer who became a famous American naval commander. (1747–1792)
62.

Jones, Rufus Matthew, American Quaker leader, and inspirational writer. (1863–1948)
783, 1616, 2241.

Jones, Thomas S., Jr., American poet. (1882–1933)
257, 616, 969.

Jones, Sir William, English Orientalist. (1746–1794)
407, 924, 935, 1088, 1092, 1180, 1189, 1343, 1446, 1574, 1917, 2176, 2227.

* Jonson, Ben, English poet and dramatist. (1573?–1637)

Jordan, David Starr, American naturalist, educator and peace advocate. (1851–1931)
2088.

Jortin, John, English ecclesiastical historian. (1698–1770)
1449, 1938.

Josephus, Flavius, Jewish historian. (A.D. 37–c. 95)
886.

Joubert, Joseph, French moralist and man of letters. (1754–1824)
14, 21, 31, 43, 68, 83, 98, 101, 130, 188, 204, 217, 228, 235, 246, 256, 328, 329, 334, 339, 359, 424, 544, 654, 739, 762, 961, 1027, 1035, 1166, 1167, 1182, 1303, 1306, 1378, 1428, 1516, 1563, 1572, 1611, 1628, 1689, 1927, 1929, 1945, 1966, 1969, 1990, 2038, 2050, 2067, 2082, 2088, 2136, 2250, 2253.

Joussenel. No biographical data available.
471.

Jouvenot, F. de, and Micard, H., French dramatists. (fl. 1888)
43.

Jouy, Victor Joseph Étienne de, French playwright and librettist. (1764–1846)
2184.

Jowett, Benjamin, English educator, essayist and translator. (1817–1893)
34, 829, 1177.

Joyce, James, Irish novelist and poet. (1882–1941)
1221.

Joyce, Patrick Weston, Irish teacher and historian. (1827–1914) 1630

Judge, Jack, English actor and song-writer. (1878–1938)
996.

Jugurtha, Numidian king conquered by the Romans. (154?–104 B.C.)
125, 1739.

Julian, Flavius Claudius Julianus, The Apostate, Roman Emperor. (331–363)
263, 410, 495.

Julius III (Gianmaria del Monte), Roman Pope. (1487–1555)
818.

Junius, pseud. of the author of a series of letters which appeared in the London *Public Advertiser*, from 1769–1771, attacking George III and his ministers. His identity has never been definitely established, but there are strong reasons for attributing the letters to Sir Philip Francis, an English statesman. (1740–1818)
1, 53, 333, 588, 627, 816, 820, 988, 1043, 1168, 1468, 1541, 1927, 2099.

Junot, Andoche, Duc d'Abrantès, French general under Napoleon I. (1771–1813)
73, 719.

Justinian I, Emperor of Constantinople. (527–565)
1027, 1082, 1478.

Jusserand, Jean Adrien Antoine Jules, French statesman and man of letters. (1855–1932)
748.

* Juvenal, Decimus Junius, Roman satirical poet. (40–125)

K

Kahn, Gus, American song-writer. (1886–)
2289.

Kahn, Otto Hermann, American banker and art patron. (1867–1934)
1107.

Kaines, Joseph, English educator and lecturer.
234.

Kalidasa, "the Shakespeare of India," most illustrious of Hindu poets. (fl. A.D. 225?)
2184.

Kant, Immanuel, German metaphysician, founder of the Transcendental school of philosophy. (1724–1804)
148, 1721, 1914.

Karr, Alphonse, French novelist. (1808–1890)
1378, 1489, 2274.

Kauffman, Reginald Wright, American journalist and miscellaneous writer. (1877–)
294, 1067, 1867.

Kazinczy, Francis, Hungarian poet and translator. (1759–1831)
3.

Kearney, Denis, American labor agitator. (1847–1907)
1066.

Keats, John, English poet. (1795–1821)
28, 83, 89, 116, 124, 133, 136, 142, 171, 290, 321, 415, 422, 453, 479, 496, 512, 522, 566, 578, 603, 612, 633, 634, 684, 689, 692, 745, 799, 823, 832, 842, 880, 912, 924, 964, 966, 969, 986, 989, 1017, 1033, 1145, 1162, 1189, 1192, 1196, 1198, 1208, 1247, 1261, 1264, 1291, 1295, 1300, 1302, 1303, 1309, 1315, 1317, 1337, 1341, 1343, 1363, 1364, 1365, 1366, 1374, 1401, 1405, 1406, 1417, 1442, 1455, 1471, 1500, 1516, 1531, 1533, 1559, 1584, 1610, 1628, 1743, 1744, 1746, 1772, 1773, 1782, 1794 1825, 1826, 1844, 1873, 1878, 1885, 1886, 1901, 1903, 1913, 1952, 1974, 1995, 2000, 2003, 2038, 2055, 2095, 2140, 2153, 2154, 2157, 2187, 2195, 2232, 2265, 2269.

Keble, John, English divine and poet. (1792–1866)
26, 49, 81, 94, 157, 158, 171, 242, 264, 281, 391, 403, 505, 507, 514, 637, 661, 684, 790, 810, 877, 905, 912, 936, 944, 1000, 1012,

1025, 1124, 1165, 1219, 1271, 1347, 1364, 1384, 1385, 1386, 1405, 1422, 1500, 1516, 1533, 1576, 1587, 1659, 1660, 1707, 1755, 1773, 1827, 1847, 1873, 1874, 1902, 1903, 1914, 1931, 1973, 1974, 1983, 2004, 2093, 2207, 2230.

KEENE, CHARLES SAMUEL, English humorous artist. (1823–1891)
1637.

KEENE, THOMAS WALLACE, American actor. Real name, THOMAS R. EAGLESON. (1840–1898)
9.

KELLER, HELEN ADAMS, American, blind, deaf and dumb, who became a writer and educator. (1880–)
1038.

KELLEY, HUBERT, contemporary American poet.
2150.

KELLEY, THOMAS. No biographical data available.
264, 514.

KELLOGG, JOHN HARVEY, American surgeon; founder of the health food industries. (1852–1943)
38, 2018.

KELLY, GEORGE, contemporary American dramatist. (1890–)
1912.

KELLY, JAMES, Scottish writer and compiler. No biographical data available.
468, 613.

KELLY, JOHN W., American song-writer.
1638, 2289.

KEMBLE, FRANCES ANNE, English actress and poet. (1809–1893)
3, 23, 1128, 1218, 1352, 2047, 2161.

KEMBLE, WILLIAM H., American politician. (fl. 1867)
1555.

KEMP, HARRY HIBBARD, American poet. (1883–1960)
397, 796, 938, 1025, 1587.

KEMPIS, THOMAS À, see THOMAS À KEMPIS

KEN, or KENN, THOMAS, English divine and devotional writer. (1637–1711)
314, 370, 793, 1150, 1890.

KENDALL, TIMOTHY, English compiler of epigrams. (fl. 1577)
2105, 2188.

KENDRICK, WILLIAM, English dramatist. (d. 1777)
1613.

KENNEDY, EDWARD DAVID, American poet. (1901–)
27.

KENNEDY, GEOFFREY ANKETELL STUDDERT-, English clergyman. (1883–1929)
262.

KENNEDY, HARRY, American ventriloquist and song-writer. (1855–1894)
1455, 2289.

KENNEY, JAMES, Irish dramatist. (1780–1849)
1347.

KENYON, JAMES BENJAMIN, American Methodist clergyman and verse-writer. (1858–1924)
203, 1066, 1125, 1128, 1244, 1370, 1431, 1534, 1892, 2140.

KEPLER, JOHANN, German astronomer. (1571–1630)
795, 1673.

KEPPEL, LADY CAROLINE, Scottish poet. (1735– ?)
3.

KEPPEL, DAVID, American writer of religious works. (1846– ?)
2044.

KERNAHAN, COULSON, English writer. (1858–1943)
274, 2257.

KERR, SOPHIE [MRS. SOPHIE KERR UNDERWOOD], American miscellaneous writer. (1880–)
1802.

KETHE, WILLIAM, English Protestant divine. (? –1608?)
793.

KEY, FRANCIS SCOTT, American jurist and author of *The Star-Spangled Banner*. (1779–1843)
51, 674, 2046.

KEY, THOMAS HEWITT, English Latin scholar. (1799–1875)
1314.

KHAYYÁM, see OMAR KHAYYÁM

KIERAN, JAMES M., American newspaperman. (1901–1952)
1555.

KIERKEGAARD, SÖREN, Danish scholar. (1813–1855)
1118.

KILLIGREW, THOMAS, English dramatist. (1657–1719)
1639.

KILMER, ALINE MURRAY [MRS. JOYCE KILMER], American poet. (1888–1941)
41, 756, 1193, 1216, 1352, 2101.

KILMER, JOYCE, American poet. (1886–1918)
275, 1869, 1879, 1914, 2037.

KIMBALL, HARRIET MCEWEN, American poet. (1834–1917)
688.

KING, BEN[JAMIN FRANKLIN], American humorist. (1857–1894)
586, 1410, 1414, 1578.

KING, HARRIET ELEANOR [MRS. HAMILTON KING], English poet. (1840–1920)
1128, 1850.

KING, HENRY, English divine and poet. (1592–1669)
684, 2277.

KING, JOHN, Bishop of London. (1559?–1621)
1615.

KING, STODDARD, American newspaper columnist and song-writer. (1890–1933)
481, 2257.

KING, WILLIAM, English writer. (1663–1712)
129, 315, 450, 522, 987, 1167, 1223, 1478.

KINGLAKE, ALEXANDER WILLIAM, English historian of the Crimean War. (1809–1891)
1863.

KINGSLEY, CHARLES, English poet and novelist. (1819–1875)
6, 34, 72, 220, 223, 231, 258, 263, 280, 282, 306, 332, 425, 453, 506, 561, 616, 671, 723, 764, 793, 807, 821, 893, 897, 943, 1061, 1062, 1129, 1133, 1140, 1274, 1283, 1296, 1444, 1556, 1560, 1570, 1640, 1668, 1732, 1733, 1764, 1832, 1940, 1953, 1962, 2001, 2017, 2123, 2131, 2165, 2231, 2234, 2235, 2262, 2264, 2282.

KINGSMILL, HUGH (pseud. of HUGH KINGSMILL LUNN), English critic and biographical writer. (1889–1949)
531, 579, 580, 1496, 1593, 1685.

KINGSTON, RICHARD, English political pamphleteer. (fl. 1700)
954.

KINNEY, COATES, American journalist and verse-writer. (1826–1904)
1351, 1669.

KINSOLVING, SALLY BRUCE, American poet. (1876–) 1813.

KIPLING, RUDYARD, English poet and short-story writer. (1865–1936)
19, 56, 69, 103, 126, 174, 204, 211, 238, 275, 280, 294, 325, 330, 332, 335, 368, 441, 455, 461, 464, 472, 505, 513, 514, 534, 545, 547, 551, 552, 555, 556, 561, 586, 614, 618, 627, 675, 707, 708, 716, 725, 730, 754, 756, 765, 767, 789, 852, 879, 936, 956, 957, 973, 991, 995, 999, 1022, 1042, 1045, 1046, 1102, 1128, 1151, 1157, 1185, 1198, 1203, 1212, 1224, 1226, 1229, 1252, 1276, 1277, 1352, 1392, 1465, 1470, 1481, 1502, 1503, 1506, 1525, 1543, 1549, 1590, 1604, 1628, 1629, 1636, 1665, 1707, 1736, 1742, 1756, 1773, 1779, 1814, 1815, 1830, 1833, 1850, 1857, 1864, 1865, 1866, 1867, 1869, 1880, 1930, 1947, 1957, 1961, 1963, 1968, 1981, 2019, 2027, 2045, 2059, 2082, 2101, 2102, 2116, 2121, 2187, 2188, 2191, 2205, 2209, 2217, 2220, 2232, 2234, 2243, 2273, 1246, 2298m, n, o, 2299c, g.

KIRK, RICHARD RAY, American poet. (1877–)
143, 309, 740, 1357.

KIRKMAN, FRANCIS, English writer and bookseller. (fl. 1674)
1676.

KISER, SAMUEL ELLSWORTH, American editor and verse-writer. (1862–1942)
705, 2145.

KITCHENER, HORATIO HERBERT, first EARL KITCHENER, English field-marshal. (1850–1916)
557.

KLEISER, GRENVILLE, American inspirational writer. (1868–1953)
1847, 1992.

KNAPP, JUNE, American girl ten years old when her poem was printed in *The Conning Tower.*
2262.

KNATCHBULL-HUGESSEN, EDWARD HUGESSEN, first BARON BRABOURNE, English statesman. (1829–1893)
573

KNIBBS, HENRY HERBERT, American poet. (1874–1945)
80, 2102.

KNIGHT, CHARLES, English writer and publisher. (1791–1873)
127.

KNIGHT, THOMAS, English actor and dramatist. (? –1820)
441, 1581.

KNOTT, JAMES PROCTOR, American politician and Governor of Kentucky. (1830–1911)
275.

KNOWLES, FREDERICK LAWRENCE, American poet. (1869–1905)
206, 378, 387, 888, 1048, 1049, 1077, 1220, 1384, 1401, 1879.

KNOWLES, F. M., American humorous writer. 488, 619, 910, 1112, 1262, 1440, 2099.

KNOWLES, JAMES SHERIDAN, English dramatist. (1784–1862)
86, 221, 649, 734, 739, 1062, 1299, 1307, 1352, 1895.

KNOX, HENRY, American Major-General and Secretary of War. (1750–1806)
2122.

KNOX, ISA CRAIG, Scottish poet. (1831–1903)
1143, 1877.

KNOX, J. MASON, American humorist. (fl. 1900)
1862.

KNOX, JOHN, Scottish Protestant reformer, theologian and historian. (1505–1572)
218, 2188

KNOX, WILLIAM, Scottish poet. (1789–1825)
828, 1607.

KOCK, PAUL DE, French novelist. (1794–1871)
194, 252, 1103.

KOLLOCK, SHEPARD, American journalist and publisher. (1750–1839)
810.

KÖPFEL, WOLFGANG FABRICIUS, see CAPITO

KOSSUTH, LOUIS, Hungarian revolutionary leader. (1802–1894)
1379.

KOTZEBUE, AUGUST FRIEDRICH FERDINAND VON, German dramatist. (1761–1846)
967, 1887.

KREYMBORG, ALFRED, American poet. (1883–)
555, 684, 778, 890, 1397, 1489, 1802, 1812, 1834, 2120, 2147.

KRUMMACHER, FRIEDRICH ADOLF, German theologian. (1768–1845)
966.

KRUTCH, JOSEPH WOOD, American miscellaneous writer. (1893–)
354, 1056, 1059, 1125, 1345, 1623.

KUMMER, CLARE, contemporary American playwright.
2183.

KYD, STEWART, English politician and legal writer. (? –1811)
319.

KYD, or KID, THOMAS, English dramatist. (1557?–1595?)
320, 1264, 1398, 1443.

L

LABERIUS, DECIMUS, Latin writer of farces. (105–43 B.C.)
193, 918.

LABOULAYE, ÉDOUARD RENÉ LEFEBVRE, French historical writer and satirist. (1811–1883)
932, 1462.

* LA BRUYÈRE, JEAN DE, French writer and moralist. (1644–1696)

LA CHAUSSÉE, PIERRE CLAUDE NIVELLE DE, French dramatist. (1692–1754)
1727.

LACORDAIRE, JEAN-BAPTISTE HENRI, French preacher and publicist, founder of new order of Dominicans. (1802–1861)
47.

LA COSTE, MARIE RAVENEL DE, American writer. (1849–1936)
410.

LACTANTIUS, LUCIUS CŒLIUS FIRMIANUS, Latin Father and rhetorician. (d. c. 325)
1481, 2052.

LACY, JOHN, English dramatist and comedian. (? –1681)
257, 2180.

LACYDES, Greek philosopher. (fl. c. 241 B.C.)
1098.

LAFFAN, WILLIAM MACKAY, American journalist and art connoisseur. (1848–1909)
1741.

LA FOLLETTE, ROBERT MARION, American legislator. (1855–1925)
1541, 2048.

LA FONTAINE, JEAN DE, French fabulist and poet. (1621–1695)
86, 112, 145, 146, 161, 207, 254, 349, 421, 454, 463, 465, 516, 540, 584, 588, 676, 692, 712, 713, 734, 765, 780, 787, 821, 835, 963, 990, 992, 1024, 1057, 1097, 1128, 1180, 1303, 1320, 1424, 1462, 1513, 1604, 1650, 1730, 1736, 1785, 1789, 1803, 1810, 1821, 1902, 1962, 2059, 2070, 2076, 2231.

LA GIRANDIÈRE, French editor and collector of epigrams.
695.

LA GUARDIA, FIORELLO H., American lawyer, Mayor of New York City. (1882–1947)
1112.

LA HARPE, JEAN FRANÇOIS DE, French critic and poet. (1739–1803)
2050.

LAIGHTON, ALBERT, American lawyer and verse-writer. (1829–1887)
116, 1494.

LAIGHTON, OSCAR, American Unitarian clergyman. (1839– ?)
283.

LAIRD, DONALD ANDERSON, American psychologist. (1897–)
1241.

LAIRD, WILLIAM (pseud. of WILLIAM LAIRD BROWN), American poet. (1888–)
644.

LAMACHUS, Athenian general. (470–414 B.C.)
2108.

LAMARTINE, ALPHONSE DE, French poet and politician. (1790–1869)
432, 445, 470, 593, 899, 1148, 1185, 1198, 1238, 1471, 1539, 1786.

LAMB, ARTHUR J., American song-writer. (1870–1928)
1268, 2289, 2290.

LAMB, CHARLES, English essayist and poet. (1775–1834)
2, 5, 83, 86, 153, 162, 182, 189, 191, 194, 199, 219, 238, 240, 283, 289, 326, 375, 401, 402, 415, 441, 491, 512, 516, 522, 597, 631, 634, 702, 731, 751, 774, 860, 866, 903, 940, 955, 1012, 1020, 1108, 1167, 1177, 1218, 1271, 1489, 1572, 1587, 1603, 1632, 1654, 1666, 1675, 1676, 1696, 1769, 1788, 1826, 1859, 1895, 1936, 1942, 1944, 1952, 1979, 1986, 2017, 2019, 2056, 2071, 2235, 2238, 2250, 2254.

LAMB, CHARLES and MARY, English writers and collaborators. (1775–1834), (1764–1847)
79, 121, 2074.

LAMB, WILLIAM, second VISCOUNT MELBOURNE, English statesman. (1779–1848)
1542.

LAMBARDE, WILLIAM, English historian of Kent. (1536–1601)
646, 936, 2177.

LAMBERT, [MRS.] MARY ELIZA TUCKER, American miscellaneous writer. (1838– ?)
713.

LAMPTON, WILLIAM JAMES, American newspaperman. (1859?–1917)
1034.

LANCASTER, G. E. No biographical data available.
1046.

LANDON, LETITIA ELIZABETH, English poet. (1802–1838)
91, 251, 603, 604, 1222, 1297, 1566, 1687, 2086.

LANDOR, WALTER SAVAGE, English poet and essayist. (1775–1864)
3, 29, 34, 47, 79, 104, 145, 185, 203, 266, 274, 308, 346, 387, 399, 401, 408, 410, 422, 502, 552, 594, 623, 626, 628, 636, 678, 682, 697, 740, 766, 806, 817, 823, 832, 834, 848, 878, 881, 903, 964, 990, 1027, 1032, 1049, 1148, 1204, 1260, 1268, 1269, 1376, 1377, 1386, 1424, 1450, 1456, 1521, 1609, 1612, 1654, 1667, 1689, 1696, 1737, 1772, 1781, 1807, 1853, 1867, 1871, 1876, 1879, 1918, 1927, 1936, 1942, 2053, 2064, 2206, 2230, 2258.

LANE, FRANKLIN KNIGHT, born in Canada; American Secretary of the Interior under Woodrow Wilson. (1864–1921)
18, 674, 1382, 1503, 1782.

LANE, GEORGE MARTIN, American educator. (1823–1897)
2290.

LANG, ANDREW, English scholar, folklorist, poet and man of letters. (1844–1912)
37, 124, 181, 185, 188, 276, 334, 399, 636, 708, 904, 911, 934, 1009, 1156, 1198, 1565, 1601, 1907, 2011, 2095, 2268.

Langbridge, Frederick, American miscellaneous writer. (1849–1923)
1434.

Langford, G. W. No biographical data available.
766.

Langford, John Alfred, English antiquary and journalist. (1823–1903)
186.

Langhorne, John, English poet. (1735–1779)
633, 1020, 1023, 1031, 1320, 1460, 1880.

Langhorne, William, English poet and translator. (1721–1772)
1198.

Langland, William, English poet, author of *The Vision of Piers the Plowman.* (1330?–1400?)
11, 131, 145, 169, 201, 223, 242, 243, 246, 256, 300, 330, 375, 493, 498, 646, 751, 787, 818, 910, 961, 1019, 1058, 1063, 1086, 1094, 1155, 1170, 1173, 1233, 1298, 1392, 1416, 1461, 1462, 1539, 1566, 1580, 1592, 1595, 1639, 1666, 1679, 1760, 1809, 1984, 1985, 2004, 2049, 2054, 2104, 2133, 2148, 2167, 2225.

Langtoft, Peter, English rhyming chronicler. (? –1307?)
1046.

Lanier, Sidney, American poet and critic. (1842–1881)
51, 261, 263, 284, 514, 1367, 1386, 1732, 1941, 2003.

Lanigan, George Thomas, journalist and humorous poet, born in Canada, died at Philadelphia, Pa. (1845–1886)
65, 1369, 1399.

Lannes, Jean de, Duke of Montebello, French Marshal. (1769–1809)
415.

Lao-tsze (the Venerable Philosopher), Chinese teacher, philosopher and reputed founder of Tâoism. (fl. 6th century B.C.)
148, 297, 310, 352, 447, 773, 885, 994, 1060, 1189, 1319, 1467, 1723, 1786, 2039, 2057, 2090, 2218, 2229, 2243.

La Place, Pierre Simon, Marquis de, French mathematician. (1749–1827)
114.

Lapraik, John, Scottish innkeeper and poet. (1727–1807)
2140.

Lapsley, W. S. No biographical data available.
847.

Laramore, Vivian Yeiser [Mrs. Robert Eugene Laramore], American poet. (1891–)
2021, 2201.

Larcom, Lucy, American poet. (1824–1893)
309, 674, 1283, 1780, 1818, 1846, 2036.

Lardner, Ring, American short-story writer. (1885–1933)
1056.

* La Rochefoucauld, François, Duc de, French epigrammatist. (1613–1680)

La Rochfoucault-Liancourt, François, Duc de, French philanthropist, social reformer. (1747–1827)
60, 1714.

Larochejaquelin, Louis du Verger, Comte de, French insurgent leader in La Vendée. (1777–1815)
663.

Lathbury, Mary Artemisia, American poet and hymn-writer. (1841–1913)
1128.

Lathrop, George Parsons, American littérateur and verse-writer. (1851–1898)
1361, 2122.

Lathrop, Mary T., first woman member of the American Bar Association.
366, 2184.

Latimer, Hugh, English churchman, Bishop of Worcester. (1485?–1555)
169, 216, 252, 344, 443, 850, 921, 928, 1293, 1960, 2036, 2057.

Latrobe, Charles Joseph, Australian Governor and traveller. (1801–1875)
1034.

Laud, William, English Archbishop. (1573–1645)
415, 948.

Lauder, Sir Harry, Scottish comedian and writer of songs. (1870–1950)
494, 1729, 1925.

Lawlor, Charles, American song-writer. (1852–1925)
2290.

Laurier, Sir Wilfrid, Canadian statesman. (1841–1919)
545.

Law, Andrew Bonar, English statesman and Premier. (1858–1923)
2108.

Law, Edward, first Baron Ellenborough, English Lord Chief-Justice. (1750–1818)
1874, 2060.

Lawrence, Saint, Spanish saint. (d. c. 258)
415

Lawrence, David Herbert, English poet and novelist. (1885–1930)
55, 723.

Lawrence, Sir Henry Montgomery, English general. (1806–1857)
506.

Lawrence, James, American naval commander. (1781–1813)
62.

Layard, Sir Austen Henry, English explorer and politician. (1817–1894)
1549.

Lazarus, Emma, American poet. (1849–1887)
1012, 1397.

Leacock, Stephen Butler, Canadian political economist and writer of humorous stories. (1869–1944)
931, 1166, 1452, 1479, 1619, 1753, 2046, 2189.

Lear, Edward, English artist and writer of nonsense verse. (1812–1888)
127, 1157, 1399, 1410, 1411.

Learned, Walter, American verse-writer. (1847–1915)
708.

LEONARDO DA VINCI, Italian painter, sculptor, architect, musician and natural philosopher. (1425–1519)
1064.

LEONIDAS OF TARENTUM, Greek poet. (c. 275 B.C.)
502, 907, 912.

LEOPOLD OF ANHALT-DESSAU, see ANHALT-DESSAU

LE ROUX DE LINCY, A. J. V., archæologist. (1806–1869)
469, 470.

LE ROW, CAROLINE BIGELOW, American compiler and verse-writer. (1843– ?)
1786.

LE SAGE, ALAIN RENÉ, French novelist and dramatist. (1668–1747)
86, 155, 216, 222, 649, 676, 780, 939, 1010, 1167, 1176, 1606, 1686, 1966, 1986, 2127, 2199.

LESLIE, AMY (pseud. of MRS. LILLIE WEST BROWN BUCK), American dramatic critic. (1860–)
1875.

LESLIE, PAUL, American song-writer.
2290.

LESSING, GOTTHOLD EPHRAIM, German critic and dramatist. (1729–1781)
6, 144, 193, 352, 615, 774, 806, 880, 885, 891, 1016, 1059, 1078, 1581, 1798, 1815, 1948, 2049, 2182, 2191.

L'ESTRANGE, SIR ROGER, English Tory journalist and pamphleteer. (1616–1704)
126, 178, 593, 1028, 1081, 1333, 1456, 1596, 1899, 1921, 1958, 2177, 2180.

LETTS, WINIFRED [MRS. W. H. FOSTER VERSCHOYLE]. Irish poet. (1882–)
196, 1064.

LETTSON, JOHN COAKLEY, English physician. (1744–1815)
468.

LEVER, CHARLES JAMES, Irish novelist. (1806–1872)
962, 1856.

LEVERIDGE, LILLIAN, contemporary Canadian poet.
907.

LEVESON-GOWER, GRANVILLE GEORGE, second EARL GRANVILLE, English statesman. (1815–1891)
452.

LEVIS, PIERRE MARC GASTON, DUC DE, French writer of maxims. (1764–1830)
72.

LEWES, GEORGE HENRY, English miscellaneous writer. (1817–1878)
759, 832, 841, 1359, 1560, 1621.

LEWIS, GILBERT NEWTON, American chemist. (1875–1946)
1086.

LEWIS, HENRY T., American politician. (fl. 1896)
204, 1594.

LEWIS, MATTHEW GREGORY, English novelist. (1775–1818)
1206, 1232, 2141.

LEWIS, SAM M. (1883–1959) and YOUNG, JOE, American song-writers.
2284.

LEWIS, SINCLAIR, American novelist. (1885–1951)
53, 1643, 1692, 1970.

LEWISOHN, LUDWIG, American critic and miscellaneous writer. (1882–)
106, 328, 433, 1498, 1910.

LEYBOURNE, GEORGE, English song-writer.
2296.

LEYDEN, JOHN, Scottish physician and poet. (1775–1811)
2038.

LÉZAY-MARNÉSIA, CLAUDE FRANÇOIS ADRIEN DE, French statesman and poet. (1735–1800)
44.

LIBANIUS, Greek sophist and rhetorician. (314–393)
2114.

LICHTWER, MAGNUS GOTTFRIED, German fabulist. (1719–1783)
2269.

LIDDELL, CATHERINE C., English miscellaneous writer. (1848– ?)
261.

LIDDELL, HENRY THOMAS, first EARL OF RAVENSWORTH, English statesman, poet and translator. (1797–1878)
639.

LIGNE, KARL JOSEPH, PRINCE DE, Austrian general and witty writer. (1735–1814)
360.

LILIENTHAL, JOSEPH. No biographical data available.
1046.

LILIUS GREGORIUS GYRALDUS (GIGLIO GREGORIO GIRALDI), Italian scholar and poet. (1479–1552)
566.

LILLO, GEORGE, English dramatist. (1693–1739)
992, 1018, 1123, 1366, 2011, 2214, 2229.

LILLY, WILLIAM, English grammarian. (1466–1523)
1901.

LINCOLN, ABRAHAM, sixteenth President of the United States. (1809–1865)
54, 57, 59, 71, 100, 234, 271, 304, 319, 421, 427, 432, 455, 470, 530, 574, 575, 589, 598, 612, 663, 787, 816, 941, 1028, 1066, 1067, 1092, 1103, 1159, 1160, 1236, 1303, 1333, 1350, 1352, 1395, 1418, 1431, 1459, 1479, 1481, 1488, 1555, 1564, 1619, 1661, 1726, 1792, 1823, 1841, 1842, 1867, 1869, 1966, 2006, 2083, 2099, 2106, 2115, 2122, 2181, 2225, 2231, 2277.

LINDSAY, or LYNDSAY, SIR DAVID, Scottish poet. (1490–1555)
201, 2092, 2108.

LINDSAY, JENNIE, American song-writer.
2290.

LINDSAY, NICHOLAS VACHEL, American poet. (1879–1931)
46, 284, 401, 441, 627, 801, 823, 879, 883, 1005, 1034, 1067, 1114, 1159, 1230, 1238, 1397, 1405, 1570, 1733, 1888.

LINDSAY, WALTER (pseud. of ROBERT BURNS ANNANDALE), biographical writer. (1889–)
275.
LINGARD, WILLIAM HORACE (real name WILLIAM THOMAS), English actor and song-writer. (1837–1927)
2290.
LINK, ROBERT H., alleged American inventor of "boon-doggle."
1556.
LINKLATER, ERIC, English poet. (1899–)
53.
LINLEY, GEORGE, English verse-writer and musical composer. (1798–1865)
3, 429, 484, 1796.
LINNÆUS, CARL, Swedish botanist. (1707–1778)
1382.
LINSCHOTEN, JAN HUGH VAN, Dutch voyager. (1563–1633)
1813.
LISSAUER, ERNST, German poet. (1882–1937)
2300i.
LISZT, FRANZ, Hungarian composer, pianist and abbé. (1811–1886)
1044, 1148.
LITHGOW, WILLIAM, English traveller. (1582–1645?)
497.
LIVINGSTONE, DAVID, English missionary and explorer in Africa. (1813–1873)
964.
LIVY, TITUS LIVIUS, Roman historian. (59 B.C.–A.D. 17)
16, 19, 46, 166, 178, 274, 295, 337, 429, 565, 593, 654, 663, 681, 712, 749, 810, 844, 863, 916, 1001, 1060, 1064, 1073, 1080, 1089, 1236, 1322, 1333, 1336, 1393, 1483, 1625, 1639, 1737, 1738, 1809, 1865, 1932, 1945, 2033, 2040, 2041, 2045, 2050, 2111, 2119, 2168, 2191, 2192, 2209, 2227, 2231, 2247, 2264.
LLOYD, DAVID, English divine and poet. (1752–1838)
850, 1429, 1488, 1901.
LLOYD, ELIZABETH. No data available.
1305.
LLOYD, ROBERT, English poet. (1733–1764)
10, 2097.
LLOYD GEORGE, DAVID, English statesman. (1863–1945)
536, 1381, 1464, 2114.
LOCKE, JOHN, English philosopher. (1632–1704)
6, 356, 419, 420, 577, 593, 606, 814, 871, 946, 958, 997, 1020, 1062, 1087, 1382, 1427, 1623, 1667, 1676, 1678, 1689, 1803, 1989, 2053, 2066, 2218, 2237.
LOCKE, JOHN, Irish poet. (1847–1889)
997.
LOCKER-LAMPSON, FREDERICK, English poet. (1821–1895)
109, 121, 346, 645, 708, 711, 827, 1102, 1120, 1168, 1296, 1410, 1413, 1529, 1817, 1861, 2014, 2075, 2242.
LOCKHART, JOHN GIBSON, Scottish writer, biographer of Sir Walter Scott. (1794–1854)
403, 446, 490, 839, 1033, 1430, 1769.
LOCKHART, ROBERT HAMILTON BRUCE, English journalist. (1887–)
194.
LOCKIER, FRANCIS, English divine and essayist. (1667–1740)
1769.
LODBROK, REGNER, or RAGNAR, semi-legendary Norse Viking. (fl. A.D. 800)
1774.
LODGE, HENRY CABOT, American statesman and historian. (1850–1924)
1159, 2275.
LODGE, THOMAS, English poet and romance writer. (1558?–1625)
223, 444, 1208, 1413, 1632, 1874, 1952, 2036.
LODGE, THOMAS, and GREENE, ROBERT, English poets and collaborators. (1558?–1625), (1560?–1592)
1686.
LOGAN, JAMES, Scottish writer and antiquary. (1794?–1872)
1352.
LOGAN, JOHN, Scottish divine and poet. (1748–1788)
116, 346, 388, 591, 1274, 1361.
LOGAU, FRIEDRICH, BARON, German poet and epigrammatist. (1604–1655)
170, 875, 1148, 1337, 1708, 1829, 2050.
LOINES, RUSSELL H. No biographical data available. 1884.
LONDON, JACK, American novelist. (1876–1916)
2298i:1.
LONG, HANIEL CLARK, American poet. (1888–) 211.
LONG, JOHN DAVIS, American legislator, Secretary of the Navy, Governor of Massachusetts. (1838–1915)
1104.
LONGBRAKE, ARTHUR, American song-writer.
2290.
* LONGFELLOW, HENRY WADSWORTH, American poet and scholar. (1807–1882)
LONGFELLOW, SAMUEL, American Unitarian clergyman and poet. (1819–1892)
1128.
LONGINUS, DIONYSIUS CASSIUS, Greek philosopher and critic. (c. 210–273)
105, 1927.
LONGINUS, LUCIUS CASSIUS, Roman tribune. (c. 90 B.C.)
1081.
LONGWORTH, [MRS.] ALICE ROOSEVELT, daughter of Theodore Roosevelt. (1884–)
1553.
LOOS, ANITA, American writer. (1893–)
848.
LORENS, FRÈRE, medieval French moralist.
519, 1628.
LORRIS, GUILLAUME DE, French author of first part of *Roman de la Rose*. (fl. 1250)
2145.
LOTHARIUS I, German Emperor. (c. 795–855)
230.
LOUIS XI, King of France. (1423–1483)
815, 1039, 1608.

Louis XII, King of France. (1462–1515)
766.
Louis XIII, King of France. (1601–1643)
346, 719.
Louis XIV, King of France. (1638–1715)
415, 1044, 1045, 1354, 1548, 1579, 2117, 2140.
Louis XV, King of France. (1710–1774)
719.
Louis XVI, King of France. (1754–1793)
415, 1056.
Louis XVIII (Stanislaus Xavier), King of France. (1755–1824)
328, 548, 1044.
Louis-Philippe, King of France, the "Citizen King." (1773–1850)
1556.
Lounsbury, Thomas Raynesford, American philologist. (1838–1915)
1312.
Love, Robertus Donnell, American journalist. (1867–1930)
71.
Lovelace, Richard, English Cavalier and poet. (1618–1658)
136, 565, 608, 644, 878, 917, 1613, 1855, 2155, 2157.
Loveman, Robert, American poet. (1864–1923)
1436.
Lover, Samuel, Irish song-writer, novelist and painter. (1797–1868)
121, 123, 479, 601, 776, 1170, 1227, 1463, 1464, 1663, 1778, 1857, 1991, 2136, 2188, 2211, 2255.
Lovibond, Edward, English poet. (1724–1775)
71.
Lowe, John, Scottish poet. (1750–1798)
1343.
Lowe, Robert, first Viscount Sherbrooke, English politician. (1811–1892)
528.
Lowell, Abbott Lawrence, American educator and writer on government. (1856–1943)
531.
Lowell, Amy, American poet, essayist and biographer. (1874–1925)
40, 102, 180, 184, 756, 854, 1143, 1155, 1515, 1559, 1917, 2120, 2226, 2264.
* Lowell, James Russell, American poet and critic. (1819–1891)
Lowell, Robert Traill Spence, American Episcopal clergyman and verse-writer. (1816–1891)
1766.
Lowndes, William, English, Secretary to the Treasury. (1652–1724)
1998.
Lowth, or Louth, Robert, Bishop of London and littérateur. (1710–1787)
1457.
Loyson, Charles Jean Marie (Père Hyacinthe), French pulpit orator. (1827–1912)
768.
Lubbock, Sir John, see Avebury, Lord
* Lucan, Marcus Annæus Lucanus, Latin poet. (A.D. 39–65)
Lucas, Edward Verrall, English essayist and writer of travel-books. (1868–1938)
409, 660, 755, 1129, 1768.
Lucas, Jimmy, American song-writer.
2290.
Lucas, St. John, English writer. (1879–1934)
472.
Luce, Morton, English poet. (1849–1943)
1183, 1880.
Lucian, Greek satirist. (c. 120–180)
19, 92, 112, 127, 408, 632, 679, 799, 1062, 1117, 1328, 1348, 1354, 1395, 1816, 1901.
Lucilius, Latin satirist. (148–103 B.C.)
228, 465, 659, 776, 1056.
Lucretius, Titus Lucretius Carus, Roman poet. (fl. 96–55 B.C.)
35, 69, 84, 310, 377, 384, 516, 798, 807, 892, 909, 920, 1018, 1054, 1127, 1148, 1150, 1185, 1310, 1311, 1313, 1322, 1323, 1414, 1415, 1499, 1501, 1511, 1518, 1539, 1692, 1717, 1780, 1784, 1798, 1888, 1938, 1953, 2022, 2050, 2067, 2078, 2126, 2167, 2173, 2185, 2238.
Lucullus, Lucius Licinius, Roman consul and epicure. (110?–57? B.C.)
449.
Ludlow, Fitzhugh, American journalist. (1836–1870)
1074.
Luhrs, Marie, contemporary American writer and reviewer.
2228.
Lulham, Habberton, contemporary English poet.
1274.
Lummis, Charles Fletcher, American editor and western writer. (1859–1928)
1489.
Lunt, George, American journalist. (1803–1885)
675.
Lupton, Donald, English miscellaneous writer. (fl. 1583)
1398.
Luther, Martin, German leader of the Reformation. (1483–1546)
268, 272, 300, 515, 779, 784, 875, 1221, 1227, 1262, 1266, 1430, 1581, 1582, 1695, 1699, 1722, 1752, 1799, 1831, 1984, 2195, 2224, 2255.
Luttrell, Henry, English wit and poet. (1765–1851)
1967.
Luxburg, Count Karl von, German Chargé d'Affaires at Buenos Aires, 1914.
768.
Lyall, Sir Alfred Comyn, Anglo-Indian administrator and writer. (1835–1911)
1996.
Lyall, Edna (pseud. of Ada Ellen Bayly), English novelist. (1857–1903)
287.
Lycurgus, Greek law-giver. (fl. c. 820 B.C.)
274, 431, 847, 1232.
Lydgate, John, English poet. (1370?–1451?)
87, 166, 167, 169, 171, 248, 290, 360, 380, 420, 441, 465, 504, 607, 699, 713, 836, 849,

952, 999, 1193, 1268, 1283, 1295, 1328, 1333, 1476, 1568, 1617, 1633, 1666, 1686, 1699, 1709, 1726, 1744, 1766, 1950, 2001, 2009, 2126, 2159, 2173, 2221, 2244, 2264.

* LYLY, JOHN, English dramatist and author of *Euphues*. (1554?–1606)

LYNN, ROSS W., American lawyer, living in New York City.
124.

LYON, GEORGE W., American journalist. (1879–)
1644, 2245.

LYSAGHT, EDWARD, Irish song-writer. (1763–1811)
1330.

LYSAGHT, SIDNEY ROYSE, contemporary Irish miscellaneous writer. (c. 1874–1941)
483, 2168.

LYSANDER, Greek general and statesman. (? – 395 B.C.)
46, 717, 1418, 1781.

LYTE, HENRY FRANCIS, English hymn-writer. (1793–1847)
28, 793, 1815.

LYTLE, WILLIAM HAINES, American poet. (1826–1863)
376.

LYTTELTON, GEORGE, first BARON LYTTELTON, English poet and statesman. (1709–1773)
138, 139, 291, 602, 924, 944, 956, 984, 1170, 1176, 1182, 1203, 1266, 1446, 1513, 1526, 1651, 1698, 2140, 2180, 2188, 2205.

* LYTTON, EDWARD GEORGE EARLE LYTTON BULWER-, first BARON LYTTON, English novelist and dramatist. (1803–1873)

LYTTON, EDWARD ROBERT BULWER, first EARL OF LYTTON, see MEREDITH, OWEN

M

MAB, or MABBE, JAMES, English scholar. (1572–1642?)
112, 471, 922, 1185, 1442, 1807, 1816, 2226.

MCALLISTER, SAMUEL WARD, American society leader. (1827–1895)
1859.

MACALPINE, JAMES, contemporary Irish-born American poet.
167.

MACARTHUR, DOUGLAS, distinguished American general. (1880–)
2298d, 2298h.

* MACAULAY, THOMAS BABINGTON, first BARON MACAULAY, English historian, scholar and critic. (1800–1859)

MCBAIN, HOWARD LEE, American educator and writer on government. (1880-1936) 964.

MACBEATH, F. J., contemporary American writer. 315.

MACCALL, WILLIAM, Scottish writer. (1812–1888) 507.

MCCARTHY, DENIS ALOYSIUS, Irish-born American poet. (1870–1931)
996.

MACCARTHY, DENIS FLORENCE, Irish poet. (1817–1882)
1283.

MCCARTHY, JUSTIN HUNTLY, English novelist. (1861–1936)
985.

MCCLELLAN, E. N., Major in the U. S. Marine Corps in 1932.
67.

MCCLINTOCK, CHARLES WARREN, English song-writer.
2290.

MCCORD, DAVID (THOMPSON WATSON), American poet and essayist. (1897–)
572.

MCCORMICK, ELSIE, contemporary American miscellaneous writer.
759.

MCCORMICK, VIRGINIA TAYLOR [MRS. J. JETT MCCORMICK], American poet. (?–1957)
1856.

MCCRAE, JOHN, Canadian poet. (1872–1918)
1559, 1869.

MCCREERY, JOHN LUCKEY, American journalist and verse-writer. (1835–1906)
412.

MACDONALD, London *Times* staff correspondent. (c. 1855)
2184.

MACDONALD, BALLARD, American song-writer. (1882–1935)
880, 2290.

MACDONALD, E. M. No biographical data available.
1955.

MACDONALD, GEORGE, British poet and novelist. (1824–1905)
31, 114, 121, 131, 138, 162, 200, 260, 268, 275, 413, 475, 507, 510, 603, 605, 616, 618, 655, 692, 697, 731, 734, 773, 785, 787, 824, 882, 913, 1018, 1026, 1095, 1321, 1390, 1403, 1419, 1610, 1727, 1907, 1941, 1972, 2041, 2046, 2054.

MACDONALD, JAMES RAMSAY, English statesman and Prime Minister. (1866–1937)
442.

MACDONNELL, JAMES FRANCIS CARLIN, see CARLIN, FRANCIS

MCDONOUGH, PATRICK, Irish poet. (1902–)
378.

MACDOWELL, EDWARD ALEXANDER, American composer. (1861–1908)
481.

MCDUFFIE, GEORGE, Governor of South Carolina. (1790–1851)
63.

MACFADDEN, BERNARR ADOLPHUS, American editor and writer on health subjects. (1868–1955)
460.

MCFARLAND, WILMA KATE, contemporary American writer.
2071.

MCFEE, WILLIAM, English novelist, resident of U. S. since 1911. (1881–)
1487.

McGaffey, Ernest, verse-writer, born in Canada, but long a resident of the United States. (1861–)
2199.

McGee, Thomas D'Arcy, Irish-Canadian statesman and poet. (1825–1868)
1671.

McGlennon, Felix, American song-writer.
848, 907, 2290.

Machiavelli, Niccolo di Bernardo dei, Florentine statesman and political philosopher. (1469–1527)
711, 985, 1020, 1257, 2016, 2106, 2115.

Macintosh, Douglas Clyde, Scottish clergyman and educator. (1877–)
531.

McIver, Charles Duncan, American educator. (1860–1906)
2193.

Mackail, John William, Scottish literary historian. (1859–1945)
348, 1166.

Mackay, Charles, English poet and journalist. (1814–1889)
413, 447, 565, 893, 1029, 1042, 1133, 1303, 1436, 1473, 1777, 1854, 1978, 1992, 2295.

Mackaye, Percy, American poet and dramatist. (1875–1956)
719, 1844.

McKenna, William J., American song-writer. (1881–1949)
2290.

Mackenzie, Donald Alexander, Scottish writer, folklorist and archæologist. (1873–1936)
2149.

Mackenzie, Sir George, English jurist. (1636–1691)
629.

Mackenzie, Orgill, contemporary English writer.
1743.

McKim, John Cole. No biographical data available.
944.

McKinley, William, twenty-fifth President of the United States. (1843–1901)
64, 66, 416, 507, 821, 970, 1458, 1544.

Mackintosh, Sir James, British philosopher. (1765–1832)
507, 816, 953, 1056, 1427, 1627, 1659.

Maclaren, Ian (pseud. of John Watson), Scotch Presbyterian divine and writer of fiction of the "Kailyard school." (1850–1907)
961, 2296.

McLennan, Murdoch, Scottish poet. (fl. 1715)
456.

Macklin, Charles, English actor, dramatist and stage-manager. (1697?–1797)
681, 973, 1082.

MacLagan, Alexander, Scotch-Canadian poet. (1818–1896)
1767.

McLaurin, Anselm Joseph, American legislator. (1848–1909)
1545.

MacLeish, Archibald, American poet. (1892–)
1516.

Macleod, Fiona, see Sharp, William

Macleod, Norman, Scottish divine. (1812–1872)
937.

McLuke, Luke (pseud. of James S. Hastings), American newspaper columnist. (1868–1921)
45, 1730.

MacMahon, Marie Edme Patrice Maurice de, French Marshal and President. (1808–1893)
2109.

MacManus, Theodore F., American verse-writer. (1872–)
563, 1653.

McNabb, Father Vincent, American Catholic priest and writer. (1868–)
150.

MacNally, Leonard, Irish playwright and political informer. (1752–1820)
1212.

Macpherson, James, Scottish poet and reputed translator of the Ossianic poems. (1736–1796)
1940.

Macrobius, Ambrosius Theodosius, Latin grammarian. (fl. 5th century)
1082, 1637.

McSwiney, Terence, Irish patriot. (1879–1920)
1466.

MacWhite, Michael, Irish Free State Minister to the United States. (1883–)
1008.

Macy, John Albert, American writer on literary subjects. (1877–1932)
158, 168, 446, 734, 1128, 1166, 1452, 1514, 1559, 1683, 2147.

Madariaga, Salvador de, Spanish critic, essayist, poet and novelist. (1886–)
56, 102, 1071, 2112, 2194.

Madden, Samuel, Irish miscellaneous writer. (1686–1765)
987, 2227.

Madison, James, fourth President of the United States. (1751–1836)
57, 416, 1622.

Mæcenas, Caius Cilnius, Roman statesman and patron of letters. (c. 70–8 B.C.)
923.

Maeterlinck, Maurice, Belgian poet and dramatist. (1862–1949)
386, 748, 798, 1032, 1943, 2127.

Magee, William Connor, English prelate, Archbishop of York. (1821–1891)
1324.

Maginn, William, British poet, journalist and miscellaneous writer. (1793–1842)
1631, 1639.

Mahābhārata, sacred book of the Hindus; longest epic of the world; composed c. 200 B.C.
1245.

Mahomet, or Mohammed, Arabian religious and military leader, founder of the Moslem religion. (c. 570–632)
114, 488, 789, 945, 1451, 1763.

MAHOMET II, Sultan of Turkey. (1430–1481)
2061.

MAHONY, FRANCIS SYLVESTER (FATHER PROUT), Irish writer and humorist. (1804–1866)
997, 1733.

MAINTENON, FRANÇOISE D'AUBIGNÉ, MARQUISE DE, secret wife of Louis XIV of France. (1635–1719)
148, 1177, 1790.

MAISTRE, JOSEPH MARIE, COMTE DE, French writer. (1753–1821)
815, 1930.

MAITLAND, FREDERIC WILLIAM, English professor, and writer on legal and miscellaneous subjects. (1850–1906)
2101.

MALHERBE, FRANÇOIS DE, French poet and critic. (1555–1628)
1704, 1745, 1887.

MALINES, JOSEPH, English editor. No biographical data available.
1286.

MALKIN, BENJAMIN HEATH, English educator, historian, and writer on historical and miscellaneous subjects. (1769–1842)
1668.

MALLET (originally MALLOCH), DAVID, English poet, dramatist, and miscellaneous writer. 1705?–1765)
16, 49, 91, 601, 844, 1185, 1193, 1329, 1442, 2139, 2218.

MALLOCH, DOUGLAS, American poet and syndicate writer. (1877–1938)
413, 514, 857, 948, 966, 1145, 1592, 1832.

MALONE, EDMUND, English critic. (1741–1812)
272.

MALONE, WALTER, American judge and poet. (1866–1915)
370, 474, 1159, 1431, 1686.

MALORY, SIR THOMAS, English writer, author of the *Morte d'Arthur*. (c. 1430–c. 1471)
328, 353, 647, 680.

MANCINI, MARIA ANNA, niece of Cardinal Mazarin. (1649–1714)
1973.

MANDALE, W. R. No biographical data available.
1333.

MANDEVILLE, BERNARD, English fabulist and wit. Born in Holland. (1670?–1733)
660, 1092, 2132.

MANDEVILLE, SIR JOHN, English traveller, supposed writer of books of travel. (1300–1372)
1019.

MANGAN, JAMES, commonly called James Clarence Mangan, Irish poet. (1803–1849)
998.

MANILIUS, Latin poet in the reign of Augustus and Tiberius.
407, 593, 785, 797, 934, 1064, 1083, 1130, 1311, 1774, 2005.

MANLEY, [MRS.] MARY DE LA RIVIERE, English writer, author of the *New Atlantis*. (1663–1724)
1185, 1599, 2005.

MANN, HORACE, American philanthropist and educator. (1796–1859)
527, 530, 934, 958, 1058, 1494, 1655, 2083, 2088.

MANNERS, LORD JOHN JAMES ROBERT, seventh DUKE OF RUTLAND, English politician and poet. (1818–1906)
70.

MANNERS-SUTTON, CHARLES, English Archbishop. (1755–1828)
563.

MANNING, RICHARD IRVINE, Governor of South Carolina. (1789–1836)
64.

MANNING, WILLIAM THOMAS, American Episcopal Bishop. (1866–1949)
1688.

MANNINGHAM, JOHN, English diarist. (? –1622)
936, 2180, 2204.

MANNYNG, ROBERT (ROBERT DE BRUNNE), English poet and Gilbertine monk. (fl. 1288–1338)
167, 256, 376, 560, 699, 737, 825, 1014, 1433, 1937.

MANRIQUE, JORGE, Spanish poet. (c. 1440?–1479)
1372.

MANSFIELD, EARL OF, see MURRAY, WILLIAM

MANSFIELD, RICHARD, American actor. Born in England, came to the United States in 1874. (1857–1907)
51.

MANTUANUS (JOHANNES BAPTISTA SPANOLO), Latin writer of Mantua. (1448–1516)
1210, 1231.

MANUEL, DON JUAN, PRINCE OF CASTILE, Spanish military leader and author of political works. (1282–1349)
19.

MANWOOD, SIR ROGER, English judge. (1525–1592)
319.

MANZOLLI, PIER ANGELO (PALINGENIUS STELLATUS), Latin poet. (fl. 1540)
419, 1737.

MAPES, OR MAP, WALTER, English writer and wit. (fl. 1200)
496.

MARBURY, ELISABETH, American theatrical agent. (1856–1933)
1177.

MARCUS AURELIUS ANTONINUS, Roman Emperor and religious philosopher. (121–180)
4, 8, 13, 81, 105, 131, 143, 149, 186, 208, 225, 231, 289, 309, 352, 374, 384, 391, 405, 427, 439, 465, 541, 623, 625, 763, 798, 800, 807, 857, 971, 1096, 1120, 1123, 1131, 1238, 1250, 1309, 1311, 1323, 1328, 1383, 1414, 1424, 1425, 1427, 1435, 1488, 1612, 1645, 1647, 1678, 17C3, 1792, 1827, 1991, 2004, 2056, 2066, 2067, 2068, 2234.

MARCY, WILLIAM LEARNED, American lawyer and statesman. (1786–1857)
1555.

MARIA THERESA, Queen of Hungary. (1717–1780)
416.

Marie Antoinette, Queen of France. (1755–1793)
1571.

Marie Josephine. No biographical data available.
2238.

Marion, David Graves, American song-writer. (1861–1934)
236, 2291.

Marius, Gaius, Roman general. (155–86 B.C.)
1081, 1287, 2083.

Markham, Edwin, American poet. (1852–1940)
84, 184, 202, 273, 368, 403, 507, 640, 643, 789, 966, 1066, 1152, 1159, 1160, 1514, 1670, 1774, 1892, 1975, 2098.

Markham, Gervase, or Jervis, English scholar and agricultural writer. (1568?–1637)
705, 1428.

Markham, [Mrs.] Lucia Clark, American poet. (1870–)
688.

Marks, Edward B., American music publisher and song-writer. (1865–1945)
11, 1351, 2291.

Marlborough, Duke of, see Churchill, John

Marlowe, Christopher, English dramatist. (1564–1593)
48, 119, 139, 360, 441, 643, 700, 730, 889, 917, 1012, 1013, 1030, 1047, 1170, 1205, 1212, 1509, 1640, 1692, 1704, 1718, 1732, 1747, 1870, 1952, 1955, 2021, 2039, 2072, 2088, 2174, 2192.

Marmion, Shackerley, English dramatist. (1603–1639)
42, 221, 246, 350, 411, 632, 835, 1018, 1907, 2081, 2264.

Marmontel, Jean François, French dramatist, novelist and critic. (1723–1799)
1725.

Maro, Publius Vergilius, see Vergil

Marot, Clément, French Protestant poet. (1497–1544)
237, 318.

Marquis, Donald Robert Perry (Don Marquis), American journalist, humorist and poet. (1878–1937)
26, 74, 110, 223, 277, 282, 325, 335, 369, 435, 439, 586, 644, 666, 679, 864, 867, 1010, 1051, 1109, 1113, 1116, 1137, 1145, 1268, 1283, 1521, 1525, 1614, 1681, 1877, 2252.

Marryat, Frederick, English naval captain and novelist. (1792–1848)
119, 126, 260, 331, 973, 1281, 1292, 1645, 1691, 1793, 2083.

Marsden, William, English Orientalist and numismatist. (1754–1836)
2023.

Marshall, John, American jurist. (1755–1835)
431, 1967.

Marshall, Thomas Riley, American lawyer and Vice-President of the United States. (1854–1925)
307, 977, 1547, 2019.

Marston, John, English dramatist and divine. (1575?–1634)
286, 388, 648, 697, 1252, 2043.

Marston, Philip Bourke, English poet. (1850–1887)
1137, 1222.

* Martial, Marcus Valerius Martialis, Latin poet. (43–104)

Martin, Ada Louise, contemporary American poet.
1845.

Martin, Edward Sandford, American editor, critic and poet. (1856–1939)
270, 1257, 1572, 1928.

Martin, Everett Dean, American sociologist. (1880–1941)
152.

Martin, Sir James, English Chief-Justice of New South Wales. (1815–1886)
2228.

Martin, John No biographical data available.
1826.

Martineau, Harriet, English miscellaneous writer. (1802–1876)
416, 1887.

Martineau, James, English Unitarian divine. (1805–1900)
1726.

Marvel, Ik, see Mitchell, Donald Grant

Marvell, Andrew, the younger, English poet and satirist. (1621–1678)
8, 49, 121, 170, 246, 344, 549, 684, 723, 756, 782, 810, 828, 904, 999, 1173, 1213, 1311, 1361, 1420, 1437, 1596, 1776, 1792, 1871, 1918, 1975, 2006, 2037.

Marvin, Frederic Rowland, American clergyman and poet. (1847–1918)
563.

Marx, Karl, German founder of international socialism. (1818–1883)
973, 1229, 1689, 2298.

Mary, Queen of England. (1516–1558)
416.

Mary, Queen of Scotland. (1542–1587)
1587.

Marzials, Sir Frank Thomas, English writer of biography. (1840–1912)
376.

Marzials, Théophile Julius Henry, English poet. (1850–1920)
1777, 1914.

Masefield, John, English poet and novelist. (1878–)
50, 93, 110, 130, 136, 139, 201, 202, 246, 251, 257, 332, 381, 384, 403, 481, 496, 499, 644, 789, 798, 855, 878, 884, 932, 1116, 1122, 1138, 1145, 1156, 1173, 1183, 1188, 1224, 1280, 1294, 1311, 1336, 1389, 1469, 1487, 1582, 1587, 1620, 1708, 1745, 1775, 1814, 1833, 1894, 1918, 1953, 1968, 1981, 1983, 2009, 2056, 2079, 2102, 2103, 2117, 2153, 2167, 2188, 2192, 2201, 2260.

Mason, Agnes Carter, American verse-writer. (1835–1908)
121.

Mason, Caroline Atherton, American verse-writer. (1823–1890)
1160, 2291.

MASON, GREGORY, American journalist and anthropologist. (1889–)
67.
MASON, JOHN, English nonconformist divine and devotional writer. (1706–1763)
1607.
MASON, WALT, American humorist and rhymester. (1862–1939)
399, 526, 869, 873, 1137, 1538, 1981, 2023, 2040.
MASON, WILLIAM, English poet. (1724–1797)
634, 641, 663, 841, 1576, 1954, 1966, 2123.
MASON-MANHEIM, MADELEINE, contemporary English writer.
1351.
MASSEY, GERALD, English poet. (1828–1907)
35, 75, 121, 171, 202, 408, 552, 555, 834, 875, 886, 927, 1016, 1036, 1043, 1198, 1274, 1616, 2241.
MASSIEU, JEAN BAPTISTE, French ecclesiastic. (1742–1818)
823.
MASSILLON, JEAN BAPTISTE, French pulpit orator. (1663–1742)
1611.
* MASSINGER, PHILIP, English dramatist. (1583–1640)
MASSINGER, PHILIP, and FIELD, NATHANIEL, English dramatists and collaborators. (1583–1640), (1587–1633)
976, 1486.
MASSON, THOMAS L., American journalist and humorist. (1866–1934)
228, 975.
MASTERS, EDGAR LEE, American poet and novelist. (1869–1949)
512, 1136, 1160, 1825, 1893.
MATHER, COTTON, New England Congregational clergyman and religious writer. (1663–1728)
670, 1677, 1963.
MATTHEWS, JAMES BRANDER, American essayist and critic. (1852–1929)
528, 996, 1362, 1412, 1506.
MATURIN, CHARLES ROBERT, English novelist and dramatist. (1782–1824)
458, 1207, 2144.
MAUGHAM, WILLIAM SOMERSET, English novelist. (1874–)
129, 356, 758, 1304, 1687, 1888, 2259.
MAULE, SIR WILLIAM HENRY, English judge. (1788–1858)
206.
MAUPASSANT, GUY DE, French novelist. (1850–1893)
141, 876, 977, 1046, 1102, 1270, 1277, 1463, 2180, 2234.
MAUPERTUIS, PIERRE LOUIS MOREAU DE, French mathematician. (1698–1759)
1926.
MAURICE, FREDERICK DENISON, English divine and educator. (1805–1872)
187.
MAUROIS, ANDRÉ (ÉMILE HERZOG), French novelist, biographer and essayist. (1885–)
969.
MAURUS TERENTIANUS, Latin poet, native of Carthage. (fl. A.D. 180)
182.
MAXIMILIAN, FERDINAND JOSEPH, Archduke of Austria, Emperor of Mexico. (1832–1867)
416.
MAY, JULIA HARRIS, American verse-writer. (1833–1912)
403.
MAY, THOMAS, English poet and historian. (1595–1650)
3, 1080.
MAYHEW, HENRY, English miscellaneous writer. (1812–1887)
679, 1266.
MAYNARD, THEODORE, English poet and educator, resident of U. S. since 1920. (1890–)
1880, 2157.
MAYNE, JASPER, English Archdeacon and dramatist. (1604–1672)
1003, 2005.
MAZARIN, JULES (GIULIO MAZARINI), French statesman and Cardinal, Sicilian by birth. (1602–1661)
719, 2003.
MAZZINI, GIUSEPPE, Italian patriot. (1805?–1872)
507, 707, 783, 1114, 1379.
MEDLEY, SAMUEL, English Baptist minister and hymn-writer. (1738–1799)
790.
MEDWALL, HENRY, English writer of interludes. (fl. 1486)
2171, 2246.
MEE, WILLIAM, English poet and journalist. (1788–1862)
139.
MEEN, GEORGE, American song-writer.
2291.
MEIGS, CHARLES DELUCENA, American physician and medical writer. (fl. 1792)
158, 1588.
MEILHAC, HENRY, and HALÉVY, LUDOVIC, French composers and dramatists. (1831–1897), (1834–1908)
945, 1398.
MELANCHTHON (pseud. of PHILIP SCHWARZERD), German humanist and professor of Greek. (1497–1560)
242.
MELBANCKE, BRIAN, English euphuistic writer. (fl. 1583)
103, 160, 898, 922, 1047, 1811, 2188.
MELBOURNE, LORD, see LAMB, WILLIAM
MELCHIOR, see POLIGNAC, MELCHIOR DE
MELDENIUS, RUPERTUS, German (possibly pseudonymous) author of treatise appearing in Germany c. 1630 without place of publication or date.
242.
MELEAGER, Greek poet and epigrammatist. (fl. c. 80 B.C.)
350, 512.
MELLEN, GRENVILLE, American lawyer and verse-writer. (1799–1841)
2117.

MELTON, SIR JOHN, English politician and political writer. (? –1640)
468, 1318, 1821, 1947.

MELVILLE, HERMAN, American novelist. (1819–1891)
322, 1126, 1907.

MELVILLE, SIR JAMES, English autobiographer. (1535–1617)
283.

MELVILLE, WALTER, American song-writer.
2033.

MEMMIUS, GAIUS, Roman jurist. (fl. 110 B.C.)
1084, 1839.

MÉNAGE, GILLES DE, French philologist. (1613–1692)
376.

MENANDER, Greek dramatic poet. (342–291 B.C.)
17, 28, 35, 112, 156, 176, 215, 218, 228, 254, 256, 288, 289, 291, 299, 315, 325, 376, 409, 457, 477, 479, 632, 646, 651, 695, 702, 728, 734, 800, 807, 840, 847, 848, 871, 896, 947, 980, 994, 1076, 1080, 1088, 1118, 1185, 1197, 1258, 1262, 1264, 1268, 1274, 1306, 1348, 1352, 1396, 1400, 1408, 1481, 1568, 1570, 1588, 1678, 1718, 1720, 1726, 1790, 1822, 1827, 1839, 1843, 1977, 2045, 2057, 2064, 2148, 2164, 2188, 2193, 2217, 2220, 2226.

MENCIUS, Chinese philosopher. (370?–290? B.C.)
423, 831, 1080, 1492, 1611, 1832.

MENCKEN, HENRY LOUIS, American journalist and satirist. (1880–1956)
27, 79, 107, 132, 343, 348, 433, 478, 507, 565, 578, 616, 640, 656, 662, 798, 938, 951, 968, 992, 1032, 1145, 1174, 1276, 1345, 1380, 1422, 1479, 1500, 1516, 1529, 1534, 1542, 1545, 1556, 1570, 1597, 1598, 1623, 1682, 1698, 1715, 1720, 1911, 1925, 1971, 2055, 2111, 2208, 2230, 2231, 2250, 2258.

MENENNIUS AGRIPPA (LANATUS), Roman patrician and senator. (fl. 493 B.C.)
155.

MENKEN, ADAH ISAACS, American actress and poet. (1835?–1868)
257.

MERCHEL, WILHELM VON, German writer. (1803–1861)
431.

MERCIER, LOUIS SÉBASTIEN, eccentric French dramatist and miscellaneous writer. (1740–1814)
597.

MERCURIUS AULICUS. No biographical data available. (fl. 1648)
1635.

MEREDITH, GEORGE, English novelist and poet. (1828–1909)
31, 167, 200, 217, 231, 280, 329, 333, 356, 437. 449, 512, 559, 578, 609, 619, 633, 648, 661, 708, 823, 978, 998, 1003, 1013, 1047, 1072, 1128, 1143, 1145, 1209, 1213, 1224, 1248, 1254, 1274, 1276, 1307, 1317, 1358, 1396, 1421, 1423, 1427, 1496, 1510, 1517, 1536, 1541, 1586, 1594, 1629, 1652, 1656, 1659, 1671, 1678, 1712, 1731, 1736, 1763, 1796, 1821, 1826, 1829, 1855, 1872, 1880, 1889, 1891, 1915, 1917, 1990, 1999, 2050, 2056, 2079, 2153, 2157, 2165, 2178, 2193, 2195, 2201, 2203, 2207, 2209, 2249.

MEREDITH, OWEN (pseud. of EDWARD ROBERT BULWER-LYTTON, first EARL OF LYTTON), English statesman and poet. (1831–1891)
43, 105, 225, 226, 231, 238, 245, 315, 361, 427, 439, 449, 507, 512, 602, 710, 762, 782, 831, 833, 851, 937, 981, 1005, 1006, 1126, 1141, 1142, 1146, 1193, 1205, 1213, 1289, 1371, 1399, 1402, 1444, 1446, 1659, 1677, 1704, 1707, 1788, 1801, 1803, 1823, 1915, 1930, 1975, 1989, 2006, 2009, 2046, 2055, 2109, 2236.

MEREDITH, WILLIAM TUCKER, American journalist. (1839– ?)
2000.

MERES, FRANCIS, English divine and writer. (1565–1647)
1487.

MERITON, or MERRITON, GEORGE, English poet and legal writer. (1634–1711)
152, 458, 621, 737, 928, 1047.

MERMET, CLAUDE, French poet. (c. 1550–1605)
729

MERRICK, JAMES, English poet and scholar. (1720–1769)
100, 1423, 1588, 1964.

MERRIMAN, HENRY SETON (pseud. of HUGH STOWELL SCOTT), English novelist. (1862–1903)
531, 721, 1731, 2193.

MERRYMAN, MILDRED PLEW [MRS. CARL M. MERRYMAN], contemporary American poet.
251.

MESSINGER, ROBERT HINCKLEY, American poet. (1811–1874)
42.

METASTASIO (pseud. of PIETRO BONAVENTURA TRAPASSI), Italian poet. (1698–1782)
143, 297, 305, 459, 622, 1118, 1152, 1660, 2273.

METELLUS, QUINTUS CÆCILIUS (MACEDONIUS), Roman general. (d. 115 B.C.)
1293.

METRODORUS, Greek philosopher. (fl. 168 B.C.)
1446, 1561.

METTERNICH, KLEMENS WENZEL NEPOMUK LOTHAR, PRINCE, Austrian diplomat and statesman. (1773–1859)
1001, 2023.

MEURIER, MEURIR, or MURIER, GABRIEL, Flemish philologist. (? –1587?)
590.

MEYER, BARON DE, French style expert.
491.

MEYNELL, [MRS.] ALICE CHRISTIANA [THOMPSON], English poet and essayist. (1850–1922)
31, 263, 269, 998, 1076, 1213, 1475, 1774, 1845, 1907, 1990, 1999, 2185.

MEYNELL, FRANCIS, English poet. (1880–1941)
889.

MICHAELIS, ALINE, American journalist and verse-writer. (1885–)
1161.

MICHELANGELO (MICHELANGELO BUONARROTI), Italian sculptor, painter and poet. (1475–1564)
129, 391, 1190, 1311, 1485, 1771, 1786.

MICKLE, WILLIAM JULIUS, Scottish poet. (1735–1788)
4, 131, 1213, 1341.

MIDDLETON, CHRISTOPHER, English translator and poet. (1560?–1628)
1668.

MIDDLETON, SCUDDER, American poet. (1888–)
640, 702, 1462, 2232.

MIDDLETON, THOMAS, English dramatist. (1570?–1627)
5, 6, 28, 36, 225, 248, 370, 411, 439, 443, 479, 542, 595, 679, 837, 850, 914, 988, 1004, 1026, 1027, 1028, 1062, 1080, 1135, 1169, 1173, 1174, 1176, 1195, 1324, 1341, 1347, 1633, 1638, 1651, 1671, 1722, 1922, 1952, 2027, 2029, 2039, 2042, 2050, 2069, 2098, 2136, 2138, 2183, 2203, 2222, 2228, 2240.

MIDDLETON, THOMAS, and DEKKER, THOMAS, English dramatists and collaborators. (1570?–1627), (1570?–1641?)
136 1196, 1828.

MIDDLETON, THOMAS, and MASSINGER, PHILIP, English dramatists and collaborators. (1570?–1627), (1583–1640)
1082, 1099, 1324, 1722, 1785, 2057.

MIDDLETON, THOMAS, and ROWLEY, WILLIAM, English dramatists and collaborators. (1570?–1627), (1585?–1642?)
597, 660, 1182, 1412.

MIFFLIN, LLOYD, American poet. (1846–1921)
1421, 1520.

MILES, JOSEPHINE, American verse-writer.
769.

MILES, WILLIAM PORCHER, American legislator. (1822–1899)
2278.

MILHAUD, JEAN BAPTISTE, French revolutionary general. (1766–1833)
376.

MILL, JOHN STUART, English philosopher. (1806–1873)
68, 356, 464, 565, 575, 637, 722, 758, 978, 979, 1066, 1103, 1229, 1419, 1427, 1428, 1429, 1441, 1544, 1918.

MILLAY, EDNA ST. VINCENT [MRS. EUGEN BOISSEVAIN], American poet. (1892–1950)
130, 176, 216, 242, 374, 399, 481, 635, 796, 827, 991, 1136, 1174, 1201, 1624, 1907, 1987, 2103, 2136, 2241, 2267.

MILLER, ALICE DUER [MRS. HENRY WISE MILLER], American writer. (1874–1942)
102, 1257.

MILLER, E. E. No biographical data available.
1067.

MILLER, EMILY HUNTINGTON, American poet. (1833–1913)
2262.

MILLER, HARRY S., American song-writer.
2291.

MILLER, J. CORSON, American poet. (1883–)
1141.

MILLER, JOAQUIN (pseud. of CINCINNATUS HINER MILLER), American poet. (1841–1913)
26, 284, 293, 365, 374, 391, 612, 623, 697, 773, 803, 883, 899, 1023, 1049, 1111, 1115, 1153, 1198, 1343, 1352, 1390, 1442, 1453, 1488, 1719, 1823, 1832, 1834, 1890, 1940, 2014, 2052, 2084, 2103, 2201.

MILLER, MARION MILLS, American educator and publicist. (1864–)
985.

MILLET, JEAN FRANÇOIS, French painter. (1814–1875)
101.

MILLIKEN, RICHARD ALFRED, Irish poet. (1767–1815)
997.

MILLS, JOHN, English banker. (fl. 1878)
391.

MILLS, OGDEN LIVINGSTON, American politician, former Secretary of the Treasury. (1884–1937)
2103.

MILMAN, HENRY HART, English divine and historian. (1791–1868)
828, 1025, 1770, 1771, 2176.

MILNES, RICHARD MONCKTON, first BARON HOUGHTON, English statesman and poet. (1809–1885)
200, 266, 463, 876, 885, 887, 898, 1034, 1218, 1325, 1501, 1583, 1685, 1716, 1885, 1989, 2003, 2194.

* MILTON, JOHN, English epic poet. (1608–1674)

MIMNERMUS, Greek elegiac poet. (fl. 630–600 B.C.)
29, 565.

MINCHIN, JAMES GEORGE COTTON, contemporary English writer.
1542.

MINER, CHARLES, American journalist and essayist. (1780–1865)
207.

MING-HSIN PAO-CHIEN, or MING-LUM PAOU-KEËN in the Cantonese transcription, is sometimes given as a person's name, but is really the title of a small collection of moral citations, of which neither author nor date is known. The title may be translated as *Precious Mirror to Enlighten the Heart*, and the collection plays the rôle in the East that the *Imitation of Christ* does in the West. It was translated into Spanish as early as 1592. The quotations given here are from the translation made by the Rev. William Milne, and published in the *Indo-Chinese Gleaner* for August, 1818.
311, 958.

MINSHULL, or MYNSHUL, GEFFRAY, English miscellaneous writer. (1594?–1668)
1003.

MIRABEAU, VICTOR DE RIQUETTI, MARQUIS DE (L'AMI DES HOMMES), French eccentric and economic writer. (1715–1789)
416, 631, 722, 971.

MIRBEAU, OCTAVE HENRI MARIE, French dramatist. (1850–1917)
207.

MIRÆUS, AUBROTUS (AUBERT LEMIRE), Flemish compiler. (1573–1640)
832.

MISSON, FRANÇOIS MAXIMILIEN, French descriptive writer. (1650?–1722)
2017.

MITCHEL, JONATHAN, New England divine. (1624?–1668)
838.

MITCHELL, DONALD GRANT (IK MARVEL), American essayist. (1822–1908)
318, 459, 1720.

MITCHELL, J. F., American song-writer.
2202, 2291.

MITCHELL, MARIA, American astronomer and educator. (1818–1889)
1390.

MITCHELL, SILAS WEIR, American physician, poet and novelist. (1829–1914)
665, 1932.

MIZNER, ADDISON, American miscellaneous writer. (1872–1933)
632.

MODESTUS, Roman general. (fl. 250 B.C.)
1052.

MOFFETT, MOUFET, or MUFFET, THOMAS, English physician and scientific writer. (1553–1604)
198, 345, 450, 458, 518, 834.

MOHAMMED, see MAHOMET

MOIR, DAVID MACBETH, English physician and miscellaneous writer, known as DELTA (Δ). (1798–1851)
167, 408, 685, 689, 1156, 1746, 1912, 1950.

MOLESCHOTT, JACOB, Dutch physiologist. (1822–1893)
1989.

MOLIÈRE (pseud. of JEAN BAPTISTE POQUELIN), French dramatist. (1622–1673)
98, 119, 137, 147, 172, 210, 224, 226, 231, 253, 294, 310, 352, 381, 420, 434, 446, 449, 517, 564, 576, 596, 601, 697, 742, 764, 802, 820, 852, 863, 947, 1056, 1069, 1070, 1078, 1167, 1178, 1181, 1183, 1188, 1197, 1199, 1269, 1270, 1286, 1324, 1349, 1453, 1469, 1494, 1506, 1526, 1630, 1648, 1650, 1678, 1829, 1897, 1899, 1902, 1927, 1963, 2081, 2089, 2093, 2126, 2169, 2171, 2175, 2208, 2246.

MOLLER, GEORG, German architect and writer on architectural subjects. (1784–1852)
95.

MOLTKE, HELMUTH KARL BERNARD, COUNT VON, German Field-Marshal. (1800–1891)
1970.

MONKHOUSE, WILLIAM COSMO, English poet and critic. (1840–1901)
121, 188, 257, 1743, 1782.

MONNOYE, or MONNOIE, BERNARD DE LA, French poet and critic. (1641–1728)
1095.

MONRO, HAROLD, English poet. (1879–1932)
1405.

MONROE, H. R., American song-writer.
1557.

MONROE, JAMES, fifth President of the United States. (1758–1831)
59.

MONSELL, JOHN SAMUEL BEWLEY, English writer of hymns and religious verse. (1811–1875)
1593.

MONTAGU, MRS. ELIZABETH, English essayist and letter-writer. Epithet "blue-stocking" first applied to her. (1720–1800)
1563.

MONTAGU, LADY MARY WORTLEY, English letter-writer and poet. (1689–1762)
328, 356, 450, 476, 536, 629, 640, 702, 951, 1016, 1141, 1350, 1442, 1692, 1758, 1802, 2202, 2205, 2217.

MONTAGUE, BASIL, English legal and miscellaneous writer. (1770–1851)
1542.

MONTAGUE, CHARLES EDWARD, Irish journalist. (1867–1928)
2109.

* MONTAIGNE, MICHEL EYQUEM DE, French philosopher and essayist. (1533–1592)

MONTANDRÉ, see DUBOSCQ-MONTANDRÉ

MONTANUS, Phrygian originator of schismatic movement in Christian church. (fl. 130)
1696.

MONTENAEKEN, LÉON LOUIS MOREAU CONSTANT CORNEILLE VAN, Belgian poet. (1859– ?)
1137.

MONTESQUIEU, CHARLES LOUIS DE SECONDAT DE, French writer and philosopher. (1689–1755)
15, 433, 702, 723, 814, 816, 902, 1088, 1438, 1481, 1484, 1675, 1858, 1918, 1930, 2061, 2171.

MONTGOMERIE, ALEXANDER, Scottish poet. (1540–1607)
1486, 2009.

MONTGOMERY, JAMES, English poet. (1771–1854)
141, 167, 284, 291, 301, 358, 388, 403, 445, 476, 578, 622, 689, 691, 722, 740, 750, 781, 782, 794, 809, 827, 843, 884, 887, 905, 922, 924, 937, 945, 966, 1017, 1018, 1057, 1061, 1073, 1104, 1133, 1148, 1311, 1390, 1402, 1417, 1451, 1465, 1510, 1560, 1582, 1583, 1689, 1707, 1743, 1772, 1862, 1894, 1944, 2002, 2013, 2086, 2248.

MONTGOMERY, LUCY MAUD, contemporary Canadian novelist.
582, 1521, 2253.

MONTGOMERY, ROBERT, English divine and poetaster. (1807–1855)
395, 512, 1227, 1391, 1731, 1773, 1912.

MONTGOMERY, ROSELLE MERCIER (MRS. JOHN S. MONTGOMERY), American poet. (1874–1933)
398, 644, 1199, 1207, 2190.

MONTLUC, ADRIAN DE, French writer. (fl. c. 1735)
243.

MONTOLIEU, JEANNE ISABELLE DE BOTTENS, BARONNE DE, Swiss novelist. (1751–1832)
2098.

MONTROSE, MARQUIS OF, see GRAHAM, JAMES

MONTROSS, PERCY, American song-writer.
2291.

MONVEL, JACQUES MARIE BOUTET, French actor and dramatist. (1745–1812)
2094.

MOODY, DWIGHT LYMAN, American evangelist. (1837–1899)
234.

MOODY, WILLIAM VAUGHN, American poet and dramatist. (1869–1910)
781, 799, 826, 885, 1384, 1457, 1542, 2011, 2247.

MOOR, MICHAEL, Irish educator; provost of Trinity College, Dublin. (1640–1726)
2239.

MOORE, CHARLES LEONARD, American lawyer and verse-writer. (1854–1940)
1907.

MOORE, CLEMENT CLARKE, American professor, poet and lexicographer. (1779–1863)
155, 270.

MOORE, EDWARD, English fabulist and dramatist. (1712–1757)
136, 291, 705, 753, 754, 993, 1008, 1063, 1183, 1234, 1524, 1565, 1574, 1718, 2201, 2265.

MOORE, FRANCIS, English astrologer and almanac-maker. (1657–1715?)
2113.

MOORE, GEORGE, British novelist and essayist. (1853–1933)
10, 103, 181, 182, 260, 341, 435, 632, 720, 787, 896, 996, 1129, 1148, 1174, 1240, 1278, 1334, 1513, 1599, 1685, 1701, 1989, 2040, 2074, 2185, 2260.

MOORE, MARIANNE CRAIG, American poet. (1887–)
1518.

* MOORE, THOMAS, Irish poet. (1779–1852)

MOORE, VIRGINIA, American poet. (1903–)
1948.

MORDAUNT, MAJOR THOMAS OSBERT, British officer. (1729–1809)
781.

MORE, EDWARD, English poet. (1537?–1620)
2183.

MORE, HANNAH, English religious writer. (1745–1833)
238, 345, 493, 533, 620, 656, 678, 824, 846, 909, 956, 962, 1007, 1029, 1088, 1141, 1228, 1238, 1506, 1512, 1586, 1820, 1880, 2042, 2194.

MORE, HENRY, English theologian. (1614–1687)
1152, 1309, 1795.

MORE, MARGARET, daughter of Sir Thomas More, English diarist. (fl. 1524)
921.

MORE, SIR THOMAS, English wit, philosopher and statesman. (1478–1535)
40, 98, 219, 345, 416, 469, 569, 584, 668, 885, 929, 987, 1075, 1093, 1155, 1333, 1394, 1452, 1518, 1634, 1635, 1960.

MOREHOUSE, FREDERICK COOK, American editor. (1868–1932)
432.

MORELAND, JOHN RICHARD, American poet. (1880–1947)
263, 264, 388, 827, 883, 1051, 1534, 1975.

MORELL, THOMAS, English classical scholar. (1703–1784)
896.

MORESCO. No biographical data available.
129.

MORGAN, ANGELA, contemporary American poet.
130, 225, 270, 325, 1162, 1889.

MORGAN, JOHN PIERPONT, American financier and art collector. (1837–1913)
66, 532, 2048.

MORGAN, JUNIUS SPENCER, American financier. (1813–1890)
66.

MORGAN, SYDNEY, LADY MORGAN, Irish novelist. (1783–1859)
1414, 2100.

MORLEY, CHRISTOPHER DARLINGTON, American editor, poet and essayist. (1890–1957)
100, 251, 275, 470, 499, 512, 518, 535, 566, 759, 906, 951, 1015, 1122, 1160, 1239, 1243, 1317, 1370, 1498, 1516, 1529, 1594, 1618, 1689, 1759, 1828, 1845, 1883, 1928, 1984, 2004, 2041, 2049, 2059, 2132, 2222, 2226.

MORLEY, JOHN, first VISCOUNT MORLEY OF BLACKBURN, English statesman, critic and man of letters. (1838–1923)
98, 205, 235, 538, 566, 586, 720, 807, 891, 1102, 1119, 1165, 1238, 1381, 1541, 1621, 1691, 1826, 1861, 2207, 2230.

MORRIS, CHARLES, English song-writer. (1745–1838)
195, 276, 1168.

MORRIS, GEORGE POPE, American poet and journalist. (1802–1864)
57, 158, 905, 1397, 2036, 2067, 2182.

MORRIS, SIR LEWIS, Welsh poet. (1833–1907)
8, 368, 618, 860, 1061, 1208, 1726, 1727, 1907, 1932, 2238.

MORRIS, WILLIAM, English poet, artist and socialist. (1834–1896)
119, 202, 226, 231, 365, 366, 372, 384, 411, 413, 507, 512, 540, 602, 660, 665, 708, 752, 843, 908, 924, 991, 1018, 1065, 1119, 1131, 1139, 1196, 1213, 1229, 1261, 1294, 1375, 1386, 1451, 1520, 1534, 1572, 1605, 1609, 1635, 1657, 1684, 1754, 1771, 1772, 1827, 1959, 1961, 1975, 1999, 2043, 2045, 2047, 2161.

MORRISON, ROBERT F. No biographical data available.
202.

MORROW, DWIGHT WHITNEY, American banker and diplomatist. (1873–1931)
1544.

MORSE, E. MALCOLM, American physician.
1354.

MORSE, SAMUEL FINLEY BREESE, American artist and inventor of the electric telegraph. (1791–1872)
535.

MORTIMER. THOMAS, English economic writer. (1730–1810)
1696.

MORTON, DAVID, American poet. (1886–1957)
130, 2038, 2184.

MORTON, OLIVER PERRY, American lawyer, Governor of Indiana 1861-1867. (1823-1877)
1823.
MORTON, THOMAS, English dramatist. (1764?-1838)
870, 980, 1579, 1861.
MOSES, GEORGE HIGGINS, American politician. (1869-1944)
2278.
MOSLEY, SIR OSWALD ERNALD, English labor leader. (1896-)
769.
MOSS, THOMAS, English poet. (? -1808)
145, 1799.
MOTHERWELL, WILLIAM, English poet. (1797-1835)
770, 1051, 1201, 1206, 1295, 1384, 1999, 2153.
MOTLEY, JOHN LOTHROP, American historian. (1814-1877)
1228.
MOTT, LUCRETIA COFFIN, American Quaker preacher and reformer. (1793-1880)
2051.
MOULTON, LOUISE CHANDLER, American poet. (1835-1908)
94, 392, 1148, 1401, 1752.
MOULTRIE, JOHN, English poet. (1799-1874)
708.
MUGFORD, CAPTAIN JAMES, American naval commander. (d. 1776)
62.
MUHLENBERG, WILLIAM AUGUSTUS, American Episcopal clergyman, poet and devotional writer. (1796-1877)
1140.
MUIR, JOHN, American scientist and explorer. (1838-1914)
2037, 2211.
MUIS, BISHOP CORNELIS, Dutch priest and poet. (1503-1572)
346, 1872.
MÜLLER, KARL OTFRIED, German educator and historian. (1797-1840)
1507.
MÜLLER, NIKLAS, German printer and poet. (1809-1875)
685.
MULLIGAN, JAMES H., American jurist. (1844-1916)
1034.
MULLINS, EDGAR YOUNG, American clergyman and educator. (1860-1928)
964.
MULOCK, DINAH MARIA, see CRAIK
MUMFORD, LEWIS, American miscellaneous writer. (1895-)
646.
MUNBY, ARTHUR JOSEPH, English poet and civil servant. (1828-1910)
2213.
MÜNCH-BELLINGHAUSEN, ELIZIUS FRANZ JOSEPH VON, Austrian poet and dramatist. (1806-1871)
1181.
MUNDAY, ANTHONY, English poet and playwright. (1553-1633)
424, 954.
MUNRO, H. H. (SAKI), English miscellaneous writer. (1870-1916)
1637, 2204.
MÜNSTER, ERNST FRIEDRICH HERBERT, COUNT VON, Hanoverian politician. (1766-1839)
1359.
MUNTHE, AXEL, Swedish physician, psychiatrist, and writer. (1857-1949)
585, 1401, 1800.
MURAT, JOACHIM, French Marshal, King of Naples. (1771-1815)
416.
MURPHY, ARTHUR, English actor and playwright. (1727-1805)
250, 559, 936, 1889, 2151, 2171, 2220.
MURPHY, JOSEPH JOHN, Irish poet. (1827-1894)
439, 579.
MURPHY, PATRICK FRANCIS, American orator and humorist. (1860-1931)
1965.
MURPHY, ROBERT XAVIER, Irish editor and Orientalist. (1803-1857)
1340.
MURPHY, STANLEY, American song-writer.
2291.
MURRAY, ADA FOSTER, see ALDEN, ADA
MURRAY, ROBERT FULLER, American-born verse-writer, living in England. (1863-1894)
342.
MURRAY, WILLIAM, first EARL OF MANSFIELD, English judge. (1705-1793)
681, 723, 1020, 1030, 1841.
MUSONIUS, RUFUS, Stoic philosopher. (fl. A.D. 70)
1312.
MUSSET, LOUIS CHARLES ALFRED DE, French poet, novelist and dramatist. (1810-1857)
423, 1182, 1199, 1295, 1326.
MUSSOLINI, BENITO, Italian Dictator. (1883-1945)
1918.
MYERS, FREDERIC WILLIAM HENRY, English poet and essayist. (1843-1901)
121, 368, 1349, 1775, 1777.
MYSON, Greek philosopher. (c. 600 B.C.)
98.

N

NADAUD, GUSTAVE, French poet and musician. (1820-1893)
109.
NÆVIUS, GNÆUS, Latin playwright. (c. 265-204 B.C.)
1579.
NAIDU, [MADAME] SAROJINI, Hindu poet. (1878-1949)
1906.
NAIRNE, CAROLINA, BARONESS NAIRNE, Scottish ballad-writer. (1766-1845)
29, 68, 636, 669, 884, 1843.
NANCY, LORD. No biographical data available.
1056.

NAPIER, SIR CHARLES JAMES, English general. (1782–1853)
298, 1377.
NAPIER, SIR WILLIAM FRANCIS PATRICK, English general and historian. (1785–1860)
557.
NAPOLEON I, NAPOLEON BONAPARTE, Emperor of the French. (1769–1821)
43, 45, 73, 114, 215, 266, 337, 452, 530, 535, 542, 544, 588, 594, 625, 663, 726, 866, 902, 947, 962, 971, 973, 1002, 1037, 1117, 1186, 1280, 1285, 1350, 1378, 1391, 1398, 1413, 1430, 1453, 1466, 1505, 1582, 1601, 1689, 1700, 1714, 1725, 1760, 1793, 1863, 1867, 1869, 1918, 1946, 1955, 1962, 1999, 2040, 2051, 2106, 2115, 2117, 2180, 2198.
NAPOLEON III, (CHARLES) LOUIS NAPOLEON BONAPARTE, King of France. (1808–1873)
719, 1863.
NASH, OGDEN, American humorist. (1902–)
280, 497, 524, 904, 1217, 1410, 1954, 2072.
NASHE, or NASH, THOMAS, English satirist. (1567–1601)
13, 136, 273, 286, 329, 350, 539, 1062, 1091, 1155, 1305, 1371, 1640, 1642, 1722, 1907, 2028, 2179, 2222, 2238.
NASO, PUBLIUS OVIDIUS, see OVID
NATHAN, GEORGE JEAN, American essayist and critic. (1882–1958)
102, 107, 112, 135, 150, 338, 761, 855, 1174, 1257, 1463, 1474, 1479, 1794, 1875, 1909, 2251.
NATHAN, ROBERT, American poet and novelist. (1894–)
121, 129, 842, 1077.
NAYLOR, JAMES BALL, American physician and novelist. (1860–1945)
1038.
NEALE, JOHN MASON, English divine and hymn-writer. (1818–1866)
515.
NEAVES, LORD CHARLES, English jurist. (1800–1876)
586, 1082, 1767, 2125, 2194.
NECKER, MADAME (SUSANNE CURCHOD), Swiss leader in literary circles. (1739–1794)
464.
NEELE, HENRY, English poet and miscellaneous writer. (1798–1828)
1146.
NEIHARDT, JOHN GNEISENAU, American poet. (1881–)
320, 332, 397, 425, 1162, 1245, 1452.
NELSON, ED. G., American song-writer.
1636.
NELSON, HORATIO, VISCOUNT NELSON, English admiral. (1758–1805)
506, 545, 2083.
NEPOS, CORNELIUS, Latin historian. (fl. 75 B.C.)
397, 533, 584, 716, 814, 1111, 1258, 1599.
NERO, CLAUDIUS CÆSAR DRUSUS GERMANICUS, Roman Emperor. (37–68)
416, 521, 1962, 2259.
NESBIT, EDITH [MRS. HUBERT BLAND], English poet and novelist. (1858–1924)
2038.
NESBIT, WILBUR D., American verse-writer. (1871–1927)
674, 1065, 1297.
NETHERSOLE, SIR FRANCIS, English scholar and political writer. (1587–1659)
1458, 1477.
NEUMANN, HERMANN KUNIBERT, German romantic poet. (1808–1875)
875.
NEVINS, ALLAN, American educator and biographer. (1890–)
280.
NEWBOLT, SIR HENRY JOHN, English poet. (1862–1938)
202, 225, 328, 556, 557, 673, 754, 998, 1038, 1375, 1396, 1422, 1474, 1767, 1779, 2116, 2232.
NEWCASTLE, DUCHESS OF, see CAVENDISH, MARGARET
NEWCOMB, EZRA BUTLER, American clergyman. (1852– d.)
977.
NEWELL, PETER SHEAF HERSEY, American humorist and illustrator. (1862–1924)
682, 683, 1370.
NEWELL, ROBERT HENRY, American journalist, poet and humorist. (1836–1901)
649.
NEWLAND, ABRAHAM, English banker. (1730–1807)
573.
NEWMAN, JOHN HENRY, CARDINAL, religious leader in Church of England; later Roman Catholic prelate and writer. (1801–1890)
181, 231, 281, 403, 469, 763, 811, 884, 972, 1152, 1239, 1293, 1609, 1797, 1993, 1995, 2003.
NEWTON, BYRON R., American newspaperman and publicist. (1861–1938)
2277.
NEWTON, SIR ISAAC, English philosopher and mathematician. (1642–1727)
1399, 1995, 2244.
NEWTON, JOHN, English divine and hymn-writer. (1725–1807)
413, 1753.
NEWTON, JOSEPH FORT, American clergyman. (1878–1949)
797.
NEY, MICHEL, French Marshal under Napoleon. (1769–1815)
413, 1377.
NICÆNETUS, Greek epigrammatic poet. (c. 250 B.C.)
2157.
NICANDER, Greek physician, grammarian and poet. (fl. c. 150 B.C.)
177.
NICARCHUS, Greek epigrammatic poet.
373, 1047, 2137.
NICEPHORUS, Emperor of Constantinople. (d. 811)
720.
NICHOLAS I, Emperor of Russia. (1796–1855)
2061.

NICHOLS, DUDLEY, contemporary English writer.
655.

NICHOLS, J. B. B., contemporary English writer.
1503.

NICHOLS, ROBERT, English poet. (1893–1944)
1869.

NICOLL, ROBERT, Scottish poet. (1814–1837)
131.

NICOLSON, ADELA FLORENCE, see HOPE, LAURENCE

NICOLSON, JOHN URBAN, American poet. (1885–1944)
4, 384.

NIETZSCHE, FRIEDRICH WILHELM, German philosopher. (1844–1900)
242, 246, 286, 831, 1239, 1240, 1293, 1393, 1539, 1547, 1597, 1807, 1845, 2054, 2111, 2112, 2119.

NISBET, J. F. No biographical data available.
759.

NOBLES, MILTON, American actor and playwright. (1848–1924)
2085.

NOCK, ALBERT JAY, American writer and educator. (1873–1945)
67.

NODIER, CHARLES, French philologist, novelist and poet. (1780–1844)
189.

NOEL, RODEN BERKELEY WRIOTHESLEY, English poet. (1834–1894)
264, 1780.

NOEL, THOMAS, English poet. (1799–1861)
747, 1212, 2161.

NOLAN, MICHAEL, Irish song-writer.
2291.

NONNUS, Greek epic poet. (fl. A.D. 380)
2207.

NORRIS, FRANK, American novelist. (1870–1902)
2048.

NORRIS, JOHN, English divine and religious writer. (1657–1711)
76, 306, 453, 784, 1018, 1676.

NORRIS, WILLIAM EDWARD, English novelist. (1847–1925)
1900.

NORTH, CHRISTOPHER (pseud.), see WILSON, JOHN

NORTH, DUDLEY, fourth BARON NORTH, English economic writer. (1602–1677)
936.

NORTH, GEORGE L., contemporary American writer.
1223.

NORTH, ROGER, English lawyer and historian. (1653–1734)
824, 1260, 1951, 2132, 2177.

NORTH, SIR THOMAS, English translator. (1535?–1601?)
702, 1677.

NORTHBROOKE, JOHN, English preacher and writer against the theatre. (fl. 1568–1579)
764, 1249, 1721, 1948.

NORTHCOTE, JAMES, English painter and miscellaneous writer. (1746–1831)
1095.

NORTON, CAROLINE ELIZABETH SARAH, English poet. (1808–1877)
403, 738, 1178, 1195, 1357, 1510, 1801, 1869, 2097.

NORTON, DELLE W., American poet. (1840–?)
1735.

NORTON, GEORGE A., American song-writer.
2291.

NORTON, GRACE FALLOW, American poet. (1876–)
1845.

NORWORTH, JACK, American actor and song-writer. (1879–)
1455, 2291.

NOTCH, FRANK K., contemporary American miscellaneous writer.
43, 1145, 1484.

NOUE, ODET DE LA, French officer and poet. (d. 1618)
249.

NOVALIS (pseud. of FRIEDRICH LEOPOLD VON HARDENBERG), German poet and novelist. (1772–1801)
158, 478, 559, 979, 1429, 1531.

NOVELLO, IVOR (1894–1951), and FORD, LENA GUILBERT, English actor and American poet.
282, 1881.

NOYES, ALFRED, English poet. (1880–1958)
362, 463, 481, 673, 794, 1155, 1191, 1212, 1343, 1370, 1734, 1736, 2062, 2113, 2153, 2235.

NOYES, EDWARD FOLLANSBEE, American general and Governor of Ohio. (1832–1890)
2119.

NUGENT, ROBERT, EARL NUGENT (assumed surname CRAGGS), English politician and poet. (1702–1788)
576, 1200, 1236, 1513, 1739.

NYE, EDGAR WILSON (BILL NYE), American journalist, humorous writer and lecturer. (1850–1896)
1362, 2160.

O

O. HENRY (pseud. of WILLIAM SYDNEY PORTER), American short-story writer. (1862–1910)
313, 415, 1116, 1397, 1554, 1977, 2098, 2178.

OATES, TITUS, English perjurer, preacher and pamphleteer. (1649–1705)
1113.

O'BRIEN, JOHN P., American lawyer and former Mayor of New York City. (1873–1951)
1604.

O'CONNELL, DANIEL, Irish orator and political agitator. (1775–1847)
462, 1056, 1082.

O'DONNELL, CHARLES LEO, American educator and poet, President of Notre Dame University. (1884–1934)
966.

O'HARA, GEOFFREY, American song-writer. (1882–)
2296.
O'HARA, KANE, Irish burlesque writer. (1714?–1782)
771, 1023, 1631, 1657.
O'HARA, THEODORE, American poet. (1820–1867)
1034, 1869.
O'KEEFFE, ADELAIDE, English poet and novelist. (1776–1855?)
211.
O'KEEFFE, JOHN, Irish actor and dramatist. (1747–1833)
233, 237, 287, 648, 914, 941, 1070, 1099, 1258, 1593, 1701, 1866, 2042.
O'KELLY, DENNIS, Irish gambler, owner of race-horse Eclipse. (1720?–1787)
1632.
O'REILLY, MILES, see HALPINE, CHARLES GRAHAM
OLDHAM, EDWARD. No biographical data available.
49.
OLDHAM, JOHN, English poet. (1653–1683)
209, 346, 400, 780, 1146, 1147, 1216, 1217, 1361, 1527, 1537, 1566, 1579, 1657, 1718, 1758, 1828, 1892, 1932, 1989, 2247, 2253, 2258.
OLDMIXON, JOHN, English Whig historian and pamphleteer. (1673–1742)
2197.
OLDYS, WILLIAM, English antiquary. (1696–1761)
693, 1131.
OLIPHANT, [MRS.] MARGARET, English novelist and historical writer. (1828–1897)
961.
OLIPHANT, THOMAS, English musical composer. (1799–1873)
552.
OLLIVIER, ÉMILE, French minister of state and political writer. (1825–1913)
718.
OLNEY, RICHARD, American lawyer and statesman. (1835–1917)
58.
OLSON, TED, contemporary American journalist and verse-writer.
2060.
O'MALLEY, FRANK WARD, American journalist. (1875–1932)
1116.
OMAR IBN AL-KHATTAB, second Calif of the Mussulmans. (c. 581–644)
1433.
OMAR KHAYYÁM (Khayyám means tent-maker), Persian poet and astronomer. (d. 1123)
100, 226, 384, 389, 401, 495, 496, 498, 682, 893, 926, 1108, 1120, 1121, 1131, 1139, 1141, 1152, 1213, 1243, 1244, 1370, 1405, 1600, 1646, 1699, 1745, 1834, 1871, 1906, 1940, 2021, 2067, 2157, 2158.
O'MEARA, BARRY EDWARD, Irish surgeon to Napoleon in St. Helena, author of memoirs. (1786–1836)
2116.
O'NEIL, GEORGE, American poet. (1897–)
233, 2161.
O'NEILL, EUGENE GLADSTONE, American dramatist. (1888–1953)
381, 1813.
O'NEILL, MOIRA (pseud. of MRS. NESTA HIGGINSON SKRINE), contemporary Irish poet.
1174.
O'NEILL, ROSE CECIL, American artist and poet. (1875–1944)
2120.
ONSLOW, ARTHUR, English statesman; Speaker of the House of Commons. (1691–1768)
1693.
OPIE, [MRS.] AMELIA, English novelist and poet. (1769–1853)
732, 1220.
OPIE, JOHN, English portrait and historical painter. (1761–1807)
1447.
OPPENHEIM, EDWARD PHILLIPS, English writer of mystery stories. (1866–1946)
236.
OPPENHEIM, GARRETT, contemporary American poet.
2274.
OPPENHEIM, JAMES, American poet. (1882–1932)
31, 798, 859, 945, 1160, 1213, 1239, 1397, 1771, 1839, 2119.
O'REILLY, JOHN BOYLE, Irish revolutionist, journalist and poet; banished to Australia and escaped to America in 1869, where he afterwards resided. (1844–1890)
108, 243, 476, 484, 594, 595, 735, 777, 920, 1035, 1315, 1474, 1822, 2175.
O'REILLY, MILES, see HALPINE, CHARLES GRAHAM
O'RELL, MAX (pseud. of PAUL BLOUET), French journalist, lecturer and critic. (1848–1903)
317.
ORIGO, Latin dramatist. (fl. 75 B.C.)
2138.
ORLÉANS, DUCHESSE DE, French noblewoman of the time of Louis XIV.
1962.
ORMONDE, DUKE OF, see BUTLER, JAMES
ORR, HUGH ROBERT, contemporary American writer. (1887–)
402.
ORRERY, EARL OF, see BOYLE, ROGER
OSBORN, SELLECK, American journalist and poet. (c. 1782–1826)
764.
OSBORNE, FRANCIS, English miscellaneous writer. (1593–1659)
589, 1674.
OSGOOD, [MRS.] FRANCES SARGENT, American verse-writer. (1811–1850)
661, 1064, 2087.
O'SHAUGHNESSY, ARTHUR WILLIAM EDGAR, English poet and herpetologist. (1844–1881)
43, 202, 389, 1369, 1972.
O'SHEEL, SHAEMAS, American poet. (1886–1954)
93, 484, 613.

Osler, Sir William, Canadian physician, resident in the United States 1884–1904; at Oxford, Eng., 1904 until his death. (1849–1919)
35, 2049.

Osorio, Jeronymo (Hieronymus Osorius), Portuguese ecclesiastic and scholar. (d. 1580)
2090.

Ossian, or Oisin, semi-legendary Gaelic warrior and bard. (Supposedly fl. 3rd century)
613, 1152, 1878, 2119.

O'Sullivan, John L., American editor. (fl. 1845)
64.

Otis, James, American patriot and orator. (1725–1783)
1103, 2297.

Otway, Thomas, English dramatist. (1652–1685)
169, 254, 326, 532, 680, 742, 789, 826, 915, 918, 1028, 1204, 1213, 1246, 1455, 1491, 1712, 1948, 2159, 2185, 2188.

Ouida (pseud. of Marie Louise de la Ramée), English novelist. (1839–1908)
266, 627, 924, 990, 1090, 1475, 1637, 1761, 1875.

Oungst, Webb M., American song-writer.
1558.

Ouseley, Thomas J., English poet. (d. 1874)
1450.

Overbury, Sir Thomas, English poet and victim of court intrigue. (1581–1613)
72, 83, 105, 137, 180, 313, 713, 850, 1185, 1209, 1876, 2051, 2180, 2202, 2218, 2228.

Overstreet, Harry Allen, American educator. (1875–)
133, 960.

* Ovid, Publius Ovidius Naso, Roman poet. (43 B.C.–A.D. 18)

Owen, Anita. No biographical data available.
358.

Owen, John, English epigrammatist. (1560?–1622)
230, 443, 467, 715, 2021, 2029.

Owen, John, English theologian. (1616–1683)
467.

Owen, Robert, English socialist and philanthropist. (1771–1858)
273, 1060.

Owens, Mary, Abraham Lincoln's early sweetheart.
1160.

Oxenford, Edward, contemporary English miscellaneous writer.
542.

Oxenham, John (pseud. of William Arthur Dunkerley), English poet and novelist. (1861–1941)
282, 667, 858, 1433.

Oxford, Edward, Lord, see Vere, Edward de

Ozell, John, English translator. (d. 1743)
935, 1075, 1414, 1566.

P

Pacuvius, Marcus, Latin poet. (c. 220–129 B.C.)
320.

Page, H. A. (pseud. of Alexander Hay Japp), English writer and publisher. (1837–1905)
1003.

Page. O. F., contemporary American. No biographical data available.
1644.

Page, William Tyler, American, retired clerk of the House of Representatives. (1868–1942)
54.

Paget, Catesby, English hymn-writer. No biographical data available.
264.

Pailleron, Édouard, French poet and dramatist. (1834–1899)
2238.

Pain, Barry Eric Odell, English novelist and humorist. (1864–1928)
962.

Paine, Albert Bigelow, American novelist and biographer of Mark Twain. (1861–1937)
1707.

Paine, Robert Treat, American poet. (1773–1811)
1840.

Paine, Thomas, English political writer and freethinker, who came to America in 1774. (1737–1809)
62, 114, 145, 225, 235, 320, 335, 622, 700, 723, 725, 816, 817, 949, 1105, 1174, 1605, 1689, 1694, 1725, 1792, 1948, 2093, 2122.

Painter, William, English writer and adapter. (1540?–1594)
222, 743, 939, 1269, 1271, 1432, 1648, 1712.

Palafox y Melzi, José de, Duke of Saragossa, Spanish general. (1780–1847)
2107.

Paleotti, Gabriel, Italian Cardinal and devotional writer. (1524–1597)
273.

Paley, William, English prelate and theological writer. (1743–1805)
788, 1855.

Palgrave, Francis Turner, English poet and critic. (1824–1897)
827, 1121, 2012, 2230.

Palingenius Stellatus, see Manzolli

Palladas, Greek epigrammatist. (fl. A.D. 400)
6, 155, 163, 176, 377, 381, 405, 420, 564, 713, 714, 1125, 1126, 1131, 1143, 1146, 1419, 1430, 1565, 1572, 1719, 1820, 1823, 1973, 2006, 2142, 2188.

Palmer, Alice Freeman, American educator and poet. (1855–1902)
211.

Palmer, George Herbert, American educator. (1842–1933)
527.

Palmer, Gretta, contemporary American journalist.
855.

Palmer, John F., American song-writer.
360.

Palmer, John Williamson, American physician and poet. (1825–1906)
1005, 2065.

Palmer, Ray, American Congregational clergyman and hymn-writer. (1808–1887)
2274.

PALMER, SAMUEL, English essayist and biographer. (1741–1813)
224, 532, 656, 1006, 1458, 1711, 1760, 1985.

* PALSGRAVE, JOHN, English chaplain and compiler. (1480–1554)

PANAT, CHARLES LOUIS ÉTIENNE, CHEVALIER DE, French naval officer. (1762–1834)
304.

PANNONIUS, JANUS (JOHANNES JESSINGE, or CISINGE), Hungarian poet who wrote in Latin. (1434–1472)
569, 1820.

PARACELSUS (pseud. of PHILIPPUS AUREOLUS THEOPHRASTUS BOMBASTUS AB HOHENHEIM), Swiss alchemist and charlatan. (1493–1541)
465.

PARDOE, JULIA, English novelist and historical writer. (1806–1862)
875, 1043.

PARIS, GASTON BRUNO PAULIN, French educator and writer on literary subjects. (1839–1903)
1924.

PARIS, MATTHEW, English chronicler. (d. 1259)
1393.

PARK, ANDREW, Scottish poet. (1807–1863)
1732.

PARKER, [MRS.] DOROTHY ROTHSCHILD, American poet and satirist. (1893–)
102, 108, 176, 374, 517, 569, 779, 1042, 1204, 1276, 1850, 2087, 2204, 2287.

PARKER, EDWARD GRIFFIN, American lawyer and writer. (1825–1868)
1438.

PARKER, GEORGE, English soldier, actor and lecturer. (1732–1800)
177, 914.

PARKER, HUBBARD, contemporary American writer.
674.

PARKER, JOSEPH, English writer and divine. (1830–1902)
264.

PARKER, MARTIN, English ballad-monger. (d. 1656?)
83, 861, 1648, 1780, 2151.

PARKER, THEODORE, American Unitarian clergyman and abolitionist. (1810–1860)
183, 266, 431, 618, 758, 823, 836, 951, 957, 964, 980, 1245, 1541, 1690, 1842, 2034, 2054, 2055.

PARKHURST, DR. CHARLES HENRY, American Presbyterian clergyman and reformer. (1842–1933)
616, 882, 890, 904, 1061, 1388, 1660, 1827.

PARKINSON, RICHARD, English agriculturist. (1748–1815)
60.

PARMENIDES, Greek Eleatic philosopher. (fl. 450 B.C.)
2068.

PARMENIO, Macedonian general under Alexander. (fl. 335 B.C.)
891.

PARNELL, CHARLES STEWART, Irish political leader. (1846–1891)
1871.

PARNELL, THOMAS, Irish poet. (1679–1718)
374, 695, 895, 1179, 1199, 1258, 1263, 2014.

PARROT, HENRY, English epigrammatist. (c. 1578–c. 1633)
2133.

PARSONS, THOMAS WILLIAM, American dentist, translator and poet. (1819–1892)
117, 365, 2005.

PARTON, JAMES, American journalist and biographer. (1822–1891)
1008.

PARTON, MRS. SARAH PAYSON, see FERN, FANNY

PASCAL, BLAISE, French mathematician, physicist and moralist. (1623–1662)
68, 82, 147, 334, 529, 533, 536, 584, 625, 699, 727, 756, 768, 785, 797, 882, 1010, 1021, 1027, 1056, 1102, 1107, 1141, 1231, 1238, 1239, 1250, 1251, 1316, 1390, 1412, 1428, 1429, 1500, 1660, 1693, 1731, 1788, 1823, 1874, 1989, 2040, 2051, 2068, 2074, 2128, 2225, 2252.

PASQUIER, ÉTIENNE, French lawyer and man of letters. (1529–1615)
972.

PATER, WALTER HORATIO, English critic and essayist. (1839–1894)
1727.

PATMORE, COVENTRY KERSEY DIGHTON, English poet. (1823–1896)
138, 430, 474, 482, 947, 1049, 1051, 1119, 1201, 1254, 1276, 1765, 1796, 1827, 1870, 1899, 2052, 2178, 2188, 2206, 2216, 2241.

PATRICIUS, Bishop of Gæta. (fl. A.D. 450)
520.

PATRICK, JOHN, English Protestant controversialist. (1632–1695)
1556.

PATTEN, WILLIAM, English historian. (fl. 1548–1580)
2231.

PATTISON, MARK, English miscellaneous writer. (1813–1884)
188.

PAUL I (PAVLOF, PETROVITCH), Emperor of Russia. (1754–1801)
1920.

PAUL III (ALESSANDRO FARNESE), Roman Pope. (1468–1549)
891.

PAUL, JOHN, see JONES, JOHN PAUL

PAULDING, JAMES KIRKE, American naval officer and miscellaneous writer. (1778–1860)
61.

PAULET, or POULET, SIR AMIAS, English courtier and custodian of Mary Queen of Scots. (1536?–1588)
863.

PAULET, PAWLET, or POULET, SIR WILLIAM, MARQUIS OF WINCHESTER, English courtier. (1485?–1572)
327.

PAULINUS, PONTIUS MEROPUS, SAINT, Bishop of Nola. (fl. c. A.D. 340)
267.

PAULUS JOVIUS, Lombard historian. (c. 720–c. 800)
559, 1492.

PAULUS SILENTIARIUS, Greek poet. (fl. 6th century)
1771.

PAUSANIAS, Spartan general. (fl. 479 B.C.)
468.

PAXTON, DR. JOHN RANDOLPH, American clergyman. (1843–1923)
631.

PAYN, JAMES, English novelist. (1830–1898)
453, 1464, 1859.

PAYNE, JOHN, English poet. (1842–1916)
407, 1138.

PAYNE, JOHN HOWARD, American actor and playwright. (1791–1852)
906.

PAYNE, PERCY SOMERS, Irish poet. (1850–1874)
1825.

PEABODY, GEORGE, American philanthropist. (1795–1869)
53.

PEABODY, JOSEPHINE PRESTON [MRS. LIONEL SIMEON MARKS], American poet and dramatist. (1874–1922)
535, 2233.

PEACH, ARTHUR WALLACE, American poet. (1886–)
2267.

PEACOCK, THOMAS LOVE, English novelist and poet. (1785–1866)
98, 333, 359, 364, 366, 369, 381, 422, 496, 502, 569, 659, 685, 769, 1267, 1278, 1393, 1410, 1433, 1438, 1486, 1599, 1640, 1687, 1811, 1983, 2012, 2095, 2123, 2139, 2182, 2267.

PEALE, REMBRANDT, American painter and writer on art subjects. (1778–1860)
293.

PEARSE, MARK GUY, English miscellaneous writer. (1842–1930)
2044.

PEARSON, JOHN, English prelate, Bishop of Chester. (1613–1686)
825.

PEASE, HARRY, American song-writer.
1636.

PECK, FRANCIS, English antiquary. (1692–1743)
1339.

PECK, HARRY THURSTON, American educator and man of letters. (1856–1914)
367, 2236.

PEELE, GEORGE, English dramatist. (1558?–1597?)
325, 507, 512, 917, 930, 1047, 1172, 1207, 1464, 1960, 2014, 2114.

PEGGE, SAMUEL, THE ELDER, English antiquary. (1704–1796)
890, 1857.

PEGLER, WESTBROOK, American newspaper columnist. (1894–)
1571.

PELLICO, SILVIO, Italian dramatist. (1788–1854)
1863.

PELLISSON-FONTANIER, PAUL, French historical writer. (1624–1693)
1613.

PEMBERTON, SIR FRANCIS, English jurist. (1625–1697)
1082.

PEMBERTON, HARRIET L. CHILDE, contemporary American playwright.
1116.

PEMBROKE, EARL OF, see HERBERT, HENRY

PENN, WILLIAM, Quaker and founder of Pennsylvania. (1644–1718)
36, 80, 88, 89, 100, 165, 267, 299, 314, 403, 432, 526, 598, 730, 741, 743, 937, 1023, 1111, 1284, 1440, 1444, 1480, 1577, 1677, 1691, 1694, 1820, 2050, 2051, 2079.

PEPLER, HILARY DOUGLAS C., contemporary English writer.
1094.

PEPYS, SAMUEL, English diarist. (1633–1703)
43, 125, 141, 167, 365, 449, 451, 469, 471, 487, 561, 592, 641, 832, 853, 942, 998, 1043, 1044, 1052, 1073, 1162, 1272, 1334, 1413, 1437, 1472, 1551, 1591, 1594, 1595, 1709, 1929, 2015, 2072, 2135, 2146, 2180.

PERCIVAL, JAMES GATES, American poet and scholar. (1795–1856)
509, 687, 1743, 1842, 1949, 1992, 2241.

PERCY, THOMAS, English prelate, Bishop of Dromore, editor of the *Reliques of Ancient English Poetry*. (1729–1811)
1015, 1202, 1203, 1338.

PERCY, WILLIAM ALEXANDER, American lawyer and poet (1885–1942)
162, 1559.

PERIANDER, Greek tyrant; one of the Seven Sages. (665?–585 B.C.)
433, 657, 736, 845, 1337, 1512, 1637, 1651, 1723, 1821.

PERICLES, Greek statesman and military commander. (fl. 460 B.C.)
1440, 2003.

PERRONET, EDWARD, English hymn-writer. (1721–1792)
264.

PERRY, NORA, American poet and story-writer. (1832–1896)
253, 1203, 1289.

PERRY, OLIVER HAZARD, American naval commander. (1785–1819)
62, 63.

PERSES, King of Macedonia. (fl. 179 B.C.)
1282.

PERSIUS, AULUS PERSIUS FLACCUS, Latin satirist. (34–62)
90, 112, 124, 127, 135, 155, 160, 209, 221, 230, 379, 435, 449, 459, 493, 519, 613, 627, 651, 695, 722, 861, 876, 879, 1056, 1136, 1288, 1414, 1517, 1526, 1536, 1584, 1593, 1708, 1788, 1855, 1889, 1899, 1927, 1963, 2023, 2089.

PERSOV, ANNE. No biographical data available.
861.

PESCHEL, OSKAR FERDINAND, German geographer. (1826–1875)
1970.
PÉTAIN, HENRI PHILIPPE, French Marshal. (1856–1951)
2109.
PETERSON, FREDERICK (PAI TA-SHUN), American physician and poet. (1859–1939)
813, 1748.
PETEVAL, FRANÇOIS DE, French writer. (fl. 1734)
1082.
PETIGRU, JAMES LOUIS, American statesman. (1789–1863)
1231.
PETRARCH, FRANCESCO PETRARCA, Italian poet and Platonic lover of Laura, wife of Hugues de Sade. (1304–1374)
25, 98, 138, 149, 187, 392, 579, 1149, 1209, 1405, 1471, 1600, 1819, 1853, 1926, 2091.
PETRE, MAUD D. M., contemporary English writer. (?–1942)
724.
PETRONIUS, CAIUS (ARBITER), licentious writer and director of pleasures (*arbiter elegantiæ*) at the court of Nero. (d. A.D. 66)
78, 89, 112, 119, 138, 140, 232, 236, 238, 330, 334, 383, 462, 465, 470, 477, 479, 491, 496, 528, 565, 633, 650, 704, 760, 772, 800, 803, 824, 850, 876, 946, 1092, 1097, 1131, 1133, 1224, 1231, 1242, 1281, 1487, 1564, 1572, 1583, 1681, 1687, 1756, 1784, 1795, 1886, 1927, 1940, 1966, 1987, 2021, 2030, 2041, 2138, 2151, 2155, 2188, 2258, 2277.
PETTIE, GEORGE, English writer of romances. (1548–1589)
246, 320, 1143, 1632, 2191.
PEYRAT, ALPHONSE, French political writer. (1812–1891)
1592.
PHÆDRUS, Latin fabulist. (fl. A.D. 20)
13, 18, 19, 86, 119, 138, 152, 174, 178, 184, 218, 287, 288, 346, 461, 502, 510, 519, 533, 584, 588, 621, 651, 678, 697, 744, 748, 885, 953, 963, 986, 993, 1057, 1100, 1150, 1162, 1236, 1252, 1258, 1281, 1307, 1312, 1354, 1407, 1432, 1480, 1506, 1527, 1570, 1572, 1575, 1626, 1682, 1710, 1801, 1901, 1931, 2046, 2064, 2070, 2124, 2134, 2158, 2165, 2171, 2250.
PHALÆCUS, Greek epigrammatic poet.
1778.
PHELPS, AUSTIN, American Congregational clergyman and devotional writer. (1820–1890)
190.
PHELPS, EDWARD JOHN, American publicist and diplomatist. (1822–1900)
1543.
PHELPS, ELIZABETH STUART, see WARD, ELIZABETH STUART PHELPS
PHELPS, MARION. No biographical data available.
1046.
PHELPS, WILLIAM LYON, American educator and man of letters. (1865–1943)
558.
PHILEMON, Athenian comic poet. (c. 361–263 B.C.)
290, 465, 1027, 1840.
PHILIP OF MACEDON, King of Macedonia and father of Alexander the Great. (382–336 B.C.)
112, 218, 1838.
PHILIP II, King of Spain. (1527–1598)
2003.
PHILIP, JOHN WOODWARD, American naval officer. (1840–1900)
66.
PHILIPPUS OF THESSALONICA, epigrammatic poet. (fl. A.D. 100)
164, 912, 1771.
PHILIPS, AMBROSE, English poet. (1675?–1749)
137, 1099.
PHILIPS, JOHN, English poet. (1676–1709)
491, 549, 746, 750, 858, 1816.
PHILIPS, KATHERINE, English verse-writer. (1631–1664)
1693.
PHILLIPS, CHARLES, Irish barrister and miscellaneous writer. (1787?–1859)
1378.
PHILLIPS, HENRY WALLACE, American novelist. (1869–1930)
2208.
PHILLIPS, STEPHEN, English poet and dramatist. (1864–1915)
42, 139, 345, 413, 478, 608, 613, 617, 765, 837, 848, 1095, 1143, 1201, 1213, 1290, 1468, 1576, 1666, 1743, 2095, 2155.
PHILLIPS, SUSAN K., American poet. (1870–)
1746.
PHILLIPS, WENDELL, American orator and abolitionist. (1811–1884)
72, 307, 527, 817, 1023, 1090, 1105, 1106, 1236, 1240, 1280, 1395, 1426, 1501, 1507, 1542, 1575, 1597, 1602, 1617, 1659, 1696, 1714, 1842, 1919, 2034, 2127.
PHILLPOTTS, EDEN, English novelist. (1862–)
1138, 1230, 1793, 1906, 2068.
PHILO-JUDÆUS, Jewish philosopher, born in Alexandria. (c. 20 B.C.– ?)
347.
PHILOSTRATUS, Greek sophist, rhetorician and biographer, resident at Rome. (c. 181–250)
601, 1987.
PHINEHAS-BEN-JAÏR, Jewish rabbi. No biographical data available.
279.
PHOCION, Athenian general and patriot. (402?–317 B.C.)
1091, 1480, 1897.
PHOCYLIDES, Greek gnomic poet. (fl. 560 B.C.)
1329, 1349, 1484, 1986, 2026.
PHRYNE, a celebrated Athenian courtesan. (fl. 350 B.C.)
1771.
PIATT, DONN, American journalist. (1819–1891)
542, 543, 831, 897, 899, 1483.
PIATT, JOHN JAMES, American poet. (1835–1917)
630, 909.

PIATT, SARAH MORGAN BRYAN, American poet. (1836–1919)
211.

PIAVE, F. M., Italian librettist. (fl. 1850)
2198.

PIBRAC, GUY DU FAUR, SEIGNEUR DE, French jurist and poet. (1529–1584)
1098.

PICKTHALL, MARJORIE LOWRY CHRISTIE, English poet. (1883–1922)
384.

PIERCE, EDWARD LILLIE, American publicist. (1829– ?)
1556.

PIERCE, [MRS.] GEORGE, contemporary American writer.
1516.

PIERPONT, JOHN, American Unitarian clergyman and poet. (1785–1866)
498, 878, 975, 1153, 1501, 1583, 2098, 2116.

PIIS, ANTOINE PIERRE AUGUSTIN, French dramatist and song-writer. (1755–1832)
1138.

PIKE, ALBERT, American journalist and Confederate general. (1809–1891)
64, 2116.

PILPAY, or BIDPAI, famous Oriental fabulist. Bidpai is a corruption of bidbah, the appellation of the chief scholar at the court of an Indian prince. *The Fables of Bidpai* is the title of an Arabic version of a lost original of the *Panchatantra,* a celebrated Sanskrit collection of fables, the source of much European folklore. Date unknown.
69, 224, 302, 327, 680, 730, 758, 804, 1080, 1520, 1709, 1744.

PINCKNEY, CHARLES COTESWORTH, American soldier and diplomat. (1746–1825)
63.

PINDAR, Greek lyric poet. (c. 522–442 B.C.)
627, 787, 792, 802, 856, 922, 1029, 1295, 1332, 1458, 1522, 1649, 1720, 2002, 2124, 2176.

PINDAR, PETER, see WOLCOT, JOHN

PINERO, SIR ARTHUR WING, English dramatist. (1855–1934)
41, 710, 746, 808, 944, 990, 1008, 1188, 1278, 1453, 1460, 1582, 1637, 1911, 1981, 2100, 2127, 2180, 2192.

PINKNEY, EDWARD COOTE, American poet. (1802–1828)
604, 2185.

PINKNEY, WILLIAM, American statesman. (1764–1822)
2064.

PIOZZI, HESTER LYNCH [MRS HENRY THRALE], English author and friend of Dr. Samuel Johnson. (1741–1821)
30, 232, 465, 923, 2208.

PIPER, EDWIN FORD, American educator and poet. (1871–1939)
1613.

PIRON, ALEXIS, French poet, playwright and wit. (1689–1773)
1507.

PITKIN, WALTER BOUGHTON, American psychologist and publicist. (1878–1953)
467, 1480, 1547.

PITT, CHRISTOPHER, English poet and translator. (1699–1748)
1594, 1895.

PITT, WILLIAM, first EARL OF CHATHAM, English statesman. (1708–1778)
60, 296, 328, 818, 936, 1082, 1574, 1603, 1696, 1999, 2063, 2264.

PITT, WILLIAM, THE YOUNGER, English statesman and Prime Minister. (1759–1806)
318, 416, 536, 556, 581, 1152, 1393, 1438, 1464, 1534, 1748.

PITTACUS, Greek statesman and poet, one of the Seven Sages. (c. 652–569 B.C.)
420, 502, 506, 710, 807, 1089, 1267, 1298, 1392, 1431, 1512, 1548, 1634, 1838, 2142.

PIXLEY, FRANK, American librettist and song-writer. (1867–1919)
2292.

PLANCHÉ, JAMES ROBINSON, English playwright. (1796–1880)
95, 167, 224, 350, 419, 872, 1268, 1631, 1763, 1929, 2177.

PLATO, Greek philosopher. (428–347 B.C.)
31, 73, 98, 129, 132, 146, 280, 391, 405, 433, 452, 662, 748, 771, 772, 783, 784, 785, 787, 811, 816, 817, 819, 820, 845, 860, 983, 987, 1027, 1054, 1060, 1084, 1162, 1190, 1224, 1240, 1241, 1252, 1255, 1303, 1312, 1362, 1420, 1438, 1440, 1464, 1498, 1508, 1511, 1512, 1534, 1588, 1607, 1634, 1771, 1786, 1804, 1843, 1872, 1877, 1888, 1894, 1917, 1935, 1959, 1969, 2002, 2013, 2043, 2049, 2058, 2073, 2084, 2089, 2091, 2092, 2125, 2167, 2168, 2245.

PLATT, JOHN, engineer, born in England, resident of U. S. since 1888. (1864–1942)
2123.

PLATT, THOMAS COLLIER, American politician, Republican "boss" of New York. (1833–1910)
2280.

* PLAUTUS, TITUS MACCIUS, Roman dramatist and poet. (fl. 254–184 B.C.)

PLAYFORD, JOHN, THE ELDER, English musician and publisher. (1623–1686)
220.

PLINY, CAIUS PLINIUS SECUNDUS, THE ELDER, Roman naturalist. (fl. 62–113)
2, 16, 20, 70, 114, 124, 126, 147, 163, 184, 227, 229, 347, 355, 370, 411, 498, 510, 518, 596, 605, 606, 636, 647, 688, 904, 969, 1075, 1110, 1141, 1227, 1246, 1249, 1250, 1282, 1306, 1313, 1357, 1415, 1416, 1433, 1476, 1506, 1709, 1756, 1775, 1798, 2000, 2001, 2155, 2165.

PLINY, CAIUS PLINIUS CÆCILIUS SECUNDUS, THE YOUNGER, Latin letter-writer and advocate. (b. A.D. 61)
125, 199, 234, 313, 352, 355, 370, 372, 386, 397, 421, 443, 569, 594, 630, 645, 652, 814, 900, 901, 926, 929, 955, 986, 1009, 1089, 1102, 1165, 1313, 1340, 1372, 1388, 1420, 1438, 1440, 1462, 1469, 1527, 1560, 1561, 1581, 1626, 1674, 1702, 1710, 1763, 2006, 2085, 2096, 2254.

PLOTIUS FIRMUS, Roman soldier and philosopher (fl. A.D. 60)
177.

PLUNKETT, JOSEPH MARY, Irish patriot and poet. (1887–1916)
264.

PLUTARCH, Greek moralist and biographer. (fl. A.D. 66)
1, 2, 46, 70, 74, 81, 138, 145, 161, 199, 213, 221, 234, 256, 275, 288, 298, 354, 356, 370, 420, 422, 447, 502, 528, 542, 565, 577, 580. 591, 642, 677, 727, 797, 801, 803, 807, 826, 863, 876, 901, 963, 982, 984, 1028, 1030, 1040, 1109, 1131, 1134, 1141, 1170, 1273, 1292, 1332, 1354, 1398, 1440, 1450, 1457, 1488, 1490, 1541, 1547, 1579, 1665, 1669, 1678, 1687, 1739, 1775, 1790, 1817, 1824, 1863, 1888, 1901, 1919, 1964, 1973, 2000, 2034, 2066, 2076, 2089, 2090, 2096, 2114, 2120, 2126, 2130, 2143, 2152, 2243, 2248.

POCOCK, ISAAC, English painter and dramatist. (1782–1835)
2208.

POE, EDGAR ALLAN, American poet, essayist and short-story writer. (1809–1849)
17, 83, 96, 140, 152, 154, 285, 366, 385, 395, 411, 422, 463, 481, 483, 484, 525, 673, 822, 918, 1206, 1213, 1218, 1235, 1303, 1322, 1352, 1425, 1516, 1534, 1624, 1672, 1697, 1723, 1746, 1879, 1989, 2175, 2242.

POINCARÉ, RAYMOND NICHOLAS LANDRY, French statesman, Premier and President. (1860–1934)
545.

POLE, REGINALD, English Cardinal and Archbishop of Canterbury. (1500–1558)
2106.

POLIGNAC, MELCHIOR DE, French Cardinal, statesman and poet. (1661–1742)
41.

POLING, DANIEL V., American clergyman and prohibition leader. (1865–)
2113.

POLLARD, JOSEPHINE, American poet. (1843–1892)
713.

POLLOCK, CHANNING, American dramatist. (1880–1946)
342, 855.

POLLOCK, EDWARD, American verse-writer. (1823–1858)
1455.

POLLOK, ROBERT, Scottish poet, author of *The Course of Time*. (1798–1827)
121, 158, 505, 629, 662, 730, 740, 861, 949, 1293, 1298, 1368, 1585, 1773, 1836, 1972.

POLYBIUS, Greek historian. (c. 204–122 B.C.)
433.

POMFRET, JOHN, English poet. (1667–1702)
354, 398, 405, 529, 576, 789, 1058, 1715, 1924, 2158.

POMPADOUR, MADAME DE, JEANNE ANTOINETTE POISSON D'ÉTIOLES, MARQUISE DE POMPADOUR, mistress of Louis XV of France. (1721–1764)
416, 1632.

POMPEY (CNEIUS POMPEIUS), Roman general. (106–48 B.C.)
983, 1939.

POMPONIUS LÆTUS, JULIUS, Roman antiquarian and historian. (1425–1497)
826.

POOLE, JACOB, English antiquary. (1774–1827)
813.

POOLE, JOHN, English dramatist. (1786–1879)
352, 1638.

* POPE, ALEXANDER, English poet and critic. (1688–1744)

POPE, FRANCES E. No biographical data available.
32.

POPE, WALTER, English astronomer. (d. 1714)
1330.

POQUELIN, JEAN BAPTISTE, see MOLIÈRE

PORPHYRY, Greek Neo-Platonic philosopher. (c. 233–304)
1117.

PORSON, RICHARD, English Greek scholar. (1759–1808)
99, 503, 1655, 2017.

PORTER, DAVID, American poet. (1790–1871)
708.

PORTER, HENRY, English dramatist. (fl. 1596–1599)
218, 330, 589, 853, 914, 1627, 1997.

PORTER, HORACE, American general and diplomat. (1837–1921)
1551.

PORTER, KENNETH WIGGINS, American historian and miscellaneous writer. (1905–)
363.

PORTER, NOAH, American Congregational clergyman and educator. (1811–1892)
1674.

PORTER, WILLIAM SYDNEY, see O. HENRY

PORTEUS, BEILBY, English prelate and doctrinal writer. (1731–1808)
1135, 1147, 1359, 1474.

POSIDIPPUS, Greek comic dramatist. (fl. 289 B.C.)
1120, 1432.

POSIDONIUS, Greek Stoic philosopher. (c. 135–51 B.C.)
680, 702, 1080, 1097, 1723.

POTTER, CHARLES FRANCIS, American lecturer and humanistic writer. (1885–)
2109.

POTTER, HENRY CODMAN, American Protestant Episcopal Bishop. (1835–1908)
56, 1553, 2093.

POULLET, PIERRARD, French poet. (fl. 1590)
874.

POUND, EZRA, American poet. (1885–)
1166, 1572.

POUNDS, JESSIE BROWN, American song-writer.
2292.

POWELL, SIR JOHN, English jurist. (1633–1696)
1079.

POWYS, JOHN COWPER, English novelist and essayist. (1872–)
348, 960, 1121, 1129, 1178, 1489, 1517, 1691, 1704.

PUTTENHAM, GEORGE, English writer, reputed author of *The Arte of English Poesie* (c. 1530–c. 1600, although *The Dictionary of National Biography* asserts that it was more probably by his scapegrace elder brother, RICHARD PUTTENHAM (c. 1520–c. 1601). Both were the sons of Robert Puttenham.
1068, 1163, 2119, 2183.

PYM, JOHN, English parliamentary statesman. (1584–1643)
2228.

PYPER, MARY, Scottish poet. (fl. 1870)
1123.

PYRRHO, Greek philosopher and skeptic. (c. 376–270 B.C.)
1861.

PYRRHUS, King of Epirus. (381–272 B.C.)
2083.

PYTHAGORAS, Greek philosopher and mathematician. (582–500 B.C.)
14, 356, 504, 728, 741, 876, 1086, 1119, 1259, 1457, 1584, 1585, 1678, 1771, 1788, 1792, 1824, 1840, 1894, 1922, 1956, 2002, 2088, 2138, 2279.

PYTHEAS, Greek mariner of Marseilles. (c. 330 B.C.)
1923.

Q

QUARLES, EDWIN, contemporary American poet.
137, 1214, 1584.

QUARLES, FRANCIS, English poet and devotional writer. (1592–1644)
21, 48, 78, 267, 302, 306, 341, 369, 375, 377, 379, 400, 468, 570, 571, 599, 660, 681, 690, 732, 736, 774, 784, 794, 810, 841, 874, 877, 884, 887, 890, 892, 1058, 1116, 1123, 1125, 1134, 1149, 1150, 1156, 1228, 1231, 1237, 1239, 1251, 1261, 1275, 1300, 1310, 1340, 1399, 1640, 1699, 1705, 1734, 1772, 1791, 1794, 1823, 1867, 1894, 1911, 2009, 2013, 2015, 2021, 2024, 2029, 2145, 2146, 2160, 2216, 2239, 2242, 2243, 2277.

QUAY, MATTHEW STANLEY, American politician. (1833–1904)
1555.

QUILLEN, ROBERT, American editorial writer and columnist. (1887–1948)
958.

QUILLER-COUCH, SIR ARTHUR, English educator, essayist and novelist. (1863–1944)
446, 512, 1163, 1494, 1704, 2142, 2170.

QUILLINAN, DOROTHY WORDSWORTH, see WORDSWORTH, DOROTHY

QUIN, DAN, English humorist. (1860–1938)
1275.

QUINAULT, PHILIPPE, French poet and dramatist. (1635–1688)
2164.

QUINCY, JOSIAH, American statesman and educator. (1772–1864)
58, 725.

QUINTILIAN, MARCUS FABIUS QUINTILIANUS, Roman rhetorician. (fl. 35–95)
13, 48, 90, 107, 147, 510, 537, 594, 651, 702, 739, 749, 760, 846, 913, 921, 954, 972, 1024, 1036, 1076, 1107, 1112, 1152, 1306, 1393, 1396, 1618, 1681, 1750, 1816, 1835, 1876, 1897, 1952, 1970, 2056, 2088, 2092, 2107, 2135, 2169, 2223, 2224, 2254, 2259.

QUINTUS CURTIUS RUFUS, Roman historian. (fl. c. 2nd century)
320, 471, 656, 667, 824, 846, 863, 867, 1393, 1563, 1617, 1625, 1679, 1731, 2035, 2084, 2089, 2126.

R

RABBETTE, LEO J., contemporary American journalist.
2187.

* RABELAIS, FRANÇOIS, French humanist and satirist. (1494–1553)

RABIRIUS, CAIUS, Roman defended by Cicero. (fl. 54 B.C.)
774.

RACINE, JEAN BAPTISTE, French poet and dramatist. (1639–1699)
389, 395, 792, 917, 919, 929, 987, 990, 1078, 1279, 1326, 1333, 1821, 2081, 2135.

RADCLIFFE, ANN, English novelist. (1764–1823)
644, 1153, 1815.

RAE, JOHN, English arctic explorer. (1813–1893)
2087.

RALEIGH, OR RALEGH, SIR WALTER, English navigator, naval commander, poet and historical writer. (1552?–1618)
247, 272, 318, 388, 392, 398, 416, 436, 521, 529, 620, 622, 624, 837, 865, 895, 899, 900, 917, 1185, 1196, 1209, 1212, 1218, 1220, 1457, 1605, 1607, 1648, 1894, 1918, 2014, 2087, 2159, 2168, 2199, 2202, 2228.

RALEIGH, SIR WALTER, THE YOUNGER, English educator and writer. (1861–1922)
1246, 1406, 1532, 1736, 1938.

RALPH, JULIAN, American miscellaneous writer. (1853–1903)
1601.

RAMÉE, MARIE LOUISE DE LA, see OUIDA

RAMSAY, ALLAN, Scottish poet. (1686–1758)
38, 110, 217, 636, 738, 905, 1097, 2025, 2213.

RAMSAY, EDWARD BANNERMAN, Scottish educator, Dean of the University of Edinburgh. (1793–1872)
745.

RANDALL, JAMES RYDER, American poet. (1839–1908)
411, 2054, 2064.

RANDOLPH, JOHN, OF ROANOKE. American statesman. (1773–1833)
63, 2129, 2279.

RANDOLPH, THOMAS, English poet and dramatist. (1605–1635)
28, 79, 289, 539, 916, 1031, 1164, 1254, 1269, 1501, 1582, 1618, 1669, 1720, 2155, 2212, 2244, 2269.

RANDS, WILLIAM BRIGHTY, English writer of verse for children. (1823–1882)
695, 1143, 1989, 2241.

RANKIN, JEREMIAH EAMES. American poet. (1828–1904)
122, 793, 1501.

RANSFORD, EDWIN, English vocalist and actor. (1805–1876)
2102.
RANSOM, JOHN CROWE, American educator and poet. (1888–)
1595.
RAPER, JOHN W., American newspaper columnist. (1870–1950)
401.
RAPIN, RENÉ, SIEUR DE, French Jesuit and writer of Latin poetry. (1621–1687)
1261.
RAVENEL, BEATRICE WITTE [MRS. PRIOLEAU G. RAVENEL], American poet. (1870–)
1347.
RAVENSCROFT, EDWARD, English dramatist. (fl. 1671–1697)
1637.
RAVENSCROFT, THOMAS, English musician. (1592?–1635)
1412.
RAVENSWORTH, LORD, see LIDDELL, HENRY THOMAS
RAVIGNAN, GUSTAVE DELACROIX, PÈRE DE, French Jesuit writer. (1795–1858)
1110.
RAVISIUS-TEXTOR, JEAN, or JOHANN, generally known as JEAN TIXIER DE RAVISI, French humanist. (c. 1480–1524)
596.
RAY, JAMES, English chronicler. (fl. 1745–1746)
457.
* RAY, JOHN, English naturalist and collector of proverbs. Spelled name Wray until 1670. (1628–1705)
RAYMOND, WILLIAM LEE, American writer. (1877–1942)
1726.
RAYNAL, GUILLAUME THOMAS FRANÇOIS, French Jesuit and writer. (1713–1796)
1741.
READ, THOMAS BUCHANAN, American poet. (1822–1872)
930, 1401, 1451, 1774, 1890, 2118.
READE, CHARLES, English novelist and dramatist. (1814–1884)
84, 125, 442, 662, 761, 845, 867, 1284, 1631, 1636, 1686, 1736, 1921, 2252.
REALF, RICHARD, poet, born in England, resident of U. S. after 1854. (1834–1878)
107, 401, 425, 774, 991, 1143, 1544, 2212.
RECORDE, ROBERT, English mathematician and writer. (1510?–1558)
804.
REDFORD, JOHN, English poet and dramatist. (c. 1485–c. 1545)
1809.
REED, DAVID, JR., American song-writer.
2292.
REED, JAMES A., American lawyer and politician. (1861–1944)
2279.
REED, JOHN, American journalist and revolutionary. (1887–1920)
166, 1397.
REED, THOMAS BRACKETT, American politician; Speaker of the House of Representatives. (1839–1902)
648, 817, 846, 970, 1236, 1482, 1544, 1545, 1551, 1552, 1627, 1741, 1919, 2048.
REESE, LIZETTE WOODWORTH, American poet. (1856–1935)
93, 180, 259, 269, 335, 357, 392, 484, 619, 624, 889, 1072, 1144.
REEVES, BILLY, American song-writer.
2292.
REGNARD, JEAN FRANÇOIS, French comic poet and dramatist. (1655–1709)
324, 1217, 1562, 1631.
REGNIER, ABBÉ RENÉ FRANÇOIS, French priest. (1794– ?)
396.
REID, THOMAS, English philosopher. (1710–1796)
797.
REIS, LINCOLN. No biographical data available.
2132.
RÉMI, or RÉMY, SAINT, French apostle and Bishop of Rheims. (c. 437–533)
265.
RENAN, JOSEPH ERNEST, French skeptical writer and critic. (1823–1892)
69, 416. 1792.
RENARD, JULES, French littérateur. (1864–1910)
107.
RENTOUL, [REV.] JOHN LAWRENCE, Australian writer and poet, born in Ireland in 1846.
1465.
REPPLIER, AGNES, American essayist. (1858–1950)
779.
REXFORD, EBEN EUGENE, American verse- and song-writer. (1848–1916)
39.
REYNIÈRE, GRIMOD DE LA, ALEXANDRE BALTHASAR LAURENT, French wit and gastronome. (1758–1838)
532.
REYNOLDS, FREDERIC, English dramatist. (1764–1841)
390, 419, 2004, 2188.
REYNOLDS, JOHN HAMILTON, English poet. (1796–1852)
603.
REYNOLDS, SIR JOSHUA, English portrait-painter. (1723–1792)
339, 416, 607, 758, 963, 980, 1447.
RHOADES, JAMES, English poet, translator and writer. (1841–1923)
1075.
RHODES, CECIL JOHN, English imperialist, promoter and benefactor. (1853–1902)
104, 561.
RHODES, HUGH, English miscellaneous writer. (fl. 1550)
521, 591, 678, 1729, 1970.
RHODES, JAMES FORD, American historian. (1848–1927)
1377.

RHODES, WILLIAM BARNES, English dramatic writer. (1772–1826)
411, 480, 505, 926, 1186, 1410, 1875, 2198.

RHYS, ERNEST, English editor and poet. (1859–1946)
1376, 2226.

RICE, CALE YOUNG, American poet. (1872–1943)
434.

RICE, GRANTLAND, American journalist and sports writer. (1880–1954)
754.

RICE, RUTH MASON, American verse-writer. (1884–1927)
2082.

RICE, SIR STEPHEN, chief Baron of Irish exchequer. (1637–1715)
1082.

RICE, WALLACE DE GROOT CECIL, American poet and editor. (1859–1939)
251, 551, 921.

RICH, BARNABE, English soldier and miscellaneous writer. (1540?–1617)
200, 1192, 1413, 1811, 2189, 2201, 2212, 2237.

RICHARD I (CŒUR-DE-LION), King of England. (1157–1199)
546.

RICHARDS, AMELIA B. No biographical data available.
547.

RICHARDSON, ROBERT, Australian poet. (1850–1901)
570.

RICHARDSON, SAMUEL, English novelist. (1689–1761)
20, 254, 443, 580, 695, 861, 914, 1014, 1038, 1046, 1077, 1180, 1197, 1636, 1639, 1712, 1715, 1921, 1997, 2024, 2206, 2212.

RICHELIEU, ARMAND JEAN DU PLESSIS, DUC DE, French Cardinal and statesman. (1585–1642)
325, 543, 1039, 2259.

RICHE-SOURCE, JEAN DE SOUDIER, SIEUR DE, French rhetorician, self-styled "Moderator of the Academy of Orators." (fl. 1661–1687)
1505.

RICHMOND, DUKE OF, see STUART, JAMES

RICHMOND, CHARLES ALEXANDER, American clergyman and educator. (1862–1940)
2300j.

RICHTER, JOHANN (JEAN) PAUL FRIEDRICH, German novelist. (1763–1825)
35, 236, 424, 452, 548, 677, 724, 784, 865, 1078, 1124, 1138, 1149, 1184, 1329, 1331, 1394, 1570, 1665, 1744, 1784, 1843, 1875, 1974, 2044, 2062, 2076.

RICKER, MARILLA M., American lawyer, humanitarian. (1840–1920)
1110, 1446.

RIDDELL, HENRY SCOTT, Scottish poet. (1798–1870)
1767.

RIDER, WILLIAM, English miscellaneous writer. (1723–1785)
3.

RIEUX, MADAME DE CHATEAUNEUF (RENÉE DE RIEUX), called LA BELLE, a French dame, favorite of the Duc d'Anjou. (1550–1587)
1262.

RIIS, JACOB AUGUST, social reformer, born in Denmark, came to U. S. 1870. (1849–1914)
1119, 2238.

RILEY, JAMES WHITCOMB, American poet. (1849–1916)
116, 168, 448, 494, 636, 674, 779, 879, 906, 938, 1025, 1170, 1207, 1290, 1476, 1578, 1954, 2071, 2128, 2152, 2175.

RIMBAUD, JEAN ARTHUR, French poet. (1854–1891)
2109.

RINEHART, DAISY. No biographical data available.
613.

RIVAROL, ANTOINE, called COMTE DE, French critic, translator and satirical writer. (1753–1801)
427, 2173.

RIVERS, LORD, see WOODVILLE, ANTHONY

RIVES, AMÉLIE, see TROUBETZKOY, AMÉLIE RIVES

ROBBINS, LEONARD, American writer. (1877–1947)
573, 629, 1236.

ROBERT OF GLOUCESTER, English historian. (fl. 1260–1300)
1057.

ROBERT, HUMPHREY, English miscellaneous writer. (fl. 1572)
421.

ROBERTS, CHARLES GEORGE DOUGLAS, Canadian poet and novelist. (1860–1943)
93, 2007.

ROBERTS, HARRY, English writer. (1871–1946)
175.

ROBERTS, RICHARD, English divine and inspirational writer. (1879–1945)
1174.

ROBERTSON, EILEEN ARBUTHNOT [MRS. HENRY ERNEST TURNER], English novelist. (1903–)
580.

ROBERTSON, FREDERICK WILLIAM, English divine and educational writer. (1816–1853)
262.

ROBERTSON, THOMAS WILLIAM, English actor and dramatist. (1829–1871)
1897.

ROBERTSON, WILLIAM, English lexicographer. (d. 1686?)
579

ROBESPIERRE, ISIDORE MAXIMILIEN DE. French Jacobin and revolutionary leader. (1758–1794)
532, 1038, 2094

ROBINSON, AGNES MARY FRANCES [MADAME JAMES DARMESTETER]. English poet born in 1857 and long a resident of Paris, France
1138, 1764, 2062.

ROBINSON, CLEMENT, English song-writer. (fl. 1566–1584)
1699, 2160.

ROBINSON, CORINNE ROOSEVELT [MRS. DOUGLAS ROBINSON], American poet. (1861–1933)
1118.

ROBINSON, EDWIN ARLINGTON, American poet. (1869–1935)
83, 95, 232, 272, 300, 385, 394, 493, 613, 947, 1043, 1160, 1183, 1504, 1516, 1687. 1816, 1824, 2008, 2014, 2181, 2203, 2236, 2246, 2263.

ROBINSON, EDWIN MEADE, American humorous verse-writer. (1878–1946)
1157, 1213, 1412, 1413.

ROBINSON, ELOISE, contemporary American writer.
378.

ROBINSON, JOHN, Speaker of the Virginia House of Burgesses. (fl. 1734)
2122.

ROBINSON, JOSEPH TAYLOR, American politician. (1872–1937)
1619.

ROBINSON, LILLA CAYLEY. No biographical data available.
782.

ROBINSON, VICTOR, American physician and medical historian. (1886–1947)
1957, 2136.

ROBINSON, WILLIAM ALEXANDER, American professor of political science and biographer. (1884–)
66.

ROCHE, SIR BOYLE, Irish baronet and politician. (1743–1807)
995, 1564.

ROCHE, JAMES JEFFREY, Irish-American journalist and verse-writer. (1847–1908)
102, 396, 507, 554, 1085, 1103, 1728, 1839, 2104, 2122.

ROCHEFOUCAULD, see LA ROCHEFOUCAULD

ROCHESTER, EARL OF, see WILMOT, JOHN

ROCKEFELLER, JOHN DAVISON, American capitalist and philanthropist. (1839–1937)
464.

RODGER, ALEXANDER, Scottish minor poet. (1784–1846)
150.

RODMAN, THOMAS P., American minor poet. (fl. 1777)
62, 630.

ROE, or ROWE, SIR THOMAS, English statesman and ambassador. (1581?–1644)
2061.

ROGERS, ALEX, American miscellaneous writer. (1876–)
1415.

ROGERS, DANIEL, English divine. (1573–1652)
126, 442, 1469.

ROGERS, JAMES EDWIN THOROLD, English political economist. (1823–1890)
805, 1092, 1460, 2296.

ROGERS, JOHN, English Protestant preacher and martyr. (1500?–1555)
794.

ROGERS, ROBERT CAMERON, American minor poet. (1862–1912)
1183, 1214.

ROGERS, SAMUEL, English poet. (1763–1855)
16, 26, 28, 132, 153, 162, 192, 212, 239, 252, 403, 424, 525, 576, 608, 634, 766, 775, 905, 1001, 1002, 1083, 1211, 1214, 1242, 1266, 1291, 1292, 1306, 1330, 1340, 1343, 1362, 1512, 1515, 1578, 1679, 1687, 1762, 1781, 1786, 1819, 1874, 1902, 1941, 1972, 1977, 1989, 2062, 2141, 2258, 2266.

ROGERS, WILL, American humorist. (1879–1935)
56, 529, 666, 938, 959, 1058, 1541, 1545, 2099, 2181, 2279, 2293.

ROGERS, WILL B. No biographical data available.
2181.

ROHMER, SAX (pseud. of ARTHUR SARSFIELD WARD), English writer of mystery stories, author of the Fu Manchu tales. (1883–)
1125.

ROLAND, MADAME JEANNE PHILIPON (wife of Jean Marie Roland de la Platière), French sympathizer with Republicans and Girondists during the Revolution, and finally guillotined. (1754–1793)
470, 1104.

ROLLAND, ROMAIN, French essayist, novelist, biographer and polemical writer. (1866–1945)
2023.

ROLLE, RICHARD DE HAMPOLE, English hermit and religious writer. (1290?–1349)
72, 1174.

ROLLESTON, THOMAS WILLIAM, Irish poet. (1857–1920)
997.

ROLLIN, CHARLES, French historian. (1661–1741)
2035.

ROMAINE, HARRY, American poet. (fl. 1895)
335.

ROMANES, GEORGE JOHN, English scientist. (1848–1894)
49.

ROMANI, FELICE, Italian librettist. (fl. 1875)
1214.

RONELL, ANN, American song-writer. (1908–)
2177.

RONSARD, PIERRE DE, French poet. (1524–1585)
2010.

ROONEY, JOHN JEROME, American jurist and verse-writer. (1866–1934)
1863.

ROOSEVELT, FRANKLIN DELANO, thirty-second President of the United States. (1882–1945)
249, 635, 1932, 1967, 2265, 2279, 2281, 2298.

ROOSEVELT, PHILIP JAMES, American broker. (1892–)
1741.

ROOSEVELT, THEODORE, twenty-sixth President of the United States. (1858–1919)
55, 56, 164, 207, 220, 319, 416, 435, 540, 575, 581, 663, 1028, 1064, 1089, 1113, 1119, 1235, 1304, 1382, 1464, 1466, 1471, 1542, 1545, 1598, 1644, 1685, 1717, 1787, 1832, 1864, 2111, 2150, 2169, 2189, 2279, 2280.

ROOT, EDWARD MERRILL, American miscellaneous writer. (1895–)
331.

ROOT, ELIHU, American statesman. (1845–1937)
1554.

ROOT, GEORGE FREDERICK, American song-writer. (1820–1895)
674, *2292*.

ROSCOE, THOMAS, English writer and translator. (1791–1871)
1343.

ROSCOMMON, EARL OF, see DILLON, WENTWORTH

ROSE, ALEXANDER MACGREGOR, Scottish expelled minister, who spent his last years as a journalist in America. (1846–1898)
768.

ROSE, BILLY (real name WILLIAM S. ROSENBERG), American song-writer and theatrical producer. (1901–)
708, 2296.

ROSEBERY, LORD, see PRIMROSE, ARCHIBALD PHILIP

ROSENBERG, CHARLES GEORGE, contemporary American miscellaneous writer.
798.

ROSENFELD, MONROE H., American song-writer. (1862–1918)
649, 1881, *2292*.

ROSS, ALEXANDER, Scottish poet. (1699–1784)
1272.

ROSS, DAVID, and COATES, ARCHIE, American song-writers.
434.

ROSS, WILLIAM STEWART (SALADIN), British secularist. (1844–1906)
1353.

ROSSETTI, CHRISTINA GEORGINA, English poet. (1830–1894)
25, 269, 321, 395, 401, 405, 482, 515, 560, 582, 616, 668, 734, 777, 808, 877, 922, 966, 1146, 1193, 1214, 1220, 1255, 1297, 1349, 1352, 1403, 1406, 1445, 1451, 1559, 1569, 1594, 1684, 1728, 1744, 1771, 1792, 1824, 1833, 1880, 1907, 1949, 1957, 2153, 2166, 2274.

ROSSETTI, DANTE GABRIEL, English painter and poet. (1828–1882)
11, 92, 140, 205, 374, 439, 512, 517, 542, 885, 926, 1059, 1139, 1151, 1294, 1343, 1448, 1659, 1687, 1772, 1781, 1883, 1894, 2098, 2159, 2191.

ROSTAND, EDMOND, French dramatist. (1868–1918)
233, 533, 537, 867, 881, 961, 1046, 1376, 1893, 2058.

ROSTAND, JEAN, French littérateur. (1894–)
841, 1491.

ROTHENSTEIN, WILLIAM, English artist. (1872–1945)
107, 498.

ROTHSCHILD, NATHAN MEYER, Jewish financier and merchant. (1777–1836)
1661.

ROTROU, JEAN DE, French poet and dramatist. (1609–1650)
1403.

ROUGET DE L'ISLE, CLAUDE JOSEPH, French soldier and song-writer. (1760–1836)
719.

ROUS, FRANCIS, English Puritan writer. (1579–1659)
459, 609, 1225, 1582, 1801, 2089.

ROUSSEAU, JEAN-JACQUES, Swiss social and political philosopher. (1712–1778)
6, 130, 132, 172, 184, 251, 277, 299, 362, 416, 559, 638, 649, 745, 814, 855, 873, 926, 951, 1060, 1068, 1090, 1096, 1119, 1314, 1355, 1391, 1462, 1571, 1617, 1691, 1697, 1791, 1995, 2029, 2134, 2194, 2236.

ROUTH, MARTIN JOSEPH, English divine and educator. (1755–1854)
1668.

ROUX, JOSEPH, French priest and epigrammatist. (1834–1886)
533, 563, 584, 593, 596, 608, 633, 638, 640, 727, 741, 745, 797, 809, 917, 925, 937, 947, 1018, 1028, 1032, 1166, 1174, 1178, 1181, 1319, 1320, 1331, 1438, 1439, 1516, 1581, 1629, 1668, 1763, 1787, 1836, 1871, 1873, 1973, 2013, 2228, 2253.

ROWE, NICHOLAS, English poet and dramatist. (1674–1718)
140, 173, 392, 398, 677, 824, 837, 844, 914, 917, 978, 1289, 1374, 1738, 1915, 1946, 2076, 2105, 2106, 2141, 2149, 2195, 2201, 2215.

ROWLAND, EDWARD C. H., English song-writer and theatre manager. (1883–1955)
2292.

ROWLAND, HELEN, American miscellaneous writer. (1876–) 1262.

ROWLANDS, RICHARD (alias VERSTEGEN), English antiquary. (fl. 1565–1620)
779, 1854.

ROWLANDS, SAMUEL, English writer of tracts in prose and verse. (1570–1625)
370, 509, 813, 1281, 1513, 1637, 2057.

ROWLEY, RICHARD, contemporary American writer.
1534.

ROWLEY, SAMUEL, English dramatist. (d. 1633)
636, 863.

ROWLEY, WILLIAM, English dramatist. (1585?–1642?)
69, 479, 827, 1225, 1886, 2244.

ROY, PIERRE CHARLES, French satirist and dramatic poet. (1683–1764)
950.

ROYDON, MATTHEW, English poet. (fl. 1580–1622)
608, 1485.

ROYER-COLLARD, PIERRE PAUL, French philosopher and statesman. (1763–1845)
1691.

RUBINSTEIN, ANTON GREGOR, Russian-Jewish pianist and composer. (1829–1894)
561.

RUFUS, M. CŒLIUS, Roman orator. (86–48 B.C.)
1709.

RUHL, ARTHUR BROWN, American miscellaneous writer. (1876–)
978.

RULHIÈRE, CLAUDE CARLOMAN DE, French epigrammatist and anecdotist. (1735–1791)
290, 1294.

RUMBOLD, RICHARD, English soldier and conspirator. (1622?–1685)
1067.

RUNKLE, BERTHA [MRS. LOUIS H. BASH], contemporary American novelist.
2071.

RUSKIN, JOHN, English critic, artist and social reformer. (1819–1900)
95, 102, 107, 182, 188, 232, 278, 294, 348, 362, 472, 491, 507, 537, 548, 570, 584, 662, 669, 690, 702, 762, 763, 779, 826, 833, 961, 1067, 1100, 1103, 1239, 1309, 1346, 1354, 1380, 1425, 1447, 1449, 1453, 1462, 1470, 1481, 1577, 1605, 1610, 1622, 1668, 1674, 1689, 1717, 1731, 1771, 1820, 1835, 1840, 1983, 2012, 2058, 2060, 2076, 2100, 2182, 2206, 2231.

RUSSELL, BENJAMIN, American journalist and politician. (1761–1845)
63, 2280.

RUSSELL, BERTRAND ARTHUR WILLIAM, English philosopher and mathematician. (1872–)
56, 152, 266, 433, 475, 527, 529, 534, 646, 854, 893, 1100, 1116, 1174, 1216, 1229, 1270, 1473, 1685, 1787, 1827, 1861, 1993, 2043.

RUSSELL, DORA WINIFRED BLACK, contemporary English writer on sociological subjects.
164, 857, 1225, 1429, 1859, 2094.

RUSSELL, GEORGE WILLIAM (A. E.), Irish poet and artist. (1867–1935)
131, 997, 1445, 1685, 1829, 2062, 2152.

RUSSELL, GEORGE WILLIAM ERSKINE, English statesman and miscellaneous writer. (1853–1919)
929.

RUSSELL, IRWIN, American journalist and minor poet. (1853–1879)
1679.

RUSSELL, JAMES S., American song-writer.
2292.

RUSSELL, JOHN, English writer. (fl. 1450)
1326, 1848.

RUSSELL, LORD JOHN, first EARL RUSSELL, English historian, orator and statesman. (1792–1878)
2, 431, 1472, 1629.

RUSSELL, SIR WILLIAM HOWARD, English war correspondent. (1820–1907)
1863.

RUTHERFORD, SAMUEL, Scottish divine. (1600–1661)
1085.

RUTLAND, DUKE OF, see MANNERS, LORD JOHN

RUTLEDGE, JOHN T., American song-writer.
2291.

RYALL, WILLIAM BOLITHO, see BOLITHO, WILLIAM

RYAN, ABRAM JOSEPH, American Roman Catholic priest and poet. (1839–1888)
1522, 1975.

RYDER, ARTHUR WILLIAM, American educator, translator and poet. (1877–1938)
318, 2195.

RYSWICK, or RYSWYK, JAN VAN, Dutch poet. (fl. 1840)
1818.

S

SABATINI, RAFAEL, Italian-English novelist and dramatist. (1875–1950)
1076.

SABIN, EDWIN LEGRAND, American verse and juvenile writer. (1870–)
2044.

SABIN, PAULINE MORTON [MRS. CHARLES SABIN], American club woman and political leader. (1887–)
1619.

SACKVILLE, CHARLES, sixth EARL OF DORSET, English courtier and poet. (1637–1706)
2171, 2253.

SACKVILLE, [LADY] MARGARET, Scottish poet. (1881–)
2060.

SACKVILLE, THOMAS, first EARL OF DORSET and BARON BUCKHURST, English statesman and poet. (1536–1608) 219, 1570, 1849.

SADI (Nom de plume of SHAIKH-'A-DIN), Persian Mohammedan poet, author of the *Gulistan*. (fl. c. 1200)
99, 155, 306, 657, 734, 862, 945, 1019, 1057, 1165, 1462, 1487, 1744, 1779, 1824, 1838, 2030, 2081, 2142, 2177.

SAINTE-BEUVE, CHARLES AUGUSTIN, French critic and poet. (1804–1869)
43, 338, 474, 2055, 2225.

SAINT-ÉVREMOND, CHARLES DE MARGUETEL DE SAINT-DENIS DE, French courtier, wit and littérateur. (1610–1703)
559.

ST. JOHN, HENRY, first VISCOUNT BOLINGBROKE, English statesman, orator and political writer. (1678–1751)
114, 578, 899, 900, 1144, 1379, 1390, 1677, 2055, 2103, 2245.

SAINT-JUST, ANTOINE LOUIS LÉON FLORELLE DE, French revolutionary leader. (1767–1794)
1042, 1787.

SAINT-SIMON, LOUIS DE ROUVROY, DUC DE, French courtier, diplomat and writer of memoirs. (1675–1755)
44, 1478.

SAINTINE, XAVIER (pseud. of JOSEPH FRANÇOIS BONIFACE), French miscellaneous writer. (1798–1865)
229.

SAINTSBURY, GEORGE EDWARD BATEMAN, English educator, literary critic and connoisseur. (1845–1933)
496, 497, 1196, 1429, 2022, 2155, 2277.

SAKI, see MUNRO, H. H.

SALA, GEORGE AUGUSTUS HENRY, English journalist and novelist. (1828–1896)
570, 2101.

SALE, GEORGE, English Orientalist, translator of the *Koran*. (1680–1736)
1879.

SALIS-SEEWIS, BARON JOHANN GAUDENZ VON, Swiss lyric poet. (1762–1834)
394, 924, 1120.

SALISBURY, MARQUESS OF, see CECIL, ROBERT ARTHUR TALBOT GASCOYNE

SALLE, JACQUES ANTOINE DE, French jurist. (1712–1778)
1174.

SALLUST, CAIUS SALLUSTIUS CRISPUS, Roman historian. (86–34 B.C.)
8, 70, 81, 119, 155, 177, 214, 239, 325, 361, 419, 537, 622, 629, 656, 714, 730, 741, 846, 861, 903, 918, 954, 1021, 1042, 1106, 1123, 1129, 1134, 1141, 1314, 1393, 1464, 1543, 1575, 1611, 1620, 1737, 1831, 1929, 1962, 2033, 2073, 2091, 2092, 2106, 2107, 2108, 2118, 2119, 2194, 2225, 2248.

SALVANDY, M. LE COMTE DE, French statesman. (1795–1856)
360.

SAMS, G. E. No biographical data available.
778.

SAND, GEORGE (pseud. of ARMANDINE LUCILE DUPIN, BARONNE DUDEVANT), French novelist. (1804–1876)
140, 416, 855, 1307, 1383, 1651.

SANDBURG, CARL, American poet. (1878–)
67, 84, 176, 188, 206, 251, 401, 613, 694, 822, 1078, 1094, 1160, 1220, 1458, 1516, 1772, 2023, 2071, 2226.

SANDFORD, JOHN, English poet and grammarian. (1560?–1629)
1998.

SANDYS, SIR EDWIN, English statesman. (1561–1629)
913.

SANDYS, GEORGE, English poet. (1578–1644)
1591.

SANGSTER, [MRS.] MARGARET ELIZABETH, American minor poet and writer for children. (1838–1912)
392, 1353, 1908, 2132.

SANNAZZARO, JACOPO, Italian poet. (1458–1530)
213, 584, 1991, 2194, 2198.

SANTAYANA, GEORGE, born in Spain; brought to America at age of nine; educated at Harvard University and teacher of philosophy there for many years; later a resident of England; finally living at Rome, Italy. A philosophical writer and essayist. (1863–1952)
25, 26, 103, 107, 129, 152, 165, 199, 278, 284, 338, 348, 395, 407, 448, 507, 534, 584, 618, 633, 665, 698, 759, 806, 855, 888, 951, 968, 975, 1059, 1078, 1116, 1121, 1129, 1166, 1201, 1233, 1264, 1308, 1362, 1418, 1458, 1477, 1489, 1514, 1535, 1607, 1629, 1721, 1736, 1755, 1789, 1859, 1891, 2049, 2064, 2068, 2074, 2168, 2238, 2241, 2263.

SANTEUL, JEAN DE, French priest and writer of Latin hymns. (1630–1697)
1079, 1370.

SAPPHO, Greek lyric poet. (fl. 610 B.C.)
92, 132, 985, 1211, 1406, 1916.

SARETT, LEW, American poet. (1888–1954)
376, 378, 1942

SARGENT, EPES, American journalist and minor poet. (1813–1880)
1402, 1466, 1777.

SARPI, PIETRO (FRA PAOLO), Italian scholar and theologian. (1552–1623)
2077.

SASSOON, SIEGFRIED, English poet. (1886–)
1870.

SAUNDERS, FREDERICK, American librarian and essayist. (1807–1902)
234, 2220.

SAUNDERS, JOHN, English novelist and minor poet. (1810–1895)
602.

SAURIN, BERNARD JOSEPH, French dramatist. (1706–1781)
934, 1402.

SAURIN, WILLIAM, English politician. (1757?–1839)
1082.

SAVAGE, RICHARD, English poet and "volunteer laureate." (1698–1743)
72, 80, 464, 625, 836, 1089, 1154, 1294, 1548, 1622, 2192, 2203, 2204, 2247.

* SAVILE, SIR GEORGE, MARQUIS OF HALIFAX, English political pamphleteer and statesman. (1633–1695)

SAXE, JOHN GODFREY, American humorous poet, journalist and lecturer. (1816–1887)
9, 35, 131, 192, 220, 291, 422, 449, 525, 535, 696, 848, 1049, 1051, 1109, 1138, 1264, 1268, 1272, 1372, 1572, 1730, 1844, 1928, 1984, 1989, 2204.

SAYERS, HENRY J., American song-writer.
2292.

SCARBOROUGH, G. L. No biographical data available.
308.

SCARRON, PAUL, French burlesque dramatist and novelist. (1610–1660)
417, 457, 570.

SCHAUFFLER, ROBERT HAVEN, American poet, biographer and compiler. (1879–)
707, 797, 1116.

SCHEFFLER, JOHANN (ANGELUS SILESIUS), German poet. (1624–1677)
382.

SCHELLING, FELIX EMANUEL, American educator. (1858–1945)
527.

SCHELLING, FRIEDRICH WILHELM JOSEPH VON, German philosopher. (1775–1854)
95.

SCHIDONI, BARTOLOMEO, Italian painter. (1560–1615)
94.

* SCHILLER, JOHANN CHRISTOPH FRIEDRICH VON, German poet and dramatist. (1759–1805)

SCHLEGEL, AUGUST WILHELM VON, German poet, Orientalist and critic. (1767–1845)
903.

SCHLEIERMACHER, FRIEDRICH ERNST DANIEL, German scholar, critic and orator. (1768–1834)
1821.

SCHNECKENBURGER, MAX, German song-writer. (1819–1849)
767, 1716.

SCHNEIDER, GEORGE J., American Congressman 1923–33. (1877–1939)
1618.

SCHOONMAKER, BLANCHE W., contemporary American poet.
1162.

SCHOPENHAUER, ARTHUR, German pessimist philosopher. (1788–1860)
247, 328, 422, 624, 759, 969, 1335, 1341, 1667, 2010, 2194, 2238.

SCHOULER, JAMES, American lawyer and historian. (1839–1920)
620.

SCHREINER, OLIVE EMILIE ALBERTINA, South African novelist. (1855–1920)
107.

SCHUMACHER, B. G., German song-writer.
767.

SCHUPPIUS, or SCHUPPE, JOHANN BALTHASAR, German scholar and satirist. (1610–1661)
1896.

SCHURZ, CARL, German orator and general who emigrated to the United States in 1852, served with distinction in the Civil War and was afterwards U. S. Senator from Missouri. (1829–1906)
63.

SCHWAB, CHARLES M., American capitalist and steel manufacturer. (1862–1939)
1489, 2233.

SCHWARZERD, PHILIP, see MELANCHTHON

SCHWENDI, LAZARUS VON, German statesman and general. (1522–1584)
2114.

SCIPIO AFRICANUS MAJOR, PUBLIUS CORNELIUS, Roman general and consul. (237?–183? B.C.)
545, 698, 1874.

SCOLLARD, CLINTON, American poet. (1860–1932)
93, 481, 484, 1001, 1005, 1193, 1214, 1283, 1514, 1908, 2122, 2153.

SCOPAS, Greek sculptor and architect. (395–350 B.C.)
1228.

SCOT, or SCOTT, SIR JOHN, Scottish lawyer and patron of letters. (1585–1670)
254.

SCOTT, ALEXANDER, Scottish minor poet. (1525?–1584?)
2195.

SCOTT, CLEMENT WILLIAM, English journalist and dramatic critic. (1841–1904)
2293.

SCOTT, DUNCAN CAMPBELL, Canadian poet. (1862–1947)
2261.

SCOTT, G. FORRESTER, see HALSHAM, JOHN

SCOTT, HUGH STOWELL, see MERRIMAN, HENRY SETON

SCOTT, JOHN, first EARL OF ELDON, English scholar and jurist. (1751–1838)
92, 862.

SCOTT, JOHN, English Quaker poet. (1730–1783)
2113.

SCOTT, JOSEPH S., American lawyer. (1867–)
1558.

SCOTT, MARTIN J., American clergyman and devotional writer. (1865–1954)
267.

SCOTT, or SCOT, REGINALD, or REYNOLD, English writer on witchcraft. (1538?–1599)
480.

SCOTT, THOMAS, English poet and political writer. (1580?–1626)
702.

SCOTT, THOMAS, English divine and hymnwriter. (1705–1775)
515.

* SCOTT, SIR WALTER, Scottish novelist and poet. (1771–1832)

SCOTT, WILLIAM, BARON STOWELL, English maritime and international lawyer and scholar. (1745–1836)
451, 464, 1087.

SCOTT, WINFIELD, American general. (1786–1866)
65.

SCRIBE, AUGUSTIN EUGÈNE, French comic dramatist. (1791–1861)
1863.

SCRIBE, AUGUSTIN EUGÈNE, and DELAVIGNE, JEAN FRANÇOIS CASIMIR, French dramatists and collaborators. (1791–1861), (1793–1843)
803.

SCROPE, or SCROOP, SIR CARR, first BARONET, English versifier and man of fashion. (1649–1680)
1478.

SCRUGGS, ANDERSON M., American poet and educator. (1897–)
481.

SCUDDER, HORACE ELISHA, American editor, littérateur and miscellaneous writer. (1838–1902)
689.

SCUDÉRY, MADELEINE DE, French novelist. (1607–1701)
2084.

SEAMAN, SIR OWEN, English editor and writer of light verse. (1861–1936)
105, 224, 694, 1110, 1567, 1653, 2047, 2147.

SEAMON, CHARLES, American song-writer.
2293.

SEARS, EDMUND HAMILTON, American minor poet. (1810–1876)
269, 1473.

SEBASTIANI, HORACE FRANÇOIS DE LA PORTA, COUNT, Corsican general and diplomat. (1772–1851)
1441.

SECUNDUS, CAIUS PLINIUS, see PLINY

SEDAINE, MICHEL JEAN, French popular dramatist and poet. (1719–1797)
1038.

SEDGWICK, ANNE DOUGLAS [MRS. BASIL DE SELINCOURT], American novelist, resident in England. (1873–1935)
1055.

SEDLEY, SIR CHARLES, English wit and dramatist. (1639?–1701)
376, 456, 717, 749, 870, 968, 1019, 1199, 1201, 1205, 2115.

SEDULIUS, CÆLIUS, Latin poet and Biblical commentator. (fl. c. 480)
1315.
SEEGER, ALAN, American poet. (1888–1916)
131, 381, 397, 1017, 1143.
SEELEY, SIR JOHN ROBERT, English historian and essayist. (1834–1895)
96.
SEGAR, or SEAGER, FRANCIS, English translator and poet. (fl. 1549–1563)
959, 1326.
SEIBERT, T. LAURENCE, American song-writer.
2293.
SEIFFERT, MARJORIE ALLEN [MRS. OTTO S.], contemporary American poet.
1225.
SEITZ, DON CARLOS, American journalist and biographer. (1862–1935)
1661.
SELDEN, EDGAR, American song-writer.
2293.
SELDEN, JOHN, English jurist and juridical writer. (1584–1654)
123, 159, 256, 442, 462, 502, 543, 615, 677, 693, 738, 764, 816, 818, 937, 957, 1043, 1044, 1058, 1082, 1088, 1090, 1096, 1262, 1264, 1279, 1335, 1440, 1478, 1497, 1542, 1575, 1595, 1596, 1694, 1705, 1822, 2010, 2142, 2171, 2180, 2220.
SELVAGGI, Italian poet. (fl. 1650)
1305.
SELWYN, GEORGE AUGUSTUS, English prelate, Bishop of Lichfield. (1809–1878)
1080.
SEMPILL, FRANCIS, Scottish ballad-writer. (1616?-1682)
738.
SÉNANCOURT, ÉTIENNE PIVERT DE, French novelist, author of *Obermann*. (1770–1846)
579, 1386.
* SENECA, LUCIUS ANNÆUS, Roman Stoic philosopher, moralist and dramatist. (c. A.D. 5–65)
SENECA, MARCUS ANNÆUS, Latin rhetorician, father of Lucius Annæus. (c. 54 B.C.–A.D. 39)
298.
SERTORIUS, QUINTUS, Roman military commander. (121?–72 B.C.)
1488.
SERVICE, ROBERT WILLIAM, Canadian poet and novelist. (1874–)
398, 587, 613, 790, 1125, 1138, 1353, 1707, 1854, 1942, 2103.
SETOUN, GABRIEL [THOMAS NICOLL HEPBURN], Scottish poet. (1861–1930)
2241.
SEVERUS, LUCIUS SEPTIMIUS, Roman Emperor. (146–211)
12, 417.
SÉVIGNÉ, MARIE DE RABUTIN-CHANTAL, MARQUISE DE, French letter-writer. (1626–1696)
364, 1166, 2114, 2171.
SEWALL, [MRS.] HARRIET WINSLOW, American writer of religious verse. (1819–1889)
109.
SEWALL, JONATHAN MITCHELL, American lawyer and verse-writer. (1748–1808)
1575.
SEWARD, ANNA, English poet and letter-writer. The "Swan of Lichfield." (1747–1809)
1015.
SEWARD, THOMAS, English divine. (1708–1790)
911.
SEWARD, WILLIAM HENRY, American statesman and miscellaneous writer. (1801–1872)
307, 434, 1714, 1842.
SEWELL, WILLIAM, English divine and miscellaneous writer. (1804–1874)
1022, 1827.
SEYMOUR, WILLIAM KEAN, English poet. (1887–)
1406.
SHACKLOCK, RICHARD, English Roman Catholic divine and theological writer. (fl. 1575)
179, 326.
SHADWELL, CHARLES, English dramatist. (fl. 1710–1720)
1650, 1792.
SHADWELL, THOMAS, English dramatist and poet. (1642?–1692)
160, 249, 302, 516, 824, 862, 919, 1179, 1276, 1287, 1333, 1770, 1819, 1960, 2218.
SHAFTESBURY, LORD, see COOPER, ANTHONY ASHLEY
SHAIRP, JOHN CAMPBELL, English poet and essayist; professor of poetry at Oxford. (1819–1885)
129.
SHAIRP, MORDAUNT. No biographical data available.
107.
* SHAKESPEARE, WILLIAM, English poet and dramatist. (1564–1616)
SHAMS-ED-DINMUHAMMAD, see HAFIZ
SHANE, ELIZABETH, contemporary Irish poet.
730.
SHANKS, EDWARD, English poet. (1892–1953)
613.
SHARP, WILLIAM (FIONA MACLEOD), English poet and romanticist. (1855–1905)
435, 482, 1137, 1173, 1475, 1845, 2001, 2153, 2192, 2261.
SHARPE, R. L., American writer. (fl. 1890)
1127.
SHARPHAM, EDWARD, English dramatist. (fl. 1607)
697, 2182.
SHAW, FRANCES WILLS, American poet and dramatist. (1872–1937)
908.
SHAW, GEORGE BERNARD, British dramatist, novelist, critic and publicist. (1856–1950)
34, 60, 76, 87, 92, 107, 108, 136, 140, 152, 209, 235, 248, 251, 256, 271, 272, 274, 278, 341, 377, 383, 392, 412, 422, 434, 435, 452, 471, 493, 518, 527, 531, 542, 547, 556, 557, 561, 585, 594, 613, 656, 677, 696, 754, 756, 763, 786, 804, 810, 817, 825, 835, 855, 857, 860, 865, 871, 891, 896, 903, 905, 913, 930, 943, 946, 951, 952, 956, 957, 969, 991, 994,

SIEYÈS, EMMANUEL JOSEPH, COUNT, French politician and publicist. (1748–1836)
296, 376, 718, 721, 724, 1379.

SIGISMUND, King of Hungary and Emperor of Germany. (1368–1437)
820.

SIGOURNEY, LYDIA HUNTLEY, American poet. (1791–1865)
284, 846, 977, 1353, 1789.

SILIUS ITALICUS, TITUS CATIUS, Latin poet and imitator of Vergil. (25–101)
429, 956, 2007, 2073, 2091.

SILL, EDWARD ROWLAND, American poet. (1841–1887)
292, 387, 395, 492, 613, 696, 700, 1138, 1595.

SILLERY, CHARLES DOYNE, Irish poet. (1807–1837)
400.

SILVER, ABBA HILLEL, Jewish rabbi, born in Lithuania, resident of U. S. (1893–)
407.

SILVER, FRANK (1892–1960) and COHN, IRVING (1898–1961), American song-writers.
2293.

SIMEONIS, SYMON, Irish Franciscan and traveller. (fl. 1322)
959.

SIMMS, WILLIAM GILMORE, American novelist and poet. (1806–1870)
1261.

SIMONIDES OF CEOS, Greek lyric poet. (556–468 B.C.)
377, 397, 398, 570, 1447, 2141, 2183.

SIMS, GEORGE ROBERT, English journalist and dramatist. (1847–1922)
71, 1168, 2188, 2245.

SINGLETON, MARY MONTGOMERIE, BARONESS CURRIE (VIOLET FANE), English poet. (1843–1905)
756, 1074, 1218, 1491.

SIRMOND, JEAN, French poet. (1589?–1649)
496.

SIWARD, EARL OF NORTHUMBERLAND, probably came to England with Canute. (d. 1055)
417.

SIXTUS V (FELIX PERETTI), Roman Pope. (1521–1590)
1741.

SKELTON, JOHN, English poet. (1460?–1529)
160, 170, 190, 256, 442, 471, 813, 1004, 1056, 1357, 1470, 1518, 1608, 1631, 1635, 1671, 1688, 1751, 1992, 2005, 2009, 2027, 2144, 2177, 2237, 2239, 2262.

SLATER, W. M. No biographical data available.
968.

SLICK, SAM (pseud. of THOMAS CHANDLER HALIBURTON), Nova Scotian jurist and humorist. (1796–1865)
1228, 1451, 1859, 2191, 2213.

SMART, CHRISTOPHER, English poet. (1722–1771)
784, 1564, 1664.

SMEDLEY, FRANCIS EDWARD, English novelist. (1818–1864)
1176, 1633.

SMILES, SAMUEL, English homiletical writer and social reformer. (1812–1904)
74, 159, 209, 235, 267, 328, 443, 505, 520, 713, 925, 999, 1090, 1100, 1262, 1504, 1792, 1932, 1952, 1985, 1997, 1998, 2039, 2148, 2226.

SMITH, ADAM, English political economist. (1723–1790)
286, 548, 1241, 1335, 1764, 1860.

SMITH, ALEXANDER, Scottish poet, author of *Dreamthorp*. (1830–1867)
93, 122, 180, 187, 235, 292, 358, 363, 374, 376, 383, 582, 620, 624, 709, 777, 838, 857, 1108, 1124, 1208, 1280, 1290, 1293, 1447, 1459, 1502, 1509, 1519, 1521, 1785, 1890, 1891, 1915, 1926, 2008, 2020, 2037, 2040, 2042, 2071, 2242, 2256, 2275, 2297.

SMITH, ALFRED EMANUEL, American politician, Governor of New York State. (1873–1944)
56, 59, 1644, 2281, 2298o.

SMITH, ARABELLA EUGENIA, American verse-writer. (1844–1916)
609, 1578.

SMITH, CHARLOTTE, English poet and novelist. (1749–1806)
1283, 1949.

SMITH, EDGAR, American playwright and librettist. (1857–1938)
778.

SMITH, EDMUND, English poet. (1672–1710)
1362.

SMITH, EDWARD, English compiler. (fl. 1727)
316.

SMITH, EDWARD CONRAD, American professor of political science. (1891–)
2280.

SMITH, ELIZABETH OAKES, American miscellaneous writer. (1806–1893)
613, 616.

SMITH, GEOFFREY. No biographical data available.
270.

SMITH, HARRY B., American librettist and song-writer. (1860–1936)
2293.

SMITH, HENRY. No biographical data available.
1993.

SMITH, HORATIO (HORACE), English verse-writer and parodist. (1779–1849)
11, 20, 30, 83, 105, 243, 267, 305, 374, 526, 686, 715, 1156, 1340, 1593, 1724, 1845, 1940.

SMITH, HORACE and JAMES, English parodists and collaborators. (1779–1849), (1775–1839)
92, 241, 350, 362, 420, 819, 835, 931, 996, 1039, 1046, 1303, 1348, 1369, 1527, 1623, 1624, 1996, 2008, 2095.

SMITH, CAPTAIN JOHN, English adventurer, President of Virginia Colony. (1579–1631)
539, 1896.

SMITH, JOHN, English Platonist and educator. (1618–1652)
6.

SMITH, LANGDON, American journalist and versifier. (1858–1908)
586.

SMITH, [MRS.] LANTA WILSON. American writer. (1856–)
1704.
SMITH, LESLIE. No biographical data available.
1160.
SMITH, LOGAN PEARSALL, American littérateur, living in England. (1865–1946)
25, 31, 368, 587, 641, 855, 1062, 1129, 1225, 1237, 1264, 1308, 1663, 1676, 1685, 1723, 1760, 1862, 1884, 1889, 1895.
SMITH, [MRS.] MARY LOUISE RILEY, American verse-writer. (1842–1927)
312, 1139, 1436.
SMITH, NATHANIEL, English Quaker. (fl. 1669)
2137.
SMITH, SAMUEL FRANCIS, American Baptist clergyman and poet, author of *America*. (1808–1895)
52.
SMITH, SEBA, American journalist. (1792–1868)
1353.
SMITH, SYDNEY, English clergyman, wit and essayist. (1771–1845)
1, 5, 13, 18, 45, 47, 54, 61, 82, 181, 289, 294, 297, 304, 314, 316, 319, 321, 322, 335, 448, 451, 489, 513, 524, 550, 558, 581, 620, 637, 671, 742, 743, 748, 749, 782, 856, 858, 905, 931, 955, 960, 996, 999, 1028, 1029, 1057, 1079, 1087, 1119, 1229, 1294, 1308, 1314, 1366, 1399, 1420, 1565, 1576, 1577, 1589, 1593, 1654, 1684, 1691, 1764, 1767, 1768, 1769, 1802, 1810, 1855, 1859, 1866, 1898, 1918, 1924, 1926, 1937, 1951, 1968, 1996, 2030, 2128, 2129, 2138, 2171, 2254, 2255, 2281.
SMITH, WALTER CHALMERS, English poet and preacher. (1824–1908)
751, 900, 1898, 2001, 2204.
SMITH, WILLIAM HENRY, Scottish philosopher and poet. (1808–1872)
710, 743, 1068.
SMOLLETT, TOBIAS GEORGE, English novelist. (1721–1771)
50, 94, 169, 282, 375, 382, 419, 448, 455, 543, 572, 607, 611, 632, 974, 976, 1015, 1096, 1105, 1178, 1179, 1186, 1189, 1224, 1227, 1231, 1353, 1463, 1492, 1570, 1571, 1633, 1652, 1659, 1694, 1705, 1733, 1768, 1778, 1779, 1859, 1860, 1932, 1987, 2110, 2166, 2171, 2238, 2260.
SMUTS, JAN CHRISTIAAN, Dutch statesman and general in the Boer War. (1870–1950)
1436, 2150, 2151.
SMYTH, WILLIAM, English educator, lecturer and poet. (1765–1849)
1501, 1764.
SNELL, BERTRAND H., American politician and member of Congress. (1870–1958)
59.
SNYDER, TED, American song-writer. (1881–)
1279.
SOBIESKI, JOHN, King of Poland (JOHN III). (1624–1696)
298.
SOCRATES, Greek philosopher. (469–399 B.C.)
11, 99, 137, 261, 276, 309, 320, 417, 516, 624, 731, 780, 807, 913, 940, 1060, 1100, 1175, 1267, 1328, 1427, 1623, 1663, 1896, 1950, 1994, 2031, 2053, 2104, 2208.
SOLON, Athenian legislator. (c. 638–559 B.C.)
20, 29, 39, 236, 275, 288, 405, 411, 440, 504, 574, 627, 728, 729, 1030, 1085, 1098, 1110, 1228, 1231, 1267, 1319, 1326, 1420, 1452, 1513, 1544, 1573, 1662, 1679, 1723, 1774, 1784, 1897, 2065.
SOMERVILLE, JAMES. No biographical data available.
1748.
SOMERVILLE, WILLIAM, English poet. (1675–1742)
14, 368, 550, 603, 622, 731, 942, 1044, 1249, 1332, 1496, 1591, 1998, 2005, 2137.
SOPHOCLES, Greek tragic poet and dramatist. (495–406 B.C.)
30, 32, 38, 87, 229, 327, 406, 411, 423, 461, 511, 577, 580, 717, 731, 751, 753, 777, 787, 816, 842, 921, 960, 1032, 1036, 1109, 1190, 1205, 1232, 1243, 1321, 1335, 1353, 1392, 1406, 1418, 1430, 1452, 1459, 1483, 1624, 1625, 1629, 1639, 1678, 1804, 1845, 1867, 1899, 1931, 1973, 1992, 2003, 2005, 2024, 2053, 2057, 2065, 2120, 2127, 2168, 2176, 2177, 2210, 2229.
SORLEY, CHARLES HAMILTON, Scottish verse-writer. (1895–1915)
2040, 2119.
SOULE, JOHN L. B., American editor. (fl. 1851)
2131.
SOUTH, ROBERT, English divine. (1634–1716)
515, 840, 1112, 1902, 1982.
SOUTHERNE, THOMAS, Irish dramatist. (1660–1746)
47, 385, 394, 711, 728, 918, 929, 990, 1180, 1222, 1271, 1284, 1612, 1867, 2016.
SOUTHEY, MRS. CAROLINE ANNE [BOWLES], English poetaster. Wife of Robert Southey. (1786–1854)
1651.
* SOUTHEY, ROBERT, English poet and man of letters (1774–1843)
SOUTHWELL, ROBERT, English Jesuit and devotional poet. (1561?–1595)
229, 232, 836, 1202, 1307, 1311, 1380, 1432, 1433, 1849, 2001, 2036, 2229.
SOZOMEN (SOZOMENOS HERMIAS), Greek ecclesiastical historian. (fl. 440)
669.
SPAETH, SIGMUND, American musician and writer on musical subjects. (1885–)
1881.
SPALDING, [MRS.] SUSAN MARR, American verse-writer. (1841–1908)
643, 1187.
SPEARE, DOROTHY [MRS. CHARLES J. HUBBARD], American miscellaneous writer. (1898–)
610.
SPELMAN, WILLIAM, English traveler and antiquary. (fl 1595)
167, 1958.
SPENCER, HERBERT, English philosophical writer. (1820–1903)
81, 114, 132, 137, 202, 278, 304, 307, 433,

527, 587, 696, 755, 759, 804, 811, 812, 816, 855, 873, 897, 951, 959, 1031, 1044, 1059, 1117, 1236, 1303, 1310, 1346, 1380, 1387, 1426, 1501, 1540, 1542, 1597, 1617, 1672, 1684, 1726, 1759, 1859.

SPENCER, WILLIAM ROBERT, English poet and wit. (1769–1834)
633, 2007, 2189.

SPENDER, J. ALFRED, English journalist. (1862–1942)
703, 1060, 2166.

* SPENSER, EDMUND, English poet. (1552?–1599)

SPEYER, LEONORA [MRS. EDGAR SPEYER], American poet. (1872–)
110, 1154.

SPILGER, FLORENCE B. No biographical data available.
117.

SPINGARN, JOEL ELIAS, American poet and critic. (1875–1939)
1559, 1802.

SPINOZA, BENEDICT (BARUCH) DE, Dutch-Jewish pantheistical philosopher. (1632–1677)
1252, 1795.

SPOFFORD, HARRIET PRESCOTT, American novelist and verse-writer. (1835–1921)
93, 122, 137, 482, 821, 1567, 1744, 1747.

SPOONER, WILLIAM A., English educator, Warden of New College, Oxford, 1879.
1039.

SPRAGUE, CHARLES, American banker and verse-writer. (1791–1875)
107, 162, 464, 1105, 1602, 1760, 1807, 1911, 2019.

SPRAT, THOMAS, English divine and miscellaneous writer. (1635–1713)
624, 1515.

SPRING-RICE, CECIL ARTHUR, English diplomatist. (1859–1918)
2277.

SPROAT, NANCY DENNIS, American writer of verse for children. (1766–1826)
255.

SPURGEON, CHARLES HADDON, English Baptist minister and pulpit orator. (1834–1892)
17, 84, 85, 86, 111, 151, 155, 193, 197, 204, 206, 256, 261, 267, 330, 458, 500, 613, 652, 677, 718, 737, 753, 790, 812, 871, 904, 908, 928, 930, 937, 939, 953, 958, 959, 993, 1019, 1056, 1073, 1091, 1110, 1273, 1302, 1336, 1358, 1445, 1457, 1470, 1488, 1492, 1585, 1589, 1600, 1620, 1621, 1638, 1650, 1686, 1811, 1817, 1854, 1884, 1947, 1959, 1985, 2042, 2060, 2085, 2126, 2152, 2183.

SQUIRE, [SIR] JOHN COLLINGS, English journalist and critic. (1884–)
162, 556, 1452, 1524, 1619, 2170.

STAËL, MADAME ANNE LOUISE GERMAINE DE, French novelist and woman of letters. (1766–1817)
95, 218, 527, 707, 710, 758, 759, 760, 856, 1175, 1184, 1253, 1307, 1321, 1362, 1464, 1517, 1536, 1583, 1659, 1691, 1773, 1945, 2004, 2052, 2171, 2193.

STAFFORD, ANTHONY, English devotional writer. (1587–1645?)
888.

STAFFORD, WENDELL PHILLIPS, American jurist. (1861–)
1162.

STALLINGS, LAURENCE, see ANDERSON, MAXWELL

STAMFORD, JOHN, American song-writer.
2293.

STANBRIDGE, JOHN, English grammarian. (1463–1510)
315, 773, 1371, 1413, 2170.

STANDISH, JOSEPH W., American song-writer.
1852.

STANHOPE, PHILIP DORMER, fourth EARL OF CHESTERFIELD, see CHESTERFIELD

STANISLAUS LESZCZYNSKI, King of Poland. (1677–1766)
429, 447, 475, 1691, 1764, 2174.

STANLEY, MRS. A. J. No biographical data available.
1928.

STANLEY, EDWARD GEORGE GEOFFREY SMITH, fourteenth EARL OF DERBY, English statesman. (1799–1869)
1554.

STANLEY, EDWARD JOHN, second BARON STANLEY OF ALDERLEY and first BARON EDDISBURY OF WINNINGTON, English statesman. (1802–1869)
1544.

STANLEY, SIR HENRY MORTON, English explorer, administrator and journalist. (1841–1904)
2283.

STANLEY, THOMAS, English scholar and writer. (1625–1678)
1037, 1594.

STANTON, COLONEL C. E., American soldier. (1859–1933)
67.

STANTON, EDWIN MCMASTERS, American lawyer and statesman; Secretary of War. (1814–1869)
1160.

STANTON, FRANK LEBBY, American editor and verse-writer. (1857–1927)
4, 122, 674, 890, 1488, 1744, 1745.

STANYHURST, RICHARD, English historian and translator. (1547–1618)
2219.

STARBUCK, VICTOR, American poet. (1887–1938)
909.

STARK, JOHN, American Revolutionary general. (1728–1822)
61, 62.

STARKEY, THOMAS, English divine and devotional writer. (1499?–1538)
502, 539, 1081, 1420.

STARR, HATTIE, American song-writer.
1847, 2293.

STATIUS, PUBLIUS PAPINIUS, Latin poet. (61–c. 96)
80, 321, 371, 423, 653, 708, 712, 800, 864, 971, 1017, 1293, 1298, 1575, 1705, 2022, 2089, 2135.

STAUNFORD, SIR WILLIAM, English jurist. (1509–1558)
936.

STEAD, WILLIAM FORCE, American educator and poet. (1884–)
93.

STEALEY, O. O., American politician. (fl. 1912)
1548.

STEDMAN, EDMUND CLARENCE, American banker, poet and man of letters. (1833–1908)
103, 203, 341, 574, 759, 884, 919, 1050, 1096, 1160, 1252, 1290, 1397, 1496, 1515, 1532, 1984.

STEELE, SIR RICHARD, English essayist, dramatist and politician. (1672–1729)
10, 91, 166, 314, 450, 456, 509, 528, 534. 631, 641, 655, 716, 831, 852, 955, 982, 1050, 1076, 1101, 1263, 1314, 1319, 1423, 1478, 1486, 1541, 1563, 1638, 1648, 1653, 1722, 1874, 1925, 1998, 2022, 2146, 2182.

STEERS, FANNY. No biographical data available.
1202.

STEEVENS, GEORGE WARRINGTON, English journalist. (1869–1900)
60

STEFFENS, JOSEPH LINCOLN, American journalist. (1866–1936)
2048.

STEIN, GERTRUDE, American novelist and literary eccentric. (1874–1946)
1743, 1898.

STENDHAL, see BEYLE, MARIE HENRI

STEPHEN, JAMES KENNETH, English poet. (1859–1892)
1115, 1655.

STEPHEN, SIR LESLIE, English editor, man of letters and philosopher. (1832–1904)
1496, 1962.

STEPHENS, JAMES, Irish poet and story-writer. (1882–1950)
129, 141, 682, 1784.

STEPHENS, JOHN, English essayist. (fl. 1615)
853.

STEPHENSON, ISABELLA S., contemporary English poet.
1588.

STEPNEY, GEORGE, English diplomatist and poet. (1663–1707)
1280, 1676.

STERLING, ANDREW B., American song-writer. (1874–1955)
1779, 1882, 2284, 2288, 2293, 2294.

STERLING, GEORGE, American poet. (1869–1926)
368, 1402, 1421.

STERLING, JOHN, English miscellaneous writer. (1806–1844)
421, 992, 1243, 1408, 1532.

STERNE, LAURENCE, English novelist and sentimentalist. (1713–1768)
21, 68, 75, 100, 202, 227, 300, 329, 339, 377, 399, 458, 466, 544, 561, 602, 646, 710, 720, 721, 789, 871, 922, 978, 999, 1010, 1055, 1059, 1116, 1174, 1197, 1314, 1372, 1424, 1447, 1471, 1478, 1490, 1595, 1633, 1674, 1802, 1840, 1866, 1872, 1876, 1951, 1961, 1997, 2014, 2015, 2029, 2052, 2074, 2110, 2166.

STERNHOLD, THOMAS, English versifier of the Psalms. (? –1549)
693, 796, 1835.

STEVENS, ABEL, American Methodist clergyman and editor. (c. 1815–1897)
328, 1061, 2206.

STEVENS, GEORGE ALEXANDER, English lecturer. (1710–1784)
1776, 2152.

STEVENS, WALLACE, contemporary American poet.
136, 374, 1362, 2192.

STEVENSON, ALEC BROCK, American poet. (1895–)
1223.

STEVENSON, MRS. ROBERT ALAN MOWBRAY. No biographical data available.
1878.

STEVENSON, ROBERT LOUIS, English poet, novelist and essayist. (1850–1894)
3, 25, 35, 36, 73, 77, 90, 97, 116, 142, 179, 187, 191, 197, 202, 208, 232, 255, 258, 278, 293, 299, 323, 325, 331, 339, 356, 403, 434, 452, 464, 467, 493, 501, 520, 594, 626, 651, 654, 662, 696, 710, 722, 738, 764, 788, 794, 829, 856, 857, 858, 874, 875, 926. 955, 974, 978, 1006, 1015, 1110, 1122, 1126, 1129, 1166, 1207, 1233, 1262, 1266, 1267, 1270, 1271, 1272, 1276, 1277, 1278, 1279, 1337, 1346, 1396, 1437, 1507, 1541, 1560, 1586, 1588, 1629, 1633, 1664, 1677, 1725, 1728, 1729, 1730, 1781, 1783, 1795, 1801, 1802, 1856, 1897, 1898, 1909, 1920, 1932, 1962, 1966, 1982, 2017, 2020, 2029, 2031, 2049, 2051, 2075, 2082, 2103, 2111, 2119, 2128, 2141, 2194, 2213, 2241, 2260, 2263, 2265, 2267, 2268.

STEVENSON, ROBERT LOUIS, and HENLEY, WILLIAM ERNEST, English writers and collaborators. (1850–1894), (1849–1903)
501, 534, 570, 899, 1461.

STEVENSON, R. L., and OSBOURNE, LLOYD, English and American writers and collaborators. (1850–1894), (1868–1947)
1233.

STEWART, GEORGE DAVID, American surgeon. (1862–1933)
1583.

STICKNEY, JOSEPH TRUMBULL, American poet. (1874–1904)
887.

STILL, JOHN, English prelate, reputed author of *Gammer Gurton's Needle*. (1543?–1608)
45, 497, 599, 914, 1114.

STILLINGFLEET, BENJAMIN, English botanist and writer on natural history. (1702–1771)
314, 1010, 1761.

STILPO, Greek philosopher. (c. 300 B.C.)
1561.

STIRLING, EARL OF, see ALEXANDER, SIR WILLIAM

ST[illegible]erican naval officer and writer. (1872–1948)
2119.

STOBÆUS, JOHANNES, Greek classical compiler. (fl. 5th century)
640, 1098, 1810.

STOCKTON, ROBERT F., American naval officer and Senator. (1795–1866)
2281.

STODART, MARY A., English poet. (fl. 1850)
1884.

STODDARD, HENRY LUTHER, American journalist. (1861–1947)
2281.

STODDARD, RICHARD HENRY, American journalist and minor poet. (1825–1903)
39, 76, 138, 253, 436, 453, 836, 952, 1019, 1129, 1160, 1386, 1404, 1508, 1936, 2158, 2267.

STODDART, THOMAS TOD, Scottish angler and writer. (1810–1880)
1999.

STONE, JOHN TIMOTHY, American clergyman and devotional writer. (1868–)
1685.

STOREY, VIOLET ALLEYN, American poet. (1900–)
409.

STORRS, EMERY ALEXANDER, American lawyer. (1835–1885)
1463, 1545, 1813, 2125.

STORY, JOSEPH, American jurist and legal author. (1779–1845)
432, 1083, 1602.

STORY, WILLIAM WETMORE, American sculptor and poet. (1819–1895)
103, 230, 613, 618, 887, 1170. 1447, 1476, 1526, 1820, 1931, 2084, 2087, 2095, 2215.

STOUGHTON, WILLIAM, American colonist, Governor of Massachusetts. (1630?–1701)
1324.

STOWE, [MRS.] HARRIET ELIZABETH BEECHER, American novelist. (1812–1896)
75, 164, 1775, 2135.

STRACHEY, EVELYN JOHN ST. LOE, English man of letters. (1901–)
1526.

STRATFORD, E. W. No biographical data available.
784.

STRAUS, NATHAN, American merchant. (1848–1931)
777.

STREET, ALFRED BILLINGS, American verse-writer. (1811–1881)
1503.

STREET, JULIAN, and FLAGG, JAMES MONTGOMERY, American writer and artist. (1879–1947), (1877–1950)
1411.

STRINGER, ARTHUR, American novelist and poet. (1874–)
137, 1024.

STROBEL, MARION [MRS. JAMES HERBERT MITCHELL], American poet. (1895–)
2036.

STRODE, WILLIAM, English poet and dramatist. (1602–1645)
1047. 1858.

STRONG, [REV.] GEORGE AUGUSTUS, American writer. (1832–1912)
1411.

STUART, JAMES, fourth DUKE OF LENNOX and first DUKE OF RICHMOND, English courtier. (1612–1655)
1031.

STUART, LESLIE (real name THOMAS AUGUSTINE BARRETT), English organist and song-writer. (1864–)
1233.

STUART, MURIEL, contemporary English writer.
889.

STUBBS, CHARLES WILLIAM, English divine and writer. (1845–1912)
302.

STUBBS, or STUBBES, PHILIP, English Puritan pamphleteer. (fl. 1583–1591)
764.

STULTS, R. M., American song-writer.
2293.

SUBHADRA BHIKSHU, author of the *Buddhist Catechism,* published in 1888. (d. 1917)
583, 1756.

SUCKLING, SIR JOHN, English poet. (1609–1642)
90, 236, 361, 436, 501, 592, 609, 705, 880, 917, 960, 1023, 1164, 1176, 1202, 1204, 1205, 1221, 1458, 1719, 1831, 2004, 2213, 2247.

SUE, MARIE JOSEPH EUGÈNE, French novelist. (1804–1857)
2094.

SUETONIUS, CAIUS TRANQUILLIUS, Roman historian. (70?–140?)
213, 298, 632, 718, 1479, 1639, 1922, 2254.

SULLA, LUCIUS CORNELIUS, Roman general and dictator. (138–78 B.C.)
457.

SULLIVAN, JOHN LAWRENCE, American pugilist. (1858–1918)
9, 303, 765.

SULLIVAN, JOSEPH J., American song-writer.
491.

SULLIVAN, MARK, American journalist. (1874–1952)
955, 2151, 2281.

SULLIVAN, TIMOTHY DANIEL, Irish poet. (1827–1914)
997.

SULLIVAN, TIMOTHY DANIEL (BIG TIM), New York Tammany politician. (1862–1913)
1454, 2281.

SULLY, MAXIMILIEN, DUC DE, French statesman. (1560–1641)
560.

SULPICIUS, RUFUS SERVIUS, Roman jurist and orator. (106–43 B.C.)
843.

SULPICIUS SEVERUS, Latin historian. (c. 365–425)
465.

SUMNER, CHARLES, American statesman and abolitionist. (1811–1874)
297, 626, 1380, 1473, 1550, 1841, 1842.

SUMNER, WILLIAM GRAHAM, American political economist. (1840–1910)
2281.

SUNDAY, WILLIAM ASHLEY, American evangelist. (1863–1935)
1618.

SURREY, EARL OF, see HOWARD, HENRY

SURTEES, ROBERT SMITH, English sporting novelist. (1803–1864)
1905.

SUTRO, ALFRED, English dramatist. (1863–1933)
280, 661, 720, 854, 890, 951, 1656, 1895, 1911, 2046, 2208.

SUTTNER, BERTHA, BARONESS VON, German novelist. (1843–1914)
894.

SUWARROW, or SUVÓROFF, ALEXANDER VASILIEVITCH, Russian general. (1729–1800)
298.

SWAIN, CHARLES, English poet. (1801–1874)
1018, 1061, 1312, 1426.

SWAIN, JOHN D. No biographical data available.
1687.

SWAMWRA, Turkish mystic. (fl. 675)
1801.

SWAN, JOHN, English writer. (fl. 1635)
270.

SWANN, WILLIAM FRANCIS GRAY, American physicist. (1884–)
2068.

SWEDENBORG (SWEDBERG), EMANUEL, Swedish scientist, philosopher and theologian. (1688–1772)
241, 299, 585, 784, 791, 812, 884, 888, 1175, 1179, 1581, 1689, 1791, 1904, 1989.

* SWIFT, JONATHAN, English divine, satirist and man of letters. (1667–1745)

* SWINBURNE, ALGERNON CHARLES, English poet. (1837–1909)

SWOPE, HERBERT BAYARD, American editor and publicist. (1882–1958)
1932, 2298h.

SYLVA, B. G. DE, American song-writer. (1895–1950) 1297.

SYLVESTER II (GERBERT), Roman Pope. (c. 940–1003) 1481.

SYLVESTER, JOSHUA, English poet and translator. (1563–1618)
310, 1215, 1328, 1677, 1938, 2089.

SYMONDS, JOHN ADDINGTON, English miscellaneous writer. (1840–1893)
799, 968, 1883, 1890.

SYMONDS, SYMON, English, Vicar of Bray. (fl. c. 1500) 1546.

SYMONS, ARTHUR, English journalist and poet. (1865–1945)
339, 1366, 1486.

T

TABB, JOHN BANISTER, American gnomic poet. (1845–1909)
363, 587, 938, 1183, 1344, 1514, 1999, 2087.

TABRAR, JOSEPH, American song-writer.
2294.

TACITUS, CAIUS CORNELIUS, Latin historian. (c. A.D. 55–c. 117)
2, 20, 81, 84, 147, 156, 208, 218, 248, 274, 376, 431, 455, 457, 463, 465, 466, 536, 544, 594, 626, 627, 655, 657, 676, 678, 712, 726, 731, 760, 784, 797, 816, 865, 867, 901, 955, 970, 985, 986, 990, 994, 1011, 1013, 1021, 1083, 1084, 1090, 1095, 1096, 1104, 1105, 1107, 1240, 1258, 1286, 1287, 1328, 1329, 1333, 1357, 1370, 1373, 1474, 1480, 1537, 1564, 1573, 1575, 1585, 1596, 1618, 1625, 1652, 1656, 1666, 1682, 1713, 1736, 1737, 1751, 1754, 1826, 1837, 1838, 1863, 1866, 1867, 1909, 1918, 1966, 1993, 2014, 2029, 2032, 2033, 2034, 2060, 2070, 2073, 2079, 2084, 2085, 2107, 2115, 2119, 2124, 2169, 2191, 2210, 2229, 2258.

TAFT, WILLIAM HOWARD, twenty-seventh President of the United States. (1857–1930)
202, 1473.

TAGGART, GEORGE, American song-writer.
2294.

TAGORE, SIR RABINDRANATH, Hindu poet and mystic. (1861–1941)
121, 368, 463, 602, 822, 932, 1141, 1347, 1391, 1495, 1512, 1586, 2186, 2240.

TAINE, HENRI (baptized HYPPOLYTE ADOLPHE), French historian and critic. (1828–1893)
1859.

TAIT, JOHN, Irish poet. No biographical data available.
1733.

TALFOURD, SIR THOMAS NOON, English judge and classical writer. (1795–1854)
239, 1021, 1786, 2126.

TALIESIN, Welsh bard. (fl. 6th century)
1772.

TALLEMANT DES RÉAUX, GÉDÉON, French littérateur and writer of gossip. (c. 1619–1700)
1413.

TALLEY, ALFRED JOSEPH, American lawyer. (1877–)
53.

TALLEYRAND-PÉRIGORD, CHARLES MAURICE DE, French politician, diplomat and wit. (1754–1838)
147, 219, 316, 337, 373, 664, 728, 971, 1175, 1378, 1429, 1902, 2269.

TALMUD, THE, 205, 215, 236, 279, 286, 461, 497, 666, 743, 788, 804, 1105, 1445, 1562, 1568, 1577, 1621, 1698, 1820, 1831, 1835, 1985, 2023, 2139, 2145, 2181, 2186, 2199, 2234.

TANAQUIL, PAUL (pseud. of J. G. CLEMENCEAU LE CLERCQ), American poet. (1893–)
1495.

TANEY, ROGER BROOKE, American Supreme Court jurist. (1777–1864)
1395.

TANNAHILL, ROBERT, Scottish song-writer. (1774–1810)
1289.

TARKINGTON, NEWTON BOOTH, American novelist. (1869–1946)
856, 1059, 1764, 2138.

TARLTON, RICHARD, English comedian. (? –1588)
2024.

TARQUIN, LUCIUS (SUPERBUS), King of Rome. (6th century B.C.)
737.

TOWNLEY, JAMES, English teacher and writer of farces. (1714–1778)
1510, 2156.
TOWNSEND, AURELIAN, English poet. (fl. 1601–1643)
1852.
TOWNSEND, MARY ASHLEY, American verse-writer. (1832–1901)
1220.
TRACY, LOUIS, English novelist. (1863–1928)
1347.
TRACY, WILLIAM, American song-writer. (1883–1957)
1881, 2284.
TRAHERNE, THOMAS, English writer of religious works. (1634?–1704)
315, 994, 1175, 2236.
TRAPASSI, PIETRO BONAVENTURA, see METASTASIO
TRAPP, JOHN, English divine and Bible commentator. (1601–1669)
1648.
TRAPP, JOSEPH, English divine, poet and pamphleteer. (1679–1747)
2069.
TRAVERS, WILLIAM R., American stock-broker and wit.
665.
TREITSCHKE, HEINRICH VON, German militarist and historian. (1834–1896)
2112.
TRENCH, HERBERT, Irish poet. (1865–1923)
992, 1025.
TRENCH, MELESINA [MRS. RICHARD TRENCH], English writer. (1768–1827)
648.
TRENCH, RICHARD CHENEVIX, Archbishop, English philologist, theologian and poet. (1807–1886)
15, 193, 585, 786, 794, 1068, 1132, 1304, 1325, 1583, 1708, 1731, 1759, 1973, 2196, 2218.
TRENT, WILLIAM PETERFIELD, American educator and writer on literary subjects. (1862–1939)
317.
TREVELYAN, G. O., English miscellaneous writer. (1838–1962)
1859.
TRÉVILLE, M. DE, French soldier. (fl. 1635)
2172.
TRINE, RALPH WALDO, American publicist and writer on social science. (1866–)
845, 2068.
TRIPTOLEMUS, mythical son of King Eleusis, and patron of agriculture.
82.
TRIVULCE, TEODORO, Italian general. (1441–1518)
2114.
TROLLOPE, ANTHONY, English novelist. (1815–1882)
36, 180, 490, 880, 1207, 1488, 1676, 1857, 1923.
TROLLOPE, [MRS.] FRANCES, English novelist. (1780–1863)
521, 1691.
TROUBETZKOY, AMÉLIE RIVES, American novelist and poet. (1863–1945)
1019.
TROWBRIDGE, JOHN TOWNSEND, American novelist and poet. (1827–1916)
25, 42, 50, 112, 165, 251, 282, 310, 473, 627, 694, 794, 1160, 1257, 1451, 1539, 1716, 1732, 1936, 2236.
TRUMBULL, JOHN, American satirist and poet. (1750–1831)
499, 599, 1083, 1564, 1585, 1711.
TRUSLER, JOHN, English divine, literary compiler and medical empiric. (1735–1820)
1257.
TUCKER, JOSIAH, English economist and divine. (1712–1799)
548.
TUCKER, MARY F., see LAMBERT
TUCKERMAN, HENRY THEODORE, American critic, essayist and poet. (1813–1871)
108, 1200.
TUER, ANDREW WHITE, English publisher and miscellaneous writer. (1838–1900)
1071.
TUFTS, GEORGE, American educator. (fl. 1869)
1114.
TUGWELL, REXFORD GUY, American educator and economist. (1891–)
2160.
TUKE, SIR SAMUEL, first BARONET, English playwright. (? –1674)
706, 726, 744.
TULL, JEWELL BOTHWELL, contemporary American writer.
318.
TUNNELL, SOPHIE LETITIA, American poet. (1884–)
654.
TUPPER, MARTIN FARQUHAR, English moralist, author of *Proverbial Philosophy*. (1810–1889)
25, 79, 122, 129, 182, 186, 201, 296, 421, 526, 576, 650, 790, 797, 814, 985, 1000, 1028, 1067, 1154, 1253, 1292, 1329, 1370, 1560, 1576, 1609, 1691, 1707, 1790, 1823, 1843, 1989, 1991, 2003, 2042.
TURBERVILLE, or TURBERVILE, GEORGE, English poet. (1540?–1610?)
88, 938, 954, 1335, 1608.
TURENNE, HENRI DE LA TOUR D'AUVERGNE, VISCOUNT DE, French general. (1611–1675)
298.
TURGENEV, IVAN SERGEYEVICH, Russian novelist. (1818–1883)
89, 124, 974, 2021.
TURGOT, ANNE ROBERT JACQUES, French financier and publicist. (1727–1781)
722, 1542.
TURNBULL, MARGARET, American writer and dramatist. (c. 1890–1942)
645, 1256.
TURNER, CHARLES TENNYSON, English poet, brother of Alfred Tennyson; changed name to Turner in 1830. (1808–1879)
144, 581, 1670, 2120.

TURNER, NANCY BYRD, American poet and editor. (1880–)
378, 668, 898.

TURNER, WALTER JAMES, British poet, born in Australia. (1889–1946)
1175, 1481.

TURVEY, HILTON, see HILTON-TURVEY

TUSSER, THOMAS, English agricultural writer and poet. (1524?–1580)
45, 90, 94, 125, 128, 270, 301, 310, 471, 520, 604, 636, 637, 660, 668, 739, 752, 862, 906, 908, 940, 1087, 1149, 1265, 1281, 1328, 1332, 1441, 1470, 1639, 1648, 1800, 1954, 2001, 2005, 2010, 2143, 2151, 2170, 2180, 2265.

TUVILL, D., English compiler. (fl. 1638)
472, 913, 1611, 1938.

TWAIN, MARK (pseud. of SAMUEL LANGHORNE CLEMENS), American humorist. (1835–1910)
12, 20, 60, 72, 80, 92, 103, 194, 195, 293, 342, 353, 355, 385, 392, 395, 471, 502, 530, 532, 534, 561, 570, 611, 632, 637, 698, 699, 707, 720, 735, 737, 745, 747, 753, 755, 760, 769, 829, 853, 873, 915, 959, 961, 971, 980, 1002, 1010, 1011, 1019, 1042, 1084, 1110, 1111, 1112, 1114, 1119, 1149, 1237, 1239, 1241, 1246, 1257, 1330, 1341, 1346, 1412, 1428, 1449, 1565, 1603, 1608, 1618, 1629, 1646, 1652, 1691, 1701, 1781, 1789, 1808, 1828, 1852, 1890, 1920, 1927, 1943, 1952, 1982, 1986, 2051, 2058, 2060, 2085, 2092, 2104, 2128, 2223, 2235, 2265, 2298i:4.

TWEED, WILLIAM MARCY, American political "boss." (1823–1878)
2099.

TWEEDY, HENRY HALLAM, American theologian. (1868–)
653.

TYDINGS, MILLARD E., American legislator and ex-U. S. Senator. (1890–)
1726.

TYERS, THOMAS, English political writer. (1726–1787)
1148.

TYLER, JOHN, tenth President of the United States. (1790–1862)
1215.

TYMNES, Greek epigrammatic poet.
473.

TYNAN, KATHERINE, see HINKSON, KATHERINE TYNAN

TYNDALE, WILLIAM, English translator of the Bible. (? –1536)
1648, 1960.

TYNDALL, JOHN, English natural philosopher. (1820–1893)
667.

U

UDALL, or UVEDALE, JOHN, English Puritan and controversial writer. (1560?–1592)
1431.

UDALL, LYN, American song-writer.
2294.

UDALL, or UVEDALE, NICHOLAS, English dramatist and scholar. (1505–1556)
146, 197, 822, 1177, 1301, 1318, 1811.

UFFORD, EDMOND SMITH, American evangelist and hymn-writer. (1851–1929)
202.

UHLAND, JOHANN LUDWIG, German poet. (1787–1862)
767, 1905.

ULLMAN, SAMUEL. No biographical data available.
2263.

UMBERTO I (HUMBERT I), King of Italy. (1844–1900)
1043.

UNAMUNO, MIGUEL DE, Spanish educator and philosophical writer. (1864–1936)
111, 133, 277, 481, 655, 710, 759, 775, 787, 846, 921, 964, 967, 971, 979, 1176, 1197, 1280, 1426, 1680, 1764, 1765, 1876, 1897, 1930, 1973, 1989, 2054, 2163.

UNDERDOWN, THOMAS, English poet and translator. (fl. 1566–1587)
1934.

UNDERWOOD, OSCAR WILDER, American politician. (1862–1929)
1090, 1620, 1685.

UNTERMEYER, LOUIS, American poet, critic and anthologist. (1885–)
294, 475, 614, 1182, 1402.

UPHAM, JAMES BAILEY, American publicist and miscellaneous writer. (1845–1905)
2275.

UPTON, RALPH R., American educator and publicist. (1868–1935)
2120.

URMY, CLARENCE, American poet. (1858–1923)
611, 1025.

USHER, JOHN, Scottish poet. (1809–1896)
2019.

USK, THOMAS, English allegorical writer. (d. 1388)
1068, 1822, 1851, 2058.

USTERI, JOHANN MARTIN, Swiss poet. (1763–1827)
2010.

V

VALDEMAR IV (ATTERDAG), King of Denmark. (c. 1320–1375)
2023.

VALERIUS MAXIMUS, Roman historian. (fl. A.D. 25)
502, 1221, 1452, 1709.

VANBRUGH, or VANBURGH, SIR JOHN, English dramatist and architect. (1664–1726)
187, 302, 415, 668, 745, 1006, 1075, 1202, 1256, 1258, 1457, 1561, 1607, 1699, 1702, 2091, 2196, 2203, 2219.

VANBRUGH, SIR JOHN, and CIBBER, COLLEY, English dramatists and collaborators. (1664–1726), (1671–1757)
1636, 2219.

VAN BUREN, MARTIN, eighth President of the United States. (1782–1862)
588.

Vance, John Frazier, contemporary American writer.
2126.
Van de Water, Frederic Franklyn, American miscellaneous writer. (1890–)
399.
Vanderbilt, Cornelius, Jr., American socialite and journalist. (1898–)
1918.
Vanderbilt, William H., American financier and railroad executive. (1821–1885)
1480.
Van der Leeuw, Jacobus Johannes, English theosophical writer. (1893–)
1117.
Vandersloot, F. W., American song-writer.
1207.
Vandiver, William Duncan, American legislator. (1854–1932)
1636.
Van Doren, Carl, American editor and critic. (1885–1950)
1679, 1696.
van Dyke, Henry, American Presbyterian minister, poet and essayist. (1852–1933)
32, 52, 150, 336, 348, 469, 668, 672, 905, 934, 964, 979, 1033, 1064, 1078, 1114, 1149, 1176, 1194, 1306, 1475, 1529, 1679, 1744, 1812, 1891, 1930, 1943, 1971, 1983, 2036, 2037, 2103, 2110, 2230.
Vandyke, Harry Stoe, English writer of prose and verse. (1798–1828)
660, 1370.
Vane, Sir Henry, the younger, English statesman. (1613–1662)
417.
van Loon, Hendrik Willem, American journalist and miscellaneous writer, of Dutch birth. (1882–1944)
566, 899, 1280, 1383, 1395, 1617.
van Swieten, Geraard, Dutch physician. (1700–1772)
918.
Vardill, Anna Jane [Mrs. James Niven], English writer. (1781–1852)
1834.
Varenne de Fenille, Philibert Charles, French writer on agricultural and domestic subjects. (d. 1794)
316.
Varro, Marcus Terentius, Latin scholar and miscellaneous writer. (116–27 B.C.)
29, 277, 471, 812, 913, 1401.
Vaughan, Henry (the Silurist), English physician and poet. (1622–1695)
161, 181, 184, 372, 392, 402, 579, 732, 967, 1107, 1239, 1348, 1478, 1582, 1670, 1729, 1890, 1995.
Vaughan, William, English poet and colonial pioneer. (1577–1641)
150, 1443.
Vauvenargues, Luc de Clapiers, Marquis de, French moralist. (1715–1747)
280, 300, 438, 534, 592, 698, 952, 1032, 1064, 1127, 1423, 1462, 1498, 1625, 1629, 1927, 1991.
Vaux, Thomas, second Baron Vaux of Harrowden, English poet. (1510–1556)
27, 310, 825, 1824.
Vedder, David, Scottish poet. (1790–1854)
1387.
Vedder, Miriam, contemporary American poet.
798.
Vegetius, Flavius Vegetius Renatus, Roman military writer. (fl. c. A.D. 375)
1599.
Velleius, Gaius, Roman senator and Epicurean philosopher. (fl. 50 B.C.)
783.
Venable, William Henry, American historian and poet. (1836–1920)
1503.
Venning, Ralph, English nonconformist divine and theological writer. (1621?–1674)
137, 256.
* Véprie, J. de la, French compiler and littérateur.
Vere, Sir Aubrey, see De Vere
Vere, Edward de, seventeenth Earl of Oxford, English poet. (1550–1604)
608, 1725, 2207.
Vergennes, Charles Gravier, Comte de, French statesman. (1717–1787)
2040.
Vergil, Polydore, Italian historian and ecclesiastic. (1470?–1555)
921, 1257.
* Vergil; Publius Vergilius Maro, Latin epic poet. (70–19 B.C.)
Verrucosus, Quintus Fabius Maximus, see Fabius
Very, Jones, American poet. (1813–1880)
162, 692, 1808.
Vespasianus, Titus Flavius (Vespasian), Roman Emperor. (40–81)
370, 1044, 1336.
Vest, George Graham, American legislator. (1830–1904)
473, 1552.
Victoria (Alexandrina Victoria), Queen of Great Britain and Ireland, Empress of India. (1837–1901)
67, 417.
Vida, Marco Giralamo, Italian prelate and miscellaneous writer. (1480–1566)
1927.
Vielé, Herman Knickerbocker, American novelist and poet. (1856–1908)
709, 988.
Viennet, Jean Pons Guillaume, French littérateur. (1777–1868)
1086.
Vigny, Alfred Victor, Comte de, French poet, dramatist and novelist. (1797–1863)
831.
Villari, Pasquale, Italian historian. (1827–1917)
833.
Villars, Claude Louis Hector, Duc de, French general and diplomat. (1653–1734)
544, 734.

VILLIERS, ABBÉ DE, French writer. (1648–1728)
1595.

VILLIERS, GEORGE, second DUKE OF BUCKINGHAM, English courtier, poet and dramatist. (1628–1687)
178, 700, 1219, 1271, 1373, 1414, 1815, 1990, 2220.

VILLON, FRANÇOIS, French poet. (1431–1484?)
372, 570, 1050, 1182, 1358, 1453, 1789, 1857.

VINAL, HAROLD, American poet and publisher. (1891–)
1162.

VINCENT DE BEAUVAIS, French Dominican encyclopedist. (d. c. 1264)
1565, 1566, 2189.

VINCENTIUS LUPANUS. No biographical data available.
1039.

VINCI, LEONARDO DA, see LEONARDO

VINES, RICHARD, English Puritan divine. (1600?–1656)
1754.

VITELLIUS, AULUS, Roman Emperor. (A.D. 15–69)
544.

VITRUVIUS POLLIO, Italian architect. (fl. c. 15 B.C.)
1928.

VIVES, JOHANNES LUDOVICUS, Spanish scholar at the English court. (1492–1540)
137.

VIZÉ, JEAN DONNEDY DE, French dramatist and littérateur. (c. 1640–1710)
1791.

VLAMINCK, MAURICE DE, French critic. (1876–)
1447.

VOGAN, A. J. No biographical data available.
614.

VOGELWEIDE, WALTER VON DER, German minnesinger. (c. 1168–1230)
2181.

VOITURE, VINCENT, French poet and wit. (1598–1648)
712.

VOLNEY, COMTE DE, see CHASSEBŒUF, CONSTANTIN FRANÇOIS

VOLTAIRE (pseud. of FRANÇOIS MARIE AROUET), French philosopher and dramatist. (1694–1778)
1, 43, 73, 97, 103, 140, 147, 182, 184, 192, 193, 228, 248, 332, 338, 340, 350, 375, 417, 419, 421, 428, 438, 440, 466, 467, 511, 546, 550, 554, 560, 561, 576, 578, 654, 700, 702, 710, 721, 724, 728, 742, 757, 777, 788, 797, 806, 815, 880, 900, 901, 902, 904, 945, 946, 988, 1024, 1032, 1061, 1064, 1107, 1120, 1200, 1227, 1228, 1256, 1263, 1280, 1288, 1306, 1326, 1374, 1375, 1388, 1430, 1435, 1457, 1465, 1507, 1529, 1569, 1576, 1586, 1593, 1596, 1663, 1691, 1694, 1700, 1701, 1706, 1737, 1758, 1760, 1791, 1795, 1798, 1808, 1809, 1810, 1836, 1840, 1859, 1889, 1902, 1927, 1928, 1931, 1944, 1945, 1972, 1989, 2001, 2027, 2049, 2055, 2057, 2065, 2089, 2114, 2194, 2225, 2253, 2258, 2276.

VONVED SVEND, Hamlet-like hero of a Danish folk ballad, "Vonved" meaning mad. 1928.

VOORHEES, DAYTON, a Princeton student in 1902.
1157.

VOSS, JOHANN HEINRICH, German poet and critic. (1751–1826) 2160.

W

W., A. It has been suggested that these initials stand for ANTHONY WOTTON (1561–1626). Davison's *Poetical Rhapsody* was published in 1602.
144, 750.

WACE, ROBERT, Anglo-Norman poet. (c. 1100–1175)
1741.

WADE, JOSEPH AUGUSTINE, English composer. (1796?–1845)
1289.

WAGER, LEWIS, English rector and author of *Repentaunce of Marie Magdalene.* (fl. 1566)
1633, 2190.

WAGER, WILLIAM, English writer of interludes. (fl. 1566)
97, 952, 1633.

WAGNER, CHARLES, Alsatian pastor and inspirational writer. (1851–1918)
1136, 1826.

WAGNER, WILHELM RICHARD, German musician, composer and poet. (1813–1883)
1369.

WAKEFIELD, [MRS.] NANCY PRIEST, American verse-writer. (1836–1870)
402.

WALKER, FELIX, American politician, member House of Representatives 1817–1823. (1753–1828)
2281.

WALKER, JAMES J., American lawyer, former Mayor of New York City. (1881–1946)
331, 1074, 1216, 1685, 1882.

WALKER, JOHN, English lexicographer and compiler. (1732–1807)
35, 270.

WALKER, [MRS.] KATHERINE KENT, American essayist and religious writer. (1840– ?)
1645.

WALKER, MARSHALL, American verse-writer.
2294.

WALKER, STANLEY, American journalist. (1898–)
1398.

WALKER, WILLIAM, English schoolmaster. (1623–1684)
1673.

WALL, JAMES CHARLES. English archaeologist. (1860–1943)
1317.

WALLACE, EDGAR, English novelist. (1875–1932)
528, 890, 1532.

WALLACE, HORACE BINNEY, American scholar and littérateur. (1817–1862)
707.

WALLACE, JOHN AIKMAN. No biographical data available.
1583.

WARTON, THOMAS, THE YOUNGER, historian of English poetry, and poet. (1728–1790)
862, 1510, 1849, 2186.

WASHINGTON, BOOKER TALIAFERRO, Negro educator. (c. 1859–1915)
1430.

WASHINGTON, GEORGE, American general and first President of the United States. (1732–1799)
54, 59, 60, 61, 62, 63, 200, 214, 298, 417, 540, 732, 738, 753, 815, 816, 881, 915, 1028, 1104, 1247, 1335, 1467, 1597, 1701, 1842, 1863, 1864, 2052, 2110, 2122.

WASSON, DAVID ATWOOD, American Unitarian clergyman, essayist and verse-writer. (1823–1887)
2000.

WATERMAN, NIXON, American verse-writer. (1859–1944)
849, 1019, 1578, 2045.

WATKYNS, ROWLAND, English writer and compiler. (fl. 1662)
164, 271, 302, 462, 871, 1134, 1162, 1269, 1282, 1333, 1701, 2144.

WATSON, JOHN, see MACLAREN, IAN

WATSON, JOHN BROADUS, American psychologist. (1878–)
466, 1888.

WATSON, JOHN WHITAKER, American journalist and verse-writer. (1824–1890)
1858.

WATSON, SYDNEY. No biographical data available.
1478.

WATSON, THOMAS, English poet. (1557?–1592)
1175.

WATSON, WALTER, Scottish poet. (1780–1854)
1132.

WATSON, SIR WILLIAM, English poet. (1858–1935)
6, 26, 61, 88, 93, 116, 171, 206, 212, 244, 284, 304, 368, 379, 454, 473, 482, 556, 557, 614, 621, 629, 635, 722, 783, 797, 798, 865, 888, 897, 923, 954, 964, 992, 996, 999, 1016, 1030, 1060, 1067, 1073, 1115, 1125, 1130, 1149, 1170, 1201, 1248, 1260, 1283, 1306, 1370, 1380, 1445, 1463, 1468, 1474, 1486, 1490, 1521, 1532, 1535, 1548, 1617, 1707, 1709, 1716, 1762, 1772, 1782, 1812, 1826, 1853, 1879, 1885, 1942, 1983, 2051, 2099, 2147, 2186, 2196, 2223, 2230, 2242.

WATTERSON, HENRY, American editor and journalist. (1840–1921)
144, 280.

WATTLES, WILLARD AUSTIN, American educator and poet. (1888–1950)
262, 336.

WATTS, ALARIC ALEXANDER, English poet and journalist. (1797–1864)
38, 1525, 1804, 1862.

WATTS, [MRS.] ALARIC ALEXANDER, English poet. (1799–1873)
1804.

WATTS, ISAAC, English hymn-writer. (1674–1748)
144, 158, 161, 196, 231, 255, 269, 385, 394, 487, 541, 553, 649, 698, 794, 804, 827, 828, 845, 850, 883, 884, 885, 888, 890, 898, 908, 954, 980, 1068, 1112, 1125, 1242, 1307, 1349, 1368 1377, 1452, 1465, 1567, 1609, 1699, 1700, 1746, 1789, 1792, 1810, 1831, 1843, 1847, 1939, 1987, 2005, 2274.

WATTS-DUNTON, WALTER THEODORE, English critic, novelist and poet. (1832–1914)
97, 270, 283, 284, 732, 1051, 1169, 1176, 1220, 1404, 1524, 1883.

WAYLAND, FRANCIS, American Baptist clergyman, educator and metaphysician. (1796–1865)
912.

WEATHERLY, FREDERIC EDWARD, English verse-writer. (1848–1929)
879, 1779, 1870, 2102.

WEAVER, JOHN VAN ALSTYN, American poet and novelist. (1893–1938)
482, 2268.

WEBB, CHARLES HENRY, American journalist. (1834–1905)
741, 1780, 1781.

WEBB, "HOPPY." No biographical data available.
1987.

WEBBE, CHARLES, English poet. (fl. 1675)
1202.

WEBBER, BYRON, English writer and journalist. (1838–1913)
171.

WEBSTER, DANIEL, American statesman and orator. (1782–1852)
38, 54, 58, 63, 64, 158, 266, 274, 296, 334, 431, 508, 547, 607, 638, 674, 723, 816, 974, 980, 1028, 1031, 1055, 1066, 1083, 1104, 1106, 1307, 1312, 1340, 1415, 1419, 1427, 1458, 1466, 1715, 1933, 1967, 1990, 1995, 2061, 2069, 2110, 2123, 2129.

WEBSTER, JOHN, English dramatist. (1580?–1625?)
42, 50, 235, 327, 375, 380, 426, 463, 486, 539, 680, 772, 871, 890, 915, 988, 1030, 1066, 1154, 1256, 1278, 1484, 1625, 1735, 1777, 1884, 1885, 2190.

WEBSTER, JOHN, and MARSTON, JOHN, English dramatists and collaborators. (1580?–1625?), (1575?–1634)
446, 704.

WEBSTER, JOHN, and ROWLEY, WILLIAM, English dramatists and collaborators. (1580?–1625?), (1585?–1642?)
732.

WEBSTER, NOAH, American philologist and lexicographer. (1758–1843)
1068.

WEDGWOOD, JOSIAH, English potter. (1730–1795)
1605, 1841.

WEEMS, MASON LOCKE, American biographer and miscellaneous writer. (1759–1825)
2123.

WEIGALL, ARTHUR, English Egyptologist. (1880–1934)
762.

WEINBERGER, HARRY, American lawyer. (1886–)
1728, 2276.

WEISS, JOHAN, American Unitarian minister and writer on literary topics. (1818–1879)
938, 1000, 1075.

WEISSE, CHRISTIAN FELIX, German lyric poet and writer for children. (1726–1804)
2021.

WELBY, [MRS.] AMELIA COPPUCK, American verse-writer. (1819–1852)
1155, 1297, 1915.

WELDON, SIR ANTHONY, English historical writer. (d. 1649?)
1472.

WELLER, CHARLES E., American typewriter expert. (1840–1925)
2282.

WELLES, WINIFRED [MRS. HAROLD A. SHEARER], American poet. (1893–1939)
176.

WELLESLEY, ARTHUR, first DUKE OF WELLINGTON, see WELLINGTON, DUKE OF

WELLESLEY, HENRY, English scholar and antiquary. (1791–1866)
569.

WELLINGTON, ARTHUR MELLEN, American engineer. (1847–1895)
1764.

WELLINGTON, DUKE OF; ARTHUR WELLESLEY, first DUKE OF WELLINGTON, English Field-Marshal. (1769–1852)
274, 557, 581, 846, 865, 977, 983, 1325, 1378, 1848, 1862, 1864, 1867, 2085, 2110, 2117, 2127.

WELLS, CAROLYN [MRS. HADWIN HOUGHTON], American humorist and writer of mystery stories. (1868–1942)
360, 1157, 2002, 2186, 2203, 2296.

WELLS, CHARLES JEREMIAH, English poet. (1799?–1879)
1171, 1698.

WELLS, HERBERT GEORGE, English novelist and social reformer. (1866–1946)
60, 388, 557, 562, 641, 732, 751, 794, 896, 951, 969, 1006, 1116, 1146, 1229, 1325, 1337, 1467, 1571, 1680, 1808, 1983, 2099, 2110, 2180, 2298g:2.

WELLS, ROLLIN J. American poet. (1848– ?)
29.

WENDELL, JACOB, JR., American playwright and actor. (1869–1911)
360.

WENDELL, MARY ANN, American, daughter of Jacob Wendell. (d. 1931)
236.

WERNER, CARL, contemporary American writer.
258.

WESLEY, CHARLES, English Methodist divine and hymn-writer. (1707–1788)
253, 264, 269, 271, 407, 515, 618, 791, 887, 1124, 1696, 1744, 1890, 1891, 2181.

WESLEY, JOHN, English evangelist and leader of Methodism. (1703–1791)
150, 278, 496, 862, 1124, 1315, 1458, 1493, 1842, 2110, 2298i:2.

WESLEY, SAMUEL, THE ELDER, English divine and poet. (1662–1735)
198, 492, 829, 876, 1149, 1178, 1349, 1767.

WEST, BENJAMIN, American painter; lived in England. (1738–1820)
1448.

WEST, GILBERT, English miscellaneous writer. (1703–1756)
589, 1045, 1300, 2016.

WEST, REBECCA (pseud. of MRS. CICELY FAIRFIELD ANDREWS), English novelist. (1892–)
1166.

WEST, RICHARD, English poet. (1716–1742)
826, 1248.

WESTCOTT, EDWARD NOYES, American novelist. (1847–1898)
471, 804.

WESTERN, HUGH (pseud. of ALFRED E. HAMILL), American poet. (1883–)
567.

WESTON, R. P., American song-writer.
2284.

WHARTON, EDITH JONES, American novelist. (1862–1937)
473, 2076.

WHARTON, SIR GEORGE, first BARONET, English astrologer. (1617–1681)
471.

WHATELY, RICHARD, English scholar and prelate; Archbishop of Dublin. (1787–1863)
70, 226, 592, 860, 914, 1595, 1846, 2054.

WHEELER, JOHN HILL, American historian. (1806–1882)
2282.

WHEELOCK, JOHN HALL, American poet and editor. (1886–)
276, 512, 513, 1218, 1600.

WHETHAM, SIR WILLIAM CECIL DAMPIER-, English educator and scientific writer. (1867–)
1765.

WHETSTONE, GEORGE, English miscellaneous writer. (1544?–1587?)
289, 607, 822, 1723, 2236.

WHEWELL, WILLIAM, English philosopher and educator. (1794–1866)
82, 706, 1724.

WHICHCOTE, or WHITCHCOTE, BENJAMIN, English divine, educator and religious writer. (1609–1683)
735, 1690, 1696, 2051.

WHICHER, GEORGE MEASON, American educator and miscellaneous writer. (1860–1937)
899.

WHIPPLE, EDWIN PERCY, American essayist and critic. (1819–1886)
186, 251, 759, 762, 1000, 1106, 1828.

WHISTLER, JAMES ABBOTT MCNEILL, American painter and etcher, living in London. (1834–1903)
99, 102, 103, 105, 106, 108, 340, 341, 486, 544, 727, 1157, 1414, 1447, 1581, 2147.

WHITAKER, ROBERT, American clergyman and verse-writer. (1863–1944) 1161.

WHITCOMB, SELDEN LINCOLN, American educator. (1866– d.) 1445.

WHITE, ANDREW DICKSON, American diplomat and educator. (1832–1918)
2298i:2.

WHITE, ELWYN BROOKS, American miscellaneous writer. (1899–) 1175, 1668.

WHITE, HENRY KIRKE, English poet. (1785–1806)
221, 311, 579, 856, 1138, 1291, 1321, 1344, 1610, 1748, 1749, 1814, 2004, 2092.

WHITE, JAMES TERRY, American editor and poet. (1845–1920)
945.

WHITE, JOSEPH BLANCO, English theological writer. (1775–1841)
1149, 1402.

WHITE, RICHARD GRANT, American Shakespearean scholar and critic. (1821–1885)
2097, 2219.

WHITE, WILLIAM ALLEN, American editor and publicist. (1868–1944)
891, 1644, 2042, 2069.

WHITEHEAD, PAUL, English satirist. (1710–1774)
318, 917, 1576.

WHITEHEAD, WILLIAM, English Poet Laureate. (1715–1785)
1056, 1241, 1532, 1978, 2081, 2167.

WHITING, GEORGE, American song-writer.
2143.

WHITLOCK, RICHARD, English writer. (fl. 1654)
181.

WHITMAN, [MRS.] SARAH HELEN POWER, American critic and verse-writer. (1803–1878)
582, 687, 688, 1401, 1672, 2087.

WHITMAN, WALT, American poet. (1819–1892)
25, 32, 40, 52, 54, 55, 82, 87, 88, 111, 114, 159, 176, 191, 202, 210, 237, 275, 287, 305, 378, 393, 399, 407, 433, 438, 574, 579, 581, 590, 606, 614, 635, 675, 690, 733, 775, 784, 785, 812, 822, 855, 951, 955, 967, 970, 1033, 1063, 1088, 1095, 1149, 1155, 1156, 1161, 1167, 1176, 1239, 1245, 1247, 1294, 1316, 1344, 1364, 1387, 1397, 1398, 1402, 1404, 1441, 1443, 1471, 1473, 1490, 1503, 1517, 1530, 1539, 1563, 1613, 1652, 1690, 1718, 1774, 1804, 1814, 1826, 1835, 1859, 1873, 1889, 1893, 1915, 1939, 1957, 1983, 2068, 2103, 2113, 2123, 2163, 2231, 2237, 2241.

WHITMELL, [MRS.] C. T., contemporary English writer.
263.

WHITNEY, [MRS.] ADELINE DUTTON TRAIN, American novelist and verse-writer. (1824–1906)
26.

WHITNEY, GEOFFREY, English poet. (1548?–1601?)
1035, 2031.

WHITSON, BETH SLATER, American song-writer.
484.

WHITTEN, WILFRED ("JOHN o' LONDON"), English editor. (c. 1876–1942)
1168.

* WHITTIER, JOHN GREENLEAF, American poet. (1807–1892)

WHUR (or WHAURR), CORNELIUS. No biographical data available.
742.

WHYTE-MELVILLE, GEORGE JOHN, English novelist and poet. (1821–1878)
931, 988, 1208, 1225, 1512.

WICKERSHAM, GEORGE WOODWARD, American lawyer and statesman. (1858–1936)
905, 1619.

WICKHAM, ANNA [MRS. PATRICK HEPBURN], English poet. (1884–)
12, 248, 940, 1223, 1277, 1539, 2139, 2146, 2193, 2216.

WICKLIFFE, CHARLES A., American politician. (1788–1869)
1644.

WIDDEMER, MARGARET, American poet and novelist. (1880–)
374, 427, 1915, 2193.

WIELAND, CHRISTOPH MARTIN, German poet. (1733–1813)
593, 644, 778, 1512.

WILBERFORCE, SAMUEL, English prelate; successively Bishop of Oxford and Winchester. (1805–1873)
1324.

WILBYE, JOHN, English madrigal composer. (fl. 1598–1614)
309.

WILCOX, CARLOS, American Congregational clergyman and verse-writer. (1794–1827)
402.

WILCOX, ELLA WHEELER, American poet. (1855–1919)
24, 35, 336, 368, 378, 404, 446, 454, 464, 737, 810, 872, 981, 1037, 1051, 1077, 1115, 1197, 1218, 1277, 1421, 1435, 1445, 1458, 1585, 1727, 1760, 1813, 1854, 1928, 2091, 2181, 2244.

WILDE, GEORGE JAMES DE, English journalist. (1807–1871)
903.

WILDE, OSCAR O'FLAHERTIE WILLS, Irish wit, poet and dramatist. (1856–1900)
9, 20, 33, 41, 53, 56, 61, 69, 85, 99, 101, 102, 103, 106, 108, 129, 133, 136, 144, 181, 203, 218, 242, 244, 257, 300, 302, 322, 340, 347, 348, 352, 357, 368, 417, 432, 451, 454, 491, 508, 544, 548, 556, 562, 594, 595, 642, 661, 662, 663, 686, 694, 704, 706, 754, 760, 765, 810, 865, 874, 877, 879, 903, 928, 944, 946, 991, 1008, 1039, 1074, 1110, 1116, 1119, 1132, 1143, 1150, 1166, 1182, 1184, 1192, 1195, 1202, 1204, 1205, 1207, 1240, 1256, 1258, 1262, 1265, 1271, 1277, 1278, 1279, 1280, 1318, 1325, 1327, 1344, 1346, 1350, 1358, 1366, 1370, 1416, 1448, 1453, 1476, 1494, 1508, 1510, 1539, 1545, 1562, 1567, 1586, 1601, 1602, 1603, 1614, 1615, 1617, 1665, 1679, 1736, 1755, 1759, 1760, 1788, 1791, 1808, 1825, 1833, 1835, 1859, 1860, 1884, 1925, 1928, 1942, 1963, 1971, 1978, 1981, 1982, 1996, 2020, 2046, 2100, 2104, 2110, 2123, 2144, 2147, 2178, 2181, 2183, 2194, 2196, 2207, 2230, 2235, 2237.

WILDE, RICHARD HENRY, American lawyer and verse-writer. (1789–1847)
1142.

WILDER, THORNTON NIVEN, American novelist and educator. (1897–)
1166.

WILHELM I, King of Prussia and Emperor of Germany. (1797–1888)
768.
WILHELM II, third Emperor of Germany. (1859–1941)
557, 768, 2120, 2147.
WILKES, JOHN, English politician. (1727–1797)
6, 471.
WILKINS, GEORGE, English dramatist and pamphleteer. (fl. 1607)
499, 2183.
WILKINSON, MARGUERITE [MRS. JAMES G. WILKINSON], American poet. (1883–1928)
164, 194.
WILLARD, EMMA HART, American educator and poet. (1787–1870)
1777, 2182.
WILLARD, FRANCES ELIZABETH, American temperance leader. (1839–1898)
1620.
WILLIAM THE CONQUEROR, King of England. (1027?–1087)
213.
WILLIAM THE SILENT, PRINCE OF ORANGE, founder of the Dutch republic. (1533–1584)
1489, 1797.
WILLIAM II (WILLIAM RUFUS), King of England. (? –1100)
417, 1044.
WILLIAM III, PRINCE OF ORANGE, later King of England. (1650–1702)
417, 1467, 2110.
WILLIAMS, BERTYE YOUNG [MRS. KARL H.], American writer. (?–1951)
133.
WILLIAMS, FRANCIS HOWARD, American editor and poet. (1844–1922)
2132.
WILLIAMS, HARRY, English song-writer. (1874–1924)
92, 366, 2294.
WILLIAMS, HELEN MARIA, English miscellaneous writer. (1762–1827)
1588.
WILLIAMS, ISAAC, English poet and theologian. (1802–1865)
845.
WILLIAMS, JAMES, contemporary English writer.
964.
WILLIAMS, JOHN SHARP, American politician. (1854–1932)
818.
WILLIAMS, ROGER, American colonist and apostle of toleration. (c. 1600–1683)
1921.
WILLIAMS, SARAH (SAIDIE), English verse-writer. (1841–1868)
1932.
WILLIAMS, THEODORE CHICKERING, American verse-writer. (1855–1915)
374, 1126.
WILLIS, NATHANIEL PARKER, American poet, essayist and dramatist. (1806–1867)
50, 110, 379, 388, 398, 627, 888, 1026, 1057, 1208, 1268, 1588, 1830, 1859, 1917, 2097, 2141.
WILLSON, BRYON FORCEYTHE, American verse-writer. (1837–1867)
1290.
WILMOT, HENRY, first EARL OF ROCHESTER, English soldier and courtier. (1612?–1658)
1415.
WILMOT, JOHN, second EARL OF ROCHESTER, English poet. (1647–1680)
29, 72, 80, 194, 244, 306, 332, 652, 1498, 1532, 1680, 2143, 2186, 2207.
WILMOT, SIR JOHN EARDLEY-, English jurist. (1709–1792)
540.
WILSON, ALEXANDER, English ornithologist. (1766–1813)
417, 868, 2210.
WILSON, ANNE ELIZABETH, contemporary American writer.
1202.
WILSON, CHARLES A., American song-writer.
1833, 2294.
WILSON, H. SCHÜLTZ. No biographical data available.
212.
WILSON, HARRY LEON, American novelist. (1867–1939)
12, 45, 778, 892, 1376, 1398, 1573, 2234.
WILSON, JOHN, English playwright. (1627?–1696)
224, 345, 377, 717, 1664.
WILSON, JOHN (CHRISTOPHER NORTH), Scottish editor and poet. (1785–1854)
163, 208, 281, 547, 554, 1036, 1075, 1088, 1256, 1362, 1383, 1443, 1444, 1545, 1653, 1750, 1820, 1898, 1920, 1991, 2149, 2171, 2223.
WILSON, JOHN, English bookseller. (c. 1875)
189.
WILSON, MCLANDBURGH, contemporary American writer.
1434, 1741.
WILSON, ROBERT, THE ELDER, English actor and playwright. (? –1600)
145, 497, 1818.
WILSON, ROBERT BURNS, American poet. (1850–1916)
643, 1261.
WILSON, THOMAS, English scholar, Secretary of State. (1525?–1581)
125, 382, 409, 497, 1070, 1134, 1292, 1461.
WILSON, THOMAS, English prelate, Bishop of Sodor and Man. (1663–1755)
8, 97, 120, 243, 267, 373, 489, 599, 620, 623, 743, 747, 773, 806, 888, 938, 1210, 1280, 1424, 1608, 1713, 1991.
WILSON, THOMAS WOODROW, American educator, historian, and twenty-eighth President of the United States. (1856–1924)
54, 55, 58, 60, 65, 66, 67, 204, 235, 304, 431, 433, 436, 508, 666, 675, 698, 723, 725, 742, 768, 815, 975, 1008, 1023, 1028, 1080, 1083, 1104, 1106, 1153, 1161, 1225, 1308, 1379, 1380, 1470, 1471, 1472, 1541, 1546, 1548,

1550, 1558, 1578, 1612, 1618, 1717, 1856, 1860, 1865, 2048, 2050, 2066, 2099, 2110, 2113, 2282.

WINCHELSEA, COUNTESS OF, see FINCH, ANNE

WINCHESTER, MARQUIS OF, see PAULET, WILLIAM

WINDHAM, WILLIAM, English statesman. (1750–1810)
1229, 1453.

WINDOM, W. H., American song-writer.
2295.

WINFIELD, ALAN T. No biographical data available.
601.

WINGATE, PHILIP, American song-writer.
1883.

WINKLER, JOHN K., American writer of biography. (1891–)
66, 1600, 1601.

WINN, MARY DAY, contemporary American writer.
1802.

WINSLOW, ANNE GOODWIN [MRS. E. E. WINSLOW], American poet and novelist. (1875–1959)
1197.

WINSLOW, EDWARD, English Governor of Plymouth Colony. (1595–1655)
198.

WINTER, BANKS, American song-writer. (1855–1936)
2295.

WINTER, WILLIAM, American dramatic critic and poet. (1836–1917)
50, 884, 1037, 1139, 1171, 1257, 1387, 1496, 1808, 1939, 2229.

WINTHER, CHRISTIAN, Danish lyrical poet. (1796–1876)
1406.

WINTHROP, JOHN, New England colonist, Governor of Massachusetts. (1588–1649)
1104.

WINTHROP, ROBERT CHARLES, American statesman and orator. (1809–1894)
57, 58, 64, 530, 1463, 1492.

WINTLE, WALTER D. No biographical data available.
1931.

WIRT, WILLIAM ALBERT, American educator. (1874–1938)
1715.

WISDOM, ROBERT, English prelate, Archdeacon of Ely. (? –1568)
2017.

WISE, STEPHEN SAMUEL, Jewish rabbi, born in Hungary. (1874–1949)
1691.

WISHART, GEORGE, Scottish reformer. (1513?–1546)
417, 1821.

WISTER, OWEN, American novelist and miscellaneous writer. (1860–1938)
324, 492, 2298j:1.

WITHER, or WITHERS, GEORGE, English poet and pamphleteer. (1588–1667)
17, 85, 221, 270, 271, 360, 873, 958, 1081. 1177, 1261, 1354, 1403, 1506, 1526, 1884, 1991, 2017, 2199.

WITHERSPOON, JOHN, Scottish-American Presbyterian divine and educator, President of the College of New Jersey, now Princeton University. (1723–1794)
2219.

WODROEPHE, JOHN, English commentator. (fl. 1623)
84, 118, 245, 726, 728, 923, 1511, 1650.

WOEPCKE, FRANZ, German Orientalist. (1826–1864)
1539.

WOLCOT, JOHN (PETER PINDAR), English satirist and poet. (1738–1819)
92, 124, 125, 126, 146, 221, 302, 343, 455, 473, 522, 524, 580, 592, 626, 642, 676, 766, 803, 903, 1015, 1035, 1297, 1327, 1332, 1480, 1522, 1550, 1564, 1665, 1737, 1852, 2016, 2052, 2055, 2166, 2250.

WOLFE, CHARLES, Irish poet. (1791–1823)
394, 402, 709, 1870.

WOLFE, HUMBERT, English poet. (1885–1940)
167, 402, 692, 1156, 1250.

WOLFE, JAMES, English general. (1727–1759)
260, 417, 1517.

WOLSEY, THOMAS, English Cardinal and statesman. (1475?–1530)
534, 1801.

WOMBAT, R. T., American verse-writer.
865, 955, 1434, 1788.

WOOD, CLEMENT, American poet and miscellaneous writer. (1888–1950)
1115.

WOOD, [MRS.] HENRY (ELLEN), English novelist. (1814–1887)
1663.

WOOD, J. T., American song-writer. (fl. 1880)
282.

WOODBERRY, GEORGE EDWARD, American critic, editor and poet. (1855–1930)
52, 136, 181, 197, 203, 321, 400, 555, 1462, 1688.

WOODBRIDGE, BENJAMIN, English divine; first graduate of Harvard College. (1622–1684)
572.

WOODBRIDGE, FREDERIC JAMES EUGÉNE, American educator. (1867–1940)
1391.

WOODFALL, HENRY SAMPSON, English printer and journalist. (1739–1805)
247.

WOODLOCK, THOMAS FRANCIS, Irish-born American financial writer. (1866–1945)
1084.

WOODRUFF, [MRS.] JULIA LOUISE MATILDA [W. M. L. JAY], American writer and compiler. (1833–1909)
391.

WOODVILLE, ANTHONY, BARON SCALES and second EARL RIVERS, English statesman and compiler. (1442?–1483)
732, 1701.

WOODWARD, JOSIAH, English writer. (fl. 1770)
953.

WOODWARD, WILLIAM E., American miscellaneous writer: author of *Bunk*. (1874–1950)
60, 64, 637.

WOODWORTH, SAMUEL, American journalist and verse-writer. (1785–1842)
252, 1394, 2126, 2205.

WOOLLCOTT, ALEXANDER, American essayist and dramatic critic. (1887–1943)
1369.

WOOLSEY, JOHN MUNRO, American jurist. (1877–1945)
1263.

WOOLSEY, SARAH C., see COOLIDGE, SUSAN

WOOLSON, CONSTANCE FENIMORE, American poet and novelist. (1848–1894)
603.

WOOLTON, JOHN, English divine, Bishop of Exeter. (1535?–1594)
417.

WORDSWORTH, CHRISTOPHER, English educator and divine. (1774–1846)
515.

WORDSWORTH, DOROTHY [MRS. EDWARD QUILLINAN], English poet, daughter of William Wordsworth. (1804–1847)
2160.

WORDSWORTH, DAME ELIZABETH, English poet. (1840– ?)
280.

* WORDSWORTH, WILLIAM, English poet. (1770–1850)

WORK, HENRY CLAY, American printer and song-writer. (1832–1884)
1878, 2295.

WOTTON, SIR HENRY, English diplomatist and poet. (1568–1639)
271, 342, 402, 452, 546, 633, 672, 853, 974, 1002, 1136, 1345, 1561, 1604, 1668, 1744, 1787, 2090, 2199.

WRANGHAM, FRANCIS, English classical scholar and miscellaneous writer. (1769–1842)
757.

WREN, CHRISTOPHER, English biographer. (1675–1747)
95, 1340.

WRIGHT, FRANCES A. [MADAME D'ARUSMONT], Scottish reformer, who settled in the United States in 1830. (1795–1852)
1829.

WRIGHT, LEONARD, English controversialist. (fl. 1591)
120, 466, 735, 738, 750, 2179.

WRIGHT, THOMAS, English philosopher. (fl. 1604)
237, 648.

WRIGHT, THOMAS, English antiquary. (1810–1877)
442, 604, 1047.

WRIGHT, WILLARD HUNTINGTON (S. S. VAN DINE), American novelist and miscellaneous writer. (1888–1939)
2199.

WRIOTHESLEY, CHARLES, English herald and chronicler. (1508?–1562)
874.

WYATT, SIR THOMAS, English poet. (1503?–1542)
177, 289, 327, 570, 602, 712, 714, 1226, 1615, 1851, 1992, 2011, 2032, 2170, 2193, 2199, 2221.

WYCHERLEY, WILLIAM, English dramatist. (1640?–1716)
71, 173, 174, 208, 218, 351, 462, 465, 471, 479, 1007, 1091, 1266, 1270, 1325, 1394, 1537, 1580, 1701, 1980, 2016, 2139, 2145, 2159, 2172, 2220.

WYCLIFFE, JOHN, English theologian and religious reformer. (? –1384)
243, 431, 1491, 1635, 1822, 2026.

WYKEHAM, WILLIAM OF, English prelate, Bishop of Winchester and founder of New College, Oxford. (1324–1404)
1258.

WYLDE, ROBERT, English Puritan divine and poet. (1609–1679)
162.

WYLIE, ELINOR HOYT, American poet and novelist. (1885–1928)
133, 399, 1218, 1873, 2193, 2226, 2261.

WYNDHAM, SIR WILLIAM, third BARONET, English politician. (1687–1740)
1605.

WYNNE, JOHN HUDDLESTONE, English miscellaneous writer. (1743–1788)
859.

WYNNE, DR. SHIRLEY WILMOTT, American physician and former Health Commissioner of New York City. (1882–1942)
461.

X

XENOCRATES, Greek philosopher. (396–314 B.C.)
1825.

XENOPHANES, Greek philosopher and poet. (c. 576–480 B.C.)
333, 473, 1059, 2049, 2166.

XENOPHON, Grecian general, historian and essayist. (c. 430–355 B.C.)
45, 1578, 1626, 1874.

Y

YALDEN, THOMAS, English poet. (1670–1736)
463, 1049.

YARRANTON, ANDREW, English engineer and agriculturist. (1616–1684?)
1304, 1798.

YATES, EDMUND, English poet, playwright and journalist. (1831–1894)
609, 663, 1857.

YATES, JOHN HENRY, American poet. (1837– ?)
694.

YATES, SIR JOSEPH, English judge. (1722–1770)
951.

YEATS, WILLIAM BUTLER, Irish poet and dramatist. (1865–1939)
37, 136, 152, 484, 806, 877, 889, 898, 1630, 1743, 1872, 1975, 2007, 2261.

YEATS-BROWN, FRANCIS, English journalist. (1886–1944)
651.

INDEX OF AUTHORS OF ADDED QUOTATIONS

BALDWIN, STANLEY, English statesman. (1867-1947)
2298w.
BALL, GEORGE WILDMAN, American lawyer and diplomat. (1909-)
2299g.
BANVILLE, THÉODORE DE, French poet and parodist. (1823–1891)
2300m.
BARKLEY, ALBEN WILLIAM, American politician; Vice-President of the United States. 1949–1953. (1877–1956)
2299t.
BARRINGTON, BISHOP SHUTE, English divine and religious writer. (1734–1826)
2298x.
BARRYMORE, ETHEL, American actress. (1879–1959)
2298j.
BARTON, BRUCE, American editor and advertising executive. (1886-)
2298j.
BARUCH, BERNARD MANNES, American financier. (1870–1965)
2298k, 2298p, 2299d, 2299e, 2299r, 2299t, 2300f.
BEAVERBROOK, WILLIAM MAXWELL AITKEN, first Baron Beaverbrook, Anglo-Canadian newspaper publisher and government official. (1879–1964)
2298t, 2298w.
BEERBOHM, SIR MAX, English critic and caricaturist. (1872–1956)
2298z, 2300l.
BEN SYRA (SIRA), collector of proverbs from the Hebrew. (c. 190 B.C.)
2298u.
BENN, ANTHONY NEIL WEDGWOOD, British politician. (1925-)
2298w.
BENTON, THOMAS HART, American painter. (1889-)
2298s.
BERLIN, IRVING, American song writer. (1888-)
2300d, 2300e.
BEVERIDGE, ALBERT JEREMIAH, American politician and historian. (1862–1927)
2299u.
BIERCE, AMBROSE, American journalist and satirist. (1842–1914?)
2299n.
BIGGERS, EARL DERR, American novelist and playwright. (1884–1933)
2298u.
BOHLEN, CHARLES EUSTIS, American diplomat. (1904-)
2298u.
BONAPARTE, NAPOLEON, see Napoleon I.
BONE, DAVID DRUMMOND, Scottish journalist. (fl. 1875)
2300c.
BONHAM CARTER, VIOLET (Lady Asquith of Yarnbury), British political leader and arts patron. (1887-)
2299u.
BOULTON, HARRY EDWIN, British poet. (1859–1935)
2300m.
BRADFORD, GAMALIEL, American poet and biographical writer. (1863–1932)
2299c.
BRALEY, BERTON, American journalist and publicist. (1882–1966)
2298t.
BRANN, WILLIAM COWPER, American journalist. (1855–1898)
2299q.
BRAUN, WERNHER VON, rocket engineer, born in Germany and resident in the United States after World War II. (1912-)
2300c.
BRISBANE, ARTHUR, American journalist. (1864–1936)
2299i.
BROGAN, DENIS WILLIAM, British political scientist and writer. (1900-)
2299n.
BROOKS, VAN WYCK, American critic and literary historian. (1886–1963)
2299l.
BROWN, JOHN MASON, American critic, essayist, and lecturer. (1900-)
2298j.
BRYAN, WILLIAM JENNINGS, American politician and government official. (1860–1925)
2299c, 2299u.
BURNS, ROBERT, Scottish poet. (1759–1796)
2300h.
BUTLER, NICHOLAS MURRAY, American educator. (1862–1947)
2298x.
BUTLER, SAMUEL, English novelist and satirist. (1835–1902)
2298k, 2298t, 2298x, 2299a, 2299c, 2299d, 2299h, 2299k, 2299l, 2299m, 2300a, 2300c, 2300f, 2300m.

C

CABELL, JAMES BRANCH, American novelist and poet. (1879–1958)
2298k, 2298v, 2298y, 2299j, 2299k, 2299l, 2300d, 2300f, 2300l.
CALHOUN, JOHN CALDWELL, American statesman. (1782–1850)
2299z, 2300m.
CANTOR, EDDIE, American comic actor. (1892-)
2300f.
ČAPEK, KAREL, Czech novelist and dramatist. (1890–1938)
2298y.
CARLYLE, THOMAS, British essayist and historian. (1795–1881)
2300m.
CARMAN, HARRY JAMES, American historian. (1884-)
2298q, 2299u.
CARNEGIE, DALE, American lecturer and writer. (1888–1955)
2299c.
CARTER, VIOLET BONHAM, see Bonham Carter, Violet.

CATULLUS, QUINTUS VALERIUS, Latin lyric and heroic poet. (87–54? B.C.)
2299k.

CAWEIN, MADISON JULIUS, American poet. (1865–1914)
2299h.

CHURCH, FRANK, American politician. (1924–)
2298k.

CHURCHILL, SIR WINSTON LEONARD SPENCER, British statesman. (1874–1965)
2298j, 2298t, 2298v, 2298w, 2299a, 2299b, 2299e, 2299g, 2300b, 2300e, 2300h, 2300i, 2300k, 2300m.

CLARK, THOMAS CAMPBELL, American jurist. (1899–)
2300a.

CLAY, HENRY, American statesman. (1777–1852)
2299u.

CLURMAN, HAROLD EDGAR, American theatrical director and critic. (1901–)
2300c.

COLBERT, JEAN BAPTISTE, French statesman and financier. (1619–1683)
2300f.

COLLINS, LEROY, American politician and government official. (1909–)
2298k, 2299b, 2299h, 2300a.

COPLAND, AARON, American composer. (1900–)
2299n.

CORWIN, THOMAS, American politician and government official. (1794–1865)
2300h.

COTY, RENÉ, French statesman. (1882–1962)
2299a.

D

DALADIER, ÉDOUARD, French statesman. (1884–)
2300h.

DAVIS, ELMER HOLMES, American journalist and broadcaster. (1890–1958)
2299a.

DAY, CLARENCE, American miscellaneous writer. (1874–1935)
2298v.

DE GAULLE, CHARLES ANDRÉ JOSEPH MARIE, French general and statesman. (1890–)
2298t, 2299b.

DE MILLE, AGNES, American dancer and choreographer. (1905–)
2298n.

DÍAZ ORDAZ, GUSTAVO, Mexican statesman. (1911–)
2298y, 2300d.

DIRKSEN, EVERETT MCKINLEY, American politician. (1896–)
2299m.

DONNE, JOHN, English poet and divine. (1573–1631)
2298o.

DOUGLAS, LORD ALFRED BRUCE, English poet. (1870–1945)
2300i.

DOUGLAS-HOME, SIR ALEXANDER FREDERICK, British statesman. (1903–)
2298s.

DOWSON, ERNEST, English poet. (1867–1900)
2299d, 2299k, 2300k.

DULLES, JOHN FOSTER, American government official; Secretary of State, 1953–59. (1888–1959)
2298l, 2300b, 2300i, 2300o.

DUNNE, FINLEY PETER, American humorist. (1867–1936)
2298s.

DWIGHT, TIMOTHY, Congregational clergyman, educator, and miscellaneous writer; president of Yale College. (1752–1817)
2300m.

E

EASTMAN, MAX FORRESTER, American editor and writer. (1883–)
2298p.

EISENHOWER, DWIGHT DAVID, American general and thirty-fourth President of the United States. (1890–)
2298l, 2298q, 2298x, 2298y, 2299b, 2299c, 2299e, 2299g, 2299q, 2299r, 2299u, 2300c, 2300e.

EISENHOWER, MILTON STOVER, American educator and government official. (1899–)
2298v, 2299j, 2300b.

ELLIS, HENRY HAVELOCK, English physician and psychologist. (1859–1939)
2298q.

ERNST, MORRIS LEOPOLD, American lawyer and critic. (1888–)
2298s, 2299s.

EVANS, ROBLEY DUNGLISON, American admiral. (1846–1912)
2300i.

F

FAULKNER, WILLIAM, American novelist and short-story writer. (1897–1962)
2299b, 2299l, 2299t, 2300l.

FIELDING, HENRY, English novelist. (1707–1754)
2299k.

FISKE, JOHN, American essayist and historian. (1842–1901)
2298l.

FOCH, FERDINAND, French marshal. (1851–1929)
2300i.

FORD, HENRY, American automobile manufacturer. (1863–1947)
2300i.

FORD, LENA GUILBERT, American poet. (fl. 1915)
2300i.

FRANCE, ANATOLE (pseudo. of JACQUES ANATOLE THIBAULT), French novelist, dramatist, and poet. (1844–1924)
2299j.

FRANKFURTER, FELIX, American jurist. (1882–1965)
2298r.

FRANKLIN, BENJAMIN, American philosopher and statesman. (1706–1790)
2298s, 2298x.

FROST, ROBERT, American poet. (1874–1963)
2299b, 2299e, 2299t, 2299x.

FULBRIGHT, JAMES WILLIAM, American politician and educator. (1905–)
2299a, 2299c, 2299q, 2299z, 2300f.

G

GARNER, JOHN NANCE, American politician; Vice-President of the United States, 1933–1941. (1868–)
2299u.

GOLDBERG, ARTHUR JOSEPH, American jurist and government official. (1908–)
2298r, 2299r.

GOLDWATER, BARRY MORRIS, American politician. (1909–)
2298q, 2298t, 2298u, 2298y, 2299e, 2299n, 2299r, 2299u, 2300g.

GOLDWYN, SAMUEL, American motion-picture producer and executive, born in Poland. (1882–)
2298y.

GOODWIN, J. CHEEVER, American librettist. (1850–1912)
2298y.

GRAHAM, HARRY JOCELYN CLIVE, English poet and dramatist. (1874–1936)
2300m.

GRAHAM, WILLIAM FRANKLIN (Billy), American evangelist. (1918–)
2299g.

GUEDALLA, PHILIP, English miscellaneous writer. (1889–1944)
2298w.

GUINEY, LOUISE IMOGEN, American poet. (1861–1920)
2299j.

GUINNESS, SIR ALEC, English actor. (1914–)
2298j.

H

HAMILTON, ALEXANDER, American statesman. (1757–1804)
2299l, 2299m, 2299u, 2300a, 2300i, 2300k, 2300m, 2300n, 2300p.

HARDING, WARREN GAMALIEL, twenty-ninth President of the United States. (1865–1923)
2299d.

HARDWICKE, SIR CEDRIC WEBSTER, English actor. (1893–1964)
2298w.

HARDY, E. J., American clergyman. (fl. 1910)
2299l.

HARLAN, JOHN MARSHALL, American jurist. (1899–)
2298r.

HARRIS, SYDNEY JUSTIN, American journalist. (1917–)
2299e.

HARRISON, ALBERTIS SYDNEY, JR., American lawyer and politician. (1907–)
2299v.

HART, MOSS, American dramatist. (1904–1961)
2299n, 2300e.

HASKINS, MINNIE LOUISE, English educator. (1875–1957)
2300n.

HAVEMANN, ERNEST CARL, American journalist. (1912–)
2299k.

HAYDON, BENJAMIN ROBERT, English historical painter and lecturer. (1786–1846)
2299z.

HEENAN, JOHN CARMEL, English clergyman, Archbishop of Westminster. (1905–)
2298o.

HEMINGWAY, ERNEST MILLER, American novelist. (1899–1961)
2300m.

HENRY, O., see O. HENRY

HERBERT, SIR ALAN PATRICK, English humorist and novelist. (1890–)
2298z.

HERFORD, OLIVER, American humorist, poet, and illustrator. (1863–1935)
2300l.

HERSHFIELD, HARRY, American monologist and toastmaster. (1885–)
2299p.

HEWART, GORDON, Viscount, British jurist; Lord Chief Justice of England, 1922–1940. (1870–1943)
2299h.

HIGHET, GILBERT, American educator, born in Scotland. (1906–)
2299m.

HITLER, ADOLF, German dictator. (1889–1945)
2300n.

HOGG, QUINTIN MCGAREL, British government official. (1907–)
2299m.

HOLMES, JOHN HAYNES, American clergyman, publicist, and reformer. (1879–)
2300a, 2300g.

HOLMES, OLIVER WENDELL, American essayist, poet, and physician. (1809–1894)
2300n.

HOLMES, OLIVER WENDELL, American jurist. (1841–1935)
2300f.

HOOVER, HERBERT CLARK, thirty-first President of the United States. (1874–1964)
2298l, 2298o, 2298q, 2298r, 2298s, 2299c, 2299l, 2299v, 2300a, 2300f.

HOUSTON, SAMUEL, American general and statesman. (1793–1863)
2298z.

HUGHES, CHARLES EVANS, American jurist; Chief Justice, 1930–1941. (1862–1948)
2298r.

HUMPHREY, HUBERT HORATIO, JR., American politician; Vice-President of the United States, 1965– (1911–)
2299i, 2299l, 2299v, 2300a, 2300e.

HURDIS, JAMES, English educator and poet. (1763–1801)
2300n.

HUXLEY, THOMAS HENRY, English physiologist and naturalist. (1825–1895)
2298v.

I

ICKES, HAROLD LE CLAIRE, American government official. (1874–1952)
2299v.

Ionesco, Eugène, Rumanian playwright resident in France. (1912–)
2298s.

Irwin, Wallace, American poet and novelist. (1875–1959)
2298z.

J

Jackson, Helen Hunt, American novelist and poet. (1831–1885)
2298z.

James, Henry, Jr., American novelist, essayist, and critic, who became a naturalized British subject. (1843–1916)
2298q, 2298w, 2298x, 2298z, 2299k, 2299l, 2299q, 2299v, 2300l, 2300n.

James, William, American psychologist. (1842–1910)
2299d, 2300g.

Jefferson, Thomas, third President of the United States. (1743–1826)
2298k, 2298l, 2298q, 2298r, 2298x, 2299d, 2299h, 2299j, 2299k, 2300f, 2300k, 2300l, 2300n.

John XXIII (Angelo Giuseppe Roncalli), Pope, 1958–1963 (1881–1963)
2298q.

Johnson, Claudia Alta Taylor (Mrs. Lyndon B. Johnson). (1912–)
2298j, 2300d.

Johnson, Gerald White, American journalist. (1890–)
2299v, 2300n.

Johnson, Lyndon Baines, thirty-sixth President of the United States. (1908–)
2298j, 2298l, 2298m, 2298n, 2298p, 2298q, 2298r, 2298s, 2298u, 2298v, 2298x, 2299a, 2299b, 2299c, 2299e, 2299f, 2299i, 2299j, 2299k, 2299n, 2299o, 2299q, 2299s, 2299v, 2299y, 2299z, 2300a, 2300b, 2300d, 2300e, 2300g, 2300i, 2300l.

Johnson, Philip Cortelyou, American architect. (1906–)
2298n.

Johnson, Samuel, English lexicographer and poet. (1709–1784)
2300f.

Jolson, Al, American actor and singer, born in Russia. (1886–1950)
2298z.

Joyce, John Alexander, American poet and essayist. (1842–1915)
2299m.

K

Kaufman, George S., American dramatist. (1889–1961)
2299n, 2300e.

Keats, John, English poet. (1795–1821)
2299i.

Keller, James G., American clergyman; founder of the Christophers. (1900–)
2300n.

Kennan, George Frost, American diplomat. (1904–)
2298m.

Kennedy, Charles Rann, American actor and playwright, born in England. (1871–1950)
2300a, 2300n.

Kennedy, Jacqueline Lee Bouvier (Mrs. John F. Kennedy). (1929–)
2299l.

Kennedy, John Fitzgerald, thirty-fifth President of the United States. (1917–1963)
2298m, 2298o, 2298p, 2298s, 2298t, 2298u, 2298v, 2298x, 2299c, 2299f, 2299g, 2299h, 2299i, 2299j, 2299m, 2299n, 2299o, 2299q, 2299s, 2299t, 2299v, 2299y, 2299z, 2300a, 2300b, 2300c, 2300d, 2300e, 2300g.

Kerr, Jean, American humorist. (1923–)
2299l.

Kerr, Walter F., American dramatic critic. (1913–)
2300e.

Kettering, Charles Franklin, American electrical engineer and inventor. (1876–1958)
2299g.

Khrushchev, Nikita Sergeyevich, Soviet Russian statesman. (1894–)
2298n, 2298o, 2299e, 2299f, 2299g, 2299p, 2299w, 2300a, 2300b, 2300i.

King, Martin Luther, Jr., American clergyman and civil-rights leader. (1929–)
2298p, 2299b, 2299o.

Kipling, Rudyard, English poet and short-story writer. (1865–1936)
2298u, 2298w, 2298z, 2300j, 2300l, 2300n.

Kirk, Grayson Louis, American educator. (1903–)
2300a.

Knebel, Fletcher, American journalist. (1911–)
2299w.

Koussevitzky, Sergei Alexandrovich, musician and conductor, born in Russia and long resident in the United States. (1874–1951)
2299n.

Kronenberger, Louis, American critic and educator. (1904–)
2300d.

Krutch, Joseph Wood, American critic, essayist, and naturalist. (1893–)
2300b.

L

La Guardia, Fiorello Henry, American politician. (1882–1947)
2299w, 2300o.

Lampton, William James, American journalist. (1859?–1917)
2299m.

Larson, Arthur, American government official and educator. (1910–)
2299w.

LeMay, Curtis Emerson, American general. (1906–)
2300d.

Lewis, Sinclair, American novelist. (1885–1951)
2298z.

Liebling, Abbott Joseph, American journalist. (1904–1963)
2299y, 2300o.

N

NAPOLEON I, NAPOLEON BONAPARTE, Emperor of the French. (1769–1821)
2298s.
NASH, OGDEN, American humorist. (1902–)
2298x.
NATHAN, GEORGE JEAN, American essayist and critic. (1882–1958)
2300e.
NEHRU, JAWAHARLAL, Indian statesman; first prime minister of the Republic of India. (1889–1964)
2299s.
NIEBUHR, REINHOLD, American theologian. (1892–)
2298s.
NIETZSCHE, FRIEDRICH WILHELM, German philosopher. (1844–1900)
2298u.
NIMITZ, CHESTER WILLIAM, American admiral. (1885–)
2300c.
NIXON, RICHARD MILHOUS, American politician; Vice-President of the United States, 1953–1960. (1913–)
2298t, 2299w.
NUREYEV, RUDOLF, Russian ballet dancer. (1938–)
2298t.

O

O. HENRY (pseud. of WILLIAM SYDNEY PORTER), American short-story writer. (1862–1910)
2298v, 2298z.
OCHS, ADOLPH SIMON, American newspaper publisher. (1858–1935)
2300o.
OGILVY, DAVID MACKENZIE, American advertising executive, born in England. (1911–)
2298k.
O'KEEFE, PATRICK F., American publicist. (1872–1934)
2299a.
ORDAZ, GUSTAVO DÍAZ, see DÍAZ ORDAZ, GUSTAVO.
OVERSTREET, BONARO WILKINSON, American writer and lecturer. (1902–)
2298y.
OVERSTREET, HARRY ALLEN, American writer and educator. (1875–)
2298y.

P

PACKARD, VANCE OAKLEY, American miscellaneous writer. (1914–)
2298k.
PAIGE, LEROY (SATCHEL), American baseball player. (c. 1910–)
2299j.
PATRICK, JOHN, American playwright. (1905–)
2299q.
PAUL VI (GIOVANNI BATTISTA MONTINI), Pope, 1963– . (1897–)
2298u, 2299f, 2299g, 2300j.
PEALE, NORMAN VINCENT, American clergyman. (1898–)
2300f.
PEGLER, JAMES WESTBROOK, American journalist. (1894–)
2299a.
PENN, WILLIAM, Quaker and founder of Pennsylvania. (1644–1718)
2300j.
PENNEY, SIR WILLIAM GEORGE, British scientist and government official. (1909–)
2298x.
PHILIP, PRINCE OF THE UNITED KINGDOM (PHILIP MOUNTBATTEN); Duke of Edinburgh, consort of Queen Elizabeth II. (1921–)
2299e, 2299n.
PINDAR, Greek lyric poet. (c. 522–442 B.C.)
2299i.
PITT, WILLIAM, first Earl of Chatham, English statesman. (1708–1778)
2299y.
PITT, WILLIAM, THE YOUNGER, English statesman. (1759–1806)
2299q.
POLLARD, JOSEPHINE, American poet. (1843–1892)
2299m.
PROUST, MARCEL, French novelist. (1871–1922)
2299f.

R

RABI, ISIDOR ISAAC, American physicist and educator. (1898–)
2300c.
RANSOM, JOHN CROWE, American poet and educator. (1888–)
2299t.
RENAN, JOSEPH ERNEST, French skeptical writer and critic. (1823–1892)
2299d, 2299j.
RESTON, JAMES BARRETT, American journalist. (1909–)
2298u, 2299p.
RICHMOND, CHARLES ALEXANDER, American clergyman and educator. (1862–1940)
2300j.
RICKENBACKER, EDWARD VERNON, American aviator and airlines executive. (1890–)
2298s.
RILEY, JAMES WHITCOMB, American poet. (1849–1916)
2299m.
ROCKEFELLER, JOHN DAVISON, American capitalist and philanthropist. (1839–1937)
2299f.
ROCKEFELLER, NELSON ALDRICH, American politician and government official. (1908–)
2298o, 2298p, 2298y, 2300g.
ROMNEY, GEORGE, American industrialist and politician. (1907–)
2299w, 2300b.
ROOSEVELT, ANNA ELEANOR (MRS. FRANKLIN DELANO ROOSEVELT), American essayist and lecturer. (1884–1962)
2298n, 2298q, 2299b, 2299k.
ROOSEVELT, FRANKLIN DELANO, thirty-second President of the United States. (1882–1945)
2299w, 2300j, 2300k.

THOMSON, ROY HERBERT (BARON THOMSON OF FLEET), British journalist, born in Canada. (1894–)
2299z.
THOREAU, HENRY DAVID, American naturalist, poet, and essayist. (1817–1862)
2299k, 2300p.
TODD, MICHAEL, American theatrical and motion-picture producer. (1909–1958)
2299y.
TOYNBEE, ARNOLD JOSEPH, English historian. (1889–)
2298q, 2299f.
TRENCH, RICHARD CHENEVIX, Archbishop, English philologist, theologian, and poet. (1807–1886)
2298w, 2299g.
TREVELYAN, GEORGE MACAULAY, English historian. (1876–1962)
2298q.
TREVOR-ROPER, HUGH REDWALD, English historian. (1914–)
2299z.
TRUMAN, DAVID BICKNELL, American educator. (1913–)
2298v.
TRUMAN, HARRY S., thirty-third President of the United States. (1884–)
2298k, 2298p, 2299g, 2299p, 2299x, 2300j.
TUCKER, SOPHIE, American cabaret singer. (1884–1966)
2299k.
TWAIN, MARK (pseud. of SAMUEL LANGHORNE CLEMENS), American humorist. (1835–1910)
2299a, 2299i, 2299j, 2299n, 2299r, 2299x, 2299y.
TYNAN, KENNETH, English dramatic critic. (1927–)
2298t.

U

UDALL, STEWART LEE, American government official. (1920–)
2299e.
UPSON, MAXWELL MAYHEW, American engineer and industrialist. (1876–)
2299n.
UREY, HAROLD CLAYTON, American scientist. (1893–)
2298t.

V

VANDENBERG, ARTHUR HENDRICK, American politician and journalist. (1884–1951)
2299h.
VANDERBILT, CORNELIUS ("COMMODORE" VANDERBILT), American financier. (1794–1877)
2298x.
VIDAL, GORE, American novelist and dramatist. (1925–)
2298j, 2298t.
VOLTAIRE (pseud. of FRANÇOIS MARIE AROUET), French philosopher and dramatist. (1694–1778)
2300p.

W

WANAMAKER, JOHN, American merchant. (1838–1922)
2298k.
WARREN, EARL, American jurist; Chief Justice, 1953– . (1891–)
2299a.
WASHINGTON, BOOKER TALIAFERRO, American educator. (c. 1859–1915)
2299i, 2299p.
WATTERSON, HENRY, American journalist. (1840–1921)
2299x.
WAUGH, EVELYN ARTHUR ST. JOHN, English novelist. (1903–1966)
2300m.
WEBSTER, DANIEL, American statesman. (1782–1852)
2299i, 2299j.
WELLS, HERBERT GEORGE, English novelist and social reformer. (1866-1946)
2300k, 2300p.
WESLEY, CHARLES, English Methodist divine and hymn writer. (1707–1788)
2299d.
WESTCOTT, EDWARD NOYES, American novelist. (1847–1898)
2299a, 2299m.
WHEELER, POST, American journalist and diplomat. (1869–1956)
2299z.
WHITE, WILLIAM ALLEN, American journalist. (1868–1944)
2299a, 2299x.
WHITTIER, JOHN GREENLEAF, American poet. (1807–1892)
2299h.
WILDE, OSCAR O'FLAHERTIE WILLS, Irish wit, poet, and dramatist. (1856–1900)
2299a, 2299k, 2299l, 2299m.
WILLKIE, WENDELL LEWIS, Amercian lawyer, businessman, and politician. (1892–1944)
2299x.
WILSON, CHARLES ERWIN, American industrialist and government official. (1890–1961)
2298p.
WILSON, FRANK WILEY, American jurist. (1917–)
2299h.
WILSON, THOMAS WOODROW, twenty-eighth President of the United States. (1856-1924)
2298w, 2299j.

INDEX AND CONCORDANCE

SUGGESTIONS FOR THE USE OF THE CONCORDANCE

THE CONCORDANCE is a word-index to all the quotations in the book, grouped alphabetically by leading words and phrases, with a reference not only to the page on which the quotation may be found, but also to its number on the page, so that it may be turned to instantly. The first entry in the index on the following page is 39:13, which means the thirteenth quotation on page 39. Identifying words and phrases are generously given, in order that a quotation which is not exactly remembered may be traced through any one of a number of channels.

Let us suppose that the phrase which is being sought is, "The conscious water saw its God, and blushed." Perhaps all that is remembered of it is that it has something to do with water seeing God, or with water blushing. In either case it would be evident that the place to look for it is under "Water." It could of course be looked for in the text under that subject, where it would be found (2124:14), with a cross-reference to "Miracle," where the whole quotation, together with several variations, has been placed, because it has to do with the miracle of turning water into wine. But the easier way would be to look under "Water" in the CONCORDANCE, where two entries referring to it will be found, "conscious water saw its God," and "saw its God and blushed," both referring directly to the main quotation, 1315:14. And it will also be found under "Blushed" ("saw its God and b."), in case any one should happen to look there first.

So with every quotation in the book. The word selected for the index entry is always the noun—if there is a noun—which is the subject of the sentence, in the above case "Water." But many others are thrown in for good measure, as "Blushed" is in this instance, so that the quotation may be found even if the principal noun is incorrectly remembered. "Chip of the old block," for example, is entered under both "Chip" and "Block." Where there is no noun, the principal adjective or verb is used. "Absent one from another" will be found under "Absent." "Who excuses accuses" will be found under both "Accuses" and "Excuses." An effort has also been made to include all unusual words and phrases by which a quotation might stand out in the memory. "A biscuit or two with Brie" is naturally indexed under "Biscuit," but it will be found also under "Brie."

The only exception to this detailed indexing is where the subject is a very short one. The black-letter lines in the CONCORDANCE indicate subject-headings in the body of the book, and where the subject runs less than a column of text, such as "Abstinence," the quotations under this subject carrying this word are not indexed separately unless they are unusually important, and the reader should turn at once to the subject itself and run through the entries under it—a matter of a moment. Where the same key-word occurs in quotations under other headings it is, of course, indexed. Thus, under the black letter subject-heading "Abstinence" in the CONCORDANCE will be found two entries from quotations on other pages. This system was adopted in order to keep the CONCORDANCE free from unnecessary entries, and to hold it within manageable proportions.

Some niceties of the alphabetical arrangement should perhaps be explained. Under each subject the singular noun comes first ("God," for example); then the singular possessive ("God's"); then the hyphenated compounds ("God-like"); then the plural ("Gods"); and finally the plural possessive ("Gods' "). Proper nouns precede common nouns. All foreign-language quotations follow the English ones, even if the key-word is identical, so that the French entries beginning with "Art," for instance, will be found immediately after the English ones beginning with the same word. It should also be remembered that a word is sometimes spelled in different ways, as "blessed" and "blest." Cross-references call attention to this, and both spellings should be consulted, as the text follows the style used by the author.

All entries necessarily are very brief, but an effort has been made to give sufficient context to enable the reader to identify the quotation readily. It should be pointed out, however, that the mind of the reader will not always run exactly in accord with the mind of the indexer, and the phrase which springs to the reader's memory may not be the exact one which the indexer has chosen, in which case a little perseverance may be necessary to turn up the quotation desired.

No one can get the full benefit of this book without understanding thoroughly the use of the CONCORDANCE, for it is the key to its contents, and if the reader will spend a little time familiarizing himself with the suggestions given above he will find the book much more useful and satisfactory than it could otherwise be.

INDEX AND CONCORDANCE

See also page 2811 for index to recent additions.

Apparel, *continued*
oft proclaims the man 491: 1
shapes 485: 6; 332: 2
Apparelled in celestial light 2266:11
in more precious habit 1297: 4
Apparere: non a. si sumas potest 1998: 2
Apparition
See also Ghost
a lovely A. sent 2186: 7
horrid a., tall 769:14
Apparitions and prodigies 1944:16
seen and gone 1018: 2
thousand blushing a. 173: 5
which are, and are not 2002: 5
Appeal from ballot to bullet 2099: 2
no a. against judgment 1022:12
of truth to time 812: 9
to Philip sober 502:20
unto Cæsar 212:10
woe to him who has no a. ..1022:12
Appear: not what I a. 86: 2
Appearance 85
appoint a. and return 300: 2
bears away the bell 85:11
good a. recommendation 85: 5
imposing a. no brain 86:10
judge not according to a. ..86: 8
of neatness 485:21
of not hearing insult 1651: 8
outward a. of virtue 948:10
preferred to reality 720: 5
those of evil a. best 86:11
thou hast a grim a. 609:16
Appearances: always scorn a. 88: 3
concerned for outward a. ..88: 7
don't judge by a. 2287: 3
guess at women by a. ..2179: 3
judge by appearances 85:15
keep up appearances 88: 1
no trusting to a. 86: 8
of four kinds 88: 4
resist a. 88: 2
terrible doubt of a. 88: 9
those awful goddesses 88: 6
to save, his only care 88: 1
very deceitful 86: 8
Appetence: lustful a. 2105: 4
Appetens: alieni a., sui profusus 119:13
Appétit vient en mangeant ..89:13
Appetite 88
abhorring in my a. 89: 2
all requires skill but a. ..1833:17
allay their a. with gust 452:14
bent a. beyond sphere 89: 8
best sauce 88:10
but no food 88:16
comes with eating 89:13
doth not the a. alter 89:18
even as a. play the god ..981: 2
flemeth discretion 90: 5
for grief 1491: 3
from judgement stands aloof 90:11
fruitful mother of a. 230:16
goes to bed with me 89:13
govern well thy a. 90: 7
grown by what it fed on ..89:16
hath he to eat a mouse 223: 1
how quaint an a. in woman 2208: 9
hungry edge of a. 962: 8
if thou be given to a. 90: 8
leave with an a. 88:11
makes eating a delight 90: 2
men have ever likerous a. 1223: 9
mortified a. never wise 90:12
nature gives an a. 517: 3
no wish to spoil my a. ..522: 4
no wish to waste a. 89: 9
nothing more shameless 89: 4
over-nice a. 89:14
prophetic eye of a. 88:13
rise from banquet with a. ..88:11
seek a. by toil 89: 6
sharpen with sauce 315:15
sick man's a. 89:16
stop short of a. 518:19
surfeiting, a. may sicken 1365:15
taste confounds the a. 89:12
Appetite, *continued*
well-govern'd and wise a. 808: 2
where a. stands cook 88:15
whose name was A. 90: 1
Appetites bigger than bellies 89:15
cloy the a. they feed 2076:16
fools create new a. 1328: 3
ruled by sight above 438:14
subdue your a. 90: 6
subject to reason 90: 6
to make our a. keen 89:19
were hearty 88:12
Appetitus rationi 90: 6
Applaud a man's speech ..293:10
contented to a. myself ..118:13
to the very echo 466: 2
us when we run 1616: 7
Applause 90
attentive to his own a. 13:12
deserved a. 90:19
dismiss me with a. 1124:17
echo of a platitude 90:13
from none but self a. ..1126:13
give us your a. 91: 6
has ruined him 90:23
ill-timed a. wrong speaker 1260: 2
in spite of faults, due ..2253: 6
less blessing than snare 91: 8
makes head giddy 91: 5
neglect a. of multitude ..831:10
of a single human being 90:18
of listening senates 91: 1
popular a. 90:21
satiate of a. 31:14
sole proprietor of just a. ..91: 7
spur of noble minds 90:15
thence a., hence profit 1979:15
was without art 90:20
Apple 91
a day keeps doctor away ..91:10
all evil brought by a. 92: 2
art thou topmost a. 92: 4
better given than eaten 91:11
eat a. on going to bed 91:10
egg, orange, nut 91:11
fruit of human sin 499:11
how the devil got the A. in ..92:10
is an excellent thing 1475:17
like than a. and oyster ...1155: 2
lost with a., won with nut ..91:16
Newton saw a. fall 1400: 1
of his eye 597:12
pares a. cleanly feed 91:14
pie and cheese 92: 5
pluck a. from branch 92: 3
rotten a. spoils others 982:10
rotten at the heart 949: 8
was the a. applesauce 11:13
where the a. reddens 352:12
which reddens on topmost bough 92: 4
will not wed, eat cold a. 91:10
Apple's: for the a. sake 12: 2
Apple-cart: upset the a. 92: 1
Apple-dumpling: refuses a. ..522: 7
Apple-Dumplings sew 92:10
Apple-pie and cheese 92: 5
causes 92: 5
Apple-tart: carv'd like a. ...489: 5
cream to eat with a. 331: 8
Apple-tree: let us plant a. 2036: 6
you shan't climb our a. ..2295: 2
Apple-trees: melancholy old a. 91:13
Apples: bad to eat a. 12: 2
bloom of sciential a. 1108: 8
burned among leaves 116: 9
eat no green a. 254:14
from the tamarisk 746: 9
greater charm to early a. 1415:17
happy a. when south winds ..91:12
how we a. swim 91: 9
lie scattered 92: 8
love-a. that bloom 92: 2
of gold in pictures 2220: 5
on other side sweetest 91:15
on the Dead Sea's shore .452:14
quench flame of Venus 91:10
small choice in rotten a. .260:14
smelt most sweet 659:19
Apples, *continued*
stolen be your a. 1618: 2
sure as God made little a. .226:10
that are bitter-sweet 91:13
Applesauce: was the apple a. ..11:13
Appliance your disease requires 1980: 3
Application: bearing lies in a. 1897:13
Appointment: behold fine a. he makes 1790:11
not by a. 1016: 7
Appomattox: its apple tree 821: 4
Apprehension: in a. how like a god 1239: 5
of peril, danger 363:17
of the good 811:16
suffered more from a. ..2044:14
Apprehensions come in crowds 657: 7
greater as unknown 2045: 8
shut their a. up 2042:17
Apprenticeship to renunciation 1115: 4
Appris: ils n'ont rien a. ..304: 3
Approbation from Sir Hubert Stanley 1579: 2
gave the bays 1580: 6
of mankind 1701:13
thirst for a. 1577: 8
Appropriate as difficult as to invent 1507: 2
Appropriation Clause 1919: 8
Approval of the people 90:21
to secure own a. 1789: 9
Approve: men of sense a. ..14:10
April 92
an A. day in the morning ..93:15
in her eyes 93:11
in her face 133:19
in the west wind 2153: 2
laugh thy girlish laughter ..93:18
make me over, Mother A. ..92:14
misted A. 92:14
of her prime 25: 4
proud-pied A. 93:12
sweet wild A. 93:16
till A.'s dead 873: 1
warms the world anew 93:17
well-apparel'd A. 93:12
when they woo 1274: 5
April's amazing meaning 93: 3
Apron: make a. for Miss Eve 1908:12
smell of the a. 1923:10
Apron-strings: hold by a. 1630: 7
look upon her a. 2180:10
Aprons: fig-leaves for a. ...487:10
greasy a. 1066:12
to go in leather a. 70:16
Apros capiam duos 160: 8
sibi totos ponit a. 519:12
Aptam dimittere noli 15: 3
Aptitude: each man has a. 1962: 1
Aptus: beatissimus qui totus a. ex sese 1785:13
cras minus a. erit 1131:10
qui non est hodie 2010:14
Aqua: molli saxa caventur a. 2126:10
Aquam a pumice 119: 9
et polentam 518: 1
Aquas: quærit a. in acquis 1987:12
Aquila non capit muscas 509: 8
non fa' guerra ai ranocchi ..509: 8
Aquilæ: neque progenerant a. columbam 69:13
Aquilam volare doces 510: 9
Arab at his prayers 434: 9
with guest 1016: 4
Arabesque: graceful a. of vines 1502: 4
Arabia: all A. breathes ..1487: 5
Arabie the blest 1487: 5
Ararat: with Andes and ..95:14
Aratro jugera regiæ 1041:15
Arberi grandi piu ombra ..2035:11
Arbiter elegantiæ 1966: 4
Arbitrament of swords ..1956: 8
Arbitrate: who shall a. 1966: 5

Art, *continued*
of Writing 2249: 5
of writing billet-doux 686:16
old masters not a. 102:21
one way possible of speaking truth 101: 6
only a. her guilt to cover .2201:16
path of creator to his work .101:11
perfection of nature 105: 6
plagiarist or revolutionist .102:19
popularity in a. 106:14
preservative of arts 1612:13
pursued with view to money 2250: 8
Puseyism in a. 103: 5
quickens nature 136:14
reaching for vagrant beauty 102: 4
read a. and wisdom rare .2240:12
repays with grand triumphs 101: 9
represents things truly 102: 6
requires entire self-devotion 101: 9
revelation of man 105: 2
right hand of nature 105: 8
sacrifice and self-control ..102: 3
seasons beauty 140: 5
science in the flesh 101: 8
secret of life is in a. 101: 5
shadow of humanity 101:17
shall love true love 51: 9
should never be popular ..106:14
so vast is A. 104: 5
specimen of a. peculiarly English 559: 9
strives for form 101: 3
strong, mimetic a. 761:12
supplies where strength may fail 717:19
supreme a. of teacher ..1969:11
temple of a. built of words 101:13
tender strokes of a. 10: 2
that can immortalize 102:16
that nature makes 105:10
theirs is the kingdom of a. .103: 9
theory of a. 107: 9
thou hast many infamies 2113: 1
to blot 505:10
to conceal a. 103:10
to dissemble a. 103:10
tongue-tied by Authority ..103:13
too precise in every part ..487:12
vain the lessons of a. 105:11
vaunted works of a. 104:15
venerate a. as a. 102:14
violated every rule of a. ..446:13
way to success in art 106:14
what a. can a woman ..1351:11
what a. wash guilt away 2201:16
what thou a., thou a. 236:11
which adds to nature 105:10
which is grand and yet simple 101: 3
whose A. was Nature 570: 1
would better Nature's best 105: 9
Art de vous taire 2027: 6
Art's perfect forms 130: 8
Arta decet sanum 13: 5
Arte Dio quasi è nipote 105: 4
magistra 1833:21
perennat amor 1224: 7
vostra quella 105: 4
Artem: libens censebo exerceat a. 1424:15
quam quisque norit a. 106: 5
vitam est, longam a. 104: 1
Arteries: man as old as a. ..38: 7
Artes emollit mores 1923:16
hæ tibi erunt a. 1738:16
omnes a. habent vinculum 101: 7
theatrales a. 1909:19
Artful Dodger, the 1377: 6
to no end 318: 9
Arthur str ts 9: 1
Arthur's: in A. bosom 886: 5
Article: to last a. ..... .743: 3
Articles de foy 619:12
Artifex: qualis a. pereo 416:11
Artifice disdain 703:11
Artificer: great A. 2141: 7
lean, unwashed a. 1066:12
Artificer, *continued*
of death 1854: 4
of own happiness 859:15
word-mosaic a. 2230:11
Artifices arte perire sus ..1710:10
Artificium nunquam moritur 528:13
Artillery: heaven's a. 2000: 7
infallible a. 1589: 2
love's great a. 1188:11
of words 2225: 6
Artisan and artist 1715: 8
Artist 106
and censor differ 107:11
born to pick and choose ...106: 1
choice is what separates a. 107:14
confuse man and a. 107:11
dips in his own soul 106: 8
envies what a. gains 564:23
fashions beauty out of chaos 129: 6
first an amateur 106:16
free to create any image ..106:13
gleaned from many faces ..108: 1
grasps the flame 107:18
great a. the simplifier 106: 3
greatest a. follows nature .105: 2
greatest a. greatest ideas .107:13
half a. and half anchorite .719:16
hired an a. to curse 353: 9
idle for want of a. 107:15
in accord with himself ...340: 2
is a dreamer 107:14
is a great thing 106: 6
is a rare, rare breed 191:12
judge better than people .1912: 7
makes a bad husband ...101: 9
may visit a museum 1477: 1
needs no religion 107: 4
never dies 107: 7
no man is born an a. 672: 4
nothing from a. that is not in the man 107: 8
of the Universe 796: 6
or as artisan 105: 2
paints his own nature 106: 8
planet for pedestal 107: 1
regenerated into poetic a. 1532:11
scratch an a. 107: 5
sets down his vision 107: 6
should be artic late ,......107:19
though he have not tools ..107: 2
torpid a. seeks inspiration .106:15
was forgotten 107: 7
what an a. the world is losing 416:11
will let wife starve 107:17
without sentiment 106: 6
writes autobiography 106: 8
Artist's jealousy 142:10
throbs the a. heart 107:10
what is the A. duty 106: 2
Artistic: never a. period ..103:18
Artists, authors, actors 108:11
must be sacrificed to art ..106:16
revealed to one another 108: 5
Artless catch the game 317:11
Artos rodere casses 135:15
Arts: all a. are brothers ..103:17
all A. are vain 349:14
all a. linked together 101: 7
Babblative and Scribblative 2223: 9
copiers of nature ... .105: 4
divorced from truth 102:13
great a. now, no poetry ..1517:10
in a. of death outdoes Nature 2113: 6
in which the wise excel .2253: 4
inglorious a. of peace 344: 8
jugglin' hocus-pocus a. ..1558:13
meretricious a. of dress ...485:11
new a. destroy the old .102:17
no a., no letters 233:14
of building from bee 144: 1
of deceiving 420:14
theatrical a. 1909:19
vain without fortune 349:14
well fitted in a. 239: 4
which I lov'd 1923:18
Arvina orationis 1927:12
Aryan: hustle the A. brown .513:15
Ascend, I follow thee 1420: 2
Ascending thorough just degrees 903:21
Ascolta chi la nota 1165: 3
Ase: sits poking in the a. ..222: 3
Ashamed: more a. more respectable 1706: 5
of our naked skins 1810: 3
to say what you think 217: 7
were not a. 1416: 9
Ashes: chew'd bitter a. 452:14
I wish my a. to repose ..1378: 4
in a. live wonted fires 667: 2
of my chance 78:14
of Napoleon Bonaparte ...1378: 4
of roses these 1687:16
raked-up a. of the past 34: 6
sow in a., reap in dust ...1491:10
that are left behind 2017:12
thou these a., little brook 2135:14
throw a. on their heads ...67: 5
to a. 964:19
to the taste 452:14
turn to a. on the lips 452:14
wouldst find my a. 190:12
Ashlar: new-cut a. 2232: 5
Asia's groaning millions ..675: 5
Asile: éternité deviens a. ..579: 3
Asinum non potest, stratum cædit 112:12
Asinus: ex auribus cognoscitur a. 112:11
Ask, and it shall be given 1586:10
don't a. for what you'll wish you hadn't got ..2169: 7
not to be denied 144:16
only for high things 1585:10
to a. is highest price 145:9; 1605: 6
who fears to a. 2215: 5
Askelon: publish it not in 1496:16
Asketh: every one that a. receiveth 1586:10
Asking highest price 145: 9
what they knew 1665: 6
Asleep in lap of legends ...83: 3
in the deep 2289:11
neither fear nor hope ..1844: 5
not good for anything 1843:12
we are all equal 1843: 4
Asno sufre la carga 111: 8
Asp: let a. with adder fight 1614: 1
Asparagi: celerius quam a. cocuntur 316: 6
Asparagus 522: 7
inspires gentle thoughts ..522: 7
quicker than 316: 6
Aspect: close a. of his 1698: 4
of such vinegar a. 1853: 9
sweet a. of princes 1611:20
sweet, grave 608: 9
Aspen: shake like an a. 2038: 1
Aspen-trees tremble 2038: 1
Aspens show light and shade 608:15
Aspera: per a. ad astra ..1913: 9
silvis 472:15
Asperitas agrestis 1260: 3
Aspersion: babbler's trade 1760:11
upon my parts of speech ..820:15
Aspersions throw a stone 1836: 8
Aspersius nihil est 115: 3
Aspes: as an a. leaf she 'gan to shake 657:14
Asphodel: ankles sunken in a. 688: 1
flowering meads 688: 2
Aspiration 108
cannot prove an a. 1621:11
failed, in a. vast 614: 3
I drink wine of a. 109: 6
lifts him from the earth ...110:11
men overbold in a. 109:11
of man sacred 285:17
sees only one side 1560:18
should be fulfilled 572:10
Aspirations are my only friends 110: 2
old loves, old a. 41:13
outlive men's lives 41:13

Bell, *continued*
surly sullen b. 405:10
thou soundest merrily 153: 4
to the prompter's b. 11: 3
toll'd by earthquake 2097: 9
vesper b. from far 153: 5
warning b. 2120:16
who will b. the cat 222:19
Bell-boy: comic b. 783: 7
Bell-wether to the rest 388:14
Bella! horrida bella 2113:10
justa b. quibus necessaria 2111:10
man: letumque gero 2120:10
matribus detestata 2112:15
ob eam causam in pace ..2118: 4
placuit nullos triumphos .2114: 2
Belle dame sans merci 123:11
gentle b. reject a Lord ..1856:14
Lou'siana B. 2286: 5
vain to be a b. 138: 5
Bellerium: from old B. 546: 1
Bellican: mouth holds more than b. 1477: 9
Bellies: appetites bigger than b. 89:15
stuff b. with ache 517: 4
swell with dropsy 460:12
Bellies': for their b. sake ..155:11
Bellis: omnia misera in b. civibus 2113:14
Bello: ibis redibis non morieris in b. 1436:11
in b. plurumum ingenium 2106:17
nulla salus b. 2119:13
pejor est b. timor 2109: 9
Bellerophonte: melior B. ..931:10
Bellorophontem tebellas ..1102: 8
Bellow of the blast 152: 4
Bellows of the mind 1006: 1
puff with pair of b. 2256:13a
Bells: angels' music 1752:12
are best of preachers 153:12
are music's laughter 153:10
are voice of the church 153:11
bid the merry b. ring 154: 7
call others 153: 7
cheerful Sabbath b. 153: 1
down in the b. and grass ..11:12
have been anointed 153:11
knows how to ring the b. 1055: 9
like ringing of church b. ..153: 1
love not noise of b. 153: 6
may ring their b. now 154: 9
mellow wedding b. 152:20
music nearest heaven 153:10
no wedding b. for her ..2291:10
of Shandon 1733: 6
on Christmas Day 270: 6
Play uppe, O Boston b. ..153: 9
ring out, wild b. 2262: 8
ringeth to evensong 372: 8
sound to call others 1677: 4
sounds of village b. 153: 3
sweet b. jangled out of tune 1313: 5
that rang without a hand 771: 3
they tune like b. 152:19
those evening b. 154: 1
ting, ting, that's how the b. go 2280: 3
Bellum striketh 2247:21
Bellum: civile avertite b. ..2114: 2
diu apparadum est b. 2106:14
inexpertis 2111: 6
justum est b., quibus necessarium 2111:10
magis desierat 2119:12
nisi pax quæsita 2118: 4
ostendite modo b. 2118:13
Belly **154**
all well with b.. feet 871: 5
began to cry cupboard 940: 3
breaks chastity down 155:10
cannot make respectable ..155: 6
carries the legs 155: 5
cook although the b. ache 1183:13
deny everything except the b. 155: 6
disappointed b. 154:17
dispenser of genius 155: 3
Belly, *continued*
do not mourn with the b. 155: 4
fair round b. with capon 2240: 5
fat b. not fine sense 647:11
for a single b. all this food 315:14
full b. makes dull brain 155: 7
given up to the b. 1123: 3
God send thee ale 45: 1
great b. but no palate 1169: 9
gross b. 154:15
has a wolf in 's b. 2177: 5
has no ears 154:12
his wit in his b. 156: 2
hungry b. barks for food 1310:20
in the b. of the grape 2156: 6
little round b. 155:19
many kept busy to humor b. 155:18
mother of all evil 155:10
never let back be warm 155: 8
no barricado for a b. 156: 2
no clock more regular 155:14
not filled with words 155:13
O importunate b. 156: 6
robs the back 155: 8
seat of empire 155:12
slaves to the b. 81:13
something a round b. 164: 4
spent under Devil's b. 155:15
vilest of beasts 154:15
what the b. asketh 498: 4
when b. fall, bones at rest ..156: 3
who does not mind his b. ..154:16
whose God is their b. 155:11
will not listen to advice ..154:12
with bad pains 155:17
with nothin' in 'is b. 1864:14
woman with a big b. 129: 3
your b. chimes 155:14
Belly-naked: saw him b. 11: 8
Belly-timber: founded on your b. 155:12
Bellyfull is b. 155:16
of fighting 665: 8
Belongings of others 1986: 4
Beloved by none 1184:14
over all 1465: 6
Belshazzar had a letter .1101: 8
Beltane: blooming at B. ..1552: 1
Belted you and flayed you 1252: 9
Belua: constat leviori b. ...1537: 5
multorum es capitum 1484: 1
Ben: ah B.! Say how 1015:13
my old hero 1322:11
Ben Battle was a soldier bold 1654:18
Ben Bolt: don't you remember sweet Alice, B. B. 1296: 9
Ben trovato 995: 2
Bench: mourner's b. 1691:18
Benches: anxious b. 1691:18
Bend: rather b. than break 1650: 4
Bene: good for bootless b. 1585:18
Bene facere, male audire ..1040: 6
malo b. facere periculum ...653:10
merenti mala es 810: 7
nati, b. vestiti 764:14
pro b. cum mali metas 987: 4
quod b. potes facere noli differre 1614: 2
si b. quid facias, facias cito 774: 7
si quid facias, nec meminisse 156: 8
si vales b. est. ego valeo ...870:17
vult nisi bene fac't 994:17
Benedick the married man 1264: 2
Benediction
See also Blessing
of these heavens 168:19
out of heaven's b. 1634: 1
perpetual b. 1214:17
that follows after prayer 1877: 9
with God's b. upon her ..131:19
Benedictions: celestial b. ...16: 9
Benefacit: sibi b. qui b. amico 739: 7
Benefactor: first great b. of race 12: 4
Beneficence of friendship ..743:18
Beneficent easier than just 1031:11
Beneficia excidunt hærent injuriæ 987: 6
læta sunt 156:17
nemo scribit 427:16
Beneficium accipere et reddere nescit 156:13
accipere, libertatem vendere 156:14
bis dat, qui dat celeriter ..775:11
clericorum 1590: 4
collocari puto 1036:16
dando accepit 653:11
dignis, omnes obliges 156:15
ingratum est b. 775: 6
non in eo quod fit 156:16
qui dare nescit 653:11
qui dedit b. taceat 156: 8
Benefit: accept b., sell freedom 156:14
cited as reproach 987: 5
consists not in what is done 156:16
distinguish between b. and injury 1791: 8
equivalent to injury 987: 5
he who confers a b. 156: 7
hook in every b. 156:14
is a good office 156:16
of Clergy 1590: 4
they whom I b. 984:13a
writes itself on wave 987: 1
Benefits **156**
are in common set 728:14
chief source for evils 156:12
common among friends ..728:15
disable b. of own country 2032: 6
excite hatred 156:17
forget b. cling to injuries 987: 6
forgot 984:15
please like flowers 156:11
sow b. reap injuries 987: 4
too great to be repaid 156:17
write b. in marble 156:10
write b. upon the wave ...987: 1
Benevolence
See also Philanthropy
characteristic of man ...1492:16
display b., not state 1329:10
does most harm or good ..1494:10
in trifles 328: 5
'tis for b. one loves people 2208: 6
Benevolent assimilation ...970:10
one-sided and fussy 1494:13
Benighted walks 2134:19
Benignitas: ne b. major esset 777: 6
Benignitate benignitatis ..1036: 6
Benignitatis: me ditavit ..1035:13
Benizon: without our b. ..353:15
Benjamin: sweet B. 2024:19
Bennett: that's May B. 120: 8
Bent: follow your own b. ..973:10
you all are b. 1642:22
Beq eath: what can we b. .1562: 7
Berkeley: Bishop B. said ..1314:13
destroyed world 1314:15
Bermoothes: still-vex'd B. .1643:13
Berries on one stem 2067: 3
Berry: bright b. from naked thorn 2261:15
brown as a b. 1631: 6
God could have made better b. 672:6; 1921:13
O sweeter than the b. 2213: 9
Beryl-rimmed rebecs 1879: 2
Besognios: pilfering b. 1641:21
Besom won't board you 1226:13
Best: all is for the b. 1435: 4
bad's the b. of us 1247: 4
began b., can't end worst .1434: 8
believed the b. 152:17
better in one general b. 1194: 6
choose what is b. 356: 4
corrupted are worst 319:15
created of every creature's b. 1485:17
die first 380:12
does the b. he can 324:21
folks hae done their b. ...1956:13
from worst 290:12
he doubtless did his b. 2011: 7
he has done his b. 1:12
is b., if never intermix'd 2055: 2

Bird, *continued*
thou art a bitter b. 1671:11
thou never wert 1073: 1
wasn't black, was yellow 1157:13
whom Man loves best 1735:12
whose tail's a diadem 1476: 5
with the broken pinion 290:13
with the red stomacher 1735: 8
with the wisp of straw 1909: 2
Bird-song: gush of b. 93:15
Bird-songs in hearts 1568: 3
Birdie: what does b. say ..162:12
with a yellow bill 1730:14
Birmingham: night we went to B. 1734: 5
Birds 160
are flown 160:11
are silent in their nest 1941: 4
breed not vipers 1527: 7
bury me where b. will sing 417:18
call for their mates 2071: 6
can fly, an' why can't I ..694: 2
catch old b. with chaff 160: 4
confabulate or no 160: 9
couple too, this day 2071: 9
dame Nature's minstrels .161:12
do not sing in caves 910: 7
eagle suffers little b. 510: 4
false b. can fetch wind ..604:14
go north again 291: 9
have God for caterer 160: 6
in last year's nests 160: 7
in little nests agree 161: 8
joyous the b. 1273: 8
know when friend is nigh 162:13
little b. sang east 161:10
long-tailed b. of Paradise 1551: 9
made b. in moment merry .162: 2
may pick dead lion 1163:19
melodious b. sing madrigals 1732: 4
met b. and justled 799:11
mugwumps, long-tailed b. 1551: 9
named all b. without gun 149:10
never lim'd no fear 989:16
nor sow nor reap 161: 7
of a feather 289: 2
of the air have nests 910:11
other men catch the b. 99: 1
sing on a bare bough 151:14
singing b. musicians 962: 7
sit brooding in snow 2161:10
somewhere the b. are singing 1347: 2
strange b. are on the air ...161:14
sweetly did sing 162: 1
that cease to sing 4: 5
that tune their morning's joy 162: 1
their paramours find 2071: 8
these are unchanging 162:11
to man's succour flee 363: 9
two b. sitting on fence ..753: 3
two b. with one stone 160: 8
where late the sweet b. sang 36: 3
without despair to get in 1278:16
would sing and think it were not night 604: 8
Biretta in mano 328:15
Birth 163
all-embracing b. 261: 5
and ancestry scarcely our own 70:11
compels it 72:12
death and b. are one 407:16
end of b. is death 407: 5
from b. begin to die 407:20
high b. never disparaged ..70:15
impulses of deeper b. 1871:18
in a famous city 275: 2
life, and death 1148:12
my love is of b. as rare ..1213: 1
new b. of freedom 432: 1
new b. of our new soil 1150: 6
noble b. imposes obligation .72:12
nothing but death begun .1150: 8
nothing where virtue not ..2003: 6
our b. is but a sleep 164:10
Saviour's b. is celebrated ..233: 7
Birth, *continued*
some glory in their b. 1606:11
was of the womb 164: 2
what can b. bestow 71: 6
Birth's invidious bar 69: 2
Birth-pangs of nations 1714: 4
Birth-Stones 165
Birthday 164
different dooms our b. 164:12
dry America's first b. ...1618: 7
my b. 165: 1
of eternity 413: 9
of your eternity 967: 1
yo r b. to me is dear 165: 2
Birthdays: count your b. ..164:13
Birthplace: for b. moans ...907: 6
of song 1767: 8
true man's b. grand 165:12
Birthright 165
grudge you not the b. 2070:21
high and holy 71: 6
sell b. with liberty 1106: 12
sold his b. unto Jacob 165:10
thank God for such a b. ..165:12
Birthrights: bearing their b. 165:13
Bis dat qui dat celeriter 775:11
Biscay: in the Bay of B., O 1813:15
Biscay's sleepless bay 1775: 4
Biscuit or two with Brie ...933: 8
twice baked 316: 1
Bishop: hypocrisy of a b. ...53: 9
I would not the good b. be 1589:15
looked grave at his jest ..1592: 7
no marble b. on his tomb ..1502: 4
of His Reverence 1593: 7
ought to die on his legs ...417: 9
should die preaching 417: 9
to cry No B. 1683: 3
Bishops: by b. bred 210:13
divide, clergy 1589:11
Bit by him that comes behind 1536:18
ev'ry little b. added to what you've got 2285: 3
golden b. no better horse 1718: 6
Bitch biteth ill 472: 3
Bitch-goddess, Success 1931: 9
Bitches: you sons of b. 67: 5
Bite: bark worse than b. ..471:15
dead men b. not 377: 1
hand that fed them 984: 2
killing dog cure b. 470:10
now you can't see to b. ..679: 6
though mad, I will not b. .1231: 5
Biter should be bit 1710: 3
wit to bite the b. 1710: 3
Bites him to the bone 1664: 5
Tartar b. the ground 375:12
the bloody sand 375:12
two b. of a cherry 1631:15
Bits in certain jaws 1918:10
Bitter but I like it 876:19
end 539: 5
for sweet and sweet for b. .810: 9
goes before the sweet 1952:19
muse how b. can spring up 1953: 1
o'er flowers its venom ...1018:13
past, more welcome sweet 1953: 9
to endure, sweet remember 1293:18
to look into happiness 860: 5
to some b.. to others sweet 1953: 4
to sweet end 1285: 8
with b. chase sweet 634:17
Bittern booming in the weeds 1749: 5
Bitterness in heart of devout 1694:14
in midst of wit, b. 2173: 7
of your galls 36: 1
say not so in b. 1175: 8
thou art in the gall of b. ..583: 1
worse than b. of death 927: 2
Bitterns: habitation of b. .1749: 3
Bitters of love 1197: 4
Bivalve we call the mind ..1516:12
Bivouac: in b. of Life 897: 5
of the dead 1869:11
Blab: they must b. 1642:25
Blabbed: why have I b. 1900:12
Black 166
above b. there is no colour .166: 2
and blue 166: 6
and burning as a coal 602:15
as any coal 167: 1
as ebony 166: 8
as hell 166: 6
as ink 167: 2
as the damning drops 75:10
as the devil 167: 4
as thunder 167: 4
but none too shady 778:10
diamonds 283: 8
down in b. and white 776: 7
eyes for being blind 170: 7
how well you looked in b. 2075:20
hung be heavens with b. ..747:10
in b. and white ..166:4; 1561: 6
is a pearl 166: 1
is as good as the white ...1124: 6
is b. so base a hue 166: 9
is the badge of hell 166: 7
is there no b. or white 2081: 7
it stood as night 444:17
not so b. as painted 444: 3
not so very b. 293:13
only white and b. 166: 4
sheep we cry 1023:19
will take no other hue 166: 3
Black-lettered list 633: 5
Black-Monday 1947: 2
Blackberries: plentiful as b. 1681: 1
sit and pluck 511:12
Blackberry would adorn parlors of heaven 1387: 4
Blackbird 167
Blackbird 1395:10
Blackbirds: again the b. sing 1908:13
four-and-twenty b. 1875: 3
have their wills 1908: 7
Blackcoat: stand away, b. ...1564: 4
Blacket of them all 344:14
Blackface: get away, b. ..1564: 4
Blackguard: dirty little b. 1033: 6
Blackguards: accomplished b. 705: 7
both 94: 7
Blackness no deformity ...1828: 6
of that noonday night 1151:13
Blacks: two b. not white ..1728: 1
two b. do not make a white 1395: 8
Blacksmith, see Smith
Bladder: blows up like a b. 1819: 5
one blue b. 2225: 4
Bladders filled with hope .1953:14
how we b. strut 1242: 6
of philosophy 1498:20
swimming on b. 1953:14
that swim on b. 782: 1
Blade: bloody blameful b. .1933:12
care-defying b. 1302: 4
carves casques of men ..1660: 4
ilka b. o' grass 1647: 1
not alone for b. was bright steel made 1854: 4
trenchant b., Toledo trusty 1955: 2
your own good b. 1956: 3
Blades: beware of treacherous b. 2032:11
brightest b. grow dim 1752: 4
ten razor b. in one neat case 1558:15
two b. of grass 638:13
we are double-edged b. ..2081:18
Blaine, James G. 1554: 9
continental liar 1557: 9
Blaize: lament for Madam 1576:13
Blake, William 167
Blake, Homer, Job 1518: 9
Blame: alike reserv'd to b. ..13:12
careless of b. 1786: 3
culture not soil 640:10
nor blame the writings, but the men 341: 1
safer than praise 340: 9
teasing with b. 1579:17
where you must 340: 9
without or praise or b. 1580: 2
withouten b. or blot 141: 2

Blâme: préférer le b. a la louange 1580: 7
Blame-all, praise-all 339: 9
Blameless: how we wish ..1662:15
Blanc: monarch of mountains 1355:15
thy awful head 1355:15
Blanch the most resplendent hair 848:15
Bland, passionate 573:15
Blandishments of wine 2158: 5
soft b. 603: 2
will not fascinate 725:16
Blanditia viscus merus 678:11
Blanditiæ: insidias b. 1901:16
mali 678:11
Blanditias molles 2214:10
Blandus: qui large b. est ...676:21
Blank cheque 1554: 3
her history, a b. 900:11
Blanket by night, plaid by day 908:14
under b., black good as white 1224: 6
wrong side of b. 2260:17
Blarney: the groves of B. .907: 3
Blasphemer: escape the rod 1952: 6
Blasphemous to dispraise ..340:14
Blasphemy: flat b. 1867: 6
mad with b. 1831:17
shrink not from b. 340: 6
Blast: misfortune's eastern b. 1321:10
monitory b. wails 117: 3
of that dread horn 983: 3
of vain doctrine 469: 1
of War's great organ 1472:16
one b. upon his bugle 983: 3
Blasts: howling b. drive ...436:20
wait on tender spring 811:16
Blaze: let b. laugh out 666:21
no spectacle nobler 666:21
of Eloquence 1812:12
of reputation dies in socket 1700:11
Blazon: any such nauseous b. 1376:13
evil deeds 336:15
give five-fold b. 764:14
in posterity 1563: 3
on a coffin-lid 624:10
Bleak: look b. i' the cold wind 240:11
Bleared eyes with books ..1676:20
Bleat: you have his b. 69:13
Bled in Freedom's cause ...51: 6
Bleed awhile then fight again 665:13
many to enrich few 2113: 7
'tis sweeter to b. 725:13
Bleeding: he hated b. 2108: 8
Blemish: let b. be undisguised 41: 4
no b. but mind 1310:12
Blemishes are hid by night 1224: 6
in the world's report 1701: 6
Blend of mirth and sadness 1159: 7
Blending of all beauties ..1716:13
Bless: except thou b. me 75:13
God b. us every one 168: 8
God b. you, my dear 415:17
my heart, liver, lungs 169: 2
the bed that I lie on 141:11
thy secret growth 150: 8
Blessed are the innocent ..103: 9
are the merciful 1298: 7
are the peace-makers 1471: 8
are the pure in heart 1659:16
are the sleepy 1845: 5
are the valiant 168: 5
be the name of the Lord .163:15
be ye poor 1568: 8
come what may, I *have been* b. 1560:15
cometh in name of Lord ..168:15
he that considereth poor .1492:14
he who expects nothing ..592: 6
he whom thou blesseth is b. 168:14
I b. them unaware 168: 6
in blessing others, b. 168:12
Blessed, *continued*
is he that blesseth thee ...168:14
is he who gets gift 772:15
is he who leads country life 321: 8
judge none b. before death 411: 9
more b. to give 773: 6
nothing b. in every respect 168:13
shall be thy basket 168: 7
that are not simple men .1826: 5
that endureth temptation 1981: 2
that nought expect 592: 6
they that have not seen ..151:14
who has found his work .2233: 4
wholly b. in thee alone ..2139:11
with good fortune 712: 3
with virtuous wife 2140: 1
See also Blest.
Blessedness dwells in human breast 1451: 1
instead of happiness 858: 2
of being little 17: 1
perfect b., vision of God 2095:15
single b. 1278: 8
Blesses: as it b., blest 168:12
Blesseth him that gives ..1298:19
with loud voice 1730: 3
Blessing 168
age not the least b. 32: 2
and a name unstained 985:14
and cursing 168:14
dismiss us with thy b. ..1587: 7
double b., double grace ..168:20
greatest b. or plague 2182: 8
hold it fast till it gives its b. 75:13
I'll b. beg of you 168:20
inestimable b. of vanity 2075:10
is he can't be curst 945:3a
most need of b. 168:20
national debt a b. 62:10
no b. lasts forever 168:17
of earth is toil 1064: 7
of idleness 2235: 6
of the years 51: 7
of your heart 44:14
out of b. into warm sun .1634: 1
rarest b. good woman 245: 9
steal immortal b. from her lips 1164:13
too much of mother's b. ..1350: 7
Blessings: break in b. on your head 2045: 4
brighten as fly 168: 9
from whom all b. flow 793: 7
have banished fear 168:16
in disguise 16: 9; 1586:19
infinite 169: 3
light upon thy back 169: 1
many b. do years bring 31: 5
memory of abundant b. ...30:10
no one small 311:14
not valued till gone 168: 9
on him that invented sleep 1844: 4
on the falling out 1197:14
on thee, little man 196:13
on whoever invented books 181:10
on your frosty pow 38: 9
public praise attend 47:12
scatter'd b. with wasteful 1000:17
star forth for ever 352:18
such b. Nature pours 1387: 8
thousand, thousand b. 552: 8
three b. for which I am most grateful 169: 3
wait on virtuous deeds ...2091: 7
wife, children, friends 633: 5
Blessure est pour vous 2247:18
Blest as immortal gods 1211: 7
be those how mean soe'er ..168:19
call no mortal b. 411:10
I have been b. 1560:15
no end of actions b. 834: 4
no man b. till his end 411:12
they are supremely b. 413: 6
today is as completely so ..168:18
we shall be b. 1144:13
what know we of b. above 884:14
See also Blessed.
Blew and snew 2128: 7
in power by the river 1365: 1
Blind and Black George ...2279: 3
Blight of life—thought ... 591:11
Blighted, past retrieving ..151:16
Blind: all ye b., behold 261:10
among enemies 170: 8
among the b. the one-eyed is king 169:17
and wailing, and alone 121: 3
as a bat at noon 169: 8
as to future destiny 749:12
bargain 125:18
better b. than see ill 169:10
cannot forget eyesight lost .170:11
cannot judgen well in hues 169: 7
did Cupid rise 350: 9
eat many a fly 169:15
eyes to the b. 169:13
follow b. side of him 169: 5
fortune is b. 713: 1
in their own cause 169:11
justice is b. 1028: 6
lead the b. 169:16
love is b. 1179:13
may catch a hare 1225:22
none so b. as they that won't see 169:12
of colors all wrong deemeth 169: 7
of the halt and the b. 201:22
old and b. 1305:13
poor man is 170:12
prone to go it b. 1596: 7
to former as future fate ..968: 6
to Heaven's gifts 777:21
to Some-one I must be 170: 5
too b. to have desire to see 169:12
when maddened by love ..1179:17
with too much light 1151:11
Blind-man's holiday 170: 2
Blinded alike from sunshine 1743:13
boy, that shoots 351: 3
Blinder: be a little b. 1036:17
who is b. than he that will not see 169:12
Blindness 169
and the inward light 1305: 6
first-born of Excess 170: 3
from all b. of heart 1981: 8
is a dark profound 32:15
reproach them of b. 1479: 6
to the future 749:13
we may forgive 1542:18
worse than chains 170: 8
Blinkard: no b. heathen stumbling 259: 4
one-eyed b. reigns 169:17
Blinking like goose in rain .812:12
Bliss 170
all night 1275: 1
all that poets feign of b. ..345:14
all the b. they know 2273: 3
antedate the b. above 1364: 8
bathe in b. 310:14
betwixt them two 1274: 7
bordering upon woe 1795:22
bowers of b. 14: 2
breaks at every breeze 171: 6
certainty of waking b. ...226:15
connubial b. real jam up 1451:21
domestic b. of happy ignorance 49: 3
e'en of a moment 170:14
how exquisite the b. 201: 5
in possession will not 1017:26
in that dawn to be alive ..2266:11
indistinctly apprehend a b. 170:16
is b., then, such abyss 170:17
is the same in subject or in king 171: 4
mighty b. is fugitive 2267:11
momentary b. bestow 898: 8
never to have tasted b. ..1218:17
no greater b. than such ..859: 1
no wealth can bribe 1185: 1
O mother, what is b. 1210: 8
of ignorance 059:23
of men below 2077: 9
of solitude 1294:17
some place b. in action ..1098: 2

Bliss, *continued*
such b. beggars enjoy 310: 7
sum of earthly b. 171: 3
that never past thro' pain 1445:18
that simplest b. 1143:13
too avid of earth's b. 212: 6
unalloyed for none 109: 9
where ignorance is b. 959:22
which centres in mind ..1307:14
Blisses about my pilgrimage 439: 6
Blissful: more b. to give ...773: 6
something b. and dear 4:16
Blister in light 947:16
Blithe as the lark 2022:15
buxom and debonair 2263:17
Block: chip of the old b. ...69:12
hew the b. off 527: 4
may soak gore 612: 2
Blockhead
See also Fool
Athenian b. worst 1925: 5
bit by fleas 679: 6
bookful b. 1677: 6
British b. 557: 6
enough to have me 1160: 5
learned b. greater 1097:17
no man but b. ever wrote except for money 2250: 8
nothing but a genius 758: 7
ridiculous when he talks ..699:17
rubs thoughtless skull 702: 8
Blockheads copy each other 106:10
imbeciles, idiots 697:19
read what b. wrote 1674: 2
Blocks are better cleft 1408:12
cut b. with a razor 205: 6
Blonde and the brunette .1234:16
strawberry b. 360: 6
Blood **171**
all b. alike ancient 73: 5
ancient but ignoble b. 72: 4
and iron 2107: 3
and judgment commingled 1023:12
and revenge hammering .1713:19
bring the b. into cheek 172:14
by b. king, at heart clown 1042: 9
cold in b. 2265: 2
quenched in fraternal b. .. 58: 2
faith than Norman b. 73:10
farewell to Norman b. 941:14
freeze thy young b. 658: 5
from country's bosom ...1465:13
gentle b. generous might .258:13
gentle b., gentle manners 1259:14
gipsy b. to gipsy b. 2102: 3
hath been shed ere now ..1360: 1
hath bought b. 1155: 8
hey-day of the b. 35:16
had so much b. in him 171:14
heal'st with b. the earth .2106: 3
her snowy cheeks did dye .172: 3
his b. be on us 171:12
his b. began to change 172: 3
His b., down dropping ..1735: 7
his b. is freedom's eucharist 1158:13
I have nothing to offer but b. 2298c: 1
I see His b. upon the rose 264: 4
I'll not shed her b. 1834: 6
in b. stepp'd in so far 171:14
in our own veins 1781: 7
inclined to mirth 650: 3
is all of a color 171:10
is an inheritance 2093: 2
is the life 171: 7
is very snow-broth 240:11
let my b. cement your happiness 415:25
like b., like goods 1267: 6
like pelican, tapp'd out ...1477: 8
loud-tongued b. demands supplies 243:18
made of one b. all nations 1379:15
make thick my b. 346:12
milder b. the scaffold wet 1280:23
mixes b. with his colors .1447:12
more stirs 325:18
move a man's b. to blush ..172:14
my b. doth quicker shoot .872:10
Blood, *continued*
my b. is liquid flame 1711:11
never dies 1359:12
no b. stains limpid glass 2125:12
noble b. accident 1407:15
Norman b. 73:10; 941:14
not like wine 74: 4
nothing like b. 70: 9
nuptial to webbed bottle .1763: 4
obligation of our b. forbids 1731: 4
of a fellow citizen 1008:14
of a king 376:19
of all the Howards 72: 4
of Bayard be my own 398:15
of Christians fresh seed ..1280:18
of martyrs seed of church 1280:18
of Old Brown 203: 4
of our martyrs sanctifies 1465:19
of queens and kings 171:11
of the Lamb 883:14
of tyrants natural manure 1104: 5
of unjust king pleasing .1042: 8
old b. is bold b. 171:19
one in b. established 2064:20
one raised in b. 2064:20
out of a turnip 119: 9
patriot's b. seed of freedom 1466: 3
potent b. hath modest May 1282:16
pure and eloquent b. 173: 5
red b. reigns 1908: 3
repast them with my b. ..1477: 8
ruddy drop of manly b. ..1188:15
ruined b. improved flesh ..69: 4
sacrilegious taste of b. ..524:17
smell b. of Englishman ..546: 4
speaks to you in my veins 2219: 7
stirs the b. in an old man's heart 2097:14
stuffed in skins 521:19
swam thro' seas of b. ...2063: 3
their tongues have spilt ..1093: 9
thence did spring gentle b. .73: 1
thicker than water 171:18
thicks man's b. with cold 1147: 8
to freeze the b. 1539: 9
to know the gentle b. 68:13
toil, tears and sweat ... 2298c: 1
washed in b. of the Lamb .883:14
watered by b. of tyrants .1104: 5
what boots ancient b. 71: 8
whispered, like the stream 1223: 3
whoso sheddeth man's b. .1708: 2
will draw unto b. 171:16
will follow knife 303: 8
will have b. 1708:2
will tell 73:13
with b. that letters enter .1673: 1
with b. paint ground 2113: 5
world's fresh b. runs fleet 1939:15
young b. must have its course 2264: 2
Blood-sister to the clod ...1384:12
Blood-suckers: damned b. .1643: 2
Bloodhound at his heels ..1708:14
Bloodhounds from the slip ..48:12
Bloodless lay untrodden snow 1733: 4
Bloodstone to their grave ..165:14
Bloody Ground of Kentucky 1034: 3
luxurious, avaricious 240:11
with spurring 863:15
Bloom: burst to b. you proud, white flower ...251: 3
of a rose passes quickly ..1745: 1
of young desire 1221:10
of youth 141: 5
short b. of brief life 1140: 7
sort of b. on a woman 244: 8
tender b. of heart 461:16
trust not to your b. 136:15
wherefore waste rose's b. 1578: 9
Bloomed fairer as they grew 1525: 1
Bloomers 489:12
Blooms: summer's lingering b. 2085: 6
too thick for fruit 2075: 5
Bloomsbury: eye pleased in B. 1168:13
Blossom as the rose 434: 7
enchantingly shy 2087: 2
fairer seems b. than fruit 1561: 1
fairest b. of garden dies .1646: 5
in purple and red 1215:11
on the plum 1260:17
rather have one b. now ..1578:12
so fair and tender 2151: 8
sweet b. of Humanity 121:13
that hangs on bough 1301: 7
thou winged b. 211: 4
which the wind assails 1174: 1
Blossom-bald 363: 2
Blossoms: Hope's tender b. .924:17
of humanity 252: 6
of my sin 1359:16
opening to the day 1659:13
'twixt page and page 188:10
Blossoms': apple b. shower .91:17
Blot: Creation's b. 773: 8
on the script of Time ...2147:12
out, correct, insert 1526: 9
what they discreetly b. ..1526: 9
Blotches: crimson b. 2210:20
may offend 340:11
on a beetle's back 1345: 5
Blotted it out forever 75:11
never b. line 1807: 1
the fine out 75:11
Blow: afraid to b. too much 2152:14
and swallow at same time not easy 971:10
first b. half the battle ..1598: 6
for a b. 767: 3
for b. 664:15
in cold blood 256:17
knock-down b. 79: 9
remember swashing b. ...665: 2
second b. makes the fray 1638: 9
smiling gives the b. 1853: 5
that innocence can give ..989: 8
that liberates the slave ..1839:18
thou winter wind 984:15
wait the sharpest b. 1704:14
who does not return b. ..1474:13
with word deeper than sword 2224: 3
word and a b. 97: 6
Blower of which blast is she 2151:11
Blowing his own strumpet 1581:10
trumpet of own praise ...1581:10
trumpet of own virtues ..1581:10
Blown with restless violence 983:12
Blows: adventures find b. ..15:15
almost came to b. 100: 9
and buffets of the world 1321: 4
Apostolic b. and knocks ..1589: 2
fell only on crime 338: 7
good b. o' both sides 2116: 1
great guns 2151: 2
have answer'd b. 1155: 8
heal the b. of sound 1825:10
never b. so red 384:10
of circumstance 274:15
strike b. for power 84: 9
Blue: a-feelin' b. 4: 8
and the Gray 1869: 1
black and b. 166: 6
Bonnets over the border .1767:11
darkly, deeply blue 1834:10
distinguish b. from yellow 502:17
put b. into their line 1559:13
Ribbon of the Turf 1631: 2
two little girls in b. 2287: 6
Blue-bottles: caught b. ...148:10
Blue-stocking a scourge ..2194: 4
resolute sagacious b. 1042: 3
will remain spinster 2194: 4
Bluebells swaying 688: 9
Bluebird carried sky 162:14
Blues of mental wear 331:17
Blunder
See also Error, Mistake
frae monie a b. free us ..1788: 7
or plunder 1553: 8
worse than a crime 337: 3
youth a b. 23: 8

Blunderbuss against religion 240: 8
Blundered on some virtue ..1259:15
Blunderer sturdy as a rock 1924:15
Blundering and plundering 1553: 8
Blunders: God make b. wise 284: 7
Irish b. never of heart 996: 5
of youth 23: 8
Blunt tools sometimes of use 217:14
Bluntness: prais'd for b. ..1260:10
Blurb: it's bold b. 1644: 1
Blush and cry, "guilty" ..173: 4
as red as turkey-cock 171:21
at being thought sincere 1833: 4
beautiful as woman's b. ...91:17
beautiful, inconvenient ...172:10
because they understand. 172:11
better a b. on the cheek ..172: 2
canst thou say all this and never b. 173: 7
excuse the b. 1103: 1
happy maiden 1048: 2
her b. is guiltiness 173: 5
I b. for thee, Ben 1322:11
in the rose 326:13
is guiltiness 173: 5
is no language 172: 9
less for their crimes 172:12
maiden b. bepaint my cheek 173: 6
nor b. to shed a tear 1961:14
of maiden shame 2213: 6
rather see a young man b. 172: 2
shall not b. in knowing ..1407: 8
she looked down to b. 601: 8
so to be admired 138: 5
sudden b. devours them .171:22
that kindles in thy cheeks .173: 2
that virgin fears impart ..172: 6
to cheek of young person .172: 7
to find it fame 625:11
to give it in 75: 7
to see you so attir'd 660: 6
while Brutus standeth by .172:11
yet will she b. 173: 6
Blushed as he gave it in 75:11
Miss frown'd, b. 1271:13
saw its God, and b. 1315:14
we never b. before 172: 5
with blood of queens 171:11
Blushes: animal that b. ..1241:18
badges of imperfection ...173: 9
become a pale face 173: 1
conscious b. into wine ...1315:14
he b.: all is well 173: 8
in a rattle-trap 174: 7
not quite a brute 172: 8
one way, feels another . 2190: 7
quench your b. 173: 7
who b. is guilty 172:13
Blushing 171
hue of virtue 172: 8
like scarlet 75:11
like the morn 1273: 8
sign of guilt 171: 4
to whites of his eyes 172: 7
Bluster: bully's b. coward's fear 1652: 7
sputter, cavil 1091: 1
Blut ist ein ganz besondrer Saft 171: 7
Bo: say bo to a goose 813:11
Bo-peep has lost her sheep 1811: 7
play at B. 705: 4
Boar chafed with sweat ..2200: 6
held by dog 470:13
fly b. before b. pursues ..681:10
Board consumes more 520:10
festal b. 2185: 7
heap high the b. 1983:13
hospitable b. 934: 1
I will b. her tho' she 2200: 6
mirthful b. 2223:20
with saints 1755:10
Board-wages 1985: 8
Boarding-house: polyglot b. .55: 9
Boars served for himself ..519:12
two b. in one brake 160: 7
Boast: could'st thou b. ...1982:13
great b. and small roost ..173:12
of heraldry 826:13
Boast, *continued*
such is the patriot's b. ..1467: 3
when he rides in style 174: 7
Boasters: great men not b. ..833: 9
ye deedless b. 173:18
Boasting 173
in one street 2088: 8
of b. more than bomb afraid 1864: 2
show their scars 174: 8
where b. ends dignity begins 174:13
Boasts: indecipherable b. .1421: 7
Boat
See also Ship
at midnight sent alone 4: 3
in the same b. 287:2; 1813: 3
is on the shore 500:13
of stone 1813: 7
often in the selfsame b. 1813: 3
on a sea of wisdom 184: 8
shaped like crescent moon 2210: 2
to Charon's b. for exile ..383:15
tug in a little b. 1683:13
Boats: little b. 1651:14
shallow bauble b. 1774:13
Bobolincon, Wadolincon ...174:17
Bobolink 174
Bobolinkon: there flew a B. 174:14
Bobtail: tag rag and b. ..1478:12
Bocks: drink our b. 2018: 5
Bode: what should that b. ..865: 3
Bodice aptly laced 489: 1
lace my b. blue 3: 6
swelled with bosom's thrill .70: 8
Bodies bore wounds in front 2248: 4
devoid of mind statues ..1313:11
die, souls return 389: 9
doomed to die 968: 2
fat b. lean brains 647:11
fat wet b. 362: 6
given up to pleasure 1123: 3
human b. are sic fools ..2045: 2
little b. have great souls 1893: 3
no subsistence without mind 1314:11
of lovers forms of desire 1175:13
o r b. do not fit us 175: 7
our gardens 176: 6
pay with our b. 435:16
perish thro' excess of blood 2171:11
pile the b. high 822: 4
present b. living sacrifice 1792:16
subject to change 1348: 8
trunks for worms 136:19
two b., one seduction 1830:17
two b. with one soul 726: 6
two seeming b. but one heart 2067: 3
why are our b. soft, weak 2192:12
Body 175
absent in b. 2: 2
always little and sweet 566:17
and soul of woman frail .2192: 5
and soul united jar 1275:10
assailed by force of time ..35: 2
beautiful passionate b. ...176: 7
big and mightly pight 1417:13
borrows from whole world 175: 7
but a swallowing grave ..1563:14
charms because of soul ...132:13
chest of tools 175: 7
chinks of her b. 28:10
commits his b. to painful labour 945: 1
couched in a curious bed 1611:19
covered with his b. 325: 7
dead b. revenges not 543: 4
demd damp moist b. 240: 3
did contain a spirit 50: 1
drags down the soul 1891:15
every b. is mortal 175: 4
fair was her sweet b. 131:21
faultless b., blameless mind 1313:12
feeble b. enfeebles mind .1314: 1
fill'd and vacant mind ..1850:16
fretted pigmy b. to decay 1891:11
Body, *continued*
gave his b. to earth 259: 4
gets its sop 2055:18
gin a b. meet a b. 1051: 4
give my b. to be burned ..241: 9
good for b. is work 2234:11
grow more fragile in b. 31: 8
hairy b. manly soul 846:18
head aches, b. worse 870: 6
healthy b. guest-chamber ..870: 8
her b. thought 173: 5
here in the b. pent 887:11
his b. is under hatches 568: 4
if a b. kiss a b. 1051: 4
in what condition b. will be 175: 4
incurable b. 458:21
indulge b. little 873: 8
indulge b. only for health 1313:17
is an affliction of soul 176: 1
John Brown's b. 203: 2
keep under my b. 175: 5
lean b. and visage 1891:11
leprous b. of Christianity 1788: 1
little b. mighty heart 552: 8
little b. mighty mind 1313:12
loved the b. of a woman ..176: 9
magazine of inventions ...175: 7
make less thy b. hence ..1980: 3
make to yourself perfect b. 1892: 3
Nature is, and God soul ..1390:14
nought cared b. for wind 2266: 3
not a home but an inn ..1123: 4
not b. to cover mind 1314: 6
of a weak woman 1664:14
of dead enemy smells sweet 544: 2
of soul, b. form doth take 1892: 1
of this death 376:11
old in b., not spirit 23: 1
old mind, young b. 22: 4
omnibus 69: 8
on the oblong bed 176: 8
packed with sweet 1213:12
passed into spirit 1050:12
patch up thine old b. 1686: 7
perfect b. itself soul 1891:18
points of beauty in 129: 9
politic 814:11
precious earth and root ..251:12
quick to decay 1285:11
repaired and supported ..1313:17
rest free from evil 406:10
rumple b., rumple mind .1314: 8
sickness-broken b. 28:10
socket of the soul 1891:18
sooner dressed than soul 1891:14
sound b. at root of excellence 175: 8
sound b. product of mind .871: 4
sound mind in sound b. ..871: 4
strong b. above wealth 870:21
strong b., strong mind ..1313:13
suffers, soul profits 1891:17
tasted her sweet b. 960: 2
temple of Holy Spirit 175:10
that does me grievous wrong 33:12
this b. is your country ..1468: 5
this tumultuous b. 882:22
though the b. starve 106:14
thy b. at its best 1891: 9
thy b. packed with sweet 1213:12
to kick 319: 8
vile b. 176: 3
virtue fairer in fair b. 85:13
well but purse sick 467:16
with b. I thee worship ...1271:10
woman's b. is sacred 176: 9
woman's b. is the woman 4:12
worthy of worship 175:10
wounded b. shrinks 656:15
young and cool 176: 2
young b. with old head ..870: 1
Bœotum in crasso ære 1925: 4
Boerhaave: health with B. .396:13
Boets and Bainters: hate .1537: 2
Boffkin: vengeful Mrs. B. ..69: 9
Bog: o'er b. or steep 444:19
Serbonian b. 889:15
Boggler: a b. ever 1925:13
Bogie, National Anthem ...546:15

Brain, *continued*
shallow b. behind mask ..1436:12
silly, half-baked b. 2297: 1
sows not corn, thistles ..1312: 6
turns b. like cat in pan ..2018: 3
tyrant with a rose 1465:15
visionary b. 37:14
whatever comes from b. 882:11
which b. makes of fumes 2095:10
Brain-storm: paranoia 1084: 9
Brain-trust 1555: 6
Brain-women, heart-women 2193:11
Brainless as a March hare 1230: 7
Brains: confuse b. in college 528:18
cudgel thy b. no more ..1308: 5
cumbered up with b. ..2193:17
do it with their native b. ..1507: 1
enemy in mouth to steal b..498:15
enough to make fool of self 2265: 8
evident they have little b. 2194:13
fat bodies, lean b. 647:11
fumbles for his b. 1310: 3
his b. could not move 1676:15
I abhor b. 1307:16
knock out her b. 377: 1
made of gingerbread 1310: 4
mix them with b. 1447: 4
mod'rate portion of b. ...2131:1a
most b. reflect crown of hat 1310: 6
no b. yet 39:14
publish to world lack of b. 1310: 1
rack b. for lucre 1523:13
seventy-year clocks 1306:17
shaken up like coppers 929: 6
strains from hard-bound b. 1524: 8
ta'en out and buttered ..2039: 9
to be a real fool 697:14
unhappy b. for drinking ..498:14
were only candle-grease 1309:19
when b. were out, man die 770:14
who rack their b. 1308: 5
Brains-trust 1555: 6
Brainsickly: think so b. ..1996:14
Brake that virtue must ..1838: 1
Bramble-dew: gold and b. .2141: 7
Bran: can of shredded b. ..873:10
Branch better that bowen will 1650: 4
cut is the b. 1870: 4
goodly verdure flings 71: 4
Branches: all arts b. on one tree 103:17
hide a lost spirit 2150: 1
rarely into the b. 74: 5
superfluous b. 746:13
Brand: bring a b. from heaven 1455:10
him who will 1836:13
Brands: pleasant are b. 905:12
Brandy and lemon juice 499: 4
and the water 499: 8
distilled damnation 499: 6
fou o' b. 499: 3
how b. lies 499: 7
Latin for a goose 216: 6
sipped b. and water 499: 5
Bransle: tout ce qui b. 622: 3
Brass: become as sounding b. 241: 9
bold as b. 177:10
monumental b. 1339:12
Brasses: knightly b. of the graves 1340:11
Brat: castle-bred b. 72: 5
lest stolen b. be known ..1505: 8
Brauch gedeiht in einem Lande 355: 5
Brauchen: tiefer Sinn in den alten B. 354: 9
Brave able to bear envy ..565:19
all b., many generous, some chaste 728: 4
born from the b. 324: 2
deserves the fair 323:17
fortune favors the b. 717: 4
how sleep the b. 1868: 9
is not therefore b. 324: 5
know how to forgive 710:12
love mercy 1298: 4
men b. from first 323:15
Brave, *continued*
men were living before Agamemnon 1521:10
seeks not applause 324:21
tomorrow to be b. 664:13
unreturning b. 1866: 9
what's b., what's noble 325:18
who would not sleep with b. 1868: 7
Brave des braves 1377:13
Bravery
See also Courage
but a vain disguise 486:12
never out of fashion 324:11
of his grief 842:14
with all her b. on 488: 8
with the bravest 323:10
Bravest are the tenderest 1870: 6
at the last 1934: 7
fall by hands of cowards 2073:10
frightened by terrors 655: 6
not to seem b., but to be 1831:19
of the brave 1377:13
where the b. fall 630: 3
Bravo! Field-marshal! Catherine! 298: 5
was decisive 342:12
Braw bricht moonlicht nicht 494:11
Bray: vicar of B. 1546: 8
Bray: if a donkey b. 112: 1
time for thee to b. 112: 1
you in a mortar 98:10
Brays: when a lion b. 112:10
Breach of promise 2217: 7
once more into the b. ..2116:10
who can an open b. defend ..245:11
Bread 197
and butter glad to eat 197:16
and cheese and kisses 1047:16
and cheese two targets 198: 4
and circuses 197:19
and Gospel is good fare ..158: 1
and oil and wine 478: 5
ask b., give stone 198: 5
beg bitter b. thro' realms 1867: 2
bitter b. of banishment ..591:19
brown b. and an onion 1107: 3
cramm'd with distressful b. 1850:16
crust of b. and liberty ..1107: 3
eat b. by weight 198: 1
eat b. his own hand earns 1395: 5
eat b. to the full 534:21
eat b. with your pudding ..198: 4
eaten b. is forgotten 197: 9
eaten in secret pleasant ..1618: 2
eaten your b. and salt ..1756: 5
eateth not b. of idleness 2143:10
eats b. without washing ..279: 7
from mould we reap b. ..383:10
give him b. while living ..2256:14
give us this day daily b. ..198: 3
good as ever broke b. 914:18
half-penny-worth of b. ..2155:14
he took the b. and brake it 262:13
home-made b., putty, lead 909:14
humour of b. and cheese ..939: 1
in sorrow ate 1885: 8
is buttered on both sides 197:18
is not to be had 197: 5
like morning b. 198: 2
live by b. alone 197:12
loaf of b. sell half 945: 4
look for better b. 197: 8
made b. from bump of wonder 2209: 3
made of stone 198: 5
man earn b. and eat 2233:10
man who bites his b. 521: 6
men break is broke to them 197:14
neither eating b. nor drinking wine 440:11
never touch b. till it's toasted 518:17
not give the b. of life ...1589: 7
nourisheth the body 945: 4
of affliction 16: 7
of all smells, b. 197:17
of one day 728: 8
plain b. and butter 1793: 6
Bread, *continued*
quarrel with b. and butter 1648:16
salt savor b. of others ..1468:13
secure of b. as of light 197:13
seek b. with the plough ..637: 5
she baked the b. 1657:11a
she was cutting b. and butter 1204: 3
smell of b. and butter 778: 6
soon want b. 817: 8
spoil'd the b. 2188: 8
staff of life 198: 1
staff of your b. 198: 1
to the soul 2166:24
to the wise 1930: 8
upon the waters 197:14
we eat b. another sows ...803: 5
which side b. buttered 197:18
whole stay of b. 198: 1
wholesomeness of oaten b. 1768: 7
will it bake b. .... .1652: 9
with b. all sorrows less ..1884:11
with b. let him eat it 197:11
with one fishball 2290: 1
without industry they find 2071: 4
wond'ring for his b. 847: 1
Breadth of heaven betwixt you 1172: 4
preached upon "b." 2022: 5
Break, break, break 1995:13
best we get is an even b. 1143:17
her betimes 2145: 4
the ice 950: 1
the staff of bread 198: 1
Breaker of God's own peace 2147:11
of proverbs 444: 7
Breakers: hug his b. 1773: 6
roar beneath 1815: 6
wanton'd with thy b. 1773: 6
Breakfast: arg'ed the thing at b. 100: 4
dinner, and tea, oh 1797:15
eat b. on lip of lion 679: 8
makes good memory 518: 8
one doth but b. here ..1122:10
unsubstantial b. 939: 6
wholesome hungry b. 518: 8
Breaking of windows or laws 1088: 4
sorry b. up 26: 4
Breast against a thorn 162:18
and back as either should be 1434: 9
arm th' obdured b. 1462:13
bare her b. of snow ...359:10
bared b. she curls inside ..851: 5
boiling bloody b. 1933:12
cold b. and serpent smile ..353:11
covered with wounds 2248: 4
deep in b. secret wound 2248:16
depth of her glowing b. ..1744: 1
ease my b. of melodies ..1451:12
hath marble been to me 1339:17
lean'd b. up-till a thorn ..1404:12
many a swan-like b. 997:13
marble of her snowy b. ..2105: 3
my fair one's ripening b. 1192: 8
ne'er learned to glow ..2176:14
read thy own b. right ..1788: 2
soothe a savage b. 1362:17
tamer of the human b. 17: 8
that music cannot tame ..1362:17
to Chloe's b. 350: 2
what his b. forges 217: 8
where roses could not live 394: 4
with wound riven 2248: 4
within this filial b. 3:12
Breast-high amid the corn 1235: 2
Breastplate than heart 879: 6
Breasts: come to my woman's b. 346:12
lovely b. September claims .133:19
your cruel b. assuage 929: 1
Breath: abundance of superfluous b. 1900:11
against the wind 1586:17
and bloom of the year ..1048: 8
boldest held his b. 1825: 6
can make them 1611: 5
ceasing of a sweeter b. ..2269:18

Burgundy: an aged B. runs with a beardless Port 2157:10
milk of B. 2156: 1
waterish B. 1234: 3
Burial: in one red b. blent 2120: 1
of an ass 112: 5
Buried by upbraiding shore 364:15
Burke, Edmund 205
and Hare: but an' ben ..1360: 5
Burlesques on the art of argument 100:10
Burn: better to marry than to b. 1265:15
candle at both ends 216: 7
make him fit to b. 791:12
to be great 833: 2
Burning no answer 97:12
not improved by b. 152: 6
quenched by fire 246:13
questions 1554: 4
Burns, Robert 205
Burnt, and so is meat 316:13
child dreads fire 595:19
Burr, Aaron 366: 8
Burrow and build 108:17
Burrs: stick like b. 633:18
stick where thrown 2212:14
when you stick on 314: 3
Burst in ignorance 959:13
Burthen was thy birth 122: 3
public b. of nation 1043: 6
Burton built on Trent 44:13
Bury: helped to b. whom he helped to starve 835: 1
Bush afire with God 511:12
beat about the b. 99: 1
bonnie briar b. 1767: 5
burning b. 115:14
burning b. still burns 1390: 8
debate and beat the b. 972: 8
each b. we see's a bear 302: 5
feareth every b. 656:13
good wine needs no b. ..2155:10
if you can't be tree 1832:18
in b. with God may meet 1390: 8
supposed a bear 962: 5
who aims but at a b. 110:14
worth two in the b. 161: 3
Bushel: candle under a b. ..216:10
Bushes: beat the b. 161: 4
burning b. fired of God ..1050:12
Busier than he was 209:19
Business 206
after dinner 451:11
always above his b. 208: 5
asketh silent secrecy 1784: 3
at his b. before he rises 207: 2
big b. 207:17
bloody b. of the day 2120: 3
called by particular b. 236: 6
chief b. is to pay 2281: 8
consists in persuading 207:11
derned sight better b. 74:11
despise rewards of b. 207:18
did my b. 602: 1
diligent in his b. 208:20
dispatch b. quickly 209:13
dispatched is well 209:16
do b. in great waters 1779: 7
do your own b. 208: 7
drive thy b. 207: 1
easy to escape from b. 207:18
every man has b. 207:19
everybody's b. nobody's b. .208: 9
fig for the cares of b. 209: 1
for sake of being busy ...210: 4
for the sake of leisure 2118: 4
hath little b. become wise ..1100: 4
hurried is ill done 209:16
I go to my pleasure, b. 208:11
if b. calls 14: 2
importunity of b. 2235: 1
is b. 207:13
keeps mind steady 208:18
let's banish b. 2020:16
life's b. terrible choice ...259:14
leave b. to idlers 1509:11
like man to double b. 972:17
make b. a pleasure 1509:11
man's b. does not fit him ..209: 6
Business, *continued*
men some to b. 1255: 3
mind his own b. 207: 7
my b. is to live 1128:13
neither above nor below ..208: 5
never fear want of b. 207: 8
no better c..re than b. 955:17
no feeling of his b. 207:19
not slothful in b. 207:16
object of b. to make money .208:13
of life is to enjoy it 1130: 8
of life to be, to do 1119: 1
of life to go forward 1118:11
of your life is love 1182:18
other people's b. 207: 7
other people's money 207: 5
postponed serious b. 208: 8
salt of life 208:15
some plunge in b. 714:14
to b. that we love 208:21
to please the throng 1032: 3
tomorrow 206: 6
try to do a little b. 42:13
was his aversion 208:11
weighty b. 207:19
will never hold water 206:13
with an income 208:14
without any b., is forever busy 210: 3
woman's b. to get married 1266: 2
your own foolish b. 206:12
Businesses turn on pin ..2041: 8
Busk thee, my winsome marrow 2140: 5
Buskin: shuffle off the b. ..291:10
strait and terse 1525: 7
Buss and be friends 1046:20
give flattering b. 1050: 1
gives a smacking b. 237: 5
the clouds 96:11
Busses: flattering b. 1050: 1
Bust and temple rise 2204: 1
animated b. 389: 2
crumbling b. 49:11
of marriages 662: 2
outlasts the throne 102:20
raise tardy b. 1339:19
Buste survit à la cité 102:20
Busters: bunk among b. ..1434: 3
Bustle: various b. of resort 1871:18
Busts: smoke-begrimed b. ..71: 8
then we are b. 629: 9
Busy as bees 142:12
as fool and knave 700:10
be b. and you will be safe 1187: 1
have no time for tears ..1884:10
idly b. rolls their world ..953:14
is modest maid's holiday 979: 9
no one so b. 210: 5
nowhere so b. a man 209:19
to be too b. is danger 1284:15
too b. gets contempt 210: 2
too b. with crowded hour 2233:11
wants to be b. 1099:12
when corn is ripe 711:12
who more b. than he with least to do 210: 1
Busybodies: be no b. 1284:13
speaking things 1761:15
Busybody: the world's b. ..553: 7
Busyness 209
extreme b. 955: 6
Busyrane: gates of B. 178: 3
But me no buts 08:14
But yet: do not like b. 474:20
Butcher 210
of a silk button 505:15
that devil's b. 210:10
that served Shakespeare 1804: 9
with an axe 1621:15
Butcher'd to make Roman holiday 903: 9
Butchers: begot by b. 1525: 3
whose hands are dy'd 210: 7
B tler: on B. who can think 780: 2
Butt: here is my b. 378:13
of traveling salesman 1174: 5
Butt-shaft: Cupid's b. 350:15
Butter and eggs and cheese 122:13
and eggs and pound of ..1409: 2
Butter, *continued*
bread on both sides 1547:12
in lordly dish 522:13
not all b. from cow 330: 7
smell of bread and b. 254: 1
smoother than b. 2223:18
that makes temptation ..1981: 3
would not melt in mouth ..947: 4
wouldn't melt in mouth 1358: 9
Butter-and-egg man 1631: 8
Buttercup 210
I'm called little B. 210:20
wakes to the morn 121:12
Buttercups across the field ..210:18
and daisies 210:21; 684: 4
and daisies spun 683: 8
little children's dower 210:16
stoop for b. 2074:13
yellow japanned b. 684: 2
Buttered: which side my bread b. 197:18
Butterflies all gold 211: 2
there will be b. 211: 7
Butterfly 211
as idle thing 211: 8
Balkis talked to a b. 211: 6
crush b. or brain gnat ..1015: 9
dies in a day 1745: 1
don't shoot b. with rifles 2042:16
fly away, b., fly away 211:13
gray b. 1813:12
I'd be a b. 211: 1
mere court b. 327:15
preaches contentment 19: 9
seed that's cast 617:24
suggestions 100: 5
we saw a snow-white b. ..211: 5
who breaks b. upon wheel 1758: 7
Buttocks: fits all b. 124:15
Button: drop a b. in the hat 949: 3
eminent b. maker 47:17
I found a bachelor's b. ..757: 2
not care a b. 978: 1
not have to buy a b. 718:11
on fortune's cap 715:11
that little bronze b. 1864: 9
Button-hole lower 1642: 1
miss the first b. 147:11
Button-maker: my father an eminent b. 47:17
Buttons: gold b. now are sewn 363: 1
of a Roman's breeches ..1737:16
soul above b. 47:17
taken of his b. off 852:15
Buxom, blithe, debonaire 2269:17
Buy: how many things there are to b. 1826:16
never b. because cheap 1604:15
now I can b. the meadow and hill 165: 8
what I'll never pay for ...194: 5
with you 1597:15
Buyer: timely b. hath cheaper 125:17
Buying and the selling 208:23
Buys and lies 125: 3
Buzz of multitude bloody 1484: 9
Buzzard: blind b. 169:14
is no fowl 100: 2
Buzzards all gentlemen 763:11
By and by easily said 1614: 3
and by never comes 1614: 3
Bye-and-bye: menace of the b. 1131: 1
By-blow: but for the b. ..210: 6
By-blows are world and we 2013: 6
By-ways: take no b. 245:18
Byers: the accusing B. 75:11
Bygone only last 1459:14
Bygones: let b. be b. 1458: 4
Byre: peace to the 269: 4
Byron, George Gordon ..211
was eternally farewelling ..635: 9
Bystanders hope he dies ..1322:14
Byword among all nations 1628: 5
among all people 1012: 4
I am their b. 1875:10
of all years to come 2086: 4
Byzantine Logothete 2150:10

C

Charles II: light-hearted Majesty C. 2283: 4
Charlie: Flying C. 1161: 6
you can't lose me, C. 2291: 5
Charlotte having seen his body 1204: 3
Charm 244
about the old love still ..1207: 9
ache with air 245: 2
adds a c. 244: 9
air to give a sound 2175:18
any Scotsman without c. 1768:10
by sages often told 311: 2
by thought supplied 1385: 1
by way of a prayer 244:18
dissolves apace 245: 3
for every woe 924: 3
hast thou a c. to stay 1355:15
he that can draw a c. ..1384: 3
in melancholy 1291: 4
incommunicable c. 244:13
it's that damned c. 244: 8
modest c. of not too much 1327: 2
nothing could a c. impart 1974:13
of all the Muses 2223:10
of earliest birds 1347:11
of his talk 1963:20
of poetry and love 357:12
one native c. 244:10
secret of their c. 56: 2
soon the c. will pass 136:15
sort of bloom on a woman 244: 8
steps over burning marle 1510:19
that lulls to sleep 743:20
to stay morning-star 1355:15
touching with c. of poetry 1518:11
unforgotten every c. 3:12
wasted on the earth 691: 9
way to c. not by writing 2193: 7
what c. can soothe her melancholy 2201:16
with all c. of woman 1255:12
wondrous c. of sex 1802: 9
Charmed it with smiles 244:15
Charmer of an idle hour ..2018:13
t'other dear c. away 317: 8
whether c. sinner it 2198: 6
Charmers charming never so wisely 244:17
Charming: all c. people spoiled 244:14
he saw her c. 1331:20
people c. or tedious 810: 8
saying what is c. 244:14
Charms alas! that won me 1212: 8
all spread their c. 1795:21
and the man I sing 534:13
are frail 487:11
by accepting 2143:11
for distant admiration 244:11
he must behold no more 4: 5
her modesty concealed ..1331:20
honored well c. to sell ..1268: 3
nature's c. 1384:1; 1385: 4
strike sight, merit soul ..1300: 2
strong magnetic c. 306:13
sweet, seducing c. 90:21
Charnel-houses and our graves 1340: 9
Charnels: stone-covered ..1024:18
Charon, seeing, may forget 399:14
Charrue devant les bœufs 1631:10
Chart: got its c. from Columbus 284: 3
no c. save faith 284:10
white on the c. 235: 9
Chartæ: perituræ parcere c. 2255: 9
Charter: large as the wind 1105: 2
Chartier rompit son fouet ..714:16
Chartres: said of C. 1758: 8
Chase, The
See also Hunting
days spent in the c. 590:17
I follow far 942: 2
o'er hills, dales 942:10
seek out some other c. ..941: 7
sport of kings 942: 6
sulky leaders of the c. 941: 6
wild bear c. 941:17
Chase, *continued*
wild-goose c. 1643: 7
with hurrying c. 794:11
Chased them up to heaven .628: 8
with more spirit c. 1560:16
Chasm: bloody c. 58: 3
Chaste as ice 215:4; 248:10
as is the bud 247:14
as morning dew 410: 3
as picture in alabaster ..247:11
as the icicle 247:11
as unsunned snow 247:11
but charity is wanting . 1591:15
call'd her c., too soon 1342: 9
in morals 246: 8
many generous, some c. ..728: 4
nothing so c. as nudity ..1416: 8
to husband, frank to all 1325:10
what care I how c. she be 247: 4
when no fear of detection .246:16
who was never asked 246:15
whom no one has asked ..246:15
woman does not dye hair ..847:12
you, virtuous you 1033: 5
Chastely: if not c., cautiously 246:17
keeps c. to husband's side 246: 1
Chasteneth: whom the Lord loveth He c. 789: 4
Chastens whom he loves . ..17: 3
Chastest you can choose ..2142:10
Chasteté: par la c. l'âme respire 246: 3
Chastised you with whips 1657:17
Chastises what best loves 1276:13
whom he likes 789: 4
Chastity 245
abstinence or continence ..248: 4
and Beauty deadly foes ..245:12
beauty flower of c. 120: 1
chief of heavenly lights ..248: 2
clothed on with c. 248: 5
dear to heaven 246:12
enables soul to breathe pure air 246: 3
fruitless c. 247:16
hymn in praise of C. 1903: 4
it was married c. 1563:12
jewel of our house 247: 8
like an onion 245:17
live in perfect c. 247: 2
my white stole of c. 247:12
no art can repair c. 2201:16
not c. enough in language 1069: 9
of honor 245: 5
poor women without c. ..1718: 8
presuming upon merit of c. 245: 4
sacred rays of c. 246:12
'tis c. my brother, c. 246:12
very ice of c. 247:11
virtue in some, in many vice 246:14
without charity chained ..246: 5
Chasuble: he wore, a c. ..1747: 3
Chat: couldn't c. together ..313: 4
on various subjects 1495: 3
where'er I come 2026:14
Chat: à bon c. bon rat 224:16
n'eveille point c. qui dort ..224: 6
Chatham, sword undrawn 1664: 4
Châtiment des mauvais princes 1611:10
Chatouille qui ne pince ...1446: 3
Châtre: billet qu'a La C. .1620:12
Chatter: I c. c. as I flow ..200:16
in c. excellent 1898:15
it's only idle c. 313: 4
of frivolity 313: 4
Chatterboxes: women justly accounted c. 2200: 2
Chatterton, marvelous Boy 1524:11
Chaucer, Geoffrey 248
at Woodstock 31: 9
is a rough diamond 249: 2
Chaucer's: rich as C. speech 55:14
worst ribaldry 2258: 6
Chaussetier mal chaussé ..1817:13
Chauvin: j'suis C. 1463:13
Chauvinism: entered into c. 1463:13
Che sera, sera 1704:10
Cheap: all good things c. 2247:13
all things were c. 83: 5
as lies 1977:16
esteem too lightly 725:14
ill ware is never c. 207:15
not how c., but how good 1605: 7
obtain too c. esteem too lightly 725:14
sitting as standing 1631:14
Cheaper: make worse and sell a little c. 1605: 7
Cheapest: things called dear, c. 1605: 7
Cheaply bought 189:11
obtain c., esteem lightly ..1604:16
Cheapness: competition for c. cause of decay 1605: 7
never buy because of c. 1604:15
Cheapside is the best garden 756: 8
Cheat at play 249:12
his neighbor 804: 7
I must c. as women can ..2216:11
lowering of money a c. ..1551: 3
me in price not goods 249:12
one c. can gull all these ..249: 7
so lucrative to c. 249: 6
successful c. of love 1204:10
to a c. a c. and a half....250: 3
to c. a man is nothing ...2205:13
Cheated: better be c. 1218:15
honest man when c. retires 249:14
I will not be c. 1016:23
if c. by great, say nothing 249:14
in horse, wig, wife 249:11
most c. who cheats himself 249: 4
not c. who knows he is c. 249: 9
Cheater: old bald c., Time 2002:16
Cheateth in small things ..249:12
Cheating 249
thousand methods of c. ..249:10
Cheats: every man c. 915:12
horse and foot 250: 2
Check: he writes his c. ..1333:10
political blank c. 1554: 3
Cheek: bashful maiden's c. 1577:10
be ready with a blush ..173: 7
bear'st c. for blows 2015: 7
by jole 1642:23
by jowl 1031: 8
daisy's c. tipp'd with blush 358: 6
damask c. 1209:17
give this c. a little red 2076: 3
hangs upon c. of night ..140:11
he that loves a rosy c. ..1200: 7
Helen's c., not heart 889: 4
her c. all purple 139: 2
his native c. 1091: 1
in each c. pretty dimple ..448:19
leans c. upon her hand ..851:14
marching c. by jowl 1031: 8
never stain a c. 172:11
of parchment, eye of stone 1761:16
of the young person 172: 7
turn the other c. 937: 3; 1708: 1
upon her c. the red rose dawned 1206: 7
Cheeks: blushing c. 652: 7
crack your c. 1921: 5
fresh as rose in June 318:11
his c. should flame 79: 9
his rawbone c. 1570:14
how wan her c. are 86:13
lean sallow c. 455:12
of sorry grain 910: 3
ruby of your c. 323: 3
so rare a white 609: 4
vermeil red did shew 141: 2
vying with rose leaves 120:11
white as the flour de lys ..1157: 3
whose c. are pink 40:10
wide c. o' the air 2000:18
Cheel that can tell 252: 9
Cheer: be of good c. 250:14
but not inebriate 1968: 7
don't c., poor devils dying ..66: 8
for glad New Year 2261:16
small c. and great welcome 660: 3
up 250:13
wedding c. to burial feast .747:10
when victory's near 1854: 3

Cheer, *continued*
yet they made good c. 2125:13
you do not give the c. ..932:14
Cheered up himself with verse 250: 6
Cheerful at morn 250:10
without mirth 858: 1
Cheerfully: look c. upon me 250:18
Cheerfulness 250
befits us 250: 9
feel a deep c. 250:11
ingredient in health 250: 5
let c. abound 1558:10
more spent, more remains 250: 8
no man poet without c. 250: 9
result of discipline 250:20
sign of wisdom 250:15
Cheerless, dark, dreary ..1885: 4
Cheese: after c. nothing ..522:14
and garlic 192:16
apple pie and c. 92: 5
bread and c. 198: 4
digestive c. 523: 1
king's c. lost in parings 1043: 1
like crusted foam 933: 8
moon made of green c. 1341: 6
pound of c. 122:13
table's closing rite 522:14
take chalk for c. 86: 5
you Banbury c. 1642:12
Cheese-paring: made of a c. 1246:11
Chelsea: Elsie from C. ..2284: 6
Chemin: aucun c. de fleurs à gloire 780: 6
est long du projet 147:13
Chemins: tous c. vont à Rome 1736:10
Chemise: dernière c. 316:16
Cheops: not a pinch remains 1339: 7
Cheque, *see* Check
Chequer-board of Nights ..1121:16
Cherchez la femme 2206: 4
Chères qui plus cousté ...1605: 4
Cherish hearts that hate ..150: 5
Cherished: better c. nearer death 379:12
Cherries fairly do enclose 2027: 9
kissing c. 1164: 5
Cherry: like to a double c. 2067: 3
loveliest of trees 2038: 5
ripe do cry 608: 3
ripe, I cry 1164: 5
ruddier than the c. 2213: 9
three bits of a c. 1631:15
Cherry-stones: carved on 1959: 4
Cherry-trees: blossoming c. 2038: 5
Cherub Contemplation 307:14
in the shape of a woman ..215: 4
musical c., soar singing 1072:11
rode upon a c. 693:20
that sits up aloft 1778: 2
who had lost way 408:10
Cherubim: helmed C. 76:12
Cherubin: hatch'd a c. 568: 2
young and rose-lipped c. 1462:17
Cherubins: young-eyed c. ..1367:10
Cherubs: childless c. 1452: 6
Chess: life too short for c. ..754: 5
only wasting time 754: 5
Chessboard is the world ..1121:16
we called the c. white ..113: 8
Chest: bed by night, c. by day 908:14
Dead Man's C. 493:14
listen to his doubtful c. ..466: 1
military c. insolvent 2114: 7
Chesterfield: courtly C. ..942:10
only devil can make a C. ..764:10
Chestnut: Arcadians were c. eaters 94: 3
horse c. and c. horses 100:10
in a farmer's fire 2200: 6
much told joke 1009: 7
only color 848:11
Chestnut-eaters: Arcadians ..94: 3
Chestnut-tree: Under a spreading c. 1854: 9
Chestnuts, lavish of gold 2038: 6
pull c. from the fire 223:16
Cheval emblé, ferme l'estable 2168:21
volant 930:15
Chevalier sans peur 259:12
Chew and choke as much as possible 1488: 5
on fancy's food 634:17
upon this 1682:17
Chewed, swallow'd 338: 2
thrice-turn'd cud 79: 3
Chewing the food of sweet and bitter fancy 634:17
Chewing-gum: Americans spend more for c. 56: 5
Cheverel consciences 300:19
skins stretch 300:19
Chez nous: partout comme 2238:12
Chicago, Ill. 251
Chick of the old cock 69:12
Chicken in pot on Sundays .516: 3
is the country's 275: 6
she's no c. 41: 9
who dat say c. 2285: 7
Chicken-pox: avoid the c. ..254:14
Chickens: all my pretty c. .409: 1
count c. before hatched ...694:17
eat c. in the shell 533: 1
Chide as loud as thunder ..2200: 6
him for faults 650: 3
him from our eaves 1880:14
if she do c. 2215: 9
no breather 651:11
Chiding: better a little c. ...256: 7
of the winter's wind 2161: 8
Chief: brilliant c. irregularly great 97:14
hail to the c. 297:11
of a thousand for grace ..819: 5
of Pyramid and Crocodile 1406:15
Chief-inquisitor: recording c. 1284: 6
Chief-justice, rich, quiet ..1021: 2
Chieftain: great C. who takest such pains 2131:1a
Chieftains and bards 392: 7
Chield's amang you takin' notes 1603:14
Chiels: best o' c. 987:10
that winna ding 611: 7
Chien de mieux dans l'homme 470:18
est à moi 768: 7
mal éveiller c. qui dort ..470: 9
qui m'aime, aime mon c. ..469: 9
Chiens: plus j'admire c. ..470:18
Chiffon du papier 767: 7
Chilblains fell 460:11
Child amang you takin' notes 1603:14
and weak 257:13
around c. bend Graces ...819:18
art thou a c. of tears 1973: 5
be a c. o' the time 2014:11
become as a little c. 1057: 3
become as this little c. 252:17
better c. should cry than father 256:12
blessed vision! happy c. ...253:16
burnt c. dreads the fire . 595:19
christom c. 397:11
come forth from womb 391:11
each has been little c. 257:19
every c. may joy to hear ..1537: 9
exquisite c. of the air 211:10
fair and sinless c. of sin 1222:15
flies into a passion 2240: 5
for little c. little mourning 253: 3
for such c. I bless God ...252:17
foul c. and fair hound 256: 3
give a c. his will, ill 256: 3
give c. what he will crave .256: 3
governed by a c. 252: 8
great with c. to speak . .2251:10
happy English c. 552:12
he that cockers his c. 255:12
he who gives a c. a treat ..251:12
he's a c. in mind 361:12
humble himself as this little c. 252:17
Child, *continued*
I was a c. and she was c. 1206:14
I was a city c. 275:20
I'd rather be thy c. 1368:17
if I am Devil's c. 441: 4
imposes on the man 529: 3
instructed in virtue 256: 2
is father of the man 251:13
is it well with the c. 252:13
is known by his doings 255:2
is not mine as first was 257:10
kiss c. for nurse's sake ..1047:19
leave a c. alone 255:13
lie down like tired c. 221:12
little c. born yesterday 121: 2
Little Lost C. 2291: 2
maid's c. best taught 252:10
make me a c. again 2011: 1
may say amen 1587: 1
Monday's c. fair of face ..164:11
must teach the man 253:15
my c. said such a witty thing 313:16
naked new-born c. 407:11
never-wean'd, though favor'd c. 1374: 1
New World's c. 248:18
not a c. in arms 26: 1
of grandmother Eve 2178:15
of many prayers 1118:14
of misery, baptised in tears 1320:18
of mortality 1348: 5
of Nature, learn 1382: 9
of the skies 51: 5
of these tears lost 1972:10
owes parents no gratitude 1452: 8
put another's c. in your bosom 257: 9
respect the c. 255:15
Rowland to the dark tower 546: 4
saved little c. that shall lead them 2150:11
saving a little c. 74:11
says what it heard by fire 257: 3
should always say what's true 255: 8
simple child 409: 6
soothed its c. of air 171: 2
spare the rod and spoil the c. 256:12
spirit of a little c. 253:13
spoiled by the world 2098:10
spoilt c. never loves mother 255:12
stoop to heal that only c. ..74:10
strike c. in anger 256:17
teach c. a trade 1061:14
teach c. to hold tongue 257: 1
thankless c. 254:11
that is not clean and neat ..255: 6
this only c. 254:11
thy king is a c. 252: 8
train up the c. 256: 5
twice a c. 27:19
weep bramble's smart 1976: 6
when I was a c. I spake as a c. 251: 7
whom many fathers share 743:20
wise c. that knows father ..645:23
with laughing look 257:19
you see me with c. 245:10
young years of little c. 251:12
Childhood 251
and youth are vanity 251: 8
days of c. days of woe 251:19
eye of c. fears painted devil 657: 2
has no forebodings 251: 9
how my c. fleeted by 251:15
is health 251:10
is the sleep of reason 251:16
may do without purpose ..1661: 8
scenes of my c. 252: 1
second c. 27:19
shows the man 251:13
stage in remanufacture of the Life Stuff 251:18
whose happiness is love 251:11
Childhood's hour 452:15
Childishness: second c. 2240: 5
Childless: best works from c. men 252: 4

Childless, *continued*
seldom misfortune to be c. 645:20
with her children 985:11
Children 252
age after age the c. give ..1064: 9
all Adam's c. 485: 7
anchors hold mother 1353: 7
and chicken always pickin' 252:10
and chickens ever eating ..520: 4
and fools cannot lie 1109:15
and fools speak true 2057: 6
arise and call her blessed 1352: 7
as one wishes c. to be, they are 256: 9
bachelor's c. always young 252:11
begin by loving parents ..257:15
bills of charges 632:11
bind c. by respect not fear 256: 8
blessings seem, torments are 254: 7
blest with many c. by you 2143: 9
born of fairy stock 614:13
born of thee are sword and fire 2113: 9
bring innumerable cares ..254: 2
bring their own love 254: 4
climbing for a kiss 909:10
cruel c., crying babies ...255: 4
disliked of c. 252:15
divine who love them 252:14
do anything with c. 255:11
do not make mothers 1350:14
do ye hear c. weeping 1064: 9
doing nothing, doing mischief 254:17
dream not first half year ..480: 1
education of c. 531:15
e'en c. followed 1590: 8
enjoy the present 254:20
fall out, and fight 255: 9
gath'ring pebbles on shore 1399:14
gets to share poverty 254: 6
good and bad c. 255: 1
hanging on my neck ... 1351:10
happy in his c. 257: 7
have wide ears 257: 2
heritage of the Lord ...253:12
his c. hang upon his kisses 909:10
hostages to fortune 632:10
I have four nice c. 1352:11
if c. were no more 253:11
in praise of little c. 253: 6
keys of paradise 253:13
know friend and foe 252:14
late c. early orphans 257: 6
learn to creep ere go 255:17
let c. play 827:12
lisp of c. 1510:19
little c., little sorrows 254: 8
little c. of the wind 2153:12
little c. saying grace 255: 7
living poems 253:11
make parents fools 254: 8
may be strangled 427: 8
most divine are c. 253: 6
most imaginative 252:16
mothered by the street 252: 6
need models not critics 256: 1
no c. nowadays 253: 1
no parents think c. ugly .1452:13
not to be forced by whipping 256: 4
of life are we 1127: 3
of light 2166:10
of necessity 1392:15
of splendor and fame ...1248:10
of swift joy 191: 7
of the brain 180:14
of the crucible 55: 3
of the present spouse 257: 9
of the sun 1711:12
of this world wiser 2166:10
of yesterday 1128: 6
olive plants 253:12
pale c. of feeble sun 802: 5
pick up words as pigeons peas 257: 5
poor men's riches 253: 9
reflect constant cares 254: 1
seen, not heard 254:15
suck mother when young ..254: 8

Children, *continued*
suffer the little c. 252:17
sweeten labours 253:17
symbol of marriage 253: 8
torment, nothing more .. .254:13
unruly c. make sire stoop 254:12
use the fist 254:16
vexation to your youth ..254:12
we of smiles and sighs ..1139:12
what sweeter than c. 253: 7
when c. stand still, ill 254:17
where c. are not heaven is not 253:14
wicked c. wake and weep . 255: 1
Chill and shadow 392: 9
then stupor 386: 1
Chilly and grown old 847:19
Chimborazo under the line 1533: 6
Chime: faintly as tolls .1776:10
let your silver c. 1367: 7
midnight c. sounds 1302: 9
musical as c. of rills 947: 2
of sweet Saint Charity ..515: 2
patchwork pastoral c. 1982:15
Chimera buzzing in space .1410:11
what a c. then is man . 1238:16
Chimeras huge 635: 3
Chimes at midnight .... .1303: 6
manifold soft c. 1401:11
your belly c. dinner 155:14
Chimney: dirty c. on fire ...60: 4
in my father's house . ..1621:15
looking up a c., fine day ..558: 8
on roof and c. 1526:15
smoked like a c. 2017: 1
that won't smoke 95: 4
Chimney-side of prudence 1142:11
Chimney-sweepers: as c., come to dust 382: 5
black 166: 8
Chimneys: good grove of c. .276: 2
were blown down 1946:14
Chimpanzee from which we sprang 586: 7
near c. 1482: 5
Chin: alas poor c. 128: 5
chuck o' the c. 2027: 7
cloven c. 448:18
new reaped . .. .124:16
small show of man on c. ..127: 6
stands for purpose 606: 2
with beard supplied 455:12
with the dimpled c. 26: 9
your c. double 36: 1
China ancient and blue ...1565: 2
China-crackers on the fifth of July 2207: 8
Chinafy this country 1471: 6
Chinee: heathen C. 349:10; 1066: 2
Chinese have two eyes 597: 4
Chink in the world above 1586:16
wise are swayed by c. 818: 1
Chinks of her body ..... .28:10
shall have the c. 478: 4
so we get the c. 1336:15
that time has made 28:10
Chinning to the fourteenth line 2071: 5
Chintz: charming c. 2076: 3
exceeds mohair 977:16
Chip: carried c. on shoulder 1378: 6
fall in your eye 49: 1
of the old block 69:12
Chips: let c. fly where ..1726:11
Chisel: ne'er did Grecian c. trace 140: 9
Chiselers: we know there are c. 249:15
Chit-chat of the day . ..1761: 8
small talk 313: 4
Chivalry 253
age of c. is gone 258: 6
Cervantes smiled c. away .227:10
lacking in our land 258:11
male c. had perished 258: 5
redeem the fight 258:13
with England's c. 1474: 8
Chloe: I could do without you, C. 977:14
is my real flame 318:10

Chloe, *continued*
wants a heart 881:19
work of C. 2136:10
Chloris: I saw fair C. ...1858: 5
Chloroform after sixty 35: 6
of the mind 180: 2
Choice 259
and occasion return no more 1433: 1
between dark and light ..423: 4
between truth and repose 259:16
between two evils 1541: 5
difficulty is the c. 260:13
growth lies in c. 259:15
is what separates artist ..107:14
leave the c. to me 30: 3
makes friends 729: 2
most c. forsaken 2093:17
no c. no difficulty 260: 9
not number, c. of friends 728:21
of difficulties 260:15
of evils 260:17
of evils rather than goods ..261: 1
of profession 209: 4
of the prudent 1872: 3
of working or starving ..1103:11
on c. of friends name depends 729: 3
people's c. was just 2123: 5
small c. in rotten apples .260:14
well-made c. of friends ..185: 9
Choices: better c. not to be had 261: 1
Choir: first of all starry c. 1940: 6
invisible 981:11
when c. got up to sing ..1880: 2
Choirs: bare ruin'd c. 36: 3
Choix fait les amis 729: 2
Choke a poor scamp for the glory of God 852:16
Choler: aggravate your c. ..78:17
drunk with c. 78:17
let's purge this c. 78:17
Choose: cannot c. but err 576:19
do not c. 260: 1
friends like books 729: 4
I do not c. 1552: 9
rather c. I should die ...1624:16
thine own time 403: 3
those who pick and c. ..1507: 1
what is best 356: 4
what many men desire ..1482:10
Choosers: beggars no c. 145: 7
Choosing: each c. each 1187: 8
Chops and changes 2242: 9
and Tomato sauce 2217: 7
Choragus: coryphæus or c. .538:11
Chord or Self 1183: 6
one clear c. 1539: 7
Chorda qui semper oberrat eadem 1635: 2
Chords: dissonant c. beget divinest harmonies 860:21
in the human mind 1956:16
mystic c. of memory 57:11
smite the c. rudely 1528:13
that tenderest be 123:11
vibrate sweetest pleasure 1445:16
Chore done by the gods 109: 4
Chortled in his joy 1409: 8
Chorus: tormenting fantastic c. 2223:13
value of kindly c. 677:16
what a c. 697:13
Chorus-ending in Euripides .113: 8
Chose: plus c'est la même c. 2274: 1
Chosen between love and gold 1271:10
Chrematistic art 1336: 4
Christ 261
and Longfellow, both dead 1861: 6
awhile to mortals given ...515:10
Birth of C 267
bless thee, brother 265:14
brings Saviour C. again to Earth 251:12
came gently 883:14
child of Nazareth 269: 3
child stood at Mary's knee 261:11
crystal C. 263:11

Cloud, *continued*
one c. can hide sunlight........ 281: 1; 2041:13
only disperse the c. 281: 4
overcome us like a summer's c. 2209:10
pillar of the C. 280:17
round-topped c. 281: 2
sable c. 282: 4
sits in a foggy c. 1905: 6
spher'd in a radiant c. ..1151: 7
that wraps the present 15:19
that's dragonish 281:20
that's mine too 309:14
turn c. inside out 282: 8
under the c. 280:16
were I a c. I'd gather 280:15
what a scowl of c. 1914: 3
yon little c. of gray 1941:13
Cloud-continents of sunset-seas 281:19
Cloud-folds of her garments 1858: 1
Cloudlet: over the c. dim ..1072:11
Clouds 280
after greatest c., sun 282: 9
and darkness are around Him 65:11
are big with mercy 2045: 4
at her bidding disappear ..925: 5
base contagious c. 1686: 6
billowy c. 282: 2
birds that never sleep 281: 3
black, weather clear 282: 9
chequering the eastern c. 1347:16
come o'er the sunset 33: 4
consign treasures to fields ..281:16
fair, frail palaces 281:19
fancy c. where none be ..1491: 2
far c. of feathery gold 282: 2
fear not c. will always lour 311:11
gaudy c. like courtiers 372:13
have wept and died 1834:11
he that regardeth c. 861:11
her form environ 212: 1
humorous lining to c. 282: 6
I saw two c. at morning ..280:14
if no c. not enjoy sun 281:11
impregns the c. 1853:17
in the c. 281:10
in thousand liveries dight ..281: 7
like rocks and towers 281: 2
look black 1669: 3
looks when c. are blowing 1775:13
make c. what you please 282: 1
maketh c. his chariot 796: 3
may drop down titles 2164: 1
mountains and cliffs in c. ..281: 2
never doubted c. would break 1434: 9
of life's tempestuous hours 2182: 4
on balmy zephyrs silver c. 2269:16
pack, c., away 1730:12
play i' th' plighted c. 615: 5
praise the evening c. 281:12
replenish'd from below 281: 9
rolling c. are spread 1590: 8
scatter the c. that hide ...886:10
silver lining 282: 4
sleep in thy c. 1940: 2
that gather round the setting sun 281:17
their chilly bosoms bare ..1857:12
through c. I'll never float 2210: 2
thy c. all other c. dispel ..2019:11
tops do buss the c. 96:11
trailing c. of glory 164:10
turn my c. about 282: 5
uglier seem the c. 281:14
undaunted by c. of fear ...887: 9
wait till the c. roll by 282:13
were really to blame 282:11
when c. appear, wise men 1921: 6
when c. in autumn crack 2200: 6
which seem pavilions 48: 7
ye so much dread 2045: 4
Clout: change not a c. 1283:17
Clover 282
broidery of purple c. 686: 6
in the c. or the snow 1868: 6
is aristocracy 71: 5

Clover, *continued*
may I in c. lie snug 1348:14
to be in c. 283: 3
Clover-bloom and sweet-brier 283: 6
Clown: gie a c. your finger .631: 6
make c. become gentleman .764:10
mated with a c. 1277: 7
Clowns: let those that play c. .10: 6
Clowns' fawnings 697:10
Cloy: best things beyond their measure c. 89: 5
hungry edge of appetite 89: 5
Cloyless sauce 315:15
Club: assembly of good fellows 1860:14
cleft his c. to make fire ..2142: 4
her best c. is the home ..2204:15
scene of savage joys 1860:14
Club-mate: adulterer be your c. 288:15
Clubs cannot part them ..1205:13
typical of strife 219:13
Clue: Labyrinth's single c. 1677:16
lost c. regain 868:16
Clues: simple c. 474:19
Clusters load the lilac-bushes 1155:13
Clutter up the Universe ..968:17
Clyde: young fellow of C. ..747:15
Clyde's meandering stream 1732:15
Coach: built c., lost use of feet 278:11
drive c. and six 1082:17
go, call a coach 212: 9
good company is c. 289: 4
in the baggage c. ahead 1350:21; 2284: 7
with four horses 2212: 5
Coach-makers: fairies' c. ...615:11
Coachman likes to hear whip 845:10
Coal 283
black diamonds 283: 8
black is better 166: 9
dead c. of wars 2106:18
living c. his heart was 879:14
making c. for Baer 1065:11
whole world turn to c. 1892:12
Coal-barges: ten dark c. ...350:12
Coal-black and grizzled 1065: 7
is better 166: 9
Coalition: between victor and vanquished, c. 2084:19
Coals of fire 543: 8
thereof are c. of fire 1007:13
to Newcastle 283: 7
Coarse: every thing nat'ral is c. 1653: 6
I'm c. when terse 2252: 2
Coast: gain the c. of bliss ..158: 8
of Bohemia 1815: 1
stern and rockbound c. ..1775: 7
was clear 1632: 2
what c. knows not our blood 171: 9
Coast-storm in a shawl 1160: 4
Coat bare of nap 490: 8
cut c. after cloth 13: 5
his c. was red 444:10
leathern c. 943: 2
loves a scarlet c. 1866: 4
man who wears laced c. ..1717:18
of many colors 485: 8
old c. like old friend 490: 8
poor c. that I love 490: 8
so smooth and bare 490: 8
spoil c. with scanting 119:15
take off your c. 106:14
turn'd his c. 2034:10
walks in a c. of darkness 2258:16
wear the old c. 100: 1
Coats: silken c. and caps ..489: 4
Cob was the strongest 930:11
Cobble-stones: talking c. ..1963: 6
Cobbler apron'd 714: 3
better than king 1817:12
I am but a c. 1818: 7
keep to your leather 1817:11
let c. stick to his last 1817:11

Cobbler, *continued*
mock not the c. 1818: 5
puts off considering cap ..1990: 3
Cobblers
See also Shoemakers
must thrust their awls ..1818: 8
ye tuneful c. 1818: 1
Cobweb fashion 945:10
Cobwebs out of my eyes ..994: 1
swept 315:17
weave fine c. 1638: 2
Cock 232
and bull tale 1960: 7
caused the sun to rise 233: 4
chick of the old c. 69:12
crows in the morning 1729: 3
early village c. 233: 6
God Almighty's c. 161: 9
hath sung 1442:11
he's welly like a c. 233: 4
hight Chauntecleer 232:18
may craw, day may daw ..45: 4
of the hat 864:16
on his own dunghill 980:21
owe c. to Æsculapius 417: 5
that's silent, hen crows ..2145:10
that treads them 2197:12
this is a c. 1448:14
to Æsculape 458:19
trumpet to the morn 233: 6
with lively din 233: 1
Cock-a-diddle-dow 233: 8
Cock-crow: at first c. 769:19
Cock Robin: who killed ..1359: 9
Cockaigne: haunts of old ..1168: 5
wondrous land 1741: 4
Cocked: into a c. hat 204: 3
Cockle: sow'd c., no corn .1709:12
wild oats, rough burs 2130: 3
Cockles of my heart 876:16
Cockloft empty 1309:17
unfurnished 1309:17
Cockney-poetry 1033: 6
Cockpit of Europe 150:11
Cockroach: gods i am pent 1525:12
Cocktail: brandy c. 499:10
Cocleas tibi habe 522: 4
Cocoon of its thoughts 1311: 6
spins toiling out of c. ..2245: 1
Cocus domini debet habere gulam 315:10
Cod: Boston c. 194:15
Code of life and conduct ..150: 1
sublime c. of morals 265:22
Codlin's your friend 727: 1
Codling when almost apple 2265: 7
Codlings: ye c. peep 670: 6
Cœlum Imperium 888:11
qui c. possit nisi nosse 797: 2
ruat c. 1031: 2
vituperant 885:13
See also cœlum
Cœnam: post c. ambulabis ..872: 7
s b c. inambula 872: 7
Cœpisti melius quam desinis .147:14
Cœpit: quidquid c. et desinit 147:17
Cœur: à c. vaillant rien d'impossible 971: 6
a ses raisons 882:17
dit du bien de son c. 882:12
dur c. qui en Mai n'aime 1283:16
mon c. comme un tambour .827:18
quand on aime, c. juge ..1182:10
sent rarement 1901: 9
Cœurs: qu'il reste encore ..881:21
Coffee: I will not take any more c. 2280: 2
makes politician wise 1547:18
o'er cold c. trifle 2198: 6
Coffee-house: go to the c. ..735:15
Coffin: care to our c. adds a nail, no doubt 221:15
every c. "Whither"? 1139: 3
nailed his c. down 203: 4
no useless c. enclosed 1870: 9
Coffin-lid: blazon on 624:10
Coffins stood round 2175: 9
Cog, face and lie 1113:15
smooth, deceive 678:20

Country, *continued*
our c. to be cherished 64: 2
praise me not the c. 276: 1
serves his c. best 1544: 8
that draws fifty foot of water 904: 6
title of their mother c. ..1463:10a
to love c., c. lovely 1463:11
tremble for my c. 1464: 4
undiscover'd c. 389:11
unmapped c. within us ...235: 9
vow to thee, my c. 2277: 4
when right, to be kept right 63: 6
where I may live well 320: 3
where one is well off 320: 3
wherever his abode 320:15
who loves c. cannot hate .1463:12
who serves his c. best 1465: 5
will not love his c. 1465:13
woman-c., wooed not wed 1000:19
Country's, God's, Truth's ..150: 5
my c. be the profit 1465: 3
Country-presses labor with poets 1528:12
Country-seat: old-fashioned c. 2013: 7
Countryman too much of a child 640:12
Countrymen: sequester himself from c. 2029:17
Countryside: no one knows 321: 6
Couple: found c. still the same 1797: 8
must c. or die 1225:12
one c. more 1253:19
to c. is a custom 1225:12
with my valentine 2071: 9
Coupled and inseparable ...287:14
together for sake of strife 2096:13
Coupler-flange to spindle-guide 1814: 3
Couplet: delivered of c. ..2254:14
Couplets: golden c. are disclosed 1824:17
Coups d'épingle 2040:11
de fourches ni 1424: 9
gisent beau c. 15:15
Cour: loin de la c. 326: 6
ne rend pas content 326:11
vu la C., vu du monde 326:11
Courage 322
all goes if c. goes 323: 7
bad man's c. 323:14
best c. flashes of genius ..322: 9
best gift of all 322:16
brother, do not stumble ..937: 2
brutal thing called C. 455:14
can't answer for one's c. ..324: 4
caused by fear 654:23
champions cause of right ..322: 7
conquers all things 322:15
contagious 324: 6
dangerous profession 1862:19
destitute of c. 174: 5
Dutch c. 494: 3
equality to problem 322: 9
fear father of c. 653:15
footstool of virtues 323: 4
from going much alone ..1871:14
from hearts, no numbers ..324:14
goes before 323:16
have c. of my opinions ...1554: 3
highest gift 322:11
his c. and mercy strive ..1298:11
in danger half battle 324: 5
is generosity 322: 8
keen and polished 506: 1
leads starward 323: 2
mightier than the sun 325: 6
most vulgar virtue 322:14
mounteth with occasion ...324: 8
never to submit 325:14
no c. but in honest cause .990:19
no c. but in innocence 990:19
of having done thing before 322: 9
of my opinions 1554: 3
of opinions of others 2147: 7
of the negro 1395: 7
of unshaken root 1030:13
peace tries best 279:14
Courage, *continued*
puts new face on everything 323:21
quick for war 324:14
rather than live in snuff ..388: 8
scorner of fear 323: 3
scorns death it cannot shun 323:20
should have eyes 324: 1
that endureth long 325: 4
to appear good 1245: 5
to ask questions 1665: 9
to bear defeat 322:12
to bear others' afflictions .1322:15
to do without witnesses ..322:13
to endure and to obey ...2141: 8
to expose our ignorance ..1665: 9
to face difficulty 447:24
to face ultimate defeat 323: 5
to live rather than die ...1140:13
to take hard knocks 323: 1
to the sticking-place 326: 2
want of c. 331:13
want of c. not to be content 309: 4
weak in c. strong in cunning 349: 3
which heart did lend it ..1934: 7
yet c., soul 617:23
yet was his c. green 38: 2
Courir: rien ne sert de c. .146:14
Course: compulsive c. 1713:19
daily c. of duty run 1890:17
fight the c. 665:10
I have run the c. 1133: 5
I must stand the c. 1704:14
middle c. is best 1327: 3
my c. be onward still 507: 2
my constant c. I bear 248: 2
of ages begins anew 43:18
of empire takes its away 52: 6
of Nature c. of death 1387:11
of nature has its pains ...739:20
of Nature is art of God ..1391: 6
of true love never did run smooth 1195:10
steer a middle c. 436:20
university c. convinces 287:21
wise c. to steer 14: 2
Courser: winged c. 1526: 3
Coursers of ethereal race ..505: 7
Courses even with the sun .1942:11
Court 326
abounds in lords 327: 2
at c. everyone for himself 326: 8
does not make us happy ..326:11
happy that never saw c. ..327: 1
her c. was pure 2082:14
her in conqueror's style ..2215: 6
holy water 326: 8
like marble palace 326:11
live turmoiled in c. 326:14
liveth in c. die in straw ..327: 5
virtuous c. draws world ..326:10
who has seen c. seen world 326:11
Courted and jilted 2217: 4
by all the winds 488: 8
in your girls be c. 257:16
Courteous out of self-respect 559:14
so very c. and well-bred 329:15
sweet c. things unsaid ..932: 7
though coy 329: 6
to all 738:13
to strangers 320: 4
Courtesan: cool a c. 2133:16
Courtesies: small, sweet c. .329:13
Courtesy 327
always time for c. 328:14
and forbearance becoming 329: 5
apish c. 678:20
be not a beast in c. 503:18
candy deal of c. 329:20
costs nothing 328:15
dissembling c. 2064:14
evil and insolent c. 1608: 4
glozing c. 948:14
grace of God is in c. 327:20
grows chill 227:12
grows in court 314: 2
Courtesy, *continued*
has done its most 933: 4
ideal of c. 238: 3
less c. more of purse 330: 1
much c., much subtlety ..329:18
nothing more valuable 329:14
of C. it is much less 327:20
scant this breathing c. ...933:10
sooner found in sheds 329:12
strain curt'sy c. 543:14
sweet and gracious is c. ...329: 8
was in him more 328:19
wins women all as well ..2215: 1
whole of chivalry in c. 258: 9
would seem to cover sin ..329:20
Courtier extraordinary 873: 3
young, beggar old 327: 5
Courtiers beggars in age ..327: 5
foreign c. and whores 244: 4
Courts and camps the only places to learn world ..2243: 6
and cities seen 1258: 7
for cowards were erected 1105: 2
seats of good-breeding 326: 5
to cities and c. repair 277: 4
Courtship
come to c. as to prayer ..2212: 4
dream in c., in wedlock wake 2139: 6
employ chiefest thoughts to c. 2212:10
hours of c. 1274: 5
in c. of repose 1850: 4
perpetually varying 2211:15
pleasant the snaffle of C. 1276: 6
when widow returns from funeral 2136:19
Cousin-germans: serve their c. 904: 6
Cousins: not ashamed of c. 586:17
Cove: quiet old c. 65: 3
Covenant between all and One 1670: 9
between me and the earth 1670: 9
God's glowing c. 1670: 9
of salt for ever 1756: 5
with death 381:6; 1841: 7
Covenants: open c. of peace 1471:17
Covent Garden to Peru ...1423:11
Coventry: sent to C. 1632: 4
Cover in phrenzie guards ..949: 7
Covered: one man allowed to stand c. 864: 6
Coverlet: grassy c. of God .385:10
stretch according to c. ...1648:11
Covers: who c. discovers ..1632: 5
Covet earnestly best gifts .776: 2
thou shalt not c. 209: 2
Covetize: thro' pride or c. 1522: 6
Covetous does nothing well 118: 4
I am not c. for gold 919: 4
never has money 1615:11
of others' property 119:13
Covetousness: age and c. ...36: 9
breaks the sack 117:14
brings man to a morsel ...118: 1
bursts the bag 117:14
cracks sinews of faith 117:15
excess of wealth cause ...119: 3
furnishes constant grief ..311:17
has blinding power 120: 1
root of all evil 120: 2
Covets: who c. always poor .118: 1
Cow 330
bid the c. consider 331: 3
cross c. holds up milk 330: 6
cursed c. short horns 330: 8
does not gaze at rainbow ..330: 5
good animal in field 330:12
good c. hath evil calf 330:10
is in the hammock 978: 8
kill a c. for beef 939:16
killed the parson's c. 1595: 4
like c., like calf 1154: 9
lowing c. forgets calf 331: 1
moo-cow-moo 331: 5
my c. milks me 1621:20
Purple C. 331: 4
surpasses any statue 1387: 4

Curious, *continued*
be not c. about God 797:15
more c. than devout 43:21
Curiousness a perpetual wooing 351:18
Curis: interpone gaudia c. 1510:12
quis solutis beatius c. 1706:12
Curl: barter c. for c. 1889: 8
even as thou twinest c. ..2013:15
scornful and malignant c. 1766: 4
that winter c. 41: 4
Curls: ambrosial c. 799:14
drowned in Tyrian dews ..109: 4
Currency: debased c. a cheat 1551: 3
Current: heart's c. 878:14
make him c. to the world 2016: 5
of my days 1803:13
smooth c. of domestic joy 909: 1
take c. when it serves ..1433: 8
that with gentle murmur glides 1732: 6
turn c. of woman's will 2204: 5
with noiseless c. strong ..660:20
Currents of this world ..1083:19
two such silver c. 1274: 6
Currus: finge datos c. 1938: 2
Curs bark when fellows do 543:14
not regarded 1163: 9
of low degree 470: 6
shall tame each other 1607:19
Curse 352
and be cursed 352: 2
and lie and steal 255:10
artistry's haunting c. 748: 1
attends woman's love 2207: 7
beneath the c. of Cain ..1359: 1
causeless shall not come ..353: 3
common c. of mankind 958:13
concludes with Cupid's c. 1207: 4
counted a c. to him 1730: 3
his better angel 75: 2
I know how to c. 1951:10
is like a cloud 352:18
launch the c. of Rome 353: 1
like a very drab 1952: 8
like stone flung to heaven ..352:20
loser's c. 753: 6
man's state necessary c. 1231:21
never was heard such c. 353:13
of an aching heart 982: 8
of an evil deed 585: 6
of crushed affections 354: 3
of greatness 837:17
of kings to be attended ..1043:10
of marriage 1277: 2
of Rome 353:13
of this country 537: 2
on man who business 209: 8
pillowed on a c. too deep 1697: 2
shall be on thee 1851: 2
thee by a parent's outraged love 354: 3
'tis the c. of service 1868: 4
upon your venom'd stang 2028: 1
with a c. annex'd 336:18
with book, bell, candle ..353:13
Cursed be the social wants ..354: 4
he c. him at board 353:13
is he that curseth thee 168:14
that rascally thief 353:13
with granting of prayer ..1585:10
See also Curst.
Curses bestowed on cooks ..316: 2
come home to roost 352:20
how can c. keep him yours 1197:15
mutters coward c. 1952: 2
not loud but deep 36: 3
rigg'd with c. dark 1815:12
sort of prayers 1368:16
Cursing: blessing and c. ..168:14
clothed himself with c. ..353: 4
returneth again 352:20
Curst from his cradle 1120: 7
she is intolerable c. 2189: 7
that moves my bones 1808:10
to all succeeding ages c. ..240: 4
See also Cursed.
Curtain: draw c. and show picture 609: 1
Curtain, *continued*
draw the c., farce played 416:15
iron c. 2298g:24
lecture 2146: 4
let the thick c. fall 614: 4
lift c. from common 761: 3
never outward swings 393: 4
of fir woods and heather 614:11
of repose 1707: 6
twilight lets her c. down 2061:15
undrawn no more .... .389:13
withdraw the c. 1992:12
Curtain's mystic fold 1910: 7
Curtain-lecture 2146: 4
Curtains: feathery c. stretching 282: 2
of the East 368: 7
of thine eye 599: 7
shakes c. with advice 2146: 9
Curtius Rufus descended from himself 74: 2
Curtsey while thinking 328:11
Curva trahit mites 1691:21
Curve: red c. of her lips 139:14
Curves of a perfect mouth 1358:11
Curzon, George Nathaniel 534:13
Cushion: never had a c. ..1228: 6
threadbare with prayers ..1588:13
Cushions on which knaves 915:20
Cushla-ma-chree: world's C. 996:12
Custard: eat c. of day 479: 5
Custards for supper 522: 6
Custodes: quis custodiet ipsos c. 2144:17
Custom 354
and convention govern ...1861:12
as the c. is 355: 3
bad c. like good cake 356:13
cannot conquer nature....355: 1
deadliest foe to love 355:14
dogs bark from c. 471:21
follow c. where you are ..1737:19
force of nature 355:17
gives sin lovely dye 1828: 6
good c. surer than law ..354: 8
guide of human life 355:20
hath not old c. made 2211: 2
in sin gives sin lovely ..1828: 6
is another law 354: 6
is another nature 354:10
is before all law 354: 6
is but ancient error 354: 9
jadeth 2261:12
loathsome to the eye 2018: 7
makes all things easy ...356: 4
makes dancing necessary ..359:13
makes one do unjust things 356: 6
master of all things 355:16
meets us at the cradle 355:21
men dupes to c. 356: 8
mistress of language 1069: 3
more honour'd in breach 355: 8
never can c. conquer nature 1391: 9
of Branksome Hall 355: 6
of his trade 209: 4
of the country 5 2:19
only basis of ethics 354:11
plague of wise 354:14
power to fashion us 356: 1
reconciles to everything ..355:15
rotten c. 356: 7
rules the law 354: 6
second nature 354:10
severe taskmistress 857:15
stand in the plague of c. ..355: 9
suffers naught to be strange 354: 5
that monster, c. 356: 4
that unwritten law 354: 7
thing of c. 355: 9
'tis the coward's plea 354:15
tyrant c. 355:19
violent schoolmistress 356:13
what c. hath endeared 355:13
what c. wills 356: 5
what humanity abhors c. reconciles 355:23
what is done against c. ..356: 2
world's great idol 354:13
Custom's idiot sway 356: 8
Custom-house experience ..1554: 6
Customer: tough c. 97:13
Customers' yachts 665:20
Customs change like leaves ..355: 2
differ 354:12
do not thrive in foreign soil 355: 5
more popular than laws ..354: 6
new c. follow'd 356: 5
nice c. curtsey 355: 9
not easily broken 355:22
of large numbers 1618: 6
to break off c. 149:12
with c. we live well 1080: 7
Cut: always take short c. 1678:18
and come again 219:17
by the higher orders 2274: 5
off one's nose 1413: 8
unkindest c. of all 984:16
Cute: te intus in c. novi ..1056: 9
Cutpurse of the empire ..1986:12
Cuttlefish: ink of the c. . .565: 3
like c., hide in own ink ..2225: 5
Cutty-stool 1699: 4
Cybele: she looks a sea C. 2076:18
Cycle and epicycle 2068: 3
new c. shame old 43:20
of Cathay 581: 8
Cyclone in a smile 1160: 4
Cyclopedia: a living c. ...1677: 1
Cygnea cantio 1950: 4
Cygnet to this pale faint swan 1950: 8
Cygnus cantator funeris ipse sui 1950: 4
Cymbal: tinkling c. 241: 9
Cynara: faithful to thee, C. 1198: 3
non sum qualis 231: 3
Cynic can chill with a word ..356:16
royal c. 356:15
Cynicism 356
hate c. worse than devil ..356:19
intellectual dandyism 356:18
Cynosure of neighboring eyes 598:12
Cynthia came riding 1342: 4
her new journey runs . 1341:12
mistress of the shade ..1442:12
of this minute 2198: 6
regent of night 1341: 4
Cyrus: epitaph 571: 1
Cytherea: rich-crowned C. 2077:13
Cytherea's breath 2087: 8

D

D: never use a big D. 1951: 3
D. T.'s: alcoholic psychosis 502: 6
Da locum melioribus 937:16
luego D., d. dos veces 775:11
Dab at an index 976: 2
Dachs-hond, Geist 472: 4
Dad: brother's father 2225: 7
Daddies: than their auld d. 22:10
Daddy wouldn't buy me a bow-wow 2294: 1
Dadivas quebrantan penas 772: 2
Dads: raw d., fat lads 646: 9
Dæmon: ægrotat D. 443: 2
Daffadowndillies 686: 3
Daffodil is doorside queen ..357: 1
tiny yellow d. 357:10
Daffodils 357
beneath the trees 93: 8
brazen helm of d. 683: 1
come before swallow 685: 9
fair d., we weep to see 357: 5
it's raining d. 1435:14
lady April bringing d. 93: 6
mirth of d. 93:10
raiment all of d. 93:16
small keen flames 357: 7
watching my windy d. ...756:10
when d. begin to peer ...357: 8
Daffy-down-dilly 357: 9
Dagger: air-drawn d. 2095:11
is this a d. which I see ..2095:11
muzzled lest it bite 258: 1
of the mind 2095:11

Dagger, *continued*
wear d. with braver grace 2266: 9
wear not d. in mouth ..2228:20
Daggers: at d. drawing ..1663: 9
breech'd with gore 1360: 1
give me the d. 657: 2
in men's smiles 1853: 8
rain d. with points down 1669: 1
speak d. to her 1898: 1
you have spoken d. 1898: 1
Dainties bred in books ..1676: 3
of his chaste desire 2215: 9
spiced d. every one 1952:11
who dainties love, beggars
prove 519: 4
Daintiest last 32: 2
Dainty of leave-taking ...1258:10
Dairy: this I call my d. ...682: 3
Dairy-maid inquires 352: 3
Daisies infinite uplift 358: 4
myriads of d. 357:12
pied 685: 8
plant d. at his head 401: 7
said she would be d. 358:11
smell-less yet quaint 358: 5
that little children pull 358:13
that men callen d. 358: 3
turned up to the d. 252: 5
won't tell 358: 9
Daisy **357**
fresh as a d. 1633:14
give me answer true 1211: 9
is for simplicity 357:13
leaped at a d. 853:17
lowly d. sweetly blows 357:13
makes comparison 609: 4
protects the dew-drop 1801: 9
show'd like April d. 851:13
Daisy-chain: trouble of ..2043: 3
Dale: every hill hath d. 898:10
Dalliance: primrose path 1596: 3
too much rein 1225: 6
Dallies: who d. is dastard ..63: 9
with innocence of love 123:10
Dam: two-penny d. 977: 9
Dame: behold yond d. 949: 6
belle d. sans merci 1878:5; 2187:16
he that will win his d. 2214: 3
I've lived without a d. ..1278:14
Dame: Notre D. des Neiges 1857: 6
Dames: elder d. thy haughty
peers 58: 6
in whom he did delight ..2031: 6
of ancient days 37:12
Persian d. umbrella's 2065:12
taught by cottage d. 157: 2
willing d. enough 2105:11
Damn and perjure rest ..1836:17
better off a d. sight 2168:18
braces; bless relaxes 1951:15
cared not d. for damning 1696: 2
for falling short 1696:15
her at a venture 1632:12
like a parson's d. 1950:13
literary fellers 1552: 3
the torpedoes 65: 9
those authors never read ..342:13
what do not understand ..340:15
with faint praise 13:12
Damna: esse solent d.
minora bono 751: 8
minus consueta movent 16: 2
Damnant quod non intel-
ligunt 1024: 3
Damnation: deal d. 937: 7
distilled d. 499: 6
nothing to d. add 437:15
of his taking-off 2093:18
pleading for d. of race .1603:10
wet d. 499: 6
Damnations: syllable d.
round 2096:12
twenty-nine distinct d. 159: 4
Damnatos: odit d. 1483: 3
Damned: all others will be
d. 1696:15
all silent and all d. 1822: 3
beneath all depth in hell ..1032:17
better d. than mentioned
not 626: 7
Damned, *continued*
common d. shun society ..1933: 5
ere I'ld challenge him 505:17
for despairing to be saved 1757: 3
for never king's son 353: 5
genteelly d. beside a Duke 1856:12
he who doubts is d. 63: 9
his fate 642:23
irretrievably d. 969: 6
to everlasting fame 344: 9
to fame 625:10
what do d. endure 436:19
without redemption 354: 2
world for standing up 808: 5
you'll be d. if you do ..1696:15
Damnifications of humanity .586: 2
Damning: no hint of d. 790: 3
Damns: love man that D. us 1595: 3
Damnum: profecto d. præ-
stet 751: 9
Damozel: blessed d. 885:15
Damsel lay deploring 1775: 6
strolling d. 1702:15
with a dulcimer 483:11
with swelling breasts 1451:13
Dan to Beersheba 1632:13; 2029:12
Danaë, in a brazen tower 1191: 6
Danaos: timeo D. 838:16
Dance all night 610:10
along Death's icy brink ..1130: 6
and Provençal song 1317:19
and sing, be gaily drest .2178:17
at the end of a rope 853:16
attendance 327:14
attendance here 1643: 3
barefoot among thorns 359:14
barefoot on wedding day ..85: 3
before England's hearse ..753: 6
decent measur'd d. 1367: 4
hand hath liberty in the d. 362: 3
is a measured pace 359: 1
light, for my heart 360:14
light is the d. 1469:11
like a d. of snow 2183:12
like an angel 359: 6
more skillfully than honest
woman 361:13
move easiest who d. 2253:12
no more at holiday 1978:13
of death 1362:11
of plastic circumstance ..1124: 6
of Time 379:17
of youth 439: 5
on with the d. 359:11
pressed in the d. 361:14
Pyrrhic d. 839: 1
raindrops' showery d. 1669:16
the antic hay 360: 3
those that d. must pay 1469:11
tipsy d. and jollity 659:14
to every fool's pipe 359:17
to every tune 239: 3
upon a jig to heaven 154: 4
when you do d. I wish you
a wave of the sea 361: 5
will not d. because I will
not d. 2203: 1
won't you join the d. 359:12
Danced along the dingy
days 183:11
like a gentleman 360:18
till doom day 1469:11
until day 978: 6
without theatrical pretence .360:18
Dancer: like d. in the fair ..333: 6
the greater fool, the better
d. 362: 4
Dancers ennoble what is
coarse 359:19
Dances: dizzying d. 361: 1
in what ethereal d. 484: 3
midnight d. 32:9; 747: 4
such a way 361: 6
well to whom Fortune pipes .360: 9
with the daffodils 1294:17
Dancing **359**
by the pale moonlight 499:18
child of Music 359: 2
days are done 360:11
in the chequer'd shade ...361: 3
Dancing, *continued*
in yonder green bower ..361: 1
is a touchstone 359: 4
of savage origin 361:10
Oh, Heaven, her d. 361: 2
on volcano 360:13
ridiculous act 359:13
when d. fires 247: 1
who comes d. over the
snow 2261:17
with heavy shoes 1953:14
Dancing-days are done 1223:10
past our d. 360:11
Dancing-school: no need of
d. 176: 2
Dandelion **362**
Dandelions: golden kisses ..362:12
star-disked d. 684: 2
Dandin: George D. 434:17
Dandolo: one hour of D. ..982:14
Dandy
See also Fop
future belongs to the d. ..706: 8
Dandy-despot 705: 6
Danger **363**
absent d. appears greater ..656:10
all your d. in discord 2066:21
and delight on one stalk ..363:15
and life and love 724:15
another's d. soothes 1322:17
beard shook with d. 127:15
best remedy of d. 363:20
certain d. doubtful prize 1715:13
deadliest d. beneath sweetest flowers 364: 1
despised comes sooner 363:19
deviseth shifts 364: 7
fear'd no d. 989:11
fears d. seldom feels it 363:12
few accepted d. 20:21
free from d. if on guard 1651:19
great d. great courage 326: 1
hath honor 323:16
he that loveth d. 363:9a
if d. seems slight 363: 3
if without d. without glory ..297:17
in delay 429: 5
in reckless change 230:19
in the deed 918:15
is in discord 455: 3
less fear less d. 654:21
levels man and brute 363: 6
natural aversion to d. 455:14
nature shrinks from 322: 5
near, remote disappear 363: 9
nearest we least dread 364: 5
neither shape of d. 239:13
never overcome without d. ..363:20
next door to security 363:12
of representative govern-
ment 433:13
on the deep 1647: 1
on utmost edge 363:14
out of this nettle, d. 1754: 9
outweighs hope 456:18
past, God forgotten 364: 2
past, saint cheated 443: 7
past, works delight 363:16
send d. from east to west ..364: 7
share one d., one safety 2067: 4
soon as life, there is d. ..363:10
spur of all great minds 363: 7
sweet is d. 363:15
there's d. on the deep 1774:16
to give advice 19:10
who sees d. perishes 363:17
wink on opportunity 363:18
without d. game cold 754: 7
Dangereux: personne d. 364: 6
Dangerous: have in me
something d. 1979: 5
no person not d. for someone 364: 6
Dangers bring fears 363: 4
foreseen sooner prevented ..363:12
great d., great courage 324: 8
loved me for d. passed ..1186: 7
needless d. 363:13
no d. fright him 1892:13
nor stepped aside for d. ..1705: 3

Dawn, *continued*
is loud with battle 2199: 7
is overcast 368:20
merely a sob of light 1152: 2
nearer d. darker night 291:13
never see the D. 368:11
of ampler life 2047:4a
of light, ne'er seen before 394:10
of morning after 504:15
of music, poetry, art 1189: 1
on the hills of Ireland 997: 2
rare roseburst of d. 991:16
restored her light 368:16
Salutation of the D. 2020:10
sleeps on shadowy hills ...368:14
slow buds the pink d. 368: 1
to sunset's marge 408:14
what is d. without dew ..1853:15
white still d. 368: 6
with silver-sandalled feet ..368:19
yours is d. of morning ..1074:16
Dawning and the dew 1207: 7
Dawnlight: seen d. run ..1346:11
Dawns: two break at once ..284: 6
Daws: for d. to peck at 876:13
Day 368
after d. of cloud and wind 1941:12
All Fool's d. 93: 1
and the way we met 1455:12
April d. in the morning 93:15
as it fell upon a d. 1282:10
at the close of the d. 581:13
babbling, remorseful d. ..372:17
becomes more solemn 32: 4
begins to break 369:11
believe every d. your last 1127:12
better d. await wretched 1319:10
better d., better deed 370: 7
blabbing and remorseful d. .372:17
boils at last 369: 3
breaketh 75:13
breaks not, it is my heart .369: 4
bright d. brings the adder 1798: 3
brings its petty dust 707:14
brought back my night ..770: 7
busy d. peaceful night ..1063:13
clear as the d. 1632: 1
come d., come night 1403:14
comes the supreme d. 382:12
commend fine d. 566: 2
compare thee to summer's
d. 1215: 1
conflux of two eternities ..371: 9
cram in a d. 27: 2
darkest d. pass'd away ..372: 6
death-bed of a d. 581:12
despised d. of small things 2040:10
differs not from eternity ..370: 9
each d. a separate life ..1131:14
each d. is like a year 1614: 1
each d. thy last esteem 370: 6
each has his appointed d. ..382:13
each lost d. patron saint 2268: 6
each time d. comes round ..165: 1
entertains the harmless d. 1136: 6
every d. best d. in year ..370: 6
every d. brings a ship ..1101:12
ev'ry d. he had to live ..1150:11
every d., in every way 872: 3
every d. we live 1150: 3
every god has his d. 470: 8
every man hath ill d. 371:12
fairest d. sets in night ..1018:14
flutter thro' life's d. 1240: 2
follows murkiest night 293: 3
for gods to stoop 371: 5
forever and a d. 2:13
full-blown and splendid ..1404: 7
general all-ending d. 2053: 6
glimmer'd in the east ..1343:13
glory of an April d. 93:13
goes by like a shadow 1454:12
gone molten down throat ..233: 3
good d. good words 371: 2
goodly d. tomorrow 1942: 6
hail D. of days 514: 8
happy d. to be enrolled ..371:15
hath put on his jacket ..2062: 1
hath roused ribald crows ..369:12
how troublesome is d. 369:10

Day, *continued*
I hate the d. 371:19
I have lost a d. 370:12
I know not when d. shall
be 1187: 8
I was thinking d. splendid 1914:15
if in d. of battle I forget 1864: 4
immortal in its dying 372: 7
in April never came so
sweet 1209: 9
in d. of adversity consider 1625:16
in d. of prosperity joyful 1625:16
in serene enjoyment spent 1510:15
in thy courts is better 887: 2
is cold and dark 1670: 1
is done and the darkness 1403: 9
is gone and all its sweets ..1455: 1
is great and final 1403: 7
is miniature eternity 370: 9
is short, work much 104: 6
is snow-white dove 369: 1
is the Child of Time 1404: 3
keep somewhat for rainy d. 1997: 5
last d. as happy as first ..2188: 9
like a tired monarch 372:13
like a weary pilgrim 582: 7
lit camp-fires 372:11
live each d. as if thy last 1127: 4
livelong d. 370:10
long to be remembered ...371: 4
long bright d. is done ..1846: 1
long d. wanes 372:20
longed for d. 371: 6
longest d. has end 372:15
lost without laughter 1075:13
love the perfect d. 26: 3
lucky d. 371: 3
make d. out of night 439: 4
make each d. a critique ...370: 5
makes July's d. short 982: 2
man's posthume d. 181: 1
marked with white stone ..370:15
more d. to dawn 369:13
most calm, most bright ..1752:13
neither dread last d. 388: 3
never-setting d. 965: 5
next d. never so good 371:15
no d. passeth without grief 371:12
no d. which has not night ..373: 2
no d. without its line 370: 4
no d. without sorrow 1887: 7
nor night unhallow'd pass 824:21
not to me returns d. 170: 8
now's the d. and hour ..1432:15
O d., if I squander 369:15
O frabjous d. 1409: 8
O, such a d. 371: 3
O summer d. beside sea .1936: 8
of adversity 1625:16
of all the week the best ..1752:13
of crumbling 954: 9
of fortune harvest d. 711:12
of glory! Welcome d. 975: 6
of marriage 1271:11
of resurrection ..514:13; 1724:11
of salvation 1756:16
of small things 2040:10
of sunny rest 292:14
of the east wind 2151:14
of the Lord, as all days ..1753: 1
of wrath, d. of burning ..1025: 9
on which one has not
laughed 1075:13
one d. equal to every d. ..369:18
one d. gives, another takes 371:22
one d. in the country 321:14
one d. time enough 370: 1
one d. well spent 369:16
one d., with life, and heart 370: 1
out of Eternity the new d.
is born 2020: 2
parting d. dies 372: 5
passed as if it were last ..370: 6
peevish April d. 1138: 9
perverse and adverse d. 371:14
Policeman D. 1850:10
present d. has no value ..2023:10
proud d. 369:11
pushed out by d. 371:23
rainy d. 1271:11; 1997:5; 2065: 9

Day, *continued*
rare as a d. in June 1026: 2
red-letter d., dead-letter ..903:11
returns and brings us 1588:10
rise! for d. is passing ..2020: 4
scholar of yesterday 370: 5
seems a year 22:11
shall not be up 15:16
shall yet be fair 618:15
shineth unto perfect d. ..1030: 2
shrouded d. retreats 1914: 2
sighed to lose a d. 370:12
single d. among learned ..1097:10
single d. in life of wise ..702:10
single d. of innocence 990: 2
so cool, so calm 372:10
so foul and fair a d. 371:17
some d., some d. of days 1289: 8
some d.—some sweet d. ..1434: 6
something against rainy d. 1271:11
spent with approbation ..1701:13
spy d. at a little hole 2039:17
stage on life's journey 30: 1
stands tip-toe 369:12
sufficient unto the d. 2023: 5
sullies flowers 1729: 9
tedious is this d. 489: 4
tenderly the haughty d. ..369: 5
that housed annual grain 1983:18
that I loved, night here ..1403: 5
that is dead 371:20
that sees Him rise 515:10
think that d. lost 370:13
thinking d. most splendid 1914:15
this d., of all our days 1275: 8
this is another d. 325: 3
this is my busy d. 370: 3
this was the "D." 2147:11
thou art my single d. 2261:13
thy d. without a cloud 399:11
tired at close of d. 29:13
to childhood seems a year ..22:11
to come longer 372: 2
to divide d. from night ..1912:13
to the d. 2299c: 4
too bright is D. 992: 3
turned and departed 371:24
unlucky d. changing name 1272: 3
unpleasant d. for journey 719: 4
unto d. uttereth speech ..1403:13
warm precincts of d. 386: 3
wasted half my d. 1587: 9
wear out d. and night ..1404: 5
what d. may bring forth ..2023: 9
what hath d. deserv'd 371:16
when first we met 1747: 3
when I must die 439:13
wherein I was born 163:13
which crowns Desire 1436: 6
white d. from white bean .370:15
whose better d. is over 1375: 2
wild was the d. 1501: 7
Day's: golden day's decline ..32:12
Day-book open till sunset 75: 9
Day-breaking: full d. 618:20
Day-Dreams 484
Day-labor, light denied 170: 9
Day-spring: shot a d. 1305: 9
Day-star arise in your hearts 1916: 5
like the d. in the wave 897: 3
so sinks the d. 1939:12
Day's-eye: daisy 358: 3
Daybreak everywhere 369: 6
white, tremendous 369: 2
Daylight and the sun grow
painful 2241:14a
and truth meet 901:19
of honest speech 217:19
pure d. of honest speech ..217:19
through very small holes ..2039:17
we burn d. 1642:13
Dayrolles: give D. a chair 414:17
Days: abridge my doleful d. 395:11
adieu to salad d. 38:10
afternoon of best d. 41: 8
all d. are nights to see ... 4: 7
all my d. are trances 484: 3
all the d. and hours 3: 8
all our d. are numbered ..1935: 2
among the dead 184:13

Death, *continued*
nothing break bond but D. 1274:15
nothing call our own but d. 1562: 7
nothing more beautiful ..393: 3
nothing, save d., mute ..2116:13
nothing terrible in d. 395: 3
O D., all eloquent 1220: 3
O D. in life 231:12
o'ertakes man who flees ..375:13
of a dear friend 740:15
of all pain the period 393: 5
of d. to d. 262: 8
of friendship, love 409: 8
of old men honorable 397: 6
of the flowers 683: 2
of the righteous 397: 5
often a gift 374: 8
often fled from man 375:19
on ev'ry wave appears ..1775: 9
on his pale horse 376:10
on shadowy feet 380: 8
once dead, no more dying .406:16
one should never think of d. 1147:12
only an old door 378: 1
only binds us fast 1219:20
only immortal who treats us all alike 385: 9
openeth gate to fame 399: 3
pain without peace of d. 2:16
pale D. knocks 383:13
pale priest 373:14
passed from d. unto life ..412:11
path that must be trod 374: 6
pays all debts 377:11
peak of a life-wave 407:16
pleasant road to fame 399: 3
plucks my ear 1132: 7
poor man's dearest friend 390: 3
precious is d. of saints ...1755:12
preferable to slavery 1840: 5
privilege of nature 392: 8
proud d. 385: 6
puts out the flame 375: 9
quits all scores 377:11
rather than toilsome life ..389:14
receipt for all ills 389:15
regarded without flinching 388: 1
report of d. exaggeration ..395: 1
respects age nor merit ...384: 1
rest from misery 390: 8
reveals the eminent 383: 8
rides on every breeze 379: 2
rids me of my pains 392: 3
rock me asleep 395:11
routs life into victory 413: 2
run to d. for fear of d. ..1933:16
sable smoke 373:15
salt of states 373:12
says, "School is dismissed" 408: 4
scion of house of hope 374: 5
secret house of d. 1933:10
secret of Nature 374: 2
see they suffer d. 1655:15
seek a glorious d. 142:15
seems in word farewell ...635:11
seven inches from d. 1778:11
shall give to age its toys ..388: 5
shameful d. dreadful 376: 6
shun d. is my advice 456:15
shuts up the day of life ..1849:14
sisters D. and Night ...1473:12
sleeping partner of life ...374:11
snatch me from disgrace ..461: 5
softens all resentments ...406: 7
softly d. succeeded life ..393:11
sometimes a punishment .374: 8
speak me fair in d. 406: 3
stands above me 387:18
stands ready at door 379:19
stepped tacitly 374:23
still draws nearer 381:20
strange that d. should sing 1950: 8
studied in his d. 397:12
sudden d. sudden joy 392:15
sure physician. d. 389:15
sure retreat from infamy .918: 7
sweet bosom of d. 402: 2
sweet is d. to those who weep 392: 1

Death, *continued*
swift d. or victory 2083:14
take up little room in d. ..385: 7
takes no denial 380:15
takes toll of beauty 2056: 9
tavern on our pilgrimage ..403: 9
that cuts in marble 399: 7
that feeds on men 406:16
that hath suck'd 400: 2
that makes life live 1147: 4
that tyrant grim 376: 9
the healer 389:15
the journey's end 1122: 7
there is no D. 412:12
they die an equal d. 383:14
think not disdainfully of d. 391:11
this is d. and sole d. 396: 9
thou shalt die 406:16
thou wast not born for d. .1405: 3
through hollow eyes of d. .413:10
timid and brave alike 384: 6
'tis a sunset 373:15
to be carnally minded d. .1224:12
to do with cruel D. 410:13
to drown in ken of shore ..612: 9
to falter, not to die 398:14
to monumental stones 380: 6
to the happy terrible 390: 3
too great price for praise .1530: 6
universal tyrant 385: 1
unloads thee 1573: 2
unrolls the awful lot of numberless generations 1262:9a
untangles mortal mesh 390:12
until d. all is life 923: 6
valley of the shadow of d. 388: 6
visits each and all 382: 4
votes alike for high, low ..383:15
wander away with D. ..1148:20
was a harbor 378:10
was not the worst of all ..1466:17
was safety 391:12
way to dusty d. 2262:12
ways of D. are soothing ..391: 4
we flee from d. 27:12
we turn to thee, D. 398: 3
wears us away 382: 4
welcome as May 390: 7
welcome at journey's end ..390: 3
were d. denied even fools would wish to die 374:16
were great joy 389:14
what hadst thou to do with cruel D. 410:13
what should it know of d. .409: 6
when D. makes his arrest .381:13
where d. and glory meet ..781:13
where is thy sting 412: 7
which long for d. 391: 7
who cares naught for d. ..387:11
who gives us life 387:17
who hath abolished d. 966: 6
who sets all free 377:10
whom D. hath sundered ..413:12
why do we then shun d. ..1149:15
why fear d. 398: 4
will bring us all up 382: 9
will disappear with sin ..1827:16
will find me 385:16
will have his day 387: 1
will seize the doctor too ..382: 5
wish for d. coward's part 1935:10
wistful she is 399:12
with d. doomed to grapple 1113: 2
with his thousand doors ..380: 1
with might of sunbeam 412: 2
without death's quiet 34:13
without dying 1849: 5
without peace of d. 2:16
without phrases 376:19
woodland d. that kills ...1241: 5
working like a mole 379: 4
worse things than d. 392:14
yet d. we fear 1149: 9
Death's approach terrible ..386:13
couriers. Fame and Honour 2115:13
head often in your dish ..2136: 5
inexorable hand 389:13
knocking at d. door 28: 4

Death's *continued*
pale flag 400: 2
truer name "Onward" ..374:13
untimely frost 410: 1
Death-bed: detector of the heart 413:15
dreads d. like slave 324: 5
gone to his d. 1219:10
no lesser than thy land ..1703: 4
of a day 581:12
of fame 2120: 2
repentance 1699: 6
Death-hymn: wild swan's d. 1950:12
Deaths: all d. I could endure 1213: 6
many are the d. 388: 2
unknown to fame 399: 5
Debate
See also Argument
and beat the bush 972: 8
brief and bitter the d. 98:10
destroys despatch 97:11
masculine 312: 9
Rupert of d. 97:14
settle without d. 98:11
Debauch: whiff of stale d. ..501:14
Debauchee of dew 991:10
of dews 142:14
Debauchees: gloomy-visaged d. 606: 3
Debauchery and Drinking 1618: 5
without business d. 208:16
Debility: senile d. 28: 2
Debita: naturæ d. pro patria 1466: 4
Debitio: dissimilis est d. et gratiæ 418: 3
Debitorem: æs d. leve 193:11
Debonair: deft and d. 311:12
Deboshed on every tomb ..920:18
Debt 417
all must pay 377: 8
ambition's d. is paid 50: 1
and gratitude different ...418: 3
cancel my d. 418: 7
double d. to pay 908:14
due to death 377:10
gets out of d. grows rich ..418:14
grievous bondage 418:24
large d. makes enemy 419: 5
live out of d. and danger .2177:17
mother of folly 418: 8
national d. a blessing 62:10
of nature 377:9; 1466: 4
of the Maker of Universe 2067:14
of thought to mankind 418: 9
out of d. out of danger ..418:14
pay every d. 418:10
pays the d. of nature 1466: 4
poor man's d. 418:11
produce d. instead of their discharge 72: 7
public d. a blessing 62:10
speak not of d. unless to pay 418:12
to be out of d. 31: 2
to Nature's quickly paid ..377:13
two ways of paying d. ..418: 2
until the Judgment Day ..193: 5
what nearer d. in humanity 2141: 5
which cancels all others ..377:11
worst poverty 418:11
Debtes et mensonges 418:15
Debtor: be d. for a rood ..1062: 2
no d. but accounts to Fate 1469:14
no man's d. 418:23
small sum makes a d. 193:11
Debtors are liars 418:15
creditors better memories .194: 7
Debtorship: Immense D. ..1796: 6
Debts and lies mixed 418:15
better than grudges 419: 8
deny their honest d. 1708:16
forgive us our d. 709:22
he that dies pays all d. 377:15
I pay my d. 326:13
may his d. torment him ..418:22
my d. are large 1586:12
new way to pay old d. 419: 8
of honor 419: 3
other d. than of honor ..753:14

Deeds, *continued*
who doeth ill d. vile 427: 3
with d my life filled 424: 9
you wrought not in vain ..897: 1
Deep: asleep in the d. 2289:11
calleth unto d. 1772:11
down, down beneath the d. 1815:11
in lowest d a lower d. 893: 5
maketh d. to boil like pot 1775:10
moans with many voices ..372:20
rocked in cradle of the d. 1777:13
under every d. lower d. 1772:11
vasty d. 1905: 4
where it's d., awful cold ..178:14
where never care nor pain 392: 1
wind-obeying d. 1772: 1
young man 1423: 2
Deep-drenched in sea of care 221: 9
Deep-search'd with saucy looks 1924:10
Deep-tangled wild-wood 252: 1
Deeper the sweeter 1538: 6
Deer: herd-abandoned d. ..943: 2
I must hunt this d. 941: 7
I with the d. 1384: 8
let stricken d. go weep ..2238:16
my own stricken d. 1213: 7
such small d. 516:14
that left the herd 943: 2
Deer-stealers best park-keepers 1985:12
Deering: even his name N. D. 1654:13
Defacing first, then claiming 1505: 8
you with defame 811:10
Defalcation, the dishonesty 2281: 1
Defamation a necessity ..1835:16
vile cur 215: 4
would bark at angel's train 215: 4
Defamed by every charlatan 765:10
Defaming and defacing ..1837: 6
breathed d. to my ears ..428:10
Défaut: connoit le d. d'un homme 649:17
d'un homme veut plaire ..2127:16
Défauts de ses qualités 649: 3
grands hommes grands d. 649:15
montrer d. à un ami 739:11
n'avouons de petits d. 650: 9
n'avouons jamais nos d. ..649:16
n'avions point de d. 650:11
plaisons par nos d. 2082: 2
Defeat
See also Failure
croaking d. in triumphs 1671:15
does d. end in victory of death 381:16
ennobled by d. 533:14
in d. defeated not 2123: 4
learn not to know d. 611:12
no d. save from within ..611:13
no more d., faith 1474: 8
of wounds and sore d. ..2247:24
sublimed d. 612: 4
Defeats more triumphant 2084:16
Defeatures in my face 607: 5
Defect: fair d. of nature 2188: 7
glory from d. arise 780:14
heroical d. of thought 115: 1
in brain absence of mind 1310: 6
make d. perfection 1485:13
of character 235:12
of life in America 60: 3
quarrel with grace 652: 8
rapt red with d. 343: 8
single redeeming d. 779:16
Defects of doubt 812: 5
of great men 831:14
of his qualities 649: 3
reckon d. not attainments 1788: 9
Defence: at one gate 305: 7
in war a weak d. 1865: 9
last and best d. 438: 6
millions for d. 63: 2
not defiance 428: 5
stand in your own d. 326: 2
Defences thou hast round me set 1980:13
Defend: by all means d. ourselves 1787:16
me from my friends 734: 4
me from myself 1981:11
open breach d. 245:11
your departed friend 739: 1
Defender: faith's d. 1037: 9
Defendit numerus 726:20
Defense, *see* Defence
Deference most elegant of compliments 328: 8
Defiance 428
breathed d. to my ears 428:10
sings d. to the wheel 713:11
Défiance justifie la tromperie 420:13
Deficit omne quod nascitur 147:17
Defienda me Dios de my 1981:11
Defier de ses amis 732:18
Defile: nothing from without can d. 520:15
the pleasant streams 1385:11
Defilement from within ..1827: 4
Define: divide and d. 428:14
he that can d. best man ..428:14
Definitio periculosa est 428: 1
Definition: every d. dangerous 428:15
no great opinion of a d. ..428:12
of the word liberty 2277: 1
so clear, of victory 2084:13
Definitions 428
I hate d. 428:13
Deformed, crooked, old ...240:11
none d. but the unkind ..2070: 1
Degeneration: fatty d. 1262:19
Degradation: living d. 1466:12
Degrades another d. me ...202:13
Degree conceals ears 2069: 6
differing but in d. 447: 1
priority, and place 1441: 2
take but d. away 1369: 5
Degrees: prohibited d. of kin 818: 8
render sweet harmony 860:12
scorning base d. 50: 4
Dei: nil facimus non sponte D. 787: 1
Deil could na skaith thee ..607:19
take the hindmost 863:14
Deils: clever d. he'll make them 1970:10
Deities: eternal D. 643:10
for d. held 1373:11
to vulgar d. descends 1456:12
Deity believ'd joy begun ..795: 1
man's genius a deity 758:11
perfectly well-bred 798: 9
why seek D. further 795:14
Dejected: never d. while another's bless'd 1957:13
Déjeuner fait mémoire 518: 8
Delators: pickthank d. 1838: 6
Delay 428
fatal to those prepared 429: 6
gives strength 429:10
great procuress 429: 8
I must not d. 1493: 7
is always hurtful 429: 6
leads impotent beggary ..429:13
long that postpones joys ..429: 9
naught of d. nor repose ..429:17
no d. too long 429: 4
of justice injustice 1032:13
often injury wrought 429: 5
preferable to error 429: 3
prevents performance 429: 2
remedy for anger is d. 81: 6
reprov'd each dull d. 1595:13
restored the state 428:17
sweet, reluctant d. 429: 7
tear thyself from d. 429: 2
what we dare not refuse ..429:11
will not brook d. 207:18
wise cunctation 1649: 5
you may d., time will not 2005:14
Delays have dangerous ends 429: 5
thousand d. to be endured 1086: 9
Delectable Mountains 1354: 1
Delectantia: quod d. scribere 2251: 5
Delenda est Carthago...... 1695:8; 2108: 1
Deliberamus: dum d. serum 972:15
quando incipiendum 147: 3
Deliberando perit occasio ..972:14
Deliberandum est diu 1652:16
est sæpe 423: 6
Deliberates: woman that d. is lost 1187: 6
Deliberation: deep on front .448: 6
Delicacies I contemn 777: 2
Delicacy: flattering with d. .676: 5
if person has no d. he has you in his power 2100: 1
to love 1177:18
Delicates: prince's d. 1611:19
Délicats sont malheureux .454: 8
Deliciæ populi, quæ 1453:16
Delicious: how d. winning 1018:11
Delight 429
all day give and take d. ..2105: 5
and dejection 292:13
bathe spirits in d. 496: 5
enjoy d. with liberty 211:12
for dear d. another pays .359:18
go to 't with d. 208:21
in having pleased self 430: 3
in misfortunes of others.. 1322:12; 1323: 1
in proper young men 2265: 8
in sorrowing soul poured d. 429:20
in your arms was still d. 1210:11
lock me in d. awhile 1844:10
lordly d. of the dead 829: 9
lost days of d. 1687:11
my ever new d. 2140:13
never too late for d. 430: 2
not by appointment do we meet D. 1016: 7
of a critic to praise 338:16
of mental superiority 1309: 7
of more d. than hawks ..1215: 1
of new course of reading 1675: 6
of the Valleys of Dream ..482: 2
one whom D. flies 212: 6
over-payment of d. 409: 2
rootless flower 430: 6
sacred and home-felt d. ..171: 3
she that was world's d. 2078: 2
sole d. to vex 2183: 1
sweet d. quiet life 1135:10
temple of impure d. 5:13
that consumes desire 430: 6
that lives an hour 430: 6
that they may mend mankind 1969: 9
they never knew 1104: 9
to knock a thing down 665: 7
turn d. into sacrifice 1517:12
was all in books 188:12
weighing d. and dole 949: 5
woman's d. to wound ..1255:10
Delights: all d. are vain ..430: 5
palative d. 1511: 2
violent d., violent ends 430: 5
which to achieve 430: 1
Delightsome: most d. of all 659: 8
Delilah: long sleeps D. ...1066: 5
Delinquencies: thine own d. 651:10
Delinquency: unpunished 1031:16
Delirium: love's d. haunts 1222: 9
Delitti: per d. non sia 336: 9
Delivery: management of d. 1439: 7
Delphian airs have died 991: 4
Delphic sword 1436:11
Delphinorumque columnas .352: 2
Deluder: thou great D. ...1181: 8
Deluge: after us the d. 1632:14
Delusion: darling d. of mankind 1616: 5
greatest d. that evils can be cured by legislation 817:14
hence, dear d. 2095:13
Messianic d. 938:19
mockery and snare 1081:13
of youth 23: 8
that distance creates 463: 3
Delve when dawn is nigh ..484:16
Delver in earth's clod 408:10

Deus, *continued*
regnator omnium 784: 7
si pro nobis 785:20
vetat dominans in nobis d. 1935: 3
verius cogitatur D. 796: 7
virorum bonorum habitat d. 808: 4
Deutschen: des D. Vaterland 767: 1
wollen regiert sein 769: 2
Deutschland in den Sattel ..768: 1
über alles 767: 2
Deux et n'avions qu'un cœur 1182: 3
Development: arrested d. ..586: 8
Deviation from nature ...1382:15
Device: dull not d. by coldness 429:13
perish under d. 2033:10
poor d. of man 797:15
Devices for cheapening labor 1229:15
for preservation of virtue 2094: 7
still are overthrown 644: 7
Devil, The 440
a saint would be 443: 2
a-walking the D. is gone ..444:10
abash'd the D. stood 445: 1
always builds a chapel ...272:15
and deep sea 364:11
and Doctor Faustus 440:18
and no monster 440:17
and witch of Endor 1052: 6
as a roaring lion 443:13
at everything 1: 3
at the helm 1813: 7
author of confusion 1441: 4
author of confusion and lies 443: 9
behind the cross 440:15
behind the glass 1317: 9
black as the d. 167: 4
both a d. and a saint ..810:11
brooding in miser's chest ..118: 5
builds a chapel 272:13
by the tail 785: 8
can cite Scripture 949: 8
can the d. speak true ..2057:15
careful d. still at hand 443:10
climbs into the belfry ..1590: 3
consorts with solitude 1873: 7
corrects sin 442:14
cross my prayer 1582:20
dear old d. 443:18
defy the d. 442:13
diligent at his plough 443:12
divides the world 114: 1
drunkenness to d. wrath 650: 7
enters prompter's box 1125:10
eternal d. to keep state ..1730:15
ever God's ape 272:18
every d. not cloven foot ..440:19
every one, God or d. 237: 1
fears a painted d. 657: 2
fiddles all the way 443:17
first rebel 1681:16
fly away with fine arts ..102:13
for all 441: 9
give d. his due 442: 8
go, poor d. 693:10
go to d. where he is known 441:15
goes share in gaming 753: 5
good when pleased 444: 9
had d. by the tail 785: 8
has care of his footmen ...443:16
has not any flower 682: 6
hath eleven points of law .1080:12
hath power to assume 444: 6
hath some good in him 444: 3
have all the good tunes ..1362:10
he could not skaith thee ..607:19
he hath a d. 440:11
he is not ugly, lame 444: 2
head d. 1542:19
how like a mounting d. ...50:12
how the d. they got there 46:16
if d. catch man idle 441:11
I'll trust the d. first 2196:16
I'm a d., I'm a d. 440:20
in every berry of grape 2158:13
in private brawls 1663:16
in the moon for mischief 1342: 9
Devil, *continued*
invented dicing 753: 5
is an ass 441:16
is an egotist 441:12
is dead 442:18
is in dice 753: 5
is waiting for them 892:19
keep d. at the door 441:10
kind to his own 443:16
laughing d. in his sneer ..1855:12
lawful to combat d. 441: 5
lawful to employ d. 540: 3
let d. wear black 442: 7
let us call thee d. 2158:13
live from the D. 441: 4
made sin 443: 1
make a moral of the d. ..142:11
may be respectable 890: 1
meet the d. in private ..1872:10
most devilish when respectable 440:14
most diligent bishop 443:12
needs go that d. drives ..441:20
no man means evil but d. .443:14
not so black as painted ..444: 3
of a man 2066: 1
one d. is like another 440:16
painted tail pea-green 491: 1
prophet still if bird or d. 1624:10
raise the d. 441: 6
renounce d. and all his works 440:13
reproving sin 442:14
resist the d., and he will flee 441:14
rides upon a fiddlestick ..442: 9
rise to meet the d. 441: 2
rul'd the woman 2194:17
said to Simon Legree 441:19
scampering as if D. drove 441:20
seldom outshot 442: 6
sends cooks 315:18
shall have his bargain 444: 7
shame the d. 217:4; 2057:15
sooner raised than laid 441: 6
swear d. out of hell 1951: 7
take the hindmost 440:12
talk of the d. 441: 5
taught women to dance ..362: 2
tempts us not 1980:18
though d. lead the measure 1915:12
to pay 442:19
told me I did well 426: 4
turned precisian 442: 2
understands Welsh 444: 7
was piqued 1981:13
was sick and crazy 443: 4
when the d. was sick 443: 2
will not have me damned .648:16
will shake her chain 1946:10
will take his own 442:16
wipes tail with poor pride 1566:21
with d. damn'd 1249: 4
world. and flesh 440:13
worship the d. too 2245:14
would have him about women 1178: 6
would I were a d. 443:15
you the blacker d. 77: 9
young saint, old d. 1755:13
Devil's: got over D. back ..155:15
if I am D. child 441: 4
leavings 36: 7
pictured beuks 220: 3
spent under d. belly 155:15
toward D. House we tread 2187:11
Devil-and-all to pay 442:19
Devilish to remain in error 576:16
when respectable 440:14
Devils: all d. respect virtue 2089: 5
all the d. are here 891: 5
as d. Scripture quote 442:12
as many d. as tiles 1227: 6
being offended 2183: 3
cast out seven d. 442: 1
casting out d. juggling 442: 1
charcoal d. used as fuel ..890: 5
poor d. are dying 66: 8
some d. ask parings 1946:10
Devils, *continued*
sometimes d. to ourselves 1982: 3
soonest tempt 1981:17
'tis d. must print 1612:17
will the blackest sin 87: 3
Devised by the enemy 541:23
Devoir des Juges 1020:15
est vertu heroique 194:11
rien leur d. 194: 8
Devomas: ut d. vult 1008: 2
Devon was heaven to him ..551: 4
Dévot sous un Roi athée, athée 1684: 6
Devotedness of woe 4: 2
Devotee when soars the Host 1016: 4
Devotion 445
daughter of astronomy ..1917:13
enough to do our small d. 1753: 4
given to princes 1611: 9
has mastered the hard way 445: 7
last full measure of d. ...432: 1
mother of obedience 445: 5
of a married woman 1265: 4
wafts the mind above 1193: 2
Dévotion aux princes amour-propre 1611: 9
Devotion's every grace 881:16
Devout: more curious than d. 43:21
no man ever d. enough ...1690: 1
yet cheerful 239: 1
Dew 445
as the d. to the blossom 1297: 7
diamond d. so pure 445:22
extracts healing d. 142:11
fades awa' like morning d. 1202:13
fall on me like silent d. 1669:19
fall on their heads like d. ..168:19
for one d., hare-bell 1280: 7
glist'ring with d. 1347:11
he lived upon d. 445:11
honey-heavy d. of slumber 1846:11
is cold upon the ground ..1442:11
keeps its ain drap o' d. 1647: 1
kept d. of my youth 1871:15
like the d. on the mountain 401:14
lovely varnish of d. 445:16
midst d.-fall of tears 897: 3
morn set a-sparkle 2268: 3
morning d. drops pearls 1669:19
of Pulpit Eloquence 1595: 1
of thy youth 164: 2
of true repentance 1697: 3
passed like morning d. ..393:10
reflects a sky 445:15
shall weep thy fall 372:10
shed a honeyed d. 1451: 4
shut in lily's core 1952:13
silently, as d. on roses ..1974:12
silver drops of morning d. 1242: 5
stars of morning 554:20
that on violet lies 604: 7
timely d. of sleep 1845: 3
'tis of the tears 445: 9
walks o'er the d. 1347:10
was falling fast 494: 5
Dew-bead, Gem of earth ..445:14
Dew-fall of a nation's tears 897: 3
Dew-note had lilac in it ..1156: 1
Dewdrop clinging to the rose 445:19
from lion's mane 351: 4
had a whole heaven within it 445:15
in the breeze of morn 445:21
paints a bow 445:15
time's corrosive d. 2012:10
Dewdrops: gems of morning .445:13
I must go seek some d. ..446: 1
Nature's tears 445: 9
Dewey was the admiral ..446: 2
Dews: brushing the d. away .445:18
debauchee of d. 142:14
drip earthward 2086:18
of heaven fall thick 168:19
of summer night did fall 1341: 4

Die, *continued*
'tis but to d. 398:11
'tis right to d. 1656: 8
to d. before my hour 387:10
to d. debt due to nature 377: 9
to d. is different 407:18
to d, is gain 204: 3
to d. is landing on silent shore ..378: 6
to d. is to begin to live 412: 1
to d. is to live 1147:15
to d.; to sleep 395:10
to d. without fear 388:10
to-morrow we d. 517:14
to save charges 117:17
to stop criticism 340: 1
to the sound of music 416: 8
two months ago 1340:10
upon a kiss 1049:11
upon hand I love so well 888:14
upon the walls of Zion 398: 1
vile thing to d. 386:13
was now cast 975:8; 1464:16
we all must d. 396: 8
we can d. but once 61:10
we do not d. wholly 1150: 4
we must 382: 7
we who are about to d. 212:18
we will d. free men 725:16
well chief virtue 397:14
what can old man do but d. 29: 1
when dream is past 1172: 4
when he is best of name 396:12
when you will 399:15
where his father before 396:10
where thou diest, will I d. 1199: 5
who can rightly d. 392: 4
who would not d. with brave 1868:7
whom the gods love d. young 409: 7
will show you how to d. 1591: 5
with a full belly 154:13
with music in them 1879: 4
without dying sweet to d. 1849:18
you d. with envy 1203: 3
Die: bona verba d. 371: 2
quaque id promisit 370: 3
Diebe: kleine D. hängt man 1986:10
Died and come to life again 2210:19
as game as Christyan martyrs 852:10
as He d. to make men holy 1841:10
fearing God 397:12
full of years and honors 397: 6
he d. a gallant knight 259: 2
he that d. o' Wednesday 919:12
he who d. at Azan 404: 5
I d. for my country 414: 9
I only d. last night 1904:12
if I had thought thou couldst have d. 402:13
in beauty, like a rose 400: 3
liked it not, and d. 402:15
men have d. from time to time 1220: 8
of medicable wounds 2247:16
quietly and without fear 397:11
she d. in beauty 400: 3
she d. singing it 2150: 2
so he d. standing 417: 9
they d. in bed 740:16
to make verse free 1525:12
to save us all 262: 3
while ye were smiling 201: 3
with nothing done 955:15
with their swords in hand 1870: 5
without a rood his own 1379: 2
Diem: carpe d. 1600: 8
metuas d. nec optes 311:19
O d. lætum 370:15
omnem crede d. supremum 1127:12
perdidi 370:12
summum nec metuas d. 388: 3
Dies and makes no sign 402: 2
as he sings he d. 1950: 3
before he calls for death 396: 6
but something mourns 1356:13
every day 873:16
every minute d. a man 407:17

Dies, *continued*
he that d. pays all debts 377:15
he who d. for virtue 2092:14
in nature nothing d. 412:12
like a dog 675: 2
man d. as he loses friends 739:21
meaner part that d. 413: 5
never sick d. first fit 458: 9
no man d. for love 1220: 8
not how he d., but lives 1148:10
this year, quit for next 377:15
to himself unknown 1789: 5
when a great man d. 809: 7
when she d. with beauty d. her store 140:11
who d. if England live 551:11
who d. in youth, d. best 410: 9
with a song of rapture 1950: 4
Dies adimit ægritudinem 2011: 9
æterni natalis est 413: 9
agit et agit-r velox d. 2007: 5
discipulus est prioris posterior d. 370: 5
exspectata d. aderat 371: 6
iræ, dies illa 1025: 9
longissimus d. cito 372:15
nec revocare potes, d. 26:14
nulla d. mærore caret 1887: 7
nulla sine linea 370: 4
O longum memoranda d. 371: 4
opinionum commenta delet d. 2012: 3
optima d. prima fugit 36:12
pervorsus, advorsus d. 371:14
pulchra d. nota 370:15
quem lapida candidiore 370:15
quid non imminuit d. 2012: 3
singulos d. singulas vitas 1131:14
stat sua cuique d. 382:13
truditur d. die 371:23
unus d. bene actus 369:16
unus par omni est 369:18
unus plus patet 702:10
venit summa d. 382:12
Diet cures more than doctors 872: 2
Dr. D., Dr. Quiet 872: 2
his sickness 944:16
of onions 1972:12
sober in your d. 2205: 8
Dieth: man d. and wasteth away 381: 9
Dieu aide et prête sa main 787:17
est le poète 2239:10
et mon droit 546: 2
je crains D. 792: 2
mesure le froid 789: 2
modère tout 789: 2
pour les gros escadrons 2114:13
si D. n'est pas dans nous 797:13
si D. n'existait pas 788: 1
t'a fair pour l'aimer 797:11
Dieux ont soif 799:10
Differ, all agree 1440:18
Difference between happiness and wisdom 2162: 8
between ordinary company 1858:13
between Peter and Peter 1491:14
between talent and genius 762: 7
between us and dead friend 747:14
between wise and fool 703: 9
between young women 2181: 2
betwixt King and me 446:20
by d. is in order found 2244: 8
distinction without a d. 446:18
great d. in beholders 1423: 9
is as great between 447: 2
makes no d. 447: 6
Nature's d. keeps nature's peace 858:12
no d. between life, death 1147:13
not in deed but doer 428: 4
of man and man 1240:19
of opinion alienates 1426:14
of opinion makes horse-races 1426:14
of religion breeds quarrels 1696: 3
seasons' d. 2161: 8
to me 402:14

Difference, *continued*
'twixt covetous and prodigal 1615:11
'twixt Tyrian and Trojan 447: 7
'twixt wake and sleep 1846:11
what a d. in the morning 2290:12
what d. does it make 978: 8
wide which the sheets will not decide 1197:12
Differences 446
are policies 1544:11
full of most excellent d. 765: 7
no social d. till women come in ...2180:14
political than religious 1693:15
Different: by d. methods d. men excel 1485: 1
taste in d. men prevails 1966:13
Differtur, vita transcurrit 1614:13
Difficile tristi fingere 1010:18
Difficilia: non quia d. sunt 296: 5
Difficilis gloriæ custodia est 781:21
Difficilius: quo d. hoc præclarius 447:12
Difficult: all things d. before easy 447:14
not impossible 971: 7
nothing so d. 1703:19
to appropriate as invent 1507: 2
to design prove easy 447:18
to keep a secret 447:11
to retain glory 781:21
when done with reluctance 447:25
worth while must be d. 447:21
Difficulties are indeed great 59: 4
choice of d. 260:15
show what men are 447:13
Difficulty 447
and labour hard 447:20
comes from lack of confidence 296: 5
daughter of idleness 447:17
every d. yields 447:15
greater d., greater glory 447:12
in life is choice 260:13
raiseth spirits 447:13
severe instructor 447:10
there's d. 447: 9
whene'er a d. may impend 2044: 8
Diffidence dies away in man 1330:14
with best desert goes d. 1331: 6
with time d. dies 1330:14
Diffusion of knowledge among people 530:10
Dig grave with teeth 520: 5
Dig.: infra d. 448:14
Digest hard iron 448:12
to d. divine 448: 1
Digested: meat not d. 155: 2
Digestion 447
appetite and quick d. 89:17
good d. to you all 89:17
good d. turneth all to health 448: 1
great secret of life 448: 3
like Love and Wine 315: 8
mostly matter of mind 883:10
no trifling will brook 315: 8
prove in d. sour 1953:11
question about my d. 215:10
wait on appetite 89:17
Digestions: unquiet meals make ill d. 516:13
Digitalis of failure 1435:12
Digitis a morte remotus 1778:11
Digito: monstror d. 627:10
Digna eveniunt dignis 2247: 1
sacra populi d. est 1481: 3
Dignified: something d. and effective 1556: 5
Dignitas: facilius crescit d. 448: 8
Dignitate: otium cum d. 1099:14
Dignitatem: infra d. 448:14
quicumque amisit d. 621: 9
Dignities: by indignities men come to d. 1444: 4
double-charge with d. 448:11
indignities lead to d. 836: 9

Dolor animi gravior quam corporis 1314: 2
flagrantior æquo non debet d. 840: 9
in lacrimas verteret merum 2159: 9
in longinquitate levis 291: 6
innocentes cogit mentiri d. 1444:16
jocundus d. est 1196:16
levis est d. qui capere consilium 842:13
malvagio il buono scerne il d. 1700: 2
morbusque 458: 8
non facit finem 843:17
plerumque d. 986: 8
quem non temporis minuat 843:18
strangulat inclusus 842: 9
Dolore alterius 596: 4
nessun maggiore d. 1295: 2
sine d. non vivitur in amore 1195:14
supervacuum est d. 841: 8
Dolorem: fortis vero d. 322: 7
infandum renovare d. 841:15
lucrum est d. exstinguere 1444:15
Dolores: in amore d. 1195: 5
posituro morte d. 392: 3
Dolori: quid juvat d. suo occurrere 2044:11
Dolphin: dies like the d. ..372: 5
useless d. might 1303:15
Dolphin-chamber 2217: 7
Dolts: become mere d. 1230: 5
Domains of tender memory 1297: 8
Dome: fir'd Ephesian d. ...624:14
him of Western d. 537:14
no gilded d. swells 2121:11
of many-colored glass 1143:12
of nobler span 617:21
of thought 1834: 7
re-echoes to his nose 1856: 5
rounded Peter's d. 95:14
upon some manly d. 1052: 5
well-proportion'd d. 96: 1
Domes involv'd in rolling fire 2114: 3
of sheeted spray 1942: 7
Domesticity in excelsis 2082:14
Domi habuit unde disceret 2032: 1
Domina: omnium arta d. ..536:13
Dominam: ad d. emacem ..2192: 4
Dominandi: cupido d. flagrantior 1751: 2
Dominate dinner-table 706: 8
Domination: female d. 2195:10
Dominatione: omnia serviliter pro d. 1575:17
Dominatus: in servitute d. 1281: 3
Domine, dirige nos 786:14
inter pontem et fontem ...788: 9
Domini est dirigere gressus .787: 3
pudet, non servitutis 1800:15
Dominion absolute 1839:19
I traversed a d. 1429:13
of the sea 547: 7
Old D., mother of us all 2087:14
sunset of d. 555:10
Dominions of the sun 513:11
thought's d. 96: 8
Domino: sicut a d. agresti profugi 30:11
Dominoes: animated d. ...753: 5
Dominum videre plurimum 1281:12
Dominus domo honestanda est 1281: 2
nisi D. frustra 275:15
omnium est 1038:19
providebit 790:11
qualis d., talis 1281:17
Domo: ex d. in domum migrare 397: 4
Domum: celebrantes d. lugere 163: 9
dulce d. 906: 1
intra d. sævus est 947:18
Domus accipiet te læta 909: 5
ante oculos errant 1297: 1
casta pudicitiam servat d. .909:10
et placens uxor 909: 2
his d., hæc patria est 908: 4
Domus, *continued*
redet argento d. 1717:17
servis est plena superbis 1799:11
stat fortuna d. 633: 8
Don de la familiarité 631: 7
Don Quixote of one generation 1859:15
wish longer 1674: 7
Done: a' is d. in vain 611:19
and can't be undone 426:22
and said 2229: 6
and undone 426:19
been and gone and d. 295:11
by man been d. 1:17
by the rule 1750:11
cannot be amended 426:22
for another d. for oneself 1492:17
has d. and might have d. ..426:21
he is d. for 48: 3
I am d. for 388:22
if d. when 'tis d. 424:19
it couldn't be d. 1931: 5
much to be d. little known 1058:19
nothing d., doth not all ..424: 6
nothing d. while aught remains 424: 6
so little d. 104: 7
that which is d. 1415:11
that which was our duty ..1799:14
things we ought not 426:19
well and with a care 426: 3
well d. better than well said 2227:14
well d. soon enough 423:19
well d., thou good and faithful servant 1799:17
well begun is half d. 146: 6
well it were d. quickly 424:19
what should be d. must be learned 424:16
what's d. is d. 426:22
what's d. we may compute 1980: 9
when all is d. and said 310:14
ye have d. it unto me 242:13
Donkey 111: 9
because a d. brays 112: 1
that's a dead d. 375: 6
thought himself a deer 111:18
Donkey's: about a d. taste ..111:12
Donna è mobile 2197:14
Dono infelice di bellezza ..1001: 2
Donor: what costs to be a d. 1188: 3
Dons d'un ennemi 777: 4
Don't: advice on marriage 1266:14
Donum exitiale Minervæ ...777: 5
Doo & Dairet 1488: 2
Doom clipp'd Time's wings 1471:11
elder brother, D. 644:20
ignorant of coming d. 749: 9
irrevocable d. of Jove 423: 8
is to be beautiful 1743: 2
is to despair 621: 2
mitigate their d. 1031:14
nor at home escape d. 438: 9
of fate's decree 297:20
regardless of their d. 254:20
walk darkling to their d. ..438:15
wove your d. 439: 9
Doomsday: every day is d. 370: 6
is near 379:12
then is d. near 915:23
Doomsmen: deeds our d. ..427:17
Doomsters: purblind d. ...439: 6
Doon: banks and braes ..220: 6
Door: at any d. I knock ..932: 3
at the d. of life 392:14
came out by the same d. ..100:11
charmèd d. of dreams ...1850: 1
double-leaf d. for mouth 1164: 8
double-lock the d. 1948:18
either shut or open 423: 2
every d. barred with gold .802:17
gone upstairs and shut d. .404: 3
I am the d. 1757: 1
just next d. 1395:16
knocking at my d. 24: 5
landlord's hospitable d. ..1567: 6
leaves d. upon latch 409: 1
let the d. be locked 2086: 8
make d. upon woman's wit 2193:15
Door, *continued*
must be open or shut 423: 2
of Darkness 389: 8
of the toes 362: 5
one d. shuts out the snow ..206: 1
open d. 66: 9
open soul and open d. 55: 6
shut the d. after you 1259: 6
shuts, another opens 1430: 7
slam d. on doctor's nose ..873: 4
sliding down your cellar d. 2295: 2
stand at d. of thought ...1994:14
sweep against own d. 588: 2
that time unlocks 2023: 1
to which I found no Key 1370:16
will open at a touch 933:13
Door-keeper in house of God 887: 2
Door-nail: dead as a d. 375:18
Door-plates not so brazen .1376:13
Doorband strong enough ...933:13
Doors: adamantine d. 2160:14
all d. open to courtesy 329: 9
death's thousand d. 380: 1
dovecote d. of sleep 1845: 3
hingeless d. 1105:13
keep shut d. of mouth ...1821: 7
noiseless d. close after us 438:15
of breath 1220: 9
of death ever open 380: 2
open your living d. 2244: 6
shut d. against setting sun 1939:11
that opened of themselves ..771: 3
to let out life 379:20
Doorstep to wisdom 2168:14
Doorway: low d. of my tent ..76: 1
Dora: Leave to her poet ..106:11
Dorcas 242: 1
Doris, the Shepherd maiden 2213:10
Dormire: sex horis d. sat est 1848: 9
Dormit: bene d. non sentit male dormiat 1843:13
Dorothy Q. 70: 8
Dors bien sinon au sermon 1843:14
Dos est magna parentium virtus 1452: 9
est uxoria lites 2142: 7
in conjugis fit noxia 477:11
Dot it well 589:13
Dotage: senile debility 28: 2
terms so 1425:18
what d. will not vanity maintain 2074:18
Dote on his very absence 2: 9
Dote imperium vendidi 477:13
inde faces ardent a d. 477:18
Dotes yet doubts 1007:10
Doth as most men do 1705:22
Dots: no d. over i's 1998:14
Double in words and meaning 2033: 8
toil and trouble 2043:22
Double-charge thee 448:11
Double-darken gloomy skies 1436: 1
Double-lock the door 1948:18
Double-minded: man who is .420:10
Double-shade the desert 1402: 9
Doubles of those whose way .611:20
Doublet and hose courageous 2138: 2
fashion of a d. 491: 5
goes in d. leaves off wit ..2175: 7
new d. before Easter 514:16
Doublets: no more d. than backs 485:18
Doubly-dead so young 411: 2
Doubt 474
academic d. 475: 5
accomplice of tyranny 475:23
and discord 454:15
as to constitutionality ..2279: 7
beacon of the wise 475:18
beginning of wisdom 475:12
brother devil to Despair ..476: 7
clouded with d. 475: 2
desolate shores of d. 2176: 7
dimmed heaven with d. 336: 2
diversified by faith 113: 8
easier to believe than d. ...152: 1
every d. that can retard ..2163: 5

Drinking, *continued*
no d. after death 495: 7
not blamed but excess 502:15
oceans dry 971: 8
red-hot with d. 503:11
sluggish men improved by d. 493: 2
takes drunkard out of society 502: 4
thirst departs with d. 89:13
two reasons for d. 496: 7
unhappy brains for d. 498:14
will make man quaff 497: 8
Drinks: bottled windy d. ..500: 5
intoxicating d. 1619:10
like a funnel 493:13
long time between d. 494: 6
support of health 498: 7
well, sleeps well 497: 7
who d. on to hell may go ..503:17
Dripping hollows rock 2126: 7
Drivel: ropy d. 1408:15
Driven: hardly d. easily led 1424: 4
into desperate strait 436:20
Driving like Jehu 931:11
Drollery called representative government 433: 9
Drone: glorious, lazy d. ..956: 5
like cloistered d. 956: 5
Drones: better ten be fed ..243: 9
like stingless d. 956: 5
who waste labor 956: 5
Drop: last d. empties water-clock 1921: 8
in Ocean's boundless tide 1242: 3
nor any d. to drink 1987:11
of a bucket 1380: 6
of pleasure 1446: 2
of pure and pearly light ..1972: 2
prove crocodile 1977:20
ruddy d. of manly blood 1188:15
silver d. hath fallen 848:19
take a d. in water 1285: 4
take a d. too much 2154:18
vaporous d. profound ...1344: 1
Dropping: continual d. in rainy day 2146:12
will wear hard rocks 2126:11
Dropping-down-deadness ...1589:10
Drops: blood d. 1745: 8
damning d. that fall 75:10
holy and pure d. 1272:14
liquid d. of tears 1974: 7
little d. of water 2040:19
make a cat a ghost 2016:17
minute d. from off eaves ..2153: 3
of water hollow stone 2126:10
sacred pity engender'd ..1976: 1
store of childish d. 1976: 2
that make a lakeful 1851: 4
these foolish d. 1976:12
what precious d. are those 1974:12
Dropsy grows apace 460:12
Dropt: Mrs. Montagu has d. 1859:11
Dross costs ounce of gold 1605: 2
enure to dirty d. 2105:14
for Duchesses 1522: 3
Drought: after d., rain ...1512: 1
Drown in ken of shore 1816: 5
incontinently d. myself ..1933:13
to save his board 529: 4
what pain it was to d. 483: 6
Drowned: third degree of drink 504:12
Drowning: no d. mark upon him 852:14
Drowns for want of skill ..1954: 5
Drowsiness shall clothe with rags 956:10
Drowsy as the clicking of a clock 313: 5
make heaven d. 1174:15
Drowsyhed: land of D. ...482:10
Drudge, like Selden 1924: 7
Drudgery at desk's dead wood 2254: 9
gray D. that grinds 643:17
no d. in ordered world ...1229:15
unremitting d. and care ..1422: 2
Drug of illusion 109: 6
will give no d. 2274: 3
with words 184: 4
Drugs do not heal 1285: 2
no use in d. 1285: 3
Druid: in yonder grave a D. lies 1623:16
Drum: beat the d. 1850:17
ecclesiastic 1593:19
follow thy d. 2113: 5
hoarse d. would sleep 1042:13
made of his skin 982:13
noise of threatening d. ..2117: 7
not a d. was heard 1870: 9
of the world's ear 1373: 6
quick alarming d. 2116: 3
sit like unbraced d. 1533:12
spirit-stirring d. 636:11
stormy music in the d. ..1363:12
unto d. did groan 2115:14
when hollow d. has beat ..1342:12
Drum's discordant sound 2113: 3
sad roll has beat 1869:11
Drum-beat: morning d. 547: 3
Drumfires: walking into the d. 67: 5
Drummer soldier with a drum 1862:14
Drums: maddening d. 2117: 3
of three conquests 1706:10
of time 2008: 2
of war, d. of peace 2119:11
rum-tumming ev'rywhere 2284: 2
worn out with martial din 455:12
Drunk as a lord 501:13
as a piper 501:13
as a Plymouth fiddler 501:13
as a tinker 501:13
as an Englishman 561: 6
do not think I am d. 502:17
gloriously d. 503: 5
great as a king 503: 2
half-d. half-dressed 504: 6
he that killeth, d. 502:11
not d. is he 502:17
on a winter night 502: 8
partly she was d. .... .1223: 6
to be d. business of day ..502: 2
to Frankfort and got d. ..503: 9
with choler 78:17
with dream of conquest ..297:23
Drunkard: in the mouth of the d. 504: 5
one d. loves another 502:16
reel in d., reel out saint 2080: 6
reeling from a feast 505:12
when he prays 2201: 8
Drunkards: beget d. 502:13
by planetary influence ...1915:10
have fools' tongue 503:15
more old d. than doctors ..465:16
Drunken as a rat 501:13
but not with wine 2154:20
may his mother kill 503:18
of things Lethean 263:12
what's d. man like 504:12
Drunkenness 501
darling fav'rite of hell 503:14
discovers faults 504:10
does not create vice 504:10
identical with ruin 504: 8
immoderate affection 504:14
insulated us in thought ...503: 6
is eke a foul record 503:12
is very sepulture 503:12
root of all sins 2018: 7
unlocks secrets 504: 1
voluntary madness 504: 9
where d. reigneth 503:12
wine one thing, d. another 2154:20
Drury's: happy boy at D. ..196: 8
Drusa receives her visitants in bed 248:10
Dry as stubble wheat 1747: 4
we d. away 389: 3
Dryden, John 505
Dryfoot: draws d. well ..1540:15
Dubbiar: non menche saver, d. m'aggrata 475:10
Dubitando ad veritatem 475:11
Dubitatione facinus inest ..972: 5
Dubius, a scrupulous good man 808: 6
Dublin City, there's no 997:11
Ducat: dead for a d. 376:15
Ducats: O my Christian d. .367: 1
Duce: me d. damnosas 1095: 1
Duchess: that's my last D. 1448:11
what think you of a d. ..2016: 8
Ducis: propriæ d. artes ...1867: 3
Duck: lame d. 1556: 6
played at d. and drake ...1615: 3
served whole 523: 3
Ducks and drakes 1615: 3
deem it d. and drakes 978: 8
Dude: Yankee dude'll do ..705:18
Dudgeon: civil d. 1662:13
Dudley, Thomas: epitaph ..572: 8
Due: give the devil his d. ..442: 8
render to all men their d. 1253: 3
Duel in which artist cries ..106: 7
Duelling 505
Duello he regards not 505:15
Dues: render to all men ..1028:18
simple d. of fellowship 458: 1
Duke Humphrey: dine with 449: 3
Duke of Argyle: God bless 1770:14
Dukedoms: we grant no d. ..53: 9
Dukes of waterish Burgundy 1234: 3
Dulce amarumque misces .1953: 6
domum resonemus 906: 1
et decorum est pro patria mori 1466: 9
est desipere in loco 702: 2
etiam fugias 1953: 7
Dulcimer: on her d. she played 483:11
Dulcius: quid d. hominum 253: 7
Dull as alderman at church 1925: 3
as ditch water 375:10
as Dutch commentator ..1925: 3
construed to be good ...1925:11
fill d. man to the brim 1924:13
if d., design in it 1925:15
man is always sure 1925: 7
she is not bred so d. 2144: 1
smoothly d. 192:13
thus I am never d. 109: 6
venerably dull 1676:10
Dull-eyed diplomatic corps ..451:16
Duller nature triumphant 1662:14
Dullness
See also Stupidity
blest fertile D. 1925:16
cause of d. in others 1925: 6
declares wit dull 2174:16
ever loves a joke 1925:10
if D. sees grateful day ..1044: 5
marked him for mayor ..1924:14
nobody reads on account of d. 1928: 1
of the fool whetstone 698: 4
portion of truly blest 1924:12
sacred in sound divine ...1592: 4
whose good old cause 1925: 9
with d. was he cursed 1925:14
Dum vivimus, vivamus 1132:10
Dumb and deaf as post 373: 3
art of acting d. 1652: 7
as drum with hole 1821:13
in midst of arms 1081: 4
throng to see him 1560:10
to Homer, d. to Keats 1341:19
too clever is d. 280: 3
Dumb's a sly dog 349: 7
Dumb-bells: hard-boiled d. 2069:14
why use d. 590:22
Dumm: mir wird so d. 1900: 4
Dumpling: turning the d. ..92:10
Dumps: doleful d. 897: 7
doleful d. oppress 1364:13
Dun of all the duns 386: 5
Dunblane: Bob of D. 456:20
Duncan Gray came here ..2213: 7
Dunce awakens d. 696:18
graduated d. 1969:10
nobody calls you d. 280: 3
sent to roam 910: 6
with best of intentions 994:15
with wits 2173: 3

Emperors only husbands ..943:14
Emphasis: spoiled by e. 1899: 3
Empire and liberty 970:13
for e. kings ambitious fight 835:10
great e., little minds 1541:16
great e. of the west 51:12
intellectual e. imperishable 839:11
it is peace 719: 6
it is the sword 719: 6
of the Heavens bright 297:20
of the sea 548: 1
of thy perfect bliss 1213: 9
power in trust 1574: 7
rule e. of himself 1787:10
too narrow for two kings 1042:11
trade's proud e. 286: 3
trample an e. down 202: 8
westward the course of e. ..52: 6
what an e. we inherit ..1245:13
where now the haughty E. 1739:13
wide as Shakespeare's 55:14
Empire au phlégmatique ..1787: 3
c'est la paix 719: 6
c'est l'épée 719: 6
Empire Day: meaning of ..970: 6
Empires are far below thy aims 2121:13
day of e. 1380:19
die of indigestion 1918: 9
if changing e., rose or fell 1797: 8
in their brains 970: 9
not maintained by timidity 2014:16
unimagined E. draw 1502:13
wax and wane 2012:12
Empiric's gains 1662:12
Emplois: digne des e. qu'on n'a pas 1549:10
Employ: unknown Power's e. 438:12
Employed: innocently e. ..1336: 1
Employment meriting no praise 410:10
prevents melancholy 1290:12
Employments: chase brave e. 1864:12
how various his e. 954:18
occupied in highest e. 1:12
who gives me e., master ..1281: 8
Emptiness: dreaming e. ..662:14
in the affairs of men 221: 2
of art 107: 3
of love 1200: 4
seems at the heart of all things 462: 2
Emptio: nam mala e. semper ingrata 125:10
Empty is the cradle 2289:10
vessel giveth greater sound 174: 3
Empty-hearted: nor are these e. 1833: 1
Empyrean rung 1753: 2
Emulation: bloodless e. ..566: 1
gory e. 'twixt us twain 1731: 4
shouting their e. 91: 2
Enamoured: hung over her e. 140: 1
Encampment on plains of night 1914:14
Enchant a fair Sensitive Plant 317: 2
thine ear 314:17
Enchanting Objects set 2:11
Enchantment: distance lends e. to the view 463: 1
sails through magic seas 1342:10
waves her potent wand ..1675: 5
Enclosure: temporary e. ..969: 8
Encomiums: deprive boaster of his e. 174: 1
Encounter of our wits 2174: 6
Encounters at the bar ..1093: 6
Encourage the others . ..546: 6
Encourager les autres 546: 6
Encumbers him with help 1468:14
End 538
A' made a finer e. 397:11
all things have an e. . ..416:18
all things move to their e. ..539: 6
and beginning 147: 8
End, *continued*
apathetic e. 1146: 7
at e. of love 392: 2
at tongues' e. 2024:14
better e. than beginning ..147:10
bid all men watch life's e. ..411:14
bitter e. 539: 5
cables veered out to the better e. 539: 5
consider their latter e. ..375: 5
crowns all 539:13
crowns every action 539:16
directs means 540:10
everything hath e. 538:15
fairest have fleetest e. ..1745:15
from e. new beginnings ..147:16
good onset bodes good e. 148: 1
he made a good e. 397:11
he makes a swan-like e. 1950: 9
her e. bitter as wormwood 2133:13
hope a prosperous E. 1584:12
if e. be well, all well 538:12
inferred from beginning ..147:18
is come of pleasant places 1845:16
is hard to reach 1901: 7
is not yet 539: 4
is the renown 538:12
justifies the means 539:19
keeps one e. in view 538:13
lawful, means lawful 539:19
let the e. try the man 539: 7
linked to beginning 407:12
make me to know mine e. 1141: 8
make the e. sweet 32: 2
must justify the means 540: 3
my last e. be like his 397: 5
of a feast better 660: 4
of a fray 660: 4
of a perfect day 372:12
of childhood fears 657: 2
of good is an evil 810:13
of life is not knowledge 7:16
of poor Jenny 853:22
of prayer and preaching 1388:19
of the beginning 11: 9
of things is at hand 539: 4
of this day's business 539: 8
of what we fear 656: 2
of woman's being 1352:10
of your nose 1413:14
one must consider the e. ..540:16
original and e. 783: 3
preëxists in the means 225:22
regard the writer's e. ..2253: 6
remember Milo's e. 1710: 2
remember the e. 540:12
stay we may e. sooner ..863: 8
that crowns, not the fight ..539:13
wise taketh heed to the e. ..148: 2
wrong e. of stick 2260:14
Endearment: fond e. tries ..161:13
Endearments: connubial e. ..550: 5
Endeavor: all thy good e. ..394: 3
to do thy duty 507:17
Enderby: brides of E. 153: 9
Ending of the day 372:14
still e., and beginning 147: 9
wait to see life's e. 411:15
where all things end 1961:12
Endow a college or a cat ..224: 5
Ends: all the e. thou aim'st at 150: 5
all well that e. well 538:12
at fingers' e. 666:16
by our beginnings know 2263: 9
everything e. 147:17
in everything 1645:13
make both e. meet 1997:12
means, not e. 49:13
more are men's e. mark'd ..32: 3
noble e. by noble means 831: 6
prosperous e. 74: 6
stolen out of holy writ ..949: 8
things will work to e. 539:12
virtuous e. by virtuous means 539:21
we have some private e. ..1742:11
will make him greatest 7: 6
worldly e. 1312:16
Endurance 540
crowning quality 1462:11
every lot overcome by e. ..541: 7
nobler than strength ...1462:11
Endure and die 1146: 2
and persist 1489: 1
bear with and e. all men ..541: 5
more able to e. 541: 8
their going hence 382: 8
unto the end 541: 2
what can't be mended 541:14
Endured: much and long have I e. 541: 3
Endures: he that e. is not overcome 541: 2
Enemies: afraid of making e. 733:22
blind among e. 170: 8
care in choice of e. 544: 8
civilized man has no e. ..543: 1
come nearer truth in judgments 542:11
defend myself from e. ..734: 4
fallen among our e. 542:20
friends and e. 733: 3
giving e. the slip 544: 1
heed e. reconciled 543: 5
I deserved my e. 733:10
just friends brave e. 59: 3
laws e., e. to laws 1086: 1
like village-curs 543:14
little e. not despised 543: 2
love him for the e. he has made 279:13
make my e. ridiculous ..1586:13
many e. when back to wall 542: 3
no e., no following 543: 1
no man without e. 542: 8
of e. fewer the better 541:21
one of my intimate e. 542:15
rather my e. envy me than I my e. 565:17
rising man cannot count e. 837: 9
shall lick the dust 542:22
tell you your faults 542: 6
their e. were targets 1865:12
there are your e. 62: 6
think seldom of your e. 1475:12
time's e. may not have ..1433: 8
to their own life 1831: 8
will tell the rest 542: 7
your majesty's e. 544: 6
Enemigos los menos 541:21
Enemy 541
and friend to hurt heart .735: 9
anger is a sworn e. 80: 3
best friend blundering e. 734: 7
bridge for flying e. 544:18
calumniating e. 541:23
came, was beaten 298: 5
common e. oppressor of all 1088:11
dead e. smells sweet 1712:15
devised by the e. 541:23
do not undervalue e. 543:11
each man his own e. 544: 9
evil to trust the e. 542:17
finding e. so curst 543:14
for friendship's sake 733: 7
give e. road for flight 545: 1
give us a good e. 542: 6
God send me an e. 735:10
God's e., Hell's friend ..1618: 7
greatest e. to man is man 1248:19
guard e. from oppression 1105: 1
hardly a warm personal e. left 544: 7
hath done this 542:13
hath ever been God's e. 2064:20
he has no e., you say 543: 1
he who has one e. 735: 6
helps a fallen e. 543: 8
how goes the e. 2004: 1
if thine e. hunger, feed him 1711:11
in a man's own breast ..544:16
in their mouths 498:15
is at hand 544: 5
is within our gates 1786:11

Equitem: post e. sedet atra
Cura 220:14
Equity in law, spirit 1090: 5
is a roguish thing 1090: 5
prompt sense of e. 1029:17
Equivocate: I will not e. 1705: 6
Equivocation half lying ..1111:13
of the fiend 2060:12
Equo ne credite, Teucri ..930: 6
Equum Sejanum 928:11
solve senescentem e. 929: 7
tenera docilem cervice 1969:14
Equus: fortis e. reserato ..929:14
Era of good feeling 63: 7
smoking e. 2017: 9
Eras: new e. in brains 56: 3
Erasmus, great injur'd
name 1593: 9
Erato harmonizes foot and
song 800:11
Erbteil wie herrlich 2003:14
Ercle's vein; tyrant's vein 2064:19
Erebus: lowest bottom of 889:15
Erect: Godlike e. 1254:17
Eremite beneath his moun-
tain's brow 1157: 5
Eremites and friars 1593:10
Erin
See also Ireland
dear E., how sweetly 996:12
go bragh 996: 1
go bread and cheese 996: 1
mavournin 997:12
Erin's: honor and E. pride 997: 5
starving E. pallid cheek ..675: 5
Eripe te moræ 429: 2
Eripitur persona, manet
res 2050:20
Eripuit Jovi fulmen 722: 3
Ermined and minked 1860:16
Eros older than Saturn ..1523: 1
remind not E. of wings 1201: 7
Eroses: bevy of E. 1203:18
Err but once, undone for-
ever 2138:14
in company with Hume 575:10
in company with Lincoln 575:10
in different ways 575:20
in things too high 886: 2
most may e. as grossly ..1482: 3
those who e. follow poets 1531:18
to e. in opinion human 577: 1
to e. is human 577: 2
upon the sober side 1958: 5
when I e. every one can see 1109:12
when thousands e. 1058:20
with learned error 576:14
with millions on thy side 1725:15
with Plato 575:10
with Pope 575:10
Errand: sleeveless e. 1851: 6
Errands of supernal grace ..76: 2
run willing e. 704:14
Errandum causas honestas ..576: 2
Erranti monstrat viam 1493:18
Errare: cujusvis hominis ..576:17
humanum est 577: 2
malo cum Platone 575:10
Errasset: si non e., fecerit
illa minus 1324:15
Errata: without e. 571:10
Erred and repents 577: 3
through wine 498: 2
Erreur a ses martyrs 1024: 7
a son merite 576:12
Erreurs: plus courtes 575:25
Erro: Si in hoc e. 965: 8
Error 575
acquires honor 475:24
all men liable to e. 576:20
also has its merit 576:12
and truth 577: 5
basis of disease 459:17
belongs to libraries 577:14
by his own arms 575:24
cannot be believed sin-
cerely 577:19
classify disease as e. 459:17
conquer e. by denying its
verity 577:12
Error, *continued*
deep as hell I count his
e. 1751: 3
defended only by e. 577:20
double e. sets us right 575:22
dubious waves of e. 575:14
father truth 578: 3
force that welds 578: 4
giant e., darkly grand 576: 6
gross e. held in schools ..717:10
has its martyrs 1024: 7
has no end 575: 4
honest e. to be pitied 575: 9
if e. causes honorable 576: 2
if this be e. 1175: 3
in endless e. hurl'd 1239: 3
in multitude of words ..2224:15
in which I find delight ..965: 8
is a hardy plant 576:11
is discipline 575: 8
is hell or mischief as bad 1441: 6
is prolific 575:17
last e. worse than first ...575:22
learns e. in maturer years 2263: 8
lives ere reason born 1680: 4
man protesting e. 577:10
melancholy's child 576: 8
mistake of our judgement 577:22
mountainous e. 576: 7
natural accompaniment ...576:19
needs support of govt. 817: 8
no one who lives in e. free .575:16
no vehement e. can exist ..575:18
O e. soon conceived 576: 8
of eye directs mind 576: 8
of head, not heart 882: 3
of opinion tolerated 577: 1
of the mind 575:19
one thing to show man e. ..577:22
progress of man to e. 576:13
superficial e. 577:15
that's all an e. 1944: 1
there is no e., sin, death 1188:14
to be exposed 578: 1
troops of e. 577: 7
very e. of the moon 1344: 4
what damned e. but some 1693: 3
which truth may stay 619: 1
worse than ignorance 575: 3
wounded, writhes in pain ..577: 8
Error sed variis partibus ..575:20
suus cuique attributus est
e. 651: 7
utinam aliquando e. finiatur 1740: 1
Error's hidden side is truth 577:17
poisoned springs 576: 1
Errore imperitæ multitudinis 1482:13
Errorem, quo delector 965: 8
Errors: faults breed e. 649: 1
learn more from e. 575: 2
like straws, upon the surface flow 575:15
little e. lead soul away 2040:19
our wild e. be forgiven ..1588:13
own your e. past 1686: 3
perplex'd in e. 1645:7a
profit by his e. 595:14
shortest e. best 575:25
some female e. fall 608:14
theological e. 1918:17
they defend their e. 575: 6
think not of e. now 236:20
who can discern his e. 576: 5
yesterday's e. 575:13
Errs in her own grand way 576:10
quickly, quick in correcting 575: 1
who e. and mends 575: 7
Erubescit: sordido vehiculo
e. 174: 7
Erubuit: salva res est 173: 8
Eruditissima: belle e. 1096:10
Eruditus: cum errat e. 576:14
Eruption to our state 1946:11
Ervo: tenui solabitur, e. ..1107: 3
Esau selleth his birthright ..165:10
Esau's hands 420: 5
Escam malorum 1511:12
Eschewed: what can't be e. .541:12
Escurial: my house to me E. .906: 5
Esel schimpft den andern
Lang-ohr 113: 1
Espace d'un matin 1745: 7
stature de Dieu 2067:13
Esperables: toutes choses e. .923:13
Espérance et la crainte ...927: 5
je cultivais e. 926: 4
toute trompeuse 925:19
Esperances infinies 2061: 1
Esponge: je ne boy en plus
qu'une e. 493: 8
Espoused to death 397:12
Esprit brille aux dépens de
sa mémoire 1010:15
conçoit avec douleur 2253: 5
de discernement 1013: 7
de l'escalier 2172: 3
de son age 43:19
dupe du cœur 882:13
est atmosphère de l'âme ..1306:15
grand e. imagine grandes
choses 1309: 8
humain fait progrès 1307: 4
livre De l'E. 2276: 1
nous sert à faire des sottises 2173: 6
nul n'aura de l'e. hors nous 2175: 5
qu'une sorte d'e. 2171: 4
votre e. en donne aux
autres 2174: 2
Esprits: beaux e. lernen
einander 2174: 2
beaux e. rencontrent 2172:16
médiocres 1288: 9
petits e. trop blessés 1308:15
Esse quam videre 1831:19
Essen: nach dem E. sollst du
stehen 872: 7
Essence: divine e. love 791: 1
glassy e. 1245:19
love is God's e. 790:10
of all vulgarity 1715: 8
of humor sensibility 938:12
of good and evil 809:17
of life is divine 1143: 9
of poetry invention 1516: 5
Essences: sweetest e. in
smallest glasses 1486:19
Essentials: bored by e. ..1310: 5
Estate: adapt thyself to e. ..13: 6
fallen from high e. 621: 8
fleeting e. of man 1250: 2
fourth e. of the realm ..1601:10
goes before steward 432: 8
grown to man's e. 255: 5
his e. possesses him 1621:20
left religion for e. 1690: 5
poor e. scorns fortune ..310: 7
praise a great e. 637: 4
real e. foundation of guilt 1622: 5
sinks in a quarry an e. ...95:10
Third E. 718:10
this is thy hard e. 1065:10
which wits inherit 629: 2
Estates: Four E. of the Island 1601:12
Esteem: honest bard's e. ...14: 4
a man as highly 534: 7
merit our e. 876: 9
never to be sold 803: 4
our own e. 1127:14
Esteemed: if one wishes to
be e. 288: 3
Estimates: city e. of great
and small 2210:20
Estimé: si l'on voulait être e. 288: 3
Estimer: difficile d'e. 534: 7
Esto perpetua 2077: 3
Estridges: all plumed like e. 1865: 2
Estuary: in you the e. 32:10
Et tu, Brute 2032:10
Et tu, Brute filii 984:16
État c'est moi 1044: 1
tout l'é. est en lui 1044: 1
Eternal Feminine 2179:18
forever if at all 785:17
not ourselves 856:16
sense of the e. 578:17
with E. to be deem'd 444:16

Evil, *continued*
communications 288:11
covetousness root of e. 120: 2
deeds 426:11
deliver us from e. 1981: 8
doeth e. hateth light 583:24
every e., but not e. wife ..2145:2a
fear of one e. leads to worse .583: 3
fittest to consort with e. ..584: 3
fog of good and e. 21: 7
for every e. remedy 584:20
for good, good for e. 810: 7
for his good repay 810: 7
from religious conviction 1693: 1
from seeming e. good 812: 6
genius 74:12
greatest e., greatest good 1509: 5
half-cured cause we know .583: 9
harms plotter most 1710: 8
has appetite for falsity ..585: 5
hastening to merge itself ..812: 8
I will fear no e. 388: 6
in an ivory setting 129:16
in bud easily crushed 583:10
inadvertently said e. 1480: 3
into mind of God or man ..584: 8
is easy 584:11
is null, is nought 809:11
known e. best 584:12
like a rolling stone 585: 7
love of money root of e. 1337: 2
manfully fronted ceases ..583: 5
must come of e. 1708: 2
neighbor to good 811: 3
no e. great which is last ..584:10
no e. man happy 583:26
no e. so terrible as woman 2187: 8
no e. without compensation .292: 1
no e. without remedy 584:20
no e. without some good ..810: 2
no inspiration in e. 1902: 7
no man enjoyed e. 583:26
no nature hath 583:17
no time too brief for e. ..584:22
often triumphs 584:19
one e. rises from another .585: 6
one that eschewed e. 238:10
only good perverted 810:15
only one e., ignorance ..1060: 2
out of e. bring good 811: 1
overcome of e. 583:14
partial e., universal good .811: 6
rather e. than nothing ..1581: 1
recompense no man e. 584:18
resist not e. 1708: 1
shall admit no cure 1687:10
shall back recoil 584: 7
springs up 584: 5
submit to present e. 584:12
sufficient unto day is e. ..2023: 5
tends to disappear 812: 8
that e. well deserves 583: 8
that good may come 539:20; 540: 4
that men do lives after ...811:13
to avoid an e. 540: 6
to depart company of living 1860: 8
to him who thinks e. 585: 8
too far advanced to avoid ..583:10
welcome e., if alone 583: 7
when e. advantageous 584:15
which admits no cure ..1276:14
which I would not 149: 1
why do you thus devise e. 1223:11
write e. in marble 987: 2
wrought by want of thought 583:20
Evil-speaker, evil-doer 1835:14
Evils: accidental e. 1498:18
choice of e. 260:17
choose least 260:17
cured by contraries 583:23
desperate e. make calm ..585: 1
equal when extreme 583:11
from doctors flow 872: 3
'gainst minor e. pray 2245:10
if e. come not fears vain ..584: 9
imaginary e. 583:15
least of e. 584:13
lesser of two e. 261: 2
Evils, *continued*
many e. has religion caused 1692:17
of sensual sloth 2062:10
of two e. choose neither ..261: 3
present e. triumph 1500: 5
shuns e., does good 812: 3
that never arrived 2045: 6
that take leave 585: 3
these fix'd e. sit so fit 240:11
twelve e. of the age 240: 5
two weak e., age, hunger ...35:15
Evolution 585
ever climbing 587: 4
not a force but a process ..586:13
others call it God 585:12
sounding watchword "E." 587: 4
Ewe and a lamb 1720:19
when hurt resists 2244:16
will not hear lamb 1068: 1
Ewer: safe in a golden e. 1589: 1
Ewig-Weibliche zieht hinan 2179:18
Ex tempore 1439: 8
Exactitude, politesse des rois 328:18
Exactness of peculiar parts ..129:12
Exagère: affaiblit tout ce qu'on e. 2050:18
Exaggeration always weakens 2050:18
in conversation 312:15
report of death an e. 395: 1
Exalteth: whoever e. 937: 1
Examinations formidable .1969: 8
Example 587
and precept 589: 2
as e. to deter 588: 9
by e. men may do 588: 1
custom, fear 1980:13
does the whole 588:16
follow e. of time 2002: 3
good e. best sermon 1595:12
greatest of seducers 588: 4
is a dangerous lure 588:11
lesson all men can read ..589: 1
let e. be obey'd 588: 3
more efficacious 589: 6
more harm by evil e. 587:10
of great duties done 2122: 7
one e. more valuable 589: 3
presents great e. great ..1380:20
profit by their e. 2033:18
salutary influence of e. ..980:19
school of mankind 587: 7
set a good e. 588: 7
you with thievery 1987: 1
Examples draw 1595:12
evil e. in household 588:10
fair e. of renown 628: 9
noblest e. from crimes ..1090:11
to give bad e. 27:13
work more forcibly 589: 6
Exceedingly well read 1676: 2
Excel: thou shalt not e. ..2124:17
'tis useless to e. 138: 5
Excellence 589
constant in wondrous e. ..589:16
fair divided e. 1274: 6
great or bright not e. 589:14
lamed by his e. 589:13
long in maturing 589:15
settled by time and place ..2088: 8
that angels love men with 1199: 9
without definition 589:11
Excellences: by e. measure great man 832: 2
Excellency: definition 589:11
Excellent in neither 1247: 4
ought was e. assayed 447:23
to have giant's strength ..1922:16
Excels: everyone e. in something 1:15
in what we prize 896: 6
Excelsior 110: 1
Exception proves the rule 1750: 5
Excès en tout est un défaut 2094: 6
Excess
See also Moderation
best things to e. 1327: 1
better e. than defect 178: 3
Excess, *continued*
between e. and famine ...1327: 4
blasted with e. of light ..1305:11
brings trouble to mankind 1327: 3
by e. of evil, evil dies 584:21
clogged with e. 519: 9
desire of power in e. 241: 6
distribution should undo e. 1328: 7
every e. causes defect ..1953:12
give me e. of it 1365:15
in anything is a defect ..2094: 6
in literature 1166: 8
is opposed to nature 1327: 1
lapse into shameful e. 67: 8
leads to wisdom 1327: 9
libertine e. 460:10
nothing in e. ..1326:15; 1629:17
nothing succeeds like e. 1327: 9
nothing to e. 1326:15
of glory obscur'd 444:14
of joy weeps 1018: 7
surprise by a fine e. 1516: 7
to be blamed 502:15
wasteful and ridiculous e. 1327: 8
where e. begs all 1794:12
Excesses of our youth 2264: 5
Exchange is no robbery ..1985:19
Exchequer of the poor 823:15
rob me the e. 1986:13
Excidit: tamen e. ausis 613: 3
Excise: hateful tax 1967:13
Exciseman: bustling about like an e. 1718: 2
De'il awa wi' e. 492: 4
Exclamations: cured with e. 1952: 5
Excludes: not till sun e. ..202:18
Excommunication 1954: 9
Excrement: to me is e. ..1486:18
Excusare: quam miser e. sibi non potest 590: 7
Excuse 589
beauty is its own e. 691: 9
better bad e. than none 589:19
coy e. 391:15
excellence perfect e. 589:13
is a lie guarded 590:11
most easily idleness 953: 2
must needs e. 340:11
never e. 590:10
no e. for crime 336:13
pitiable who cannot e. self ..590: 7
prove e. for the glass 501: 5
sleeveless e. 1851: 7
stoop not to poor e. 590: 2
to tyrant no e. 2064: 9
your e. is out of season ..2289: 5
Excuses: don't make e., make good 590: 2
find e., for you are woman 2191: 5
find e. for myself 590: 7
for another 590:10
who e. accuses 590: 8
Excusing of a fault 649:23
Execution: one that rode to 429: 4
Executioner: very expert ..414: 8
Executions in naked country 1358:20
Executors: let's choose e. 1562: 7
Exempla debet æquo animo pati 1656: 4
sua quisque e. debet 588:15
vitiorum e. domestica 588:10
Exemple plus grand de séducteurs 588: 4
Exemples: donner de mauvais e. 27:13
Exemplis: hodie e. tuemur 1596:14
vitiorum e. recedendum ...650: 1
Exemplo malo 427:13
plus nocent 587:10
quod e. fit 588: 1
Exemplum dei quisque 785:15
omne magnum e. 1656:11
Exempt from action's test ..279:16
from talking nonsense ..1408:16
Exemption: I ask e. from nothing 1704: 6

Fat, *continued*
fair and fifty 41: 7
fair and forty 41: 7
fry the f. out of manufacturers 2281: 5
grow f. and look young 648: 5
his f., his suet 210: 8
his soul, make body lean .1584: 1
is in the fire 648: 2; 1633: 7
knoweth not what lean thinketh 648: 8
no sweeter f. than mine ..979: 5
plump and juicy 870:16
resolved to grow f. 41: 7
waxed f. and kicked 648: 3
with feasting there 316:12
with the lean 648: 4
Fat, sots croient homme de mérite 697:12
Fat-frier: Hanna was a f. 2281: 5
Fata data secutus 644:10
ducunt volentem 642:16
prospectant paria 2085: 1
quo f. trahunt sequamur .643: 4
sed quo trahunt 642:21
nullo excludere 644: 2
obstant 644:11
ubi vocant 642:21
viam invenient 643: 4
Fatal to be loved 1194:13
Fate 642
all things produced by f. ..643: 8
and this is F. 1187: 8
as f. has willed 643: 6
behold f. of a reformer ..1685:14
belief in brute F. 439: 3
best cannot suspend f. 809: 6
big with the f. of Cato 368:20
blackest ink of F. my lot .1373: 5
boldly meet our f. 178: 4
brave hearts to adverse f. .325:12
cannot harm me 451:12
cannot rob of applause 90:19
chain of causation 643: 5
chance decides f. 229:16
come upon f. while shunning f. 644: 6
cropped him short 411: 4
curst f. of all conspiracies ..305:15
deeds in prior existence ..642:18
did f. begin Weaving 439: 9
drags him who resists 642:16
each cursed his f. 642:23
eagle's f. and mine, one ..509: 2
fears his f. too much 177: 4
fix'd f., free will 100:11
found a rare soul pliant ..1514: 6
hard f. of man 2176: 2
has carried me mid arrows 643: 7
has wove thread of life ..1250:10
has written a tragedy 1125:10
hath little to inflict 645: 3
holds the strings 643:13
how wayward decrees of F. 835: 5
in the storms of f. 18: 4
in vain from F. I fly 1189: 6
inextricable 2149:10
is ruled by chance 1127:13
is the gunman 644: 1
is unpenetrated causes 642:18
it shall be high 51: 8
knocks at the palace 383:14
laughs at probabilities 642:13
leads the willing 642:16
man's f. and woman's 1253: 9
monarchs must obey 380:13
my f. cries out 645: 4
never wounds more deep ..993:11
no armour against F. 385: 7
no one so accursed by f. ..1957:11
not option Nature gave ..1381: 3
O f. of fools 696:19
of books 182:18
of fighting cocks, kings ..1602:13
of his f. is never wide 644: 6
one common f. we must prove 1203: 3
ordains that dearest friends must part 1454:10
Fate, *continued*
seem'd to wind him up 396:17
shall yield to chance 233:17
show thy force 644: 8
sits on these dark battlements 644: 5
steals with silent tread 643: 9
stern f. and time 380:12
Strong-arm Worker 644: 1
that flings the dice 643:10
thrifty, not a needy, f. ...1997:13
'tis my f. to write 2258: 3
to bear is to conquer f. 644:17
to rich f. sends gold 1562:11
too vast orb of her f. 555: 2
tried to conceal him 1854:11
unpitied, rites unpaid ...1794: 4
we're steered by F. 1931: 6
what shall be maiden's f. 1233:21
whatever limits us 642:17
who can control his f. 645: 6
who shall shut out F. 644: 2
whom f. ruins, makes mad 1232: 4
will leave loftiest star 642:14
wisest f. says no 644:11
your spindles fill 643:14
Fated: 'twas f. so 642:22
Fates are just 1709:14
equal f. alone may bless ..1267: 5
lead, let us follow 643: 4
lead, Virtue follows 642:21
not quite obdurate 644: 4
say us nay 644:11
supp'd with F. and Furies 196: 8
their gifts allot 643:12
three were the f. 643:17
we are our own f. 427:17
what f. impose men must needs abide 644: 8
whither the F. call 642:21
will find a way 643: 4
Father 645
Abraham: we are coming 1158:12
and a mother 195:11
behooves f. to be blameless .646: 6
cannot give holier name ..645:16
composed your beauties ..646:14
dear f., come home with me now 2295: 4
deny thy f. 1372:18
everybody works but f. ..2290:10
follows f. with unequal steps 74: 7
for hoarding went to hell ..119:16
for judge, safe to trial 645: 8
forgive them 709:21
got me strong 164: 9
hearken unto thy f. 1452:12
he follows his f. 74: 7
he took my f. grossly 1359:16
her f. loved me 15:17
Holy F., in thy mercy ...1588: 9
honor thy f. and mother ..1452: 4
I am going to your f. 416: 4
I had it from my f. 1964:18
is rather vulgar 1652:20
is watching the sheep 1847: 8
like f. like son 74:7; 1155: 1
methinks I see my f. 1308: 4
more than schoolmasters ..645:10
my F. made them all 1390: 5
my true-begotten f. 645:13
night my f. got me 646: 1
no more like my f. 290: 8
no one knows own f. 645:23
of a family 645:12
of all, in every age 704: 3
of courage 653:15
of English criticism 505: 8
of good news 1399: 7
of his country 647: 4
of his land 647: 8
of nations 2123: 7
of rosy day 1939:19
of the People 2122: 3
of trusts 2048: 6
of your country 2122: 3
of Waters 1733: 9
one f. govern hundred sons 645:22
one moment makes a f. ..1452:11
Father, *continued*
our fair f. Christ 264: 6
should be as a god 646:14
struck f. when son swore .256:10
to me thou art and mother 944: 9
to the bough 646: 3
to the poor 1492:14
was a friar 1624: 5
was born before him 646:16
which art in heaven 789:13
which is in heaven 588:14; 1485: 7
who would be a f. 645:14
wise f. knows own child ..645:23
with whom no variableness 777:20
your F. knoweth 1586: 9
Word, and Holy Ghost 783:11
Father's dust is left alone .402: 5
Fathered: being so f. 944: 9
Fatherland: call country f. 1464: 7
contended for their f. 1465: 7
dear F., no danger thine ..767: 4
focuses a people 1464:15
his is a world-wide f. 165:12
this is the German's f. 767: 1
where most I prosper 320: 3
Fatherless and widows ...1689:11
seldom misfortune to be f. 645:20
Fathers: admire f. too much 646: 7
brave and free 1839:15
criticise f. for being narrow 646: 7
few f. care for sons 645:20
foolish over-careful f. 119:15
gathered to his f. 376: 1
had helped to gild 1488: 6
harsh judges 647: 1
have been fools so long 72: 4
have eaten sour grapes ...821:14
in war f. bury sons 2118: 9
lean'd not on his f. 1786: 7
shame f. by virtue 646: 7
that wear rags 646:13
thy f. watching the sheep 1847: 8
want children to be credit 646:10
we think our f. fools 646: 7
were thy f. gentle 74: 8
were under the cloud 280:16
what unjust judges f. are 647: 1
worshipt stocks, stones ...957: 7
your f., where are they ..1624:20
Fathom deep in love 1214: 7
full many a f. deep 1815: 3
Fathom-deep the place 404: 7
Fati: sit cæca futuri 749:12
Fatigatio modulatione solatur 1876: 9
Fatigue of idleness 955:18
of supporting freedom 723: 9
Fatiguée: devez être f. 414: 1
Fatis: quam brevibus pereunt ingentia f. 2041: 1
sic erat in f. 642:22
Fatness 647
of these pursy times 2081:13
Fats: in thy f. our cares be drowned 2157: 2
Fattings for the worms 379:15
Fatuity of idiots 998:15
Fatum: multi ad f. venere ..644: 6
Fatuum: præ litteras f. esse 1097:12
Fault: all f. who hath none 652:15
as great as faulty 649:15
clung to their first f. 1609: 6
concealed by virtue 649:20
confessed half amended ..295:12
confessed half redressed ..649: 8
every f. condemned 650: 5
every man has his f. 916: 3
faultless to a f. 652:10
find f. with individuals ..1258:1a
find f. with yourself 1788: 3
flint and hardness of f. ...878: 5
glorious f. of angels 47: 8
greatest f. conscious of none 652:11
he has no f. 652:15
her only f. faults enough 2189: 7
hint a f. 13:12
if friend telleth thee a f. ..219:10

Fault, *continued*
is not in our stars 650: 4
is of place 649:21
it was a grievous f. 50: 5
like my brother's f. 1789: 6
maintain a f. double f. ..649:12
mark everything a f. 1182:11
Nature's f., not thine 2197:11
no f. in women 2191:10
nobody but has his f. 1588: 6
not *my* f. if *others* hurt
you 1711:13
of the ass 112:12
of the Dutch 285:11
once excused twice committed 649: 7
one f. seeming monstrous .650: 1
overlook f. invite f. 649:22
sooner found than mended 649: 6
that is hidden 41: 4
'tis a f. to Heaven 650: 2
'tis not a f. to love 1187: 6
understanding to find f. . 1685:20
unknown as though unacted 650: 8
where the f. springs 1022:19
which humbles a man . ..938: 3
wicked heinous f. 1698: 4
will remain forever 1656: 5
without f., not a friend 652:14
worst f. given to prayer ..1588: 6
Faultily faultless 652:18
Faultless monster 652:17
to a fault 652:10
whoever thinks f. piece ...2253: 6
Faults 648
abounds in sweet f. 651: 4
all f. that may be named 2189: 6
all his f. observed 651:12
all men make f. 650:13
allied to excellence 650:16
allow a few f. in himself ..649: 4
bad excuse their f. 649:14
be to her f. a little blind ..2194: 3
bear f. of friend 739:13
breed errors 649: 1
brought their excuse 651: 3
copy f. want of sense 1505: 9
correct f. in second edition 1133: 8
could I her f. remember .1182:13
critics dare not mend 2173: 6
done by night 649:10
double we see those f. 41: 4
earth covereth 468: 6
every man has his f. 651: 7
excellencies in excess 2253: 6
first f. theirs that commit ..649: 5
fool perceives f. of others .651: 8
for which responsible 648:18
from seeming free 650: 5
great men have great f. ...832: 2
have such charm 652: 5
hidden f. and follies known 652: 1
in other men we f. spy ..1024:11
know f. of a man 649:17
leave behind pattern of f. ..650: 1
lie gently on him 650: 3
lie open to laws 650: 3
like her for her f. 649: 2
loves him better for f. ...650:16
make death a gain 650:14
man must have f. 650:12
men do not suspect f. 649:13
men have many f. 2189: 3
men still had f. 652:13
needs to thank f. 650:15
no one without f. 650:10
nor seek slight f. to find ..341: 1
not to show f. to friend ..739:11
of his own liking 651:13
of others 651: 7
people who please with f. .1299:15
prejudicial to friends 744:17
proceeding on distemper ..338: 2
proud to find f. 343: 8
publish not men's f. 1838:13
rich men have no f. 1720:16
see all others' f. 2168:11
seldom to themselves 651:14
smack of good qualities ..559: 5

Faults, *continued*
stripped of f. 288:15
survey f. and study them 649:18
tell me all my f. 677:12
that are rich are fair 650: 6
thick where love thin 649:11
tho' f. were thick as dust 1035:13
thou hast no f. 652:12
to make us men 651: 5
tolerate f. of others 652: 3
vile, ill-favour'd f. 650: 6
want a person's f. 651:16
we cite our f. 650: 9
who cover f. shame derides 349:18
with all her f., she is my
country still 545: 7
with all her f. I love her
still 2292: 6
with all my f. to love me
still 2138: 7
with all thy f., I love thee
still 545: 7
write to excuse my f. 649:23
Fauna of civilization 2243:12
Faustus: devil and Dr. F. ..440:18
I thought, like Dr. F. 107: 3
Fautes: excuser mes f. 649:23
sues que de nous 337:11
Fauts: twa f. or maybe three 648:20
Faux pas: had made a 1324:14
Favete linguis 2027: 2
Favitorum qui recte facit ..1468:16
Favor 652
accept f., confer one 653: 2
by a hard man 653: 3
doing f. for bad man 653:10
don't ask f. you can take ..653:14
easier to get than keep 712: 9
falleth out of own f. 611:14
good man sheweth f. 193:13
greater f. greater obligation 653: 1
he whom I f. wins 545:10
I court no f. 653: 7
in author's cap a feather .1559:14
is deceitful 138: 8
king's f. no inheritance ..1038: 6
of her face 608: 9
of great no inheritance 653: 5
of ignoble men 653:12
refuse a f. gracefully 653: 6
regain f. with myself 533:16
relaxing of strictness 653: 4
they whom I f. thrive 653: 9
to repay debt 419: 7
to this f. must she come ..382: 6
Favorem: via ad f. ferat ..1560: 9
Favorite: fortune's f. 711:20
has no friends 727: 2
mark his f. flies 734:19
Prodigal's f. 440:10
was never heard of 1553: 3
Favorites in danger of falling 327: 7
Favoritism governed kissage 1046: 9
Favors but like the wind ..2197: 8
confer f. generously 653: 8
hangs on princes' f. 1611:20
hospitable f. 932:13
pleased with f. given 1704: 4
prince's f. 1029:11
secret, sweet and precious 652:19
slowly granted 774: 7
steep'd in f. 653:13
your f. nor your hate ...1623:10
Fawn at his feet if he flings
bone 2236: 8
on any man 1801:18
to f., to crouch, to wait ..1802: 2
Fawned like man 472:11
on every fool alive 949:13
Fawning and flattery 676: 7
Fays and fairies dwell 616: 1
Fealty: forget your f. 708:21
Fear 653
akin to Death 654: 1
all men slaves to f. 1840: 3
and be slain 656: 4
and Shame without 1830:14

Fear, *continued*
anticipates many evils 653:23
Arch F. 387: 9
argues ignoble minds 655: 8
as bad as falling 655:14
at my heart, as at a cup ..657:15
beadle of the law 653:21
begin in f. end in folly ..1541:18
believes the worst 656: 2
betrays like treason 654: 5
brought gods into world ..800: 4
came upon me 658: 5
can make coward valiant ..331:16
can neither fight 657: 3
concessions of f. 2127: 8
direst foe of courage 655:14
dismiss your f. 654:15
do not f., my little darling 2291: 2
dreadful f. of hell 892:21
drives wretched to prayer 1582:18
early and provident f. ...1648: 5
every day surmount f. ...654:11
father of courage 653:15
feels no pity 654: 8
first brought gods 800: 4
first made gods 653:23
first put on arms 654:14
fleeter than wind 655:10
follows hope 927:11
gave wings to his feet 655: 9
God, honor the King 792: 2
God, keep commandments .791: 8
good to f. the worst 656: 2
greater than his haste 655:10
hate that we often f. 867:15
hath a hundred eyes 655:11
heavy with f. 31: 6
herald of revolutions 653:20
highest fence 654:26
him who fears thee 657:12
hindrance to virtue 653:22
hope and f. 927: 5
I f. no foe with Thee 793:10
I to fall 622: 7
increased with tales 387: 7
invites danger 655:12
is affront 2204: 7
is an ague 653:16
is fire that melts 653:18
is my vassal 388:11
is sharp-sighted 655:11
keeps men in obedience ..1419: 9
keeps the garden better ..654:26
kills more than disease ..654:16
know not what we f. 1751:12
last of all evils, f. 926:17
lay aside sad f. 324:13
less base the f. of death ..1935:13
less f. less danger 654:21
less, hope more 149:12
like a cloak 654: 4
loosens every power 656: 6
loves idea of danger 654:20
made her daring 654:23
made her devils 927: 9
made the gods 800: 4
many whom many f. 657:11
may break faith 655: 5
most afraid of f. 655:18
mother of safety 653:15
no f. in love 1216:11
no f. of God before eyes ...785:19
no f. without hope 927: 5
no pleasure attached to ...564:10
nobility is exempt from f. 1408: 8
not 654:15
not a teacher of duty 653:17
not spoke of in Scotland .1767:11
not them that kill body 791:14
not to swear anything 1418: 1
nothing so rash 655:10
nothing terrible save f. 655:15
of death damps my brow ..388:16
of death like f. beyond ..388: 4
of doing ill does nought ..972:13
of future doubt 390:13
of hell 888:15
o' Hell's hangman's whip .892:18
of his shadow 656:12
of Lord beginning of 792: 2

Fly, *continued*
when we f. them, they pursue 2216: 2
within bead of amber 46:12
Flying 693
amorous f., fond pursuing 2216: 1
came f. all abroad 693:20
Dutchman 2175:12
what pursues 2216: 4
Foam: blew off the f. because unhealthy 852:11
grasp the f. 747:16
new as f. 1515:11
of the grapes 1845:15
on Ocean's f. to sail 440: 3
Fodder in the shock 116:12
whose delight is 519:20
Foe
See also Enemy
and more than a f. 1045:10
arm us 'gainst f. 1598:16
avowed, erect, manly f. ..219: 7
base insulting f. 542: 3
call no man f. 149:11
dares not praise a f. 1576:11
each brave f. a friend ..734: 3
fear no f. in armor 542:18
from f. comes good 734:16
has knock'd under 1322:11
homely f. 542:12
I was angry with my f. 78:13
lodge their deadliest f. ...2273: 3
met dearest f. in heaven ..543:10
ne'er find nobler f. 543: 9
neither seeks nor shuns f. 542: 3
never made themselves f. ..733:22
no man's f. but his own ..1615:12
no man's f. else 544: 9
of mice as well as men 452:13
of tyrants, friend to man 2048:17
open f. may prove curse ..733:20
rush'd to meet insulting f. 2073: 3
that comes with fearless eyes 225: 2
that hurts not 735:11
they come! they come 544: 5
tim'rous f. 13:12
to God ne'er friend to man 735:12
unrelenting f. to love 715:15
was folly, weapon wit 568:13
we lose a f. 31: 2
whom I would wish friend 733:11
yourself your greatest f. ..544:14
Foeman's: spills foremost f. life 1598: 6
Foemen worthy of steel 543: 9
Fœnum habet in cornu 78: 4
Foes: admiring f. 734: 6
by my f. I profit 112:17
cruel f. their peace molest 2273: 3
fouls hands with dirty f. 541:19
greatly his f. he dreads ..733:11
in the forum 735: 8
of his own household 542:12
tell me I am an ass 112:17
thrice he routed all his f. .173:14
whom he laughs at 735: 3
wish them to stay 542: 9
worst of public f. 2143: 3
worthy f. 543: 9
Fog 694
as black as Acheron 694:10
comes on little cat feet 694: 8
in my throat 387: 9
not dispelled with fan 694: 5
of dilettantism 341: 4
of man's mind 1309:18
rubs back on window-panes 694: 7
the magician 694: 4
wisp of f. 1144:13
yellow f. came creeping down 694:11
Fogs: fen-suck'd f. 353:15
Foi dans la bouche des rois 1040:12
je n'y adjouste point de f. 619:14
qui m'assurait de Dieu 151:10
Foibles: in a stranger 651:15
Foil: put it to the f. 652: 8
to set it off 1686: 6
Foining o' nights 1686: 7
Fol: une fois f. 702: 3
Fold: but one f. 1810:18
Foliage: October's f. yellows 1425: 7
Folie: qui vit sans f. 701:23
Folies: courtes f. meilleures 695: 1
Folio of four pages 1601: 2
Folk: let f. bode weel 110: 8
merry f. who give pleasure .9: 2
simple labouring f. 2233: 8
you poor f. in cities 1026: 5
Folks are better than angels 1481:15a
are sure to tumble 255:17
hae done their best 1956:13
let white f. rule it 2285: 7
old f. at home 907: 2
ten thousand dollars for the f. back home 2295:10
that ride a bit of blood ...942:15
young f. are smart 22:10
Follies: all f. alike did seem 695:18
fight against yourself 656: 4
into what new f. run 1789:17
knows f. in youth 695: 3
laid him low 205:11
may cease with youth 2264:14
mimic f. of a farce 1911: 9
miscalled crimes 695: 9
not so much as hint at f. ..219: 7
of the wise 701:22
or crimes of others 2266: 1
others' f. teach us not ...596: 6
shift f. on another's head ..695:14
shortest f. are the best 695: 1
sprang from generous blood 227:13
that are amusing 227:15
that themselves commit ..1179:18
travel faster than coach ..695: 5
whipt with own f. 595: 7
youthful f. 35:12
Follow as night the day ..2058:16
I f., f. still 109:11
if they run we f. 542: 9
it and it will f. thee 2216: 4
never f. anything 1607:18
Oh, f., f., f. me 2154: 1
some must f. some command 1565: 4
thou shalt win 2154: 1
throughout the world 664: 3
thy nose 1413:15
to f. thou art bound 944:12
with truth and loyalty 664: 3
young Lord Paris 1095: 3
Followed when he walked before 1095: 3
Follower of the sun 1944: 6
Followers: more f. than thief 596: 8
Follows but for form 1794: 5
that which f. ever conforms 225:25
Folly 694
accounted dangerous f. ...811:15
adding f. to our pain 1490:21
all they taught me 2195:13
always loathes itself 696: 1
and ignorance 958:13
and innocence so alike 989: 9
anger and f. walk cheek ..80: 2
at full length 694:14
born moment after woman 2189: 8
chief disease 695: 8
cloak of knavery 699:21
common curse of mankind 958:13
covering discretion with f. 456: 7
current f. proves ready wit 2171:12
dram of f. in mixture 701:23
enjoys the f. of fray 858: 6
fathomless abyss of f. 695: 2
fills the town 1602:13
grows without watering ...695: 8
harmless f. of the time ..1284: 1
helped her to heir 138: 9
if f. grow romantic 2198: 6
in a mean man 702: 1
in reputation for wisdom ..693: 1
in youth is sin 695: 3
is a butt for all 695:16
is f. then so old 2189: 8
is low, abject 696: 2
Folly, *continued*
is pursuit of happiness 696: 5
little f. desirable 702: 4
long a doing 351:18
loves martyrdom of fame 625:15
more followers than discretion 694:16
none exempt from f. 698:17
not to be fool 699: 6
of others ridiculous 695: 5
of our pursuits 1145: 2
of the Farce is done 390:13
of world confounds wisdom 701:20
often goes beyond bounds 1260: 4
often sick of itself 696: 1
passed with youth away ..2079: 8
prettiest word 696: 5
profit by f. of others 596: 3
rival f. of credulity 334: 6
self-chosen misfortune 695:13
self-pleasing F. 695: 6
shoot f. as it flies 1251:13
sprinkle f. among neighbors 1324:21
superfluous f. 703: 2
that ever love did make ..1181: 6
that seeks through evil ..540: 6
'tis f. to be wise 959:22
to be wives 2137: 8
to complain of wind 2151:17
to expect men to do all 592:14
to flee from f. wisdom ..2163: 4
vain laughter of f. 701: 1
where human f. sleeps 829: 1
which you think wit 2172: 4
who lives without f. 701:23
whom F. pleases 695:17
would F. ere be taught ..1609:11
yet do not my f. reprove 2199: 2
Folly's: in F. cup still laughs 695:17
slave 24: 6
Fond: I am too f. 1214:12
if we grow f. they shun us 2216: 2
none more f. than she ..2216: 5
of setting things to rights 1684:10
so f. are mortal men 1749: 7
thing vainly invented 995: 1
too f. to rule alone 13:12
Fonte ancor vicino è torbino cosi 1660: 3
de f. leporum surgit amari aliquid 1511:10
Fontes ipsi sitiunt 1987: 8
Food
See also Eating
alike for worms 383:12
always choose plainest f. 872:10
beauty buys no f. 128:16
but no appetite 88:16
crops the flowery f. 1067:14
doth choke the feeder 519: 7
earth's true f. for men ..1952:20
enjoyment for healthy ...517:19
fair fancy's f. 634:17
feed me with f. convenient 1329: 2
fills the wame 494:12
for powder 1863:10
for Roman Emperors 521:14
for soul in cultivating mind 1312: 5
for the gods 521:14
for the soul 1108: 2
hard f. for Midas 801:18
human nature's daily f. .2186: 7
hungry man's f. 2017: 4
judge of wholesome f. 184:11
make not flesh your f. ..524:17
most delicious f. 2186: 2
not f. but content 449: 4
nothing to eat but f. 1414: 9
nourish with vegetable f. 524:17
nourished by the sickly f. ..90:21
of Acheron 376: 8
of study and learning 1096: 3
of sweet and bitter fancy .634:17
one's f. another's poison ..516: 8
sweet f. of knowledge 1057:11
'tis not the f. 449: 4
to restore strength 518:14
what f. thickets yield 1388:15

Food, *continued*
which gives new appetite ..89: 1
win his f. from desert rude 1502:13
worms' f. fine end of living 2244:17
Foods: support life by tasteless f. 1510:19
Fool 696
a madman, an ass 2281: 1
always finds a greater 14: 3
among knaves 700:18
and his money 1332: 4
and his words 2219: 9
and knave with different views 699:20
and wise man alike 701:16
announced himself wise ..702: 6
any f. can carry on 701: 7
any f. can destroy trees ..2037: 8
any f. can make a rule ...820:17
answer f. according to his folly 702:11
at fifty a f. 26:11
at forty 699:10
at woman's service 700:16
athletic f. 590:13
be merciful to me, a f. ..1595: 4
beckons f. 696:18
beholdeth only beginning ..148: 2
better a witty f. 2174:11
better f. than knave 700:13
between f. and sage 25:15
bigger f. than you look 697:19
blind f., Love 1179:18
bray f. in a mortar 698: 1
call me not f. 697: 5
can dance without fiddle ..697: 3
can not sit still 696:17
choose f. for wife 2139: 1
cometh into Market to be seen 2256: 5
consistent 1457: 5
contends that God is not 755:12
Court f.: the plaintiff ..1090:16
digests philosophy into folly 2069:11
disease incurable 697:11
doth his business 455:19
doth think he is wise 703: 3
drop into thyself and be f. 1765:14
dull moral f. 1117:10
eats till sick 520: 3
every f. is not a poet 1528: 9
every f. will be meddling 1284:12
fiddle to the company 697: 3
finds a bigger f. 696:13
first step toward wisdom ..701:21
fortune's f. 717:13
from want of sensibility ..697: 9
getting ready to live 1130:12
gilded f. 1569: 6
gives counsel 697:18
gives good advice 18: 9
gives good counsel 697: 4
God Almighty's f. 705:12
great f. better dancer 362: 4
great way f. 240:11
greater f. greater liar 1112:18
greatest f. may ask 1969: 8
happy he knows no more 702: 8
hath f. in his sleeve 699: 2
hath said in his heart ..114:13
he is a f., shun him 1060: 5
heart of f. in mouth 876: 8
he who at fifty is a f. 699:10
he's a f. that marries ..1266:17
hid in inconsistencies 305: 8
holding peace, wise 1822:17
honesty's a f. 916: 2
I am a f., I know it 2174:11
I met a f. i' the forest ...698: 5
I'm a ding-dang f. 80: 6
I'm a f. for thinking 1996:13
if f. she'll wed knave 699:20
in fashion 698:15
in his devotions 114: 9
in three letters 697:17
inherits, wise get 985: 5
is he that comes to prate 1595: 5
is he that shadows seeks ..2159: 5
it isn't every f. fit 1112:19
Fool, *continued*
known by his tongue 699:18
knows more in own house ..701: 4
let a f. hold his tongue ..1822:17
let gulled f. war pursue ..2113: 7
let me play the f. 1318: 2
lies here 513:15
lunatic lean-witted f. 698: 6
make a f. of himself 2265: 8
make money, wise to spend 1336:13
marry a f. 1266:17
may ask more questions ..702:13
may guide wise man 701: 5
may throw stone in well ..701: 2
me no fools 696:14
me to top of my bent 281:20
moral f. 1346: 4
more f. more knave 831: 6
more hope of a f. 294:16
motley f. 698: 5
must now and then be right 1727: 7
neglect merit, admire f. ..1299:14
never f., never wise 703:10
no f. like an old f. 699:11
no f. silent over cups 504:13
noble f. never in fault 72: 3
none is f. always 699: 3
none so busy as f. 700:10
not a f. who holds his tongue 1820:16
not altogether a f. 703: 5
now and then be right 697: 4
only f. in the world 698:20
of fate, man 1238:10
of nature 697: 1
often fails 612: 5
one f. in every couple ...1263:10
or a physician 700:21
part of f. to give advice ..19:19
perseveres in error 576:17
persist in folly 700:22
play f. at cheaper rate 418: 5
play f. in own house 698: 7
play'd the f. 1784:11
possessed of talent 1022:23
praise f., water folly 1576:21
prosperous f. heavy load .696:11
resolved to live a f. 2226: 1
returneth to his folly 698: 1
sees faults of others 651: 8
sees not same tree 700:24
sees only mischiefs past ..2168:18
selfish smiling f. 700:23
shall not enter heaven 703:14
smarts so little 697:21
so wise a sermon made ..1595: 4
so yoked by a f. 1181: 7
some people all the time ..421: 2
speaks naught but proverbs 1627:11
squint-eyed f. 564:16
strong f. breasts flood 697:16
talent, never judgment ..1022:23
tells secrets because f. ..1784: 6
that eats till he is sick 1595: 4
that far is sent 2030:16
that makes doctor heir 465:15
that provokes a woman ..2203: 8
that wears title lies 2016:13
that will endanger body 1203:15
that will forget himself ..1794:10
the more f. I 2031:10
there is a greatest f. 696:16
there was 2217: 6
to give advice 19:19
to his master 1969:17
to make me merry 595:11
to play f. be learned man .700:13
to reason with a f. 698: 9
trust wild f. and woman ..2196:16
very scandalous thing 696:11
walketh in darkness 701:12
wanders, wise man travels 2028:12
wasp-stung, impatient f. 2025: 9
weak f. turns his back 697:16
what a f. honesty is 916: 4
what f. invented kissing 1047:17
when we play the f. 697:13
who feels the pulse 700: 2
Fool, *continued*
who thinks himself wise ..702: 6
who tried to hustle East ..513:15
will laugh at nought 1076:15
wisest f. in Christendom ..701:18
with judges 705:10
would needs be virtuous .2094: 9
you silly old f. 206:12
you're a sweet little f. ..1215: 7
Fool's bolt is soon shot 689:16
Fool's-cap: deserves a f. ..695:12
Fool's Paradise 703
Foolery: as much f. as I have 703: 5
little f. governs world 818: 2
shines everywhere 696: 3
wise men have 703: 3
Fooling: she is f. thee 318: 4
Foolish: better f. with all ..701:19
if others had not been f. ..694:13
never f. that was fair 138: 9
never says a f. thing 244: 7
once f. never wise 702: 3
things of the world 701: 8
to pluck out one's hair 848:20
when he had not pen 805: 2
wiser and more f. 27:14
Foolishness excommunicates world 698: 2
with God 2167:14
Fools admire 702: 7
afraid of what knaves invent 749:14
all men are f. 698:20
all the f. in town 699: 1
ambition's honour'd f. 48:13
and babes tell true 2057: 6
and knaves 699:20
and knaves better paid ...434:14
and poets run ahead 702: 2
and wise equally harmless 701:17
and wise men 700:21
April f. 93: 1
are fond o' flittin' 2031: 8
are mad, if left alone 2215: 9
are made for jests 697: 2
are my theme 1757:10
are never uneasy 697: 6
are not mad folk 698: 6
are stubborn in their way 1424: 2
beans in flower f. in power 93: 1
bite one another 701:19
book-learnèd f. 1676:13
bubbled f. 1500:10
by heavenly compulsion .1915:10
cannot hold tongue 699:16
caught with silken shows 696:20
choose f. for their wives 2139: 1
conceal their open wounds 2247:22
consult interpreters 479: 4
count themselves wise 702: 6
create new appetites 1328: 3
decoyed into our condition 1272: 2
ever since the Conquest ..72: 4
fanatic f. 633:15
fill world with f. 696: 9
flannelled f. at wicket 754:13
for arguments use wagers 97: 7
fortune favors f. 717:11
game which knaves pursue 700:11
give f. their gold 638:16
grow without watering 697: 3
hated by f., f. to hate 867: 9
have fortune 697: 5
have itching to deride 697: 8
have their own Paradise ..704: 2
how many f. to make a public 1481:20
if all f. wore white caps ..699: 2
let f. the studious despise 1057: 6
live poor to die rich 1770: 8
make a mock at sin 1828: 9
make the banquets 659: 3
make the text 1690: 2
maketh wise men f. 366:20
making f. than lovers 319: 1
may not speak wisely 703: 3
men called f. in one age 1059: 6
mere f. or good physicians 700:21
more f. than knaves 700: 4
mostly f. 562:13

Fools, *continued*
name of loyalty divide 456: 4
never perceive ill-timed ..696:18
none but f. will dally 711:12
of art and memory 25:18
of fortune 2035: 4
of our own woes 698:18
of present 1739: 5
old f., bigger f. 699:12
old men are f. 22:13
one of love's April f. ..1908:15
one-half the world f. 266: 9
out of favor 915:14
petty f. of rhyme 1982:15
play f. with time 703: 4
prate of right and wrong 700: 1
prov'd plain f. at last 344: 1
rush in 697:22
set out f., and return so ..2030:16
set stools 701: 2
suckle f. 2180:19
tedious old f. 35:15
tell commonly truth 2057: 6
thankful for the f. 698:11
they are f. who roam 906:13
this great stage of f. 164: 5
to keep own contrive 752: 3
to make a public 1481:20
to talking ever prone 699:16
trifling with literary f. ..1015: 6
what f. these mortals be 699: 7
what gift to f. avails 776: 6
when f. pipe he may dance 227: 6
who came to scoff 1590: 8
who have wit troublesome 2173: 5
who kiss and tell 2027: 3
will still be f. 697: 7
wise in affairs of women ..701:15
you will always be f. 562:19
Foolscap: every leaf turned to f. 2255: 8
Foot 704
advancing his firm f. 1030:13
and hand go bare 45: 1
best f. forward 704:20
better bare f. than none ..704: 9
better f. before 704:20
better to go on f. than ride and fall 1651: 5
black ox hath trod on f. 1442:15
chancellor's f. 1090: 5
crow's f. is on her eye ..1442:15
deformity of which 212: 2
dish yer rabbit f. 1226:16
feeble of f. 26: 9
forty-second F. 1099: 6; 1654:18
from the f., Hercules 704:10
fuddled f. 502:18
god-like f. there trod 1261:17
gotten God by the f. 785: 8
her f. speaks 318:13
his very f. has music in't 1213: 5
home with staggering f. ..502:10
in no wise faint of f. 176:10
inaudible and noiseless f. of time 2006: 8
is on my native heath ..1372:12
is upon a hero 896:10
it featly 361: 4
lazy f. of Time 2008: 4
less prompt 32:12
loose f. of the wanderer ..2102: 7
more light 140: 9
must not put my f. amiss 170:17
noiseless f. of time 2006: 8
noiseless falls f. of time 2007: 9
on cradle, hand on distaff 2205: 4
one f. he centred 2244: 6
one f. in flannels 2139: 5
one f. in sea and one on shore 1201:15
one f. in the ferry boat 826: 5
one f. in the grave 826: 5
prettiest f. 705: 4
set but a f. 353:13
set my f. on 's neck 1193:14
set not f. to make blind ..1036:13
sets f. upon a worm 729: 1
silent as f. of time 2006: 8
so light a f. 705: 1

Foot, *continued*
sow'd them [flowers] with her odorous f. 704:13
spurn him with his f. 2073: 5
stamped her angry f. ..1898:16
stood a spell on one f. ..2213: 7
to each f. its own shoe ..1817: 2
use another's f. to kick a dog 1651:13
went up with thwack 1034:12
whenever I stamp my f. ..983: 2
with sportive f. to beat the earth 495:13
with staggering f. 502:10
withdraw thy f. from neighbor's house 1396:10
Foot-ball: base f. player ...754:13
Foot-in-the-grave young man 705:15
Foot-licker: for aye thy f. 1801:17
Foote: ever-laughing F. 9: 1
Footed the streets, bills ...1654:10
Footfall, footfall 439: 5
eve's silent f. steals 1914: 9
Foothold: mortis'd in granite 399: 1
Footing: missed her f. 1740: 7
Footman cannot swear like a lord 1951:12
Footpath to Peace 1475:12
Footprints directed towards thy den 704:11
of departed men 383: 4
of their age 1600:11
Nature's f., light and fleet 105: 2
on the sands of time 588:13
Footstep: more than face ..588:13
furthest f. never strayed ..2070:19
slow and noiseless f. 770: 7
where thy f. gleams 484: 3
Footsteps of a throne 1999: 6
of illustrious men 588:19
of the master 636:17
Footstool: earth is my f. ..511:22
my f. earth 1606:10
of humility 937: 5
of the stronger kind 2181:12
of virtues 323: 4
Footways laurel-strewn ...1731: 1
Fop 705
cherishes heart of a f. 763: 7
recommend another 706: 3
solemn f. 705:10
some fiery f. 505:12
their passion 318: 9
Fopperies: has death his f. 377: 7
Foppery atones for folly ..705:11
of the world 1915:10
Fopplings grin to show ..2250:16
Fops help nature's work ...705:12
positive persisting f. 1686: 3
For: I am for you 747: 7
we are for you 1640:14
Forbear: bear and f. 709:15
Forbearance ceases to be virtue 1462:23
pray'd me oft f. 1331:18
Forbearing: by long f. ...1490:10
Forbid us, that desyren we 1617:12
Forbidden because hurtful 1617:13
fruit sweetest 1617:12
have secret charm 1617:17
striving for things f. 1617:17
wanted because f. 12: 2
Force 706
always room for man of f. 1574: 9
and fraud cardinal virtues 2108:12
because persuasion fails ..765:11
brute f. 1679: 9
driven by the same f. 383:15
finds a way 706:19
from f. must ever flow ..1709:13
is not a remedy 706:11
is of brutes 324:21
joint f. of all 129:12
Life F. 1240:17
move us to gentleness 765:13
music's f. tame beast 1363: 2
natural f. abated 37: 8
no f. can bend me 423: 8
no f. however great 706:20
of arms 706:12

Force, *continued*
of merit 199:11; 1299: 6
of necessity irresistible ..1391:19
of words to know men ..2219:22
opulent f. of genius 1158: 3
overcome by f. 706:12
present he is a f. respected 1489:15
such f. should fight 1775:12
surpris'd by unjust f. 2091: 9
virtue's f. 716:14
we love f. 706:14
what f. cannot, fraud shall 706:13
who overcomes by f. 706:17
without fore-cast 706:15
works on servile natures ..706:16
Force et le droit règlent ..1303:16
supporter maux d'autrui 1322:15
Forces: bring all f. 2215:10
centripetal and centrifugal f. 1263: 2
opposing and enduring f. 1842: 4
Forcible: how f. are right words 2222: 9
Forcibly if we must 58: 1
Fore-spurrer: this f. 1209: 9
Forefathers: all same number of f. 73: 8
rude f. of the hamlet 829: 3
Forefinger of all Time 1520:12
Forehead: brazen f. 1554: 9
gate of the mind 1306: 8
God-like f. 1735: 7
instantly your f. lowers ..1008: 6
low, receding f. 2297: 1
of man 335: 7
of our faults 1083:19
of the fool 354: 4
of the morning sky 1939:12
profound his f. was 283:15
with unbashful f. 37:18
Foreheads of Islam bowed as one 1449:13
villainous low 2085:13
Foreigners 707
are contemporary posterity 707: 5
excel in dancing 360:18
spell better than pronounce 707:12
Foreknowledge absolute 100:11
Forelock: occasion's f. 1432: 3
take time by the f. 1432: 9
Foreman takes out his watch 1026:16
Foremost leads herd 588:16
Forenoon, afternoon, night 1138: 7
wear out good wholesome f. 1094: 1
Foresight
See also Prudence
half as much f. 2168:18
Forest
See also Woods
below London Bridge 1983: 9
is long time growing 2210: 9
is my loyal friend 1384: 6
looks as nightingales 2210:17
this is the f. primeval 2210: 8
who can impress the f. ..2210:10
Foresters: Diana's f. 580: 5
Forests and enchantments drear 510:17
if I cannot carry f. 1962: 2
of America delight to God 2211:1a
thousand f. one acorn 1238: 4
with shadowy f. riched ..2211: 3
wond'ring f. dance again 1877:10
Forever and a day 2:13
but I go on f. 200:16
do you want to live f. 67: 5
it may be f. 1454: 6
man has F. 1132:10
never, f. 2103: 7
'tis a single word 1409: 3
vast F. 387: 3
Forewarned, forearmed ..1597:20
forearmed 2120:14
Forge: flaming f. of life ..1128: 7
guilty f. of vain conceit ..294:20
one who at the f. 1854:10
quick f. of thought 1991: 3
Forget because we must ..707:14
best sometimes f. 708:21
better by far f. and smile 1297:14

Forget, *continued*
cannot f. things 1297:17
cannot quite f. me 711: 4
don't f. your mother 2293:10
expedient to f. 708:20
me not 731:22
forgive and f. 711: 1
go, f. me 709: 5
hardest science to f. 1199: 4
I shall not f. 1297:16
I'll not f. you, darling 636:15
if I f. thee, O Jerusalem ..708:19
if thou wilt, f. 405: 7
knew we should both f. ..1455:12
lest we f. 545:11
oneself is to be happy 857:17
source that keeps it filled 708:12
that I remember 1297: 9
thee—if to dream 708:15
thee, never 709: 2
them, or forgive 652: 3
thou shalt not f. 708: 3
thy self to Marble 708:13
we never do f. 708: 4
we shall all f. 708: 5
were it not better to f. ..1297:13
what grief I should f. 843:19
Forget-me-not: blue f. 689: 5
Forget-me-nots of angels ..1912:11
Forgetful of your own kin 708:16
Forgetfulness 707
enshaded in f. divine 1844:14
find f. in thine 708: 2
grows over it like grass ..708:22
life's last balm 707:15
makes life possible 1297:10
not in entire f. 164:10
of grief I yet may gain ..1196:11
privilege of dead 391: 2
sweets of f. 581:13
to dumb f. a prey 386: 3
Forgets: taught, he ne'er f. 1244: 7
Forgetting: if this thou call'st f. 708:15
my people 708: 7
no such thing as ultimate f. 708: 4
sleep and a f. 164:10
woman's greatest art 2190: 2
Forgive and forget 711: 1
but don't forget 2282: 5
do not quite f. giver 774:14
enemies their virtues 710:16
everyone is cruelty 709:12
father, f. them 709:21
good to f. 711: 2
how many will say, "f." ..710:15
I f., you can't help self ..709:13
I f. you, you f. me 709: 8
makes powerful 710: 6
more noble to f. 1711: 9
others often, self never ..590:10
our friends 733:15
she knows not to f. 2204: 1
that you may be forgiven ..710: 7
they who f. most 709: 7
to err human, to f. divine 577: 2
to f. is beautiful 710: 6
to understand is to f. 710:11
Forgiven and forgotten between us 711: 4
come back and be f. 710: 1
Forgiveness 709
best revenge 1711: 9
better than revenge 710: 3
man's f. give and take ..709:16
to injured doth belong 986:17
who asks f. should give ..709:18
Forgives everything, f. nothing 710:11
readily invites offense 709:12
Forgo me now, come to me soon 318:11
Forgot: but thou art not f. 4: 9
in your sweet thoughts f. ..405:10
more than we remember 1297:11
that thou couldst mortal be 402:13
to quite forget 708:11
was Britain's glory 1178:18
Forgot, *continued*
what "No" meant 708:10
you f. to remember 1881: 5
Forgotten even by God ...611:16
if you've f. my kisses 709: 1
inside of a church 271:13
learned nothing and f. nothing 304: 3
must have f. myself 708:10
of all men altogether 392:14
Forgotten Man 2281: 8
Foris ut mos est 355: 7
Fork commonly rake's heir 985:17
with f. I will scatter 985:17
Forked: a f. one 1203:14
Forks: fingers made before 521:12
Form better than face 148:11
fain would I dwell on f. ..293: 9
finer f. or lovelier face 140: 9
formal with your f. 1655: 1
had not lost brightness ..444:14
heaven-labour'd f. 176: 9
his dear f. she never saw 2289: 5
his f. was ponderous 2165:10
human f. divine 175: 9
is the Golden Vase 1926: 4
it seemed to hide 488: 1
of life and light 139: 2
of manliest beauty 1778: 4
repeat f. of progenitors 69:10
semblance of f. divine 132: 2
so fair 2185: 7
stanzaic f. 2277: 2
thou, most awful F. 1355:15
wear another f. 399:15
what is f., what is face 85:10
Forma bonum fragile est ..137: 1
dei munus 128: 5
egregia f. 141: 5
grataque f. sua est 140: 3
in f. pauperis: sue 1584: 8
magna pudicitiæ 137:13
nulli non sua f. placet ..2192: 5
nullo exercente senescit ..138: 5
raram cum sapientia f. ..138: 7
raro admodum f. 137:13
virginibus grataque f. est .779: 3
viros neglecta decet 491: 2
Formalities: get f. right ..1920: 5
Formality: prim f. 1177: 6
Formarum: cottidianarum harum f. 2181: 4
Formas: cui placet impares F. 2077:14
Format: we like the little f. 189: 8
Formicæ sua bilis inest 693: 9
tendunt ad inania 736:12
Formosa fores minus 132:17
Formosam quamlibet illa facit 1224: 6
Formosos sæpe inveni pessimos 86:11
Formosum Pastor Corydon 1522:13
Forms as fair as Eve's ..1496:13
beyond f. of faith 617:17
for f. of government let fools contest 814: 3
O sacred f. 1354: 4
of ancient poets 615: 7
outward f. inward man reveal 85:10
that once have been 1459: 7
Formula for greatness 831: 4
which expresses 1390:12
Formulas: cased in f. 1861: 5
clear myself of f. 946:18
Fors æqua merentes 712:18
et virus miscentur 228: 6
quem F. dierum dabit ..749:10
quod f. feret 229: 4
Forsaken his sins 1829: 6
Forschers: Der Blick des F. 352:11
Forster, John P.: fat-frier 2281: 5
Forsworn on "mere necessity" 1393:16
Fort: deliver up our f. ...1935: 8
give up the f. 63: 3
hold the f., I am coming ..65:10
in this blemish'd f. 1934:11
truth's f. laugh shall win 1078:11
Forte più che il morire 1146:13
Fortes adjuvat ipsa venus ..717: 6
creantur fortibus 324: 2
etiam f. subitis terreri 655: 6
in fine consequendo 766: 8
vivite 325:12
Forth: mazy F. unravelled 1734: 2
Fortis: invidiam ferre f. potest 565:19
re secunda f. est 1626: 7
Fortiter ille facit qui miseresse potest 1935: 7
in re 766: 8
Fortitude is loyalty 322: 6
Fortitudo contemptrix timendorum 323: 3
pro æquitate 322: 7
Fortress: a mighty f. is our God 784: 2
I can march up to f. 2212: 8
no f. too strong for money 1334: 7
Forts of folly fall 611:11
Fortuitous combination 274: 1
concourse of atoms 6:12
Fortuna arbitriis tempus ..229:13
audentis juvat 717: 3
brevis est magni f. 429: 2
cui f. secunda est 736:10
cum blanditur 712: 8
cum maribus immutatur 1611:17
dura vocat 715:16
efficit cæcos complexa 713: 2
ex humili ad fastigia extollit 714: 2
facimus F. deam 714:10
fortes metuit 177:18
fortis adjuvat 717: 4
humana fingit 714:13
in nos incurrit 712:10
in omni re dominatur 714: 4
magna servitus magna f. 1723: 9
maximis virtutibus F. parcit 17: 9
minimum eripit F. 1568:10
minor in parvis furit 715:10
miserrima est f. quæ inimico caret 543: 1
miserrima tuta est 1754: 4
multis dat nimis 712: 5
multos f. liberat poena ..1657: 4
non est tuum, f. quod fecit tuum 228:18
non mutat genus 1332:16
obesse nulli contenta est semel 711: 7
omnis f. ferendo est 541: 7
opes auferre 712:12
plus quam consilium valet 714:15
quam nemo videt 711: 8
quem vult perdere 1232: 4
quidquid in altum 714: 5
quod fecit tuum 712:11
quod non dedit f., non eripit 712:11
raro virtutibus F. parcit ..715: 9
regum casus rotat 714:17
si f. juvat, nihil laboris ..1625:12
stultum facit 717:12
velox F. 713:18
viris invida fortibus 715: 9
vitrea est 713:17
Fortunæ: cætera F., non mea, turba 736:10
cetera mando 712: 6
ex mediocritate f. 1329: 5
facere cedere magnæ f. ..1336: 9
filius 711:20
in f. qui casibus omnia ponant 114: 4
solent mutarier 713:13
Fortunam atque obsequentem 712: 7
bene ferre discam 716:16
citius reperias 712: 9
extra f. donatur amicis ..773:15
intra f. debet 311:19
posteraque in dubio est f. 2022:12
potest cavere 712:12
quod mihi f., si non uti ..1335:14
raro simul bonam f. bonam mentem 712: 3
reventur habe 711: 5
ut tu f. 1625: 4

Freedom, *continued*
from her mountain height 673:11
glory of the state 433: 3
hallows with her tread 724:13
has thousand charms 724:14
he ever warr'd with f. ..766:12
he only earns his f. 725: 9
he sighs for f., she power 1255: 3
is a noble thing 722: 4
is pursuing own good 722: 9
is the pledge of all 724:14
justice reigns, f. to obey 1028:19
let f. ring 51:12
let idea of f. go to seed ..2069:14
love not f. but licence 724: 4
lovers of f. free 723:11
makes old brave 724: 7
mistaking for f. paper preamble 974:12
needs all her poets 725:12
ne'er overcome by force ..724:10
new birth of f. 432: 1
New F. 1558: 6
no f. who deny to others ..724: 1
no f. without virtue 723: 1
not caprice 722: 5
not f. where all command ..723: 3
not fair young girl 722: 6
O F., if to me belong 725:17
of a freeborn people 725: 7
of old sat F. on heights ...724:21
of speech 726: 1
of the press 53: 8
of the will 2149: 7
of thought 52: 5; 1992:15
once thy flame hath fled ..725:13
only in land of dreams 724: 6
our pain 723:14
political power in fragments 723: 4
pray you use your f. 1685: 2
princes owe people 1610:19
re-created year by year ..723: 7
regained f. with a sigh 723:13
retained by acquiescence .2064: 7
right to live as we wish ..722: 9
shrieked as Kosciusko fell 725: 8
sober-suited F. chose 552:11
suckled by f. 724:20
suppressed 723:13
sweetest f. honest heart ..723:17
takes care of government 723: 9
their battle-cry 725: 4
those who deny f. to others 1842: 5
to slave, f. to free 1841:11
to think 1992:20
to worship God 1501: 9
unchartered f. 725: 1
under government 814: 8
upon the seas 1471:17
use your f. 724: 3
waste the gifts of F. 55:12
what avail if f. fail 53: 9
what is f. 723: 7
where bastard F. waves ..675: 5
while state exists no f. ..1918:9a
who stands if F. fall 551:11
work out your f. 724: 9
Freedom's banner streaming .673:11
oak forever thrive 304: 7
thou art F.'s now 1373:13
Freehold of Content 310: 3
Freeman: better mortal f. than immortal slave ..1840: 5
of nature 433: 3
thou art Nature's f. 211: 5
whom truth makes free . 2052:11
with unpurchased hand ..2098:17
Freemason for secrecy 1417:12
Freemasonry of genius 760: 5
Freemen: Come, F., come! 2116: 3
worst slaves 1839:11
Freewill: Necessity and F. 1689: 6
settle F. by vote 2022: 7
Freeze beneath the Pole ..1570: 8
thou bitter sky 984:15
Freezes up heat of life 658: 3
Freight: of value is thy f. ..52: 4
Freiheit Reich der Träume 724: 6
von der F. gesäugt 724:20
Frein au scélérat 788: 1
French all slaves 721: 2
and Russian matter not ..767: 3
disguise their shapes 720:22
dislike F. from vulgar antipathy 721: 9
distribute medals 720:14
faithful in love of change..720: 7
give laws for pantaloons ..641:11
give praise to F. ladies ..1453:14
Guards never fire first 2108:11
have F. for friends 720:10
how frantically acted 61: 2
language of insincerity ..720:18
leave: take F. leave 1257:18
seems fool and is wise 702:16
she spake full fair 720:15
smutty and contemptible ..720:20
speech of clear, cheerful ..720:17
to smatter F. meritorious 1069:11
who think 559: 3
wiser than they seem 2162: 6
with equal advantage content 285:11
Frenchman always playing to gallery 720: 5
brilliant F. 2098: 6
easy, debonair 720:21
feels an easy mastery 720:16
flippant F. speaks 2098: 5
loves his mother 721: 5
must be always talking ..559: 6
Frenchmen: fifty million F. 721: 3
sin in lechery 560: 5
Freni: non faciunt meliorem equum aurei f. 1718: 6
Freno: fugiunt f. non remorante dies 2006:14
Frenos imponit linguæ conscientia 300:12
Frenzy: demoniac f. 460:14
in fine f. rolling 1535: 3
what f. dictates 1008: 5
Frères: soyons f. 201:19
Fresh as a daisy 1633:14
as an angel 2265: 2
as Dian's visage 1702:16
as flowers in May 1633:14
as month of May 1282:12
as morning rose 1633:14
as paint 1633:14
as rainbow of July 1773: 7
changeful, constant 878:18
Freshness of character 236:12
of the heart can fall 877:10
Freslons: irriter les f. 1663:10
Fret of restless passions ..1887: 3
though you can f. me 973:13
Fretted the pigmy body ..240: 4
Freud and his three slaves 1802: 7
I've been reading F. 479:8a
Freude macht drehend 1016:21
Freuden sondern Hoffnungen aufhören 35: 9
Freunde Eifer 734:17
Friar had goose in sleeve 1985:18
I will be 1338: 3
of orders gray 1338: 5
well as holy f. 1593: 8
Friars and their hoods 1338: 6
Friction: better performed 466: 3
iteration, like f., likely to generate heat 99:16
Friction-matches incendiary 151: 7
Friday fell all mischance ..1945:11
too, the day I dread 1945:14
Friend 726
after f. departs 740: 9
ahoy! Farewell 635:15
all men's f. no f. 726:16
among a hundred 728: 8
and associate of this clay 1893: 9
and brother 202: 4
at a sneeze 1856: 2
be a f. to man 1495: 8
be f. to one 149:11
be slow in choosing f. 728: 6
because it pays 736:15
becomes her lover 745: 7
best f. blundering enemy ..734: 7
best f., bravest enemy 542: 6
Friend, *continued*
better new f. than old foe 735: 4
better one f. than many ..726:15
boyhood's f. hath fallen ..740: 3
candid f. 219: 7
chid away my f. 738:17
constant f. rare 727:13
damned good-natured f. ..739:18
dangerous as ignorant f. ..734: 6
delightful is f. restored .738: 4
down inside of me 1792: 3
everybody's f. but his own 544:12
expell'd the f. 465:14
faithful f.: advice of 995: 9
faithful f. from faltering foe 737: 6
fat f: at house 727:17
firm f. of human kind 1841: 2
forsake not an old f. 738: 1
fortune's f. mishap's foe ..712:21
gain'd from Heaven a f. 730: 1
give and keep your f. 193:10
good f. for Jesus' sake ..1808:10
good f. never offends 731:17
good f. that does thee good 732: 2
good man is best f. 729: 7
grant me f. in my retreat 1872: 1
greatest blessing 730:11
hard found, soon lost 732:16
he is f. that helps me 732: 2
he rose without a f. 733:21
he was my f., faithful and just 732: 3
he who betrays a f. 2032:15
himself and f. the same ...726: 6
hollow f. 734:19
hope of the heart 726: 9
I was angry with my f. 78:13
I would be f. to all 239:10
if thou require soothing ..731:22
in a pinch 737:13
in corner 731:15
in court aye better is 326: 3
in court worth a penny ..1081: 1
in name only 732:12
in need 737:15
indeed help in need 737: 6
is a second self 726:14
judicious f. better 739:10
keep thy f. under key 730:16
keep f., lose your money ..193:10
known in necessity 737: 5
lend and lose your f. 193:10
lies full of rest 405: 6
like a f. He walked 263: 5
long a-getting, soon lost ..732:16
lose f. rather than jest ...739:15
make thine own self f. 1789: 7
make use of ev'ry f. 734: 9
makes no f. no foe 733:22
married f. is f. lost 745: 8
masterpiece of nature 726: 9
may profess yet deceive ..732: 9
medicine of life 726: 7
mine own familiar f. 727:14
more divine than all 729:14
more precious than gold ..731: 2
must hate man injures me 743:13
must not be wounded 739:14
'neath every one a f. 35: 1
neither make f. equal brother 731:21
never do f. dirty trick 150: 1
never lack a f. 734:19
never rais'd themselves f. 733:22
never want f. or bottle ..731:10
new f. as new wine 738: 1
newest f. is oldest f. 738: 5
no f. a f. till he prove ..737:17
no f. like a sister 1833: 9
no good thing unknown to f. 726:18
not a f. in the world 733:22
not a f. to close eyes 621: 8
not one f. to take fortune 621: 8
nothing better than firm f. .731: 2
nothing but heaven better than a f. 730:11
O, be my f. 149:10
of every country but own 1467:13
of man, to vice a foe 1495: 1

Gaul: insulting G. 720:13
Gaunt as wolf of Languedoc 2177:10
Gauntlet of the mob 527:18
with a gift in't 1585:20
Gave: I never g. you aught 775:12
what we g. we have 774: 5
Gawds: new-born g. 1416: 3
Gay as gilded summer sky ..366: 7
as summer morn 366: 7
guiltless pair 162:10
in gems and wanton dress 488: 7
without frivolity 42: 8
Gaze: gone from my g. 3:13
upon her unaware 139: 1
Gazelle: never nursed a g. 452:15
Gazettes and Ledgers swarm 1603: 2
Gazing: by g. to multiply 600:14
Gear: gather g. by every ..973: 2
soon-speeding g. 1540: 7
Geben Sache des Reichen ..772: 5
Gedanken sind zollfrei 1992:15
Gedge, Peter: epitaph 572: 2
Geese
See also Goose
all our g. are swans 813: 7
and gabies 255: 4
are getting fat 271: 2
more g. than swans live 1491:12
old lady picking g. 1857: 8
Rome's ancient g. 813:10
wild g. sailing high 116: 1
with g., women with women 2199:14
Gefallen: vielen g. ist schlimm 1513:12
Geflügelte Worte 2226: 7
Gefühle: herrliche G. 661: 3
Gegenwart mächtige Göttin 1599: 6
Gehalt bestimmt seinen Werth 1125: 8
Gehenna: down to G. 1277:16
Geist, their little friend ...472: 4
Geist: hoher G. in engen Brust 1893: 3
Gelebt und geliebet 1133: 2
Geliebt: lang genug g. ...1217:16
Gem: best g. upon her zone ..95:14
froze into a g. 1858: 5
instinct with music 1073: 5
of earth and sky begotten 445:14
of purest ray serene 1422: 3
of the old rock 69:12
set g. above flower 326:13
that twinkling hangs 1975:14
thou bonie g. 357:12
when others pick it up ..1013: 9
Gemeine: alle bändigt 1288: 7
Gemimus: naturæ imperio g. 1356:18
Geminos anxia mater alit ..1649:12
Gems add grace to thee ..140: 2
have life in them 1013: 6
in g. and wanton dress ..2185: 4
no g., no gold she needs ..138:13
of Heav'n, starry train ..1401:13
of morning dew 1912:15
pave thy radiant way 368:12
rich and rare were the g. 1013:13
winter's crystal g. 2160:15
General came in new tin hat 2110:13
clean hands make real g. 1867: 3
disdained 566: 1
every g. voted himself first 719:15
good g. talks of success ..1867: 3
greatest g. fewest mistakes 1867: 3
is hard to find 1868:5a
sorry it was not a g. 1867: 4
yesterday corporal today 1420: 7
General Deux Sous 977: 9
Generalities: glittering g. ..974:11
spacious liberty of g. 1439: 5
Generalize is to be an idiot 1448:13
Generals: despite your g., prevail 1867:6a
examining our g. 335: 8
out of mud 1867: 3
send a barrel to other g. 1867: 4
who gain successes dictators 1867: 7
wish he would bite other g. 1867: 4
Generation needs regeneration 1686: 9
now descends new g. 261:10
of all things through change 231: 7
on shoulders of g. 1505:15
one g. passeth away 511:18
pride in coming g. 2265: 1
unto third and fourth g. 1830:12
wrong-headed g. 1537: 4
younger g. comes knocking 24: 5
Generations: loud sound of g. 570: 8
no hungry g. tread thee 1405: 3
pass while trees stand ..1348: 7
press on g. 926:13
three g. from shirtsleeves 74: 6
vast g. are come forth ..1024:18
Genere: eo sum g. gnatus ..68:10
indignus g. 74: 8
Generosity
See also Gifts and Giving
flower of justice 777:10
freaks of g. 234:16
good-humor and g. 777:15
never a g. 554: 1
should not exceed means ..777: 6
Generosus: qui est g. 68:13
Generous: few capable of g. 237: 6
forget they have given ..743: 4
is the truly wise 773:12
nothing g. unless just 776:13
pays for what is given ..776:17
pleasant to be g. 777: 8
ready for what is g. 13:10
when he has little 777: 9
Genesis: set you square ..151: 2
Genevieve, sweet Genevieve 1296: 8
Génie: c'est la patience ..757:11
commence beaux ouvrages .762: 8
ist Wahrheits-Liebe 760: 4
Genitum: nec sibi sed totium g. 1496: 3
Genius **757**
an affair of energy 757: 7
and enthusiasm 563: 6
and its rewards 759:19
and talent 761:14
beauty is higher than g. ..129:18
begins great works 762: 8
best plain-set 760: 9
bright and base 762:13
but excites 762: 1
can never despise labour ..758: 1
capacity for evading work 759: 1
capacity for taking pains ..758:12
character above g. 234:15
creates 762: 1
delight of mankind 761: 5
discovered in proverbs ..1627: 9
disease of glands 759: 6
do nothing against one's g. 149:12
does not herd with g. 760: 7
draws up the ladder 760: 3
eagle portion of g. 509: 4
energy which collects 757: 7
European and American g. ..53: 3
evil g. 74:12
excels in expression 758:10
father of heavenly line ..980: 5
fire is g. 759: 5
fit for some peculiar arts 1380: 8
for g. renown endures 760:14
for repose 61: 1
fostered by industry 758: 1
German and a g. 769: 9
goes and Folly stays 760: 2
greatest good and harm ..758: 7
has somewhat of infantine 757: 9
hath electric power 761: 1
highest miracle of g. 761: 8
impatient of harness 758: 9
in a reverend gown 1589:11
in g. rejected thoughts ..758: 5
is a vagabond 2297: 4
is character too 757:10
is essentially creative 759:11
is like gold 757:13
is lonely 758: 6
is master of man 762:11
is nothing but labour 758: 1
Genius, *continued*
is of no country 759:17
is patience 757:11
is predominance of sensibility 759: 9
is religious 758: 5
is with sighing sent 1356:20
life never commonplace to g. 761: 6
man apart 759:13
man who observes grows into g. 757:12
married to science 759:10
master of nature 762: 5
melts many ages into one 761: 4
mind of large powers 759: 3
must be born 758: 3
never drops from skies ..760:10
never g. without madness 761:10
nothing against one's g. 149:12
nothing to declare except g. 760:19
of these lands 2121:13
oft but perseverance 757: 8
one per cent inspiration ..758: 4
only g. can say the banns 1525: 5
power to be boy again 757: 9
power to do right thing ..759: 2
premature g. 760:15
presiding g. of the place 801: 9
proof of g. great poem 1518:12
punished, fame exalted ...760:18
ramp up my g. 218:15
ruined only by itself 760:11
rusts for want of use 760: 6
secret to itself 759:15
see things in advance 761:13
slow of growth 759: 4
so shrinking and rare 868:17
sparkles from eyes 600: 8
survives 760:14
talent of man who is dead 758: 8
talk with man of g. 760:17
thine own g. gave the blow 1710: 1
three fifths of him g. 1514: 8
thus g. rose and set 1305: 9
to make common marvelous 1534: 3
to raise the g. 10: 2
two kinds of g. 761: 7
two sorts possess g. 2253: 9
true g. is but rare 342: 6
unsettles 762: 1
wanting art is dumb 760:12
what an impostor g. is ...761:12
without education 759:10
Genius loci 801: 9
Genius' proud career 343: 4
Geniuses create wonders ..762: 4
greatest g. lie hidden 760:13
in trade 285:16
shortest biographies 758: 6
Genoese: immortal G. 284:13
Genres: tous les g. bons ..1927: 9
Gens d'esprit sont bêtes ..2172:13
les faux honnêtes g. 649:16
pas de g. plus affairés 210: 5
plus honnêtes g. du monde .559: 3
qui ressemblent aux vaudevilles 123: 3
sans bruit dangereux 1821: 4
superstitione obnoxia 1013: 1
Gent: military g. I see ...1863:15
Genteel in personage 1259: 3
no dancing bear was so g. 1259: 9
so exceedingly g. 313: 5
thing is g. 764: 4
Genti: lascia dir le g. 2237: 7
Gentian-flower: blue g. 689: 7
Gentilhomme qui vit mal monstre 764: 9
Gentility: ancient riches 68: 9
no afternoon g. 117: 5
nor stand on your g. 71: 7
stand upon g. 1609: 1
Gentle and merciful and just 1158: 6
as lamb 2141: 9
as zephyrs 766: 5
Craft 1818: 9
in manner 766: 8
is that g. does 766: 7
now we are gentlemen 762:14

Gentle, *continued*
peace to the g. 568: 6
tender, and forgiving 944:15
to others 766: 4
that doth g. deeds 762:15
therefore to be won 2212:13
yet not dull 1983: 5
Gentleman 762
absolute g. 765: 7
affable and courteous g. ..765: 8
all the world over 764: 1
and scholar 763:12
be each, pray God, a g. ...765: 2
bears him like portly g. ..764:13
bees in a concatenation ..764: 4
by creation 764:10
calculating adventurer 763: 7
disposed to swear 1951:18
dunghill g. 764:16
earth bears not so stout a g. 765: 8
fine-paced g. 764: 7
fine puss-g. 1486:18
fineness of nature 763: 9
finished g. top to toe 765: 4
first true g. that ever breathed 261:13
fleshly g. 1927:12
flowering of civilization ..763: 2
frequent in England 763: 1
God Almighty's g. 265:16
grand old name of g. 765:10
I know a discontented g. ..454:12
I'll be sworn thou art ..764:14
is not in your books 462:11
Jack would be a g. 1004: 5
kind and affable 762:14
kinder g. treads not 765: 8
king cannot make a g. 764:10
knows quite enough 765: 3
large-minded g. 1551: 7
learn from Bible to be g. 764: 8
leave world untainted 763: 8
let him storm town 764: 6
lord of himself, inborn g. 1158: 5
make a g. of you 764:12
Manhattan g. 1396:20
may make a king 764: 5
more active-valiant 765: 8
myself one of these days ..764: 2
never inflicts pain 762:15
no g. ought to pay them ...209: 9
no g. weighs over 200 ...648:13
no g. will ask as a favor ..653:14
not essential g. think 763: 4
not gay coat makes g. ..763: 3
of blood and breeding ..764:13
of the first head 764:16
of the press 1604: 3
of very first house 505:15
once a g. always a g. 764: 1
our well-dressed g. 1964:12
stainless g. 765:10
sweeter and lovelier g. 765: 8
travel abroad, dwell home 2028:12
true breeding of a g. ..1259: 8
true g. may swear it 1419: 5
true heroic English g. 558:11
understands self-love 763: 6
very simple g. 916: 4
very valiant g. 999: 8
was fond, lady fair 1325: 5
what's g. but his pleasure ..763: 5
when you've said a g. 763:17
who could calculate eclipse 1008:18
who lives ill a monster 764: 9
who was then the g. 73: 1
written on his brow 763:14
young g. is deceased 411: 6
Gentlemanliness: humanity 762:14
Gentlemen: all g. melancholy mad 1076: 8
by g. for g. 765: 2
can't-be g. 1968: 3
gentlemen's g. 1800: 3
good morning, g. both ..1959: 1
in stays, stiff as stones ...705: 7
most Gothic g. of Spain 70: 3
must risk their skin 1223: 8
no. g. but gardeners 12: 3
Gentlemen, *continued*
of the French Guard 2108:11
of the shade 580: 5
prefer blondes 848:10
two single g. rolled 763:13
unafraid 765: 5
venison in heaven 764:11
who wrote with Ease 2253:12
ye g. of England 1780:14
Gentleness 765
better than violence 765:13
imposed to gentle men 765:12
of all the gods 766: 6
of rain in the wind 1670: 3
strong enforcement be 765:13
this milky g. 766: 5
touch'd with human g. 766: 5
with deeds requite thy g. 1716: 3
your g. shall force 765:13
Gently down hill 931:11
to bear with men 541: 5
Genus et virtus vilior alga 1720: 6
immortale manet 633: 8
irritabile vatum 1537: 4
male voli solatii g. 1320: 7
qui g. jactat suum 68:14
rarum g. 1415: 9
vix nostra voco 70:11
Geographers crowd into maps 2243: 8
in Afric maps 2243: 8
Geography: in America g. sublime 56: 1
Geology, ethnology 620:16
Geometrician: God is a g. 783:14
Geometry: axioms of g. ..1726: 1
no royal road to g. 528: 2
only science 1763:15
George 766
if his name be G. 1376:15
King G. will be able to read that 62: 2
let G. do it 766:14
when G. the third was king 2264:10
George, St.: ever on horseback, yet never rideth ..748: 3
he was for England 585: 8
of Merry England 546: 8
the dragon hath killed 546: 8
George Dandin: vous l'avez voulu 434:17
George Washington: my commander was G. W. 2286: 4
Georges four 766: 9
Georges: laissez faire a G. ..766:14
Georgia: marching through 1878:11
German and a genius 769: 9
life too short to learn G. 769: 7
no little G. state 556: 3
people chosen of God 2147:12
shout for help in G. 769: 6
to the matter 173:10
will claim me as G. 1011:20
Germans are honest men ..769: 8
boors of Europe 768: 9
chosen of God 2147:13
dullest nation G. 995:17
fear God but nothing else ..768: 1
want to be governed 769: 2
Germany 767
diseased world's bathhouse 769:10
hands of men in G. 768: 9
lovely place 769: 5
Germens: all g. spill 1486:13
Germs of good in every soul 334:17
Gerry: Elbridge G. 2280: 5
Gerrymander 2280: 5
Gertrude, Ep and Ein 1377: 1
Geschichte: alte G. immer neu 1206: 8
Geschickes: Willen des G. 644:12
Gesetz: kein G. was hat nicht ein Loch 1085:10
und Rechte: es erben sich 1086: 5
Gestores: pendeant g. linguis 1838:11
Gesture: in every g. dignity 599:19
is too emphatic 1591: 9
Gestus: est quiddam g. edendi 521: 9
Get before forget 708: 6
by giving 773: 9
don't care how, g. it 1622: 4
what you can ..1562: 2; 1997:10
what you desire 1929: 8
Getting and spending 434:15; 2244: 2
with g. get understanding 2066:10
Gettysburg address 432: 1; 1869: 5
Gettysburg: 'tis grown ...628: 8
Get-up: you've got to g. ..1729:10
Ghost 769
alas, poor g. 770:10
applaud the hollow g. 32:12
besprent with April dew ...770: 3
came g. to Marg'ret's door 771: 4
escapes from pyre 966:16
especially the g. 9: 8
gave up the g. 375:15; 1109: 4
giveth up the g. 381: 9
haunted by husband's g. 1910:10
I'll make a g. of him that lets me 770:11
invites my steps and points .770: 3
it is an honest g. 770:13
needs no g. to tell this ..1053: 4
no g. should be allowed ..770:12
of a shadow 478:15
of a summer that lived ..1936: 7
of Hamlet's Father 770:12
of his eternity 1765:13
Scipio's g. walks unavenged 769:11
stubborn unlaid g. 246:12
vex not his g. 392:11
Voltaire's g. 770: 2
who shall be nameless 342: 9
Ghost-writers 2250:12
Ghosts and forms of fright 770: 4
are in very deed, G. 769:16
between the lines 69: 9
dead men's g. do not haunt 388:19
did shriek and squeal ..1946:12
don't believe in g. 770: 2
from an enchanter fleeing 2153:13
make the g. gaze 970: 1
must be all over the country .69: 9
never speak till spoke to ..769:13
of dead renown 630: 7
of defunct bodies 769:15
of our foes are many ..2119: 5
of those that once have been 191:10
shoals of visionary g. 770: 1
troop home to churchyards 1940:12
Ghouls: they are G. 2175:13
Giant 771
brazen g. of Greek fame 1397: 5
Despair 436:14
domestic Irish g. 436:14
fling but stone, g. dies ..590:20
keeps his height 771:11
Little G. 1377:16
loves the dwarf 771: 5
race before the flood 771: 8
this g. of mankind 1158: 9
upon air will live 917: 7
use it like a g. 1922:16
Western g. smiles 550: 9
will starve 771: 7
Giants in the earth 771: 8
in their promises 834:17
to slay 1003:10
work great wrongs 771: 9
Gibbets keep the lifted hand in awe 1359: 4
Gibes: where be g. now ..1010:10
Gibson girl 1644: 7
Giddy: more g. and unfirm 1265:11
thinks world turns 534: 3
Giff-gaff makes friends 772:17
Gift 771
and not an art 312:12
anticipates no return 772:12
April's g. to April's bees ..92:11
back of g. the giving 774: 3
blindeth the wise 776:16
born with g. of laughter 1076: 2
deadly g. of Minerva 777: 5
derives value from rank ..775: 7
destroyeth the heart 776:14
doth stretch itself 20:12

God, *continued*
hath said what shall betide 2022: 1
hath share in little house 906: 5
hath two wings 789: 7
have no opinion of G. 796: 8
have you made peace with G. 2298i: 5
he findeth G. finds earth . 511:13
he for G. only 1254:17
he trusts in G. 113:12
he vainly sought is himself 795: 5
he's a g. or painter 610:12
heals, doctor takes fee 465: 2
helps everyone 787:11
helps the brave 324: 9
helps them who help selves 787:10
helps us do our duty 507:12
hesitates to say her nay ..2195:14
hides some souls away ..1025: 1
himself can't kill them 2226: 5
himself is the best poet ..1515: 1
his own interpreter 113:15
honest G. noblest work ..914:12
how G. employed Himself 351: 9
I am becoming a g. 417:10
I believe in one G. 334:17; 966: 2
I came from G. 413: 3
I fear G., but not afraid ..792: 2
I know of I shall ne'er 797:13
I know that G. is good 791: 4
I never spoke with G. 883: 4
I want to meet G. awake 416: 3
I wish that G. were back 797:16
if G. for us, who against 785:20
if G. is not in us 797:13
if not good g., good devil 812: 7
in babe's disguise 120: 6
in every good man G. dwells 808: 4
in G. is our trust 674: 3
in his harmony 2195: 7
in his own coin to pay ..784:14
in making man intended 1243: 7
in man 261: 5
in three persons 793: 1
incorporeal, divine 783: 6
inspiring G. 795:14
iron hands, leaden feet ...789: 9
is a circle 273: 4
is a spirit 783:11
is above all 113:10; 1890: 2
is abroad 795:10
is alpha and omega 784: 3
is an unutterable sigh 784: 4
is and all is well 1435: 1
is as fates assign 335: 6
is at the anvil 1941:18
is at work on man 1244:15
is forgotten 443: 6
is guide 2245: 4
is in his heaven 1905:13
is its author, not man ..1363: 9
is law, say the wise 1083:20
is light 784: 1
is living, working still 2233: 6
is love 790:14
is mind, and G. is all ..1306:16
is more there than thou ..271: 8
is not dumb 114: 7
is not mocked forever ..1483:10
is our fortress 784: 2
is the author 2239:10
is the best Poet 1515: 1
is the One Miracle 1238:11
is the only King 794:16
is the perfect poet 782:17
is their belly 155:11
is thy law, thou mine 2143: 7
is true 1084: 1
is yet with us 251: 6
isn't G. upon the ocean ..794: 4
jolly g. in triumph comes .495: 5
laid His fingers 394: 7
lends a hand 176:18
lends a helping hand 787:10
let G. do it 787:16
let us worship G. 2245:11
lets no sin be hidden ..1831: 7
light never darkened 784: 1
lips say G. be pitiful 114:13

God, *continued*
little greatest g. 351: 5
live among men as if G. beheld you 1583:16
lives and reigns 65:11
long as thy G. is G. above ..51: 9
looked down and smiled ..335: 9
looked upon front of G. ..75:15
loves adverbs 786:11
loveth cheerful giver 774:12
made all pleasures innocent 1510:16
made it all 2240: 9
made man 443: 1
made man to hear praise 1243: 7
made mothers 1350:18
made my lady lovely 140: 7
made no death 377: 6
made the country 321: 7
made thee perfect 1485: 9
made them high or lowly 1646: 4
made two great lights ..1942:12
make a g. of religion 1691: 4
make thee beautiful within 1588:2a
makes not the poet 1532:10
makes sech nights 1401:12
makes, tailor shapes 1958:10
man proposes, G. disposes 787: 7
may be had for asking ...885: 4
may consent for a time ..786:17
may emerge at last 798: 8
may forgive, I never 709:14
mighty fortress is our G. ..784: 2
mindful of right, wrong ..792: 5
moderates all 789: 2
more truly imagined 796: 7
moved by prayer 1586: 7
moves in a mysterious way 795: 7
must laugh 196: 6
must transcend what is ..783:12
my G., my father 377: 3
my G. will raise me up ..2014: 5
my soul's earth's g. 1469: 2
naught but G. can satisfy ..784:10
nearer, my G., to Thee ..792: 7
necessary to invent 788: 1
necessary to man 787:19
ne'er afflicts us 434:15
ne'er dooms to waste 788:10
never had a church 272:16
never imposes duty 507:18
never made his work 872: 5
never made mouth without meat 788:10
never meant that man 796: 9
never pardons 710:10
never repents decision 786: 1
never speeds him well 1093: 2
never wants a voice 787: 1
no G. but G. 786: 9
no g. but is worthy 335: 7
no g. dare harm a worm 1029:13
no one against G. except G. 785: 7
no respecter of persons ...784: 9
none but G. can satisfy ..794:12
nor G. too much a man ..1251: 3
nor let a g. intervene 799:19
not a cosmic bell-boy 783: 7
not body but semblance ..783: 1
not given spirit of fear ..1307:18
not G.! in gardens 755:12
not serve G. if devil bid 1490:15
not we, the poem makes 1534:15
nothing G. cannot effect ..784:11
nothing is void of G. 796: 5
now G. be thanked 1200: 4
of avenues and gates 801: 4
of Christian gardens 1942:18
of G., ye cannot overthrow it 785:20
of granite and rose 795: 9
of Harvest 862: 6
of life and poesy 1938:13
of love 1188: 9
of Music dwelleth 1361: 5
of my idolatry 957:11
of our fathers 545:11
of talking cowards 351: 6
of the Congo 801:6a
of Things as They Are 2233:15
of worlds brocading 793: 3

God, *continued*
often visits us 797:18
on our side 1083: 4
on side of big battalions .2114:13
on side of stronger 2115: 3
one G. and Father of all ..2066:15
one G., one law, one element 2068:12
one great G. looked down 335: 9
one morning laughed 121: 4
one that feared G. 238:10
one that would circumvent G. 1548: 2
only asks you to be good 807:15
only G. can make a gentleman 764:10
only G. can make a tree ..2037: 8
only G. can make us poor 1571: 4
only God is great 1421: 5
only G. is in the sky 1834:11
only G. may be had for the asking 885: 4
or guardian angel 467: 4
or something very like him 114:13
other to the altar's G. ..1585: 4
others call it G. 116:1; 783: 4
our fathers' G. 794:17
our help in ages past 794:15
palter'd with Eternal G. 2054: 1
pardon all good men 808: 5
patted G. on head 325: 2
permanently interesting ..797: 3
plagiarized the clay 1514:11
poor G. 1345:12
praise G., from whom all 793: 7
pray to G., pray to love ..1584: 6
preaches, noted clergyman 1594: 5
preacheth patience 1462: 4
president of the day 2129: 8
presume not G. to scan ..1251:14
rabbit's G. and man's 783: 8
refuge and strength 784: 2
reigneth, all is well 1435: 1
reigns, Government lives ..65:11
rejects all Prayers 1585: 6
remains 793: 8
render unto G. the things that are God's 212:15
rest ye, little children 269: 3
rest you merry, gentlemen ..269:10
ridiculous to believe 114:12
ripes the wine and corn 1283:13
said, I am tired of kings 1041: 9
save all here 933: 6
save regent, church, king 1546: 2
save the king 546:13
save the mark 785:18
saw G. divide the night ..1154: 2
screens from ideas 950:15
seek G. in a garden 756:17
seen G. in the stone 1390: 1
sees and hears 792: 1
sees flowers growing 1494: 5
sees G. in clouds 976:10
seldom think upon our G. ..281:12
send you a good night ...1074:16
sends cold according to cloth 789: 2
sends curst cow 330: 8
sends meat 315:18
sent his Singers 1518:10
serve G. if devil bid 442:13
set G. apart from mortal men 795: 3
set upon my lips a song 1879: 5
shall be my hope 783: 3
shall G. of Nature govern by his own laws 1316: 6
shall wipe away all tears 1973: 8
she knows G. 1856:13
shepherd's awe-inspiring g. 1450: 2
shines through all 28:10
sifted a whole nation 1324: 5
sifted three kingdoms 260: 7
smites with thunderbolt ..836: 8
so near is G. to man 506:14
sparing of His talk 2027: 1
spell G. with wrong blocks 2236:11
sphere which we call G. 2068: 5
stand alone with G. 1356: 7

God, *continued*
stands winding lonely horn 2007:14
strikes not both hands 789: 5
strikes with his finger 789: 5
strive to know thy G. 1242:13
surely like a g. 800: 8
tailor and g. mercer 1958:14
take care, G. is here 116: 1
take G. from Nature 1391: 6
takes a text 1462: 4
talks to Jones 194:15
tempers wind to lamb 789: 2
thank G. every morning ..2234: 7
that is within us 1143:15
the herdsman goads them 2261:12
the ruler of all 784: 7
the soul 1390:14
their severance rul'd 1796: 9
there is a G. 795: 8
there is a g. within us ..1534: 8
there is no G. 114:13
there is no g. but G. ..1583: 4
there is no G., no man-made G. 797:17
there's G. to wonder at ..2208:16
they serve G. well 1801:10
this g. did shake 460:15
this thing is G. 1130: 1
thou art love 790:14
though in the germ 585:10
thought about me 121:10
thought on me, his child 439: 9
'tis G. gives skill 1833:12
'tis hard to find G. 796:10
to be g., set up as a g. 46:10
to G. by nature joined 787: 1
to G. should tend the soul 306:12
to G. the Father 794:14
to man speaks in solitude 1871:11
to plough them under 794: 9
to punish and avenge 792: 5
to the Unknown G. 801: 9
treat G. as father's friend 797:18
truth, light his shadow 784: 1
turns a school-divine 1305:14
understand nothing of G. 797: 5
unto G. things that are God's 1028:18
unutterable sigh 784: 4
us ayde 154:10
vindicate G. to man 1251:13
vine-wreathed g. 262:14
waited six thousand years 1673:13
walks among the pots and pipkins 2276: 3
walks with us as of old ..1390: 8
warms his hands 1582:11
was bored by him 1378: 7
we are, because G. is 784: 6
we won't let G. help 787:18
what G. hath joined together 1272: 1
what great G. is this 414:19
what hath G. wrought 535: 8
what I call G. 1390: 1
whatever we see is G. 795:14
when G. is to be served 786: 7
where G. calls follow 787: 9
where G. is merry 785:11
whether g. or hero speaks 1438: 7
while G. is marching on ..725:11
who could but read or spell 1590: 4
who gave life, gave liberty 1103:10
who is our home 164:10
who loveth all His works ..282:12
who rules mankind 1421: 5
who sends the wound, sends the medicine ...1286: 5
who's in Heav'n 1586: 6
whom G. aids no man hurt 785:20
whom G. hath joined 885:18
whom G. loveth best, taketh soonest 409: 9
whose approval he won 2150: 4
will estimate Success ...1929: 2
will give right upper hand 1726: 3
will go to sleep 787:16
will not love thee less ...1560:14

God, *continued*
will provide 790:11
willing it 787: 8
wise man who invented G. 787:19
with G. be the rest 403: 4
with those who persevere ..1488: 7
with us 261: 7
won by humblest offering 799: 1
works in moments 1315: 6
works wonders now and then 1091: 9
worship G. from fear 2245:14
worshipp'd G. for spite ..1658: 8
worshipped with pure mind 794: 8
wrestled with him 786: 8
wrote his loveliest poem ..2038:14
wuz on his throne 1435: 1
ye good den 786: 2
yellow g. forever gazes ..957: 6
God's Acre: Saxon phrase 829: 6
afterthought 12: 5
caught at G. skirts 1583: 1
Christmas tree 270: 8
gifts put man's to shame 777:17
house is rotting 175: 3
on G. side 2115: 6
own image bought and sold 1842:11
wisdom and G. goodness 782:16
God-like all sin to leave ..1829: 9
erect 918:19
Goddam! j'aime les Anglais 550:12
Goddaughter: fiend's g. 1624: 5
Goddess: art a g. of dainty thought 102: 8
by her gait 799:15
clasp'd g. in his arms 1273: 6
ev'n the proudest g. 1456:12
excellently bright 1343: 3
had somehow flown 991: 4
I never saw a g. go 2101: 6
of my idolatry 957:11
reeling g. with zoneless waist 1511: 6
she moves a g. 799:15
shone before 799:15
that g. blind 713: 5
thou G. fair and free 1317:20
to keep the G. constant ..1523: 9
violated 1105:15
with zoneless waist 1511: 6
Godfather can give a name 1765:15
Godfathers of heaven's lights 1765:15
Godhead fires, soul attains 991:15
sole G. rose complete 1449:14
Godhead's benignant grace 508:13
Godlike to create 1108:17
Godliness: cheerful g. 1136: 4
profitable 591: 5
Gods 798
all the g. go with you 2084: 6
and poets only can create 1534: 9
appear 798:15
are athirst 799:10
are dead 476: 7
are just 2079:16
are kind 924:13
are we, Bards 1573:11
are with me 800: 2
as far remov'd from G. ..798: 4
behold the punishment ...1655:15
cannot recall gifts 772:19
careful about great things 799: 7
claim the right to decide 1931: 6
despise enforced offerings ..799: 1
Ethiop g. have Ethiop lips 785: 2
even the g. dwelt in woods 2210:13
even the g. must go 1519: 9
ever-gentle g. take breath 1935:12
fade, but God abides 799: 3
false g. fell down 1449:14
first set world at odds 1694:13
first taught artist's craft ..106: 4
Grecian g. like Greeks ..785: 2
grew dumb and pale 1450: 3
hate indifferent poet 1537: 1
he makes g. who prays ..1583: 4
hear hands before lips 850:20
I have said, ye are g. 382: 1
if we meet no g. 799:12

Gods, *continued*
implore not, plead not 1433: 1
knees of the g. 799:16
law unto themselves 800: 3
leave the g. to decide 1586: 9
little tin G. on wheels 1549: 9
make sport with men 800: 5
meet g., and justle 799:11
of all g. most invincible ..1191: 5
of fable shining moments 798:12
of the Copybook Headings 1628:19
of the Market Place 1628:19
of your own desire curse g. 799: 4
on the knees of the g. 799:16
play games with men 800: 5
pleasant to die, if g. 798:16
possess form of man 783: 1
profit the man 800: 2
protect the poor 1568: 9
see deeds of righteous ..426: 1
see everywhere 96: 5
sell all things for work ..2233:12
sell best goods cheapest ..1401:15
sell us all good things ..1061:15
shaped in his image 335: 7
shining moments of men 798:12
so many g. 1037:4a
so willed it 787: 8
there is a race of g. 798:13
there ought to be g. 798:11
to please thy g. 2269: 4
upon their spheres 1574:11
we stand by 798:14
when half-g. go, g. arrive 799: 9
who hearkens to the g. ..1586: 7
who worship dirty g. 804: 2
whom g. love dies young 409: 7
whom the g. destroy, they first make mad 1231:23
worship g. of the place ..1738: 2
would you placate the g. .800: 7
Godward: look up G. 1535: 9
open on g. side 723: 7
Goebel: bullet that pierced 1229:16
Goers-between, Pandars ...2105:13
Goes: one who g. happier 1455: 4
Goethe at Weimar 31: 9
Goethe's creed 2078: 3
sage mind 2229:17
Goggles: eh, dull g. 670: 5
Going: always somebody g. 2028: 6
out with the tide 2001:11
seem coming are g. 452: 2
stand not upon order of your g. 863: 6
sure it's not the g. 378:11
to and fro in the earth 2029: 4
Gold **801**
age of g. 44: 3
all men worship g. 803: 4
all not g. that glisters 87:15
all that glitters not g. 87:11
almighty g. 803: 3
and lead 801:12
and riches cause wars 2107: 4
and silver becks me on ..1981:13
and silver pass all the world over 2015:14
and silver turn to dirt ...804: 2
ass laden with g. 112:13
begets in brethren hate ..802:12
bright and yellow 802:17
burnt in my pocket 1333: 8
but muck 803:13
by g. love is procured 803: 4
California g. 639: 4
can a path clear 802:18
can do much, beauty more 135: 3
can g. calm passion 2167:13
child of Zeus 802: 6
crying is a cry for g. 358:12
deep-persuading orator ...803: 8
doing more murders 804: 1
first g. in childhood's purse .362:11
for g. we love impotent 1268: 3
for which other men die 801:16
from drossiest volume 184: 8
gild refined g. 1327: 8
gives a look of beauty ..802: 8
gives only worthless g. ..775: 2

Good, *continued*
man and a just 238:10
man as g. as he has to be 1254: 9
man best friend 729: 7
man happy is a common g. 807:16
man is contented 309: 7
man nearest g. at home ..907: 7
man seeks his own g. ..1793: 1
man sheweth favour 193:13
me no goods 808: 5
men are a public g. 1478:15
men give g. things 808: 2
more communicated, grows 807:19
most g. to whom no ill ...810: 1
must associate 1235: 7
must merit God's care 808:16
my son, be g. 19: 2
Nature's g. and God's ..1890:14
needs fear no law 1080: 3
never be one lost g. 809:11
never done no g. to me ..2243:13
never g. unless obstinate 1424:12
no g. apart from pleasure 1509: 2
no g., no bad 809:11
no g. of life but love 2206:16
no g. of telling truth 2055: 6
no g. we can say ours 811:16
no g. without ill 810: 2
no man suddenly g. 812: 2
no more g. than nation ..1683:16
none but g. love freedom ..724: 4
none that doeth g. 808:17
nor can it come to g. 809: 2
not enough to be g. 807: 3
not g. is not delicious 808: 2
not long g. that knows not
why 806:13
not present g. or ill 749:13
not too g. to be true 1398: 8
nothing either g. or bad ..1991:22
nothing g. or evil save will 2148: 5
nothing g. they say 2189: 3
nothing itself g. or evil ..2070: 8
nothing so g. as seems 453: 2
object of life to do g. 208:13
of ancient times 84: 2
of subjects end of kings ..1045: 2
old summer time 1936:11
only noble to be g. 73:10
only one g., knowledge ...1060: 2
opposite to every g. 585: 2
out of g. to find evil 811: 1
own g. before neighbor's 1793:17
people are scarce 808:10
Pleasure, Ease, Content ..855: 3
provoke to harm 1363: 4
public g. 807:16
Queen Bess: image of ...802:17
rail at g. practise ill 2080: 6
rather g. than fortunate ..807: 5
received, giver forgot 774:10
right g. from a book 1672:12
said our g. things before 1507:11
say not that g. are dead ..809: 5
say nothing g. of self 1581: 8
seek to be g. 2205: 8
she was g. as she was fair 1210:15
smallest actual g. 2228: 7
smallest g. by worst evil 2090: 7
so g. no one better 238: 8
so harsh to the clever 280:13
so much g. in worst of us 1023:21
so she's g. what does it signify 245: 6
solid g. 1128:12
some g., most bad 1247: 6
somehow g. 812: 5
something g. in you 694: 9
suffers, bad prevails 810: 6
supreme G. 1135: 5
Supreme G. in soul 1888:14
take the g. the gods provide thee 309: 3
that does me g. 806: 3
that I can do 1660: 6
that I would, I do not 149: 1
that love me, though few 806:19
that woman sometimes rules 2195: 7
that's in the worst of us .1024: 6

Good, *continued*
the pure, the beautiful 158:13
thing do not defer 1614: 2
think of emulating 809:15
those who were g. and great 72: 4
to be g. believe you are bad 805: 6
to be happy needs be g. ..856:17
to be merry and wise 806:12
to be noble we'll be g. ..1407:17
to fall 614: 3
to fear the worst 656: 2
to g., nothing evil 811: 4
to gain the day 614: 3
to have friends 737:16
to himself g. to friend 729: 7
to greatest number 859: 4
to public g. private respects must yield 1478:15
to study household g. 2143: 7
too g. for great things ..834: 5
too g. to be true 1398: 8
too g. to be unkind 790: 8
too much of a g. thing 1327: 7
touched up with evil 809:14
try, then know, the g. 184:11
unlooked-for streams of g. 1647:13
vacillating, inconsistent ..809: 4
walks on crutches 1398:13
we never miss 808: 7
we trust that somehow g. 812: 5
what g. came of it at last 2084:10
what g. is it 1081: 6
what g. thing you do, do not defer it 1493: 3
when he gives 1586:19
where it would do most g. 1551: 4
which belongs to prosperity 1626:11
who is g. is beautiful 132: 6
why is g. with evil mixt ..809:12
wiser being g. than bad ..1861: 3
within range of abilities 1: 5
without effort 807:12
without pretence 569: 8
woman g. to some man ..1255: 9
woman hidden treasure ..245: 9
work together for g. 790:19
wos wery g. to me 807:13
ye are and bad 812: 4
you do, do not defer 1493: 3
you were g. as you look ..1023:17
you're not g. for me 808:18
young until they die 409:10
zealously affected in g. 805: 8
Good-breeding: courts seats of g. 326: 5
differs 1738: 2
is best security 1259: 4
necessary 329: 3
Good-bye: kiss me, and say g. 636: 2
my Fancy 635: 5
proud world 2242: 4
say g. er howdy-do 1290: 5
there is no word 636: 2
to the bar 1145:10
Good-for-nothing: curly-headed g. 253: 5
Good-humor, and a Poet ..1522: 3
Good-looking, not good 2183: 2
Good-morning: bid me g. ..403: 3
in brighter clime, bid g. 1146:16
Good-morrow: bids blithe g. 1072: 6
bids not himself g. 1582: 7
give my Love g. 1730:12
to my Valentine 2071:11
Good Name: invisible thing 1700: 8
Good-nature cheapest commodity 1177:12
Good-natured, and civil 978: 6
Good-night, good-night ...1453:18
dear heart 570: 3
I have to say g. 1453:18
if he fall in, g. 1641:10
ladies 636: 9
my native land—G. 591: 8
say g. till it be morrow ..1455:11
say not g. 403: 3
to all, to each, a fair g. ..1846:10
Good-Sense 1795

Good-wife oped the window wide 1908:10
Good-will makes intelligence 994: 2
mightiest force 1035:11
of the rain 1670: 3
Goodliness is as flower 1348:14
Goodly: he that g. doeth ..424: 8
Goodman: as g. saith, so say we 2145:12
of the house 1986: 8
Goodness 805
all the g. of a good egg 532: 8
and he fill one monument 1340: 8
aspiring to God in g. 790: 6
blackens g. in its grave ..1761:16
cause of g. in others 807:19
cherish g. 1611:13
dare not check thee 2064:17
delighteth to forgive 709:10
did disdain comparison ..1484:16
dies in his own too much 809: 2
does not perish 809: 6
find so much of g. 1023:21
funambulatory track of g. 806: 9
how awful g. is 445: 1
is love in conduct 1174: 9
is something to love 1177: 1
makes its own heaven ..1830:11
more g. in little finger 239: 8
never fearful 2090:13
not so absolute in g. 1021:14
not tied to greatness 834: 9
nothing but indolence 808:11
of soul gathers in eyes 602: 9
saw the g. not the taint ..1496: 6
so-called g. of God 798: 3
special kind of truth 133: 7
springs from heart 805: 6
that ye may do today, do 1493: 4
thinks no ill 1948:11
Time's rude hand defies ..1748: 3
will to become good 806: 4
you hypocrite come out ..812: 7
Goods: all my g. are with me 1561: 6
American dry g. 663: 2
bad piece of g. 2182:10
bestow my g. to feed poor 241: 9
evil g., evil spent 750:19
he gave his g. away 570:12
he who bestows his g. 242: 6
ill-gotten g. seldom prosper 751: 2
laid up for many years ..1889:14
she is my g., my chattels 2145: 1
with all my worldly g. ..1271:10
Google: Barney G. 2296: 7
Gooms: tortur'd g. alang .2028: 1
Goose 812
among melodious swans ..1539: 3
as deep drinketh g. as gander 812:16
bee and calf govern world 1477:18
carries not the fox 456:10
comes back quack-quack ..2031: 4
eat king's g., choked 1038:16
every g. a swan 2264: 2
every g. can 1: 8
every g. is cackling 1406: 5
for his discretion 456:10
-gander, gosling, one thing ..813: 4
hangs high 813:12
here may you roast g. 813: 5
is a g. still 813: 9
of today is memory's swan 812:11
royal game of g. 754: 9
shoe the g. 813: 3; 1284:10
so screams a g. 813:10
sound on the g. 2282: 3
steal g. from off common 1085: 9
steal g., give giblets 772: 9
that laid golden eggs 813:12
there swims no g. so grey 2208: 8
thus you silence g. 812:17
too much for one 813: 1
when g. winketh 813: 6
where gottest that g. look 813: 5
wild g. cosmopolite 813: 8
Goose-pen: write with a g. 1758:12
Goose-quill: my grey g. ..1477:13
Goose-quills: afraid of g. ..1478: 8

Grace, *continued*
more beautiful than beauty 819: 4
more of g. than gifts 1136: 6
my g. is sufficient 818: 9
never say g. to his meat ..90: 3
of a day that is dead 1459: 9
of deities 2247:11
of God to man manifested 790:13
of God gear enough 786:13
of heaven enwheel thee ..818:16
orders her actions 819:11
prevenient g. descending ..818:14
raised by aunts à la g. ..2204:14
religion never to say g. 90: 3
saving g. in poverty 1871:14
sister of virtue 819: 8
soft and pensive g. 140: 9
sweet attractive g. 1254:17
sweet attractive kind of g. 608:16
tender g. of a day 371:20
that won who saw 819: 7
there, but for g. of God ..818: 7
to body judgment to mind 819: 6
to give the countersign 1910:12
to g. a gentleman 764:14
to groan 818:16
to listen well 1165: 1
to pardon all my sin 158:11
unbought g. of life 258: 6
under the common thing
the hidden g. 2147: 5
was in all her steps 140: 1
was seated on this brow ..239: 4
when once g. we have forgot 818:16
within his soul reigned ..1885:11
worth of the g. of God ..133:10
ye are fallen from g. 818:12
Grace: bonne g. est au corps 819: 6
Graces, The 819
adorn yourself with g. 820: 1
and beauties of virtue ..2089: 6
are four 820:2; 2077:8a
Batavian g. 819:14
Faith, Hope, Charity 819:18
follow in proper places ..1673:20
four are the G. 820: 2
in my love do dwell 1196:10
king-becoming g. 1040:16
lapt in men's good g. ..1548: 6
lead these g. to the grave ..247:16
long g. keep stomachs 90: 3
malice are his g. 24:11
no fabled g. 1525: 1
not at his cradle 819:15
number all your g. 600: 5
other g. will soon fill up ..819:13
outward g. 132:18
remember the G. 820: 1
sacrifice to the G. 820: 1
shot forth peculiar g. 140: 1
three sweet G. 24:11
Gracious to all 216:15
Graculo: nil cum fidibus g. 1362: 6
Gradations: cold g. of de-
cay 393:13
no pale g. quench 1942: 1
of their decay 33: 8
Graduate of field or street ..196: 7
Graduates: sweet girl-g. 779:11
Graduating up in spiral line 101: 5
Græca mercamur fide 1333: 9
Græcam: non possum ferret
G. urbem 1737: 1
Græce: omnia G. 1070: 2
Græcia capta ferum victorem 839: 6
Mæonidam 1305: 9
Græcos: inter G. græcissimus 838:11
Græculus esuriens 939:17
Græcum est, non potest legi 1070: 5
Grafted them to grow there 2224: 2
Grain: against the g. 1634: 8
first bird gets first g. 160: 5
fruitful g. of counsels 748: 2
of gold in every creed ..334:17
of our blessed gold 639: 4
of salt being added 1756: 8
of wit, g. of folly 1953:12
send choice g. 1324: 5
'tis in g., sir 1643:20
to the last g. of dust 2246:16
Grains: little g. of sand ..2040:19
of titillating dust 1856: 5
Grammaire, sait régenter ..820:13
Grammairiennes: la plus
part des troubles 820:14
Grammar 820
above g. 820:16
grave of letters 820:11
heavenly g. did I hold ..1071: 5
lords it over kings 820:13
subservient to success ..1929: 9
why care for g. 820:18
Grammar-school: erecting ..531: 7
Grammar-Tree: who climbs
G. 820:12
Grammarians at variance ..820:10
race of g. 820: 4
Grammatical and dull 2068: 8
Grammaticam: supra g. 820:16
Grammatici certant 820:10
Grand and comfortable ...284:15
as doomsday 2194:12
as rich man's funeral 746: 1
gloomy and peculiar 1378:10
Grand-jurymen since before
Noah 1026:15
Grandad, viewing earth's
worn cogs 2278: 1
Grandam: authorized by her
g. 2015: 9
little less in love 1353: 2
might have been g. 1301: 9
Grandam-talk and nursery-
hymn 388:21
Grandee: perfumed g. 1551: 7
Grandeur derived from
Heav'n alone 344: 5
false g. meanness 2191:15
flee g. 310:16
has heavy tax to pay 838: 7
hear with disdainful smile 1567:16
in growling of gale 1367: 2
lies in our illusions 832:10
men of infamy to g. soar 838: 5
so nigh is g. to our dust ..506:14
that was Rome 140: 6
what is g., what is power 1574: 3
Grandeur: donne la g. aux
autres 990: 8
Grandfather: don't know g. 71: 9
Grandfathers: friends with
g. 646: 7
take thy g. and go 71: 8
Grandmother Eve 2178:15
Grands: j'avais vu les g. ..835: 6
ne sont g. que parceque
nous sommes à genoux 835: 2
Grandsire cut in alabaster 1318: 2
gay g. 37:12
our g. Adam 11: 8
young g. cut his throat 1933:13a
Gran'thers they knowed
sunthin', tu 22:10
Granite: mountain of g. 94:11
Grant, Ulysses S. 821
biger man than old G. ..1553: 7
is shrined 1867:6a
Granta: O G.! sweet G. ..1099:14
Granted: part g., part denied 1586: 8
take for g. 226:11
Grape 821
burst Joy's g. 1291: 6
foaming g. of eastern
France 2156: 1
gains purple tinge 963: 3
little more g. 64: 3
long life to the g. 2156: 5
purple from another g. 963: 3
red g. in lands of song 2156: 1
stained with blood of g. ..115:13
that can with Logic 2157:13
winter g. sour 821:11
Grape-shot: whiff of g. 2107:11
Grape-stone as thunder 380:10
or a hair can kill 381:21
Grapeism: sour g. 821:10
Grapes are sour 821: 8
brought forth wild g. 821:15
deceived with painted g. ..821:17
Grapes, *continued*
eaten sour g. 821:14
gleaning of g. of Ephraim 821:16
of thorns 303: 4
pluck the g. 2010:13
sanguine g. of pain 1455:12
their flowers unmask 1906:12
whence be g. of wine-
press 2116: 8
Grapevine: this fertile old g. .503: 1
Gras comme un cochon 647:10
Grasp not at much 1651: 1
of thought 1990:13
reach should exceed g. ..108:17
Grass 821
afraid of every g. 656:13
all flesh is g. 1348:14
almost hear it growing 822:10
and hay, all mortal 1348:14
blade of g. always blade of g. 822: 8
clothing the earth 822: 5
cut from under feet 1632:17
down in the bells and g. ..11:12
floweth like a stream 822: 9
go to g. 821:18
green g. growing all around 2295: 9
groweth, horse starveth ..822: 3
grows above all graves ..822: 4
grows not upon highway ..822:11
have not let g. grow 822:14
horse while g. grows may
starve 822: 3
I am the g., I cover all ..822: 4
I can push the g. apart 796: 1
ilka blade o' g. 1647: 1
is growing upon you 410: 6
leaf of g. is no less 1387: 4
leave the g. 416:24
long has g. been growing 2237:13
lush and lusty g. looks 822:12
make spot of green g. on
prairie 1065:17
make two blades of g. grow 638:13
may grow in winter 866: 5
no g. on my heel 822:14
of England once again 553: 4
on carpet with sunbeam ..822:13
roots 2279: 4
snake in the g. 1798: 7
springeth not 822: 6
stoops not 704:13
what is the g. 822:15
while the g. grows 822: 3
wonderful g. upon breast 2241: 9
you ate g. 613: 8
Grass-blade no easier 2252: 6
Grasses of the ancient way 2117:13
Grasshopper 822
shall be a burden 823: 1; 2075:18
takes lead in summer luxury 823: 3
your fairy song 512:22
Grasshoppers: chirping like g. 39:20
like g. rejoice 39:20
Grata dolore venit 1446: 4
Grate: ponderous g. and
massy bar 2109: 8
Grateful can never forget ..743: 4
Gratia: beneficiorum g.
sempiterna 824:16
ingratium g. tarda facit ..774: 7
levior pluma est g. 823:14
magna habendast g. 419: 7
malorum infida 1560: 7
pro rebus merito 824:13
Gratiam: mecum facile
redeo in g. 533:16
Gratis anhelans 748: 4
Gratitude 823
akin to hate 825: 3
cannot be bought 823: 7
charge upon inheritance .. 823:17
debt and g. different 418: 3
English g. is such 553:12
for benefits eternal 824:16
fruit of cultivation 823: 8
greatest virtue 823: 6
hope of receiving favors ..823:10
is a burden 823: 5
is expensive 1711:15
is lighter than a feather ..823:14

Head, *continued*
to contrive 1: 7
turned by success 1929:22
turnin' back for counsel ..19:16
ugly is h. without hair ..849: 7
uneasy lies the h. 1848: 2
unmellow'd 595:13
what could woman's h. contrive 2191: 5
when h. acheth all body worse 870: 6
when your h. did ache ..1037: 1
where to hide my h. 2000:23
where to lay his h. 910:11
which statuaries loved ...212: 2
who touches a hair of yon gray h. 675: 2
who washes ass's h. 111:13
whole h. is sick 458:15
wise h. as low as ours 385:11
with h. touch stars 1538: 5
with my exalted h. 109: 4
with roses crowned 109: 4
without h. or tail 869: 4
Head-dress: variable h. 487: 3
Head-off! head-off 869: 3
Head-winds right 895:13
Headache of the morn 504:16
you wake with h. 504:17
Headaches: lose sick h. at fifty 31: 2
Headings: Gods of Copy-book H. 1628:19
Headlight on behind 1310:16a
Heads be full of bees 143: 8
bow, knees bend 327: 6
cut h. out of cherry stones 1305:12
empty h. with empty sound 1895: 4
fat h., lean brains 647:11
fired by h., by tails 1966:13
hide ignominious h. 869:17
hide their diminished h. 1938:17
houseless h. 1321: 4
how high you lift your h. 1354: 4
hush'd h. 1666: 2
I win, tails you lose 249:16
many h. but no brains 1483:20
of future things appear ..2096: 1
or tails 2242: 5
scabby h. love not comb ..869: 8
so little no room for wit ..869: 9
so many h. and so many wits 869:7; 1427:24
some brown, some bald ..847: 7
some h. easily blown away 869:10
that have no wit at all 869: 7
their h. never raising 81:12
thousand h., thousand tastes 1427:22
to get money 1336: 3
two h. better than one ..869:14
young h. giddy 2263: 8
Headstone: you come not to 405: 1
Headstones: milestones into h. change 35: 1
thicken along the way 35: 1
Headstrong as an allegory 1424:11
Heal: how do drugs h. ..1285: 2
Healing for every pain ..290:13
in his wings 1372: 6
of most High cometh h. ..466:11
that night has shed 2262:14
Health 870
above all gold 871:11
abused not my h. 38: 1
and cheerfulness beget each other 870: 7
and h. on both 89:17
and high fortune 543: 9
and hope have gone the way of love 437:13
and intellect blessings 871: 8
and money go far 870:14
and virtue gifts 321: 7
and wealth create beauty 870: 9
answers its own ends 871: 1
appurtenance unto life ..872: 1
beginning of h. 458: 4
better than wealth 871: 9
blessing money cannot buy 871:13
Health, *continued*
condition of wisdom 250: 5
consists with temperance 873: 5
destroys h. by preserving 874: 3
felt not at all 458:10
first good lent to men ...871: 3
foundation for State 870:19
frolic h. 2257: 7
from h. contentment 311:10
genius, honour 1262:9a
give me h. and a day ..870:12
grant me but h. 871:11
greatest wealth 871:14
he that will this h. deny ..500:17
healthy know not of their h. 870:10
here's to your h. 501: 2
hunt for h. unbought 872: 5
importing h. and graveness 25: 3
interested in her own h. ..874: 4
is the first muse ..590:17; 872: 8
look to your h. 871:13
lose h. like spendthrift 874: 2
lost, something lost 236:14
mental joys and mental h. 310:17
my nerves and fibres brace 871:12
not a condition of matter 870:11
not valued till sickness 870:10
of body, peace of mind 1330: 2
of the people 870:19
of the poor 871: 6
owe h. to a disease 873:17
Peace, and Competence ..873: 5
precious thing 870:18
preservation of h. a duty ..873: 9
prodigal of h. 1495: 1
rosy-compexion'd H 590:19
ruddy h. loftiest Muse 872: 5
safeguard h. of body 872: 6
silliest word in language ..874: 4
Sir Condy's good h. 500:18
spreads her rosy wing 873:13
step toward h. to know the disease 458: 4
that snuffs morning air ...870:13
this moment perfect h. 410: 3
to all those that love us ..501: 8
to the nut-brown lass 501: 6
to them that's awa 500:12
unbought h. 872: 5
unto the happy 1435:14
vital principle of bliss ..871:12
where h. and plenty cheer'd 2085: 6
who hath good h. is young 870: 9
with h. pleasure flies 871: 2
without h. life not life 871: 7
without money ague 870:14
Healths, Drinking 500
drink h. amplifying diseases 500:15
drink h., drink sickness ..500:15
drink h., spoil own 500:15
five-fathom deep 483: 6
when h. and draughts go free 2157: 8
Healthy by exercise 238:20
by temperance 238:20
happy and wise 872: 4
know not of their health .870:10
Heap high farmer's wintry hoard 640: 1
o' livin' 904:16a
o' payin' 904:16a
struck me of a h. 1639: 7
Hear as well as see 1798: 8
could ever h. by tale or history 1195:10
ears to h. 510:15
I shall h. in heaven 414: 7
me for my cause 225: 5
neither h. nor see 169:12
see, and be silent 1822:11
still I see thee, still I h. 3: 7
still stood fix'd to h. 2097: 1
swift to h. 149:13
time will come when you will h. me 1902: 8
to h., not see play 1912: 3
to h. with eyes 191: 5
Hear, *continued*
twice as much as speak 511:10
what he does not wish 218:10
what you deserve to h. 165: 2
with patience h. 1461: 4
Hear Hims: proud of his 1437:15
Heard and seen of none ..828: 8
for their much speaking ..1900: 8
I will be h. 1705: 6
when h. less keen than seen 604:15
Hearer: never was better h. 1165: 1
Hearing
See also Ears
heard of thee by h. 605: 2
no h. on prudent side 178: 8
where h. should not latch 2223: 6
Hearings: younger h. are quite ravished 1302: 5
Hearkeners seldom hear good 1165: 5
Hears but half who h. one 1019:15
Hearse and flowers 2006: 6
grim one-horse h. 747: 6
laureate h. 684:13
thy grandam's h. 567:12
underneath this sable h. 567:12
with scutcheons blazon'd 746:16
Heart 874
accept with light h. 718:11
all h. they live 1905: 1
always doing lovely things 878:19
and hand both open 259: 5
and mind, and thoughts! ..828:14
and not the brain 882:14
angel h. of man 878:18
apply my h. to wisdom ..2165:17
arise, and h. to h. 1730: 7
as far from fraud 879: 6
as soft, a h. as kind 880:14
as my h. is set will I wive 1269:15
as sound as a bell 217: 8
as warm h. as ever beat ..879: 4
ask h. what it doth know 1789: 6
asks if this be joy 1016:19
asks pleasure first 874:10
at leisure from itself 878: 9
at mouth for fear 876: 8
awake, O h. 92:11
ay's the part ay 875:11
be calcined into dust 354: 3
be still, sad h. 282:11
beat hot and strong 110: 4
beat upon mine, little h. 1352: 3
beating of her restless h. 1921: 2
beats on forever 875: 7
because his h. was true ..2132:13
because my h. I proffered 1184: 8
because my h. is pure ..1660: 4
being dried with grief 878: 5
benevolent and kind 1036:11
bestuck and bleeding h. ..2071:11
betray thy h. to woman 2208:11
better poet's h. than brain 882:16
bitter h. that bites 881: 2
blessed are pure in h. ..1659:16
bloody hand, hard h. 851:12
bold h. storms 1431:10
bowed down by weight of 927:16
brave impetuous h. 881:24
break, my h. 437:16
build on human h. 1535: 4
can ne'er transport know 1446: 2
cannot heal throbbing h. 295: 5
cannot heave h. in mouth 880: 9
carries color of birthplace 882:11
Catholic, stomach Lutheran 515:17
caused widow's h. to sing 2136: 6
cease repining 282:11
chicken h. so tender 406: 9
cleanse h. with tears 1973:14
cleft my h. in twain 878: 5
cold is the h., fair Greece 838:17
cold is thy hopeless h. 243:16
comes from h. goes to h. 2250:15
cometh from h. go to h. ..880: 2
concealing it will break ..2024:22
create in me a clean h. 879: 3
cruel h. ill suits manly mind 346: 3
daily his own h. he eats 895:13

Heart, *continued*
deceitful above all things 881: 7
deep Poetic h. 1521: 4
desert h. is set apart 434:10
desires, hand refrains 991:15
did not our h. burn 876: 3
doth need a language 993: 5
each h. is Freedom's shield 2116: 8
eat not thy h. 876:21
eat thy h. 876:19
embracing h. entire 730:13
envious h. mickle smart ..566: 4
ever at your service 876:14
ever new 878: 8
every h. is a sawdust ring 1888: 6
every h. its own ache 877:12
every h. its sorrow 291: 9
every h. to heaven aspires 887:17
every h. vibrates to that 1785:15
every h., when sifted well 881:14
every human h. is human 875: 7
every one speaks of h. 882:12
faint h. ne'er won fair lady 2215: 2
faithless h. betrays head ..881:23
falls back to Erin's Isle 2:15
far from eyes, far from h. ..5: 5
father's h. was broken ..1350:21
feels ice 620:16
firm as a stone 881: 8
for any fate 1705:10
for better lore 197: 2
for every fate 644:16
for falsehood framed 1113:16
for many an honest h. may beat beneath a ragged coat 2287: 3
form'd for softness 881: 3
found sky in your eyes ..602: 2
free and fetterless 875: 4
from h. of very h. 933:10
full h.'s a Psalter 878:16
furnace-burning h. 1978:11
gathered to thy h. 1213: 4
generous h. repairs 878:15
gentle h. tied easy 765:15
gets speeches by it 1902:12
give me back my h. again 1202:15
give me the h. to fight ..613:18
give, oh, give me back my h. 880:22
give us this day good h. 2116: 1
giving h. to dog to tear ..472:13
good h. better than head 806:11
good h. helps 879: 2
good h. letter of credit 85: 7
good h.'s worth gold 879: 5
governs understanding ...882: 4
great as the world 878:12
grateful h. 824:18
grown cold 392:13
grows old with body 876: 4
hangeth on a joly pin ...1300:15
happiest h. that ever beat 858: 3
hard h. does not love in May 1283:16
hard was the h. 1164:17
hardeneth his h. 654:25
hardest in softest climes ..881: 9
hardness of the human h. 1600:15
has arguments 882:17
has eyes 882:17
has its reasons 882:17
has learned to glow 1957: 7
hath its own memory 874:14
hath one poor string 877:21
hath treble wrong 2024:22
he that hardeneth his h. ..654:25
he whose h. hath tried ...593:12
heathen h. that puts 789: 8
heavy h. bears not 880: 9
held h. in his hand 876:19
her conscious h. glow'd .1221:10
her h. adrift with one 1818: 6
her h. is not of ice 2202: 6
her h. was voluble 880:17
hid with flowering face 87: 2
his aching h. assails 1809:14
his flaw'd h. burst 878: 6
his h. as great as world ..1158:11
Heart, *continued*
his h. kept goin' pitty-pat 1180:11
his h. should glow 79: 9
his h. was rich 242:19
his h. was true to Poll ..1198: 3
hold me in thy h. 159:17
home is where the h. is 904:19
honest, humble h. 880: 1
how dear to this h. 252: 1
how the h. listened 538: 2
how variable and vain 881:10
how weak the h. of woman 2190: 3
human h. is a mirror 874: 8
humble and contrite h. ...879:24
humblest of h. 1503:13
hush, my h. 93: 8
I am sick at h. 1492:18
I give my h. and my hand 975: 8
I have a beggar h. 1202:11
I thought to undermine h. 880:23
if h. of man depressed ..2184: 4
if thy h. fails thee 622: 7
imbued with virtue 879: 1
in each h. tiger, pig 874: 6
in his h. my h. is locked .1214: 5
in laughter h. sorrowful .1077:16
in lowliness of h. 448:13
in my h. of h. 1457:10
in my mouth 876: 8
in the right place 1535:12
in unison with mankind ..201:12
indomitable h. and arm .2123: 4
innocent h. brittle 877:23
is a kicking horse........879:16
is a letter of credit 85: 7
is a small thing 874: 9
is cramm'd with arrogancy 881:13
is his mouth 217: 8
is its own fate 644:14
is like a rhyme 115:17
is like a singing bird 877: 6
is like an apple-tree 877: 6
is like an instrument 874:15
is like some fortress 1183: 9
is slow to learn 1174: 1
is snares and nets 2187: 7
is true as steel 879: 7
is turn'd to stone 877: 20
is turning home again 52: 2
is wax to be moulded 875:12
it is h. that judges 1182:10
it nerves my h. 2220: 9
just another broken h. ...2295: 1
keeps persistency still 1170: 1
kind and gentle h. he had 1495: 4
kind h. loseth nought 1035: 9
knoweth its bitterness 877:18
lack of h. 881:18
lad's h. is to a lad's h. ...202:19
lady's h. beggar's purse .2191:11
laments that virtue 2091: 2
largest h. soonest broken .878: 3
last thing that moves 2023:17
lay battery to her h. 2215:10
left no bolder h. behind ..1870: 3
less bounding 32:12
let me hold thee to my h. 1211:13
let me wring your h. 876:12
let my h. be fresh 878:18
let not your h. be troubled 877:11
let thy h. cheer thee 2266: 4
let us lift up our h. . ..876: 1
lies under your feet 360:14
light h. in fat body 648:11
light h., light foot 31: 6
light h. lives long 1301: 9
light h., thin breeches 877: 3
lightest h. heaviest mourning 1357: 1
like a millstone 875: 1
like a muffled drum 827:18
likened to *one* flower 1944: 1
live in my h. pay no rent 2211:14
look in thy h. and write ..2251:10
lose his h. with dignity ..1176:13
lose not h. in temptation ..1981: 4
lost h. preserv'd sheep ..1203:11
lowly h. wins love 938: 2
lurking-place of crime 602: 9
made callous by many blows 343: 6
Heart, *continued*
make h. dance with joy 598:14
makes fathers and sons ..646:11
makes h. in love with night 1343: 5
makes men eloquent 537: 9
man after his own h. 1252:13
man lose h. with dignity .1176:13
man's h. deviseth way ...787: 3
many a h. is aching 2288: 1
may give lesson to h. 882: 7
may wish at will 739:19
mean h. that lurks 881:12
merry h. continual feast ..877: 5
merry h. goes all the day .877: 8
merry h. like medicine ..877: 5
merry h. maketh cheerful 1301: 6
mine is a soft h. 878:20
mine is h. at your feet ..1185: 7
miss old h. in myself 35: 8
mother h. within me 1352:19
mother's h. child's school 1350: 1
mother's h. is weak 1352:14
must rule, head obey 436: 4
my h. beat in my brain 881:25
my h. ferments not 335: 5
my h. has bled 169: 3
my h. is Catholic 515:17
my h. is dead 1880:13
my h. is exceeding heavy ..944:20
my h. is feminine 306:10
my h. is fixed 876:10
my h. is heavy 877:13
my h. is in my prayer ...1584: 7
my h. is weary waiting ..1283: 6
my h. leaps up when I behold 1670:15
my h. led me past 880:16
my h. like a muffled drum 827:18
my h. moves with thine .1957:12
my h. springs up anew ..1909: 5
my h. still light 38: 2
my h. untravell'd turns 3: 3
my h. waketh 1843:20
my h. with pleasure fills 1294:17
my h. would hear her ...1215:11
my h.'s in the Highlands 1768: 2
my old h. is crack'd 878: 6
my poor resistless h. 880:24
my very h. faints 1487:11a
naked human h. .... .876:17
nature's h. beats strong ...898:11
near h. to be loved 11:11
needs no preparation .880: 6
never ached with a h. ..176: 7
never grows better 33: 9
never jumpeth with h. 87: 3
new h. also will I give you 1685:16
no matter from the h. 2225: 6
not far from h. to mouth 2228:16
not made of horn 876: 7
now cracks a noble h. 878: 6
nowhere beats h. so kindly 1768:07
O h. of little faith 1182:20
o'erflowing h. 880:12
of a coquette 318: 1
of a frog 763: 7
of a King 1664:14
of a man to h. of a maid ..2102: 4
of emperor for silly worm 2244:17
of fool is in his mouth 876: 8
of friendship colder 35: 7
of God takes in 790:16
of ice, a soul of fire 1247:12
of itself but little 874: 9
of man is restless 792:10
of man place Devil's in ..881: 1
of melancholy beats in thee 998: 1
of my h., O come with me 1212: 1
of nature music 1361: 5
of oak 1417: 2
of such fine mould 242:19
of the citizen hissing in war 1474:15
of the mighty mountains 1732:16
of the wooer is warm 2212: 3
old as one's h. 38: 7
on her lips 599:17

Heart, *continued*
once h. of maiden is stolen 1233:15
one h. another h. divines 1206:12
one h., one bed 1182: 2
one h. one hope, one flag ..57: 7
open, brave and free 879: 4
open not h. to every man 1650:10
our h. is in heaven 887: 8
out of h. mouth speaketh 1897:17
out of h. shortly 1699:18
out-worn h. 877:23
pass, thou wild h. 26: 8
passionate h. of poet 1537: 6
pierced through ear 2220:18
place where devil dwells ..893: 3
posing for photograph ...875: 5
pour out the h. 1103: 1
praise h., pity the head ..1589: 1
preaching down daughter's h. 366:17
pregnant with celestial fire 2218: 6
"prima donna's" tuneful h. 342:12
promised what the fancy drew 2266: 8
proud h. and beggar's purse 1607: 2
pulses of her iron h. 1921: 2
rapturous h. of things ..1812: 9
reconciles contradictions ..874:13
reflect without sullying ..874: 8
resolves matter in trice ..2079: 6
reveal presence of love ..1208:14
rocked its babe of bliss 171: 2
roving h. gathers no affections 21: 9
runs away with head 882: 6
sad h. of Ruth 1405: 3
saddest h. pleasure take ..1382: 6
sailed world of his own h. .874:11
sair for Somebody 877: 9
same h. beats 875: 7
sank into my boots 875: 8
say not Woman's h. is caught 2208: 7
seated h. knock at ribs ...657:19
seek to soften Jewish h. .1012:13
seldom feels what mouth 1901: 9
selfish h. deserves pain ..1794: 8
send me back my h. 880:22
set h. on goal, not prize 1716: 11
set my poor h. free 1050: 2
set not h. upon riches ..1722:10
sets my h. a clickin' 116:12
shall break into flaws 1978:11
shall thank you 824: 5
should be only guide 880:13
sighing of a contrite h. ..1818:10
sinful h., feeble hand ...1828:10
sleep, mournful h. 1846: 1
small h. small desires 879:23
so full a drop o'erfills ...858: 9
so full of emotion 661: 7
so high, of heroic rage ...237: 3
so manly and so kind 879: 4
so simple is h. of man ..877: 1
so the h. is right 416:16
soft as woman's love 878:13
something h. must have ..875: 1
soon forgets 5: 6
soonest awake to flowers 1116: 9
sore-tried 393: 4
speak to his h. 2093:12
speaks what's in his h. 78:15
splitted the h. 1934: 7
steady of h. 879:17
sticks to good red bricks .275:20
stop one h. from breaking 1036:17
stout h. and open hand ..879:17
stout h. breaks bad luck ..323:12
stout h. that has no fear ..1584:10
strong h. of her sons 562: 9
stubborn h. shall fare evil 1424: 5
subduing a greedy h. ...1786:15
sweetest freedom honest h. 723:17
take back the h. thou gavest 1881: 4
take h. of grace 875: 9
teach my h. to find way ..937: 7
tear out one's h. 875:10
that keeps its twilight hour 1995:11

Heart, *continued*
that loved never forgets .1198:18
that music cannot melt .1363: 8
that never feels a pain ...291:14
that understands 1957:14
that was humble 1475: 7
that watches and receives .879: 9
then be content, poor h. ..312: 4
then burst his mighty h. .984:16
thinketh, tongue speaketh 880: 5
thinking h. 446:13
thinks, tongue speaks 217: 8
tho' my h. be at the root ..875:10
tho' my h. was at sea ..1270: 9
though 'tis savage one ...881: 4
thus the h. will break 878: 1
thy h. is in thy hose 875: 8
thy h. was generous 212: 4
tired h. shall cease 31: 9
to conceive 1: 7
to h., lips to lips 1454: 2
to mend the h. 10: 2
to my dead h. run them in 858:16
to pity, hand to bless 1503:14
to resolve 1: 7
toil on, sad h. 507: 4
too great for what contains it 1113:16
triumphs in struggle with understanding 874: 7
trust to thy h. 960:13
undermine the h. 2213: 3
unlock h. with sonnet key 1883:17
unpack h. with words ...1952: 8
unstable h. of man 874:15
valiant h. of youth 22:5
was as great as the world 1158:11
was hot within him 879:14
was in his work 876: 2
was swollen 1609: 7
way to man's h. through stomach 515:18
we shut our h. up 875:15a
wear h. upon my sleeve ..876:13
what eye sees not, h. rues not 598: 7
what female h. can gold despise 2191: 7
what h. can endure shame 1810:12
what h. could have thought you 1858: 2
what the h. did think 880: 5
when h. inclines to h. ..2216: 2
when h. is a fire 880: 4
when we love, h. judges 1182:10
where h. is failed 2215: 4
where h. is treasure 876: 2
which others bleed for ..1184:11
who stabs at my h. 1468: 5
who with a fervent h. goes forth 2241: 4
whole h. is faint 458:15
whole of woman 874: 7
whose h. is snares 2179: 1
whose love is innocent ..2184: 5
wild h. of youth 26: 8
will find more than the eye 1826:16
willing h. adds feather ..2148: 7
wiser than intellect 882:10
with a h. for any fate ..1705:10
with a h. that is true 92: 9
with all my h. 876:18
with h. eye doth see 636:13
with h. in concord beats ..134: 3
with h. new-fired 664: 3
with Nature's h. in tune 1384:14
with own h. confer 678:16
with pity filled 618: 9
with pity tear my h. 1536: 3
with room for every joy . 877: 1
with strings of steel ... 1588: 5
with women h. argues ...2190: 3
within blood-tinctured 203: 7
without a stain 879: 8
without rich h. beggar ..1721: 8
woman's h. grows chill ..2191:12
woman's h. precious 2184: 6
woman's h., woman's life 2184: 6
wounded h. hard to cure .877:13
you have a merry h. 1302: 6

Heart, *continued*
you would eat in private ..420:11
young h. under winter 22: 4
Heart's core 1457:10
desire 435:22
Heart-ache: all cases of h. 1187: 2
we end the h. 395:10
Heart-beat at my feet 473: 8
hot and strong 110: 4
Heart-break: full of 927:20
in thy song 167: 8
Hill 1886:14
of the sea 1183: 4
Heart-stain: ne'er carried h. 1812:13
Heart-strain: remedy h. ...1583:11
Heart-strings are a lute ..1879:10
Heart-throb in the sky ...1072:15
Heart-throbs: count time by h. 1134: 5
Heart-whole and soul-free 2141: 7
I'll warrant him h. 880:20
Heart's-ease: most rare ..1450: 9
one could look 1450: 8
or pansy 1450:12
that the poets knew 1450:10
Hearth: bless the h. 168:11
clean h. 219:16
for h. and home 908: 8
genial h. 934: 1
gladden our domestic h. ..739:23
his h. the earth 2166:20
no h. without a woman ..2205: 5
no more the blazing h. 909: 5
nor sitting by his h. 438: 9
of home 905: 4
room about her h. 55: 6
smoldering h. 24: 3
Hearth-stone: clean h. 905:15
going to me own h. 2242: 4
round the h. of home 905:15
Hearts agree though heads differ 882: 9
apply our h. unto wisdom 2165:17
are fresh and simple 618: 4
are hard and sour 877:15
are steeped in gall 881:11
are still our own 327: 6
bowed be our h. to think 1917: 9
brave h. and clean 876: 6
broken h. die slow 878: 1
cherish h. that hate thee ..866:19
cold are yearning h. 410:15
cold h. freeze allegiance ..2024:12
confess the saints elect ..242:21
dry as summer dust 809: 8
ensanguined h. 219:13
feel your great h. throbbing 186: 1
fortunes, beings blend ..1275: 5
give true h. but earth ..1384:10
glad h. without reproach .508:13
gentle-humoured h. 2026:14
have as many fashions 875: 3
he fashioneth h. alike 875: 7
her favorite suit 219:16
home-keeping h. happiest .907:14
honest h. chainless hands 1786: 6
humble h. have humble desires 435: 9
in gall and vinegar 946: 8
in love use own tongues .2214:13
in the right place 875:15
just as pure and fair 913: 6
kind h. more than coronets .73:10
knit your h. with an unslipping knot 880:19
let your h. be strong 325:10
like doors, ope with ease .329: 9
like muffled drums 827:18
little group of wise h. 702:15
live by being wounded 877:22
lo now, what h. have men 1255:13
long-enduring h. 2127: 3
maidens' h. always soft ..1233: 5
may bruise and beat 2299c: 4
melts the most obdurate h. 1872: 2
men led by their h. 882: 4
million h. wait our call ..535:10
mother h. beset with fears 1352:18
of flint 1504: 5

Heaven, *continued*
to the hand of h. submit ..1420: 2
to the Virtuous 1716: 1
treasury of everlasting joy 884:10
trims our lamps 1844: 2
turn'd h. unto hell 1196:10
'twas whispered in h. ...1724: 5
upon earth to the weary head 141:17
vain toil surveys 49:12
vaulty h. 1072:16
visible as we have eyes to
see 884:16
vision of fulfill'd Desire ..893: 6
was all tranquillity 1815:13
was her help 596: 1
was in him 888: 1
was not H. if Phaon 885: 5
we are all going to h. 415: 5
we can't have h. crammed 1696:15
we had needs invent h. ..788: 2
we storm h. itself 49: 5
were not h. 592:10
were there no h. nor hell .915: 3
wha'll gang up the h. ..1072: 2
what h. is love; what hell 1196:10
what matter how h. we gain 887:16
what they do in h. 1264:15
what's a H. for 108:17
when good deed done 888:10
when the h. is shut up .1669: 2
who can know h. 797: 2
who seeks for h. alone ..1194: 3
why, to h. I trust 1869: 9
will bless your store 145:13
will protect working-girl ..778:12
will take our souls 987:16
wills our happiness 885:16
with thee its lot has cast ..590: 2
without good society 885: 5
would I were h. to look 1917: 5
would no bargain drive ..885: 4
writ in climate of h. 76:11
Heaven's help better than
early rising 1729:11
Heaven-directed to the poor 985:11
Heaven-faring: sent me H. 1161:10
Heavens: all I ask, the h.
above 2103: 5
are just 1030: 8
began their march sublime 1940: 6
behold the h. and the earth 2031:11
blaze forth the death of
princes 146: 1
covered by h. 1340: 1
declare the glory of God 1834:18
fought 2109:10
from yon blue h. 73:10
he bowed the h. also 796: 4
man should scale the h. ..2167:15
most ancient h. 508:13
my wide roof-tree 910: 9
of parchment made 791: 6
road to the h. remains 110: 8
starry h. and moral
law 1345:5; 1891:6; 1914: 8
stretchest h. like curtain 796: 3
though the h. fall 1030:16
thundered, air shone fire 1154: 4
to suit taste of all 1624: 7
Heavier by the weight of
a man 944:20
Heaviness: chilling h. of
heart 1780:20
foreruns good 1945:13
life-harming h. 250:18
of heart breaketh strength 877:11
of stomach 1780:20
pleasing h. 1846:11
take no h. to heart 877:11
what means this h. 1843:24
Hebe Autumn fills 116:10
flies from those 2216: 6
Hebetudo et duritia cordis 881: 9
Hebreu pour moi 1070: 5
Hebrew: it is H. to me ..1070: 5
will turn Christian 265:12
Hebrides: among the far-
thest H. 2097:11
in dreams behold the H. .1767: 9
Hecademus: divine H. 1096: 6
Hector: know of H. 16:10
toss her head and h. 2146: 4
like H. in field to die ..178: 3
Hectora quis nosset 16:10
Hecuba of Troy ran mad 1231:12
what's H. to him 10: 5
Hedge keeps friendship ..1395:12
pull not down your h. ..1395:12
time to h. 752:11
to h. and to lurch 919:15
vainly you h. him 380: 5
will look upon h. 580: 7
Hedge-sparrow 347: 3
Hedgehog only one trick ..717:15
rolled wrong way 1697:10
Hedgehogs dressed in lace 454:18
Hedgerow: set him before a
h. in a lane 1383:20
Hedges his own way 2039: 8
Hee-haws: dry h. 1035: 7
Heed: take h. how you look
back 173:11
Heel: despot's h. 2064:12
I will begin at thy h. 217:11
lifted h. against me 727:14
of limping winter 93:12
of the North-East Trade .1814: 3
tread each other's h. 2177: 3
Heels as high as head 955: 2
grow out at h. 715:11
may kick at heaven 1359:16
show it fair pair of h. ..1641:14
take to one's h. 681: 9
Heidelberg, dear H. 2291:13
Heifer: ploughed with my h. 1723:13
run with halter 772: 1
sacrifice h. to Juno 2139: 2
who finds the h. dead 1621:15
Height: cannot reach the h. 110: 2
of human happiness 858: 5
of prophetic spirits 1623:12
so hard is h. 345:12
Heightening of money a
cheat 1551: 3
Heights by great men
reached 830: 9
for Freedom's battlement ..65:11
hazardous to the weak head 836:10
more h. before him 1355: 6
other h. in other lives ..1522:11
soul is competent to gain 1893: 5
trod the sunlit h. 1539: 7
undreamed of yore 404: 3
which the soul gains 108:14
Heir
See also Inheritance
absent shall not be h. 2: 5
born the free h. 1247: 2
Creation's h. 2237:14
follows h. as wave 985: 8
impatient h. 985: 4
looks to be h. 985: 7
make doctor his h. 465:15
of all the ages 43:16
scarce to third h. descends ..74: 6
suspected and hated 985:15
Heiresses: all h. beautiful 134: 9
Heirloom: its h. is the heart 1466: 2
Heirs: more h. at love 645:17
of all eternity 579: 5
of habits and customs ..1428:22
of more than royal race ..2232: 4
of tomorrow 1128: 6
of truth and delight ...1536: 6
of universal praise 630: 2
Shakespeare's h. 1306: 2
to h. unknown 985:11
to some six feet of sod 826:16
Held, Anna: is dead 401:13
Helen, thy beauty is to me 140: 6
where H. lies 1221: 3
Helen of Troy 888
fair-haired mother of H. 1191: 6
like another H. 888:19
past ruined Ilion H. lives 1521:11
ravish'd H., Menelaus'
queen 889: 5
sweet H., make me im-
mortal 1047: 1
with wanton Paris sleeps .889: 5
Helen's: one hair of H.
tress 135:13
Helicon quaffed like beer 1528:12
Helicon's harmonious springs 200:10
Heliotrope: turns to sun ..1198:18
Hell 889
afloat in lovers' tears 1204:16
all h. broke loose 890:20
all places shall be h. 889:14
an' Maria 890:20
and heaven are near man 888:14a
ascended into h. 50: 3
bade all its millions rise ..241: 9
bid him to h. to h. goes ..939:17
black as h. 166: 7
bosom-h. of guilty man ..301:14
both sides of the tomb ..890: 1
broke loose on butterfly ..336:12
came to h. without cause ..892: 6
cannot stop invincible 891: 3
circle about unbelieving ..889:12
contains no fouler fiend 2187:14
cunning livery of h. 949: 7
don't half enough go 1324: 1
earth ante-room of h. 512: 3
fiery gulf of h. 892: 3
fifteen minutes of h. 888: 9
for his destination 1813: 7
for the inquisitive 351: 9
from beneath is moved 890:19
full of good intentions ..891: 9
full of musical amateurs 1362: 3
full of the ungrateful 984: 1
given up reluctantly 892:20
gives us art to sin 1830:13
go to h. without perspiring 1597:11
grew darker at frown 78: 7
has wholly boiled away . .890:14
hath no limits 889:14
he'll visit you in h. 1446:13
hot from h. 2109:11
Hull and Halifax 890:15
in their smile 2197: 5
I was never afraid of h. ..892:17
I will move all h. 891: 7
in h. alone individuality .969: 6
in h. they reign 441: 8
in the dark heart 888:10
is doing evil 888:14a
is empty 891: 5
is gaping for them 892:19
is the wrath of God 889: 8
itself breathes out 1303: 5
live as quiet in h. 2142: 4
made before world 351: 9
might sit for H. 1089:16
milk of concord in h. 234: 2
mocking laughter of h. ...1078:21
more bearable than nothingness 890:11
myself am h. 893: 5
never mentions h. 580: 3
no h. for authors 2256:13
no h. frighten from sin 892:20
no h. like bad conscience ..301:10
no h. save earth 517:10
no lady can bear 1263: 3
no other but soundless pit 889:11
nor h. a fury like woman 2203:11
of horses 549: 1
of waters 1775: 4
old H. of the Bible 890: 3
on the feet 451:19
pain of h. and Paradise 1445: 2
paint gates of H. 949:12
paved with good intentions 891:11
paved with granite blocks 891:10
paved with scholars' skulls 1763: 2
paved with skulls 891:12
pot threatened h. 2187:12
profoundest h. 444:12
rather out of date 890:14
rides through h. to save ..2109:16
ridiculous 888:13
roofed with lost oppor-
tunities 891:12
send to h. across lots 891: 8
shall stir for this 891: 7
stands abashed 1373:19
tell him to go to h. 974: 6

History, *continued*
of England 552: 2
of individual a Bible ...979: 1
of liberty, h. of resistance 1104: 4
of women h. of tyranny ..2196: 2
owes excellence to writer 903: 1
pageant not philosophy 899: 4
Philosophy from examples .899:10
pleasanter to read h. than live it 900:14
prospects by starlight 901:13
read h. in nation's eyes ..2080:13
record of quest for bread and butter 899:16
register of crimes 902: 8
repeats itself 821: 7; 901: 4
represent events themselves 902:13
resolves into biography ..899: 6
shall not dare to state anything false 900:15
should be a Bible 158: 7
strange, eventful h. 2240: 5
teaches everything 899:15
tells what man has done 1054:16
that is ancient h. 900: 1
they who live in h. 900: 6
triumphed over Time 900: 8
unrolled scroll of prophecy 899:12
what he hit is h. 941: 4
what's her h.? a blank 900:11
with supernatural element 901: 9
writes h. of the world ..2249: 7
History's purchased page 296:12
Histrionem: quod fere totus mundus h. 2240: 6
Hit: as it may h. 1448:14
don't h. at all 2280: 3
never h. soft 2280: 3
palpable h. 1641: 8
that brings runner in 893:14
Hitch your wagon to a star 109: 4
Hitched: gettin' h. 1263: 5
into a rhyme 1522: 8
Hitherto shalt thou come ..1772: 5
Hive: bad for the h. 143:13
braided h. 144: 5
stock and tend your h. 41: 2
this great h., the city ...276:11
Hives: fill our h. with honey 347:10
Hoard and life together 215: 9
with a little h. of maxims 366:17
Hoarding: do not discourage h. 1998: 1
went to hell 119:16
Hoards: after h. 119: 1
Hoarse with having little else to do 76:14
Hoarseness caused by swallowing gold 199:10
Hob nob is the word 1663:16
Hob-and-nob with brother Death 959:15
with Death 376:23
Hobbard de hoy 2265: 7
Hobbes clearly proves 2106: 1
Hobbes' voyage 415:11
Hobbledehoy stage 2265: 7
Hobbs hints blue 1559:13
Hobby: each man bestride 1489:12
Hobby-horse is forgot 567: 6
Hobgoblin of little minds 304:12
Hobnails: but tintacks 820: 7
Hobo builds palaces 2070:20
Hoboken: Heaven, Hell or H. 67: 6
Hobson's choice 260:16
Hoc ego, tuque sumus ...1489:10
erat in votis 1329:12
est corpus meum 2221: 8
single syllable, H. 2221: 8
Hock-carts, wassails, wakes 1538: 2
Hodie mihi, cras tibi 2021:11
quod h. non est, cras erit 2277: 2
vivendum 1130:13
Hodierno manum injeceris 2021: 9
Hoe his row 1488:10
Hoeder, blind old god 1825:14
Hoffen: besser h. 927:19
Hog: fattest h. in Epicurus' sty 1954:13
from Epicurus' herd 648: 9
Hog, *continued*
go the whole h. 1645: 6
in sloth 954: 3
like h. or dog 1793:18
root, h., or die 1954: 8
steal h., give feet 772: 9
that ploughs not 1954:16
Hog-butcher of the world 251: 5
Hogarth: epitaph 568:16
Hoghton: he who would see old H. right 1342:19
Hogmanay, like all festivals 658: 8
Hogs: keep h. and eat husks 1615:19
Höhe: ungewohnter H. nicht zu schwindeln 837: 3
Hohngelächter der Hölle ..1078:21
Hoi polloi 1479: 1
Hoist with his own petar 1710:15
Hoity toity 77:17
Hokum: let them eat h. ..1571: 3
Holbein: of seven lords ..764:10
Hold: makes nice of no vile 1393:14
mine to have and to h. 1271:10
never will you h. me ..1211:10
take better h. 1488: 5
thee to my heart 1211:13
to have and to h. 1271:10
Holdfast is the only dog ..470:17
Holds with glittering eye 597: 9
Hole: hath but one h. 1357:14
in a' your coats 1603:14
little h. of discretion 456: 9
see day at little h. 2039:17
to keep wind away 385: 5
too open under the nose 1358: 3
what h. in hell 1300: 4
where tail came through ..444:10
Holes: square pegs in round h. 1119:15
where eyes did once inhabit 1816: 5
yourselves have made 343: 5
Holiday 903
blind-man's h. 170: 2
give the boys a h. 414: 3
never see it but a h. 903:16
on a sunshine h. 903:13
perpetual h. hell 903:15
Roman h. 903: 9
take much h. 903:18
Holiday-time of my beauty 1103: 2
Holidays: holiest of h. 903:12
Holily: that wouldst thou h. 972:18
Holiness 903
confers a certain insight ..903:21
consummate h. 903:21
of serene nature 903:20
plan on which God buildeth 904: 5
Holland and the Hollanders 904
Hollander: swag-bellied H. .561: 8
Holler: no use to h. 1499: 2
Hollow: all false and h. ..86: 9
fearful h. of thine ear ..1406: 5
man, who has become h. ..1476:19
murmur of ocean-tide ...1773: 8
profound man h. 1476:19
Hollowness of human life 1490:18
reverbs no h. 1833: 1
Hollows where those flowers grew 2293: 2
Holly: green winter of the h. 37:15
Holly Tree 2038:11
Hollyhock: flaring h. 756: 1
Hollywood war 2120: 5
Holmes: "Common-place," said H. 2209: 5
Holy, divine, good, amiable 2185: 5
fair and wise is she 2185:10
give not h. unto dogs 1476:13
holy, holy 793: 1
Love, however brief 1174: 1
neither h. nor Roman ..1737:15
Holy Ghost: Father, Word 783:11
Holy Grail is found 1390: 8
Holy Land: hangs midway 482: 6
Holy-water: court h. in dry house 2125: 5
of court 326: 9
Holystone the decks 1779:12
Homage is due to kings ..1044: 1
of a sigh 134:13
of a tear 1975:16
of thoughts unspoken ...1374:20
to a king 327:11
to rising dawn 1944: 4
Hombre pone y Dios dispone 787: 7
Home 904
all things have h. 910:12
and a pleasing wife 909: 2
and certainty and sanctity are best 1735: 6
and its duties 2205:10
any more at h. like you 1233:12
art gone and ta'en wages 401:15
at h. in a better place ..2031:10
at h. like devils they be 2183: 4
at h. secure and safe 945: 1
at last 907: 9
be it never so homely ...906: 2
be thou thine own h. 909:12
Christian, steer h. 1651: 7
city, pass before my eyes 1297: 1
cling to thy h. 907:12
come h., father 2295: 4
come h. to men's bosoms ..206: 8
come we in weariness H. 905: 8
country h. a cemetery ..829:11
creep h. and take place ..34:14
deep imag'd in soul 907: 8
even in his own country 320:11
every one for his h. 1793: 2
father, dear father, come h. with me now 2295: 4
first best country, h. 1467: 3
from one h. to another ..397: 4
from the lonely cities 52: 2
from which to run away ..95: 2
gilded walls never make h. 905:18
great object of life 904:17
hath no fellow 906:10
he that doth live at h. ..907: 5
he that lives always at h. 910: 6
here is our h. 908: 4
holiest spot 905:15
homely features keep h. ..138: 5
I am nearer h. today ...887:11
I left my old Kentucky h. for you 2288: 5
I wouldn't leave my h. if I were you 2288: 5
I'd leave ma happy h. for you 2288: 5
I'm afraid to come h. in the dark 2294: 7
interprets heaven 904:14
is anywhere for me 320:13
is everywhere 320: 5
is h. 906:12
is high in heaven 509:12
is on the deep 547: 8
is the air 361: 2
is the Kingdom 908:15
is the sailor 570: 9
is where the heart is 904:19
leave thy h., O youth ..2030: 8
left me at h., deserted ..2291: 2
live at h. at ease 1780:14
Maggie Murphy's h. 933: 5
man goeth to his long h. ..823: 1
man nearest good at h. 907: 7
my eternal h. 887: 8
my h., the city 1297: 1
my old Kentucky h. 1454:12
never h. came she 2001: 8
no h. whose h. is everywhere 320:12
no place like h. 906: 7
no place like home, and many glad of it 910: 1
nursery of infinite 904:14
of lost causes 224:17
of the Arts 1001: 4
of the bean and the cod ...194:15
of the brave 674: 3
of the brave and the free 51:5; 548: 3
of the Truth and Light ..194:15
of thy rest 403: 4
oh, to be h. again 907: 1

Hoop: grown into a h. 2175:19
his body with embraces ..1997: 4
of gold, a paltry ring 1013:13
Hooping: out of all h. 2209:10
Hoops of steel 730:16
Hoosier State of Indiana ..977: 3
Hop for his profit exalt 45: 2
of a wild rabbit 117:11
Hop-o'-my-thumb 771: 9
Hope 921
abandon h. ye who enter ..922: 2
against h. 922:17
adorns and cheers way ...924: 7
all h. falls 621:12
all h. of never dying 1348: 9
alone 'mongst mortals dwelleth kindly H. 925: 3
and fear alternate 927:10
and fear inseparable 927: 5
and fear keep step 927:11
and Fortune farewell 569: 4
and Joy, pleasure's train 1312:14
and patience remedies 924: 2
and Youth are children of one mother 924:19
assassin of our joy 928: 6
auspicious h. 924: 3
bade world farewell 725: 8
balm and lifeblood 923:23
best to h. the best 928: 3
better good h. than bad ..921:16
beyond shadow of dream ..969:13
brighten days to come ..1460:11
brightest from fears 927:10
build h. on incense 469: 7
but sad despair 437:11
but speculations 88: 9
buy h. with money 922:20
Cape of Good H. 27: 1
celestial influence 924:11
changed for despair 437:17
charmer, linger'd still 924: 3
cheap as despair 927:19
cheers e'en misery 924: 4
congenial h. 924: 3
corrupt him with h. 1543: 2
could have no fear 927: 3
cozening h. 926: 8
creates from its own wreck 1129: 9
cure of all ills 921: 5
day-star of might 966: 3
deceives 925:10
deferred 922:15
delayed h. afflicteth heart ..922:15
doubtful of the future 926:12
dying but not dead 923: 7
elevates, Joy brightens ...924:13
enchanted smil'd 922: 1
enchantress fond and kind .924: 1
entertaining h. 926:17
every man's h. in himself 1786: 8
Faith, H., Charity 24:11
fallen from what high h. ..622:15
farewell h., farewell fear ..927: 3
floods my heart 966: 3
for all help is myself 1786: 2
for another day of existence .30: 1
for ever on the wing 926:15
for every woe 1017:23
for happiness beyond 334:17
for living, none for dead ..923:16
for Tomorrow 2022:15
for years to come 794:15
frustrate h. severer than despair 2:17
gay H. is theirs 634: 4
good breakfast, ill supper .923:19
good h. better than bad possession 924: 5
great deceiver as she is ...925:19
had perish'd long ago 436:16
hath happy place 965: 7
he that wants h. poorest ..922: 5
heavenly h. is all serene ..925:12
high h. for low heaven 922:19
high h. to relapse 462. 1
I cultivated h. 926: 4
I don't intrude 352:11
I h. I fear, resolved 475:22
I thus do exalt 45: 2
Hope, *continued*
I'll build a Christian's h. ..469: 7
if h. were not, heart would break 923:24
illusions of h. 925:13
immortal h. dispels gloom 964:16
in action is charity 921:13
in death h. sees star 964: 7
in h. to merit heaven 888: 8
incline to h. than fear 927: 7
inspires poetic lays 924: 8
is a kind of cheat 925:11
is a lover's staff 924:18
is a waking dream 921: 2
is but the dream 921: 2
is flat despair 437:11
is like a harebell 922:16
is like the sun 925: 1
is there any hope 798: 6
is there no hope 467:16
keeps the heart whole 923:24
keeps the spark alive 923:17
knows not if fear speak truth 550: 3
less clear than dew 2007:14
less h. hotter love 1186: 9
less quick to spring 32:12
let not h. prevail 926:16
like a cordial 925: 6
lined himself with h. 926: 8
lives on h., die fasting 923:22
long h. fainting soul 922:15
Love's leman is 436:16
mainspring of patriotism .1464: 6
maintains mankind 921:12
makes fettered miner live .924:15
makes shipwrecked sailor strike out 924:15
maketh not ashamed 924:16
man is saved by h. 17:17
man of h. and forward-looking mind 1308:11
may succor 1193:14
may vanish but die not 292: 4
mighty to inspire h. 2157: 3
most befriends us here ...925: 6
most hopeless of all 925: 8
most universal thing 925: 2
mounts on swiftest h. 862:16
my own h. is a sun 1434: 8
never comes 925:18
never leaves wretched 922: 4
no change, no pause, no h. 437:18
no h. left, no fear 927: 3
no h., no endeavor 921:11
not necessary to h. in order to undertake 1489: 2
nurse of young desire 921: 4
of a good dinner 451: 4
of all who suffer 1028: 4
of being good 922: 2
of life returns 1118:12
of my spirit 306:11
of the half-defeated 1540:10
of the world 51: 7
on h. the wretch relies 923:10
one leaf is for h. 1227: 2
other h. had she none 238:14
our fathers saw 675: 4
our greatest good 926:17
paramount duty 921:14
parent of faith 921: 3
patent medicine for sin ..921: 5
poor man's bread 921: 8
poor salad 923:20
putrid eggs of h. 437: 1
returns with the sun 923:11
rules land for ever green ..925: 5
second soul of the unhappy .921: 7
sees a star 964: 7
silver-tongued H. 861:22
so lives inveterate h. 923: 3
sows what Love shall 926: 5
species of happiness 921:11
springs eternal 922:14
springs exulting 922:14
spur to industry 980:10
star of life's ocean 921:10
starves without a crumb .1434: 6
supports each noble flame .924: 8
Hope, *continued*
survives worst disease ..1094: 2
sweet h., nurse of eld 922:12
sweetest of all plums 924: 9
swells my sail 924:13
take h. from heart of man .924:14
tender leaves of h. 1146: 5
that points to heaven 238: 9
these have not h. of death ..375: 4
thing with feathers 921: 6
thou not much 927:14
though h. were lost 927:15
thus H. me deceived 925:10
to h. till H. creates 1129: 9
to inherit in the grave 828:14
to meet again 1796:13
to the end 922:11
to the fainting heart 686:15
told a flattering tale 926:16
traitor of the mind 926: 9
travels thro', nor quits us 923:14
treacherous goddess 925:19
triumph h. over experience 1279: 9
true h. is swift 924:18
unhappy, h. 921:15
universal liar 921: 5
unsatisfied 109: 7
walks with golden shoon ..369: 7
we h. and h. 29:17
well and have well 922: 9
what is h. but deceiving ..449:10
what was dead was h. 928: 5
when h. was high 109:12
where h. is coldest 592: 7
whereof he knew 1999:12
while there's life, there's h. 923: 5
white-handed H. 618: 6
who bids me h. 924:12
will make thee young 924:19
with honey blends cup 924:10
with lofty h. we came 1374:21
without an object 927:17
worldly h. men set 926: 6
worse than despair is h. ..928: 2
worth any money 924: 5
wrong guide, good company 925:19
you never bade me h. 1620: 8
Hope's: condemned to H. delusive mine 1145: 8
deluding glass 463: 4
perpetual breath 925: 5
star to man grows dim .2182:12
Hoped for better things 922:10
Hopeful in adversity 1626: 3
Hopeless, lays his dead away 967: 8
Hopers go to hell 925:16
Hopes are all with thee 52: 4
belied our fears 393:12
called her Small H. 1014: 4
called waking dreams 921: 2
catch hold of h. 1921: 9
dearest h. in pangs born ..927:22
extravagant h. of the future 42:13
faded h. and h. agleam ..2101:15
far-reaching h. 926: 7
fondest h. decay 452:15
for constant love 2198: 2
give h. of bliss or dig my grave 1202:15
great h. make great men ..830:13
greater numbers lost by h. .927: 1
her h., her fears, joys 927:10
his h. became a part 237: 3
how buoyant are thy h. ..2266: 6
if h. were dupes 927: 2
in heaven do dwell 887:14
like towering falcons 926: 3
lost in far distance 921: 2
mighty h. make us men ...924: 6
more than half my h. came true 25:16
not always realized 922:10
of golden rules 1500:10
of honest men 893:17
of thy house 923: 2
our h. belied our fears ...393:12
put aside trifling h. 925:14
raises false h. 925:15
that fall like flowers 617:24
undimmed for mankind ..205: 8

Hound-dog to scent out evil 1685:11
Hounds make welkin answer 526: 1
of Sparta 942: 4
of spring 1908: 6
run with the h. 421:14
Hour: abode his destin'd h. 1141: 9
ago since it was nine 934: 8
appointed h. 967: 1
bad quarter of an h. 719: 3
blessed h. of dinner 449:10
busied with crowded h. ..934:10
cannot ward inevitable h. .826:13
catch the transient h. ...2009:12
children's h. 253:11
consecrated h. 1588:12
enjoy shining h. of sun ..1130: 6
enjoy the present h. 311:19
evening's calm and holy h. 581:16
every h. a miracle 1316:14
every h. approaches death 382: 4
fleeting h. has brought ..1458:19
flies 379: 8
flies the inconstant h. 713:18
happen in one h. 934:12
I also had my h. 111: 9
I have had my h. 1132:16
improve each shining h. ..144: 6
in each man's life 1432:11
in one h. what anguish 934: 3
in the morning 934:13
inevitable h. 826:13
is come but not the man ..934:16
make coming h. o'erflow 1017:15
many things happen in h. .714: 6
may destroy what an age was a building 934:12
may lay it in the dust 1918: 2
nor lose the present h. .. 1327:10
not for just an h. 1881: 5
nothing can bring back h. 1459: 4
O heavy h. 2141: 4
o' night's arch keystane ..1302: 8
of destruction's near 745: 8
of Fate's serenest weather 1436: 6
of inward thought 448:13
of justice does not strike 1032:14
of lead 386: 1
of love worth age of living 1182:15
of pain long 934: 3
of that Dundee 983: 7
of virtuous liberty 1106:10
once in a golden h. 2130:12
one crowded h. of life 781: 4
one h. in doing justice ..1029: 6
one h. of youthful joy 196: 2
one loving h. for many years of sorrow 1953:13
one self-approving h. 629: 1
pernicious h. 353: 6
present h. alone man's ..1599: 8
serve the future h. 1801: 8
short h. ayont the twal 934: 2
some wild wakening h. 602:17
that sweeten'd life 934:17
that wakens fond desire ..582: 4
the poet loves....572: 3
this h.'s the very crisis ..934: 9
Time and the h. 371:17
'tis all a transient h. 1141: 7
'tis the h. of prayer 1587: 2
to fill the h. 854: 5
to sing, love and linger ..1137:10
to weep in 1137:4a
torturing h. 1697:12
wait th' appointed h. 1935: 3
what better than happy h. .855:19
when lovers' vows 581:17
when pleasure blooms ...582:11
when rites unholy 1587: 2
when the soul emerges 391:11
wherein man might be happy 855:20
which gives us life 1150: 7
which has gone never returns 2009: 2
Whirlwind H. 1159: 8
wisely tell what h. of day 1097: 1
witching h. of night 1303: 5

Hour, *continued*
you laughed and kissed ..1874: 9
you were born in merry h. 1302: 6
Hour-glass run gold-dust ..2008:16
Hour-hand of truth 2059:21
Hours 934
are as miser's coins 1142: 3
are golden links 934:14
are long, pay small 1066:16
are Officers brave 2009:12
are passing slow 934: 3
are Time's shafts 1943:16
canonical h. 873: 6
chase the glowing h. 359:11
count only h. serene 1943:12
creeping h. of time 2211: 2
evil h. may end in good ..147: 8
feathered with flying h. ..2005:12
fly, flowers die 1943: 8
fly in a circle 934: 5
give me no changeless h. .2008: 9
golden h. of vision 860:13
golden h. on angel wings 1210:15
happy h. employ'd upon my books 189: 1
hath not known god-like h. 1245:13
hotter h. approach 1937: 7
how many h. bring day ..2007: 7
how soon h. are over 697:13
I do not count the h. 1384: 6
I mark h. by shadow 1943: 6
I only mark sunny h. 1943:12
I spent with thee 1214: 2
in love have wings 2:18
jolly h. lead on 1405: 8
lo! where rosy bosom'd h. 1906:15
long h. do pass away 1943:19
lost h. and days 1687:11
love, all the h. are long ..1214: 6
love reckons h. for months ..2:18
made for man 934:15
make use of thy salt h. ..1756:11
merry H., smile instead ..2262: 7
none but cloudless h. 1943:12
of brightness gone 1295: 2
pass inoffensive h. away 1275: 1
passionate young h. 1456: 1
six h. enough for work ..1062:17
slowly pass the h. 934: 3
so many h. must I rest 935: 1
social h., swift-wing'd ...1860: 2
softly, O midnight h. 1846: 6
spend long h. talking 1963:24
steal a few h. from night 1403:15
sly slow hours 591:18
talk with our past h. 1788:17
that I throw away 934:11
these h. redeem Life's ill 1192: 6
to play the lover 697:13
twilight h. flew by 1914:15
two golden h. 934: 6
undelightful h. 878:19
unheeded flew the h. 2007: 9
unnumbered h. of pain ...290:14
were cups of sack 2008: 5
what peaceful h. I enjoy'd 1293:19
whose indefatigable h. ..1143: 2
will take care of themselves 1315: 4
winged h. of bliss 76: 3
wingless crawling h. 934: 3
House 935
and woman suit 909: 2
appointed for all living 825:14
best for secrecy 1783:16
better h. too little 935: 7
better to h. of mourning .1356:16
bless this little h. 168:11
bloody h. of life 1043:10
built by the wayside 935:11
built h. upon the sand 695:12
built on another's ground 935:14
but not a dwelling 910: 4
by the high-road 1495: 8
by the side of the road ..1495: 8
carry h. upon her back ..2205: 3
cast h. out at window 935: 3
choose not h. near inn 935: 8
clear fullest h. 537:16
confines the spirit 909:13
dark h. and detested wife 1275:10

House, *continued*
divided against itself 455: 4
each should in h. abide ..906:14
eaten out of h. and home 516:17
every h. where Love abides 905:18
fare you well, old h. 905: 5
find h. a master 909:13
for fools and mad 562:17
founded upon a rock 935:10
full of books 904:18
full of sacrifices 1666:14
get out of my h. 97: 8
goes mad when women gad 2205: 1
great source of happiness .905:17
handsome h. to lodge a friend 1329:12
he breaks up h. 1871:16
he kept no Christmas-h. ..932:10
he that buys h. ready wrought 935: 6
he that in neat h. will dwell 935: 5
his h. is sweet to him 905: 7
I am in the h. 1489:13
is a prison 1388:13
is made of glass 1650: 7
is not a small h. best ...906: 4
join h. to h. 118:15
laughs with silver 1717:17
laws favor privacies of h. 936: 1
leave to those to come the h. itself 1503: 5
let me mind h. of dust 825:13
little h. well filled 906: 8; 1721:11
man's h. his castle 936: 4
may I have a warm h. 1330: 3
more to my taste than a tree 276: 2
my h. is my castle 935:15
my h. to me Escurial 906: 5
nearer my Father's h. ...883:12
no baby in the h. 122: 7
no h., lie in yard 935: 9
no h. without mouse 1357:16
not built with hands 33:12
not made with hands 905: 5
of Christmas 268: 7
of clay for to be made 825:10
of dreams in which I live .483:12
of dreams untold 481:10
of feasting 1356:16
of flesh and blood 175: 3
of have and h. of want ...1616: 6
of laughter, h. of woe ..1078: 9
of Lords 555:13
of six by two 825: 9
of sticks and mud 175: 3
one's vacant h. of life 160: 3
Prison H. of Pain 1444: 7
ready-made 935: 6
return no more to his h. ..375:14
secret h. of death 1933:10
secret H. of Shame 754: 3
set h. on fire to roast eggs 1790: 4
set thine h. in order 1598: 7
shall be called h. of prayer 1986: 7
shows the owner 935: 4
small h. and large garden 1329: 8
spoil h. to save town 667:11
t' make it home 904:16a
this mortal h. I'll ruin ..1933:10
though thou art small 906: 5
to be let for life 877:19
to me my castle 936: 4
to put his head in 935:12; 1855: 3
trimmed 315:17
untiled 910: 2
upon an ill seat 94: 9
was built of stone 96: 3
was known to all 2070:17
where I was born 1297: 1
where there is plenty 316: 6
whinstone h. my castle is 935:16
whose h. is of glass 1650: 7
why build my h. by road 1495: 8
with lawns enclosing it 191: 6
with Montaigne now 932: 3
with starry dome 2242:14
withdraw thy foot from in thy neighbor's h. ..1396:10
worse than a smoky h. 192:16
wretched h. of They 1760:10

Inch, *continued*
give i., take ell 1635:12
importance of a mile 1015: 9
not an i. further 1641:13
of joy, ell of annoy 1018:19
of our territory 718:11
refuse to budge an i. 1616:11
Inch-meal: by i. a disease ..353:15
Inch-rule of taste 1965:14
Inches: tell what thou art by i. 217:11
Incidente del mertiere ...1043: 4
Incipere multost facilius ..147:15
Incitantur enim homines ..352: 9
Incivility not vice of soul 1260: 5
Inclinata: in te omnis domus i. 923: 2
Inclination: overcome your i. 1981:12
treach'rous i. 1223: 6
Inclinations avowed by eye 597:15
of own nature 1391:14
Inclose: what we i. you i. 1517: 4
Income twenty pounds 1997: 7
Incommodis alterius commoda 1323: 5
Incomplete: artistry's curse 748: 1
Incompleteness: flowed around our i. 792:15
Inconsistencies in principle 1929:11
of opinion 1427:21
Inconsistency
See also Consistency
imputed i. for changing mind 304:11
of human nature 1308:17
only thing consistent 305:10
Inconstancy
See also Constancy
I loathe i. 305:19
Inconstant as the seas ..2197: 9
call one another i. 1200:12
more i. than the wind 479: 6
Inconstantiam: mutationem consilii i. 304:11
Incontinent before marriage 1205:13
to be continent 246:13
Inconvenience: better mischief than i. 1319: 4
Inconvenient to be poor ..1565:12
Incorporate two in one ..1272: 7
Incorpsed and demi-natured 931:13
Incorruptible: Sea-green I. 1377:15
Incorruption: put on i. ..965: 9
Increase: God gave i. 636:18
our Maker bids increase 1273: 8
Incredible more credible 1481:13
Incrédules plus crédules ..334:10
Incredulity first step to philosophy 475:11
loses knowledge of divine 476: 5
vulgar i. 476:10
wit of fools 476: 1
Incredulous are the most credulous 334:10
Increment: unearned i. 464:15
unearned i. of Madeira ..2154:10
Ind: from east to western 1013:11
rude and savage man of I. 1758:19
Indecision 972
brings its own delays 972: 7
in i. grief 972: 5
Indefatigable: Old I. 1771:15
who more i. than a friend 729:13
Indemnity for the past ..1460: 7
Indentation: conscientious i. 2041: 5
Indentures, covenants 1094: 3
Independence 973
Britons prize too high 973: 6
Hail! I.. hail! 974: 2
is a rocky island 973:11
let i. be our boast 51: 6
now and i. forever 974: 7
of principle 1612: 8
thy spirit, I., let me share 973:15
to remain true to myself ..973: 3
Independence Day 974
Index 975
best book owes most to i. 975:10
face but the soul's i. 85:10
Index, *continued*
marble i. of a mind 1400: 3
necessary implement 976: 1
of the heart 606: 8
soul's i. 606: 8
thunders in the i. 8:15
to joy and mirth 606: 8
Index: tolliter i. 844:13
Index-learning turns no student pale 976: 4
Indexes although small pricks 976: 5
India: an I. in itself 658:13
India's prehistoric clay 586:10
Indian (American) 976
dances to prepare 359: 5
like a base I. 1476:16
Lo, the poor I. 976:10
make I. of white man 976:12
only good I. dead I. 976:11
ruins of mankind 976: 8
summer 1936: 3
to see a dead I. 1615:14
Indian-like, adore 216:13
Indiana 977
Indians without govt. happy 817: 8
Indictment against a whole people 61: 4
Indifference 977
and hypocrisy 978: 7
buttressed with i. 977:15
cold i. came 978: 3
don't produce distress 977: 8
full of a sweet i. 977: 7
half infidelity 1690: 2
Harvard i. 978: 4
infernal i. 79: 4
moral i. malady 977: 7
nymph I. bring 977:13
Indifferency: preaches i. ..977:12
Indifferent: nothing i. 1492:21
Indifferentism: mild i. 977: 7
Indigent: how i. the great ..837: 4
hundred i. 1567: 4
Indigestion 978
and loss of sleep 30: 9
makes a coward 895:10
of i. bred 478:18
reality and i. therewith ..960:15
sows hurry and reaps i. ...978:11
Indignatio: facit i. versum 1524: 2
ubi sæva 570:10
Indignation
See also Anger
can no longer tear heart 570:10
incens'd with i. 444:18
moral i. jealousy halo ..1006:10
spit forth iron i. 2118: 2
Indignities: by i. to dignities 836: 9
Indignor quicquam reprehendi 340:10
Indirections: by i. find directions out 421: 5
Indiscretion: green i. 240: 6
innocence 991: 1
without i. no lover 2207:13
Indiscrétions: femmes pardonnent grandes i. 2207:13
Indissoluble union 57: 2
Individual always mistaken 978:12
every i. strives to grow ..978:14
end of the Universe 979: 2
I announce great i. 979: 4
insulate the i. 978:13
it ain't the i. 1862:18
not an i., a species 1258:12
underneath all, i. 979: 4
Individualism poison 979: 3
rugged i. 978:15
Individuality 978
justified in i. 978:13
matter of psychology 1978:14
retained in hell alone 969: 6
salt of common life 979: 3
Individuals guided by reason 1484:11
may form communities ..1379:10
Indocti discant et ament ..960: 8
surgunt 958:18
Indolence
See also Idleness
fight off your i. 953: 5
is King for life 956:11
is the sleep of the mind ..952: 6
is the true state of man ..955: 1
makes a person honest ..913:18
nor i., nor pleasure 1887: 3
philosophy of i. 2132: 8
sort of suicide 952: 8
such dread was i. 972:12
was called wisdom 955: 9
Indolence sommeil des esprits 952: 6
Indolent: delightful condition of doing nothing .955: 3
Indoor: who will stay i. ..941:16
Indostan: six men of I. ..535:15
Indulged perhaps too much 2268:10
Indulgence: demoralised by i. 1086:15
for weaknesses 2074:15
his weak i. will accuse 2204:10
of grief blunder 840: 6
Indulgences: most sweet i. ..31: 4
Industries: infant i. 1965: 8
Industry 979
all things easy to i. 954: 1
and little conscience 980: 6
avarice spur of i. 118:14
by i. stor'd 310:16
can do anything 979: 6
fortune's right hand 980: 6
fosters genius 758: 1
God gives all to i. 980: 3
improves talents 980: 7
is a loadstone to draw 979: 8
is mother of fortune 979:11
is soul of business 979:13
mother of genius 758: 1
need not wish 979:16
nobility abateth i. 70:16
of artificers 994:21
supplies deficiencies 980: 7
supplies place of genius ..758: 1
supports us all 980: 1
Inebriate: cheer but not i. 1968: 7
of air am I 991:10
Inebriated with exuberance of own verbosity 779:16
Inelegance of poverty 1568:17
Inequalities: life's i. 204: 4
Inequality dear to American 574: 5
glorious i. of talent 527:15
measure of progress 527:15
Inertiæ dulcedo 955: 8
Inertis est nescire liceat ..1082:19
Inevitable: arguing with i. ..98:12
each of us i. 1245:12
Inexactitude: terminological i. 1840:14
Inexpressibles 580: 9
Infallible: none i. 577: 4
Infamia: immortalis 461:12
mendax i. terret 214:12
non nella pena è la i. 1657: 5
quid salvis i. nummis ..1336: 8
senza i., et lodo 1288: 4
Infamous fond of fame 625:16
through love of praise ..1578: 4
to be poor 1570:15
Infamy: eternal i. 48:16
give i. renown 1962: 9
never incurred 461: 6
prefer i. to taxation 1968: 1
to die and not be missed 402:11
to prefer life to honor ..918: 9
what is i. if money safe 1336: 8
Infancy: heaven lies about us in i. 252: 3
lay folded in i. 251:13
not only around our i. ..884:17
shadow-peopled i. 967: 2
wayward was thy i. 122: 2
Infant: as soon as sent forth, lies naked 163: 4
crying in the night 748: 8
manufactures 1965: 8
mewling and puking 2240: 5
well-educated i. 428:16
when it gazes on lig ..1016: 4

Intellect, *continued*
essence of age 31: 7
fragments of i. good 1307: 1
gigantic, well-proportioned 1308:17
great only by comparison 1309: 3
growth of i. spontaneous 1306:10
hitting below the i. 1679: 9
improperly exposed 1314: 6
is not replenished 1676: 3
let not conceit of i. 1370:18
may subdue women 2207: 1
nothing more excellent than i. 1511: 1
obscures more than illumines 1308:12
one-story i. 1591:14
our wayward i. 1390: 5
parts of i. whetstones 757:10
unconscious i. 1805: 2
Intellects: one-story i. 1308:14
Intellectual all-in-all 1477: 5
sense and souls 2143: 8
Intellectus qui plura intelligit 1309:10
Intellegendo: faciuntne i. 1058:21
Intellexeram si tacuisses 1823:10
Intelligence 993
all things slaves to i. 994: 6
and courtesy not combined 328:17
bright i. whose flame 795:14
enlarge the horizon 994: 5
higher i. than ours 2204:15
is tongue that discerns ..994:10
look of i. in men beauty 1254:11
more easily stamped out 1096:20
star-eyed i. 1602: 7
to perceive things in germ 994: 4
trained i. trusted 529: 5
Intelligent have a right 994: 2
we are not i. 994: 3
Intelligible: aim at being ..760: 8
is to be found out 218:11
Intemperance
See also Drunkenness
in nature is a tyranny ...504:11
no tyrant like i. 502: 5
Intemperantia litterarum .1166: 8
Intender needs only a voice 994:18
Intent: with carnal i. 1272: 2
working out a pure i. 2106: 4
Intention 994
good i. sudden power 994:14
Intentions: friends with the best i. 733: 8
good i. vicious results 994:15
hell paved with good i. ..891:12
stain not fair acts with foul i. 994:12
Intents savage-wild 1662: 3
wicked or charitable 770:10
Interchange: venal i. 286:11
Intercourse between living 770: 2
of daily life 1037: 6
speed the soft i. 1103: 1
Interdecit ne cum meleficio 288:12
Interest: agricultural i. 639: 7
always will prevail 1493:16
and fear, two levers 1793: 8
and vanity usual source of misfortunes 1321:19
better to earn i. 464:19
governs councils of men 1793: 8
natural i. of money 464:14
nine parts of i. 1494:16
savors of private i. 888:15
take i. in nothing 1414:6a
that keeps peace 1470:18
vested i. 75:11
wise man's i. to be seen ..703:11
world ruled by i. alone 1793: 8
Interested in others 14:12
Interesting: aim at being i. 192:17
people 67:10
Interests: powerful i. 2048: 8
which divinities honor 109: 4
Intérêt et la vanité 1321:19
Interêts: divisés d'i. 338: 6
Interior: report i. of nation 707:13
Interlocutor: each i. stands before us 185:10
Intermixture of the rattle 1222: 7
Internationalism another name for money juggling 60: 2
Internationalists: group of i. 59: 8
Interpolate: when exposition fails, i. 1019:17
Interpres: malignus i. 1011: 6
optimus i. legum 1092:17
Interpretation: more ado to interpret i. 186: 6
private i. 1624: 8
will misquote our looks ...87: 1
Interpreter: each may be his own i. 2221:11
every man own 617: 8
hardest of two 1070: 9
ignorant, base i. 340:13
of life 538:10
one sole: of Humanity ...783:13
thy best i. a sigh 1194:13
Intérressant plutot qu'exact 192:17
Interrogation of custom 356:10
Intervals: lucid i. 1230: 4
Interview: first i. the best 1289: 2
Intestina poetæ 1537: 5
Intestines of agile cat ..1369:13
smaller i. 1989:17
Intimate: be i. at home ..1789: 7
be i. with few ..631: 8; 738:13
Intimate the whole 1526: 7
Intolerable, not to be endured 541: 4
Intolerance
See also Tolerance
form of egoism 534: 2
in support of toleration 2022: 4
intolerant only of i. 2022: 4
Intonuere poli 1154: 4
Intoxicated: as with new wine i. both 2157:11
with eloquence 537: 1
Intoxication: best of life but i. 504:17
Intrinsical to himself 1489: 3
Intristi: tute hoc i. 1711: 3
Introduce me to the girl ..2290:11
Introduction to literary work 2249: 6
Introitum unum ad vitam ..380: 2
Introrsum turpem 948:10
Intrude: hope I don't i. ..352:11
Intruder: unmannerly i. ...352:11
Intruders: kicks i. 1684:11
Intuition: known by i. ..1807: 8
Intuta quæ indecora 1258:14
Inustatis atque incognitis 1370:12
Inutile: il n'est rien d'i. ..2070:13
Invectives 'gainst the officers 331:16
Invent: fitter to i. 2263: 2
necessary to i. him 788: 1
necessary to i. it 376: 7
something I must i. 1449: 2
we had needs i. heaven 788: 2
what some i., rest enlarge 1751: 8
Inventé par l'ennemi 995: 3
Invented: fond thing vainly i. 995: 1
if not true, well i. 995: 2
wise man who i. God 787:19
Inventer: il faudrait i. 376: 7
Invention 994
all admir'd 995:12
anger raiseth i. 78: 2
breeds i. 995: 8
essence of poetry 1516: 5
exquisite i. this 686:16
flags 436:18
in applying a thought 1666:22
man's i. and his hand 995:15
mere i. somewhat cheap 2249:10
my own i. 995: 2
necessity mother of i. ..1394: 2
of God 787:19
really a threat 1668: 7
weak i. of the enemy 541:23
Inventions: ages will beget new i. 995: 5
have not lightened toil 1229:12
in times of ignorance 995:17
many i. 995: 6
only its costume 102:17
Inventions, *continued*
submit i. to censure 995: 9
true rules for old i. 227: 9
Inventor knows to borrow 995: 8
of harmonies 1305:15
of history 853: 1
of kissing 1047:17
to read well 1673: 7
Inventors ashamed of 56: 1
Investigate systematically 1703:15
Investigation better than faith 620: 5
broadens 1703:15
Investment in knowledge .1054: 4
Invictus enim morior 296:20
Invideo: non i.; miror magis 2210: 1
Invidia: cæca i. est 1236:13
fanno 220:20
loquitur quod videt 1236:16
mordax 1236:15
non majus tormentum 565: 1
Invidiam placere virtute relicta 565: 4
summa petere 565: 9
Invidus macrescit 565: 2
Invincible in arms 238: 1
in peace 2119: 3
who is i. 322:10
Invisible as nose on face 1010:14
in war 2119: 3
worshipped the i. alone ..1355:15
Invitus: quam i. facias ..2149: 3
Inwardness, mildness 1792:10
Inwariable: glass o' the i. ..45: 6
Io: castles in the air 109:11
Ipse dixit 1897:11
Ira: adjuvat i. manus 79:14
furor brevis est 80: 5
gravis i. regum 1038: 8
lente i. deorum 1708:15
lento divina procedit i. ..1708:16
prohibenda est i. in puniendo 1655:18
quæ tegitur nocet 78:13
ruinis simillima 80:10
servorum i. cecidisse 1840: 6
trux decet i. feras 1471:10
ut fragilis glacies 78:10
vim suscitat i. 79:14
Iracundi hominis iracunda oratio 1899:12
Iracundia: ita i. obstitit oculis 78:11
Iræ: amantium i. 1197:14
inde i. et lacrimæ 1973:13
pone i. frena modumque ..81: 3
qui non moderabitur i. 80: 4
Iram atque animos a crimine cumunt 2201: 4
sævæ memorem Junonis ob i. 867:20
Iras: plumbeas i. gerunt ..823:14
Iratus: putat facere quam possit 79:16
Ire: full of i. 241: 1
he must be without i. 79:16
he that hath great i. 79:16
of sin 301:10
Ireland 995
bane of England 998: 8
gives England soldiers ..998:10
Glorious I. 997:10
green and sad 998: 3
I'll not forget old I. 997: 8
in state of social decomposition 996: 3
is a little Russia 996: 7
nothing in I. lasts long except miles 996: 7
wedded but never won 999: 1
Ireson: poor Floyd I. 1658: 4
Iris all hues 684:13
changes on dove 477: 9
Irish Brigade 1868:10
bulls, calves in Greece ...995:18
fair people 999: 6
more I. than the I. 999:12
now the I. are ashamed 999: 7
tormenting I. lay 1463: 2

Jam tomorrow, j. yesterday 2020:13
Jamaica: I'm for right J. 499:18
James, Henry: cosmopolitanism 320:11
poor Henry J. 2258:20
James: King J. to the fly ..693:11
Jane was good as gold 148:10
Jangled: sweet bells j. 154: 6
Janua lethi 377:19
surda sit oranti 772:14
Januam hanc Orci, obsecro 922: 2
January gray is here 1283:10
not till a hot J. 1231: 9
snowy, February flowy ..1783: 1
wedded be until this J. 1268:11
weds May 1268:11
will have May in bed 1268:15
Janus am I 801: 4
Japed with Jewen silver ..1019:12
Jar: folks out in front 609:11
into his heart's great j. 1158: 4
will long keep fragrance 1746: 3
Jardin: il faut cultiver j. ..756:20
Jargon: brutish j. 1071: 5
murders with j. 468: 1
o' your schools 529: 1
Jars were made to drain 2158: 5
women's j. breed wars ..1254: 2
Jas in Arab language 1005: 7
Jasmine **1005**
Jasper: better than gold ..245: 9
tips the spear 1736: 1
Jaw: ponderous rock-like j. 1381: 7
that never yields 1488: 5
Jawing: apt word 1069: 1
Jaws: American j. must wag 56: 5
of danger and of death 2111:16
of darkness do devour it 1153:19
of death 375: 8; 2115:14
ponderous and marble j. 828:12
Jax: William J. quickly taught 2282: 1
Jay: some j. of Italy 1201:12
Jay's: go at once to J. 38:10
Jealous: beggar j. of beggar 145: 5
each j. of the other 1008:11
for they are j. 1006: 7
grows j., and with cause ..1276: 1
in honor 2240: 5
more j. than cock-pigeon 1008:10
none but j., j. can know 1007:12
one not easily j. 1006:24
view him with j. eyes 13:12
Jealousy **1005**
artist's j. 1539:11
beware j. of the gods 799:13
bred in the bone 1006:13
carry-tale, dissentious J. 1007: 2
consequence of love 1006: 8
cruel as the grave 1007:13
dislikes world to know ..1006:14
doth call himself sentinel 1007:11
friends tincture of j. 1006:15
full of artless j. 844:14
green-eyed j. 1007:10
green-eyed monster 1007:10
hydra of calamities 1006:11
inborn in women's hearts 1008: 4
injur'd lover's hell 1006: 5
is a city passion 1006: 9
is bellows of the mind 1006: 1
is born with love 1006: 3
is nourished by doubt 1006: 3
is offspring of Love 1006: 2
is the greatest evil 1006: 3
its venom once diffuse 1007:13
judgment cannot cure 1007: 8
love's curse 1007: 1
love's enemy 1006:21
mad j. 1007: 8
magnifier of trifles 1006: 6
never satisfied 1006:16
of someone's heir 1455: 8
self-harming j. 1007: 8
shapes faults are not ..1007: 9
shuts one door, opens two 1006:22
to the bride 1006:12
tyrant, tyrant J. 1005:12
ugliest fiend of hell 1007: 7
Jealousy, *continued*
will be ruin of you 1006:20
with groundless j. repine 1007: 4
Jealousy's peculiar nature 1008: 1
Jean: bonny J. 1205:16
Jeanie: artless J. 1222: 8
dear J. Morrison 1295: 5
Jebb, Richard: epitaph 572: 6
Jecur ansere majus 523: 8
Jeer: meaning another when yourself you j. 2172: 4
Jeerers taste of own broth 1724: 7
Jefferson, Thomas **1008**
on Christianity 265:22
Jeffersonian simplicity 56: 8
Jehovah has triumphed 535: 1
Jove, or Lord 794: 3
name of the Great J. 61: 8
no superiority to Jupiter ..1694: 7
saw world was good 2244: 9
they depose 798: 9
Jehu, son of Nimshi 931:11
Jejune: flat, j. modern 83: 4
Jelly: distill'd to j. 657:18
like a bowlful of j. 155:19
Jenny kissed me 1049: 4
wi' the airn teeth 1846:14
Jeptha's daughter 367: 6
Jephthah's oath 1418:10
Jericho; go to J. 1635:14
tarry at J. 127:11
Jerkin: wear it like a leather j. 1427:17
Jerusalem
See also Heaven
and we have seen J. 1142: 6
building New J. 96: 3
if I forget thee O J. 708:19
my happy home 888: 5
New J. 2013: 5
new J., when it comes 885: 1
next to the New J. 2291:12
the golden 886: 9
till we have built J. 554:16
Jeshurun waxed fat 648: 3
Jesse James had a wife 1360: 6
Jesse's root a branch 261:10
Jessie: give 'em J. 1557: 4
Jest: all is but j. 1680: 5
all things big with j. 1009:14
an the ship sinking 1009: 4
and youthful Jollity 1010: 2
answer j. with earnest 98: 1
bitter j. 1011: 8
breaks no bones 1009:17
cruel j. 1011: 4
dry j., sir 1010:14
duller than witling's j. 2241: 7
fashion j. with sad mind 1010:18
for all mankind 713:15
good j. for ever 100:17
he had his j. 1615: 6
hold the sweet j. up 2160:11
I am a Merry J. 1009:18
intermingle j. earnest 1008:20
is clearly to be seen 2251:14
lose friend for a j. 739:15
mirth-loving j. 1302: 5
never failed to have j. ..1009: 4
not only find the j., but the laugh 1009:13
pass your proper j. 340: 6
poisoned j. 1011: 7
rather lose friend than j. 1008:21
scornful j. 1011: 5
stabs you for a j. 505:12
such a paltry humbug j. ..1653:14
tell j. but omit oaths 1009:12
tells j. without smile 932:11
threadbare j. 1009: 1
unseen, inscrutable 1010:14
which will not bear examination 938:17
Jest-book better than nothing 184: 8
Jester: a bad character ..1010: 3
and jestee 1010:16
at the court of death 1219:21
fool and j. 39: 8
scurril j. 1161: 5
Jester's motley garb 1010: 1
Jesters oft prove prophets 1010: 8
Jesting **1008**
ill j. with edge-tools 1011: 9
leave j. while it pleaseth ..1009:15
often cuts hard knots 1009:16
putting j. aside 1009:15
savage j. 1011: 3
with edged tools ..364:8; 1633: 1
without bitterness 1011: 6
Jests: gleaned j. at home 1009:17
made of dead men's flesh 405:15
no time to break j. 1010:18
of rich successful 1720:17
that give pain no j. 1011: 2
tho' his j. are coarse 930: 2
two sorts of j. 1009: 3
Jesuit: sow a J., reap revolter 1741: 2
Jesuites une épée 1741: 2
Jesuits of the Revolution 1741: 2
sword whose handle is at Rome 1741: 2
Jesus Christ **261**
and Barabbas 2040: 9
gentle J., meek and mild 252:17
gentleman J. 261: 5
good paragon 263:11
good *sansculotte* J. 165: 6
hath risen 515: 9
I know how J. could liken .253: 7
influence for good 263: 3
is in a garden 756:13
is risen today 515:12
King of Glory 515:11
listened at home 263: 3
little J., wast Thou shy ..261:11
little Lord J. 268:17
lover of J. and truth 111: 1
lover of my soul 264:18
loves me 2274: 2
loves thee best 394:16
on the rood 783: 4
ploughed into history 263: 3
shall reign 2274: 2
Socrates and J. 262:12
that gentleman J. 261: 5
then came J. forth 261:14
thought he was J. C. 2150:11
wept; Voltaire smiled 277:18
Jet: black as j. 167: 3
Jets under advanced plumes 307:16
Jeu: dans le j. tout arrive ..752: 4
ne vaut pas la chandelle ..754:15
Jeune sans être belle 138: 1
Jeunesse dorée 2264:7a
ivresse continuelle 2263:14
si j. savoit 23:14
vit d'espérance 24: 7
Jew **1011**
an Ebrew J. 1012:12
damned J. 1011:14
dripping with blood 1450: 3
has nothing revolting 1012: 5
hath not a J. eyes 1012:13
if a J. wrong Christian ..1713:17
of humble Parentage 1015:12
proud to be a J. 1011:14
rather had I, a J., be hated 1012: 7
rich as a J. 235: 8
ruled by J. and prostitute 2277: 3
that Shakespeare drew ..1012: 9
to be J. is a destiny 1011:11
to praise Jehovah's name ..335: 9
you question with the J. .1012:13
Jewel **1013**
best enameled 1013:12
called her his j. 1540: 9
consistency a j. 304:10
has hung twenty years 2141: 2
heavenly j. 1013:18
immediate j. of their souls 1701:20
in an Ethiope's ear 140:11
in barred-up chest 178: 1
no Indian mines can buy ..309: 1
no j. is like Rosalind 1013:11
no j. like chaste woman 245: 8
of gold and pearl 1013: 3
of gold in swine's snout 2202: 1
of the just 392:18
of life robbed and ta'en .1013:18

Joy, *continued*
making fools 319: 1
may be a miser 1019: 7
mingle shades of j., woe 1124:12
momentary j. breeds pain 1018: 9
no j. so great 232:10
not a j. world can give ...461:16
of heart colors face 877: 4
of heaven to earth come .791: 3
of life and work 53: 2
of mind marks strength ..1311:16
of meeting not unmixed .1289: 4
of old j. new remembrance 1295: 2
of the marriage night 2188: 9
of this world 1017:21
of youth and health 599:20
one hour of youthful j. ..196: 2
or power, not both 1574: 3
out of breath with j. 2152:14
over sinner that repenteth 1699: 9
present j. breeds annoy ..1511: 8
rises in me like morn .. .1017:10
rul'd the day 1016:17
scatter j. not pain 1493:17
shipmate, j. 378:15
shivers in the corner 300:13
shuts up passages of j. 34: 9
slenderly equipped for j. 1018:10
snatch a fearful j. 1016:18
so seldom weaves chain ..1018: 1
solemn is j. 131: 5
stern j. warriors feel 543: 9
such a j. in June 1026: 3
such j. ambition finds 48: 5
sweet j. through sorrow ..1019: 6
Temperance and Repose ..873: 4
that endless j. 888:16
that fleets away 1018:16
that lasteth evermo' 1274: 7
that moves the pinion ... 1016: 8
that slights the claim 1294:16
that springs from labor ..1064: 2
that triumph brings 2275:1a
that's shared j. doubled ..1019: 1
there is no j. but calm ..1797: 2
thing of beauty is a j. forever 135:20
three-parts pain 15:19
to him that toils 908:13
to the face sent 605:15
to the world 2274: 2
was duty, and love law ..1272:13
weak is j. never wearied .1016:12
what j. awaits you 211:14
whose hand is ever at lips 1291: 6
wish you all the j. 1017: 4
with its searing-iron 130:13
without canker or cark ..1565: 2
worldly j. is soon ago ..1018: 9
writh'd not at passed j. ..1295: 2
Joy's delicious springs 1018:13
Joy-bells chime 975: 1
ring in Heaven's street ..251:12
Joy-riding: financial j. . .666: 8
Joy-song of the crocus 93:10
Joyful and free from blame 2087: 9
Joyfulness prolongeth days 855:22
Joyous: be henceforth j. ..1879:18
Joys are bubble-like 1017:18
augments his j. 1275: 1
briefly die their j. 254:10
do not abide ... .1017:25
fairest j. give most unrest 1196: 8
flow where Fate concealed 749: 7
great j. are silent 1018:15
great j. weep 1018: 7
grow up between crosses 1019: 9
guilty j. of the mind 1308: 9
hence, vain deluding j. ..1016:22
how fading are the j. ..1018: 2
human j. swift of wing ..1017:22
imaginary j. 1017:17
impregnate 1018: 7
joy of j. 32:17
melancholy j. of evil 583:19
mental j. and mental
health 1721: 5
nor postpone your j. 1130:17
nor wedded j. nor sorrows
knew 410:10
Joys, *continued*
not j. but hopes cease 35: 9
of battle 2107: 5
of marriage heaven on
earth 1274: 7
of sight, smell, taste 1796: 3
old j. fade 31:12
present j. more to flesh ..1016: 6
purest j. wear out 856: 1
redoubleth j. 741: 3
remember'd j. never past 1017:26
remembered sharpen ill ..1296: 1
rich man's j. increase ...1571:11
sacred j. of home 909: 6
season'd high ... .1017: 7
sweeter for past pain 1018:12
that faded like morning
dew 1296: 6
that fortune bring 1722: 6
too exquisite to last ...1017:26
vanish with the day 1846: 1
visionary j. 221:13
wanton in fulness 1019: 5
who bathes in worldly j. ..1016:18
with age diminish 1142: 4
with health are flown 1905:14
withered like the grass ..713:16
Jucundi acti labores 1061:16
Jucundum tamen nihil agere 955: 3
Jucundus acerbus es idem 237: 4
Judah and Israel dwelt
safely 907:11
Judas 1019
betrayest thou 2033: 3
had given them the slip 2033: 3
hanged on an elder 1019:12
so J. kiss'd his master ..2033: 3
sold himself, not Christ ..1605:10
to a tittle 609:10
Judases: three J. 354: 2
Judee: down in J. 1547:13
Judex damnat improbanda 1021: 6
damnatur cum nocens ab-
solitur 1021: 4
honestum prætulit 1020:13
male verum examinat cor-
ruptus j. 1020:13
subtilis veterum j. 82: 9
transit in legislatorem ..1019:17
Judge .... .1019
according to appearance 86: 8
according to results 1022: 4
among fools a j. 705:10
an upright j., a learned j. 1021:12
be wary how ye j. 1023: 3
becomes a law-maker 1019:17
between the high and low 1845:11
business of j. to find out
truth 1020: 5
by appearances 85:15
by their merits 83:15
by what they might be ..1022: 7
condemned when guilty
acquitted 1021: 4
corrupt j. 1019:17
decides as he can 1020: 6
delays justice 1020:15
don't j. by appearances ..2287: 3
forbear to j. 1023: 3
grows tender-hearted 1021: 4
I see the j. enthron'd ...1025:11
if you j., investigate . ..1021: 7
me by myself 1022:11
no j. but self, condemns
self 1020: 1
no one j. in own cause ...1021: 3
none j. so wrong 1023: 7
nor can man of passions j. 1456: 2
not that ye be not judged 1023: 3
O wise young j. 1021:12
of all the earth 785: 6
of matters of taste 1966: 4
of quick and dead 1019:14a
on side of compassion ..1020: 4
ourselves by capacity 1024:14
prefers what is right 1020:13
righteous judgment 1022:21
sober as a j. 1020: 8
sole j. of truth 1239: 3
that no king can corrupt 1645:19
Judge, *continued*
that pardon'd guilty ...1021: 4
they'll j. like Britons 1805: 3
upright j. condemns crime 1021: 6
was much deafer 373: 6
when j. puts on robes 1020: 9
who has j. for father 1020: 3
will read each work 341: 1
you are a worthy j. 1021:12
you as you are 1024:17
Judges answer question of
law 1026:17
best at the beginning 1021:13
bought for gold 803: 4
cannot make law 1087: 3
he only j. right 1021:16
hungry j. sentence sign ..1026:16
man j. from partial view 1024: 8
obliged to go armed 1020: 7
of a-size 1020:12
of fact, not j. of laws ..1026:13
ought to remember Roman
Tables 1079: 9
ranged, a terrible show ..1091:11
should be many j. 1020:18
when j. have been babes ..122: 1
without informing himself 1020:16
Judging by appearances 86: 8
Judgment 1022
affection bends the j. 21: 4
conscience and j. same 299: 5
cruel and cold is j. 1023:18
drops damning plummet .1022: 3
every event j. of God 1645:19
falls upon a man 462: 8
few have j. 1439: 6
fled to brutish beasts 1024: 5
for j. behold oppression ..2064: 1
fortune more than j. 714:15
ground of writing well ..2252:17
guide his bounty 772:13
has been bought for gold ..803: 4
hasty j., first repent 1023: 9
in discerning art 103: 2
in j. old 22: 4
in my j. 1022:20
in old men j. found 30:10
in their features lies 600: 8
man's erring j. 1609:16
my j. wars with itself ..1022: 5
nor is people's j. always
true 1482: 3
of character 236:15
of man is fallible 1024: 1
of the human mind 1308:16
of the King of kings 1645:19
of their own 341: 1
oft cause of fear 655: 3
one cool j. worth 1023:16
overheard j. of posterity .1563:11
picks the sober way 634: 1
rawness of j. 1022:18
reserve thy j. 1023:11
returns to own door 1711: 6
right of private j. 52: 5
righteous or unrighteous j. 1023:14
ripe j. 595:13
surrender j. hoodwinked .1374:12
suspension of j. 1022:17
weak prejudice is strong 1023: 4
what j. shall I dread 1023:13
when day of j. comes ..1677:10
when I was green in j. ..2265: 2
with critic j. scan 1299: 8
Judgment Day 1024
Judgment-signal's spread .1024:18
Judgments: none go alike 1023: 8
of mob worthless 1483: 4
parcel of their fortunes ..1022: 8
prepared for scorners 1657:11
revised without ceasing ..1764: 2
sway with fortune 1022:13
weak, prejudice strong ..1597:10
wholesale j. loose 1022: 6
with j. as with watches ..1023: 8
Judicando: in j. criminosa
est celeritas 1023: 9
Judicas: si j., cognosce ..1021: 7
Judicat: cito qui j. 1024: 2
securus j. orbis terrarum .2236:18

Justos: veces j. por pecadoes 1830: 8
Justum et tenacem propositi virum 1661: 9
Justus ut palma florebit ..1728:18
Juvat ipso labor 1064: 2
Juvenci: veniunt ad aratra j. 1442:19
Juveni parandum 39:13
Juvenis: angelicus j. 23:13
Juventam: senilem j. prœmaturæ mortis signum ...411: 1
Juventus: force of j. 2264:11
fugit 2267: 3
vitio parentum rara j. ...2116: 6
Juvenum discrimina 24:10
Juxtaposition: anatomical .1045:20

K

Kailyard: bonnie brier bush 1767: 5
Kaiser dream He was Prussian 2147: 9
Kaiser auf der Vaterland 2147:10
Kaiser's: to see K. epitaph 2147: 8
Kalendas Græcas 838:10
Kalends Greek 838:10
Kammerdiener keinen Helden 898: 2
Kammern: zwei K. hat das Herz 875: 2
Kampf: der rasche K. verewigt 2111: 7
Kangaroo: fairies' K. 823: 4
Kann: ich k. nicht anders 1227: 5
Kansas raising hell 891: 1
what's the matter with K. 891: 1
Kathleen Mavourneen 1454: 6
Kathleen ni Hoolihan 996: 9
Katie Connor: sweet K. C. 2284: 6
Katterfelto: this new K. ..1814: 2
with hair on end 2209: 3
Katy: K-K-Katy 2296: 6
Katydid **1033**
Kavanagh receives to-night 933: 8
Kean: to see K. act 9: 1
Keats, John **1033**
and Shelley sleep at Rome 1001:12
criticism of 343: 6
dirty little blackguard ..1033: 6
him—even 1341:19
kill'd off by one critique 1033: 6
out-glittering K. 1982:15
the real Adonis 1033: 3
what porridge had John K. 1559:13
Kedron: thou soft-flowing 1733: 5
Keel: on even k. 1776:13
thrill of life along her k. 1814: 4
Keen: exquisitely k. 2172: 1
for change 232: 6
Keenness of practised eye 1094: 9
of thy sharp envy 565:21
Keep a-goin' 1488:20
all you have 1794: 9
only things we ever k. 773: 7
they k. who can 1562: 8
thing seven years 1998: 4
well as win 1997: 6
what you have got 584:12
yourself within self 1787: 8
Keep-clean better than ten make-cleans 278:20
Keeper is only a poacher ...943: 1
my brother's k. 201:11
Keepers: who shall keep k. 2144:17
Keeping: in thy gracious k. 394:17
Keepsakes: precious k. 874:14
Keer: take k. of yourself ..636: 2
Kelly and Burke and Shea .999: 4
from the Emerald Isle ..2290:13
Kelson of the creation 1176: 2
Ken: far as angels' k. 76:13
I always own I dinna k. ..217:21
Kennst du das Land 1001: 3
Kens: what a man K. he cans 1:14
Kent: everybody knows K. .551: 4
Kentucky **1034**
fly away K. Babe 1847: 2
my old K. home 1454:12

Kentucky, *continued*
old K. shore 2284: 1
ran in K. hills 1034: 7
Kept: little well k. 1293: 5
Kerensky of this revolution 1714:17
Kerke: to k. the narre 272: 3
Kernel: eat k. crack shell ..1062: 6
of instinct 529:10
who will eat k. 515: 1
Kerns and gallowglasses 996: 8
rough rug-headed k. 998:14
uncivil k. of Ireland 998:14
Kerse: not worth a k. 2167:20
Kettle called the pot black 1564: 4
had a k., let it leak 1968:11
how agree k. and pot 1564: 6
let k. to trumpet speak 501: 4
Polly, put the k. on 1968: 8
sings song of family glee 2136: 9
Kew: Highness' dog at K. 470:16
in lilac-time 1155:12
Key of knowledge 1057:19
of life opes gates of death 378: 2
of the fields 1934: 1
right k. to Paradise 1451: 9
sought k. of heaven bent 1741: 3
that golden k. 110: 6
turn k. and keep counsel 1784: 3
turn the k. of time 2004: 8
used k. always bright 2070: 5
which passions move 134:16
with easy k. open life 2261: 5
you shall keep the k. 1293:14
Key-note of all harmonies 1363: 9
Keyboard contains all music 106: 1
Keyhole of the cash box ..319: 2
out at k. 2174: 1
Keys: clutch golden k. ...1999: 3
of all the creeds 1804: 3
of Paradise 1451: 9
of some great instrument 2153: 2
of this breast 135: 2
till Peter's k. some Jove .1741: 1
two massy k. he bore 387: 2
Keystone of human progress 814: 1
Kibe: galls his k. 43:13
Kibitzer 1284:16
Kick **1034**
a fallen man 1034:11
against the pricks 1703:20
he's quite the k. 705: 9
I await the sixth k. 832: 3
I should k. being kick'd ..1035: 1
in that part more 1034:13
man when he is down ..1322:11
may kill a sound divine ..1034:14
she gimme a k. 1657:11a
the bucket 1035: 2
the wind 853:15
their owners over 1711: 4
why k. me downstairs 1035: 3
Kicked until they feel shoe 1657:10
waxed fat and k. 648: 3
Kicker: hate to be a k. ..2132: 1
Kicking you seems the lot of common curs 2273: 2
Kickshaws: pretty tiny k. ..522: 5
Kickshawses: good at k. 68: 6
Kicky-wicky: hugs his k. .2111:15
Kid: I love my wife, but oh you k. 2290: 9
snow-white k. tomb of Homer marks 913: 1
turns k. to goat 2267:12
where's that k. o' your own 2205: 7
you lucky little k. 1817: 7
Kidney: man of my k. 1642:19
Kidneys: mortal men have .499:13
peeping elegantly 210: 8
Kids: don't neglect k. 490:14
when we were a couple of k. 2283: 5
Kiebitz nein singvogel 1284:16
Kill: all men k. the things 1359: 7
all the lawyers 1091:21
as good almost k. a man as k. a book 180: 9
could only k. once 375: 2
him honestly 1358:17

Kill, *continued*
him in the shell 532:21
hundred and fifty ways ..1359: 5
it by cullying it 1035:17
thee, and love thee after 1359: 5
things they do not love ..867: 8
thou shalt not k. 1358:22
twa at a blow 1769: 3
two birds with one stone ..160: 8
wife with kindness 1035:17
with right, save with pity .789: 3
Killers: light ones may be k. 2019:10
Killing as canker to rose ..459: 8
less k., soft, or kind 1035:10
must be done 1229:16
no Murder 1359: 8
Kills: each man k. the thing he loves 1195:15
me to look on it 599: 4
Kin: help thy k. 243: 2
more than k. 1035:18
Kind: art of being k. 1037:42
as kings on coronation day 1038: 2
be k., and touch me not ..231:12
be k. to my remains 739: 1
belie nature when not k. 1035: 4
cannot be k. for an hour .1237: 5
cruel only to be k. 346:10
each after his k. 161:13
he was k. and she was k. 1037: 4
he was so k. 262: 2
I'll be k. and true 2285: 6
is not therefore k. 8:10
less than k. 1035:18
make haste to be k. 1036:10
of k. the same 447: 1
she was jes' the quiet k. 2184:12
things seek their k. 289: 3
to each other for an hour 1237: 5
to k. 1562:13
what care I how k. she be 2199: 5
will creep 1177:10
Kind: besser das K. weine 256:12
Kinder: be a little k. 1036:17
Kindness **1035**
any k. that I can show ..1493: 6
begets k. 156: 9
begetter of k. 1036: 6
consists in loving 1035:15
counterfeiting absent love 1194:16
destroys vigor 1036: 3
distinguishes God's gentleman 763: 2
easily forgotten 987: 7
for k. owe good turn 1036: 4
for many generations ..2036: 9
give him all k. 735: 1
have you had k. shown ..1036:12
in another's trouble 1120:10
in women shall win love .1037: 3
is produced by k. 1036: 6
is sunshine virtue grows 1035:14
is the word 1035:19
is wisdom 1035: 4
kill with k. 1035:17
kind overflow of k. 1036: 4
loving k. 131: 7
loving-k., pity's kin 1036: 7
milk of human k. 217:13
nobler ever than revenge 1037: 1
nothing popular as k. 1035: 8
once done you a k. 156: 9
out of k. or knavery 1052:22
postmortem k. 1578:13
repay k. while receiving ..824:17
tempered every blow 1037: 5
there's no dearth of k. ..1036:19
to good investment 1036:16
to lead the drunk 502: 7
to refuse immediately 1687: 3
very indigestible 1036: 8
who does k. not kind 1036: 1
worth more than beauty ..131:18
Kindnesses which make me wiser 729: 7
Kindred: greater k. less kindness 1035:18
Milton's k. 1306: 2
with the skies 1797: 7

L

Labored more abundantly 1061:12
not for myself only 1970:16
Laborem: studio fallente l. 1063:15
suave alterius spectare l. 1322:17
Laborer: European l. superperless 1598: 8
little recks 1063:10
sett'st weary l. free 1915:14
worthy of his hire 1066: 8
worthy of his reward 1715: 7
Laborer's task is o'er 378: 4
Laborers are few 861:17
count clock oftenest 1066:15
draw hame at even 1936: 8
poor because numerous ..1065:12
Labores: jucundi acti l. ..1061:16
tolerate l. 24: 1
Laboring in the winter ...1062:12
Laboris: quæ regio non plena l. 1062:14
Labors for the toys we seek 1065: 5
he that l. spins gold 1062: 7
lighten l. by song 1876: 9
of the poor 1572:15
our fruitless l. mourn 628:14
rest from their l. ..390:2; 397: 8
tax our l., excise brains 1967: 1
till it clouds itself 2255: 6
who l., prays 1063: 2
Laborum dolorum efficit faciliorum 1063:12
dulce lenimen 1063:15
homo nascitur ad l. 1065: 9
Labra: similem habent l. lactucam 111:12; 1154:12
Labris: non a summis l. venerunt 2219: 2
Laburnam dropping gold ..683:10
pink lays cheek 682:16
Labyrinth of the mind ..1766: 1
of uncertainty 1533:11
wat'ry l. 1421: 2
without a clew 976: 1
Labyrinths of error 340: 8
of treason 2033:19
Lac senum 2156:5a
Lace: at distance eyes the l. 1866: 4
has charm for fair 1866: 4
Lacerti: stulto l. 590:22
Lâche fuit en vain 375:13
Lâches: honnêtes gens sont des l. 1706: 6
Lack of heart 881:18
of money 1333:6; 1333:12; 1337: 2
they l., I lend 1329: 9
Lacked and lost 1561: 2
Lackest: what thou l. 309:15
Laconic—an Olympian ...1160: 6
Laconically suffering 986: 3
Lacrima: nihil citius arescit 1972: 9
Lacrimæ animum profusæ levant 1974: 6
hinc illæ l. 1973:13
inimico exstincto non habent l. 543: 4
pondera vocis habent 1976:15
prosunt 1977:10
sunt l. rerum 1973:16
Lacrimandum, non plorandum 405: 8
Lacrimas fundunt ut ostendant 1977:13
lacrimis miscere 1320: 8
Lacrimis admanata movebis 1977:10
corrumpis ocellos 1977: 9
egeriturque dolor 1974: 4
nemo me l. decoret 1519:11
neve puellarum l. moveare 1977:11
quis temperet a l. 1976: 4
semper paratis 1977: 6
Lacrimula: una falsa l. ..1978: 2
Lacrymarum: movendarum l. 1438:15
Lacte: quam l. lacti est ..1155: 6
Lactuca inchoat nostras cenas 523: 7
movendo utilis 523: 7
post vinum 523: 6
valebis 522: 4
Lactucam: similem habent labra l. 111:12; 1154:12
Lad: dear-lov'd l. 1223: 6
I used to be 257:18
my old l. of the castle ..988:11
of mettle, a good boy 1004: 1
that is gone 258: 2
we shall meet again 262: 7
whom the jungle 2265: 7
Lad's love's a busk of broom 1179:10
Ladder by which we rise ..109: 8
down l. to choose wife ..2139: 8
draw the l. after me 1341:15
Fame's l. 627:16
go up the l. to bed 853:20
is easy to climb 626:17
leaning on the cloud 2266: 6
lowliness ambition's l. ...50: 4
make a l. of our vices ..2078: 3
of Saint Augustine 2078: 3
step after step l. ascended 1488: 4
unto l. turns his back 50: 4
with corded l. fetch her 2215: 8
Ladders: golden l. rise 76: 5
Laddie's dear sel' he lo'es dearest 1790: 5
Laddies: beardless l. 22:10
Ladies call him sweet 1560:10
Cambridge l. 1861: 6
fairest l. love the blackest men 1176:10
fairy l. danced 1226: 2
far fetched good for l. ..2180: 5
fond of company of l. ..2200: 1
grieve not, l. 41:10
if l. be but young . ..2192:11
intellectual 943:11
like variegated tulips 2198: 6
look after the l. 452: 6
masked are roses 608:18
now make pretty songs .1529: 3
of most uneasy virtue 943:12
of Saint James's 610: 6
old l. of both sexes 1802:11
pleased the l. round him ..647: 8
ride with hawk on wrist ..258:12
shortest l. longest men ..1176:10
supreme among amusements 2194:16
Ladroni: Italiani tutti 1002: 4
Lads: golden l. and girls ..382: 5
unremembered l. 1201: 4
Lady: all because a l. fell in love 2207: 2
Bountiful 1492:12
Colonel's L. and Judy O'Grady 1833: 8
doth protest too much 844:18
ev'ry l. would be queen ..1255: 3
from Philadelphia 1644:10
gentle l. married to Moor 2141: 4
God made my l. lovely ..140: 7
in the case 2206: 6
in the sun 2181: 6
is angry without cause ..2190:13
lent his l. to his friend ..1223: 8
let's have done with "l." 2181: 7
lovely young l. I mourn 978: 6
make a l. of my own 409: 5
met a l. in the meads ..2187:16
never shows underwear ..2178: 6
no l. ever a gentleman ..2179: 6
of a certain age 40:15
of incisive features 609:13
of my delight 2185: 3
Old L. in Threadneedle Street 1167:15
old, old, old, old l. 22: 9
our L. of Pain ..1416:13; 2094:11
our L. of the Snows 1857: 6
our l. of the twilight 2062: 5
perfect l. 1233:12
richly clad was she 488: 7
shall say her mind freely 2200: 6
some love l., some Joan 1224: 6
such a l. God's mother 261:12
sweet and kind 1211:14
this coal black l. 2289: 4
when a l.'s in the case ..2206: 6
Lady, *continued*
with a Lamp shall stand 2184:11
with her daughters 366: 7
with one hand thrust l. from 2214: 3
Lady-smocks all silver white 685: 8
Ladyship: her humorous l. ..332:12
Lædaris: ne l. alterum 804:13
Læditur: nemo l. 986:15
Læsæ majestatis 1043:12
Læseris: odisse quem l. 986:10
Læserunt et oderunt 986:10
Læsit: aut imbecillior l. ..986:22
Lætus sorte tua 311:15
Lafayette, we are here 67: 4
Lag-end of my life 312: 2
Laggard: ill-fated l. in rear 531: 9
Laggards: not for l. doth contest wait 176:10
Lagniappe 1630:10
Laigle of the oration 490: 8
Laird did address her 2214: 2
Lairdie: wee, wee German 769: 1
Laissez faire 1552: 7
à Georges 766:14
Laissez passer 1552: 7
Lak-a me, I lak-a you 2284: 3
Lake of Winnipissiogie ...1285: 4
where Sodom flam'd 452:14
Lalage: Brown's for L. ..1376: 1
Neara, Chloris 1375:16
seeks for husband 944: 7
Lamb: rather be Charles L. than Charles XII 2256: 9
Lamb 1067
behold the L. of God 1067:13
ewe l. 1067:15
God tempers wind to l. ..789: 2
I would bring a l. 2274: 2
in the house, lion in field 1068: 3
like l. to the slaughter ..1067:12
Mary had a little l. 1067:11
never gentle l. more mild ..1068: 2
of God, I come 264:11
one dead l. is there 401: 8
quiet as a l. 1666:12
Thou L. of Calvary 2274: 2
thy riot dooms to bleed ..1067:14
to bed with l. ...... .1729: 6
to the slaughter 16: 6
white ewe l. of Europe ..150:12
you are yoked with a l. .78:19
Lambe them, lads 1636: 1
Lambkin: my pretty cosset l. 1847: 4
welcome heavenly l. 268: 5
Lambs could not forgive ..1759:14
run sporting about 1068: 4
that did frisk in sun 990:16
to their friends 1068: 3
Lambskin goeth to market 1810:16
Lame: do not limp before l. 328:20
dogs over stiles 893:13
duck 1556: 6
feet was I to the l. 169:13
he is not l. 444: 2
live with, limp 288:13
poor fellow l. 464:20
who reproves l. 1022:16
Lament by ordinance of Nature 1356:18
for a golden age 44: 8
weaker to l. 1698:18
Lamentation
See also Mourning
bury me with l. 1519:11
no l. can loose 388:18
no need of l. 405: 4
prop of suffering 1356:11
right of the dead 405: 9
Lamented in thy end 238:21
Lamentings heard i' the air 1946:14
Lamp appears a lion 302: 5
by passion slain 1126: 9
deep sunk l. of light 1941:10
ere Homer's l. appeared ..1305: 9
glorious l. of heaven 1938:14
had I but Aladdin's l. ...1018: 3
Hesper's l. begins to glow 582: 3
I press God's l. 965: 3

Law, *continued*
of Medes and Persians 1084: 6
of nations 1084: 4
of nature and of nations 1083:11
of nature, l. of nations 1388: 9
of sacrifice, duty 1792:14
of the Yukon 587: 2
old father antic, the l. 1082:20
on divine l. divination 1083:18
only a memorandum 1089:12
only aristocratic element 1093: 4
Physic and Divinity 819:18
preserves the earth 1083:17
reign of l. 1083: 8
road to highest stations 1092:16
seat is bosom of God 1083:14
seven hours to l. 935: 1
shall scorn him trial 1088: 7
should be brief 1080: 8
shows her teeth 1083: 9
sometimes great injustice 1032:18
speaks in general terms 1080: 1
speaks too softly 1081: 4
State's collected will 1088:17
stepping-stone in politics 1092:16
strictest l. greatest injustice 1032:18
sumptuary l. 1084:11
sword l. 1955:16
that veils Future's face 749:11
the lawyers know about 1094: 2
to take care of raskills 1079:13
to the l. and testimony 1086:16
today, none tomorrow 1081: 3
transgressing nature's l. 2209: 4
tyrant of mankind 1086: 7
ultimate, angels' l. 1083:12
unjust to ourselves 1089:18
unwritten l. 1084: 9
violated a demoralizer 1619: 7
voice from heaven 1080: 8
what is l. if those who make it 1088:11
what is the l. of God 1704: 6
what l. demands, give 1419:18
whatever is boldly asserted 1079: 7
whereof you are a pillar 1021:12
which moulds a tear 1083:17
who breaks no l. 1087: 9
who can give l. to lovers 1191: 8
who to himself is l. 1081: 8
whoso loves l. dies mad 1080:13
will admit of no rival 1083:4a
will never be strong 1087:11
windy side o' the l. 1083: 3
with honor hold by l. 1087:15
yet all be l. 1093:15
you of the l., can talk 1093:13
Law-breaker 1088:11
Law-giver: stern l. 508:13
Law-maker not law-breaker 1088:11
without notion of l. 1087:18
Lawful: made what pleased her l. 1081: 7
that law bar 1090: 8
to do what I will 1561:15
what is l. no charm 1617:17
where nothing l. 1089: 5
Lawless: except slave 1839:12
Lawn: climbs upland l. 1944: 4
dew-scented l. 500:10
white as snow 489: 6
Lawrence, Henry: did duty 506: 2
Lawrence, James 62: 1
Laws above the prince 1089: 2
all l. useless 1080: 3
all things obey fixed l. 1083:15
are like cobwebs 1085: 7
are spiders' webs 1085: 7
are with us 1083: 4
attention, orators none 1437:11
bad l. worst tyranny 1086: 1
base l. of servitude 724:16
best l. for benefit of good 1090:11
better no l. than so many 1089:20
biting l. 1086:11
blue l. 1084: 8
brain may devise l. 79: 1
cares not who makes l. 123:2; 1875:13
Laws, *continued*
civil l. are cruel 2113: 5
cold, material l. 1765: 2
curse on all l. 1270:11
defective l., morals 1090: 6
die, books never 181: 9
do not persuade by threat 1088: 6
dumb in midst of arms 1081: 4
established l. just 1027:14
eternal l. 1083:13
eternal l. of justice 336:14
exact l. fabulous 1086:17
execute l. royal office 1550: 6
for imaginary commonwealths 1499:12
generally found to be nets 1085: 6
give his Senate l. 13:12
give l. to the peoples 1089: 4
go as kings like 1081: 7
go hand in hand with progress 307: 5
good l. by bad manners 1082:11
good l. trample bad l. 1090: 2
government of l. 813:13
grind the poor 1085: 1
he who hold no l. in awe 1087:12
his self-made l. 1126:13
human l. copies of eternal 1083:13
I know not whether l. be 1614: 1
laughable 1082: 2
lay up his l. in heart 794: 7
lean on one another 1079: 6
like spiders' webs 1084:13
made for men in general 1079:18
made to be broken 1088:10
men must not obey l. 1087:14
more l., more offenders 1082: 6
must embody public opinion 1088: 3
nature's l. 1400: 2
necessary for good manners 1257: 1
necessary for men 1085:13
never apologize 590:12
no l. can be so plain 1089:11
no l. can make idle industrious 1090: 9
no restraint upon freedom of good 1080: 3
not masters but servants 1087:10
nullified by immorality 1089:17
obey custom 1080: 7
of art convertible 102:16
of beauty and utility 1388: 6
of conscience born of custom 299: 8
of England bounded by four seas 2297: 2
of God, the l. of men 1087:16
of gravity, chemistry 1765: 4
of nature 1388: 5
of Nature God's thoughts 1388:10
of necessity 1087:17
petty l. breed great crimes 1090: 1
place safety of all first 1079: 9
pressed by heavy l. 1018: 4
punish by justice 1655:18
repeal bad l. by execution 1087:11
so many l., so many creeds 1037:4a
so many l. so many sins 1080: 5
spring from instinct 1079:17
tend to gravitate 1089: 6
that torture men 1085:12
too gentle seldom obeyed 1082: 4
unequal l. for rich, poor 1089:16
unnecessary l. traps 1089:15
unvaried l. preserve 1083:16
useful to those who have 1090: 3
useless when men pure 1080: 3
vain, if kings destroy 1088:15
which first herself ordain'd 1388:11
who studies ancient l. 1924: 7
wise as Nature 1083:16
would complain of lawyers 1091:13
your curb and whip 1083: 2
Lawsuits consume time 1080:13
Lawyer 1090
an Honest L. 1091: 9
as a peacemaker 1092:18
bribe scarce hurts l. 199:17
Lawyer, *continued*
from l. keep not truth hidden 465: 1
good l., bad neighbor 1091: 8
good l. gets you out of scrape 1092:14
has spoiled the statesman 1093:10
he saw a l. killing viper 1093: 7
lives by quarrels 2257:11
Philadelphia l. 1091:24; 2276: 4
unfee'd l. 1092:13
when a l. cashes in 1094: 4
without history 1091:20
Lawyers: as l. go to heaven 1964: 1
be they knaves or fools 1092:16
bring l. to thy bar 1093: 9
good when young and new 1091:10
let's kill all the l. 1091:21
mountebanks of state 1093: 9
no bad people, no good l. 1091: 2
one hundred and fifty l. 1093:14
plead cause in hell 1093: 5
ready to get man trouble 1093:12
take what they would give 1091:14
twist words and meanings 1093:11
whose trade is talking 1093:14
with the greater ease 1089: 9
woe unto you also, ye l. 1093:16
Lawyers' gowns lined with wilfulness 1090:16
houses built on heads of fools 1090:16
Lax in their gaiters 241: 3
labours, excise brains 1967: 1
Laxantes jucundis sermonum 314: 9
Laxity: Parisian l. 2274: 5
Lay: he l. low 1650:15
imperishable l. 1521: 3
loud and welcome l. 167:14
me down in peace 1847:12
me down to sleep 1847:12
oh, leave me l. 1729:12
some merry l. he sung 1878:13
unpremeditated l. 1538:12
warbling his Doric l. 1879: 8
Lays: carolled l. of love 1880: 9
constructing tribal l. 1525:11
old melodious l. 1530: 3
Lazar-house it seemed 460:14
Laziness travels slowly 956:10
Lazy: if long, l. 237:11
liftin' the l. ones 1592: 7
man gets round sun 955:14
man is a bad man 955:20
too l. to investigate 618: 9
too l. to write well 2254: 8
Lead: full of l. 1291:12
lapp'd in l. 739:22
of those who do not believe in men 1095:8a
scald like molten l. 17:12
to l. or brass 2015:15
Lead and be victors still 202: 8
horse to water 930: 9
kindly light 1152:15
me where Thou wilt 1704: 6
neither l. nor tell way 1094:11
O for a living man to l. 1095: 5
Thou me on 1152:15; 1609:10
when we think we l. 1094:10
Lead-pencils: manufacturer of l. 1988: 2
Leaden-eyed: limp and l. 1570: 3
pale, and l. 1924: 8
Leader 1094
in camps, a l. sage 258:14
lives no greater l. 1095: 4
of leaders 1095: 4
vagrant l. of the mind 1427:19
Leaders of the blind 169:16
Leads clanging rookery home 345: 5
he l. himself 1424:11
Leaf: days are in yellow l. 33: 4
every l. a miracle 1155:14
fade as doth a l. 1349: 4
greenest l. turns serest 744: 6
I sing the first green l. 1908: 1
is on the tree 905:10
last l. upon tree 27: 9
one l. is for hope 1227: 2

Life, *continued*
ended when honor ends ..918:10
ends with Revelations ...1119:17
enlarge my l. 1145: 9
eschew the idle l. 954:14
eternal l. 964:18
eternal l., Happiness 855:13
eternal war with woe 1120: 6
even eternal life 966: 6
every form of l. romantic 1735:16
every l. tragedy at last ..1144: 4
evermore is fed by death 1148: 8
every man holds dear 918:12
external l. beyond our fate 1530:11
fairy-tale written by God 1125:11
fardel of l. 121: 8
fed by bounty of earth ...639: 9
festival only to the wise .1142:11
fie upon this quiet l. 174:10
find l. crude, leave it raw 663: 1
flowed in eternal kiss 1051: 1
flower of a blameless l. .1041: 1
following l. thro' creatures 1703:17
for friend l. too short 729:15
for l. for death 1172: 4
for l. I had never cared ..1145: 3
for the living 1130: 6
for the sake of other 1119:10
for which is bought renown 630: 6
Force 1240:17
foremost foeman's l. 1598: 6
fortified by friendships ...743:16
found that l. was Duty ..507: 4
free from sorrow 1884:12
from day to day 1833:11
full of kindness and bliss 1143: 6
future l. 963:16; 968: 1
future l. matter of faith ..968: 7
game of whist 1122: 3
gift of immortal gods 1499:10
given to be used 1127: 1
gleam between eternities 1123: 6
glorious l., or grave 1864:12
golden l. in iron age 1119: 6
good only when magical .1142:11
grandest l. ever lived 262: 1
greatens in later years ..2020: 9
grinds the bread of l. ...1124:14
grows insipid 1105: 6
grows sadder 35: 1
half my l. full of sorrow .1124:10
happy after course is run 411:14
happy l., a quiet l. 854: 4
happy l. consists in tranquillity 854: 4
hardly tasted L. at all ..1136:15
has flowed from its mysterious urn 239: 9
has given me of its best ..1137: 8
has its heroes 1125: 3
hath more awe than death 1146:16
hath no joy like his 732: 5
hath quicksands 1118:14
hath set no landmark 1125:15
have little care that l. ..1928: 5
have we loved 1139: 5
he lived *his* l. 1133: 4
her quiet l. flowed on ...1136: 4
here find l. in death 283:10
here my l. must end 1141:12
heroic poem of its sort....159:13
his l. a breath of God 108:13
his l. a watch or a vision 1250: 3
his l. is Christ 1755: 9
his l. was gentle 1252:15
holds disappointment 1146: 8
holds matter together 1117: 5
hovers like a star 1138:12
how good is man's l. 1142: 4
how human l. began 1139: 4
how pleasant thy morning 2266: 1
how short is l. 1139:18
how short this L. 1117:11
I bear a charmed l. 1119:14
I gave my l. for freedom 1466: 7
I have had my span of l. ..414:30
I have led a happy l. 415: 9
I have set l. upon a cast ..752:16
I spy l. peering 413:10

Life, *continued*
I want free l. 724:15
if l. did ride upon a dial's point 1129: 7
if l. were always merry ..1078: 8
if l. were merchandise ...2236: 1
if whole in l. 807:14
ill whose cure is death ..1121: 4
imaginary l. in minds of others 2074: 3
imitating l. so near 1448: 7
in America without savour 60: 3
in l. lie hid moe deaths ..1149: 9
in low estate began 834: 1
in others' breath 629: 2
in the decline of l. 31: 8
in the downhill of l. 1329: 7
in the midst of l. 378:17
in the Old Land yet 552: 3
in youth standeth still 22:11
incurable disease 1121: 1
inferior gift of heav'n ..1105:10
insane dream we take ...1121: 7
integrated into l. 2132: 7
is a battle 1120: 2
is a boundless privilege 1114:10
is but a span ..1249:16; 1865: 1
is a cheat, a fake 1143:17
is a diary 1115: 6
is a dream 1114:12
is a dream worth dreaming 1121: 8
is a dusty corridor 1115:11
is a fatal complaint 1121: 2
is a flame 1114:14
is a fleeting breath 1148:20
is a fortress 1117: 4
is a game 1121:15
is a game of whist 1122: 3
is a heroic poem 1515: 5
is a hollow bubble 1120: 9
is a jest 1115:15
is a kind of sleep 1121: 9
is a ladder 1114: 8
is a leaf of paper white ..1116: 6
is a living lie 462:14
is a loom 1114:12
is a mission 1114:13
is a narrow vale 1123:10
is a perilous voyage 1126: 2
is a pill needs gilding .. .1145: 7
is a predicament ... .1116:12
is a pure flame 1114: 6
is a series of surprises ..1114:10
is a short summer 2009:12
is a shuttle 1116:14
is a smoke that curls ...1115:17
is a sorry mélange 1116:13
is a spent dream 1121: 6
is a stage 1125: 4
is a step toward grave ...1150: 5
is a tragedy 1125: 1
is all we must endure 969: 7
is an archer 1114:15
is an arrow 1114:15
is an ecstacy 1114:10
is an empty dream 1121: 7
is an experiment 1114:10
is apprenticeship 1115: 4
is art of drawing conclusions 1115:10
is barren enough 1145: 8
is better l. 387: 4
is brief and irrevocable ...382:13
is but a day at most 1141: 7
is but a play 1137:13
is but a wraith 613:18
is but an empty dream ...1121:14
is but jest 1137:13
is but thought 1114: 9
is changeable 713:13
is checkered 1118:14
is delight, away dull care 1143: 8
is dream-storms' breath ..1114:12
is dying 1147:15
is eating us up .... .1117:17
is ever lord of Death 967: 8
is fading fast away 39: 7
is fair 439: 5
is far too important 1119:17
is in labor 855:12

Life, *continued*
is in the loom! Room for it 1128: 6
is joy 251:12
is like a cup of tea 1115: 6
is like a scrambled egg ..1116: 7
is like game of dice 1122: 3
is like the autumn leaf ...1142: 1
is like the sea 899:18
is long enough 1134: 9
is long if it is full 1134:11
is much flatter'd 1150: 1
is nearer every day to death 1150: 5
is never the same again ..2041:13
is not a dream 1121:14
is not to be purchased ..1116: 3
is only a document 1115: 4
is patchwork 1124: 5
is perfected by death 1147: 3
is preparation for future .1114:11
is probation 1114: 7
is profession of faith 587: 6
is protracted woe 34: 9
is real, l. is earnest 1150: 9
is school of probability ..1115: 5
is short and wears away ..693:10
is short, art long 104: 1
is so dreary and desolate 1144: 9
is sturdy 348: 3
is sweet and joyful thing 1143:14
is sweet, brother 1142: 3
is sweet to everyone 1143: 8
is tendency 1116:18
is the desert 383: 5
is the gift of the gods 1499:10
is the test of us 1118: 1
is thought 1991:17
is to most a nauseous pill 1145: 7
is too strong for you 1136:13
is vain; a little love 1137:13
is war with woe 1120: 6
is well enough 1117:17
is whatever God wills it ..1137:13
isn't all beer, skittles 1118: 7
journey to death 1150: 7
Joy, Empire, Victory 1129: 9
jump the l. to come 1359: 5
just a stuff to try soul on 1114: 7
just one damned thing after another 1116: 4
keeps none against will ..1119:11
kind of stage play 1125: 1
kindlier l. or sweeter 239: 7
large as l., twice as natural 1636: 4
last year's Nightingale ..1115:17
lay down l. for a friend ..727:11
leading a double l. 946:13
learn to make most of l. 1130:11
learnt l. from the poets ..1536: 4
lengthened while growing 1991:15
let l. burn down 1149:10
let my l. sing 1435: 6
let us bestow 629:12
let us cherish 2010:18
levels all men 383: 8
liberty and happiness 975: 4
liberty, property 975: 4
lies about us dumb 662: 6
lies all within present ..1123:12
like a dome of many-colored glass 1143:12
like a froward child 1116:16
like a Japanese picture ..1114:11
like a library 1117: 1
like a lily her l. did close ..408:13
like a loan 1127: 1
like following life 1139: 7
like playing violin 1115:10
like stroll upon the beach 1136: 2
like to this fading flower 1141: 7
like unto a winter's day ..1122:10
like unto summer day 573:11
live out thy l. 1130: 1
live the l. of brutes 2089: 3
lived for others 1126:10
livelier than l. 1448:12
lives only in success 1930: 2
lives well, l. good 1131: 3
long if it is full 1134:11
long lesson in humility ..1115: 6

Life, *continued*
'tis from high l. 72: 3
to come 966:17
to destroy for fear to die 1933:16
to destroy l. easy 1118:16
to have its sweets 1953: 5
to measure l., learn thou 1128:12
to sea thy l. flowed on 1170: 3
to the last enjoy'd 1142: 7
to whom l. heavy, earth
light 406:15
toddles half an hour 1142: 1
too late tomorrow's l. 1131: 5
too near paralyses art 102:17
too short for anxieties ...1129: 7
too short for distant aim .629:15
too short to waste 1129: 7
tragedy of errors made ..1125:10
treads on l. 1144: 7
true name is trial 1144: 1
true to poles of nature ..1142:12
twelve o'clock of l. 26: 3
two things to aim at in l. 1129:10
unhappy l., to have failed 1129: 3
unspotted l. in old age ..2167:12
unspotted l. is age 32:11
used to say l. was truth 2268: 5
useless l. early death 1148: 2
uttered part of l. 1820:11
vacant house of l. 160: 3
value from use alone 1131: 3
varied l. steal unper-
ceived 1704: 7
virtuous l. maketh dear ..1596: 4
voyage homeward bound .1126: 1
waking l. dream controlled 1121:11
was in the right 617: 6
was like the violet sweet 1660: 5
waste of wearisome hours 1116: 9
wastes his l. and blood ..2255: 6
we call this l. 966:11
we come, we cry, that is l. 1137: 2
we love l. 27:12
we praise that does excel 1134:11
wears on so wearily 1145: 5
weary of worldly bars 1934:10
web of l. of mingled yarn 1119:13
weep away the l. of care ..221:12
well-written l. rare 159:13
we've been long together 1146:16
what a l. were this 2007: 7
what is l. but Art 961: 2
what is l.? even a vapour 1140: 5
what is l. of man 1116:15
what is l. wanting love ..1182:17
what is one l. in the af-
fairs of a state 1918: 4
what is the simple l. 1136: 3
what l. shall man choose 1120: 7
what signifies l. of man ..2184: 2
what without love 1183: 2
when I consider L. 1144:13
when l. flows like a song 1854: 3
when l. knocks at door ...381:13
when l. leaps in veins 1142:13
when L. was slain 262: 4
where living is extinct ..1130:15
which flows along 1135:11
which is of all l. centre ..404: 4
while there's l., hope 923: 5
who can get another l. 456:15
whose l. is a bubble 1242: 2
whose l. is a span 1249:14
whose l. was all men's
hope 1146:14
whose L. was Love 262: 4
whose plot is simple 1136: 2
whoso lives holiest l. 1148:22
why should l. all labor be 1065: 8
wipe l. out like a sponge 1217: 4
with honor at the close ..1143: 2
with l. as with a play 1125: 8
without a plan 1127: 5
without friend Death 730: 3
without love is load 1182:19
without vanity impossible 2075:10
woman's is a secluded l. 1183: 9
worth living 1118: 1
would be a ship 1183: 3
would come gladly back ..1220:14

Life, *continued*
you take my l. 935:13
Life's best wine last 32: 2
blotted from l. page 33: 1
busy l. bewildered way ..1135: 4
double l. fading space ..805:11
dying taper burns 1905:14
enchanted cup 33: 3
fitful fever 395:12
flag is never furled 403: 8
inequalities and woe 204: 4
long night is ended 1187: 8
poor play is o'er 68: 5
richest cup love's to fill ..1183: 4
road so dim and dirty 165: 6
succeeding stages 22:11
tumultuous sea 1883:16
uncertain voyage 1126: 4
ungarlanded expense 2234: 6
unresting sea 1890:17
Life-blood: my l. seemed to
sip 657:15
of our enterprise 459: 4
of the great 384:10
of the state 1917:15
warm its creeping l. 34: 6
Life-current: deep l. 1158: 3
Life-drop of bleeding breast 509: 2
Life-illusion 960:14
Life-line: throw out the l. ..202: 4
Life-tide: ebbs the crimson l. 376:14
Life-weary taker may fall
dead 1540: 7
Lifeless, faultless 652:16
Lifetime of happiness 860: 6
Lift himself above himself .111: 1
laugh, love 239:10
people l., and lean 810: 8
Lifting the lazy ones 1592: 7
Light 1150
a benediction 339: 7
and leading 546: 7
and not heat 1153: 5
apparelled in celestial l. ..2266:11
as any wind that blows ..704:13
as putrefaction breeds ..1683: 7
as with a garment 796: 3
blasted with excess of l. ..1305:11
borrowed from the ancients 2257:14
burning and shining l. ..1152: 4
candle to the sun 215:20
casting dim religious l. 96: 6
coverest thyself with l. 796: 3
darkness rather than l. ..1152: 3
dear as l. that visits 289:10
dies before thy word 234: 1
dispenses l. from far 1938:16
dissolves in supernatural l. 1680: 4
do we stand in own l. 1803:14
doeth evil hateth l. 583:24
don't turn out the l. 415:11
Ethereal, first of things ..1151: 7
even through pollution ...1150:18
every l. has its shadow ..1803:16
faithful to l. within 1726: 7
first creature of God 1151: 1
from above 469: 6
from her eyelids outspoke 599:15
gains heavy purses 750: 1
garmented in l. 140:14
give l. and let us die 281: 4
gladsome l. of jurispru-
dence 1081:10
glimmering l. often suf-
fices 1152:10
God said "Be l." 884: 3
God's eldest daughter 1151: 1
great L. that haloes all 109: 2
great world of l. 1152: 6
he leaves behind him 809: 7
Heaven's l. forever shines 1143:12
I am moved by the l. 1943: 5
I am the l. of the world ..1152: 4
is come into the world 1152: 3
is mingled with gloom 292:12
is the first of painters 1151: 6
is thine element 1944: 5
it giveth l. to all in the
house 216:10
lambent easy l. 1151: 4

Light, *continued*
Lead, Kindly L. 1152:15
leave l. of hope behind 924: 3
let our prayer be for l. ..1584:10
let there be l. 1151: 7
let your l. so shine 588:14
like gem its l. may smile ..761:12
little l. because so high ...313: 3
little more toward the l. 38:10
living l. eternal 965: 6
love l. in your eye 600:11
makes some things invis-
ible 1151: 2
men of inward l. 1788: 8
mild l., and by degrees ..170: 7
much l. shadows deepest 1151: 9
my l. is spent 170: 9
name the bigger l. 1942:14
no l. in earth or heaven ..1916: 2
no l. in Natur when she
winks 554: 7
of a pleasant eye 2097:14
of bright world dies 1187:11
of dark eye in women 603:12
of duty shines 508:11
of Heav'n restore 170: 6
of love, purity of grace ..1221:10
of midnight's starry heaven 604: 3
of my own effigies 1553: 5
of other days is faded ..1293:19
of praise shall shine 1579:15
of somewhat yet to come 2184: 8
of Terewth 2049: 3
of that celestial fire 2105:14
of the body is the eye 598:11
of the heaven she's gone to 257:10
of the land and the sea ..1211:12
of the Mæonian star 912: 7
of the moon 33: 4
of the Muses 913: 3
of the sense 1151: 1
of the world 131:3; 1152: 4
of thy countenance 607:10
offspring of Heav'n first-
born 1151: 1
one True L. 1152:16
only l. of heaven pure ...1151:10
or life, or breath 2:16
out of l. profit 1152:18
out of l. that dazzles me 1892: 9
prime work of God 1151: 1
purple l. of love 436: 5
put out the l. ....
361:11; 416:21; 1153: 2
reason's l. with falling ray .32:15
rule of streaming l. 1152:11
sadder l. than waning
moon 422:13
seek the l. I cannot see ..1151: 3
seeking l. 1153: 1
shineth in darkness 1152: 3
shineth unto perfect day .1152: 3
silently wrapping all 967: 7
sown for the righteous ..1152:19
star to star vibrates l. ..1890: 8
sweetness and l. 347:10
take care how you l. 50:14
teach l. to counterfeit 1152:11
that Failed 1151:11
that hath no name 1942: 7
that lies in woman's eyes 2212: 3
that made darkness itself 1151: 2
that never was 1153: 6
that shone when Hope
was born 1347:19
that visits these sad eyes .2141: 2
these lights shall l. us 31: 6
they made l. of it 2042:12
thickens 1403:18
this thing called l. 170: 4
though my l. be dim 1670: 9
to guide, a rod 508:12
to l. Tom Fool to bed 1915:10
to seek the l. of truth 2056:13
to them that sit in darkness 1152: 8
tolerance and equity of l. 1152: 9
translateth night 513:10
true l., which lighteth ..1152: 3
truly the l. is sweet 1151: 5
unto my path 158: 9

Lord, *continued*
thy L. and master see 350: 8
thy L. is risen 514:10
thy l. shall never die 1522: 6
to crown Him L. of all ..264:17
trust ye in the L. for ever 793: 6
unless L. keepeth the city 275:15
watch between me and thee ..2: 4
went before them by day ..280:17
who gave us Earth 798: 2
whom L. loveth chasteneth 789: 4
whose hand must take ..944:16
your l. will soon return ..2144: 6
Lord Chief Justice dwells 1679:12
Lord Mayor: mad life to be 1142: 9
Lord's Prayer: the sublime 1582:12
Lordlings and witlings 327:13
Lords and Commons 545: 5
are lordliest in wine 2155: 6
feeble and forlorn 71: 1
God save House of L. ..555:13
new l. new laws 1081: 3
of creation 100: 1
of creation men we call 1750:16
of humankind 1750:16
of ladies intellectual 943:11
of the visionary eye 2096: 1
of the wide world 2143: 8
our L. on high 1480:12
reveling like l. 1986:14
whilst l. continue fools ..71:11
Lore: laugh at the l. 1390: 8
Shakespeare's rich and varied l. 1807: 9
skill'd in gestic l. 37:12
Lorenzos of our age 68: 7
Lose: better l. jest than friend 739:15
cannot l. what never had 1170:13
dost l.? rise up 752: 5
easier to l. than resign 1170:12
honor, l. myself 918:11
if I do l. thee 1129: 8
in the moment you detect 1139: 7
it that do buy it 2244: 2
itself in a fog 694:10
men take pains to l. 1490:12
neither l. nor gain 163:15
no happy day 1130:11
none but shamefaced l. ..1808:14
that which we l. we mourn 1171: 5
thee were to l. myself 1262: 7
thou art sure to l. 755: 2
to l. by keeping 773: 9
upon the square 249:16
what we l. we have 773:19
whatever l. of no account 1170:17
Loser: cheerful l. a winner 1170: 9
let l. have his word 219:18
Losers full of suspicion ..1948:15
must have leave to speak 1170: 7
with l. sympathize 751:15
Loseth: nothing that l. 785: 9
that despairs to win 438: 4
Losing is true dying 400:15
Losing Loadum: playing at 1760:11
Loss 1170
a total l. 11:13
and gain 751: 4
better little l. 1170:10
better to incur l. than make gain 751: 9
embraceth shame 1171: 3
half l. at time whole gain 2106: 7
has its compensation 290:13
is no shame 1171: 3
leave a l. so large 408:14
man's l. from gain 396: 9
most patient man in l. ..752:15
my l. may shine yet 751:13
no one knoweth l. or gain 1137: 7
of friends only grief 740: 7
of heaven pain in hell ..888: 9
of wealth l. of dirt 1568: 2
outweighed by gain 751: 8
prefer l. to dishonest gain 750:18
total l. 11:13
unknown l. no l. at all ..1170:17
what l. feels he 1986:20
Loss, *continued*
whose l. our eternal gain ..567:11
worse l. than l. of youth 2267:13
Losses: God bless all our l. 751: 5
huddled on his back ..1171: 2
laughed at my l. 1012:13
strung l. on rhyming ...1537:12
Lost a day 370:12
all and found myself 1170: 5
all is l. save honor 917:15
better to have fought and l. 612: 3
better to have loved and l. 1218:20
by what is lawful 1086:15
I have l. a day 370:12
I have l. my all 1170: 5
in depths of the grave ..828: 9
in the multitude 182:20
is his God, his country ..327:11
missed it, l. it forever 1432:14
my oil and my labor ..1062:19
not l. all if one cast left 1170:18
not l. but gone before ..402:16
shouted l., l., l. 1170:19
to the world 828: 8
to virtue 1871:10
today won tomorrow 2020:14
"we are l.!" the captain shouted 794: 4
we have l. all 917:15
what is l. is found again 291: 7
whatsoever got is l. 751: 4
who is l. to shame 1809: 9
woman that deliberates is l. 1187: 6
Lot: another's l. 453: 9
assigned to every man ..1647: 6
blameless vestal's l. 1422:10
certainly decreed 440: 4
change common l. to rare 439: 2
enjoy your own l. 1132: 6
of man but once to die ..375: 2
of man: to suffer and die 1250:10
policeman's l. is not a happy one 1540:14
saddest l. of all 1295:11
thinks his l. worst 204: 6
unequal to vast desires ..170:13
why lament the common l. 1804: 5
Lot's wife........352: 5; 1756: 1
Loth to depart 853: 2
Lothario: gallant, gay L. .2105: 6
Lotium: non valet l. suum 1756: 6
Lots: admiring others' l. ..453: 9
are cast into the urn 383:15
Lottery: fortune's false l. 1933:16
Lotus 1171
eat l. of the Nile 521:15
never the l. closes 556:14
Lotus-dust is blown 1171:12
Louange en grec 1070: 3
Louanges: le refus des l. 1577:15
Loud: not as l. had spoken 1429:13
not l. but deep 301:13
so l., it deafens 1367: 1
yet was never l. 2026: 1
Loue: on l. et blâme parce que c'est la mode 1580: 7
on ne l. que pour étre loué 1577:15
Louer: l'art de l. 1576: 8
Louerais: je vous l. davantage 1579:10
Louise: Baby L. 120:16
Lounging: makes for l. ...2017:11
Loup: pour ranger le l. ..2177:20
Lour: smile she or l. 2143: 8
Louse 1171
drive a l. a mile 118: 8
flay a l. for skin 118: 8
sue a beggar, get a l. 145: 2
upon threadbare cloth ..1958: 7
Lou'siana Belle 2286: 5
Lovable for bad qualities 236:19
Love 1171
a bright particular star ..110:10
a cross to bear 300:13
above King or Kaiser ..1189: 7
absence conquers l. 4: 9
absence is enemy of l. 4:13
absent l. vanishes 5: 1
Love, *continued*
adds seeing to the eye 1174:15
aids the hero 1190:16
alabaster boxes of l. 1578:13
alas the l. of woman 1183: 8
all except American 60: 9
all for l., or Lost Pleiad 1917: 9
all for l., world well lost 1176:15
all is fair in l. and war 1176: 9
all l. gives words 1209:11
all l. is but this 1200: 4
all l. is sweet 1185: 5
all l. like generous wine 1172: 6
all mankind l. a lover ..1177: 2
all that I ask is l. 2293: 5
all, trust a few 150: 5
allured by gentle eyes 601: 6
alone can fate defy 1189:17
alone makes fetters please 1269: 9
alternate joy and woe ..1195:18
alters not 1175: 3
ambassador of loss 1219: 2
ambition combats l. 51: 1
among the daughters 141: 1
an unbounded weakness ..1217: 9
and a cough cannot be hid 1177: 8
and ambition no bounds 1188:13
and ambition no fellowship 1178: 3
and desire and hate ..1137: 4
and envy bewitch 563:19
and friendship are the same 745: 7
and friendship exclude each other 744:17
and grief and motherhood 2193: 4
and I were well acquainted 1203: 4
and marriage rarely combine 1269:12
and murder will out 1177: 8
and pease porridge 1177: 7
and pity twins 1180: 8
and pots of ale 926:16
and pride stock Bedlam ..1177: 5
and red nose cannot be hid 1177: 8
and scandal sweeten tea 1968: 6
and sorrow twins 1194: 8
another country, damn me 1468: 9
another l. overhangs heart 1187: 4
appetite of generation ..1175: 6
apples in his eyes 92: 2
are you so much in l. ..1518: 3
armed with l. 1473:11
as a relation ruined 1270:13
as any spirit free 1191: 9
as the angels may 1172: 4
as though some day hate 1217: 8
as wise men say 1174: 4
as you loved me then ..2215: 4
ask not of me what is l. 1172: 1
asks faith 617:12
at first sight 1205: 9
awaits at journey's end 1193:14
bade me write 1809:15
bane of generous souls ..1196: 6
banished from the heart ..1201: 3
base and building of my l. 1190:10
based upon impossible view of women 1174: 3
be but sworn my l. 1372:18
be sweeter for work 1210:12
be swift to l. 1036:10
be wise not given to god 1181: 4
beginning of Knowledge 1172: 8
begins to sicken and decay 1201:14
begins with l. 1185: 4
begot of l. 1222:15
begot of plenty and penury 1178:17
being in l. 1185: 5
being naked, promote suit 1270: 1
believes in miracles 1178: 4
believes the impossible .1178: 4
best of passions, l. 1190:16
best say least 1178: 9
best to be off wi' old l. 1207: 3
best to l. wisely 1219: 1

Love, *continued*
in hut, with water, crust 1208: 6
in idleness 955: 4
in l. inhere war and peace 1173:12
in l. one deceives oneself 1205: 8
in l. there is no lack ..1630: 2
in l. we see no faults ..744:17
in silence with thy soul 1208:13
in spite of what they are 1182:14
in the lowliest cot 1208: 9
in thy youth, fair maid ..1192:12
in your heart as idly burns 1200: 6
increase or diminish 1173: 6
indeed is anything 1173:21
infinite, ever-present L. ..1188:14
inordinate l. of riches 117:16
insidious l. 1186: 2
inspires with strength ..1715: 6
is a beautiful dream 1173:18
is a boy by poets styl'd 1203:18
is a credulous thing 1178: 4
is a devil 1174:15
is a familiar 1174:15
is a fire, a coal 1172: 9
is a fiend, a fire 1172: 2
is a flame 133:23
is a kind of warfare 1174: 7
is a lie, fame a breath ..1148:15
is a light burden 1174:11
is a miser 745: 2
is a sour delight 1175: 1
is a talkative passion ...1210: 5
is a tumble-about thing ..1115:14
is all in all 1193:13
is all in fire 1173:21
is all truth 1225: 7
is an April's doubting day 1175: 5
is an egotism of two 1174:13
is an unerring light 508:13
is anterior to life 1219:15
is at home on a carpet ..1208:11
is best 1193: 1
is blind all day 1179:12
is child of illusion 1175:14
is death's brother 1175:14
is different with us men 1183: 7
is disguised in hate 1217: 4
is doomed to mourn 926:16
is duty 2240: 9
is ever sick 1173:21
is faithless 1204:17
is flower-like 33:12
is full of busy dread 1216:10
is full of fears 1216:13
is God 1183: 1
is God's essence 790:10
is greater than illusion ..1220:11
is he that alle thing bind 1188: 9
is heaven and heaven is l. 1190: 7
is his own avenger 1194:13
is hurt with jar and fret 1197:13
is indestructible 1199:10
is instinct 1270: 5
is King of Kings 1192:16
is law of the school 1971: 6
is liberal 1176: 7
is life, and Death at last 1220: 4
is life's end 1173: 4
is light from heaven 1172: 7
is like a dizziness 1189:12
is like a lovely rose 1193:13
is like fire 1194: 9
is like our life 411:12
is like the measles 1177:13
is loadstone of l. 1184:10
is L. a lie 1148:15
is l. for evermore 1199:12
is l. in beggars and kings 1179: 6
is love's reward 1185: 9
is master where he will ..1189: 5
is Nature's second sun ..1188: 8
is no more than the wide blossom 1174: 1
is not getting, but giving 1176: 1
is not in l. 1866: 6
is not l. a Hercules 1190: 9
is not l. when mingled with regards 1175: 3
is not l. which alters 1175: 3
Love, *continued*
is of sae mickle might ..1187:10
is only chatter 744: 7
is same in everyone 1179: 6
is self-giving 1183: 1
is something awful 1188: 2
is soul of true Irishman ..999:11
is sparingly soluble 1209: 5
is spiritual fire 1175: 8
is still an emptier sound 1203: 5
is still miraculous 251: 6
is strong as death 1220:11
is such a mystery 1176: 6
is sunshine 1118:14
is sweet for a day 263:12
is swift of foot 1189: 9
is that orbit 1172: 3
is the fairest guest 1174:11
is the King 908:15
is the object of l. 1184:15
is the salt of life 1175: 4
is the secret sympathy 1174:14
is to be tasted 1048:12
is uniform 2211:15
is unreturning 1207:11
is without law 1192: 2
is your master 1181: 7
isn't always two souls ..1953: 5
it is a pretty thing 1172: 9
it is a prick, a sting 1172: 9
it is an ever-fixèd mark ..1175: 3
it is l. that is sacred 1270: 5
jealous l. lights torch ..1007: 3
jewel that wins the world 1174: 6
keeps his revels 1182: 1
keeps the cold out 1173:16
keeps the door of heaven 791: 5
kelson of the creation ..1176: 2
kills happiness 1197: 3
kindest, hath most length 1184:19
king who loves the law ..1039:13
knew how to l. himself 1791: 8
knightly l. blent with reverence 1173: 2
knoweth no laws 1191:12
knows no mean or measure 1191:10
knows no order 1192: 1
knows no rule 1191:11
knows no winter 1909: 8
lad's l.'s a busk of broom 1179:10
laid upon her garment-wise 2078: 2
last year's Rose 1115:17
lasts as long as the money 1208: 2
laughs at locksmiths 1178:16
laughs glad in paths aside 1193: 4
law, die mad or poor 1080:13
leads to present rapture 1196: 9
led by l. of novelty 486: 9
leech of life 1173:15
lent me wings 391:12
less rare than friendship 744:18
lessens woman's delicacy 1184: 1
let in L. and let out Hate 1218: 8
let l. be free 1192: 4
let l. clasp grief 1195:14
let l. have his way 1176:14
let those l. now who never loved before ...1179: 9
let thy l. be younger ..1265:11
let us l. so well 1210:12
leveller of mankind 1219:11
lies hidden in every rose 1212: 1
lies in eyes 601:13
lieth deep 1179: 1
life better than figs 1143:11
life's one joy 1176: 2
light in her eye 600:11
lights more fire than hate 1218:13
like a landscape 463: 5
like a shadow flies 2216: 4
like champagne 744:16
like l. to hatred turn'd ..2203:11
like mine must have return 1184: 8
like ours can never die 1198:11
like the flies 1173:13
like Ulysses, a wanderer 1207:11
limb-unnerving l. 601: 1
Love, *continued*
lisped the same l. 2152:12
little emptiness of l. 1200: 4
little l., a little trust 1136:16
little l. and laughter ..1137: 7
little sane l. all right ..1181: 2
lives in cottages 1208: 7
lives in gardens 756: 5
lock than linketh minds .1173: 9
longs for life beyond 968: 1
looks for l. again 1184:10
looks not with eyes, mind 1179:18
lord of truth and loyalty 1190:15
lost but upon God alone 790: 7
lost in men's minds 1183:11
loveliest embalmed in tears 1743:13
lures thee to shame 1188:12
lurks about sheepcote ..1208: 7
made l. to waiting-women 1498: 2
made manifest 396: 9
made of sighs and tears 1174:15
made those hollows 448:19
madness most discreet ..1175: 1
magician, enchanter 1189:14
maintained by wealth ..1208: 5
make l., and pay taxes ..2242: 5
makes a beast a man ..1190: 9
makes a drunken master 1188: 1
makes a good eye squint 1188:13
makes all men orators ..1188:13
makes anew this heart 37:10
makes dog howl in rhyme 1523: 2
makes eke one will 1182: 3
makes l. at all seasons ..1242: 1
makes l. with knees 237: 5
makes people inventive ..1188:13
makes the time pass 1191: 4
makes the world go round 1191: 4
makes those young whom age doth chill 1188: 8
makes us beggars 2159:10
maketh wit of fool 1188:13
malady without a cure ..1186:14
man who feigned to l. ..1186: 1
man's l. is of man's life 1183: 9
man's l. is strong 1183:12
marked by embarrassment 1201: 1
marrow of friendship ..1102:14
master of the wisest 1181: 8
may transform to oyster 1443:15
me and the world is mine 2292: 3
me for myself alone 1215: 7
me if I live 1213:14
me less or l. me more ..1202:15
me little, l. me long 1198: 8
me l. my dog 469: 9
men because not women 1253:12
men l. or need our l. ..2207:12
merely a madness 1174:15
merely to make l. romantic 1007: 4
mightier far than nerve .1191: 3
mighty lord 1190:11
mind's strong physic ..1173:21
moderately; long l. doth 1198: 8
more happy, happy l. ..1192: 9
more just than justice ..1176:11
more l. or more disdain ..1202:15
more than great richesse 1193:10
most concealed 1208:14
most, say least 1210: 4
most serious thing in world 1197: 2
mother's l. outlives all ..1352: 4
must cling 1193:12
must kiss that mortal's eyes .94: 4
must needs be blind 1179:14
must not ridicule l. 1177:14
mutual l., heaven 1263: 4
my l. as deep 1214:14
my l. he loves another l. 1202:14
my l. he purloined her away 2296: 1
my l. is come to me 877: 6
my l. is like a red rose 1211: 2
my l. is of a birth 1213: 1
my l.-lies-bleeding 1194:15
my l. lies in gates of foam 1220:15
my l., my l. loves me ..1072: 7

Love, *continued*
my l., my own 1048: 7
my l. of thee 1185: 7
my l. was passionless ...1222: 1
my old l. comes to meet
me 1207: 7; 1909: 5
my only l. from only hate 1218: 6
mysterious l. uncertain ..1195:17
naked is complete 351: 7
name of honor 918:12
native of the rocks 1177:14
natural in youth 24:15
Nature's oracle, first l. ..1206: 1
ne'er ebb to humble l. ..1713:19
neither for l. nor money 1179:11
never did run smooth ..1195:10
never dies of starvation 1201: 2
never doubt I l. 1214: 9
never link'd to deserver 1483: 5
never l. unless you can 1182: 5
no evil angel but l. 1174:15
no gift grateful as wings 1201: 7
no good of life but l. 2206:16
no great l. in beginning 1270:14
no l. lost between us 1176:12
no l. to a father's 645:10
no l. without jealousy ..1006: 4
no l. without suffering ..1195:14
no man 420:11
no man can temper L. ..1189: 5
no man dies for l. 1220: 8
no more than gold or fame ..15: 9
no passages of l. 1225:11
no remedy for l. but l.
more 1187: 2
noblest hateful l. 1217:20
none but L. to bid us laugh 1219: 8
none knew but to l. thee ..740: 3
nor lordship no fellowship 1178: 3
not constrained by mas-
tery 1191: 9
not cured by herbs 1186:15
not, hapless sons 1195: 6
not hood but eye-water ..1179:16
not l. but superstition 1172:11
not Time's fool 1175: 3
not to be reason'd down 1187: 6
not to know l. is not to live 1182:19
not where most profest 1210: 2
nothing grows again more
easily than l. 1208: 1
nothing like making l. ..1192: 6
nothing more hateful than
l. 1217:20
nothing so sweet as l. ..1217:19
nothing when l. ingrate ..984:11
nowhere less than Divine 790:17
nuptial l. maketh man-
kind 1171:18
O lyric l., half angel ..1193: 1
O unexampl'd l. 790:17
object of l. is to serve ..742: 6
o' mutton beat l. o' sheep 1793: 6
of a servant-maid 1224: 6
of beauty is taste 1966: 1
of books, golden key 188:15
of country 1463: 5
of country prevents crime 1467:11
of economy root of evil ..821:10
of equality 433: 1
of fame 625:19
of flattery in men 678: 2
of food 518:11
of future fame 626: 5
of gold, meanest amour ..802: 7
of higher things 989: 8
of justice fear of injus-
tice 1032:12
of lads soon out 1179:10
of liberty is l. of others 1103: 8
of liberty with life giv'n 1105:10
of life's young day 1206:13
of man? Exotic flower ..1183:10
of money root of all evil 1337: 2
of pleasure eldest-born ..1510:22
of pleasure, l. of sway ..2192: 8
of praise 1577: 5
of servant no disgrace ..1224: 6
of singularity 1489: 5
of the beautiful 130:16

Love, *continued*
of the l. of greatness 831:13
of the populace 1559:15
of the turtle 2061: 8
of woman and bottle of
wine 2159:17
of you made flesh 1210: 9
of your work 107:13
often chang'd the sweeter 1200:13
often fruit of marriage ..1270: 7
Oh L.! young L.! 1192: 6
old l. is gold l. 1207: 2
old l. is little worth . ..1207: 6
once extinguished 1207:10
once fled, never returns 1207:10
once gone, goes forever ..1207:10
once gone never returns ..1207:12
once possess'd 133:21
once when l. is betrayed ..1222:17
one can't choose when l. 1189:13
one l., one hope 975: 5
one l., 1000 imitations ..1177:16
one of many passions ..1173:14
one person all your life ..1202: 7
one returns to first l. ..1206: 5
one should always be in l. 1271: 4
only l. remedyless 1186:14
only parents' l. can last ..1452: 5
only priest 854:11
other pleasures not worth 1196: 1
our land for what she is ..52: 2
our l. as endless prove ..1198: 7
our l. is like our life 411:12
our l. is principle 1172:12
our l. was like most other 1201: 9
over head and ears in l. ..950: 1
overflows honey and gall 1196:12
owe little duty and less l. 508: 1
owes nature his charms ..105:11
passing the l. of women 1184: 3
passionate l. of right ..1727:19
penny-weight of l. 1082: 5
people for good we do ..807:10
perfect l. casteth out fear 1216:11
picks locks at last 133:23
picks twenty locks 1178:16
platform all ranks meet 1173: 7
pleasanter the colder 1172: 6
pleasing but various clime 1175: 5
prays devoutly for l. 1184:10
present for mighty king 1189: 0
privilege of emperors ..1174: 5
prone to l. as sun to shine 1175:12
pronounce but l. and dove 1214:12
prove so hard a master 1188: 1
purple light of l. 436: 5
put out religion's eye ..1696: 9
rather l. than be in l. ..1185: 5
real l. of a lie 1112:20
reality in imagination ..1175: 9
reckons hours for months ..2:18
reflects thing beloved ..1184: 9
reflection of worthiness .1173: 3
repulsed returneth 292: 4
resembles hate 1217:18
resist l. at outset safe ..1190: 8
resistless in battle 1190:14
returns with l. to lover 1218:11
right to dissemble l. 1035: 3
ripe fruit of lifetime 1198:12
ruined by legitimacy 1270:13
rules the court, the camp 1190: 7
rules without a sword ..1189:10
sacrifices all things 1172: 5
said to be a child 1179:18
satisfied, charm gone ...1221: 5
say not woman's l. bought 2208: 7
say that you l. me not 1195: 8
say that you l. me still ..2289:11
scorn no man's l. 543: 2; 1189: 9
secret l. break my heart 1210:15
secret l. is sheer ruin ..1224: 9
seeks a guerdon 744:13
sees no faults 1182: 8
seldom haunts the breast 1763: 8
sever l. from charity 241:14
she never told her l. 1209:17
shone impartial as sun ..1160:12
shot which ever hits 1175: 1
should have no wrong ..2213: 6

Love, *continued*
show thou l. to win l. ..1184: 6
shows but one shaft 1215: 9
shut our eyes 1222: 7
sickness full of woes ..1172:13
silently wrapping all 967: 7
sincere refines upon taste 1198: 2
sits long 1194: 2
slighted l. sair to bide ..1195: 9
smoke raised with sighs 1175: 1
so dear I l. him 1213: 6
so I could eat ye 1178:10
so very timid when 'tis
new 1206: 1
society invented l. 1174: 3
some day L. shall claim ..1434: 6
some l. is light 1201: 6
soonest hot, soonest cold ..1177: 9
sought is good 1178:15
sour delight 1175: 1
sparingly soluble 1209: 5
spends all, hath store ...1176: 7
spice dish with l. pleases 1178: 5
still boy, oft wanton is ..1203:18
still has something of sea 1201:11
still is Nature's truth ..1220:16
stirs in the heart of a boy 1909: 9
stolen l. pleasant to man 1224: 7
stoops as fondly as soars 1179: 7
stops at nothing 1222: 6
strange bewilderment ...1175:11
strikes where it doth l. 1885:12
strong as death 1220:11
such l. as Spirits feel 1194: 5
sunny hour of play 1174: 4
sunshine, hate shadow ..1118:14
sunshine mixed with rain 1196:15
surfeiting in joys of l. ..1273:10
surfeits not 1225: 7
surviving gift of Heaven 1172: 7
sweet is true l. 1194: 1
Sweet L. dead 1219: 3
sweetest joy, wildest woe 1195:18
sweetest thing on earth ..507:17
sweetness, goodness in
her 2140:14
swift, sincere, pious 1175:10
take away l. earth a tomb 1210:14
take l. from life 1183: 2
take l. sublimely 245:16
takes the meaning 990:15
taste the bitters of l. 1197: 4
taught him shame 1809: 4
taught me to rhyme 1203:13
teach me to l. you 2285:11
teaches letters 1177: 3
tell l. it is but lust 1894: 3
tell me, do you l. me 2293: 1
tell me if this be l. 1176: 6
ten men l. what I hate 1966: 5
thank heaven, fasting,
for l. 1193:15
that asks no questions ..2277: 4
that came down shower-like .33:12
that cannot brook delay ..2101:15
that dies untold 1209: 5
that endures for a breath 1239:11
that lives a day 430: 6
that lives on beauty 2261:12
that l. of yours was mine 1211: 6
that loves a scarlet coat 1866: 4
that makes world go round 1191: 4
that never found earthly
close 1195:13
that of every woman's
heart 1183: 9
that no return doth crave 1216: 3
that passes l. of woman ..202:19
that scorns lapse of time 1198: 1
that took an early root 1195: 3
that watched from afar 1189: 6
that would seem hid 1208:14
that's linked with gold ..1178: 2
the master 1188: 9
the midnight through 517:15
the name of honour 918:12
thee as good l. heaven ..1212: 8
thee for heart that's kind 882: 8
thee like pudding 1178:10
them for what they are ..737:19

Love, *continued*
there L. lived 448:19
they happy are and l. ..884:14
they l. indeed who quake 1210: 1
they l. least that let ..1209:12
they l. they hate 2198: 6
things we once hated ...232:10
this lady too too much ..1215: 3
those who admire us 14:12
those who l. cannot age 1188: 8
thou art my l., my life ..1211:14
thou art not king alone ..1188: 4
thou blind fool, L. 1179:18
thou hast left thy first l. 1206:15
thou shalt l. thy neighbor 1396:13
though l. repine 1754:13
through l. of self he slew 1791: 1
through l. to light 1151: 8
thy l. is better than 1215: 1
thy l. to me was wonderful 1184: 3
thyself last 150: 5
'tis brief as woman's l. 2198: 8
'tis l. that makes me bold 1191: 5
'tis woman's whole existence 1183: 9
'tis youth's frenzy 1186:11
to be beloved, l. 1184: 5
to fear l. is to fear life ..1216:15
to his soul gave eyes ..1121: 9
to know her was to l. her 132: 4
to l. again and be undone 1183: 9
to l. alone luxury known 1183: 5
to l. and to be loved 743:16
to l. and be beloved 1184:13; 1192:13
to l. and to cherish 1271:10
to l. and win the best 1219: 1
to l. but little loved 1185:12
to l. but l. in vain 1195:18
to l. foolishly better 1219: 1
to l. her was a liberal education 982: 4
to l. is human 1178: 7
to l. is to believe 1176: 2
to l. is to choose 1174:12
to l. is to know sacrifices 1173:11
to l. oneself is a life-long romance 1791:15
to l. us now and then ..1203: 1
to pour l. through deeds 1160: 4
to see her is to l. her ..2184: 1
tomorrow l. for loveless 1179: 9
too much, hate too much 1217:17
too much that die 1186:13
too precious to be lost ..1179: 1
too violent a passion 1270:16
too young to know what conscience is 1178:14
took up the harp of life 1183: 6
trembling, pure, was l. 1205:16
true l. grounded on esteem 1271: 3
true l. has been my death 1220:12
true l. never did run smooth 1195:10
true l. to God 790: 9
tunes shepherd's reed ...1190: 7
turns to sourest hate 1218: 6
turns upon a wheel 1202: 8
two souls, one flesh 745: 3
tyrant l. 1180:22
tyrant of the heart 1173: 4
unchanged, will cloy 1201: 2
understands l. 1209: 3
union of two minds 1181:12
united to jealous thought 1007: 6
using l. as episode 2071: 5
vanquished by succeeding l. 1187: 2
varnished l. 1217:10
very god of evil 1194:13
waly, gin l. be bonny ..1202:13
wanton l. corrupteth 1171:18
was aye between them twa 1222: 8
was but a name 1223: 2
was her guardian Angel ..393:10
was like the liberal air ..1496: 8
was pearl of his oyster ..1443:17
wayward is this foolish l. 1203:16

Love, *continued*
we all l. great men 897:12
we always l. those who admire us 14:12
we are all born for l. 1182:18
we live to l., meet to part 1290: 7
we l. as one 2299c: 4
we l. but while we may ..1207: 8
weary l. is thine 1887: 6
wedded l. founded on esteem 1271: 3
wee little whimpering L. 2019: 9
weightier business of man 1182:18
well, whip well 2179:10
what can pay l. but l. ..1185: 9
what costs us pains 2208: 9
what hours thine and mine 1194: 1
what is the l. of men 1201: 8
what l. can do dares l. ..1190:10
what silent l. hath writ ..191: 5
what we lack ourselves 453: 9
when a man talks of l. ..1204:13
when I l. thee not, chaos 1214:11
when l. first came to earth 1747: 7
when l. for you died 1220: 8
when l. in the faint heart 1688: 1
when l. is liberty 1222: 4
when l. is unerring light 1216: 4
when l. links two people 1223: 8
when l. pleads admission 1187: 6
when l. speaks harmony 1174:15
when L. was loveliest .1401:14
when they should fight ..1174: 7
where beauty is 133:20
where I l., I profess it ..1217:21
where L. and Wisdom dwell 1435: 5
where l. draws hate 1218: 7
where l. fails 649:11
where l. is, marriage 1269:18
where l. is, no lack 1176: 7
where no l. all faults 649:11
where shall we find such l. 1757: 2
which rules heaven 1192:15
while l. shall last 1130:11
while you are able 1221: 9
who l. their fellow-men ..1493:10
who says "I l. not," in l. 1186: 2
whose month is ever May 1909: 4
whose shafts of fire 1189: 2
why am I crying after l. .134: 1
will conquer at the last ..1191: 1
will creep in service 1177:10
will dream 404: 1
will find out the way 1191: 5
will hallow it all 2204:13
will long for absent 4: 4
will make man dare to die 1190: 5
will never die 1219: 4
will not be drawn, led ..1192: 3
will still be lord 1189: 7
will you l. me in December 1216: 1
winning l., risk losing 1195: 2
winter-l. in dark corner 1028: 1
wiser than ambition 51: 4
with all her faults I l. her still 2292: 6
with all thy faults, I l. thee still 649: 2
with fear the only God ..1420: 3
with gall and honey 1196:12
with true l. as with ghosts 1198:13
without l. no joy 1193: 7
without marriage 1269:18
woman complimented by l. 2206:15
woman's l. is but a blast 2199: 8
woman's l. is mighty 1352:14
woman's l. writ in water 2196:15
woman's whole existence 1183: 9
woman's wonderful l. ...2184: 6
worse fate 1195: 6
years of l. have been forgot 1218: 2
yet I l. her till I die 1211:14
yield up, O l., thy crown 1218: 5
you all the day 899: 1
you can l., and think 1989:11
you for what you are ...2207: 1
you I l., and you alone ..1630: 1

Love, *continued*
you long for l. that is surer 2288: 1
you may l. screaming owl 1176: 3
you'll l. me yet 1214:13
your enemies 542: 6
your neighbor's wife 212: 3
Love's best habit soothing tongue 1209:16
dreams 483:11
except for l. sake only ..1184: 7
law out of rule 1191:11
lesson to please eye 600:10
reason's without reason ..1181: 1
stories written in l. book ..601:11
tongue is in the eyes 600:17
very pain is sweet 1197: 1
Love-apples that bloom 92: 2
Love-at-first-sight: old miracle—L. 1205:12
Love-chant: utter forth his l. 1404:15
Love-ditties passing rare ..1203:13
Love-feat wilt advance 1325:12
Love-in-idleness 690
Love-knot: my l. on his spear 259:10
Love-letters made of flowers 686:16
'scaped l. 1103: 2
to great women 1102:15
Love-lies-bleeding 1194:15
Love-like: low and l. 201:20
Love-making: do it best ..1176: 8
Love-match for happiness 1269:17
Love-matches, month of honey 1269:10
Love-philtre: one genuine l. 1185:14
Love-quarrels oft in concord end 1197: 7
Love-song I had somewhere read 1878:10
learned to relish l. 1735: 9
shot through the ear with a l. 605: 6
Love-star of March 357: 2
Love-suit: plead his l. 2212: 8
Loved a love not blind 1180: 1
all her l. that looked upon her face 2204:14
and hated, sought and feared 236:22
better to have l. and lost ..1218:20
by none who loves none 1184:14
had we never l. sae kindly 1194:12
hath any l. you well 388:22
I have lived and l. 1133: 2
I have l. not wisely 1222:18
I l. him for himself 1215: 7
I l. him too as woman l. 1222:16
I only know we l. in vain 635: 9
I prefer to be l. 1216:14
I saw and l. 1185:10
if you would be l. love ..1184: 5
long since and lost awhile 403:12
me for the dangers 1186: 7
men l. beyond wisdom ..1180:18
much, hoped little 1331:10
no sooner looked but l. ..1205:13
no sooner l. but sighed ..1205:13
not at first sight 1205: 9
not wisely but too well ..1222:18
once, when I l. 1217: 4
one isn't l. every day ..1193:12
she never l. who durst not 1221: 8
so long, sees no more 402:17
that I had l. smaller man 1248: 9
the blue-eyed maid 2211:17
though l. you well, I woo'd you not 2216: 2
three whole days together 1202: 5
to be l. needs only to be known 321: 8
to be l. needs only be seen 2053:12
too late I l. Thee 130: 3
who never l. at all 1218:19
who never l. never lived 1182:19
you ere I knew you 1213: 3
Lovelier than seas are strong 997:10
Loveliest and the best 401:10
of lovely things 1745: 3
Lovelight in her eye 600:11
in your eyes 1852:16

Loveliness: all her majestic l. 105: 2
April's rare l. 93:13
beyond completeness 120: 8
born upon a thorn 1744:13
dim and solitary l. 1401: 7
essential l. 131: 3
her l. I never knew 139: 4
is enough 2240:10
lay down in her l. 1844: 7
long'd-for l. 1486: 5
majesty of L. 134:13
needs not aid of ornament 490: 4
of perfect deeds 264: 7
of woman 1253:13
stands for aye in l. 104:17
when I approach her l. ..2185: 5
Lovell our dog 545: 8
Lovely as the day 139:10
crumpled, but l. still 40:10
grow l., growing old 40: 5
grow more l. growing wise ..30:12
in a lonely place 1844: 8
in their lives 402:15
make you l. to be loved 133:20
she's l., she's divine 139:15
things that are l. 134:18
to the last 399:11
what is l. never dies 135:17
whatsoever things are l. ..2090:10
Lover: accepted l. lost charm 1206: 4
adventurous l. successful 2215: 7
all mankind love a l. 1177: 2
every l. is a soldier 1174: 7
every man l. of truth 2053:14
find me reasonable l. 1181: 2
forsaken, new love get ..1186:13
great l. of the ladies 1178: 6
has become her friend 745: 7
I am the Last L. 374:14
in husband may be lost ..1266:12
in vain you tell parting l.1455: 9
is beloved 134: 3
let every l. be pale 1224: 7
miracle to find l. true ..1200: 9
not l. who does not love 1198: 5
of blest and unblest 135: 2
of hospitality 932:10
of letters loves power too 2250: 2
of Liberty at heart 1305:16
of meadows and woods ..1385: 1
of self, without rival 1790: 8
of the good old school ..1201:14
of things that change ..2274: 1
of wine and minstrelsy ..1868: 1
pants upon her breast 977:16
pressing l. seldom wants 2215: 7
rooted stays 1188:15
see Helen's beauty 1179:18
shall join hater 1137: 7
should give 1178: 2
sighing like furnace 2240: 5
the man outlives the l. ..1200: 8
thou wilt be like a l. 2225: 8
to listening maid 2213: 6
too shuns business 1187: 1
using a l. well 2207:11
value l. according to gifts 1178: 2
what mad l. ever died ..1220: 8
who can deceive a l. 1179: 4
who will find l. for Death ..399:12
why has l. cast noose ..1186:13
Lover's eyes gaze eagle blind 601:11
Lovers and ministers seldom true 2180:18
are fools 1177:11
are given to poetry 1523: 4
bide at home 906:14
cannot see 1179:18
clumsy summer-flies 1204: 2
derive pleasures from misfortunes 1196: 3
diocesans of Bishop Valentine 2071:11
dream a rich and long delight 1194:17
falling-out, falling in 1197:14
holding death in scorn ..1502:12
live by love 1185: 3
love the western star 1917: 6

Lovers, *continued*
make two l. happy 1182:20
more l. than husbands 134: 8
of freedom free 723:11
old l. are soundest 42: 6
pity l. more than seamen 2203:10
remember all things 1199: 4
run into strange capers ..1181: 6
should guard strangeness 1206: 4
sight of l. feedeth love ..1186: 5
such as I am all true l. are 1215: 2
swear more performance 1205: 4
sweet l. love the spring .1909: 3
tell me if l. are losers ..1220: 7
thus l. tie their knot 3: 4
unafraid of heaven 1222:12
what can l. wish for more 1204:18
which l. ever found her true 2243: 1
Lovers' oaths 1204: 7
Loves as gay and fleeting ..2156:12
but half the earth 512:15
enough that does not hate 1630: 1
great l. have pulses red 1219:19
great l. live on 1198:17
he l. me for little 1217:15
he l. me not 358: 7
he that l. but half earth ..1494: 8
he that l. himself 2073: 4
he that l. not wife 633: 6
him who l. always one ..1200:10
him with that excellence 1199: 9
his l. are brazen images ..904: 3
I sing of little l. 1193: 9
little who l. by rule 1191:11
new l. are sweet 1207: 8
nobody l. a fat man 647: 9
nobody l. me 1195:11
none l. king better 1468: 7
of all my l. the last 1198: 9
one l. without reason 1217: 7
one that l. his fellow-men 1495:10
other l. may come to us ..1207: 9
remain, perfect and pure 1156:12
she l. and l. forever 2208: 7
so much cannot forget ..1199: 4
somebody l. me 2293: 9
sorry her lot who l. too well 1222:18
ten thousand little L. 2071:11
that meet in Paradise ...1451:20
to be flattered 677:19
to be trodden underfoot ..16:13
two human l., one divine 1182: 3
well that makes weep 1973: 1
what he lacks in himself 1176:10
who early l. is wise 24:15
who gave us nobler l. 1536: 6
who l. me follows me 663: 7
who l. not women, wine and song 2160: 1
whoso l. believes impossible 1178: 4
with fortunes change 1201:13
you better than his horse ..930: 2
Lovest: an thou lovest me 1178:13
whate'er thou l. thou must become 382: 1
Loveth and maketh a lie ..1113:13
downward, and not up 350: 6
prayeth best who l. best 1584: 2
who l. nought is here as dead 1183: 1
Loving: all I want is l. 2293:10
are the daring 1870: 6
comes by looking 1185:10
goes by haps 351: 2
he's had no l. for a long, long time 2284: 2
is a painful thrill 1195:18
living, l. and loved today 2183:12
me the l., you the loth ..2216: 1
oh, fear to call it l. 1172: 4
practiced l. long enough 1217:16
so l. and so lovely 2207: 2
thy mournful face 244: 1
Loving-jealous of his liberty 1455:11
Loving-kindness: crowneth thee with l. 790: 1
pity's kin 1036: 7

Low: had an amiable l. 69:13
happy l., lie down 1848: 2
lay him l., lay him l. ...1868: 6
they feared the l. 561:17
though I am 622: 5
Low-fallen from high estate 621: 9
Lowe, Robert: epitaph 573: 4
Lowell: I've never seen a L. walk 194:15
Lowells talk to Cabots 194:15
won't speak to the Cohns 194:15
Lower than the angels 1243: 8
Lowering of money a cheat 1551: 3
Lowest: goes l. builds safest 1753:13
Lowliness ambition's ladder .50: 4
base of virtue 936: 6
of heart 448:13
Loyal: be l. to one's friends 744: 6
to profession of medicine 2274: 3
Loyalties: impossible l. 224:17
life's fine l. 227:12
Loyalty
See also Fidelity
holiest good 664: 1
may be blind 742: 6
room for but one l. 55: 9
to petrified opinion 1428:17
to Truth be sealed 1128: 9
we, too, friends to l. 1039:13
well held to fools 664: 2
where is l. 664: 2
Lubin fears that he may die 1276:15
while L. is away 3: 6
Lubricos: sublimi maxime l. 838: 3
Luce: ex l. lucellum 1152:18
Lucem: ex fumo dare l. ..1152: 1
Lucernam olet 1923:14
Luchyn, Lady: epitaph 570: 2
Lucid intervals 1230: 4
Lucidus ordo 1926:13
Lucifer: it is L. 444: 4
son of morning 621:13
Luck 1225
as good l. would have it 1226: 6
bad l. often brings good ..1226:10
bad L. she is never a lady 1226:13
for fools 1225:13
for l. cast old shoe 1226:17
frees from punishment ..1657: 4
give a woman l. 1225:16
good l. befriend thee 1226: 2
good l. covereth faults ..1225:20
good l. go with thee 1226: 2
good l. never too late 1225:17
good L. she is never a lady 1226: 1
has come to many a hopeless man 1226: 3
here's l. 1796:12
is a lord 1225:18
just like my l. 1226: 7
knocks at his door 1431:10
let us seek what l. 2103: 4
little is l. I've had 1226:11
makes madness wisdom ..1225:21
may look after the rest ..1128: 5
mistook for art 1225:14
nae l. aboot the house 3:15
ounce of l. better 1226: 5
reaches farther than arms 1225:20
shallow men believe in l. 1225:19
stay alive by l. 195:12
there's l. in odd numbers 1227: 3
'tis an affair of l. 672: 3
too good to share 240: 2
what evil l. soever 1226:11
what l. 672: 3
when good l. comes, take ..1225:15
will turn 24: 5
you never know your l. ..228:14
Lucky: better l. than wise 1226: 5
born so late 84: 2
fifty per cent l. 1140: 1
to be born 407:18
to die as to be born 407:18
Lucre: greedy of filthy l. .1337:20
lofty l. of renown 627:14
savour of l. is good 1336:15
Lucri quidquid est 1562: 2
Lucro: præter spem esse in l. 592:11

Lucrum malum æquale dispendo 751: 1
non omnino l. utile 750:12
sine damno alterius 751:10
Lucullus dines with L. 449: 8
Lucus a non lucendo 1152:20
est l. uni cuique suus ..1504:19
umbra opacus 1152:20
Lucy: linger longer, L. ..2295: 6
Sir Thomas L. 941: 9
when L. ceased to be 402:14
Lucy Locket lost her pocket ..61: 7
Ludas: ut l. creditores 249:10
Ludendi quidam modus retinendus 67: 8
Ludis me obscura canendo 1423: 4
Ludo: quæramus seria l. ..1009:15
Ludos: nullos l. spectasse 1909:11
Ludum: pudet non incidere l. 695:10
Ludus animo debet 1312:12
enim genuit trepidum 754:11
Lues Boswelliana 14: 9
Lugete, O Veneres 1356:14
Luggage of life 2143:4a
Lukewarmness I account no sin 1200:11
Lull of treacherous sea ...1772: 3
Lullaby Time is singing ..2011:10
Lumbago jumps upon his back 1900: 5
Lumber: loads of learned l. 1677: 6
of the schools 1500:10
Lumen siccum optima anima 1306:14
Luminaries: moral l. 1685: 8
Luminary: great l. aloof ..1938:16
Lumine: a l. motus 1943: 5
Luminous but not sparkling 604: 6
Lump of death 233:10
Luna: fortune's fickle L. ..716:12
the moon 1343:18
Luna: micat inter ignes l. minores 1913: 6
Lunacies earth can boast 1609: 5
Lunacy linked with sanity 1024: 6
Lunatic fringe 1685: 6
lover, l. 1181: 3
lover, poet 962: 5
Lunatics rather than of lovers 1181: 3
Lunch: after l. rest 872: 7
Lune: au clair de la l. ...1345: 3
garder la l. des loups ..1341:13
Lunes: at his old l. 944:18
Lung-protector: he wears ..212: 7
Lungs began to crow 1075: 4
heaving of my l. 1852: 6
it opens the l. 1973:21
of London 1453:17
offend'st l. to speak loud 1898: 3
to wet the l. 491: 9
Lupo ovem commisisti 1811:14
Lupum: auribus teneo l. 2177:18
Lupus est homo, non homo 1249: 5
hac l., hac canis 364:11
in fabula 441: 5
in sermone 2177:12
languebat 443: 2
Lure within lovely tresses ..11:10
Luscum: inter cæcos l. regnare posse 169:17
Luscus: cæcorum in patria l. 169:17
Lusor: non cessat perdere l. 752:12
Lust
See also Love and Lust
accursed l. for gold 802: 7
and rank thoughts 2189: 6
and wine plead pleasure 1952: 3
burning l., brutish passion 1223: 7
by unchaste looks 1224: 5
charms all womankind ..1224:10
cistern of my l. 2105:11
cursed l. of gold 802: 1
deathless l. of song 1518: 6
doth pollute and foul 245:18
for pleasure 1511: 1
harsh and cruel master 30:11
here hath l. domination 90: 5
holds despotic sway 1511: 1
Lust, *continued*
into ashes all my l. 246: 9
like a glutton dies 1225: 7
loathly sinful L. 1190:15
new l. gives lecher thrill 1224: 3
no l., because no law ..1090:10
of gain 1474:15
of gold, unfeeling 802: 4
oldest lion of them all ..1225: 4
right thing to extinguish l. 1223: 5
rule l., temper tongue ..1787: 4
sacred l. of praise 1577:17
tempest after sun 1225: 7
was driv'n from men ..1270: 6
will lull them all to sleep 1225: 2
wretched l. of praise 629: 2
Lust: kurze L. die Quelle langer Schmerzen 1512: 3
und Liebe die Fittige ...1173: 8
Lustest: hotly l. to use her 949: 6
Lustre: dark l. of thine eyes 604: 7
dies away 1683: 7
in its sky 32: 4
ne'er could any 601:14
never lost her l. 2141: 2
with diminished l. shone ..833: 6
Lustres: reflected l. play ..1941:17
Lusts of body scandalize soul 1225: 8
troublesome l. 30:11
Lusty: strong and l. 37:18
Lutanist and lute 1137:10
Lute, The 1368
Apollo's l. 1368:13
lascivious pleasing of a l. .362: 9
let warbling l. complain ..1368:11
play upon a l. 1:15
riven l. shall sound 1244: 3
sighs whispering l. 1369:13
silent is the l. now 402:12
take time-worn l. away ..1368:10
warbling l. 1367:13
whose leading chord is gone ..4: 3
Lute-player: some dead l. 1368:14
Luther, Martin 1227
crucified 1695: 2
destroyed the roof 1741: 5
guilty of two great crimes 1227: 8
prison of flesh 1889: 9
rough old Martin L. 1227: 7
Lutheran: spleeny L. 1695: 9
Lux: Fiat L. 1151:13
in tenebris 1152: 3
mundi 1152: 4
orta est 1152:19
per immunda non inquinatur 1150:18
Luxe: vain l. environne 712: 1
Luxor: winds of L. 383: 7
Luxuria: sævior armis L. incubuit 1474: 4
Luxuriant animi rebus ...1606: 9
Luxuries demanded by women 2107: 4
give us l. and we dispense with necessaries 1228:15
hindrances 285: 7
stole too deep into soul ..1228:13
Luxurious, avaricious 240:11
falsely l. 1228:20
Luxury 1227
all their l. doing good 806:17
and riot 1474: 7
anger is expensive l. 77:14
blesses stars, thinks it l. 1227:13
ceases to be innocent 1228:10
curs'd by heaven's decree 1228: 5
enjoy the l. of thought ..1789: 7
enslaves 1228:14
greatest l. of riches 1571:13
hath sting in her tail ..1228:16
in self-dispraise 1331:14
is like a wild beast 1228:12
more cruel than warfare ..1474: 4
more perilous to youth ..1228:14
never satisfied 1327:14
of disrespect 635: 6
of doing good 659: 5
of false religion 1691:14
of giving 772: 5
Luxury, *continued*
of grief 841:16
of self-sacrifice 2193: 1
of woe 841:16
sick of night's debauch ..505: 3
there is limit to l. 1228: 9
to learn 1969:13
we can do without l. 1228: 6
what will not l. taste 521:19
Lyæo: narrabis multa L. ..504: 7
Lydia: in heart a L. 573: 9
Lydian: lap me in soft L. airs 1365:12
Lying at home or abroad ..452: 7
becomes none but tradesmen 1111:15
but kind of self-denying 1111:21
for its own sake 1110:11
how world is given to l. 1113:17
is thy sustenance 2060: 5
let me have no l. 1111:15
no vice so mean 1111:11
not so easy by half as l. 1729:14
one form of l. forbidden ..1111: 1
putting away l. 2057: 9
rides upon debt's back ..418:15
second vice is l. 418:15
shows force of truth 2059:11
that cannot be laid hold of 1109: 8
three sorts of people l. ..2032: 4
to liars 1109:16
whole way to hell 1111:13
Lympha pudica Deum 1315:14
Lymphis: non sua purpura, l. 1315:14
Lynnhaven 1733: 8
Lynx envers nos pareils ..1024:13
Lynx-like is his aim 941:10
Lyræ: Romanæ fidicen l. ..627:10
Lyre: deaf to the l. 1362: 6
formed the seven-chorded l. 1854: 8
heaven-taught l. 1526: 9
Horace's l. is unstrung ..1519:12
Milton's golden l. 1305: 5
my l. within the sky 1534:11
Orpheus strikes trembling l. 1363: 1
wak'd to ecstasy living l. 851: 8
welcome at feasts 1368: 2
what has ass to do with l. 112: 8
Lyric: I would be the l. 1517: 6
perfect l. is a deed 425: 8
risk fame upon one l. 1519: 4
splendid ecclesiastical l. ..335: 1
Lyrical: each little l. 206: 2
Lyrics for me 1517: 6
Lyrist of Roman race 627:10
Lysander: principle of L. ..1418:13

M

M.D.: worth one D—M. ..468: 3
Ma, ma, where's my pa ..1557: 8
Maas: nur M. ihm Reiz ..1329: 3
Mab, Queen 615:11
the Mistress-Fairy 615:11
Mab's ethereal palace 282: 2
Mabel: ain't it awful, M. 9:11; 2288: 4
Macadam on its wings ..1025:16
Macassar: incomparable oil 2093:10
Macaulay, Thomas Babington 1229
is like a book in breeches ..1229: 1
Macaulay's New Zealander 1740:13
Macbeth does murder sleep 1845: 9
Maccabæus: ycliped M. ..1019:14
McCloskey: throw him down M. 2289: 9
Macdonald: where M. sits .832: 5
Macduff: lay on, M. 428: 9
Macedonians: rude M. ..218:16
McFlimsey: Miss Flora ...487: 4
McGinty: down went M. 2285:13
McGregor: my name is M. 1372:12
where M. sits 1504:13
Machiavel, Nick 1377:10
writes what men do 427: 4
Machiavelian holy maxim 1543: 1

Man, *continued*
you're a better m. than I 1252: 9
young m. married is m. marred 1277: 1
young m. with touch of age 23: 1
Man's best things nearest him 463: 7
reach should exceed grasp 108:17
Man-and-Mammon worship 1856:17
Man-at-arms only man 1864:13
Man-beast is the worst 1248:16
Man-Child: conceived 163:13
when the m. is born 1714: 4
Man-despot: oppressive m. 1086: 3
Man-like to fall into sin 1829: 9
Man-of-letters and manners 2257: 3
Man-of-war best ambassador 1598: 1
Man-shaped like thee 1188:12
Man-slaughter and isolated murder 2113: 4
infinite m. 2111:13
Man-slayer: physician and m. 446:15
Man-stealing takes rights 1842:10
Manage: he will not m. her 2195:16
Manager: your m. is in love 1214:10
Manchester fight with 1472:13
shortest way out of M. 499:13
Mandalay: come you back to M. 1212: 6
road to M. 368: 5
Mandates of fate 1893: 6
Mandide madeam 502:12
Mandragora: give me to drink m. 1850:19
Mandy Lee, I love you 1883: 1
Mane: grasped the m. 1654:14
is like a river flowing 930:13
laid hand upon thy m. 1773: 6
of every wind 681:12
Manes: mittunt insomnia M. 478:21
quisquis suos patimur M. 1657: 8
Manger: away in a m. 268:17
cradled in a m. 269: 5
dog in the m. 471: 6
for his cradle stands 269: 8
is heaven 261: 4
of Bethlehem 268:11
Manger pour vivre 517: 2
Manges: dis moi ce que tu m. 515:13
Mangeurs: les grands m. 647:11
Mangler in a million 2179:12
Manhattan: mighty M. 1397:11
Manhattan's a hell 1397: 4
Manhood breathes in every line 205:16
ere we dream of m., age is nigh 2006: 8
find thy M. all too fast 26: 4
in battle 22:15
is a struggle 23: 8
learning, gentleness 239: 4
melted into courtesies 293: 9
misled by wandering fires 1609:10
of nine tailors 1958:18
over our m. bend skies 1386: 5
robs me of my m. 1956:17
there was m. in his look 1245: 8
troubled m. followed 238: 2
what makes m. great 206: 3
what m. bids thee do 1126:13
Manhood's simple level 238:15
tossing waves 967: 2
Mania of owning things 82: 3
Maniæ infinitæ sunt species 1231: 3
Manibus pedibusque 2027:17
Manichean god 800: 4
Manières: deux m. de s'elever 1930:12
Manifest destiny 64: 1
not be made m. 1784:12
Manifestoes: any one can issue m. 2280: 2
Manipulators: unscrupulous m. 1543:17
Manis: quisque suos patimur M. 440: 6
Mankind: all doings of m. 190:16
all m. love a lover 1177: 2
asses who pull 546:10
countless species of m. 1240:12
crucify m. on cross of gold 1551:10
despise m. in all its strata 1246: 4
easier to know m. than man 1251:11
falls down before money 1334: 3
fell in Adam 144: 9
good opinion of m. 1428: 4
happier for having been 1294:13
has ceased to torture 1932:19
has honoured destroyers 1246: 6
have been women's fools 2187:12
how beauteous m. is 1245:11
in original perused m. 1251: 3
incorrigible race 957: 1
leave m. unknown 187: 7
need not be to hate m. 1870:12
our countrymen 320:10
proper study of m. is man 1251:14
reveres your sires 72:11
rushes on through every time 337: 6
survey m. from China to Peru 1423:11
think myself one of best 1246: 4
to help m. begin at home 60: 2
unfit for own government 1247: 1
way to generate m. 2188: 7
will not be reasoned 1492: 5
will take advice 20:20
wisest, meanest of m. 122:11
wish m. only one neck 1394: 3
Manlike to fall into sin 1829: 9
Manliness: silent m. of grief 842: 4
wrongs m. by laughing 1076:14
Mann: here lies Anne M. 573: 5
Mann des Schicksals 439:14
Manna: drop m. in the way 2185: 4
of popular liberty 1106: 7
was not good 1729: 9
Manner: affable m. wins affections 312:11
answered in roundest m. 1260:10
dislike m. not matter 1897:20
dropping-down-deadness m. 1589:10
good bedside m. 464:24
her coaxing m. 1258: 6
is all in all 2251:14
kind m., gentle speech 1036:16
of primitive man 124:11
of speaking important 1898:11
speak after the m. of men 1899:10
suit your m. to the man 1258:15
superior m. 561:15
to the m. born 355: 8
vulgar of m., overfed 1398: 2
Mannerly: behave m. 255: 8
Manners 1256
after you is good m. 1258:12
all who saw admired 329: 6
and money make gentleman 763: 3
are not idle 1257:10
before morals 1258:18
bred ere m. in fashion 904: 8
catch m. as they rise 1251:13
chastises m. with a laugh 1079: 1
consideration for others 1257: 4
degenerate m. 1260: 7
differ in their beauty 1257: 7
dignity of m. necessary 448: 5
do shape fortune 716: 7
evil communications corrupt m. 288:11
evil m. grow up quickly 1260: 7
evil m. live in brass 987: 1
external m. of laments 2176:17
fine m. need support 1257:20
flower of noble character 1257:11
forget a lady's m. 1260: 9
gentle, compelling 568:12
good m. and soft words 1258:17
good m. at the court 1257: 8
Manners, *continued*
good m. be your speed 1259:13
good m. sacrifices 1259: 7
greater than laws 1256:13
happy ways of doing things 1256:13
her m. had not the repose 1260:12
here's a million of m. 1258:11
his salon m. 1260:13
honors change m. 921: 1
ill m. produce good laws 1082:11
in eating 521: 9
in his m. insolence 559: 2
in the face 607: 4
learning of high m. 2030: 9
make laws 1082:11
make the man 1258:19
man bewray'd by his m. 1259:14
mildest m., gentlest heart 1259: 8
more m. than he ought 1257:19
must adorn knowledge 1256:10
no m. at all 1259:16
not good m. to mention 580: 3
not learning, but m. 1258:16
not men, but m. 1258:1a
nothing settled in m. 1256:13
observed m. of men too little 1423:15
of a Marquis 70: 6
of a' nations bad 1256:14
of different nations 1256:14
of every age 1258:1a
of m. gentle 238:21
of many men and their cities 2029: 2
of women 431: 1
old m. 41:13
one's m. make one's fortune 1258: 5
polish'd m. and fine sense 729: 1
practise m. of the time 1257: 3
pursuits, peoples 901: 5
puts on Mayfair m. 1259: 2
same m. for everyone 1257: 9
saw the m. in the face 568:16
simple m. 83:16
soft and bland 647: 8
stately m. of the old school 1259: 1
such high-bred m. 1259:10
table m. 521: 5
take tincture from our own 1257: 6
that they never mend 1861:11
their m. noted 2029: 1
to keep fools at distance 1256:13
to mention 580: 3
uncouth m. 52: 6
unruly m. 1260: 2
what times! what m. 1257:17
where m. ne'er preached 1260:10
with fortunes 232: 3
your m. are familiar 1258: 1
Manners': for m. sake 521: 5
Mannikin: one little m. 164:12
Mano: una m. lava l'altra 850:11
Manor: goodly m. for a song 1875:16
Mansion have those vices 2081:15
in our Father's m. 883:12
making a perpetual m. 1123: 4
of aching hearts 2289:11
Summer's nimble m. 828:19
village preacher's modest m. rose 1590: 8
Mansions: build thee more stately m. 1890:17
Father's many m. 404: 3
in my father's house are many m. 883:12
in the skies 883:12
where all God's m. be 883:12
Mansuetudo est remedium 346: 9
Mantica: spectatur m. tergo 651: 7
Manticæ: non videmus m. 651: 7
Mantis: saint among vermin 1970:18
Mantle: fame's m. a pall 630: 3
golden m. her attire 848:10
how is night's sable m. 1402: 7

Mantle, *continued*
in russet m. clad 1347:10
night's m. covers all 1400: 6
of the Prophet seems 1941:13
o'er dark her silver m. threw 582: 9
prophet's m. 1623:14
saffron-colored m. 1346:19
wrap thy form in m. grey 1404: 2
Mantles: daisied m. 358: 2
Mantuan, divinely sweet ..244:13
Manu: qua vincit 297:12
Manufactories of drama ..2068:16
Manufactures: foster certain infant m. 1965: 8
home m. 1965: 8
never purchase foreign m. 1965:10
Manum: osculantur qua sunt oppressi m. 1801:16
Manure: blood of tyrants natural m. 1104: 5
of m. wagon-load 1015: 9
Manus hæc inimica tyrannis 2065: 1
longos regibus esse 1038:13
manum lavat 850:11
nostra perfecit m. 2250:12
nulla m. pura est 1020:17
nullum laborem recusant m. 850:12
puras non plenas m. 850: 8
qui m. armaverit 457: 5
sed etiam mentes puras ..279: 7
timidas non habuisse m. ..850: 7
vacuæ m. temeraria 145: 6
Manuscript: whoever dipped in her m. 1389:11
youth's sweet-scented m. .2267: 5
Manuscripts of God 1389:13
Many are called few chosen 260:11
are governed by the few ..814: 6
from m. to make one 56:12
incompetent m. 434: 3
make the household 909: 4
safe from the M. 238:16
too m., yet how few 400:10
Many-headed monster-thing 1484: 5
Many-twinkling feet 359:15
Map me no maps, sir 2243: 8
of busy life 1124: 8
roll up that m. 581: 3
Maples: scarlet of m. can shake me 115:17
Mar curious tale in telling 1959:13
we m. what's well 50: 6
Maranatha 1418: 4
Marasmus 460:14
Marathon: age spares grey M. 82: 8
looks on the sea 839: 1
mountains look on M. 839: 1
Maraviglia: niuna m. dura più che tre giorni 2209: 7
Marble and recording brass decay 1339: 3
as the m. wastes, the statue grows 1771: 1
every block of m. contained statue 527: 4
forget thyself to m. 708:13
keeps cold memory 1340: 4
leapt to life a god 1771:10
like a man sawing m. ..329:21
like Niobe, we m. grow 2176: 5
not by m. graven 1339:18
not m. nor gilded monuments 1519:11
not m. shall outlive 1519:11
of her snowy breast 2105: 3
soften'd into life 1771:10
stricken m. grows to beauty 1770:17
there wants no m. for a tomb 1339:17
to her tears 1977:19
to retain 875:12
under this m. 1558: 9
work upon m. will perish 1312:19
Marble-constant 306: 5
Marble-limbed: beauty m. ..335:12
Marbles keep not themselves 1158: 7
mossy m. rest 401: 1
where speaking m. show 2131:11
Marblestone: seldom mosseth the m. 1639: 3
Marcellus exiled feels 629: 1
young M. sleeps 411: 3
March 1260
beware ides of M. 2120:15
comes in like lion 1260:15
dry M. and dry May ...2128:15
has its hares 1654:11
mad as a M. hare 1230: 7
March: day's m. nearer home 887:11
does not m. but dance ..360: 1
forced m. of bullocks 531: 9
in life's morning m. 2266: 2
of human mind is slow 1307: 9
of intellect 1307: 9
of that eternal harmony ...374:13
of time goes on 416:17
without noise of drum ..2117: 7
Marche: mais il danse 360: 1
Marched without impediment 2117: 7
Märchen aus alten Zeiten .1959: 3
speist man mit M. 615: 4
Marches: solemn m. fill nights 2120: 4
Marches: battant des m. funèbres 827:18
Marching as to war 267: 8
in endless file 371:24
Marcus: buy M. at price he is worth 533:11
Marcus Aurelius married ill 1278:10
Mare: grey m. better horse 929:13; 2145: 4
grey m. ill to live with ..2145: 4
money makes the m. trot 1332:11
rode upon a sorry m. 931: 9
shanks's m. 2101:12
Mare commune omnibus ..1782: 1
cum m. compositum 1774:12
exitio est avidum m. nautis 1778:11
in m. fundis aquas 667:13
per m., per terras 1780:13
Mare's nest: find a m. 1636: 9
Maréchal: comment meurt un m. de France 413:17
Margate beach 2136: 4
Margin: broad m. of leisure 1100:20
Mæander's flowery m. ...1950: 3
meadow of m. 190: 4
Mari qui veut surprendre 945: 3
sers m. comme maitre 944:13
teneat, necesse rerum potiri 1782: 2
Maria: Dear M. 2280: 3
hurrah for M. 1557: 8
Maria montisque polliceri 1620:15
Sancta M. ad Nives 1857: 6
Maria Theresa: epitaph ...571: 6
Mariage fortresse assiégée 1279: 1
Mariages: bons m. 1276: 7
se font au ciel 1271: 5
Mariana of moated grange 1642: 5
Marianne: voilà la M. 719: 9
Marie: come to me, sweet M. 2294: 6
Marigold 1261
sun-observing m. 690: 8
to bed with sun 685: 9
Marin: un m. naufragé ..1157: 9
Marine: loyal M. Regiment 2283: 4
Mariner: steer, bold m. on 284:11
Mariners: relations of m. ..334: 3
slow sail'd the weary m. 1300:11
Marines have landed 1636:10
tell it to m. 1636:10; 2283: 4
Marionette: Japanese 327: 8
Maritum: petet Lalage m. ..944: 7
regnat poscitque m. 2146: 1
Mark: aim above m. 1661: 4
archer little meant 2226:10
ever-fixed m. 1175: 3
Mark, *continued*
fair as breast of foe 541:20
fairest m. is easiest hit 1757: 9
God save the m. 1129: 7; 1641: 9
good humor's m. 569: 6
he was m. and glass 1252:15
lion's m. is always there 2230: 8
make his m. equal to 2259: 3
missing the m. 1925: 1
of the elect 339: 1
shoot not beyond m. 456:14
upon his lip is wine 248:12
vain m. of humility 2074:11
was a Pill 1268: 1
where she stands 353:13
Mark Antony: my own M. A. 1176:15
Mark Hopkins: a pine bench with M. H. 2069: 4
Marked: him for his own 239:11
with whitest stone 370:15
Market: best of a bad m. 125: 8
earth's great m. 1017:14
friend in the m. 729:18
glutted m. makes provision cheap 2208: 9
is the best garden 756: 8
of his time 1241:14
one who on m. day 501:12
place where men deceive 208:22
Market-gardener: sure to marry m. 452:15
Marks upon a blushing face 172: 6
Marksmen: you are all m. ..61: 9
Marley was dead 375:18
Marlowe, Christopher .1261
made by Kit M. 1212:11
Webster, Fletcher, Ben ..1529:18
Marmalete 1852:17
Marmion: last words of M. 2084: 4
Marmora: non incisa notis m. 1339:18
Marquis: manners of a M. ..70: 6
Marred: man that's m. 1277: 1
Marreth what he makes ..1580: 3
Marriage 1261
all m. in repentance ends 1269: 8
and buried 756: 4
and love nothing in common 1270: 5
antagonistic coöperation 1263: 2
belongs to society 1269:16
best state for man 1266: 8
common butt of railleur 1263:11
concluded for beauty's sake 1270: 8
consisting of two slaves ..1262: 1
demands insincerity 1261:19
domesticates Recording Angel 1276: 4
far from natural 1276: 3
field of battle 1262:19
first bond of society, m. ..1262: 4
for young man not yet 1265:17
from love, like vinegar ..1269:10
genuine m. hallowed by love 1271: 2
given in m. 1264:15
given in m. to wife 2138:10
good m. between blind and deaf 1264:16
hallowed by love 1271: 2
has no relation to love ..1269:16
hasty m. seldom well 1269: 7
honorable to all 1263:18
image of Heaven and Hell 1263: 4
in m. three is company ..1265: 3
in m. two things allowed .2188: 9
instances that second m. move 1279:12
is a desperate thing 1279: 2
is a fetter, is a snare ..1263: 3
is a law of nature 1262:10
is a lottery 1262:17
is destiny made in heaven 1271: 6
is law, love is instinct 1270: 5
is the life-long miracle ..1274:13
it won't be a stylish m. 1211: 9
Keeley cure for love 1262:13
laws mark of incompetence 2094: 7

Marriage, *continued*
leapeth upon the saddle ..1269: 8
least concerns others 1264: 9
like beleaguered fortress 1279: 1
like public building 1265: 5
made in heaven 1271: 5
makes deception necessary 1261:19
makes one unselfish 1277: 9
maximum of temptation 1264:13
minimum of temptation ..1264:13
most horrible of means to bind the noble 1262:16
necessary evil 1262:11
not at all heroic 1262:19
nothing but civil contract 1262:14
O curse of m. 1277: 2
objects in m. love, money 1267:14
of so much use to woman 1266: 2
of soul with nature ...1383:12
of true minds 1264: 5
one long conversation ..1262:18
only adventure open to the cowardly 1263: 1
pair of stairs to m. 1205:13
physic against incontinence 1262:10
public virtue 1464: 9
refuses company of love 1270: 8
running fight with m. 15: 9
shows people up 1263:15
step grave and decisive 1262:19
sympathy or conquest 1262: 6
terrible thornbit of m. ..1276: 6
the happiest bond 1270: 2
those in wish to get out 1278:16
trial m. of thirty days ..1264: 3
turns staff into stake ..1275:16
weakens the will 1262: 2
who are happy in m. ..1276: 8
who heard of m. deterred 1272: 5
with peace, Paradise 1263: 4
without love, love without m. 1269:18
women happy in first m. ..1279: 5
world-without-end bargain 1262:15
worse than cross I win 1276:16
Marriage-bed and pew 1207: 7
Marriage-feast: sweeter than the m. 1587: 4
Marriage-robes for heaven .874:15
Marriage-tomb: upon their m. 1276: 9
Marriages: convenient m. 1276: 7
done in heaven 1271: 5
made by Lord Chancellor 1263:20
we will have no more m. 1264:10
Married at leisure 1278:15
best m. that dies m. young 1277: 3
dreadfully m. 1265: 2
if only m. when in love 1270:16
kind of bilboes to be m. ..1275:16
longer tarried before m. ..1269: 4
man dies in good style 1278:12
man tempest-tossed 1277:10
men viler than bachelors ..944:14
never m., and wish father never had 1278:14
not well m. lives m. long 1277: 3
once a man is staked ..1275:16
once m., must be good 1277: 6
one never m.; that's hell 1277:13
past redemption 1263: 9
she m. another 1279:14
to a full man 2146:14
to immortal verse 1365:12
to my country 1464: 9
to tie knot with tongue ..1263:14
well-m., man is winged 1263: 4
when you're m., Samivel 1275:14
woman's business to get m. 1266: 2
young man m. is man marred 1277: 1
Marries first, love will come 1270: 7
no matter whom one m. ..1266:16
to love better 1270: 7
when he is poor 1268: 2
when man m. again 1279:15
when man m., friends lost 1277: 4

Marries, *continued*
when man m. trouble begins 1277:11
who m. does well 1266: 7
Marrons: tirer les m. 223:16
Marrow: my m. burning ..680:12
Persuasion's m. 1559:17
winsome m. 1734: 2
Marrowbone Stage 2101:12a
Marry above rank, sell liberty 1267: 7
be wary how you m. a widow 2136: 5
better to m. than to burn 1265:15
doänt thou m. for munny 1268: 6
easv to m. rich as poor 1268: 6
first and love will follow 1270: 7
for love invites tragedy 1269:13
for love, work for siller 1270:12
for wealth sell liberty ..1267:16
honest men m. quickly ..1265:17
I should m. twenty . ..944:17
if need m., m. a fool 1266:17
in haste, repent at leisure 1269: 6
in Lent, live to repent 1266:15
in May, repent alway ..1266:15
in one's own degree 1267: 5
likely to m. country girl ..2139: 7
men m. because tired ..1265: 6
Monday, for wealth .. .1267: 4
neither m., nor are given in marriage 1264:15
or not, you will repent 1267: 1
quite prepared to m. again 1279: 7
son when you will 1266: 5
that Echion may become a father 1276: 5
the girl first 1272: 8
they that m. ancient people .... .1275:18
to m. young no man repents 1266:10
to please ourselves 1265:12
too soon, repent too late ..1269: 6
when shall I m. me 1263:12
where I m., cannot love 1270: 9
while ye may, go m. 2010:11
wisely, m. your equal ..1267: 9
with a suit of clothes 488: 2
woman who lives near ..1266: 6
Marrying: cannot be without women 1262:10
their cousins 69: 4
to increase love 1270: 7
Mars gave sign of war ..2116: 8
might quake to tread 324:18
of malcontents 454:11
rages throughout 2110: 5
red disk of M. 1473:13
red planet M. 1916: 2
Mars sævit toto M. impius 2110: 5
Marseillaise, La 719: 2
Marshal of France: see how a M. of F. can die 413:17
Marshall has made his decision 1555: 2
Marshes, candid and simple 1386: 4
Marte: suo m. 1574: 2
Martem accendere cantu 1878: 1
Martha: sons of M. 2232: 7
thou art careful 2232: 7
Martial airs of England ..547: 3
could M. rival one of these 143:11
in his air 1864: 8
Martin Elginbrodde 572:10
Martineau: existence of M. 416: 5
Martinmas to every pig 1708:10
Martirio a questa pace 1280: 2
Martyr 1279
burned while votes counted 1236: 3
calm m. of a noble cause ..367: 8
cannot be dishonored 1280: 4
die m. to sense 1795: 4
in his shirt of fire 1280:16
king hath made me m. ..1279:17
Love's M. when heat past 1195:16
to mild enthusiasm 1970: 9
to the cause of man 1158:13

Martyrdom: all have not gift of m. 1280: 3
from m. unto this peace ..1280: 2
life-long m. 2100:10
of our passions 409:12
to reformers 1541: 4
Martyrs by pang without palm 1280:17
for bad causes 1280:19
groaning m. toil'd 1739:11
if we loved God 1280:22
look on m. as mistakes ..1280:10
noble army of m. 1279:18
of a fallen cause 1869: 1
or Nero 2084:18
or reformers 1279:20
plaintive m. 1279:19
to vice exceed m. to virtue 2080: 7
who create faith 1280:19
who left for reaping 1280:11
Marvel: men will cease to m. 1415:16
no m. he is so humorous ..444: 7
now we look behind 2268: 9
of human soul 1891: 6
of the universe 535:11
Marvell's graceful song ...725:17
Marvelous for the first time 1415:16
nothing know but what is m. 2210: 3
Marvels: Orient's m. 115:14
which pencil wrought 108: 4
Mary: Bloody M. 802:17
had a little lamb 1067:11
hath chosen that good part 260: 8
kept belt of love 1210: 6
little M. 154:11
ma Scotch Blue-Bell 1212: 7
my sweet Highland M. 1210:15
of whom gentleman Jesus 261: 5
passion for name of M. 1375:14
sinful M. walks more white 1830: 2
sons of M. 260:8; 2232: 7
spare his Highland M. 206: 4
to M. Queen praise be given 1844: 6
Mary, Virgin 261
Mary-buds: winking m. ..1730:13
Maryland: heart of M. 880:18
my M. 2064:12
Mascots: from Paradise ..1226:14
Mask a king in weeds 761: 3
lift not the festal m. ..2176:16
of brooses blue and green 2247:21
of night is on my face ..173: 6
put off the m. 1125: 4
strip the m. from men 86:13
Masks: deluded by ancient m. 71: 8
lift their frowning m. 75:15
outrageous and austere ..2261:10
Mason and Dixon line 63: 8
Mason asks narrow shelf 618:17
Masonry: literary m. 2250:10
north wind's m. 1857:14
pendant on naught 795:13
Masquerades: midnight m. ..247: 1
Masques: I delight in m. and revels 68: 6
Mass are animal, in pupilage 1482: 5
devil's m. 441:17
never equals best member 1484:13
of brick and smoke 1168:16
of things to come 976: 5
Paris is worth a M. 1453: 6
that matters 1740: 3
Massa ob de sheepfol' 1810:18
Massa's in de cold, cold ground 2286: 5
Masses and Classes 1479:15
butter bread with the M. 1547:12
of men 1095:8a
rude, lame, unmade 1482: 5
Mässigkeit reines Glück ..1328:12
Massive and concrete 9: 7
Mast of some great ammiral 444:13
Master 1281
absent, the house dead ..1281: 1

Maze, *continued*
wander in that m. 484:20
wildering m. of Eternity .1993: 3
Mazes: in wand'ring m.
lost 100:11
of metaphorical confusion 820:10
puzzled in m. 1645:7a
Mazzard: knocked about the
m. 1834: 8
Me: cheapest, nearest 1490: 2
judice 1022:20
only Me 2286: 1
Mead: shun not the m. 494:5a
Meade, and barren field ...1654:15
Meadow: by m. and stream ..3:13
of margin 190: 4
painted m., purling stream 1385: 4
that cuts thrice a year 719:14
Meadows have drunk
enough 1669:10
infinite m. of heaven 1912:11
paint m. with delight 685: 8
trim with daisies pied ..1385: 4
wide are m. of night 1912:11
wide unrolled 683: 8
Meads: now hedged m. re-
new 1909: 5
yellow m. of asphodel ..688: 2
Meal: barrel of m. wasted
not 516: 6
each m. Supper of Lord ..632:19
handful of m. in a barrel 516: 6
large, grace short 520:16
one m. a week will serve 2030: 3
she sifted the m. 1657:11a
smallest grain of m. 516: 6
Meals: lengthen life, lessen
m. 518:16
make no long m. 754: 9
of beef and iron 1863:11
short are his m. 88:15
three m. a day in guarantee 1498:15
unquiet m. 448: 2
Mean: all men m. well 994:20
between excess and fam-
ine 1327: 4
cultivate the golden m. ..1326:10
golden m. free from trips 1326: 9
golden m. proper bliss ..1548: 6
happy the golden m. 837: 8
hold fast golden m. 1326:10
how m. we seem 1129: 2
more than he says 1239:16
no m. happiness to be seated
in the m. 1326: 7
nothing is m. or irksome 2204:13
people make life m. 288: 8
there's a m. in morals ...1326: 3
what I say 1897:10
Meander's margent green ..525:11
Meandering: let us have
no m. 2070:15
Meanest have their day 624: 2
of mankind 122:11
Meaning: deep m. in old customs 354: 9
double m. 1653:15
gilded want of sense 994:19
honest m. of itself a law 1092: 1
in every object m. 597: 5
no m. but sound clever 1895:11
no m. to what is termed
good 854: 6
not m. any harm 1416:12
one sole m. still same 104:17
outmastered the meter 991:16
read life's m. 1187: 8
suited to his mind 1388:16
thinking right and m.
well 1383: 5
to find its m. is my meat
and drink 2240: 9
Meanings: beautiful m. ...348:16
two m. have fantasies 634:11
two m. in one word 2223: 7
wagon-load of m. for
word 2221: 8
Meanness of being a hypo-
crite 946:12
often found in a preface ..2250:14
Meannesses too mean even
for men 2189:10
Means and End 539
and ends 225:22
and leisure, civilizers 1100: 1
bad m. and bad men 225:17
hard things by easy m. ..447:18
humble m. match not 454:12
intensely, and m. good ..2240: 9
live beyond my m. 2280: 6
proportion'd to end 540: 2
spotless as ends 540:11
swift m. to radiant ends 2230:11
think on m., manner, end .540:15
to do ill deeds 1981:16
to gratify the will 1716:19
to live 1132: 1
well 994:17
Meant: here lies one who m.
well 570: 8
more than meets the ear ..510:17
Measles: if so, how many .461: 4
Measly gum-drop name ..1376:11
Measure: anon we'll drink a
m. 1317:15
good m. pressed down 773:14
in all things 1326: 3
in everything lieth m. ..1326: 3
is a merry mean 1326: 3
is medicine 498: 4
is treasure 1326: 3
last full m. of devotion ...432: 1
make themselves m. of mankind 1581: 4
moderate m. most perfect 1325:15
of a happy life 1135: 1
of a master 830: 8
of an unmade grave 826: 9
of life not length 913: 8
of life, well-spending ...1134: 7
of my days 1141: 8
of my wrath 78:20
still for m. 863:17
tread a m. 360:10
with what m. ye mete ...1708: 4
Measured to you again ..1708: 4
Measures: new m. and new
men 1616:14
not men 1543: 7
short m. perfect 805:10
Meat 523
and drink to me 521: 3
anger's my m. 78:16
bones bring m. to town ..179: 9
eaters of m. ferocious 559:13
fire and clothes 1722: 9
first to be eaten 450: 6
for thy health's sake 2104: 3
for thy master 680: 5
full as egg of m. 533: 3
hae m. and cannot eat 88:16
have m. and lack stomach 1319: 7
heed m. twice boiled 543: 5
I cannot eat but little m. .497: 3
loves m. in his youth 89:18
made for mouths 1627:11
make my brother to of-
fend 524:16
new m. begets appetite 90:10
not digested 155: 2
not the m. but appetite 90: 2
one man's m. another's
poison 1539:16
out-did the m. 523:12
she biled the m. 1657:11a
sits at m. with publicans ..288: 6
smelt roast m. 523: 9
some love m., some to pick
bone 1672:13
stolen m. sweetest 1618: 2
strong m. 523:11; 1304: 4
sweet m., sour sauce 1953: 3
they have no other m. ..197:16
too good for any but anglers 523:14
upon what m. doth this our
Cæsar feed 214: 3
want m. for stomachs 88:16
was made for mouths 940: 6
Meats: funeral baked m. ..1998: 5
sweetest m. soonest cloy 2076:10
Mecca backed by Nazareth 581: 7
of the mind 205:16
saddens at delay 429:16
Méchanceté vient de fai-
blesse 2134:20
Méchants sont toujours surpris 280:12
Mécontent de son esprit ..711:11
Medal has two sides 291:12
leather m. his reward ..1716: 5
man breaks not the m. 57: 7
Medals: God will not look
for m. 1025: 4
Meddle and muddle 1553: 8
I'll not m. 1284:15
with what you have to do 1284: 8
Meddled: everybody m. ...1284: 5
Meddler 1284
Meddles: whoso m. 1284:10
Medea gather'd enchanted
herbs 1287:17
slaughter her children ...1910:15
Medea: nec pueros coram
populo M. trucidet ..1910:15
Médecin: après la mort le m. 465: 4
Tant-pis 465: 6
Medendo: ægrescitque m. 1287: 7
Medes and Persians: law ..1084: 6
Medias: in m. res 1636:11
Medically: lives m. 837:12
Medicamen: contra mortis
non est m. 380: 9
Medice, cura tiepsum 465: 8
Medici: Miniver loved the
M. 83: 8
Medicina ægro, non regio 1286:17
modo dat m. salutem 1285: 9
monstra contingunt in m. 1286: 9
ne insanabiles 1285:10
sera m. paratur 1286:14
temporis ars m. fere est 1285: 9
tollere nescit m. podagram 1285: 9
Medicinal as light 1152: 7
Medicine 1284
against Death no m. 380: 9
becomes a heroic art 466:12
bed is a m. 142: 9
bitter m. oft helpful 1285: 8
by m. life prolonged 382: 5
collection of uncertain prescriptions 1285: 7
confession a m. 295: 2
every m. an innovation ..1285: 1
for every mood 182:22
for the mind 1108: 2
frequent change of m. hinders cure 1285:10
grief is a m. 840: 5
increases the disease 1287: 7
loyal to the profession of
m. 2274: 3
men have always flour-
ished 466: 6
more professed than la-
boured 1284:17
no m. but only hope 921: 5
no m. for troubled mind 1313: 6
no m. to remove gout ..1285: 9
not scenery, for sick man 1286:17
one m. makes other neces-
sary 1286:10
out, loathed m. 1287: 1
question of timeliness ..1285: 9
same m. harms and cures 1286:13
sometimes injures 1285: 9
took his m. as it came ..1524:10
true m. is philosophy 1497: 7
try one desperate m. more 1287: 9
what m. can disease re-
move 1218: 7
who grief imparts 843:12
worse than the disease ..1287: 3
Mediciners: defy the m. ..520:18
Medicines: created m. out of
earth 1287:15
many m., few cures 1286: 6
of our great revenge ... 1712: 9
to make me love 288:16
Medicum: dulce lenimen m. 1361:11
hæredem facit 465:15

Memory, *continued*
man's real possession ...1293: 1
morning-star of m. 139: 2
most delicate and frail ..1292:14
mystic chords of m. 57:11
necessary to lying 1112:12
no less requires the bit ..1761:14
nothing but majestic m. 1293:17
nothing to lose but m. 29: 6
of a dream 484: 2
of all he stole 1506: 6
of Earth's bitter leaven .1299: 4
of fire and brimstone 2094: 4
of genius immortal 760:14
of happiness 1295: 2
of our lives long 1129: 4
of past folly 701: 6
of past troubles pleasant 2043: 8
of past will stay 1293:19
of sorrow brings delight 1293:18
of the just is blessed 1029:15
of the just survives 1029:18
of the past 1464:17
of the red man 977: 1
of well-spent life eternal 1133:13
oft requires the bit 1010:15
O M., thou fond deceiver 1295: 3
owes charm to "far away" 1293: 2
place in thy m., dearest 1296:10
plays an old tune on heart 1296: 7
pluck from m. a rooted sorrow 1313: 6
qualification of prophet ..1623:18
remarkable m., yours 1293:11
silent shore of m. 1294:16
soft as m. of buried love 2184: 3
some call her M. 1292:10
soul of joy and pain 1294:11
storehouse of the mind ..1292:17
sweet is m. of past labor 1061:16
sweet M., wafted by thy 1294: 9
'tis in my m. lock'd 1293:14
to enjoy m. to live twice ..805:11
to m. dear 3:12
treasure of the mind 1292:17
wandering through M. Lane 1297: 6
warder of the brain 504:11
what wonders it performs 1292:15
where is now thy youth .2268: 5
while m. holds a seat 1295: 8
will bring back feeling ..1214: 4
will endure if lives deserved 1340: 4
will then be pang'd by me 1698: 1
wore my heart away 4: 2
yet hath night of life m. 1295: 7
Men about me that are fat 648: 1
act with original views ..1428:20
age of great m. going 42: 7
aged m., full loath and slow 35:12
all contemptible 1246: 3
all m. are bad 1247: 7
all m. are liars 1113:13
all m. are mad 1231:17
all m. chloroformed at sixty .35: 6
all m. cowards 332:17
all m. created equal 975: 4
all m. desire immortality 964:11
all m. equal as m. 431:17
all m. have their price ..1605:11
all m. make faults 650:13
all m. poets at heart 1531:15
all m. possible heroes 895: 7
all m. women's property 2181:11
all sorts conditions of m. 1240: 5
all things to all m. 12:13
almost all m. are fools 699: 4
always trust my word ...2046:16
and women merely players 2240: 5
and women must pass lives together 1263:20
and women not same language 1253: 4
angels are m. 77: 4
angry m. seldom want woe ..80: 9
are all inventors 1238: 6
are April when they woo 1274: 5

Men, *continued*
are as the time is 1956: 6
are led by trifles 2040: 4
are liable to error 576:20
are like musical glasses ...492: 7
are m. 708:21
are m. needs must err 576:18
are not angels, nor brutes 1243: 8
are not common 727:13
are ripe of Saxon kind ..1918: 6
are still m. 2063:16
are the city's fortress 274:18
are the devil 1908:16
are used as they use 804:11
are what they can be 1380: 1
as angels without feminine 2188: 7
as proper m. as ever trod 1818: 7
at court cunning 327: 9
become old not good 33: 9
begotten in night 1403: 6
behind the guns 1863: 5
best m. moulded of faults 651: 5
best of all m. 20:25
best of m. a sufferer 261:13
best of m. that e'er wore earth 261:13
better than sheep or goats 1588:11
better than theology 1984: 8
better than they seem ..1245: 5
black m. are pearls 1176:10
brave m. and patriots 110: 6
brave m. ne'er warred with dead 406: 1
by nature unequal 574: 5
by themselves are priced 1605:10
by whom impartial laws 1595:13
cannot learn m. from books 187: 7
chaste m. with one wife ..248: 9
childless m. 252: 4
children of larger growth 1242: 9
children of larger size ..1242:11
clever m. are tools 1052:15
climb hills to suffer 898:16
clothes darker 485: 9
condemned to thunderbolts 1230: 5
constitute a state 1917:15
cunning m. pass for wise 349: 1
dare trust selves with m. 1249: 7
dead m. rise up never ..1149:10
dead m. tell no tales 377: 5
deal with life as children 1126:11
deteriorate 230:22
determine, gods dispose ..786:15
developed from monkeys ..586:14
differ as Heaven and Earth 1255:13
dig the earth for gold 802: 5
disputatious m. 1695: 6
divided into two parties ..430:15
do not suspect faults 649:13
do not vary much in virtue 2080:17
draw m. as they ought to be 1448: 7
drop so fast 35: 1
educated m. superior 528: 8
England's true m. we are .557:10
faint-hearted m. 2014:16
fear raging poet 1537: 2
fell out, knew not why ..1662:13
few honest m. better than numbers 914: 4
fewer m., greater honor ..919: 4
fighting m. city's fortress 1917:15
fighting m. city's walls ..1917:15
first fishes 585: 9
first m. that Saviour dear 670:14
fished for women 498:12
following those who do not believe in m. 1095:8a
give us m. 1252: 7
given up to belly 155:11
glorious m. scorn of wise .836: 9
go farthest smoothest 452: 8
God's m. and women still 1247:10
golden race of speaking m. 1243:11
good and bad m. 86: 4

Men, *continued*
good m. and true 1253: 1
good m. are the stars 807:16
good m. make me poor ..811: 5
great m. are guide-posts ..833: 3
great m. are true m. 830: 1
great m. have great faults 649:15; 832: 2
great m. have greater faults 832: 2
great m. models of nations .833: 3
great m. not always wise .834:12
great m. not great scholars 1763: 3
great m. only m. 834:13
great m. solitary towers ..833:14
great m. still admirable ...833: 5
great m. too often unknown 836:13
greater than noblemen ..2016: 7
greatest m. simplest 833:11
group of wilful m. 67: 1
grow better as the world grows old 1218:13
guilty m. escape not 844: 6
happiest of m. 11: 7
have all m. bound 2195:15
have come and gone 2126:12a
have lost their reason 1024: 5
have many faults 2189: 3
have marble minds 1255: 7
have more privilege than mountains 1374: 6
have not heard 886:15
have reputation by distance 1700:14
hid and inaccessible 1108: 3
high-minded m. 1917:15
honest in disgrace 915:14
honest m. and knaves same cloth 915:14
honest m. marry quickly .1265:17
honest m. soft cushions ..915:20
how much more are m. than nations 1380: 3
how vainly m. themselves amaze 49:10
if m. saved by merit 1300: 4
if m. unselfish as women 1253:15
in a hurry to hate 867: 6
in catalogue ye go for m. 473: 1
in great place servants 836: 9
in single state should tarry 1266: 2
jugs with spirits in them 1243:17
keeping m. off keep on ..317: 9
learn to hate wives 1452: 5
learn while they teach 1970: 2
learned m. without wit ...1166:20
let greater m. strike loftier notes 1538: 9
like butterflies 735:20
like conventions 1861:15
like musical glasses 492: 7
literary m. perpetual priesthood 2256:15
live in their fancy 634: 2
lived like fishes 668:13
love m. because not women 1253:12
love to wonder 1763:14
loved beyond wisdom 1180:18
made by nature unequal ..574: 5
made for kings 1042:14
made the manners 1258:19
make laws, women manners 1254: 5
many m. have many minds 2204:12
married m. laugh at single 1254: 8
married m. viler than bachelors 944:14
marry because tired 1265: 6
may be read too much 596:17
may come and m. may go 200:16
may live fools 699: 9
may perish, but not their songs 1519:12
may say more, swear more 1205: 4
medicine m. have always flourished 466: 6
meet, greet, and sever 1289:15
melancholy m. most witty 1290: 9
merriest when from home ...4:16

Meteor, *continued*
swift-flitting m. 1607:11
that had lost its way 1514: 5
Meteors: coruscations of m. 958:17
fright fixed stars 1946:14
with different name 373:15
Method good in all things 1441: 4
having my m. by the end 2251:12
in his madness 1230:17
in man's wickedness 2134:17
mother of memory 1292:13
of making a fortune 199:14
requisite in writing 312: 8
to please in m. 1015:14
Methodist: morals of a M. 70: 6
would not do for M. 1695: 9
Methodists love your big sinners 1696:13
Methuselah: has M. before him 29:18
Methusalem: I may not be M. 26: 1
slept in open 1848: 3
Métier: chacun son m. 1061:14
mon m. c'est vivre 1128:13
sur m. remettez ouvrage 2254: 3
Metiri se suo modulo 1794:11
Metre: stretched m. of song 1878: 7
Metres: not m. make poem 1525: 5
Metropolis: noble spirit of 1168: 3
Mettle enough to kill care 221:16
there's m. in thee 324: 9
Metu: credenda proni m. 656: 2
ex m. credita 2032: 9
exemplique m. torqueor 588:15
Metuant: oderint, dum m. 867:13
Metuas vincere quod nequeas 654: 6
Metui: nolo ego m. 1216:14
Metuit: perisse cupit 654:22
Metum: pone m. 654:15
Metus futuri 749: 1
improbos compescit 654:26
malus est custos m. 655:13
Metuunt, oderunt 654:12
Meum and tuum 1986: 3
est 1674: 8
est autem tuom 1562: 3
Meurs: je m. content 415:20
Meurt tous les jours 873:17
Mewling and puking 2240: 5
Micat inter omnes iulium sidus 1913: 6
Micawber: never desert 1198: 4
Mice desert building about to fall 1357:15
rats and such small deer 516:14
schemes o' m. an' men 452:13
when cat is away m. will play 223: 7
Michael Angelo for breakfast 102:21
irregularities of M. A. 339: 8
talking of M. A. 347:13
Miching mallecho 1319: 2
Mickle: many a little 2039:11
Microcosm of public school 531: 2
Microscopes are prudent 619: 7
patent double m. 598: 9
Mid-air: in m. wings 1072:14
Mid-harvest: e'en in m. 640:14
Midas: hard food for M. 801:18
rocked the cradle 163:14
Midas' golden touch 2104: 1
Midday: in m. give counsel 1127:10
Middle class: safety 560: 1
have the best 1329: 1
honey'd m. of the night 1401: 8
life's m. state 1329: 1
of my heart 876:11
of the road 2258:15
once went down the m. 359:16
Middle-aged person 26: 2
Middleman: man who plunders 285:13
Middlesex: acre in M. 551: 4
Middleton, Dr. 449: 9
Midge and the nit 1421:11
Midnight 1302
and yet no eye 1303: 9
at m. held your head 1037: 1
at m., in his guarded tent 2061:10a
brought on dusky hour 1303: 1
dark and drear 1815: 9
dead of m. noon of thought 1302: 7
dreadful dead of dark m. 1303: 4
filled slumbers with song 991: 4
intoxicates human swine 1302: 9
iron tongue of m. 1303: 7
is mine 1302: 9
let's mock the m. bell 1303: 3
look as black as m. 78: 7
made of her own hair 848:12
not to be abed after m. 1729: 8
O wild and wondrous m. 1302:14
of her hair 848:13
once upon a m. dreary 1303: 2
one hour's sleep before m. 1848: 4
outpost of advancing day 1302:13
pale M. on her starry throne 1303: 8
solemn m. centuries ago 268: 8
thy dark pencil, m. 1303:10
'tis now dead m. 379:13
turn to me at m. with a cry 1201: 4
upon the m. clear 269: 6
yet not a nose 1303: 9
Midriff: shake m. of despair 1075: 5
Midst of the matter 1636:11
Midsummer madness 1231:13
Midwife: fairies' m. 615:11
Miel: haceos m. 676:10
Mien carries more invitation 982: 4
distant m. 85: 8
Mieux: je vais de m. en m. 872: 3
Miggs: kept Miss M. awake 351:13
Might 1303
and justice yoke-fellows 1030:11
and Right and sovran Zeus 1303:11
and right govern everything 1303:16
by m. or sleight 1303:12
do it with thy m. 423:16
God's m. to direct us 795: 2
half slumb'ring 1516: 7
in God's own m. 1304: 3
is right 1303:21
it m. have been 1687:22
makes right 1303:21
no m. in mortality 215: 6
of the gods 799:13
of one fair face 1190: 3
of trivial things 1877: 5
overcometh right 1303:21
that makes a title 1303:13
unaw'd by lawless m. 1303:12
was measure of right 1303:19
we m. have been 1687:22
where m. is, the right is 1304: 2
Might-have-been: my name is M. 1687:16
Mightiest in the m. 1298:19
Mightst: what thou m. have been 290: 7
Mighty are brought low 2041:11
haste to destruction 1931:11
how are the m. fallen 622:10
how m. and how free 1354: 4
nay, al-m. gold 803: 3
to inspire new hopes 2157: 3
Mignonette 690
delicate odor of m. 686:14
Frenchman's darling 690: 9
pitcher of m. 690:10
Mil: le moindre grain de m. 516: 6
Milch der frommen Denkart 1035: 7
Mild as she is seeming so 1503:19
Mildness and gentleness more manly 81: 4
Mile: measured many a m. 360:10
Scottish m., two English 1768: 9
Miles: mirk m. broad 168: 2
twelve m. from a lemon 321:19
Miles gloriosus 1865:12
malus m. qui gemens 1868: 2
Milestone: past my next m. 165: 9
Milestones into headstones change 35: 1
Militant: true Church M. 1589: 2
Militare est credere post mortem nisi cadaver 1868:13
Militarism is a spirit 2113:11
uses armies for aggression 2113:11
Milites: nescire quædam m. 1863:14
Militia: black m. of pen 2258:11
of the lower sky 1904:15
Milk 1304
adversity's sweet m. 16:11
alike as two drops of m. 1155: 6
as bids remember 553: 2
babe fed with m. 121: 2
better buy m. than keep cow 330:11
comes frozen in pail 2161:10
cow that is near 330:18
crying over spilt m. 1304: 7
does marble good 2123: 8
drunk the m. of Paradise 1451: 4
land flowing with m. 321: 9
masquerades as cream 86:12
mother's m. scarce out 2265: 7
of Burgundy 2156: 1
of concord in hell 234: 2
of human kindness 217:13; 1035: 7
of human kindness ran 1495:11
oh, Milk and Water 989:10
on mother's m. fed 121: 2
says to wine, welcome 2154:16
standing cow 330:18
such as have need of m. 523:11
sweet m. of concord 234: 2
take my m. for gall 346:12
to soak my bread 331: 9
turn m. of kindness into curds 1684:11
tyrant-hating m. 2033:18
useth m. unskilful 1304: 4
wash m. from your liver 1304: 5
Milk-liver'd man 2015: 7
Milk-teeth of babes 1351:11
Milkmaid half divine 1208:11
Milkmaids: when merry m. 1442:11
Milksop 1644:12
Milk-soup domestic bliss 1276:12
Milkweed and buttercup 682: 3
Milkwhite is the slae 683: 3
Milky Way: God be thanked for M. W. 1914: 9
our planet in the M. W. 1874: 5
Mill 1304
cannot grind 1304:10
charge were it but a m. 227:12
goes toiling slowly around 1304:11
grains in pieces tear 17: 6
I wandered by the m. 200:13
in for m. in for million 1637: 7
Mill-Boy of the Slashes 1377:16
Mill-wheel whirled in head 1900: 4
Millenniums against the grave 1745: 4
Miller grinds more corn 1305: 3
he hecht her a heart 2214: 2
honest m. has golden thumb 1304: 9
sees not all the water 1305: 2
there was a jolly m. 1302: 3
Millers: two m. thin, Bone and Skin 1304: 8
Millinery: jewell'd mass of m. 705: 6
Million: aiming at a m. 1660:10
of manners 1258:11
Millions for defence 63: 2
from love of brandy 1967: 5
now alive 142: 1
tear-wrung m. 464:11
tired m. toil unblest 1067: 9
twenty-seven m. mostly fools 562:13
we mortal m. live alone 1873: 6
Mills and women ever want 2180: 2
of God grind slowly 1708: 5
Millstone about his neck 252:15
and human heart 875: 1
nether m. 881: 8
see into m. 1819:11
see through a m. 598: 9
wept when he beheld m. 1708: 8

Milo's lurking smile 1853:11
remember M. end 1710: 2
Milton, John **1305**
damp fell round path of M. 1883:17
devil according to M. 444:11
here many a rustic M. ..1422: 2
mighty M.'s gift divine 725:17
New World honors him ..1306: 3
one sound test of a M. 1422: 2
our Homer of war in Heaven 2230: 8
prince of poets 1305: 7
sacrificed to devil 1306: 1
seem'st a M. 2098:11
sightless M. with his hair 1808: 8
some mute, inglorious M. 1422: 2
Milton's gift divine 725:17
wormwood words 2055:12
Miltons: no mute inglorious M. 1422: 2
Mimæ, balatrones, hoc genus omnes 9:13
Mime: endless m. goes on 1125: 2
Mimicry of noble war 942: 2
Mimum vitæ commode 1124:17
Minantis: nulla m. auctoritas apud liberos ..1996:21
Minantur: non persuadent, quia m. 1088: 6
Mince the matter 1642:24
they dined on m. 1410: 6
Mince-pie: mince-piety ...270: 2
you must eat more m. ..1035:12
Mince-pies and other luxuries 522: 6
Mind **1306**
absence of m. 5:10
aided by body's purity ..248: 7
all in the state of m. ..1931: 5
all of one m., and one m. good 2066:20
alone cannot be exiled ..1311:17
always makes progress ..1307: 4
amongst the maids 155:10
and matter 1314:12
as m. pitch'd, ear pleas'd 1364: 1
at peace with all below ..2184: 5
atmosphere of soul 1306:15
bad m., bad heart 1308: 7
be ye all of one m. 1307:19
beauty allays an angry m. 134:10
beholds at every turn ..1174: 1
bent to holiness 904: 3
bettering of my m. 1312:16
both m. and money 1335:15
brave m. hard hand 850:17
breaks down 35: 2
bungalow m. 1308:10
calf-paths of the m. 1596: 7
can dwell a hermit 1311: 6
cannot be burned or wounded 1311:17
care and labor of his m. ...28:10
celebrates a triumph 1308: 1
changed his m. 305: 8
clear your m. of cant 946:18
conceives with pain 2253: 5
conscious of guilt 301:15
conscious of innocence ..1761:12
conscious of rectitude ..1309:11
content both crown and kingdom is 310: 7
contented m., that best of blessings 310: 8
contented m. enjoys life ..310:10
control m. by force tyrant 1307:15
decays with the body ..1313:15
decent m., indecent body 107:11
deficient in humor 938:14
diseased 1313: 6
disordered m. 1313: 2
distinguish men by m. ..1308: 3
does not create 1307:10
doth newly fashion 1190:15
each m. has own method 1307:20
embarks in great courses 295:21
encyclopedic m. 1056: 8
ennobles, not blood 1308: 2
entwined about hearer's m. 1437:15
every m. is a tent 1888: 6
Mind, *continued*
fair terms and villain's m. 2085:16
fairer was her m. 131:20
farewell tranquil m. 636:11
feed m. in wise passiveness 1312:18
feeling m. 446:13
filled with inborn worth ..1407: 7
filling my wintry m. 878:19
first destroys their m. ..1232: 1
flash of a fiery m. ...... .78:16
forbids to crave 1310:20
forward-looking m. 1308:11
frame your m. to mirth 1318: 7
free from over-weening joy 1797: 4
free m. though slave ...1839:18
free, whate'er afflict man 1307:11
free-born lover's m. 209: 8
freedom and peace of m. 723: 8
from sinner's m. the sin 1827: 4
full of scorpions is my m. 1698: 6
full of superstition 1306: 6
gentle m. by gentle deeds 1259:14
give the m. perfect dye 1098: 1
golden m. stoops not 1309:15
good m. possesses kingdom 1310:21
grand prerogative of m. 1996: 3
grateful m. by owing ...824:12
great lever of all things 1307: 6
great m. calm 1797: 9
great m. conceives great 1309: 8
great m. good sailor 1309: 3
great m. great fortune ..1309:14
grows sicker than the body 1314: 1
has a thousand eyes 1187:11
has broken down barriers 1311: 7
has only feared and slept 1241:19
hasn't any m. 1310:16a
hath no horizon 1311:14
he has a nasty m. 1239:13
he hath a month's m. ..1339: 2
his m. his kingdom 1310:19
hoggish m. 1310:14
honest m. and plain 451:20
how active springs the m. 2262:11
human m. in ruins 1232: 6
human m. wrote history ..900: 3
idle m. knows not wants 956: 1
if for a tranquil m. you ask 1838:15
ignorant of fate 749: 9
immortal m. remains 1311: 5
improper m. a perpetual feast 1308: 9
in his right m. 1307:18
incapable of conceiving soul 1888: 8
interior of any man's m. impossible to find 1308: 6
is a very citadel 1311: 9
is clouded with doubt 475: 2
is fruit 251:12
is in doubt 475: 3
is its own place 1311:13
is like a bow 1312:10
is the man 1306: 7
is unsworn 2023:20
keep m. alert and free 335:12
known by its company ..288: 4
larger than crown of tears 1307:17
lays down its burden 1706:12
less in m., lesser pain 4:14
let extend thy m. 2167: 2
let m. relaxation take 1682:11
like clock running down 1306:13
like sheet of white paper 1306:12
look to the m. 86: 1
maintain a quiet m. 310: 5
makes marriage lasting ..1264: 5
makes the body rich 1314: 5
man but chang'd his m. 1307:21
man's m. makes him slave 1839:18
man's unconquerable m. 897:11
may color all things gray 1992: 1
minister to a m. diseased 1313: 6
mirror of heavenly sights 1307: 3
Mind, *continued*
more developed in winter 1782: 4
most perfect m. dry light 1306:14
mostly in your m. . ... .482:12
moves matter ... .1314:16
much sufferance o'erskips 843: 8
my m. to me a kingdom is 1310:20
my m. to me an empire is 1310:22
my own m. is my church 1689:18
my wooing m. 217: 9
nasty m. 1239:13
nature's first great title 1306: 9
never lose presence of m. 862:20
noble m. disdains to hide 1309: 4
noble m. free to all men 1308: 2
noblest m. best content ..310:11
not in my perfect m. ...36: 2
not of sound m. 1313: 2
nothing can withstand m. 1311: 8
nothing great but m. . ..1245: 7
nothing old but m. 1307:12
O mighty m. 212: 5
O m. of man, ignorant ..1310:16
of firm yet placid m. 2138: 7
of gentleman, emotions of bum 1257: 5
of more value than hand 1313:16
of the people like mud 1481:16
of true genius clear 761:10
of worm, claws of dragon 2064:13
oh, the fetterless m. 1993: 3
old m., youthful body 22: 4
our ancestral m. 1597: 5
our m. is God .... .1306:16
past hope, heart shame ..882:15
persuaded in his own m. 1307:19
philosophic m. 321:5; 1308:11
power, love and sound m. 1037:18
presence of m. 323:19; 862:20
presence of m. and courage 1930: 7
presence of m. tests man 1786:20
preserve an even m. 1797: 4
princely m. undo family 1615: 8
qualities of m. avail most in war 2106:17
quiet m. 310: 6
releas'd from anxious ...1721:21
remains unshaken 1705:19
restrain your m. 1312: 7
rich m. lies in sun 7:10
rule your m. 1312: 7
ruler of the universe ..1312: 1
runs from toil to pleasure 1510: 5
sad m. forge merry face 1077: 8
saw visage in his m. 606:10
sea's my m. 1457:18
serene for contemplation 919:17
serene, impenetrably just 2122: 7
shall banquet 642:11
shall say her m. freely ..2200: 6
sharp m. in velvet sheath 1750:17
she had a frugal m. 526:13
sick m. affects body 1314: 1
sick m. no harshness 1312:11
single-track m. 1308:10
sitting in my m. 1873:15
soars to the lofty 1308:13
soft, contemplative 634: 8
sound m. in sound body 871: 4
so various is human m. ..463: 3
standard of the man 1307: 5
stay at home in your m. 1428:20
strength of m. exercise ..952:14
strikes darkness from light 1311: 4
sublime elevates the m. 101: 4
talking with my m. 1307: 8
teach the m. its proper face .10: 6
that builds for aye 1383:16
that cannot yield 1424: 7
that little world, the m. ..1306:19
that maketh good or ill 1312: 3
that museth upon many things 1314: 9
that ocean where each kind 1311:10
that temple, thy fair m. 1307: 2

Mohammed
See also Mahomet
religion a promise 266: 8
Mohammed's truth lay in holy Book 266: 8
Moi: le m. est haissable ..533:15
Moisture: all my body's m. 1978:11
Moitié du monde ne sçait ..1119: 5
Molasses: slick ez m. 1547:12
Mole: blind as a m. 169: 8
learn of the m. to plough 1388:15
show that m. on your neck 1655: 5
Molehill: make m. mountain 1353:14
Moles: comfortable m. 1434: 5
to ourselves 1024:13
Moles: auditis tollere m. ..2154: 3
Molestations of Marriage 1274:10
Molestum: nihil m. non desideres 435: 6
Moley and the brain trust 1555: 6
Molinos de viento: acometer 747:16
Molly dear, I cannot linger 2286: 2
Molly Stark: or M. S. is a widow 62: 6
Mollycoddles 1644:12
Moloch, horrid King 171:13
Moly 690
Mome raths outgrabe 1409: 8
Moment
See also Minute
by the fates assigned 579: 1
calmer m. would be afraid to answer 2269: 7
crowded world one m. may contain 1315: 2
each m. is a day 1315: 2
face some awful m. 239:13
for one transcendent m. .110: 3
golden m. of opportunity 1430:18
great m. triumph of enthusiasm 563: 7
improve each m. as it flies 2009:12
improve the present m. ..1315: 1
in the middle of a m. 708:10
life's sovereign m. battle 2111: 9
make my m. fine 690:14
may with bliss repay 290.14
myself and the lucky m. ..1315: 3
of finding fellow-creature 950:14
of happy lover's hour 1182:15
one m. knelled woe of years 2176: 1
one m. makes a father ...1452:11
one m. of thy dawn 1388:17
parted from eternity 1238:17
passing m. is an edifice ...1599: 5
precise psychological m. 1825: 2
present m. is our ain 1315: 1
seizes the m. 1430:15
shining m. is an edifice ..1315: 5
standing still for ever ...578:19
to decide 423: 4
trap m. before it's ripe ..1432:13
unamus'd a misery 68: 7
when all would go smooth 710: 1
when I ought to die 397:15
who seizes the m. right ..1430:15
Momentary as a sound ..1895: 5
how m. is life 81: 4
in the mind 136: 2
Momentous to himself 1490:12
Moments big as years ..2003:19
flowering m. of the mind 1899: 1
golden m. flit 45: 5
golden m. fly 429: 2
how swift the m. fly 2005: 9
leave dead m. to bury ..2006:13
let us husband them 1315: 5
one by one the m. fall ..1315: 9
seek immortal m. 108:16
shining m. of great men ..798:12
sweetest m. at dawn 368:17
'tis grand m. that signify 1315: 6
worth purchasing with worlds 1315: 2
Monachum: cucullus non facit m. 1338: 7
Monachus esse volebat 443: 2
Monaco: strength of M. ...752: 4
Monarch
See also King
alone he can command ..1038: 5
every m. subject 1044: 8
forest's m. throws 868:10
illustrious m. of Iberia 1896: 1
of a shed 908:15
of all I survey 1038:19
of all it surveys 1038:19
of the brook 672: 2
of the vine 2157: 2
scandalous and poor 244: 6
upon whom sun never sets 1896: 2
who plays m. be a king 1832:11
Monarch-Reason sleeps 478:20
Monarchies end through poverty 815:17
Monarchs could ye taste the mirth 1042:13
ill can rivals brook 1730:15
laugh at m. to their face 1041: 7
must redress 1045: 5
righteous m. 725: 5
seldom sigh in vain 2211:11
show their state abroad ..2065:12
whom rebellious dreams affright 31: 6
Monarchy consists in base things 1042:16
is a merchant-man 430:10
like man-of-war 430:10
sounder than democracy ..814: 5
tempered by songs 719: 5
universal m. of wit 2172:15
world's m. designed 548: 2
Monboddo: knew as well ..587: 5
Monday for wealth 1267: 4
I drive the coach 2004:11
parson's holiday 903:17
St. M. 979:14
they that wash on M. 2121: 6
Monday's child fair of face 164:11
Monde è fatto a scale 2236: 2
elle était du m. 1745: 7
est le livre des femmes ..2236: 3
m'embarasse 788: 7
n'est plus fat 2239: 3
n'est qu'une bransloire ..2236: 9
où l'on s'ennuie 2238: 9
se passer de tout le m. ..2238: 2
se paye de paroles 2225: 3
tout le m. en parle 1198:13
Mondes: meilleur des m. possibles 1435: 4
Mondo è un bel libro 2236: 3
Monet: qui m. adjuvat 20: 1
qui m. nulli nocet 20: 6
Money 1332
advise to spare m. 1333: 2
and a friend 727: 6
and nothing to do 1103:11
and time heaviest burdens 204:11
answereth all things 1334: 9
are you able to save m. ..1930:10
as m. grows, care grows 1723: 1
bane of bliss, source of woe 1337:11
before m. all ways open .1335: 3
best foundation in world 1334: 5
borrowed soon sorrowed ..193: 7
breeds m. 1335:17
bribes a senate 1337:17
brings honor, friends ..1334:16
brought in manners 707: 8
by any means m. 1336: 5
cheated out of m. 1335:18
clean out o' m. 1109:19
"cole" is m. 1333:16
cures melancholy 1335: 2
deception and disappointment 1337:22
do everything for m. 1332:13
eggs for m. 533: 2
employed getting m. 1336: 1
enough is enough 1333:17
everybody of same religion 1333:18
find m. for mischief 1318:18
finishes man 1332: 2
first of games making m. 548:10
fool and his m. ..698:10; 1332: 4
Money, *continued*
for that which is not bread 2123:13
get m., m. still 1336: 5
get m., still get m., boy ..1336: 7
gets women 1223: 5
god of our time 1334: 6
got no m. but a good excuse 2287:10
has better end of staff ..1333: 4
has no smell 1336:15
he that plays his m. 752: 7
he that wants m. 2104: 5
heightening of m. a cheat 1551: 3
how pleasant to have m. 1334: 8
I don't want m. 1883: 4
I don't want your m. 2293:10
I had m. and a friend 727: 6
if I'd as much m. 1523:16
if you want a man's m. ..944:11
immoral m. 707: 8
in my chest 118:13
in purse in fashion 1332: 8
in Three per Cents 464:10
is a beautiful dowry 478: 1
is a beautiful gift 1333:11
is a good soldier 1335: 3
is ace of trumps 1334:10
is honey 1334:12
is omnipotent 134: 8
is sinews of affairs 1332: 3
is their plogh 1334: 6
is trash 1335: 8
keep m. to look at 1335:20
lack of m. 1333: 6
lack of m. root of evil 1337: 2
lack of m. trouble 1333:12
lends out m. gratis 193:14
let us despise m. 1337: 9
lies nearest the grave 36: 9
like drops of blood 119:12
loath to lay out m. 117:17
loss of m. more than death 1333: 3
love of m. root of evil ...1337: 2
lowering of m. is only a cheat 1551: 3
make m. their pursuit 60:12
makes a man laugh 1335: 2
makes mastery 1334: 9
makes m. before gets wit 1332: 4
makes the man 1332: 1
makes the mare go 1332:10
makes the pot boil 2250:13
maketh horses run 1332:10
making m. 1336: 1
mankind falls down before 1334: 3
masters all things 1334: 9
means freedom 1334: 2
more m., always m. 2114: 9
most charming of all things 1334:11
most important thing in the world 1335: 4
necessary as coat of mail 1334:15
never cometh out of season 1332: 8
never do anything for m. 1337:16
never made any man rich 1337:13
no m. gave me better value 496:10
no m., in mouth honey ...1333:19
no m. in your purse 1332: 9
no m. need no purse 1332: 9
no one work for m. 2233:15
not contemptible stone 118:10
not good except spread ..1335: 6
not long for borrowed m. ..193: 5
not required for necessities 1718:10
not to be avaricious m. 1721: 7
nothing but m. counts ..1334:16
of very uncertain value ..1337: 8
other people's m. 207: 5
our pleasures to fulfil ..1335: 7
pay for m. in liberty ..1337:19
put m. in thy purse 1336:12
queen of all delights 1334: 1
ready m. Aladdin's lamp 1334: 3
reap m., sow m. 1335:11
ruling spirit of all things 1335: 1
sacks cities 1335: 5
see what m. can do 1334:17
sinew of love as well as war 2114: 8

Moon, *continued*
looks bloody on the earth 1946:14
looks on many brooks ...1343:11
looks upon many flowers 1343:11
lover's lamp 1342: 7
made of green cheese 1341: 6
maiden m. that sparkles .1344:13
maker of sweet poets 1341:10
may draw the sea 1344:14
meet m. upon the lea 1999:18
minions of the m. 580: 5
moving m. went up the sky 1342:11
my sweetheart's the man in the m. 2294: 3
new m. with auld in arm 1345: 2
no planet is of mine 306: 5
not seen where sun shines 1341:14
not the crescent m. 34:16
not the time of the m. 580: 6
of Mahomet arose 267:15
of the tides of men 1397: 9
outglows lesser light 1913: 6
pale-faced m. 919: 3
pull'd off veil of light 1342: 8
put forth a little peak ..1343: 4
rains out her beams 1073: 1
returns, and spring 1207:10
riding near highest noon .1343: 8
rising in clouded majesty 582: 9
rising m. beholds sun 1942:10
rising m. break from clouds 1342:16
rose o'er the city 1302:13
sailing where waters fill .1342:17
saw the m. was round 593:12
shone the wintry m. 1584:11
silver pin-head vast 1342: 3
sits arbitress 615: 5
slow m. climbs 372:20
small m. lightens more ..581:14
so called, of honey 1273: 7
so silver and cold 1273: 7
stars, and cloudless sky ..1834:11
suddenly the m. withdraws 1344:18
swear not by the m. 1344: 6
sweet regent of sky 1341: 4
takes up wondrous tale .1342: 2
that nothing does but shine 1344:14
thou art man in the m. ..2139:17
thou fair M. 1343: 8
to the red rising m. 1405: 3
upon the corner of the m. 1344: 1
wan M. 1344: 9
was a ghostly galleon ...1343:12
what is there in thee, M. .1343: 4
when m. shone, no candle 781: 5
will wax, m. will wane ..2021: 5
with how sad steps, O M. 1344: 9
worn thin to width of quill 1344:12
yon dead world the m. ..1473:10
yonder fire! it is the m. .1343: 5
young m. has fed her horn 1344: 8
Moon-calf: how now, m. .1341:17
Moon-mountains African ..1406:15
Moonbeam dwells at dewy e'en 1205:16
Moonbeams kiss the sea ..1050: 5
on a river 165: 8
Moonlight: by m. at her window sung 1880:14
fair to-night along Wabash 977: 2
filled them with glamours 1223: 3
how sweet the m. sleeps ..1344: 2
in de ebening by the m. ..1881: 7
is softest in Kentucky ..1034: 8
like m. o'er troubled sea 1343:10
march out by m. cheerily 1342:12
meet me by m. alone ..1289:14
of a perfect peace 1475: 9
on still pools 134:18
Moonlight's ineffectual glow 1344: 8
Moonrise wakes the nightingale 1406: 2
Moons: no lapse of m. can canker Love 1199:11
shall wax and wane no more 2274: 2
Moonshine: hours of m. smile 1342: 9
transcendental m. 1408:19

Moquer de tous 1077: 5
Moquerie l'indigence d'esprit 1724:12
Mora dat vires 429:10
longa m. quæ gaudia differt 429: 9
longa properanti m. est ..429: 9
maxima lena m. est 429: 8
nec m., nec requies 429:17
remedium est iræ 81: 6
Moral: doomed to be m. ..1345:16
everything has a m. 1345: 7
is that gardeners pine ..1687:22
let us be m. 1345:10
make a m. of the devil ...811:12
no one m. till all are m. ..202:13
of time's vicissitude 91:13
point a m. or adorn tale .1373:14
whate'er story, m. true ..1345: 7
when uncomfortable 561: 3
within bosom of rose 1743: 4
Morale of armies from lies .2112:16
Moraler: too severe a m. ..1346: 4
Moralist: canting m. 1345: 9
great English m. 1014:13
no sterner m. than pleasure 1511: 3
teach rustic m. to die 904: 1
Moralité: aiment la m. 1484:12
Moralities: thousand new m. 481:13
Morality 1345
absolute m. 1346: 5
as English as beefsteak ..1014:13
attitude we adopt 1346: 9
foundations of m. 1345: 6
golden principle of m. 804: 9
is kindness to the weak ..1345:11
men talk of mere M. 1345:12
modern m. 1346: 9
no boundaries or race ...1346: 5
no m. so pure as Jesus' ..265:22
no such thing as m. 1346: 8
not in purple patches 1770:4a
of art 102: 9
periodical fits of m. 2274: 5
physical m. 873: 9
procure m. which suits ..1345:15
sees farther than intellect 1345:14
standing jest 619: 6
was made for man 1346:10
what is pure m. 1346: 1
wholesome sharp m. 340:13
with religion 1345:19
Moralize his pensive road 1389: 1
two meanings in one word 2223: 7
Moralizing: to denounce m. 1345: 9
Morals corrupted by riches 1720: 4
dreary m. are wrong 1346: 6
his musty m. 706: 7
if m. good, place fortified ..274:18
like all m., melancholy ...1345: 7
manners before m. 1258:18
of a harlot 1258:18
of a Methodist 70: 6
personal affair 1346: 7
which Milton held 553: 4
world is wide, so are m. ..179:12
Moras nocuit differe paratis 429: 6
pelle m. 429: 2
Morbi: pallentes 890: 7
perniciosiores sunt animi ..459:16
Morbid, all bile and verjuice 1697:10
Morbis: in m. minus 1285: 4
Morbo: hoc m. cupiditatis .351: 8
venienti occurrite m. 459: 1
Morbos: innumerabiles esse 315:14
non eadem sentire et demere m. 467: 3
Morbum: hunc habet m. ..1853: 7
non corpore sed loci 460: 3
occultare m. 459:13
si m. fugiens incidis in medicos 468:12
Morbus: gravissimus est m. a capite 814:10
More abundant grows 807:19
better the m., than less ..178: 3
he cast away, m. had 773: 7
I want some m. 1636:13
it changes 230: 6

More, *continued*
man hath m. desireth 119: 1
no m. of that 1178:13
pineth still for m. 119: 1
the merrier 1301: 5
More-having would be sauce 940:10
Mores: ætatis m. 1258:1a
cuique sui fingunt fortunam 716: 4
corrupti m. admiratione divitiarium 1720: 4
deteriores increbescunt ..1260: 7
disparis m. disparia studia 1256:11
et studia et populos 901: 5
fingunt fortunam 716: 4
fuerant vitia m. sunt 1257:17
hominum ostendere 1258:1a
hominum m. perspexi parum 1423:15
mali succreverunt 1260: 7
qui m. hominum vidit ...2029: 2
temporibus m. 13: 2
turpes m. collinunt 149: 2
Morgan buys his partners ..206: 9
J. P. M. "Jupiter" 1377:12
Lady M. makin' tay 997:11
Morgen, nur nicht heute ..2021:14
Morgenstunde hat gold ...1346:17
Mori: bene m. aut male 397:10
bene m. est libenter m. 1149: 7
bene m. non vetat 1149: 7
est felicis 396: 6
felix esse m. 391:10
honestius m. quam occidere 2113: 4
mallem m. quam mutare 1424: 9
timore mortis m. 1933:16
usque adeone m. miserum est 394:12
Moria pur quando vuol ...399:15
Moriar: cum m., medium inter opus 2231:15
non omnis m. 966: 4
Moribus: de m. ultima fiet quæstio 1720:21
multa injusta fiunt m. 846:14
Moris: nigris prandia m. finiet 523:15
Morituri salutamus 212:18
Morn and cold indifference .978: 3
beloved, it is m. 1346:18
blessed m. has come again 1347: 3
breaks from thine eyes ..1730:10
fair laughs the m. 2268: 4
from m. to noon he fell ..621:13
furthers man on his road .1346:17
genial M. appears 1976:16
greets the dappled M. 941:13
grey-eyed m. smiles 1347:16
heavenly airs of m. 233: 9
hues of rich unfolding m. 1347: 5
I came at m., 'twas spring 1123: 2
incense-breathing m. 1346:13
in russet mantle clad 1347:10
in the white wake 1348: 1
is the source of sighs 1347: 1
is up again, dewy m. 1346:13
like pensive Beauty 1346:14
meek-eyed M. 1348: 1
nice M. on th' Indian steep 1347: 9
not waking till she sings 1071:14
now m., her rosy steps ..1347:12
prosperous m. in May ..1283:15
rise, happy m. 1347:19
ris'n on mid-noon 1411:11
rosy-fingered is the m. ..1744: 2
rosy-finger'd m. 1346:19
salute the happy m. 268: 4
September m. 178:14
this is the happy m. 269: 2
unbarr'd gates of light ...1347:12
was fair, skies clear 1347: 4
went out with Sandals grey 1347:10
with the m. those angel faces smile 77: 1
without eve 967:12
Morning 1346
after 504:15
all is illusion till m. bars 1346:16
always m. somewhere ...1347: 2

Murder, *continued*
runs in families 1359: 3
sooner m. than unacted desires 435: 5
thou shalt do no m. 1360: 3
though it have no tongue 1359:14
to m. thousands 1359: 4
unpunished m. 1031:16
whiles I smile 947:19
will out, certain 1359:10
woe, want and m. 48:12
Murdered: all m. 1043:10
both his parents 1028:16
Murderer: hate m. less than claimant 1469: 5
Murderers walk the earth 1359: 1
Murdering: art of m. 1361: 1
Murders, rapes, and massacres 338: 3
too terrible for the ear 1360: 1
twenty mortal m. 770:14
Mure: hath wrought the m. .28:10
Murem peperit 1354: 5
Murex: who fished the m. 1559:13
Murmur at possessors of power 42:13
from growing grass 822:10
of bee a witchcraft 142:14
of the breaking flood 1781: 7
of the ocean-tide 1773: 8
of world beyond grave 969: 1
rustic m. of their bourg ..2085:12
unsleeping m. like a shell 1781: 6
Murmuring of innumerable bees 1895: 6
Murmurings whereby 1781: 9
Murmurs: as the ocean m. 1781: 6
in hollow m. die away 1365: 4
never touch the gods ...799: 8
of the poor 1573: 7
Murus æneus esto 989:16
Mus: nascetur ridiculus m. 1354: 5
Musa: dignum laude virum 1521: 9
gratia, M., tibi 1518:13
Musca splenem 693: 9
Musæo contigens cuncta lepore 1518:11
Musam: tenui m. meditamur avena 1768: 8
Musas: inanes desere M. .1477:14
Muscle: keep thy m. trained 1705:11
Muscles: highly developed m. 531: 6
orbicular oris m. 1045:20
Muscular: his Christianity was m. 265: 5
Muse benignant and serene 1169:17
in a crowd all day 1172: 4
made prostitute the M. ..1528:11
meditate thankless M. 956: 4
migrate from Greece 1530:10
my M., though mean 1505:13
no M. proof against gold 1523:13
O for a M. of fire 1535: 2
o'er flood and fell 1384: 1
of the English strain 1530: 5
on thee by day 708:15
such, poets, is the M. 1532:16
Tenth M. 1377:16
thanks, M., to thee 1518:13
tho' hamely in attire 991: 7
Tragic M. first trod 10: 2
unless you can m. in a crowd all day 1172: 4
unlettered m. 1521: 8
was born of woman 205:16
whose early voice 1526: 3
worst-natured m. 1532: 6
Muses are ten 820: 2
forsake the useless m. 1477:14
loved the m. and the sex ..1325: 5
old maid tabbies, the M. 2230: 4
pallidest of m. 6: 8
ragged as one of the M. ..487: 5
some say the M. are nine .820: 3
ten is the number of M. ..2077:8a
where stray ye, M. 1534:14
whole circle of m. 800:11
Mushroom: race of the m. ..869:18
Mushrooms: morning m. ..1250: 4
Mushrumps: leave to grow 836: 5
Music 1361
and banquet and wine 658:13
and moonlight and feeling 1879:14
and poesy use to quicken 1924: 3
and rhythm find their way 1362:13
and the flying cloud 1891: 4
and wine are one 2156: 6
arch-reformer 1364:11
architecture frozen m. 95: 1
arose with its voluptuous ..600: 9
art irrational as m. 102: 4
art most nigh to tears ..1366:15
at the close 32: 3
audible to him alone 1367:11
away with funeral m. ...1122: 4
beckon lost m. from lute 2009: 4
brandy of the damned ...1362: 3
breathing from her face ..1221:10
bright as soul of light 1366: 4
built out of m. 1808: 6
by M. minds equal temper 1364: 8
can soften pain to ease ..1364: 8
can tame furious beast ..1363: 2
cannot be prostit ted 1361:12
carry m. in their heart ..1364: 6
ceasing of exquisite m. ..131:19
celestial m. 1367: 8
cordial of troubled breast 1361:11
creation of man 1361: 5
crept by me upon waters 1365:14
cunning in m. 1971:10
does our joys refine 1361:11
ear's deep-sweet m. 1369: 4
essentially useless 1362:14
exalts each joy 1363: 6
exquisite m. of a dream ..1364: 7
fading in m. 1950: 9
feedeth what it findeth ..1363: 7
fiercest grief can charm,..1364: 8
fled is that m. 1405: 3
floods of delirious m. 162:17
for m. any words good ..1876:12
for the time doth change his nature 1363: 5
from chords of life 1119: 3
from Life's many frets ...874:15
give her m. o' mornings ..1364: 9
God is its author 1363: 9
God's voice 129: 4
goes 'round and around ..2296: 4
good as a wheelbarrow ..1362: 9
greatest good that mortals know 1361: 2
had the heat of blood 1366: 6
has died away 2095:13
hath charms to soothe ...1362:17
hath no m. in himself 1363: 8
haunted dreams by day ...991: 4
hear a sky-born m. still ..1367: 5
Heav'nly Maid 1363:13
helps not toothache 1364: 4
horse-hairs and calves'-guts 1369:13
how irksome is this m. 861: 2
how sour sweet m. is 1369: 5
I cried for madder m. 1198: 3
I shall hate sweet m. 1366: 5
if M. and Poetry agree ..1361:17
if m. be the food of love .1365:15
in all growing things 1361: 5
in his soul 1362:13
in my heart I bore 1366: 8
in note Cupid strikes 1192:17
in sighing of a reed 1367: 2
in sweet m. is such art ..1363: 3
instrument of God 1364:14
is dreamy 360: 6
is feeling, not sound 1362: 5
is the Prophet's art 1361:15
is what awakes from you 1364:12
jocund m. charm ear 615: 5
keep step to the m. 57: 3
least disagreeable noise ..1361:14
let me have m. dying 1365: 9
let the m. knock it 1370: 3
let the sounds of m. 1365:14
light quirks of m. 154: 4
like m. to heart it went ..1214: 3
liquid m. of her voice ...1880:10
Music, *continued*
low m. for the guest 434: 9
makes sweet m. with the 1732: 6
medicine of mind 1361:11
melted in the throat 1877: 4
moody food 1362: 2
more of m., less of words 2097:13
mosaic of the air 1361:16
most eloquent m. 1367:15
my m. in the future 1863: 1
nearest heaven 153:10
no m. in a rest 1100:16
no m. in Nature 1361: 5
no m. more for him 401:11
no m. to dramas of life ..1125: 7
no m. with woman in concert 2187: 6
of all sorts 1880:14
of her face 608: 11
of his own vain tongue ..2025: 9
of men's lives 1369: 5
of still ho..rs 1883:15
of the brook 200:11
of the Gospel leads 157:13
of the moon 1406: 8
of the spears 1367: 9
of the Spheres 1366:16
of the tongue 2025:12
of their motion may be ours 1915: 6
of those village bells 153: 3
of wonderful melodies ...1534: 2
of zither, flute, lyre 1368: 5
oft hath such a charm 1363: 4
only art of originality 1361:13
only universal tongue 1362: 1
only unpunished rapture ..1366: 2
pant for the m. divine ..1366: 1
perfect m. unto noble words 1255:15
planet-like m. of poetry ..1517:19
pleasure without vice 1361:14
poor man's Parnassus 1361: 7
pours on mortals 1362: 8
precious m. of heart 1878: 4
purely religious art 1362:16
real melojous m. 2285: 7
refresh mind of man 1364: 9
religious heat 1363: 6
resembles poetry 1361:17
rich m. of a summer bird 2097:15
sea-maid's m. 1877:11
sent up to God 108:17
shrill m. reach'd them 1300:11
simpler m. ne'er heard ..2097:13
slander m. more than once 2097: 8
slumber in the shell 1781: 8
so delicate, soft 945: 8
soars within little lark ..1072: 3
soft charm of heav'n 1362: 4
something of Divinity 1363:10
speech of angels 1361: 4
sphere-descended maid ..1361: 6
still sad m. of humanity .1251: 1
still sweet fall of m. 1365: 4
stormy m. in the drum ..1363:12
such m. as shall save 1146:14
sweeps by as messenger .1362: 6
sweet m. of alluring eyes .600:13
sweet m. of speech 1899: 2
sweet m. softer falls 1366: 7
sweeter than their own ..1539: 9
tells no truths 1361: 3
that brings sweet sleep ..1366: 7
that can deepest reach ...1898:14
that would charm forever 1366: 7
they were thy chosen m. ..2097:12
thing of the soul 1361:10
thy m. like river rolls 2230:10
to hear sea-maid's m. ...1300:10
uninform'd by art 1368:18
universal language 1362: 1
Wagner's m. is better than it sounds 1362:15
waste m. on savage race .1387: 8
we are the m.-makers 1369:11
when M., Heav'nly Maid 1363:13
where M. no mischief ..1362: 7
wherever harmony 1366:16
while m. wakes around ..1908: 9

Music, *continued*
wild sounds civilized 1361: 8
wilt thou have m. 1365:14
with her silver sound ...1364:13
with th' enamell'd stones .200:15
wonderful effect of M. ...1364: 1
you delight not in m. 1362: 6
Music's: bells are M. laughter 153:10
force tame furious beast ..1363: 2
Music-box: played upon m. 1370: 2
that plays 875:15a
Music-Grinders, crusaders 1369: 1
Music-land of dreams 481: 3
Music-makers: we are the m. 1369:11
Musica: donde hay M. no mala 1362: 7
mentis medicina 1361:11
Musicæ: occultæ m. nullum respectum 1962: 6
Musical as Apollo's lute ..1499: 8
as the chime 947: 2
glasses: men are like 492: 7
most m., most melancholy 1405: 6
Musician 1369
an admirable m. 1877:11
hath forgot his note 1369: 8
he is dead, the sweet m. ..1369:10
keeps false time 1083: 5
no better m. than wren ..1406: 5
Musicians: best of all m. 1369:10
never know when to end 1370:10
sound for silver 1364:13
we m. know 1369: 6
Musing: fire burned.......667:17
full sadly 1292: 6
Musique celeste 1367: 8
Musis: aversis utinam carmina M. 1534: 7
Musk and amber in revenge 1712:15
in a dog's kennel 1486:20
Money M. 1034: 3
Musk-rose: sweetened every 1746: 5
Musketeer: Pomeranian m. 2246:3a
Muskets flung their pills ..2117:11
kick owners over 1711: 4
Muslin: pretty bit of m. ..2181: 5
Mussulman, abstain from pork 1954: 9
Must: it m. not be again ..2112:11
we are what we m. 439:11
we m. do the thing we m. 1419:10
what I m. do 506:13
whither I m., I m. 1393:12
Must's for the king 115: 9
Mustard bites the tongue ..151: 7
Muster: take a m. speedily 379:12
Muta: perchè m. lato 623: 7
Mutability: nought may endure but m. 232: 9
or mistress synonymous ..1325: 5
Mutantur: omnia, nihil interit 231:14
omnia, tempora 230:22
Mutare: mallum mori quam m. 1424: 9
Mutat quadrata rotundis ..231: 1
Mutatio: omnia m. loci 232: 7
Mute and broken-hearted ..828:10
and magnificent 1978: 6
as a fish 1821:13
as m. had thought 1429:13
I, in love, m. and still ...1209:13
Muthigen: dem M. hilft Gott 324:10
Mutine in matron's bones 1809:20
Mutinied against the stomach 155: 1
Mutter: die M. schenk' ich 366:13
Mutton: eat m. cold 205: 6
evil communications corrupt good m. 288:11
leg of m. and trimmings ..523:10
love of m. beat love of sheep 1793: 6
of all birds, m. 523:16
old and claret good 1767: 1
very good treat 771:14
Muzzle mouth of the ox ..1442:13
Myrrh sweet-bleeding 2037:15
whose the gift of m.......774:11
Myrrhs and Mochas of mind 218: 5
Myrtle 691
and bay shoot fresh 2053: 4
and ivy of two-and-twenty 2266: 1
us for plain m. 503: 1
winding m. round your shed 1523:15
Myrtles brown, with ivy ..1002:12
Myrto: simplici m. 503:22
Myself: all to m. I think of you 1296:15
am Heav'n 893: 6
am Hell 893: 5
and me 1900:14
and the lucky moment ...1315: 3
as I walked by m. 572: 7
hope for all my help, m. 1786: 2
I celebrate m. 979: 5
I must mind most 440:12
I say that I am m. 1145: 4
Lord deliver me from m. 1788: 5
only m. to give 1128: 5
to m. dearer than friend 1791:10
to m. do I owe fame 624:16
when young 100:11
Mysteries: know all m. 130:13
lie beyond thy dust 392:18
love's m. in souls do grow 1221: 7
that cups of flowers 686:11
Mysterious not miracles ..1316: 4
Mystery 1370
all the rest is m. 1102: 4
Asian m. 819:14
before, reticence behind ..2152:11
begins, justice ends 1027: 3
begins, religion ends 1027: 3
essence of worship 1688: 3
every m. is dissipated ..1459:7a
for each m. find a key ..1139: 9
hid under Egypt's pyramid 534:17
I love not m. or doubt ...475: 9
leads millions by nose 578: 2
lucrative business of m. 1370:11
nine times folded in m. 1385:14
no m. in immortality 964: 3
now comes the m. 414: 5
of folded sleep 1842:12
of life not solved 1117: 8
of mysteries 158:10; 848: 2
of sex subject of jest ...1802:13
of the world the visible ..2235: 9
of Time 2002: 5
pluck out heart of my m. ..973:13
purple m. of dawn 368: 8
question of drainage 1370:15
that great m. of Time ...2002: 5
this life remains the M. ..1139:10
what he missed is m. 941: 4
which cannot be reasoned away 656: 5
Mystical better things 109: 7
Mystics hope science will overtake them 1764:17
Mystification for mastery ..341: 4

N

N.R.A. me down to sleep ..1847:12
Nabis sine cortice 1954: 3
Naces: non con quien n. ..1257:16
Naïad: guardian N. of the strand 1165: 7
Nail 1371
care to coffin adds a n. 221:15
drive not a second n. ..1371: 1
driven out by another 845:14; 1371: 1
every n. rivet in universe 1371:10
fabricate a n. 1422: 2
for want of n. shoe lost ..2041: 7
hittest n. on the head 1371: 9
in the wound 1371: 2
one n. by strength 1187: 4
polished to the n. 1258: 2
so high his name 2012: 7
Nailed colors to the mast ..673: 4
Nails: cut your n. on Monday 1371:12
even with ends of fingers 1371:12
hard as n. 235: 8
Nails, *continued*
keep free of dirt 491: 3
like gold n. in temples 538: 9
stronger than mine eyes ..1371: 6
which were taper 1654:16
white speck upon n. 1371:11
Naissance n'est rien 2093: 6
Naked and not ashamed ..1416: 9
and unashamed 2051:19
as a needle 1416: 9
as my nail 1416: 7
as shorn sheep 1416: 7
as a worm was she 1416: 7
as truth 1416: 7
beauty more adorned 1416: 9
came I out of womb 1416: 4
duke addressing n. house 1416: 6
every day he clad 1495: 4
he is born n. 163: 4
I alighted on earth 163:15
I seek the camp 1416:10
in December snow 962: 8
in nothing should woman be 1331:22
left me n. to my enemies 1801:13
tho' locked in steel 1030:14
to the hangman's noose ..852:15
upon the earth 163: 4
was I born 163:15
we came into the world ..1416: 4
went n. to hungry shark ..2195: 9
with her friend in bed ..1416:12
Nakedness
See also Nudity
general n. 338:12
not in utter n. 164:10
of indigent world 485:10
of woman work of God ..1416: 5
truth's best ornament 2051:17
with presented n. 1416:12
Namby-Pamby: called, after his name, N. 2278: 2
is your guide 1525: 2
Name 1371
and also an omen 1372: 3
at which world grew pale 1373:14
awakens all my woes 1102:16
beat n. on drum of world 1373: 6
begrimed and black 1702:16
Ben Adhem's n. led rest 1495:10
bequeathed to son good n. 1701:17
borrow n. of the world ...1759: 4
breathe not his n. 1375: 1
bright n. hallow song 1374: 7
builds himself a n. 95:10
by any other n. would smell as sweet 1373: 1
call everything by n. 218: 6
calleth by Christian n. 631: 4
change n. and not letter ..1265:14
clumsy n. 1372: 1
conspicuous and sublime 1374: 5
de good Lawd know my n. 1745:13
demanding thy n. on paper 1947: 6
descending with all time .2123: 3
died before the man 628:15
don't recall your n. 1258: 1
dreaded n. shall sound 1373: 9
even his n. "N. Deering" 1654:13
ever-living n. 1375:11
every godfather can give n. 1765:15
ev'ry sacred n. in one 726:12
fading n. 50:13
fair-seeming n. 1371:17
famous n. heavy burden .1374: 4
far babbled n. 1375: 2
fascination of a n. 340: 8
fast anchored in abyss ...1374: 5
filches my good n. 1701:20
finds his crackt n. 1374:16
float upon sea of time 1371:15
for ever sad 1372: 5
for my n. and memory ..1374: 6
forever memorize 1522: 6
forgotten his n. 1170: 3
give a dog ill n. 469:16
give n. to every fixed star 1765:15
give them everlasting n. .1374:17
giving n. poetic art 1515: 6
good n. a second life 1701:10

Name, *continued*
good n. better than ointment 1701:10
good n. better than riches 1701:11
good n. endureth forever .1701:12
good n. in man or woman 1701:20
good n. is worth gold ..1701:10
good n. keeps lustre in dark 1701:18
good n. ne'er retriev'd ...1703: 9
good n. rather than riches 1701:10
good n. seldom got by oneself 174:12
good n. unstained 1701:14
good n. white as tulip 1701:14
grand old n. of gentleman 765:10
graved in the white stone 1373: 7
great in story 2266: 1
great n. never pass away 1373: 7
great example stands 344: 5
great n. of England 552:10
greater the n., more guilt 1831:12
Greek and Roman n. 1374:14
halloo your n. 526: 2
have left a n. behind 1374:15
he loved to hear 401: 1
him and he's always near 441: 5
his first n. was Jupiter ..1377:12
holy n. of grief 840: 3
I had a silvery n. 1405: 5
I have no n. 120:10
I've forgotten your n. ..709: 1
if n. is to live at all 1521: 2
if n. up, lie in bed 1701:18
ill wound cured, not ill n. 1703:10
illumined by patriot's n. ..1466:13
illustrious and ancient n. 1373:17
in the n. of the Prophet ..664:12
ineffable N. 1369: 6
invisible thing called Good N. 1700: 8
is on your waters 977: 1
keep your good n. 245: 6
king's n. a tower 983: 5
king's n. twenty thousand 983: 5
leave a living n. behind 50:10
left Corsair's n. 1374: 9
lend his n., that other men may buy 1662:12
let be my n. 1373: 4
let him n. it who can 1372: 1
live in people's hearts 1521: 2
lived and died without n. 1522: 6
local habitation and a n. ..1535: 3
love lord and not his n. ..1372:18
love's suspected n. 745: 7
lustrous n. of patriot 1468: 8
measly gum-drop n. 1376:11
my good n. unstained 1701:14
my n. ends with me 1372:11
my n. is Benjamin Jowett 1056:15
my n. is Legion 1372: 3
my n. is MacGregor 1372:12
my n. shall live 1374:18
my n. shall never die 1519:11
my unsoil'd n. 215: 5
no n. in country's story ..1161: 3
no n. shall but your own 2037:10
none nail so high his n. ..2012: 7
nothing but a n. 1374: 8
obnoxious to no pun 1654: 7
of Annabel Lee 1206:14
of chamber was Peace ...1475: 2
of death never terrible ..1148:22
of friend is common 744: 1
of friendless n. a friend .1496: 2
of Lord strong tower 1372: 6
of the Great Jehovah 61: 8
of the Prophet—figs 664:12
of the wicked shall rot ..1029:15
of which was Beautiful ...130: 5
one great n. can make 1373:12
one N. above all names 264:14
our n. shall be forgotten ..1421:10
patriot's all-atoning n. ..1468: 2
rather make n. than inherit 1373: 4
sacred n. of friendship ...741:15
scrawl, as I do here, n. ..1374:21
serene companion, good n. 1703:11
shouts louder empty n. ..1375: 2

Name, *continued*
sound of sweetheart's n. .1375:15
stain'd his n. 205:11
starlike-immortal shines thy n. 1158:10
stolen both office and n. ..1372:13
sweet n. from Rome 1375:16
sweet n. of liberty 1104: 8
swiftly fades thy n. 1604: 2
take good n., take life ..1703: 1
take not God's n. in vain 1951:14
take not His n. in vain ..1952: 3
taunts of scorn they join thy n. 58: 6
tender of her own good n. 1702:13
that dwells on every tongue 1372: 2
that's never spoken 1375:13
thy n. expanded flies 1375: 5
thy n. shall shine 51: 9
to be washed out 1372:14
to live and die for 2122: 4
to see one's n. in print 190:10
to such a n. for ages long 1374: 3
unmusical 1372:13
very naked n. of love 1190:11
waft thy n. beyond sky 1588: 3
was writ in water 1033: 9
we must have your n. 982:11
what a wounded n. 1372:14
what is your n. 1376: 7
what n. Achilles assumed 1665: 5
what's in a n. 1373: 1
when thou hast heard his n. 1221:12
which before thee 1378: 4
which you know by sight 1376:17
whistling of a n. 344: 9
whistlings of a n. 1374:11
whose n. blisters tongues 2064:16
whose n. was traced in sand 1034: 1
whose n. was writ in water 1033: 9
whose n. well spelt 1376:10
will not perish in dust ...1375: 7
with good n. rich 1701:16
without an echo 1375: 3
worth age without a n. ...781: 4
wounded n. 1372:14
writ n., made blot 1373: 5
write your glorious n. 1375: 8
writes his n. upon wall ..1372: 8
wrote her n. upon strand 1375: 8
yes, that is my n. 2283: 3
your n. hangs in my heart 1376: 6
Name's: for his n. sake ..790:18
Named: better never n. than ill spoken of 1700:16
Nameless and dead these centuries 107: 7
here for evermore 1235: 5
in dark oblivion 1421: 3
in worthy deeds 427:16
Names are old sad stories ..613: 2
at which Fame blushes ...625: 1
athwart the dusk 780: 4
commodity of good n. ...1701:19
deathless n. defiled 221:20
distinguish but by n. 1155: 8
distinguished n. 1373: 8
fair n. and famous 402: 3
familiar in his mouth 1375: 6
few n. even in Sardis ..1372: 9
fools' n., like faces 1372: 8
gleam like sun 780: 4
great n. debase 1373:15
he love to hear 401: 1
may live through time 781:12
more force in n. 1371:17
more n. than shirts 2016: 2
of great dowry of nation ..833: 3
of music linger 977: 1
of things belov'd are dear 1376: 8
one of few, immortal n. 1373:13
proud n. who once reins ..2131:11
put n. to their books 625:17
put no new n. on virtues 2080: 2
saved others' n. 1372:12
skilful to invent n. 1765:15
strange n. rustics give ..1376:12
that among the noblest are 1761:16

Names, *continued*
that hast forgot their n. ..1373:10
that men remember 1374: 2
that must not wither 425:12
their very n. shine still ..1374: 5
those rugged n. 1373:18
to carve our n. 48: 2
to hide its ignorance 1765:15
to such n. sounding 1804:14
true things by wrong n. ..1371:13
twenty more such n. 1376:16
unpronounceable awful n. 1376:12
victorious n. 1373:11
what are n. but air 1375:16
women's n. keep murmuring 1376: 3
woundy luck in n. 1371:17
Nancy: lang-tochered N. 1790: 5
Nantes in gurgite vasto 1816: 7
rari n. in gurgite vasto 1772:21
Nantucket: old man of N. 1157:17
sunk and here are we 1778: 7
Nap after dinner 1848: 6
beauty n. 778: 8
Napa, petty gratuity 1630:10
Napkin: send for n. 1074: 6
Napkins: dip n. in blood ...824:22
Naples, Paradise of Italy .1000:18
see N. and die 1000:18
sitteth by the sea 1000:18
to whom all N. is known 1056:10
Napoleon **1378**
called Cent Mille 982:15
deems not that great N. ..980:25
equal to 40,000 men 982:15
healed through sword 1378: 5
impostor and rogue 1378: 2
incarnate Democrat 1378: 2
is thoroughly modern 1378: 2
of the realms of rhyme ..211:16
one thought he was N. ..2150:11
the little 1379: 4
was a man 1378: 2
were I not N. 45:16
Napoli: vedi N., e poi muori 1000:18
Napping: ta'en you n. 1643:12
Narcissus 691: 5
is the glory of his race 819:12
nourisheth the soul 945: 4
Narcotics: numbing pain ..843: 3
Naribus: minus aptus acutis N. 1855:15
nimis uncis N. indulges ..1855:18
Narines de feu 930:15
Narr sein Leben lang 2160: 1
Narrando: nihil quin n. possit depravarier 1760: 8
Narration: mixed n. 2251:12
Narrative of designs 1250:13
with age 39:20
Narrow: criticise fathers ..646: 7
Narrower by going farther 2031: 3
Nasci miserum, vivere pœna 1144: 5
Nasty mind 1239:13
Nasum nidore supinor ...1487: 1
non datum habere n. 1413: 5
Natalis grate numeras 164:13
Nathan said to David 1252:13
Nati natorum 1564: 3
Natio comœda est 2240: 6
Nation **1379**
better a brutal n. 110: 5
boast themselves ancient n. 904: 8
brutal, starving n. 554: 8
conceived in liberty 574: 9
does not import religion ..1690:13
earth's greatest n. 53:11
foreign n. is contemporary posterity 707: 5
happy n. without history .902: 9
ignorant and free 1380: 7
institutions create n. 1379:10
is hammer or anvil 84: 8
lives and acts like man ..1379:11
made army, navy, n. 367: 9
never falls but by suicide 1380:13
never use the word N. 57: 1
never was art-loving n. ...103:18
never was a n. great 1380:16

Navy

Night, *continued*
and day, both sweet things 1142: 3
another n., another day ..1145: 6
awaits us all 381: 3
azure robe of n. 673:11
bare-bosom'd n. 1402: 6
before Christmas 270: 7
before some festival 489: 4
bend low, O dusky N. ..1401:14
best-beloved N. 1401:11
beyond the n., across day 1199: 5
black bat, n., has flown ..756:19
blindman's holiday 350:13
blue n. with white moon ..378:12
brave n. to cool courtesan 2133:16
brings out the stars 290:11
brings troubles to the light 1402:14
broods over the deep 1401: 4
burn n. with torches 1400:15
but daylight sick 1404: 1
by n. an atheist believes 114:20
by n. blemishes hid 365: 4
Christian, what of the n. ..619:18
collied n. 1153:19
come, seeling n. 1403:16
cometh at last 372: 8
cometh when no man can work 2232: 2
comfort-killing N. 1403: 2
cowlèd N. 1402: 3
cut short the n. 1403:15
dark is the n. 908:15
dark n. strangles 1403:17
dark-eyed n. 1401: 1
darksome n. be passed ..1706:15
day's elder born 1404: 4
dead vast and middle of n. 1303: 4
death's dateless n. 1976: 3
defining n. by darkness ..428:11
does the rich gem betray 1013: 4
doth love her 212: 1
drunken n. cloudy morn ..505: 1
dusky n. rides down sky ..941:12
each n. revers'd toils of day 2234:15
each n. we die 1849:19
empty-vaulted n. 76:12
fall dark 1745:13
followed, clad with stars 2062: 9
forespent n. of sorrow ...371:10
getting up in the middle of the n. 1730: 2
had been unruly 1946:14
has a thousand eyes 1187:11
hath a thousand eyes 1400:10
hath been familiar face 1401: 7
hath set her silver lamp 1923: 1
haunted chambers of N. 1401:11
he has the n. 1443: 3
holds keys of day 1404: 6
honey'd middle of the n. 1401: 8
how beautiful is n. 1401:16
how beautiful this n. 1401:16
how long n. to pain 1402:12
how pleasant is Saturday n. 255: 3
in banqueting spent 660: 5
in the lonesome October ..1425: 6
infolds the day 1941:14
is beginning to lower 253:11
is for the day 1403: 7
is mother of the day 419:17
is mother of thoughts 1400:11
is the outlaw's day 1403:11
is the time for rest 1707: 6
is the time to weep 1402:10
isn't more n. than day 293: 2
it is a dreary n. 1402:13
joint-laborer with day 863:13
know not what n. will bring 1401: 3
last out a n. in Russia ..1402:12
let's have another gaudy n. 1400:15
life's long n. is ended 1187: 8
long n. folds them all 2130: 2
long n. of her deep hair ..848:14
long n. of winter 2161: 3
long that never finds day 1403:18
love n. more than day ..1403: 3
lovely as a Lapland n. 38: 5
loving, black-brow'd n. ..1401: 1

Night, *continued*
love's n. is noon 1208:14
low'ring N. 1403:12
mad naked summer n. ..1402: 6
made for loving 33: 4
made wanton the n. 2105:12
magnetic nourishing N. ..1402: 6
majestic presence of N. 1401:11
make n. brighter than day 2140:10
makes the n. morning 1884: 6
making n. hideous 1400:16
mask of n. is on my face 173: 6
mine is the n. 1401: 5
miserable n. 483: 6
misery's blackest n. 1319:10
most beautiful and rare 1401:16
mother of counsels 1400:11
muffles up the day 1403:16
my father got me 646: 1
mysterious n. 1402: 5
naughty n. to swim in ..1403: 1
no day but has its n. 373: 2
not sent for slumber 1400:12
O holy N. 1401:11
of an unknown hereafter 2005:11
of error 201: 5
of life some memory 1295: 7
of love and beauty 1195: 4
of memories and sighs ..401: 6
of south winds 1402: 6
of tears 1402: 8
of the grave 1905:10
oft in the stilly n. 1293:19
older than day by day ..1404: 4
one n. awaits us all 381: 3
one n. went betwixt 809:12
out of n. that covers me 1892: 9
pass n. with wine-cup ..2158: 3
passed a miserable n. ...1851: 1
pities nor wise nor fool ..1403: 1
sabbath of mankind 1400: 4
sable goddess 1402: 7
sable N., mother of dread 1401: 1
sable-vested n. 1400: 6
sad and solemn N. 1914: 4
sadder than daylight 1402:11
see how the cowlèd n. 1402: 3
seems termless hell 277: 7
shades of n. were falling 110: 1
shall be filled with music 220:18
ships that pass in the n. ..1290: 2
showery n. and still 362:13
shows stars and women 1400: 5
silent N. 1401:13
sink discouraged into n. ..110: 2
sober-suited matron 1400: 6
starlit hall of N. 1401:15
stealthy evil Raven 1400:13
sum up at n. day's deeds 1788:17
sweeps along the plain 1138: 9
sweeps up the hours 159:15
that baleful burning n. ..2046: 4
that had no morrow 1402:12
that no morn shall break 395: 8
the dark-blue hunter 2062: 8
the shadow of light 1239:11
things that love n. 1403: 1
this little strip of n. 2021:16
this n. in banqueting 660: 5
'tis a fearful n. 1647: 1
'tis a wild n. 1403: 1
trailing garments of N. 1401:10
unpleasant sort of n. 1403: 1
unto n. sheweth knowledge 1403:13
upon the cheek of n. 140:11
very witching time of n. 1303: 5
walked down the sky ..1401: 9
wan n., shadow-goer 1401: 6
was drawing her curtain 2062: 1
was our friend 438: 2
watchman, what of the n. .1400: 8
we'll add n. to the day 1403:15
what is the n. 1400: 8
when deep sleep falleth ..481: 8
when evils are most free ..305:16
when N. is on the hills ..992: 2
when no man can work 1400: 9
whose pitchy mantle 369:11
will blossom as the rose 2166:24
will hide joys no longer ..369:12

Night, *continued*
windy n. rainy morrow ..1887:11
winter-seeming summer's n. 1194:17
with her sullen wings ..1402: 9
with her train of stars ..1941: 9
with him fled shades of n. 1400:14
with power to silence day 1403:10
Night-cap deck'd brows ..908:14
Night-caps: better or not 1843: 8
Night-crow cried 1946:13
Night-dress: lectures in her n. 2146: 9
Night-school: had been to 529: 4
Night-shirts: as credentials 87: 4
Night-watchman: wurruks as n. 1431:10
Night-watches: lone n. 1245:12
Nightfall: we wait for n. 29: 6
when one may rest 29: 6
Nightingale, Florence 2184:11
Nightingale 1404
act the part of a n. 13: 3
amorous descant sung ...582: 9
and not the lark 1406: 5
as soon as April bringeth 1406: 7
bemoans a life 1404: 8
cease from enamour'd tale 1406: 6
Chinese n. 1405: 5
dies for shame 1404:13
Hark! ah, the n. 1404:11
has a lyre of gold 167: 9
heard the bird himself ..963: 9
if she should sing by day 1406: 5
in the sycamore 191: 6
is singing from the steep ..1405: 3
last night n. woke me 1406:10
leave to n. her shady wood 1073: 5
love-lorn n. 1406: 8
mellow-throated n. 1406: 3
mourning her ravish'd young 1405:11
never n. so singeth 1405: 1
no prize at poultry show 1406: 1
O n. thou surely art 1406:12
Oh n.! What doth she ail 1404:14
one n. for twenty 1743: 8
plain eggs of the n. 1406: 8
rapt in her song 756:19
sings round it 1405: 9
sits alone in sorrow 1405: 2
telling self-same tale 1406: 2
that in the branches sang 1405:10
that on yon bloomy spray 1405: 8
there is no music in n. 1199: 9
'tis the merry n. 1404:15
'tis the ravish'd n. 1404:12
we vivisect the n. 960: 9
Nightingale's lament 1404: 9
Nightingales: constancy from n. 306: 4
sing only in the spring 1274:10
that sing to rose of life 180: 7
till the n. applauded 1342: 6
twenty caged n. do sing 1365:14
thy n. live on 894: 3
Nightmare Life-in-Death .1147: 8
Nights: all days are n. 4: 7
banished from realms of sleep 1697: 2
devoid of ease 1534: 2
gay-spent festive n. 111: 2
God makes sech n. 1401:12
in careless slumber spent ..310: 7
lee-lang n. 220: 3
lie ten n. awake 1958: 9
merry n. and sorry days ..1270:12
on gossamer n. 614:10
soft n., solid dinners 1755:10
starless n. 1935: 3
three sleepless n. 1311: 7
two n. to every day 1582: 7
wakey n. 1851: 5
waste long n. in discontent 1802: 2
Nighty: follow in her n. 2206:14
Nigræ: lanæ n. nullum colorem 166: 3
Nihil ab illo vacat 796: 5
esse 1415: 5
Nihilist does not bow down 974: 4

Nihilist, qui nil amat 1318:14
Nihilo: ex n. nihil fit 1414:10
Nihilum: det nihilo n. 1414:10
redit ad n. res ulla 1414:10
Nil admirari 14:13
de nilo posse fatendum ..1414:10
Nil ultra: here I fix 858: 5
to hopes 925:17
Nile, The 1406
can water the earth 1406:13
dam the waters of N. 52: 8
forever new and old 1406:16
mouths of fertile N. 808:10
overflowing N. presageth famine 1407: 1
Nili: facilis sit N. caput invenire 1407: 5
Nilus: higher N. swells ..1407: 1
word of monk N. 1406:13
Nimini-pimini 1652:20
Nimirum hic ego sum 1489:10
Nimis: ne quid n. 1326:15
Nimium: nil n. 1326:14
Nimrod: proud N. 941: 3
the mighty hunter 941: 3
Nine lives instead of one ..224: 3
make a clamor 450:14
Ninepence in ready money 313: 2
only n. in my pocket 805: 2
Ninepunce a day fer killin' 1866:10
Ninety-and-nine just persons 1699: 9
that safely lay 1810:18
Ninety-eight: who fears ..997: 1
Nineveh: should not I spare N. 849:20
Niobe dissolves into a tear 1977: 3
like a new N. 1936:13
like N., all tears 1977: 3
of nations 1739: 2
Nipples: beauty spot 1351:17
red as cherries 2105: 3
Nirvana: in rest of N. 1414: 1
Nitor in adversum 1617: 2
Nitre: windy n. 2118: 3
Nives: capitis n. 39: 5
No: could not pronounce 1687: 2
forgot what "No" meant ..708:10
from the mouth of woman 2212: 8
in winter easy to say No 1908:16
is no negative in woman 2202:16
lass saith no, and would 2202:10
never say no 1288:12
never take No for answer 2202: 8
others said, No 190: 8
sayers of no 423: 1
spell no for me 2202:18
waspish word as No 2202:17
when we can say No, say Yes 2149: 6
No tangas letras como un si 1687: 2
No-man's-land 1904:12
Noah often said to his wife 2158:10
ordained fast 642: 8
Papa N. 861: 8
to the Zebra 1073: 7
when he had anchored ..2158:10
Nobilem: non facit n. imaginibus 71: 8
Nobilitas sola est virtus 1407:17
Nobilitate: quid est in n. bonum 72: 9
Nobility 1407
all was noble save N. ..1407:11
but ancient riches 68: 9
constrains us 72:12
finds blazon in posterity ..1563: 3
graceful ornament 70: 2
hereditary n. 68:12
imposeth necessity 72: 9
in pain 612:16
leave our old n. 70:10
more nobly to repay 149:10
my n. begins in me 73:11
of ascent 2093: 7
of birth 70:16
of labor 1061:17
O lady, n. is thine 1273: 5
scorns leather aprons 70:16
that hands show no fear ..850: 7
Nobility, *continued*
transmissible n. 72: 6
true n. exempt from fear 1408: 8
Nobis meminisse relictum 1293:17
Noble and nude and antique 1416:13
be n. in every thought ..1408: 1
better not be than not n. 1408: 9
experiment 1618:11
fool never in fault 72: 3
how n. in reason 1239: 5
more n., more humble 1408: 4
must nobly meet fate 72:10
of Nature's own creating 1408:10
only n. to be good 73:10
that hath n. conditions ..1408: 4
those who think nobly are n. 1407: 7
to be n. we'll be good ..1407:17
to grant life 1298:14
too n. for this place 1408: 7
unto n. everything good 1407:12
who has a priority 1407:10
Noble-minded: be n. 917: 5
Noble-mindedness 993:17
Nobleman: busts do not make a n. 71: 8
dar'st thou brave a n. 322:12
is he 1407: 7
like a turnip 72: 1
Noblemen do nothing well 70:16
Nobleness: not beauty but n. witcheth 1273: 5
royal n. 1408: 7
that lies in other men 1408: 2
to try for 2122: 4
Nobler: nought n. is than to be free 722: 8
of us two 1407: 9
to something n. we attain 1459: 1
Nobles bended as to Jove's statue 1560:10
by earlier creation 68:11
lose the race 72: 7
so many great n. 1748: 7
Noblesse est une dignité 68:12
oblige 72: 8
Noblest things find vilest 810:10
Nobly: how n. they live ...1408: 6
Nobody cares for thee 572: 7
does, and why should you ..70: 5
I care for n., not I 1302: 3
knows when begun 586: 9
loves me 2293: 9
there's n. at home 2174:14
Nocendum: nulli n. 986: 6
Nocens: nemo fit fato n. ..643: 1
non sponte est n. 1827:10
se judice nemo n. absolvitur 1657: 1
Nocentes: florere n. 987:10
Nocere: miserius est n. 986: 5
Nocte: in n. consilium ..1400:11
latent mendæ 1224: 6
Noctem: sic n. patera 2158: 3
Noctemque diemque fatigunt 1404: 5
Noctes, cenæque deum 1400: 7
tecum longas requiescere n. 1215:13
Noctis erant placida 1401: 2
Nocturna versate manu ..1674: 5
Nocturne in Black and Gold 1449: 4
Nod: affects to n. 799:14
as good as a wink 2160:13
from a good man 1579:11
gives the n. 799:14
Homer himself observed to n. 911:16
land of N. 1843:21
tremble with his n. 799:14
Noddin': nid, nid, n. 1843:11
Noddle: comb your n. 870: 4
Noddles: smite his n. 1642:17
Nodosities of character 234:16
of the oak 1014: 6
Nods and becks 1010: 2
French n. 678:20
Nodum: in scirpo n. quæris 2044:10
Noes: honest kersey n. 217: 9
valiant n. spoken 7:11
Noise as the shrouds make ..91: 2
come, bring with a n. 270: 1
dire was n. of conflict 2117: 4
dreadful n. of waters 1816: 5
enough in the world 625: 9
flicterin' n. an' glee 908: 6
like that of a hidden brook 200: 7
like that of a water-mill ..1944:16
musicians make tuning ..2252: 9
of hammer and anvil 84: 5
of many waters 2125: 1
of the moon 1838: 6
over a good deed 427:16
power of n. to move 1364: 8
stab upward with your n. 233: 3
yearning to make a n. 2250: 8
Noiseless as fear 1825:12
Noises: discordant n. 455: 2
Noisy man always right 97:10
Noisyville-on-the-Subway .1397: 2
Nokes outdares Stokes 1559:13
Noles: nimio celerius veniet quod n. 2043:19
Noli me tangere 1639:14
Nolunt ubi velis 2199: 3
Nom trop fameux, un poids 1374: 4
Nombre: mas vale el buen N. que riquezas 1701:11
Nome: scolpire olte quel termine nostro n. 48: 2
Nomen: æternumque tenet n. 1375:11
amicitia est 743:20
amicitiæ sanctum et venerabile n. 741:15
atque omen 1372: 3
clarum et venerabile n. ..1373:17
dulce libertatis 1104: 8
foristan nostrum n. 1375: 4
ne hodie malo n. 1272: 3
teneo melius ista quam n. 1056: 9
toto sparget in orbe 1373:17
Nomina: honesta n. prætendebant 1373: 3
ponto 1730:21
Nominated: if n. I will not accept 2281: 1
in the bond 1086:19; 1272: 1
Nomination decided in a smoke-filled room 1553: 1
I will not accept n. 2281: 1
Nominanza: é color d'erba 628:10
Nomine: mutato n. de te fabula 1959:15
Nominis: stat magni n. umbra 1373:16
superstitione n. 1373: 3
Noms: grands n. abaissent 1373:15
Non possumus 1637:11
putarum 698: 3
tibi spiro 1513:13
Non sequitur: conclusion a n. s. 1663: 1
you're a n. s. 1663: 1
Non-combatant: no fury like that of n. 2109: 6
Non-conformist: man must be a n. 973: 5
Non-flunky: one n. 895: 9
Non-possession of much ..1565: 5
Non-resistance ties cravat 1684:11
Nonage: in my n. 2264: 3
Nonchalance of death 412: 9
Nonpareil: thou art the n. ..1485:15
Nonsense 1408
daring n. seldom fails to hit 1408:12
dullest n. most profound 1408:12
his n. suits their n. 1408:12
little n. now and then ..1408:20
may be good law 1090: 4
no biggodd n. about her 1408:14
of their stone ideal 1770:16
one word n., two nothing 1898:15
only n. set to music 1876:11
privilege of aristocracy ..1479:16
round the corner of n. 1927:14
swallows n., and a lie ..2242: 1
throned in whiskered hair 1795: 5
to dispute about a hue 602:13
varnish n. with sound ..1876:11

Nook: booke and a shadie n. 189: 4
grant him some noble n. 1856:12
rocky n. with hilltops ..194:17
shady n., babbling brook .2287: 5
with a book 189: 3
Nooks: by many winding n. 200:15
sequestered n. 189: 3
to lie and read in 189: 3
Noon 1411
novelty of n. out of date 1415:14
O sweet, delusive N. ..1411:10
shameless n. 1411:13
she comes not when n. 992: 3
very n. of night 1302:10
who left off at n. 73: 3
Noon-glory: sun's n. 1944: 5
Noonday: clearer than n. ..1632: 1
in the bustle 1434: 9
Noontide: when n. wakes anew 210:16
Noose: forc'd his neck into a n. 1225:14
struggled with marriage n. 1276:14
Noosing of rich people 1271:14
Norfolk: Duke of N. deals in malt 207: 6
Normalcy: not nostrums but n. 67: 7
Norman's Woe: reef of ..1815: 9
Norn Mother saw 1159: 8
North and South together brought 58: 3
no N., no South, no East ...57: 5
points to the needle 475: 4
tender is the n. 237: 9
tyrannous breathing of n. 1052: 2
North Carolina: governor of 494: 6
North Pole: damn the N. P. 1898: 6
Northern men loveth fight ..999: 2
Northwest Territory: no slavery in N. T. 1841: 5
Nor'wester's blowing, Bill 1780: 1
Norval; on Grampian hills 1811:18
Nosce te 1790: 2
Nose 1412
and chin threaten ither ...609: 9
any n. may ravage rose 1412: 4
assert n. upon his face his own 1412: 6
becomes all n. 1996:17
betrays porridge 1413: 4
blow n. differently 2021:18
bor'd through the n. 1413: 1
change laws of empire ..1412:10
choose man with long n. ..1413: 7
cock to her n. 1413: 3
curl up n. for savory smell 1487: 1
cut off n. to spite face 1413: 8
did not like to turn n. 1413: 5
dipped his Roman n. 2157: 1
dog's n. ever cold 469:15
down his innocent n. 1975: 7
e'en at thy father's n. ..1486:18
embellished with rubies ..1413:10
fell a-bleeding 1947: 2
follow thy n. 1413:15
foot of n. 477:19
haughtily he cocks n. ..1056:14
his n. should pant 79: 9
hold n. to grindstone ...1412:13
if a man's n. bleeds 1947: 2
innocent n. 943: 2
insinuated n. 473: 7
into every platter 1284: 7
jolly red n. 1412: 2
led by the n. 1412:12
led by the n. with gold 115:12
like a coal of fire 1413:12
like a waxen n. 1413:16
loses n. loses character ..1176:13
many an Aldermanic n. 1412: 1
Marian's n. looks red ..2161:10
means will 606: 2
never thrust n. into other men's porridge 1284: 7
not a n. among twenty ..1413:15
of nice nobility 1412: 6
often wipe a bloody n. ..1664: 5
of wax 1413:16
on a man's face 1010:14
Nose, *continued*
paying through the n. 1413: 1
put n. out of joint 1413: 9
seek no further than end of n. 1413:14
snipe-like n. 455:12
snuffing with writhed n. 705:13
speaks through his n. 1591: 9
that has great n. 1412:11
that wakeful nightingale, his n. 1412: 1
that's his precious n. 1412:14
thrust n. into platter ...1284: 7
tip-tilted like flower 1413: 3
tumbles on his n. 472:18
turn up his n. 1412: 7
under n. of envious 565:14
use your turned-up n. ..1724:13
was sharp as a pen 1413:12
why does n. look so blue 1932:23
why n. is in middle 1413:13
wipe it down, not up 1412: 3
wipe n. of neighbor's son 1492: 8
wiped n. on sleeve 1412: 3
wipes child's n. kisseth mother 257: 8
Nosegay of others' flowers 1668: 1
Nosegays: leave for waking 480:14
Noses: bloody n. 665: 9
crook'd n. 214: 1
diplomats have long n. ..451:18
follow n. led by eyes ..1413:15
people ought to guard n. 1284:11
wearing our own n. 552: 7
Nosse volunt omnes 1056: 5
Nostri nosmet pænitet ..1791:11
Nostril: stretch the n. wide 2116:10
through prest n. 1880: 1
upturn'd n. wide 1413: 6
Nostrils: curved n. 1855:18
Not-day: saw the n. 1914:15
Not-incurious in God's handiwork 1242: 3
Notches on the blade 1956: 9
Note and to observe 352: 2
dreadful n. of preparation 2117: 6
not a n. worth the noting 1603:14
now sinks the n. of fear ..1815: 2
silent n. Cupid strikes ..350: 3
soft is n., sad the lay ...1357: 3
sparrow's n. from heaven 1896: 7
take no n. of time 2010: 6
when found, make a n. of 731:10
why then a final n. prolong 1879:12
Noteless as race 1372:12
timeless, tuneless fellow ..1880: 1
Notes by distance made more sweet 1290:16
chield's amang you takin' n. 1603:14
do beat the vaulty heaven 1072:16
ever-ready n. of ridicule ..162:17
few n. but strong 167:14
loosen n. in silver shower 1366: 1
necessary evils 2251: 3
praised unblushingly her n. 1880: 5
resembling stars 1999:14
such sweet soft n. 1365: 2
that close eye of day 1405: 8
thick-warbl'd n. 1508: 6
thousand blended n. 1995:16
tuned to her sad estate ..1405:11
Nothing: begins and n. ends 1445:10
better do n. 953: 9
better than a good woman? N. 245: 9
better to know n. 959:19
brings me all things 460: 6
brought n. into world 163:15
but a rose 1747: 4
can be known 1060:13
can be made of n. 1414:10
can touch him further 395:12
did n. in particular 427: 1
doing n. with skill 953:11
do n. and get something 750: 5
do n. at all 953:13
do n. emphatically 1589:14
do n. for ever and ever ..573:12
Nothing, *continued*
do n. is in every man's power 953: 1
do n. is way to be n. 956: 7
do n. to nobody 1414:12
does n. at all 952:21
doing n., never do amiss 1548: 6
either good or bad 1991:22
elder brother to shade ..1415: 4
for me to-day 2291: 6
for n. 1414:11
from n. I was born 1415: 6
from n. to n. I travel 1414:6a
gives to airy n. 1535: 3
has no savor 1414: 3
having n., possessing all 1414: 6
here lies one who was n. ..571: 7
hundred years hence 1335:21
I come from n. 1990:24
I that am n. 137:11
in the world to do 1811:15
is altered 718: 8
is but what is not 1415: 2
is changed 718: 8
is given for n. 1414:11
is had for n. 1414:11
is hid 2051: 7
is it n. to you 1887: 2
is no good 2279: 5
is right and n. is just ..1491:10
is stolen 1505:13
is there to come 1599:14
is too late 31: 9
it set out from 1141: 9
know n., doubt n. 959: 6
knowing n. is sweetest ..960: 3
laboriously doing n. 953:12
learning to say n. cleverly 2249:12
left'st me n. in will 985:14
let n. disturb thee 793: 8
make no use of n. 1414:10
matters 1414: 7
nearby it is n. 463: 6
new or true 1414: 7
of n. comes n. 1732: 1
out of n. comes n. 1414:10
proceeds from nothingness 1414:10
really perishes 230: 6
returns to nothingness ..1414:10
said that has not been said before 1507:11
so absurd or vain 1500:19
something made of n. ..1045:19
stake, nothing draw 752: 8
that cannot happen 970:18
there's N. Like It 2292: 6
they do n. laboriously ..953:15
they that have n. 1414: 5
they that n. know 959: 4
to do but work 1414: 9
to do n. at all 955: 5
to do n. in every power ..953: 1
to have n. is not poverty 1566: 2
to look backward to 612:10
to say n., to do n. 1414:12
to say, say n. 1824: 1
to the purpose 99:16
to wear 487: 4
to what I could say 1897:10
to write about 1102: 9
turns to a wild of n. 1415: 2
under heaven so blue ...2031:12
undertaketh, n. achieveth ..176:17
ventures 176:17
was born, n. will die 232:13
when n. in, n. can come out 1414: 5
when you are used to it ..355:10
where n. is, n. can come 1414: 8
which we don't invite 1710: 5
who does n. with better grace 819:12
who have n. little to fear 1567:11
will come of n. 1414:10
without leave of God 787: 1
Nothingness 1414
hell better 890:11
in sleep's n. relief 1844:13
my n., my wants 1588: 8
on one who loves nothing 1318:14
whole substantial thing ..1387:11

O

Opinion, *continued*
public o. vulgar tyrant 1429:14
puffs up fools 1427:18
queen of the world 1428: 7
reacts on utterer 1426:18
rules the world 1428: 3
says hot and cold 1426:16
sole o. having none 1426:15
stifling o. an evil 1427:11
think last o. right 1427:14
this is my o. 1426:19
to err in o. is human 577: 1
too great o. of ability 533:13
unjust than public o. 1429:14
vain O. all doth sway 2239:11
weigh not self in own o. 1788: 4
weigh o. against Providence 1646:11
which on crutches walks 1429: 2
world's master 1428: 5
Opinion: bonne o. que l'homme a de soy 1426: 5
plus d'esprit que Napoléon 1429:19
reine du monde 1428: 7
Opinone: omnia ex o. 1426: 8
quam re laboramus 2045:12
Opinionem: nimiam o. ingenii 533:13
præstat nullam diis o. 796: 8
Opinions: adopts o. of others 1429: 4
always wish to punish o. 1683:19
do not differ as supposed 1429: 1
effervescing o. 1426:22
establish our o. 97: 5
give o. name of Conscience 1428:11
halt between two o. 1427: 4
hold such absolute o. 1428:12
I have bought golden o. 1427:16
in love with their own o. 1428:11
in o. look not back 305: 2
men never so good as o. 1427: 7
never retract their o. 1428:14
never two o. alike 1427:23
new o. always suspected 1427: 6
popular o. often true 1429:17
stiff in o., always wrong 1428:10
they would die for 1689:14
tormented by o. 1427:12
we inherit our o. 1428:22
worth more than arguments 1426:21
Opis: maxime o. indigeat 893:11
Opium: key of Paradise 1451: 9
of the people 1689:14a
rivals o. and his brides 2019: 7
spares o. or nepenthe 1385:14
succor spirits by o. 106:15
Oportet: quod o. non pudebit 2191:16
Opportunitas non potuit 1431: 2
Opportunities lost never regained 1433: 6
seldom labelled 1431: 7
small o. beginnings 1430: 8
wise man will make o. 1430: 5
Opportunity 1429
age is o. no less 31: 9
America means o. 53: 3
best captain 1430: 4
danger will wink on o. 363:18
dust of servile o. 1431: 9
fleeting 104: 1
for doing mischief 1430: 3
has hair on her forehead 1432: 3
has power everywhere 1430:20
is a god 1430: 2
is bald behind 1432: 1
is easily lost 1431: 3
is my name 1433: 5
keep thou from O. 1430:14
knocks at ivry man's dure 1431:10
know your o. 1431: 1
makes a thief 1430: 6
man must make o. 1430: 5
man's extremity God's o. 1430:12
neglected o. 1433: 1
observe the o. 1430: 9
of a noble death 375: 2
plays anvil chorus 1431:12
Opportunity, *continued*
snatch o. from the day 1430:16
strong seducer, O. 1429:20
thy guilt is great 1430: 3
time's o. 1459: 5
unfecundated egg 1429:21
want of o. 1430:10
well taken 1431: 8
whoredom's bawd 1429:20
Opposite of best worst 319:15
to every good 585: 2
Opposites cured by o. 1285: 4
Opposition: duty to oppose 1544:19
of the stars 1173:19
rankles into enmity 100: 9
Oppression
See also Tyranny
allow o. share the crime 2063: 8
and sword-law 1955:16
guard enemy from o. 1105: 1
in prison's o. 1587:13
irresponsible power 2064:11
of a minority 1235:13
tall 771: 9
Oppressor: blended lie o. 826:19
every man his own o. 430:16
Opprobria: aliena o. absterrent vitiis 588: 6
fingere sævus 1761:10
pudet hæc o. nobis 993:14
Optibus: non o. mentes 1722:12
Optics seeing objects seen 447: 3
turn o. in upon't 1788: 8
Optimism 1434
best possible world 1435: 2
declaring all is well 1435: 4
digitalis of failure 1435:12
sadly at variance 1436: 5
Optimist and pessimist 1434: 3
says black is white 1434: 7
Optimus modus 1325:15
Optuma: nam o. nulla potest eligi 2182:10
Opum furiosa cupido 1718:16
Opus: crescens pectore fervet o. 2253: 5
divisum sic breve fiet o. 2231: 8
hoc o., hic labor est 1062:14
hoc o., hoc studium 2166:22
magnum in manibus 2256: 4
nec multo o. est nec diu 2104: 7
non o. est magnis 1518:13
propositum perfice o. 2231:15
quod nec Jovis ira, nec ignis abolere 2256: 4
quod non o., asse carum 1604:15
suum ipse implet 796: 5
Or: à la touch l'on epreuve l'or 801:19
donne aux plus laids 802: 8
est une chimère 803:17
même a la laideur 802: 8
tout n'est pas or 87:10
Ora: quæ caret o. cruore nostro 171: 9
Oracle 1436
every man's reason his o. 1677:14
fast by o. of God 1436:13
I am Sir O. 1436:14
Nature's o., first love 1206: 1
no truth in the o. 1436:14
shall contents discover 1436:14
within an empty cask 1436:12
Oracles are dumb 1436:13
God's o. can never lie 965:12
Orange 1437
I get o. after food 1437: 9
squeeze o., throw away rind 1437: 2
where o. blooms, man foe of man 723:16
Orange-tree: if I were yonder o. 1437: 6
song of o. 1437: 4
Orange-trees, fruit and blossoms 1437: 7
Orare: laborare est o. 1063: 2
Orat: qui o. et laborat 1063: 3
Orateurs: ce que manque aux o. 1438:10
Oratio: brevis o. penetrat cælum 1584:14
odiosa est o. 99: 1
regulam non habet 1927: 6
Oratione: quid beneficium esse o. 2228:14
Orationem: ex ore o. eripis 2218:17
Orationis: lepos et festivitas o. 1963:20
Orations: for fear o. should giggle 1439:12
make no long o. 195: 3
Orator 1437
boy o. of the Platte 204: 1
charm us, o. 1439: 4
deep-persuading o. 803: 8
good o. is despised 1438: 2
I'll play the o. 1439: 2
man becomes an o. 1438:16
mouth of a nation 1438:16
no o. as Brutus is 1438:19
no true o. not a hero 1438: 7
persuades and carries all 1437:16
says what he thinks 1437:13
too green 1439: 2
Orator fit poeta nascitur 1532: 8
spernitur o. bonus 1438: 2
Orator's virtue to speak truth 1438:14
Orators: compared o. to winds 1437:11
dumb when beauty pleads 135: 6
loud-bawling o. 1438: 3
shoot blank cartridges 974:10
thence to famous O. repair 1438: 9
what o. lack in depth 1438:10
when out, will spit 1437:18
Oratory 1439
first part of o. 1439:10
mild heat of holy o. 1440: 9
object of o. persuasion 1440: 3
power of beating down arguments 1439:16
Orb of her fate 555: 2
of one particular tear 1977:18
quail and shake the o. 237: 7
that mighty o. of song 1306: 4
within orb 600: 6
Orbe: nihil est toto 231:14
quicquid in o. fuit 140: 4
Orbis: rebus cunctis o. 1083:15
si fractus inlabatur o. 325: 1
unus Pellæo non sufficit o. 46: 4
Orbit of the restless soul 1172: 3
roll lucid o. 599: 8
Orbity: most dreaded 252:12
Orbs: all these shining o. 1913: 2
empty their o. 1916:14
folded o. would open 1220:14
nor to their idle o. doth sight appear 170: 9
these spacious o. 1912:15
what are ye o. 1912: 8
Orchard flings an apple 92: 8
good is an O. 2211: 4
Orchestration of platitudes 1166:12
Orcum: apud O. te videbo 885:14
Orcus: bottomless pits of O. 1888: 8
Ordainer: faith in an O. 1693:10
Order 1440
and beauty of the universe 795: 4
arrived in alphabetic o. 1073: 7
beauty from o. springs 129: 5
breeds habit 1440:10
foundation of all 1440:13
from disorder sprung 1440:17
gave each thing view 1441: 1
Heaven's first law 1440:18
in graceful o. 1507: 1
in variety we see 1440:18
is a lovely thing 1440:12
is heavenly 1441: 6
man's greatest need 1440:11
matter better in France 720: 4
means light and peace 1440:11
of the day 1792:1a
old o. changeth 232:14
reigns in Warsaw 1440:19
stand not upon o. of going 863: 6
teach the act of o. 142:15

Owl, *continued*
thought own birds fairest 1442: 1
virtuous o. 1442: 9
wailing o. screams solitary 1442: 3
was a baker's daughter 1442: 7
white o. in belfry sits 1442:11
wise old o. lived in an oak 1825: 4
Owlet's 'larum chilled 324:18
Owls: drunk as o. 501:13
fashionable o. 1442:12
in St. Peter's choir 1169: 7
make o. pass for eagles 1505:14
no o. in whole island 1797:15
only look wise 1970:19
to Athens 283: 7
Own: came unto his o. 591:12
my o. shall come to me 1797: 1
Owner bring honor to house 935: 4
not o. of morrow 1140: 4
Ox 1442
as ox to slaughter 1443: 2
black ox had not trod 1442:15
black ox hath trod on her toe 2261:12
fat ox desires trappings 453: 9
has spoken 1443: 5
is taken by horns 1442:14
knoweth his owner 1442:17
look'd to fell an ox 210: 9
old ox straightest furrow 1442:16
stalled ox and hatred 449:15
take heed of ox before 1650:11
that treadeth out corn 1442:13
where shall ox go 1442:16
whose ox is gored 1644:16
Oxen come to the plough 1442:19
let strong o. plough 639:14
ten teams of o. draw less 135:13
that rattle the yoke 1443: 3
who drives fat o. 725: 5
years like great black o. 2261:12
Oxford of whom the poet said 224:17
to O. sent horse 2069:12
Oxygen: indebtedness to o. 535: 7
Oyster 1443
as an apple doth an o. 1155: 2
bold man first eat o. 1443:14
from granite to o. 586: 3
is a gentle thing 1444: 2
made an uncommon fine o. 1443:13
may be cross'd in love 1443:17
months with letter R 1443: 8
on desert shore 1443: 7
open o. without knife 1092: 5
sick o. possesses pearl 1443:16
too-long opened o. 604: 9
transform me to an o. 1443:15
'twas a fat o. 1092: 5
two travellers found an O. 1092: 5
world's mine o. 2238:18
wounded o. 650:15
Oyster-knife that hacks 1758: 4
Oyster-women lock'd their fish up 1683: 3
Oysters are a cruel meat 1444: 3
are amatory food 524:13
eaten without grace 1444: 3
four young o. hurried up 1443: 9
had often eaten o. 1444: 1
no end to eating o. 1444: 1
Ozymandias, king of kings 1421: 7

P

P: going to pronounce P. 1653: 1
P's: mind your P's and Q's 1637: 5
Pabulo: animal p. lætum 519:20
Pabulum Acheruntis 376: 8
studii doctrinæ 1096: 3
Pace: middling p. I own 1328:17
silent and dejected p. 1344: 9
you are driving 931:11
Pace: e venni dal martirio 1280: 2
in p. aptarit bello 1599: 2
prospicere in p. 1598:13
Pacem: disice compositam p. 1474:14
exarsi in p. tuum 1474:18
iniquissimam p. 2118: 8
miseram p. vel bello bene 1474:14
Pacem, *continued*
qui desiderat p. 1599: 2
seu p. seu bella geram 2046:20
te poscimus 2119:13
Paces: two p. room enough 50: 1
Paces: con quien p. 515:14
Paciencia y barajar 1460:16
Pacientes vincunt 1462: 8
Pacifism: only one vice 2107: 1
Pacifists in pleasure 1474:13
Pacings: long, mechanic p. 1146: 7
Pacis: patimur longæ p. mala 1474: 4
Pack and label men for God 1452: 3
horse thinks own p. heaviest 204: 6
pour out p. of matter 1399: 6
when it begins to rain 1794: 5
Pack-horse: sin's p. 2012:15
Pack-thread not embroidery 340:12
Pact of Paris 1473:15
Pactum non pactum est 125: 9
Padd in the straw 1798: 7
Paddle your own canoe 973: 9
Padlock: clap your p. on her mind 2194: 3
Padlocks on Truth's lips 2053: 5
Pady, James: epitaph 572: 5
Paese: non esce dal p., pieno pregiudizi 2030: 4
Pæte, non dolet 1933: 9
Pagan: primitive P. 538: 9
suckled in creed outworn 267: 7
Pagan's homage to sun 335: 5
Paganini comb 1369: 7
Pagans: to chase these p. 264: 5
Page: beautiful quarto p. 190: 4
blotted from life's p. 33: 1
come hither, my little p. 1775: 3
every p. an ample marge 190: 4
preserving thy invaluable 190: 5
spangle life's p. 2008: 8
sporting p. 1676:14
to serve his witt 1808:11
Pageant: insubstantial p. faded 2095:12
of a day 1609: 4
of passing days 683: 5
of the skies 1835: 7
Pageantry of a king 53: 9
Pages: from Nature's golden p. 1386:11
of God's book 362:16
Pagina: dicit tibi tua p. "Fur es" 1505:14
Pagoda: by old Moulmein P. 1212: 6
Paid: he was p. for it 1524: 1
him very large 200: 6
in her own coin 1469: 8
in our own coin 1710:13
more p. than she'll demand 419: 6
the uttermost farthing 1469:15
well p. that is well satisfied 1469:18
Pail: full dinner p. 1558: 4
Pain 1444
a little p. little pleasure 1138: 1
Alpine summits of great p. 1001: 7
and grief to me 1821: 6
and pleasure at strife 1196:14
aromatic p. 1746: 8
at her side 870: 6
between p. and Paradise 1445: 2
burden'd with p. 17:10
by which purchased heaven 1280:17
change place but keep p. 231: 4
cruel to prolong a p. 1019: 4
every p., but not heart p. 1445: 6
fierce, unutterable p. 1697:11
for every p. a plaster 1186:14
forces innocent to lie 1444:16
forgotten where gain comes 1444:18
go in company with p. 1394: 1
greatest evil 322: 7
if severe not prolonged 1445: 3
in elbow short 2135:18
in my heart stirs quiet p. 1201: 4
Pain, *continued*
is hard to bear 1444:14
is no evil 1444:12
is not fruit of p. 1444: 5
is perfect misery 1444:13
is pleasure if p. be love 1196:16
is price on all things 1444:10
is superficial 1280: 5
joy three-parts p. 15:19
least p. in little finger 1793: 4
lessen'd by another's 843: 9
light if long 291: 6
lives there who loves p. 893: 1
love's very p. is sweet 1197: 1
mighty p. to love it is 1195:18
mosaics of p. 40:18
narrows not his cares 2010: 5
no fiery, throbbing p. 393:13
no gain without p. 750:13
no p. death does not end 2011: 4
no p., no palm 267:14
not p. when past 1444:14
nought said of years of p. 996: 2
of a little censure 339:12
of a new idea 950:12
of death would hourly die 1143:11
of finite hearts 1455:16
of mind worse than p. of body 1314: 2
of truth 2055:10
only folks who give us p. 1445:13
Our Lady of P. 1416:13; 2094:11
over p. to victory 1405: 1
past p. is pleasure 1445:22
pity-wanting p. 842:16
Prison House of P. 1444: 7
prunes my twigs with p. 1445: 1
purchase p. with joy 1131:12
rusts into beauty too 1444: 6
shall reach innocent heart 392: 1
superflux of p. 346:13
that monster callèd P. 1445: 7
the bliss of dying 1893: 9
thorny bed of p. 460: 7
those who do not feel p. 1444:11
till thought grew p. 4: 2
touches not a corpse 389:15
turns with ceaseless p. 3: 3
unjustly suffered p. 987:13
unnumbered hours of p. 290:14
unusual p. 1364: 9
us least when keen 2172: 1
vindictive P. 1511: 6
way to rest is p. 1734:15
weighs heavily 618:15
what p. it was to drown 1816: 5
when p. can't bless 1445:14
when p. ends, gain ends 1444:18
with the thousand teeth 1445:11
without peace of death 2:16
Pain manque 197: 5
Painch: pit their p. in 1569: 7
Paine, Thomas 1446
Pains: all p. are nothing 1885:13
and penalties of idleness 956:13
by their p. and aches find 1445: 6
double p., double praise 1445: 8
feels nor fears ideal p. 1462: 2
for their sweat 1062:20
how we lose our p. 1445: 4
if p. be a pleasure 1445:23
little p. yield profits 750:13
long p. light ones 291: 6
men come to greater p. 836: 9
mitigates his p. 1275: 1
no p., no gains 1444:17
of body 1570: 8
of love be sweeter far 1196: 5
of power are real 1574: 3
taking p. 340: 4
wages of ill pleasures 1445:25
when p. grow sharp 29:19
with p. come into world 407: 8
Paint character and spirit 103:20
fresh as p. 1633:14
gates of hell 949:12
ground them all into p. 1508: 5
he best can p. them 2176:15
he fain would p. 453: 6
let her p. an inch thick 382: 6

Paint, *continued*
like nature 105:12
me as I am 1447:10
my picture truly 1447:10
pot of p. in public's face 1449: 4
skin but not bones 2002:1a
such a sin to p. 610:10
the devil foul 444: 3
truest praise most 1447: 7
what men p. themselves ..947:16
Paint-brush: first part ...1446:17
Painted as it may hit 1448:14
in water colours 573:15
let me be vilely p. 1264: 2
to the eyes 610: 6
wrought he not well that p. 1448:12
you both p. be 610: 7
Painter: but a landscape p. 1448: 2
figure p. loves beauty 107:13
is hinted and hidden 107:10
landscape p. loves hills 107:13
life among pictures no p. 1447: 6
love of gain never made p. 1447: 8
Nature's sternest p. 1525: 1
no handless p. 107:19
we praise the p. now 610: 8
without colors 106: 6
would surpass the life 105:10
Painters and poets have leave to lie 1449: 6
and poets have licence ...1527:11
Painting 1446
almost the natural man ..1448:12
amateur p. innocent mind 1448: 1
and sculpture but images ..96: 4
between thought and thing 1446:17
good p. like good cooking 1447: 5
more than p. can express .140: 8
mountains in a mist 113:11
not life 103:16
nothing but noble language 1447: 2
on p. and fighting look afar 1447:11
pretty mocking of life 1447: 3
resource of misanthropy .1449: 1
silent poetry 1447: 3
then I stopped my p. 1860:11
two styles of portrait p. ..1448:15
Paintings: allegorical p. ..1449: 3
Paints best who feels most 1447: 7
she that p. is a whore 2133:18
the creak and strain 103:15
white and red the moors 1385:14
Pair: blest p. happiest ...1274:16
gay, guiltless p. 162:10
kindest and happiest p. ..1275:12
of stairs to marriage 1205:13
youthful, loving, modest p. 1192: 6
Pairing: vicious practice 1542:13
Paix à tout prix 1471: 6
Palace and prison on each hand 2076:18
be thine own p. 909:12
built upon the sand 635: 1
cannot make cheap p. ...1605: 1
dwell in such a p. 87: 2
fair and stately p. 96: 8
keeps p. of soul serene ..1968:14
King Bradmond's p. 97: 3
Mab's ethereal p. 282: 2
name was Beautiful 130: 5
of Eternity 110: 6
of learning 976: 4
of the soul 1834: 7
pine in a p. alone 1208: 8
radiant p. rear'd head 96: 8
such a gorgeous p. 87: 2
where luxury dwells 712: 1
windowless p. of rest 1869: 5
Palaces are crumbling to the shore 2076:18
in Kingdom come 251:12
in such green p. first kings 2211: 5
'mid pleasures and p. 906: 7
those golden p. 2095:12
Palam mutire plebeio 1480: 2
Palate: reason for living ..517: 6
that needs will taste 90:11
Palates both for sweet and sour 2144:17
we our p. urge 89:19
Palato: in solo vivendi causa p. est 517: 6
Pale and pettish 237:11
as his shirt 657:18
for weariness 1344: 7
in her fading bowers 1936:13
why so p. and wan 1204: 1
Paleozoic bigot 1552: 2
time 586:16
Paley: simile of watch 788: 5
Palfreys black as jet 167: 3
Palindromes 1411: 7
Palinodiam canere 1637:19
Pall Mall: sweet shady side of P. M. 1168: 8
Pallas, take away thine Owl 702: 2
Pallets: upon uneasy p. 1848: 2
Palliation of a sin 1829:12
Pallor, squalor, hunger ..1924: 9
that lovers ever prize 1222:11
Palm 1449
bear the p. 1449:10
expect the p. prize of victory 1449:10
in Athens again 1449:10
is a gift divine 1449:13
itching p. 200: 2
like some tall p. 96: 3
sweating p. 850:17
to win the p. 49:10
Palm-leaf: human p. 851: 4
Palm-tree standeth so tall 1449: 8
Palm-trees, with branches fair 1449:11
Palma non sine pulvere ..1715: 3
Palmæ: meritæque expectent præmia p. 1449:10
Palmam qui meruit, ferat 1449:10
Palmas: dum numerat 920:13
Palmistry: in p. he deals .1624:11
Palms before my feet 111: 9
callous p. of laborer 1066: 4
fold thy p. 394: 6
fronded p. in air 791: 4
of Paradise 395:15
Palpable and familiar 368: 9
Palsy and not fear 323: 6
may God p. 353:12
you have the p. 953: 8
Palter with us in a double sense 1621: 5
Palumbes; congessere 776:11
Palumbi inguina tardent ...524:14
Pan 1449
best of leaders, P. 1450: 2
great P. is dead 1449:14; 1450: 3
half a beast is the great god P. 1536:11
in Wall Street 1397:10
laughed the great god P. 1365: 1
of the garden 1449:14
this Concord P. 1987:18
to Moses lends Pagan horn 1741: 1
Pan: buscar P. de trastigo .197: 8
comido y la compania deshecha 197: 9
con su P. se la come 197:11
Pan-Germanism 768: 6
Pancake: flat as a p. 1633:10
Pandars: brokers-between 2105:13
Pandion is dead 739:22
Pandolf's: Fra P. hands ..1448:11
Pandora: more lovely than P. 489:16
Pane: sale lo p. altrui 595: 2
Panegyrics here provide ..678: 2
mingled with poppy 678:15
Panem et circenses 197:19
ostentat altera 198: 5
quæramus arato 637: 5
Panes of quaint device 2154: 5
Pang as great as when a giant dies 388:13
is in parting 366:16
my bosom dare not 708: 2
of bitter self-reproach ..1855:13
of despised love 1195: 9
of hope deferr'd 922:15
preceding death 923:10
quick-returning p. 1699:12
there is no future p. 1697: 2
Pangs arthritic 460:10
cannot hold out these p. 28:10
in love as shells 1195: 5
in sweet p. of it remember 1215: 2
inward p. of secret woe ..2273: 3
of deep regret 2288: 1
of despised love 1934: 9
of poetic birth 1531:13
of soul 1570: 8
Panic: blind p. 364: 4
fear 655: 3
what p. in thy breastie ..1357: 9
Panis: frusto p. conduci potest 199:10
Panjandrum: grand P. ...1409:12
Pannus: tenuis pravia p. habet 1572: 8
Panochœa: heavenly P. ..2222: 3
Panorama of a year 2261: 2
Pansies: beauteous p. rise 1450:11
for ladies all 1450: 5
I send thee p. 1450:10
that's for thoughts 687: 3
Pansy 1450
brings thoughts 1450: 4
for lover's thoughts 1450: 6
freakt with jet 684:13
Pantaloon: slipper'd p. 2240: 5
Pantaloons and Antics 2235: 8
Panting: for ever p. 1192: 9
Pantisocracy he cried 2034:10
Pantler, not so eminent ..1840: 7
Pants: grandpa's p. 1557:12
leave p. to men 2145: 8
neither vest nor p. 1705:21
who p. for glory 781:20
with all it granted 880:12
word for "gents" 490: 7
Papa: another p. on the Salt Lake Line 2293: 4
his dear p. is poor 255: 6
mama, kiss and be friends 2294: 8
potatoes, poultry 1652:20
Papa: dove è il P., ivi è Roma 1741: 6
Papa's having not like having one's self 1562:10a
Papacy ghost of Roman Empire 1740: 9
Paper appears dull 1925:15
government 817: 1
kept from p., pen, and ink 2253: 9
learn anything from a penny p. 1602:14
order p. punctually served 1602: 5
reading the morning p. ..1603:10
scrap of p. 767: 7
spare p. doomed to perish 2255: 9
to write whore upon 2134: 2
Paper-blurrers: company of 2258: 8
Paper-credit: blest p. 333:20
Paper-mill: built a p. 1613: 3
Papers: let them read the p. 1603: 4
wrote for certain p. 1604: 7
Papilia, wedded 2198: 6
Papillæ of a man 216: 5
Pappy out of cherry-bruises 116:16
Parables are not lies 1112: 4
in which lay hid gold 1926:11
Parade: make ostentatious p. 2194: 1
of pain 1445: 9
sic p., sic pomp an' art ..1016:14
Paradise 1451
Adam had p. at will 11:15
blooms nowhere but in P. 1975:19
blundered into P. 1452: 3
break oath to win p. 1419: 3
charming climate in P. ..1451:21
curiosity lost P. 351:10
descent into P. 50: 3
did the p., persuaded 1221:12
drives from some P. 1451:10
earthly P. as this 1451:18
ev'n in P. unbless'd 11: 8
fool's p. ....703:12, *et seq.*
for a sect 633:14
for p. break faith, troth ..1205: 2
gate of P. 1451:18
hath room for you and me 1451:20

Paradise, *continued*
heavenly p. is that place ..608: 3
hence the fool's p. 2095: 8
how grows in P. our store 403: 6
how has she cheapen'd P. 2188: 8
I was taught in P. 1451:12
in some canine P. 472:14
inhabited with devils 1002: 2
knew the seat of P. 12: 6
lighten earth from P. 395:16
lives retired still in P. ..1451: 2
long-tailed birds of P. 1551: 7
made her man p. forego 2196: 9
make earthly p. 1493: 9
must I leave thee, P. 1451:14
'neath the palms of P. 395:15
no P. on earth so fair ..844: 3
not in mine eyes alone is P. 1451: 5
of fools ....703:13, *et seq.*
of the four seas 549:14
of women 549: 1
one little glimpse of P. ..1451: 3
paint Hell with P. 949:12
plant a tub and call it P. 1398: 2
purple hills of P. 1451:19
quire of blest Souls 1451:11
right key to P. 1451: 9
steer to P. 2235: 9
stood formed in her eye ..599:19
to him are opening p. 460: 7
to P., the Arabs say 1476: 7
to what we fear of death ..386:14
under wall of P. 1451:19
unto you is P. opened 1451: 7
what was p. is now a broken home 2287: 2
who doth not crave for rest 1451: 8
with P. devise Snake 709:16
you were in P. the while .1852: 8
Paradises: two P. 'twere 1871:17
Paradox comforts while it mocks 1931:16
how strange a p. is true ..1522: 6
in pride 1608:23
too strict 426:17
Paradoxes make fools laugh 1010:14
useful 566: 7
Paragon: an earthly p. 77: 8
of animals 1239: 5
of her sex seeming p. ..2185: 7
Paragons description 1234: 8
Paragraphs of praise 1578: 6
Parallax: star that has no p. 1542: 5
Parallel: admits no p. 1484:16
none but itself 1484:16
perfect past all p. 1484:16
Parallels in beauty's brow 2014: 7
Paralytic: crawls a p. 628:11
Paramours: to call forth p. 1908: 5
Paranoia of millionaire ..1084: 9
Parapet: dare not peep over p. 1980:13
Parasite 145:17
Parasites or sub-p. 1382:16
smooth, detested p. 2035: 4
Paratus fuit quadrantem ...119: 6
Parchment: no virtue in p. or wax 1080:14
put your p. in the closet ..1525: 8
should undo a man 1080:14
Pardon
See also Forgiveness
all but thyself 710: 5
as God shall p. me 710: 8
for p. cry, held sinner ..1829: 5
God p. all good men 709: 9
God's best attribute 790: 2
if life were bitter, p. 395:16
know all and p. all 710:11
like a p. after execution ..285: 6
ne'er p. who have done the wrong 986:17
no sin, no p. 1829:13
nobler to p. than condemn 709:11
not p. but applause 340:10
ready to p. mankind 234:14
still the nurse of second woe 1298:17
the fault 649:21
the word for all 710: 8
Pardon, *continued*
to understand is to p. 710:11
Pardoned and retain offence 710: 9
Pardonne: qui p. aisément 709:12
tant que l'aime 709:20
Pardonner ses ennemis les vertus 710:16
Pardonnons ceux qui nous ennuient 192: 9
Pardons as one loves 709:20
Pare: cum p. contendere, anceps est 99: 5
Parean l'occhiaje anella ..604:10
Paree: after they've seen P. 2284: 2
Parem: quæris Alcides p. 1485:12
quando inveniet p. 1252: 8
Parens: magna p. frugum 1001:13
patriæ 647: 6
rerum 226: 6
Parent: everything dear to p. 1452:13
of good 796: 2
of his country 647: 6
of manners 1689: 1
of the universe 226: 6
one p. from the sky 1351: 4
privilege of a p. 1452:10
Parentes: diligere p. prima lex 1452: 4
stulti 1097:19
Parents 257, 1452
child owes p. no gratitude 1452: 8
conduct toward p. 1452: 7
few p. act in such manner 1452:10
happy the p. of so fair a child 247:16
have the most reverence 1452: 8
if p. want honest children 1452:10
reverence for p. 1452: 4
taught to read and write 1097:19
the Lord knows who 71: 3
to watch over me 257:14
Pares cum paribus 289: 1
Paresse: demeurons plus aisément 953: 2
plus de p. dans l'esprit ..953: 2
Pari: omnes sorte nascimur 574: 7
par p. jugator conjunx ..1267:12
par p. respondet 1712: 7
Parietes: utrosque p. linunt 946: 7
Parings of one's nail 1946:10
Paris 1452
an immense hospitality ..1453: 7
as far as P. for fashion ..641:11
at P. it was 1453: 2
café of Europe 1453: 7
city where great ideas perish 43: 1
common shore of P. 1169:10
derisive of absurd pretensions 1453: 4
fair fantastic P. 1453: 1
from P. to Peru 1423:11
good Americans go to P. 1452:14
half Angel, half grisette .1168: 4
in P. queer little man ..1302: 2
insist on seeing P. 2138: 4
is worth a Mass 1453: 6
perfumed 178: 3
plainest city in Europe ..1453: 8
slept on 888:18
unites utile and dulce 1453: 3
what's P. but a circus ..1453: 7
who have not been to P. —go 1453:12
with wanton P. sleeps 889: 5
woman's paradise 1453:11
Paris: tout P. va voir 1453: 9
vaut bien une Messe 1453: 6
Parisienne 721: 1
Park 1453
how charming is a p. 2198: 6
Neptune's p. ribbed 549:16
proud p. takes dwellings ..1453:16
sovereign for a cold 460:15
Parks be lungs of London 1453:17
Parla troppo non parlar bene 1964:11
Parle peu quand la vanité ne fait pas parler 1899: 4
qui p. beaucoup 1964: 8
Parlent toujours d'eux-mêmes 1177:16
Parler aux yeux 2259: 4
difficile de bien p. 1899: 4
pour tromper 421:12
Parley of provocation 600: 3
Parlez tout comme un livre 1963: 4
Parliament meeting of idle 816:16
of man 1473: 9
Parlor: prison'd in a p. ..2030: 2
walk into my p. 1903:10
Parmenio: if I were P. 45:17
Parnasse est desuni 289:15
Parnassus: climb P. by dint o' Greek 528:18
Oh, thou P. 1355:10
one top sacred to Bacchus 497: 4
only one peak sacred to Apollo 497: 4
placard To Let 1530:10
Parochial: worse than provincial, p. 1988: 4
Parody of an angel 77:12
profane p. of Old Testament 1925:19
Parole: art de peindre la p. 2259: 4
pour déguiser la pensée ..1902: 4
pour exprimer sa pensée ..1901:15
son femmine 2227:13
Paroles: dit beaucoup en peu de p. 1069: 4
en peu de p. beaucoup ..2225:16
Paroquet repeats one note 2261: 2
Parritch: halesome p. 1768: 7
Parrot: drunk, speak p. 504:11
Pars: quorum p. magna fui 1321: 6
ultima pungit 1691:21
Parsimonia: magnum vectigal sit p. 526:10
sera p. in fundo est 527: 2
Parsnips: words butter no 2220:16
Parsimonious: age is p. 34: 1
Parsimony worst profusion 526:17
Parson: in arguing, too, the p. own'd his skill 100: 8
knows enough 1589:13
much bemused in beer ...677:18
never spare 520:12
oh! illustrious spark 1592:16
would like to be Pope ...1593:14
Part: act well your p. 917: 2
but p. we see, not whole 1251:13
few shall p. 2120: 2
great p. of which I was 1321: 6
his blessed p. to heaven ..395:12
I am p. of all you see 1384: 2
I have forgot my p. 10: 3
my soul's far better p. ..2137:18
no more in the wind 1772:13
of all that I have met ...592:15
play the maid's p. 2202:15
put beside his p. 10: 3
since well I've play'd p. .1124:17
so he plays his p. 2240: 5
take your own p. 1787:17
'tis hard to p. 1146:16
to p. is to die a little 1454: 9
to tear a cat in 10: 9
we only p. to meet again 1290: 1
we p. with pain 1455: 5
we play 1125: 8
Partaker as bad as thief ..1835:14
earth make us p. 1057:10
Parte tamen meliore 966:15
Parted: he p. well 397:12
in silence and tears 1454: 4
Parthenon: earth wears P. ..95:14
Parthians: more lying than 1109:16
Partial for observer's sake 1423:16
voice of fame p. 625: 1
Particulas ac lanciamus ..1129: 6
Parties die of own lies ..1543:12
High Contracting P. 1473:15
I name no p. 1372: 4
names of p. cease 1544: 4
two great p. 1544: 5
two p., want and have ..1571: 5
Parting 1453
all we know of heaven ..1454: 7
image of death 1454: 9

Peace, *continued*
at-almost-any-price 1471: 6
at any price ..1471: 6; 1557: 5
at what cost p. of globe 1598: 3
be p. on earth 270:13
be to my sable shroud 391:15
be to this house 1471: 7
be to you 1475: 4
be within thy walls 1471: 7
begins where ambition ends 1475:13
between two spirits 739: 3
bleeds and hope expires ..513: 3
can we dig p. from mine 2167:13
cannot be kept by force ..1472: 9
carry gentle p. 150: 5
celestial p. in her look ..2184: 5
churchyard's p. 829: 8
courts his hand 1471: 4
dear nurse of arts 1470: 9
depart in p. 65:1; 394: 1
desire of life, P. 435:11
disadvantageous p. 2118: 8
disarmed p. is weak 1598: 5
duty and the prize 1470: 7
ef you want p., fight 1598: 9
enjoyed p. valor won 51: 6
every gale is p. 1387: 1
every man endeavor p. ..2118:11
fight for p. 1598: 2
for p. do not hope 1474: 9
forever hold his p. 1823: 9
from martyrdom unto this p. 1280: 2
get p. in heaven 1470:10
getter of bastard children 2119: 7
gives tranquillity 1471:16
go in p. 1470:14
God gave her p. 2082:14
God, give us p. 1598: 9
good will toward men 793: 9
grave's most holy p. 969: 7
guide feet into way of p. 1152: 8
happy shade, be thine ..1471: 7
hath balsamed Pain 1171: 6
hath her victories 2118: 7
hath higher tests of manhood 2118: 7
healing and elevating 1470:12
hold my little p. 1475: 6
hold your p. 1822:11
I am for p. 2119: 6
I labour for p. 2119: 6
if there's p. to be found 1475: 7
in Europe 1472: 7
in Freedom's hallowed shade 2065: 1
in love's unselfishness ..2186: 5
in our minds 723: 8
in p. provides 'gainst war 1599: 2
in p. sons bury fathers ..2118: 9
in p. there's nothing 2116:10
in time of p. prepare for war 1599: 2
in time of p. thinks of war 1597:19
inglorious arts of p. 344: 8
invincible in p. 2119: 3
is all thy own 873: 5
is always beautiful 1471:15
is beauty in action 1027: 7
is becoming to men 1471:10
is better than war 2118: 9
is it p. or war 1474:15
is liberty in tranquillity .1470: 6
is poor reading 1474: 2
is what I seek 1474:17
keeps all nature's p. 447: 2
lay me down in p., and sleep 1847: 9
let us have p. 821:2; 1471: 1
like quiet night 1475: 8
love p. as means to war 2119: 2
made p. with no less honour 1472: 4
maintained with honour ..1472: 3
make desert, call it p. 1470:13
make p. sword in hand ..1598: 4
maker of cuckolds 2119: 7
makes plenty, plenty makes pride 2119: 7

Peace, *continued*
more destructive 1471: 6
must be on earth 1470:10
name of chamber was P. 1475: 2
nature of a conquest 1470:11
no p. unto the wicked ..2134:14
no p. within himself 1475: 5
not hard for old to keep p. ..35:16
not thus doth P. return 1472: 5
nothing bring p. but yourself 1474:18
nothing but to rust iron ..2119: 7
nurse of Ceres 1470: 9
nurse of drones 1474: 6
of Allah abide with you ..1588:14
of God which passeth ..1475: 4
of great books 188:10
of mind 723: 8
of my conscience 168: 3
offspring is of power 1599: 1
oh, that p. may come 417:11
on earth, good will 270: 6
on earth p., good will 793: 9
only a breathing-time 2106:11
only just enjoys p. 1028:11
over all the earth 1473: 5
pain without p. of death 2:16
passeth human knowing ..514:13
passing all understanding 264: 8
patched-up p. 1474:14
pipe on pastoral hillock 1471:14
poison of premature p. ..1474:16
prate of blessings of p. ..1474:15
prefer most unjust p. ..2118: 8
preferable to civil war ..2114: 1
prize of his toil 344: 5
progress's bitter foe 2119: 7
provide in p. needs of war 1598:13
rest and sleep 392:14
right more precious than p. 54: 7
rules the day 1470:17
seek p. and follow it 1470: 8
shall be in patience 1475:11
should be p. at home 908:12
should not so dull a kingdom 1598:16
smooth-faced p. 1471:13
so by my grave my p. 827:15
soft p. she brings 241:13
sweet p. conduct his soul ..886: 6
thank God for p. 1470:15
that is balm for tears ..2132:15
they are at p. 1869: 5
thrice my p. was slain ..409: 1
to corrupt 1474: 7
to happy Britain brings ..552: 6
to the mighty dead 399: 4
translated into thy p. ..1474:18
universal p. is near 1473: 6
universal P. lie like 1473: 9
until p. the storm 2119:10
uproar the universal p. ..234: 2
victory to both sides 1470:19
war in masquerade 1474: 1
weak piping time of p. ..1474:12
what p. in silence 1825: 8
when for to hold his p. 1824:20
when there is no p. 1471: 3
where p. is perfect 884:12
where there is p. God is ..785: 9
which follows duty 508: 5
which passeth human knowing 514:13
which world cannot give 1474:18
win p. or buy it 1470:10
with dishonor 1472: 6
with honor 1472: 1
with p. and honour 1472: 2
without a worm in it ..1470:18
without victory 1471:17
Peace-maker: if the only p. 1663:15
Peace-makers: blessed are the p. 1471: 8
Peaceably if we can 58: 1
Peaceful penetration 2297: 5
shalt thou end 28:11
Peach 1475
little p. in orchard grew ..1475:15
once a bitter almond 1257:13

Peach, *continued*
peel p. for enemy 1476: 2
ripest p. highest 1476: 3
that such a P. should marry such a prune ..1268: 1
will have wine 1475:16
Peaches brought out of Persia 1476: 1
it's p. and creamy 360: 6
Peacock 1476
feathered like a p. 778:10
in everything but beauty 1476:10
in his pride 1476: 9
sweep along his tail 1476: 8
Peacock's feet 704:18
Peak: hear its p. 1654:17
lofty p. smitten with thunder 836: 8
Peaks: loftiest p. most wrapt in clouds 837: 9
old age's lambent p. 32:10
pearl-white p. uplift 282: 3
Peal on p. 1154: 2
one full p. of praise 1386:12
Pealing: slow and silver p. 1025:10
Peanut: half a salted p. ..1996: 4
Peanuts and cracker-jack 2291:11
Pear basking over the wall 2217: 2
Cath'rine p. 609: 4
Pear-tree: blossomed p. ..1999: 7
Pearl 1476
as p. in foul oyster 915:22
barbaric p. and gold 444:15
black is a p. 166: 1
Christian p. of charity ..242:21
crested Fortune wears 1975:14
devotion's p. might sanctify 1694: 9
disease of oyster 1516:12
dropt from eyelids of morn 1347: 8
enough for a swine 1954:18
fair p. in bosom of sea 1422: 3
for each p. eyes wept 1975: 4
hang p. in cowslip's ear ..446: 1
has p. less whiteness 1476:11
in toad's head 1476:11
not in Indian but Empyrean ocean 859: 9
of great price 1476:14
of soul may be melted 1894: 1
pure as p. 1659:10
rises with his p. 15:10
sow'd earth with orient p. 1347:12
threw a p. away 1476:16
treasure of an oyster 1476:15
waiting one more plunge 1931:14
whose price hath launch'd 889: 5
will always wear 165:14
with p. and ruby glowing 525:13
Pearl-gift thrown to hogs 1459: 5
Pearls at random strung 1520:12
black men p. 1176:10
cast p. before swine ..1476:13
drops p. into the bosom 1669:19
from diamonds dropp'd ..1854: 2
must dive below 575:15
of morning's dew 389: 3
of thought 1520:12
pierced the fair p. 1520:12
some ask'd how p. did grow 2027: 9
string stars for p. 4: 4
which a Peri 1975: 4
ye strowen to hogs 1476:13
Pears: expect p. from elm 746: 9
pear-tree for p. 746: 9
Peas: eat with knife 521: 6
Peasant approaches divinity 638: 6
loves nothing 640:12
may believe as much 638: 6
nourishest man 638:11
poetic and triumphant p. 205:10
sullen payer 640:12
we greet the monarch-p. ..205:16
when the Himalayan p. ..2187:17
Peasant-born: mightiest p. .829: 2
Peasant-Prince 1159: 7
Peasantry their country's pride 638: 5

Pleasant: easy enough to be p. 1854: 3
it is to have money 1334: 8
to play madman 1408:17
to see one's name in print 190:10
too, to think on 2185: 2
Pleasantness: ways of p. ..1471:12
Please against his will 341: 9
at once both p. and preach 1911:13
difficult to p. all 1513:14
everything having eyes ..1233:10
I do not exist to p. you 1513:13
just as he p. 1188: 9
rather p. one good man ..1512:19
rise early to p. everyone 1513: 7
the gentle and the good 191: 9
they p. Him best 1473:14
they who are pleased themselves must always p.1513: 1
to be happy learn to p. ..857:11
to p. many is bad 1513:12
'twas natural to p. 1513: 6
who seeks to p. all men ..1513: 7
with faults 1299:15
Pleased against will 98: 9
by not studying to please 1513: 9
he who is p. with nobody 1318:13
if thou lament 2208:14
makes people p. with him 1513: 1
more had p. 1512:18
to the last 1067:14
too little or too much 596:15
when p. nourished 1510:13
Pleases everyone except self 1512:20
many must have merit ..2252:10
no one thing p. all 1966:12
one against his will 341: 9
Pleasing a man's self 311:13
lascivious p. of a lute 362: 9
live on hope of p. 922: 8
needs only the desire 1513: 1
Pleasure 1508
absence of pain 1508:14
after p. commyth payne .1512: 1
all his p. praise 895: 3
at the helm 2268: 4
attracts each one 1510: 7
bait of sin 1511:12
balanced by pain 1446: 8
bought by pain harmful 1445:25
brief not a true p. 1512:12
brings remorse, sorrow ..1511: 6
but fantastical 1445:17
by p. unseduc'd 1303:12
cannot be trapped 1509:14
carnal p. deadly curse ..1511: 1
carnal p. hinders deliberation 1511: 1
comes, but not to stay ..1512:16
compassed round by p. ..1510:21
crush the lees of p. 1455:12
deferred is keenest 1509:17
departed from ear to eye ..605: 1
drop of p. for sea of woe 2176: 2
drown the brim 1017:15
enslaves the will 1511: 6
even of kings 68: 4
exceeding p. out of pain 1446: 9
fell all present p. 1511: 8
first and kindred good ..1508:14
fly from p. 1509:16
fly p. that bites tomorrow 1511: 8
follow p., p. flees 1509:14
for one p. thousand griefs 1511: 9
for to sit at ease 1780:10
frail like a dewdrop 1512:15
from p. refrain 1509:17
go to your business, p. ..208:11
greatest evil or good 1509: 5
has neighboring disgrace 1511: 4
has sting in its tail 1512: 2
he who must have p. 1514: 1
highest good 322: 7
honour bring but trouble 2239: 8
howe'er disguis'd by art 1510: 3
I have no p. in them ..2266: 4
if p. not followed by pain 1446: 1
if you knew the pensive p. 1819: 1
immense p. to come 1510: 6
imperial p. 1510:22

Pleasure, *continued*
in doing good 2091: 5
in indulging grief 842: 3
in my bath 125:19
in p. bitterness 1511:10
in poetic pains 1537:15
in praise 1577: 9
in the pathless woods 1384: 1
incentive to evil 1511:12
increases with danger ..1618: 3
indeed a pleasant thing ..1509: 9
is a sin, sin's a p. 1511:12
is according to the man ..1508:13
is an inciter to vileness ..1511:12
is in lovers coy 317: 3
is labor too 1511: 6
is man's chief good 1509: 5
is reciprocal 1513: 1
is the aim 1509: 6
is the end and aim of life 1508:14
it is p. to remember 1294: 8
itself cannot spoil 1100: 3
know what p. means 1569: 6
leads and peace attends ..540:11
lies in moderation 1329: 6
life's p. hath he lost 410:10
little p. in the house 3:15
love of p. into pain betrays 1578: 4
loves p., for p. fall 1509:18
make hours seem short ..934: 3
make p. a business 1509:11
may perfect us 1508:11
men of p. have none 1513:16
miss'd her, scandal hit ..1762: 3
mistress of ethereal powers 1510:22
more perfect the thing, the more p. 1445:19
more sharp than pain ...1538: 8
most pointed p. take 858:16
must succeed to p. 1445:15
my lawful p. she restrained 1331:18
my occupation 1509:11
nests upon the ground .1606:14
never is at home 634: 9
never p. without repentance 1512: 1
never to blend our p. 1493: 2
no keener p. than love ..1224: 8
no man regrets p. 1510: 9
no p. in aught eunuck has .2105: 7
no p. in envy and fear ..564:10
no p. in itself evil 1511: 7
no p. like the pain 1196:13
no p. to be awakened 968: 1
no p. unalloyed 1511:11
no profit where no p. 1924: 3
no sterner moralist than p. 1511: 3
not a minute without some p. 1510:18
not even p. to excess good 1511: 5
nothing so hateful as p. ..1511: 1
of being cheated great 249: 8
of fishing them out 728: 3
of having it over 1860:17
of love is in loving 1185: 5
of making new mistress ..1325:14
of the act of love brief .1224: 8
of the fleeting year 4: 7
of the game 754:17
of the greatest number 859: 5
of the pain 1196: 2
oft eludes our grasp 1509:14
on p. bent 526:13
one p. to come 1510: 6
only p. to be displeased ..1513: 5
other p. not worth pains 1196: 1
over, disgrace remains 461:12
pain and p. 1445:15
painful p. to pleasing pain 1446: 7
pay every p. with pain ..1445:24
punish not thyself with p. 1511: 2
relief and reward 1508:12
removal of pain 1445:21
rock people split upon 1511: 4
safe less valued 1510: 1
scraps of p. 1124: 5
seldom found where sought 1509:14

Pleasure, *continued*
seldom give p. when not pleased 1513: 1
shock of p. to frame 2125:18
short p., long lament 1512: 1
siren that lures 1511: 3
slight p. from misery ..1320: 7
soon shall fade 811:10
sov'reign bliss 1508:14
stolen being sweetest ...1618: 2
such as leaves no sting ..1512: 2
such is our good p. 1043:16
sure in being mad 1230:15
sweet is p. after pain 495: 5
sweet p. from other's pain 1446: 4
sweeter as recreation 1509: 4
taking p. in my bath 125:19
tempers the spirit 1510:17
that is born of pain 1446: 3
that most enchants us ..1512:17
that reeling goddess 1511: 6
the alpha and omega 1508:14
the servant 1509: 1
there is in life itself 1143:16
those call it p. 1098: 2
to be deceived 420:14
to frown at p. 1446:12
to save fellow-man 1494: 7
too, to remember 1294: 8
treads paths which reason shuns 1512: 4
turn to p. all they find ..1510:14
under p., pain lies 1445:20
vantage-ground for p. ..1041: 1
virtue's gayer name 1509: 1
was his business 208:11
we may well spare 311:16
what p. is Pursuit 1561: 1
which carries no reproach 1057:12
which is akin to pain 1446: 3
who gives p. charitable ..1513:10
wins his heart 2094:14
with pain for leaven 1239:11
without one p. or pain ..1446:10
work thou for p. 106:14
Pleasure's devious way ..1509: 8
smiling train 291:18
Pleasure-house: lordly p. 1510:20
Pleasure-seekers never find 1509:14
Pleasures: all the p. prove 1212:11
are not worth its pains ..1196: 1
are transient 1512:13
banish pain 884:15
devoid of sensual p. 30:11
doubling p., cares dividing 2140:17
earn p. by business 1513:16
ever in hands or eyes ..1510: 2
first our p. die 377:16
forbidden p. loved 1617:17
fresh-revolving p. 2076:10
from research and education 527:17
from their misfortunes ..1196: 3
have mutable faces 1512: 5
in unreproved p. free 1317:20
intellectual p. 1127:14
interfering with p. of others 1685: 8
like poppies spread 1512: 6
look on p. as they go 1512:10
make scanty p. less 1704: 2
mid p. and palaces 906: 7
more delight when shared 286:18
nor do I call p. idleness 1508:12
not protracted 1942:18
of a gentleman 1513:16
of a parent 1452: 6
of a rational being 1508:12
of all the spheres 887: 2
of beautiful form 1509: 2
of man of fashion 1508:12
of rich bought with tears of poor 1571:10
of taste 1509: 2
of the Mahometans 662: 7
of the present day 1132:10
of the table 1513:16
of youth 22:12; 34:15
of youth are flowers 1132:11
only three p. in life 1509: 3

Pomp, *continued*
painted p. 2211: 2
take physic p. 594: 6
their golden p. 668: 8
this midnight p. 1402: 7
vain p. and glory of world 2242:10
what is p., rule, reign 382: 7
wisdom's sullen p. 2167:18
Pompadour, Madame de ..719: 4
Pompe des enterrements ...746:16
Pompeia: he took to wife P. .213: 2
Pomps and vanity of world 2075:14
Pond before full to brim 1329:10
mantle like a standing p. ..294:18
Poniards: she speaks p. ..1898: 1
Pons asinorum 113: 2
Pont d'argent à vos ennemis 545: 1
Pontem: inter p. et fontem 788: 9
Pontic: like to P. sea 1713:19
Pontifex: chief builder ..1740:12
either P. Maximus or an exile 213: 1
Pontificem: nisi p. 213: 1
non reversurum 213: 1
Pontiffs: line of supeme P. 1740:13
Pontus: nihil est nisi p. et aër 1776: 1
Pooh-Bah paid for services 1750:14
Pooh-pooh this plan 2227:16
Poodle: the king's p. 356:15
Pool: crystalline p. 112:18
sour and turbid 723: 8
Pools of art and memory ..25:18
Poop was beaten gold 1814: 7
Poor always with you 1567: 5
and content is rich 1573: 4
and independent impossible 1569:16
and liberal 772: 5
and proud 1566:21
are ox-like 1570: 3
arise to serve Mammon ..1566:24
as church mice 1566: 9
as Job 1014: 3
as Job's turkey 1014: 5
at heart all your life ..1568:16
be not p., but break it 1573: 4
because numerous 1065:12
become purse-proud 1571: 7
blessed be ye p. 1568: 8
blind man is a p. man 170:12
brother hateth thee if p. 1569: 3
but honest 1566:19
can sleep with windows shut 1573: 6
change nothing but masters 1570: 9
Constance: they said, poor C. 978: 6
days of the p. are evil ..1568:16
destruction of the p. 1570:11
distinguish by virtues ..1572: 1
do anything for the p. ..1566:23
enough to be a wit 2174:11
few save p. feel for p. ..1566:10
found'st me p. at first ..1523:19
gets just as sick as rich ..1781: 2
God only can make us p. 1571: 4
gods protect the p. 1568: 9
grind the faces of the p. 1566:11
he who bestows upon p. ..1493:13
how apt p. are to be proud 1566:21
how many p. I see 1567: 9
I am even p. in thanks ..824:20
if p., brother hateth 735:16
in abundance 454:14
in gear, rich in love 1193:10
in my own money 418:17
inconvenient to be p. ..1565:12
inur'd to drudgery 1569: 6
is never free 1569:16
is not believed 1570: 6
laughs loudest of all 1495: 6
lay their wrongs away ..1850:10
live independent lives ..1568:13
live miserably every way 1570:10
love country and be p. ..1464:11
make no new friends 1569: 3
makes friends of enemies ..734:19
makes me p. indeed 1701:20
Poor, *continued*
man has no credit 333:11
man is despised 1570: 1
man who craves more, p. 1565: 5
may sing before thieves ..1568: 6
must be wisely visited ...1492:14
must labor while life lasts 1570: 6
must work their passage 1571:16
naked, barelegg'd p. 948: 9
no one so p. as born 1566:18
not p. if love liberty 1106: 1
not p. who has enough ..1566: 1
nothing more luckless 1570: 5
now, always p. 1562:12
one changeless race, the p. 1567: 2
resolve not to be p. 1998: 1
rest I leave to the p. 985:14
sings before the thief ..1568: 6
sold p. for pair of shoes ..2032:9a
that desireth much 1565: 5
that God hates 791: 2
that lack ablution 1567: 9
though p., honest 914:10
'tis infamous to be p. ..1570:15
to be p. never to rise ..1570: 2
unemployed p. 638: 9
unfriended p. 1492:14
virtuous p. not admired 1566:25
what can a p. man do ..1569: 4
who are cheerful 1571: 6
who does not flatter 1571: 6
with nothing but gold ..803:14
work miracles every day 773:16
Poorer and baser you appear 2030: 3
Poorest lived in abundance 1572: 3
Poorhouse is vanishing ..1554: 8
over the hill to the p. ..1566: 6
Poorly—poor man—he liv'd 1903: 2
Poorness of spirit 1903:13
Pop goes the weasel 1333: 7
my inside is going p. 978:10
the question 2212: 6
Pope, Alexander 1558
Pope, The
See also under Rome
condemned the P. 1227:12
drives handsome chariot ..505: 8
fancy I am the P. 962: 1
man may come to be P. ..1740: 5
more than P. of Rome ..959:16
sit in Rome, strive with p. 1738: 5
where P. is, Rome is 1741: 6
who crowned Pepin 1740:13
Popery man or horse 1740: 8
no p. 1740: 8
Popes: when P. damn P. ..1694:12
Popinas: habitare ne inter p. 498:13
Popish tricks 299:11
Poplar: edg'd with p. pale 1356:20
old, looks young 2038:14
tall silver p. 2038:14
Poplar-trees shadows throw 2013: 7
Poppies: drink p. of Cathay 521:15
for the twilight 2102: 2
lays p. on the bruise 1385:14
overcharged with rain 410: 8
pleasures like p. spread ..1512: 6
scatter thy drowsiest p. ..1845:12
showed scarlet coats 1559: 4
Poppy 1559
infusion of p. 678:15
not p., nor mandragora ..1850:19
Poppy-seeds of slumber ...365:12
Populace cannot understand bureaucracy 817:15
love of the p. 1559:15
of Heaven 1912: 9
Popular applause 90:21
Popularité, gloire en gros sous 1560: 3
Popularity 1559
disarms envy 1560: 2
empty and ugly thing ..1560:12
enfeoff'd himself to p. ..1560:11
glory in copper pieces ..1560: 3
in art 106:14
is crime when sought 1560: 1
of a bad man 1560: 7
to some, p. suspicious ..1560: 4
Popularity, *continued*
when Fortune favors, P. bears company 1560: 8
Poplars: gently rock yon p. 2038:14
Population: agricultural p. bravest 637:15
Populi: ad juga cur faciles p. 1481:12
contemnere voces 1479: 8
imperium juxta libertatem 1104: 1
Populo nos damus 1480: 5
numquam volui p. placere 1482:16
quilibet esse potest 1489:10
quis placere p. potest 1482:10
Populus esuriens 940: 5
me sibilat 118:13
vult decipi 420: 7
Porcelain of human clay ..1243:16
Porcum: Epicuri de grege 648: 9
Porcupine: respected, not loved 235:13
Pork: abstain from p. 1954: 9
dreamed of eating p. 1591: 4
raise the price of p. 265:13
Pork-eaters: grow to be p. ..265:13
Porpentine: fretful p. 658: 5
Porphyrogenitus 163:10
Porridge: comfort like cold p. 285: 6
spare breath to cool p. ..1821:16
tell me of mess of p. 1961:13
we have water and p. 518: 1
what p. had John Keats 1559:13
Porro unum est necessarium 2131: 3
Port after stormy seas ..1707:13
any p. in a storm 1920:16
came to p. last Sunday ..120:12
he knows not where 951:20
his was the lofty p. 85: 8
humble p. to imperial Tokay 2156: 3
hymns to conservatism ..1763: 4
I've found the p. 569: 4
in p. and speech Olympian 2129: 9
more p. than portable ..2154:18
no wind that has no p. ..1661:16
poisoned her with p. 1767: 1
speaks wisdom 2157:10
such a graceful p. 1259: 1
yourself in p. you'll surely find 880:13
Port: vom sichern P. rathen 19: 9
Portæ: sunt geminæ Somni p. 478:21
Portal: deaf to prayers 772:14
Portals Night and Day ..1141: 9
of our earthly destinies ..438:15
of the night 2062:1a
twain: one all of horn ..478:21
Porte: ouvre moi ta p. ..1345: 3
soit ouverte ou fermé 423: 2
sublima 2061:14
Porter and skittles 1118: 7
at the door of thought ..1994:14
bends beneath load 204: 7
Porters of the Posterns ..2054:13
Portion: equal p. to all mankind 1467: 3
not large indeed 1327:10
what prodigal p. have I spent 1615:19
Portmanteau words 2221: 5
Porto Rique: sail for P. ..143: 1
Portrait: cowlèd p. dear ..1580:15
of artist 1448: 3
of bright angels' hue 141: 2
of dog that I know 1449: 3
take Death's p. 374:17
to sit for one's p. 1447:15
Portraits inside of heart ..1448: 8
Ports and happy havens ..887: 3
beyond the stars 378:10
keep'st the p. of slumber 221: 6
pale p. o' the moon 1344:15
Portum: inveni p. 569: 4
Poscænia: vitæ p. celant ..1784: 2
Posies: thousand fragrant p. 1747: 7
Position, see Place
Positive pronounce without dismay 1022:14
weighs more 99: 2

Prayer, *continued*
swears a p. or two 483: 6
that craves is vicious 1585: 4
that p. is enough 1588:2a
try everything—even p. .1582:14
unceasing, earnest p. 1584:10
was "Light" 1151:13
what an asylum has soul in p. 1583:14
whatsoever ye shall ask in p. 1583:4a
when P. is of no avail 1585:18
who rises from p. better 1586:11
will remedy heart strain 1583:11
ye have no need of p. 162:10
yet this will P. 1583: 6
Prayers and praises spotless lambs 1581:18
and provender hinder no journey 1582: 8
and wishes all I can return 1584: 7
angry p. of enemies 734:18
beseech with childish p. 1585: 7
costly to buy with p. 1582:19
disease of will 335: 3
few and short were the p. 1870: 9
first let thy P. ascend 1584:12
grant folly's p. 1586: 5
I grant your p. forthwith ..309:12
make mention of you in p. 1588: 3
make of your p. sacrifice 1588: 5
not words duly hallowed 1584: 7
of Abel linked to Cain ..1585: 3
only righteous p. heard ..1585:14
past all comforts but p. ..285: 6
plough not 1582: 4
stronger in unison 1583: 8
sweet ambassadors 1581:20
that all men may hear ..1583:16
three hours a day 2198: 6
to heal her wrongs 987:12
where p. cross 1981:18
yield to my holy p. 442: 1
Prayeth well who loveth well 1584: 2
Praying against temptation 1982: 6
end of preaching 1594:12
past p. for 1582:20
Prays: teaches to deny that faintly p. 2015: 6
to human form divine 1297:19
truth is what p. 1581:13
who p. and works 1063: 3
without confidence 1585: 5
Pre-Adamite ancestral descent 68:10
Pre-eminence and all the large effects 1040:16
Preach as we will 1253: 9
because you have something to say 1595: 6
for ever, but in vain 1594: 3
gospel to every creature ..1594:16
let us p. and pray 1593:16
long, loud and Damnation 1595: 3
not ourselves but Christ 1589: 5
practise what you p. ..1595:15
respectable mythology ...1594: 2
to the storm 1321: 7
Preached as a dying man ..1593:16
doubters down 1595: 2
Preacher **1589**
he too is no mean p. 2000: 3
judge not the p. 1589: 5
make a p. lay his Bible down 2294: 5
met p. there I knew 1590: 6
powerfulest p. 501: 1
should live perfectly 1595: 9
speaks through his nose ..1591: 9
who praught 1409:11
would I describe a p. 1590: 7
Preacher's merit or demerit 1589: 1
Preachers: bells best of p. 153:12
best of all the p. 1595:10
with Pride the P. dwelleth 1591:16
Preaches patience 124:17
well who lives well 1595:10
Preaching down a daughter's heart 366:17

Preaching, *continued*
exceed not an hour in p. 1594: 3
foolishness of p. 1594: 1
for profit of the belly 1591:16
God calleth p. folly 1589: 5
good p. praise Saviour 1594: 9
much, but more his practice wrought 1595:11
Preamble: long p. of tale .1961: 7
Precando: deum flecti p. ..1585:16
Precari: semperque eadem p. 145:14
Precaution better than cure 1648: 7
Prece: in p. totus eram ..1582:13
Precedent **1086, 1596**
codeless myriad of p. 1087: 8
embalms a principle 1087: 5
fatal p. will plead 2166:22
for poor men's facts ..1772:18
from p. to p. 552:11
I'll show thee a p. 1596:11
is not P. a King of men ..1596:13
nor are we to judge by any p. 1:16
one p. creates another ..1087: 4
recorded for a p. 1087: 6
shunned by p. 596: 5
Precedents: create good p. 1596: 5
Precept and Example ..**589**
begins 589: 8
ending with some p. deep 1963:25
let your p. be "Be easy" 2022:10
must be upon p. 2040: 1
path of p. long 589: 9
Précepte commence 589: 8
Precepts from Cynic tub 1498:13
love p. for teacher's sake 335:4; 1490: 4
no p. profit a fool 697:11
Preces: conjunctas fortius ire p. 1583: 8
neque a Diis nisi justas p. audiri 1585:14
Precibus: nulla carius constat quam p. empta ..1582:19
Precincts of the cheerful day 386: 3
Precious: more p. than before 404: 2
Precious-dear than life 918:12
Precise in promise-keeping 1621: 3
Precisian: devil turned p. ..442: 2
Predecessor: illustrious p. .588:19
Predestination far removed 1695: 7
in the stride of yon 1814: 3
Predestined to be good ...1893: 2
Predica quien bien vive ..1595:10
Predicting the future 749: 8
Prediction prove a lie 1624:16
Predominance: is 't night's p. 1403:17
Preface: meanness found in 2250:14
Preëminence: painful p. ...837:14
sorry p. 1339: 4
Prefer et obdura 1489: 1
to know what you 974: 1
Preferment goes by letter 1868: 4
is disgrace 653: 7
through each p. 1868: 4
Preferments at a court 326:12
Preferre ac pati omnes 541: 5
Preghi: caro costa p. 145: 9
Pregnant with celestial fire 875:16
Prejudice child of ignorance 1597: 7
full of vulgar p. 1596:17
greatest enemy of truth ..2050: 7
here let p. depart 1597:14
nothing stronger than p. 1597:13
opinion without support ..1596:16
pass for reason 1596:19
renders virtue habit 1596:18
Prejudiced is weak 1597:10
we are all p. 1597:16
Prejudices against a nation 707: 7
bundle of p. 1597: 8
contribute to order 1481:21
I respect honest p. 2297: 4
never too late to give up p. 1597:17
our mistresses 1596:19
passion of his p. 1597: 1

Prejudices, *continued*
props of civilization 1597: 4
take origin in intestines ..1597:12
Préjugés: chassez les p. ..1597: 3
sont les rois du vulgaire 1597:18
Prelate saith life is sweet 1143: 8
Prelude: play p. of our fate 1888: 7
Preludes: life but series of p. 1148
Premature expenditure ...1615: 6
Première: n'avez pas été 1630: 5
Premises are strong 100: 5
Preordained from eternity 439: 9
Preparation: dreadful note of p. 2117: 6
without p. failure 1928: 6
Preparations should be maintain'd 1598:16
Prepared for war 1597:21
is half the victory 1597:20
Preparedness **1597**
broomstick p. 1598:15
Prepoceras: something less p. 1410: 1
Prerogative of innocence ..990: 3
of mind 1996: 3
of place 73: 2
the last p. 1677:17
Prés, ce n'est rien 463: 6
Presage of your own decay 419:15
Presagers: dumb p. 191: 5
Presbyter but old priest ..1593: 4
Presbyterian true blue 1589: 2
Prescription most solid ...2015:11
to die 1121: 5
Presence: bodily p. is weak 1101: 5
conspicuous by its p. 2: 1
feasting p. full of light ..140:11
how many ships p. worth 982:12
into the P. flattening 472:13
majestic p. of the Night ..1401:11
My Lady's p. makes the roses red 1164: 3
noble p. in himself 1484:16
of mind 323:19; 862:20
of mind and courage 1930: 7
of mind tests man 1786:20
overpowering p. 957: 4
scanter of your maiden p. 1233:20
stood in p. of Master 397:16
strengthens love 3: 2
Present, The **1599**
act in the living p. 8: 4
be joyful in the p. 1600: 9
big with the future 1600:10
by losing p. we lose all 2009: 8
can make no man wretched 1599:11
changes so quickly 1599:10
contains only the past ...1459:13
enough for common souls 1600:11
ever-frowning P. 1697: 3
for the p. live 1599: 3
glory of the p. 52: 2
in spirit 2: 2
indivisible point 1599: 4
interests me more 1600: 5
is all thou hast 1599:12
is our own 1599:10
is the same for all 1131: 4
judge of p. by past 1459:12
never a happy state 1599:11
no imperfection in p. 393: 3
only p. love demands 1184:10
past and p. 1459:12
praised p. abused past 1460: 3
product of the past 1599: 7
read aright the p. 2163: 3
seize the p. 1600: 8
sum-total of the past 1459:13
take desponding view of p. 44: 4
things p. worst 1460: 1
thinketh only of p. 1600:15
thou to God hast sent 408:15
though absent, p. to desire ..3: 1
we fling from us 1132: 5
wisely improve the P. 1460:10
Présent est gros d'avenir 1600:10
Presentment: counterfeit p. 239: 4
Presents endear absents 2: 7
giving p. to a woman 2214:15
to the mother 366:13

Presents, *continued*
who makes p. expects p. ...776:21
with female virtue prevail 2202: 2
Preservation: times of p. ..2004:11
Preserve, protect, and defend 1418:12
President: any child may be P. 1431: 4
I do not choose to run for P. 1552: 9
office of P. 1548: 8
office of P. not difficult ..1557:13
one more P. in protection 1965: 3
pays dear for his White House 1549: 5
rather be right than P. ..1552: 5
two terms as p. 63: 5
who tries to mind own business 1552: 9
Presidency: third term 63: 5
Presiding genius 801: 9
Press, The 1600
Arkymedian Leaver 1602: 3
chartered libertine 1603: 8
damp from the p. 1603: 2
free from force p. remains 1601:16
freedom of the p. 53: 8
more instruction from P. 1675:10
of gaping faces 607:13
on, while yet ye may 110: 1
people's right maintain .1601:19
prove vehicle of virtue ..1601: 1
pulpit and stage 42:17
puts into the p. 1604:11
spring of endless lies ...1602:15
takes place of rack 1603:11
then hail to the P. 1602:11
when the p. is free all is safe 1601:17
with vigour on 969:10
Press-men: slaves of lamp 1603:12
Pressed from the grape its fine blue 361:14
in the dance 361:14
Pressure of public opinion 1429:15
pig-of-lead-like p. 1591: 9
Presume not that I am the thing I was 231: 3
Presumption: most it is p. 1646:13
or meanness in preface ..2250:14
ruins many 436:21
Pretence
See also Hypocrisy
of friendly ends 948:14
robe P. was wearing 946:18
Sleeveless P. 1851: 7
to piety and godliness 948: 4
Pretend: mighty to p. 947: 2
Pretender begins to love truly 1186: 1
who p. is and who king ..1037: 9
Pretending to be wicked ..946:13
Preter: divine est p. 194:11
et emprunter 194:11
Pretesti: non mancano p. ...420: 8
Pretexts never wanting ..420: 8
Pretio: in p. pretium 1334:16
Pretioso gloriabitur 174: 7
Pretium: in pretio p. nunc est 1622: 8
ob stultitiam fero 696: 9
Pretty to walk with 1234:10
you are p., young, rich ..1581: 2
Preussen über alles 767: 2
Preuve: la p. en est connue ..73: 3
Prevail or perish 1030:13
Prevails who nobly dares ..176:13
Prevarication: last dyke of 1109: 7
Prevention better than cure 496:7; 1286:15
daughter of intelligence .1648: 7
past help beyond p. 541:13
Prey: anger seeks its p. 80: 1
his p. was man 941: 3
of rich on poor 581: 2
on others, or become a p. 1792:1a
Priam: ancient P. 39:20
doting P. 2046: 1
Priapus thy father 1416:13
Price 1604
advice is beyond p. 19: 4
all men have their p. 1605:11
buy at p. he is worth 533:11
every man has his p. 1605:11
her p. is fall'n 1605: 8
highest p. is to ask 145: 9
I know my p. 1605: 8
in proportion to skill 1605: 7
is far above rubies 245: 9
no mortal thing can bear so high a p. 1605: 5
of a laugh too high 1076:17
of every man 1605:11
of everything 356:20
of great p. 1904: 6
of labor 1061:15
of votes 199:11
of wisdom above rubies ..2166:23
of your voice 1092: 7
people who consider p. ..1605: 7
sign of slavery to have p. 1840: 8
too great for peace 1471: 6
too high p. for knowledge 1147:11
vigilance p. of liberty ..1106: 2
what p. glory 1640: 4
what p. Salvation 1640: 4
without money, without p. 1333: 1
Prices: all have p. 1605: 9
Prick us, do we not bleed ..1012:13
Prick-song: sing p. 505:15
Pricket: pretty pleasing p. 1410:13
Pricking of my thumbs ...1947: 1
on the plain 259: 7
Pricks: kick against p. 1703:20
Principles in which bred ...1694: 6
Pride 1606
age pulls down p. 32:14
aiming at bless'd abodes ..1609:17
all our p. but a jest 2239:11
and conceit original sin ..1606: 7
and poverty ill met 1607: 2
angered p. makes a noise ..986: 3
answers " 'Tis for mine" 1606:10
at bottom of all mistakes 1610: 2
breakfasted with Plenty ..1607: 4
brings want 1607: 9
builds among the stars ..1606:14
burning p. and high disdain 1713:15
cause of allē woe 1609:13
cleric p. no contradiction 1591:13
costs more than hunger ..1607: 9
daughter of riches 2107: 4
deep, interminable p. ...1609: 7
down with your p. of birth 1245: 9
Envy, Avarice 1606: 5
Envy, Malice are his Graces 819:18
feels no cold 1607: 7
fell with my fortunes ...1608:11
fly p., says peacock 1476: 9
fond p. of dress 486:16
gaudy p. corrupts age ..1607:10
goes before, shame after 1608:14
goeth before destruction 1608:10
goeth forth on horseback 1608: 9
great p. or little sense 2042:12
grows by reflection in mirror 1317: 4
grows greater in prosperity 1606: 9
had rather go out of way 1607: 5
handsome, economical ..1608:23
hated stands 1609: 4
hath no other glass 1608: 1
high-blown p. broke 1608:11
his p. becomes him 1609: 2
how blind is p. 1609: 9
I have loved p. and praise 1609:10
in coming generation 2265: 1
in darkness soars 1606:14
in making dinner cost little 450:12
in prosperity, misery 1607: 6
in reasoning lies 1680:10
in reasoning p., error lies 1609:17
in saucy p. 665:20
in seeming not proud ..1607: 1
in their port 1750:15
in this coming generation 2265: 1
Pride, *continued*
is his own glass 1610: 3
is littleness 1606:12
is the life of woman 2191: 7
is the spring of malice ..1606: 8
lives with all 1376:12
lose by p. attained by grace 1608: 5
loud a beggar as want ..1607: 8
made the devil 443: 1
most dangerous fault ..1609:17
mother's p. father's joy ..257:12
must have a fall 1608: 8
must tarre mastiffs on ..1607:19
never feels pain 1607: 7
no higher than the Desk ..1015:12
no mean factor in State 1380:17
no p. like p. of intellect ..1606: 6
of a butterfly dies in day 1240: 2
of kingly sway 1043:10
of rich make labor of poor 1572:15
of summer passing by ..1936:14
of the peacock 1476: 9
of victory corrupts 2084:11
our p. misleads 1608: 6
overdone p. makes naked .1607: 9
parent of many virtues 1608:21
pomp and circumstance ..636:11
proud provoked by p. ...1607: 3
recruits of needful P. ..1609:16
rides, shame lacqueys 1608:16
root of seven sins 1828:22a
ruled my will 1609:10
save me alike from foolish P. 1610: 1
self-adoring p. 1609: 8
self-pleasing p. 1609: 3
so barbarous as p. 1606: 4
solemn vice of greatness 1609:14
steps in to our defence ..1609:16
still is aiming 1609:17
Stoic's p. 1239: 3
struck out new sparkles 1609:10
such aim at Heaven p. ...972:12
sure of shameful fall 1608:12
swells a haughty worm ..1609: 5
sworn enemy to content 1609:11
that apes humility 1607: 1
that dies on vanity 1607: 4
that impartial passion 1606:14
that licks the dust 1607:13
that pulls country down 491: 6
there is of rank 1606: 6
'tis p., rank p. 1606: 1
to pampered priesthood dear 1591:13
to p. oppose 1608: 4
towering in p. of place 1505: 4
under thread-bare coat ...1607: 2
vainglory and hypocrisy ..1981: 8
vice of fools 1609:16
waits on beauty 2192: 5
was ever P. contented 1609:11
was never made for man ..679: 3
waxes in prosperity 1606: 9
went before 1607:18
when p. cometh, then shame 1608:19
when p. is in the saddle ..1608:18
where was then p. of man 72:13
who cries out in p. 1609: 2
will have a fall 1608: 8
withered in their p. 1609: 6
without dignity 834:14
Priest
See also Preacher: Priest
always in alliance with despot 1593: 2
always with the herd 1593: 3
chanted Brahma's might ..335: 9
delicate-handed p. 1593:13
earthly spirit of the p. ..1592:14
fiddling p. 1592:12
for an enemy 1592: 5
forgetteth he was clerk ..1592:16
God's true p. always free 1591: 7
he merry is and blithe ..1592:12
hostile to liberty 1593: 2
if a p. be foul 1595:10
lays curse on fairest joys 1592: 9

Problem, *continued*
of land 1067: 7
wait till I finish my p. 414: 4
Problems: insoluble p. 1497: 1
Probos: ad p. propinquitate .288:14
Proboscis: wreath'd lithe p. .535:14
Probum: gratis pænitet esse p. 915:21
Proceedings: subsequent p. 1851:16
Procerem: agnosco p. 1407:17
Procès est plus court 1081: 1
Process of unsinning sin ..1829: 7
Processes of legal change ..1618: 6
Procession: in plumed p. 76: 9
move in a mournful p. 9:14
Proclaim one honest man ...914:19
Procrastination **1614**
is the thief of time 1615: 1
keeping up with yesterday 1614:11
nothing so perilous 1614: 7
Procreation common to all 2140:13
Procuress to Lords of Hell 806: 7
Prodigal course like the sun's 1615:15
doth nature seem 362:16
give what they despise ..776:19
killed for the P. 1615:20
like p. doth she return ...1615:21
of ease 1100: 2
of health 1495: 1
returning p. not to be exchanged for gold 1615:18
robs his heir 1615: 7
should waste 1615: 7
thriftless p. of smiles ...1126:11
within compass of guinea 1615: 9
Prodigality **1615**
framed in p. of nature ..765: 8
of the rich 241:12
Prodigals come from swinekeeping 1615:20
when p. return 1615:18
Prodigies: they told of p. 2032: 9
Prodigiis terras implerunt 1946: 2
Prodigus et stultus donat ..776:19
Prodigy: calls it a p. 631: 5
in learning 1096:18
round-faced p. 1441:17
Proditores invisi sunt 2033:13
Proditori: nemo sapiens p. credentum 2034:11
Produce of immortal Mind 1812:12
Producing: everyone is p. .2297: 4
Product of English school 531: 6
of lively imagination 1960: 7
of scoffer's pen 2253:10
Proelio minus pepercissent 2108: 8
Profanation: foul p. 835:11
Profane: let no p. enter ..1108: 2
Profanely: not to speak it p. 10: 6
Profani: procul este p. ...1479: 7
Profanity relief denied to prayer 1951:19
Profectus velle proficere ..1617: 6
Profess most least sincere 1691:16
Profession: Adam's p. 12: 3
debtor to p. 417:21
is to keep secrets 1589: 3
loyal to p. of medicine ...2274: 3
men of your large p. 1093:15
panted for liberal p. 47:17
they admit the p. 9:14
Professions: one of p. that is full 809: 3
Professor
See also Teacher
high-cheek-boned P. 1970: 9
mere p., spite of cant ..1970:18
of books 182: 3
Professors: all such false p. 1971: 8
American p. cold, pure ..1970:20
men, women and p. 1802: 8
of the Dismal Science ...1970:13
Profeti armati vinsero 2115: 8
Profit by folly of others 596: 3
by losing of prayers 1586:19
first p. is to spare 1998:3a
greatest p. least price ..1605: 3
it will p. me nothing ..619:14
more p. and less honor ..750:16
Profit, *continued*
no one ruined by p. 750:16
no p. but the name 297:18
no p. grows where is no pleasure ta'en 1924: 3
no p. if outlay exceeds receipts 750:13
of their shining nights ...1765:15
out of light a little p. 1152:18
seek out own p. 1795: 1
small p. and small loss ..2223:21
to p. from advice 19:13
to p., learn to please 1513: 3
what p. hath man of labor 1064:11
Profitable as snow in harvest 1857: 3
Profound of love to man ..795: 1
while merely hollow 1476:19
Profundis: de p. 792: 3
Profundity: vast p. obscure 2244: 6
Profusion apes noble part 1615: 5
Prog from pole to pole ...2029: 9
Progenitors: do as your p. have done 70:14
four-footed p. 586:17
Progeny of learning 1096:18
of light 76:12
Prognostics do not prove ..1624:19
Progrès en spirale 1307: 4
Progress **1616**
begins with a crime 1616:10
calls each fresh link P. ..553: 5
depends on unreasonable 1679: 6
exchange of one nuisance for other 1616: 3
from scaffold to scaffold 1617: 3
from stake to stake 1280:13
golden p. in the east 1940:11
heat instead of p. 99:16
in spirals 1307: 4
is an unfolding 1054: 7
is not real 1616: 6
is the desire to p. 1617: 6
is the law of life 1616: 2
long-continued slow p. 965:11
man's distinctive mark ..1616: 2
means suffering 1617: 3
of long decay 419:12
of man to error 576:13
part of nature 1617: 7
realization of Utopias ..1617:11
social p. binds all 1616: 6
that's what p. is 124: 4
what p. by society 42:13
world's best p. springs ...454: 2
Progressive for certain time 978:17
in religion 1616: 5
knows where he is going .1545:16
recognizes new facts 1545:16
who never progressed 204: 2
yet no change 1777:11
Prohibition **1617**
divided the nation 1619: 3
made nothing but trouble 1619: 1
nation-wide scandal 1618: 8
result of European War ..1619: 9
will injure temperance ..1619:10
world benefited by banishment of intoxicants ..1619:10
Projects: fitter for new p. 2263: 2
pink 455:20
Prolixity, thinness, endless dilution 2230: 1
Prologue: excuse came p. 590: 9
foolish to make long p. 1961: 7
is the grace 1912: 1
or posy of a ring 2198: 8
what's past is p. 1458:13
Prologues are loss of time 1910:14
precede the piece 1910:14
Promenades: pensive p. ...1136: 9
Prometheus: like P. bring fire 2054:11
like P. devise methods and expedients 109:11
Promettons selon nos espérances 1620:20
Promise **1620**
according to our hopes ..1620:20
and performance 1620:17
Promise, *continued*
apt to p., apt to forget ..1620: 7
be sure to p. 1620:14
beyond the p. of his age ..325: 8
breach of p. 2217: 7
broken or kept 1620: 6
failed the bright p. 1011:19
great p., small performance 1620:18
is a p. 1620: 9
is debt 1620: 5
leaned on wavering p. ..926:11
let us keep our p. 1620:17
little, perform much 1621:6a
makes his p. good 1621: 3
most given, least said 1620: 4
mountains, perform molehills 1621: 6
much and perform little ..1621:6a
not to do a thing 1618: 4
of a soul's allegiance 1045:23
of celestial worth 2247:15
of matrimony 704: 3
of the year 1610:13
of your early days 612:13
Oh, p. me 2293: 2
seas and mountains 1620:15
soul of advertisement 1620:14
spare not to p. anything 1418: 1
that He hath promised ..966: 6
to men in grief 1620:13
where is p. of my years ..257:20
where sleeps that p. now ..257:20
you'll be true 2295: 6
Promise-keeping: precise in 1621: 3
Promises: broken p., cracked oaths 1638: 2
don't fill the belly 155:13
fair p. avail little 1620:16
for pleasure of breaking ..1620:10
giants in their p. 834:17
green p. of youthful heat ..23: 7
like a merchantman 1620: 7
like Adonis' gardens 1621: 3
made to be broken 1620:16
many p. impair confidence 1620:11
may get friends 731:14
mighty, performance nothing 1621: 4
of impossibilities 2228: 7
of youth 334: 8
supplement p. with deeds 1621: 2
Promising very air o' the time 1621: 4
want for no p. 1620:14
Promissa: multa fidem p. levant 1620:11
Promittere: nihil p. parcunt 1418: 1
quid enim p. lædit 1620:14
Promontories: Lesbian p. ..2105:15
Promontory—death 400: 7
once I sat upon a p. 1300:10
Promote: one-third p. 666: 5
Promoter of mutual acquaintance 1101:11
Promotion cometh neither from east 1929:20
none sweat but for p. 1799:17
Prompt at every call 1590: 8
Prompters: how many p. ..697:13
Promptings of each heart 2273: 3
Promptitude à l'erreur nous expose 863: 7
Pronas fluminis esse vias ..2220:11
Pronounce with the vulgar 2250: 3
Pronuntiatio est vocis 1439: 7
Proof **1621**
best p. is experience 593:11
give me the ocular p. ..1621:16
incapable of p. 1621:10
is called impossibility ..2148:17
of beneficence 795:11
of pudding is eating 515:19; 1621: 8
to bolster his opinion ..1427: 1
to vouch this, is no p. 1621:16
Proofs: all p. sleeping else 1948:19
four valid as dozen 1621:13
of beneficence 795:11
of holy writ 1007:10

Questioning not the mode among gentlemen 1665:11
too much q. offends 1665: 8
Questionings: obstinate q. of sense 1796: 2
Questions are then the Windlass 2052: 5
ask me no q. 1109:13
begs the simplest q. 100: 5
burning q. 451:15
burning q. of the day ...1554: 4
hard q., hard answers ..1665:13
never indiscreet 1665:17
puzzling q. 1665: 5
when great q. end 1543:13
Qui s'excuse, s'accuse 590: 8
Quibble and quiddity 313: 4
Quick and the dead 1019:14a
as greyhound's mouth ..2173:15
as lightning 1153: 8
hurries q. to join dead ..378:18
touch to the q. 1639:15
with the q. 1148: 1
Quicken with kissing 1049:14
Quickly enough if well ..862:11
Quickness: too much q. 1131:12
Quicksand: halts on a q. ..2034:12
of deceit 421: 5
Quicksands of politics ...1542: 6
Quicksilver: hard to hold as q. 1398: 4
Quid dem? quid non dem 772:11
for Quo 1298:16
nec q. nec quare 1681: 7
Quiddists or quids 1545: 1
Quiddities: where be his q. 1091:21
Quiddity: quibble and q. ..313: 4
Quien Canta males espanta 1876: 7
las sabe las tañe 1055: 9
Quies: dulcis et alta q. ..1849:17
inquieta est 1666:15
secura q. 1707:16
una q. operum 1062:16
Quiet 1665
all q. along the Potomac ..65: 5
anything for a q. life 1135: 8
as a lamb 1666:12
as a Nun 582:17
as a street at night 1666:12
conscience 300:20
dispassionate and cold ..1794: 7
Doctor Q., Diet 872: 2
have I found thee here ..756:12
I keep q. 1650:15
in q. she reposes 393: 7
in q. true joy 854: 4
is an unquiet thing 1666:15
is mankind's concern ...1984: 5
noonday q. holds the hill 1411:14
Lethe's gloom without its q. .2:16
of this holy ground 829:12
only stay q. 1294: 4
scallop-shell of q. 398:10
study to be q. 208: 7
to quick bosoms is a hell 1666: 1
Quietam: cur quæris q. ...1065: 9
Quietem possit pati 955:18
Quietis in tumultum 1666:15
Quietness and confidence 1666:10
blue q. above 1835: 6
dry morsel and q. 1666:14
is best 1666: 9
true q. of heart 1457:14
Quiets: hallowed q. of past 1458: 8
Quietude: speaking q. 1401:16
Quietus make with bodkin 1934: 9
Quill from angel's wing ..1477:11
rams his q. with scandal 1762: 1
sucks substance through q. 2254: 9
Quillets: cases, tenures ...1091:21
nice q. of the law 1090: 7
Quills: tender stops of various q. 1879: 8
Quimus: ut q. quando 1651:13
Quinapalus: what says Q. 2174:11
Quince: Solon bade bride eat q. 1273: 5
Quinces: Othmanee q. 521:16
Quinn, James: epitaph ...568:11
Quinque advocavi 450:15
Quinsy: silver q. 199:10
Quintessence of dust 1239: 5
of perception 2066: 8
pure 1151: 7
Quintilian: made Q. stare 1373:18
Quintus Horatius 503: 1
Quip modest 1110:19
Quips: all her sudden q. ..1215: 3
and thy quiddities 1010:11
Cranks, wanton Wiles ...1010: 2
Quire: full voic'd q. 1365:12
Quiring to the young-eyed cherubins 1367:10
Quirks: light q. of music ..154: 4
of blazoning pens 1234: 8
Quis custodiet 2144:17
Quisquilia: cetera q. omnia 1795:11
Quit ourselves like men ...2066:16
yourselves like men 1922:13
Quitter: God Almighty hates a q. 331:17
Quiver full of them 253:12
Quixote, see Cervantes
Quixotic sense of honor ..918:21
Quo vadis, domine 1637:16
Quod est eo decet uti 1921:17
expendi habui 774: 5
Quorum pars magna fui 1820:7a
Quotation 1666
advantage in q. 1667: 9
confesses inferiority 1667: 4
every q. contributes 1667: 9
fine q. a diamond 1668: 5
pardon q.; I hate it 1667:11
parole of literary men ..1667: 8
requires delicacy 1666:22
Quotations: always verify 1668: 4
of q. not to be relied on 1667:12
sham q. *peri hupsos* 1667:12
to patch-work q. allied ..1668: 6
Quote: by necessity all q. 1667: 4
easier to q. 1558:11
others to express myself ..1668: 1
quotation on quotation ..1667:12
till one compiles 1667: 2
who never q. seldom quoted 1667: 2
Quoted by others 2257: 8
to be q. is fame 1667: 7
Quotes: great man q. bravely 1667: 6
Quoth the Raven, "Nevermore!" 1672: 2

R

Rabbi Ben Karshook 1698:11
Rabbit: hop of a wild r. 117:11
Rabbit's God and man's ..783: 8
Rabbits: companionable like r. 2001:18
Rabble: all the r. of the ship 1478:12
base r. are enraged 1480:11
cowardly r. 1480: 9
envious r. 1479: 7
miscellaneous r. 1482: 8
now a r. rages 1169:10
values rumor above truth 1482: 1
Rabiem livoris acerbi 564: 9
Rabies miseranda ducis ..1095: 2
omnibus armatur r. 80: 1
Race: a despicable r. 9:13
an iron r. 1094: 8
bloodless r. 39:20
by vigor won 1930: 8
could save one-half labor 1683:18
despicable r. 9:13
fascinating r. emigrated ..615: 7
Flora's brilliant r. 692: 6
golden r. of speaking men 1243:11
good-bye to Anglo-Saxon r. 941:14
he ran his godly r. 1590: 8
he ran his r. 403:16
heavenly r. demands thy zeal 969:10
homeless r. 1012: 3
honest horse r. 752:10
how fur we've gone in r. ..586: 9
I wish I loved the Human R. 1246: 4
idiot r. to honor lost 766: 9
Race, *continued*
is run by one and one 1277:16
is won 390:10
joy is in the r. 754: 4
lamplit r. 202:16
life's r. well run 391:14
life's uncertain r. 927:10
mixed with every r. 1011:13
mongrel half-bred r. 560: 7
naught can deform human r. 1865: 7
noble r. and brave 977: 1
not to the swift 1930: 8
of delight is short 1512: 5
of hero spirits 897: 4
of honor in America 508:10
one changeless r., the poor 1567: 2
over wildest Alps 49: 7
primeval r. was run 83:10
purblind r. of men 421:10
remains immortal 633: 8
runs well, runs twice his r. 805:11
sceptred r. 401: 6
servile r. in folly nursed 999:10
suicide 164: 3
thank God for r. and sod 999: 4
that binds body in chains 1616: 3
that noble r. and brave ..977: 1
to win a r., timely start 146:14
took suffering human r. .1251: 3
triumphant r. 1011:19
without a goal 967:12
Races: fighting r. don't die out 999: 4
Rachel, shedding tears ..1972: 8
weeping for her children 408: 9
Racine passera comme café 1166: 2
Raciness of his qualities ..651: 2
Rack and torture for his sins 1830: 7
helps pass hour or two 2250: 3
leave not a r. behind ...2095:12
men had the r. 1603:11
never put anyone on r. ..1758: 6
of a too easy chair 956:13
of this tough world 392:11
put on r. by biting poem 1758: 6
you speak upon the r. ..1444:16
Racking of the brains 2254: 5
Racks, gibbets, halters ...1932:20
Raconte: je n'enseigne point, je r. 1969: 1
Radiance of eternity 1143:12
Radiancy: edged with intolerable r. 282: 2
Radiant: all r. with the glory 75:15
Radical: be very r. and rich 1545: 2
one who goes too far 1545:16
Radicalism 304: 6
Radish: like a forked r. 1246:11
Rafael, see also Raphael
made century of sonnets 1883: 6
of the dear Madonnas 1188: 3
Ratt: democracy a r. 430:10
Rafter: sounding r. 1868:11
Rag and bone and hank 2217: 6
bloomin' old r. 547: 3
moth-eaten r. 675: 9
tag, r. and bobtail 1478:12
Rag-bag of the world 1685:17
Rag-time: hello! ma r. gal 2288: 8
Rage
See also Anger
but not talent, to abuse 1758: 4
by civil r. and rancor fell 1768: 1
cold r. seizes one 2051:22
divides a friendship 744: 2
flash of that satiric r. ..1758: 9
for fame 626: 7
for saying something 1900: 6
Heaven's fell r. 40:12
hence r. and tears 1973:13
how with this r. shall beauty 137: 3
in r. deaf as the sea 241: 1
inextinguishable r. 78: 8
is any Panther's r. so furious 2203:11
no r. like love to hatred 2203:11
of biting envy 564: 9
of shining to subdue 314: 6

Relics: scattered r. of the day 2094:17
Relief: certain r. in change 231: 4
for this r. much thanks 1492:18
hold out; r. is coming 65:10
is there no r. for love ..1937: 3
poor r. we gain 231: 4
sure r. of prayer 1583:14
Religentem esse oportet ..1691:11
Religio: minimis r. inserit deos 1945: 8
peperit divitias 1692:11
peperit scelerosa 1692:17
tantum r. potuit malorum 1692:17

Religion 1688
adverse to knowledge 1688: 5
adversity reminds of r. 16: 8
always a crab fruit 1689: 3
and eye not to be touched 1691: 6
animated only by faith ..1691: 8
artist needs no r. 107: 4
as much r. as my William likes 2138:12
at best anxious wish 1690: 7
attempt to suggest realities 1689:16
attracts devotion 1688: 3
best armour in world ..1691: 1
breathing household laws 1136: 5
brought forth riches 1692:11
brought shameful actions 1692:17
can bear no jesting 1691: 6
can no more degrade its Devil 441: 3
cannot make r. for others 1693:13
clears mind from desires 1689:20
cloaked crimes 633:15
comfort to distressed 1692:9a
conform to any r. 1690: 5
conscientious men of one r. 1693: 9
consists in obedience 1688: 7
consists not of doubt 1688: 9
converts despair 1692: 3
cordial to the sick 1692:9a
daughter of Hope 1688: 6
delight and duty 1689:12
destroyed by bigotry 1695:10
does not censure 1690: 9
domination of the soul ..1689:17
done love great service ..1177: 4
effeminates, demoralizes .1689: 3
elder sister of Philosophy 1689:12
enough r. to make hate ..1696:10
ethics of holy person 1689: 5
every man has his r. ..1694: 4
everybody of same r. 1333:18
everywhere of one r. 1694: 2
false r. conflict with nature 1691:14
fashion of country 1689:14
fit to match his learning ..1589: 2
friend of friendless 1689:15
good that teaches good ..1694: 1
grey with age becomes r. 2011:15
grown infant with age ..1316: 3
harsh, intolerant 1689: 1
has nothing more to fear 1691:15
hath no landmarks 1691:19
hides many mischiefs ...1692:18
if abbé had spoken of r. ..1056: 8
if your r. is Roman 1738: 3
in heart, not knee 1691: 7
is a stalking-horse 1689: 9
is all 1692:10
is life 1688:11
is low 531: 3
is my name 1693: 5
is what life has taught ..1693:13
judged others' r. by lives 1693:14
left r. for an estate 1690: 5
Liberty, and Law 1601:19
like the fashion 1694: 4
look on no r. scornfully ..1693: 6
make all of one r. 1694: 3
makes fools of men 1692:15
man's r. chief fact 1688: 9
men of sense of one r. ..1693:16
mother of dreams 1689: 8
mother of Form and Fear 1689: 2
must have spice of devil ..809:14
needs only to be seen ..1692: 4

Religion, *continued*
never to say grace 90: 3
never told my r. 1693:14
New Englander's r. 1694: 7
no need of r. 1692:16
no r. binds men 2034:14
not a hearsay 1689:20
not dogma but service ..1689:10
not impossibilities enough in r. 1688: 3
of Jesus a threat 266: 8
of Mohammed a promise ..266: 8
of one age poetry of next 1689:12
of one madness to another 1694:15
of solitude 1871: 3
of well-doing and daring 1693: 9
of the brave and good ..1693:12
one r. true as another ..1693: 7
opium of the people 1689:14a
organized for slaves 1692:13
pure r. and undefiled 1689:11
rather gamble than insurance 1691:20
rational people of one r. 1694: 3
reduced Spain to guitar .1692:14
relates to life 1689:11
relation of soul to God ..1695:10
restraint on wicked 1692:9a
sense of ultimate reality 1688:10
should be rule of life 1690:10
should extinguish strife ..1695: 5
sides with poverty 1692: 6
sigh of the oppressed ...1689:14a
spawn'd a various rout ..1694:18
speaks language of heart 1692: 1
stab r. with side-thrust ..2098: 6
stands on tiptoe in land ..1691: 5
substantially good 1693:14
superstition and r. 1945: 2
there is only one r. 1694: 5
'tis r. to be true 1199: 7
to do good 320:14
troubled with dyspepsia ..1695: 9
true policy befriends 1693: 2
true r. built upon rock ..1688: 5
truth he lives habitually 1689:13
value of r. its challenge 1692: 8
veils her sacred fires 1696: 7
voice of deepest experience 1688: 4
we are all of same r. 1694: 8
well defends 1695: 6
went to Rome 1740:10
what treasure untold 2218: 9
which allies with injustice 1689: 7
whoso fighteth for r. 1691: 9
wise men are of same r. ..1693:16
with one commandment ..1690: 9
without a prelate 1658:10
without joy, no r. 1690: 9
without mystery ceases ..1688: 3
without r. clever devils ..1691: 3
wrangle for r. 1695: 4
Religion's: pale Reason at R. sight 1680: 4
put out R. eye 1696: 9
Religions: all r. tolerated 1693:11
but two possible r. 1689: 6
die of one disease 1691:10
ejaculations of men 1689: 5
many r., one morality 1346: 3
measure r. by civilizing 1690:13
northern r., harsh, bitter 1693: 4
of the world 1689:14
sixty different r. 554:13
thirty two r. 316:10
up from soil r. pass 512:22
we call false once true ..1690:12
Religiosæ: stultæ et misere r. 2193: 3
Religiosity: shun r. 1691:11
Religiosus ne fuas 1691:11
Religious after manner of this platform 1556: 5
I know thou art r. 299:11
if not r., superstitious 957: 9
life a struggle 1691:17
test 1550: 9
Reliquiæ: tales cum sint r. 2158: 1

Relish him more in the soldier 217: 8
his r. grown callous 757: 4
is so sweet 592: 9
no r. of salvation in't 1359:16
that inviteth 2018:16
Relishes: what one r. nourishes 89: 3
Relligio: cadebat R. 987:10
Relume: can thy light r. ..1153: 2
Rem: facias r., si possis, recte 1336: 5
tu strenuus auge 1622: 6
Rembrandt: house of R. ..1446:17
Remedia faciunt dolorem .1287: 8
graviora sunt r. periculis 1287: 5
non prosunt 1285:10
tardiora sunt r. quam mala 1285:11
Remedies: efficacious r. cause pain 1287: 8
extreme r. for diseases ..1287:10
more grievous than offence 1287: 6
more slow than disease 1285:11
new r., or new evils 1285: 1
oft in ourselves do lie ...1286:18
past, griefs ended 843:20
worse than the disease ..1287: 5
Remediis: gravior r. quam delicta 1287: 6
Remedio: si hay r. porqui ..584:20
Remediorum creora mutatio 1285:10
Remedium tumultus fuit alius 1682: 6

Remedy
See also Medicine
best r. for danger 363:20
for democrats is soldiers ..431:11
for everything but death ..380: 9
for injuries to forget 986:21
in his sleeve 2234: 8
for men diseased 126: 5
no evil without r. 584:20
no r. against death 380: 9
no r. for fear 332:15
no r. for love 1187: 2
no r. for time misspent ...956:17
of a defect 486:12
of books 179:16
sovereign r. to all diseases 2016:16
'tis a sharp r. 416:16
without r. without regard .426:22
worse than the disease ..1287: 5
Remedyless: only love r. ..1186:14
Remember 414:15
and be sad 1297:14
both food and drink 89: 4
cannot but r. such things 1295: 8
hard to bear, sweet to r. .1293:18
I r., I r. 196:3; 251:15; 684:3; 1297: 1
if I do not r. 1293:12
if thou wilt, r. 405: 7
me when I am gone away 401:12
one thing to r., another to know 1054:20
the end 540:12
the Maine 66: 5
thee 1295: 8
then you'll r. me 1296: 4
there's no other 2293:10
till thou r. and I forget 1949:10
to r. to forget to ask 1297:18
way we parted 709: 1
we found a lonely spot 1881: 5
while light lives yet 1297:16
ye may r. what ye will ..708:14
you are but a man 379: 8
you must die 379: 8
Remembered by a song 1521: 2
those who deserve to be r. ..901: 1
twice read r. 1673:11
Rememberer as well as remembered 625: 7
Remembering: teach me not art of r. 1297:17

Remembrance
See also Memory
age lives on r. 24: 7
and reflection how allied 1682:15
by their deserts 435: 2

Remembrance, *continued*
fallen from heaven 1239:11
fond r. hidden deep 1296: 3
have our works in r. 1421:10
honor with r., not tears ...404: 8
how sharp point of r. is 1295:10
let us not burden our r. 1295:10
no r. which time does not 2011: 4
of a generous deed 1952:18
of a weeping queen 1295: 9
of his dying Lord 259: 4
of joys departed painful 1295: 1
of my former love 1187: 4
of things past 1295:10
sweet is r. of troubles ..2043: 8
sweet r. of the just 1029:18
wakes with her busy train 1295: 3
writ in r. more 32: 3
Remembrances embellish life 1297:10
poor r. are statues 1339:15
Reminiscence: not a r. of the land alone 191: 8
sing 1294:15
Remis adice vela tuis 862:18
velisque 862:18
Remission: gain thee no r. 2134:20
Remnants of history 82: 5
Remords s'endort 1697:14
Remorse 1697
abandon all r. 1698: 7
access and passage to r. ..346:12
as heart in which it grows 1697: 3
begets reform 1697: 6
evil when promotes despair 1697: 6
fatal egg by Pleasure laid 1697: 5
feel thy pangs, R. 1697:15
for yesterday 2020:12
goes to sleep 1697:14
haply with r. 1703:11
is memory awake 1697: 8
is penitence 710:10
O that r. had voice to warn 1698: 8
Remote from towns 1590: 8
unfriended 2028:13
Remould it nearer to the ..2067: 5
Remove: by every r. I drag chain 3: 3
Rempublicam æternam ...1918:19
Remuer: decider sans r. 98:11
Renard qu'une poule aurait pris 1810: 5
Rendezvous: I keep Life's r. 381: 6
with death 381: 6
with life 381: 6
Rendezvous: voyez le beau r. 1790:11
Renegadoes double knaves 1544: 3
Renomme better than richesse 1701:10
Renommée: je ne dois 624:16
Renounce for fear of losing 1170:16
Renovates and lives 1844:14
Renown
See also Fame
all fair examples of r. ..1319: 8
all hit or miss 627: 1
and glory: difference 624: 7
content with judgments ..1700:13
extend r. by deeds 426: 7
ghosts of dead r. 630: 7
is this your r. 1322:11
life for which is bought r. 630: 6
lofty lucre of r. 627:14
mother of virtues 623: 3
not child of repose 954: 7
of riches frail 2092:15
on earth 626:16
poor r. of being smart ..1758: 6
praise rendered good man .624: 6
small town, great r. 47:13
without one ripple of r. ..1890:18
Renowned be thy grave 826: 8
Rent envious Casca made ..984:16
her r. is sorrow 877:19
millions—why? for r. 464:11
murdering r. for bit of soil 996: 2
what you goin' to do when the r. comes 'round ..2293:10
who paid the r. 1882: 2
Rent-roll Cupid 558: 7
Rents: anticipated r. 418: 5
Repaired: what cannot be r. not regretted 541: 9
Repartee: argue, or to r. ..2200: 3
Repast: neat r. shall feast us 659:15
sweet r. and calm repose ..582: 6
Repeateth: he that r. 1837:11
Repent: first to r. and regret 2201: 7
for doing good 807: 8
I'll r. and that suddenly 1699:18
it from my very soul 428: 1
never r. of having eaten too little 518:17
never to r., wisdom 1698:18
never too late to r. 1699:13
noble mind disdains not to r. 1699: 5
of good behavior 812: 7
one day before your death 1698:11
sure to die, would r. 1585: 2
weak alone r. 1698:18
what's past 295:18
Repentance 1698
all save silence bring r. 1822:16
always comes behind 1699:14
death-bed r. 1699: 6
give r. to her lover 2201:16
good, innocence better ..1699: 3
he who seeks r. 1698:11
I decline to buy r. 1698:17
is the form you see 1433: 5
long years of r. 1016:23
more than remorse 1700: 3
no r. in the grave 1700: 4
of hypocrite hypocrisy ...945:13
of thy thousand lies 214:10
rears her snaky crest 1699:12
stand in stool of r. 1699: 4
swift counsel drags r. 19:17
to do it no more 1699:10
treads on their heels 80: 2
try what r. can 1699:18
virtue of weak minds ..1698:18
want of power to sin 1699: 1
whip of his own r. 1657: 5
winter-garment of r. fling 1699:11
with morning cool r. came 1699:16
ye sorrowed to r. 1698:15
Repented but of three things 1698:14
never r. anything 1698:11
often r. 1825: 3
Repenting in coach and six 1267:17
Repentir n'est pas tant un regret du mal 1699: 8
Repents: age r. too soon 32:13
he that r. of his own act is a fool 1699: 2
world not believe man r. 1700: 1
Repetitia: occidit miseros crambe r. 450: 3
Repetition kills the wretch 450: 3
use not vain r. 198:12
Replication prompt 2025:20
Reply Churlish 1663:15
for r. too mad 1925:10
I pause for a r. 1665:13
in few words 198:10
theirs not to make r. 2115:14
Répondre de son courage ..324: 4
Report: but I'll r. it 1604:11
evil r. and good r. 809:16
good r. makes men live long 1701:12
knew great men by r. 327: 1
makes crows blacker 344:14
of death an exaggeration ..395: 1
sell me your good r. 200: 4
stifle in your own r. 215: 5
Repos en soi-même 1475: 5
est un bon chose 193: 1
Repose: boredom its brother 193: 1
curtain of r. 1707: 6
earned a night's r. 1063:13
fair-dream'd r. 974: 2
foster nurse of nature ..1285: 3
genius for r. 61: 1
Repose, *continued*
God has given us this r. ..1707:15
his last r. 12: 6
men have ever loved r. 1666:18
perpetual r. unendurable 955:18
statue-like r. 393: 6
sweet repast and calm r. 582: 6
sweet r. and rest 1846:10
that ever is the same 725: 1
Reprehensa proverbio est ..461: 7
Reprehension: checked with r. 48: 7
Representation: taxation without r. 2297: 2
Representative depends upon people 432: 8
Repression seed of revolution 1715: 1
Reproach and everlasting shame 1809:20
cuts deeper than sword .1697: 4
listen to fool's r. 696:12
of a few 1479:17
of making world miserable 2180: 9
receives r. of being 1702: 1
without fear and without r. 259:12
Reproaches: idle and poor r. 956: 8
of his own heart 1697: 1
Reprobation: fall to r. 75: 2
Reproches qui louent 1580: 7
Reproduction of mankind a great marvel 1221:13
Reproof: bear r. who merit praise 1580:10
is half lost 1684: 8
on her lip 601: 8
useful r. to praise 1580: 7
Valiant 1663:15
Reproofs make friendship distant 738:17
Reprove: avoid what you r. 1832: 7
her when she's right 2183: 1
Reptile: let the r. live 1855: 5
Reptiles: breed r. of the mind 1428: 9
Republic
See also Democracy
bloom forever, O R. 1160: 2
climate of civilization 430:14
is a raft 430:10
of letters 1167: 4
of mediocrity 759:12
tortured for the R. 1280: 2
Republica: corruptissima r. 1090: 6
Republican: acrimonious and surly r. 431: 7
form of government 431:10
highest form of government 433: 4
mail handed out by R. ..1548:12
only form of government 432:13
party 1545:11
Republicanism of the family 632:18
Republicans split 1545:11
stalwart R. 1545:11
we are R. 1552: 2
Republics end through luxury 815:17
exist by being agitated 1106: 7
République des lettres ...1167: 4
Républiques finissent par le luxe 815:17
Repudiate the repudiators 1557: 6
Repugnance to paying 1470: 2
Repulse: take no r. 2202:14
Reputation: at every word a r. dies 1700:17
better than my r. 1701: 5
blaze of r. dies in socket 1700:11
bleeds in every word 1837: 7
but no money 1701: 7
contemporaneous r. 624: 7
demands words 1700:13
difficult to win r. 1700: 9
easily cracked 1703: 8
false r. 1761: 7
for veracity 921: 5
good r. is a fair estate 1701:11
great r. great noise 1700:12

Riddles still bid us defiance ... 1765: 7
Ride a bit of blood ... 942:15
booted and spurred to r. 1067: 5
for curing melancholy ... 1291:11
just came for the r. ... 747:15
man, sit easy and light 931: 8
more than thou goest ... 1931: 1
not free horse to death ... 928:16
we r. them down ... 1255:14
well could he r. ... 931:13
Ride, si sapis ... 1076: 1
Rideau: tirez le r. ... 416:15
Ridenda aut flenda ... 1078: 5
Ridentem: audit dulce r. ... 1211: 7
Ridentibus arrident ... 1077:13
Rider
See also Horsemanship
and horse—friend, foe ... 2120: 1
he had a r. on his back 931: 6
unequalled ... 931:14
Riders in a race do not stop 39:12
Rides behind must not guide ... 1094:14
upon the storm ... 795: 7
Rides: plus des r. en l'esprit ... 35: 5
tecum ipse r. ... 1078:13
Ridge that tempts ambition .49: 7
Ridgepole: held the r. up ... 1159: 8
Ridicule ... **1724**
checks what is absurd ... 1724:15
he who laughs bears r. ... 1724: 7
hold them up to r. ... 60:13
philosophy philosophical .1500:14
sacred to r. his life long 1724:14
test of truth ... 1725: 5
to r. philosophy philosophical ... 1500:14
turning others into r. ... 1724: 8
Ridicule des méchants originaux ... 963: 5
touche au sublime ... 1725:11
Ridiculous and magnificent 1725:10
for qualities he pretends ... 946: 2
touches sublime ... 1725:11
Ridiculousness ... **1725**
Ridiculum acri fortius ... 1009:16
Riding, fencing, gunnery 531:17
good r. at two anchors ... 1649:12
Rien: ci-gît qui ne fut r. ... 571: 7
n'arrive pour r. ... 1414:11
Riez donc, beau rieur ... 1078:22
Rifiuto: il gran r. ... 1686:14
Rift between the sexes ... 1802:12
within the lute ... 1368:15
Rigadoon: ancient r. ... 361:11
Rigdom Funnidos ... 1409: 5
Rigging: his r. refitted ... 572: 3
Riggish: when she is r. ... 2076:16
Right ... **1725**
after death all men r. ... 565:10
all goes r. and nothing wrong ... 1491: 4
all seem wrong and r. ... 99:17
all's r. with the world ... 1905:13
and wrong become one ... 643:16
and wrong exist in nature 1727:12
as a line ... 1725:18
as a ram's horn ... 1725:18
as a Ribstone Pippin ... 879:11
as a trivet ... 1725:18
as my glove ... 1725:18
as my leg ... 1725:18
as snow in harvest ... 1857:10
as rain ... 558:3; 1725:18
as soldier, wrong as man 1865:15
be sure you are r. ... 1725:17
better than law ... 1726:15
both are r. ... 25: 8
by force of beauty ... 131:10
claim as r. what you can ask ... 653:14
constitutional r. ... 57:10
defend your r. to say it ... 2276: 1
divine of kings to govern wrong ... 1044: 5
divine r. of government ... 814: 1
divine r. of kings ... 814: 1
divine r. of plutocrats ... 1065:11

Right, *continued*
do r. and get no thanks ... 1727: 6
do r. and leave consequences ... 1726:11
equal r. to use of land ... 1066: 1
foot first ... 704:19
give every r. you claim 2022: 6
God and my r. ... 546: 2
God will give r. upper hand ... 1726: 3
greatest r. in world ... 1728:7a
he's all r. ... 1557:11
heaven still guards the r. ... 77: 3
hew to line of r. ... 1726:11
hooking r. and wrong ... 1094: 5
I am r. and you are r. ... 1726: 4
I see the r. ... 149: 1
I shrank from what was r. 972:12
if mankind had wished for r. ... 1726: 6
in r. with two or three 1839:15
is in our swords ... 1955:13
is more than might ... 1304: 3
is overcome by might ... 1303:21
is r. ... 1725:16
it don't seem hardly r. ... 59: 6
it must be r. ... 845:13
makes might ... 1303:18
mashing of r. and wrong 1727: 5
might and r. ... 1303:11
might and r. govern ... 1303:16
more precious than peace ... 54: 7
more r. than wrong ... 1727: 4
my r. has been rolled up 2108: 5
natural r. to be free ... 1103:10
never do r. by mistake ... 1727:13
never valued r. and wrong ... 1092: 3
not satisfied to be r. ... 1727:11
nothing r. until beautiful 131:15
now ain't I r. ... 2290: 7
now is wrong ... 1728: 4
of earlier creation ... 68:11
of excessive wrong ... 1727: 3
of ignorant man ... 530: 5
of poets ever was ... 1527:11
of private judgment ... 52: 5
of roaming ... 2070:21
one goes to r., other left ... 575:20
or wrong: our country ... 63: 6
overborne of wrong ... 1728: 5
people's r. remains ... 1483:11
pray that God defend R. 555:15
prove r. is wrong ... 1728: 1
rather r. than President 1552: 5
refuse with r. take with left ... 199:12
revolutionary r. to dismember ... 57:10
seizes the r. and holds it 2167:13
shall be the r. ... 1727: 3
spake much of r. and wrong ... 1727:18
speak r., denounce wrong 1727:17
still in the r. to stay ... 937: 7
swift-footed to uphold r. 1728: 3
tends to universal good 1726: 9
that r. should overcome might ... 1304: 1
to acquire property ... 1622: 7
to be a cussed fool ... 699: 5
to be happy ... 857:12
to be his own oppressor 430:16
to be in this world ... 1728:12
to be wrong ... 1728:7a
to begin with ... 2244: 5
to censure, heart to help 1023: 5
to consume happiness ... 857:14
to dissemble love ... 1035: 3
to live as we wish ... 722: 9
to portion of earth ... 1728:12
to see r. and not do it ... 331:13
to square inch of soil ... 1464: 1
to use of land ... 1728:12
to yield to truth ... 2053: 3
tried hard to do r. ... 279:12
true idea of r. ... 1726:14
until it is settled r. ... 1726:20
what r. have we to happiness ... 854:10

Right, *continued*
what r., what true ... 2054: 3
whatever is, is r. .1435:8; 1726:17
who can be secure of r. 1303:14
with firmness in the r. 1726:12
with two or three ... 1839:15
you all are r. and wrong 1423:14
Righteous are bold as lion 2134:22
be not r. over much ... 1728:15
flourish like palm tree 1728:18
forsaken ... 145:10
hath hope in his death ... 413: 8
in his own eyes ... 1728:16
not seen the r. forsaken ... 145:10; 1728:18
pay for the sinners ... 1830: 8
promise little, perform much ... 1621:6a
rigid R. is a fool ... 1728:15
sold the r. for silver ... 2032:9a
tormented ... 987:10
Righteousness ... **1728**
and peace have kissed ... 1298:12
choose r. ... 1471: 6
exalteth a nation ... 1728:17
for r., but behold a cry 2064: 1
in the way of r. ... 38: 8
unskilful in r. ... 1304: 4
what is all r. ... 1728:14
Rightness expresses of actions ... 1726:18
Rights are still transmitted 1086: 5
equal r. for all ... 53: 8
for which one hand fights 304:13
God-given r. ... 1728:11
no r. to respect ... 1395: 9
of Man ... 1728: 8
of mankind ... 432:13
of men to govern self ... 813:15
of the laboring man ... 1065:11
only when our r. invaded ... 59: 7
that cost sires' blood ... 558:13
unalienable r. ... 975: 4
what r. are his ... 1728:13
with all r. in their hands 432: 4
Rigmarole: learn'd call r. .1899:19
Rigol: golden r. ... 395:11
Rigor and no law ... 1948:19
of penal law ... 1088: 3
of the game ... 219:16
of the law ... 1086:19
want of sufficient r. ... 2062:13
Riled: gittin' r. ... 79: 4
what vexed and r. him ... 79: 4
Riley: life of R. ... 1636: 7
Rill: in every r. sweet instruction ... 1389: 3
Siloam's shady r. ... 1156: 9
sing who will of r. ... 275:20
sun-loved r. ... 200:11
Rills: pure gurgling r. ... 1387: 8
their mazy progress take ... 200:10
Rim: Sun's r. dips ... 365:10
Rimarum: plenus r. sum ... 1785: 4
Ring: bright gold r. on hand 1013:13
for liberty ... 975: 9
I'll buy the r. ... 2289: 3
iron r. worn by use ... 2070: 6
of Wedded Love ... 1274:15
out the false ... 2262: 8
that looked like ruby ... 490:13
with this r. I thee wed ... 1271:10
your wedding r. wears ... 1274: 9
Ringing in the ears ... 2: 8
Ringlet of thin gray hair 2294: 4
Ringlets: all the wanton r. loop ... 848: 2
in wanton r. wav'd ... 847:14
Rinsings of unclean imagination ... 60:10
Rio: roll down to R. ... 1779: 1
Riot: his rash fierce blaze of r. ... 563:16
Rip: let her r. ... 1644:11
to manhood grew ... 1971: 4
Rip Van Winkle: when R. V. W. went away 1882: 2
Ripe as the melting cluster 2213: 9
for exploits ... 2265: 5
not r. till rotten ... 1638: 3

Ripe, *continued*
soon r. soon rotten 1638: 3
we r. and r. 934: 8
Ripeness is all 382: 8
Ripple of renown 1890:18
Rire est le propre 1077:17
Rise at five, dine at nine 873: 6
betimes 1266:10
by things under feet 1616: 9
early to please all 1513: 7
like feather'd Mercury ..931:13
let it r., let it r. 1340:12
never r. to fight again ..457: 3
of empires and their fall 795:10
of empires, fall of kings 792:13
of every man 587: 5
of the second Adam 11: 9
perchance to fall 1040: 2
some r. by sin 2082: 8
sooner fall than r. 622: 9
to r. by others' fall 1380:13
we fall to r. 621: 6
we r. by raising others ..1492: 7
with the lark 1071: 8
you early in morning ..1729: 1
Riser: early r. may sleep 1729: 5
Rises but to fall 419:14
early to do wrong 1403:11
on the toe 110:11
one never r. so high 1929: 4
Riseth first, first dressed 1729: 4
up again 1488:11
who r. late 1729: 2
Risibility: what provokes
you to r. 1480: 3
Rising 1728
early in the morning 1730: 3
seem'd pillar of state 448: 6
to a man's work 2234: 7
unto place laborious 836: 9
with Aurora's light 1526: 9
Risk all in one day 456:18
must pay for gain 752: 8
sweetened by r. 363:15
Riso dell' universo 1851:13
Risu: nam r. inepto 1076: 5
Risum teneatis, amici ..1078:18
Risus: nimium r. pretium
est 1076:17
Rite: outworn r. 949: 1
Rites mysterious of love 1273: 8
to jocund Flora dear ..1911:10
Ritual means throwing away
something 1691:13
truth of religion is in its r. 1691:13
Rival: each upon his r.
glared 1731: 4
in the wrong 698:15
keeps jealous lookout 1730:18
Rivalem patienter habe ..1731: 1
Rivalry 1730
in valor spurred them
on 2072:13
is good for mortals 1730:19
unresentful r. 58: 3
Rivals dwell on same river 1731: 5
not r. in command 201:15
tightly belted for the race 1731: 1
Rivalship: nothing done
beautifully in r. 1731: 3
Rivaux: qui s'aimait sans
avoir de r. 1730:20
River 1731
at my garden's end 1329:12
beyond r. I-forget 709: 4
blame some crystal r. ..988: 2
cosiest of friends 1731: 6
did not bring r. and sky 1896: 7
fill r. with my tears 1975: 9
floats upon the r. of his
thoughts 2195: 3
follow r. and find sea ..1731:12
fruitful r. in the eye ..2176:17
glideth at own sweet will 1168:14
has its individuality 1731: 9
let us cross the r. 1005: 4
like thee, noble r. 1143: 3
living r. by the door ...191: 6
never seen a r. 1731:10
O r. of rest 1845: 6
River, *continued*
of his thought 2195: 3
of Oblivion 1421: 2
of ten thousand masts 839:11
of thy thoughts 300:23
ol' man r. 2287: 8
over the r. they beckon 402: 8
passed and God forgotten 785:10
sea-green r., proud to lave 1732: 8
seek a r. for companion 1731:12
she by the r. sat 1975: 9
that bears on its bosom ..595:10
there is r. in Macedon ..1732: 5
thousand years hence r.
will run 1731: 7
thronged r. toiling to
the main 1983: 4
to join the brimming r. ..200:16
winds somewhere safe to
sea 1149:10
Rivers: all r. run into sea 1771:14
benefaction to towns 1731: 8
bitter r. 2033:14
deepest r. make least din 2126: 3
deepest r. flow with least
sound 2126: 5
from bubbling springs ..2042: 2
not so rapid as error 576:13
roads that move 1731:11
see the r. how they run 1732: 2
shallow r., to whose falls 1732: 4
which are still in motion,
stay 1739: 6
Rivières chemins qui mar-
chant 1731:11
Rivos: claudite jam r. 1669:10
Rivulet: drinking at a r. ..201: 2
of text 190: 4
Rivulets hurrying thro'
lawn 200:10
Roach: timid r. 518: 5
Road 1734
and the r. below me 2103: 5
any r. leads to end of world 1734: 8
because r. was steep 1879: 5
Best R. of All 1735: 1
give enemy r. for flight ..545: 1
grows strange 35: 1
had you seen r. before
made 1735: 3
hard-beaten r. to house 630: 8
human being travels 1622:12
I take to the open r. 2103: 5
it's the white r. westwards 2103: 1
keep common r., safe ..1734:10
life's r. so dim and dirty ..165: 6
life's unfinished r. 1933: 5
live by side of the r. ..1495: 8
my r. shall be r. I made 1708: 3
no easy r. from earth to
stars 1913: 9
no expeditious r. 1452: 3
no flowery r. to glory ..780: 6
on beaten r. tolerable traveling 1734: 4
only r. to highest stations 1092:16
pursued a lonely r. 1251: 3
reeling r., a rolling r. ..1734: 5
rolling English r. 1734: 5
rough r. to greatness 838: 2
rough that has no friend 730:17
straggling r. in Spain 227:11
surest r. to health 872: 3
that has room to spare for
one 1277:16
that leads to God knows
where 1735: 1
this r. not jackassable ..1734: 6
to arrive follow single r. 1661:15
to heaven near by water 885:19
to hell easy to travel 892: 4
to Mandalay 368:5; 1212: 6
to the heavens remains ..110: 8
to resolution lies by doubt 1734:15
to ruin always in repair 1749: 9
to vice steep 2079:12
up-hill all the way 1146: 3
upon the r. to Romany ..2102: 2
was a ribbon of moonlight 1734:14
whence no one returns ..389: 1
Road, *continued*
where r. bends, short steps 1649:14
wherever my r. shall lie ..439:13
which we must travel too 389: 8
who passes by r. so late 259:11
whose dust is gold 1734:13
windin' mile after mile 2102: 6
Road's last turn best 32: 8
Roads: all r. end at grave 825:21
countless r. to hell 892: 5
crooked r. of genius 759:16
endure 1734: 9
great r. the Romans built 1734: 9
there are fifty r. to town 1696: 8
thousand r. lead to Rome 1736:10
to our last abode 966: 5
various the r. of life 1148:14
Roam: ever let the Fancy
r. 634: 9
which best, to r. or rest 2101: 9
Roamed o'er many lands ..708: 1
Roamer: sweetest r. 197: 1
Roamin': vacant, careless r. .32:17
Roaming in thought 812: 8
we own the right of r. ..2070:21
with a hungry heart 2029: 2
Roar all like bears 126:11
as 't were nightingale ..2097: 7
gently as sucking dove ..2097: 7
loosen'd aggravated r. ..1154: 2
nature says, r. 1444: 9
Roast beef of old England .522: 9
great boast and little r. 173:12
rule the r. 1751: 5
Roast-meats and pilaus 523: 9
Roasting of eggs 532:16
Rob lady of her fortune 1267:15
Peter 1491:19
Peter, and give it Paul ..1491:20
Rob was lord below 510: 8
Rob Roy rule 1598: 3
Robbed: he that is r., not
wanting 1986:20
that smiles 1986:19
Robber, see Thief
Robbers spring up by night 1985:20
Robbie asked for bread 198: 5
Robe: azure r. of night 673:11
down flow'd her r. 1099: 1
giant's r. upon dwarfish
thief 2016: 8
golden r. to queen it in ..2234: 3
if any naked be 263: 4
majestic r. of earth 176: 9
of flesh 28:10
purple r. 11: 2
ye weave, another wears 1506: 9
Robert: believe the experienced R. 594:12
Robert of Lincoln 174:16
Roberto: experto crede R. ..594:12
Robes and furr'd gowns 2079:15
in their ostents 489: 9
loosely flowing 488: 4
new r. and may not wear 489: 4
purple r. cause watchful
nights 1723: 9
your tyrants wear 1067: 7
Robin 1735
and the wren 161: 9
help one fainting r. 1036:17
in a cage 1735: 5
our little English R. 1735:12
Redbreast 1735: 4
thou wert there upon day 1735: 7
took from crown one thorn 1735: 7
Robin Adair 3: 9
Robin Hood and Little John 122:14
ballad-singers joy 122:14
tales 1960: 8
Robin's not here 3: 9
Robin-redbreast and the
wren 1735:11
Robinson, Sir Thomas 1875: 6
Robinson Crusoe 184: 9
Robs on business principles 561: 9
Rock engirdled by the sea 428: 6
founded as the r. 657:20
founded upon a r. 271:11
gem of the old r. 69:12

Rock, *continued*
me to sleep, mother 2011: 1
no r. so hard but that ..2042: 4
of Ages 792:14
of Israel, of salvation ..792:14
of national resources ...334: 1
of offence 1425:15
sharp-edged r. of poverty 2094:10
stood the sea's shock 1775:12
struck and cleft for me 792:14
this r. shall fly 428: 6
turn r. into a garden 1622:15
upon this r. 271:11
what is harder than r. ..2126:10
Rocked in the cradle of the deep 1777:13
Rocket in the air 228:17
risen like a r. 446:12
rose like a r. 205: 9
Rocking-horse: they sway'd upon r. 1529: 2
Rocks: from r. to roses ..1963:25
impregnable not so stout 2014: 8
look for r. ahead 1625: 8
proclaim approaching Deity 261:10
rich in gems 1356: 9
to sit on r. 1384: 1
unscalable 549:16
whereon greatest men 1560: 5
Rod and thy staff 285: 5
for him void of understanding 1657:11
for the back of him 1657:11
for the fool's back 697:23
have a r. in pickle 1657:20
his r. revers'd 1575: 1
is a long instrument 671: 8
kiss the r. 1203:16
let the r. have a rest ..1971: 6
of criticism 339: 7
of empire 851: 8
of iron 1750:20
spareth r. hateth son 256:16
spare the r. and spoil the child 256:14
throw away thy r. 791:10
twelve feet long 671: 5
would a man scape the r. 1698:11
you must kiss the r. 1047:20
Rode madly off in all directions 931:12
Roderick: where was R. ..983: 3
Roderick Dhu: I am R. D. 1766:18
Rods of fortune-tellers ..2125:15
Roe: similar r. 108:11
Roederer: scent of the R. 1746: 3
Rogare: nisi quod r. possis palam 1583:16
noli r. quod inpetrare 1585:10
postea noli r. quod nolueris 2169: 7
Rogat: qui r., ille facit ..1583: 4
qui timide r. docet negare 2015: 6
Rogatæ: gaudent esse r. ..2208: 5
Roger is my dog 473: 4
Rogue 1735
and peasant slave am I 1840: 7
ev'ry inch not fool is r. 700: 9
frosty-spirited r. 1053: 5
in grain a r. amain 1052:21
is only a fool 700:20
may dig the grave 827: 8
no den to hide a r. 1656:13
one r. to usher in other 1052:16
præternotorious r. 1052:12
roundabout fool 700: 8
satirical r. 35:16
some busy, insinuating r. 1837:15
still suspects another ...700: 7
thorough-paced r. 346: 8
with venison 451: 1
Rogued: I've r. an' I've ranged 1224: 2
Roguery of alchemy 1500:10
Rogues by retail 1484:12
live with r. and fools 700: 2
only r. feel law 1080: 3
such smiling r. as these 1053: 5
who could not hide their tricks 626:17
Roi est mort. Vive le r. ..1043:15
le R. le veut 1043:16
malheureuse 718: 9
O Richard, O mon r. ...1038:18
premier r. soldat heureux ..74: 3
regne, ne gouverne pas ..1039:11
Rois: ces malheureux r. ..1040: 5
Role: act this r. adroitly ..1124:19
play well the r. 1124:19
who cast you for the r. ..1125: 4
Rolet un fripon 1371:13
Roll of common men 832:15
on, thou ball 2237:13
Roller: heavy r. of Democracy 1556: 4
steam r. 1556: 4
Rolling: he just keeps r. 1733: 9
he keeps on r. along 2287: 8
Rolls it under his tongue 2024: 4
mouldy r. of Noah's Ark 2016: 1
Roma: á R. por todo 1736:13
cuando á R. fueres 1738: 1
frangitur R. superba bonis 1739:12
locuta est 1740: 1
neque uno est condita R. die 1737: 6
prima urbes inter, aurea R. 1738: 7
Romæ: altæ mœnia R. ..1737:13
cum fueris R., Romano vivito more 1737:18
fumum et opes strepitumque R. 1738:10
omnia R. cum pretio 1737: 2
omnia venalia R. 1737: 2
quando R. sum, jejuno Sabbato 1737:18
quid R. faciam 1737: 1
rus optas 454: 7
Tibur amem 454: 7
Romam: fortunatam natam me consule R. 1736:16
urbem quam dicunt R. 1739: 1
Roman: go forward like a stoic R. 2203: 5
high R. fashion 325:18
I'm a R. for that 1467:10
is was a noble R. 1734: 4
more an antique R. 1737: 7
nature of R. to suffer bravely 1737: 4
noblest R. of them all 1737: 9
Old R. 1377:16
thou art R., be not barbarous 1737:10
would have turned back 1946: 3
Romana manus contexuit 1739: 4
Romanam: tantæ molis R. condere gentem 1737:14
Romance 1735
brought up the nine-fifteen 1736: 1
cold and grey without r. 1735:13
Farewell, R. 1736: 1
full of truths 662: 5
grace and glimmer of r. 1533:10
is always young 1736: 6
leaves one so unromantic 1736: 7
like ghost, eludes touching 1735:15
love affair other than domestic 1736:4a
parent of golden dreams 1735:14
quantity production 1174: 5
makes woman look a ruin 1265: 5
should begin with science 1736: 7
spirit of adventure 1736: 5
to be a man's last r. 1207: 1
to love oneself is a lifelong r. 1791:15
what world calls r. 1736: 8
who avoid r. escape title of fool 1736: 3
Romances: like r. read ..1221: 5
paint wooings 662: 2
Romane: hae tibi erunt artes R. 1738:16
imperio populos, R. 1738:16
Romani: terrore nominis R. 1736:14
Romanism: rum, R. and rebellion 1552: 2
Romanorum ultimus 1737:11
Romanos, rerum dominos 1738:16
Romans: blunt, flat people 1737: 3
do as R. do 1738: 6
last of the R. 1737:11
man who first ruined R. 1739:10
were like brothers 202: 1
Romanum: facere et pati fortiter R. 1737: 4
Romanus: civis R. sum ..1736:14
Senatus Populusque R. ..1737:17
Romany lass to R. lad ..2102: 3
road to R. 2102: 2
Romanza: singing his sweet r. 1364:12
Rome 1736
and I 533: 9
at R. hanker for country 454: 7
built of mud 1736:12
cherished humanity as sons 1738: 8
church of R. fallen into mire 1740: 7
city of the soul 1739: 2
could never make island 550: 7
curse of R. 353:13
doth conquered R. inter 1739: 6
every one comes round by R. 1736:13
first among cities 1738: 7
found R. brick 1736:12
found R. of brick 1089: 8
gate of holy R. 1741: 4
gave to R. my rendezvous 1738:11
grave, city, wilderness ..1739:13
has spoken 1740: 1
her own sepulchre appears 1739:11
in R. do as Romans do ..1737:18
launch the curse of R. ..353:13
loved R. more 213: 8
no place like R. 454: 7
of R. hath victory 1739: 6
only R. could make R. tremble 1738: 9
only to R. compared be 1738: 9
queen of nations 1738: 7
second at R. 47:13
square stones of R. 268: 7
thousand roads lead to R. 1736:10
upon it sun never sets 1738: 8
victorious in mourning ..1738:14
was not built in a day 1737: 6
when at R., do after dome 1738: 4
yet perished fated R. 1739: 9
your mother never at R. ..68: 8
Rome ne fut pas faite ..1737: 6
Rome's far-reaching bolts 1227: 9
gross yoke 1740: 4
Romeo cut up into stars ..1214:15
give me my R. 1214:15
if dead 1214:15
wherefore art thou R. ..1372:18
Romore: mondam r. 623: 7
Romulus and Remus had suckled 83:10
Romulus æterne nondum formaverat urbis 1737:12
Rood maintained its man ..638: 5
Roof fretted with fire 2068:10
high embossed r. 96: 6
thatched r. covered free men 1329: 4
under one r. with me ..2032:15
Roofs as Piety could raise 271:17
some of the r. are plumcolor 1783:15
Rooks, Committee-men or Trustees 100: 2
Room: ample r., verge enough 890:18
better than company 287: 6
darkened r. to muse invite 2255:11
every r. hath blaz'd 1300:17
for honest men to live 62: 4
for yours sincerely 1102: 6
genial r. to treat friend 1329:10
in wooden house golden r. 328:17
little r. of dreams 481: 9
old log cabin r. 2293:10
serve to fill a r. 697:20

Room, *continued*
smoke-filled r. 1553: 1
to swing a cat 223: 3
uppermost r. worst 1309:17
very r. seemed warm ...981:13
without books, soulless ..181:12
Rooms for ambition too low 310:16
of thy native country 2028:11
Roosevelt, Theodore ...1741
will walk on the waters 1741: 7
Roosevelt is only Kerensky 1714:17
Rooshans: some people R. 558:15
Roosian: might have been a R. 558:15
Roost: great boast small r. 173:12
Rooster 232
crimson Gallic r. 719:12
hungry r. don't cackle ..939:11
Root: call a r. a r. 1898:16
for the home team 2291:11
have we eaten insane r. 1231:11
hog, or die 1954: 8
in the right soil 1743:14
is hard to loose 690:13
lacking r. in homely earth 1812:10
love of money r. of evil 1337: 2
more pernicious r. 119:17
of all our woe 1617:16
of daffodil 1213:15
of forget-me-not 684:10
of honesty and virtue 528:14
of the matter 224:22
tho' my heart be at the r. ..875:10
unfix his earth-bound r. 2210:10
Root, Elihu: head devil ..1542:19
Rootlets up through fibres 2036: 8
Roots: blind deep-buried r. 1906: 3
broad on r. of things ..108:17
grass r. 2279: 4
if the r. are deep 2035:10
of cruelty 355:23
of education bitter 528: 8
Ropa: no da cienca 485:20
Rope: climbs the r. 360: 8
enough to hang himself ..852:13
for a keepsake 853:10
intended to stretch a r. ..1547:13
knit a r. of sand 1638: 2
loath to lay out money on r. 117:17
makes a r. his life to end 1997:11
must not be mentioned ..852: 7
of sand could twist 1638: 2
throw r. after bucket ..1650: 1
twist a r. of sand 1683:10
Ropes are taut with dew ..2102: 5
made with sand 1638: 2
Rore vixit more cicadæ 445:11
Rosa flos veneris 1742:11
riget amissa spina relicta r. 1744: 8
Rosaleen: my dark R. 998: 2
Rosarum: quam una dies, ætas r. 1744:20
Rosary: my r. 1214: 2
Rosas: collige, virgo, r. ..2010: 9
Rose 1742
ah! may the red r. live alway 2286: 2
Alpine r. 1743:16
awful r. of dawn 798: 6
because the r. must fade 1745: 6
blendeth with violet 684: 5
bloom of a r. passes quickly 1745: 1
brain a tyrant with a r. 1465:15
breedeth a burr 1744: 5
budding r. 1743:13
by any other name 1373: 1
by r. I strip the leaves 1745: 2
choked in the grass 1144:13
crimsonne r. is drooping 945: 6
distils a healing balm ..1746: 6
earthlier happy r. distill'd 1278: 8
Eden R. 1746: 6
fairest when 'tis budding 1743:13
flamelike r. of verse 1812:10
for every thistle 491: 9
gather the r. in prime ..2010:17
go, lovely r. 1748: 3
great is the r. 1745: 4
Rose, *continued*
half-blown r. 138:12
has but summer reign ..358: 8
has one powerful virtue 1746: 9
how fair is the r. 1746: 9
I have lived with the r. 1746: 2
I marked 1747: 9
I'll pu' the budding r. ..1746: 1
in hand of ugly 1487: 7
in snowy milk bashful r. 608: 3
is a r. is a r. is a r. 1743: 6
is fragrant 686: 7
is red, violet blue 2072: 2
is sweet 1745:13
is sweeter in the bud ..1743:13
is the flower of Venus ..1742:11
it had no thorn 49:15
it is written on the r. 1745: 7
joy of heaven 1743:16
just like love yonder r. 1194:14
keep my r. for a wintry day 2286: 2
kissed me today 1049: 1
leaves upon the briar 1744: 6
like nymph to the bath ..1744: 1
like to the damask R. 2277: 2
looks fair 1746: 9
lovely is the r. 1670:16
lover's r. is dead 2149:16
might be a throat 1367:14
mighty lak a r. 122: 5
must fade and beauty lose 1745: 5
my little Irish r. 2292: 8
never blows so red the r. ..384:10
no r. has been original ..1441: 7
no r. without thorn 1744: 5
nothing but a r. I gave her 1747: 4
of all the World 1743: 6
of the Desert 1743: 1
of the desert, thou art ..1746:15
of the Garden 1743: 1
of Yesterday 1745:10
old R. is dead 400:16
on my right side 1946: 1
one r. but one 1050: 9
one r. makes a gown 883: 3
perishes, thorn is left ..1744: 8
queen of flowers 138:12
queen r., so fair and sweet 1746: 2
raise the milk-white r. ..1747: 1
red as a r. is she 1272:14
red r. on triumphant briar 1747: 1
reddens to a r. 1535: 7
rose-leaves, when r. is dead 1293: 9
royal-hearted r. 683: 6
sad R. of all my days ..1743: 6
secret, and inviolate r. ..1743: 6
shall sing thee lullabies ..1847: 4
shut and be bud again ..1743:13
smell a r. through a fence 1747: 5
speaks all languages 586: 4
spoken under the r. 1783: 8
sweet as r. that died 1743:15
sweet is the r. but grows upon a briar 1953:12
sweet r., fair flower 1745:12
sweetest r. has prickle 1511:11
sweetest r., where all 138:12
that all are praising 1743: 7
that challenges the crypt 1745: 4
that lives its hour 1745: 3
that's the r. for me 1743: 7
thou art sweetest flower ..1743:16
though r. have prickles ..2215: 9
through thee r. is red ..729:16
'tis the last r. of summer 1745: 9
to the living is more ..1578: 8
under the r. 138:12; 1742:11
vast as the heavens 1940: 3
voted R. Queen of flowers 1742:13
vying with the r. 120:11
was Heaven to smell 1743:10
waxed as red as r. 172: 3
wears a r. in her hair 138:12
wears the r. of youth 2265: 3
Wee White R. 408:14
when I have pluck'd the r. 1745:11
where Cæsar bled 384:10
where fall tears of love 685: 3
Rose, *continued*
where leaves the R. of Yesterday 1745:10
white r. in red rose-garden 609: 5
white r. meant surrender 1747:13
white r. of all the world ..408:14
who dares to name thee ..1747: 4
whose hue, angry and brave 1745: 7
will repeat its story 136: 3
with a broken stem 1747:10
with leaves yet folded ..138:12
withers, Blossom blasteth 2277: 2
yet a R. full-blown 261: 6
your mouth the mystic R. 1747: 8
Rose: je ne suis pas la r. 1746: 2
Rose Aylmer 401: 6
Rose's: one day the r. life 1744:20
wherefore waste r. bloom 1578: 9
Rose-bloom fell on her hands 1584:11
Rose-bush: best r. 1744:19
Rose-crossed into darkness .398: 5
Rose-crowned into the darkness 398: 5
Rose-dew: born of r. 336:12
Rose-grove: I come from r. 1748: 2
Rose-in-Bloom: pet of the harem, R. 521:16
Rose-leaves fall into billows 1940: 3
Rosebud and a pair of gloves 1201: 9
set with wilful thorns 2185: 2
white r. for a guerdon ..1746:10
Rosebuds: crown ourselves with r. 2010:19
fill'd with snow 2027: 9
gather ye r. 2010:11
in the morning dew 1743: 9
scarcely show'd their hue 1743: 9
warm r. below 37:10
yellow and red 1747: 2
Roseburst of dawn 991:16
Rosemary 691
for remembrance 687: 3
Rosen: himmlische R. 2185: 9
pflücke R. weil sie blühn .2010:10
Roses all that's fair adorn 1744: 2
and raptures of vice 2081:16
are beauty 1745: 8
ashes of r. these 1687:16
at first were white 1746:14
bade me gather her blue r. 1203: 7
bread, but give us r. 945: 4
but ain't the r. sweet ..1744:17
by Bendemere's stream ..1405: 9
do r. stick like burrs ..1227: 7
first came red 1746:14
first r. of year shall blow 827:13
for the flush of youth 25: 1
fresh-blown r. 2269:17
friends again with r. 1743: 3
gather r. while they bloom 2010:10
gather the r., maiden ..2010: 9
gather r. of your youth 2010:15
give me my r. now 1578: 8
heavenly r. in earthly life 2185: 9
how r. first came red ..1538: 2
I sent my love two r. 1747:13
I will make thee beds of r. 1747: 7
in a bed of lilies shed 141: 2
in the lilies' bed 172: 3
it was r. r. all the way ..1742: 8
it was the time of r. 1743:11
it will never rain r. 1742:12
keep not r. for dead brow 1578:11
kindled into thought 172: 3
knotted oaks adorn 46:15
make world so sweet 1026: 3
may fade 1296:11
musky-breathed 686: 5
newly wash'd in dew 2200: 6
of eighteen 947:15
of pleasure 1512:11
on your thorny tree 683: 3
over-washed with dew 1164: 3
plenty, r. plenty 1743: 8
prickly thorn often bears soft r. 1744: 9
red and r. white 1203: 7
red and violets blue 686: 3

Safety, *continued*
by ourselves s. bought 58: 9
in multitude s. 20: 5
in numbers 726:20
in patience there is s. ..1462: 7
lies in middle course 1754: 5
Lord makest me dwell in s. 1847: 9
no s. in war 2119:13
of all before s. of few ..1079: 9
of people highest law 1478:15
of state highest law 1478:15
only hope of s. in boldness 178: 4
only s. is to expect no s. 1754:12
pluck this flower, s. 1754: 9
pot of ale and s. 44:17
preserve s. by innocence .990:20
public s. supersedes private 935:15
razor blades 124:12
sought s. in flight 457: 1
strike against public s. ..1065:15
temporary s. 1106:14
Sagacious, bold, and turbulent 240: 4
Saftest of the fam'ly 1925: 6
Sagacity: homeopathic s. ..2269: 3
Sage best of all herbs 1288: 1
between fool and s. 25:15
experience made him s. 39: 3
in France, madman in Japan 2162: 6
its signet s. 26: 6
make the s. frolic 2158:12
no better than the fool ..1794:10
of Greystone 1377:16
of Monticello 1377:16
of Wheatland 1377:16
why die who has s. 1288: 1
without hardness be s. 42: 8
Sage avec sobriété 1678:21
évite le monde 1859:23
plus s. qu'il re le faut ..2164:10
pour les autres 2165: 9
qui ne pense point l'être 2168: 6
qui se croit s. 702: 6
Sages: sayings of the Seven S. 1629:17
would have died to learn 157: 2
Sagesse à l'âme, santé ...2163:10
aimer le vin 2159:10a
de Bonaparte 1378: 8
Said anything you understand 1480: 3
as well s. as if I had s. it 174:11
easier s. than done 2227: 1
if I s. so, it was so 2057:11
inadvertently s. some evil thing 1480: 3
it that knew it best 1055: 5
least s. soonest mended ..1821:15
less s. the better 1454: 1
never s. foolish thing 244: 7
not what we s. but are ..2229: 9
our good things before us 1507:11
so much, done so little ..2228: 9
sooner s. than done 2227: 1
that's well s. 174:11
was it something s. 1194:10
whatever well s. is mine .1507: 8
Sail: all s. and no ballast 2190:13
and s., and let 'er knit ..1778:12
before the wind 1543:15
direct my s. 1646:14
good to s. upon the sea ..1776:13
gray s. against the sky ..1813:12
he spreads for Heav'n ..1696: 4
is shifted accordingly 1546: 9
never weather-beaten s. ..1706:10
O farther, farther s. 1893: 4
o'er silent seas again 1455: 5
on! s. on! and on 1488: 9
phantom s. 1344:11
quiet s. noiseless wing ..1776: 6
seen from deserted shore ..129: 1
thou too, s. on 52: 4
through life towards death 740: 1
thy best, ship 52: 4
to take in s. 27: 6
we s. "outward bound" 1430:17
whirring s. goes round ..1442:11
white s. of his soul 400: 7
Sail, *continued*
wind-filled s. 129: 3
with the stream 2243: 7
Sail-yards tremble 1776: 8
Sailed: never s. with me before 1785:12
Sailor
See also under Sea
bring'st s. to his wife ..1814: 8
buried on this shore 1816: 3
every inch a s. 1779: 9
here comes a s. 1779: 9
home is the s. 570: 9
like drunken s. on a mast 1779: 8
speaks of winds 1899:12
take care 2289:11
true-hearted s. 1009: 6
wonder any sane man s. 1778: 6
Sailors born for all weathers 2151: 2
but worldly men 1778: 9
get money like horses ...1779: 9
should never be shy 1778: 9
three s. of Bristol City ..1779:10
Sails: add s. to oars 862:18
behold the threaden s. ..1777:10
easy to spread s. in calm 1774:12
fill'd with lusty wind 1776: 8
majestic with swelling s. 1814: 8
ripp'd, seams op'ning wide 436:20
set thy s. warily 1651: 7
sets s. to suit wind 1779: 5
to spread s. of fate 643: 3
where s. are blossoming 1733: 8
wisely reef thy s. 1651: 7
with full-spread s. 439: 1
with s. of silver by 1835:10
Saint **1754**
able to corrupt a s. 288:16
abroad, devil at home 947:18
black-leg s. 1755: 7
by doing lovely things ..2276: 3
by getting meals 2276: 3
by whom no mercy is shown 1754:16
Christ's chosen s. 1755: 9
dead sinner revised 1754:14
designed a s. above 1754:17
devil a s. was he 443: 2
earthly S. 1350:20
every s. has past 1755:18
every s. his own candle ..1755: 3
every s. superfluous 1754:18
greatest s. may be sinner 1755: 6
grey-haired s. may fail ..1219:20
he weren't no saint 507: 1
he who says what is mine is yours is a s. 1562: 3
in crape 72: 3
in the church 2183: 3
like s., like offering 1755: 3
little S. fits little Shrine 2039:16
make s. of libertine 1755:13
or murderer, the same ...852:10
patron s. in armour 190: 5
person of heroic virtue ..1755:14
savage, sage 334:15
sceptic once in twenty-four hours 1754:18
seem s. when most devil ..949: 8
self-elected s. 1606: 6
she could make of me a s. 1202:16
she'll not appear a s. 2193: 6
so like the rest of us ..1024: 6
sustained it 569: 8
there ain't Another S. ..2072: 2
threadbare s. in wisdom's school 1569: 5
twice a s. in lawn 72: 3
'twould a s. provoke 1755:15
weakest s. upon his knees 1583: 2
who works no miracles 1755: 2
young s. old devil 23:13; 1755:13
Saint Agnes' Eve 1442: 4
Saint George ever on horse backe 748: 3
he was for England 546: 8
hoist standard of S. G. ..2108: 6
that swinged the dragon ..748: 3
the dragon hath killed 546: 8
Saint James's: low S. J. 1336: 5
St. John mingles with my friendly bowl 659:18
Saint Leon raised his kindling eye 1351: 9
St. Louis: meet me in St. L. 2293:10
Saint Martin's summer ..1936: 3
Saint Paul's loomed like a bubble 694:11
ruinous portico of S. P. 1749: 6
ruins of S. P. 1740:13
what built S. P. cathedral .157: 6
where stood S. P. 1749: 3
Saint Peter: give not S. P. so much 1491:16
judge far off 1023: 6
sat by celestial gate 1491:13
very well at Rome 1740: 6
who praiseth S. P. 1491:17
St. Stephen fell asleep 580: 8
Saint Swithin christening the apples 1669:11
Saint Vitus' dance 2235: 4
Saints: all not s. that go to church 1754:15
are more stiff-necked 1754:16
board with s. 1755:10
by all the s. 442: 1
come ye s., look here 514:15
contracting with s. 1755: 1
errant s. 1589: 2
fanatics make s. 633:10
frets s. in heaven 458: 1
great may jest with s. ..835:11
in church they be 2183: 6
in church with s. 287: 3
must be in heaven 1754:17
never S. in Heaven 1754:15
nor Philip Sidneys 499:13
only have such faces 608:10
plaster s. 1866:11
praise dead s. 1755: 8
precious is death of s. ...1755:12
really religious 1684: 4
reforming s. 1753: 8
self-constituted s. 1591:15
silver s. 271:17
stern s., tortured martyrs 1280:15
taught and led the way ..1595:13
teaches s. to tear 2268:15
which God loves best 1755: 5
will aid if men will call ..1586: 3
will sometimes be 773: 5
with s. dost bait hook 1755:17
with the s., a saint 1546: 8
women in churches, s. 2183: 6
Saintship of an anchorite .2031: 6
Sait rien, comprend tout ..2066: 1
Sake: for his belly's s. 154:14
for his name's s. 790:18
for labor's s. against nature 1062: 3
for manners' s. 521: 5
for their bellies' s. 155:11
for old sake's s. 1296: 3
Saki: Eternal S. 1120:12
Sal Atticum 1756: 7
Salaam Aleikum 1588:14
Salad: adieu to song and s. .38:10
and eggs and lighter fare .524: 5
four persons wanted 524: 4
herbaceous treat 524: 6
lobster s. 1923: 4
my s. days, when I was 2265: 2
our Garrick's a s. 757: 4
Salamander? Call it Gerrymander 2280: 5
nourished in the fire 1201: 3
Sale of chapmen's tongues ..129:14
things of s. 208: 1
Salesmanship: learning s. ..529: 5
principles of s. 529: 5
Salgama non noc sunt 1487:12
Salinas, salt pits 1627: 8
Salis: additio s. grano 1756: 8
cum grano s. 1756: 8
multos modios s. simul edendos 737:18
nemini fidas nisi s. absumpseris 1755:23
plus s. quam sumptus 659:15

Satan, *continued*
stood up against Israel ..442: 4
thence in Heaven call'd S. 442: 4
trembles when he sees ...1583: 2
was now at hand 444:17
wiser than of yore 1981:13
Satanas: vade, S. 442: 3
Satanic old age 23:13
school 530: 2
Satchel: carry my s. still 1070:15
Sate at the board of kings ..2275:1a
Satietas: studiorum s. vitæ
facit satietatem 1424:13
voluptatibus vicina s. 90: 9
Satiety follows pleasures .1511: 5
giveth occasion of s. 1284: 4
neighbor to pleasure 90: 9
no s. in study 1923: 3
of occupation s. of life ..1424:13
of large possessions 1561: 9
Satiram: difficile est s. non
scribere 1758: 2
Satire 1757
always virtue's friend ...1757:13
business of the stage 1910: 4
care for s. or epigram 1758:11
has always shone 1757:17
implicit s. on mankind ..1316:15
is a sort of glass 1758:13
is lonely occupation 1757:14
is my weapon 1758: 8
let s. be my song 1757:10
my s. seems too bold 1758: 8
runs him through 1758: 5
should wound with touch 1758: 4
some s., keen and critical 1758:10
when s. flies abroad 1757:13
wit enough to write S. ..1757:10
Satire ment pendant leur
vie 1758:14
Satirical upon thing so small 1758: 7
Satirist: a would-be s. 1604: 1
Satis: desideratem quod s.
est 1328:14
jam s. est 1328: 4
non s. est puris verbis ..1516: 3
quod s. est cui contigit 1328:13
Satisfaction in being poor 1568:15
in work well done 1957:14
is death 2104: 6
no s. without companion ..286:18
the word is S. 1758: 5
to our blood 596: 5
windy s. of the tongue ..2024:15
Satisfied: I hope you're s. .982: 8
no one s. with fortune ..711:11
three things never s. 828:11
well paid that is well s. ..1469:18
with life, not with self ..150: 1
with my own country 707: 3
with your possessions ..1475:12
Satisfy: nothing can s. ..2210: 3
one friend 728: 5
Saturated with moral law ..1324: 1
Saturday no luck at all ..1267: 4
Saturn, Jupiter, Mars 1912:11
Satyrs grazing on the lawn 360: 3
I would live with s. 248: 9
in white and black 362: 6
Sauce: appetite stands cook .88:15
appetite the best s. 88:10
cloyless s. 315:15
for goose, s. for gander ..812:15
green s. 315:15
her with bitter words 2224: 8
hunger is the best s. 940: 9
in England only one s. 554:13
most sharp s. 2173:15
tabasco s. of sex 1802:14
to his good wit 1260:10
to make me hunger more ..940:10
Sauces: sundry s. dangerous 518:20
Sauciness: impudent s. 178:13
Saul also among prophets 1624:12
and Jonathan 740:13
Saunter à la Sainte Terre 2101: 7
Sausage: first tried German 769: 4
Saut: je fais s. perilleux ..417:12
Savage as a bear with sore
head 126:15
Savage, *continued*
at home a s. 947:18
roam'd the gloomy wild ..1758:17
with sparks of genius 1808: 4
Savageness: begets s. 1759: 2
in blood 1312: 2
Savagery 1758
Savages converse in figures 1758:18
dirty s., extemporizing ..1758:18
we call them 976: 9
Savannah: fair S. is ours 2115: 9
Savants ont peu d'esprit ..1166:20
Save: both get and s. 24: 1
man from his friends 734: 1
what we s. we lose 773:19
Saved by want of faith 620:18
in vulgar company 1856:12
what must I do to be s. 1756:13
Saves: he who s. should enjoy 1561:11
or serves the state 831:11
Saving
See also Thrift
is getting 1998: 3
of s. cometh having 1998: 3
prove s. in the end 751:14
remember that sore s. 1723: 6
Saviour comes, by bards
foretold 261:10
of 'is country 1866:11
of silver-coasted isle 2131: 2
of society 1859:15
sacred feet of her S. 238:14
there is born 268: 9
which is Christ the Lord ..268:16
with their S. rest 413: 6
Saviour's birth is celebrated 233: 7
Savium prius quam abis ..1051: 2
Savoir a son prix 1057: 6
Savor: genial s. of stews ..523: 9
I know your s. 198: 2
not in s. lies pleasure 518: 2
of lucre is good 1336:15
of old Adam 235:16
of others' bread 595: 2
suffer no s. to scape 2156: 6
Saw: all of which I s. 1820:7a
I find thy s. of might 1205: 9
just tell them that you s.
me 2285: 5
more he s. less he spoke 1825: 4
nor no man ever s. 1376:16
nothing save his own 1562: 9
who s. life steadily 1117:12
with my own eyes 151: 5
Sawbones: a surgeon 466: 7
Saws: full of wise s. 2240: 5
toothless s. 566:14
Saxa cavantur aquis 2126:10
Saxe as Saxy: pronounces 1372:10
Saxpence: bang went s. ...1766:17
Saxum: sine nomen s. 1372: 1
Say and speak thick 1897:21
anything but what you are 235:11
can s. a neat thing myself 2172:11
can't s. fairer than that 1897:15
disapprove of what you s. 2276: 1
harder to s. than do 2227: 1
having nothing to s. 1901: 1
hedn't no gret things to s. 1900: 7
I had a thing to s. 1899:15
if men knew what others
s. 727:12
it that should not s. it ..1897: 8
it with flowers 2285:15
just what I think 216:14
let them s. 1760:10
little things nobly 1899: 3
not afraid to s. his s. 217:17
nothin' you can be held tu 1901: 4
nothing but think more ..1993:17
nothing have to s. 1900:10
one thing and mean an-
other 216:14
one thing, think another 1901:18
perfectly correct thing 946:10
some older nothing 1526: 8
something to remember ..1897:16
still s. what I said at first 1424: 8
talk most least to s. 1900:10
Say, *continued*
that I said so 1642: 4
they s. is half lie 1760:10
thou dost love me 1208:13
well good, do well bet-
ter 2227:6; 2229:12
what mere friends s. 744: 6
what thou seest yond 599: 7
what we feel 1832:21
what we s. we feel 660:20
what you mean 1897:10
what you think 1994: 4
you do not like it 340: 4
Say-nought-at-all beaten ..1657:16
Saying: ancient s. is no
heresy 1265: 7
and doing quarreled 2227:14
and doing two things 2226:13
as the s. is 1638:4a
deed of s. out of use 1621: 4
every wise s. has opposite 1629: 5
faithful s. worthy acceptation 2058: 6
good thing 2170:19
I can tell thee where that
s. was born 1629:10
keeps on s. 1773:11
long step from s. to doing 2227: 3
old-world s. 411:15
short s. much wisdom ..1629:11
that was a man 1629:10
what he likes 218:10
Sayings and doings of others 1475:11
don't go believing in s. ..1628:12
my s. are my own 244: 7
of philosophers 250: 6
of the seven sages 1629:17
Say'st undisputed thing ..1507:14
Says: everybody s., nobody
thinks 1993:18
he s. but little 2174:14
just nothing 1594: 3
little, thinks less 952:21
much in few words 1069: 4
never s. a foolish thing 244: 7
what everyone s. must be
true 1429: 8
Scab of error 271:14
of one sheep 1810:17
of the church 271:14
Scabie: unius s. 1810:17
Scabies: occupet extremum
s. 440:12
Scaffold: on s. high 396: 7
will be dead 1244:12
whether on the s. high ..997: 9
Scaffoldage: footing and
s. 10: 9
Scaffolds: take all your
s. down 1638:15
Scalam: de vitiis nostris s. 2078: 3
Scales: village s. 339: 8
Scaliger in fit of gout 566:19
Scaligeri quod fuit 566:19
Scallop-shell of quiet 398:10
Scallop-shells so many bring 1528:12
Scalp: behind s. is naked 1432: 8
covered with painted locks 849: 6
Scalping-knife: critic's s. ..343: 7
Scamander: by S. side 888:18
Scan from head to foot 160: 2
gently s. brother man 2022: 2
learn thyself to s. 679: 3
Scandal 1759
about Queen Elizabeth ..1760: 5
about whom s. fears to lie .245: 4
and the cry 160: 2
assail'd by s. 1760:14
blackest s. of the age 781:17
caused by dearth of s. ..1603: 4
fierce to invent s. ...... .1761:10
gossip made tedious 1759:10
greatest part of offence ..1828:23
greatest s. waits on 1760: 5
has new minted an old lie 1757:16
makes the offence 1829: 3
no s. like rags 1569:10
no s. while you dine 450:10
of others mere dirt 214: 6

Scandal, *continued*
rubs out like dirt 1759:18
sweetener of female feast 1762: 4
they s. have at will 1761: 9
though s. should ensue ...627: 2
tickling in our ear 1761: 8
to save his blood from s. ..2143: 3
we read the s. 2274: 5
Scandale fait l'offense 1829: 3
Scandalized and foully spoken of 1760: 3
Scandalous: never s. tale without foundation ...1760: 6
Scandals: on eagles' wings s. fly 1760:14
subjects for dissection ..1759:12
Scanderbeg's sword 1955:8a
Scanter of your maiden presence 1233:20
Scapegoat 1638: 5
Scapegoats for our sins ..1646: 1
Scar although wound healed 2247:21
livery of honor 2248: 6
on a little lonesome star ..251: 3
on the conscience 300:11
that will remain 2247:21
wound leaves s. behind ..2247:21
Scarcity: all this s. 1968: 2
Scare worth more than advice 654:18
Scarecrow of the law 1088: 8
Scared into heaven 1945: 2
out of seven senses 655: 1
Scares: nothing s. them 324:18
Scarf up tender eye 1403:16
veiling beauty 87: 3
Scarfs, garters, gold 68: 5
Scarlet: clad in silk and s. ..84:16
of the maples can shake ..115:17
Scarron, Paul: epitaph 570: 5
Scars: boasting show their s. 174: 8
honorable s. 2248: 6
jests at s. who never felt 2248:14
my s. I carry with me 412: 7
show unaching s. 174: 8
they mean negroes' s. 675: 5
Sçavant n'est pas s. par tout 2165:15
Scavenger and king same to me 2016:12
Scelera: honesta s. successus facit 337:19
per s. semper sceleribus ..2135: 5
sæpe in magistrum s. redierunt 1710:14
tuta s. esse possunt 1831: 3
Sceleratis sol oritur 2135: 6
Scelerum: omnis s. formas 338: 5
Scelestissimum te arbitror 1052:20
Scelus aliqua tutum, nulla securum 1831: 3
cui podest s. is fecit 338: 1
ingenio abesse meo 994:16
intra se tacitum qui cogitat 337: 9
nec ullum s. inpunitum est 1657: 5
nullum s. rationem habet 337:12
nunquam s. scelere vincendum 337:17
properum s. virtus vocatur 337:19
scelere velandum est s. ..337:17
semper timibum 2135: 9
suum quemque s. agitat ..336:16
Scena sine arte fuit 1909:13
Scene: forest's shady s. ..1384: 1
in a Divine Drama 966:10
in life's last s. 384: 3
last s. of all 2240: 5
lofty s. be acted o'er 749: 3
noisy s. of crowds 1860:15
solitary, silent, solemn s. 829: 1
tenebrific s. 1288:22
who would tread again s. 1133:10
Scenery: to disparage s. ..340: 7
Scenes: Arcadian s. that Maro sings 94: 2
changing s. of life 1124:15
feign'd Arcadian s. 1569: 6
gay and festive s. 660: 8
Scenes, *continued*
in strong remembrance set 1296: 5
long for rural s. 908: 5
of crowded life 1423:11
Scent: amber s. of odorous 1487: 6
best s. no s. 1487:18
I s. the morning air 1347:16
if my s. be good 683:11
of Eden's roses 1108:10
of meadowlands 1936: 4
of that alluring fruit 92: 2
of the Eden Rose 1746: 6
of the roses will hang ...1293: 9
one s. to hyson 1381: 3
penny s. a sweeter thing .1487: 3
rose's s. is bitterness 1745:15
wich pays the best 1546: 7
Scents: away with s. 1487:12
sweet unmemoried s. 682:15
Sceptic, see Skeptic
Scepticism attribute of critic 338:11
Sceptra: ferulæque tristes, s. pædagogorum 1971: 6
mox s. tyrannis 722: 3
valida s. tenere manu 1039:18
Sceptre and crown must tumble down 385: 7
barren s. in my gripe 345:15
hold s. with a firm hand 1039:18
leaden s. 1402: 6
or an earthly sepulchre ...2083:14
shall have passed from England 839:11
shows temporal power ..1298:19
snatched s. from tyrants .722: 3
to control world 27:17
unwieldy s. 1043:10
Sceptres crooked at the top 814:10
have no charms for thee ..2121:13
stolen s. anxious hands ..1038:20
Scheldt: lazy S. 2028:13
Schein soll nie die Wirklichkeit 952: 1
Scheme: grasp this sorry s. of things entire 2067: 5
none can achieve his s. ...748: 1
of merriment 1301: 3
of social amelioration ...2281: 8
talks of s. and plan 797:15
Schemes: adventurous s. . 863: 5
best-laid s. 452:13
die fast away 628: 4
inferior to goddess 714:13
o' mice and men 452:13
reforming s. none of mine 1683:13
Scheming: soul-harden'd s. 1761:16
Scherzando! ma non troppo 1880: 2
Schicksals: der Mann des S. 439:14
des S. Zwang ist bitter ...644:12
Schiesskugeln: die Menschen gehen wie S. 452: 8
Schimpf: uns den S. 993:13
Schismatics: long-winded s. 1685:12
Schlaf: lange S. des Todes 1149: 6
Schmerz: kurz ist des S. 1019: 3
Scholar **1762**
among rakes 2173: 3
and a soldier 1763: 9
at court, ass among apes ..1763: 6
Christian and a brute ..1014:11
could presage 9: 5
drawn white lot in life ..1762: 8
every man a s. potentially 1762: 9
gentleman and s. 763:12
in society sees fair face ..1862: 4
is student of world 1762:10
little s. poor enough 570:12
mere s., mere ass 1763: 6
must embrace solitude ..1763: 1
no s. but a gentleman 531: 6
office of s. to guide 1762:10
poor s. foots it 1762: 6
rake, Christian, dupe ...237: 2
ripe and good one 1763: 9
secret of true s. 1762: 9
so simple, so sincere 1763: 7
to this day every s. poor 1762: 6
where should s. live 1763: 1
who cherishes comfort ..1762: 7
Scholar, *continued*
without good-breeding, pedant 329: 3
Scholars: play s. who can't play men 1763: 8
so many senseless s. 1677: 5
who become politicians ..1547:15
Schön: lieber s. als fromm sein 139:11
Schönheit für ein fuhlend Herz 133: 8
School
See also Education
Common S. great discovery 530:13
go to s. on summer morn 532: 2
goeth to s., not to travel ..2029:17
instructed in woman's s. 2203:12
I pray you, s. yourself ..1787: 8
nothing so horrible as a s. 531: 8
of coquettes 317: 7
of coarse good-fellowship 1860:14
to mediocrity 1541: 7
toward s. with heavy looks 1185: 6
School-boy: cruel as s. 346:14
whining s. with satchel ..2240: 5
what every s. knows 1056:14
whips his taxed top 1967:18
School-days, school-days ...2283: 5
School-divine 1305:14
School-house by the road ..530: 9
larger than church 530: 9
Schooled by female lips and eyes 1970:12
Schooling in Pleasures ...1509:19
Schoolman's subtle art 238:20
Schoolmaster: average s. an ass 1971: 1
is abroad 1970:11
of the Republic 1377:16
over land is advancing 359: 7
Prussian over Austrian s. 1970:11
should walk wonderingly 1970: 8
Schoolmasters fit to instruct youth 1971:10
let s. puzzle their brain ..495: 9
Schoolmen: babbling s. ...1245:12
Schoolroom a cell 1388:13
Schoolrooms: better build s. 530: 6
Schools: nurseries of vice ..531: 7
public s. abomination 531: 1
scene of solemn farce 1969:10
sophist s. 1390: 8
they want profoundness ..529: 9
Schooner in the offing ...2101:16
Schritt: dreifach ist der S. der Zeit 2008: 3
Schulmeister: preussiche s. 1970:11
Schultern nach der Bürde 204:12
Schuylkill: alone by the S. 1733:13
Schwarz auf weiss besitzt 1561: 6
Schweigt in sieben Sprachen 1821:17
Science **1763**
and art belong to world ..1763:12
and logic he chatters 1765:14
antidote to enthusiasm ..1764: 5
art is s. in the flesh 101: 8
bright-eyed S. watches ..1764:11
bright searchlights of s. .1765: 7
brings little happiness ..1765: 3
by false s. betray'd 1764:18
calls the adventure s. . ..1764: 1
cemetery of dead ideas ..1764: 9
destroyed favorite son ..1765:10
dismal s. 1763:11
doing well with one dollar 1764:10
enough of S. and of Art ..879: 9
every s. has been outcast 1764:12
exchange of ignorance ..1765: 1
falsely so called 1765: 5
for those who learn 1763:10
from Creation's face 1765: 2
frown'd not on humble birth 1291: 2
furniture for upper-chamber 1764: 8
genius married to s. 1764: 6
good sense and reason ..1764: 8
handicraft of the mind ..1763:10

Science, *continued*
hardest s. to forget 708:17
hocus-pocus s. 1082:10
how s. dwindles 216: 1
in s. read newest books ..1674: 1
is to modern world 1763:12
its own reward 1764:13
lawless s. of our law 1087: 8
mount where S. guides ..1765:14
moves, but slowly 1764:17
no s. without religion 723: 1
nothing but perception ..1764: 3
of fools with long memories 1763:11
of forgetting 707:15
of sciences 1497: 8
one S. only will one genius fit 104: 5
opened by the sword 297:19
organized knowledge 1764: 7
proper S. for man himself 1251: 6
ranks as monstrous 76:10
robs men of wisdom 1765: 6
sees signs 1515:14
soar on wings of s. 1765: 8
social s. 1763:11
star-eyed S. 1765: 2
teaches to doubt 1764: 1
topography of ignorance .1764: 1
truth shall know 51: 9
uncertain guess 1764: 1
Sciences may be learned by rote 2166: 8
most of all the abstruse ..1095:10
which should become country 1764:15
Scientia nostra, tuæ comparata 1058:14
potestas est 1057:15
scientiarum 1497: 8
Scientiam: futuram rerum s. 749: 7
Scientific management ...1764: 6
Scies: quod s. nesciveris ..455:21
Scilurus on his death-bed 2066:21
Scintellez, petits astres ...1157: 9
Scintilla: parva sæpe s. ...667:21
Scion: a most eminent s. ...72: 4
herself the solitary s. 1563: 7
Scipio Africanus: first shaven S. A. 124:14
Scipionism of Scipio 832: 4
Scire est nescire 1056: 7
nec s. fas est omnia 1056: 2
tuum nihil est 1056: 7
vere s. esse per causas s. ..225:20
Scirpo nodum quæris 2044:10
Scis: tu pol quod s. nescis 455:21
Scissors nicks him 124:17
Sciunt plerique omnes 951: 1
Scoff, remained to pray ..1590: 8
Scoffer always on the grin .113: 9
Scoffing not of wisdom ..1725: 2
Scolded: how oft she s. ..2146: 2
Scolding from Carlyle 291:10
Scope turns to restraint ...292: 2
Scorn **1766**
always s. appearances 88: 3
exposing men to grinning s. 1570: 1
is bought with groans ..1195:12
makes after-love the more 2215: 9
O what a deal of s. 1766:12
of her s. the maid repented 2217: 1
one should s. s. 1766: 7
salt s. 1756:10
sound of public s. 1766: 5
tempering wrath 1766:13
them, but they sting 1837:18
though lips of s. 2286: 2
to point his finger at 1766:11
Scorned: be s. again 1766: 3
by one that I scorn 1766:14
Scorner of his Maker's laws 113:15
thou s. of the ground 1073: 1
Scornful: seat of the s. ..1766: 6
Scorning to revenge an injury 986:16
Scorpion died of the bite ..1798:10
epigram like s. 566: 8
Scorpions: chastise with s. 1657:17
full of s. is my mind 1698: 6
Scot fight for Christ's Kirk 2258: 6
paid s. and lot 1469:12
trust yow no S. 1769: 2
we will not lose a S. 1769: 9
will not fight 1769: 3
Scot-free: never come off s. 1638: 6
Scotch: ardent disposition of S. 1768:12
knew enough to go in 1768: 6
name swept ultimate seas 1769: 8
nation of gentlemen 1769:10
soft with women 1768:12
tulip planted in dung 904:10
void of wit 1769:16
Scotched the snake 1798: 4
Scotchies: Arcades ambo. S. both 94: 7
Scotchman: beggarly S. 240: 8
gangs till he gets it 561: 3
if he be caught young 1769:11
of sense leaves country ..1769:12
sees highroad to England 1769:12
Scotchmen: trying all my life to like S. 1769:13
Scotia! my native soil 1767: 7
Scotland **1766**
change S. for Strand 1169:10
drink a cup of S. yet 1767: 9
had noble prospects 1769:12
land of Calvin, oat-cakes 1768: 4
let me see it ere I die 1767: 6
renown'd for sanctity ..1740:11
stands S. where it did ..1767: 2
to no interest true 1768: 4
Scotorum: perfervidum ingenium S. 1768:12
Scots are poor 1769: 6
are steadfast 1769: 4
few industrious S. 1769: 5
kills S. at a breakfast 174:10
wha hae 1769: 3
Scotsman: bring S. frae his hill 1769: 3
loose with three hundred pounds 1768:11
moral attribute of S. 1769: 1
on the make 1768:11
without charm 1768:10
Scott, Sir Walter **1770**
Scoundrel and a coward ..240: 8
anoint s. he will wound you 1987: 3
bed before twelve is a s. ..142: 4
deceives by lying 1111: 4
discover worse s. 2086: 5
every man over forty a s. ..34:11
greatest s. on two legs ..2085:13
illness makes a s. 458:16
lowest s. of s. kind 2085:13
Scoundrels ever since the flood 72: 4
Scourge and torturing hour 1697:12
calls to penance 1697:12
from conceit 294:20
iron s. 17: 8
of God 1339:14
of rough and knotted cords 1757:15
one may even s. me 1838: 1
Scourged by the winds 211:17
Scout: babbling Eastern s. 1347: 9
Scowl of heaven 607: 1
Scramble: things you must s. for 1928: 9
Scrap of paper 767: 7
Scraper never a brave man 118:10
Scrapped to make room ..392:12
Scraps of pleasure and despair 1124: 5
stolen the s. 1069: 8
Scratch my back 824:14
my head, Peaseblossom ..1770:12
the very dead for spite ..1982:15
up to the s. 1638: 7
when it itches 1770:11
Scratcheth with a bear 126: 8
Scratching **1770**
had the s. of thee 1770:13
Scrawl: worse s. better dose 468: 8
Scrawls with desp'rate charcoal 677:18
Screams of horror rend skies 1357: 2
strange s. of death 1946:14
Screech-owl with ill-boding cry 1442: 5
Screw: arrant s. 1012: 9
Scribam: nihil est quod s. 1102: 9
Scribas vide plane et probe 2259: 7
Scribbler: every busy little s. 2257: 2
now a s., once a man 2258:11
who shames a s. 2255:10
Scribblers accustomed to lie 2112:16
and statesmen 628:17
call for more pens 2255: 8
Scribbling: craze for s. ..2255: 7
Scribe aliquid magnum ..2252:15
Scribendi: bene ac velociter s. 2259: 8
cacoëthes 2255: 8
calet uno s. studio 2255: 7
piger s. ferre laborem 2254: 8
Scribendo disces scribere 2252:15
scribendi crescit 2255: 8
Scribentem juvat ipse labor 2253: 5
Scribere: aliud s., aliud sentire 2252: 8
Scribes and Pharisees 946:5; 948:13
not as the s. 115: 6
Scribit: non s., nemo legit 1532: 3
Scrip: beggar's s. never filled 146: 5
of joy, immortal diet 398:10
with s. and scrippage 1640:11
Scripsi: quod s., s. 2250: 6
Scripta ferunt annos 2256: 7
Scriptores fœdo splendida facta linunt 1521: 7
Scriptoria dicente vox populi 1481: 4
Scripture
See also Bible
authentic, uncorrupt by man 1913: 3
devil can cite S. 949: 8
foretells glorious liberty 81:11
like an open town 159:11
nor lard with S. 159: 6
rammin' S. in our gun ...159: 8
rule the S. 159: 3
warp'd from its intent 159: 2
was his jest-book 159: 2
with a piece of S. 810: 7
Scripturas: scrutamini 159:10
Scriptures are uncorrupt ..157:10
Holy S. 158: 3
of the skies 1912: 8
Scritto: in fronte s. 220:20
Scrivener notched and cropt 2254: 9
Scrofula, lymph, impotence ..69: 5
Scrofulous French novel ..720: 8
Scroll contain the whole 791: 6
Scruple: some craven s. ...972:17
Scruples dark and nice ...1984: 4
Scrupulous about words ...2218:10
not suited to affairs 1542:17
Scrutantibus gehennas parabat 351: 9
Scullion: away, you s. 1641:17
Sculptor: and you, great s. 106:11
does not work for anatomist 1771: 9
O thou s., painter, poet ..2251: 4
soul of the s. bidden 107:10
who carves in snow 8:20
wields the chisel 1770:17
Sculpture **1770**
is more than painting 1770:19
more like Nature 1770:19
painting and s. images 96: 4
with bossy s. graven 96: 7

Sheet: a wet s. 1776:11
of livid flame 1154: 2
Sheets and leaves could turn with care 2240:12
canvass thee between a pair of s. 1225: 5
difference is wide that s. will not decide 1197:12
privy to your wishes ..2105: 7
three s. in wind 492: 8
Sheffield: Brooks of S. 280: 5
he comes from S. 280: 5
Shelf: laid upon the s. 437:17
Shell: coiling s. of petty cares 1855: 6
dwell forever in s. 1443:10
from the ocean-beach 1781:10
mends with pearl 650:15
must break 161:13
of clean salt 1329:11
pink whorl of s. 1526: 6
rose-lipped s. 1361:10
shaved with a s. 124:11
Shell-scarred face 2150: 9
Shelley, Percy Bysshe 1812
did you once see S. plain 1812: 5
Shells: magical s. 180: 7
picking up s. 1399:14
sinuous s. of pearly hue 1781: 6
Shelter: earth's the best s. 511:21
for the hunted head 55: 5
from the summer shower 2036: 6
in next stage coach 2030: 2
what s. to grow ripe 1144: 2
Shelters: naught s. them..794:11
Shepherd 1811
of mortals, here behold ..263: 7
on the plains of Assyria ..1894: 6
shiten s. and a cleane sheep 1595:10
sleepest or wakest thou, jolly s. 1812: 2
tells his tale 868:13
woe to idle s. 956: 5
Shepherdess of sheep 2185: 3
Shepherds and ministers ..1455:15
dread no poison 1811:17
in Judea 267:17
lame s. they 1593:15
run, s., run 268: 9
shun the noonday heat ..1937: 3
Sheridan, Richard Brinsley 1812
Sheridan: hurrah for S. ...930:14
twenty miles away 2118: 1
Sheriff-Muir battle was 456:20
Sherman marched down to the sea 2115: 9
Sherry: bottle of s. 494: 1
Shibboleth 1638:10
Shield against shafts of doubt 619: 1
for s. self 1490: 1
of faith 617:10
of some fair-seeming name 1371:17
too late I grasp s. 1074: 1
Shieling: from the lone s. 1767: 9
Shift: bad s. better than none 197: 6
every man s. for all 202:12
from side to side 231: 4
we s. and bedeck us 1416:13
Shiftings of every fashionable gale 1546: 9
Shifts: while she s. 248:10
Shill I, shall I 2136:18
Shillelagh: sprig of s. 999:11
Shilling: not s. counts 775:15
spent idly by a fool 1997: 8
Splendid S. 858:11
took a s. out 243:14
Shilly shally 972: 4
Shine: few qualified to s. ..1258:13
we endeavor to s. 2074: 3
with reflected light 2257:14
without scorching 2170:12
Shines: good deed s. 426: 4
in the second rank 1288:11
Shineth unto the perfect day 1152: 3
Shingle: waiting on the s. ..359:12
Shining: beyond the s. 390: 4
Shins: break s. against wit 2173:15
Ship 1812
all I ask is a tall s. 2102: 8
and woman great trouble .488:10
being on s. is in jail ..1778:13
build a s. of Truth 2056: 9
capital s. for ocean-trip ..1813:14
commit thy s. unto wind 2197: 6
divine s. sails divine sea 1814:11
don't give up the s. 62: 1
ever in need of repair ..1813: 5
every s. brings a word ..1101:12
fasten s. to one anchor ..922: 3
great s. asks deep waters 1813: 2
hangs hovering on verge 1815: 6
has weather'd every rack 1161: 2
helmless s. 985:14
in harbor safe 1754:13
is anchor'd safe 1161: 2
is more than the crew ..754:14
of democracy may sink ..431: 3
of Democracy, sail thy best 52: 4
of state 52: 4
one s. drives east 1813:10
our s. is swift and strong 1775: 3
plant s. when we plant tree 2036: 5
scuttle s. or cut a throat 1259: 8
sooner rigged than woman 488:10
speed on the s. 1814:12
stately s. is seen no more 1520: 5
that is waiting for me 378: 7
that sails the ocean 1813: 8
there was a s., quoth he ..1812:14
this is the s. of pearl ..1814: 1
thy s. wants sea-room ..1894: 2
to crazy s. winds contrary 2151: 7
to furnish s. requires trouble 2180: 2
true s. is ship builder 1813: 1
under sail, beautiful 129: 3
was cheered 1776: 9
way of s. in midst of sea 2209: 8
what is s. but prison 1778:13
with sails all set 378: 8
with s. in battle meets ..1449:10
would not travel due west 1777: 4
Ship-shape and Bristol fashion 1812:14a
Ships and deep friendship 1389: 5
are but boards 1778:11
are lying in the bay 2101: 8
as s. becalmed at eve ..1813:16
came home from sea 1812:15
dim-discovered dropping from the clouds 1814:10
down to the sea in s. ..1779: 7
draw far places near ..1813:11
from fir'd s. man leaps 363: 9
have been drown'd 1780: 5
how many s. is my presence worth 982:12
I have at sea 1812:15
launched a thousand s. 889: 1
met like s. upon the sea 1290: 2
reclining on the sea 1813: 4
rest upon the beach 1813: 8
sail wherever billows roll 1781:13
she 'as s. on the foam 2082:12
stately s. go on 402: 4
tall s. ribbed with brass 1777:14
that have gone down at sea 1815:13
that pass in the night ..1290: 2
that sailed for sunny isles 1813:14
unanchored s. 1890:18
we've got the s. 1464: 3
we come like s. 163:12
were British oak 562: 8
when great gray s. come in 1470:15
wooden walls 1813: 8
Shipwreck 1814
common s. is a consolation 1816:10
each makes his own s. 1815:10
he who has suffered s. fears to sail 1815: 7
make s. in port 1816: 2
makes s. second time ..1816: 1
on the coast of Bohemia ..1815: 1
suffer s. unawares 1625: 8
they make glorious s. 1815:10
Shipwrecked, kindles on the coast 1816: 8
man fears every sea 595:17
Shipwrecks of time 82: 5
Shire: heart of England ..551: 4
Shirt: bloody s. 65:12
Bryan O'Lynn had no s. 1411: 2
happy man's without a s. 1568: 2
martyr in s. of fire 1280:16
merits of a spotless s. ..1891: 5
nearer than coat 1793:12
of Nessus is upon me ..1932:22
rich, al had he not a s. ...1568: 2
sending ruffles when wanting s. 771:14
song of the s. 1571:17
stuffed s. 1645: 1
Shirtsleeves to s. 74: 6
Shirts: converting s. into sugar 1381: 6
no banners but bloody s. 65:12
poisonous Nessus s. 946:18
Shive: of cut loaf steal s. 1985:21
Shiver and shake 1932:23
Shoal of time 1359: 5
Shoals of visionary ghosts ..770: 1
Shock: better sink 612: 1
misfortune's rudest s. 211:17
Shock, pride of kind 472:11
Shocking must thy summons be 385:14
Shocks of passion prepare ..134: 4
thousand natural s. 395:10
Shod like a mountaineer 1208:11
with Kentucky steel 879:16
Shoe 1816
cast an old s. after 1226:17
cast aside worn out s. 984:12
great s. for little foot 1817:10
has power to wound 705: 4
made on own last 1817: 2
never yet trod s. awry ..245:13
same s. on every foot ..1817: 2
shines beneath oily hand 1817: 4
to each foot its own s. ..1817: 2
too large for foot 1816:14
where my s. pinches 1817: 1
will hold with sole 1817: 6
wooden s. going up 2298i: 1
Shoeblack-seraph authors 2256:14
Shoe-leather: honest s. 914:14
Shoe-string: careless s. 487:12
Shoe-strings: for poetry ..1524:10
to get s. 640: 6
Shoemaker 1817
makes a good shoe 1818: 4
quietly stick to last 829: 7
with bad shoes 1817:13
Shoemakers gentlemen of the gentle craft 1818: 9
Shoes: all s. fit not all feet 1817: 2
and ships and 1962:17
dead-men's s. 1816:12
make pair of s. rightly ..1818: 2
makes s., goes barefoot ..1817:13
no more s. than feet 485:18
nothing broader than his s. 107: 1
o'er s., o'er boots 1637: 7
old s. easiest on feet 738:10
over s. in love 1203:14
sitting to have s. polished 1554: 7
their s. were on their feet .031: 2
too short the modish s. ..1816:14
were clean and neat 1443: 9
Shoestrings: to get s. he speculates 640: 6
Shoon: by his sandal s. ..1203: 9
wait for dead men's s. ..1816:12
Shoot folly as it flies 695:16
great men s. over 110:14
him on the spot 64: 9
if you must, this old gray head 675: 2
in heaven's name 417:16
teach young idea how to s. 1970: 6
the way you shout 1832:19
you s. a fellow down 2112:12
Shoots at the midday sun 110:14
higher 110:14
of everlastingness 967: 5

Shadows, *continued*
for true substances 841: 9
from lofty mountains ..1354:10
grow more dreary 34:16
have power to shake me ..657: 7
have struck more terror ..302: 9
he walked with s. 1514:10
hunter of s. 1803:10
in a shadowy band 402: 9
lengthening as vapors rise 1941: 7
lengthening s. wait 2062: 1
longer s. from lofty mountains 1804: 4
not substantial things 385: 7
of eternity 579:10
of hates 866:23
of his stormy life 203: 5
of the grave 828:16
pointed cedar s. drowse ..1803:11
see only their own s. 1804: 2
shift 1139:16
some there be that s. kiss 1803:17
that showed at noon 1804: 5
to the unseen grief 2176:17
vanish in Light of Light 1151:13
what s. we pursue 1803: 5
wove on their aerial looms 1907: 5
Shadwell never deviates into sense 1924:16
Shaft: Cupid's fiery s.....350:16
in heel overthrew bravest 2041: 9
many a s. at random sent 2226:10
when I had lost 752:17
winged s. of fate 643: 7
Shafts: thy fatal s. 1189: 9
Shake, Mulleary, and Goethe 1531:11
was dramatist of note ..1804:15
Shake: first s. with you ..850:18
like aspen leaf 2038: 1
off the dust 1632:16
off the very dust 277: 1
Shaken: so s. as we are 221: 5
when taken 1286: 3
Shaker of o'er-rank states 2106: 3
Shakes: brace of s. 1631: 4
like a reed 212: 5
so s. the needle 306:10
Shakespeare 1804
and musical glasses 1963:21
he had said it all 1807: 3
heartrending reading ...1807: 6
is it not sad stuff 1537: 2
made use of it first 1506:12
myriad-minded S. 1805: 4
not of an age but for all time 1806: 8
puts them all down 1808: 9
reading S. by lightning 9: 1
subtract S., trash remains 1530: 4
sweet Swan of Avon 1806: 8
sweetest S., fancy's child 1807: 4
the less S. he 1883:17
try to be S. 1660: 8
weeps with me 2098: 5
when S. passes by 1957: 3
with this key S. unlocked heart 1883:17
Shakespeare sauvage avec de génie 1808: 4
Shakespeare's magic could not copied be 1805: 8
Shalimar: beside the S. 851: 9
Shall: his absolute s. 115: 9
not when he will 1433:11
shill I, s. I. 2136:18
that s. be, s. be 438:13
Shallop of crystal ivory-beak'd 1203:18
Shallow: all alike s. 1144:14
in himself 1677: 3
last s. charted 1587:14
murmur, deep are dumb 1457: 8
Shallows where lamb could wade 158: 2
Sham: wind-bag and a s. ..87: 5
Shame 1808
ain't dat a s. 1882: 6
and dishonor sit 1810: 2
and ostracism of poverty 1569:15
arises from fear of men ..1809:11
ashamed with noble s. ..453:15
be mine the s. 1609:10
checks first attempts 2079: 5
daughter of uncleanness 1810:10
deep in his heart boils s. 1810:11
deterred by another's s. ..588: 6
erring sister's s. 2205:11
fall on Asolo 369:15
false s. of fools 1809:10
flexible in s. 13:10
followed s., and woe woe 2177: 4
foul s. and scorn 1084: 1
hath a bastard fame 1809:20
his poor word with deed ..425:11
in s. no comfort 1810: 4
is as it is taken 1808:12
is in the crime 1809: 2
is ornament to young 1808:13
is s. whether thou think'st 1810: 6
knows no return 1809:19
leaves us by degrees 1809:19
let s. say what it will 1976: 9
make thy s. thy glory ..173:17
makest thou s. thy pastime 1810: 1
mark of base man 1808:13
me from my sneer 1161: 5
needless s. 172: 6
new s. of old sins 1828: 1
no maiden s. 1331:19
no s., no conscience 1809: 7
no s., no honour 1809: 7
not to be shameless 1808:14
O s., where is thy blush 1809:20
of poverty the worst 1809:13
on shameful thing s. attends 1809: 6
paint mortal s. of nature 2251:11
pride's cloak 1608:13
proclaim no s. 1809:20
put off s. with clothes ..1273:11
secret and heavy 1586:12
secret House of S. 754: 3
shroud of s. 396:12
smites nothing sharp as s. 1809:12
so much glory and s. 780: 2
stings sharpest of worms 1810: 9
such as never yet 160: 1
the devil 217: 4; 2057:15
this is the bloodiest s. ..1759: 1
to him whose striking 651:13
to say of s., what is it ..1827:11
to them that think s. ..1809: 8
upon his brow s. ashamed 1810: 2
walks with s. 1703:11
what s. is there 1991:22
where s. is there is fear 1809:14
where s., virtue 1809:18
which is glory and grace 1809: 5
whilst s. keeps watch 1809: 1
with words of s. 58: 6
yield to such inevitable s. 462:10
Shameful: why s. 1808:12
Shamelessness and Spite ..984:13a
Shames: hold a candle to my s. 216:11
thousand innocent s. 173: 5
Shamrock
See also Ireland
green, immortal S. 998: 5
is forbid by law 998: 6
sweet little s. 998: 5
three-leaved S. grows 2292: 8
Shan-van-Voght 998: 6
Shandon: bells of S. 153:13
Shank: shrunk s. 2240: 5
Shanks's mare 2101:12
Shannon: banks of S. 472: 8
where the River S. flows 2292: 8
Shape alone let others prize 1313: 8
assume a pleasing s. 444: 6
execrable s. 770: 6
harmony of s. express 489: 1
her s. her own 1224:11
his s. o'ertakes me 14: 2
Shape, *continued*
lick them into s. 126:16
mould into any s. 981: 2
neither s. of danger can dismay 239:13
questionable s. 770:10
that s. had none 770: 6
two of far nobler s. 1254:17
you'd improve its s. 1412: 3
Shapen: when a thing is s. .438:13
Shapes of foul disease 459:12
sublime and beauteous s. ..482: 4
that come not 2096: 1
Shard: iron s. 789: 8
Share: chief s. Lion's 1162:18
friends s. in common 728:11
like a punished soldier 125: 1
lion's s. 1162:18
most s., best enjoyed 2167:11
not what we give, but s. 775: 2
wouldst thou s. alike 309:12
Shares: bubble s. 1723: 5
Sharp as two-edged sword 2133:13
is the word 862:17
somebody's s. 280: 5
too s. for its body 2170:12
Sharper: not damn the s. ..754: 1
than serpent's tooth 254:11
Sharpers so rich 853:21
Sharps: unpleasing s. 1369: 4
Shass caffy: and a s. c. 494: 1
Shave a lion 1162:19
dry s. 125: 1
hard to s. an egg 532:11
learn to s. by shaving ..124:17
like a goat 490:14
narrow s. 1635:11
two do not s. alike 124: 8
Shaved with a shell 124:11
Shaven: first that was s. ..124:14
well lathered is half s. ..124: 9
Shaving: barber kept on s. ..341:12
daily plague 127: 5
reasons for s. 124: 6
Shawl: coast-storm in a s. 1160: 4
She: chaste, unexpressive s. 247:10
cruell'st s. alive 247:16
that not impossible s. ..2195: 4
whom I love 1213: 2
She-bear thus accosted 2187:17
She-tyrant: submit to a s. 1276: 5
Sheaf: lay thy s. adown ..2211:14
Shears of destiny 440: 2
Sheen of polished ivory 478:21
silver s. of famine 659:12
Sheep 1810
always flock together 509: 9
are happier of themselves 1089:20
be in the corn 1812: 2
before her shearers 16: 6
black s. a biting beast ..1810:14
black s. in every fold 87:12
black s. we cry 1023:19
Colchian s. wore golden fleece 639: 7
divide s. from goats 1811: 2
every s. hath fellow 1810:15
foolish s. makes wolf confessor 1811:13
hanged for s. as lamb ..1811: 5
he that makes himself s. 1811:11
in credulity 1696:12
most foolish animals 1811: 4
mountain s. are sweeter 1811: 3
my s. are thoughts 2185: 3
my s., is dey all come in 1810:18
now I have s. and cow ..1720:19
one s. follows another ..1811: 4
one sickly s. infects flock 1810:17
other s. not of this fold 1810:18
quiet, fond and few 1811:15
scabbed s. infecteth fold 1810:17
shepherded moonlit s. 394:19
that have not shepherd ..1811: 1
when s. are in the fauld 1846:15
with his s. securely fold you 793: 7
without, wolf within 946:16
Sheeps' guts hale souls ..1369:13
Sheepish as a fox 1810: 5
eye 600:18

Sigh, *continued*
forgotten how to s. 1850:11
God an unutterable s. 784: 4
hast ever weigh'd a s. ..1972: 6
homage of a s. 134:13
hush'd be that s. 1978:12
in thanking God 824: 2
like Tom o' Bedlam 1292: 4
meaning of a s. 393:10
meet us with a s. 1885:17
never s., but send 1819: 7
no more, ladies 1201:15
not a s. nor a tear 1974:12
not only s. but roar 1444: 9
of the oppressed creature 1689:14a
passing tribute of a s. 1818:18
prompts eternal s. 855: 3
she looked up to s. 601: 8
smiling with a s. 1854: 1
so piteous and profound 1819: 4
some s. for this and that ..2019: 8
subterraqueous s. 1443:17
that rends thy constant heart 1818:17
the absent claims 3: 5
the lack of many a thing I sought 1295:10
to s., yet feel no pain 1818:14
to s., yet not recede 1818:15
to those who love me 644:16
waft a s. from Indus ..1103: 1
what! s. for toothache ..2028: 5
when he is gone, I s. with grief 1818:16
wherefore s. and whine ..1007: 4
with pity 659: 5
Sighed and look'd and s. again 1818:11
and wept 1818:12
for love of a ladye 1880: 8
had s. to many 1818:11
man s. till woman smiled 2184: 4
Sighing for the far-off, unattain'd 109: 5
like furnace 2240: 5
lovely s. of the wind 2153: 1
of a contrite heart 1818:10
plague of s. and grief ..1819: 5
where's the use of s. 2006: 1
woos it with enamour'd s. 2153: 4
Sighs: easy s. 1818:13
growing deeper in my s. 35:10
heart-sore s. ...1190:11; 1195:12
her s. will make a battery 2195:16
Joy stole from Sorrow ..1819: 1
language of the heart ..1819: 3
made of s. and tears 1174:15
not such sorrowful s. ..1818:13
on pensive bed 870: 6
she knows all s. 1774: 2
Sight **1819**
blessings of the s. 170: 4
could not want s. who taught world to see 911:14
credit most our s. 604:15
fairer s. perchance 1748:10
for sore eyes 1820: 5
hath strength of a lion ..1819:12
is keenest of senses 1819:12
love at first s. 1205: 9
O, loss of s. 170: 8
of lovers feedeth love ..1186: 5
of man hath force of lion 1819:12
of vernal bloom 170: 8
out of s., out of mind .4:15; 5: 4
ruled by the s. above 438:14
sad s. is human happiness 860: 9
second s. dispels love ..1205:15
splendid s. to see 1819: 8
things out of s. 4:11
tho' lost to s. 3:12
to delight in 1819: 8
to dream of, not tell 1819: 8
to make old man young ..779:12
Sights as youthful poets dream 130:14
bleared s. 1560:10
ugly s. and ghastly dreams 1851: 1
ugly s. of death 483: 6
Sign brings customers 207:10
by this s. thou shalt conquer 267: 9
that Shakespeare knew ..1808: 1
to know the gentle blood ..68:13
Signa: certis rebus certa s. præcurrent 1945:13
Signal: Nature's s. of retreat 374: 1
Signatum præsente nota ..1926:14
Signet of all-enslaving power 803: 9
Signet qui marque la page 1714:13
Signo: in hoc s. vinces 267: 9
Signs foretell death of kings 1946:14
no believing old s. 865: 3
of the times 1623: 7
of trades 2129: 2
precede certain events ..1945:13
Silence **1820**
accompany'd 582: 9
after grievous things 1824:18
all save s. brings repentance 1822:16
all s. an' all glisten 1401:12
and modesty valuable 1820:16
and the wakeful stars ..1124:13
answers yes 1822: 6
art of conversation 1820:16
as their benediction 75:15
at last s. comes 1159: 6
back of sound, s. 774: 3
be check'd for s. 1824:16
best answer to calumny ..214:15
best ornament of woman 2200: 9
better than any speech ..1824:13
breaking s. twenty-three years 1824:19
broods like spirit on brae 2117:13
by s. seems more learn'd 1820:14
come then, expressive S. 1823: 8
commendable in maid ..1821:21
conversation with Englishman 559: 6
Death and Sleep 1825: 5
deep as death 1825: 6
deep as Eternity 1823:12
denotes the lover 1209: 6
earth's s. lives, throbs ..1361: 5
eloquence of s. 314:19
eloquent in love 1823: 3
end of every song 1823:12
eternal duty of man 1820:10
eternal s. be their doom ..1821:14
even from good words ..1821: 6
feet are shod with s. 1825:14
fine jewel for a woman ..1821: 8
flashes of s. 1229: 2
froze me into s. 1822: 2
full of potential wisdom ..1822:13
gives consent 1822: 5
gives grace to women 2200: 9
golden S., bid our souls 1825: 8
grand orchestral s. 1910:11
gratitude of affection 1821: 3
great Empire of S. 1820:10
great, sweet s. 1821:12
harms no one 1838: 7
has no end 1824:19
healing for all ailments ..1820: 8
his mother-tongue 1821: 9
his s. will sit drooping ..1824:17
how dead 1402: 7
I'll speak to thee in s. ..1823: 6
in love betrays more woe 1209:14
in s. God brings all ..1822:15
in the churches 2199:12
in woman like speech in man 2200: 1
inch by inch, is there 1395:10
is a duty and a doom 405:15
is confession 1822: 6
is gain to many 1820: 8
is strength 1820:17
is sufficient praise 1577: 4
is the perfect whole 1823: 5
is the sharper sword 1824:10
is the soul of war 1821: 1
is virtue of fools 1820: 9
it moves, in mystic s. ..1733: 8
keep s. because I approve 1822: 4
Silence, *continued*
kindly s. when they brawl 1822:19
like a poultice, comes ..1825:10
like a sense of pain 525:10
listen to the s. 2006: 7
looked at her s. 599:15
love s., even in the mind 1820:17
man's chief learning 1820:14
may do good 1822: 9
melts away 525: 4
more eloquent than words 1822:20
more majestical than arms 1939:14
more musical than song ..1823:12
most noble till the end ..1824:18
mother of Truth 1820:12
never betrays you 1822:16
never harmful 1822:10
of friend treachery 2032:14
of neglect can ne'er appall 1578: 6
of people lesson for kings 1821: 5
of that dreamless sleep ..394:14
of the hours of dew 445:17
of the receding world 1554: 9
of the stars and sea 1825:15
often of pure innocence 1823: 7
out of s. picked welcome 1822: 1
perfectest herald of joy ..1821: 2
portends dread event 842:18
propagates itself 313: 5
reply to calumny 1822:19
rest of the mind 1820:17
safer than speech 1824: 6
safest rule 1822:14
scarce more than s., sound 1206:12
seldom hurts 1822: 9
sleeping on a waste of ocean 1825:16
solvent that destroys 1820:13
stand shadowless like S. ..117: 8
stillborn s. 1820:15
sweeter is than speech ..1823:12
taught by misfortunes ..1821:19
tenable in your s. 1785: 1
that accepts merit 90:16
that is in starry sky 1389: 1
that spoke 1490: 6
the rest is s. 1821:20
there is an eloquent s. ..1823: 4
thunders of white s. 1770:15
time to keep s. 2004:11
'tis s. all 592:12
to s. another, be silent ..1821:18
uttering love 1210: 3
very small virtue 1824:12
was pleas'd 582: 9
well-timed s. 1822:20
what better than s. 1824:11
when S. speaks for Love 1209: 1
where hath been no sound 1825:11
which was almost pain ..1825: 1
wisdom's best reply 1820:14
wit of fools 1820: 9
Silence est l'esprit des sots 1820: 9
et la modestie commodes 1820:16
grand talent pour s. 559: 6
leçon des rois 1821: 5
parti le plus sûr 1822:14
Silences: grand orchestral s. 1910:11
three s. there are 1825: 5
Silent: all s. and all damn'd 1822: 3
all with one accord s. ..1824:21
as the grave 1825:17
as the moon 1942:13
as the shadows 1825: 5
bad cause should be s. ..225:16
be s. if would be loved ..2146:14
better s. and thought fool 1823:10
great joys, griefs, s. 1018:15
I am s. and curb my mouth 1821: 7
impossible to be s. 1823:11
in seven languages 1821:17
is the lute now 402:12
majority 382:15
naught so s. as foot of time 2006: 8
over Africa 550:13
people are dangerous 1821: 4
people more interesting ..1824: 3
think highly of themselves 1821:10

Silent, *continued*
three things are ever s. 1825: 5
upon a peak in Darien 912: 2
when there is need 1823: 9
when you doubt sense 1824:14
you shall not say I yield being s. 1822: 8
Silentia: exigua virtus præstare s. 1824:12
quid s. cogis rumpere ..1824:21
Silentio: est fideli s. merces 1822:12
Silentium: regionis s. 978:10
Silere: alium s., primus sile 1821:18
alium s. quod voles 1784:18
Silet: qui s. est firmus 1820:17
Silhouette sublime 627:15
Silk: in s. and scarlet ..2133: 8
makes the difference 485: 7
purse of a sow's ear 1954:8a
rustling in unpaid-for s. 1607:17
so women could go naked 488: 1
ye sall walk in s. attire ..488: 1
Silken coats and caps 489: 4
Silks put out kitchen fire 486:15
weave no more s. 2120: 4
whenas in s. Julia goes ..488: 1
Silkworm: so spins the s. 2255: 6
Siller in every blossom ..1386: 1
scraping s. 220:17
Silliness when to live is torment 1121: 5
Silly: it is s. sooth 123:10
neither extraordinarily s. 562:16
nothing more s. than s. laugh 1076: 5
Siloam's shady rill 1156: 9
Silvæ: Ipsæ concedite s. ..2210:14
Silvam: in s. non ligna feras 283: 7
Silvas Academi 2056: 5
Silver: an everywhere of s. 1779:15
and gold have I none 775:17
and gold not only coin ..2090:12
can't have bushel of s. ..2104: 1
fight with shafts of s. 2114:11
he that loveth s. 2074:20
is the king's stamp 1256: 6
just for handful of s. ...2229:19
livery of advised age 39: 8
not free s., free men 1555: 4
pure s. of Pope's line ...1558:12
threads among the gold ...39: 7
to s. creep and wind 1562:13
uses s. as earthenware 831: 8
with borrowed s. shine ..1344:10
Silver-sandalled feet 368:19
Silver-sweet sound 1209:16
Silvia: except I be by S. ..1199: 9
who is S. 2185:10
Silvis: in s. invenies quam in libris 1389: 5
Simia quam similis nobis 84:15
tu fai come la s. 84:13
Simile: no s. runs on all fours 1069: 7
one s. that solitary shines 1519: 4
with a long tail 330:17
Simile: nullum s. quatuor pedibus 1069: 7
Similem habent labra 111:12
Similes like songs in love ..99: 2
sit and play with s. 1069: 7
unsavoury s. 1069: 7
Similia similibus curantur 1285: 4
Similitude: worst s. in the world 1731:18
Similitudes 2095: 2
Simon: old S. the cellarer 2156: 3
old S. the King 497: 8
Simon Legree: Devil said to S. L. 441:19
Simon Pure: the real S. P. 1638:12
Simonides bore off the prize ..31: 9
Simple: beauty of the s. ..129: 7
blissful are the s. 1826:15
in elegance 488: 4
life 1136: 3
modest, manly true 238:16
so s. is heart of man 877: 1
that are not s. men 1826: 5
to be s. is to be great ..1826: 4
Simpleness and gentleness 765: 5
and duty tender it 1826:13
Simples: compounded of many s. 1291:13
many s. operative 1850:18
of thousand names 1287:16
that have virtue 1540: 4
Simplex munditiis 847:11
Simplicitas ac liberalitas ..218: 9
ævo rarissima nostro S. ..1826:11
beata s. 1826:15
sancta s. 1826:15
Simplicite: Sister S. 1850: 6
Simplicity 1826
and liberality 1826:14
blessed s. 1826:15
cultivate s. 1826: 8
hail! divine lady S. 1826: 3
holy s. 1826:15
in his s. sublime 2131: 2
in s. a child 238:21
in the face of a fool 1826: 5
is a state of mind 1826:17
is the art of art 1826:19
is unconsciously audacious 1826: 9
most rare in our age ..1826:11
no hindrance 1826:10
not the rage 488: 6
of living 1135: 5
of the three per cents 464:17
pity my s. 252:17
talks of pies 1208:11
tongue-tied s. 1826:13
what power has white s. 1826: 7
Simplify, s. 1826:16
Simulacrum: damnedest s. ..87: 6
Simulation of the painted scene 1910:11
Simulator: sæpe cœpit s. amare 1186: 1
Simulatum: nec s. potest diuturnum 779:19
Sin 1826
against our dearest 961: 5
and death abound 1451:16
and her shadow, Death 1830:19
be sure your s. will find you out 1830:20
besetting s. 1828: 7
better eschew s. 1828:20
better flee s. than death 377: 2
black spot against sun ..1827: 6
blackest s. put on 87: 3
blush to give it in 75: 7
bright. beautiful s. 1051:12
brought death 1827:16
by that s. fell the angels 50: 3
can be well-guarded 1831: 3
cleared with absolution ..1829:14
conceived and born in s. ..73: 4
confess their s. 295:15
confessed half forgiven 1829:14
custom gives s. lovely dye 1828: 6
devil corrects s. 442:14
done for things there's money in s. 1336:10
draw s. with cart rope ..1828: 4
dulled eyes with s. 336: 2
each man bears his own s. 1827:18
e'er remark another's s. 1024:10
e'er s. could blight 408: 3
ere s. threw a blight 410:14
every day takes out patent 1828: 1
falls into s. is a man 1829: 9
falter not for s. 23: 3
familiar s. 1010:13
fell the angels 50: 3
fixed as some darling s. ..845:16
fools make a mock at s. 1828: 9
for me to sit and grin 485:13
for one s. no forfeit 1830:21
for plebeian to grumble ..1480: 2
forgive what seemed my s. 2247:12
forgiven by Christ 1830: 3
forsaken by s. 1829: 6
forsaketh s., ere s. you forsake 1829: 6
free to s., less s. 1827: 5
fresh s., fresh penance ..1830: 9
geographical; illusory ...1827: 8
Sin, *continued*
good man's s. 75: 7
grant one s. in safety ..1830:21
great s. to swear unto s. 1418:10
has many tools 1111: 9
he that is without s. 1828:11
if it be s. to covet honor ..919: 4
if thou wilt, but secret ...88: 1
in blossoms of my s. .. .1359:15
in others is experiment for us 1827: 1
in state, majestically ...1828: 8
in wine or wantonness ..173:17
is a state of mind 1827: 4
is in being found out 1829: 1
is in itself excusable 1828:24
kills the sinner 1831:6a
lawful for no one to s. 1826:21
lay not this s. to their ..1827:12
lest S. surprise thee 90: 7
lewd and lavish act of s. 1224: 5
lieth in the scandal .. .1828:23
lose s., keep the sense 1425:11
love's fruit to steal 1209: 8
made a s. of abstinence ...5:14
make white one single s. 1587:11
makes its own hell 1830:11
merely in the noise . . 1829: 3
monuments of s. 755:11
most inhibited s. in the canon 247: 7
naught that delights is s. 1827: 1
no s. but stupidity 1925:17
no s. but to be rich 146: 2
no s. love's fruit to steal 1209: 8
no s. to labor in vocation 1062:10
no s. to look at a girl .. .779:12
none of us is without s. 1828:11
nor numbers make less s. 1827: 3
not accidental, a trade ..1828:16
not forbid s. encourages 1828:13
not hurtful forbidden ..1827:19
of omission .... .1827: 2
of self-love 1791:10
one little drop of s. 1827:17
one s. will destroy sinner 1830: 5
one slough and crust of s. 1831:17
Original S. 1827:13
palliation of a s. 1829:12
piercing pain, killing s. . .858:16
plate s. with gold .... .1029: 1
process of unsinning s. ..1829: 7
punishment for s. 1831: 4
put not another s. 79: 2
result of collaboration ..1830:17
securely s., safely never 1831: 3
sits s., to seize the souls 1430: 3
smacking of every s. 240:11
so much of s. and blot . 1023:21
some rise by s. 2082: 8
sometimes s.'s a pleasure 1511:12
speaks punishment at hand 1830:10
struck down like an ox ..1831: 5
teach s. carriage of saint 949: 5
than s. hath snares 157: 9
that amends patched 2082: 9
that doth belie dead 406: 3
that neither God nor man can well forgive 1830: 1
through s. reach light ..1828: 3
to do s. is mannish 1829: 9
to s. biass'd nature leans 443:10
to s. in loving virtue 1981:20
to s. is human 1829: 9
to which I had descended 1980:13
that undying s. we shared 1392:18
too dull to see beyond ..1828:19
touches not man so near 1810: 9
wages of s. is death 1831: 2
we can but kiss it 1827:11
we have explained away 1831: 9
what record of s. awaits ..2021:19
what s. to me unknown ..2255:11
when thy lovely s. has been wasted in despair 1829:15
who tell us love can die 1199:10
who's free to s. sins less 1827: 5
whoever plots the s. 1430: 3
win who plays with s. ..754: 3

Sin, *continued*
without delight 113:13
writes histories 1827:20
ye do by two and two ..1830:17
you're by s. undone 1985:21
Sin-absolver 591:19
Sin-no-more task too hard 1699:10
Sinai: find'st not S. 114: 7
Sinais: we S. climb 884:17
Sinbad was in bad all the time 2291: 8
Sincere: dangerous to be s. 1833: 2
every man alone is s. ...1832: 9
every s. man is right 1832: 9
knew to be s. 1651:17
more eloquent less s. 537:10
sagacious, melancholy 1160:13
tho' well bred, s. 238:20
without weakness, s. 1651:17
Sinceritas: ad perniciem solet agi s. 218: 7
Sincerity **1831**
allowed only to highest ..1832: 9
bashful s. and comely love 1982: 2
his sheet anchor is s. 1832: 9
in his speech 2230: 1
little s. dangerous 1833: 2
loss of s., loss of power ..1832: 5
merit of originality 1441: 9
must pervade whole being 1832:15
only basis of talent 1961:20
private s. is public welfare 1832: 2
sincere alone recognise s. 1832: 6
small s. of mirth 1077: 9
wrought in a sad s. 95:14
Sincerum est nisi vas 278:21
Sinecures for worthless people 243:10
Sinew of the soul 79: 8
Sinews: crack my s. 919: 6
of new-born babe 1588: 5
of war 2114: 5
sell s. to be wise 628:11
stiffen the s. 2116:10
to make catlings on 1369:13
Sinful: we are all s. 1828:12
Sinfulness greater than use 2158:15
Sing: alas for those that never s. 1879: 4
as I shall please 1526:10
because I must 1539: 1
but as linnet sings 1539: 1
do not s. unbidden 1879:17
he knew himself to s. 1879: 1
I cannot s., I'll weep 1885: 2
I heard a bird so s. 160:10
I may not s. of love 1880:13
I s. of little loves 1193: 9
I s. of May-poles 1538: 2
it not in mournful numbers 1121:14
let's s. our sang 716:12
like birds i' the cage 1613:12
me a Song of the South 2291:10
me, I s. as I must 399: 7
more merrily 1950:11
no sad songs for me 405: 7
of Beauty, Death and Love 1514:10
of thee I s. 51:12
or paint or carve 106:14
out of tune 339:15
savageness out of bear ..1877:11
self-taught I s. 1538: 4
that I may seem valiant ..323:18
thee, ever thee I s. 52: 3
they s. and love 884:14
they s., they will pay 1876: 8
thy praise 1579: 5
till the rafters ring 2161: 4
to the Lord with cheerful voice 793: 7
well poor accomplishment 362: 8
when I but hear her s. ..1877: 6
Sing-song: carry s. 1838:12
Singe: plus le s. s'elève 84:13
Singed the beard 1895:20
the king's beard 127: 9
Singer: as a s., great dancer 1875:11
belongs to a year 1519:12
Singer, *continued*
clear, sweet s. 2132:14
idle s. of an empty day ..1520:10
New World's sweetest s. 1169:16
of an empty day 1534: 6
of undying songs is dead 1983: 2
with the crown of snow 2132:14
Singers: first of earthly s. 200:11
God sent S. upon earth 1518:10
in tavern corners 1142: 6
never leave off 1880: 4
singing s. with vocal voices 1878:14
sweetest of all s. 1369:10
Singest: in vain s. 1532: 3
Singet nicht in Trauertönen 1121:14
Singeth low in every heart 400:13
with breast against thorn 1405: 1
Singillatim mortales 964:17
Singing as a bird mourns 1539: 1
as little waters do 200:11
bring back the s. 1936: 4
in the bath 126: 2
in your heart 1353: 3
merrily s. on brier and weed 174:16
somehow, s. 398: 9
till his heaven fills 1072:12
Singist not a success 1878:12
Single gentlemen double ..1277:14
nothing in world is s. ...1215: 6
one s. can its end produce 1251:13
Singleness is bliss 2137: 8
set in for s. 1233:17
Sings: alway something s. 1367: 5
as sweetly as nightingale 2200: 6
several times faster 123:11
to one clear harp 2078: 3
when Malindy s. 1879:2; 2285: 7
who s. scares away woes 1876: 7
Singula: quæ non prosunt s. 2040: 5
Singular and rash 2269: 4
Singularity: love of s. 1489: 5
must not go abroad 1489: 8
ruins many 1429:12
trick of s. 236: 5
Singulos: notare s. 1258:1a
utilitate publica rependitus 1656:11
Sink or swim, live or die 975:8; 1464:16
or s. or swim 1954: 4
ship except on even keel ..663:18
Sinne: fest auf dem S. ...2148: 3
Sinned and repented 1698:13
some have s. with safety ..1831: 3
we have all s. 285: 1
would have s. incessantly 83: 8
Sinner and sin mightily ..1831:13
it or saint it 2198: 6
be merciful to me, a s. ..789: 8
every s. has future 1755:18
feels remorse 1697:15
made s. of his memory ..1113:19
man, the hungry s. 448:22
more angry with s. than heretic 2268:14
must pray for himself 1588:13
no s. like young saint ..1831:10
one s. that repenteth 1699: 9
only s. has right to preach 1594:17
or I of her a s. 1202:16
too weak to be a s. 2125:17
vilest s. may return 1699:13
Sinners are wishful to pray 1592: 7
bed with s. 1755:10
despised by saints 948: 9
dear s. all, the fool began 1595: 4
if s. entice thee 1981:14
of all unhappy s. 295:11
that grow old in sin 1831:18
to blot out score 2134: 6
Sinning: more sinn'd against than s. 1828:14
official s. 1543: 6
this is the end of our s. .2288: 1
Sinon: like a S. take Troy 2046: 2
Sins all forsake him 1829: 6
are washed out 75: 6
Sins, *continued*
be all my s. remembered 1588: 3
compell'd s. 1827:10
compound for s. they are 1658: 8
do bear their privilege ..1828:15
few love to hear the s. ..1828:17
few s. to answer for 2186:13
first dislik'd, belov'd 2079: 5
forgive us our s. 709:22
frown upon Saint Giles's s. 1828: 2
he s. against this life 964:15
highway of our virtue ..1828:21
in the regenerate 1827: 7
increase, hairs fall 1831:11
leaving her s. to Saviour 1829:11
like to our shadows 1831: 6
little s. make room for ..1827:17
many s. pass unpunished 1830:18
my s., my contrition 1588: 8
no s. to be forgiven 162:10
not by my s. wilt Thou judge me 1707: 3
of our friends 651: 7
of the fathers visited upon the children 1830:12
oldest s. newest kind ..1828: 1
one of seven deadly s. ...1828:22a
our own proper s. 651: 7
punished by, not for, s. ..1830:15
scarecrow s. at home 1944:10
seven deadly s. 1335: 4
their s. armed against them 1831: 8
they sinned in Eden 1828: 1
thinkin' on their s. 1827:14
to be forgiven 162:10
visited in this poor child 1830:12
weep for their s. 82: 3
were scarlet 190: 7
when drunk 502:11
who never s. can little boast 1830: 2
who s. and mends commends 1829: 8
who s. not because she dares not 246:16
with all their scarlet s. ..1359:16
without intent 1827:10
Sip from goblet of delight .429:18
Sipping only what is sweet 143: 1
Sir-come-spy-see 1340:14
Sir Loin: one fat S. L. 522:11
Sire: graceless s. 46: 3
his sword bequeathing ..2110: 9
thy s. was a knight 1847:10
Sireland: sweet face of s. ..997: 2
Siren: part s. and part Socrates 719:16
sing, s., for thyself 1879:13
sings sweetest 1980:11
song of ambition 48:11
waits thee, singing 1879:13
who lures men to ruin ..1776:12
Sires renowned for virtue ..70: 4
strong were our s. 771: 8
Sisera: stars fought against S. 1616:12; 1915: 9
Sister **1833**
little s. of the poor 1572: 4
no friend like a s. 1833: 9
Susie's sewing shirts 2284: 2
thine azure s. of Spring ..2153:13
thou of the stars 511:15
turned mother 1350: 3
vain s. of the worm 1242:13
Sisters and his cousins and his aunts 632:16
ever serving Truth 2054:13
saw you the weird s. 2175:17
Seven S. 2048: 9
sphere-born harmonious s. 1875:12
the birds 160: 6
those s. rare 1833: 6
three fatal s. wait 1830:14
two s. from the same old home 1833:11
under their skins 1833: 8
wayward s. depart in peace 65: 1
weird s. 1833:11

Slaughter and knocking on the head 1865: 8
as lamb to the s. 16: 6
as an ox goeth to s. 1443: 2
he that made the s. 1621:15
men for glory's sake 1473: 2
wade through s. to throne 2080:13
Slaughter-house: Europe's dynastic s. 581:10
march through s. into open-grave 280: 1
Slaughters of the race 439: 9
Slave albeit of free birth ..327:16
as s. departs, man returns 1839: 2
base is the s. that pays 1469:17
better devil's than woman's s. 2195:11
cogging, cozening s. 1837:15
every sixth man a s. 60:14
false s. to false delight 2012:15
feel equality with saints 1839: 8
God makes no man s. 1103:15
half-s., half-free 1841: 6
hard to be s. to passions 1457: 7
has but one master 49: 8
I would not have a s. ..1839: 7
if there breathe a s. 1839:15
in his father's stead 1043: 2
kings among ancestors 73: 7
man in debt a s. 418:24
many a purchased s. 1840: 8
never possess another s. ..1842: 9
never s. but in body 175: 6
no s. is here 1842: 3
no s. who has not king ..1038: 9
nothing lawless except s. 1839:12
nought but folly's s. 24: 6
O that the s. had forty thousand lives 1713:18
of circumstance 971:15
of gross appetite 1998: 1
of my thoughts 1477:13
of philosophy 1499: 6
of the Most High 888:11
of the wheel of labor 640: 7
one man's s. free from none 1839: 3
one who can be bought ..300: 1
open mouth beneath the closed 1358:14
ordained the s. of man ...1839: 2
passion's s. 1457:10
peasant s. am I 1840: 7
play s. to gain tyranny ..949:12
priest-ridden s. 1135: 2
rests from his labours 829: 1
shackled s. 49: 8
show me man who is not s. 1840: 3
singing hymn to liberty ..1876: 8
sovereign s. of care 1388:17
takes half his worth 1839:14
they set the s. free 1839:18
thou wast my S. 350: 8
to an old hag 1840: 3
to fame 625:19
to no sect 1390:15
to oneself 1840: 4
to the flesh 680: 7
unto Mammon 1237:10
useless to be s. 1839:16
wall-eyed s. 1643:16
what a s. art thou 332:10
who cannot live on little 1327:12
wretch, coward 332:12
Slave-drivers whipped underground 829: 7
Slave-trade: villainy 1842:10
Slaver kills, not the bite ..1232:13
Slavery 1838
ancient as war 1840:12
but half abolished 530:15
declares man a chattel ..1842: 5
enchains a few 1840: 4
endure s. with patience ..1839:10
get rid of s. or freedom 1841: 6
if s. not wrong, nothing 1841: 3
in the Light of Political Economy 64: 6
makes s., freedom freedom 1839: 8
Slavery, *continued*
most onerous s. to oneself 1840: 4
no s. but ignorance 958:14
of tea and coffee 1968: 5
of women 1839: 8
sign of s. to have price ..1840: 8
thou art bitter draught ..1840: 9
violation of institutions ..1842: 2
was not in his chains 1839:18
weed of every soil 1839: 1
where S. no Liberty 1841: 6
Slaves: all are s. to gold .2246:15
all but savages were s. ..1758:16
all s. of opinion 1428: 2
born s., bred s. 1838:16
bought with a price 1839:10
cannot breathe in England 1840:15
five-and-thirty black s. ..1370: 7
foreign s. free in France 1840:16
ignorant are s. 725:15
in a land of light and law 1842:11
mechanic s. 1066:12
nations of s. 1838:16
of a legendary virtue 896:17
of chance 229:15
of custom 356: 9
of gain 276:11
of the Lamp 1603:12
of their own vaunts 836: 9
poor s. in metre 1536:14
shock'd at purchase of s. 1839: 5
so we are s. 1838:16
that apes would beat 332: 9
that take their humors ..1043:10
to beauty of riches 1720: 6
to fear 723:17
to musty rules 341: 7
to the belly 81:13
who fear to speak 1839:15
wholly s. or wholly free 1841: 6
will ye give it up to s. 2116: 9
willing s. to custom old ..857:15
would be tyrants 2063: 9
Slay: pity to s. meanest thing 1358:19
thing so fair 1358:19
Slayer: if the red s. 406:18
of the winter 1260:19
oft is slain 2108:16
soon follows slain 382: 4
Sleary babies develop S.'s fits 69: 9
Sleek-headed men 648: 1
Sleep 1842
after luncheon not good 1848: 8
after toil 1707:13
allow not s. to draw near 1788:17
and Death twins 1849:14
and if life was bitter 395:16
an' let me to my wark ...1846:14
and restoring darkness ..1404: 7
and take thy rest 394:16
and S. shall obev me 1851: 2
baby, s. 1847: 8
balmy s. 1846: 3
beauty bright 1847: 1
before death 1848:13
before midnight 1848: 4
before you fight 664:13
beneath the shadows 394:20
best of rest is s. 395:13
better than medicine 1845:13
bless man who invented s. 1730: 4
blessings on him that first invented s. 1844: 4
broke s. with thoughts ...119:15
brother of death 1848:11
but a short death 1849: 9
but to s. and feed 1241:14
calm, unbroken s. 1411:12
came at length ... .1850:13
cannot s. a wink 1850:14
care-charmer S. 1848:12
certain knot of peace 1845:11
come, gentle s. 1849:18
come, S., and with thy ..1844:10
comfortably at sermon ..1843:14
cool S., thy reeds 1844.16
counterfeited Death 1849:12
Sleep, *continued*
Cousin of Death 1849: 1
cure for waking troubles 1844: 5
day out of countenance ..1404: 5
death-counterfeiting s. ..1849:14
death's ally 1849:15
Death's twin brother 1849: 3
death-like s. 395: 2
deep s. falleth on men ...481: 8
dewy-feather'd s. 1845: 3
disports with shadows too 478:15
do I s.? do I dream 2095: 1
does not disdain cottage 1848: 1
doth sin glut 1729: 9
driven s. from mine eyes 770: 4
dwell upon thine eyes ...1846:11
end of all, the poppied s. .1845:16
exposition of s. 1843:18
falls like snowflakes 1849: 7
first s. last repose 12: 6
flattering truth of s. 480: 8
folds them in for s. 2185: 3
fresh dew of languid love 1845:10
friend of Woe 1845:14
from pure digestion bred 1848: 7
full of sweet dreams 135:20
gave Nature restorative 1848:11
give s. to mine eyes ...1850:12
gives his name 478:21
gives us s. for last time 2006:12
God must give 1845:16
golden dew of s. 483: 6
golden s. 2245: 9
grant us the gift of s. 1588:10
great gift of s. 1941: 9
hath its appointed s. 1843:19
hath its own world 1843: 3
he giveth his beloved s. ..395: 6
he slept an iron s. 1868: 6
holy thing is s. 1844:12
hours of s. 1848: 9
how s. the brave 1868: 9
I can get nane 1850: 3
I do not dare to s. 1647: 1
I lay me down to s. 1847: 6
I must s. now 414:12
I s., but my heart waketh 1843:20
I will s. in the air 1848: 3
if an endless s. He wills ..395: 6
image of chill death 1849:11
in Old England's heart ..1870: 8
in pity thou art made ...1844:11
in the night 369:14
innocence and purification 1844: 2
inviting s. 1846: 2
is awful 1843: 2
is like death 1849: 4
it is a gentle thing 1844: 6
kinsman thou to death ..1849: 3
last to come where wanted most 1850: 7
let me s. alway 1850: 5
liest thou in smoky cribs 1848: 2
like a top 1843: 5
like closing flowers 2021: 1
like Death be deep 1850: 2
like hare with eyes open 1843: 6
little more s. 1843:22
long s. of death 1149: 6
makes darkness brief ...1843: 9
meat for the hungry 1844: 4
medicines all pain 395:14
midday s. short 1848: 8
monstrous forms in s. 478:20
much s. not medicinal ..1848: 8
mystery of s. 1842:12
Nature's soft nurse 1850:16
never s. the sun up 1729: 9
no s. till morn 359:11
not s. that made him nod 1944: 3
now I lay me down to s. 1847:12
O, come, benignest s. ..1850: 2
O magic s. 1844:14
O soothest S. 1844:14
O such another s. 1252:14
of death closes scars 1149: 6
of laboring man sweet ..1847:15
of the just 395: 7
old men s. longest 1121: 9
on and smile 121: 1

Sleep, *continued*
on both ears 1843:10
on in peace 77: 2
on the grass to weary ..1519: 3
on their s. may rise 395:16
one hour's s. before midnight 1848: 4
only medicine gives ease 1845:13
our daily healer 1844: 2
poppied s. 1845:16
preservation from immoderate s. 1015: 2
resolve to s. no more 986: 3
rock me to s., mother ...2011: 1
rock thy brain 1846:11
rounded with a s. 1141:11
season of all natures 1845: 9
shake off this drowsy s. ..1849:14
she belike hath drunken s. 1844: 7
Silence' child 1844: 9
sing me to s. 1850: 6
six hours for a man 1848: 9
six hours to s. 935: 1
sleeps the holy s. 394:15
slept an iron s. 1868: 6
so long at last is s. 1219: 8
soft embalmer 1844:14
sole comforter of minds 1844: 9
sooner it's over, sooner to s. 2234:18
sovereign gift of God 1845: 2
still let me s. 482:18
stole on me unawares 1850: 9
sweet harlot of the senses 1845: 4
sweet s. be with us 480:11
sweet within this quiet ..1846: 7
sweetly in humble graves 1869: 1
that from this golden rigol 395:11
that is among the lonely hills 1389: 1
that knits up the ravell'd sleave of care 1845: 9
that knows no waking ..379:10
that knows not breaking .1870: 3
that no pain shall wake ..395: 8
that shall ne'er know waking 379:10
that shuts up sorrow's eye 1845: 9
think of them that s. 1815: 3
third of life passed in s. .394:14
this s. is sound indeed 395:11
thou ape of death 1849:13
thou rest of all things ..1845: 7
till the end, true soul 396: 3
timely dew of s. 1845: 3
to be enjoyed must be interrupted 1843:15
to s. and feed 519:20
to s. and not to know it .1843:13
to s. for a season 482: 7
to s., perchance to dream .395:10
to soft S. we give 480:10
to wake 1434: 9
'twill only be a s. 395:15
two gates of s. there are ..478:21
undisturb'd as death 183: 8
visit her, gentle S. 1846: 5
we term s. a death 1849: 6
well and peacefully 406:15
what hath night with s. .1400:12
when work is done 1138:10
where care lodges, s. will never lie 221: 6
who can wrestle against s. 1843:22
who do not care to s. ...1850: 7
whole night through 1848: 5
will not be commanded .1850: 4
wish friend as sound a s. 394:19
with eyes open 1843: 6
without supping 418:13
wonted s. 1811:17
would I were s. and peace 1846:11
Sleepeth: she is not dead but s. 395: 1
with dogs, rise with fleas 470: 4
Sleeping are men 1147:15
away the unreturning time 2267: 4
enough in the grave 1849:10
if s. wake 1431:11
when she died 393:12
Sleepless to give readers sleep 1534:12
yet do lie s. 1851: 4
Sleeps by day More than wild-cat 1843:16
she s.! My lady s. 1846:9; 1917: 3
well who knows not 1843:13
who s. longest happiest ..394:18
upon his watch 506: 7
well, think well 497: 7
with the rose 384:10
Sleepy-head: ain't you 'shamed, you s. 1730:14
Sleet: whistling s. and snow 1815: 9
Sleeve guise of messengers 1851:10
laugh in your s. 1078:13
like a demi-cannon 489: 5
without s. no errand 1851:10
Sleeveless 1851
some and shirtless 9:13
Sleeves: tie up my s. 3: 6
Sleight: admire s. of hand ..249: 8
either by might or s. 1303:12
Sleights and subtleties ..2197:13
Slept and dreamed that life was Beauty 507: 4
not s. one wink 1850:14
reasonably 417: 2
securely, dreamt of more 1843:10
we still have s. together ..287:14
whilst Adam s. 12: 6
Slide: greatness loves to s. .48:18
Kelly, s. 1638:14
Slight is the field of toil ..781:16
not strength 1922: 5
Slime: proud s. 1574:19
wastes of cosmic s. 586:11
Slimepit and the 'mire 892:13
Sling: little s. may destroy .543: 2
Slings and arrows 1934: 9
Slinks through dark Oblivion's gate 367:12
Slip: every s. not a fall ..621:10
giving enemies the s. 544: 1
many a s. 6:16
of the foot recovered 2024: 1
Slip-shod: go s. 2173:15
Slipper: compose s. and song 1818: 1
we only hunt a s. 1509:14
wear s. for a glove 2246: 8
well-worn s. feels 291:10
Slippers to put on when you're weary 2204:13
Slippery: topmost point ...838: 3
Slipping: no s. up hill 612:10
Slipt like him 651:13
you would have s. 651:13
Slithy means lithe, slimy .2221: 5
Slop over 2123: 2
Slope of faces 607:13
Sloth 953
See also Idleness, Indolence
banish your s. 953: 5
brings in all woe 954: 2
cares and woe of s. 1067: 6
finds down pillow hard ..1847:15
impotent to rise 626:12
is foe to virtuous deeds ..954: 3
is tempter that beguiles ..953:19
is the devil's pillow 954:10
like rust, consumes 954: 1
makes all difficult 954: 1
Mother of Doom 954: 9
must breed a scab 954: 3
never suspected of s. 48: 7
shake off dull S. 1890:17
shameful Siren, s. 954: 4
sustains the trade 464:23
triumphs over energy 43:22
turns the edge of wit 954: 3
Slothful: not s. in business 207:16
Slothfulness: detestation to all s. 112: 3
Slouch becomes a walk ..1864: 8
Slough of Despond 1826:20
Slough: casted s. 1314: 4
one s. and crust of sin ...1831:17
Slovenliness no part of religion 278:16
Slow and steady wins 1488: 7
as the elephant 535:16
but precious sure 227: 1
to smite, swift to spare ..1158: 6
to speak 149:13
Slow-worm could see 1798: 8
Slowness: beaten the snail in s. 1855: 9
is sure 227: 1
Sluggard wiser in own conceit 954: 6
Sluggardized: dully s. 910: 6
Slugs despise the worms ..1609: 5
leave their lair 955:19
that come crawling 1765: 9
Slumber everywhere 1850: 1
honey-heavy dew of s. 1846:11
I must s. again 953:21
if you seek to s. 1851: 4
into dreadful s. lull'd 1843: 2
keepst the ports of s. open wide 221: 6
let not s. close your eyes 1788:17
lie still and s. 1847:11
light 31: 6
little sleep, little s. 395: 5
of a decided opinion 1428:18
poppy-seeds of s. 365:12
to mine eyelids 1850:12
Slumbering in background of time 2004: 2
Slumbers: balmy s. 1846: 3
golden s. kiss your eyes ..1847: 3
hast thou golden s. 1847:14
infant's s. pure and bright 1847: 7
made all our s. soft 1590: 9
my s. are not sleep 1850: 4
sweet are s. of virtuous ..1844: 1
sweet thy mercy send us 1846:13
waked with strife 1865: 3
Slut: am not a s. 2133:15
eat after a s. 91:11
Sluts: foul s. in dairies ..614:12
Smack and tang of elemental things 1159: 8
of observation 1423:20
some s. of age 26: 7
Smacks of something greater 1408: 7
Small and early 1859: 9
escape notice 837:11
few are so s. 2041: 9
he hath made s. and great 1248:13
he that contemneth s. things 2041: 4
how s. very great are 835: 5
many s. maken great 2039:11
matters win commendation 2040:16
no great and no s. 835: 8
no perfect thing too s. 1486: 3
one a strong nation 2041:10
suffered for great 835:11
things are best 2039:13
things make base men proud 2042:10
these are s. things 2040: 2
things to the s. 2039:10
to greater matters 2042:13
very s. very great are 835: 5
Small-pox 460:10
charm'd the s. 610:10
Smart: men feel s. 2079: 6
smarteth most who hideth s. 1607:14
some of us will s. for it .1658: 2
Smartness of an attorney's clerk 947:13
Smatch: some s. of honor ..919: 5
Smattering of everything .529: 8
Smear: sceptred S. 2147:12
Smell a fox 1651: 9
grateful s. 1777: 3
he that doth s. so sweetly 1487:14
him that's stinking 1413:15
it on the tree 1745:11
like a washing-day 524: 2
neither to s. rank 1487:12

Soil, *continued*
out of which men are made 53:11
richest s., rankest weeds .2130: 6
think there thy native s. ..944:12
was barren, hearts hard ..943: 5
where first they trod 1501: 9
where s. is, men grow 1247:13
Soils: rich s. often weeded 1900:16
Sol crescentis duplicatum-
bræ 1804: 5
etiam cæcat 1938: 1
matutinus s. 1940: 8
occubuit; nox nulla 1038: 7
quando annotta, il S.
tramonta 1896: 2
Solace for everything 1461: 1
sweet s. of labor 1063:15
truest s. to act no sin 1317:17
whence comes s. 481: 7
which busy world dis-
dains 1583: 8
Solamen miseris socios 1320: 4
Solar system has no anxiety
about its reputation ..1702: 2
Solatia: centum s. curæ ..2030: 7
Sold: all are to be s. 1605: 9
cheap what is most dear ..237: 8
himself unto himself he s. 1794: 7
many things he might have
s., and did not sell ..2298h: 1
myself for dowry 477:13
to be so bought and s. 78:16
Soldat: quel plaisir d'être 1863: 7
Soldier **1862**
American s. known but to
God 1864: 4
among sovereigns 1378:11
an' sailor too 1636:10
and statesman 2122: 7
and unapt to weep 1865: 3
arm'd with Resolution ...2215: 3
armed with sword, gun ..1865: 7
bad s. who grumbles 1868: 2
be a s. without dying 1862: 9
Ben Battle was s. bold ..1654:18
but a man 1865: 1
deserving s. makes way ..1868: 4
did not lay aside citizen 1864: 3
didst very right as a s. ..1865:15
elder s., not a better 1863:12
every s. carries baton ...1430:19
farewell, honest s. 1870: 5
fed on beef and beer 1863:11
fie! a s. and afeard 1863:13
fit to stand by Cæsar 1865: 3
fitting for s. ignorant ..1863:14
for a s I listed 1866:10
full of strange oaths 2240: 5
God and the s. we alike
adore 1867: 1
God's s. be he ...1870:5; 2248: 4
how happy's the s. 1866:10
I did not raise boy to be
a s. 1864: 7
I raised my boy to be a s. 1864: 7
in army of liberty 1992:19
is an anachronism 1865:14
kindly bade to stay 1864:11
let a s. drink 496:12
little toy s. is red with
rust 408: 1
living, dying, heroic s. .1869: 9
mere recreant prove 1866: 6
negro s. in trenches 53: 3
never expect s. to think 1865:14
never keep unnecessary s. 1965: 9
not exempt from saying a
foolish thing 1865:15
nothing but a plain old s. 2286: 4
of the King 556:15
of the Legion 1869:10
old revolutionary s. 2286: 4
raised himself to be s. ..1864: 7
rest, thy warfare o'er ..1870: 3
shall I ask brave s. 335: 8
should be fear-inspiring ..1864:15
should be modest as maid 1864: 2
successful s. first king 74: 3
summer s. 62: 4
teach a s. terms 2212: 8
Soldier, *continued*
tell me, tell me weary s. ..2286: 4
thou more than s. 781:14
what delight to be a s. ..1863: 7
when falls the s. brave ..1522: 4
when s. was the theme ..1863: 9
without ambition no spurs 1862:10
worse man, better s. 1863: 2
Soldier's debt 377: 9
Soldiers accustomed to
plunder 2112:16
all not s. that go to war ..1862:16
all s. run away 1864: 1
and chiefs of Irish Bri-
gade 1868:10
are becoming too popular 2231: 2
are citizens of death's ...1870: 2
are easily got 1868:5a
ate three s. 1555: 6
best s. France ever had ..1395: 7
commanded ten s., ate
three 1555: 6
good s. but also good men 1865: 5
in peace like chimneys ..1862:12
marching all to die 1863:10
may not quit the post ..1935:11
miserly s. monsters 1864: 6
not ceased to be citizens 1864: 3
of America have killed ..1865:10
old s. are surest 42: 6
old s. never die 2298h: 4
onward, Christian s. 267: 8
remedy against democrats 431:11
ten good s. wisely led 1863:16
unnam'd s. fallen 614: 3
when s. brave death 1869: 8
why should Spanish s.
brag 1896: 5
ye living s. of mighty war 1864: 9
Sole as a flying star 801: 3
Sole juvant umbræ 1509:17
Sole-leather: preferable to
s. 929: 6
Sole-sitting by the shores 1736: 9
Solecism of power 1573:12
Solecisms never pardoned 1856: 8
Soleil: fait élever le s. 233: 4
ma place au s. 768: 7
voir pour la dernière fois 416:23
Solem enim e mundo tol-
lere 743: 9
qui in s. venit 1938: 4
quis dicere falsum 1938: 7
Solemn as an ass 829:14
Soles: firm, well hammer'd
s. 1816:14
Soles occidere et redire 968:16
Solicit for it straight 338: 3
Solicitor: our best-moving 1093: 3
whose s. given me brief 1091:12
Solicitude of weak mortality 1945: 6
Solid and sound 979: 5
Solitary as an oyster 1443:11
be not s., be not idle 952:18
Solitude **1870**
affects like wine 1872: 4
audience-chamber of God 1870:15
best nurse of wisdom ..1871:18
dangerous to reason 1872: 7
feels his s. peopled 1363:11
hail, mildly pleasing S. .1872: 2
how passing sweet is s. ..1872: 1
if I must with thee dwell 1873: 2
impracticable 1862: 4
in s. dew of youth 1871:15
in s. what happiness 1872: 8
in s. when least alone ..1873:13
is sweet 1872: 1
is very sad 1862: 1
is within us 1873: 3
love tranquil s. 1862: 7
made perfect 202:15
makes s., calls it peace ..1470:13
needful to imagination ..1862: 5
no place can ever be s. ..1216: 4
no such thing as s. 1873: 7
nurse of enthusiasm 1871:13
O s. where are the charms 1872: 5
of his originality 1378:10
Solitude, *continued*
pasturage for suspicion .1872: 7
prompts to all evil 1872:10
proud, society vulgar 1482: 5
sacred s., divine retreat .1872: 3
secret of s. no s. 1870:13
should teach us to die ..1871:11
sometimes is best society 1862: 6
soul's best friend 1871:12
sweet retired S. 1871:18
teaches what conscience is 298:14
think it s. to be alone ..1871:10
this is not s. 1384: 1
vivifies 1871: 7
whoso walketh in s. 1384: 6
whosoever delighteth in s. 1870:11
worst s. to have no true
friends 743: 7
would ripen despots 1872: 9
Solitudinem faciunt, pacem
appellant 1470:13
Solitudo: O beata s. 1872: 1
omnia nobis mala s. 1872:10
Sollicitudines: neque mordaces aliter diffugiunt
s. 2157: 2
Solomon, he liv'd at ease ..1100:11
in all his glory 1156:15
laid hold of folly 701:16
listened to many 678: 1
never dressed 161: 7
of saloons 450:19
wrote the Proverbs 1038:11
Solon compared people unto
the sea 1437:11
saved one king 411:14
wished everybody ready ..1437:11
Solum: minus s. quam
solus 1874: 3
Solus: to mihi s. eras 408:16
Solute: soft harmonies 860:22
Solventur risu tabulæ 1078:19
Solvitur ambulando 2101: 7
quod jessu alterius s. ...1492:17
Somebody: can't beat s.
with nobody 2281: 6
how dreary to be s. 837: 1
loves me 2293: 9
Something attempted 1063:13
better than nothing 197: 6
for nothing 750: 5
given that way 1640: 2
has some savour 1414: 3
in the autumn 115:17
made of nothing 1045:19
real s. yet to be known 88: 9
rich and strange 232: 8
to be contented with 312: 7
very like him 443: 3
will come of this 171: 8
will turn up 592: 4
would turn up 1435: 9
Sometime: it shall be done
s., somewhere 1586: 1
someday, somewhere 1882: 2
somewhere, some day 1216: 6
Somewhat: an unfathom-
able s. 992: 6
I have s. against thee ..1206:15
which we name 797:14
Somewhere 121:12
beautiful Isle of S. 2292: 1
Sommeil des justes 395: 7
Somne, quies rerum 1845: 7
Somni: geminæ S. portæ ...478:21
Somnia: ægri s. vanæ 478: 8
ludunt temeraria nocte 479: 7
me terrent veros imitantia 483: 3
nec sint mihi s. vera 483: 7
post mediam noctem, s. vera 480: 4
sed sibi quisque facit 479: 4
sub aurora s. vera 480: 4
Somnium narrare vigilantis
est 1829:16
Somnus agrestium 1848: 1
faciat breves tenebras 1843: 9
mortis imago 1849:11
non bonust s. de prandio 1848: 8
nullus s. meridianus 1848: 8
sollicitas deficit 1851: 3

Sons, *continued*
of Care always s. of Night 1321:12
of Columbia 1840: 1
of Edward sleep 886: 6
of freedom, wake to glory 719: 2
of honor, follow and obey 918:17
of Mary seldom bother ..2232: 7
of the Empire 556: 4
of the morning 1587: 8
of the wild jackass 2278: 6
seldom s. succeed father 1874: 8
strong s. of thine 56:11
with purple death expire 2114: 3
ye s. of light 76:14
your s. shall prophesy 2095: 3
Sooner the better 1641:22
Socple: be s., Davie 452: 9
Sooth: it is silly s. 123:10
oft in game s. said 2050: 5
Soothe: born to s. and entertain 2194:16
Soothers: tongues of s. 678:19
Soothes be not to say 2058:13
Soothfast: forever to me ..590: 2
Soothsayings 1623: 2
Sop for Cerberus 1631:13
o' the moonshine 1997: 4
Sophism of all sophisms ..1901:17
Sophist: dark-brow'd s. ..1901:17
schools 294:13
Sophisticated: three on's ..2244: 1
within the s. 23: 1
Sophistries of June 116: 2
optimistic s. 1434: 5
Sophistry: lively s. and exaggeration 312:15
with s. sauce they sweeten 1954: 9
Sophocles wrote his grand Œdipus 31: 9
Sophonisba, O! 1376: 4
Sopor: consanguineus Leti S. 1849:14
fessis in gramine 1519: 3
Soporific on listless ear 1439: 9
Soprano, basso, contra-alto 342:12
Sorbonist: learned S. 1638: 2
Sordello's story told 1959: 5
Sore: for every s. a salve 1186:14
if friends are s. 1078:23
lanceth not the s. 1886: 6
rub s. when bring plaster 1286: 7
same old s. breaks out ..1571: 5
which no man healeth ...881:18
Sores: different s., salves 1286: 7
mobs of cities 276:15
to strange s. strain cure 1286: 7
Sororum: qualem decet esse 1155: 4
Sorrel: low-growing s. 523: 7
Sort fait les parents 729: 2
Sors: certa si decreta 440: 4
cui placet alterius 453: 9
Sorte: utere s. tua 229: 6
Sorrow 1884
and a care that killed 1887: 3
and death may not enter 886:15
and disease 458: 8
and sighing shall flee away 1886: 2
and silence are strong ..540:23
and the scarlet leaf 117:10
any s. like unto my s. 1887: 2
breaks seasons 1884: 6
breeds s. 220:11
brief is s. 1019: 3
bring down gray hairs with s. 848:16
calls no time that's gone 1978:13
can wait 2166:21
canker s. eat my bud ..1887:10
cheered by being poured 1885:17
clamorous s. wastes itself 842:18
come then, S., sweetest S. 1885:10
comes unsent for 1884:13
concealed doth burn heart 1886: 8
couch'd in seeming gladness 1887:12
crazy s. saith 386: 3
crown of s. remembering 1295:11

Sorrow, *continued*
death-bed s. rarely shows man 1699: 6
eighty odd years of s. 1019: 5
eldest child of sin 1884: 7
enough in hell 1849:10
enough in natural way ..472:13
excess of s. laughs 1018: 7
fail not for s. 23: 3
fat s. better than lean ..1884:11
first great s. 436:12
flouted at is double death 1886: 9
followeth glory 782: 4
for husband short 2135:18
fore-spent night of s. 371:10
free from s. as from sin 2196: 9
give s. words 842:15
gnarling s. less power ..1886: 6
good for nothing but sin 1884: 7
great idealizer 1884: 5
hang s. 221:16
hardly leisure for great ..621:15
has cross'd the life-line ..851: 7
hath killed many 1886: 1
heavy s. that bows head 1886:16
Hecuba ran mad for s. ..1231:12
I found more joy in s. ...1019: 8
I have a silent s. here ..1887: 1
I shall not let a s. die 595:15
I walked a mile with S. 1885: 9
if s. can admit society ...1886: 7
in wooing s. let's be brief 1886: 6
is a kind of rust 1884: 4
is a woman a man may take 1884: 2
is knowledge 1884: 1
lean s. hardest to bear ..1884:11
let s. lend me words 842:16
like a mighty river 1704:15
little s., little pleasure ..1138: 8
longest s. finds relief 1886: 3
makes us wise 1884: 1
men die but s. never dies 1886:14
miss the artist's s. 106:12
more beautiful than beauty 1885:10
more in s. than in anger 1885: 3
my old s. wakes and cries 1886:19
nae s. there, John 884: 6
need not come in vain ..1885:11
never comes too late 1886:17
never long without ease ..1886: 2
no day without s. 1887: 7
no greater s. than recall 1295: 2
no s. in thy song 346:19
no s. like a love denied ..1221:11
no s. rankles 405: 6
no wisdom in hopeless s. 1884: 3
nothing too soon but s. ..1884: 9
O, s.! why dost borrow .1886:20
of the meanest thing ...1493: 2
one s. brings an heir ..1322: 9
only sorrow's shade 1887:15
play fool to s. 209:11
pluck from memory rooted s. 1313: 6
pluck out hair for s. 848:20
preys upon its solitude ..1884:10
proportion'd to our cause 1884: 6
ransom for offence 1699:19
remove s. from thee 1886: 1
return'd with the morn ..1886:13
sefish S. ponders on past 1886:12
showers of s. lot of all 840:10
shows us truths 290:11
shunned with averted eye 1885:14
sing away s. 1885:16
sit thee down, s. 1626:12
smit with exceeding s. ...1884:15
so royally in you appears .1887:13
solitary s. best befits 842: 7
some natural s., loss 1887:16
struck so many blows ...1887:10
suffocating s. 1887:14
take no s. of thing lost ...1704: 1
teach me to believe this s. 1887: 9
teach s. to make me die ..1887: 9
that bides 1018:16
that's shared but half 1019: 1
there is only s. in my heart 1216:12

Sorrow, *continued*
this s. heavenly 1885:12
thy s. and the s. of sea 998: 1
to show an unfelt s. 1885: 5
to S. I bade good morrow 1886:20
to s. must I tune my song 1878:12
too great to share 27:11
touch'd by Thee, grows bright 1151: 2
tracketh wrong 1887: 5
true s. makes a silence ..842:14
wear a golden s. 312: 2
well-feigned s. to belie 421: 4
whate'er there be of S. .1018: 5
whatever crazy s. saith ..386: 3
when she's here with me .117: 7
when s. sleeps wake it not 1884:14
when young I said to S. 1886:15
where s., holy ground ..1884: 8
wherever s. is, relief 1886: 5
whisper s. into sleep 200: 7
wild s., avenging care 890: 7
wilt thou rule my blood ..1887:15
with night we banish s. ..1730:12
without door let s. lie 1884:14
Sorrow's eye glazed with tears 840:13
Sorrowed to repentance ..1698:15
Sorrowful: don't be s. 293: 2
Sorrowing: goeth a-s. 193: 7
Sorrows: all s. less with bread 1884:11
anticipate our s. 1933:16
are like thunderclouds ..2044: 8
come in battalions 1887: 8
describe another's s. 1322:16
ease our s. to reveal 1885:17
encompass the tomb 404:12
every man has secret s. ..1887: 3
few s. with good income 1884:11
great s. laugh 1018: 7
half the s. of women ...2199:16
here I and s. sit 1887: 9
hundred thousand s. 2112:11
I will indulge my s. 436:12
instruct s. to be proud ..1887: 9
joys impregnate, s. bring 1018: 7
little s. sit and weep 1847: 1
man of s. 261: 8
new s. strike heaven 1887: 7
of a poor old man 145:13
of death compassed me .386:12
of vanity 2075: 3
our portion are 1886:18
past s. moderately lament 1885: 6
pick s. from joys 1018:11
pierced themselves with s. 1337: 2
remembered sweeten joy 1293:18
sharing each other's s. 2290:12
short that gain bliss 1885:13
thy s. hush 2179:19
visitors without invitation 1884:13
whose s. matched my own 1887: 2
why anticipate s. 1933:16
woven with delights 1887: 4
Sorry for himself 1791:11
for what you haven't done 426: 2
I'm s. I made you cry ..1883: 2
Sors: certa si decreta s. est 440: 4
cui placet alterius sua odio s. 453: 9
Sort fait les parents 729: 2
Sorte: utere s. tua 229: 6
Sortem: nemo s. contentus vivat 309:11
Sorts and conditions of men 1240: 5
Sospetto: lasciare ogni s. ..464: 1
Sot: their prize a S. 318: 9
Sot: admirer un s. 1299:14
avec de l'esprit 1022:23
comme un anglais 561: 6
en trois lettres 697:17
se croit riche de peu 698:12
trouve un plus s. 696:13
Sots: what can ennoble s. ..72: 4
Sots: combien faut-il de s. 1481:20
font le texte 1691: 2
qui ont de l'esprit 2173: 5
sont en majorité 699: 1

Sovereigns may sway materials 41: 4
sceptered s. 833: 4
Sovereignty of man 1057: 3
of self-governing people 54: 5
representative s. 432: 6
what your sex desire is S. 2195: 5
Sow: barren s. not good to pigs 1350:17
comparing s. to Minerva 173:13
returns to her mire 1628:19
snapped at a gnat 2042: 1
wrong s. by the ear 1324:13
Sow and seed 1992:12
and sing and reap 1135: 7
as you s. ye shall reap ..1709: 4
directed from Washington when to s. 817: 8
dry and set wet 756:15
in ashes and reap in dust 1491:10
in morning s. thy seed ..861:11
that you may reap 640:13
wild oats 1640: 5
Soweth: whatsoever a man s. 1709: 7
Sown in barren ground 968:13
Sows against the wind ..2198: 2
he that speaks s. 1824: 8
he who s. ground 639: 1
who s. a field 638:16
Space as nothing to spirit ..425: 9
desolate wind-swept s. ...1904:12
enough in such a prison 1613:11
out of S., out of Time ..463:14
stature of God 2067:13
that's in tyrant's grasp 2085:16
Spaces: great open s. 223:10
sun-swept s. God made 1387: 2
wide s. and the open air ..240: 2
Spade: don't call me s. ..219: 2
Spades are Spades 218
emblem of graves 219:13
Spain 1895
all evil comes from S. ..1895:17
beard of the King of S. ..127: 9
over the sea lies S. 1895:19
renown'd romantic land 1895:14
Spake: never s. but do wisely 2228:12
one thing thought another 1901:12
the word he meant 216:15
Span: life but a s. 1249:14
of life is short 1129: 4
world's uncertain s. 1340: 6
Spangles deck the thorn ..233: 2
Spaniard is bad servant 1895:11a
Spaniards seem wiser than they are 2162: 6
Spaniel: play the s. 2025:18
Spaniel-like, the more she 1215: 3
Spaniels of the world 471:10
Spanish fan 1766: 8
I must learn S. 1376: 9
Spare and have 1997: 8
all I have, take life 117:17
bid him go and s. not ..1455:14
Spared a better man 636:10
Sparing is the first gaining 1998:3a
Spark: ae s. o' Nature's fire 991: 7
conceited, talking s. 1964:14
from Heaven's bright throne 322:11
from little s. mighty flame 2041: 3
no s. of honor bides 919:13
of aboriginal savage 235:16
of never-dying flame 1887:19
shows a hasty s. 78:19
small s. mighty conflagration 667:21
thou s. of life 211: 4
unburied 965: 6
vital s. of heavenly flame 1893: 9
vocal s. 1073: 5
Sparkle of his swarthy eye 604: 7
Sparkled, was exhal'd 410: 3
Sparkling and bright 2156:12
Sparks: as the s. fly upward 2043:13
from central fire 1727:19
more s., worse match 2214: 7
that are like wit 2174: 5

Sparks, *continued*
that kindle fiery war 2115:13
unnumber'd s. 1914:12
Sparrer-grass: look lak s. ..85:15
Sparrow 1896
better a s. in the hand ..161: 3
cannot fall without God ..718:12
caters for the s. 1647: 7
my lady's s. is dead ..1896: 6
now my little s. gone 1896: 6
providence in fall of s. ..1647: 7
take off hat to the s. 1896: 8
Sparrows chirped as if still proud 1896: 9
two s. sold for farthing ..1647: 7
when s. build 1886:19
Sparta: hath many worthier 211:16
Spartan: just as S. ladies 943:12
Spartans: ask where enemy 544: 5
at Thermopylæ: epitaph . 570: 7
Spass verliert Alles 1009:13
Spät kommt ihr, doch kommt 1074: 3
Spatio debilitatur amor 4:13
Spats: he has thrown away 705:18
Spawn innumerable 1386: 6
Speak according to rules ..355:12
after the manner of men 1899:10
all this I s. in print ... 1613: 2
ancients without idolatry ..83:15
and purpose not 217: 9
and sweetly smile 1852: 8
as having seen 1820: 6
as small as you will 1898: 4
as the common people do 1993:12
as you think 726: 4
be ready to s. your mind 217:12
before your time 1899:15
begin low, s. slow 1440: 2
boldly and s. truly 217: 4
by permission 1897:12
by tears, before tongue 1974:16
by the card 1641: 5
cannot s. but judges self 1896:10
clearly if at all 1898:16
daggers to her 1898: 1
difficult to s. well 1899: 4
every man can s. eloquently 1898:11
for yourself, John 1209: 9
from your folded papers 1520: 3
gently, 'tis a little thing ..766: 3
hear all men s. 464: 5
I only s. right on 1438:19
if thou wilt s. aright 1900:14
ill of the absent 2: 8
know when to s. 19:10
leave others turns to s. ..1900:15
less than thou knowest ..1931: 1
low, if you s. love 1209:16
low to me, my Saviour ..262:10
may s. thing he will 552:11
me fair in death 406: 3
men shall s. well of you 1702: 6
no ill of the dead 405:13
no more s. fast than run 1899: 5
no more than truth 2058: 1
not till there is silence 1824:15
not till you have somewhat to s. 1900:17
not to s. it profanely 10: 6
o' the devil 441: 5
of love aright 152:21
of me as I am 1237: 1
of whom you s., to whom 1838:15
one's mind 218: 3
or be for ever silent 1823: 9
out 217: 6
plain and to purpose 217:10
roughly to your boy 255:14
say, and s. thick 1897:21
slow to s., slow to wrath ..149:13
so well, be so ill 2227: 8
softly, carry big stick ...1598:15
softly s. and sweetly smile 1211: 7
something notable 1897:16
sweetly, man 1953: 8
ten millions wrong 1236: 2
that I may see thee 1896:10
that we do know 1055: 5

Speak, *continued*
that which is not 218: 1
that which you will wonder 2209: 9
thing I shall repent 2027: 5
to a dead man 1897:18
to every cause 1093:15
to me, Lord Byron 212: 1
to s. and purpose not 946: 9
to s. and to offend 1899: 3
to s. his thoughts 726: 3
to s. much not to s. well 1899:13
to the earth 512: 1
to the meanings of each other 312:13
to the point or be still ..494:5a
to thee in silence 1823: 6
to whom you s., of whom 1900:14
we never s. as we pass by 2285: 8
we s. not what we mean 1902: 2
well of no man living ..565:10
what he means 1876:13
what should we s. of 1897:21
what you think to-day 304:12
when he is spoken to 255: 8
when I s. they are for war 2119: 6
when you are spoken to ..254:19
where we are both known 1838: 1
why don't you s. for yourself, John 1209: 9
with me 146: 3
with seeming diffidence ..1824:14
with tongues of men 241: 9
without a tongue 526: 5
ye who best can tell 76:14
you s. upon the rack 1444:16
your mind 217:12
Speaker: I am truest s. ..1833:10
of my living actions 159:17
Speaketh more honestly than can do 2226:11
Speaking: heard for much s. 1900: 8
much, saying nothing 2225:10
much sign of vanity 2228:10
nor have I readiness in s. 1899: 7
of misfortunes a relief ..1323:10
often repented s. 1825: 3
to deceive 421:12
well consists in lying 1111:22
while I am s., hour flies 2006: 6
Speaks best who hath the skill 1824:20
he s. holiday 903:16
he s. home 217: 8
he that s. lavishly 1900: 3
her foot s. 318:13
like a small woman 1898: 4
little without vanity 1899: 4
me fair and loves me not 1901:19
never s. but mouth opens 1897:19
often s. but never talks 1964:12
plain cannon fire 1898: 2
she s. poniards 1898: 1
three or four languages 1070: 4
through his nose 1591: 9
very shrewishly 2265: 7
well of everybody 2047: 5
what's in his heart 78:15
without care, sorrow 1901: 2
Spear: cast s. 2046:10
he walked with 444:13
idle s. and shield hung ..1473: 3
slander's venomed s. 1837:15
snatch'd s. but left shield 2073: 3
Spears and swords unblest 1931: 7
Species: not an individual, a s. 1258:1a
Species cogitur ire pedes 1762: 6
quanta s. cerebrum non habet 86:10
Specimen fuisse humanitatis 238: 3
Speck: smallest s. seen on snow 137:11
this s. of life 1124: 1
Spectacle afforded by fellow-creatures 1245:16
more grand than sea 300: 4
no s. so ridiculous 2274: 5

Spirals: human mind makes progress in s. 1307: 4
Spire: every village marked with little s. 2085:11
that out-towers crag 2036: 5
Spire-steeples point 272: 9
Spires **272**
million s. are pointing 336: 7
Spirit **1903**
accusing S. 75:11
all compact of fire 1248:11
all save s. of man divine 2061: 8
American s. in literature 1166: 4
ancient s. of Englishmen 559: 1
and senses grow dead 348: 7
bend up every s. 2116:10
best-condition'd s. 1037: 2
black earthly s. 1592:14
blooms timidly 2241: 2
bold s. in loyal breast ..178: 1
brave s. helps misfortune 1323:13
break her s. or her heart 2146: 7
breaking s. of a law 1086:13
burning but unbent 1698:18
cabin'd, ample s. 393: 7
carping s. of mankind 84: 3
commits itself to yours ..2144: 1
curb thou the high s. 1664: 7
dauntless s. of resolution 177:20
doubtful public s. 531:16
each of us suffers own S. 1657: 8
earthy s. of the priest 1592:14
every s., as it is more pure 1892: 1
every s. is of character 1904:10
every s. makes its house 909:13
extravagant and erring s. 1905: 3
fairer s. 14: 2
familiar s. 2194: 6
felt with s. so profound 1995:16
fervent in s. 207:16
flies and with it all 1906: 7
flits chameleon-like 1002: 6
foolish extravagant s. 961: 7
free s. of mankind 52: 7
full of s. as month of May 1865: 2
giveth life 1903:15
grew robust 183:11
grieving of the S. 1904:10
hail to thee, blithe S. 1073: 1
half-extinguished s. 378:19
haughty s. before a fall 1608:10
haunts year's last hours 2262: 8
he that ruleth his s. 1787: 1
her s. is devout 957: 4
his s. grew robust 183:11
holy s. of the Spring 1907: 7
humble, tranquil s. 261:13
I am thy father's s. 770:12
I look for s. in her eyes 1313: 8
I resign my s. to God 415:16
I would you had her s. 2142:15
ill s. have so fair a house 132:10
immense and brooding S. 1502:13
in heaven a s. doth dwell 1879:10
in which gift is rich 774:11
into thy hands I commend my s. 1904: 3
invisible s. of wine 2158:13
is upon you 107:13
is willing 680: 4
it is S. that quickeneth 1903:15
labour to draw S. to us 1904:10
let not worser s. tempt 1935:12
lies under the walls 1451:19
little, little thing 1904:11
long shaping for sublime 2150: 6
man's s. hath operative faculties 798:10
may be the devil 444: 6
meek and quiet s. 1904: 6
mellows 42: 5
more brightly s. shine ..1904: 2
must brand the flesh 1829:12
my little s., see 1905: 6
my s. drank repose 1302:13
new s. will I put within you 1685:16
nimble, stirring s. 1301: 9
noble s. of metropolis 1168: 3
not of letter, but of s. ..1903:15

Spirit, *continued*
not willing to live 1129: 5
O s. of love! how quick ..1193:17
of a child that waits 258: 4
of a little child 253:13
of a tapster 207:20
of antiquity 83: 3
of Beauty 131: 3
of Christianity 265: 8
of discernment rare 1013: 7
of divinest Liberty 1105: 9
of God brother of my own 1176: 2
of health or goblin damn'd 770:10
of his age 43:19
of inquiry 352:10
of mortal be proud 1607:11
of my own s. let me be ..1904: 5
of nationality 997: 7
of Night 1402: 1
of one happy day 371: 7
of proselytism 633:11
of Saint Lo is 1161: 8
of self-sacrifice 1792:22
of s. so still and quiet ..1234: 8
of the chainless Mind ..1106:13
of the Summer-time 309: 2
of the Times 1989: 5
of the worm 2244:12
of Twilight 2062: 3
of unspiritual conditions 1689:14a
of Wine sang in my heart 2156:11
of youth begins betimes 2267: 8
of youth in every thing 93:12
old in s. never 23: 1
only can teach 1970:17
paint character and s. 103:20
pard-like s., beautiful ..1905: 8
pardon s. of liberty 1104: 6
perturbed s. 1707:11
pour out my S. upon all 2095: 3
present in s. 2: 2
prone to strife 39: 4
pure, sweet s. 1170: 3
renew a right s. within me 879: 3
seems our comrade yet 240: 2
serve in newness of s. ..1086:18
shall return unto God 965:14
shallow s. of judgement 1090: 7
sink not in s. 110:14
sister S., come away 1893: 9
sliding through tranquillity 1666:13
soaring s. is prime delight 251: 1
stab my s. broad awake ..858:16
strongest and fiercest S. ..444:16
superior to every weapon 1904: 5
supernal 551: 3
that is one 334:15
that its author writ 341: 1
that on life's rough sea ..1776: 8
their s. walks abroad 612: 2
there is a s. in the woods 2211: 6
thou s. of contradiction 1663: 7
thou s. of Summertime ..1936: 4
'tis a blushing shamefast s. 302: 8
too much s. to be at ease 1996:12
truly is ready 1904: 4
walks of every day 373: 1
when his s. is departed ..404:10
where S. of the Lord is, liberty 1103: 4
which prized liberty 54: 2
why should the s. of mortal be proud 1607:11
willing, but flesh weak 1904: 4
with more s. chased 1560:16
without experience 593:14
wounded human s. turns .2253: 5
wounded s. that loved 708:18
wounded s. who can bear 1904: 7
yet a woman too 2186: 7
yet a S. still, and bright 2186: 7
zealous as he seem'd 1251:12
Spirit-level: pure s. 1089:16
Spirit-world around this world of sense 1904:16
Spiriting: do my s. gently 1905: 7
Spirits **1904**
aërial s., by Jove design'd 1904:15
are in Heaven 409: 6

Spirits, *continued*
are we not S. 769:16
black s. and white 1905: 5
bravest s. base born 71: 3
by our own s. deified 1524:11
call s. from vasty deep ..1905: 4
can either sex assume ..1905: 1
congenial s. part to meet 1290: 1
cull'd fiery s. from world 2111:16
dancing upon needle's point 1904:11
enslaved that serve evil ..585: 4
familiar s. cull'd 893:21
float who watch and wait 1846: 4
for happy s. to alight ..1670: 6
great s. have great aims ..830:13
I like congenial s. 2296:10
jump with common s. ..1482:10
keep up your s. 440:20
like outcast s. 77:10
lost s. to the end 1277: 6
master s. of this age 1904: 8
never with bodies die 809: 7
of just men made perfect 1904: 1
raise no more s. 1905: 2
rush'd together 1050:10
snuff of younger s. 24: 5
some s. so atheistical 114:16
stride before events 1945:13
thousand s. in one breast 428:10
thy s. all of comfort 636: 8
touch'd but to fine issues 1904: 9
twain have crossed with me 1905: 9
unnumber'd S. round thee fly 1904:15
vital in every part 1905: 1
wanton s. look out 318:13
we are but s. clad in veils 1242:14
we s. have just natures ..1904:14
Spiritual determines material 1903:14
Spiritualism: distrust s. ..770: 2
Spiritum: in manus tuas commendo s. meum ..1904: 3
latius regnes avidum dominando s. 1786:15
mente cæca torques s. 119: 8
Spiritus autem vivificat ..1086:14
intus alit 795:14
quidem promptus est 1904: 4
sedibus ætheriis s. ille venit 1534: 8
Spiro: non tibi s. 1513:13
Spit: bid memory s. upon him 221:20
God of Love turn the s. 1208:10
good orators will s. 1437:18
I s. at him 428:10
in my face 1110: 5
in my hands 1488: 5
on the harvest 861: 8
upon my Jewish gabardine 1012:12
Spite: bow thy head in gentle s. 1156:13
in erring Reason's s. 1435: 8
loving s. 1197: 8
of his teeth 2027:16
of wind or tide 33:12
rival's or eunuch's s. 344: 1
Spits against Heaven 1952: 4
man only animal that s. 1241:11
which turn round 988:15
Spitting from lips once sanctified by hers 2273: 2
in your face 678: 3
Spittle: cast your s. 1385:11
death to serpents 1798:11
Spitzkugeln: lieber S. 2107: 7
Spleen: cook'd his s. 79: 3
fly hath his s. 693: 9
his heart possessed 866:26
mind's wrong bias, S. 590:20
particular and private s. 340:13
so much s. about thee 237: 4
turning to milk sophist's s. 1901:17
which only seizes on lazy 1318:12
Splendid and a happy land 1571:11
everything s. is rare 1485: 2
tho' not s., clean 1327: 4
Splendidly isolated 545: 9

Stafford: Lord S. mines for coal 207: 6
Stag: catch before skinning 1649:16
poor sequester'd s. 943: 2
runnable s. 941:11
this day a s. must die 941:18
Stage 1909
allotted to play the sage ..697:13
black s. for tragedies 1403: 2
drown the s. with tears....10: 5
echoes the public voice ..1912: 2
great s., the world 9: 4
if in the s. I seek to soothe my care 14: 2
is time 1108:10
last s. of all 32:12
life is a s. 1125: 4
life's little s. 2240: 8
me to their eyes 91: 4
never trod the s. 10: 3
on every s. from youth to age 453: 4
on s. natural, simple 757: 4
poor degraded s. 1911: 4
press, pulpit and s. 42:17
smaller world the s. 2240: 2
so gloomed with woe 1911: 1
then to well-trod s. anon 1807: 4
this great s. of fools 164: 5
was unadorned 1909:13
where every man must play 2240: 5
world he meant to say ..2240: 2
Stage-coach: travelling in a s. 231: 4
Stage-coaches: most people sulk in s. 289: 8
Stage-playing: world must practice s. 2240: 4
Stage-successes 2242: 3
Stages: life's succeeding s. ..22:11
Stagger like drunken man 2173:11
so much alike 502: 3
Staggered down the stairs 1815: 6
Staghound: every s. bayed 1595: 4
Stagnation, cold, and darkness 1140: 2
Stagyrite: ethical work by the S. 1592: 7
stout S. 2056:10
wise and bright 86:10
Stagyrites: planets, fill'd with S. 1807: 5
Stain: felt a s. like a wound 245: 5
from a woman's name 1747:10
goodly vermeil s. 1272: 9
in honor 917:12
mental s. 1313: 1
upon his silver down 345: 4
Stains of our humanity ..1319:11
such s. there are 2258:17
Stair: hied down the s. ..864: 4
Staircase: on the s. you ..483:12
Stairs: climb another's s. ..595: 2
kicked the s. 1136:10
kiss his feet 1560:10
make thieves and whores ..94:13
staggered down the s. ..1815: 6
vaulted up four pair of s. 2264:10
Stairway of surprise 1451: 6
Stake all in defense of honor 1379: 8
bear to the s. 126: 7
I am tied to the s. 1704:14
manage the last s. 27: 3
nothing s. 752: 8
tied me to a s. 665:10
Stalactites bright 950: 2
Stale: a common s. 2133: 9
poor I am s. 1201:12
Staled by frequence 632: 9
Stalks up and down like peacock 1476: 8
Stall: we could not s. 1730:15
Stallion shod with fire 2215: 4
Stalwart for the right 1407:17
Republicans 1545:11
Stamboul: magnificent in S. 2019: 7
Stamp cannot make metal better 2016:11
of kings imparts no more 2015:15
of nature 6: 7
Stamped: when I was s. ..646:12
Stamps God's own name upon lie 209: 3
Stampin', an' he's jumpin' 1591:10
Stanch and valiant, and free 51:11
Stand by us in hour of need 556: 4
fiercely s., or fighting fall 2120: 1
give me where to s. 1573:10
how they may s. or fall 623: 2
in your own light 1151:12
inside yourself 1490: 1
out of my sun 1937:12
pat 1554: 5
united we s. 56:13
we will s. by each other 731: 9
with anybody that stands right 1726:12
Stand-patters 1554: 5
Standard: each man s. to himself 588: 5
plant a s. 324:19
to which wise can repair ..54: 1
true s. of quality 1407: 7
Standers-by: not for s. to curtail oaths 1951:18
Stands: so s. the pole 306:10
Stanley, Sir Hubert: praise 1579: 2
Stanley: on, S., on 2084: 4
Star 1912
after s. from heaven's high arch 233:12
as still to the s. of its worship 306:11
beck of a baleful s. 2070:14
black s. riding sky 1491: 2
bright particular s. 110:10
bright S., would I were 1913:11
caught a s. in its embrace 1914:15
curb a runaway young s. ..76:14
evening s., love's harbinger 1916: 3
evening s. so holy shines 1390: 8
follow but thy s. 1916:12
for every state 58: 5
gone like a s. 212: 4
grapples with his evil s. ..1916:17
hitch your wagon to a s. ..109: 4
hope's s. grows dim 2182:12
I await my s. 1916:11
knew you and named a s. 1033: 4
knock at s. with head ..109: 4
like to the falling of a s. 1242: 5
lovers love western s. ..1917: 6
most auspicious s. 1916:16
my s., God's glow-worm 1916:10
name to every fixed s. ..1765:15
never s. was lost here 1917: 8
no more sailing by s. 2061:13
no s. is ever lost 1917: 8
no s. without influence 1915: 3
nor any s. pursue 149:11
now the bright morning s. 1283: 8
of Eternity 158: 8
of spangled earth ...... .782: 6
of the unconquered will 1797: 6
one s. another far exceeds 427:10
one s. differeth from another in glory 1914: 6
our jovial s. reigned 1916:16
pinned with a single s. ..2061:15
separate s. seems nothing 1914:13
she would infect north s. 2194: 9
shines out the Julian s. 1913: 6
so white a virgin's 1914:10
stoop sometimes to s. 1916:13
that bids shepherd fold ..1916: 3
that bringest home the bee 1915:14
that has no parallax 1542: 5
that rose at ev'ning bright 1916: 3
that ushers in the even 1916: 8
that's fallen 136:12
their s. is a world 1916:10
there was a s. danced ..1302: 6
there's a s. in the sky 268:11
thou art that s. to me 1215:14
to every wandering bark 1175: 3
to guide thy feet 370: 2
to guide the humble 937: 2
to s. vibrates light 1890: 8
to steer her by 2102: 8
Star, *continued*
twinkle, twinkle, little s. 1913:12
unfolding s. calls shepherd 1916: 7
violate a s. 219: 2
was there no s. 74:10
wat'ry s. 1344: 3
we call the sun 1942: 8
were a s. quenched on high 809: 7
westward s. of empire 52: 6
whose beam so oft 1917: 4
wind each ticking s. 1681:19
you may be lustrous as s. 1981: 7
Star-chamber matter 1784: 3
Star-dust in his hair 2102: 7
or sea-foam 135:17
Star-gleam on a stone 1138: 6
Star-inwrought 1404: 2
Star-spangled banner 674: 3
Stare: stony British s. 561:11
Stark, John 61:9; 62: 6
Molly S. a widow 62: 6
Starlight: behind the cloud the s. 925: 4
by cloudless s. treads 1914:11
by s. and by candle-light 992: 3
Stars: all the s. looked down 261:11
among the s. a star 571: 2
and you, ye s. 1913:16
are Daisies that begem 1912:11
are for religion's sake ..1690: 1
are forth 1401: 7
are golden fruit 1912:12
are images of love 1916:18
are poor books 158: 3
blind, he sings of s. 1533:15
break up the Night 1914:13
bright sentinels of skies 1912:14
build beneath the s. 109: 4
buttoned it with s. 2061:15
by the luckiest s. 1226: 6
came otherwise 1341: 1
certain s. shot madly 1300:10
chaste s. 226: 3
clouded lamps relume 364:17
come forth to listen 1914: 9
continuous as the s. 357:11
count of s. an endless number 1851: 4
cry out upon the s. 1915: 5
cut up into little s. 1214:15
daisy s. 358: 6
different lots s. accord 1916:15
doubt thou s. are fire ..1214: 9
ere s. were thundergirt ..439: 9
fairest of s., last in the 1916: 3
fiery s. will drop 233:15
first pale s. of twilight ..2062: 1
fought against Sisera 1616:12; 1915: 9
gazing at the s. 1915:12a
give little light because high 1499:12
glows in the s. 1390:14
go down to rise 412:12
govern our conditions ..1915:12
half-quenched in mists 604: 6
have instruction given 158:11
have lit welkin dome 673:11
he reads the s. 107:18
he that strives to touch s. 1913:10
heav'n sentry, wink 1912:14
hide their diminished heads 1938:17
I care not for the s. that shine 2292: 3
I have loved s. too fondly 1913:14
in heaven invisible 1151: 2
kinship with the s. 31:11
large white s. rise 1154: 2
lie in apparent confusion 1914: 4
look at s. procures solitude 1870:14
look out upon the s. 604: 6
made the s. and set them 1912:15
mansions built by nature 1913: 2
more s. than a pair 1913: 4
morning s. sang together 1367: 6
my good s., my guides 1916:14
Night's blue arch adorn 1975:14
nor sink those s. 403: 5
not in high s. alone 1367: 5
now the frosty s. are gone 368:15

Stars, *continued*
of evening glow 925:12
of heaven are free 722: 8
of human race 1094:13
of its winter 196: 1
of midnight shall be dear 1387: 7
of morning 445:20
of night will lend light 1917: 1
of the summer night ..1917: 3
one sees the mud, one s. 1434: 3
pitch the golden tents ..1914:14
poetry of Heaven 1915: 6
preserve the s. from wrong 508:13
quenchless s. 1912:14
rejoice to watch thee 687: 6
rent into shreds of light 1915: 4
rule men, God rules s. ..1915: 7
see s. down well at noon 2052: 5
sentinel s. set their watch 1912:14
sets like s. that fall 2201:16
seven s. and solar year ..1489: 6
shall fade away 969: 9
she made s. of heaven more bright 400: 6
shine for comforting 1915: 1
shine through cypress-trees 967: 8
shooting s. attend thee ..604: 2
shot madly from spheres 1877:11
stand thick as dewdrops 1914: 1
steal to their sovran seats 1914: 2
stretching hand for s. ..109: 5
strives to touch the s. ...1913:10
Syrian s. look down 262: 4
take s. for money 109: 4
ten thousand s. in sky ..1914:15
that fight in their courses 674: 1
that have most glory ..1914: 6
that in earth's firmament do shine 684:10
that nature hung in heaven 1912:15
their clouded lamps relume 364:17
their s. more in fault ..2201:17
then s. arise, night holy 1914: 9
they fell like s. 2248: 6
thou lookest on s., my Star 1917: 5
through hardship to s. ..1913: 9
through his cypress-trees 967: 8
two s. keep not motion ..1730:15
unmuffle, ye faint s. 1343: 8
unutterably bright 1401:16
we all gaze at the s. 109: 5
when s. are in quiet skies 1916:19
when s. are shining clear 614: 7
who can count the s. of heaven 1915:13
wholesome s. of love 602: 2
whom gentler s. unite ..1275: 5
with trains of fire 1946:12
yonder s. so bright 2262: 6
Start afresh 146:12
anybody can s. something 147:15
timely s. 146:14
Starts: she s., she moves 1814: 4
Starve before he stole ..238:12
for want of impudence 178: 9
joyless dignity to s. 448:12
with nothing 1326: 7
Starved, feasted, despaired 1130: 7
go s. to bed 410:12
Starveling in scanty vest ..358:14
Starving: hold out at 540:22
State **1917**
all were for the s. 202: 1
and family ever at war ..632:21
arguments of s. 99: 8
association, not men 1918:12
best s. least talked of ..902:12
but a golden prison 1918:14
cannot be sever'd 1262: 7
cannot get a cent 2281: 8
corrupt s., many laws ..1090: 6
every actual s. corrupt ..817: 6
falling with a falling s. 18: 4
for every star 58: 5
foul swarm of s. 817: 6
founding a firm s. 1918:10
grant me a middle s. ..1329:12
happy must be the S. ..1573: 7
his s. is kingly 793:11
I am the S. 1044: 1
State, *continued*
ideal social s. 1717: 4
in a parlous s. 1640:10
in perfect, purple s. 1048: 7
is always poor 1478:13
keeps middle s. 1329: 1
last s. worse than first 1250:14
man's wretched s. 1349: 6
meddle not with matters of s. 2279: 2
one vast insane asylum ..1231:19
O ship of s. 52: 4
pillars of the s. 70:13
pre-existent s. 968: 6
safety of the S. the highest law 1478:15
saves or serves the s. 508: 6
spider S. set web for Man 1918: 8
stable changeless s. 230: 9
strange s. of being 1843: 2
tenants of life's middle s. 1329: 1
thousand years scarce serve to form a s. ..1918: 2
to educate wise, S. exists 1918: 5
to guard, t' adorn the s. 1045: 1
to rot in s. 1339: 4
what constitutes a S. ..1917:15
when one S. refuses 57: 9
while S. exists no freedom 1918:9a
without a King 1658:10
without kings or nobles 1658:10
worth of s., worth of individuals 1918:11
State-business cruel trade 1542:16
Statecraft was the Golden Rule 804:18
Statement: no s. too absurd 1499:14
States dissevered, discordant 58: 2
equal and sovereign s. 57: 1
free and independent s. ...974: 8
free S. from obligation 58: 1
have growth, manhood, decay 1918: 9
in duty S. find welfare ..1918:18
indestructible s. 57: 2
monumental S. 1503: 3
move slowly 1918: 1
no more slave S. 1841: 5
not made, nor patched ..1918:10
social s. of human kinds 1311:11
sovereign nation of s. 53:12
were better s. unseen 453:10
with others' ruin built ..1380:13
Statesman **1918**
great s. sublime poet 1919: 1
makes the occasion 1919: 7
man of common opinions 1918:20
should be on his guard ..1919:12
standard of a s. 1919: 2
successful politician dead 1919: 7
three ends of s. 1919: 2
too nice for a s. 205: 6
truth from American s. ..1919:15
yet friend to truth 569:10
Statesmen always sick of one disease 1919: 6
and beauties 33: 8
at her council met 1920: 3
have long noses 1919: 4
liable to give account 1919:16
O S., guard us 1920: 3
talked with looks profound 1398: 6
who survey 1571:11
whom democracy had degraded 1919: 7
Statesmen's kindnesses 1919:12
Station: give me private s. 919:17
in the file 1868: 3
is nought 1731: 1
like the herald Mercury ..239: 4
midway s. given 1670: 6
post of honour private s. .919:17
woman's noblest s. retreat 2205: 8
Stations bring woes 836:11
high s. create tumult 838: 9
know our proper s. 1424:14
Statistics: lies and s. 1112: 9
testify for either side ..1112: 8
Stato mutar per mutar loco 1424: 9
Statuam statui ex auro ..1340: 3
Statue
See also Monument
ask why I have no s. 1339: 9
beautiful when incomprehensible 1770:18
dotes on a gilded s. 136:18
doth wait, thralled 1535: 7
embraced the cold s. 1090:15
erected by national subscription 86: 9
falls from the pedestal 901:17
into s. that breathes 107:10
magic s. standing deathless 1771: 3
not a man but a s. 1771: 6
on pedestal of scorn 1766:11
raise her s. in pure gold 1340: 2
that enchants the world 1770:15
to this man a s. of gold 1340: 3
Statuendum est semel 423: 6
Statues and pictures grand 103:16
many s. must come down 1862:16
poor remembrances are s. 1339:15
Statuit aliquid parte inaudita 1019:15
Stature: erect his s. 1243:12
shorten s. of my soul ..1421:12
small s. can be perfect ..1134:11
undepressed in size 38: 6
Statute is a currency 1089:12
take the s. from the mind 1918: 6
Statutes: strict s. 1086:11
Stavano bene; per star meglio 1770: 1
Stavo bene; per star meglio 468:13
Stay a little longer 416:14
at home is best 907:14
here I am, here I s. ...2109: 1
is a charming word 933: 3
must you s. 1639: 1
standeth at a s. when others rise 70:16
the poor man's s. 1496: 9
the s. and the staff 198: 1
Steadfast as a tower 325:10
to a dream 2095: 4
Steady of heart 879:17
Steal: did not s., but emulate 2258:13
don't s., cheat 249: 6
few hours from the night 1403:15
learn'd to s. no more 1985:14
not this book 190: 6
out of your company ..1986:17
thou shalt not s. 249: 6
us from ourselves away ..2261: 5
Stealing
See also Thief
will continue s. 1986: 5
Steam **1920**
enemy of space and time 1920: 8
exceptin' always S. 1814: 3
greater power than Napoleon 1920: 9
is a tyrant 1920:11
strong-shouldered s. 1920: 8
that great civilizer 1920:10
unconquer'd s. 1920: 7
Steam-engine in trousers .2129: 8
Steam-roller 1556: 4
Steed: bonny white s. 929:19
of matchless speed 2115:13
stolen, shut stable door ..2168:21
threatens s. 2117: 6
was black as raven 167: 4
why vent on s. your rage 929: 1
Steeds: curb thy fierce s. 1937: 1
decked with purple 931: 3
Steel: amorous s. 306:13
clad in complete s. 246:12
forge the s. which slays ..1249: 3
is beneath your hand 2132: 1
is prince or pauper 206:10
make s. with men 206:10
smoke and blood of s. 206:10
true as s. 663: 6
Steel-true, blade-straight ..2141: 7
Steeple: church and no s. ..272:10
leap a s. from a bore 192: 8
Trinity's undaunted s. ..1397:10

Steeple-towers and spires ..272: 9
Steeples loud in their joy ..153: 8
Steer a middle course 436:20
bear up and s. onward ..170: 9
ill-mated s. 1267: 9
right onward 618: 7
Steerage of my course ..1646:14
Steers-mate at the helm ..1095: 2
Steersmen: grow good s. 1128:11
Stein: there's a wonderful family, S. 1377: 1
Stein: cold s. for mine ..1882:19
on the table 933: 8
Stella: se tu segui tua s. 1916:12
Stemmata duid faciunt 71: 8
Stench remains 1683: 7
Stenches: two and seventy s. 1716:14
Step: cannot see one s. 2044: 5
first s. that costs 146:11
first s. which one makes ..147: 6
hardest s. over threshold 146:11
inadvertent s. 1855: 5
keep s. to the music 57: 3
once a s. above her 982: 8
one false s. damns her ..2201:16
one false s. ne'er retrieved 1651:15
see not a s. before me ..2044: 5
single s. and all is o'er ..1933:13
stalks with Minerva's s. ..324:18
they were all out of s. but Jim 2284: 2
to s. aside is human ..2022: 2
watch your s. 980: 4
we miss thy small s. 408:14
Step-dame: like to a s. ..1344: 3
to her son 2197: 4
Step-mother: complaining to s. 1638:17
kindly s. 1350:17
stony-hearted s. 2069:15
Stephen was a worthy peer .491: 6
Stephen Sly and John Naps 1376:16
Stepping-stone in political line 1092:16
Stepping-stones of their dead selves 2078: 3
Steps: beware of des'prate s. 372: 6
Creation's golden s. 795: 6
fifteen s. he made but three 864: 4
her s. are of light 361: 2
her s. take hold on hell 2133:13
mincing s. into manly stride 2266: 9
no s. backward 325:11
of our ancestors 70:11
that upwards lead gradual 795: 6
will lead my s. aright ..1434:11
with a tender foot 704:13
with how sad s., O Moon 1344: 9
Stereotyped despair 437:20
Sternhold out-Sternholded 1730:17
Stew in my own grease ..1633:15
Steward: backward s. for the poor 1237:12
old hereditary bore 192:14
one honest man and he's a s. 914:19
Stewards: Goddes s. all ..784:13
Stewart: injured S. line ..766: 9
Stewed 503: 1
Stick: Big S. rides before 1741:10
carry a big s. 1598:15
come down like a s. 446:12
dressed up 485: 1
fell like a s. 205: 9
filth will s. 214: 6
make crooked s. straight 1686: 2
right end of the s. 1333: 4
something is sure to s. 214: 6
watch for that s. 446:12
Sticking-place 326: 2
Sticks: two dry s. 563: 8
Stiff-necked people 1424: 5
Stigma to beat dogma 1984:11
Stigmatical in making 240:11
Stile: I'm sitting on the s. 1796:16
Stile-a: merrily hent s. 877: 8
Stiles: helping lame dogs over s. 893:13
Stilicidio: nemo multum ex s. 1170:18
Still as a mouse 1666:12
as the grave 1825:17
he came all so s. 269:11
he that is s., granteth 1822: 2
Still-born: inherit 985:16
Stillicidi casus lapidem cavat 2126: 8
Stillness and the night 861: 3
horrid s. invades the ear 1825: 9
in s. oft magic power 1797: 7
modest s. and humility ..2116:10
perfect s. when they brawl 1822:19
reigneth evermore 1775:13
wilful s. 294:18
Stilo oltra l'ingegno non si stende 1926: 8
Stilts: emotional s. 9:15
on Bible s. 159: 6
Stilum: sæpe s. vertas 2254: 8
Stimmenmehrheit 1235:15
Stimulis: parce puer, s. 931:11
Stimulos pugnis cædis 1703:20
si s. pugnis cædis 1703:20
Sting: draws s. of life and death 915:11
each s. that bids not sit ..15:19
guarded with a s. 143:12
in her tail 143:12
in tail of pleasure 1512: 2
in the tail 1512: 2
is not so sharp 984:15
leaves no s. behind 496: 6
lieth in the tail 566: 8
of a reproach 339:12
sharper than the sword's 1837:15
should be felt in tail 566:17
within brother's heart 1758: 6
Stinger: had a s. 1638:18
Stinging of a heart 1757:11
Stings and motions of sense 240:11
armed in their s. 142:15
defended by thousand s. 143:12
wanton s. of sense 240:11
Stink and be forgotten ...1958:13
Stipulis: in s. magnus ignis 668: 6
Stir: fretful s. unprofitable 2242:15
more you s. worse 1638:19
of the great Babel 2237: 5
what should not be stirred 1284: 9
Stirrer: an early s. 1729: 8
Stirring as the time 177:20
man that's fond of s. 1729:14
Stirrup and ground 788: 9
Stitch here and there 787:14
in time saves nine 1650:14
Stitcher: cross-legged s. ..383:11
Stock from which I spring 68:10
of a very old s. 72: 4
Stock-dove: I heard the s. ..477:10
Stockholders: working for my s. 1480:10
Stocking: said shoe to s. ..1816:11
Stockings: tinge of blue improves s. 2194: 4
Stockish, hard 1363: 5
Stocks instead of breeches 948: 9
will fall or rise 304: 4
Stoic: every S. was a S. ...266:11
of the woods 976: 7
Stoicism: cased in s. 977:15
Romans call it s. 1606: 1
Stoics austere 451: 1
Stole: white s. of chastity 247:12
Stolen what we do fear to keep 1987: 2
Stomach
See also Belly
and no food 715:12
burden to a full s. 89:12
empty s. bad adviser 940: 5
full s. turns from honey ..89:12
good s. excels them all 89:11
gratifying the s. 154:11
he hath excellent s. 520: 1
hold more than mine 118:12
hungry s. common food ..939:15
Lutheran s. 515:17
make hearer's s. rise 1579: 3
Stomach, *continued*
man of unbounded s. 520: 1
mutiny against the s. 155: 1
my s. is not good 497: 3
no s. bigger than another 88:14
no s. to the fight 665: 8
of my sense 2225: 8
of the judicious epicure ..516: 7
pinch s. or fingers 1622:10
pleasure, golden sleep ..2245: 9
seldom empty 89: 7
serves instead of clock ..940: 3
sets us to work 939: 8
surcloys s. with cates ..1677: 9
to digest his words 1260:10
to have s. and lack meat 1319: 7
way to man's heart 515:18
Stomach's solid stroke 940: 3
Stomached: high-s. are they 241: 1
Stomacher: red s. 1735: 8
Stomachi: fastidientis s. ...89:14
Stomachs: best s. not best thinkers 1989:17
lazy folks' s. don't tire 516: 2
like ostriches 448:1a
make what's homely savory 939:15
mithridatic s. 1491: 3
that would fall to 90: 3
they are all but s. 1255: 6
two s. like a cow 524: 9
want s. for meat 88:16
Stomachus: jejunus raro s. vularia temnit 939:15
Stone: ask bread, give s. ..198: 5
at his heels a s. 401:15
base foul s. made precious 2064:20
beneath this s. I lie 248:11
beneath your heels 2132: 1
choosing each s. 1918:10
every s. one lifts by day 1614: 1
for a heart within 1476: 4
he that rolleth a s. 1710: 4
heaviest s. melancholy can throw 1290:10
hollowed out by water ..2126:10
in one hand a s. 198: 5
inserted in the body of Italy 1070:15
intestine s. 460:14
is senseless 1339:11
Jackson standing s. wall 1005: 2
leave no s. unturned 1639: 2
let him cast the first s. ..1828:11
lily blossoming in s. 94:11
lucky escape for the s. ..766:12
make a s. a flower 211: 3
many a rich s. 1422: 3
mark with white s. 370:15
no s. without its name ..1372: 1
not a s. tell where I lie ..1422:11
of Heraclea 983:11
of s. grew I within 1978: 8
philosophers have sought 1498:14
roll s. from grave 413:13
rolling restless s. 713: 5
rolling s. gathers no moss 21:9; 1639: 3
seek water from a s. 119: 9
set in the silver sea 550: 1
sinking s. a circle makes ..273:12
skin a s. for penny 118: 9
that is rolling 1800:18
that turneth all to gold ..801:14
the gout or s. 33: 4
the twenty-first 987: 8
there is a s. there 997: 3
throw s. at head of others 1836: 8
to beauty grew 95:14
to emulate in s. 96:10
to make a s. a flower 211: 3
turn lead into gold 1997:10
two birds with one s. 160: 8
very plain brown s. 2104: 1
which builders refused 96: 9
will be rolled away 293: 1
without a s. a name 384: 4
you cannot flay a s. 118: 9
Stone's: within a s. throw 1639: 4
Stone-cutter or a painter 1958:16
Stonehenge 1373:10

Streams, *continued*
gliding pale s. 1939: 1
headlong s. 1877:10
lapse of murmuring s. ...200:14
large s. from little 1438: 4
meander level with fount 1731:18
mellifluous s. 1437:14
most sweet 252: 1
of dotage flow 384: 3
of truth roll through us ..1142:12
polluted s. again are pure 2201:15
purling s. 1220: 8
rejoic'd that winter's work is done 200: 9
rise not above source ..1732: 1
shallow s. run dimpling .1853: 7
talk of cowslips 200: 9
that keep a summer mind 1732: 3
various race supply 670: 7
wan prophets tent beside 134:14
which fretted be 474:14
Street as false as church ...272: 1
crooked s. goes past my door 481: 5
every s. has two sides ..2263: 4
great s. paved with water 1983: 7
houseless s. 985:14
in Paris famous 1453:13
New S. of the Little Fields 1453:13
of dreams 481: 5
queer s. full of lodgers ..1230:10
somewhat back from the village s. 2013: 7
Street-song: bawling s. 124: 4
Streets of Rome and Troy ..196: 8
old s. a glamour hold 40: 5
to rumbling wheels unknown 2077: 1
Tory brick-built s. 1168:13
Strength **1921**
acquire s. we have overcome 1922: 3
all below is s. 818:10
all your s. is in union ..2066:21
and color of life 291:18
anger brings back s. 79:14
brute s. bereft of reason 1922: 5
everlasting s. 792:14
excellent to have giant's s. 1922:16
for climbing 108:14
from hope and despair ...438: 8
from s. to s. advancing ..964:18
gain s. of temptation 1980:12
giant's unchained s. 52:7
great s. of feeble arms ..2066:16
great s. use lightly 1922:16
holy s. of mind 2184: 5
in a true heart 879:15
in Lord everlasting s. ..793: 6
in Saxon s. 96:10
is as the s. of ten 1660: 4
is so tender 868:17
let s. be law of justice ..1922:19
like s. from hope 927:19
lose s. with woman 1922:15
love's s. standeth 1128: 4
lovely in your s. 603:12
made perfect in weakness 818: 9
match'd with s. 1155: 8
maugre thy s., youth ..2035: 3
no s. to repent 1699:18
not s. but weakness 34:16
not s. to follow reason ..1678:16
of body 175: 4
of mind is exercise 952:14
of the strongest kings ..414:19
of twenty men 1922:17
profaned God-given s. ..1922:15
silence, simpleness 2066:14
spend their s. in action ..109: 3
strengthens with his s. ..459:19
surpassing s. 1240:17
sympathizing with my s. 1921:16
their s. is to sit still ..1922: 6
they go from s. to s. 1922:12
thy s. is small 16:12
to bear others' misfortunes 1322:15
to bear our portion 1584:10
to do your work 2234: 5
Strength, *continued*
to meet sorrow 661:10
true s. of guilty kings ...1041: 2
unbend your noble s. 1996:14
united more powerful ..2067: 1
what is s. without wisdom 1922: 5
what though s. fails 177:13
while s. permits, endure labor 24: 1
will with burden grow ..205: 4
yet is their s. labor and sorrow 1141: 8
Strenua inertia 952:23
Strepitus: polularis vincentem s. 1484:10
Stretch and strive 863:13
sides o' the world 214: 2
Strewings: give her s. 408: 7
of the ways 2078: 2
Strict accountability 66:13
Stride: at one s. comes the dark 365:10
of Time 2008: 3
Strife **1922**
See also Discord, Quarrelling
among professors of one faith 1696: 9
and the discouragement ...16: 9
artificial s. lives 1448:12
between brothers 202: 7
betwixt man and wife ..1263: 4
dire immeasurable s. 1124:14
dowry with a wife 2142: 4
elemental s. 1457: 3
ignoble s. 1135: 4
immanity and bloody s. ..1696: 9
it is to fast from s. 866: 7
let there be no s. 1663: 2
man of s., of contention ..1663: 3
never, business seldom ..207:14
none worth my s. 29: 3
of disputatious men 1695: 6
of frail humanity 508:12
of little natures 208:23
of tongues 2024: 8
of Truth with Falsehood ..423: 4
petty s. which clouds 909: 6
relentless s. law of life ..2111: 3
Strike against the public safety, no right to 1065:15
below the knee 2033: 7
but hear 1461: 8
home 1372:16
now, or else the iron cools 1000: 4
now or never 1432:12
till last armed foe expires 1464:14
too soon is oft to miss ..1920: 5
up the band 1779: 9
while iron is hot 999:19
with vengeful stroke 433: 6
yet afraid to s. 13:12
Strikes hour very correctly 313: 8
three s. you're out 2291:11
where it doth love 1885:12
String after s. is severed from the heart 402: 6
all bound round with woolen s. 2293: 3
always on same s. 1635: 2
attun'd to mirth 1291: 3
few can touch magic s. ..1879: 4
harp not on that s. 1635: 2
harp on frayed s. 1635: 2
two-fold s. 1649:13
untune that s. 1369: 5
which hath no discord ..2199:13
Strings: hung round with s. 2016: 6
in human heart 875:13
of life began to crack 841: 9
two s. to his bow 1649: 7
when such s. jar 861: 2
Stripe: red s. blazoned forth 674: 5
Stripes: black s. on yellow ground 2001:18
cut his s. away 852:15
for the back of fools 1657:11
forty s. save one 1657:11
Stripped: I'm s. to the buff 2280: 2
Strive against stream 1639: 6
and hold cheap the strain 15:19
mightily 1094: 6
to do their best 110: 8
to sit out losing hands ..752: 5
to s., to seek, to find 879:20
with an equal 99: 5
with things impossible ..971:11
Striving to better, oft we mar what's well 50: 6
Stroke: achieved the grand s. 2252: 6
of tongue breaketh bones 2026: 8
terrible and nimble s. ..1153:17
Strokes: calumnious s. 2091: 2
imitative s. 962:13
little s. fell great oaks 2041: 5
many s., though with little axe 2041: 5
Strolling: go s. about 1051:14
Strong and unimpaired 37: 7
as a bull moose 2279: 8
be thou s. 1922: 8
but to damn 1071: 5
easy to be s. as weak ...1922: 3
I would be s. 239:10
land and goods to s. 1562:13
make s. themselves by ill ..147: 4
only the S. shall thrive .587: 2
only to destroy 800: 4
suffer and be s. 19:6; 325:13
to be s. is to be happy 854:15
together continue s. 2066:21
until he feels alone 1873: 8
upon the stronger side ..332:12
without rage 1983: 5
yet I am s. and lusty 37:18
Strong-arm worker 644: 1
Strong-box: build for yourself a s. 2042:17
Strong-souled for my fate 1732:16
Stronger always succeeds 1922:11
than hosts of Error 1030:12
Strongest wander farthest 1932:19
who stands alone 1871: 3
Strongholds shall be like fig trees 664:10
Strongly it bears us 1527: 4
Strove: I s. with none 29: 3
who s. and failed 613:17
Struck me of a heap 1639: 7
Struggle deeper peace than sleep 1457: 1
for Existence 586: 1
irrepressible s. 1842: 4
is the prize 1121:15
manhood a s. 23: 8
of discordant powers ...1368:17
say not the s. nought availeth 612: 3
shun not the s. 325: 9
through s. and wars 438:12
with abuses strong 279:16
Strugglers against tyranny, martyrs 2034:13
Struggling in storms of fate .18: 4
with adversity 18: 3
Strumming at doors of inns 1368: 3
Strumpet: blowing own s. 1581:10
have heard I am a s. 2133:15
not to be a s. 2134: 3
Strut: insufferable s. 1044: 1
turkey-gobbler s. 1551: 7
Struts and frets his hour ..1125: 9
his dames before 233: 1
Stuart: Mary S. 719: 8
Stubble before the wind 2134:16
Stubble-land at harvest-home 124:16
Stubborn: too s. grown for school 26:11
Stubbornness: with noble s. 1468: 2
Stud: that trusty old s. 572: 8
Student on one end of a log 2069: 4
Students of words 529: 4
their own victims 1924: 9
Studia: abeunt in mores ..845: 6
colendi s. teneamus 39:11
doctrinæ 1098: 9
quare liberalia s. 528:15

Studies: common s. form country 1924: 1
crafty men contemn s. 1922:21
happy that composed book 189:13
liberal s. defined 528:15
pleasing, useful s. 1924: 2
serve for delight 1923:16
too much time in s. sloth 1924: 6
worthy of a gentleman 528:15
Studiis florentem ignobilis oti 1100:21
Studio minuente laborem 2029: 2
Studiorum: non est ulla s. satietas 1923: 3
quot capitum, totidem s. 1966: 5
Studios: God's Eternal S. 875: 5
Studious: be s. and be learned 1930:10
of laborious ease 1099:17
their own victims 1924: 9
to please 339:13
Studium famæ mihi crevit honore 626: 1
Study 1922
black despair succeeds brown s. 436:18
brown s. 1923: 6
but little on the Bible 158:14
discovers our ignorance 1059: 1
evermore is overshot 1924:10
faithful s. of liberal arts 1923:16
full of books 1097: 8
had made him very lean 1924: 8
his s. is his tilt-yard 904: 3
I am slow of s. 1923: 9
is like the sun 1924:10
live to s., not s. to live ..1922:22
my favorite s. is man ...1251: 5
night is time for s. 1923: 1
of imagination 1297: 4
of the beautiful 106: 7
of words distemper 2222:10
proper s. of mankind.... 1251:14
was but little on the bible .158:14
what is the end of s. 1924: 3
what you most affect 1924: 3
with those to s. 451: 1
Stuff as madmen tongue ..483: 5
is it not sad s. 1537: 2
made of s. so flat 127:15
on what strange s. 48:15
penetrable s. 876:12
skimble-skamble s. 100:17
such s. as dreams 1141:11
such s. world is made of 2237: 5
to make me love him 1186: 6
what masquing s. 489: 5
why s. for fools 160: 3
Stuffed man: no less than 949: 9
Stuffed shirt 1645: 1
Stuffing: she asked for s. ..819: 2
Stulta maritali porrigit 1276: 5
Stulti, stolidi, fatui 697:19
Stultique prope omnes 699: 4
Stultis videri eruditi volunt 702:12
Stultitia ad sapientam erepit 703: 1
ducere invitos canes 941: 5
humilis res est s. 696: 2
laborat 696: 1
semper incipit vivere 1130:12
senilis s. 28: 2
tanta s. mortalium est 699: 7
Stultitiam: misce s. consiliis brevem 702: 2
monere 696: 8
patiuntur opes 1720: 6
Stulto intellegens quid interest 703: 9
Stultum: aliis consilium dare s. 697:18
est vicinum velle ulcisci incendio 1713:10
Stultus: præter speciem s. es 697:19
Stumble before he sleepeth 1648:20
do not s. 937: 2
that run fast 227: 1
to s. twice disgrace 461: 7
Stumbled coming down stairs 1945:14
Stumbler stumbles least ...447:14
Stumbles through existence 1310:16a
Stumbling-block in way ..1981:15
or stepping-stone 1127: 3
Stumbling-stone and rock .1425:15
Stump: extatic s. 2028: 3
me to a fight 59: 6
Stump-o'-the-Gutter 771: 9
Stump-oratory 2281: 9
Stumps: fought upon his s. 897: 7
hard row of s. 1488:10
Stupid about death 390:12
as educated man 529: 9
at wondrous things he saw 2209: 4
thing from noblest motives 1925:18
too stupid about death 390:12
Stupidest of London men 1168:17
Stupidity 1924
against s. gods contend ..1925:12
confirm'd in full s. 1924:16
excess of s. not in Nature 1925: 6
for his throne trembled ..362: 7
great admiration for s. ..1925:18
is without anxiety 697: 6
no sin but s. 1925:17
Sturm ist Meister 1776: 1
Stygian shores 467:12
ye S. set 399:14
Style 1925
base is the s. 1928: 3
beyond genius never dares 1926: 8
can least be changed 1926: 5
chaste and lucid s. 1926: 1
dress of thoughts 1926: 9
elegant not ostentatious ...13:11
fame's great antiseptic ..1926: 6
familiar but not coarse 13:11
fleshy s. full of suet 1927:12
flowery s. 1927:15
formed early in life 1926: 5
gives value to thought ..1926: 9
grand s. in poetry 1524:14
has no fixed laws 1927: 6
higher s. than man 48: 6
his s. is chaos 1928: 4
how the s. refines 72: 3
immortal in literature ..1926:10
is mind's voice 2096: 2
is the man himself 1925:19
Johnson's turgid s. 1015: 9
of author image of mind 1926: 3
of remarkable fullness ..1928: 1
our s. bewrays us' 1926: 1
shifts s. oftener than clothes 2251:13
so wicked and free 441:19
strict and succinct s. ...1926:12
theirs for s. I'll read ...1523: 5
towering s. 1982:16
vehicle of the spirit 1926: 9
wheedling and soft their s. 1928: 2
Style est l'homme même ...1925:19
Styles: all s. good save tiresome 1927: 9
Stylus: turn s. to erase ..2254: 8
virum arguit 1926: 1
Suavitur in modo 766: 8
Sub-deb: argot of the s. ..1802:14
Sub rosa 1742:11
Subdue: learn'd himself to s. 1787: 2
Subject: edge about to s. ..313:16
for an angel's song 896:26
long and wish to be s. ...1045:15
longed to be a king 1045:15
made to your hand 203: 8
of controversy 98: 5
one of great difficulty 1619: 1
ponder well your s. 2251: 2
suited to your strength ..2251: 2
Subject-matter lacks logic 1591: 9
Subject-theme may gang ..1875: 5
Subjection: marked for s. 1067: 5
Subjects by oppression bold 1045: 4
hated by s. cannot be king 1045:13
may grieve 1045: 5
treat humble s. with delicacy 536: 1
Sublime and ridiculous ..1725:14
as Milton's theme 55:14
dashed to pieces 1927:14
elevates the mind 101: 4
from s. to ridiculous 1725:12
most helpful to morals ..101: 4
'tis the s. of man 1245: 3
Sublime: du s. au ridicule 1725:12
Sublime Porte 2061:14
Sublimity blended with ridicule 1725: 9
Submission: dishonorable, vile s. 1419:14
to thy will 389:12
to wrong and injustice ..1379: 8
yielded with coy s. 1222: 2
Submit: taught to s. 1420:19
Submitting: by s. sways ..2143:11
Subordinate finds fault ..1801:14
Subordinates utterly unknown 2281: 1
Subservience to none 59: 1
Subservient: to none s. 216:15
Substance: brags of his s. 294:18
call'd that shadow seem'd 770: 6
of the common Earth 1244: 3
superstantial 783: 1
wasted s. with riotous living 1615:18
we know not s. 1803: 5
Substantiam ultra s. 783: 1
Substantives that answer Who 1449: 2
Substitute shines brightly 963:12
Subtilitatem: militaribus ingeniis s. deesse 1866: 1
Subtilité: trop grande s. ..1256:17
Subtle, cruel and unconstant 1246: 7
discerning, eloquent 1002: 6
though polished, s. 1526: 2
Subtlety may deceive 420: 3
of the American joke 1010:19
wanting in military genius 1866: 1
Subtract faith from fact ..577:16
Suburb of straw-built citadel 1921:10
of the life elysian 412:12
Suburbs: go into the s. 1277: 7
spangled s. 884: 8
Succeed: all things s. amiss ..2: 3
by merit, not by favor ..1300: 1
I s. him; no one replace 721:15
in small things 49: 9
to s. appear fool 702: 5
to s. seem fool 1930:15
well, if I don't s. 1931:17
who best can pay 199:11
Succeeds: nothing s. like success 1929: 5
where he s., merit's his ..1299: 8
Succès depend combien de temps 1930:16
rien ne réussit 1929: 5
sert aux hommes de piédestal 1929:15
tout obeit au s. 1929: 9
Success 1928
be strew'd before feet ..2084: 6
begins with will 1931: 5
bitch-goddess, S. 1931: 9
born for s. he seemed 1930: 9
brought many to destruction 1931:13
cannot give formula for s. 1932:7a
child of Audacity 1928: 7
criterion of wisdom 1929: 1
depends upon preparation 1928: 6
dismaller than failure ..1931:15
does not depend on numbers 1929:10
doing well whatever you do 1930:13
forever good 1929: 6
God will estimate S. 1929: 2
hard to bear 1931: 8
has ruined many 1931:13
head turned by s. 1929:22
Heaven's to give s. 1929:13
I believe in S. 150:14

Swiss: no money, no S. ..1333:13
Swithin: St. S. day rain 1669:11
Switzerland an inferior Scotland 1767: 3
Swivel rakes the staggering wreck 1684:11
Swoon: that divine s. 1189:14
Swoop: at one fell s. 409: 1
Sword **1954**
always beaten by mind ..1955:18
and sceptre rust 826:11
anger sets edge on s. 79: 6
another's s. laid him low 2120: 2
arrest the lifted s. 236:20
beating our deadly s. 1955:11
bringer of women 1954:20
by no s. save her own falls Liberty 1106: 5
Delphic s. 1436:11
despite thy victor s. 2035: 3
draw s. against oppression 1612: 3
draws s. to attain quiet ..2065: 1
drew s. threw away scabbard 2106:10
eats s. it fights with 2073: 4
fallen by edge of the s. ..2026: 8
false measure of truth ..2051:15
famous by my s. 1522: 1
first to produce s. 1955:11
flesh his virgin s. 1955: 9
forsook for sake of church 2104:14
glued to my scabbard ..1955:14
good s. in poor scabbard 1955: 8
grac'd with s., worthier fan 1955: 5
hack thy s. 332:10
he flung the s. away 888:18
he who s. of heaven bears 1021:10
he with the s. 1583:12
I give to him 412: 7
in hand of Justice 1028:14
it steels my s. 2220: 9
laid to my throat 788: 9
leaden s. ivory scabbard 1955: 8
less hurt than pen 1478: 5
let not Man withhold s. ..2109:15
let the s. decide 1956: 8
like s. in scabbard 2170:12
Love, Song, Honor, Sleep 1137: 9
never give s. to madman 1955:19
never out of fashion 1955: 1
no s. in hand of justice 1028:14
of Common Sense 1795:10
of God in his hand 263: 5
of heaven not in haste ..1656:12
of justice first lay down 1045: 2
of metal keen 2115:13
one s. keeps another sheathed 1598:14
outwears its sheath 1955: 4
pen mightier than s. 1478: 3
perish with the s. 1955:15
protects the prince 1611:18
put up again thy s. 1955:15
rescued by his pen 1478:10
ruled all things 1956: 2
sets s. back in sheath 227:11
shining s. of light 368:10
should end it 505:16
sleep in my hand 554:16
stir fire with the s. 1956: 1
take away the s. 1955: 1
that severs all 1276: 9
they that take the s. 1955:15
this is his s. 1956: 3
though made of lath 1956: 5
tied little fellow to s. 1955: 5
to lay my hand to 2199: 7
two-edged s. of craft ..1089: 8
two-edged s. of God's word 1009:10
upon s. sit victory 2084: 6
was servant unto right ..1956: 7
what rights the brave? The s. 1954:20
with his own s. cut throat 1711: 2
with silver hilt 706: 9
with s. quarter'd world ..1956: 3
within its scabbard sleeps 1741:15
Sword-arm of justice 1602:11
Swords: died s. in hand ..1870: 5
into ploughshares 1472:14
measured s. and parted ..1956: 4
more eloquent than words 1955:17
more s. and shields 157: 9
of Sheffield steel 562:10
our s. shall play orators ..1955:13
sheathed s. for lack of argument 1956: 4
yet were they drawn s. ..2223:18
Swordsmanship: no skill in 1955:19
Swore: knew not what to say, s. 1950:13
like a trooper 1950:14
terribly in Flanders 1951:11
Sycamore: sighing by s. tree 2150: 2
Sycorax: foul witch 2175:19
Sylla proceeded by persuasion 1490: 8
Syllabes: still may s. jar with time 1518: 1
Syllable: chase panting s. 2221: 8
last s. of recorded time ..2023:13
Syllables govern world ..2220: 1
slow archangel's s. 412: 9
word-catcher lives on s. 2221: 8
Syllabubs: endless host ...522: 6
Syllogisms hang not on my tongue 1727: 7
steps we walk by 1628: 6
Sylph: 'tis but their S. 247: 1
warn'd by the S. 1233:18
Sylphs: fifty chosen s. 488:11
Sylva: momento fit cinis: diu s. 1748:11
Sylvæ: nobis placeant s. ..2211: 5
nunc frondent s. 1908:11
Sylvas habitarunt di 2210:13
Sylvia: for S. gain the prize 601: 6
Symbol of coming Springs 812:18
of past power 1421: 7
welcome gift to man 1070:15
Symmetry: fearful s. 2001:15
Sympathy **1956**
cold to distant misery 1957: 4
craving for s. 1957: 6
homely s. that heeds the common life 1957:20
in souls s. with sounds ..1364: 1
just to teach us s. 1956:12
keeps love awake 1270: 2
melts with social s. 1957: 1
mild and healing s. 1383:19
no s. because of work ..1064: 5
of love unite thoughts 608:18
of mind keeps love awake 1270: 2
of Sire and Sons 647: 2
sink as we rise through s. 1956:20
walks furlong without s. 1957:19
what a s. of woe is this 2177: 1
without relief like mustard 1957: 2
world in anguish to teach us s. 1956:10
Symphonies: dulcet s. 96: 3
playing celestial s. 2153: 2
Symphony: angelic s. 1367: 7
of spring 347: 5
this is my s. 1126:15
Symptoms of good or evil mind 606:12
Syne: auld lang s. 738:11
Synods mystical bear-gardens 1694:18
Synthesis of truth 348:12
Syon: urbs S. aurea 886: 9
Syrian stars look down ..262: 4
Syrops: lucent s. 522: 2
Syrup, lotion, drop, or pill 1662:12
Syrups: drowsy s. of the world 1850:19
System, The 1554: 6
how s. into s. runs 2068: 7
Nature's s. of divinity ..1913: 3
System-grinder hates truth 1597: 2
Système: ce s. sublime est necessaire 788: 1
Systems: brutal s. give place 1616:12
crush 233:12
into ruin hurl'd 749:13
social s. among bees 142:15

T

T: fitted him to a T. 1154:10
performed to a T. 1154:10
Ta-ra-ra-boom-de-ay 2292: 9
Tabac, dont mon âme est ravie 2017: 8
Tabagie: ignoble t. 2017:11
Tabbies: we're not as t. are 2016:17
old maid t. 2230: 4
Tabella: picta vultum mentemque t. 1448: 8
pulchrior in terris nulla t. foret 103:20
Taberna: meum in t. mori 496: 3
Tabernacle: earthly t. 1314: 9
Tabitha, called Dorcas 242: 1
Table: crowd not your t. ..450:14
depends on other's t. 451: 6
good t. always right 1559:18
I know the T. Round 248: 6
keep a good t. 452: 6
number at t. 450:13
of my memory 1295: 8
robs more than thief 516: 4
round t. no dispute 450:17
three-legged t. 1329:11
what's a t. richly spread 2186: 3
what's on the t. 450: 4
Table: bonne t., toujours raison 1559:18
tenez bonne t. 452: 6
Table Round, my friends ..728: 4
Table-talk: serve for t. ..1963:13
Table-talker rich in sense 1963:12
Tablecloth: great deal of t. 516:16
Tables were stor'd full ..518:10
Tablet of thoughts 605:13
Tace: Latin for candle 216: 6
Tacent: cum t. clamant ..1823: 3
satis laudant 1577: 4
Tacere cogi, quod cupias loqui 1784:16
multis discitur malis 1821:19
Tacet: qui t., consentire ..1822: 5
Tacitum silvas inter reptare salubres 2210:21
Taciturnitas pro sapientia 1822:17
Taciturnitus acerbi 1330:10
Taciturnity: glory in their t. 1963:16
Tacuisse: nulli t. nocet 1838: 7
nunquam me t. pœnitet ..1825: 3
Tadpole: when you were t. 586:16
Tædia: dedecet ingenuos t. ferre sui 192:12
mille ferenda T. 1086: 9
Tædium vitæ 1117:13
Tag and ragge 1478:12
just a little brass t. 1869: 2
rag and bobtail 1478:12
Tag: auf den T. 2299c: 4
wird es auf die dickste Nacht 293: 3
Tag-rag people 1478:12
Tail: at lovers wagg'd my t. 471:13
cod's head for salmon's t. 2167: 7
dock the tail of Rhyme ..1369: 1
downhill like calf's t. 330:15
hangs down behind 330:15
joins on back 1034:12
kiss her t. 716:18
lecherous t. 2105: 5
like a peacock sweep along his t. 1476: 8
more he shows his t. 84:13
must wag the dog 103: 7
of the lions 286:15
of the noble hoss 1369:13
piece lion with fox's t. ..717:19
scaly horror of folded t. ..445: 3
subdued in armed t. 143:12
such a little t. behind 535:12
takes in his teeth 670: 3
that wagged contempt 473: 7
their t. the rudder 104:13
treading on my t. 1409: 6
turnin' to the t. 19:16
what a monstrous t. 222:18
whose t. you may go by 1801:17
without head or t. 869: 4

Talking, *continued*
don't forget you're t. to a Lady 1881: 8
he will be t. 40: 1
I profess not t. 2228:20
indice of a fool 699:16
is not always to converse 312:12
like playing on harp 1962:12
of love is making it 1186: 4
passion of a woman 2199: 9
sat t. with my mind 1307: 8
seldom repent t. too little 1825: 3
tall and tactless 1113:10
'tis their exercise 2199: 9
with my mind 1307: 8
Talking-machine: red tape 1437:17
Talks about the weather 2128:14a
familiarly of lions 1163: 9
hum-drum "long t." 2281: 9
money t. 1333:20
much and says just nothing 1594: 3
much says foolish things 1964: 8
much t. in vain 314: 1
to unburthen his mind ..1962:13
while he t. he is great ..805: 2
Tall: divinely t. 139: 9
great is T. 1552: 1
to reach the Pole 1307: 5
Tam saw an unco sight 2175: 9
was glorious 2083: 6
Tamer of the human breast ..17: 8
Tammany: great is T. 1552: 1
Tammany, Big Chief sits ..1882: 4
Tandem triumphans 1930: 5
Tañe: quien las sabe las t. 1055: 9
Tangibility: no t. but they haunt us 69: 9
Tangle: tomorrow's t. 2157:13
Tangles of Neæra's hair ..956: 4
Tankards: cheerfu' t. foamin' 32:17
no Sunday t. foam 1753: 8
Tanlings: hot summer's t. 1938: 4
Tanned: walketh in sun, t. 1938: 4
Tantale, nullæ aquæ 1987:12
Tantalus a labris sitiens 1987:12
Tanto buon che val niente 808: 6
Tao, method of 148:15
Tape: red t. 2281: 3
red t. talking-machine ...1437:17
Taper: exulting in their t. 216:13
hallow'd t. trembling 397: 7
hold to sun my little t. ..216: 1
husband out life's t. 1666: 6
life's dying t. burns 1905:14
light t. at neighbor's fire 2105: 5
lights t. at mine 951: 5
midnight t. 629: 9
of conviviality 731:10
Tapers: hold glimmering t. to the sun 216: 1
like t. clear 1917: 1
of the sky 1913: 1
till there's nothing left ..2044: 8
Tapestry: wrong side of Turkey t. 2250:17
Tapeworm of Europe 580:12
Tar: if you fool around with t. 1981: 7
loved not savour of t. ..1770:13
Tar-baby ain't sayin' nuthin' 1650:15
Taradiddles: I will tell t. 71: 1
telling t. 1109:13
Tarantulated by a tune ..1362:17
Tard: mieux t. que jamais 1073: 7
Tarditudine: vicistis cochleam t. 1855: 9
Tares: corn-cumbring t. ..2130: 3
of discord and division ..1838: 6
seed-wheat-kennel t. 2130: 3
Tariff 1965
customs t. law 2048: 6
Gulf Stream of politics 1965:12
is a local question 1965: 7
Tarre the mastiffs on 1607:19
Tarred and feathered 1658: 4
Tarriers: drill, ye T., drill 1882:10
Tars are Fortune's sport ..1778: 2
true-hearted t. love 1778: 3
Tartar: caught a T. 1639:10
Tartness of his face 609:17
Tartuffe opened shop 548:12
Task: all her t. to be sweet 2186: 4
delightful t. 1970: 6
each morning sees t. begun 1063:13
every t. is noble 2233:13
for fortitude and delicacy 1129:11
go thou to thy learned t. 1765:12
hard is t. of justice 1031: 5
lay hold of today's t. ..2021: 9
light t. when many share 2231: 8
my great t. of happiness 858:16
my t. accomplished 398: 8
my t. is smoothly done 1061:16
noble t. to rescue from oblivion 901: 1
strange t. of living 1126: 9
this is the t. 1062:14
trivial round, common t. ..507: 5
unglad t. ever plies 441:18
Tasks are done and tears shed 2262:14
equal to your powers 1584:10
little t. large returns 1098: 8
Taskwork: unmeaning t. ..1144: 3
Tassel-time of Spring 1907: 3
Tassels and an ostrich plume 398:15
no t. you can lure 1268: 3
of the maple flowers 1908:13
Tasso's echoes are no more 2076:18
Taste 1965
appreciates pictures 1446:19
confounds the appetite 89:12
cultivating t. while filling belly 316:10
dark brown t. 504:15
different t. in different men 1966:13
enough of learning 529: 6
every man to his t. 1966:11
for collecting shells 1781:11
for fact amounts to disease 2057:10
forgot the t. of fears 657:20
from the t. obscene 13:12
here was sacrilege 1966:10
in weaving words 1926:14
inch-rule of t. 1965:14
judge of matters of t. ..1966: 4
last t. of sweets 32: 3
literary conscience of soul 1966: 7
loathe t. of sweetness 1952:15
love of beauty is T. 1966: 1
mongrel product 1966:14
my *anno domini* 27: 7
never t. who always drink 1964: 9
not to be spared 1965:16
of Attic t. 659:15
of devil's broth 441:13
of mobs, now of lords ..1911:13
of pleasure unpursued ..1510:21
of you burnt my mouth ...198: 2
of your quality 236: 5
offended t. rejected 452:14
rear'd by t. 1525: 1
sans t. 28: 5
sate the curious t. 1386: 6
seldom critic's share 342: 6
shocking to t. 1966: 2
sweet to t., digestion sour 1953:11
touch not; t. not 5:12
want of t. 1965:15
whose mortal t. 12: 4
Tasted: universally t. 1559:11
Tasteless and ill-bred 42:15
if not enjoy'd with thee 1199: 9
Taster for himself and master 315:10
Tastes: as many t. as men 1966: 5
high æsthetic t. 1966: 2
may not be the same 804:15
men have not all same t. 1966: 5
no disputing about t. 1966:15
simple t. and mind content 2104: 1
sweet t. have sour closes 1699:12
Taters: there's where t. grow 2087:13a
Tatter to her tail 487: 5
Tatters: tear a passion to t. 10: 6
Tattle: subject of t. 313:16
Tattlers also, busybodies ..1761:15
Tattoo: soldier's last t. ..1869:11
Tattooed Man 1377:16
Tattycoram: count five-and-twenty, T. 80:16
Taught: as if you t. them not 1969:20
as one having authority ..115: 6
by self, fool for master 1969:17
but followed himself 589: 4
lowly t. 1136: 5
say I t. thee 1971: 9
that profits by teaching 1969: 2
us how to live 413:17
Taupes envers nous 1024:13
Tauri: fortes invertant t. 639:14
Taurus: patiens fit t. aratri 1442:19
sun with T. rides 143:15
Tautology: prophet of t. 2258:14
Tavern: capital t. 989: 3
eat at Terré's t. 522:12
from t. to t. youth dances 2268: 1
I intend to die in t. 496: 3
O miraculous t. 988:15
producer of happiness 989: 3
what paradise it is 988:15
within the T. caught 1152:16
Tavernes: tout aux t. 493: 3
Taverns: knew the t. well ...988: 5
Tawny-throated 1404:11
Tax and please impossible 1966:17
false income t. return ..1967:10
on humbug 1967:15
power to t., to destroy ..1967:16
single t. upon land 1967: 8
Taxation must not take ..1967: 7
requiring trivial oaths ..1967: 7
unnecessary t. unjust 1967:11
without representation ...2297: 2
Taxed bridle, on a t. road 1967:18
Taxes 1966
death and t. 226:13
fall upon agriculture 640: 4
men least willing to pay t. 1967: 4
milks dry 1967:14
on everything on earth ..1967:18
one class imposes t. 1966: 7
paid in sweat 1967:14
people over-laid with t. ..1966:16
true as t. is 1967: 6
what is't to us if t. rise or fall 1967: 1
widows, wooden legs, debt 2113: 3
Taxi: refused to pay a t. 1988: 2
Taxing machine 813:16
Tay: Lady Morgan makin' t. 997:11
some'll swallow t. 1968: 5
Taylor: General T. never surrenders 64: 4
let T. preach 1729:14
Shakespeare of divines ..1589:15
Tea 1968
coffee and other slopkettle 1968: 5
discharge their t. 580: 7
does our fancy aid 1968:14
favorite beverage of the intellectual 1968: 9
go on drinking t. 2263:11
haven't had t. for week 1968:11
having t. just too far 2258:20
Lady Morgan makin' tay 997:11
nor take t. without stratagem 1968:15
retired to t. and scandal 1968: 6
sip their elemental t. ..1968:12
spill her solitary t. 2198: 6
sweetens t. with scandal 1762: 4
thank God for t. 1968:13
thou soft, thou sober, sage 1968: 4
we'll have t. and toast ..522: 6
women for t. forsook spinning 500: 4
Tea-cup times 488: 6
Teach: and gladly t. 1970: 2
easier t. twenty 1596: 3
fain would t. the world ..867: 2
him how to live 1147:11
if aught can t. us 16: 3

Teach, *continued*
ingenuous youth of nations 256:11
me more than Hell to shun 300:10
me to live that I may dread 1150:15
men to die, and to live ..1147:11
not t., only tell 1969: 1
others who themselves excel 342: 6
Spirit only can t. 1970:17
still pleas'd to t. 238:20
the hundredth part 197: 2
them how to die 1147:11
them how to live 1147:11
to t. a teacher 1970: 5
who themselves excel 1971: 7
with sour and pale faces 1970: 3
young babes gently 256: 4
young idea how to shoot 1970: 6
Teacher and taught are young 1970:12
art of the t. 1969:11
experience the best t. 594:17
I am not a t. 1971:11
let Nature be your t. ..2000: 3
should be sparing of smile 1970:14
spare your simple flock 1971: 6
young t. who taught 1409:11
Teachers of the law 1093: 1
of the little taught 182:23
woods and rills 1389: 1
Teaches: he t. who gives 1970:17
he who cannot, t. 1971:12
Teaching 1969
makes the difficulty 1970: 1
nature's t. 1388:19
what he didn't know 1971: 4
Teachings: Nature's t. ...1388:13
Team: heavenly-harness'd t. 1846:11
Teamwork: everlastin' t. ..1862:18
Tear 1971
but ay the t. comes 2:15
chase the pensive t. 496: 6
counterfeited t. 327: 4
did not think to shed t. 1976:11
down childhood's cheek ..1972: 9
drop a t. 1047:12
dropped a t. on the word ..75:11
drying up a single t. 1493:14
every t. becomes a babe ..1971:17
fallen a splendid t. 1215:11
flows down Virtue's cheek 1975:14
for all that die 1975:13
for thee t. be duly shed ..1356:15
forgot as soon as shed ..634: 4
from virgin steal a t. 1534:13
gave to misery a t. 730: 2
great interpreter 1972: 4
he hath a t. for pity 242:18
here did she fall a t. ..1295: 9
hypocritic t. 404:11
in Beauty's eye 1976:16
in grave rained many a t. 828:12
in her eye 601: 8
is an intellectual thing ..1279:16
let fall a t. 1976: 1
made it deeper by a t. ..1975: 9
man without a t. 976: 7
never a t. bedims the eye 1972: 9
not a t. must o'er her fall 395: 6
nothing dries sooner than a t. 1972: 9
of Saturn 1070:15
of the sisters of Phaëton 46:14
on that grave drop not a t. 404: 7
one small pretended t. ..1978: 2
sacred, shed for others ..1975:12
scarcely a t. to shed 1219: 3
shed no t. 1974:18
so limpid and so meek ..1975:19
sympathetic t. 1853:13
that is wip'd with address 1977: 2
that we shed 1293:13
thou couldst not hide 1978: 1
timid t. in Cleopatra's eye 1977: 1
unanswerable t. 1977: 1
wakest the sleeping t. ..1972:14
was in his eye 2034:16
which sinner had shed 75: 6
with a t. in every line ..1296:13
Tears: accept these grateful t. 1957: 7
after t. joy may return ..1973:17
are dim with t. 196: 3
are for the conquered ..1973: 6
are in the falling rain ..1977: 7
artificial t. 947:19
best brine 1977:14
big round t. 943: 2
blessings, let them flow ..1974: 1
bring me your t. 1975: 1
but handsells of our joys 1971:18
conscious of the t. I shed 1350:23
coursed one another 943: 2
crocodile t. 1972:11
did he break into t. 1976:13
drawing others' t. 11: 1
drop t. as fast as the Arabian trees 1976:13
drop t. at command 1977:10
ease the soul 1974: 6
embalm'd in t. 1196:17
feign'd t. 2188: 7
few t. and some laughter 1078: 3
few t., but friendly 405: 5
for his love 1716: 1
for misfortune 1973:16
from the depth 1975:10
funeral t. 1976: 5
gain respite for suffering 1977: 8
give me thy t. 1975: 1
glazed with blinding t. ..840:13
happier in t. than smiles 1853:18
have run colors from life 1974: 9
he who has but t. to give 740:10
hence these t. 1973:13
her t. to the windflower 1746:11
honor me with t. 1519:11
how lovely in her t. 1976:16
hung on every tree 2236: 5
idle t., I know not 1975:10
idleness of t. 1144:13
if you have t. prepare ..1973:10
in his eyes 10: 5
in t. I was born 1973: 5
in youth, t. without grief 1973: 9
inexperienced t. 1222:11
iron t. down Pluto's cheek 1877:10
its dewy leaves disclose ..1194:14
lady's t. silent orators ..1976:15
lament in fruitless t. ..2260:21
language of affection 1972: 1
last a day 25:11
little while t. and laughter 1137:10
live in an onion 1972:12
loose me from t. 392: 7
lovelier than smile 1976:16
my t. gainsay 1976:10
my t. must stop 1974:17
no t., but t. of wine 2159: 9
no t. can wash out shame 1809:17
no t. dim the sweet look 1382: 6
no t. when enemy dies ..543: 4
noble language of the eye 1971:18
nothing is here for t. ..1978:11
of all the angels 2186:13
of an heir laughter 985:13
of bearded men 1976: 6
of boyhood's years 196: 9
of fallen women 446: 8
of it are wet 1972:11
of mournful eve 445:13
of poison 1697: 3
of repentance 1432:13
of Saints more sweet ..1755: 4
of the first morn 333: 8
of the human race 1477:9a
of the sky 445:12
of the young 25:11
of warlike men 1976: 6
of woe 1432:13
only t. that ever burst ..1978: 7
our t. not yet brew'd 1973:10
pleasant laughing-stock 25:16
prove holy water on thee 1976: 2
raining t. of lamentation 1972: 8
run down dappled face ..943: 2
salt t. 1756:10; 2150: 2
sang t. into his eyes 1880:10
scald like lead 17:12
Tears, *continued*
scare me with thy t. 1978: 1
shed t. for show 1977:13
silent language of grief 1972: 5
sinner's brine 1971:18
skilled in moving to t. ..1438:15
so lively acted with my t. 1076: 3
soothe suffering eyes 1974: 5
stanch thy bootless t. 405:12
stand congeal'd 2176: 5
stood on her cheeks 1977:17
such as angels weep 1976: 7
supply of t. always ready 1977: 6
sweet April's t. 93:14
sweet to mingle t. with t. 1320: 8
sympathetic t. 1975:15
that comes through t. 1854: 3
that speak 2218: 8
their triumphs, o'er 391: 1
tired of t. and laughter 1845:15
to drop thy foolish t. 405:11
to human suffering due ..1933: 4
Tommy's t., Mary's fears 2015:10
tragic t. bedim the eye ..388: 2
waste not t. over griefs 1973: 3
water-power 1077:12
weep thy girlish t. 93:18
weep your t. into channel 1975: 9
weighty as words 1976:15
wept each other's t. 1212: 5
what heavy t. 86:13
when our bitter t. o'erflow 2176:12
which stars weep 445: 9
who can refrain from t. 1976: 4
will pierce into marble heart 2195:16
with t. brought forth 840: 7
with t. melt iron 1977:10
with your t. moist it 2254:13
Teary round the lashes ..1853:16
Teasing: always t. others 1513: 5
Technocracy 1764: 6
Techstone: war's red t. ..2120: 7
Teddy-bear 1741:16
Tedious about trifles 861:13
as a tired horse 192:16
as twice-told tale 1125:12
Tediousness [is soul of] the limbs 199: 5
Tedium of idleness 955:18
Teen: each joy wrecked ..1019: 5
Teeter-board of life 1115:14
Teeth: aching t. ill tenants 2028: 4
armed to the t. 722: 6
as black as jet 167: 3
barrier to check words 2027:11
bid them keep t. clean ..279: 4
chattering t. for cold ..2161:13
children's t. set on edge 821:14
cleaning with knife 521:13
dig grave with t. 520: 5
free of rust 491: 3
I will give thee bloody t. 2027:15
in spite of his t. 2027:16
in the t. of tomorrow ..2020:20
Læcania white t. 2027:14
now set the t. 2116:10
of a gift horse 773: 1
of emulation 2091: 2
pick a halfpenny out of the dirt with his t. 119: 6
sans t., sans eyes 2240: 5
set my t. on edge 123: 7
show t. by way of smile 1853: 9
sit melancholy and pick t. 1291: 5
skin of my t. 2027:13
to restrain words 2027:11
white t. everlastingly smiling 1853: 7
Teetotaller: never marry t. 1267: 2
Tehee, quoth she 2154: 6
Tela: perfida t. cave 2032:11
Telegraph my baby 2284: 2
printing, gas are little events 995:11
Telegraph-wire: high harp 1364:10
Telescope: fancy's t. 634: 5
put by the t. 1765:13
wherever we point t. we see beauty 2241: 2

Tell: just t. them that you saw me 2285: 5
me that beautiful story 2289:11
the world 1641:16
us and you t. town 2199:15
wise men never t. 1693:16
Teller: bad news infects t. 1399: 5
no common t. of news ..1838: 6
Telling: I am t. you 99:12
us all that they think 218: 4
Tellus: æqua t. 383:14
Tema esce il diletto 657: 6
Temeritas est florentis ætatis 22:15
Temeritate: ex t. spes 1754:11
Temper: because she lost her t. 2232: 7
cheerful t., chief good 250: 9
cheerful t. with innocence 250: 4
from his dinner 449:16
good t. estate for life 1978:17
he of t. was so absolute 1252: 5
hot t. leaps cold decree ..79: 1
keep me in t. 1232:15
lose t. in defending taste 1965:17
of her own 1978:17
of heroic hearts 879:20
open and noble t. 250: 5
softens down the t. 1973:21
stubborn t. of the man ..1424:11
tart t. never mellows ..2026:11
uncertain t. 1978:17
whose unclouded ray 250:16
Temperament 1978
makes women chaste 1979: 2
matter of sensation 1978:14
solid base of t. 1979: 9
vortex of his t. 1979: 3
Tempérament font la vertu des femmes 1979: 2
Temperance 1979
and labor true physicians 873: 5
ask God for t. 1980: 3
be rein'd again to t. 78:15
beget a t. 10: 6
controls our desires 1980: 2
driven into t. 1979:13
guess what t. should be ..1980: 3
healthy by t. 238:20
holy dictate of spare T. 1980: 1
in pet of t. feed on pulse 1979:19
is a bridle of gold 1979:12
is the regimen for all ..1979:11
moderation in good things 1620: 2
nurse of chastity 1980: 5
reason over passion 1979:14
Tempérance et travail deux vrais médecins 873: 5
Temperantia prætermittendis voluptatibus corporis 1979:14
rationis in libidinem 1979:14
Temperate in every place 1979:15
in love and wine 1305: 7
lovely and more t. 1215: 1
Temperatures differ 1979: 1
Tempers: bad t. surely worst 1978:17
different t. run 1966: 5
lose t. in defending taste 1965:17
Tempest: after t. come calms 1797: 2
dropping fire 1921: 5
foretells a t. 2153:10
in a glass of water 1920:15
in a teapot 1920:15
poetical t. arises 1537: 4
windy t. of my heart ..1976:10
Tempest-toss'd, sails ripp'd .436:20
Tempest-tost: it shall be t. 1816: 4
Tempestas: poetica surgit t. 1537: 4
quo me rapit 932: 3
Tempests: looks on t. 1175: 3
on his naked head 837: 9
when scolding winds 1921: 5
when t. tear the main ..1322:17
where t. never beat 883: 7
whistle round 908:14
Tempête: dans un verre d'eau 1920:15
Templa: sapientum t. serena 2166:24
Temple: favored t. humble heart 879:21
good, a holy place 1695:15
half as old as Time 1001:10
near t. insult the god 632: 8
no sooner is a t. built to God 272:17
not made with hands 1594:13
nothing ill in such t. 132:10
of art built of words 101:13
of fame 627:11
of fame on grave 629:11
of great men 832: 6
of silence, reconciliation 1168: 6
of virtue was she 2093:10
she's a t. sacred by birth 2178:6a
that t., thy fair mind ..1307: 2
there is t. in ruin stands 2012: 6
where a God may dwell 1834: 7
where men go to weep 1973:15
where's the need of t. 271:15
Temple Bar to Aldgate Street 2076: 1
Temple-walls to shut thee in 336: 2
Temples ascend the skies ..272:12
crumble to dust 1312:19
gray t. at twenty 39: 1
grew as the grass 104:15
in one's own breast 794: 8
mortal t. of a king 345:15
of God abound in riches ..939: 9
of the Holy Ghost 939: 9
serene t. of the wise 2166:24
talk not of t. 1387: 3
throb, pulses boil 1923: 4
while sacred t. burn 42:14
Tempo: perder t. a chi più 2008:13
Tempora: adsiduo labuntur t. motu 2004:16
consumere longa loquendo t. 1963:24
mutantur 230:22
O t.! O mores 1257:17
perde precando 1585: 7
si fuerint nubila, solus eris 736:12
stare putes adeo procedunt t. 2008: 1
tarde t. norrando fallat ..1963:24
vocis et silentii t. nosse ..1823: 9
Tempore: ex t. 1439: 8
Tempori parce 2008:19
Temporis medicina fere est 2011: 9
quicquid transit t. perit 2007: 3
respice celeritatem t. 2007: 4
velocitas t. 2007: 4
Temps: bon t. si malheureux 1294: 1
c'était le bon t. 1294: 1
fait passer l'amour 1191: 4
fuit et nous traine 2006: 6
le mieux employé 2010: 3
louast le t. passé 84: 1
perdu mon t. et mon labor 1062:19
souverain médecin 2011:12
Tempt not a desperate man 1982: 3
the dark abyss 1703:18
Temptanda via est 626: 6
Temptaris: aut non t., aut perfice 1929:18
Temptation 1980
above t. in low estate 238:21
comes in fine gay colours 1980:17
lead us not into t. 1981: 8
let us not lose heart in t. 1981: 4
man that endureth t. 1981: 2
never resist t. 1982: 4
resist everything except t. 1982:14
safe from t. 413: 1
strength to yield to 1981: 1
strong t. and the need ...1023: 1
that doth goad us on 1981:20
that way going to t. 1981:18
that ye enter not into t. 1981: 9
to get rid of t. yield 1982:14
to have tricked t. 1980:10
to see too much 1434: 8
tries a just man 1982:10
why comes t. but for man 1980: 8
ye're aiblins nae t. 1223: 6
Temptations hurt not 1980:18
not good to be without t. 1980: 6
Temptations, *continued*
of today 2020:1a
to belong to other nations 558:15
were strong t. planted ..1982:13
Tempted: no man t. 1980:18
one of the t. 1981:19
Tempter or the tempted ..1981:19
saw his time 1981:13
so gloz'd the t. 1981:10
subtlest t. smoothest style 1980:11
Tempts by making rich ...1981:13
your wandering eyes 87:14
Tempus abire tibi est 24: 5
Æquo stat t. 2005: 5
breve et inreparabile t. ..382:13
da t. ac spatium tibi 429:12
edax rerum 2007:16; 2012: 3
erit 41: 5
fugit inreparabile t. 2009: 2
in agrorum cultu dulce ..639:12
ipsa mortis t. indignius ..386: 8
nec præteritum t. revertitur 2009: 2
omnia revelat 2051: 7
perditum non redit t. 2009: 2
quam bonum t. in re mala 2004: 3
qui t. accepit 2008:18
quod antecedit t. 1656: 7
tanto brevius felicius t. ..2006:15
tantum nostrum est 2004: 4
venit ineluctabile t. 382:12
Ten struck the church clock 141:14
Upper T. 1859: 9
Ten Commandments: where there aren't no T. C. ..513:14
will not budge 1986: 5
Ten-to-oners in rear 1553: 3
Tenants of life's middle state 1329: 1
we are but t. 381: 8
Tend him, nurse him, mend him 2140: 3
Tendance: touch'd by her t. 684:13
Tendency: stream of t. 586: 6
Tender as woman 402:10
for another's pain 1932:12
so t., yet so true 1961:14
Tender-handed stroke a nettle 177: 7
Tender-minded does not become sword 1956: 6
Tenderness best quality in man 1974: 2
flute fantastic t. 949:12
repose of passion 21:10
Tendresse repos de la passion 21:10
Tenement: clayey t. 825:10
of clay 1891:11
Teneriff, unremov'd 1922:10
Tenets same at last 100:14
Tengomenas facimus 491: 9
Tennis: faith they have in 755: 4
Tennis-balls: stuffed t. 128: 2
Tennis-court: in that vast 440: 3
Tennyson, Alfred 1982
Tenor: noiseless t. of way 1135: 4
Tense: set up the present t. 299: 3
Tent: guarded t. 2061:10a
have struck Heaven's t. ..76: 1
is struck 76: 1
let the t. be struck 415:23
low green t. 393: 4
nightly pitch my moving t. 887:11
pitched'st thy golden t. 1937: 1
stands in a garden 755:13
that little t. of blue 1835:10
to live in a t. 2284: 2
when I have folded up t. .378: 9
whose curtain never outward swings 393: 4
Tentes: aut nunquam t., aut perfice 1929:18
Tents and starry skies 1136: 7
dwell in t. below 887: 8
fold their t. like the Arabs 220:18
of wickedness 887: 2
Tenui musam meditamur avena 1768: 8
Tenuitas: tuta est hominum t. 1572: 8
Tenure: unsure the t. 629: 2
Tereu, t.! by and by 1404:12

Term: third consecutive t. 2280: 2
Terminations: terrible as t. 2194: 9
Terminum: spectare vitæ t. 411:14
Terms: define your t. 428:16
fair t. and villain's mind 2085:16
litigious t. 1092:10
sweetest t. 452: 9
too deep for me 1423: 2
Terpsichore: a maid 361:11
governs the emotions 800:11
Terra incognita 874:11
malos homines 584: 1
quando t. iter facere possis 1779:13
qui jacet in t. 621: 3
sit super ossa levis 406:15
sit tibi t. levis 406:12
Terram: ex alto procul t. conspiciunt 1779: 6
Terras: omnes t. viris natura aperuit 2029:15
quid t. alio calentes 2031: 7
Terret: qui t., plus ipse 657:10
Terribilis: multis t. caveto multos 657: 8
Terrible as a meteor 673:12
as an army with banners 2113: 8
to many, beware of many 657: 8
Terror
See also Fear
causes real misery 656:18
closes ears of mind 656:17
death armed with new t. 159:12
grisly t. 386: 6
haunts the guilty mind ..844:20
in her tier 1813:13
no t. in your threats 1997: 3
of the Roman name 1736:14
one species of t. 462:10
only rules by t. 1751: 3
paralysing t. 325: 5
to the soul of Richard 302: 9
where t. stalks 1587: 5
Terror: major ignotarum rerum t. 2045: 8
Terrore nominis Romani ..1736:14
Terrors of living, not the dead 385:18
of the earth 1713:16
of the main 1780:14
one of new t. of death ..159:12
sudden t. 655: 6
the king of t. 386: 6
Tertium quid 1545: 1
Tertullian: rule of faith ..152:14
Test: bring me to the t. 1233: 3
made of my metal 2247: 9
no religious t. 1550: 9
of a first-rate work 179:12
of a vocation 1062:10
of civilization 277:13
of ridicule 1725: 7
of success simple 1930:10
of the heart is trouble 1854: 3
of the poet is love 1523: 2
to man, propose this t. ..1891: 9
Testa: imbuta recens 1796: 3
pallida t. 522: 8
servabit odorem T. diu ..1746: 3
Testament: New T. a Pauliad 159: 4
of bleeding war 2113: 5
of noble-ending love 397:12
Old T. tribal 158:16
purple t. of bleeding war 2113: 5
thou makest a t. 1562:14
Testamur: quod vidimus t. 1055: 5
Tester I'll have in pouch 1336:12
Testes: superos contemnere t. 844: 7
Testify that we have seen 1055: 5
Testimonies are my meditation 2066:11
Testimony against them ..1632:16
like an arrow 97: 4
of a good conscience 301: 6
pitch t. out of window ..1026:16
to the law and t. 1086:16
Testudo: grata t. Jovis ..1368: 2
Testy: old men are t. 34: 1
Tetchy and wayward 122: 3
Tête: faire tomber la t. 621: 3
Tetegit non ornavit 536:16
Teucer as leader 1095: 1
Teufel ist ein Egoist 441:12
Texas and Hell 891: 6
Text: approve it with a t. 1693: 3
fools make the t. 1691: 2
holy t. of pike and gun ..1589: 2
inspires not them 991:11
many a holy t. 904: 1
neat rivulet of t. 190: 4
old, orator too green 1439: 2
one unquestioned t. 790:14
read ev'ry t. and gloss over 1499:13
that looks a little blot ..190: 4
will suit any sermon 1595: 4
you are now out of your t. 609: 1
Texts in their favor 1691: 2
so much the worse for the t. 1691: 2
Texture: liquid t. 1905: 1
Thackeray flattered aristocracy 1856:17
Thalatta! Thalatta 28: 8
Thalia rejoices in comedy 800:11
Thames, The 1983
overgrown with weeds ..1749: 3
set fire to the T. 667: 8
sweet T., run softly 1272: 9
what my T. affords 670: 7
with no allaying T. 2155:13
Thank: always t. we God therefor 825: 7
heaven, fasting 1193:15
me no thankings 825: 2
the God I know to be ..1892: 9
thee for that word 2220: 9
whatever gods may be ..1892: 9
you for nothing 824: 4
Thanked: not t., t. enough 824: 7
Thankful for what ye have not 825: 7
Thankfulness of heart 1983:16
Thanks are justly due 824:13
as fits a king 824:19
exchequer of the poor ..823:15
glad he t. God 824: 2
I give as one near death 824:19
I'll flow in t. 825: 4
in everything give t. 825: 5
in part of thy deserts ...1716: 3
late t. ever best 823:16
not forthcoming 775: 6
of millions yet to be ..897: 3
old t., old thoughts 41:13
small t. for my labour ..1062:21
small t. market price 18:13
take the t. of a boy 792:11
to give t. is good 395:16
unto the harvest's Lord ..1983:13
Thanksgiving Day 1983
Thanksgiving doth invite ..824: 9
presarved fr'm th' Puritans 1658:11
to the vine 2156: 8
Thanksgivings for the golden hours 1984: 2
That that is is 643: 6
That alles, nichts Ruhm ..1716: 9
Thatch: sheltered by t. ..1571:18
Thaten: nur T. geben Stärke 423:21
Thaw: if there comes a ..1906: 9
Theatre
See also Stage
everybody has his own t. ...9:10
for diverting representation 1911:11
is the House of Life 1125:10
of everlasting generations 1458:14
of stateliest view 2037:11
Théâtre des ris 141:13
Theban: this same learned T. 1963: 8
Thebes, or Pelops' line 2045:17
Thee: neither with t. nor without 237: 4
Theft: great t. who robs self 1985:13
most base 1987: 2
Theism: atheism last word of t. 113:16
Theme: be t. and hearing ever 214: 1
Theme, *continued*
give me a t. 1535: 4
glad diviner's t. 2095: 3
Homer's t. but a dream ..912: 8
my t.! my inspiration 795: 1
no such thing as dirty t. 2251: 7
Themes: ignoble t. 1525: 1
of war 2113:10
strain celestial t. 1880: 1
Themselves: kept to t. 561:17
pass t. by 2030:14
Theodore: in the reign of T. 1741:10
with all thy faults 1741:11
Theologian: up comes a t. 1984: 4
Theologic wars 1984:17
Theologie ist Anthropologie 1984: 9
Theologies: village t. 1984: 6
Theology 1984
attempt to explain a subject 1984:10
cure for false t. motherwit 1984: 7
get t. out of education ..1984:11
into t. a humane spirit ..1985: 2
sent worst to heaven ..1984:11
stringent t. 531: 3
vexed me ten score times 1984:12
Theorem: big perilous t. ..514: 1
Theoric: bookish t. 190: 3
Theorie: grau ist alle T. ..1143: 1
Theories: all t. are gray ..1143: 1
cramm'd with t. 2194:12
frigid t. 43: 1
Theory: condition, not a t. 1965: 3
over practice 43:22
possession for life 951: 2
There: here and t. 971:10
I'll never go t. any more 2289: 1
over t. 2284: 2
we'd both been t. before 2292: 1
Thermometers: friends are 735:20
Thermopylæ: pass of T. ..900: 2
to make a new T. 839: 1
Thersites to Hercules 1551: 7
Thesaurus stultis in lingua situs 2024: 6
Theseus went to hell 2147: 3
Thespis, first professor 122: 1
Thetis, image of eternity ..579: 7
in the lap of T. 1940: 9
They: everyone else is t. ..707: 4
say; let them say 1760:10
terrible family "They" ...1760:10
Thick: through t. and thin 1528:11; 1639:12
Thick-and-thinnite 1554: 5
Thief: bankrupt t. 342: 7
call one t., he will steal 1985:10
each thing's a t. 1987: 1
hang t. when young 1986:11
if t. has no opportunity ..1985: 5
impenitent t. who died upon the cross 462:14
in what watch t. would come 1986: 8
knows a t. 1985:16
myself, know tracks of t. 1985: 9
of venison keep forest ..1985:12
once t., ever in danger ..1985:14
one t. knoweth another ..1985:16
sacrilegious t. 1986:12
said last word to Christ 1985: 7
save a t. from gallows ...1987: 3
seek for t., robbed 1980: 7
set t. to catch t. 1985:12
so clomb this first t. 1592: 2
steals from himself 1985:13
whether you're honest or t. 1091:12
who drank a pot of beer ..852:11
Thievery: example you with t. 1987: 1
petty, picking t. 1985: 8
Thieves: all not t. dogs bark at 1985: 4
are hangmen made 341:11
at home must hang 1986:10
at t. I bark'd 471:13
big t. lead away little ..835:11
do not break through 885:10
fell among t. 1986: 6

Thieves, *continued*
for robbery authority ..1021: 9
great t. hang little ones ..1986:10
honest to one another ..1985:11
never rogues among selves 1985:11
receiver, stealer both t. ..1986: 9
when t. cannot be true ..1985:11
when t. fall out 1985:15
Thieving 1985
Thigh: smote them hip and t. 1635: 6
Thimble: wooed wench with silver t. 2212: 5
Thin as Banbury cheese ..1642:12
red line 1863: 6
Thine: only call me t. 1375:16
what is t. is mine 728:16
what is t. own hold 1562: 2
Thing: empty t. that they would wish to be 1576: 8
face the grisly T. 397: 3
good-conceited t. 1876: 1
I am the t. I was 231: 3
I had a t. to say 1899:15
I have done one braver t. 1331: 0
I was born to do 423:18
if it isn't one t., tother 1116: 4
never says a foolish t. ..244: 7
no evil t. that walks by night 246:12
no great t. done by great effort 833:18
no new t. under the sun. 1415:11
no the t. I should be 948: 3
of beauty is a joy for ever 135:20
of shreds and patches 1039:1; 1879: 3
of temperament not of art 1978:15
one rich t. that morn 1744:16
passive t. 239: 3
poor little fluttering t. ..1893: 9
saved some trifling t. ..1296: 3
that fills me with wonder 1223: 1
that hath been 1415:11
the one inexorable t. 439: 8
weak churchyard t. 28: 3
wee t. makes us think 222: 3
Things: aggregate of little t. 909: 6
all earthly t. above 2277: 4
all t. are changed 230: 6
all t. have their place ...1504:18
all t. look older 35: 7
all t. must change 231: 6
all t. taken from us 2007:12
all t. to all men 12:13
all t. to one man 12:13
all t. touch'd with Melancholy 1291: 3
all t. work together for good 790:19
ancient and holy t. fade 1140: 7
and actions what they are 302:14
are in the saddle 1229: 6
are sons of heaven 2227:13
are t. what they seem 2095: 1
are where t. are 643: 6
better t. to say 1101:13
brave translunary t. 1261:15
breed thoughts 1991: 7
change them to the contrary 231: 7
curious and unfamiliar ...82: 9
day of small t. 2040:10
despiseth small t. 2041: 4
determined t. to destiny ..440: 1
dishonest t. have bitter rivers 2033:14
do not happen 228: 7
done without example 426: 3
dying t. turn to West 2131: 4
either are what they appear 88: 4
eternal fitness of t. 1440:14
first made, then words ..2218: 3
hard t. by easy means 447:18
his best t. done in a moment 1315: 7
how many t. I do without 1328: 2
I have been all t. 417: 3
I put away childish t. 251: 7
ill-got had bad success ..751: 2
impossible of attainment ..970:15
in the breast 455:20
it may annihilate 865: 9
Things, *continued*
less dreadful than seem ..87: 7
little t. affect little minds 2042:10
little t. go lessening 2040:18
little t. great to little man 2042:10
little t. on little wings 2039:13
make vile t. precious 1393:15
man's best t. are nearest him 463: 7
more t. in heaven and earth 1498:18
my liberal t. shall he stand 1545: 5
not what they seem 1121:14
of to-day 425:12
old, unhappy, far-off t. ..1459:10
order t. better in France 720: 4
precious t. are free 1826:16
refuse to be trifled with 1083:15
render unto God the t. that are God's 212:15
seldom what they seem ..86:12
show t. as they are 216:17
standing thus unknown ..1372:14
that are 579: 2
that are lovely 134:18
that are most excellent ..454: 1
that didn't occur 2045: 5
that little children suffer ..251:12
that ne'er were, nor are ..236: 8
three t. are ever silent ..1825: 5
vilest t. become themselves 2076:16
we do not need to buy ..1826:16
what they appear to be 88: 4
whatsoever t. are honest 2090:10
when t. are small 1927: 8
which I have seen 232:16
which I regret 1687:16
won are done 424:21
won't-you-let-me-help-you t. 2041: 6
Think according to nature 355:12
all to myself I t. of you 1296:15
all you speak 1900:18
alone, all places friendly 1994:19
amiably-disposed, I don't t. 1639:11
and ne'er disclose mind ..455:18
as wise men do 1993:12
bad form to t. 951:13
can because they t. they can ..1:14
don't t. foolishly 946:18
for two minutes together 1996: 3
for yourselves 2276: 1
hardest task to t. 1996: 2
him so, because I t. him so 2203: 6
how few t. justly 1996: 3
how many never t. 1996: 3
I t., therefore I am 1991:14
in fashion of period 1429: 6
in the morning 369:14
lawful to t. what you wished 1903: 4
learn to t. imperially 970: 5
less t., more talk 1964: 9
likely, mister 1049: 8
more, act less 1992:10
much, speak little 1993:17
nobler privilege to t. 1108:17
none but dull rogues t. ..1996: 6
not I am what I appear 86: 2
not what people t. 506:13
of myself looking at you 708:10
of things we used to do 1296:15
on him that's far awa 2:15
on these things 2090:10
on things impossible 484:20
one thing, another tell ..420:10
so because others t. so ..1060: 5
so brainsickly of things ..1996:14
that dares not speak 1993:15
that you mightn't 1224: 2
thinking men t. for self 1429: 1
those who greatly t. 1715:14
those who t. must govern 814: 2
those who t. nobly noble 1407: 7
till I weary of thinking 1996:11
to be happy 2167: 3
to t. and to feel 758: 2
to t. is to act 7:10
to t. to converse with self 1989:16
today, speak tomorrow ..1993:13
too little, talk too much ..1964: 9
Think, *continued*
truly and thy thoughts ..2057: 4
unless you can t. when the song is done 1172: 4
twice before you speak 1901: 3
we t. as others t. 1428:19
what do you yourself t. ..186:13
what is true 1726:10
what people t. other people t. 1429: 7
what thoughts were best ..1995:12
what we t. we feel 660:20
what you t. makes world 1992: 1
what you t. of yourself ..1789: 4
when I t. I must speak 2199:11
without confusion clearly .150: 7
would it were not as I t. 2170: 7
you would t. otherwise ..1427:20
Thinker: arrival of a t. ..1994:11
God lets loose a t. 1994:11
no t. with memory too good 1293: 8
profound t. suspects 1994:17
thought of mathematical t. 2067:12
Thinkers help others think 1989: 5
Thinketh: as a man t., so is she 2206:13
as he t. in his heart, so is he 1991:18
Thinking: avoid real labor of t. 1996: 1
do not craze yourself with t. 348: 3
hardest work there is 1996: 2
he's t. upon naething 222: 3
high t. 1136: 5
idle waste of thought 1996:15
leave off t. cause of errors .575:23
makes it so 1991:22
men suffer from t. 1996:16
moment's t. hour in words 1994:22
never thought of t. for myself 1543:18
of the old 'un 943:17
paid it off with t. 1993:19
right and meaning well 1383: 5
thoughts after thee 795:10
too much t. to have thought 1996:12
troublesome effort of t. ..1995:17
'twas her t. of others 1035: 5
what is little one t. about ..121: 3
what to say 1996: 6
where we ought to feel ..1324:10
Thinkings are below moon 1995: 9
speak to me as to thy t. 1993:21
Thinks amiss concludes worse 1996: 9
as a man t. 1992:17
best man t. for self 1428:21
everybody t., nobody says 1993:18
he t. too much 648: 1
like a Tory 1545:14
most interesting thoughts 1994:18
not well that t. not again 1993: 9
says what honestly t. 980:17
what a baby t. 121: 3
what man t. in spirit 1989:15
who t., must mourn 164: 1
Thinner: if you wish to grow t. 518:17
Thirst 1987
and a man can raise a t. 513:14
comes with drinking 493: 6
cup in hand 1987:14
departs with drinking 89:13
dry t. burns the throat 1987:11
dry t. of honor 47: 2
for fame 625:20
for fruit of flowers 2056:10
for gold, beggar's vice ..802: 2
go not to pot for every t. 1987:10
greater is t. for fame than for virtue 625:20
he slakes at brook 88:15
master t., master health 1987:10
no wine so wonderful as t. 1987:13
of greatness 1187: 6
of praise 48:16
pines with t. amidst waves 1987:11
scorches in the breath ..1987: 7
slaked t. at wells of thought 184: 6

Thoughts, *continued*
give thy t. no tongue 1993:21
give worst t. worst words 1993:21
glance quick as lightning 1993:20
go blowing through them 2190: 1
good t. do not perish 1989:12
great t. become great acts 1992:11
great t., great feelings ..1989: 8
great t. hallow labor 1063: 9
great t. in crude verse.. 1524:13
great t. need no trumpet 1990: 5
had rest in heaven 1590: 8
have a high aim 1995: 5
have no depraved t. 1994:13
hide not thy t. 217: 6
high-erected t. 1995: 5
his dunghill t. 2105:14
his t. were heaving 1209: 9
hit roofs of palaces 1991: 1
how many noble t. 2012: 4
I have such sweet t. 413:18
in a flower bell curled 1994:20
in black and white 2251:12
in t. more elevate 100:11
legible in the eye 606:12
like rose-leaves scattered 1991: 9
link'd by hidden chain ..1989:13
lo, my t. of white 1156:11
make not t. prisons 1996:14
might have good end 1995:12
mightier than strength ..1992: 6
moan from soul of the pine 1994:20
my recollectest t. 1409:10
my t. are my companions 1990:16
my t. are not your t. ..1990:18
my t. remain below 1585:11
naked t. that rove about 1995: 4
new t. thrilled dead bosoms 1990:22
o' bygane years 1295: 5
of Christ, the living bread 1590: 6
of God borne inward 395: 6
of God pause but for moment 785: 4
of happier years 927:13
of mortality cordial 1348:13
of the best minds 1860: 5
of youth are long, long t. ..196: 7
old thanks, old t. 41:13
on hospitable t. intent 933: 9
only conceivable prosperity 1989: 1
our t. are our own 1992:18
our t. are ours 644: 7
over-busy t. 1846: 2
perplexing t. 1135: 9
pious t. as harbingers 28:10
pleasant t. bring sad t. 1995:16
responsible for evil t. 584: 8
rule the world 1991:21
second t. are wisest 1993: 7
second t. often worst 1993:11
select most nutritive t. ..2252: 1
shut up want air 1990: 2
slaughterous t. 657:20
so all unlike each other ..1994:12
so sudden, that they seem 1992: 2
sober and second t. 1993: 8
solicit not thy t. 1940: 5
sow t., reap actions 845: 6
strange t., strange deeds 1992:14
talent to conceal my t. ..216:14
that arise in me 1995:13
that ascend like angels ..1995:11
that breathe 634: 4
that dwell in great men ..830: 4
that have tarried in mind 1989: 7
that mould the age 1992: 3
that savour of content 310: 7
that shall not die 1294:16
that thick my blood 982: 2
that wander eternity 386:10
that will glad two or three 2251: 4
their own t. sublime 58: 9
then feed on t. 1990:25
to memory dear 1297: 3
to nobler meditations 1148: 3
toll-free, not hell-free 1992:15
too deep for tears 687: 5
too deep to be expressed 1991:11
transcend our dreams ..1995:15

Thoughts, *continued*
undying t. I bear 1990:24
unexpressed fall back dead 2226: 5
united t. and counsels ...2067: 4
unsought t. most valuable 1989: 7
unstain'd t. do seldom ..989:16
unthought-like t. 1989: 7
vagrant as the wind 240: 6
were always downward bent 1237:11
were of another world ..1994: 7
when dark t. 924:11
whirled like potter's wheel 1991: 4
white t. stand luminous 1849: 4
who knows t. of child 253: 2
whose very sweetness ..1366: 7
worse than we are 1990:15
Thousands at his bidding speed 793:11
Thracian dog: Zoïlus 342: 4
Thraldom: single t. 2141:12
Thrale: Mrs. T. 1015: 5
Thrall in person free in soul 1840:10
Thread: hang by slender t. 229:13
of his verbosity 99: 6
of human life 1124:12
of life we spin 1831:11
of life would be dark ...730: 8
of my days 1133: 6
of our life is spun 1124: 5
pluck one t. web ye mar 981: 4
shot through with golden t. 2038: 8
weave their t. with bones 123:10
which holds them together 1668: 2
Threadbare topics of half wits 313: 4
Threadneedle St.: old lady 1167:15
Threads of life are twisted 1126: 8
silver t. among gold 39: 7
turn to cords 845: 8
Threat 1996
Threaten the threat'ner 177:20
with death unlawful 1997: 3
Threatened folk live long 1997: 2
more t. than stricken 1997: 2
Threateners do not fight ..1996:22
Threatens many 986: 2
while he quakes 1996:22
Threats: man does not die of t. 1997: 2
to freemen, t. impotent ..1996:21
to use t. is womanish 1996:20
with wind of aery t. 1996:25
without power 1996:18
Three bear record in heaven 783:11
can make planets sing 202: 8
is a crowd 287: 4
is company, two none .. .1265: 3
is trumpery 287: 4
men riding together 202: 8
not fewer than t. 450:13
number t. fortunate 1227: 3
sheets in the wind 492: 8
that never quit the chase ..643:17
things t. are needful 2104: 3
we t. meet again 1289:11
with a new song's measure 202: 8
Three per cents: simplicity 464:17
Three-and-thirty: I have dragged to t. 165: 6
Thresher of the wheat 387: 6
Threshold high enough 933:13
Thrice he assay'd 1976: 7
is he arm'd 1030:14
slew the slain 173:14
Thrice-blessed 1278: 8
Thrift 1997
base respects of t. 1279:12
Horatio 1998: 5
I am about t. 2124: 3
may follow fawning 677:10
philosopher's stone 1997:10
waxes thin 1998: 8
when t. and you fell 1997:15
when t. is in the town ..1615: 2
Thrifty and thoughtful of others 980: 2
Thrill: into t. and shine ...392: 9
of a happy voice 2097:14

Thrill, *continued*
of life along her keel 1814: 4
one electric t. 2053: 5
Thrive rise at five 1729: 3
Thrives: none t. upon dream 482:15
Throat: brazen t. of war 1474: 7
cut his t. 1933:13a
cut your t. for own sake 1217: 3
if down his t. a man 1409: 4
in t. give the lie 1113:12
lofty and shrill-sounding t. 233: 6
open sepulchre 677: 3
open thy t. to wine 2160: 1
put a knife to thy t. 90: 8
they cut his t. 1360: 9
Throats: begin slitting t. ..79:13
nor cut each others' t. 81:10
richest of all singing t. ..167:12
wash t. before eyes 873: 7
Throbbings and burnings ..109: 7
Throe: never grudge the t. ..15:19
simulate a t. 2051: 9
Throne 1998
any t. except t. of grace 1998:15
beat upward to God's t. ..841:18
but gilded wood 1999: 2
circle his t. rejoicing 76:14
doubtful t. ice 1999: 4
fiery-wheeled t. 307:14
Great White T. of God ..1582: 1
heads bow around a t. 327: 6
here is my t. 1887: 9
in mercy t. established ..1999: 1
in the spirits of men 1057: 2
legs of t., plough and oar 1998:16
living T. sapphire blaze ..1305:11
loafing around the t. 74:11
nearer the great white t. ..883:12
no brother near the t. 13:12
no t. without thorn 1999: 4
of bayonets 297: 6
of Denmark 882:19
of Mammon grey 1237: 7
of royal state 444:15
of the invisible 1773: 4
power behind the t. 1999: 3
royal t. of kings 550: 1
something behind t. 1999: 3
through slaughter to a t. .1998:17
too hot to hold her 1895:12
Thrones, Dominations, Princedoms 76:12
hold all t. in scorn 206: 1
sink to dust 419:12
who shall talk of t. 1917: 9
Throng: one of a restless t. 2289:11
Throssil whusslit sweet ..1999:16
Throstle
See also Thrush
how blithe t. sings 2000: 3
sing clear, O t. 1999:16
with his note so true 1999:16
Throw: greater from weaker 753: 1
him down, McCloskey ..2289: 9
within a stone's t. 1639: 4
Thrummed: ne'er so t. 2225: 7
Thrush 1999
aged t. frail, gaunt 1999:12
blow softly, t. 1999:20
enraptured t. 1715: 6
God's poet 1999: 9
hark to the brown t. 2000: 2
Hermit T. 1999:19
only a t. could sing 137: 2
rarely pipes mounted t. ..2000: 1
sing on, dear T. 1999: 9
sing, sing on, O t. 1999:11
that never spoke 1999: 8
that sings loud 2000: 3
Thrushes: I question not if t. sing 1936: 6
Thrust: madman's t. 1232: 8
Thud: dull and sickening 1645: 3
Thuggery: Glasgow t. 1052: 9
Thule: there was king of 1040:13
ultima T. 463:14
ultimate dim T. 463:14
Thumb: bite your t. at us 1083: 4
biting t. to quick 78:11
he had t. of gold, pardie 1304: 9

Time, *continued*
stands with impartial law 2005: 5
steals on our youth 2006: 6
stood still 2008: 1
stuff life is made of 2008:14
subtle thief of youth 165: 5
such a t. is this 1379: 7
suppresseth wrongs 1030: 8
surest poison is t. 1539:13
swift-footed T. 2012:13
swiftest of things 2007: 4
take a little t. 80:16
take no note of t. 2010: 6
take t. and delay 80:12
take t. by the forelock ..1432: 9
take t. enough 819:13
take t. in t. 2009:11
takes away grief 2011: 9
takes them home 402: 3
tassel-t. of spring 1907: 3
teaches all things 2003: 2
teaches wisdom of silence 2003: 3
tell t., it is but motion ..1894: 3
that aged nurse 2003:18
that bald sexton, T. 2002:16
that bears no fruit 1135: 3
that lights and quenches men 239: 7
that old bald cheater, T. 2002:16
that shall outgrow all flowers 1943: 4
that t. of year thou mayst ..36: 3
that was the good t. 1294: 1
the avenger 2011: 3
there is no t. like Spring 1907:18
there was a t. when meadow 252: 3
there'll come a t. some day 2288: 1
there's a good t. coming .1436: 2
this doth fit the t. 641:19
this thy golden t. 25: 4
thou must untangle 447:22
'tis t. to be gone 24: 5
tithing t. draws near 1592:12
to be born, and t. to die ..2004:11
to be earnest 29:12
to be happy is now 334:17
to be old 27: 6
to choose t. is to save t. ..2003: 4
to every purpose 2004:11
to keep silence 2004:11
to love, t. to wed 2004:11
to spare from own affairs 1284:16
to stand and stare 1099:18
to T. I'm heir 2003:14
to turn out 1848:10
to weep and t. to laugh ..2004:11
toil'd after him in vain ..1806: 6
too slow for those who wait 1943: 9
torn half the leaves 2014: 1
touch us gently, T. 1126:3; 2011: 6
travels in divers paces ..2008: 5
tries troth 2005: 4
trieth truth 2005: 4
truth which cunning t. puts on 87: 3
turn amber locks to grey .2013:15
unfolds Eternity 513:10
very shadow that passeth 2007:13
waiting t. hardest t. 2100: 7
was dumb within that ..2003:16
was made for slaves 2003: 8
was, t. shall be 2005: 9
waste t. making money ..1337: 6
wasted is existence 2010: 7
wastes too fast 2013:15
we have t. in store 1484:14
we know not of 439: 9
we live in t. 1458: 7
we take no note of t. 934: 2
weak piping t. of peace ..1474:12
weakens love 744:15
wears his locks before ..1432: 8
weary-wearing t. 29:16
what an empty vapor 'tis .2006:10
what foolish thing is t. ..2008: 9
what hast thou with t. ..2008: 5
what lovely t. they had 83:18
what will not t. subdue ..1816:15
when meadow, grove 252: 3

Time, *continued*
when T. hath spoken 2165: 3
when you will hear me ..1902: 8
where t. and eternity meet 29:13
whereof memory of man 2003: 5
who has leisure to cozen .2262: 2
who hath t. hath life 2003: 4
who hath t., loses t. 2003: 4
who murders T. 2013:14
who steals our years away 1293:19
who subdueth all things .1432: 5
why meet we on bridge of T. 1290: 1
will bring healing 2011: 9
will come when every change shall cease ...1599:14
will come when you will hear me 1902: 8
will doubt of Rome 1739: 2
will explain it all 1963: 1
will make thee colder 1192:12
will no man bide 2005:10
will not come again 2008:21
will not be stayed 2007:10
will reveal the calyxes of gold 312: 4
will run back 2003:22
will unfold 349:18
witching t. of night 1303: 5
with a gift of tears 1239:11
with his silent sickle 2012: 8
withers on the stalk 2010:12
wonderful stream is River T. 2005: 1
would never be 2003:15
writes no wrinkle 1773: 5
you old gipsy man 2006: 4
Time: te sine teste t. 426: 9
Time's best jewel from T. chest 2014: 8
by T. slow finger written 1749: 2
corrosive dew-drop 2012:10
dark events 393: 1
deformed hand 607: 5
devouring hand 2012: 3
fatal wings do ever fly ..1150: 3
iron feet print no trace 1773: 5
mark T. rapid flight 1943:10
noblest offspring is the last 52: 6
revolving wheels 579: 1
wingèd chariot 2006:11
Time-servers and blockheads 817: 6
Timeam: quid ignoro 656:15
Timeat: necesse est multos t. 657:11
Timendo: nemo t. ad summum 177:14
Timens: omnia tuta t. 656: 7
Timere: multos t. debet 657:11
nolite 654:15
quod vitari non potest 656: 1
si vultis nihil t. 655: 2
Times: accusing t. excusing selves 590: 3
are big with tidings 2014:12
are not alike 2014: 9
bad t. have value 16: 4
better t. are coming 2287: 1
change, and we with them 230:22
daily change 4:11
do shift 230:20
former t. shake hands ..1527: 9
giddy-paced t. 123:10
go by turns 232:10
good old t. 1458: 6
hopes better t. 988:16
how merry are the t. 1782: 6
I hate all t. 2007:11
more aged than earlier 82: 6
most remote from birth ..82: 6
new t. demand new measures 1616:14
not the t. are bad 42: 9
of preservation 2004:11
old t. 41:13
old t. were changed 244: 3
our t. are in his hand 30: 7
scorn to the new 83:13
signs of the t. 1623: 7
still succeed former 34: 5

Times, *continued*
that try men's souls 62: 4
that were are better 42:13
there's t. when you'll think you mightn't ..1224: 2
these costermonger t. 2073: 6
these t. ancient t. 82: 6
trans-shifting 1538: 2
true old t. are dead 83:11
when t. were not hard ..1336: 2
wherein we now live most ancient 82: 6
why slander the t. 42: 9
Times [London] more information than Thucydides 1602: 8
Timid and brave must die ..384: 6
calls himself cautious 2015: 3
never set up trophy 2014:16
then shriek'd the t. 1815: 2
to t. everything impossible 2015: 5
Timidi est optare necem ..1935:10
nunquam trophæum 2014:16
Timidissimis: oratio t. audax 1902:15
Timidity 2014
Timidus: pericula t. non sunt videt 2015: 3
se vocat cautum 2015: 3
Timon will to the woods ..1036: 5
Timor animi auribus officit 656:17
audacem fecerat 654:23
degeneres animos t. arguit 655: 8
in vota miseros cogit t. ..1582:18
initium sapientiæ t. Domini 792: 2
misericordiam non recipit .654: 8
mortis morte pejor 388: 7
non magister 653:17
pedibus addidit alas 655: 9
pessimus augur 653:23
primus deos fecit t. 800: 4
virtutis impedimentum 653:22
Timoris: quo t. minus est 654:21
Timorous yield to despair ..177:12
Timotheus yield the prize ..77: 7
Timothy: agree about T. ..335: 8
learnt sin to fly 1830: 4
Timour-Mammon grins ...1474:15
Tincture in the blood 2063: 9
perfumed t. of roses 1487:10
Tinfoil of pretense 1501: 2
Ting, ting, that's how the bells go 2289: 3
Tingling: a whoreson t. 461: 3
Tinker Bell 614: 6
Tinker: drunk as a t. 501:13
how could a little 291: 2
to Evers to Chance 755:7; 2297: 6
Tinkers: take it as t. do ale 2016:16
Tinkling of innumerable feet 1669:16
of the camel-bell 1126:13
Tinnitu aurium 2: 8
Tinsel: you talk of t. 1982:15
Tinte: viel Wasser in die T. 1528:14
Tintinnabulation 154: 3
Tintinnabulum: nunquam ædepol temere tinnit t. 154: 2
Tints of rainbow hue 1450:11
to harmonize 2062: 7
visionary t. 116:10
Tip is jewel of the ear 1013:17
missed my t. 1637:14
of his subduing tongue ..2025:20
Tip-toe: jocund day stands t. 369:12
stand a t. 1465:12
Tippecanoe and Tyler too .1556: 7
Tipperary: long way to T. ..996: 6
sweet is T. 996: 6
Tipple a bit 497: 9
Tippler leaning against sun 991:10
Tire: early t. gets tack 1728:10
Tired at close of day 29:13
how t. you must be 414: 1
of London, t. of life 1168: 2
the sun with talking 894: 3
Tires that spurs too fast ..863:19

U

Vice, *continued*
flee v. beginning of virtue 2080:15
from no one v. exempt 308:10
gather'd every v. 581: 5
gets more than piety 2080: 1
how soft and voluptuous 2078: 6
indulged, or overcome ..2078:20
is a failure of desire 2078:18
is habitual 2078: 8
is virtue well concealed .2080: 6
its own punishment 2079:16
lashed v. but spared name 1237: 4
laughed at his v. 2079:13
lost half its evil 2078: 4
loves v. for its own sake 2079:13
low v., curiosity 351:11
makes virtue shine 2080:12
misery of every creature 2080: 4
monster of frightful mien 2079: 5
must have variety 2078: 6
never-failing v. of fools ..1609:16
never yields fruits 2080: 1
no v. but beggary 146: 2
no v. but is woman's part 2189: 6
no v. so mean 1111:11
no v. so simple but assumes 2081:14
not v. unless 'tis known ..2080: 6
nourished by concealment 2079: 9
of impiety 352: 8
of our leading parties ..1544: 5
of the age 1758: 9
old-gentlemanly v. 36: 9
on Christian ground 581: 5
one v., two children 2078:11
or Virtue there is none 2081: 7
pernicious v. of gaming ..753:18
repeated is like the wandering wind 2079:17
shall dignity of V. be lost 2081: 7
shame of v. 33: 5
should not correct sin ..2079: 4
smack of this v. 2079:10
so clear too of other v. ..1686: 1
sold tools, yet kept v. ..1854: 6
stings even in pleasures 2080: 7
subject to v. of lying ..1113:17
that reverend v. 2079:14
they keep people from v. ..68: 2
to sanction V. 2080: 5
to virtue a just equinox 2081:14
triumphs over virtue 43:22
when v. prevails 919:17
which offends no one 2079: 3
world can ill spare any v. 2078: 5
wrap up v. with words ..2080:14
you have a v. of mercy 1299: 1
Vice: il n'est v. qui n'offense 2079: 3
j'aime mieux un v. commode 2081: 6
Vice-President: elected V. and nothing ever heard of him again 1547:14
Vices are now manners ...1257:17
at heels of virtues 2082:10
combatting one another ..2078:13
conquered by his v. 2082: 6
creep in as virtues 2082: 5
dispersed by occupation ..1424:17
do not feel in ourselves ..1024:12
enter into virtues 2082: 3
good to be without v. 1980: 6
great men's v. virtues ..2081: 5
hate him that my v. telleth me 2078: 7
helped by their v. 2079:11
if v. were profitable 2080: 1
indebted to his v. 2079:11
instruments to plague 2079:16
intertwined with virtues .2082: 7
learned without a master 2078:12
less dangerous than virtues 1590: 2
less serious when open ..2079: 9
let thy v. die before thee 2078:11
make ladder of our v. 2078: 3
men should his v. tell 219: 8
my v. telleth me 219: 8
next-door to virtues 2082: 5
of a scoundrel 1508:12
Vices, *continued*
of kings cannot be hid ..1042:15
of mankind, not of times 2079:10
of the time 2079:10
of world's nobler half ..2079: 1
once v. but now manners 1257:17
people bear being told v. 2127: 9
please more by v. 2082: 2
redeemed v. with virtues 2081:20
see my own v. without heat 2078: 9
so v. brag 152:21
tainted with thousand v. 2079:14
tempt by rewards 584:22
vanquished by their v. ..2079:18
very good patriots 1967: 5
when our v. leave us 2078:19
Vices: quand les v. nous quittent 2078:19
Vicia negotio discuti 1424:17
Vicinum: mali v. malum .1396: 1
stultum est v. 1713:10
Vicious, ungentle, foolish 240:11
would base-born call 1407:12
Vicissitudes in all things ..1322: 4
man used to v. 16: 2
of fortune 715: 4
of sects and religion 1694:11
of woe 802: 5
sad v. of things 1876:10
wild v. of taste 1966: 6
Vicissitudo: omnium rerum v. est 231: 7
Vicisti Galilæe 263:12
Victi vicimus 297:15
Victim: dress the v. to the offering 949:12
o' connubiality 1275:14
of perpetual slight 439: 2
ready at hour of sacrifice 1466:16
ruined and heart-broken .2274: 5
Victims: little v. play 254:20
Victis: væ v. 2083:19
Victoire me suit 2084: 5
prieray pour vostre v. ...1349:11
Victor exchanges war 2119: 8
from vanquish'd issues ..2084:19
Hail! thou as v. crowned ..767: 5
over death and pain 1029:13
to v. belong the spoils ..2278: 4
Victor nec longum lætabere 2085: 1
pace bellum mutavit 2119: 8
victorum cluet 297:15
Victore: contendere durum est cum v. 297: 5
Victorem captiva sequar ..2144: 7
Victores victosque fide 2084:19
Victoria, Queen 2082
Victoria: hæc te v. perdet 2084:17
rivalitatem non amat v. ..2084: 2
semper est v. ubi concordia 2084: 2
uti nescis 2083: 4
Victoriæ: quam v. pudeat 2084: 3
Victoriam: ipsam v. vicisse videris 2083: 8
malle quam pacem 2084:11
Victorians, Tudorians 303:10
Victorias: no V. in twentieth century 2082:15
Victories of peace 2118: 7
of right born of strife 1726:16
Victorious: o'er a' the ills o' life v. 2083: 6
on lips of men 626: 6
Victors by victories undone 2083:13
give the v. way 2084: 9
in defeat 612:11
who are Life's v. 2084:18
Victory 2083
all things follow v. 2084: 5
and defeat at hands of self 1786:21
and defeat of same price 2084:14
another v. and we are undone 2083:13
both win the v. 1583:12
brings a v. in pocket 2084: 7
but 'twas a famous v. 2084:10
celebrate the v. 414:18
does not like rivalry 2084: 2
Victory, *continued*
ends in defeat of death 381:16
floated to v. on sea of oil 2083: 9
for humanity 2083:17
fruit of skill or fortune ..2083: 2
greatest v. is defeat 2084:14
hardest v. over self 1786: 9
I will not steal a v. 2083: 1
if not v. is yet revenge ..1712: 4
in believing 151:16
in dying well 1466: 3
is a spirit 2083:12
is said to be one-handed 1470:19
kiss him with glorious v. 2084: 8
let v. fall where it will ..2083:11
life's v. won 391:14
mine is the v. 2083: 7
nothing so dreadful as v. 2085: 2
of endurance born 540:21
of Prussian schoolmaster 1970:11
of the tomb 412: 7
only v. over love is flight 1186:12
or else a grave 2083:14
peace without v. 67: 1
pleased Cato 2083:16
pray God for your v. 1349:11
preferred v. to peace 2084:11
silent, so is defeat 2084:12
suicidal to victors 2084: 1
there be the v. 2084: 8
they only the v. win 2084:18
thing of the will 2083:12
to Heaven the v. 2109:15
twice itself 2084: 9
vanquished v. itself 2083: 8
where there is unanimity 2084: 2
white flower of v. 821: 1
whose v. was Peace 1473:13
will be your ruin 2084:17
with V. on thy left 52: 3
Victrix causa diis placuit ..2083:16
Victuros agimus semper ..1130:12
Vida es sueño 1121: 7
Vide inquiunt 267: 5
Videaris: tandem v. unus esse 1832:16
tibi v. quam qualis aliis 1789: 4
Videndi: acerrimum esse sensibus v. 1819:12
Videntur: non semper sunt quæ v. 86:12
Video meliora proboque ..1727:20
Videre: non expedit omnia v. 1425:16
Videris: ne v. quod v. 455:21
Videto: cui des v. 772: 4
de viro cui dicas v. 1838: 9
Vidi: quæque ipse v. 1820:7a
Vie: don't v. with me 13: 5
Vie est brève 1137:13
est telle que dieu la fit ..1137:13
la v. est vaine 1137:13
longue et cruelle maladie 1121: 1
ma v. a son secret 1210: 7
ma v. est un combat 1120: 2
meilleure partie de leur v. 1118:13
qu'est-ce qu'une grands v. 831:12
un pas vers la mort 1150: 5
Vieillard abecedaire 39:13
Vieillards aiment à donner des bon préceptes 27:13
Vieillesse est un tyran 34:15
l'on craint la v. 27:12
n'ôte à l'homme d'esprit ..31: 7
quelle triste v. 219:19
Vieillissant: on devient plus fou 27:14
Vienna: looker on here in V. 1820: 2
Vieux: ensemble nous devenons v. 490: 8
savent être v. 26:13
View: horizon's grander v. 1128: 8
long last lingering v. 591: 8
of these hush'd heads ...1666: 2
Views: adopt new v. so fast 575:21
distant v. of happiness ...463:18
future v. of better or worse 749:13
mercenary v. 1523:14

Virtue, *continued*
always against the law ..2089: 4
always in a minority 2094:16
and conscience of worth 2212: 2
and cunning endowments greater than nobleness 349:19
and funds seldom seen ..2094:13
and happiness Mother and Daughter 2092: 4
and learning need polish 1256:10
and riches seldom together 1722:15
and sense are one 2087:18
and trade best inheritance 2093: 4
and vanity 2094: 3
and vice bad bound'ries .2080: 8
and vice equally distributed 2030: 3
as gold to silver, V. to gold 1336: 5
asserts itself in adversity 2089:12
assume a v., if you 2089:18
attired in women see 1802: 4
bears the bell 152:21
beauty and v. 132: 2
beauty and v. strangers ..137:13
beauty is flower of v. 132: 3
beauty of the soul 131:14; 2092: 1
becomes o. trageous 2274: 5
belov'd contented thing ..2092:10
best plain set 2087:19
best v. some vice 2082: 3
better set without gold ..2087:19
betwixt two vices v. lies 2081:19
blooms on wreck of life ..2092:17
blunder'd on some v. 1259:15
bold, goodness never fearful 2090:13
but a word 2088: 7
but at second hand 172:11
can surmount evils 1810:12
chok'd with ambition 50: 2
choose high or low degree 2092:10
consoles us in pains 2080: 7
could see to do 2090: 9
debases in justifying 2089:22
disgrace to envy v. 2089: 1
distinguished alone by v. ..574: 7
doth reside in books 188:17
doubly pleasing 2090:14
ends v. or begins vice ..2082: 3
engages his assent 2094:14
every v. kindred vice ..1511: 4
every v. mayst behold 766:10
ev'ry v. under heaven 2093: 9
fairer in a fair body 85:13
false v. hypocrisy 2191:15
finds no friends 2094: 9
first v. vices to abhor ...2080:15
flies from and disdains ..2081: 8
flies when love blows 246: 7
flourish in old cravat 864:12
follow v. for v.'s sake 2091:12
fount whence honor springs 2088:12
fugitive and cloistered v. 2088:19
give V. scandal 1534:13
gives herself light 2090: 9
goes quietly to sleep 2274: 5
greatest of all monarchies 2088:16
habit of the mind 2088: 3
happiness, vice misery ..2080: 4
has degrees, so has vice ..2081: 9
has vanity at her side 2094: 3
hate V. while it lives 2089: 9
he married public v. 1464: 9
he must delight in v. 2091:15
health of the soul 2088:10
how far from easy is v. 2090:17
hue of v. 172: 8
if seen, would win love ..2089:14
if there be any v. 20 0:10
in almost every vice 915:13
in ambition is violent 2087:20
in conscious v. bold 10: 2
in distress, vice in triumph 2080: 9
in her shape how lovely ...445: 1
in v. are riches 2090:12

Virtue, *continued*
in women 246: 6
is according to nature ...2081:11
is an angel, a blind one .2088:11
is an empty boast 2081: 7
is at hand 2088: 4
is beauty 2088:14
is enough 834: 3
is harmony 2088:13
is honor 2016:11
is height 2088: 5
is its own reward 2091: 5
is like precious odours ..2087:19
is not hereditary 2093: 7
is not malicio s 2090: 1
is the roughest way 2090:19
is v. found in voices 2099: 3
it is not v., wisdom, valor 1185:15
itself turns vice 2081:15
knelt with v. 1514: 5
languishes, pleasure fails 2065: 7
learn v. from me 2089:21
learned v. of the vicious 2081:10
let v. be as wax 1809:20
lies in the struggle 1716: 8
linked with one v. 1374: 9
lives beyond the grave ..2092:16
lives when beauty dies ..1748: 3
love v.; she alone is free .2092: 8
love V., while they fall ..1697:11
loves herself 2090: 2
loves children she beats ..2089: 8
magnetic v. in woman ..2184: 3
make a v. of necessity ..1393: 7
make v. almost natural ...2080: 2
makes life harmonious ..2091:14
makes the bliss 2092: 3
makes them most admired 2192:11
many praise v., do no more 2249: 9
may barefaced take field 2080: 6
may be assail'd never hurt 2091: 9
may be gay with dignity 2089:19
may flourish in old cravat 864:12
mean between vices 2088: 6
men do not vary in v. ..2080:17
most pleasing possession 2090:12
much v. in 'if' 1663:15
mysterious v. of wax 1080:14
needs no defence 2090: 6
never aided by a vice 2081: 2
never grows old 2092:12
no freedom without v. 723: 1
no ready way to v. 2090:16
no v. in himself 2089: 1
no v. like neces ity 1393: 7
no v. poverty destroyeth not 1569:11
no v. which is final 2080:10
not birth, makes noble ...2093: 3
not desiring vice 2088:15
not in action, vice 2088:19
not left to stand alone ..2088:19
not sufficient for govt. ..1080: 4
not suns, mind matures 2090:15
nothing if not difficult ..2091: 1
nothing v. cannot reach ..2089:11
O V.! I have followed thee 2094: 1
of expediency v. of vice 2082: 1
of her lively looks 2195:13
of kings is justice 1040:14
of parents great dowry ..1452: 9
of the devil 444: 5
of the soul 1027: 1
of vice must pardon beg 2081:13
of woman to obey 2205:10a
often merely local 2088: 8
or vice emit breath 2080: 3
panting v. 14: 1
passes current all over ..2090:12
peace, O V. 873: 5
perfected by education ..2088: 2
political v. in man 1541: 8
popular regard pursue 728:21
pours each human v. 13:12
proceeds through toil 1061:17
progressive v. 1136: 1
rate their v. high 218: 1
redeem us from v. 2094:11
repose of mind 2088:17
remains bright and eternal 2092:15

Virtue, *continued*
requires no reward 2091:12
requires rough passage ..2090:19
saint-like v. 1111:21
'scapes not calumnious strokes 2091: 2
seek v. first, be bold 1336: 5
seek v. for its own sake ..2091:14
seldom spared by fortune .715: 9
sell not v. for wealth ...2089: 6
should be practised 2088:19
show v. her feature 10: 6
sign of noble soul 2089:24
sina qua non of pleasure 1509: 1
social v., pigs in litter ..1859: 5
some by v. fall 2082: 8
song to cheer God along 2233: 8
starves while vice is fed 2081: 8
stronger guard than brass 2088:18
struggles after fame 2091: 3
such v. hath my pen ..1522: 5
sufficient for happiness ..2092: 9
suspect those who affect one v. 1684: 4
takes root in any place ..2089:16
that possession would not 1561: 2
that transgresses 2082: 9
tho' in rags, will keep me warm 1568: 4
thou simular man of v. ...949: 6
through v. road to peace 2092: 7
'tis v., wit, and worth ..2246: 4
to conserve friendship 743: 5
to repent 1460: 4
to restrain tongue 2026:15
to soul as health to body ..2088:10
to v. no way ill 2089:17
to withstand highest bidder 200: 5
too painful an endeavor ..422:18
treads paths that end not 2092:13
tries our v. by affliction 15:19
trips on poverty 2094:10
unadulterated v. 1106: 6
valour, wisdom sit in want 653: 9
verily found in voices ..2099: 3
victorio.s resi tance 2088: 1
what v. breeds iniquity ..811:16
when concealed no value 2089: 2
when was public v. found 1467:14
where does v. go to lodge 2089:10
whet v., straps our vice ..2081:18
which alone is free 2090: 5
which depends on opinion 2093:21
which requires to be guarded 2094: 2
who would embrace v. 625:20
whose v. is a song 2233: 8
will catch by contact ...2080: 3
will endure to posterity ..2092:14
will keep me warm 1568: 4
wins eternal fame 2091: 6
with v. conquer world ..2090: 8
withers without opposition 2094: 8
without v. no happiness ..2092: 6
woo the Angel V. 1698:11
wrapped in my v. 1568: 4
wrapt in my v. 311: 6
Virtue's: age is v. season ...24:15
force can cause obey 716:14
steely bones 240:11
Virtues: all the v. but one 2201:11
atone her husband's sins 2144: 4
authentic v. 2080: 2
be to her v. very kind ..2194: 3
but vices in disguise 2081: 3
court v. highest rate 326:13
curse on his v. 2093:20
despise who have no v. ..2081: 3
do not distrust thy v. ...1919: 9
dying never 1522: 6
fam'd for v. he had not ..2094:12
for several v. women 652: 8
formed magic of song 1536: 7
from passions shoot 1457: 3
greatest v. splendid sins .2081:17
his v. plead like angels ..2093:18
his v. were his arts 2093: 9
if v. did not go forth 588:17
implanted by nature 2088: 2
joined to dwindled soul ..976: 8

Water, *continued*
inspir'd w. warmth of wine 1315:14
lead a horse to w. 930: 9
like w. from duck's back 1639:19
like w. off duck's back ..2043:10
little drops of w. 2040:19
make w. run up hill 1683:10
more w. glideth by mill ..1305: 2
never miss w. till well dry 2124:12
no worse w. than w. sleeps 2126: 4
noblest element 2124:20
now in the w. 1443:10
of affliction 16: 7
only makes you wet 45:14
owns a power divine 1315:14
past cannot make mill go 1304:10
pure w. best of gifts 2125:16
saw its God and blush'd ..1315:14
seek w. from a stone 119: 9
seeks w. in the sea 2125: 3
soft w. hollows rock 2126:10
spilt on the ground 2125: 4
that drives mill, decayeth 1305: 1
that pours silver 2124:13
to give a cup of w. 2125:18
too much of w. hast thou 1976: 9
turn'd to wine 1315:14
unstable as w. 2124:17
washes everything 2125: 2
we have w. and porridge ..518: 1
when w. chokes you ..2125: 9
where least expected 2125: 7
whose name was writ in w. 1033: 9
will tell how deep 2124:21
will wear away stone 2126: 7
willy-nilly flowing 1139: 6
wonderful w. curled 2241: 9
would certainly wet us ...1628:19
Water-breaks: dancing down thy w. 201: 1
Water-carrier when old 492: 2
Water-drinkers: let w. tell 2052: 3
Water-drops: melt myself away in w. 1039: 4
women's weapons, w. 1977:18
Water-gruel, healing power 872:10
Water-land of Dutchmen ..904: 7
Water-Mill: listen to the W. 1304:10
Water-right 1731: 5
Water-tanks: song heard at w. 2071:4a
Water-wagon is the place for me 504:15
Waterbrooks: hart panteth 108:12
Waterflies, diminutives ...2242:11
Waterloo **2126**
every man meets his W. 2127: 1
fatal W. visible 2127: 1
put back the clock 2126:13
won on playing-field of Eton 2127: 5
world-earthquake, W. 2127: 3
Waterloo's ensanguined plain 1770: 4
Waterman, looking one way 420: 2
Waters are Well of Life ..792:14
as cold w. to thirsty soul ..1398:10
by sweet w. where dove sips 1989: 6
by the w. of Life we sat 1212: 5
calm the troubled w. 2125: 8
deep w. noiseless are 842: 5
earth's width of w. span ..874:15
fishing in troubled w. 670:11
from Rio Grande's w. ..2116: 9
he drinketh strong w. 499:15
how fleet the w. flash 22:11
I cast thee on the w. 191: 4
leadeth me beside still w. ..790:18
many w. cannot quench love 1190:13
moving w. of his mind ..1534: 5
noise of many w. 2125: 1
o'er the glad w. of sea 1776: 7
oil on troubled w. 1775: 1
on a starry night 37: 4
once more upon the w. ..1776: 6
returning 21: 2
Waters, *continued*
smooth w. run deep 2126: 5
smoothly the w. kist 2152:10
still w. run deep 2126: 2
stolen w. are sweet 1618: 2
till w. refuse to glisten ..202:18
time's w. will not ebb .. .2004:14
unpath'd w. 1772:18
walks w. like thing of life 1813:13
wear the stones .. ... .2126:11
were winding-sheet 629: 7
with w. past impel mill ..1304:10
Watt who told King George 1574:10
Wattle, Captain 492: 9
Watts: put W. into 'em ...62: 8
Wave: ambition like the w. ..47:11
blind w. break in fire ..1502:13
every w. with dimpled face 1914:15
for a winding sheet a w. 1815: 5
from which no return 389:11
glassy cool translucent w. 848: 4
more credit in a w. 2197: 6
never was w. more just ..1815:14
past cannot be called back 2009: 2
quickly lost in sea ... .. .625: 7
salt w. 1772:17
that echoes round the world 2085:12
that has passed 1459: 3
that reflects in bosom 874: 8
walk o'er western w. 1402: 1
Wavering, sooner lost 1265:11
Waves breaking on a farther shore 1554: 9
breaking w. dashed high ..1775: 7
but came the w. 1375: 8
came shining up 585:15
clasp one another 1050: 5
contentious w. 1954: 5
dance to the music 2241: 8
like as the w. make toward the pebbled shore 1315: 9
number w. of the sea 971: 8
of thy sweet singing 1889: 1
of woe 2176: 7
over-matching w. 1949:18
salt w. dashing o'er him 1815:11
smooth flow the w. 1852:19
tainted with death 2064:22
though the ocean w. divide ..2:14
thy proud w. be stayed ..1772: 5
what are wild w. saying . 1773:11
wherever w. can roll 1777:14
wild w. whist 361: 4
Waving the bloody shirt 65:12
Wawl and cry 164: 5
Wax and parchment 1080:14
frequent in tapers 1654:16
if we are w. or tallow 375: 9
man of w. 1246:11
'tis the bee's w. 143:12
to be moulded 875:12
to receive 875:12
Waxed as red as rose 172: 3
Way: always a best w. ..532: 9
broad is the w. to destruction 892: 9
clear the w. 1992:12
dim and perilous w. 1311: 7
dull w. which leads to nothing 1414:6a
every w. makes my gain ..750:14
farthest w. about 1734:15
fret w. at last to sea 474:14
he'll find a w. 1: 3
heav'n's wide pathless w. 1343: 8
high w. and a low 1433: 4
himself will choose 20:17
I'll find a w. or make one 1734: 4
it is God's w. 416: 1
lead the w. 589: 7
let the w. wind up hill ..2103: 7
lies where God knows ..1215: 9
life's bewildered w. 1135: 4
long is the w. and hard ...892:10
long, uncomfortable w. ..1734:11
longest w. round 1640: 1
lovely w. to slimepit 892:13
make w. for liberty 1104: 7
making the hard w. sweet 314:16
marshall'st me the w. 1095: 7
Way, *continued*
must be straight out 1832:20
narrow is the w. to life ...892: 9
never in the w. 1799: 4
next w. home 1734:15
no ready w. to virtue 2090:16
no w. barred to virtue ..2089:11
noiseless tenor of their w. 1135: 4
o' wisest men 217:21
of a man with a maid ..2200: 8
of a serpent upon a rock ..2209: 8
of a young man 2209: 8
of all earth 375:17
of all flesh 375:17; 680:14
of sinners made plain 1830:11
of superior man threefold 1245: 4
of transgressors is hard ..1831: 1
out of the world's w. 1421: 8
pleasing w. not right 887:13
pleasure's devious w. 1509: 8
pretty Fanny's w. 1258: 6
primrose w. 892:13
right w. to go 1727: 2
see my w. as birds 1434:11
spring-like w. 41: 4
Stonewall Jackson's w. ..1005: 3
surest w. to get 1562: 8
surest w. to hit a woman's heart 2214: 8
takes her listening w. 525: 4
that I find the w. 378:11
that leadeth to destruction 892: 9
that leads from darkness 1151: 8
that w. madness lies 1231: 8
that's the eftest w. 863:18
there lies your w., due west 2131: 6
thorny w. to heaven 1596: 3
to be happy 334:17
to dusty death 2262:11
to God by ourselves ..785: 5
to Heaven of like length ..885:17
to Hell's a Heaven 892:11
to rest is pain 1734:15
was long and weary 1168:11
went her unremembering w. 1455:13
whence I shall not return 389: 5
wrong w. more reasonable 2260:16
wrong w. to the wood ..2260:15
you've such a w. wid you 1592: 7
Way-station between too little and too much 855: 2
Ways: God's w. seem dark 292:12
hard are w. of truth ...2055:13
he of their wicked w. ..1591: 1
Heaven's w. 885: 9
justify God's w. 44:13
justify w. of God to men 793:12
loved the good old w. 618:20
many w. to fame 625: 2
neither are your w. my w. 1990:18
nine and sixty w. 1525:11
of Death are soothing 391: 4
of Heav'n dark 1645:7a
of hoar antiquity 83:12
of men must sever 1796:12
of pleasantness 1471:12
of the gods are slow 1708:12
old w. safest and surest ..303:12
parting of the w. 260: 3
sixty-seven w. in which woman can like a man 2208:13
that are dark 349:10
that wind and wind 1037:4a
there are w. and means ..294: 4
there be triple w. to take 1814:3; 2209: 8
to have thee slain 346:13
two w. of getting on 1930:12
uncertain w. unsafest 476: 2
vindicate w. of God 1251:13
windy w. of men 496:12
world's w. 989: 8
Wayward is this foolish love 1203:16
We: all people we like 707: 4
put it down a we 2221:10
say ve for we 769: 3
Weak and the gentle 981: 5
apt to be cruel 346: 2

Wed: December when they w. 1274: 5
neither plight nor w. 394:13
or cease to woo 2217: 4
some ladies w., some love 2179:14
would not w. her for gold 2189: 7
Wedded all the world ...1485:18
if w., much discomfort ..1120: 7
she was some years 943:12
Wedden after their estate 1268:12
Wedding
See also Marriage
is destiny 1265: 7
just another fatal w. 2295: 1
never w., ever wooing ..2217: 4
Wedding-banquet to skies ..1508: 4
Wedding-bells: hear the mellow w. 152:20
no w. for her 2291:10
Wedding-garment: ours is w. 291: 1
Wedding-ring: circle of a w. 1275:11
Weddings: fair weather w. 1272:15
make a lot of people sad ..2289: 8
Wedges of gold 1816: 5
pearl-white w. 2027: 9
Wedlock and padlock same 1273:13
brings to nightcap 33:11
calls it w., veils sin 1265: 1
compared to public feasts 1278:15
desire and repent of w. ..33:11
forced but a hell 2144: 8
hath likened been 1278:15
holy w. in a happy wife 1275: 3
honest w. glorious thing 1275: 1
in w. wake 2139: 6
is a padlock 1262:12
lane no turning 1262: 5
never laid claim to w. 1265: 1
of minds 1264: 5
of silence and light 688: 6
tames man and beast 33:11
very awful thing 1276: 2
without love, some say ..1269:11
women angels, w. devil ..1275: 7
Wednesday: he that died o' 919:12
is Wheeson week 2217: 7
Weed 2130
basest w. outbraves dignity 2130:11
duller than the fat w. ..1925:13
evil w. is soon grown 2130:13
flower in disguise 2130: 5
forego the Indian w. 2019: 9
he that bites on every w. 2130: 7
I am as a w. 440: 3
ill w. groweth fast 2130:13
Indian w. withered quite 2017:12
o'ergaes the corn 2130: 7
one ill w. mars pottage ..2130: 7
pernicious w., whose scent 2018: 3
soon prospers vicious w. 2130:13
what I thought flower only w. 2130: 4
who art so lovely fair 2130: 9
Weeds and tares of my brain 1441: 8
are shallow-rooted 2130: 8
away with slavish w. 1802: 1
bred among w. of my brain 2250:17
call us not w. 2130: 1
discern w. 184:11
great w. do grow apace ..2130:10
grow in sustaining corn ..2130: 3
idle w. fast in growth 2130:10
in sable w. appear 747: 4
of vice without power ..2079: 8
scented wild w. 822:12
settled age his w. 25: 3
suck soil's fertility 2130: 8
take root with flowers 811:16
that strewed victor's way ..628:13
wind-shaken, remain 1744:18
winter w. outworn 512:19
Week is forever and a day ..2:13
keep a w. away 4: 7
of teen 1019: 5
Week-days trail 1752:13
Weep and waste within ..2176:17
and you w. alone 1077:13
Weep, *continued*
away the life of care 221:12
awhile if ye are fain 404: 4
better to w. at joy 1973:11
but not wail 405: 8
for joy kind of manna ..1018: 7
I w. for you, Walrus said 1974:10
I will w. for nothing ...1977:15
I'll w., and word it 1885: 2
if thou wilt 1972:13
man may w. on wedding day 1272: 6
more because w. in vain 1974:14
no more, my lady 1034:6; 1978:13
no more, nor sigh 1978:13
not for those 410:14
not, my wanton 1974:15
not, O friend 405: 6
some w. because they part 1453:18
such a little thing to w. 1974:11
to w., to sleep 1138: 5
when we are born 407: 4
why do you w. 415:24
why sit still and w. 3: 6
with them that w. 1886: 9; 1957:15
ye not for the dead 404:10
Weeper: make the w. laugh 2025:20
Weeping
See also Tears
and gnashing of teeth ...2027:12
comes in w. 1242: 2
disperses our wrath 1974: 4
I have full cause of w. 1978:11
is the ease of woe 1973:20
learn w., laugh gaining ..1077:11
make little w. for dead ...404:10
may endure for a night ..1018:18
mocking your untimely w. 2262: 7
no w. save when died ..1040: 8
of an heir laughter 985:13
they are not long, the w. 1137: 4
thou sat'st 407:11
thy w. is in vain 405:12
with w. and with laughter ..83:20
Weeping Cross: come home by W. C. 1325: 9
Weeps before maiden's bier 2263:16
each w. for himself 843: 4
why these w. 1973:13
Weib: das W. Meisterstücke 2182: 3
hat tausend Schritt voraus 2187:11
Weiber, Wein und Gesang 2160: 1
Weiberkopf: was hatt ein W. erdacht 2191: 5
Weigh, not count, judgments 1023:10
Weighed in the balances ..612: 7
Weight: able to pull his w. ..56: 9
bends beneath w. of thought 122:10
bird's w. breaks infant tree 2035: 8
bosom-w., stubborn gift 1498:21
bowed by w. of centuries 1066: 9
burden'd with like w. of pain 17:10
of any misery 592: 3
of chance-desires 725: 2
of too much liberty 1107:11
owes all its w. to lead 2174:14
pay for offence by w. 115:10
thrice their w. in gold 189:11
worth thy w. of gold 2246:17
Weights: sink with their own w. 2172:14
Weird may be her ain, jo ..1222: 8
Weisheit in der Wahrheit 2162:10
Weiss hat viel zu sorgen 1059:11
man w. nichts als selbst erfahrt 593:20
Weke, weke! so cries pig 1954:19
Welcome
See also Hospitality
all wonders 261: 5
as breath of flowers 329: 8
as flowers in May 681:25; 932: 6
bear w. in your eye 932:14
bids you a w. adoo 1454:11
coming, speed parting guest 932: 2
deep-mouth'd w. 908: 7
ever smiles 2007: 8
Welcome, *continued*
general w. from his grace 933:10
Highland w. 1767: 4
his w. was the same 2275:1a
is the sweet 1953: 9
makes a merry feast 660: 3
old sea w. waiting 1779: 4
out of silence pick'd a w. 1822: 1
peaceful evening in 582: 1
thee, and wish thee long 1283: 8
to our house 933:10
unclouded w. of a wife 2141:10
warmest w. at an inn ..989: 6
Welcomes: hundred thousand w. 933:10
little fishes in 947: 1
Welfare: country's w. first concern 1465: 5
of a people 58: 9
Welkin: amaze the w. 2116:10
made the w. ring 2281: 4
make w. answer 526: 1
starry w. 694:10
Well: all is not w. 1948:16
all w. if life remains 923:12
all w. that ends w. 538:12
every man w. or ill 308:22
I was w. 468:13
if you are w., it is w. ..870:17
is it w. with the child 252:13
let w. alone 1640: 3
never get w. if you pick 1542: 4
not how w. but how much 2253: 8
not so deep as a w. 2248:12
of eloquence 248:18
of English undefiled 248:18
of homely life 1568:14
of lofty thought 238: 9
of love 139: 4
of music and melody 1367: 4
of true wit truth itself ..2050:12
say you are w. 872: 3
till the w. runs dry 2124:11
to do better than w. 48: 3
what will be will be w. ..1436:10
where Truth keeps court 2052: 4
where truth lies hidden ..2051:23
word of malice 1580: 3
Well-born: who is w. 68:13
Well-bred and ill-bred 1256:16
everyone thinks self w. 1258: 8
to needless scrupulosity .1259: 9
Well-connected: scorn the w. .70: 5
Well-doing: weary in w. ..807: 6
weary in w. 1494: 3
Well-dressed: in good spirits when w. 485:22
man 491: 2
sense of being w. gives feeling of tranquillity 485:22
Well-favoured: very w. ...2265: 7
Well-informed: to be w. ..1057: 9
Well-read man 1675: 7
Well-spring in wilderness 729:14
Weller's knowledge of London 1169: 4
Wellington, Duke of ..2130
Wells of thought 184: 6
purest w. of English undefiled 248:18
spider-peopled w. 1026: 1
Welt: nimm die W. wie sie ist 2238:11
will betrogen sein 420: 7
Weltering in his blood 621: 8
Weltgeschichte Weltgericht 900:10
Wench: brown w. lay kissing 2105: 9
in flame-coloured taffeta ..2008: 5
misbehav'd w. 454:11
pretty w. no land 607:11
take heed of a young w. 2179:19
Wench's: white w. black eye 605: 6
Wencher marries to live better 1270: 7
Wenches for the marriage-day 1283:13
Went: she came and w. ..76: 1
we w. across, but they won't come across 1553: 4

Whited sepulchres 948:13
Whitee man-cipation 1841: 9
Whiteness: in angel w. 173: 5
not w. of years 1345: 4
of his soul 725:6; 1890:12
Whiter than driven snow 489: 6
than snow on raven's back 1857: 5
Whitewash 1645:11
Whitewashed 1547:13
Whither away 247:16; 1642:20
away so fast 2089:20
goest thou 1637:15
willy-nilly blowing 1139: 6
Whiting to a snail 1409: 6
with tail in mouth 597: 1
Whitman, Walt 2132
once said to me 968:15
Whittier, John Greenleaf 2132
rather W. than I 1687:22
Whittle the Eden Tree 103: 7
Whittler: American hero ..955: 7
Whoa! Emma 2290: 8
Whole and perfect 1465:14
as the marble 657:20
call the w. a part 107: 3
equal to scum of parts 430: 8
in himself 831: 2
need not a physician 465:10
one beautiful perfect w. 1187: 8
parts of one stupendous W. 1390:14
Wholesome as air 329: 8
Wholesome-profitable 740:14
Whom are you 529: 4
Whoopee: makin' w. 2289: 8
Whore 2133
and a bottle 1960: 7
be strong in w. 2134: 4
bought name of w. dearly 2133:16
ever your fresh w. 2133:17
I cannot say "w." 2134: 3
is proud 2134: 7
like a w., unpack my heart with words 1952: 8
made a noble dame a w. ..49:13
man who makes w. keeps woman 2133:11
most noted w. alive 71: 3
once a w., ever a w. 2133:10
passion drive thee to w. 2080: 6
she cries w. first 2133: 3
why dost thou lash w. ..949: 6
world postponed to w. ...2134: 5
young w. old saint 1755:13
Whoremaster: abandoned w. 1513:16
of man 1915:10
Whores: back-doors make w. 94:13
of kings 2016: 6
only w. go to plays 1910: 9
till all w. burnt alive 2133:12
used painting 2133:18
Whoresons: sly w. 1876: 3
Whoring: fruit of w. 2134: 4
tokens of w. 2133: 8
Whorl: pink w. of shell ..1526: 6
Why and wherefore 1681: 4
and wherefore in all 226: 3
and W. not knowing 1139: 6
is this thus 1645: 2
not knowing 1139: 6
plain as way to parish church 1681: 8
should the beautiful ever weep 2286: 2
should the spirit 1607:11
Wicked all at once 2134:17
always ungrateful 984: 3
cause I's w. 2135:10
cease from troubling 391:6; 886: 9
flee when no man pursueth 2134:22
go astray and fall 2135:11
God bears w., not forever 2134:10
God cannot procure good for w. 2135:12
God help the w. 2155:14
Wicked, *continued*
have their proper Hell ..704: 1
how w. we are 810: 5
let but thy w. out go ..1169: 2
let w. forsake his way ..2134:14
little better than one of the w. 288:16
man his own hell 2134:11
name of the w. shall rot ..1029:15
never w. man was wise .2134:12
never wonder to see men w. 1810: 8
no peace unto the w. 2134:14
people go to hell 892:14
seen w. in great power ..2135: 1
something w. this way comes 1947: 1
surprised to find 280:12
to wish to appear w. 2135: 2
was their mind 715:14
Wickedness 2134
all the w. in our convent 1760:15
all w. is weakness 2134:20
be sweet in his mouth ..2024: 4
call w. by its own terms ..218:15
comes of ill teaching ...2063:16
ever to flee 257:14
felicity and flower of w. ..2134: 9
how cowardly w. is 2135: 9
licentious w. 2135: 8
method in man's w. 2134:17
of luxury 2062:10
proceedeth from wicked 2135: 4
of woman 2187: 7
ye have ploughed w. 2134:13
Wickersham report 1619: 1
Wickliffe, John 2135
Wicks: three w. to life ..1140: 2
Wider: no w. than heart is wide 2241: 6
Widow 2135
and the orphan 464:13
at Windsor 2082:12
better soldier's w. 1862: 8
comes to cast her weeds ..2136: 4
has firm faith 617:19
he that will woo w. 2136:18
he'll have a lusty w. now 2137: 2
husbandless w. 657: 1
live no longer than w. weeps 1340:10
Machree 2136: 9
Malone 2136: 9
marries w. and two daughters 2136: 3
marry w. before she leaves mourning 2136:19
marry w. make fortune ..2136: 8
Molly Stark's a w. 62: 6
must be a mourner 2136:17
never w. say him nay ..2136:15
of doubtful age 2136: 2
some undone w. 1955:14
that has cast rider 2136: 5
thou must be mine 2136:18
to one safe at home 2136:12
woo w. day and night ..2137: 1
woo w. must not dally ..2136:18
Widow-comfort: my w. ...1874: 6
Widower can't be too careful 2136:16
matrimony w. escapes ...1262: 9
prove a w. shortly 2135:17
Widowhood is pitiable 2136:17
way to have a w. 2136:20
Widows against second marriage 1279: 6
be very careful o' w. 2135:16
bereaved and relieved ..2136:14
each morn new w. howl 1887: 7
from undone w. derive wit 2136:11
grass w. 2136:14
most perverse creatures ..2135:16
too wise for bachelors ..2136:13
we'll play at w. 2136: 1
what creatures w. are 2135:18
Width: not w. but weight 1134:11
Wife 2137
affectionate and fair 2138: 7
affectionate to your w. ..2144:10
Wife, *continued*
all the world and his w. 2237: 6
alone unsullied credit wins 2144: 4
always at home as if lame 2143:12
and children charges 632:11
and children disciplining .632:11
and he separate rooms ..1761: 4
and health man's wealth ..2140:16
at my side 908:15
bad w. bitterest curse 2141: 6
baker's w. bite of a bun 1800: 6
barren w. endears to friend 2137:15
be w. and widow but once 2136: 7
best or worst fortune 2141: 6
better half 2137:18
better your w. be musical 2139: 4
blessed that hath virtuous w. 2140: 1
burden imposed by law .2137:19
Cæsar's w. 213: 2
cheerful w. joy of life ...2140:16
children and friends 633: 5
choose w. by your ear ..2138:11
choose w. upon Saturday 2138:15
choosing good or ill w. 2138:14
circumspection in choosing w. 2138:14
cleave unto his w. 1262: 7
common to have foolish w. 2143: 1
complaining of servants 1799: 2
constellation of virtues 2139:17
cursed with ugly w. 2142: 8
damn'd in a fair w. 2142:13
dead w. under the table 2147: 4
dearer than the bride 2140:12
domestic, good and pure 2205: 3
down ladder choosing w. 2139: 8
easily govern thy w. 2144:14
enjoy fair w. 1270: 8
every w. to see Paris ..2138: 4
fair helpmates 2137:18
fair, rich and young 2200: 5
fair w. without fortune 2138:10
forever reckoning merits 2142: 5
from a black man keep w. 1650: 5
from Adam's w. that proved a curse 2187: 2
gentle, loving, trusting w. 2140:10
give w. a yard, she'll take an ell 2144:12
giving honor unto w. 2138: 2
good w. and health, wealth 871:10
good w. is a good portion 2140: 1
good w. never grumbles 2143:12
grows flippant 1276: 1
half so delightful as w. 2139:16
hath w. hath strife 2142: 1
he that loves not w. 633: 6
he that takes w. takes care 2142: 1
here lies my w. 2147: 2
his w. wore the breeches 2145: 5
honeysuckle w. 2142: 4
I hae a w. o' my ain ..2139:12
I need not blush to show 2138: 8
ideal w. has ideal husband 2138: 5
in choosing w. trust not 2138:13
in election of a w. 2138:14
in every port a w. 1778: 3
in wedding-sheets and shroud 2188: 9
is fair, feeds well 1006:17
is key of the house 2137:13
keep your w. indoors 2137:16
kill a w. with kindness ..1035:17
lawful plague of life ...2142: 9
lawfully begotten w. 2137:14
lets his w. abroad 695:12
lets w. go to every feast ..2144:15
light w., heavy husband ..2143: 1
little w. well-willed 1721:11
looking-glass to husband 2143: 9
love your neighbour's w. ..212: 3
loving w. best possession 2140: 2
luck to find modest w. ..2139: 2
make me your w. 2292: 6
makes false w. who suspects her 2137: 6
makes husband her apron 2143:11
man who strikes his w. 2179: 8

Wife, *continued*
me wrong with all 864: 5
my w. gone to the country 2143: 4
my w. my plague 2142: 9
my w. won't let me 2290: 3
neither doat nor doubt w. 1266:13
next to no w. 633: 9
next to no w., good w. 2140: 3
nice w. and a back door 2124: 6
no better than she should
be 2138: 6
no remedy against a w. ..2141:15
no such comfort as w. ..2139:13
not to be chosen by eye 2138:11
not too lettered 2139: 3
nothing better than w. ..2139:10
nothing half so delightful 2139:16
oblig'd to Heat a W. 945:3a
of earthly goods, w. best 2141: 6
of Englishman blessed ..549: 4
of patient man, patient ..2137: 7
of thy bosom 2139:18
of twenty years 728: 8
one good w. in world 2139:14
one w. too much for most 2142: 2
peculiar gift of heaven 2140:15
preaches in her gown ..2146: 9
prudent w. from the Lord 2140:15
right to see Paris 1453:11
Roy's w. of Aldivallock ..2142: 3
rules husband by obeying 2143:11
rules the roast 2146: 1
safest by husband stays 2143: 7
servingman's w. may
starve 1800: 6
seventh w. being buried 2147: 3
should be another's w. ..1007:15
should keep within door 2205: 3
sleep with his w. 2137:19
sovereign bliss, a w. 2139:10
stay from w. seven years 1275:13
sweet wee w. o' mine 2139:12
teacher, comrade, w. 2141: 7
tell w. all he knows 2144:13
tells his w. news 2144:13
thanked God my w. was
dead 2273: 2
that galling load, a w. ..2141:14
that pretty w. of thine ..2160: 1
thy w. hath dream'd 2095: 3
tin canister tied to tail 2141:14
to be husband's judge ..2143: 6
to please a w., when her 2142:10
to solace fatigues of life 2140: 4
to soothe his years 2140: 3
to take w. as companion 2138: 9
true and honorable w. ..2141: 2
true and humble w. 2143: 9
ugly w. will be bane ..1265:13
uncumbered with a w. ..2137: 9
was pretty, trifling, weak 2146: 8
weaker vessel 2138: 2
well-choosing of his w. 2138:14
what can you want with
young w. 2139: 5
what do you want with my
w. 97: 8
what w.? I have no w. 2141: 4
when his w. talks Greek 2139: 3
when w. is May, husband
June 1269: 1
when w. lives as in jail 1277: 5
white horse and fair w. 1006:17
who from his w. will run 2145: 3
who hath fair w. needs
eyes 2142:13
who never caused me grief 2140:11
whom he knows false 2143: 3
whoso findeth a w. 2140:15
why blind man's w. paint 2075:23
wicked w. not chasted ..910: 2
widowed w., wedded maid 1234: 6
with such a wit 2173:15
with w. two days pleasure 2188: 9
worst that may be 2141:13
you, my w. govern me ..816: 6
Wig: first part of oratory 1439:10
that flowed behind 490:10
Wight: if ever such w. were 2180:19
she was a w. if ever 2180:19

Wight, *continued*
to graceless w. by graceless
squire 46: 3
who reads not 2221: 8
Wights: O scaly, slippery
w. 670: 5
Wigwam built of shamrocks
green 2285: 6
Wild as any hare 1230: 7
by starts 'twas w. 436:17
exquisitely w. 253:16
madly w. or oddly gay ..1258: 6
that no man knows 377:21
with all regret 1687:19
Wild-beast of force 706:10
Wild-cat: sleeps more than
w. 1843:16
Wild-cats in your kitchens 2183: 3
Wild-fowl: fearful w. 1163:12
opinion concerning w. ..1894: 9
Wild-geese fly that way ..2161: 9
Wild-goose chase 1643: 7
Wild-wood: deep-tangled w. 252: 1
Wilde, Oscar 2147
jokes on Oscar W. 1010: 6
Wilder, the more virtuous .1240: 8
Wilderness: in such a w.
as this 1213: 9
in w. a lodging place 1873: 2
in w. never alone 1873: 7
of drifting sands 434:10
of faults and follies 652: 9
of human flesh 2277: 3
of single instances 1087: 8
of steeples peeping 1168:16
of sweets 1952:12
were Paradise enow 1213: 9
what w. earth appears ..2242: 6
Wildernesses: desert w. ...634:13
Wildflower: one w. he's
plucked 316:16
Wildings of husband's
heart 1262:19
of nature 683: 4
Wilds: sandy perilous w. ..246:12
Wile: evil habit's earliest
w. 846: 3
Wiles and guiles 2197:13
of foreign influence 59: 9
pretty infant w. 120: 9
reconciles by mystic w. ..1188:15
skilled in w. 349:15
subtle w. 2188: 7
Wilful will do't 2148: 1
Wilhelm II 2147
Wilkinson: Mr. W., a
clergyman 1590: 1
Will 2148
all is possible to w. 2148: 3
and Mary on the coin 545: 6
be there w., wisdom finds
way 2148: 6
bow before the Awful W. 1705: 1
boy's w. is the wind's ..196: 7
by reason sway'd 1679:19
can do anything 2148: 3
cannot be compelled 2149: 7
compel all to my w. 2149: 2
complies against his w. ..1426:13
deliver w. from wilfulness 2149:11
determines, not intellect 2149: 4
do it against your w. 2149: 3
doing the w. of God 1419:19
each has his w. 1240:12
education of the w. 2148: 4
Emperor's w. is law 768: 7
enkindled by mine eyes ..2148:16
fleshes w. in honor 680: 8
for deed I accept 2148: 9
freedom of w. 2149: 9
had w. but power 1493:12
have w. though w. woe
win 2148: 8
he w. not when he may 1433:10
Heaven's all-subduing w. 1646: 3
His w. be done 1704: 8
if she w., she w. 2204: 5
impartial is w. of heaven 1149: 3
in his w. is our peace ..1475: 3
inflexible 2148:11

Will, *continued*
iron w. of one stout heart 296: 8
is over-ruled by fate 643:18
is the cause of woe 2148: 8
is the man 2149: 5
is the rudder 1253:20
left free the human w. 2149:10
let my w. stand for rea-
son 1680:14
let not thy W. roar 2148:15
man has w., woman way 2204: 8
nae w. to say him na' 1222: 8
no one can rob of free w. 2149: 7
not even in sleep is w. resigned 481:17
not gift makes giver 774:15
not my w. but thine 1704: 8
of man cannot be taken ..2149: 7
of man in his happiness 859:14
of man is free 2149: 9
of the people 1479: 3
or not we w. have w. 2148:10
or wit to do amiss 808:11
over-ruled by fate 643:18
roll'd onward like a wheel 2148: 2
say not w. of man is free 2149: 9
she'll have her w. 1276: 1
sign your w. 379: 5
State's collected w. 1088:17
stripling W. 1804:16
subdued the w. to live 1148: 5
take the w. for the deed 2148: 9
them as w. kin 292: 5
theory against freedom of
w. 2149: 9
thy w. be done 1704: 2
thy w. by nature free 2149:10
thy w. not mine be done 792: 6
'tis what you w. 2148: 3
to be saved means much 1757: 3
to believe 475:16
to deny freedom of w. ..2149: 8
to do, soul to dare 26: 6
to doubt 475:16
to him that w., ways 2148: 6
to husband's w. thine shall
submit 944:12
to incline His w. 1583: 6
to undergo labor win goal 2148:13
to w. what God doth w. 1704: 9
to your w. conformable ..2143: 9
'twas His w.: it is mine ..1704: 9
'twixt w. and w. not 972:19
unbridled w. 1194: 6
unconquerable w. 325:14
voucher for the deed 2148: 9
was his guide 2149: 1
well whose w. is strong 2149: 2
what he w. he does 2148:17
what I w., I w. 2204:11
what I w. is Fate 645: 2
what w. be shall be 1704:10
where there's a w. 2148: 6
where w. ready, feet light 2148: 7
wide as his w. 790:12
without power 2148: 1
you w. and you won't 1696:15
Wille: des Menschen W.,
das ist sein Glück 859:14
nicht die Gabe 774:15
William: you are old,
Father W. 38: 1
Willie is no good 1452:13
Willie's dwelling in the
skies 2286: 3
gone to Heaven 2286: 3
Willing: Barkis is w. 2211:12
I'm w. to learn 2285:11
no one more w. to send me
out of life 415:21
Willingly as kill a fly 692:14
nothing troublesome done
w. 2149: 3
Willow 2149
all under the w. tree 1219:10
and the rose 1137:10
had a song of w. 123: 9
make weeping w. laugh ..2147: 8
not an oak 327:19
shall be thy garland 2150: 2

Winds, *continued*
tempestuous w. of words 2221: 1
that come and go 1139: 2
that never moderation knew 2152:14
to seas are reconciled ..1776: 5
use all w., shift sail 2151: 7
viewless w. 924: 3
wail their feeble moan ..2152: 5
were love-sick with them 1814: 7
what manner w. guideth you 2151: 3
what w. can happy prove 1455: 9
when south w. blow 91:12
where shrill w. whistle ..1777: 1
wild as the w. 2153:11
wild w. of power 30:13
winter w. wearily sighing 2262: 8
with melody are ringing ..1889: 1
with wonder whist 2152:10
wither'd in stagnant air ..365: 8
Windward of the law 1083: 3
Windy side o' the law ..1083: 3
Wine 2154
age gives tone to w. 42: 5
and beasts supplied feasts 659:16
and wassail so convince ..504:11
and wenches empty purses 2159:17
and women into apostasie 2159:16
and women, two plagues 2159:11
bored with good w. 2154:13
bright at goblet's brim ..2159: 3
bring me w. 2156: 6
by savor, bread by heat ..2154:14
cannot know w. by barrel 2154:16
catches you by the feet 2159: 1
counsels seldom prosper ...20:10
cup of hot w. 2155:13
doth God's stamp deface .503:18
drank red w. through helmet 1865: 1
drink w. and have gout ..2154:10
drowned more than the sea 2158:10
drunk my share of w. ..1132:17
erred through w. 498: 2
few things surpass old w. 2159:12
fills the veins 2158: 7
for old w., a new song 1875:16
for thy stomach's sake ..2158: 6
from w. sudden friendship 2156: 7
give me a bowl of w. 2155:16
gives a man nothing 2158:14
gives us liberty 2159:10
golden w. is drunk 437:13
good Falernian w. 2157: 1
good familiar creature ...2155:16
good w. needs no bush ..2155:10
grudge myself good w. ..2156: 3
had warm'd the politician .467:10
has play'd the Infidel 2157:13
I rather like bad w. 2154:13
in bottle does not quench thirst 2154:16
in, murder will out 497:11
in w. there is truth 2155: 9
is a mocker 2159: 2
is drawn 337: 3
is horse of Parnassus 496: 6
is like rain 2156:10
is poured 1711: 3
is the illustrious example 2019: 1
is the milk of Venus 2157: 6
Jug of W., Loaf of Bread 1213: 9
keeps secrets nor promises 2158: 9
kindles wrath 2159: 4
leads the mind forth 2156: 9
let us have w. and women 2159:12
life's best w. last 32: 2
life's heart-warming w. ..1529: 6
like red w. and honey 198: 2
look not on w. when red 2159: 2
makes all sorts at table 2158:11
makes man pleased with self 2158:14
makes men apt for passion 2159: 8
makes us princes 2159:10
maketh a man contemptible 2159: 2
master's w. butler's gift 2155: 7
mellow, like good w. 42: 4
Wine, *continued*
milk of age 2156:5a
mirror of heart 2154: 8
mystic w. of night 1402: 4
never spare parson's w. ..520:12
new w. into old bottles ..2155: 4
no laughter; drinks no w. 2155:15
no w. no love 2159: 6
of aspiration 109: 6
of life is drawn 437:13
of Life keeps oozing 1141: 9
of love is music 1194: 2
of Nature's bottling 499: 1
of their wits wise beguile 2158:12
old w. darkling in the cask 1906:12
old w. desireth new 42: 1
old w. to drink 41:11
old w. wholesomest 42: 6
one friend to dine best w. 2155: 3
open thy throat to w. 2160: 1
out-did the frolic w. 1015:13
pays for his lodging 2154:16
poet's horse accounted ..2157: 6
pour forth cheering w. ..2156: 8
pour out four year old w. 2157: 1
prepares heart for love 2159: 8
racked by w. and anger 504: 2
red w. first must rise 1964:19
sans w., sans song 1131: 9
set forth w. and dice 1132: 7
shows mind of man 2156: 2
smack of every sort of w. 2156: 3
so priceless should not die 2155: 2
some fond of Spanish w. 1968: 5
some liked the w. 1158: 4
Spirit of W. sang in heart 2156:11
strong w. red as blood 523: 4
superiority of w. over Venus 2157:10
supplied our feasts 659:16
sweet is old w. in bottles 2156: 4
sweet w. of youth 409:13
taste no other w. 1017:16
tells of many things 504: 7
that goeth down sweetly 2156: 2
that maketh glad the heart 2158: 4
that quenches every thirst 2002:10
they that tarry long at w. 2159: 2
throws man out of self ..504:10
timely given helps 1285: 9
to madness doth incline ..135: 9
to poet wingèd steed 2157:12
too good to drink 2155: 2
transformeth man to beast 2159: 2
true old man's milk 738: 6
turns man inside outwards 2158:11
turns w. to water 1315:14
unnerves the limbs 2158:12
use a little w. for thy stomach's sake 2158: 6
warmed with the new w. 232:20
was made to drink 2158: 5
wasn't w., 'twas salmon 2154:12
water'd was my w. 1180: 1
what were w. without song 2155: 8
when w. is in, wit is out ...497:11
whets the wit 2158: 2
which belongs to another ..492:10
which Music is 2156: 6
who after w. prates of hardships 495:12
will taste of cask 2155:3a
with w. their whistles wet 491: 9
with w. to extinguish light 1412: 2
women, war 1518: 6
women, w., and song 2160: 1
wondrous good cheer ...2269:17
Wine's old prophetic aid ..2154:15
Wine-bearer draws sweet drink 659: 8
Wine-cellar into book-seller 2154:19
Wine-counsels seldom prosper 20:10
Wine-cup and song 2158: 3
Wine-lees and democracy 218:12
Wine-press of the wrath of God 791:13
trodden w. alone 1874: 1
Wine-skins: made old w. new 1518: 9
Wines: home-made w. that rack the head 909:14
known to Eastern princes 521:16
mislike thy taste 933: 4
of Nature's bottling 499: 1
rich-clust'ring rise 500: 6
some are fond of red w. ..499:18
that had suck'd the fire 2156:13
Wing: always on the w. ..2028:16
Death's imperishable w. ..374:21
fend you with his w. ..724:17
he asks no angel's w. 976:10
high-soaring w. 1477:11
imperfect w. to soar upon ..4: 3
of friendship 2154:11
of friendship never moults 731:10
on the w. of all occasions 2216: 4
one likes pheasant's w. ..1966:13
one w. and Lee other 367: 7
pruned her tender w. ..1526: 3
quill from angel's w. 1477:11
Wings and no eyes 1179:18
and the Boy 1161: 8
are fictions 76:10
as if an angel shook w. ..77: 5
call for their w. 693:17
clap her sooty w. 455: 9
clip his w. 1640:5a
cut the w. of hopes 922: 7
fastened with wax 1730:21
fear gave her w. 655: 9
find w. waiting there 108:14
fine w. made him vain 211:11
fit their light w. 693:14
float upon w. of silence 76:12
fluttering of silken w. ..1206:11
fly upon w. of wind 2151:19
from my w. are shaken ..281:15
held tightly want to go ..318:15
in vale perfumes his w. ..2269:14
knowing that he has w. 162: 4
like a dove 477: 4
mealy w. 735:20
mount with w. as eagles 509:10
of a wren 509: 9
of borrowed wit 1506:10
of false desire 436: 8
of love lose a feather 745: 1
of man's life plumed with feathers of death 429: 2
of the morning 1347:14
of the wind 2151:19
of time black and white ..291: 3
on parchment w. acres fly 1615:10
one black, one white 628:18
one feels bird has w. 161: 1
plumed her shining w. ..1431:11
sailing on obscene w. 113:14
scarlet w. flit once 1202: 9
show not their mealy w. 735:20
soars with his own w. 108:15
soul's w. never furled ..230: 9
that which hath w. 160:10
time's fatal w. fly 1150: 3
to thy speed add w. 863: 6
walketh on w. of the wind 796: 3
White W. 2295: 3
winnowed by w. of liberty 1895:16
with love's light w. did I 1190:10
with rustling w., she 1431:11
Wink and couch 615: 9
as good as a nod 2160:13
at human frailty 2021:18
each at the other 2160:11
hard must he w. 599: 1
in a w. false love turns ..1218:10
not slept one w. 1850:14
there's a time to w. 2160: 4
though I w., not blind ..2160:10
when most I w., then do eyes best see 2160:12
with both our eyes 1596: 6
with weakest eye 2160: 5
you may w. and choose ..2160: 9
Winketh: when the cat w. 223: 9
Winking 2160
at each other w. 1993:19
Winkings of prudence 1652: 9

Wise above that which is written 2164:15
after the event 2168:18
amazed, temperate 1979: 7
among fools 702:12
and discreet withdrew 456:17
and wary was noble pere 2165:10
are swayed by chink 818: 1
as a man of Gotham 2164:21
as far as beard 127: 4
as serpents 2165:12
as she is fair 474:19
be lowly w. 886: 2
be merry and w. 1301:10
be w. today 2166:22
be w. with speed 26:11
be ye w. as fair to see ..2166:17
bearing caught 288:17
before not after the event 2168:17
being w. in time 2169: 2
but fools in love 1180:21
by experience w. 238:20
by rule and experience ..2162: 5
consider the w. rich 1588:2a
dare to be w.; begin 1130:17
darkly w. and rudely great 1239: 3
defer not to be w. 2166:22
design'd by Nature w. 701:10
discovered he is fool 2168:12
does everything nobly ...2162: 7
does not lay up treasure ..773:13
do ne'er live long 411: 1
draws advantage from enemies 701:14
easier to be w. for others 2165: 9
eat and be w. 516:10
enough to play the fool ..701:11
equally w., equally foolish 1058:14
every man wishes to be w. 349:12
few w. by own counsel ..1969:17
foolish and more w. 27:14
foolish things confound w. 701: 8
for himself unwise 2164:18
fortified against attack ..703: 1
free from perplexities ..1245: 4
go where will, w. at home 2166:20
greatly guilty never w. ...843:22
grow w. for spite 2183: 1
grow w., trust woman ..2047: 1
half as w. as he looks ..2129: 8
he is w., follow him 1060: 5
his own best assistant ..2166: 2
how cautious are the w. ..474:13
how w. are fools in love 1180:21
if a minister 72: 3
if we be made content ..616:11
in his own conceit 294:16
in proportion to experience 594: 8
in their own craftiness ..2165: 7
in their own eyes 2165: 6
in words only 2163: 1
is master of his mind ...1312: 7
is not w. in everything ..2165:15
knows himself a fool ...703: 3
learn from their foes 2164: 2
least w. govern most w. ..817: 9
let thy words show thee w. 1823:10
like bees, do grow 184:11
listen to pretty lies 678: 1
little w. best fools 701:11
lived yesterday 1131: 5
loses nothing 1170:14
make jests, fools repeat ..1010: 9
make proverbs 1628: 7
make thyself over w. 1728:15
man does no wrong 13: 2
man is great wonder 2164:20
man is strong 1058: 2
man shuts his door 702: 2
man stays at home 2031: 2
many w. in their own ways 2162: 5
may think what hardly fools say 703: 8
men and fools 700:21
men came from the East ..513:12
men learn by others 701: 3
men profit from fools 701: 3
more happy if less w. 855:17
more lovely growing w. 30:12
Wise, *continued*
more of fool than w. 698:19
ne'er sit and wail 1171: 1
never attempts to govern ..815:14
never does a w. one 244: 7
no man can be w. and love 1180:17
no man ever w. by chance 2166: 3
no man is born w. 2003:10
no one w. at all hours 2165:15
none is born w. 2164:20
none so w. but fool o'ertakes 701:19
nor ever did a w. one 244: 7
not to cherish anger 2162: 3
not to w., the light 1930: 8
not w. in everything 2165:15
nothing lost by being w. 1057: 6
obscurely w., coarsely kind 1036:18
on exercise depend 872: 5
one was w., one was fair 1833: 6
only shows bright side ..2164:13
only w. and good are happy 2092: 6
only w. knows how to love 1181: 5
only w. possess ideas 950:13
only wretched are the w. ..960: 1
out of reach of fortune ..2163: 8
pause awhile to be w. 1058: 7
plead causes, fools decide them 1026: 7
professing themselves w. ..702:14
profit by others' mistakes ..596: 2
rather by ears than eyes ..1912: 3
reckon w. to be wealthy ..2167:2a
reputed w. for saying nothing 1823:10
resist pleasures 1509:13
say nothing in danger ...1822:18
send the w. and say nothing 2218:18
she can be as w. as we ..2193:14
sit in clouds and mock 703: 4
so w. so young do ne'er live long 411: 1
some deemed him w. 2164: 3
some w., some otherwise 2166: 7
takes w. to recognize w. ..2166:13
those who drink old wine 2163:12
through excess of wisdom 701:13
through time 39:20
tired of being always w. 2167:17
'tis folly to be w. 959:22
'tis vulgar to be w. 71:11
to be w. and love 1181: 4
to learn, godlike to create 1108:17
to talk with past hours ..1788:16
too jealous are 701: 9
too w. do ne'er live long 411: 1
too w. to be mistaken 790: 8
too w. to err 790: 8
turns chance to good fortune 2163: 8
twenty w. equal one fool ..703: 6
upright, valiant 1751: 4
venture to be w. 177: 9
wax w. by experience 593:10
what is it to be w. 2168:11
when others we admonish 1024: 9
who can be w. amazed ..1979: 7
who can instruct us 1969: 3
who in heat of blood was w. 2166:14
who invented God 787:19
who knows useful things w. 2162: 3
who reasons wisely not w. 1680:10
who refuse to govern 817:13
who rejoices in what he has 2162:12
who soar but never roam 1073: 5
who wickedly is w. 831: 6
whoever is not too w. is w. 2165:11
will live within w. 2170:12
wisest of w. may err 576:15
wisest who is not w. 703:10
with history of own heart 2022: 7
with w. consort, w. become 2164:19
you look w. 86:10
Wiseacredom both high and low 227:12
Wisely and slow 227: 1
not w. but too well 1222:18
Wiser: be w. than others if you can 2164:10
by always reading 1676:11
by the event 2168:19
every year 1587:12
grew no w. from the past 572:11
grow w. and better 1330: 3
in his own conceit 954: 6
in midst of adversity 1626:10
never seem w. than company 1259: 4
no w. than a daw 1090: 7
no w. than before 1058: 5
not wise to be w. than necessary 2164:10
sadder and a w. man 2164:12
than the children of light 2166:10
today than yesterday 2260:18
we are w. than we know 2164:17
Wisest does not fancy he is so 2168: 6
generally greatest fool ..2162: 8
grieve at loss of time 2008:13
masters ev'n the w. 2194:17
may well be perplexed ..972: 3
men have erred 2201: 7
of the wise 678: 1; 755: 5
preaches no doctrines ...2163:16
sometimes acts weakly ..2165:15
to entrap the w. 421: 6
virtuousest, discreetest ..2185: 5
who is not wise at all 2168:16
Wish 2169
all your w. is woman to win 26:10
believe what we w. 151: 3
eager w. to soar 110: 4
every w. like a prayer 2169: 4
evil w. evil to wisher 2169:11
father to the thought 2169:21
fickle w. ever on wing ..2170: 9
for what does happen 2170: 4
for what I faintly hope 484:20
hopeless w. to flee from certainty 226:17
if a w. wander 5:13
me no worse than I w. thee 2170: 5
no w. profan'd my heart 1227:13
not that which I w. 1588: 1
not to live long 1134:10
not what we w. but want 1588: 1
pious w. 133:11
selfish w. to govern 1684:13
that all men could be free 1841:11
that failed to act 614: 4
to appear clever 280: 8
to earn applause 90:22
to live well 1127:11
to scatter joy, not pain ..1493:17
to sin entails penalty 1830:16
virgin's w. without her fears 1103: 1
warmer days 2161: 8
we w. it ours again 1561: 2
what most we w. fancy near 2169: 5
what you can do 2170: 4
who would w. to die 1142: 3
you have your w. 2169:17
you should w. as we w. ..2169:17
Wished in youth, in old age has 2169: 9
Wishers and woulders 2170: 3
were ever fools 2169:19
Wishes: be my vain w. stilled 1588:12
followed his own w. 20:22
half w. double troubles ..2169: 8
"he w. well" worthless ..2228:14
his restless w. tower 49: 5
if w. were buttercakes ..2169:18
if w. were horses 2169:18
lengthen as sun declines .2170: 9
let w. run away with them 2169:10
never can fill a sack 2170: 3
never filled the bag 2170: 3
never learnt to stray 1135: 4
pays thee naught but w. ..2022:16

Woman, *continued*
what w. can resist praise 1577:10
what w. says to lover 1204: 8
when a w. means mischief 2180:10
when a w. woos 2212:13
when did w. ever invent 2194:14
when lovely w. stoops to 2201:16
when she weeps 2201: 8
when to ill thy mind 2187:14
when w. says she loves ..1184: 7
when w. wants her way ..2195:14
when w. writes confession 2201: 2
where Nature made female 1174: 3
whistling w., crowing hen 2145:11
who always was tired 573:12
who can find virtuous w. 245: 9
who did not care 2217: 6
who did not know 2187:18
who has lost chastity 248: 3
who is the chaste w. 245: 4
who is 't can read a w. ..2179: 3
who knows birth-pangs ..120: 6
who makes her own will 1082:13
who meditates, evil 2192: 9
who teaches w. letters ..2193:12
who tells her real age 40:22
who to w. trusts peace ..2197: 2
who understands 2187:18
whole family 2193:13
why should I sing of w. 2199: 7
wicked w., full of subtlety 2186: 9
will have last word 2200:10
will or won't, depend on 't 2204: 7
wise in short avysement ..2196: 8
wise w. twice a fool 2193: 9
wisely a w. prefers 1200:15
wish is w. to win 26: 9
with a big belly 129: 3
with a past has no future 2181: 9
with brawling w. in house 2200: 4
with cut hair filthy spectacle 847:18
with passion for lying ..2192: 4
with the heart 1255:15
with the Serpent's Tongue 1761:16
with West in her eyes ...1253:14
without a laugh in her ..2189:11
witty w. a treasure 2193:15
wordless w., silent thunder 2199:10
worth purest gold 245: 9
writes mind in postscript 1101: 2
wronged can cherish hate 2203:11
yet think him an angel ..1256: 1
you will be w. set apart 1353: 3
Woman's adventure is man ..15: 9
ambition: to be fair 139:11
behavior is a surer bar.. 2202:12
curiosity 352:17
envy and bigot's rage 564:18
faith and w. trust 2196:15
glories is the heart 1183: 9
lot to be wooed and won .1183: 9
oaths are wafers 1418:16
portion when she loves ..1183:13
story history of affections 1183: 9
story told in eyes 599:22
'tis our w. trade 2190: 7
Woman-adventurer all love or hate 15: 9
Woman-country, wooed not wed 1000:19
Woman-friend! he that ...2197: 2
Woman-hater: there was a w. 2183: 2
Womanhood and childhood 1235: 3
heroic w. 2184:11
illogical nature of w. 2190: 7
Womankind: first that fell of w. 139: 2
more joy discovers 2207:11
one rosy mouth 1018:10
thinks the worst of w. 2187:13
two good days hath she 2188: 9
Womanliness means motherhood 1351:12
Womanly: pure w. 2201:14
Womb: bears in w. seeds of change 231:14
filling w. with heat 1907: 8

Womb, *continued*
forth from mother's w. ..163: 8
holds us for ten months 967: 1
into the virgin's w. 261: 4
of its mother 163: 4
of morning dew 164: 2
of pia mater 961: 7
of the morning 164: 2
of uncreated night 386:10
sin-conceiving w. 1830:12
through foul w. of night 2117: 6
when frae mither's w. 889: 9
Wombs: good w., bad sons 1875: 1
Women adore failures 2207: 1
alas! the love of w. 1183: 8
all w. are ambitious 2192: 2
all w. born so perverse ..2187: 2
all w. can be caught 2208: 4
all w. coquettes 318: 2
all w. fair in the dark ..138: 4
all w. love great men 2207: 1
all w. we need inside 1273:12
American w. 56: 2
and care and care and w. 2239: 9
and coquetry 318: 2
and cowards on land may lie 1780: 2
and elephants never forget 2204: 4
and music never be dated 2180: 1
and wine do make a man 2159:13
and wine, game and deceit 2159:14
are angels, wooing 2212:14
are as roses, whose fair ..1265:11
are door-mats 2178: 5
are dressed in rags 2197: 1
are like pictures 2178: 7
are the gate of hell 2186:12
are w. books 2178: 9
arm selves with weaknesses 2190: 5
as soon as w. belong to us 1221: 5
as w. wish to be who love 1352: 2
ashamed w. are so simple .2144: 3
beat men in evil counsel 2196:12
because of men, w. dislike each other 1254:12
become like mothers 1350:13
being weaker vessels 2138: 2
below men, above children 2178: 3
better or worse than men 2182: 9
bevy of fair w., richly gay 2185: 4
blot all w. out of mind ..2181: 4
born of delay itself 2192: 7
buy cat in the bag 1264: 4
by nature fickle 185: 5
by w. been deceived 2201: 7
can neither do nor say well 2189: 3
can true converts make ..1490: 4
cannot live without 'em ..2188: 5
can't do otherwise than lie 2200:11
chaste w. often proud 245: 4
children of larger growth 2178: 3
chilly w. 558: 1
coloring matter 2185: 6
commend a modest man .1254: 2
counselling of w. 2196: 3
created for comfort of men 2178:13
dally not with other w. ..2179:16
dear, dead w., with such hair, too 847:19
delicate as peaches 1475:18
delight in revenge 2203: 9
delights w. to be asked ..2208: 5
desire what flees them ...2216: 8
desiren liberty 2190:10
dey does de talkin' 1254: 7
discreet w. no ears 455:18
do not spell it so 2202:18
do w. never bear children 2179: 7
done wondering at w. ..2208:16
easily caught by birdlime 2190:11
eat more sparingly 2191:13
English w. not slaves 549: 5
enjoy'd are like romances read 1221: 5
ever thrust to the wall ..2138: 2
ever want something 2180: 2
expect life given to them 1253: 6

Women, *continued*
faded for ages 2183:12
fair w. and brave men ..658:13
feeblest idea of poetry ..1517:11
female pulchritude 132:16
find few friends 2180:18
flattery of w. 2178: 3
framed to make w. false .2198:10
full of wile 2187: 3
giddy w. 2198: 3
good w. bore one 2183: 2
good w. weary of trade ..246: 6
guide the plot 2195:18
happiest w. have no history 2179:15
happy in first marriage ..1279: 5
hard for w. to keep counsel 2199:15
hardly fit for theology ..1984:14
have been devil's tools ..2187:12
have little brains 2194:13
have little difference 2193: 8
have mental reservation ..2190:12
have no characters at all 2192: 8
have no rank 2180:14
have no souls 2190: 8
have no wilderness in them 2190: 6
have one object 141:10
have talent but no genius 2194: 8
have taught eyes to weep 1977:11
have to wait 1254: 4
have tongues of craft 2197: 5
have wills while live 2204: 9
he chose for their looks ..185:11
he's not so much for w. ..2181: 4
her w. fair 551: 1
horses, power and war ..1963:23
however well-bred 1171:16
hydrogen derivatives 2178:12
I learned about w. from 'er 2191:14
I suggest, should marry ..1266: 2
I've seen much finer w. ..1770:16
if w. could be fair 2207: 2
if w. were humbler, men would be honester 1256: 4
in churches, saints 2183: 6
in East w. conceal faces ..2194:13
in their first passions, w. love the lover 1200:18
intelligent w. marry fools 1266:17
jealous of ships 1813: 4
jealous w. are mad 1008: 7
knight-errants to last 258: 5
know no perfect love 1183:14
know that I don't know w. 2199: 3
know to rear children 255:12
laugh up their sleeves 1254: 8
laugh when they can 1977: 5
learned w. to be found ..2194:14
let your w. keep silence 2199:12
liars since world began ..2201: 6
like China-crackers 2207: 8
like men who are docile 2208: 2
like to marry Poem 1264: 1
live under a hard law ..1255: 2
lovely w. dear to rhyme ..2183:12
made to give eyes delight 2178:13
make manners 1254: 5
make stoutest men turn tail 2195: 2
manners of w. 431: 1
many things that w. know 2190: 1
many w., many words ..2199:14
married w. are kept w. ..1264:14
marry because curious ..1265: 6
marry don't want to work 1263:16
may fall, when no strength 1255: 8
men mar in profiting 2178:13
men see you as w. 1813: 4
miles of shopping w. 2192: 4
models of their sex 1705:20
money and wine pleasure 2160: 2
more impressionable 1256: 2
most w. have small waists 2189:12
must trust somebody 2180:18
nature framed w. to be won 2212: 9
necessary evils 2188: 5

Wooing, *continued*
time I've lost in w. 2212: 3
to cross their w. 1915: 5
wedding, and repenting ..1269: 7
Wool: all cry and no w. ..748:10
go for w., come home shorn 1710: 6
he had no w. on de top ob de head 2286: 5
of bat, tongue of dog 245: 1
Wool-gathering: ran a w. 5: 9
Woolen: odious in w. 2076: 3
rather lie in w. 128: 2
Woolen-drapers: wretches .209: 9
Word: acute w. cuts deeper 2224: 3
and a blow 97: 6
as good as his bond 2229:13
as good as his w. 2229:15
as good as the Bank 2229:13
before using fine w. 1927: 2
better one living w. 2218:14
better speak one simple w. 2251: 4
brave w. that I failed to speak 332: 5
bring in new w. by head 2222:14
by seers or sibyls told ..157:12
carve every w. 1898:16
choice w., measured phrase 1899:16
coins new w. with peril ..1926:14
dictatorial w. 79: 9
do not render w. for w. ..2252: 3
drops like a pebble 661: 7
easy to recall stone as w. 2226: 8
enough to raise mankind 2224: 5
every act and w. 8: 6
every fool can play upon w. 1654: 5
every w. becomes poetic .2222: 1
every w. echoes in skies ..2220: 3
every w. once a poem 1515:10
every w. stabs 1898: 1
fitly spoken 2220: 5
flowering in a lonely w. ..2223:10
for lackeys 2181: 7
for me is Joy 1017: 9
for one w. deemed wise ..2219:22
for this you've my w. ..2018:12
found as true as any bond 2229:13
give me right w. 1573:10
good soldier-like w. 2221: 5
grand w., woman 2181: 7
had breath, and wrought 264: 7
have the last w. 2200:10
he was the w. that spake it 262:13
he will perform each w. ..791: 7
honeying at w. of a lord 1856:16
honor his own w. 2229:16
I failed to speak 332: 5
I have thy mother's w. ..1874:11
I thank thee for the w. ..2220: 9
I'll take thy w. for faith 1419: 4
if my w. be sterling yet 1317: 8
ill w. empoisons liking ..1837:11
in earnest good as speech 2218:11
in season like silver apple 2228:15
in season spoken 2220: 4
in your ear 2219:13
is thrall, thought free 2024:20
it is a w. unsaid 855:13
keep the w. of promise ..1621: 5
king's w. King's bond ..1040:11
king's w. more than oath 1040:11
lamp unto my feet 158: 9
laugh'd his w. to scorn ..2098: 6
leave no tender w. unsaid 1130:11
like arrow shot from bow .981: 3
man's physician 2217: 9
many a w. at random spoken 2226:10
men always trust my w. ..2046:16
must accord with deed ..2227: 4
never sincere w. lost 1832: 9
never wanted a good w. 1576:13
no simple w. shall make ..2223:20
no such w. as fail 611:18
nor can one w. be chang'd 1926:12
not spoken does no mischief 2225:13
of fear 347: 4
of "never to return" 591:18

Word, *continued*
of the Lord endureth 158: 8
of whom no w. we hear ..1522: 6
once spoken not revoked 2226: 5
one kind w. to think upon 1455: 7
one short pathetic w. 1951: 3
one w. that's in tune 343:16
passed barrier of teeth ..2027:11
say one w., heart may break 2041:13
second w. makes bargain 1638: 9
seldom is heard a discouraging w. 2296: 5
shall speak for me 1393:16
shame w. with nobler deed 425:11
single w. great design ..2220: 6
skin of a living thought 2217:15
slave debosh'd on tomb ..920:18
some with a flattering w. .1195:15
spake the w. he meant 216:15
spoken arrow let fly 2226: 6
spoken beyond recall 2226: 8
spoken in due season 2220: 5
spoken w. better than books 1440: 5
spoken w. never recalled 2226: 8
stab me with a w. 1824:10
subsides the infrequent w. 2225:18
suit the action to the w. 10: 6
sweet and gentle w. 774:16
tempted with w. too large 1982: 2
there's a fine new w. 2221: 5
they wish to hear 1101:12
thy w. is a lamp 158: 9
to each w. a warbling note 1876: 3
to the wise enough 2172:16
to the wise sufficient 2218:18
torture one poor w. 2221: 8
tricksy w. 2223: 7
true w. spoken in jest 1010:8; 2050: 5
two-edged sword of God's w. 1009:10
unspoken is thine 2024:21
unto the prophet spoken ..157:12
weathercock for ev'ry wind 2221:11
well culled, sweet, apt ...1927: 7
what is w. but wind 2221: 1
whatsoever w. thou speaketh 2224: 7
whose w. no man relies on 244: 7
why waste a w. 1886:11
wisest w. the humblest ..936: 8
without deed vain 2229:11
Word-catcher lives on 2221: 8
Words 2217
acrid w. 1035: 7
actions speak louder than w. ..8: 5
admirable rich w. 1876: 1
all ears took captive 2224: 2
all w., no performance ..2228: 9
alone last forever 2220: 3
and feathers wind carries 2220:13
and performances no kin 2228:22
apt and gracious w. 1302: 5
apt w. have power 2220: 4
are but empty thanks 824: 5
are but wind 2221: 1
are music in my ear 1589:15
are things 2219:19
are thorns to grief 843: 2
are women, deeds are men 2227:13
art is built of w. 101:13
as hard as cannon balls ..304:12
as lucent as the morn ..1520:12
at random flung 1520:12
ate and drank the precious w. 183:11
be roof against the rain ..2099: 3
become thee as thy wounds 2228:21
bedded in good Logic-mortar 2219:20
belly not filled with w. ..155:13
bereft me of all w. 2219: 7
bethump'd with w. 2225: 7
bind w. in double meanings 2223: 2
bolder than deeds 2228:17
borrowed of antiquity ..1927: 1

Words, *continued*
breathe their w. in pain 2051: 9
build no walls 2220:21
burning w. 730:13
but direct 589: 2
but fragments of the glass 1823: 5
but signs of ideas 1068: 9
but wind 1417:16; 2221: 1
but w. are w. 2220:18
butter no parsnips 2220:16
by foolish w. men foolë ken 699:18
by ten w. too long 1911: 2
by thy w. condemned ...2218:16
by winning w. conquer ..1490: 7
by w. mind excited 2219:16
carried new strength 217: 6
clatter of w. pours from 2200: 2
can no man trust 420:10
cannot be cured by w. 2248: 7
care in weaving w. 1926:14
careful with w. 2226: 5
clamor and dissonance ..2217:14
cloth'd in reason's garb ..1100:21
coin what w. they please 1527:11
come forth awrye 1209: 7
come from you in crowd 2224:11
command old w. to wake 2222:16
comprehending much in few w. 198: 7
congeal'd in northern air 2048:16
contentious never lacks w. ..97:10
contradict thoughts 2190:13
copiousness of w. 536: 9
copy my w. into books ...1506: 4
cousin to the deed 2227: 4
cram w. into my ears ..2225: 8
dally nicely with w. 2223: 8
daughters of earth 2227:13
dealt w. like blades 2224: 6
deceive with vain w. 420: 6
decocted into few w. 1628:11
distract more than noises 2220: 8
divide and rend 1824:18
divine of poet 51:10
don't break bones 2220:21
don't chink 2220:17
dread fair w. 678:12
dress of thoughts 2221: 7
dressing old w. new 2222:16
droon the ideas 2223:13
drowsy part of poetry ...1515:12
eat your w. 2219:10
empty w. 2225: 9
enhance gifts with w. 775:14
enough, but little wisdom 2225: 6
enough man shall find ..2221: 2
evil w. corrupt good manners 1258: 4
fair w. break never bone 2224: 1
fair w. butter no cabbage 2220:16
fair w. fat few 1620:21
fair w. make fools 1630: 2
fair w. make me look to purse 2223:17
fair w. never hurt tongue 2223:16
familiar as household w. .1375: 6
fantastical banquet 217:10
far-fetched w. 2221: 3
feather'd with heavenly w. 2196: 7
few were his w. 198: 9
few w. but to effect 2223: 5
fill not the belly 2220:16
fine w., you stole 'em 1506: 8
flow with ease 2253:11
follow upon things 2218: 3
foot-and-a-half long 2222: 3
for music always trash ..1876:14
for your punishment 1658: 3
foul w. and frowns 2215: 9
from airy w. alone 2219:20
from edge of the lips 2219: 2
from good w. thyself refrain 1957:10
from his sweet tongue 1590: 9
from lives not from w. ..1693:14
from sharp w. no fruit ..2224:10
from w. to blows 100: 9
full of w. as a woman 40: 1
give ear to my w. 794: 7

Words, *continued*
glad w. of prose or rhyme 1687:22
glisten and rustle 202:18
good from w. of love 2228:21
good w. and ill deeds 2227: 8
good w. anoint a man 2218:13
good w. cool more than water 2220: 4
good w. fill not sack 2220:17
good w. worth much 2218:13
grievous w. stir anger 78:12
grown so false 2220:19
harsh w., though pertinent 2222: 4
have their colors too 2226: 3
have undone the world 159:10
he had wished unsaid ...1687:15
he spareth his w. 2225:16
he w. me, girls 2219: 3
hearts true, w. few 880: 3
his w. are bonds 2229:13
his w. are half battles ..1227:11
his w. softer than oil 2223:18
hold fast form of sound w. 2222: 9
holy as deed they cover ..2229: 1
Homer's w. costly 1533: 5
how forcible are right w. 2222: 8
howl'd out in desert air ..2223: 6
I do not know the w. ..1878: 3
I love smooth w. 2226: 4
idle w., servants to fools 2218: 5
if my w. seem treason ...2033:18
ill w. kill a man 2218:13
immodest w. admit no defence 422:14
in a silent look 598:14
in place of gifts 2223:21
in w. are valiant 2229: 4
in w. as fashions 2222:16
in w. great gifts gave ..2223:21
jesting w. become merry ..2222: 8
kind w. are benedictions 2220: 4
large, comfortable w. 2218: 6
last w. of Marmion 2084: 6
lavish of w. niggard in deed 2228:10
lead to things 2219:19
learn'd by rote 312:12
led by woman's gentle w. 2195: 7
less needful to sorrow 842: 6
let thy w. be few 2225:14
let thy w. show thee wise 1823:10
like cloud of snakes 2224: 9
like gods, deeds like lice 2228: 5
like leaves 2225: 4
like Nature, half reveal ..843: 3
like wildfire 2224:11
little gift of w. 1757:15
little w. are hard and cold 2224: 4
little w. of love 2040:19
long-tailed w. in osity ..2222: 3
look how you use proud w. 2226: 9
loud w. are so little worth 1901: 7
low w. please us when the theme is low 1927: 8
loyal w. heal grief 2220: 4
maketh not a man holy 1596: 4
many w. like cuttle-fish 2225: 5
many-syllabled w. 1830:14
may be false, full of art 1819: 3
may be greatly revenged 1713: 6
mean so many things ...2221: 6
meaningless torrent of w. 2224:13
mere w., not from heart 2225: 6
Milton's wormwood w. ..2055:12
modest w. for immodesty 579:15
more avail than deeds ..2227:11
more sincere and hearty 1543:15
most powerful drug 2220: 2
most w. in smallest ideas 2225: 2
move slow 1528:15
multiplieth w. without knowledge 2224:15
my w. are little jars 2226: 2
my w. are only w. 2220:20
my w. fly up 1585:11
my w. shall not pass away 2220: 3
nice grand w. to say 2218: 9
no choice of w. for him who sees truth 2222: 1

Words, *continued*
no need of w.; trust deeds 2228:13
no w. can paint 238:18
no w. suffice soul to show 2218: 7
noblest group of w. 570: 7
not things themselves ...2218:2a
not w. alone pleas'd her ..944:12
obsolete and old-fashioned w. 1928: 2
ocean of w. 2224:14
of affection 2223:15
of all sad w. of tongue ..1687:22
of death grave and sweet ..391: 4
of glozing courtesy 948:14
of learned length 100: 8
of love then spoken 196: 9
of Mercury harsh 2219: 6
of shame 58: 6
of so sweet breath 775:12
of the wise as goods 2218:12
of truth and soberness ..2218: 6
of truth paradoxical 2057: 2
on a good day good w. 371: 2
or I shall burst 2222: 2
ought to have weight 1585: 6
our w. are our own 2225:12
our w. have wings 2226: 7
pay no debts 2228:22
pegs to hang ideas on ..2217:11
pervert the judgment 2219:17
perverteth w. of righteous 776:16
phrases pass away 2220:12
physicians of mind diseased 2217: 9
plausive w. 2224: 2
poisoned w. that wildly fly 1761:16
portmanteau w. 2221: 5
pouring w. into sieve 2219: 1
power of w. 1490: 9
pregnant with celestial fire 2218: 6
pretty w. that make no sense 255:12
proper w. in proper places 1927: 7
prove w. by deeds 2228:18
provoke to wrath 2219:15
puny things are w. 2226: 2
quench fire of love with w. 1209:18
razors to wounded heart 2224: 8
reconciling w. 1901:17
repeated have another sense 2222:13
rob me of certainty 2220:11
rob the Hybla bees 676:10
sauce her with bitter w. 2224: 8
say much in few w. 2225:16
scatter my w. among mankind 1518:14
scattered like seed 2220: 7
scrupulous about w. 2218:10
seemed to them idle tales 2220:14
serve to conceal 1901: 8
serve your will 2223: 4
set betwixt two charming w. 1052: 2
sharp w. make wounds ..2224: 3
short in w., long in wit ..1628:11
shy and dappled 2226: 4
signs of ideas only 2218:2a
simple are the w. of truth 2057: 2
sincere w. not grand 2218: 2
slavish w. 1801:18
sleeveless w. 1851: 9
slow in w. woman's virtue 2200: 7
smell of the apron 1923:10
smooth w., smooth ways 2224: 1
smoother than butter 2223:18
smoothing w. 2224: 2
snared with w. of mouth 1947: 6
snatch w. from my mouth 2218:17
so beautiful as w. 2226: 1
soft creeping w. on w. ..1525:10
soft w. break no bones ...2224: 1
soft w. hurt not mouth ..2223:16
soft w. win hard hearts 2223:16
solemn and holy w. 2264: 9
soul's ambassadors 2218: 1
sound w. Timothy to use 1926:11
speak a few reasonable w. 348: 7
speaking w. of endearment 2223:15
speaks the kindest w. 420:14
stamped with mark of day 1926:14
strangest w. at your beck 2223:13

Words, *continued*
striking, high-sounding w. 1928: 2
stuff with chaff of w. 160: 3
suffered corruption since Chaucer 2222:12
Sunday-school w. 2223:12
superfluous w. flow away .198:10
sweet are w. of love 1209: 1
sweet as honey 2223:18
ten low w. one dull line 1527: 6
that are set to music 1877: 1
that bore semblance of worth 2222:13
that burn 634: 4
that dropped from his sweet tongue 1590: 9
that gender things 2219:19
that have been so nimble 2226: 1
that kindle glory 426: 2
that may become alive ...2220: 2
that my w. were written ..182: 5
that never lie or brag ...1361:12
that now you speak 2288: 1
that weep 2218: 8
that will solace 2223:15
that wise Bacon or Raleigh spake 2222:16
three w. with charity 2223:19
through w. and things 1311: 7
thy w. are bigger 2228:20
thy w. need an army 173:10
tire with book of w. 2225: 8
to veil their design 1901:17
tokens for conceits 2217:10
too much of w. 1451: 3
too sweet for w. 1899: 8
traverse the heavens 535:11
trip about him at command 2222:13
two w. have undone world 159:10
two w. to that bargain 125:16
tyrants quake to hear 1440: 3
uncouth w. in disarray ..1525: 9
unpleasant'st w. 2224: 8
uplandish w. 2222: 7
use w. with economy 1523:20
vain sound of w. 1439:17
vain w. of men 2052:14
weasel w. 2218: 5
weigh'st thy w. 2225:17
well-chosen w. 1516: 3
well-placed w. 2219:21
wench-like w. 2223: 3
were meant for rhyme ...2222:15
were simple w. enough ..2222:11
what difference who spoke the w. 1519:12
what need is there for w. 2219:11
what so wild as w. 2224:11
what w. or tongue of seraph 2220:15
what w. won't do, gold ..803:10
where honied w. prevail 1384: 8
which delight the ear 2214:10
which Moses spake 1708: 1
whose w. all ears took ..2224: 2
why should I spare w. ...2225:11
wild and whirling w. 2224: 8
wild w. wander here and 2223:10
will naturally flow 2252:17
winged w. 2226: 7
wise men's counters 2217:10
with nothing in them 1877: 2
with w. we govern men ..2220: 1
without anything in them 2222: 6
without deeds are rushes 2227:15
without knowledge 2224:15
without thoughts never to 1585:11
worth more than silence 1824: 2
writ in waters 2220:12
y-clad with majesty 2218:12
you can cut with w. 184: 4
you reply in few w. 198:10

Wordsworth, William ..2229
bell with wooden tongue ..2230: 2
chime his childish verse ..2229:20
in sonnet is classic too ..2230: 6
not to vulgar W. stoop ..2229:20
out-babying W. 1982:15
true philosopher and poet 2230: 5
Wordsworth's healing power 2229:17

Work 2230
a little w., a little play ..1137:13
a little w., a little sweating 1137:12
all in the day's w. 2231:18
all things w. together for good 790:19
all w. and no play 1003: 9
all w. is noble 2233: 4
always w., and yet more w. 2230:14
an unknown good man does 981: 7
and acquire 228: 11
and for what pay 1067: 7
and play, w. and play ..2233: 8
and rest shall be won ...2233: 6
and thou wilt bless day 2233: 6
and wait 1462: 4
and your house be fed ..2233: 6
appraising w. of others ...343:18
as close as we may 407:13
at his dirty w. again 2255:10
bears witness who does well 2231:10
best investment 2233: 9
best prize life offers 1064: 5
best w. hasn't been done 2233: 1
better for our love 1210:12
better than whiskey 2233: 9
by my own w. before night 2232: 5
by w. one knows workman 2231:10
composes soul of man 1063: 4
consider w. you have done 174: 2
considered w. important 534: 1
cure for all maladies ...2233: 4
day is short, w. long 104: 6
day's w. is a day's w. 2231:18
demon, behold your w. ..441: 1
dirty w. at the crossroads 2033: 4
divided is shortened 2231: 8
do devil's w. for nothing .441: 7
do his dirty w. 2257:18
do the w. that's nearest ...893:13
do thy w. and know it not 508:13
done squarely 2234: 6
enough w. to do 2234: 5
establish w. of our hands 2232:13
every man's w. manifest 2231: 3
excelled the material 2231:14
find w. for hands to do ..954:11
finish w. in hand 2231:15
fire nor sword have power to destroy w. 2256: 4
first and then rest 2231: 7
first best w. of Creator ..2184:10
for immortality 964: 6
for ourself and a woman 2232: 6
for the work's sake 106:14; 2233: 3
for your own amusement 2234: 1
forced to w. and do your best 2234: 7
free men freely w. 2233: 2
genuine w. alone eternal 2233: 4
get leave to w. 2233: 2
give us this day our w. 2234: 7
gives flavor to life 2232:16
go to bed to w. 141: 1
God's own w. to do on earth 2232: 4
gods sell all things for w. 2233:12
goes bravely on 2231: 1
goes merrily with song ..1876: 6
great w. from poor cradles 2250: 9
hard and dirty w. 1067: 7
he who defers this w. ..1614:10
his six days' w., world ..2244: 6
how best to avoid w. ...2231: 5
how w. grows play 855:16
I have great w. in hand 2256: 4
I want w. 174:10
I'll do no w. this day ..1882: 6
if any would not w. neither should he eat 2231:19
in morning of life, w. ..1127:10
is done 39:12
is not a good 2235: 3
is prayer 1063: 4
left w. but just begun ..1587: 9
lends dignity to man 2234:10a
let your w. be a fight ...2111:16
life's w. well done 391:14
like a digger 106:14
Work, *continued*
like a man 2231: 7
like other men do 2071:4a
little w., a little sweating 1137:12
looks to w. for reply 2233:11
love of your w. 107:13
make the day's w. happy ..53: 2
man goeth forth to w. ..2232: 2
man hath his daily w. ..2232:11
man must find his w. 2232: 1
man must finish off w. ..2232: 6
man's w. is to labour 2233: 3
man's w. lasts till set of sun 2180:17
many hands make light w. 851: 3
men must w., women must weep 1145:10; 2234:18
more we w., more we may 2235: 5
more w., and always w. 7:8; 2230:14
my w. is done, I'll go to bed 2180:17
never done a stroke of w. 2231: 5
never w. without reward 2231:12
no disgrace 2231: 6
no substitute for w. 2233: 0
no w. nor device in grave 828: 6
noblest w. is reckoned 929: 2
noblest w. of God 2015:14
not design, but destiny ..439:11
nothing to do but w. 1414: 9
of Chloe 2136:10
of noble w. silent part best 1820:11
of skill, surpassing sense 1390:14
of world must be done ..2232:12
or lose power to will 2233: 6
other w. in hand 2231:17
outlives him,—there's his glory 107: 7
perishes fruitlessly 2124: 1
pleasant and clean w. ..1067: 7
proud w. of human skill 1473:14
rejoicing in his w. 2233:10
returns to husbandman ..639:15
serious w. for fame 626: 9
she plied 2234:15
sit and look at w. 2231: 5
so bravely done, so rich 2234:10
something you want done 2234: 1
source of human welfare 2234:12
suffering from lack of w. 2164:14
sustenance of noble minds 2234: 9
taken in midst of w. ...2231:15
that smells of oil 1923:15
that tells a story 95: 3
the w. some praise, some the architect 96: 7
their w. continueth 627: 4
there is always w. 2232: 9
thou for pleasure 106:14
three words of counsel, w., w., w. 2230:14
too great for fame 1604: 2
useful w. is worship 2234: 4
wanted yet the master w. 1243:12
wanting to w. is rare ...2231:11
was strong and clean 1818: 7
well and hastily 862:12
what endless w. have I ..2256: 4
what w. have you in hand 1556: 5
who first invented w. 2235: 1
who is to do no w. 1067: 7
will lead to song 1972:13
with stout heart 1064: 3
without Hope 927:17
without w., unemployment 2231: 4
without w., without food 2231:19
woman's w. is never done 2180:17
your w. and labor of love 2233:15
Worked like a galley-slave 2230:15a
Worker: strong-arm W. 644: 1
to w. God lends aid 787:12
Workers get so little 1718:15
Working as hen lays eggs 2230:16
I've been w. on the railroad 2295:13
like a horse 2230:15a
love w. and reading 980:11
that makes workman 2230:16
Working-girl: heaven will protect the w. 778:12
Workman: American w. and foreign 1065:17
bad w. same wages as good 1066:11
never doth refuse meanest tool 543: 2
not ashamed 2231: 6
was no cobbling clown ..1816:14
Workmanship and value ..2234:10
Works after his own manner 2234: 1
all these his wondrous w. 1251:12
are the mirror 427: 7
best w. from childless men 252: 4
by which of thy good w. 1022:10
everybody w. but father 2290:10
faith without w. is dead ..620:11
find righteous judgment 1023:14
full of good w. 242: 1
golden chords of good w. 425:20
good w. in husband 2143: 7
good w. make the man ..2227: 7
greatest w. of any poet ..348: 7
have our w. in remembrance 1421:10
he w., plots, fights 344: 6
imperial w. 552: 6
last and best of God's w. 2185: 5
more one w., more willing 2230:16
noblest w. from childless men 252: 4
of malice in another style 810:14
of moderns, better 187:19
of the Lord 1779: 7
of women are symbolical 2204:13
rich in good w. 238:10
ripples on the sea 539:11
so fleet w. of men 1140: 7
son of his own w. 716: 3
their w. do follow them ..397: 8
thy w. and alms 394: 3
thy w. outlive thy tomb 1806: 8
to recount almighty w. ..2220:15
which of thy good w. ..1022:10
with mercy doth embrace 790:20
work the w. of him that sent me 2232: 2
Workshop of Nature 1381:13
of the world 548: 8
Worky-days are the backpart 1752:13
World 2235
a better w.'s in birth 1066:17
a bubble 1120: 7
a jest, joy a trinket 1115:15
a mass of folly 24: 6
a scene of changes 305:20
advances 1616:14
affords no law to enrich 2242:11
ah, love, the w. is fading 1140: 8
aids w., in aiding mind ..1312:17
all sorts to make w. 2237:19
all the sad w. needs 1037:42
all the w. a stage 2240: 5
all the w. and his father 1513: 8
all the w. and his wife ..1859:20
all the w. can't find me out 273:13
all the w. was Adam 11:14
all w. lulled to rest 1401: 2
all's right with the w. ..1905:13
almost whole w. players 2240: 6
always equal to itself ..2237:11
an inn 1122: 7
an ugly w. 1861:11
and all the w. was gay ..1852:19
and I shall ne'er agree ..276:11
and the flesh 440:13
another and a better w. ..967: 6
anywhere out of the w. ..437: 3
appears unkind 675: 7
are you so grey 2242: 3
assembly of beings 2236: 7
at best but a bubble 2239: 7
aureoled in mystery 2132: 6
averse to all the truth ..2242: 1
beautifully dressed 2241: 9
begins lying about us 884:17
begins with a garden 274:19
belongs to those who act 2237:17

Wrong, *continued*
private, not public w. 1712: 1
rules the land 2260: 3
something is w. 230: 8
speak ten millions w. ...1560: 6
suffer w. than do it 2047: 2
that needs resistance ...1660: 6
that never wrongeth 2260:12
they do me w. 1431:12
to do him w. was to beget
a kindness 242:19
was his who complain'd ..2259:14
when everyone is w.,
everyone is right 1727:14
when people agree 99:13
who does no w. needs no
law 1080: 3
who treasures up a w. ...1708: 9
wrought no w. to any 2260: 4
you are i' the w. 1899:15
you w. our friendship 728:14
Wrongdoing to turn us pale 989:16
Wronged me in nicest point 2260: 7
Wronger: to wrong the w. 2012:15
Wrongs 2259
beget new mischiefs 2259:16
darker than death 1129: 9
heaviest w. get uppermost 2241:17
ingrate w. I read 284:12
make his w. his outsides 2073: 5
makes people's w. his own 1493:16
not w. done to us harm
us 2260: 1
of base mankind 2260: 5
on adamant w. engrave ..987: 1
public w. popular rights 1728:10
righting w., writing verses 1529: 3
some write w. in marble 987: 2
two w. do not make a
right 1728: 1
unredressed 2260:11
unrequited w. 156:17
unspeakable 2260:11
which flesh and blood cannot endure 2259:13
Wrote drop by drop 2254:14
for the man of wit 938:18
he w. for certain papers 1604: 7
like an angel 805: 2
no man but blockhead ever
w. except for money 2250: 8
what he w. all his own ..2258:13
whatever he w. did it better 805: 3
Wroth: then sudden waxed
w. 1206:16
with one we love 1197: 5
Wrought: first he w. 589: 4
Wunder: es geshehen keine
W. mehr 1316:12
ist des Glaubens liebstes
Kind 1316: 4
Wurzburger: down where
the W. flows 1882: 3
Wy: he'll find a wy 1: 3
Wynken, Blynken and Nod 1847: 5

X

Xanadu: in X. did Kubla 1732:10
Xantippe made her good
man 2146: 2
Xenophon at New York 52: 6
Xerxes the great did die ..385:13
the splendid 384: 2

Y

Y.M.C.A.: sat alone in the
Y.M.C.A. 2294: 7
Yachts: where are the c-cus-
tomers' y. 665:20
Yak: so negligee 1410: 1
Yale, Elihu: epitaph 571: 8
Yankee Doodle 61: 7
in a flyin' ship 694: 3
peddling, tuppenny Y. 721:12
Yanks are coming 2284: 2
Yap that drags 'em round ..71:10
Yaptown-on-the-Hudson ..1397: 2
Yard: I don't want to play
in your y. 2295: 2
she had enclosed 232:18
Yards: few y. in London
cement 1859:17
Yarn: of a mingled y. ...1119:13
Yarrow: see the Braes of ..1734: 2
thy genuine image 1294:17
Yawcob Strauss: leaf dot 122: 5
Yawn: everlasting y. 956:13
we y., we go 1137: 2
which sleep cannot abate 192: 2
Yawning make another
yawn 587: 8
Yawns: one y., procras-
tinates 1614: 4
Yawp: my barbaric y. 1539: 5
Yea: let your y. be y. ...198:12
Year 2260
another y. has burst 2262: 5
at the spring 1905:13
come to Forty Y. 26: 9
comes in at one y. 510:20
doth nothing but open and
shut 2261: 4
each passing y. robs us 2012: 9
flows on harmoniously ..2275: 2
goes wrong 1434: 6
grows rich as it groweth old 31: 1
Heaven's eternal y. 887: 7
if all y. was playing holidays 903:15
in my sixtieth y. 29: 8
is all but done 2262: 3
is but asleep 2262: 7
is dying in the night 2262: 8
is going, let him go 2262: 8
leading up the golden y. ..371: 5
liberal y. laughs out 862: 8
life's y. begins and closes ..42: 4
live one more y. 29:15
many a y. ago 1206:14
merry y. is born 2261:15
my eightieth y. 29:12
no contemptible portion of
existence 2261: 3
not y. or two shows man ..1255: 6
of joy, another of com-
fort 1275: 4
of rest unto land 637: 6
of the Age of Gold 995:11
of the rose is brief 1745:14
of wonders 2260:23
old y. is with the past 2261:14
old y. lies a-dying 2262: 8
on her deathbed 2262: 7
Orphan Hours, Y. is dead 2262: 7
pleasure of the fleeting y. 4: 7
rolling y. is full of Thee 1782: 6
smiles as draws near
death 1425: 2
so rolls the changing y. ..1782: 8
sweet o' the y. 1908: 3
that's awa' 731:11
three-and-twentieth y. ...165: 5
'tis leap y. lady 2216: 2
usher in the circling y. ..2262: 6
wake the purple y. 1906:15
whose days are long 1614: 1
wonderful glad New Y. 2261:17
Yearn not for soft things ..2169: 7
Yearning: nobler y. never
broke 2178:17
to make money 2250: 8
Years: alas! my fifty y. 32:15
all one a hundred y. hence
............1635:10; 1797: 3
and y. and donkey's ears 2261:11
before the beginning of y. 1239:11
behind us in death's hands 382: 4
being only four y. old ..121:14
better fifty y. of Europe 581: 8
bless the middle y. 25:16
bring blessings 2261: 5
bring philosophic mind ..1498:21
count a man's y. 27: 5
crowding y. in one brief
moon 196:13
cuts off twenty y. 1934:10
eighty odd y. of sorrow 1019: 5
Years, *continued*
exile us into dreams 481: 2
find us the same 231: 3
first y. provision for last 1651: 4
forty y. on 26: 9
f lfil y. of his life 2140: 1
full of y. and honors ...397: 6
glide swiftly by 2006: 5
go by in single file 2261:10
golden y. return 512:19
hath done this wrong 2255: 4
have hardier tasks 2260:20
his y. but young 595:13
how flash the y. along 2005: 9
how many y. mortal live 2007: 7
hundred y. from now 1635:10
hundred y. of gloom ..2156:13
it may be for y. 1454: 6
keep a thing seven y. ..1998: 4
know more than books ..187:10
leave us and find us same 231: 3
like great black oxen 2261:12
long y. of repentance ..1016:23
most important earliest y. 2264: 4
nine y. a-killing 1359: 5
noisy y. seem moments ..1825:19
not y., but actions 1134:10
of anguish crowd 934: 3
of discretion 456:13
of fading strength 22:11
of men are in the looms 1128: 6
of toil and soil 2186: 5
only the y. are strong 2150: 3
pass like water 1131:10
quench not thirst of glory .781:11
sae monie changefu' y. 33: 1
set is the sun of my y. ...35: 4
seventy y. young 37:13
shall right the balance ..2150: 3
should teach wisdom 2165: 3
sigh not over vanished y. 2260:21
since last we met 1882: 8
six y., six drops of time ..2260:19
six y. thou shalt sow 637: 6
slow y. pass 2261: 6
spend our y. as tale that is
told 2261: 8
steal fire from mind 33: 3
steal something every day 2014: 4
steal us from ourselves ..2261: 5
summit of my y. 28: 8
swift y. slip and slide 2261: 6
teach much the days never
knew 2261: 1
that are past 1459: 4
thousand y. as a moment 2261: 7
thousand y. as yesterday 2261: 7
thousand y. scarce serve
to form a state 1918: 2
three years she grew 409: 5
three-score y. and ten ..1141: 8
to mother bring distress 1353:13
unknown to fame 1422: 8
uselessness of men above
sixty y. 35: 6
vale of y. 27:16
watch y. that hasten by 2260:21
we waste, tears we waste 2187:18
what y. could us divide ..740: 1
whole y. in absence to deplore 4: 5
will not let y. run over me 2261: 9
with y. richer life begins ..42: 5
Yesterday's Sev'n Thou-
sand Y. 2021: 6
young in y., old in hours 2263: 2
young y. of little child ..251:12
Yeas: ruinous y. 7:11
russet y. 217: 9
Yeast: God made y. 45: 7
Yelk of an addled egg 103: 7
Yell of savage rage 2117: 9
Yellow: his bill's so y. 167:16
journalism 1600:18
learn from Y. an' Brown 1224: 2
literary atmosphere 1600:18
'tis a color she abhors 491: 7
to jaundic'd eye 1948:14
your perfect y. 128: 1
Yellows of the quitter 331:17

INDEX TO ADDED QUOTATIONS

Politicians, *continued*
tin-horn p. 2299x: 9
Politics 2299t
if you can't tell who's for you 2299v: 7
is a profession 2299u: 7
is like football 2299v:17
non-partisan in p. 2299x: 4
of partisanship 2299v: 8
of responsibility 2299v: 8
practical p. 2299v: 5
science of who gets what 1541: 6
seldom think of p. more than 18 hours a day 2299v: 9
Poor: never p., only broke 2299y: 7
society cannot help the many who are p. ..2299y: 3
wall between rich and p. 2299y: 1
Posterity: let p. choose ..2298t: 3
Poverty 2299y
keeps together homes ..2299y: 5
tap root is ignorance ..2299y: 2
there is inherited p. 2299y: 4
war on p. 2298m: 2
worst of crimes 2299y: 6
Power 2299y
apt to abuse it 2299y:12
I do not find impressive 2299y: 9
is legitimate only 2299y:11
is sweet, a drug 2299y:14
of positive thinking 2300f:10
unlimited p. corrupts ..2299y:13
when p. corrupts, poetry cleanses 2299t: 9
Praise: bores me 2298t: 6
Lord, pass ammunition 2298d: 7
Prejudices eradicate 23000:12
President of all the people 2299s:14
President's hardest task .2299v:14
Press, The 2299y
dictators seek to control 2299z: 4
free p. a necessity 2299y:17
wayward p. 2299y:16
Pride: man thinking too highly of himself ..23000:18
Problems of victory 2298c: 1
we [can] solve together 2300g: 5
Progress: alliance for p. 2298m:13
Progressive who is prudent 2299v.10
Promise must never be broken 2300n: 1
Promises: vote for man who p. least 2299t:14
Property seeks protection 2299z: 6
Prosperity: profitless p. ..2299a: 4
Public office, few attractions 2299u:12
the p. interest 2299s:13
who molds p. sentiment 2299p: 1
Purposes: in name of noble p. 2299z: 8

Q

Quarantine [aggressors] 2300j: 8
Quisling 2298f:10
Quoted: seldom q. correctly 2300d: 4

R

Radical has feet in air....2298a: 6
the r. Right 2299x:2
Read between lines 2298x: 7
Reappraisal: agonizing r. 2298l: 1
Reason 2299z
inclines to mildness 23000:12
let us r. together 2299z: 11
live by guidance of r. ..2299z:13
Reforms: no r. come easy 2300a: 2
Religion: priests not necessary 2300a: 4
Remember the Alamo 2298z: 3
Republican party is size I like 2299v:12
Respect: covet nothing but 2298c: 1
Responsibility: divided r. 2298e: 5
is price of greatness ..2298c: 1
Retaliation: massive r. ...2300i: 2
Return: I shall r. 2300j: 2
Revolution 2300a
no r. in Germany 2300n: 4
our "permanent r." 2300a: 9
remedies are not r. 2300a: 8
stop r. at beginning 2300a:11
Revolutions are not exportable 2300a:10
Riddle in a mystery 2300b: 3
Right: state's r. to default on national duty ..2298k:16
the radical R. 2299x: 2
to be heard, to be taken seriously 2300e: 6
to vote, basic 2300g:11
wrong to be too r. 2300m: 8
Rights 2300a
exist only under law ...2300a:13
from hand of God 2300a:16
men, their r. and nothing more 2300a:12
not from old parchments 2300a:14
only people have r. 2300b: 1
right to interfere with r. of others 2300a:17
states have no r. 2300b: 1
women, their r. and nothing less 2300a:12
Roar: luck to give r. 2298w: 6
Rudeness, imitation of strength 2300n: 6
Rugged individualism 2298l: 6

S

Sanctuary: privileged s. ..2300j: 1
Santa Claus: nobody shoots 2299a: 6
Say it with flowers 2299a: 2
Scare: don't let them s. you 2299a:23
Schools need to learn 2298v:15
Science 2300b
contributes to culture ..2300c: 2
invoke wonders of s. ...2300b:17
is a great game 2300c: 5
language is universal ..2300c: 1
neither potential for good or evil 2300c: 6
tells what is possible, not what is right 2300b:14
Seabees welcome Marines 2298f: 4
Security: business of state 2300e:21
no one ever had s. 2298q: 3
no s., only opportunity 2299q: 5
Segregation on deathbed ..22990:11
Self-criticism is mark of social maturity 2298t: 8
Self-preservation, first principle 2300m:19
Sense: let's talk s. 2299w:12
Sex on the brain 2298w:12
Ship 2300c
referred to as "she" ...2300c:11
strength is service 2300c:10
Shoot: don't s. pianist ...2299a:16
Shoots at Santa Claus 2299a: 6
Show business 2300e: 9
Shroud: no pocket in s. ..2299m:16
Sidney: clear everything with S. 2298: 6
Siegfried: hang washing on S. line 2298f: 5
Silence 2300c
is the greatest sin 2300d: 1
tact is golden, not s. ...2300c:13
Silver at noon of day 2298x:16
Sin 2300d
always been ugly word 2300d: 6
I believe in forgiveness of s. 2300d: 7
Sincerity subject to proof 2300d:10
Sins I had no opportunity to commit 2300d: 5
Smell: sweet s. of success 2300f: 3
Socialism seeks to pull down wealth 2299e: 1
Society 2300d
Great S. ...2298m: 8, 2299v:13, ...2300d:14
who killed s. 2300d:12
Soldier prays for peace ..2300e: 3
Solid South 2299a: 1
Space: no national sovereignty rules in outer s. 2300b:15
Specialist: trained but uneducated 2298v:18
Speech like love affair ...2299q: 7
U.S., land of free s. ...2300e: 5
Speeches: submit to s. ...2299q: 8
Speed: all deliberate s. ...2299a: 8
Spirit of '76 ....2299a:17
State's right to default on national duty 2298k:16
Status seekers 2298k:11
Strength 2300e
speak for itself 2300e:17
today is not problem ...2300e:16
Sub: sighted s., sank same 2298e: 6
Success 2300f
bitch-goddess 2300n:12
nothing fails like s. 2300f: 4
sweet smell of s. 2300f: 3
takes 20 years to make an overnight s. 2300f: 2
where s. comes before work 2299i: 2
Summit: only s. meeting that can succeed ..2298u: 7
Sure: dull man always s. ..2299l: 8

T

Take: can't t. it with you 2299m:16
Talk sense to people 2299w:12
Tastes: no accounting for t. 2298z: 7
Taxation: art of t. 2300f: 5
Taxes, for civilized society 2300f: 6
Teach: too honest to t. ..23000:17
Teetotaller: beer t. 2298v: 8
Theatre: hold up burial of t. 2300e:12
is cliffhanger, phoenix ..2300e:12
it is destiny to struggle 2300e:15
last free institution 2300e:13
march toward extinction 2300e:12
want to create t., not build 2300e:14
which depends on immediate smash hits 2300e:10
Think about "unthinkable" 2300f: 9
Thinking: power of positive t. 2300f:10
Ticker tape ain't spaghetti 23000: 1
Tiger: riding the back of t. 2299y:10
Tigers: dictators ride t. ..2300m:15
Time great legalizer 23000: 9
Tin-horn politicians 2299x: 9
Tinker to Evers to Chance 2300m: 3
Tongue: all [but] t. gets tired 2300c:12
Torch passed to new generation 2298m:12
Treason: 20 years of t. ..2299w: 7
Trenches: out of the t. ...2300i: 6
Truth 2300f
any fool can tell t. 2300f:14
in honest lies 2300f:13
often unpopular 2300g: 2
stop telling t. about them 2299j: 6
stronger than error 2300g: 1
Tyranny is normal pattern 2299c:11